Who Was Who in America®

Who Was Who in America®

with world notables

2006-2007
Volume XVIII

890 Mountain Avenue, Suite 300
New Providence, NJ 07974 U.S.A.

Who Was Who in America®

Marquis Who's Who®

Published by Marquis Who's Who LLC.

For information, contact:
Marquis Who's Who
890 Mountain Avenue, Suite 300
New Providence, New Jersey 07974
908-673-1001
www.marquiswhoswho.com

International Standard Book Number	978-0-8379-0269-2	(20-Volume Set)
	978-0-8379-0266-1	(Volume XVIII)
	978-0-8379-0267-8	(Index Volume)
	978-0-8379-0268-5	(Volume XVIII and Index Volume)
International Standard Serial Number	0146-8081	

Manufactured in the United States of America.

Table of Contents

Preface

Marquis Who's Who is proud to present the 2006-2007 Edition of *Who Was Who in America*. This 18th edition features over 4,000 profiles of individuals who had previously been profiled in *Who's Who in America* and other Marquis Who's Who publications, but who have died since the publication of the last edition of *Who Was Who in America* in December, 2006.

Among the notable Americans profiled in this volume are individuals as influential and diverse as Merv Griffin, Norman Mailer, Luciano Pavarotti, Arthur M. Schlesinger, Jr., and Anna Nicole Smith. The impact of these individuals during their lifetimes was enormous and their influence is certain to live on.

Of course, not every person profiled in this volume is a household name. These pages include the profiles of doctors, lawyers, entrepreneurs, researchers, inventors, and other prominent achievers who have died in the last two years.

The biographical information included in the profiles that follow was gathered in a variety of manners. In most cases, those listed had submitted their personal biographical details during their lifetime.

In many cases, though, the information was collected independently by our research and editorial staffs, which use a wide assortment of tools to gather complete, accurate, and up-to-date information.

Who Was Who in America is an important component of the Marquis Who's Who family of publications. Along with *Who's Who in America* and *Who's Who in the World*, Marquis Who's Who also publishes a number of specialized and regionalized volumes. These include *Who's Who of American Women*, *Who's Who in American Law*, *Who's Who in Medicine and Healthcare*, and *Who's Who in the East*, to name a few.

It has been an honor to compile this edition of *Who Was Who in America*. It is our hope that the biographical profiles will do justice to the individuals memorialized on the pages that follow.

Table of Abbreviations

The following is a list of some of the most frequently used Marquis abbreviations:

A

A Associate (used with academic degrees)
AA Associate in Arts
AAAL American Academy of Arts and Letters
AAAS American Association for the Advancement of Science
AACD American Association for Counseling and Development
AACN American Association of Critical Care Nurses
AAHA American Academy of Health Administrators
AAHP American Association of Hospital Planners
AAHPERD American Alliance for Health, Physical Education, Recreation, and Dance
AAS Associate of Applied Science
AASL American Association of School Librarians
AASPA American Association of School Personnel Administrators
AAU Amateur Athletic Union
AAUP American Association of University Professors
AAUW American Association of University Women
AB Arts, Bachelor of
AB Alberta
ABA American Bar Association
AC Air Corps
acad. academy
acct. accountant
acctg. accounting
ACDA Arms Control and Disarmament Agency
ACHA American College of Hospital Administrators
ACLS Advanced Cardiac Life Support
ACLU American Civil Liberties Union
ACOG American College of Ob-Gyn
ACP American College of Physicians
ACS American College of Surgeons
ADA American Dental Association
adj. adjunct, adjutant
adm. admiral
adminstr. administrator
adminstrn. administration
adminstrv. administrative
ADN Associate's Degree in Nursing
ADP Automatic Data Processing
adv. advocate, advisory
advt. advertising
AE Agricultural Engineer
AEC Atomic Energy Commission
aero. aeronautical, aeronautic
aerodyn. aerodynamic
AFB Air Force Base
AFTRA American Federation of Television and Radio Artists
agr. agriculture
agrl. agricultural
agt. agent
AGVA American Guild of Variety Artists
agy. agency
A&I Agricultural and Industrial
AIA American Institute of Architects
AIAA American Institute of Aeronautics and Astronautics
AIChE American Institute of Chemical Engineers
AICPA American Institute of Certified Public Accountants
AID Agency for International Development
AIDS Acquired Immune Deficiency Syndrome
AIEE American Institute of Electrical Engineers
AIME American Institute of Mining, Metallurgy, and Petroleum Engineers
AK Alaska
AL Alabama
ALA American Library Association
Ala. Alabama
alt. alternate
Alta. Alberta
A&M Agricultural and Mechanical
AM Arts, Master of
Am. American, America
AMA American Medical Association
amb. ambassador
AME African Methodist Episcopal
Amtrak National Railroad Passenger Corporation
AMVETS American Veterans
ANA American Nurses Association
anat. anatomical
ANCC American Nurses Credentialing Center
ann. annual
anthrop. anthropological
AP Associated Press
APA American Psychological Association
APHA American Public Health Association
APO Army Post Office
apptd. appointed
Apr. April
apt. apartment
AR Arkansas
ARC American Red Cross
arch. architect
archeol. archeological
archtl. architectural
Ariz. Arizona
Ark. Arkansas
ArtsD Arts, Doctor of
arty. artillery
AS Associate in Science, American Samoa
ASCAP American Society of Composers, Authors and Publishers
ASCD Association for Supervision and Curriculum Development
ASCE American Society of Civil Engineers
ASME American Society of Mechanical Engineers
ASPA American Society for Public Administration
ASPCA American Society for the Prevention of Cruelty to Animals
assn. association
assoc. associate
asst. assistant
ASTD American Society for Training and Development
ASTM American Society for Testing and Materials
astron. astronomical
astrophys. astrophysical
ATLA Association of Trial Lawyers of America
ATSC Air Technical Service Command
atty. attorney
Aug. August
aux. auxiliary
Ave. Avenue
AVMA American Veterinary Medical Association
AZ Arizona

B

B Bachelor
b. born
BA Bachelor of Arts
BAgr Bachelor of Agriculture
Balt. Baltimore
Bapt. Baptist
BArch Bachelor of Architecture
BAS Bachelor of Agricultural Science
BBA Bachelor of Business Administration
BBB Better Business Bureau
BC British Columbia
BCE Bachelor of Civil Engineering
BChir Bachelor of Surgery
BCL Bachelor of Civil Law
BCS Bachelor of Commercial Science
BD Bachelor of Divinity
bd. board
BE Bachelor of Education
BEE Bachelor of Electrical Engineering
BFA Bachelor of Fine Arts
bibl. biblical
bibliog. bibliographical
biog. biographical
biol. biological
BJ Bachelor of Journalism
Bklyn. Brooklyn
BL Bachelor of Letters
bldg. building
BLS Bachelor of Library Science
Blvd. Boulevard
BMI Broadcast Music, Inc.
bn. battalion
bot. botanical
BPE Bachelor of Physical Education
BPhil Bachelor of Philosophy
br. branch
BRE Bachelor of Religious Education
brig. gen. brigadier general
Brit. British
Bros. Brothers
BS Bachelor of Science
BSA Bachelor of Agricultural Science
BSBA Bachelor of Science in Business Administration
BSChemE Bachelor of Science in Chemical Engineering
BSD Bachelor of Didactic Science
BSEE Bachelor of Science in Electrical Engineering
BSN Bachelor of Science in Nursing
BST Bachelor of Sacred Theology
BTh Bachelor of Theology
bull. bulletin
bur. bureau
bus. business
BWI British West Indies

C

CA California
CAD-CAM Computer Aided Design–Computer Aided Model
Calif. California
Can. Canada, Canadian
CAP Civil Air Patrol
capt. captain
cardiol. cardiological
cardiovasc. cardiovascular
Cath. Catholic
cav. cavalry
CBI China, Burma, India Theatre of Operations
CC Community College
CCC Commodity Credit Corporation
CCNY City College of New York
CCRN Critical Care Registered Nurse
CCU Cardiac Care Unit
CD Civil Defense
CE Corps of Engineers, Civil Engineer
CEN Certified Emergency Nurse
CENTO Central Treaty Organization
CEO Chief Executive Officer
CERN European Organization of Nuclear Research
cert. certificate, certification, certified
CETA Comprehensive Employment Training Act
CFA Chartered Financial Analyst
CFL Canadian Football League
CFO Chief Financial Officer
CFP Certified Financial Planner
ch. church
ChD Doctor of Chemistry
chem. chemical
ChemE Chemical Engineer
ChFC Chartered Financial Consultant
Chgo. Chicago
chirurg., der surgeon
chmn. chairman
chpt. chapter
CIA Central Intelligence Agency
Cin. Cincinnati
cir. circle, circuit
CLE Continuing Legal Education
Cleve. Cleveland
climatol. climatological
clin. clinical
clk. clerk
CLU Chartered Life Underwriter
CM Master in Surgery
cmty. community
CO Colorado
Co. Company
COF Catholic Order of Foresters
C. of C. Chamber of Commerce
col. colonel
coll. college
Colo. Colorado
com. committee
comd. commanded
comdg. commanding
comdr. commander
comdt. commandant
comm. communications
commd. commissioned
comml. commercial
commn. commission
commr. commissioner
compt. comptroller
condr. conductor
conf. Conference
Congl. Congregational, Congressional
Conglist. Congregationalist
Conn. Connecticut
cons. consultant, consulting
consol. consolidated
constl. constitutional
constn. constitution
constrn. construction
contbd. contributed
contbg. contributing
contbn. contribution
contbr. contributor
contr. controller
Conv. Convention
COO Chief Operating Officer
coop. cooperative
coord. coordinator
corp. corporation, corporate
corr. correspondent, corresponding, correspondence
coun. council
CPA Certified Public Accountant
CPCU Chartered Property and Casualty Underwriter
CPH Certificate of Public Health
cpl. corporal
CPR Cardio-Pulmonary Resuscitation
CS Christian Science
CSB Bachelor of Christian Science
CT Connecticut
ct. court
ctr. center
ctrl. central

D

D Doctor
d. daughter of
DAgr Doctor of Agriculture
DAR Daughters of the American Revolution
dau. daughter

DAV Disabled American Veterans
DC District of Columbia
DCL Doctor of Civil Law
DCS Doctor of Commercial Science
DD Doctor of Divinity
DDS Doctor of Dental Surgery
DE Delaware
Dec. December
dec. deceased
def. defense
Del. Delaware
del. delegate, delegation
Dem. Democrat, Democratic
DEng Doctor of Engineering
denom. denomination, denominational
dep. deputy
dept. department
dermatol. dermatological
desc. descendant
devel. development, developmental
DFA Doctor of Fine Arts
DHL Doctor of Hebrew Literature
dir. director
dist. district
distbg. distributing
distbn. distribution
distbr. distributor
disting. distinguished
div. division, divinity, divorce
divsn. division
DLitt Doctor of Literature
DMD Doctor of Dental Medicine
DMS Doctor of Medical Science
DO Doctor of Osteopathy
docs. documents
DON Director of Nursing
DPH Diploma in Public Health
DPhil Doctor of Philosophy
DR Daughters of the Revolution
Dr. Drive, Doctor
DRE Doctor of Religious Education
DrPH Doctor of Public Health
DSc Doctor of Science
DSChemE Doctor of Science in Chemical Engineering
DSM Distinguished Service Medal
DST Doctor of Sacred Theology
DTM Doctor of Tropical Medicine
DVM Doctor of Veterinary Medicine
DVS Doctor of Veterinary Surgery

E

E East
ea. eastern
Eccles. Ecclesiastical
ecol. ecological
econ. economic
ECOSOC United Nations Economic and Social Council
ED Doctor of Engineering
ed. educated
EdB Bachelor of Education
EdD Doctor of Education
edit. edition
editl. editorial
EdM Master of Education
edn. education
ednl. educational
EDP Electronic Data Processing
EdS Specialist in Education
EE Electrical Engineer
EEC European Economic Community
EEG Electroencephalogram
EEO Equal Employment Opportunity
EEOC Equal Employment Opportunity Commission
EKG electrocardiogram
elec. electrical
electrochem. electrochemical
electrophys. electrophysical
elem. elementary
EM Engineer of Mines
EMT Emergency Medical Technician
ency. encyclopedia
Eng. England
engr. engineer
engring. engineering
entomol. entomological
environ. environmental
EPA Environmental Protection Agency
epidemiol. epidemiological
Episc. Episcopalian
ERA Equal Rights Amendment
ERDA Energy Research and Development Administration
ESEA Elementary and Secondary Education Act
ESL English as Second Language
ESSA Environmental Science Services Administration
ethnol. ethnological
ETO European Theatre of Operations
EU European Union
Evang. Evangelical
exam. examination, examining
Exch. Exchange
exec. executive
exhbn. exhibition
expdn. expedition
expn. exposition
expt. experiment
exptl. experimental
Expy. Expressway
Ext. Extension

F

FAA Federal Aviation Administration
FAO UN Food and Agriculture Organization
FBA Federal Bar Association
FBI Federal Bureau of Investigation
FCA Farm Credit Administration
FCC Federal Communications Commission
FCDA Federal Civil Defense Administration
FDA Food and Drug Administration
FDIA Federal Deposit Insurance Administration
FDIC Federal Deposit Insurance Corporation
FEA Federal Energy Administration
Feb. February
fed. federal
fedn. federation
FERC Federal Energy Regulatory Commission
fgn. foreign
FHA Federal Housing Administration
fin. financial, finance
FL Florida
Fl. Floor
Fla. Florida
FMC Federal Maritime Commission
FNP Family Nurse Practitioner
FOA Foreign Operations Administration
found. foundation
FPC Federal Power Commission
FPO Fleet Post Office
frat. fraternity
FRS Federal Reserve System
FSA Federal Security Agency
Ft. Fort
FTC Federal Trade Commission
Fwy. Freeway

G

GA, Ga. Georgia
GAO General Accounting Office
gastroent. gastroenterological
GATT General Agreement on Tariffs and Trade
GE General Electric Company
gen. general
geneal. genealogical
geog. geographic, geographical
geol. geological
geophys. geophysical

geriat. geriatrics
gerontol. gerontological
GHQ General Headquarters
gov. governor
govt. government
govtl. governmental
GPO Government Printing Office
grad. graduate, graduated
GSA General Services Administration
Gt. Great
GU Guam
gynecol. gynecological

H

hdqs. headquarters
HEW Department of Health, Education and Welfare
HHD Doctor of Humanities
HHFA Housing and Home Finance Agency
HHS Department of Health and Human Services
HI Hawaii
hist. historical, historic
HM Master of Humanities
homeo. homeopathic
hon. honorary, honorable
House of Dels. House of Delegates
House of Reps. House of Representatives
hort. horticultural
hosp. hospital
HS High School
HUD Department of Housing and Urban Development
Hwy. Highway
hydrog. hydrographic

I

IA Iowa
IAEA International Atomic Energy Agency
IBRD International Bank for Reconstruction and Development
ICA International Cooperation Administration
ICC Interstate Commerce Commission
ICCE International Council for Computers in Education
ICU Intensive Care Unit
ID Idaho
IEEE Institute of Electrical and Electronics Engineers
IFC International Finance Corporation
IL, Ill. Illinois
illus. illustrated
ILO International Labor Organization
IMF International Monetary Fund
IN Indiana
Inc. Incorporated
Ind. Indiana
ind. independent
Indpls. Indianapolis
indsl. industrial
inf. infantry
info. information
ins. insurance
insp. inspector
inst. institute
instl. institutional
instn. institution
instr. instructor
instrn. instruction
instrnl. instructional
internat. international
intro. introduction
IRE Institute of Radio Engineers
IRS Internal Revenue Service

J

JAG Judge Advocate General
JAGC Judge Advocate General Corps
Jan. January
Jaycees Junior Chamber of Commerce
JB Jurum Baccalaureus
JCB Juris Canoni Baccalaureus
JCD Juris Canonici Doctor, Juris Civilis Doctor
JCL Juris Canonici Licentiatus
JD Juris Doctor
jg. junior grade
jour. journal
jr. junior
JSD Juris Scientiae Doctor
JUD Juris Utriusque Doctor
jud. judicial

K

Kans. Kansas
KC Knights of Columbus
KS Kansas
KY, Ky. Kentucky

L

LA, La. Louisiana
LA Los Angeles
lab. laboratory
L.Am. Latin America
lang. language
laryngol. laryngological
LB Labrador
LDS Latter Day Saints
lectr. lecturer
legis. legislation, legislative
LHD Doctor of Humane Letters
LI Long Island
libr. librarian, library
lic. licensed, license
lit. literature
litig. litigation
LittB Bachelor of Letters
LittD Doctor of Letters
LLB Bachelor of Laws
LLD Doctor of Laws
LLM Master of Laws
Ln. Lane
LPGA Ladies Professional Golf Association
LPN Licensed Practical Nurse
lt. lieutenant
Ltd. Limited
Luth. Lutheran
LWV League of Women Voters

M

M Master
m. married
MA Master of Arts
MA Massachusetts
MADD Mothers Against Drunk Driving
mag. magazine
MAgr Master of Agriculture
maj. major
Man. Manitoba
Mar. March
MArch Master in Architecture
Mass. Massachusetts
math. mathematics, mathematical
MB Bachelor of Medicine, Manitoba
MBA Master of Business Administration
MC Medical Corps
MCE Master of Civil Engineering
mcht. merchant
mcpl. municipal
MCS Master of Commercial Science
MD Doctor of Medicine
MD, Md. Maryland
MDiv Master of Divinity
MDip Master in Diplomacy
mdse. merchandise
MDV Doctor of Veterinary Medicine
ME Mechanical Engineer
ME Maine
M.E.Ch. Methodist Episcopal Church
mech. mechanical
MEd. Master of Education
med. medical
MEE Master of Electrical Engineering
mem. member
meml. memorial
merc. mercantile
met. metropolitan
metall. metallurgical
MetE Metallurgical Engineer

meteorol. meteorological
Meth. Methodist
Mex. Mexico
MF Master of Forestry
MFA Master of Fine Arts
mfg. manufacturing
mfr. manufacturer
mgmt. management
mgr. manager
MHA Master of Hospital Administration
MI Military Intelligence, Michigan
Mich. Michigan
micros. microscopic
mid. middle
mil. military
Milw. Milwaukee
Min. Minister
mineral. mineralogical
Minn. Minnesota
MIS Management Information Systems
Miss. Mississippi
MIT Massachusetts Institute of Technology
mktg. marketing
ML Master of Laws
MLA Modern Language Association
MLitt Master of Literature, Master of Letters
MLS Master of Library Science
MME Master of Mechanical Engineering
MN Minnesota
mng. managing
MO, Mo. Missouri
moblzn. mobilization
Mont. Montana
MP Member of Parliament
MPA Master of Public Administration
MPE Master of Physical Education
MPH Master of Public Health
MPhil Master of Philosophy
MPL Master of Patent Law
Mpls. Minneapolis
MRE Master of Religious Education
MRI Magnetic Resonance Imaging
MS Master of Science
MSc Master of Science
MSChemE Master of Science in Chemical Engineering
MSEE Master of Science in Electrical Engineering
MSF Master of Science of Forestry
MSN Master of Science in Nursing
MST Master of Sacred Theology
MSW Master of Social Work
MT Montana
Mt. Mount
mus. museum, musical
MusB Bachelor of Music
MusD Doctor of Music
MusM Master of Music
mut. mutual
MVP Most Valuable Player
mycol. mycological

N

N North
NAACOG Nurses Association of the American College of Obstetricians and Gynecologists
NAACP National Association for the Advancement of Colored People
NACA National Advisory Committee for Aeronautics
NACDL National Association of Criminal Defense Lawyers
NACU National Association of Colleges and Universities
NAD National Academy of Design
NAE National Academy of Engineering, National Association of Educators
NAESP National Association of Elementary School Principals
NAFE National Association of Female Executives
N.Am. North America
NAM National Association of Manufacturers
NAMH National Association for Mental Health
NAPA National Association of Performing Artists
NARAS National Academy of Recording Arts and Sciences
NAREB National Association of Real Estate Boards
NARS National Archives and Record Service
NAS National Academy of Sciences
NASA National Aeronautics and Space Administration
NASP National Association of School Psychologists
NASW National Association of Social Workers
nat. national
NATAS National Academy of Television Arts and Sciences
NATO North Atlantic Treaty Organization
NB New Brunswick
NBA National Basketball Association
NC North Carolina
NCAA National College Athletic Association
NCCJ National Conference of Christians and Jews
ND North Dakota
NDEA National Defense Education Act
NE Nebraska
NE Northeast
NEA National Education Association
Nebr. Nebraska
NEH National Endowment for Humanities
neurol. neurological
Nev. Nevada
NF Newfoundland
NFL National Football League
Nfld. Newfoundland
NG National Guard
NH New Hampshire
NHL National Hockey League
NIH National Institutes of Health
NIMH National Institute of Mental Health
NJ New Jersey
NLRB National Labor Relations Board
NM, N.Mex. New Mexico
No. Northern
NOAA National Oceanographic and Atmospheric Administration
NORAD North America Air Defense
Nov. November
NOW National Organization for Women
nr. near
NRA National Rifle Association
NRC National Research Council
N S Nova Scotia
NSC National Security Council
NSF National Science Foundation
NSTA National Science Teachers Association
NSW New South Wales
nuc. nuclear
numis. numismatic
NV Nevada
NW Northwest
NWT Northwest Territories
NY New York
NYC New York City
NYU New York University
NZ New Zealand

O

ob-gyn obstetrics-gynecology
obs. observatory
obstet. obstetrical
occupl. occupational
oceanog. oceanographic
Oct. October
OD Doctor of Optometry

OECD Organization for Economic Cooperation and Development
OEEC Organization of European Economic Cooperation
OEO Office of Economic Opportunity
ofcl. official
OH Ohio
OK, Okla. Oklahoma
ON, Ont. Ontario
oper. operating
ophthal. ophthalmological
ops. operations
OR Oregon
orch. orchestra
Oreg. Oregon
orgn. organization
orgnl. organizational
ornithol. ornithological
orthop. orthopedic
OSHA Occupational Safety and Health Administration
OSRD Office of Scientific Research and Development
OSS Office of Strategic Services
osteo. osteopathic
otol. otological
otolaryn. otolaryngological

P

PA, Pa. Pennsylvania
paleontol. paleontological
path. pathological
pediat. pediatrics
PEI Prince Edward Island
PEN Poets, Playwrights, Editors, Essayists and Novelists
penol. penological
pers. personnel
PGA Professional Golfers' Association of America
PHA Public Housing Administration
pharm. pharmaceutical
PharmD Doctor of Pharmacy
PharmM Master of Pharmacy
PhB Bachelor of Philosophy
PhD Doctor of Philosophy
PhDChemE Doctor of Science in Chemical Engineering
PhM Master of Philosophy
Phila. Philadelphia
philharm. philharmonic
philol. philological
philos. philosophical
photog. photographic
phys. physical
physiol. physiological
Pitts. Pittsburgh
Pk. Park
Pky. Parkway
Pl. Place
Plz. Plaza
PO Post Office
polit. political
poly. polytechnic, polytechnical
PQ Province of Quebec
PR Puerto Rico
prep. preparatory
pres. president
Presbyn. Presbyterian
presdl. presidential
prin. principal
procs. proceedings
prod. produced
prodn. production
prodr. producer
prof. professor
profl. professional
prog. progressive
propr. proprietor
pros. prosecuting
pro tem. pro tempore
psychiat. psychiatric
psychol. psychological
PTA Parent-Teachers Association
ptnr. partner
PTO Pacific Theatre of Operations, Parent Teacher Organization
pub. publisher, publishing, published, public
publ. publication
pvt. private

Q

quar. quarterly
qm. quartermaster
Que. Quebec

R

radiol. radiological
RAF Royal Air Force
RCA Radio Corporation of America
RCAF Royal Canadian Air Force
Rd. Road
R&D Research & Development
REA Rural Electrification Administration
rec. recording
ref. reformed
regt. regiment
regtl. regimental
rehab. rehabilitation
rels. relations
Rep. Republican
rep. representative
Res. Reserve
ret. retired
Rev. Reverend
rev. review, revised
RFC Reconstruction Finance Corporation
RI Rhode Island
Rlwy. Railway
Rm. Room
RN Registered Nurse
roentgenol. roentgenological
ROTC Reserve Officers Training Corps
RR rural route, railroad
rsch. research
rschr. researcher
Rt. Route

S

S South
s. son
SAC Strategic Air Command
SAG Screen Actors Guild
S.Am. South America
san. sanitary
SAR Sons of the American Revolution
Sask. Saskatchewan
savs. savings
SB Bachelor of Science
SBA Small Business Administration
SC South Carolina
ScB Bachelor of Science
SCD Doctor of Commercial Science
ScD Doctor of Science
sch. school
sci. science, scientific
SCV Sons of Confederate Veterans
SD South Dakota
SE Southeast
SEC Securities and Exchange Commission
sec. secretary
sect. section
seismol. seismological
sem. seminary
Sept. September
s.g. senior grade
sgt. sergeant
SI Staten Island
SJ Society of Jesus
SJD Scientiae Juridicae Doctor
SK Saskatchewan
SM Master of Science
SNP Society of Nursing Professionals
So. Southern
soc. society
sociol. sociological
spkr. speaker
spl. special
splty. specialty
Sq. Square
SR Sons of the Revolution
sr. senior
SS Steamship
St. Saint, Street
sta. station

stats. statistics
statis. statistical
STB Bachelor of Sacred Theology
stblzn. stabilization
STD Doctor of Sacred Theology
std. standard
Ste. Suite
subs. subsidiary
SUNY State University of New York
supr. supervisor
supt. superintendent
surg. surgical
svc. service
SW Southwest
sys. system

T

Tb. tuberculosis
tchg. teaching
tchr. teacher
tech. technical, technology
technol. technological
tel. telephone
telecom. telecommunications
temp. temporary
Tenn. Tennessee
TESOL Teachers of English to Speakers of Other Languages
Tex. Texas
ThD Doctor of Theology
theol. theological
ThM Master of Theology
TN Tennessee
tng. training
topog. topographical
trans. transaction, transferred
transl. translation, translated
transp. transportation
treas. treasurer
TV television
twp. township
TX Texas
typog. typographical

U

U. University
UAW United Auto Workers
UCLA University of California at Los Angeles
UK United Kingdom
UN United Nations
UNESCO United Nations Educational, Scientific and Cultural Organization
UNICEF United Nations International Children's Emergency Fund
univ. university
UNRRA United Nations Relief and Rehabilitation Administration
UPI United Press International
urol. urological
US, USA United States of America
USAAF United States Army Air Force
USAF United States Air Force
USAFR United States Air Force Reserve
USAR United States Army Reserve
USCG United States Coast Guard
USCGR United States Coast Guard Reserve
USES United States Employment Service
USIA United States Information Agency
USMC United States Marine Corps
USMCR United States Marine Corps Reserve
USN United States Navy
USNG United States National Guard
USNR United States Naval Reserve
USO United Service Organizations
USPHS United States Public Health Service
USS United States Ship
USSR Union of the Soviet Socialist Republics
USTA United States Tennis Association
UT Utah

V

VA Veterans Administration
VA, Va. Virginia
vet. veteran, veterinary
VFW Veterans of Foreign Wars
VI Virgin Islands
vis. visiting
VISTA Volunteers in Service to America
vocat. vocational
vol. volunteer, volume
v.p. vice president
vs. versus
VT, Vt. Vermont

W

W West
WA, Wash. Washington (state)
WAC Women's Army Corps
WAVES Women's Reserve, US Naval Reserve
WCTU Women's Christian Temperance Union
we. western
WHO World Health Organization
WI Wisconsin, West Indies
Wis. Wisconsin
WV, W.Va. West Virginia
WY, Wyo. Wyoming

X, Y, Z

YK Yukon Territory
YMCA Young Men's Christian Association
YMHA Young Men's Hebrew Association
YM & YWHA Young Men's and Young Women's Hebrew Association
yr. year
YT Yukon Territory
YWCA Young Women's Christian Association

Alphabetical Practices

Names are arranged alphabetically according to the surnames, and under identical surnames according to the first given name. If both surname and first given name are identical, names are arranged alphabetically according to the second given name.

Surnames beginning with De, Des, Du, however capitalized or spaced, are recorded with the prefix preceding the surname and arranged alphabetically under the letter D.

Surnames beginning with Mac and Mc are arranged alphabetically under M.

Surnames beginning with Saint or St. appear after names that begin Sains, and are arranged according to the second part of the name, e.g., St. Clair before Saint Dennis.

Surnames beginning with Van, Von, or von are arranged alphabetically under the letter V.

Compound surnames are arranged according to the first member of the compound.

Many hyphenated Arabic names begin Al-, El-, or al-. These names are alphabetized according to each biographee's designation of last name. Thus Al-Bahar, Neta may be listed either under Al- or under Bahar, depending on the preference of the listee.

Also, Arabic names have a variety of possible spellings when transposed to English. Spelling of these names is always based on the practice of the biographee. Some biographees use a Western form of word order, while others prefer the Arabic word sequence.

Similarly, Asian names may have no comma between family and given names, but some biographees have chosen to add the comma. In each case, punctuation follows the preference of the biographee.

Parentheses used in connection with a name indicate which part of the full name is usually omitted in common usage. Hence, Chambers, E(lizabeth) Anne indicates that the first name, Elizabeth, is generally recorded as an initial. In such a case, the parentheses are ignored in alphabetizing and the name would be arranged as Chambers, Elizabeth Anne.

However, if the entire first name appears in parentheses, for example, Chambers, (Elizabeth) Anne, the first name is not commonly used, and the alphabetizing is therefore arranged as though the name were Chambers, Anne.

If the entire middle name is in parentheses, it is still used in alphabetical sorting. Hence, Belamy, Katherine (Lucille) would sort as Belamy, Katherine Lucille. The same occurs if the entire last name is in parentheses, e.g., (Brandenberg), Howard Keith would sort as Brandenberg, Howard Keith.

For visual clarification:

Smith, H(enry) George: Sorts as Smith, Henry George
Smith, (Henry) George: Sorts as Smith, George
Smith, Henry (George): Sorts as Smith, Henry George
(Smith), Henry George: Sorts as Smith, Henry George

Who Was Who in America®

AARON, BENJAMIN, law educator, arbitrator; b. Chgo., Sept. 2, 1915; s. Henry Jacob and Rose (Weinstein) A.; m. Eleanor Opsahl, May 24, 1941; children: Judith, Louise. AB, U. Mich., 1937; LL.B., Harvard U., 1940; postgrad., U. Chgo., 1940-41. With Nat. War Labor Bd., 1942-45; mem. labor adv. com. to Supreme Comdr. Allied Powers, Tokyo, 1946; research assoc. Inst. Indsl. Relations; lectr. labor law, dept. econs. UCLA, 1946-51, assoc. dir., 1957-60, dir., 1960-75, prof. law, 1960-86, prof. emeritus, 1986—2007. Faculty mem. Salzburg (Austria) Seminar in Am. Studies, 1958, 67; arbitrator labor-mgmt. disputes, 1946—2007; pub. mem. WSB, Washington, 1951-52; mem. Statutory Arbitration Bd. in R.R. Dispute, 1963-64; chmn. Calif. Farm Labor Panel, 1965-66; mem. Nat. Commn. on Tech., Automation and Economic Progress, 1965-66; pub. mem. Adv. Council on Employee Welfare and Pension Benefit Plans, 1966-68; vis. prof. Harvard U., 1972, U. Mich., 1979; mem. pub. rev. bd. U.A.W., 1975—2007; mem. arbitration services adv. com. Fed. Mediation and Conciliation Service, 1974-82; mem. ILO Com. of Experts on Application of Convs. and Recommendations, 1986-94; charter emeritus fellow Coll. of Labor and Employment Lawyers, 1996-2007. Author: Legal Status of Employee Benefit Rights Under Private Pension Plans, 1961; Editor: The Employment Relation and The Law, 1957, Labor Courts and Grievance Settlement in Western Europe, 1970, Comparative Labor Law jour, 1979-85; co-editor: Industrial Conflict: A Comparative Legal Survey, 1972; Public-Sector Bargaining, 1979; mem. editl. bd. Internat. Labor Law Reps., 1974—2005. Fellow Ctr. for Advanced Study in Behavioral Scis., 1966-67; vis. fellow Clare Hall, Cambridge (Eng.) U., 1973, Australian Nat. U., 1982; named First Southwestern Legal Found. Rsch. Fellows Disting. Scholar in Residence, 1971; first Howard W. Wissner Meml. Lectr. Tulane U., 1971; Phi Beta Kappa vis. scholar, 1978-79 Mem. ABA (sec. sect. labor rels. law 1975-76), AAUP, Internat. Soc. Labor Law and Social Security (chmn. U.S. nat. com., internat. exec. com. 1967-83, v.p. N.Am. region 1982-85, pres. 1985-88, hon. pres. 1988—), Nat. Acad. Arbitrators (pres. 1962, bd. govs.), Indsl. Rels. Rsch. Assn. (exec. bd. 1965-68, pres. 1972, mem. CCH labor law reports panel of experts 1987-92), Am. Arbitration Assn. (mem. adv. coun. L.A. 1975-76, Disting. Svc. award 1981). Home: Santa Monica, Calif. Died Aug. 25, 2007.

AARON, ILENE BONDER, speech pathologist; b. Bklyn., May 7, 1920; d. Daniel and Esther (Kroll) Bonder; m. Abraham Aaron, June 29, 1943; children— Ellen, Cynthia Henry-Steven. B.A. magna cum laude, Queens Coll., 1975; M.A., L.I. U., 1977. Grad. asst. C.W. Post Coll., 1976-77, Herbert G. Birch Sch. for Exceptional Gifted, Queens, N.Y., 1976; speech pathologist Mexia State Rehabilitative Sch., Tex. State Mental Health-Mental Retardation Dept., 1978-79; speech pathologist Suffolk Devel. Ctr., N.Y. State Dept. Health, Melville, 1979—; acting speech coordinator speech dept. Creedmoor Psychiat. Ctr., Queens, 1984—. Mem. Am. Speech and Hearing Assn., L.I. Speech and Hearing Assn., Bus. and Profl. Women's Club, Alpha Sigma Lambda (pres. Upsilon chpt. 1973-74). Died June 20, 2006.

AARONSON, HUBERT IRVING, metallurgical engineering educator; b. NYC, July 10, 1924; s. Robert Benjamin A. BS, Carnegie Mellon U., 1948, MS, PhD, 1954. Research metallurgist Metals Research Lab., Carnegie Inst. Tech., 1953-57; supr. phase transformation sect. dept. metallurgy, sci. research staff Ford Motor Co., Dearborn, Mich., 1958-72; sr. vis. fellow U. Manchester, 1972; prof. dept. metall. engring. Mich. Tech. U., Houghton, 1972-79; R.F. Mehl prof. Carnegie-Mellon U., 1979. Editor: Decomposition of Austenite by Diffusional Processes, 1962, Phase Transformations, 1970, Diffusion, 1972, Procs. of Internat. Conf. on Solid-Solid Phase Transformations, 1983; contbr. numerous articles to profl. jours. Served to 1st lt. USAAF, 1943-46. Decorated Air medal with oak leaf cluster. Fellow Am. Soc. Metals (tech. div. bd. 1976-80, chmn. tech. div. bd. 1978-80, chmn. materials sci. div. 1976-78, Edgar C. Bain award Pitts. chpt. 1983, Albert Sauveur Achievement award 1987); mem. Minerals, Metals and Materials Soc.-AIME Champion H. Mathewson Gold medal 1968, Inst. Metals lectr. 1990, R.F. Mehl award 1990), Am. Soc. Metals, Inst. Metals (U.K.), Internat. Metall. Soc., Sigma Xi. Jewish. Died Dec. 13, 2005.

ABBOTT, BERNARD CYRIL, biology educator; b. E. Coker, Eng., Oct. 13, 1920; came to U.S., 1957, naturalized, 1977; s. Frederick B. and Daisy J. (Hawkins) A.; m. Doris Pontin, Oct. 4, 1944; 1 dau., Pauline. BS, Univ. Coll., London, 1941, PhD in Physiology, 1950. Lectr. biophysics and physiology Univ. Coll., 1946-53; prin. sci. officer Marine Biol. Assn., U.K., Plymouth, 1953-57; assoc. prof. zoology UCLA, 1957-62; prof. biophysics and physiology, head div. biophysics U. Ill., Urbana, 1962-68; prof. biol. scis. U. So. Calif., 1968-85, prof. emeritus, from 1985, chmn. dept. biol. scis., 1968-82. Instl. rep. Assn. Systematics Collections, 1972— Contbr. articles to profl. jours. Bd. dirs. Allan Hancock Found., 1968-82. Served to maj. Brit. Army, 1942-46. Fellow Inst. Physics London, Royal Soc. Medicine; mem. Am. Heart Assn. (Distinguished Scientist award 1975), Internat. Soc. Toxicology (council 1972—), Soc. Gen. Physiology (council 1964-77), Orgn. Tropical Studies (council 1969-73), Physiol. Soc. London, Am. Physiol. Soc., Biophys. Soc. (council 1968-72), Soc. Exptl. Biology, Marine Biol. Assn., Am. Soc. Zoologists, Biomed. Engring. Soc., Sigma Xi. Episcopalian. Died Jan. 20, 2006.

ABBRUZZESE, CARLO ENRICO, physician, writer, educator; b. Rome, May 28, 1923; came to U.S., 1951, naturalized, 1959; s. Aurelio and Maria (Sbriccoli) A.; m. Silvia Ramirez-Lemus; children: Marco A., Carlo M., Eric L., Christopher E., Romana S., Kevin R., Alvaro L. Liceo-Ginnasio, Dante Alighieri, Roma, 1935-43; Facoltà di Medicina e Chirurgia, Università di Roma, 1943-49; DSc, London Inst. Applied Rsch., 1973. Lic. med. dr. Italy, European Community, Calif. Resident in tropical subtropical diseases U. Rome, 1950-51; intern Woman's and Highland Park Gen. hosps., Detroit, 1951-53; resident in family practice Saratoga Gen. Hosp., Detroit, Columbus Hosp., Newark, 1953-57; gen. practice occupational and sport medicine Rome, 1949-51, Oakland, Calif., 1958-75, Santa Ana, Calif., 1975-84. Dir. emergency and outpatient depts. Drs. Hosp. Santa Ana, Calif., 1975-77; dir. North Bristol Family Med. Clinic, Rsch. and Diagnostic Lab. Author: Storia della Psicologia, 1949, Roma, L'ascoltazione Stetoscopica del cuore, RCA italiana, 1953, L'ascoltazione stetoscopica, 1955, 56, 83, 86, Roma, 1986, Esercitazioni di diagnostica ascoltatoria, 1983, 86; founder, pub., editor-in-chief ESDNA, Rome, 1983, ESDI, Rome, 1986; pub. Med. Newsletter, 1987; contbr. articles to profl. jours. Founder, leader polit. youth movements, Rome, 1943-47; co-founder, nat. chmn. U.S. divorce reforms orgns., 1975; UN rep. on violation of due process and domestic human rights, 1977; exec. officer Men Internat., Calif.; active Nat. Italian Am. Found. Decorated Commendatore di Merito, 1950, Gran Croce Merito del Lavoro, Internat. Bus. Corp., 1981; Fulbright fellow, 1951-53. Fellow Am. Acad. Family Physicians; mem. AMA, Calif. Med. Assn., Orange County Med. Assn., Ordine dei Medici di Roma, Societá Italiana di Chirurgia, Union Am. Physicians, Am. Acad. Family Practice (co-founder). Home: Beaverton, Oreg. Died Mar. 22, 2006.

ABEL, BRENT MAXWELL, lawyer, director; b. Washington, May 6, 1916; s. Charles and Susan Alice (Maxwell) A.; m. Georgiana Powell, May 17, 1941 (div. 1972); children: Brent Maxwell, Molly Abel Warner; m. Corinne W. VanHorne, Nov. 2, 1973. AB, Harvard, 1937, LL.B., 1940. Bar: N.Y. 1940, Calif. 1946. Assoc. Cravath, Swaine & Moore, NYC, 1940-41, McCutchen, Doyle, Brown & Enersen and predecessors, San Francisco, 1946-54, ptnr., 1954-86, of counsel, from 1986. Vis. lectr. law U. Calif., 1955-60; trustee U.S. Trust Co. N.Y., 1979-88; mem. overseers com. to visit Harvard Law Sch., 1967-68, chmn., 1977-82 Bd. dirs. San Francisco chpt. Am. Cancer Soc., 1957-63, pres., 1959-60; trustee Anna Head Sch., Oakland, Calif., 1962-71, Phillips Exeter Acad., Exeter, N.H., 1959-75, 80-84, bd. overseers Harvard U., 1975-81. Served with USNR, 1941-46; Capt. Res. Decorated Navy Cross, Navy Unit commendation ribbon. Mem. Phillips Exeter Acad. Gen. Alumni Assn. (pres. 1964-66), Bar Assn. San Francisco (pres. 1964), Am. Bar Assn., State Bar Calif. (bd. govs. 1972-75, pres. 1974-75), Harvard Law Sch. Assn. No. Calif. (pres. 1961), San Francisco Legal Aid Soc. (pres. 1967-68), Asso. Harvard Alumni (pres. 1971-72) Clubs: Bohemian (San Francisco), Bankers (San Francisco), Pacific Union (San Francisco); Harvard (N.Y.C.). Home: San Francisco, Calif. Died Dec. 26, 2005.

ABEL, ROBERT BERGER, science administrator; b. Providence, July 21, 1926; s. Abraham Lincoln and Betty Ruth (Berger) A.; m. Nancy Marilyn Klein, Oct. 4, 1953; children: Alan Stewart, Deborah Jane. BS in Chemistry, Brown U., 1947; MEA, George Washington U., 1961; PhD, Am. U., 1972. Chemist Woods Hole (Mass.) Oceanographic Inst., 1947-50; oceanographer U.S. Navy Hydrographic Office, Suitland, Md., 1950-55; asst. to dir. U.S. Navy Hydrog. Office, 1955-60; asst. research coordinator Office Naval Research, Washington, 1961-64; exec. sec. Interagy. Com. Oceanography, 1960-67; asst. exec. sec. Nat. Council Marine Resources and Engring. Devel., 1967-68; dir. Nat. Sea Grant Program, Dept. Commerce, 1966-77; asst. v.p. Tex. A&M U., 1977—80; v.p. N.J. Marine Scis. Consortium, Fort. Hancock, 1979-81, pres., 1981-93; sr. sci. Stevens Inst. Tech., Hoboken, NJ, 1993—2007. Instr. oceanography USNR Officers Sch., 1960-65, Fairleigh Dickinson U., 1966-83, U. Va., 1976-77; instr. ocean mgmt. Rutgers U., 1980-84; dir. Israel Oceanographic and Limnol. Rsch. Ltd., Inc.; mem. panel Nat. Acad. Scis.; mgr. Cooperative Marine Tech. Program for Middle East, 1980-2007; mem. N.J. Marine Fisheries Coun., 1993-2007; mem. N.J. Aquaculture Adv. Coun.; chmn. adv. com. Jersey Shore Partnership; cruise lectr. Cunard, Crystal, Holland Am., Celebrity, Lindblad and Seabourne Lines. Pres. Cris-Mar Manor Civic Assn., 1957-61; bd. dirs. Tantallon Civic Assn., 1973-74, Ctr. Ocean Law and Policy; v.p. Jewish Congregation; chmn. Zoning Bd., Shrewsbury, N.J., 1990-2001. Active duty USN, 1945—46, recruiting officer USN, 1946—47, RI, instr. Naval Reserve Officers Sch. USN, 1960—66, active USNR, 1945—65. Recipient Spl. award Prince of Monaco, 1952, Superior Civilian Svc. award Navy Dept., 1963, Disting. Svc. award, 1967, Disting. Alumnus award George Washington U., 1983, Compass Disting. Svc. award, 1987, Disting. Svc. award Egyptian Nat. Inst. Oceanography and Fisheries; Gold medal Dept. Commerce, 1973; named Man of Yr. Nat. Sea Grant Program, 1977; decorated Order Jules Richard, Monaco, 1951. Mem. Am. Chem. Soc., Rsch. Soc. Am. (past pres. chpt.), Marine Tech. Soc. (pres. 1974-75), Am. Geophys. Union, Am. Soc. Oceanography (pres. 1971-72), Cosmos Club (Washington), Brown Club NJ, B'Nai Israel Congregation (bd. trustees). Jewish. Home: Shrewsbury, NJ. Died Oct. 10, 2007.

ABELES, THEODORE LILLIEN, lawyer; b. NYC, July 23, 1934; s. Theodore Jerome and Ethel Harriet (Lillien) A.; m. Joan Susan Riemer, Apr. 8, 1967; children: Marc, Scott, Robyn. BS in Fgn. Svc., Georgetown U., 1953; LLB, NYU, 1956. Bar: N.Y. 1957, N.J. 1957. Assoc. Lum Brunno & Tompkins, Newark, 1956-64, ptnr., 1965-83, Lum Hoens Abeles Conant & Danzis, Roseland, N.J., 1983-89, Sills Cummis Zuckerman Radin Tischman Epstein & Gross, Newark, 1989-93, Tompkins, McGuire & Wachenfeld, Newark, from 1993. Pres. Suburban Investment Co., West Orange, N.J., 1978—, Cummings Realty Co., West Orange, 1978; bd. dirs. Liberty Optical Mfg. Co., Newark, ADM Corp., Middlesex, N.J. Assoc. editor NYU Law Rev., 1955-56. Pub. bd. dirs. Bankers Nat. Life Ins. Co., Parsippany, N.J., 1973-74; chmn., vice chmn. West Orange Zoning Bd., 1986—; chmn. bd. trustees Woodland Cemetery, Newark, 1980—. Mem. ABA, N.J. Bar Assn. (fellow 1979-80), N.Y. State Bar Assn., Essex County Bar Assn., West Orange Tennis Club. Jewish. Avocation: painting. Home: West Orange, NJ. Died May 12, 2006.

ABELOFF, MARTIN DAVID, medical administrator, educator, researcher; b. Shenandoah, Pa., Apr. 4, 1942; s. Aaron Harry and Cele (Freid) A.; m. Diane Kaufman, Jan. 7, 1967; children: Elisa, Jennifer. Student, Franklin and Marshall Coll., 1959-61; AB, Johns Hopkins U., 1963, MD, 1966. Diplomate Am. Bd. Internal Medicine, subspecialty in med. oncology. Intern U. Chgo. Hosps. and Clinics, 1966-67; clin. assoc. Balt. Cancer Rsch. Ctr., 1967-69; sr. asst. resident in medicine Beth Israel Hosp., Boston, 1969-70; fellow in clin. hematology New Eng. Med. Ctr., Boston, 1970-71; fellow in clin. oncology Sch. Medicine Johns Hopkins U., Balt., 1971-72, instr. in medicine, 1972-75, asst. prof. oncology, 1974-79, asst. prof. medicine, 1975-80, prof. medicine, 1990—2007, Eli Kennerly Mashall Jr. prof. oncology, dir., Sidney Kimmel Comprehensive Cancer Ctr., 2000—07; prof. & dir. Johns Hopkins Oncology Ctr., Balt., 1992—2007. Numerous vis. professorships and lectrs. including Institut Jules Bordet, Brussels, Milton S. Hershey Med. Ctr., Nat. Cancer Inst., U. Ariz., SUNY, Stony Brook, U. So. Calif., U. Chgo., U. Md., Boston U., Mayo Clinic, others; advisor St. George's Soc., Am. Cancer Soc., 1974-84; chmn. psychosocial com. Ea. Coop. Oncology Group, 1979-83; cons. reviewer for clin. oncology rev. com. divsn. cancer treatment Nat. Cancer Inst., Bethesda, Md., 1980-2007. Editorial bd. Lung Cancer, 1985-2007, PDQ, NCI, 1986-88, Cancer Rsch., 1993; assoc. editor Jour. Clin. Oncology, 1987-96, Oncology, 1987-2007; assoc. editor, editorial bd. Cancer Treatment Reports, 1980-83; editor Clin. Oncology, 1992-2007, Oncology News Internat.; sect. editor Annals of Surg. Oncology, 1993-2007; adv. bd. The Med. Letter, 1991-2007; mem. editorial adv. bd. Health After 50, 1989-2007; contbr. numerous articles to profl. jours., chpts. to books. Bd. dirs. Md. divsn. Am. Cancer Soc., 1985-86. Mem. Am. Soc. Clin. Oncology (mem. ednl. com. 1978-80, mem. program com. 1981-83, chmn. program 1983-84, bd. dirs. 1984-87, chmn. com. on patterns of care 1986-87, chmn. ad-hoc com. for FDA liaison 1988-89, pres. 1991-92), Am. Assn. Cancer Rsch., Internat. Assn. for Study of Lung Cancer, Am. Assn. Cancer Edn., Phi Beta Kappa. Died Sept. 7, 2007.

ABERNATHY, ROBERT SHIELDS, medical educator; b. Gastonia, NC, Nov. 18, 1923; s. Thomas Jackson and Emma Frances (Glenn) A.; m. Rosalind Gower Smith, Apr. 2, 1949; children— Robert S., David S., Susan G., Thomas G., Douglas L. Student, Davidson Coll., 1941-43, MIT, 1943-44, Yale U., 1944; BS, MD, Duke U., 1949; PhD, U. Minn., 1957. Diplomate: Am. Bd. Internal Medicine. Intern U. Minn., 1949-50, fellow in medicine, 1950-51, 53-54, research fellow, 1954-55, instr. medicine, microbiology and lab. medicine, 1955-57; asst. prof. medicine and microbiology U. Ark. Med. Center, Little Rock, 1957-60, assoc. prof., 1960-66, prof., from 1966, chmn. dept. medicine, 1967-76, dir. infectious diseases, from 1976. Cons. VA Hosp., Little Rock.; Mem. regional adv. group Ark. Regional Med. Program, 1966—; panel mem. NRC, 1966-68; mem. com. Nat. Heart and Lung Inst., 1970-72; cons. USPHS, 1966— Editorial cons., various med. jours. Served with M.C. AUS, 1943-45, 51-53. Borden grantee Duke U., 1949; ACP fellow, 1954-55 Fellow A.C.P. (gov. 1971—); mem. Am. Thoracic Soc., Infectious Disease Soc., Assn. Profs. Medicine, Sigma Xi, Alpha Omega Alpha. Research brucellosis, bacterial endotoxins, autoimmunity in neurologic diseases, other. Home: Little Rock, Ark. Died Feb. 21, 2007.

ABRAMS, EDWARD MARVIN, construction company executive; b. South Bend, Ind., Mar. 13, 1927; s. Alfred Robert and Sara Lee (Kaufman) A.; m. Ann Uhry, Oct. 11, 1953; children: Alan Ralph, Laurie, James Andrew. Student, Ga. Inst. Tech., 1947-48; BS cum laude, U. Notre Dame, 1950; grad., Naval Officer Candidate Sch., 1951. Pres. Abrams Industries, Inc., Atlanta, 1953-95, chmn. bd. dirs., 1995-98, chmn. exec. com., 1998—2004, chmn. emeritus, from 2004. Mem. faculty Univ. of Shopping Ctrs., Ga. adv. bd. Liberty Mut. Ins. Co. Mem. interreligious affairs com. Am. Jewish Com., 1969—, chmn. Atlanta chpt., 1971-73, mem. nat. task force on social club discrimination; mem. adv. council Coll. Arts and Letters, U. Notre Dame, 1972—, chmn., 1977-78; co-chmn. Ga. region NCCJ, 1977-78; active United Way Metro Atlanta. Served with USN, 1945-47, 50-52. Mem. Internat. Council Shopping Centers, Ga. Engring. Soc., Atlanta C. of C. (chmn. aviation task force com. 1981, adv. bd. 1999-2000), Notre Dame Alumni Assn., Commerce Club (Atlanta), Notre Dame Club (Atlanta). Home: Atlanta, Ga. Died Feb. 22, 2007.

ABZUG, MALCOLM, flight mechanics engineer; b. NY, Apr. 13, 1920; BS, Mass. Inst. Tech., 1941; MS, Univ. Calif., 1959, PhD, 1962. Asst. aeronautical engr. aircraft lab. U.S. Air Corps, 1941-43; project engr. flight control dept. Sperry Gyroscope Co., 1949-52; aerodyn. engr. stability & control group Douglas Co., 1946048, design specialist, 1952-55, supr., 1955-62; chief astrodyn. br. Missile & Space Systems Divsn., Santa Monica, 1963-64; sr. staff engr. TRW System, Inc., 1962-67; cons., from 1976. Cons. Cambridge Univ. Press, 1951-57, guest lectr. Univ. Calif., L.A., 1958; adj. prof. Univ. Southern Calif., 1980-86. Recipient Douglas Aircraft Co. award, 1957, 64. Fellow Am. Inst. Aeronautical & Astronautical; mem. Nat. Acad. Engring. Home: Pacific Palisades, Calif. Died May 23, 2007.

ACKERMAN, BETTYE LOUISE (MRS. SAM JAFFE), actress; b. Cottageville, SC, Feb. 28, 1924; d. Clarence Kilgo and Mary Mildred (Baker) A.; m. Sam Jaffe, June 7, 1956 (dec.). Student, Columbia Coll., 1945; BA, Columbia U., 1946-50; student, Otis Art Inst., 1964-68, Theatre Wing, NYC, 1954-56, Stella Adler Sch., 1956-58; L.H.D. (hon.), Drew U., 1983; D.F.A. (hon.), Columbia Coll., 1986. Stage appearances include Pheelie in No 'count Boy, 1954, Elmire in Tartuffe, 1955, 56, Antigone In Sophocles Trilogy, N.Y.C., 1956, tour of The Lark, 1956-57, Portia in Merchant of Venice, Dickinson (N.D.) State Coll., 1971, An Evening with Edna St. Vincent Millay, Wesleyan Coll., Macon, Ga., 1986, A Pure Desire, Georgia O'Keeffe Centennial Celebration, Columbia (S.C.) Coll., 1987; (films) Face of Fire, 1958, Rascal, 1969, Love and Venice, 1989, Pre-Hysteria II, 1994; (TV movies) Companions in Nightmare, 1968, Heat of Anger, 1971, Murder or Mercy, 1974, The Feather and Father Gang, 1977, The Yeagers, 1979, Confessions of a Married Man, 1982, A Day of Thanks on Walton's Mountain, 1982, others; appeared as Maggie Graham on Ben Casey TV series, 1961-66; as Anne Frazier in TV series Bracken's World; appeared in over 400 television shows, numerous guest appearances Good Morning America; numerous others; tchr. body movement, Lucy Feagin Sch. Drama, N.Y.C., 1953, recorded Salome and School for Scandal; lectr., demonstrator ethnic dances, Louise Gifford Pantomime classes Columbia U., 1954-56; one-woman art shows, Erskine Coll., Due West, S.C., 1970, 76, 82, 96, Lambert Gallery, Los Angeles, 1970, Columbia Coll., 1971, 86, Monterey Peninsula Mus. of Art, 1980, Drew U., 1982, U.S. Internat. U., 1982, Wesleyan Coll., 1986; retrospective show Atrium Gallery, Augusta, Ga, 1992, one woman Art Show, Heritage Gallery Los Angeles, Calif., 1996,; group shows, Gallery 8, Claremont, Calif., 1976, Galleria Beretich, Claremont, Calif., 1981, Ambassador Galleries, Inc., N.Y.C., 1996, Heritage Gallery, Los Angeles Calif., 1996, United States Internat. U., San Diego Calif., 1985, Two Person Art Shows Include; Harvey Mudd Coll., Claremont, Calif., 1993, Galleria Beretich, Claremont, Calif., 1993, 87, 81. West Coast campaign chmn. Muscular Dystrophy Assn., 1963-69; sec., bd. dirs. Hollywood Motion Picture and TV Mus. First woman grand marshall I Am An American and Constitution Day Parade, Balt., 1972. Home: Beverly Hills, Calif. Died Nov. 1, 2006.

ACKERMAN, BRUCE DAVID, pediatrician, neonatologist, educator; b. N.Y.C., Mar. 12, 1934; s. John and Ida (Waldman) A.; m. Jean M. Pedevill, Mar. 16, 1957 (div. June 1976); children— Lisa, Stacy. A.B., NYU, 1954; M.D., U. Chgo., 1958. Diplomate Am. Bd. Pediatrics, Am. Bd. Neonatal and Perinatal Medicine. Intern Geisinger Med. Ctr., Danville, Pa., 1958-59, resident in pediatrics, 1959-61; fellow in neonatology U. Pitts., 1963-65; instr. pediatrics U. Calif.-Irvine, 1965, asst. prof., 1966-71, assoc. prof., 1971-72; dir. neonatology L.I. Jewish Med. Ctr., N.Y.C., 1972-74, Beth Israel Med. Ctr., N.Y.C., 1974-75; assoc. dir. pediatrics, dir. neonatology Maimonides Med. Ctr., Bklyn., 1975—. Contbr. numerous articles to profl. jours. Campaign worker Congl. campaign of Charles Schumer, Bklyn., 1980. Served to capt. U.S. Army, 1961-63. Mem. Soc. for Pediatric Research, N.Y. Perinatal Soc., Physicians for Choice, N.Y. Friends of Peace Now. Democrat. Jewish. Avocations: travel; chess; photography; Spanish literature. Home: New York, NY. Died Oct. 16, 2006.

ACKERMAN, JAY (JOHN CHARLES ACKERMAN), former state legislator; b. Morton, Ill., Nov. 23, 1933; m. Joann Rhoades Ackerman; 4 children. Student, U. Ill. Mem. Ill. Ho. Reps. from Dist. 89, 1979—82, 1987—99. Mem. Agr., Urban Redevel., Econ. Devel., Elem. and Secondary Edn. and Pub. Utilities, Registration and Regulation Coms.; farmer. Mem. Ill. Sportsman's Caucus (co-vice chair). Died July 23, 2007.

ACOSTA, HERNANDO, architect; b. Bogota, Columbia, July 23, 1928; came to U.S., naturalized, 1968; s. Lissandro and Merceds (Sanchez) A.; m. F. Margot Schroedel, Dec. 28, 1965; 1 son, Paul H. D.Arch. Nat. U. Colombia, 1954. Cert. Nat. Council Archtl. Registration Bd. Pres., ARK Ltd., Bogota, 1953-55; chief designer Rufus Nims, Architect, Miami, Fla., 1956-59; chief designer Robert B. Browne, Architect, Miami, 1959-66; ptnr. Irani & Acosta, Architects & Engrs., Miami, 1967-68; ptnr. Treister & Acosta, Architects, Miami, 1968-73; owner Hernando Acosta, Architects, P.A., Miami, 1973—; lectr. architecture Miami-Dade Community Coll. Mem., City of Miami Com. on Ecology and Beautification. Served as lt. Colombian Army, 1953-54. Mem. AIA, Fla. Assn. AIA, Sociedad Colombiana de Arquitectos Club: Coconut Grove Sailing. Designer award winning pub. housing in U.S. and Caribbean; award winning comml. bldgs. in Fla. Home: Miami, Fla. Died Oct. 21, 2006.

ADAMS, ARTHUR EUGENE, former university official; b. Indianola, Iowa, Apr. 11, 1917; s. Arthur Henry and Armenia (James) A.; m. Ouida Janet Steckelberg, Aug. 9, 1942; children: Russell James, Joan Catherine. BA, U. Nebr., 1942; PhD, Cornell U., 1951. Ford faculty postdoctoral fellow Harvard U., 1954-55; prof. history Mich. State U., 1951-70, chmn. Russian and Eastern European studies program, 1963-70; prof. history, dean Coll. Humanities, Ohio State U., 1970-77, prof. history, asso. provost, 1977-78, vice provost, 1978-82, coordinator univ. research complex, 1982-84, prof. emeritus, from 1984. Cons. on Soviet Union affairs Radio Free Europe, 1961-63, NEH, 1966-70; bd. dirs. Midwest Univs. Consortium for Internat. Activities, 1977-83; mem. commn. on accreditation Am. Council Edn., 1978-82; mem. adv. group on adult edn. Coll. Bd., 1980-82 Author: An Historical Atlas of Russia and East Europe, 1967, Bolsheviks in the Ukraine (Borden award Hoover Inst. and Libr. 1963), Men Versus Systems: Agriculture in the USSR, Poland and Czechoslovakia, 1971, Stalin and His Times, 1972, Quimby, 1988, (with Ronald Suny) The Russian Revolution and Bolshevik Victory, 1960, 3d edit., 1989. Mem. Commn. for a Greater Columbus, 1979-84, Radio Free Europe/Radio Liberty Bd., 1978-82. Served to maj. AUS, 1942-46. Social Sci. Research Council grantee, 1956; Carnegie Corp. Inter-Univ. travel grantee to USSR, 1957; recipient Outstanding Prof. award Mich. State U., 1959, Ohio State U. Disting. Service award, 1986. Mem. Am. Hist. Assn., Mich. Acad. Arts and Scis. (chmn. Russian studies sect. 1960-61, 65-66), Am. Assn. Advancement Slavic Studies (bd. Midwest Slavic Conf. 1968-69), Phi Beta Kappa, Phi Kappa Phi, Delta Tau Kappa. Home: Columbus, Ohio. Died Aug. 6, 2007.

ADAMS, DANIEL NELSON (NELSON ADAMS), lawyer; b. Dec. 30, 1909; m. Diana Gerli (dec. 1995); 1 child, Daniel Jr. AB in History & English, Yale U., 1932; LLB, Harvard U., 1935. Bar: N.Y. 1937. Law clk. to Hon. Leonard Hand US Ct. Appeals (2nd cir.), 1935—36; assoc. Davis Polk & Wardwell, NYC, 1936—49, ptnr., 1949—70, head tax dept., 1950—77, mng. ptnr., 1970—77, sr. counsel, 1977—2007. Served in Army Air Corps. Mem. ABA, N.Y. State Bar Assn., Assn. of Bar of City of N.Y., N.Y. County Lawyers Assn., Am. Law Inst. Died May 31, 2007.

ADAMS, DOUGLAS GLENN, religious studies educator; b. DeKalb, Ill., Apr. 12, 1945; s. Glenn Hammer and Harriet Foote (Engstrom) A.; m. Margo Alice Miller, June 7, 1968. BA, Duke U., 1967; MA, MDiv, Pacific Sch. of Religion, 1970; ThD, Grd. Theol. Union, 1974. Ordained United Ch. of Christ, 1970. Asst. pastor Arlington Community Ch., Kensington, Calif., 1968-70; pastor Coll. Heights Ch., San Mateo, Calif., 1970-72; asst. prof. religion dept. U. Mont., Missoula, 1975-76; asst. prof. Pacific Sch. Religion & Grad. Theol. Union, Berkeley, Calif., 1976-79, assoc. prof., 1979-84, prof., 1984—2007. Editorial bd. mem. Modern Liturgy, San Jose, Calif., Church Teachers, Durham, N.C. Author: Humor in the American Pulpit, 1975, Meeting House to Camp Meeting, 1981, Transcendence with the Body in Art, 1991; editor: Art as Religious Studies, 1987, Dance as Religious Studies, 1990. Pres. Internat. Sacred Dance Guild, N.Y., 1977-79. Named Overseas Fellow Third Internat. Congress of Religion Art & Architecture, Jerusalem, 1973, Vis. Theologian, The Rockwell Found., Univ. Houston, Tex., 1986; recipient of Post-doctoral Fellowship in Art History, Nat. Mus. Am. Art, Smithsonian Instn., Washington, 1974-75. Fellow Soc. for the Arts, Religion and Contemporary Culture, N. Am. Acad. of Liturgy (chmn. fine arts com.); mem. Am. Acad. Religion (chmn. arts sect. 1984-86), Am. Acad. Homiletics, Coll. Art Assn. Democrat. Home: Richmond, Calif. Died July 24, 2007.

ADAMS, MARK, artist; b. Ft. Plain, NY, Oct. 27, 1925; s. Earl D. and Edith (Wohlgemuth) A.; m. Beth Van Hoesen, Sept. 12, 1953. Student, Syracuse U., 1943-46, Hans Hofmann Sch. Fine Arts, 1946-48, Jean Lurcat, 1955. Instr. San Francisco Art Inst., 1961; panelist Internat. Symposium on Tapestry, San Francisco, 1976; disting. vis. prof. U. Calif. at Davis, 1978; painter in residence Am. Acad. in Rome, 1963 Book: Mark Adams, 1985; one-man shows include deYoung Mus., San Francisco, 1959, Portland (Oreg.) Mus., 1961, Calif. Palace of Legion of Honor, San Francisco, 1961, retrospective, 1970, San Francisco Mus. Modern Art, 1962, French & Co., N.Y.C., 1964, John Berggruen Gallery, San Francisco, 1978, 80, 82, 83, 85, 87, 90, 94, Graham Modern, N.Y.C., 1981, 84, Jane Haslem Salon, Washington, 1989, Palo Alto (Calif.) Cultural Ctr., 1990; exhibited in numerous group shows including Mus. Contemporary Crafts, N.Y.C., 1957, 58, 62, 65, Dallas Mus., 1958, Internat. Biennial of Tapestry, Lausanne, Switzerland, 1962, 65, St. Louis Art Mus., 1964, Norfolk Mus., 1966; represented in permanent collections San Francisco Mus. Modern Art, Dallas Mus. Fine Arts, Chase Manhattan Bank, N.Y.C., San Francisco Pub. Library, Legion of Honor Mus., San Francisco; maj. archtl. commns. include tapestries, Bank of Calif., San Francisco, Weyerhauser Co., Tacoma, Wash., Fairmont Hotel, Dallas, San Francisco Internat. Airport, Luth. Brotherhood, Mpls., stained glass, Temple Emanu-el, San Francisco, St. Thomas More Cath. Ch., San Francisco, St. Andrews Episcopal Ch., Saratoga, Calif. Died Jan. 24, 2006.

ADAMS, NATHANIEL JAMES, architect; b. Buhl, Idaho, July 16, 1921; s. William C. and Naomi K. (Bristow) Adams; m. Sally Louise Lake, Mar. 21, 1948; children: Thomas Lake, John William. BS in Architecture, U. Oreg., 1950. Lic. arch., Idaho. Pres., owner Nat J. Adams & Assocs., Archs., Boise, Idaho, from 1955. Bd. dirs. St. Luke's Hosp., Boise, 1962—79. Lt. comdr. USN, 1942—46, PTO. Mem.: AIA (chpt. bd. dirs. 1966—67, chpt. pres. 1965—66), Arid Club (bd. dirs. 1971—72), Rotary (bd. dirs. 1979—80). Home: Boise, Idaho. Died Aug. 21, 2007.

ADAMS, RICHARD D., state legislator; b. Mar. 10, 1943; BS, JD, U. Ky. Mem. Ky. State Senate, Frankfort, from 1999, mem. agri. and natural resources com., mem. econ. devel. and tourism com., judiciary com., mem. labor and industry com. Previously atty. Active Boy Scouts Am., Big Bros./Big Sisters, Am. Heart Assn., Am. Cancer Soc., YMCA, Habitat for Humanity. Fellow Lafferty Soc. U. Ky. Coll. Law. Fellow Ky. Bar Found. Democrat. Baptist. Home: Madisonville, Ky. Died Apr. 3, 2006.

ADAMS, RICHARD EDWARD, management consultant, former aerospace company executive; b. Springfield, Ohio, Aug. 14, 1921; s. Fred Curren and Carrie (Miller) Adams; m. Grace Butler, Nov. 17, 1945; children: Richard Winfield, Elaine Butler Adams Hall, Anne Curren. BSME, Purdue U., 1942, DEng (hon.), 1977. Registered profl. engr., Calif., Tex. With Gen. Dynamics, Inc., from 1951, v.p. engring. Convair div. San Diego, 1970—71, v.p., gen. mgr., 1971—74, corp. v.p., 1974—81, corp. exec. v.p. Aerospace Ft. Worth, 1981—87; cons. in engring., from 1987. Bd. dirs. Exec. Svc. Corp., Tarrant Co., Ft. Worth. Mem. adv. coun. McDonald Obs. U. Tex., Gen. Dynamics bd., 1981—87; past mem. tech. adv. bd. So. Meth. U. Found. Sci. and Engring.; bd. dirs. Tarrant County United Way, Ft. Worth Arts Coun., N. Tex. coun. Boy Scouts Am., Tex. Christian U. Research Found., YMCA Met. Ft. Worth, Carter Blood Ctr. Named Silver Knight NMA. Mem.: NAE. Christian Ch. Home: Fort Worth, Tex. Died Feb. 17, 2007.

ADAMS, VERA GERTRUDE, market research data collection company executive; b. Denver, June 25, 1920; d. Hubert Charles and Margaret (Dawson) Farrow; m. Lawrence Elmer Adams, Dec. 30, 1937; children— George Gordon, Bettie Ann, Lawreen Edna. Student Metro State Coll., Denver, 1975-80. Interviewer Linda Calloway, Denver, 1948-62; supr. Knop Interviewing, Lakewood, Colo., 1962-71; owner Adams Research, Denver, 1971-72; mgr. Quality Controlled, Denver, 1972-75; pres. Info. Research, Denver, 1975—. Mem. Am. Mktg. Assn., Market Research Assn. Methodist. Club: Deer Creek Assn. (treas. 1984—) (Bailey, Colo.). Home: Littleton, Colo. Died July 8, 2006.

ADAMS, WILLIAM LEROY, petroleum company executive; b. Clay Center, Kans., May 23, 1929; s. Glenn Cook and Elizabeth (Osenbaugh) A.; m. Betty Ann Froehlich, Aug. 29, 1954; children: Glenn A., Craig W., Drew H., Kenneth P. BS, U. Kans., 1951; MS, UCLA, 1956; A.M.P., U. Va., 1970. Cert. petroleum geologist. With Amoco Prodn. Co., 1956-81; v.p. exploration Amoco Prodn., Chgo., 1975-79, regional v.p. New Orleans, 1979-81; exec. v.p. Champlin Petroleum Co. (now Union Pacific Resources Co.), Ft. Worth, 1981-82, pres., chief operating officer, 1982-86, chmn., chief exec. officer, 1986-91, chmn., from 1991, also dir. Ft. Worth. Bd. dirs. Am. Petroleum Inst., Mid-Continent Oil & Gas, The Van Cliburn Found., Tex. Rsch. League. Mem. nat. exec. bd. Boy Scouts Am., Irving, Tex.; trustee Tex. Christian U.; mem. adv. bd. Edwin L. Cox Sch. of Bus. at So. Meth. U.; bd. dirs. Downtown Ft. Worth Assn. Served to lt. USN, 1951-54, Korea. Recipient Best Tech. Paper award Am. Assn. Petroleum Geologists, 1963 Mem. Am. Petroleum Inst., Am. Assn. Petroleum Geologists, Mid-Continent Oil and Gas Assn., Kansas Univ. Geology Assocs., Nat. Petroleum Council. Clubs: Fort Worth, Fort Worth Wildcatters, Shady Oaks Country; Petroleum, Century II, Ridglea Country. Republican. Home: Fort Worth, Tex. Died Feb. 12, 2007.

ADLER, ROBERT, electronics engineer; b. Vienna, Dec. 4, 1913; came to U.S., 1940, naturalized, 1945; s. Max and Jenny (Herzmark) A.; m. Mary F. Buehl, 1946 (dec. Jan. 1993); m. Ingrid C. Koch, 1998. PhD in Physics, U. Vienna, 1937. Asst. to patent atty., Vienna, 1937-38; lab. Sci. Acoustics, Ltd., London, United Kingdom, Assoc. Rsch., Inc., Chgo., 1940-41; research group Zenith Radio Corp., Chgo., 1941-52, assoc. dir. research, 1952-63, v.p., 1959-77, dir. research, 1963-77, EXTEL Corp., Northbrook, Ill., 1978-79, v.p. research, 1979-82; tech. cons. Zenith Electronics Corp., 1982-97, Motorola, 1997—2001, Elo Touch Sys., 1997—2007. Contbr. articles to profl. jours. Co-recipient Emmy award, Nat. Acad. Television Arts & Sci., 1997; recipient Outstanding Technical Achievement award, Inst. Radio Engineers, 1958. Fellow IEEE (Edison medal 1980); mem. Nat. Acad. Engring. Achievements include 200 patents: invention of ultrasonic remote control for TV sets, electromechanical I.F. filter, electron beam parametric amplifier, ultrasonic touch system using rayleigh waves; research on improved touch system using Love waves. Home: Northbrook, Ill. Died Feb. 15, 2007.

ADLER, STUART OWEN, computer systems specialist; b. NYC, Mar. 27, 1935; s. Millard D. and Sydell L. (Levine) Adler; m. Marilyn Cynthia Leitner, Oct. 27, 1957; children: Deborah Ann, Michael Evan, Lorraine Carol. BS, NYU, 1957. Sys. programmer NY Life Ins. Co., 1957—59; competitive analyst Univac, 1960; sys. engr. IBM Corp., 1960—69; prin. mem. tech. staff Xerox Corp., 1969—71; computer sys. cons., 1972—75; sys. specialist Western Bancorp Dada Processing Co., 1976—77; sr. sys. analyst Litton Energy Control Sys., 1977—79; sys. analyst Worplex Corp., 1979—80; pres. Adler Computer Tech., Woodland Hills, Calif., from 1980. Cons. computer sys. housing aiding computer hardware and software selections to profls. and small bus. Author programming sys. Pres. Temple Solael Mr. and Mrs. Club. Mem.: Woodland Hills C. of C. Home: Woodland Hills, Calif. Died Apr. 9, 2006.

ADRI, (ADRI STECKLING COEN), fashion designer; b. St. Joseph, Mo. Student, Sch. Fine Arts, Washington U., St. Louis, Parson Sch. Design. With B.H. Wragge; owner, pres. Adri Studio, Ltd., NYC, from 1983. Critic Parsons Sch. Design, 1982—; with Claire McCardell in 2-person showing, Innovative Contemporary Fashion, Smithsonian Instn., Washington, 1971. Two-woman show (with Claire McCardell) Smithsonian Instn., Washington, 1972. Recipient Coty award, 1982, Internat. Best Five award, Tokyo, 1986. Died Nov. 5, 2006.

ADUJA, PETER AQUINO, lawyer, business executive; b Vigan, Philippines, Oct. 19, 1920; came to U.S., 1927, naturalized, 1944; s. Dionicio and Francisca (Aquino) A.; m. Melodie Cabalona, July 31, 1949; children— Jay, Rebecca. BA, U. Hawaii, 1944; JD, Boston U., 1951. Bar: Hawaii 1953, U.S. Supreme Ct. 1983. Individual practice law, Hilo, Hawaii, 1953-60, Honolulu, from 1960; dep. atty. gen. State of Hawaii 1957-60; judge Hawaii Dist. Ct., 1960-62; prin. broker AAF Realty, Inc., Honolulu, from 1970; pres. Aduja Corp., Las Vegas, Nev., from 1972, Travel-Air Internat., Honolulu, from 1975. Mem. Hawaii Ho. of Reps., 1954-56, 66-74; del. Hawaii Constl Conv., 1968; sec.-treas. Melodie Aduja, Inc., 1979—. Troop committeeman Aloha council Boy Scouts Am., 1959—; active ARC; chmn. Salvation Army Adult Rehab. Center, Honolulu 1965—, Goodwill Industries, 1972; chair Kaneohe Neighborhood Bd., 1991—. Served with U.S. Army, 1944-46. Mem. Bar Assn. Hawaii, Hawaii Bd. Realtors. Democrat. Methodist. Home: Kaneohe, Hawaii. Died Feb. 19, 2007.

AGOSIN, MOISES KANKOLSKY, zoology educator; b. Marseilles, France, Dec. 1, 1922; came to U.S., 1968, naturalized, 1973; s. Abraham W. and Rachel S. (Kankolsky) A.; m. Frida Halpern, June 19, 1948; children— Cynthia Regina, Marjorie Stella, Mario Daniel. MD, U. Chile, 1948. Intern Salvador Hosp., Santiago, Chile, 1946, resident parasitology and med. entomology, 1948; Rockefeller Found. fellow NIH, Bethesda, Md., 1952-54, research assoc., 1955; head biochemistry sect., dept. parasitology U. Chile, 1957-59, chmn. dept. chemistry, prof. chemistry, 1960-67; research prof. zoology U. Ga., Athens, from 1968. Vis. prof. U. Calif., Berkeley, 1960, U. London, 1964; hon. prof. U. Cayetano Heredia, Peru, 1984 cons. in field. Contbg. author: The Physiology of Insecta, 1974, Comprehensive Insect Biochemistry, Physiology, Pharmacology, 1985; mem. editorial bd.: Exptl. Parasitology, 1967-73, Archives Insect Biochemistry and Physiology, 1982-86; contbr. articles to profl. jours. Recipient Lamar Dodd award for creativity in rsch. U. Ga., 1989; grantee USPHS, 1958—, WHO, 1963-67, Wellcome Trust, 1966, NSF, 1974, U.S.-Israel bi-nat. Sci. Found., 1976, Conicit, Chile, 1996; Fulbright scholar, Peru, 1991, Fondecit (Chile) grant, 1996. Fellow Am. Acad. Microbiology; mem. Am. Soc. Biol. Chemists, Biochem. Soc. (London), AAAS, N.Y. Acad. Scis., Am. Soc. Parasitology (Bueding-von Brand Meml. award 1990), Chilean Acad. Scis.(rsch. prof. emeritus 1992). Home: Athens, Ga. Died July 18, 2006.

AHLBERG, CLARK DAVID, educator, former university president; b. Wichita, Kans., May 23, 1918; s. Grant and Sue McGuire A.; m. Rowena Osborn, Aug. 8, 1941; children: Val Jeanne, Thomas G., John C. AB, U. Wichita, 1939; MA, Syracuse U., 1942, PhD, 1951, LL.D., 1969. Grad. fellow, instr. polit. sci. Syracuse U., 1940-42, research dir. Washington Office, 1948-51, asst. dean Coll. Engring., 1951-54, asst. prof., 1951-54, v.p. adminstrn. and research, 1959-68, prof. polit. sci., Maxwell Citizenship and pub. Affairs, 1959-68; personnel asst. Panama Canal, 1942-43; mem. staff adminstrv. mgmt. div. VA, 1946-47; mem. staff. President's Sci. Research Bd., Washington, 1947; personnel researcher Nat. Bur. Standards, Washington, 1947-48; dep. dir. N.Y. State Budget Div., Albany, 1954-57, dir. budget, 1957-59; 1st dept. controller N.Y. State Dept. Audit and Control, Albany, 1959; pres. Syracuse U. Research Corp., 1959-68, Syracuse U. Press, 1959-68, Wichita State U., 1968-83, Univ. prof., from 1983. Dir., interium chancellor U. Alaska, Anchorage, 1986-87 Author: (with John C. Honey) Attitudes of Scientists and Engineers About Their Government, 1950; editor: Agency and Departmental Statements on Research and Development Administration, 1947; contbr. articles to ednl. jours. Bd. dirs. Wichita Sedgwick Devel. Commn.; bd. dirs. Kans. Region NCCJ, NIH. Served with AUS, 1944-46. Mem. Am. Assn. State Colls. and Univs., Am. Council on Edn., Assn. Urban Univs., Inst. Internat. Edn., Inst. Logopedics. (trustee), Kans. Assn. Colls. and Univs., Nat. Council for Tchr. Accreditation, North Central Assn. Colls. and Secondary Schs., Wichita State U. Library Assocs., Phi Eta Sigma, Phi Kappa Phi Clubs: Wichita Books and Authors. Home: Gig Harbor, Wash. Died Jan. 26, 2007.

AHRENS, THOMAS H., communications executive; b. NYC, Oct. 25, 1919; BA magna cum laude, U. Buffalo, 1938; JD, Harvard U., 1941; certificate in Culinary Arts, N.Y.C. Tech. Coll., 1953. Bar: N.Y. 1944. Dir. Edward F. Gallaher Prodns., from 1946; lectr. wines and beverages N.Y.C. Tech. Coll., 1953-55, prof. hotel and restaurant mgmt., from 1971; dir. rsch., security analyst Templeton, Dobbrow and Vance, 1962-64; pres. Chef Phillip, Inc., 1956-69. Author radio and TV scripts on wines, gastronomy and music, 1946—. Mem. chmn.'s coun. Lincoln Ctr. for Performing Arts. 2d lt. AUS, 1942-45. Decorated officer Chaine des Rotisseurs; Confrerie Saint Etienne d'Alsace; Chevaliers du Tastevin; Commanderie des Cordons Bleus de France; Medaille de la Ville de Paris, 1976 Mem. ABA, N.Y. Soc. Security Analysts, Phi Beta Kappa. Clubs: Harvard, Paris-American, Met., Met. Opera (all N.Y.C.); Travellers, Cercle de l'Union Interalliée (Paris). Died Oct. 4, 2005.

AIROLA, JOE ANTONIO, retired academic administrator; b. Fairbanks, Tex., July 13, 1928; m. Jannette Rutledge; children: Cathy, Mark, Jim BS, U. Houston, 1950, MEd, 1954, EdD, 1972. Tchr. Cypress-Fairbanks Jr. High Sch., Houston, 1948-50, Meml. Dr. Elem. Sch., 1950-52, prin., 1952-55, Spring Br. Jr. High Sch., 1955-60; dep. supt. for instr. Spring Br. Sch. Dist., 1960-68, acting supt., 1968, supt. instrn., 1968-71; dir. instructional svcs. Region IV Edn. Svc. Ctr., Houston, 1971-73; v.p., dean instrn. N. Harris County Coll., Houston, 1971-82, chancellor, 1982-91. Chancellor emeritus N. Harris County Coll., 1991-2007; vis. prof. Coll. of Edn., U. Houston, 1991-2007; workshop cons.; lectr. in field; dir. Interfirst Bank, Greenspoint. Recipient Disting. Alumni award, U. Houston Coll. Edn., 1985, Citizen of the Yr., Houston N.W. C. of C., 1988. Mem. Tex. Assn. Jr. and Community Coll. Instructional Officers (past pres.), Tex. Assn. Instructional Suprs. (past pres.), Tex. Jr. Coll. Tchrs. Assn., N.W. C. of C. (bd. dirs.). Home: Huntsville, Tex. Died Jan. 13, 2007.

AJL, SAMUEL JACOB, microbiologist, biochemist; b. Poland, Nov. 15, 1923; came to U.S., 1939, naturalized, 1943; s. Joseph and Celia (Hertz) A.; m. Adele Davis, Sept. 15, 1946; children— Stephen Ira, Diane Francis, Leslie Judith. BA, Bklyn. Coll., 1945; PhD, Iowa State Coll., 1949; L.H.D. (hon.), Dropsie U. Asst. prof. bacteriology Washington U. Sch. Medicine, St. Louis, 1949-52; on leave with Rockefeller U., 1951; chief microbiol. chemistry sect. Walter Reed Army Inst. Research, 1952-56, asst. chief dept. bacteriology, 1956-58; prof., dir. metabolic biology NSF, 1959-60; dir. research Albert Einstein Med. Center, Phila., 1960-71, Nat. Found.-March of Dimes, White Plains, N.Y., 1971-73, v.p. for research, 1973-91, cons. White Plains, N.Y., from 1991; prof. dept. biology Temple U., 1960-71; research prof. microbiology Sch. Medicine, 1960-71; Mem. metabolic biology panel NSF, from 1959. Chmn. exec. bd., bd. govs. Dropsie U. Hebrew and Cognate Studies, Phila., 1966, acting pres., 1966-67 Contbr. articles profl. jours., papers.; Editor: Microbial Toxins, 1970, Archives of Biochemistry and Biophysics, 1969. Bd. dirs. Am. Jewish Com.; bd. dirs. Nat. Found. Jewish Culture. Recipient commendation for superior service U.S. Army, 1955; NSF sr. postdoctorate fellow Jerusalem, Israel, Oxford, Eng., 1958; recipient Alumus Honors award for outstanding scientific achievements Bklyn. Coll., 1964 Fellow N.Y. Acad. Sci., Biochem. Soc. (Eng.); mem. Soc. Biol. Chemists Am., Soc. Microbiology, Soc. Exptl. Biology and Medicine, Am. Acad. Microbiology, Jewish Publ. Soc. Am. (v.p. 1969, dir.), Sigma Xi. Home: Philadelphia, Pa. Died June 2, 2006.

AKAISHI, TADASHI, publishing executive; b. Sendai, Japan, Jan. 22, 1925; came to U.S., 1949, naturalized, 1961; s. Yoshiaki and Yasu (Yamamoto) A.; m. Amy Nagata, Jan. 29, 1955; children— Carolyn Keiko, Janet Akemi. B.D., San Francisco Theol. Sem., 1950, Th.M., 1951, Th.D., 1957. Ordained to ministry Presbyn. Ch., 1953; pastor Christ Presbyn. Ch., Los Angeles, 1957-61; asso. editor John Knox Press, Richmond, Va., 1961-66; editor Harper & Row, 1966-67, editor-mgr., 1967-69; asst. pub. Harper & Row Pubs., Inc., NYC, 1969-70, v.p., pub., 1970-76, group v.p., pub., 1973-76; v.p., pub. Barnes & Noble Books, 1971-76; v.p., dir. Kodansha Internat. U.S.A., 1977-86. Author: Annotated Bibliography of New Testament Literature (1925-1955), 1955. Home: Eastchester, NY. Died Feb. 28, 2007.

ALBERT, CALVIN, sculptor; b. Grand Rapids, Mich., Nov. 19, 1918; s. Philip and Ethel (Schlacht) A.; m. Martha Neff, Dec. 25, 1941; 1 dau., Jill. Student, Art Inst., Chgo., 1936-37, Inst. Design, 1937-39. Mem. faculty N.Y.U., 1949-51, Bklyn. Coll., 1948-49, Inst. Design, Chgo., 1942-47; prof. art Pratt Inst., Bklyn., 1950-85, head grad. sculpture program, 1960-85, prof. emeritus, from 1985. Exhibited in one man shows at, Theobald Gallery, Chgo., 1941, Grand Rapids Art Gallery, 1943, 48, Puma Gallery, N.Y.C., 1944, Art Inst., Chgo., 1945, California Palace of Legion of Honor, San Francisco, 1947; exhibited in one man shows at, Laurel Gallery, N.Y.C., 1950, Light Gallery, Southampton, N.Y., 1981, Phoenix Gallery, Washington, 1982, Ingber Gallery, N.Y.C., 1983, Bologna-Londi Gallery, East Hampton, N.Y., 1983, Ingber Gallery, N.Y.C., 1985, Benton Gallery, Southampton, N.Y., 1986, Vered Gallery, East Hampton, N.Y., 1988, Ground Zero, Gallery, Miami Beach, Fla., 1988, Gaumann Cicchino Galery, Ft. Lauderdale, Fla., 1989, Boca Mus., Boca Raton, Fla., 1990, Peter Drew Gallery, Boca Raton, 1991; exhibited in traveling show, Des Moines Art Center, U. Mich., Grand Rapids Art Gallery, Mich. State U., 1957, Grace Borgenicht Gallery, N.Y.C., 1952, 54, 56, 57, Stable Gallery, N.Y.C., 1959, 64, Jewish Mus., N.Y.C., 1960, Galleria George Lester, Rome, Italy, 1962, Landmark Gallery, N.Y.C., 1974, 77, Benson Gallery, Bridgehampton, N.Y., 1975; exhibited in retrospective, Guild Hall Mus., East Hampton, N.Y., 1979, group shows at, Houston Mus. Fine Arts, 1958-59, Addison Gallery, 1959, Galerie Claude Bernard, Paris, 1961, Art Inst. Chgo., 1962, Sculpture Biennale, Cararra, Italy, 1962, Pa. Acad., Phila., 1963, FAR Gallery, N.Y.C., 1964, Whitney Mus., 1954-57, 60, 62, 64, U. Ill., 1965; rep. permanent collections, Whitney Mus., Bklyn. Mus., Art Inst. Chgo., Detroit Inst. Arts, Met. Mus., Jewish Mus., U. Nebr., Chrysler Mus. Art, Wm. Rockhill Nelson Gallery Art.; author: (with D.G. Seckler) Figure Drawing Comes to Life, 1957, 2nd edit., 1987. Recipient Haass prize Detroit Inst. Arts, 1944, Forst award for sculpture Audubon Artists Annual, 1954, Anonymous Prize for sculpture Audubon Annual, 1957, Fulbright Advanced Research grant Italy, 1961-62, Tiffany grant, 1963, 65, Guggenheim fellowship, 1966, Am. Inst. Arts and Letters award, 1975 Died June 4, 2007.

ALBRIGHT, RALPH NATHANIEL, JR., lawyer; b. Nov. 24, 1942; m. Susanne Albright; children: Lisa, Emily. BBA, U. Pitts., 1964; JD, Am. U., 1968. Bar: D.C. 1968, Md. and Pa. 1984. Ptnr. Morgan, Lewis & Bockius, Washington, 1987—2007. Died July 20, 2007.

ALBRITTON, ROBERT SANFORD, life insurance executive; b. St. Paul, Feb. 19, 1914; s. Elmer Sanford and Mary (Bierer) A.; m. Helen Richards, Mar. 14, 1938; children— David Richards, Robert Rapp. BS, Northwestern U., 1935; MBA, U. Pa., 1937; C.L.U., 1947. Agy. supr. Minn. Mut. Life Ins. Co., Mpls., 1937-40; agt. Provident Mut. Life Ins. Co., Phila., Los Angeles, from 1940; pres. Albritton, Frank & Co., from 1961; chmn. ins. ops. com. Empire Gen. Life Ins. Co., 1963-78; pres. Million Dollar Round Table of Nat. Assn. Life Underwriters, 1960, Million Dollar Round Table Found., 1962-64. Mem. Phi Delta Theta. Clubs: Rancho Bernardo Golf. Home: San Diego, Calif. Died Feb. 21, 2006.

ALCORN, MERRITT OAKNEY, pathologist; b. Wynne, Ark., Nov. 5, 1920; s. Merritt Oakney and Martha Ellen (Keelty) A.; children: Merritt Keelty, George Lawrence, Mary Ellen Cox Caughran, Charlotte Lee Alcorn Daughhetee. BS in Chemistry, U. Ark., 1941, MD, 1950. Diplomate Am. Bd. Pathology. Intern U. Ind., 1951; resident in pathology U. Louisville, 1962; engr. U.S. Army Ordinance, Hope, Ark.; pvt. practice Madison, Ind.; pathologist Madison and Lawrenceburg, Ind., 1962-92; CEO Pathology Computer Systems, Madison. With USN. Home: Madison, Ind. Died June 16, 2007.

ALDOUS, ELAINE MARIE, blood bank facility administrator; b. Isabell, S.D., Aug. 6, 1931; d. August G. Opp and Julia Elizabeth (Samuelson) Nightengale; m. Richard Robert O'Leary, July 23, 1946 (div. 1953); children— Sherry, Kathy, Vicky; m. 2d, James Henry Aldous, June 6, 1964 (dec.). Cert. in motel-hotel mgmt. Whitcomb Sch. Ltd., Clearwater, Fla., 1968; A.A., Fla. Jr. Coll. at Jacksonville, 1975; B.A. cum laude, U. North Fla., 1978. Self-employed in clerical mgmt., Aberdeen, S.D., 1947-50; gen. office mgr. Lavigne Ranches, Calexico, Calif., 1950-56; office mgr. Stan's Furniture Inc., El Centro, Calif., 1956-60; cashier mgr. Interstate Bakeries Corp., Glendale, Calif., 1960-64; acctg. tax/price cons. Standard Oil of Calif., Jacksonville, Fla., 1965-69, Louisville, 1969-73; personnel mgr. Jacksonville Blood Bank, 1976—. Mem. U. North Fla. Found. Inc., Jacksonville, 1978—; treas. Springfield Preservation and Restoration Soc., Jacksonville, 1982; activities dir. El Centro Recreation Dept., 1958-60. Mem. Am. Soc. Personnel Adminstrn. (cert.), N.E. Fla. Hosp. Personnel Assn., Jacksonville Personnel Women, Tiquana Jr. C. of C. of Mex. (hon.). Home: Jacksonville, Fla. Died July 13, 2006.

ALDRIDGE, JOHN WATSON, language educator, writer; b. Sioux City, Iowa, Sept. 26, 1922; s. Walter Copher and Nell (Watson) A.; m. Leslie Felker, Dec. 10, 1954 (div. June 1968); 1 son, Geoffrey; children by previous marriages: Henry, Stephen, Leslie, Jeremy; m. Alexandra Bertash, July 13, 1968 (div. Dec. 1982); m. Patricia McGuire Eby, July 16, 1983. Student, U. Chattanooga, 1940-43; fellow, Breadloaf Sch. English, summer 1942; BA, U. Calif.-Berkeley, 1947. Lectr. English U. Vt., 1948-50, asst. prof., 1950-53, 54-55; lectr. Christian Gauss Seminars Criticism, Princeton, NJ, 1953-54; mem. lit. faculty Sarah Lawrence Coll., also New Sch. Social Research, 1957; prof. English Queens Coll., 1957; Berg prof. English NYU, 1958; Fulbright lectr. U. Munich, Fed. Republic of Germany, 1958-59; writer-in-residence Hollins Coll., 1960-62; Fulbright lectr. U. Copenhagen, Denmark, 1962-63; prof. English U. Mich., 1964-91, prof. emeritus, 1991—2007; book critic N.Y. Herald Tribune Book Week, 1965-66, Saturday Review, 1970-79. Staff Bread Loaf Writers Conf., 1966-69; chief regional judge Book-of-the Month Writing Fellowship Program, 1966-67; spl. adviser for Am. studies U.S. Embassy, Germany, 1972-73; spl. adviser for Authors Am. Sta. WETA, 1990-2007; book commentator McNeil/Lehrer News Hour, 1983-84. Author: After the Lost Generation, 1951, Critiques and Essays on Modern Fiction, 1952, In Search of Heresy, 1956, The Party at Cranton, 1960, Time to Murder and Create, 1966, In the Country of the Young, 1970, The Devil in the Fire, 1972, The American Novel and the Way We Live Now, 1983, Talents and Technicians, 1992, Classics and Contemporaries, 1992; also articles.; editor: Selected Stories by P.G. Wodehouse, 1958. Served with AUS, 1943-45, ETO. Decorated Bronze Star; Rockefeller Humanities fellow, 1976-77 Mem. Authors Guild and League of Am., MLA, Nat. Book Critics Circle, P.E.N. Home: Madison, Ga. Died Feb. 7, 2007.

ALEXANDER, CHARLES WILLIAM, psychologist, consultant; b. Zanesville, Ohio, Feb. 13, 1951; s. Charles and Doris (Paxson) A.; B.S., Denison U., 1973; M.A., Bowling Green State U., 1975, Ph.D., 1978. Psychol. intern Southwestern Med. Sch., Dallas, 1977-78; asst. prof. psychology Wichita (Kans.) State U., 1978-83; pvt. practice clin. psychology, Wichita, 1979—; cons. Roots & Wings Foster Care Project, Mental Health Assn. Sedgewick County, also residential mental retardation and psychiat. facilities. Mem. Am. Psychol. Assn., Soc. Behavioral Medicine, Soc. Psychophysiol. Research, Mental Health Assn. Sedgewck County, Southwestern Psychol. Assn., Wichita Psychol. Assn. Author: (with Richard and Muriel Saunders) The Small Home Handbook: A Kansas Guide to Develop, Fund, and Operate Small Residential Facilities for the DD Adult. Home: Wichita, Kans. Died June 24, 2006.

ALEXANDER, LLOYD CHUDLEY, author; b. Phila., Jan. 30, 1924; s. Alan Audley and Edna (Chudley) A.; m. Janine Denni, Jan. 8, 1946; 1 dau., Madeleine (Mrs. Zohair Khalil). Student, West Chester State Coll., Pa., 1942, Lafayette Coll., 1943, U. Paris, 1946. Free-lance writer and translator, 1946—2007; cartoonist, pianist, advt. writer, mag. editor, from 1948; author-in-residence Temple U., 1970. Author: And Let The Credit Go, 1955, My Five Tigers, 1956, Janine is French, 1958, August Bondi, 1958 (Isaac Siegel Meml. award 1959), My Love Affair with Music, 1960, Aaron Lopez, 1960, Time Cat, 1963, Fifty Years in the Doghouse, 1964, (with Dr. Louis J. Camuti) Park Avenue Vet, 1962, The Book of Three, 1964 (A.L.A. notable book 1964), The Black Cauldron, 1965 (A.L.A. notable book 1965), Coll and His White Pig, 1965, The Castle of Llyr, 1966 (A.L.A. notable book 1966), Taran Wanderer, 1967, The Truthful Harp, 1967, The High King, 1968 (Newbery medal 1969), The Marvelous Misadventures of Sebastian, 1970 (Nat. Book award 1971), The King's Fountain, 1971, The Four Donkeys, 1972, The Foundling, 1973 (A.L.A. notable book 1973), The Cat Who Wished to be a Man, 1973 (A.L.A. notable book), The Wizard in the Tree, 1975, The Town Cats, 1977 (ALA notable book 1977), The First Two Lives of Lukas-Kasha, 1978, Westmark, 1981 (Am. Book award 1982), The Kestrel, 1982, The Beggar Queen, 1984, The Illyrian Adventure, 1986, The El Dorado Adventure, 1987, The Drackenberg Adventure, 1988, The Jedera Adventure, 1989, The Philadelphia Adventure, 1990, The Remarkable Journey of Prince Jen, 1991, The Fortune-tellers, 1992, The Arkadians, 1995, The House Gobbaleen, 1995, The Iron Ring, 1997, Gypsy Rizka, 1999, How the Cat Swallowed Thunder, 2000, The Gawgon and the Boy, 2001, The Rope Trick, 2002, The Xanadu Adventure, 2005, Dream-of-Jade the Emperor's Cat, 2005; translator from French: (Paul Eluard) Selected Writings, 1950, (Jean-Paul Sartre) The Wall, 1951, Nausea, 1953, (Paul Vialar) The Sea Rose, 1951. Bd. dirs. Carpenter Lane Chamber Music Soc., Phila. Served with AUS, World War II. Recipient Golden Cat award, 1984, Regina medal, 1986, Carolyn W. Field medal, 1987, Otter award, 1993, Horn Book-Boston Globe award 1993; World Fantasy Life Achievement award, 2003, Lifetime Achievement award Gov. Pa., 2005. Mem. Authors League Am., P.E.N. Died May 17, 2007.

ALFORD, JACK LELAND, mechanical engineer, educator; b. Long Beach, Calif., Nov. 19, 1920; s. Leon Otto and Ethelind (Humphrey) A.; m. Edith Elizabeth Humann, Mar. 8, 1944; children: Christopher John, Margaret Ann. Student, U.S. Naval Acad., 1937-39; BS, Calif. Inst. Tech., 1942, MS, 1946, PhD, 1950. Registered profl. engr., Calif. With Turbodyne Corp., Hawthorne, Calif., 1948-50; postdoctoral fellow Calif. Inst. Tech., 1950-52; research engr. Jet Propulsion Lab., 1957-59; head engring. div. U.S. Naval Ordnance Test Sta., 1952-55; asst. to tech. dir. Technicolor Corp., 1955-57; prof. Harvey Mudd Coll., Claremont, Calif., 1959-65, James Howard Kindelberger prof. engring., from 1965, chmn. dept. engring., 1967-72, 73-79. Served to lt. USNR, 1942-46. Mem. Am. Soc. M.E., Earthquake Engring. Research Inst., Am. Soc. Engring. Edn., Am. Assn. U. Profs., Sigma Xi, Tau Beta Pi. Died Feb. 11, 2006.

ALFORD, NEILL HERBERT, JR., retired law educator; b. Greenville, SC, July 13, 1919; s. Neill Herbert and Elizabeth (Robertson) Alford; m. Elizabeth Talbot Smith, June 26, 1943; children: Neill Herbert III, Margaret Dudley, Eli Thomas Stackhouse. BA, The Citadel-Mil. Coll. S.C., 1940; LLB, U. Va., 1947; JSD, Yale U., 1966. Bar: Va 1954. Mem. faculty law U. Va. Law Sch., Charlottesville, 1947—74, 1976—90, Doherty Found. prof., 1966-74, spl. cons. to pres. univ., legal adviser to rector and bd. dirs., 1972-74; Joseph Henry Lumpkin prof., dean U. Ga. Law Sch., Athens, 1974-76; Percy Brown Jr. prof. law U. Va., 1976-90; state reporter Supreme Ct. Va., 1977-84; counsel Woods, Rogers & Hazelgrove, Charlottesville, 1991-97. Spl. counsel Va. Code Comn., 1954—57; dir. Va Bankers Asn Trust Sch, 1958—61; prof., chair internat. law Naval War Coll., 1961—62, consult, 1962—68; summer tchr. George Washington U., U. NC, U. Ala.; chmn. bd. dirs. U. Va. Press, 1970—74, 1987—89, prof. law emeritus, 1990—2007; Lehmann disting. vis. prof. law Washington U., St. Louis, 1991; Hofstedler prof. Ohio State U. Law Sch., 1992; prof. Washington and Lee Law Sch., 1992. Author: (book) Modern Economic Warfare: Law and the Naval Participant, 1967, Cases and Materials on Decedents Estates and Trusts, 8th edit, 1993; contbr. articles to profl jours. Comdr. civil affairs group USAR, 1947—66, lt. col. AUS, 1941—46, ETO, col. AUS. Decorated Bronze Star, Combat Inf Badge; fellow Ford, U. Wis., 1958; Sterling fellow, Yale U., 1950—51. Fellow: Am. Bar Found., Va. Law Found.; mem.: ABA, Raven Soc., Va. Bar Assn., Va. State Bar, Am. Law Inst., Am. Judicature Soc., Am. Soc. Legal Hist., Selden Soc., Colonnade Club, Order Coif, Omicron Delta Kappa, Phi Alpha Delta. Home: Charlottesville, Va. Died Oct. 20, 2007.

ALJIAN, JAMES DONOVAN, investment company executive; b. Oakland, Calif., Nov. 5, 1932; s. George W. and Marguerite (Donovan) A.; m. Marjorie L. Townsend, Oct. 17, 1959; children: Mark Donovan, Mary Anne, Reed Townsend. BS, U. Calif., Berkeley, 1955; MBA, Golden Gate U., 1965. Office mgr. Uniroyal Co., San Francisco, 1957-60; audit supr. Ernst & Ernst, San Francisco, 1960-65; sec.-treas. Tracy Investment Co., Las Vegas, 1965-73, Internat. Leisure Corp., Las Vegas, 1967-70; sr. v.p. fin. MGM, Culver City, Calif., 1973-79; pres. Tracinda Corp., Las Vegas, 1979-82; sr. v.p. fin. planning MGM/UA Entertainment Co., Culver City, Calif., 1982-85; exec. v.p., CFO Southwest Leasing Corp., Los Angeles, 1985-87; with Tracinda Corp., Las Vegas, Nev., 1987—2007. Mem. shareholder com. Daimler Chrysler AG, 1998-00; bd. dirs. MGM Mirage Inc., 1988-2007 With AUS, 1955—57. Mem. Am. Inst. C.P.A.s, Calif. Soc. C.P.A.s., Acad. Motion Picture Arts and Scis. Home: Marina Del Rey, Calif. Died Apr. 12, 2007.

ALKER, HAYWARD ROSE, political scientist, educator; b. NYC, Oct. 3, 1937; s. Hayward Rose and Dorothy (Fitzsimmons) Alker; m. Judith Ann Tickner, June 3, 1961; children: Joan Christina, Heather Jane, Gwendolyn Ann. BS, MIT, 1959; MS, Yale U., 1960, PhD, 1963. From instr. to assoc. prof. Yale U., New Haven, 1963-68; prof. polit. sci. MIT, 1968-95; John A. McCone prof. internat. rels. U. So. Calif., LA, 1995—2005, prof., 2005—07. Vis. prof. U. Mich., 1968; Olaf Palme vis. prof. U. Stockholm, U. Uppsala, 1989; adj. prof., scholar Brown U., 1996, 2003—07; chmn. Math. Social Scis. Bd., 1970—71; mem. exec. com. Internat. Social Sci. Coun., 1990—92. Author: (non-fiction) Mathematics and Politics, 1965; co-author: World Handbook of Political and Social Indicators, 1966; co-author: (with Russett) World Politics in the General Assembly, 1966; co-author: (with Bloomfield and Choucri) Analyzing Global Interdependence, 1974; co-author: (with Hurwitz) Resolving Prisoner's Dilemmas, 1981; co-editor, co-author: book Journeys Through Conflict, 2001; author: Rediscoveries and Reformulations, 1996; editor: Honors Theses in International Relations, 2003; editor: (mem. bd.) (jour.) Jour. Interdisciplinary History, 1969—71, Internat. Orgn., 1970—76, Quality and Quantitiy, 1974—2007, Internat. Studies Quar., 1980—89, European Jour. Internat. Rels., 1995—99, Review of Internat. Polit. Econ., 1995—2007, Internat. Rels. of Asia Pacific, 2000—07, Internat. Rels., 2003—07, Jour. Lang. and Politics, 2006—07. Congl. intern Office of Chester Bowles, 1960. Fellow, Ctr. Advanced Studies in Behavioral Scis., 1967—68. Mem.: Am. Assn. Artificial Intelligence, Internat. Studies Assn. (v.p. 1990—91, pres. 1992—93), Internat. Peace Rsch. Assn., Internat. Polit. Sci. Assn., Am. Polit. Sci. Assn. Home: Santa Monica, Calif. Died Aug. 24, 2007.

ALLAIN, EMERY EDGAR, retired paper company executive; b. Northbridge, Mass., Oct. 22, 1922; s. Emery and Florida (Pelletier) A.; m. Florance Chabot, Feb. 10, 1945 (dec. Mar. 1995); children: Amy Louise Lester, John Emery; m. Patricia Sheehan Flemming, Feb. 15, 1997. Student, Bentley Coll., 1939-41, Northeastern U., 1941-43. C.P.A., Mass., Me. With Arthur Andersen & Co., Boston and NYC, 1944-49; contr. Royal Lace Paper Works, 1949-51, treas., 1951-54; with Great No. Paper Co., 1954-87, contr., 1962-68, v.p. fin., 1968-69; v.p. fin., chief fin. officer Gt. No. Nekoosa Corp., 1970-87, exec. v.p., 1987, ret., 1987. Mem. AICPA, Inst. Mgmt. Accts., Fin. Execs. Inst., Williams Club (N.Y.C.). Home: Greenwich, Conn. Died Oct. 19, 2006.

ALLEMAN, RAYMOND HENRY, multinational company executive; b. Yonkers, NY, Sept. 18, 1934; s. William A. and Ann L. (White) A.; m. Beverly I. Schmidtendorff, 1984; children: Mark, Brian, Bruce, Gregg, Paul, Blair, Lynn, Janet. BBA, Manhattan Coll., 1956. CPA, N.Y. Audit mgr. Arthur Andersen and Co., NYC and Newark, 1956-65; controller Oneida Paper Products/Deerfield Glassine Co., Clifton, N.J., 1965-67; v.p., dep. controller ITT Corp., NYC, 1978-84, sr. v.p., contr., from 1985. Sr. v.p., bd. dirs. ITT Industries, Internat. Standard Electric Corp., ITT Holdings, Inc. Mem. Am. Inst. CPA's, Nat. Assn. Accts., Machinery and Allied Products Inst. (fin. council II), Am. Mgmt. Assn. Roman Catholic. Home: Stamford, Conn. Died June 29, 2007.

ALLEN, CHARLES JOSEPH, II, advertising agency executive; b. Providence, June 8, 1917; s. John Alfred and Emily (Smith) A.; m. Fay Eleanore Manne, Nov. 19, 1941; children: Linda Fay (Mrs. Marc D. Constant), June Lee (Mrs. Michael L. Traviolia). AB with honors, U. Pitts., 1939. Corporate sales service mgr. Kroger Co., Cin., 1945-52; v.p. Gardner Advt., Inc., St. Louis, 1952-56, McCann-Erickson, Inc., Chgo., 1956-58; chmn. bd., chief exec. officer Allen, Anderson, Niefeld & Paley, Inc., Chgo., 1958-69; pres. Charles J. Allen & Assos., Woodridge, Ill., from 1970; v.p., dir. Grabin-Shaw Advt., Milw., 1960-73; pres., dir. A A Gift Shopper Plan, Elmhurst, from 1970. Dir. EFS Service Corp., Elmhurst, Sales Force Cos. Chgo., Elmhurst Fed. Savs. & Loan, A/C/T Enterprises, Chgo., Press Syndicate Service, Pitts.; cons. in field, 1960— Contbr. articles to profl. jours.; Speaker in field. Pres. bd. dirs. Village IV Orgn., Woodridge, Ill., 1978-82. Mem. Assn. Food Execs. (pres. 1967—), Chgo. Assn. Commerce and Industry, Elmhurst C. of C. (dir., past pres.), U. Pitts. Alumni Assn., Am. Marketing Assn. (past dir.), Indsl. Advt. Club. Clubs: Chicago Press, Executives, Itasca (Ill.) Country. Home: Woodridge, Ill. Died Apr. 9, 2007.

ALLEN, DONALD MCGOWAN, retired lawyer, retired financial management company executive; b. Pitts., Aug. 11, 1925; s. Donald M. and Helen (Gessford) A.; m. Louise Colgan, June 18, 1949; children— Amy Louise Benson, Michael Andrew, David Colgan BA, Washington and Jefferson U.; LL.B., U. Pa. Bar: Pa. Assoc. Anderson & Anderson, Donora, Pa., 1952-53; with trust dept. Fidelity Bank, Phila., 1953-56; atty. Del. Mgmt. Co. Inc., Phila., from 1956, sec., from 1961, v.p., 1965-86, ret., 1986. Trustee Washington and Jefferson U., 1984—. Served as lt. (j.g.) USNR, 1943-46 Republican. Presbyterian. Home: Newtown Square, Pa. Died May 14, 2007.

ALLEN, RAY MAXWELL, college dean, educator; b. Memphis, Dec. 16, 1922; s. Harry Davis and Louise (Martin) A.; m. Julia Wellford, Apr. 3, 1948; children— Julia, Ray, Katherine. B.A., Rhodes Coll., 1944; B.D., Duke U., 1947, Ph.D., 1953. Dir. Memphis State U. Wesley Found., 1947-49; dir. Duke U. Meth. Student Movement, Durham, N.C., 1950-52; asst. prof. Wofford Coll., Spartanburg, S.C., 1953-56; prof. Lambuth Coll., Jackson, Tenn., 1956-63; dean, prof. Rhodes Coll., Memphis, 1963—. Home: Memphis, Tenn. Died Feb. 27, 2007.

ALLEN, SHEILA ROSALYND, screenwriter, novelist; b. Elmira, N.Y., Mar. 8, 1942; d. Charles Judson and Doris Elizabeth (Beers) A. Ptnr. Allen & Ukra, Los Angeles, 1974-75; owner Allen Enterprises, Venice Beach, Calif., 1975-84; pres., chief exec. officer S.R.A., Inc., Venice Beach, 1984—, also bd. dirs.; writer Columbia Studios TV, 1983-84, Aaron Spelling Prodns., 1984; mem. adv. bd. Whole Ocean Catalog, Dana Point, Calif., 1986, Insight for Learning, Ventura, Calif., 1978; bd. dirs. We the People, Santa Monica; speaker pub. TV, 1982. Author: (books) Fire and Innocence, 1984, Victoria's Secret Masquerade of Hearts, 1986, The Mars Kill, 1987; author: (screenplay) Honeymoon, 1986; author: (TV series) Cops and Riders, 1987, also movies of the week, documentaries and films. Speechwriter Calif. Dem. Kick-Off Campaign, 1976. Recipient Teacher's award Insight for Learning, Ventura, 1978, Silver award Houston Film Festival, 1984; named Best New Novelist, R.T. Book Conf., N.Y.C, 1986. Mem. Writers Guild Am. (west arbitrator credits 1984-86), Authors Guild, Authors League, Romance Writers Am. (awards judge 1986-87), Mystery Writers Am., Nat. Writers Club (critiquing cons). Anglican Catholic. Club: Rose Ave. Beach (Venice, Calif.). Avocations: painting, cycling, volunteer programs for disadvantaged would-be writers, classical music, culinary arts. Home: Santa Monica, Calif. Died Jan. 6, 2006.

ALLEN, VERNON EUGENE, retired marketing executive; b. Cleve., Dec. 24, 1919; s. Vernon L. and Beatrice (Figgins) A.; student pub. schs., Cleve.; m. Florence Wilma Stanard, Mar. 5, 1942; children— Vernon William, Carol Jean Allen Holmes, Gregory, Holly L. Allen May. Machine operator, Tinnerman Products Inc., Cleve., 1938-42; devel. engr. Eaton Corp., Cleve., 1946-47, sales supr., 1947-70, sales mgr., 1970-72, div. mktg. mgr., 1972-80, dir. community affairs, 1980-82. Capt. of Ohio Hwy. Patrol Aux., 1968-70; chmn. bd. Hospice Found., Inc.; mem. Ret. Execs. Adv. Panel. Served with C.E., U.S. Army, 1940-46; PTO, ETO. Decorated Bronze star. Mem. Eaton Soc. Inventors, Am. Arbitration Assn., Am. Legion, VFW. Republican. Home: Clearwater, Fla. Died June 20, 2007.

ALLER, JAMES CURWOOD, retired science foundation executive, instrumentation company executive; b. Yakima, Wash., Aug. 19, 1921; s. Curtis Cosmos and Igna Pauline (Olson) A.; m. Mary Bramble, Aug. 1943; children: Charles C., James David, Robert C., Mary Suzanne, Cynthia Jane Aller Kelly. BS, US Naval Acad., 1942; MA, Harvard U., 1949, MES, 1954; DSc, George Washington U., 1968. Commd. ensign, US Navy, 1942, advanced through grades to comdr., 1962; with Ctr. for Naval Analyses, 1963-67; fellow USPHS Lab., Washington, 1967-68; prof. Naval War Coll., Newport, RI, 1968-70; assoc. prof. George Washington Med. Sch., Washington, 1970-73; sr. assoc. Ketron, Arlington, Va., 1973-75; program dir. NSF, Washington, 1975-86; pres. Aller Assocs., 1989—; cons. Office Mgmt. Budget, Washington, 1971; cons. various groups, 1986—. Editor (with others) Biosalin Concept; contbr. chpts. in sci. books. Treas. Falls Church council Boy Scouts Am., 1963-68, also Cub Scout pack chmn., Oxnard, Calif. Recipient letter of appreciation Cinc Pac Fleet, 1967; spl. achievement award NSF, 1978, 82, Meritorious Service award, 1980. Fellow AAAS; mem. IEEE (life, sr.). NY Acad. Scis. Home: Charlottesvle, Va. Died Jan. 5, 2007.

ALLER, ROBERT OLEN, aerospace engineer, consultant; b. Dayton, Ohio, Mar. 26, 1930; s. Olen A. and Carolyn R. (Lewis) A.; m. Nancy B. Rife, June 5, 1953; children: Cynthia Thornett, Carole Brennan, Robert C. BS, U.S. Naval Acad., 1953; MS, U. Mich., 1960. Commd. 2d lt. USAF, 1953, advanced through grades to capt., 1959; mgr. Philco Ford, Houston, 1963-64; dep. program mgr. NASA, Washington, 1964-78, div. mgr., dir. The Space Network, 1978-83, assoc. adminstr. space ops., 1983-89; cons. Aller Assocs., Washington, 1989—2006. Contbr. articles to profl. jours. Recipient Exceptional Svc. medal (2), NASA, Space Flight award, Am. Astronautical Soc., 1989. Fellow Am. Astronautical Soc.; assoc. fellow AIAA. Republican. Lutheran. Died May 17, 2006.

ALLERY, ALAN J., health science association administrator, consultant; b. Cando, ND, July 29, 1947; s. Louis E. and Ermaline P. (Krebsback) A.; m. Margaret J. DeMers, Aug. 2, 1969; children: Chris, Aaron, Gina. BS in Physical Edn., Bus., Mayville State U., 1970; M in Sch. Adminstrn., Northern State U., 1975; MHA, U. Minn., 1981. Educator Lansford (N.D.) Pub. Sch., 1970-72; adminstr. United Tribes N.D., Bismarck, 1972-73; educator Northern State Coll., Aberdeen, N.D., 1973-75; health adminstr. Indian Health, Aberdeen, 1975-84, Bemidji, Minn., from 1984. Republican. Roman Catholic. Home: Bemidji, Minn. Died July 14, 2007.

ALLEY, FREDERICK DON, hospital executive; b. May 27, 1940; s. William Dezell and Rita Mae (Bartlett) A.; children: Kirk Frederick, Nicole Kathleen BS in Bus. Adminstrn., Ferris State Coll., 1962; MS, Columbia U., 1965. Adminstrv. resident Hackensack Hosp. Assn., Hackensack, N.J., 1963-64, asst. adminstr., 1965-68; assoc. dir. The Bklyn. Hosp., N.Y., 1968-77, exec. dir., chief exec. officer N.Y., 1977-82; pres., chief exec. officer The Bklyn. Hosp-Caledonian Hosp., Bklyn., from 1982. Adj. assoc. prof. L.I. U.; lectr., Columbia U. Contbr. articles to profl. jours. Bd. dirs. Bklyn. Soc. Prevention Cruelty to Children, 1985; bd. dirs. Kings County Health Care Rev. Orgn., 1985; mem. Bklyn. Adv. bd. to Police Athletic League, 1985 Fellow Am. Coll. Hosp. Adminstrs.; mem. Greater N.Y. Hosp. Assn. (bd. govs., exec. com. 1985), Bklyn. Lung Assn. (bd. dirs. 1985), Am. Hosp. Assn., Council of Teaching Hosp., Assn. Am. Med. Colls., Am. Pub. Health Assn., N.Y. Pub. Health Assn. Clubs: Brooklyn (bd. govs.), Municipal; Brooklyn Heights Casino. Died Mar. 23, 2007.

ALLEY, ROBERT SUTHERLAND, humanities educator, author; b. Richmond, Va., Jan. 5, 1932; s. Reuben Edward and Mary Elizabeth (Sutherland) A.; m. Norma Franklin Crane, Aug. 17, 1957; children: Robert Sutherland Jr., John Reuben. BA, U. Richmond, 1953; BD, So. Bapt. Sem., 1956; MA, Princeton U., NJ, 1960, PhD, 1962. Asst. prof. religion William Jewell Coll., Liberty, Mo., 1961-63; with U. Richmond, from 1963, prof., chmn. religion dept., 1973-78, prof. humanities, chmn. area studies dept., from 1978. Vis. prof. rhetoric and communications U. Va., Charlottesville, 1986, 89. Editorial advisor Free Inquiry mag., Buffalo, 1986—; cons. Va. Festival Am. Film, Charlottesville, 1987—. Organizer Richmond chpt. ACLU, 1965; mem. Henrico County Dem. Com., Richmond, 1965-66; treas. Virginians for McCarthy, Richmond, 1968; bd. dirs. James Madison Meml. Com., Buffalo, 1985—; mem. nat. adv. bd. Americans United for Separation of Ch. and State. Va. Found. for Humanities grantee, 1976, 78-79, Markle Found. grantee, 1979. Mem. Com. for Sci. Study of Religion (bd. dirs. 1985—), Religion and Bibl. Criticism Rsch. Project (steering com. 1985—). Avocations: photography, videography. Home: Richmond, Va. Died Aug. 14, 2006.

ALLINGTON, ROBERT WILLIAM, instrument company executive; b. Madison, Wis., Sept. 18, 1935; s. William B. and Norma Evelyn (Peterson) A.; m. Mary Lynn Kaylor, Sept. 4, 1976. BS, U. Nebr., 1959, MS, 1961, ScD (hon.) in Chemistry, 1985. CEO, chmn. Isco, Inc., Lincoln, Nebr., from 1961. Inventor in field; contbr. numerous articles to profl. jours. Active Lincoln/Lancaster Planning Commn., 1968-88, chmn., 1978-85; bd. dirs. League Human Dignity, Lincoln, 1981—, Nebr. Rsch. and Devel. Authority Lincoln, 1986-94, chmn., 1990-94; mem. Gov.'s Com. on Employment of the Handicapped, Lincoln, 1983; mem. Indsl. Adv. Bd., Dept. Chemistry, U. Nebr., 1988—; bd. dirs. Lincoln Cmty. Found. Inc., 1989-96; chmn. Nebr. EPSCOR Com., 1991—. Named Handicapped Nebraskan of the Yr., Gov. of Nebr., 1972, Outstanding Engrng. Achievement Profl. Engrs., 1975, Nat. Small Bus. Person of the Yr., SBA, 1985, Exec. of the Yr., R&D Mag., 1991, U. of Nebr. Outstanding Alumnus, 1993, Entrepreneur of Yr. Nebr. Ctr. Entrepreneurship Lincoln Coll. Bus. Adminstrn. U. Nebr., 1998; recipient Disting. Svc. award Kiwanis, 1978, Support of Rsch. award Sigma Xi, 1986. Fellow Am. Inst. Chemists; mem. IEEE, Am. Chem. Soc., Instrument Soc. Am., Nat. Soc. Profl. Engrs., Analytical and Life Sci. Sys. Assn. (bd. dirs. 1992-95), Nebr. Club, The Club. Episcopalian. Avocation: sci. and tech. history. Home: Lincoln, Nebr. Died Mar. 2006.

ALLINSON, GARY DEAN, Japanese studies educator; b. Webster City, Iowa, Aug. 12, 1942; s. Everette John and Grace Lucille (Winnie) A.; m. Patricia S. Bush, Dec. 27, 1965; 1 child, Robin John. BA, Stanford U., 1964, MA, 1966, PhD, 1971. Asst. prof. to prof. U. Pitts., 1971-83; Ellen Bayard Weedon prof. east Asian studies U. Va., Charlottesville, from 1983. Author: Japanese Urbanism, 1975, Suburban Tokyo, 1979, Political Dymanics in Contemporary Japan, 1993; contbr. articles to profl. jours. Fulbright fellow U.S.-Japan Edn. Commn., 1974-75, Japan Found. fellow, 1978-79; recipient Policy Study award Japan-U.S. Friendship Commn., 1990. Mem. Assn. Asian Studies, Am. Hist. Assn., Am. Polit. Sci. Assn. Democrat. Avocations: running, gardening, tennis, swimming, travel. Home: Charlottesville, Va. Died Sept. 14, 2006.

ALLISON, LAIRD BURL, business educator; b. St. Marys, W.Va., Nov. 7, 1917; s. Joseph Alexander and Opal Marie (Robinson) A.; m. Katherine Louise Hunt, Nov. 25, 1943 (div. 1947); 1 child: William Lee; m. Genevieve Nora Elmore, Feb. 1, 1957 (dec. July 1994). BS in Personnel and Indsl. Relations magna cum laude, U. So. Calif., 1956; MBA, UCLA, 1958. Chief petty officer USN, 1936-51, PTO; asst. prof. to prof. mgmt. Calif. State U., LA, 1956-83; asst. dean Calif. State U. Sch. Bus. and Econs., LA, 1971-72, assoc. dean, 1973-83, emeritus prof. mgmt., from 1983. Vis. asst. prof. mgmt. Calif. State U., Fullerton, 1970. Co-authored the Bachelors degree program in mgmt. sci. at Calif. State U., 1963. Mem. U.S. Naval Inst., Navy League U.S. Ford Found. fellow, 1960. Mem. Acad. Mgmt., Inst. Mgmt. Sci., Western Econs. Assn. Internat., World Future Soc., Am. Acad. Polit. Social Sci., Calif. State U. Assn. Emeriti Profs., Calif. State U. L.A. Emeriti Assn. (program v.p. 1986-87, v.p. adminstrn. 1987-88, pres. 1988-89, exec. com. 1990-91, treas. 1991—), Am. Assn. Individual Investors, Am. Assn. Ret. Persons, Ret. Pub. Employees Assn. Calif. (chpt. sec. 1984-88, v.p. 1989, pres. 1990-92), Am. Legion, Phi Kappa Phi, Beta Gamma Sigma, Alpha Kappa Psi. Avocations: history, travel, photography, hiking. Home: Covina, Calif. Died May 14, 2007.

ALLMON, JOSEPH THURMAN, retired textiles executive; b. Mize, Miss., Mar. 20, 1921; s. William Richard and Susan Elizabeth (Huff) Allmon; m. Vauda Carolyn Burson, Sept. 25, 1945; 1 child, Warren Douglas. Student, East Ctrl. Jr. Coll. 1938—40; BA, Miss. Coll., 1942; ThM, So. Bapt. Sem., 1945 postgrad., N.Y. U., 1948. V.p. indsl. rels. Riegel Textile Corp., 1969—73, v.p. Greenville, SC, 1973—84; pres. Effective Orgns., Inc., from 1984. Disting. lectr. mgmt. U. S.C., Columbia, from 1984. Editor: How to Organize and Conduct a Management Development Group, 1950. Pres. Greenville Urban League, 1974—76, Greenville Symphony Assn., 1982—83; chmn., bd. trustees Ednl. Resources Found., 1976—78; civil svc. commr. Greenville, 1977—82; chmn., bd. dirs. Ednl. Resources Found., from 1986; pres. bd. dirs. YMCA Blue Ridge Assembly, 1983—85; bd. dirs. So. Indsl. Relations Conf. With USNR, 1945—46. Republican. Unitarian. Died Aug. 17, 2007.

ALPEN, EDWARD LEWIS, biophysicist, educator; b. San Francisco, May 14, 1922; s. Edward Lawrence and Margaret Catherine (Shipley) A.; m. Wynella June Dosh, Jan. 6, 1945; children: Angela Marie, Jeannette Elise BS, U. Calif., Berkeley, 1946, PhD, 1950. Br. chief, then dir. biol. and med. scis. Naval Radiol. Def. Lab., San Francisco, 1952—68; mgr. environ. and life scis. Battelle Meml. Inst., Richland, Wash., 1968—69, assoc. dir., then dir. Pacific N.W. divsn., 1969—75; dir. Donner Lab., U. Calif., Berkeley; also assoc. dir. Lawrence Berkeley Lab., 1975—87; prof. biophysics emeritus U. Calif., Berkeley, from 1975, prof. radiology emeritus San Francisco, from 1976, dir. U. Calif. Study Ctr. London, 1988—90; councillor, dir. Nat. Coun. Radiol. Protection, 1969—92; exec. v.p., tech. dir. Neutron Tech. Corp., Berkeley, 1990—93. Mem. Gov. Wash. Coun. Econ. Devel., 1973-75; bd. dirs. Wash. Bd. Trade, 1973-76 Author books, papers, abstracts in field Served to capt. USN, 1942-64 Recipient Navy Sci. medal, 1962, Disting. Svc. medal Dept. Def., 1963, Sustaining Members medal Assn. Mil. Surgeons, 1971; fellow Guggenheim Found., 1960-61; sr. fellow NSF, 1958-59 Fellow: Calif. Acad. Scis.; mem.: Biophys. Soc., Radiation Rsch. Soc., Am. Philat. Soc., Bioelectromagnetics Soc. (pres. 1979—80), Sigma Xi (nat. lectr. 1994—96). Episcopalian. Home: Richmond, Calif. Died Nov. 3, 2006.

ALPERT, GORDON MYLES, lawyer; b. Charlotte, NC, May 7, 1944; s. Benjamin and Rose (Wilfand) A.; m. Judith Landon, Aug. 20, 1967; 1 child, Ivanya. AB, Harvard U., 1966; LLB, M in Urban Studies, Yale U., 1970. Bar: N.Y. 1971. Assoc. Marshall, Bratter and others, NYC, 1970-77, ptnr., 1977-82, Rosenman & Colin, NYC, from 1982. Mem. ABA (real property, probate and trust law sect., comml. leasing com.), N.Y. State Bar Assn. (comml. leasing com.), Assn. of Bar of City of N.Y. (real property com.). Home: New York, NY. Died May 23, 2006.

ALPERT, WARREN, oil industry executive, foundation administrator; b. Chelsea, Mass., Dec. 2, 1920; s. Goodman and Tena (Horowitz) Alpert. BS, Boston U., 1942; MBA, Harvard U., 1947; DBA (hon.), Bryant Coll. Mgmt. trainee Std. Oil Co. of Calif., 1947—48; fin. specialist The Calif. Oil Co., 1948—52; pres. Warren Petroleum Co., 1952—54; founder, pres., chmn. bd. Warren Equities, Inc., 1954. Chmn. emeritus Ritz Tower Hotel, 1995—2007; chmn. bd. Kenyon Oil Co., Inc., Mid-Valley Petroleum Corp., Puritan Oil Co., Inc., Drake Petroleum Co., Inc.; mem. U.S. Com. for UN, 1958; exec. com. Small Bus. Adminstrn., 1958; adminstr. for adminstrn. U.S. AID, 1962; former trustee, mem. exec. com. Boston U.; trustee Emerson Coll.; former v.p. Petroleum Mktg. Edn. Found.; bd. dirs., life mem. Assocs. of Harvard Bus. Sch., Mass.; mem. com. for resource and devel. Harvard Med. Sch. bd. fellows. Bd. dirs. World Coun. Synagogues; bd. overseers Albert Einstein Med. Sch.; founder Warren Alpert Found.; bd. fellows Harvard Med. Sch.; former trustee Boston U., Emerson Coll. Named Harvard Med. Sch. Rsch. Ctr. Bldg. named in his honor, 1993; recipient Andrew Wellington Cordier fellow Sch. Internat. Affairs, Columbia U. Mem.: Am. Petroleum Inst. (dir. mktg. divsn.), Young Pres. Orgn. (past dir.), Univ. Club, Met Club, Marco Polo Club, Harvard Club (N.Y.C. mem. house com.), Am. Petroleum Industry 25 Yr. Club, Harvard Bus. Sch. Club (exec. com., dir., bd. govs., pres. 1960—61). Died Mar. 3, 2007.

ALPHER, RALPH ASHER, physicist, educator; b. Washington, Feb. 3, 1921; s. Samuel and Rose (Maleson) Alpher; m. Louise Ellen Simons, Jan. 28, 1942; children: Harriet Alpher Lebetkin, Victor. BS, George Washington U, 1943, MS, 1945, PhD, 1948; ScD (hon.), Union Coll., 1992, Renssalaer Poly. Inst., 1993. Physicist Bur. Ordnance and Naval Ordnance Lab., USN, Washington, 1940-44, Applied Physics Lab., Johns Hopkins U., Silver Spring, Md., 1944-55, GE R&D Ctr., Schenectady, NY, 1955-86; disting. rsch. prof. physics Union Coll., Schenectady, 1986—2004, prof. emeritus, 2004—07. Adj. prof. aero engring. Renselaer Poly. Inst., 1958—63, adj. prof. physics, 1986—92. Contbr. chapters to books, articles to profl. jours. Bd. dirs. Mohawk-Hudson Coun. Ednl. TV, 1974—80, 1982—87, chmn., 1978—80, 1986—87; bd. dirs. Dudley Obs., Union U., Albany, NY, 1968—72, 1980—86, v.p., 1983—86, adminstr., disting. sr. scientist, from 1987. Recipient Magellanic Premium, Am. Philos. Soc., 1975, Georges Vanderlinden prize, Belgian Royal Acad. Scis., Letters and Fine Arts, 1975, John Price Wetherill medal, Franklin Inst., 1980, Phys. and Math. Scis. prize, NY Acad. Scis., 1981, Disting. Alumnus award, George Washington U., 1987, Henry Draper medal, NY Acad. Scis., 1993, 2005 Nat. Medal Sci., NSF, 2005. Fellow: AAAS (sect. B physics steering com. 1982—86), Am. Acad. Arts & Scis., Am. Phys. Soc. (councillor-at-large 1979—82, mem. exec. com. 1980—81); mem.: Internat. Astron. Union, Am. Astron. Soc., Fedn. Am. Scientists, Internat. Torch Club, Sigma Xi. Home: Austin, Tex. Died Aug. 12, 2007.

ALSBERG, DIETRICH ANSELM, electrical engineer, consultant; b. Kassel, Germany, June 5, 1917; came to U.S., 1939, naturalized, 1943; s. Adolf and Elisabeth (Hofmann) A.; m. Glenna Rose Le Baron, Nov. 6, 1942; children: Peter Allyn, Ronald Ashley, Terry Wayne, David James (dec.). BS in E.E, Tech. U., Stuttgart, 1938; postgrad., Case Sch. Applied Sci., Cleve., 1939-40. Engr. Wright Tool and Forge Co., Barberton, Ohio, 1940-41, Bridgwater Machine Co., Akron, Ohio, 1941-43; with Bell Labs., Holmdel, Murray Hill, Whippany (NJ) and NY, 1945-82, head various depts., 1965-82. Author: (autobiography) A Witness to a Century, 1999; contbr. articles to profl. jours. and books; patentee in field of comms., electromagnetic waves, missile and space guidance and civil engring. Mem. Berkeley Heights (N.J.) Bd. Edn., 1955-58; chmn. Environ. Commn., Berkeley Heights, 1971-76; various office positions local Meth. Ch. With U.S. Army, ETO, 1943-45. Fellow IEEE (life). Lutheran. Home: Carmel, Calif. Died Feb. 27, 2007.

ALSCHULER, ALFRED SAMUEL, psychology educator; b. Chgo., Aug. 14, 1939; s. Alfred Samuel and Helen Nancy (Adler) A.; m. Irene Ultika Hystrom, June 21, 1964 (div. Aug. 1976); children: Lisa, Brigette, Alfred; m. Cathryn Fishman, Aug. 21, 1981; 1 child, Elena. BA, Amherst Coll., 1961; MA, Harvard U., 1963, PhD, 1966; LHD (hon.), John F. Kennedy U., 1978; DPsych. (hon.), Rosebridge Grad. Sch., 1989. Diplomate N.Y. Bd. Psychology. Asst. prof. Harvard Grad. Sch. Edn., Cambridge, Mass., 1966-69; assoc. prof. SUNY, Albany, 1969-71; prof. U. Mass., Amherst, Mass., 1971-89; pres. John F. Kennedy U., Orinda, Calif., 1989-90, Inst. Transpersonal Psychology, Menlo Park, Calif., 1990-92; dean Appalachian State U., Boone, N.C., 1992-94, prof., from 1992. Pres. Devel. Rsch. Assocs., Cambride, 1966-69; bd. trustees Traveling Sch. Internat., Santa Cruz, Calif., 1989—; and many other bds. Author: (books) Teaching Achievement Motivation, 1970, School Discipline. 1980, Teacher Burnout, 1982, Weapons of Construction, 1989, Recipient 3 pre-doctoral grants, NIMH, 1960-66; 2 Fulbright fellowships, Holland, Norway, T. Scott Rogo award Parapsychology Found., N.Y.C., 1994. Home: Raleigh, NC. Died Aug. 3, 2006.

ALSTADT, DONALD MARTIN, manufacturing executive; b. Erie, Pa., July 29, 1921; s. Rheinhold L. and Jean M. Alstadt; m. Judith Carlow, Nov. 23, 1984; 1 child, Karen. BS, U. Pitts., 1947; Sc.D. (hon.), Thiel Coll., 1980. With Lord Corp., Erie, from 1961, v.p., gen. mgr., 1964-66, exec. v.p., 1966-68, pres., 1968-75, also chmn. bd., chief exec. officer, 1982-91, now chmn. bd., from 1993. Cons. Carborundum Co., Transistor Products Co. of Boston, 1952-56; dir. Keithley Instruments Inc.; cons. Lincoln Project, 1952-53, NSF, 1980—; guest lectr. Internat. Inst. Mgmt. Sci. Ctr., Berlin, 1979; vis. scientist MIT, 1986. Contbr. articles to profl. jours. Chmn. bd. overseers Franklin Pierce Law Ctr., 1981—; mem. adv. bd. Ctr. for Advanced Engring. Study, MIT, 1981—; mem. Pa. Sci. and Engring. Found., 1980—; bd. advisors Case Western Res. Sch. Mgmt., Cleve., 1970—; bd. visitors U. Pitts. Grad. Sch. Bus., 1972—; trustee Poly. Inst. N.Y., Bklyn., 1973—, Kolff Found., Cleve., 1974—, Hamot Med. Center, Erie, Pa., 1973-78, Rose Poly. Inst., 1976-79; mem. adv. bd. Mellon Inst. Research; met. chmn. Nat. Alliance of Businessmen, 1969; mem. president's council Tulane U., 1976—; mem. vis. com. Sch. Engring., M.I.T., 1980—, Sch. Engring., Duke U., 1980—; mem. policy com. Pa. Bus. Council, 1979—; dir., pres. Lord Found. of N.C., Lord Fond. of Calif., Lord Found. of Mass., Lord Found. of Pa., Lord Found. of Ohio. Recipient Medal of Merit Edinboro State Coll., 1979; Univ. medal Pa. State U., 1981; Disting. Service award Sch. Engring. Duke U., 1985, Adhesives and Sealant Council, 1985; named Hon. Football Coach, U. So. Calif. Fellow Am. Inst. Chemists; mem. Am. Phys. Soc., Am. Chem. Soc., Faraday Soc. of Eng., Electrochem. Soc., Chemists Club N.Y., N.Y. Acad. Scis., Inst. Mgmt. Sci., Am. Security Council, Swedish Royal Acad. Engring. Sci. (guest lectr. 1984), Acad. Applied Sci. Republican. Presbyterian. Avocation: fishing. Died Feb. 19, 2007.

ALTHOUSE, ERNEST E., utility executive; b. Strausstown, Pa., Sept. 24, 1904; s. Adam Joseph and Minnie (Burkey) A.; m. Elizabeth Righter Plank, May 29, 1935. E.E., Lehigh U., 1926. Registered profl. engr., N.Y., Pa. With Central Hudson Gas & Electric Corp., Poughkeepsie, N.Y., 1928-86, pres., 1968-75, vice chmn., 1975-86, also dir. Mem. IEEE, Soc. Gas Lighting. Clubs: Mason. Home: Willow Street, Pa. Died Apr. 6, 2006.

ALTIERI, JEANNETTE CORVINO, accountant; b. Bridgeport, Conn., May 8, 1937; d. Christopher C. and Julia Marie (Carbonara) Corvino; m. Mario Dominic Altieri, Mar. 29, 1954; children: Jeanmarie, Michael, Lisa Ann, John Christopher. Student, U. New Haven, 1975, Air Traffic Controller Sch., 1976, Housatonic Community Coll. Office mgr. Sportsmen Accessories, Inc., Bridgeport, Conn., 1972-76, New Haven Travel Service, Inc., 1976-79; acct. mgr. Warnaco Outlet Stores div., Warneco Inc., Bridgeport, 1977-87; mgr. Internat. Acctg. Warnaco, Inc., Bridgeport, from 1979; mgr. internat. acctg. Warnaco, Inc., Bridgeport, from 1987. Execc. adviser Jr. Achievement, 1980—. Mem. Nat. Assn. Female Execs., Am. Soc. Profl. and Exec. Women. Home: Mooresville, NC. Died June 17, 2007.

ALTMAN, LYLE D., communications company executive; b. Mpls., Oct. 12, 1930; s. Clayton E. and Gladys B. (Rathbun) A.; m. Jean L. Meehl, Sept. 24, 1952; children: Ann, Don, Elizabeth, Kurt, Eric. BSBA cum laude, U. Nebr., 1952. Mktg. mgr. IBM, LA, 1954-65; v.p. mktg. Control Data Corp., Mpls., 1965-70; pres. Fabri-Tek Inc., Mpls., 1970-76; chmn., chief exec. officer Network Systems Corp., Mpls., from 1976. Bd. dirs. BMC Industries, St. Paul. Capt. USAF, 1952-54. Mem. Phi Beta Kappa, Beta Gamma Sigma, Sigma Nu (comdr. U. Nebr. chpt.). Home: Naples, Fla. Died Jan. 11, 2007.

ALTMAN, ROBERT (ROBERT BERNARD ALTMAN), film director, producer, scriptwriter; b. Kansas City, Mo., Feb. 20, 1925; s. B.C. and Helen Altman; m. LaVonne Elmer, 1947 (div.), 1 child, Christine; m. Lotus Corelli, 1954 (div.), children Stephen, Michael; m. Kathryn Reed, 1959, children Robert, Matthew R.; 1 stepchild, Konni Corriere Student, U. Mo., 3 years. Owner Sandcastle 5 Prodns. Dir.: (films) The Delinquents, 1957, Countdown, 1968, That Cold Day in the Park, 1969, M*A*S*H, 1970 (Grand Prix award Cannes Film Festival 1970, Best Film, Nat. Soc. Film Critics 1970), Popeye, 1980, Come Back to the 5 & Dime, Jimmy Dean, Jimmy Dean, 1982, Streamers, 1983, Beyond Therapy, 1987, Vincent & Theo, 1990, The Gingerbread Man, 1997; dir., prodr., writer: (films) Three Women, 1977, HealtH, 1979, Gosford Park, 2001 (nominee Best dir. and Best Picture Acad. award 2002, Best dir. in Motion Picture Golden Globe award 2002, Dir. of Yr. AFI. Film Award 2002, BAFTA award, Evening Std. Brit. Film award NSFC award NYFCC award, Best Dir./Best Film Silver Ribbon award 2002), Paint, 2005; dir., prodr.: (films) Nashville, 1975, A Wedding, 1978, Quintet, 1979, A Perfect Couple, 1979, Secret Honor, 1985, The Player, 1992 (Best Dir. citation Cannes Film Festival, 1992), After Glow, 1997, The Company, 2003; dir., writer: (films) Brewster McCloud, 1970, McCabe and Mrs. Miller, 1971, Images, 1972, The Long Goodbye, 1973, Thieves Like Us, 1974, California Split, 1974, Buffalo Bill and the Indians, 1976, Fool for Love, 1985, Short Cuts, 1993 (nominee Best Dir. Acad. award 1993), Ready to Wear (Prêt-à-Porter), 1994, Kansas City, 1996, Cookie's Fortune, 1999, Dr. T and the Women, 2000, The Company, 2003, A Prairie Home Companion, 2006; dir., prodr.: (TV films) Precious Blood, 1982, Rattlesnake in a Cooler, 1982, The Laundromat, 1984, The Dumb Waiter, 1987, The Room, 1987, Caine Mutiny Court Martial, 1987, Tanner '88, 1988, Tanner on Tanner, 2004; dir. (plays): (Broadway) Come Back to the 5 & Dime, Jimmy Dean, Jimmy Dean, 1982, (Lyric Opera of Chgo.) McTeague, 1993, Resurrection Blues, 2006; prodr.: (films) The Late Show, 1977, Welcome to L.A., 1977, Rich Kids, 1979, Remember My Name, 1979, Mrs. Parker and the Vicious Circle, 1994; exec. prodr.:(films) Roads & Bridges, 2001; co-prodr.: (films) The James Dean Story, 1957; actor (films) Dr. T & The Women (Golden Lion award 2000); (TV movies) Frank Capra's American Dream, 1997. Served with AUS, 1943-47. Named 17th Greatest Director of all time, Entertainment Weekly; recipient Lifetime Achievement award, 2000, Hon. Golden Berlin Bear award, 2002, Hon. Award for Lifetime Achievement, Acad. Motion Picture Arts & Sciences, 2006. Mem. Dirs. Guild Am. Died Nov. 20, 2006.

ALTON, ELAINE VIVIAN, mathematics educator; b. Watertown, NY, Aug. 30, 1925; s. Keith Earle and Gladys Louise (Freeman) A. AB, SUNY-Albany, 1946; M.Ed., St. Lawrence U., 1951; MA, U. Mich., 1958; PhD, Mich. State U., 1965. Tchr. math. Fultonville High Sch., NYC, 1946-48; assoc. prof. math. Ferris State Coll., Big Rapids, Mich., 1948-62; asst. instr. math Mich. State U., East Lansing, Mich., 1962-64; prof. math. edn. Ind.-Purdue U., Indpls., 1964-90, prof. emeritus, from 1990. Author: (with J.A. Gersting) Vol. SI-the Metric System, 1977, (with J.A. Gersting and J.E. Kuczkowski) filmstrip-cassette course, Trigonometry, 1980, (with Lucreda A. Hutton and J.E. Kuczkowski) Success with Algebra, 1986; contbr. articles in field to profl. jours. NSF grantee, 1970-73 Mem. Nat. Council Tchrs. Math., Assn. Tchr. Educators, Math. Assn. Am., Am. Math. Assn. Two Year Colls., Ind. Council Tchrs. Math. Clubs: Pilot (Indpls.). Home: Indianapolis, Ind. Died Aug. 11, 2006.

AMBRISTER, JOHN CHARLES, lawyer; b. Norman, Okla., June 21, 1944; s. Charles Alexander and Rebecca Louise (Scott) A.; divorced; 1 child, Charles Scott; m. Roni Miller, Sept. 3, 1977. BA, Tulsa U., 1962-66; JD, Washington U., St. Louis, 1969. Bar: Mo. 1969, Ill. 1978. Sole practice, St. Louis, 1969-73; corp. atty. Sargent Welch, Skokie, Ill., 1973-74; corp. counsel, asst. sec. Bell and Howell, Chgo., 1974-80; gen. counsel, sec. Dayton Walther, Ohio, 1981; sr. exec. v.p., gen. counsel, sec. AM Internat., Chgo.; gen. counsel Floral Transworld Delivery (FTD); exec. v.p., COO Beitler Real Estate Corp. Mem. ABA, Ill. Bar Assn., Mo. Bar Assn., Am. Soc. Corp. Secs. Avocation: golf. Home: Chicago, Ill. Died July 6, 2007.

AMBROSINO, RALPH THOMAS, JR., retired telecommunications executive; b. Gloversville, NY, Aug. 5, 1940; s. Ralph Thomas and Mary Agnes (Peters) A.; m. Roberta Joy Goldman, Nov. 1, 1970; children: Robin, Jill. BS in Acctg., U. Buffalo, 1961. With Gen. Telephone Co., 1968-74; gen. comml. mgr. Upstate N.Y., Johnstown, 1968-70, gen. service office mgr., 1970-74; regulatory matters mgr. GTE Service Corp., Stamford, Conn., 1974-76, revenues and earnings mgr., 1976-78; dir. regulatory affairs Gen. Telephone Co. of Calif., Santa Monica, 1979-81; dir. regulatory matters GTE Service Corp., Stamford, 1981-84, v.p. investor relations, 1984-87, v.p. external affairs, 1987. Mem. Investor Relations Assn. Home: Southport, Conn. Died Apr. 27, 2007.

AMENTA, MICHAEL JOSEPH, accountant; b. NYC, Apr. 21, 1933; s. Angelo and Jessie Catherine (Purpura) A.; m. Antoinette M. Florio, Feb. 20, 1955; children: Michael, Marie, Theresa. BBA, CUNY, 1955. CPA, N.Y.; cert. specialist in real estate securities. Nat. real estate ptnr. Laventhol & Horwath, NYC, from 1958. Editor: (newsletters) Real Estate Insight, 1984—, laventhol & Horwath Real Estate Newsletter, 1978-89; mem. editorial bd. Real Estate Securities Jour., 1980—, Real Estate Fin., 1983—, Limited Partnership Investment Rev., 1985—, Jour. Acctg. and Fin., 1990—, Perspective, 1978—. Mem. bd. overseers L.I. U., 1989—; mem. Real Estate Inst. C.W. Post Coll., 1989—; mem. bd. appeals and zoning Village of Port Washington North, 1960-70; pres. Cath. League Nassau County, N.Y., 1980-82; assoc. trustee North Shore U. Hosp., N.Y., 1975—. With U.S. Army, 1955-57. Mem. Real Estate Securities and Syndication Inst. (pres. N.Y. state chpt. 1982-84, exec. com. 1988-89, gov. 1989-90), Urban Land Inst. (mktg.-pub. affairs com.), Internat. Coun. Shopping Ctrs., Nat. Assn. Home Builders, AICPA, N.Y. State Soc. CPAs, Nat. Assn. Realtors (urban affairs com.), Nat. Assn. Indsl. and Office Parks, Plandome Country Club. Avocations: lapidary, golf, photography, gardening. Home: Roslyn, NY. Died Dec. 22, 2005.

AMES, LINCOLN, manufacturing executive; b. Glen Ridge, NJ, Aug. 8, 1932; s. Wyllys Pitman and Anna (Lincoln) A.; m. Aubin Wells Zabriskie, Nov. 26, 1960; children: Hyla Lincoln, Mark Zabriskie, David Wyllys. BS, Yale U., 1954; MBA, Harvard U., 1960. Sr. v.p., dir. corp. fin. Blyth & Co., Inc., NYC, 1960-72; exec. v.p., chmn. capital markets group Dean Witter Reynolds, Inc., NYC, 1972-84, also bd. dirs.; also mem. exec. com., chmn. Dean Witter Reynolds Overseas, Ltd.; sec.-treas. Lumintech, Inc., Irvington, N.J., from 1986; pres. Universal Mfg. Co., Inc., Irvington, from 1988; chmn. Hammer Mfg. Co., Inc., Linden, N.J., from 1986. Bd. dirs. Montclair (N.J.) Savs. Bank, 1986—. Trustee Montclair Art Mus., 1982—, Mental Health Resource Ctr., Montclair, 1986—. Lt. (j.g.) USNR, 1954-57. Mem.: Montclair Golf, The Brook (N.Y.C.), Hartwood (Forestburg, N.Y.). Republican. Presbyterian. Avocations: reading, sports, travel. Home: Montclair, NJ. Died Feb. 22, 2006.

AMES, THOMAS TREES, steel company executive; b. New Kensington, Pa., Mar. 12, 1924; s. Francis Edward and Mary Agnes (Trees) A.; m. Rena June Connor, July 19, 1946; children— James Connor, Howard Francis. Student Va. Poly. Inst., Blacksburg, 1946-49. With Aluminum Co. of Am., New Kensington, Pa., 1949-56; plant mgr. Gen. Electric Co., New Kensington, 1956-66; mgr. ops. conduit div. Jones & Laughlin Steel Corp., Niles, Ohio, 1966-75, works mgr., Hennepin, Ill., 1975—. Bd. dirs. Citizens Gen. Hosp., New Kensington, 1963-66, YMCA, New Kensington, 1963-66. Served with USAAF, 1942-45. Mem. Assn. Iron and Steel Engrs., C. of C. Clubs: Elks, Bureau Valley Country. Home: Bonita Springs, Fla. Died Sept. 17, 2006.

AMICONE, JOSEPH ANTHONY, food company executive; b. Malden, Mass., June 18, 1927; s. Joseph and Lucia (De Cesare) A.; student public schs., Malden; m. Josephine Antonucci, July 3, 1949; children: Joseph, Cheryl Ann. Owner, operator bakery, Malden, 1952-55; sales mgr. Vanco Products, Stoneham, Mass., 1956-62; chief exec. officer, treas. J. Amicone Co. Inc., Malden, 1962— (now merged with Internat. Multi Foods, Mnpls.); cons. bakery field. Capt., a.d.c. to gov. of Mass. Served with USN, 1945-48; ETO. Mem. New Eng. Bakers' Club. Republican. Roman Catholic. Club: Ancient and Hon. Arty. Co. Mass. Home: Melrose, Mass. Died Apr. 7, 2007.

AMSEL, ABRAM, experimental psychologist, educator; b. Montreal, Que., Can., Dec. 4, 1922; came to U.S., 1946, naturalized, 1957; s. Aaron Harry and Annie (Levitt) A.; m. Tess Steinbach, June 11, 1947; children: Steven David, Andrew Jay, Geoffrey Neal. BA, Queen's U., Kingston, Ont., 1944; MA, McGill U., Montreal, 1946; PhD, U. Iowa, 1948. Mem. faculty Tulane U., 1948-60, U. Toronto, 1960-69; vis. prof. U. Calif., Berkeley, 1962; NSF sr. postdoctoral fellow University Coll., London, 1966-67; prof. exptl. psychology U. Tex., Austin, from 1969, Ashbel Smith prof., from 1981. Philips lectr. Haverford Coll., 1970; vis. prof. U. Pa., 1974-75, U. Oxford, Eng., fall 1979; D.E. Berlyne lectr. U. Toronto, 1986; I.E. Farber lectr. U. Ill., Chgo., 1987; MacEachran lectr. U. Alta., 1987; Horsley Gantt lectr. Pavlovian Soc., 1991. Author: (with M.R. Rashotte) Mechanisms of Adaptive Behavior: Clark Hull's Theoretical Papers With Commentary, 1984, Behaviorism, Neobehaviorism and Cognitivism in Learning Theory, 1989, Frustration Theory: An Analysis of Dispositional Learning and Memory, 1992; editor Psychonomic Sci., 1970-72; founding editor Animal Learning and Behavior, 1972-76; mem. editorial bd. Jour. Exptl. Psychology, 1963-69, Internat. Jour. Psychophysiology, 1982-90; contbr. articles to profl. jours., monographs. Recipient Disting. Grad. award U. Iowa, 1992; rsch. grantee NSF, 1956-83, 87-90, NRC, Can., 1962-69, NIMH, 1979-83, Nat. Inst. Child Health and Human Devel., 1983-86, Nat. Inst. Alcohol Abuse and Alcoholism, 1987—; fellow Ctr. Advanced Study in Behavioral Sci., Stanford, Calif., 1986-87. Fellow AAAS (chmn. electorate nominating com. divsn. J 1990, chair-elect divsn. J 1995); mem. NAS, Internat. Brain Rsch. Orgn., Internat. Soc. Devel. Psychobiology, Soc. Exptl. Psychologists (chmn. 1976, chair Warren medal com. 1983, 95, Howard Crosby Warren medal 1980), Soc. Neurosci., Psychonomic Soc. (chmn. governing bd. 1978), Southwestern Psychol. Assn., So. Soc. Philosophy and Psychology. Home: Austin, Tex. Died Sept. 1, 2006.

AMSTADTER, LAURENCE, retired architect; b. Chgo., Apr. 9, 1922; s. Frank J. and Irene B. (Black) A.; m. Erma Jacqueline Kallen, Mar. 8, 1948; children: John Kallen, Marc Robert. BA in Architecture, Chgo. Tech. Coll., 1948; postgrad., Northwestern U., Evanston, Ill., 1948-49. Registered architect, Ill., 20 other states. Architect Ford Bacon & Davis Inc., Chgo., 1949-50, Skidmore Owings & Merrill, Chgo., 1950-51, Sidney Morris & Assocs., Chgo., 1951-52, Chgo. Housing Authority, 1952-53; sr. v.p. A. Epstein and Sons Inc., Chgo., 1953-87; cons., 1987—2006. Mem. Exec. Svc. Corps of Chgo. With Air Corps, U.S. Army, 1941-45, ETO. Mem. AIA (corp.), Svc. Corps Ret. Execs., Soc. Am. Registered Architects, Chgo. Com. on High Rise Bldgs. Democrat. Home: Flossmoor, Ill. Died Dec. 29, 2006.

AMSTER, ADOLPH B., chemist, researcher; b. NYC, Nov. 22, 1924; s. Milton M. and Jennie (Feigin) Amster; m. Shirley Selma Mallin, Sept. 1, 1947 (dec. Apr. 1948); m. Ruth Irene Mittleman, June 1, 1953; 1 child, Kenneth. BS, CCNY, 1943; AM, Columbia U., 1947; PhD, Ohio State U., 1951. Chemist Nat. Bur. Stds., Washington, 1951—54, Naval Ordnance Lab., Silver Spring, Md., 1954—60; chmn. phys. and inorganic chemistry Stanford Rsch. Inst., Menlo Park, Calif., 1960—68; dir. chemistry divsn. energetic materials Naval Sea Sys. Command, Washington, 1968—78; head chemistry divsn. Naval Weapons Ctr., China Lake, Calif., 1978—85, sr. scientist, from 1985. Contbr. articles to sci. publs. Lt. US Army, 1943—45, ETO. Fellow: AIAA; mem.: Am. Phys. Soc., Combustion Inst., Sierra Club (mem. outing com. from 1983). Home: Ridgecrest, Calif. Died Oct. 24, 2006.

AMSTUTZ, DANIEL GORDON, agricultural products executive, consultant, retired federal agency administrator, grain company executive; b. Cleve., Nov. 8, 1932; s. Gordon M. and Elizabeth (Kiss) Amstutz. BS, Ohio State U., 1954. Trainee Cargill, Inc., Mpls., 1954-55, grain mcht. Ft. Worth, 1959, sr. grain mcht. Mpls., 1960-72; grain mcht. Tradax Can., Ltd., Montreal, Que., 1955-56, Tradax Geneva S.A., 1956-57; mgr. Deutsche Tradax GMBH, Hamburg, Germany, 1957-58; pres. Cargill Investor Svcs., Inc., Chgo., 1972—78; ptnr. Goldman, Sachs & Co., NYC, 1978-82; undersec. Dept. Agr., Washington, 1983-87; pres. Cmty. Credit Corp., Washington, 1983-87; amb., chief trade negotiator for agr. USDA, Washington, 1987-89; exec. dir. Internat. Wheat Coun., London, 1992-95; pres., CEO N.Am. Export Grain Assn., Inc., Washington, 1995-2000; pres. Amstutz & Co., Washington, from 2000; sr. ministry adv. agrl. Iraq, 2003—04. Mem. U.S. Agrl. Policy Adv. Com., 1998—2003, U.S.-Russian Joint Commn. Econ. and Tech. Coop., 1996—2000; bd. dirs. U.S. Feed Grains Coun., 1967—72. Mem.: Nat. Grain and Feed Assn. (bd. dirs. 1973—82), Ohio State U. Found. (bd. dirs. from 1998), Ohio State U. Alumni Assn. (v.p. 1989, co-chair fund raising campaign 1990—99). Home: Arlington, Va. Died Mar. 20, 2006.

ANDERS, DAN RANEY, judge, government administrator; b. State College, Miss., Aug. 22, 1933; s. Charles B. and Ruth (Raney) A.; m. Camille Shephard, Sept. 3, 1994. B.S., Millsaps Coll., 1954; J.D., U. Miss., 1958. Bar: Miss. 1958, U.S. Dist. Ct. (no. dist.) Miss. 1958, U.S. Ct. Claims 1974, U.S. Supreme Ct. 1966. Field claims atty. State Farm Mut. Ins. Co., Shreveport, La., 1958-59; gen. atty. VA, Shreveport, 1959-63, mgmt. specialist, Washington, 1963-64, asst. dir. investigation and security service, 1966-73, dir. contract compliance service, 1973-74, adminstrv. judge/vice chmn. Bd. Contract Appeals, 1974—; dep. to dir. compliance EEOC, Washington, 1964-66. Served to sgt. U.S. Army, 1954-56; Korea. Mem. bd. contract Appeals Judges Assn., Miss. State Bar Assn., Kappa Sigma. Home: Carrollton, Ga. Died Jan. 4, 2006.

ANDERSON, CHESTER GRANT, language educator; b. River Falls, Wis., Dec. 8, 1923; s. C.A. Chester and Inga Amelia (Grant) A.; m. Carole Nygard, Apr. 23, 1945; children: Stephen, Mark, Jonathan. Student, St. Olaf Coll., 1941-43; MA, U. Chgo., 1948; PhD, Columbia U., 1962. Asst. prof. English Creighton U., Omaha, 1948-50, asst. prof., 1954-57, Fordham U., NYC, 1951-52; dir. State Soc. Services, AICPAs, 1952-54; assoc. prof. Western Conn. State U., 1957-63; asst. prof. Columbia U., 1963-68; prof. English U. Minn., Mpls., 1963-96, prof. emeritus, from 1996; Fulbright prof. Helsinki (Finland) U., 1963-64. Semester-at-Sea prof., 1987; W.B. Yeats Internat. Summer Sch. prof., Sligo, Ireland, 1987; vis. prof. Odense U., Denmark, 1977-78, Curtin U., Australia, 1989. Author: James Joyce and His World, 1967, translation in Portugese and Italian, 1989, Spanish, 1990, Chinese, 1999, Critical Edit. of James Joyce's A Portrait of the Artist, 1968, corrected 1992, Growing Up in Minnesota, 1976. Ensign AC, USNR, 1943-45. Mem. MLA, MLA Helsinki, Acad. Am. Poets, James Joyce Found. Home: Mount Dora, Fla. Died May 29, 2006.

ANDERSON, DAVID EDMOND, telecommunications company executive; b. Sioux City, Iowa, Nov. 17, 1926; s. David E. and Ella S. (Geneva) Anderson; m. Marilyn G. Hoefer, May 28, 1949; children: Susan Sonye, Nancy J. BSEE, Iowa State U., 1948. Plant engr. Gen. Telephone Wis., Sun Prairie, 1948, divsn. mgr. Black River Falls, 1961, chief engr. Sun Prairie, 1965—67, Gen. Telephone Ohio, Marion, 1967—68; v.p. ops. Gen. Telephone Ill., Bloomington, 1968—77, pres., 1978—79; v.p. network engring. and constrn. Gen. Telephone Calif., Santa Monica, 1977—78; pres., CEO, 1979; now ret. Bd. dirs. Barclays Bank Calif., San Francisco. Chmn. 1982 HIspanic Woman's Coun. awards dinner; chmn. ann. awards dinner Nat. Hispanic Scholarship Fund, 1983; bd. dirs. Calif. State U. Found., Long Beach, from 1982, INd. Colls. So. Calif., from 1982, L.A. United Way, Calif., L.A. Opera Theatre, Calif. With USN, 1944—46. Mem.: NSPE, L.A. Area C. of C. (bd. dirs., chmn. 1985), Calif. C. of C., Calif. Roundtable (bd. dirs.). Methodist. Home: Pacific Palisades, Calif. Died May 28, 2006.

ANDERSON, ERNEST WASHINGTON, manufacturing executive; b. Corydon, Ind., Feb. 22, 1922; s. Roscoe Irvin and Orpah (Dick) A.; m. Jeanne Elizabeth Schoonover, July 12, 1944 (dec. Sept. 1991); children— Thomas, Carol, Steven, Jane; m. Lucille De Boer, Nov. 7, 1992. BS, Ind. U., 1943. With Gen. Motors Corp., Detroit, 1948-52; with Fed.-Mogul Corp., Detroit, 1952-86, v.p. corp. affairs, sec., from 1986. V.p., sec. advisory bd. Providence Hosp.; bd. dirs. Citizens Research Council Mich. Served to capt. AUS, 1943-48. Mem. Tax Execs. Inst. (nat. v.p., treas., dir., chpt. pres.), NAM, U.S. C. of C., Fin. Execs. Inst., Am. Soc. Corp. Secs., Mich. C. of C. (dir.), Southfield C. of C. (dir.), Detroit C. of C. (dir.), Briarwood Country Club (dir.). Home: Sun City West, Ariz. Died Mar. 30, 2006.

ANDERSON, GEORGE FREDERICK, educator, former association executive; b. Buffalo, Sept. 15, 1914; s. Gustaf Edmund and Harriett Manelva (Paulding) A.; m. Julia Jane Ackley, Nov. 26, 1942; children: Lois A. Ezell, Cheri A. Goodson. BS, SUNY, Cortland, 1940; MS, Syracuse U., 1947, Ed.D., 1950. Tchr. phys. edn., coach, vice prin. Gorham (N.Y.) Central Sch., 1940-43; instr. Syracuse U., 1947-48, dual prof. liberal arts and edn., 1948-51; asso. exec. sec. Am. Alliance Health, Phys. Edn., Recreation and Dance, Washington, 1951-74, exec. v.p., 1974-80, dir., 1974-80; ret., 1980. Dir. Center for Ednl. Assns., 1974-80 Contbr. articles to profl. jours. Served with USNR, 1943-46. Mem. NEA (life), Am. Alliance Health, Phys. Edn., Recreation and Dance (life), Am. Soc. Assn. Execs., Soc. State Dirs. of Health, Phys. Edn. and Recreation. Republican. Lutheran. Home: Silver Spring, Md. Died Aug. 26, 2006.

ANDERSON, JACK WAYNE, marine science researcher, administrator; b. San Diego, Mar. 15, 1938; s. Neil S. Anderson and Ethel (Wills) Archer; m. Marilyn Sue Wallace, Sept. 1964 (div. 1974); m. Mary Linda McLain, Feb. 19, 1978; children: Amanda Lynn, Jacquelyn Lindsey. AA, El Camino Coll., 1960; BA, Calif. State U., Long Beach, 1964, MA, 1966; PhD, U. Calif., Irvine, 1969. Asst. prof. Tex. A&M U., College Station, 1969-74, assoc. prof., 1974-76; sr. research scientist Battelle Northwest Lab., Sequim, Wash., 1976-83, assoc. mgr. Marine Research Lab., 1983-85; dir. So. Calif. Coastal Water Research Project, Long Beach, from 1985. Cons. EXXON Prodn. Research Co., Houston, 1973-76; chmn. com. biol. effects program NSF/IDOE, 1974-75; mem. 5 man NOAA adv. com. on Amoco Cadiz oil spill, 1978-81; mem. sci. adv. com. U.S. Sec. of Interior, 1979-81. Author 5 books on marine science; founding co-editor Marine Environ. Research, 1978-80; contbr. over 80 articles to profl. jours. Grantee Am. Petroleum Inst., U.S. Dept. Energy, Sea Grant, NSF, 1974-76. Mem. Am. Soc. Zoologists, AAAS, Western Soc. Naturalists, So. Calif. Acad. Scis., Sigma Xi. Avocations: skiing, windsurfing, volleyball. Home: San Marcos, Calif. Died Feb. 21, 2007.

ANDERSON, JON MAC, lawyer, educator; b. Rio Grande, Ohio, Jan. 10, 1937; s. Harry Rudolph and Carrie Viola (Magee) A.; m. Deborah Melton, June 1, 1961; children: Jon Gordon, Greta. AB, Ohio U., 1958; JD, Harvard Law Sch., 1961. Bar: Ohio 1961. Law clk. Hon. Kingsley A. Taft Ohio Supreme Ct., Columbus, 1961—62; assoc. Wright, Harlor, Morris & Arnold, Columbus, 1962—67, ptnr., 1968—76, Porter, Wright, Morris & Arthur, Columbus, from 1977. Adj. prof. law Ohio State U. Law Sch., Columbus, 1975-83; bar examiner State of Ohio, 1971-76, chmn., 1975-76; lectr. tax and estate planning insts.; bd. dirs. White Castle System, Inc. Trustee Columbus Mus. of Art, 2003—, Berea Coll, Ky., 1976-2000, Pro Musica Chamber Orch., Columbus, 1980-98, Opera Columbus, 1985-88, 1st Congl. Ch., Columbus, 1979-83, Greater Columbus Arts Coun., 1989-99; chmn., 1996-98; mem. adv. coun. The Textile Mus., 1996-2002. Mem. ABA, Ohio State Bar Assn., Columbus Bar Assn., The Columbus Club, Rocky Fork Hunt and Country Club. Democrat. Avocations: music, art, literature, antiques. Home: Columbus, Ohio. Died May 14, 2007.

ANDERSON, KENNETH OSCAR, film company executive; b. Rembrandt, Ia., Dec. 23, 1917; s. Oscar Frank and Ethel Mae (Anderson) A.; student Wheaton Coll., 1936-37, 45-51, Northwestern U., 1947-48; m. Doris Ilene Jones, Nov. 16, 1938; children— Naoma (Mrs. Larry Clark), Margaret (Mrs. T. Landon Mauzy), Donn, Lane, Max, Ken D., Melody. Editor, Campus Life Mag., Wheaton, Ill., 1945-51; with Gospel Films, Muskegon, Mich., 1949-61, exec. producer, 1949-61; pres. Ken Anderson Films, Winona Lake, Ind., 1963—; dir. Master Investments Corp., Warsaw, Ind.; dir. Internat. Films, London, 1969-72, Reach & Teach, London; vis. instr. Haggai Inst., Singapore, 1974—; vis. lectr. St. Xavier's Coll., Bombay, 1979. Mem. pres.'s com. Grace Coll., Winona Lake, 1972—; adv. com. League for the Handicapped, Walworth, Wis., 1965—; bd. dirs. Youth Haven Ranch, Rives Junction, Mich., Crusade Evangelism, London, Ont., Can. Named Evang. Press Assn. Writer of Year, 1962; Nat. Evang. Film Found. award as Dir. of Year, 1970. Mem. Gidions Internat. Presbyterian (elder 1963—). Author: Himalyan Heartbeat, 1966; Stains on Glass Windows, 1969; Adjustable Halo, 1969; Satan's Angels, 1975, Contemporary Concordance, 1988; (with Tony Mockus) I'm Learning from Protestants How to be a Better Catholic, 1975; producer, dir. film of book Pilgrim's Progress, 1977, film Christiana, 1978, Some Through the Fire (Uganda), 1980, Hudson Taylor, 1981; dir. Mud, Sweat and Cheers, 1984; Fanny Crosby, 1984. Home: Warsaw, Ind. Died Mar. 12, 2006.

ANDERSON, MARY JANE, library director, consultant; b. Des Moines, Jan. 23, 1935; d. William Kenneth and Margaret Louise (Snider) McPherson; m. Charles Robert Anderson, Oct. 21, 1965 (div. Oct. 24, 1989); 1 child, Mary Margaret. BA in Edn., U. Fla., 1957; MLS, Fla. State U., 1963. Elem. sch. librarian Dade County Schs., Miami, Fla., 1957-61; children's/young adult librarian Santa Fe Regional Library, Gainesville, Fla., 1961-63; br. librarian Jacksonville (Fla.) Pub. Library, 1963-64, chief of children's services, 1964-66, head of circulation, 1966-67; pub. library cons. Fla. State Library, Tallahassee, 1967-70; dir. tech. processing St. Mary's Coll. of Md., St. Mary's City, 1970-72; coordinator children's services Balt. County Pub. Library, Towson, Md., 1972-73; exec. dir. young adult services div. ALA, Chgo., 1973-75, exec. dir. assn. for library service to children, 1973-82; pres. Answers Unltd., Inc., Deerfield, Ill., 1982-92; dir. Wilmington (Ill.) Pub. Libr., 1993-97; dir. media svcs. Newark (Ill.) County Sch. Dist., 1997-98; dir. Maud P. Palenske Pub. Libr., St. Joseph, Mich., 1998-2000; coord. Sr. Net Learning Ctr., Ariea IV Agy. Aging, St. Joseph, 2000—03; libr. cons., from 2000. Instr. and cons. in field; part-time faculty No. Ill. U., 1985-86, Nat. Coll. Edn., Evanston, Ill., 1989; head youth svcs. Waukegan (Ill.) Pub. Libr., 1988-93; mem. exec. com. U.S. sect. Internat. Bd. on Books for Young People, 1973-82; mem. adv. bd. Reading Rainbow, TV series, 1981-84; mem. sch. bd. Avoca Sch. Dist. 37, 1985-87; mem. ALSC Newbery Medal Com., 1991. Editor: Top of the News, 1971-73, Fla. State Library Newsletter, 1967-70, Nor'Easter (North Suburban Library System Newsletter), 1984-88; contbr. articles to profl. jours. Bd. dirs. Child Devel. Assocs. Consortium, 1975—83, Coalition for Children and Youth, 1978—80; downtown redevel. commn. City of Wilmington, 1996—98; coun. mem. Episcopal Diocese Chgo. Diocese, 1988—94, standing com., 1994—97, dep. to gen. conv., 1997, Bishop's search com., 1997—98, province V rep., 1998—99; mem. vestry St. Thomas' Episcopal Ch., Morris, Ill., 1996—98; active Episcopal Diocese West, Mich., Diocesan cons. team, from 1999, alt. dep. to gen. conv., 2003; deanery rep. St. Paul's Episc. Ch., St. Joseph, Mich., 2000—01, lay eucharistic min., from 1999, mem. vestry, 2003—05. Mem. ALA (coun. 1992-2000, com. on orgn. 1999-01), Rotary (sec.-treas. 1994-96, pres. 1996-97), Wilmington C. of C. (bd. dirs. 1996-97, sec. 1997), Caxton Club (Chgo.), Beta Phi Mu, Sigma Kappa. Episcopalian. Home: Saint Joseph, Mich. Died May 23, 2006.

ANDERSON, RICHARD WILLIAM, retired psychiatrist, educator; b. Brainerd, Minn., Sept. 11, 1919; s. John Peter and Christine (Erichsen) A.; m. Bette Ann Simonson, July 31, 1943; children: Peter, John, Erik. Student, Carleton Coll., 1936-38; BS, U. Minn., 1941, M.B., MD, 1943. Diplomate: Am. Bd. Psychiatry and Neurology. Intern U.S. Marine Hosp., Seattle, 1943; grad. tng. Mass. Mental Health Center, 1946-47, part-time 1949-50; resident psychiatrist Baldpate, Inc., Georgetown, Mass., 1947-50; dep. commr. mental health Minn., 1950-51; pvt. practice St. Paul, 1951-53; mem. faculty U. Minn. Med. Sch., 1953-75, prof. psychiatry, 1961-75; chief psychiatry service Mpls. Gen. Hosp., 1953-57, dir. adult psychiatry clinic, 1958-70, chief clin. services, dept. psychiatry, 1970-75; sr. cons. Scripps Clinic, La Jolla, Calif., 1975-93; ret., 1993. Contbr. articles to profl. jours. Served with AUS, 1943-46. Commonwealth Fund fellow Ipswich, Eng., 1963-64 Fellow Am. Psychiat. Assn. (life) Home: La Jolla, Calif. Died June 5, 2007.

ANDERSON, ROBERT, retired manufacturing company executive; b. Columbus, Nebr., Nov. 2, 1920; s. Robert and Lillian (Devlin) A.; m. Constance Dahlun Severy, Oct. 2, 1942 (div.); children: Robert, Kathleen D.; m. Diane Clark Lowe, Nov. 2, 1973. BS in Mech. Engring, Colo. State U., 1943, LLD (hon.), 1966; M Automotive Engring., Chrysler Inst. Engring., 1948; DHL (hon.), U. Neb., 1985; JD (hon.), Pepperdine U., 1986; D of Engring. (hon.), Milw. Sch. Engring., 1987. With Chrysler Corp., 1946-68, v.p. corp., gen. mgr. Chrysler-Plymouth div., 1965-67; with Rockwell Internat., 1968-93, pres. comml. products group, 1968-69, v.p. corp., 1968-69, exec. v.p., 1969-70, pres., COO, 1970-74, pres., 1974-79, CEO, 1974-88, chmn., 1979-88, chmn. exec. com., 1988-90, chmn. emeritus, 1990—2006. Bd. dirs. Timken Co., Canton, Ohio, Optical Data

Systems, Richardson, Tex., Gulfstream Aerospace Corp., Savannah, Ga. Trustee Calif. Inst. Tech.; chmn. bus.-higher edn. forum Am. Coun. on Edn., 1982-84; chmn. We. Hwy. Inst., 1983-84; trustee, bd. visitors John E. Anderson Grad. Sch. Mgmt. UCLA. Capt. F.A., U.S. Army, 1943-46. Named Exec. of Yr. Nat. Mgmt. Assn., 1980 Mem. Phi Kappa Phi, Tau Beta Pi, Sigma Nu. Died Oct. 28, 2006.

ANDERSON, THOMAS HAROLD, agricultural products executive; b. Toledo, Jan. 21, 1924; s. Harold and Margaret Mary (Meilink) A.; m. Mary Pat Adamshick, Sept. 13, 1952; children: Mary, Andrew, Margaret, Anthony, Matthew, Janet, Ellen, Ted, Frederick, Alex, Katherine, Thomas, Angel. BS, Mich. State U., 1966. Asst. gen. mgr. The Andersons, Maumee, Ohio, 1947-87, chmn., from 1987. Chmn. Med. Coll. Ohio, Toledo, 1984-89; pres. Toledo Zool. Soc., 1985-86, Internat. Ctr. Preservation Wild Animals, Columbus, Ohio, 1985—. Served to 2d lt. USAAC, 1943-45. Named Trustee of Yr., Ohio Library Trustees Assn., 1971. Mem. C. of C. (chmn. Toledo area 1989—). Lodges: Rotary (pres. Maumee club 1951-52). Avocation: wildlife photography. Home: Whitehouse, Ohio. Died Nov. 30, 2006.

ANDERSON, THOMAS JEROME, educational administrator, orchestra conductor; b. Atlanta, Feb. 28, 1943; s. Farris Furman and Suzelle (Bergren) A.; children— Scott Thomas, Kristen Sue. B.A., Duke U., 1965; Mus.M., Fla. State U., 1967, Ph.D., 1977. Chmn. div. fine arts DeKalb Coll., Clarkston, Ga., 1971—; condr. DeKalb Symphony Orch., Atlanta,1979—. Mem. Met. Assn. for Performing Arts, Inc. (exec. dir. 1984—). Home: Atlanta, Ga. Died Oct. 29, 2005.

ANDERSON, WARREN MATTICE, lawyer; b. Bainbridge, NY, Oct. 16, 1915; s. Floyd E. and Edna (Mattice) Anderson; m. Eleanor C. Sanford, June 28, 1941 (dec. Sept. 1996); children: Warren David, Lawrence, Richard, Thomas; m. Ruth W. Bennett, Aug. 25, 2001. BA, Colgate U., 1937; JD, Albany Law Sch., 1940, LLD (hon.), 1979, Hartwick Coll., 1976, Coll. of New Rochelle, 1979, Fordham U., 1980, Union Coll., 1981, Colgate U., 1982, Hamilton Coll., 1985, Clarkson U., 1987, St. Lawrence U., 1988, Elmira Coll., 1989, St. Francis Coll., 1991; LHD (hon.), Hofstra U., 1987. Bar: N.Y., 1940. Practice in Binghamton; asst. county atty. Broome County, NY, 1940-42; assoc. Hinman, Howard & Kattell LLP, 1949-52; ptnr. Hinman, Howard & Kattell, 1952—2007; mem. N.Y. State Senate, 1953-88, chmn. fin. com., 1966-72, pres. pro tem, majority leader, 1973-88. Del. Rep. Nat. Conv., 1972, 76, 80, 84, 88, mem. platform com., 1972; trustee Colgate U., 1964-70, Cornell U., 1973-88, Elmira Coll., 1989-95; hon. life mem. NY State Commn. on Jud. Nominations; mem. adv. com. Govt. Law Ctr., Albany Law Sch.; mem. bd. overseers Nelson A. Rockefeller Inst. Govt. With AUS, 1943-45, lt. JAGD, 1945-46. Recipient Alumni award Colgate U., 1972 Fellow Am. Bar Found.; mem. ABA, Broome County Bar Assn. Clubs: Binghamton; Oteyokwa Lake (Hallstead, Pa.). Presbyterian. Home: Binghamton, NY. Died June 1, 2007.

ANDERSON, WILLIAM HENRY, JR., clergyman, sociologist; b. Dover, N.J., Sept. 21, 1921; s. William Henry and Gaynell J. A.; B.A., Wheaton Coll., 1943; Th.M., Pitts. Sem., 1949; Ph.D., NYU, 1960; m. Lucile Whieldon Thomas, June 11, 1948; children— William W., Nadyne G., Anders C. Ordained to ministry United Presbyn. Ch., 1949; pastor, Ohio, N.Y. and Pa., 1949-64; prof. sociology Va. Union U., 1964-74; cons. sociology, Richmond, Va., 1974—. Mem. Richmond Democratic Com., 1971-88. Served to lt. col., USAFR, 1942-77. Fellow AAAS, Am. Anthrop. Assn., Am. Sociol. Assn.; mem. Archeol. Soc. Va., Phi Delta Kappa. Died Aug. 15, 2006.

ANDERSON, WILLIAM ROBERT, retired congressman, retired military officer; b. Bakerville, Tenn., June 17, 1921; s. David Hensley and Mary (McKelvey) A.; m. Yvonne Etzel, June 10, 1943 (div. Apr. 1979); children: Michael David, William Robert; m. Patricia Walters, Dec. 26, 1980; children: Jane Hensley, Thomas McKelvey Grad., Columbia Mil. Acad., 1939; BSEE, U.S. Naval Acad., 1942; DSc, Defiance Coll., 1958. Commd. ensign USN, 1942, advanced through grades to capt., 1960; assigned submarines Tarpon, Narwhal, Trutta and 11 Pacific combat patrols, World War II; postwar service submarine Trutta, Sarda; comdr. attack submarine USS Wahoo, Pearl Harbor, 1953-55; head tactical dept. Submarine Sch., 1955-56; staff naval reactors br. AEC, Washington, 1956-57; comdr. USS Nautilus, 1957-59; ret. USN, 1962; mem. US Congress from 6th Tenn dist., 1965—73; co-founder Pub. Office Corp. Author: Nautilus 90 North, 1959, First Under the North Pole, 1959, The Useful Atom, 1966; Contbr. articles to nat. mags. and profl. publs. Decorated Bronze Star, Legion of Merit; recipient Stephen Decatur prize Navy League U.S., Distinguished Service award N.Y.C., Christopher Columbus Internat. Communications award Genoa, Italy; Elisha Kent Kane medalist Geog. Soc. Phila., 1959; Patron's medal Royal Geog. Soc., 1959; Leadership award Freedoms Found., 1960, Lowell Thomas award The Explorers Club, N.Y.C., 1997; featured in Greatest Adventures of All Times spl. edit. Life mag. Died Feb. 25, 2007.

ANDLAUER, EDGAR LOUIS, hotel company executive; b. Newark, Mar. 10, 1923; s. Frederick Charles and Anna Maria (Lowenberg) A.; m. Audrey Virginia Brown, Nov. 3, 1956 (dec. 1979); children: Phillip, Lynn, Eric; m. Patricia Catherine Farley, June 6, 1982. BS in Bus. Adminstrn., Rutgers U., 1948, MBA, 1954. CPA, N.Y., N.J. Mgr. Price Waterhouse & Co., NYC, 1948-65; asst. treas. Howard Johnson Co., North Quincy, Mass., 1965-69, v.p., treas., 1970-75, sr. v.p., treas., chief fin. officer, from 1975. Dir. Multibank Fin. Corp., Dedham, Mass., South Shore Bank, Quincy. Served with U.S. Army, 1943-46, ETO Mem. AICPAs, Fin. Execs. Inst., Boston Treas.' Club. Clubs: Wellesley. Republican. Home: Jupiter, Fla. Died Apr. 23, 2006.

ANDRESEN, MALCOLM, lawyer; b. Medford, Wis., July 26, 1917; s. Thomas Whelen and Ethel (Malkson) A.; m. Ann Kimball, 1942 (div. 1968); children: Anthony M., Susan A. Bridges, Abbott K.; m. Barbara Brown, 1971 (div. 1976); m. Nigi Sato, 1979. BA, U. Wis., 1940, LLB, 1941. Bar: Wis. 1941, N.Y. 1946, U.S. Supreme Ct. 1958. Acct. J.D. Miller & Co., NYC, 1946-47; jr. tax acct. Peat Marwick Mitchell & Co., NYC, 1947-48; assoc. Davis Wagner Hallett & Russell, NYC, 1948-52; tax counsel, then sr. tax counsel, sr. govt. rels. adviser Mobil Oil Corp., NYC, 1952-70; dir. tax legal affairs Nat. Fgn. Trade Coun., NYC, 1970-73; of counsel Delson & Gordon, NYC, 1973-77, Whitman & Ransom, NYC, 1977-86; pvt. practice NYC, from 1986. Trustee, fin. v.p. Nat. Urban League, 1959-65; trustee, treas. Cathedral Ch. of St. John the Divine, N.Y.C., 1977-84. Capt. USMCR, 1942-46. Decorated Bronze Star medal. Mem. Assn. of Bar City of N.Y., Internat. Fiscal Assn. (coun. U.S.A. br. pres. 1971-72), Univ. Club (coun. mem. 1985-89, co-chair com. women mem. admission 1988). Democrat. Episcopalian. Home: New York, NY. Died Nov. 27, 2006.

ANDREW, ROBERT HARRY, agronomist; b. Platteville, Wis., Aug. 2, 1916; s. Harry Roscoe and Lu (Howery) A.; B.A., U. Wis., Madison, 1938; Ph.D., 1942; m. Nancy H. Wright, Apr. 15, 1944; children— Stephen, Elizabeth, Sarah, Martha, Charles. Agronomist Wis. Expt. Sta., 1942-46; asst. prof. agronomy U. Wis., Madison, 1946-52, asso. prof., 1952-58, prof., 1958-84, prof. emeritus, 1984—; vis. Fulbright lectr. U. Wageningen (Netherlands), 1953-54; vis. prof. Porto Alegre, Rio Grande do Sul, Brazil, 1968; cons. Padang, West Sumatra, Indonesia, 1986, Medan, North Sumatra, 1987, Kharkov, Ukraine, Krasnodar, U.S.S.R., 1987. Fellow AAAS, Am. Soc. Agronomy, Crop Sci. Soc. Am.; mem. Sigma Xi, Phi Sigma, Gamma Sigma Delta, Phi Beta Kappa, Gamma Alpha. Methodist. Contbr. articles to profl. jours. Home: Madison, Wis. Died Dec. 25, 2006.

ANDREWS, BENNY, artist; b. Madison, Ga., Nov. 13, 1930; s. George Clevel and Viola (Perryman) A.; children: Christopher, Thomas Michael, Julia Rachael; m. Nene Humphrey, June 14, 1986. Student, Ft. Valley State Coll., 1948-50, U. Chgo., 1956-58; BFA, Chgo. Art Inst., 1958. Instr. art New Sch. Social Rsch., NYC, 1967-70, Queens Coll., NYC, from 1969; dir. visual arts program Nat. Endowment for Arts, Washington, 1982—84. Vis. artist Calif. State Coll. Hayward, 1969; vis. art critic Yale U., 1974. Author: Between the Lines, 1978; illustrator: Applachee Red (Raymond Andrews), 1978, Rosebell Lee Wildcat Tennessee (Raymond Andrews), 1980; contbr. articles on black art, culture to profl. jours.; assoc. editor (art): Encore mag.; one man shows Kessler Gallery, Provincetown, Mass., 1960-70, Forum Gallery, NYC, 1962-64-66, Henri Gallery, Alexandria, Va., 1963-64, Studio Mus., NYC, 1970, ACA Gallery, N.Y.C., 1972, U. Md., 1972, Aronson-Midtown Gallery, Atlanta, 1973, Lerner-Heller Gallery, NYC, 1979, 80, 81, Gallery of Sarasota, 1979, Savannah Coll. Art and Design, 1983, Sid Deutsch Gallery, NYC, 1983, Merida Galleries, Louisville, 1984, Michael Rosenfeld Gallery, NYC, 1997-98, ACA Galleries, 2000-01, others; exhibited in group shows at Detroit Inst., 1959, Phila. Acad. Art, 1960, Bklyn. Mus., 1963, Butler Inst. Am. Art, 1967, Mus. Modern Art, NYC, 1968-71, High Mus., Atlanta, 1971, Wadsworth Atheneum, 1979, Art Inst. Chgo., 1979, Los Angeles County Mus. Art, 1982, ACA Galleries, NYC, 1995-97, 2000-01, Wichita Art Mus., Wichita, Kans., 1996-97, others; represented in permanent collections Mus. Modern Art, N.Y.C., High Mus., Atlanta, African Mus., Washington, Norfolk Mus., Va., Butler Inst. Am. Art, Youngstown, Ohio, Chrysler Mus., Provincetown, Mass., La Jolla (Calif.) Mus., NYU, NYC, Detroit Inst. Art, U. Kans. Art Mus., Lawrence, U. Wyo. Art Gallery, Laramie, Joslyn Mus. Art, Omaha, Bklyn. Mus., Joseph H. Hirschhorn Mus., Ohara Mus., Japan, Edwin A. Ulrich Mus., Wichita, Kans. Co-chmn. Black Emergency Cultural Coalition, 1969—; bd. dirs. Children's Art Carnival, MacDowell Colony, Artists Talk on Art, Provincetown Work Ctr., Creative Drama Soc., Atlanta Bur. Cultural Affairs Gallery. staff sgt. USAF, 1950-54. John Hay Whitney fellow, 1965-67; Dorne Professionship U. Bridgeport, Conn., 1970; NY Coun. Arts grantee, 1971; fellow Nat. Endowment for Arts, 1974-81, NY Coun. on Arts, 1971-1981, MacDowell Colony fellow, 1973-73, 75-78, Academician NAD, 1997. Died Nov. 10, 2006.

ANDREWS, JAMES EDGAR, church official, minister; b. Whittenburg, Tex., Dec. 29, 1928; s. Bryan McEvrie and Rose Ellen (Simpson) A.; m. Sarah Elizabeth Crouch, Sept. 16, 1962; children: Charis Megan, Bryan Hugh. BA, Austin Coll., 1952, MA, 1953, DD, 1974; BD, Austin Presbyn. Theol. Sem., 1956. Ordained to ministry Presbyn. Ch. U.S., 1956. Asst. minister St. Andrews Presbyn. Ch., Houston, 1956-58; info. officer World Alliance of Ref. Chs., Geneva, 1958-60; dir. pub. relations and asst. to pres. Princeton (N.J.) Theol. Sem., 1960-71; asst. to stated clk. Presbyn. Ch. U.S., 1971-73, stated clk., 1973-83; interim co-stated clk. Presbyn. Ch. (U.S.A.), 1983-84, stated clk., from 1984. Home: Decatur, Ga. Died Mar. 7, 2006.

ANDREWS, WILLIAM HENRY, hospital administrator; b. Wellston, Mo., Oct. 16, 1919; s. William H. and Viola (Williams) A.; B.S. in Edn., Lincoln U., 1941; M.H.A., Washington U., 1954; m. Mildred E. Joyce, Aug. 7, 1943; children— William H., Brenda J. Asst. adminstr. Homer G. Phillips Hosp., 1941-52; adminstr. People's Hosp., 1954-55, George W. Hubbard Hosp., Meharry Med. Coll., 1955-59; adminstr. Forest City Hosp., 1959-64; asst. dir. Cleve. Met. Gen. Hosp., later dep. dir., dir., 1969—, sr. v.p., 1981—; adminstr. Kaiser Permanente Med. Center, Cleve., 1981-84; sr. staff assoc. Kaiser Permanente Med. Ctr., Cleve., 1984-86. Mem. faculty health services adminstrn. Grad. Sch. Ohio State U.; mem. council Nat. Inst. Arthritis and Metabolic Diseases, 1968-71; mem. physicians clin. asst. adv. com. Cuyahoga Community Coll.; mem. personnel adv. com. and Social Service clearing house com. Cleve. Fedn. for Community Planning. Mem. Catholic Interracial Council, Cleve. Arthritis Found. Trustee Cleve. Hemophilia Found., Hough Norwood Family Health Care Program. Commonwealth Fund fellow, 1952. Life fellow Am. Coll. Hosp. Adminstrs. (examiner); mem. Wash. U. Alumni Assn. (treas.), Nat. Assn. Health Services Execs (2d v.p.), Ohio Hosp. Assn. (shared services com. and social work adv. panel), Am. Hosp. Assn. (life), Greater Cleve. Hosp. Assn. (exec. com., blood bank com., house staff com.), Kappa Alpha Psi. Club: Rotary. Home: Cleveland, Ohio. Died Mar. 2, 2006.

ANDRISANI, PAUL J., business educator, management consultant; b. Wilmington, Del., Oct. 19, 1946; s. Paul and Mary (Tavani) A.; m. Barbara Lee Frank, Nov. 23, 1968; children: Nathan, Damian, Danielle. BS, U. Del., 1968, MBA, 1970; PhD, Ohio State U., 1973, postgrad., 1973-74. Sr. rsch. assoc. Ctr. for Human Resource Rsch. Ohio State U., Columbus, 1973-74, vis. rsch. assoc., 1979; asst. prof. Sch. Bus., Temple U., Phila., 1974-76, assoc. prof., 1977-83, prof., from 1983; dir. Bur. Econ. Rsch., Phila., 1977-78, Ctr. for Labor and Human Resource Studies, from 1987; co-dir. Ctr. for Competitive Govt., Phila., 1997—2002, assoc. dean, 1989-91, chmn. dept. mgmt., 1993-95. Pres. Paul J. Andrisani Mgmt. Cons. Svcs., Wilmington, Del., 1974—, St. Anthony's Edn. Fund, 1986—; pres. West End Neighborhood House Social Svc. Agy., 1995-97; cons. Price Waterhouse, U.S. EEOC, UPS, U.S. Army Recruiting Command, Acme Markets, CBS, Coca-Cola, City of Tucson, City of Phila., Chevron, Chrysler, Olsten, La. Power and Light, La. Land and Exploration, PanAm, Smith Kline, Carpenter Tech., The Aerospace Corp. of Am., Boeing Co., Dynalectron Corp., Lukens Steel, Nordstrom, Phila. Police Dept., Shoney's Inc., Martin Marietta, CIGNA, Airline Pilots Assn., Prudential Ins., Traveler's Ins., Suffolk County Police Dept., Internat. Comms. Agy., N.Y. Times, U.S. Steel, Readers Digest, K-Mart, Wal-Mart, Russell Sage Found., United Food and Comml. Workers Union, Del. Econ. and Fin. Adv. Com., New Orleans Pub. Svc. Inc., Disability and Pension Rev. Com., Rockwell Internat., ARCO, Nationwide Ins., ICI Ams., DuPont, Witco Chem., Westinghouse, GTE, Inco, Gould Electronics, Chrysler, Dollar Bank, Rhone-Poulenc Rorer, Ohio Edison, Delmarva Power, LaSalle Univ., Carter Wallace, Nortel Networks, Enterprise Rent-a-Car, Gulfstream Aerospace Technologies, We. Digital, govt. agys., others; lectr. Internat. Comms. Agy., Japan, Portugal, Italy, Can., Brandeis U., Pa. State U., Columbia U., William and Mary Coll., U. So. Calif., U. Pa., Nat. Employment Law Inst., San Francisco and Washington; testimony before U.S. Congress, 1991; presentation on new economy to Pa. Legis., 2000. Author: Pre-Retirement Years, vol. III, 1973, vol. IV, 1974, Career Thresholds, 1975, Work Attitudes and Labor Market Experience, 1978, Making Government Work, 2000; mem. editl. bd. Jour. Econs. and Bus., 1979-83; reviewer U. Mich. Press, Ohio State U. Press, Temple U. Press and various scholarly jours.; contbr. over 40 papers to profl. jours. and socs. Temple U. Law Sch. Bd. Visitors, 1997—. With U.S. Army, 1972-73. Recipient Wilmington Man of Yr. award, 1995, West End Neighborhood House Leadership award, 1997, Prof. of Yr. award Temple U. Chpt. Soc. for Advancement of Mgmt., 1997, awards for vol. svc., Thomas J. Reese award for cmty. svc., 2000, U. Del. Alumni Hall of Fame award, 1999; Salzburg fellow, Roosevelt Youth Policy fellow; grantee U.S. Dept. Labor, 1974-77, Nat. Commn. for Employment Policy, 1979-83, Adminstrn. on Aging, 1981-82, Social Sci. Rsch. Coun., 1982, U.S. Dept. Army, 1986, 98, Human Resource Rsch. Orgn., 1989-90, PriceWaterhouse Coopers Endowment for the Bus. of Govt., 1998-2000. Mem. Am. Econs. Assn., Indsl. Rels. Rsch. Assn., Acad. of Mgmt., Soc. Labor Economists, Strategic Mgmt. Soc., U. Del. Alumni Assn. (bd. dirs. 2001—). Died Mar. 12, 2006.

ANNAND, JAMES EARLE, university dean, minister, educator; b. Glendale, Calif., May 23, 1929; s. David Earle and Wilma (Aver) A.; m. Connie Lou Cousins, Aug. 22, 1953; children: David, Paul, Priscilla. BA, Occidental Coll., 1951; BD, Yale Div. Sch., 1954, STM, 1956; DD (hon.), Yale U., 1975. Ordained to ministry Episc. Ch., 1954. Vicar Ch. Holy Spirit, Monterey Park, Calif., 1956-58; rector Christ Ch., Westerly, R.I., 1958-69, St. Paul's Ch., Greenwich, Conn., 1969-74; interim rector St. Luke's Ch., Darien, Conn., 1975-77, St. Peter's Ch., Narragansett, R.I., 1978, St. Paul's Ch., Fairfield, Conn., 1979-80; lectr. Berkeley Divinity Sch., Yale U., New Haven, 1981-82, acting dean, 1982, dean, 1983-91. Canon Christ Ch. Cathedral, Hartford, Conn., 1985—. Fellow Coll. Preachers. Home: Greenville, Del. Died Sept. 1, 2006.

ANNESE, DOMENICO, retired landscape architect; b. NYC, June 9, 1919; s. Fedele and Antonia (Angelini) A.; m. Serafina Villanova, July 16, 1944; children: Donald F., Loretta S. Student, SUNY Coll. Environ. Sci. and Forestry, 1942; BS in Landscape Architecture, Syracuse U., 1942. Registered landscape architect, N.Y., Pa., Conn., Mass., Ohio, Tenn. Landscape architect Clarence C. Combs, NYC, 1946-50, asso., 1955-56; asst. chief landscape architect Nat. Capital Parks, Washington, 1950-55; asso. Clarke and Rapuano, Inc., NYC, 1956-72, v.p., 1972-91. Vice chmn. N.Y. State Bd. Landscape Architects, 1961-67, chmn., 1967-71; mem. Pleasantville (N.Y.) Parks and Recreation Bd., 1974-83; adj. prof. urban landscape architecture CCNY, 1975-76; vis. prof., lectr. in landscape architecture Sch. Planning and Architecture, New Delhi, India, 1977; pres. Landscape Architecture Found., 1973-1975; dir. N.Y. State Coun. Landscape Architects; dir. coll. environ. sci. and forestry ESF Found., 1987-2000; dir. N.Y. Parks and Conservation Assn., 1991-1995 Served with Coast Arty., F.A. U.S. Army, 1942-46, ETO. Fellow Am. Soc. Landscape Architects, Sigma Lambda Alpha. Lutheran. Home: Pleasantville, NY. Died May 16, 2007.

ANTHONY, ROBERT NEWTON, retired management educator; b. Orange, Mass., Sept. 6, 1916; s. Charles H. and Grace (Newton) A.; m. Gretchen Lynch, Aug. 28, 1943; children: Robert N., Victoria Stewart; m. Katherine Worley, Aug. 4, 1973. AB, Colby Coll., 1938, MA (hon.), 1959, LHD (hon.), 1963; MBA, Harvard U., 1940, DCS, 1952. Mem. faculty Bus. Sch., Harvard U., 1940-42, 46-67, 68-83, Ross Graham Walker prof. mgmt. control, prof. emeritus, 1983—2006. Pres. Mgmt. Analysis Ctr., Inc., 1955-63; asst. sec., contr. US Dept. Def., 1965-68; prof. Mgmt. Devel. Inst., Switzerland, 1957-58; with Stanford Exec. Devel. Program, 1962; mem. adv. com. IMEDE, Switzerland, 1961-65, 68-77; spl. asst. to chmn. Price Commn., 1971-73; mem. educators cons. com. GAO, 1973-87; dir., chmn. audit com. Carborundum Co., 1971-77; dir. Warnaco, Inc., 1971-86; mem. adv. com. Kyoto Rsch. Inst., 1987-90, IPMI (Jakarta), 1983-90. Author: Management Controls in Industrial Research Organization, 1952, (with Dearborn and Kneznek) Shoe Machinery: Buy or Lease?, 1955, (with Reece) Accounting, Text and Cases, 1956, 11th edit. (with Hawkins and Merchant), 2004, Office Equipment, Buy or Rent?, 1957, Essentials of Accounting, 1964, 8th edit., 2003, (with Leslie Breitner) Accounting

Principles, 1965, 7th edit., 1995, Planning and Control Systems: A Framework for Analysis, 1965, (with Govindarajan) Management Control Systems, (With Vijay Govindarajan) 11th edit., 2004, (with Hekimian) Operations Cost Control, 1967, Plaid in Management Accounting, (with Welsch) Fundamentals of Financial Accounting, 1974, Fundamentals of Management Accounting, 1974, (with Young) Management Control in Nonprofit Organizations, 1975, 7th edit., 2003, Accounting for the Cost of Interest, 1976, Financial Accounting in Nonbusiness Organizations, 1978, Tell It Like It Was, 1983, Future Directions for Financial Accounting, 1984, Teach Yourself the Essentials of Accounting (computer software), 1999; (with Anderson) The New Corporate Director, 1986, The Management Control Function, 1988, Should Business and Nonbusiness Accounting Be Different?, 1989, Rethinking the Rules of Financial Accounting, 2003; editor Richard D. Irwin, Inc.; mem. bd. Harvard Bus. Rev., 1947-60; contbr. articles to profl. jours. Trustee Colby Coll., 1959-74, 75-2006, chmn., 1978-83; trustee Dartmouth Hitchcock Med. Ctr., 1983-93, treas., 1993; town auditor Town of Waterville Valley, N.H., 1976-92; mem. audit com. City of N.Y., 1977-85. Lt. comdr. USNR, 1941-46. Recipient Disting. Leadership award Fed. Govt. Accts. Assn., Disting. Pub. Svc. medal Dept. Def., Disting. Svc. award Harvard Bus. Sch., Marriner Disting. Svc. award Colby Coll., Meritorious Svc. award Exec. Office of Pres., CINPAC Letter of Commendation, Baker Scholar; named to Acctg. Hall of Fame. Fellow Acad. Mgmt.; mem. Am. Acctg. Assn. (v.p. 1959, pres. 1973-74, Outstanding Acctg. Educator of Yr. 1989, acctg. sect. Lifetime Achievement award 2003), Fin. Exec. Inst., Inst. Mgmt. Accts. (chmn. cost concepts subcom., mgmt. acctg. practices com.), Assn. Govt. Accts., Am. Soc. Mil. Compts., Cosmos Club, Phi Beta Kappa, Pi Gamma Mu, Beta Alpha Psi. Home: Hanover, NH. Died Dec. 1, 2006.

ANTON, GEORGE LOUIS, direct marketing executive; b. Savannah, Ga., Nov. 2, 1923; s. Louis George and Pauline (Constantine) A.; m. Sophia Andrianopoulou, Sept. 9, 1951; children: Louis George, Charles John. BS in Indsl. Engring., Ga. Inst. Tech., 1949, MS in Indsl. Engring., 1952. Cert. prof. engr., Calif. Supr. insl. engring. Ethyl Corp., Baton Rouge, 1952-59; dir. indsl. engring. U.S. Borax & Chem. Corp., Los Angeles, 1959-62, dir. prodn. planning, 1963-65, dir. mfg., 1965-70; asst. to pres. Oxford Paper subs. Ethyl Corp., Richmond, Va., 1970-74; v.p. ops. Capitol Products Corp. subs. Ethyl Corp., Harrisburg, Pa., 1974-79, exec. v.p., gen. mgr., 1979-86; chmn. bd. Comtrad Market Network Inc., from 1987. Spl. editor, Jour. Indsl. Engring., 1954-59. Pres., bd. dirs. United Cerebral Palsy Ctr., 1981-83, chmn. bd. dirs., 1984-85; cub master Cub Scouts Am., Arcadia, Calif., 1961-65; pres. Civic Assn., Richmond, 1972, Harrisburg, Pa., 1987-89; mem. Gov. Reagan's Com. Efficiency and Cost Control, 1967; mem. indsl. engring. adv. bd. Va. Inst. Tech.; mem. Susquehanna Township Planning Commn., 1989—. Served with U.S. Army, 1943-46, ETO. Decorated Bronze Star; decorated Croix de Guerre (unit) Fellow Am. Inst. Indsl. Engrs. (dir. mgmt. div. 1982-83, chpt. pres. Los Angeles and Baton Rouge); mem. Am. Mgmt. Assn., West Shore Country Club (Camp Hill, Pa.), Rotary. Greek Orthodox. Home: Harrisburg, Pa. Died May 25, 2006.

ANTON, HARVEY, textile company executive; b. NYC, Nov. 10, 1923; s. Abraham J. and Byrdie (Casin) A.; student Western State Coll. Colo., 1941, Savage Sch. Edn., 1941-42; BS, NYU, 1949; m. Betty L. Weintraub, Dec. 18, 1949; children: Bruce Norman, Lynne Beth. Pres., Anton Yarn Corp. (merged with Robison Textile Co. to form Robison-Anton Textile Co. 1959), NJ, 1949-50, chmn. bd., 1989—; v.p. Arrow Spinning, Susquehanna, Pa.; adv. bd. 1st Jersey Nat. Bank; v.p. Mid-Valley Textile; sec. Bloomsburg Dye; chmn. bd. Robison-Anton Textile Co. Trustee Erza Charitable Found.; pres. Anton Found.; bd. dirs. Pascock Valley Hosp., Westwood, NJ Served to 1st lt. AUS, 1943-46. Clubs: Masons, KP; Leonia Tennis; NY Univ. Letter (NYC). Home: Emerson, NJ. Died Feb. 2, 2006.

ANTON, MARK J., chemical company executive; b. Newark, Feb. 12, 1926; s. Mark and Adele (Buecke) A.; m. Elizabeth Flower, Oct. 31, 1953. BA, Bowdoin Coll., 1951. Various mgmt. positions Suburban Propane Gas Corp., Whippany, N.J., 1951-58, v.p., 1958-61, exec. v.p., 1961-63, pres., chief exec. officer, 1963-79, chmn., pres., chief exec. officer, 1979-83, chmn., pres., 1983-88; exec. v.p. Quantum Chem. Corp. (acquired Suburban Propane Gas Corp., 1983), Whippany, N.J., 1987-89. Bd. dirs. Chem. Bank N.J., Morristown, Home Life Ins. Co., N.Y.C., Pittston Co., Greenwich, Conn. Lt. USN, 1944-46. Mem. Nat. Propane Gas Assn. (bd. dirs.), Nat. Assn. Corp. Dirs., 25-Yr. Club Petroleum Industry, Baltusrol Golf Club (Springfield, N.J.), Short Hills Club (N.J.), Mill Reef Club (Antiqua, W.I.), Bay Head Yacht Club (N.J.), John's Island Club (Vero Beach, Fla.). Avocations: flying, golf, sailing. Home: Short Hills, NJ. Died May 10, 2006.

ANTON, THOMAS JULIUS, political science and public policy educator, consultant; b. Worcester, Mass., Sept. 28, 1934; s. Julius and Irene (Dupsha) A.; m. Barbara Jane Lindblom, June 22, 1957; children: Lynn Allison, Leslie Carol, Thomas Rolf. AB, Clark U., 1956; MA, Prnceton U., 1959; PhD, Prnceton U., 1961. Lectr. U. Pa., Phila, 1960-61; asst. prof. U. Ill., Urbana, 1961-63, assoc. prof. Urbana, Chgo., 1964-67; from assoc. prof. to prof. U. Mich., Ann Arbor, 1967-83, dir. PhD program in urban planning, 1977-80; prof. polit. sci., dir. A. Alfred Taubman Ctr. for Pub. Policy and Am. Instns. Brown U., Providence, from 1983, dean of faculty, 1990-91. Vis. prof. U. Stockholm, 1968, 71; cons. State of Ill., Springfield, Chgo., 1963-70, State of Mich., Lansing, 1972-83, HEW, Washington, 1976-80, Brookings Instn., Washington, 1970-—; cons. NAS, Washington, 1976-80, panel mem., 1981-82; mem. Swedish Fulbright Commn., Stockholm, 1971; vice chmn., bd. trustees Clark Univ., 1995-2001. Author: The Politics of State Expenditure in Illinois, 1966, Governing Greater Stockholm, 1975, Moving Money, 1980, Administered Politics, 1980, American Federalism and Public Policy: How the System Works, 1989; editor: Policy Scis., Amsterdam, 1977-80. Commr. Providence Housing Authority, 1986—, chmn., 1990—. J.F. Kennedy fellow Gov. of Sweden, 1977; NSF grantee, 1980; recipient Individual Recognition award HUD, 1992. Mem. Am. Polit. Sci. Assn. (Gladys M. Kammerer award 1989, Disting. Federalism scholar award 2000), Assn. Pub. Policy and Mgmt., Midwest Polit. Sci. Assn., Nat. Acad. Pub. Adminstrn. (panel on info. mgmt. 1993—), Princeton Club (N.Y.C.), Phi Beta Kappa. Democrat. Home: Orleans, Mass. Died June 6, 2006.

APPEL, IRVING H(AROLD), optical manufacturing company executive; b. NYC, Jan. 8, 1917; s. Ralph and Ada (Ader) Appel; m. Gertrude Matlin, Jan. 16, 1938; children: Michael E., Bonnie A., Kathy S. Grad., U.S. Army Air Force Aviation Cadet Sch., 1943. Inventory clk. Nat. Container Corp., Long Island City, NY, 1935—36; prodn. mgr. Kraft Corrugated Containers, Inc., Bayonne, NJ, 1936—42; gen. mgr. Republic Container Corp., Jersey City, 1945—49, San Miguel Brewery Carton Plant, Manila, 1949—56; v.p. Cleghorn Folding Box Co., Lowell, Mass., 1957—64; pres. Lowell Corrugated Container Corp., 1959—64; exec. v.p. Prince Macaroni, Lowell, 1960—64, also bd. dirs.; pres., founder Welling Internat. Corp., Milford, Conn., 1964—79, chmn. bd. dirs., 1979—84, chmn. emeritus, from 1984. Cons. Darier Asia Ltd. div. of Darier & Co, Geneva, 1988; bd. dirs. Conn. Bank & Trust Co., New Haven, Orange Nat. Bank., Conn. Trustee Conn. Visual Health Ctr., Bridgeport, chmn., 1984; bd. dirs. Lake Copake Conservation Soc., Copake Lake, NY; pres. ARMDI, Golan; bd. trustees New Eng. Coll. Optometry, Boston, 1988. 1st lt. USAAF, 1943—45, ETO USAAF, NATOUS. Decorated D.F.C. Air medal with 5 oak leaf clusters; named Largest Individual Fund Raiser, Korea/Vietnam Meml., 1987; recipient cert. Appreciation, Conn. Visual Health Ctr., Inc., 1975, Pres.'s award, 1977, Recognition award Flying Tigers, 1975, Recognition award, Ambassador's Soc. Bd. Trustees, 1981, State of Israel, 1980, Pub. Health award Conn. Visual Health Ctr., 1987, Mission of Mercy award, ogen David Adam, 1987. Mem.: Air Force Assn., 2d Air Div. Assn., 8th Air Force Hist. Soc., Aircraft Owners and Pilots Assn. Home: Hallandale, Fla. Died May 27, 2006.

APPELSON, WALLACE BERTRAND, academic administrator; b. Bklyn., June 9, 1930; BS, NYU, 1951, MA, 1952; Ed.D., Columbia U., 1959. Chief X-ray technician Samaritan Hosp., Bklyn., 1951-52; tchr. art White Plains Pub. Schs., NYC, 1954-57; research asst. Inst. Adminstrv. Research (Columbia U.), 1957-58; asst. prof. ednl. adminstrn. Rutgers U., 1958-60; coordinator terminal program N.J. State Dept. Higher Edn., 1960-65; dean acad. affairs Bucks County Community Coll., Newton, Pa., 1965-70; pres. Atlantic Community Coll., Mays Landing, N.J., 1970-73; dean faculty LaGuardia Community Coll., CUNY, 1973-76; pres. Truman Coll., Chgo., from 1976. Editor: Associated Public Schools System Yearbook, 1958, Toward Higher Education Newsletter, N.J. Div. Higher Edn., 1960-65; contbr. articles to profl. jours. Pres. bd. dirs. North Bus. and Indsl. Coun. Chgo., Orchard Mental Health Ctr., Skokie, Ill.; v.p. Uptown C. of C.; bd. dirs. Ravenswood Hosp. Med. Ctr., Chgo., Uptown Commn., Chgo. Mem. Am. Assn. Sch. Adminstrs., Am. Assn. Higher Edn., Am. Assn. Community and Jr. Colls., Phi Delta Kappa, Kappa Delta Pi. Died Jan. 12, 2007.

APPLBAUM, RONALD LEE, academic administrator; b. Charleroi, Pa., Dec. 14, 1943; s. Irwin and Marion (Caplan) A.; m. Susan Joy Stone, July 4, 1968; 1 child, Lee. BA, Calif. State U., Long Beach, 1965, MA, 1966; PhD, Pa. State U., 1969. Prof. Calif. State U., Long Beach, 1969-76, assoc. dean, 1976-77, dean, 1977-82; v.p. U. Tex.-Pan Am., Edinburg, 1982-90; pres. Westfield (Mass.) State Coll., 1990-96, Kean U., Union, NJ, 1996—2002, Colo. State U., Pueblo, from 2002. Mem. bd. examiners Dept. Edn., 1997—; dir. N.J. Alliance, Inc., 1998—. Author: Fundamentals of Human Communication, 1973, Process of Group Communication, 1979, Organizational Communication, 1981, Business and Professional Speaking, 1982; co-author 7 textbooks; editor textbook series ModComm, Mass-Com, ProCom, 1973-80; contbr. articles to profl. jours. Bd. dirs.Temple Emanuel, McAllen, Tex., 1983-90, pres., 1987-89; v.p. McAllen chpt. B'nai Brith, 1984-89. Mem. Internat. Comm. Assn., World Comm. Assn. (sec.-gen. 1982-91, pres. 1991-95), Ea. Comm. Assn. (reviewer 1991-93, exec. coun. 1994-96), Speech Comm. Assn., Mass Comm. Assn., Assn. Comm. Adminstrs. (editor JACA 1992—), Westfield C. of C. (bd. dirs. 1991-96, vice-chair 1992-94, chair 1994-95), Westfield Comty. Devel. Corp. (pres. 1994, 95), Westfield Kiwanis (v.p. 1992-95, pres. 1995-96), Phi Kappa Phi (pres. Calif. State U. Long Beach chpt. 1976-77, Westfield State Coll. chpt. 1992-93), Union County Alliance (exec. bd. 1997—), Union County Twp. C.C. (bd. dirs. 1997—). Home: Pueblo, Colo. Died Nov. 16, 2006.

APPLETON, MYRA, magazine editor, writer; b. Phila., Dec. 21, 1934; d. Joseph and Sylvia (Pouls) Magid; m. John Johnston Appleton, July 29, 1962 BA, Temple U., 1955. Researcher TV Guide, Phila., 1956-61; assoc. editor Show Bus. Illustrated, Chgo., 1961-62; contbg. editor Show mag., NYC, 1962-64; free-lance writer NYC, 1964-68; sr. editor Cosmopolitan mag., NYC, 1968-88; editor Lear's mag., NYC, 1988-92, editorial cons., 1992-93; sr. articles editor Cosmopolitan Mag., NYC, from 1993. Author various mag. articles, film scripts; editl. dir. various one-shot mags. Mem. Womens Media Group, Am. Soc. Mag. Editors. Died Jan. 27, 2007.

ARCHIBALD, REGINALD MAC GREGOR, pediatrician, endocrinologist, chemist, educator; b. Syracuse, NY, Mar. 2, 1910; s. Eben Henry and Minnie (Archibald) A.; m. Evelyn Stroh, June 12, 1948; children: Ruth, Lawrence. BA, U. B.C., 1930, MA, 1932; PhD, U. Toronto, Ont., Can., 1934, MD, 1939. Tchr., rsch. asst. U. B.C., 1930-32; tchg. and rsch. asst. U. Toronto, 1932-33, fellow pathol. chemistry, 1933-35; intern pathology Hosp. for Sick Children, Toronto, 1937, surgery, 1938, medicine, 1939; intern Toronto Gen. Hosp., 1939-40; fellow divsn. med. scis. NRC, 1940-42; asst. resident physician Rockefeller Inst. Hosp., 1941-46; assoc. Rockefeller Inst. Med. Rsch., 1946, mem., from 1948; prof. Rockefeller U., 1955-80, prof. emeritus, from 1980; sr. physician Rockefeller Hosp., 1955-80. Prof. biochemistry Sch. Hygiene and Pub. Health Johns Hopkins U., 1946-48; mem. adv. bd. Hosp. of Rockefeller U., 1992-93. Mem. editl. bd.: Jour. Biol. Chemistry, 1948-58, Jour. Clin. Endocrinology and Metabolism, 1952-60, Child Devel., 1954-56; adv. bd.: Analytical Chemistry, 1957-60. Mem. Am. Chem. Soc., Am. Soc. Biol. Chemists, Harvey Soc., Med. and Chirug. Faculty Md., Endocrine Soc., Soc. Rsch. in Child Devel., Brit. Biochem. Soc., Lawson Wilkins Soc. Pediatric Endocrinology, Soc. Adolescent Medicine, Nat. Acad. Clin. Biochemistry, N.Y. Met. Pediatric Endocrine Soc., Internat. Assn. for Adolescent Medicine, Explorers Club, Sigma Xi. Achievements include medical research in pediatric endocrinology and biochemistry; development of clinical laboratory methods; study of influence of hormones on enzymes, problems of physical growth and maturation of children. Home: Rochester, Minn. Died May 10, 2007.

ARENT, ALBERT EZRA, retired lawyer; b. Rochester, NY, Aug. 25, 1911; s. Hyman J. and Sarah (Weller) A.; m. Frances Feldman, Nov. 23, 1939; children: Stephen Weller, Margery Arent Safir. AB, Cornell U., 1932, LL.B., 1935. Bar: N.Y. 1935, D.C. 1945. Rsch. asst. N.Y. State Law Revision Commn., 1934; atty. U.S. Bur. Internal Revenue, 1935-39; spl. asst. to Atty. Gen. U.S., 1939-44; chief trial atty. Alien Property Unit, U.S. Dept. Justice, 1942-44; pvt. law practice specializing in taxation; ptnr. firm Arent, Fox, Kintner, Plotkin and Kahn and (predecessor firms), Washington, 1944-86; counsel, 1986—2003; lectr. taxation Am. U., 1948-52; prof. taxation Georgetown Law Sch., 1951-73; ret. Also lectr. tax subjects before Practising Law Inst., NYU, U. Chgo. tax insts., Am., Fed., various local and state bar assns.; prosecuted leading fgn. agt. registration act cases, World War II.; chmn. adv. coun. Cornell Law Sch., 1979-82 Contbr. articles to legal publs. Vice pres. Jewish Cmty. Coun. of Greater Washington, 1953-57, pres., 1957-61; chmn. Commn. on Social Action of Reform Judaism, 1973-77; chmn. Cornell Law Sch. Fund, 1975-77; mem. steering com. Nat. Urban Coalition, 1970-77, mem. exec. com., 1970-72; mem. governing bd. and exec. com. Common Cause, 1970-72; bd. dirs. Overseas Edn. Fund of LWV, 1961-79; vice chmn. Nat Jewish Cmty. Rels. Adv. Coun., 1967-70, chmn., 1970-73; vice chmn. Conf. Pres.'s Major Jewish Orgns., 1970-73; trustee Cornell U., 1978-83, trustee emeritus, 1983—; 1st v.p. Washington Hebrew Congregation, 1978-80; v.p. United Jewish Appeal Fedn. Greater Washington, 1979-81. Recipient Stephen S. Wise medallion award Nat. Capital chpt. Am. Jewish Congress, 1965, Vicennial medal Georgetown U., 1971, Humanitarianism award B'nai Brith, 1975, Disting. Alumnus award Cornell U. Law Sch., 1982, award for outstanding svc. Overseas Edn. Fund, 1983, Disting. Svc. award Washington Lawyers Com. for Civil Rights Under Law, 1987, Judge Learned Hand award Am. Jewish Com., 1991. Mem. ABA, Am. Law Inst., Fed. Bar Assn., D.C. Bar Assn., Telluride Assn., Phi Beta Kappa, Phi Kappa Phi. Home: Boca Raton, Fla. Died Oct. 31, 2006.

ARENTZ, ANDREW ALBERT, management consultant; b. Chgo., May 12, 1928; s. Andrew A. and Ruth J. (Gulbransen) A.; B.S.C.E., Ill. Inst. Tech., 1950; J.D., John Marshall Law Sch., 1960; m. Lillian Regina Ivanovsky, Sept. 1, 1950; children—Andrew Anton, Alethea Ruth, Paul David. Supr. ops. research AMF, Niles, Ill., 1959-62; assoc. dir. advanced transp. planning Gen. Am. Transp. Corp., Chgo., 1963-66, asst. to v.p. corp. planning, 1966-68; pres., chief exec. officer GARD, Inc., Niles, 1968-77; dir. planning and devel. GATX Corp., Chgo., 1977-83, spl. asst. to v.p. fin., 1983-84, dir. pers. rsch. and benefits planning, 1984-86; pres. Arentz and Assocs., 1986—; Bd. dirs. Chgo. Bot. Garden, 1979-82, Luth. Sch. Theology, Chgo., 1972-78; mem. Synod Coun. Met. Chgo. Synod, Evang. Luth. Ch. Am., 1987-90, South-Ctrl. Synod Wis., 1995—; trustee Village of Riverwoods, 1969-73, 87-90. With AUS, 1952-54. Died July 20, 2006.

ARMAN, ARMAND PIERRE, sculptor; b. Nice, France, Nov. 17, 1928; came to U.S., 1961, naturalized, 1972; m. Corice Canton-Arman, July 13, 1971; children: Yasmine Valentine, Philippe Alexandre. Student Ecole Nat. d'Art Decoratif de Nice, 1946-49; MA in Art History, Ecole du Louvre, Paris, 1949-51. Exhibited one-man shows, Walker Art Ctr., Mpls., 1964, Musees des Arts Decoratifs, Paris, 1969, La Jolla Mus. Contemporary Art, Calif., 1974, Albright-Knox Gallery, Buffalo, 1975, Kunstmuseum, Hannover, Fed. Republic Germany, 1981, Pablo Picasso Mus., Antibes, France, 1981, Hessisches Landesmuseum, Darmstadt, Fed. Republic Germany, 1982, Tel Aviv Mus., Israel, 1982, Tubingen Kunstmuseum, Fed. Republic Germany, 1983, Wichita State U., Ulrich Mus. Arts, Kans., 1986, Mus. des Beaux Arts, Nimes, 1988, Lunds Konstall, Lunds, 1989, Mus. Fine Arts, Houston, 1991, Bklyn. Mus., N.Y.C., 1992, Detroit Inst. Arts, 1992; group shows include Mus. Modern Art, N.Y.C., 1961, Kaiser Wilhelm Mus., Krefeld, Fed. Republic Germany, 1963, Tate Gallery, London, 1964, Janis Gallery, N.Y.C., 1964, Nat. Mus. Modern Art, Tokyo, 1969, Kunsthaus, Zurich, 1979, Westfalishes Landesmuseum, Munster, Fed. Republic Germany, 1980, Stedelijk Mus., Amsterdam, Netherlands, 1982; represented in permanent collections, Albright-Knox Gallery, Buffalo, Guggenheim Mus., N.Y.C., Met. Mus. Art, N.Y.C., Musee des Arts Decoratifs, Louvre, Paris, Kaiser Wilhelm Mus., Krefeld, Israel Mus., Jerusalem, Hirshhorn Mus. and Sculpture Garden, Washington, Nat. Gallery, Canberra, Australia, La. Mus. Modern Art, Mus. Fine Arts, Houston, Mus. de Arte Contemparanea de Caracas. Named Commander Arts and Letters, 1984; recipient Legion of Honor, 1989. Died Oct. 22, 2005.

ARMITAGE, RICHARD, former university official; b. Ravenna, Ohio, Apr. 15, 1918; s. Harry and Inez (Hughes) A.; m. Janet Plummer, Mar. 28, 1942 (div. 1978); children: Bruce, Suzanne, Barry, Daniel, Douglas, John; m. Mary Beth Snyder, July 29, 1978; 1 child, David AB, Oberlin Coll., 1939; MA, Ohio State U., 1940, PhD (Univ. scholar 1940-41), 1945; postdoctoral student, U. Tex., 1951-52. Faculty Ohio State U., Columbus, 1941-70, 71-78, prof. Romance langs., 1966-70, 71-78, asst. dean Coll. Arts and Scis., 1954-55, asst. dean Grad. Sch., 1956-60, assoc. dean, 1960-63, dean, 1963-70, univ. ombudsman, 1971-73, v.p. student services, 1973-78, v.p. emeritus, from 1978; provost, dean faculties U. Mo., Kansas City, 1970-71; vice chancellor student affairs U. Calif., San Diego, 1978-81; dir. student acad. services UCLA, 1981-82; mgmt. cons., from 1982. Vis. prof. Kenyon Coll., fall 1947; cons. Minn. State Coll. Bd., 1968, Inst. Internat. Ed., 1967-80; mem. Grad. Record Exam. Bd., 1973-78, chmn., 1976-77; Chmn. region VIII Woodrow Wilson Fellowship Found., 1961-65; bd. dirs. Ohio State U. Research Found.; chmn. editorial bd. Ohio State U. Press Author: (with W. Meiden) Beginning Spanish, Fundamentals of Spanish Grammar; also articles, revs. Trustee Children's Hosp., 1967-70; mem. adv. com. on grad. programs Ohio Bd. Regents, 1965-70. Recipient Disting. Svc. award, 1990; Ford Fellow, 1951-52. Mem. Am. Assn. Tchrs. Spanish and Portuguese. Died May 26, 2007.

ARMSTRONG, GENE LEE, systems engineer, consultant, retired aerospace transportation executive; b. Clinton, Ill., Mar. 9, 1922; s. George Dewey and Ruby Imald (Dickerson) A. m. Lael Jeanne Baker, Apr. 3, 1946; children: Susan Lael, Roberta Lynn, Gene Lee. BS with high honors, U. Ill., 1948, MS, 1951. Registered profl. engr., Calif. With Boeing Aircraft, 1948—50, 1951—52; chief engr. astronautics divsn., corp. dir. Gen. Dynamics, 1954—65; chief engr. Def. Sys. Group TRW, Redondo Beach, Calif., 1956—86, pvt. cons. sys. engring., 1986; pres., CEO Armstrong Sys. Engring. Co, Westminster, Calif., from 1986. Mem. NASA Rsch. Adv. Com. on Control, Guidance & Navigation, 1959-62 Contbr. chpts. to books, articles to profl. publs. 1st lt. USAAF, 1942-45 Decorated Air medal; recipient alumni awards U. Ill., 1965, 77 Mem. Am. Math. Soc., AIAA, Nat. Mgmt. Assn., Am. Def. Preparedness Assn., Masons. Home: Westminster, Calif. Died Nov. 27, 2006.

ARMSTRONG, ROBERT ARNOLD, petroleum company executive; b. Chgo., Feb. 17, 1928; s. Arnold Gustave and Lillian (Laver) A.; m. Jane Victoria Colestock, May 13, 1951 (dec. 1964); children: Michael, Richard, Patricia, Casey; m. Margaret Soden, Nov. 17, 1973; children: Gregory, Jennifer. Student, Mo. Sch. Mines, 1946-48; BS, Stanford U., 1951; postgrad., Colo. Sch. Mines, 1956-58; MS, U. So. Calif., 1961, postgrad., 1961-64. Petroleum engr. S.Am.; with Standard Oil Co. of Calif., 1951-58; research engr. Chevron Research Labs., La Habra, Calif., 1958-61; sr. evaluation engr. Union Oil Co., Los Angeles, 1961-63; v.p. Lee Keeling & Assocs., Los Angeles, 1963-65; pres. Armstrong Petroleum Corp., Newport Beach, Calif., from 1965, West Newport Oil Co., from 1983, also bd. dirs.; pres. Los Amigos de Aviones, Tram Tower Comm. Assn. Bd. dirs. Armstrong Petroleum, Calif. Ind. Oil Producers; dir., pres. West Newport Oil Co., Newport Beach, Calif., Angel Flight; vis. prof. engring. U. So. Calif., Los Angeles, 1960-65 Patentee in field of subsea prodn. systems. Mem. adv. bd. Stanford Bus. Sch.; chmn. U.S. Internat. U., Africa, chmn., San Diego. Mem. AAAS, Ind. Oilman's Assn., Calif. Conservation Commn., Am. Inst. Mining Engrs. (pres. jr. group, petroleum br. 1960-61), Am. Petroleum Inst., Orange County Petroleum Assn. (bd. dirs.). Home: Newport Beach, Calif. Died Aug. 21, 2006.

ARMSTRONG, ROGER JOSEPH, cartoonist, educator; b. LA, Oct. 12, 1917; s. Roger Dale and Elizabeth Theresa (Eliason) Armstrong; 1 child, Julia Ann Vance. Student, Pasadena City Coll., 1932—38, Chouinard Art Inst., 1938—40, student, 1948—50; PhD (hon.), Art Inst. So. Calif., 1990. Illustrator, writer children's books and comic books Western Pub. Co., 1940—49, cartoonist Little Lulu comic strip, 1964—66; cartoonist Ella Cinders comic strip United Feature Syndicate, 1950—60; cartoonist, writer Napoleon and Uncle Elby comic strip Times Mirror Syndicate, 1950—61; dir. Laguna Beach Mus. Art, Calif., 1963—66; instr. Laguna Beach Sch. Art, 1967—85; pvt. instr., 1985—2007. Cartoonist Scamp comic strip Walt Disney Prodns., 1978—88; mem. faculty Orange Coast Coll., Costa Mesa, Calif., 1980—90, So. Calif. Art Inst., 1988—2007, Irvine Coll. Fine Arts Ctr., 1995—2007. One-man shows include Ettinger Gallery, Laguna Beach, 1980—82, Challis Galleries, 1982, Anaheim (Calif.) Cultural Ctr., 1983, City Hall gallery, Buena Park, 1986, AFSC Gallery, Pasadena, 1992, Aguajita del Sol, Ariz., 1992, Newport Beach Ctrl. Libr., 1996, exhibited in group shows at Dalzell Hatfield Galleries, LA, 1975, Desert Mus., Palm Springs, Calif., 1981, Irvine Fine Arts Ctr., 1992, Stary-Sheets Gallery, Irvine, from 1992, Primera Bienal Internacional de Acurela, Mexico City, 1994, Anderson Art Gallery, Sunset Beach, 1995, 1996, Represented in permanent collections Laguna Beach Art Mus., Smithsonian Instn., Washington, Ohio State U., Banking House Rothschild, San Francisco, City of Sante Fe Springs, City of Pico Rivera; author: How to Draw Comic Strips, 1990. With US Army, 1944. Recipient 1st prize for Oil Painting, Pico Rivera Festival Arts, 1967, 1st Bicentennial award for Meritorious Achievement, Cypress (Calif.) Coll., 1976, Golden award, Motion Picture Screen Cartoonists, 1992. Mem.: Comic Artists Profl. Soc., Nat. Cartoonists Soc., Artists Equity, Nat. Watercolor Soc. (pres. 1984—85). Home: Laguna Hills, Calif. Died June 7, 2007.

ARNESON, GEORGE STEPHEN, manufacturing executive, management consultant; b. St. Paul, Apr. 3, 1925; s. Oscar and Louvia Irene (Clare) A.; children: George Stephen, Deborah Clare, Diane Elizabeth, Frederick Oscar. BS in Marine Transp., U.S. Mcht. Marine Acad., 1945; BEE, U. Minn., 1949. Certified mgmt. cons. Sales engr. Hubbard & Co., Chgo., 1949-54; cons. Booz, Allen & Hamilton, Chgo., 1954-57; mgr. mktg. cons. services, dir. mktg., plant mgr. Borg-Warner Corp., Chgo., 1957-60; asst. gen. mgr., then v.p., gen. mgr. Delta-Star Electric div. H.K. Porter Co., Inc., Pitts., 1960-63, v.p., gen. mgr. elec. divs., 1963-65; v.p. mktg. Wheeling Steel Corp., 1965-66; pres., chief exec. officer Vendo Co., Kansas City, Mo., 1966-72, also dir., chmn. exec. com.; pres., chmn. Dun-Lap Mfg. Co., Newton, Iowa, 1973-77; pres. Arneson & Co., Overland Park, Kans., from 1974. Contbr. articles on mgmt. cons., bus. valuation and appraisal of mgmt. to profl. jours. Chmn. adv. bd. Kans. Dept. Corrections, Topeka, 1980-92. Lt. (j.g.) USNR, 1943-46. Recipient Outstanding Alumnus award U.S. Mcht. Marine Acad., 1968, Past Dir. award Automatic Merchandising Assn. Mem. Phi Gamma Delta (life), Alpha Phi Omega (life). Clubs: Masons, KT, Shriners. Presbyterian. Home: Leavenworth, Kans. Died May 30, 2006.

ARNHEIM, RUDOLF, psychologist, educator; b. Berlin, July 15, 1904; came to U.S., 1940, naturalized, 1946; s. Georg and Betty (Gutherz) A.; m. Mary Elizabeth Frame, Apr. 11, 1953; 1 dau., Margaret. PhD, U. Berlin, 1928; D.F.A. (hon.), R.I. Sch. Design, 1976, Kansas City Art Inst., 1985, Mass. Coll. Art, 1985, Albion Coll., 1987; Litt.D. (hon.), Bates Coll., 1981, Marquette U., 1984, Sarah Lawrence Coll., 1985. Asso. editor publs. Internat. Inst. Ednl. Films, Rome, 1933-38; lectr., vis. prof. Grad. Faculty, New Sch. Social Research, NYC, 1943-68; mem. faculty Sarah Lawrence Coll., 1943-68; prof. psychology of art Carpenter Center for Visual Arts, Harvard U., 1968-74, prof. emeritus, 1974—2007. Vis. prof. U. Mich., Ann Arbor, 1974-84 Author: Art and Visual Perception, 1954-74, Film as Art, 1957, Picasso's Guernica, 1962, Toward a Psychology of Art, 1966, Visual Thinking, 1969, Entropy and Art, 1971, Radio, 1971, The Dynamics of Architectural Form, 1977, The Power of the Center, 1982, 2d rev. edit., 1988, New Essays on the Psychology of Art, 1986, Parables of Sunlight, 1989, To the Rescue of Art, 1992. Recipient Disting. Svc. award Nat. Art Edn. Assn., 1976; Guggenheim fellow, 1941-42; decorated Grand Cross of Merit, Order of Merit, Fed. Republic of Germany, 1989. Fellow Am. Psychol. Assn. (pres. div. psychology and arts 1957-58, 65-66, 70-71), Am. Acad. Arts and Scis.; mem. Am. Soc. Aesthetics (pres. 1959-60, 79-80), Coll. Art Assn. Home: Ann Arbor, Mich. Died June 9, 2007.

ARNOLD, JOHN HUDSON, bank executive; b. Plain Dealing, La., Oct. 7, 1931; s. Edward H. and Edna (Teutsch) A.; m. Wilda Kennon Arnold, Sept. 2, 1955; children: Steve Richard, J. Mark. BS, East Tex. Bapt. U., 1957; MS, New Orleans Bapt. Theol. Sem., 1959. Owner Church Supply Co., Houston, 1961-63; mgr. Ada Oil Co. Union, Houston, 1963-65, Monsanto Choc. Bayou Fed. Credit Union, Alvin, Tex., 1965-73; v.p. Tex. Credit Union League, Dallas, 1974-76; pres., chief exec. officer S.W. Corp. Fed. Credit Union, Dallas, from 1976. Chmn. credit com. U.S. Cen. Credit Union, Kansas City, 1985—; chmn. corp. forum Assn. Credit League Union Execs., Madison, Wis., 1980-82. Chmn. fin. com. East Tex. Bapt. U., Marshall, 1985—, also trustee. Home: Addison, Tex. Died July 17, 2006.

ARNOLD, PETER VAUGHN, aviation, marine and civil engineering consultant; b. Gardner, Mass., May 1, 1933; s. Elsworth Vaughn and Lois Arelia (Nichols) A.; B.C.E., New Eng. Coll., 1959; m. Geraldine Ann Avellar, June 6, 1953; children— Deborah Lee, Kevin Vaughn. Engr., Morrison Knudsen & G.A. Fuller Co., 1959-61; gen. mgr. Astro Technology, Mountain View, Calif., 1961-65; contract adminstr. Nat. Accelorator Labs., Stanford, Calif. and Batavia, Ill., 1965-72; pres. Constellation Aeros., Tallahassee, 1961—, also Admiralty Marine Service, Tallahassee. Mem. CAP, Coast Guard Aux. Served with USCG, 1951-59. Mem. U.S. Naval Inst., Am. Boat and Yacht Council, Fla. Engrs. Soc., Nat. Soc. Profl. Engrs., ASCE, Soc. Mil. Engrs., Soc. Naval Architects and Marine Engrs., Sigma Phi Delta. Clubs: Moose, Masons. Patentee in field. Died June 21, 2006.

ARNOLD, RICHARD KEITH, forester, educator; b. Long Beach, Calif., Nov. 17, 1913; s. Park and Mayme F. (Swan) A.; m. Helen Louise DuBose, Feb. 7, 1942 (dec. Jan. 1970); children: Bruce Gaillard, Richard Park, Jay Ross; m. Lillian Chandler DeAngelis, Oct. 27, 1970 (dec. Sept. 1985); m. Ruth Stroud, May 29, 1986. AA, Glendale Jr. Coll., 1935; BS, U. Calif.-Berkeley, 1937; M.F., Yale U., 1938; PhD, U. Mich., 1950. Assoc. in forestry U. Calif.-Berkeley, 1939-41, asst. prof. forestry, 1946-51, 53-55; forester Forest Service U.S. Dept. Agr., Berkeley, 1951-53, chief of fire research, 1955-57; dir. Pacific S.W. Forest Expt. Sta., 1957-63; dir. div. Forest Protection Research, Forest Service U.S. Dept. Agr., Washington, 1963-66, dep. chief research, 1969-73; dean Sch. Natural Resources, U. Mich., Ann Arbor, 1966-69; assoc. dean Lyndon B. Johnson Sch. Pub. Affairs, U. Tex., Austin, 1974-76; asst. v.p.-research U. Tex., 1976-79; dir. div. natural resources and environ. Lyndon B. Johnson Sch. Pub. Affairs, U. Tex., 1974-76. Cons. CD and fire research State of Calif., 1949-54; U.S. mem. FAO Com. on Forestry Edn., 1968-69; mem. adv. com. Yale U. Sch. Forestry, 1969—; chmn. fire working group N.Am. Forestry Commn., 1965-66 Mem. Mich. Gov.'s Commn. on Urban Affairs, 1968. Served to lt. USNR, 1942-46. Fellow Soc. Am. Foresters (pres. 1975-77); mem. Internat. Union Forestry Research Orgns., Internat. Union Socs. Foresters, AAAS, Am. Forestry Assn., Sigma Xi, Phi Beta Kappa. Clubs: Kiwanis. Home: Hot Springs National Park, Ark. Died Apr. 22, 2006.

ARONSON, DAVID, retired chemical and mechanical engineer; b. Bklyn., Sept. 24, 1912; s. Oscar and Amy (Maas) A.; m. Hannah Unger, Feb. 11, 1945; children: Deborah, Judith. BS, Cooper Union Sch. Engring., 1936; BSChemE, Poly. Inst. Bklyn., 1944. Chem. engr. Sanderson & Porter, Pine Bluff, Ark., 1942-43, Kellex Corp., NYC, 1943-45, Elliott Co., Jeannette, Pa., 1945-51; staff engr. Worthington Corp., Harrison, N.J., 1951-54; ptnr. Deutsch & Loonam, NYC, 1954-55; pvt. practice Montclair, N.J., 1995; ret., 1995. Cons., dir. R & D Worthington Corp., Harrison, N.J., 1955-70; cons. engr. David Aronson Assocs., 1995, Upper Montclair, N.J., 1970-94. Contbr. articles to profl. jours. Chmn. cmty. relations com. Congregation Shomrei Emunah, 1971-90. Inducted into the N.J. Inventors Congress and Hall of Fame, 1995. Fellow ASME; mem. AIChE, Sigma Xi, Tau Beta Pi. Achievements include numerous patents on cryogenic systems power generating systems using low grade heat, and on large capacity water chillers both mechanical compression and chemical absorption; development of simplified techniques used to control production barrier for separation of uranium hexafluoride isotopes. Died July 19, 2006.

ARTHUR, MACON MICHAUX, lawyer; b. Goldsboro, NC, Mar. 1, 1922; s. Joseph Dogan and Sarah Borden (Michaux) A.; m. Marianne de Roubaix, Sept. 16, 1950; children: Patrick, Danielle, Elizabeth. BA, U. Va., 1947, LL.B., 1948. Bar: D.C. 1949, Md. 1959, Ill. 1961. Assoc. Adair, Ulmer, Murchison, Kent & Ashby, Washington, 1948-58, ptnr., 1958-61, Mayer, Brown & Platt, Chgo. and Paris, from 1961. Trustee Eastern Mineral Law Found., Morgantown W.Va., 1983—. Served to capt. U.S. Army, 1942-46, ETO, PTO; served to maj. USAR, 1946-66. Mem. ABA, Chgo. Bar Assn. Clubs: University (Chgo.), Metropolitan (Chgo.). Home: Pawleys Island, SC. Died Apr. 9, 2006.

ASH, MAJOR MCKINLEY, JR., dentist, educator; b. Bellaire, Mich., Apr. 7, 1921; s. Major McKinley Sr. and Helen Marguerite (Early) A.; m. Fayola Foltz, Sept. 2, 1947; children: George McKinley, Carolyn Marguerite, Jeffrey LeRoy, Thomas Edward. BS, Mich. State U., 1947; DDS, Emory U., 1951; MS, U. Mich., 1954; MD (hon.), U. Bern, 1975; PhD, Walsingham U., 2006. Instr. sch. dentistry Emory U., Atlanta, 1952—53; instr. U. Mich., Ann Arbor, 1953—56, asst. prof., 1956—59, assoc. prof., 1959—62, prof., 1962—89, chmn. dept. occlusion, sch. dentistry, 1962—89, dir. stomatognathic physiology lab., sch. dentistry, 1969—89, dir. TMJ/oral facial pain clinic, sch. dentistry, 1983—89, Marcus L. Ward prof. dentistry, 1984—89, prof. emeritus, rsch. scientist emeritus, 1989—2007; cons. N.E. Regional Dental Bd., 1988—92. Vis. prof. U. Bern, 1989, U. Tex., San Antonio, 1990-98; pres. Basic Sci. Bd., State of Mich., 1962-74; cons. over the counter drugs FDA, Washington, 1985-89. Author, co-author 70 textbooks, 1958-2007; editor 4 books; contbr. over 190 articles to profl. jours. Served to tech. sgt. Signal Corps, U.S. Army, 1942-45, ETO. Grantee, Nat. Inst. Dental Rsch., 1962—85. Fellow Am. Coll. Dentists, Internat. Coll. Dentists, European Soc. Craniomandibular Disorders, European Soc. Oral Physiology; mem. AAAS, ADA (cons. coun. on dental therapeutics 1982-2007, cons. coun. sci. affairs 1995-2007), N.Y. Acad. Scis., Washtenaw Dist. Dental Soc. (pres. 1963-64), Phi Kappa Phi. Presbyterian. Avocations: photography, birdwatching. Died Mar. 21, 2007.

ASHE, JAMES S., entomologist, educator; b. Charlotte, Feb. 23, 1947; BS, U. N.C., 1969; MA, Appalachian State U., 1972; PhD, U. Alta., 1982. Vis. curator entomology Am. Mus. Natural History, NYC, 1983; acting div. head invertebrates Field Mus. Natural History, Chgo., 1986-87, acting chmn. zoology, 1985, 87-88, div. head insects, 1985-88, asst. curator, then assoc. curator insects, 1982-88; assoc. prof. entomology, systematics and ecology U. Kans., Lawrence, from 1988, dir. Snow Entomol. Mus., from 1988. Asst. curator, session instr. U. Alta., Edmonton, 1978-79; lectr. evolutionary biology U. Chgo., 1984-88. Sci. editor Fieldiana, 1988; contbr. articles to profl. jours. With U.S. Army, 1970-72. Rice grantee, MacArthur Found. grantee, BBC grantee, 1986-89, NSF grantee, 1988—. Mem. Soc. Systematic Zoology (coun. mem. 1985-88, rep. A.S. Coll. 1988), Entomological Soc. Am. (sec., sec.-elect 1988-89, sect. A chmn. 1990-91), Coleopterists Soc. (pres., pres. elect 1989-90). Died Dec. 27, 2005.

ASHLEY, JAMES WHEELER, lawyer; b. Chgo., Sept. 23, 1923; s. Frederick and Elizabeth (Wheeler) A.; m. Courtney Collidge, Dec. 27, 1947 (div. 1975); children: James W., Cooper S., Courtney, Christopher R., John M.; m. Joan Allbright, Sept. 25, 1975. Student, Fordham U., 1941-43; JD, Northwestern U., 1948. Bar: Ill. 1948. Asst. sec. Continental Ill. Nat. Bank, Chgo., 1948-57; assoc. McDermott, Will & Emery, Chgo., 1957-59, ptnr., 1959-88, of counsel, from 1989. Bd. dirs. Madison-Kipp Corp., Key Trust Co., 1988-93; chmn. Y-Mut. Ins. Co., 1987-92; dir. Chgo. Tube & Iron Co., Globe Corp. Contbr. articles to legal jours. Bd. dirs. Chgo. YMCA, 1964-85, chmn., 1974-75, mem. nat. bd. dirs., 1975-90, chmn., 1985-87; bd. dirs. Bus. and Profl. People Pub. Interest, Chgo., 1973-89, pres., 1982-86; trustee Village of Hinsdale, 1969-72; justice of peace State of Vt., 1989-91; treas. Dem. Com. Vt., 1991—. Capt. USAAF, 1943-45, ETO. Mem. ABA, Ill. Bar Assn., Chgo. Bar Assn., Chgo. Coun. Lawyers, Monroe Club Chgo. (pres. 1980-88, bd. dirs. 1976-88). Home: Norwich, Vt. Died Apr. 2, 2007.

ASPATURIAN, VERNON VARAZTAT, political science educator, consultant, author; b. Armavir, Kuban, USSR, Feb. 16, 1922; s. Serop and Gayane (Ohanesian) A.; m. Suzanne Lee Dohan, Aug. 29, 1948; children: Heidi Jeanne, Nancy Lee. AB with highest honors, UCLA, 1947, PhD, 1951. Evan Pugh prof. polit. sci. Pa. State U., University Park, 1952-92, dir. Slavic and Soviet Lang. and Area Ctr., 1965-89, sr. dir., 1989-92, Evan Pugh prof. emeritus polit. sci., from 1992. Vis. prof. Johns Hopkins U. Sch. Advanced Internat. Rels., UCLA, Columbia U., Rand Grad. Sch., Naval Postgrad. Sch., grad. Inst. Internat. Affairs, Geneva, Inst. Advanced Studies, Vienna, Austria, Christian Albrechts U., Kiel, Germany; lectr. univs. in U.S., Europe, Latin Am., E. Asia; cons. Rand Corp., Santa Monica, Calif., 1961-68, HEW, U.S. Dept. State, U.S. Dept. Commerce, HRB-Singer, State Coll., Pa., 1970-71, CIA, Army War Coll., Carlisle, Pa., USIA, Pacific-Sierra Corp., Washington, 1981-82; adv. bd., Kennan Inst., Washington, U. Miami Grad. Sch. Internat. Affairs; expert witness com. on fgn. affairs U.S. Ho. Reps. Author: The Union Republics in Soviet Diplomacy, 1960, The Soviet Union in the World Communist System, 1966, Process and Power in Soviet Foreign Policy, 1977; co-author: Foreign Policy in World Politics, 1958, 7th rev. edit., 1988, Modern Political Systems: Europe, 1963, 6th rev. edit., 1986, New Trends in Kremlin Policy, 1971; co-author, co-editor: Eurocommunism Between East and West, 1980, The Soviet Invasion of Afghanistan: Three Perspectives, 1980; guest commentator TV, radio stas.; contbd. to more than 150 books; contbd. to profl. jours. Recipient Smith Mundt award Govt. U.S., 1958-59; Inter-Univ. Com. travel grantee, 1958; Joint Com. on Ea. Europe conf. grantee, 1976, 80; Rockefeller Found. rsch. fellow, 1956-67. Mem. Polit. Sci. Assn. (pres. conf. on comparative communist studies 1972-73), Am. Assn. for Advancement Slavic Studies (exec. coun. 1973-74, chmn. Shulman prize com. 1987-92), Internat. Studies Assn., Internat. Polit. Sci. Assn., Am. Coun. Learned Socs. (mem. joint com. on Ea. Europe), Phi Beta Kappa, Pi Gamma Mu, Pi Sigma Alpha. Democrat. Episcopalian. Avocations: stamp collecting/philately, ancient coins, antique maps, archaeology. Home: Laguna Niguel, Calif. Died Aug. 1, 2007.

ASTOR, BROOKE, foundation administrator, philanthropist, writer; b. Portsmouth, NH, Mar. 30, 1902; d. John Henry and Mabel (Howard) Russell; m. J. Dryden Kuser 1916, div. 1930; m. Charles Marshall 1932 (died 1952); m. Vincent Astor 1953 (died 1959); s. Anthony Dryden Marshall. LLD (hon.), Columbia U., 1971, Brown U., 1980; LHD (hon.), Fordham U., 1980, NYU, 1986; PhD in Biomed. Sci. (honoris causa), Rockefeller U., 1986. Pres., trustee Astor Home for Children; trustee Hist. Hudson Valley, Marconi Internat. Fellowship; trustee and hon. chmn., mem. devel. com., mem. exec. com. N.Y. Pub. Libr., NYC; life trustee, mem. conservation com. N.Y. Zool. Soc.; trustee emeritus, mem. coun. of fellows Pierpont Morgan Libr. Trustee emeritus, chmn. vis. com. dept. Asian art, mem. acquisitions com., exec. com. ex officio Met. Mus. Art, N.Y.C.; life trustee Rockefeller U. Author: Patchwork Child, 1962, rev. edit., 1993, The Bluebird Is at Home, 1965, Footprints, 1980, The Last Blossom on the Plum Tree, 1986; feature editor: House and

Garden, 1946-56, cons. editor, 1956-93. Mem. N.Y. State Pk. Commn., 1967-69. Decorated dame Venerable Order of St. John of Jerusalem; recipient Anniversary medal Astor, Lenox and Tilden Founds. of N.Y. Pub. Libr., 1961, award Sisters of Good Shepherd and Children of Madonna Heights Sch. for Girls, 1963, Client Award cert. N.Y. State Assn. Architects, 1964, award Pk. Assn. N.Y.C. Inc., 1965, Honor award HUD, 1966, cert. of appreciation City of N.Y., 1967, Albert S. Bard Merit award City Club N.Y., 1967, Award of Honor, Women's Aux. N.Y. chpt. AIA, 1968, Rector's award St. Phillip's Ch., 1968, Michael Friedsam medal Archtl. League N.Y., 1968, award Brotherhood-In-Action, Inc., 1968, Outstanding Contbn. award Am. Soc. Landscape Architects, 1968, Spirit of Achievement award Albert Einstein Coll. Medicine, Yeshiva U., 1969, Good Samaritan award P. Ballentine & Sons, 1969, Good Samaritan award Prospect Block Civic Assn., 1969, Disting. Svc. award N.Y. region Rotary, 1970, YWCA honor, 1970, Housing award N.Y. Met. chpt. Nat. Assn. Housing and Redevel. Officials, 1971, $24 award Mus. City of N.Y., award N.Y. Pub. Libr., 1972, Albert Gallatin medal NYU, 1972, spl. citation AIA, 1973, Medal of Merit award Lotos Club, 1973, commendation Neighborhood Com. for the Asphalt Green, 1975, commendation ARCS Found., 1976, Pres.'s medal Mcpl. Art Soc. N.Y., 1976, Gold Medal award N.Y. Zool. Soc., 1978, Elizabeth Seton Humanitarian award N.Y. Foundling Hosp., 1978, Little Apple award Met. Mus. Art, Little Apple award Morgan Library, Little Apple award N.Y. Public Library, Little Apple award N.Y. Zool. Soc., Little Apple award Rockefeller U., Little Apple award South St. Seaport and Sta. WNET-TV/Channel 13, 1978, New Yorker for N.Y. award Citizens Com. for N.Y.C., 1980, 1st Myer Myers Cultural award City of N.Y., award Citizens Housing and Planning Coun., 1980, Bishop's Cross, Diocese of N.Y., 1980, Forsythia award Bklyn. Bot. Garden, 1981, award Pks. Coun., 1981, Woman of Conscience award Appeal of Conscience Found., 1981, commendation Lower Manhattan Cultural Coun., 1984, Disting. New Yorkers award Bowery Savs. Bank, 1984, Gov.'s Arts award State of N.Y., 1985, Am. Acad. and Inst. Arts and Letters award, 1986, Marconi Internat. Fellowship Coun. award, 1986, landmark plaque and medallion N.Y. Landmarks Preservation Found., 1987, Gold medal St. Nicholas Soc., N.Y.C., 1987, Fashion Industry award Coun. of Fashion Designers Am., 1988, Presdl. Medal of Freedom, Pres. Reagan, 1988, Nat. Medal of Arts, Nat. Endowment for the Arts, 1988, World Monuments Fund The Hadrian award, 1991, annual humanitarian award ARC of Greater N.Y., 1993, Eleanor Roosevelt medallion City of N.Y., 1993, 8th Annual Town & Country Most Generous American award, The Hearst Corp. and Hearst Mags., 1993, The Mayor's award of Honor and Culture, City of N.Y., 1993, 10th Annual Humanitarian award N.Y., 1993, Richard Rodgers award for Disting. Svc., Profl. Children's Sch., 1994, Scroll of Honor, N.Y. coun. Navy League of U.S., 1994; Brooke Astor Day proclaimed by Mayor of N.Y.C., March 5, 1992. Fellow Am. Acad. Arts and Scis.; mem. Mcpl. Art Soc. N.Y., Pilgrims U.S., Venerable Order St. John of Jerusalem (dame), The Century Assn., Colony Club, Knickerbocker Club, N.Y. Yacht Club, Sleepy Hollow Country Club. Died Aug. 13, 2007.

ATHERTON, CHARLES HENRY, federal commission administrator; b. Kingston, Pa., June 24, 1932; s. Thomas Henry and Mary A.; m. Mary Bringhurst Davis, Dec. 15, 1967; children: Sarah Scott, Thomas Henry, Charles Henry. BA summa cum laude, Princeton U., 1954, MFA, 1957. Registered architect, D.C. Asst. sec. Fine Arts Commn., Washington, 1960-64, sec., adminstrv. officer, 1964—2004; ret., 2004. Trustee Nat. Child Rsch. Ctr., 1975-79; v.p. Washington Hist. Soc.; bd. dir. Hist. Am. Bldg. Survey Found. (elected fellow 2003), Navy Art Found.; mem. Citizens Commemorative Coin Adv. Com., 1994-2003; bd. dirs. Heurich House Found., 2003—. Lt. (j.g.) USNR, 1957—60. Recipient Martin Luther King Leadership award D.C. Pub. Libr. Sys., 1992, Centennial medal Washington chpt. AIA, 1993, Lifetime Achievement award Comm. of 100 on the Federal City, Mayor's award lifetime achievement in hist. preervation, 2004, Thomas Jefferson award for pub. architecture AIA, 2005; inductee Washington D.C. Hall of Fame, 2004. Mem.: Cosmos Club, Potomac Boat Club. Home: Washington, DC. Died Dec. 15, 2005.

ATKERSON, JOANNE RUTH, radio announcer, news director; b. Lewis Station, Mo., Jan. 18, 1933; d. John Logan and Carolyn Ruth (Schneider) Gill; m. Virgil Riley Atkerson, Jan. 16, 1955; 1 child, Teresa Susan Atkerson Muhs. Grad. high sch., McAlester, Okla. Lic. FCC Hostess cable show Sta. KBLE, McAlester, 1973-76; staff announcer Sta. KNED, McAlester, 1974-86, news dir., 1983-86. Active Tiak council Girl Scouts U.S.A., 1962-70, McAlester PTA, 1962—; vice-chair bd. dirs. McAlester Pub. Library, 1984-88, chair, 1988—; bd. dirs. McAlester Alcoholism Bd., 1982-83, Girls' Club Bd., McAlester, 1982-83; adv. Kiamichi Vo-Tech Sch. Bd., McAlester, 1976-83; vice chair McAlester Pub. Library Bd., 1984—. Recipient Meritorious Service citation Am. Legion Post 79, 1981; DJ of Yr. Runner-up, Kiamichi Country Tourism Group, 1979; Named DJ of Yr. Little Dixie Hayride, 1980. Republican. Baptist. Lodge: Optimists (bd. dirs. McAlester club 1988—). Avocations: swimming, wood carving, painting, reading, embroidery, crocheting. Home: Mcalester, Okla. Died June 2, 2006.

ATWATER, FRANKLIN SIMPSON, business executive; b. New Britain, Conn., Aug. 24, 1916; s. George Franklin and Ida (Simpson) A.; m. Marion Jane Brian, May 9, 1947; children: Mary-Jane, Brian, Sally. BS, MIT, 1938. Mem. staff MIT, 1938-39; with Fafnir Bearing Co. (div. Textron Inc.), New Britain, 1939-75, prodn. engr., indsl. engring. mgr., asst. gen. works mgr., gen. works mgr., 1956-59, v.p. mfg., 1959-63, v.p. ops., 1963-67, exec. v.p., 1967-69, pres., 1969-75, Homelite, Charlotte, N.C., 1975-76, chmn., 1976-77. Bus advisor Internat. Exec. Svc. Corps, 1981-88; bd. dirs. Fusion Sys. Corp., Fairbanks, Inc. Author: (with L.L. Bethel and others) Industrial Organization and Management, 1945, Essentials of Industrial Management, 1954, Production Control, 1942. Home: Clover, SC. Died Aug. 1, 2007.

ATWELL, ROBERT JAMES, emeritus medical educator; b. Gary, Ind., Sept. 1, 1919; s. Oswald B. and Helen N. (Neuding) A.; m. Paula Mozelle Mitchell, Apr. 28, 1945; children: Robert, David M., Paul N. AB, Duke U., 1941, MD, 1944. Intern Duke Hosp., 1944-45, resident, 1945-47, Bellevue Hosp., NYC, 1947-48; chief med. service Ohio Tb Hosp., Columbus, 1950-66; mem. faculty Coll. Medicine Ohio State U., 1951-83, prof., 1966-83; acting dean Coll. Medicine, 1972-73; dir., prof. Sch. Allied Med. Professions Ohio State U., 1966-83, prof. emeritus Sch. Allied Med. Professions, from 1983. Mem. attending staff U. Hosp., Columbus, 1952—; cons. asst. sec. health affairs HEW, 1971-74, Nat. Libr. Medicine, 1970-74, AMA, 1969-83, Regional Med. Programs, 1969-72, Bur. Health Manpower Edn., NIH, 1968-70, Nat. Inst. Arthritis and Metabolic Diseases, 1962, VA 1954-86; chmn. med. adv. com. State Tchrs. Retirement Sys., 1965-97, Sch. Employees Retirement Sys., State of Ohio, 1966—. Contbr. articles to profl. jours. Fellow A.C.P.; mem. Assn. Schs. Allied Health Professions (sec.-treas. 1969, pres. 1971), Central Soc. Clin. Research. Home: Columbus, Ohio. Died May 11, 2006.

AUGELLO, WILLIAM JOSEPH, lawyer; b. Bklyn., Apr. 5, 1926; s. William J. and Catherine (Ehalt) A.; m. Elizabeth Deasy, July 1, 1950; children: Thomas, Charles, Patricia, William, Peggy Ann, James. LLB, Fordham U., 1950; BA, Dartmouth Coll., 1946. Bar: N.Y. 1951. Individual practice law, NYC, 1953-71; mem. firm Augello, Deegan & Pezold, Huntington, NY, 1971-78; sr. mem. firm Augello, Pezold & Hirschmann, Huntington, 1978—98; adj. prof. U. Ariz., from 2001. Treas., dir. Transp. Arbitration Bd., Inc., 1978-96; chmn. accreditation com. Certified Claims Profl. Accreditation Council, Inc., Washington, 1981-96; exec. dir. Transp. Consumer Protection Coun. Inc., Huntington, 1974-2003; exec. dir., gen. counsel Freight Transp. Cons. Assoc.; adv. com. pvt. internat. law study group maritime matters Dept. State; co-chmn. uniform liability regime working group Ctr. Inter-Am. Trade; adj. prof. U. Ariz.; former faculty U. Denver Intermodal Transportation Inst., bd. dirs. Inst. Logistical Mgmt.; lectr. in field. Author: Freight Claims in Plain English, 1979, 3d edit., 1995, Transportation Insurance in Plain English, 1985, Defending and Avoiding Undercharge Claims and Suits, 1991, Doing Business Under the New Transportational Law: The Negotiated Rates Act of 1993, 94, How to Read Tariffs to Avoid Surprises, 1994, Shippers Domestic Truck Bill of Loding, 1996, A Guide to Transportation After the I.C.C., 1996, Protecting Shippers Interests, 1997, Corporate Procedures for Shipping and Receiving, 1998, Transportation, Logistics and the Law, 2001, 04; co-author: Freight Claim Prevention in Plain English, 1985, Transportation Contracts in Plain English, 1991, Q & A in Plain English, 1999. Served with USN, 1944-46. Recipient Harry E. Salzberg Medallion award Syracuse U., 1994, Transp. Educator of Yr. award Operation Stimulus, 1996; named Nat. Transp. Man of Yr., Delta Nu Alpha, 1979-80. Mem. Maritime Law Assn., Transp. Lawyers Assn. (Disting. Svc. award 1988), Suffolk County Bar Assn., Assn. Transp. Law, Logistics and Policy, El Con Conquistador Country Club (Tucson), Delta Nu Alpha. Republican. Roman Catholic. Died Nov. 9, 2006.

AURELI, GILES, industrial design educator; b. Phila., Jan. 8, 1926; s. Gaetano and Julienne (Bellenger) A.; m. Eileen Johns, Sept. 13, 1951. B.Arch., Pratt Inst., Bklyn., 1950, M.Arch., 1958. Archtl. designer numerous firms, NYC and Chgo., 1950-65; partner Aureli-Jeffe Design, White Plains, N.Y., 1965-67; project dir. Katz, Waisman, Weber, NYC, 1968-85; chmn., instr. indsl. design dept. Pratt Inst., from 1956. Author: Steel in Home Building, 1964, Reducing Costs of Public Housing, 1966. Served with U.S. Army, 1943-46. Recipient Unesco Design award, 1962 Mem. Indsl. Designers Soc. Am. Died May 7, 2007.

AUSTRIAN, ROBERT, internist, medical educator, department chairman; b. Balt., Apr. 12, 1916; s. Charles Robert and Florence (Hochschild) Austrian; m. Babette Friedmann Bernstein, Dec. 29, 1963 (dec. 2000); stepchildren: Jill Bernstein, Toni Amber. AB, Johns Hopkins U., 1937, MD, 1941; DSc (hon.), Hahnemann Med. Coll., 1980, Phila. Coll. Pharmacy and Sci., 1981, U. Pa., 1987; DSc (hon.), SUNY, 1996. Diplomate Am. Bd. Internal Medicine. House officer Johns Hopkins Hosp., 1941—50, asst. dir. med. out-patient dept., 1951—52; assoc. prof. medicine, then prof. medicine SUNY Coll. Medicine, 1952—62; John Herr Musser prof., chmn. rsch. medicine U. Pa. Sch. Medicine, 1962—86, prof. emeritus, chmn. emeritus, 1986—2007. Attending physician Hosp. U. Pa.; Tyndale vis. lectr. and prof. Coll. Medicine U. Utah, 1964; spl. rsch. on infectious diseases, bacterial genetics; mem. Meningococcal Infections Commn., 1964—72, Commn. on Acute Respiratory Disease, 1965—72, Commn. Streptococcal and Staphylococcal Diseases, 1970—72, Armed Forces Epidemiol. Bd.; cons. surgeon gen. U.S. Army R&D Command, 1966—69; mem. subcom. streptococcus and pneumococcus Internat. Com. Bacteriol. Nomenclature; mem. allergy and immunology study sect. Nat. Inst. Allergy and Infectious Diseases, 1965—69, mem. bd. sci. counselors, 1967—70, chmn., 1969—70; mem. WHO Expert Adv. Panel Acute Bacterial Diseases, 1979—2001. Mem. editl. bd.: Jour. Bacteriology, 1964—69, Am. Rev. Respiratory Diseases, 1963—66, Bacteriol. Rev., 1967—71, Jour. Infectious Diseases, 1969—74, Antimicrobial Agents and Chemotherapy, 1972—86, Infection and Immunity, 1973—81, Revs. of Infectious Diseases, 1979—89, Vaccine, from 1983, guest editor: Drugs and Aging, 1999. Trustee Johns Hopkins U., 1963—69. Capt. M.C. US Army, 1943—46. Recipient US Typhus Commn. medal, 1947, Albert Lasker Clin. Med. Rsch. award, 1978, Phila. award, 1979, Willard O. Thompson award, Am. Geriatric Soc., 1981, Lifetime Sci. award, Inst. Advanced Studies in Immunology and Aging, 1997, Pasteur Merieux MSD award, 1st Internat. Symposium on Pneumococci and Pneumococcal Diseases, 1998, Maxwell Finland award, Nat. Found. for Infectious Diseases, 2001. Master: ACP (James D. Bruce Meml. award 1979); fellow: AAAS (chmn. sect. on med. scis. 1975), Am. Acad. Microbiology, NY Acad. Scis.; mem.: NAS, Am. Osler Soc., Johns Hopkins Soc. Scholars, Infectious Disease Soc. Am. (pres. 1971, Maxwell Finland lecture award 1974, Bristol award 1986), Interurban Clin. Club (pres. 1970), Coll. Physicians Phila. (pres.-elect 1986, pres. 1988—89, Meritorious Svc. award 1980, Disting. Svc. medal 1997), Philadelphia County Med. Soc. (Strittmatter award 1979), NY Acad. Medicine (sec. sect. microbiology 1961—62), Am. Assn. Immunologists, Balt. Med. Soc., Inst. Medicine, Am. Fedn. Clin. Rsch., Harvey Soc., Soc. Exptl. Biology and Medicine, Am. Philos. Soc., Am. Soc. Microbiology (v.p. NY br. 1961—62), Am. Clin. and Climatol. Assn. (pres. 1984), Am. Soc. Clin. Investigation, Assn. Am. Physicians, 14 W. Hamilton St. Club, Omicron Delta Kappa, Alpha Omega Alpha, Sigma Xi, Phi Beta Kappa. Home: Philadelphia, Pa. Died Mar. 25, 2007.

AUTIO, RUDY, artist, educator; b. Butte, Mont., Oct. 8, 1926; BS, Mont. State U., 1950; MFA, Wash. State U., 1952; DFA, Md. Inst. Coll. Art, Balt., 1986. Resident artist dir. Archie Bray Found., 1952-56; asst. curator Mont. Mus. Hist. Soc., 1955; prof. ceramics and sculpture U. Mont., 1957-84. Author: About Drawing, 1985; one-man shows include Henry Gallery, U. Wash., Seattle, 1963, Toledo Art Mus., 1965, Retrospectives, Am. Crafts Mus., N.Y., 1983, John Michael Kohler Art Mus., Sheboygan, Wis., 1983, Bellevue Art Mus., Wash., 1983, Mont. Horses, Ryijy Tapestry, Taideteollisuusmuseo, Helsinki, 1985, Everson Mus., Syracuse, 1964; group shows include Chgo. Art Mus., 1968, Am. Studio Potters & Victoria & Albert Mus., London, 1972, San Francisco Mus. Modern Art, 1972, Mus. Contemporary Crafts, N.Y., 1974, Seattle Art Mus., 1979; retrospectives includes Am. Crafts Mus., N.Y. and Bellevue Mus. Seattle, 1984, Western States Arts Found. 3d Ann. Exhbn. Bklyn. Mus., 1986, Contemporary Am. Ceramics, Nat. Mus. Modern Art, Seoul, 1987; prin. works exhibited Renwick Gallery, Smithsonian Mus., Everson Mus., Syracuse, N.Y., Victoria & Albert Mus., London, Nat. Mus. Stockholm, Taideteollisusmuseo, Helsinki. Recipient Tiffany Found. award, 1963, Purchase award Everson Mus., 1964, Ceramic Art award, Am. Ceramic Soc., 1978, NEA, 1980, 1st Gov.'s award in Visual Arts' Most Outstanding Artist, 1980, Disting. scholar award U. Mont., 1984. Fellow Am. Craftsmen Coun. (gold medal 1999), Archie Bray Found. (trustee 1974), Internat. Ceramic Soc. Geneva; mem. Nat. Coun. Edn. Ceramic Arts. Died June 20, 2007.

AVEDISIAN, EDWARD, artist; b. Lowell, Mass., 1936; Student, Boston Museum Sch. Art. Artist-in-residence U. Kans., 1969; instr. Sch. Visual Arts, N.Y.C., 1969-70, U. Calif. Irvine, 1972, U. La., 1973. One-man shows include Boyston Print Ctr. Gallery, Cambridge, Mass., 1957, Hansa Gallery, 1958, Tibor de Nagy Gallery, 1959, 60, Robert Elkon Gallery, N.Y.C., 1962-75, Galerie Zigler, Zürich, 1964, Nicholas Wilder Gallery, L.A., 1966, 68, 69, Kasmin Gallery, London, 1966, 67, Bucknell U. Art Gallery, 1970, Walter Moos Gallery, 1971, Jack Glenn Gallery, Corona del Mar, Calif., 1971, Janie C. Lee Gallery, Houston, 1974, Carriage House, Buffalo, 1975, 78, Fishback Gallery, 1979, Jason McCoy, Inc., N.Y.C., 1984, Mitchel Algus Gallery, 1995; exhibited in group shows at Tibor de Nagy Gallery, Tony Shafrazi, 1987, Boston Mus. Art, Mus. Modern Art, Washington, Whitney Mus. Art, Dayton (Ohio) Art Internat., Kasmin Gallery, Mus. Modern Art, N.Y.C., Jewish Mus., N.Y.C., Larry Aldrich Mus., San Francisco Mus. Art, Paintings From Expo '67, Boston Inst. Contemporary Art, Berkshire Mus., 1980; represented in permanent collections at Guggenheim Mus., Whitney Mus. Art, Mus. Modern Art, L.A. Mus. Art, Pasadena (Calif.) Mus. Art, Larry Aldrich Mus., Wadsworth Atheneum, Met. Mus., N.Y.C., others. Died Aug. 17, 2007.

AVNER, LOUIS LEONARD, drug company executive, director; b. California, Pa., Apr. 22, 1915; s. Samuel and Rose (Hoffman) A.; m. Helen L. Huffman, Feb. 22, 1941; children: Constance (Mrs. Bruce Buchanan), Robin. BA, U. Mich., 1936, postgrad., 1937. V.p. Thrift Drug Co., Pitts., 1945-62, exec. v.p., 1962-68, pres., 1968-80; chmn. bd. Apex Resources Inc., from 1980, R&A Devel. Inc., from 1980; dir. Union Nat. Bank Pitts. Bd. dirs. Montefiore Hosp., Am. Friends of Hebrew U. Mem. Beta Gamma Sigma. Home: Pittsburgh, Pa. Died Apr. 7, 2006.

AXON, DONALD CARLTON, architect; b. Haddonfield, NJ, Feb. 27, 1931; s. William Russell Sr. and Gertrude L. (Ellis) A.; m. Rosemary Smith, Sept. 1952 (div. Oct. 1967); children: Donald R., James K., Marianne Axon Flannery, Darren H., William R. II; m. Janice Jacobs, Mar. 16, 1968; stepchildren: Jonathan Lee, Elise Marie. BArch, Pratt Inst., 1954; MS in Arch., Columbia U., 1966. Registered architect, NY, Pa., Calif. Designer, drafter Keith Hibner, Assoc., Hicksville, NY, 1954-56; designer Charles Wood, Riverhead, NY, 1956-59; architect, prin Donald C. Axon, Assoc., Wantaugh, NY, 1959; ptnr. Bailey-Axon & Assoc., Long Beach, NY, 1960-66; project mgr. Caudill Rowlett Scott, Houston, 1966-69; in-house arch. Kaiser Permanente Hosp., LA, 1969-75; dir. med. facilities Daniel Mann Johnson Mendenhall, LA, 1975-78, Lyon Assoc., LA, 1979-80; pres. Donald C. Axon, FAIA, Inc., LA, from 1980. Tchr. bldg. sci. program U. So. Calif., 1978-82; lectr. in field; profl. advisor dept. architecture U. Tex., 1968-69; advisor to chmn. Sch. Architecture Rice U., Houston, 1968-69; profl. dir. Future Architect Am., 1965-66. Mem. Crestwood Hills Assn., bd. dir. 1971-75, pres., 1973-75, archtl. rev. com., 1987—; bd. dir. Brentwood Community Fedn., 1973-75, v.p., 1974-75. Recipient LA Beautiful award KPH Norwalk Hosp. Fellow AIA, Royal Soc. Health, Health Facilities Inst., Am. Coll. Healthcare Arch. (founding fellow),(Calif. regional bd. dir. 1987-89, mem. various subcoms., chair steering com. 1980, liaison 1991—, bd. dir. L.A. chpt. 1983-84, pres. 1986, chair com. on architecture for health 1974, chair health facilities com. Calif. coun. 1975, Disting. Svc. citation 1992), mem. Am. Soc. Healthcare Engr., Archtl. Found. LA (founding, v.p. 1985-89, pres. 1989-90), Internat. Conf. Bldg. Ofcl., Am. Hosp. Assn., Forum for Health Care Planning (bd. dir. 1982—, pres. 1993-94). Died May 6, 2007.

AYAD, JOSEPH MAGDY, retired psychologist; b. Cairo, May 21, 1926; arrived in U.S., 1949, naturalized, 1961; s. Fahim Gayed and Victoria Gabour (El-Masri) Ayad; m. Widad Fareed Bishai, May 29, 1954; children: Fareed Merritt, Victor Maher, Michael Joseph, Mona Elaine. BA in Social Scis., Am. U., Cairo, 1946; MA in Clin. Psychology, Stanford U., 1952; PhD in Clin. Psychology, U. Denver, 1956. Trans. Hoover Inst. War and Peace Stanford U., 1950—51; asst. to chief psychologist Colo. Psychopathic Hosp., 1952—54; cons. Child Guidance Clinic State Dept. Pub. Welfare, Denver, 1953—56; cons. psychologist Dept. Pub. Welfare State of Tex., 1957—72; cons. psychologist Dept. Insts. Social and Rehab. Svc. State of Okla., 1960—72; cons. psychologist N.Mex. Dept. Pub. Welfare, 1960—72; lectr. Fitzsimmons Army Hosp., Denver, 1953—54; vis. psychologist

Child Guidance Clinic State Dept. Pub. Welfare, Pueblo, Colo., 1953—54; staff psychologist Cons. Psychol. Svc., Denver, 1956—57, High Plains Neurol. Ctr., Amarillo, Tex., 1973—2002; pres. JMA Cattle Co., Amarillo, 1973—2002; v.p., treas. Filigon Inc., Amarillo, 1962—75, pres., 1976—2002, ret., 2002. Mem. profl. adv. bd. Amarillo Mental Health Assn., 1968—69. Contbr. articles to profl. jours. Mem. Amarillo Child Welfare Bd., 1961—63; area chmn. U. Denver Fund Raising Campaign, 1963; mem. profl. adv. bd. St. Paul's Meth. Ch. Sch. for Children with Learning Disabilities, Amarillo, 1969—70. Recipient Grad. Sr. award in philosophy, Am. U. at Cairo, 1946. Mem.: APA, Calif. Psychol. Assn., Tex. Psychol. Assn., Potter-Randall County (Tex.) Psychol. Soc. (pres. 1974), Am. Assn. Marriage and Family Therapists, Internat. Assn. Applied Psychology, Am. Psychol. Soc., Amarillo Country Club. Presbyterian. Home: Nashville, Tenn. Died Aug. 7, 2006.

AYERS, THOMAS G., retired utilities executive; b. Detroit, Feb. 16, 1915; s. Jule C. and Camilla (Chalmers) A.; m. Mary Andrew, Nov. 25, 1938 (dec.); children: Catherine Mary Ayers Allen, Thomas G., William Charles, Richard James, John Steven. AB, U. Mich., 1937; LL.D., Elmhurst Coll., 1966. With Pub. Service Co. No. Ill., 1938-52, mgr. indsl. relations, 1948-52; asst. v.p. Commonwealth Edison Co., Chgo., 1952, v.p., 1953-62, exec. v.p., 1962-64, pres., 1964-73, chmn., pres., CEO, 1973-80. Bd. dirs. Chgo. Pacific Corp., Zenith Radio Corp., Gen. Dynamics Corp. Chmn. Dearborn Park Corp.; chmn. Met. Crusade of Mercy, 1969, Leadership Council for Met. Open Communities; chmn. bd. trustee Northwestern U., Chgo. Symphony Orch. Mem. Chgo. Assn. Commerce and Industry (dir., past pres.) Clubs: Chicago, Mid-Day, Commercial, Tavern (Chgo.); Glen Oak Country; Pauma Valley Country (Calif.). Home: Glen Ellyn, Ill. Died June 8, 2007.

BABLER, WAYNE E., lawyer, retired utilities executive; b. Orangeville, Ill., Dec. 8, 1915; s. Oscar E. and Mary (Bender) B.; m. Mary Blome, Dec. 27, 1940; children: Wayne Elroy Jr., Marilyn Anne Monson, Sally Jane Sperry. BA, Ind. Cen. Coll., 1935; JD, U. Mich., 1938; LLD, Ind. Cen. U., 1966. Bar: Mich. 1938, N.Y. 1949, Mo. 1955, Wis. 1963, U.S. Supreme Ct. 1963. Assoc. Bishop & Bishop, Detroit, 1938-42, ptnr., 1945-48; atty. AT&T, 1948-55; gen. solicitor Southwestern Bell Tel. Co., St. Louis, 1955-63, v.p., gen. counsel, sec., 1965-80, ret., 1980; v.p., gen. counsel Wis. Tel. Co., Milw., 1963-65. Bd. dirs., chmn. St. Louis Soc. Crippled Children; bd. dirs. St. Louis Symphony Soc. Mem. ABA (chmn. pub. utility sect. 1978-79), Fed. Comms. Bar Assn., Mo. Bar. Assn. Home: Saint Louis, Mo. Died Dec. 15, 2006.

BACHE, THEODORE STEPHEN, recording company executive; b. NYC, Dec. 19, 1936; s. Max Isselbacher and Leona (Rose) Hammel; m. Sheila Gottehrer, Oct. 18, 1959 (div. 1967); children: Mona Sharon, Caryl Michelle; m. Suellyn Kaplan, Feb. 18, 1968; children: Paul Michael, David Eric. BBA, Pace U., 1957, MBA, 1970; cert. in bus. adminstrn., Columbia U., Harriman, NY, 1973. CPA, N.Y. Auditor Orenstein & Bernstein, 1956-58; sr. auditor Klein, Katcher & Co., 1958-61; sr. internal auditor Rexall Drug and Chem. Co., 1961-64; supervising internal auditor CBS Inc., 1964-65, asst. to dir. acctg. TV network div., 1965-66, asst. dir. acctg. TV network div., 1966-68, dir. acctg. TV network div., 1968-69, asst. contr. TV network div., 1969-71, asst. contr., 1971-76, v.p. fin. specialty stores div., 1976-79; v.p. fin. and adminstrn. records div. CBS Inc. (changed to Sony Music Entertainment Inc.), 1979-94; v.p., cons. Sony Music, NYC, from 1995. Pres. Hickory Consulting Group. Former mem. adv. bd. Mt. Sinai Diabetes Edn. Svc. Honoree Thyroid Found. Am. Tri-State chpt., 1996. Mem. AICPA, Fin. Exec. Inst., N.Y. Soc. CPAs. Jewish. Home: Stamford, Conn. Died Aug. 18, 2006.

BACKSTROM, JAMES W., lawyer; b. Mobile, Ala., Aug. 29, 1942; BBA, U. Miss., 1964, JD, 1967. Mem Bryan, Nelson, Schroeder, Backstrom, Castigliola & Banahan. Mem. ABA, Fed. Bar Assn., Jackson County Bar Assn., Miss. Defense Lawyers Assn., Assn. Trial Lawyers Am., Defense Rsch. Inst., Phi Delta Phi. Died Jan. 3, 2006.

BACON, ROGER, physicist, researcher; b. Cleve., Apr. 16, 1926; s. Francis Rogers and Edith Melrose (Farquhar) B.; m. Irene Louise Prischl, June 2, 1951 (div. 1968); children: Elizabeth Bacon Fox, William Farquhar Bacon; m. Agnes Maria Kormoczy, Apr. 15, 1972. BA, Haverford Coll., Pa., 1951; PhD, Case Western Res. U., 1956. Rsch. scientist Union Carbide Corp. (acquired by Dow Chem. Co.), Parma, Ohio, 1955-62, rsch. group leader, 1962-86; sr. rsch. assoc. Amoco Corp., Parma, 1986-90; sr. rsch. assoc., polymers group Amoco Corp. (now BP plc), Alpharetta, Ga., 1990—98. Physics instructor Baldwin Wallace Coll., Berea, Ohio, 1959—71. Author: (chpt.) Carbon Fibers from Rayon Precursors, 1973; contbr. over 20 articles to profl. jours. Recipient Medal of Excellence in Composite Materials, U. Del., Benjamin Franklin medal in Mech. Engring., Franklin Inst., 2004. Mem. Am. Carbon Soc. (adv. bd. 1989), Am. Phys. Soc. Achievements include research in potential of graphite filaments to achieve high young's modulus and tensile strength; patents for graphite whiskers and high performance carbon fibers from rayon precursors. Home: Oberlin, Ohio. Died Jan. 26, 2007.

BAER, BYRON M., retired state legislator; b. Pitts., Oct. 18, 1929; m. Linda Pollitt; children: David, Laura, Roger Pollitt, Lara Pollitt. Student, Cornell U. Mem. NJ Gen. Assembly, Trenton, 1972—94, asst. minority leader, 1986-93; mem. NJ State Senate from Dist. 37, Trenton, 1994—2005. Alt. del. Dem. Nat. Conv., 1984. Recipient Assemblyman of Yr. award N.J. Coun. Chs., Equal Justice medal Legal Svcs. Corp. and N.J. Bar Assn., Legislator of Decade award N.J. Tenants Orgn., 1981. Mem. Anti Defamation League, Nat. Assn. Jewish Legislators (sec. 1985-87), Nat. Consumer Congress (bd. dirs. 1973-76), Holocaust Meml. Com. Died June 24, 2007.

BAERG, RICHARD HENRY, podiatrist, surgeon; b. LA, Jan. 19, 1937; s. Henry Francis and Ruth Elizabeth (Loven) B.; children from previous marriage: Carol Elizabeth, William Richard, Michael David, Niccolo, Monica, Arianna, Mia, Reagan. AA, Reedley Coll., 1956; BS, Samuel Merritt U., Sch. Podiatric Medicine, 1965, DPM, 1968, MSc in Foot Surgery, 1970; MPH in Med. Adminstrn., U. Calif., Berkeley, 1971; ScD (hon.), N.Y. Coll. Podiatric Medicine, 1980; LittD (hon.), Ohio Coll. Podiatric Medicine, 1984; postgrad. Sch. Edn. and Pub. Health, U. Mich., 1973—74; postgrad. Sch. of Bus. and Sch. of Edn., Harvard U., 1975. Diplomate Am. Bd. Podiatric Surgery (foot and ankle surgery), Am. Bd. Podiatric Orthopedics and Primary Podiatric Medicine (exec. dir. 1980-90), Am. Bd. podiatric Pub. Health (bd. dirs. 1980-89). Intern Highland Alameda County Gen. Hosp., Oakland, Calif., 1969; resident in surgery Pacific Coast Hosp., San Francisco, 1970; acad. dean N.Y. Coll. Podiatric Medicine, NYC, 1971-74; v.p., dean Samuel Merritt U., Sch. Podiatric Medicine, Oakland, Calif., 1974-76; chief podiatric medicine Los Angeles County-U. So. Calif. Med. Ctr., 1976-78; dir. So. Calif. Podiatric Med. Ctr., 1976-78; pvt. practice Beverly Hills, Calif., 1976-78; dean Roseland Franklin U. Coll. Podiatric Medicine, Chgo., 1978-79; mem. spl. med. adv. group to sec. Dept. Vets. Affairs, Washington, 1976-79, dir. podiatric service, dept. medicine and surgery, 1979-84, acting dir., 1984-86; health resources adminstrn. cons. Dept. Health and Human Svcs., Washington, 1974-88; chief podiatry VA Med. Ctr., Loma Linda, Calif., 1984-89; dir. residency tng. Loma Linda Foot Clinic, 1990; exec. v.p., med. dir. Dr. Footcare Corp., Montclair, Calif., 1988-90; faculty podiatry U. N.C. Hosps., Chapel Hill, from 1992; clin. prof. Sch. of Podiatric Medicine Barry U., Miami, Fla., from 1993; clin. prof. Med. Sch., U. N.C., from 1992; staff podiatrist Morehead Hosp., Eden, NC, 1997-2000. Mem. podiatric staff Chapel Hill Surg. Ctr., 1993—; chief of podiatry Umstead Hosp., Butner, N.C., 1997-2000, VA Med. Ctr., Huntington, W.Va., dir. residency tng. chief podiatry sect., 2000-02; assoc. clin. prof. Stanford U. Med. Sch., 1974-76; clin. prof. Temple U. Coll. Podiatric Medicine, 1979-86, Des Moines U. Medicine and Health Sci., 1984-, U. NC Sch. Medicine, 1980-90; prof. dept. surgery Marshall U. Sch. Medicine, Huntington, W.Va., clin. prof. podiatric medicine and surgery Pikeville Coll. Sch. Osteopathic Medicine; pres. Baerg & Assocs.; cons. foot surgery, Las Vegas, 2002—; mem. podiatry adv. panel NAS Inst. Medicine, 1974; mem. bd. podiatric medicine Calif. Dept. Consumer Affairs, 1989-90, chmn. residency, edn. and hosp. inspection com. Contbg. author: (text) Podiatric Medicine and Public Health, 1987; mem. editl. bd. Jour. Podiatric Edn., Yearbook of Podiatric Medicine and Surgery, Mil. Medicine Jour.; contbr. over 30 articles to profl. jours., 3 chpts. to textbooks. With M.C. U.S. Army and USN, 1958-64. Mead-Johnson fellow, 1968-69. Fellow USPHS, Am. Podiatric Med. Assn. (com. on pub. health 1971-84, coun. podiatric edn. 1975-84, chmn. profl. edn. com. 1977-78, com. on hosp. 1980-85, Kenison award 1984, cert. appreciation 1990, com. on pub. health and preventive medicine), Am. Coll. Foot and Ankle Surgeons, Am. Coll. Foot & Ankle Orthopedics and Medicine (exec. dir. 1980-90), Acad. Ambulatory Foot Surgery; mem. APHA (governing coun. 1977-80, chmn. podiatric health sect. 1991-94, chmn. nominating com. 1994-96), Am. Acad. Podiatric Adminstrs. (exec. dir. 1990-91), Nat. Bd. Podiatric Med. Examiners (bd. dirs.), Assn. Podiatrists in Fed. Svc., Am. Assn. Colls. Podiatric Medicine (exec. com. 1973, pres. 1980-81), Assn. Mil. Surgeons U.S., Nat. Acads. of Practice (podiatric medicine 1985), N.C. Foot and Ankle Soc. (bd. dirs. ins. com. 1994-97, cons. 1997-2000, chmn. zone III 1994-97, rep. N.C. Health Care Reform Com. 1994-97), Coun. Med. Sch. Affiliated Podiatrists (bd. dirs., dir. region 10), N.C. Symphony Assn., Palm Mortuaries (Las Vegas), Mason (Scottish Rite, 32 degree), Sigma Pi Epsilon, Pi Delta. Republican. Died June 19, 2006.

BAHNAK, JOHN J., JR., lawyer; b. Mpls., Minn., Jan. 6, 1947; BA, St. John's U., 1969; JD cum laude, St. Louis U., 1972. Lawyer Greensfelder, Hemker & Gale PC, St. Louis, Mo. Mem. ABA (mem. comml. leasing com., sect. real property, probate and trust law), Ill. State Bar Assn., The Bar Assn. of Metro. St. Louis (chmn. real property and devel. com. 1991-92), Alpha Sigma Nu, Delta Theta Phi, Order of Woolsack. Died Aug. 17, 2007.

BAHNIUK, EUGENE, mechanical engineering educator; b. Weirton, W.Va., Mar. 10, 1926; s. Michael and Mary (Sikora) B.; m. Margaret J. Hilton, June 11, 1977; children— Douglas Eugene, Joy Ruth, Barbara Jane, Becky Lynn, David Robert BS, Case Inst. Tech., 1950, MS, 1961; PhD, Case Western Res. U., 1970. Registered profl. engr., Ohio. Devel. engr. Air Brake, Watertown, N.Y., 1950-54; project engr. Lear Corp., Elyria, Ohio, 1954-56; supr. Borg Warner Corp., Bedford Heights, Ohio, 1956-61; mgr. research and devel. Weatherhead Corp., Cleve., 1961-68; faculty Case Western Res. U., Cleve., from 1970, prof. mech. engring., from 1972. Contbr. articles to profl. jours.; patentee in field Served to 1st lt., inf. U.S. Army, 1944-46 NIH fellow, 1969-70, NSF fellow, 1968-69, NASA fellow, 1982 Fellow ASTM (award of merit 1988); mem. Am. Soc. Biomechanics, Internat. Soc. Ski Safety, Sigma Xi Home: Gates Mills, Ohio. Died May 25, 2007.

BAIL, JOE PAUL, agricultural educator emeritus; b. Herold, W.Va., May 12, 1925; s. Alva Edward and Prudence (Wood) B.; m. Nelma Louise Rapp, Oct. 20, 1945; 1 son, David Joe. BS, MS, W.Va. U., 1947; PhD, Mich State U., 1958. Tchr. agr. Spencer (W. Va.) High Sch., 1947; head dept. agr. Glenville (W. Va.) State Coll., 1948-51; asst. prof., assoc. prof. agrl. edn. W.Va. U., 1951-57; asst. prof., then assoc. prof. Cornell U., Ithaca, N.Y., 1957-67, prof. agrl. edn. div., 1967-90, prof. edn. emeritus, from 1990, chmn. agrl. edn. div., 1963-71, chmn. dept. edn., 1978-87. Vis. prof. U. Ariz., U. Fla.; Cons. pub. schs., N.Y., Mass., W.Va., Ariz., Fla.; mem. com. Nat. Acad. Scis.; field review officer U.S. Office Edn. Contbg. author: Teacher Education in Agriculture, 1967, 79; contbr. articles to profl. jours. Dist. chmn. Boy Scouts Am., 1972-73; mem. Ch.-Community Action, Inc., 1968—; past pres. N.Y. Council on Rural Edn. Served to 1st lt. USAAF, 1943-45, ETO. Decorated Soldier's medal, Air medal with four oak leaf clusters; recipient 30-yr. award in agrl. edn. N.Y. Assn. Tchrs. Agr., 1977, Outstanding Educator award N.Y. State Rural Schs., 1987, Outstanding Alumni award W.Va. U., 1990; named Hon. Am. Farmer Future Farmers Am., 1978, Paul Harris fellow. Mem. Am. Vocat. Assn. (past nat. com. chmn.), Assn. Higher Edn., N.Y. Assn. Deans of Edn. (coun.), Rotary (past pres.), Alpha Zeta, Kappa Delta Pi, Delta Tau Delta, Alpha Tau Alpha. Democrat. Baptist. Died May 7, 2006.

BAILEY, GLENN WALDEMAR, manufacturing executive; b. Cleve., May 8, 1925; s. Harry W. and Elizabeth B.; m. Cornelia L. Tarrant, June 12, 1952. BS, U. Wis., 1946; MBA, Harvard U., 1951. Project engr. Thompson Ramo Wooldridge, Cleve., 1946-49; fin. staff Ford Motor Co., Dearborn, Mich., 1951-54; mgr. fin. analysis Curtiss Wright Corp., 1954-57; asst. to v.p., gen. mgr. Overseas div. Chrysler Corp., Detroit, 1957-60; group gen. mgr. ITT Corp., NYC, 1960-67; chmn. bd., pres. Keene Corp., NYC, 1967-81 and from 90, Bairnco Corp., NYC, 1981-90. Bd. dirs. Genlyte Group, Inc., Union, N.J. Ensign USNR, 1943-46. Home: Louisville, Ky. Died Aug. 19, 2006.

BAILEY, HENRY JOHN, III, retired lawyer; b. Pitts., Apr. 4, 1916; s. Henry J. and Lenore Powell Bailey Cahoon; m. Marjorie Jane Ebner, May 30, 1949 (dec. July 1998); children: George W., Christopher G., Barbara W., Timothy P. Student, U.S. Naval Acad., 1934-36; BA, Pa. State U., 1939; JD, Yale U., 1947. Bar: N.Y. 1948, Mass. 1963, Oreg. 1974. Ins. investigator Liberty Mut. Ins. Co., NYC, 1941-42; atty. Fed. Res. Bank of N.Y., NYC, 1947-55; asst. v.p. Empire Trust Co., NYC, 1955-56; atty., legal dept. Am. Bankers Assn., NYC, 1956-62; editor Banking Law Jour., Boston, 1962-65; asso. prof. law Willamette U., Salem, Oreg., 1965-69, prof., 1969-81, prof. emeritus, from 1981, adj. prof., 1981-83, scholar in residence, 1987; counsel firm Churchill, Leonard, Brown & Donaldson, Salem, 1981-85; vis. prof. sch. law U. Akron, 1983-84; vis. prof. coll. of law Fla. State U., 1984-85; vis. prof. sch. law Rutgers U., Camden, N.J., 1985-87. Cons., lectr. to bar and banking groups; lectr. Banking Sch. of South, Baton Rouge, 1972, 73, 75. Author: Brady on Bank Checks (The Law of Bank Checks), 1960, 3d edit., 1962, 4th edit., 1969, 5th edit., 1979, 6th edit., 1987 and periodic supplements, 7th edit. (with Richard B. Hagedorn), 1992, (with Richard B. Hagedorn) rev. edit. 2 vols., 1997, periodic supplements, Uniform Commercial Code Forms, 1963, (with Clarke and Young) Bank Deposits and Collections, 1972, UCC Deskbook: A Short Course in Commercial Paper, 1973, (with Robert D. Hursh) The American Law of Products Liability, 2d edit, 1984, (with William D. Hawkland) The Sum and Substance of Commercial Paper, 1976, 80, 88, Secured Transactions in a Nutshell, 1976, 2d edit., 1981, 3d edit. (with Richard B. Hagedorn), 1988, (with Richard B. Hagedorn) 4th edit., 2000, Oregon Uniform Commercial Code, 3 vols., 1983, 84, 86, 88, 2d edit. 3 vols., 1990, New 1990 Uniform Commercial Code: Article 3, and 4, periodic supplements; contbr. articles on sales, products liability, comml. paper and secured transactions to legal jours. 1st lt. USAAF, 1942-45; lt. col. Res.; ret. Mem. Am. Bar Assn. (chmn. subcom. on comml. paper 1965-66, 79-81), Am. Law Inst. (mem. editorial bd. The Practical Lawyer 1981-93, emeritus mem. editorial bd. 1993—, 50 Yr Commemorative medal, 2004), Oreg. State Bar, Lambda Chi Alpha. Republican. Roman Catholic. Home: Salem, Oreg. Died Apr. 28, 2006.

BAILEY, MILTON, chemist; b. N.Y.C., May 20, 1917; s. Abraham and Lillian (Ruderman) Bialek. B.B.A., CCNY, 1940, M.S., 1949; cert. Pratt Inst., 1951; postgrad. Bklyn. Coll., 1958-61; m. Lucille Rubin, Jan. 9, 1954; 1 child, Joseph Adam. Editor newspaper and ednl. materials Adj. gen.'s office Dept. Army, 1941-43; feature editor S. Pacific Daily News, 1945-46; chem. supt. Ruderman Inc., N.Y.C., 1946-52; leather chemist U.S. Naval Supply Rsch. and Devel. Facility, 1952-67; phys. sci. adminstr. USN Clothing and Textile Rsch. Unit, Natick, Mass., 1967-89; lectr. CCNY, 1951-52, N.Y.C. Community Coll., 1953-61. Arbitrator, Am. Arbitration Assn., 1973; sec. Am. Leather Chemists Assn.-ASTM, 1960-64; chmn. subcom. safety shoe com. Am. Nat. Standards Inst., 1973. With AUS, 1943-46. Recipient commendation Undersec. Navy, 1964; Presdl. citation for accomplishment in field, 1980. Mem. Soc. Fed. Labor Rels. Profls., Am. Leather Chemists Assn., ASTM (chmn. safety and traction for footwear com. 1978-81, chmn. Footwear leather subcom. 1982), Boston Orgn. Devel. Network, Soc. Profls. Dispute Resolutions, Mass. Assn. Mediation Programs (chmn. Wayland Pers. Bd., 1990), Am. Legion, Internat. Assn. Quality Circles (chmn. Navy Clothing and Textile Research Facility steering com. 1982), N.Y. Acad. Sci, Mass. Mcpl. Quality Network. Club: Toastmasters (area gov. Bklyn. 1963). Patentee in field. Home: Wayland, Mass. Died Mar. 20, 2006.

BAILHE, RICHARD FREDERICK, financial planner; b. Ft. Wayne, Ind., Jan. 18, 1925; s. Gaston and Lois (Gemmill) Bailhe; m. Helen Kane, Nov. 8, 1952; children: Richard, Rosemary, Maryanne. AB in Speech, U. Mich., 1947. CLU Am. Coll. of Life Underwriters, 1957. Regional group sales mgr. Lincoln Nat. Life Ins. Co., Ft. Wayne, 1948—58, nat. pension sales mgr., 1958—62, dir. advanced underwriting, 1962—66, gen. agt. Detroit, 1966—73; pres. Richard F. Bailhe & Assocs., Birmingham, Mich., 1973—81; income funding Cons. P.C., Troy, Mich., from 1981. Qualifying mem. Million Dollar Round Table, Chgo., 1981—82, 1983—84. Mem.: Mich. Life Ins. Counselors, Nat. Assn. Life Underwriters (bd. dirs. Detroit chpt. 1975—79), Am. Soc. Chartered Life Underwriters (pres. Ft. Wayne chpt. 1965), Lions (past pres. Birmingham 1978, dist. chmn. youth exchange program Mich. 1983—84). Roman Cath. Home: Birmingham, Mich. Died Nov. 28, 2006.

BAILY, ALFRED EWING, environmental engineer; b. Carmichaels, Pa., Jan. 20, 1925; s. Richard L. and Alta (Hebel) B.; student Waynesburg (Pa.) Coll., 1943, Bethany (W.Va.) Coll., 1943-44; B.S. in Physics, Duke U., 1945, B.S. in Civil Engring. magna cum laude, 1949; m. Hannah Jane Drake, Sept. 1, 1946; children: Judith Ann, Frank Henry, Louise Jane, Nancy Lee. With Chester Engrs., Moon Township, Pa., 1949—, ptnr., 1965, dir. mcpl. svcs., 1974, 77—, pres., chmn., CEO, 1992, ret., vice chmn. bd. dirs. Mem. Scott Twp. Planning Commn., 1963-64; elder Presbyn Ch. Served from ensign to lt., USNR, 1943-46, 52-53. Registered profl. engr., Pa., Fla. Fellow ASCE; mem. Water Environ. Fedn., Tau Beta Pi. Home: Tampa, Fla. Died May 25, 2006.

BAINBRIDGE, JOHN SEAMAN, retired lawyer, retired academic administrator; b. NYC, Nov. 1, 1915; s. William Seaman and June Ellen (Wheeler) Bainbridge; m. Matharine Barker Garrett, Feb. 3, 1943 (div. July 24, 1968); 1 child, John Seaman; m. Elizabeth Kung-Ji Liu Bainbridge, May 13, 1978. BS,

Harvard U., 1938; LLB, JD, Columbia U., 1941. Bar: NY 1941, Md 1946, US Dist. Ct./Md. 1946, US Supreme Ct. 1946, US Dist. Ct. (so. dist.)/NY 1948. Gen. practice law, Md., 1945—56, NY, 1945—56; asst. dean Columbia U. Law Sch., 1956—65; assoc. dir. Internat. Fellows Program, 1960—62; asst. to pres. Columbia U., 1965—66; dir. Project on Staffing of African Instns. of Legal Edn. and Rsch., 1962—72; assoc. dir. Ctr. Adminstrn. of Justice, Wayne State U., Detroit, 1972—74; dir. planning Sch. Law, Pace U., Westchester County, NY, 1974—76; assoc. dean, dean, prof. law No. Ill. U. Coll. Law, Glen Ellyn, 1976—81; vis. prof., assoc. dean Del. Law Sch., Wilmington, 1981—82; dean, prof. law Touro coll. Sch. Law, Huntington, NY, 1982—85. Cons. Edward John Noble Found., 1959—61, Inst. Internat. Edn., 1962—67. Author: The Study and Teaching of Law in Africa, 1972. Lt. comdr. USNR, 1940—46. Mem.: ABA, African Law Assn. in Am., Inc., Peace Corps Lawyers Project, Sons of Revolution, Harvard (NYC). Sr Presbyn. Home: Kennett Square, Pa. Died Jan. 25, 2006.

BAIRD, WILLIAM DAVID, retired anesthesiologist; b. Dallas, Feb. 17, 1922; s. John B. and Sue S. B.; m. Virginia Claye Sanders, June 27, 1948; children: Linda B. Moore, Cynthia B. Matthews, C. Sanders Baird, Ginger B. Stark, J. Davies Baird. BA, Rice Inst., Houston, 1949; MD, U. Tex., 1953. Diplomate Am. Bd. Anesthesiologists. Intern U. Tex. Med. Br. Hosps., Galveston, 1953-54, resident in anesthesiology, 1954-56, fellow, instr. anesthesiology, 1956-57; pvt. practice anesthesiology Garland, Tex., 1957-80; med. cons. Garland Cmty. Hosp., 1980-81, Branson & Misko, 1981-93. Clin. instr. U. Tex. SW Br., 1963-80; chief anesthesiology Garland Clinic and Hosp., 1957-75, Garland Meml. Hosp., 1975-78; exec. staff com. Meml. Hosp. Garland, 1975-78; adv. bd. Presbyn. Hosp. Dallas, 1969. Author: Some Descendants of John Baird, A Genealogy, 1997; editor, pub.: The 17th Sortie Newsletter of the 17th Bomb Group/Wing Reunion Assn. Precinct chmn. Rep. party, Garland, 1969-74; bd. dirs. Garland YMCA, 1972-74. Fellow Am. Coll. Anesthesiologists; mem. AMA, Am. Soc. Anesthesiologists, Tex. Med. Assn., Dallas County Med. Soc., Tex. Soc. Anesthesiologists, Dallas County Anesthesiology Soc., Dallas County Hist. Soc., Dallas County Pioneer Assn., Marauder Men of Metroplex, B-26 Marauder Hist. Soc. Republican. Avocations: genealogy, farming, hunting, fishing, history. Home: Dallas, Tex. Died Mar. 15, 2006.

BAKER, BARBARA JEAN, media specialist; b. Chattanooga, Tenn., July 20, 1931; d. James L. and Idaline (Turner) Bookout; m. Richard L. Bajker, May 25, 1952; children— Vance P., Matt R. Mus.B., Samford U., 1953; M.A. in Edn., U. Ala., 1976, postgrad. specialist degree, 1981. Media specialist Woodlawn High Sch., Birmingham, Ala., 1972-74, Kennedy Elem. Sch., 1974-76, Central High Sch., Lawrenceville, Ga., 1976-81, Brookwood High Sch., Snellville, Ga., 1981—. Mem. Ga. Assn. Educators, ALA, Ga. Library Media Dept., Phi Delta Kappa. Home: Duluth, Ga. Died Aug. 18, 2006.

BAKER, BERNARD ROBERT, state district court judge; b. Chgo., Apr. 5, 1937; s. Bernard F. and Pearl L. (Beesley) B.; m. Caroline Spanier, Mar. 22, 1958; children: Susan Caroline, Deborah Ann, Pamela Ruth. BSBA, Northwestern U., 1958; JD, Ind. U., 1964. Bar: Colo. 1968, Ind. 1964, U.S. Supreme Ct. 1969, U.S. Ct. Mil. Appeals 1965, U.S. Dist. Ct. Colo. 1968, Ind. 1964; ins. counselor Equitable Life Ins., N.Y.C., 1958-60; acct. Chevrolet div. Gen. Motors Corp., Indpls., 1960-61; claims investigator, supr. Allstate Ins. Co., Indpls., 1961-64; assoc. Agee & Fann, Colorado Springs, Colo., 1968; dep., chief dep. dist. atty. Office Dist. Atty., State of Colo., 1968-75; dist. ct. judge 4th Jud. Dist., State of Colo., Colorado Springs, 1976—; guest prof. Nat. Jud. Coll., Reno, Nev., 1982—. Pres., Citizens Lobby for Sensible Growth, 1974; bd. dirs. Salvation Army, 1973-78, Mental Retardation Found., 1972-76. Capt. JAG Corps, U.S. Army, 1965-67. Decorated Army Commendation medal; recipient Presdl. citation Colo. Health Dept., 1975. Mem. ABA, Colo. Bar Assn., El Paso County Bar Assn., Am. Judicature Soc., Moose. Contbg. editor, bd. editors Colo. Environ. Law Handbook, 1971-72. Democrat. Methodist. Died Mar. 7, 2006.

BAKER, HASTINGS WYMAN, lawyer and business exec. b. Stovall, NC, June 12, 1914; s. Hastings Wyman and Sallie (Younger) B.; m. Beverly Higgins, July 7, 1938; children— Hastings Wyman III, Barry. Student, Harvard, 1932-33, Western Res. U., 1933-34, Wittenberg U., 1934-35, George Washington U., 1935-37, Coll. City N.Y., 1937, Columbia, 1937; LL.B., Fordham U., 1941. Bar: N.Y. State bar 1941. Law clk., asso. atty. Chadbourne, Hunt, Jackel & Brown, NYC, 1939-43; asst. to head legal dept. Mathieson Chem. Co., 1943-44; corp. counsel, asst. sec. Tubize Rayon Corp., 1944-46; with Beaunit Mills, Inc., NYC, from 1947, sec., treas., dir., from 1959, head legal dept., from 1947; various positions to sec.-treas. and head legal dept. Skenandoa Rayon Corp., Nat. Weaving Corp., N.Am. Rayon Corp.; also dir.; mng. dir. Sta. Reps. Assn., Inc., from 1964. Pres. Care Centers, Inc.; dir. Tyrex, Inc. (subsidiaries 20th Century Fox Film Corp.) Home: Darien, Conn. Died Oct. 2, 2005.

BAKER, JACKSON ARNOLD, container shipping company executive; b. Saltville, Va., May 1, 1938; s. Joseph Arnold and Katherine Kimmons (Seale) B.; m. Carolyn Josephine Cantrell, Dec. 27, 1957; children— Allison Kimmons, Elizabeth Arnold. BS in Indsl. Mgmt, Ga. Inst. Tech., 1960. Dock foreman Roadway Express, Atlanta, 1960-63; asst. terminal mgr. Waterman of P.R., Mobile, Ala., 1963-65; with Sea-Land Service, Inc., 1965-90; v.p. west coast SeaLand Service, Inc., Seattle, 1972-75, exec. v.p. Alaska div., 1975-84; group v.p. Atlantic div. Sea-Land Service, Inc., Iselin, N.J., 1984-86, vice chmn., chief operating officer, 1986-87, pres., chief operating officer, 1987-89; pres. JAB Internat. Inc., Bellevue, Wash., 1990-93; pres., CEO Intrenet, Inc., Milford, Ohio, from 1993. Died Aug. 20, 2007.

BAKER, NORMAN HODGSON, JR., astronomy educator; b. Fergus Falls, Minn., Oct. 23, 1931; s. Norman Hodgson and Jeannette (Lieber) B.; m. Doris Blum Nagel, Jan. 16, 1976. BA, U. Minn., 1952; PhD, Cornell U., 1959. Vis. fellow Max-Planck Inst. for Physics and Astrophysics, Munich, Germany, 1959-61; staff scientist Convair Sci. Research Lab., San Diego, 1961; research fellow Goddard Inst. for Space Studies, NASA, NYC, 1961-62; 63-64; mem. Inst. for Advanced Study, Princeton, N.J., 1962-63; vis. lectr. astronomy Yale, New Haven, 1963-64; research asso. physics dept. N.Y. U., 1964-65; asst. prof. dept. astronomy Columbia, NYC, 1965-67, asso. prof., 1967-71, prof., from 1971, chmn. dept., 1972-76. Co-editor: The Astron. Jour, 1967-72, 75-79; editor, 1979-83; co-editor: Bull. of Am. Astron. Soc, 1975-79; editor, 1979-82. NSF grantee, 1966-79 Mem. Am. Phys. Soc., Am. Astron. Soc., Internat. Astron. Union. Died Oct. 11, 2005.

BAKER, RICHARD GRAVES, geologist, palynologist, educator; b. Merrill, Wis., June 12, 1938; s. Dillon James and Miriam Baker; m. Debby J.Z. Baker; children: Kristina Kae, James Dillon, Charity Ann. BA, U. Wis., 1960; MS, U. Minn., 1964; PhD, U. Colo., 1969. Asst. prof. geology U. Iowa, Iowa City, 1970-75, assoc. prof., 1975-81, prof., from 1981, chmn. dept., 1992-95, prof. botany, 1988-92, prof. biol. scis., 1992-2000, prof. emeritus, from 2000. Contbr. articles to profl. jours., chapters to books. Chmn. Iowa chpt. Nature Conservancy, Des Moines, 1981-82. Grantee NSF, 1984-86, 88-90, 94-97, NOAA, 1992-93; recipient Disting. Scientist award Iowa Acad. Sci., 2001. Fellow Geol. Soc. Am., Iowa Acad. Sci.; mem. Am. Quaternary Assn. (disting. career award 2005), Ecol. Soc. Am. Home: Atalissa, Iowa. Died Nov. 21, 2006.

BAKER, SHIRLEY CLAIRE, distributing company executive; b. Melrose, Mass., Oct. 21, 1934; d. John Charles and Ruth Marie (Hodgson) Martin; m. Joseph William Bucci, June 7, 1952 (div. 1962); 1 child, Joseph James; m. Richard William Baker, Aug. 18, 1968 (div. 1979); m. Frank Bernard Mesmer, July 4, 1983. A.S. with high honors, Foothill Jr. Coll., Palo Alto, Calif., 1972. Office export mgr. Atomium, Inc., Billerica, Mass., 1961-63; office mgr., bookkeeper Geo Space Gravity, Woburn, Mass., 1963-64; sales office mgr. Amicon Corp., Lexington, Mass., 1965-68; treas., mgr. Berghof/Am., Bend, Oreg. and Derry, N.H., 1974-79; pres. Berghof Am., Raymond, N.H., 1980—. Mem. Am. Chem. Soc. (assoc.), Derry C. of C. (bd. dirs.). Republican. Avocations: sailing, theater, painting, reading, cooking. Home: Bedford, NH. Died May 16, 2006.

BAKEWELL, STANLEY ELLSWORTH, personnel consultant; b. Eagle Bend, Minn., Apr. 10, 1920; s. Benjamin Levis and Eva Mary (Macaulay) B.; B.S. in Fgn. Service, Georgetown U., 1947-49; B.S. in Edn. and Animal Industry, U. Minn., 1943. Econ. asst., vice consul U.S. Fgn. Service, Am. embassy, Mexico City, Mexico, 1949-52; sr. market analyst Kimberly Clark Corp., Neenah, Wis., 1952-60; mgr. market research Forest Products div. Owens-Ill. Glass Co., Toledo, 1960-64; project dir. indsl. research Elrick & Lavidge, Chgo., 1964-66; pres., gen. mgr. Bryant & Bakewell Marketing Services div. Bryant Assos., Chgo., after 1967, now exec. v.p. Trustee Bakewell Investment Trust. Served to lt. (j.g.) USNR, 1944-46. Mem. Chgo. Symphony Soc., Am. Mktg. Assn., Am. Iris Soc., Chgo. Council Fgn. Relations, Alpha Gamma Rho. Republican. Episcopalian. Clubs: Chgo. Athletic Assn., Whitehall, Georgetown (Chgo.); Mason, Shriner, K.T. Author: Bakewell History-Genealogy, Part I, 1980, Part II, 1983. Home: Joliet, Ill. Died Mar. 13, 2006.

BALCER, CHARLES LOUIS, retired academic administrator; b. McGregor, Iowa, May 23, 1921; s. Ludwig Frank and Iva (Vaughan) B.; m. Martha Elizabeth Belgum, Jan. 6, 1944; children— Mary Elizabeth, Mark Lewis, Beth Louise, Brian Charles. BS, Winona State Tchrs. Coll., Minn., 1942; MA, State U. Iowa, 1949, PhD, 1954; DHL (hon.), Augustana Coll., 2003. Tchr. Minn. and Iowa high schs., 1942-43, 46-47; instr. State U. Iowa, 1947-50; high sch. prin. Detroit Lakes, Minn., 1950-54; assoc. prof. speech St. Cloud (Minn.) State Coll., 1954-56, prof., acad. dean, 1958-64; prof. speech SUNY-Oswego, 1956-57; pres. Augustana Coll., Sioux Falls, SD, 1965-80, pres. emeritus, 1980—2007, Disting. Service prof., 1980-95, interim chair edn. dept., 1999-00. Interim pres., CEO Good Samaritan Soc., 1997-98. Author: (with H. F. Seabury) Teaching Speech. Bd. dirs. Evang. Luth. Good Samaritan Soc.; active Marquette Bank SD, Sioux Falls Symphony Assn. Served with AUS, 1943-46 Decorated knight 1st class Royal Order St. Olav (Norway); named to S.D. Hall of Fame, 2003. Mem. Speech Communication Assn. Am., Central States Speech Assn. (pres. 1954), NEA, Assn. Higher Edn., Delta Sigma Rho, Kappa Delta Pi, Phi Delta Kappa. Democrat. Home: Sioux Falls, SD. Died July 26, 2007.

BALDWIN, DAVID RAWSON, retired academic administrator; b. New Haven, Nov. 2, 1923; s. Albert A. and Hilda (Rawson) B.; m. Dorothy Elizabeth Sonstrom, June 19, 1948; children: Dwight Rawson, Brian Mark, James Albert. BS in Govt., U. Conn., 1947; M.P.A. (Volker fellow 1948-49), Wayne State U., 1949. Research asst. Conn. Pub. Expenditure Council, Hartford, 1948-50; exec. sec. Fayette County br. Pa. Economy League, Uniontown, 1950-51; chief assessor Fayette County, 1952-56; fiscal adv. Gov.-elect George Leader State of Pa., 1954; research asso. Pa. Economy League, Pitts., 1956-59; budget sec. State of Pa., 1959-64, exec. asst. to treas., 1964-65; asst. sec. for adminstrn. US Dept. Commerce, 1965-69; v.p. bus. & fin. Wayne State U., Detroit, 1969-71; assoc. v.p. for fin. affairs, asst. treas. Temple U., Phila., 1972-85, ret., 1985. N.E. regional dir. Nat. Assn. State Budget Officers, 1962-64; cons. HEW, 1964 Served to lt. (j.g.) USNR, 1944-46. Mem. Am. Soc. Pub. Adminstrn., Nat. Assn. Coll. and U. Bus. Officers (chmn. com. on ins. 1970-72), Theta Xi (pres. 1947) Presbyn. (ruling elder). Home: Jenkintown, Pa. Died June 4, 2007.

BALE, DONALD CHARLES, publisher; b. Madison, S.D., Aug. 20, 1937; s. Burtes Donald and Eleanor Maude (Schmidt) B. BA, State U. S.D., 1959; MS, Columbia U., 1960. Writer KELO-TV, Sioux Falls, S.D., 1962; pres., owner Bale Books & Bale Publs., New Orleans, 1963—. Author: Complete Guide for Profitable Coin Investing and Collecting, 1963; columnist Money Maker mag.; contbr. articles to profl. jours. Recipient Customer Service award Krause Publs., 1983. Mem. Phi Beta Kappa. Methodist. Avocation: numismatics. Home: New Orleans, La. Died Nov. 9, 2006.

BALL, CHARLES ELIHUE, association consultant; b. Minter, Tex., Feb. 8, 1924; s. Albis Elihue and Eula May (Terry) B.; m. Ruth Carlton Kimball, June 7, 1947; children— Charles E. Jr., Mary Ann Ball Rhys; m. Dawn L. Cooley, Nov. 24, 1990. BS, Tex. A&M U., 1947; MS, Iowa State U., 1948. Cert. assn. exec. Assoc. editor Farm and Ranch Mag., Nashville, 1948-49, mng. editor, 1950-51; regional editor Farm Jour., Dallas, 1952-72; exec. v.p. Tex. Cattle Feeders Assn., Amarillo, 1972-88; assn. cons., from 1989. Author: Saddle Up, 1970, The Finishing Touch: A History Of Cattle Feeding, 1992, Building the Beef Industry, 1997; contbr. articles to Farm Jour., Sat. Eve. Post, Readers Digest. Bd. dirs. U.S. Meat Export Fedn., 1981-95, Beef Promotion and Rsch. Bd., Denver, 1988-93, Nat. Cattlemen's Assn., Denver, 1988-91, Internat. Stockmen's Ednl. Found, 1991—; pres. Dallas Agrl. Club, 1958, Tex. Agrl. Workers Assn., 1963, Tex. Comml. Agriculturist Coun., 1964. Capt. U.S. Army, 1943-46, ETO. Recipient Outstanding Agriculturist award Tex. Tech. U., 1971, Hall of Merit award Am. Polled Hereford Assn., 1979; named Man of Yr. in Agr., Tex. Assn. County Agts., 1973, Man of Yr. in Tex., Agr. Progressive Farmer, 1983, Disting. Agrl. Alumni, Tex. A&M, 1993, One of 25 Who Made A Difference in the U.S. Beef Industry in the Last 25 Years, Beef Mag.; inducted into Internat. Livestock Congress Hall of Fame, 1991. Fellow Am. Soc. Agrl. Engrs.; mem. Am. Soc. Assn. Execs., Rotary. Home: Amarillo, Tex. Died June 4, 2006.

BALL, ROY ORVILLE, food corporation engineer, educator; b. Washington, Oct. 24, 1945; s. Rura O. and Dorothy R. (Toynton) B.; m. Jacqueline Sue Childress, Apr. 4, 1970; children: Christian, David. BS in Civil Engring., U. Fla., 1967; MS in Environ. Engring., U. Tex., 1972; PhD, U. Del., 1976. Registered profl. engr., Del., Minn., Iowa, Ill. Facilities engr. U.S. Armor Ctr., Fort Knox, Ky., 1967-69; IBM, Fishkill, N.Y., 1970-71; environ. engr. DuPont, Newark, Del., 1972-77; asst. prof. engring. U. Tenn., Knoxville, 1978-80; mgr. process design Roy F. Weston, West Chester, Pa., 1980-81; prin. ERM, Chgo., 1981—; adj. faculty mem. Villanova U. (Pa.), 1980, Drexel U., Phila., 1980, Marquette U. Co-author: Engineers Guide to Hazardous Waste Management, 1985; editl. bd. Hazardous Waste Mgmt., 1994; contbr. articles to profl. publs. Holy Cross Sch. Bd., 1987-89. Served to 1st lt. U.S. Army, 1968-69. Davis fellow, 1975-77. Mem. Inst. Chem. Engrs., Air and Waste Mgmt. Assn., Water Pollution Control Fedn. Republican. Avocations: harpsichord, boating. Home: Deerfield, Ill. Died Dec. 27, 2006.

BALLARD, LOUIS WAYNE, composer; b. Miami, Okla., July 8, 1931; s. Charles Guthrie and Leona Mae (Quapaw) B.; m. Ruth Sands, Dec. 6, 1965; children by previous marriage: Louis Anthony, Anne Marie, Charles Christopher. B.Mus. and Music Edn., U. Tulsa, 1954; M.Mus., 1962; D.Mus. (hon.), Coll. Santa Fe, 1973; D.Mus. (hon.), William Jewell Coll., 2001. Dir. vocal and instrumental music Nelagoney (Okla.) Public Sch., 1954-56; dir. vocal music Webster High Sch., Tulsa, 1956-58; pvt. music tchr., 1959-62; music dir. Inst. Am. Indian Arts, Santa Fe, 1962-65, dir. performing arts, 1965-69; nat. dir. music edn. curriculum and rev. Bur. Indian Affairs, Washington, 1969-79. Lectr., clinician, 1960—; pres. First Am. Indian Films, Inc., 1969—; disting. vis. prof. music Wm Jewell Coll., Liberty, Mo., 2000—. Composer, Santa Fe, 1979—; guest composer West German Music Festival, Saarbrü, 1986, Musik im 20 Jahrhundert, Ariz. State U., 1992, U. Ill. at Champagne, 1992, Ea. Music Festival, Greensboro, N.C., 1994, 95, 96; gala concert Carnegie Hall, 1992; full concert in Beethoven Chamber Music Hall, Bonn (first Am. composer), 1989; (ballet) Koshare, 1964, The Four Moons, 1967, Maid of the Mist and the Thunderbeings, 1991; (orchl. music) Fantasy Aborigine, Nos. I, II, III, IV, V; (chamber music) Rhapsody for Four Bassoons, Incident at Wounded Knee, Desert Trilogy, Ritmo Indio, Katcina Dances for cello-piano suite; (choral cantatas) The Gods Will Hear, Portrait of Will Rogers, Thus Spake Abraham; (oratorio) Dialogue Differentia text in Latin, Lakota-Sioux, English, Live On, Heart of My Nation (choral cantate with native Am. dialect), Manitoo, Gitche Manitoo (Am. Indian Doxology); (band works) Nighthawk Keetowa; (percussion) Cecega Ayuwipi, Music for the Earth and the Sky; (guitar) Quetzalcoatl's Coattails, 1992, The Lonely Sentinel, 1993, The Fire Moon (string quartet), A City of Silver, A City of Fire, A City of Light (piano concert pieces), numerous others.; commd. writer Lila Wallace Reader's Digest Arts Ptnrs./Meet the Composer, 1991; commd. writer (opera) Ministry Lower Saxony (Germany), 1993-94; author: The American Indian Sings, Book 1, 1970, Book 2, 1991, American Indian Chants for the Classroom, Oklahoma Indian Chants for the Classroom, 2004, also articles. Recipient 1st Marion Nevins MacDowell award chamber music, 1969, Nat. Indian Achievement award, 1972, Catlin Peace Pipe award Nat. Indian Lore Assn., 1976, ASCAP award, 1966-88, Lifetime Music Achievement award First Americans in Arts, 1997; F.B. Parriott grad. fellow, 1969; grantee Ford Found., 1970; grantee Nat. Endowment Arts, 1967, 69, 76, 79; commd. by Martha B. Rockefeller Found., 1969, Am. Composers Orch., 1982, commd. by Ministry Lower Saxony for Opera in Norden Gymnasium, West Germany, 1994; named to Okla. Music Hall of Fame, 2004. Mem. ASCAP, Music Educators Nat. Conf. (chmn. minority concerns com. for N.Mex. 1976), Am. Symphony Orch. League, Internat. Soc. for Polyaesthetic Music Edn. and Performance (lectr.), Phi Beta Kappa (alumni mem. Beta chpt. Okla. 1999). Lodges: Masons, Scottish Rite (32d degree). Died Feb. 9, 2007.

BALLES, JOHN JOSEPH, banker, business consultant; b. Freeport, Ill., Jan. 7, 1921; s. Louis J. and Kathleen P. (O'Connor) B.; m. Mira Jane Knupp, June 16, 1944; children: Nancy, Janet. BS, State U. Iowa, 1942, MA, 1947; PhD, Ohio State U., 1951. Instr., then asst. prof. econs. and bus. adminstrn. Ohio State U., 1947-54; sr. economist, then v.p. in charge credit dept. Fed. Res. Bank Cleve., 1954-59; sr. v.p. in charge econ. and corp. planning Mellon Nat. Bank & Trust Co., Pitts., 1959-72; pres. Fed. Res. Bank San Francisco, 1972-86. Cons. World Bus. divsn. SRI Internat., 1986-88, Pacific Gas and Electric Corp., 1988-92. Author: (with Richard W. Lindholm and John M. Hunter) Principles of Money and Banking, 1954. Bd. dirs. Meyer Friedman Inst., 1980-93. Served with AUS, 1943-46. Decorated Bronze Star with oak leaf cluster. Mem.

Am. Finance Assn. (dir. 1962-63), Am. Bankers Assn. (govt. relations council 1970-72), Nat. Assn. Bus. Economists (council 1964-66), Pa. Bankers Assn. (pres. 1965-66), Am. Econ. Assn. Died Oct. 3, 2005.

BALLIETT, WHITNEY, writer, critic; b. NYC, Apr. 17, 1926; s. Fargo and Dorothy (Lyon) B.; m. Elizabeth Hurley King, 1951; children: Julia, Blue, Will; m. Nancy Kraemer, 1965; children: Whitney, Jamie. BA, Cornell U., 1951. Mem. editl. staff New Yorker mag., NYC, 1951—2001, successively collator, proofreader, reporter, 1951-57, staff writer, 1957—2002; columnist on jazz; book, movie, theater and art reviewer, reporter. Author: The Sound of Surprise, 1959, Dinosaurs in the Morning, 1962, Such Sweet Thunder, 1966, Super-Drummer: A Profile of Buddy Rich, 1968, Ecstasy at the Onion, 1971, Alec Wilder and His Friends, 1974, New York Notes, 1976, Improvising, 1977, Night Creature, 1981, Jelly Roll, Jabbo, and Fats, 1983, American Musicians: Fifty-Six Portraits in Jazz, 1986, American Singers: Twenty-Seven Portraits in Song, 1988, Barney, Bradley and Max: Sixteen Portraits in Jazz, 1989, Goodbyes and Other Messages: A Journal of Jazz, 1981-90, 91, American Musicians II: Seventy Two Portraits in Jazz, 1996, Collected Works: A Journal of Jazz, 1954-2001, 2002, New York Voices, Fourteen Portraits, 2006; contbr. to N.Y. Rev. Books, 1998-2007. Recipient Acad. award in lit. Am. Acad. Arts and Letters, 1996. Mem. Century Assn. Died Feb. 2, 2007.

BALOWS, ALBERT, microbiologist, educator; b. Denver, Jan. 3, 1921; s. Lazerus and Anna (Kleiner) B.; m. Patricia Ann Barker, Oct. 7, 1956; children: Eve Ellen, Daniel Scott. BA in Biology (Lowell scholar), Colo. Coll., 1942; MS in Microbiology, Syracuse U., 1948; PhD (Haggin fellow), U. Ky., 1952. Diplomate: Am. Bd. Med. Microbiology. Microbiologist St. Joseph Hosp., Lexington (Ky.) Clinic, 1952-69; dir. bacteriology div. Ctrs. Disease Control, USPHS, Atlanta, 1969-81; asst. dir. lab. sci. Ctrs. Disease Control, USPHS (Ctr. Infectious Diseases), 1981-88; dir. emeritus Ctr. Disease Control, USPHS (Ctr. Infectious Diseases), 1988. Asst. prof. medicine U. Ky. Med. Ctr., Lexington, 1960-63, assoc. prof. medicine and cell biology, 1963-69; prof. lab. medicine Emory U. Sch. Medicine, 1970-98, prof. lab. medicine emeritus, 1998; prof. biology Ga. State U., Atlanta, 1970—89; lectr. Am. Soc. Microbiology Found., 1974-76; cons. clin. microbiology VA Hosp., Good Samaritan Hosp., Lexington, 1965-69; Med. Svc. Corps Dept. Army, 1973-79; chair expert panel WHO Internat. Collaborating Ctr. for Rsch. Syphilis Serology and Immunology, 1974-82; bd. dirs. WHO Internat. Collaborating Ctr. for Rsch. and Ref. in Antibiotic Susceptibility Testing, 1975-82, WHO Internat. Collaborating Ctr. for Rsch. and Ref. in Diagnostic Methods and Materials, 1985-88; mem. expert panels bacterial diseases, biol. standardization, lab. sci. WHO, Geneva, 1977-88. Founding editor-in-chief Jour. Clin. Microbiology, 1974-79, Current Microbiology, 1982—2005; editor Applied Microbiology, 1965-74, Ann. Rev. Microbiology, 1979—, C.C. Thomas med. microbiology series, 1964-90; author, editor over 75 books on microbiology and infectious disease; mem. editorial bds. 6 sci. jours.; editor: The Prokaryotes, 1981, sr. editor: The Prokaryotes, 2d edit., 1991; gen. editor: Topley & Wilson's Microbiology & Microbal Infections, 9th edit., 1998 (winner Advanced Edited Book category Med. Soc. London 1998); contbr. articles to profl. jours. Bd. dirs. Lexington chpt. NCCJ, 1960—64. With US Army, 1943—46, with M.C. US Army, 1943—46, ETO. Named Lab World Microbiologist of Yr., 1980; recipient Becton-Dickinson award in clin. microbiology, 1981, Silver medallion for outstanding contbns. to clin. microbiology Italian Soc. Microbiology, 1983, Louis T. Benezet Disting. Alumni award Colorado Coll., 1988, Abbott Labs. award for devel. of rapid lab. diagnostic techs., 1990, Disting. Profl. Recognition award, Am. bd. Med. Microbiology, 1997, bioMerieux Sonnenwirth award for exemplary leadership in clin. microbiology, 1999; named to Alumni Hall Fame, Palmer H.S., 2004 Fellow Am. Acad. Microbiology (bd. govs. 1973-77, 89-95, chmn. 1975-76), N.Y. Acad. Scis., AAAS, Am. Pub. Health Assn., Infectious Disease Soc. Am., Am. Acad. Lab. Physicians and Scientists; mem. Am. Soc. Microbiology (pres.-elect 1979-80, pres. 1980-81, council, also mem. council policy com. 1974-82, P.R. Edwards award for outstanding service furthering high profl. ideals and standards in microbiology from S.E. br. 1987, elected hon. mem. 1988), Am. Soc. Clin. Pathology, Soc. Gen. Microbiology, AAUP, Med. Mycol. Soc. Am., Soc. Applied Bacteriology, Am. Veneral Disease Assn., South Ctrl. Assn. Clin. Microbiology (hon.), Assn. State & Territorial Pub. Health Lab. Dirs. (hon.), Sci. Writers Guild, Sigma Xi, Blue Key, Omicron Delta Kappa, Tau Kappa Alpha, Zeta Beta Tau, B'nai B'rith. Died Sept. 23, 2006.

BALTHAZOR, ALBERT, JR., optometrist; b. Fond du Lac, Wis., Jan. 11, 1925; s. Albert Francis and Ernestina Alvina (Smith) B.; m. LaVerne R. Nelson, Aug. 30, 1952; children: Loren, Dean, Michael, Timothy Student, U. Wis., 1942-43, 46-47; OD, Ill. Coll. Optometry, 1949. Gen. practice optometry, Fond du Lac, 1949-76, Apache Junction, Ariz., 1976-82, Mesa, Ariz., from 1982. Cons. Fond du Lac County Mental Health Ctr., 1973-76; vision screening on Seattle Mariners baseball team, U.S. Olympic archery team Bd. dirs. Fond du Lac County Republican party, 1965-67; county chmn. Wis. Congress Conservatives; mem. sch. bd. Christ the King Sch., Mesa, 1982-85. Served with USAF, 1943-46; to capt. USAFR, 1950-58 Fellow Coll. Optometrists in Vision Devel. (state dir.), Coll. Syntonic Optometry; mem. Am. Optometric Assn., Cen. Area Optometric Soc. (pres. 1981-82), Optometric Extension Program, Nat. Acad. Sports Vision, Internat. Acad. Sports Vision, Jaycees (Outstanding Mem. Fond du Lac 1961), VFW (past commdr. Post 1904), Am. Legion, DAV, Lions, KC (Mesa) Roman Catholic. Home: Mesa, Ariz. Died July 18, 2007.

BALZER, WILMA H., retired association executive; b. Newton, Kans., Nov. 21, 1916; d. Jacob Frank and Jennie Alieda (Van Der Smissen) B. BA, Carleton Coll., 1938; MA in Edn. of Deaf, Columbia Tchrs. Coll., 1940; MSW, N.Y. Sch. Social Work, 1950. Tchr. deaf-blind students, dir. deaf-blind dept. N.Y. Inst. Edn. Blind, NYC, 1938-42; mem. recreation staff Jones ctr. Children's Aid Soc., NYC, 1942-43; dir. co-ed teen program west side br. YWCA, NYC, 1943-48; asst. dir. sch. community ctr. N.Y.C. YWCA and N.Y.C. Bd. Edn., 1946-48; dir. teen program East Liberty br. Pitts. YWCA, 1950-51; YWCA dir./ctr. coord. Amsterdam Houses Community Ctr., NYC, 1951-55; asst. dir. group work and recreation N.Y.C. Youth Bd., 1955-60; family case worker Family & Children's Svc., Omaha, 1960-62; met. assoc. exec., dir. downtown br. Houston YWCA, 1962-73; cons. orgn. devel. nat. bd. dirs. YWCA U.S.A., NYC, 1974-82; ret., 1982. Mem. NASW. Avocations: community theater, art/design projects, adult literacy tutoring, local industrial and ethnic history projects. Home: Bethlehem, Pa. Died Apr. 30, 2006.

BAMFORD, THOMAS TRUMAN, b. Ipswich, Mass., June 10, 1926; s. Robert and Isabel (Nutt) B.; m. Calypso Giantis, Apr. 21, 1974; children— Sandra, Shiela, Robert, William, Deidre, Tracy. BS in Chem. Engring, Worcester Poly. Inst., 1949, MS, 1950. Research engr. Lever Brothers Co., Cambridge, Mass., 1950-52; mem. sr. staff Arthur D. Little, Inc., Cambridge, 1952-74; pres. Bamford Assocs., Ipswich, 1974-79; v.p. research and devel. FMC Corp., Chgo., from 1979. Dir. IMRX, Inc., Phila., Centocor, Inc., Malvern, Pa.; assoc. prof. mgmt. of tech. U. N.H., 1971-72 Author: Executive Zoo, 1974. Served with USN, 1944-46. Mem. Indsl. Research Inst. Clubs: Mid-America, Courtside, Forest Country. Died Oct. 13, 2005.

BAMPTON, ROSE ELIZABETH, opera singer, voice educator; b. Cleve., Nov. 28, 1907; d. Samuel and Henrietta (Hunt) B.; m. Wilfrid Pelletier, May 24, 1937 (dec. 1982). MusB, Curtis Inst. Music, Phila., 1932; LHD, Drake U., 1940; HHD (hon.), Hobart and William Smith Colls., 1950. Prima donna Met. Opera, NYC, 1932-50, Covent Garden Opera, London, 1937-38, San Francisco Opera, 1942-45, Teatro Colon, Buenos Aires, 1945-50; tchr. Manhattan Sch. Music, 1963-79, N.C. Sch. of Arts, Winston-Salem, 1964-69, Conservatoire of Music, Montreal, Que., Can., 1972-74, Juilliard Sch., NYC. Chmn. bd. dirs. Bagby Found.; mem. Sullivan Found.; mem. profl. com. Met. Opera Co., N.Y.C. Avocations: theater, tennis, swimming. Home: Bryn Mawr, Pa. Died Aug. 21, 2007.

BANDROFCHECK, JOSEPH, b. Hunker, Pa., Sept. 1, 1920; s. Paul and Catherine (Kukla) B.; m. Mary Kay Wesbecher, Oct. 27, 1951; children— Charles Paul, Susan Kathleen, Mark Joseph. Extension student, U. Pitts. With Robertshaw Controls Co., Richmond, Va., from 1941, asst. controller, 1959-69, treas., from 1969. Served with USNR, 1944-46. Mem. Nat. Assn. Accts. (past pres.), Fin. Execs. Inst. (past pres.), Budget Execs. Inst. (past pres.) Republican. Roman Catholic. Home: Richmond, Va. Died Dec. 31, 2006.

BANKS, ROBERT J., bishop; b. Winthrop, Mass., Feb. 26, 1928; s. Robert Joseph and Rita Katherine (Sullivan) B. AB, St. John's Sem., Brighton, Mass., 1949; STL, Gregorian U., Rome, 1953; JCD, Lateran U., Rome, 1957. Ordained priest Roman Cath. Ch., 1952, ordained titular bishop of Taraqua, 1985. Prof. canon law St. John Sem., Brighton, Mass., 1959-71, acad. dean, 1967-71; rector St. John's Sem., 1971-81; vicar gen. Boston Archdiocese, 1984; aux. bishop Boston, 1985-90; bishop Diocese of Green Bay, Wis., 1990—2003; ret., 2003. Roman Catholic. Died May 30, 2007.

BANKS, WILLIAM DRESSEL, publishing executive, book retailer, educator; b. St. Louis, May 3, 1938; s. W. Jack and Louis (Dressel) B.; m. Susan B. Bay, Aug. 19, 1961; children— Kevin, Steve. Grad. Webster High, Webster Groves, Mo., 1956. Student Coll. of Wooster, 1956-57; B.S., Washington U., St. Louis, 1960, B.A., 1960. Salesman, H. J. Heinz, St. Louis, 1960-62; agt. Gen. Am. Life, St. Louis, 1962-70; pres. Impact Books, Inc., Kirkwood, Mo., 1971—; owner, mgr. Successful Life Bookstore, Kirkwood, 1971—; tchr. New Wine Ministries, Kirkwood, 1971—, president, 1973—. Author: Alive Again!, 1977; Ministering to Abortion's Aftermath, 1982, other books including Deliverance From Childlessness, 1990, Three Kinds of Faith for Healing, 1992, Everything is Possible, 1995, How to Tap into the Wisdom of God, 1996. Editor numerous books on religion. Recipient Man of Yr. award Kirkwood C. of C., 1982. Republican. Home: Saint Louis, Mo. Died Apr. 16, 2007.

BANNING, LANCE GILBERT, historian, educator; b. Kansas City, Jan. 24, 1942; s. E. Willis and Marie G. B.; m. Lana J. Sampson, July 11, 1964; 1 child, Clinton E. BA, U. Mo., Kansas City, 1964; MA, PhD, Washington U., St. Louis, 1971. Prof. history U. Ky., Lexington, from 1973. John Adams prof. U. Groningen, The Netherlands, 1997. Author: The Jeffersonian Persuasion, 1978, The Sacred Fire of Liberty, 1995, Jefferson and Madison, 1995. Fellow Guggenheim Found., Fullbright, Nat. Humanities Ctr.; recipient Internat. Book award Phi Alpha Theta, 1979, 1996, Merle Curti award Orgn. Am. Historians, 1996. Died Jan. 31, 2006.

BARAGWANATH, ALBERT KINGSMILL, curator, writer; b. Lima, Peru, July 20, 1917; s. John Gordon and Leila Radcliff (Morris) B.; m. Eileen Mary Flanagan, Sept. 1, 1943; children— Joan Baragwanath Shaw, Janice, John Blackburn, Patricia. Grad., Hill Sch., Pottstown, Pa., 1936; BA, Princeton, 1940; MA in Am. History, Columbia, 1952. With traffic and sales dept. Eastern Air Lines, NYC, 1946-50; librarian Mus. City N.Y., 1952-58, curator prints and portraits, from 1959, sr. curator, 1963-79, sr. curator emeritus, from 1980. Mem. N.Y.C. Mayor's Task Force on Municipal Archives, 1966; mem. adv. com. Mus. Am. Folk Art, 1969— Author: More Than a Mirror to the Past: The First Fifty Years of the Museum of the City of New York, 1973, 50 Currier & Ives Favorites, 1978, 100 Currier & Ives Favorites, 1978; New York Life at the Turn of the Century in Photographs, 1985; contbr.: New York City Guide, 1964, Currier and Ives, Chronicles of America, 1968. Served from pvt. to capt. AUS, 1941-46, ETO; Served from pvt. to capt. AUS, PTO. Decorated Combat Inf. badge. Mem. Am. Hist. Print Collectors Soc. (dir.) Home: Larchmont, NY. Died Nov. 24, 2006.

BARBER, HUGH REMEGIUS KILROE, gynecologist, obstetrician, educator; b. Erie, Pa., July 23, 1918; s. Thomas Francis and Elizabeth Frances (Kilroe) B.; m. Mary Louise McAuley, July 5, 1954. BA, Columbia U., 1941; MD, Columbia U. Coll. Physicians and Surgeons, 1944. Diplomate Am. Bd. Ob.-Gyn., Am. Bd. Gynecol. Oncology. Asst. prof. U. Oreg. Med. Sch., Eugene, 1951-52; prof., chm. Ob-Gyn. N.Y. Med. Coll., Valhalla, 1979-86; dir. div. Ob-Gyn. Westchester County Med. Ctr., Valhalla, 1979-84; assoc. dean for cancer programs N.Y. Med. Coll., Valhalla, 1981-86; adj. prof. clin. ob-gyn. Cornell U. Med. Ctr., NYC, 1979-89, prof. clin. ob-gyn., 1989; dir. Dept. Ob-Gyn. Lenox Hill Hosp., NYC, from 1963. Author 20 books and more than 400 sci. articles; editor The Female Patient, 1976— (Hammond award for excellence in med. journalism 1982). Pres. Am. Cancer Soc., N.Y.C. Div., 1973-77 (Ann. Nat. Divisional award 1977). Lt. (j.g.) USN, 1946-48. Recipient Silver Anniversity All Am. award, 1965, Outstanding Program Dir. award Dist. II, Am. Coll. Obstetricians and Gynecologists, 1986, The Wholeness of Life award Hosp. Chaplaincy, N.Y.C., 1988. Fellow Am. Gynecol. and Obstet. Soc.; founding mem. N.Y. Gynecol. Soc.; mem. Soc. Pelvic Surgeons (past pres.), Soc. Gynecol. Oncologists (past pres.), N.Y. Obstet. Soc. Died Dec. 26, 2006.

BARBER, RUSSELL BROOKS BUTLER, television producer; b. Tacoma, Wash., Nov. 4, 1934; s. Russell Brooks and Verga Merrill (Lesher) Butler. BA, U. Puget Sound, 1957; AM, Stanford U., 1959; PhD, Northwestern U., 1963. Exec. prodr. Sta. WCBS-TV, NYC, 1964-71; religion editor Sta. WNBC-TV, 1973-90, media lectr., 1993—2007. Adj. prof. pub. comm. Nova Southeastern U., Ft. Lauderdale, Fla., from 2002. Author: Among First Patriots, 1976. Advisor Templeton Found., London, 1976-2007; dir. Coun. Chs. NYC, 1979-2007; mem. comms. com. Am. Cancer Soc. NY, NYC, 1978—, NYC Mission Soc., 1979-2007, Laymen's Nat. Bible Com., NYC, 1983-2007, Conn. Diocese Episcopal Ch., Hartford, 1984-2007, media cons., prodr., host Diocese Armenian Ch. of Am., 1992-2007; established Barber Scholars, U. Puget Sound, Tacoma, 1978-2007, Nat. Lecture Tours on Media; bd. dirs. Inst. for Religion & Pub. Policy, Washington, DC, 1998. Recipient Faith and Freedom award Religious Heritage Am., St. Louis, 1982, Emmy awards NATAS, N.Y.C., 1984, 85, 88, U. Thant Peace award UN Peace Meditation, 1986, Gabriel award Nat. Cath. Assn. for Broadcasters and Communicators, 1987, Trisccort award Roman Cath. Ch., 1988, Nat. Cmty. Svc. award, U. Puget Sound, 2003; named Knight Comdr. Order St. John of Jerusalem, N.Y.C., 1985. Mem. NATAS, World Assn. Christian Comms., Am. Fed. TV and Radio Artists. Avocations: travel, antiques, reading, writing, golf. Home: Fort Lauderdale, Fla. Died June 4, 2007.

BARBERA, JOSEPH ROLAND, motion picture and television producer, cartoonist; b. NYC, Mar. 24, 1911; s. Vincente and Frances Barbera; m. Sheila Holden; children: (by former marriage) Lynne Meredith, Jayne Earl, Neal Francis. Grad., Am. Inst. Banking. Banking clk. Irving Trust Co., NYC, 1930-32; storyboard writer, sketch artist Van Beuren Studio, NYC, 1932-34; animator Terrytoons, New Rochelle, 1934-37; head animation dept. MGM, 1955-57; co-founder with William Hanna Hanna-Barbera Prodns., from 1957. Dir. with Hanna of short animated films including Puss Gets the Boot, 1940 (Academy award nomination best animated short subject 1940), The Nightmare Before Christmas, 1941 (Academy award best animated short subject 1941), Yankee Doodle Mouse, 1943 (Academy award best animated short subject 1943), Mouse Trouble, 1944 (Academy award best animated short subject 1944), Quiet, Please!, 1945 (Academy award best animated short subject 1945), The Cat Concerto, 1946 (Academy award best animated short subject 1946), Dr. Jekyll and Mr. Mouse, 1947 (Academy award nomination best animated short subject 1947), The Little Orphan, 1948 (Academy award best animated short subject 1948), Hatch Up Your Troubles, 1949 (Academy award nomination best animated short subject 1949), Jerry's Cousin, 1950 (Academy award nomination best animated short subject 1950), The Two Mouseketeers, 1951 (Academy award best animated short subject 1951), Johann Mouse, 1952 (Academy award best animated short subject 1952), Touche, Pussy Cat, 1954 (Academy award nomination best animated short subject 1954), Good Will to Men, 1955 (Academy award nomination best animated short subject 1955), One Droopy Knight, 1957 (Academy award nomination best animated short subject 1957); animated programming series with Hanna include The Ruff and Reddy Show, 1957-60, The Huckleberry Hound Show, 1958-62 (Emmy award 1960), Yogi Bear, 1958-62, The Quick Draw McGraw Show, 1959-62, The Flintstones, 1960-66 (Golden Globe award 1965), Top Cat, 1961-62, Lippy the Lion, 1962, Touche Turtle, 1962, Wally Gator, 1962, The Jetsons, 1962-67, 69-76, 79-81, 82-83, 85, The Adventures of Jonny Quest, 1964-65, 67-72, 79, 80-81, The Magilla Gorilla Show, 1964-67, The Peter Potamus Show, 1964-67, Tom and Jerry, 1965-72, 75-78, 80-82, The Atom Ant/Secret Squirrel Show, 1965-68, Sinbad, Jr., the Sailor, 1966, The Abbott and Costello Cartoon Show, 1966, Laurel and Hardy, 1966-67, Space Kiddettes, 1966-67, Space Ghost, 1966-68, Frankenstein, Jr. and the Impossibles, 1966-68, Sampson and Goliath, 1967-68, Birdman and the Galaxy Trio, 1967-68, The Herculoids, 1967-69, Moby Dick and the Mighty Mightor, 1967-69, Shazzan!, 1967-69, The Fantastic Four, 1967-70, The Wacky Races, 1968-70, The Adventures of Gulliver, 1969-70, The Perils of Penelope Pitstop, 1969-71, The Cattanooga Cats, 1969-71, Dastardly and Muttley in Their Flying Machines, 1969-71, Scooby-Doo, Where Are You?, 1969-74, Where's Huddles?, 1970-71, The Harlem Globetrotters, 1970-73, Josie and the Pussycats, 1970-76, Pebbles and Bamm Bamm, 1971-72, Help! It's the Hair Bear Bunch, 1971-72, The Funky Phantom, 1971-72, Wait Til Your Father Gets Home, 1972, Sealab 2020, 1972-73, The Roman Holidays, 1972-73, The Amazing Chan and the Chan Clan, 1972-74, The Flintstones Comedy Hour, 1972-74, Josie and the Pussycats in Outer Space, 1972-74, Speed Buggy, 1971-74, Butch Cassidy and the Sundance Kids, 1973-74, Peter Puck, 1973-74, Inch High, Private Eye, 1973-74, Yogi's Gang, 1973-75, Jeannie, 1973-75, Goober and the Ghost Chasers, 1973-75, The Addams Family, 1973-75, Super Friends, 1973-83, Wheelie and the Chopper Bunch, 1974-75, The Partridge Family: 2200 A.D., 1974-75, Hong Kong Phooey, 1974-76, These Are the Days, 1974-76, Devlin, 1974-76, Valley of the Dinosaurs, 1974-76, The Scooby-Doo/Dynomutt Hour, 1976-77, Mumbly, 1976-77, Jabberjaw, 1976-78, The Skatebirds, 1977-78, The Tom and Jerry/Great Grape Ape Show, 1977-78, Scooby's All-Star Laff-a-Lympics, 1977-78, Fred Flintstone and Friends, 1977-78, Captain Caveman and the Teen Angels, 1980, The Scooby-Doo and Scrappy-Doo Show, 1980-82, The Drak Pack, 1980-82,

Fonz and the Happy Days Gang, 1980-82, The Richie Rich Show, 1980-82, The Kwicky Koala Show, 1981-82, Trollkins, 1981-82, Laverne and Shirley in the Army, 1981-82, The Smurfs, 1981-90 (Emmy award 1982, 83), Laverne and Shirley with the Fonz, 1982-83, Scooby, Scrappy, and Yabba Doo, 1982-83, Snorks, 1984-86, The Funtastic World of Hanna-Barbera, 1986-87,87-88, Pound Puppies, 1986-87, The Flintstone Kids, 1986-87, Wildfire, 1986-87, Foofur, 1986-87, Popeye and Son, 1987-88, The Completely Mental Misadventures of Ed Grimley, 1988-89; animated spls. include Alice in Wonderland, 1966, Jack and the Beanstalk, 1967 (Emmy award 1967), Last of the Curlews, 1972 (Emmy award 1973), My Smurfy Valentine, 1982, Smurfily-Ever-After, 1985, The Flintstones' 25th Anniversary Celebration, 1986, The Jetsons Meet the Flintstones, 1987, Hanna-Barbera's 50th: A Yabba Dabba Doo Celebration, 1989, I Yabba Dabba Doo!, 1993; live action spls. include The Runaways, 1974 (Emmy award 1974); live action TV movies include Hardcase, 1972, Shootout in a One-dog Town, 1974, The Gathering, 1977 (Christopher award 1978, Emmy award 1978), The Gathering Part II, 1979, Stone Fox, 1987; animated feature films include Hey There, It's Yogi Bear, 1964, A Man Called Flintstone, 1966, Charlotte's Web, 1973 (Annie award 1977), Heidi's Song, 1982, Once Upon a Forest, 1993; live action feature films C.H.O.M.P.S., 1979, The Flinstones, 1994; co-creator Huckleberry Hound, Yogi Bear, Flintstones, Jetsons, Top Cat, Jonny Quest, Scooby-Doo; co-author: (with Alan Axelrod) My Life in Toons: From Flatbush to Bedrock in Under a Century, 1994. Recipient TV Acad. Gov.'s award, 1988, Hall of Fame award Acad. Arts and Scis., 1993, Movie Guide award Tom & Jerry the Movie, 1993, The Flintstones, 1994. Home: Studio City, Calif. Died Dec. 18, 2006.

BARBOUR, ARTHUR J., artist; b. Paterson, NJ, Aug. 23, 1926; One-man shows include Beumont Mus. Art, Tex., 1965, exhibitions include Nat. Acad. Design, NYC, Am. Watercolor Soc., Am. Artists Profl. League, Wolf Gallery, Franklin, NJ, 1973, Fritchman Galleries, Boise, Idaho, 1974, U.S. Navy Dept., Marietta Coll., Norfolk Mus. Arts and Sci., Prudential Life Ins. Co., others; author: Watercolor: The Wet Technique, 1978, Painting Buildings in Watercolor, 1973, Painting the Seasons in Watercolor, 1980. Recipient Silver Medal Honor, Audubon Artists, 1988. Mem.: Nat. Soc. Painters Casein and Acrylic, Allied Artists, Painters and Sculptors Soc. NJ, NJ Watercolor Soc., Am. Watercolor Soc. (Gold Medal 1965, Mary S. Litt award 1983). Died Mar. 12, 2006.

BARCLAY, ALLAN GENE, psychologist, educator; b. Masonville, Iowa, Dec. 22, 1930; s. Otho R. and Marian (Lee) B.; student U. Louisville, 1949-50; A.B. cum laude, U. Tulsa, 1955; postgrad. U. Iowa, 1955-56; Ph.D., Washington U., St. Louis, 1960; children— Lisa, Allan. Clin. psychologist Mental Hygiene Clinic, VA Regional Office, St. Louis, 1959-60; faculty St. Louis U., 1960—, prof. psychology, 1965—, assoc. univ. research adminstr., 1968-72, dir. program in developmental psychology, 1965—, dir. Sch. Medicine Child Devel. Clinic, 1972—; chief psychologist dept. pediatrics Cardinal Glennon Meml. Hosp. for Children, St. Louis, 1960—, asso. dean acad. affairs Sch. of Profl. Psychology, Wright State U., Dayton, Ohio, 1979—. Cons. to hosps., govt. agys.; spl. adviser Pres.'s Com. on Mental Retardation; councilor Joint Commn. on Hosps., Accreditation Council on Facilities for Mentally Retarded. Bd. dirs., pres., mem. adv. com. New Hope Found. St. Louis, 1977-79. Served with AUS, 1948-52. Grantee USPHS, 1961-79, U.S. Children's Bur., 1960-68, Joseph P. Kennedy, Jr. Found., 1965, Children's Research Found., 1965, Office Econ. Opportunity, 1965-68, Social Rehab. Service, 1972—; Am. Psychol. Found., 1980; diplomate Am. Bd. Examiners in Profl. Psychology; mem. Nat. Register Health Service Providers in Psychology. Fellow Am. Assn. on Mental Deficiency; Soc. for Rorschach Research and Projective Techniques, Mo. Psychol. Assn., Internat. Council Psychologists (past pres.); mem. Am. Psychol. Assn. (fellow div. clin. psychology, fellow div. developmental psychology, chmn. bd. profl. affairs, sec.-treas., past pres. div. clin. psychology, past pres. div. mental retardation), Ill. Psychol. Assn., Mo. Psychol. Assn., Ohio Psychol. Assn., AAAS, AAUP, Am. Assn. Mental Deficiency, So. Soc. Philosophy and Psychology, Soc. Research in Child Devel. Inter-Am. Soc. Psychology, Internat. Council Psychologists (past pres.), Am. Pub. Health Assn., AMA, Sword and Key, Sigma Xi, Pi Gamma Mu, Psi Chi (nat. pres.), Phi Gamma Kappa. Editor: Jour. Profl. Psychology; contbr. articles to publs. Home: Dayton, Ohio. Died Feb. 6, 2006.

BARD, JAMES W., dermatologist; b. New London, Wis., Mar. 12, 1934; s. Everett K. and Gertrude (Chapiewsky) B.; m. Elaine D. Winter, Sep. 14, 1957; children— Paul, Stephen. M.D., Med. Coll. Wis., 1958. Diplomate Am. Bd. Dermatology. Intern, Yale-New Haven Hosp., 1958-59; resident in dermatology Mayo Clinic, 1962-65; sect. head Lexington Clinic, Ky., 1965-80, v.p., 1980-85, pres., 1985—. Contbr. articles to profl. jours. Exhibited in group shows Ky. Photographers, 1983. Served to capt. U.S. Army, 1959-62. Recipient Humanitarian service award AMA, 1971. Fellow Am. Acad. Dermatology; mem. Noah Worcester Dermatol. Soc. (sec., treas. 1981-86, pres. 1987—), Cin. Dermatol. Soc. (pres. 1985-86), Ky. Dermatol. Soc. (pres. 1977-78). Lodge: Rotary. Avocation: photography. Home: Lexington, Ky. Died Nov. 22, 2006.

BARE, BRUCE, retired life insurance company executive; b. Pierson, Iowa, May 26, 1914; s. Edward E. and Myrtle Viola (Sloan) B.; m. Adaline Light, June 14, 1936; children: Bruce Jr., Barbara Bare Spaulding, John. BA, Grinnell Coll., Iowa, 1935; LL.D. (hon.), Westmont Coll., Santa Barbara, Calif., 1971. C.L.U. With New Eng. Mut. Life Ins. Co., 1935—, gen. agt. Los Angeles, 1946-80, field v.p., 1979-82. Trustee Westmont Coll., 1947—, chmn., 1965; past pres. Fuller Evangelistic Found., Pasadena, Calif.; chmn. bd. trustees African Enterprise Internat., 1979-84. Recipient Farrell award Los Angeles C. of C., 1968; named to Hall of Fame Gen. Agts. and Mgrs. Assn., 1977 Mem. Am. Soc. C.L.U.'s (pres. 1964, trustee 1974), Life Underwriters Assn. (past pres. Los Angeles chpt.), Los Angeles Life Ins. Mgrs. Assn. (past pres.) Presbyterian. Home: San Diego, Calif. Died Oct. 30, 2005.

BARHAM, MACK ELWIN, lawyer, former state supreme court justice; b. Bastrop, La., June 18, 1924; s. Henry Alfred and Lockie Izorie (Harper) B.; m. Ann LeVois, June 3, 1946; children: Bret L., Megan. JD, La. State U., 1946; postgrad., U. Colo., 1964-65. Judge City Ct., Bastrop, 1948-61, 4th Jud. Dist. Ct., Parishes of Ouachita and Morehouse, 1961-67, 2d Circuit Ct. of Appeal, 1967-68; assoc. justice La. Supreme Ct., 1968-75; prof. Tulane Sch. Law, 1975-78; counsel Lemle, Kelleher, Kohlmeyer & Matthews, 1975-78; pres. Barham & Churchill, 1979-88; founder Barham & Arceneaux, New Orleans, 1988—2006. Mem. faculty Am. Acad. Jud. Edn., U. Ala., 1968-73. Chmn. Ouachita Valley council Boy Scouts Am. Recipient award Freedoms Found. at, Valley Forge, 1969; Outstanding Service award ACLU, 1976; Creative Intelligence award Am. Found. Sci., 1976 Mem. La. Juvenile Judges Assn. (past pres.), La. Law Inst. (council), Internat. Acad. Estate and Trust Law, Scribes, Kiwanis, Blue Key, Order of Coif, Omicron Delta Kappa, Lambda Chi Alpha, Phi Delta Phi, Phi Alpha Delta. Home: Houston, Tex. Died Nov. 27, 2006.

BARICKMAN, JAMES HALL, advertising agency executive; b. Mpls., Oct. 5, 1924; s. Mary (Barickman); m. Mary Mischler, Jan. 26, 1974; children: Nancy Barickman Greenley, James Hall, Julie King, Robert, Daniel. BS in Fin, U. Minn., 1947. With Northwestern Nat. Bank, Mpls., 1947-50; West Coast advt. mgr. Pillsbury Co., 1950-51; account exec. Brewer Advt., Kansas City, Mo., 1951-59; with Barickman Advt., Kansas City, 1959-80, pres., 1959-80; (co. merged with Doyle Dane Bernbach Internat.), 1980, former chmn. bd., now chief exec. officer; chmn. bd. Barkley & Evergreen Advt., from 1985. Dir. Columbia Union Bank, Kansas City.; Adv. bd. Research Med. Center, Kansas City Pres. Kansas City Jr. C. of C., 1958-59; pres. Kansas City Jr. Achievement, 1963-65. Served with AUS, World War II. Recipient Ann. Silver medal Am. Advt. Fedn., 1976 Mem. Am. Assn. Advt. Agys., Am. Mktg. Assn., Affiliated Advt. Agys. Internat. Clubs: Kansas City, Carriage; La Quinta (Calif.); Country; Hillcrest Country (Bartlesville, Okla.); Moss Creek Country (Hilton Head, S.C.); Williams, Friars (N.Y.C.); Indian Hills Country, Wolf Creek Country. Republican. Presbyterian. Home: Overland Park, Kans. Died Jan. 13, 2006.

BARKER, DAVID BENTON, marine corps officer; b. Needham, Mass., Jan. 11, 1930; s. Charles F. and Mildred R. (Benton) B.; m. Priscilla Farrant, Apr. 20, 1953; children— Laurel, Howard, David, Sandra. BS in Chemistry and Biology, Tufts Coll., 1951; MA in Personnel Adminstrn, George Washington U., 1966. Commd. 2d lt. U.S. Marine Corps, 1951, advanced through grades to gen., 1980; comdg. gen. Marine Corps Base, Camp Lejeune, N.C., 1978-81; dep. chief of staff for tng. Hdqrs. U.S. Marine Corps, Washington, 1981-82; chief of staff Hdqrs. U.S. Forces, Japan, 1982-84; comdg. gen. 4th Marine Div., from 1984. Mem. exec. bd. East Carolina council Boy Scouts Am., 1978-81; exec. v.p. Far East council Boy Scouts Am., 1982-84; mem. exec. bd. Keep N.C. Beautiful, 1979-81; exec. dir. Mil.-Civilian Community Council, Jacksonville, N.C., 1970-81. Decorated Legion of Merit with combat V and gold star, Navy Commendation medal with combat V. Mem.: Semper Fidelis, Scottish Rite. Methodist. Died Jan. 15, 2006.

BARKER, RICHARD GORDON, former corporate research and development executive; b. Rochester, NY, Feb. 8, 1937; s. Richard I. and Laura (Gordon) B.; m. Nancy Heiligman, Sept. 7, 1957 (dec.); children: Laurie Frances, Richard, Jonathan David; m. Mary Kathryne Simpson, Sept. 16, 1995. AB, Hamilton Coll., 1958; MS, Inst. Paper Chemistry, 1960, PhD, 1963. Research scientist Union Camp Corp., Princeton, N.J., 1962-69, group leader, 1969-71, sect. leader, 1971-74, dir. research and devel. projects, 1974-79, lab. dir., then corp. dir. research and devel., from 1979. Rep., trustee Pulp and Paper Found., Maine, pres., Miami, U. Pulp Paper Found. Contbr. articles to profl. jours.; patentee in field. Mem. Empire State Paper Rsch. Assn. (chmn. rsch. steering com. 1975-82, v.p. N.Am. chpt. 1982-90, pres. 1990-96), TAPPI (bd. dirs., chmn. bd. dirs. publs, com., chmn. rsch. mgmt. com.; v.p. 1997—), Inst. of Paper Chemistry (past chmn., exec. council, past chmn. pulping and bleaching subcom. rsch. adv. com.), Princeton C. of C., Am. Chem. Soc., Soc. Rsch. Adminstrs., R & D Coun. N.J. (bd. dirs.). TAPPI Rsch. Mission Com. (chmn.). Home: Ocean City, NJ. Died Aug. 22, 2006.

BARKSDALE, RICHARD DILLON, civil engineer, educator; b. Orlando, Fla., May 2, 1938; s. William Spruil and Lucile Dillon B.; m. Bonnie Alice McClung, Nov. 16, 1962; children— Cheryl Lynn, Richelle Denise. A.S., So. Tech. Inst., Marietta, Ga., 1958; B.C.E., Ga. Inst. Tech., 1962, MS, 1963; PhD, Purdue U., 1966. Registered profl. engr., Fla., Ga., S.C., N.C., Ala., Tenn., La. Asst. prof. civil engring. Ga. Inst. Tech., Atlanta, 1965—69, assoc. prof., 1969—75, prof., 1975—95, prof. emeritus, from 1995. V.p. Soil Systems, Inc., Marietta, 1972-79, Soil Systems of the Carolina, 1976-79; spl. lectr. So. Tech. Inst., 1958-60; mem. com. longterm pavement performance Strategic Hwy. Rsch. Program. Contbr. articles in field to profl. jours. Co-pres. Briarcliff High Sch. Booster Club, 1983-84, Briarcliff High Sch. PTA, 1985-86 Recipient Ga. Engring. Soc. award, 1961, ICAR/AFTRE Disting. Rsch. award, 2003; co-recipient Croda prize Instn. Highway Engrs., 1989; NSF grantee, 1966-67; rsch. fellow Brit. Sci. and Engring. Rsch. Coun., 1988. Mem. ASCE (Norman medal 1978, pres. Ga. sect. 1975-76, chmn. nat. com. structural design of roadways), Nat. Stone Assn. (prof. of yr. 1996), Appalachee Sportsman Club (pres. 1974-95), Phi Kappa Phi (pres. Ga. Tech. chpt. 1979). Republican. Baptist. Home: Atlanta, Ga. Died Jan. 14, 2007.

BARNES, DAVID K., JR., lawyer; b. Bloomington, Ind., Mar. 24, 1944; JD, Detroit Coll. Law, 1972. Bar: Mich. 1972, U.S. Dist. Ct. (ea. dist.) Mich. 1973, U.S. Ct. Appeals (6th cir.) 1983. Lawyer Sachs, Waldman, O'Hare, Helveston, Hodges & Barnes PC, Detroit. Mediator Wayne County Mediation Tribunal Assn., 1978—. Mem. Am. Arbitration Assn. (panel arbitrators 1979), Assn. Trail Lawyers Am., State Bar Mich., Mich. Trial Lawyers Assn. (lect. in law seminars 1980, 82, 84), Detroit Bar Assn. Died Feb. 22, 2006.

BARNES, MARTIN MCRAE, entomologist; b. Calgary, Alta., Can., Aug. 3, 1920; s. Harry Olan and Vida (Killian) B.; m. Julia Butts, Aug. 31, 1946; children— Wayne, Martin, Delia, Brian. BS, U. Calif., Berkeley, 1941; PhD, Cornell U., 1946. Mem. faculty U. Calif., Riverside, from 1946, prof. entomology, 1962-91, prof. emeritus, from 1991, chmn. dept. entomology, 1988, entomologist agrl. rsch. expt. sta., 1946-91. Contbr. articles to profl. jours. Fellow AAAS, Entomol. Soc. Am. (hon., pres. Pacific br. 1976-77); mem. Sigma Xi. Democrat. Achievements include research in deciduous orchard and vineyard entomology, conservation of invertebrates. Home: Riverside, Calif. Died Apr. 22, 2007.

BARNES, MYRTLE SUE SNYDER, retired editor; b. Farmville, Va., July 14, 1933; d. George McClure and Alma White (Hillsman) Snyder; m. Shelton W. Barnes, Dec. 23, 1954 (dec. Aug. 1979); children: Donna Barnes Boulter, David Brian. BJ, Northwestern U., 1955. Reporter Times-Herald, Newport News, Va., 1956-60, 67-72, city editor, 1972-75, asst. mng. editor, 1975-82; mng. editor Daily Press & Times Herald, Newport News, 1982-87; adminstrv. editor Daily Press, Newport News, Va., 1987-95, reader editor, 1995-96, ret., 1996. Mem. jury for Pulitzer prize Columbia U., 1977, 78; mem. Accreditation Coun. on Edn. in Journalism and Mass Comm., 1986-91. Past pres., now treas. Newport News Libr. Friends. Named to Va. Comm. Hall of Fame, 1993; recipient Founding Dir.'s award Va. Coalition on Open Govt., 2000. Mem. AP Mng. Editors (chmn. com. 1986-88, bd. dirs. 1988-91, Meritorious Svc. award 1993), Va. AP Newspapers (chmn. 1987), Nat. Fedn. Press Women (bd. dirs. 1972-74, numerous awards for writing and editing), Va. Press Women (pres. 1970-72, Press Woman of Yr. 1973, numerous awards for writing and editing), Soc. Profl. Journalists (pres. Tidewater chpt. 1978, George Mason award Richmond chpt. 1986), Nat. Congress Parents and Tchrs. (life). Avocations: reading, travel, theater, handwork. Home: Hampton, Va. Died Feb. 8, 2007.

BARNES, THOMAS JEFFERSON, JR., pharmacist; b. Baxley, Ga., June 23, 1926; s. Thomas Jefferson Sr. and Merle Fenton (Johnson) B.; m. Barbara Lynn Tollison, Dec. 12, 1954; children— Barbara Karen Barnes Yonchak, Mark Tollison, Jane Ellen Howard. BS in Pharmacy, U. Ga., 1949. Lic. pharmacist, Ga. Pharmacy intern Roy G. Williams Drug, Macon, Ga., 1949-50; pharmacist employee Barnes Drug Store, Baxley, 1950-59, owner, pres., 1959-82, Barnes Prescription Shop, 1974-82; ptnr. Barnes Drug Store, Baxley, 1982—, Barnes Prescription Shop, 1982—; cons. in field. Mem. sch. bd. Appling County Schs., Baxley; mem. city council City of Baxley; mem. Appling County Bd. Health. Served with USN, 1944-46. Mem. Appling County C. of C. (past bd. dirs., past pres.), Ga. Pharm. Assn., Nat. Assn. Retail Pharmacists, Am. Pharm. Assn. Baptist. Avocations: fishing; hunting; golfing. Home: Baxley, Ga. Died Jan. 9, 2007.

BARNHART, CHARLES ELMER, zoology educator; b. Windsor, Ill., Jan. 25, 1923; s. Elmer and Irma (Smysor) B.; m. Norma McCarty, Dec. 28, 1946 (dec. Dec. 25, 1970); children: John D., Charles E., Norman R.; m. Jean M. Hutton, Jan. 12, 1973; stepchildren: Mark, David, Bonnie, Beth Hutton. BS in Agr., Purdue U., 1945; MS, Ia. State U., 1948, PhD, 1954. Mem. faculty U. Ky., Lexington, from 1948, assoc. prof. animal sci., 1955-57, prof., 1957-88, prof. emeritus, from 1988, dean, dir. exptl. sta. and coop. extension service, 1969-88, dean emeritus, from 1988. Pres. So. Assn. Agrl. Scientist, 1982-83 Patentee in field. Bd. dirs. Ky. Bd. Agr., 1966-88, Ky. State Fair and Expn. Ctr., 1969-88, Ky. Tobacco Rsch. Bd., Farm Credit Svcs. Mid Am., 1988-93, Ky. Farm Bur., 1969-76; mem. Gov.'s Coun. on Agrl., 1971-80. Named Man of Yr. in Ky. Agr. Progressive Farmer, 1962, Man of Yr. for Ky. Agr. Ky. Agrl. Communicators, 1979; elected to Saddle and Sirloin Portrait Gallery, 1987. Mem. Am. Soc. Animal Sci., Ky. Hist. Soc., Farmhouse Fraternity, Masons (32 deg.), Shriners, Epsilon Sigma Phi, Gamma Sigma Delta., Omicron Delta Kappa, Sigma Xi. Methodist. Home: Venice, Fla. Died Apr. 1, 2007.

BARON, ALMA FAY S., management educator; b. Pitts., July 26, 1923; d. Max J. and Emma C. (Aronson) Spann; m. Lee A. Baron, Dec. 23, 1944; children— Ellen J., Michael A., Jill S. BA, U. Pitts., 1943; PhD, U. Wis-Madison, 1974. Advt. mgr. Kaufmann's, Pitts., 1943; head copywriter Levy Bros., Houston, 1945; fashion coordinator Baron's, Madison, Wis., 1946-54; host TV Talent, Sta. WMTV, Madison, Wis., 1953-54, Sta. WQED, Pitts., 1954-58, Sta. KORN, Mitchell, S.D., 1958-66, Sta. KELO, Sioux Falls, S.D., 1959-66; co-owner Lee Baron's Women's Store, Madison, 1966-71; instr. U. Wis. Mgmt. Inst., Madison, 1974-77, assoc. prof. mgmt., 1978-81, prof. mgmt., 1981-88, prof. emeritus, from 1988. Mem. internat. Bd. Inst. Cert. Profl. Secs., 1977—81; vis. faculty La. State U., Baton Rouge, Pa. State U., Univ. Park, U. Okla., Norman, Purdue U., W. Lafayette; lectr., Scandinavia, England, India, Kuala Lumpur, Malaysia, Hong Kong, Jakarta, Singapore, Bangkok, Australia, New Zealand; started Sr. Class TV program. Author: Assertiveness in the Business Environment, 1979, Nonverbal Communication, 1981, Women in Management: Strategies for Success, 1995; host, prodr.: (TV show) Mature; contbr. articles to profl. jours. Pres. Madison Civic Music Assn., 1971—73; v.p. YWCA, Madison, 1973—76; pres. Madison Civice Club, 1985—86; chmn. bd. advisers St. Mary's Hosp., from 1986; chmn. blue ribbon millennium com. U. Wis. Ret. Assn.; pres. U. Wis. Faculty-Staff Assn., 1999—2000. Recipient Woman of Achievement award This is Madison, 1977, Outstanding Women award Select mag., 1976, Madisonian award Wis. State Jour., 1975, Sales and Mktg. award Sales Mktg. Execs., 1977, Meritorious Ind. Study Course award Nat. Univ. Extension Assn., 1980, Disting. Service award U. Wis. Extension, 1982, Outstanding Prof. award U. Wis.-Madison, 1985, Robert A. Jerred award U. Wis. Sch. Bus., 1988, Women of Distinction award YWCA, 1993, U. Wis. Disting. Alumni award, 1995, Jean Harris Rotary Dist. award, 1998. Mem. AAUW, Am. Bus. Comm. Assn., Am. Soc. Tng. and Devel. (mem. sr. faculty symposium 1980), Wis. Internat. Women's Forum (initiator 1987—), Gen. Semantics Assn., Wis. Acad. Arts and Scis., Assn. Platform

Speakers, Nat. Telemedia Coun. (Journalist award 1996), U. Wis.-Madison Ret. Faculty Assn. (1st pres.), B'nai B'rith, Blackhawk Country Club, Zeta Phi Eta. Home: Middleton, Wis. Died Oct. 12, 2006.

BARONE, JOHN ANTHONY, academic administrator emeritus; b. Dunkirk, NY, Aug. 30, 1924; s. John A. and Josephine (Audino) B.; m. Rose Marie Pace, Aug. 23, 1947. BA, U. Buffalo, 1944; MS, Purdue U., 1948, PhD, 1950; ScD (hon.), Fairfield U., 1992. Research fellow Purdue U., 1948-50; instr. Fairfield U., Conn., 1950-51, asst. prof. Conn., 1951-56, assoc. prof. Conn., 1956-62, prof. chemistry Conn., 1962-92, dir. rsch. and grants Conn., 1963-66, v.p. planning Conn., 1966-70, provost Conn., 1970-92, emeritus Conn., from 1992. Mem. rev. and evaluation com. Conn. Regional Med. Program, 1970-76; dir. NSF In-Service Inst., 1961-69; mem. steering com. comprehensive health planning United Community Svc.; bd. dir., mem. Corp. Conn. Blue Cross, 1973-77; bd. dir., mem. exec. com. Blue Cross-Blue Shield Conn., 1977-94; project mgr. HUD New Rural Soc. contract, 1972-76; mem. adv. com. on fed. matters Conn. Commn. for Higher Edn., 1974-77; pres. UN Assn. Conn., 1970-72; mem. Conn. Health and Edn. Facilities Authority, 1987-2001, vice-chmn., 1988-2001; mem. adv. com. Conn. Dept. Health Svc., 1987-93. Contbr. articles profl. jour. Trustee Conn. Coun. for Sci. Edn., Hall-Brooke Found., St. Vincent's Coll., Ctr. for Fin. Studies, vice chmn., 1977-94; bd. dir. Jesuit Rsch. Coun. Am., chmn., 1968-70; bd. dir. Higher Edn. Ctr. for Urban Studies, Health Systems Agy. S.W. Conn., 1977-84; mem. Conn. Statewide Health Coordinating Coun., 1979-87, chmn., 1984-87. Served with AUS, 1944-46. Barone Campus Ctr. at Fairfield U., Barone Resource Ctr. at St. Vincent's Coll. named in his honor, 1992; cancer rsch. grantee NIH, dir. NSF undergrad. rsch. program, 1961-67. Fellow AAAS; mem. Am. Chem. Soc. (chmn. western Conn. sect. 1966), AAUP (1st pres. Fairfield U. chpt.), Newcomen Soc., Phi Beta Kappa, Sigma Xi, Phi Lambda Upsilon. Clubs: Algonquin. Democrat. Roman Catholic. Home: Fairfield, Conn. Died June 1, 2007.

BARR, IRWIN ROBERT, retired aeronautical engineer; b. Newburgh, NY, May 16, 1920; s. Abraham Herman and Esther (Reibel) B.; m. Florence Lenore Skliar, Oct. 19, 1941 (dec. Feb. 1957); children: Mary Barr Megee, Betty Barr Mackey, Joan Barr Blanco, Alan Howard; m. Dorothy Friendly Weeks, Sept. 20, 1958. Cert. aero. engring., Inst. Aeros., 1940. Registered profl. engr., Md. Design group engr. Glenn L. Martin Co., Balt., 1940-50; chief ordnance engr., then pres. and chief exec. officer AAI Corp., Hunt Valley, Md., 1950-89, chmn. bd. emeritus, from 1989. Patentee rocket stblzn. and control sys., aircraft, weapons, wheels, suspensions, bearings, solar energy collectors, med. catheter, heart pump, aluminum-powered batteries. Served with USAAF, 1944-46. Named to Ordnance Hall of Fame, Aberdeen Proving Ground, Md., 1985 Home: Cockeysville Hunt Valley, Md. Died Oct. 10, 2005.

BARR, JAMES, retired foreign language educator; b. Mar. 20, 1924; s. Allan B.; student Daniel Stewart's Coll., Edinburgh, Scotland; MA, Edinburgh U., 1948, BD, 1951; MA, Oxford (Eng.) U., 1976 DD, 1981; DD (hon.), Knox Coll., Toronto, Ont., Can., 1964, U. Dubuque, 1974, U. St. Andrews, 1974, U. Edinburgh, 1983, U. South Africa, 1986, Victoria U., Toronto, Ont., Can., 1988, Faculté de Théologie Protestante, Paris, 1988, U. Oslo, 1991, U. Helsinki, 1997; MA (hon.), U. Manchester, 1969; m. Jane J. S. Hepburn, 1950; 3 children. Minister of Ch. of Scotland, Tiberias, Israel, 1951-53; prof. N.T. lit. and exegesis Presbyn. Coll., Montreal, Que., Can., 1953-55; prof. Old Testament lit. and theology Edinburgh U., 1955-61, Princeton Theol. Sem., 1961-65; prof. Semitic langs. and lits. Manchester (Eng.) U., 1965-76; Oriel prof. interpretation Holy Scripture, and fellow Oriel Coll., Oxford U., 1976-78, hon. fellow, 1980; Regius prof. Hebrew, Oxford U. and student Christ Ch., 1978-89; prof. Hebrew bible, Vanderbilt U., Nashville, 1989-94; disting. prof., 1994-98; ret., 1998; vis. prof. Hebrew U., Jerusalem, 1973, U. Chgo., 1975, 81, Strasbourg U., 1975-76, Brown U., Providence, R.I., 1985, 94, U. Otago, New Zealand, 1986, U. South Africa, 1986, Vanderbilt U., 1987-88; lectr. Princeton U., 1962-63, Union Theol. Sem., 1963; Currie lectr. Austin Theol. Sem., 1964; Guggenheim Meml. fellow for study Biblical semantics, 1965; Cadbury lectr. Birmingham U., 1969; Croall lectr. Edinburgh U., 1970; Grinfield lectr. on Septuagint, Oxford U., 1974-78; Firth lectr. Nottingham U., 1978; Sprunt lectr. Union Theol. Sem., Richmond, Va., 1982; Schweich lectr., Brit. Acad., 1986; Cole lectr. Vanderbilt U., 1988; Sarum lectr. Oxford U., 1989; Read-Tuckwell lectr. Bristol U., Eng., 1990; Gifford lectr. Edinburgh U., 1991; Hensley Henson lectr. Oxford U., Eng., 1997. Served as pilot RNVR (Fleet Air Arm), 1942-45. Fellow Brit. Acad., SOAS (hon.; mem. governing body 1980-85), Am. Acad. Arts and Scis., Am. Philos. Soc.; mem. Soc. O.T. Studies (pres. 1973), Brit. Assn. Jewish Studies (pres. 1978), Göttingen Acad. Scis. (corr.), Soc. Biblical Lit. U.S.A. (hon.), Norwegian Acad. Sci. and Letters, Swedish Royal Acad. Sci. Uppsala. Author: The Semantics of Biblical Language, 1961; Biblical Words for Time, 1962; Old and New in Interpretation, 1966; Comparative Philology and the Text of the Old Testament, 1968; The Bible in the Modern World, 1973; Fundamentalism, 1977; The Typology of Literalism, 1979; Explorations in Theology 7: The Scope and Authority of the Bible, 1980; Holy Scripture; Canon, Authority, Criticism, 1983; Beyond Fundamentalism, 1984, Variable Spellings of the Hebrew Bible, 1989, The Garden of Eden and the Hope of Immortality, 1992, Biblical Faith and Natural Theology, 1993; editor Jour. Semitic Studies, 1965-76, Oxford Hebrew Dictionary, 1974-80; contbr. articles to profl. jours. Died Oct. 14, 2006.

BARRIE, JEFFREY EDWARD, marketing executive, consultant; b. Balt., Jan. 6, 1941; s. Seymour Theodore and Minna (Rankin) B.; m. Frances Evans, Dec. 29, 1963 (div. Sept. 1973); children: Marc Evans, Brian Evans; m. Maureen Linnea, Jan. 1, 1977. BA in Lit., The Citadel, 1963; MA in Soviet Studies, Fordham U., 1970. Advanced through ranks to lt. col. U.S. Army, 1968-83; project mgr. div. personal computer Satra Corp., Moscow, 1984-86; project mgr. Mosaic Rsch. U. Ariz., Tucson, 1987-88; dir. Kniga Printshop Joint Venture, Moscow, 1989-90; pres. Satra Aerospace, Moscow, 1990-91, Barrie Assocs., Marblehead, Mass., Moscow, from 1992. Cons. Satra Corp., N.Y.C., 1984-91, Apple Corp., Cupertino, Calif., 1985-87, PAC Aviation, Pompano Beach, 1987-91, Trace Worldwide, Torrance, Calif., 1991. Editor The Barrie Newsletter, 1989-91; contbr. articles to profl. jours. Nat. dir. Young Execs. Nat. Defense Transp. Assn., Washington, 1974. Mem. U.S. Parachuting Assn., Exptl. Aircraft Assn., Internat. Aerobatics Club. Avocations: flying, parachuting, motorcycling, computers. Home: Marblehead, Mass. Died Mar. 8, 2007.

BARROW, CHARLES WALLACE, university dean; b. Poteet, Tex., Sept. 22, 1921; s. Hunter Denson and Lillie Ozella (Crouch) B.; m. Sugie Williams, Aug. 25, 1943; children—Charles Wallace, John D., David W., James H. JD, Baylor U., 1943. Bar: Tex. 1943, U.S. Supreme Ct. 1955. Practice law, San Antonio, 1945-59; mem. firm Moursund Ball Bergstrom & Barrow, 1946-58; judge 45th Jud. Dist., San Antonio, 1959-62; assoc. justice 4th Ct. Civil Appeals, San Antonio, 1962-66, chief justice, 1967-77; justice Tex. Supreme Ct., Austin, 1977-84; dean Baylor U. Sch. Law, Waco, Tex., 1984-91. Served to capt. USNR, 1942-45, 50-52. Mem. Tex. Bar Assn., San Antonio Bar Assn. Clubs: Masons, Kiwanis, Hermann Sons. Democrat. Methodist. Home: San Antonio, Tex. Died June 25, 2006.

BARSON, JOHN, college president, medical educator; b. Glassport, Pa., Sept. 11, 1928; s. John and Anna (Sin) B.; m. Eleonora Margaret Buta, Oct. 21, 1950; children— John V., Thomas R., Eleonora M. BA, Eastern Mich. U., 1950; M.Ed., Wayne State U., 1957, Ed.D., 1962. Cert. secondary edn., Mich. Assoc. prof. Wayne State U., Detroit, 1959-63; prof. med. edn. Mich. State U., East Lansing, 1963-73, assoc. dir. med. edn., 1968-70, assoc. dean, 1969-73; founding pres. Okla. Coll. Osteo. Medicine, Tulsa, 1973-86; v.p. health professions and biomed. scis. U.S. Internat. U., San Diego, from 1986. Cons. div. medicine USPHS, 1968—; exchange prof. U.S. Dept. State, 1969; dir. Bank of Okla. S.W. Tulsa Author: (with others) Educational Psychology, 1970; also tech. reports Vice-pres. bd. dirs. Tulsa Philharm. Soc., 1981-84; pres. bd. Tulsa Council on Alcoholism, 1982-84; mem. nat. council Met. Opera, N.Y.C., 1981—; co-dir. Okla. Met. Opera Auditions, Tulsa, 1980— Recipient Commendation award Okla. State Regents for Higher Edn., 1980, John Barson Adminstrn. Bldg. named and dedicated in his honor, 1978 Mem. Am. Assn. Colls. Osteo. Medicine (bd. govs. 1973—, pres. 1984-85), Am. Osteo. Assn. (assoc.) Clubs: Tulsa, Summit (Tulsa). Lodges: Rotary (Tulsa). Avocations: classical music; flying; computer programming; boating. Died Feb. 17, 2006.

BARTHOLOMEW, GEORGE ADELBERT, retired biology educator; b. Independence, Mo., June 1, 1919; s. George A. and Esther Orpha (Carstensen) B.; m. Elizabeth Burnham, Nov. 7, 1942; children— Karen, Bruce AB, U. Calif., Berkeley, 1940, MA, 1941; PhD, Harvard U., 1947; DSc, U. Chgo., 1987. From instr. to prof. dept. biology UCLA, 1947-87. Contbr. more than 150 papers on behavior and physiology to profl. publs. Mem. Am. Acad. Arts and Scis., Nat. Acad. Scis. Home: Greenbrae, Calif. Died Oct. 2, 2006.

BARTHOLOMY, JOHN MARTIN, college president; b. May 13, 1935; m. Mary Jo McCabe; children: Lezlee, Matthew, Andrew. Grad., USAF SAC Leadership Sch., 1956; BS, Western Mich. U., 1962, MA, 1963; PhD, Ohio U., 1969. Mem. faculty, v.p. univ. services Murray State U., 1974-77; pres. Drury Coll., 1977-80, William Woods Coll., Fulton, Mo., from 1980. Named Outstanding Instr. Ohio U., 1968 Mem. Am. Speech and Hearing Assn., Speech Communications Assn. Died Nov. 9, 2006.

BARTLETT, GORDON E., state legislator; b. Springfield, Mass., Apr. 24, 1926; m. Martha Bartlett; 1 child. BS, Babson Coll., 1950. Exec. dir. Rep. State Com., 1975-78; N.H. state rep. Dist. 6, from 1991; mem. transp. com. N.H. Ho. of Reps. Mem. N.H. Police Assn. (assoc.), Gilford Police Relief Assn. Died Sept. 8, 2006.

BARTLETT, RICHMOND JAY, soil chemistry educator, researcher; b. Columbus, Ohio, Sept. 23, 1927; s. Claude Jay and Cecil Jane (Richmond) R.; m. Martha Louise Harry, Feb. 16, 1952 (dec. Apr. 1987); children: Amy, Anne, Ellen, Samuel. BA, Ohio State U., 1949, PhD, 1958. Newspaper reporter, Indpls. and Columbus, 1950-52; promotional writer Peoria (Ill.) and Columbus, 1952-55; asst. soils sect. Ohio State U., Columbus, 1955-58; from asst. prof. to assoc. prof. U. Vt., Burlington, 1958-67, prof. soil chemistry, 1967-97, prof. emeritus, from 1997. Cons. chemistry environmental soil, water and plant nutrition. Contbr. articles to profl. jours., 1958—. Sgt. U.S. Army, 1946-48 Japan. Fellow AAAS, Am. Soc. Agronomy, Soil Sci. Soc. Am.; mem. Internat. Soil Sci. Soc., Phi Beta Kappa, Sigma Xi, Gamma Sigma Delta, Phi Lambda Upsilon. Progressive. Home: Silver Spring, Md. Died Dec. 20, 2005.

BARTON, LARRY K., city manager; b. Kansas City, Mo., Dec. 7, 1934; BS in Acctg., U. Mo., 1956; postgrad. in mgmt. devel., Harvard, 1970; MBA, Auburn U., 1974. Commd. USAF; advanced through grades to col.; fighter pilot; vice-comdr. Weapons Ctr. Nellis AFB; dep. city mgr. City of Las Vegas, city mgr., from 1993. Died Jan. 30, 2007.

BARUH, MORTON GOLDMAN, liquor company executive; b. San Francisco, Mar. 15, 1923; s. Harold F. and Doris (Goldman) B.; m. Marilyn Felix, Aug. 10, 1944; children: Barry F., Terye Baruh Levy, Randie (dec.). Student, Marin Jr. Coll., 1940-41, San Francisco Inst. Accountancy, 1941-42. Treas., merchandising mgr. Goldman's Store, Oakland, Calif., 1946-53; treas. Goldman's Hayward, Inc., Calif., 1952-53; v.p. Baruh Liquors, Inc., San Jose, Calif., 1953-60, exec. v.p., 1960-69, pres., 1969-70; v.p. E. Martinoni Co., San Francisco, 1954-69, pres., 1969-79, chmn. bd. dirs., 1979-86; v.p. Goldman's Walnut Creek, Inc and Goldman's Alameda, Inc., 1958-79; pres. James A. Robertson of Wash., Seattle, 1969-79, chmn. bd. dirs.; ptnr. Baruh Spirits Co. Chmn. bd. Am. Constrn. Assocs., Menlo Park, Calif., 1962-64. Bd. dirs. Randie Lynn Baruh Research Found. for Leukemia; nat. bd. trustees Leukemia Soc. Am., 1980-84; pres. No. Calif. chpt. Leukemia Soc., 1984-85. Served with USAAF, 1943-45. Decorated Air medal. Mem. Calif. Wholesale Liquor Distbrs. Assn. (pres. 1969), Calif. Distilled Spirits Rectifiers Assn. (pres. 1973—). Clubs: St. Francis Yacht, Villa Taverna. Lodges: Masons. Died Sept. 30, 2006.

BARZANTI, SERGIO, history and international studies educator; b. Rome, Oct. 4, 1925; came to U.S., 1955, naturalized, 1961; s. Domenico and Pierina (Casadei) B.; m. Gabriele A. Stormer, Oct. 24, 1968 (div. 1973); children— Simonetta, Paul, Mark, Lorenzo. Baccalaureat, Liceo, Rome, 1943; Dr. J., U. Rome, 1947; MA, N.Y. U., 1958, PhD, 1962; postgrad., U. Paris, 1959. Mem. faculty Fairleigh Dickinson U., Rutherford, N.J., from 1963, asst. prof., 1964-67, asso. prof., 1967-75, prof. history and internat. studies, from 1975. Author: The Underdeveloped Areas Within the Common Market, 1965. Fulbright grantee, 1965 Died Oct. 24, 2005.

BARZILAY, ISAAC EISENSTEIN, historian, educator; b. Vilkovishky, Lithuania, USSR, Mar. 15, 1915; came to U.S., 1946; s. Simon Eisenstein and Taube (Rosenthal) B.; m. Helly Frost, Sept. 20, 1949; children— Joshua Israel, Sharonah Barzilay Graff. MA, Hebrew U., Jerusalem, 1940; PhD, Columbia U., 1955; DHL (hon.), Jewish Theol. Sem., NYC, 1981. Instr. Herzliyah Tchrs. Sem., NYC, 1947-58; instr. Bklyn. and Queens Coll., NYC, 1955-56; asst. prof. Wayne State U., Detroit, 1957-59; assoc. prof. Columbia U., NYC, 1959-67, prof. Hebrew Lit. and Jewish History, 1967-87, prof. emeritus, 1987. Mem. editorial bd. Hadoar Hebrew Weekly, 1979-86, Hebrew Ann. Rev., Ohio State U., 1978-86, Jewish Social Studies, N.Y.C., 1983—; editor Proc. of Am. Acad. Jewish Research, N.Y.C., 1975-88; author books; contbr. articles to profl. jours. Fellow Am. Acad. Jewish Research (pres. 1982-88) Democrat. Home: New York, NY. Died Apr. 15, 2006.

BASFORD, ROBERT EUGENE, retired biochemistry educator, researcher; b. Montpelier, ND, Aug. 21, 1923; s. Eugene M. and Bertha (Cudworth) B.; m. Carol Kaufman Phebus, Dec. 23, 1965; 1 child, Lee A. Phebus BS, U. Wash., 1951, PhD, 1954. Postdoctoral fellow U. Wis.-Madison, 1954-58; asst. prof. U. Pitts., 1958-63, assoc. prof., 1963-70, prof., 1970-93, prof. emeritus, from 1993. Cons. Mine Safety Appliance Co., Pitts., 1966-69; mem. neurol. scis. study sect. NIH, Washington, 1977-80. Home: Fountaintown, Ind. Died Mar. 11, 2007.

BASOLO, FRED, retired chemistry professor; b. Coello, Ill., Feb. 11, 1920; s. John and Catherine (Marino) Basolo; m. Mary P. Nutley, June 14, 1947; children: Mary Catherine, Freddie, Margaret-Ann, Elizabeth Rose. BE, So. Ill. U., 1940, DSc (hon.), 1984; MS, U. Ill., 1942, PhD in Inorganic Chemistry, 1943; LLD (hon.), U. Turin, 1988; Laurea Honoris Causa (hon.), U. Palermo, Italy, 1997. Rsch. chemist Rohm & Haas Chem. Co., Phila., 1943—46; mem. faculty Northwestern U., Evanston, Ill., from 1946, prof. chemistry, from 1958, Morrison prof. chemistry, 1980—90, chmn. dept. chemistry, 1969—72; Charles E. and Emma H. Morrison prof. emeritus Nortwestern U., Evanston, Ill., 1990—2007. Guest lectr. NSF summer insts.; chmn. bd. trustees Gordon Rsch. Conf., 1976; pres. Inorganic Syntheses, Inc., 1977—81; mem. bd. chem. scis. and tech. NRC-NAS; adv. bd. Who's Who in Am., 1983; cons. in field. Co-author (with Ralph G. Pearson): (books) Mechanisms of Inorganic Reactions, A Study of Metal Complexes in Solution, 1958, 1967; co-author: (with Ronald C. Johnson) Coordination Chemistry, 1964; co-author: (with John L. Burmeister) On Being Well-Coordinated, A Half Century of Research on Transition Metal Complexes, 2002; author: (autobiography) From Coello to Inorganic Chemistry, A Lifetime of Reactions, 2002. Recipient Ballar medal, 1972, So. Ill. U. Alumni Achievement award, 1974, Dwyer medal, 1976, James Flack Norris award for Outstanding Achievement in Tchg. of Chemistry, 1981, Oesper Meml. award, 1983, IX Century medal, Bologna U., 1988, Mosher award, 1990, Padova U. medal, 1991, Distinction Bicentenaria medal, Univ. Los Andes, Merida, 1991, Chinese Chem. Soc. medal, 1991, G.C. Pimental award, 1992, Humboldt Sr. US Scientist award, 1992, Gold medal, Am. Inst. Chemists, 1993, Joseph Chatt medal, Royal Soc. Chemistry, 1996, Inauguration mem. Hall of Fame, Chem. Dept. So. Ill. U., 1996, SIU Obelisk Leadership award, 2000; fellow Guggenheim, 1954—55, NSF, 1961—62, NATO sr. scientist, Italy, 1981. Fellow: AAAS (chmn. chemistry sect. 1979), NAS, Am. Acad. Arts and Scis.; mem.: Am. Inst. Chemists, Nat. Acad. Lincei (Italy), Italian Chem. Soc. (hon.), Royal Soc. Chemistry (Joseph Chatt medal 1996), Am. Chem. Soc. (assoc. editor jour. 1961—64, chmn. divsn. inorganic chemistry 1970, pres. 1983, bd. dirs. 1982—84, award for rsch. in inorganic chemistry 1964, N.E. regional award 1971, Disting. Svc. award in inorganic chemistry 1975, award in chem. edn. 1992, Chem. Pioneer award 1992, Gold medal 1993, Josiah Willard Gibbs medal 1996, Priestly Medal 2001), Sigma Xi (Monie A. Ferst medal 1992), Kappa Delta Phi, Phi Kappa Phi, Alpha Chi Sigma, Phi Lambda Upsilon, Phi Lambda Theta (hon.). Home: Glenview, Ill. Died Feb. 27, 2007.

BASS, JOHN F., state senator; b. St. Louis, July 18, 1926; s. Dee and Alma (Brown) B.; m. Frieda Whitmore, Mar. 20, 1946; 1 child, Jill Triplett. B.B.A., Lincoln U., 1959; M.A., Washington U., St. Louis, 1962, also postgrad. Comptroller, City of St. Louis, 1973-77; mem. St. Louis Bd. Aldermen, 1978-79; dir. Mo. Dept. Transp., 1979-81; mem. Mo. State Senate, 1981—. Mem. rules com. Democratic Nat. Conv., 1980; sec.-treas. Nat. Black Caucus of Local Elected Ofcls., 1975-77; del. Democratic Nat. Conv., 1976, 84; mem. adv. council St. Louis Mcpl. Employment Pension Bd., St. Louis Agy. on Tng. and Employment, St. Louis Pub. Schs. Vocat. Tech. Edn.; mem. adv. bd. Mathews-Dickey Boys Club; social human resources advisor Cardinal Ritter. Bd. dirs. Mo. Mcpl. League, St. Louis Police Pension Bd.; trustee Parson Blewett Found. Served with USNR, 1944-46. Mem. NAACP, St. Louis Ambassadors, Urban League, Mcpl. Fin. Officers. Assn., Am. Legion, Lincoln Univ. Found. Democrat. Roman Catholic. Clubs: Royal Vagabonds, Anniversary. Died Feb. 25, 2007.

BASS, RAY DEAN, state highway director, engineer consultant; b. Slocomb, Ala., Dec. 19, 1933; s. Alexander Bell and Ellie (Warr) B.; m. Clara Nell Smith, Dec. 21, 1957; children: Elizabeth, Thomas, Joan. B.C.E., Auburn U., 1959. Registered profl. engr. County engr.; contractor W. O. Smith Constrn. Co., Montgomery, Ala., 1965-67; county engr. Montgomery County (Ala.), 1967-71; state hwy. dir. Ala. Hwy. Dept., Montgomery, 1971-79, 83—; cons., engr. Monn-Bass, Inc., Tuscaloosa, Ala., 1981-83. Served with U.S. Navy, 1951-54. Mem. Am. Soc. Profl. Engrs., Nat. Assn. County Engrs. Democrat. Methodist. Home: Montgomery, Ala. Died Mar. 22, 2007.

BASSETT, WOODSON WILLIAM, JR., lawyer; b. Okmulgee, Okla., Nov. 7, 1926; s. Woodson William and Bee Irene (Knerr) B.; m. Marynm Shaw, Dec. 16, 1950; children: Woodson William III, Beverly M., Tod Corbett. JD, U. Ark., 1949. Bar: Ark. 1949. Employed in New Orleans and Monroe, La., 1949-51; claims examiner Employers Group Ins. Cos., 1949-51; mgr. Light Adjustment Co., 1951-56; v.p. legal dept. Preferred Ins. Cos., 1957-62; sr. partner Bassett Law Firm, from 1962. Spl. chief justice Ark. Supreme Ct., 1991—; mem. Ark. Bd. Law Examiners Mem. editorial staff: Ark. Law Review, 9. Pres. Sherman Lollar Boys Baseball League, 1962; v.p. Babe Ruth Baseball Assn., 1968; chmn. bd. dirs. Fayetteville Public Library, 1975-79. Served with AUS, 1950-51. Fellow Am. Coll. Trial Lawyers; mem. ABA, Ark. Bar Assn., Washington County Bar Assn. (pres. 1973-74), Am. Bd. Trial Advs., Delta Theta Phi, Kappa Sigma. Home: Fayetteville, Ark. Died Jan. 10, 2006.

BASTEDO, HELEN WILMERDING, civic worker; b. N.Y.C., Jan. 5, 1917; d. Lucius and Helen (Cutting) Wilmerding; ed. pvt. sch.; m. Philip Bastedo, Feb. 4, 1937; children— Russell, Bayard, Cecily, Christopher. Active Planned Parenthood of Manhattan, Bronx, 1937-66, chmn. 1952-55; active Planned Parenthood N.Y.C., 1966—; chmn. fund raising com. Planned Parenthood Fedn. Am., 1952-53, vice chmn., 1968-71; mem. Women's Aux. Union Settlement, 1939-58; mem. Women's bd. Women's Hosp., 1954-58; vice chmn. Women's com. Lincoln Center for Performing Arts, 1958-63, co-chmn. seat endowment com. 1960-63; mem. Assn. Vol. Sterilization, 1951-73. Episcopalian. Club: Cosmopolitan. Died Apr. 27, 2006.

BATES, JOSEPH CLARK, aluminum company executive; b. Sparta, Ill., June 26, 1920; s. Joseph C. and Anna Ella (Reinhardt) B.; m. Millicent Anne Simonds, June 28, 1947; children: Jan M. Wheeler, Joseph C. III, Maya A. Roderick, Leslie K., Robert W. BS in Mech. Engring, U. So. Calif., 1943; post., MIT, 1945-46. With Bates Engring. Co., Newhard Cook, 1946-61; v.p., gen. mgr. Aluminum Container Corp., St. Louis, 1961-65; works mgr. Aluminum Co. Am., Richmond, Ind., 1966-68; mng. dir. Alcoa Australia Ltd., Melbourne, 1968-71; gen. mgr. diversified products Aluminum Co. Am., Pitts., 1975-76, v.p. internat., 1976-78, exec. v.p. internat., 1978-82, exec. v.p. allied products, 1982-84; v.p. tech. Allegheny Internat., Pitts., 1985-86. Cons. Mitsubishi Internat. Corp.; dir. Pitts. Des Moines Corp., C-Cor Electronics Inc. Served with submarines USN, 1941-45. Decorated Silver Star. Mem. ASME. Clubs: Allegheny Country, Duquesne, Harvard-Yale-Princeton, Rolling Rock. Republican. Presbyterian. Home: Sewickley, Pa. Died Nov. 18, 2005.

BATSON, LARRY FLOYD, author; b. Aguilar, Colo., Feb. 17, 1930; s. Ernest C. and Myrtle Mae (Diskin) B.; m. Laurel A. Larson, Apr. 19, 1951; children— Ernest, William, James. Student, U. Nebr. Reporter, news broadcaster, editor Star Herald, Scottsbluff, Nebr.; asst. mng. editor Omaha World Herald; news and sports editor Mpls. Tribune, also columnist and nat. corr. Contbr. articles to mags.; works include The Hills Are Theirs. Served with USAF, 1950. Mem. Sigma Delta Chi. Home: Minneapolis, Minn. Died Jan. 30, 2006.

BAUER, ROBERT PAUL, financial executive; b. Cin., Oct. 19, 1920; s. Elmer John and Ione (Koehne) B.; m. Alice M. Miller, Sept. 23, 1944; children: Barbara Jo, Peggy Lou, Gus. BBA, U. Cin., 1949. CPA, Ohio. Pub. acct. Haskins & Sells, CPAs, Cin., 1947-51; div. contr. Baldwin-Lima-Hamilton Corp., Lima, Ohio, 1951-57, gen. contr. exec. office Phila., 1957-61; treas., contr. Cessna Aircraft Co., 1961-67, v.p., treas., 1967-69, sr. v.p., 1969-82. Chmn. bd. Firm One Securities Inc., 1982—; bd. dirs., chmn. Cessna Fin. Co., Cessna Fluid Power Ltd., Scotland; pres., chmn. Cessna Internat. Fin. Corp. Named Outstanding Young Man of Yr., Lima, 1956. Mem. AICPA. Home: Mcallen, Tex. Died June 2, 2007.

BAUGH, JOHN FRANK, retired wholesale company executive; b. Waco, Tex., Feb. 28, 1916; s. John Frank and Nell (Turner) B.; m. Eula Mae Tharp, Oct. 3, 1936; 1 child, Barbara. Student, U. Houston, 1934-36. With A & P Food Stores, Houston, 1932-46; owner, operator Zero Foods Co., Houston, 1946-69; with Sysco Corp., Houston, 1969-98, chmn. bd., 1969-85, sr. chmn. bd., 1986-98, ret., 1998. Bd. dirs. Bank of Houston Founding trustee Houston Bapt. U.; chmn. deacons Bapt. Ch., Houston, 1954-55, chmn. bd. trustees, 1966-86; trustee, bd. regents Baylor U. Mem. Lakeside Country Club. Home: Houston, Tex. Died Mar. 5, 2007.

BAUMAN, JEROME ALAN, lawyer; b. NYC, July 7, 1931; s. Melville J. and Tillie (Cohn) B.; m. Esme Pamela Joseph, July 4, 1966; children— David Meredith, Oren Reid. BS in Chemistry, Queens Coll., 1953; LL.B. cum laude, Harvard U., 1958. Bar: N.Y. bar 1959, Fla. bar 1971. Asso. counsel firm Levin, Rosmarin & Schwartz, NYC, 1958-62, Sperry, Weinberg & Cutler, NYC, 1962-64; gen. counsel Inland Credit Corp., NYC, 1964-66; assoc. counsel firm Golenbock & Barell, NYC, 1966-68; assoc. counsel GAC Corp., Allentown, Pa., Miami, Fla., 1968-72; v.p., gen. counsel GAC Properties, Inc., Miami, 1970-72, Gulfstream Land & Devel. Corp., Plantation, Fla., 1972-78; ptnr. Bauman, Wurtenberger & Schottenfeld, 1979-90; pvt. practice law Plantation, from 1990. Pres. Plantation Jewish Congregation, 1975-79; mem. campaign cabinet Fedn. Jewish Philanthropies New York N.L.D., 1963-65. Served with U.S. Army, 1953-55. Mem. N.Y., Fla. bar assns. Home: Fort Lauderdale, Fla. Died May 10, 2007.

BAUMAN, ROGER ALAN, radiologist; b. West Bend, Wis., May 28, 1937; s. Howard Albert and Elizabeth Edmunds (Wolff) B.; m. Margaret Lang, May 11, 1968; children: Karen Lang, Margaret Sprague, David Westcott. Diplomate Am. Bd. Radiology, Am. Bd. Nuclear Medicine. Commd. med. officer USPHS, 1962, advanced through grades to sr. surgeon, intern Seattle, 1962-63, med. officer USC & GSS Pioneer, 1963, med. officer USCG Air Sta. Annette, Alaska, 1963-65, dir. Alaska Native Health Clinic Metlakatla, Alaska, 1963-65; resident in radiology Balt. USPHS Hosp., 1965-68, chief nuclear medicine, staff radiologist, 1968-69; clin. fellow in radiology Mass. Gen. Hosp., Boston, 1969-70, staff Lab. Computer Sci., 1969-72, clin. asst. radiology, 1970-72, clin. assoc. radiology, 1972-74, asst. dir. radiology Lab. Computer Sci., 1972-78, asst. radiologist-in-chief, 1974-85, assoc. radiologist, 1975-77, radiologist, from 1978, assoc. radiologist-in-chief, from 1985, dir. radiology digital imaging group, 1985-91. Clin. instr. radiology Harvard Med. Sch., 1971-74, instr. radiology, 1975-76, asst. prof. radiology, 1976-85, assoc. prof. radiology, 1985—; observer nuclear medicine Johns Hopkins Hosp., 1969, NIH Clin. Ctr., 1989; radiologist Bur. Radiol. Health, 1969-74; mem. standing com. internat. symposium Planning of Radiology Depts., 1986-92; lectr., instr. confs., soc., symposia worldwide. Editor-in-chief Jour. Digital Imaging, 1987—; mem. editorial bd. European Jour. Radiology, PACS and Digital Radiology, 1993—; contbr. articles to profl. jours., abstracts. Chmn. Town of Winchester Sch. Com., 1980-82, mem. capital planning com., 1978-82, mem. sch. com., 1978-84, mem. com. on names, 1981-83, chmn. 1983-84, mem. housing partnership bd., 1989—, mem. com. govtl. regulations, 1991—; chmn. subcom. srs. housing First Congregl. Ch. of Winchester, 1986—; mem. Winchester Town Meeting, 1979—; mem. ancillary task force Joint Mass. Blue Shield/Mass. Hosp. Assn., 1981-84. Fellow Am. Coll. Radiology (computer divsn. 1970-75, computer info sys. com. 1970-73, chmn. computer assisted instrn. and diagnosis com. 1971-75, computer sys. in clin. practice com. 1973-75, computers com. 1975-89, 92—, computer of commn. on edn. 1981, 92—, systematized refresher courses com. 1988-91), Am. Coll. Med. Informatics; mem. IEEE, AMA, AAAS, Assn. Computing Machinery, Soc. Nuclear Medicine, Radiol. Soc. N.Am., Mass. Radiol. Soc. (adv. com. to dept. pub. health 1977-79, chmn. 1979—), Am. Coll. Physician Execs., Am. Inst. Ultrasound in Medicine, Mass. Med. Soc., Am. Coll. Nuclear Physicians, Am. Roentgen Ray Soc., Am. Coll. Nuclear Physicians,, Internat. Soc. Optical Engring., Soc. Computer Applications in Radiology (dir. 1988—), New Eng. Roentgen Ray Soc., Commd. Officer's Assn. USPHS. Mem. United Ch. of Christ. Avocations: genealogy, photography, model railroading. Home: Winchester, Mass. Died Nov. 1, 2005.

BAUMEL, JULIAN JOSEPH, anatomy educator; b. Sanford, Fla., July 26, 1922; s. Samuel S. and Sadye (Zelmenovitz) B.; m. Lenora Golipsky, July 1945 (dec. 1969); children: Robert, Dinah, Felicia; m. Mary B. Laya, Aug. 1983. BS, U. Fla., 1947, MS, 1950, PhD, 1953. Instr. U. Fla., Gainesville, 1952-53, Creighton U., Omaha, 1953-56, ast. prof., 1956-60, assoc. prof., 1960-64, prof. anatomy, 1964-95, prof. emeritus, from 1995; vis. scholar U. Wash., Seattle, from 1993. Author, editor: Nomina Anatomica Avium, 1970, Handbook of Avian Anatomy, 1993; contbr. articles to profl. jours. With U.S. Army, 1942-45. Mem. Am. Assn. Anatomists, Internat. Com. Avian Anatomical Nomenclatur(gen. chmn. 1964—), World Assn. Vet. Anatomists, Am. Ornithologists Union, Am. Soc. Zoologists, Assn. Avian Veterinarians. Home: Seattle, Wash. Died Jan. 25, 2006.

BAUMLER, JEAN ANN, nurse; b. West Union, Iowa, Apr. 22, 1951; d. Melvin John and Rita Theresa (Lansing) Baumler; B.S.N., Viterbo Coll., LaCrosse, Wis., 1973; M.S., San Jose (Calif.) State U., 1980. RN, Hawaii; cert. gerontol. nurse., ANCC, gerontol. nurse practitioner, San Jose State U., arthritis self-help instr. Arthritis Found., Health supr. Camp Ehawee Scout Camp, LaCrosse, 1973; staff nurse, then asst. head nurse Letterman Army Med. Ctr., San Francisco, 1972-75; charge nurse Palo Alto (Calif.) VA Hosp., 1975-83, mem. inservice com. Extended Care Service, 1981-83; adult day health program coordinator Kuakini Med. Ctr., Honolulu, 1983-87, mem. various coms. 1984-87; quality assurance nurse analyst, Straub Clinic & Hosp., Honolulu, 1987-88, dir. nursing svcs. Laniolu Good Samaritan Ctr., 1988-91, on-call case mgmt., nurse cons. Community Long Term Care Svcs., 1987-91, on-call nurse Hospice Hawaii, 1991—. Treas. Fair Oaks 90 Homeowners Assn., 1980-83. Served with Nurse Corps, U.S. Army, 1972-75. Recipient Incentive award VA, 1978, Components Achievement medal USAR, 1981, First Lady's Outstanding Vol. award Hawaii, 1987. Mem. Geront. Soc. Am. (student rep. to biol. sci. sect. 1980), Hawaii Pacific Gerontol. Soc., Alzheimer's Disease & Related Disorders Assn. (founding mem., cons. San Jose and Menlo Pk, Calif. chpts. 1982-83, bd. dirs. Honolulu chpt., 1984-91, also chair edn. and pub. com. 1984-91, long term care com. 1987-92). Contbr. articles to profl. jours.; author book revs. and brochure. Died July 18, 2006.

BAUSCH, JAMES JOHN, foundation executive; b. New Brunswick, NJ, May 1, 1936; s. Charles John and Colette (Perdoni) B.; m. Janet Ellen Safer, May 22, 1970; children: Jennifer, David. Student, Fordham U., 1953-54; BS, St. Peter's Coll., 1955-58; postgrad., Emory U., 1958-61, Wharton Sch., U. Pa., 1977. Lectr. in social sci. Emory U., Ga. Inst. Tech., Atlanta, 1958-61; vol. U.S. Peace Corps, Bangladesh, 1961-63; chief U.S. Peace Corps South Asia div., Washington, 1965-69; dir. tng. Experiment in Internat. Living, Brattleboro, Vt., 1963-64; dir. edn. Coun. on Internat. Ednl. Exch., NYC, 1964-65; program officer Ford Found., NYC, 1969-71, 73-76, rep. Jakarta, Indonesia, 1971-73; v.p., sec. The Population Coun., NYC, 1976-88; pres. Save the Children Fedn., Westport, Conn., 1988-92; vice chmn. A.T. Hudson & Co., Oradell, N.J., 1992-94; pres. J.J. Bausch Cons. Svcs., River Vale, N.J., 1992-94, Nat. Charities Info. Bur., NYC, 1994-99; cons. in philanthropy, from 1999. Trustee, mem. exec. com., chmn. fin. com., chmn. investment com., co-chmn. N.Y. Assocs. World Learning, Inc., Brattleboro, Vt., 1980-88; trustee, sec.-treas. Internat. Child Health Found., Columbia, Md., 1985-87, chmn. bd. trustees, 1987-94; mem. fin. com. Population Coun. 1976-88; trustee Ctr. Pvt. Vol. Orgns./Univ. Collaboration, N.C., 1990-92, Ind. Sector, Washington, 1991-93. Chmn. UNICEF Action for Children, NYC, 1985—89; mem. Bretton Woods Com., Washington, from 1991; chmn. bd. advisors U. South Fla. Sr. Acad., from 2003; trustee Selby Bot. Gardens, from 2001, sec. bd. trustees, 2002—03. Mem. N.Y. Acad. Scis., Population Assn. Am., Am. Pub. Health Assn., Nat. Coun. Internat. Health (mem. exec. com. 1991-92), Carnegie Coun. on Ethics and Internat. Affairs, Nat. Peace Corps Assn. Democrat. Home: Sarasota, Fla. Died July 13, 2006.

BEACH, MORRISON HOWARD, insurance company executive; b. Winsted, Conn., Jan. 10, 1917; s. Howard Edmund and Edith (Morrison) Beach; m. Evelyn R. Harris, Sept. 6, 1942; children: Howard, Linda, Deborah. BA magna cum laude, Williams Coll., 1939; postgrad., MIT, 1942; JD, U. Conn., 1954; PhD (hon.), U. Hartford, Thiel Coll. Bar: Conn. With Travelers Corp., Hartford, Conn., 1939, asst. actuary, 1950—54, assoc. actuary, 1954—57, actuary, 1957—59, v.p., actuary, 1959—62, 2d v.p, 1962—64, v.p., 1964—65, sr. v.p., 1965—70, exec. v.p., 1970—71, pres., chief adminstrv. officer, 1971—73, chmn-.,CEO, 1973—82, chmn. exec. com., 1982—87, also dir. Dir. numerous Travelers subs.; mem. Conn. Natural Gas Corp.; participant White House Conf. on Aging, 1981. Mem. nat. adv. com. Nat. Multiple Sclerosis Soc.; chmn. Conn. Higher Edn. Loan Authority, 1982—87; trustee Horace Bushnell Meml. Hall Corp.; corporator Hartford Sem. Found, Inst. of Living, Winsted Meml. Hosp.; bd. dirs. Hartford Hosp., Greater Hartford chpt. ARC, Hartford YMCA, Old State House Corp. Maj. USAF, ETO. Recipient Corp. Leadership award; MIT. Fellow Soc. Actuaries. Mem.: Conn. Conf. Bd. Home: West Hartford, Conn. Died Dec. 5, 2006.

BEACH, ROBERT PRESTON, accountant, fraternal organization executive; b. Portland, Oreg., Jan. 29, 1916; s. Henry Edward and Olga Ruth (Lindblad) B.; m. Barbara Frances Harvey, July 12, 1941; 1 dau., Barbara Anne Beach Meek. BS, U. Calif., Berkeley, 1938; MBA, Harvard U., 1940. CPA, Mass. Acct. Coopers & Lybrand, Boston, 1940-42, 46-53; sec. corp. Brown & Sharpe Mfg. Co., Providence, 1953-55; bus. mgr. Metcalf & Eddy, Boston, 1956-60; prof. practice acctg. Boston, from 1961. Corporator First Am. Bank for Savs., Boston, 1974-86; guest lectr. Boston U., 1966-67. Treas. Rep. Town Com., Natick, Mass., 1948-53; clk. First Congl. Ch. in Wellesley Hills (Mass.), 1967-72; mem. corp. New Eng. Bapt. Hosp. Corp., Boston, 1964—; trustee Leonard Morse Hosp., Natick, 1950-53. Lt. comdr. USN, 1942-46, PTO. Fellow AICPA, Mass. Soc. CPAs (various coms.); mem. SAR (treas. Mass. chpt. 1975-77, 94-95), Conf. Grand Secs. in N.Am. (sec.-treas. 1976-85, pres. 1985-86), Harvard Club, Masons (editor publs. 1966-88, grand sec. 1968-88, 33d degree, D.S.M. and Henry Price medals 1963, 66, Philip C. Tucker medal 1983, past presiding officer many orgns., trustee Masonic Edn. and Charity Trust 1982-89), Beta Alpha Psi. Died Mar. 9, 2007.

BEACH, WALTER EGGERT, retired publishing organization executive; b. North Adams, Mass., Aug. 24, 1934; s. W. Edwards and Liselotte Josephine Sophie (von Usedom) B. BA, Dickinson Coll., 1956; MA, George Washington U., 1961. Staff assoc., asst. dir. Am. Polit. Sci. Assn., Washington, 1965-80; sr. staff mem. Brookings Instn., Washington, 1980-90; dir. Heldref Publs. Helen Dwight Reid Ednl. Found., Washington, 1990-97. Treas. D.C. Dem. Party, 1981-84; mem. adv. bd. Hubert H. Humphrey Inst. Pub. Affairs, U. Minn., Mpls., 1990-99; trustee Dickinson Coll., 1984—, Mt. Vernon Coll., 1971-97, Helen Dwight Reid Ednl. Found., 1982—; pres. Internat. Eye Found., 1993-95; bd. dirs. Hillwood Mus. and Gardens, 2001—; mem., bd. dirs. various polit. coms. With U.S. Army, 1956-58. Recipient Disting. Alumni award Dickinson Coll., 1991. Mem. Internat. Polit. Sci. Assn., Am. Polit. Sci. Assn. (Frank Goodnow award 1998), Ctr. Study Presidency, Hist. Soc. D.C., Midwest Polit. Sci. Assn., Nat. Capital Area Polit. Sci. Assn., Policy Studies Orgn., So. Polit. Sci. Assn., UN Assn. Nat. Capital Area, Western Polit. Sci. Assn., Cosmos Club, Pi Sigma Alpha. Democrat. Unitarian Universalist. Home: Washington, DC. Died Nov. 14, 2006.

BEACHELL, HENRY MONROE, agriculturalist; b. Waverly, Neb., Sept. 21, 1906; s. William Albert and Alice Leona (Degler) B.; m. Edna Mary Payne, Sept. 17, 1983. BS in Agr., U. Neb., 1930; MS in Plant Breeding and Genetics, Kans. State U., 1933; postgrad., Tex. A&M U., 1939; PhD Agr. (hon.), Seoul Nat. U., Korea, 1970, U. Neb., 1972. Rice breeder Agr. Research Service U.S. Dept. Agr., Beaumont, Tex., 1931-63, Rockefeller Found. Internat. Rice Research Inst., Los Banos, Philippines, 1963-72; rice breeder, cons. Internat. Rice Research Inst., Bogor, Indonesia, 1972-82, RiceTec, Inc., Alvin, 1982—2006. Cons. Brit. Supply Delegation, George Town, Brit. Guana, 1949, Atomic Energy Agy. UN, Internat. Rice Research Inst., Los Banos, 1983, Winrock Internat., Colombo, Sri Lanka. Breeder numerous types of rice, 1940-81. Recipient Indsl. Service Merit Bronze Tower award, Korea, 1978, Japan prize Sci. and Tech. Found. Japan, 1987, John Scott medal Honor City of Phila., 1969, award Internat. Rice Research Inst. Los Banos, 1972, Disting. Service award Tex. A&M U., 1981, World Food prize, 1996 Fellow AAAS, Am. Soc. Agronomy; mem. Golf Crest Country Club. Republican. Episcopalian. Avocations: golf, travel. Home: Pearland, Tex. Died Dec. 13, 2006.

BEAGHEN, STANTON PEABODY, business executive; b. New Rochelle, N.Y., Dec. 23, 1938; s. George and Augusta (Stanton) B.; m. Katrina X. Hartford, June 9, 1962; children— Peter, Jonathan, Kristin, Jared. Student Colgate U., 1956-60, NYU Grad. Sch. Bus., 1960-62. Exec. trainee Hanover Bank, N.Y.C., 1960-62; sales and product mgr. Drackett Co., Cin., 1965-70; account exec. to sr. v.p. Lewis & Gilman, Phila., 1970-82; from sr. v.p. to exec. v.p. Maher Hartford, Conn., 1982—. Served to lt. USCG, 1962-65. Republican. Presbyterian. Avocations: outdoor sports; music; camping. Home: West Chatham, Mass. Died June 20, 2006.

BEAN, LARRY L., lawyer, partner; b. Salina, Kans., Nov. 19, 1935; s. Lawrence L. and Stella Vivian (Sias) B.; M. Carole Bierdeman Booth, July 1961 (div.); m. Jane Ryan, June 5, 1982; childrem: Scott L., Marla L. BS cum laude, Kans. State U., 1957; JD cum laude, So. Methodist U., 1960. Bar: Tex. Assoc. Jackson & Walker, Dallas, 1961-66; ptnr. Jackson & Walker L.L.P., Dallas, from 1967. Bd. dirs. Larry & Jane Harlan Found., Dallas, Caleum Moor Found., Dallas; chmn. Southwest Legal Found. (taxation divsn.) Dallas, 1970-73. Contbr. articles to profl. jours. Bd. dirs. Dallas Helps Found., 1992—, Dallas Coun.

Alcoholism adn Drug Abuse, 1980-86. 1st Lt. U.S. Army, 1960-67. Mem. ABA (natural resources com., chmn. sect. taxation 1974-76), Tex. Bar Assn., Dallas Bar Assn. (com. chmn. 1986-87). Presbyterian. Avocations: tennis, golf. Died Oct. 15, 2006.

BEAN, VERNALD FLOYD, manufacturing executive; b. Monida, Mont., Aug. 8, 1929; s. Farmer Floyd and Ethel Marie (Blake) B.; m. Patricia Jane Powers, Apr. 24, 1954; children: John J., David J., Thomas E. Student pub. schs. With NCR Corp., from 1952, field engr., 1952-66, dir. field engring. services, 1966-71, ops. mgr. internat. mfg., 1971-75, dir. internat. mfg., 1974-77, v.p. components and support div., 1977-80, v.p. corporate field engring., 1980-83, v.p. customer services, from 1983. Served with U.S. Army, 1947-50. Mem. Dayton C. of C. Clubs: KC. Republican. Roman Catholic. Home: Dayton, Ohio. Died Sept. 3, 2006.

BEAR, CHARLES BENSON, magazine publisher, sports executive; b. Washington, Iowa, Mar. 12, 1919; s. Charles H. and Grace (Benson) B. BA, Grinnell Coll., 1939; MA, Fletcher Sch. Law and Diplomacy, 1940. With Gallup Poll, Am. Inst. Pub. Opinion, Princeton, N.J., 1940-41; adminstrv. asst. Office Govt. Reports, Chgo., 1941-42; bus. mgr. Time-Life Internat., 1945-49, dep. mng. dir., 1960-64, mng. dir., 1965-68; bus. mgr. Fortune mag., 1949-53, assoc. pub., 1953-60; gen. mgr. Archtl. Forum, 1954-60; v.p. internat. Time Inc., 1965-69, adminstrv. v.p., 1969-72; group v.p., sec. 1972-84, dir., 1977-84. Dir. Mktg. and Sales Devel. Corp., Lyndhurst, N.J. Trustee Grinnell Coll.; mem. exec. bd. Support Ctr.; bd. dirs. Friends of Earth Found.; mem. U.S. Olympic Com.; v.p. L.A. Olympic Organizing Com., 1984—; chmn. Maj. League Baseball Properties Corp., 1984-87; trustee Asia Soc., Nat. Arts Stabilization Bd.; bd. dirs. Creative Arts Rehab. Ctr.; bd. dirs. Ethics Resource Ctr., Washington; bd. dirs., treas. The New 42nd St. Inc. Capt. USAAF, 1942-45. Mem. Internat. C. of C. (trustee U.S. council). Baptist. Home: New York, NY. Died June 21, 2007.

BEARD, GEORGE BRECKENRIDGE, physics educator; b. Marblehead, Mass., Feb. 22, 1924; s. Daniel Breed and Anna Louise (Curran) B.; m. Eveline Louise Roehling, Jan. 29, 1955; children: Kevin, William, Glenn, Louisa, Randall. Student, Yale U., 1944; AB, Harvard U., 1947; postgrad., MIT, 1945; MS, U. Mich., 1948, PhD, 1955. Instr. physics Mich. State U., East Lansing, 1954-55, asst. prof., 1955-60; assoc. prof. Wayne State U., Detroit, 1960-65, prof., from 1965, chmn. dept. physics, 1973-77, 80-81, acting chmn. dept. computer sci., 1984-85, assoc. dean Coll. Liberal Arts, 1986. Research appointee dept. nuclear physics U. Mich., Ann Arbor, 1961; resident research asst. Argonne (Ill.) Nat. Lab., summers 1963-65, resident assoc., 1969-70; vis. scholar U. Melbourne, Australia, 1981-82. Co-author: Quantum Mechanics With Applications, 1970; contbr. articles to profl. jours. Served to 1st lt. USAAF, 1943-46. Predoctoral fellow U.S. Atomic Energy Commn., 1951-53; grantee Air Force Office Sci. Research, 1957-60, NSF, 1961-72. Fellow Am. Phys. Soc.; mem. Mich. sect. Am. Assn. Physics Tchrs. Avocations: reading, outdoor activities, handyman repairs. Home: Southfield, Mich. Died Jan. 15, 2007.

BEATON, ROY HOWARD, retired nuclear energy industry executive; b. Boston, Sept. 1, 1916; s. John Howard and Mary (LaVoie) B.; m. Margaret Marchant, July 22, 1939 (dec. Oct. 4, 1978); m. Leora Lauer Schier, June 26, 1982; children: Constance Beaton Fegley, Roy Howard, Patricia Schier Briselden, Susan Schier Craig, Mary Schier Rieber. BS, Northeastern U., 1939, DSc (hon.), 1967; DEng, Yale U., 1942. Registered profl. engr., Wash., Wis., Fla., Calif. With E.I. DuPont, 1942-46, plant tech. supr. Manhattan (Nuclear Bomb) Project, 1943-44; chief chem. devel., chief engr., gen. mgr. constrn. engring. GE, Richland, Wash., 1946-56, gen. mgr. neutron devices dept. Milw., 1957-63; gen. mgr. Apollo Systems, Daytona Beach, Fla., 1964-68; v.p., gen. mgr. def. electronics systems div. GE, Syracuse, NY, 1968-74, v.p., gen. mgr. energy systems and tech. div. Fairfield, Conn., 1974-75; sr. v.p., group exec. Nuclear Energy Group, San Jose, Calif., 1975-81. Chmn. industry div. United Way Campaign, Santa Clara County, Calif., 1978-79. Fellow AAAS, Am. Inst. Chemists; mem. NSPE, Nat. Acad. Engring., Am. Ordnance Assn., Am. Nuclear Soc., Am. Inst. Chem. Engrs., IEEE, AIAA, Navy League U.S., Air Force Assn., Soc. Mil. Engrs., Santa Clara County Mfg. Group, Sigma Xi, Tau Beta Pi Died Jan. 7, 2007.

BEATTIE, NORA MAUREEN, insurance company executive, actuary; b. Bklyn., July 10, 1925; d. Robert G. and Eileen (Geaney) B. BA summa cum laude, St. John's U., 1947, MS, 1949, D.C.S. (hon.), 1983. Asst. actuary N.Y. Life Ins. Co., NYC, 1960-63, asso. actuary, 1963-67, actuary, 1967-71, 2d. v.p., 1971-74, v.p., actuary, 1974-88, ret., 1988. Fellow Am. Acad. Actuaries, Soc. Actuaries; mem. Bus. and Profl. Women's Club (treas. Wall St. Br. 1969-71, Woman of Yr., N.Y. br. 1968), N.Y. Guarantee Assn. (treas. 1981-86) Clubs: N.Y. Actuaries. Home: Short Hills, NJ. Died Apr. 28, 2006.

BEAUBIEN, DAVID JAMES, electronics company executive, consultant; b. Montague, Mass., Sept. 20, 1934; s. Arthur and Helen Agnes (Moreau) B.; m. Mary Ann Robert, Sept. 21, 1957; children: Arthur F., Patricia M., Mark C. BSEE, U. Mass., 1957. Registered profl. engr., Mass. Pres., founder Cambridge Systems, Inc., Newton, Mass., 1959-67; asst. to pres. EG&G, Inc., Bedford, Mass., 1967-77, v.p. Wellesley, Mass., 1977-82, sr. v.p., from 1982. Bd. dirs. Kidder Peabody Family Mut. Funds, N.Y.C. Vice chmn. then chmn. Bd. Regents Pub. Higher Edn., Boston, 1980-88; trustee U. Mass., 1979-80. Recipient Disting. Alumnus award U. Mass., 1983. Mem. Am. Meteorol. Soc., Sigma Xi. Roman Catholic. Home: Montague, Mass. Died Apr. 20, 2007.

BECK, ABE JACK, retired business executive, retired air force officer; b. Dallas, May 24, 1914; s. Jacob S. and Mollie (Pollock) B.; m. Anne Gilaire Michlin, Oct. 21, 1945; children—Stephanie Jo, Melanie Gilaire, Darcy Jane, John Dallas. LL.B., So. Meth. U., 1939. Bar: Tex. bar 1939. Pvt. practice law, Dallas, 1939-40; joined USAAF, 1940; grad. Flying Sch., 1941; commd. 2d lt. USAAF, 1941; advanced through grades to maj. gen. USAF, 1963; tactical officer, engring. officer, also pilot instr. Air Cadet Advanced Flying Sch., Luke Field, Ariz., 1941-42; aide Hdqrs. 5th Air Force, later; operation officer 374th Troop Carrier Group, New Guinea, 1942-43; asst. chief staff A-3, 54th Tactical Wing, New Guinea; also ops. officer Hdqrs. 5th Air Force, New Guinea; and later asst. chief staff A-3, 310th Bomb Wing and chief staff 310th Bomb Wing, SW Pacific, 1943-45; student Command and Gen. Staff Sch., 1945; officer charge classification and assignment br. A-1, Office Records Br., 400th AAFBU, San Francisco, 1946; resigned, 1946-47; re-joined USAF, 1947; staff legal officer, later asst. staff judge adv. Hdqrs. 8th Air Force, Ft. Worth, 1947-48; chief air judge adv. sect., personnel and adminstrn. SAC, Andrews AFB, Md., 1948, chief air judge adv. sect., personnel and adminstrn., also project officer, command sect. Hdqrs. Offutt AFB, Omaha, 1948-52; dep. comdr., then comdr. 3902d Air Base Wing, Offutt AFB, 1952-54; comdr. 340th Bomb Wing, Sedalia AFB, Mo., 1954-57, 4082d Strategic Wing, Goose AFB, Labrador, 1957-59; chief staff, command sect. Hdqrs. 8th Air Force, SAC, Westover AFB, Mass., 1959-61; comdr. 817th Air Div., Pease AFB, N.H., 1961-63; insp. gen. Hdqrs. SAC, Offutt AFB, 1964, dir. materiel, 1964-66; sr. air force mem. weapon systems evaluation group, directorate def. research and engring. Office Sec. Def., 1966-68; comdr. Warner Robins Air Materiel Area, 1968-72; ret., 1972; exec. v.p. Morris Industries, Inc., Omaha, 1972-74; v.p. Zale Corp., Dallas, 1974-78, sr. v.p., 1978-80. Decorated D.S.M., Legion of Merit with 2 oak leaf clusters, D.F.C., Air medal with 3 oak leaf clusters, Air Force Commendation medal; British Mil. Cross (Australia). Home: Dallas, Tex. Died July 2, 2006.

BECK, JAMES HENRY, art historian, educator; b. New Rochelle, NY, May 14, 1930; s. Samuel and Margareth (Weisz) B.; m. Darma Tercinod, Apr. 9, 1956; children: Eleonora M., Lawrence C. BA, Oberlin Coll., 1952; MA, NYU, 1954; PhD, Columbia U., 1963. Asst. prof. U. Ala., Tuscaloosa, 1958-59; asst. prof. Ariz. State U., Tempe, 1959-61; faculty Columbia U., NYC, 1961—2007, prof. art history, 1972—2007, chmn. dept. art history, 1984-90. Vis. assoc. prof. Princeton U., 1970 Author: Marioano di Jacopo detto il Taccola, 'Liber tertius', 1969, Jacopo della Quercia e San Petronio, 1970, Michelangelo: A Lesson in Anatomu, 1975, Raphael, 1976, Masaccio, the documents, 1978, Leonardo's Rules of Painting: An Unconventional Approach to Modern Art, 1979, Italian Renaissance Painting, 1981, The Doors of the Florentine Baptistry, 1985, The Sepulcral Monument for Ilaria del Carretto by Jacopo della Quercia, 1988, 89, Jacopo della Quercia, 2 vols., 1991, The Tyranny of the Detail, 1992, The Culture, the Business and the Scandal, 1993, rev. edit., 1996, Rephael, The Camera della Segnatura, 1993. Recipient grants-in-aid Am. Philos. Soc., 1969, 72, 75; Herodotus fellow Inst. for Advanced Study, Princeton U., 1967; fellow Harvard U. Center for Italian Renaissance Studies, 1967-68, 72; vis. scholar Harvard U. Center for Italian Renaissance Studies, 1983; Guggenheim fellow, 1973-74 Mem. Renaissance Soc. Am., Mediaeval Acad. Am., Coll. Art Assn., Artwatch Internat. (former pres.). Home: New York, NY. Died May 26, 2007.

BECK, ROD (RODNEY ROY BECK), retired professional baseball player; b. Burbank, Calif., Aug. 3, 1968; m. Stacey Beck; 2 children. With Oakland (Calif.) Atheletics, 1986-88; pitcher San Francisco Giants, 1988-98, Chgo. Cubs, 1998-99; relief pitcher Boston Red Sox, 1999—2001, San Diego Padres, 2003—04. Mem. Nat. League All-Star Team, 1993, 94. Died June 23, 2007.

BECKEN, BRADFORD ALBERT, engineering executive; b. Providence, Oct. 5, 1924; s. Albert R. and Ruth M. (Stephenson) B.; m. Gaynelle M. Lane, Nov. 30, 1946; children: Bradford Albert, Brian A., Christian L., Anne Tracey. Student, U. R.I., 1942-43; BS, U.S. Naval Acad., 1946; BS in Electronics, U.S. Naval Postgrad. Sch., 1952; MS, UCLA, 1953, PhD, 1961. Commd. officer USN, advanced through grades to comdr.; cons. Airtronics-Spl. Warfare Lab., 1967; mgr. systems engring. lab. submarine signal div. Raytheon Co., Portsmouth, R.I., 1967-70, mgr. engring., 1970-82, dir. tech. Portsmouth Engring. Lab., 1982-94; cons., 1994—97. Author: Advances in Hydroscience, 1964. Trustee Newport Hosp., 1977, chmn. bd., 1979-84; chmn. bd. dirs. Newport Health Care Corp., 1984-93; treas. Newport Hist. Soc., 1993-94, pres., 1994-2001. Recipient Asst. Chief Bur. Ships award, 1963, Am. Def. Preparedness Assn. Gold medal, 1995, Navy Undersea Warfare Ctr. Decibel award, 1997, Capt. George W. Ringenberg award, 1999. Fellow Acoustical Soc. Am.; mem. Nat. Def. Indsl. Assn., Naval War Coll. Found., U.S. Naval Inst., U.S. Naval Acad. Alumni Assn. Episcopalian. Home: Portsmouth, RI. Died Sept. 22, 2006.

BECKER, GEORGE FRDERICK, retired labor union administrator; b. Granite City, Ill., Oct. 20, 1928; s. George and Frances Becker; m. Jane Goforth; children: Gregory, Matthew, George. Staff rep. United Steelworkers of Am., Ill., 1965-75, safety and health technician Pitts., 1975-85, internat. v.p. adminstrn., 1985-94, internat. pres., 1994—2001. V.p. exec. coun., chmn. econ. policy com. AFL-CIO; mem. exec. com. Internat. Metalworkers Fedn., Geneva; chmn. world rubber coun. Internat. Fedn. Chem., Energy, Mine and Gen. Workers' Unions, Brussels; apptd. by Pres. Clinton to Pres.'s Export Coun.; confirmed by congress to U.S. Trade and Environ. Policy Adv. Com., Washington. Served in USMC, 1946—48, served in US Army, 1950—56. Died Feb. 3, 2007.

BECKHAM, WILLIAM ARTHUR, bishop; b. Columbia, S.C., Apr. 29, 1927; s. Francis Morgan and Maud Elizabeth (Guthrie) B.; m. Harriet Louise Wingate, Dec. 17, 1948. B.S., U. S.C., 1951; M.Div., Va. Theol. Sem., 1954, D.D. (hon.), 1980; D.D. (hon.), U. of South, 1985; D.H.L. (hon.), U. S.C., 1989; DL (hon.) St. Augustine's Coll., 1994. Ordained to ministry Episcopal Ch. Rector, Trinity Edgefield, S.C., 1954; asst. sec. Conv. of Our Savior Ch., Trenton, S.C., 1954-57; priest-in-charge Union & Calvary, Glenn Springs, 1957-58; rector, Resurrection, Greenwood, S.C., 1958-64; archdeacon Upper S.C., 1964-79; bishop of Upper S.C., 1979—; mem. Ch. Pension Fund and Affiliates Bd., chmn. 1991—. Trustee U. of South, 1963-69, 79—, Voorhees Coll., 1979—. Died Dec. 24, 2005.

BECKMAN, JOSEPH ALFRED, research and development administrator; b. Macomb, Ill., Oct. 30, 1937; s. Alfred Jacob and Mary Jeanette (Botts) B.; m. Peggy Ann Miller, Feb. 1, 1938; children: Bruce, Jill. AB in Chemistry, Western Ill. U., 1960; PhD in Organic Chemistry, Iowa State U., 1965. Various research positions The Firestone Tire & Rubber Co., Akron, Ohio, 1964-74, mgr. elastomer research, 1974-80, asst. dir. research, 1980-87; v.p. research & devel. DSM Copolymer, Inc., Baton Rouge, from 1987. Mem. Indsl. Rsch. Adv. Com. La. Bd. Regents, Baton Rouge, 1989-91, Indsl. Adv. Com. Adv. Com. Dept. Polymer Sci., U. So. Miss., Hattiesburg, 1989-93. Patentee in field. Mem. Am. Chem. Soc., Akron Rubber Group. Republican. Avocations: gardening, golf, woodworking, reading, tropical fish. Home: Baton Rouge, La. Died Dec. 22, 2005.

BEDELL, GEORGE NOBLE, internist, educator; b. Harrisburg, Pa., May 1, 1922; s. George Harold and Elsie Clair (Noble) B.; m. Betty Jane Goldzier, Nov. 4, 1950 (dec. Mar. 1970); children: David, Mark, Barbara, Bruce; m. Mirriel Shields Hummel, Oct. 17, 1970; step-children: Judy, Jeffrey, Eric, Deborah, Andrew. BA, DePauw U., 1944; MD, U. Cin., 1946. Intern U. Iowa, 1946-47, resident in pathology, 1947-48, resident in internal medicine, 1950-52, research fellow in internal medicine, specializing in cardiology, 1952-54; research fellow physiology Postgrad. Sch. Medicine, U., Pa., 1954-55; asst. prof. dept. medicine Coll. Medicine, U. Iowa, 1955-59, asso. prof. dept. medicine, 1959-68, prof., from 1968; dir. Pulmonary Disease div. Dept. Medicine, 1968-81. Cons. VA Hosp., Iowa City, 1954—; mem. staff U. Hosps., Iowa City Contbr. articles to profl. jours. Mem. Johnson County Democratic Central Com., 1956-69, treas., 1958-64. Served with AUS, 1948-50. NIH Spl. fellow, 1954-55; recipient Career Devel. award, 1960-70, Walter L. Bierring award Am. Lung Assn. Iowa, 1973 Mem. ACP, Am. Lung Assn. (dir. 1972-80), Am. Lung Assn. Iowa (dir. 1971-81), Am. Fedn. Clin. Research, Am. Thoracic Soc., Iowa Thoracic Soc. (v.p. 1960-61, pres. 1962-63), Iowa Tb and Health Assn. (dir. 1961-65, 67-71), AMA (vice chmn. sect. council on diseases of chest 1971-73, chmn. sec. council diseases of chest 1974-76, Am. Thoracic Soc. del. to AMA 1979-85), Iowa, Johnson County med. socs., Soc. Exptl. Biology and Medicine, Iowa Clin. Soc. Internal Medicine, Central Soc. Clin. Research, Am. Coll. Chest Physicians, Am. Physiol. Soc., Am. Soc. Clin. Investigation, A.C.P., Central Clin. Research Club. Democrat. Unitarian Universalist. Home: Iowa City, Iowa. Died Jan. 20, 2007.

BEDELL, JOAN GRIFFITHS, career consultant; b. Bronxville, N.Y., June 15, 1928; d. Richard and Mabel (Jeynes) Griffiths; children: Hollis, Jeffrey, Randall, Lauren, David. Student U. Oreg., NYU, Smith Coll. Dir. Johnson O'Connor Research Found., Atlanta, 1973-78; co-founder, pres. Ability Potentials, Inc., 1979-85; pres. Resource Devel., Inc., 1985—. Mem. Mensa, Intertel, Am. Personnel and Guidance Assn., Am. Soc. Tng. and Devel., Nat. Aptitude Measurement Soc., NOW, ACLU, Smithsonian Assos. Quaker. Died Mar. 20, 2006.

BEDNAREK, ALEXANDER ROBERT, mathematician, educator; b. Buffalo, July 15, 1933; s. Alexander G. and Bertha (Wlodarz) B.; m. Rosemary Anderson, Aug. 29, 1954 (dec.); children: Robert A., Andrew R., Thomas C., Eugene P. BS, SUNY, Albany, 1957; MA, SUNY, Buffalo, 1959, PhD, 1961. Sr. mathematician Goodyear Aerospace Corp., Akron, Ohio, 1961-62, cons. info. scis. dept., 1963-65; asst. prof. math. U. Akron, 1962-63, U. Fla., Gainesville, 1963-66, assoc. prof., 1967-69, prof., from 1969, chmn. dept. math., 1969-86, interim chmn., winter 1988, co-dir. Center Applied Math., 1974-92, prof. dept. math. Gainesville, 1993—96, prof. emeritus, from 1996. Vis. staff mem. Los Alamos Sci. Lab., 1976-85; mem. adv. bd. CRC Handbook Math. Tables; NAS exchange prof., Warsaw, Poland, 1972 Editor (with L. Cesari) Dynamical Systems, Vol. I, 1977, Vol. II, 1982; contbr. to Ency. of Libr. and Info. Sci., Vol. 3, 1970; editor (with F. Ulam) Analogies Between Analogies, 1990; contbr. articles to profl. jours. Served with U.S. Army, 1952-54. Mem. Math. Assn. Am. (past chmn. Fla. sect.). Home: Gainesville, Fla. Died Mar. 19, 2007.

BEDROSSIAN, PETER STEPHEN, lawyer, business executive; b. Hoboken, NJ, Sept. 15, 1926; s. Nishan and Helen (Jamagotchian) B.; m. Jean M. Reynolds, Jan. 1951 (div. Oct. 1962); children: Peter, Alice Marie; m. JoAnn H. Thorpson, Nov. 16, 1962 (div. July 1986); children: Stephanie Ann, Jennifer Ann. BBA, St. Johns U., 1949, JD, 1954. Bar: N.Y. 1954, Calif. 1973. Chief acct. Stauffer Chem. Co., NYC, 1948-58, dir. taxes, 1958-76, asst. treas., 1961-76; mem. firm Dobbs, Berger & Molinari, San Francisco, 1976-80; pres. Parrot Ranch Co., San Francisco, from 1982. V.p., dir. Stauffer Chem. Internat., Geneva, Switzerland, 1959-62; Vice chmn. Nitron Inc., Cupertino, Calif.; dir. Kali-Chemie Stauffer, Hannover, Germany, Stauffer Chem. Co. Internat. Served with AUS, 1944-46. Mem. Am., N.Y., Calif. bar assns., Tax Execs. Inst. (pres. N.Y. chpt.), Internat. Assn. Assessing Officers, Am. Electronics Assn., Am. Legion, Phi Delta Phi, Alpha Kappa Psi. Clubs: N.Y. Athletic (N.Y.C.); Beach and Tennis (Pebble Beach, Fla.). Died June 12, 2007.

BEENERS, WILBERT JOHN, retired speech professional, minister; b. Lennox, SD, May 19, 1921; s. William and Sophie (Schmidt) B.; m. Dorothy Presnell, Sept. 18, 1948 (div. June 1993); children: Susan Corinne, Brian Edward, Sally Beeners Tanis; m. Hanna C. Boekhoff, Oct. 2, 1993. BA, U. Dubuque, 1943, DD, 1960; BD, Princeton Theol. Sem., 1948; Studies with Maud Scheerer, NYC, 1946-61. Ordained to ministry Presbyn. Ch., 1948. Instr. Princeton (N.J.) Theol. Sem., 1949-51, asst. prof., 1951-53, assoc. prof., 1953-58, prof., dir. speech program, 1958-91; acting dean Princeton Theol. Sem., Princeton, N.J., 1968-70. Vis. prof. New Brunswick (N.J.) Theol. Sem., 1949-75, Salvation Army Tng. Sch., N.Y., 1958-87, U.S. Army Chaplaincy Tng. Prorgam, 1968-87; cons. Sta. WANE TV, Ft. Wayne, Ind., 1966-67, 71; mem. Coun. on Mass Media, 1963-68, Coun. on Theol. Edn., 1968-71 United Presbyn. Ch. U.S.A.; cons. and lectr. in personal communication for bus. and industry; seminar leader in ins. field; pvt. coach voice prodn. and interpretative speech; speaker profl. orgns. and civic clubs; narrator audio-visual presentations. Producer-narrator radio program The Bible, 1956-57. With U.S. Mcht. Marines, 1944-46, ETO, PTO. Mem. Religious Speech Communications Soc. Am. Democrat. Avocations: woodworking, landscape gardening. Home: Columbus, NJ. Died June 26, 2007.

BEEZLEY, GILBERT GERALD, management consultant; b. St. Louis, Nov. 3, 1935; s. Vernon Edward and Alta Cynthia (Dahle) B.; children: John Gilbert, Katherine Lynn. Attended, Riverside Coll., 1956—57, U. Riverside, 1956, Pasadena City Coll., 1958—61. Loan officer Home Savs. & Loan, Arcadia, Calif., 1958—61; tract loan agt. T.J. Bettes Co., LA, 1961—65; br. mgr. Bankers Mortgage, Oxnard, Calif., 1965—71; owner, mgr. Ventura Properties, Oxnard, from 1966, Boathouse, from 1973; cons. travel agt., from 1975; loan officer County Savs. Bank, Santa Barbara, 1984; founder Calif. Paralegals, 1984. Cons. Bus. Cons., from 1980. Chmn. Citizens Polit. Action Com., from 1983; trustee Jason Gair Found., Beverly Hills, from 1983; bd. dirs. Heritage/Family Tree Tours. With USAF, 1953—57. Mem.: Ventura County Assn. Legal Assts., World Wide Travel Writers Assn., Pacific Area Travel Assn., Ventura Geneal. Soc., Nat. Geneal. Soc., Heritage Fraternities of Am. Libertarian. Died Sept. 29, 2006.

BEGANDO, JOSEPH SHERIDAN, retired university chancellor, educator; b. Roseland, Kans., Jan. 7, 1921; s. James and Bessie (Barcus) B.; m. Virginia DeVillo Suttee, Aug. 6, 1943; children: DeVillo Begando Janecek, Dana Ann Begando Rodziewicz, Darcy V. BS, Pitts. State U., Kans., 1942; MS, U. Ill., 1947, PhD, 1951. Asst. in mktg. U. Ill., 1946-47, instr., 1948-51; instr. commerce Pittsburg State U., 1947-48, asst. prof. econs., summer 1951; asst. prof. mktg. U. Kans., 1951-53; asst. dean, asso. prof. pharmacy adminstrn. U. Ill., Chgo., 1953-58, asst. to pres., 1958-61, v.p. univ., 1961-66; chancellor U. Ill. Med Center, Chgo., 1966-83, chancellor emeritus, from 1983, prof. health resources mgmt. Sch. Pub. Health, 1982-95. Citizen fellow Inst. Medicine, Chgo., 1985. Served to lt. (s.g.) USCG, 1942-45. Recipient Meritorious Achievement award Pittsburg State U., 1959, Disting. Service award U. Ill. Alumni Assn., 1983 Mem. Assn. Acad. Health Centers (pres. 1976-77), Assn. Am. Med. Colls., Pi Omega Pi, Beta Gamma Sigma, Alpha Kappa Psi, Rho Chi, Delta Kappa Sigma, Phi Delta Chi. Clubs: Univ. (Chgo.). Home: Saint Charles, Ill. Died May 2, 2007.

BEGLEY, CHARLES M., state legislator, educator; b. Lawrence, Mass., Feb. 7, 1927; s. John P. and Isabel (Vose) B.; m. Jeanne Frye, 1953; children: Mary (Mrs. Bhard), Charles M. Jr., Paul F., Mark W. AB, Bowdoin U. Tchr., adminstr., 1949-87; mem. from dist. 20 Maine State Senate, 1993-95, mem. from dist. 16, from 1995. Treas. Lincoln County, Maine, 1989-92; chmn. Lincoln County Rep. Com., 1991-92; pres. Waldoboro Pub. Libr., 1963-77. Ford Found. fellow, 1968-69. Mem. Maine Tchrs. Assn., Waldoboro Lions Club (v.p. 1962, pres. 1963). Died Feb. 3, 2007.

BEHAN, ROBERT FRANCIS, retired bank executive; b. New Haven, May 16, 1933; s. Edmund Joseph and Marie (Ridinger) B.; m. Patricia Sanders; children: Carolyn Ann, Katherine Louise. BA, Yale U., 1955; MBA, Columbia U., 1959. With Conn. Bank & Trust Co., Hartford, 1959-91, regional mgr. New Haven region, from 1970, exec. v.p., from 1982. Bd. dirs. Hosp. of St. Raphael, New Haven, 1982-92, Albertus Magnus Coll., chmn. bd. trustees, New Haven, 1980-87; bd. dirs. Shubert Performing Arts Ctr., 1987-93, Jr. Achievement S.E. Conn., 1987-93, Scranton Meml. Libr., 1994—, VNA Cmty. Care, Madison Ct., chmn. bd. dirs. Recipient Americanism award Anti-Defamation League of B'nai B'rith, New Haven, 1984, Disting. Community Service award YMCA Greater New Haven, 1987. Mem. Greater New Haven C. of C. (bd. dirs. 1980-88, chmn. bd. 1985-87), Madison Country Club, Mory's Club. Home: Madison, Conn. Died Apr. 24, 2007.

BELDEN, RICHARD O., state legislator; b. Derby, Conn., Aug. 13, 1934; s. Elbridge F. and Margaret (Cowles) B.; m. Bertha M. Kurtyka, 1956. Student, U. Philippines, 1960-61. Factory worker Sponge Rubber Products, 1952-55; ret. exec., mgr. Sikorsky Aircraft Divsn. United Tech., 1961—99; mem. Dist. 113 Conn. Ho. of Reps., from 1975, past asst. minority leader, dep. spkr., 1985, dep. minority leader/dean of house. Mem. Rep. Town Com., Shelton, Conn., 1964—, mem. Bd. Apportionment and Taxation, 1967-71, alderman, 1972-73, mem. bldg. com., 1972-73, mem., vice chmn. Shelton Sewer Com., 1972-75, mem. Bd. Tax Rev., 1974; trustee St. Margaret Mary Ch., 1978—; dir. Conn. Resource Recovery Authority, 1985-02; chmn. bd. Conn. Inst. Mcpl. Studies; mem. Citizen Adv. Bd., Emmett O'Brien Tech. Sch.; corporator Griffin Hosp. & Hewitt Meml. Hosp., LNV Boys and Girls Club; mem. Shelton Hist. Soc.; chair Valley Substance Abuse Action Coun. With USAF, 1956-61. Home: Shelton, Conn. Died Aug. 20, 2007.

BELDEN, ROBERT ADAMS, management consultant; b. Columbus, Ohio, Aug. 18, 1920; s. Charles Lee and Dorothy (Adams) B.; m. Wilanne Emily Schneider, Oct. 14, 1948; 1 child: Leigh Schneider. BS, U.S. Naval Acad., 1942; MBA, Harvard U., 1948; JD, U. San Diego, 1961. CPA Calif. Budget analyst Convair, San Diego, 1948—54, staff asst., v.p. engring. adminstrn., 1955—56, schedules engr. Astro div., 1956—60; mgr. bid analysis Stromberg Carlson, San Diego, 1960—62; mng. ptnr. Microlabels, San Diego, 1962; mgmt. cons. Robert A. Belden & Assocs., San Diego, from 1963; lectr. bus. Calif. Western U.S. Internat. U., San Diego, 1963—76; lecr. San Diego State U., from 1976. Film advisor San Diego United Schs., 1970—75; tchr. U. Calif.-San Diego, 1973; tchr. filmmaking La Jolla Mus. Modern Art, 1974—75. Editor (photographer): (slide-sound publicity film) Schools for Tomorrow, 1972; author: (booklet) Strategy Toolkit, 1983. Cons., dir. San Diego Ballet, 1977. Lt. USN, 1942—46. Mem.: Assn. MBA Execs., Am. Soc. Bus. and Mgmt. Cons., Am. Film and Media Educators, Info. Film Prodrs. Assn., Harvard Bus. Sch. Assn. San Diego. Republican. Episcopalian. Home: San Diego, Calif. Died Oct. 2, 2006.

BELK, JOHN MONTGOMERY, retired retail executive, former mayor; b. Charlotte, NC, 1920; BS in Economics, Davidson Coll., 1943. Various mgmt. positions Belk Stores Svcs., Inc. and Belk, Inc., 1945—54, CEO, 1954—81; mayor City of Charlotte, NC, 1969—77; CEO, chmn. Belk Stores Svcs., Inc. and Belk, Inc., 1981—2004. Bd. mem. PMC, Inc.; former bd. mem. Wachovia Corp., Lowe's Co., Coca-Cola. Juvenile Diabetes Found.; Carolina Citizens Freedom Found.; chmn. The Belk Found. Lt. US Army. Mem. Nat. Retail Fedn. (bd. dirs.). Died Aug. 17, 2007.

BELL, HARRISON BANCROFT, publishing executive, consultant; b. Bangor, Maine, May 9, 1925; s. Charles Edward and Dorrice Clement (Robinson) B.; m. Martha Louise Denton, Aug. 7, 1948; children: Sally R. (Mrs. John A. Fink), Martha (Mrs. Robert A. Bell), Judith, Charles Edward II (dec.). BA, Cornell U., 1949, MA, 1951. Tchr., Templeton, Mass., 1952-53, Greenwich, Conn., 1953-60; sr. editor Holt, Rinehart & Winston, Inc., NYC, 1960-66; editor-in-chief Noble & Noble Pubs., Inc., NYC, 1966-69; v.p., editor-in-chief Silver Burdett Co., Morristown, N.J., 1969-75; v.p., pub. sch. div. Harper & Row, NYC, 1975-81; editor-in-chief McCormick-Mathers Inc., 1981; asst. to pres. Amsco Sch. Pubs., Inc., 1981-82; pres. Ten-Thirty Corp. Pres. HarCroft Pub. Co. Author: Spelling for You, 1968. Treas., council for bd. edn., Greenwich, Conn., 1957-60. Served with USNR, 1943-46, 51-52. Mem. Phi Delta Kappa. Home: Hancock, Maine. Died July 18, 2006.

BELL, JUANITA L., state legislator; b. Youngstown, Ohio, Feb. 26, 1923; m. Silas Joseph; 2 children. Degree, Wilberforce U. U. N.H. Sec. Rockingham County Democrats, 1980-86, vice chmn. 1985-88, Portsmouth City Democrats, 1972, Dem. State Com., 1982—. Mem. NEA (N.H. mem. bd. dirs. 1976-88), NAACP, LWV, New England Assn. Black Educators (pres. 1975—), Assn. Portsmouth Tchrs. (bldg. rep., cmty. rels. chmn. 1975-88), New Hope Baptist Ch. Avocations: bridge, music, reading, travel. Home: Portsmouth, NH. Died Apr. 13, 2006.

BELL, MARION SEDWICK, copper company executive; b. Grayson County, Ky., Apr. 28, 1923; s. John Sedwick and Gladys Elizabeth (Collard) B.; m. Annette Koerner, Dec. 26, 1946; children— Greg, Alexis, Mark. Metall. Engr. Colo. Sch. Mines, 1949. With Phelps Dodge Refining Corp., from 1949, v.p., gen. mgr., 1976-79, pres. NYC, 1979-87, Phelps Dodge Copper Products, NYC, 1982-87. Patentee in field. Past pres. United Way El Paso County, Tex., El Paso Indsl. Betterment Council, Jr. Achievement El Paso; past regional v.p. Tex. Assn. Bus. Served to 2d lt. USMCR, 1942-46. Recipient Van Diest Gold medal Colo. Sch. Mines, 1961 Mem. Selenium and Tellurium Devel. Assn. (pres. 1979), Mining and Metall. Soc. Am., Metall. Soc. Clubs: Mining (N.Y.C.). Republican. Roman Catholic. Home: Santa Teresa, N.Mex. Died July 26, 2006.

BELL, PHILIP WILKES, accountant, economist, educator; b. NYC, Oct. 24, 1924; s. Samuel Dennis and Miriam Ball (Wilkes) B.; m. Katharine Elizabeth Hubbard, June 16, 1945 (div. May 1980); children: Susan, Geoffrey, Mary Ellen, James; m. Virginia Wood Crozier, June 14, 1980 (dec. Nov. 1998); stepchildren: Thomas, Steven, Peter; m. Jean Grady Wyeth, Oct. 24, 1999. BA, Princeton U., 1947; MA, U. Calif., Berkeley, 1949; PhD, Princeton U., 1954. Instr. Princeton (N.J.) U., 1948-51; rsch. assoc. Inst. for Advanced Study, Princeton, 1951-52; asst. prof. Haverford (Pa.) Coll., 1952-56, assoc. prof., then prof., 1960-68; assoc. prof. U. Calif., Berkeley, 1957-60; prof. Merrill Coll., U. Calif., Santa Cruz, 1968-79, provost, 1968-72; William A. Kirkland prof. Rice U., Houston, 1979-89; prof. acctg. and econs. Boston U., 1989-92; ret. Assoc. dir. Rockefellor Found., 1963-68; chmn., prof. econ. Makerere U. Coll., Uganda, 1963-65; chmn. econ., Fisk U., 1965-66; dir. Edn. Abroad Program U. Calif., Kenya, 1972-74; vis. prof. Univ. Sains Malaysia, Penang, 1976-77, Norges Handelshoyskole, Bergen, Norway, spring 1982, U. Pa., Phila, fall 1982. Author: Sterling Area in the Postwar World, 1956, Toward Greater Logic and Utility in Accounting: The Collected Writings of Philip W. Bell, 1997; co-author: (with Edgar O. Edwards) Theory and Measurement of Business Income, 1961, (with Edgar O. Edwards and L. Todd Johnson) Accounting for Economic Events, 1979, (with Michael H. Granof) Financial Accounting: Principles and Issues, 1992; contbr. articles to profl. jours. 2d lt. USAF, 1943-45. Social Sci. Rsch. Coun. rsch. fellow, London, 1956-57, Ford Found. fellow, Berkeley, 1959. Mem. Am. Acctg. Assn., Brit. Acctg. Assn., European Acctg. Assn., Royal Econ. Soc. (U.K.), Acctg. Assn. Australia and New Zealand (elected to Acctg. Hall of Fame, Columbus, Ohio, 2003). Mem. Soc. Of Friends. Died Aug. 1, 2007.

BELL, RICHARD, state supreme court justice; b. Iva, SC, July 5, 1920; s. Frank Montgomery and Margaret (Blaine) B.; m. Naomi Whittemore, 1954; children: Richard, Carol Anne, Naomi Jean and Margaret Jane (twins) BS, Presbyn. Coll. S.C., 1943; LLB, Emory U., 1949. Bar: Ga. 1950. Rep. Ga. Gen. Assembly from DeKalb County, 1950-52; solicitor City Ct. of Decatur, 1954-56; solicitor gen. Stone Mountain Jud. Cir., 1956-76; exec. dir. State Bar Ga., 1976-80; judge Superior Ct. Stone Mountain Jud. Cir., 1981-82; assoc. justice Ga. Supreme Ct., Atlanta, from 1982, presiding justice, from 1992. Past mem. Jud. Coun. Ga.; past adminstrv. judge 4th dist.; emeritis dist. atty., 1976—. Capt. U.S. Army, World War II, PTO, lt. col. Res. ret. Mem. ABA, State Bar Ga. (bd. govs. 1963-71, treas. 1971-76), Ga. Dist. Attys. Assn. (pres.), Nat. Dist. Attys. Assn. (bd. dirs.), Decatur-DeKalb Bar Assn., Old Warhorse Lawyers Club, Atlanta Lawyers Club, Masons, Lions. Home: Decatur, Ga. Died Nov. 28, 2005.

BELLIS, DAVID JAMES, public administration educator; b. Nashville, May 1, 1944; s. Carroll Joseph and Helen Louise (Jett) B.; m. Ann Seagreaves, Dec. 23, 1972; 1 child, James. BS, UCLA; MA, U. So. Calif., 1969, PhD, 1977. Dir. narcotics prevention project, Los Angeles, 1970-72; dir. West End drug abuse control Ontario, Calif., 1972-75; cons. Project Heavy, Los Angeles, 1975-78; dir. econs. Telacu, Los Angeles, 1978-80; asst. dir. Youth Gang Services, Los Angeles, 1980-81; councilman City of Signal Hill, Calif., 1980-86, mayor Calif., 1983-84; assoc. prof. pub. adminstrn. Calif. State U., San Bernardino, 1985-89, prof. pub. adminstrn., from 1989. Cons. San Bernadino County Sheriff's Dept., 1993-95, San Bernadino Police Dept., 1993-95, U.S. Dept. State, 1992-94, San Bernardino County Dept. Pub. Social Svcs., 1995—. Author: Heroin and Politicians, 1983. Avocation: flying. Home: Cedar Glen, Calif. Died June 29, 2006.

BELTZ, CHARLES ROBERT, retired engineering executive; b. Pitts., Feb. 23, 1913; s. Charles Fred and Ester (Johnston) B.; m. Amy Margaret Ferguson, Oct. 23, 1935; children: Charles R., A.M. Bonnie Beltz Hatch, Homer F., William T., Carol E. Beltz Marks, M. Joy Beltz O'Keefe. Student, Greenbrier Mil. Sch., 1930-33; MSE, Cornell U., 1934; MS in Aero. Engring., U. Pitts., 1937. Engr. Crane Co., 1937-39; design engr. Stout Skycraft Corp., 1939-43; project engr. Cycle-Weld Labs., 1943-44; project engr., mgr. Fairchild E&A Corp., Roosevelt Field, 1944-46; corp. engr. Chrysler Corp., 1946-47; pres. Charles R. Beltz & Co., Detroit, 1947-85, Beltz Engring., 1950-2001, Beltemp, Inc., 1969-81. Author: Ice Skating, Skating Weather or Not, ABC's Air-conditioning, Roatable Aircraft; designer in field. Mem. Nat. Aero. Assn. (past pres.), Air Conditioning Inst. (past pres.), Inst. Aero. Scis. (vice chmn.), ASHRAE (contbg. author), Engring. Soc. Detroit, Air Force Assn., Grosse Pointe Hist. Soc., English Speaking Union, Air Force Found., Yankee Air Force, Toledo Zool. Soc., Am. Philatelic Soc., Aero Club (bd. dirs.), Econ. Club, Curling Club (Detroit), Grosse Pointe Yacht Club, Lost Lake Woods Club. Died Jan. 1, 2007.

BENEDICT, MANSON, retired chemical engineer, educator; b. Lake Linden, Mich., Oct. 9, 1907; s. C. Harry and Lena I. (Manson) Benedict; m. Marjorie Oliver Allen, July 6, 1935 (dec. 1995); children: Mary Hannah (Mrs. Myran C. Sauer, Jr.), Marjorie Alice (Mrs. Martin Cohn). B in Chemistry, Cornell U., 1928; MS, MIT, 1932, PhD, 1935. NRC fellow chemistry, 1935—36; rsch. assoc. geophysics Harvard, 1936—37; rsch. chemist M.W. Kellogg Co., 1938—43; in charge process design gaseous diffusion plant for uranium-235 Kellex Corp., 1943—46; dir. process development Hydrocarbon Rsch., Inc., 1946—51; tech. asst. to gen. mgr. AEC, 1951—52; prof. nuclear engring. MIT, 1951—69, Institute prof., 1969—73, prof. emeritus, from 1973, head dept. nuclear engring., 1958—71; dir. Burns & Roe, Inc., 1979—85. Sci. advisor Nat. Rsch. Corp., 1951—58, dir., 1962—67; mem. gen. adv. com. AEC, 1958—68, chmn., 1962—64; dir. Atomic Indsl. Forum, 1966—72; mem. energy R & D adv. coun. FEA, 1973—75. Co-editor: Engineering Developments in the Gaseous Diffusion Process, 1949; co-author: Nuclear Chemical Engineering, 1981. Recipient Indsl. and Engring. Chemistry award, Am. Chem. Soc., 1962, Perkin medal Soc. Chem. Industry, Robert E. Wilson award in nuclear chem. engring., 1968, Fermi award, AEC, 1972, John Fritz medal, Engring. Founder Socs., 1974, Nat. Medal Sci., 1975, Henry D. Smyth Nuclear Statesman award, Atomic Indsl. Forum, 1979, Washington award, Western Soc. Engrs., 1982. Fellow: AIChE (William H. Walker award 1947, Founders award 1965), Am. Philos. Soc., Am. Acad. Arts and Scis., Am. Nuclear Soc. (pres. 1962—63, Arthur H. Compton award); mem.: NAS, Nat. Acad. Engring. (Founders award 1976), Country Club Naples (Fla.), Weston Golf Club (Mass.), Sigma Xi. Died Sept. 18, 2006.

BENNETT, ROBERT MCARN, retail executive; b. Cheraw, S.C., Apr. 13, 1932; s. Russell Evans and Mary Ella (Gandy) B.; m. Mary Murray Paulling, Aug. 1, 1953; children— Robert McArn, D. Paulling, J. McCauley. Student, Duke U., 1950-52; A.B., U. S.C., 1954. Pres., Bennett Motor Co., Cheraw, 1954—; v.p. Russell Bennett Chevrolet-Buick-Mazda, Rockingham, N.C., 1973—; dir. 1st Fed. Savs. & Loan; adv. mem. 1st Citizens Bank & Trust. Ruling elder, clk. First Presbyterian Ch., Cheraw; trustee Pee Dee Presbytery, U. S.C. Mem. Chevrolet Dealer Council, Oldsmobile Dealer Council, Buick Dealer Council, Jr. C. of C. (past pres.). Clubs: Cheraw Country (past pres.), Country of N.C., So. Pines, Palmetto (Columbia, S.C.) Home: Cheraw, SC. Died Jan. 19, 2007.

BENNETT, RUSSELL ODBERT, lawyer; b. Dexter, Mo., July 11, 1915; s. Corna Lewman and Nelle (Odbert) B.; m. Patricia Birch, June 26, 1948; children: Birch Odbert, Russell Andrew. AB, U. Okla., 1936; LLB, Harvard, 1939. Bar: Ill. 1939. Assoc. firm Taylor, Miller, Busch & Boyden, Chgo., 1939-41, Carney, Crowell & Leibman, Chgo., 1946-52; partner firm Leibman, Williams, Bennett, Baird & Minow, 1952-72; partner successor firm Sidley & Austin, Chgo., 1972-85, of counsel, 1986-90, ret., 1990. Bd. dirs. Lawrence Hall Youth Svcs., 1949-91, pres., 1960-63; chancellor Seabury-Western Theol. Sem., Evanston, Ill., 1973-95. Served to maj. AUS, 1941-46. Mem. Internat., Am., Ill., Chgo. bar assns., Am. Law Inst., Chgo. Council Fgn. Relations, Phi Beta Kappa, Phi Gamma Delta. Clubs: Law, Legal, Economic, Mid-Day (Chgo.); Indian Hill (Winnetka, Ill.); Westmoreland Country (Wilmette, Ill.). Republican. Episcopalian. Home: Winnetka, Ill. Died May 19, 2007.

BENNETT, SAUL, public relations agency executive; b. NYC, Oct. 21, 1936; s. Philip and Ruth (Weinstein) Ostrove; m. Joan Marian Abrahams, Aug. 15, 1965; children: Sara (dec.), Charles, Elizabeth. BS in Journalism, Ohio U., Athens, 1957. Engaged in pub. rels., from 1963; from acct. supr. to v.p. Rowland Co., NYC, 1965—74; from v.p. to sr. v.p. Robert Marston and Assocs., NYC, 1974—78, exec. v.p., 1978—86, ptnr., from 1979, sr. exec. v.p., from 1986; pres. Robert Marston Mktg. Communications Inc., from 1996. Cons. in field. Author: (poems) New Fields and Other Stones, Jesus Matinees and Other Poems, 1998, Harpo Marx at Prayer, 2000. With USAR, 1958-59, 61-62. Mem. Pen Am. Ctr. Home: Woodstock, NY. Died Aug. 6, 2006.

BENTON, ARTHUR LESTER, psychology educator; b. NYC, Oct. 16, 1909; s. James Edward and Anna Esther (Touster) Bernstein; m. Rita Rosenfeld, Sept. 24, 1939 (dec. Mar. 1980); children: Raymond S., Abigail Benton Sivan, Daniel J. AB, Oberlin Coll., 1931, AM, 1933; PhD, Columbia U., 1935; DSc (hon.), Cornell Coll., Mt. Vernon, Iowa, 1978; D. Psychology (hon.), U. Rome, 1990. Diplomate Am. Bd. Profl. Psychology. Asst. in psychology Oberlin (Ohio) Coll., 1931-33, N.Y. State Psychiat. Inst., NYC, 1933-36; psychologist N.Y. Hosp., NYC,

1936-69, attending psychologist Westchester div. White Plains, 1939-41; assoc. prof. U. Louisville Sch. Medicine, 1946-48; prof. psychology U. Iowa, Iowa City, from 1948. Counsellor CCNY, 1939-41. Author: Right-Left Discrimination, 1959, Neurobehavioral Consequences of Closed Head Injury, 1983, Studies in Neuropsychology, 1985. Served with USN, 1941-46. Recipient Samuel T. Orton award Orton Dyslexia Soc., 1984. Fellow Am. Orthopsychiat. Assn. (pres. 1964-65); mem. APA (Disting. Profl. Contbn. award 1978), Am. Neurol. Assn., Internat. Neuropsychol. Assn. (pres. 1970-71, Disting. Sci. Contbn. award 1981), Am. Acad. Neurology, Nat. Acad. Neuropsychology, Am. Assn. for History Medicine. Avocation: research in history of neurology and neuropsychology. Home: Glenview, Ill. Died Dec. 27, 2006.

BERAN, WALTER FRANK, retired accounting company executive; b. The Grove, Tex., Apr. 20, 1926; s. Frank Walter and Selma (Nowotnik) B.; m. Sharon Annette Lott, May 28, 1948; children: John David, James Paul BBA cum laude, Baylor U., 1948; LL.D. (hon.), Calif. Luth. Coll., 1978. C.P.A. With Ernst & Whinney, 1948-86, ptnr. in charge San Antonio, Austin, Corpus Christi and Laredo offices Tex., 1960-65, ptnr. in charge client relations, nat. office Cleve., 1965-72, vice chmn. 23 western region offices, mem. 7-man managing com. Los Angeles, 1972-86, cons., 1986—2007. Chmn. bd. councilors Sch. Bus. Adminstrn., U. So. Calif. Named one of four exceptional leaders, Los Angeles, 1983, Order of Rising Sun award Govt. Japan, 1986. Mem. Am. Inst. C.P.A.s, Calif. Soc. C.P.A.s, Los Angeles C. of C. (past-chmn.). Clubs: Los Angeles Country, California, Regency. Home: Venice, Calif. Died June 3, 2007.

BERG, JOHN PAUL, manufacturing executive; b. Grasston, Minn., Apr. 16, 1920; s. Alf F. and Mary Berg; m. Helen Berg, June 19, 1941; children: Barbara, Roxanne. Student, U. Minn., 1946—50. Chief indsl. engr. Kickernick Inc., Mpls., 1946—57; indsl. engr. Greif Bros., St. Paul, 1957—62, mgr. mfg., 1962—70, v.p., div. gen. mgr., 1970—79, pres., from 1979. Served to capt. US Army, 1942—46. Mem.: Paper Shipping Sack Assn. (past pres.), Rotarian. Roman Cath. Home: Eden Prairie, Minn. Died May 19, 2007.

BERG, LEONARD, retired neurologist, educator, researcher; b. St. Louis, July 17, 1927; s. Jacob and Sara (Kessler) B.; m. Gerry Saltzman, Mar. 25, 1948; children: Kathleen, John, Nancy. AB cum laude, Washington U., St. Louis, 1945, MD cum laude, 1949. Diplomate: Am. Bd. Psychiatry and Neurology (dir. 1978-85, pres. 1985). Intern Barnes Hosp., St. Louis, 1949-50, resident, 1950-51, Neurol. Inst., NYC, 1951-53; clin. assoc. Nat. Inst. Neurol. Diseases and Blindness, NIH, 1953-55; mem. faculty Washington U. Med. Sch., 1955—98, prof. clin. neurology, 1972-89, prof. neurology, 1989-98, prof. emeritus, 1998—2007. Attending neurologist Barnes Hosp., Jewish Hosp., St. Louis; dir. Alzheimer's Disease Rsch. Ctr., Washington U., 1985-97; expert U.S. FDA, 1992-96; mem. U.S. Congress Adv. Panel on Alzheimer's Disease, 1993-96, Leonard Berg Annual Symposiums Nat. Spkrs. Co-author: Atlas of Muscle Pathology in Neuromuscular Diseases, 1956. Bd. dirs. Temple Israel, St. Louis, 1972-74, Jewish Center for Aged, 1981-98, hon. dir., 1999-2007; With USPHS, 1953-55. Recipient Lifetime Disting. Rsch. on Alzheimer's Disease and Related Disorders award, 7th World Alzheimer's Congress, 2000, Robert E. Schlueter Leadership award, St. Louis Met. Med. Soc., 2001, 2d Century award, Washington U. Mem. AMA, Am. Acad. Neurology, Am. Neurol. Assn. (1st v.p. 1988-89), Soc. for Neurosci., Alzheimer's Assn. (Chgo.) (bd. dirs. 1989-95, 96-98, chair med. and sci. adv. bd. 1991-95), Phi Beta Kappa, Sigma Xi, Alpha Omega Alpha. Home: Saint Louis, Mo. Died Jan. 15, 2007.

BERGAN, JOSEPH ANTHONY, surgeon; b. South Bend, Ind., Mar. 30, 1920; s. William N. and Ellen (Hagerty) B.; m. Marvada Ann French, May 16, 1953; children— Bridget, Joseph, Patrick, Mary, Susan, Thomas, James, George, Peter. B.S., U. Notre Dame, 1942; M.D., Loyola U., 1945. Diplomate Am. Bd. Surgery. Chief surgery St. Anthony Hosp., Michigan City, Ind., 1967-69, 1974-76, pres. staff, 1969-70; practice medicine specializing in surgery Michigan City, 1949-88. Served to capt. U.S. Army, M.C., 1946-48. Fellow Internat. Coll. Surgeons, Pan Pacific Surg. Assn., Am. Geriatric Soc.; mem. AMA, Ind. State Med. Assn. Roman Catholic. Clubs: Serra (pres. 1959-60), Notre Dame (pres. 1957-58) (Michigan City). Home: Lake Dallas, Tex. Died Nov. 30, 2005.

BERGÉ, CAROL, writer; b. NYC, 1928; d. Albert and Molly Peppis; m. Jack Bergé, June 1955; 1 child, Peter. Asst. to pres. Pendray Public Relations, NYC, 1955; disting. prof. lit. Thomas Jefferson Coll., Allendale, Mich., 1975-76; instr. adult degree program Goddard Coll., 1976; tchr. fiction and poetry U. Calif. Extension Program, Berkeley, 1976-77; assoc. prof. U. So. Miss., Hattiesburg, 1977-78; vis. prof. Honors Ctr. and English dept. U. N.Mex., 1978-79, 87; vis. lectr. Wright State U., 1979, SUNY, Albany, 1980-81; tchr. Poets and Writers, Poets in the Schs. (N.Y. State Council on Arts), 1970-72, Poets in the Schs. (Conn. Commn. Arts). Summer writing confs. Squaw Valley, Ind. U., U. Calif., Santa Cruz, 1975-1980; propr. Blue Gate Gallery of Art and Antiques, 1988-2003. Author: (fiction) The Unfolding, 1969, A Couple Called Moebius, 1972, Acts of Love: An American Novel, 1973 (N.Y. State Coun. on Arts CAPS award 1974), Timepieces, 1977, The Doppler Effect, 1979, Fierce Metronome, 1981, Secrets, Gossip & Slander, 1984, Zebras, or, Contour Lines, 1991; (poetry) The Vulnerable Island, 1964, Lumina, 1965, Poems Made of Skin, 1968, The Chambers, 1969, Circles, as in the Eye, 1969, An American Romance, 1969, From a Soft Angle: Poems About Women, 1972, The Unexpected, 1976, Rituals and Gargoyles, 1976, A Song, A Chant, 1978, Alba Genesis, 1979, Alba Nemesis, 1979, (reportage) The Vancouver Report, 1965; editor Center Mag., 1970-84, pub., 1991-2007; editor Miss. Rev., 1977-78, Subterraneans, 1975-76, Paper Branches, 1987, Light Years: The N.Y.C. Coffeehouse Writers and Multimedia Artists of the 1960s, 2005; contbg. editor Woodstock Rev., 1977-81, Shearsman mag., 1980-82, S.W. Profile, 1981, Caprice, 2000-05; editor, pub. Center Press, 1970-93; pub.: Medicine Journeys (Carl Ginsburg), Coastal Lives (Miriam Sagan), 1991; co-pub.: Zebras (Carol Berge). Nat. Endowment Arts fellow, 1979-80 Mem. Authors' League, Poets and Writers, MacDowell Fellows Assn., Nat. Press Women Home: Santa Fe, N.Mex. Died Feb. 16, 2006.

BERGER, GUSTAV ADOLPHE, art conservator; b. Vienna, July 28, 1920; s. Rudolph P. and Julia Lily (Ullmann) B.; m. June 7, 1946; children— Ron A., Raphael Student civil engring., Tech. Inst., Haifa, Palestine, 1938-40; student, Art Students League, NYC, 1954-57. Interpretor aerial photographs Photogrammetric Inst., Jerusalem, 1949-51; interpretor aerial photographs Dept. Agr., Tel-Aviv, 1952-54; paintings conservator Julius Lowy Co., NYC, 1954-56, S.H. Kress Collection, NYC, 1956-64, William Suhr Studio, NYC, 1964-67; pres., chief conservator Berger Art Conservation, Inc., NYC, from 1967; research dir. Art Conservation Research Found., Ltd., NYC, from 1982. Inventor BEVA adhesive for restoration, self-adjusting, continuous-tension stretcher; contbr. 58 articles to profl. publs. Recipient award of excellence Atlanta Urban Design Commn., 1982, Spl. medal of Merit Govt. Polish People's Republic, 1986, Austrian Cross of Honor, 1st class, 1990; grantee S.H. Kress Found., 1968, 69, 74, 83, 88, 89, The Brown Found. Inc., 1985, 86, Nat. Endowment for Arts, 1973, Joseph E. Seagram Found., 1982, 85, 88. Fellow Internat. Inst. Conservation, Am. Inst. Conservation; mem. Internat. Council Museums, Appraisers Assn. Am. Died Mar. 6, 2006.

BERGER, ROBERT ARMIN, dermatologist; b. N.Y.C., Feb. 7, 1932; s. Arthur and Rose (Haberman) B.; m. Ann Fletcher, June 16, 1967 (div. 1977). Student Harvard U., 1948-51, Washington U. Sch. Medicine, St. Louis, 1951-53 M.D., NYU, 1955. Diplomate Am. Bd. Dermatology. With Orentreich Med. Group, N.Y.C., 1960-68; practice medicine specializing in dermatology, N.Y.C., 1968—; attending staff Mt. Sinai Hosp., N.Y.C. Fellow Dermatologic Soc. Greater N.Y., Am. Acad. Dermatology, Am. Soc. Dermatologic Surgery, Am. Assn. Cosmetic Surgeons, Am. Soc. Facial Plastic Surgery. Jewish. Avocations: bridge; fox hunting; skiing; polo. Home: New York, NY. Died Feb. 18, 2007.

BERGMANN, ROBERT LEWIS, data processing executive; b. St. Louis, Jan. 21, 1926; s. William G. and Elvera O. (Baum) B.; m. Dorothy E. Thoma, July 24, 1954; children: Laura A., Alice M., Thomas C., Karen S. BS in Commerce cum laude, St. Louis U., 1949. CPA, Mo.j. Sr. auditor Arthur Andersen and Co., St. Louis, 1949-55; mgr. adminstrv. data processing McDonnel Aircraft Corp., St. Louis, 1955-64; v.p. data processing Mercantile Trust Co., St. Louis, 1964-73, sr. v.p. ops. and date processing, 1973-80, exec. v.p. ops. and date processing, from 1980. Chmn. bd. dirs. Payment and Adminstrv. Communications Corp., N.Y.C., 1980-83, Payment and Telecommunications Corp., N.Y.C., 1980-86, Monetary Transfer System, 1983—; bd. dirs. Payment and Adminstrv. Communications Corp., Payment and Telecommunications Corp.; mem. ABA/Fed. Res. 1st V.P. Banker Contact Program, St. Louis, 1981—. Served with U.S. Army, 1944-45. Mem. Am. Inst. CPA's, Data Processing Mgmt. Assn. (St. Louuis chpt.), Assn. Systems Mgmt. (pres. 1968-69 St. Louis chpt., Achievement award 1982), The Backstoppers. Clubs: Mo. Athletic (St. Louis). Lodges: KC. Home: Saint Louis, Mo. Died Dec. 12, 2006.

BERGONZI, FRANK MICHAEL, former retail drug store chain finance executive; b. Lebanon, Pa., Aug. 2, 1945; s. Michael D. and Dorothy M. (Burkholder) B.; m. Polly Ann Mayhoffer, June 24, 1967 (div. Apr. 1985); children: Megan Ann, Peter Michael; m. Gail Elizabeth Forbes, Nov. 25, 1986. BSBA, Susquehanna U., 1967. CPA, Pa. Staff acct. Main Hurdman, Harrisburg, Pa., 1967-69; asst. v.p., asst. controller Rite Aid Corp., Harrisburg, 1969-77, v.p., 1977-85, sr. v.p. fin., 1985—99. Home: Hummelstown, Pa. Died June 8, 2007.

BERLE, PETER ADOLF AUGUSTUS, lawyer, media director; b. NYC, Dec. 8, 1937; s. Adolf Augustus and Beatrice (Bishop) B.; m. Lila Sloane Wilde, May 30, 1960; children: Adolf Augustus, Mary Alice, Beatrice Lila, Robert Thomas. BA (Knox fellow), Harvard U., 1958, LLB, 1964; LLD (hon.), Hobart Smith Coll., 1977, L.I. U., 1993, So. Vt. Coll., 1996; LLB (hon.), North Adams Tchrs. Coll., 1988. Bar: N.Y. 1964, U.S. Dist. Ct. (so. and ea. dists.) N.Y. 1966, U.S. Ct. Appeals (2d cir.) 1966, U.S. Supreme Ct. 1973. Assoc. Paul, Weiss, Rifkind, Wharton & Garrison, NYC, 1964-71; ptnr. Berle, Butzel & Kass, NYC, 1971-76; commr. environ. conservation State of NY, 1976-79; ptnr. Berle, Kass & Case, 1979-85; pres., CEO (pub. Audubon mag.) Nat. Audubon Soc., 1985-95; dir., host The Environment Show N.E. Pub. Radio, 1995—2001, weekly commentator, 2001—07; pres. Sky Farm Prodns. Inc., from 2002; trustee Twentieth Century Fund, Inc., 1971—2007, chmn., 1982-87. Tchg. fellow econs. Harvard Coll., Cambridge, Mass., 1963-64; assoc. adj. prof. Sch. Urban Affairs Hunter Coll., 1974, 84; vis. prof. environ. sci. and forestry SUNY, 1980. Author: Does the Citizen Stand a Chance, 1974. Mem. N.Y. State Assembly, 1968-74; chmn. N.Y. Gov.'s Transition Task Force on Environment, 1974-75; commr. N.Y. State Moreland Act Commn. on Nursing Homes, 1975-77; bd. dirs. Clean Sites, Inc., 1986-93; chmn. Commn. on the Adirondacks in the 21st Century, 1989-90; mem. EPA adv. group on biotech., 1989-92, EPA adv. grout air quality; mem. nat. com. environ., 1991-92, nat. commn. superfund, 1992-94; mem. joint pub. adv. com. N.Am. Commn. on Environ. Coop., 1994-2002; dir. N.Y. Ind. Sys. Operator, 1999-2007; adv. bd. Harvard U. Com. on Environment; mem. commn. internat. environ. law World Conservation Union; pres. Stockbridge Land Trust, 2001—07. 1st lt. USAF, 1959-61. Decorated Commendation medal; named Outstanding Legislator Eagleton Inst. Politics, 1971 Mem. ABA, N.Y. State Bar Assn., Assn. of Bar of City of N.Y. (environ. law com., profl. responsibility com., energy policy com., internat. human rights com., internat. environ. law com.). Episcopalian. Home: Stockbridge, Mass. Died Nov. 1, 2007.*

BERMINGHAM, JOHN HANIFAN, lawyer; b. Port Chester, NY, May 13, 1921; s. Thomas Valentine and Katherine Josephine (McDonald) B.; m. Berthe M. Reny, May 20, 1950; children— Thomas V. II, Maryclaire Bermingham Fouse, Paula Bermingham Filippone, Amy G., John Hanifan Jr., Jerrold G. AB, Fordham Coll., 1943; LL.B., Harvard U., 1948; LL.M., NYU, 1961. Bar: N.Y. 1949. Atty. RCA Corp., NYC, 1949-63, counsel, 1963-73, staff v.p., counsel corp. affairs, 1973-78, staff v.p., gen. atty., 1978-80, v.p., gen. atty., 1980-85, v.p., dep. gen. counsel, 1985-86, sr. v.p., gen. counsel, 1986. Bd. dirs., pres. Scarsdale Family Counseling Service, N.Y., 1964-73; mem. Mayor's Adv. Com. on Human Relations, Village of Scarsdale, 1965-71; mem. personnel com. White Plains Hosp., N.Y., 1983—. Served to sgt. USAF, 1943-46 Mem. Assn. Bar of N.Y.C., ABA, Nat. Assn. Mfrs. (lawyers adv. com. 1981—), Am. Corp. Counsel Assn. (founding mem., bd. dirs. 1982-83) Clubs: Wykagyl Country (New Rochelle, N.Y.). Democrat. Roman Catholic. Avocation: bridge. Home: Scarsdale, NY. Died Apr. 5, 2006.

BERNARD, ROBERT F., consulting company executive; s. Charles and Sandy Humola; m. Elisa Fryer; children: Kendal Elisabeth, Bryce Robert. Founder Whittman-Hart (later March-First), Chgo., 1984, CEO, chair bd. dirs.; founder, CEO, pres. WhitmanHart Inc., Chgo., 2006—07. Chmn. edn. subcom. Chgo. Mayor's Coun. Tech. Advisors; bd. dirs. Marklund Children's Home, divine InterVentures Inc., WynWyn.com., Form & Function Capital, WebStreet.com., B&B Investment Group LLC. Featured in (articles) Crain's Bus. Chgo., 2006. Named one of 40 Under 40, 1997, Regional Entrepreneur of Yr. for Bus. Svcs. in Ill./N.W. Ind., Ernst & Young, 199; named Ill. High-Tech Entrepreneur of Yr., KPMG Peat Marwick, 1992. Died Feb. 2, 2007.

BERNHARDT, HARVEY EVAN, pathologist, educator; b. Bronx, N.Y., July 27, 1944; s. Harry and Gertrude (Solomon) B.; m. Regina Therese Wakin, Sept. 30, 1967; children— Wesley Joseph, Monica Denise, Harrison Bradley. B.S., Queens Coll. CUNY, 1964; M.D., U. Louisville, 1968. Diplomate Am. Bd. Pathology. Intern, Jackson Meml. Hosp., Miami, 1968-69; resident in pathology Los Angeles County Harbor Gen. Hosp., 1969-71, Mt. Sinai Hosp., Miami, Fla., 1973-74; dir. clin. labs. Univ. Hosp., Jacksonville, Fla., 1974-76; pathologist Meth. Hosp., Jacksonville, 1976-79; chief exec. officer Am. Med. Labs., Jacksonville, 1979-81; chmn. dept. pathology, dir. clin. labs. Jacksonville Gen. Hosp., 1981—; med. dir. Smith Kline Biosci. Labs., Jacksonville, Fla.; clin. assoc. prof. U. Fla. Med. Sch., 1975—; adj. prof. U. North Fla., 1982—. Bd. dirs. Duval County Republican Exec. Com., 1974-76. Served to lt. comdr. USNR, 1971-73. Mem. AMA (Physicians Recognition award 1973, 76, 80, 85), Fla. Soc. Pathology (Alfred L. Lewis award 1974), Duval County Med. Soc. (Beals award 1978), Fla. Med. Assn., Coll. Am. Pathologists, Internat. Acad. Pathologists, Assn. Clin. Scientists, Am. Soc. Clin. Pathologists. Jewish. Contbr. articles to profl. jours. Died Jan. 9, 2007.

BERNHEIM, PEGGY, judge; b. Newark, Feb. 2, 1929; d. Charles E. and Eva (Kempner) B. A.B., U. Miami, Coral Gables, Fla., 1950; LL.B., NYU, 1965. Bar: N.Y. 1965, U.S. Dist. Ct. (so. dist.) N.Y. 1968, U.S. Ct. Appeals (2d cir.) 1968. Mdse. exec. A. Bohrer, Inc., 1956-66; staff atty. Civil Legal Aid, 1966-70; law sec. to Civil Ct. Judge, 1970-73, to Supreme Ct. Justice, 1973-78; civil ct. judge, Bronx County, N.Y., 1978—; acting justice, 1st Dept., N.Y. Supreme Ct., N.Y.C., 1980—. State Democratic committeewoman 82d Dist. N.Y., 1970-74. Mem. ABA, Nat. Assn. Women Judges, N.Y. State Bar Assn., Bronx County Bar Assn. (dir.), N.Y. State Trial Lawyers Assn., NYU Law Alumni, Nat. Council Jewish Women, Delta Phi Epsilon (nat. exec. council). Democrat. Jewish. Home: Bronx, NY. Died Nov. 21, 2006.

BERNSTEIN, DONALD CHESTER, brokerage house executive, lawyer; b. St. Louis, July 29, 1942; s. Michael Charles and Laura (Schmidt) B.; m. Estelle Marla Cohen, Jan. 17, 1946; children: Kimberleigh, Chad, Aaron. BSBA, Washington U., 1964, JD, 1967; LLM, U. London, 1968. Bar: Mo. 1967. V.p., counsel A.G. Edwards & Sons, Inc., St. Louis, from 1969. Mem. Mo. Bar Assn., Bar Assn. Met. St. Louis. Republican. Jewish. Home: Saint Louis, Mo. Died Dec. 4, 2006.

BERNSTEIN, ROBERT, retired physician, retired military officer; b. NYC, Feb. 20, 1920; s. Morris and Rose (Gordich) B. BA, Vanderbilt U., 1942; MD, U. Louisville, 1946. Diplomate Nat. Bd. Med. Examiners, Am. Bd. Internal Medicine. Commd. 2nd lt. U.S. Army, 1942, advanced through grades to maj. gen., 1973; intern Grasslands Hosp., Valhalla, NY, 1946-47; resident Walter Reed Army Med. Ctr., Washington, 1952-55, dep. comdr., 1972-73, comdg. gen., 1973-78; surgeon U.S. Mil. Assistance Command, Vietnam, 1970-72; ret., 1978; commr. for spl. health svcs. State of Tex., Austin, 1978-80, commr. health, 1980-91. Adj. prof. U. Tex. Health Sci. Ctr., 1982—. Contbr. articles to mil. and med. jours. Decorated D.S.M. with oak leaf cluster, Legion of Merit with two oak leaf clusters, Bronze Star with oak leaf cluster, Purple Heart. Fellow ACP; mem. Soc. Med. Consultants to Armed Forces, Internat. Soc. Internal Medicine, Phi Delta Epsilon, Phi Kappa Phi, Alpha Epsilon Pi, Alpha Omega Alpha. Home: Austin, Tex. Died July 23, 2007.

BERRY, DEAN LESTER, lawyer; b. Chgo., Jan. 20, 1935; s. Ruben W. and Leonore C. (Nelson) B.; m. Donna J. Zack, Nov. 16, 1962 (dec.); children: Megan, Thomas. BA with distinction, DePauw U., 1955; JD with distinction, U. Mich., 1960. Bar: Ohio 1961, U.S. Dist. Ct. (no. dist.) Ohio 1962. Assoc. Squire, Sanders & Dempsey L.L.P., Cleve., 1960-70, ptnr., 1970—2002, counsel, 2002—03. Lectr. various programs, Order of Coif. Author: Local Government in Michigan, 1960; contbr. articles to profl. jours.; participant in Quiz Kids radio program, 1945-47. Mem. council City of Rocky River, Ohio, 1967-71; mem. cen. com. Cuyahoga County Rep. Orgn., Ohio, 1963-75, mem. exec. com., 1969-2001. Served to 1st lt. USAF, 1955-57. Mem. Ohio State Bar Assn., Portage County Bar Assn., Greater Cleve. Bar Assn. (com. chmn. 1978), Soc. Profl. Journalists. Avocations: travel, crossword puzzles. Home: Aurora, Ohio. Died Mar. 31, 2007.

BERRY, JOE WILKES, academic administrator, English educator; b. Ft. Worth, Feb. 9, 1938; s. Joe Wilkes and Pearl Elleen (Meggs) B.; m. June Massengale, Dec. 20, 1960; children: Elizabeth Berry Trahan, Alicia Berry Hubbard. BA, Abilene Christian U., 1960; MA, Rice U., 1962, PhD, 1964. Asst. prof.

English Tex. Tech U., Lubbock, 1964-68, assoc. prof., 1968-73, prof., 1973-81, chmn. dept., 1977-81; dean Coll. Humanities and Fine Arts, prof. English Tex. Woman's U., Denton, 1981-89, assoc. v.p. acad. affairs, from 1987. Home: Denton, Tex. Died Jan. 17, 2006.

BERTRAND, ALVIN LEE, rural sociologist; b. Elton, La., July 6, 1918; s. Jacob William and Ludie (Treme) B.; m. Mary Nic Ellis, Aug. 29, 1941; Children— William Ellis, Mary Lynne. BS, La. State U., 1940, PhD, 1948; MS, U. Ky., 1941. Mem. faculty La. State U., 1940-42, 46-78, prof. rural sociology, Boyd disting. prof., prof. emeritus, from 1978; founder, pres. Socio-Tech. Cons., Inc., from 1980; head levels living sect., farm population and rural life br. Dept. Agr., 1957-58. Vis. prof., internat. chair Va. Poly. Inst. and State U.; adj. prof. Tulane U.; mem. nat. sci. adv. com. Nat. Park Service; cons. in field. Author books, monographs, bulls., articles in field. Served with USAAF, 1942-46. Fellow Am. Sociol. Assn.; mem. Rural Social Soc. (Disting. Service award), So. Assn. Agrl. Scientists (Disting. Service award rural sociol. sect.), Southwestern Sociol. Soc., Population Assn. Am., La. Acad. Scis., AAUP, Am. Country Life Assn., La. Hist. Assn., European Congress Rural Sociology, Community Devel. Soc., Assn. Latino-Americana De Sociologia Rural, Internat. Rural Sociol. Assn., Nat. Parks and Conservation Assn., Mid-South Sociol. Assn., Gamma Sigma Delta (merit award), Phi Kappa Phi, Alpha Gamma Rho, Alpha Kappa Delta, Alpha Delta, Alpha Sigma Lambda. Democrat. Baptist. Died Feb. 26, 2006.

BETTY, GARRY (CHARLES GARRY BETTY), Internet company executive; b. Huntsville, Ala., Mar. 4, 1957; m. Kathy Betty. BChemE, Ga. Inst. Tech., 1979. Joined IBM, 1980; sr. v.p. sales, mktg. and internat. ops. Hayes Microcomputer Products, 1984-89; pres., CEO Digital Comm. Assocs., Inc., 1990—96; pres., COO Earthlink, Inc., Atlanta, 1996; CEO EarthLink, Inc., Atlanta, 1996—2006. Chmn. Ga.'s High Tech Month, 1993; bd. dirs. Equifax, DBT OnLine, allAutoRepair.com., Global Payments, Inc; chmn. Physician's Data Corp. Bd. dirs. Carter Center Bd. of Councilors; external adv. bd. School Chemical & Biomolecular Engrng., Georgia Tech. Inst. Recipient IBM's Pres. Excellence award, 1982, Engrng. award from the Council of Outstanding Young Engineering Alumni, Ga. Inst. Tech., 1994, Disting. Alumni award, Coll. Engr. Ga. Tech, 2000, Tech. Leadership award, Los Angeles C of C, 2001; named Young Alumnus of the Year, Ga. Inst. Tech., 1993, Top 40 Under 40 list in Atlanta's bus. cmty., Outstanding Young Person, Atlanta Bus. Chronicle, Coll.; named one of Elite 100, Upside Mag., 1999, Most Influential Atlantans, Atlanta Business Chronicle, 2004; inducted into Ga. Tech. Hall of Fame, 2005. Died Jan. 2, 2007.

BEVAN, JOHN A., pharmacologist, educator; b. London, Apr. 24, 1930; came to the U.S., 1955; s. John and Florence (Barrett) B.; m. Rosemary D. Prior, June 12, 1955; children: Christopher, Heather, Diane, Alison. BS with spl. honors, U. London, 1950, MB, BS, 1953. Lectr. in physiology Regent St. Poly., London, 1950-52; acting chmn. pharmacology UCLA Med. Ctr., 1961, assoc. prof., 1962, mem. brain inst., 1963, prof. pharmacology, 1967-83; prof., chmn. U. Vt., Burlington, from 1983. Vis. scientist dept. pharmacology Hoffman LaRoche, Basel, Switzerland, 1970-71; vis. prof. U. Basel, 1970-71; house surgeon Westminster Hosp., 1950, house physician, 1954; honorary demonstrator St. Bartholomew's Hosp. Med. Sch., London, 1950-52; adv. com. cardiovascular rsch. program U. Mich., 1978-81, Johns Hopkins Med. Sch. Program Cerebrovascular Control, 1984-85; cons. Australian Nat. Health and Med. Rsch. Coun., 1974-77, FDA, 1976, NHLBI, 1972, 76, 78, 85, 89, NIH. Editor: Blood Vessels, 1975-91. Major Royal Air Force, 1954-56. NIH grantee, 1983, 84. Mem. Am. Soc. Pharmacology and Experimental Therapeutics, Am. Physiol. Soc., Western Pharmacological Soc., Internat. Soc. Hypertension, Microcirculatory Soc., Am. Heart Assn., Royal Soc. Medicine. Home: North Ferrisburg, Vt. Died Feb. 14, 2007.

BEVAN, WILLIAM, retired foundation executive; b. Plains, Pa., May 16, 1922; s. William and Elizabeth Merle (Jones) B.; m. Dorothy Louise Chorpening, Feb. 17, 1945; children: William III, Mark Filbert, Philip Ross. AB with honors, Franklin and Marshall Coll., 1942, ScD, 1979; MA, Duke U., 1943, PhD, 1948, LLD, 1972; ScD, Fla. Atlantic U., 1968, Emory U., 1974, U. Md., 1981, Kans. State U., 1987; DHL, So. Ill. U., 1989. Instr. psychology Duke U., 1947, William Preston Few prof. psychology, 1974-92, prof. emeritus, from 1992, provost, 1979-83; instr., then asst. prof. psychology Heidelberg Coll., Tiffin, Ohio, 1946-48; mem. faculty Emory U., 1948-59, prof. psychology, 1958-59; prof. psychology, chmn. dept. Kans. State U., 1959-62, dean arts and scis., 1962-63, v.p. acad. affairs, 1963-66; fellow Center for Advanced Study Behavioral Scis., Stanford, Calif., 1965-66; sr. postdoctoral fellow NSF, 1965-66; v.p., provost Johns Hopkins U., Balt., 1966-70, prof. psychology, 1966-74; exec. officer AAAS, 1970-74, pub. Science, 1970-74; mem. adv. bd. Univ. Coll., U. Md., 1978-86; bd. govs. Research Triangle Inst., 1979-82; v.p. John D. and Catherine T. MacArthur Found., Chgo., 1983-91, ret., 1991. Mem. adv. bd. Ctr. Advanced Study U. Va., 1976-89. Editorial adv. bd.: Am. Men and Women of Sci., 12th edit, 1972, Social Sci. Citations Index, 1972-77; contbr. articles to profl. jours. Trustee Human Resources Research Orgn., 1968-88, Franklin and Marshall Coll., 1971-76, Coll. Retirement Equity Fund, 1972-90, Ctr. for Creative Leadership, 1972-79, Biosis. Info. Svc., 1974-80, Am. Psychol. Found., 1970-77, 83-89, Assn. Advancement of Psychology, 1974-78, William T. Grant Found., 1977-90, HumRRO Internat. Inc., 1985-89, Jackson Meml. Lab., 1986-90. With USNR, 1944-70. Recipient Franklin & Marshall Coll. Disting. Alumni award, 1966, Duke U. Disting. Alumni award, 1997-98; Fulbright scholar U. Oslo (Norway), 1952-53. Fellow: AAAS, APA; mem.: Am. Psychol. Soc., Soc. Exptl. Psychologists, Am. Acad. Arts and Scis., History of Sci. Soc., So. Soc. Philosophy and Psychology, Psychonomic Soc., Inst. Medicine of Nat. Acad. Sci., Cosmos Club (Washington), Sigma Xi, Phi Beta Kappa. Home: Durham, NC. Died Feb. 26, 2007.

BEZANSON, PETER FLOYD, retired banking and finance company executive; b. Mpls., Apr. 2, 1915; s. Harry B. and Lillian M. (Zwicker) B.; m. Lorrayne B. Bing, June 17, 1939; children: Judith Rae, Randall Peter. BA, U. Wis., 1937; postgrad., Columbia U., 1960. Chmn. bd. MorAm. Fin. Corp., Cedar Rapids, from 1953; chmn. MorAm. Capital Corp., from 1958, MorAm. Mktg. Inc., MorAm. Realty Co.; pres., bd. dirs. Bezanon Property Inc. Bd. govs. Nat. Assn. Small Bus. Investment Assn., 1961-68; v.p., chmn. bd. Am. Indsl. Bankers Assn., 1966-68. Nat. vice chmn. fund drive ARC, 1959-60; trustee Installment Banking Sch., U. Colo., 1962-72, Coe Coll., Cedar Rapids, 1974-85; pres. Hawkeye area coun. Boy Scouts Am., 1976-78. With USAAF, 1944-45. Mem. Cedar Rapids Country Club, Masons, Shriners, Elks, Rotary, Chi Phi. Presbyterian (elder). Home: Cedar Rapids, Iowa. Died Feb. 26, 2006.

BICKEL, HERBERT JACOB, JR., corporation executive; b. Evanston, Ill., Feb. 20, 1930; s. Herbert Jacob and Jean (Meadows) B.; m. Joan Hough, July 17, 1954; children: David Alan, Daniel Wayne, John Douglas. BS in Bus. Adminstrn, U. Fla., 1952; MS in Indsl. Mgmt, Ga. Inst. Tech., 1955; postgrad., Mass. Inst. Tech., 1955-56. Prin. economist Tex. Eastern Transmission Corp., Houston, 1957-66, treas., 1966-80, v.p., 1971-80; sr. v.p. fin. Saxon Oil Co., Dallas, 1980-85; pres. Resource Savs. Assn., 1985-86, May Petroleum Inc., 1986-87, Statlab Med. Products, 1987-95. Instr. Ga. Inst. Tech., 1955, Centenary Coll., Shreveport, 1958; vis. lectr. Pa. State U., 1964 Author: (with others) National Fuels and Energy Study, Competition and Growth in American Energy Markets, 1947-1985, 1968. Served to 1st lt. AUS, 1952-54. Mem. Fin. Execs. Inst., Soc. Petroleum Engrs., Houston Soc. Fin. Analysts (pres. 1970-71) Home: Frisco, Tex. Died Dec. 2, 2005.

BIESEL, DUANE MACDONALD, manufacturing company executive; b. Chgo., June 9, 1931; d. Lorne Evan and Marie Eileen (Lyness) MacDonald; m. Garnett Biesel, May 1, 1954 (div. June 1970). B.S., Monmouth Coll., 1952; postgrad. Northwestern U., 1956-57. Chemist, Underwriters Lab., Inc., Chgo., 1952-56; Toni Co. div. Gillette Co., Chgo., 1956-61; chemist Gillette Co., Chgo., 1964-74; product devel. mgr., Boston, 1974-87; research and devel. dir. Frank Fuhrer Internat., Pitts., 1987—. Patentee in hosiery field. Mem. Soc. Cosmetic Chemists. Avocations: reading; classical music; travel; golf. Home: Pittsburgh, Pa. Died Mar. 13, 2007.

BIGELOW, DONALD NEVIUS, educational association administrator, historian, consultant; b. Danbury, Conn., Aug. 19, 1918; s. Harry R. and Bessie M. (Nevius) B.; m. Louise M. Fournel, Sept. 21, 1957; 1 son, Pierre Nevius. BA cum laude, Amherst Coll., 1939, MA, 1945; PhD, Columbia U., 1950. Spl. agt. Inland Marine Ins., North Brit. and Merc. Ins. Co., NYC and Detroit, 1939-43; with U.S. Engr. Dept., Fairbanks, Alaska, 1942; instr. history Amherst Coll., 1943-45; instr. Columbia U., 1947-50, asst. prof., 1951-55; assoc. prof. Brandeis U., 1955-60; chief lang. and area ctrs. program Office Edn., HEW, Washington, 1961-64; head task force NDEA Title XI Inst. Program, 1964-65, dir. divsn. ednl. pers. tng., 1965-67, dir. divsn. program adminstrn., 1967-68; dir. divsn. coll. programs Bur. Ednl. Pers. Devel., 1968-71; dir. Northeast divsn. Nat. Ctr. for Improvement Ednl. Sys., 1972-74; spl. asst., assoc. commr. for Instl. Devel. and Internat. Edn., 1974-76; chief grad. tng. Office of Postsecondary Edn., Dept. Edn., Washington, 1976-82; sr. adminstr. The Nat. Faculty, Atlanta, 1985-88; spl. asst. to dep. asst. sec. Office of Postsecondary Edn., US Dept. Edn., Washington, 1988-93, sr. exec. Ctr. Internat. Edn., 1993; program mgr. Dwight D. Eisenhower Leadership Devel. Act of 1992 Office of Postsecondary Edn., U.S. Dept. Edn., Washington, 1993-96. Exec. dir. Javits Fellowship Bd., 1996-2000, spl. asst. Office Internat. Edn. & Grad. Edn. Office Higher Edn., 1998—, sr. advisor, 2002; vis. Fulbright prof. Am. civilization U.S. Ednl. Fund, India, U. Baroda, U. Lucknow, 1954-55; prof. humanities NY Sch. Music, 1949-56; vis. prof. U. So. Fla., 1969; postdoctoral rsch. fellow George Washington U., 1970-71; lectr. U. Va., 1973; adj. prof. Am. U., 1975; cons. Ford Found., 1957, Carnegie Corp., 1958, U.S. Office Edn., 1959-60; moderator ABC TV series Seminar, 1953-54, PBS WGBH TV series on ethnicity, 1956-57; assoc. dir. com. lang. and area ctrs. Am. Coun. Edn., 1960-61; book reviewer Nat. Pub. Radio series Options in Education, 1976-77. Author: William Conant Church and the Army and Navy Journal, 1952, (with Joseph Axelrod) Resources for Language and Area Studies, 1960, (with Lyman Legters) Language and Area Centers, 1964, (with others) Non-Western Studies in the Liberal Arts College, 1964; editor: (with Hiram Haydn) Makers of the American Tradition Series, 4 vols., 1953-55, The Annals (The Non-Western World in Higher Education), 1964, The Liberal Arts and Teacher Education: A Confrontation, 1971, Schoolworlds '76, New Directions for Educational Policy, 1976, Democracy at Risk: "Leadership and Education", an Unpublished Report on the Eisenhower Leadership Program, 1992-96, 1999. Home: Washington, DC. Died June 7, 2007.

BIGGER, MORTON, JR., oil company executive; b. Dallas, Feb. 9, 1924; s. Morton, Sr. and Mildred (Lowrey) B.; m. Anita Byrde Craddock, Dec. 27, 1947 (div. 1967); children— Mildred Anne Bigger Nixon, Margaret Morton Bigger Tarrance, Carolyn Byrde Bigger Peck; m. Catherine Rhody, Sept. 30, 1967. Student Washington and Lee U., 1942-43, Kenyon Coll., 1943-44; B.S., U. Tex., 1947. Geologist, Chevron Oil Co., New Orleans, 1947-49; asst. to v.p. Republic Nat. Gas Co., Dallas, 1949-51; v.p. subs. Union Oil Co. of Calif., Trucial Coast, Africa, Norway, 1966-75; v.p. Transcontinental Oil Corp., Shreveport, La., 1975-80; sr. v.p. Latham Exploration Co., Shreveport, 1981-83; pres. Atakora Corp., Shreveport, 1980—; petroleum cons., Dallas, 1951-66, Shreveport, 1980-81. Served with U.S. Army, 1943-44. Decorated chevalier l'Ordre Nationale du Dahomey, 1972. Mem. Am. Assn. Petroleum Geologists, Shreveport Geol. Assn., West Tex. Geol. Assn., Dallas Geol. Soc., Sigma Gamma Epsilon. Republican. Presbyterian. Clubs: Shreveport Country, Les Ambassadeurs (London). Avocations: hunting; golf; painting. Home: Shreveport, La. Died Aug. 16, 2006.

BIGGS, J. O., lawyer, manufacturing executive; b. Kansas City, Mo., Feb. 17, 1925; s. John Olin and Parilee Catherine (Story) B.; m. Marilyn Frances Sweeney, Dec. 27, 1947; children— Melissa Anne, John Kevin, Brian Sweeney. AB, U. Kans., 1947, LLB, 1949. Bar: Kan. bar 1949, Mo. bar 1950, Ia. bar 1953. With legal dept. Kansas City Life Ins. Co., 1950-51; exec. asst. to industry members Regional Wage Stblzn. Bd., 1951-52; dir. labor relations Meredith Pub. Co., 1952-58; with Gustin-Bacon Mfg. Co. (merger into Certain-teed Products Corp. 1966), from 1958, v.p., asst. to pres., 1962-63, pres., chief exec. officer, 1963-66; exec. v.p. Ardmore, Pa., 1966-69; pres. Thermo-Kinetic Corp., 1969-76; mem. firm Wagner, Leek & Mullins, from 1976. Cons. in field; sr. v.p., gen. counsel Exec. Hills, Inc., Shawnee Mission, Kans., 1979—. Active Big Bros. of Tucson. Mem. Am., Mo., Kans., Johnson County bar assns., Kansas City Met. Bar Assn., Am. Mgmt. Assn., Sigma Alpha Epsilon, Phi Alpha Phi. Clubs: Skyline (Tucson), Country (Tucson); Carriage (Kansas City). Republican. Presbyterian. Home: Shawnee Mission, Kans. Died Feb. 26, 2006.

BIGMAN, ANTON W., lawyer; b. Braddock, Pa., Apr. 6, 1929; AB cum laude, U. Pitts., 1951; LLB, Harvard U., 1954. Bar: Pa. 1955, U.S. Supreme Ct. 1965. Pvt. practice, Pitts., from 1955. Solicitor Braddock Sch. Dist., 1956-71, No. Braddock Sch. Dist., 1957-69; No. Braddock Sch. Bldg. Authority, 1960-69, Gen. Braddock Area Sch. Dist., 1971-72, 1980-81. Chmn. Braddock Borough Parking Authority, 1958-59; v.p. Beth Hamedrash Hagadol-Beth Jacob Congregation, Pitts., 1986—. Mem. ABA, Pa. Bar Assn., Allegheny County Bar Assn., Assn. Trial Lawyers Am., B'nai Brith, Harvard-Yale-Princeton Club (Pitts.). Home: Pittsburgh, Pa. Died Feb. 15, 2006.

BILL, MARY FOURNIER, theater director, retired; b. Cleve., Jan. 13, 1925; d. Frederick Joseph and Clara Margaret (Custer) Fournier; m. Charles Bill, July 5, 1952; children: Kate, Anne, Matthew. BA, Western Res. U., 1946; MA, Bowling Green State U., 1949; postgrad., Cath. U. Am., 1949-50. Theater instr. Notre Dame Coll., South Euclid, Ohio, 1950-53; theater dir. St. Joseph Acad., Cleve., 1960-70; mng. dir. Great Lakes Theater Festival, Cleve., 1971-93; retired, 1993. Head theater panel Ohio Arts Coun., Columbus, 1973-74, mem. presenting panel, 1978-81. Playwright An Infinite Deal of Nothing, 1969, The Welcoming, 1970. Recipient Profl. Woman of Achievement award YWCA, Cleve., 1991, Gov.'s award for arts adminstrn., State of Ohio, 1993, Faith and Svc. award Kappa Gamma Pi, 1993; named Woman of Achievement, Women's City Club, Cleve., 1993. Democrat. Roman Catholic. Avocations: gardening, cooking. Died Dec. 4, 2006.

BINGHAM, WALTER D., retired minister; b. Memphis, June 3, 1921; s. Willie and Lena (Allen) B.; m. Rebecca T. Bingham; stepchild, Gail Elaine Bingham. BA, Talladega Coll., Ala., 1945; MDiv, Howard U., 1948, postgrad., 1948-49; DD, Christian Theol. Sem., Indpls., 1969; LHD, Drury Coll., Springfield, Mo., 1972; LLD, Transylvania U., Lexington, Ky., 1973. Ordained to ministry Disciples of Christ Ch., 1947. Campus minister, instr. religion Jarvis Christian Coll., Hawkins, Tex., 1949-57; minister Pine St. Christian Ch., Tulsa, 1957-61; pastor 3d Christian Ch., Louisville, 1961-92, pastor emeritus ecumenical, from 1992; v.p. Christian Ch. Commn. Jefferson County, Ky., 1965-66, pres., 1978-81; mem. gen. bd. Christian Ch., 1979-87, chair coun. on Christian unity, 1981-85; pastor ecumenical emeritus Third Christian Ch., Louisville, from 1986; pres. Christian Ch. Ky., 1966-67; moderator Disciples of Christ Ch., U.S. and Can., 1971-73; mem. gov. bd. Nat. Council Ch., 1969-73; mem. nat. steering com. on covenant Christian Ch.-United Ch. of Christ, 1982-85; Christian Ch. del. Consultation on Ch. Union, 1988-91. Fraternal visitor for Christian Ch. to Japan, Hong Kong, Thailand, India, 1972; del. 5th Assembly, World Council Chs., Nairobi, Kenya, 1975, 6th Assembly, World Coun. Chs., Vancouver, B.C., Can., 1983. Mem. Louisville and Jefferson Air Bd. Citizens Com., 1971-74; bd. dirs. Vols. Am., 1965-71; trustee Jarvis Christian Coll., 1971-75, Lexington Theol. Sem., 1969-89, elected emeritus, 1990. Recipient Outstanding Community Leadership award Phi Beta Sigma, 1969, Humanitarian award Kappa Alpha Psi, 1992; named Ky. Col., 1967, Pastor of Yr., Sta. WLOU, 1970, Disting. Citizen Louisville, 1971, Patron of Christian Unity, Disciples of Christ Coun. on Christian Unity; The Walter D. Bingham Leadership award Scholarship named in his honor Lexington Theol. Sem., 1990. Mem. NAACP, Urban League, Omega Psi Phi. Home: Louisville, Ky. Died Apr. 12, 2006.

BINGMAN, HARRY DAVID, geology educator; b. Richardson, W.Va., Mar. 15, 1921; m. Eleanor Frances Smith, June 21, 1942; children: Harry David III, Stephen Michael. AB, Marietta Coll., 1948; MA, W.Va. U., 1964; postgrad. Rice U. Tchr. Wirt County H.S., Elizabeth, W.Va., 1948-50, Parkersburg High Sch., W.Va., 1950-59; dir. Wood County Planetarium, Parkersburg, 1959-64; instr. W.Va. U.-Parkersburg Ctr., 1965-72; instr., div. chmn. Parkersburg C.C., 1972-65, prof. emeritus, 1965—; part-time instr. astronomy W.Va. U., Parersburg Ctr., Marietta Coll., 1965-80. Served as sgt. U.S. Army, 1942-46. Mem. W.Va. Acad. Sci., Nat. Assn. Geology Tchrs., Soc. Econ. Paleontologists and Mineralogists, Ohio Valley Gem and Mineral Assn. (pres. 1976-78), Phi Delta Kappa. Republican. Lodges: Mason, Elks. Avocations: boating; mineral and fossil collecting; music. Home: N Parkersburg, W.Va. Died June 20, 2007.

BIRCH, WILLIS DANIEL, lawyer; b. Chgo., Feb. 13, 1925; s. Arthur Lee and Estrid (Holthe) B.; m. Ruth E., Aug. 7, 1948; children— Thomas C., Robert W., Martha M. B.S. in Commerce and Law, U. Ill., 1949; LL.B., Cornell U., 1951, LL.D., 1969. Bar: N.Y. 1952, U.S. Dist. Ct. (no. dist.) N.Y. 1952. Assoc. Deyo, Turnbull, Turner & Normile, Binghamton, N.Y., 1951-53, Chernin & Gold, Binghamton, 1953-56; ptnr. Night, Keller & Birch, Binghamton, 1957-63; sole practice Willis D. Birch, P.C., Binghamton, 1963—. Town Justice Town of Fenton, Broome County, N.Y., 1953-70; pres. Chenango Valley Cemetery Assn., Binghamton, 1983-84. Served with USN, 1943-45. Former mem. N.Y. State Trial Lawyers Assn. Republican. Presbyterian. Lodge: Rotary (charter mem., past pres. chpt.). Home: Binghamton, NY. Died Feb. 19, 2006.

BIRD, FRANK EDWARD, JR., educational institute administrator; b. Netcong, N.J., Dec. 19, 1921; s. Frank Edward and Virginia (Goebel) B.; m. Esther Savidge, Nov. 6, 1948; children— Frank Edward, Susan Bird Arnold, Bille, David John, John Mark. B.S., Albright Coll., Reading, Pa., 1950; postgrad. NYU, 1956-57. Supr. safety Lukens Steel, Coatesville, Pa.,

1953-68; dir. engring. services Ins. Co. N.Am., Phila., 1968-71; exec. dir. Internat. Safety Acad., Macon, Ga., 1971-73; pres. Internat. Loss Control Inst., Inc., Atlanta, 1974-91; adj. prof. Ga. State U. Author: Damage Control, 1966; co-author: Management Guide to Loss Control, 1974, Loss Control Management, 1976, Management Guide to Mine Safety, 1984, Practical Loss Control Leadership, 1985, Commitment, 1988, Profits are in Order, 1989, Safety Strategies with Power, 1994, Safety and the Bottom Line, 1996, The Property Damage Accident, 1997; patentee in field; originator internat. safety rating system. Chmn. safety Chester County Council Boy Scouts, Phila., 1955-64; mem. instrn. tng. bd. ARC, Phila. regional officer 1965-71; pres. Chester County Safety Council, 1958-71. Served with USN, 1942-46. Recipient Gold award Royal Soc. Prevention of Accidents, Eng., Pub. Service award U.S. Dept. Interior, 1971; named Optimist of Yr., 1967; inducted Safety and Health Hall of Fame, 1988. Fellow Am. Soc. Safety Engrs.; mem. Nat. Safety Mgmt. Soc., Ind. Occupational Prevention Assn. Ont. (hon. life), Can. Soc. Safety Engrs. (hon.), New Zealand Soc. Safety Profls. (hon.) Soc. Systems Safety Soc. Methodist, Am. Legion (post 293). Died June 28, 2007.

BIRDLEBOUGH, HAROLD, dentist; b. Yakima, Wash., May 4, 1928; s. Otis Theodore and Elizabeth (Brown) B.; m. Donna Mae Vensel, June 18, 1977; children: John Michael, Elizabeth, William Powers, Marcia; step: Steve Hassenfratz, Nancy Hassenfratz, Keith Fontel. DDS, U. Wash., 1959. Practice dentistry, Seattle, 1959—61, King County, Wash., from 1961. Mem. dental adv. com. Blue Cross Ins. Co. With USNR, 1948—52. Mem. ADA, Wash. Dental Assn., Snohomish County Dental Soc., Gen. Acad. Dentistry, U. Wash. Dental Alumni, Soc. Preservation and Encouragement Barbershop Quartet Singing in Am., Delta Sigma Delta, Alpha Delta Phi (1st v.p. local alumni assn., del. nat. constl. conv. 1968), Elks Club. Republican. Episcopalian (Sr. Warden). Died Mar. 20, 2006.

BIRMINGHAM, MARTIN F., banker, retired; b. Rochester, NY, Oct. 30, 1921; s. Edward M. and Mary Elizabeth (Egleton) B.; m. Ann Louise Bayer, Sept. 30, 1950; children: Katherine J., Mary L., Mark R., Martin K. V.p. Abstract & Title Ins. Co. (now div. Title Guarantee Co.), Rochester, 1940-54; with Marine Midland Bank, Rochester, from 1954, 1968-73, pres., from 1973, regional chmn., from 1987, also dir., exec. v.p. NYC. Bd. dirs. United Way Rochester, St. John Fishers Coll., Gannet Found., Inc., St. Ann's Home and Heritage, Strong Mus., Genessee Country Mus.; bd. dirs., chmn. Exec. Svc. Corps, Rochester. With USAAF, 1943-45. Mem. Greater Rochester C. of C. (bd. dirs.), Clubs: Automobile of Rochester, Country of Rochester, Oak Hill Country, Genessee Valley. Home: Pittsford, NY. Died June 9, 2006.

BISCHOFF, KENNETH BRUCE, chemical engineer, educator; b. Chgo., Feb. 29, 1936; s. Arthur William and Evelyn Mary (Hansen) B.; m. Joyce Arlene Winterberg, June 6, 1959; children: Kathryn Ann, James Eric. BS, Ill. Inst. Tech., 1957, PhD, 1961. Asst. to assoc. prof. U. Tex., Austin, 1961-67; assoc. prof., then prof. U. Md., 1967-70; Walter R. Read prof. engring. Cornell U., 1970-76, dir. Sch. Chem. Engring., 1970-75; Unidel prof., biomed. and chem. engring. U. Del., 1976-98, emeritus, from 1998, chmn. dept. chem. engring., 1978-82. Mem. NRC Bd. on Chem. Scis. and Tech., 1984-86, various coms., 1984—; cons. Exxon Rsch. and Engring., NIH, Gen. Foods Corp., W.R. Grace Co., Koppers Co., DuPont Co. Author: (with D.M. Himmelblau) Process Analysis and Simulation, 1968, (with G.F. Froment) Chemical Reactor Analysis and Design, 1979, 2d edit., 1989; chmn., editor: (with R.L. Dedrick and E.F. Leonard) The Artificial Kidney, Process 1st. Internat. Symposium Chem. Reaction Engring., 1970, (with R.M. Koros and T.R. Keane) Process 9th Symposium, 1986; mem. editorial bd. Advances in Chemistry Series, 1973-76, 78-81, Jour. Bioengring., 1976-80, Jour. Pharmacokin, Biopharmaceutics, 1975-92, Biotech. Progress, 1987-2000, Advances in Chem. Engring., 1981-2000. Recipient Ebert prize Acad. Pharm. Scis., 1972, Founders award Chem. Indsl. Inst. Toxicology, 1992, Disting. Alumni award Ill. Inst. Tech., 1996, Profl. Achievement award, 1997; Shell Found. fellow, 1959, NSF fellow, 1960, U. Ghent fellow, 1960-61, NAE fellow. Fellow AAAS, AIChE (dir. 1972-74, chmn. food, pharm. and bioengring. divsn. 1985, chmn. nat. program com. 1978, Profl. Progress award 1976, Food Pharm. and Bioengring. divsn. award 1982, 34th Ann. Inst. lectr. 1982, R.H. Wilhelm award 1987); mem. Am. Inst. Chem. Engr., Am. Chem. Soc., Am. Soc. Artificial Internal Organs, Engrs. Coun. for Profl. Devel. (bd. dirs. 1972-78), Coun. Chem. Rsch. (governing bd. 1981-84, chmn. 1985), Catalysis Soc., AAUP, N.Y. Acad. Scis., Sigma XI, Tau Beta Pi, Phi Lambda Upsilon, Omega Chi Epsilon, Alpha Chi Sigma. Home: Rehoboth Beach, Del. Died 2006.

BISHOP, JOEY (JOSEPH ABRAHAM GOTTLIEB), comedian, actor; b. NYC, Feb. 3, 1918; s. Jacob and Anna (Siegel) Gottlieb; m. Sylvia Ruzga, Jan. 14, 1941 (dec. Sept. 21, 1999); 1 child, Larry. Student pub. schs., Phila. Comedian Ea. burlesque cir., 1938-42, Vine Gardens, N.J., 1948-49, Chez Paree, Chgo.; actor: (films) The Deep Six, 1958, Onionhead, 1958, The Naked and The Dead, 1958, Ocean's Eleven, 1960, Pepe, 1960, Sergeants Three, 1962, Johnny Cool, 1963, Texas Across the River, 1966, A Guide for the Married Man, 1967, Valley of the Dolls, 1967, Who's Minding the Mint?, 1967, The Delta Force, 1986, Betsy's Wedding, 1990, Mad Dog Time, 1996; (TV movies) Esther Williams at Cyrpress Gardens, 1960, Glory Years, 1987; (TV appearances) Toast of the Town, 1949-58, Cavalcade of Bands, 1951, Frankie Laine Time, 1955, The Dinah Shore Chevy Show, 1957, The Frank Sinatra Show, 1958, Keep Talking, 1958, The Jack Paar Show, 1958-62, Keep Talking, 1959-60, Richard Diamond, Private Detective, 1959, The Dupont Show of the Month, 1960, The Jack Benny Program, 1960-64, What's My Line?, 1960-66, The Andy Williams Show, 1963-65, The Dick Powell Show, 1963, The Hollywood Palace, 1967, Get Smart, 1967, The Smothers Brothers Comedy Hour, 1969, The Barbara McNair Show, 1969, Rowan & Marin's Laugh-In, 1968-71, The Dean Martin Show, 1970-74, The Hollywood Squares, 1972, Tonight Show Starring Johnny Carson, 1971-88, Celebrity Sweepstakes, 1975, Match Game PM, 1975, Break the Bank, 1976 Chico and the Man, 1976, Liar's Club, 1976, Dinah!, 1977, The Merv Griffin Show, 1978, Trapper John, M.D., 1981, Hardcastle and McCormick, 1985, Murder, She Wrote, 1985; host (TV series) The Joey Bishop Show, 1961-65;(theatre) Who Was That Lady I Saw You With?, 1960, Sugar Babies, 1981. Served in US Army, 1942-45. Jewish. Died Oct. 17, 2007.

BISHOP, JOHN FREDERICK, manufacturing executive; b. Yenangyuang, Burma, Jan. 3, 1924; (parents Am. citizens); s. Fay and Florence Louise (Larson) Bishop; m. Ann Rix, Nov. 4, 1945; children: Caren Lee Bishop McDonald, John Bradford, Kimberly Ann Bishop Rothwell, Suzann Louise Burke. BSME, U. Calif., Berkeley, 1945; MBA, Harvard U., 1948. With market rsch. and distbn. dept. Owens-Corning Fiberglas Corp., LA, 1948—51; divsn. gen. mgr. Beckman Instruments, Inc., Fullerton, Calif., 1951—59; exec. v.p. Textron Electronics, Inc., Santa Ana, Calif., 1959—60; chmn. bd. dirs. EIP Microwave, Inc., Newport Beach, Calif., from 1960, Cushman Electronics, Inc., Newport Beach, from 1960. Bd. dirs. ECCO, Inc., Baker Internat. Corp. Trustee Webb Sch. Calif., 1970—73, Claremont Men's Coll., 1972—75; founding pres. UCI (U. Calif., Irvine) Found., 1968—69. Lt. (j.g.) USNR, 1943—47. Mem.: IEEE, ASME, Mchts. and Mfrs. Assn. (bd. dirs. 1968—70), Chief Execs. Orgn., World Bus. Coun., Young Presidents Orgn., Am. Electronics Assn., Instrument Soc. Am., Indian Wells Club, The Vintage Club, Big Canyon Country Club, Calif. Club. Republican. Episcopalian. Home: Newport Beach, Calif. Died Nov. 28, 2006.

BISHOP, ROBERT MILTON, former stock exchange official; b. Elmira, NY, June 5, 1921; s. Milton W. and Florence E. (Crofutt) B.; m. Anne Selene Rowan, Oct. 30, 1943; children: Donald M., Anne Selene (Mrs. Donald R. Bennett), Elizabeth M. (Mrs. Thomas H. Speed), Robert Milton, Regina J.M. (Mrs. David P. Bergeland), Rowan J.S. AB, Union Coll., Schenectady, 1943; AM, Trinity Coll., Hartford, Conn., 1955. Asst. dir. pub. relations Union Coll., Schenectady, 1945-47; dir. pub. relations Trinity Coll., 1947-55; mem. staff N.Y. Stock Exchange, 1955-86. Dir. dept. mem. firms liaison, asst. dir. dept. mem. firms, 1961-63, v.p., assoc. dir. dept. mem. firms, 1963-65, v.p., dir. dept. mem. firms, 1965-73, sr. v.p. mem. firm regulation and surveillance group, 1973-81, sr. v.p. regulatory svcs. group, 1982-84, sr. v.p. regulatory quality rev. and long-range planning, 1984-86; cons. Lloyds of London, USAID, World Bank, Capital Markets Authorities and Stock Exchs. of Bulgaria, Dominican Republic, Egypt, Jamaica, Kazakhstan, Kenya, Hungary, Morocco, Pakistan, Serbia, Siberia, Singapore, Slovenia, Sri Lanka, Tunisia, Uganda. Author booklets, securities tng. manuals, and model basic rules for a stock exch. Trustee Cathedral Symphony at Cathedral Sacred Heart, Newark, 1984-92, Union Coll., 1989-93. With USAF, 1943-45. Mem.: India House, Stock Exchange Luncheon, Mohawk. Episcopalian. Home: Maplewood, NJ. Died May 10, 2007.

BIXLER, DAVID, medical and dental educator, genetic counselor; b. Chgo., Jan. 7, 1929; s. David Clare and Mary Wilhelmina (Wall) B.; m. Betty Ann Foxworthy, Feb. 3, 1952; m. Gloria Ann Greenen, Feb. 5, 1964; children— David, Kathy, Scott, Laurie, Brian, Michelle AB, Ind. U., 1950, PhD, 1956, D.D.S., 1959. Diplomate Am. Bd. Med. Genetics. USPHS postdoctoral fellow Ind. U. Sch. Dentistry, Indpls., 1956-58, asst. prof., 1959-66, assoc. prof. basic sci. and med. genetics, 1967-75, prof. oral-facial and med. genetics, from 1976, prof., chmn. oral-facial genetics (dentistry), from 1972, prof. med. genetics (medicine), from 1976, prof. emeritus, from 1993; retired. Cons. Procter & Gamble, Beecham Co., NIH; lectr. Nat. Found. March of Dimes Contbr. chpts. to textbooks, articles to sci. publs. Served with USAF, 1949-51 Recipient career devel. award NIH, 1967-72 Mem. AAAS, Am. Soc. Human Genetics, Soc. Craniofacial Genetics, Sigma Xi, Omicron Kappa Upsilon Home: N Fort Myers, Fla. Died Nov. 15, 2005.

BLACK, DANIEL JAMES, chemical company executive; b. Asbury Park, NJ, Dec. 31, 1931; s. Daniel Joseph and Julia (Palmer) B.; m. Marilyn Russo, Apr. 23, 1960; children— Daniel, Deborah, Peter. Student, Cooper Union, St. John's U., 1950-52; BS, N.Y. U., 1956. Asst. to treas. Frederick Snare Corp., NYC, 1954-60; pres., chief operating officer Carter-Wallace Inc., NYC, from 1960, also dir., mem. exec. com. Bd. trustees Mt. Holyoke Coll., 1994—; bd. overseers Stern Sch. Bus. NYU, 1994—. Served with AUS, 1952-54. Mem. Tax Execs. Inst. (v.p. 1967-71), Fin. Execs. Inst., Sands Point Golf Club, Manhasset Bay Yacht Club, Met. Club, Univ. Club. Roman Catholic. Home: New York, NY. Died May 11, 2007.

BLACK, LYDIA T., anthropologist, educator; b. Kiev, USSR, Dec. 16, 1925; came to U.S., 1950; m. Igor A. Black, Jan. 12, 1947 (dec. 1969); children: Anna Black Treiber, Maria Black McEvoy, Zoe M. Black Pierson, Elena. BS in History, Northeastern U., 1969; MA in Social Anthropology, Brandeis U., 1971; PhD in Social Anthropology, U. Mass., 1973. Asst. prof. to prof. anthropology Providence Coll., 1973-85; prof. anthropology U. Alaska, Fairbanks, 1985—98. Instr. anthropology U. Mass., 1972; vis. lectr. Am. Anthrop. Assn., 1974-76; cons. various orgns. Author: The Journals of Iakov Netsvetov-The Atkha Years, 1980, Aleut Art, 1982, Atkha-Ethnohistory of the Western Aleutians, 1983, The Journals of Iakov Netsvetov. The Yukon Years: 1845-1863, 1984, The Round the World Voyage of Hieromonk Gideon, 1803-1809, 1989, Glory Remembered: Wooden Headgear of Alaska Sea Hunters, 1991, Lovtsov's Atlas of the North Pacific Ocean, 1991; translator: Notes on the Islands of Unalaska District (by Ioann Veniaminov), 1984; contbr. numerous articles to profl. jours. Mem. Icon Preservation Task Force, Anchorage, 1986-2007. Eastern Orthodox. Avocations: poetry, reading mystery novels, walking, hiking in alaskan mountains. Home: Kodiak, Alaska. Died Mar. 12, 2007.

BLACK, PRESTON ROBERT, pediatric surgeon; b. High Springs, Fla., May 26, 1949. A.B., Harvard Coll., 1971, M.D., 1975. Diplomate Am. Bd. Surgeons. Resident in surgery Peter Bent Brigham, Boston, 1975-80; research fellow Brigham and Women's Hosps., Boston, 1980-82; fellow in surgery Children's Hosp., Boston, 1982-84, asst. surgery, 1984—87; asst. prof. surgery Harvard Med. Sch., 1984—87, Loyola U. Med. Ctr., 1987-97, pvt. practice, 1997-2007 Died Feb. 13, 2007.

BLACK, SAMUEL HAROLD, microbiology and immunology educator; b. Lebanon, Pa., May 1, 1930; s. Harold William and Beatrice Irene (Steckbeck) B.; m. Elisabeth Martha Zandveld, Aug. 16, 1961 (dec. Aug. 1997); children: Vicki Ann, Alisa Jo. Student, Hershey Jr. Coll., 1948-50; BS, Lebanon Valley Coll., 1952; postgrad., U. Pa., 1952-54; MS, U. Mich., 1958, PhD, 1961. NSF fellow Tech. U. Delft, The Netherlands, 1960-61; instr. U. Mich., Ann Arbor, 1961-62; asst. prof. Baylor Coll. Medicine, Houston, 1962-67, assoc. prof., 1967-71, Mich. State U., East Lansing, 1971-73, prof., 1973-75; prof. microbiology and immunology Tex. A&M U., College Station, from 1975, head dept. med. microbiology and immunology, 1975-90, asst. dean for curriculum and undergrad. med. edn., 1985-87, interim dean Coll. Medicine, 1987-88, assoc. dean Coll. Medicine, 1988-91, prof. humanities in medicine, from 1998. Lectr. U. Houston, 1964-66; vis. prof. Swiss Fed. Inst. Tech., Zurich, 1969-70 Served with M.C., U.S. Army, 1954-56. Recipient citation Lebanon Valley Coll. Alumni Assn., 1981. Fellow Am. Acad. Microbiology; mem. Am. Soc. Microbiology, Am. Soc. Cell Biology, Soc. Gen. Microbiology, Electron Microscope Soc. Am., Soc. Invertebrate Pathology Home: College Station, Tex. Died Mar. 30, 2007.

BLACKMAR, CHARLES BLAKEY, retired state supreme court justice; b. Kansas City, Mo., Apr. 19, 1922; s. Charles Maxwell and Eleanor (Blakey) B.; m. Ellen Day Bonnifield, July 18, 1943 (dec. 1983); children: Charles A. (dec.), Thomas J., Lucy E. Blackmar Alpaugh, Elizabeth S., George B.; m. Jeanne Stephens Lee, Oct. 5, 1984. AB summa cum laude, Princeton U., 1942; JD, U. Mich., 1948; LLD (hon.), St. Louis U., 1991. Bar: Mo. 1948. Pvt. practice law, Kansas City; ptnr. Swanson, Midgley and predecessors, 1952-66; profl. lectr. U. Mo. at Kansas City, 1949-58; prof. law St. Louis U., 1966-82, prof. emeritus, 1982—2007; spl. asst. to atty. gen. State of Mo., 1969-77; judge Supreme Ct. Mo., 1982—92, chief judge, 1989-91, sr. judge, 1992; labor arbitrator, active sr. judge, 1992—2007. Chmn. Fair Pub. Accommodations Commn. Kansas City, 1964-66; mem. Commn. Human Rels. Kansas City, 1965-66. Author: (with Volz and others) Missouri Practice, 1953, West's Federal Practice Manual, 1957, 71, (with Devitt) Federal Jury Practice and Instructions, 1970, 3d edit., 1977, (with Devitt, Wolff and O'Malley) 4th edit., 1988-92; contbr. numerous articles on probate and corp. law to profl. publs. Mem. Jackson County Rep. Com., 1952-58; mem. Mo. Rep. Com., 1956-58. 1st lt., inf. AUS, 1943-46. Decorated Silver Star, Purple Heart. Mem. Am. Law Inst., Nat. Acad. Arbitrators, Mo. Bar (spl. lectr. insts.), Disciples Peace Fellowship, Scribes (pres. 1986-87), Order of Coif, Phi Beta Kappa. Mem. Christian Ch. (Disciples Of Christ). Died Jan. 20, 2007.

BLACKMER, ALFRED M., agronomy educator; b. Fall River, Mass., Dec. 11, 1943; s. Randolph C. and Edna (Chaffee) Blackmer; m. Dianne Smith, Nov. 27, 1965; children: Tracy, Julie, Darcy. BS, U. Mass., Amherst, 1971, MS, 1973; PhD, Iowa State U., 1977. Asst. prof. Iowa State U., Ames, 1979-83, assoc. prof., 1983-89, prof., from 1989. Contbr. articles to sci. jours. or books. With U.S. Army, 1966-69. Fellow Am. Soc. Agronomy (Robert E. Wagner award 1993); mem. AAAS, Am. Soc. Microbiology, Soil Sci. Soc. Am. (Soil Sci. Applied Rsch. award 1994). Home: Jefferson, Iowa. Died Jan. 28, 2006.

BLACKMORE, JOSIAH H., II, retired academic administrator, law educator; b. Marietta, Ohio, Nov. 26, 1934; m. Joyce Blackmore; children: Anne, Alex, Josiah III. BA, Miami U., Oxford, Ohio, 1956; LHD (hon.), Miami U., 1989; JD cum laude, Ohio State U., 1962; HHD (hon.), Capital U., 1986. Bar: Ohio 1962. Pvt. practice law, 1962—70; assoc. prof. Capital U., Columbus, Ohio, 1970—73, acting dean, 1979—80, dean, 1980—87, interim pres., 1987—88, pres., 1988—98; mem. med. malpractice arbitration panel Ct. of Common Pleas, Franklin City, Ohio; staff counsel evidence rules coun. Ohio Supreme Ct., 1975—78; lectr. Ohio Jud. Conf., 1975—77; pres. Higher Ed. Coun. of Columbus, 1991—92; bd. dir. Right From the Start Early Childhood Ed., 1991. Adj. prof. law Capital U. Law Sch., 1969—70; vis. prof. U Pitts., 1978—79. Author: Ohio Trial Evidence, 1981. Served USN, 1956—59. Named an Outstanding Prof., Capital U. Law Sch., 1977; recipient Ohio Mcpl. League award, Golden Achievement award, Doctors Hosp., Living Faith award in Edn., Met. Area Church Coun., 1992, Presdl. award for Lifetime Svc., Columbus Bar Found., 2005. Mem.: Ohio Found. Ind. Coll. (bd. dir. 1988), Order of Coif, League of Ohio Law Sch. (pres. 1977—78), Ohio Acad. Trial Lawyers (pres. award 1977), Columbus Bar Assn. (bd. gov. 1987—91, Liberty Bell award), I Know I Can, Ohio Mcpl. League (dir. gen. offense code project 1973), Columbus C. of C. (co-chair internationalization com. 1990), Luth. Ednl. Conf. of N.Am. (bd. dir.), Cen. Ohio coun. Boy Scouts Am. (mem. 1990), Children's Hosp. (trustee), Rotary. Died Sept. 26, 2007.

BLAKE, ELIAS, JR., retired academic administrator; b. Brunswick, Ga., Dec. 13, 1929; s. Elias and Ruth (Thomas) B.; m. Mona Williams, June 13, 1963; children: Michael, Elias Ayinde. BA, Paine Coll., 1951; MA, Howard U., 1954; PhD, U. Ill., 1960; degree (hon.), Paine Coll., 1983. Asst. prof. Howard U., Washington, 1959-66; dir. S.E. Upward Bound program Inst. for Service to Edn., Washington, 1966-77, pres., 1969-77, Clark Coll., Atlanta, 1977-87; former dir. ednl. policy studies Howard U., Washington. Vice chmn. Nat. Citizens Commn. for African-Am. Edn.; past chmn. Nat. Adv. Com. of Black Higher Edn., Carnegie Found. for Advancement of Teaching. Contbr. writings to profl. publs. Chmn. council of pres. United Meth. Ch., 1986-87. Served with U.S. Army, 1951-53. Recipient outstanding tchr. award Student Council Coll. Liberal Arts, Howard U., 1964; Disting. achievement awards Ohio State U., 1981, Tenn. State U., 1982, Southern U., 1986. Mem. Nat. Assn. for Equal Opportunity in Higher Edn. (past chmn.), Ga. Assn. Pvt. Colls. and Univs. (pres. 1985-87). Home: Washington, DC. Died June 11, 2007.

BLAKE, JEREMY, artist; b. Ft. Sill, Okla., 1971; BFA, Sch. Art Inst. Chgo., 1993; MFA, Cal-Arts, 1995. One-man shows include One Hit Wonder, Work on Paper Inc., LA, 1999, Bungalow 8, Contemporary Arts Ctr., Cin., 2000, Angel Dust, XYZ, Toronto, Can., 2001, Mus. Contemporary Art, San Diego,

2002, Am. Mus. Moving Image, Astoria, NY, 2003, The 59th Minute: Video Art, Time Sq. Astrovision, NYC, 2003, Autumn Almanac, Feigen Contemporary, NY, 2003, Sister, LA, 2004, Galerie Ghislaine Hussenot, Paris, 2004, Centro de Arte Caja de Burgos, Spain, 2004, exhibited in group shows at Heaven's in the Backseat of My Cadillac, Name Gallery, Chgo., 1995, History of Glamour, Works on Paper Inc., LA, 1998, Fifteen, Lobby Gallery, Deutshe Bank, NY, 1999, Maximal Minimal, Feigen Contemporary, NY, 2000, Whitney Biennial Am. Art, Whitney Mus. Am. Art, 2000, 2002, 2004, BitStreams, 2001, Looking at Am., Yale U. Art Gallery, New Haven, Conn., 2002, Animations, Kunst-Werke, Berlin, 2003, Breathtaking, Art Inst. Boston, Lesley U., 2004, One Channel Only, Atrium Gallery, U. Conn. Sch. Fine Arts, 2004, Floor to Ceiling/Wall to Wall, Wadsworth Atheneum Mus. Art, Hartford, Conn., 2004. Recipient Interactive Design Rev. Medal, I.D. Mag., 1999, 79th ann. Directors Club Award for Broadcast Design & Animation, 2000; NY Found. Arts Fellowship, 1999. Died July 17, 2007.

BLAKE, PETER JOST, architect; b. Berlin, Sept. 20, 1920; came to U.S., 1940, naturalized, 1944; Student, U. London, 1938; student in architecture, Regent St. Poly., London, 1939, U. Pa., 1941; BArch, Pratt Inst., 1949. Apprentice to Serge Chermayeff, Architect, London, 1938-39, George Howe, Oskar Stonorov and Louis Kahn, Architects, Phila., 1940-42; curator dept. architecture and indsl. design Mus. Modern Art, NYC, 1948-50; assoc. editor Archtl. Forum, NYC, 1950-61, mng. editor, 1961-64, editor-in-chief, 1965-72; ptnr. Peter Blake & Julian Neski, Architects, NYC, 1956-60, James Baker & Peter Blake, Architects, NYC, 1964-71; contbg. editor New York mag., NYC, 1968-76; editor-in-chief Architecture Plus, NYC, 1972-75; chmn. Sch. Architecture, Boston Archtl. Ctr., 1975-79; chmn. dept. architecture and planning Cath. U. Am., Washington, 1979-86, prof. architecture, 1986-91; prin. Peter Blake Architect, Washington, 1979-93; prof. emeritus Cath. U. Am., Washington, 1991—2006. Vis. critic, lectr. Harvard U., Cambridge, Mass., Yale U., New Haven, Cornell U., Ithaca, N.Y., Washington U., St. Louis, Tulane U., New Orleans, Pratt Inst., Cooper Union, New Sch. for Social Rsch., Bennington Coll., Columbia U., N.Y.C., Ill. Inst. Tech., U. Mich., Ann Arbor, also schs. of architecture in Hamburg, Aachen, Hanover, Braunschweig, and West Berlin, Fed. Republic of Germany, Vienna, Zurich, Halifax, N.S., Can., Maracaibo, Venezuela, Milan, and Hong Kong; chmn. Alcoa Conf. on Future of Housing, Boca Raton, Fla., 1957; chmn. Internat. Design Conf., Aspen, Colo., 1962, bd. dirs., 1965-73, advisor to bd., 1974-91; chmn. adv. panel on quality of Iranian housing, urban devel. and new town planning Shah of Iran, 1976; mem. U.S. del. Internat. Conf. on Theater Design, Berlin, 1960; participant Internat. Conf. on Urban Design, New Delhi, 1965, U.S./Yugoslav Conf. on Housing, Zagreb, 1974, Iran Internat. Congress on Architecture, Persepolis, 1974, U.S. del. Helsinki Cultural Forum, Budapest, Hungary, 1985; spkr. at seminar in Chandigarh, India, 1994. Author: The Master Builders, 1960, God's Own Junkyard, 1964, Form Follows Fiasco: Why Modern Architecture Hasn't Worked, 1977, No Place Like Utopia: Modern Architecture and the Company We Kept, 1993; contbr. articles to mags. and newspapers; important works include Hollis Unitarian Ch., Queens, N.Y., offices and warehouse, Queens, Temple Emanu-El, Livingston, N.J., Ford Found. Ideal Theater, Darrow Sch. Libr., New Lebanon, N.Y., Berlin-Tegel Airport Project, Manistee (Mich.) Town Planning Project, Max Planck Inst. Project, Berlin, Rehab. Ctr., Binghamton (N.Y.) State Hosp., Roundabout Theater, Stage One, N.Y.C., Neely Exptl. Theatre, Vanderbilt U., Nashville, P.R. Traveling Theatre, N.Y.C., Apt. Bldg., I.B.A., St. Lukas Ch., West Berlin; collaborator with Kevin Roche in Dept. State competition design new U.S. Embassy in Berlin, 1995. Served with AUS, 1943-47, ETO. Recipient Howard Myers award for archtl. journalism, 1960; Graham Found. Advanced Studies in Fine Arts fellow, 1962, several grants; Ford Found. grantee, 1960; disting. design fellow Nat. Endowment for Arts, 1984. Fellow AIA (Architecture Critics medal 1975). Died Dec. 5, 2006.

BLANK, IRWIN MAURICE, adult education educator, rabbi; b. NYC, Dec. 6, 1925; s. Philip and Dora (Rubinstein) B.; m. Elinor Grace Mintz, Nov. 11, 1952; children: Joshua, Daniel, Rebecca Ann, Myer Abraham. BS, CCNY, 1946; B in Hebrew Lit., Hebrew Union Coll., 1948; MA, Columbia U., 1950, EdD, 1958. Ordained Rabbi, 1950. Asst. rabbi Congl. Emanu-El, NYC, 1950-56; rabbi Temple Sinai, Tenafly, N.J., 1956-73; sr. rabbi Temple Ohabei Shalom, Brookline, Mass., 1973-78; dir. adult edn. B'nai B'rith Internat., Washington, 1978-83; Isaac C. Rosenthal prof. Balt. Hebrew U., from 1984. Pres. Synagogue Coun. Am., 1973-75; chmn. bd. ministry Harvard U., Cambridge, Mass., 1974-75. Contbr. articles to profl. jours. Mem. Cen. Conf. Am. Rabbis, Assn. Jewish Communal Svc., Am. Sociol. Assn., Jungian Soc. Democrat. Avocations: camping, acting. Home: Washington, DC. Died Mar. 15, 2006.

BLAYNEY, KEITH DALE, university administrator, consultant; b. Anamosa, Iowa, Feb. 8, 1937; s. Darrell Price and Evelyn Mae (Thompson) B.; m. Joyce Ann Bryan, Sept. 14, 1958 (div. 1978); children— Michael Bryan, Steven Price. B.Sc., U. Iowa, 1959, M.S., 1961, Ph.D., 1966. Adminstr. U. Ala. Hosps., Birmingham, 1969-71; dean Sch. Community and Allied Health U. Ala., Birmingham, 1971—; hosp. adminstr., cons. to China Project HOPE, 1983—. Contbr. articles to profl. jours. Hon. bd. dirs. Xian Med. U., People's Republic of China, 1984. Served to 1st lt. USAF, 1961-64. Recipient 50th Anniversary commendation AMA, 1978; Am. Soc. Allied Health Professions fellow, 1984. Fellow Am. Coll. Hosp. Adminstrs. Unitarian. Avocation: fishing. Home: Birmingham, Ala. Died July 1, 2007.

BLECKE, ARTHUR EDWARD, retired principal; b. Oak Park, Ill., Sept. 21, 1926; s. Paul Gerard and Mathilda (Ziebell); m. June Audrey Eckholm, Jan. 22, 1949; children: William, Robert, Carol; m. Marilyn J. Black, Jan. 1, 2005. BS in Phys. Edn., U. Ill., 1950; M.Edn., Loyola U., 1967. Tchr., coach Buckley High Sch., Ill., 1951-52, Paxton High Sch., Ill., 1952-53; tchr., coach, dept. chmn. Luther High Sch. North, Chgo., Ill., 1953-65; asst. coach football and basketball Elmhurst Coll., Ill., 1965-66; dean, prin. Antioch Community High Sch., Ill., 1966-91. Cons. in field; lectr. Contbr. articles to profl. jours. Mem. sanitary dist. Village of Lindenhurst, Ill., 1968-92, chmn., 1972-92; planning commn., 1967-77; chmn. long range planning com. and bldg. com. Bella Vista Luth. Ch. Served with U.S. Army, 1945. Recipient Hon. Mention Those Who Excel, Ill. State Bd. Edn., 1980; named Prin. of Yr. for Ill. Nat. Assn. of Secondary Sch. Prins., The Coun. of Chief State Sch. Officer, and The Burger King Corp., 1987. Mem. Ill. Prins. Assn. (dir. 1980-81, 83-84, Herman Graves award, 1991), Nat. Assn. Secondary Sch. Prins. Lutheran. Avocations: golf, reading. Home: Bella Vista, Ark. Died May 19, 2006.

BLEE, MYRON ROY, educator, state official; b. Paw Paw, Ill., Feb. 25, 1917; s. Roy T. and Martha (Fox) B.; m. Charlotte Marie Leverenz, Jan. 1, 1941; 1 dau., Kathleen Marie Blee Ashe. B.E., No. Ill. State Tchrs. Coll., 1938; MA in Polit. Sci, U. Ill., 1939, Ed.D., 1958. Tchr., also teaching prin. elementary schs., Lake County, Ill., 1939-42; asso. dean men, instr. Am. Govt. No. Ill. State Tchrs. Coll., 1946-48; asst. supt. instruction Community Unit Sch. Dist. 271, Ashton, Ill., 1948-52; asso. dir. Fla Legis. Reference Bur., Tallahassee, 1952-54, Council Study Higher Edn. in Fla., 1954-56; ednl. and research officer Fla. Bd. Control Higher Edn., 1956-62; dir. Fla. Inst. Continuing Univ. Studies, Tallahassee, 1962-65; asso. dean academic affairs Fla. Atlantic U., 1965-66; dep. dir. Office Emergency Planning, Exec. Office of Pres., 1966-67; pres. Jr. Coll. Broward County, Ft. Lauderdale, Fla., 1967-68, Asso. Consultants in Edn., Inc., 1968-74; adj. prof. higher edn. Fla. State U., 1970-73; assoc. dir. for program div. community colls. Fla. Dept. Edn., 1972-82, spl. asst. to commr., 1982-86. Mem. Fla. Ednl. TV Commn., 1960-66; Mem. bd. edn. Fla. Ann. Conf. Methodist Ch., 1960-68; trustee Bethune Cookman Coll., Daytona Beach, 1961-68 Served to lt. comdr. USNR, 1942-46, PTO. Mem. Fla., Adult edn. assns., World Future Soc., Council for Advancement of Exptl. Learning (trustee 1980-82), Kappa Delta Pi, Phi Delta Kappa. Democrat. Home: Glenville, NC. Died Apr. 14, 2007.

BLESSING, EDWARD LEE, construction executive; b. Ft. Wayne, Ind., Nov. 21, 1935; s. Luther Charles and Olinda Amanda (Meitz) B.; m. Mildred Mae Cheyney, Nov. 18, 1961; children: Jerry, Carol, Catherine. AA, Concordia Coll., 1955. Tech. engr. Kaiser Engrs., Richland, Wash., 1960—62; chief surveys Seattle City Light, Metaline Falls, 1962—68; v.p. Gen. Constrn. Co., Seattle, from 1968. Mem. Jaycees, 1961, Tacoma C. of C., Kennewick Jaycees, bd. dirs., 1961; pres. St. Lukes Lutheran Ch., Federal Way, Wash., 1975, 1976, 1979. With US Army, 1957—60. Recipient Outstanding 1st Yr. Jaycee, Kennewick Jaycees, 1961. Republican. Home: Apache Jct, Ariz. Died June 12, 2007.

BLEVINS, MERRILL MAYHALL, consultant, former foreign service officer; b. Somerset, Ky., June 9, 1916; s. David Blucher and Nellye (Mayhall) B.; m. Esther Merriam, Sept. 14, 1946 (dec. 1968); children: Karen Lee, Katheryn Mary Anne; m. 2d, Susan Patricia Groom, Mar. 24, 1972. A.B., U. Ky., 1938; postgrad. U. Chgo., summer 1961. Personnel mgr. War Dept., 1940; joined U.S. Fgn. Service, 1947; asst. attaché, Brussels, also The Hague, Luxembourg, 1947-48; econ. commr. Office Spl. Rep. for ECA, 1948-49; assigned Dept. State, 1949-51; attaché, Bonn, Germany, 1951-52, Bern, Switzerland, 1952-54, New Delhi, India, 1954-55; 1st sec., consul, Canberra, Australia, 1956-60; fgn. affairs officer Dept. State, 1961-65; U.S. dep. rep. to food agys. FAO, UN, Rome, 1965-68; ret., 1968; spl. asst. to asst. dir.-gen. for adminstrn. and fin. FAC, Rome, 1968-71, protocol officer, chief protocol, 1972-79; cons., Alexandria, Va., 1979—; treas., dir. internat. relations Advanced Devel. Distribution, Inc., Alexandria, 1986—; adminstr. Va. Trust Historic Preservation; asst. for presdl. visits abroad Dept. State, 1962-63; asst. to sec. Dept. Interior, 1964-65; sec.-gen. Internat. Symposium on Water Desalination, 1964-65. Served to capt. USAAF, 1942-46. Decorated Air medal with palm, Purple Heart; recipient Meritorious Service award Dept. Interior, 1965; named Ky. col., 1955. Mem. Diplomatic and Consular Officers Ret., Res. Officers Assn. of U.S., RAF Assn. London, SAR, Soc. of the Lees of Va., George Washington's Fire Engine Co., Delta Tau Delta, Pi Sigma Alpha, Phi Mu Alpha. Episcopalian. Club: Caterpillar (London). Home: Ranchos De Taos, N.Mex. Died Aug. 27, 2006.

BLINDER, MARTIN S., management consultant, art dealer; b. Bklyn., Nov. 18, 1946; s. Meyer and Lillian (Stein) Blinder; m. Janet Weiss, Dec. 10, 1983. BBA, Adelphi U., 1968. Acct. exec. Bruns, Nordeman & Co., NYC, 1968-69; v.p. Blinder, Robinson & Co., Westbury, NY, 1969-73; treas. BHB Prodns., LA, 1973-76; pres. Martin Lawrence Ltd. Edits., Van Nuys, Calif., 1976-94, chmn., 1986-94, bd. dirs., from 1994; dir. AZ/NY Gallery, Scottsdale, Ariz., from 2000. Pres., dir. Corp. Art Inc., Visual Artists Mgmt. Corp., Art Consultants Inc.; pres., owner, founder MSB Fine Art, Phoenix, 1994—; lectr. bus. symposia. Contbr. articles to mags. and newspapers; appeared on TV and radio. Mem. Dem. Nat. Com., benefit com. AIDS project, L.A., 1988; bd. dirs. Very Spl. Arts, 1989—; chmn. visual arts Internat. Very Spl. Arts Festival, 1989; patron Guggenheim Mus., N.Y.C., Mus. Modern Art, N.Y.C., L.A. County Mus. Art, L.A. Mus. Contemporary Art (hon. founder), Whitney Mus. Am. Art, Palm Springs Mus. Art, Hirschorn Mus., Washington, Skirball Mus., L.A., Diabetes Found. of City of Hope, B'nai B'rith Anti-Defamation League, 1999, Very Spl. Arts, Scottsdale (Ariz.) Ctr. for the Arts, Scottsdale Mus. Contemporary Art (lectr. on Keith Haring); mem. Citizens for Common Sense; bd. dirs., pres. Rsch. Found. for Crohns Disease; mem. benefit com. Art Against AIDS, 1989; co-chair artists com. for Don't Bungle the Jungle Companions of Arts and Nature, 1989; prin. sponsor, ann. fundraiser AIDS Project, L.A., 1990; patron Ariz. Stat U. Art Mus., Sylvia Plotkin Mus. Recipient resolution of commendation L.A. City Coun., 1983, State of Calif. resolution for contbn. to arts in Calif., 1983, Merit award Republic Haiti for contbn. to arts, 1985, U.S. Senate commendations, 1983, County of L.A. Bd. Suprs. resolution for contbn. to arts in So. Calif., 1983, Gov. of R.I. resolution for contbns. to arts, 1985, commendation County of L.A.-Supr. Ed Edelman, 1991, commendation for contbns. to the arts and the healing arts City of L.A., 1991, commendation for contbns. to arts and philanthropy Mayor David Dinkins, N.Y.C., 1992; Nov. 18, 1985 declared Martin S. Blinder Day in L.A. in his honor by Mayor Tom Bradley, spl. award San Diego Youth and Cmty. Svcs., Bruin Bear award for establishing Blinder Rsch. Found., UCLA Sch. Medicine, 1994. Mem. Fine Art Pub.'s Assn. (bd. dirs. 1990-94), Med. Art Assn. at UCLA. Home: Paradise Valley, Ariz. Died Mar. 15, 2007.

BLISS, CARMAN ARTHUR, university dean; b. Olds, Alta., Can., Dec. 10, 1923; came to U.S., 1949, naturalized, 1966; s. Walter Franklin and Minnie (Cheeseman) B.; m. Mary Watson Farmer, Aug. 23, 1952; children— Kevin, Allison. BS in Pharmacy, U. Alta., 1949; MS in Pharmacy, Purdue U., 1952, PhD in Pharm. Chemistry, 1954. Asst. prof. Coll. Pharmacy, U. So. Calif., 1954-56, assoc. prof., 1956-66, Coll. Pharmacy, U. Sask., Can., 1966-69, prof., 1969-70; prof., dean Coll. Pharmacy and Dental Programs, U. N.Mex., Albuquerque, from 1970, acting dir. dental programs, 1973-74. Author: chpt. in Pharmaceutical Chemistry, 1969; also articles on plant chemistry and biochemistry. Served with Canadian Army, 1944-45. Am. Found. Pharm. Edn. fellow, 1952-54 Mem. Am. Pharm. Assn., Sigma Xi (pres. U. So. Calif. chpt. 1961-62), Skull and Mortar, Rho Chi, Phi Lambda Upsilon, Phi Delta Chi, Kappa Sigma. Clubs: Rotarian. Died Oct. 22, 2005.

BLOCH, ROBERT WAGNER, public relations and marketing consultant; b. NYC, Mar. 21, 1928; s. Maurice and Madeline (Neuberger) B.; m. Deborah Garfunkel, June 23, 1955; 1 child, Alexandra Bloch Jeydel. BS in Mktg., NYU, 1949. Rsch. asst. The Biow Co., Inc., NYC, 1945-49; TV features producer Stark Layton Prodns., Inc., NYC, 1949-51; acct. exec. Dine-Kalmus Pub. Rels., NYC, 1954-56; pres. Robert W. Bloch Internat., NYC, from 1956. Vis. lectr. in field. Trustee Am. Jewish Soc. for Svc., N.Y.C.; mem. bd. electors Wadsworth Atheneum, Hartford, Conn.; vice chmn. pub. information com. Congregation Emanu-El City of N.Y.; mem. pub. rels. and mktg. com. Jewish Mus., N.Y.C. Staff sgt. USMC, 1951-53. Mem. Internat. Radio TV Soc., Pub. Rels. Soc. Am., Nat. Acad. TV Arts and Scis., Inst. for Pub. Rels. (London), Univ. Club (N.Y.C.). Democrat. Jewish. Avocation: antiquarian book collecting. Died Oct. 14, 2006.

BLOCK, DUANE LLEWELLYN, physician; b. Madison, Wis., Dec. 27, 1926; s. Cecil Jay and Josephine Amanda (Holten) B.; m. Mary Jane Lohrman, Sept. 10, 1949 (dec. Oct. 1980); children: Susan Block Rupe, Jeffrey Holten; m. Kathleen Sylvia Smith, June 5, 1982. BS, U. Wis., 1949, MD, 1951. Diplomate: Am. Bd. Preventive Medicine. Intern Harper Hosp., Detroit, 1951-52; resident Gen. Motors Occupational Medicine Tng. Program, 1952; plant physician Cadillac div. Gen. Motors Corp., Detroit, 1952-54; med. dir. Gen. Motors Tech. Ctr., Detroit, 1954-55; physician in charge Rouge Med. Ford Motor Co., Dearborn, Mich., 1955-70, med. dir., from 1970. Cons. prof. health scis. Oakland U. Center Health Services, Rochester, Mich., 1978—; clin. asst. prof. Wayne State U. Sch. Medicne, Detroit, 1960—; clin. assoc. prof. U. Wis. Health Scis., 1980—; non-resident lectr. U. Mich. Sch. Pub. Health, Ann Arbor, Mich., 1960— Trustee Mich. Heart Assn., Detroit, 1971-80; mem. policy council Mich. Cancer Found., 1974—; dir. Mental Health Assn. Mich., 1982—; trustee Maplegrove-Henry Ford Hosp., 1981—; trustee, vice-chmn. Rehab. Inst., 1973—. Served with USN, 1945-46. Recipient Pres. award Mich. State Med. Soc., 1969; recipient Weisfeldt Meml. award Med. Coll. Wis., 1976 Fellow Am. Occupational Med. Assn. (pres. 1969 meritorious service award, pres. William S. Knudsen award), Am. Acad. Occupational Medicine (Robert A. Kehoe award 1981), Am. Coll. Preventive Medicine (editorial bd. 1982—); mem. Am. Bd. Preventive Medicine (chmn. 1977-84), AMA, Mich. State Med. Soc., Wayne County Med. Soc. Republican. Presbyterian. Home: Bloomfield Hills, Mich. Died Jan. 3, 2007.

BLOCK, LEONARD NATHAN, drug company executive; b. Bklyn., Dec. 21, 1911; s. Alexander and Tillie (Goetz) B.; m. Adele Goldberg, Oct. 8, 1936; children: Peggy Davis (Mrs. Richard M. Danziger), Thomas Roger. BS, U. Pa., 1933; L.H.D. (hon.), Mt. Sinai Sch. Medicine, 1985. Sr. chmn. Block Drug Co., Inc., Jersey City, from 1933. Mem. N.Y.C. Com. of Foster Care of Children, 1966-69; mem. Bd. Social Welfare, 1969-77, vice chmn., 1974-77; treas. Child Welfare Info. Services, 1972-84; bd. dirs. Welfare Research, Inc., 1980; Bd. dirs. Fedn. Jewish Philanthropies, 1953—, asso. chmn. bd., chmn. distbn. com., 1958-63, chmn. communal planning com., 1964-68; bd. dirs., treas. Lincoln Ctr. for the Performing Arts, 1977-84. Recipient award N.Y. State Welfare Conf., 1972, Naomi and Howard Lehman award, 1974, Disting. Service award Fedn. Jewish Philanthropies, 1984 Mem.: Harmonie, Hollywood Golf, Ocean Beach, Lyford Cay Club. Home: New York, NY. Died Nov. 9, 2005.

BLOOM, NORMAN DOUGLAS, JR., lawyer; b. Albuquerque, Apr. 6, 1928; s. Norman Douglas and Rose (Conway) B.; m. Janet Pierce, June 11, 1949 (div. June 1970); children— Ellen Clarie, Nancy Rose, Verna Madge; m. Betty Minter, Aug. 8, 1970; children— Dorothy Jane, Norma Jo, Deborah Kay, Brenda, Nathan Dean, Norman Douglas III. B.A., U. Colo., 1952; J.D., U. N.Mex., 1966; postgrad. Nat. Dist. Attys. Coll., 1972. Bar: N.Mex. 1966, U.S. Dist. Ct. N.Mex. 1966, U.S. Ct. Appeals (10th cir.) 1975, U.S. Supreme Ct. 1977, U.S. Ct. Claims 1979. Ptnr. Fettinger, Bloom & Overstreet, Alamogordo, N.Mex., 1966-71; dist. atty. 12th Jud. Dist., Otero and Lincoln Counties, N.Mex., 1971-75; ptnr. Fettinger & Bloom, Alamogordo, 1975-94, Fettinger, Bloom & Quinlan, P.C., 1994—. Organizer, founder La Placita Children's Home, Alamogordo, 1972, pres., 1975—. Served with AUS, 1946-47; PTO. Recipient Service to Mankind awards Sertoma Club, 1978, Sertoma Internat. of South N.Mex.-S.W. Tex., 1978, Greater Rocky Mountain Region, 1978. Mem. N.Mex. State Bar Assn. Otero County Bar Assn. (sec.-treas. 1967-68, pres. 1971-72, 84-85). Lodges: Kiwanis (bd. dirs. 1968-70, 76-78, Elks (trustee 1967-70) (Alamogordo), So. N.Mex. Am. Inns of Ct. (master bencher). Home: Alamogordo, N.Mex. Died Jan. 7, 2007.

BLOOSTEIN, ALLAN JEROME, retail executive; b. Passaic, NJ, Dec. 23, 1929; s. Elias Meyer and Rose (Slutsky) B.; m. Sally Boxer, April 13, 1951; children: Oren, Jonathan, Ellen. BA in History, CCNY, 1953. Trainee to mdse. mgr. home furnishing B. Gertz Dept. Stores, NYC, 1956-60; gen. mdse. mgr. home furnishing Stern Bros., NYC, 1960-64, exec. v.p. mdse. and sales promotion, 1964-65, pres., 1965-68; pres., chief exec. officer The Hecht Co., Washington, 1970-80; vice chmn., bd. dirs. The May Dept. Stores Co., NYC, 1980-87. Retail cons.; bd. trustees Shearson-Lehman Spl. Income and Equities Portfolios, N.Y.C., 1985—; bd. dirs. Crystal Brands, Inc., Southport, Conn.; gen. ptnr. Shearson-Lehman Multiple Opportunities Portfolios, N.Y.C. Recipient The Good Scout award Boy Scouts Am., N.Y.C., 1967, Torch of Learning award Hebrew U. in Jerusalem, 1968, Presdl. medal for Disting. Community Service, Cath. U. Am., Washington, 1975. Died Feb. 8, 2007.

BLOTNER, NORMAN DAVID, lawyer, real estate broker, corporate financial executive; b. Boston, Dec. 6, 1918; s. Leon and Sarah B.; m. Helen I. Whitman (dec.), Aug. 13, 1954; 1 son, James B. McClain (dec.). AB, Harvard U., 1940, JD, 1947. Bar: N.Y. 1948. Mem. firm Spiro, Felstiner, Prager & Treeger, NYC, 1947-52; with Lane Bryant Inc., NYC, 1953-82, sr. v.p., gen. counsel, sec., dir., 1968-82, ret., 1982. Bd. dirs. Better Bus. Bur. Met. N.Y., until 1982. Lt. comdr. USNR, 1941—46. Named Lacrosse All-am., 1940. Mem.: Assn. Bar City NY, Harvard Varsity Club, New Rochelle Tennis Club. Republican. Home: New Rochelle, NY. Died June 23, 2006.

BLOUNT, WILBUR CLANTON, ophthalmologist; b. Columbus, Ohio, Feb. 5, 1929; s. Percy Hammond and Bayetta (Dent) B.; m. Elsie M. Paradis; children: Angela Diane, Wilbur S., Elizabeth Rachel, Jacqueline Rebecca; 1 stepchild, Michael C. Paradis. BSc in Bacteriology, Ohio State U., 1951, postgrad., 1951-52, MD, 1959. Intern U. Ill. Rsch. and Ednl. Hosps., Chgo., 1959-60; gen. practice medicine Williamson, W.Va., 1960-62; resident dept. ophthalmology Coll. Medicine, Ohio State U., Columbus, 1964-67, instr. ophthalmology, 1970-71, clin. asst. prof., from 1977. Spl. NIH fellow in retinal surgery U. Minn., 1967-69; practice medicine specializing in ophthalmology, especially surgery and diseases of the retina; staff Lexington VA Hosp., 1971-77, attending staff Grant Hosp., 1977—; courtesy staff Mt. Carmel Med. Ctr., 1977—; asst. prof. surgery, dept. ophthalmology U. Ky. Med. Ctr., Lexington, 1971-77, dir. retinal svc.; mem. nat. adv. coun. Nat. Eye Inst., NIH, 1991-93; mem. bd. nominations Nat. Aviation Hall of Fame, 1998—. Trustee Urbana U., 1994—, Ohio History of Flight Mus. Served to 1st lt. USAF, 1954-56; col. Air N.G., 1984—. Fellow ACS, Aerospace Med. Assn. (assoc.), Am. Soc. Laser Medicine and Surgery, Internat. Coll.; mem. AMA, Nat. Med. Assn., Ohio Med. Assn., Acad. Medicine Columbus and Franklin County, Soc. USAF Flight Surgeons, Am. Acad. Ophthalmology, Assn. Mil. Ophthalmologists, Columbus Ophthalmology/Otolaryngology Soc., Ohio Ophthalmol. Soc., Am. Soc. Cataract and Refractive Surgery, Ophthalmic Photographers Soc., Ohio State U. Alumni Assn. (life), Ohio State U. Coll. Medicine Alumni Assn. (life), Assn. Naval Aviation (life), Aerospace Med. Assn. (life), Exptl. Aircraft Assn. (aeromed adv. coun. 1993), Civil Aviation Med. Assn., Tuskegee Airmen Inc., Air Force Assn. (life), N.G. Assn. (life), Ohio State U. Pres.'s Club, Lins. Home: Columbus, Ohio. Died May 8, 2006.

BLOUT, ELKAN ROGERS, retired biological chemistry professor, retired dean; b. NYC, July 2, 1919; s. Eugene and Lillian B. Blout; m. Joan E. Dreyfus, Aug. 27, 1939; children: James E., Susan, William L.; m. Gail A. Ferris, Mar. 29, 1985; 1 child, Darya L.M. AB, Princeton U., 1939; PhD, Columbia U., 1942; AM (hon.), Harvard U., 1962; DSc (hon.), Loyola U., 1976. With Polaroid Corp., Cambridge, Mass., 1943—62, successively rsch. chemist, assoc. dir. rsch., 1948—58, v.p., gen. mgr. rsch., 1958—62; rsch. assoc. Harvard U., Cambridge, 1950—52, 1958—60, lectr. on biophysics, 1960—62, prof. biol. chemistry, 1962—90, Edward S. Harkness prof. biol. chemistry, 1964—90, Edward S. Harkness prof. emeritus, 1990—2006, head dept. biol. chemistry, 1965—69; dean for acad. affairs Harvard Sch. Pub. Health, 1978—89, chmn. dep. environ. sci. and physiology, 1986—88, dir. divsn. biol. scis., prof., 1987—91, prof. emeritus, 1991—2006. Rsch. assoc. Children's Hosp. Med. Ctr., Boston, 1950—52, cons. chemistry, 1952—89; mem. conseil de surveillance Compagnie Financière du Scribe, 1975—81; trustee Bay Biochem. Rsch., Inc., 1973—83; mem. exec. com. divsn. chemistry and chem. tech. NRC, 1972—74, mem. assembly of math. and phys. scis., 1979—82; mem. sci. adv. com. Ctr. for Blood Rsch., Inc., 1972—92, emeritus trustee, 1992—2006, also mem. bd. dirs.; mem. rsch. adv. com. Children's Hosp. Med. Ctr., 1976—80, 1984—90, chmn., 1987—90; mem. vis. com. dept. chemistry Carnegie-Mellon U., 1968—72; bd. visitors Faculty Health Scis. SUNY, Buffalo, 1968—70; overseer Boston Mus. Sci.; trustee Boston Biomed. Rsch. Inst., 1990—2006, v.p., 1990—94; bd. govs. Weizmann Inst. Sci., Rehovot, Israel, 1978—90, gov. emeritus, 1990—2006; bd. dirs. Nat. Health Rsch. Found., ESA, Inc.; bd. dirs., sec.-treas. Nat. Acads. Corp.; gen. ptnr. Gosnold Investment Fund Ltd. Partnership, 1985—95; bd. dirs., investment mgr. Auburn Capital Corp., 1985—2006; sci. advisor Affymax Rsch. Inst., 1988—92; sr. sci. adv. FDA, 1991—99; mem. sr. adv. bd. The Ency. of Molecular Biology, 1991; mem. coun. visitors Marine Biol. Lab., 1992—2006; pres., trustee Inst. for Internat. Vaccine Devel., 1997—2006. Mem. adv. bd.: Jour. Polymer Sci., 1956—62, mem. editl. bd.: Biopolymers, 1963—85, hon. founding editor:, from 1985, mem. editl. bd.: Am. Chem. Soc. Monograph Series, 1965—72, Internat. Jour. Peptide and Protein Rsch., 1978—89, mem. editl. adv. bd.: Macromolecules, 1967—70, Jour. Am. Chem. Soc., 1978—82; contbr. articles to profl. jours. Recipient Princeton Class of 1939 Achievement award, 1970, Nat. Med. Sci. award, 1990, John Phillips award, Phillips Exeter Acad., 1998, Prof. Emeritus award for merit, Harvard Sch. of Pub. Health, 2000; fellow NRC, 1942—43. Fellow: AAAS (fin. com. 1977—84, com. on investments 1984—2001, chmn. budget com. 1988—92, treas. 1992—98), Optical Soc. Am., N.Y. Acad. Arts and Scis. (past pres. New Eng. sect.); mem.: NAS (adv. com. USSR and Eastern Europe 1979—84, treas. 1980—92, mem. com. sci. engring. and pub. policy 1992—95, treas. emeritus from 1992, audit com. 1994—2000), Fedn. Am. Socs. Exptl. Biology (investments adv. com. 1981—85), Internat. Orgn. Chem. Scis. in Devel. (coun. 1981—2005, chmn. fin. com. 1982—2005, v.p. 1982—2005, treas. 1985—2005, bd. dirs. 1985—2005), Commn. on Phys. Scis., Math., and Resources of NRC, Biophys. Soc., Am. Soc. Biol. Chemists (fin. com. 1973—82), Am. Chem. Soc. (nat. councillor 1958—61, Ralph F. Hirschmann award 1991), Russian Acad. Scis. (fgn.), Inst. Medicine. Achievements include patents in field. Home: Cambridge, Mass. Died Dec. 20, 2006.

BLUEFARB, SAMUEL MITCHELL, retired physician; b. St. Louis, Oct. 15, 1912; s. Sol and Pauline (Brown) B.; m. Grace Parsons, Jan. 1, 1944; 1 son, Richard Alan; m. Leah Rose Vendig Pollock, Jan. 24, 1968; children: Fred, Nancy Pollock. BS, U. Ill., 1936; MD, 1937. Diplomate Am. Bd. Dermatology and Syphilology. Intern Cook County Hosp., Chgo., 1937-38; resident Bellevue Hosp., NYC, 1939-41; practice medicine specializing in dermatology, 1941-78; sr. attending dermatologist, chmn. dept. Cook County Hosp., 1952-58; attending dermatologist VA Lakeside Hosp., 1954-78; sr. attending staff Chgo. Wesley Meml. Hosp., Passavant Hosp. Prof., chmn. dept. dermatology Northwestern U. Med. Sch., 1962-78; prof. dermatology U. South Fla., 1985-88; chmn. dept. dermatology Bay Pines VA Hosp., Fla., 1984-87. Author books and articles. Fellow Am. Acad. Dermatology and Syphilology (dir. 1969), ACP; mem. AMA, Ill. Med. Soc. (past pres. dermatol. sect.), Chgo. Med. Soc., Soc. Investigative Dermatology, Chgo. Dermatol. soc. (past pres.)., Am. Dermatol. Assn., Noah Worcester Dermatology Soc. Died June 7, 2007.

BLUM, ALBERT ALEXANDER, finance educator; b. NYC, Apr. 5, 1924; s. Morris and Estelle (Kaplan) B.; m. Roslyn Silver, Jan. 16, 1949; children: Steven, David. BS, CUNY, 1947; MA, Columbia U., 1948, PhD, 1953. Asst. prof. labor rels. Cornell U., Ithaca, N.Y., 1958-59; assoc. prof. labor rels. Am. U., Washington, 1959-60; prof. labor rels. Mich. State U., East Lansing, 1960-74; prof. pub. affairs Lyndon B. Johnson Sch. U. Tex., Austin, 1974-78; dean sch. bus. Ill. Inst. Tech., Chgo., 1978-82; George Wilson prof. internat. mgmt. U. Pacific, Stockton, Calif., 1982-84; prof. mgmt. N.Mex. State U., Las Cruces, from 1985. Chmn. internat. bus. dept. Am. U., Paris, 1987-89; prof., dir. Ctr. for Bus. Studies U. Witwatersrand, Johannesburg, S. Africa, 1991-92; exec. sec. commn. labor mgmt. rsch. NAS, Washington, 1973-74; rsch. assoc. Econ. of Social Rsch. Inst., Dublin, Ireland, 1968, Danish Nat. Inst. Social Rsch., Copenhagen, 1968, Internat. Labor Office, Geneva, 1967-68. Author: Drafted or Deferred, 1967, Teacher Unions and Associations, 1968, White Collar Workers, 1971, A History of American Labor, 1992, 2 edits. With USAF, 1943-45. Grantee Social Sci. Rsch. Coun., 1958-59, Lyndon B. Johnson Found., 1975-76, Fulbright Commn., 1967-68, U.S. Dept. Labor, 1974-76. Mem. Internat. Indsl. Rels. Assn., Internat. Conflict Mgmt. Assn., Indsl. Rels. Rsch. Assn., Am. Arbitration Assn., Fed. Mediation Arbitration Panel, Southwest Labor Studies Assn. (exec. bd. 1965-75). Home: San Francisco, Calif. Died May 10, 2007.

BLUMBERG, ARNOLD, historian, educator; b. Phila., May 9, 1925; s. Louis and Rose Y. (Bleecher) B.; B.S., U. Pa., 1947, M.S., 1948, Ph.D. in European Diplomatic History, 1952; m. Thelma Lillian Alpert, Dec. 26, 1954; children— Raphael David, Eva Rebecca, Michael Seth. Tchr. social studies Phila. Public Schs., 1950-58; faculty Towson State U., Balt., 1958—, prof. history, 1964—; vis. lectr., library cons. Mohawk Valley Community Coll., Utica, N.Y., summers 1963, 64; vis. prof. history U. R.I., summer 1967; researcher public and pvt. archives U.S., Gt. Brit., France, Israel. Bd. mem., historian Congregation Shearith Israel, Balt. Served with U.S. Army, 1943-45. Danforth Found. grantee, 1961; grantee Johnson Fund, Am. Philos. Soc., 1966; ann. rsch. grantee rsch. com. Towson State U., 1963-89. Mem. Am. Hist. Assn. (life), So. Hist. Assn. (life mem. European Div.), Soc. French Hist. Studies, AAUP, Phi Alpha Theta (charter Theta Beta chpt.), DAV (life). Democrat. Editorial cons. publs. including Am. Hist. Rev., Historian, Pacific Coast Hist. Rev.; reviewer, abstracter various jours.; author: Diplomacy of the Mexican Empire, 1863-1867, 71, 87, 2d edit., 1987, A View from Jerusalem, 1849-1858, 1980, Zion before Zionism, 1838-1880, 1985, A Carefully Planned Accident; the Italian War of 1859, 1990; editor-in-chief: Great Leaders/Great Tyrants: Opposing Views of People Who Have Influenced History, 1995; contbr. articles to jours. Home: Baltimore, Md. Died July 10, 2006.

BLUMEL, JOSEPH CARLTON, university president; b. Kansas City, Mo., Mar. 3, 1928; s. Joseph F. and Lillian M. (Spinner) B.; m. Priscilla Bryant, June 16, 1961; children— Christina, Carolyn. BS, U. Nebr., 1950, MA, 1956; PhD, U. Oreg., 1965; LL.D. (hon.), U. Hokkaido, Japan, 1976. Prof. econs. Portland (Oreg.) State U., 1968, dean undergrad. studies, asso. dean faculty, 1968-70, v.p. acad. affairs, 1970-74, pres., 1974-86, pres. emeritus, disting. sr. prof., from 1986. Served with U.S. Army, 1951-53. Mem. Phi Kappa Phi, Alpha Kappa Psi, Beta Gamma Sigma. Home: Portland, Oreg. Died Apr. 2, 2007.

BOARDMAN, SEYMOUR, artist; b. Bklyn., Dec. 29, 1921; s. Joseph and Bessie (Warren) B. BSS, CCNY, 1942; postgrad., Ecole des Beaux-Arts, Paris, 1946-47, Atelier Fernand Leger, 1948, Art Students League, NYC, 1949-50, Ecole de la Grande Chaumiere, 1950-51. One-man shows, Galerie Mai, Paris, 1951, Martha Jackson Gallery, N.Y.C., 1955, 56, Stephen Radich Gallery, N.Y.C., 1960-61, 62, A.M. Sachs Gallery, N.Y.C., 1965, 67, 68, Dorsky Gallery, N.Y.C., 1972, Aaron Berman Gallery, N.Y.C., 1978, Anita Shapolsky Gallery, N.Y.C., 1987, 91, Anderson Gallery, Buffalo, 1994; group shows include, Carnegie Internat., Pitts., 1955, Whitney Mus. Am. Art, 1955, 61, 67, Nebr. Art Assn., 1956, Kunsthalle, Basel, Switzerland, 1964, Santa Barbara Art Mus., 1964, Albright-Knox Gallery, Buffalo, 1967, Cornell U., 1971, Anita Shapolsky Gallery, N.Y.C., 1986, David Anderson Gallery, Buffalo, 1991-92; represented in permanent collections, Whitney Mus. Am. Art, Guggenheim Mus., Walker Art Ctr., Mpls., Santa Barbara Mus. Art, NYU. Served with USAAF, 1942-46. Longview Found. grantee, 1963; Guggenheim Found. fellow, 1972-73; Adolph and Esther Gottlieb Found. grantee, 1979, 83; Pollock-Krasner Found. grantee, 1985-86, 91, 98, 2001, 2003. Died Oct. 3, 2005.

BOARDMAN, SHELBY J., geologist, former dean; b. Akron, Ohio, Nov. 7, 1944; s. William J. and Nancy (Jett) Boardman; m. Jean Boardman; children: Steven, Dave. BA in Geology with honors, Miami U., Ohio, 1966; MS in Econ. Geology, U. Mich., 1969, PhD in Petrology, 1971. Mem. geology dept. Carleton Coll., Northfield, Minn., 1971—2007, Charles L. Denison prof. geology, chair geology dept, 1977—83, assoc. dean, 1994—98, acting dean, 1997, dean, 2002—05. Vis. scholar/rsch. assoc. U. Glasgow, Scotland, U. Kans., U. Ariz.; assoc. dir. Associated Colls. Midwest Geology in the Rockies Program, 1978, dir., 80, Keck Geology Consortium Project, Colo., 1988, faculty mem., Colo., 99; pres. geology coun. Coun. on Undergrad. Rsch., 1987—89. Editor: (volume of essays) Revolution in the Earth Sciences; contbr. articles to profl. jours. Fellow: Geol. Soc. Am.; mem.: AAAS, Am. Mineral. Soc., Am. Geophysical Union, Nat. Assn. Geoscience Tchrs., Sigma Xi. Died Jan. 19, 2007.

BODANSZKY, MIKLOS, chemist, educator; b. Budapest, Hungary, May 21, 1915; came to U.S., 1957, naturalized, 1964; s. Lajos and Maria (Friedner) B.; m. Agnes A. Vadasz, Apr. 21, 1950; 1 child, Eva. Diploma in chem. engring, Tech. U. Budapest, 1939, DSc, 1949. Sr. lectr. Tech. U. Budapest, 1950-56; research assoc. Cornell U. Med. Coll., 1957-59; sr. research assoc. Squibb Inst. Med. Research, New Brunswick, N.J., 1959-66; prof. chemistry and biochemistry Case Western Res. U., Cleve., 1966-83, Charles Frederic Mabery prof. research in chemistry, 1978-83, prof. emeritus, from 1983. Author: Peptide Synthesis, 1966, 2d edit., 1976, Principles of Peptide Syntheses, 1984, 2d edit, 1993, The Practice of Peptide Synthesis, 1984, 2d edit., 1994, Greek transl., 1984, Indonesian transl., 1998, Peptide Chemistry, 1988, 2d edit., 1993, The World of Peptides, 1991; mem. editl. bd. Jour. Antibiotics, 1971-87, Internat. Jour. Peptide Protein Rsch., 1978-89. Recipient Pierce award, 1977; Morley medal, 1978; A. von Humboldt award, 1979 Mem. Am. Chem. Soc., Am. Soc. Biol. Chemistry, Hungarian Acad. Scis. (fgn.). Achievements include research in Nitrophenyl ester method of peptide synthesis, 1954; first synthesis gastrointestinal hormone secretin, 1966; synthesis vasoactive intestinal peptide, 1973. Home: Princeton, NJ. Died Feb. 7, 2007.

BODDIE, LEWIS FRANKLIN, retired medical educator; b. Forsyth, Ga., Apr. 4, 1913; s. William F. and Luetta T. (Sams) Boddie; m. Marian Bernice Claytor, Dec. 27, 1941; children: Roberta Boddie Miles, Lewis Jr., Bernice B. Jackson, Pamela, Kenneth, Fredda, Margaret Boddie Lewis. BA, Morehouse Coll., 1933; MD, Meharry Med. Sch., 1938. Diplomate Am. Bd. Ob-Gyn. (proctor parti exam L.A. area 1955-63). Intern Homer-Phillips Hosp., St. Louis, 1938-39, resident in ob-gyn, 1939-42; mem. attending staff Grace Hosp., Detroit, 1944-48, Parkside Hosp., Detroit, 1944-48; sr. mem. attending staff Queen Angels Hosp., LA, from 1949, chmn. dept. ob-gyn, 1968—70; mem. attending staff L.A. County Gen. Hosp., 1952-79; asst. clin. prof. U. So. Calif. Sch. Medicine, LA, 1953-79, asst. clin. prof. emeritus, 1979—2007; assoc. clin. prof. U. Calif., Irvine, 1956-81. Sec. Verndro Med. Corp., 1952—90. Steward African Meth. Episc. Ch., LA, from 1949; vice chmn. bd. mgrs. 28th St YMCA, LA, 1960—75. Fellow: ACOG (life), ACS (life), L.A. Ob-Gyn. Soc. (life); mem.: Child Welfare League Am. (bd. dirs. 1969—76), Children's Home Soc. (bd. dirs. 1952—89, v.p. 1963—68, pres. 1968—70, trustee 1989—2007), L.A. United Way (stds. com. 1987—95, new admission com. 1988—95, priorities and allocations coms. 1989—95). Republican. Home: Los Angeles, Calif. Died Sept. 11, 2007.*

BODVARSSON, GUDMUNDER, research scientist; BS in Physics and Math., Catawba Coll., Salisbury, NC, 1974; MS in Civil Engring., NC State U., Raleigh, 1976; PhD in Hydrology, U. Calif., Berkeley, 1981. Dep. group leader reservoir engring. and hydrology earth scis. divsn. Lawrence Berkeley Nat. Lab., Calif., 1991—93, dept. head nuc. waste dept. earth scis. divsn., 1993—98, program head nuc. waste program earth sciences divsn., 1993—2006, dir. Earth Sci. divsn., 2001—06. Dept. head unsaturated zone sci. studies Yucca Mountain Mgmt. and Operation Contractor, TRW, Las Vegas, Nev., 1997—2001, Yucca Mountain Mgmt. and Operation Contractor, Bechtel SATC, Inc., Las Vegas, Nev., 2001—02, lab. lead Lab. Coun. Chief Sci. Officer, 2001—06; cons. in field. Recipient Task Achievement award, Civilian Radioactive Waste Mgmt. Sys. Mgmt. and Operating Contractor, 2000, Outstanding Performance award, Lawrence Berkely Nat. Lab., 2000, Cert. Appreciation, Nat. Def. U., Indsl. Coll. of Armed Forces, 2003. Died Nov. 29, 2006.

BOEHLER, HURLEY KIRCHMAN, pilot; b. Montgomery, Tex., Oct. 17, 1918; s. Fritz J. and Ethel M. (Turner) B.; 1 child from previous marriage: Barbara Ann; m. Maria Cristina Pinero, June 30, 1966 (div. 1976); 1 child, Terry. Student U. Ala., 1944. Lic. comml. pilot. Mechanic, Johnson Chevrolet Co., 1936-39; with Civil Svc., Kelly, Fla., 1940-43, Barsdall Oil Co., 1945-50; corp. pilot Standard Oil Co., 1950-77; mgr., pilot Eagle Aviation, Tulsa, 1977-80; mgr., test pilot Iliff Aircraft Co., Tulsa, 1980—; aviation cons.; aircraft insp.; ground inst. Tulsa, Voteck; flight instr. Tulsa N. Airport, 1950-77. Served with USAAF, 1943-45. Mem. Christian Motorcycle Assn., Exptl. Aircraft Assn. Baptist. Clubs: Cactus, Masons. Inventor in field; Tulsa Aviation Booster Day named for him. Home: Claremore, Okla. Died Nov. 20, 2006.

BOESCH, FRANCIS THEODORE, electrical engineer, educator; b. NYC, Sept. 28, 1936; s. Victor and Margaret (Wright) B. BS, Poly. Inst. N.Y., 1957, MS, 1960, PhD, 1963. Instr., then asst. prof. elec. engring. Poly. Inst. N.Y., 1957-63; mem. mil. research staff Bell Telephone Labs., 1963-68, mem. research staff, 1969-79; prof. elec. engring. and computer sci., dept. head Stevens Inst. Tech., Hoboken, NJ, 1979-88, dean of faculty, 1988-93, prof. elec. engring., from 1993. McKay prof. elec. engring. and computer sci. U. Calif., Berkeley, 1968-69. Author: Large-Scale Networks, 1976; editor-in-chief: Networks, 1970-81; editor: Graph Theory, 1978-81; contbr. articles to profl. jours. Vice pres. Fair Haven (N.J.) Little League, 1974; scoutmaster Fair Haven council Boy Scouts Am., 1973-78, dist. commnr. Monmouth council, 1978-80. Fellow IEEE, N.Y. Acad. Scis.; mem. Assn. Computing Machinery, Am. Math. Soc., Sigma Xi, Eta Kappa Nu. Home: Fair Lawn, NJ. Died Mar. 27, 2007.

BOGDONOFF, MAURICE LAMBERT, physician; b. Chgo., May 11, 1926; s. Harry A. and Mary Ivy (Grogan) B.; m. Diana Edith Rauschkolb, June 29, 1956; children: Vivian, Gregory, Audrey. BS, Tufts U., 1948; MD, Yale U., 1952. Intern U. Ill. Rsch. and Edn. Hosp., Chgo., 1952-53; resident in internal medicine Boston City Hosp., 1953-54; resident in radiology Columbia-Presbyn. Med. Ctr., NYC, 1955-57; asst. prof. to assoc. prof. radiology to prof. U. Ill., Chgo., 1958-69; attending radiologist Rush-Presbyn.-St. Luke's Med. Ctr., Chgo., pres. med. staff, 1975-77; prof. radiology and medicine Rush Med. Coll., Chgo., 1970-88, 1969-88, prof. emeritus, 1988—2007. Cons. Argonne (Ill.) Nat. Lab., 1963-88; cons., health dir. Canal Zone Panama, 1973-80; vis. lectr. nuclear power engring. Maine Maritime Acad., 1989. Contbr. articles to profl. jours. Pres. Wheaton (Ill.) Dist. 36 Sch. Bd.,1964-67; bd. visitors Coll. of DuPage Radio and TV Sys., Glen Ellyn, Ill., 1987-94. With USN, 1944-46. Fellow Am. Coll. Radiology, Inst. Medicine, also others; mem. Chgo. Lit. Club. Republican. Avocations: boating, astronomy, classics. Home: Wheaton, Ill. Died Jan. 15, 2007.

BOHANNAN, PAUL JAMES, anthropologist, retired dean, writer; b. Lincoln, Nebr., Mar. 5, 1920; s. Hillory and Hazel (Truex) B.; m. Laura Marie Smith, May 15, 1943 (div. 1975); 1 child, Denis Michael; m. Adelyse D'Arcy, Feb. 28, 1981. BA, U. Ariz., 1947; B.Sc., Oxford U., Eng., 1949, DPhil, 1951. Lectr. social anthropology Oxford (Eng.) U., 1951-56; asst. prof. anthropology Princeton (N.J.) U., 1956-59; prof. Northwestern U., Evanston, Ill., 1959-75, U. Calif., Santa Barbara, 1976-82; prof., dean social scis. and communications U. So. Calif., Los Angeles, 1982-87, prof. emeritus, 1987—2007. Author: Justice and Judgement, 1957, Africa and Africans, 1964, 4th edit., 1995, Divorce and After, 1970, We, the Alien, 1991, How Culture Works, 1995. Served to capt. U.S. Army, 1941-45. Decorated Legion of Merit; Rhodes scholar. Mem. Am. Anthrop. Assn. (pres. 1979-80), Am. Ethnol. Soc. (dir. 1963-66), African Studies Assn. (pres. 1963-64), Social Sci. Research Council (dir. 1962-64) Home: Visalia, Calif. Died July 13, 2007.

BOHL, ROBERT WALTER, consulting metallurgist; b. Peoria, Ill., Sept. 29, 1925; s. Francis John and Ella (Ziegenbein) B.; m. Florence Marie Reace, May 30, 1947; children— Nancy (Mrs. Theodore Williams), Betty (Mrs. Vance Kepley, Jr.), Barbara, Robert F. BS, U. Ill., 1946, MS, 1949, PhD, 1956. Faculty U. Ill., Urbana, from 1946, now emeritus prof. metall. and nuclear engring. Cons. Caterpillar Tractor Co., U.S. Steel Co., Argonne Nat. Lab., Battelle Meml. Inst. Contbr. articles profl. jours. Bd. dirs. Univ. YMCA. Fellow Am. Soc. Metals; mem. Am. Soc. Engring. Edn., Am. Inst. Mining, Metall. and Petroleum Engrs., Sigma Xi, Tau Beta Pi, Phi Kappa Phi, Alpha Sigma Mu. Home: Urbana, Ill. Died Mar. 18, 2006.

BOILEAU, OLIVER CLARK, JR., retired aerospace transportation executive; b. Camden, NJ, Mar. 31, 1927; s. Oliver Clark and Florence Mary (Smith) B.; m. Nan Eleze Hallen, Sept. 15, 1951; children: Clark Edward, Adrienne Lee, Nanette Erika, Jay Marshall. BS in Elec. Engring., U. Pa., 1951, MS, 1953; MS in Indsl. Mgmt., MIT, 1964; LLD (hon.), U. Wyo., 2006. With Boeing Aerospace Co., 1953-79, mgr. Minuteman, v.p., 1968, pres., 1973-79; pres., vice chmn. Gen. Dynamics Corp., 1980-88; pres., COO Grumman Corp., 1994—95. Bd. dirs. Centerre Bank, Northrop Corp. (gen. mgr. B-2 divsn.); trustee The Conf. Bd.; mem. vis. com. aeronautics and astronautics MIT, chmn. Lincoln Lab. Adv. Bd.; cons. Gen. Dynamics, 1989. Mem. Corp. Lawrence Inst. Tech.; trustee Ranken Tech. Inst.; v.p. exec. bd. St. Louis Area coun. Boy Scouts Am.; bd. overseers U. Pa.; vis. bd. MIT, U. Pa., So. Methodist U.; trustee St. Louis U. Served with USN, 1944-46, World War II. Sloan fellow, MIT, 1963-64 Mem. AIAA, NAE, Navy League Air Force Assn., Am. Def. Preparedness Assn., Assn. U.S. Army, Nat. Aeronautic Assn., Nat. Space Club, Naval War Coll. Found., Old Warson Country Club (St. Louis), St. Louis Club, Calif. Club, Old Baldy Club (Saratoga, Wyo.), N.Y. Acad. Scis., Confrerie des Chevaliers du Tastevin (L.A.), Eta Kappa Nu, Sigma Tau, Theta Xi. Home: Saint Louis, Mo. Died July 27, 2007.

BOLGER, ROBERT JOSEPH, retired trade association administrator; b. Phila., Aug. 9, 1922; s. Harold Stephen and Edna (Adams) B.; m. Helen Siegfried, May 22, 1954; children: Robert, Mary T., Cynthia A., Ann M., Catherine B., David A. BS, Villanova U., 1943; postgrad., Northwestern U., 1945-46, U. Pa., 1946-47, U. Geneva, 1948-49; DS in Pharmacy (hon.), Mass. Coll. Pharmacy, 1983. Salesman Container Corp., Phila., 1947; supr. sales Kraft Food Co., Phila., 1949-52; overseas mgr., dir. retail rels. Smith, Kline Beckman Corp., Phila., 1952-62; asst. to exec. v.p. Nat. Assn. Chain Drug Stores, Inc., Arlington, Va., 1962-67, pres., 1967-87; ret., 1987. Founder, developer Robert J. Bolger Assocs., 1988—2007; bd. dirs. Barr Labs., Pomona, NY, Am. Pharm. Inst., Washington, Am. Found. Pharm. Edn., Nat. Drug Trade Conf., pres., 1974—82. Co-author: Chain Drug Retailing, 1980. Bd. dirs. Nat. Coun. on Patient Info. and Edn.; hon. bd. dirs. Nat. Assn. Chain Drug Stores Inc.; Nacos Edn. Fedn. Lt. comdr. USNR, 1943—46, PTO. Decorated Air medal; named Man of Yr. Cosmetic and Toiletry sect. United Jewish Appeal, 1972, Chain Exec. of Yr., Chain Drug Rev., 1979; recipient Torch of Learning award Am. Friends of Hebrew U., 1987, Chain Drug Rev. Bd. Lifetime Achievement award, 1988, Robert B. Begley award, 1988. Mem. Am. Pharm. Assn., Com. of 100, U.S. C. of C., Cen. Coun. Nat. Retail Assns. (chmn.), Am. Retail Fedn. (bd. dirs.), Nat. Assn. Cmty. Pharmacists, Joint Commn. Pharmacy Practitioners, Pharmacists Against Drug Abuse (bd. dirs. 1986-2007), Am. Soc. Assn. Execs. (life), Nat. Assn. Execs. Club (bd. dirs.), Am. Druggist Bd. Advisers, Key Exec. Industry Coun., Alexandria Chief Execs., Belle Haven Country Club. Died Oct. 7, 2007.

BOLOGNA, GIACOMO JOSEPH, management consultant, lawyer; b. Detroit, Mich., Jan. 1, 1929; s. Salvatore and Cristina (Randazzo) Bologna; m. Jean A. Kolar, Feb. 16, 1957; children: James, Michael, Anne, Mary, Paul, Janine. BBA in Acctg., Detroit Inst. Tech., 1951; JD, U. Detroit, 1957; DSc (hon.), Ind. No. U., 1980. With Nat. Bank of Detroit, 1950—52, Arthur Young & Co., 1953—54; with various U.S. govt. agys., 1955—68; v.p. Performance Sys., Inc., 1969—70, Intertel, Inc., Washington, 1971—73; pres. George Odiorne Assocs., Inc., Plymouth, Mich., from 1973, Computer Protections Sys., Inc., Plymouth, from 1980. Asst. prof. mgmt. Siena Heights Coll., Adrian, Mich.; officer, dir. various profl. cons. groups, from 1972. Author: Computer Crime: Wave of the Future, Corporate Fraud: Prevention and Detection, Forensic Accounting Guidelines; editor: Forensic Acctg. Rev.; contbr. articles to profl. jours. Chmn. citizen's adv. coun. Plymouth Ctr. for Human Devel.; mem. sch. bd. com. Our Lady of Good Counsel Ch. Mem.: Nat. Assn. Accts., N.Am. Soc. Corp. Planning, Data Processing Mgmt. Assn., Am. Mgmt. Assn., Am. Soc. Bus. and Mgmt. Cons. Home: Plymouth, Mich. Died Mar. 10, 2006.

BOLTON, ELLIS TRUESDALE, marine scientist; b. Linden, NJ, May 4, 1922; BS, Rutgers U., 1943, PhD, 1950. Mem. faculty Coll. Marine Studies, U. Del., Newark, from 1975, prof. marine biology, from 1975; dir. Coll. Marine Studies, U. Del. (Center Mariculture Research), from 1977. Dir. dept. terrestrial magnetism Carnegie Instn., Washington, 1966-74 Author numerous articles, reports in field. Died Jan. 6, 2006.

BOLTON, LEON LESLIE, plastic surgeon; b. Memphis, Sept. 4, 1954; BA summa cum laude, U. Tenn., 1976; MD, U. Tenn., Memphis, 1980. Diplomate Am. Bd. Surgery, Am. Bd. Plastic Surgery. Resident in gen. surgery Emory U. Hosps., Atlanta, 1980-83, U. Ky. Hosps., Lexington, 1983-85; resident in plastic and reconstructive surgery U. So. Calif., LA, 1985-87; pvt. practice Aesthetic Surgery Ctr., Long Beach, Calif., from 1987. Clin. instr. surgery U. So. Calif., L.A., 1987—; spkr. in field. Contbr. articles to profl. jours. Fellow ACS; mem. AMA, Am. Assn. for Accreditation of Ambulatory Surgery Facilities (chair oper. com. 1995—), Am. Soc. Plastic and Reconstructive Surgeons, Am. Soc. Aesthetic Plastic Surgery, Calif. Soc. Plastic Surgeons, Lipoplasty Soc. N.Am., Los Angeles County Med. Assn., Calif. Med. Assn., Phi Beta Kappa, Phi Kappa Phi, Alpha Omega Alpha. Avocations: skiing, water-skiing, tennis. Home: Long Beach, Calif. Died Oct. 11, 2006.

BOND, EPPERSON ELLIS, chemist, retired; b. Nashville, Apr. 5, 1923; s. Epperson Porter and Margaret (Reed) B.; m. Marian Ruth Philips, June 9, 1950; 1 child, Michael Ellis BA, Fisk U., 1944, postgrad., 1945, DePaul U., 1946. Research assoc. Glidden Co., Chgo., 1946-47; research assoc. Med. Sch., U. Ill., Chgo., 1947-50, Northwestern U., Chgo., 1950-53; chemist VA Hosp., Hines, Ill., 1953-88, retired, 1995. Chmn. credit com. Hines Fed. Credit Union, 1963-73, pres., 1973-85; chmn. EEO com. Hines Hosp.; chmn. EEO program council Med. Dist. 17 Bd. dirs., pres. Roseland Heights Cmty. Assn.; mem. cmty. adv. coun. Chgo. State U., 1984-88; lay reader Meth. Ch. Fellow Am. Inst. Chemists; mem. Am. Assn. Clin. Chemists (bd. dirs.), Am. Chem. Soc., Ill. Kidney Found., Am. Assn. Ret. Persons (Abbott Park chpt. chmn., bd. dirs. mem. com.), Alpha Phi Alpha Methodist (vice chmn. bd. stewards). Club: Men's (Chgo.) Home: Chicago, Ill. Died Apr. 24, 2007.

BONDAR, ANDREW ARTHUR, dentist; b. Manchester, N.H., Oct. 23, 1914; s. Arthur George and Anna (Greneshen) B.; student U. N.H., 1932-34; D.M.D., Tufts U., 1938; diploma U.S. Army Med. Field Service Sch., 1969; cert. Command and Gen. Staff Coll., 1972; m. Ellen Ferguson Stewart, July 24, 1953; 1 dau., Billie Arlene. Pvt. practice dentistry, Manchester, 1939-42, 46-49; dentist VA Hosp./Dental Service, 1949-82. Lectr., clinician dist. and local dental socs. in N.H., N.Y., Que., Can. Asst. coach Jr. Am. Legion Baseball Team, Manchester, 1947-49; nat. chmn. Nat. German Prisoner of War Meml. Service, Ft. Custer, Mich., 1973-75. Served to capt. AUS, 1942-46, now col. Res. ret. Fellow Am. Acad. Gen. Dentistry, Midwest Acad. Prosthodontics; mem. ADA, Tufts Coll., U. N.H. alumni assns., Assn. Mil. Surgeons U.S., Am. Soc. Geriatric Dentistry (nat. treas. 1975-81), Am. Legion, VFW, DAV, Res. Officers Assn. (del. to United War Vets' Council of Greater Battle Creek, Mich., cert. commendation, 1979), Mil. Order of World Wars, Vets. of Battle of the Bulge, Res. Officers Assn. U.S. (brigade of vols., past pres. chpt.; dental surgeon Mich. dept. 1973-77, 79—), 40 and 8. Lodges: Elks, Eagles. Home: Rochester, NH. Died Aug. 6, 2007.

BONE, ARTHUR ELLSWORTH, retired gas industry executive; b. Pontiac, Mich., Oct. 11, 1913; s. Stephen Arthur and Enid Mary (Jewel) Bone; m. Sarah Elizabeth Williford, Oct. 18, 1944; 1 child, William Lewis. Student, Mich. State U., 1933. Midwest regional supr. Phillips Petroleum Co., Detroit, 1936—45; asst. to pres. uburban Propane Gas Corp., Whippany, NJ, 1945—51; pres. Eastern Propane Corp., Malvern, Pa., 1951—59; with UGI Corp., Valley Forge, Pa., 1959—84; pres. Ugite Gas Inc., 1959—68, exec. v.p., 1968—70, pres., CEO, 1971—79, chmn., 1979—84, ret., 1984. Mem. pres.'s adv. coun. Eastern Colls., 1977—84, chmn., 1979—83; bd. dirs. Pennsylvanians for Effective Govt., chmn., 1978—81; bd. dirs. Chester County, Pa. Economy League. With USNR, 1943—45. Recipient Am. Gas Assn. Disting. Service award, 1979, Silver Beaver award Boy Scouts Am., 1967, Disting. Eagle award, 1978, Silver Antelope award, 1973. Mem.: Pa. C. of C. (dir. 1974, chmn. bd. dirs. 1980—82), Am. Gas Assn. (past dir., treas., chmn. fin. com.), Pa. LP Gas Assn. (past dir, past pres.), Pa. Gas Assn., Nat. LP Gas Assn. (dir. 1955—68, pres. 1958—59), Merion Golf, Pine Valley Golf, Country of N.C. Republican. Presbyn. Home: Pinehurst, NC. Died Mar. 4, 2007.

BONHORST, CARL WILLIAM, chemist, educator; b. Van Metre, SD, Dec. 31, 1917; s. Charles Wilhelm and Minnie (Grupe) B.; m. Harriet Emma Witmer, Oct. 12, 1945; 1 dau., Lena Marie. BS, S.D. State U., 1943; MS, Pa. State U., 1947, PhD, 1949. Research asso. pharmacology U. Va., Charlottesville, 1951-52; asso. biochemist S.D. State U., Brookings, 1952-56; mem. faculty dept. chemistry U. Portland, Oreg., 1949-51, 56-81, prof., 1966-81, chmn. dept., 1968-73. NSF faculty fellow, 1962-63 Mem. Am. Chem. Soc., Sigma Xi, Gamma Sigma Delta. Home: Portland, Oreg. Died Dec. 24, 2006.

BONSAL, RICHARD IRVING, textile marketing executive; b. Palmyra, NJ, June 19, 1920; s. Alonzo Felten and Jennie (Weart) B.; m. Jean Caven, Oct. 18, 1947; children: Julia Lynn, Sarah Bonsal Miller, Martha Bonsal Day. BE in Mech. Engring., Yale U., 1942. Lic. profl. engr., N.Y., N.J. Rsch. supr. E.I. DuPont de Nemours & Co., Inc., Wilmington, Del., 1942-47; with Joshua L. Baily & Co., Inc., Hoboken, N.J., from 1947, pres., from 1967. Bd. dirs. Mayfair Mills, Arcadia, S.C.; ATMI rep. gen. arbitration coun. of textile industry, 1993—. Commr. Town of Montclair (N.J.), 1972-80, dep. mayor, 1972-76; trustee Montclair Pub. Library, Mountainside Hosp. Found., Mt. Hebron Cementary. Recipient Cmty. Svc. award Montclair Jaycees, 1992, Citizenship award Svc. Clubs Coun., Montclair, 1985, Associated Physicians of Montclair and Vicinity Health Citizen of Yr., 1993. Mem. ASME (life), Am. Textile Mfg. Inst. (past chmn. textile market com., rep to gen. arbitration coun. of textile industry), Am. Arbitration Assn. (arbitrator), Montclair Golf Club, Union League Club, Princeton Club, Bradford Bath and Tennis Club, Upper Montclair Country Club (pres. 1969-71), Sigma Xi (assoc.), Tau Beta Pi. Avocations: golf, barbershop quartet singing. Home: Upper Montclair, NJ. Died July 20, 2006.

BOODMAN, DAVID MORRIS, management scientist; b. Pitts., July 4, 1923; m., 1948; 2 children BS, U. Pitts., 1944, PhD in Phys. Chemistry, 1950. Sr. staff mem. Ops. Eval. group MIT, Cambridge, 1950-60, sr. staff mem. Ops. Research sect., 1960-72; v.p. Arthur D. Little, Inc., Cambridge, from 1972, mgr. artificial intelligence sect., until 1989, ret.; pvt. cons., from 1989; ops. analyst, mem. staff Comdr.-in-Chief Pacific Fleet, USN, 1951, mem. ops. devel. force, 1953-54, mem. staff, 1958. Fellow AAAS; mem. Inst. Mgmt. Sci., Ops. Research Soc. Am. Home: Lexington, Mass. Died Dec. 14, 2006.

BOOHER, JACOB ORIAL, journalist; b. Birmingham, Ala., Sept. 20, 1937; s. Jacob Orial and Sue Lenore (Ellis) B.; m. Mary Ruth Girod, May 8, 1968; children— Joel Hendrik, Neil Erik BS, U. Tenn.-Knoxville, 1960. News editor Harriman Record, Tenn., 1960; pub. relations specialist White Sands Missile Range, N.Mex., 1961-64; newsman AP, Albuquerque, NYC and Salt Lake City, 1964-76, bur. chief Louisville, 1977-81, Columbus, Ohio, from 1981. Served with U.S. Army, 1961-62 Mem. Sigma Delta Chi Died Mar. 26, 2007.

BOOTH, PHILIP, poet, educator; b. Hanover, NH, Oct. 8, 1925; s. Edmund Hendershot and Jeanette (Hooke) B.; m. Margaret Tillman, Aug. 3, 1946; children: Margot, Carol, Robin. AB, Dartmouth Coll., 1948; MA, Columbia U., 1949; LittD (hon.), Colby Coll., 1968. Instr. Bowdoin Coll., Brunswick, Maine, 1949-50; asst. to dir. admissions Dartmouth Coll., 1950-51, instr., 1954; instr. to asst. prof. Wellesley Coll., 1954-61; assoc. prof. Syracuse (N.Y.) U., 1961-65, prof., 1966-86. Author: Letter from a Distant Land, 1957, The Islanders, 1961, Weather and Edges, 1966, Beyond Our Fears, 1968, Margins, 1970, Available Light, 1976, Before Sleep, 1980, Relations, 1986, Selves, 1990, Pairs, 1994, Trying to Say It: Outlooks and Insights on How Poems Happen, 1996; editor: The Dark Island, 1960, Syracuse Poems, 1965, 70, 73, Syracuse Stories and Poems, 1977, 83; contbr. poems and essays to jours. Served with USAAF, 1944-45. Recipient Hokin prize Poetry mag., 1955, Lamont prize 1956, Saturday Rev. Poetry award, 1957, Phi Beta Kappa Poet Columbia, 1962, Emily Clark Balch prize Va. Quar. Rev., 1964, award for poetry Nat. Inst. Arts. and Letters, 1967, Theodore Roethke prize Poetry Northwest mag., 1970, Friends of Witherle Library award, 1985, Maurice English Poetry award, 1987; Guggenheim Meml. fellow, 1958-59, 65; Rockefeller fellow, 1968, Nat. Endowment for Arts fellow, 1980; Acad. Am. Poets fellow, 1983. Home: Castine, Maine. Died July 2, 2007.

BOPP, EMERY, art and design educator, artist, sculptor; b. Corry, Pa., May 13, 1924; s. Emery Jacob B. and Katherine Ann Woodward; m. Marian Edith Meyer, May 29, 1948; children: Sue Ann marie, Laurie Kay, Jay Morgan. Cert. Illustration, Pratt Inst., 1949; BFA, Yale U., 1951; student, Inst. Fine Arts 1951-52; MFA, Rochester Inst. Tech., 1967. Prof. art Bob Jones U., Greenville, S.C., 1951-55 and from 94, chmn. divsn. art 1955-94, chmn. emeritas, from 1994. Co-founder, pres. bd Hamptos III Gallery Ltd., Taylors, S.C., 1970—. With USNR 1943-46. Recipient Best In Show Hunter Gallery Regional Chatto, Tenn., 1966, Mus. Purchase award Greenville County Mus. Art, S.C., 1967, Select award Southeastern Regional H.S. Atlanta, 1970. Home: Greenville, SC. Died Feb. 1, 2007.

BOREHAM, ROLAND STANFORD, JR., electric motor company executive; b. LA, Sept. 2, 1924; s. Roland S. and Anita K. (Brown) B.; m. Judith P. Boreham; children: Debra Rhea Anita Katherine. BA in Physics, UCLA, 1947, postgrad., 1951-54; PhD (hon.), U. Ozarks, 1986, U. Oklahoma City, 1991. Ptnr R.S. Boreham & Co. (mfr.'s rep. for Baldor Electric Co.), LA 1948-61; v.p. sales Baldor Electric Co., Ft. Smith, Ark., 1961-70, exec. v.p., 1970-75, pres., 1975-81, CEO, chmn. bd., from 1975. Trustee U. Ozarks, Clarksville, Ark., 1981—, Sparks Regional Med. Ctr., Ft. Smith, 1981—; dir. United Way, Ft Smith, 1984-87, Gov.'s Commn. on Literacy, Little Rock 1989—. 1st lt. USAAF, 1943-46, PTO. Mem. Am. Bus. Conf (bd. dirs.). Republican. Presbyterian. Home: Fort Smith, Ark Died Feb. 5, 2006.

BORIE, ARTHUR, retail company executive; b. Phila., June 6 1926; s. Louis and Mollie (Zeitz) B.; m. Norma D. Duck, Dec 30, 1955; 1 child, Randy Harwood. BBA, U. So. Calif., 1950 Gen. mdse. mgr. Lucky Stores, Los Angeles, 1951-60; gen mdse. div. mgr. Boys Markets, Los Angeles, 1961-72; v.p. Pic'N'Save Corp., Carson, Calif., 1972-79, exec. v.p., chief operating officer, from 1980. Served with USN, 1944-46, PTO. Avocations: golf, watch collector, music collector. Home: Long Beach, Calif. Died Jan. 10, 2006.

BORROR, DONALD A., retired construction company executive; b. July 15, 1929; m. Joanne Borror, 1952; children Douglas, David, Donna. Grad., Ohio State U., Columbus, 1950 JD, Ohio State U. Sch. Law, Columbus, 1954. With Summer & Co. Inc., Columbus, Ohio, 1956-71; founder The Borror Corp Dublin, Ohio, 1971—99, pres., 1976-82; chmn. The Borror Realty Co. (formerly The Borror Corp.), Dublin, 1994-97

Dominion Homes Inc. (formerly The Borror Realty Co.), Dublin, 1997—99; chmn. emeritus Dominion Homes Inc. (formerly The Borror Corp.), Dublin, 1999—2006. With USAF. Died Dec. 31, 2006.

BORTOLAZZO, JULIO LAWRENCE, education educator; b. Santa Barbara, Calif., Sept. 17, 1915; s. Santo and Vittoria (Raccanello) B.; m. Alyce Corbin, Sept. 11, 1940; children— Richard Alan, Gerald William, Paul Lawrence. BA, Santa Barbara State Coll, 1936; MS, U. So. Calif., 1939; Ed.M., Harvard U., 1942, Ed.D., 1949. Tchr. Santa Barbara Jr. High Sch., 1936-41; tchr., counselor San Francisco City Coll., 1946; prin. Ainsworth Elem. Sch., Portland, Oreg., 1946-48, Jefferson High Sch., Portland, 1948-50; Faculty grad. sch. edn. Harvard U., 1948; faculty San Diego State Coll., 1949; extension center U. Oreg., 1949-52; supt. schs. Lake Oswego, Oreg., 1950-52; faculty summer session U. Maine, 1946, U. Wash., 1951, 53; pres. Stockton Coll., 1952-56; supt. San Mateo Jr. Coll. Dist.; also pres. Coll. San Mateo, 1956-68; supt., also pres. San Joaquin Delta Coll., 1968-69, Santa Barbara City Coll., from 1969; exec. dir. Tech. Edn. Centers, S.C., 1971; ednl. cons., lectr. Cons. to Italian Govt. in Vocat. Edn., 1955; Ford Found. Study of Italian Edn., 1960; ICA ednl. cons. in vocat. tech., Liberia, 1959; mem. Commn. Accreditation of Service Experiences, Am. Council Edn., 1961—, Vocat. Edn. Study Adv. Com., Commn. Acad. Affairs, 1965—; mem. jr. coll. adv. panel Calif. Bd. Edn.; mem. Calif. Postsecondary Edn. Commn., 1974—; cons. higher edn. Colombia, 1966—; dir. Blue Cross So. Calif., 1979, exptl. med. policy; designer Ultracare; chmn. Ultracare liaison com. to Blue Cross Calif., 1980-87. Pres. Boys and Girls Aid Soc., Portland; chmn., co-covenor Gray Panthers of Santa Barbara County; mem. Calif. Joint Legis. Com., Am. Assn. Ret. Persons and Nat. Ret. Tchrs. Assn.; sr. senator Calif. Sr. Legislature, 1982; bd. dirs. Pilgrim Terr. Coop. Homes 1987—, pres. 1988-89. Served as lt. USNR, 1942-46. Mem. Am. Legion., NEA, Calif. Jr. Coll. Assn. (pres. 1966-67), Am. Assn. Jr. Colls., Am. Assn. Sch. Adminstrs., Calif. Tchrs. Assn., Phi Kappa Phi, Phi Delta Kappa, Kappa Delta Pi, Sigma Alpha Kappa. Clubs: Mason, Commonwealth of Calif, Kiwanis. Died Apr. 29, 2006.

BOSLAUGH, LESLIE, retired judge; b. Hastings, Nebr., Sept. 4, 1917; s. Paul E. and Ann (Herzog) B.; m. Elizabeth F. Meyer, Aug. 10, 1943; children: Marguerite Ann, Sarah Elizabeth, Paul Robert. BBA, U. Nebr., 1939, LL.B., 1941. Bar: Nebr. 1941. Mem. staff Nebr. Statute Revision Commn., 1941-43; pvt. practice law Hastings, 1946-47; asst. atty. gen. Nebr., 1947-48; mem. firm Stiner & Boslaugh, Hastings, 1949-60; judge Nebr. Supreme Ct., Lincoln, 1961-94. Served to lt. AUS, 1943-46. Mem. Nebr. Bar Assn., Order of Coif. Home: Lincoln, Nebr. Died Feb. 16, 2006.

BOSTROM, HARVEY RADER, clergyman, college president; b. Chgo., Jan. 1, 1919; s. Albert and Ruth (Hawkinson) B.; m. Naomi Butcher, Aug. 24, 1944; children— Stephen, Daniel. B.S. Econs. and Bus. Wheaton Coll., 1940; diploma in missions Nyack Coll., 1943; M.A. Christian Ed., Wheaton Coll., 1944; Ph.D. in Higher Ed. Adminstrn., N.Y. U., 1960. Ordained to ministry Christian and Missionary Alliance, 1947. Missionary, Christian Missionary Alliance, Ecuador, 1945-58; faculty Wheaton Coll., Ill., 1960-65, Trinity Coll., Deerfield, Ill., 1967-72; v.p. adminstrn. Trinity Evang. Div. Sch. & Trinity Coll., Deerfield, 1973-75; v.p. devel. and pub. relations Trinity Coll., Deerfield, 1976-80; pres. Fort Wayne Bible Coll., Ind., 1980—. Lodge: Rotary. Home: Fort Wayne, Ind. Died Jan. 22, 2006.

BOTHWELL, JOSEPH CONRAD, JR., electronics company executive; b. Palmer, Mass., Aug. 2, 1923; s. Joseph Conrad and Katherine Louise (Utley) B.; m. Maureen Rhona Gilbride, Sept. 24, 1949; children: Brian J., Bruce A., Douglas J. AB, Harvard U., 1944, MBA cum laude, 1949. Sr. v.p. M/A Com., Inc., Burlington, Mass., from 1952. Industry advisor ICC, 1989; bd. dirs. Spectran Corp., New Eng. Household Moving and Storage. Bd. dirs. Boston Heart found., New Eng. Deaconess Hosp. 1st lt. U.S. Army, 1942-46, PTO. Mem. Internat. Communications Conf. (chmn. fin. com. 1978, industry advisor 1989). Clubs: Harvard (Boston), Univ. (Boston). Avocations: photography, writing, travel. Home: Boston, Mass. Died July 1, 2006.

BOTTNER, IRVING JOSEPH, cosmetic company executive; b. Bronx, NY, Jan. 15, 1916; s. Sigmund and Rose (Habercorn) B.; m. Elaine Schiff, Sept. 8, 1940 (div. Aug. 1958); children— Barbara, Jeffrey; m. Roslyn Ailene Miller, Feb. 14, 1961. BS, NYU Sch. Commerce, 1937; MS, NYU Grad. Sch. Bus., 1939. C.P.A., N.Y. CPA Seidman & Seidman, NYC, 1938-41; v.p., treas. Lewyt Corp., NYC, 1941-56, Revlon, Inc., NYC, 1956; pres. Kno-Mark Esquire Shoe Polish (subsidiary Revlon), 1959; group v.p. in charge of subsidiaries Revlon, Inc., NYC, 1965-68; pres. Revlon Profl. Products Group, 1968-91; sr. v.p. Revlon, Inc., NYC, 1980-91; chmn. Revlon Profl. Products, 1991-92; cons. Revlon, Inc., from 1992. Pres. Revlon-Realistic; chmn. Roux Labs., Gen. Wig (subs.); bd. dirs. Henry Colomer Co. Barcelona, Spain, Revlon Profl. Products Inc. Can. (all subs. Revlon), Howtek, Inc., Hudson, N.H.; inventor "through-the-wall" air conditioner, vacuum cleaner; Revlon Sensor Perm and MP-200 Hair Conditioner. Inventor "through-the-wall" air conditioner, vacuum cleaner; Revlon Sensor Perm and MP-200 Hair Conditioner Named Man of Yr. City of Hope, N.Y. State Chpts., 1965 Mem.: Friars (N.Y.C.); Hampshire Country (Mamaraneck, N.Y.); Del-Aire Country (Delray Beach, Fla.). Republican. Jewish. Avocations: golf; tennis. Home: Delray Beach, Fla. Died May 31, 2006.

BOTTOMLEY, CHARLES GREGORY, research administrator; b. Joliet, Ill., Jan. 26, 1935; s. Edward John and Louise (Seipp) B.; m. Karen Gerhardt, Sept. 7, 1957; children— Gregory, David, Janet, Edward BS in Chemistry, U. Ill., 1957; PhD in Chemistry, Cornell U., 1961. Research chemist E.I. DuPont de Nemours and Co. Inc., Wilmington, Del., 1961-68, research supr. Waynesboro, Va., 1969-72, tech. supt. Camden, S.C., 1973-75, lab. dir. Wilmington, Del., 1975-81, research dir., from 1982. Mem. Am. Chem. Soc., Indsl. Biotech. Assn. Home: Morehead City, NC. Died Mar. 5, 2007.

BOTTORFF, JAMES, state legislator; b. Jeffersonville, Ind., July 28, 1944; m. Carlene Bottorff; children: Christopher, Robert. Student, Ind. U. Treas. Clark County, 1979-86, assessor, 1987-90; mem. Ind. State Rep. Dist. 71, from 1990; chmn. commerce com., mem. local govt., fin. instns. Ind. Ho. of Reps., county and twp. fin. inst. and natural resource coms.; former chmn. Clark County Dem. Ctrl. Com.; real estate appraiser. Charter chmn. Clark County Dem. Men's Club; mem. First Christian Ch. Mem. Elks, Moose, Eagles, Farm Bur. Home: Jeffersonville, Ind. Died Dec. 6, 2005.

BOTWINICK, JACK, psychology educator, researcher; b. Bklyn., Jan. 9, 1923; s. Samuel Meyer and Annie (Leibson) B.; m. Joan Betty Garfein, Sept. 9, 1956; children— Laura, Karen, Paula BA, Bklyn. Coll., 1946, MA, 1949; PhD, NYU, 1953. Rsch. psychologist Lab Psychology, NIMH, NIH, Bethesda, Md., 1955-63; assoc. prof., prof. med. psychology Duke U., Durham, N.C., 1963-69; prof. psychology Washington U., St. Louis, 1969-88, prof. neurology, 1982-88. Cons. VA, Washington, 1981-85; prof. emeritus Washington U., St. Louis, 1988—. Author: Cognitive Precesses in Maturity and Old Age, 1967; co-author: Memory, Aging & Related Functions, 1978; author: We are Aging, 1981; Aging and Behavior, 1984 Served with U.S. Army, 1943-45 Fellow Am. Psychol. Assn. (pres. div. 20 1962, Disting. Contbn. award 1979), Gerontology Soc. Am. (pres. behavioral and social sci. sect. 1963, Kleemeier award 1979, Brookdale award 1984) Home: Saint Louis, Mo. Died Feb. 12, 2006.

BOURKE, THOMAS GILMOUR, retired bank executive; b. Memphis, Oct. 13, 1919; s. Ernest Walter and Nettie (Gilmour) B.; m. Virginia Bass, Dec. 20, 1948; children: Michael, Patricia. BS, Stanford U., 1947. Nat. bank examiner U.S. Treasury Dept., San Francisco, 1949—55; v.p. Pacific Nat. Bank, San Francisco, 1955—64, 1st Security Bank Idaho, Boise, 1968—70, sr. v.p., 1970—72, exec. v.p., 1972—75, pres., 1975—83. Dir. 1st Security Corp., Salt Lake City. Dir., past pres. Idaho Coun. Econs. Edn.; pres. Boise C. of C. Lt. comdr. USN, 1941—45. Mem.: Idaho Bankers Assn. (pres.), Boise Club, Rotary Club. Home: Boise, Idaho. Died Feb. 11, 2007.

BOUSEMAN, JOHN KEITH, entomologist, naturalist; b. Clinton, Iowa, Aug. 11, 1936; s. Thomas Elmer and Kathryn Teresa (Van Buer) B.; m. Barbara Ann Busby, Aug. 21, 1956; children— Karen, David, Thomas, Lynn, Paul; m. 2d, Tamara Faye Moore, Oct. 15, 1977; 1 child, William. B.S. in Entomology, U. Ill., 1960, M.S. in Entomology, 1962. Registered profl. entomologist, Ill. Expdn. entomologist Am. Mus. Natural History, Uruguayan Expdn., 1963, Bolivian Expdn., 1964, 65; instr. U. Ill., Urbana, 1965-66; asst. entomologist agrl. entomology Ill. Agrl. Expt. Sta., Urbana, 1972—; asst. entomologist Ill. Natural History Survey, Champaign, 1972-84, assoc. entomologist, 1984—; entomol. expdns. to Bolivia, Brazil, Paraguay, Zambia, Uruguay, Venezuela, W.I., Mex.; cons. Zambia Ministry Agr. and Water Devel., 1984; mem. tech. adv. com. on mgmt. Ill. Nature Preserves Commn., 1985—. Sci. Research Soc. Am. grantee, 1961; NSF grantee, 1982. Mem. Soc. Entomol. Am., Coleopterists Soc., N.Y. Acad. Sci., N.Y. Entomol. Soc., Internat. Soc. Hymenopterists, Mich. Entomol. Soc., Entomol. Soc. Washington, Kans. Entomol. Soc., Sigma Xi. Club: Ill. Field Entomologists (Champaign). Contbr. numerous publ. to profl. jours. Died May 13, 2006.

BOVEE, EUGENE CLEVELAND, protozoologist, emeritus educator; b. Sioux City, Iowa, Apr. 1, 1915; s. Earl Eugene and Martha Nora (Johnson) B.; m. Maezene B. Wamsley, May 18, 1942 (div. 1967); m. Elizabeth A. Moss, May 9, 1968; children— Frances, Gregory, Matthew; stepchildren— Lynne, Lisa. BA, U. No. Iowa, 1939; MS, U. Iowa, 1948; PhD, UCLA, 1950. Instr. zoology Iowa U., 1940-41; biology tchr. Greene (Iowa) H.S., Iowa, 1941-42; instr. biology U. No. Iowa, 1946-48; journalist Iowa Recorder, Greene, 1945—46; instr. zoology UCLA, 1948-50, research zoologist, 1962-68; asst. prof. biology Calif. Poly. U., 1950-52; assoc. prof. zoology, dept. chmn. N.D. State U., 1952-53; asst. prof. biology U. Houston, 1953-55; assoc. prof. U. Fla., 1955-62; prof. physiology and cell biology U. Kans., Lawrence, 1968-85, prof. emeritus, from 1985. Co-owner arts and crafts bus., 1985-96; cons. Am. Type Culture Collection, 1980-82, W.C. Brown, Pub., 1978-82. Author: (books of poems) Give Back My Body, 1994, To Tartarus and Back, 1999, Sette Bellos, 2000, A Cinquain Zoo, 2000, Old Olympian Games, 2000, Pundamonium, 2001, Biblical Limericks, 2002, Sonnets for Various Reasons, 2002, Historical Limericks, 2003, The Common Gene Pool, 2003; co-author: Historical Limericks II, 2004, Selected Poems, 2004, Various Poems, 2004, Double-Dactyl Fun, 2004; co-editor, co-author: An Illustrated Guide to the Protozoa, 1985; co-author: How to Know the Protozoa, 2d edit., 1979; Microscop. Anat. Invert., Vol. 1, 1991; editor Kans. Sci. Bull., 1974-79; contbr. chpts. to books, articles to sci. jours.; contbr. to small press lit. jours. 1st lt. MIS, U.S. Army, WWII. Research grantee NIH, 1957-62, NSF, 1970-74, NIH, NSF and ONR, 1962-68, Kans. Fed. Water Resources Inst. and U. Kans., 1968-81; recipient Disting. Alumni award U. No. Iowa, 1980. Fellow Iowa Acad. Sci.; mem. Soc. Protozoologists (hon., pres. 1979-80, v.p. 1970-71, treas. 1972-78, exec. com. 1970-81), Am. Microscop Soc. (mem.-at-large exec. com. 1959-62), Western Soc. Naturalists, Kans. Acad. Sci. (life mem., pres. 1979-80, exec. com. 1975-81), Acad. Am. Poets, Poetry Soc. Am., Kans. State Poetry Soc., Kans. Authors Club (Writing Achievement award 1996), Nat. Woodcarvers Assn., United Amateur Press Assn. Am., Sigma Xi. Home: Olathe, Kans. Died Oct. 20, 2005.

BOWEN, WILLIAM AUGUSTUS, financial consultant; b. Greenville, NC, Jan. 17, 1930; s. Joseph Francis and Dorothy Lee (Simmons) B.; m. Hilda Carolyn Rowlett, June 8, 1952; children: Carol Bowen Bernstein, Elizabeth Lee Bowen Jones, William Augustus Jr., Mary Jane Bowen Sullivan. BS in Bus. Adminstrn, U. N.C., 1951, grad. exec. program, 1965. With Wachovia Bank & Trust Co., Charlotte, N.C., 1955-79, regional v.p., mgr. So. region, 1970-79; pres., chief operating officer, dir. First Tulsa Bancorp., Tulsa, First Nat. Bank & Trust Co., Tulsa, 1980-84; chmn., CEO First Nat. Bank and Trust Co., Tulsa, 1984-87; pres. The Bowen Co., from 1987. Bd. dirs. AAON, Inc., Tulsa. Pres. Met. Tulsa Econ. Devel. Found., 1987-88—; chmn. Tulsa Area United Way,, 1986, campaign chmn., 1985. Lt. USNR, 1951-55. Mem. DeBordieu Club Inc. (Georgetown, S.C.), Phi Beta Kappa, Beta Gamma Sigma (pres. 1950-51). Home: Georgetown, SC. Died June 18, 2006.

BOWERS, JOHN WILLIAM, church official; b. Martinsburg, W. Va., Nov. 17, 1933; m. Betty Pittman. Grad., L.I.F.E. Bible Coll., 1956; DD (hon.), Int. Ch. Foursquare Gospel, 1988. Ordained to ministry, 1959. Field sec. ea. dist. Foursquare Chs., 1962-65; from asst. to nat. dir. youth & Christian edn. to nat. dir. Foursquare Hdqs., 1965-80; bd. dirs. Internat. Ch. of Foursquare Gospel, 1980-82, asst. to gen. supr., 1982-87, corp. sec., from 1987. Mem. Foursquare Cabinet; mem. adv. com. Foursquare World Advance mag.; tchr. Mt. Vernon Bible Coll., 1962-65. Mem. Rosemead (Calif.) Pub. Sch. Bd., pres. Home: Pico Rivera, Calif. Died Sept. 14, 2006.

BOWES, BETTY MILLER, painter, art consultant; b. Phila, July 30, 1911; d. George Washington and Elizabeth (Dawson) Miller; m. Thomas David Dowes, June 22, 1946 (div. 1981). ED., Moore Coll. Art., Phila., 1932. One-man shows, Phila. Art Alliance, 1954, 60, 65, Woodmere Gallery, 1958-64, group shows; art cons., Sun Oil Co., Radnor, Pa., mem. exhbn. com, Woodmere Gallery, Designer tapestry, (paintings reproduced in art books). George W. Elkins European fellow, 1932; Dolphon fellow; recipient numerous awards Mem. Am. Watercolor Soc., Phila. Art Alliance, Phila. Watercolor Soc. Republican. Roman Catholic. Home: Wynnewood, Pa. Died Sept. 12, 2007.

BOWES, EDWARD (BUD), superintendent of schools; b. Feb. 21, 1941; s. Edward Carpenter and Margaret Ann (Zerbe) B.; m. Sharon Gail Burd, Aug. 17, 1963.; 1 child, Jennifer. BS in Secondary Edn., Lock Haven U., 1963; MS in Secondary Edn., Ind. U., 1967, EdD in Sch. Adminstrn., 1971. Tchr. English and social studies Ben David Jr. H.S., Indpls., 1963-67, asst. prin., in-svc. coord., 1967-69; adminstrv. asst. Ind. Sch. Bds. Assn., Bloomington, 1969-71; asst. supt. East Brunswick (N.J.) Pub. Schs., 1971-74; supt. Rahway (N.J.) Pub. Schs., 1974-78, Met. Sch. Dist. Wayne Twp., Indpls., 1978-95, North Penn Sch. Dist., Lansdale, Pa., from 1995. Cons. on planning and goal setting to bds. edn.; adj. prof. Butler U., Indpls.; bd. visitors Ind. U. Sch. Edn., Bloomington; mem. adv. bd. Ind. Prins. Assessment Ctr.; mem. and mem. exec. com. curriculum coun. adv. com. Ind. Bd. Edn.; mem. task force on performance and accountability, task force for innovations in learning, supt.'s adv. com., biennial plan for secondary and adult vocat. edn. com. Office Ind. Supt. Pub. Instrn.; bd. dirs., 1st pres. Ind. Pub. Sch.-Univ. Partnership. Bd. dirs., v.p., pres. Project I-STAR, drug abuse prevention project; vice chmn., chmn. local bd. 31, SSS; bd. dirs., chmn. curriculum com. Ruth Lilly Ctr. for Health Edn.; bd. dirs. Cmty. Svc. Coun. Met. Indpls., Jr. Achievement Ctrl. Ind., Indpls. Campaign for Healthy Babies, Ind. Congress Parents and Tchrs., Inc.; chmn. edn. div. campaign Indpls. United Way; mem. noise abatement project adv. bd. Indpls. Internat. Airport; mem. Indpls. Mayor's Tax Increment Financing Task Force. Recipient Sagamore of Wabash award State of Ind., Disting. Educator award Lock Haven U.; named One of 100 Best Sch. Adminstrs. in N.Am., Exec. Educator, 1993; Paul Harris fellow Rotary Internat. Mem. Am. Assn. Sch. Adminstrs., Ind. Assn. Pub. Sch. Supts., Mid-Am. Assn. Sch. Supts., Midwest Suburban Supts. Orgn., Assn. for Advancement Internat. Edn. (bd. dirs., v.p., pres.), PTA (hon. life), Century Club, Phi Delta Kappa. Avocations: tennis, reading, fishing. Home: Indianapolis, Ind. Died Nov. 17, 2006.

BOWSER, ANITA OLGA, state senator, education educator; b. Canton, Ohio, Aug. 18, 1920; d. Nicholas B. Alby and Emile Stobbe. AB, Kent State U., 1945; LLB, William McKinley U., 1949; MS, Purdue U., 1967; MA, U. Notre Dame, 1972, PhD, 1976. Instr. Kent (Ohio) State U., 1945-46; prof. Purdue U. North Cen. Campus, Michigan City, Ind., from 1950; mem. Ind. Ho. Reps., 1980-92, Ind. Senate from 8th dist, 1992—2007. Mem. Delta Kappa Gamma. Home: Michigan City, Ind. Died Mar. 4, 2007.

BOWYTZ, ROBERT B., lawyer; b. Pitts., Apr. 21, 1938; BS, U. Va., Pa. State U., 1959; JD, U. Pitts., 1962; LLM, George Washington U., 1969. Bar: Pa. 1962, D.C. 1968, Md. 1976. Ptnr. Keck, Mahin & Cate, Chgo. Mem. ABA (legis. coord. com. model procurement code 1975-84, vice chair pub. contract law sect., vice chair socio econ. policies and regulation com.), Fed. Bar Assn., D.C. Bar (chair procurement com. 1982-85), Md. State Bar Assn. (chmn. pub. contract law com.). Died Oct. 15, 2006.

BOYD, ALAN CONDUITT, lawyer; b. Indpls., Aug. 19, 1926; s. Alan Wilson and Dorothy Rodman (Lee) B.; m. Anne Crete Fuller, Aug. 30, 1947; children: Anne Margaret Boyd McKisson, Amy Lucretia Boyd. BBA, U. of Mich., 1947, JD cum laude, 1951. Bar: Ind. 1951, Ohio 1958. Assoc., Barnes, Hickam, Pantzer & Boyd, Inpls., 1951-58; atty. Owens-Illinois, Toledo, 1958-77, asst. gen. counsel and asst. sec., 1977-83, assoc. gen. counsel and asst. sec., 1983-85; sec., assoc. gen. counsel, 1985-87; ptnr. Fuller & Henry, Toledo, 1987-92, of counsel, 1992—. Hon. dir., Lucas County Unit Am. Cancer Soc., Toledo; sec. Com. of 100. Mem. ABA, Ohio State Bar Assn., Toledo Bar Assn. Republican. Club: Inverness (Toledo) Home: Toledo, Ohio. Died Oct. 29, 2005.

BOYD, GORDON, retired insurance company executive; b. Maplewood, NJ, Mar. 14, 1918; s. James and H. Estelle (Boyd) B.; m. Betty Bleakney, Apr. 4, 1941; children— Randall Bleakney, Gordon Reed. BS in Econs, U. Pa., 1940; MBA, N.Y. U., 1949. Mortgage investments exec. James Boyd, Inc., NYC, 1940-42; with financial div. Socony-Vacuum Oil Co., NYC, 1946; with Mut. Benefit Life Ins. Co., Newark, from 1946, treas., 1956-72, v.p., treas., 1972-83, ret., 1983. Dir. FMI Fin. Corp. Vice pres. Robert Treat council Boy Scouts Am., 1965-81; Trustee, mem. finance com. Overseas Ministries Study Center, Ventnor, N.J., 1960-85. Served to lt. USNR, 1942-46. Mem.: Bond (N.Y.); Treas.'s (N.Y.C.); Money Marketeers (N.Y. U.); Suburban of U. Pa; Baltusrol (Springfield, N.J.); Essex (Newark). Home: Convent Station, NJ. Died Feb. 27, 2006.

BOYD, JOSEPH ARTHUR, JR., lawyer, retired state supreme court justice; b. Hoschton, Ga., Nov. 16, 1916; s. Joseph Arthur and Esther Estelle (Puckett) B.; m. Ann Stripling, June 6, 1938; children: Joanne Louise Boyd Goldman, Betty Jean Boyd Jala, Joseph Robert, James Daniel, Jane N. Ohlin. Student, Piedmont Coll., Demorest, Ga., 1936-38, LLD, 1963; student, Mercer U., Macon, Ga., 1938-39; JD, U. Miami, Coral Gables, Fla., 1948; LLD, Western State U. Coll. Law, San Diego, 1981. Bar: Fla. 1948, U.S. Supreme Ct. 1959, D.C. 1973, N.Y. 1982. Practice law, Hialeah, 1948-68; city atty., 1951-58; mem. Dade County Commn., Miami, Fla., 1958-68, chmn., 1963; vice mayor Dade County, 1967; justice Fla. Supreme Ct., Tallahassee, 1969-87, chief justice, 1984-86. Mem. Hialeah Zoning Bd., 1946-48; juror Freedoms Found., Valley Forge, Pa., 1971, 73 Bd. dirs. Bapt. Hosp., Miami, 1962-66, Miami Coun. Chs., 1960-64; emeritus trustee Piedmont Coll. Recipient Nat. Top Hat award Bus. and Profl. Women in U.S. for advancing status of employed women, 1967 Mem. ABA, Fla. Bar Assn., Hialeah-Miami Springs Bar Assn. (pres. 1955), Tallahassee Bar Assn., Hialeah-Miami Springs C. of C. (pres. 1956), Am. Legion (comdr. Fla. 1953-54), VFW, Shriners, Masons (33 deg.), Lions, Elks, Iron Arrow, Phi Alpha Delta. Democrat. Baptist (deacon). Home: Tallahassee, Fla. Died Oct. 26, 2007.

BOYD, LEONA POTTER, retired social worker; b. Creekside, Pa., Aug. 31, 1907; d. Joseph M. and Belle (McHenry) Johnston; m. Edgar D. Potter, July 16, 1932 (div.); m. Harold Lee Boyd, Oct. 1972. Grad., Indiana State Normal Sch, Pa., 1927; student, Las Vegas Normal U., N.Mex., 1933; student Sch. Social Work, Carnegie Inst. Tech., 1945, U. Pitts., 1956-57. Tchr. Creekside Pub. Schs., 1927-30, Papago Indian Reservation, Sells, Ariz., 1931-33; caseworker, supr. Indiana County (Pa.) Bd. Assistance, 1934-54, exec. dir., 1954-68; ret., 1968. Bd. dirs., hon. life mem. Indiana County Tourist Promotion; former bd. dirs. Indiana County United Fund, Salvation Army, Indiana County Guidance Ctr., Armstrong-Indiana Mental Health Bd.; cons. assoc. Cmty. Rsch. Assocs., Inc.; mem. Counseling Ctr. Aux., Lake Havasu City, Ariz., 1978-80; former mem. Western Welcome Club, Lake Havasu City, Sierra Vista Hosp. Aux., Truth or Consequences, N.M. Recipient Disting. Svc. award Indiana Jaycees, 1965, Bus. and Profl. Women's Club award, 1965. Mem.: AARP, Daus. Am. Colonists. Lutheran. Died Oct. 2, 2006.

BOYER, ROBERT ALLEN, physics educator; b. Hummels Wharf, Pa., Aug. 27, 1916; s. H. Alvin and Jennie (Saurers) B.; m. Eleanor Rae Moyer, June 24, 1939; children— Patty Rae (Mrs. William H. Hinkle), Stephen C. AB summa cum laude, Susquehanna U., 1938; MA, Syracuse U., 1940; PhD, Lehigh U., 1952; DSc (hon.), Muhlenberg Coll., 1981. Instr. physics Clarkson Coll. Tech., 1940-41; instr. physics, acting dept. head Muhlenberg Coll., 1941-52, prof. physics, head dept., 1952-81, prof. emeritus, from 1981; adj. prof. Cedar Crest Coll., 1981-86. Vis. prof. summer grad. sch. Conn. Wesleyan U., 1963-72, 75 Lay speaker Eastern Pa. Synod, Lutheran Ch., 1969-70. Recipient Lindback award, 1961; Alumni Achievement award Susquehanna U., 1984, Disting. and Exceptional Service to Muhlenberg Coll., 1987—. Mem. Am. Assn. Physics Tchrs. (pres. Central Pa. sect. 1956-57, Disting. Service award, 1987—), Acoustical Soc. Am., AAUP, Assn. Am. Boyers (pres. 1981—) Home: Reading, Pa. Died Jan. 30, 2007.

BOYKIN, NANCY MERRITT, academic administrator; b. Washington, Mar. 20, 1919; d. Matthew and Mary Gertrude (White) Merritt; m. Ulysses Wilhelm Boykin, Apr. 17, 1965 (dec. 1987); 1 child from previous marriage, Tauyna Lovell Banks. BS, D.C. Tchrs. Coll., 1939; MA, Howard U., 1940, MSW, 1956; PhD, U. Mich., 1976. Employee rels. counselor Office Chief of Fin., U.S. Army, Washington; adminstrv. asst. to civilian aide Sec. of Def., Washington; policewoman Met. Police Dept., Washington; social worker Dept. Pub. Welfare, Washington; adminstrv. asst. to dir. Active Cmty. Teams, Inc., Detroit, 1965—66; dir. continuing edn. for girls program Detroit Pub. Schs., 1966—87; ednl. cons. and cmty. outreach coord. New Health Ctr., Livonia, Mich., 1988—90. Presdl. appointee Nat. Adv. Coun. on Extension and Continuing Edn., 1973—80; cons. U.S. Dept. Edn., 1982. Mem. Mich. Bd. Examiners of Social Workers, 1978—83; gov.'s appointee Mich. Youth Adv. Com., 1984—87, Commn. on Svcs. to Aging, 1992—2006; mem. Nat. Black Republicans, 1972—2006, Mich. Rep. Com., 1975—80, 1983—2006; sec. 1st Rep. Dist., 1973—77; presdl. appointee to nat. adv. bd. C.C. of Air Force, 1984—2006. Named Educator of Yr., Nat. Black Women's Polit. Leadership Caucus, 1981, Hon. Lt. Col. Aide De Camp in Ala. Militia, Gov. Wallace, 1986, in her honor, The Nancy Boykin Continuing Edn. Ctr., Detroit Pub. Sch. Bd., 1993; recipient Spirit of Detroit award, 1979, Nat. Kool Achiever's award in Edn., Brown and Williams Tobacco Co., 1987, Outstanding Contbns. to Cmty. award, Assn. Black Judges Mich., 1988—90, Cmty. Svc. award, YWCA, 1992, Pioneer award, Frederick Douglas Soc., 1994, others. Mem.: Detroit Assn. Univ. Mich. Women, Detroit Orgn. Sch. Adminstrs., Nat. Assn. Black Sch. Educators, Nat. Assn. Supervision and Curriculum Devel., Profl. Women's Network, Mich. Assn. Concerned with Sch. Age Parents (past pres., Recognition award 1986, Outstanding Svc. award 1993), Wayne State U. Sch. Edn. Alumni Assn. (bd. govs.), U. Mich. Alumnae Assn., Phi Delta Kappa, Alpha Kappa Alpha, Eta Phi Beta (Outstanding Profl. Women award 1992). Died Jan. 28, 2006.

BOYLAND, JOSEPH FRANCIS, corporate controller; b. NYC, Sept. 29, 1931; s. Joseph Francis Sr. and Veronica Rita (Jennings) B.; m. Janeane Alene Folk, Feb. 1959; children: Theresa, Joseph III, Stephen, Mary, Timothy, Regina. BBA, St. John's U., Bklyn., 1952. With Foster Wheeler Corp., Clinton, N.J., from 1955, now asst. contr.; v.p., contr. Foster Wheeler Energy Corp.; contr. Foster Wheeler World Svc. Corp.; contr., treas. Foster Wheeler Constructors Inc., also bd. dirs. Sg. U.S. Army, 1952-54, Korea. Mem. VFW. Roman Catholic. Avocations: sports, fishing, gardening. Home: Whippany, NJ. Died Jan. 10, 2006.

BOYLE, PETER, actor; b. Phila., Oct. 18, 1935; m. Loraine Alterman, Oct. 1977; children: Lucy, Amy. BA in English, La Salle U., Phila., 1957; Degree (hon.), La Salle U., 1993. Former Monk Christian Bros. order. Actor in Off-Broadway shows, N.Y.C., also Second City group, Chgo., and TV commls.; (films) The Group, 1966, The Virgin President, 1968, Medium Cool, 1969, The Monitors, 1969, Joe, 1970, Diary of a Mad Housewife, 1970, T.R. Baskin, 1972, The Candidate, 1972, Ghost in the Noonday Sun, 1973, Steelyard Blues, 1973, Slither, 1973, The Friends of Eddie Coyle, 1973, Kid Blue, 1973, Crazy Joe, 1974, Young Frankenstein, 1974, Taxi Driver, 1976, Swashbuckler, 1976, F.I.S.T, 1978, The Brink's Job, 1978, Hardcore, 1979, Beyond the Poseidon Adventure, 1979, In God We Tru$t, 1980, Where the Buffalo Roam, 1980, Hammett, 1980, Outland, 1981, Yellowbeard, 1983, Johnny Dangerously, 1984, Turk 182, 1985, Surrender, 1987, Walker, 1987, Red Heat, 1988, The In Crowd, 1988, Speedzone, 1989, Funny, 1989, The Dream Team, 1989, 27 Wagons Full of Cotton, 1990, Solar Crisis, 1990, Men of Respect, 1991, Kickboxer 2: The Road Back, 1991, Nervous Ticks, 1992, Death and the Compass, 1992, Honeymoon in Vegas, 1992, Malcolm X, 1992, The Shadow, 1994, The Killer, 1994, Exquisite Tenderness, 1994, The Santa Clause, 1994, Katie, 1995, Born to Be Wild, 1995, While You Were Sleeping, 1995, Death and Compass, 1996, Final Vendetta, 1996, That Darn Cat, 1997, Milk % Money, 1997, Species II, 1998, Dr. Dolittle, 1998, Monsters Ball, 2001, The Adventures of Pluto Nash, 2002, The Santa Clause 2, 2002, Scooby-Doo 2: Monsters Unleashed, 2004, The Santa Clause 3: The Escape Clause, 2006; (TV movies) The Man Who Could Talk to Kids, 1973, Tail Gunner Joe, 1977, From Here to Eternity, 1979, Conspiracy: The Trial of the Chicago 8, 1987, Ehoes in the Darkness, 1987, Disaster at Silo 7, 1988, Guts and Glory: The Rise and Fall of Oliver North, 1989, Challenger, 1990, Poochinski, 1990, The Tragedy of Flight 103: The Inside Story, 1990, In the Line of Duty, Street War, 1992, Taking the Heat, 1993, Royce, 1994, In the Lake of the Woods, 1996, A Deadly Vision, 1997, Master Spy: The Robert Hanssen Story, 2002; (TV series) Joe Bash, 1986, Comedy Tonight, 1970, Everybody Loves Raymond, 1996-2005 (nominee Outstanding Supporting Actor in Comedy Series Emmy award 1999-2001, nominee Funniest Supporting Male Performer in TV Series Am. Comedy award 2000); (TV appearances) Cagney & Lacey, 1988, Midnight Caller, 1990, Flying Blind, 1992, 93, The Hopeless Romantic, 1993, Philly Heat, 1994, NYPD Blue, 1994, 95, Lois & Clark: The New Adventures of Superman, 1994, 95, The X Files, 1995 (Emmy award for Outstanding Guest Actor in a Drama Sereis 1996), The Single Guy, 1996, 97, Cosby, 1997, The King of Queens, 1998, Roswell, 2005. Recipient Emmy award, 1996, Shining Star award, La Salle U., 2005. Died Dec. 12, 2006.

BOYNTON, ROBERT MERRILL, retired psychology professor; b. Evanston, Ill., Oct. 28, 1924; s. Merrill Holmes and Eleanor (Matthews) B.; m. Alice Neiley, Apr. 9, 1947 (dec. Oct. 15, 1996); children: Sherry, Michael, Neiley, Geoffrey; m. Sheleah Maloney, Oct. 17, 1998. Student, Antioch Coll., 1942-43, U. Ill., 1943-45; AB, Amherst Coll., 1948; PhD, Brown U., 1952. Asst. prof. psychology and optics U. Rochester, N.Y., 1952-57, assoc. prof., 1957-61, prof., 1961-74, founder, dir. Ctr. for Visual Sci., 1963-71, chmn. dept. psychology, 1971-74; prof. psychology U. Calif., San Diego, 1974-91, prof. emeritus, 1991—2006, assoc. dean grad. studies & rsch., 1987-91. Guest researcher Nat. Phys. Lab., Teddington, Eng., 1960-61; vis. prof. physiology U. Calif. Med. Center, San Francisco, 1969-70 Author: Human Color Vision, 1979, 2d edit., 1996; chmn. bd. editors Vision Research, 1982-86; contbr. articles to profl. jours. Served with USNR, 1943-45. Recipient Charles F. Prentice award Am. Acad. Optometry, 1997. Fellow AAAS, Optical Soc. Am. (dir.-at-large 1966-69, Frederick Ives medal 1995), APA, Assn. for Rsch. in Vision and Ophthalmology (trustee 1984-89); mem. NAS. Home: Del Mar, Calif. Died Sept. 4, 2006.

BOYSE, EDWARD ARTHUR, retired microbiologist, medical researcher; b. Worthing, Sussex, Eng., Aug. 11, 1923; arrived in US, 1960; s. Arthur and Dorothy Vera (Mellersh) Boyse; m. Judith Bard; children: Conrad, Adrienne. MB, BS, U. London, 1952, MD, 1957. Mem. med. staff various hosps., England, 1952—57; researcher Guy's Hosp., London, 1957—60, Sch. Medicine, NYU, 1960—71, adj. prof., 1971—2007; prof. Cornell Grad. Sch. Med. Sci., NYC, 1969—89; assoc. scientist Meml. Sloan-Kettering Inst., NYC, 1962—64, assoc. mem., 1964—67, mem., 1967—89; Disting. prof. U. Ariz., Tucson, 1989—94, prof. emeritus, 1994—2007. Affiliated scientist Monell Chem. Senses Ctr., Phila. Contbr. articles to profl. jours. With RAF, 1941—46. Recipient Isaac Adler award, Rockefeller U., 1976, Harvard U., 1976. Fellow: Nat. Acad. Sci., Am. Acad. Arts & Sci., Royal Soc. Home: Tucson, Ariz. Died July 14, 2007.

BRACALI, GIAMPAOLO, composer, conductor, pianist, music educator; b. Rome, May 24, 1941; came to U.S., 1969; s. Enrico and Luigia (Recchioni) B.; m. Bretta Van Nes, June 1, 1970 (div. 1976); m. Barbara Beth Gersch, July 28, 1977; 1 child, Julian. Diploma in Piano, Santa Cecilia, Rome, 1960, diplomas in Composition and Conducting, 1963; diploma in Composition (hon.), Accade Mia Chigiana, Siena, Italy, 1964. Asst. prof. music Santa Cecilia Conservatory, Rome, 1963-65; scholar French Govt. Paris Conservatoire, 1965-67; pvt. scholar Brit. Council, London, 1967-68; Fulbright scholar Manhattan Sch. Music, NYC, 1968-69, asst. condr., 1969-71, prof. composition, from 1971, prof. conducting, from 1983. Condr. Metro Lyric Opera, N.J., 1981—, Opera Lyrics, N.J., 1982—, Treasure Coast Opera Soc., Ft. Pierce, Fla., 1983—, Nat. Grand Opera, L.I., N.Y., 1985—, Bklyn. Philharm., 1987, Conn. Opera, 1988, Riverside (Calif.) Opera, 1989—, Radio Television Orch. of Hungary, 1990—, Hungarian State Orch., 1991, Hong Kong Philharm. Orch., 1992-93, Shangai Symphony Orch., 1992-94, Beijing Ctrl. Symphony Orch., 1992-94, Singapore Symphony, 1993—. Recipient Napolitano prize Conservatory of Naples, Italy, 1963, Bonaventura Somma prize Accademia Chigiana, 1964, Boulanger Fund award, 1967, Prince Pierre Competition award, 1968, 80. Avocations: soccer, baseball, sailing. Home: Bronx, NY. Died Dec. 16, 2006.

BRACE, FLORENCE HILGERMANN, retired librarian; b. Milw., Aug. 4, 1914; d. George and Mary Jane (Higgins) Hilgermann; m. Sears Webster Brace, Nov. 30, 1940 (div. 1950). Student, Gulf Park Jr. Coll., U. Minn., 1932-36, 1953, U. Houston, 1968-70. Copywriter Dayton's Store, Mpls., 1937-40, sr. fashion copywriter, 1951-59; sr. fashion copywriter, promotion adviser Stix, Baer & Fuller, St. Louis, 1943-48; mgr. advt. and pub. relations Mindlin's Fashion Store, Kansas City, Mo., 1948-50; librarian rsch. for promotions Friendswood Devel. Co. subs. Exxon Co., Houston, 1981-84. Past bd. dirs., fundraiser Women's Advt. Clubs, St. Louis, Mpls., and Kansas City, Mo., past vol. fundraiser for various charities, Cuernavaca, Mex.; past vol. ARC. Mem. NAFE, DAR, Tex. Assn. Realtors, Meml. Wo men's Assn., Delta Gamma. Republican. Episcopalian. Clubs: Univ.; Yankee Women's Service (Edmonton, Can.); Mpls. Women's. Home: Excelsior, Minn. Died May 25, 2006.

BRACEWELL, RONALD NEWBOLD, engineering educator; b. Sydney, July 22, 1921; s. Cecil Charles and Valerie Zilla (McGowan) Bracewell; m. Helen Mary Lester Elliott; children: Catherine Wendy, Mark Cecil. BSc in Math. and Physics, U. Sydney, 1941, B in Engring., 1943, M in Engring. with 1st class honors, 1948; PhD, Cambridge U., Eng., 1950. Sr. rsch. officer Radiophysics Lab., Commonwealth Sci. and Indsl. Rsch. Orgn., Sydney, 1949—54; vis. asst. prof. radio astronomy U. Calif., Berkeley, 1954—55; mem. elec. engring. faculty Stanford U., from 1955, Lewis M. Terman prof. and fellow in elec. engring., 1974—79, Terman prof. emeritus elec. engring., 1979—2007. Pollock Meml. lectr. U. Sydney, 1978; Tektronix Disting. Visitor, 81; Christensen fellow St. Catherine's Coll., Oxford, 1987; sr. vis. fellow Inst. Astronomy; fellow commoner Churchill Coll., Cambridge U., 1988; Bunyan lectr. Stanford U., 1996; mem. adv. panels NSF, Naval Rsch. Lab., Office Naval Rsch., NAS, Nat. Radio Astronomy Obs., Jet Propulsion Lab. Adv. Group on Radio Experiments in Space, Advanced Rsch. Projects Agy.; cons. in field. Author: The Fourier Transform and Its Applications, 1965, 2000, The Galactic Club: Intelligent Life in Outer Space, 1974, The Hartley Transform, 1986, Two-Dimensional Imaging, 1995, Fourier Analysis and Imaging, 2003, Trees of Stanford and Environs, 2005; co-author: Radio Astronomy, 1955; translator: Radio Astronomy (J.L. Steinberg and J. Lequeux); editor: Paris Symposium on Radio Astronomy, 1959; former mem. editl. bd.: Internat. Jour. Imaging Sys. and Tech., Planetary and Space Sci., Proceedings of the Astron. Soc. Pacific, Cosmic Search, Jour. Computer Assisted Tomography, mem. bd. ann. rev.: Astronomy and Astrophysics, 1961—68; contbr. articles and revs. to jours., chapters to books. Recipient Duddell Premium, Instn. Elec. Engrs., London, 1952, Inaugural Alumni award, Sydney U., 1992; Fulbright travel grantee, 1954, William Gurling Watson traveling fellow, 1978, 1986. Fellow: AAAS, IEEE (life Heinrich Hertz Gold medal 1994, Jim Wolfensohn Suguna award 1996), Am. Acad. Arts and Scis., Astron. Soc. Australia, Royal Astron. Soc.; mem.: Order of Australia (officer), Internat. Sci. Radio Union, Astron. Soc. Pacific (life), Internat. Astron. Union, Am. Astron. Soc. (past councilor), Inst. Medicine of NAS. Home: Stanford, Calif. Died Aug. 12, 2007.

BRACKEN, PEG, writer; b. Filer, Idaho, Feb. 25, 1918; d. John Lewis and Ruth (McQuesten) B.; m. John Hamilton Ohman, June 15, 1991; 1 child from previous marriage, Johanna Bracken. AB, Antioch Coll., 1940. Author: The I Hate to Cook Book, 1960, The I Hate to Housekeep Book, 1962, I Try to Behave Myself, 1963, Peg Bracken's Appendix to The I Hate to Cook Book, 1966, I Didn't Come Here to Argue, 1969, But I Wouldn't Have Missed It for the World, 1973, The I Hate to Cook Almanack - A Book of Days, 1976, A Window Over the Sink, 1981, The Compleat I Hate to Cookbook, 1986, On Getting Old for the First Time, 1996. Home: Portland, Oreg. Died Oct. 20, 2007.*

BRADFIELD, RICHARD HAROLD, retired architectural firm executive; b. Lincoln, Nebr., Apr. 22, 1933; BS, Ga. Inst. Tech., 1959. Registered arch., Ala., Ga., Fla., Miss., Ohio, Ky., Tenn., Tex., N.C., S.C., V.I.; cert. Nat. Coun. Archtl. Registration Bds. CEO, ptnr. Bradfield, Richards & Assocs., Archs., Inc., Atlanta. Past pres., bd. dirs. com. for coll. architecture Ga. Inst. Tech.; mem. adv. group Intervarsity Christian Fellowship, Atlanta; tech. advisor Ministries to Women, U.S.A., Inc. Fellow AIA (chair nat. housing com., chair affordable housing task force, bd. dirs. Atlanta chpt., edn. commr., housing commr., nat. bd. dirs. 1996, Honor award); mem. Soc. Am. Mil. Engrs. Died Mar. 13, 2007.

BRADFORD, G. ERIC, animal science educator emeritus; b. Kingsey, Que., Can., Nov. 2, 1929; came to U.S., 1957, naturalized, 1989; m. Elizabeth Ann Engelke, June 19, 1954; children: Anne, Kenneth, Margaret, Ellen. BSc in Agr., McGill U., Montreal, 1951; MS, U. Wis., 1952, PhD, 1956. Asst. prof. McGill U., 1955-57, U. Calif. Davis, 1957-64, assoc. prof., 1964-69, prof. animal sci., 1969-93, chair dept. animal sci., 1973-78, 90-93, prof. emeritus, from 1993, dir. Animal Agr. Rsch. Ctr., 1993-95. Vis. asst. prof. Cornell U., Ithaca, N.Y., 1963; vis. scientist Am. Breeding Rsch. Orgn., Edinburgh, 1970-71, Winrock Internat., Morrilton, Ark., 1978-79. Author some 135 articles on animal sci. and animal genetics. Bd. dirs. Internat. House, Davis, 1993—. Recipient Svc. awrd Calif. Wool Growers Assn., 1990. Fellow AAAS; mem. Am. Soc. Animal Sci. (Rockefeller-Prentice award 1984), Brit. Soc. Animal Sci., Coun. Agrl. Sci. and Tech. Presbyterian. Avocations: gardening, travel, environmental interests. Home: Davis, Calif. Died July 29, 2007.

BRADLEY, ED (EDWARD RUDOLPH BRADLEY JR.) news correspondent; b. Phila., June 22, 1941; s. Edward R. and Gladys Bradley; m. Diane Jefferson, 1964 (div.); m. Priscilla Collidge, 1981 (div. 1984); m. Patricia Blanchet, 2004 BA in Edn., Cheyney State Coll., Pa., 1964. Radio news reporter Sta. WDAS, Phila., 1963-67, Sta. WCBS, NYC, 1967-71; stringer CBS News, Paris, 1971-73, prin. corr., 1971, Saigon, 1972-74 1975, Washington, 1974—75, Phnom Penh, 1975, White House corr., 1976—78; prin. corr. CBS Reports, 1978-81, "60 Minutes", 1981—2006; anchorman CBS Sunday Night News, 1976-81; anchor CBS News magazine "Street Stories", 1992—93 Anchorman: various documentaries including What's Happening to Cambodia, 1978, The Boat People, 1979, Blacks in America: With All Deliberate Speed, 1979, The Boston Goes to China, 1979, In the Belly of the Beast, 1983, Lena, 1983 Schizophrenia, 1985, Caitlin's Story, 1992, In the Killing Fields of America, 1995 Recipient Overseas Press Club award, 1975 Disting. Commentator award NY Chapter Nat. Assn. Medi

Women, 1975, Assn. Black Journalists award, 1977, Alfred I. Du Pont-Columbia U. award for Broadcast Journalism, 1978, 80, 97; George Foster Peabody Broadcasting award U. Ga., 1979, 97, Edward R. Murrow award, 1979,Emmy award, 1979 (3), 1983 (2), 1985, 86, 92, 93, 95 George Polk Journalism award, 1980, Sol Taischoff award, 1993, NCAA Anniversary award, 1989, Sol Taischoff award, 1993, Robert F. Kennedy Journalism award, 1995, Paul White award Radio Television News Directors Assn., 2000, Lifetime Achievement Emmy award, 2002 Died Nov. 9, 2006.

BRADLEY, FRANCIS XAVIER, aluminum company executive; b. NYC, Aug. 25, 1915; s. Francis Michael and Estelle Veronica (McQuade) B.; m. Mary Ann Flynn, Sept. 10, 1940; children: Robert S. and Bruce (twins), Patricia Bradley Greene. BS, U. Ala., 1937; MA, Columbia U., 1951. Planning specialist Martin Co., Balt., 1959-61, gen. sales mgr., 1961-63; v.p. Martin Marietta Aerospace, Denver, 1963-70; v.p. mktg. and planning Martin Marietta Aluminum, Torrance, Calif., 1970-72, exec. v.p. Washington, 1973, pres., chief operating officer, 1974, pres., chief exec. officer, 1975-80; v.p. Martin Marietta Corp., 1973-80; pres., chief exec. officer Halco Mining Inc., 1980-84; chief exec. officer Tara Tape Corp., from 1987, also chmn. bd. dirs. Dir. Martin Marietta Corp. Served with AUS, 1937-59. Mem. Aluminum Assn., Internat. Primary Aluminum Inst. Clubs: George Town, Army-Navy, Army-Navy Country, Pisces, Duquesne, San Diego Yacht. Home: Washington, DC. Died Mar. 23, 2007.

BRADLEY, MITCHELL HUGH, retired professional society administrator, retired career officer; b. Birmingham, Ala., Apr. 27, 1935; s. Samuel Brice and Mildred (Maiche) M.; m. Carol Nason Sexton, Mar. 23, 1963; children: Susan, Carin. BS in Mech. Engring., Auburn U., 1957; MS in Mech. Engring., Stanford U., 1964. Commd. 2d lt. USAF, 1957, advanced through grades to lt. col., ret., 1977; mng. dir. ASME, Washington, 1977-89; exec. dir. Am. Assn. Engring. Socs., Washington, 1989-95. Chmn. Indsl. Devel. Authority, Manassas, Va., 1970-80. Mem. ASME, Tau Beta Pi, Omicron Delta Kappa, Pi Tau Sigma. Home: Centreville, Va. Died July 13, 2007.

BRADLEY, WILLIAM BRYAN, cable television regulator; b. Charleston, W.Va., Feb. 12, 1929; s. Floyd England and Florence Clara (O'Bryan) B.; m. Virginia Vanderhoof Logan, Oct. 27, 1951; children: Christopher, Thomas, Michael, John, Mary Clare (dec.), Mary Ellen, Ann. BA in Journalism cum laude, U. Notre Dame, 1950. Supr., indsl. engr. Martin Co., Denver, 1958-61, 62-65; cons. Reynolds, Ward & Carey, Denver, 1961-62; analyst Denver City Coun., 1965-69, staff dir., 1969-82; dir. Office of Telecommunications, Denver, 1982-94; sr. assoc. Media Mgmt. Svcs., Inc., 1994-99. Co-founder, dir., vice-chmn. Greater Metro Cable Consortium, 1992; initiated joint city-industry cable TV Tech. Stds., 1987, adopted by FCC, 1992. Participant Japanese-Am. conf. on Globalization and Cable TV, Suwa, Japan, 1991. Co-founder Nat. Assn. Telecomm. Officers and Advisors, Washington, 1980, bd. dirs., 1983-88, pres., 1985-87; chmn. telecomm. subcom. Colo. Mcpl. League, Denver, 1985-86; bd. dirs. Denver Cmty. TV, 1996-98; charter mem. The Cable Ctr., 1998. Line Officer USN, 1950-53. Roman Catholic. Avocations: chess, books. Died May 13, 2007.

BRADY, GENE PAUL, investment firm executive; b. Wexford, Pa., July 8, 1927; s. John Authur and Frances Augusta (Aven) B.; m. Helena Marie Real, Feb. 1, 1958. B.S., U.S. Naval Acad., 1950; M.B.A., U. Pa., 1958. Commd. ensign U.S. Navy, advanced through grades to lt., 1956; security analyst Laird, Bissell and Meeds, N.Y.C., 1958-61, Orvis Bros., N.Y.C., 1962-66, W.E. Hutton, N.Y.C., 1967-74, Reynolds and Co., N.Y.C., 1975-78; asst. v.p. research Dean Witter Reynolds, N.Y.C., 1979—. Author: Tripling Your Money in the Stock Market with Techno Fundamental Strategies, 1975; A Master Plan for Winning in Wall Street, 1976. Mem. N.Y. Soc. Security Analysts. Republican. Roman Catholic. Home: Briarcliff Manor, NY. Died Jan. 31, 2007.

BRADY, JOHN PAUL, psychiatrist; b. Boston, June 23, 1928; s. James Henry and Evelyn Louise (Rice) B.; m. Christeen Nelson, Mar. 19, 1963; children— James Palmer, Pamela Eros, June Pamela, David Duncan. AB, Boston U., 1951, MD, 1955; MA (hon.), U. Pa., 1967. Intern Gorgas Hosp., Panama, 1955-56; resident in psychiatry Inst. of Living, Hartford, 1956-59; rsch. psychiatrist Ind. U. Med. Sch., Indpls., 1959-63; faculty U. Pa. Med. Sch., Phila., from 1963, prof. psychiatry, from 1968, Kenneth Appel prof., from 1974, chmn. dept., 1974-82. Co-founder, asso. editor Behavior Therapy, 1970— Author: An Introduction to the Science of Human Behavior, 1963, Classics of American Psychiatry, 1975, Psychiatry: Areas of Promise and Achievement, 1977, Voyage to Inishneefa, 1987; co-editor: Controversy in Psychiatry, 1978, Behavioral Medicine; Theory and Practice, 1979, Psychiatry at the Crossroads, 1980, also articles. Recipient Research Scientist award NIMH, 1963-74; Strecker award Inst. of Pa. Hosp., 1972 Fellow Am. Psychiat. Assn., Indian Psychiat. Soc.; mem. Assn. Advancement Behavior Therapy (past pres.), Soc. Biol. Psychiatry (pres. 1979-80), Psychiat. Research Soc. (program chmn. 1973), Soc. Behavioral Medicine (dir. 1980-81), Soc. Interam. de Psicologia, Am. Psychosomatic Soc. Home: Haverford, Pa. Died June 21, 2006.

BRAGG, CLARENCE CORDER, manufacturing executive, electrical engineer; b. Duffy, W.Va., Apr. 13, 1915; s. George William and Arcelia Mitilda (Pickens) Bragg; m. Mary Barbara McLain, July 1, 1938; children: Douglas M., Michael J., Steven M. BSEE, W.Va. U., 1947. Registered profl. engr., W.Va., Oreg. With Westinghouse Electric Corp., 1936—39, 1942—46, gen. foreman Emeryville, Calif., 1945—46; gen. mgr. Indsl. Electric Co., Clarksburg, W.Va., 1947—51; prodn. supt. Lear, Inc., Grand Rapids, Mich., 1951—52; dept. supt. top secret security clearance Dow Chem. Co., Denver, 1952—53; mgr. mfg. Schwager-Wood Corp., Portland, Oreg., 1953—60; founder, dir. and v.p. mfg. Powerdyne, Inc., Lake Oswego, 1960—65; exec. v.p. and gen. mgr. Portland Chain Co., Portland, 1965—67; gen. mgr. and dir. Williams Air Control, Portland, 1967—68; pres., CEO and chmn. bd. Eltec, Inc., 1968—76; regional mgr. elec. sales Willamina Lumber Co., 1974—81; owner and pres. Gus Gragg & Assoc., 1981. Dist. advancement chmn. Pioneer Dist. Portland Area coun. Boy Scouts Am.; mem. citizens budget com. Lake Oswego Pub. Schs. Recipient Golden Hammer award, Mechanix Illus. Mem.: IEEE (life), Shiners, Masons, Kappa Mu Alpha, Eta Kappa Nu, Phi Sigma Kappa. Meth. Achievements include patents for garage door opener. Home: Portland, Oreg. Died Feb. 16, 2006.

BRAIBANTI, RALPH JOHN, political scientist, educator; b. Danbury, Conn., June 29, 1920; s. Daniel Vincent and Jane Helena B.; m. Lucy Kauffman, Feb. 19, 1943; children: Claire, Ralph Lynn. BS, Western Conn. State U., 1941, LHD (hon.), 1995; A.M., Syracuse U., 1947, PhD, 1949. Asst. prof. polit. sci. Kenyon Coll., 1949-52, assoc. prof., 1952-53; adv., civil adminstr. Ryukyu Islands, 1950; adj. lectr. George Washington U., 1951; asst. dir. Am. Polit. Sci. Assn., Washington, 1950-51; cons. Govtl. Affairs Inst., 1950-51; assoc. prof. polit. sci. Duke U., Durham, NC, 1953-58, prof., 1958-68, James B. Duke prof. polit. sci., 1968-90, James B. Duke prof. emeritus, from 1990, founding dir., program on so. Asia, 1962—82; vis. asst. prof. Trinity Coll., 1952; adj. lectr. Am. U., 1956; vis. asst. prof. Utica Coll., 1949; founding dir. Islamic and Arabian devel. studies, 1977-89. Scholar-in-residence Rockefeller Found., Bellagio Ctr., Italy, 1967; cons. AID, 1958-59, Ford Found., 1972, UN, 1974, Govt. Saudi Arabia, 1974—, UNESCO, 1977, Islamic Secretariat, 1980, World Bank, 1987; vis. prof. U. Kuwait, 1984; advisor on adminstrv. reform Pakistan, Malaysia, South Africa, Lebanon, Morocco, Saudi Arabia, Bangladesh; cons.; bd. advisors Nat. Coun. U.S.-Arab Rels., Moroccan-Am. Found., Mid East Policy Coun.; founding pres. Am. Inst. Pakistan Studies, 1973-78, 86, 88, Am. Inst. Yemeni Studies; bd. dirs. U.S. Mid-East Performing Arts Coun., 1995—; chmn. nat. selection com. Joseph J. Malone Postdoctoral Fellowships in Arabian Affairs; King Faisal Disting. Internat. lectr. Am.-Arab Affairs Coun., 1989-91; mem. internat. adv. com. Global Forum of Spiritual and Parliamentary Leaders on Human Survival, 1996—. Author: Research on the Bureaucracy of Pakistan, 1966, The Nature and Structure of the Islamic World, 1995, revised edit., 2000, Chief Justice Cornelius of Pakistan: Analysis, Letters, Speeches, 1999; co-author, editor: Political and Administrative Development, 1969, Pakistan: The Long View, 1976, Asian Bureaucratic Systems Emergent from the British Imperial Tradition, 1966, Tradition, Values and Socio-Economic Development, 1961, Administration and Economic Development in India, 1963, Evolution of Pakistan's Administrative System: The Collected Papers of Ralph Braibanti, 1987; co-compiler, co-editor: (with Lucy Kauffman Braibanti) The Collected Poems of Charles Henry Kauffman, 2001; gen. editor 7 vol. series on comparative adminstrn., 1968-73; bd. editors Middle East Policy, Studies in Contemporary Islam, Jour. South Asian and Mid. Ea. Studies, Comparative Politics, Politikon, Asian Forum, Jour. Pakistan Studies, Internat. Jour. Islamic and Arabic Studies. Served to capt. U.S. Army, 1942-47. Recipient citation outstanding prof. Duke Student Assn., 1972, alumni award disting. undergrad. teaching, 1979; Maxwell fellow Syracuse U., 1949, Ford Found. fellow, 1955-56, Social Sci. Rsch. Coun. fellow, 1955-56; decorated commendation medal U.S. Army, 1947. Fellow Internat. Assn. Mid. Ea. Studies (mem. exec. com. 1991—); mem. Internat. Studies Assn.-South (pres.), Am. Inst. Pakistan Studies (founding pres. 1975-77, pres. 1986-90), Internat. Cultural Soc. Korea (hon.), Am. Council for Study Islamic Socs. (bd. dirs.) Died Nov. 24, 2005.

BRAKKE, MYRON KENDALL, retired research chemist, educator; b. Fillmore County, Minn., Oct. 23, 1921; s. John T. and Hulda Christina (Marburger) B.; m. Betty-Jean Einbecker, Aug. 16, 1947; children: Kenneth Allen, Thomas Warren, Joan Patricia, Karen Elizabeth. BS, U. Minn., 1943, PhD, 1947; DSc (hon.), U. Nebr., 1996. Rsch. assoc. Bklyn. Bot. Garden, 1947-52; rsch assoc. U. Ill., 1952-55; rsch. chemist U.S. Dept. Agr., Lincoln, Nebr., 1955-86. Prof. plant pathology U. Nebr., Lincoln, 1955-86. Editor: Virology, 1960-66; contbr. articles to profl. jours. Fellow AAAS, Am. Phytopath. Soc. (Award of Distinction 1988); mem. Am. Chem. Soc., Nat. Acad. Scis., Sigma Xi, Phi Lambda Upsilon, Gamma Sigma Delta, Alpha Zeta. Home: Bellingham, Wash. Died June 15, 2007.

BRANAN, JOHN MAURY, psychology educator, counselor; b. Tallahassee, Fla., Oct. 25, 1933; s. Roger Leo and Lala Marian (Crapps) B.; m. Mar. 23, 1957; children: John Maury Jr., Penny Michelle. BA, U. Fla., 1955, M in Rehab. Counseling, 1957, EdD, 1965. Lic. counselor, Ga. Rehab. counselor State of Fla., Gainesville, 1956-61; asst. prof. psychology Berry Coll., Mt. Berry, Ga., 1962-66; dir. counseling, asst. prof. psychology Valdosta (Ga.) State Coll., 1966-67, prof. psychology, dept. head, 1967-72, prof. psychology, counseling and guidance, from 1972. Author: The Future Makers, 1971; contbr. articles to profl. jours. Mem. Am. Psychol. Assn., Southeastern Psychol. Assn., Am. Assn. Marriage and Family Therapy (clin.), Am. Assn. for Counseling and Devel., Am. Assn. Clin. Hypnosis (clin.), Internat. Club (pres. Valdosta chpt. 1973-74), Kiwanis, Phi Kappa Phi. Home: Valdosta, Ga. Died Apr. 18, 2007.

BRANDEMUEHL, DAVID A., state legislator; b. Dec. 7, 1931; Student, U. Wis. State assemblyman dist. 49 State of Wis., from 1986. Mem. transp. project com. and legis. coun. farm safety com.; farmer. Former mem. local sch. bd.; pres. Regional CESA. Died Sept. 26, 2006.

BRANDIMORE, STANLEY ALBERT, lawyer, holding company executive; b. Highland Park, Mich., Aug. 20, 1927; s. Albert James B. and Genevieve (McCormick) Weideman; m. E. Kennedy Greene, Dec. 27, 1952; children: Vanessa Brandimore Lund, Darrell Stanley. BBA in Acctg., U. Miami, Fla., 1954; JD, U. Miami, 1957. Bar: Fla. 1957, U.S. Supreme Ct. 1968. Instr., lectr. acctg. U. Miami, 1954-57; atty. Fla. Pub. Service Com., Tallahassee, 1957-59, Fla. Power Corp., St. Petersburg, 1959-63, asst. gen. counsel, 1963-68, v.p., gen. counsel, 1968-75, sr. v.p., gen. counsel, 1975-83; exec. v.p., gen. counsel Fla. Progress Corp., St. Petersburg, from 1983. Trustee St. Petersburg Jr. Coll. With USN, 1945-48, 50-52. Mem. St. Petersburg Bar Assn. (treas. 1964-65), Fla. Bar Assn., ABA, St. Petersburg C. of C. (bd. govs.), St. Petersburg Jr. Coll. Alumni Assn. (bd. dirs.). Clubs: Suncoasters, Tiger Bay, Presidents; Treasure Island Tennis and Yacht (Fla.) (bd. govs., rear commodore). Republican. Home: Saint Petersburg, Fla. Died Nov. 29, 2005.

BRANDON, CLEMENT EDWIN, paper science and engineering educator; b. Oct. 3, 1915; s. David Clement and Mary (Van Tilburgh) B.; m. Marian Steingass, June 25, 1939; children: Ralph Edwin, William Lee. AB, Defiance Coll., 1936; MS, SUNY, 1942. Chemist Aetna Paper Co., Dayton, Ohio, 1937-40; chief chemist Howard Paper Mills, Dayton, from 1941, tech. dir., until 1958; prof. dept. paper sci. and engring. Miami U., Oxford, Ohio, from 1958, now prof. emeritus, exec. dir. Pulp and Paper Found., 1960-88, chmn. dept., 1961-81. Contbg. author: Pulp and Paper, Vol. III. Recipient alumni achievement award Defiance Coll and 1986 Alumni Citation for acad. excellence. Fellow Am. Inst. Chemists, TAPPI (chmn. testing div. 1958-61, mem. testing adv. bd. 1961—, past chmn. microscopy, precision and acad. adv. coms., Silver medal testing div.); mem. ASTM (chmn. com. D-6 on paper 1970-72, chmn. precision and sampling com. 1975—), Internat. Standards Orgn. (mem., past chmn. U.S. adv. com. tech. com. 6 on paper, U.S. rep. to meetings 1965—), Am. Nat. Standards Inst. (mem. com. P-3 on paper), Paper Industry Mgmt. Assn. Home: Lebanon, Ohio. Died Jan. 31, 2007.

BRANDT, EDWARD NEWMAN, JR., physician, educator; b. Oklahoma City, July 3, 1933; s. Edward Newman and Myrtle (Brazil) Brandt; m. Patricia Ann Lawson, Aug. 29, 1953; children: Patrick James, Edward Newman III, Rex Carlin. BS, U. Okla., Norman, 1954, MD, 1960, PhD, 1963; MS, Okla. State U., Stillwater, 1955; LHD (hon.), Med. U. S.C., Rush U., Chgo.; DSc (hon.), NY Inst. Tech., Old Westbury. Intern Oklahoma City VA Hosp., 1960—61; resident U. Okla. Hosps., 1961; from instr. to prof. preventive medicine and pub. health U. Okla. Med. Ctr., Oklahoma City, 1961—70, prof., chmn. dept. biostatistics Sch. Health, 1967—68, assoc. dean Sch. Medicine, assoc. dir., 1968—70; dean Grad. Sch., prof. preventive medicine and cmty. health U. Tex. Med. Br., Galveston, 1970—72, prof., 1970—84, prof. family medicine, 1973—84, acting dean, 1972—74, assoc. dean clin. affairs, 1972—73, acting dean medicine, 1973—74, dean medicine, 1974—76, exec. dean, 1976—77; vice chancellor health affairs U. Tex. Sys., Austin, 1977—81; asst. sec. health US Dept. Health & Human Services, Washington, 1981—84; pres., prof. epidemiology and preventive medicine U. Md., Balt., 1985—89; prof. internal medicine, exec. dean Coll. Medicine U. Okla., Oklahoma City, 1989—92, prof. health adminstrn. Coll. Pub. Health, 1989—96, Regents prof., 1996—2004, Regents prof. emeritus, 2004—07, dir. Ctr. Health Policy, 1992—2004, chair dept. health adminstrn. and policy Coll. Pub. Health, 2000—02. Mem. primate ctr. rev. com. NIH, 1975—79, chmn., 1978—79, mem. rsch. career devel. award com., 1968—72, mem. adv. com. on rsch. in women's health, 1995—99; bd. regents Nat. Libr. Medicine, 1985—89, chmn., 1987—89; mem. exec. bd. WHO, 1982—84; chmn. adv. com. on injury control CDC, 1988—93; chmn. adv. coun. on food FDA, 1992—2000. Editor, contbr. Proc. of Conf. at U. Okla. Med. Ctr., 1968, editor Continuing Education for the Family Physician, 1974—77, AIDS and Pub. Polic Jour., 1988—91. Recipient Superior Performance award, VA Hosp., Oklahoma City, 1961, Lloyd M. Southwick Meml. award for med. writing, 1974, 1975, Spl. Appreciation award, Tex. Acad. Family Physicians, 1974, Leone award for adminstrv. excellence, 1976, Outstanding Alumni Svc. award, U. Okla. Coll. Medicine, 1977, Disting. Svc. award, U. Tex. Med. Br., 1977, 19th Ann. Stoneburner lectr., Med. Coll. Va., 1966, Disting. Leadership award, HHS, 1984, Disting. Pub. Svc. award, Dept. Def., 1986, Pub. Health award, Am. Acad. Family Physicians; scholar Triennial, Phi Kappa Phi, 1998—2001. Fellow: AAAS (chair med. scis. sect. 1992—93), Am. Coll. Cardiology (hon.); mem.: AMA (chmn. sect. on med. schs. 1979—81, chmn. com. accreditation continuing med. edn. 1979—81), Inst. Medicine NAS (governing coun. 1986—92), Philos. Soc. Tex., Okla. Acad. Family Physicians, Am. Acad. Family Physicians, Okla. Med. Assn. (chmn. com. on family violence 1993—98, chmn. coun. on state legis. 1994—2007), Assn. Am. Med. Colls. (exec. coun. 1986—89, Spl. Recognition award 1985), Alpha Omega Alpha, Sigma Xi, Mu Epsilon, Phi Sigma Pi, Phi Kappa Phi (nat. scholar), Alpha Epsilon Delta, Phi Eta Sigma. Home: Oklahoma City, Okla. Died Aug. 25, 2007.

BRANNON, TERENCE C., bank executive; b. Mobile, Ala., Jan. 1, 1938; m. Sybil Jean Brown, June 7, 1958; 1 child, J. Michael Brannon. AB in Econs. and Bus. Adminstrn., Birmingham So. Coll., 1960. V.p. Cen. Bank of South, Birmingham, Ala., 1970-74, sr. v.p., 1974-75, pres., 1977-88, also bd. dirs., vice chmn., from 1989; exec. v.p. Cen. Bancshares of South, Inc., Birmingham, 1975-77, pres., 1977-88. Bd. dirs. Salvation Army, Birmingham, 1984—; former dir. Birmingham Assn. of Home Builders; former dir. ARC. Republican. Methodist. Avocations: travel, fishing, reading. Home: Birmingham, Ala. Died Sept. 16, 2006.

BRANSCOMB, LEWIS CAPERS, JR., retired librarian, educator; b. Birmingham, Ala., Aug. 5, 1911; s. Lewis Capers and Minnie Vaughn (McGehee) Branscomb; m. Marjorie Berry Stafford, Jan. 15, 1938 (dec. 1999); children: Lewis Capers III(dec.), Ralph Stafford(dec.), Carol Jean, Lawrence McGehee. Student, Birmingham-So. Coll., 1929-30; AB, Duke U., 1933; AB in Libr. Sci., U. Mich., 1939, AM in Libr. Sci., 1941; postgrad., U. Ga., 1940; PhD, U. Chgo., 1954. Clk. Young & Vann Supply Co., Birmingham, 1933-38; order libr. U. Ga., 1939-41; libr. Mercer U., 1941-42; libr., prof. libr. sci. U. S.C., 1942-44; asst. dir. pub. svc. depts., assoc. prof. libr. sci. U. Ill., 1944-48; assoc. dir. librs., prof., 1948-52; dir. librs., prof. Ohio State U., Columbus, 1952-71, prof. Thurber studies, 1971-81, prof. emeritus, from 1981. Mem. faculty compensation and benefits com. Ohio State U., 1981-90; chmn. Adv. Coun. on Libr. Svcs. and Constrn. Act, Ohio, 1967-70; cons. Punjab Agrl. U., India, 1967, Mansfield (Ohio) Pub. Libr., 1977; mem. adv. coun. Hitachi Found., 1985-88. Author: Ernest Cushing Richardson Research Librarian, Scholar, Theologian, 1993; editor: The Case for Faculty Status for Academic Librarians, 1970; contbr. articles to profl. jours. Mem. Ohio Commn. to Abolish Capital Punishment, 1960-69; bd. dirs. Ctr. for Rsch. Librs., 1953-64, mem. exec. com., 1954-56, chmn. bd. dirs., 1961-62, mem. coun., 1965-71; chmn. bd. trustees Ohio Coll. Libr. Ctr., 1968-70, vice chmn., 1970-72. Mem. AAUP (sec.-treas. U. Ill. chpt. 1947-48; sec.-treas. Ohio State U. chpt. 1948-52, pres. 1953-54; nat. council 1952-55, co-author History of the Ohio Conf. 1949-74, chmn. com. E 1979-91, mem. exec. com. 1981-91), ALA (chmn. nominating com. 1954-55), Assn. Coll. and Research Libraries (dir. 1953-55, v.p. 1957-58, pres. 1958-59), Ohio Library Assn. (chmn. coll. and univ. sect. 1952-53, chmn. library adminstrn. sect. 1969-70, chmn. local conf. com. 1970, chmn. awards and honors com. 1974-75, chmn. notable Ohio librarians com. 1978-79, award of merit 1971, Hall of Fame 1982), Franklin County Library Assn., Acad. Library Assn. Ohio, ACLU (exec. com. Central Ohio chpt. 1958-60, 64-66), Common Cause, Thurber Circle, Thurber House (bd. trustees emeritus 1985—), Friends of Ohio State U. Libraries, Ohio State U. Retirees Assn. (exec. bd. 1983-92), Beta Phi Mu (exec. council 1955-58), Sigma Alpha Epsilon. Democrat. Home: Columbus, Ohio. Died 2006.

BRANSDORFER, STEPHEN CHRISTIE, retired lawyer; b. Lansing, Mich., Sept. 18, 1929; s. Henry and Sadie (Kohane) B.; m. Peggy Ruth Deisig, May 24, 1952; children: Mark, David, Amy, Jill. AB with honors, Mich. State U., East Lansing, 1951; JD with distinction, U. Mich., 1956; LLM, Georgetown U., Washington, DC, 1958. Bar: Mich. 1956, US Supreme Ct. 1959, US Dist. Ct. (we. dist.) Mich. 1959; cwert. mediator US Dist. Ct. (we. dist.) Mich., 1995-2003. Trial atty. Dept. Justice, Washington, 1956—58; atty., editor Office of Public Info., Office of Atty. Gen., 1958—59; spl. asst. US Atty. for DC, Washington, 1958—59; assoc. Miller, Johnson, Snell & Cummiskey, Grand Rapids, Mich., 1959—63, ptnr., 1963—89; dep. asst. atty. gen. civil div. US Dept. Justice, Washington, 1989—92; pres. Bransdorfer & Bransdorfer, P.C., Grand Rapids, 1993—2000; ptnr. Bransdorfer & Russell, LLP, Grand Rapids, 2000—03; ret. Pres. State Bar of Mich., 1974-75, commr., 1968-75, chmn. sr. lawyers sect., 1994-95; pres. Grand Rapids chpt. Am. Inns of Ct., 1995-96; trustee Am. Inns of Ct. Found., 1997-2001; chmn. Mich. Civil Svc. Commn., 1977-78, mem., 1975-78; adv. com. 6th Cir. Jud. Conf., 1984-89; co-chair Mich. polit. leadership program Mich. State U., 1992-94; mem. comml. panel Am. Arbitration Assn., 1998-2001. Asst. editor: U. Mich. Law Rev, 1956. Pres. Grand Rapids Child Guidance Clinic, 1969-71; chmn. Kent County Coms., Griffin for Senator, 1972, Lenore Romney for Senator, 1966; mem. council legal advisers Rep. Nat. Com., 1981-89; Rep. candidate for atty. gen., Mich., 1978; trustee, v.p., Mich. State Bar Found., 1985-87, chmn., fellows, 1987-89; chmn. Mich. State Bd. Canvassers, 1985-87, Commn. on Future Directions in Health Care, West Mich., 1987-89; trustee Hist. Soc. for US Dist. Ct. (we. dist.) Mich., 2002—07. With US Army, 1951-53. Recipient Superior Performance Spl. award, Civil Divsn., U.S. Dept. Justice, 1990, Robert P. Hudson award, State Bar Mich., 2005. Fellow: Am. Bar Found.; mem.: FBA (pres. West Mich. chpt. 1984, Disting. Life. Svc. award 1989), ABA, Mich. Rep. Party (Svc. award 1989), Rep. Nat. Lawyers Assn. (bd. govs. 1985—89), 6th Cir. Jud. Conf. (life; mems. com., sr. counsel to 6th cir. ct. from 1999), Grand Rapids Bar Assn. (Donald R. Worsfold Disting. Svc. award 2005), Cascade Hills Country Club, Rotary, Phi Kappa Phi. Presbyterian. Home: Ada, Mich. Died Mar. 15, 2007.

BRASEL, JO ANNE, pediatrician, educator; b. Salem, Ill., Feb. 15, 1934; d. Gerald Nolan and Ruby Rachel (Rich) B. BA, U. Colo., 1956, MD, 1959. Diplomate in pediatrics and pediatric endocrinology Am. Bd. Pediatrics. Pediatric intern, resident Cornell U. Med. Coll.-NY Hosp., NYC, 1959-62; fellow in pediatric endocrine Johns Hopkins U. Sch. Medicine, Balt., 1962-65, asst. prof. pediats., 1965-68; asst. prof., then assoc. prof. pediatrics Cornell U. Med. Coll., NYC, 1969-72; assoc. prof., then prof. pediats. Columbia U. Phys. and Surg., NYC, 1972-79; prof. pediats. Harbor-UCLA Med. Ctr./UCLA Sch. Medicine, from 1979, program dir. Gen. Clin. Rsch. Ctr., 1979-93, prof. medicine, 1980—2005; Joseph W. St. Geme, Jr. prof. pediats. UCLA Sch. Medicine, 1999—2005, prof. emeritus pediatrics, from 2005. Mem. adv. com. FDA, Rockville, Md., 1971-75; mem. nutrition study sect. NIH, Bethesda, Md., 1974-78; mem. select panel for promotion of child health HEW, Washington, 1979-80; mem. life scis. adv. screening com. Fulbright-Hays program, Washington, 1981-84; mem. digestive disease and nutrition grant rev. group NIADDK, 1985-89; mem. US Govt. Task Force on Women, Minorities and the Handicapped in Sci. and Tech., 1987-89. Recipient Rsch. Career Devel. award NIH, 1973-77, Irma T. Hirschl Trust Career Sci. award, 1974-79, Sr. Fulbright Sabbatical Rsch. award, 1980. Mem. Soc. Pediatric Rsch. (sec.-treas. 1973-77, v.p. 1977-78, pres. 1978-79), Am. Fedn. Clin. Rsch., Endocrine Soc., Am. Soc. Clin. Nutrition, Am. Inst. Nutrition, Western Assn. Physicians, Lawson Wilkins Pediatric Endocrine Soc. (bd. dirs. 1972-74, v.p. 1991-92, pres. 1992-93), Western Soc. Pediatric Rsch., Phi Beta Kappa, Alpha Omega Alpha. Home: San Pedro, Calif. Died May 14, 2007.

BRATTEN, JOHN EDWARD, retail executive; b. Ft. Worth, Aug. 11, 1924; s. Philip Mace and Ruth Wilhelmina (POwell) Bratten; m. Meta Alice Keith, May 28, 1954; children: Keith Edward, Adelaide Elizabeth. Student, U. Dayton, 1941—42, Drexel Inst., 1943—44; BA, Cornell U., 1947. With Montgomery Ward, Danville, Ill., 1948—52; mdse. mgr. The Fair, Ft. Worth, 1952—55; acct. exec. O'Ryan Advt., Memphis, 1955—57; v.p. corp. ops. Cummins Lighting Co., Ft. Worth, 1957—84; ranching, oil and gas investments, from 1984. Mem. exec. bd. Boy Scouts Am., Ft. Worth, 1968—88; v.p. Camp Fire Girls, 1968—81; deacon Presbyn. Ch., Ft. Worth, 1968—74; bd. dirs. Tarrant County Cancer Soc., 1980, Tex. Boys Choir, 1982—88. With US Army, 1943—45. Decorated Bronze Star; recipient Luther Halsey Gulick award, Camp Fire Girls, 1979, Ernest Thompson Seton award, 1978, Sebago award, 1976, award of merit, Boy Scouts Am., 1974, Silver Beaver; Paul Harris fellow, Rotary, 1980—81. Mem.: Rotary, Phi Gamma Delta. Republican. Home: Fort Worth, Tex. Died June 14, 2007.

BRATTON, JOSEPH KEY, retired military officer; b. St. Paul, Apr. 4, 1926; s. John Smith and Maude Katherine (Keys) B.; m. Louise Skelly, Sept. 30, 1950 (dec. 2006); children: Joseph Key, John (dec. 1993), Mary, Anne, James. BA, U.S. Mil. Acad., 1948; MS in Nuclear Engring., MIT, 1959. Commd. 2d lt., C.E. US Army, 1948, advanced through grades to lt. gen., 1980, sec. to Joint Chiefs of Staff, 1970-72, dir. nuclear activities SHAPE Belgium, 1972-75; dir. Div. Mil. Application US Dept. Energy, Washington, 1975-79; chief US Army C.E., 1980—84; sr. v.p. Ralph M. Parsons Corp., Pasadena, Calif. Decorated Disting. Svc. medal, Legion of Merit with 2 oak leaf clusters, US Army Distng. Svc. medal, Bronze star (2) Mem. Soc. Am. Mil. Engrs. Clubs: Army Navy Country. Roman Catholic. Died June 2, 2007.

BRAUN, RICHARD LANE, lawyer, university administrator; b. Los Angeles, Oct. 18, 1917; s. Joseph George and Vera Louise (Lane) B.; m. Anne Clautice, Feb. 16, 1991; children from previous marriage: Susan, Richard L., Jeffrey. BA, Stanford U., 1941; JD, Georgetown U., 1951, LL.M., 1953. Bar: D.C. 1951, Calif. 1961, Va. 1963, Mich. 1969, Ohio 1974, N.C. 1982. Commd. 2d lt., pilot U.S. Marine Corps, 1942, advanced through grades to lt. col., ret., 1961; prof. Georgetown U. Law Sch., 1961-64; practice law Springfield, Va., 1963-65; dep. U.S. asst. atty. gen. Dept. Justice, 1965-68; dir. govt. relations and info. Automobile Mfrs. Assn., 1968-70; prof., dean U. Detroit Law Sch., 1970-74; dean U. Dayton Law Sch., 1974-80; prof. law sch. Campbell U., Buies Creek, N.C., 1980-93. Trustee Aviation Hall of Fame; mem. N.C. Commn. on Criminal Law, 1981; reporter N.C. Superior Ct. Judges Pattern Instrns. to Jury Com.; commr. Nat. Conf. Uniform State Laws, 1985-93. Contbr. articles to profl. jours. Decorated D.F.C. (6), Bronze Star, Air medals (22). Mem. ABA, Ohio Bar Assn. (chmn. spl. com. law related edn. 1976-80), Dayton Bar Assn., N.C. Bar Assn., Dayton Public Def. Assn. (vice chmn. 1974-77), Am. Law Inst. Methodist. Home: Scottsdale, Ariz. Died Aug. 13, 2006.

BRAUTIGAM, DANIEL CORY, foundry executive, writer, educator; b. Shelby County, Ohio, Feb. 10, 1918; s. Ervin D. and Mary (Cory) B.; m. Beulah Arlene Clay, Oct. 9, 1937; children— Marian Nelle Brautigam Desch, Albert Clay, John Philip. A.B., DePauw U., 1939; postgrad. U. Ill. M.Ed., Wittenberg U., 1965. Tchr. English, high sch., Catlin, Ill., 1939-42; foundryman Sidney Aluminum Products (Ohio), 1942-48, supt., 1948-67, personnel dir., 1967-69; instr. bus. mgmt. Wittenberg U., Springfield, Ohio, 1969-71; supt. Quincy Foundry div. Warren Tool, Quincy, Ohio, 1971-83; operator Tropics Aquarium, Pemberton, Ohio, 1968-80; free-lance newspaper columnist, humorist, Lavonia, Ga., 1983—. Rector scholar DePauw U., 1935-39. Republican. Author: Tropical Fish For Fun and Profit, 1982. Home: Lavonia, Ga. Died Feb. 23, 2007.

BRAVO, LEONORE MCCRYSTLE, biologist, psychologist, conservationist; b. Vallejo, Calif., July 14, 1914; d. Arthur Bernard and Geraldine Marie (Winslow) McCrystle; B.A., San Francisco State U., 1934; M.A., U. Calif., Berkeley, 1947; m. Ignacio Bravo-Caro, Aug. 2, 1939; children— Nacho E., Michael A. Tchr. Indian schs. in Nev. and Calif., 1937-40; tchr., adminstr. schs. in Calif., 1940-47; head psychologist Sacramento County schs., 1948-51; tchr. San Francisco secondary schs., 1953-62; asst. prin. Indio (Calif.) High Sch., 1962-63; psychologist Oakland (Calif.) pub. schs., 1963-72, cons., 1972—; lectr. San Francisco Community Coll. Dist., 1975-87; exec. sec. Tamalpais Conservation Club, 1974-77, bd. dirs., 1974-88; pub. mem. Calif. Cling Peach Processors Adv. Bd., 1975-79; mgr. honeybee exhibit San Francisco Flower Show, 1979—; participant Biennial Internat. Congresses of Apiculture, 1979—. NSF fellow, 1957, 59-62; scholar intergroup relations Stanford U. NCCJ, 1959; fellow OAS, 1970. Mem. Am., Interam., Calif. psychol. assns., Calif. Tchrs. Assn., Calif. Acad. Scis., Calif. Sch. Psychologists Assn., Western Apicultural Soc. (charter), People for Preservation of the Natural and Wild in Bay Area Open Space (founder, pres. 1977), San Francisco Beekeepers Assn. (founder 1976, pres. 1978, exec. sec. 1977-79), Women's Internat. League Peace and Freedom, Common Cause, Amnesty Internat., Calif. Wilderness Coalition, Am. Beekeeping Fedn., Calif. State Beekeepers Assn., San Francisco Democratic Women's Forum (dir. 1978-81, v.p. 1979), San Francisco Women for Peace, ACLU, Tamalpais Conservation Club (v.p. 1984, pres. 1986), Am. Friends Service Com., Friends of Earth, UN Assn., Wilderness Soc., Calif. Native Plant Soc., Save the Redwoods League (life), U. Calif. Alumni Assn. (life), San Francisco State U. Alumni Assn., Consumers Coop. Berkeley. Author articles. Home: Bayside, Calif. Died Feb. 4, 2006.

BRAWLEY, ROBERT JULIUS, artist, art educator; b. Brainerd, Minn., Apr. 24, 1937; s. Julius Augustus Brawley and Evanelle (Rogers) Johnson; m. Vivian Ruth Strom (dec. June 1968); children: Robert Eric, David James, Elisabeth Giuliana; m. Judith Carol Cramer, Aug. 15, 1969. Student, Cen. Wash. State U., 1955-56, U. Wash., 1957-59; BFA, San Francisco Art Inst., 1963, MFA, 1965; postgrad., Academia de Belli Arti, Florence, Italy, 1965-66. Asst. prof. Ferris Stâte Coll., Big Rapids, Mich., 1967-69; dir. Acad. Art Coll., San Francisco, 1969-71; chmn. art dept., grad. dir. Lone Mountain Coll., San Francisco, 1971-78; artist lectr. art dept. St. Mary's Coll., Moraga, Calif., 1981-88; prof., chmn. art dept. U. Kans. Sch. Fine Arts, Lawrence, from 1988; represented by Mongerson-Wunderlich Galleries, Chgo., from 1981, Capricorn Galleries, Bethesda, Md., from 1981. Represented in numerous exhbns. and collections, including AAAL, San Francisco Mus. Modern Art, Butler Inst. Am. Art, San Francisco Art Inst., Nat. Portrait Gallery, Washington, Los Angeles County Mus. Art, Nat. Mus. Am. Art, Washington, Art Inst. Chgo., Nelson-Atkins Mus., Kansas City, Mo., Mulvane Art Mus., Topeka. Recipient numerous awards for paintings; Fulbright fellow, Florence, Italy, 1965. Home: Lawrence, Kans. Died Apr. 12, 2006.

BRAY, CHARLES WILLIAM, III, former foundation administrator, former ambassador; b. NYC, Oct. 24, 1933; s. Charles William and Katherine (Owsley) B.; children: Charles W., David C., Katherine M. AB, Princeton U., 1955; postgrad., Univ. de Bordeaux, France, 1955-56, U. Md., 1966-67. With US Dept. State, 1958-77, 81-88, dep. asst. sec. for inter-Am. affairs, 1976-77, dir. Fgn. Svc. Inst., 1987-88; dep. dir. Internat. Communication Agy., Washington, 1977-81; US amb. to Senegal US Dept. State, 1981-85; pres. The Johnson Found., Racine, Wis., 1988—99. Adj. lectr. U. Georgetown. With U.S. Army, 1956-58. Recipient Disting. Svc. award Pres. of U.S., 1984; Fulbright fellow, 1955-56; Presdl. fellow, 1966-67. Home: Milwaukee, Wis. Died July 23, 2006.

BRAY, RALPH, physics educator; b. Moghilev, Bylorussia, U.S.S.R., Sept. 11, 1921; s. Harry and Pauline (Ginzberg) B.; m. Felice Sandra Tannenbaum, Feb. 1, 1948; children: Stephen, Peter, Sharon. BA, Bklyn. Coll., 1942; MS, Purdue U., W. Lafayette, Ind., 1945, PhD, 1949. Instr. Purdue U., W. Lafayette, 1945-50, asst. prof. physics, 1950-57, assoc. prof., 1957-65, prof., 1965-88, prof. emeritus, from 1989. Vis. prof. Becton Ctr., Yale U., New Haven, 1970, Christ Ch./Oxford U., Eng., 1969-70, Hebrew U., Jerusalem, 1978; NRC fellow Tech. U. Delft, Holland, 1951-52; vis. scientist Gen. Atomics Rsch. Lab., LaJolla, Calif., 1960-61; cons. in field. Contbr. numerous articles to profl. jours.; editorial bd. Jour. Applied Physics, 1967-69. Recipient Vis. Scientist award Japan Soc. for Promotion of Sci., 1977, von Humboldt Sr. Scientist award Max Planck Inst., Stuttgart, 1985-86; Guggenheim fellow, 1969-70. Fellow Am. Phys. Soc.; mem. Sigma Xi, Sigma Pi Sigma. Home: West Lafayette, Ind. Died Sept. 28, 2006.

BRAZIER, DON ROLAND, retired railroad executive; b. Pittsburg, Kans., Mar. 30, 1921; s. Hosie O. and Lola Frances (Tow) B.; m. June Darla Harr, Nov. 8, 1941. B.C.S., Benjamin Franklin U., Washington, 1950, M.C.S., 1951. Civilian budget officer Ordnance Corps, Dept. Army, 1940-43, 46-53; OFC asst sec. def., 1953-67; comptroller Def. Supply Agt., 1967; dep asst. sec. Army, 1967-68; prin. dep. asst. sec. def.-comptroller 1968-74; treas. AMTRAK, 1974-75, v.p. fin., treas., 1975-82 exec. v.p. fin. and adminstrn., 1982-86. Dir. Washington Union Terminal; pres., dir. Chgo. Union Sta. With USAAF, 1943-46 maj. AUS ret. Decorated Meritorious Service medal; recipient Def. Disting. Civilian Service award, 1971, 73, 74 Died Aug. 23 2006.

BRECKER, MICHAEL, saxophonist; b. 1949; m. Susan Brecker; children: Jessica, Sam. Student, U. Ind. Founder jazz-rock group Dreams, 1970; saxophonist Horace Silver Quintet, 1973; co-founder (with brother, Randy) The Brecker Brothers, 1974; co-mgr. (with brother) Seventh Avenue South jazz club, NYC; co-founder (with Mike Maineiri, Eddie Gomez, Steve Gadd, & later Peter Erskine) Steps Ahead band, 1979 Musician: (albums) Michael Brecker, 1987 (Jazz Album of Yr. Downbeat mag., Jazz Album of Yr., Jazziz mag.), Don't Try This At Home (Grammy award), Now You See It (Now You Don't), 1990, Return of the Brecker Brothers, 1992, Out of the Loop, 1994 (Grammy award), Tales From the Hudson, 1997 (Grammy award), Two Blocks From the Edge, 1998, Time Is Of The Essence, 1999, Nearness of You: The Ballad Book (Record of Yr., Swing Jour. (Japan), 2 Grammy awards), Directions in Music-Hancock...Brecker...Hargrove..., 2002 (Grammy award best jazz instumental album), Wide Angles, 2003 (2 Grammy awards, 2004, Best Jazz Record of Yr.), (album appearances Herbie Hancock's The New Standard, McCoy Tyner's Infinity Named Arts of Yr., Swing Jour., Best Soloist of Yr., JazzLife mag., Jazz Man of Yr., Swing Jour.; recipient Grammy award Best Jazz Instrumental Performance, 1996, 1997, Grammy award Best Jazz Instrumental Solo, 1996—97, 2002. Died Jan 13, 2007.

BREDESEN, DOROTHY LOUISE ANTIL, rehabilitation counselor, community activist; b. N.Y.C., July 20, 1929; d. Michael Charles and Mary (Holman) Antil; BA, Syracuse U. 1951, MA (scholar), 1956; postgrad. (scholar) U. Chgo., 1962 64; cert. advanced study, 1964; m. Nov. 1952 (div. Dec. 1972) children: Karen Louise, Mark Jon, Eric Tod. Social worker Maricopa County Welfare Dept., Phoenix, 1957; lectr. speech Ariz. State U., Tempe, 1957-59; instr. speech Memphis State U. 1960-62; vol. worker Christ Child Settlement House, 1964-65 rehab. counselor D.C. Rehab. Services Adminstrn., Washington 1965-86. Chmn. working adv. com. New Brent Sch., 1967-68 mem. exec. com. Brent Elem. Sch., 1965-68. Panel chmn. Dist Tng. Sch.'s 9th ann. conf. Mental Retardation, 1968; mem internat. study tour profl. seminar, U.S.S.R., 1986. mem. coun selor advisory com. Occupational and Tng. Center, 1971-75 mem. counselor adv. com. D.C. Evaluation Unit, 1972-73 Pres.'s com. on Employment of Handicapped, Washington 1988; bd. dirs. Friends of Reston Community Center, 1981— treas., 1982, 87, 88, 89, 90, Liaison to RCC bd. gov. 1997, asst treas., 1983, pres., 1989-94, 96—; Recipient cert. of apprecia tion Help for Retarded Children, Inc., 1967, D.C. Dept. Vocat Rehab., 1968, D.C. Rehab. Counseling Assn., 1977, 79, D.C Assn. for Retarded Citizens, 1983, Very Spl. Arts, Reston, 1989 Betty L. Hardy Haney Meml. award, 1982; cert. of recognition D.C. Dept. Human Services, 1983, Cert. of award, 1984; United Black Fund Community Service award, 1986; cert. rehab counselor, Recognition and Appreciation Plaque County o Fairfax, 1989. Mem. Adult Edn. Assn. Greater Washington (dir 1967-68, rec. sec. 1968-69, 2d v.p. 1970-71, chmn. long-range planning 1974-75), Am. Sociol. Assn., Nat. Rehab. Assn. (pro gram com. 1975, co-editor D.C. chpt. Newsletter 1976, bd mem. nat. congress on rehab. of homeward bound and institu tionalized persons 1977-78), Nat. Rehab. Counseling Assn. (dir D.C. chpt. 1971-72, sec. 1978-80, Cert. of Award 1979), Am Assn. Counseling and Devel., Capitol Hill Community Counci (pres. 1968-69), AFSCME-AFL-CIO (treas. local affiliate D.C Commn. Social Service Employees 1977-80, v.p., chief stewar local affiliate 1980-81, steward local affiliate 1981-86, del. 26th internat. conv. San Francisco 1984), Delta Sigma Rho, Alph Omicron Pi. Democrat. Roman Catholic. Home: Reston, Va Died Jan. 3, 2007.

BREGMAN, PAULA JEAN, publishing company executive; b Chgo., Feb. 1, 1947; d. Fredrick and Florence (Silavin) B.; m Alfred Donald Morris, May 16, 1981. BA, U. Wis., 1969; MA U. Chgo., 1977; MBA, DePaul U., 1987. Researcher, Menaker Dangerfield & Wright, Chgo., 1974-78; research supr. Harshe Rotman & Druck, Chgo., 1978-80; research analyst G. D. Searl & Co., Skokie, Ill., 1980-81, asst. product mgr., 1981-83, assoc product mgr., 1983-85, product mgr., 1985-86; dir. mktg. Ran McNally Map Services Co., 1986-91; v.p., gen. mgr. Creativ Sales/Am. Map, Chgo., 1991—. Mem. Friends VOA Assn Chgo., 1992—. Home: Bayside, NY. Died Oct. 21, 2006.

BREMNER, JOHN MCCOLL, agronomy and biochemistry educator; b. Dumbarton, Scotland, Jan. 18, 1922; came to U.S., 1959; s. Archibald Donaldson and Sarah Kennedy (McColl) B.; m. Eleanor Mary Williams, Sept. 30, 1950; children: Stuart, Carol. BS, Glasgow U., 1944, DSc, 1987; PhD, U. London, 1948, DSc, 1959. With chemistry dept. Rothamsted Exptl. Sta., Harpenden, Eng., 1945-59; assoc. prof. Iowa State U., Ames, 1959-61, prof. agronomy and biochemistry, 1961-75, C.F. Curtiss disting. prof. agriculture, prof. agronomy, biochemistry, 1975-93, disting. prof. emeritus, 1993—2007; ret., 1986. Tech. expert IAEA, Austria, 1964-65, Yugoslavia, 1964-65. Author or co-author over 300 publs. including 30 chpts in sci. monographs. Recipient Outstanding Research award First Miss. Corp., 1979, Alexander Von Humboldt medal Alexander Von Humboldt Found., Fed. Republic of Germany, 1982, Gov.'s Sci. medal State of Iowa, 1983, Harvey Wiley award U.S. Assn. Ofcl. Analytical Chemists, 1984, Spencer medal Am. Chem. Soc., 1987, Burlington No. Found. Faculty Achievement award for Research, Gamma Sigma Delta award of merit for disting. service to agriculture, Regents award for faculty excellence, 1992, Award for Advancement of Agrl. & Food Chemistry, Am. Chem. Soc.; fellow Rockefeller Found., 1957, Guggenheim Found., 1968. Fellow AAAS, Am. Acad. Microbiology, Am. Soc. Agronomy (Agronomic Rsch. award 1985, Environ. Quality Rsch. award 1990), Soil Sci. Soc. Am. (Achievement award 1967, Bouyoucos Disting. Career award 1982, Disting. Svc. award 1993), Iowa Acad. Sci. (disting.); mem. NAS, Am. Soc. Microbiology, Brit. Soc. Soil Sci., Internat. Soil Sci. Soc., Phi Kappa Phi (centennial medalist 1997), Sigma Xi, Gamma Sigma Delta. Achievements include patent for nitrification inhibitor; development and evaluation of nitrification and urease inhibitors for control of adverse transformations of fertilizer nitrogen in soils; development of methodology for research on the nitrogen cycle and environmental problems related to agriculture; research on microbial, enzymatic, and chemical processes responsible for nitrogen transformations in soils, such as nitrification, denitrification, chemodenitrification, and urease activity. Home: Palm Desert, Calif. Died July 25, 2007.

BRENDLE, DOUGLAS DAVID, retail executive; b. Elkin, NC, July 4, 1928; s. James David and Edna (Arnold) B.; m. Lydia Jane Underwood, Aug. 21, 1954; 1 child, Adelia Jane. Student, Wake Forest U., 1947; BS in Acctg., Bowling Green U., 1950. Buyer/salesman Brendle's Cash Wholesale, Inc., Elkin, N.C., 1952-55, buyer/salesman, sec.-treas., 1956-66, sec., treas., 1956-84, pres., chief exec. officer, 1984-89, chief exec. officer, chmn. bd. dirs., from 1989. Trustee Bapt. Childrens' Homes, Thomasville, N.C., Wake Forest U., advisor bus. sch.; advisor Campbell U., Appalachian State U., Boone, N.C. Sgt. U.S. Army, 1950-52. Democrat. Baptist. Home: Winston Salem, NC. Died Feb. 11, 2006.

BRENNAN, JOHN EDWARD, manufacturing executive; b. NYC, July 12, 1928; s. Michael J. and Catherine T. (Mallon) B.; m. Carol Claire Kissell, Oct. 27, 1956; children: Susan Lynn, Nancy Carol, Pamela Ann, Karen Claire. B in Elec. Engring., Manhattan Coll., 1952; MBA, NYU, 1955. Registered prof. engr., N.Y. Application engr. Westinghouse Electric, NYC, 1952-55; asst. v.p. atomic power Babcock & Wilcox, NYC, 1955-60; asst. to pres. Garlock Inc., Palmyra, N.Y., 1960-64, mgr., 1964-66, v.p. mech. power Rochester, N.Y., 1966-76, sr. v.p., 1976-90; pres. Garlock Spl. Products, Rochester, 1976-90; group pres. Coltec Industries, Inc., Rochester, from 1990; dir. Garlock GmbH, Garlock Overseas Corp. Served with U.S. Army, 1946-48. Mem. Soc. Plastics Industries, Nat. Fluid Power Assn., IEEE, Am. Nuclear Soc. (N.Y. sec. chmn. 1959-60) Roman Catholic. Died Apr. 5, 2006.

BRENT, WALTER RUDOLF, retired non-ferrous metals company executive; b. NYC, Aug. 2, 1919; s. Rudolf Emil and Katherine (Mossbacher) B.; m. Dolores M. Germaine, Feb. 15, 1953; children— Alison, Wayne, Andrew. BBA, CCNY, 1942. C.P.A., N.J. Sr. accountant Scovell Wellington & Co., NYC, 1946-49; asst. treas. Bacardi Imports, NYC, 1950-51; controller Standard Electronics Corp., Newark, 1952-57; sec., asst. treas. Revere Copper and Brass Inc., NYC, 1958-85. Served with U.S. Army, 1942-46. Mem. AICPA, Inst. Mgmt. Accts. Republican. Presbyterian. Home: Pittsboro, NC. Died June 3, 2006.

BRESKY, H. HARRY, agricultural products executive; b. 1925; Pres. Seaboard Corp., 1967—2001; treas. Seaboard Fluor Corp., 1973—2002, pres., 1987—2002; chmn., pres., CEO Seaboard Corp., 2001—06, chmn., from 2006. Died Mar. 11, 2007.

BRESNAHAN, WILLIAM JOSEPH, SR., insurance company executive; b. Phila., Apr. 12, 1928; s. William Joseph and Agnes (Baker) B.; m. Sophie Bernadette Hermanowicz, Dec. 29, 1945 (dec. 1978); children— Bernadette Dianne, William, Jr., Thomas, Mary; m. Helen Marie McCann, Jan. 19, 1980; stepchildren— Robert, Daniel, Susan. Student Temple U. Dairyman first class Supplee Milk Co., Phila., 1949-52; police insp. Phila. Police Dept., 1953-80; bldg. services mgr. Provident Mut. Life Ins. Co., Phila., 1981—. Served with USAAF, 1946-47. Mem. Internat. Assn. Police Chiefs, Southeastern Assn. Pa. Police Chiefs, Delaware Valley Police Chiefs Assn., Internat. Police Officers Assn., Bldg. Owners and Mgrs. Assn., Irish Soc. Republican. Roman Catholic. Lodges: Lions, K.C. (4th degree). Avocations: traveling; fishing. Home: Warminster, Pa. Died Mar. 1, 2007.

BREWER, JAMES WILLIAM, mathematics educator; b. West Palm Beach, Fla., May 29, 1942; s. William Ferrell and Martha Elizabeth (Grimes) B.; m. Deborah Ann Phelps, Dec. 27, 1973 (div. Mar. 1987); m. Virginia Gayle Ganther, Aug. 5, 1989; children: Deborah Lynn, Jill Diane, Amy Webb, James C.B., David R., Thomas. AB, Fla. State U., 1964, MS, 1966, PhD, 1968. Asst. prof. math. Va. Polytech. Inst., Blacksburg, 1968-70; prof. math. U. Kans., Lawrence, 1970-85, Fla. Atlantic U., Boca Raton, from 1985. Author: Power Series Over Commutative Rings, 1981; co-author: Linear Systems over Commutative Rings, 1986; co-editor: Proceedings of the Kansas Commutative Algebra Conference, 1973, Emmy Noether: A Tribute to Her Life and Work, 1981; contbr. articles to profl. jours. Mem. Am. Math. Soc. Avocations: golf, running. Home: Boynton Beach, Fla. Died Sept. 23, 2006.

BRIARE, BILL (WILLIAM H. BRIARE), former mayor; b. Long Beach, Calif., July 13, 1930; m. Jo Briare (dec. 1988); children: Linda, Bill, Don, Bob, Tim, Jim; m. Susan R. Briare; 1 stepchild, Lori. Mem. Nev. State Legis., 1960—62, Clark County Commn., 1962—68; mayor City of Las Vegas, 1975—87. Died Dec. 8, 2006.

BRICKER, WILLIAM HAROLD, oil and gas producing and refining company executive, private investor; b. Detroit, Jan. 29, 1932; B.S. in Agr., Mich. State U., 1953, M. Hort., 1954; m. Doris Arlene Bricker, Apr. 30, 1955. With Diamond Shamrock Chem. Co., Dallas, 1969—, v.p. biochems., 1969-72, pres., 1973-74; v.p. Diamond Shamrock Corp. (name changed to Maxus Energy Corp., 1987), Dallas, 1973-74, chief operating officer, 1974-75, pres., 1975-76, 86—, chief exec. officer, 1976-79, 86-87, chmn. bd., 1979-87; chmn., chief exec. officer Skyline Investments, Inc., 1987—, D.S. Energy Svcs.; bd. dirs. Lloyd West Corp., Am. Ball Mfg. Corp., LTV Corp., Blue Coral, Inc., Trammell Crow Real Estate Investors. Bd. govs.; bd. dirs. Kent Waldrep Nat. Paralysis Found.; past mem. communications com. Dallas Citizens Coun., Dallas Mus. Fine Arts, Dallas Symphony Mus.; mem. ARC, bus. adminstrn. and devel. coun. Tex. A&M U. Mem. Dallas Petroleum Club. Clubs: Preston Trail Golf, Brook Hollow, Tower (bd. govs.). Died Mar. 7, 2006.

BRIDGES, ROBERT LYSLE, retired lawyer; b. Altus, Ark., May 12, 1909; s. Joseph Manning and Jeffa Alice (Morrison) B.; m. Alice Marian Rodenberger, June 10, 1930; children: David Manning, James Robert, Linda Lee. AB, U. Calif., 1930, JD, 1933. Bar: Calif. 1933, U.S. Supreme Ct 1938. Pvt. practice, San Francisco, 1933-92; assoc. firm Thelen Marrin Johnson & Bridges, 1933-39, ptnr., 1938-92. Trustee, former chmn. U. Calif. Berkeley Found.; trustee, hon. dir. John Muir Found., from 1992. Mem. ABA, Calif. Bar Assn., San Francisco Bar Assn., Commonwealth Club of Calif., Pacific Union Club, Claremont Country Club (Oakland). Republican. Home: Lafayette, Calif. Died July 18, 2006.

BRIEFF, FRANK, conductor; b. New Haven, Apr. 19, 1912; m. Anabel Hulme, Oct., 1939; children: JoAnne, Geraldine, Madeleine. BS, N.Y. U., 1933; postgrad., Juilliard Sch., 1934-38. Conductor, violist Columbia Broadcasting, NYC, 1945-47, NBC Symphony, NYC, 1948-52, New Haven Symphony, 1952-74, Waterbury (Conn.) Symphony, 1974-94. Conductor Manhattan Sch. Music, N.Y.C., 1951-53; judge Mitropolous for Conductors, N.Y., 1945-48, Naumbert, N.Y., Chopin, Miami, Pianists, Montreal. Violist with Guilet String Quartet, 1942-48, recordings, 1962-68; conductor Mahler First Symphony, 5 Movements, 1968 (Mahler-Bruckner Soc. award 1968, Toscanina award 1987). Fellow Yale. Avocations: painting, tennis. Home: Wallingford, Conn. Died Nov. 22, 2005.

BRIERLEY, GERALD P., chemistry professor; b. Ogallala, Nebr., Aug. 14, 1931; s. Phillip and Myrtle (Shireman) B.; m. Miriam Grove, Apr. 17, 1971; children: David, Steven, Glenn, Lynn. BS, U. Med.-Coll. Park, 1953, PhD, 1961. Asst. prof. U. Wis., Madison, 1962-64; faculty mem. Ohio State U., Columbus, from 1964, prof. physiol. chemistry, from 1969, chmn. dept., 1981-95, prof. emeritus, chmn. emeritus of dept. med. biochemistry, from 1996. Capt. USAF, 1953-56. USPHS grantee to study ion transport by heart mitochondra, 1965—; USPHS grantee to study pathology mitchondria in ischemia, 1977— Mem. Am. Soc. Biol. Chemistry, Biophys. Soc., Am. Heart Assn. Home: Dublin, Ohio. Died Oct. 22, 2006.

BRILL, KENNETH GRAY, JR., geology educator, researcher; b. St. Paul, Nov. 16, 1910; s. Kenneth Gray and Laura (Cooke) B.; m. Priscilla Ritchie, July 28, 1939; children— David, Thomas. B.A., U. Minn., 1935; postgrad. Yale U., 1935-37; M.S., U. Mich., 1938, Ph.D., 1939. Inst., asst. prof. U. Chattanooga, 1939-45; geologist U.S. Geol. Survey, Washington, 1942-44; from asst. prof. to prof. St. Louis U., 1946-79, prof. emeritus, 1979—; contract geologist Gulf Oil Corp., Tulsa, summer 1952, 54, 55, 56, Pan Am. Petroleum Corp., Tulsa, summer 1961, 62, 63, 65; spl. coal cons. Econ. Cooperation Adminstrn., Republic of Korea, 1949; Fulbright lectr. U. Tasmania, Hobart, 1952, hon. research assoc., 1978. Contbr. articles to profl. jours. James Dwight Dana Fellow Yale U., 1935-36. Fellow Geol. Soc. Am. (emeritus; sec., treas. North Central sect. 1980—), AAAS (council mem. 1952-53); mem. Paleontol. Soc. (emeritus), Am. Assn. Petroleum Geologists, Mo. Acad. Sci. (pres. 1968), Sci. Tchrs. Mo. (Sci. Educator award 1974-75), Explorers Club. Episcopalian. Home: Newark, Del. Died Aug. 12, 2007.

BRINE, JOHN JOSEPH, bank executive; b. Boston, July 15, 1931; s. Clarence M. Brine and Margaret L. (Flanagan) Niles; m. Elizabeth Anne Willey, Apr. 24, 1934; children: Denise K., Eveline L., John S. AB, Harvard U., 1953, MBA, 1958. Asst. controller Chem. Bank, NYC, 1958-63; v.p. Keefe, Bruyette & Woods, NYC, 1963-67; sr. v.p., chief fin. officer, pres. of subs. First Bank System, Mpls., 1967-74; exec. v.p., chief fin. officer First Interstate Bancorp., Los Angeles, 1974-79, First Pa. Corp./First Pa. Bank N.A., Phila., 1979-81, sr. exec. v.p., chief fin. officer, 1981-88, vice-chmn., dir., 1988-90. Bd. dirs. service subs. of Phila. Stock Exchange. Bd. dirs. Episc. Community Svcs. Mem. Fin. Exec. Inst. (Phila. chpt. bd. dirs.), Harvard Club of Phila., Harvard Bus. Sch. of Phila (bd. dirs.), Union League, Merion Cricket Club (Pa.), Harvard Club (Boston). Home: Pocasset, Mass. Died June 30, 2007.

BRINK, FRANK, JR., biophysicist, former educator; b. Easton, Pa., Nov. 4, 1910; s. Frank and Lydia (Wilhelm) B.; m. Marjory Gaylord, May 1, 1939; children— Patricia Brink Mayer, David Warner BS, Pa. State Coll., 1934; MS, Calif. Inst. Tech., 1935; PhD, U. Pa., 1939; D.Sc. (hon.), Rockefeller U., 1983. Instr. physiology Cornell U. Med. Coll., NYC, 1940-41; instr. biophysics Johnson Research Found., U. Pa., Phila., 1941-49; assoc. prof. biophysics Johns Hopkins U., Balt., 1949-53; prof. biophysics Rockefeller U., NYC, 1953-81, dean grad. studies, 1958-72, Detlev W. Bronk prof., 1974-81, prof. emeritus, from 1981. Cons. to sec. of war Dept. Army, Washington, 1941-44; mem. com. for biology and medicine NSF, Washington, 1953-59; chmn. Pres.'s Com. for Nat. Med. Sci., Washington, 1963-64 Editor Biophysics Jour., 1960-64; mem. editorial bd. various jours., 1955-71; contbr. articles on phys. chemistry of nerve cells to profl. jours. Johnson scholar U. Pa., 1935-38; Lalor Found. fellow U. Pa., 1939-40 Fellow AAAS (life); mem. AAAS, NAS, Biophys. Soc. (charter), Soc. Gen. Physiologists, Am. Acad. Arts and Scis. Avocations: reading, cycling, travel. Home: Doylestown, Pa. Died June 6, 2007.

BRINKMEYER, LOREN JAY, data processor, college administrator; b. Udall, Kans., Apr. 21, 1925; s. William Frederick and Verna Christina (Mead) B.; student U. Kans., 1943, 50-51, U. Wis., 1943-44; D. Mus. Dramatics, U. Heidelberg (Germany), 1954; D. Internat. Comml. Law, U. Poitiers (France), 1964; B.S.B. with honors, Emporia State U., 1972, M.S.B. with honors, 1978; Ph.D. in Computer Info. Systems, Loyola U., Paris, 1983; also student numerous data processing and computer sci. courses; m. Helen Josephine Walkemeyer, Mar. 10, 1946; 1 son, Karl Phillip. Served as enlisted man U.S. Army, 1943-45, commd. 2d lt., 1945, advanced through grades to lt. col., 1962; data processing supr., Hawaii, 1945-51, W. Ger., 1951-54, U.S., 1955, 60-61, Alaska, 1956-59, France, 1962-64, ret., 1964; dir. data processing Butler County Community Coll., El Dorado, Kans., 1964—; cons. data processing. Pres. El Dorado Mcpl. Bd., 1971-83; mem. choir United Methodist Ch., El Dorado, 1964—; mem. Kans. U. Alumni Band, 1972—. Decorated Army Commendation medal, Bronze Star with two oak leaf clusters, Purple Heart. Mem. NEA, Kans. Higher Edn. Assn., Am. Vocat. Assn., Kans. Vocat. Assn., Kans. Bus. Occupations Assn., Kans. Bus. Edn. Assn., Kans. Bus. Computerized Student Follow-up (adv. bd.), Data Processing Edn. Kans., Assn. Ednl. Data Systems, Data Processing Mgmt. Assn. (cert.), Assn. Computing Machinery, Soc. Data Educators, Internat. Assn. Computer Programmers, Ret. Enlisted Assn., Ret. Officers Assn., 96th Inf. Div. Assn., Nat. Assn. Uniformed Services, Am. Legion, VFW. Independent Republican. Author: Electrical Accounting Machines, 2d edit., 1964; Automated Inventory and Financial Systems, edit., 1976; Punched Card Business Data Processing, 3d edit., 1974. Home: El Dorado, Kans. Died Jan. 8, 2006.

BRITT, JOHN ROY, banker; b. LA, Oct. 9, 1937; s. Roy Arthur and Virginia Alice (Vaughn) B.; children: Jeffrey John, Belinda Lynn, Gregory Scott. BA, Claremont McKenna Coll., 1959; grad., Pacific Coast Banking Sch., U. Wash., 1973, Managerial Policy Inst., U. So. Calif., 1978. Diplomate Am. Bd. Forensic Examiners. With Security Pacific Nat. Bank, 1959-83, regional v.p. Los Angeles, 1972-74, sr. v.p., 1974-83, adminstr. Mid City-Eastern div., 1978-83; instr. Essentials of Banking Sch., U. Notre Dame, 1979; sr. v.p. Coast Savs. and Loan, Los Angeles, 1983-85; exec. v.p., chief operating officer Pacific Inland Bank, Anaheim, Calif., 1985-86, pres., chief exec. officer, 1986-89; pres. JRB Assocs., from 1990; pres., chief exec. officer United Citizens Nat. Bank, LA, 1992. Mem. pres.'s adv. coun. Claremont McKenna Coll., 1993; past chmn. bd. dirs., mem. exec. com. Commuter Transp. Svcs., Inc., L.A. Capt. USAR, 1959-67. Mem.: Risk Mgmt. Assn., Am. Coll. Forensic Examiners (bd. cert.). Republican. Methodist. Died Aug. 27, 2007.

BRITTAIN, PERRY GEORGE, electric utility company executive; b. Center, Tex., Mar. 10, 1925; s. Zack B. and Donnie (Matthews) B.; m. Martha Nelle Black, Dec. 30, 1945; children: Jennifer Margaret, Martha Katharine. BS, U. Tex., 1949. Registered profl. engr., Tex. With Dallas Power & Light Co., 1949-72, v.p. engring., purchasing, 1968-72; exec. v.p. Tex. Utilities Services, Inc., 1972-73, pres., 1973-81, chmn. bd., chief exec., 1981-83; exec. v.p. Tex. Utilities Co., Dallas, 1974-81, pres., 1981-83, chmn. bd., chief exec. officer, 1983-87, ret., 1987, also dir.; pres. Tex. Utilities Generating Co., Dallas, 1974-81, chmn. bd., chief exec. officer, 1981-83; pres. Tex. Utilities Fuel Co., 1974-81, chmn. bd., chief exec. officer, 1981-86, Tex. Utilities Mining Co., 1984-86; chmn. bd. Basic Resources Inc., 1983-86, Chaco Energy Co., 1983-86; dir. Edison Electric Inst., 1984-87, Atomic Indsl. Forum, 1984-87, Am. Nuclear Energy Council, 1984-87. Trustee Tech. Edn. Research Ctr., 1978-84; bd. dirs. Ctr. for Occupational Research and Devel., 1980-86, Southwestern Med. Found., Met. Dallas YMCA; mem. Dallas Citizens Council. Served with USAAF, 1943-46. Recipient Disting. Grad. award U. Tex. Coll. Engring., 1976 Mem. IEEE, Tex. Soc. Profl. Engrs. (Engr. of Year award 1977) Home: Dallas, Tex. Died Feb. 7, 2007.

BRITTON, ROBERT BYRON, gas industry executive; b. Olney, Ill., Dec. 3, 1937; s. Byron C. and Margaret L. (Lewis) Britton; m. Carol Ann Bartruff, Dec. 7, 1962; children: Lisa Ann Britton Stoltz, David E. Mem. material control dept. Pure Oil Co., Olney, 1955—58; owner, operator R. B. Britton Oil Properties, Olney, from 1958, A. V. Well Svc. 1st lt. USAR, 1960—70. Mem.: Am. Legion. Republican. Methodist. Home: Olney, Ill. Died Apr. 16, 2007.

BROADBENT, ROBERT KENNETH, JR., sales executive; b. Middleboro, Mass., Nov. 21, 1926; s. Robert and Alice (Laflamme) B.; student pub. schs.; m. Emily Pratt, Oct. 12, 1947; children— Linda, Joan, Karen, Cindy, Douglas, Kenny, Hazel. Salesman, Ralston Purina Co., St. Louis, 1965-70; sales mgr. Agway Inc., Syracuse, N.Y., 1971—, dist. mgr., 1971—. Mem. Cape Cod Mgrs. Assn. Republican. Baptist. Clubs: Mitchel Meml. (Middleboro, Mass.); P.G.A. Golf (Palm Beach, Fla.). Home: Lakeville, Mass. Died Aug. 22, 2006.

BROADBENT, THOMAS RAY, surgeon; b. Heber, Utah, Aug. 4, 1921; s. Charles N. and Sarah Jane (Wood) B.; m. Edith Stovall, June 3, 1950; children— Kenneth Ray, Stephanie, Catherine, Lisa Anne. BA, Brigham Young U., 1943; MD, Duke, 1946. Diplomate: Am. Bd. Surgery, Am. Bd. Plastic Surgery (examiner, vice chmn. 1972-73). Intern Duke U. Hosp., 1947, gen. surgery residency, 1948-50, plastic surgery residency, 1950-52; instr. surgery Duke, 1951-52; asso. clin. prof. U. Utah Sch. Medicine, 1955; active staff Primary Children's Hosp., Salt

Lake City, W.H. Groves Latter-Day Saints Hosp., Salt Lake City, also dir. residency program, dept. plastic surgery, from 1957, pres., 1974-75. Trainee Nat. Cancer Inst., 1950-52; B. K. Rank traveling prof. Royal Australasian Coll. Surgeons, 1982; sec. gen. 3d Internat. Congress Plastic Surgery, 1963 Served to 1st lt. AUS, World War II. Recipient prize on original research Found. Am. Soc. Plastic and Reconstructive Surgery, 1958; Distinguished Service award Brigham Young U., 1969 Fellow ACS, Internat. Coll. Surgeons (vice regent 1959-60); mem. AMA, Utah Med. Assn., Calif. Soc. Plastic Surgery, Am. Soc. Plastic and Reconstructive Surgery (gen. sec. 1958-63, pres. 1968-69, asso. editor jour. 1964-70, travelling prof. Ednl. Found. 1979-80), Internat. Confedn. Plastic Surgeons (exec. com. 1964-75), Am. Assn. Plastic Surgery, Plastic Surgery Research Council (chmn. 1957), Am. Soc. Aesthetic Plastic Surgery, Salt Lake Surg. Soc. (pres. 1968-69), Alpha Omega Alpha. Mem. Lds Ch. Home: Salt Lake City, Utah. Died Aug. 12, 2007.

BROCKWAY, DUNCAN, librarian, clergyman; b. Manchester, NH, July 23, 1932; s. Walter Priest and Eleanor (Duncan) B.; m. Lois Simpson, Jan. 19, 1957 (div. 1974); children: Peter, Andrew, Ellen, Catherine; m. Ruth Pensiero, Sept. 6, 1975 (dec. Sept. 1981). BA, St. John's Coll., Annapolis, Md., 1953; student, Harvard Div. Sch., 1953-55; B.D., Princeton Theol. Sch., 1956; MA in L.S, Rutgers U., 1960. Ordained to ministry Presbyn. Ch., 1956; pastor in Windham, N.H., 1956-58; order librarian Speer Library, Princeton Theol. Sem., 1958-62; pastor in Frenchtown, N.J., 1962-65; with Case Meml. Library, Hartford Sem. Found., 1965-76, librarian, 1967-76; pastor Colebrook (Conn.) Congregational Ch., 1971-77; dir. library services Sch. Theology, Dubuque, Iowa, 1977-88, U. Dubuque, 1981-88; pastor Centralia (Iowa) Presby. Ch., from 1982. Stated clk. Presbytery Conn. Valley, 1973-77, John Knox Presbytery, 1986—; sec. W. Hartland Fire Dept., 1966-72; mem. Hartland Bd. Edn., 1970-71. Democrat. Died Jan. 22, 2007.

BRODERICK, EDWIN B., bishop emeritus; b. Bronx, NYC, Jan. 16, 1917; s. Patrick J. and Margaret M. (O'Donnell) B. AB, St. Joseph's Coll., Yonkers, NY, 1938; PhD in English, Fordham U., 1951; L.H.D., L.I.U., 1968, Cath. U. Am., 1982; LL.D., Siena Coll., 1969. Ordained priest Roman Catholic Ch., 1942; tchr. Cardinal Hayes High Sch., 1943-47; asst. pastor St. Patrick's Cathedral, NYC, 1947; dir. radio-TV Archdiocese, N.Y., 1951-54; sec. to Cardinal Spellman, 1954-64; pres. St. Joseph's Sem. and Coll., Yonkers, 1964-68; consecrated bishop, 1967; bishop of Albany, N.Y., 1969-76; exec. dir. Cath. Relief Services, NYC, 1976-84. Conclavist Papal election, 1958; trustee Key Trust Co., Albany. Theol.; cons. to Danforth Found.; Chmn. N.Y. State Cath. Bishops' Liaison with N.Y. State Cath. Colls.; chmn. N.Y. State Cath. Conf., 1968-76; mem. U.S. Bishops' Com. on Edn.; mem. adminstrv. bd. U.S. Cath. Conf., 1972-75; U.S. rep. Cor Unum. Author: Your Child and Television, 1954, Your Place in Television, 1953. Mem. McKay Commn. to investigate Attica Riot, 1971; mem. adv. com. Yale Div. Sch., 1978-83, Hoffstra U. Sch. Law, 1983; pres. Interfaith Hunger Appeal, 1978-80; chmn. Horn of Africa Ecumenical Coalition, 1980-82; trustee Coll. Mt. St. Vincent, Riverdale, N.Y., 1985—. Recipient LaSalle medal Manhattan Coll., 1971; decorated grand knight Grand Cross Holy Sepulchre. Mem. MLA, Met. Opera Club, Equestrian Order Knights Malta. Clubs: Friars. Home: New York, NY. Died July 2, 2006.

BRODERICK, JOHN DOUGLAS, bank executive; b. NYC, Feb. 26, 1942; s. John Patrick and Mary Ellen (McElroy) Broderick; m. Mary A. Savage, Jan. 20, 1962 (div. 1977); children: Mary Alice, Kristin Ann. BBA, Pace Coll., 1966; MBA, U. Chgo., 1974. Asst. v.p. Chase Manhattan Bank, NYC, 1959—65; v.p. Citicorp, NYC, 1965—77; exec. v.p. Crocker Nat. Bank, San Francisco, 1977—83; dir. Interlink Network Inc., San Francisco, 1983. Dir., CEO CNC Ins. Co., San Francisco, 1982. Home: Tiburon, Calif. Died June 26, 2006.

BRODMAN, ESTELLE, librarian, retired educator; b. NYC, June 1, 1914; d. Henry and Nettie (Sameth) B. AB, Cornell U., 1935; BS, Columbia U., 1936, MS, 1943, PhD, 1954; postdoctoral study, UCLA, 1959, U. N.Mex., 1960; D.Sc. (hon.), U. Ill., 1975. Asst. librarian Cornell U. Sch. Nursing Library, NYC, 1936-37; asst. med. librarian Columbia Libraries, NYC, 1937-49; asst. librarian for reference services Nat. Library Medicine, Washington, 1949-61; librarian, assoc. prof. med. history Washington U. Sch. Medicine, St. Louis, 1961-64, librarian, prof. med. history, 1964-81, librarian, prof. med history emerita, from 1981; documentation expert UN Tech. Assistance program UN, Central Family Planning Inst., New Delhi, 1967-68, WHO, New Delhi, 1970, Manila, 1983, ECAFE, Bangkok, 1973, AID, 1975, UNFPA, 1976. Mem. Pres.'s Commn. Libraries, 1968-70, Mo. Gov.'s Adv. Commn. Libraries, 1977-78; study sect. NIH, 1971-75, chmn., 1973-75; instr. Columbia U., 1946-52, 84, Cath. U. Am., 1957; vis. prof. Keio U., Tokyo, 1962, U. Mo., 1971, 73, Washington U. Med. Sch., 1964-81 Author: Development of Medical Bibliography, 1954, Japanese translation, 1994; author: Bibliographical Lists for Medical Libraries, 1950; editor: Bull. Med. Libr. Assn., 1947-57; guest editor N.J. Medicine, 1988. Recipient Holloway award Archivists and Librs. in History of Health Sci., 1993. Mem. Med. Libr. Assn. (pres. 1964-65, spl. award 1957, Noyes award 1971, Gottlieb award 1977, Frank B. Rogers info. advancement award 1985, centennial award 1998), Spl. Librs. Assn. (bd. dirs. 1949-52, John Cotton Dana award 1981), Am. Assn. History Medicine, N.J. Med. History Soc. (treas. 1985-88, v.p. 1988-92). Home: Hightstown, NJ. Died Mar. 1, 2007.

BRODSKY, ISADORE, oncologist, hematologist; b. Phila., Apr. 27, 1930; s. Max and Alice Brodsky; m. Estelle Lea Tobin, June 17, 1956; children: David, Jeffrey, Robert. BA, U. Pa., 1951, MD, 1955. Asst. instr. U. Pa., Phila., 1956-57; sr. asst. surgeon USPHS, NIH, Bethesda, Md., 1957-59; research collaborator Brookhaven Nat. Lab., 1959-61; assoc. in medicine U. Pa., Phila., 1961-62; asst. prof. medicine Hahnemann U., Phila., 1962-65, assoc. prof., 1965-69, prof., 1969—2007, dir. Cancer Inst., 1963-78, dir. Inst. for Cancer & Blood Diseases, 1978—2007, prof., chmn. dept. neoplastic diseases, 1986—2007, pres. med. staff, 1990-92; chief hematology & oncology dept. Drexel U. Coll. Med. Cons. USPharmocoeia Commn. on Revision; cons. mem. ad hoc rev. com. NIH, Bethesda, Md.; rep. AMA, Chgo. Co-author articles in med. jours. Mem. Dean's Cancer Coordinating Com. of Phila., Gov.'s Task Force on Cancer, Phila., 1974-77, N.J. Commn. on Cancer Rsch.; chmn. Phila. Coop. Cancer Group, Phila., 1974-76. Fellowship, Am. Cancer Inst.; recipient Torch of Learning award Am. Friends of Hebrew U., Phila., 1981. Fellow Coll. of Physicians; mem. Phila. County Med. Soc. (bd. dirs.-at-large), Am. Soc. Hematology. Jewish. Home: Narberth, Pa. Died Oct. 6, 2007.

BRODY, THEODORE MEYER, pharmacologist, educator; b. Newark, May 10, 1920; s. Samuel and Lena (Hammer) B.; m. Ethel Vivian Drelich, Sept. 7, 1947; children— Steven Lewis, Debra Jane, Laura Kate, Elizabeth. BS, Rutgers U., 1943; MS, U. Ill., 1949, PhD, 1952. Instr., prof. dept. pharm. U. Mich. Med. Sch., Ann Arbor, 1952-66; prof. pharmacology Coll. Medicine, Mich. State U., East Lansing, 1966-90, prof. emeritus, 1990—2007, founding chmn. dept., 1966-86. Cons. NIH, 1969-73, NIDA, 1975-79, Internat. Soc. Heart Rsch., 1973—2002; mem. sci. adv. com. Pharm. Mfrs. Assn. Found., 1973—2002; U.S. rep. Internat. Union Pharmacology, 1973-76; mem. bd. Fedn. Am. Socs. for Exptl. Biology, 1973-76; mem. Com. Sci. Soc. Presidents. Mem. editl. bd. Jour. Pharmacology and Exptl. Therapeutics, 1965-80, specific field editor, 1981-92; mem. editl. bd. Rsch. Comm. in Chem. Pathology and Pharmacology, Molecular Pharmacology, 1972-90; editor: Human Pharmacology Molecular to Clinical, 1991, 94, 97, Ed Brody's Human Pharmacology, 4th edit., 2005; cons. Random House Dictionary of English Lang., 1964-2007; contbr. 300 articles to profl. jours. Served with AUS, 1943-46. Recipient Disting. Faculty award, Mich. State U., 1984; Disting. scholar, NSF-U. Hawaii, 1974. Mem. Am. Soc. Pharmacology and Exptl. Therapeutics (John Jacob Abel award 1955, mem. council 1969-72, sec.-treas. 1970, pres. elect 1973, pres. 1974, past pres. 1975, Torald Sollmann award in pharmacology 1995), Internat. Soc. Biochem. Pharmacology, Am. Coll. Clin. Pharmacology, Assn. Med. Sch. Pharmacologists (sec. 1984-86), Soc. Toxicology, Soc. Neurosci., Japanese Pharmacology Soc., AAUP, Sigma Xi, Rho Chi, Phi Kappa Phi. Home: East Lansing, Mich. Died June 11, 2007.

BROEHL, WAYNE GOTTLIEB, JR., educator; b. Peoria, Ill., Aug. 11, 1922; s. Wayne G. and Dimple (Rush) B.; m. Jean Kirby, Aug. 4, 1944; children— David Robert, James Richard, Michael Kirby. BS, U. Ill., 1946; MBA, U. Chgo., 1950; D.Sc. in Bus. Adminstrn, Ind. U., 1954; MA (hon.), Dartmouth, 1958. Staff labor relations dept. Western Electric Co., 1946-48; asst. prof., asst. dean Coll. Commerce, Bradley U., 1948-51; faculty lectr. Sch. Bus., Ind. U., 1951-54; prof. bus. Amos Tuck Sch. Bus., Dartmouth, from 1954. Vis. prof. bus. history U. Coll., Dublin, Ireland, 1960-61; vis. prof. U. Buenos Aires, 1962, Internat. U. Japan, 1990. Author: Trucks, Trouble and Triumph, 1954, Precision Valley, 1959, The Molly Maguires, 1964, The International Basic Economy Corporation, 1968, The Village Entrepreneur, 1978, John Deere's Company: A History of Deere & Company and its Times, 1984, Crisis of the Raj: The Revolt of 1857 Through British Lieutenants' Eyes, 1986, Cargill: Trading the World's Grain, 1992, Cargill: Going Global, vol. 2, 1998; co-author: Administering the Going Concern, 1962, Business Research and Report Writing, 1965, Hospital Policy; Process and Action, 1966. Mem. Am. Econ. Assn., Am. Hist. Assn., Econ. History Assn., Acad. Mgmt., Beta Gamma Sigma, Beta Theta Pi. Home: Hanover, NH. Died June 28, 2006.

BROIDO, ARNOLD PEACE, music publishing company executive; b. NYC, Apr. 8, 1920; s. Samuel S. and Ruth (Lewis) B.; m. Lucille Janet Tarshes, Mar. 5, 1944; children: Jeffrey, Laurence, Thomas. BS magna cum laude, Ithaca Coll., 1941, DMus (hon.), 1990; MA, Columbia U., 1954. Tchr. instrumental music East Jr. H.S., Binghamton, NY, 1941—42; editor, prodn. mgr. Boosey & Hawkes Inc. (music pub.), 1945—55; v.p., gen. mgr. Century Music & Mercury Music Corp., 1955—57; edn. dir. Edward B. Marks Music Corp., 1957—62; dir. publs. and sales Frank Music Corp., 1962—69; v.p. Boston Music Co., 1968—69; pres. Theodore Presser Co., 1969—95, chmn., 1995—95, Elkan-Vogel Inc., 1970—2007. Pres. Music Industry Coun., 1966-68, v.p., 1969-70; dir., sec. Harry Fox Agy., 1989-2000, sec.-treas., 2000-07. Co-author: Music Dictionary, 1956, Invitation to the Piano, 1959; assoc. editor: Univ. Soc. Ency. of Piano Music; contbr. articles to profl. jours. Mem. Nassau County (NY) Dem. Com., 1952-63; bd. dirs. NY Citizens Com. for Pub. Schs., 1963-68, Am. Music Ctr., 1968-72, 78-83, 85-91, Am. Music Conf., 1979-80, Nat. Music Coun., 1979-85, 93-2007, Music Educators Nat. Conf., 1966-68; trustee ASCAP Found., 1976-2007, treas., 1990-2007; trustee Union Free Sch. Dist. 21 Bd. Edn., Rockville Centre, NY, 1963-69, sec., dist. clk., 1966-67, v.p., dist. clk., 1967-69. With USCGR, 1942-45. Recipient Disting. Alumnus award Ithaca Coll., 2001; Lowell Mason fellow MENC, 2003. Mem. ASCAP (bd. dirs. 1972-2007, bd. rev. 1980-82, asst. treas. 1989-90, treas. 1990-2007), Music Pubs. Assn. U.S. (pres. 1972-74, 80-82, bd. dirs. 1980-82, 83-92, 96-2005), Nat. Music Pubs. Assn. (bd. dirs. 1980-2007, sec. 1989-2007, treas. 2000-07), Internat. Pubs. Assn. (v.p. sect. music 1972-73), Internat. Confederation Music Pubs. (v.p. 1978-88, bd. dirs. 1992-07, pres. 1993-94, chmn. 1994-96, pres. 1996-98, chmn. 1998-2003, v.p. 2003-07), Internat. Fedn. Serious Music Pubs. (v.p. 1978-93, 2003-07, pres. 1993-2003), Music Industry Mfrs. Assn. (dir. 1980-82), Charles Ives Soc. (bd. dirs. 1985-2003), Phi Mu Alpha Sinfonia. Home: Haverford, Pa. Died Oct. 25, 2007.

BROMBERG, ROBERT SHELDON, lawyer; b. Bklyn., May 3, 1935; s. Jack and Bertha (Toskey) B.; m. Barbara W. Schwartz, Apr. 1, 1978; children: Jason, David. AB, Columbia U., 1956, LLB, 1959; LLM in Taxation, NYU, 1966. Bar: N.Y. 1960, D.C. 1972, Ohio 1972, U.S. Ct. Claims 1976, U.S. Supreme Ct 1975. Practiced law, NYC, 1960-66; atty. exempt orgns. br. IRS, Washington, 1966-70, Office Chief Counsel, 1970-72; partner firm Baker, Hostetler & Patterson, Cleve., 1972-79; prin. Robert S. Bromberg, L.P.A., Cleve., 1979-81, Paxton & Seasongood, Cin., 1981-85; sole practice Cin., from 1985. Lectr. tax and health law confs. Author: Tax Planning for Hospitals and Health Care Organizations, 2 vols., 1979; cons. editor: Prentice Hall Tax Exempt Organizations Service, 1973-84; nat. adv. bd. Integrated Healthcare Report; adv. bd. The Exempt Organization Tax Review; contbr. articles to profl. jours. Recipient award (5) Dept. Treasury, 1966-72, citation Am. Assn. Homes for Aged, 1973 Mem. Am. Health Lawyers Assn. (pres. 1986-87, program chmn. Ann. Tax Inst. 1975-95). Died Mar. 19, 2006.

BROMSEN, MAURY AUSTIN, historian, writer, rare book dealer; b. NYC, Apr. 25, 1919; s. Herman and Rose (Eisenberg) B. BSS cum laude with spl. honors, CCNY, 1939; MA, U. Calif., Berkeley, 1941, Harvard U., 1945, doctoral postgrad. in history, 1945-50; LHD (hon.), Northeastern U., 1987. Vis. lectr. Am. history Cath. U., Santiago, Chile, 1942; instr. history CCNY, 1943-44; founding editor Inter-Am. Rev. Bibliography, 1950-53; editor, sect. chief dept. cultural affairs Pan Am. Union, Washington, 1950-54; on leave, 1953-54; adv. editor, U.S. rep. Inter-Am. Rev. Bibliography; founder, dir. Maury A. Bromsen Assocs. (rare book, manuscript and fine art dealers), Boston, 1954—2005; pres., treas. Maury A. Bromsen Assocs., Inc. (rare book, manuscript and fine art dealers), 1963-89; proprietor, dir. Maury A. Bromsen Co., 1990—2005; hon. curator Latin Americana Collections Boston Pub. Libr., 1977—2005; hon. curator, bibliographer Latin Americana John Carter Brown Libr. Brown U., Providence, 1996—2005. Vis. prof. U. Chile, Santiago, 1947; exec. sec. Medina Centennial Celebration, Washington, 1952; adv. coun. univ. librs. U. Notre Dame, 1981-84, emeritus adviser, 1984-2005; bd. govs. Am. Jewish Hist. Soc., 1987-92; est. Maury A. Bromsen-Simon Bolivar Room John Carter Brown Libr., Providence, 1999. Author: Simón Bolívar: A Bicentennial Tribute, 1983; editor: José Toribio Medina, Humanist of the Americas: an Appraisal, 1960, Spanish transl., 1969; research and publs. in history and bibliography of Ams. Established Medina and Harrisse rare book collections, U. Fla. Library, 1958, 63. Endowed Archibald Bromsen Meml. scholarship, CCNY, 1964; endowed Bromsen lectureship in Humanistic Bibliography, Boston Pub. Library, 1970, Maury A. Bromsen Latin Am. Acquisitions Fund, 1976, Bromsen Fund, Mass. Gen. Hosp. (Health Scis. Lib.), 1983. Decorated Orden al Mérito Bernardo O'Higgins, Knight Comdr. (Chile), Orden de Francisco de Miranda, First Class (Venezuela); elected Colonial Soc. Mass., 1985; Carnegie Endowment for Internat. Peace and U.S. Govt. Exch. fellow U. Chile, 1942; Harvard Woodbury Lowery Travelling fellow, 1946-47, Social Sci. Rsch. Coun. fellow, 1946-48; recipient Brown U. President's Medal, 2003. Mem. Antiquarian Booksellers Assn. Am., Am. Hist. Assn., ALA, Bibliog. Soc. Am., Manuscript Soc. (charter), Conf. on Latin Am. History, Academia Nacional de la Historia, Buenos Aires (corr.), Latin Am. Studies Assn., Bibliog. Soc. (London), Bibliog. Soc. U. Va., Boston Athenaeum, Harvard Coll. Library Friends, Boston Pub. Library Assocs. (hon.), Boston U. Library Assocs. (life), Iowa Library Assocs. (patron), Bell (Minn.) Library Assocs., Clements (Mich.) Library Assocs., Yale Library Assocs., Am. Hist. Soc., Am. Jewish Hist. Soc., Va. Hist. Soc (life), N.Y. Hist. Soc., Sociedad Chilena de Historia y Geografía The Countway Libr. of Medicine (Harvard Med. Sch., Rare Books & Special Collections subcommitte, 2003-05) Filson Club (life), Phi Beta Kappa. Clubs: Harvard (Boston), Boston Athenaeum (Boston). Died Oct. 11, 2005.

BROOKS, HARRIETT BURCH (MRS. FRANCIS EARL BROOKS), nursing administrator; b. Deland, Fla., May 24 1924; d. William A. and Mary (Cadwallader) Burch; diploma Grady Meml. Hosp. Sch. Nursing, Atlanta, 1945; B.S. in Pub Health Nursing, U. N.C., 1962; m. Francis Earl Brooks, Mar. 6 1946; children— Mary Anne, Eleanor Susan. Inst. staff nurse Hernando County Hosp., Brooksville, Fla., 1945-47; staff pub health nurse Citrus County Health Dept., Inverness, Fla., 1951-60; field supr. pub. health nursing Palm Beach County Health Dept., West Palm Beach, Fla., 1962-64; dir. nursing service Leon County Health Dept., Tallahassee, 1964-77; family planning program mgr. Dist. II, Fla. Dept. Health and Rehab Services, Gainesville, 1977-80; dir. nurses Eastbrook Health Care Center, 1983—; asst. prof. Fla. State U., 1972-73. Sec continuing edn. com. Fla. Bd. Health, 1966-69, chmn. conf adminstrs., suprs. and educators, 1969—. Bd. dirs. Tallahassee Leon County Community Action Program, 1967-72. Mem. Fla Nursing Assn. (dist. 1st v.p. 1967-68), Fla. Pub. Health Assn (sec. 1969, 1st v.p. 1972, dir. 1973-74, pres.-elect 1975, pres 1976—), Leon County Assn. Community Services. Baptist Home: Floral City, Fla. Died Sept. 10, 2006.

BROOKS, JEROME BERNARD, English and Afro-America literature educator; b. Houston, Mar. 20, 1932; s. Osbur Bernard and Agnes (Harrison) B. BA, Holy Cross Sem., Chgo 1956, MA, 1960, Notre Dame U., 1962; PhD, U. Chgo., 197 Instr. English Holy Cross Sem., 1962-66; lectr. English CCNY 1968-72, asst. prof., 1972-75, assoc. prof., 1985-90, prof 1991-95, chmn. dept. English, 1985-88, acting dean U. Affairs 1988-89, dep. to the pres., 1991-95, prof. emeritus, from 199 Cons. NEH, Washington, 1985, U. Mo. Press, Columbia, 198 bd. dirs. N.Y. Alliance for Pub. Schs., Transp. Rsch. Consortium Rice H.S.; vis. prof. English, Bard. Coll., Annandale-on Hudson, N.Y. Author: Black Women Writers 1950-80, 198 contbr. World Authors Encyclopedia, 1986, The Paris Review 1994; co-editor Continuities mag., 1973-76. NEH grantee, 197 named Fulbright Sr. Lectr. at U. Madagascar, USIA, 1976-7 Mem.: Princeton Club, Univ. Club of Chgo. Democrat. Roma Catholic. Avocation: play classical piano. Home: New York, N Died Jan. 31, 2007.

BROOKS, KEITH, retired speech communication educator; Tigerton, Wis., May 14, 1923; s. Oscar Derby and Henriet (Mierswa) B.; m. Laquata Sue Walters, Dec. 29, 1951; childre Todd Randall, Craig William. BS, MS, U. Wis., 1949; Ph Ohio State U., 1955. Mem. faculty Eastern Ky. State U Richmond, 1949-53, Ohio State U., Columbus, 1953-87, pr communication, 1968-87, prof. emeritus, from 1987, chm dept., 1968-75. Comms. cons. Procter & Gamble, Ohio B Regents, Mead World Hdqs., U.S. Dept. Agr., Ohio Bell Tel phone, Ea. R.R. Assn., Shaw U., Raleigh, N.C. Author: (wi Bahn and Okey) Literature for Listening, 1968, The Commur cative Act of Oral Interpretation, 1967, 2d edit., 1975, Tl Communicative Arts and Sciences of Speech, 1967, (wi Dietrich) Practical Speaking, 1969. With USNR, 1945-46. Mer Speech Communication Assn. (chmn. interpretation div., vi chmn., sec.), Internat. Communication Assn. (co-editor Newsletter 1979-80), Cen. States Speech Assn. (editor Jour. 1958-61), Am. Ednl. Theatre Assn. (bd. dir. 1958-60) Home: Dublin, Ohio. Died Feb. 7, 2007.

BROTCHNER, RICHARD RAYMOND, industrial and mechanical engineer, consultant; b. Mpls., Feb. 25, 1944; s. Robert J. and Dorothy I. (Goldblum) B. B.S., Calif. State U.-Northridge, 1967; M.P.A., U. So. Calif., 1975. Ops./shift supr. The Flying Tiger Line, San Francisco, 1971-73; manpower controller Am. Airlines' Sky Chief Subs., 1973; dir. Manpower Devel. and Tng. Co., Merced, Calif., 1974; cons., group mgr. United Research Corp., Wofac, Inc., 1973-77; manpower cons. Orange County-Long Beach Health Consoritum, Calif., 1974-75; mgr. hub and ramp operating systems, mgr. plans and programs Fed. Express Corp., Memphis, 1977-79, mgr. advanced tech. and research, 1979—. Spl. and res. dep. Shelby County Sheriff's Dept., Shelby County, Tenn. NASA postgrad. fellow, 1968-75; grad. teaching asst. Calif. State U., Northridge, 1966-68. Mem. Soc. Automotive Engrs., Air Cargo Handling Com., Blue Key, Pi Sigma Alpha. Lodge: Grand Krewe of Osiris. Home: Memphis, Tenn. Died Jan. 12, 2007.

BROUILLETTE, DONALD G., grain company executive; b. Fowler, Ind., Nov. 7, 1930; s. Fred G. and Estella (Steinmetz) Brouillette; m. Marilyn Strasburger, Aug. 11, 1956; children: Michelle, JoAnn, Michael, Tim, Susan. Student, St. Joseph's Coll., 1949—50. Pres., CEO Demeter, Inc., Fowler, Ind., 1973. Bd. dirs. Bank One, Lafayette, Ind. Mem.: Nat. Grain and Feed Assn. (past pres.). Died Jan. 27, 2007.

BROUN, PAUL C., retired state legislator; b. Mar. 1, 1916; widowed; children: Paul, Jr., Conway, Michael. BS in Agrl. Engring., U. Ga. Pres. Athens Tire and Supply Co.; mem. Ga. State Senate, Atlanta, 1963—2001; chmn. econ. devel., tourism and cultural affairs com.; sec. higher edn. com.; mem. appropriations, banking and fin. instn. coms. Ga. rep. econ. and cultural devel. com. So. Legis. Conf.; mem. Regional Edn. Bd. Active Emanuel Episcopal Ch. Lt. col. U.S. Army. Recipient Abraham Baldwin award U. Ga., Alumni Merit award, 1994, Legis. Svc. award Ga. Mcpl. Assn., 1995. Mem. Athens C. of C. (past bd. dirs.), Exch. Club (past pres.), City Club (past pres.), Pres. Club, Gridiron Secret Soc. Died Feb. 14, 2005.

BROWN, ARTHUR WAYNE, former college dean, educator; b. Sheshequin, Pa., Apr. 20, 1917; s. Arthur L. and Helen E. (Laclair) B.; m. Dorothy C. Johnston, Sept. 17, 1938; children—Anne (Mrs. Allan Root), Margaret (Mrs. Frank O'Neill), Michael, Patricia (Mrs. Eugene Crabbe), Thomas, Arthur, Mary, Deborah. AB, U. Scranton, 1937; MA, Cornell U., 1938; PhD, Syracuse U., 1950. Prof. English Utica Coll. of Syracuse U., 1955-63; prof. English, chmn. dept., dir. Inst. Humanities, Adelphi U., 1963-65, pres., 1965-67; dean faculties, dean Grad. Sch., Fordham U., 1967-68, v.p. for acad. affairs, 1968-69; pres. Marygrove Coll., Detroit, 1969-72; dean Sch. Liberal Arts and Scis., Baruch Coll., CUNY, 1972-77; dean Coll. Arts and Scis., U. Miami, Coral Gables, Fla., 1977-85, prof. English, 1985-89, dir. collegiate studies, from 1989. Westchester dir. 1st Nat. City Bank. Author: Always Young for Liberty, 1956, William Ellery Channing, 1960, Margaret Fuller, 1964; Co-editor: series Great American Thinkers, 1964-73, World Leaders, 1973-83. Sec. Catholic Commn. on Intellectual and Cultural Affairs, 1970—; exec. com. Mich. Colls. Found.; bd. dirs. Catholic Charities, Utica, 1960-62, United Fund, L.I., Fla. Endowment for Humanities; chmn. bd. dirs. St. Elizabeth Sch. Nursing, Utica, 1961-62; trustee Molloy Coll., L.I., 1969-73; bd. govs. St. Paul's Sch., Garden City, 1968-69, 73-74; v.p. Council on Edn. for Public Health, 1979-85. Am. Council Learned Socs. grantee, 1961-62 Mem. AAUP, MLA, Phi Beta Kappa. Died Jan. 12, 2006.

BROWN, CHARLES WINSTON, army officer, cattle rancher; b. Rushville, Nebr., June 15, 1932; s. Charlie Wilson and Elenore (Winston) B.; m. Sherry Church; children— Stephan Charles, Christi Jeanne BS, N.Mex. Mil. Inst., 1953; M.P.A., Pa. State U., 1975. Commd. 2d lt. U.S. Army, 1953, advanced through grades to lt. gen., 1987, comdr. support command 2d armored div. Ft. Hood, Tex., 1976-78, dir. material mgmt. Communications-Electronics Command Ft. Monmouth, N.J., 1978-80, comdr. 200th Theater Army Materiel Mgmt. Command Federal Republic Germany, 1980-82, comdr. 2d support command, 1982-84, asst. dep. chief of staff, logistics Washington, 1984-87, dir. defense security assistance agy. Recipient mil. valor and merit awards Dept. Def., 1963-74; research grantee U.S. Army Research Inst., Washington, 1974-75 Fellow Armed Force and Soc. (Citation 1976); mem. Am. Def. Preparedness Assn., Assn. of U.S. Army. Avocations: fishing; hunting; golf; racquetball. Died Feb. 15, 2007.

BROWN, EPHRAIM TAYLOR, JR., lawyer; b. Birmingham, Ala., Aug. 31, 1920; s. Ephraim Taylor and Lida (Otts) B.; m. Clara DeBardeleben Ebaugh, Oct. 21, 1949; children: Ephraim Taylor III, Clara DeBardeleben, Lida Otts. AB, Princeton U., 1941; LLB, Cornell U., 1943. Bar: Ala. 1943. Pvt. practice, Birmingham; assoc. Cabaniss, Johnston, Gardner, Dumas & O'Neal, 1943-52, ptnr., 1952-91; of counsel, from 1992. Chmn. spl. com. Revision Probate Laws Ala., 1967; chmn. bd. bar examiners Ala. State Bar, 1967-79. Bd. dirs. Childrens Fresh Air Farm; trustee, elder, deacon local Presbyn. ch. Fellow Am. Coll. Trust and Estate Counsel; mem. ABA, Ala. Bar Assn. (pres.), Birmingham Bar Assn., Ala. Law Inst. (mem. counsel), Birmingham Country Club, Sigma Alpha Epsilon. Home: Birmingham, Ala. Died Oct. 10, 2006.

BROWN, GERALD CURTIS, retired military officer, engineering executive; b. Worcester, Mass., Aug. 10, 1942; s. Victor Curtis and Ethel (Dean) B.; m. Alelaide M. Forshey, June 28, 1964 (div.); children: Deborah Ann, Suzanne Marie; m. Jean Jennings, Aug. 1, 1998. BS, U.S. Mil. Acad., West Point, NY, 1964; MS, U. Ill., 1970. Registered profl. engr., Tex., Md., D.C., Fla., Ill. Commd. 2d. lt. U.S. Army, 1964, advanced through grades to brig. gen., 1988; capt. 18th Engr. Brigade, Vietnam, 1966-67; maj. 1st Air Cavalry Div., Vietnam, 1970-71; assoc. prof. history U.S. Mil. Acad., West Point, 1974-77; bn. comdr. 2d Combat Engr. Bn., Bamberg, Fed. Republic Germany, 1978-80; dist. engr. Balt. Dist., Corps Engrs., 1982-84; staff engr. U.S. Army Tng. and Doctrine Command, Ft. Monroe, Va., 1984-86; mil. exec. Office Undersec. Army, Washington, 1986-88; fellow Harvard U., Cambridge, 1988-89; comdg. gen. U.S. Army Corps Engrs., North Atlantic Div., NYC, 1989-92; dir. Environ. programs Dept. of Army, The Pentagon, Washington, 1992-94; ret. U.S. Army, 1994; v.p. Sverdrup Civil, Inc., Falls Church, Va., 1994-95; v.p., mgr. Ea. Ops. Sverdrup Environ., Inc., Balt., 1995-98; v.p. Sverdrup Civil, Inc., Falls Church, 1998-99; program mgr. Parsons Brinckerhoff, London, 2000—01; assoc. dir. for ops. Fermi Nat. Accelerator Lab., Batavia, Ill., 2001—05; ret., 2005. Natl. Defense Exec. Reserve; Fed. Emerg. Mgmt. Agency, chmn. bd. of vis., fed. Emerg. Mgmt. Inst., Md., 1998-2000; founder, pres. Army Corps Engrs. Meml. Corp. Contbr. articles to mil. jours. Fellow Soc. Am. Mil. Engrs. (v.p. 1989-92, bd. dirs. 1993-96, founder, chmn. Acad. Fellows 1995-96); mem. ASCE, Army and Navy Club (Washington). Avocations: golf, opera, reading. Home: Geneva, Ill. Died July 28, 2006.

BROWN, HARRY MATTHEW, English language educator; b. Newark, Ohio, Jan. 24, 1921; s. Marlin Alexander and Elizabeth Gertrude (Cahill) B.; m. Jeanette Karen Hoegstrom, Aug. 25, 1951; children: Michele, Inga, Karren, Kit. BTH, Malone Coll., 1945; BA, Baldwin-Wallace Coll., 1946; MA, Case Western Res. U., 1948, PhD, 1955. Instr. Baldwin-Wallace Coll., Berea, Ohio, 1946-50; teaching fellow Case Western Res. U., Cleve., 1950-53; asst. prof. Shepherd Coll., Shepherdstown, W.Va., 1953-56; assoc. prof. La. Polytech. U., Ruston, 1956-63; asst. prof. Calif. State Polytech. U., Pomona, 1963-66; prof. Midwestern State U., Wichita Falls, Tex., from 1966, dean humanities dept., 1968-78, dir. humanities dept., 1982-92, prof. English, from 1992. Author: Contemporary College Writings, 1977, How to Write, 1978, Business Report Writing, 1980. Named Piper Prof. of 1981, Minnie Stevens Piper Found., Midwestern State U., Hardin Prof., Hardin Found., 1994. Mem. Modern Lang. Assn., Nat. Coun. Tchrs. of English (judge ann. essay awards Urbana, Ill. chpt. 1968—), South Cen. Modern Lang. Assn., Conf. Coll. Tchrs. of English of Tex. Home: Fort Worth, Tex. Died Nov. 9, 2006.

BROWN, JAMES, singer, performer; b. Pulaski, Tenn., June 17, 1928; Former pres. J.B. Broadcasting, Ltd., James Brown Network. Chmn. James Brown Enterprises, James Brown Prodns. Leader musical group, Famous Flames, from 1956; now solo performer, rec. artist with cos.including King, Smash Records, Polydor; recs. include At the Apollo, Pure Dynamite, Original Disco Man, Please, Please, Raw Soul, Sex Machine, I Got You (I Feel Good), Get on the Good Foot, The Popcorn, There It Is, I Got the Feelin', Soul on Top, Hot on the One, Poppa's Got a Brand New Bag, Gravity, The Big Payback, Living in America; more than 75 albums including: Live At The Apollo, 1962, Hot Pants, 1971, Best Of, 1975, Body Heat, 1977, Special, 1981, Soul Syndrome, 1980, Bring It On, 1983, Gravity, 1986, I'm Real, 1988, Love Overdue, 1991, Love Power Peace: Live at the Olympia, Paris 1971, 1992, Papa's Got a Brand New Bag, 1992, A Payback, 1992, Universal James, 1992, The Greatest Hits of the Fourth Decade, 1992, Try Me, 1996, Hooked on Brown, 1996; U.S. tours include performances at Apollo, NYC, Howard U., Washington; author (autobiography) I Feel Good: A Memoir of a Life of Soul, 2005. Recipient 44 Gold Record awards; Grammy award, 1965, 1986; inducted into Rock and Roll Hall of Fame, 1986. Died Dec. 25, 2006.

BROWN, JAMES ANDREW, naval architect; b. Columbia, Tenn., Aug. 19, 1914; s. Charles Allen and Martha (Crawford) B.; m. Frances Adelaide Jones, June 7, 1941 (dec.); children: James Andrew, Martha Janet; m. Mary Julia Hargroves Greene, Feb. 16, 1973. BS, U.S. Naval Acad., 1936; MS, MIT, 1941. Registered profl. engr., Va. Commd. ensign U.S. Navy, 1936, advanced through grades to rear adm., 1963; jr. officer in USS W.Va., 1936-38; asst. hull supt. charge new constrn. Boston Naval Shipyard, 1942-45; mem. staff Comdr. Service Force Pacific, 1945-47; with Bur. Ships, Dept. Navy, 1947-50, project officer destroyer types, 1950- 51, head hull design, 1955-59, asst. chief design, shipbldg. and fleet maintenance, 1963-65; prof. naval architecture MIT, Cambridge, 1951-54; comdg. officer ship repair facility Subic Bay, P.I., 1954-55; planning officer N.Y. Naval Shipyard, 1959, prodn. officer, 1959-61; supr. shipbldg. U.S. Navy, Camden, N.J., 1961-63; comdr. Norfolk Naval Shipyard; also supr. shipbldg. 5th Naval Dist., Portsmouth, Va., 1965-70; ret., 1970; prodn. mgr. J.L. Smith Constrn. Co., Portsmouth, 1970-77; pres. CDI Marine of Va., 1978-81; mgr. Hampton (Va.) Office, 1979-80; sr. engr. QED Systems Inc., 1981-87, chief engr. shipsystems group, 1987-90. Pres. Tidewater Fed. Exec. Agy., 1968; exec. bd. Inter Agy. Bd. Examiners Civil Service for Va., 1968-70; mem. Supplemental Fire and Police Retirement Bd., City of Portsmouth, 1978-86, chmn., 1980-86; bd. dirs. Portsmouth Community Action, 1969-70, 78-79; mem. Panel Spl. Advisers Auditor Gen. U.S.A., 1972, citizen adv. com. transit devel. study Southeastern Va. Planning Dist. Commn.; commr. Tidewater Transit Dist. Commn., 1978-86; bd. dirs. Portsmouth United Fund, 1965-77; coord. for vol. tutors, Portsmouth Sch. Bd., 1991-92. Decorated Legion of Merit; recipient Commendation medal Sec. of Navy; named Disting. Grad. Class of '31 Peabody Demonstration Sch., Nashville, 1986. Mem. Am. Soc. Naval Engrs. (coun. 1959), Naval Inst., Naval Archs. and Marine Engrs. (coun. 1968-69, chmn. Chesapeake sect. 1959, chmn. Hampton Rds. sect. 1969-70, v.p. 1969-70), Am. Philatelic Soc., World Affairs Coun. Greater Hampton Rds. (v.p. 1969-70, pres. 1971, 72), English Speaking Union, Portsmouth Hist. Soc. (hon., dir. 1977—, 1st v.p. 1987—), Portsmouth C. of C. (chmn. urban affairs com., v.p. for urban affairs 1972-73, chmn. com. hwys. and mass transit 1974-75, 76-78, bd. dirs. 1971-73, 79-82), Portsmouth C. of C. (mil. affairs com. 1970-95, transp. com. 1983-87), Navy League, Portsmouth Execs. Club (bd. dirs. 1975-76, 78-79, 79-82, 83-87, mem. ship structure com. 1963-65, chmn. subcom. 1955-59, 87-88), Sigma Xi. Died July 29, 2006.

BROWN, JAMES JOSEPH, manufacturing executive; b. NYC, Apr. 4, 1928; s. Peter J. and Mary (O'Neil) B.; m. Mary E. McKeon, Dec. 30, 1961; children: Patricia, James, Carolyn, Denise, Erin. BS, Fordham U., 1952. C.P.A., N.Y. Acct. Touche, Ross, Bailey & Smart (C.P.A.s), NYC, 1952-54; sr. acct. Price Waterhouse & Co. (C.P.A.s), Caracas, Venezuela and NYC, 1954-63; mgr. internal audit Litton Industries, 1963-65; sr. v.p., chief fin. officer dir. Kidde, Inc., 1965-82; chmn. bd. Am. Desk Mfg. Co., 1982-97. Served with AUS, 1946-48. Named Alumni Man of Year, Fordham U. Coll. Bus. Adminstrn., 1971 Mem. AICPA, N.Y. State Soc. CPAs, Econ. Club N.Y. Clubs: Treasurers of N.Y, Ridgewood Country, N.Y. Athletic. Home: Wyckoff, NJ. Died Feb. 18, 2006.

BROWN, JAMES K., lawyer; b. Boston, Sept. 17, 1942; AB, Harvard Coll., 1965; JD, U. Colo., 1968. Bar: Mass. 1968, N.H. 1993. Mem. Foley, Hoag & Eliot, Boston. Editor U. Colo. Law Rev., 1967-68. Died May 4, 2007.

BROWN, JOHN CONARD, dentist; b. Cedar City, Utah, Mar. 27, 1926; s. John Middleton and Althea (Lund) Brown; m. Mary Morris, May 20, 1950; children: Conard Lee, Douglas Morris, Carol Ann. AA, So. Utah State Coll., 1951; DDS, U. So. Calif., 1961. Gen. practice dentistry, Claremont, Calif., 1961—97; dir. Dentists Ins. Co., Sacramento, from 1997. With USN, 1944—46. Recipient Dentist of Yr. award, So. Calif. Acad. Gen. Dentistry, 1979. Fellow: Pierre Fouchad Acad., Am. Coll. Dentistry, Internat. Coll. Dentistry, Acad. Gen. Dentistry (master, nat. pres. 1988—89); mem.: ADA, Am. Orthodontic Soc., Flying Dentists Assn., Tri County Dental Assn., Calif. Dental Assn. (trustee from 1990), Kiwanis. Republican. Mem. Lds Ch. Home: Claremont, Calif. Died Apr. 11, 2007.

BROWN, OGDEN, JR., psychologist, educator; b. Evanston, Ill., Apr. 1, 1927; s. Ogden and Frances Louise (Falck) Brown; m. Alyce Marie Whitesides, May 1, 1953; children: Marsha Brown Whitesides, Lynda Brown Dunne, Ogden III, Tarleton II. Psychometrician U.S. Employment Svc., Washington, 1950—51; commd. 2d lt. USAF, 1951, advanced through grades to col., 1971; from instr. to assoc. prof. U.S. Air Force Acad., 1961—68; asst. for edn. and tng. Office of Sec. of Air Force, Washington, 1968—71; comdr. 3415 Spl. Tng. Group, Lowry AFB, Colo., 1971—73; ret., 1973; pres. Mgmt. Devel. Assocs., Colorado Springs, Colo., from 1973. Exec. v.p. Am. West Enterprises, Colorado Springs, 1973—78; from asst. prof. to prof. human factors, dir. sys. mgmt. program Inst. Safety and Sys. Mgmt. U. So. Calif., LA, 1978—87; prof., dir. sys. mgmt. program Coll. Sys. Sci. U. Denver, from 1987. Editor: Human Factors in Organizational Design and Management I, 1984, 1986, 1990; contbr. articles to profl. jours. Decorated Legion of Merit, Meritorious Svc. medal, Commendation medal. Mem.: APA, Rocky Mountain Psychol. Assn., Soc. Indsl. and Orgnl. Psychology, Internat. Ergonomics Assn., Human Factors Soc., Ergonomics Soc., Am. Psychol. Soc., Am. Mgmt. Assn., Am. Evaluation Assn., Acad. Mgmt., Elks, Delta Phi Alpha, Omicron Delta Kappa, Psi Chi, Sigma Xi. Republican. Episcopalian. Home: Florissant, Colo. Died July 15, 2007.

BROWN, PAUL SHERMAN, lawyer; b. June 26, 1921; s. Paul Michael and Norma (Sherman) Brown; m. Ann Wilson, Feb. 7, 1959; 1 child, Paul S. BS in Commerce, St. Louis U., 1943, JD cum laude, 1951. Bar: Mo. 51, U.S. Dist. Ct. (ea. dist.) Mo. 51, U.S. Ct. Appeals (8th cir.) 51, U.S. Supreme Ct. 66. Shareholder Brown & James, P.C., St. Louis, from 1980. Instr. St. Louis U. Night Law Sch., from 1978; lectr. in field; mem. com. on civil pattern jury instructions Mo. Supreme Ct. Contbr. articles to profl. jours. Fellow: Internat. Soc. Barristers, Internat. Acad. Trial Lawyers, Am. Coll. Trial Lawyers; mem.: ABA (vice-chmn. com. consumer products liability 1977—78), Am. Judicature Soc., Bar Assn. Met. St. Louis (pres. 1970—71), Lawyers Assn. St. Louis, Am. Bd. Trial Advocates, Mo. Bar Assn. (bd. govs. 1963—67), Order of Woolsack, St. Louis Amateur Athletic Assn. (bd. dirs. 1974—76, pres. 1976—78), Alpha Sigma Nu. Roman Catholic. Home: Saint Louis, Mo. Died Apr. 5, 2006.

BROWN, REGINALD JUDE, federal agency administrator; BS, U.S. Mil. Acad., 1961; MPA, Harvard U., 1965. Dir. adminstrn. Mitre Corp., McLean, Va., 1972-73; dep. adminstr. Office of Food, Cost of Living Coun., Washington, 1973-74; assoc. dir. Def. Manpower Commn., Washington, 1974-75; prin. analyst Congl. Budget Office, Washington, 1975-77; exec. dir. Pres.'s Commn. on Mil. Compensation, Washington, 1977-78; dir. Energy Div., Office of Price Monitoring, Coun.on Wage and Price Stability, Washington, 1979; exec. v.p. DECA Group Inc., Miami, Fla., 1979-81; sr. fellow Ctr. for Strategic and Internat. Studies, Washington, 1982-89; asst. adminstr. U.S. AID, Washington, 1989—93; asst. secy. army manpower reserve affairs U.S. Dept. Defense, Washington, from 2001. Co-author: The Lessons of Wage and Price Controls, 1977; contbr. articles to jours. in field. Decorated Bronze Star, Meritorious Svc. medal. Republican. Home: Alexandria, Va. Died Dec. 17, 2005.

BROWN, RICHARD BRUCE, infectious disease physician; b. NYC, May 22, 1944; s. Seymour Michael and Norma M. (Lipchansky) B.; m. Bonnie M. Morganstein, Oct. 11, 1970; children: Scott M., Robin D. BS, Tufts U., 1965; MD, George Washington U., 1969. Diplomate internal medicine and infectious diseases Am. Bd. Internal Medicine. Resident in medicine New Eng. Med. Ctr. Hosp., Boston, 1969-71, fellow infectious diseases, 1973-75, Peter Bent Brigham Hosp., Boston, 1975-76; chief infectious disease divsn. Baystate Med. Ctr., Springfield, Mass., from 1976. Interviewer Tufts U., Medford, Mass., 1991—; prof. medicine Tufts U. Sch. Medicine, 1995; co-dir. Wound Healing and Hyperbaric Medicine Program Baystate Med. Ctr., Springfield, Mass., 1994—. Editor: Infections in Outpatient Practice, 1988, Clinical Problems in Infectious Diseases, 1999. Fellow ACP, Infectious Disease Soc. Am. Avocations: photography, travel, wine. Home: Longmeadow, Mass. Died Sept. 30, 2006.

BROWN, RICHARD JAMES, banker; b. Glen Ellyn, Ill., Aug. 17, 1944; s. Edward Henry and Bernice (Brummel) B.; m. Carolyn Beal, Aug. 19, 1967; children: David M., Daniel P., Kathleen M. BBA, U. Notre Dame, 1966; MBA, Dartmouth Coll., 1968. Banking officer Harris Trust & Savs. Bank, Chgo., 1968-70, asst. v.p., 1970-79, v.p. London, 1979-84, sr. v.p. Chgo., from 1985, v.p. London, Eng., 1981-84. Cons. Ill. State

Banking Bd., Springfield, 1986—. Mem. exec. bd. dirs. Boy Scouts Am., Chgo., 1985—; bd. dirs. Boys Hope. Mem. Am. Bankers Assn., Bankers Club Chgo., Bankers Assn. for Fgn. Trade (edn. com. 1985—), Chgo. Athletic Assn. Home: Northfield, Ill. Died Feb. 1, 2007.

BROWN, RICHARD W(ILLITS), paper company executive; b. Downingtown, Pa., Mar. 11, 1921; s. Ellis Y. and Mary (Godley) Brown; married, Sept. 23, 1944; children: Peter, Anne, Philip. BS in chemistry, Haverford Coll., 1942; MS, PhD, Inst. Paper Chemistry, 1948. Rsch. chemist Rohm and Haas Corp., Phila., 1942—44; with Hammermill Paper Co., Erie, Pa., 1950, asst. v.p., dir. rsch., 1968—69, v.p.-rsch., 1969—75, v.p.-tech., 1975—86; pvt. practice cons. Erie, from 1986. Bd. dirs Pa. Sci. and Engring. Found.; chmn. rsch. com Nat. Council of Paper Industry for Air and Stream Improvement, Inc., 1975—77, gov., mem. operating com., 1975; mem. rsch. adv. com. Inst. Paper Chemistry, 1979—83, chmn., 1981; sec., acting chmn. Erie County (Pa.) Solid Waste Authority, 1969—75. Served to lt. (j.g.) USN, 1944—46. Fellow: TAPPI (chmn. div. rsch. and devel. 1965—68, dir. 1973—76); mem.: Erie. Republican. Home: Erie, Pa. Died July 4, 2006.

BROWN, ROBERT DELFORD, artist; b. Portland, Colo., Oct. 25, 1930; s. Robert Delford and Faye (Kelly) B.; m. Harriett Rhett Gurney, Mar. 21, 1963. BA, UCLA, 1952, MA, 1958. One-man shows Drawings, N.Y.C., 1959-70, Bob Brown and His Friends (photography), 1965-69, Wall Hangings, 1973, Ceramics, 1973, Tinted Photographs, 1973, The Great Building Crackup, 1967, Leonard Perlson Gallery, N.Y., 1986, Pub. Sch. 1, Long Island, N.Y., Nahan Contemporary, N.Y.C., 1990, Fondazione Mudima, Milan, 1992; retrospective exhbn., 1958-81, Phyllis Kind Gallery, N.Y.C., BAC, London, 1994; other exhibits Originale, Judson Hall, N.Y.C., 1964, Meat Show, N.Y.C., 1964, Gallery of Modern Art, Washington, 1965, Kansas City Art Inst., Mo., 1971, Moore Coll. Art, Phila., 1973, 85, U. Bridgeport, Conn., 1976, 77, R.I. Sch. Design, Providence, 1978, San Diego State U., 1978, Phila. Art Alliance, 1981, Pitts. Ctr. for Arts, 1981, Pratt Inst., 1981, Phyllis Kind Gallery, 1983, Bard Coll., N.Y.; author: Hanging, 1967, First Class Portraits, 1973, Ulysses, An Altered Plagiarism, 1975, Teachings of the First National Church of the Exquisitepanic, Inc., 1991; founder First Nat. Ch. of Exquisite Panic Inc., 1964 Acadia Found. fellow, 1990. Died July 2, 2007.

BROWN, ROBERT WAYNE, physician; b. Atwood, Kans., June 27, 1923; s. Paul D. and Florence (Sawer) B.; m. Julia L. Potochnick, Dec. 15, 1945; children— Sandra S., Craig. BA, U. Colo., 1949; MD, Kans. U., 1955. Intern Kans. U. Med. Center, 1955-56, resident, 1956-59; practice medicine specializing in internal medicine Kansas City, Kans., from 1959; mem. faculty Kans. U., 1959-61; chief med. service Kansas City (Kans.) VA Hosp., 1961-64, cons., from 1964; asst. prof. endocrinology and metabolism Kans. U. Med. Center, 1965-68, prof. internal medicine, from 1969. Dir. Kans. Regional Med. Program, Kansas City, 1968-76, Salina Health Edn. Found.; program dir. Salina Family Practice Residency Program, 1977-82; cons. USAF. Served to 1st lt. USAAF, 1943-46. Fellow ACP; mem. AMA Phi Beta Pi, Alpha Omega Alpha. Home: Salina, Kans. Died Jan. 22, 2006.

BROWN, RUTH, rhythm and blues singer; b. Portsmouth, Va., Jan. 12, 1928; m. Earl Swanson, 1955; 2 children. Known as Miss Rhythm, 1950's; star original Paris prodn. Black and Blue; first major artist signed to Atlantic Records, recorded Teardrops from My Eyes, 1950 (No. 1 Billboard Hit); later No. 1 hits include I'll Wait For You, 1951, I Know, 1951, 5-10-15 Hours, 1952, Mama Treats Your Daughter Mean, 1953, Oh What a Dream, 1954, Mambo Baby, 1954, Don't Deceive Me, Lucky Lips; albums include Have a Good Time, Help a Good Girl Go Bad, Miss Rhythm, Blues on Broadway, 1989, (Grammy awd., 1990), Fine and Mellow, 1991, The Songs of My Life, 1993; co-author: (with Andrew Yule) Miss Rhythm, 1995 appeared on stage in Guys and Dolls, Aladdin Theatre, Ruth Brown and Friends, Gilded Cage, Las Vegas; played role of Mahalia Jackson in stage play, Selma, L.A.; European and Asian tours with Monterey Jazz Festival; actor (films)Under the Rainbow, 1981, Hairspray, 1986, True Identity, 1991; (TV films) Black and Blue, 1993, Shake Rattle and Rock, 1994; (TV series) Hello Larry, 1979-80; (TV appearances) The Jeffersons, 1981, American Playhouse, 1993; star off-Broadway in Staggerlee; host nat. syndicated radio series Harlem Hit Parade Sta. WGBO Jazz 88; star That Rhythm Those Blues for PBS; co-author (with Andrew Yule) Miss Rhythm, 1995 Recipient Antoinette Perry award for performance by leading actress in a mus. for Black and Blue, 1989; profile in Down Beat, Mar. 1990; inducted Rock and Roll Hall of Fame, 1993. Died Nov. 17, 2006.

BROWN, STRATTON SHARTEL, lawyer; b. Ann Arbor, Mich., Sept. 13, 1923; s. William Ellis and Eleanor York (Shartel) B.; m. Joyce Laughlin Hall; children: Paula Brown Gray, Duncan Hall. BA, U. Mich., 1947, JD, 1949. Bar: Mich. 1949. Instr. USN Midshipman Sch., Columbia U., NYC, 1944; assoc. Miller, Canfield, Paddock and Stone P.L.C., Detroit, 1949-58; ptnr. Miller, Canfield, Paddock & Stone, Detroit, 1958-89, mng. ptnr., 1973-81, adminstrv. ptnr., 1978, of counsel, from 1989. Mem. Gov.'s Commn. on Bed Reduction, Lansing, Mich., 1979, Mayor's Fiscal Stabilization Commn., Detroit, 1981; gen. sec. Southeastern Mich. Regional Transp. Coord. Coun. Lt. (j.g.) USNR. Mem. ABA (chmn. transp. subcom. urban law), State Bar Mich., Detroit Bar Assn., Govt. Fin. Officers Assn., Nat. Inst. Mcpl. Law Officers, Nat. Assn. Bond Lawyers, Orchard Lake Country Club, Belvedere Country Club, Order of the Coif. Episcopal. Home: Bloomfield Hills, Mich. Died Nov. 7, 2006.

BROWN, VIRGINIA, system program manager; b. Knippa, Tex., Nov. 13, 1933; d. Ralph and Hedwig Deely; stepfather James L. Stevenson; m. Larry Foster Keith, Nov. 30, 1957 (div. 1965); children— William Scott, Joyce Marie, Bradford Jay, Keith Brown; m. James Clarence Brown, June 25, 1965 (div. 1979). Clk., Ft. Sam Houston, Tex., 1951-58, Kelly AFB, Tex., 1964-67; clk. Aero. Systems div. Wright-Patterson AFB, Ohio, 1973-74, chief adminstrv. orders, 1974-76, program analyst Avionics Lab. Air Force Wright Aeronaut. Labs., 1976-81, program analyst Directorate Aircraft Modification, 4950th Test Wing, 1981-83; fin. specialist Aero. Systems div. Wright-Patterson AFB, Ohio, 1983-84. Mem. Am. Soc. Mil. Comptrollers, Engring. Mgmt. Soc. (exec. com.), Am. Bus. Women's Assn. Lutheran. Home: Dayton, Ohio. Died May 31, 2006.

BROWN, WILLIAM JOSEPH, insurance company executive; b. Flushing, N.Y., May 21, 1947; s. William Charles and Mary Alice (Black) B.; m. Patricia Jane Riordan, Dec. 27, 1969; 1 child, William E. B.S. in Ins. Adminstrn., U. Conn., 1972; M.S. in Fin. Scis., Am. Coll., Bryn Mawr, Pa., 1985. C.L.U., Ordained permanent Cath. deacon, 1988. Mgmt. trainee Conn. Mut. Ins. Co., Hartford, 1968-70; life underwriter Aetna, Hartford, 1970-73, pension sales mgr., Rochester, N.Y., 1973-79; mgr. sales adminstrn. Hartford Ins. Group, 1979-81; assoc. dir. Keogh mktg. Conn. Mut. Ins. Co., Hartford, 1981-82; v.p. Diversified Ins. Services Am., Hartford, 1982-86; regional v.p. CWS Holdings Ltd., 1986—. Vice pres., treas., pres. Bowers Sch. PTA, Manchester, Conn., 1980-82; pres. Townwide PTA Council, Manchester, 1984-85; mem. advancement com., bd. rev., chmn. troop com. 25 Boy Scouts Am., Manchester, 1985—. Served with U.S. Army, 1966-68. Recipient Alumni Assn. award U. Conn. Sch. Ins., 1971. Mem. C.L.U. (pres. Hartford chpt. 1987—), Life Mgmt. Inst. Assn. Central New Eng. Republican. Roman Catholic. Clubs: Toastmasters Internat., Friendship Force (ambassador and host). Home: Manchester, Conn. Died May 1, 2006.

BROWN, WILLIAM PAUL, investment executive; b. Detroit, Oct. 23, 1919; s. Paul Joseph and Adele (LaFerte) B.; m. dau., Barbara (Mrs. Boyd Kenyon Knowles). AB, U. Detroit, 1941. Vice pres. Baker, Simonds & Co., Detroit, 1945-64; instl. sales mgr. E.F. Hutton & Co., Inc., Detroit, from 1964; v.p. Smith & Barney, from 1965; treas. Detroit Stock Exchange, 1964. Served to lt. (s.g.) USNR, 1941-45, PTO. Decorated Bronze Star medal. Mem. Investment Bankers Assn. Am. (gov. 1969—); chmn. Mich. group (1967), Bond Club Detroit, Security Traders Assn. Detroit (pres. 1955) Clubs: Country of Detroit, University of Detroit (pres. 1973 bd. govs.), Detroit Athletic Club. Home: Williamsburg, Va. Died Aug. 19, 2007.

BROWN, WOOD, III, lawyer; b. New Orleans, Jan. 13, 1936; s. Wood and Martha Hyland B.; m. Sandra Anne Brown, July 30, 1960; children— Carolyn, Charles, Martha, Claiborne. BA, Tulane U., 1958, LL.B., 1961. Bar: La. 1961, U.S. Supreme Ct. 1980. Assoc. Montgomery, Barnett, Brown & Read, New Orleans, 1961-66, ptnr., from 1966. Mem. adj. faculty Tulane U. Law Sch., 1977-82, dean's council, 1974—; mem. faculty Ins. Counsel Trial Acad., 1985; mem. com. on disciplinary enforcement U.S. Dist. Ct. (ea. dist.) La. Editor La. Bar Jour, 1971-73. Mem. New Orleans Civil Service Commn., 1977-83, chmn., 1981-83; bd. dirs. YMCA Greater New Orleans, Protestant Home for Aged. Served with U.S. Army, 1958-59. Recipient Monte Lemann award La. Civil Service League, 1981. Fellow Am. Coll. Trial Lawyers, Internat. Acad. Trial Lawyers; mem. ABA, La. Bar Assn. (ho. of dels. 1964-70, 73-87, sec.-treas. 1971-73, pres.-elect 1987-88, pres. 1988-89; com. bar admissions 1974-78, com. on profl. responsibility 1975-85), New Orleans Bar Assn., Am. Law Inst., Am. Judicature Soc., Internat. Assn. Def. Counsel, Def. Research Inst., La. Assn. Def. Counsel. Clubs: Boston, Stratford. Democrat. Presbyterian. Home: Mandeville, La. Died May 11, 2006.

BROWNE, JOHN ROBINSON, banker; b. Ft. Worth, Aug. 29, 1914; s. Virgil and Maimee Lee (Robinson) B.; m. Elizabeth Anne Hargett, Sept. 1, 1945 (dec. June 1990); children: John Robinson, Ann Browne (Mrs. John M. Dunker); stepchildren: Bob Allen Street, David H. Street; m. Christine H. Anthony, Mar. 20, 1992 (dec. May 1993); m. Barbara C. (Conner) Edwards, Nov. 18, 1994 (div. Apr. 2001). AB, Okla. U., 1938, JD, 1939; postgrad., Harvard Grad. Sch. Bus. Adminstrn., 1939-40; grad., Rutgers U., 1965. Bar: Okla. bar 1939. With Liberty Nat. Bank & Trust Co., Oklahoma City, 1945-46, 60-71, sr. v.p., 1960-71; gen. mgr. Coca-Cola Bottling Co., Colorado Springs and Pueblo, Colo., 1946-59; chief exec. officer Union Bancorp., Inc., Oklahoma City, 1971-89; chmn. bd. dirs. Sterling Sugars Co., Franklin, La., 1989-96, Cheyenne Propagation Co., Colo. Springs, Colo., from 1989. Mng. gen. ptnr. Glencoe-Vacherie Plantation Ltd., Okla., 1972—. Served from 2d lt. to lt. col., F.A. AUS, 1940-45. Mem. Okla. Bar Assn. Died Nov. 14, 2005.

BROWNE, ROSCOE LEE, actor; b. Woodbury, NJ, May 2, 1925; Student, Lincoln U.; postgrad., Middlebury Coll., Vt. Columbia. Nat. sales rep. Schenley Import Corp., 1952-56; instr. French and lit. Lincoln U. Performed with NY Shakespeare Festival, 7 seasons; performed various Shakespearian roles for, Canadian Broadcasting Co., Toronto; guest artist, Spolato Festival Two Worlds; reader classics and modern poetry in univs. throughout U.S.; (with Anthony Zerbe in) ann. tour Behind The Broken Words; appeared in Broadway plays: The Ballad of the Sad Cafe, 1963, The Cool World, 1960, General Seeger, 1962, Tiger, Tiger Burning Bright!, 1962, The Connection, 1962, Black Like Me, 1964, The Old Glory, 1964-65, My One and Only, 1983, Two Trains Running, 1992 (Tony nomination); actor, dir. (Broadway plays) A Hand is On The Gate, 1966, The Blacks, 1961, Aria de Capo, 1958; actor (films) The Connection, 1962, Terror in the City, 1964, Black Like Me, 1964, The Comedians, 1967, Uptight, 1968, Me and My Brother, 1969, Topaz, 1969, The Liberation of L.B. Jones, 1970, The Cowboys, 1972, Cisco Pike, 1972, The World's Greatest Athlete, 1973, Superfly T.N.T., 1973, Uptown Saturday Night, 1974, Logan's Run, 1976, Twilight's Last Gleaming, 1977, Double Take, 1979, Nothing Personal, 1980, (voice only) The Nativity, 1986, Jumpin' Jack Flash, 1985, Legal Eagles, 1986, (voice only) Oliver & Company, 1988, The Mambo Kings, 1992, Eddie Presley, 1992, Naked in New York, 1993, The Beast, 1995, (voice only) Babe, 1995, Last Summer in the Hamptons, 1995, Muppet Treasure Island, 1996, The Pompatus of Love, 1996, Dear God, 1996, Forest Warrior, 1996, Judas Kiss, 1998, (voice only) Babe: Pig in the City, 1998, Morgan's Ferry, 1999, Sweet Deadly Dreams, 2002, (voice only) Treasure Planet, 2002, Behind the Broken Words, 2003, (narrator) Epic Movie, 2007; actor (TV films) The Rex Harrison Presents Stories of Love, 1974, The Big Rip-Off, 1975, Dr. Scorpion, 1978, The Haunting of Harrington House, 1980, For Us the Living: The Medgar Evers Story, 1983, (narrator) Night Angel, 1989, Stuck with Each Other, 1989, Lady in the Corner, 1989, Moon 44, 1990, Colombo: Rest in Peace, Mrs. Columbo, 1990, Open Windows, 1991, You Must Remember This, 1992, The Notorious 7, 1997, Hard Time: The Premonition, 1999, (voice only) Tales of a Fly on the Wall, 2004; (TV mini-series) King, 1978, Space, 1985; (TV series) McCoy, 1975, Miss Winslow and Son, 1979, Foofur, 1987, Ring Raiders, 1989, Hamlet, 2000; (TV appearances) East Side/West Side, 1963, Espionage, 1963, NET Playhouse, 1967, Mannix, 1968, The Invaders, 1968, The Outcasts, 1969, The Name of the Game, 1969-70, Insight, 1971, Bonanaza, 1972, Sanford and Son, 1972, The Streets of San Francisco, 1973 All In the Family, 1972-73, Good Times, 1974, Planet of the Apes, 1974, Barney Miller, 1975, Starsky & Hutch, 1977, Maude, 1977-78, Once Upon a Classic, 1978, Benson, 1980, Hart to Hart, 1980, Soap, 1980-81, Magnum P.I., 1983, Head of the Class, 1986, 227, 1987, The Cosby Show, 1986-87, Visionaries: Knights of the Magical Light, 1987, (voice only) The Real Ghostbusters, 1988, Highway to Heaven, 1988, Falcon Crest, 1988, A Different World, 1988-92, Father Dowling Mysteries, 1990, Baby Talk, 1991, Law & Order, 1992, 2003, SeaQuest DSV, 1993-94, (voice only) Batman, 1994, Freakazoid!, 1995, New York Undercover, 1996, Cosby, 1996, (voice only) Spider-Man, 1995-98, ER, 1999, Hope Island, 1999, (voice only) The Wild Thornberrrys, 1999, The Shield, 2002, Static Shock, 2003-04, Will & Grace, 2004, Independent Lens, 2006, Garfied: A Take of Two Kitties, 2006; Author poems, short stories. Trustee Millay Colony Arts, N.Y., Los Angeles Free Pub. Theatre, KPFK, Pacifica Radio, Los Angeles. Track champion (1000 yard indoors) Amateur Athletic Union, 1949, 51; twice named All-American; recipient Obie award for best actor in Benito Cereno 1964-65, Los Angeles Drama Critics award for Best Actor, Dream on Monkey Mountain 1971, Emmy award Best Actor in Drama or Comedy Show, The Cosby Show, 1986. Died Apr. 11, 2007.

BROZMAN, TINA LESSER, lawyer, former federal judge; b. Oct. 7, 1952; m. Andrew Brozman; children: Nicholas, Alix, Wallis. BA, NYU, 1973; JD, Fordham U., 1976. Ptnr. Anderson Russell Kill & Olick, 1976—85; judge US Bankruptcy Ct. So. Dist. NY, NYC, 1985—96, chief judge, 1996—2000; ptnr. Bingham McCutchen LLP, NYC, 2000—07, chairperson fin. restructuring practice group. Lectr. Practicing Law Inst., 1987. Named an The 50 Most Influential Women Lawyers in Am., Nat. Law Jour., 2007. Fellow: Am. Coll. Bankruptcy (second cir. nominating com.); mem.: Bankruptcy Appellate Panel US Ct. Appeals, second cir., Assn. Bar City NY (bankruptcy & corp. reorganization com.), Am. Bankruptcy Inst., Nat. Conf. Bankruptcy Judges (former second cir. governor), Internat. Insolvency Inst. (elected), Am. Law Inst. (elected), UN Commn Internat. Trade Law, INSOL Internat. (founder & former chairperson Judge's divsn.). Died June 26, 2007.

BRUCE, CATHERINE MARY, savings and loan company executive; b. Indpls., Nov. 15, 1943; d. George Thomas and Mary Jo (Carton) O'Connor; m. Curtis Brian Bruce, Dec. 28 1963; children— Krista, Kylie, Brian. Real estate agt. Realty World, Escondido, Calif., 1976-78; in pub. relations Blackshea Ltd., Okinawa, Japan, 1978-79; dir. pub. relations Am. Income Richmond, Va., 1980-81; nat. trainer Nat. Fitness Virginia Beach, Va., 1981-83; ctr. mgr. Carnation Health & Nutrition San Diego, 1983-84; dist. coordinator 1st Nationwide Savs. and Loan Assn., San Diego, 1984—. Pres. Marine Wives, San Diego 1968-69. Mem. Community Services Commn., San Marcos Calif., 1983—; bd. dirs. North San Diego County Community TV Found., Calif., 1985. Mem. Nat. Assn. Female Execs Avocations: oil painting; flower arranging. Home: Escondido Calif. Died Jan. 22, 2006.

BRUDVIG, GLENN LOWELL, retired library director; b. Kenosha, Wis., Oct. 14, 1931; s. Lars L. Brudvig and Ann Elizabeth (Hillesland) B. Lovejoy; m. Myrna Winifred Michael Oct. 1, 1953; children: Gary Wayne, Lee Anthony, James Lowell, Kristin Elizabeth BA in Edn., U. N.D., 1954, MA, 1956 MALS, U. Minn., 1962. Tchr. pub. schs. Mahnoman and Herman, Minn., 1954-55, 56-58; librarian, archivist U. N.D Grand Forks, 1958-62, asst. librarian, 1962-63; supr. dept libraries U. Minn., Mpls., 1964, dir. bio-med. libr., 1964-83; di libr. Calif. Inst. Tech., Pasadena, 1983-95, ret., 1995. Inst library sci. U. N.D., Grand Forks, 1962-63; asst. dir. for rsch. & devel. U. Minn., Mpls., 1968-79, instr. library sci., 1968-71, di Inst. Tech. Libraries, 1982-83; cons. Nat. Library of Medicine Bethesda, Md., 1971-75. Contbr. articles to profl. jours. Serve with U.S. Army, 1951-52 Nat. Library of Medicine grante 1967-79. Home: Saint Paul, Minn. Died Jan. 26, 2007.

BRUES, ALICE MOSSIE, physical anthropologist, educato b. Boston, Oct. 9, 1913; d. Charles Thomas and Beirne (Barret B. AB, Bryn Mawr Coll., 1933; PhD, Radcliffe Coll., 194 Faculty U. Okla. Sch. Medicine, 1946-65, prof., 1960-65; vi prof. anthropology U. Colo., Boulder, 1965-66, prof., fro 1966, chmn. dept. anthropology, 1969-71. Asso. editor: Am Jour. Phys. Anthropology, 1962-66; Author: People and Race 1977, contbr. articles to profl. jours. Mem. Am. Assn. Phy Anthropologists (v.p. 1966-68, pres. 1971-73), Soc. Study Evo lution, Am. Acad. Forensic Scis., Soc. Naturalists, Sigma X Home: Boulder, Colo. Died Jan. 14, 2007.

BRUMFIELD, JOAN HARDY, small business owner; Tulsa, Aug. 6, 1949; d. Homer Dwight Jr. and Phyllis Jo (Love) Hardy; m. Jerry L.R. Mowery, July 11, 1980 (div. Jun 1987); 1 child, Scott Weston Mowery; m. James R. Brumsfiel BBA, Okla. U., 1971; MBA, So. Meth. U., Dallas, 1979. Ac exec. Dean Witter Reynolds, St. Louis, 1976-78; internal audit The Williams Cos., Tulsa, 1979-80; fin. analyst Peabody Co Co., St. Louis, 1980-81; assoc. auditor Chevron Oil Co., S Francisco, 1981-82, analyst telecommunications, 1982-84, co trols analyst, Warren Petroleum div., Tulsa, 1985-86, analy mfg. reporting Wareen Petroleum div., 1986-87; pres. Sm Bus. Services, Inc., Salem, Va., 1988—; v.p., bd. dirs. World A Services, Tulsa, 1978—. Advisor Tulsa chpt. Jr. Achievemen

1985; mem. adv. bd. Domestic Violence Intervention Services, Tulsa, 1986-87, Community Services Council, Tulsa, 1987; treas. adv. bd. Women's Treatment Ctr., Tulsa, 1987. Republican. Methodist. Mem. Jr. League Tulsa, Kappa Alpha Theta. Avocations: needlepoint, skiing, reading. Died Oct. 10, 2006.

BRUNALE, VITO JOHN, aerospace engineer; b. Mt. Vernon, NY, July 2, 1925; s. Donato and Antoinette (Wool) B.; m. Joan Florence Montuori, Apr. 23, 1949; 1 child, Stephen. AAS, Stewart Aero. Inst., 1948; BSAE, Tri-State U., 1958; MSME, U. Bridgeport, 1966; DSc, Nev. Inst. Tech., 1973; PhD (hon.), Internat. U., Spain, 1987; DSc, Pacific Western U., 1984. Rsch. engr. Norden Labs., White Plains, NY, 1948-55; instr. Tri-State U., Angola, Ind., 1955-58; engring. cons. Norden Div. United Aircraft, Norwalk, Conn., 1958-67; chief engring. cons. Singer-Kearfott Corp., Pleasantville, NY, 1967-73; chief engr. Diagnostic/Retrieval Systems, Mt. Vernon, NY, 1973-76; tech. problem mgr. Fairchild Republic Co., Farmingdale, NY, 1977-87; sr. tech. expert Sikorsky Aircraft, from 1987. Cons. in field; engring. tutor to coll. students; v.p. Lithoway, Inc., 1969-73; lectr. in field; tech. guest speaker numerous tech. soc. meetings.; participant engring. exchange program, USSR, People's Republic China. Contbr. articles to profl. jours. including Product Engring., Aviation Week, Environ. Scis. Participant U.S.A. Citizen Amb. Program. Served with USAAF, 1943-45. Decorated Purple Heart (3), Air medals, D.F.C. Tri-State U. tcht. fellow, 1955-58; NSF grantee; recipient Aircraft Design award, 1948, Inst. Aero. Sci. Lecture award, 1948, Norden Rsch. award, 1963, Cost Reduction award, 1965, Singer Engring. award, 1970, 72, Fairchild outstanding achievement award, 1985, 86, 87, Fairchild award of excellence, 1984, Am. Biographical Inst. and Research Assn. Outstanding Performance award, 1989, Aircraft Recognition award, 1986, citation N.Y. State Assembly, 1988, Conspicuous Service Cross N.Y. State, 1988, Prisoner of War medal, 1988, others; honoree Nat. Air and Space Mus.; named to Wisdom Hall of Fame, 1998. Mem. AIAA (award 1973, Aviation award 1994, Sr. Mem. award 1994, Merit award 1998, membership award 1998, award 1998), VFW, DAV, K.C., U.S. Naval Inst., Air Force Assn., Am. Ordnance Asssn., Inst. Environ. Sci., Nat Space Inst., Newman Club, Internat. Students Assn., Internat. Platform Assn., World Inst. of Achievement. Roman Catholic. Achievements include patent (with others) for Bearing Spin Rail Test; development of method of discriminate displacement for equilibrium of structures, of the position point vibration isolation technique, of the vapress vibration system, of advanced techniques for structural and vibration analyses, of the Doppler-Inertial-Loran system, of state of the art mathematical and structural analyses techniques, of Mars Doppler Lander system, computer time studies, anti-corrosion methods; resolution of 140 technical problems on the Fairchild A-10 aircraft, of more than 30 technical problems with the Saab-Fairchild 340; solution of Grumman A-6A radar tracking problem in Vietnam; elimination of technical problems on LEM inertial guidance; rsch. in mfg. productivity, co-planer structural analyses. Home: Brewster, NY. Died Sept. 21, 2006.

BRUNE, DAVID HAMILTON, finance company executive, lawyer; b. Long Beach, Calif., Apr. 23, 1930; s. Stephen J. and Rebecca (Welch) B.; m. Eleanor Goode, Jan. 29, 1957; children: Claudia Ann, Elizabeth Burr. Student, Tex. Christian U., 1948-50; BA, U. Tex., 1953, JD, 1958. Bar: Tex. 1958. From assoc. to ptnr. Sawtelle, Hardy, Davis & Goode, San Antonio, 1958-62; gen. counsel San Antonio River Authority, 1963-66, mgr., 1966-68; gen. mgr. Trinity River Authority, Arlington, Tex., 1968-79; exec. officer, bd. dirs. Southland Fin. Corp. and 2 key subs. (Las Colinas Corp., Southland Land & Cattle Co.), 1979-89; exec. v.p., chief devel. officer, gen. counsel Las Colinas, Inc., Irving, Tex., 1989-92; assoc. Hutchison Boyle Brooks & Fisher, 1992; mng. dir. and corp. counsel Faison-Stone Las Colinas, Inc., Irving, 1993-99; sr. v.p., corp. counsel Cousins Stone, Irving, from 1999. Pres.-elect Tex. Water Conservation Assn., Austin, 1978-79; bd. dirs. North Tex. Commn., 1984-88, 91-92; pres., CEO, Dallas County Utility and Reclamation Dist., 1981—; bd. councillors U. Dallas. Decorated knight grand cross Order Holy Sepulchre (Jerusalem); recipient Preservation, Conservation & Utilization award San Antonio Conservation Soc., 1966, Unselfish Svc. award Soil Conservation Soc. Am., 1966, Hon. Membership award, 1971. Mem. ABA, State Bar Tex., Dallas Bar Assn., Greater Dallas C. of C. (bd. dirs. 1980-84), Irving C. of C. (bd. dirs. 1990-94, chmn.-elect 1991-92, chmn. 1992-93), U. Dallas Serra Club (past pres.), Las Colinas Country Club, LaCima Club, Phi Alpha Delta. Roman Catholic. Home: Crowell, Tex. Died Jan. 13, 2007.

BRUNNER, EDOUARD, retired diplomat; b. Istanbul, Turkey, Feb. 24, 1932; BA in Law, U. Geneva. Dep. permanent observer to UN Govt. of Switzerland, 1975—78, sec. state fgn. affairs, 1984—89, amb. to the US Washington, 1989—93; spl. envoy to the Middle East UN, 1991; spl. rep. of UN sec.-gen. UN Observer Mission in Georgia. Died June 24, 2007.

BRUNS, G(ERALD) THOMAS, state representative, pharmacist; b. Kansas City, Mo., Dec. 20, 1931; s. Samuel Frank and Sarah Veronica (Riggs) B.; m. Judith Ann Heavner, Oct. 15, 1968. BS in Pharmacy, U. Mo., Kansas City, 1958. Registered Pharmacist, Kans. Pharmacist, mgr. John S. Watkins, Prairie Village, Kans., 1958-59, Sunset Pharmacy, Kansas City, Kans., 1959-61; pharmacist, owner Bruns Pharmacy, Kansas City, from 1961; state rep. State of Kans., from 1992. Sgt. U.S. Army, 1951-54. Mem. Nat. Assn. Retail Druggists, Kans. Pharm. Assn., Optimists (new bull. writer 1967-68), Leavenworth Rd. Bus. Revitalization (pres. 1987-93). Democrat. Roman Catholic. Avocation: gourmet cooking. Home: Kansas City, Kans. Died Aug. 15, 2006.

BRUNSDALE, ANNE E., federal official; b. Mpls., Oct. 1, 1923; BA, U. Minn., 1945, MA, 1946, Yale U., 1949. With CIA, 1947, 50-56, Craig-Hallum Corp., Mpls., 1957-65, v.p. rsch., 1964-65; assoc. dir. publs. Free Soc. Assn., Washington, 1966-67; rsch. assoc. Am. Enterprise Inst. for Pub. Policy Rsch., Washington, 1967-70, dir. of publs., 1970-77, mng. editor Regulation, 1977-85, resident fellow, 1984-85; apptd. mem. U.S. Internat. Trade Commn., Washington, 1986-93, acting chmn., 1988-89, chmn., 1989-90, acting chmn., 1990-91, vice-chmn., 1990-92. Died Jan. 20, 2006.

BRUSHWOOD, JOHN STUBBS, Latin American literature educator; b. Glenns, Va., Jan. 23, 1920; s. John Benson and Evelyn (Stubbs) B.; m. Carolyn Darrach Norton, May 19, 1945; children: David Benson, Paul Darrach. BA, Randolph-Macon Coll., 1940, Litt.D. (hon.), 1981; MA, U. Va., 1942; PhD, Columbia, 1950. Instr. Romance langs. Va. Poly. Inst., 1942-44; from instr. to prof. Spanish U. Mo. at Columbia, 1946-67; Roy A. Roberts prof. Latin Am. lit. U. Kans., 1967-90, prof. emeritus, from 1990; reviewer Latin Am. books Kansas City Star, 1967-79 and from 86. Fulbright lectr. Colombia, 1974 Author: The Romantic Novel in Mexico, 1954, Breve historia de la novela mexicana, 1959, Mexico in Its Novel, 1966, Spanish edit., 1974, Enrique Gonzalez Martinez, 1969, Los ricos en la prosa mexicana, 1970, The Spanish American Novel: A Twentieth Century Survey, 1975, Genteel Barbarism: New Readings of Nineteenth-Century Latin American Novels, 1981, Spanish edit., 1988, La novela hispanoamericana del siglo xx: una visión panorámica, 1984, La novela mexicana (1967-1982), 1985, Narrative Innovation and Political Change in Mexico, 1989, Una elegancia especial: narrativa mexicana del porfiriato, 1998; also articles.; Translator: (with Carolyn Brushwood) The Precipice (by Sergio Galindo), 1969, Don Goyo (by D. Aguilera-Malta), 1981, Mexican Masquerade (by Sergio Galindo), 1984 Fellow Fund Advancement Edn., 1951-52; grantee Am. Philos. Soc., 1957; grantee Am. Council Learned Socs., 1961; grantee Social Sci. Research Council, 1971; grantee Nat. Endowment for Humanities, 1976; scholar-in-residence Bellagio Study and Conf. Center, 1978, 87; Balfour Jeffrey award for research in the humanities and social scis.; Louise E. Byrd Grad. Educator award, 1986. Mem. MLA, Instituto Internacional de Literatura Iberomericana, Am. Assn. Tchrs. Spanish and Portuguese, Hispanic Soc. Am. (corresponding), Phi Beta Kappa, Sigma Delta Pi, Phi Sigma Iota. Home: Lawrence, Kans. Died May 27, 2007.

BRYAN, COLGAN HOBSON, aerospace engineering educator; b. Trenton, SC, Oct. 7, 1909; s. John William and Mary (Hobson) B.; m. Sara Lucille Turbeville, June 18, 1938 (dec. Nov. 17, 1975); 1 son, Colgan Hobson; m. Carol Lindsay Smelley, July 14, 1979 (dec. Sept. 20, 1993). BS in Elec. Engring, U. S.C., 1932; M.Ed., Duke U., 1940; MS in Aero. Engring, Ga. Inst. Tech., 1948. Registered profl. engr., Ala. Faculty U. Ala., from 1942, prof. aerospace engring., from 1948, chmn. dept., from 1952; research scientist NASA, 1962; on leave with U. Tenn. Space Inst., 1968-69. Cons. to industry, 1941-. Mem. Ala. Aero. Commn., 1944-48. Recipient Charles Henry Ratcliff award for excellence in teaching, 1976, Outstanding Faculty award Delta Tau Delta, 1976, George H. Denny Outstanding Faculty award Sigma Chi, 1976, Disting. Engring. fellow, 2002; established Colgan H. Bryan Aerospace Engring. Scholarship, 1991. Fellow AIAA (assoc.; Disting. Svc. award 1980, Disting. fellow 2002, award for excellence in tchg. 2003); mem. NSPE, ASME, AAUP, NEA, Am. Soc. Engring. Edn., Am. Ordnance Assn., Ala. Soc. Profl. Engrs. (Engr. of Yr. award Tuscaloosa chpt. 1990), Ala. Edn. Assn., Acacia (life), Kiwanis (pres. Tuscaloosa 1966, Service award 1966, Disting. Service award 1977), Pi Tau Chi (faculty adviser). Episcopalian. Achievements include research projects in theoretical and applied aerodynamics, energy (solar and wind). Home: Tuscaloosa, Ala. Died Jan. 4, 2006.

BRYAN, JAMES EDMUND, library consultant; b. Easton, Pa., July 11, 1909; s. William Whitely and Florence (Shimer) B.; m. Helen Elizabeth Lamb, July 2, 1938 (dec. Nov. 21, 1973); children— James Edmund, Arthur Lamb; m. Eunice Ankeney von Ende, May 1, 1976. B.S., Lafayette Coll., 1931; B.L.S., Drexel Inst. Tech., 1932; M.A., Am. U., 1937; Litt. D.(hon.), Rutgers U., 1964. Library asst. Public Library, Washington, 1932-36; librarian Public Library, Easton, 1936-38; head adult lending dept. Carnegie Library of Pitts., 1938-43; asst. dir. Newark Public Library, 1943-58, dir., 1958-72, cons. on library bldgs., 1972—. Contbr. to profl. periodicals. Chmn., Middle Atlantic States Regional Library Conf., 1949; chmn. adv. bd. Grad. Sch. Library Service, Rutgers U. Recipient 70th Anniversary Alumni citation Drexel Inst. Tech., 1961; George Washington Kidd award Lafayette Coll., 1974. Mem. ALA (council, exec. bd. 1961-64, pres. 1962-63), Public Library Assn. (pres. 1959-60), N.J. Library Assn. (pres. 1952- 54), Delta Upsilon, Beta Phi Mu. Democrat. Presbyterian. Club: Kiwanis. Home: Peterborough, NH. Died May 10, 2007.

BRYAN, ORPEN W., education educator; b. Chgo., Mar. 17, 1931; s. Roland and Alberta (Davis) B.; m. Mary L. Washington, Aug. 21, 1967. A.A., Wilson Jr. Coll., 1950; B.Ed., Chgo. Tchrs. Coll., 1952; B.E., Loyola U., Chgo., 1959, M.Ed., 1963; Ed.D., Nova U., 1975. Cert. tchr. and prin., Ill. Elem. tchr., Chgo. Bd. Edn., 1954-61, counselor, asst. prin., 1961-65, prin., 1965-73, dist. supt., 1973-81, dep. supt., 1981-85, asst. supt., 1985-90; adj. prof. Chgo. State U., Roosevelt U., 1991—; former mem. State of Ill. Edn. Adv. Council, 1976-81. Pres. Joint Negro Appeal; bd. dirs. Beatrice Caffrey Youth Services, Inc., Abraham Lincoln Ctr. Served with U.S. Army, 1952-54. Recipient Outstanding Service award State of Ill. Commn. on Delinquency, 1979. Mem. Am. Assn. Sch. Adminstrs., Nat. Assn. Black Sch. Educators, Urban League, NAACP, Am. Legion, Phi Delta Kappa. Methodist. Died Dec. 7, 2006.

BRYAN, RICHARD RAY, retired real estate and construction executive; b. Centerville, Iowa, Apr. 15, 1932; s. Ashley Chester and Celia Mildred (Wright) B.; m. Shirley Erline Wilson, Dec. 17, 1955; children: Scott Douglas, Shari Kay. BS, Tex. A&M U., 1956; MS, Stanford U., 1957; postgrad., Harvard U., 1986. Registered profl. engr., Tex. Project mgr. H.B. Zachry Co., San Antonio, 1957-63, 69-70, v.p., 1985-87, sr. v.p., mem. exec. com., 1987-93, exec. v.p., 1993-99, also bd. dirs., exec. com.; project mgr. Zachary Internat., Lima, Peru, 1964-68; gen. mgr. Trans-Pecos Materials Co., Odessa, Tex., 1968-69; project mgr., v.p. Gerald D. Hines Interests, Houston, 1970-75, sr. v.p., 1979-80; bd. dirs., gen. mgr. Hines Overseas Ltd., Athens, Greece, 1976-78; sr. v.p. Cadillac Fairview, Urban Devel. Inc., Houston, 1981-85. Pres. Meth. Healthcare Ministries of South Tex. Wtih USAF, 1950-52, Korea. Fellow ASCE, former mem. Constrn. Industry Inst. (adv. bd., exec. com., chmn. 1993), Natl. Geographic Soc., Giraud Club, Dominion Country Club. Home: San Antonio, Tex. Died Dec. 8, 2006.

BRYANT, DONALD LOYD, insurance company executive; b. Orchard, Iowa, Jan. 30, 1919; s. Lester E. and Bessie (Farless) B.; m. Eileen Galloway, May 11, 1941; children: Donald Loyd, Hedy E. Bryant Garlock, Brenda K., Becky Bryant Hubert. B.Ed., So. Ill. U., 1940. With War Manpower Commn., Mt. Vernon, Ill., 1940; agt., dist. mgr. Equitable Life Assurance Soc. U.S., Elgin and Carbondale, Ill., 1946-54, agy. mgr. St. Louis, 1954-69, v.p., chief agy. staff ops. NYC, 1969-71, v.p. corp. relations, 1971-72, sr. v.p. corp. relations, 1972-74, exec. v.p., spl. asst. to pres., 1974-78, exec. v.p., 1978-81. Bus exec.-in-residence Tex. Christian U., Ft. Worth, 1980—; cons. Nat. Exec. Services Corp.; bus. exec.-in-residence So. Ill. U. Served to lt. USN, 1942-46. Recipient Alumni Achievement award So. Ill. U., 1964, 88. Mem.: Quail Ridge Golf and Tennis (Boynton Beach, Fla.). Presbyterian. Died May 22, 2007.

BUCHAN, RONALD FORBES, internal and preventive medicine physician; b. Concord, NH, Sept. 24, 1915; s. Robert and Mary Jean (Forbes) B.; m. Maureen O'Regan, June 17, 1940; children: Robert Bruce, Joan Dallas Fleming, Ian Forbes Morgan. AB, U. NH, 1936; MD, CM, McGill U., 1942; postgrad., Princeton U., 1958. Diplomate Nat. Bd. Med. Examiners, Am. Bd. Preventive Medicine. Reporter Concord Daily Monitor, 1936; asst. exec. sec. Unemployment Compensation Commn., NH Dept. Labor, 1937; sanitarian City of Concord and Ea. Health Dist. NH, 1938; chief, med. unit Bur. Indsl. Hygiene, Conn. Dept. Health, 1943-46; dir. Hartford (Conn.) Small Plant Indsl. Med. Svcs., 1946; clin. dir., asst. prof. indsl. medicine Yale U. Inst. Occupl. Medicine and Hygiene, 1946-48; assoc. clin. prof. indsl. medicine NYU Bellevue Postgrad. Med. Sch., 1948-57; assoc. med. dir. Prudential Ins. Co. Am., 1948-49, dir. employee health, 1949-57, med. dir., v.p. med. svcs. Boston, 1957-74, cons. occupl. medicine, environ. medicine, toxicology, from 1974. Chief med. dir., v.p. Mediscreen, 1974-87; propr. Portsmouth (NH) Athenaeum; assoc. clin. prof. preventive medicine Tufts U. Sch. Medicine, 1958-74; vis. lectr. numerous med. schs., 1948-89. Narrator (audio hist. tour) The Freedom Trail, Boston, (audio visual hist. survey) Shipbuilding on the Kennebec-Maine Maritime Mus.; author: Industrial Toxicology; contbr. Oxford Medicine, Current Therapy, Occupl. Medicine, Encyclopedia-Medico-Chirurgicale (Paris); also numerous articles to profl. and lit. jours. Chmn. rsch. adv. com. Brattleboro (Vt.) Retreat, 1960-70; mem. sci. adv. bd. Office Chief Staff USAF, chmn. life scis. human factors facilities, 1960-65, protocol rank, lt. gen.; cons. RI Group Health Assn., 1973-75, Harvard Cmty. Health Plan, 1972-75; bd. dirs. Met. Boston chpt. ARC, 1971-73, chmn. com. on safety, 1972-74; founding mem. Challenger Space Ctr., 1987; trustee Miles Meml. Hosp., Damariscotta, Maine, 1988-91. Sr. asst. surg., USPHS, 1943-46; surgeon-lt. York (Maine) Militia-Gov.'s Footguard, 1971—. Recipient Honor award Wisdom Soc., 1970. Fellow Am. Coll. Occupl. and Environ. Medicine (past pres.), Am. Coll. Preventive Medicine (chmn. com. on clin. procedures 1972-74), Am. Acad. Occupl. Medicine (past pres.), Acad. Medicine NJ (past pres.); mem. AAAS, Am. Indsl. Hygiene Assn., Am. Acad. Ins. Medicine, AMA (assoc. editor Archives Environ. Health), Assn. Internationale Pour La Medicine Du Travail (permanent commn. 1965-74), Mass. Med. Soc., Ramazzini Soc., Academie Europeene des Arts, Sciences et des Lettres, Am. Assn. Sr. Physicians, NY Acad. Scis., Nat. Trust Hist. Preservation, Soc. for Preservation of New Eng. Antiquities, John Buchan Soc. (Edinburgh), Osler Libr. (patron McGill U., Montreal), Soc. for Protection of NH Forests, North Country Authors and Scientists League (past pres.), Newcomen Soc. N.Am., St. Andrew's Soc. of Maine, Can. Hist. Soc., NH Hist. Soc., Clan Buchan U.S.A., Clan Forbes U.S.A., U. NH Alumni Assn. (gen. awards com. 1987-90, sec. U. NH class of '36, 1981—, pres.'s coun. 2000—), McGill U. Alumni Assn., Friends of Bowdoin Coll., Friends of Mt. Holyoke Coll., Friends of Middlebury Coll., Strawberry Bank Mus. (patron), Black Heritage Tr. Portsmouth, NH (patron). Home: Manchester, NH. Died Jan. 2007.

BUCHANAN, GEORGE FRANCIS, retired book wholesaling company executive; b. Phila., Sept. 21, 1924; s. Charles Joseph and Mary Veronica (White) B.; m. Patricia Rose Earley, Apr. 3, 1948; children— Geraldine, James, Mary, George, Hugh, Brian, Matthew, Regina, Michael, David. BS, St. Joseph's U., 1950; MA, Temple U., 1952. Instr. indsl. psychology St. Joseph's U., 1950-52; with RCA, Cherry Hill, N.J., 1952-68; v.p. distbn. Random House, Inc., Md., 1968-75; exec. v.p. Baker & Taylor Co., NYC, 1975-86; pres. Blackwell N.Am., Inc., Blackwood, N.J., 1987-92, ret., 1992. Served with U.S. Army, 1943-46. Mem. Systems & Procedures Assn., Am. Mgmt. Assn. Home: Mount Laurel, NJ. Died June 23, 2006.

BUCHMANN, ALAN PAUL, lawyer; b. Yonkers, NY, Sept. 5, 1934; s. Paul John and Jessie Gow (Perkins) B.; m. Lizabeth Ann Moody, Sept. 5, 1959. BA summa cum laude, Yale U., 1956; postgrad, U. Munich, 1956-57; LLB, Yale U., 1960. Bar: Ohio 1960, U.S. Dist. Ct. (no. dist.) Ohio 1963, U.S. Ct. Appeals (6th cir.) 1968, U.S. Supreme Ct. 1977, Fla. 1996. Assoc. Squire, Sanders & Dempsey, Cleve., 1960-70, ptnr., 1970-96; pvt. practice St. Petersburg, Fla. Contbr. articles to profl. jours. State chmn. Ohio Young reps., 1970-71, nat. committeeman, 1971-74; exec. com. Cuyahoga County Reps., 1969-95, fin. com., 1987-94; mem. Selective svc. Bd., 1967-75; trustee Cleve. Internat. Program, 1979-82, 94-95; pres. English Speaking Union, 1981-83. Recipient Robert A. Taft award Young Reps., 1969, Outstanding State Chmn. award, 1971, James A. Rhodes award, 1974; Fulbright fellow U. Munich, 1956-57. Mem. ABA (chmn. pub. utility law sect. 1989-90, sect. del. 1996-2005, coord. com. on legal edn. 1991-97, nominating com. 2003-05, mem. credentials com. 2004-05), Fla. Bar Assn., Ohio State Bar Assn., St. Petersburg Bar Assn., Hillsborough County Bar Assn. Home: St Pete Beach, Fla. Died Sept. 25, 2005.

BUCHOLZ, KURT S., state representative; b. Omaha, Nov. 5, 1950; m. Laura Bucholz; children: Bessie, John. BA, Colo. Coll., 1979; DVM, Colo. State U., 1979. Veterinarian Lexington

Animal Clinic, 1979—82; pres. XH Land and Cattle Co., Saratoga, Wyo., from 1982; state rep. dist. 47 Wyo. Ho. of Reps., Cheyenne, from 2002. Pres. Corbeti Med. Found., from 1995, Platte River Basin Agrl. Alliance, from 1997; treas. Highline Watershed Improvement Dist., from 1999; vice chair Carbon County Sch. Dist. # 2, from 1996; bd. dirs. Old Baldy Corp., from 2001. Mem.: Wyo. Stockgrowers Assn., Upper North Platte Water Users Assn. (pres. 1990—2002). Republican. Died Dec. 5, 2006.

BUCK, ROBERT REINHART, lawyer; b. Oklahoma City, Dec. 29, 1928; s. Arthur M. and Margaret A. (Rinehart) B.; m. Anne S. Scharlach, July 29, 1957; children— Carol, Alison, Monica, Leslie; m. 2d, Betty R. Cain, Dec. 27, 1978. B.S., Okla. State U., Stillwater, 1951; LL.D., U. Okla., 1956. Bar: U.S. Dist. Ct. (we. dist.) Okla. 1958, U.S. Supreme Ct. 1975. With Buck & Crabtree, Oklahoma City; to 1979; ptnr. Buck & Hoyt, Ltd., Oklahoma City, 1979—; lectr. U. Okla. Law Sch., Oklahoma City U., Law Sch., Tulsa U. Law Sch., Law Sci. Inst., Okla. Trial Lawyers, Okla. Hwy. Safety Office. Former dir. Urban League of Oklahoma City; leader Boy Scouts Am.; family life dir. diocese, Roman Catholic Ch.; Served to capt. USAF, 1951-63. Mem. ABA, Oklahoma Bar Assn., Oklahoma County Bar Assn., Assn. Trial Lawyers Am. (former state del.), Okla. Trial Lawyers Assn. (v.p. 1972, pres. elect 1973, pres. 1984). Democrat. Roman Catholic. Died May 30, 2006.

BUDKE, CHARLES HENRY, secondary school educator; b. Beloit, Kans., Nov. 17, 1924; s. William Joseph and Margaret Helen (Koster) B.; m. Cecilia Ann Meyer, May 27, 1952; children: Marilyn, Luci, Carl, Earl, Robert, Barb, Diane, Dennis, Nancy, Mary, Charlene, Chuck, Cecilia Terese. BA, Benedictine Coll., Atchison, Kans., 1954; MS, Fort Hayes State U., Kans., 1965, postgrad., 1970. Cert. tchr. history, adminstr. Tchr. history St. John's High Sch., Beloit, 1954-56; tchr. English Esbon (Kans.) High Sch., 1956-59; tchr. social studies Damar (Kans.) High Sch., 1959-63; tchr. Thomas More Prep-Marian, Hays, Kans., 1963-91, chmn. dept. social studies, 1981-91. Mem. acad. coun., 1981-91. Contbr. articles to profl. jours. Pres. PTA, Hays, 1965; Spl. Olympics Kans. State Basketball Tourney, 1980—. Named to Kans. Tchrs. Hall of Fame, 1991. Mem. KC (Grand Knight 1982-84, Knight of Yr. Coun. 1325 1985, dist. dep. 1984-88, state retention chmn. 1995), Toastmasters (pres. 1969), High Plains Barbershop Chorus (chmn. logopedics 1978—, Dist. awards 1978—). Roman Catholic. Avocations: writing, counseling, golf, walking, reading. Home: Hays, Kans. Died Sept. 14, 2006.

BUERKLE, RICHARD LOUIS, commercial real estate executive; b. Jonesboro, Ark., Jan. 11, 1947; s. Bill and Marvine (Matthews) B.; B.B.A., Ark. State U., 1971; M.B.A. with honors, So. Meth. U., 1972; m. Lena Ann Weston, Aug. 14, 1971; children— Richard Louis II, Ryan Lee. Comml. loan officer Glenn Justice Mortgage Co., Dallas, 1971-72, Equitable Life Assurance Soc. U.S., Dallas, 1972-73; v.p. s.w. div. Alpert Investment Corp., Dallas, 1973-76; chmn. bd., pres. Buerkle Investment Corp., Arlington, Tex., 1976—; guest lectr. numerous real estate seminars, univ. classes, banquets; dir. Real Estate Today TV series; expert witness before cts. and city govts. Exec. com. bus. adv. council U. Tex., Arlington, 1978-82; dir. Women's Haven of Arlington; bd. deacons 1st Bapt. Ch. of Arlington; Ark. state chief Order of Arrow, Boy Scouts Am., 1966, mem. Eagle Scout, Vigil. Served with USMC, 1966-68; Vietnam. Lic. real estate broker, Tex. Mem. Internat. Council Shopping Centers, Dallas and Ft. Worth Apt. Assn., Beta Gamma Sigma. Republican. Home: Arlington, Tex. Died Dec. 4, 2006.

BUFFINGTON, LOUIS DELL, communications executive; b. Jan. 15, 1928; s. John F. and Ellen M. (Watson) Buffington. BA, Iowa State U., 1950. V.p. corp. comm. Minnegasco Inc., Mpls., from 1981. Bd. dirs. Mpls. Aquatennial, Mpls., 1984, Minn. Dance Theatre, 1984, St. Paul Chamber Orch., 1984. Mem.: Am. Gas Assn. (comm. com. from 1982), Mpls. Athletic Club. Died Oct. 23, 2006.

BUJAKE, JOHN EDWARD, JR., beverage company executive; b. NYC, May 23, 1933; s. John E. and Mary (Muzyka) B.; m. Gail E. Cruise, Aug. 1, 1964; children: John Edward III, Laura, Jacquelyn, William. BS, Manhattan Coll., 1954; MS, Holy Cross Coll., 1955; PhD, Columbia U., 1959; MBA, NYU, 1963. Rsch. assoc. Lever Bros., Edgewater, N.J., 1959-68; dir. R & D Foods div. Coca Cola Co., Houston, 1968-72; dir. foods R&D, Quaker Oats Co., Barrington, Ill., 1972-77, dir. R&D, 1977-78; v.p. R&D, Seven Up Co., St. Louis, 1978-87; v.p. R&D Brown-Forman Beverage Co., Louisville, 1987-98; cons., from 1998. Indsl. adv. bd. Speed Sch., U. Louisville. Mem. editl. bd. Research Mgmt, 1976-77, 97-98; contbr. articles to profl. jours. Mem. Indsl. Rsch. Inst., Am. Chem. Soc., Inst. Food Technologists, Internat. Life Scis. Inst., Calorie Control Coun. Died Apr. 28, 2006.

BULLA, CLYDE ROBERT, writer; b. King City, Mo., Jan. 9, 1914; s. Julian W. and Sarah Ann (Henson) B. Columnist Tri-County News, King City, Mo., 1942-47. Author 70 books for young people, White Bird, 1966, Shoeshine Girl, 1975, A Lion to Guard Us, 1981, A Place for Angels, 1995, The Paint Brush Kid, 1999, A Grain of Wheat, 2005. Recipient Commonwealth Children's Book award Commonwealth Club, Calif., 1970; recipient Christopher award The Christophers, 1972, Sequoyah Book award Okla. Sch. Children, 1978, Charlie May Simon award Ark. Sch. Children, 1976, book award S.C. Sch. Children, 1980, Focal award L.A. Pub. Libr., 1991. Mem. Soc. Children's Book Writers, Authors Guild Home: Warrensburg, Mo. Died May 23, 2007.

BULLOCK, J(IMMIE) BRUCE, agricultural economics educator, researcher; b. Lindsay, Okla., June 23, 1940; s. Roland E. and Lois E. (McKinzie) B.; m. B. Louise Adams, May 24, 1959; children: Athena, Angela, Roland. BS, Okla. State U., 1962, MS, 1964; PhD, U. Calif., Berkeley, 1968. Economist econ. research service USDA, Washington, 1964-68; asst. prof. N.C. State U., Raleigh, 1969-74, assoc. prof., 1974-76; research mgr. Farmbank Services, Denver, 1976-79; assoc. prof. Okla. State U., Stillwater, 1980-81; prof., dept. chair U. Mo., Columbia, 1982-88, assc. dean Coll. Agr., assoc. dir. Mo. Agrl. Expt. Sta., from 1988. Contbr. numerous articles to research jours. Mem. Am. Agrl. Econs. Assn., So. Agrl. Econs. Assn., Western Agrl. Econs. Assn. Home: Columbia, Mo. Died May 10, 2006.

BURCHFIELD, HARRY PHINEAS, JR., retired biochemistry consultant, science writer; b. Pitts., Dec. 22, 1915; s. Harry Phineas and Florence Faye (Fearl) B.; m. Eleanor Emerett Storrs, Nov. 29, 1963; children: Sarah Storrs, Benjamin Hyde. AB, MA, Columbia U., 1938, PhD, 1956. Chemist, Nat. Oil Products Co., Harrison, N.J., 1938-40; research scientist Uniroyal Corp., Naugatuck, Conn., 1940-50, dir. plantations research dept. Indonesia and Malaysia, 1951-52; asso. dir. Boyce Thompson Inst. Plant Research, Yonkers, N.Y., 1952-61; inst. scientist, mgr. S.W. Research Inst., San Antonio, 1961-65; chief pesticides research lab. USPHS, Perrine, Fla., 1965-67; sci. dir. Gulf South Research Inst., New Iberia, La., 1967-76; adj. prof. chemistry U. Southwestern La., 1967-77; prof. chemistry, head div. molecular biology Med. Research Inst., Fla. Inst. Tech., Melbourne, 1977-81; charter mem. Soc. Univ. Fellows, 1978, ret. Prin. scientist Research Assos., 1976—; trustee Gulf Univs. Research Consortium, 1971-76; mem. carcinogenesis panel of secs. HEW Commn. on Pesticides, 1969; mem. nat. tech. adv. com. pesticides EPA, 1971-72, project reviewer research grants, 1972; cons. carcinogensis Nat. Cancer Inst., 1965-67; cons. leprosy Pan Am. Health Orgn., WHO, 1974, EPA, 1976— Author: (with Eleanor E. Storrs) Biochemical Applications of Gas Chromatography, 1962, (with D.E. Johnson and Eleanor Storrs) Guide to the Analysis of Pesticide Residues, 1965; contbr. chpts. to books, articles to profl. jours., crossword puzzles to books. Recipient award Chgo. Rubber Group, 1946; EPA grantee, 1969-76; Nat. Inst. Environ. Health Scis. grantee, 1977— Mem. Am. Chem. Soc. (lecture tour speaker 1972-77), Soc. Toxicology, Am. Inst. Biol. Scis., AAAS. Episcopalian. Died July 12, 2006.

BURDETTE, WALTER JAMES, surgeon, educator; b. Hillsboro, Tex., Feb. 5, 1915; s. James S. and Ovazene (Weatherred) B.; m. Kathryn Lynch, Apr. 9, 1947; children: Susan, William J. AB, Baylor U., 1935; A.M., U. Tex., 1936, PhD, 1938; MD, Yale, 1942. Diplomate: Am. Bd. Surgery, Am. Bd. Thoracic and Cardiovascular Surgery. Intern Johns Hopkins Hosp., 1942-43; Harvey Cushing fellow surgery Yale, 1943-44; resident staff surgery New Haven Hosp., 1944-46; instr., asst., assoc. prof. surgery La. State U., 1946-55; vis. surgeon Charity Hosp. of La., 1946-55; cons. Touro Infirmary and So. Baptist Hosp., 1952-55, Oak Ridge Inst. Nuclear Studies Hosp., 1953-59; vis. investigator Chester Beatty Inst. Cancer Research, Brompton, and Royal Cancer Hosp., London, 1953, Max Planck Institut Fuer Biochemie, Tuebingen, Germany, summer 1955; prof., chmn. dept. surgery U. Mo., 1955-56; prof. clin. surgery St. Louis U. Sch. Medicine, 1956-57; prof., head dept. surgery U. Utah, 1957-65; dir. lab. clin. biology, surgeon-in-chief Salt Lake Gen. Hosp., 1957-65; chief surg. cons. VA Hosps., Salt Lake City, 1957-65; prof. surgery, assoc. dir. U. Tex-M.D. Anderson Hosp. and Tumor Inst., Houston, 1965-72; prof. surgery U. Tex. Sch. Medicine at Houston, 1971-79; adj. prof. pharmacology U. Houston, from 1975. Chief surgery Univ.Hosp., U. Mo., 1955-56, St. Louis U. Svc., John Cochran VA Hosp., 1956-57; chief thoracic and cardiovascular surgery Park Pla. Hosp., 1990—; pres. Nat. Biomed. Found., 1972—; cons. St. Luke's Hosp., 1975—, Park Plaza Hosp., 1976—, Meth. Hosp., 1976—; Gibson lectr. advanced surgery Oxford U., 1966; vis. prof. U. Oxford, spring 1965; ofcl. U. Congo, summer 1968 Editor, author: Etiology, Treatment of Leukemia, 1958, Methodology in Human Genetics, 1962, Methodology in Mammalian Genetics, 1962, Methodology in Basic Genetics, 1963, Primary Hepatoma, 1965, Carcinoma of the Alimentary Tract, 1965, Viruses Inducing Cancer, 1966, Carcinoma of the Colon and Antecedent Epithelium, 1970, Planning and Analysis of Clinical Studies, 1970, Invertebrate Endocrinology and Hormonal Heterophylly, 1974, Cancer: Etiology, Diagnosis and Treatment, 1997; editl. bd. Surg. Rounds, Yale Jour. Biology and Medicine, Cancer Rsch.; contbr. over 200 articles to med. and sci. jours. Chmn. genetics study sect., mem. morphology study sect. NIH; cons. Nat. Cancer Inst.; mem. Nat. Adv. Cancer Council, Nat. Adv. Heart Council, Surgeon General's Com. on Smoking and Health; chmn. U.S.A. nat. com. Internat. Union Against Cancer; mem. transplantation com. Nat. Acad. Scis.; chmn. working Cadre on cancer large intestine Nat. Cancer Inst.; deacon, elder Christian Ch. Rockefeller travel fellow USSR and Ea. Europe, summer 1957; Disting. Grad., Yale U. Fellow ACS; mem. AAAS, Soc. Surgery Alimentary Tract, Am. Assn. Cancer Research (dir., v.p.), Am. Cancer Soc. (chmn. research adv. council, mem. council on analysis and projection), Am. Surg. Assn., Soc. Clin. Surgery (treas.), Soc. U. Surgeons, Soc. Exptl. Biology and Medicine, Genetics Soc. Am., Utah Genetics Soc. (pres.), Western Soc. Clin. Research, Am. Assn. Thoracic Surgery, Transplantation Soc., N.Y. Acad. Sci., Soc. Am. Naturalists, New Orleans, St. Louis, Salt Lake City, Houston surg. socs., Tex. Med. Soc., Harris County Med. Soc., So., Western surg. assns., So. Thoracic Surg. Soc., Peruvian Cancer Soc. (hon.), Am. Soc. Clin. Oncology, Am. Soc. for Cancer Edn., Tex. Surg. Soc., Assn. Yale Alumni in Medicine (exec. com. 1977), Soc. Internat. de Chirurg, Am. Guild Organists, Yale Club of Houston (pres. 1989-91), Phi Beta Kappa, Sigma Xi, Alpha Omega Alpha Home: Houston, Tex. Died Apr. 18, 2006.

BURDITT, JOHN FREDERIC, retired manufacturing executive; b. Newton, Mass., Apr. 4, 1918; s. Frederic Macgregor and Florence Lovejoy (Willey) B.; student Buckingham Browne and Nichols Sch., Cambridge, Mass.; B.A., Yale U., 1940; D.Sc. in Bus. Adminstrn. (hon.), Clarkson U., 1978; m. Jane Spaulding Nye, Sept. 6, 1947; children— Faraday Nye Burditt de la Camara, Frederic Macgregor, John Carver, Timothy Nye, Benjamin Ames. With Chem. Bank & Trust Co., N.Y.C., 1945-48; with ACF Industries, Inc., N.Y.C., 1948-83, asst. treas., 1948-52, treas., 1952-63, v.p., 1963-65, exec. v.p., 1965-67, chmn. bd., chief exec. officer, 1967-83; trustee Dorset Theatre Festival. Lt. comdr. USNR, 1941-46. Mem. Elwanok C. of C., Yale Club (N.Y.C.), Dorset Field Club (Vt.) Home: Manchester Center, Vt. Died May 24, 2007.

BURGERT, THEODORE PHILIP, public relations executive; b. Bklyn., Aug. 16, 1931; s. Philip Theodore and Margaret (Bullock) B.; student Bklyn. Coll., 1949-51; m. Patricia Helen Hollahan, Feb. 4, 1956; children— Stephen, Theodore J., Kenneth. With The Eastern Underwriter, 1949-51, Bill Communications Publs., 1956-60; with Borden, Inc., N.Y.C., 1960-70; v.p. Hill & Knowlton, N.Y.C., 1970-75; account supr. Burson-Marsteller, N.Y.C., 1975-79; exec. v.p. Holder Kennedy & Co., N.Y.C., 1979-84; pres Theodore Burgert Assocs., Old Bridge, N.J., 1985-97. Served with USAF, 1951-55. Home: Beverly Hills, Fla. Died Mar. 1, 2006.

BURGESS, JOHN FRANK, retired utilities executive; b. Lanett, Ala., Nov. 18, 1917; s. John Frank and Mary Catherine (Heard) B.; m. Helen Hamby, Aug. 26, 1939; children: Beverly, Barbara, Frank. BS, Auburn U.; MA, George Washington U. Commd. 2d lt. U.S. Army, 1941, advanced through grades to col., ret., 1969; regional v.p. Consol. Edison Co. of N.Y., Inc., NYC, 1969-83; cons. mgmt. Melville, NY, 1983-85; assoc. cons. Power Mgmt. Assocs., Inc., Groton, Conn., 1985-87; Columbia, Md., 1985-89. Active bds. various civic and profl. orgns., Queens, N.Y., 1969-83. Decorated Legion of Merit with 2 oak leaf clusters; named Man of Yr. Queens County Bldg and Contractors Assn., 1977 Episcopalian. Home: Roswell, Ga. Died June 19, 2007.

BURGESS, LLOYD ALBERT, construction company executive; b. Culver, Oreg., Oct. 4, 1917; s. Estell Elmer and Arrista (Ditterline) B.; m. Wanda Marie Gregory, Dec. 18, 1955; children— Gregory Scott, Elizabeth Anne, Jeffrey Lloyd; 1 son by previous marriage, Jason M. B.C.E., Oreg. State U., 1939. Engr. C.E., Portland, Oreg., 1939-40, 41; engr. Douglas Aircraft Co., 1940-41, Tidewater Asso. Oil Co., 1941-42; pres. Burgess Constrn. Co., Fairbanks, Alaska, 1946-69, Spruce Equipment, Inc., Fairbanks, 1955-64, Grove Inc., Fairbanks, 1955-64, Alaska Freight Lines, 1959-60, Burgess Internat. Inc., Seattle; chmn. Burgess Intercontinental, Inc., 1969-72, Burgess Overseas Sales Corp., Burgess Interstate, from 1972. Dir. Alaska Title & Guarantee Co., Canon— Holosonics, Tokyo, Holosonics, Richland, Wash., Earth Resources Co., Dallas, Simasko Prodn. Co., Denver, Pacific Alaska Airlines, Fairbanks. Chmn. Alaska Rep. Fin. Com., 1958-62; del. Rep. Nat. Conv., 1968, mem. nat. platform com., 1968; mem. Nat. Rep. Com. from Alaska, 1964-69. Served to lt. comdr. USNR, 1942-46, PTO. Mem. Asso. Gen. Contractors (pres. Alaska 1960) Home: Mercer Island, Wash. Died Mar. 3, 2006.

BURGIN, E. J., natural gas pipeline company executive; b. White Pine, Tenn., Sept. 27, 1927; s. Martin Lee and Virginia (Bailey) B.; m. Barbara Jean Inman, Dec. 28, 1971; 1 dau., Stacey Jean. BSM.E., U. Tenn., 1955; postrad., Stanford U., 1981. V.p. So. Ga. Natural Gas Co., Thomasville, 1955-58; gen. supt. ops. Fla. Gas Transmission Co., Winter Park, 1959-73, v.p. ops., 1974-77, v.p. mktg., 1978-81, exec. v.p., 1981-85, dir., from 1979; pres., corp. engring Enron Pipeline Services, Houston, 1986-87; pres. and chief ops. officer Enron Gas Pipeline Operating Co., from 1987. Served to capt. U.S. Army, 1951-59. Mem. Am. Gas Assn. (award of merit 1975), So. Gas Assn., Fla. Natural Gas Assn. (dir., pres. 1987), Inst. Gas Tech. (dir.), Rolling Hills Country Club (pres. 1979-81), Mason. Republican. Died Dec. 3, 2006.

BURKE, JOHN, science technology company executive; b. LA, Oct. 14, 1947; s. Robert J. and Virginia Lee (Albany) B.; m. Myriah Lennox, May 25, 1990. BS in Engring., UCLA, 1969, MS in Engring., 1973; postgrad., Calif. State U., San Diego, 1974-78. Sect. mgr. Logicon, Inc., San Pedro, Calif., 1970-73 program mgr. Sci. Applications Inc., La Jolla, Calif., 1973-75; div. mgr. SAI Comsystems Corp., San Diego, 1975-77, v.p., 1977-81, Sci. Applications Internat. Corp., San Diego, 1981-87 corp. v.p., 1987-88, group sr. v.p., 1988-89, sector v.p., 1989-90; pres. SAIC Tech. Svcs. Co., San Diego, 1990-92, sector v.p., from 1992. Democrat. Avocations: travel, wine collecting Home: La Jolla, Calif. Died July 22, 2006.

BURKE, RICHARD KITCHENS, lawyer, educator; b. Helena, Ark., Aug. 21, 1922; s. James Graham and Myrtie May (Kitchens) B.; m. Bonnie Beth Byler, Jan. 21, 1946; children: Charles, Bonnie Louise. Student, U. Va., 1939-40; BA, U. Ark. 1942, LLB, 1947; PhD, Vanderbilt U., 1957. Bar: Ark. 1947 Ariz. 1959, S.D. 1974. Ptnr. Burke, Moore & Burke, Helena 1947-52; asst. prof. polit. sci. U. Ariz., 1957-60; ptnr. Robertson Childers, Burke & Drachman, Tucson, 1960-67; prof. polit. sci U. Southwestern La., 1967-69; U.S. atty. Dist. Ariz., Dept. Justice, 1969-72; dep. asst. atty. gen. U.S. Dept. Justice, Washington, 1972-73; prof. law U. S.D. Sch. Law, 1973-84, dean 1974-80; prof. law U. Ark., 1984-86, prof. emeritus, from 1986 Mem. Ariz. Rep. State Com., 1963-67; Rep. congl. candidate So Dist. Ariz., 1962; chmn. citizen's adv. com. Ampitheater Sch Dist., Tucson, 1964-66. With USN, 1942-45, 53-54. Decorated Air medal; Ford fellow Vanderbilt U., 1957. Mem. Am. Bar Assn., State Bar S.D., State Bar Ariz., Ark. Bar Assn. Republican. Mem. Christian Ch. Home: Cherokee Village, Ark. Died June 12, 2007.

BURLESON, CLAUDE ALFRED, communications company executive; b. Danville, Ill., July 21, 1924; s. Claude Harold and Grace Alma (Carter) B.; m. Norma J. Zitani, Feb. 6, 1946 children: Ronald, Susan, Neil. BS, Rutgers U., 1950; MBA, U N.Y., 1957. Asst. tax mgr. St. Regis Paper Co., NYC, 1950-55 asst. treas. Merritt-Chapman & Scott, NYC, 1955-61; asst controller taxes GTE Corp., NYC, 1961-76, v.p. taxes Stamford Conn., 1976—. Dir. GTE Reins. Co., Ltd.; chmn. The Bus Roundtable Taxation Coordinating Com., 1979-84; mem. adv bd. Tax Mgmt. Inc. Bd. dirs. Musician Emergency Fund 1983—, Inst. for Research on Econs. of Taxation. Mem. Nat Assn. Mfrs. (taxation com.), Tax Exec. Inst., Nat. Tax Assn., Tax Inst. Am., Internat. Assn. Assessing Officers, U.S. Telephone Assn. (taxation com.), Wash. State Research Council, Stamford Tax Assn. (pres., founder) Clubs: Stamford Yacht. Home: Boca Raton, Fla. Died Oct. 13, 2005.

BURLESON, IRA LEE, insurance company executive, director; b. Athens, Ala., June 6, 1920; s. Luther A. and Marie (Witt) B.; m. Anna Kate Givens, Sept. 7, 1948 (dec. 1982). BS, Florence State Coll., Ala., 1940; postgrad., U. Ala., 1941; LL.B., U. Va., 1948. Bar: Ala. 1948. Of counsel Spain, Gillon, Grooms & Young, Birmingham, 1948-50 and from 86; with Liberty Nat. Life Ins. Co., Birmingham, from 1950, v.p., 1967-73, sec., gen. counsel, from 1967, sr. v.p., from 1973, also sec. to bd. dirs., dir., now vice-chmn. bd., gen. counsel. Sec., dir. Brown Service Funeral Homes Co., Inc., 1960—, Liberty Nat. Fire Ins. Co., 1971—; vice chmn. bd., gen. counsel Torchmark Corp., 1979—; dir. Globe Life Ins. Co., United Am. Ins. Co., Am. Life & Accident Ins. Co. Contbr. articles to legal jours. Trustee Birmingham-So. Coll., 1979; bd. dirs. Assoc. Industries Ala., United Funds Inc. Served to comdr. USNR, 1942-46, PTO. Mem. ABA (vice chmn. com. life ins. law), Ala. Bar Assn. (vice chmn. sect. corp. law), Assn. Life Ins. Counsel (pres. 1980), Am. Soc. Corp. Secs., Am. Life Ins. Assn. (chmn. legal sect. 1973), Am. Council Life Ins., U.S. C. of C. (antitrust council), Ala. C. of C. (dir.) Methodist (chmn. ofcl. bd. 1964-66). Clubs: The Club, Shoal Creek Country, Country of Birmingham (Birmingham). Lodge: Kiwanis. Home: Birmingham, Ala. Died Aug. 13, 2006.

BURNELL, BATES CAVANAUGH, engineering and construction company executive; b. Portland, Oreg., Aug. 15, 1923; s. Ray Lawrence and Beatrice (McIndoe) B.; m. Shirley Eugenia Banks, Sept. 1, 1945; children: Bates C. Jr., Michael L. (dec.), Barbara B., Stuart M. BS, U.S. Mil. Acad., 1945; MS, MIT, 1949. Registered profl. engr., Wis. Commd. 2d lt. U.S. Army, 1945, advanced through grades to maj. gen., 1971, ret., 1979, dep. dir. spl. studies, 1966-68; troop command engr. C.E. U.S. Army, 1968-69; div. engring. Huntsville, 1969-73; comdr. BMDSCOM U.S. Army, Huntsville, 1973-75; dir. mil. constrn. C.E. U.S. Army, Washington, 1975-77, asst. dep. chief staff logistics, 1977-78, dep. chief engrs., 1978-79; v.p. Morrison-Knudsen Co. Inc., Boise, Idaho, 1979-84; chmn., mng. dir. Morrison-Knudsen Internat. Co., Boise, 1984-88, ret.; sr. assoc. Lemley & Assocs., Boise, from 1989. Contbr. articles to profl. jours. Decorated D.S.M., Legion of Merit with two oak leaf clusters, Bronze Star with two oak leaf clusters, others. Fellow ASCE, Soc. Am. Mil. Engrs.; mem. Am. Underground Space Assn. (bd. dirs.), Sigma Xi (assoc.). Clubs: Hillcrest Country, Arid. Lodges: Moles, Beavers. Republican. Episcopalian. Avocations: skiing, golf. Home: Boise, Idaho. Died Apr. 5, 2007.

BURNHAM, WILLIAM A., wildlife conservation organization executive; b. Pueblo, Colo., Oct. 5, 1947; s. William H. and Bertha (Nemier) B.; m. Patricia Ann Wood, July 9, 1966; 1 child, Kurt Kristopher. BS, U. So. Colo., 1973; MS, Brigham Young U., 1975; PhD, Colo. State U., 1984. Tech. assoc. Cornell U., Colo. and Idaho, 1974-88; dir. World Ctr. for Birds of Prey, Boise, Idaho, from 1984; pres., CEO The Peregrine Fund, Boise, Idaho, from 1986. Adj. faculty Boise State U., 1986—, trustee, 1985—; bd. dirs. Philippine Eagle Found. and Raptor Breeders Assn.; bd. advisors Disney's Animal Kingdom. Contbr. articles to profl. jours. Mem. Cooper Ornithological Soc., Am. Ornighologists' Union, Wilson Ornithological Soc., Raptor Research Found., Arctic Inst. of N. Am., The Ottawa Field-Naturalists' Club, The Wildlife Soc., Sigma Xi. Avocations: fly fishing, falconry, diving. Home: Boise, Idaho. Died Oct. 16, 2006.

BURNIM, KALMAN AARON, retired theater educator; b. Malden, Mass., Mar. 7, 1928; s. Jack K. and Sadie (Levy) B.; m. Verna Ruth Lesser, June 6, 1928; children: Ira, Judith, Esther Burnim Ouray. BA in Drama magna cum laude, Tufts U., 1950; MA in Theater, Ind. U., 1951; PhD, Yale U., 1958. Mng. exec. New England Adding Machine Co., Boston, 1951-55; asst. prof. Valparaiso (Ind.) U., 1958-59, U. Pitts., 1959-60, Tufts U., Medford, Mass., 1960-61, assoc. prof., dir. theater, 1961-65, prof. drama, 1965, chmn. dept. drama, exec. dir. theater, 1966-75, Fletcher prof. oratory and drama, 1971-87, emeritus prof., from 1987. Rsch. prof. English George Washington U., Washington, 1975-76, 85-86; mem. nat. screening com. for theater Fulbright Commn., Washington, 1985-89; mem. exec. com. Internat. Fedn. for Theatre Rsch., 1979-83, 91-95; cons. Folger Shakespeare Libr., 2002-05; panelist, del. various confs. Author: David Garrick, Director, 1961; co-author: (with William Appleton) The Prompter, An Eighteenth Century Theatrical Paper, 1966, The Biographical Dictionary of Actors, Actresses, Dancers, Managers, and Other Stage Personnel in London Stage, 1660-1800, 16 vols., 1973-93, (George Freedley Meml. award Theatre Library Assn. 1979, 94), Pictures in the Garrick Club. A Catalogue, 1997, (with P.H. Highfill Jr.) John Bell, Patron of Theatrical Portraiture, 1998, (with Andrew Wilton) The Richard Bebb Collection in the Garrick Club, 2001; editor: The Letters of Sarah and William Siddons to Hester Lynch Thrale Piozzi, 1969, The Complete Plays of George Colman the Elder, 6 vols., 1983, (with John Baskett) Brief Lives, Sitters and Artists in the Portraits in the Garrick Club, 2003; assoc. editor Ednl. Theatre Jour., 1968-70; contbr. articles to profl. jours. Guggenheim fellow, 1964-65, Folger Library fellow, 1957-58, 69, 71; Sterling fellow Yale U., 1957-58; Am. Council for Learned Socs. grantee, 1966, 71; NEH grantee, 1967-68, 70, 74-76, 85-86; Tufts faculty research grantee, 1960-81. Mem. Am. Soc. for Theatre Rsch. (pres. 1985-91, mem. exec. com. 1960-63, 64-69, 72-75, 83-86, program chmn. 1963-65, 76, chmn. publs. com. 1975-76, 79-82, del. to Am. Coun. Learned Socs. 1976-82, spl. citation 1994), Brit. Soc. for Theatre Rsch., Am. Soc. for Eighteenth-Century Studies, IREX (chmn. commn. on Am.-Soviet theatre exchs. 1988-91), Coll. Fellows Am. Theatre, Phi Beta Kappa (pres. Tufts chpt. 1983-85), Garrick Club. Died July 10, 2006.

BURNS, CHESTER RAY, retired medical educator; b. Nashville, Dec. 5, 1937; s. Leslie Andrew and Margaret (Drake) B.; m. Ann Christine Griffey, Aug. 31, 1962; children: Christine, Derek. BA, Vanderbilt U., 1959, MD, 1963; PhD, Johns Hopkins U., 1969. Asst. prof. history medicine U. Tex. Med. Br., Galveston, 1969-71, James Wade Rockwell asst. prof. history medicine, 1971-75, James Wade Rockwell assoc. prof., 1975-79, James Wade Rockwell prof., from 1979; ret., from 2006. Cons. Nat. Ctr. for Health Svcs. Rsch., Washington, 1976-78; mem. nat. bd. cons. NEH, Washington, 1978-83. Editor: Humanism in Medicine, 1973, Legacies in Ethics and Medicine, 1977, Legacies in Law and Medicine, 1977; co-editor: Philosophy of Medicine and Bioethics: A Twenty Year Retrospective and Critical Appraisal, 1997; co-editor: Proceedings of the 37th International Congress on the History of Medicine, 2002, Saving Lives, Training Caregivers, Making Discoveries A Centennial History of the University of Texas Medical Branch at Galveston, 2003, Practicing the Medical Humanities, 2003; author numerous essays. Bd. dirs. The Grand 1894 Opera House, Galveston, 1986—88. Mem. Am. Assn. for History of Medicine (exec. coun. 1972-75), Soc. for Health and Human Values (pres. 1975-76), Am. Osler Soc. (bd. govs. 1984-87, 2002—, pres. 2004—05), Internat. Soc. for History of Medicine (treas. 1991—2003), Tex. State Hist. Assn. (exec. coun. 1993-97), Tex. Oral History Assn. (bd. dirs. 2005—), Rotary (pres. Galveston club 1980-81, gov. Dist. 5910, 1993-94). Democrat. Methodist. Avocations: swimming, photography. Died Dec. 27, 2006.

BURNS, JOHN JOSEPH, pharmacology educator; b. Flushing, NY, Oct. 8, 1920; s. Thomas F. and Katherine (Kane) B. BS, Queens Coll., 1942; MA, Columbia U., 1948, PhD, 1950. With lab. chem. pharmacology Nat. Heart Inst., 1950-60, dep. chief lab., 1957-60; head sec. clin. pharmacology, also adj. asst. prof. biochemistry NYU research service Goldwater Meml. Hosp., Welfare Island, N.Y., 1950-57; dir. research pharmacodynamics div. Wellcome Research Labs., Burroughs Wellcome & Co. (U.S.A.) Inc., Tuckahoe, N.Y., 1960-66; v.p. for research Hoffmann-LaRoche Inc., Nutley, N.J., 1967-84. Vis. prof. pharmacology Albert Einstein Coll. Medicine, 1960-68, Cornell U. Med. Coll., 1996—; adj. prof. Cornell U. Med. Coll., 1969-84, Rockefeller U., 1984-94; adj. mem. Roche Inst. Molecular Biology, 1984-96; cons. pharmacology and toxicology programs NIH; chmn. com. problems drug safety Drug Rsch. Bd., 1965-72. Contbr. articles to profl. jours. Served with AUS, 1944-46. Fellow Am. Inst. Chemists; mem. Inst. Medicine, Nat. Acad. Scis., N.Y. Acad. Scis. (v.p. 1964-65), Am. Soc. Pharmacology and Exptl. Therapeutics (pres. 1972-73), Am. Soc. Biol. Chemists, Am. Inst. Nutrition, Am. Coll. Neuropsychopharmacology, Internat. Union Pharmacology (pres. 1975-78) Achievements include research in metabolism drugs, vitamins and carbohydrates. Home: Westport, Conn. Died July 29, 2007.

BURNS, RICHARD MICHAEL, public utility company executive; b. Somerville, Mass., July 18, 1937; s. James Edward and Helen May (Arnold) B.; m. Carol Ann, Nov. 15, 1964; children: Robert, Karen, Gary, Kevin. BS in Bus. Adminstrn., Boston Coll. CPA, Mass. Audit mgr. Alexander Grant & Co., Boston, 1962-74; comptroller Eastern Utilities Assocs., Boston, from 1974. Bd. dirs. Eva Svc. Corp., Eva Cogenex Corp., Lowell, Mass., Montaup Electric Co., Boston. Served with U.S. Army, 1960-62. Mem. Mass. Soc. of CPAs, Edison Electric Inst. (acctg. mgmt. com., taxation com.). Democrat. Roman Catholic. Avocations: golf, basketball. Died May 13, 2006.

BURRIS, CONRAD TIMOTHY, chemical engineering educator; b. Edmonton, Can., May 17, 1924; came to U.S., 1950, naturalized, 1956; s. James Edward and Mary Elizabeth (Salzl) B. B.Chem. Engring., U. Alta., 1946, M.Chem. Engring., 1948; PhD, Cath. U. Am., 1955. Asst. prof. Manhattan Coll., Bronx, N.Y., 1958-61, assoc. prof., 1961-63, prof., 1963-89, head dept. chem. engring., 1961-71, 83-89, dean engring., 1971-80, professorial lectr., 1989—2007. Mem. Am. Inst. Chem. Engrs., Am. Soc. Engring. Edn., Am. Chem. Soc., Sigma Xi, Tau Beta Pi, Omega Chi Epsilon Died Feb. 9, 2007.

BURT, RICHARD MAX, lawyer, director; b. Phila., Dec. 8, 1944; s. Joseph Frank and Louise Esther (Kevitch) Burt; m. Katherine Anne Hedrick, Apr. 25, 1965 (div.); children: Corinne, Julie; m. Susan Adamson Burt, Mar. 2, 1990. BA, Gettysburg Coll., Pa., 1965; JD, Dickinson Sch. of Law, 1969. Bar: NY 1970, US Dist. Ct. (so. dist.)/NY 1972, US Ct. Appeals (2d cir.) 1972. Assoc. Donovan, Leisure, Newton & Irvine, NYC, 1969—73; asst. counsel Sandoz, Inc., East Hanover, NJ, 1974—78, v.p., sec. NYC, 1978—88; sec. Sandoz Nutrition Corp., Mpls., 1983—88, Master Builders Inc., 1985—88; v.p. fin. and develop., chief fin. officer Sandoz Pharm. Corp., East Hanover, NJ, 1989; gen. counsel, sec. Asea Brown Boveri, Inc., Stanford, Conn., from 1989; bd. dir. ABB Lummus Crest, Inc. Mem.: Am. Corp. Counsel Assn., Internat. Bar Assn., Westchesterfield Corp. Counsel Assn., Am.-Swiss Assn. (bd. dir.), Am. Arbitration Assn. (bd. dir.), ABA. Died Mar. 26, 2007.

BUSSEY, CHARLES DAVID, military officer; b. Edgefield, SC, Dec. 8, 1933; BS in English, N.C. Agrl. and Tech. State U., 1955; MA in Journalism, Ind. U., 1970; MS in Communication Sci., Shippensburg State U., 1974. Commd. 2d. lt. U.S. Army, 1955, advanced through grades to maj. gen., 1984; comdr. 2d bn. 504th Inf. 82d Airborne div., Fort Bragg, N.C., 1970-71; comdr. 2d brigade 2d Inf. div., Korea, 1976-77; dep. comdr., chief of staff 172d Inf. Brigade, Ft. Richardson, Alaska, 1980-82; chief personnel actions inf. br. Mil. Personnel Ctr., Alexandria, Va., 1972-73; exec. officer to chief legis. liaison Dept. Army, Pentagon, Washington, 1974-76, chief policy and plans, office chief of pub. affairs, 1977-80, dep. chief pub. affairs, 1982-84, chief pub. affairs, 1984-87; dep. chief of staff, personnel HQ Army Materiel Command, Alexandria, Va., 1987-89; sr. counsel Manning, Selvage & Lee, pub. rels., Washington, from 1990. Mem. adj. faculty U. Md. Coll. Journalism, 1989—. Contbr. numerous articles on leadership, tng., discipline, mgmt. and pub. affairs maintenance to mil. jours. and comml. newspapers. Chmn. bd. trustees N.C. A&T State U. Named Outstanding Alumnus N.C. Agrl. and Tech. State U., 1982, Disting. Alumnus Ind. U., 1983; named to Order of the Palmetto, Gov. of S.C.; mem. ROTC Hall of Fame, N.C. Agrl. and Tech. State U., 1965. Mem. Assn. U.S. Army, Pub. Rels. Soc. Am., Internat. Platform Assn. Democrat. Episcopalian. Avocations: writing, athletics. Home: Springfield, Va. Died June 22, 2007.

BUTLER, ARTHUR D., retired economics educator; b. Detroit, Oct. 13, 1923; s. Dwight and Gertrude Mae (Byers) B.; m. Kathleen Lehman, Sept. 3, 1945; children: Terese Kay, Pamela Ann, Sandra Sue. BA, Manchester Coll., Ind., 1944; MA, U. Minn., 1946; PhD, U. Wis., 1951. Lectr. U. Buffalo, 1949-52, asst. prof. econs., 1952-57, assoc. prof., 1957-61, prof., 1961—89, acting dean, 1960-63; provost social scis. SUNY-Buffalo, 1973-78; cons. U.S. Senate, Washington, 1976-78; ret., 1989. Author: Labor Economics and Institutions, 1961, Impact of the Fiscal System, 1968, State and Local Government Payrolls, 1968; editor: Selections in Economics, 1958. Bd. dirs. Housing Opportunities Made Equal, Buffalo, 1983—. Fulbright prof. U. Zambia, 1978-79; recipient Outstanding Alumnus award Manchester Coll., 1982 Fellow Japan Soc. for Promotion Sci. Home: Buffalo, NY. Died Oct. 23, 2006.

BUTLER, GEORGE BERGEN, chemistry educator; b. Liberty, Miss., Apr. 15, 1916; s. Benjamin Franklin and Estelle (McGehee) B.; m. Josephine Eldridge, June 4. 1944; children: George Bergen, Barbara Butler Ward. Cert., S.W. Miss. Jr. Coll., 1936; BA, Miss. Coll., 1938, DSc (hon.), 1986; PhD, U. N.C., Chapel Hill, 1942. Instr. organic lab. Miss. Coll., Clinton, 1937-38; instr. analytica lab. U. N.C., Chapel Hill, 1938-40, rsch. fellow, 1940-42; rsch. chemist Rohm & Haas Co., Inc., Phila., 1942-46; prof. chemistry, rsch. prof. U. Fla., Gainesville, 1946-90, dir. Ctr. Macromolecular Sci. and Engring., 1970-90, prof. emeritus, from 1990. Mem. panel on nation's potential for basic rsch. in chemistry Nat. Rsch. Coun., Washington; cons. Chemstrand Corp., PCR Inc., Atlantic Refining Inc., Calgon divsn. Merck, Inc., Allied Chem. Co., Internat. Minerals and Chem. Co., Proctor and Gamble, indsl. and govtl. labs. Editl. bd. Macromolecular Syntheses, 1961-95, Jour. Macromolecular Sci.-Chemistry, 1966-90; adv. bd. Jour. Polymer Sci., 1966-86; organizer, co-editor Jour. Macromolecular Sci. - Reviews, 1966-98, Reviews in Macromolecular Chemistry, 1967-68; editl. adv. bd. Macromolecules, 1968-69. contbr. articles to profl. jours. Recipient Fla. Blue Key award, 1965, Disting. alumnus award Miss. Coll., 1993. Fellow Am. Inst. Chemists (pres. Fla. chpt.); mem. AAAS, Am. Chem. Soc. (councilor Fla. sect. 1949-51, chmn. 1954-55, gen. chmn. 1958, award for Outstanding Rsch. and Tchg. 1963, Herty medal 1978, Polymer award 1980, Stone award 1983, So. chemist 1985, Flory Polymer Edn. award 1990), Fla. Acad. Scis. (bd. dirs., medal 1982), Sigma Xi (pres. 1962-63, award 1961), N.Y. Acad. Scis. Republican. Presbyterian. Avocations: weekend farming, fishing, travel. Home: Gainesville, Fla. Died June 7, 2007.

BUTT, JOHN BAECHER, chemical engineering educator; b. Norfolk, Va., Sept. 10, 1935; s. Willoughby Joseph and Mary Angela (Baecher) B.; m. Regina Elizabeth Roche, June 29, 1963; 1 son, John Baecher (dec.). BS, Clemson U., 1956; M.Engring., Yale, 1958, D.Engring., 1960. Registered profl. engr., Conn. Instr. chem. engring. Yale, 1959-60, asst. prof., 1960-63, asst. prof. engring. and applied sci., 1963-64, assoc. prof., 1964-69; prof. chem. engring. Northwestern U., Evanston, Ill., from 1969, Walter P. Murphy Prof., from 1981. Vis. prof. U. Tex., summer 1961, U. Calif. at Davis, spring 1967; Solvay vis. prof. U. Libre, Brussels, Belgium, 1971; chmn. Gordon Conf. on Catalysis, 1979; chmn. Internat. Symposium on Catalyst Deactivation, 1991. Assoc. editor: Catalysis Reviews, Chem. Engring. Jour.; contbr. articles to profl. jours.; patentee applied chemistry. Alexander von Humboldt sr. U.S. scientist award, 1985 Fellow Am. Inst. Chem. Engrs. (A.P. Colburn award 1968, Profl. Progress award 1978, dir. 1975-77); mem. Am. Chem. Soc. (petroleum research fund adv. bd. 1973), AAAS, Catalysis Soc. (E.B. Maxted award 1997), Va. Hist. Soc. Home: Prescott, Ariz. Died Aug. 15, 2007.

BUTTOLPH, JOHN, retired company executive; b. Dec. 24, 1928; Pres. Sholodge Franchise Sys., Inc., Hendersonville, Tenn., from 1993; v.p. Sholodge, Inc., Hendersonville, from 1993. Died July 18, 2007.

BYE, JAMES EDWARD, lawyer; b. Thief River Falls, Minn., May 2, 1930; s. Morris and Ida Mathilda (Dahl) B.; m. Patricia Ann Nadolski, Dec. 27, 1952; children: David Stanley, Anne Elizabeth. BBA with distinction, U. Minn., 1951; LLB cum laude, Harvard U., 1956. Bar: Colo. 1957, U.S. Tax Ct., U.S. Ct. Appeals (10th cir.), U.S. Supreme Ct. 1992. Assoc. Holme Roberts & Owen, Denver, 1957-61; ptnr. Holme, Roberts & Owen LLP, Denver, from 1961. Editor Harvard U. Law Rev. Chmn. continuing legal and jud. edn. Colo. Supreme Ct., Denver, 1977-78; chmn. Alexis de Tocqueville Soc. Met. Denver, 1986-89, Met. Denver GIVES, 1986-91; trustee Loretto Hts. Coll., Denver, 1977-88, Regis. Coll., 1988-92, The Two Percent Club, 1991—, Alliance Health Found., 2002—, Children's Hosp., 1993-95; exec. bd. Denver Area coun. Boy Scouts Am., 1992—, The Spot, 1996—; Tointon Inst. Adv. Bd., 2000—; bd. dirs. Mex. Cultural Ctr., U. Colo. Blue Ribbon Commn. Diversity, Cmty. Health Quality Partnership, 2002-. Recipient Silver Beaver award, Boy Scouts Am., 1996, Whitney M. Young Jr. Svc. award, 1999, Disting. Svc. to Humanity award, Vols. of Am., 1996, Pub. Svc. award, U. Colo. Grad. Sch. Pub. Affairs, 1996, Alex de Tocqueville Soc. award, United Way, Reconocimiento Ohtli award, Sec. of Fgn. Rels. of Mex., 1998, William Funk award, Colo. Assn. Nonprofit Orgns., 1998, Ally award, Women's Vision Found., 1999, Maverick Thinker's award, Urban Peak, 2001, Daniel L. Ritchie Ethics in Bus. award, U. Denever, 2004, Cmty. award, Arthistis Found., 2005, Philanthropic Leadership award, Denever Found., 2005. Fellow Am. Bar Found. (life), Colo. Bar Found.; mem. ABA (natural resources com. tax sect.), Colo. Bar Assn., Denver Bar Assn. (bd. regents), Am. Coll. Tax Counsel, Denver Estate Planning Coun., Greater Denver Tax Counsel Assn. Avocation: golf. Home: Englewood, Colo. Died Apr. 24, 2007.

BYRNE, RICHARD HILL, counselor, educator; b. Lancaster, Pa., Aug. 3, 1915; s. Jacob Hill and Mary Deborah (Allwein) B.; m. Magdalene Antoinette Wardell, June 12, 1954; children—Christopher, Mary, Matthew, Peter AB, Franklin and Marshall Coll., 1938; MA, Columbia U., 1947, Ed.D., 1952. Tchr. several sch. systems, Lancaster County, Pa., 1939-42; counselor Allegany County Schs., Cumberland, Md., 1949-50; state guidance supr. State of N.H., Concord, 1950-51; assoc., then prof., chmn. counseling dept. U. Md., College Park, 1951-82, prof. emeritus, from 1983, resident grad. prof. Upper Heyford, Eng., 1982-84, Boston U., Germany, 1984-86. Cons. U.S. Dept. Labor, Washington, 1964-68; cons. in guidance numerous sch. systems, Md., Pa., Va., 1951-82; dir. interpoll. research ctr. on pupil services, College Park, Md., 1963-68 Author: The School Counselor, 1963, Guidance: A Behavioral Approach, 1977, Becoming a

Master Counselor, 1994. Served to capt. U.S. Army, 1942-46, ETO Mem. Am. Psychol. Assn., Md. Personnel and Guidance Assn. (1st pres. 1957-58) Home: Tarpon Springs, Fla. Died July 29, 2006.

BYRNES, ARTHUR FRANCIS, retired federal official; b. NYC, June 28, 1917; s. Arthur I. and Barbara (Young) B.; m. Anne Louise Schug, Dec. 24, 1941; children: Arthur Everett, Suzana, John Mitchell. BS, Manhattan Coll., 1940; MEd, Springfield Coll., Mass., 1942; PhD, NYU, 1951. Asst. prof. orgn., adminstrn. and mgmt. Springfield Coll., 1940-42; supt. schs. Monroe, Ind., 1945-49; prof., dir. communications Eastern Ill. State U., Charleston, 1949-53; dir. research, 1953-55; ICA cons. Ministry Edn., Govt. Brazil, 1955-57; div. chief AID, Dept. State, 1957-62, dep. dir. mission Northeast Brazil, 1962-63, dir. mission, 1963-64, asst. dir. Rio de Janeiro Brazil, 1964; dep. dir. U.S. U.S. AID, dir. mission Quito, Ecuador, 1966; also attaché, econ. and social devel. Am. Embassy, Quito, 1965; with U.S. Army War Coll., Carlisle, Pa., 1966-67; dir. internat. and regional programs AID, Washington, 1967-70, dir. office internat. tng., 1970-75; dir. internat. programs U.S. Dept. Agr. Grad. Sch., 1975-85; pres. Ednl. Cons. Internat., from 1985, World Ctr. for Devel. and Tng., from 1985. V.p. Am. Inst. Rehab., Edn. and Employment, Washington, 1987—. Mem. Fulbright Brazilian-U.S. Exchange Commn., 1957-64; acad. affairs com. Escola Americana, Rio de Janeiro, 1960-64. Served to capt. USAAF, 1942-45. Decorated Cruziero do Sul Brazil, 1960; named to Hall of Fame, Manhattan Coll., 1986. Mem. Am. C. of C., Am. Soc., AAUP, Fgn. Service Assn., Soc. Internat. Devel., Phi Delta Kappa. Home: Mc Lean, Va. Died Dec. 15, 2005.

CADDY, EDMUND H.H., JR., architect; b. NYC, Apr. 17, 1928; s. Edmund Harrington Homer and Glenna Corinne (Garratt) C.; m. Mary Audrey Ortiz, Dec. 22, 1951; children—Edmund Harrington Homer III, Mary Elizabeth. BA, Princeton, 1952, M.F.A. (grad. sch. fellow), 1955. With Louis E. Jallade, NYC, 1949-53, Eggers & Higgins, NYC, 1953-55; dir. design Dalton-Dalton Assocs., Cleve., 1955-60; assoc. Raymond & Rado, NYC, 1960-68; gen. ptnr. Raymond & Rado and Ptnrs., NYC, 1968-72, Raymond, Rado, Caddy & Bonington, P.C., NYC, 1972-80, pres., 1980-83; project mgr. Robinson, Mills & Williams, San Francisco, 1983-87, McCue, Boone, Tomsick, San Francisco, 1987-88, O'Brien-Kreitzberg, San Francisco, 1988-90; Sverdrup Corp., 1990-94; archtl. design cons., from 1994. Apptd. by Pres. John F. Kennedy to adv. com. arts John F. Kennedy Ctr. Performing Arts, 1963-70; mem. archtl. adv. commn. N.Y.C. C.C., CUNY, 1979-83. Works include Suburban Hosp, Cleve., 1957, J.M. Smucker Co, Salinas, Cal., 1957, Brookpark (Ohio) City Hall, 1959; Cleve. Transit System addition, 1959, adminstrn. bldg., Met. Water Treatment System, Saigon, 1960, Franklin D. Roosevelt High Sch, N.Y.C., 1963, Crown Heights Intermediate Sch, N.Y.C., 1966, engring. complex design, Stony Brook Campus, State U. N.Y., 1970, Sibley's dept. stores, Syracuse, N.Y., 1973, Rochester Downtown Devel. Study, 1975, R.H. Macy & Co. dept. store, Stamford, Conn., 1979; project mgr. Main Postal Facility, San Francisco, 1985, Univ. Ctr., U. Calif., Irvine, 1987, Santa Clara (Calif.) County CourtHouse, Ft. Mojave Resort Devel., 1991-94. Pres. bd. trustees Montclair (N.J.) Cmty. Hosp., 1973-80. Served with USMC, 1946-48, USMCR, 1948-53. Mem. AIA, Tower Club (Princeton), Racquet and Tennis Club (N.Y.C.) Home: Bolingbrook, Ill. Died Apr. 17, 2006.

CADIGAN, GEORGE LESLIE, bishop; b. Mt. Vernon, NY, Apr. 12, 1910; s. Edward J. and Christine (Lindbloom) C.; m. Jane Jones, Aug. 15, 1944; children— Peter, David, Rufus, Christine. BA cum laude, Amherst Coll., 1933, also D.D.; student, Episcopal Theol. Sch., 1935, Jesus Coll., Cambridge U., 1936; D.D., Hobart Coll., U. South, Hofstra U. Ordained deacon P.E. Ch., 1935, priest, 1936; curate Grace Ch., Amherst; chaplain Amherst Coll.; rector St. Paul's Ch., Brunswick, Maine, 1937-42, Grace Ch., Salem, Mass., 1942-48, St. Paul's Ch., Rochester, N.Y., 1948-59; bishop Diocese of Mo., 1959-75. Dir. religious activities Amherst Coll., 1975-86. Dep. Episcopal Gen. Convs., 1955, 58; mem. Commn. on Alcoholism, Episcopal Ch., 1955-59; past trustee St. Luke's Episcopal-Presbyterian Hosps., Episcopal-Presbyn. Found. for Aging, Barnard Free Skin and Cancer Hosp., Thompson Retreat and Conf. Center, Mo. Botanical Gardens, all St. Louis; past pres. chpt. Christ Ch. Cathedral, Episcopal City Mission Soc., CARE and Counseling, Inc., Met. Ch. Fedn. Greater St. Louis; past chmn. bd. Grace Hill Settlement House, Neighborhood Health Center, Ednl. Center, all St. Louis; mem. agenda com., chmn. adv. com. to suffragan bishop to armed forces House of Bishops, Episcopal Ch., 1959-75. Named Distinguished Citizen of Yr. St. Louis Jewish Council Community Relations, 1973; Named Distinguished Citizen of Yr. St. Louis Urban League, 1974 Died Dec. 14, 2005.

CAHILL, WILLIAM WALSH, JR., lawyer; b. St. Louis, Oct. 29, 1927; s. William Walsh and Estelle Mary (Conley) C.; m. Patricia Denise McVey, Aug. 19, 1950; children: Patricia Denise, Kathleen Mary, Tracey Ann. BS, Loyola Coll., Balt., 1947; JD, Georgetown U., 1950. Bar: Md. 1950. Sr. ptnr. Weinberg & Green, Balt., from 1951. Chmn. bd. trustees Pub. Defender System, Balt., 1971—. Mem. ABA (ho. dels. Chgo. 1988-90), Md. State Bar Assn. (bd. govs. 1987-88), Bar Assn. of Balt. City (pres. 1974-75). Democrat. Roman Catholic. Died Feb. 20, 2007.

CAIN, DONALD EZELL, retired judge; b. San Marcos, Tex., Oct. 8, 1921; s. Erie Montclair and Betty Belle (Howell) C.; m. Betty Anne Culberson, June 14, 1952; children: David, Dale Cain Husen, Donald Ezell, Randolph. A.S., North Tex. Agrl. Coll., 1941; BBA, U. Tex., 1943, LL.B., 1948; postgrad., Nat. Jud. Coll., Reno, 1974, 78, 82. Bar: Tex. 1948. With contracts dept. Convair, Ft. Worth, 1948-50; pvt. practice law Pampa, Tex., 1951-76; county atty. Gray County, Tex., 1955-68; county judge, 1971-77; dist. judge 223rd Dist. Ct. Tex., 1977-91; sr. dist. judge State of Tex., from 1991, ret. Pres. Adobe Walls coun. Boy Scouts Am., 1957-59; bd. dirs. Pampa United Fund, 1956-60. Lt. USNR, 1943-46, WWII; lt., 1950-51, Korea Recipient Silver Beaver award Boy Scouts Am., 1958 Fellow Tex. Bar Found.; mem. ABA, Tex. Bar Assn., Gray County Bar Assn. (pres. 1968), Am. Judicature Soc., Tex. Judges and Commrs. Assn., Panhandle County Judges and Commrs. Assn. (pres. 1975), Pampa C. of C. (dir. 1959-60), Phi Alpha Delta. Clubs: Masons, Rotary (pres. 1958-59), Pampa Country. Democrat. Baptist. Home: Pampa, Tex. Died July 3, 2007.

CAIN, RAYMOND FREDERICK, landscape architect, planning company executive; b. Harrisburg, Ill., Sept. 13, 1937; s. Raymond Ransome and Edna (Kirkham) C.; m. Galen S. Short, Sept. 13, 1965 (div. 1971); m. Lois A. Kiehl, Dec. 27, 1981. BA, U. Ill., 1959, MA, 1962. Cert. profl. landscape architect, Md., Hawaii. Landscape architect W.J. Spear & Assoc., Houston, 1962-66; landscape architect Belt, Collins & Assoc., Honolulu, 1966-76, dir. landscape architecture, from 1976, v.p., from 1981. Speaker Urban Devel. Seminar, Singapore, 1980, Fiji Hotel Assn., Nandi, Fiji, 1981; lectr. Tourist Mgmt. Sch., Honolulu, 1978 Mem. Hawaii Year 2000, Honolulu, 1971; advisor Outdoor Cir., Honolulu, 1976; mem. Waikiki Improvement Assn., Honolulu, 1973 Recipient Nat. Landscape award Mauna Kea Beach Hotel, Hawaii, 1976; Nat. Design award Kona Surf Hotel, Hawaii, 1980, Mauna Lani Golf course, 1982, Aga Khan award Tanjong Jara Hotel, Malaysia, 1983 Fellow Am. Soc. Landscape Architects (treas. 1975-76); mem. Am. Planning Assn. (assoc.) Clubs: Outrigger (ground chmn. 1976-77), Honolulu, Oahu Country (ground chmn. 1972-73). Home: Honolulu, Hawaii. Died Nov. 11, 2005.

CAIRNS, FRANK ELMER, insurance company executive; b. Steger, Ill., Nov. 4, 1924; s. Frank Elmer and Leta Amanda (Blattner) Cairns; m. Gladys Marie Pfahler, Sept. 1, 1951; children: Gregory Bruce, Jeffrey Peter, Deborah Ann. BS, Duke U., 1947, MF, 1950; diploma, Ins. Inst. Am., 1972. Forrester State of Wis., Madison, 1950—55; supr. bodily injury claims Home Indemnity, NYC, Chgo., 1955—62; N.W. claims rep. Rural Ins. Co., Madison, Wis., 1962; with Farmers Mut. Ins., Juneau, 1974—79; owner Indianhead Claim Svc., Eau Claire, Wis., from 1979. Assoc. mem. Eau Claire County Farm Bur., 1962—74. With USNR, 1943—46, advance through grades to lt. USNR, 1946—66. Decorated Victory medal. Mem.: Rural Ins. Co. Claims Bd. (pres. 1970—71, sec. 1968—69), Ins. Inst. Am. (first coord. Eau Claire Chpt. 1968—70), Indianhead Adjusters Assn. (social chmn. 1968—69, pres. 1969—70, v.p. 1982—82), Ret. Officers Assn. Home: Eau Claire, Wis. Died June 12, 2006.

CALHOUN, CALVIN LEE, SR., physician; b. Atlanta, Jan. 7, 1927; s. Robert and Mary L. (Huff) C.; m. Evelyn Greene, Feb. 14, 1948; 1 son, Calvin Lee BS, Morehouse Coll., 1948; MS, Atlanta U., 1950; MD, Meharry Med. Coll., 1960. Instr. biology Morehouse Coll., 1950-51; intern G.W. Hubbard Hosp., Nashville, 1960-61, resident in medicine, 1961-62; resident in neurology U. Minn. Med. Center, Mpls., 1962-65, fellow in neurology, 1965-66; instr. anatomy Meharry Med. Coll., Nashville, 1951-57, asst. prof. anatomy, 1961-62, assoc. prof. anatomy, 1966-72, prof. anatomy, 1972-91, prof. medicine, 1973-91, dir. div. neurology, 1966-91; chief neurology sect. Meharry Med. Coll., Hubbard Hosp., 1968-90, prof. anatomy, neurology emeritus, from 1991. Dir. div. neurology, 1966—, acting chmn. dept. anatomy, 1968-71, chmn., 1971-81; chief neurology service Meharry Med. Coll.-Hubbard Hosp., 1968, dir. neurodiagnostic lab., 1966; vis. prof. U. W.I., 1975; mem. adv. bd. Epilepsy Found. Am., Davidson County chpt. ARC. Contbr. chpts. to books, articles to profl. jours. Chmn. bd. deacons 1st Baptist Capitol Hill Ch.; mem. life membership com. NAACP; mem. adv. council Pro Musica. Served with U.S. Army, 1945. Fellow Stroke Council of Am. Heart Assn.; mem. Am. Acad. Neurology, Nat. Med. Assn., AAAS, Am. Assn. Anatomists, R.F. Boyd Med. Soc., Tenn. Med. Assn., Tenn. Anatomical Bd., So. Clin. Neurological Soc., Phi Beta Kappa, Alpha Omega Alpha, Beta Kappa Chi, Kappa Alpha Psi. Clubs: Nashville, Sportman's, Apollo, 100 Black Men of Middle Tenn. Home: Nashville, Tenn. Died Dec. 23, 2005.

CALHOUN, LILLIAN SCOTT, public relations company executive; b. Savannah, Ga.; d. Walter Sanford and Laura (McDowell) Scott; m. Harold William Calhoun, Sept. 20, 1950; children: Laura, Harold, Walter, Karen. BA, Ohio State U., 1944. Columnist, feature editor Chgo. Defender, 1963-65; assoc. editor Jet, Ebony, mags., 1961-63; reporter Chgo. Sun-Times, 1965-68; mng. editor Integrated Edn. mag., 1968-71; info. officer, acting info. dir. Dept. Labor, 1971-73; co-editor Chgo. Reporter, 1973-76; pres., prin., founder Calmar Communications, Inc., Chgo., 1978-93; columnist Crain's Chgo. Bus., 1978-80, Chgo. Journalism Rev., 1969-74. Vice-chairperson Ill. Commn. on Human Relations, 1973-75; mem. Gov.'s Commn. on Status of Women, 1965-67, Gov.'s Adv. Council on Manpower, 1973-75. Recipient YWCA Leader award, 1984. Mem. Soc. Midland Authors, Chgo. Network, Alpha Gamma Pi. Episcopalian. Clubs: Chgo. Press, Publicity, Arts. Home: Chicago, Ill. Died Jan. 25, 2006.

CALI, JOSEPH JOHN, librarian; b. Amsterdam, NY, Oct. 17, 1928; s. Joseph and Jennie (Natoli) C. BA, Union Coll., Schenectady, 1951; MSL.S., Western Res. U., 1952; postgrad., U. Mich., 1957-65. Serials librarian Antioch Coll., Yellow Springs, Ohio, 1954-65, pub. services librarian, 1965-69, assoc. librarian, 1969-83, head librarian, from 1983. Served as sgt. arty. U.S. Army, 1952-54 Mem. ALA, Am. Beethoven Soc., U.S. Trotting Assn. Died Feb. 14, 2007.

CALKINS, CARROLL CECIL, editor, freelance; b. Springfield, Oreg., Oct. 7, 1918; s. Herman Cecil and Gladys (Riggs) C.; m. Ruth Geneva Monroe, Sept. 27, 1947; children: Christopher Carroll, Robin Ruth, Melissa Howard; m. Barbara Pfeffer, Apr. 5, 1981. BA, U. Oreg., 1946. Self employed comml. photographer, Eugene, 1949-53; N.W. editor Sunset mag., 1953-56, asso. editor, 1956-57, House Beautiful mag., 1957-67; editor-in-chief Home Garden mag., 1967-69; sr. staff editor Readers Digest Books., 1969-88; ind. freelance writer, from 1988. Author: (with Jerome A. Eaton) How to Garden, 1979; project dir. 12 books mostly on gardening, landscaping and travel. Served to maj. USAAF, 1941-45. Decorated D.F.C., Air medal with 5 oak leaf clusters. Home: New York, NY. Died May 21, 2006.

CALLAHAN, LESLIE GRIFFIN, JR., engineer educator; b. Pocomoke City, Md., July 27, 1923; s. Leslie Griffin Sr. and Ruth (Parks) C.; m. Annette Hodges, Dec. 20, 1994 (dec. June 1988); children: Susan Ruth, Leslie Griffin III; m. Dorothy Warren, Oct. 21, 1989. Student, Washington Coll., 1940-41; BS, U.S. Mil. Acad., 1944; MSEE, U. Pa., 1951, PhD, 1961. Advanced through grades to col. U.S. Army, 1944-69, ret., 1969; prof. engring. Ga. Inst. Tech., Atlanta, from 1969. Mem. Ops. Rsch. Soc. Am., Armed Forces Comm. Assn. Republican. Episcopalian. Home: Atlanta, Ga. Died Oct. 21, 2006.

CALLAHAN, ROBERT L., JR., soft drink executive; b. Bklyn., Oct. 11, 1932; s. Robert L. and Edna (Peterson) C.; m. Mary Byrne Carolan, mar. 5, 1955; children: Robert, Thomas, Kevin, Maureen, Ann, Sheila, Neal, John, Megan, Dennis. BSS, Georgetown U., 1954, JD, 1960, LLM, 1961. Bar: DC 1960. Deputy counsel solicitor of labor U.S. Dept. Labor, Washington, 1961-64; gen. counsel Nat. Soft Drink Assn., Washington, 1964-68; v.p. The Coca-Cola Co., Atlanta, from 1968. Dir., sec. Calorie Control Council, Atlanta; mem. Internat. Food Council, Washington, U.S. Council for Internat. Bus., N.Y.C. Dir. Ga. Easter Seals, Atlanta. Served to 1st lt. US Army, 1954-56. Recipient St. Thomas More scholarship St. John's Law Sch., Bklyn, 1954, E. Barrett Prettyman fellowship Georgetown Law Sch., 1961. Mem. ABA, Fed. Bar Assn., Internat. Bar Assn., Inter-Am. Bar Assn., Atlanta Bar Assn., Am. Corporate Counsel Assn. (pres. 1985-87). Clubs: Commerce, Georgetown (Atlanta). Roman Catholic. Home: Cleveland, Ga. Died July 31, 2006.

CALLANAN, DANIEL FRANCIS, JR., insurance company executive; b. Brighton, Mass., Nov. 14, 1931; s. Daniel Francis and Dorothea Jane (Daly) Callanan; m. Lois Anne O'Laughlin, Oct. 8, 1955; children: Gail, Patricia, Mary, Nancy. AB in econs., Boston Coll., 1953. Cert. Bentley Coll., 1959. Div. mgr. John Hancock Mut. Life Ins. Co., Boston, 1963—66, asst. contr., 1966—71, v.p. acctg. ops., 1971. Dir. John Hancock Distbrs., Inc., Boston, John Hancock Realty Services Corp., Boston. Team leader Mass. Gov.'s Mgmt. Take Force, 1975—76; bd govs. Com. of 1000 for support Boys and Girls Clubs Boston 1982; trustee John Hancock Charitable Trust, Boston. Fellow: Office Mgmt. Inst. (life); mem.: Office Mgmt. Assn. (life; mem cost acctg. com. 1982, fin. planning and control coun. 1982) Died Nov. 22, 2005.

CALLOWAY, ROBERT QUINCY, school supply company executive; b. Logansport, Ind., Oct. 14, 1927; s. Charles Quincy and Gladys Fern (Maxson) C.; m. Patricia Louise Sims, Nov. 12 1950; children— Cynthia Louise, Carol Ann, James Quincy Student Ind. U., 1948. Founder, pres. Imperial Enterprises Corp. Lafayette, Ind., 1961—, Imperial Ednl. Programs Co., Lafayette 1970—, Imperial Travel Service, Lafayette, 1974—; dir Marengo State Bank, Milltown Nat. Bank, Rushville Nat. Bank Served with USN, 1945-46; ETO. Mem. Nat. Sch. Supply and Equipment Assn., Ind. Sch. Distbrs. Assn. Republican. Lodges Masons, Shriners, Elks. Home: Lafayette, Ind. Died Nov. 17 2006.

CALVIN, LYLE DAVID, statistician, educator; b. Dannebrog Nebr., Apr. 12, 1923; s. David A. and Muriel (Harvey) C.; m Shirley Jeanne Schmidt, Apr. 19, 1952; children— James Arthur Ronald David, Janet Lee. Grad., Parsons Jr. Coll., Kans., 1943 BS in Meteorology, U. Chgo., 1948; BS, NC State U., 1947 PhD, 1953. Biometrician G.D. Searle & Co., Chgo., 1950-52 asst. statistician N.C. State U., Raleigh, 1952-53; assoc. prof stats. Oreg. State U., 1953-57, prof., 1957-88, chmn. dept. stats 1962-81; dir. Survey Rsch. Ctr., 1973-85; dean Grad. Sch. Oreg State U., 1981-88, prof., dean emeritus, from 1989. Vis. prof. U Edinburgh, 1967, Inst. Stat. Studies and Rsch., U. Cairo 1971-72; chmn. Com. of Pres. of Statis. Socs., 1985-91. 1st l USAAF, 1943-46. Fellow AAAS, Am. Statis. Assn.; mem Internat. Statis. Inst., Biometric Soc. (pres. WNAR 1964-65 gen. sec. 1980-84), Am. Statis. Assn. Home: Corvallis, Oreg Died Oct. 8, 2006.

CAMPBELL, BEBE MOORE, writer; b. Phila., Feb. 18, 1950 d. Doris Moore; m. Tiko Campbell (div.); 1 child, Maia; m. Ellis Gordon Jr., 1984; 1 stepchild, Ellis Gordon III. BS in Elem Edn., U. Pitts., 1971. Author: (non-fiction) Successful Women Angry Men: Backlash in the Two-Career Marriage, 198 (memoir) Sweet Summer, Growing Up With and Without M Dad, 1989, (novels) Your Blues Ain't Like Mine, 1992 (N Times Notable Book of Yr., NAACP Image award for Lit. Brothers and Sisters, 1994, Singing in the Comeback Choi 1998 (NY Times Bestseller list), What You Owe Me, 2001 (N Times Bestseller list, LA Times Best Book, 2001), 72 Hou Hold, 2005, (children's books) Sometimes My Mommy Ge Angry, 2003 (Nat. Alliance for Mentally Ill Outstanding Li award, 2003), Stomping at the Savoy, 2006; contbr. articles NY Times Mag., Washington Post, LA Times, Essense, Ebon Black Enterprise, others; regular commentator on NPR's Morn ing Edition. Mem. Nat. Alliance for Mentally Ill (NAMI founding mem. NAMI-Inglewood, Calif. Died Nov. 27, 2006

CAMPBELL, DONALD K., theological seminary administr tor, educator; b. Ft. Wayne, Ind., July 6, 1926; s. Dwight V. ar Evelyn G. (Pfeiffer) C.; m. Beatta Ruth Carlson (dec. 1991 children: Stephen, John Timothy, Mary Joy, Jonathan; Lavonne Bernice Jensen; children: David, Thomas, James. A in History with highest honors, Wheaton Coll., 1947; ThM wi high honors, Dallas Theol. Sem., 1951, ThD in Bible Expositio 1953; DD, Liberty U., 1989; D Humanities, Dallas Bapt. U 1993. Tchr. Dallas Bible Inst., 1951-53; chmn. dept., asst. pro Bryan Coll., Dayton, Tenn., 1953-54; registrar Dallas Theo Sem., 1954-67, asst. prof. Bible exposition, 1954-61, acti chmn. Bible exposition, 1960-61, acad. dean, 1961-84, exe v.p., 1985-86, vice chmn. faculty, 1961-86, pres., 1986-94, pre emeritus, from 1994. Author: Nehemiah: Man in Charge, 197 Joshua: Leader Under Fire, 1981, Daniel: God's Man in Secular Society, 1988, Judges: Leaders in Crisis Times, 198 editor: Walvoord: A Tribute, 1982, A Case for Premillennialis A New Consensus, 1992; contbr. to Bible Knowledge Comme tary, Old Testament edit.: Book of Joshua, 1985, N.T. edit.: Bo of Galatians, 1985, Essays in Honor of J. Dwight Pentecost: T

Church in God's Prophetic Program; cons. editor: Chafer's Systematic Theology, abridged edit., vols. 1 and 2; contbg. writer: Baker Encyclopedia of the Bible; also articles and revs. Bd. advisors Dallas Assn. for Decency, Dallas Christian Leadership, Barnabas Internat., Rockford, Ill., Fair Park Friendship Ctr.; mem. steering com. Citizens for Dallas; mem. bd. reference Found. for Thought and Ethics, Richardson, Tex., Family Ministry, Little Rock, Ark., Outreach Inc., Grand Rapids, Mich., Patkai (India) Christian Coll., Uppsala (Sweden) Theol. Sem., Capturing Poland for Christ, Nashville Bible Coll. Mem. Wheaton Coll. Scholastic Honor Soc., Pi Gamma Mu. Home: Dallas, Tex. Died Sept. 7, 2006.

CAMPBELL, HELEN ZOTT, writer, lecturer; b. Des Moines, Feb. 7, 1919; d. John Henry and Perna A. (Jones) Zott; m. Robert A. Campbell Jr. (dec. 2004); children: Karen, Debra; student Fairmont Jr. Coll., 1938, Strayer Bus. Coll., 1939-40, George Washington U., 1943-45, Orgn. Mgmt. Inst., U. Del., 1973, Mgmt. Inst., Notre Dame U., 1978; m. Robert A. Campbell, Jr., Sept. 4, 1948; children— Karen Leigh, Debra Arlene. Acctg. clk. George Washington U., Washington, 1940-46; sec., bookkeeper NEA, Washington, 1946-47; sec., acct. W. E. Cumberland, Washington, 1947-52; acct. Am. Apparel Mfrs. Assn., Inc., Arlington, Va., 1967-72, asst. treas., 1972-79, dir. fin. services, 1973-79; free-lance artist, writer and lectr., 1979—. Jr. bd. George Washington U. Hosp., Washington, 1948-50, pres., 1950-52; bd. govs. English Speaking Union, Sydney, Australia, 1963-65. Recipient citation Philippine Govt., 1958, citation Children of Libya, 1963. Mem. Nat., Am., Washington socs. assn. execs., Nat. Assn. Execs. Clubs, Soc. Preservation Va. Antiquities, Assn. Fgn. Service Women, Arlington C. of C. (assn. council 1975-79), Zonta Internat., Kappa Delta. Republican. Presbyterian. Clubs: Capital Speakers, Washington, Nat. Press, Capitol Hill. Died Feb. 11, 2007.

CAMPBELL, JAMES R., transportation executive; b. July 16, 1941; s. Ray E. and Anne Louise (Wooten) Campbell. BS, U. Houston, 1965; postgrad., Case Western Res. U., 1967-68, Yale U., 1990. Personnel asst. The Standard Oil Co., Cleve., 1966-68; dir. equal opportunity programs Turner Constrn. Co., Cleve., 1968-73; employment project dir. Nat. Assn. Drug Abuse Problems, NYC, 1973-74; exec. dir. The Cuyahoga Plan Ohio, Cleve., 1974-77; dir. EEO compliance and cmty. activities the continental Group, Inc., Stamford, Conn., 1978-85; cons. human resources James Campbell & Assocs., Inc., 1985-88; asst. v.p. strategic human resource planning MTA N.Y.C. Transit, Bklyn., 1990—93, acting dep. v.p. employee resources, 1993—96, asst. v.p. employee resources, 1988—90; v.p. adminstrn. MTA Long Island Bus, Garden City, NY, 1996—2007. Expert witness HUD, 1970, U.S. Ho. of Reps. subcom., 1972. Contbr. Chmn. task force, mem. steering com. Cleve. Fedn. Cmty. Devel. Manpower Planning & Devel. Commn., 1971—73; mem. cmty. adv. bd. Cleve. Press, 1972; mem. Pres.'s com. Employment of People With Disabilities, 1985—91. With USAF, 1958—62, Japan. Recipient Key to City, Cleve., 1970, Outstanding Cmty. Svc. award, Urban League Cleve., 1972. Mem.: ASTD, Nat. Tartan Day N.Y. Com. (treas. 2005), N.Y. Human Resources Planning Soc., Pers. Accreditation Inst., Soc. Human Resources Mgmt. (life-time profl. cert. advanced level), Human Resource Assn. N.Y., St. George's Soc. N.Y., St. Andrew's Soc. N.Y. State, Clan Campbell Edn. Found. (trustee from 2000), Clan Campbell Soc. (dep. commr. N.Y.C. 1998—2000, trustee from 2000, N.Am. chpt.), N.Y. Caledonian Club (chieftain 1999, trustee 2000—02, chief 2001—02), Omicron Delta Kappa (circle v.p. 1965, Gold Key 1965). Died Feb. 9, 2007.

CAMPBELL, JEFFERSON HOLLAND, English language educator; b. Beaumont, Tex., Jan. 19, 1931; s. William Holland and Eula Mildred (Owens) C.; m. Shelia Ann Trapp, Sept. 4, 1952; children: Cary Elizabeth, Susan Holland, William Charles. AA, Lamar Coll., 1950; BA, So. Meth. U., 1952; BD, Perkins Sch. Theol., 1955; PhD, Duke U., 1963. Prof., chmn. English dept. Southwestern U., Georgetown, Tex., 1962-74, Midwestern State U., Wichita Falls, Tex., from 1974. Chmn. faculty devel. com. Humanities CLEP Exam., Princeton, N.J., 1972-77; chmn. writing exam Tex. Acad. Skills Coun., Austin, 1986-88. Author: John Howard Griffin, 1970, Updike's Novels: Thorns Spell Word, 1987. Mem. MLA (south ctrl. sect. chmn. 1972, 75, 91), Am. Studies Assn. Tex. (pres. 1971, v.p., councillor), Conf. Coll. Tchrs. English (pres. 1974, councillor). Democrat. Methodist. Home: Wichita Falls, Tex. Died June 30, 2006.

CAMPBELL, LEONARD M., lawyer; b. Denver, Apr. 12, 1918; s. Bernard Francis and May (Moran) C.; m. Dot J. Baker, Sept. 23, 1944; children: Brian T., Teri Pat, Thomas P. AB, U. Colo., 1941, LLB, 1943. Bar: Colo. 1943. With Gorsuch, Kirgis, 1948-88, sr. ptnr., 1951-88; city atty. Denver, 1951-53; of counsel Gorsuch, Kirgis LLC, 1989—2004. Cons. pub. utility matters Colo. Mcpl. League. Mem. Denver Charter Com., 1947; mgr. Safety and Excise for Denver, 1947-48; chmn. Denver Com. Human Relations, 1954; mem. Denver Planning Bd., 1950-51; mem. Bd. Water Commrs., Denver, 1965-70, pres., 1968-69; mem. Gov.'s Com. on Jud. Compensation, 1972; chmn. U. Colo. Law Alumni Devel. Fund, 1962. Served with USAAF, 1943-46. Mem. ABA, Colo. Bar Assn. (pres. 1978-79, Award of Merit 1967), Denver Bar Assn. (pres. 1969), Am. Coll. Trial Lawyers, Cath. Lawyers Guild Denver (pres. 1962, St. Thomas More award 1978), Nat. Inst. Mcpl. Law Officers (v.p. 1952), Colo. Judicial Inst. (Chancellor Chester Alter award 1987), Denver Athletic Club (sec. 1960-61, pres. 1962). Democrat. Roman Catholic. Died July 16, 2006.

CAMPBELL, PATTON, stage designer, educator; b. Omaha, Sept. 10, 1926; s. Ralph Harold and Frances Lorraine (Patton) C. BA, Yale U., 1950, MFA, 1952. Instr. costume design and history Barnard Coll., 1955-57; instr. scenery, costume design and history NYU, 1962-67; assoc. prof. Columbia U., 1967-91, SUNY, Purchase, 1975—2002; vis. lectr. Bklyn. Coll., 1973-74, 80, 86-89, Brandeis U., 1975-76, 82-83. Faculty New Sch., 1985; vis. prof. So. Methodist U., 1986, SUNY, Stony Brook, 1987; lectr. O'Neill Ctr., Suffolk Community Colls., 1987, Ohio U., 1996, So. Meth. U., Dallas, 1996, 97, Easton, Conn. Libr., 1997. Designer: costumes for plays and operas including 27 Wagons Full of Cotton, Playhouse Theatre, 1955, Trouble in Tahiti, 1955, Fallen Angels, 1956, A Hole in the Head, Plymouth Theatre, 1957, All American, Winter Garden Theatre, 1962, Wuthering Heights, N.Y.C. Opera, 1959, The Mikado, 1959, The Inspector General, 1960, Natalia Petrovna, 1964, Katya Kabonova, 1964, Capriccio, 1965, Lizzie Borden, 1965, La Traviata, 1966, The Pirates of Penzance, 1968, Carry Nation, 1969, Susannah, 1971, The Ballad of Baby Doe, 1988 (PBS), La Belle Helene, 1976, The Student Prince, 1980, La Traviata, 1981, Il Tabarro, Gianni Schicchi, Juilliard Opera Theatre, N.Y.C., The Lady from Colorado, 1964, Madame Butterfly, Central City (Colo.) Opera, 1964, After The Fall, Nat. Co., Wilmington, Del., 1964, Oliver!, 1964, Man of La Mancha, ANTA Washington Square, 1965 (Tony award nominee), On A Clear Day You Can See Forever, Nat. Co. Cleve., 1966, Loot, Biltmore Theatre, 1968, Der Rosenkavalier, Santa Fe Opera, 1968, Tosca, Santa Fe Opera, 1969, Cosi Fan Tutte, 1969, The Fisherman and His Wife, Opera Co. of Boston, 1970, Scarlett, Imperial Theatre, Tokyo, 1970, Between Time and Timbuktu (on PBS), 1972, Gone With The Wind, Drury Lane Theatre, London, 1972, Regina, Houston Grand Opera, 1980, Merry Wives of Windsor, So. Meth. U., The Mighty Casey and Gianni Schicchi, Glimmer Glass Opera Theatre, Cooperstown, N.Y., 1986, Teddy and Alice, Omaha Playhouse, 1990; costumes and scenery The Rake's Progress, Santa Fe Opera, 1957, Ariadne auf Naxos, 1957, La Boheme, 1958, Capriccio, 1958, Falstaff, 1958, Fledermaus, 1959, The Abduction From The Seraglio, 1959, The Makropoulos Affair, N.Y.C. Opera, 1970, H.M.S. Pinafore, 1975; exhibited in shows at Wright Hepburn Gallery, 1969, Praha Quedrennial, 1985, 89, Omaha Playhouse, 1986, Gone with the Wind Mus., 1993. Served with USN, 1944-46. Mem. United Scenic Artists. Episcopalian. Died Sept. 28, 2006.

CAMPBELL, RICHARD JOHN, air conditioning manufacturing company executive; b. Rochester, NY, Dec. 21, 1929; s. Eugene S. and Margaret (Lurz) C.; m. Mary Ann Hinders, July 18, 1958; children: Richard, Ann, John. Student, Rochester Inst. Tech., 1948-50; B Welding Engring., Ohio State U., 1955. Registered profl. engr., Wis., Ohio. Welding engr. ACF Industries, Berwick, Pa., 1957-59, Gen. Electric Co., Cin., 1959-61; with Trane Co., La Crosse, Wis., 1962-66, 68—, mrg. mgr. Societe Trane, Epinal, France, 1966-68, v.p., gen. mgr. comml. div., 1973-77, pres., chief operating officer, from 1977; sr. v.p. Am. Standard, Inc. (parent co.), NYC, from 1985. Bd. dirs. Trane Co. Can. Ltd. Bd. dirs. U. Wis.-La Crosse Devel. Found., Aquinas Found., La Crosse. Served to 1st lt. USAF, 1955-57. Hon. recipient James F. Lincoln Welding award Lincoln Electric Co., Cleve., 1961; named Outstanding Engring. Alumnus Ohio State U., 1973 Mem. ASME (boiler code), Am. Welding Soc., Am. Soc. Metals, Nat. Assn. Purchasing Mgmt., Am. Soc. Heating, Air Conditioning, Refrigeration Engrs. Roman Catholic. Home: West Salem, Wis. Died Feb. 16, 2006.

CAMPBELL, ROBERT HALLER, educational administrator; b. East Alton, Ill., Nov. 13, 1939; s. Joseph A. and Margaret R. (Haller) C.; m. Edith Marlene Leonard, Apr. 9, 1960; children— Susan Marie, Jeffrey Robert. A.B., McKendree Coll., 1961; M.A., Carnegie Inst. Tech., 1967; postgrad. So. Ill. U., 1972-73. Cert. tchr. supr., adminstr., Ill. Tchr. High Mount Sch., Belleville, Ill., 1961-63, Roxana Pub. Schs. (Ill.), 1964-66; gifted program dir. Community Unit Sch. Dist. No. 2, Marion, Ill., 1967-71, dir. curriculum and instructional services, 1973—, area service ctr. dir. John A. Logan Coll., Carterville, Ill., 1971-73. Active United Way, YMCA, Methodist Ch. commr. Marion Park Dist., v.p., 1982-83. Recipient Disting. Service award Marion Jaycees, 1972. Mem. Assn. Supervision and Curriculum Devel., Ill., Assn. Supervision and Curriculum Devel., Nat. Assn. for Gifted Children; Marion C. of C. (Citizen of Yr. award 1979), Schoolmasters, Phi Delta Kappa. Lodge: Kiwanis (pres. Marion 1978-79). Home: Marion, Ill. Died Mar. 5, 2006.

CAMPBELL, WILLIAM HENRY, geologist; b. Kansas City, Mo., Sept. 20, 1923; s. Myers D. and Wilma (Morris) C.; m. Virginia Hargus, Oct. 8, 1955; children: Constance Lyn, William Arthur. BA, Kans. U., 1947; BS in Geology, Mo. State U., 1950, MS, 1960; PhD in Archaeology, U. Biarritz, France, 1965. Cons. geologist and oil field operator various locations, 1951-55; mining engr. Batesville, Ark., 1955-57; geologist, v.p. A.R. Jones Oil & Operating Co., Kansas City, Mo., 1957-58, also bd. dirs.; pres. Jones & Campbell, Inc., Shawnee Mission, Kans., from 1958, chmn. bd., 1960. Lectr. paleontology Mo. State U., 1960; geologist Lotus & Trojan Oil Co., Kansas City, Mo., 1957-58 Contbr. articles on paleontology and mineralogy to sci. jours. Chmn. United Fund, Kansas City, Mo., 1957; mem. Energy Adv. Council, State of Kans., 1976-78; bd. dirs. Gillis Home for Children. Served to capt. U.S. Army, 1943-46, ETO. AAU 3-meter diving champion, 1940 Mem. Am. Assn. Profl. Geologists (lic.), Am. Assn. Petroleum Geologists, Soc. Mining Engrs., Smithsonian Assos., Aircraft Owners and Pilots Assn., Air Force Assn., Am. Legion, VFW, Sigma Chi, Phi Sigma Epsilon. Clubs: University (Kansas City, Mo.); Exchange, Bounders, Masons. Episcopalian. Home: Shawnee Mission, Kans. Died Apr. 30, 2006.

CAMPBELL, WILLIAM STEEN, publishing executive, writer, chaplain; b. New Cumberland, W.Va., June 27, 1919; s. Robert N. and Ethel (Steen) C.; m. Rosemary J. Bingham, Apr. 21, 1945 (dec. Dec. 1992); children: Diana J., Sarah A., Paul C., John W. Grad., Steubenville Bus. Coll., Ohio, 1938. Ordained minister Progressive Universal Life Ch., 2002. Cost acct. Hancock Mfg. Co., New Cumberland, 1938-39; cashier, statistician Weirton Steel Co., W.Va., 1939-42; travel exec. Am. Express Co., NYC, 1946-47; adminstr., account exec. Good Housekeeping mag., 1947-55; pub. Cosmopolitan mag., 1955-57; asst. dir. circulation Hearst Mags., NYC, 1957-61; gen. mgr. Motor Boating mag., 1961-62; v.p., dir. circulation Hearst Mags., 1962-85; pres. Internat. Circulation Distbrs., 1978-81, Mags., Meetings, Messages, Ltd., from 1986. With Periodical Pubs. Svc. Bur. subs. Hearst Corp., Sandusky, Ohio, 1964-85, v.p., chief exec., 1964-69, pres., chief exec., 1970-85; dir. Audit Bur. Circulations, 1974-86, Nat. Mag. Co., Ltd., London, Randolph Jamaica Ltd., Omega Pub. Corp. Fla., Hearst Can. Ltd., 1964-85; former chmn. Ctrl. Registry, Mag. Pubs. Assn.; chmn. bd trustees Hearst Employees Retirement Plan, 1971-85; mem. pres.'s coun. Brandeis U., 1974-81; chmn. nat. corp., found. com. U. Miami, 1979-85; dir. Broadway Assn., 1985-90, v.p., 1988-90; keynote spkr. Hospitality Industry Luncheon, Santa Barbara, Calif., 1996 Bd. dirs. Santa Barbara Rep. Club, 1993-94, Lobero Theatre Found., 1994-96, v.p., 1995-96. Lt. col. USAF, 1942-46, ETO. Recipient Lee C. Williams award Mag. Fulfillment Mgrs. Assn., 1974, Torch of Liberty award Anti-Defamation League, 1979. Mem. Campbell Clan Soc., Mil. Order of World Wars (chaplain), Masons, Cosmopolitan Club (chaplain). Died Nov. 26, 2006.

CAMPION, ROBERT THOMAS, manufacturing executive; b. Mpls., June 23, 1921; s. Leo P. and Naomi (Revord) C.; m. Wilhelmina Knapp, June 8, 1946; 1 son, Michael. Student, Loyola U., Chgo., 1939-41, 46-48. C.P.A., Ill. With Alexander Grant & Co., Chgo., 1946-57, ptnr., 1954-57; with Lear Siegler, Inc., Santa Monica, Calif., from 1957, pres., 1971-85, chief exec. officer, dir., 1971-86, chmn., 1974-86; pvt. investor, from 1987. Served with AUS, 1942-46. Mem. AICPA, Ill. Soc. CPAs, Bel Air Country Club, Jonathan Club, La Quinta Country Club. Republican. Died May 1, 2006.

CANEDY, CHARLES EDWIN, retired military officer; b. Buckland, Mass., Nov. 11, 1931; s. Charles Edward and Gladys Sunshine (Baker) C.; m. Fredrica Hazel Dole, June 21, 1953; children: Susan Canedy Wyland, Carol Canedy Guillory, Charles Dole. BA, Norwich U., 1953. Commd. 2d lt. U.S. Army, 1953, advanced through grades to brig. gen., comdr. world's first air cav. brigade, 1973-75, dir. army aviation, 1975-80, asst. div. comdr. 3d Armored Div. NATO, 1980-81, chief of staff 5th U.S. Army, 1981, ret., 1981. Decorated D.F.C., D.S.M., Purple Heart, Silver Star, Legion of Merit, Air medal with 23 oak leaf clusters. Mem. Army Aviation Assn. Am. (bd. dirs.), Daedalions (bd. dirs.). Home: San Antonio, Tex. Died July 29, 2007.

CANNON, ROBERT EMMET, consumer products manufacturing company executive; b. Greenville, Miss., Nov. 18, 1929; s. Robert Emmet and Louise (Hill) C.; m. Kathryn Gracey, Aug. 28, 1955; children: Katherine, Howard, Hall. B.M.E., Ga. Inst. Tech., 1951. With Procter & Gamble Co., 1954-91, sr. v.p. Memphis, 1989-91; chmn. & CEO Buckeye Technologies Inc., Memphis, 1993—2003. Pres. Chickasaw coun. Boy Scouts Am., 1978-80, bd. dirs., 1975—; bd. dirs. United Way Greater Memphis, Future Memphis, Inc., Lebonheur Children's Hosp.; mem. nat. adv. bd. Ga. Inst. Tech., mem. adv. bd. Sch. Mech. Engring.; past pres., bd. dirs. Memphis Orchestral Soc.; officer Shady Grove Presbyn. Ch., Memphis. Served with USN, 1951-54. Mem. Chickasaw Country Club. Home: Memphis, Tenn. Died Mar. 14, 2007.

CANNON, WILLIAM BERNARD, retired academic administrator; b. Cascade, Iowa, Nov. 10, 1920; s. Charles Bernard and Irma (White) C.; m. Jeanne Adair Ketchum, Aug. 16, 1944; children: Julia, Dominic, William, Robert. Ph.B., U. Chgo., 1947; MA, 1949. Budget examiner Bur. Budget, 1951-54, 59-62; asst. v.p. U. Chgo., 1954-59, v.p. programs and projects, 1968-74; dean Lyndon B. Johnson Sch. Pub. Affairs, U. Tex. at Austin, 1974-75; v.p. bus. and fin. U. Chgo., 1976-83, prof., 1976-89, prof. emeritus, from 1989. Asst. chief, office legis. reference for health, edn. and welfare programs Bur. Budget, 1962-65, chief edn., manpower and sci. div., 1965-67; dep. chmn. Nat. Endowment for the Arts, 1968 Mem. selection com. Rockefeller Pub. Service Awards, 1976-81; mem. Midwest selection com. H.S. Truman Scholarship Program, 1977-87. Served with AUS, 1943-46. Mem. Phi Beta Kappa. Home: Davis, Calif. Died July 1, 2006.

CANTELLA, VINCENT MICHELE, securities trader, director; b. Boston, Oct. 27, 1917; s. Michele and Josephine (Sapienza) C.; m. Josephine R. Castanien, Nov. 19, 1944; children: Betsy Ann, David V., Steven M. BS, Boston U., 1939. Mng. ptnr. Cantella & Co., Boston, 1952-74; ptnr. Josephthal & Co., Boston, 1974-78, 1974-78; pres. Cantella & Co. Inc., 1979, 1979-97, chmn., 1997—2007. Mem. Boston Stock Exch., 1953—2005, bd. govs., mem. exec. com., 1963—74, 1979—91, chmn. exec. com., 1971—73, chmn. bd. govs., 1973—74; pres. Boston Stock Exch. Clearing Corp., 1964—68; mem. Midwest Stock Exch., 1965—72, Pacific Coast Stock Exch., 1965—78, N.Y. Stock Exch., 1969—78, Detroit Stock Exch., 1963—76, P.B.W. Stock Exch., 1970—73, Am. Stock Exch., 1972—75. Ret. Maj. USMC, World War II. Mem.: The N.Y. Stock Exc. Luncheon Club, Boston Athletic Club. Home: Boston, Mass. Died May 4, 2007.

CANTOR, ELI, writer, novelist, playwright, poet, typographic company executive, management consultant; b. N.Y.C., Sept. 9, 1913; s. Sol M. and Bertha (Seidler) C.; BS, N.Y. U., 1934, MA (Ogden Butler fellow in Philosophy), 1935; JD, Harvard, 1938; m. Beatrice Mink, Oct. 4, 1942; children: Ann, Fred. Of counsel CBS, N.Y.C., 1939; mem. editorial staff Esquire, Coronet mags., Chgo., 1940-41; editor-in-chief Rsch. Inst. Report, Rsch. Inst. Am., Inc., N.Y.C., 1951-61; pres. The Photo-Composing Room, Inc., N.Y.C., 1961-65; chmn. bd. The Composing Room, Inc., 1965-71, chmn. emeritus, 1971—; chmn. bd. Printing Industries Met. N.Y., 1971-73; chmn. bd. Printing Industries Am., 1973-74; mem. printing and journalism adv. commns. Bd. Edn., N.Y.C., 1972—; chmn. exec. com. Advt. Typography Assn., N.Y., 1967-70; chmn. rsch.-tech. com. Graphic Arts Tech. Found., 1971-76; cons. fed. graphics Nat. Endowment Arts, 1975—; industry rep. before Congress. Pres. Columbian Hook and Ladder Co., Croton Fire Dept., 1951; trustee Croton Free Libr.; bd. dirs. Chamber Music Am., Asolo Theatre, Sarasota; mem. nat. adv. coun. Fla. Music Festival, Sarasota, Sarasota County Arts Coun. Named to O'Brien Roll of Honor, N.Y. Printers Hall of Fame, 1981; Yaddo fellow. Mem. PEN, Author's Guild, Poets and Writers, Harvard Club of Sarasota. Author numerous short stories, articles, poems for popular publs. TV plays NBC. Author: (plays) Candy Store, The Golden Goblet, (novels) Enemy in the Mirror, Love Letters; (under name Gregory A. Douglas) The Rite; (film) The Nest, 1987; commencement speaker U. South Fla., Sarasota, 1992; lectr. and educator in fields of econs., bus., graphic arts, lit. Home: Sarasota, Fla. Died Oct. 17, 2006.

CANTOR, SAMUEL C., lawyer; b. Phila., Mar. 11, 1919; s. Joseph and Miryl (Ginzberg) C.; m. Dorothy Van Brink, Apr. 9, 1943; children: Judith Ann Stone, Barbara Ann Palm. BSS, CCNY, 1940; JD, Columbia, 1943. Bar: N.Y. 1943, U.S. Dist. Ct. (so. and ea. dists.) N.Y. 1951, U.S. Supreme Ct 1969, D.C. 1971. Asst. dist. atty., NYC, 1943-48; legislative counsel N.Y. State Senate; counsel N.Y.C. Affairs Com. N.Y. State Senate, 1949-59; mem. firm Newcomb, Woolsey & Cantor, Newcomb & Cantor, NYC, 1951-59; 1st dep. supt. ins. State of N.Y., 1959-64, acting supt. ins., 1963-64; 2d v.p., gen. solicitor Mut. Life Ins. Co. N.Y., 1964-66, v.p., gen. counsel, 1967-72, sr. v.p., gen. counsel, 1973-74, sr. v.p. law and external affairs, 1974-75, sr. v.p. law and corp. affairs, 1975-78, exec. v.p. law and corp. affairs, 1978-84; counsel Rogers & Wells, 1984-89. Bd. dir. Mut. Life Ins. Co N.Y., Mony Reins. Corp., Monyco, Inc., Key Resources, Inc., Mony Advisors, Inc.; chmn. exec. com. N.Y. Life Ins. Guaranty Corp., 1974-84; mem. spl. com. on ins. holding holding cos. N.Y. Supt. Ins., 1967, N.Y. State select com. pub. employee pensions, 1973 Contbr. articles to Golf and other mags., legal and ins. jours. Fellow Am. Bar Found.; mem. Ins. Fedn. N.Y. (pres. 1967-68), Am. Bar Assn., N.Y. State Bar Assn., Am. Life Conv. (v.p. N.Y. State 1965-70), Am. Coun. Life Ins. (chmn. legal sect. 1977, chmn. legis. com. 1977-78, N.Y. State v.p. 1977-84), Health Ins. Assn. Am. (chmn. govt. rels. com. 1975, chmn. health care com. N.Y. State 1974-80), Assn. Life Ins. Counsel (dir.), Am. Judicature Soc., Bar Assn. City N.Y., N.Y. Law Inst., Nat. Attys. Assn., N.Y. State Dist. Attys. Assn., Union Internationale des Avocats, Columbia U. Law Sch. Alumni Assn. (dir.) Clubs: Mason. (N.Y.C.), University (N.Y.C.); Met., Univ. (Washington); Fort Orange (Albany, N.Y.); Sawgrass Country, Marsh Landing, Ponte Vedra (Fla.); La Costa Country (Carlsbad, Calif.); Confrérie des Chevaliers du Tastevin; Fairview Country (Greenwich, Conn.); Royal Dornoch Golf (Scotland), Am. Seniors Golf Assn., U.S. Golf Assn. (committeeman). Home: Greenwich, Conn. Died June 8, 2007.

CAPEL, GUY B., lawyer, banker; b. Brussels, Mar. 26, 1938; came to US, 1941; s. Maurice and Lola (Low) C.; m. Anna Krakoski, Nov. 10, 1975 (div. Apr. 1982); 1 child, Abigale Julia; m. Margaret Elizabeth French, Oct. 17, 1987; children: James Matthew, Leila Katherine. BA, Columbia U., 1962, JD, 1964. Bar: NY 1965, Vt. 1987. Assoc. Milbank Tweed, Hadley & McCloy, NYC, 1969-71; assoc. gen. counsel NY State Banking Dept., NYC, 1971-74; v.p., gen. counsel Savs. Banks Assn. of NY State, NYC, 1974-77; sr. v.p., gen. counsel Apple Bank, NYC, 1977-86, Long-Term Credit Bank of Japan - NY br., NYC, 1997—2000; counsel Downs, Rachlin and Martin, Burlington, Vt., 1986-88; pvt. practice Burlington, 1988-91; sr. v.p., gen. counsel, sec. Bank Leumi Trust Co., NYC, 1991-93; ptnr. Fink Weinberger P.C., NYC, 1993, Emmet, Marvin & Martin, NYC, 1993-97; v.p., assoc. gen. counsel HSBC Equator Bank (USA) Inc., Glastonbury, Conn., from 2000. Chmn. Banking Roundtable, Vail, Colo., 1983-88; bd. dirs. NY League for Hard of Hearing, 1982-87. Mem. ABA, Vt. Bar Assn. Avocations: music, tennis, skiing. Died June 2, 2006.

CAREY, ERNESTINE GILBRETH (MRS. CHARLES E. CAREY), writer, educator; b. NYC, Apr. 5, 1908; d. Frank Bunker and Lillian (Moller) Gilbreth; m. Charles Everett Carey, Sept. 13, 1930 (dec. 1986); children: Lillian Carey Barley, Charles Everett. BA, Smith Coll., 1929. Buyer R. H. Macy & Co., NYC, 1930-44, James McCreery, NYC, 1947-49. Carey writer and lectr. Book reviewer, 1949-2006, syndicated newspaper articles, 1951, (with Lillian Moller Gilbreth) (McElligott medallion Assn. Marquette U. Women 1966); author: Jumping Jupiter, 1952, Rings Around Us, 1956, Giddy Moment, 1958, Off and Away, 1998, Blubby, 1999; co-author (with Frank B. Gilbreth, Jr.) Cheaper by the Dozen, 1948 (Prix Scarron French Internat. Humor award 1951, more than 54 translations), Belles on Their Toes, 1950; contbg. author: Smith Voices—Selected Works by Smith College Women, 1990, 99; lifetime papers represented in collections at Smith Coll.; also mag. articles and book revs. Bd. dirs. Right to Read, Inc., 1968-2006, co-chmn., 1967; lay adv. com. Manhasset (N.Y.) Bd. Edn.; trustee Manhasset Pub. Libr., 1953-59, v.p., 1956-59; trustee Smith Coll., 1967-72; active in care-preservation and current student use of Frank B. and Lillian M. Gilbreth lifetime papers at Purdue U., Smith Coll. and internationally. Montgomery award Friends of Phoenix Pub. Libr., 1981, honored guest Ariz. Lib. Friends, 1994; recipient Internat. Mgmt. award: the Gilbreth Medal, Soc. for Advancement of Mgmt., 1996. Mem. Authors Guild Am. (life mem., mem. guild council 1955-60), PEN, North Shore Club, Smith Coll. Club (asst. chmn. scholarship com. L.I. chpt. 1950-59), Smith Coll. Club (vice chmn. scholarship com. Phoenix chpt.). Home: Reedley, Calif. Died Nov. 4, 2006.

CAREY, RON (RONALD J. CICENIA), actor; b. Newark, Dec. 11, 1935; s. John and Fanny Cicenia; m. Sharon Boyeronus, Nov. 11, 1967. BA, Seton Hall U., 1958. Appeared on numerous TV variety shows including The Steve Allen Show, The Clifton Davis show, The Melba Moore Show, The Jack Paar Show, The Merv Griffin Show, The Mike Douglas Show, The Johnny Carson Show; actor (TV series)The Corner Bar, 1972-73, The Montefuscos, 1975, Barney Miller, 1976-82, Have Faith, 1989, Lucky Luke, 1993; (TV appearances) Alice, 1977, Benson, 1982, New Love, American Style, 1986; (films) The Out of Towners, 1970, Who Killed Mary What's Her Name, 1971, Made for Each Other, 1971, The Silent Movie, 1976, High Anxiety, 1977, Fatso, 1980, History of the World Part I, 1981, Johnny Dangerously, 1984, Lucky Luke, 1991, The Fight Before Christmas, 1994, The Good Bad Guy, 1997, Food for Thought, 1999; performer (comedy albums) The Slightly Irreverant Comedy of Ron Carey, 1966. Mem. Screen Actors Guild, AFTRA, Equity. Democrat. Roman Catholic. Home: Los Angeles, Calif. Died Jan. 16, 2007.

CARL, JOHN L., former insurance company executive; b. Huntington, Ind., Feb. 22, 1948; m. Brook Swanson, Aug. 30, 1969; children: Brian, Erin. BS, Purdue U., 1970; MBA, Ind. U., 1972. Fin. analyst Am. Hosp. Supply Corp., Glendale, Calif., 1972-73, plant contr., 1973-74, Milledgeville, Ga., 1974-75, dir. fin. planning Irvine, Calif., 1975-76; v.p., contr. McGraw Labs divsn., Irvine, 1976-81, Hosp. Sector divsn., Evanston, Ill., 1981-86; v.p., corp. contr. Kraft Foods Inc., Glenview, Ill., 1986-89; v.p., CFO Nat. Computer Sys., Mpls., 1989-90; v.p., corp. contr. Amoco Corp., Chgo., 1991-94, exec. v.p., CFO, 1994-99; sr. v.p., CFO Allstate Corp., Northbrook, 1999—2002. Active Dean's Adv. Coun., Sch. Bus., Ind. U.; bd. dirs. Evanston (Ill.) Hosp., United Way of Chicago Coun. Mem. Fin. Execs. Inst., Am. Petroleum Inst. Home: Lake Forest, Ill. Died Feb. 10, 2006.

CARLINER, DAVID (ABRAHAM DAVID CARLINER), lawyer; b. Washington, Aug. 13, 1918; s. Louis and Cassie (Brooks) C.; m. Miriam Kalter, Jan. 24, 1944 (dec. Aug. 9, 1994); children: Geoffrey Owen, Deborah Joan (Mrs. Robert Remes). Student, Am. U., 1935-36, U. Va., 1936-38, student in law, 1938-40; LLB, Nat. U., 1941. Bar: Va. 1940, D.C. 1946, US Supreme Ct. 1953. Atty. JAG Office Army Dept., Washington, 1946; Washington rep. New Coun. Am. Bus., Washington, 1946-48; pvt. practice, 1948-50; ptnr. Wasserman and Carliner, 1950-67; of counsel Chapman Duff and Lenzini, 1968-74; ptnr. Carliner and Gordon, 1974-84, Carliner and Remes, PC, Washington, from 1984. Vis. lectr. Fgn. Svc. Inst., Dept. State, USIA, Harvard U., 1985. Author: Rights of Aliens, 1977; co-author The Rights of Aliens and Refugees, 1990. Nat. bd. dirs. ACLU, 1965-83, gen. counsel, 1976-79; chmn. Internat. Human Rights Law Group, 1978-86, Washington Home Rule Com., 1966-70; co-chmn. D.C. Com. for Re-Orgn. Plan, 1967-68; chmn. Washington chpt., mem. nat. exec. coun. Am. Jewish Com., 1969-71; mem. nat. adv. coun. Amnesty Internat., 1969—2007; Bd. dirs. Am. Coun. for Nationalities Svcs., 1977-89, Internat. League for Human Rights; trustee Washington Inst. Values in Pub. Policy, 1984-88. With AUS, 1941-45. Recipient Oliver Wendell Holmes award, 1966, Human Rights award Ctr. for Human Rights and Constl. Law, 1994, Isaiah award Am. Jewish Com., 1998. Mem. ABA (chmn. immigration and nationality com. adminstrv. law sect. 1979-83, mem. coun. adminstrv. law sect. 1983-87, Brookings Instn. coun., Washington 1995-2007), Fed. Bar Assn. (chmn. com. immigration and naturalization 1961-62), D.C. Bar (vice chmn. opinions com. ethics 1974-76, bd. dir. 1980-83), Va. State Bar, Am. Law Inst., Am. Immigration and Naturalization Lawyers Assn. (Jack Wasserman Meml. award 1994), Cosmos Club (Washington). Died Sept. 18, 2007.

CARLSON, ARTHUR EUGENE, accounting educator; b. Whitewater, Wis., May 10, 1923; s. Paul Adolph and Dorothy Adeline (Cooper) C.; m. Lorraine June Bronson, Aug. 19, 1944; 1 child, George Arthur. EdB, U. Wis., Whitewater, 0943; MBA, Harvard U., 1947; PhD, Northwestern U., 1954. Instr. Ohio U., 1947-50; lectr. Northwestern U., 1950-52; from asst. prof. to prof. acctg. Washington U., St. Louis, 1952-88, prof. emeritus, from 1988. Vis. prof. U. Hawaii, 1963-64. Author: College Accounting, 1967, 7th edit., 1993, Accounting Essentials, 1973, 5th edit., 1991. Chmn. Robert Meml. Endowment Fund, University City, Mo., 1972-2004, trustee Police and Fire Pension Bd., 1979-88. Mem. Inst. Mgmt. Accts. (past pres.), Assn. Sys. Mgmt. (past pres., Disting. Svc. award 1973), Soc. Profs. Emeriti Washington U. (pres. 1995, disting. bus. alumni awards com. 1998—), Kiwanis (pres. 1969). Republican. Episcopalian. Avocations: bowling, gardening. Home: Saint Louis, Mo. Died Jan. 15, 2006.

CARLSON, CHARLES A., retired information technology executive; b. Mpls., Jan. 28, 1933; s. Clifford and Loretta M. (Sengir) C.; m. Marlene G. Carlson, Nov. 1, 1969; children: Susan, Anne, Richard, Patricia, Andrew. BA in English, Coll. St. Thomas, St. Paul, 1954; postgrad., U. Iowa. Retail store mgmt. positions Sears Roebuck & Co., Mpls., 1955-66, dept. mgr. positions Chgo., 1966-76, territorial data processing mgr. Atlanta, 1976-80, nat. mgr. computers and comm. Chgo., 1980-81, v.p. data processing and comm., 1981-89; pres. Sears Tech. Svcs., Inc., Schaumburg, Ill., 1989-93; retired, 1993. Bd. dirs. Jr. Achievement Chgo., 1985-89. Woodrow Wilson fellow, 1955 Mem. Nat. Retail Mchts. Assn. (bd. dirs. info. systems div. 1981-89). Republican. Lutheran. Avocations: civil war interests, sports. Home: Antioch, Ill. Died Aug. 12, 2006.

CARLSON, ROBERT GEORGE, pharmaceutical company executive, veterinarian, consultant; b. Grand Rapids, Mich., Apr. 1, 1922; s. Harry and Hilda (Carlson) Chapman; m. M. June Bryant, Sept. 14, 1942; children— Margaret Anne, Carrie Jean. D.V.M., Mich. State U., 1952; M.S., Purdue U., 1954, Ph.D., 1956. Diplomate Am. Coll. Vet. Pathologists, Am. Coll. Lab. Animal Medicine. Instr., asst. prof. Purdue U., West Lafayette, Ind., 1952-56; research scientist Upjohn Co., Kalamazoo, Mich., 1956-61, sect. head, 1961-74, dir. pharm. research and devel. Japan Upjohn Ltd., Tokyo, 1974-85, research mgr., 1978-80, group mgr., 1980-84, dir., 1984-87, ret. 1987. Served to capt. USAAF, 1943-45, ETO. Mem. Am. Coll. Vet. Pathology, Am. Coll. Lab. Animal Medicine, Soc. Toxicology, Euorpean Soc. Toxicology. Home: Kalamazoo, Mich. Died July 4, 2006.

CARLTON, ALWIN HORATIO, mechanical engineer; b. Birmingham, Ala., Feb. 24, 1933; s. Basil Brown and Nannie Hope (Lee) C.; B.S., Auburn U., 1960; postgrad. U. Tenn., 1965-67; m. Dorothy Emma Bowles, Sept. 16, 1952; children— Patricia Ann, Linda Jane, James Alwin, Robert Duane. Mech. engr. Holston Def. Corp., Kingsport, Tenn., 1960-72, chief engr., 1972-79, supt. utilities, 1979-83, supt. mfg. services, 1983—. Bd. dirs. Community Chest Kingsport, 1974—. Registered profl. engr., Tenn. Mem. ASME, Tenn. Soc. Profl. Engrs. (dir. Upper East Tenn. chpt. 1978-79, pres. Upper East Tenn. chpt. 1983—). Baptist (deacon). Clubs: Bays Mountain Flying, Elks. Home: Kingsport, Tenn. Died Oct. 19, 2006.

CARLTON, CATHERINE KENNEY, osteopathic surgeon; b. Oct. 20, 1915; d. Charles Francis and Helene (Larmoyeux) K.; m. Elbert P. Carlton, June 11, 1941 (dec. 1972); children: Cathy Carlton Landon, Helen McFall, Jane Carlton Toone; m. Eugene Hightower, May 23, 1974 (dec. 1992). Student, Incarnate Word Coll., San Antonio, 1933, U. Tex., Arlington, 1934; DO, Kirksville Coll. Osteo. Med., Mo., 1938. Cert. in gen. practice Am. Acad. Osteopathy. Practice medicine specializing in osteopathy, from 1939; mem. staff Ft. Worth Osteo. Hosp., from 1946. Prof. Tex. Coll. Osteo. Medicine, 1970-75, clin. prof., 1975-96; lectr., demonstrator osteo. manipulative technique 1st Internat. Congress Osteo. Medicine, Brussels, 1984; cons. and lectr. in field. Editor: A History of St. Mary of the Assumption Catholic Church 1908 to 1988, 1988; contbr. articles to profl. jours. Mem. NCCJ, Ft. Worth, 1984-93; eucharistic min. St. Mary Assumption, San Antonio, 1987, active in hist. places registration, 1984; mem. St. Mary's Parish Coun., Ft. Worth Diocese; pres. Nat. Coun. Cath. Women, 1952-53. Named Outstanding Alumnus, Kirksville Coll. Osteo. Medicine, 1965, Gen. Practitioner of the Yr., Tex. Assn. Osteo. Family Practitioners, 1997, Family Physician of Yr., Tex., 1997; recipient Meritorious Svc. award Tex. Coll. Osteo. Medicine, 1975, Outstanding Hosp. Staff Mem. award Osteopathis Med. Ctr., Tex., 1989, Edna Gladney Aux. Svc. award, Ft. Worth, 1978, Hist. Medallion award Tex. Hist. Commn., 1979, Founders medal Tex. Coll. Osteo. Medicine Bd. Regents, 1983, Profl. Woman award Ridglea Bus. & Profl. Women, 1984, Humanitarian Disting. Svc. award 4th degree KC, 1986. Mem. Am. Acad. Osteopathy (pres. 1976-77), Kirksville Coll. Osteo. Medicine Alumni Assn. (sec. Tex. chpt. 1965-87, pres. 1979-80), Tex. Acad. Osteopathy (pres. 1969-88, sec.-treas. 1971-87), Tex. Coll. Osteo. Medicine Found. (sec. 1986-88), Zonta (Outstanding Profl. Accomplishments award 1976), Rotary (1st v.p. Ft. Worth club 1986-87), Knights & Ladies of the Holy Sepulchre (lady commr.), The Serra Club (pres. Ft. Worth club 1999-00, rep. internat. meeting Glasgow, Scotland 1999). Republican. Avocations: swimming, walking, reading. Home: Colleyville, Tex. Died Aug. 22, 2006.

CARMACK, MILDRED JEAN, retired lawyer; b. Folsom, Calif., Sept. 3, 1938; d. Kermit Leroy Brown and Elsie Imogene (Johnston) Walker; m. Allan W. Carmack, 1957 (div. 1979); 1 child, Kerry Jean Carmack Garrett. Student, Linfield Coll., 1955-58; BA, U. Oreg., 1967, JD, 1969. Bar: Oreg. 1969, U.S. Dist. Ct. Oreg. 1980, U.S. Ct. Appeals (9th and fed. cirs.) 1980, U. S. Claims Ct. 1987. Law clk. to Hon. William McAllister Oreg. Supreme Ct., Salem, 1969-73, asst. to ct., 1976-80; asst. prof. U. Oreg. Law Sch., Eugene, 1973-76; assoc. Schwabe, Williamson & Wyatt, Portland, Oreg., 1980-83, ptnr., 1984-96, ret., 1996. Writer, lectr., legal educator, Oreg., 1969—; mem. exec. bd. Appellate sect. Oreg. State Bar, 1993-95. Contbr. articles to Oreg. Law Rev., 1967-70. Mem. citizen adv. com. State Coastal Planning Commn., Oreg., 1974-76, State Senate Judiciary Com., Oreg., 1984; mem. bd. visitors Law Sch. U. Oreg., 1992-95; mem. Oreg. Law Commn. Working Group on Conflict of Laws, 2000. Mem. Oreg. State Bar Assn., Order of Coif. Home: Ukiah, Calif. Died June 7, 2007.

CARMONY, MARVIN DALE, retired linguist, educator; b. nr Richmond, Ind., Feb. 27, 1923; s. Harry Edgar and Eller (Brown) C.; m. Mary Joan Nicholson, May 31, 1947; children— Ronald Dee, Kathryn Lynn. Student, Valparaiso Tech. Inst. 1941-42, Olivet Nazarene U., 1947-49; AB, Ind. State U., 1950 MA, 1951; PhD, Ind. U., 1965. Radio operator Am. Airlines Chgo., 1942-44; tchr. high schs. Pendleton and Shelbyville, Ind. 1953-59; from instr. English to assoc. prof. English and linguistics Ind. State U., Terre Haute, 1959-69, prof., 1969-88, assoc dean Coll. Arts and Scis., 1970-86. Co-founder Ind. Place Names Survey, 1968, dir., 1968-70; co-founder Ind. Names (now Hoosier Folklore), 1970, gen. editor, 1970-88. Author (with D.F. Carmony) Indiana Dialects in Their Historical Setting, 1972, rev. edit., 1979, (with Ronald Baker) Indiana Place Names, 1975; also articles. Trustee Olivet Nazarene U., 1967-70, mem. alumni bd. dirs., 1995-2000. With U.S. Mcht. Marine 1944-46; vet. USCG. Am. Council Learned Socs. fellow 1964-65 Mem. Am. Dialect Soc. (adv. bd. publs. 1972-77 82-86, pres. 1981-82), Soc. Wireless Pioneers, Am. Names Soc (editorial bd. Names 1977-84), Linguistic Soc. Am., Nat. Soc XVII Century Colonial Dames (Disting. Svc. award 1975), Phi Delta Lambda, Phi Delta Kappa, Sigma Tau Delta. Methodist Died Dec. 27, 2006.

CARNEY, ROBERT ALFRED, retired health care administrator; b. Winnipeg, Man., Can., Feb. 24, 1916; s. Thomas Alfred and Opal Edna (Fogle) C. (parents Am. citizens); m. Jacquelin Briscoe, May 15, 1943; children: Thomas A., Roberta L. Richard D. BA, Denison U., 1938. Lic. hosp. and nursing hom adminstr. Accountant Nat. Cash Register Co., 1938-41; accountant, auditor, controller Miami Valley Hosp., Dayton, O., 1941-47; asst. dir. Ochsner Found. Hosp., New Orleans, 1947-48 adminstrv. dir. Jewish Hosp., Cin., 1948-61, assoc. exec. dir 1961-68, exec. dir., 1968-78; cons. mgmt. and employee relations Children's Hosp. Med. Center, Cin., 1979; adminst Marjorie P. Lee Home for Aged, Cin., 1980-89; dir. spl. project Twin Towers Retirement Community, Cin., 1989-92; interim adminstr. Auglaize Acres County Nursing Home, Wapakoneta Ohio, 1990-91; adminstr. Lincoln Ave. and Crawford's Hom for the Aged, 1993-96; cons. Drake Ctr., 1996-97; ret., 199 Adj. assoc. prof. hosp. adminstrn. Coll. Pharmacy U. Cin 1969-78; adj. faculty mem., grad. program hosp. adminstr Xavier U., Cin., 1970-78; trustee Health Careers Greater Cin 1956-85, 1st v.p., 1970-85; mem. exec. com., trustee Healt Careers of Ohio, 1973-81, treas., 1976-79; trustee Am. Nurse Assn. Nat. Retirement Plan, 1973-75; pres. Withrow H.S. PTA 1969-71; mem. bd., pres. Bapt. Home Benevolent Soc., 197- 88; mem. bd. Jewish Fedn. Cin., 1969-70, 72-73; mem. raci isolation task force Cin. Pub. Schs., 1972-73, mem. adv. com for sch. lic. practical nursing, 1973; mem. home health svcs. ad com. Cin. Dept. Health, 1972—, chmn., 1974-76, 96-99; mer adv. com. Lic. Practical Nurse Assn. Ohio, 1979-85; mem. Oh Commn. Nursing, 1973-75, Am. Bd. Med. Specialists, 1977-8 sec. Ohio Coun. on Nursing Needs and Resources, 1978-81; b dirs., sec., treas. Fedn. for accessible Nursing Edn. and Lice sure, 1984-98; chmn. Greater Cin. Nursing Home assn., 198 98. Trustee emeritus Assn. Ohio Philanthropic Homes, 199 Recipient Outstanding Preceptor award Xavier U., 1974 Mer Am. Coll. Hosp. Adminstrs. (life), Am. Hosp. Assn. (life), Oh Hosp. Assn. (life), Nat. League for Nursing (dir. 1977-81), Oh League for Nursing (dir. 1968-76, v.p. 1973-76), Greater Ci Hosp. Council, Am. Pub. Health Assn., Assembly of Hosp. Sch Nursing (chmn. bd. 1977-78), Eagle Scout Assn. (life), Sign Chi, Phi Mu Alpha. Lodges: Masons. Baptist. Died Nov. 2 2005.

CARR, JOHN WESLEY, communications system executiv b. Indpls., Dec. 21, 1945; s. Lowell Russell and Mary Ja (Morris) C.; m. Rebecca Susan Wilfong, Apr. 30, 1981; childre Allison, Catherine. BS, Purdue U., 1968. Prodn. supr. Colli

Radio Corp., Cedar Rapids, Iowa, 1968-70; equipment supr. Ind. Bell Tel., Indpls., 1970-74, account exec., 1974-78, svc. mgr., 1978, sales mgr., 1979-82, Am. Bell, Indpls., 1983; mktg. mgr. nat. accounts AT&T, Chgo., 1984-85; 2d v.p., dir. corp. tech. systems Lincoln Nat. Corp., Ft. Wayne, Ind., 1985-87, v.p., dir. corp. tech. svcs., 1987-89, v.p., dir. corp. systems devel., from 1989. Mem. customer adv. coun. Digital Cons. Inc., 1990—, IBM-Image Plus, 1990—. Dir. Learning and Devel. Ctr., Ft. Wayne, 1986—, IPFW Bus. Coun., Ft. Wayne, 1989—. Mem. No. Ind. Telecom. Assn. Avocations: golf, downhill skiing. Died May 14, 2006.

CARR, MARIE BERNICE, communications educator; b. Aberdeen, SD, Oct. 13, 1917; d. James Michael and Minnie (Harder) C. BA, San Jose State U., 1939; MA, Stanford U., 1942, PhD, 1957. Instr. San Jose State U., 1939—43, asst. prof., 1947—51, assoc. prof., 1951—57, prof. comm. studies, 1957—81, prof. emeritus, from 1981, chmn. dept., 1975—86. Editor numerous textbook revisions. U.S. civil svc. rep. 12th Civil Svc. region, San Francisco, 1943—46, Monterey, 1943—46; tchr. Latter Day Saints Ch., 1st Ward, San Jose, 1982—85. Mem.: AAUP, Speech Comm. Assn., Western Speech Comm. Assn., Chi Omega. Republican. Home: San Jose, Calif. Died Jan. 15, 2006.

CARROLL, EDWARD ELMER, JR., nuclear engineering educator, consultant; b. North Bergen, N.J., Feb. 13, 1930; s. Edward Elmer and May Rita (Sullivan) C.; m. Joann Marie Harrington, Dec. 27, 1959 (dec. 1971); children— Cynthia, Megan, Edward, III; m. 2d, Thuy Thanh Tong, Dec. 12, 1975; children— Thanh-Mai, Giang Thanh. B.A., Harvard U., 1950; M.S., U. Pa., 1952, Ph.D., 1959. Sr. scientist Westinghouse Bettis Lab., West Mifflin, Pa., 1959-64; fellow scientist Westinghouse Electric Corp., Pitts., 1964-66; assoc. prof. nuclear engrng. U. Fla., Gainesville, 1966-70, asst. dean Coll. Engrng., 1971-74, acting chmn. nuclear engring., 1976-79, prof. nuclear engrng. scis., 1972—. vis. staff mem. Los Alamos Nat. Lab., 1970-71. Bd. dirs. Cath. Charities, Inc., North Fla., 1980—. Served to lt. (j.g.) U.S. Navy, 1952-55. Mem. Am. Phys. Soc., Am. Nuclear Soc., Soc. Photo Optical Instrumentation Engrs., Sigma Tau, Tau Beta Pi. Contbr. articles to profl. publs.; patentee in field. Home: Gainesville, Fla. Died May 16, 2006.

CARROLL, GEORGE JOSEPH, pathologist, educator; b. Gardner, Mass., Oct. 14, 1917; s. George Joseph and Kathryn (O'Hearn) C. BA, Clark U., Worcester, Mass., 1939; MD, George Washington U., 1944. Diplomate Am. Bd. Pathology. Intern Worchester City Hosp., 1944-45; resident in medicine Doctors Hosp., Washington, 1945-46; resident in pathology Sibley Hosp., Washington, 1948-49, VA Hosp., Washington, 1949-50; asst. pathologist D.C. Gen. Hosp., 1950-51, assoc. pathologist, 1951-52; pathologist Louise Obici Meml. Hosp., Suffolk, Va., from 1952, sec. med. staff, 1956-59, chief of staff, 1959-60, 67-69; pathologist Chowan Hosp., Edenton, NC, 1952-71, Southampton Meml. Hosp., Franklin, Va., from 1952, Greensville Meml. Hosp., Emporia, Va., from 1961. Instr. pathology Georgetown U. Sch. Medicine, 1950-52; instr. bacteriology Am. U., Washington, 1950-51; assoc. clin. prof. pathology Med. Coll. Va., Richmond, 1968-70; clin. prof. pathology Va. Commonwealth U., 1970—; prof. dept. pathology Eastern Va. Med. Sch., Norfolk, 1974—; sec.-treas. Va. Bd. Medicine, 1967-86, treas., 1971-86. Contbr. articles to med. jours. Served with U.S. Army, 1946-48. Fellow ACP, Coll. Am. Pathologists, Am. Soc. Clin. Pathologists (bd. dirs. 1969—, pres. 1977—), Internat. Acad. Pathology; mem. AMA, So. Med. Assn. (Va. councilor 1965-70, pres. 1973-74), Med. Soc. Va., 4th dist. Med. Soc. (pres. 1968-70), Seaboard Med. Soc. (pres. 1957), George Washington Med. Soc., Tri-County Med. Soc. (pres. 1971-73), Am. Soc. Clin. Pharmacy Therapeutics, Va. Soc. Pathology (pres. 1973-74), Soc. Nuclear Medicine, Am. Assn. Blood Banks, Am. Cancer Soc. (bd. dirs. Va. div. 1955-62), Va. Med. Svc. Assn. (bd. dirs. 1960-71), Rotary. Died Jan. 8, 2007.

CARROLL, SEAN B., geneticist, biologist, educator, researcher, writer; b. Sept. 17, 1960; m. Jamie Carroll; 2 children; 2 stepchildren. BA in Biology, Washington U., St. Louis; PhD in Immunology, Tufts U., 1983. Postdoctoral rschr. U. Colo., Boulder; faculty mem. to prof. molecular biology, genetics and med. genetics U. Wis., Madison, from 1987; investigator Howard Hughes Med. Inst., from 1990. Contbr. articles to sci. jours.; co-author: From DNA to Diversity: Molecular Genetics and the Evolution of Animal Design, 2004; author: Endless Forms Most Beautiful: The New Science of Evo Devo and the Making of the Animal Kingdom, 2005, The Making of the Fittest, 2006. Named one of 50 Future Leaders 40 and Under, Time mag., 1994; recipient Presdl. Young Investigator award, NSF, Shaw award, Milw. Found., Herbert W. Dickerman award, Wadsworth Ctr., NY State Dept. Health. Mem.: NAS, AAAS. Home: Fitchburg, Wis. Died Feb. 7, 2007.

CARRUTH, GORTON VEEDER, editor; b. Woodbury, Conn., Apr. 9, 1925; s. Gorton Veeder and Margery Tracy Barrow (Dibb) C.; m. Gisele Leliet, Dec. 28, 1955; children: Gorton Veeder III, Hayden III, Christopher Leliet. Ph.B., U. Chgo., 1948; BA, Columbia U., 1950, MA, 1954. Editor ref. books Thomas Y. Crowell Co., NYC, 1954-63; exec. editor McGraw-Hill Book Co., NYC, 1963-68; editor-in-chief Funk & Wagnalls, NYC, 1968-71; pres. Morningside Editorial Assocs., Pleasantville, N.Y., from 1971. Founding mem., v.p. Hudson Group, Inc., Pleasantville, 1972— Author: The Encyclopedia of American Facts and Dates, 9th rev. ed, 1993, The Encyclopedia of World Facts and Dates, 1993, The Young Reader's Companion, 1993; co-author: Where to Find Business Information, 1979, 2d edit., 1982, Oxford Am. Dictionary, 1980, The VNR Dictionary of Bus. and Fin, 1980, The Oxford Illustrated Literary Guide to the United States, 1982, The Encyclopedia of Historic Places, 1984, The Complete Word Game Dictionary, 1984, The Transcriber's Handbook, 1984, The New York Times Concise Crossword Puzzle Dictionary, 1987, The Bird Watcher's Diary, 1987, The Harper Book of American Quotations, 1988; editor-in-chief: The Volume Library, 1982—, The Student Handbooks, 1985—, The Family Handbook, 1985—. Mem. Linnaean Soc., Lab. Ornithology Cornell U. (hon.), Phi Beta Kappa. Home: Pleasantville, NY. Died Jan. 30, 2006.

CARRUTHERS, PAUL MATTHEW, textile company executive; b. Greensboro, NC, Apr. 6, 1921; s. Joseph Tinnie and Ethel (Williamson) C.; m. Carlotta Marsh, Feb. 23, 1957; children— Nora Evelyn, Paul Matthew. AB, Duke, U., 1947; MS, U. Ill., 1948; JD, U. N.C., 1954. Bar: N.C. 1954; C.P.A., N.C. Tax accountant A.M. Pullen & Co., Greensboro, N.C., 1948-52; asst. counsel R.J. Reynolds Tobacco Co., Winston-Salem, N.C., 1955-59; counsel, controller Wunda Weve Carpet Co., Greenville, S.C., 1959-61; sec., gen. counsel Callaway Mills Co., La Grange, Ga., 1961-68; sec. Deering Milliken Inc., Spartanburg, S.C., 1968-71; sec.-treas. Dan River, Inc., Greenville, S.C., 1971-75, v.p., sec., 1975-84; of counsel Rainey, Britton, Gibbes & Clarkson, Attys., Greenville, from 1985. Pres. City-County Hosp. Bd., La Grange, Ga., 1967-68. Served to capt. USAAF, 1942-46. Mem. Am. Inst. C.P.A.s, Am. Bar Assn. Clubs: Poinsett, Greenville Country. Home: Greenville, SC. Died July 31, 2007.

CARTER, ARTHUR LINWOOD, JR., savings and loan executive; b. Washington, June 27, 1948; s. Arthur Linwood and Doris (Fullerton) C.; m. Leah Kidd, Jan. 13, 1973; children: Michelle Lynn, Rebecca Anne. BA, George Mason U., 1970. Asst. controller Piedmont Fed. Savs. & Loan Assn., Manassas, Va., 1970-80, savs. officer, 1980—, v.p., 1981—. Sec.-treas. Prince William Multiple Sclerosis Soc., Manassas, 1980. Mem. Fin. Mgrs. Soc., Prince William-Greater Manassas C. of C. (pres. 1983-84, Mem. of Yr. 1978-79). Club: Sudley, Inc. (bd. dirs. 1987—). Lodge: Kiwanis (1987-88). Home: Manassas, Va. Died July 23, 2006.

CARTER, CHARLES EDWARD, lawyer; b. Springfield, Ohio, June 20, 1925; s. Brindley and Mary Bess (Smoot) C.; (div.); children: Bette Charlene Brown, Norman Brindley. BA, Miami U., Oxford, Ohio, 1950; LLB, Ohio State U., 1957. Bar: Ohio 1957. Ptnr. Cobb & Carter, Springfield, 1957-58; asst. law dir. City of Springfield, 1958-60, prosecutor, 1960-61, law dir., 1961-69; gen. counsel Mahoning County Legal Svc., Youngstown, Ohio, 1969-71; assoc. gen. counsel NAACP, NYC, 1971-86, corp. counsel Balt., 1986. Home: Springfield, Ohio. Died Oct. 1, 2005.

CARTER, JAMES HARVEY, psychiatrist, educator; b. Maysville, NC, May 11, 1934; s. Thomas and Irene (Barber) C.; m. Jettie Lucille Strayhorn, Aug. 21, 1957 (dec. Sept. 1987); 1 child, James Harvey; m. Elsie Richardson, Aug. 26, 1988; 1 child, Saunia Carter-Wilson BS, N.C. Ctrl. U., Durham, 1956; MD, Howard U., 1966; MDiv, Shaw U., Raleigh, NC, 1999. Diplomate Am. Bd. Psychiatry and Neurology, Am. Bd. Forensic Examiners. Rotating intern Walter Reed Army Hosp., Washington, 1967; resident in gen. adult psychiatry Dorothea Dix/Duke Med. Ctr., Raleigh-Durham, NC, 1969-70; assoc. dept. psycihatry Duke U., Durham, 1971-74, asst. prof., 1974-78, assoc. prof., 1978-83, prof., from 1983; sr. psychiatrist Dept. Correction, Raleigh, from 1974. Lectr. N.C. Found. for Alcohol and Drug Studies, U. N.C., Wilmington, 1989-95. Editor Epikrisis. Bd. dirs. Gov.'s Inst. on Alcohol and Substance Abuse, 1992-94; co-founder Drug Action of Wake County, Raleigh. Served to Col. M.C., U.S. Army, 1958-94. Decorated Order of Mil. Merit; recipient Profl. Designation A, U.S. Army Surg. Gen., 1985, Order of the Oak Leaf Pine Gov.'s award, 1999, Salomon Carter Fuller award, Am. Psychiatric Assn., 2003; E.Y. Williams clin. scholar, 1994; Josiah Macy Faculty fellow, 1970-74; Falk fellow, 1971-72. Fellow Am. Psychiat. Assn. (life; disting.; Solomon Carter Fuller award 2003); vice chair com. on chronic mental illness), Orthopsychiat. Assn.; mem. AMA, N.C. Med. Soc. (life), Alpha Kappa Mu, Alpha Omega Alpha. Achievements include founding of various drug awareness programs. Home: Raleigh, NC. Died Mar. 8, 2007.

CARTER, JOHN ROBERT, retired physician; b. Buffalo, Apr. 21, 1917; s. John Harvey and Gertrude Ann (Buckpitt) C.; m. Adelaide Briggs, May 8, 1943; children: Marilyn Anne, Jeanne Catherine. BS, Hamilton Coll., 1939; MD, U. Rochester, 1943. Diplomate: Nat. Bd. Med. Examiners. Intern State U. Iowa, 1943-44, resident, 1944-48, asst. dept. pathology, 1944, from instr. to asso. prof., 1944-55, prof., 1955-59; prof., chmn. dept. pathology and oncology U. Kans. Med. Center, 1960-66; prof. pathology dept. orthopedics Case Western Res. U., Cleve., 1981—2001, dir. Inst. Pathology, chmn. dept. pathology, 1966-81, prof. emeritus, 1987—2007. Cons. VA Hosp., U.S. Army Hosp., U.S. Penitentiary, Watkins Meml. Hosp.; Past chmn. pathology study sect. NIH; mem. pathology tng. grant com. Nat. Inst. Gen. Med. Scis.; mem. pathology adv. council Central VA Office; mem. sci. adv. bd. Armed Forces Inst. Pathology.; Bd. dirs. Univs. Asso. Research and Edn. Pathology; past pres. Mem. editorial bd.: Am. Jour. Pathology. Served to lt. USNR, 1946-48. Mem. AMA, AAAS, Cleve. Acad. Medicine, Path. Soc. Gt. Britain and Ireland, Am. Assn. Pathologists and Bacteriologists (past pres.), Internat. Acad. Pathology, Am. Soc. Clin. Pathology, Am. Soc. Exptl. Pathology, Am. Soc. Investigative Pathology, Coll. Am. Pathologists, Soc. Exptl. Biology, AAUP, Central Soc. Clin. Research, Phi Beta Kappa, Sigma Xi, Alpha Omega Alpha. Home: Willoughby, Ohio. Died Aug. 25, 2007.

CARTER, RICHARD, publisher, writer; b. NYC, Jan. 24, 1918; s. Samuel J. and Alice (Kulka) C.; m. Gladys Chasins, Oct. 20, 1945; children: Nancy Jane, John Andrew. BA, Coll. City N.Y., 1938. Music editor Billboard mag., 1940-46; staff organizer N.Y. Newspaper Guild, 1946-47; writer N.Y. Daily Mirror, 1947-49, N.Y. Daily Compass, 1949-52; pres. Millwood Publs., Inc., 1971-80; columnist The Racing Times, 1991-92, Daily Racing Form, 1992—2007. Author, contbr. mags., 1952—; Author: The Man Who Rocked the Boat, 1956, The Doctor Business, 1958, The Gentle Legions, 1961, Your Food and Your Health, 1964, Breakthrough: The Saga of Jonas Salk, 1966, Superswine, 1967, (with Curt Flood) The Way It Is, 1971, (under pseudonym Tom Ainslie) The Compleat Horseplayer, 1966, Ainslie's Jockey Book, 1967, Ainslie's Complete Guide to Thoroughbred Racing, 1968, The Handicapper's Handbook, 1969, Theory and Practice of Handicapping, 1969, Ainslie's Complete Guide to Harness Racing, 1970, Ainslie's Complete Hoyle, 1975, Ainslie's Encyclopedia of Thoroughbred Handicapping, 1978, How to Gamble in a Casino, 1979, (with Bonnie Ledbetter) The Body Language of Horses, 1980. Served with USAAF, 1942-45, PTO. Recipient George Polk Meml. award, 1952 Mem. Authors Guild, Nat. Assn. Sci. Writers, Nat. Turf Writers Assn. Died Sept. 1, 2007.

CARTLAND, JOHN EVERETT, III, investment executive; b. Paterson, NJ, Dec. 11, 1944; s. John Everett Jr. and Klazina Dirk (Kuiken) C.; m. Lucy Anne Campbell, July 12, 1969; children: Kathryn Allerton, Elizabeth Fairgreives. BA, Bowdoin Coll., 1966; JD, Georgetown U., 1969; MBA, Harvard U., 1972. Bar: Conn. 1970. Assoc. Robinson & Cole, Hartford, Conn., 1972-74; atty Aetna Life & Casualty Co., Hartford, 1974-77, investment officer, 1977-80, asst. v.p., 1980-87, mng. dir., v.p., from 1987. Dir. Hartford Capital Corp., Local Initiatives Mgmt. Assets Corp., N.Y.C. Trustee Grace Blass Trust, Hartford. Mem.: Hartford Golf. Home: West Hartford, Conn. Died Apr. 7, 2007.

CARTWRIGHT, HELEN MORRIS, philosophy educator, writer; b. Ferndale, Mich., July 18, 1931; d. Robert Edmondson and Winifred Jane (Matthews) Morris; m. Richard L. Cartwright, Mar. 28, 1959. BA, U. Mich., 1954, MA, 1957, PhD, 1963. Adj. asst. prof. philosophy Wayne State U., Detroit, 1965-67; asst. prof. philosophy Tufts U., Medford, Mass., 1968-73, assoc. prof. philosophy, 1973-84, prof. philosophy, from 1984. Contbr. articles to profl. jours. Vis. fellow Clare Hall, Cambridge U., 1981-82. Mem. Am. Philosophica Assn. (ea. divsn.). Avocation: philosophy. Home: Boston, Mass. Died May 14, 2006.

CARWILE, STUART FREDERICK, lawyer; b. Lynchburg, Va., Aug. 26, 1942; s. Lewis Frederick and Dorothy Marie (Davis) C.; m. Andrea Barton, Feb. 13, 1988; children: Charles, Elizabeth, William, Frederick. BS in Comm. with distinction, U. Va., 1964, LLB, 1967. Ptnr. Carwile, Kudravetz & Krumm, Charlottesville, Va., 1973-82, Kirkland & Ellis, Washington, 1982-83, Wiley, Rein & Fielding, Washington, from 1983. Bd. suprs. Albemarle County, Charlottesville, 1971-75; mem. Thomas Jefferson Regional Planning Commn., Charlottesville, 1972-75, chmn., 1972-74. Avocation: sailing. Home: Charlottesvle, Va. Died Apr. 16, 2007.

CARY, CHARLES OSWALD, aviation executive; b. Boston, July 10, 1917; s. Charles P. and Adeline J. (Oswald) C.; m. Jean M. Cochran, May 8, 1948. Student, Northeastern U., 1937-39, MIT, 1941-42. With comml. airlines, 1936-44; supt. ops., gen. traffic mgr. Alaska Star Airlines, 1943-44; exec. asst. to chmn. CAB, 1944-46; spl. asst. to asst. sec. navy for air, 1946-48; mem. Civil Transp. Aircraft Evaluation and Devel. Bd., 1948-49; exec. sec. Air Coordinating Com., 1949-54; gen. sec. Air Transp. Moblzn. Survey, Nat. Security Resources Bd., 1950-51; dep. adminstr. Def. Air Transp. Adminstrn., 1951-54; dir. marketing & sales electronics div. Curtiss-Wright Corp., 1954-63; v.p. Hazeltine Corp., 1963-65; asst. adminstr. dept. transp. internat. aviation affairs FAA, 1965-78, spl. rep. of adminstr. Brussels, Belgium, 1978-79; ret., 1979; sr. lectr., dir. internat. studies Flight Transp. Lab., MIT, 1979-95. Mem. U.S. del. 1st assembly Provisional Internat. Civil Aviation Orgn., 1945, U.S. dels. assemblies, 1947, 51, 53, 70, 74, 77; cons. to adminstr. FAA, 1963; bd. govs. Flight Safety Found., Washington, 1979-93; vice chmn. State of N.H. Aviation Users Adv. Bd., 1986-89, chmn., 1989-92. Fellow AIAA (assoc.); mem. Diplomatic and Consular Officers Club Ret. (Washington), Lake Sunapee Yacht Club. Home: Sunapee, NH. Died Jan. 23, 2007.

CARY, ELTON MIKELL, banking and insurance company executive; b. Savannah, Ga., Jan. 28, 1929; s. Theron Elton Mikell and Nellie (Johnson) Walker; m. Ilene Joyce Cary; children: Mikell, James, Jennifer Lee. BS, U. Ga., 1950; postgrad., Emory U., 1950-51. Ins. agt., chmn. Adae & Hooper, Miami Beach, Fla., from 1950; chmn. Gen. Ins. Co., Miami Beach, 1973-93, Cary Marine, 1967-74, Wometco Enterprises Inc. and Wometco Cable TV Inc., Miami, 1983-84; CEO, chmn. bd. dirs. Fin. Fed. Savs. & Loan Assn., 1986-91. Dir., exec. com. Fin. Fed. Savs., Miami, 1983; chmn. Sentinal Info. Mgmt. Systems, 1991—. Trustee Papenicolaou Cancer Research Inst., Miami, 1975-79. Mem. Fla. Assn. Domestic Ins. Cos. (vice-chmn. 1978—). Democrat. Methodist. Died Sept. 22, 2006.

CARY, JOHN MILTON, physician; b. Ewing, Mo., July 11, 1932; s. Milton Madison and Alice (Sells) C.; AB, Cen. Coll. Mo., 1954; MD, St. Louis U., 1958; m. Barbara Ann Dorsey, June 4, 1955; children: Kimberly Anne Cary Kelce, John Madison. Diplomate Am. Bd. Internal Medicine. Intern, Barnes Hosp., St. Louis, 1958-59, resident in internal medicine, 1959-60, subsequently mem. staff; resident in internal medicine St. Lukes Hosp., St. Louis, 1961-62, subsequently mem. staff; fellow in hematology Washington U., St. Louis, 1960-61; practice medicine specializing in internal medicine, St. Louis, 1962—; mem. staff St. Johns Mercy Med. Ctr.; clin. instr. Washington U., 1966—. Mem. ACP, N.Y. Acad. Scis., St. Louis Soc. Internal Medicine, Mo. Med. Assn., St. Louis Med. Soc., Alpha Omega Alpha. Congregationalist. Home: Chesterfield, Mo. Died Mar. 15, 2007.

CARY, WILLIAM JEWELL, JR., trade association executive; b. Independence, Mo., Oct. 19, 1924; s. William Jewell and Mildred Elizabeth (Crews) Huserik; m. Genevieve Campbell, Sept. 7, 1947; children: William J., Christopher C. BJ, U. Mo.; MSc in Journalism, Northwestern U. Mng. editor Orange Daily News, Calif., 1954—56; owner, pub. Tri-Town Times, Fallon, Nev., 1956—69; bus. editor Oreg. Jour., Portland, Oreg., 1959—67; dir. pub. affairs Western Wood Prodn. Assn., 1967—72; asst. dir. pub. info. Georgia-Pacific, 1972—79; exec. v.p. Pacific Logging Congress, Portland, Oreg., 1979—86. Mem. bd. overseers Lewis and Clark Coll., from 1969; chmn. dept. comm. Episcopal Diocese Oreg., Portland, from 1982; priest Episcopal Ch., from 1973. 1st lt. US Army, 1942—46, 1st lt. US Army, 1951—53, PTO. Mem.: Pub. Relations Round Table Portland, Pub. Relations Soc. Am. (pres. Columbia River chpt. from 1984, pres. 1972), Masons Lodge, Kappa Tau Alpha. Republican. Episcopalian. Home: Portland, Oreg. Died June 22, 2006.

CASDIN, JEFFREY WHITMAN, investment company executive; b. Worcester, Mass., Feb. 27, 1940; s. Joseph Charles and Miriam (Whitman) C.; m. Sharon Blaisdell Jones, Sept. 12, 1964; children: Adam, Alexander, Eli. AB, ScB, Brown U., 1962; MBA, Harvard U., 1967. Electrical engr. Texas Instruments, Attleboro, Mass., 1962-67; acct. exec. Oppenheimer & Co., NYC, 1967-70, mgr., dir., from 1988; pres., owner Source Securities, NYC, 1970-82. Home: New York, NY. Died Oct. 23, 2005.

CASE, CHARLES WARREN, university dean, education educator; b. Rochester, NY, May 14, 1938; s. Paul Wilfred and Wava Katherine (Hamlin) C.; m. Karen Ingebretsen, Oct. 7, 1988; 1 child, Amanda Alyce. BS, LeMoyne Coll., 1960; MS, Syracuse U., 1965; Ed.D., U. Rochester, 1969. Asst. to pres. SUNY Agrl. and Tech. Coll., Morrisville, 1964-66; asst. to dean U. Rochester, 1966-69; assoc. prof., dept. chmn. U. Vt., Burlington, 1969-74; assoc. dean, prof. edn. Cleve. State U., 1974-76; dean Coll. Edn., prof. U. Wis.-, Oshkosh, 1976-80; dean Coll. Edn., prof. edn. U. Iowa, Iowa City, 1980-87; dean Sch. Edn., prof. edn. U. Conn., Storrs, from 1987. Author, editor: (with J. Brubacher and T. Reagan) Becoming a Reflective Educator, (with W.A. Matthes) Trends in Professional Education, (with P.A. Olson) The Future-Create or Inherit, 1974; contbr. more than 50 chpts. to books, articles to profl. jours. Mem. Assn. Colls. and Schs. Edn. in State Univs. and Land Grant Colls. (sec. 1982, pres.-elect 1983, pres. 1984, past pres. 1985), Am. Ednl. Rsch. Assn., Holmes Group, Am. Assn. Coll. Tchr. Edn. Died Apr. 30, 2006.

CASE, KENNETH MYRON, physics educator; b. NYC, Sept. 23, 1923; SB, Harvard U., 1945, MS, 1946, PhD, 1948. Rsch. assoc. Lawrence Radiation Lab., 1949-50, U. Rochester, 1950-51; prof. U. Mich., 1951-69, Rockefeller U., 1969-88, prof. emeritus, from 1988. Adj. prof. Inst. Nonlinear Studies, U. Calif., San Diego, 1988—, vis. prof., 1981-82, Lawrence Radiation Lab., 1956, 61, MIT, 1963-64; scientist Los Alamos Sci. Lab., 1944-45; mem. Inst. Adv. Study, Princeton, 1948-50, 56-57, 70-88; cons. Rand Corp., Ramo-Woolridge Corp., La Jolla Inst. & Phys. Dynamics. Recipient Guggenheim fellow, 1963. Fellow Am. Phys. Soc.; mem. Nat. Acad. Scis. Home: La Jolla, Calif. Died Feb. 1, 2006.

CASEY, RICHARD CONWAY, federal judge; b. Ithaca, NY, Jan. 1, 1933; BA, Holy Cross, 1955; JD, Georgetown U., 1958. Asst. US atty. criminal divsn. (so. dist.) NY US Dept. Justice, 1959—63, chief internal security unit, 1960—63; counsel Special Commn. State of NY, 1963—64; assoc. Brown & Wood, 1964—69, ptnr., 1970—84, of counsel, 1984—97; judge US Dist. Ct. (so. dist.) NY, 1997—2007. Served US Army, 1958, served US Army, 1961—62. Recipient Blessed Hyacinth Cormier O.P. Medal at the Angelicum in Rome, 1999. Mem.: Assn. Bar City NY, ABA. Died Mar. 22, 2007.

CASON, DICK KENDALL, physician; b. Beaumont, Tex., June 27, 1922; s. Dick Kendall and Maurine (Mills) C.; m. Maxine Skocdopole, Apr. 4, 1946; children: Dick Mills, Alma Christine. BA Rice U., 1945; MD U. Tex., 1945. Intern Kings County Hosp., Bklyn., 1945-46; med. resident Meth. Hosp. Dallas, 1948-49; gen. practice medicine, Hillsboro, Tex., 1949-94; charter mem. Am. Bd. Family Practice. Pres. Hillsboro Indsl. Devel. Found., 1955-60, 79—; past mem. regional adv. com. Dallas Civic Opera Co.; parish vis. 1st Presbyn. Ch., Hillsboro, Tex., 1994—. Served from 1st lt. to capt., AUS, 1946-48. Fellow Royal Soc. Health (Eng.); mem. Hill County Med. Soc. (pres. 1951), Tex. Med. Assn. (alt. del. to AMA 1980-84, del. 1984-94), Am. Acad. Gen. Practice, N.Y. Acad. Sci., Internat. Horn Soc., C. of C., Hill County Soc. Crippled Children. Presbyterian (elder). Clubs: Hillsboro Country, Rotary (pres. Hillsboro 1955). Contbr. articles to profl. jours. Home: Hillsboro, Tex. Died Oct. 8, 2006.

CASPER, BARRY MICHAEL, physics professor; b. Knoxville, Tenn., Jan. 21, 1939; s. Barry and Florence (Becker) C.; m. Nancy Carolyn Peterson, Aug. 25, 1979; children: Daniel Casper, Benjamin Casper, Michael Casper, Aaron Syverson, Jay Syverson, Kaarin Madigan. BA, Swarthmore Coll., 1960; PhD in Physics, Cornell U., 1966. From asst. prof. to prof. emeritus, physics Carleton Coll., Northfield, Minn., from 1966; rsch. fellow Stanford U., Calif., Minn., 1973-74, Harvard U., Cambridge, Mass., 1975-76, U. Minn., Mpls., 1976-77, MIT, Cambridge, Mass., 1980-81, U. Calif., San Diego, 1992-93. Policy advisor to U.S. Sen. Paul Wellstone, 1991. Co-author: Revolutions in Physics, 1972, Powerline: First Battle of America's Energy War, 1981; author: Lost in Washington: Finding the Way Back to Democracy in America, 2000. Dir. Nuclear War Graphics Project, Northfield, 1981-89, Minn. Nuclear Weapons Freeze Campaign, 1983-84 Recipient Pub. Citizen award Minn. Pub. Interest Research Group, 1984 Mem. Am. Phys. Soc. (nat. council 1980-83; Forum on Physics and Soc. prize 1984), Fedn. Am. Scientists (nat. council 1970-74, 80-84, 91-95). Home: Northfield, Minn. Died Jan. 27, 2007.

CASPER, WILLIAM CECIL, former university chancellor, economics and business educator; b. China Grove, NC, Aug. 6, 1927; s. Will and Mary Johnson (Goodnight) C.; m. Gladys Hope McSwain, May 25, 1951. BS, U. N.C., Chapel Hill, 1954; MA, U. S.C., Columbia, 1965. Instr., registrar Coastal Carolina Jr. Coll. br. Coll. of Charleston, Conway, S.C., 1954-60; resident dir. U. S.C., Coastal Carolina Campus, Conway, 1960-62; dir. U. S.C., Aiken Campus, 1963-78, chancellor, 1979-83, chancellor emeritus, from 1983, prof. econs. and bus., from 1983. Mem. Aiken adv. bd. Bankers Trust of S.C., N.C. Nat. Bank of S.C. Chmn. planning and evaluation com. Aiken County Community Action Commn., 1977-81, bd. mem., 1976-81. Served with USN, 1945-48, 50-51. Mem.: Rotary, Business Men's. Home: Aiken, SC. Died Dec. 11, 2006.

CASTRO, DONALD STEVEN, academic administrator, history professor; b. Bakersfield, Calif., June 27, 1940; s. Emilio Castro-Galvez and Lilia (Mayer) Castro; m. Constance Lee Picella, June 12, 1970; children: Antonia Carolina, Daniela Emilia. AB, UCLA, 1962, MA, 1964, PhD, 1970. Asst. prof. history Calif. State Poly. U., Pomona, 1967-69, assoc. prof., 1969-72, prof., 1978-87, dir. Ctr. Chicano and Am. Indian Studies, 1969-72, dean undergrad. studies, 1978-80, dean instrn. Office grad., undergrad. studies, 1980-87; assoc. dir. office internat. programs Calif. State U., Long Beach, 1972-78, prof. history, dean sch. humanities - social scis. Fullerton, 1993—2007, spl. asst. to pres., 2003—07, v.p. acad. affairs Dominguez Hills, 1999—2003. Presenter numerous confs. on Latin Am. studies; mem. gen. edn. rev. com. Calif. State U. Sys.; steering com. Calif. State U. NEXA consortium, outside evaluator Univ. Honors Program, Chico, 1985-86; cons. Office Internat. Edn. Am. Assn. State Colls. and Univs., 1972-76, on minority edn., Calif. sch. dists.; mem. social sci. adv. com. Ryan Commn. Calif. Dept. Edn., 1972-74; faculty senate rep. Sch. of Arts on Campus, 1969-72; guest lectr. Instituto Ricardo Levene, Facultad de Filosofia y Letras, U. Nacional de Buenos Aires, 1965-66; assoc. v.p. grad. student Researchand Internat. Program, Calif. State U., Northridge, 1987-88; mem. Acad. Senate on Campus, 1987-88; program rev. Internationalizing Curriculum Calif. State U. Office of Chancellor; invited participant Intenat. Conf. Rome, 1982, 86, Amsterdam, 1988. Contbr. articles to profl. jours. Community rep. Bilingual Edn. Com. Pomona Unified Sch. Dist., 1980-83; commnr. City of Claremont (Calif.) Environ. Quality Commn.; bd. govs. Fund for Pub. Edn., Claremont; mem. Claremont Unified Sch. Dist. adv. council, chmn. Fulbright fellow, 1965-67; grantee Kellogg Found., 1971; recipient Civil Rights award Calif. Assn. Human Rels. Org., 2006 Mem. Pacific Coast Council Latin Am. Studies (bd. govs. 1976-80, 1983-85, mem. exec. bd.), Council on Latin Am. Studies (founding pres. 1979-82, bd. dirs.), So. Calif. Consortium on Internat. Studies (bd. govs. 1980-88, com. Latin Am. Studies, chmn., chmn. subcom. Latin Am. Studies Coop. program 1972-79, chmn. subcom. Latin Am. Studies Outreach), Am. Hist. Assn. (conf. Latin Am. History Rio de la Plata Area studies com.), Latin Am. Studies Assn. (membership com. 1977-79), Nat. Assn. Fgn. Student Advisors, Calif. State U. Assn. Deans of Undergrad. Studies, Acad. Planning, Calif. State U. Assn. Deans of Grad. studies (chmn. com. improving grad. studies), Calif. State U. Assn. undergrad. advisors (founding mem.), Calif. State U. Consortium on Desert Studies (bd. govs. 1979-88, chmn. 1983-88, interim dir. 1983-84), Golden Key, Phi Alpha Theta, Pi Gamma Mu. Home: Claremont, Calif. Died June 11, 2007.

CASWELL, HERBERT HALL, JR., retired biology educator; b. Marblehead, Mass., May 21, 1923; s. Herbert Hall and Grace (Parker) C.; m. Ethel Claire Preble, Mar. 28, 1948; children: Hal, Martha, William, Edward, Thomas, Michael. BS, Harvard U., 1948; MS, UCLA, 1950; PhD, Cornell U., 1956. Prof. biology Eastern Mich. U., Ypsilanti, 1955-88, prof. emeritus, 1988, head dept. biology, 1974-88. Served to 1st lt. U.S. Army, 1942-46. Mem. Ecol. Soc. Am., Assn. Field Ornithol., Am. Inst. Biol. Scis., Sigma Xi. Home: Ann Arbor, Mich. Died Jan. 30, 2006.

CATE, WILLIAM CYRUS, mining investment consultant; b. San Pedro, Calif., June 1, 1938; s. William Cyrus and Isabelle Marie (Casey) C. B.A., St. Louis U., 1965, M.A., 1967; postgrad. Washington U., St. Louis, 1967-69, So. Ill. U., 1968. Explorer, developer, cons. gold mining ventures, N.Am. and Europe, 1970—; presenter seminars on mining investments; instr. Miami-Dade Jr. Coll., Miami, Fla., 1969-70, U. Mo., St. Louis, 1967-68, Forest Park Community Coll., St. Louis, 1967-69. Author: Finding California Gold, 1981; Prospector's Guide, 1982; editor, pub. Vancouver Buccaneer. Served with U.S. Army, 1961-63; Korea. Mem. Nat. Speological Soc., Calif. Cave Diving Group (pres. 1974-76), South Am. Explorer's Club. Press Club of San Francisco. Home: Pacifica, Calif. Died Apr. 11, 2007.

CAUDILL, SAMUEL JEFFERSON, architect; b. Tulsa, June 5, 1922; s. Samuel Jefferson and Maymie Starling (Boulware) C.; m. Joy Maxwell, May 31, 1952; children: Jody Caudill Cardamone, Julie Hertzberg, Samuel Boone, Robert Maxwell, Anne Goertzen BArch, Cornell U., Ithaca, NY, 1946. Registered architect Colo., Calif., Idaho, Ariz. Prin. architect Samuel J. Caudill, Jr., Aspen, Colo., 1954-59, Caudill Assocs. Architects, Aspen, 1959-80; pres. Caudill Gustafson & Assocs. Architects, PC, Aspen, 1980-87; pres., CEO Caudill Gustafson & Assocs., Architects, PC, Aspen, from 1992; pres. Caudill Gustafson Ross & Assocs., Architects, P.C., Aspen, 1987-92. Mem. Pitkin County Planning and Zoning Commn., Colo., 1955-58; mem. outdoor edn. com. Colo. Dept. Edn., 1966-68; chmn. Pitkin County Bd. Appeals, 1970; mem. Colo. Water Quality Control Commn., 1977-80. Wildlife rep. adv. bd. Bur. Land Mgmt. Dept. Interior, Grand Junction, Colo., 1969-75, 80-85; chmn. citizens adv. com. Colo. Hwy. Dept. for I-70 through Glenwood Canyon, 1975-92; chmn. Colo. Wildlife Commn., 1978-79. Recipient Outstanding Pub. Service Bur. Land Mgmt., 1975; named to Aspen (Colo.) Hall of Fame, 1998. Fellow AIA (Community Svc. award 1976, Architect of Yr. award 1992, mem. emeritus 1995); mem. Colo. Soc. Architects (pres. 1983), Colo. Coun. on Arts and Humanities, Aspen C. of C. (pres. 1956-57), Masons, Shriners (Denver). Home: Carbondale, Colo. Died May 13, 2007.

CAVAGLIERI, GIORGIO, architect; b. Venice, Italy, Aug. 1, 1911; came to U.S., 1939, naturalized, 1943; s. Gino and Margherita (Maroni) C.; m. Norma Sanford, Jan. 31, 1942. D. Archtl. Engring, Sup. Sch. Engring., Milan, Italy, 1932; student spl. city planning, Sup. Sch. Architecture, Rome, 1934. Apprenticeship N.Y. office R. Candela, Balt. offices J.O. Chertkof, also Benjamin Franklin, arch., 1934—39; propr. own firm NYC, 1946—2007; adj. prof. Sch. Architecture Pratt Inst., 1956-69. Trustee Nat. Inst. Archtl. Edn., chmn. trustees, 1957-60; academician NAD. Prin. works in Milan, prior to World War II; prin. works include in the U.S., Fenton Hall reconstrn. Fredonia (N.Y.) Coll., Astor Libr. restoration and conversion to N.Y. Pub. Theatre, N.Y. Shakespeare Festival, Jefferson Market Courthouse restoration and conversion to N.Y. Pub. Libr., Branch Libr., Riverdale, N.Y., N.Y. Pub. Libr. main bldg. Periodical Dept., Pub. Sch. 32, S.I., Kip's Bay br. libr.; assoc. arch. Pension Bldg./Nat. Mus. Bldg. Arts, Washington; arch.-in-charge Rosary Hall, U.S. Mil. Acad. Mus.; Eldridge St. Synagogue restoration, N.Y.C.; Chapel of the Good Shepherd reconstrn., Roosevelt Island, N.Y. Served with C.E. AUS, 1943-45. Decorated Bronze Star; recipient Bard award, spl. citation City Club N.Y., 1968; Illuminated scroll Mcpl. Art Soc. N.Y., 1966; Clients award N.Y. State Assn. Archs., 1964; Gold medal honor architecture Archtl. League N.Y., 1956; winner 1st prize nat. competition auditorium Rome, 1935, 3d prize competition city hosp. Cuneo, Italy., 1938, hon. mention Armed Forces bldgs. Rome World's Fair, 1938, 3d prize N.Y.C. Bd. Edn. archtl. competition for modernization Bronx Jr. H.S., 1967; cert. of merit for excellence in design N.Y. State Assn. Archs., 1976; 1st honor award ALA/AIA, 1976; Sidney L. Strauss Meml. N.Y. Soc. Archs., 1977; recipient award Excellence in Design N.Y.C. Art Commn., 1992, Design award for Preservation Gen. Svcs. Admnistrn., 1992; Outstanding Cert. for Competition N.Y.C. Bd. Edn., 1997, Lucy G. Moses award NY Landmark Conservancy, 2002, Bronze medal Fine Art Fedn. N.Y., 2002. Fellow AIA (pres. N.Y. chpt. 1970-71, House Improvement award, 1961, Honor award, 1968, Disting. Architecture award 1985, Presdl. citation 1990, Medal of Honor N.Y. chpt. 1990); mem. Mcpl. Art Soc. N.Y. (pres. 1963-65, 4th Ann. Preservation award 1992), Archtl. League N.Y. (v.p. 1961-63), Am. Soc. Interior Designers (v.p. 1984-85, 87-88, medal 1985), Fine Arts Fedn. N.Y. (pres. 1970-72, 74-76, 2000-01, Centennial Yr. honoree 1995), N.Y. Coun. Arts and Govt., N.Y.C. Victorian Soc. (Outstanding in Preservation award 1986). Democrat. Home: New York, NY. Died May 15, 2007.

CAWLEY, THOMAS J., lawyer; b. Carbondale, Pa., Oct. 7, 1943; BS, U. Scranton, 1966; LLB, U. Va., 1969. Bar: Va. 1969. Mem. Hunton & Williams LLP, Fairfax, Va., mng. ptnr., litig., intellectual property, antitrust McLean, Va. Mem. Am. Coll. Trial Lawyers. Died Aug. 8, 2007.

CEARLOCK, DENNIS BILL, research executive; b. Wenatchee, Wash., Sept. 9, 1941; s. Joseph Loy Cearlock and Gwendolyn Irene (Glascock) Endrizzi; m. Merrily Crook, Nov. 9, 1963; children: Jody, Synette, Chris. BSCE, Wash. State U., 1964, MS in San. Engring., 1965; postgrad. in math., Joint Ctr. for Grad. Study, Richland, Wash., 1965-68; PhDCE, U. Wash. 1977. Rsch. engr., mgr. geosci. and engring. dept., dir. rsch. Pacific N.W. Labs., Battelle Meml. Inst., Richland, Wash., 1965-90, v.p., gen. mgr. Health and Environ. Group, 1990-92; corp. sr. v.p. and gen. mgr. health divsn. Columbus (Ohio) ops. Battelle Meml. Inst., from 1992. Contbr. articles to profl. jours. Mem. AAAS, ASCE (Outstanding Graduating Civil Engr 1964), Sigma Tau, Tau Beta Pi, Phi Kappa Phi. Avocations skiing, golf. Home: Deer Harbor, Wash. Died July 9, 2007.

CECI, JESSE ARTHUR, violinist; b. Phila., Feb. 2, 1924; s Luigi Concezio and Catherine Marie (Marotta) C.; m. Catherine Annette Stevens, Aug. 5, 1979. BS, Juilliard Sch. Music, 1951; license de concert, L'Ecole Normale de Musique, Paris, 1954 MusM, Manhattan Sch. Music, 1971. Assoc. concertmaster New Orleans Philharm. Orch., 1953-54; violinist Boston Symphony Orch., 1954-59, N.Y. Philharm. Orch., N.Y., 1959-62, Esterhazy Orch., NYC, 1962-68; concertmaster Denver Symphony Orch. 1974-89, Colo. Symphony Orch., 1989-95. Over 50 performances of 22 major works; mem. Zimbler Sinfonietta, Boston 1957-59; participant Marlboro Festival Chamber Orch. Vt. summmers 1960-62, 65, Marlboro Festival Chamber Orch European-Israeli tour, 1965, Grand Teton Festival, Wyo., 1972 with Denver Duo, 1975—, N.Mex. Festival, Taos, 1980, Carme (Calif.) Bach Festival, 1987—, Whistler (B.C., Can.) Mozar Festival, 1989-90, Bear Valley (Calif.) Festival, 1995—, Mendocino (Calif.) Festival, 1996—; mem. faculty Congress o Strings, Dallas, 1985, N.Y. Coll. Music, 1961-71, NYU, 1971-74, U. Colo., 1975-79; guest mem. faculty Univ. Denver, 1986 mem., assoc. concertmaster Casals Festival Orch., San Juan P.R., 1963-77; violinist Cleve. Orch. fgn. tours, 1967, 73, 78 Cin. Symphony Orch. world tour, 1966; 1st violinist N.Y. String Quartet in-residence at U. Maine, Orono, summer 1969; guest violinist Fla. West Coast Symphony, Sarasota, 1993-98; concertmaster Minn. Orch., summers 1970-71, Denver Chamber Orch 1985-90; guest concertmaster Pitts. Symphony Orch., Pitts L.A., 1988, mem. N.Y. Philharmonia Chamber Ensemble in-residence at Hopkins Ctr., Dartmouth U., summer 1973; recitalist, Paris, 1963, Amsterdam, 1963, recitalist Carnegie Recita Hall, N.Y.C., 1963, Town Hall, N.Y.C., 1968, 70, Alice Tull Hall, N.Y.C., 1972; fgn. tour Pitts. Symphony Orch., 1989 soloist Royal Chamber Orch. Japan, 1997-98, appointment t concert master position of the Royal Chamber Orchestra and th Royal Metropolitan Orchestra of Japan, 1999—. Cpl. U.S Army, 1943-46, PTO. Fulbright fellow Paris, 1951-52 Democrat. Roman Catholic. Home: Denver, Colo. Died May 10, 2006

CEDARBAUM, BERNARD, b. New Haven, Sept. 1, 1928; William and Elsie (Schuster) C.; m. Miriam Rachel Goldman Aug. 25, 1957; children— Daniel Goldman, Jonathan Goldman AB, Yale, 1950, LL.M., 1956; LL.B., Harvard, 1953. Bar: Conn bar 1953, N.Y. bar 1960. Practice in, Washington, 1956-5 NYC, from 1959; atty. Dept. Justice, 1956-59; asso. Carte Ledyard & Milburn, 1959-65, mem. firm, from 1965. Mem Scarsdale (N.Y.) Bd. Edn., 1979-85. Served with AUS, 1953-5 Mem. Am., N.Y. State bar assns., Am. Law Inst., Assn. Bar Ci N.Y. Clubs: Town (Scarsdale) (pres., 1977-78). Home: Scarsdale, NY. Died Feb. 5, 2006.

CEDERQUIST, DENA CAROLINE, former educator; Madrid, Iowa, Aug. 29, 1910; d. Clarence John and Clara (Bor Cederquist; BS, Iowa State Coll., 1931, MS, 1935; PhD, Wis., 1945. Asst. dietitian Monmouth Meml. Hosp., Lon Branch, N.J., 1932-33; instr. Kans. State Coll., Manhatta 1937-41, U. Wis., 1941-42; with Mich. State U., 1944—, ass prof., asso. prof., 1944-56, prof., head dept. foods and nutritio 1956-71, prof. food sci. and nutrition, 1971-78, prof. emeritu 1978—. Mem. Am. Dietetic Assn., Am. Home Econ. Assn Sigma Xi, Omicron Nu, Phi Kappa Phi, Sigma Delta Epsilo Home: East Lansing, Mich. Died Nov. 9, 2006.

CHAMBERS, BRUCE WILLIAM, art dealer, art historian; Cin., June 22, 1941; s. William R. and Lois M. (Mathews) C.; Margaret J. Moon, Aug. 19, 1968; children— Adam Georg Nicholas William. B.A., Yale U., 1963; M.A., U. Rochest 1969; Ph.D., U. Pa., 1974. Instr. Emory U., Atlanta, 1970-7 asst. prof., 1974-76; asst. dir. curatorial services Meml. A Gallery, Rochester, N.Y., 1976-80; dir. U. Iowa Mus. Art, Iow City, 1980-81; assoc. Berry-Hill Galleries, N.Y.C., 1982-

Author: Art and Artists of the South, 1984; The World of David G. Blythe, 1980. Contbr. articles to profl. jours. Mem. Coll. Art Assn. Episcopalian. Home: Hamden, Conn. Died May 2007.

CHAMBERS, MARJORIE BELL, historian; b. NYC, Mar. 11, 1923; d. Kenneth Carter and Katherine (Totman) Bell; m. William Hyland Chambers, Aug. 8, 1945; children: Lee Chambers-Schiller, William Bell, Leslie Chambers Trujillo, Kenneth Carter. AB cum laude, Mt. Holyoke Coll., South Hadley, Mass., 1943; MA, Cornell U., 1948; PhD, U. N.Mex., 1974; LLD honoris causa, Ctrl. Mich. U., 1977; LHD (hon.), Wilson Coll., 1980, Northern Michigan U., 1982. Staff asst. Am. Assn. UN, League of Nations Assn., NYC, 1944-45; program specialist dept. rural sociology Cornell U., Ithaca, NY, 1945-46, rsch. asst. dept. speech and drama, 1946-48; substitute tchr. Los Alamos (N.Mex.) Pub. Schs., 1962-65; project historian U.S. AEC, Los Alamos, 1965-69; adj. prof. U. N.Mex., Los Alamos, 1970-76, 84-85; pres. Colo. Women's Coll., Denver, 1976-78; dean Union Inst. and U. Grad. Sch. Interdisciplinary Arts and Scis., Cin., 1979—82, mem. core faculty Grad. Sch., 1979; interim pres. Colby-Sawyer Coll., New London, NH, 1985-86. Vis. prof. Cameron U., Lawton, Okla., 1974; commr., vice-chair N.Mex. Commn. on Higher Edn., Santa Fe, 1987-91; dir. N.Mex. Endowment for Humanities, 1995-2002, sec.-treas. 2001-2002; mem. bd. dirs. Coun. Ind. Colls. and Univs., Santa Fe, 1991-2001; rep. Los Alamos County Labor Mgmt. Bd.; lectr. U. N.Mex., Albuquerque, 1986. Contbr. articles to profl. jours. Coun. treas. Sangre de Cristo Girl Scouts Am., 2002; chair Los Alamos County Coun., 1976, councilor, 1975-76, 79; Rep.candidate N.Mex. 3d Congl. Dist., 1982, lt. gov. N.Mex., 1986; chair Sec. of Navy's Advisor Bd. on Edn. and Tng., Washington and Pensacola, Fla., 1981-89; chair Citizen Bd. of U.S. Army Command and Gen. Staff Coll., Fort Leavenworth, Kans., 1989-1992; acting chair, vice-chair adminstrn. Pres. Carter's Com. for Women, Washington, 1977-80; chair Pres. Ford's Nat. Adv. Bd. on Women's Ednl. Programs, Washington, Los Alamos County Pers. Bd., 1985-90, mem. bd., 1983-90; mem. nat. adv. coun. U.S. SBA, 1990-92; mem. Los Alamos and N.Mex. Rep. Ctrl. com., 1982—; trustee Colby-Sawyer Coll., New London, N.H., 1980-89; pub. mem. U.S. Dept. State Fgn. Svc. selection bd., 1978; mem. U.S. del. UN Conf. Women, Copenhagen, 1980; bd. dirs. N.Mex. Endowment for the Humanities, 1997—. Recipient Teresa d'Avila award Coll. St. Teresa, Winona, Minn., 1978, Disting. Woman award U. N.Mex. Alumni Assn., Albuquerque, 1990, N.Mex. Disting. Pub. Svc. award Gov. and Awards Coun., Albuquerque, 1991, Zia award U. N.Mex. Alumni Assn., 2001; named Outstanding N.Mex. Woman Gov. and Com. on Status of Women, Albuquerque, 1988, 89, Lifetime Achievement award, 2003, award Internat. Women's Forum Women Who Make a Difference, 2004; named Living Treasures Los Alamos, 2003. Mem. AAUW (life, U.S. rep. coun. 1973-75, nat. pres. 1975-79, pres. Edn. Found.), DAR, Bus. and Profl. Women (Los Alamos parliamentarian and dist. parliamentarian 1991-93), Nat. Women's Polit. Caucus (gov. bd. conv., keynoter, vice-chair Rep. caucus 1971-89), Internat. Women's Forum (founding mem. Colo. forum), N.Mex. Hist. Soc. (pres.), Los Alamos Hist. Soc. (pres., Sangre de Cristo Girl Scouts "Woman of Distinction" 1996). Presbyterian. Avocations: figure skating, skiing, swimming, painting, public speaking. Home: Los Alamos, N.Mex. Died Aug. 22, 2006.

CHANDLER, ALFRED DUPONT, JR., historian, educator; b. Guyencourt, Del., Sept. 15, 1918; s. Alfred Dupont and Carol (Ramsay) C.; m. Fay Martin, Jan. 8, 1944; children: Alpine Douglass Chandler Bird, Mary Morris Chandler Watt, Alfred Dupont III, Howard Martin. AB, Harvard U., 1940, AM, 1947, PhD, 1952, LLD (hon.), 1995; PhD (hon.), U. Leuven, Belgium, 1976, U. Antwerp, 1979; LHD (hon.), Babson Coll., 1982, Ohio State U., 1987; LLD (hon.), York U., Can., 1988, New England Coll., 1992; LLD (hon.), U. Del., 2002; DBA (hon.), Northeastern U., 2002. Research assoc. MIT, 1950-51, from instr. to prof., 1951-63; prof. history Johns Hopkins U., 1963-71, chmn. dept., 1966-70, dir. Ctr. for Study Recent Am. History, 1964-71; Straus prof. bus. history Harvard U. Bus. Sch., 1971-89, prof. emeritus, 1989—2007. Vis. fellow All Souls Coll., Oxford U., 1975; vis. prof. European Inst. Advanced Studies in Mgmt., Brussels, 1979; Walker-Ames vis. prof. U. Wash., 1981; cons. U.S. Naval War Coll., 1954; mem. Nat. Adv. Council on Edn. Professions Devel., 1970-71; chmn. adv. hist. com. U.S. AEC (renamed ERDA 1974), 1969-77. Author: Henry Varnum Poor, 1956, Strategy and Structure (Newcomen award 1964), 1962, Giant Enterprise, 1964, The Railroads, 1965, The Visible Hand (Pulitzer and Bancroft prizes for 1978), Inventing the Electronic Century, 2001, Shaping the Industrial Century, 2005; co-author (with Stephen Salsbury): Pierre S. duPont, 1971; co-author: (with Herman Daems) Managerial Hierarchies, 1980; co-author: (with Richard Tedlow) The Coming of Managerial Capitalism, 1985; editor (asst.): The Letters of Theodore Roosevelt, 4 vols., 1952—54; editor: Papers of Dwight D. Eisenhower, 5 vols., 1970; co-editor: Big Business and The Wealth of Nations, 1997, The Dynamic Firm, 1998, A Nation Transformed by Information, 2000, Leviathans: Multinationals and the New Global History, 2005; subject of The Essential Alfred Chandler, 1988. Trustee Park Sch., Brookline, Mass., 1957-63, chmn. bd., 1961-63; trustee Brookline Pub. Libr., 1959-63, Roland Park Sch., Balt., 1964-70, Johns Hopkins U., 1971-81, Eleutherian Mills-Hagley Found., 1981-95, hon. trustee, 1995-2007. Lt. comdr. USNR, 1940-45. Recipient Pulitzer prize for history, 1978, Bancroft prize, 1978, award, Assn. Am. Pubs., 1991, Melamed prize, 1992, Eminent Scholar award, Acad. Internat. Bus., 2000; rsch. fellow, Harvard U., 1955, Guggenheim fellow, 1958—59. Mem. Am. Acad. Arts and Scis., Econ. History Assn. (trustee 1966-70, pres. 1971-72), Orgn. Am. Historians (exec. bd. 1969-72), Soc. for History Tech. (exec. coun. 1972-75), Am. Hist. Assn. (Scholarly Distinction award 1997), Soc. Am. Historians, Mass. Hist. Soc. (coun. 1977-83, John F. Kennedy award 2003), Bus. History Conf. (pres. 1977-78, Life Time Achievement award 2002), Am. Antiquarian Soc., Am. Philos. Soc., Brit. Acad., Japan Acad., Acad. Mgmt. (Scholarly Contbn. to Mgmt. award 1985), St. Botolph Club (Boston), Nantucket Yacht Club (Mass.). Episcopalian. Home: Cambridge, Mass. Died May 9, 2007.

CHANDLER, ELISABETH GORDON (MRS. LACI DE GERENDAY), sculptor, musician; b. St. Louis, June 10, 1913; d. Henry Brace and Sara Ellen (Sallee) Gordon; m. Robert Kirkland Chandler, May 27, 1946 (dec.); m. Laci de Gerenday, May 12, 1979 (dec.). Grad., Lenox Sch., 1931; pvt. study sculpture and harp; LHD (hon.), St. Joseph Coll., 2001. Mem. Mildred Dilling Harp Ensemble, 1934-45; prof. sculpture Lyme Acad. Fine Arts, from 1976, chair sculpture dept. Exhibited sculpture NAD, Nat. Sculpture Soc., Allied Artists Am., Nat. Arts Club, Pen and Brush, Lyme Art Assn., Mattatuck Mus., Catherine Lorillard Wolfe Art Club, Am. Artists Profl. League, Hudson Valley Art Assn., USIA, 1976-78, Lyme Art Ctr., 1979, retrospective exhbn. Lyme Acad. Fine Arts, 1987, Madison Gallery, 1987, Old State House, Hartford, Conn., 1989, Mellon Art Ctr., Wallingford, Conn., 1989, Fairfield U. Walsh Gallery, 1991, Brit. Mus., London, Am. Medallic Sculptors Assn. Traveling Exhbn., 1994, Slater Mus. Cropsey Found., 1995, Nat. Sculpture Exhbn. Lyme Acad. Fine Arts, 1995-96, Lever House, N.Y.C., 1996, America's Tower, 1996-98, Hillsdale (Mich.) Coll., 1997, Nat. Acad. Mus., N.Y.C., 1998; represented in permanent collections Aircraft Carrier USS Forrestal, Gov. Dummer Acad., James Forrestal Rsch. Ctr. of Princeton U., Lenox Sch., James L. Collins Parochial Sch., Tex., Storm King Art Ctr., Columbia U., Pace U., White Plains, N.Y., St. Patrick's Cathedral, N.Y.C., McAuley Ctr., St. Joseph's Coll., West Hartford, Conn., Nat. Acad. Mus.; designed and executed Brookgreen Gardens medal, Forrestal Meml. Medal, Timoschenko Medal for Applied Mechanics, Benjamin Franklin Medal, Albert A. Michelson Medal, Jonathan Edwards Medal, Shafto Broadcasting Award Medal, Enrichment of Life medal Soc. Medallists, Adlai Stevenson bronze bust for Woodrow Wilson Sch. of Princeton U., 250 Ann. George Washington medal,Owen R. Cheatham bronze bust for Ga. Pacific Bldg., Atlanta, Messiah Coll., Grantham, Pa., Adlai E. Stevenson High Sch., Ill., Queen Anne's County Courthouse Square, Md., Our Lady Mercy Hosp., N.Y.C., Albert A. Michelson bust in Hall of Fame for Great Americans, pvt. collections. Active mus. therapy divsn. Am. Theatre Wing, 1942-45; trustee The Lenox Sch., 1953-55; chmn. Associated Taxpayers Old Lyme, 1969-72; trustee Brookgreen Gardens, S.C., 1989-97; founder, life trustee Lyme Acad., Coll. Fine Arts, 1976, prof. sculpture, 1976—. Recipient 1st prize Bklyn. War Meml. competition, 1945, 1st prize sculpture Catherine Lorillard Wolfe Art Club, 1951, 58, 63, Gold medal, 1969, Founders prize Pen & Brush, 1954, 76, 78, Gold medal, 1957, 61, 63, 69, 74, 76, Am. Heritage award, 1968, Solo Show award, 1961, 69, 75, Thomas R. Proctor prize NAD, 1956, Dessie Greer prize, 1960, 79, 85, Sculpture prize Nat. Arts Club, 1959, 60, 62, Gold medal, 1971, Gold medal Am. Artists Profl. League, 1960, 69, 73, 75, prize, 1981, Anna Hyatt Huntington prize, 1970, 76, Harriet Mayer Meml. prize, 1961, Gold medal Hudson Valley Art Assn., 1956, 69, 74, Mrs. John Newington award, 1976, 78, Lindsey Morris Meml. prize Allied Artists Am., 1973, Gold medal, 1982, Sculpture prize Acad. Artists, 1974, Sydney Taylor Meml. prize Knickerbocker Artists, 1975, New Netherlands DAR Bicentennial medal, 1976, Pietro Montana Meml. prize Hudson Valley Art Assn., 1995, Citation, State of Conn., 1995, Govs. Arts award Conn. Commn. on the Arts, 2000, Gari Melchers award Artist's Fellowship, 2002; named Citizen of Yr., Town of Old Lyme, Conn., 1985. Fellow: Internat. Inst. Arts and Letters, Am. Artists Profl. League, Nat. Sculpture Soc. (coun. 1976—85, Tallix Foundry award 1979, John Spring Founders award 1986, John Cavanaugh Meml. prize 1991, Silver medal, citation 1992, Herbert Adams Meml. medal for svc. to Am. sculpture); mem.: NAD (academician), Conn. Comm. for the Arts (Govs. medal 2000), Am. Profl. Artists League, Coun. Am. Artists Socs., Lyme Art Assn. (pres. 1973—75), Catherine Lorillard Wolf Art Club, Pen and Brush, Am. Medallic Art Soc., Allied Artists Am., Nat. Arts Club, Fedn. Internat. de la Medaille. Home: Old Lyme, Conn. Died 2006.

CHAPMAN, HUGH MCMASTER, banker; b. Spartanburg, SC, Sept. 11, 1932; s. James Alfred and Martha (Marshall) Chapman; m. Anne Allston Morrson, Dec. 27, 1958 (dec. Mar. 1993); children: Anne Allston, Rachel Buchanan, Mary Morrison; m. Janis Felkel, Aug. 17, 2001. BSBA, U. N.C., 1955. With Citizens & So. Nat. Bank S.C., 1958-91, pres., 1971-74, chmn. bd., 1974-91; pres. Citizens & So. Corp., Atlanta, 1986-91; vice chmn. C&S/Sovran Corp., 1990-91; chmn. Nations Bank S., 1992-97; ret., 1997. Bd. dirs. Inman Mills. Trustee East Lake Fedn., Duke Endowment. 1st lt. USAF, 1955-57. Died Apr. 29, 2007.

CHAPMAN, JEAN RUSS, publishing exec.; b. Pitts., Aug. 11, 1928; d. John Monroe and Constance (Clarke) Russ; B.A., U. Mich., 1950; postgrad. L.I. U., 1969-71; m. Robert David Rust, Mar. 4, 1957 (div.); 1 dau., Constance Clare; m. 2d, Francis Allan Chapman, Mar. 11, 1972; stepchildren— Allan, Kenneth, Jeanne. Asst. to editor Ladies Home Jour., N.Y.C., 1950-51; asst. editor Child Life Mag., Boston, 1951-55; tchr., Stirling, Scotland, 1955-57; sr. editor, project mgr., then cons. Harcourt Brace Jovanovich, N.Y.C. and San Francisco, 1971-75; adminstr. dept. anesthesiology U. Wash. Med. Center, Seattle, 1976-82; chief book editor Alaska N.W. Pub. Co., Edmonds, Wash., 1982—; instr. Nassau Community Coll., part-time 1970-71. Clk., Congl. Ch., Huntington, N.Y., 1968. Mem. Network Exec. Women, Alpha Phi (chpt. pres. 1967-69). Democrat. Presbyterian. Club: Mercerwood Shore. Sr. editor, project mgr. Bookmark Reading Series, 1973-75. Home: Hadley, Mass. Died July 27, 2007.

CHARLES, CONRAD JOSEPH, manufacturing executive; b. Chicago Heights, Ill., Aug. 7, 1930; s. Conrad and Isabel (Gayton) Charles; m. Yonne Charles; children: Richard, Michael, Rhonda, Cheryl. Student parochial schs. Prodn. mgr. Childrens Press Pub., Chgo., 1969—71; v.p. adminstr. Henry Regenry Pub. Co., 1971—75, Sheed & Ward Pub. Co., Mission, Kans., 1975—77; dir. prodn. and spl. sales Raintree Pubs., Inc., Milw., 1977—84; gen. mgr. Gannett Graphics, Augusta, Maine, from 1984. Active mem. Big Bros. Big Sisters. With US Army, 1951—53. Mem.: Printing Industry Wis., Chgo. Press Club, Chgo. Book Club. Roman Catholic. Home: Augusta, Maine. Died Feb. 27, 2006.

CHASE, JAMES KELLER, retired artist, museum director, educator; b. Logansport, Ind., May 18, 1927; s. James Howard and Agnes (Keller) C.; m. Marcelle Pierard, Dec. 29, 1969; 1 son, Henrik Clovis. BS, Ball State U., Muncie, Ind., 1952, doctoral fellow, 1972-74; MA, Mich. State U., 1963. Art supr. Chili (Ind.) schs., 1952-53, Sturgis (Mich.) schs., 1953-57; asst. prof. Western Mich. U., 1957-60; tchr. edn. TV on camera Central Mich. U., 1960-65; prof., chmn. fine arts dept. Northwood U., Midland, Mich., 1964-74; dir. Saginaw (Mich.) Mus., 1975-77, Ariz. Capitol Mus., Phoenix, 1978-81, McPherson Coll., 1982-87; art instr. Maricopa County, 1982-89; ret., 1989. Vis. prof. Western Mich. U., Saginaw Valley U., Delta Coll., Saginaw, Johns Hopkins U. at Ariz. State U.; mem. Mich. Higher Edn. Commn., 1967, Mich. Creativity Com., 1966; bd. dirs. Midland Ctr. Arts, 1967-71, Thompson Draw, Tonto Nat. Forest. Author: Nine Fine, 1977; contbr. articles to edn. jours., newspapers, mags.; exhibiting artist state, regional and nat. shows. Pres. Sands East II Homeowners Assn., 1987-89, sec., 1989-96; vol. ct. vis. guardianship rev. project Ariz. Superior Ct., 1994—. Mem. Am. Assn. Museums, Ariz. Adminstrs. Assn., Central Ariz. Museums Assn., Ariz. Hist. Assn. Died Nov. 4, 2005.

CHASE, MORRIS, international management consultant; b. NYC, May 19, 1918; s. Samuel and Bessie (Rabinowitz) Cherkasky; m. Claire Pernitz, Mar. 14, 1942; children— Sylvia, Viviane. BBA, City Coll. City N.Y., 1939; student econ. sci., U. Paris, 1959. C.P.A., N.Y. State. Mem. staff several C.P.A. firms, 1939-42; asst. to dir. finance and accounting Am. Joint Distbn. Com., 1946-48; dep. controller Marshall Plan mission to France, 1949; controller, finance officer U.S. spl. econ. mission to Cambodia, Laos and Vietnam, 1950; controller U.S. spl. econ. mission to Yugoslavia, 1951; economist Office U.S. Rep. in Europe, Paris, 1952-53; chmn. Internat. Bd. Auditors for Infrastructure, NATO., Paris, 1954-60; dir. infrastructure program NATO., 1961-68, chmn. def. installations com., 1966-68, chmn. payments and progress com. Cons. NATO Air Def. Ground Environment Consortium, 1968—. Served to capt. USAAF, 1942-46; maj. Res. Mem. Am. Inst. C.P.A.'s, N.Y. State Soc. C.P.A.'s, Fed. Accountants Assn. (pres. Paris 1961-62), NATO Retired Officers Assn. (vice chmn.), Fed. Govt. Accountants Assn. Paris (pres. 1964-65), Beta Gamma Sigma. Died Mar. 28, 2006.

CHASON, JACOB (LEON CHASON), retired neuropathologist; b. Monroe, Mich., May 12, 1915; s. Ben and Ida (Beiser) C.; m. Helen Pelok, May 19, 1942; children: Steven, Ellen, David. AB, U. Mich., 1937, MD, 1940. Intern Wayne County Gen. Hosp., 1940-41, resident, 1941-42, 46-49, asst. pathologist, 1949-50; fellow in neuropathology Mayo Clinic, 1952; dir. lab. VA Hosp., Allen Park, Mich., 1950-52; asst. prof. neuropathology Wayne State U., 1952-54, asso. prof., 1954-57, prof., 1958-86, chmn. dept. pathology, 1964-78, assoc. dean Sch. Medicine, 1970-72; neuropathologist Henry Ford Hosp., Detroit, 1978-88, cons., 1989-90. Cons. in field. Contbr. articles to profl. publs. With U.S. Army, 1942-46. NIH sr. fellow, 1959-60; grantee, 1961-63 Mem. Am. Assn. Neuropathologists, Am. Soc. Clin. Pathologists, Coll. Am. Pathologists, Internat. Acad. Pathology, Am. Acad. Neurology. Home: Dallas, Tex. Died Nov. 1, 2005.

CHASTAIN, HAROLD HERMAN, savs. and loan assn. cons.; b. Grosvenor, Tex., Oct. 25, 1919; s. Homer Hardin and Dora Frances (Baugh) C.; spl. cert. Howard Payne U., 1939; student LaSalle Extension U., 1939-50; m. Mary Francis Sprinkle, Dec. 23, 1939; Bookkeeper-cashier Weatherby Motor Co., Brownwood, Tex., 1939-40; bookkeeper, teller Citizens Nat. Bank, Brownwood, 1940-42; controller Mut. Savs. & Loan Assn., Ft. Worth, 1945-47; Savs. & Loan Assn. examiner for Tex., 1947-50, for Fed. Home Loan Bank Bd., 1950-58; dist. 9 dir. Fed. Home Loan Bank Bd., Little Rock, 1958-77; savs. and loan assn. cons., Albuquerque, 1977—; dir. Security Fed. Savs. & Loan Assn., Albuquerque, 1977—, vice chmn. bd., 1981-82, chmn. audit com. of dirs., 1978-82. Served with AC, USNR, 1942-45. Recipient Outstanding Performance Service certs. Fed. Home Loan Bank Bd., 1972-73, Spl. Recognition certs. Treasury Dept., 1959-75. Mem. Am. Assn. for Ret. People, Nat. Assn. Ret. Fed. Employees, U.S. League Insured Savs. and Loan Assn., N.Mex. League Insured Savs. and Loan Assns. Republican. Club: Four Hills Country. Home: Albuquerque, N.Mex. Died Feb. 28, 2006.

CHAZEN, HARTLEY JAMES, lawyer; b. NYC, Feb. 14, 1932; s. Joseph and Helen (Jacobson) C.; m. Lois Audrey, Dec. 12, 1967; 1 child, Nicole Joanna. AB, CCNY, 1953; LLB, Harvard U., 1958; LLM, NYU, 1959. Bar: N.Y. 1959. Assoc. Hays, St. John, Abramson & Heilbron, NYC, 1959-65, Shea & Gould, NYC, 1965-68, Rosenman & Colin, NYC, 1968-70; ptnr. Monasch Chazen & Stream, NYC, 1970-82; pvt. practice NYC, 1982-88; ptnr. Chazen & Fox, NYC, from 1988; of counsel McLaughlin & Stern, NYC, 1992-2000. Lectr. in field. Capt. USAR, 1958-68. Mem. Assn. Bar City N.Y., ABA (subcom. corp. taxation 1987—), Harvard Club. Home: Greenwich, Conn. Died June 30, 2006.

CHEN, JAMES TSUNG-TSUN, radiologist; b. Shantung, China, Jan. 11, 1924; came to U.S., 1959, naturalized, 1971; s. Yi and Chung-yu (Wang) C.; m. Alice Wu, June 29, 1963. MD, Nat. Def. Med. Center, Taipei, Taiwan, 1950. Resident in medicine 1st Gen. Hosp., Taipei, 1950-52, resident in radiology, 1952-55, Hosp. of U. Pa., Phila., 1955-56, 61-62, resident in radiation therapy, 1960-61; resident in radiology Mt. Sinai Hosp., Chgo., 1959-60; intern Presbyn. Hosp., Phila., 1962-63; resident in pediatric radiology St. Christopher Hosp. for Children, Phila., 1963-64. Asst. instr. radiology U. Pa., 1956-57, 60-62; instr. radiology Nat. Def. Med. Center, 1957-59; asso. dept. radiology Duke U., Durham, N.C., 1965-68, asst. prof., 1968-71, asso. prof., 1971-75, prof., 1975—, dir. cardiopulmonary radiology, 1976—. Contbr. in field. Named Tchr. of Yr. of Radiology Dept. Duke U., 1974; recipient Thomas D. Kinney Teaching award Duke U., 1987, 90, Duke Alumni Disting. Tchr. award, 1990. Fellow Am. Coll. Radiology and Cardiology, Am. Heart Assn.; mem. Radiol. Soc. N.Am., Am. Roentgen Ray Soc., Assn. Univ. Radiologists, Alpha Omega Alpha (faculty mem.) Presbyterian. Died Jan. 20, 2006.

CHENEY, DAVID RAYMOND, English educator; b. Castle Dale, Utah, Jan. 23, 1922; s. Silas Lavell and Klara (Young) C.; student Snow Coll., 1939-41; B.A., U. Utah, 1948, M.A., 1949; A.M., Harvard U., 1951; Ph.D., U. Iowa, 1955; m. Patricia Anne Snow, Dec. 18, 1948; 1 child, Pamela. Teaching asst. in English, U. Iowa, 1953-55; instr. English, Lewis and Clark Coll., 1956-58; asso. prof. English, S.W. Mo. State Coll., 1958-63, prof., 1963-65; prof. U. Toledo, 1965—, dir. grad. studies in English, 1968-79. Advisor, youth council NAACP, Springfield, Mo., 1963-65. Served with U.S. Army, 1941-46; PTO. U. Utah research fellow, 1948; U. Toledo research fellow, 1968, 76, 79; U. Iowa grantee, 1966, 68; U. Toledo grantee, 1968, 70, 73, 74, 79, 81-84; Nat. Endowment Humanities summer grantee, 1983. Mem. Modern Humanities Research Assn., Shakespeare Assn. Am., MLA, Central Renaissance Soc. Am., AAUP, Phi Beta Kappa, Phi Kappa Phi. Mormon. Author: The Correspondence of Leigh Hunt and Charles Ollier in the Winter of 1853-54, 1976; editor: Musical Evenings or Selections Vocal and Instrumental (Leigh Hunt), 1964; research on Leigh Hunt letters, Shakespeare. Home: Toledo, Ohio. Died June 18, 2006.

CHENG, HSIEN KEI, aeronautics educator; b. Macao, June 13, 1923; came to U.S., 1948; s. Lo Sing and Teresa Sau Kit (Cheng) C.; m. Wai Laan Lee, May 31, 1956; 1 child, Linda Y. H. BS, Chiao-Tung U., China, 1947; MS in Aero. Engring., Cornell U., 1950, PhD in Aero. Engring., 1952. Aerodynamic engr. Bell Aircraft Corp., Niagara Falls, N.Y., 1952-56; rsch. aerodynamicist Cornell Aero. Lab., Buffalo, 1956-59, prin. aerodynamicist, 1959-63; vis. lectr. Stanford (Calif.) U., 1963-64; spl. lectr. U. So. Calif., LA, 1964-65, prof., 1965-93, prof. emeritus, from 1993. Cons. McDonnell Douglas Corp., Santa Monica, Calif., 1963-70, Rand Corp., Santa Monica, 1965-74, Aerospace Corp., El Segundo, Calif., 1969-74, Sci. Applications Inc., El Segundo, 1972-78, TRW Corp., San Bernardino, Calif., 1985-88, Inst. Aero. Astro, Nat. Cheng-Kung Univ., Taiwan, 1994-95, Northwestern Poly. Univ., Xi'an, People's Republic of China, 1993—; proprietor HKC Rsch., 1996—. Contbr. numerous articles to profl. jours. Grantee Office Naval Rsch., 1972-87, NSF, 1977-86, Air Force Office Sci. Rsch., 1985-92, NASA/Dept. Def., 1987-92. Fellow AIAA, Am. Phys. Soc.; mem. NAE (elected), Soc. Indsl. and Applied Math., Acad. Model Aero., Phi Tau Phi. Died July 11, 2007.

CHENG, LUNG, mechanical engineer; b. Shaoxing, Zhejiang, China, Mar. 13, 1920; s. Ren Ching and Chi Wan (Chen) C.; came to U.S., 1964, naturalized, 1972; B.M.E., Nat. Chekiang U., 1945; M.Engring., McGill U., 1961; Ph.D., U. Ill., 1969; m. Carol Dzwen-hua Dju, June 23, 1962; 1 dau., Lilie. Instr. mech. engring. Nat. Taiwan U., 1954-59; engr. Combustion Engring. Incorp., Montreal, Que., Can., 1962-64; asst. prof. mech. engring. Christian Bros. Coll., Memphis, 1969-70; supervisory mech. engr. dust control and project leader dust explosion suppression U.S. Dept. Interior, Bur. Mines, Pitts., 1970-90. Mem. ASME, AAAS. Contbr. articles to profl. publs. on nature, behavior of dusts, suppression methods. Home: Adelphi, Md. Died Jan. 10, 2006.

CHERRY, LOUIS B., food products executive; b. Poland, Aug. 18, 1927; s. H. David and Fanny (Kleiner) Cherry; m. Barbara Goldberg, Dec. 13, 1952; children: Steven, Robert, Rosanne, Michael. BA in Polit. Sci., UCLA, 1950. Pres., chmn. David Cherry's Sons & Assocs., San Francisco; pres. Coastal Investment Corp. With US Army, 1945—47. Decorated Purple Heart. Jewish. Home: San Mateo, Calif. Died Aug. 9, 2006.

CHERRY, SANDRA WILSON, lawyer; b. Dec. 31, 1941; d. Berlin Alexander and Renna Glen (Barnes) Wilson; m. John Sandefur Cherry, Sept. 24, 1976; 1 child, Jane Wilson. BA, U. Ark., 1962, JD, 1975. Bar: Ark. 75, U.S. Dist. Ct. (ea. dist.) Ark. 79, U.S. Supreme Ct. 79, U.S. Ct. Appeals (8th cir.) 79. Tchr. social studies Little Rock Sch. Dist., 1966—70; chmn. social studies dept. Horace Mann Jr. H.S., Little Rock, 1970—72; asst. US atty. US Dept. Justice, Little Rock, 1975—81, 1983—2002, 1st asst. US atty., 2002—06; commr. Ark. Pub. Svc. Commn., Little Rock, 1981—83. Adj. instr. U. Ark. Sch. Law, Little Rock, 1980; mem. 8th cir. gender fairness task force, Ark. dist. ct. magistrate selection panel, 2001. Contbr. case note to Ark. Law Rev., 1975. Pres. bd. dirs. Gaines House, Inc.; pres. U. Ark. at Little Rock Law Sch. Assn., 1980—81, bd. dirs., 1982, Jr. League Little Rock, 1974, Ark. Cmty. Found., 1997—2006, Gov.'s Mansion Assn., 1998—2004, Good Shepherd Ecumenical Ctr., 2004—06. Recipient Gayle Pettus Pontz award, U. Ark. Law Sch. Women Lawyers Assn., 1990. Mem.: Ark. Women's Forum, Little Rock C. of C., Ark. Bar Assn. (com. on the status of women and minorities), Ark. Women Lawyers Assn., Pulaski County Bar Assn. (bd. dirs. 1989—90, 1991—92, pres.-elect 1993—94, pres. 1994—2006), Ark. Bar Assn. (Ho. of Dels. 1984—86, sec.-treas. 1986—89, 8th cir. Gender Fairness Task Force 1989—94, Ho. of Dels. 1989—2006, tenured del. 1994—2006, exec. coun. chair 1995—96, pres. 2001—02, Golden Gavel award 1992), Met. Coun., Phi Beta Phi. Republican. Presbyterian. Home: Little Rock, Ark. Died Aug. 1, 2006.

CHERVENAK, JOHN JOSEPH, hospital administrator; b. Chgo., Aug. 23, 1924; s. John and Antonette M. (Jurasek) C.; m. Lillian Florence Havlik, Sept. 8, 1951; children— Sharon, Deborah. B.S. in Bus. and Econs., Ill. Inst. Tech., 1949. Cert. safety profl., internat. health care profl. Loss prevention mgr. Am. Mut. Ins. Cos., Milw., 1949-75; dir. safety, security St. Michael Hosp., Milw., 1975—. Vice-pres. Mt. Mary Coll. Parent Assn., 1975-77. Served in U.S. Army, 1943-45. Decorated Purple Heart. Mem. Am. Soc. Safety Engrs., Internat. Assn. Hosp. Security (chmn. So. eastern Wis. chpt. 1981-82, vice chmn. 1979-81), Internat. Healthcare Profls. Am., Wis. Healthcare Safety Assn., Am. Legion. Democrat. Roman Catholic. Home: Milwaukee, Wis. Died Feb. 28, 2006.

CHICKLIS, BARBARA KAREN BURAK, retired data processing executive; b. Woonsocket, RI, July 1, 1942; d. Steven and Stella Burak; m. William A. Gianopoulos, Apr. 3, 1981; children: Karen Barbara, Paul Steven. BS in Math., Suffolk U., 1964; MSEE in Computer Sci., Northeastern U., 1974. Sys. programmer Raytheon Corp., Lexington, Mass., 1965—68, ITEK Corp., 1968—71; project and staff leader Computation Ctr. Northeastern U., Boston, 1971—74; staff cons. Control Data Corp., Waltham, 1974—2005, ret., 2005. Recipient Internat. Profl. Svcs. Analyst Symposium award, 1977. Mem.: Assn. Computing Machinery. Republican. Home: Ashland, Mass. Died Mar. 7, 2007.

CHILDS, BREVARD SPRINGS, religious educator; b. Columbia, SC, Sept. 2, 1923; s. Richard A. and Reaux (Jones) C.; m. Ann Taylor, Aug. 7, 1954; children— John, Catherine. BA, U. Mich., 1946, MA, 1948; BD, Princeton, 1950; ThD, U. Basel, Switzerland, 1955; DD (hon.), U. Aberdeen, Scotland, 1984, U. Glasgow, 1992. Ordained to ministry Presbyn. Ch., 1958. Prof. O.T., Mission House Sem., Plymouth, Wis., 1954-58; prof. religion Yale U., New Haven, 1958-99, Sterling prof. div., 1992-99, ret., 1999. Author: Myth and Reality in the Old Testament, 1960, Memory and Tradition in Israel, 1962, Isaiah and the Assyrian Crisis, 1967, Biblical Theology in Crisis, 1970, The Book of Exodus, 1974, Old Testament Books for Pastor and Teacher, 1977, Introduction to the Old Testament as Scripture, 1979, the New Testament as Canon: An Introduction, 1985, Old Testament Theology in a Canonical Context, 1986, Biblical Theology of the Old and New Testaments, 1992, Commentary on Isaiah, 2000. Served with AUS, 1943-45. Guggenheim fellow, 1963-64; Nat. Endowment for Humanities fellow, 1977-78; Fulbright-Hays fellow, 1981; Deutscher Akademischer Austauschdienst fellow, 1987. Fellow Am. Acad. Arts and Scis. Died June 23, 2007.

CHILDS, DANIEL ROBBINS, brokerage house executive; b. NYC, Aug. 20, 1935; s. Frederick R. and Mary Alixandra (Hitchcock) Childs; m. Margaret Florence Burden, June 22, 1955; children: Frederick Carter, Nicholas Fairbanks, Florence C. Macdonald, Constance C. Rosengarter, Shirley C. Kelly, Hilary Thomas, Alexandra McKenzie. Assoc. Morgan Stanley & Co., NYC, 1961—66; with William A.M. Burden & Co., from 1967, gen. ptnr., from 1971. Trustee New Canaan (Conn.) Country Sch., 1966—82, chmn., 1980—82; trustee Santa Catalina Sch., 1976—82, Whitney Mus. Am. Art, 1975—79; bd. dirs. Portmouth (RI) Abbey Sch., 1970—77, chmn., 1973—77; bd. mgrs. NY Bot. Garden, from 1978; bd. dirs. Florence V. Burden Found., from 1969. Mem.: NY Soc. Security Analysts, City Midday Club (NYC), Links Club, Harvard Club. Republican. Roman Catholic. Home: New Canaan, Conn. Died Mar. 4, 2007.

CHINMOY, SRI, composer, musician; b. Shakpura, Bangladesh, Aug. 27, 1931; came to U.S., 1964; s. Shashi Kumar and Yoga Maya Ghose. Grad. high sch., Pondicherry, Bangladesh. Clk. Indian Consulate, N.Y., 1964-67; dir. Sri Chinmoy Ctrs., Sri Chinmoy Marathon Team. Composer over 7, 000 songs. Vol. hundreds of peace concerts worldwide; opening meditator P.R. World Masters Games, 1983, N.Y. Games, 1990. Named Hon. Citizen of P.R., and 27 Am. states; hon. patron Bharatiya Vidya Bhavan; 4 bridges named in his honor State of R.I. Avocations: poetry, painting, tennis, track and field. Died Oct. 11, 2007.

CHO, ALBERT I. PAO, mechanical engineer, educator; b. China, May 2, 1932; came to U.S., 1953; s. Edward I. Lai Cho and Mildred Chong Chen; m. Betty Chan, Aug. 17, 1963; 1 son, Lawrence. B.S. in Mech. Engring., U. Ill., 1958, M.S., 1959. Cert. profl. engr. Ill., Calif., Fla., Minn., Ind., Tex., Mass., Colo. Assoc. ptnr. Skidmore, Owings & Merrill, Chgo., 1959-83; v.p. Perkins & Will, Chgo., 1984—; asst. prof. Ill. Inst. Tech., Chgo., 1980—. Mem. Mech. Engring. Soc., ASHRAE, ASME, Pi Tau Sigma. Contbr. chpts. to books and articles to profl. jours. Home: Glenview, Ill. Died July 2, 2006.

CHOPEY, NICHOLAS P., editor; b. NYC, Dec. 22, 1932; s. Nicholas W. and Alice I. (Keshelak) C.; m. Katherine J. Heaney, Sept. 12, 1959; children: Nicholas, Michael, John, James. BChE, U. Va., 1955; MA in Econs., NYU, 1972. Process engr. Esso Standard Oil Co., Linden, NJ, 1955-56, 58-59; asst. assoc. editor McGraw-Hill, Inc., NYC, 1960-67, sr. assoc. editor, 1967-72, mng. editor, 1972-78, exec. editor, 1978-82, editor-in-chief, 1982-87, from 2000, exec. editor, 1987-99, Chem. Week Assocs., 1999-2000, editor-in-chief, from 2000. Adv. com. Indsl. Energy Tech. Conf., Houston, 1992—. Editor: Handbook of Chemical Engineering Calculations, 1984, 3d edit., 2003; (reprint books) Environmental Engineering in the Process Plant, 1992, Fluid Movers, 1994. 1st lt. USAF, 1956-58. Mem. AIChE (past chair com.), Am. Soc. Engring. Edn., Knights of Malta, Roselle Golf Club, Tau Beta Pi. Roman Catholic. Home: Elizabeth, NJ. Died Feb. 26, 2007.

CHOW, RICHARD HING, physics educator; b. Vancouver, BC, Can., Sept. 6, 1924; came to U.S., 1949; m. May Fong Eng, May 20, 1948; children: Victoria, Brian, James, Randall. BA, U. B.C., 1947, MA, 1949; PhD, UCLA, 1955. Assoc. in physics UCLA, 1952-53; asst. rsch. officer Atomic Energy of Can. Ltd., Chalk River, Ont., 1954-58; asst. prof. Calif. State U., Long Beach, 1958-61, assoc. prof., 1961-65, prof., 1965-86, prof. emeritus, from 1986. Richland faculty appointee N.W. Coll. and Univ. Assn. for Scientific Studies, 1968-69; faculty participant Associated Western Univs., Golden, Colo., 1980. Contbr. articles to profl. jours. Mem. Am. Phys. Soc., Am. Assn. of Physics Tchrs., Am. Nuclear Soc. Home: Long Beach, Calif. Died Jan. 26, 2006.

CHRISTENSEN, DAN (DANIEL JAMES CHRISTENSEN), painter; b. Cozad, Nebr., 1942; m. Elaine Grove; children: James, William. BFA, Kansas City Art Inst., 1964. Guest artist Whitney Mus. Sch., 1969, San Francisco Art Inst., 1971, Provincetown Workshop for Artists and Writers, 1972; instr. Ridgewood Sch. Art., 1975, 76, 77, Sch. Visual Arts, NYC, 1976-82. Exhibited one-man shows, Noah Goldowsky Gallery, N.Y.C., 1967, Galerie Ricke, Cologne, Germany, 1968, 71, Andre Emmerich Gallery, N.Y.C., 1969, Nicholas Wilder Gallery, Los Angeles, 1970, Edmonton Art Gallery, Alta., 1973, Greenberg Gallery, St. Louis, 1974, Andre Emmerich Gallery, N.Y.C., 1975, Douglas Drake Gallery, Kansas City, 1976, 84, B.R. Kornblatt Gallery, Balt., 1977, Meridith Long Contemporary Gallery, N.Y.C., 1978, 79, 80, U. Nebr. at Omaha Art Gallery, 1980, Salander-O'Reilly Galleries Inc., N.Y.C., 1981, 82, 83, 84, Ivory Kimpton Gallery, San Francisco, 1982, Lincoln Ctr. Gallery, N.Y.C., 1983, Edward Thorp Gallery, 2005, group shows, Oberlin Coll., Ohio, 1966, Whitney Annual, N.Y.C., 1967, Whitney Mus. Am. Art, N.Y.C., 1968, 71, 72, 73, Galerie Ricke, Kassel, Germany, 1968, Corcoran Mus. Biennial, Washington, 1969, Guggenheim Mus., N.Y.C., 1969, Albright-Knox Gallery, Buffalo, N.Y., 1970, Balt. Mus. Art, 1971-72, Milw. Art Ctr., 1972, Boston Mus. Fine Arts, 1972, Aldrich Mus. Contemporary Art, Ridgefield, Conn., 1973, Greenberg Gallery, St. Louis, 1974, Museo Bellas Artes, Curacus, 1975, Lehigh U., Bethlehem. Pa., 1976, Edmunton Art Gallery, 1977, U. Nebr., Omaha, 1978, Zolla Liberman Gallery, Chgo., 1979, Carson-Sapiro Gallery, Denver, 1980, Mus. Modern Art, N.Y.C., 1981, Mus. Fine Arts, Houston, 1981, La Jolla Mus. Contemporary Art, Calif., 1981, Spl. Projects at PSI, N.Y.C., 1983; represented permanent collections, Albright-Knox Gallery, Boston Mus. Fine Arts, Chgo. Art Inst., Dayton Art Inst., Denver Mus. Art, Edmunton Art Gallery, Guggenheim Mus., Hirshhorn Mus. and Sculpture Garden, Washington, Houston Mus. Fine Arts, Wallraf-Richartz, Cologne, Germany, Met. Mus. Art, N.Y.C., Mus. Contemporary Art, Chgo., Mus. Modern Art, N.Y.C., St. Louis Art Mus., Toledo Mus., Whitney Mus. Am. Art. Recipient Nat. Endowment grant, 1968, Theodoron award, 1969; Guggenheim fellow, 1969, Gottlieb Found. grant, 1986, Pollock-Krasner Found. grant, 1996. Mem. Kansas City Art Inst. (gov. 1981) Home: New York, NY. Died Jan. 20, 2007.

CHRISTENSON, MAYNARD GLASGOW, petroleum geologist; b. Superior, Nebr., Mar. 14, 1925; s. John Alvin and May (Glasgow) C.; m. Virginia A. Warren, Jan. 2, 1954; children— John Clarke, Janet Louise. B.S., U. Nebr., 1949. Geologist, U. Nebr.-Conservation and Survey Div., Lincoln, 1949-52, Cities Service Oil and Gas Co., Denver, 1952—. Contbr. articles to profl. jours. Served to Sgt. U.S. Army, 1943-46, ETO. Mem. Am. Assn. Petroleum Geologists, Rocky Mountain Assn. Geologists, Kans. Geol. Soc. Republican. Episcopalian. Home: Denver, Colo. Died June 4, 2006.

CHUN, PAUL KWAI TUNG, retail executive; b. Honolulu, Nov. 19, 1922; s. Kim Chow and Emma (Kwock) C.; m. Rachel Bow, Sept. 15, 1945; children: Paula, Patricia, Randall, Pamela, Rodney. Grad. high sch., Honolulu, 1941. Pres., chief exec. officer Chun Kim Chow Ltd., Honolulu, from 1985. Named Retailer of Yr. Retail Merchants Hawaii, Honolulu, 1987. Died June 21, 2007.

CHUPKA, WILLIAM ANDREW, chemical physicist, educator; b. Pittston, Pa., Feb. 12, 1923; s. William and Antoinette C.; m. Olive Augusta Pirani, May 21, 1955; children: Jocelyn Terese, Marc William. BS, U. Scranton, 1943; MS, U. Chgo., 1949, PhD, 1951. Instr. Harvard U., 1951-54; asso. physicist Argonne (Ill.) Nat. Lab., 1954-67; sr. physicist, 1967-75; prof chemistry Yale U., 1975-96, prof. emeritus, from 1996. Research, numerous publs. in chem. physics. Served with U.S Army, 1943-46. Guggenheim fellow, 1961-62 Mem. Am. Chem Soc. Home: Woodbridge, Conn. Died Jan. 21, 2007.

CHURCH, ARCHER EDWARD, JR., naval officer, govt. agy ofcl.; b. Bradford, Pa., Apr. 23, 1929; s. Archer Edward and Berta Marie (Unger) C.; B.S., U.S. Naval Acad., 1951; B.C.E. Rensselaer Poly. Inst., 1955; M.S., Princeton U., 1962; m. Marie Lucy Ciampitti, June 27, 1970. Commd. ensign Civil Engr Corps, U.S. Navy, 1951, advanced through grades to comdr. 1965; asst. dir. engring. Navy facilities, Southeastern U.S. 1962-63; asst. public works officer Pensacola Naval Air Sta. 1963-65; constrn. program mgr. mil. assistance, Vietnam, 1965-66; asst. dist. civil engr. 4th Naval Dist., 1966-67; chief civi engr. U.S. facilities, Antarctica, 1967-70; spl. asst. for contracts Naval Ship Systems Command Hdqrs., Washington, 1970-73 public works officer Naval Research Lab., Washington, 1973-77 chief engring. and constrn. Def. Nuclear Agy., 1977-80. Decorated Def. Meritorious Service medal, Bronze Star medal, Navy Commendation medal. Registered profl. engr., Ala. Mem ASCE, Soc. Am. Mil. Engrs., Tau Beta Pi, Chi Epsilon Episcopalian. Author: (with G. Breese et al) The Impact of Large Installations on Nearby Areas, 1965. Home: Annandale, Va Died July 7, 2006.

CHURCH, HERBERT STEPHEN, JR., retired constructio company executive; b. Framingham, Mass., July 24, 1920; s Herbert Stephen and Edith L. (Shaw) C.; m. Carol S. Orzech Apr. 2, 1945; children: Carolyn, David, Kathryn, Patricia Virginia. BS in Civil Engring, Northeastern U., Boston, 194 Constrn. insp. N.Y., New Haven & Hartford R.R., 1940-43; wit Turner Constrn. Co., 1943; from gen. supt. to v.p., gen. mg Chgo. terr., 1965-73; sr. v.p. Western region Chgo., 1974-80; s v.p. Central region, 1980-85. Dir., 1972-85 Trustee Na Commn. for Coop. Edn., 1981-90. Mem. Contractors Mut. Assn (dir. 1974-84), Builders Assn. Chgo. (dir. 1969-74), Chgo. Clu Inverness Golf Club. Roman Catholic. Home: Arlingto Heights, Ill. Died Jan. 28, 2007.

CIAMPI, MARIO JOSEPH, architect, planner; b. San Fran cisco, Apr. 27, 1907; s. Guido and Palmira (DiVita) C.; m Loretta Keane, Sept. 26, 1939 (dec. 1972); m. Carolyn Smith June 1, 1983. Grad., Harvard Sch. Architecture, 1932; D.F.A (hon.), Calif. Sch. Arts and Crafts, 1980. Lic. architect, Cali Design critic San Francisco Archtl. Club, 1935-40; practic architecture Mario J. Ciampi and Assos. (Urban Design Con sultants), San Francisco, from 1945. Lectr. various orgns. ar univs. Urban cons. San Francisco projects including, Market S Devel. Plan, 1963-79, Waterfront Study, 1958, Golden Gatewa Project, 1958, Freeway Study, 1966, Market St. Beautificatic Project, 1968-79, Yerba Buena Center Study, 1973-75, N.Wa terfront, Port Commn., 1980, South of Market Design Pla 1983. Fellow AIA (first honor awards state and nat. awarc programs, awards for Market Street beautification 1970-7 Univ. Art Mus., Berkeley, San Francisco Junipero Serra Fre way, Seton House, Los Altos, Inst. Noetic Scis., Harvard Alum Assn., various schs. and chs. San Francisco area, winner 25 y award state competition Calif. Coun. for Art Mus., Berkele Calif. Design Assocs. 1996); mem. Marin Symphony Assn Serra Club, Lagunitas Club, Palm Springs Tennis Club, Sa Francisco Archtl. Club, Rosecrucians. Clubs: Harvard, Olympi Serra, Laqunitas, Plam Springs Tennis, San Francisco Arch

Lodges: Rosecrucians. Traveler, research and study urban design, architecture N.Am., Europe, S.Am., Orient, Middle East, 1950-66; works published N.Am., S.Am., Europe, India. Died July 6, 2006.

CICENIA, RONALD J. See CAREY, RON

CICERO, MARILYN BELLE, travel consultant; b. N.Y.C., July 16, 1931; d. Sam K. and Helen (Smith) Kass; m. Arthur Bennet Cicero, Jan. 27, 1952; children: Lori Cicero Boelig, Lois Cicero Woodbury. B.B.A., CCNY, 1953. Tchr. Burlington, Mass., Pub. Schs., 1965-69; mgr. Colpitts Travel Agy., Lexington, Mass., 1969-72, exec. v.p., 1972-80, pres., 1980—; pres. Colpitts Assocs., West Roxbury, Mass., 1975-78; pres. C and L Cons., Lexington, 1981—; v.p. Nova Assocs., Dallas, treas., 1985—; mem. adv. bd. Travel Edn. Ctr., Cambridge, Mass., Pan Am. World Airways, Boston, Continental Airlines; mem. Travel Agts. Adv. Bd. Active Women's Am. Ort. Lexington (founding pres., 1960-62). Mem. Inst. Cert. Travel Agts (life), Am. Soc. Travel Agts., Brit. Airways Travel Agts. (adv. bd. 1986), Soc. Travel Tourism Educators, Lexington C. of C. (dir. 1977—, fin. chmn. 1982—). Jewish. Home: Lexington, Mass. Died Nov. 28, 2006.

CIMINO, JOSEPH ANTHONY, preventive medicine physician, educator, former city health department administrator; b. NYC, Jan. 1, 1934; m. Margaret Langan; children: Andrea, Laura, Lisa, Joseph, Linda, Margaret, John. BA in Am. History, Harvard U., 1956, M.I.H., 1964, M.P.H., 1965; MS in Biology, Fordham U., 1958; MD, U. Buffalo, 1962. Diplomate Am. Bd. Preventive Medicine. Intern Grasslands Hosp., Valhalla, NY, 1962-63; AEC fellow in environ. medicine Harvard U. Sch. Public Health, 1963-65; research assoc. health officer NYC Dept. Health, 1965-66; dir. NYC Bur. Community Safety & Occupational Health, 1968-71, dep. commr. health, 1971-72, commr. health, 1972-74; chief med. officer NYC Dept. Sanitation, 1966-69; med. dir. NYC Poison Control Center, 1966-72; dir. health and safety NYC Environ. Protection Adminstrn., 1968-71; commr. hosps. Westchester County, NY, 1974-78; pres., CEO NY Med. Coll., 1978-81, prof. preventive medicine, 1976—2007, chmn. dept. preventive medicine, 1980—2007; pres. Occupl. Medicine Assocs., 1978—2007. Assoc. prof. environ. medicine and pub. health NYU, 1971—76; prof. cmty. dynamics Pace U., 1977—78; adj. prof. pub. health and tropical medicine Tulane U., 1972—76; lectr. in pub. health Columbia U., 1973—76; vis. prof. cmty. health Albert Einstein Coll. Medicine, 1973—76, NY State Pub. Health Coun.; pres. bd. Dominican Sisters Family Health Svcs., Inc. Author: Safety: Protection from Injury, 1969, Medical Service Manual, 1971, Drug Abuse Treatment Agencies in New York City, 1972; contbr. articles to profl. jours. Chmn. Cath. Interracial Coun. of Westchester County; chief med. cons. NYC CSC, 1966-71; Civilian US Army, 1964-65; mem. exec. com. Med.Bd. West Med. Ctr., chair greivance com., NY med. Coll., mem. N.Y.S. Pub. Health Council. Recipient Honor award, Ellis Island, 2005. Fellow Am. Coll. Preventive Medicine, NY Acad. Medicine, Am. Coll. Occupational Medicine, NY Acad. Sci.; mem. APHA, AMA, NYC Pub. Health Assn., Indsl. Med. Assn., Assn. Govtl. Hygienists, Aerospace Med. Assn., Westchester County Med. Soc., NY State Med. Assn., Am. Soc. Clin. Nutrition. Home: Tarrytown, NY. Died July 1, 2007.

CION, RICHARD M., financial executive, lawyer; b. Hartford, Conn., July 27, 1943; s. Irving and Anne (Miller) C.; m. Marjorie Baum; children: Stephanie Lee, Zachary Samuel, Alexander Lucas, Nicholas Foster. AB, Princeton U., 1965; LL.B., Harvard U., 1968. Assoc., ptnr. Kaye, Scholer, Fierman, Hays & Handler, NYC, 1968-81; v.p., gen. counsel Condec Corp., Old Greenwich, Conn., 1981-82, v.p. fin. and legal affairs, 1982-85, exec. v.p., chief fin. officer, 1985-88, dir., 1983-87; dir., exec. v.p., chief fin. officer Farley Ind., Fruit of the Loom, Inc., Farley Metals, 1985-88; mng. dir. Drexel Burnham Lambert Inc., 1988-90; sr. exec. v.p. Farley, Ind., Fruit of the Loom, Inc., NYC, from 1990. Home: Westport, Conn. Died Mar. 27, 2007.

CIPRIANO, GRACE IRENE, estimator, nurse, stables owner; b. Youngstown, Ohio, May 13, 1925; d. Floyd Raymond and Ruth (Walter) Brown; m. Otto Francis Wess, June 11, 1949 (dec. Mar. 1969); children: Raymond Francis, Shannon Grace Wess Morello, Colleen Medody Wess Bloomingdale, Honey Lucile Wess Biondillo, Alyson Rae Wess King, Carol Lynn Wess Sivley; m. James L. Cipriao, June 28, 1987. Student, Bliss Bus. Coll., 1942-43; LLB, LaSalle U., 1952; grad. nurse's tng. Youngstown Hosp. Assn., 1974. Nurse's aid St. Elizabeth Hosp., Youngstown, 1938-42; traffic clk. B.F. Goodrich Co., Akron, Ohio, 1942-43; rate clk., traffic dept. Gen. Fireproofing Co., Youngstown, 1947-49; pres., co-owner Jewels by Lady Grace, Detroit, 1949-63, Grayce's Treasure Chests, Youngstown, 1949-63, Grayce's Medicine Chests, Youngstown, 1949-63; indsl. and comml. bldg. estimator Ben Rudick & Son, Inc., Youngstown, 1963-71; freelance estimator, North Lima, Ohio, 1971—; newspaper columnist, various newspapers, 1963-68; nurse, 1974—; now staff nurse Drs. Hosp., Lake Worth, Fla.; owner Grace Wess Stables, Inc., Canfield, Ohio, 1949—. Dem. candidate for Mahoning County commr., 1973; bd. dirs. Missing Children Found., Tampa, Fla.; mem. legis. com. Palm Beach County, Mothers Against Drunk Driving. Served with WAVES, 1943-47. Mem. Am. Bus. Women's Assn. (pres. 1969-70, Woman of Yr. award 1970), Youngstown Bus. and Profl. Women's Club, U.S. Trotting Assn., Canfield Harness Horsemen's Assn., Ohio Harness Horsemen's Assn., Am. Legion, VFW, Def. Supply Assn., McGuffey Meml. Assn., Women in Constrn., Constrn. Specifications Inst., Internat. Platform Assn., Home and Sch. Assn., St. Charles Altar and Rosary Soc., Mahoning County Agrl. Soc., Am. German Club of Palm Beaches (Fla.), Youngstown Playhouse, Order Eastern Star (Grand Nurse of Fla. 1986-87, Worthy Matron Lucerne chpt. 1989—), Grange. Democrat. Roman Catholic. Died May 11, 2007.

CIRIACY, EDWARD WALTER, retired physician, educator; b. Phila., Feb. 12, 1924; s. William Frederick and Elizabeth Jane McGettigan) C. BS, Pa. State Coll., 1948; MD, Temple U., 1952. Diplomate: Nat. Bd. Med. Examiners, Am. Bd. Family Practice (chmn. recertification com. 1972-76). Intern Frankford Hosp., Phila., 1952-53, surg. resident, 1953-54, Temple Hosp., Phila., 1953-54; practice medicine specializing in family practice Ely, Minn., 1954-57, 58-71, Miami, Fla., 1957-58; mem. staffs Ely-Bloomenson Community Hosp.; prof. U. Minn., 1971-98, head dept. family practice, 1971-95. Mem. adv. panel for subcom. on patient care Cancer Coordinating Com. for Health Scis. Contbr. articles to med. jours. Served with USAAF, 1944-46. Recipient Merit award Minn. Acad. Gen. Practice, 1963 Fellow Am. Acad. Family Physicians (charter); mem. Minn. Acad. Family Physicians (pres. 1975), Minn. Med. Assn. (mem. com. med. services 1970), Range Med. Soc. (pres. 1961), Babcock Surg. Soc., Assn. Am. Med. Colls., Alpha Omega Alpha Clubs: Mason. Died June 21, 2006.

CLAIBORNE, LIZ (ELISABETH CLAIBORNE ORTENBERG), fashion designer; b. Brussels, Mar. 31, 1929; came to U.S., 1939; d. Omer Villere and Louise Carol (Fenner) C.; m. Ben Schultz (div.), 1 child, Alexander; m. Arthur Ortenberg, July 5, 1954 Student, Art Sch., Brussels, 1948-49, Academie, Nice, France, 1950; DFA, R.I. Sch. Design, 1991. Asst. Tina Lesser, NYC, 1951-52, Omar Khayam, Ben Reig, Inc., NYC, 1953; designer Juniorite, NYC, 1954-60, Dan Keller, NYC, 1960-76, Youth Guild Inc., NYC, 1976-89; designer, pres., chmn. Liz Claiborne Inc., NYC, 1985-89, pres., 1976-89, chmn., COO; chmn. Liz Claiborne Cosmetics, 1985-89, cons. Guest lectr. Fashion Inst. Tech., Parsons Sch. Design; bd. dirs. Coun. of Am. Fashion Designers, Fire Island Lighthouse Restoration Com. Recipient Designer of Yr. award Palciode Hierro, Mexico City, 1976, Designer of Yr. award Dayton Co., Mpls., 1978, Ann. Disting. in Design award Marshall Field's, 1985, One Co. Makes a Difference award Fashion Inst. Tech., 1985, award Coun. Fashion Designers, 1986, Gordon Grand Fellowship award Yale U., 1989, Jr. Achievement award Nat. Bus. Hall of Fame, 1990, Frederick A.P. Barnard award Barnard Coll., 1991, Hon. Doctorate, R.I. Sch. of Design, 1991; named to Nat. Sales Hall of Fame, 1991. Mem. Fashion Group. Roman Catholic. Died June 26, 2007.

CLAIRE, FRANKLIN HOWARD, consumer products company executive; b. Bklyn., July 24, 1938; s. John Henry and Blanche (Avner) C.; m. Marilyn Judith Margolis, July 23, 1967; children— Jason Eric, Stuart Brian. A.B., Muhlenberg Coll., 1959; M.S., L.I. U., 1960. Project dir. Pepsi Cola, N.Y.C., 1963-66; product mgr. CPC, Englewood Cliffs, N.J., 1966-68; mgr. new products Borden Foods, N.Y.C., 1968-70, Squibb, Beech Nut, N.Y.C., 1970-72; dir. mktg. T.J. Lipton, Englewood Cliffs, 1972-84; pres., chief exec. officer Red Cheek, Fleetwood, Pa., 1984—; adj. prof. Bergen Community Coll., 1978-80. Pres. Jewish Community Orgn., 1974-75; v.p. B'nai B'rith, 1978-79. Mem. Am. Mktg. Assn. Republican. Club: Berleigh (Kutztown). Avocations: racquetball; tennis. Died Aug. 12, 2006.

CLARK, BOB, film director; b. New Orleans, Aug. 5, 1941; Student, Hillsdale Coll. Dir., prodr.: (films) Children Shouldn't Play With Dead Things, 1972, Dead of Night, 1974, Black Christmas, 1975, Breaking Point, 1976, Murder By Decree, 1979, Tribute, 1980, Porky's, 1982, Porky's II: The Next Day, 1983, A Christmas Story, 1983, Turk 182, 1985, From the Hip, 1987, Loose Cannons, 1990, It Runs in the Family, 1994, I'll Remember April, 1999, Baby Geniuses, 1999, Now & Forever, 2002, The Karate Dog, 2004, SuperBabies: Baby Geniuses 2, 2002; dir. (films) Emperor's New Clothes, 1966, She-Man, 1967; (TV films) The American Clock, 1993, Fudge-A-Mania, 1995, Derby, 1995, Stolen Memories: Secrets from the Rose Gaden, 1996, The Ransom of Red Chief, 1998, Catch a Falling Star, 2000, Maniac Magee, 2003; (TV episodes) Amazing Stories, 1985; exec. prodr.: (films) Moonrunners, 1975, Black Christmas, 2006, (TV films) The Dukes of Hazzard: Hazzard in Hollywood, 2000. Mem. Dirs. Guild Am. Home: Beverly Hills, Calif. Died Apr. 4, 2007.

CLARK, BRUCE BUDGE, humanities educator; b. Georgetown, Idaho, Apr. 9, 1918; s. Marvin E. and Alice (Budge) C.; m. Ouida Raphiel, Nov. 7, 1946; children: Lorraine, Bradley, Robert, Jeffrey, Shawn, Sandra. BA, U. Utah, 1943, PhD, 1951; MA, Brigham Young U., 1948. Teaching fellow Brigham Young U., 1946-47, U. Utah, 1947-50; asst. prof. Brigham Young U., 1950-55, assoc. prof., 1955-58, prof., from 1959, dir. humanities program, 1958-60, chmn. dept. English, 1960-65; dean Coll. Humanities, 1965-81. Author: The Spectrum of Faith in Victorian Literature, 1966, The Challenge of Teaching, 1966, Romanticism through Modern Eyes, 1968, Oscar Wilde, A Study in Genius and Tragedy, 1970, Brigham Young on Education, 1970, Idealists in Revolt, 1975, History of the Brigham Young U. Coll. Humanities, 3 vols., 1984, Family History, 3 vols., 1998, Selected Essays and Other Writings, 1998; Editor: Richard Evans Quote Book, 1971; anthology (Out of the Best Books, vol. 1, 1964, vol. II, 1966, vol. III, 1967, vol. IV, 1968, vol. V, 1969, Great Short Stories for Discussion and Delight, 1979; Contbr. articles to profl. jours. Served with AUS, 1944-46. Recipient Karl G. Maeser Teaching Excellence award, 1972, David O. McKay Humanities award, 1983, Brigham Young U. Presdl. citation for disting. svc., 1994. Mem. MLA, Nat. Coun. Tchrs. English, Rocky Mountain Modern Lang. Assn., Coll. Conf. on Composition and Communications, Phi Kappa Phi. Mem. Lds Ch. Home: Orem, Utah. Died July 7, 2007.

CLARK, CHARLES EDWARD, arbitrator; b. Cleve., Feb. 27, 1921; s. Douglas James and Mae (Egermayer) C.; m. Nancy Jane Hilt, Mar. 11, 1942; children: Annette S. (Mrs. Paul Gernhardt), Charles Edward, John A., Nancy P. Gonzalez, Paul R., Stephen C., David G. Student, Berea Coll., 1939-40, King Coll., 1945; JD, U. Tex., 1948. Bar: Tex. 1948, Mass. 1956, U.S. Supreme Ct. 1959. Sole practice, San Antonio, 1948-55; writer legal articles, editor NACCA Law Jour., Boston, 1955-58; legal asst. to vice chmn., chief voting sect. U.S. Commn. on Civil Rights, Washington, 1958-61; spl. counsel Pres.'s Com. on Equal Employment Opportunity, Washington, 1961-65; sr. compliance officer Office Fed. Contract Compliance, Washington, 1965-66; regional dir. Equal Employment Opportunity Commn., Kansas City, Mo., 1966-79, arbitrator, from 1979. Prof. law, asst. dean St. Mary's U. Sch. Law, 1948-55; lectr. Rockhurst Coll., 1980-91, Longview Coll., 1988—. Contbr. articles to legal jours. Active Boy Scouts Am. Served with AUS, 1943-44. Mem. VFW, Assn. Conflict Resolution, State Bar Tex., Tex. Law Rev. Assn., Am. GI Forum (D.C. vice chmn. 1962-63), Soc. Fed. Labor Rels. Profls., Indsl. Rels. Rsch. Assn. (exec. bd. Kansas City 1976-91, pres. chpt. 1986), Profl. Men's Club K.C. (treas. 2002—), Phi Delta Phi (province pres. 1951-55). Died Nov. 24, 2006.

CLARK, CHRISTINE MAY, editor, author; b. Peoria, Ill., Apr. 25, 1957; d. Darrell Ronald and Alice Venita (Burkitt) French. BA, Judson Coll., 1978. Assoc. editor David C. Cook Pub., Elgin, Ill., 1978-80; editor Humpty Dumpty, 1980-94, Jack and Jill, 1983-86, Turtle mag., from 1990; editl. dir. Children's Better Health Inst., Indpls.; assoc. editor Highlights for Children, Honesdale, Pa., 1994-96, mng. editor, 1996—2001, v.p. editl., from 1997, editor, from 2001, also bd. dirs. Recipient Journalism award EDPRESS, 1986, 87, 88, 89, 90, 92, Outstanding Reporting award Soc. Profl. Journalists, 1990; Aurora Found. scholar, 1975. Mem. Am. Soc. Mag. Editors, Soc. Children's Book Writers and Illustrators, Ednl. Press Assn., Judson Coll. Alumni Assn. Reorganized Ch. of Jesus Christ of Latter-day Saints. Avocations: piano, travel. Died Apr. 18, 2007.

CLARK, FLOYD WATSON, JR., retired advertising executive; b. Saginaw, Mich., June 21, 1924; s. Floyd Watson and Grace (Pritchard) C.; m. Donamary Henderson Clark, Sept. 15, 1956; 1 child, Bruce Alan. BA, Mich. State U., 1949. Gen. mgr. WLEW-AM, Bad Axe, Mich., 1949-50; sales rep. WSGW-AM, Saginaw, 1950-53; writer, producer Davis-Daniels Advt., Detroit, 1953-54, W.B. Doner Co., Detroit, 1954-55; account exec. Batten, Barton, Durstine & Osborn, Detroit, 1955-67, J. Walter Thompson, Detroit, 1967-68, account dir. London, 1968-72, sr. v.p. Atlanta, 1972-93. Instr., Wayne State U., 1957-67. M/Sgt. U.S. Army, 1943-46, PTO. Mem. Adcraft Club Detroit (life). Republican. Home: Dunwoody, Ga. Died July 22, 2006.

CLARK, JOHN HOLLEY, III, retired lawyer; b. N.Y.C., May 31, 1918; s. John Holley, Jr. and Mary (Angus) C.; m. Eleanor Jackson, June 4, 1964; children: Benjamin Hayden, Christopher Angus. BA with high honors, Princeton U., 1939; JD, Columbia U., 1942; MA, NYU, 1965. Bar: N.Y. 1942, U.S. Dist. Ct. (so. dist.) N.Y. 1949, U.S. Ct. Appeals (2d cir.) 1952, U.S. Ct. Mil. Appeals 1986. Assoc. Cahill, Gordon, Reindel & Ohl, N.Y.C., 1946-54; atty. Antitrust div. U.S. Dept. Justice, N.Y.C., 1954-95. V.p. N.Y. Young Republican Club, 1953-54; mem. sch. com. Cathedral Ch. St. John the Divine, N.Y.C., 1979-81. Served with USAAF, 1942-46, PTO. Democrat. Episcopalian. Home: New York, NY. Died Apr. 17, 2007.

CLARK, JOHN WALTER, JR., water transportation executive; b. Mobile, Ala., Oct. 21, 1919; s. John Walter and Mae (Kappner) C.; m. Evelyn Ruth Hamilton, Aug. 29, 1941 (dec.); children: Ann Clark (dec.), Ruth Clark Day, Susan Clark Wells; m. Sandra L. Sharp, June 21, 1977; stepchildren: Kirsten J. Acomb, Heidi J. Qualey. Grad., U.S. Mcht. Marine Acad., 1940; postgrad., Tulane U., 1950-55. Served as officer, master mariner U.S. Mcht. Marine, 1940-46; mgr. Argentina, Brazil, West Africa and Europe Delta Steamship Lines, Inc., 1946-50, asst. to pres. New Orleans, 1950-53, v.p., 1953-59, pres., 1959-79, chmn. bd., 1979-80; pres. Clark Maritime Assocs., Inc., 1979—2007. Bd. dirs. Panama Canal Commn., 1978-82; past pres., mem. exec. com., bd. dirs. World Trade Ctr. of New Orleans; maritime arbitrator New Orleans Bd. of Trade; commr., pres. Port of New Orleans, 1978-82; exec. dir. Miss. State Port Authority, 1982-85; nat. vice chmn. Coun.of Ams., 1974-80. Rear adm. U.S. Maritime Svc. Decorated Order of Crown of Belgium; Order of Star of Africa Liberia; Order of So. Cross Brazil; Comendador de la Orden de Mayo Argentina; Orden de Isabel La Catolica Spain; named Maritime Man of Year Port of New Orleans, 1965. Mem. U.S. Mcht. Marine Acad. Alumni Assn. (Alumnus of Yr. 1975, named to Hall of Fame 1998) Plimsoll Club, So. Yacht Club, Pickwick Club, Pass Christian Yacht Club, Pass Christian Isles Golf Club. Methodist. Died Apr. 5, 2007.

CLARK, RICHARD PAUL, electronics company executive; b. Lewistown, Pa., Aug. 24, 1947; s. Harry E. and Alma E. (Koons) C.; m. Beth Millington, Oct. 23, 1971; children: Brian R., Steven M. BSEE, U. Pitts., 1969. Product engr. AMP Inc., Harrisburg, Pa., 1970-72, product engring. supr., 1972-76, product engring. mgr., 1976-79, mgr. devel. engring., 1979-82, mgr. electronic divsn., 1982-83, mgr. connector products, 1983-87, dir. ops., 1987-89, dir. engring., 1989, assoc. dir. corp. devel., 1989-95; pres., CEO M/A-COM a div. of AMP Inc., Lowell, Mass., from 1995. Bd. dirs. BroadBand Techs. Inc., Durham, N.C., ADFlex Solutions, Inc., Chandler, Ariz. Mem. Pitt vis. com. U. Pitts., 1993—; coach Highland Baseball, Camp Hill, Pa., 1981-91; booster Cedar Cliff Baseball, Camp Hill, 1989-94, Cedar Cliff Football, Camp Hill, 1991-95; session mem. Christ Presbyn. Ch., Camp Hill, 1984-87, 93-95. Recipient Disting. Alumnus award in Elec. Engring., U. Pitts., 1996. Home: Mechanicsburg, Pa. Died June 9, 2006.

CLARK, ROMANE LEWIS, philosopher, educator; b. Waverly, Iowa, Dec. 3, 1925; s. Fred G. and Mildred L. (Cole) C.; m. Marilyn Jean Cash, Aug. 8, 1948; children— Ronald, Carolee, Cathleen, John. AB, State U. Iowa, 1949, PhD, 1952. Instr. State U. Iowa, 1953; successively asst. prof., asso. prof., prof. Duke U., 1953-70; prof. philosophy Ind. U., Bloomington, from 1970. Contbr. articles to acad. philos. jours. and anthologies. Served with USAAF, 1944-45. Sr. fellow Nat. Endowment for Humanities, 1974; Fulbright sr. scholar, 1981, NEH fellowship for univ. tchrs., 1989. Mem. Am. Philos. Assn., AAUP. Home: Sun City, Ariz. Died Aug. 17, 2007.

CLARK, SAMUEL KELLY, engineering educator, researcher; b. Ypsilanti, Mich., Nov. 3, 1924; s. Floyd A. and Esther L. (Kelly) C.; m. Mary Jean Battelle, Jan. 4, 1952; children— Elizabeth, Samuel, Andrew, Frederic, David. B.S. in Aero. Engring., U. Mich., 1946, Ph.D., 1951. Registered profl. engr., Ohio. Engr., Douglas Aircraft, Santa Monica, Calif., 1946-47, Borg-Warner Corp., Detroit, 1948-51, Ford Motor Co., Detroit, 1951-52; asst. prof. Case Inst. Tech., Cleve., 1952-55; from asst. prof. to prof. U. Mich., Ann Arbor, 1955—; cons. in field. Author: Dynamics of Continous Elements, 1967; editor: Mechanics of Pneumatic Tires, 1977. Served with USN, 1943-46. Fellow Soc. Automotive Engrs.; mem. ASME, Soc. Exptl. Mechanics. Episcopalian. Avocations: travel; squash; sailing. Home: Ann Arbor, Mich. Died Oct. 26, 2006.

CLARKE, FRANKLYN ROSELLE, psychiatrist, hospital administrator; b. Bridgeton, NJ, June 27, 1926; s. George Dalby and Margaret Marshall (Gundrum) C.; m. Marilyn Leone Moss, June 29, 1947; children: Charmaine, Aletha, Jeannine. BS in Clin. Psychology, Pa. State U., 1949, MS, 1950; MD, Jefferson Med. Coll., 1954; cert. in psychiat. adminstrn., U. Wis., 1969. Diplomate Am. Bd. Psychiatry and Neurology. Intern Reading (Pa.) Hosp., 1954-55; resident in psychiatry Phila. State Hosp., 1955-56, staff psychiatrist, 1960-62, clin. dir. intensive care, 1962-64, dir. profl. tng., 1964-66, asst. supt., 1966-70, supt., 1970-80; resident in psychiatry Menninger Clinic, Topeka, 1958-60. Acting supt. Fairview State Hosp., Waymart, Pa., 1975-76; cons. Riverview Home for Aged; dir. Nat. Remotivation Technique Orgn.; mem. Pa. Comprehensive Mental Health Planning Com.; asst. prof. clin. psychiatry Thomas Jefferson U.; assoc. prof. Hahnemann Med. Coll. and Hosp. Bd. dirs. Luth. Children's Bur., 1966-72, Bucks County Psychiat. Ctr., 1970-72, Penndel Psychiat. Ctr., 1971—. Lt. U.S. Maritime Svc., 1944-47; lt. USN 1956-58. Fellow Am. Psychiat. Assn., Pa. Psychiat. Soc.; mem. AMA, Pa. Med. Soc., Pa. Med. Supts. Assn. (pres.), Psi Chi. Republican. Lutheran. Home: Langhorne, Pa. Died Mar. 2, 2006.

CLARKE, GEORGE WHITAKER, state legislator, lawyer; b. Perry, Iowa, June 22, 1906; s. Fred Greene and Mabel May (Moss) Clarke; m. Helen Vinal, July 5, 1930; children: Louise, George Whitaker Jr., Keith; m. Mary Birkenmeyer, May 23, 1976; m. Ruth Roberts Jordon, Jan. 5, 1983. Bar: Wash. 27. With Clarke, Bovingdon & Cole, Seattle, 1971—85; cons. Seattle, from 1985; gen. mgr. Wash. Surveying and Rating Bur., Seattle, 1957—71; mem. Wash. Ho. Reps., 1967—71, Wash. Senate, Seattle, 1971—85. Mem. Mercer Island Sch. Bd., 1947—67. Lt. USNR, 1944—45. Mem.: Am. Bar Assn., Seattle (Wash.) C. of C. Home: Mercer Island, Wash. Died June 25, 2006.

CLARKE, LAMBUTH MCGEEHEE, retired academic administrator; b. Salisbury, Md., Oct. 4, 1923; s. Hawes Palmore and Jessie Lee (Ham) C.; m. Alice Royall Acree, July 16, 1955; children: Leighton Krips, Palmore, Jessica, Virginia Hitch. BA, Randolph-Macon Coll., 1944, LLD (hon.), 1969; MA, Johns Hopkins U., 1948; postgrad., U. Birmingham, 1948, Harvard U., 1982; LHD (hon.), Va. Wesleyen Coll., 2002. English instr. Randolph-Macon Coll., Ashland, Va., 1948-51, asst. to pres., 1951-58, v.p. devel., 1958-66; pres. Va. Wesleyan Coll., Norfolk, 1966-92, pres. emeritus, from 1992, also trustee; acting pres. Randolph-Macon Womans' Coll., 1993-94. Bd. dirs. Va. Symphony, Norfolk, 1970-88, trustee, 1990—; bd. dirs. Leigh Meml. Hosp., later Med. Ctr. Hosps., 1970-82, Norfolk Forum, 1970-80, World Affairs Coun., 1972-76, YMCA, Norfolk, 1972-78, Sta. WHRO-TV, 1972-76, Greater Norfolk Corp., 1978-92, Com. of 101-Future of Hampton Rds., Norfolk, 1983-92, Order of Cape Henry 1607, Norfolk, Va. Eye Found., Norfolk, 1973-92, Va. Coun. Chs., 1978-82; trustee Va. Found. Ind. Colls., Richmond, 1982-92, vice-chmn., 1990-92, assoc., 1992-97; trustee Randolph-Macon Womans Coll., 1992-97, hon. trustee, 1997—; univ. senate United Meth. Ch., Nashville, 1988-92, bd. dirs., gen. bd. higher edn., 1980-88, del. jurisdictional conf., 1976-96, gen. conf., 1980-92; adv. bd. DePaul Med. Ctr., Norfolk, 1988-96; bd. dirs. Lee's Friends, 1993-99, adv. bd., 1999—; bd. dirs. Tidewater Scholarship Found., 1994-2000, Westminster-Canterbury of Hampton Rds., 1995-2003, Norfolk Sr. Ctr., Portsmouth Mus. Found., Inc., 1997-2000, Norfolk Bot. Gardens Found.; chmn. adminstrv. bd. Larchmont United Meth. Ch., 1993. Lt. (j.g.) USNR, 1943-46. Recipient Brotherhood citation NCCJ, 1991, John Wesley Disting. Educator award, 1991, Francis Asbury Educator award, 1995, Jerry G. Bray Dist. Svc. medal Va. Wesleyan Coll., 1997, Lambuth M. Clarke Acad. Ctr. of Va. Wesleyan Coll., 1999. Mem. Soc. Alumni Randolph-Macon Coll. (bd. dirs. 1993-99), Soc. of the Cin., Rotary Club Norfolk, Phi Beta Kappa, Omicron Delta Kappa, Phi Kappa Phi, Lambda Chi Alpha. Methodist. Avocations: reading, music, art, stamp collecting/philately, architecture. Home: Norfolk, Va. Died Sept. 2006.

CLARKE, PHILIP REAM, JR., retired investment banker; b. Chgo., Feb. 10, 1914; s. Philip Ream and Louise (Hildebr) C.; m. Valerie Mead, Oct. 20, 1939 (dec. Sept. 1965); children: Barbara Foster, Philip Ream III; m. Jan Finan, Dec. 2, 1967; m. Barbara Schroeder, Apr. 15, 1977. AB, U. Chgo., 1937. With Glore, Forgan & Co., Chgo., 1937-42, City Nat. Bank & Trust Co., Chgo., 1946-57, asst. v.p., 1947-51, v.p., 1951-57; mgr. indsl. dept. Lehman Bros., 1957-62, dir. new bus., 1962-65; v.p., treas., dir. Bronswood Cemetery, Inc., 1966—89, chmn., from 1990; founder Chgo. Corp., 1944, sr. v.p., 1946—66, vice-chair, 1967, vice-chmn. emeritus, 1986-96; dir. Hollymatic Corp., 1965—86, pres., CEO, 1976—86, chmn., CEO, 1979-81. Mem. Midwest Stock Exchange, 1954-56; pres., treas., dir. Bronswood Cemetery, Inc., 1966—, chmn., 1990—; vice-chmn. emeritus ABN Amro Inc., 1998-2001. Bd. dirs., exec. com. Cook County Sch. of Nursing, 1958-68, v.p., 1965-68; treas., dir. Chgo. Com. on Alcoholism, 1952-56, v.p., 1957, exec. v.p., 1958, pres., 1959, chmn., 1960-61; charter mem. bd. assocs., Chgo. Theol. Sem., 1980-84; vice chmn. Chgo. Non Partisan Com. to Bring Rep. Nat. Conv. to Chgo.; Mem. Rep. Nat. Conv., 1959-60; treas. Citizens Com. to Bring Rep. and Dem. convs. to Chgo., 1952, 56; bd. govs. Hinsdale Community House, 1968-70, vice chmn., 1969, chmn., 1970, life trustee 1993—; trustee, chmn. fin. com., 1951-55, Village of Clarendon Hills, Ill., 1956-60, pres., 1961-65; bd. govs. United Rep. Fund of Ill., 1948-74, treas., 1948-62, v.p., exec. com., 1955-69; bd. dirs. Ill. council Trout Unltd., 1972-75; trustee U. Chgo. Alumni Fund, 1958-61, citizens bd., 1955-80; mem. exec. com. Citizens of Greater Chgo., 1946-61. Lt. comdr. USNR, 1942-46. Mem. Chgo. Assn. Commerce and Industry (dir., treas. 1952-53), Chgo. Zool. Soc. (governing mem. 1956-69, 79—), Nat. Council on Alcoholism (v.p. 1959-62), Alpha Delta Phi. Clubs: Chicago, Bond, Hinsdale Golf, Coleman Lake (dir. 1972-84, v.p. 1982), Plaza. Republican. Episcopalian. Home: Burr Ridge, Ill. Died Mar. 19, 2007.

CLARY, WARREN THOMAS TIMMONS, manufacturing company executive; b. Midland, Tex., Jan. 23, 1952; s. Robert Artemus and Dorothy Jean (Timmons) C. B.A. with honors, N. Tex. State U., 1975. Consumer communications asst. Sony Corp., Dallas, 1977-79; radio communications rep. Motorola, Dallas, 1979-82, sales communications mgr., 1982—; pres. elect Bus. Exchange, Dallas. Democrat. Roman Catholic. Club: Fort Worth Boat. Died Mar. 4, 2007.

CLAUSEN, WENDELL VERNON, retired classics educator; b. Coquille, Oreg., Apr. 2, 1923; s. George R. and Gertrude (Johnson) C.; m. Corinna Slice, Aug. 20, 1947; children: John, Raymond, Thomas; m. Margaret W. Woodman, June 19, 1970. AB, U. Wash., 1945; PhD, U. Chgo., 1948; A.M. (hon.), Harvard U., 1959. Mem. faculty Amherst Coll., 1948-59, assoc. prof. classics, 1955-59; prof. Greek and Latin Harvard U., 1959-82, Victor S. Thomas prof. Greek and Latin, 1982-88, Pope prof. Latin lang. and lit., 1988-93, prof. comparative lit., 1984-93, prof. emeritus, 1993—2007, chmn. dept. classics, 1966-71; ret., 1993. Vis. prof. Univ. Coll., London, 1971; Sather prof. U. Calif., Berkeley, 1982; vis. prof. I Tatti, Florence, Italy, 1989. Author: Virgil's Aeneid and the Tradition of Hellenistic Poetry, 1987, A Commentary on Virgil's Eclogues, 1994, Virgil's Aeneid: Decorum Allusion and Ideology, 2002, articles in classical philology; editor: Persius, 1956, Persius and Juvenal, 1959, rev. edit., 1992, Appendix Vergiliana, 1966, Harvard Studies in Classical Philology, 1990—92, Commentum Cornuti in Persium, 2004; editor, contbr. The Cambridge History of Latin Literature, 1982, Premio Internazionale Virgilio, 1994, assoc. editor Am. Jour. Philology, 1976—81, Style and Tradition: Studies in Honor of Wendell Clausen, 1998. William Rainey Harper scholar U. Chgo., 1946-48; fellow Am. Acad. in Rome, 1952-53, Am. Council Learned Socs., 1962-63, fellow commoner Peterhouse, Cambridge. Fellow Am. Acad. Arts and Scis.; mem. Am. Philol. Assn., Cambridge Philol. Soc., Signet Soc., Phi Beta Kappa. Home: Cambridge, Mass. Died Oct. 12, 2006.

CLAVAN, WALTER, chemistry consultant; b. Phila., Apr. 6, 1921; s. Harry E. and Rae (Holzsweig) C.; m. Sylvia Goldstein, Apr. 26, 1945; children— Barbara, Benjamin. B.S. in Chemistry, U. Pa., 1942, M.S. in Chemistry, 1947, Ph.D. in Analytical Chemistry, 1949. Group leader analytical chemistry dept. Pennwalt Corp., King of Prussia, Pa., 1956-70, dir., 1970-75, mgr., 1975-83, corp. analytical scientist, 1984—. Served with USN, 1945-46, PTO. Mem. Am. Chem. Soc., ASTM, AAAS, Geochem. Soc., Sigma Xi. Home: Wynnewood, Pa. Died Dec. 15, 2006.

CLAYTON, BILLY WAYNE, political consultant, former state legislator; b. Olney, Tex., Sept. 11, 1928; s. William and Myrtle C.; m. Delma Jean Dennis; children: Brenda Jean Clayton Smith, Thomas Wayne. BS, Tex. A&M U., 1950; LLD (hon.), Tex. Wesleyan U., 1979, Tex. Tech U., 1982; MBA, U. Tex., 1992. Mem. Tex. Ho. Reps., 1962-83, speaker, 1975-83; former pres. Capital Cons., Austin, Tex., Distbrs. of Tex. Past chmn. So. Legis. Conf., Council of State Govts.; past pres. Interstate Conf. on Water Problems; past bd. dirs. Nat. Conf. State Legislators; mem. exec. com. So. Environ. Resources Conf., 1973-74; chmn. intergovtl. rels. com. Nat. Legis. Conf., 1973; Tex. mem. Nat. Water Congress; chmn. So. States Speakers Conf., 1975-76. Mem. adv. bd. Young Ams. for Freedom; trustee High Plains Rsch. Found., Halfway, Tex.; former deacon 1st Bapt. Ch., Springlake. Named Outstanding Farmer in Lamb County Lamb County Farm Bur., 1967, Hon. Water Well Digger Tex. Water Well Assn., 1968; recipient Disting. Service to People of Tex. award Progressive Farmer Mag., 1967, Outstanding Service to Farmers in Lamb County award Earth C. of C., 1973, Disting. Service award Dem. Party Tex., 1968, commendation Tex. Water Rights Commn., 1970, Outstanding Service award in water conservation Ft. Worth Press Club, 1972, 1st award West Tex. Water Inst., 1971, Disting. Alumnus award Tex. A&M U., 1979. Mem. West Tex. C. of C. (exec. com., water resources com.), West Tex. Water Inst. (exec. bd.), Tex. A&M Former Students Assn. (pres. 1988), bd. regents Texas A&M U., Lions (past pres. Springlake club), Masons (33 deg.). Lodges: Mason. Home: Springlake, Tex. Died Jan. 6, 2007.

CLAYTON, GENE, advertising executive; b. St. Louis, Oct. 2, 1923; s. Ida (Routman) Clayton; m. Joyce Madeline Kloske, June 16, 1956; children: Craig, Brian. BA, Mich. State U., 1946. News dir. Sta. WTMV-AM, St. Louis, 1946—52; account exec. Frank Block Assocs., St. Louis, 1952—54, H. Bloch Advt. Co., St. Louis, 1954—57, Roman Advt. Co., 1957—61; advt. mgr. McCabe Powers Body Co., St. Louis, 1961—62; pres. Norge Co., St. Louis, Gene Clayton Advt. Co., St. Louis, from 1963. Mem. St. Louis coun. Boy Scouts Am., from 1970. Mem.: Mo. Pilots Assn., St. Louis Copywriters Club. Died Feb. 23, 2006.

CLAYTON, JOE TODD, agricultural and food engineering educator; b. Etowah, Tenn., Oct. 2, 1924; s. Joe Madison and Onye (Rymer) C.; m. Helen Deane Harris, Aug. 30, 1946; children— Jeffrey Todd, Jill Elaine, Joel Harris. BS in Agrl. Engring, U. Tenn., 1949, postgrad., 1949-50; MS, U. Ill. at Urbana, 1951; PhD (NSF sci. faculty fellow), Cornell U., 1962. Registered profl. engr., Ill., Mass. Instr. U. Ill. at Urbana, 1951-54, asst. prof., 1955-57, U. Conn., 1954-55; assoc. prof. U. Mass. at Amherst, 1957-61, prof. agrl. engring., 1961-66, prof., head dept. food engring., 1966-1985; prof., food engring. U Mass. at Amherst, from 1985. Vis. prof. bioengring., NATO sr. fellow sci. U. Reading, Eng., 1971—; chmn. sci. devel. Research & Devel. Assos., 1981—; vis. scientist Food Engring. Lab., U.S. Army Natick Research & Devel. Ctr., 1983-84; internat. lectr. Brit. Soc. of Chem. Industry, 1978. Editor: Jour. Food Engring. 1981-84; contbr. numerous articles to nat. and internat. profl. jours. Served with AUS, 1943-46. Japan Soc. for Promotion of Sci. fellow U. Tokyo, 1981 Fellow Am. Soc. Agrl. Engrs. AAAS,; mem Inst. Food Technologists (profl. mem.), Internat. Soc. Biometeorology, Panam. Fedn. Engring Socs. (U.S. nat. com. 1984—), N.Y. Acad. Scis., Sigma Xi, Gamma Sigma Delta, Phi Tau Sigma. Home: Sunderland, Mass. Died May 18, 2007.

CLEARY, JAMES W., retired academic administrator; b. Milw., Apr. 16, 1927; m. Janet Cleary, 1950 (dec. 2002); children: Colleen, Patricia (dec. 2000) PhB, Marquette U., 1950, MA, 1951; PhD, U. Wis., 1956. Instr., dir. forensics high sch., Wis., 1949-51; instr. speech, head coach debate Marquette U., 1951-53; from instr. to prof. speech U. Wis., 1956-63, vice chancellor acad. affairs, 1966-69; pres. Calif. State U., Northridge, 1969—92. Mem. Pres.'s Commn. NCAA Author: Robert's Rules of Order Newly Revised, 1970, 80; editor: John Bulwer's Chirologia... Chironomia, 1644, 1974; co-editor: Bibliography of Rhetoric and Public Address, 1964. Served to 2d lt. AUS, 1945-47. Recipient Disting. Alumni award U. Wis., 1990; named one of 100 Most Effective Coll. Pres. in U.S., Exxon Edn. Found., 1986; U. Wis. fellow, 1954-55. Mem. Speech Assn. Am., Am. Assn. State Colls. and Univs. (chmn. 1983), NCAA (pres.' commn., chmn. divsn. II com.). Died Apr. 28, 2007.

CLEARY, ROBERT MADDEN, electric utility company executive; b. Buffalo, July 30, 1926; s. Robert Madden and Leah (Barry) C.; m. Patricia Ann Smalley, May 7, 1955; children— Robert, Susan, Michael, William, John. B.A., Colgate U., 1950; postgrad. in exec. tng. Harvard U., 1953; postgrad. in bus. adminstrn. U. Buffalo, 1956. Adminstrv. asst. Niagara Mohawk Power Corp., Buffalo, 1950-57, comml. rep., Syracuse, N.Y., 1957-60, dist. mgr., Baldwinsville, N.Y., 1960-65, area mgr., Syracuse, 1965-70, v.p., gen. mgr., Buffalo, 1970-82, v.p. regional ops., 1982—; dir. Norstar Bank NA, Buffalo. Bd. dirs. Zool. Soc. Buffalo, ARC, Buffalo; trustee Buffalo Gen. Hosp., regent Canisius Coll., Buffalo; exec. bd. Boy Scouts Am., Buffalo; bd. govs. NCCJ, Buffalo. Mem. Buffalo C. of C. (bd. dirs.). Republican. Roman Catholic. Clubs: Buffalo (bd. dirs. 1978, 84, pres. 1985); Country of Buffalo (bd. dirs. Williamsville). Home: Buffalo, NY. Died Jan. 21, 2006.

CLEM, L(ESTER) WILLIAM, microbiologist, educator; b. Frederick, Md., June 23, 1934; s. Lester Roosevelt and Madeline Regina (Mort) C.; m. Dolores Irene Miller, Jan 20, 1957; children: Kathleen, Constance, Cynthia, Karen, Mathew. BS, West Md. Coll., 1956; MS, U. Del., 1960; PhD, U. Miami, 1963. Instr. microbiology U. Miami, Fla., 1963-66; asst. prof. microbiology and med. microbiology Coll. Medicine, U. Fla., Gainesville, 1966-68, assoc. prof., 1968-71, prof., 1971-79; prof. chmn. dept. microbiology U. Miss. Med. Ctr., Jackson, 1979-88, F.A.P. Barnard Disting. prof., from 1988. Cons. NSF, WHO, NIH. Contbr. articles to sci. publs. Served to 1st lt. USAR, 1956-64. Rsch. grantee NSF, 1970-89, NIH, 1978—. Mem. Am Assn. Immunologists, Internat. Soc. Developmental and Comparative Immunology (pres. 1991—), Am. Soc. Zoologists (chmn. comparative immunology div. 1979-81), Sigma Xi. Avocation: shark fishing. Home: Brandon, Miss. Died Nov. 9, 2006.

CLENDANIEL, ANNE LUCILLE EVANS, communications consultant; b. Harrington, Del., Aug. 30, 1918; d. John Franklin and Bertha (Collison) Evans; student U. Del., 1936-37, spl. courses in writing, leadership and communications; m. Harry Edgar Clendaniel, Jr., Sept. 6, 1941 (dec. 1985); children: Mary Catherine, John Evans. Exec. sec. Beacom Bus. Coll., 1939 legal sec., tax dept. duPont Co., 1939-45, Maguire, Voorhees & Wells, Orlando, Fla., 1943-45; vol., study group leader Great Books, 1945-61; legal sec. Young, Conaway, Stargatt, 1962-63 dir. communications Episcopal Diocese of Del., 1963-73; exec dir. Del. chpt. Arthritis Found., Wilmington, 1974-84; bd. dirs Del. Sr. Cons., 1984-86. Mem. Del. Press Women, Profl. Staff Assn. Arthritis Found, U. Del. Div. Continuing Edn. Acad. of Lifelong Learning Faculty and Council. Republican. Club Wilmington Quota (pres. 1977-78), Contbr. poetry and verse, to newspapers, mags., anthologies, 1939-55; founder, writer Communion Diocesan paper, 1967-73; author The Arthritis Report 1974-84; editor DSC newsletter, Tech. and Mgmt. Svcs. newsletter Home: Wilmington, Del. Died Mar. 19, 2007.

CLEVELAND, PEGGY ROSE RICHEY, cytotechnologist; b. Cannelton, Ind., Dec. 9, 1929; d. "Pat" Clarence Francis and Alice Marie (Hall) Richey; m. Peter Leslie Cleveland, Nov. 25 1948 (dec. 1973); children: Pamela Cleveland Litch, Paul Cleveland Bertloff, Peter L. Cert., U. Louisville, 1956, B i. Health Sci., 1984. Cytotechnologist cancer survey project NIH Louisville, 1956-59; chief cytotechnologist Parker Cytolog Lab., Inc., Louisville, 1959-75; mgr. cytology dept. Am Biomed. Corp., 1976-78, Nat. Health Labs., Inc., Louisville 1978-89; with various hosps. and labs., from 1990. Leade cytotechnologist del. to China, 1986; clin. instr. cytology Sch Allied Health, U. Louisville, 1989; ptnr. Sham Star Stabl thoroughbred horse breeding and racing. Mem. Am. Soc. Clin Pathologist (cert. cytotechnologist), Internat. Acad. Cytolog (cert. cytotechnologist), Am. Soc. Cytology (del.-person t person cytology delegation, amb. USSR 1990), Kentuckian Cytology Soc., Cytology Soc. Ind., Horseman's Benevolent an Protective Assn. Democrat. Roman Catholic. Home: Lanesville Ind. Died Jan. 25, 2007.

CLEWETT, RICHARD MONROE, marketing educator; b San Diego, Feb. 1, 1911; s. George E. and Marie E. (Rees) C m. Mary Jane Roby, Dec. 24, 1941; children: Richard Monro Jr., Barbara Jane. BA, U. Nev., 1934; MA, U. Pa., 1942, PhI 1948. With Universal Credit Co., 1934-36, Gen. Motors Accep tance Corp., 1936-37; asst. econs. U. Calif., 1937-39; inst mktg. U. Pa., 1939-42, 45-48; asst. prof. sch. bus. Northweste U., 1948-51, asso. prof., 1951-54, prof., 1954-79, prof. emeritu lectr., 1979-94, chmn. dept. mktg., 1953-58, 65-77, dir. of exe programs in mktg., 1985-95; faculty Internat. Inst. Mgm Lucerne. Participant Pres.'s Conf. on Tech. and Distbn. R search for Small Bus., 1957; cons. Orgn. European Eco Cooperation, 1958-59 Author: Marketing Channels for Man factured Products, 1953; co-author: Cases in Marketing Str egy, 1958, rev. edit., 1964, Vertical Marketing Systems, 197 contbr. to Principles of Marketing (Philip Kotler), 1980, re edits., 1983, 86, Essentials of Marketing (Philip Kotler), 198 rev. edit., 1987; co-editor: Contemporary American Marketin 1957, rev. edit., 1963; mem. editorial staff Jour. Mktg., 1950-5 Bd. dirs. Lake Forest Sch. Mgmt., 1980-83, Presbyn. Hom Evanston, Ill., 1989—. Served with USNR, 1942-45. Mer

AAAS, Am. Mktg. Assn., Am. Inst. Baking (dir.; ednl. adv. com. 1963-68), Phi Kappa Phi, Delta Sigma Pi, Beta Gamma Sigma. Home: Evanston, Ill. Died Dec. 1, 2006.

CLIFTON, ARTHUR CALVIN, insurance company executive; b. Fair Oaks, Ind., June 1, 1924; s. Arthur Francis and Myrtle Ellen (Hall) Clifton; m. Vivian Juanita Himes, Mar. 11, 1950; children: Richard Randall, Kevin Lee. BS in Bus., Ind. U., 1947. Group rep., group mgr. Washington Nat. Ins. Co., various locations, 1947—61, regional/nat. dir. Evanston, Ill., 1961—76, v.p., 1976—79, sr. v.p. exec. com., dir., 1979—83, exec. v.p., dir., mem. exec. com., from 1983; chmn. bd. dirs., mem. exec. com. Washington Nat. Life, NYC, from 1980. Trustee United Meth. Home and Svc., Chgo., 1976—82, treas., 1979—82, Trinity Ch. N. Shore, Wilmette, Ill. With US Army, 1943—46. Fellow: LOMA Life Mgmt. Inst.; mem.: CLU Assn., Am. Coun. Life Ins. (mem. group ins. com. from 1983), Health Ins. Assn. Am. (mem. group ins. com. Washington 1976—80, chmn. group forum 1979—80, mem. edn. com. from 1980), Masons, Delta Sigma Pi. Republican. Home: Wilmette, Ill. Died Apr. 24, 2006.

CLIFTON, GENE R., coal company executive; b. Owenton, Ky., Feb. 7, 1931; s. Reat Marvin and Mary Lee (Juett) C.; m. Juanita V. Clifton, June 16, 1951 (div. 1965); children— Barry Wayne, Racgenia Gail; m. Connie F. Clifton, Nov. 22, 1966. Ed., Bethany High Sch., Owenton, Ky. Sr. systems analyst Ky. Utilities, Lexington, 1957-66; dir. sales Blue Field Supply, W.Va., 1966-69, Island Creek Coal Co., Lexington, 1969-79, exec. v.p. adminstrn., 1981-82, pres., from 1982; dir. sales Oxy, Los Angeles, 1979-81. Mem. Ky. Export Assn. Avocations: Golf; fishing; farming. Home: Versailles, Ky. Died Sept. 19, 2006.

CLINE, WILBUR JAMES, educational administrator; b. Centerville, Iowa, May 28, 1918; s. Thomas C. and Nadie (Maring) C.; B.S., Iowa Wesleyan Coll., 1940; M.S. in Edn., Drake U., 1954; Specialists Degree, U. Colo., 1959; m. Olive Lucille Jones, Oct. 25, 1942; 1 dau., Marjorie Anne Cline Holland. Tchr. Centerville (Iowa) Pub. Schs., 1939-41, Ottumwa (Iowa) Pub. Schs., 1941-42, Mason City (Iowa) Pub. Schs., 1942-43; tng. officer VA, Des Moines, 1946-53; guidance counselor Davenport High Sch., Iowa, 1954-60; dir. guidance services Davenport (Iowa) pub. schs., 1960-63; dir. data processing services Scott County (Iowa) schs., 1963-66; dir. Area 9 Schs. Info. Center, Bettendorf, Iowa, 1966-70; v.p. Kempton-Cline Data Systems, Davenport, Iowa, 1970-74; asst. to dir. Bi-State Met. Computer Commn., 1974-75; guidance counselor Pleasant Valley Community Schs., Pleasant Valley, Iowa, 1975-80; vocat. cons. to Social Security Adminstrn., 1963-64. Mem. citizens adv. com. Scott County Mental Health Center, 1977, 1978-79; elder Newcomb Presbyn. Ch., Davenport, 1957-60. Served with USAAF, 1942-46; CBI, with USAF, 1950-52; lt. col. Res. ret. Mem. Iowa Edn. Assn. (life), Ret. Officers Assn., Res. Officers Assn., Am. Assn. Ret. Persons, Beta Beta Beta. Clubs: Masons (32 deg.), Moose, Shriners. Died Mar. 1, 2007.

CLINKSCALES, WILLIAM ABNER, JR., government administrator; b. Anderson, SC, Jan. 5, 1928; s. William Abner and Nancy (Jackson) C.; m. Elizabeth Fuller, Aug. 10, 1947; children: Pamela, Susan, Debra. Officer counter intelligence U.S. Army, 1951; ret., 1971; security specialist GSA, Washington, 1971-72, criminal investigator, 1972-75, dir. investigations, 1975-78, asst. insp. gen. for investigations, 1978-80, dep. dir. info. security oversite office, 1981-83, assoc. adminstr. policy and mgmt. sys., 1983-87; dir. mgmt. improvement U.S. Dept. Interior, Washington, 1987-88, dir. acquisition, constrn. and property mgmt., 1988-94, ret., 1994. Decorated Meritorious Svc. medal; recipient Cert. of Recognition, Worker's Ethics, 1983, Presdl. Rank award, 1984, Disting. Svc. award GSA, 1984, Spl. Achievement award D.C. Coun. Engring. and Archtl. Soc., 1984, citation Japanese Nat. Police, citation Republic of Korea-CIA, Grand Cross of Color award Rainbow Girls, Japanese and Korean Linguist Black Belt, Aikido. Mem. Masons, Shriners. Episcopalian. Avocations: gardening, photography. Died Sept. 11, 2006.

CLINTON, ROBERT L., association adminstrator; b. Putnam, Tex., Nov. 27, 1923; s. Robert L. and Eva Frances (Park) C.; m. Wanda Merle Lowry, Oct. 14, 1944; children— Robert Lowry, David Reagan, Ronald Dale. B.M., North Tex. State U., 1948, Mus.M., 1950; Ed.D., Tex. Tech U., 1962. Dir. music Cisco Jr. Coll., 1949-53; supr. music Snyder (Tex.) Public Schs., 1953-60; grad. asst. Tex. Tech U., 1960; prin. Snyder Ind. Sch. Dist., 1961-63, supt., 1964-67; asst. commr. jr. coll. coordinating bd. Tex. Coll. and Univ. System, 1967-70; pres. Western Tex. Coll., 1970-81; dir. Tex. Public Community/Jr. Coll. Assn., Austin, 1981-86; interim pres. Amarillo Coll., 1986-87, pres., from 1987. Served with USAAF, 1943-46. Mem. Phi Mu Alpha, Alpha Chi, Phi Delta Kappa. Methodist. Home: Austin, Tex. Died Mar. 1, 2007.

CLOUD, BRUCE BENJAMIN, SR., retired construction executive; b. Thomas, Okla., Feb. 15, 1920; s. Dudley R. and Lillian (Sanders) Cloud; m. Virginia Dugan, June 5, 1944 (dec.); children: Sheila Marie Cloud Kiselis, Karen Susan, Bruce Benjamin, Deborah Ann Cloud McKenzie, Virginia Ann Cloud Treadwell. BCE, Tex. A&M U., 1940. Registered profl. engr., Tex. With H.B. Zachry Co., San Antonio, 1940-42, 55-99, exec. v.p., 1963-87, pres., 1987-93, vice chmn., 1993-94, sr. corp. advisor, 1995-99, adv. dir., 1999—2004; ptnr., bd. dirs. Dudley R. Cloud & Son, Constrn., San Antonio, 1946-55; owner Cloud Enterprises, San Antonio; ret. Mem. adv. bd. dirs. Capitol Cement Co./Aggregate Co., 1999—2004. Mem. adv. coun. Boysville Inc., 1978—79; bd. dirs. Tex. State Tech. Coll. Found., 1983—97, from 1998, hon. life bd. dirs. Lt. col. C.E. US Army, 1942—46, ETO. Recipient Pro Deo Et Juventute award, Nat. Coun. Cath. Youth, Soyr Svc. award, 2003. Mem.: NSPE, Cons. Contractors Coun. Am. (chmn. 1989), Tex. Engring. Ext. Svc. (adv. bd. 1995—97), Tex. Transp. Inst. (adv. bd. 1993—97), Am. Mgmt. Assn., Tex. Good Rds.-Transp. Assn. (bd. dirs. 1974—79, mem. exec. com. 1975—81, 1985—89), Tex. Soc. Profl. Engrs., Nat. Assn. Gen. Contractors (mem. bur. reclamation com. 1968—97, mem. environ. com. 1971—76, mem. enrgy and materials 1976—86, bd. dirs. 1976—88, life dir., mem. exec. com. 1978—79, mem. equipment mgmt. com. 1978—97, chmn. heavy divsn. 1979, mem. ethics rules legis. com. 1979, mem. fin. com. 1979, mem. water and power resource com. 1980—81, mem. transp. policy com. 1980—95, mem. engring. documentation rev. com. 1985, mem. corps engrs. com. 1988—97, mem. quality constrn. com. 1993—96, Nat. AGC Oustanding Com. chmn. 1997), Tex. Hotmix Paving Assn. (bd. dirs. 1972), Nat. Asphalt Paving Assn., Am. Concrete Paving Assn. (v.p. 1970—74, bd. dirs., 1st v.p. 1975, pres. 1976), Am. Inst. Mgmt., San Antonio Livestock Assn. (life), Tex. Assn. Gen. Contractors (life; dir. hwy. and heavy br. 1947—48, 1972—76, pres. 1974, chmn. corps engrs. joint com. 1989—90), San Antonio C. of C. (chmn. better rds. task force 1978—79, 1985—93, bd. dirs. 1993—94), Nocturnal Adoration Soc., Holy Name Soc. (v.p. 1962—63), KC (3d degree). Died Mar. 12, 2007.

CLOUGH, RALPH NELSON, foreign affairs researcher; b. Seattle, Nov. 17, 1916; s. Ray William and Mildred (Nelson) C.; m. Mary Lou Sander, Nov. 1, 1941 (dec. Mar. 1950); m. Awana Alene Stiles, Sept. 5, 1952; children: Frederick William, Marshall Sander, Laurie, Drusilla. Student, Lingnan U., 1936-37; AB, U. Wash., 1939; MA, Fletcher Sch. Law and Diplomacy, 1940. Vice consul, Toronto, Ont., Can., 1941-42; 3d sec. embassy, vice consul Tegucigalpa, Honduras, 1942-45; vice consul, successively Kunming, Chungking, Peiping, China, 1945-47; 3d sec. embassy, vice consul Nanking, China, 1947-49; 2d sec., consul, 1949-50; consul Hong Kong, 1950-54; assigned Nat. War Coll., 1954-55; dep. dir. office Chinese affairs Dept. State, 1955-57, dir., 1957-58; counselor Am. embassy, Bern, Switzerland, 1958-59, 1st sec. London, 1959-61, became dep. chief of mission Taipei, Taiwan, 1961, also consul gen., to 1965; fellow Center for Internat. Affairs, Harvard U., 1965-66; mem. policy planning council Dept. State, 1966-69; sr. fellow Brookings Instn., Washington, 1969-75, guest scholar, 1975-77; fellow Woodrow Wilson Internat. Ctr. for Scholars, Washington, 1977-78, Inst. Sino-Soviet Studies, George Washington U., 1979-80; research assoc. Sch. Advanced Internat. Studies, Johns Hopkins U., 1983-85. Professorial lectr. Sch. Advanced Internat. Studies, Johns Hopkins U., 1974, 83-2003; adj. prof. Am. U., 1975-76 Author: Island China, East Asia and U.S. Security, 1975, Island China, 1978, Embattled Korea, 1987, Reaching Across the Taiwan Strait, 1993, Cooperation or Conflict in the Taiwan Strait?, 1999; co-author: Japan, Korea, and China: American Perceptions and Policies. Mem. Nat. Com. on U.S.-China Rels., Asia Soc., Phi Beta Kappa, Theta Delta Chi. Clubs: Rotarian (Hong Kong). Home: Arlington, Va. Died Aug. 10, 2007.

CLOYES, EUGENE HERBERT, architect; b. Santa Ana, Calif., Aug. 22, 1921; s. Frank Hebert and Leah Nora (Harris) Cloyes; m. Harriette Nichol Young, June 30, 1951; children: Cynthia Jean Damm, Nicole Dianne Graciano, David MacDonald. BArch., U. So. Calif., 1951. Registered arch., Calif., Wash., Ariz., N. Mex., Tex. Assoc. Jung Cloyes, AIA, Del Mar, Calif., 1953—80; coordinating arch. Foodmaker Inc., San Diego, from 1980. With USN, 1943—45. Mem.: AIA. Republican. Home: Solana Beach, Calif. Died Nov. 11, 2006.

COBURN, JAMES LEROY, academic administrator; b. Oak Park, Ill., Nov. 21, 1933; s. Forest Edward and Myrtle Emmaline (Clarke) C.; m. Julianne Whitty, Sept. 3, 1955; children: James, Gregory, Julie, Cheryl. BA, North Cen. Coll., Naperville, Ill., 1956; MS, No. Ill. U., 1965; EdD, Vanderbilt U., 1983. Cert. tchr., guidance counselor, supt., Ill. Tchr. Luther South High Sch., Chgo., 1956-58, Maine Township High Sch. East, Park Ridge, Ill., 1958-61, dean, counselor, 1961-64; dir. student pers. svcs. Maine Twp. High Sch. South, Park Ridge, 1964-67; asst. prin. for staff Maine Twp. High Sch. West, Des Plaines, Ill., 1967-73, prin., 1973-97; ret., 1997. Cons. Pitts. Pub. Schs., 1965; chmn. Ill. Blue Ribbon Com. on Edn., Bloomington, 1988; spkr. Internat. Ednl. Symposium, South Korea, 1996. Editor: Growth through Reading, 1960, 61. Pres. Inter-Suburban Assn.; chmn. judges 4th of July Parade, Des Plaines, 1980-86; mem. Des Plaines Beautification Com., 1987, Des Plaines Mayor's Adv. Com., 1989—; Ill. state commr. North Ctrl. Assn., 1992-95; pres. Des Plaines chpt. United Way, 1995—; twp. sch. trustee Maine, 1996—; pres. Twp. Sch. Bd. Caucus, 2002. Recipient Those Who Excel award Ill. Bd. Edn., 1977, Disting. Educator's award Idea Inst., 1984. Mem. Nat. Assn. Secondary Sch. Prins., Am. Assn. Sch. Adminstrs., Ill. Prins. Assn., Intersuburban Assn. Prins. (pres. 1986—), Des Plaines C. of C. (bd. dirs 1980-85, 92-95), Rotary (pres. Des Plaines 1976-77, Most Valuable Mem. award 1979, Paul Harris fellow 1989, John Vaughin excellence in edn. award 1997). Lutheran. Avocations: reading, travel, recreational sports, gardening. Home: Des Plaines, Ill. Died Nov. 12, 2005.

CODY, HIRAM SEDGWICK, JR., retired telecommunications industry executive; b. Nov. 1, 1915; s. Hiram Sedgwick and Harriett Mary (Collins) C.; m. Mary Vaughn Jacoby, Oct. 4, 1941; children: Margaret Vaughn, Harriett Mary, Hiram Sedgwick III, Henry Jacoby, William Collins. BS cum laude, Yale U., 1937, JD, 1940. Bar: NC 1940. With Western Electric Co., Inc., 1946-71, regional mgr. engring. and installation Chgo., 1961-64, dir. orgn. planning NYC, 1964-65, sec., treas., 1965-71; asst. treas. AT&T, NYC, 1971-80; ret., 1980. V.p. Morris-Sussex coun. Boy Scouts of Am., 1970-80; vice-chmn. Zoning Bd. Adjustment Mountain Lakes, N.J., 1968-80; boro councilman, Mountain Lakes, 1960-61; trustee, treas. Asheville (N.C.) Sch., 1974-84; trustee Asheville Symphony Orch., 1981-91, Asheville Cmty. Concert Assn., 1981-91; bd. advisors Warren Wilson Coll., 1983—, chmn., 1987-90. With USN, 1941-45, MTO, comdr. USNR, 1946. Mem. N.C. State Bar, Tel. Pioneers Am. (v.p. 1969-71, treas. 1971-78), Tau Beta Pi. Home: Black Mountain, NC. Died Oct. 16, 2006.

COE, JOHN CLARK, air transportation executive; b. Crary, ND, Mar. 12, 1924; s. James Charles and Margaret Maybelle (Calderwood) Coe; m. Joy Eames, Nov. 27, 1954; children: Robert Eames, Nancy Louise. BS in Bus., U. Colo., 1946. Flight steward, sta. agt., sta. mgr., maintenance cost acct. Monarch AirLines, Denver, 1947—80; acct. Frontier Airlines, Inc., Denver, 1950—51, dir. econ. rsch., 1952—66, staff v.p. econ. planning, 1967—68, v.p. econ. planning, 1969—81, v.p. corp. planning, from 1982. Forensic econ. analyst air transp. Active Denver Botanic Gardens, Nat. Cathedral Assn., Washington. Mem.: N.Am. Soc. Corp. Planning. Congregationalist. Home: Denver, Colo. Died Oct. 24, 2006.

COE, ROBERT STANFORD, retired management educator; b. Cin., July 9, 1919; s. Louis Herman and Alma Mary (Jenkins) C.; children: Carolyn Lee, William Ayres, Jon Bruce; m. Dorothy June Harris, Nov. 25, 1977 BS, Miami U., Oxford, Ohio, 1941; MS, U. Houston, 1948, PhD, 1957. Asst. to v.p. Dresser Industries, Dallas, 1956-58; personnel adminstr. Ling-Temco-Vought, Dallas, 1958-64; prof., grad. adviser Stephen F. Austin State U. (Tex.), 1964-69, chmn. dept. bus. adminstrn., 1969-74; mgmt. prof. Angelo State U., San Angelo, Tex., 1969-87; pres. Mgmt. Resources Assocs., San Angelo, 1970-87. Lectr. U. Tex.-Arlington, 1960-64. Contbr. articles to profl. jours. Mem. Gov.'s Com. on Goals for Tex., 1970; bd. dirs. YMCA, 1970-72, West Tex. Lighthouse for Blind, 1985-87. Served with USN, 1941-45. Mem. Am. Psychol. Assn., Acad. Mgmt., AAUP, Am. Inst. Decision Scis., Alpha Kappa Psi, Phi Kappa Phi, Pi Kappa Alpha Clubs: San Angelo Country, Rolling Hills Country. Lodges: Rotary. Presbyterian. Home: San Antonio, Tex. Died Mar. 8, 2006.

COEN, ADRI STECKLING **See ADRI**

COFFEY, THOMAS ARTHUR, college president; b. Mpls., Apr. 6, 1936; s. Patrick Joseph and Agnes Bridget (Haley) C.; m. Maureen Ann Sullivan, July 13, 1962; children: Catherine, Mary, Patrick. AB, St. Ambrose Coll., 1960; MA, Coll. St. Thomas, 1966; A.M., U. S.D., 1967, Ed.D., 1968; postgrad, Harvard U., 1979. Tchr. secondary pub. sch., Mpls., 1962-66; teaching asst. U. S.D., Vermillion, 1966-68; asst. prof. edn. and psychology Hamline U., St. Paul, 1968-71; faculty U. Colo., Boulder, summer 1971; assoc. prof. edn. Mankato State U., Minn., 1971-76; mgr. mktg. and sales Waterquip Corp., Sioux Falls, S.D., 1955-62; dir. clin. experiences Hamline U., 1968-71; dir. Urban tr. Mankato State U., 1971-76; dean div. continuing edn. Am. U., Washington, 1976-82; pres. Thomas More Coll., Crestview Hills, Ky., 1982-85, Wayne State Coll., Nebr., from 1985. Shell grantee; Mankato State U. Urban Ctr. grantee; Am. U. global studies fed. grantee Mem. Nat. Univ. Continuing Edn. Assn., Assn. Higher Edn., Am. Personnel and Guidance Assn., Am. Assn. Univ. Adminstrs., Assn. Continuing Higher Edn. (sec.-treas. region V), Assn. Supervision and Curriculum Devel., Phi Delta Kappa Died Jan. 6, 2006.

COFFMAN, JAY DENTON, internist, educator; b. Quincy, Mass., Nov. 17, 1928; s. Frank David and Etta (Kline) C.; m. Louise G. Peters, June 29, 1955; children: Geoffrey J., Joanne K., Linda J., Robert B. AB, Harvard U., 1950; MD, Boston U., 1954. Diplomate Am. Bd. Internal Medicine. Med. intern Univ. Hosp., Boston, 1954-55, asst. resident in medicine, 1955-56, chief resident in medicine, 1957-58, fellow in cardiovascular disease, 1956-57, sect. head peripheral vascular dept., from 1960; asso. in medicine Boston U. Med. Sch., 1960-65, mem. faculty, from 1965, prof. medicine, from 1970. Author: Raynaud's Phenomenon, 1989; co-author: Ischemic Limbs, 1973, Peripheral Arterial Disease, 2002. Trustee Solomon Carter Fuller Mental Health Center, Boston, 1975-81. Served to capt. M.C. USAR, 1958-60. Mem. ACP. Am. Soc. Clin. Investigation, Am. Fedn. Clin. Rsch., Am. Heart Assn., Begg's Soc., Phi Beta Kappa, Alpha Omega Alpha. Home: Canton, Mass. Died Dec. 12, 2006.

COGGESHALL, PETER COLLIN, JR., paper products manufacturing company executive; b. Darlington, SC, Sept. 22, 1915; s. Robert Werner and Mary Beulah (Walden) C.; m. Rosanne Howard, Jan. 24, 1942; children— Peter Collin, Rosanne Howard. AB, U. S.C., 1936; MBA, Harvard U., 1938. Research staff Harvard U., 1938-39; with Sonoco Products Co., Hartsville, S.C., 1939—, v.p., 1961-76, exec. v.p., 1976-85, sr. exec. v.p., from 1985. Dir. Sonoco Internat. Co. Trustee McLeod Regional Med. Center, Florence, S.C. Served as officer AUS, 1943-45. Mem. Phi Beta Kappa, Omicron Delta Kappa, Alpha Tau Omega. Clubs: Damon Gun, Rotary. Presbyterian. Home: Hartsville, SC. Died Feb. 22, 2006.

COHEN, ALFRED, historian; b. Bklyn., May 2, 1927; s. Meyer and Lisa (Gordon) C.; m. Beatrice Claire Margaretten, Nov. 24, 1955; children: Michael, Julie Marna. BA, Rutgers U., 1949; MA, NYU, 1953; PhD, Ind. U., 1961. Prof. history Trenton (N.J.) State Coll., 1959-90, prof. emeritus, from 1991, chair dept., 1969-75. Vis. prof. Hayward (Calif.) State Coll., 1964 summer, U. Frankfurt, Germany, 1964-65, Worchester (Eng.) Coll., 1973-74. Contbr. articles to profl. jours. Cpl. U.S. Army, 1951-53, seaman 1st class USN, 1945-46. Fulbright grantee, 1965. Mem. Conf. Brit. Studies. Democrat. Jewish. Home: Princeton, NJ. Died July 5, 2007.

COHEN, BERNARD IRVIN, plastic surgeon; b. Pottsville, Pa., Jan. 6, 1936; DDS, U. Pitts., 1960, MD, 1964. Cert. Am. Bd. Gen. Surgery, Am. Bd. Plastic Surgery. Intern, gen. surgery South Side Hosp., Pitts., 1964—65; resident Colo. Med. Ctr., Denver, 1965—69, Norfolk Gen. Hosp., Va., 1969—71; hosp. appointment Butler Meml. Hosp., Pitts.; asst. clin. prof. U. Pitts.; private practice Pitts., from 1971. Fellow: ACS; mem.: Am. Soc. Aesthetic Plastic Surgery, Am. Soc. Plastic Surgeons. Died Jan. 26, 2007.

COHEN, CLAUDIA LYNN, journalist, television reporter; b. Englewood, NJ, Dec. 16, 1950; d. Robert B. and Harriet (Brandwein) C.; m. Ron Perelman, 1985 (div. 1994) 1 child, Samantha. BA in Comm., U. Pa., 1972. Mng. editor The Daily Pennsylvanian; with More Mag., NYC, 1973-76; mng. editor, 1976-77; reporter N.Y. Post, NYC, 1977-78; editor, author Page Six column, 1978-80; daily columnist I, Claudia N.Y. Daily News, NYC, 1980-81; tv entertainment reporter Live with Regis and Kathie Lee, from 1983; reporter Eyewitness News WABC, 1984—89. Bd. overseers Sch. Arts and Scis. U. Pa.; mem. adv. bd. N.Y. Hosp. Cornell Med. Ctr.; adv. coun. AIDS Cmty. Rsch.

Initiative Am. Honoree Sarah Herzog Meml. Hosp. Centennial, 1995, Rita Hayworth Gala Benefit for Alzheimers, 2000; named Police Athletic League Woman of Year, 2006. Democrat. Died June 15, 2007.

COHEN, FREDERICK, lawyer; b. Phila., Dec. 8, 1935; s. Samuel and Rose (Simon) C.; m. Daniele N. Bivas, Mar. 23, 1969; children: Seth A., Philip K. BS in Econs., U. Pa., 1957, JD, 1960. Bar: Pa. 1961, U.S. Dist. Ct. Pa., 1967, U.S. Ct. Appeals (3rd cir.) 1967, U.S. Supreme Ct. 1967. Ptnr. Gold, Bowman & Korman, Phila., 1960-79, Steinberg, Greenstein, Gorelick & Price, Phila., 1979-82, Pechner, Dorfman, Wolffe, Rounick & Cabot, Norristown, Pa., 1982-87; pvt. practice Phila., 1987-89; ptnr. Blank, Rome, Comisky & McCauley, Phila., 1989-96; of counsel Obermayer Rabmann Maxwell & Hippel LLP, Phila., 1996—2007. Adj. faculty Temple U., Phila., 1986—. Served with U.S. Army. Fellow Internat. Acad. Matrimonial Lawyers, Am. Acad. Matrimonial Lawyers; mem. ABA (family law sect.), Pa. Bar Assn. (past chmn. family law sect., chmn. exec. coun. 1976—, chmn. divorce 1979-83), Joint Family Law Coun. (exec. coun. 1976—). Avocations: computer programming, tennis, photography. Home: Bala Cynwyd, Pa. Died July 24, 2007.

COHEN, GABRIEL MURREL, editor, publisher; b. Louisville, Aug. 31, 1908; s. Isaac and Jenny (Rosenbaum) C.; m. Helen Aronovitz, Sept. 22, 1938; children: Lawrence, Theodore, Miriam, Debbie, Ben-Zion, Jennie, Hermine, Rena. AB, U. N.C., 1930. Reporter Louisville Herald-Post, 1927-28, 30-31; founder, editor, pub. Ky. Jewish Chronicle (now Ky. Jewish Post and Opinion), Louisville, 1931—, Ind. Jewish Post, Indpls., 1935—, Mo. Jewish Post and Opinion, St. Louis, 1948-92, Nat. Jewish Post (now Nat. Jewish Post and Opinion), Indpls., from 1948. Founding chmn. Am. Jewish Press Assn., 1944—. Home: Indianapolis, Ind. Died Apr. 19, 2007.

COHEN, IRWIN ROBERT, motion picture theatre executive; b. Balt., Sept. 4, 1924; s. Maurice Albert and Eleanor Lee (Tankoos) C.; m. Betty Gayle Wagner, May 30, 1928; children: Ilene C. McCaffery, Jan F. Feldman, Scott Richard. LLB, U. Balt., 1948. With R C Theatres Mgmt. Corp., Reisterstown, Md., from 1960, pres., chief exec. officer. Co-founder Key Bank and Trust Co., 1960, bd. dirs., mem. exec. com., chmn. bd. loan com. Mem. ABA, Nat. Assn. Theatres Owners (dir., mem. exec. com., fin. com.), Motion Pictures Pioneers, Md. Bar Assn. Home: Pikesville, Md. Died Dec. 22, 2006.

COHEN, MAIMON M., medical geneticist, clinical cytogeneticist, educator; b. Balt., Jan. 24, 1935; Diplomate Am. Bd. Med. Genetics. Fellow in genetics U. Mich. Med. Sch., Ann Arbor, 1962-65; now prof. ob-gyn. and pediats. U. Md. Sch. Medicine, now chief divsn. human genetics. Mem. Am. Coll. Med. Genetics. Died Jan. 25, 2007.

COLBERT, CHARLES RALPH, architect; b. Dow, Okla., June 23, 1921; s. James Eden and Alice (Hendon) C.; m. Rosemary Frances Schrafft, Sept. 26, 1946 (dec. May 1954); children— Kathryn H., James Eden III, Thomas M.; m. Frances B. Stern, June 18, 1956 (dec. Apr. 1962). B.Arch., U. Tex., 1943; MS, Columbia, 1947. Asst. prof. Tulane U., 1947-49; pvt. practice architecture and city planning, from 1953; cons. prof. architecture La. State U., from 1975. Supervising architect, dir. Office Planning and Constrn., New Orleans pub. schs., 1951-53; dir. architecture div. Tex. A. and M. Coll., 1956-58; dean Sch. Architecture, Columbia, 1960-63 Author: Idea: The Shaping Force, 1987, Seeing What I Like and Liking What I See, 1991. Mem. La. Bd. Edn., 1970-77. Served to lt. (s.g.) USNR, 1943-45. Fellow AIA; mem. Royal Soc. Arts, Tau Beta Pi. Home: Metairie, La. Died Feb. 12, 2007.

COLBURN, GUY BLANDIN, JR., lawyer; b. Boston, Aug. 17, 1920; s. Guy Blandin and Caroline Hallowell (Smedley) C.; m. Ruth Budd, Sept. 8, 1946; children— Martha Ruth, Robert Hallowell. B.A., Pomona Coll., 1942; LL.B., Harvard U., 1949; Bar: Calif. 1950, U.S. Dist. Ct. (no. dist.) Calif. 1950, U.S. Ct. Appeals (9th cir.) 1950. Law clk. U.S. Ct. Appeals (9th cir.), San Francisco, 1949-50; assoc. Dunne, Phelps and Mills, San Francisco, 1950-58, ptnr. 1959-64; research atty. Calif. Continuing Edn. of Bar, Berkeley, Calif., 1964-72; staff atty. Calif. Supreme Ct., San Francisco, 1972—. Editor: (with others) Calif. Commercial Law, Vol. I, 1964; Calif. Trial Objections, 1967, 2d rev. edit. 1984; Calif. Criminal Law Practice Vol II, 1969; Calif. Marital Termination Settlements, 1971. Served with AUS, 1943-46, PTO. Mem. ABA, Bar Assn. San Francisco, State Bar Calif. Democrat. Mem. United Ch. of Christ. Home: El Cerrito, Calif. Died Aug. 1, 2006.

COLBY, PAUL SOUTHWORTH, JR., accountant; b. East Orange, NJ, July 11, 1944; s. Paul Southworth and Mary Jane (Patterson) C.; m. Shearon Ann Bailey Copeland, Sept. 28, 1967 (div. Mar. 1981); children: Allison Reve Matlock, Adrienne Colby Boose; m. Jeannie Carol Haymore, Sept. 21, 1986 BSBA, E. Carolina U., 1969; postgrad., Va. Commonwealth U., 1975; MBA, Kennedy Wester U., 1995. CPA, Tex. Sr. asst. acct., jr. asst. acct. Haskins & Sells, CPAs, Charlotte, N.C., 1969-71; tax officer, acctg. officer, tax acct. Fidelity Am. Bankshares, Inc., Lynchburg, Va., 1971-74; corp. tax officer United Va. Bankshares, Inc., Richmond, Va., 1974-75; sr. tax acct. Hanes Corp., Winston-Salem, N.C., 1975-77; asst. controller The Bowman Gray Sch. Medicine of Wake Forest U., Winston-Salem, 1978-81; v.p., gen. mgr. So. Image, Inc., Winston-Salem, 1981-82; vice chmn. bd. dirs. Wagner-Welch Assocs., Inc., Winston-Salem, 1982-84; dir. fin. and adminstrn. Probus, Inc., Winston-Salem, 1982-84; ind. bus. cons. Colby & Assocs., Winston-Salem, 1984-90; sr. v.p., CFO, sec., treas. Knightsbridge Petroleum Corp., Arlington, Tex., 1986-87; pres. Southworth Land Mgmt. Co., Inc., Arlington, Tex., 1986-87; corp. sec., asst. treas. Datafax Systems, Inc., Arlington, Tex., 1987-88; ind. bus. cons. Colby & Assocs., Winston-Salem, Hurst, N. Carolina, Tex., 1984-90; pvt. practice Paul S. Colby, Jr., CPA, Hurst, Tex., from 1990. Vol. cons. Hill City Minority Econ. Devel. Corp., 1973, Nat. Acctg. Assn., 1979, N.C. Vietnam Vets. Leadership Program, 1985; mem. adv. bd. Ind. Small Bus. Assn. Tarrant County, 1989-90. Author: (weekly bus. column) The Bus. Press, 1994—; contbr. weekly bus. syndicated articles to profl. jours. Controller, asst. treas. Horton for Congress, Winston-Salem, 1978-79. With U.S. Army, 1963-66. Named Outstanding Young Man of Am., Lynchburg Jaycees, 1972. Mem. AICPA, N.C. Assn. CPAs, Tex. Soc. CPAs, N.E. Tarrant County C. of C., Ft. Worth C. of C., Hurst Euless Bedford C. of C., Better Bus. Bur., Small Women and Minority Bus. League (Ft. Worth/Dallas). Presbyterian. Avocation: chess. Died July 27, 2007.

COLE, EUGENE ROGER, author, clergyman, religious founder; b. Cleve., Nov. 14, 1930; s. Bernard James and Mary Louise (Rogers) C. BA, St. Edward Sem., 1954; postgrad., John Carroll U., 1957; MDiv, Sulpician Sem. N.W., 1958; AB, Cen. Wash. U., Ellensburg, 1960; MA, Seattle U., 1970; LittD (hon.), 1983. Ordained priest Roman Cath. Ch., 1958. Newman moderator and cons. Central Wash. U., 1958-59; bus. mgr. Experiment Press, Seattle, 1959-60; chaplain St. Elizabeth Hosp., Yakima, Wash., 1959-61; chmn. English dept. Yakima Central Cath. High Sch., 1959-66, Marquette High Sch., Yakima, 1966-68; poetry critic Nat. Writers Club, Denver, 1969-72; poet in service Poets & Writers Inc., NYC, from 1974. Founder Godspeople, Inc., 1985, dir. 1985—, originator, anapoem, 1985; instr. contract bridge, Ind., 1975-79; freelance writer, editor, researcher, 1958—; researcher Harvard, 1970; religious counselor; antiquarian book collector; owner, pres. Grand Slam softball team, 1985—; editorial cons. Bellflower Press, 1988—. Composer: Werther: Tone Poem for Piano, 1948; Chronicle for Tape, 1960; author: The Great "O" Antiphons, 1956, Kecharitomene, 1958, Experiment in Poetry, 1959, Which End, the Empyrean?, 1959; Spring as Ballet: a broadside, 1961; Three Cycle Poems of Yeats, 1965; twopoems, 1966; Woman, you (illustrapoem), 1967, April Is the Cruelest Month, 1970; Falling Up: Haiku & Senryu, 1979; Act & Potency (poems), 1980; Ding an sich: anapoems, 1985; Uneasy Camber: Early Poems & Diversions 1943-50, 1986; A Key to Ding an sich, 1986; Godspeople: Not a Church but a People, 1987; (under pseudonym Peter E. Locré) songpoems/poemsongs: new lyrics, 1988; lyrics for male prodn. Finian's Rainbow, 1958; 3 hymns on Bach melodies, 1958; editor: Grand Slam: 13 Great Short Stories about Bridge, 1975 (pub. in Gt. Brit. as Slam: Thirteen Great Bridge Stories); In the Beginning, 1978; Litany: Cynewulf to Vachel Lindsay, 1989; assoc. editor: The Harvester, 1955; guest editor Experiment: An Internat. Rev., 1961; editorial staff This Is My Best, 1970; contbr. Your Literary I.Q. Saturday Rev., 1970-72; author religious monograph, also contbr. articles, poetry and drama to numerous lit. jours. and anthologies; interviews on radio network Stas. WJOB, WLCL and WLTH. Recipient Poetry Broadcast award, 1968, Musical Expertise award, 1970, Lorraine Harr Haiku award, 1974, Ann. Mentor Poetry award, 1974, Pro Mundi Beneficio award, 1975, Readers Union award, 1976, Diploma di Merito, 1982, Marathon award Cleve. Orchestra, 1983, Disting. Svc. award for lit. and humanities, 1988, Internat. Cultural Diploma of Honor, 1989. Mem. Authors Guild, Poetry Soc. Am. (judge 1970), Western World Haiku Soc., Acad. Am. Poets, World Acad. Poets, World-Wide Acad. Scholars, Internat. Poetry Soc., Soc. for Scholarly Pub., Internat. Platform Assn., Eighteen Nineties Soc. (London), Friends of the Lilly Library, Expt. Group, Soc. for Study of Midwestern Lit., Nat. Fedn. State Poetry Socs., Poetry Soc. (London), Sir Thomas Beecham Soc., Chgo. Symphony Orch. Assn., Cleve. Mus. Art, Ohioana Library Assn., No. Ohio Bibliophilic Soc., Century Club of Cleve. State Univ., Poets' League Greater Cleve., Am. Contract Bridge League, Kappa Delta Pi. Died July 8, 2006.

COLE, JOHN OWEN, banker; b. Forest City, NC, May 22, 1929; s. Dee Christopher and Faye (Best) C.; m. Katherine Stuart Davidson, June 27, 1953; children: Mark Davidson, D. Matthew, Chapman Stuart, Benjamin Donnell, John Owen II, Jamie Clark, Mary F. BA, Duke U., 1953. With First Nat. Bank Md., Balt., from 1956, pres., dir., from 1968, chmn. bd., 1988; now. chmn. 1st Md. Bancorp, Balt. Mem. fed. adv. council FRS; dir. U.S. Fidelity & Guaranty Co., Balt. Gas & Electric Co. Trustee Goucher Coll. Served with USMCR, 1953-56. Mem. Res. City Bankers Assn. Died Nov. 2, 2005.

COLE, JULIAN WAYNE (PERRY COLE), computer educator, consultant, programmer, analyst; b. LaFayette, Ala., Dec. 16, 1937; s. William Walter and Hattie Lucille (Berry) C.; m. Judith Elaine Riley, June 27, 1959; children— Jeffrey Paul, Jarrett David. B.S. in Bus. Adminstrn., Ariz., State U., 1967; M. in Computer Sci., Texas A&M U., 1969. Joined U.S. Air Force, 1956, advanced through grades to capt., 1970, ret., 1978; programmer/analyst Hewlett Packard Corp., Colorado Springs, Colo., 1978-79, Digital Equipment Corp., Colorado Springs, 1979-85; lectr. U. Colo., Colorado Springs, 1978-92; tng. dir. System Devel. Corp., Colorado Springs, 1979-85; tng. dir. Unisys Corp., Colorado Springs, 1986-91; computer cons., Colorado Springs, 1980—; sr. systems analyst, tech. trainer MCI, Inc., Colorado Springs, 1992—; pres. Advanced Info. Methodology and Systems, Colorado Springs, 1982—. Author: ANSI Fortran IV, 1978; ANSI Fortran IV with Fortran 77 Extensions, 1983, ANSI Fortran 77: Structured Problem Solving Approach, 1987. Mem. Assn. Computing Machinery (chmn. 1981-82), Data Processing Mgmt. Assn., Beta Gamma Sigma, Phi Kappa Phi, Upsilon Pi Epsilon. Republican. Baptist. Club: Business. Home: Colorado Springs, Colo. Died June 26, 2007.

COLE, WENDELL GORDON, speech and drama educator; b. Chgo., May 15, 1914; s. Herbert F. and Susan (Richards) C.; m. Charlotte Clarice Klein, Dec. 14, 1948. AB, Albion Coll., Mich., 1936; AM, U. Mich., 1937; PhD, Stanford, 1951. Mem. faculty Alma (Mich.) Coll., 1943-45; mem. faculty Stanford U., from 1946, prof. speech and drama, from 1963, exec. head dept., 1956-59, 64-65, 67-69, scene and costume designer, from 1945, acting chmn. dept. drama, 1972-73, chmn. dept., 1982-83. Scene designer West Bay Opera, 1975-81 Author: The Elements of Scene Design, 1962, Kyoto in the Momoyama Period, 1967, Theatre Architecture, 1970; Editor: The Story of The Meininger, 1963; contbr. Theatre West: Image and Impact, 1990. Recipient Disting. Alumni award Albion Coll., 1988, Golden Brush award Palo Alto Children's Theatre, 1989, Paul Emerson award Coun. on Arts, 1995; Wendell Cole design studio dept. drama Stanford U. named in his honor, 1995. Home: Palo Alto, Calif. Died Apr. 17, 2007.

COLEMAN, GEORGE HUNT, chemist; b. San Gabriel, Calif., Oct. 15, 1928; s. Thomas and Grace Muriel (Love) C.; AB, U. Calif., Berkeley, 1950; PhD, UCLA, 1958; m. Lois Mae Tarleton, Feb. 14, 1953; children— David Howe, Thomas George, Margaret Rose. Microanalyst, U. Calif., Berkeley, 1950-51; nuclear chemist Calif. Rsch. and Devel. Corp., 1951-53; sr. nuclear chemist Lawrence Livermore Lab., 1957-69; assoc. prof. chemistry Nebr. Wesleyan U., Lincoln, 1969-78, prof., 1979—, acting head dept., 1976-78, head dept. chemistry, 1978-80, 1989—. Mem. Am. Chem. Soc., AAAS. Democrat. Presbyterian. Home: Lincoln, Nebr. Died Feb. 15, 2006.

COLLIER, JAMES DEWEY, association executive; b. Birmingham, Ala., Oct. 18, 1926; s. Earl S. and Annie (Williams) C.; B.S., U. Ala., 1949; M.B.A. with distinction, N.Y. U., 1967. Asst. to controller cost control Freeport Sulphur Co., New Orleans, 1954-64; mgr. chpt. ednl. services Nat. Assn. Accts., N.Y.C., 1964-68, dir. mem. services, 1968-72, dir. publs., 1972-82, editor publisher Mgmt. Acctg., 1972—, mng. dir., 1982—; cons. to industry. Treas., St. Tropez Condominium, N.Y.C., 1966-70; bd. dirs. Gallery House Condominium, 1975—. Served with C.E., AUS, 1944-46. Mem. Nat. Assn. Accts., Am. Soc. Assn. Execs., UN Assn., Met. Opera Guild, Am. Acctg. Assn., Beta Alpha Psi Forum. Contbr. articles to profl. jours. Home: Miami, Fla. Died July 20, 2006.

COLLINS, BOB (ROBERT LINDSAY COLLINS), former Australian government official; b. Newcastle, Australia, Feb. 9, 1946; married. Cattle farmer, until 1965; ext. officer No. Territory Dept. of Agr., 1965-70; market gardener, 1970-73; tech. officer CSIRO Divsn. Wildlife and Rsch., 1974-77; mem. No. Territory Legis. Assembly, 1977-87, leader of the opposition, 1981-86, leader Parliamentary Labor Party, 1981-86; mem. Senate No. Territory, 1987—98; min. shipping Govt. of Australia, 1990, min. shipping & aviation support, 1990-92, min. assisting the prime min. for No. Australia, 1990-92, min. transport & comm., 1992—93, min. of primary industries & energy, 1993—96. Died Sept. 21, 2007.

COLLINS, HARKER, retired economist, manufacturing and publishing executive; b. Denver, Nov. 24, 1924; s. Clem Wetzel and Marie (Harker) C.; m. Emily Harvey, Aug. 23, 1957; children: Catherine Emily, Cynthia Lee, Constance Marie. BS, U.S. Naval Acad., 1945. Asst. buyer Montgomery Ward & Co., NYC, 1947-51; prodn. mgr. Diamond Hosiery Mills, High Point, NC, 1953-55; v.p. Vanette Hosiery Mills, Dallas, 1955-59; v.p., dir. Grote Mfg. Co., Madison, Ind., 1959-71; group v.p., gen. mgr. Bendix Corp., South Bend, Ind., 1971-73; pres., dir. Bandag, Inc., Muscatine, Iowa, 1973-78, chief exec. officer, 1974-78; pres., chief exec. officer, bd. dirs. Harker Collins & Co., Lubbock, Tex., 1978-98; pub. newsletters The Economy and You, Update, 1978-96; econ. counsel Automotive Svc Industry Assn., 1978-91; exec. v.p., bd. dirs. Indsl. Molding Corp., Lubbock, 1993-97; pres., bd. dirs. Indl. Molding Corp., Lubbock, 1997; ret., 1997. Instr. U. Denver, 1948; chmn. automotive industry liaison com. with Dept. Transp., 1968-86, automotive industry excise tax com., 1964-70, automotive industry tariff com., 1964-70, joint operating com. for automotive trade shows, 1969-77 Mem. Pres.'s Com. Hwy. Safety, 1966-68; Bd. dirs. Iowa Ind. Coll. Found., 1976-86; bd. fellows Northwood Inst., 1974—; alderman City of Rancho Viejo, Tex. 1980-87. Served to ensign USN, 1945-47; to lt. USNR, 1951-53 Recipient Automotive Industry Leadership award, 1965, 74; Fin World award as chief exec. of yr., 1975, 77 Mem. Automotive Svc. Industry Assn. (vice chmn. 1966-67, chmn. 1968-69, chmn heavy duty exec. com. 1969-71, chmn. safety and environ protection com. 1962-67, 70-78), Automotive Sales Coun. (bd dirs. 1966-67, sec. 1971-72, v.p. 1972-73, pres. 1973-74), Am. Nat. Standards Inst. (chmn. task force on used vehicle standards 1966-74), Home Products Safety Coun. (pres. 1960-63), Medicine Cabinet Mfg. Coun. (pres. 1960-63, bd. dirs. 1960-68) Truck Safety Equipment Inst. (pres. 1960-63, dir. 1960-68) Died Apr. 18, 2007.

COLLINS, WAYNE WINFORD, former protective services official; b. Balt., July 19, 1943; s. James Winford and Clyde Kellys (Braddock) C.; m. Barbara Anne Beabout, June 22, 196 (div. Jan. 1990); m. Diane Christopher, June 23, 1990; children Dane Allen, Dawn Rene. Student, Houston C.C., 1971-74, U State N.Y., 1987-88; grad., Ga. Police Acad./Ga. Fire Acad. Internat. City Mgmt. Assn. Tng. Inst.; BS in Fire Scis., Wester States U., MS in Fire Svc. Adminstrn. Cert. fire officer VI, polic officer; expert witness fire and arson investigation; pvt. investigator; cons. security and fire loss control. Firefighter City o Galveston, Tex., 1964-66; firefighter/emergency fire apparatu operator City of Houston Fire Dept., 1966-73, capt.-fire co comdr./sta. officer, 1973-77, sr. capt. ctrl. command divsn. 1977-81, tng. officer comm. divsn., 1978-79, mem. fire chief staff/divsn. chief, 1981-85, chief officer fire and emergency med svc. comm. divsn., 1985-87; fire chief City of Thomaston, Ga 1987-91, City of Columbus, Ga., 1991—99. Faculty pub. svc divsn. Houston C.C., 1979-80; appointed chmn. Ga. Firefighter Stds. and Tng. Coun., 1995; mem. Fire Safe Ga. State Commn Fire Protection, 1991; specialist cons. weapons of mass destruction; dir. arson task force Muscogee County. Chmn. mid. Ga chpt. Nat. Kidney Found., 1989; chmn. Upson County Cour Child Abuse, Ga., 1990; advisor fire explorer program Bo Scouts Am. With USN, 1960-64. Recipient Svc. award Ga. Ins Commr., 1993, Svc. award Office of Mayor of Columbus, 1994 Arron Cohn award Juvenile Cts. System, 1994. Mem. Nat. Fir Protection Assn., Ga. Firefighters Assn., Ga. Assn. Fire Chiefs Southeastern Assn. Fire Chiefs, Internat. Assn. Fire Chiefs Internat. Assn. Firefighters (mem. exec. bd. Houston chp 1973-77, editor Houston Firefighter 1976-77, mem. City Ha com., chmn. speakers bur., Internat. Labor Press Assn. Na award), Metro Fire Chiefs Assn., Fellowship Christian Firefighters Internat., Assn. County Commrs. Ga. (mem. pub. safety con 1994), Am. Legion (Vietnam era mem.), Exch. Club Columbu Avocations: hunting, fishing, travel, civil war history. Died No 14, 2006.

COLLINS, WILLIAM JAMES, manufacturing company executive; b. Grand Rapids, Mich., Dec. 1, 1915; s. Frank C. an Aileen (Cary) C.; B.S., U. Mich., 1939; m. Margery Ailee

McDevitt, Nov. 23, 1942; children— Margaret Totin, William Jeffrey, C. Casey. With Batesco, Inc., Gary, Ind., 1964—, pres., sales mgr., 1981—; pres., sales mgr. Melt Specialties Co., Gary, 1976-81. Served with AC, U.S. Army, 1942-45, USAF, 51-52. Mem. AIME, Am. Foundrymen's Soc., U. Mich. Alumni Assn., Am. Legion, 8th AF Hist. Soc., 486th Bomb Group Assn. Club: Lions. Patentee in field. Home: Gary, Ind. Died Sept. 30, 2006.

COLLIS, CHARLES, air transportation executive; b. Bklyn., Aug. 6, 1920; s. Charles and Marie (Barnaby) C.; m. Margaret Howell, July 11, 1942; children: Jane, Joy. BSMechE, Brown U., 1942. V.p. Stratos div. Fairchild Hiller Corp., 1946-65, sr. v.p. Republic Aviation div., 1965-67, exec. v.p. corp., 1967-81; pres. Fairchild Hiller-F.R.G. Corp., 1966-69, Fairchild Republic Co., 1973-75, ret., 1981; mgmt. cons. Babylon, N.Y., from 1982. Mem. grad. mgmt. engring. adv. council C.W. Post Coll., L.I., 1965-66. Served as lt. USNR, 1942-45. Mem. AIAA, L.I. Assn. Commerce and Industry (bd. dirs. 1964-66), Babylon Yacht Club, Southward Ho Country Club. Died Aug. 13, 2006.

COLVARD, DEAN WALLACE, retired academic administrator; b. Ashe County, NC, July 10, 1913; s. W. P. and Mary (Shepherd) C.; m. Martha Lampkin, July 7, 1939; children: Carol Lampkin, Mary Lynda, Dean Wallace. BS, Berea Coll., 1935; MA, U. Mo., 1938; PhD, Purdue U., 1950, DAgr (hon.), 1961; LHD (hon.), Belmont Abbey Coll., 1978; D of Pub. Svc. (hon.), U. N.C., Charlotte, 1979; LHD, Berea Coll., 2003. Instr. agr., farm mgr. Brevard Coll., 1935-37; supt. N.C. Mountain Expt. Sta., 1938-46; prof. animal sci. N.C. State Coll., 1947-48, head dept. animal sci., 1948-53; dean agr., 1953-60; pres. Miss. State U., 1960-66; chancellor U. N.C., Charlotte, 1966-78, chancellor emeritus, 1978—2007. Mng. cons. Sci. Mus. of Charlotte, 1980-81; dir. Fed. Res. Bank of Richmond, 1955-60, dep. chmn., 1959-60; dir. Mut. Savs. & Loan, 1975-91; Spl. cons. ICA, Bangkok, Thailand, 1960; mem. Gov.'s Rsch. Triangle Devel. Coun., 1957-59; co-ordinator Agr. Rsch. Mission in Peru, S. Am., 1954-60; mem. agr. adv. com. W. K. Kellogg Found., 1954-60; chmn. Miss. Gov.'s Com. on Latin Am. Edn., 1961. Author: Mixed Emotions, A University President Remembers, 1985, Knowledge is Power, 1987, University Research Park, The First Twenty Years, 1988; contbr. to publs. in animal sci., agrl. econs., ednl. adminstrn. Chmn. Miss. Rhodes Scholar Com., 1965-66; chmn. N.C. Rhodes Scholar Com., 1967, 78; mem. Miss. Jr. Coll. Commn., 1960-66; vice chmn. Dimensions for Charlotte-Mecklenburg, 1973-76; mem. N.C. Council on State Goals and Policy, 1972-76, So. Growth Policies Bd., 1977-85, Mecklenburg and Union Counties Health and Hosp. Council, 1967-76; chmn., 1974-76; bd. dirs., exec. com. U. Research Park, Charlotte, 1967-87, vice chmn., 1974-79; trustee Berea Coll., 1956-76, St. Andrews Coll., 1969-76, Cordell Hull Found. for Internat. Edn., 1961-67; chmn. bd. trustees N.C. Sch. Sci. and Math., 1978-83. Recipient Disting. Svc. award N.C. Farm Bur., 1956, Disting. Svc. award Miss. Farm Bur., 1965, Disting. Svc. award N.C. Grange, 1958, Outstanding Civilian award U.S. Dept. Army, 1966, Charlotte News Man of Yr. award, 1977, Disting. Alumnus award Berea Coll., 1980, U. N.C. Disting. Svc. award, 1989, N.C. Disting. Pub. Svc. award, 1990, Lifetime Achievement award Nat. 4H CLub Found., 1998, award Echo Found., 2004; named Man of Yr. in Agr. in N.C., 1954. Mem. Nat. Assn. State Univs. and Land Grant Colls. (co-chmn. joint com. edn. for govt. svc. 1961-65, chmn. president's coun. 1966), Am. Coun. Edn. (commn. internt. edn. 1966-68, chmn. com. higher adult edn. 1966-68), Am. Assn. State Colls. and Univs. (bd. dirs. 1978), Charlotte C. of C. (bd. dirs. 1968-70), Charlotte Country Club, Blue Key, Sigma Xi, Omicron Delta Kappa, Phi Kappa Phi, Gamma Alpha, Alpha Gamma Rho, Gamma Sigma Delta, Alpha Zeta. Clubs: Charlotte Country, Charlotte Rotary (pres. 1978, hon. 1984-2007). Home: Charlotte, NC. Died June 28, 2007.

COMBS, KINCHEON V., military officer, civil engineer; b. Fairfax, Ala., Apr. 22, 1929; s. Robert James and Mary Katherine (Adams) C.; m. Juanita Black, Nov. 11, 1950; children— Cathryn J., Robert V. II, J. Carol, Ken V., Jr., Frances D. Assoc. in Sci., Jones Jr. Coll., 1954; B.S.C.E., Miss. State U., 1956. Staff engr. Miss. Nat. Guard, Jackson, 1956-65; commd. capt. Air Nat. Guard, U.S. Air Force, 1965; advanced through grades to col., 1977; base engr. Air N.G., Gulfport, Miss., 1965-77, comdr., 1977—; advisor Regional Airport Authority, Gulfport, 1977—; mem. U.S. Atty.'s Coordination Commn. So. Miss., 1983—. Contbr. articles on mil. engring. to profl. jours. Pres. bd. trustees Gulfport Sch. Dist., Miss., 1984—; sec. Gulfport Civil Service Commn., 1970-75; pres. Miss. Coast Crime Commn., Gulfport, 1978-80. Recipient Silver Beaver award Boy Scouts Am., 1971; Thanks Badge Girl Scouts Am., 1982; citation FAA, Atlanta, 1980. Mem. Miss. Nat. Guard Assn. (pres. 1980-81, bd. dirs. 1976-79, Commendation 1981). Methodist. Lodges: Rotary (Gulfport), Kiwanis (Pres. Gulfport 1977-78), Mason (32 degree), Shriners (pres. Miss. Coast club 1972-73). Home: Gulfport, Miss. Died Feb. 13, 2007.

COMBS, RICHARD J., retired academic administrator; b. SD, 1927; m. Audrey Combs; children: Robert, Rebecca. Chancellor Purdue U. Calumet, Hammond, Ind., 1975—90. Died Apr. 8, 2007.

COMFORT, WILL LEVINGTON, writer, management consultant; b. LA, Feb. 17, 1931; s. John Duffy Comfort and Ann Theresa (Burkhardt) Winston; m. margaret Lillian Carney, Dec. 11, 1951 (div. Nov. 1985); children: Tammy Dyce, Tarin LaNice. AA, Pasadena City Coll., 1954; BS, Calif. State U., LA, 1957. Accoutantinf and office mgr. The Eldema Corp., El Monte, Calif., 1957-59; sr. accountant The Waste King Corp., LA, 1959-61; budget and cost dir. Rubber Corp. Calif., Garden Grove, 1961-64; asst. contr. Daylin Industries, Beverly Hills, Calif., 1964-65; dir. planning The Knudsen Corp., LA, 1965-69; chief fin. officer Campus Mktg. Co., Pasadena, 1969-71; v.p. fin., administrn., bus. planning The Benchmark Group, Inc., Fullerton, Calif., 1971-76; freelance mng. cons. Calif., 1976-87; freelance writer, from 1987. V.p. programs Planning Execs. Inst., L.A., 1963-64. Author, presenter numerous corp. seminars. 1978-81; contbr. articles to profl. jours. Bd. dirs. YMCA, Industry, Calif., 1977-78; trustee The Rowney Found., Santa Barbara, CAlif., 1982-85. With USN, 1948-52. Mem. Industry C. of C., Rotary. Avocations: sailing, tennis, golf, dance, swimming. Died Oct. 3, 2006.

COMMACK, WILLIAM EARL, insurance company executive; b. St. Louis, Mar. 24, 1929; s. Earl Wilfred Commack and Leona (Voigt) Messerla; m. Marietta Bartlett (dec. 1967); children: Kim Michelle, Cathy Lane; m. Alice Marie Briedenbach, Sept. 13, 1975. BS in Edn., N.E. Mo. State U., 1952. Salesman Liberty Mut. Ins. Co., St. Louis, 1954-56, dist. sales mgr., 1956-62, dist. mgr. Kansas City, Mo., 1962-69, St. Louis, 1969-76, div. sales mgr. Dallas, 1976-81, asst. v.p., asst. div. mgr., 1981-83, v.p., div. mgr., 1983-85, exec. v.p. Boston, from 1985. Bd. dirs. Liberty Ins. Corp., Delaware, 1985, Liberty Northwest, Portland, Oreg., 1987; pres. Helmsman Ltd., Boston, 1987. Cpl. USMC, 1946-48. Mem. Weston (Mass.) Country Club. Avocations: golf, fishing, gardening. Home: Dallas, Tex. Died Mar. 29, 2006.

COMPTON, JAMES RANDOLPH, real estate developer; b. Montclair, NJ, Dec. 12, 1921; s. Randolph Parker and Dorothy (Danforth) C.; m. Beverly Lucille Arnerich, May 29, 1954 (dec. Oct. 1980); children: W. Danforth, Randolph Owen, Marshal James.; m. Patricia Oakes, Sept. 11, 1982. BA, Princeton U., 1943; MBA, U. Chgo., 1948. With Minn. Mining Co., St. Paul, 1948-49, Mpls.-Honeywell Co., Mpls., 1949; personnel supr. Northwest Airlines Inc., St. Paul, 1950-51; contract adminstr. Food Machinery & Chem. Corp., San Jose, Calif., 1951-57; self-employed real estate developer San Jose, 1957—2006. Vice chmn. Danforth Found.; chmn. Santa Clara County chpt. NCCJ, 1969-70; pres. Montalvo Assn., Saratoga, Calif., 1977-83; trustee Expt. in Internat. Living; trustee Fund for Peace, chmn.; trustee Music and Arts Found. Santa Clara Valley; pres. Compton Found., 1972—2002; bd. dirs. Inst. for Med. Research of Santa Clara County, Calif. Actors Theater, 1979-82, Calif. League Conservation Voters, San Jose Mus. Art, 1987, pres., San Jose Symphony Found., San Jose Conservation Corps.; mem. No. Calif. adv. bd. United Negro Coll. Fund; mem. adv. bd. Ctr. for Def. Info.; sec. World Ctr., San Francisco; adv. bd. No. Calif. Bus. Execs. for Nat. Security. Served with USMCR, 1943-47. Recipient svc. award San Jose area Anti-Defamation League, 1974, Brotherhood award NCCJ, 1987. Episcopalian. Home: Saratoga, Calif. Died Mar. 18, 2006.

COMPTON, ROGER ELLSWORTH, clergyman; b. Dayton, Ohio, Dec. 10, 1932; s. Earl Eli and Marie (Stegman) C.; m. Sara Jo Young, Aug. 11, 1956; children: Beth Compton Neel, Lisa Compton Zimmerman, Lori Compton Smith, Eric. AB, Wheaton Coll., 1955; MDiv, No. Bapt. Theol. Sem., Oakbrook, Ill., 1958; MA, Northwestern U., Evanston, Ill., 1960; DD (hon.), Judson Coll., 1978. Ordained to ministry Bapt. Ch., 1958. Assoc. pastor Mannheim Bapt. Ch., Franklin Park, Ill., 1957-60; pastor First Bapt. Ch., Nokomis, Ill., 1960-64, Rantoul, Ill., 1964-70, sr. pastor Mattoon, Ill., 1970-79, Cen. Bapt. Ch., Springfield, Ill., from 1979. Mem. gen. bd. Am. Bapt. Chs., U.S.A., Valley Forge, Pa., 1974-79, bd. mgrs. Great Rivers region, Springfield, 1968-78, pres. Great Rivers region, 1980. Trustee Vis. Nurse Assn., Mattoon, 1970-79, Wesley Towers Retirement Ctr., Mattoon, 1974-80, Judson Coll., Elgin, Ill., 1979—, No. Bapt. Theol. Sem., 1979—; bd. dirs. Vols. in Literacy, Springfield, 1986—; commentator Sta. WCIA-TV, Champaign, Ill., 1964—, Sta. WMAY-AM-FM, Springfield, 1984—; dir. Sangamon County Sr. Citizens Commn., Springfield, 1987-89, Greater Springfield Interfaith Assn.; bd. dirs. Vols. in Literacy, 1984—. Fellow Acad. of Parish Clergy; mem. Internat. Platform Assn., Springfield C. of C., Rotary (bd. dirs. 1990). Republican. Avocations: golf, tennis, photography. Home: Surprise, Ariz. Died Nov. 14, 2005.

COMSTOCK, GEORGE WILLS, educator, epidemiologist; b. Niagara Falls, NY, Jan. 7, 1915; s. George Frederick and Ella G. (Wills) C.; m. Margaret Karr, Aug. 29, 1939 (dec. 2000); children: Gordon F., Lloyd K., Martha W. BS with honors, Antioch Coll., 1937; MD, Harvard, 1941; M.P.H., U. Mich., 1951; Dr.P.H., Johns Hopkins, 1956. Diplomate: Am. Bd. Preventive Medicine. Intern U.S. Marine Hosp., Balt., 1941-42; commd. officer USPHS, 1941-62; dir. Muscogee County Tb Study, Columbus, Ga., 1946-55; epidemiologist Tb program USPHS, 1956-62; mem. faculty Johns Hopkins Sch. Hygiene and Pub. Health, 1962—2007, prof. epidemiology, 1966—2007. Cons. Tb program USPHS, 1962—2007; disease control study sect. NIH, 1964-67; dir. Tng. Center Pub. Health Research, 1963—2007 Editor-in-chief: Am. Jour. Epidemiology, 1979—2007; author articles in field. Named to Hall of Fame Am. Lung Assn., 1980 Fellow Am. Pub. Health Assn.; mem. Am. Thoracic Soc., Am. Epidemiol. Soc., Soc. Epidemiologic Research Washington County Med. Soc., Am. Heart Assn. (fellow council on epidemiology) Died July 15, 2007.

CONARD, JOHN JOSEPH, finance company executive; b. Coolidge, Kans., June 30, 1921; s. Joseph Harvey and Jessie May (Shanstrom) C.; m. Virginia Louise Powell, Sept. 13, 1947; children— Joseph Harvey II (dec.), James Powell, Spencer Dean, John Joseph. BA, U. Kans., 1943, MA, 1947; D Internat. Law, U. Paris, 1951. Instr. polit. sci. U. Kans., 1946-49, asst. to chancellor, 1970-75; spl. asst. U.S. Mut. Security Agy., Paris, France, 1951-54; editor, pub. Kiowa County Signal, Greensburg, Kans., 1955-70; exec. officer bd. regents State of Kans., Topeka, 1976-82; pres. Higher Edn. Loan Program of Kans., Inc., Overland Park, Kans., 1982-86; v.p. Higher Edn. Assistance Found., 1982-86; legis. liaison Gov. of Kansas, 1987-88. Dir. Haviland (Kans.) State Bank. Mem. Kans. Ho. of Reps., 1959-69; mem. State Fin. Council, 1961-69; speaker of House, 1967-69; exec. asst. to Gov. Kans., 1975-76; trustee William Allen White Found., 1959—. Served to ensign USNR, 1943-45. Summerfield scholar, 1939-42; Rotary Found. fellow, 1949-50 Mem. VFW, Rotary, Am. Legion, Phi Beta Kappa, Sigma Delta Chi, Pi Sigma Alpha, Tau Kappa Epsilon. Republican. Methodist. Home: Lawrence, Kans. Died Oct. 12, 2007.

CONGER, JOHN JANEWAY, psychologist, educator; b. New Brunswick, NJ, Feb. 27, 1921; s. John C. and Katharine (Janeway) Conger; m. Mayo Trist Kline, Jan. 1, 1944; children: Steven Janeway, David Trist. BA magna cum laude, Amherst Coll., 1943; MS, Yale U., 1947, PhD, 1949; DSc (hon.), Ohio U., 1981, Amherst Coll., 1983, U. Colo., 1989. Asst. prof. psychology Ind. U., 1949—53; chief staff psychologist U.S. Naval Acad., 1951—52; mem. faculty U. Colo. Sch. Medicine, prof. psychology, 1957—88, assoc. dean, 1961—63, v.p. for med. affairs, 1963—70, dean, 1963—68, acting chmn. dept. psychiatry, 1983—84, acting chancellor, 1985—86, prof. emeritus, from 1988. V.p., dir. health program John D. and Catherine T. MacArthur Found., 1980—83, cons., 1983—85, NIH, VA, USPHS; vice chmn. Colo. Bd. Psychology Examiners, 1961—64; mem. Gov. Colo. Com. Mental Health, 1957; chmn. mental health adv. coun. Colo. Dept. Pub. Health, 1957—61; mem. tng. com. Nat. Inst. Mental Health, 1959—62; mem. Western coun. mental health rsch. & tng. Western Interstate Commn. Higher Edn., 1959—66; chmn. rsch. com. Pres.'s Com. Traffic Safety, 1960—63; vice chmn. nat. motor vehicle safety adv. coun. Dept. Transp., 1967—70; mem. inter-coun. com. constrn. univ.-affiliated facilities for mentally retarded Dept. Health, Edn. and Welfare, 1967—70, mem. sec.'s adv. com. traffic safety, 1966—69; coun. rsch. and planning Am. Hosp. Assn., 1965—68; nat. adv. mental health coun. USPHS, 1965—69; nat. adv. com. John F. Kennedy Ctr. Rsch. on Edn. and Human Devel., 1965—76, chmn., 1970—74; mem. adv. com. on undergrad. med. edn. AMA, 1969—70; adv. com. on casualty ins. Dept. Transp., 1970; mem. Pres.'s Task Force on Hwy. Safety, 1970, Pres.'s Commn. on Mental Health, 1977—78; mem. com. study nat. needs for biomed. and behavioral sci. rsch. personnel Nat. Acad. Scis., 1976—80; mem. Inst. Medicine/Nat. Acad. Scis., from 1983; bd. mental health and behavioral medicine, 1986—92; vis. scholar Inst. Human Devel. U. Calif., Berkeley, 1978. Author: Child Development and Personality, 7th edit., 1990, Readings in Child Development, 3d edit., 1984, Personality, Social Class and Delinquency, 1965, Adolescence and Youth: Psychological Development in a Changing World, 5th edit., 1997, The Shape of the Tree: Selected Poems, 1993, Basic and Contemporary Issues in Developmental Psychology, 1975, Contemporary Issues in Adolescent Development, 1975, Psychological Development: A Life-Span Approach, 1979, Essentials of Child Development and Personality, 1980; contbr. articles to profl. jours.; Applied and Preventive Psychology, from 1991. Lt. USNR, 1944—46, lt. USNR, 1951—52. Recipient Stearns Alumni medal for extraordinary svc., U. Colo., 1970, U. Colo. medal, 1986, disting. profl. achievement award, Am. Bd. Profl. Psychology, 1979; fellow, Ctr. Advanced Study in Behavioral Scis., Stanford, Calif., 1970—71; vis. scholar, Inst. Human Devel., U. Calif., Berkeley, 1978. Fellow: AAAS, APA (mem. policy and planning bd. 1967—70, rec. sec., dir. 1974—79, pres. 1980—82, award for disting. contbns. psychology in pub. interest 1986), Soc. Rsch. in Child Devel. (program chmn. 1975, fin. com. 1989—93, Disting. Contbns. to Pub. Policy for Children award 1995); mem.: Colo. Med. Soc. (Disting. Svc. award 1970), Colo. Psychol. Assn. (pres. 1959), Denver Med. Soc. (hon.), Am. Psychol. Found. (bd. dirs. 1982—86, pres. 1985—86), Sigma Xi, Phi Beta Kappa, Alpha Omega Alpha (hon.). Home: Denver, Colo. Died June 24, 2006.

CONKLE, GALEN EUGENE, accountant, corporate director; b. Clark, Ohio, Feb. 26, 1933; s. Maynard S. and Mary (Parks) C.; B.S. in Accounting, Sacramento State Coll., 1959; m. Lureen A. Edgar, Apr. 27, 1962; children— Galen John, Ramona Jean, Rebecca Lureen. Prin., Galen E. Conkle, C.P.A., Oceanside, Calif., 1963-66; ptnr. Conkle, Sigrist & Co., C.P.A.'s, Oceanside, Calif., from 1966; later ptnr. Reschly & Conkle, C.P.A.s, Escondido; prin. Galen E. Conkle, C.P.A. Escondido, Calif.; now corp. dir.; instr. accounting and fed. income taxes Palomar Coll., San Marcos, Cal., 1964-68, 75-79. Served with USNR, 1951-55. Mem. Calif. Soc. C.P.A.'s. Republican. Died Aug. 6, 2006.

CONLEY, DARLENE ANN, actress; b. Chgo. d. Raymond and Melba (Manthey) C.; m. William Woodson, Oct. 1959 (div. 1966); 1 child, Raymond; m. Kurt Hensch, 1970 (div. 1980) Actress Broadway prodns. including: The Baker's Wife, The Night of the Iguana Actress (films): The Birds, 1963, Valley of the Dolls, 1967, Faces, 1968, Captain Milkshake, 1970, Minnie and Moskowitz, 1971, Lady Sings the Blues, 1972, Play It As It Lays, 1972, Gentle Savage, 1973, Tough Guys, 1986; (TV movies) The President's Plane Is Missing, 1973, Get Christie Love!, 1974, Return Engagement, 1978, (voice only) The Stingiest Man in Town, 1978, Rudolph and Frosty's Christmas in July, 1979, The Choice, 1981, The Nashville Grab, 1981, The Fighter, 1983, I Want to Live, 1983; (TV appearances) Ironside, 1970, The Name of the Game, 1970, The Bill Cosby Show, 1970, Gunsmoke, 1970, Longstreet, 1971, Ghost Story, 1972, Mary Tyler Moore Show, 1974, The Jeffersons, 1979, Little House on the Prarie, 1981, Cagney & Lacey, 1983, Murder, She Wrote, 1985, Scarecrow and Mrs. King, 1987, Highway to Heaven, 1987; (TV mini-series) Robert Kennedy & His Times, 1985; (TV series) The Young and The Restless, 1979-80, 86-87, 2000, General Hospital, 1984, Capitol, 1984, The Bold and The Beautiful, 1988-2006. Emmy nominee for Outstanding Supporting Actress, 1991, 92; statue made for Madame Tussaud's Wax Mus., 1998. Home: Los Angeles, Calif. Died Jan. 14, 2007.

CONLEY, JAMES EDWARD, retired surgeon; b. Harrisville, RI, Aug. 10, 1913; s. Edward James and Emily Rachel (Davies) C.; m. Lillian Brandt Quirk, Sept. 16, 1941; children: Emily, James, Robert, Bruce, Ellen, William, Katherine. BS cum laude, Providence Coll., 1935; MD cum laude, Harvard U., 1939. Diplomate Am. Bd. Surgery. Intern, then resident Mass. Gen. Hosp., Boston, 1939-43; practice gen. and vascular surgery Milw., 1946-85; mem. staff Columbia Hosp., County Gen. Hosp.; prof. surgery Med. Coll Wis., 1946-85. Mem. editorial adv. bd.: Cancer Bull. Cancer Program, 1957-62; contbr. articles to profl. jours. Pres. Quirk Found., 1968—; v.p. Florentine Opera Assn., 1971. Served with USNR, 1943-46. Decorated Bronze Star (2); Recipient Disting. Service award Am. Cancer Soc., 1966 Fellow A.C.S.; mem. Internat. Cardiovascular Soc., Soc. Vascular Surgery, Midwestern Vascular Surgery Soc. (founder mem.), Central Surg. Assn., Milw. Surg. Soc. (pres. 1966-67), Milw. Acad. Medicine (pres. 1959-60), Royal Soc. Medicine. Clubs: Univ. (Milw.). Home: Milwaukee, Wis. Died Feb. 7, 2006.

CONN, DAVID PATRICK, lawyer, former prosecutor; b. NYC, 1950; m. Rosemary Conn; children: Jessica, Danielle. Grad., Hunter Coll.; JD, Columbia U. Bar: Calif. 1978. Dep. dist. atty. City of LA, 1978—97; ptnr. Jeffer, Mangels, Butler & Marmaro LLP, Century City, Calif., 1997—2001; pvt. practice LA, 2001—06. Served in USMC. Achievements include successfully prosecuting Lyle and Erik Menendez for the murders of their parents, 1997. Died Oct. 24, 2006.

CONNELLY, LEWIS BRANCH SUTTON, lawyer; b. St. Louis, Sept. 17, 1950; s. Lewis Branch and Mary Ellen (Henneberger) C.; m. Anna Kristina Cook, Oct. 15, 1977; children: Christopher Sutton, Jeffrey Scott, Sarah Elizabeth. BA, Vanderbilt U., 1972; JD, U. Tenn., 1977. Bar: Ga. 1977. Mem. Smith, Cohen, Ringel, Kohler & Martin, Atlanta, 1977-79, Cook & Connelly, Summerville, Ga., from 1979. City atty. Summerville, 1989-99; mem. magistrate selection com. U.S. Dist. Ct. for no. dist.) Ga., 1990; atty. sch. bd. Chattooga County Schs., 1989-96. Mem. staff Tenn. Law Rev., 1975-77. Mem. ABA (complex crime com. litigation sect. 1982—), consumer affairs com. corp. banking sect. 1982—), ATLA, NACDL, Ga. Assn. Trial Lawyers, Ga. Assn. Criminal Def. Lawyers. Home: Cloudland, Ga. Died Feb. 26, 2007.

CONNER, JOHN DAVIS, lawyer; b. Seminary Hill, Tex., Feb. 24, 1911; s. Walter Thomas and Blanche Ethel (Horne) C.; m. Carolyn Rose Hyatt, Nov. 17, 1934; children: Rose Mary, Jenny Lu, John Davis, Walter Thomas. AB, Baylor U., 1933; LLB, George Washington U., 1938. Bar: D.C. 1938. Ptnr. McKenna, Conner & Cuneo, Washington, from 1938. Author: Compilation of Economic Poisons Laws and Regulations, Manual of Chemical Products Liability, Product Liability Trends, Lawyers Handbook, others. Lt. USNR, 1943-46. Fellow Am. Bar Found.; mem. ABA (chmn. com. econs. law practice 1959-65), Am. Judicature Soc. (bd. dirs. 1967-70), D.C. Bar Assn. (chmn. adminstrv. law 1956-67, bd. dirs. 1957-58), Metropolitan Club, University Club (Washington), Belle Haven Country Club (Alexandria, Va.). Baptist. Home: Alexandria, Va. Died Dec. 18, 2006.

CONRAD, PAUL, mathematics educator; b. NY, Oct. 7, 1921; married; 1 child. PhD in Math., U. Ill., 1951. From asst. prof. to prof. math. Newcomb Coll., Tulane U., 1951-70; prof. math. U. Kans., from 1970, now Henry J. Bischoff Disting. prof. math. NSF sr. fellow Australian Nat. U., 1964-65; vis. prof. U. Paris, 1967. Fulbright lectr. U. Ceylon, 1956-57. Mem. Am. Math. Soc. Research in ordered algebraic systems, group theory. Died July 25, 2006.

CONWAY, CASEY ANTHONY, health and safety manager; b. Portland, Oreg., Mar. 11, 1953; s. James William and Wanna Donna (Caspers) C. AA, Orange Coast Coll., 1974; BA in Bus. Adminstrn., Calif. State U.-Fullerton, 1976; MS in Safety, U. So. Calif., 1978. Cert. instr./trainer in surface/underground mine safety, mine foreman surface uranuim, safety profl.; registered environ. assessor Calif. EPA; lic. amateur radio operator (extra class). Safety and environ. technician energy mining div. Union Oil Co. Calif., 1979, Rawlins, Wyo., safety trainer, 1979-80, safety supr., 1980-82, regulatory compliance coord. oil shale ops., Parachute, Colo., 1983-85; safety supr. UNOCAL L.A. Refinery, Wilmington, Calif., 1986; mgr. regulatory compliance, refining and mktg. div. UNOCAL, L.A., 1986-89, mgr. health and safety compliance Refining Dept., 1989-91; sr. advisor health and safety compliance Unocal 76 Products Co., 1992—, speaker and writer in field; vol. examiner FCC amateur radio lics. profl. Mem. Am. Soc. Safety Engrs. (membership chmn. Wyo. chpt. 1981-82, Wyo. safety congress com. 1982, sec. 1982-83, Western Slope chmn. 1983-86, assembly del. Orange Coast chpt. 1990-94, v.p., 1992-94, pres. 1994-95, nat. govt. affairs com. 1991—, Culbertson Outstanding Vol. Svc. award), Calif. Mfrs. Assn. (chmn. safety and health com. 1989-92), Nat. Petroleum Refiners Assn. (fire and safety com., chmn. regulatory issues group), Orgn. Resource Counselors, Western Occupational Safety Health Steering Com., Am. Indsl. Hygiene Assn., Nat. Fire Protection Assn., Am. Radio Relay League (life, asst. dir. SW div. 1986-88) Soc. Advancement Mgmt. (Outstanding mem. 1975; v.p. membership 1976), Carbon County Amateur Radio Assn. (pres. 1980), Grand Mesa Contesters (sec.-treas. 1985), Southern Calif. DX Club, Univ. So. Calif. Inst. Safety and Systems Mgmt. Alumni Assn. (bd. dirs. 1990-91), So. Calif. Contest, Cactus Radio, Orange County Trojan Club (bd. dirs. 1988—, pres. 1991-93). Roman Catholic. Lodge: Elks. Home: Newport Beach, Calif. Died Feb. 23, 2006.

CONWAY, HARRY DONALD, engineering mechanics educator; b. Chatham, Eng., Dec. 3, 1917; came to U.S., 1947, naturalized, 1956; s. John and Ada Frances (Young) C.; m. Dorothy Daphne Adams, Aug. 24, 1946 (dec. 1976); children—Geoffrey, Peter. BSc, London U., 1942, PhD, 1945, DSc, 1949; MA, Cambridge U., Eng., 1946, ScD, 1972. Sci. officer, research on high temperature properties of metals Nat. Phys. Lab., Teddington, Eng., 1942-45; univ. demonstrator engring. Cambridge (Eng.) U. and asst. dir. studies St. Catharine's Coll., 1946-47; asso. prof. engring. mechanics Cornell U., Ithaca, N.Y., 1947-48, prof. engring. mechanics, 1948-88, prof. emeritus, from 1989. Author: Aircraft Strength of Materials, 1947, Mechanics of Materials, 1950; Contbr. articles on theoretical analyses of plates and shells, elastic vibrations, lubrication, electronic packaging and contact lenses to profl. jours. John Simon Guggenheim fellow and vis. prof. Imperial Coll., London U., 1953-54; NSF sr. postdoctoral fellow, 1961-62; Julius F. Stone vis. prof. Ohio State U., 1958-59; Sir Joseph Whitworth scholar, 1941; Sir John Johnson scholar London U., 1941 Died May 31, 2007.

COOK, CLARENCE EDGAR, science administrator, consultant; b. Jefferson City, Tenn., Apr. 27, 1936; s. Edgar Marion and Lillie Grey (Hodge) C.; m. Gail O'Connor McKee, June 1, 1957; children— David Grey, Lisa O'Connor Priebe, Kevin McKee. BS, Carson-Newman Coll., 1957; PhD, U. N.C., 1961; postdoctoral, U. Cambridge, Eng., 1961. Chemist, sr. chemist Rsch. Triangle Inst., Research Triangle Park, NC, 1962-68, group leader, 1968-71, asst. dir. chem. life sci., 1971-75, dir. life sci. bioorganic chemistry, 1975-80, dir. bioorganic chemistry, 1980-85, research v.p., 1983-96, chief scientist, 1996—2004; ret., 2004. Adj. prof. Sch. Pharmacy, U. N.C., Chapel Hill, 1985-96. Mem. editorial adv. bd. Drug Metabolism and Disposition, 1977-93; mem. editl. bd. Emerging Drugs: The Prospect for Improved Medicines, 1999-2003; contbr. articles to profl. jours., chpts. to books; patentee in field. Recipient Margaret Elliott Knox Excellence award, 2003. Fellow N.Y. Acad. Scis.; mem. AAAS, Am. Chem. Soc., Am. Soc. Pharmacology and Exptl. Therapeutics, Coll. on Problems of Drug Dependence, Nat. Inst. on Drug Abuse (biomed. rsch. rev. com. 1985-89). Avocation: gardening. Home: Staunton, Va. Died Nov. 30, 2006.

COOK, JAMES IVAN, clergyman, educator; b. Grand Rapids, Mich., Mar. 8, 1925; s. Cornelius Peter and Cornelia (Dornbos) C.; m. Jean Rivenburgh, July 8, 1950; children: Mark James, Carol Jean, Timothy Scott, Paul Brian (dec.). BA, Hope Coll., 1948; MA, Mich. State U., 1949; BD, Western Theol. Sem., 1952; ThD, Princeton Theol. Sem., 1964. Ordained to ministry Reformed Ch. America, 1953. Pastor Blawenburg Reformed Ch., NJ, 1953-63; from instr. to asst. prof. bibl. langs. Western Theol. Sem., Holland, Mich., 1963-67, prof. bibl. langs. and lit., 1967-77, Anton Biemont prof. New Testament, 1977-95, prof. emeritus, from 1995; chmn. Theol. Commn., Reformed Ch. Am. N.Y.C., 1980-85; pres. Gen. Synod-Reformed Ch. Am., NYC, 1982-83. Author: Edgar Johnson Goodspeed, 1981, Shared Pain and Sorrow: Reflections of a Secondary Sufferer, 1991, One Lord/One Body, 1991; editor Reformed Rev., 1987-2002; contbg. editor: Grace Upon Grace, 1975, Saved by Hope, 1978, The Church Speaks, 1985; founding editor Perspectives: A Jour. of Reformed Thought, 1986-90, The Church Speaks, vol. 2, 2002. Served with U.S. Army, 1943-45, ETO. Recipient Disting. Alumni award, Hope Coll., 1985, Western Theol. Sem., 2004. Home: Holland, Mich. Died May 1, 2007.

COOK, THOMAS G., automotive parts executive; b. Washington Island, Wis., Apr. 4, 1927; s. Thomas and Caroline (Swenson) Cook; m. Beverley Ellen Foss, July 12, 1950; children: Gary, Debbie, Greg, Brian. BBA, U. Wis., 1950; grad. Advanced Mgmt. program, Harvard Bus. Sch., 1968. Auditor Lybrand, Ross Bros. & Montgomery, Chgo., 1950—57; supr. gen. acctg. corp. contr., treas. Walker Mfg. Co. div. Tenneco, Inc., Racine, Wis., 1957—68, pres., 1968—77; pres. automotive divsn. Tenneco, Inc., Deerfield, Ill., 1977—79, chmn., chief exec. officer, from 1979. With USNR, 1946—47. Mem.: Motor and Equipment Mfrs. Assn. Died Mar. 12, 2007.

COOK, TIMOTHY EDWIN, political science professor; b. Van Nuys, Calif., Aug. 16, 1954; s. Thomas Edwin and Audrey Eloise (Jackson) C. BA, Pomona Coll., 1976; PhD, U. Wis., 1982. Asst. prof. Williams Coll., Williamstown, Mass., 1981-88, assoc. prof., 1988-92, prof., 1992—94, chair dept. polit. sci., 1991-94, Fairleigh Dickinson Jr. prof., 1994—2002. Guest scholar Brookings Instn., Washington, 1984-85; vis. assoc. prof. in the Lombard chair Kennedy Sch. Govt., Harvard U., Cambridge, Mass., 1989-90; vis. prof. Yale U., New Haven, spring 1995, prof. mass comm. and polit. sci. Kevin P. Reilly, Sr. chair, Manship Sch. of Mass Comm., La. State Univ., 2002-. Author: Making Laws and Making News, 1989 (Benjamin Franklin award Am. Book Seller's Assn. 1990), Citizen, Candidate and the Media in a Presdl. Campaign, 1996, Don Eraber award, Am. Polit. Sci. Assn., 2003, Governing With The News, 1998. Grantee NSF, 1991. Mem. Am. Polit. Sci. Assn. (exec. coun., Congl. fellowship 1984-85), Lesbian and Gay Polit. Sci. Caucus (founding mem.). Avocation: classical music. Home: Baton Rouge, La. Died Aug. 5, 2006.

COOKE, BETTE LOUISE, retired library director; b. Emporia, Kans., Oct. 26, 1929; d. Oscar Oliver and Ada Luella (Williams) C. Student, Grinnell Coll., Iowa, 1947-49; BS in Edn., U. Mo., 1951; MA in Libr. Sci., Vanderbilt U., 1964; EdD, Ind. U., 1971. Tchr. pub. schs., Mo. & ILl., 1951-63; instr. in libr. sci. N.E. Mo. State U., Kirksville, 1964-66; asst. prof. libr. sci. Western Ill. U., Macomb, 1966-72; assoc. prof., chair dept. libr. sci. and instructional tech. Cen. Mo. State U., Warrenburg, 1972-80; prof. libr. sci., dir. libr. St. Mary of the Plains Coll., Dodge City, 1983—92; ret., 1994. Cons. sch. librs., Ill. and Mo., 1971-79; judge S.W. Kans. Project Fair Project, Dodge City, 1987—; grant evaluator Nat. Endowment for the Humanites, 1979; chair Dodge City Libr. Consortium, Dodge City, 1985. Mem. Dodge City Friends of Pub. Libr., 1987—; bd. dirs. Homeowners Assn., Dodge City, 1989k—. Ind. U. scholar, 1971; NEH/ACRL grantee, 1987. Mem. ALA, Kans. Libr. Assn., Kans. Coll. and Rsch. Librs. (program com.), Kans. Pvt. Acad. Librs., AAUW. Republican. Presbyterian. Avocations: gardening, health foods, health activities. Home: Monett, Mo. Died Aug. 17, 2006.

COOKE, JOSEPH PETER, retired construction executive; b. Balt., Feb. 3, 1947; s. Joseph Peter and Phyllis Agnes (Bowinklemen) C.; m. Dawn Lee Klinger, Sept. 22; children: Jason, Brian, Kevin. AA, Community Coll. Balt., 1972; BS in Bus. Mgmt., U. Balt., 1975. Asst. supt. So. Engring., 1967-68; finish supt. Thomas P. Harkins Inc., Silver Spring, Md., 1968-71, site mgr., 1971-73, project mgr., 1973-78, div. mgr., 1978-80, v.p. constrn., 1980-82, exec. v.p., 1982-84, pres., COO, 1984-93, owner, CEO, 1993—2002. Founding pres. Craftmasters Inc., Landover Hills, Md., 1985-86; bd. dirs. Harbor Bank of Md., Balt. Bd. dirs. St. Louis Ch., Clarksville, Md., Prince Georges (Md.) C.C., 1988-90; bd. dirs. Balt. Housing Partnership, 1985-90; bd. dirs. Associated Cath. Charities, 1988-89, Archdioces of Balt. (mem. adv. commn. on sports.), fund devel. com., chmn. Archbishop's Lenten appeal spl. gifts, 1994; chmn. Gov's Contrn. Industry Employer's Adv. Council, Chesapeake Bay Agreement 20/20 Panel of Experts, 1989; trustee Howard County Hosp. With U.S. Army, 1966-68. Mem. Associated Builders and Contractors (chmn., pres. 1984-85), Nat. Housing and Rehab. Assn. (pres. 1987, 88), Cattail Creek Country Club (bd. dirs.). Democrat. Roman Catholic. Avocations: golf, tennis, skiing. Home: Glenwood, Md. Died Oct. 2, 2007.

COOKE, KENNETH LLOYD, mathematician, educator; b. Kansas City, Mo., Aug. 13, 1925; s. Sidney Kenneth and Mildred Blanche (Brown) C.; m. Margaret Sarah Burgess, Aug. 18, 1950; children: Catherine Sarah, Robert K., Susan E. BA, Pomona Coll., 1947; MS, Stanford, 1949, PhD, 1952. Instr., then asst. prof. math. State Coll. Wash., Pullman, 1950-57; mem. faculty Pomona Coll., 1957-93, Joseph N. Fiske prof. math., 1963—2007, chmn. dept., 1961-71, W.B. Keck disting. service prof., 1985-93. Cons. RAND Corp., 1956-65; mathematician Rsch. Inst. Advanced Studies, Balt., 1963-64; NSF sci. faculty fellow Stanford, 1966-67; Fulbright rsch. scholar U. Florence, Italy, 1971-72; vis. prof. Brown U., 1978-79, Inst. Math. Applications, U. Minn., 1983, Cornell U., 1987; Fulbright lectr. U. São Paulo, São Carlos, Brazil, 1987. Author: (with Richard Bellman) Differential-Difference Equations, 1963, Modern Elementary Differential Equations, 2d edit., 1971, (with Richard Bellman and J.A. Lockett) Algorithms, Graphs and Computers, 1970, (with Donald Bentley) Linear Algebra with Differential Equations, 1973, (with Colin Renfrew) Transformations: Mathematical Approaches to Culture Change, 1979, (with Stavros Busenberg) Vertically Transmitted Diseases, 1993; co-editor: Differential Equations and Applications in Ecology, Epidemics, and Population Problems, 1981, Differential Equations and Applications to Biology and to Industry, 1995. Served with USNR, 1944-46. Mem.: AAAS, Soc. Math. Biology, Soc. Indsl. and Applied Math., Math. Assn. Am., Am. Math. Soc., Sigma Xi, Phi Beta Kappa. Mem. United Ch. Christ. Home: Claremont, Calif. Died Aug. 25, 2007.

COOKE, ROBERT JOHN, history and law educator; b. Kingston, NY, Apr. 12, 1923; s. Harry and Anna (Hyland) C.; children: Kathleen Anne, Christian Seán, Kevin Michâel, Deirdre Gobnait, Brian Patrick, Siobhán Brighid. BS in Social Sci., SUNY, 1949; A.M. in History, Columbia U., 1950; PhD in Am. Studies, Maxwell Grad. Sch. Pub. Affairs, Syracuse U., 1964. Asst. in Am. civilization Columbia U., 1949-50; tchr. social studies and English Goshen (N.Y.) High Sch., 1950-54; staff Citizens Edn. Project, Carnegie Found., 1950-54; asst. prof. social sci. Ball State U., Muncie, Ind., 1954-59; instr. Am. studies Maxwell Grad. Sch. Pub. Affairs, Syracuse U., 1960-65, dir. Chautauqua Ctr., 1960-62; assoc. Inter-Univ. Project I, Ford Found., 1962-65; prof. Am. studies and history Southampton Coll., L.I. U., 1965-83, prof. emeritus, from 1983, chmn. history dept., 1966-70, 73-83, chmn. Am. studies program, 1968-83, dir. humanities div., 1970-73, chmn. exec. com. faculty council, 1977-79, dir. pre-law program, 1975-83. Vis. lectr. Trinity Coll., Dublin, Ireland, 1974 Contbr. articles to profl. jours. and books, miscellaneous rsch. reports, essays. Mem. legis. affairs com. N.Y. State Democratic Com., 1973-75. Served to lt. USMC(Air), 1942-46, PTO. Mem. Am. Hist. Assn., Am. Studies Assn. (chmn. and editor bibliography com. 1964-65), Nat. Coun. for Social Studies (book rev. editor jour. 1964-68, chmn. standing com. on rsch., 1961-63, bd. dirs. 1966-69), Am.-Irish Hist. Soc., Am. Com. for Irish Studies, Irish Nat. Caucus, Orgn. Am. Historians, Sinn Féin (provo). Home: Westhampton, NY. Died Feb. 25, 2007.

COON, ARNOLD WILDING, cons. engr.; b. Salt Lake City, Sept. 24, 1925; s. Chester Nelson and Clara Cornelia (Wilding) C.; S.B., U. Idaho, 1943; B.S. in Civil Engring., U. Utah, 1949; m. Arlene Elenor Pesina, July 8, 1947; children— Steven, Deborah, Gregory, Gary, Lori, Mark, Heidi. Asst. project engr. Utah Constrn. Co., Lark, 1949; structural engr. H.C. Hughes Co., Salt Lake City, 1950-54; self-employed, Salt Lake City, 1955-56; cons. engr., partner Coon & King, engrs., Salt Lake City, 1956-62; cons. engr., chmn. bd. Coon, King & Knowlton Engrs., Salt Lake City, 1962-82; owner Arnold W. Coon, forensic engrs., Salt Lake City, 1982—. Dist. chmn. Republican Party; del. county and state Reps. cons. Recipient Distinguished Civil Engring. Alumnus award U. Utah, 1975. Mem. Utah Council Land Surveyors (pres. 1969-70), Cons. Engrs. Council Utah (pres. 1959; Excellence in Engring. Design award 1975), Am. Cons. Engrs. Council (dir. 1964-65), Am. Concrete Inst. Mormon. Club: Star Valley Country. Home: Salt Lake City, Utah. Died May 31, 2007.

COON, CHARLES EDWARD, construction company executive; b. Muskogee, Okla., Feb. 9, 1933; s. Claude O. and Virginia Ann (Martin) C.; m. Betty Ann Brown, Apr. 4, 1953; children: Charles E. Jr., Stephen D., Lisa A. Coon McPhee. BA in Bus., Wichita State U., 1970. Treas. Instant Auto Glass, Inc., Wichita, Kans., 1957-61; exec. v.p. Martin K. Eby Constrn. Co., Inc., Wichita, from 1961. Staff sgt. USAF, 1953-56. Fellow Constrn. Fin. Mgmt. Assn. (pres. greater Wichita chpt.), Inst. Mgmt. Accts. (bd. dirs. 1972-73). Home: Wichita, Kans. Died Mar. 4, 2006.

COOPER, CLEMENT THEODORE, lawyer; b. Miami, Fla., Oct. 26, 1930; s. Benjamin Leon and Louise (Bethel) Cooper; m. Nan Coles; children: Patricia, Karen, Stephanie, Bridgette, Jessica(dec.), Stacy. AB, Lincoln U., 1952; student, Boston U., 1954-55; JD, Howard U., 1958; PhD in Bus. Adminstrn. (hon.), Colo. Christian Coll., 1973. Bar: DC 1960, Mich. 1960, U.S. Ct. Appeals (3d, 4th, 6th, 9th and 10th cirs.), U.S. Ct. Mil. Appeals, U.S. Ct. Claims, U.S. Supreme Ct. 1963. Pvt. practice, Washington, 1960—2007. Adj. prof. Strayer U., Washington, 1991—98; former legal cons. No. Calif. Mining Assn.; arbitrator N.Y. Stock Exch.; mem., arbitrator NASD. Author: The Sealed Verdict, 1964; contbr. articles to profl. jours. Adv. coun. DC Dept. Welfare, 1963—66; adv. bd. Com. Irish Ethnicity, NYC. Served in US Army, 1952—54, Korean War. Mem.: ACLU, ATLA, ABA, Am. Judicature Soc., Nat. Bar Assn., DC Bar Assn., Internat. Platform Assn., Rocky Mountain Mining Law Found., Oxford Club, KT (Knights fellow), Am. Legion, Soc King Charles Martyr, Alpha Phi Alpha (life). Episcopalian. Died Apr. 16, 2007.

COOPER, FRANK EVANS, banker; b. Seattle, Nov. 28, 1928; s. Frank Homer and Marguerite Caroline (Madison) C.; m Erlene Rose Johnson, June 30, 1951; children: Dawn Rene Frank Evans. BBA, U. Wash., 1950; MBA, Pacific Coast Grad Sch. Banking, 1958-61. Br. mgr. Comml. Credit Corp., Eugene Oreg., 1951-58; v.p. Puget Sound Nat. Bank, Tacoma, 1958-64 pres., chief exec. officer, dir. Bank of Tacoma, 1965-68; supr banking State of Wash., Olympia, 1968-70; sr. v.p. Bank of Hawaii, Honolulu, 1970-72; pres., chief exec. officer, dir. Bank Honolulu, 1972-76; owner Frank Cooper & Assos., 1976-80, pres., chief exec. officer Equitable Savs. & Loan, Huntingtor

Beach, Calif., from 1980. Dir. Security & Gen. Bank, Ltd., Vila, New Hebrides, World Finance, Honolulu, Guardian Finance, Honolulu, Mahalo Acceptance, Honolulu, Hula Records, Ltd., Honolulu, Keehi Drydock Corp., Honolulu; internat. fin. and mgmt. cons. Chmn. Western States Commrs. Banking, 1970; dir. Nat. Assn. Bank Commrs., 1970 Mem. bd. Tacoma Community Coll., 1967-69; mem. adv. bd. Nat. Consumer Finance Assn., 1969; Del. Wash. Rep. Convs., 1958-68; precinct committeeman, Tacoma, 1950-69; del. Rep. Nat. Conv., 1964, 68; mem. Wash. Ho. of Reps., 1963-64; chmn. Hawaii Rep. Com., 1978-80; bd. dirs. Jessie Dslyn Boys' Ranch, Tacoma, Mary Bridge Children's Hosp.; trustee Annie Wright Girls' Acad., U. Wash. Grad. Sch. Banking. Mem. C. of C. Hawaii (chmn. visitor industry com.), Hawaii Bankers Assn. (exec. com.), Navy League, Sales and Mktg. Execs. Honolulu. Clubs: Oahu Country (Hawaii), Outrigger Canoe (Hawaii), Honolulu Press (Hawaii), Plaza (Hawaii), Univ. Union (Hawaii) (pres.), Pacific (Hawaii), Waikiki Yacht (Hawaii); Masons, Shriners, Jesters, Elks, Rotary, Lions. Home: Huntington Bh, Calif. Died Aug. 15, 2006.

COOPER, JANE MARVEL, poet; b. Atlantic City, Oct. 9, 1924; d. John Cobb and Martha (Marvel) C. Student, Vassar Coll., 1942-44; BA, U. Wis., 1946; MA, U. Iowa, 1954. Faculty mem., poet-in-residence Sarah Lawrence Coll., Bronxville, N.Y., 1950-87. Author: The Weather of Six Mornings (Lamont award 1968), 1969, Maps and Windows, 1974, Scaffolding: Selected Poems (Maurice English award 1985), 1984, Green Notebook, Winter Road, 1994 The Flashboat: Poems Collected and Reclaimed, 2000. Grantee Nat. Endowment for Arts, 1981-82, Ingram Merrill Found, 1971-72; Guggenheim Found. fellow, 1960-61, Bunting Inst., 1988-89; recipient award in literature AAAL, 1995; named State Poet of N.Y., 1996-97. Mem. PEN, Poets House, Poetry Soc. Am. (Shelley award 1978). Democrat. Home: Newtown, Pa. Died Oct. 26, 2007.*

COOPER, KENNETH BANKS, business executive, former army officer, retired military officer; b. Ft. Leavenworth, Kans., Nov. 12, 1923; s. Avery John and Ona Carey (Gibson) C.; m. Virginia Leah Adkins, Dec. 29, 1979; children by previous marriage: Kenneth, Robert. BS, U.S. Mil. Acad., 1944; MS, MIT, 1951. Commd. 2nd lt. U.S. Army, 1944; advanced through grades to lt. gen., 1975; assigned to Manhattan Project-Armed Forces Spl. Weapon Project, N.Mex., Eniwetok, and Washington, 1946-48; mem. nuclear weapons staff AEC, Washington, 1951-55; nuclear weapons planning officer SHAPE, Paris, 1955-58; project mgr., ballistic missile def. rsch. Advanced Rsch. Projects Agy., Washington, 1959-63; bn. comdr. Korea, 1963-64; dir. Army Nuclear Power Program, 1965-66; with Def. Com. Planning Group, 1966-68; exec. to Sec. of Army, 1968-70; brigade comdr. Vietnam, 1970-71; dep. dir. civil works Office Chief of Engrs., Washington, 1971-72, asst. chief engrs., 1972-75; dep. comdr.-in-chief U.S. Army, Europe, Heidelberg, Germany, 1975-77; dep. adviser to sec. US Dept. Def., 1977-78; ret., 1978; gen. mgr. Svc. and Constrn. Group ITT, Nutley, N.J., 1978-79; dep. asst. sec. def. for plans and resources Office Asst. Sec. Def. C3I, Washington, 1980-81; pres. SPC Internat., Arlington, Va., 1981-84; cons. BMD (Ballistic Missile Def., formerly SDI), Alexandria, Va., 1985-88, Inst. Def. Analysis, 1988-99. Served in US Army, South Pacific, World War II. Decorated Legion of Merit (2), D.S.M. (2), D.D.S.M. Mem. Soc. Mil. Engrs, Army Navy Country Club. Home: Melbourne, Fla. Died May 7, 2007.

COOPER, ROBERT H., marketing executive; b. Defiance, Ohio, Sept. 18, 1925; s. Harold G. and Dorothy A. (Yeager) C.; m. Donna I. McLain Cooper, Apr. 23, 1949. BA, Defiance Coll., 1949. Scheduler/eng. chng. cont. North Am. Aviation, LA, 1952-55; dir. mktg. North Am./Rockwell Internat., LA, 1955-67; v.p. mktg. Pacific Airmotive Corp., Burbank, Calif., 1967-70, Miami Aviation Corp., Opa Locka, Fla., 1970-74, Am. Jet Ind./Gulfstream, Van Nuys, Calif., 1974, Rockwell Internat., Oklahoma City, 1975-78, Gulfstream Aerospace, Oklahoma City, 1978-86, sr. v.p. mktg. Savannah, Ga., 1986-92, vice chmn., from 1992. 1st lt. USAF, 1943-45. Mem. Masons. Home: Savannah, Ga. Died Mar. 17, 2007.

COOPER, ROBERT SHANKLIN, engineering executive, former federal agency administrator; b. Kansas City, Mo., Feb. 8, 1932; s. Robert S. and Edna A. (Pobanz) C.; m. Benita A. Sidwell, Oct. 5, 1985; children: Jonathan A., James G. BS in Elec. Engring, U. Iowa, 1954; MS, Ohio State U., 1958; ScD, MIT, 1963, ScD (Ford Found. postdoctoral fellow), 1965. Mem. staff elec. engring. dept. Mass. Inst. Tech., 1958-65; mem. staff Lincoln Lab., 1965-72; asst. dir. def. rsch. & engring. US Dept. Def., 1972-75; dep. dir. Goddard Space Flight Ctr., Greenbelt, Md., 1975-76, dir., 1976-79; v.p. engring. Satellite Bus. Systems, McLean, Va., 1979-81; asst. sec. for rsch. & tech. US Dept. Def., Washington, 1983-85; dir. Def. Adv. Rsch. Projects Agy., Arlington, 1981-85; pres., CEO, chmn. Atlantic Aerospace Electronics Corp., Greenbelt, Md., 1985-99; pres. Titan Corp., Aerospace Electronics Div., 1999—2005. Bd. dirs. BAE N.Am., Rockville, Md., Etenna Corp.; chmn. Trimble Navigation Ltd., Sunnyvale, Calif., GEC-Marconi N.Am., Wayne, NJ, 1998—99, Talarian Corp., Mountainview, Calif., 1989—99; mem. Def. Sci. Bd. US Dept. Def., from 1996; mem. strategic adv. group US Strategic Command, 1982—99. Served with USAF, 1954-56. Westinghouse fellow, 1958; recipient Sec. Def. Meritorious Civilian Svc. award, 1975 Fellow AAAS, AIAA, IEEE; mem. Sigma Xi, Tau Beta Pi, Eta Kappa Nu. Home: Washington, DC. Died July 2, 2007.

COOPER, THOMAS LUTHER, retired printing company executive; b. Statham, Ga., Sept. 30, 1917; s. William Henry and Ovelia Jane (Arnold) C.; m. Helen Brown, Aug. 30, 1941; 1 son, Thomas Luther. Student, Ga. State U., Atlanta, 1938-39, High Mus. Art, 1946. With Constn. Pub. Co., Atlanta, 1936-50, head photoengraving and art dept., 1947-50; pres. So. Engraving Co., Atlanta, 1950-75, Photo Process Engraving Co., Atlanta, 1954-75; pres., gen. mgr. So. Photo Process Engraving Co., Atlanta, 1955-75; v.p., bd. dir. Perry Comms., 1976-90, Beck Engraving Co., Inc., Phila., 1968-75. Bd. dirs. J.M. Tull Metals Co., Inc. Mem. exec. bd. Atlanta Area coun. Boy Scouts Am., Silver Beaver award, 1972; trustee Shorter Coll., Rome, Ga.; mem. adv. coun. Ga. State U.; chmn. bd. Ga. State U. Found. Served as capt. USAAF, 1942-45. Recipient Craftsman of Year award Inland Printer and Am. Lithographer mag., 1961 Mem. Internat. Assn. Printing House Craftsmen (pres. 1959-60), Am. Photoengravers Assn. (exec. com. 1952-54), Southeastern Photoengravers Assn. (pres. 1951-52), Nat. Soc. Art Dirs., Printing Industry Assn. Ga., Advt. Club Atlanta, Mil. Order World Wars, Am. Legion, Capital City Club, Masons, Shriners, Rotary (pres. Atlanta 1975, dist. gov. Ga. dist. 6900 1981-82). Baptist. Home: Atlanta, Ga. Died Apr. 4, 2006.

COPELAND, DONALD EUGENE, research marine biologist; b. Mendon, Ohio, Feb. 6, 1912; s. Arland Murlin and Chloe (Severns) C.; m. Marjorie Groves, June 20, 1941; children: Sandra Kay, Jane Hance, Diana Sue. AB, Rochester U., 1935; MA, Amherst Coll., 1937; PhD, Harvard U., 1941. Instr. zoology U. N.C., 1941-42; asst. then assoc. prof. zoology Brown U., 1946-51; chief aviation physiologist Office Surgeon Gen., USAF, 1951-53; profl. assoc. Nat. Acad. Scis.-NRC, 1953-56; exec. sec. NIH, 1956-59; prof. zoology Tulane U., 1959-77, prof. emeritus, from 1977, chmn. dept., 1959-65; mem. (Marine Biol. Lab.), Woods Hole, Mass., from 1948, ind. investigator, from 1977. Mem. morphology and genetics study sect., physiology study sect. NIH, 1952-53 Served to capt. USAAF, 1942-46. Mem. Am. Assn. Anatomists, Am. Soc. Zoologists, Soc. Study Devel. and Growth, Am. Soc. Cell Biologists, Am. Physiol. Soc. Achievements include research in histophysiology and ultra structure salt secreting mechanisms, gas secretion in swim bladders, oxygen elevation in fish eye, secretion of aqueous humor in fish eye, cytology of luminescent organs in deepsea fish. Home: Woods Hole, Mass. Died July 14, 2006.

COPELAND, JOHN WESLEY, textile company executive; b. Greenville, NC, Aug. 19, 1935; s. Wade Dunlap and Gladys (Brigman) C.; m. Ann Frost, Sept. 28, 1935; children: Ann Shelton, John Wesley. BS, N.C. State U., 1957; MBA, U. N.C., 1960. Mktg. mgr. Carlton Inc., Cerryville-Salisbury, N.C., 1960-64; exec. v.p. Delta Thread div. (Carlton Inc.), Salisbury, 1964-70; pres. Delta Thread div., Salisbury, 1970-77; chmn. Piedmont Mill Supply, Salisbury, 1978-79; exec. v.p. Am. and Efird Mills Inc., Mt. Holly, N.C., 1979-84, pres., 1984-94, dir., from 1979; pres. Ruddick Corp., Charlotte, N.C., from 1994. Bd. dirs. Cym Corp., Salisbury, Piedmont Mill Supply, Copeland Bus. Service Inc., Gastonia, N.C., First Union Nat. Bank, Gastonia, Ruddick Corp. Chmn. fund raising com. N.C. Heart Assn., Chapel Hill, 1966; pres. Salisbury Rowan YMCA, 1977; chmn. Rowan Republican Com., Salisbury, 1964-65, Thread Inst., 1977; bd. advisors First Union Bank, 1984—, Belmont Abbey Coll., 1987—; trustee Belmont Textile Sch., 1988—. Served to 1st lt. U.S. Army, 1957-59. Recipient Gold Medalion N.C. Heart Assn., 1967 Mem. N.C. Textile Mfrs. Assn. (pres. 1989, exec. com. 1986—), Am. Yarn Spinners Assn. (pres. 1991—), Gaston County C. of C. Clubs: Gaston (Gastonia). Methodist. Home: Charlotte, NC. Died July 3, 2006.

COPELAND, WILLIAM EDGAR, SR., physician; b. Huntington, W.Va., Nov. 22, 1920; s. Orville Edgar and Clara Gertrude (Naylon) C.; m. Carolyn Ann Varin, Jan. 31, 1948; children— William Edgar, Christopher Marsh, Stephen Jeffrey MD, Med. Coll. Va., 1945. Intern Stuart Circle Hosp., Richmond, Va., 1945-46; resident in obstetrics gynecology Hosp. U. Pa., Phila., 1948-51; practice medicine specializing in obstetrics and gynecology Phila., 1951-53, Columbus, Ohio, from 1953; mem. staff Ohio State U. Hosp., Columbus, chief of staff, 1985-87; med. dir. Univ. Health Plan, 1985; mem. staff Childrens Hosp., Riverside Meth. Hos., Columbus; mem. faculty Ohio State U., 1953-90, prof. ob-gyn, 1970-87, dir. clin. div., dept., 1971-73, emeritus prof. ob-gyn, from 1987. Contbr. articles to profl. jours. Mem. adv. com. Planned Parenthood, YMCA. Served with USN, 1943-47 Fellow Am. Coll. Obstetricians and Gynecologists, ACS, Am. Soc. Study Fertility; mem. Central Assn. Obstetricians and Gynecologists, AMA, N.Am. Obstet. and Gynecol. Soc., Ohio Med. Soc., Ohio State U. Health Ctr. Med. Soc., Assn. Am. Med. Colls. Clubs: Scioto Country, Faculty, Zanesfield Rod and Gun, Grand Hotel Hunt, Ohio State U. Pres., League Ohio Sportsmen. Home: Columbus, Ohio. Died Jan. 6, 2006.

COPLEY, PATRICK O'NEIL, college president; b. Seneca, Mo., Feb. 4, 1933; s. Charles Milton and Lorraine Lida (McCoy) C.; m. Elizabeth Ann Wheeler, Nov. 8, 1953; children: Chazell, Charlene, Patrice. BA, Grand Canyon Coll., Phoenix, 1958; MA, Ariz. State U., 1959, EdD, 1967; HHD (hon.), S.W. Bapt. U., 1988. Dir. edn. and music Parkview Baptist Ch., Phoenix, 1955-59; tchr. Central High Sch., Phoenix, 1959-65; asst. dean Sch. Edn., U. Mo., St. Louis, 1965-67; dean Sch. Edn., S.W. Mo. State U. Springfield, 1967-82; pres. Mo. Bapt. Coll., St. Louis, from 1982. Dir. Christian Communications Corp. Author articles in field. Commr. Mo. Higher Edn. Loan Authority; bd. dirs. Springfield United Cerebral Palsy, Mo. Bapt. Children's Home, St. Louis; sec. edn. commn. So. Bapt. Conv. HEW grantee, 1977-81 Mem. Am. Assn. Colls. Tchrs. Edn. (council state reps.), Mo. Assn. Colls. Tchrs. Edn. (pres. 1977-79), Tchr. Edn. Council of State Colls. and Univs. (pres. 1980-81), Mo. State Tchrs. Assn., Phi Delta Kappa, Kappa Delta Phi, Alpha Phi Omega. Died Mar. 20, 2006.

CORBETT, (WINFIELD) SCOTT, author; b. Kansas City, Mo., July 27, 1913; s. Edward Roy and Hazel Marie (Emanuelson) C.; m. Elizabeth Grosvenor Pierce, May 11, 1940; 1 dau., Jane Florence. B.J., U. Mo., 1934. Tchr. of English (part-time) Moses Brown Sch., Providence, R.I., 1957-65. Author: over 60 books, latest being The Case of the Silver Skull, 1974, The Great Custard Pie Panic, 1974, The Case of the Burgled Blessing Box, 1975, The Boy Who Walked on Air, 1975, The Great McGoniggle's Gray Ghost, 1975, Captain Butcher's Body, 1976, The Black Mask Trick, 1976, The Hockey Girls, 1976, The Great McGoniggle's Key Play, 1976, The Hangman's Ghost Trick, 1977, Bridges, 1978, The Discontented Ghost, 1978, The Mysterious Zetabet, 1979, The Donkey Planet, 1979, Home Computers, 1980, The Deadly Hoax, 1981, Grave Doubts, 1982, Jokes to Tell Your Worst Enemy, 1984, Down with Wimps!, 1984, The Trouble with Diamonds, 1985, Witch Hunt, 1985 Served with inf. U.S. Army, 1943-46. Recipient Edgar Allan Poe award Mystery Writers of Am., 1962, Mark Twain award, 1975, Golden Archer award, 1979 Mem. Authors League Am., Providence Preservation Soc. Home: Providence, RI. Died Mar. 6, 2006.

CORBIN, JAMES EDWARD, feline and canine nutrition consultant; b. Providence, Ky., July 14, 1921; s. James E. and Truda Elston (Sigler) C.; m. Margaret Reed Corbin, Oct. 14, 1950 (div. Aug. 1974); children: Mark Reed, Susan Ann Guffey, Cathie, Carl James. BS in Agrl., U. Ky., 1943, MA in Animal Nutrition, 1947; PhD in Animal Nutrition, U. Ill., 1950. Dir. animal nutrition Nat. Oats Co., St. Louis, Ill., 1950-54; mgr. spl. chows rsch. Ralston Purina Co., St. Louis, 1954-59, mgr. dog rsch., 1959-67, dir. Purina Pet Care Ctr., 1967-73; prof. animal sci. U. Ill., Urbana, 1973-84, prof. emeritus animal sci., from 1984. Pres. So. Ill. Farms, Inc., Valmeyer, 1959—; bd. dirs. Am. Pet Motels, Inc., Prarie View, Menu Foods, Inc., Toronto, Can. Contbr. articles to profl. publs. Mem. med. adv. bd. Lincoln Park Zoo, Chgo., 1984—. Lt. USN, 1943-46. Recipient Outstanding Rsch. award of yr. Am. Soybean Assn., 1975. Mem. Am. Assn. Lab. Animal Sci. (pres. 1972-73), Am. Heartworm Soc., Am. Inst. Nutrition, British Small Animal Vet. Assn., Am. Soc. of Animal Scis. Achievements include patents in the field of dog and cat food production; produced and formulated world's first extruded dog and cat foods; formulated and produced world's first commercial extruded trout foods and cat fish foods. Home: Urbana, Ill. Died Mar. 1, 2007.

CORFMAN, CARIS, actress; b. Boston, May 18, 1955; d. Philip A. and Eunice (Luccock) C. BA, Fla. State U., 1977; MFA, Yale Sch. Drama, 1980. Plays include Cymbeline, Henry IV Parts I & II, Amadeus, Passion, Anna Christie, Fathers and Sons, Camino Real, The Sea Gull, Curse of the Starving Class, The Tempest, (films) Nesto Izmedu, No Mercy, Dreamchild, Night Magic, The Pickle, Funny Farm, (TV series) Nurse, The Equalizer, Tales from the Darkside, Law and Order. Avocations: dance, swimming, travel. Died Jan. 13, 2007.

CORIN, HAROLD SEYMORE, retired retail department store executive; b. Chgo., Dec. 17, 1926; s. Edwin Michael and Sophie (Radis) C.; m. Dolores Lillian Bassin, Sept. 7, 1947; 1 son, Edward Michael. BS, Roosevelt U., Chgo. Div. mdse. mgr. Fair Store, Chgo., 1954-63; v.p., gen. mdse. mgr. Richards, Miami, Fla., 1963-65, Evans Fur Co., Chgo., 1965-67; gen. mdse. mgr. soft lines Lit Bros., Phila., 1967-70; pres., chief exec. officer Bergner Weise, Rockford, Ill., 1970-82; pres. P.A. Bergner, Peoria, Ill., 1982-85. Pres. bd. dirs. Children's Devel. Center, Rockford; v.p. Winnebago County Heart Assn.; bd. dirs. No. Ill. Hospice, Ill. Heart Assn.; chmn. Winnebago County Heart Fund; v.p. United Way; mem. Republican Presdl. Task Force. Served with USNR, 1944-46, PTO. Mem. Nat. Retail Mchts. Assn., Rockford C. of C. (bd. dirs.), Am. Mgmt. Assn. Clubs: U.S. Senatorial. Jewish. Home: Rockford, Ill. Died Mar. 5, 2006.

CORLESS, HARRY, chemical company executive; b. Coppull, Eng., Oct. 6, 1928; s. Albert and Edith (Cheetham) C.; m. Jean Houghton, Jan. 24, 1953; children: John Timothy, Victoria Elizabeth, James Anthony. B in Eng., U. Liverpool, 1949. With Imperial Chem. Industries, Ltd. (various locations), 1953-89; sr. v.p. ICI Americas Inc., Wilmington, Del., 1976-79, exec. v.p., 1979-82, pres., chief exec. officer, 1982-86, chmn., 1986-89, ret. chmn., 1989, also bd. dirs. Bd. dirs. Del. Trust Co. Trustee, bd. dirs., mem. exec. com. Med. Ctr. of Del., 1980—, chmn., 1989—. 2d lt. Brit. Army, 1951-53. Mem. Soc. Chem. Industry, Nat. Assn. Mfrs. (bd. dirs. 1984). Died May 10, 2007.

CORNELISON, FLOYD SHOVINGTON, JR., retired psychiatrist; b. San Angelo, Tex., Apr. 30, 1918; s. Floyd Shovington and Nannie Lee (Brewer) C.; m. Erwina Ladelle Bode, Aug. 30, 1940 (div. 1966); 1 child, Ann Brewer; m. Ruth Reeder Williams, Sept. 17, 1966. BA, Baylor U., 1939; postgrad., Northwestern U., 1939-40, Columbia U., 1943-45; MD, Cornell U., 1950; MS, Boston U., 1958. Diplomate Am. Bd. Psychiatry and Neurology. Intern Grasslands Hosp., Valhalla, NY, 1950-51; resident in psychiatry Mass. Meml. Hosp., Boston U. Sch. Medicine, also Boston State Hosp., 1951-54; from asst. in psychiatry to instr. Boston U. Sch. Medicine, 1951-58; lectr. psychology Tufts Coll., 1954-56; successively asst. prof., assoc. prof., cons. prof. psychiatry U. Okla. Sch. Medicine, 1958-64; prof. psychiatry Jefferson Med. Coll., Thomas Jefferson U., Phila., 1962-83, hon. prof., from 1983, chmn. dept., 1962-74; past mem. staff numerous hosps.; med. staff Wilmington Med Center; cons. area hosps., from 1962. Med. dir. Freedom From Fear, Inc., 1980-83; dir. Marka T. du Pont Inst. Human Behavior, Wilmington, Del., 1971-75; initiated self-image experience, photog. confrontation technique in psychiat. rsch. Author articles; prodr. films in field. Fellow psychiat. films Med. Audio-Visual Inst., Assn. Am. Med. Colls., 1951-53; candidate Boston Psychoanalytic Inst., 1954-58 Fellow Am. Coll. Psychiatrists (emeritus), Am. Psychiat. Assn. (life), Royal Australian and New Zealand Coll. Psychiatrists (hon.); mem. AMA, Del. Psychiat. Soc., Del. County Med. Soc., New Castle County Med. Soc., Sigma Xi. Died Jan. 23, 2007.

CORNFIELD, HUBERT, filmmaker, writer; b. Istanbul, Turkey, Feb. 9, 1929; came to U.S., 1941; naturalized, 1947; s. Albert and Mary (Tsaropoulos) C.; m. Aline Bourbon, 1968 (div. 1973); children: Stephanie, Anais. Student, U. Pa., Phila. Mus. Sch. Art. Freelance graphic designer, France and U.S., 1950-54; dir., observer Actor's Studio, NYC, 1952-54; reader Allied Artists, Hollywood, Calif., 1954; ind. filmmaker, from 1955. Dir.: (films) Sudden Danger, 1955, Lure of the Swamp, 1957, Plunder Road, 1958, (TV film) Operation Cicero, 1956; writer, producer, dir. (film) The Color is Red, 1953, The Third Voice, 1960; writer, dir.: (films) Pressure Point with Bobby Darin and Sidney Poitier, 1962, Les Grand Moyens, 1976, (French film series) Temoignages, Poker d'As, 1973-74; graphic artist (film poster) All About Eve (selected to permanent collection Mus. Modern Art, N.Y.C., 1954); dir., producer (film) The Night of the Following Day with Marlon Brando, 1969. Recipient First Beatrice Wood film award, 1994. Mem. Writers Guild Am. West, Dirs. Guild Am., Acad. Motion Picture Arts and Scis. Avocation: skiing. Died June 18, 2006.

CORSBERG, DOROTHY JEAN, humanities educator; b. Greeley, Colo., July 25, 1924; d. John Hermon and Inez Christine (Salberg) Corsberg; B.A., Colo. State Coll., 1946, M.A., 1952; postgrad. U. No. Colo., 60-81. Tchr., Oakesdale Consol. High Sch., Oakesdale, Wash., 1946-49; mem. faculty Northeastern Jr. Coll., Sterling, Colo., 1949-87, dean women, 1949-62, chmn. humanities div., 1962-83, instructional dir. gen. studies, 1983-87; prof. emeritus, 1987; critical reader/reviewer for ednl. materials; N.E. Colo. field cons. Colo. Humanities Program, 1982; mem. Colo. State Dept. Adv. Bd. Social Studies, 1966-68; chmn. Anna C. Petteys Scholarship Com., 1971-86; mem. rural libraries and humanities com. Colo. Planning and Resource Bd., 1982-83. Bd. dirs. Community Concert Assn., 1971-81. Named Outstanding Female Educator, U. No. Colo., 1968, Community Coll. Faculty Mem. of Yr., State Bd. Community Colls. and Occupational Edn. in Colo., 1981-82. Mem. NEA, Colo. Assn. Higher Edn. (program chmn., dir. 1965-67, NIC rep., Colo. core transfer curriculum faculty task force 1986-87), Colo. Assn. Coll. Instructional Dirs., P.E.O. Democrat. Died July 23, 2006.

CORTESE, ARMAND FERDINAND, surgeon, educator; b. NYC, Dec. 4, 1932; m. Patricia Lange, 1975; children: Amanda Lange, Kevin Armand. AB, Columbia U., 1954; MD, Cornell U., 1958. Intern N.Y. Hosp., Cornell U., NYC, 1958, resident, 1959-66, Am./Nat. Cancer fellow, 1966-68, assoc. attending surgeon, from 1976; clin. assoc. prof. surgery Cornell Med. Coll., NYC, from 1976. Author: (with others) Care of the Adult Patient, 1971; contbr. articles to profl. jours. Lt. USN, 1960-62. Rsch. grantee Josia and Macy Found., 1958. Mem. AMA, Am. Coll. Surgery, Am. Soc. Clin. Oncology, Harvey Soc., N.Y. Surg. Soc., N.Y. Cancer Soc., N.Y. Acad. Medicine. Home: New York, NY. Died Feb. 17, 2006.

COSGROVE, JOHN FRANCIS, lawyer, mayor; b. Coral Gables, Fla., July 1, 1949; s. Francis Freheil and Vivian Adair (Rafferty) C.; m. Bernardine Elizabeth Cosgrove, Dec. 19, 1981; children: Michael, Tiffany, Colleen. AA, U. Fla., 1969, BS in Journalism, 1971; JD, Cumberland Sch. Law, 1975. Bar: Fla., U.S. Dist. Ct. (so. dist.) Fla., U.S. Ct. Appeals (5th cir.), U.S. Supreme Ct. Assoc. Hall & Hedrick, Miami, Fla., 1975-80; sole practice Miami, from 1980. Mem. Fla. Ho. of Reps., 1981-84, 1986—; gen. counsel Biscayne Coll.; columnist Miami Rev.: Juris Conspectus, 1975—; chair Nat. Conf. State Legislatures Com. on Commerce and Comm.; chair property and casualty com., mem. exec. com. Nat. Conf. Ins. Legislatures. Chmn. Coral Gables Code Enforcement Bd.; mem. Coral Gables Econ. Devel. Bd.; mem. Jr. Orange Bowl Com.; chmn. Metro-Dade Econ. Devel. Bd., Miami Budget Rev. Com.; mem. South Miami Hosp. Assocs. Mem. ABA, Fla. Bar Assn. (Jud. Selection, Adminstrn. and Tenure Com., vice chmn. jud. nominating com.), Dade County Bar Assn. (3d v.p.), Am. Judicature Soc., ATLA, Pvt. Industry Coun. Dade County, Emerald Soc. South Fla., Miami Springs-Hialeah C. of C., Coral Gables C. of C., Grtr. Miami C. of C., Blue Key, Serra Club, Viscayans Civic Club, Le Lega Civic Club, Grtr. Miami Leadership Prayer Breakfast Club, KC (grand knight Coral Gables; pres. Dade County chpt.), Kiwanis, Knight of Malta, Phi Kappa Tau. Democrat. Roman Catholic (chmn. Cath. Svc. Bur.-50th anniversary). Home: Miami, Fla. Died Apr. 20, 2006.

COSTELLO, LORETTA ELIZABETH, realty firm executive; b. Jamaica, N.Y., Aug. 11, 1941; d. Peter F. and Loretta E. (McDermott) C. B.A., U. Md., 1963. Saleswoman, Lanier Bus. Products Co., N.Y.C., 1979-80; sales real estate N.K. Benjamin Realty Co., Forest Hills, N.Y.C., 1980-83; owner Town House Mgmt. Co., N.Y.C., 1982—; owner, broker Castleberry Realty Co., Rego Park, N.Y., 1984—, Forest Hills, N.Y., 1986—; residential apt. mgr. Com. mem. Concerned Citizens for Better Bayside, Queensboro Hill Neighborhood Assn., Flushing. Recipient various realty awards. Mem. Nat. Assn. Female Execs., Nat. Assn. Realtors, N.Y. State Assn. Realtors, L.I. Bd. Realtors (appraisal div., mortgage/banking, profl. standards coms. 1985—, polit. action com.), Forest Hills C. of C. Home: Flushing, NY. Died Aug. 8, 2007.

COSTIN, JAMES D., performing arts company executive; BA in Theater, U. Calif., LA, 1959; MA in Theater, U. Mo., Kansas City, 1966. Cert. German linguist, 1956. Mgr. Fox West Coast Theatres, LA, Calif., 1954-56; German linguist Army Security Agency, U.S. Army, 1956-59; editor Great Lakes News, 1960-61; asst. stage mgr to stage mgr. Am. Ballet Theatre, 1961-62, co. mgr., 1962-63; asst. gen. mgr. Washington D.C. Ballet Guild/Am. Ballet Theatre, 1963-64; co-founder, adminstrv. dir. Mo. Repertory Theatre, U. Mo., Kansas City, 1964-67; playwright in residence U. Mo., Kansas City, 1966-67, adminstrv. dir. of theatre, 1968-72, asst. to the provost, dir. office of cultural events, 1972-76, asst provost for performing arts mgmt., 1976-79, vice provost, chief academic fiscal officer, 1979; exec. dir./playwright in residence Mo. Repertory Theatre, Inc., 1979—2000. Cons. Internat. Theatre Inst., Great Lakes Shakespeare Festival, Kansas City Ballet. Author: (play) Laity, 1964, Lee, 1966, Ageina, 1969, The Curious Adventures of Alice, 1988, Jekyll, 1989; (stage productions) Ageina, The Curious Adventures of Alice, Jekyll; (co-author play with James Lee) The Holy Terror, 1967. Com. mem. Mayor's Com. Save The Starlight Theater, Save the Phiharmonic Orchestra; bd. dirs. State Ballet Mo., Kans. City Arts Coun. Lt. USNR 1968-71. Recipient Best Playwright award UCLA, 1959, Pirouette award, 1987, Mo. Arts award, 2000. Home: Jefferson Cty, Mo. Died Jan. 25, 2005.

COTSONAS, NICHOLAS JOHN, JR., physician, medical educator; b. Boston, Jan. 28, 1919; s. Nicholas John and Louise Catherine (Lapham) C.; m. Betty Borge, Nov. 21, 1970; children by previous marriage: Nicholas III, Bruce, Elena. AB, Harvard, 1940; MD cum laude, Georgetown U., 1943. Intern D.C. Gen. Hosp., Washington, 1944, resident in chest diseases, 1946-47, asst. med. resident, 1947-48, chief med. resident, 1948-49; asst. prof. medicine Georgetown U. Sch. Medicine, 1949-53; chief med. officer, med. divsn. D.C. Gen. Hosp., 1951-53; asst. prof. medicine U. Ill. Coll. Medicine, Chgo., 1953-57, assoc. prof., 1957-62, prof., 1962-70; dean, prof. medicine Peoria Sch. Medicine, U. Ill., 1970-79; prof. medicine U. Ill., Chgo., 1979-90, prof. emeritus, from 1989, assoc. vice chancellor for acad. affairs, 1979-82. Mem. Bradley Assocs., 1972-79; bd. dirs. Ill. Heart Assn., 1972-79, pres., 1976-77; bd. dirs. Ill. Ctrl. Health Sys. Agy., 1976-79, Planned Parenthood Assn. Greater Peoria Area, 1971-79; mem. Statewide Health Coordinating Council, 1978-79; bd. dirs. Chgo. Heart Assn., 1980-82, Inst. Religion and Medicine, 1980; mem. task force on older women Ill. Council on Aging, 1985-86; chmn. Commn. on Health Resources Allocation, Peoria, Ill., 1985-87. Asst. editor: Disease-A-Month, 1960-77; asso. editor, 1977-80, editor, 1980-86, emeritus, 1987. Served to capt. AUS, 1944-46. Recipient Raymond Allen award U. Ill. Coll. Medicine, 1955, Faculty of Yr. award, 1978 Fellow ACP, Am. Heart Assn. (coun. clin. cardiology 1963), Am. Coll. Cardiology, Inst. Medicine Chgo., Am. Geriatrics Soc.; mem. Am. Fedn. Clin. Rsch., Chgo. Soc. Internal Medicine, Harvard Soc. Chemists, Sigma Xi, Alpha Omega Alpha. Home: Chattanooga, Tenn. Died July 28, 2006.

COTTON, F. ALBERT (FRANK ALBERT COTTON), chemistry professor; b. Phila., Apr. 9, 1930; s. Albert and Helen (Taylor) Cotton; m. Diane Dornacher, June 13, 1959; children: Jennifer Helen, Jane Myrna. Attended, Drexel Inst. Tech., 1947—49; BA, Temple U., 1951; PhD, Harvard U., 1955; DSc (hon.), Temple U., 1963; Dr. (hon.), Bielefeld U., 1979; DSc (hon.), Columbia U., 1980, Northwestern U., 1981, U. Bordeaux, 1981, St. Joseph's U., 1982, U. Louis Pasteur, 1982, U. Valencia, 1983, Kenyon Coll., 1983, Technion Israel Inst. Tech., 1983, U. Cambridge, 1986, Johann Wolfgang Goethe U., 1989, U. S.C., 1989, U. Rennes, 1992, Lomonosov U., 1992, Fujian Inst. Rsch., Chinese Acad. Sci., 1993, U. Pisa, Italy, 1994, U. Zaragoza, 1994, Cleve. State U., 1995, U. Crete, 1996, Mich. State U., 1996, U. Pierre and Marie Curie, 1997, U. Palermo, 1997, U. Jaume I, 2000, N.C. State U., 2000, Ohio State U., 2001, Hebrew U., Jerusalem, 2002, Drexel U., 2002. Instr. chemistry MIT, 1955—57, asst. prof., 1957—60, assoc. prof., 1960—61, prof., 1961—71; Robert A. Welch disting. prof. chemistry Tex. A & M U., College Station, 1971—2007, dir. lab. for molecular structure and bonding, 1983—2007. Cons. Am. Cyanamid, Stamford, Conn., 1958—67, Union Carbide, NYC, 1957—94; Todd prof. Cambridge U., 1985—86. Editor: Progress in Inorganic Chemistry, volumes 1-10, 1959—68; co-author (with L. Lynch and C. Darlington): Chemistry, An Investigative Approach, 1969; editor: Inorganic Syntheses, vol. 13, 1971; editor: (with L.M. Jackman) Dynamic Nuc. Magnetic Resonance Spectroscopy, 1975; author: Chem. Applications of Group Theory, 3d edit., 1990; co-author (with R.A. Walton and C.A. Murillo): Multiple Bonds Between Metal Atoms, 1992, 3d edit., 2005; co-author: (with G. Wilkinson and P.L. Gaus) Basic Inorganic Chemistry, 3d edit., 1995; editor (with R.D. Adams): Catalysis by Di and Poly Nuc. Metal Atom Clusters, 1998; author (with G. Wilkinson, C.A. Murillo, and M. Bochmann): Advanced Inorganic Chemistry, 6th edit., 1999. Named an hon. fellow, Robinson Coll. Cambridge U., Eng.; recipient Michelson Morley award, Case Western Res. U., 1980, Nat. medal Sci., 1982, King Faisal prize, 1990, Paracelsus medal, Swiss Chem. Soc., 1994, prize, Welch Found., 1994, Polyhedron Medal, 1995, John Scott medal, City of Phila., 1997, Gold medal, Am. Inst. Chemists, 1998, Lavoisier medal, French Chem. Soc., 2000, Wolf prize in chemistry, Wolf Found., Israel, 2000, Monie Ferst award, Sigma Xi, 2005. Mem.: AAAS, NAS (chmn. phys. sci. 1985—88, coun. 1991—94, gov. bd. NRC 1992—94, Cosepup 1992—94, F.A. Cotton medal Tex. A&M sect. 1995), Chinese Acad. Sci., Inst. de France Acad. Sci., Royal Soc. London, Am. Philos. Soc., Göttingen Acad. Sci. (Gaus Prof. 2002), Am. Chem. Soc. (award 1962, award in inorganic chem. 1962, Baekeland medal N.J. sect. 1963, disting. svc. inorganic chemistry 1972, award 1974, Nichols medal N.Y. sect. 1975, Pauling medal Oreg. and Puget Sound sect. 1976, Kirkwood medal N.Y. sect. 1978, Gibbs medal Chgo. sect. 1980, Richards Medal, N.E. sect. 1986, Priestley medal 1998, award in organometallic chem. 2002, George Pimentel award in Chem. Edn. 2006), European Acad. Scis. (hon.), Indian Nat. Sci. Acad. (hon.), Acad. Europe (hon.), Royal Soc. Edinburgh (hon.), Indian Acad. Sci. (hon.), Italian Chem. Soc. (hon.), Royal Danish Acad. Sci. and Letters (hon.), Royal Soc. Chemistry (hon.), N.Y. Acad. Sci. (life). Home: Bryan, Tex. Died Feb. 20, 2007.

COULTER, EDWIN MARTIN, political science educator, writer; b. Waynesboro, Va., July 18, 1937; s. Homer Preston and Eileen (Rader) C.; m. Aleta Holbrooks, June 22, 1963 (div. 1982); children: John Edwin, David Preston. BA in Polit. Sci., Furman U., 1962; PhD in Fgn. Affairs, U. Va., 1965. Instr., U. Va., Charlottesville, 1964-65; assoc. prof. Ark. State U., Jonesboro, 1965-68, Okla. Coll. Liberal Arts, Chickasha, 1968-71; prof. Clemson U., S.C., 1971—. Author: Principles of Politics and Government, 1981, 3d edit. 1987. Served with USN, 1955-58. Woodrow Wilson fellow,1962. Mem. Am. Polit. Sci. Assn., So. Polit. Sci. Assn., Raven Soc., Phi Beta Kappa. Democrat. Episcopalian. Home: Clemson, SC. Died Sept. 23, 2006.

COURSHON, ARTHUR HOWARD, lawyer, banker; b. Chgo., Feb. 21, 1921; s. Aaron H. and Beatrice (Pollak) C.; BA, U. Fla., 1942; JD, U. Miami, Coral Gables, Fla., 1947; m. Carol Biel, Feb. 20, 1943; children: Barbara Courshon Mills, Deanne. Admitted to Fla. bar, 1947; ptnr. firm Courshon & Courshon, Miami Beach, 1948—; organizer, chmn. bd. dirs. Washington Savs. and Loan Assn. Fla., Miami Beach, 1952-81; chmn. bd. Jefferson Bancorp., Inc., holding co. Jefferson Bank, Broward, Jefferson Bank Fla.; chmn., CEO Jefferson Capital Corp.; cons. savs. and loan system in Chile, ICA, 1958—; cons. housing loans to Latin Am., 1960—, Devel. Loan Fund, Inter-Am. Devel. Bank, 1961—; cons. Govt. of Peru, 1960—; mem. U.S. Govt. task force Fed. Home Loan Bank, 1961-62; mem. savs. and loan adv. council Fed. Home Loan Bank Bd., 1969; housing finance cons. Latin Am. Affairs Subcom., Senate Fgn. Relations Com., 1960-69, State of Israel, 1977-80; mem. housing and urban devel. adv. com. AID, 1965-68; pub. mem. Adminstrv. Conf. of U.S., 1968-72. Mem. Met. Dade County Urban Renewal Agy., 1963-67; bd. dirs. South Fla. Housing Found., Miami Heart Inst.; trustee Pub. Health Trust of Dade County, U. Miami, 1990; chmn. Democratic Nat. Fin. Council, 1983-84; nat. trustee John F. Kennedy Library Found. Served with USAAF, 1942-46. Recipient citation for establishment savs. and loan system in Chile, ICA, 1960. Mem. Dade County Bar Assn., Fla. Bar (banking liaison com.), U.S. Savs. and Loan Inst., Nat. Savs. and Loan League (pres. 1969, exec. com., legis. com.), Internat. Union Bldg. Socs. (devel. com., council), Nu Beta Epsilon, Pi Lambda Phi. Democrat. Jewish. Home: Miami, Fla. Died Jan. 6, 2006.

COURTNEY, JAMES EDMOND, real estate developer; b. Meadville, Pa., Dec. 28, 1931; s. Alexis James and Marian (Winans) C.; m. Eileen Patricia Alman, Nov. 2, 1970; children: Alison M., David E. AB in Econs., Dartmouth Coll., 1953, MBA in Fin. Analysis and Acctg., 1954; LLB, Harvard U., 1959. Bar: Ohio 1960. Assoc. Jones, Day, Reavis & Pogue, Cleve., 1959-62, ptnr., 1963-74; v.p. internat. M.A. Hanna Co., Cleve., 1974-78, sr. v.p. corp. devel., 1978-79, exec. v.p., 1981-90, also bd. dirs., vice chmn., 1989-90; pres. The Mariner Group, Ft. Myers, Fla., 1992-95. Chmn. First Cmty. Bank of S.W. Fla., Ft. Myers, Robb & Stuckey, Ltd., Ft. Myers. Served to lt. USN, 1954-56. Home: Fort Myers, Fla. Died Nov. 30, 2006.

COVEY, PRESTON KING, JR., education educator, university official; b. Mpls., Aug. 29, 1942; s. Preston King and Nancy (Humphrey) C.; m. Patricia Dudley, June 20, 1964 (div.); m. Kathleen Susan Maloy, Feb. 20, 1983; 1 child, Adam Justin. BA in Psychology, Stanford U., 1965, PhD in Philosophy, 1978. Asst. prof. Carnegie Mellon U., Pitts., 1977-83, assoc. prof., from 1983, vice provost, 1986-89; exec. dir. Ctr. for Design of Ednl. Computing, Pitts., from 1985, dir., 1986-92; dir. Ctr. for Advancment Applied Ethics, Carnegie Mellon U., Pitts., from 1988. Editor: Logic in Liberal Arts 1981, Design in Liberal/Professional Education 1989; author: A Right to Die (videodisc and software) 1988, articles and computer programs. Recipient: Teaching and Ednl. Svc. Award, Carnegie Mellon U., 1983, Teaching Award Fellowship, Lilly Endowment, 1979; 3.2 million in grants 1977-87. Mem. Am. Philos. Assn. (nat. com. chmn. 1986-91), Am. Soc. Criminology, Am. Soc. Law Enforcement Trainers (life), Internat. Assn. Law Enforcement Firearms Instrs., Soc. for Risk Analysis. Home: Pittsburgh, Pa. Died Sept. 18, 2006.

COVINO, CHARLES PETER, chemicals executive; b. West New York, NJ, Dec. 9, 1923; s. Isaac L. and Rose (Luongo) C.; m. Sylvia A Covino, Dec. 27, 1947; 1 child, Candida. Student, U. Ala., 1941-43; BBA, Manhattan Coll., 1951; MBA, NYU; doctorate (hon.), Philathea U., Can., 1963; DSc (hon.), Manhattan Coll., 1995. Chmn. bd., CEO Gen. Magnaplate Corp., Linden, N.J. Mem. Hoover Inst./UN Coun. for Global Polit. and Econ. Transition, 1994; lectr. in field. Contbr. over 28 articles to profl. jours. Recipient Air Force Assn. N.J. Wing award for space contbns., 1960, Royal Cross Austria Prince Rudolph, 1964, Eloy Alfaro Found. of Panama award, 1965, Manhattan Coll. Outstanding Alumni award, 1972, Vaaler award Chem. Engring. Inst., 1976, Indsl. Rsch. 100 award for Material Devels. of Yr., 1964, 68, 78, ASM award for Disting. Svc. and Contbns. to Metals Industry, 1967, Cookware Design of Yr. award Housewares Mfr.'s Assn., 1967, award of yr. Packaging Inst., 1967-68, Outstanding New Product award Popular Sci. mag., 1967, Packaging Design award Design Inst., 1968, Outstanding USA Design award U.S. Info. Agy., 1968, Italian-Am. Man of Sci. award 1978, Churchill Medal of Wisdom award, 1995, Heros of Chemistry award Am. Chem. Soc., 1996, Am. Chem. Soc. award, 1996, Thomas Alva Edison award for best N.J. invention of Yr., 1999; named to N.J. Inventors Hall of Fame, 1994-95, Manhattan Coll. Athletics Hall of Fame, 1998, N.J. Corp. Inventors Hall of Fame, 1999. Achievements include over 101 patents and trademarks; invention of non-destructive testing method for thick lead shielding in nuclear reactors, ultrasonic test method for nuclear tubing used for condensors, various metal surface enhancement processes, low-cost (permanent composite) mold form by plasma spray method; featured in Guinness World Book of Records for world's slipperiest solid lubricant. Home: Far Hills, NJ. Died Feb. 3, 2007.

COWAN, DWAINE OLIVER, chemist, educator; b. Fresno, Calif., Nov. 25, 1935; s. Oliver F. and Eva Belle (Parsons) C.; m. LaVon H. Adams, Feb. 2, 1963. BS, Fresno State Coll., 1958; PhD, Stanford U., 1962. Research fellow Calif. Inst. Tech., 1962-63; mem. faculty Johns Hopkins U., from 1963, prof. chemistry, from 1972; mem. chemistry research evaluation panel, directorate chem. scis. Air Force Office Sci. Research, 1976-80. Discoverer of the first organic metal - TTF-TCNQ, 1973; author: (with R.L. Drisko) Elements of Organic Photochemistry, 1976; also over 180 articles. Recipient Humboldt rsch. award, 1992—; Sloan fellow, 1968-70; Guggenheim fellow, 1970-71 Fellow AAAS; mem. Am. Chem. Soc., Chem. Soc. Eng., Am. Phys. Soc., Inter-Am. Photochem. Soc., Sigma Xi, Phi Lambda Upsilon. Home: Fresno, Calif. Died May 5, 2006.

COWAN, JERRY LOUIS, lawyer; b. Des Moines, May 18, 1927; s. William Lincoln and Avis I. (Spencer) C.; m. Lee Steel, June 11, 1955; children: Grant Spencer, Breck Martin. BA, Denison U., 1951; LLB, U. Va., 1956. Bar: Ohio 1956, U.S. Ct. Appeals (6th cir.) 1958, U.S. Dist. Ct. (so. dist.) Ohio 1958, U.S. Tax Ct. 1957, U.S. Claims Ct. 1966. Assoc. Frost & Jacobs, Cin., 1956-63, ptnr., 1963-94, counsel, from 1994. Contbr. articles to profl. jours. Trustee Big Bros./Big Sisters. Found. of Greater Cin., Inc., 1962-92; bd. dirs. Hoxworth Blood Ctr., Cin., 1986-92. With U.S. Army, 1945-46. Mem. ABA, Cin. Bar Assn. (chmn. tax com. 1962-64), Ohio Bar Assn., Greater Cin. C. of C. (gen. counsel 1972-84), Cin. Country Club, Univ. Club (Cin.). Republican. Episcopalian. Avocations: golf, history. Home: Cincinnati, Ohio. Died Aug. 6, 2007.

COWEN, WILSON (ARNOLD WILSON COWEN), retired federal judge; b. nr. Clifton, Tex., Dec. 20, 1905; s. John Rentz and Florence Juno (McFadden) Cowen; m. Florence Elizabeth Walker, Apr. 18, 1930; children: W. Walker, John E. LLB, U. Tex., 1928. Bar: Tex. 1928. Pvt. practice, Dalhart, Tex., 1928—34; judge Dallam County, Tex., 1935—38; Tex. dir. Farm Security Adminstrn., 1938—40, regional dir., 1940—42; commr. U.S. Ct. Claims, Washington, 1942—43, 1945—59 chief commr., 1959—64, chief judge, 1964—77, sr. judge 1977—82, U.S. Ct. Appeals (Fed. Cir.), Washington, 1982—97 Asst. adminstr. War Food Adminstrn., 1943—45; spl. asst. to sec. agr., 1945; mem. Jud. Conf. U.S., 1964—77. Mem.: FBA, ABA, State Bar Tex., Cosmos Club (Washington), Delta Theta Phi, Order of Coif. Presbyterian. Home: Washington, DC. Died Oct. 28, 2007.*

COX, ANDREW HOOD, lawyer; b. Bangor, Maine, Sept. 28, 1917; s. James F. and Mary Christine (Burns) C.; m. Constance Buffum, Dec. 30, 1950; children: Emily Cox Sinagra, Deborah Cox Marion. AB, Bowdoin Coll., 1938; LLB, Harvard U., 1941. Bar: Mass. 1941, Maine 1941. Assoc. Ropes & Gray, Boston, 1946-57, ptnr., 1958-89, of counsel, from 1990. Mem. adv. bd. Tax Mgmt. Inc., Washington, 1974—. Contbr. articles to profl. jours. Mem. Milton (Mass.) Conservation Commn., 1969-81, chmn., 1969-74. Served to capt. arty., AUS, 1942-46, ETO, PTO. Fellow Am. Coll. Tax Counsel (chmn. 1987-89); mem. ABA, Boston Bar Assn., Phi Beta Kappa. Clubs: Harvard (Boston); Sakonnet Golf (Little Compton, R.I.); Milton Hoosic. Republican. Roman Catholic. Avocations: personal computers, golf, skiing. Home: Milton, Mass. Died Jan. 25, 2007.

COX, HENRY BARTHOLOMEW, historian; b. Washington, Oct. 2, 1937; s. Paul Vernon and Elizabeth (Bartholomew) C.; m. Hannah Moberley Soaper Caffery, June 6, 1973. A.B., Princeton U., 1959; M.A., George Washington U., 1962, Ph.D. in History, 1967, J.D., 1976. Bar: Md. 1978, US Supreme Ct. 1982. Historian, US Dept. State, Washington, 1966-69; asst. exec. dir. Nat. Hist. Publs. Commn., Washington, 1969-71; chief Bicentennial Ctr., Nat. Archives, Washington, 1971-74; sole practice, Md., 1978-79; former dir. Am. Bar Assn. Study of War Powers in Am. History, Washington; instr. history George Washington U., 1964-66; Author: War, Foreign Affairs and Constitutional Power 1829-1901, 1976; lectr. in field. Recipient 1st prize Nathan Burkan Meml. Competition of ASCAP, 1976, Disting. Svc. award, US Dept. Interior, 1984; Nat. Trust for Hist. Preservation fellow, 1963. Mem. Am. Soc. for Legal History (dir. 1969-74), Soc. Am. Archivists (Gondos Meml. award 1969), Lit. Soc. Washington, Manuscript Soc. Republican. Christian Scientist. Clubs: Chevy Chase (Md.); Soc. Cincinnati. Author: War, Foreign Affairs and Constitutional Power, vol. II, 1984; contbr. articles to profl. jours. Home: Fort Washington, Md. Died Apr. 8, 2007.

COX, JAMES CARL, JR., chemist, researcher, lexicographer, consultant; b. Wolf Summit, W.Va., June 17, 1919; s. James Carl and Maggie Lillian (Merrells) C.; m. Alma Lee Tenney, Sept. 8, 1945; children: James Carl III, Joseph Merrells, Alma Lee, Elizabeth Susan Cox Unger, Albert John. BS summa cum laude, W.Va. Wesleyan Coll., 1940; MS in Organic Chemistry, U. Del., 1947, PhD in Phys. Organic Chemistry, 1949; postgrad. in law, Am. U., summer 1953, George Washington U., summer 1954; JD with honors, U. Md., 1955. Bar: Md. 1955; registered profl. sanitarian, Tex. Rsch. chemist E.I. duPont de Nemours Corp., Belle, W.Va., 1940-43; grad. instr. chemistry U. Del., Newark, 1946-49; prof. chemistry, head dept. chemistry Wesleyan Coll., Macon, Ga., 1949-51; prof. U.S. Naval Acad., Annapolis, 1951-55, Md., 1951-55; prof., rsch. dir. Lamar U., Beaumont, Tex., 1955-65; prof., head dept. chemistry, dir. div. sci. and math. Oral Roberts U., Tulsa, 1965-68; prof., head dept. chemistry Wayland Baptist U., Plainview, Tex., 1968-76; v.p., rsch. dir. Agrl. & Indsl. Devel., Inc., Plainview, 1976-79; environ. health expert Tex. Dept. Health, Plainview, 1979-84. Mem. U. Tex indsl. planning commn., commdr. 19th dist. Dept. Tex.; field rep. Bureau of Census, 1990-92; cons., quality assurer Agri-Search Corp.; lectr. U. London, U. Dublin, Heidelberg U., summer 1976, U. Glasgow; cons. in field; vis. prof. organic chemistry Middle Tenn. State U., Murfreesboro, summer 1950, U. Baghdad, Iraq, 1956-57; quality assurer Agri-Search, Inc., 1992—. Author: George WAshington, Farmer, 1941, Lives of Splendor, 1971; Patterson's German-English Chemical Dictionary, rev. edit., 1985; editor The Condenser, 1957-65; contbr. articles to profl. jours., also abstracts. Precinct chmn. Hale County Rep., Plainview, 1983-84; bd. dirs. Plainview chpt. ARC, 1969-73, United Way, Plainview, 1972-75. Served to cpl. Combat Engrs., U.S. Army, 1943-45, ETO; field rep. Bureau Labor Stats., 1992—. Named Outstanding Prof., Lamar U., 1963-64, Wayland Bapt. U., 1971-74; fellow DuPont Endowment Found., 1947-48, Carnegie Found., 1948-49, Phillips fellow, 1949-50, State of Tex., 1957-59. Fellow Tex. Acad. Sci.; mem. AAAS, AAUP, DAV (chmn. Americanism, judge adv., vice commdr., commdr.), VFW (vice commdr., commdr., quartermaster), Am. Chem. Soc., Tex. Pub. Health Assn., Tex. Environ. Health Assn. (governing coun. 1982-84), Am. Legion (adj.), Rotary (pub. rels. officer 1969-84), Confederate Air Force (col.). Methodist. Current work: Novel fuels for industry; agricultural chemicals. Subspecialties: Organic chemistry; Polymer chemistry. Home: Fort Worth, Tex. Died Feb. 23, 2006.

COX, WHITSON WILLIAM, architect; b. Crawford, Nebr., May 13, 1921; s. William Noah and Esther Mable (Stickley) C.; m. Loreen Baker, Sept. 8, 1946; children: Marilyn Cox Gendron, Teresa Cox Balick. BS, U. Oreg., 1943, BArch, 1948. Registered architect, Calif. Prin. Cox, Liske, Lionakis & Beaumont, Architects & Engrs., Sacramento, 1953-83; dir. Dept. Architecture and Constrn. State of Calif., Sacramento, 1983-86; prin. Whitson W. Cox, Architect, Sacramento, from 1986. Cons. architect Calif. State U., 1972-83, Meth. Hosp., Sacramento, 1987—; tech. cons. Capitol Area Plan, Sacramento, 1983-86. Prin. works include Mira Loma High Sch., Sacramento, 1964, Mather AFB Chapel, Sacramento, 1968, Chico (Calif.) State Health Ctr., 1969, Sacramento County Adminstrn. Ctr., 1977; paintings exhibited in one-man and group shows, 1960—. Bd. dirs., pres. Crocker Art Mus., 1964-84; commr. Sacramento Metro Arts Commn., 1982; bd. dirs. Boy Scouts Am. Golden Empire Coun., 1962—. Lt. USNR, 1943-46, PTO. Recipient Silver Beaver award Boy Scouts Am., 1964, Commendation award Calif. Arts Coun., 1986. Fellow AIA (chpt. pres. 1963, state pres. 1972, nat. bd. dirs., 1974-78, dist. svc. citation 1985); mem. Rotary Club, Arden Hills Club. Home: Carmichael, Calif. Died Apr. 14, 2007.

COYLE, DOUGLAS JEFFERSON, state official; b. Lebanon, Oreg., Mar. 14, 1943; s. Alton Jefferson and Doris Marie (Cutts) Coyle; children: Alan Jefferson, Jeanette Marie. BS, Oreg. State U., 1965. Forester Linn Fire Patrol, Foster, Oreg., 1963—67; forest insp. Oreg. Forestry Dept., Grants Pass, 1967—68, forest fire protection analyst Salem, 1968—70, unit forester Wallowa County, 1971—72, head forestry mapping, 1972—74, area mgr., 1977—88, dir. fire control, from 1988, dist. forester LaGrande, 1974—77. Fire boss statewide fire team State of Oreg., 1976—78; fire investigator specialist, from 1973; mem. Forestry/Forest Adv. Com., from 1986, chmn., 1986—88. Mem. Union County Planning Com., LaGrande, 1975—77, Econ. Devel. Dist., 1976—77; advisor curriculum Ea. Oreg. State Coll., 1977; mem. Marion County Econ. Devel. Com., 1983; bd. dirs. ReTree Internat. Mem.: Soc. Am. Foresters (chmn. 1975—76, 1980—81). Republican. Lutheran. Home: Salem, Oreg. Died June 17, 2006.

CRAFTON, THOMAS WARD, accountant; b. San Angelo, Tex., Oct. 6, 1947; s. Donald L. and Billie M. (Ward) Crafton; 1 child, Leah. Student, N.Y. Inst. Fin., 1969—70; BS, Harding U., 1976; MBA, Pepperdine U., 1980. Staff mem. E.F. Hutton, Houston and Chgo., 1968—72; acct. Houston, 1972—76; contr. Jones Lumber Co., Houston, 1973—75; acct. Omaha, 1976—78; contr. Pepperdine U., Malibu, Calif., 1979—81; pres. Coronado Group, Inc., Westlake Village, Calif., 1981—85; contr. Reynal Controls, Inc., Houston, from 1985. Vol. Am. Cancer Soc.; chmn. employer drive United Way; vol. Rep. Mem.: Nat. Assn. MBAs, Nat. Assn. Accts., Noon Lions Club, Delta Mu Delta. Mem. Ch. Of Christ. Died June 26, 2006.

CRANDALL, HOMER LEWIS, retired allergist, immunologist, pediatrician; b. Americus, Ga., Jan. 12, 1925; MD, Med. Coll. Ga., 1948; BS, Mercer U., Macon, Ga., 1944. Intern Carraway Meth. Hosp., Birmingham, Ala., 1948-49; resident pediat. Tenn. Coal-Iron Hosp., Fairfield, 1949-51, Lloyd Noland Hosp., Fairfield, 1957-58, physician, 1949-90; ret., 1990. Clin. prof. pediat. U. Ala. Fellow Am. Acad. Allergy and Immunology, Am. Acad. Pediat., Am. Coll. Allergy and Immunology; mem. AMA. Home: Birmingham, Ala. Died Jan. 30, 2007.

CRANE, THOMAS WILLIAM, physicist, researcher; b. Ft. Bragg, NC, Oct. 11, 1946; s. Herman Thomas and Minamarie Marlene (Jewell) Crane; m. Karla Sue Brum, June 21, 1969; children: Benjamin Thomas, Genevieve Marie, Nathan Karl. BS, Otterbein Coll., Westerville, Ohio, 1968; PhD, Yale U., 1974, postgrad., 1974—76. Mem. staff Los Alamos (N.Mex.) Nat. Lab., from 1976, prin. investigator, from 1976. Mem.: Am. Phys. Soc. Methodist. Achievements include patents in field. Home: Los Alamos, N.Mex. Died May 23, 2006.

CRANOR, JOHN ROSS, retired surgeon; b. Ypsilanti, Mich., Sept. 23, 1910; s. John Ross Sr. and Ethel (Koyl) C.; m. Mary Metz Cranor, Aug. 10, 1936 (dec. Mar. 1991); children: John R. Jr., Victoria, Melissa. BSc, U. Chgo., 1935; MD, Johns Hopkins U., 1939. Diplomate Am. Bd. Surgery. Resident staff Royal Victoria Hosp., Montreal, Can., 1939-40, Yale-New Haven (Conn.) Hosp., 1940-42, Cin. Gen. Hosp., 1942; fellow in surgery Lahey Clinic, Boston, 1946-47; fellow in pathology New England Deaconess Hosp., Boston, 1948; chief of surgery VA Hosp., Topeka, Kans., 1948-49, cons. Walla Walla, Wash., 1950-75; surg. staff St. Mary's Hosp., Walla Walla, 1950-75, Walla Walla Gen. Hosp., 1950-75. Lt. comdr. USN, 1942-46. Mem. AMA, Wash. State Med. Soc. Avocations: fishing, travel, visiting family and friends, reading. Home: Belleville, Pa. Died Jan. 24, 2006.

CRANSTON, FREDERICK PITKIN, physics educator; b. Denver, Aug. 28, 1922; s. Frederick Pitkin and Alta (Kinney) C.; m. Bonnie Louise Debe, Apr. 17, 1947 (div. Mar. 1971); children: Carol, Frederick, Rodney, Claudia; m. Jerneral Warren Johnson, Mar. 21, 1971; 1 child, Lawrence Duncan Crist. BA in Physics, Colgate U., 1943; MS in Physics, Stanford U., 1950, PhD in Physics, 1959. Instr. Denver U., 1946-47; staff physicist Los Alamos (N.Mex.) Nat. Lab., 1953-62; assoc. prof. Humboldt State U., Arcata, Calif., 1962-66, prof., from 1966, dept. chair, 1971-74. Cons. Lawrence Livermore (Calif.) Lab., 1964-69, Lawrence Berkeley Lab., 1970; vis. prof. U. Calif., berkeley, 1974. Pres. Los Alamos Fedn. Am. Scientists. Maj. U.S. Army, 1942-66. Mem. Am. Phys. Soc., Am. Assn. Pysics Tchrs. Democrat. Unitarian Universalist. Avocation: steam locomotive engr. Home: Trinidad, Calif. Died Sept. 12, 2006.

CRARY, PAUL DELORIMIER, radiologist; b. Covington, Ky., Jan. 24, 1939; s. Paul Delorimier and Grace Blanche (Spitzlberger) C.; m. Jo Mary Bach, Sept. 3, 1962; children: Colleen, Shannon. BS, Xavier U., 1959; MD, St. Louis U., 1963. Diplomate Am. Bd. Radiology, Am. Bd. Nuclear Medicine. Rotating entern U.S. Naval Hosp., Gt. Lakes, Ill., 1963-64, resident in radiology Phila., 1965-68, chief dept. radiology Jacksonville, Fla., 1969-71, Miles Hosp., Damariscotta, Maine, from 1989; pvt. practice, Edgewood, Ky., 1971-89; chief dept. radiology St. Andrews Hosp., Boothbay Harbor, Maine, from 1989. Dir. No. Ky. Dist. Health Dept., 1986-89. Officer M.C., USN, 1963-71; col. M.C., U.S. Army, 1984-91. Mem. Am. Coll. Radiology, Am. Def. Preparedness Assn., Soc. Med. Cons. Armed Forces, C. of C., Lions. Roman Catholic. Avocations: german police arms, photography. Died Feb. 27, 2007.

CRAWFORD, JAMES DEE, chemical distribution executive; b. Boise, Idaho, June 23, 1950; s. Glen E. and Beverly J. (Thomas) C.; m. Diane E. Crawford (Ball), July 8, 1994. BBA, Boise State U., 1972. CPA, Idaho. Staff acct. J.R. Simplot Co., Boise, 1972-75, corp. acctg. mgr., 1975-79, asst. contr. Caldwell, Idaho, 1979-80; treas. SimCal Chem. Co., Fresno, Calif., 1980-83; dir. fin services J.R. Simplot Co., Boise, 1983-85, treas., 1995—97; CFO Wilbur-Ellis Co., San Francisco, from 2000; v.p., contr. J.R. Simplot Co., Boise, 1997—2000. Bd. dirs. Micron Tech., Inc., Boise, Investors Fin. Corp., Boise. Com. chmn. St. Alphonsus Found., Boise, 1985. Named one of Outstanding Young Men Am., Jaycees, 1974. Mem. AICPA, Idaho Soc. CPAs, Nat. Assn. Corp. Treas. Clubs: Crane Creek Country (Boise), City Club of San Francisco. Republican. Episcopalian. Avocation: golf. Home: San Francisco, Calif. Died Oct. 21, 2006.

CRAWFORD, JOHN EDWARD, retired geologist, consultant; b. Richmond, Va., June 6, 1924; s. James Henry and Loretta Ellen (Bankerd) C.; m. Mary Elizabeth Ayres, May 15, 1948; children: Michelle Lorraine, Caprice Lizette. BA, Johns Hopkins, 1947. Reg. geologist, Calif. Geologist uranium exploration program U.S. Geol. Survey, 1948-51; nat. stockpile materials specialist Munitions Bd., Office Sec. Def., 1951-53; prodn. engr. AEC, 1953-54; specialist on source, feed, fissionable materials Bur. Mines, 1954-57, nuclear tech. adviser to dir., 1957-60, chief nuc. engr. for atomic rsch. programs, 1960-63; dir. Marine Mineral Tech. Ctr., Tiburon, Calif., 1963-66; pres., founder Crawford Marine Specialists, Inc., San Francisco, also Suva, Fiji, 1966-76; pres. Earth Tech. Corp., San Rafael, 1973-77; mgr. geothermal rsch. programs and Salton Sea sci. drilling project U.S. Dept. Energy Ops. Office, Oakland, Calif., 1977-89; mgr. ops. and prin. geologist Western Geologic Resources, Inc., San Rafael, Calif., 1989-90; cons. geothermal and environ. affairs, from 1990; assoc., regional mgr. Western Ops. Earth Resources Internat., L.C., Carson City, Nev., 1994-2000; ret., 2007. Author: Facts Concerning Uranium Exploration and Production, 1956; contbr. articles to govt. and profl. jours., Leaders in Am. Sci. Vol. VIII, 1968-69. Mem. Calif. Gov.'s Commn. Ocean Resources, 1966-67, Calif. Gov.'s Small Hydro Task Force, 1981-82. Served with AUS, 1943-46. Mem. Internat. Marine Minerals Soc. (Moore medal for excellence in devel. of marine minerals 1998), Geol. Soc. Am., Marine Tech. Soc. (past chmn. marine mineral resources com., past chmn. marine resources div.), Delta Upsilon. Died Apr. 20, 2007.

CRAWFORD, JOHN JOSEPH, microwave components company executive; b. Flushing, N.Y., Oct. 18, 1936; s. John and Mary Kate (Sweeney) C.; m. Margaret Rose Hauser, July 12, 1958; children— Kevin, Theresa, Thomas, John, Paul, Christopher. B.B.A., Manhattan Coll., 1958; M.B.A., NYU, 1963. Dir. materials Aurora div. Nabisco, West Hempstead, N.Y., 1970-78; v.p. ops. Narda div. Loral, Hauppauge, N.Y., 1978—. Leader, Cub Scouts, 1965-70; coach Little League, Setauket, 1972-76; tchr. Confraternity of Christine Doctrine, 1971-82; minister St. James Roman Cath. Ch., 1982—. Mem. Am. Prodn. and Inventory Control Soc. Avocation: Stained glass. Home: Port Jefferson Station, NY. Died Feb. 14, 2006.

CREAN, JOHN C., retired housing and recreational vehicles manufacturing company executive; b. Bowden, ND, 1925; married. Founder Fleetwood Enterprises, Inc., Riverside, Calif., 1950, pres., 1952-70, chmn., CEO, 1950-98. With USN, 1942, with US Mcht. Marines, 1944—45. Died Jan. 11, 2007.

CRESPIN, REGINE, soprano; b. Marseilles, France, Feb. 23, 1927; d. Henri and Margherite (DiMeirone) C. Student, Lycée Français, Conservatoire de Paris. Appeared in numerous operas including Lohengrin, Mulhouse, France, 1950, Paris, 1951, N.Y.C., 1964, Tosca, Il Trovatore, Otello, Die Walkuere, Oberon, Fidelio, Der Rosenkavalier, Marseilles, Le Nozze di Figaro, Paris, 1956, Dialogues of the Carmelites, 1957, Parsifal, 1958, Ballo in Maschera, 1958, Fedra, Milan, Italy, 1959, Die Walkuere, Vienna, 1959, Der Rosenkavalier, Berlin, 1960, as the Marshallin, London, 1961, Les Troyens, Paris, 1961, Penelope, Buenos Aires, 1961, Otello, Ballo in Maschera, Die Walkuere, Der Rosenkavalier, Vienna, also Rosenkavalier, N.Y.C., 1962, Flying Dutchman, N.Y.C., 1962, Ballo in Maschera, N.Y.C., 1962, La Vestale, N.Y.C., 1962, Herodiade, N.Y.C., 1963, Fidelio, Ballo in Maschera, Tannhauser, Fidelio, Chgo., 1963, Carnegie Hall, 1973, Met. Opera, 1973, Carmen, Met. Opera, 1975, Cavalleria Rusticana, San Francisco Opera, 1976, Dialogues of the Carmelites, Met. Opera, 1977, 78, soloist, N.Y. Philharmonic, 1964-65, appeared in recital, Hunter Coll., 1965. Died July 4, 2007.

CRETSOS, JAMES MIMIS, pharmaceutical company science information executive chemist; b. Athens, Greece, Oct. 23, 1929; came to U.S., 1946, naturalized, 1955; s. Basil D. and Chrissa B. (Thomaidou) Kretsos; m. Barbara Ann Deitz, Mar. 10, 1952; children— Maurice William, Christopher James BS in Chemistry, Am. U., 1960, postgrad., 1960-62. Research chemist Melpar, Inc., Falls Church, Va., 1961-63, info. scientist, 1963-64, head tech. info. ctr., 1964-65, mgr. info. services lab., 1965-67; dir. instructional materials ctr. Tng. Corp. of Am., Falls Church, 1966-67; dir. info. systems lab. Litton Industries, Bethesda, Md., 1967-69; head sci. info. systems dept. Merrell Dow Pharms., Cin., from 1969. Dir. Infoflow, Inc.; cons. OEO, Ohio, Ky.-Ind. Regional Library and Info. Council; lectr. U. Cin., 1973-74, U. Ky., 1976-77, 82 Editor, Health Aspects of Pesticides Abstract Bull., 1967-69. Mem. adv. bd. chem. Abstracts Service, 1981-83, mem. user council, 1983— Mem. Creative Edn. Found., Buffalo, 1967—. Served with M.C., AUS, 1954-56 Mem. Am. Chem. Soc., Am. Mgmt. Assn., Am. Soc. Info. Sci. (chmn. So. Ohio chpt. 1973-74, chmn. SIG.BC 1973-74, chmn. profl. enhancement ocm. 1974-75, chmn. 5th mid-yr. meeting 1976, Watson Davis award 1976, chmn. biomed. communications symposium 1976, chmn. membership com. 1977, exec. com. 1979, nominations com. 1980, pres. 1979, chmn. SIG/NMR 1981, chmn. SIG/SRT 1982. Clubs: Indoor Tennis. Home: Cincinnati, Ohio. Died Aug. 4, 2006.

CREVI, PETER M., lawyer; b. NYC, Nov. 16, 1941; BA, Cornell U., 1963; JD, U. Mich., 1968. Bar: N.Y. 1969. With Cravath, Swaine & Moore, NYC. Died July 25, 2007.

CREWS, ROBERT NELSON, construction company executive; b. Texline, Tex., Feb. 28, 1924; s. John S. and Elizabeth L. (Shankle) C.; m. Joy Kleck, Aug. 17, 1946; children— Robert Nelson, Elizabeth Ann, M. Lesley B.E.C.E., Tulane U., 1948. Registered profl. engr., Tex., La. Exec. v.p., dir. J. Ray McDermontt, New Orleans, 1948-74; exec. v.p. Raymond Internat. Inc., Houston, 1975-78, pres., chief operating officer, from 1978, dir. Dir. 1st City Bank Highland Village Advisor Tulane U. Coll. Engring., 1970-72; chmn. Offshore Ops. Com., 1965; mem. panel advisors to comdr. U.S. Coast Guard, 1967-72. Served with USNR, World War II Mem. La. Engring. Soc., Nat. Ocean Industry Assn. (bd. dirs., past chmn.), Moles Clubs: University, Houston, Petroleum, Tschefuncta Country. Home: Houston, Tex. Died Apr. 8, 2007.

CRITTENDEN, EUGENE DWIGHT, JR., chemical company executive; b. Feb. 27, 1927; s. Eugene Dwight and Meltina Ester (Feldkamp) C.; m. Sarah Ann Rogers, June 23, 1951; children: Sarah Ann Crittenden D'Alonzo, Susan Gray Crittenden Chambers. BS, Purdue U., 1947; MS, U. Pa., 1949, PhD, 1951. With Hercules, Inc., 1951-92; sr. engr. Rsch. Ctr., Wilmington, Del., 1951-53; asst. to dir. devel. Naval Stores Dept., 1953-55, sr. chem. engr. Brunswick, Ga., 1955-56, Wilmington, 1956-57, tech. asst. to devel. dir., 1957-60, sr. tech. rep. NYC, 1960-62, asst. dir. devel. synthetics dept. Wilmington, 1962-63, asst. to gen. mgr. internat. dept., 1963-64; dir. Hercules Europe, Brussels, 1965-66; dir. sales organic chem. divsn., synthetic dept. Wilmington, 1966-67; asst. gen. mgr. synthetics dept., 1967-68; gen. mgr. new enterprise dept., 1968-72; indsl. sys. dept., 1972-77; divsn. v.p. adminstrn. and pub. affairs, 1977-82; divsn. v.p. ops., corp. dir., mem. exec. and mgmt. com., 1982; corp. v.p. internat., 1983-87; pres., CEO Aqualon Group, 1987-89; sr. v.p., 1982-92; ret.; corp. dir. Hercules Inc., Wilmington, 1982-92. Bd. dirs. City of Wilmington and New Castle County YMCA, 1968-92, pres. 1977-82; trustee, c.p., pres. Eleutherian Mills-Hagley Found., 1981-2001; bd. dirs. World Affairs Coun., 1981-92; trustee, bd. dirs. Med. Ctr. of Del., 1978-92, vice chmn., 1990—, bd. dirs. Chritsiana Care Corp., 1992—, del. met. chmn. Nat. Alliance of Bus., 1981-82; mem. Gov.'s Internat. Trade Coun., 1984-92; mem. Del. and Ea. Pa. Dist. Export Coun., 1984-92; del. Econ. and Fin. Adv. Coun., 1977-2001, chmn. 1989-93. Mem.: AIChE, AAAS, Am. Chem. Soc., Sea Island Golf Club, Ocean Forest Golf Club, Bidermann Golf Club, Wilmington Country Club (bd. govs.), Wilmington Vicmead Hunt Club, Pine Valley Golf Club, Sigma Xi. Republican. Episcopalian. Avocations: piano, golf, tennis. Home: Wilmington, Del. Died Apr. 28, 2006.

CROMBE, WILLIAM ALBERT, retired school superintendent; b. Irondequoit, N.Y., Sept. 13, 1920; s. John Clyde and Martha (Kemp) C.; m. Ethel Jones, Nov. 17, 1945 (div. Oct. 1954); children— Diane Sue, Barry William; m. Pauline Thresher, Mar. 22, 1957. B.S., Geneseo State Coll., 1946; M.S., Buffalo State Coll., 1951; Ed.D., U. Rochester, 1968. Cert. supt., prin., supr., tchr., N.Y. Tchr. pub. schs., Ontario, N.Y., 1946-49; supr. Webster Central Sch., N.Y., 1949-68, asst. supt. schs., 1968-70; supt. schs. Wayne Central Schs., Ontario Center, N.Y., 1970-79; instr. various colls., N.Y. State, 1964-70; cons. Town of Ontario, 1981-84. Author: Why Schools Are in Trouble, 1978. Served with U.S. Army, 1942-46. Recipient T. Walsh McQuillan award State Adminstrs. Assn. N.Y., 1977. Mem. Am. Assn. Sch. Adminstrs., N.Y. State Supts. Assn. (life), PTA (life), Ontario Hist. Soc. (pres. 1982-85). Republican. Methodist. Club: September (pres. 1981-83). Lodge: Rotary. Avocations: golf, reading, cards. Home: Ontario, NY. Died Nov. 7, 2006.

CROMILLER, HAROLD LEE, retired banker, consultant; b. New Orleans, Nov. 3, 1920; s. Harold William and Nell (Lee) C.; m. Ellen Patricia Sutton, Oct. 3, 1953; children: Suzanne Marie, Cynthia Ann, Diane Patricia, Pamela Paige, Renee Magdelaine. Student, Tulane U., 1944; grad., Am. Inst. Banking, 1956. Certified internal auditor. With Hibernia Nat. Bank, New Orleans, from 1938, v.p., comptroller, 1966-72, sr. v.p., comptroller, 1972-73; treas., dir. Hibernia Bldg. Corp., 1966-73; comptroller First Met. Bank Metairie, La., 1973-75, sr. v.p., from 1973; asst. to pres. Brinson Co., Inc., Haraham, La., 1984-85. Bank specialist Stonier Grad. Sch. Banking. Adv. bd. Banking Mag. Mem. Am. Inst. Banking (pres. New Orleans 1961), Am. Bankers Assn. (ins. and protection div. exec. com.), Bank Adminstrn. Inst. (pres. New Orleans 1962), Fin. Execs. Inst., Assn. Internal Auditors (pres. New Orleans 1973) Home: Metairie, La. Died Aug. 5, 2006.

CROMLEY, RAYMOND AVOLON, syndicated columnist; b. Tulare, Calif., Aug. 23, 1910; s. William James and Grace Violet (Bailey) C.; m. Masuyo Marjorie Suto (dec. Apr. 1946); m. Helen Sue Holcomb (dec. July 1967); children: Donald Stowe, Helen Sue, Jessica Lynn, Linda Grace, William Holcomb, Mary Ann, John Austin. BS in Physics, Calif. Inst. Tech., 1933; student, Japanese Lang. Inst., Tokyo, 1936-39, Strategic Intelligence Sch., Washington, 1954. Reporter Pasadena (Calif.) Post, 1928-34, Honolulu Advertiser, 1934-35, Flintridge Sch., Pasadena, 1935-36; reporter, then financial editor Japan Advertiser, Tokyo, 1936-40; editor Trans Pacific (econ. and financial weekly), 1938-40; with Wall St. Jour., 1938-55; Far Ea. corr., 1938-47; Washington corr., 1947-55; sci. editor radio program Monitor, 1955-56; econ. and financial commentator NBC radio, 1956-57; asst. producer CBS Radio, 1957-58; mil. analyst Newspaper Enterprise Assn., 1958-64; former pres. Cromley News-Features; syndicated columnist, 1964—2003. Asst. logic, freshman English Calif. Inst. Tech., 1928-30; lectr. Air War Coll., 1952, 54, Dept. State Fgn. Service Inst., 1955, 65-67; cons. guerilla war, Asian politics, 1952— Author: Veterans Benefits, 1966, 2d edit., 1970, 3d edit., 1973, rev. edit., 1975, Educational Benefits, 1968, Ariwara Narihira and Japanese Poetry of the Heian and Nara Periods. Chmn. dist. bds. charter rev. Boy Scouts Am., 1956-60; sec. bishop's com. pastoral benefits Va. Conf. Meth. Ch., 1967-68; organizer com. estatlishment Martha Washington Libr., Mt. Vernon, Va., 1954; chmn. Inter-ch. Coun. Teen Activities and Teen Clubs, Mt. Vernon, 1955-57, World Coun. Youth, 1932-35. Prisoner of war, 1941-42; col. AUS, 1943-46; comdg. officer U.S. Mil. and Dept. State mission to Mao-Tse-tung's hdqs., Yenan, Communist China. Decorated Legion of Merit, Bronze Star medal. Mem. Nat. Trust for Historic Preservation, Asiatic Soc. Japan, State Dept. Corrs. Assn. (pres. 1954-55), White House Corrs. Assn., Ret. Officers Assn., Smithsonian Assocs., Nat. Archives Assn., Nat. Press Found., Am. Fgn. Svc. Assn., Nat. Press Club Washington, Assn.Corcoran Gallery Art, Sigma Delta Chi, Pi Kappa Delta. Republican. Methodist (lay spkr., Sunday sch. tchr.). Clubs: Tokyo Correspondents (exec. com. 1947); Overseas Writers (Washington). Died Feb. 23, 2007.

CRONON, E(DMUND) DAVID, JR., historian, retired educator; b. Mpls., Mar. 11, 1924; s. Edmund David and Florence Ann (Meyer) C.; m. Mary Jean Hotmar, May 13, 1950; children: William John, Robert David. Student, Macalester Coll., 1942-43; AB, Oberlin Coll., 1948; AM, U. Wis., 1949, PhD, 1953; postgrad., Manchester U., Eng., 1950-51. Instr., then asst. prof. history Yale U., 1953-59; assoc. prof., then prof. history U. Nebr., 1959-62; prof. history U. Wis., Madison, 1962-94, dean Coll. Letters and Sci., 1974-89, chmn. dept., 1966-69, dir. Inst. Research in Humanities, 1969-74, prof., dean emeritus, 1994—2006; lectr. for State Dept., Europe and Near East, 1966. Fulbright-Hays lectr. Moscow State U., 1974 Author: Black Moses: The Story of Marcus Garvey and the Universal Negro Improvement Association, 1955, Josephus Daniels in Mexico, 1960, Government and the Economy: Some Nineteenth Century Views, 1960, Contemporary Labor-Management Relations, 1960, The Cabinet Diaries of Josephus Daniels, 1913-1921, 1963, Labor and the New Deal, 1963, Twentieth Century America; Selected Readings, 2 vols, 1965-66, The Political Thought of Woodrow Wilson, 1965, Marcus Garvey, 1973, The University of Wisconsin: Politics, Depression, and War, 1925-45 (with John W. Jenkins), 1994, (with John W. Jenkina) The University of Wisconsin: Renewal to Revolution, 1945-71. Mem. exec. com. Wis. Am. Revolution Bicentennial Commn.; adv. bd. Franklin D. Roosevelt Library, 1971-76, Wis. Humanities Com., 1973-77, Council for Internat. Exchange Scholars, 1977-80; mem. Commn. Instns. Higher Edn. N. Central Assn. Colls. and Schs., 1978-82, cons., examiner, 1970—; bd. dirs. Council of Colls. of Arts and Scis., 1978-80, pres., 1981-82; mem. Commn. Arts and Scis., Nat. Assn. State Univs. and Land Grant Colls., 1984-88; trustee Ripon Coll., 1976-91. Served to 1st lt., inf. AUS, 1943-46. Fulbright fellow, 1950-51; Stimson fellow, 1958-59 Fellow Soc. Am. Historians; mem. Am. Hist. Assn., Orgn. Am. Historians (exec. bd.), Wis. Hist. Soc. (bd. curators, pres.), So. Hist. Soc. (exec. coun., bd. editors), Madison Opera (bd. dirs., v.p., pres.), Phi Beta Kappa (nominating com. United chpts. 1985-91), Blackhawk Club, Univ. Club. Unitarian Universalist. Died Dec. 5, 2006.

CROOKER, JOHN H., JR., lawyer; b. Houston, Oct. 26, 1914; s. John H. and Marguerite (Malsch) C.; m. Kay Berry; children: Carolyn (Mrs. W.E. Schwing), John H. III, Linda (Mrs. Barry Hunsaker, Jr.), Tara (Mrs. Alec Mize), Allison (Mrs. David R. Margrave). BA with distinction, Rice U., 1935; LL.B. with highest honors, U. Tex., 1937. Bar: Tex. 1937, D.C. 1953. Practice law, Houston and Washington, 1937-67, 70—; chmn. CAB, 1968-69. Chmn. bd. dirs. U. St. Thomas, Tex., 1974-78. Served to lt. comdr. USNR, 1941-45. Decorated Bronze Star. Mem. ABA, State Bar Tex. (past chmn. corp. sect.), Am. Law Inst. (life), Houston Bar Found. (chmn. bd. dirs. 1984), Houston C. of C. (chmn. bd. dirs. 1978-79). Home: Houston, Tex. Died May 18, 2007.

CROSS, GEORGE R., insurance consultant; b. NYC, May 9, 1923; s. George W. and Mae E. (Fish) C.; m. Shirley Jean Williams, June 24, 1950; children: Stephen, Pamela, Jeffrey, Mark. AB, Syracuse U., 1947; JD, Bklyn. Law Sch., 1951; C.P.C.U., 1960. Bar: N.Y. 1952, U.S. Supreme Ct. 1958. With Atlantic Mut. Ins. Co., 1947-49, adjuster, 1949-52; asst. gen. counsel Nat. Assn. Ins. Agts., 1952-59; with Gt. Am. Ins. Co., NYC, 1959-70, gen. atty., 1963-68, v.p., 1967-70, gen. counsel, 1968-70, sec., 1963-67, 68-70; v.p., asso. gen. counsel, sec. Crum & Forster Ins. Cos., NYC, 1970-73, v.p. govt. affairs, 1973-79, also dir., v.p. govt. affairs, 1979-88; ins. cons., from 1988. Chmn. bd. N.J. Property-Liability Ins. Guaranty Assn., 1975-87; chmn. N.J. Med. Malpractice Reins. Assn., 1979-87; dir. Va. Ins. Guaranty Assn.; pres. N.Y. Ins. Exchange Security Fund; chmn. Fla. Med. Malpractice Ins. Assn., Nat. Coordinating Com. on Med. Malpractice; bd. dirs. Nat. Com. on Ins. Guaranty Funds; chmn. bd. N.Y. Med. Malpractice Ins. Plan, 1976-87; mem. Am. Arbitration Assn., apptd. arbitrator Arbitration Forums, Inc., 1990. Mem. Nanuet (N.Y.) Sch. Bd., 1962-65. Served to 1st lt. USAAF, 1943-45, ETO. Mem. AARP, N.Y. Bar Assn., New York County Lawyers Assn., Med. Malpractice Ins. Assn. (chmn.), Mcpl. Bond Ins. Assn. (legal com. 1974-79), Am. Legion, Drug and Chem. Club, Masons. Home: Punta Gorda, Fla. Died Jan. 17, 2007.

CROSS, SAMUEL S., lawyer; b. Detroit, Oct. 19, 1919; s. Samuel Stogden and Mildred Lurline (Hay) C.; m. Jodie E. Hecht, Jan. 3, 1947 (div. 1948); 1 child, Edward T.; m. Audrey Brauneck, Nov. 25, 1950; children— Stephen W., Lauren E., Robert A., Wendy A. BS, Lehigh U., 1941; LL.B., U. Pa., 1949. Bar: N.Y. 1951, Conn. 1953, Pa. 1977. Test engr. Bethlehem Steel Co., Steelton, Pa., 1941-43; assoc. Watson, Johnson, Leavenworth & Blair, NYC, 1949-52; gen. counsel, sec. Perkin-Elmer Corp., Norwalk, Conn., 1952-64; counsel Maguire, Cole & Bentley, Stamford, Conn., 1964-68; ptnr. Cross, Brodrick & Chipman, Stamford, Conn., 1969-79, Kelley Drye & Warren, NYC, 1979-88, life ptnr., 1989-90, of counsel, from 1991. Gen. counsel Southwestern Area Commerce and Industry Assn. of Conn., Inc., Stamford, 1970-90. Author: Corporation Law in Connecticut, 1972, Connecticut Corporation Law and Practice, 1989; editor-in-chief Conn. Bar Jour., 1982-85; contbr. articles to profl. jours. Mem. Legis. Commn. on Revision of Corp. Laws, Hartford, Conn., 1957-62; pres. The Ferguson Libr., Stamford, 1977-78; trustee The Ferguson Libr. Found., 1987-94, Engring. Edn. Found., Inc., 1969—; chmn. Forum for World Affairs, Inc., 1987-89. Ltd. (j.g.) USNR, 1943-46. Mem. ABA, Am. Soc. Internat. Law, Internat. Law Assn. (Am. br.), Southwestern Legal Found. (adv. bd. Internat. and Comparative Law Ctr.), Met. Club (Washington), Tau Beta Pi. Republican. Home: Wilton, Conn. Died July 27, 2006.

CROW, BROWNING, consulting engineer; b. Kansas City, Mo., May 25, 1923; s. Weldon D. and Elizabeth (Browning) C.; m. Helen Gene Veach, Sept. 3, 1946; children— Cathleen, Robert, Nancy. BA, U. Kansas City, 1944; BS, U. Mo., 1948. With Howard, Needles, Tammen & Bergendoff, civil engr., Kansas City, 1948-50, asst. project engr., Colo., 1950-52, project engr., Ravenna, Ohio, 1952-56, project engr., Cleve., 1956-68, ptnr., from 1968. Mem. industry adv. bd. Cleve. State U., 1976-85 Served with USN, 1943-46. Mem. ASCE, NSPE, Ohio Soc. Profl. Engrs., Am. Pub. Works Assn. Clubs: Lakewood Country, Rotary. Republican. Episcopalian. Home: Johns Island, SC. Died Feb. 18, 2007.

CROW, EDWIN LOUIS, mathematical statistician, consultant; b. Browntown, Wis., Sept. 15, 1916; s. Frederick Marion and Alice Blanche (Cox) C.; m. Eleanor Gish, June 13, 1942; children: Nancy Rebecca, Dorothy Carol Crow-Willard. BS summa cum laude, Beloit Coll., 1937; Ph.M., U. Wis., 1938, PhD, 1941; postgrad., Brown U., 1941-42, U. Calif.-Berkeley, 1947-48, Univ. Coll., London, 1961-62. Instr. math. Case Sch. Applied Sci., Cleve., 1941-42; mathematician Bur. Ordnance Dept. Navy, Washington, 1942-46, U.S. Naval Ordnance Test Sta., China Lake, Calif., 1946-54; cons. statistics Boulder Labs., U.S. Dept. Commerce, Boulder, Colo., 1954-73, Nat. Telecommunications and Info. Adminstrn., Boulder, Colo., from 1974; statistician Nat. Ctr. Atmospheric Research, Boulder, Colo., 1975-82. Instr. math. extension div. UCLA, China Lake, 1947-54; adj. prof. math. U. Colo., Boulder, 1963-81; lectr. stats. Met. State Coll., Denver, 1974. Co-author: Statistics Manual, 1960; co-editor: Lognormal Distributions, 1988; assoc. editor: Communications in Statistics, 1972-98, Jour. Am. Statis. Assn., 1967-75, Current Index to Stats., 1981—; contbr. articles to profl. jours. Survey statistician Boulder Valley Sch. Dist., 1971-72; founder, pres. Boulder Tennis Assn., 1967-69, pres., 1982. Recipient Outstanding Publ. award Nat. Telecommunications and Info. Adminstrn., 1980, 82; Bronze medal U.S. Dept. Commerce, 1970, Editor's award Am. Meteorol. Soc., 1987. Fellow Royal Statis. Soc., Am. Statis Assn. (coun. mem. 1959-60, 68-69, Outstanding Chpt. mem. 1989), AAAS; mem. Am. Math. Soc., Math. Assn. Am., Inst. Math. Stats., Bernoulli Soc. for Math. Stats. and Probability, Soc. Indsl. and Applied Math., U.S. Tennis Assn., Sigma Xi, Phi Beta Kappa. Clubs: Colo. Mountain, Harvest House Sporting Assn. (Boulder). Democrat. Unitarian Universalist. Achievements include theory and applications of mathematical statistics in ordnance, radio standards, radio propagation, communication systems, weather modification, and ranking data. Home: Boulder, Colo. Died Oct. 29, 2005.

CROWE, WILLIAM JAMES, JR., former Chairman of the Joint Chiefs of Staff; b. La Grange, Ky., Jan. 2, 1925; s. William James and Eula (Russell) C.; m. Shirley Mary Grennell, Feb. 14, 1954; children: William Blake, James Brent, Mary Russell. BS, U.S. Naval Acad., 1946; MA in Edn., Stanford U., 1956; PhD in Politics (Harold W. Dodds fellow), Princeton U., 1965; LLD (hon.), U. Liverpool, George Washington U.; LLD, Knox Coll. Advanced through grades to adm USN, 1960, ret., 1989, Commd. ensign, 1946, comdg. officer U.S.S. Trout, 1960—62; comdr. Submarine Div. 31 San Diego, 1966-67; sr. adv. Vietnamese Navy, 1970-71; dep. to Pres.'s Spl. Rep. for Micronesian Status Negotiations, 1971-73; dep. dir. strategic plans, policy, nuclear systems & NSC affairs divsn. USN, 1973-75; dir. East Asia & Pacific region, Office Sec. Def. US Dept. Def., Washington, 1975—76; comdr. Middle East Force USN, Bahrain, 1976-77, dep. chief naval ops. plans & policy Washington, 1977-80, comdr.-in-chief Allied Forces So. Europe, 1980-83, comdr.-in-chief Pacific Fleet, 1983-85; chmn. Joint Chiefs of Staff US Dept. Def., 1985-89; prof. geopolitics U. Okla., Norman, 1989-94; chmn. Fgn. Intelligence Adv. Bd., Washington, 1993-94; US amb. to U.K. US Dept. State, London, 1994-97. Counselor Ctr. for Strategic and Internat. Studies, Washington, 1989-94; prof. U. Okla., 1989-94, chmn. bd. visitors Internat. Programs Ctr., Okla. U., adv. bd. mem. GlobalOptions, Inc. Author: The Line of Fire, 1993; co-author: Reducing Nuclear Danger: The Road Away from the Brink, 1993; author supr. ops. plan for repatriation of U.S.S. Pueblo crew. Trustee Princeton U., 1995-2000; dir. USNA Found., 1998-2007 Decorated Defense Disting. Svc.medal with three oak leaf clusters, Navy Disting. Svc. medal with two oak leaf clusters, Disting. Svc. medal, Legion of Merit, Bronze Star with combat V, Air medal with six oak leaf clusters, Navy Commendation medal, Humanitarian Svc. medal, China Svc. medal, Am. Campaign medal, World War II Victory medal, Navy Occupation Svc. medal with Pacific clasp, Nat. Def. Svc. medal, Vietnam Svc. medal, Humanitarian Svc. medal, Rep. of Vietnam Navy Disting. Svc. Order, Rep. of Vietnam Gallantry Cross with Palm & Brnze Star, Rep. of Vietnam Armed Forces Honor medal, Rep. of Vietnam Gallantry Cross Unit citation, Rep. of Vietnam Campaign medal, Order of the Nat. Security Merit Tong-Il medal (Rep. of Korea), Grand Cross with Cordon of the Order of the Merit of the Rep. of Italy; recipient Presdl. Medal of Freedom, 1993, Ataturk Peace & Democracy award Am. Ataturk Assn., 1998 Mem. U.S. Naval Inst., Am. Polit. Sci. Assn., Internat. Studies Assn., Coun. on Fgn. Rels., Washington Inst. Fgn. Affairs, Phi Gamma Delta, Phi Delta Phi. Home: Alexandria, Va. Died Oct. 18, 2007.*

CROWELL, RICHARD HENRY, mathematician, educator; b. Northeast, Pa., Apr. 6, 1928; s. Milton Frederick and Esther (Dary) C.; m. Marilyn Nelson, Apr. 2, 1955; children— Philip Nelson, Peter Dary. AB, Harvard, 1949; postgrad., U. Amsterdam, Netherlands, 1950-51; MA, Princeton, 1953, PhD, 1955; MA (hon.), Dartmouth, 1968. Rsch. asst. Princeton U., 1955-56; lectr. Mass. Inst. Tech., 1956-58; asst. prof. Dartmouth Coll., 1958-63, asso. prof., 1963-67, prof., 1967-93, prof. emeritus, from 1993, chmn. math. dept., 1973-79, chmn. dept. math and computer sci., 1986-89, prof. emeritus, from 1993. Author: (with R.H. Fox) Introduction to Knot Theory, 1963, (with R.E. Williamson and H.F. Trotter) Calculus of Vector Functions, 1968, (with W.E. Slesnick) Calculus with Analytic Geometry, 1968. Mem. Am. Math. Soc., Math Assn. Am., Phi Beta Kappa. Mem. United Ch. of Christ. Home: Hanover, NH. Died Aug. 5, 2006.

CROWLEY, JOHN CRANE, real estate developer; b. Detroit, June 29, 1919; s. Edward John and Leah Helen (Crane) C.; m. Barbara Wenzel Gilfillan, Jan. 12, 1945; children: F. Alexander, Leonard, Philip, Eliot, Louise, Sylvia. BA with high honors, Swarthmore Coll., 1941; MS, U. Denver, 1943. Asst. dir. Mcpl. Fin. Officers Assn., Chgo., 1946-48; So. Calif. mgr. League Calif. Cities, Los Angeles, 1948-53; mgr. City of Monterey Park, Calif., 1953-56. Founder, exec. v.p. Nat. Med. Enterprises, L.A., 1968; pres. Ventura Towne House (Calif.), 1963-96; mem. faculty U. So. Calif. Sch. Pub. Adminstrn., 1950-53; bd. dirs. Regional Inst. of So. Calif., The L.A. Partnership 2000, Burbank-Glendale-Pasadena Airport Authority; commr. Bob Hope Airport. Trustee Pacific Oaks Friends Sch. and Coll., Pasadena, 1954-57, 92-98, Swarthmore Coll., 1987—; bd. dirs. Pasadena Area Liberal Arts Ctr., 1962-72, pres., 1965-68; bd. dirs. Pacificulture Found. and Asia Mus., 1971-76, pres., 1972-74; bd. dirs. Nat. Mcpl. League, 1986-92, AAF Rose Bowl Aquatics Ctr., 1997—; chmn. Pasadena Cultural Heritage

Commn., 1975-78; city dir. Pasadena, 1979-91; mayor City of Pasadena, 1986-88; bd. dirs. Western Justice Ctr., 1992—, v.p., 1995—, LA County Commn. on Efficiency and Economy, 1994—; mem. L.A. County Commn. on Local Govt., 2000—. Sloan Found. fellow, 1941-43; recipient Arthur Nobel award City of Pasadena. Mem. Am. Soc. Pub. Adminstrn. (local chpt., Winston Crouch award 1990), Internat. City Mgmt. Assn., Nat. Mcpl. League (nat. bd. 1980-92, Disting. Citizen award, 1984), Inst. Pub. Adminstrn. (sr. assoc.), Phi Delta Theta. Democrat. Unitarian Universalist. Home: Pasadena, Calif. Died May 30, 2007.

CROWTHER, RICHARD LAYTON, architect, consultant, researcher, author, lecturer; b. Newark, Dec. 16, 1910; s. William George and Grace (Layton) C.; m. Emma Jane Hubbard, 1935 (div. 1949); children: Bethe Crowther Allison, Warren Winfield, Vivian Layton; m. Pearl Marie Tesch, Sept. 23, 1950. Student, Newark Sch. Fine and Indsl. Arts, 1928-31, San Diego State Coll., 1933, U. Colo., 1956. Registered architect, Colo. Prin. Crowther & Marshall, San Diego, 1946-50, Richard L. Crowther, Denver, 1951-66, Crowther, Kruse, Landin, Denver, 1966-70, Crowther, Kruse, McWilliams, Denver, 1970-75, Crowther Solar Group, Denver, 1975-82, Richard L. Crowther FAIA, Denver, from 1982. Vis. critic, lectr. U. Nebr., 1981; holistic energy design process methodology energy cons. Holistic Health Ctr., 1982-83; adv. cons. interior and archtl. design class U. Colo., 1982-83, Cherry Creek, Denver redevel., 1984-88, Colo. smoking control legislation, 1985, interior solar concepts Colo. Inst. Art, 1986, Bio-Electro-Magnetics Inst., 1987-88; mentor U. Colo. Sch. Architecture, 1987-88. Author Sun/Earth, 1975 (Progressive Architecture award, 1975), rev. edit., 1983, reprint, 1995, Affordable Passive Solar Homes, 1983, reprint, 1996, Paradox of Smoking, 1983, Women/Nature/Destiny: Female/Male Equity for Global Survival, 1987, (monographs) Context in Art and Design, 1985, Existence, Design and Risk, 1986, Indoor Air: Risks and Remedies, 1986, Human Migration in Solar Homes for Seasonal Comfort and Energy Conservation, 1986, 88, Ecologic Architecture, 1992, Ecologic Digest, 1993, Ecologic Connections, 1996, Colorado Architect Monographs on Environmental Themes, 1998, Environmental Sustainability, 1999. NSF grantee, 1974-75; archtl. plans, drawings, photographs, ecol. and solar writings in archibes of western history dept. Denver Pub. Libr., 2002. Fellow AIA (commr. research, edn. and environ. Colo. Central chpt. 1972-75, bd. dirs. chpt. 1973-74 AIA Research Corp. Solar Monitoring Program contract award, spkr. and pub. Colo. Ecologic Connections open forum 1996). Achievements include ecologic bio-toxic and bio-electromagnetic research; donating architectural plans, renderings, and photographs to Western History of the Denver Pub. Libr. Died Dec. 25, 2006.

CROY, SANDRA LEE, banker; b. Tulsa, May 9, 1950; d. Roy R. and Lee (Collins) C.; 1 child, Natalie. BS, U. Tenn., 1973, MBA, 1975, postgrad., 1975-76. Fin. analyst Ashland Oil, Inc., Ashland, Ky., 1976-78, mem. planning and analysis and investor rels. staff, 1978-80; dir. investor rels. First Union Corp., Charlotte, N.C., 1980-83; Instl. sales rep. Lovett Underwood Neuhaus, Houston, 1983-86; dir. investor rels. Chase Manhattan Corp., NYC, from 1986. Bd. dirs. Art N.Y., N.Y.C., 1990; mem. adv. bd. exec. mgmt. program U. Chgo.; trustee Delaware Valley Coll. Recipient Nicholson award Nat. Assn. Investment Clubs, 1982, Roalman award, Nat. Investor Rels. Inst., 1982. Mem. Nat. Investor Rels. Inst., Bank Investor Rels. Assn. (co-founder, pres.-elect 1983). Republican. Avocations: horseback riding, painting. Died Feb. 16, 2006.

CRYER, EARL WILTON, mayor; b. Morris, Ill., July 15, 1913; s. Walter Elmer and Alma E. (Lutzow) C.; m. Mary Venetia Miller, May 15, 1937 (div. 1941); children— Ernest Scott, Rodger Earl; m. 2d, Marguerite Gladys Root, June 23, 1942; children— Dennis Robert, Kenneth Owen, Bruce Allan. B.A., Bowling Green State U., 1937. C.L.U. Salesman, N.Y. Life Ins. Co., Detroit, 1938-40, Mutual Benefit Life Ins. Co., Detroit, 1940-49, asst. dir. tng., Newark, 1949-53; dir. tng. Guardian Life of Am., N.Y.C., 1953-55, supt. agencies, 1955-79; mayor Millburn Twp., N.J., 1982-84; pres. N.Y. Tng. Dirs. Assn., N.Y.C., 1954-55. Contbr. articles to life ins. publs. Mem. Police and Fire Pension Commn., Dearborn, Mich., 1947-49; mem., v.p. Millburn Bd. of Edn., 1955-67; trustee Short Hills Country Day Sch. (now Pingry) (N.J.), 1968-74; trustee, chmn. Charles T. King Student Loan Fund, Millburn-Short Hills, 1966-76; committeeman Millburn Twp. Com., 1979-84; vice mayor Millburn Twp., 1981, mayor, 1982-84; mem. long-range planning com. St. Barnabas Hosp., Livingston, N.J., 1980-84; trustee Millburn Free Pub. Library, 1982-84, Panther Valley Property Owners Assn., 1985—, Camp Merry Heart, 1985—. Recipient Spl. Field Service award Guardian Life Field Adv. Bd., 1978. Mem. Nat. Assn. Life Underwriters, Chartered Life Underwriters Assn. (C.L.U. in agy. mgmt.), Nat. Assn. Security Dealers (cert. broker-dealer), N.J. Conf. Mayors, Pi Kappa Delta (Spl. Distinction medal 1937). Republican. Unitarian-Universalist. Lodges: Kiwanis (Dearborn, Mich.) (sec. 1942-49); Rotary (Millburn) (hon. mem. 1983—). Home: Clearwater, Fla. Died Mar. 7, 2006.

CSAKY, SUSAN DISCHKA, retired law librarian, educator; b. Budapest, Hungary, July 25, 1926; came to U.S., 1948; d. Victor and Hertha (Willerstorfer) Dischka; m. Tihamer Z. Csaky, June 18, 1953; children: Catharina M. Hirt, Karl G. AB, U. Ga., 1948; MA, Johns Hopkins U., 1951; MSLS, U. N.C., 1964; JD, U. Ky., 1977. Law libr. U. Ky., Lexington, 1963-74, head govt. documents, 1975-78; dir. of law libr., prof. law U. Mo., Columbia, 1979-93, prof. emeritus law, from 1993. Lectr. Sch. Libr. Sci. U. N.C., Chapel Hill, 1960-61, Coll. Libr. Sci. U. Ky., Lexington, 1970-78; adj. instr. Coll. Law U. Ky., 1967-78; adj. prof. Sch. Libr. Sci. U. Mo., 1983-93. Author: How to Use Government Documents in Legal Research, 1979, (audiotape) Electronic Fund Transfers, 1979; editor: (microfiche with index and supplements) The Lawson Libr. of Criminal Law, 1983—. Internat. Rsch. and Exchs. fellow, 1977. Fellow Coun. on Libr. Resources; mem. Am. Assn. Law Librs., Mid-Am. Law Sch. Libr. Consortium (chair 1990-92), Internal Assn. Law Librs., Beta Phi Mu (Internat. Libr. Sci. Hon.). Home: Fort Worth, Tex. Died Apr. 12, 2006.

CUA, ANTONIO S., philosopher, educator; b. Manila, July 23, 1932; arrived in U.S., 1953, naturalized, 1971; s. Oh and Chio (So) Cua; m. Shoke-Hwee Khaw, June 11, 1956; 1 child, Athene K. BA, Far Eastern U., Manila, 1952; MA, U. Calif, Berkeley, 1954; PhD, U. Calif., Berkeley, 1958. Tchg. asst. U. Calif. Berkeley, 1955—58; instr., asst. prof. Ohio U., 1958-62; prof., chmn. dept. philosophy SUNY Coll. at Oswego, 1962-69; prof. philosophy Cath. U. Am., Washington, 1969-96, prof. emeritus, 1996—2007. Vis. prof. U. Mo., Columbia, 1974—75, U. Hawaii, 1976—77; vis. professorial lectr. Fu Jen Cath. U., 1993, Nat. Cheng-chi U., Taiwan, 1993, Nat. Tsinghua U., Taiwan, 1995. Author: Reason and Virtue: A Study in the Ethics of Richard Price, 1966, Dimensions of Moral Creativity: Paradigms, Principles, and Ideals, 1978, The Unity of Knowledge and Action: A Study in Wang Yang-ming's Moral Psychology, 1982, Ethical Argumentation: A Study in Hsün Tzu's Moral Epistemology, 1985, Moral Vision and Tradition: Essays in Chinese Ethics, 1998, Human Nature, Ritual and History: Studies in Xunzi and Chinese Philosophy, 2005; editor: Encyclpedia of Chinese Philosophy, 2003; co-editor: Jour. Chinese Philosophy; assoc. editor: Internat. Jour. Philosophy Religion, mem. editl. bd.: Am. Philos. Quar., 1972—2002, Philosophy East and West, 1985—2003, Dao: A Jour. Comparative Philosophy; contbr. articles to profl. jours. Mem.: Aristolelian Soc., Mind Assn., Soc. Asian and Comparative Philosophy (pres. 1978—79), Internat. Soc. Chinese Philosophy (pres. 1984—86), Am. Philos. Assn. Died Mar. 27, 2007.

CULBERSON, JESSIE WALLACE, fire chief; b. Williamson County Tenn., Mar. 9, 1929; s. Wallace Alexander and Robbie Ella (Hargrove) C.; m. Frankie Elsie Short, Feb. 14, 1958; 1 child, Michael Wallace. Grad. Bethesda High Sch., Williamson, Tenn. Cert. fire chief, cert. arson investigator, Tenn. Farmer, Williamson, 1947-54; laborer Tenn. Hwy. Dept., Nashville, 1954-58; salesman Interstate Ins. Co., Nashville, 1958-63; fireman Franklin Fire Dept., Tenn., 1963-69, fire prevention officer, 1969-72, asst. chief, 1972-76, chief, 1976—; bd. dirs. Tenn. Fire Chiefs, Nashville, 1980-82; commr. Tenn. Commn. Fire Fighting Standards Personnel, Nashville, 1976—. Baseball coach Franklin Optimist League, Tenn., 1970-77. Mem. Internat. Assn. Arson Investigation (pres. 1976-77), Tenn. Firemen Assn. Democrat. Baptist. Avocations: gospel singing; hunting; fishing. Home: Franklin, Tenn. Died May 6, 2007.

CULP, GERARD HUBBARD, assets protection executive; b. Reno, Nev., Jan. 16, 1930; s. W. Ray and Ruth Lee (Hubbard) Culp; m. Audrey Elizabeth Crompton, May 26, 1955 (div. Sept. 1977); children: Stephen Gerard, Heather Janeane; m. Sandra Lee Jaksina, Dec. 23, 1977. BA, U. Redlands, 1958; postgrad., U. Maine, 1966. Cert. protection profl. Enlisted USAF, 1951, advanced through grades to col., 1973, served in U.S., Can., Eng., Pakistan; dir. pers. investigations dtr. Dept. Def., Balt., 1975—76, ret., 1976; dir. corp. security Pa. Power & Light Co., Allentown, 1977—80; mgr. nuc. security Portland (Oreg.) Gen. Electric Co., 1980—88, mgr. pers. security, from 1988. Contbr. articles to profl. jours. Decorated Air Force Commendation medal with one oak leaf cluster, Meritorious Svc. medal, Joint Svc. Commendation medal, Legion of Merit. Mem.: Am. Mgmt. Assn., Am. Nuc. Soc. (security com.), Edison Electric Inst. (security com.), Inst. Nuc. Materials Mgmt., Am. Soc. Indsl. Security (chpt. chmn.), Am. Assn. Individual Investors, Geneal. Forum Oreg., Phi Kappa Phi. Home: Portland, Oreg. Died Apr. 17, 2006.

CULP, MARILYN MARGARET WAGNER, sociologist; b. Milw., Jan. 1, 1945; d. Charles Gustave and Evelyn Eve Wagner; B.A. cum laude, Baldwin Wallace Coll., 1967; M.A. with honors, Bowling Green State U., 1969; m. Ronald Edward Culp, Aug. 9, 1969. Asst. prof. sociology Cuyahoga Community Coll., Parma, Ohio, 1969-75; pvt. practice marriage counseling, 1971—; dir. victims assistance programs Multnomah County Dist. Atty.'s Office, Portland, Oreg., 1975—; instr. Bur. Police Standards and Tng.; speaker in field. Mem. Task Force on Domestic Violence, Task Force on Victims; chairperson Tri County Community Council Safety Com.; bd. dirs. Crime Victims Assistance Network, City County Pub. Safety Commn., Crime Victims United. Named Outstanding Female Prof., Cuyahoga Community Coll., 1969-75; recipient Margery Fry award for outstanding practitioner in victim services, 1983. Mem. Am. Sociol. Assn., Am., Oreg. (dir.) assns. marriage and family therapists, Am. Assn. Marriage and Family Therapists. Club: Baldwin Wallace Women's. Home: Portland, Oreg. Died June 3, 2006.

CUMMISKEY, J. KENNETH, former college president; b. Boston, Nov. 18, 1928; s. Joseph K. and Helen F. (Penney) C.; m. Joan Lydia Ross, Aug. 13, 1953; children: Lynn Anne, David Ross. BS, Springfield Coll., 1952; M.Ed., Oreg. State U., 1953; PhD, Stanford U., 1963. Tchr., coach Sweet Home (Oreg.) High Sch., 1953-55; asso. prof. edn. phys. edn., coach Oreg. Coll. Edn., 1955-65; asso. dir. Peace Corps, Morocco, 1965-66; supr. edn. programs Tng. Corp. Am.; dir. headstart tng. programs Territory of Guam, Islands of Trust Territories, 1966-68; dir. community services project Am. Assn. Jr. Colls., 1968-71; exec. dir. Nat. Council Community Services, 1970-72; v.p. acad. affairs New Eng. Coll., Henniker, N.H., 1971-73, pres., 1973-81, pres. emeritus, from 1981; fin. cons., from 1988. Mem. N.H. Postsecondary Edn. Commn., 1978-84; auditor Henniker, 1977-80; mediator N.H. Public Employee Labor Relations Bd., 1977-81; steering com. N.H. Common Cause, 1975-81; bd. advisers Merrimack Valley Coll., 1981-84; mem. N.H. Commn. to Study Impact of Tax-Exempt Non-Fed. Instl. Property on Localities, 1979-81; mem. exec. com. New Eng.-China Consortium, 1981-84. Author works in field; mem. adv. bd.: Community Edn. Jour., 1970-73; editorial bd.: Jour. Edn, 1971-73. Served with U.S. Army, 1946-48, 51-54. Fellow Royal Soc. Arts; Mem. NEA, Am. Psychol. Assn., Nat. Council Community Services and Continuing Edn., Am. Assn. Higher Edn., N.H. Coll. and Univ. Council (pres. 1979-81), Phi Delta Kappa. Clubs: Univ. (N.Y.C.); Arundel Yacht. Unitarian Universalist. Home: Gloucester, Mass. Died June 15, 2007.

CUNDIFF, EDWARD WILLIAM, retired marketing educator; b. Long Beach, Calif., Sept. 28, 1919; s. Harry Thomas and Martha Magdalene (Koltes) C.; m. Margaret Wallace Stroud, Sept. 8, 1956; children: Richard Wallace, Gregory Edward, Geoffrey William. BA, Stanford, 1940, MBA, 1942; EdD, 1952; Ford Fellow, Harvard Sch. Bus. Adminstrn., 1956. Retailing exec., 1946-48; instr. mktg. San Jose State Coll., 1949-52; asst. prof., later asso. prof. mktg. Syracuse U., 1952-58, asst. dean, 1954-58; prof. mktg., chmn. dept. mktg. adminstrn. U. Tex., 1958-73, assoc. dean Grad. Sch. Bus., 1973-76; L.J. Buchan distinguished vis. prof. U. Tex. at San Antonio, 1976-77; Charles C. Kellstadt prof. mktg. Emory U., 1977-87; John A. Beck Centennial prof. comm. U. Tex., Austin, 1987-94, John A. Beck emeritus prof. comm. dept. advt., 1994-96, emeritus prof. mktg., from 1996; ret., 1994. Vis. prof. mktg., Fontainebleau, France, Palermo, Sicily, 1960-61. Author: (with R.R. Still) Sales Management: Decisions, Policies and Cases, 5th edit, 1988, Basic Marketing: Concepts, Environment, and Decisions, 1964, rev. edit., 1970, Essentials of Marketing, 1966, 3d edit., 1986, (with R.R. Still and N.A.P. Govoni) Fundamentals of Modern Marketing, 3d edit, 1980, (with Marye Hilger) Marketing in the International Environment, 2d edit., 1988; editor: Jour. Mktg, 1973-76. Served to lt. (s.g.) USNR, World War II. Mem. Am. Mktg. Assn. (v.p. 1980—), So. Mktg. Assn. (pres. 1967-68), Beta Gamma Sigma, Delta Sigma Pi, Theta Chi. Home: Austin, Tex. Died Nov. 8, 2006.

CUNNINGHAM, JOHN FABIAN, priest, former academic administrator; b. Providence, Aug. 7, 1928; s. Hugh Stephen and Marie Cunningham. AB, Providence Coll., 1949; S.T.L., S.T.Lr., Coll. Immaculate Conception, 1954; PhD in Philosophy, Pontifical U. St. Thomas Aquinas, 1958. Joined Dominican Order, Roman Catholic Ch. Instr. philosophy St. Joseph's Coll., Ohio, 1954-55; asst. prof. St. Stephen's Coll., 1955-56; dir. humanities program Providence Coll., 1963—65, dir. residence life, 1967—70, pres. faculty senate, 1968—69, prof., 1965—2005, dean undergraduate studies, 1971-74, pres., 1985—94. Asst. dir. Liberal Arts Honor Program, Providence Coll., 1959—65, dir., 1967—68. Died Dec. 4, 2006.

CURFMAN, DAVID RALPH, neurosurgeon, educator, civic leader, musician; b. Bucyrus, Ohio, Jan. 2, 1942; s. Ralph Oliver and Agnes Mozelle (Schreck) C.; m. Blanche Lee Anderson, June 6, 1970. Student, Capital U., 1960—62; AB, Columbia Union Coll., 1965; MS, George Washington U., 1967, MD, 1973. Diplomate Nat. Bd. Med. Examiners. Asst. organist, choirmaster Peace Luth. Ch., Galion, Ohio, 1956-62; bus. mgr. Mansfield/Galion Ambulance Svc., Galion, 1962-66; with news divsn. Sta. WTOP-TV, CBS, Washington, 1965; choirmaster, assoc. organist Grace Luth. Ch., Washington, 1966-73, historian, curator, from 1969; tchg. fellow in anatomy George Washington U., Washington, 1966-67, gen. surgery intern, 1973-74, resident in neurol. surgery, 1974-78, clin. instr. neurol. surgery, 2000—07, asst. clin. prof., 2001—07; resident in neuropathology Armed Forces Inst. Pathology, Washington, 1975; resident in pediatric neurol. surgery Children's Hosp. Nat. Med. Ctr., Washington, 1976; tchg. fellow in anatomy Georgetown U., Washington, 1967-69, clin. instr. neurol. surgery, nuerol. surgeon, 1978—2007. Chief divsn. neurol. surgery Jefferson Hosp., Alexandria, Va., 1989-93, Washington Hosp. Ctr. Soc., 1992-2007, oper. room com. 1998-2003; vice-chmn. bylaws com. Providence Hosp., 1987-95, chief of neorosurgery divsn.; panelist ann. meeting ethical issues in neurol. surgery Am. Assn. Neurol. Surgery; guest spkr. Nat. Youth Leadership Forum in Medicine, 1996-2007, World Philatelic Exhbn., Washington, DC, 2006. Chmn., chief author: Physician's Reference Guide for Medicolegal Matters, 1982, Nat. Capital Astronomers' Association, 1986-87. Elected mem. DC Rep. Com., 1988-94; bd. dirs., historian The Christmas Pageant of Peace, Inc., Washington, The Leo Sowerby Found.; pres., bd. govs. Nat. Columbus Celebration Assn. Hon. mem. Quiz Kid Show, 1953; recipient Found. award Cathedral Choral Soc., 1997, Medal of Honor Nat. Soc. DAR, 2004. Mem.: SAR (bd., DC Soc. 1997-2007), AMA (Phys. Recognition award 1983-2007), DC Soc. (bd. mgmt.), Order of the Crown in Am., Assn. Mil. Surgeons U.S. (Continuing Edn. Neurosurgery award 1993-), Washington Acad. Neurosurgery (pres. 2004-06), Am. Coll. Legal Medicine, Congress Neurol. Surgeons (joint sect. neuro-trauma and critical care), Pan Am. Med. Soc. (mem. exec. bd. 1993-97, pres. 1997), Med. Soc. DC (chmn. medicine and religion com. 1981-83, chmn. medico-legal com. 1986-88), Am. Soc. Law, Medicine, and Ethics, Assn. Am. Med. Colls. (nat. student chmn. rules and regulations com. 1971-73), Heredity Soc. Cmty. USA, Nat. Gavel Soc., St. Andrew's Soc. (Washington), Hymn Soc. Am., Pilgrim Soc. Plymouth Mass. (Plymouth, Mass.), Order Three Crusades (1096-1192), The Baronial Order of Magna Carta, Mil. Hospitaller Order Saint Lazarus Jerusalem (knight), U.S. Capitol Hist. Soc. (founding supporting mem., trust mem., bd. dirs.), Nat. Cathedral Assn., Cathedral Choral Soc. (repertoire chmn. 1981-82, v.p. bd. trustees 1981-83, pres. 1984-86, found. award 1997), Am. Guild Organists (dean DC chpt. 1974-76, publicity chmn. nat. conv. 1982, state chmn. 1984-91, nat. com. long-range devel. 1990-96), Internat. Congress Organists (Washington program chmn. 1977), Royal Sch. Ch. Music (Eng.), Order of the Crown of Charlemagne (surgeon gen.), Nat. Soc. Ams. Royal Descent (councillor), Order of Ams. of Armorial Ancestry (chaplain), Nat. Soc. Children Am. Revolution (pres. Ohio 1963-64, hon. sr. nat. v.p. 1999-2004, sr. nat. officers. club historian 2003-05, sr. nat. 2d v.p. 2004-05, hon. Ohio pres.), Gen. Soc. Sons of the Revolution (chmn. bicentennial commemorative com. death of Gen. George Washington 1999, NY and DC bd. 2002-07, 1st v.p.), Hereditary Order Descendants of the Loyalists and Patriots of the Am. Revolution, Baronial Order of Magna Charta, Sons and Daus. of Colonial and Antebellum Bench and Bar, Samuel Victor Constant Soc., Order of Washington, Hospitaller Order of St. John (hon.; knight), Osler Soc., Galion Hist. Soc. (charter), Continental Soc. Sons Indian Wars, Ordor Sancti Constantini Magni, Colonial Order of the Acorn NY, Vet. Corps Arty. State NY, Am. Revolution Soc., Soc. of 1812, Nat. Soc. Children Am. Colonists (pres. gen. 2003-05), Mil. Order Loyal Legion U.S. (Aide-de-Camp to comdr.-in-chief 2003-07), Sons Am. Colonists (surgeon gen. 1997-2005, lt. gov. gen. 2005-07), Soc. Colonial Wars (surgeon 1997-2007), Order of Indian Wars in the U.S. (historian 1999-2007), Am. Polit. Items Collectors Assn., Sons/Daus. of the Pilgrims (historian gen. 1999-2001, dep. gov. gen. 2003-05, first dep. gov. gen. 2003-07), Lincoln Birthday Nat. Commemorative Com (master of ceremonies 1995-99, vice chmn.), Sons of Union Vets. Civil War (chmn. hist. Meml. Day observances 1993-2007), Sovereign Mil. Order Temple of Jerusalem (grand chirurgeon emeritus, grand comdr., Order of Merit), Mil. Order of the Crusades, Order of the Merovingian Dynasty (founding mem., surgeon gen. 2005-07), Soc. War 1812 (surgeon gen. Md. chpt., dist. dep. pres. gen., 1st v.p. DC chpt.), Columbus Philatelic Soc., Crawford County Coin Club (charter mem.), George Washington U. Club, Elks (Galion Lodge No. 1191), Sigma Xi (pres. George Washington U. chpt. 1981-82), Phi Delta Epsilon (life). Home: Washington, DC. Died July 24, 2007.

CURIE, EVE, writer, lecturer; b. Paris, Dec. 6, 1904; came to U.S., 1941. d. Pierre and Marie (Sklodowska) C.; m. Henry Richardson Labouisse, Nov. 1954 (dec. 1987). BS, PhB, Sevigne Coll.; DHL (hon.), Mills Coll., 1939, Russell Sage Coll., 1941; LittD (hon.), U. Rochester, 1941, Hartwick Coll., 1983. Pianist, Paris, 1925; music critic Candide (weekly jour.). Spl. advisor Sec. Gen., NATO, 1952-54. Author: Madame Curie, 1937 (selection of Lit. Guild, Jr. Guild, Book of the Month Club, Sci. Book of Month, Nat. Book award for non-fiction 1937), Journey Among Warriors, 1943 (selection of Lit. Guild). Served as officer women's divsn. French Army. Decorated Chevalier Legion of Honor, France, Polonia Restituta, Poland, Croix de Guerre, France. Home: New York, NY. Died Oct. 22, 2007.

CURLS, PHILLIP B., state legislator; b. Kansas City, Mo., Apr. 2, 1942; s. Fred A. and Velma E. (Wagner) C.; m. Melba Jean Dudley, 1964; children: Phillip B. II, Michael Jay, Monica Joy Bianca, Louis Brandon Audley III. BS, Rockhurst Coll., 1965. State senator dist. 9, Mo., from 1982. Del. Dem. Nat. Conv., 1980; contractor, broker and appraiser. Died May 15, 2007.

CURTIN, DANIEL JOSEPH, JR., lawyer; b. San Francisco, Jan. 7, 1933; s. Daniel Joseph and Nell Helen (Lenihan) Curtin; m. Myrtle Rose Wanke, Feb. 7, 1959 (dec. July 2005); children: Kathleen Mary, Patricia, Thomas, Carol. AB in Polit. Sci., U. San Francisco, 1954, JD, 1957. Asst. sec. State Senate Calif., Sacramento, 1959; cons., counsel Assembly Com. on Local Govt., Sacramento, 1959-60; dep. city atty. City of Richmond, Calif., 1961-65; city atty. City of Walnut Creek, Calif., 1965-82; with Williams, Caploe, Robbins & Curtin, Benicia, Calif., 1983-84; ptnr. McCutchen, Doyle, Brown & Enersen, Walnut Creek, 1984—2001; counsel Bingham McCutchen, from 2002. Mem. bd. advisors environ. affairs Boston Coll. Sch. Law, from 1987; mem. State Sen. Housing Adv. Task Force, 1983—84; instr. continuing edn. bar U. Calif. Extension, from 1973, 1975, 82, 88, Golden Gate U. Sch. Law, 1979—82, John F. Kennedy U. Sch. Law, Walnut Creek, 1983—90, U. San Francisco Sch. Law, 1988—92. Contbr. articles to profl. jours. Lt. US Army, 1958—64. Named City Atty. of the Yr., 1971, others; recipient Disting. Leadership award, Nat. Planning award, Am. Planning Assn., 1988. Mem.: ABA (chmn. land use, planning and zoning com. 1976—78, vice chair 1999, coun. chair 2001—02, sect. state and local govt. law, Jefferson Fordham Lifetime Achievement award 2003), Nat. Inst. Mcpl. Law Officer (chmn. zoning and planning com. 1969—79, regional v.p. 1979—82, Lifetime Achievement in Mcpl. Law Charles S. Rhyne award), Calif. State Bar Assn. (mem. exec. com., real property law sect. 1988—91, mem. com. environ. 1977—80), League of Calif. Cities (pres. city atty.'s dept. 1973—74), Calif. Pk. and Recreation Soc., Lambda Alpha. Democrat. Roman Catholic. Avocation: gardening. Home: Walnut Creek, Calif. Died Nov. 30, 2006.

CURTIN, JAMES BERNARD, lawyer; b. Hartford, Conn., Jan. 28, 1929; s. Edward Martin and Mary (Carr) C.; m. Jeanne Ann Fountain, Feb. 2, 1963; children: James B. Jr., Peter J., Cynthia A. BS, Trinity Coll., 1951; JD, U. Conn., 1958. Bar: Conn. 1958, U.S. Dist. Ct. Conn. 1967, U.S. Ct. Appeals (2d cir.) 1979. Atty. So. New England Telecommunications Corp., New Haven, 1961-71, sr. atty., 1972-75, gen. atty., 1975-80, assoc. gen. counsel, 1980-81, v.p., gen. counsel, from 1981. Mem. Town Dem. Com., North Haven, Conn.; bd. dirs. Housing Ptnrship., New Haven, New England Legal Found., 1977-90. Mem. ABA, Conn. Bar Assn. Roman Catholic. Home: Old Saybrook, Conn. Died Dec. 17, 2005.

CURTIN, THOMAS EDWARD, hospital administrator, physician; b. Washington, Oct. 27, 1920; s. Edward Gregory and Mary Bridget (Deenihan) C.; m. Helen Marie Fitzsimmons, June 23, 1945; children— Thomas E., Gregory P., Mary Elizabeth, Michael W. (dec.), Kathleen Mary. B.S., U. Scranton, 1942; M.D., Georgetown U., 1945. Diplomate Am. Bd. Internal Medicine. Intern Providence Hosp., Washington, 1945-46, resident in internal medicine, 1948-50, v.p. med. affairs, 1968—; pvt. practice medicine specializing in internal medicine, Washington, 1950-80; med. dir. Carroll Manor Nursing Home, Hyattsville, Md., 1984-87. Served as capt. U.S. Army, 1946-48. Recipient Gold Cane award Providence Hosp. Alumni, 1982. Fellow ACP; mem. AMA, Med. Soc.D.C. (pres. 1976), Assn. Hosp. Med. Edn. (editor newsletter 1971-74), Med. Soc. D.C. Democrat. Roman Catholic. Club: Kenwood (Bethesda, Md.). Home: Bethesda, Md. Died Jan. 7, 2007.

CUSHMAN, HAROLD ROBERT, agriculture educator; b. Ferrisburg, Vt., Dec. 21, 1920; s. Lynn Stanley and Ruth (Field) Cushman; m. Natalia Delfinado, Aug. 26, 1970; children: Richard, Robert, Janette. BS, U. Vt., 1941, MA, 1948; PhD, Cornell U., 1951. Cert. agr. tchr. Vt. Tchr. agr., Woodstock, Vt., 1946—48; asst. state supv. agr. edn. Vt., 1948—49; head agrl. edn. dept. U. Vt., Burlington, 1951—55; prof. agr. Cornell U., Ithaca, NY, from 1955. Overseas assignments, Philippines, 1958—60, Philippines, 1968—70, Western Samoa, 1972, Papua New Guinea, 1980—81. 1st lt., 1942—45. Decorated Bronze Star with three oak leaf clusters, Purple Heart. Mem.: Am. Assn. Tchr. Educators in Agr. (Outstanding Svc. award 1978), Am. Vocat. Assn., Masons. Republican. Roman Catholic. Died July 28, 2007.

CUTKOMP, LAURENCE KREMER, retired entomology educator, consultant; b. Wapello, Iowa, Jan. 24, 1916; s. Fred Morgan and Glen (Kremer) C.; children: Kay F. Cutkomp Bahan, Terry Ann Cutkomp Ostovar, Kent Jaques Cutkomp, Lee Cutkomp Ross. BA, Iowa Wesleyan U., Mt. Pleasant, 1936; PhD, Cornell U., 1942. Entomologist TVA, Wilson Dam, Ala., 1945-47; asst. prof. to prof. U. Minn., St. Paul, 1947-87, prof. emeritus, from 1987; entomologist (on leave from U. Minn.) IAEA, Vienna, Austria, 1965-67. Co-author: A Glossary of Pesticide Toxicology, 1984, How to Know the Immature Insects, rev. edit. 1992. Pres., bd. dirs. St. Anthony Park Assn., St. Paul, 1950—. Recipient rsch. award Chronobiology Labs. U. Minn., 1986. Mem. Entomol. Soc. Am. (pres. North Ctrl. br. 1976-77), Gamma Sigma Delta (merit award 1985), Omicron Delta Kappa. Unitarian Universalist. Home: Saint Paul, Minn. Died Feb. 20, 2006.

CUTLER, EDWARD I., lawyer; b. Phila., Sept. 21, 1913; s. Samuel and Elizabeth (Esterman) C.; m. Roseline Adams, Aug. 12, 1938; children: Janet Kossman, Edward, Robin Levine. AB, U. Pa., 1934, JD, 1937. Bar: Pa. 1938, Fla. 1947, U.S. Supreme Ct. 1966. Asst. law librarian U. Pa., 1937-39; law sec. to chief justice Pa., 1937-39; practiced in Phila., 1938-44; exec. asst. Hooker's Point Shipyard, Tampa, Fla., 1944-46; engaged as real estate broker Tampa, 1947; practice law, from 1948; mem. firm Carlton, Fields, Ward, Emmanuel, Smith & Cutler, P.A. (and predecessor firms), Tampa, St. Petersburg, Orlando, Tallahassee, Pensacola, West Palm Beach, Fla., from 1961, pres., 1976-79. Sec. C.W.A.G. Found., 1950-70, Indsl. Supply Corp., 1950-81; asst. procedural and equity rules coms. Supreme Ct. Pa., 1940-44; commr. Uniform State Laws, 1974—; Nat. Conf. Commn. of Uniform State Laws, 1979-81, exec. com. 1987-89; chmn. com. on Personal Property Article 2A Uniform Comml. Code Leases, 1985-94; mem. com. on uniform Ltd. Liability Cos. Act., 1991—; mem. joint editl. bd. on Uniform Unincorp. Orgn. Acts, 1995—; mem. news media com. Supreme Ct. Fla., 1975; bd. dirs. Nat. Lawyers' Com. for Civil Rights Under Law, 1976-83; mem. Fla. Bd. Bar Examiners, 1985-90, emeritus, 1994—. Note editor U. Pa. Law Rev., 1936-37; Fla. contbr. Compendium, Nat. Comml. Assn.; editorial bd. Am. Law Inst.-ABA The Practical Real Estate Lawyer, 1984—. Co-chmn. West Coast Fla. chpt. NCCJ, 1964-67; mem. exec. com. U.S. Fla. Found., 1962-66. Fellow Am. Bar Found. (50-Yr. award 1991), Fla. Bar Found., Am. Coll. Comml. Fin. Lawyers (emeritus), Am. Coll. Bankruptcy (emeritus); mem. ABA (standing com. unauthorized practice law 1970-73, co-chmn. Nat. Conf. Lawyers and Collection Agys. 1970-72, Lawyers and CPAs 1973-76,spl. com. coordination fed. jud. improvements 1976-80, chmn. 1980-83, bankruptcy task force 1982-85, mem. standing com. legal aid and indigent defendants 1983-88), Tampa and Hillsborough County Bar Assn., Fla. Bar (chmn. unauthorized practice law com. 1964-68, mem. com. on interest on trust funds 1975; lectr. on unauthorized practice of law 1968-71, on uniform comml. code 1972, lectr. continuing legal edn. on secured creditor's rights 1964—), Am. Coll. Real Estate Lawyers (charter mem. 1979—, gov. 1981—, pres. 1984-85), Am. Judicature Soc. (bd. dirs. 1988-92, chmn. nominating com. 1988-89, chmn. Amicus Curiae com. 1988-89), Comml. Law League Am., Am. Law Inst., U. Pa. Law Alumni (bd. mgrs. 1971-78, Award of Merit 1994), Justice William Glenn Terrell Inn of Ct., Univ. Club, Tampa Club, Harbour Island Athletic Club, Order of Coif, Masons, Shriners, B'nai Brith, Temple Schaarai Zedek (pres. 1957-58), Phi Beta Kappa. Home: Tampa, Fla. Died Oct. 4, 2006.

CUTLER, KENNETH ROSS, investment company and mutual fund executive; b. Tacoma, Mar. 5, 1920; s. Clarence William and Matilda Rosanne (Ross) Cutler; m. Pat Virginia Reinecke, Aug. 6, 1943; children: Geoffrey William, Craig Lee, Brooke Roxanne Cutler Ashland. Student, U. Chgo., 1941—42, UCLA, 1945. Broker William R. Staats & Co., 1945—47, Dempsey-Tegeler & Co., LA, 1950—53, Dean Witter & Co., Century City, Calif., 1966—72; pres. Calif. Fund, LA, 1953—62; investment counsel Van Nuys, Calif., 1962—66; mgr. spl. accts. dept. Paine Webber, LA, 1972—77; chmn. Cutler & Co., Inc., Medford, Oreg., 1977—96, Cutler Trust, Cutler Equity Income Fund, Cutler Approved List Fund, from 1992. Trustee Rogue Valley Med. Ctr. Found., from 1995. Mem.: Univ. Club, Rogue Valley Country Club, Phi Delta Theta. Republican. Presbyterian. Home: Medford, Oreg. Died Oct. 8, 2006.

CUTLER, LEONARD SAMUEL, physicist; b. LA, Jan. 10, 1928; s. Morris and Ethel (Kalech) Cutler; m. Dorothy Alice Pett, Feb. 13, 1954; children: Jeffrey Alan, Gregory Michael, Steven Russell, Scott Darren. BS in Physics, Stanford U., Calif., 1958, MS, 1960, PhD, 1966. Chief engr. Gertsch Products Co., LA, 1948-56, v.p. R & D, 1956-57; with Hewlett-Packard Co., Palo Alto, Calif., 1957-99, dir. physics rsch., 1969-85, dir. instruments and photonics lab., 1985-87, dir. superconductivity lab., 1987-89, disting. contbr., 1989-99; disting. contbr. tech. staff Agilent Techs., 2000—04, disting. fellow tech. staff, from 2004. Mem. adv. panels Nat. Bur. Stds.; cons. Kernco, Inc., Danvers, Mass., 1982—, others. Patentee in field. Served with USNR, 1945-46. Recipient Achievement award Indsl. Rsch. Inst., 1990, Indsl. Applications prize Am. Inst. Physics, 1993. Fellow IEEE (Morris Leeds award 1984, Rabi award 1989), Am. Phys. Soc.; mem. AAAS, NAE, Sigma Xi. Home: Los Altos, Calif. Died Sept. 4, 2006.

CZAJKOSKI, EUGENE HOWARD, education educator; b. Bklyn., July 27, 1928; s. Walter and Stephanie (Sokolowski)_C.; m. Rosalind DeLuca, Oct. 12, 1961. B degree, Syracuse U., 1948; PhD, NYU, 1964. Cert. social worker, N.Y. U.S. probation officer U.S. Dist. Ct., NYC, 1958-60; assoc. prof. Sch. of Criminology/Fla. State U., Tallahassee, 1966-70, prof., 1970-71, chmn., prof., 1971-74, dean, prof., 1974-86, dean emeritus, from 1987. Cons. in field. Assoc. editor: Jour. Drug Issues; contbr. articles to profl. jours. Home: Tallahassee, Fla. Died Feb. 16, 2007.

DABNEY, HOVEY SLAYTON, finance company executive; b. Charlottesville, Va., Sept. 18, 1923; s. Wythe Overton and Mabel (Williams) D.; m. Patricia Ann Schmidt, Feb. 14, 1948; children: Hovey Slayton, Jill Dabney Cave, Ann Dabney Wampler. BA, U. Va., 1946, LLB, 1949; grad. exec. mgr. program, U. N.C., 1962. Asst. cashier Nat. Bank, Charlottesville, 1950-56, v.p., 1956-62, exec. v.p., 1962-64, pres., from 1964, chmn. bd., 1975; pres., chief exec. officer Jefferson Bankshares, Inc., Charlottesville, 1980-94, chmn. bd., from 1994. Dir. Jefferson Data Services, Inc., Charlottesville, Jefferson Properties; chmn. bd. VBA Interstate Banking, Richmond, Va. Pres., bd. dirs. Charlottesville Parking Ctr., 1963; commr., vice chmn. Va. Pub. Sch. Authority, 1968; chmn. U. Va. Health Svcs. Found., 1979; vice-chmn., bd. dirs. Va. Indsl. Devel. Corp. 1964; mem. coun. trustees U. Va. Med. Ctr., 1987—; rector U. Va. Sgt. USAF, 1940-43, ETO. Recipient Disting. Service award Charlottesville/Albemarle Jaycees, 1957, Boss of Yr. award Charlottesville/Albemarle Jaycees, 1965, Paul Goodloe McIntire award, 1987. Mem.: Farmington Country, Redland, Boar's Head Sports (Charlottesville); Commonwealth (Richmond). Avocation: golf. Home: Charlottesvle, Va. Died Feb. 9, 2007.

DAFFIN, CAROL FARWELL, manufacturing company executive; b. Harrison, N.Y., Oct. 21, 1953; d. Edward B. and Frances R. (Brown) Farwell; student Chesapeake Coll., 1981, U. Md., 1976-77; children: Jenny Alice, Kate Frances, Paul Edward. Salesman, Easton (Md.) Pub. Co., 1973-74; sales mgr. Chesapeake Products, Inc., Easton, 1974-75; v.p. Helm Distbrs., Inc., Easton, 1975-78, now dir.; pres. Daffin Disposables, Inc., Secretary, Md., 1977-92; dir. Daffin Corp., Secretary; pres., bd. dirs. Daffin Mfg. South Inc., Miami, Fla., Secretary, Md., 1992—; pres., bd. dirs. Carolco, Inc., Easton, Md. Bd. dirs. Chesapeake Rehab. Ctr., Easton, Talbot County Devel. Com.; coun. rep. Chesapeake County Econ. Com.; chmn. EPA com. for nonwoven garment sizing, 1988. Tng. grantee State of Md., 1980, 83. Mem. NOW, Nat. Safety Coun., Nat. Assn. Women in Bus., Safety Equipment Mfrs. Assn., Nat. Safety Equipment Dealers Assn., Am. Nuclear Soc., Am. Apparel Mfrs. Assn., Indsl. Safety Equipment Assn., Talbot County Bd. Realtors, Nat. Assn. Bus. and Profl. Women (Young Career Woman award 1982), Internat. Non-Woven Dealers Assn., Ind. Safety Equipment Assn., Safety Equipment Dealers Assn., Talbot County C. of C., Dorchester County C. of C. Republican. Died Jan. 17, 2007.

D'AGOSTINO, ANGELO, psychiatrist, clergyman; b. Providence, Jan. 26, 1926; s. Luigi and Julia (Lonardo) D.'A.; B.S., St. Michael's Coll., 1945; M.D., Tufts U., 1949, M.S. in Surgery, 1953; postgrad. Sem., Woodstock Coll., 1964-67. Intern, R.I. Hosp., Providence, 1949-50, asst. resident, 1950-51; resident New Eng. Center Hosp., Boston, 1951-53; joined S.J., 1955, ordained priest Roman Catholic Ch., 1966; assoc. prof. psychiatry George Washington U., Washington, 1969-72, clin. prof., 1972—2006; dir. Center Religion and Psychiatry, Washington, 1972—2006; practice medicine specializing in psychiatry, Washington, 1962-80, 84—2006; med. dir. phanatnikhom (Thailand) Processing Ctr., 1980-81; coordinator Jesuit Refugee Service, 1982-84. Mem. Nat. Council for VA Chaplains, 1972—; liaison for Jesuit affairs, Africa, 1982. Bd. dirs. Washington Mental Retarded Group, 1974—2006, Trinity Cons. Center, 1974-75, Nat. Italian Am. Found., 1979, Samaritans of Washington. Served to capt. USAF, 1953-55. Decorated grand knight Order of Merit, Republic of Italy, 1973. Mem. D.C. Med. Soc. (chmn. com. religion and medicine 1971-72), Am. Psychiat. Assn. (vice chmn. task force religion and psychiatry 1971-75, chmn. com. religion and psychiatry 1979-80), Washington Video-Psychiat. Study Soc. (pres. 1971-72), Med. Soc. D.C. (pres. sect. psychiatry 1977-78, chmn. medicine and religion com. 1975-79), Washington Psychiat. Soc. (pres. D.C. chpt. 1977), Italian Execs. Am. (pres. 1975-77, 79-80), Alpha Omega Alpha. Club: Cosmos (Washington). Editor: Family Community and Church, 1965; sr. editor Jour. Human Devel., 1979—2006; Author numerous publs. in field. Home: College Park, Md. Died Nov. 20, 2006.

DAHLSTROM, WILLIAM GRANT, psychologist, educator; b. Mpls., Nov. 1, 1922; s. Arthur William and Elizabeth Priscilla (Baker) D.; m. Leona Erickson, Sept. 3, 1948; children: Amy Louise, Eric Lee. Student, UCLA, 1940-41; BA cum laude, U. Minn., 1944, PhD in Psychology, 1949. Instr. psychology U. Minn., 1946-48, Ohio Wesleyan U., 1948-49; vis. asst. prof. State U. Iowa, 1949-53, research assoc., summer 1957; assoc. prof. psychiatry and psychology, dir. psychol. svcs. Meml. Hosp. U. N.C., Chapel Hill, 1953-56; assoc. prof. psychology U. N.C., 1956-60, research assoc. psychiatry, 1956-60, prof. psychology, 1960-87, Kenan prof. psychology, 1987-93, Kenan prof. emeritus, from 1993, from 1993, clin. prof. psychology in dept. psychiatry, from 1960; research prof. Inst. for Research in Social Sci., from 1960, chmn. dept., 1971-76. Vis. scholar U. Calif., Berkeley, 1968, 76-77; field dir. Child Study Center U. N.C., 1962-63; chmn. mental health study sect. NIH, 1966-67 Author: (with G.S. Welsh) An MMPI Handbook, 1960, rev. edit. (with G.S. Welsh and L.E. Dahlstrom) Vol. I, 1972, Vol. II, 1975, (with E.E. Baughman) Negro and White Children, 1968, (with L.E. Dahlstrom) Basic Readings on the MMPI, 1980, (with D. Lachar and L.E. Dahlstrom) MMPI Patterns of American Minorities, 1986. Co-editor: (with J.W. Thibaut) Jour. Personality, 1959-60; Cons. editor: Jour. Cons. Psychology, 1964-78, Jour. Abnormal Psychology, 1964-70, Psychosomatic Medicine, 1982—; Contbr. articles to profl. jours. NIMH sr. postdoctoral fellow Menninger Found., Topeka, Kans., 1967-68; Co-recipient Anisfield-Wolf award for outstanding contbn. to race relations Sat. Rev. Lit., 1968; Hargrove award N.C. Found. for Research in Mental Health, 1987. Fellow Soc. Personality Assessment, APA (Disting. Profl. Contbn. to Knowledge award 1991), AAAS, N.Y. Acad. Scis.; mem. Am. Psychosomatic Soc.; Sigma Xi. Democrat. Died June 22, 2006.

DAILEY, DONALD HARRY, adult education educator, volunteer; b. Sommerville, Mass., Mar. 26, 1949; s. Walter Merle Dailey and Shirley Esma (Clarke) Davidson; m. Janet Lynn Johnson, May 25, 1974; children: Catherine Shirley, Amanda Margaret. AS in Behavioral Scis., SUNY, Albany, 1978, BS in Liberal Arts, 1987; MPA, Ball State U., 1991, M in Adult Edn., 1995. Substitute Tchrs.' Cert., Ind. Career non-commissioned U.S. Army, 1968-88; field ennumerator U.S. Census Dept., Indpls., 1990, 2000; course developer Veteran's Upward Bound, Indpls., 1994. Demographic cons. DataSource, Indpls., 1985—;

com. mem. at large INCONJUCTION; spokesman Parents Adv. Coun. Author, critical reviews: Sherlock Holmes Review, 1990—; author, editor: Media Newsletter INTERCOM: 1705, 1983-88 (Best in Orgn. 1983-85). Polit. cons. Ind. State Senate, Indpls., 1994-95; mem. sci.-fiction rsch. group First Fandom. With U.S. Army, 1968-88. Recipient Appreciation Plaque INCONJUNCTION, Indpls., 1991, 94, Cert. of Appreciation Salvation Army, Indpls., 1990-94. Mem. VFW, Mensa, Mutual Unidentified Flying Object Network, First Fandom. Republican. Lutheran. Avocations: newsletter editing/publishing, media fan organizations, literary history. Home: Georgetown, Ind. Died May 22, 2007.

DALE, CHARLES, retired trade association administrator; b. Springhill, NS, Can., Aug. 17, 1929; m. Darlene Dale (dec. 2004); children: Cameron, Charles, Steve, Cindi, Candace, Mary, Vicki. Student, Victoria U., Wellington, New Zealand. Journalist Daily Mirror, Sydney, Can. Press; treas. local chpt. Can. Wire Svc. Guild, pres.; internat. labor rep. U.S., Can., Puerto Rico, 1955-79; sec.-treas. The Newspaper Guild, Silver Spring, Md., 1979-87, pres., 1987—95. Former pres. Fedn. Guild Reps. Died Oct. 23, 2007.*

DALE, DENVER THOMAS, III, retired marine corps officer, educator; b. Santa Barbara, Calif., July 30, 1931; s. Denver Thomas Jr. and Ethel Helen (Squire) Dale; m. Elizabeth Ann Donleavy, Nov. 17, 1956 (div. Oct. 1978); children: Denver Thomas IV, Matthew J., Jeffrey N.; m. Peggy Frances Altice, Nov. 19, 1982. Student, Va. Mil. Inst., 1948—52; BA, San Francisco State U., 1959; MS, Ctrl. Conn. State U., 1969. Cert. secondary sch. educator Calif. Enlisted USMC, 1952, advanced through grades to lt. col., 1975; comdg. officer Co. K., 3d Bn., 4th Marine Regt., Kaneohe Bay, Hawaii, 1961—62; manpower mgmt. officer 1st Marine Aircraft Wing, Iwakuni, Japan and Danang, Vietnam, 1964—65; exec. officer, comdg. officer 3d Bn., 5th Marine Regt., Ana Hoa, Vietnam, 1969—70; head officer force mgmt. unit Hdqrs. U.S. Marine Corps, Washington, 1971—73; exec. officer, comdg. officer, assoc. prof. naval sci. NROTC Unit, Rice U., Houston, 1973—75; ret., 1975; project mgr. Telemedia, Inc., Teheran, Iran, 1978; sr. marine instr. Marine Corps jr. ROTC unit Portage (Ind.) H.S., 1979—81, North H.S., Bakersfield, Calif., 1981—92, chmn. dept. mil. sci., 1981—92, varsity boys tennis coach, 1983—86. Prin. speaker at numerous civic, frat., vets., high sch. and coll. groups, from 1965. Asst. scoutmaster Boy Scouts Am., 1970—73. Decorated Bronze Star with V device, Comdt. U.S. Marines commendation. Mem.: VFW, Marine Corps Assn., VMI Alumni Assn., Masons. Republican. Home: Roanoke, Va. Died Mar. 2, 2006.

DALE, PAUL ROSS, operations manager; b. LA, Calif., June 27, 1915; s. William Lester and Rose (Roth) Dale; m. Martha Goodman, Oct. 14, 1973; stepchildren: Rodney L. Ward, Bruce A. Ward;children from previous marriage: Patricia Rose, Nadine Ann. Student, San Francisco Tech. Coll., 1935—36. Asst. supt. comm. Aramco, Saudi Arabia, 1938—41, 1946—52; chief comm. engr. Mil. Advt. Group, TDC, Taipei, Taiwan, 1953—57; regional mgr. Henningsen & Co. Ltd., Seoul, Republic of Korea, 1957—58; v.p. ITT-Far East Ltd., Hong Kong, 1959—68; dir. Laboratoire Electrique et D'Automatique Dauphinois, Grenoble, France, 1968—79; ops. mgr. Sanag divsn. Sanitek Products, LA, from 1980; mgr. Corp. Mgmt. Svcs., LA, 1973—79. Contbr. articles to profl. jours. With USN, 1941—46, PTO. Mem.: IEEE, Shriners, Masons (past master). Republican. Home: Hemet, Calif. Died July 16, 2006.

DALLAS, THOMAS ABRAHAM, retired utility company executive; b. Natchez, Miss., Oct. 30, 1923; s. Freely Skyles and Virginia (Walton) D.; m. Billye Haskins, Nov. 16, 1952; children: Virginia Hilton, Thomas Walton, Sue Ellen Dallas Shepard. BEE, Miss. State U., 1948. Registered profl. engr., Miss. Engr. Miss. Power & Light Co., Brookhaven, 1948-56, mgr. Indianola, 1956-62, Jackson, 1962-80, v.p., chief engr., 1980-85, sr. v.p., 1985-88; ret., 1988. Chmn. South Cen. Electric Cos., 1982-87. Served to 1st lt. USAAF, 1943-45, ETO. Recipient Pub. Service award Nat. Weather Service, 1973. Mem. Nat. Soc. Profl. Engrs. Lodges: Kiwanis (pres. Jackson club 1981). Republican. Methodist. Avocations: hunting, fishing, golf. Home: Jackson, Miss. Died June 16, 2006.

DALSTON, JEPTHA WILLIAM, hospital administrator, educator; b. Longview, Tex., Mar. 18, 1931; BA, Tex. A&M U., 1952; MA, U. Okla., 1966, PhD in Health Adminstrn. and Polit. Sci, 1970; postgrad., Columbia U., 1963-64; MHA, U. Minn., 1969. Controller Reynolds Army Hosp., Ft. Sill, Okla., 1959-60; adminstr. Indian Hosp. USPHS, Lawton, Okla., 1960-65, chief planning and evaluation Indian Health Svc. Oklahoma City, 1969-70; asst. adminstr. Univ. Hosp. and Clinics, Oklahoma City, 1970-73, adminstr., 1973-75; dir. Univ. Hosp., Ann Arbor, Mich., 1975-85; pres., chief exec. officer Hermann Hosp., from 1985; v.p. U. Tex. Health Sci. Ctr., Houston, from 1985; prof. community health svcs. U. Tex. Med. Sch., Houston, from 1985; asst. prof. U. Okla., 1970-73, assoc. prof., 1973-76; prof. U. Mich., 1976-85; adj. prof. U. Houston, Clear Lake, from 1987. Preceptor Washington U., U. Minn. Served with U.S. Army, 1952-58; Served with Res., 1958—. Mem. Am. Hosp. Assn., Am. Public Health Assn., Am. Coll. Healthcare Execs., Am. Acad. Polit. Sci. Died Mar. 2, 2007.

DALY, ALEXANDER JOSEPH, minister; b. Jersey City, May 23, 1930; s. Alexander Joseph and Viola (Fell) D.; m. Mary Kay Baughman, Aug. 20, 1960. BA, Lenoir-Rhyne Coll., 1958; MDiv, Luth. Sch. Theol., 1962. Ordained to ministry Luth. Ch. in Am., 1962. Pastor St. James Luth. Ch., Folsom, N.J., 1962-64; assoc. pastor Trinity Luth. Ch., Lemoyne, Pa., 1964-71, Redeemer Luth. Ch., Atlanta, 1971-80; campus pastor Ga. Inst. Tech., Atlanta, from 1980. Chaplain Luth. Towers, Atlanta, 1980—; cons. Downtown Atlanta Sr. Svcs., 1983-84. Coord. Community Head Start Program, Lemoyne, 1977-78; chmn. County-Wide Meals on Wheels, Lemoyne, 1978-79. Died Mar. 10, 2007.

DALY, JOE ANN GODOWN, publishing company executive; b. Galveston, Tex., Aug. 7, 1924; d. Elmer and Jessie Fee (Beck) Godown; m. William Jerome Daly, Jr., Jan. 25, 1958 (dec.). BA in Journalism, U. Okla., 1945, BA in Piano, 1952. Asst. editor house organ Southwestern Bell Telephone, St. Louis, 1945-47; sec. to city mgr. Okla. Daily News, Oklahoma City, 1947-49; pvt. piano tchr. Alva, Okla., 1952-54; sec. to editor Prentice-Hall, Inc., NYC, 1954-55, asst. to children's book editor, 1955-58; asst. editor children's books Dodd, Mead & Co., NYC, 1963, dir. children's books, 1965-88, asst. v.p., assoc. pub. children's books, 1986-88; editl. dir. Cobblehill Books affiliate Dutton Children's Books, NYC, 1988-97, ret., 1997. Mem. Children's Book Council, N.Y.C., 1963, treas., 1969; mem. CBC/LA Com., N.Y.C., 1980, CBC/Prelude Com., N.Y.C., 1983 Active Bklyn. Heights Assn., 1976—; friend Carnegie Hall, N.Y. Philharm.; mem. Met. Opera Guild, Mus. Modern Art, Mus. Natural History. Mem. Phi Beta Kappa, Sigma Delta Chi, Theta Sigma Phi, Mu Phi Epsilon Democrat. Methodist. Home: Loganville, Ga. Died Dec. 29, 2006.

DAMON, RONALD D., income tax specialist; b. Watertown, N.Y., Oct. 16, 1931; s. Clifford Arthur and Genevieve Barbara (Farmer) D.; m. Helen I. O'Hara, Jan. 2, 1949; children— David A., Michael C., John C., James R., Christopher S., Trina C. Firefighter City of Watertown, 1953-69, fire capt., 1970-76, bn. chief, 1976-80, dep. fire chief, 1980, chief Bur. Fire Prevention, 1980-81, chief of dept., 1981-85; sec., dir. North Side League, 1965—; owner R. Damon Tax Service, Watertown, 1968—. Committeeman, 10th ward Democratic party, 1960's. Recipient Heroism/Valor award Jefferson County Fire Coordinators, 1963, City 1st Citizen award Town of Watertown, 1986, Civic Award North Side Improvement League, 1986. Mem. Internat. Assn. Firefighters (v.p., treas. Local 191 1963-64), Internat. Assn. Fire Chiefs, N.Y. State Assn. Fire Chiefs, VFW, Am. Legion. Roman Catholic. Lodge: Eagles. Served with U.S. Army, 1948-51, Korea. Home: Watertown, NY. Died July 13, 2007.

DANFORTH, WENDY, publishing company executive; b. NYC, Nov. 6, 1936; d. Harry Kalman and Ami Clifford Clapp BA, U. Richmond, 1958; postgrad., U. Edinburgh, Scotland, 1959-60, Columbia U. V.p. Allied Pubs. P and P Publs., Palm Beach, Fla., 1971-85, v.p. New Woman, 1971-84, v.p. Harold's Heralds, 1971-84, assoc. editor/pub. New Woman Mag., 1971-84, v.p., 1984-87, v.p. chief exec. officer Harold Pubs., from 1987, also bd. dirs. Author: Ickle McNoo, 1973, Whimsicals, 1984, Willoughby, 1987, Just Beyond Your Nose, 1989; contbr. articles to various mags. Mem. Soc. Profl. Journalists Republican. Episcopalian. Home: West Palm Beach, Fla. Died June 30, 2007.

DANIEL, JOHN MONCURE, JR., state pollution control official, chemical engineer; b. Alexandria, Va., Mar. 2, 1928; s. John Moncure Daniel and Marguerite (Fitz-Gerald) Williams; m. Joy Anne Beam, June 13, 1951; children— John M. III, Joy Anne. B.Ch.E., U. Va., 1949; M.S., Ga. Inst. Tech., 1951. Registered profl. engr., Va. Chem. engr. Va.-Carolina Chem. Co., Richmond, 1954-56, sr. chem. engr., 1956-57, sect. leader (fertilizer), process and mech. devel., 1957-60, tech. asst., mfg. dept., 1960-63; asst. dir., quality control, mfg. dept. Mobil Chem. Co., 1963-66, supr., material control, research and tech. dept., 1966-68, mgr., tech. sect., 1968-69; asst. exec. dir. for enforcement Va. State Air Pollution Control Bd., Richmond, 1970—. Served with U.S. Navy, 1951-54. Mem. Am. Inst. Chem. Engrs., Air Pollution Control Assn. (past chmn. South Atlantic Sec., bd. dirs.; past chmn. Central Va. Chpt.), Tau Beta Pi. Episcopalian. Home: Richmond, Va. Died Apr. 1, 2006.

DANIELS, EDWARD WILLIAM, biomedical scientist, researcher; b. Tracy, Minn., Jan. 19, 1917; s. Azro Ashley and Nellie (Bundy) D.; m. Harriet Catherine Zimmerman, Dec. 23, 1943; children: Edward, Paul, Thomas, Lynell. BA, Cornell Coll., Mount Vernon, Iowa, 1941; MS, U. Ill., 1947, PhD, 1950. Tchr. h.s. sci., 1941-43; instr., asst. prof. dept. physiology U. Chgo., 1950-54. assoc. biologist Argonne Nat. Lab., Ill., 1954-74, biologist, 1974-81; adj. prof. U. Ill. Coll. Medicine, Chgo., 1984—. Served with USN, 1943-46. Fellow U. Ill., 1949. Fellow AAAS; mem. Soc. Protozoologists, Midwest Soc. Electron Microscopy, Am. Inst. Biol. Sci., Radiation Research Soc. Avocation: swimming. Home: Naperville, Ill. Died June 30, 2006.

DANIELS, GARY L., state legislator; b. Needham, Mass., May 16, 1954; m. Loreen Daniels; 6 children. BS in MIS, N.H. Coll., 1982. Coord. Comty. Assistance Program, 1985-94; N.H. state rep. Dist. 13; mem. labor, indsl. and rehab. svc. coms. N.H. Ho. of Reps. Chmn. Milford Rep. Com., 1992-94; mem. Am. Legis. Exch. Coun. Labor and Bus. Task Force, 1990-94, Legis. for Ltd. Spending, 1990-94; engr. Dir. Peace Gospel Folk Ministry, 1986-94. Died Feb. 17, 2007.

DANIELS, JAMES DOUGLAS, retired academic administrator; b. Harmony, NC, Nov. 14, 1935; m. Marie Brown, Oct. 6, 1957; children: Christopher James, Gregory John, Susan Marie. AB, Davidson Coll., 1957; MA, U. N.C., 1962, PhD, 1968. Exec. tng. program Deering-Milliken Textile Corp., Gainesville, Ga., 1957-58; history instr. Hargrave Military Acad., Chatham, Va., 1961-62, chmn., divsn. social sci., 1962-65, dean students, summer sch., 1964-65; asst. prof. history Valdosta (Ga.) State Coll., 1968-71, assoc. prof. history, 1971-78, history prof., 1978, dean, sch. arts, sci., 1970-80; pres., prof. history Coker Coll., Hartsville, SC, 1981—2002; ret., 2002. Bd. dirs. Byerly Hosp., 1981-85; Sunday sch. tchr. First Presbyn. Ch. Hartsville, 1981—. Com. on ministry Pee Dee Presbytery of S.C., from 1985, moderator, 1985; adv. bd. Bank of Am., from 1988, Pee Dee Heritage, from 1982, Darlington County Mental Health Citizens, from 1987. With US Army, 1958—60. NDEA fellow, U. N.C., 1966-68; recipient Man and Boy award Valdosta Boys' Club Bd. Dirs., 1970. Mem. Greater Hartsville C. of C. (bd. dirs. 1982-88, v.p. 1986, pres. 1987, chmn. bd. 1988), Hartsville H.S. Acad. Boosters Club and Band Boosters, Rotary (bd. dirs. 1982-99, Citizen of Yr. award 1989), Order of Palmetto, Omicron Delta Kappa. Presbyterian. Avocations: reading, fishing. Home: Blythewood, SC. Died June 10, 2007.

DANIELS, JOHN HANCOCK, agricultural products company executive; b. St. Paul, Oct. 28, 1921; s. Thomas L. and Frances (Hancock) D.; m. Martha H. Williams, Dec. 23, 1942; children: Martha M., John Hancock, Jane P. Daniels Moffett, Christopher W. Student, St. Paul Acad., 1932-37; grad., Phillips Exeter Acad., 1939; BA, Yale, 1943; grad., Advanced Mgmt. Program, Harvard, 1957. With Archer-Daniels-Midland Co., Mpls., 1946-96, successively mem. staff linseed oil div., prodn. mgr. alfalfa divsn., mgr. feed divsn., v.p., dir., 1946-53, pres., dir., 1958-67, chmn., 1967-72, dir., mem. exec. com., 1972-96. With Mulberry Resources Inc. Author: Nothing Could Be Finer, 1996, Affectionately H, 1999, In The Boat, 2004. With Bus. Coun.; trustee Com. Econ. Devel.; chmn. 1972 Decatur United Way Campaign. Served from 2d lt. to capt. F.A., AUS, 1943-46. Decorated Bronze Star medal. Mem. Elizabethan Club, Links Club (N.Y.C.), Mpls. Club, Woodhill (Minn.) Club, Sprindale Hall Club (Camden, S.C.), Grolier Club, Lafayette Club. Episcopalian. Home: Camden, SC. Died Sept. 18, 2006.

DANIELS, LEGREE S., federal agency administrator; b. Denmark, SC, Feb. 9, 1917; d. Earl and Carlee (Sheppard) Atterbury; m. Oscar Daniels, 1948. Student, Temple U.; LHD (hon.), Clark Atlanta U. Staff asst. to Senator Hugh Scott US Senate, 1974—76; commr. election Commonwealth of Pa., 1986, dep. sec., 1986—87; asst. sec. civil rights U.S. Dept. Edn., 1987—89; bd. govs. U.S. Postal Svc., Washington, 1990—2005. Past vice chmn. Nat. Electoral Coll.; chmn. Nat. Black Republican coun., Past mem. Middle Atlanta Adv. Bd., U.S. Civil Rights Commn., Rep. Nat. Com., Pres.'s Commn. White House Fellows, Army Sci. Bd., Nat. Endowment for Democracy; bd. advisors Penn State, Harrisburg; bd. dirs. Ctr. Internat. Pvt. Enterprise, U.S. C. of C., John Heinz Harrisburg Sr. Ctr. Died Nov. 19, 2005.

DANKESE, JOSEPH PETER, membrane devel. and mfg. co. exec.; b. Somerville, Mass., Apr. 26, 1928; s. Joseph and Diana (Mercurio) D.; grad. Boston Latin Sch., 1946, Chauncy Hall Sch., 1950; B.S. in Chem. Engring., M.I.T., 1954; postgrad. Northeastern U., 1954-60; m. Sheila Mary Heffernan, Nov. 10, 1956; children— Mary E., Patricia A., Joseph Peter, Michael T., Teresa M., Catherine D., Julia B., William J. Product devel. engr. Microwave Assos., Boston, 1954-55; process design engr. Ionics, Inc., Cambridge, Mass., 1955-57; process devel. engr. Dewey and Almy Chem. Co., Cambridge, 1957-59; research and devel. engr. Arthur D. Little, Inc., Cambridge, 1959-61; heat and mass transfer engr. Gen. Electric Co., West Lynn, Mass., 1961-64; sr. project engr. U.S. Army Research and Devel. Labs., Ft. Belvoir, Va., 1964-65; area mgr. Amicon Corp., Cambridge, 1965-66; pres., chmn. bd. Dankese Engring., Inc., 1966—. Served with USN, 1946-48. Registered profl. engr., Mass. Contbr. 15 articles to profl. publs. Inventor and developer series D membrane fuel cell used on Gemini Manned Space Mission. Patentee (6) fuel cells, membranes and batteries. Home: Dorchester, Mass. Died July 25, 2007.

DANTO, HAROLD NEWTON, environmental engineer; b. Cleve., Jan. 1, 1927; s. Joseph Bernard and Anna (Stotsky) D.; m. Muriel Elaine Sobol, Sept. 6, 1947 (dec. Sept. 1986); children— Charlotte Elizabeth, Allan Howard. B.S. in Chem. Engring., Case Western Res. U., 1950. Prin., H.N. Danto Cons., Cleve., 1954-70; air pollution engr. Ohio EPA, Cleve., 1970-76; sr. environ. engr. Sherwin Williams Co., Cleve., 1976-78; v.p. Danto Environ. Corp., Cleve., 1978-84, pres., 1985-86; sec.-treas. Insulation Removal Co., from 1986, now pres., chief operating officer; also pres. D/E 3. lectr. in field. Bd. dirs. Eagle Scout Assn., Cleve., 1973-84; active Boy Scouts Am. Served with U.S. Army, 1944-46. Mem. Am. Pollution Control Assn., Water Pollution Control Fedn., Nat. Asbestos Coun., Nat. Radon Assn., Am. Radon Assn. Avocations: swimming; hiking; computer programming. Died Aug. 21, 2007.

D'APPOLONIA, DAVID J., environmental company executive, civil engineer; b. Edmonton, Alta., Can., Feb. 5, 1944; came to U.S., 1947; s. Elio and Violet Mary D'Appolonia; m. Eileen Mauclair; children: Christine C., Caroline C., Anne V. BS, Carnegie Mellon U., 1965; PhD, MIT, 1968. Asst. prof. MIT, Boston, 1967-70; prin. Lambe Assoc. Inc., Boston, 1969-72; pres. ECI Inc., Pitts., 1972-82; chief exec. officer D'Appolonia Waste Mgmt. Inc., Pitts., 1982-84; sr. v.p. Internat. Tech. Corp., Torrance, Calif., from 1984. Contbr. numerous articles to profl. jours. Trustee Winchester Thurston Sch., Pitts., 1981—. Mem. ASCE (Middlebrooks award 1968, Croes medal 1972), Young Pres.'s Orgn. Clubs: Longue Vue (Pitts.). Home: Pittsburgh, Pa. Died Nov. 19, 2006.

DARACK, ARTHUR J., editor; b. Royal Oak, Mich., Jan. 1, 1918; s. Edward Charles and Sonia (Resnikov) D.; m. Jean Claire Puttmyer, May 28, 1942; children— Glenn Arthur, Brenda Lee. Mus.M., Cin. Conservatory, 1949; PhD, Ind. U., 1951. Music editor Cin. Enquirer, 1951-61, feature writer, columnist, 1961-62, book and art editor, 1962-63; editor Dimension; Cin., monthly mag., 1963-65; asso. editor Ency. Brit., Chgo., 1967-70; sr. editor Actual Specifying Engr. (monthly mag.), from 1971; editor Consumers Digest mag., 1972-78; pres. Consumer Group Inc., from 1978. Program annotator Cin. Symphony Orch., 1952-61; adj. asso. prof. music Coll. Music, U. Cin. Author: Outdoor Power Equipment, 1977, The Guide to Home Appliance Repair, 1979, How to Repair and Care for Small Home Appliances, 1983, Taking Profits from the OEX, 1988, Consumers Digest Automobile Repair Book, Trade the OEX, 1990; co-author: The Great Eating, Great Dieting Cookbook, 1978, Playboy's Book of Sports Car Repair, 1980; author syndicated column Buy Right, 1977-81; contbg. editor, columnist: syndicated column The Money Letter, 1979—. Served with AUS, 1941-45. Mem. Pi Kappa Lambda. Died June 29, 2007.

DARLINGTON, JULIAN TRUEHEART, retired biology educator; b. Barboursville, W.Va., Mar. 18, 1918; s. Urban V.W. and Virginia Lee (Bourne) D.; m. Jeanne Matthews, Dec. 5, 1942; children: Virginia B., Patricia M. AB, Emory U., 1940, MS, 1941; PhD, U. Fla., 1952. Asst. prof. U. Ga., Atla., 1953-54; prof. biology Shorter Coll., Rome, Ga., 1954-58, Furman U., Greenville, S.C., 1958-63, Rhodes Coll., Memphis, 1964-85. Contbr. articles to profl. jours. Commdr. Mid South Ex-POWs,

Memphis, 1992-93. Lt. USAAF, 1941-45, ETO. Decorated DFC, Bronze Star. Mem. Exchange Club, Sigma Xi, Phi Beta Kappa. Episcopalian. Home: Memphis, Tenn. Died Sept. 10, 2006.

DARRAH, JOAN, former mayor; b. L.A., Apr. 6, 1935; m. James P. Darrah. BA, U. Calif., Berkeley, 1956; MA, Stanford U., 1960; MA in Edn., U. Pacific, 1974. Mayor City of Stockton, Calif., 1990—96. Author: Getting Political: Stories of a Woman Mayor. Bd. regents U. Pacific, 1976—89. Died July 27, 2007.

D'ATTORRE, LEONARDO, engineering scientist, educator, consultant; b. La Plata, Argentina, Feb. 2, 1920; arrived in U.S., 1956; s. Juan and Isabel (Gimenez) D'Attorre; m. Beatriz Elvira Machi-Zubiaurre, Feb. 26, 1949. M in Aero. Engring., Facultad Ciencias Fisicomate Maticas, La Plata, 1947; PhD in Aero. Engring., U. La Plata, 1952. Assoc. prof. fluid mechanics U. La Plata, 1952—56, prof. rational mechanics, 1954—56, prof. fluid mechanics and aerodynamics, 1961—62; staff scientist Convair divsn. Gen. Dynamics Corp., San Diego, 1956—67; mem. profl. staff TRW Electronic and Def., Redondo Beach, Calif., from 1967. Contbr. articles to profl. jours. Named to Roll of Honor, TRW Electronic and Def., 1978. Mem.: NY Acad. Scis., Am. Math. Soc. Died Oct. 8, 2006.

DAUGHERTY, BILLY JOE, retired banker; b. Timpson, Tex., Jan. 31, 1923; s. David Albert and Kate (Smith) D.; m. Martha Carroum, May 14, 1942; children: Stephen Michael, Tony Fares, Kathryn Love. Grad., Tyler Comml. Coll., 1942; postgrad., So. State Coll., 1945-47; grad., So. Meth. U., 1969; student, Nat. Credit Lending Sch., U. Okla., 1969. Asst. v.p., asst. trust officer First Nat. Bank Magnolia (Ark.), 1947-52; plant acct. Republic Steel Corp., Magnolia, 1952-54; with Union Nat. Bank, Little Rock, 1954-70, v.p., cashier, sec. to bd. dirs., 1965-70, First State Bank & Trust Co., Conway, Ark., 1970-73, pres., dir., 1973-92; vice-chmn. bd., dir. Boatmen's Nat. Bank of Conway, 1992-96; adv. dir. Bank of Am., 1997-99. Bd. dirs. Conway Devel. Corp., pres., 1991-92, v.p. 1992-94; pres. adv. bd. Main Street Conway, 1988-91; bd. dirs. Bank of Am. Bd. dirs. Ark. Banking Sch.; mem. adv. bd. Salvation Army, 1967-70; bd. dirs. Met. YMCA, Little Rock, 1966-69; chmn. Columbia chpt. ARC, Magnolia, 1952-53; mem. budget com. United Fun Pulaski County (Ark.), 1962-65; treas. City Beautiful Com. Little Rock, 1965-67; treas. Ark. br. Am. Assn. UN, 1965-67; pres. Heart of Ark. Travel Assn., 1971-74; pres., dir. United Fund of Faulkner County, 1971-73; state treas. Radio Free Europe, 1960-72; chmn. Faulkner County Heart Fund Campaing, 1971; sec. to bd. dirs., trustee Union Nat. Found.; chmn. exec. com. conv. and vis. bur. Little Rock, 1964-66; chmn. bldg. com. Immanuel Bapt. Ch., Little Rock, 1964-66; treas. Downtown Little Rock Unltd., 1966-67, Faulkner County Centennial, Inc., 1973-74; bd. dirs. Ark. Heart Assn., 197-75, chmn. bd., 1972-73; trustee Ark. Bapt. Med. Ctr., sec.-treas., 1965-74; corp. mem. Bapt. Health Inc. (formerly Bapt. Med. Ctr.); bd. dirs. Am. Heart Assn., 1976-78, Goodwill Industries Ark., 1976-94; treas. Goodwill Industries Ark., 1984-89, 1st v.p., 1989-90, pres., 1991-92; supt. Sunday sch., chmn. bldg com. Bapt. ch., 1964-66; chmn. bd. deacons 1962-63; mem. fin. com., 1960-68, chmn. stewardship com. 1968). Served as sgt. USAAF, 1942-45, CBI. Mem. Faulkner County Fair Assn. (bd. dirs. 1972-94), Little Rock Clearing House Assn. (v.p. 1969, pres. 1965-66, sec.-treas. 1967-68), Ark. Bankers Assn. (pres. jr. bankers sect. 1950; bank dirs. adv. com. 1971-72, chmn. group II, 1977-78, bd. dirs. 1979-80), Conway C. of C. (pres. 1975), Vets. of the 68th Air Svc. Group China WWII (life), The Am. Legion Post #0001 Ark. (life), Little Rock Club, Conway Country Club, Western Hills Country Club (dir., sec. 1968-69), Sertoma (pres. 1961-62, gov. Ark. dist. 1962-63, bd. dirs. Midwest region 1963-64, treas. 1964-65), Lions (pres. Conway Club 1975). Home: Conway, Ark. Died Apr. 29, 2007.

DAUGHERTY, FREDERICK ALVIN, federal judge; b. Oklahoma City, Aug. 18, 1914; s. Charles Lemuel and Felicia (Mitchell) D.; m. Marjorie E. Green, Mar. 15, 1947 (dec. Feb. 1964); m. Betsy F. Amis, Dec. 15, 1965. LL.B., Cumberland U., 1933; postgrad., Oklahoma City U., 1934-35, LL.B. (hon.), 1974; postgrad., Okla. U., 1936-37; HHD (hon.), Okla. Christian Coll., 1976. Bar: Okla. 1937. Practiced, Oklahoma City, 1937-40; mem. firm Ames, Ames & Daugherty, Oklahoma City, 1946-50, Ames, Daugherty, Bynum & Black, Oklahoma City, 1952-55; judge 7th Jud. Dist. Ct., Oklahoma City, 1955-61; U.S. dist. judge Western, Eastern and No. Dists. Okla., Oklahoma City, from 1961; chief judge Western Dist. Okla., Oklahoma City, 1972-82. Mem. Fgn. Intelligence Surveillance Ct., 1981-88, Temporary Emergency Ct. Appeals, 1983-93, Multi dist. Litigation panel, 1980-90; mem. codes of conduct com. U.S. Jud. Conf., 1980-87. Active local ARC, 1956—, chmn., 1958-60, nat. bd. govs., 1963-69, 3d nat. vice chmn., 1968-69; active United Fund Greater Oklahoma City, 1957—, pres., 1961, trustee, 1963—; pres. Community Coun. Oklahoma City and County, 1967-69; exec. com. Okla. Med. Rsch. Found., 1966-69. With AUS, 1940-45, 50-52. Decorated Legion of Merit with 2 oak leaf clusters, Bronze Star with oak leaf cluster, Combat Infantrymans badge; recipient award to mankind Okla. City Sertoma Club, 1962, Outstanding Citizen award Okla. City Jr. C. ofC., 1965, Disting. Alumni citation Samford U., 1974, Disting. Svc. citation Okla. U., 1973, Constn. award Rogers State Coll., 1988, Pathmakers award Oklahoma County Hist. Soc., 1991; named to Okla. Hall of Fame, 1969, Okla. Mil. Hall of Fame, 2000. Mem. Fed. Bar Assn., Okla. Bar Assn., Am. Bar Found., Sigma Alpha Epsilon, Phi Delta Phi, Men's Dinner Club (Oklahoma City) (pres. 1966-69), Kiwanis (pres. 1957, lt. gov. 1959), Masons (33 degree, sovereign grand insp. gen. in Okla. 1982-86), Shriners, Jesters, Order of Coif (hon. mem. Okla. chpt.). Episcopalian (sr. warden 1957). Home: Oklahoma City, Okla. Died Apr. 7, 2006.

D'AURIA, MICHAEL MARTIN, real estate developer; b. N.Y.C., Dec. 1, 1927; s. Al Joseph and Mary Ann (Lynch) D'A.; m. Joan Ann Lebkuecher, Oct. 1, 1955; 1 child, Denise Marie Roche. B.A., Hillyer Coll., 1948; LL.B., J.D., St. John's U., 1951; LL.M., NYU, 1955. L.H.D. (hon.), Shaw U., 1979. County judge Nassau County, Mineola, N.Y., 1964-65; pvt. practice law, D'Auria, Bond, Corin and DeVito, Jericho, N.Y., 1966-68, 71-74; justice Supreme Ct. State of N.Y., Mineola, 1969-71; spl. asst. provost N.Y. Inst. Tech., Old Westbury, 1976-82, sr. v.p., 1983-89, dean Ctr. Labor and Indsl. Relations, 1977-83; exec. v.p., gen. mgr. L&K Holding Corp., Woodbury, N.Y., 1989—. Author: Legal Terms and Concepts in Criminal Justice, 1979; author plays: Youth and the Law, 1965; Narcotics and Youth, 1969. Served as col. U.S. Army, 1945-47, PTO, flotilla comdr., divsn. staff officer USCG Aux., brig. gen. N.Y. Guard ret. Mem. Criminal Justice Educators of N.Y. (chmn. 1978-82) (spl. award, 1980), Northeastern Assn. Criminal Justice Educators (pres. 1980-81) (spl. awards 1979-86). Republican. Roman Catholic. Clubs: Kiwanis Internat. (internat youth coordinator 1968-70) Brookville Taxpayers Assn. (v.p./sec. 1976-80). Lodges: Knights Columbus (chmn. 1968-70), Sons of Italy (exec. com. 1965-67). Home: Glen Head, NY. Died Aug. 1, 2007.

DAVENPORT, RICHARD CAMERON, bank executive; b. Harrisburg, Ill., Aug. 8, 1921; s. Richard Comus and Elizabeth Ann (Haddon) Davenport; m. Dorothy Helen O'Rourke, Jan. 17, 1946 (dec. 1981); children: Richard K., Scott C.; m. Patricia Porter, 1985. BSBA, U. Ill., 1946. Cert. comml. lender. Asst. mgr. credit Hart Schaffner & Marx, Chgo., 1946—55; cashier Harrisburg Nat. Bank, 1955—61, v.p., 1961—73, pres., from 1973. Mem. adv. bd. Am. Banker Assn., Washington, 1981—84. Pres. Sch. Bd. Unit 3, Harrisburg, 1962—72; bd. mem. Southeastern Ill. Coll., 1968—72; chmn. Southeastern Ill. Coll. Found., 1985; capt. CAP. Capt. USMC, 1942—46. Mem.: Kiwanis (pres. 1960, lt. gov. 1961), Shriners, Masons (past master, grand rep. to Del. for grand lodge of Ill. from 1975). Republican. Presbyterian. Home: Hilton Head Island, SC. Died Feb. 19, 2007.

DAVIDSON, HERBERT M., JR., (TIPPEN), newspaper owner; b. Chgo., Aug. 10, 1925; s. Herbert Marc and Liliane (Refregier) D.; m. Josephine Field, Dec. 27, 1947 (dec. July 1995); children: Marc, Julia. Student, Juilliard Sch., 1942-43, 45-46; Mus.D. (hon.), Stetson U., 1975. Reporter Chgo. Daily News, 1949-50; city editor Daytona Beach (Fla.) News-Jour., 1951-53, mng. editor, 1953-56, gen. mgr., 1957-85, pub., 1985-98, co-editor, from 1985, pres., CEO, from 1998. Pres. Ctrl. Fla. Cultural Endeavors, Inc., Daytona Beach, 1963—; chmn. Fine Arts Coun. of Fla., 1970-75, 81-82; mem. Fla. Alliance for Arts, 1998—; mem. Fla. Arts Coun., 1998-2000; prodr., artistic dir. Seaside Music Theater, Daytona Beach, 1976—. Cpl. U.S. Army, 1942-44, PTO. Named Ambassador of the Arts, State of Fla., Tallahassee, 1982, Hon. mem. London Symphony Orch., 1989, honoree Daytona Beach Community Coll.'s Tippen and Josephine Field Davidson Endowment for the Arts, 1992; hon. officer Civil divsn. Order of the Brit. Empire, 1998. Mem. Am. Soc. Newspaper Editors Avocations: music, theater, handicraft, stamp collecting/philately. Home: Daytona Beach, Fla. Died Jan. 23, 2007.

DAVIDSON, JAMES MELVIN, academic administrator, researcher, educator; b. The Dalles, Oreg., Apr. 16, 1934; s. Melvin Archie and Kathryn Naomie (Crooks) D.; m. Margaret May Tewinkel, June 29, 1957; children: Deborah Joy, Jodi May, Michelle Anne. BS, Oreg. State U., 1956, MS, 1958; PhD, U. Calif., Davis, 1965. Asst. prof. to assoc. prof. Okla. State U., Stillwater, 1965-72, prof., 1973-74; vis. assoc. prof. U. Fla., Gainesville, 1972-73, prof., 1974-79, asst. dean for rsch., 1979-86, dean for rsch., 1986-92, v.p. agrl. nat. resources, 1992-98. Sci. adv. com. Nat. Ctr. for Groundwater Res., Ada., Okla., 1979-86; groundwater res. rev. com. EPA Sci. Adv. Bd., Washington, 1984-86; water sci. and tech. bd. Nat. Acad. Sci., Washington, 1982-86. Co-editor: Virus Aspects of Applying Municipal Waste to Land, 1976, Environmental Impact of Non-point Source Pollution, 1980, Sludge-Health Risks of Land Application, 1980, Effects of Conservation Tillage on Groundwater Quality, 1987. Grantee EPA. Fellow Am. Soc. of Agronomy (chair environ. quality 1978), Soil Sci. Soc. Am. (chair soil physics 1984); mem. Alpha Zeta, Sigma Xi. Achievements include research in movement and sorption of pesticides and other organic solutes in soil systems in order to develop, test, and modify existing conceptual mathematical models for simulating the movement of water and solutes in homogeneous and nonhomogeneous soils. Home: Gainesville, Fla. Died Sept. 26, 2006.

DAVIDSON, JOHN, financial advisory executive; b. NYC, Oct. 8, 1916; s. John and Elizabeth (Kelly) D.; m. Charlotte J. Duffy, Apr. 22, 1950 (dec.); m. Inge Riebeth, May 23, 1970; children: Jane K. Davidson Greenler, Sara G., Kirsten M. Davidson Adam. BS, NYU, 1944. With Consol. Natural Gas Company, Inc., NYC, 1943-82, tax dept., 1943, asst. mgr. tax dept., 1953-58, mgr., 1958-61, asst. treas., 1961-63, asst. v.p. adminstrn., 1963-70, sec., 1967-70, v.p. adminstrn., 1970-82; pres. Capital Creation Co. of Pa., 1982-94; retired, 1994. Mem. Council on Employee Benefits. Mem. Pitts. Field Club, U. Club Pitts., Beta Gamma Sigma Home: Verona, Pa. Died Nov. 20, 2006.

DAVIDSON, JOHN HUNTER, agriculturist; b. Wilmette, Ill., May 16, 1914; s. Joseph and Ruth Louise (Moody) D.; m. Elizabeth Marie Boynton, June 16, 1943 (dec. Feb. 2005); children: Joanne Davidson Hildebrand, Kathryn Davidson Bouwens, Patricia. BS in Horticulture, Mich. State U., 1937, MS in Plant Biochemistry, 1940. Field rschr. agrl. chems. Dow Chem. Co., Midland, Mich., 1936-42, with R&D dept. agrl. products, 1946-72, tech. adviser R&D agrl. products, 1972-80, tech. adviser govt. rels., 1980—86, cons., from 1984. Contbr. articles on plant pathology, horticulture and weed control to profl. jours. Lt. USNR, 1945. Mem. Am. Chem. Soc., Am. Soc. Hort. Sci., Weed Sci. Soc., Am. Pathol. Soc., Exch. Club of Midland, Phi Kappa Phi, Alpha Zeta. Republican. Home: Midland, Mich. Died Sept. 8, 2007.

DAVIDSON, THOMAS NOEL, metal products executive; b. Evansville, Ind., Oct. 4, 1939; s. Harry R. and Helen E. Davidson; m. Sally Anne Fries, 1958; children: Thomas N. Jr., John C., James R., Jennifer J. BSc with honors, Mich. State U., 1961. Chmn. bd. dirs. Quarry Hill Group, Nutech Precision Metals Inc., Azure Dynamics Inc. Past prin. owner Am. Brass Co., Ansonia Brass, Atco Controls, Inc., Buffalo Brass Co., Carborundum Abrasives, Inc., Cramco, Inc., Hanson Inc., Jensen Fitting Mfg., Ltd., Jensen Fittings Corp., PCL Industries Ltd., Sandbright & Co., Sklar-Peppler Furniture Inc., Stephenson's Rent-all Inc., Union Drawn Steel Ltd., Volstatic, Inc.; chmn. bd. Azure Dynamics, LP; bd. dirs. TLC Laser Eye Ctrs., MDC Corp., Occulogix Inc., Nutech Precision Metals, TLC Eye Ctr.; bd. dirs. Nat. Marine Sanctuary, Clemmer Industries; past chmn. Gen. Trust Corp., Henson Chem. Past chmn. Ocean Reef Hist. Soc., Ocean Reef Found., Hugh MacMillan Children's Found.; past chmn. Can. CPGA Golf Championship, Metro Toronto Conv. Ctr.; past bd. dirs. Con. Smythe Rsch. Found., Westhem Corp., USF&G, Can., Nat. Club, Can. Club, Silcorp Ltd., others; bd. dirs., past chmn. Ocean Reef Cmty. Found.; chmn. Ocean Reef Cultural Ctr.; founding chmn. Ocean Reef Club, Inc. Recipient Fin. Post Can. award 1979; named Entrepreneur of Yr. by Fin. Post. Mem. Soc. Plastics Engrs. (past dir.), Soc. Plastics Industry (past chmn., Man of Yr. award 1985), Variety Ability Systems Inc. (past dir.), Variety Village (past dir.), Young Pres. Orgn. (internat. pres. 1988-89), World Pres. Orgn. (bd. dirs., internat. pres. 1997), Duck Unlimited (past dir.), Can. Club (past bd. dirs., N.Y. and Toronto), Nat. Club Toronto (past bd. dirs.), Rosedale Golf Club (Toronto), Card Sound Golf Club (bd. dirs.), English Turn Golf and Country Club (New Orleans), Griffith Island Club (Wiarton, Ont., past chmn.), Ocean Reef Club (past chmn.), Bonefish and Tarpon Unltd. (founding chmn.), The Caledon Mountain Trout Club (Inglewood, Ont.), Tau Beta Pi, Pi Tau Sigma. Home: Key Largo, Fla. Died Sept. 1, 2006.

DAVIES, DAVID KEITH, geologist; b. Barry, Eng., Oct. 10, 1940; came to U.S., 1966, naturalized, 1973; s. Buller T. and Muriel G. (Champ) D.; m. Ruth Margaret Mary Gilbertson, Dec. 12, 1964; children: Mark James, John Phillip. BS, U. Wales, 1962, PhD, 1966; DSc, 1991; MS, La. State U., 1964. Asst. prof. Tex. A. and M. College Station, 1966-68, assoc. prof., 1968-70, asst. dean, 1968-70; prof. U. Mo., Columbia, 1970-77; chmn. dept. geoscis., dir. Reservoir Studies Inst., Tex. Technol. U., Lubbock, 1977-80; dir. Tex. Commerce Bank, Kingwood, from 1984; pres. David K. Davies & Assos., Inc., Houston, from 1980. Contbr. articles to profl. jours. Mem. Planning and Zoning Commn. Columbia, Mo., 1979-80. Recipient A. I. Levorsen Meml. award Am. Assn. Petroleum Geologists, 1978 Fellow Geol. Soc. Am.; mem. Am. Assn. Petroleum Geologists, Soc. Econ. Paleontologists and Mineralogists, Soc. Petroleum Engrs. of AIME (disting. lectr. 1984-85), Phi Kappa Phi. Home: Kingwood, Tex. Died Aug. 3, 2006.

DAVIES, ROBERT MORTON, consultant; b. Carmi, Ill., Sept. 22, 1920; s. John Morton and Helen (Wallace) D.; m. Elizabeth Bell, July 2, 1955; children: Henry H., Robert W., J. Wallace. BA, Wheaton Coll., Ill., 1941; MA, U. Pa., 1945, PhD, 1954; postgrad., NYU, 1955-56. Asso. prof. The King's Coll., Briarcliff Manor, N.Y., 1943-50; dean men Perkiomen Sch., Pennsburg, Pa., 1951-52; asst. prof. English, adminstrv. asst. Valley Forge Jr. Coll., Wayne, 1952-55; instr. N.Y. Maritime Coll., 1955-58; prof., chmn. English dept. and div. humanities Thiel Coll., Greenville, Pa., 1958-64; dean Ithaca (N.Y.) Coll., 1964-66, provost, 1966-72, cons., 1972-73; v.p. adminstrn. State U. N.Y. at Purchase, 1973-78; dean acad. affairs Wilmington (Del.) Coll., 1979-80, v.p. acad. affairs, 1980-82. Chief exec. officer Belle-Day Enterprises, Inc.; Del. sr. cons.; Asst. instr. English U. Pa., Phila., part-time 1946; asst. prof. English Rutgers U., New Brunswick, N.J., parttime, 1955-58 Author: The Humanism of Paul Elmer More, 1958; Contbr. articles, book revs., essays to profl. jours. Mem. Am. Mgmt. Assn., Modern Lang. Assn., Phi Beta Kappa, Alpha Psi Omega, Pi Delta Epsilon, Delta Mu Delta. Home: Parkland, Fla. Died Mar. 23, 2006.

DAVIS, ALAN JAY, lawyer; b. Phila., Feb. 4, 1937; s. Rudolph Alan and Adele (Saver) Davis; m. Roslyn Kutcher; children: Jennifer C., Michael R. BA, U. Pa., 1957; JSD, Harvard U., 1960. Bar: Pa. 1961, US Dist. Ct. (ea. dist.) Pa. 1961, US Ct. Appeals (3d cir.) 1961, US Supreme Ct. 1979. Law clk. to chief judge US Ct. Appeals (3d cir.), Phila., 1960-61; assoc. Wolf, Block, Schorr & Solis-Cohen, Phila., 1961-66, ptnr., 1968-91, chmn. litig. dept., 1987-91; chief asst. dist. atty. Office Dist. Atty., Phila., 1966-68; sr. litig. ptnr. Ballard Spahr Andrews & Ingersoll, Phila., from 1991. Spl. master to investigate prison sys. and sheriff's dept. Ct. Common Pleas, Phila., 1968—70; lectr. law U. Pa. Sch. Law, Phila., 1973—77; city solicitor City of Phila., 1980—82, chief labor negotiator, 1991—93, Southeastern Pa. Transp. Authority, Phila., 1982, Sch. Dist. Phila., 1984, 96. Chmn. met. adv. bd. Anti-Defamation League B'nai B'rith, Phila., 1986—88; mem. sch. com. Germantown Friends Sch., Phila., 1986—88; trustee Free Libr. Phila., 1995—98; mem. bd. trustees The Pew Charitable Trusts, 2004—07; chmn. Third Cir. Lawyers Adv. Com., 2007; pres. U. Pa. Law Sch. Am. Inns of Ct., 1998—2000. Fellow: Internat. Acad. Trial Lawyers, Am. Coll. Trial Lawyers; mem.: ABA, Am. Law Inst., Phila. Bar Assn., Pa. Bar Assn., Jr. Legal Club, Legal Club. Home: Philadelphia, Pa. Died May 9, 2007.

DAVIS, AUDREY BLYMAN, retired medical sciences curator, author; b. Hicksville, N.Y., Nov. 9, 1934; d. George William Blyman and Helen Rosalie Usewack; m. Miles Davis, Aug. 6, 1960; children: Laura Helen, Allan Watson. BS, Adelphi U., 1956; PhD, Johns Hopkins U., 1969. Sci. tchr. Sewanhaka High Sch., Floral Park, N.Y., 1956-58, Saugus (Mass.) High Sch., 1959-60; cons. Sci. Svc., Washington, 1966-70; curator med. scis. Smithsonian Instn., Washington, 1967-93, co-founder, Dr. Samuel D. Harris Nat. Mus. Dentistry, 1996-2001; mus. cons. U.S. Armed Forces Inst. Pathology, Washington, 1983-84; Muetter Mus., Phila., 1979-80, Med. Mus. Indpls., 1986; cons. N.J. Med. Sch., New Brunswick, 1982; Kate Hurd Mead lectr., 1985; keynote speaker Vis. Nursing Assns., Buffalo, 1985, Omaha, 1986, Richmond, Va., 1986, Arlington, 1987; tour leader Smithsonian Assocs. trips to USSR, 1985, 86, People's Rep. China, 1984, 86. Author: Medicine and Its Technology (Choice award for outstanding acad. book 1983), 1981; Bloodletting Instruments in the NMAH, 1979; The Circulation of the Blood and Medical Chemistry in England, 1650-1680, 1974; The American Dentist: A Sociological History, 1990; contbr. articles, monographs in field to publs. Recipient Excellence Award as chairperson, editor newsletter Smithsonian Instn. Women's Coun., 1982. Mem. Hist. Sci. Soc. (sec. 1982-85, coun. 1975-78), Am. Assn. Hist. Medicine (coun. 1976-79), Am. Hist. Assn., Am. Coun. Learned Socs, Conf. Secs, Bolton Swim Club, Tennis (Balt., former tennis chmn.) Club. Democrat. Roman Catholic (chair fin. com. Corpus Christi Parish, pres. parish coun. 1990-91). Home: Baltimore, Md. Died Aug. 29, 2006.

DAVIS, BERTRAM HYLTON, retired literature educator; b. Ozone Park, NY, Nov. 30, 1918; s. Hubert Edwin and Gladys (Greenidge) D.; m. Ruth Austin Benedict, Jan. 11, 1946; children: Ralph Paul, Kathryn Davis Kohler, Richard Austin. Grad., Phillips Acad., Andover, Mass., 1933-37; student, Hamilton Coll., Clinton, NY, 1937-39; AB, Columbia, 1941, MA, 1948, PhD, 1956; LLD, Dickinson Coll., 1974. Lectr. English Hunter Coll., 1947-48; instr., then asst. prof. English Dickinson Coll., 1948-57; staff assoc. AAUP, 1957-63, dep. gen. sec., 1963-67, gen. sec., 1967-74; prof. English Fla. State U., Tallahassee, 1974-85, svc. prof., 1985-90, prof. emeritus, from 1991. Author: Johnson Before Boswell, 1960, A Proof of Eminence, 1973, Thomas Percy, 1981, Thomas Percy: A Scholar-Cleric in the Age of Johnson, 1989; editor (Sir John Hawkins): Life of Samuel Johnson LL.D, 1961; editor bull., AAUP, 1960-65; field editor Twayne's English Authors Series, 1977-93; mem. editorial com. Yale Edition of Works of Samuel Johnson, 1979—. Served to capt. AUS, 1941-46. Guggenheim fellow, 1974 Mem. ACLU, MLA, Johnsonians, South Atlantic Modern Lang. Assn., Cosmos Club, Am. Soc. for 18th Century Studies. Home: Tallahassee, Fla. Died July 12, 2007.

DAVIS, CHARLES TILL, historian, educator; b. Natchez, Miss., Apr. 14, 1929; s. Frank Vincent and Sarah Knapp (Till) D.; m. Caecilia Weyer, Sept. 8, 1961; children: Bernard, Frank. BA, Davidson Coll., 1950, Oxford U., Eng., 1952, MA, 1957, D.Phil., 1956. Mem. faculty Tulane U., New Orleans, from 1956, assoc. prof. history, 1961-64, prof., from 1964, chmn. dept., 1984-86, Andrew Mellon prof., 1987. Vis. scholar Villa I Tatti, 1988; former mem. selection coms. for Rhodes, Marshall, Fulbright and NEH fellowships and scholarships. Author: Dante and the Idea of Rome, 1957, Dante's Italy, 1984; mem. editorial bd. Speculum Anniversary Monographs, 1975-80, Medievalia et Humanistica, 1969—, Sewanee Mediaeval Studies, 1988—, Dante Studies, 1991—; contbr. articles to profl. jours. Rhodes scholar Oxford U., 1950-53; Fulbright jr. grantee, Italy, 1953-55, sr. grantee, 1972; Guggenheim fellow, 1959-60; research fellow Am. Council Learned Socs., 1965-66; NEH sr. fellow, 1976-77 Fellow Medieval Acad. Am. (councillor 1973-76); mem. AAUP, Dante Soc. Am. (councillor 1966-68, v.p. 1988-91, pres. 1991—), Societa Dantesca Italiana. Episcopalian. Home: New Orleans, La. Died Nov. 26, 2006.

DAVIS, FREDERICK VERNELL, educational administrator; b. Big Island, Va., Apr. 8, 1923; s. John Henry and Ollie Elizabeth (Ware) D.; B.S., W.Va. State Coll., 1950; M.A. (NCCJ scholar), Seton Hall U., 1951; postgrad. Rutgers U., 1957, 59, N.Y. U., 1954-55, Columbia U., 1955-57. Tchr. English, Newark Bd. Edn., 1953-57; tchr. English, Thomas Jefferson High Sch., Elizabeth, N.J., 1957-68, chmn. dept. English, 1957-68, counsellor, 1968-70, vice prin., 1968-70; instr. communications Newark Coll. Engring., 1968-70; coordinator reading and libraries Bd. Edn., Elizabeth, 1970-75, coordinator reading K-12, 1975—; conv. guest speaker; moderator; co-editor high sch. and coll. texts; adviser Quid lit.- art mag.; mem. adv. bd. Prentice-Hall, Englewood Cliffs, N.J.; chmn. Minority Community Leaders Adv. Bd., Rutgers U., 1980—, appointed v.p. bd. of edn. E. Orange, N.J., 1986; cons. pub. edn. N.J. State Dept. Edn., 1993—; edn. evaluator for pub. edn. Commr. N.J. Edn. and Gov. N.J., 1993—. Served with AUS, 1943-46. Decorated Bronze Star; Ford Found. fellow, 1959. Mem. Nat. Council Tchrs. English, Coll. Conf. on Composition and Communication, Nat., N.J. edn. assns., Internat. Reading Assn., N.J. English Tchrs. Assn. (exec. bd.), Alpha Phi Alpha. Democrat. Co-editor: Human Relations Manual, 1957, Grammar and Composition, 1984; contbr. articles to edn. jours. Home: East Orange, NJ. Died Apr. 25, 2006.

DAVIS, GORDON, apparel manufacturing executive; b. N.Y.C., Feb. 23, 1940; s. Arthur and Miriam (Kastel) D.; A.A. with high honors, Fashion Inst. Tech., 1959; B.S. cum laude in Econs., Albright Coll., 1969; m. Olive Dawn Dunkleberger, June 25; children— Gale, Jed, Cliff. Engr. trainee Terre Hill Mfg. Co. (merged with Superior Lingerie Co., N.Y., 1968), Blue Ball, Pa., 1959-63, plant mgr., 1963-65, asst. gen. mgr., 1965-68, gen. mgr., N.Y.C., 1968-79, v.p. mfg., 1979; sr. v.p. Uniforms To You and Co., Chgo., 1979-88; v.p. mfg. Angelica Corp., St. Louis, 1988—; lectr. seminar on computer-aided design and mfg. Clemson U., 1987. Bd. dirs. Pa. Assn. Children with Learning Disabilities, 1976, Jewish Community Center (Reading), 1972; trustee Temple Oheb Shalom (sec. 1973); instr. aircraft flight theory and nav. CAP Berks County, 1965. Recipient Fashion Inst. Tech. mgmt. award. Lic. real estate salesman, Pa. Mem. Am. Inst. Indsl. Engrs., Aircraft Owners and Pilots Assn., Lingerie Mfrs. Assn. (negotiating com.) Democrat. Jewish. Home: Hobe Sound, Fla. Died Apr. 28, 2006.

DAVIS, HARRY ALLEN, artist, art educator; b. Hillsboro, Ind., May 21, 1914; s. Harry A. and Eva (Smith) D.; m. Lois Irene Peterson, Dec. 20, 1947; children— Joanna Ingrid Davis Marks (dec.), Mark Frederick. B.F.A., Herron Sch. Art, 1938; F.A.A.R., Am. Acad. in Rome, 1941. Artist-in-residence Beloit Coll., Wis., 1941-42; instr. Herron Sch. of Art, Ind. U.-Purdue U.-Indpls., 1946-67, assoc. prof., 1967-70, prof., 1970-83, prof. emeritus, 1983; instr. Indpls. Art League, Ind., 1983—. Exhibited one-man shows at Ind. Sesquicentennial, 1971, Segment of Hist. Ohio Valley, U.S. Bicentennial, 1976, The Italian Influence, traveling show, 1983. Served to tech. sgt. t-4 U.S. Army, 1942-46. Recipient award of distinction in Excellence of Purchase Mainstreams Internat., 1968, 1970-74; Mo. Sesquicentennial award Watercolor U.S.A., 1971; Best of show award Realism '74, 1974; recipient numerous awards nat. and regional exhibits. Fellow Am. Acad. Rome (Prix de Rome award, 1938), Ind. Acad.; mem. Ind. Artists Club, Inc., Brown County Art Guild, Inc., Hoosier Salon. Republican. Mem. Disciples of Christ. Club: The Portfolio (pres. 1971). Avocations: music, woodworking, travel. Home: Indianapolis, Ind. Died Feb. 9, 2006.

DAVIS, HOWARD ECKERT, political scientist, educator; b. Palmerton, Pa., Sept. 16, 1933; s. Howard Edward and Clara (Eckert) D.; m. Elizabeth Holbrook Forbes, June 29, 1957; children— Lisa Jeanne, Jill Rebecca, Thomas Howard. AB, Dickinson Coll., 1955; MA, Yale, 1956, PhD, 1962. Asso. prof. polit. sci. Randolph-Macon Coll., Ashland, Va., 1959-62, prof., chmn. dept. polit. sci., 1962-70; dean Randolph-Macon Coll. (Coll. and polit. sci.), 1970-77, prof. polit. sci., from 1977, dir. honors program, from 1984. Mem. Phi Beta Kappa, Sigma Alpha Epsilon. Died Oct. 2, 2006.

DAVIS, JAMES JOHN, integrated energy company executive; b. Denver, Oct. 28, 1946; m. Diane Christine Bova, June 26, 1967; children: Todd C., Kara L. BSME, U. Colo., 1968; MS in Industrial Adminstrn., Purdue U., 1969. Fin. analyst Exxon Corp., Houston, 1969-70, Gulf Oil Corp., Houston, 1970-73, mgr. fin. London, 1973-78, mgr. banking, foreign exchange Pitts., 1978-81; mgr. fin., ins. Mesa Petroleum Co., Amarillo, TX, 1981-86; v.p., treas. MAPCO Inc., Tulsa, Okla., from 1986. Republican. Roman Catholic. Died Oct. 18, 2006.

DAVIS, JO ANN, congresswoman; b. Rowan County, NC, June 29, 1950; m. Charles E. Davis II; children: Charlie, Chris. Student, Hampton Roads Bus. Coll., Va. Owner Davis Mgmt. Co., 1988, Jo Ann Davis Realty, 1990; mem. Va. State Gen. Assembly, 1997—2001, mem. gen. laws com., mem. health welfare & insts., mem. sci. & tech. com., mem. claims com., mem. Chesapeake and its tributaries com.; mem. US Congress from 1st Va. dist., 2001—07, mem. armed svcs. com., mem. internat. rels. com., mem. permanent select com. on intelligence, chair terrorism, human intelligence, analysis and counter-intelligence subcommittee, mem. def. rev. threat panel. Republican. Mem. Assembly Of God Ch. Died Oct. 6, 2007.

DAVIS, JOHN DONALD, banker; b. Sheridan, Wyo., Apr. 27, 1927; s. Walter C. and Nell O. (Williams) D.; m. Janet B. Loeffler, Mar. 18, 1946; children— Jacqueline Davis Manering, Jerry Allen. Banker, Greeley, Colo., 1945-48; Vice chmn. bd. Valley Nat. Bank, from 1988. Past pres. Phoenix Clearing House.; past pres. Tucson Econ. Devel. Corp. bd. dirs., v.p. Tucson Met. YMCA; bd. dirs. Central Ariz. Project; trustee United for Ariz.; mem. Arizonans for Jobs and Energy, Tucson Airport Authority.; chmn. nat. bd. advisor Coll. Bus., U. Ariz. Recipient Disting. Citizen award U. Ariz., 1987 Mem. Am. Bankers Assn. (governing council, state v.p., mem. govt. relations council), Ariz. Bankers Assn. (past pres.), Tucson Met. C. of C. (past pres., named Man of Yr. 1979) Clubs: Rotary, Tucson Country, Old Pueblo. Home: Tucson, Ariz. Died Jan. 30, 2007.

DAVIS, JOHN WILLIAM, philosophy educator; b. Clendenin, W.Va., July 15, 1926; s. Benjamin Hubert and Grace Louise (Counts) D.; m. Helen Revenna Gandee, Sept. 1, 1950 (div. Oct. 1970); children: Nancy Carol, Amy Elizabeth, Paul Benjamin. BA, W.Va. U., 1950; postgrad., Ohio State U., 1950-52; PhD, Emory U., 1959. V.p. sales Continental Distbg. Co., Columbus, Ohio, 1952-54; asst. prof. philosophy U. Tenn., Knoxville, 1957-63, assoc. prof. philosophy, 1963-66, head dept. philosophy, 1966-88, prof., 1966-91, prof. emeritus, from 1991. Editor: Value and Valuation, 1972; co-editor: Forms of Value and Valuation, 1991. Chmn. bd. dirs. Found. for Philosophy of Creativity, Carbondale, Ill., 1976—, Hartman Inst. for Axiology, Knoxville, 1978-91, chmn. emeritus, 1991—. With U.S. Army, 1945-46. Mem. Am. Philos. Assn., So. Soc. for Philosophy and Psychology, Am. Soc. for Value Inquiry (pres. 1970-72), Soc. for Philosophy of Creativity, Sigma Chi. Democrat. Home: Knoxville, Tenn. Died Mar. 5, 2007.

DAVIS, KEVIN WYNSTON, educator; b. Boston, Mass., Nov. 11, 1955; s. Robert Lewis and Helen Adeline (Kemp) Davis. BA, Pacific Union Coll., 1977; MA, Loma Linda U., Calif., 1982. Ordained to ministry Seventh-day Adventist Ch.; cert. tchr. Calif. Head resident asst. Pacific Union Coll., Angwin, Calif., 1977; assoc. min. Seventh-day Adventist Ch., LA, 1977—80, elem. tchr., from 1980. Hon. mem. Spl. Olympics Com. Grantee, Seventh-day Adventist Ch., 1980. Mem.: ASCD, Calif. Reading Assn., Brookinairs Club. Democrat. Died Oct. 3, 2006.

DAVIS, LELAND JAMES, geologist; b. Salem, Utah, May 18, 1924; s. Ray and Elizabeth (Christensen) Davis; m. Barbara Nielsen, Feb. 21, 1945; children: Janice, Marilyn, James Leland, Terrie Lee, Sharon Kay. BS, Brigham Young U., 1949, MS, 1951; postgrad., U. Utah, 1951—53. Exploration geologist Standard Oil of Ind., Salt Lake City, 1953—55; tchr. Salt Lake City Sch. Dist., 1956—59; cons. geologist Salt Lake City, 1955—68; sr. devel. engr. Hercules, Inc., Salt Lake City, 1959—68; chief geologist Brush Wellman, Inc., Salt Lake City, from 1968. Contbr. numerous articles to profl. jours. County del. Rep. Party, Salt Lake City, 1974; bishop LDS Ch. Lt. USAF, 1943—46. Decorated Bronze Star. Mem.: AIME (director chmn. 1981—83), Am. Assn. Petroleum Geologists, Soc. Aero. Materials Process Engrs. (sec., treas. 1970—71), Utah Geol. Assn. (pres. 1973—74, scholarship chmn. 1979—83), Outdoors Ltd., Kiwanis. Home: Salt Lake City, Utah. Died Sept. 16, 2006.

DAVIS, OTTO ANDERSON, economics professor; b. Florence, SC, Apr. 4, 1934; s. Otto and Pauline (Anderson) D.; m. Carolyn Quinn, Dec. 26, 1962; children— Craig, Wendy, Ross. AB, Wofford Coll., 1956; MA, U. Va., 1957, PhD, 1960. Asst. prof. econs. Grad Sch. Indsl. Adminstrn., Carnegie-Mellon U., Pitts., 1960-65; assoc. prof. Grad Sch. Indsl. Adminstrn. Carnegie-Mellon U., 1965-67, prof., 1967-68, prof. polit. economy Sch. Urban and Public Affairs, 1968-81, W.W. Cooper univ. prof. econs. and pub. policy, 1981—2006, assoc. dean, 1968-75, dean, 1975-81; rsch. dir. Pa. Tax Commn., 1979-82. Bd. visitors Air U., Maxwell AFB, 1980-83. Contbr. book revs. and articles to profl. jours. Fellow Econometric Soc.; mem. Public Choice Soc. (pres. 1970-72), Assn. Public Policy Analysis and Mgmt. (policy council, pres. 1982-83), Am. Econ. Assn., Am. Polit. Sci. Assn., Am. Soc. Public Adminstrn. Home: Turtle Creek, Pa. Died 2006.

DAVIS, PHYLLIS MARIE, counselling educator; b. Topeka, Aug. 27, 1923; d. Harold Morgan and Ethel Irene (Hinchsliff) Porter; m. Orville Milo Davis, Oct. 19, 1957. A.A., North Park Coll., 1943; B.S., Northwestern U., 1945, M.A., 1951. Mathematician, Northwestern U., Evanston, Ill., 1945; asst. application engr. Westinghouse Electric Corp., Chgo., 1945-58; dean girls Bremen High Sch., Midlothian, Ill., 1958-66; counselor Thornton Community Coll., South Holland, Ill., 1966—, dir. guidance, 1967. Mem. Am. Assn. Counselling and Devel., Ill. Assn. Counseling and Devel., Ill. Women Dean Adminstrs. and Counselors, Nat. Women Deans, Adminstrs. and Counselors, Suburban Women Deans and Counselors Assn. (pres. 1963), South Suburban Counselors Assn., AAUW, Phi Delta Kappa, Delta Kappa Gamma. Lodge: Order Eastern Star. Home: South Holland, Ill. Died Feb. 7, 2006.

DAVIS, ROBERT HEATER, chemical engineer, educator, dean; b. Paris, Mar. 26, 1957; arrived in US, 1957; s. Richard Malcolm and Helen (Heater) D.; m. Shirley Lynn Giles, Dec. 28, 1982. BS in chem. engring., U. Calif., Davis, 1978; MS in chem. engring., Stanford U., 1979, PhD in chem. engring., 1982. Postdoctoral fellow dept. applied math. and theoretical physics Cambridge U., England, 1982-83; asst. prof. chem. engring. U. Colo., Boulder, 1983-88, assoc. prof., 1988—92, prof., from 1992, chair chem. engring., 1992—2002, Patten Prof., Dept. Chem. Engring., from 1997, dean Coll. Engring. and Applied Sci., from 2002. Vis. prof. MIT, 1990—91, U. Calif., Santa Barbara, 1997—98. Contbr. articles to profl. jours. Bd. dirs. univ. program First. Presbyn. Ch., Boulder, 1985—. Recipient Presdl. Young Investigator Award, NSF, 1985, Jr. Faculty Devel. Award, U. Colo., 1985, Outstanding Undergrad. Tchg. in Chem. Engring. Award, Omega Chi Epsilon, 1989, Outstanding Rsch. Award, U. Colo. Coll. Engring. and Applied Sci., 1993, Outstanding Svc. Award, 1999, Outstanding Tchg. Award, 2000, Outstanding Grad. Tchg. Award, Dept. Chem. Engring., U. Colo., 1996, 2002, Outstanding Rsch. Award, U. Colo. Boulder Faculty Assembly, 2000, Svc. Award, 2003; NATO Postdoctoral Fellowship in Sci., 1982, Guggenheim Fellowship, 1990, U. Colo. Faculty Fellowship, 1997. Mem.: Soc. Indsl. Microbiology, Am. Soc. Engring. Edn. (Rocky Mountain Sec. Dow Outstanding Young Faculty Award 1990), Am. Chem. Soc., Am. Phys. Soc., AIChE (Outstanding Paper Award 1995). Republican. Avocations: hiking, bicycling. Home: Boulder, Colo. Died Mar. 22, 2006.

DAVIS, ROBERT NORMAN, hospital administrator; b. July 30, 1938; s. Norman DuBois and Geraldine Elizabeth (Sliker) D.; m. Elizabeth Ann Paine, June 15, 1985; children: Keith Robert, Kathryn Beth, Karl Thomas. BSCE, Pa. State U., 1960; MS in Mgmt., Rensselaer Poly. Inst., 1970. Dir. plant ops. Am. Hosp. Assn., Chgo., 1964-68; dir. mgmt. engring. Hosp. Assn. of N.Y., Albany, 1968-72; assoc. exec. dir. United Hosp., Portchester, NY, 1973-75; regional mgr. Arthur Young & Co., NYC, 1975, Medicus Sys. Corp., Nashville, 1976-79; assoc. adminstr. Vanderbilt U. Hosp., Nashville, 1979-81; adminstr. Meml. divsn. Charleston (W.Va.) Area Med. Ctr., 1981-83; pres. Resource Devel. Assocs., Hendersonville, Tenn., 1983—96, 2001—05; prin. Ernst & Young Health Care, 1996-2001; exec. dir. ACS-HCS, from 2005. Contbr. articles to profl. jours. Bd. dirs., treas. Mid. Tenn. Youth Soccer Inc., 1979-82. With M.S.C., USAF, 1960-63. Fellow Am. Coll. Healthcare Execs., Hosp. Info. Mgmt. Sys. Soc. (dir. 1972-75, hon. fellow 1985). Baptist. Home: Hendersonville, Tenn. Died Feb. 25, 2007.

DAVIS, S. ROBERT, business executive; b. Columbus, Ohio, Oct. 31, 1938; s. Herman and Minnie (Newman) D.; (m), 1955; 4 children. Student, Ohio State U. Founder, pres. S. Robert Davis & Co., Inc., Columbus, Ohio, 1958-68; founder, now pres. and chmn. bd. Orange Co. Inc., Columbus, 1968—; dir. M.I.F. Funds; chmn. bd. Buckeye Fed. Savs. & Loan Assn., Strata Corp. Clubs: Columbus Athletic, Scioto Country. Died Apr. 21, 2007.

DAVIS, THOMAS EDWARD, banker, economist; b. Detroit, Jan. 16, 1932; s. Edward Thomas and Margaret (Hughes) D.; m. Myra Sue Smith, Jan. 23, 1960; children: Bradley Edward, Gary Scott, Julie Elizabeth BA, Ohio Weslyan U., 1954; MA, U. Mich., 1960, PhD, 1965; postgrad., Brit. Coun. Sch., London, 1981. Asst. internat. economist Fed. Res. Bank N.Y., 1960-61; instr. U. Mich., 1964-65; with Fed. Res. Bank, Kansas City, Mo., from 1965, v.p., 1971-77, sr. v.p., dir. rsch., from 1977. Assoc. economist Fed. Res. Open Market Com., 1977-89; instr. Colo. Sch. Banking, 1968-73; trustee Livestock Mdsg. Inst., 1972—, Kans. Coun. Econ. Edn., 1980—, Mo. Coun. Econ. Edn., 1980—; chmn. conv. Allied Social Sci. Assn., 1980. With USAF, 1955-58. Mem. Am. Econ. Assn., Am. Inst. Banking, Kansas City C. of C. Home: Shawnee Mission, Kans. Died Mar. 12, 2006.

DAVIS, VICTORIA (VICKY DAVIS), men's neckwear company executive; b. Detroit, Oct. 2, 1924; d. Isadore and Gussie (Garfunkel) Wolk; m. Lawrence Davis, Mar. 6, 1949; children— Robert M., Kenneth H. Student pub. schs., Detroit. Legal sec. firm Friedman, Meyers & Keys, Detroit, 1942-49; sec. Buick Motor Co., Flint, Mich., 1949-50; engring. sec. Fisher Body Co., Detroit, 1950-52; owner, designer Chest Knots, Oak Park, Mich., 1969-74; pres., designer Vicky Davis Ltd., NYC, from 1974. Lectr. fields of fashion, bus. opportunities for women. Pres. James N. Pepper Sch. PTA, Oak Park, 1965, 66; vol. worker Juvenile Ct., Detroit; active Detroit Assn. Retarded Children, Sinai Hosp. Women's Guild. Recipient Coty Am. Fashion Critics award, 1976; 1st Cutty Sark Fashion Designers award, 1980 Mem. Men's Fashion Assn., Men's Tie Assn., Council Fashion Designers Am. Died Sept. 5, 2006.

DAVIS, WILLIAM M., pharmacist; b. Erie, Pa., Apr. 13, 1953; s. Benjamin and Goldie (Colman) D. B.S. in Pharmacy, U. Pitts., 1977. Asst. mgr. Cunningham Drug, Parma, Ohio, 1977-79; pharmacy mgr. Barney's Food and Drug, Wickliffe Ohio,

1979-83, Bernie Shulman's, Mayfield Heights, Ohio, 1983-84, St. Luke's Med. Bldg. Pharmacy, Cleve., 1984—. Mem. Phi Eta Sigma. Home: Cleveland, Ohio. Died Jan. 17, 2006.

DAWSON, CYNTHIA FORESMAN, oil company financial executive; b. Greenville, Miss., Nov. 11, 1954; d. David Laird and Evelyn Virginia (Bush) Foresman; m. Michael R. Dawson, Jan. 31, 1981. B.S., Miss. State U., 1976, M.B.A., 1978. Acct., Shell Oil Co., New Orleans, 1978-81, acctg. supr., Houston, 1981; acctg. mgr. Elf Aquitaine Petroleum, Houston, 1981—. Methodist. Home: Sugar Land, Tex. Died Jan. 4, 2006.

DAY, ANTHONY, journalist; b. Miami, Fla., May 12, 1933; s. Price and Alice (Alexander) D.; m. Lynn Ward, June 25, 1960; children: John, Julia (dec.). AB cum laude, Harvard U., 1955, postgrad. (Nieman fellow), 1966-67; LHD (hon.), Pepperdine U., 1974. Reporter Phila. Bull., 1957-60, Washington, 1960-69, chief Washington bur., 1969; chief editorial writer L.A. Times, 1969-71, editor editorial pages, 1971-89, sr. corr., 1989-95; contbg. writer L.A. Times Book Review, 1995—2007. Mem. Signet Soc. Harvard, Asia Soc., Santa Fe Coun. Internat. Rels. Home: Santa Fe, N.Mex. Died Sept. 2, 2007.

DAY, DONALD CLIFFORD, investment executive; b. Worcester, Mass., Mar. 2, 1928; s. Clifford Warren and Dorothy Seagrave (Southwick) D.; m. Suzanne Post, Dec. 31, 1953; children: Melissa, Jennifer, Geoffrey P., Peter K. (dec.). BS, Bowdoin Coll., 1949. With State Mut. of Am., Worcester, Mass., 1949-72, v.p., 1970-72, New Eng. Mut. Life Ins. Co., Boston, 1972-81, sr. v.p., from 1981; pres., dir. New England Securities, Boston, from 1972; exec. v.p. NEL Cash Mgmt. Trust, from 1978, NEL Equity Fund, from 1972; v.p. NEL Growth Fund, from 1972, NEL Income Fund, from 1973, NEL Retirement Equity Fund, from 1972, NEL Tax Exempt Bond Fund, from 1977. Mem. Nat. Assn. Security Dealers (mem. dist. com. 1976-79, vice chmn. 1979), Beta Theta Pi. Home: Dennis, Mass. Died Dec. 13, 2006.

D'AZZO, JOHN JOACHIM, electrical engineer, educator; b. NYC, Nov. 30, 1919; s. Domenick and Jacqueline (Cappello) D'A.; m. Betty G. McBride, June 13, 1953; 1 child, Dennis. BEE, CCNY, 1941; MSEE, Ohio State U., 1950; PhD, Salford U., Eng., 1978. Registered profl. engr., Ohio. Quality control engr. Western Electric Co., Kearney, N.J., 1941-42; devel. engr. Air Materiel Command, Wright Patterson AFB, Ohio, 1942-46; prof. elec. engring. Air Force Inst. Tech., Wright Patterson AFB, Ohio, 1947-98, prof. emeritus, from 1998. Head dept. elec. and computer engring. Air Force Inst. Tech., Wright Patterson AFB, 1984-95. Co-author: Feedback Control System Analysis and Synthesis, 1960, 2d edit., 1966, Linear Control System Analysis and Design, 1975, 5th edit., 2003. Served to 2d lt. U.S. Army, 1945-46. Named Outstanding Engr. Affiliate Socs. Ohio, 1962, 86. Fellow IEEE, AIAA (assoc.); mem. Am. Soc. for Engring. Edn., Sigma Xi, Tau Beta Pi, Eta Kappa Nu. Roman Catholic. Home: Beavercreek, Ohio. Died Sept. 30, 2006.

DEAKIN, JAMES, writer; b. St. Louis, Dec. 3, 1929; s. Rogers and Dorothy (Jeffrey) D.; m. Doris Marie Kanter, Apr. 14, 1956; 1 son, David Andrew. AB, Washington U., St. Louis, 1951. Mem. staff St. Louis Post-Dispatch, 1951-81, Washington corr., 1953-80, White House corr., 1955-80; adj. assoc. prof. journalism George Washington U., 1981-87. Fellow Woodrow Wilson Internat. Ctr. for Scholars, 1980-81 Author: The Lobbyists, 1966, Lyndon Johnson's Credibility Gap, 1968, Straight Stuff: The Reporters, The White House and the Truth, 1984, A Grave for Bobby, 1990; co-author: Smiling Through the Apocalypse, 1971, The Presidency and The Press, 1976, The American Presidency, Principles and Problems, vol. II, 1983, The White House Press on the Presidency, 1983; contbr. numerous articles to mags. Recipient Disting. Alumnus citation Washington U., 1973, Merriman Smith award for White House reporting, 1977; Markle Found. grantee, 1981 Mem. White House Corrs. Assn. (pres. 1974-75) Died June 2, 2007.

DEAL, BRUCE ELMER, physical chemist, educator; b. Lincoln, Nebr., Sept. 20, 1927; s. Roy Walter and Edith Alice (Fiddock) D.; m. Rachel Vera Birmingham, Sept. 3, 1950; children: Donald Bruce, Michael David, Diane Marie. AB in Chemistry, Nebr. Wesleyan U., 1950; MS in Phys. Chemistry, Iowa State U., 1953, PhD in Phys. Chemistry, 1955. Rsch. chemist Kaiser Aluminum & Chem. Corp., Spokane, Wash., 1955-59; rsch. engr. Rheem Semicondr./Raytheon Corp., Mountain View, Calif., 1959-63; mgr. R&D Fairchild Camera & Instrument Corp., Palo Alto, Calif., 1963-88; prin. technologist Nat. Semicondr., Santa Clara, Calif., 1988-89; v.p. Advantage Prodn. Tech., Sunnyvale, Calif., 1989-92. Cons. prof. elec. engring. Stanford (Calif.) U., 1976—; instr. Continuing Edn. Inst.-Europe, Finspang, Sweden, 1982-91; adj. prof. elec. engring. Santa Clara U., 1988—. Author or co-author numerous tech. publs., 1953—; holder 9 patents in field. Com. chmn. Boy Scouts Am., Palo Alto, 1965-70. Recipient Lifetime Achievement award Semiconductor Equipment and Materials, Inc., 1998. Fellow IEEE (Tech. Achievement award 1973), AAAS, Franklin Inst. (life, cert. of merit 1975), Electrochem. Soc. (v.p. 1985-88, pres. 1988-89, Tech. award Electronics Divsn. 1974, Callinan Tech. award 1982, Solid State Sci. and Tech. award 1993); mem. Materials Rsch. Soc., Cornwall Family Hist. Soc., Sigma Xi. Republican. Presbyterian. Avocations: stamp collecting/philately, genealogy, playing french horn. Home: Palo Alto, Calif. Died Apr. 17, 2007.

DEAN, WALTER NELSON, engineering consultant; b. Bklyn., Jan. 14, 1919; s. William Nelson and Edna (Griffin) D.; m. Marjorie Washburn Ball, Feb. 2, 1946; children: Marilyn, Cynthia. BS, Columbia U., 1940, MSEE, 1941. Registered profl. engr. N.Y., Ind., Calif. Engr., sect. head Sperry Gyroscope Co., Great Neck, N.Y, 1941-67; sr. staff engr. Magnavox Co., Ft. Wayne, Ind., 1967-78; pres. Verdes Engring. Co., Palos Verdes, Calif., 1978-82; v.p. engring. Arnav Systems Inc., Salem, Oreg., 1982-85, cons. Portland, Oreg., 1985-89. V.p., chief engr. Fort Wayne Pub. TV Inc., 1975-78. Contbr. articles, revs. to profl. jours. Patentee in navigation systems field. Dist. chmn. United Way, Garden City, N.Y., 1962-66. Fellow IEEE (chmn. Ft. Wayne sect. 1977); mem. Wild Goose Assn. (pres. 1985-87, dir., award of merit, 1980). Presbyterian. Home: Wilsonville, Oreg. Died Aug. 3, 2006.

DE ARMOND, DALE BURLISON, artist, illustrator; b. Bismarck, ND, July 2, 1914; s. Daniel William and Mary Irene (Brockway) Burlison; m. Robert N. De Armond, July 29, 1935; children: William Davidson, Jane Paisley. Author, illustrator: A First Collection of Prints, 1979, Juneau: A book of woodcuts, 1973, Raven, 1975. Home: Sitka, Alaska. Died Nov. 28, 2006.

DEATON, CHARLES MILTON, lawyer; b. Hattiesburg, Miss., Jan. 19, 1931; s. Ivanes Dean Deaton and Martha Sarah Elizabeth Fortenberry; m. Mary Dent Dickerson, Aug. 15, 1951; children: Diane Rossi, Dara Rogers, Charles M., Jr. BA, Millsaps Coll., 1949-51, 55-56; JD, U. Miss., 1959. Legis. asst. U.S. Ho. of Reps., Washington, 1957; assoc. Brewer, Deaton & Bowman, Greenwood, Miss., from 1958; mem. Miss. Ho. of Reps., Jackson, 1960—80, appropriations chmn., 1976—80; city atty. City of Greenwood, Miss., 1970-84; adminstrv. asst. to Govs. Wm. Winter, B. Allain State of Miss., Jackson, 1980—88; bd. dirs. Bank of Commerce, Greenwood; mem. Miss. State Bd. of Edn., from 2003. Recipient Miss Conservationist of Yr. award The Nature Conservancy, Jackson, 1991, Nat. Oak Leaf award, Arlington, Va., 1992, Sports Hall of Fame award Millsaps Coll., Jackson, Alumnus of Yr. award, 1995, others. Mem. ABA, The Nature Conservancy, Miss. Wildlife Heritage Commn., others. Avocations: cooking, hunting, fishing, conservation, gardening. Home: Greenwood, Miss. Died June 6, 2007.

DEBATT, MICHAEL R., state legislator; b. Bklyn., July 3, 1950; s. Robert and Mary (Kalenak) DeB.; m. Janet Tonge, 1976; children: Christopher, Caryn. BA, SUNY, Buffalo, 1972; MS, Ga. Coll., 1980; grad., Arnold Air Soc. Town councilman, Lincoln, R.I., 1991-94; R.I. state senator, from 1995. Asst. v.p. E. F. Hutton & Co., Providence, 1980-88; assoc. v.p. investments Dean Witter Reynolds, Providence, 1988—. Recipient Combat Readiness medal, Nat. Def. Svc. medal. Died Jan. 20, 2006.

DEE, ROBERT FORREST, retired pharmaceutical company executive; b. Cin., July 8, 1924; s. Raymond H. and Mary (Owen) D.; m. Virginia Winston Verner, Sept. 10, 1948 (div. 1979); children: Jacqueline, Robert R., John, Catherine, Thomas; m. 2d Jean T. Tanney, Jan. 2, 1980; 1 child, Patrick. AB, Harvard U., 1946; LLD (hon.), Phila. Coll. Pharmacy and Sci., 1978; LHD (hon.), Med. Coll. Pa., 1979. With SmithKline Corp., Phila., 1948-87; successively market research analyst, asst. to adminstrv. v.p., dir. Animal Health div., dir. consumer, animal and instrument products, v.p., dir. consumer, animal and instrument products, exec. v.p., pres., chief exec. officer, chmn. Bd. dirs. United Techs. Corp., Air Products and Chems. Inc.; mem. adv. bd. Volvo Internat. Bd. dirs. U.S. Council for Internat. Bus., Com. Econ. Devel.; trustee Heritage Found. Served with AUS. Mem. Nat. Assn. Mfrs. (chmn. exec. com.), Bus. Council, Conf. Bd., Council Fgn. Relations, Mgmt. Execs. Soc. Episcopalian. Died Jan. 17, 2007.

DEEDY, JOHN GERARD, JR., writer; b. Worcester, Mass., Aug. 17, 1923; s. John G. and Grace R. (McDonough) D.; m. Mary M. Noonan, Apr. 20, 1949; children: Mary Joan, John J., Justine A., Paul V. AB, Holy Cross Coll., 1948; cert., Institut du Pantheon, Paris, 1949; AB, Trinity Coll., Dublin, 1949, MA, 1957. Reporter, corr. Boston Post, Boston Globe, Worcester Telegram, 1940-51; founding editor Cath. Free Press, Worcester, 1951-59; editor Pitts. Cath., 1959-67; mng. editor Commonweal, NYC, 1967-78. Author: (with Jack Frost) The Church in Worcester New England, 1957, (with Martin Marty, David Silverman) The Religious Press in America, 1963, Eyes on the Modern World, 1965, The Vatican, 1970, What a Modern Catholic Believes About Conscience, Freedom and Authority, 1972, (with Philip Nobile) The Complete Ecology Fact Book, 1972, What a Modern Catholic Believes About the Commandments, 1975, Literary Places: A Guided Pilgrimage, New York and New England, 1978, Seven American Catholics, 1978, Apologies, Good Friends, An Interim Biography of Daniel Berrigan, S.J, 1981, The New Nuns: Serving Where the Spirit Leads, 1982, Your Aging Parents, 1984, The Catholic Fact Book, 1986 (Nat. Cath. Book award 1987), American Catholicism: And Now Where?, 1987, The Catholic Book of Days, 1989, Retrospect: The Origins of Catholic Beliefs and Practices, 1990, Matrix: Exploring the Challenges of Contemporary Life, 1992, Facts, Myths and Maybes: Everything You Think You Know About Catholicism, But Perhaps Don't, 1993, Auden as Didymus: The Poet as Columnist Anonymous, 1993, A Book of Catholic Anecdotes, 1996. Served with USAAF, World War II. Recipient Pro Ecclesia et Pontifice, Pope Pius XII, 1954. Mem. Authors Guild and Authors League of Am. Home: Rockport, Mass. Died Mar. 28, 2006.

DEES, ANTHONY ROANE, historical society executive; b. Pikeville, N.C., Sept. 19, 1937; s. Claude Edward and Lois Winifred (Jackson) D.; m. Leslie Gray McNeill, Sept. 27, 1975. B.A., U. N.C., 1959, M.S. in L.S., 1964. Catalogue librarian Washington and Lee U., Lexington, Va., 1962-67; catalogue librarian to curator manuscripts U. Ga., Athens, 1967-77, mem. faculty, 1967-77; dir. Ga. Hist. Soc., Savannah, 1977-83; asst. dir. Ga. Dept. Architecture and History, 1983—. faculty Armstrong State Coll., Savannah, 1979—. Co-editor: Selected Eighteenth Century Manuscripts, Georgia Hist. Soc. Collection, Vol. XX, 1980. Contbr. articles to profl. jours. Mem. Soc. Am. Archivists, Soc. Ga. Archivists, Southeastern Library Assn., Ga. Library Assn. Democrat. Roman Catholic. Lodge: Rotary. Home: Atlanta, Ga. Died Apr. 29, 2007.

DEFELICE, EUGENE ANTHONY, internist, educator, magician; b. Beacon, NY, Dec. 24, 1927; s. Domenick and Louise (Grippo) DeF. BS, Columbia U., 1951; MD, Boston U., 1956. Ciba fellow, lectr. pharmacology Boston U. Sch. Medicine, 1954-57; intern Newton (Mass.) Wellesley Hosp., 1957; postgrad. tng. internal medicine/psychosomatic medicine Jackson Meml. Hosp., U. Miami Sch. Medicine, Miami, Fla., 1958—61; asst. dir. clin. rsch. Warner Lambert Rsch. Inst., Morris Plains, NJ, 1961-64; dir. clin. rsch. Bristol Labs. (now Bristol Meyers Squibb), Syracuse, NY, 1965-66, Sandoz Inc. (now Novartis Inc.), East Hanover, NJ, 1967-68, exec. dir. clin. research, 1969-70, dir. sci. affairs and comml. devel., 1970—73, v.p. corp. sci. devel., 1974-77, v.p. internat. med. rsch., med. advisor, 1977-83. Prof. biochemistry, microbiology and pub. health, dir. rsch. New Eng. Coll. Pharmacy, 1956-58; practice in medicine, cons. in medicine and med. rsch., Morristown, N.J., 1961-87, East Schodack and Albany, N.Y., 1988-2003, Niagara Falls, N.Y., 2004—; clin. assoc. prof. medicine Coll. Medicine and Dentistry N.J.-Rutgers Med. Sch., 1977-84; clin. prof. medicine UMD-Robert Wood Johnson Med. Sch., 1985—2003; clin. prof. anesthesiology UCLA, 1978-83. Co-author: Angiotensin Converting Enzyme Inhibitors, 1987, Prostaglandins, Platelets, Lipids: New Developemnts in Atherosclerosis, 1981, Health and Obesity, 1983, Beta Blockers in the Treatment of Cardiovascular Diseases, 1984, The Pharmacological Treatment of Cardiovascular Diseases, 1986; author: Web Health Info. Resource Guide, 2001, Breast Cancer, 2002, Overweight, Obesity and Health, 2002, Nutrition and Health, 2003, Web Health Information Resources, 2004, Prevention of Cardiovascular Disease, 2005, Stress and Health, 2006; mem. editl. bd. Triangle, Sandorama, 1977—81; contbr. articles to profl. jours. Served with U.S. Army, World War II. Named Hon. Citizen Italy; named to Notable Italian-Am. Hall of Fame; recipient Golden Merit award Med. Soc. NJ, 2006. Fellow Am. Geriat. Soc., Acad. Psychosomatic Medicine; mem. Soc. Am. Magicians, Internat. Brotherhood Magicians; emeritus mem. numerous profl. socs. Died May 13, 2007.

DEFOREST, ROY DEAN, retired artist, sculptor; b. North Platte, Nebr., Feb. 11, 1930; m. Gloria DeForest; children: Oriana, Pascal. Student, Yakima Jr. Coll., 1949-50, Calif. Sch. Fine Arts, 1950-52; BA, San Francisco State Coll., 1953, MA, 1958. Dir. Larsen Gallery, Yakima Jr. Coll., 1958-60; instr. Calif. Coll. Arts & Crafts, Oakland, 1964-65; from asst. prof. to assoc. prof. U. Calif., Davis, 1965-82, prof., 1985-99; ret., 1999. One-person shows include Calif. Palace Legion of Honor, San Francisco, 1971, Inst. Contemporary Art, Boston, 1977, 78, Marilyn Butler Gallery, Santa Fe, 1989, Frumkin/Adams Gallery, N.Y., 1990, 93, Fuller Groass Gallery, San Francisco, 1990, Stanford Mus. Art, Calif., 1990, John Beggruen Gallery, San Francisco, 1992, Whitney Mus. Am. Art, N.Y., 1973, San Francisco Mus. Modern Art, 1974, George Adams Gallery, N.Y.C., 1997, Paris Gibson Square Museum, Gt. Falls, Mont., 1998-2007, others; exhibited works at San Francisco Mus. Art, 1957, Calif. Palace Legion of Honor, San Francisco, 1962, 63, 64, Art Inst. Chgo., 1964, Walker Art Ctr., Mpls., 1965, Oakland (Calif.) Mus., 1966, Ark. Arts Ctr., Little Rock, 1998, John Berggruen Gallery, San Francisoc, 1998, Museum of Modern Art, N.Y.c., 1997, Sawhill Gallery, James Madison U., Harrisonburg, Va., 1997, others; represented in permanent collections San Francisco Mus. Art, Art Inst. Chgo., Joslyn Art Mus., Omaha, Phila. Mus. Art, Whitney Mus. Am. Art, N.Y., others. Recipient Nealie Sullivan award San Francisco Art Assn., 1964, Purchase prize La Jolla Art Mus., 1965; grantee Nat. Endowment Arts, 1972. Mem. San Francisco Art Assn. Died May 18, 2007.

DE GERENDAY, Mrs. LACI See CHANDLER, ELISABETH

DEHN, JOSEPH WILLIAM, JR., chemist; b. Feb. 18, 1928; s. Joseph Williams and Anna Jane (McMahon) D.; m. Mary Baxevanis, June 28, 1953; children: Joseph W. III, George John. BA, Columbia Coll., NYC, 1949; MS, Stevens Inst. Tech., 1953; PhD, Poly. Inst. Bklyn., 1964. Sr. chemist Interchem. Corp., NYC, 1949-63, Clifton, N.J., 1963-64; group leader chemist Wallace & Tiernan Inc., Belleville, N.J., 1964-67; sr. scientist Shulton Inc., Clifton, 1967-70; sr. chemist Process Chem. divsn. Diamond Shamrock Corp., Morristown, N.J., 1971-87; sr. rsch. chemist Atlantic Industries divsn. Jepson Corp., Nutley, N.J., 1988-90, Pall Corp., Glen Cove, N.Y., from 1990. Patentee in field; contbr. articles to sci. jours. Mem. AAAS, Am. Chem. Soc., Am. Inst. Chemists and Colorists, N.Y. Pigment Club, Sigma Xi, Phi Lambda Upsilon. Home: Great Neck, NY. Died Mar. 17, 2006.

DELANEY, ANDREW, retired insurance company executive, consultant; b. Vienna, Ohio, Aug. 2, 1920; s. John David and Elizabeth L. (Wurstner) D.; m. Wynelle Shellhouse, Apr. 5, 1947; 1 dau., Janet Lynn; m. Pauline Mills, July 31, 1982. BA, Oberlin Coll., 1942; BS, NYU, 1942. Actuarial trainee Equitable Life Assurance Co., NYC, 1946-49; asst. actuary Union Central Life Ins. Co., Cin., 1949-54; v.p. actuary Am. Gen. Life Ins. Co., Houston, 1954-68, sr. v.p., 1968-76, sr. v.p., chief investment officer, 1976-82, vice chmn. bd., chief investment officer, 1982-85; ret., 1985. Life bd. dirs. Big Bros., Houston, 1969—; trustee Found. for Retarded, 1982—; past chmn., bd. trustees Emerson Unitarian Ch., Houston. Capt. USAF, 1942-46. Fellow Soc. Actuaries (bd. govs.); mem. Houston Racquet Club, Ramada Club, River Oaks Country Club, Horshoe Bay Club, The Forest Club. Republican. Home: Houston, Tex. Died Jan. 20, 2007.

DELANEY, CHARLES OLIVER, music educator; b. Winston-Salem, NC, May 21, 1925; s. Charles O. and Gretchen Grace (Fiegenschuh) D.; m. Carolyn Foy, June 20, 1959; m. Susan C. Sexton, Dec. 26, 1975; children: Timothy, Thomas, Teresa. BS in Psychology Edn., Davidson Coll., 1947; diploma, Lausanne Conservatory, Switzerland, 1949; MusM, U. Colo., 1950. Instr. music Earlham Coll., Richmond, Ind., 1950-52; prof. music U. Ill., Urbana, 1952-76, Fla. State U., Tallahassee, from 1976. Conductor, flute tchr., Brevard (N.C.) Music Ctr., 1947-63; dir. instrumental program, N.C. Gov.'s Sch., Winston-Salem, 1963-70; flute tchr., Ill. Summer Youth Program, Urbana, 1970-76; conductor, music dir., Albany (Ga.) Symphony, 1979-88. Author: Fundamentals of Flute Playing, 1956, The Teacher's Guide to the Flute, 1965; composer: The Marshes of Glynn, 1953, Concerto for Flute Orchestra, American Waltzes; (opera) A Very Special Date. With U.S. Army, 1944-46, ETO. Mem.

Nat. Flute Assn. (pres 1986-87), ASCAP, Phi Mu Alpha, Pi Kappa Lambda, Pi Kappa Phi. Democrat. Methodist. Avocations: hiking, tennis, gardening. Home: Tallahassee, Fla. Died July 8, 2006.

DE LA PAVA, DANIEL, plastic surgeon; b. Bogota, Colombia, Oct. 30, 1942; came to U.S., 1969; s. Daniel and Maria Mercedes (Orrego) D.; m. Vianney Perdoma, Apr. 26, 1969; 1 child, Daniel Francisco. MD, U. Nat. de Colombia, 1967. Diplomate Am. Bd. Plastic Surgery. Intern Drs. Hosp., Washington, 1969-70; resident in gen. surgery Providence Hosp., Washington, 1970-73; resident in plastic surgery Christ's Hosp., Cin., 1973-75; fellow, clin. instr. Inst. Reconstructive and Plastic Surgery, NYU Med. Ctr., NYC, 1975-76; pvt. practice Augusta, Maine, 1976-77, Sun City, Ariz., from 1980; Australia rsch. fellow, clin. asst. St. Vincent's Hosp., Melbourne, 1977-78. Bd. dirs. Thunderbird Samaritan Hosp. Burn Svc., 1994; asst. prof. Maricopa County Hosp. Plastic Surgery Residency Program, Ariz., 1980-87; organized micro-surgery unit, Taipei, Taiwan, 1978; spkr. in field; vol. surgery Yerevan, Armenia, 1993, Ctrl. and S.Am., 1970-90, Kuwait, 1991. Recipient Spl. Recognition award 10 yr. anny. celebration Taiwan Micro-Surgery Unit, 1988, Vol. Svc. award for Kuwait surgery, 1991. Mem. Am. Soc. Plastic Reconstructive Surgeons, Lipolysis Soc. N.Am., Ariz. Plastic Surgery Soc., U.S. Colombian Med. Assn., U.S. Mex. Soc., Maricopa County Plastic Surgeon Soc. (sec./treas. 1994—). Roman Catholic. Avocations: photography, swimming. Died Nov. 29, 2006.

DELAY, WILLIAM RAYMOND, communications executive; b. Texarkana, Tex., June 16, 1929; s. Raymond Wallace and Flora Thomas (Greenwood) DeL.; m. Mary Elinor Dolson, Oct. 2, 1954; children— Martha, Nancy. B.S. in Journalism, U. Kans., William Allen White Sch. Journalism, 1951; postgrad. Mead Johnson Inst., 1958-59, Counter Intelligence Corps. Sch., 1951. Reporter Kansas City Kansan, 1951; reporter, copy editor Kansas City Times, 1953-56; pub. relations mgr. Mead Johnson & Co., 1956-60; dir. pub. relations Am. Acad. Family Physicians, 1960-71, dir. communications div., 1971—, founder Am. Acad. Family Physicians Reporter, 1974; advt. promotion mgr. Am. Family Physician mag., 1962-69; instr. pub. relations U. Mo.-Kansas City, 1979; lectr. pub. relations NYU, U. Kans. U. Nev.; mem. profl. adv. coun. dept. communication Cen. Mo. State U., Warrensburg. With U.S. Army, 1951-53. Recipient U.S. C. of C. Disting. Achievement award, 1962; Gold medal N.Y. Film Festival, 1967. Fellow Pub. Relations Soc. Am. (Silver Anvil award 1980; Prism award Kansas City chpt. 1980, 85; Profl. of Year award 1982, President's award 1985); mem. Kansas City Press Club, Nat. Assn. Sci. Writers, Am. Assn. Med. Soc. Execs., Soc. Tchrs. Family Medicine, Acad. Health Services Mktg., Southwest High Sch. Found. (pres.), Sigma Delta Chi. Roman Catholic. Contbr. to book: Kansas City Out Loud. Home: Kansas City, Mo. Died Feb. 14, 2007.

DEL CAMPO, MARTIN BERNARDELLI, architect; b. Guadalajara, Mex., Nov. 27, 1922; came to U.S., 1949; s. Salvador and Margarita (Bernardelli) Del C.; m. Laura Zaikowska, May 25, 1945; children: Felicia (dec.), Margarita, Mario. BA, Colegio Frances Morelos, Mexico City, 1941; archtl. degree, Univ. Nat. Autonoma de Mexico, Mexico City, 1948. Ptnr. Del Campo & Fruiht, architects, Santa Rosa, Calif., 1955-56, Del Campo & Clark, San Francisco, 1957-63; mgr. Hotel Victoria, Oaxaca, Mex., 1964-67; pres. Gulli-Del Campo, architects, San Francisco, 1968-70; ptnr. Del Campo Assocs., San Francisco, 1977-81. Lectr. archtl. design Coll. Environmental Design, U. Calif., Berkeley, 1973-74. Archtl. works include: Calif. Med. Facility South, Vacaville, Phillip Burton Fed. Bldg. remodeling, San Francisco, Hall of Justice, San Francisco, San Francisco Airport Internat. Terminal, Mex. Heritage Gardens, San Jose, Four Seasons Tower, San Francisco. Mem. AIA. Died Jan. 14, 2007.

DELL, ERNEST ROBERT, lawyer, educator; b. Vandergrift, Pa., Feb. 6, 1928; m. Karen D. Reed, May 8, 1965; children: Robert W., John D., Jane C. BS, U. Pitts., 1949, M.Litt., 1953; JD, Harvard U., 1956. Bar: Pa. 1957, U.S. Supreme Ct. 1961; C.P.A., Pa. Ptnr. firm Reed Smith Shaw & McClay, Pitts., from 1956. Adj. prof. law Duquesne U. Law Sch., Pitts., 1960-86; bd. dirs. Atty's. Liability Assurance Soc. Inc., Chgo., Atty's. Liability Assurance Soc. (Bermuda) Ltd. Mem. ABA, Fed. Bar Assn., Pa. Bar Assn., Allegheny County Bar Assn., AICPAs, Pa. Inst. CPAs. Home: Issaquah, Wash. Died Oct. 4, 2005.

DE LOACH, ANTHONY CORTELYOU, solar physicist; b. NYC, July 9, 1934; s. Arthur Edwin and Helen Louise (Eagleton) de L. BS in Physics, U. S.C., 1961, PhD, 1966. Solar physicist NASA, from 1966; mission scientist for NASA/European Space Agy. Space Shuttle flight simulations, 1976-77; chief solar scis. Space Scis. Lab., Marshall Space Flight Ctr., Ala., 1974-80, staff scientist solar-terrestrial physics div., 1980-84, spacelab payload projects office, from 1985. Contbr. articles to sci. jours. Served with U.S. Army, 1954-56. Nat. Def. Grad. fellow, 1961-64; Oak Ridge Nat. fellow, 1964-66 Mem. AAAS. Home: Huntsville, Ala. Died Aug. 15, 2007.

DE LONE, H. FRANCIS, lawyer; b. Phila., May 8, 1915; s. Louis S. and Helena L. (Lang) De L.; m. Madeline Heckscher, June 26, 1939 (dec. 1998); children: Richard H. (dec. 1992), H. Francis, Pamela S. Rosner, Austin S. AB cum laude, Harvard U., 1937; LL.B. cum laude, U. Pa., 1940. Bar: Pa. 1942. Since practiced, Phila.; assoc. firm Dechert Price & Rhoads (and predecessors), 1940-49, ptnr., 1949-82, of counsel, 1982—2006. Mem. Fed. Jud. Nominating Commn. Pa., 1979-93. Chmn. exec. com. Phila. High Sch. Acads., Inc.; chmn. Exec. Svc. Corps of Delaware Valley, 1984-85; pres. United Way Southeastern Pa., 1978-80, Community Svcs. Pa., 1970-73, Health and Welfare Coun., Phila., 1967-68, 76-77, United Cerebral Palsy Assn., 1953-55; mem. overseers U. Pa. Sch. Social Work, 1987-92; bd. dirs. Phila. Schs. Collaborative, 1991-93. Recipient Citizen Vol. award United Way Southeastern Pa., 1982 Mem. Am. Bar Assn., Am. Coll. Trial Lawyers, 3d Circuit Jud. Conf., Pa. Bar Assn., Phila. Bar Assn. Clubs: Merion Cricket. Home: Gladwyne, Pa. Died Nov. 22, 2006.

DEMBER, WILLIAM NORTON, retired psychologist, educator; b. Waterbury, Conn., Aug. 8, 1928; s. David and Henrietta Dember; m. Cynthia Fox, Dec. 21, 1958; children: Joanna, Laura, Gregory. AB, Yale U., 1950; MA, U. Mich., 1951, PhD, 1955. Instr. dept. psychology U. Mich., 1954-56; asst. prof. Yale U., 1956-59; faculty U. Cin., 1959-98, prof. psychology, 1965-98, asst. dean, grad. sch., 1965-67, head dept. psychology, 1968-76, 79-81, dean Coll. Arts and Scis., 1981-86, disting. rsch. prof., 1989, prof., dean emeritus, 1998; ret. Author: Psychology of Perception, 1960, 2d edit., 1979, Visual Perception, 1964, General Psychology, 1970, 2d edit., 1984, Exploring Behavior and Experience, 1971, Spontaneous Alternation Behavior, 1989; contbr. articles to profl. jours. Fellow APA, Am. Psychol. Soc.; mem. Midwest Psychol. Assn. (pres. 1976). Achievements include developing and testing theory of motivation applying to behavior of human beings and animals; rsch. in visual metacontrast, optimism/pessimism, and sustained attention. Home: Cincinnati, Ohio. Died Sept. 4, 2006.

DEMELIO, JOSEPH JOHN, insurance company executive, actuary; b. NYC, Nov. 30, 1930; s. John Joseph and Anna (Scripko) DeM.; m. Lorraine M. Quinones, May 31, 1952; children: Joanne, Carol, Lorraine, Anne, Katherine. AB, Fordham U., 1952. Asst. actuary Nat. Bur. Casualty, NYC, 1952-60; sr. v.p., actuary Home Ins. Co., NYC, 1960-76; pres. JC Penney Casualty Ins. Co., Westerville, Ohio, 1976-82, vice chmn. bd. dirs., from 1982, also bd. dirs.; vice chmn. bd. dirs. JC Penney Life Ins. Co., Plano, Tex., from 1982, also bd. dirs. V.p. North Tex. chpt. Am. Liver Found.; chmn. Columbus (Ohio) Savs. Bond Drive, 1978-80; bd. dirs. Columbus United Way, 1977-81, Columbus YMCA, 1981, St. Ann's Hosp., Waterville, Ohio, 1981-82. Fellow Casualty Actuarial Soc.; mem. Am. Acad. Actuaries, Internat. Actuarial Soc. Avocation: woodworking. Home: Plano, Tex. Died Jan. 5, 2007.

DEMERS, WILFRID JAMES LEON, JR., program manager; b. Rehoboth, Mass., July 19, 1934; s. Wilfrid James Leon and Yvonne Clarise (Teautrault) D.; m. Joyce Ann Brissette, July 6, 1968; 1 child, Lynn Marie. B.B.A. in Engring., Western New Eng. Coll., 1965. Cons. engr. Profl. Design, Agawam, Mass., 1957-61, R. M. Hallam Co., Springfield, Mass., 1961-62; designer UTC Hamilton Standard, Windsor Locks, Conn., 1962-65, project engr., 1965-81, project mgr., 1981-86, program mgr., 1986—; instr. U.S. Armed Forces Inst., Agana, Guam, 1955-56. Mem. Springfield Action Com., Mass., 1960. Served with USAF, 1956-59. Roman Catholic. Avocations: design-build custom furniture; tennis. Home: Feeding Hills, Mass. Died Oct. 20, 2006.

DEMPSTER, CURT (FRANK CURTIN DEMPSTER), artistic director, producer; b. Detroit, Nov. 1, 1938; s. Frank Dudley and Anna Jeanette (Miller) D. Artistic dir. Ensemble Studio Theatre, NYC, 1965—2002. Tchr., lectr. Smith Coll., Rutgers U., Hofstra U., Columbia U., Yale U.; assoc. prodr. First Internat Festival Arts, N.Y.C., 1988. Author: (plays) Mimosa Pudica, 1978 (Best Play award 1978), Wolf Point, 1991, (short play) Leonard Peltier, 1991. Instr. climbing N.Y. Outward Bound. Mem. SAG, Am. Alpine Club. Home: New York, NY. Died Jan. 19, 2007.

DENIUS, HOMER RAINEY, electronics company executive; b. Appomattox, Va., Jan. 31, 1914; s. Frank E. and Margaret (Watters) D.; m. Grace Evelyn Pence, June 26, 1936; children— Chris F., Sandra Jeanne (Mrs. Robert Keeley), Homer R. Student U. Cin.; D.Sc. (hon.), Fla. Inst. Tech., 1964. Mgmt. exec., 1943—; chmn. bd. Electro-Sci. Mgmt. Corp., Melbourne, Fla., 1968—. Mason (32 deg.). Epicopalian. Died Apr. 20, 2006.

DENNIS, JAMES LOUDON, medical educator; b. Oklahoma City, Aug. 8, 1913; s. William Bates and Artie (Abernathy) D.; m. Virginia Roueche, June 15, 1940; children: William H., James R., Constant Marie. BS, U. Okla., 1936, MD, 1940. Diplomate: Am. Bd. Pediatrics. Intern Highland-Alameda County Hosp., Oakland, Cal., 1941-42; resident medicine Merced County (Cal.) Hosp., 1941-43; resident pediatrics U. Tex. Med. Br., Galveston, 1950-52; asst. prof. pediatrics U. Tex. Med. Sch., 1952-54; dir. edn. Children's Hosp., Med. Center No. Calif., Oakland, 1955-62; prof. pediatrics U. Ark. Med. Sch., 1962-64, prof. emeritus pediatrics, from 1980; dean, dir. U. Okla. Med. Center, 1964-70; v.p. U. Okla. Med. Center (Med. Center affairs), 1967-70; v.p. for health scis. U. Ark., Little Rock, 1970-75, chancellor, 1975-79; prof. pediatrics James L. Dennis Devel. Ctr. Ark. Children's Hosp., from 1980. Mem. Nat. Adv. Commn. Health Facilities, 1968-69; cons. Calif. Dept. Pub. Health, 1959-62, Am. Legion Child Welfare Com., 1962-69; mem. nat. com. Pediatric Research Edn. and Practice, 1961—; chmn. Okla. Commn. Med. Research, 1964-70, Okla. Commn. Handicapped, 1965-70; cons. Nat. Found., Com. Hosp. Care Children. Contbr. numerous articles in field. Bd. dirs. Okla. Med. Research Found., 1964-70, Okla. Health Sci. Fedn., 1965-70, Ark. Chamber Singers; pres. bd. dirs. Council on Aging, 1980-81. Served with M.C. USNR, 1943-46. Recipient Disting. Faculty award Caduceus Club of Med. Coll. U. Ark., 1977; Extraordinary Achievement award as chancellor U. Ark. for Med. Scis., 1977; Disting. Service award Okla. Health Scis., Found., 1980, U. Ark. Coll. Medicine, 1981; named Physician of Yr. for Acad. Medicine, Alumni Assn. U. Okla. Coll. Medicine, 1982 Fellow Am. Acad. Pediatrics; mem. AMA (council sci. assembly 1965—, chmn. sect. pediatrics 1966), So. Soc. Pediatric Research, AAAS, Am. Pub. Health Assn., Assn. Acad. Health Ctrs. (nat. pres. 1971-72), Oklahoma City C. of C. (dir. 1969-70), Ret. Execs. Assn., Sigma Xi, Alpha Omega Alpha, Alpha Kappa Kappa. Democrat. Methodist. Home: N Little Rock, Ark. Died Jan. 10, 2006.

DENNISH, GEORGE WILLIAM, III, cardiologist; b. Trenton, NJ, Feb. 14, 1945; s. George William and Mary Ann (Bodnar) D.; div. 1993; children: Andrew Stuart, Brian George, Michael John; m. Cheryl A. Henry, Aug. 6, 1993; 1 stepson, Joshua J. Morris; 1 child, Brendan William. AB magna cum laude, Seton Hall U., 1967; MD, Jefferson Med. Coll., 1971. Diplomate Nat. Bd. Med. Examiners, Am. Bd. Internal Medicine (subspecialty cert. in cardiovascular diseases), Hosp. Mgmt. UCLA. Intern Naval Hosp., Phila., 1971-72, jr. asst. resident, 1972-73, sr. asst. resident, 1973-74; fellow cardiovascular diseases Naval Regional Med. Ctr., San Diego, 1974-76, dir. coronary care unit, 1977-78; pvt. practice cardiology San Diego, from 1978. V.p. Splty. Med. Clinic, La Jolla and San Diego, 1982—; staff cardiologist Naval Regional Med. Ctr., Faculty Medicine, San Diego, 1976—; dir. spl. care units Scipps Meml. Hosp., La Jolla, 1981-88, chmn. cardiology div., 1987—; chief medicine Scripps-Encinitas Hosp., 1983-87; co-editor Cardiac CATV, 1987—; adj. asst. prof. medicine Baylor Coll., Houston, 1980-1990; clin. prof. medicine U. Calif., San Diego, 1976—. Contbr. articles to med. jours. Bd. dirs. San Diego County Heart Assn.; pres. San Diety County divsn. Am. Heart Assn., 1999-2000; founder, pres. Cardiovascular Inst., La Jolla. Lt. comdr. USNR, 1971—. Decorated Knight of Holy Sepulcre; recipient Physician's Recognition award AMA, 1974-2005. Fellow ACP, Am. Coll. Cardiology, Am. Heart Assn. (clin. coun.), Am. Coll. Chest physicians, Am. Coll. Angrology; mem. Am. Soc. Internal Medicine, AAAS, Am. Coll. Clin. Pharmacology, N.Y. Acad. Scis., Am. Fedn. Clin. Rsch., N.Am. Soc. Pacing and Electrophysiology, Soc. for Cardiac Angiography, Soc. for Cardiac Antiography and Intervention, Old Mission Players Club, K.C. Home: Del Mar, Calif. Died Jan. 25, 2007.

DENNISON, BYRON LEE, electrical engineering educator, consultant; b. Clarksburg, W.Va., Dec. 8, 1930; s. Raymond Lewis and Edna (Sturm) D.; m. Betty Jean Davis, July 4, 1954 (div. 1988); children: Diane Lee, Shirley Joanne. BS in Elec. Engring, W. Va. U., 1953; MS in Elec. Engring, Va. Poly. Inst., 1962; PhD in Elec. Engring, Worcester Poly. Inst., 1967. Registered profl. engr. Mass., W.Va. Sr. engr. govt. and indsl. div. Philco Corp., Phila., 1953-58; asst. assoc. prof. Va. Poly. Inst., Blacksburg, 1958-66; prof. Lowell (Mass.) Tech. Inst., 1966-74, adj. prof., 1974-77, head dept. elec. engring., 1967-72; vis. prof. Va. Poly. Inst. and State U., 1977-79, Southeastern Mass. U., 1979-81, adj. prof., 1982, U. Lowell, 1982-85, disting. vis. prof., 1985-87; vis. prof. Merrimack Coll., 1983-84; lectr. U. of Mass. at Lowell, 1987-95. Cons. Polysci. Corp., Blacksburg, 1961-63, Worcester Found. Exptl. Biology, Shrewsbury, Mass., 1966-68 Mem. I.E.E.E., Am. Soc. Engring. Edn., Sigma Xi, Eta Kappa Nu, Phi Kappa Phi. Research devel. math. model for motor activity of cat iris. Home: Germantown, Md. Died Mar. 13, 2006.

DEPRIT, ANDRE ALBERT, mathematician, consultant; b. St. Servais, Belgium, Apr. 10, 1926; came to U.S., 1964, naturalized, 1974; s. Max Francois and Anne-Marie Caroline (Vasse) D.; m. Andree Jeanne Bartholome, Sept. 5, 1959; 1 son, Etienne. LPh, U. Louvain, Belgium, 1948, LSc, 1953, DSc, 1957; D honoris causa, U. Zaragoza, Spain, 1989, Russian Acad. Sci., 1994. Sr. rsch. asssoc. Nat. Bur. Standards, Gaithersburg, Md., 1977-79; mathematician Nat. Inst. Standards and tech., 1979-82, sr. mathematician, 1982-83, sr. fellow, from 1983; assoc. prof. U. Kinshassa, Zaire, 1957-59, U. Louvain, 1957-61, prof., 1961-64; staff mem. Boeing Sci. Research Labs., Seattle, 1964-71; sr. research fellow NASA, Greenbelt, Md., 1971-72; prof. U. Cin., 1972-78, Charles Phelps Taft prof., 1979. Cons. Charles Stark Draper Lab., Cambridge, Mass., 1977—, Naval Rsch. Lab., Washington, 1976—, Nat. Inst. Standards and Tech., Boulder, Colo., 1974—; vis. prof. Yale U., New Haven, 1965-66, U. Liege, Belgium, 1970, U. Wis., Madison, 1975, U. Zaragoza, Spain, 1988—, U. Castellon, Spain, 1992; vis. lectr. U. Wash., Seattle, 1965-66; resident visitor Bell Tel. Labs., 1968; George Lemaître prof. U. Louvain, 1984—. Editor: Celestial Mechanics, 1969-73; contbr. articles to profl. jours. Recipient Royal Acad. Scis. (Belgium) Agathon De Potter prize, 1957, Watson medal NAS, 1972, Wettrems prize, 1971, Alan Berman award Naval Rsch. Lab., 1982, 88, Silver medal U.S. Dept. Commerce, 1982, Gold medal, 1987, Beca de Honor award, Collegio Mirafiores, Dirk Brouwer award Am. Astron. Soc., 1985, 87, 88; NATO fellow, 1963, NAS-NRC fellow, 1971-72. Mem. AIAA, AAAS, Internat. Astron. Union, Am., Royal astronom. socs., Academia de Ciencias (Zazagoza, Spain), Cosmos Club, Sigma Xi. Home: Gaithersburg, Md. Died Nov. 7, 2006.

DEPUYDT, CHERYL ANN, physical education educator; b. Marquette, Mich., Dec. 16, 1950; d. John Bernard and Yvonne Marie (Ekstedt) Dorais; m. John Daniel DePuydt, Nov. 10, 1973; children— Jenny, Paul, Matt. B.S. in Edn., No. Mich. U., 1972, M.S. in Ednl. Adminstrn., 1978. Instr. phys. edn. Mich. Tech. U., Houghton, 1972-78, basketball coach, 1974-78, volleyball coach, 1974-80, cheerleading coach, 1972-81, asst. prof., 1978—, skating sch. dir., 1972—; figure skating cons. Portage Lake Figure Skating Club, 1972—. Recipient Service award Marquette Figure Skating Club, 1980; named Disting. Tchr., Mich. Tech. U., 1982. Mem. Houghton-Hancock Bus. and Profl. Women (named Young Careerist 1977, 78, pres. 1983-84), Ice Skating Inst. Am. (instr. 1983) U.S. Figure Skating Assn. (profl. 1969—). Roman Catholic. Home: Houghton, Mich. Died Sept. 2006.

DERMODY, JOHN, oceanographer; b. Needham, Mass., Mar. 28, 1924; s. Frank J. and Frances (Frawley) Dermody; m. Tommy Anne Black, Mar. 5, 1950; children: Grant M., Robin Anne, Todd F. BS, Holy Cross Coll., 1945; postgrad., U. Wash., 1957—58, MIT, 1959. With U.S. Coast and Geodetic Survey, 1948—56; oceanographer U. Wash., Seattle, 1957—75; mgr. programs U. Alaska, Faribanks, 1976—79; lab. dir. Ocean Inst. Wash., Seattle, 1979—81; tech. mgr. Raven Sys. & Rsch., Seattle, from 1981. Contbr. articles to profl. jours. Adult leader Boy Scouts Am., Seattle, 1968—74; exec. sec. Pres.'s Commn. on Marine Sci., Engring. and Resources, 1967—68; mem. Gov.'s Tech. Com., Alaska, 1976—79. With USN, 1942—46. Recipient award of yr., U.S. Dept. Commerce, 1956. Mem.: Marine Tech. Soc., Hydrographic Soc., Inst. Navigation, Soc. Naval Archs. and Marine Engrs. Republican. Roman Catholic. Home: Seattle, Wash. Died Oct. 23, 2006.

DEROUNIAN, STEVEN BOGHOS, retired judge, former congressman; b. Sofia, Bulgaria, Apr. 6, 1918; came to U.S., 1921; s. Boghos and Eliza (Aprahamian) D.; m. Emily Ann Kennard, Aug. 20, 1947; children: Ann Ashby, Eleanor Kennard, Steven Blake. AB, N.Y. U., 1938; LL.B., Fordham U., 1942. Bar: N.Y. 1942, D.C. 1959, Tex. 1981. Practiced in, Mineola,

N.Y., Garden City, N.Y., also Washington; mem. law firm Derounian, Candee, Guardino Murphy; mem. US Congress from 2nd NY dist., 1953—65; justice NY Supreme Ct., 1969—81. Councilman, mem. bd., Town of North Hempstead, N.Y., 1948-52 Served to capt. inf., 103rd Div. AUS, 1942-46; maj. Res. Decorated Purple Heart, Bronze Star with cluster, Combat Infantryman's badge. Mem. Am., Travis County bar assns., V.F.W., Am. Legion, Delta Theta Pi. Clubs: Chowder and Marching (Washington). Lodges: Masons; Elks. Republican. Home: Austin, Tex. Died Apr. 17, 2007.

DERRICK, A. M., petroleum engr. b. Dublin, Tex., July 26, 1922; s. Alex M. and Velma W. (Thompson) D.; m. Margie Davidson, Jan. 10, 1946; children— Michael, Nancy, David, Patricia. BS in Petroleum Engring, U. Tex., 1947; MS in Petroleum Engring, U. Houston, 1956. Petroleum engr. Stanolind Oil and Gas Co., Pampa, Wink and Midland, Tex. and Tulsa, 1947-53; with El Paso (Tex.) Natural Gas Co., from 1953, sr. petroleum engr., 1953-59, mgr. reservoir engr., 1960-65, asst. v.p., 1966-71, v.p., 1972-76, sr. v.p., from 1977. Served with U.S. Navy, 1943-46. Mem. Soc. Petroleum Evaluation Engrs., Soc. Petroleum Engrs., Am. Assn. Petroleum Geologists, Am. Gas Assn., Pacific Coast Gas Assn. Clubs: El Paso Country. Republican. Baptist. Home: El Paso, Tex. Died May 8, 2006.

DE SANTIS, ANTHONY, restaurant, theatre executive; b. Gary, Ind., Jan. 5, 1914; s. Sam and Marie (DiVergilo) DeS.; m. Lucille Cuzeli, Feb. 12, 1945; children: Deborah, Diane. Student, Armour Inst., 1941. With research lab. staff Sherwin-Williams Paint Co., Chgo., 1934-39; owner, mgr. Embassy Club, Chgo., 1940-45, Martinique Restaurant, Chgo., 1946-88; owner Drury Lane Theatre, Oakbrook Terrace, Ill., 1951—2007, now pres.; co-owner Hilton Suites Hotel, Oak Brook. Bd. dirs. Standard Bank of Hickory Hills, Chgo.; vice chmn. Heritage Standard Bank & Trust Co., Oak Brook Bank; pres. Drury Ln. Prodns., Inc., Chgo., Water Tower Dilote Entertainment Inc., Chgo., Indian Creek Investors, Lincolnshire Creek Land Co. treas. Martinique-Drury Ln. Corp Mem. adv. bd. Sheriff of Cook County, Ill.; mem. citizens bd. U. Chgo.; bd. assos. De Paul U.; mem. advisory bd. Cath. Charities, Little Flower Soc.; active United Cerebral Palsy. Recipient Humanitarian award, religious awards Little Flower Soc., 1966; decorated comdr. Order Holy Sepulchre, knight of Grand Cross of Holy Sepulchre, Knight of Malta; knight comdr. Order St. John of Jerusalem; mil. honor Order St. Lazurus of Jerusalem, Order St. Augustine Filius Ordinis; knight comdr. Order St. Gregory; Order de Chasque; recipient Pope John Pontifical award, Pope Paul Pontifical awards, also 10 othr pontifical awards; recipient Disting. Service award Chgo. Police Capts. Assn., 8 Appreciation awards FBI, Chgo., 1969-78, Appreciation award Chgo. Fire Fighters, 1980; named Oaklawn Man of Yr., C. of C., 1965 Mem. Chgo. Patrolmen's Assn. (hon. life), Chgo. Conv. Bur. (1979), Lions. Clubs: Carlton, Variety (Chgo.). Home: Villa Park, Ill. Died June 6, 2007.

DESAULNIERS, RENE GERARD LESIEUR, retired optometrist; b. Danielson, Conn., Oct. 21, 1922; s. Egide A. and Rose (Regis) D.; children: Suzanne Rose Bauzys, Maureen Frances Russe, Michelle Elizabeth Van Haagen, Thomas Benedict, John Christopher. Grad., U.S. Army Mil. Intel. Sch.; student, Georgetown U., 1943, Boston U., 1944; OD, Pa. Coll. Optometry, 1948; grad., Joe Brinkman Profl. Umpire Sch., Fla. Lic. optometrist Conn., Fla., R.I. Individual practice optometry, Putnam, Conn., 1948-98; ret., 1998. Externship Gessel Inst. Child Devel. Yale U., 1964-; past pres. Conn. Bd. Examiners in Optometry, 1957-91; past pres. Internat. Assn. Bd. Examiners in Optometry; past pres. Nat. Bd. Examiners in Optometry, Washington, D.C., 1975-85; cons. American League. Life mem., former nat. dir. Am. Optometric Found.; past pres. Putnam Little League; 2d pres. Quinnebaug Valley Assn. for Retarded, 1963; past mem. Putnam Sch. Bd.; chmn. DK Hosp. Devel. Fund, 1984—85. Lt. US Army, 1943—46, maj. inf. USAR, 1946—63. Recipient Sam Levitt Meml. award, 1948; named Conn. Optometrist of Yr., 1989. Fellow: Nat. Acad. Practices (Disting. Practitioner), Am. Acad. Optometry; mem.: Conn. Assn. Optometrists, Am. Optometric Assn., New Eng. Coun. Optometrists (chmn. 42nd Congress), Conn. Approved Baseball Umpires (ea. bd. past pres. 1981—82), Am. Legion (baseball com., VFW commn.), Major League Umpires Baseball (vision cons.), Elk, KC (4th degree), Omega Delta. Home: Putnam, Conn. Died Dec. 6, 2006.

DETRE, KATHERINE MARIA, physician; b. Budapest, Hungary, Apr. 28, 1926; came to Can., 1949; d. Ignac and Irene (Lefkovits) Drechsler; m. Thomas P. Detre, Sept. 16, 1956; children: John, Anthony. Student, Pazmany Peter Med. Sch., Budapest, 1945-49; BA, Queens U., Kingston, Ont., Can., 1950, MD, 1952; MPH, Yale U., 1964, DPH, 1967. Rotating intern Kingston Gen. Hosp., Queens Kingston, Ont., 1952-53; resident in internal medicine Queen Mary Vets. Hosp. McGill, Montreal, Que., Can., 1953-56; research assoc. hematology Yale U., New Haven, 1956-60, lectr. in biometry, 1968-74; biostatistician VA Coop. Studies Program, West Haven, Conn., 1967-95; assoc. prof. U. Pitts., 1974-79, prof. epidemiology, from 1979. Mem. clin. adv. bd. NIH, Bethesda, Md., 1977-78, mem. epidemiology and disease control com., 1983-87, mem. Fogarty Internat. Ctr. adv. bd., 1994—; mem. rsch. com. B, Nat. Heart, Lung and Blood Inst., Bethesda, 1978-82. Contbr. over 434 articles to profl. jours. Named Woman in Sci. Chatham Coll., 1987; internat. student scholar Queens U., 1949-52. Fellow AAAS (disting. scientist), Am. Coll. Cardiology (hon.), Coun. on Epidemiology (chmn. 1981-83), Am. Coll. Epidemiology; mem. Am. Statis. Assn. (Statistician of Yr. 1993), Biometric Soc. (regional adv. bd. 1993), Soc. Clin. Trials (bd. dirs. 1981-85, program com. 1994-95), Am. Epidemiology Soc. Home: Pittsburgh, Pa. Died Jan. 24, 2006.

DEVENOW, CHESTER, manufacturing executive; b. Detroit, Mar. 3, 1919; s. Samuel and Bessie (Aronoff) D.; m. Marilyn Fruchtman, Apr. 20, 1947 (div. Feb. 1977); children: Mark F., Jeffrey A., Sara Devenow Abrams, Susan P.; m. Maudette Shapiro, Dec. 18, 1978. BA, NYU, 1941; postgrad., Harvard Law Sch., 1941-42; D.BA (hon.), Siena Heights Coll., Adrian, Mich., 1977. Pres. Globe Wernicke Industries, Toledo, 1954-67; pres. Sheller-Globe Corp., Toledo, 1967-72, chmn., chief exec. officer, from 1972, also bd. dirs. Bd. dirs. Toledo Edison, Toledo Trust Co., Toledo Trustcorp., Centerior Energy Corp., Knoll Internat. Holding, Inc. Bd. dirs. Tech. and Productivity Ctr. Ohio, Columbus, 1982—; trustee, chmn. bd. trustees Ohio State U., Columbus, 1972-82; mem. Labor-Mgmt. Citizens Com., Toledo, 1972; chmn. bd. Blue Cross NW Ohio, 1975-82. Served to 1st lt. U.S. Army, 1942-45 Recipient Heritage award Yeshiva U., 1971, Gov.'s award State of Ohio, 1981; named Hon. Prof., Ohio State U., 1982 Mem. Toledo Area C. of C. (pres. 1976, sr. council), Soc. Automotive Engrs., Nat. Energy Found. (bd. dirs.) Clubs: Renaissance (bd. govs. 1974—), Economic (Detroit); Toledo; Jockey (Miami, Fla.). Died Nov. 6, 2005.

DEVERS, VICTOR LEE, federal agency administrator; b. Topeka, Oct. 24, 1931; s. Milburn Lee and Ruth Catherine (Brooke) Devers; m. Constance J. Webert, Feb. 18, 1960; children: Mikel Lee, Daniel Scott. BS in Bus. Mgmt., San Diego State U., 1956; MA in Econs., U. N.Mex., 1962. Site rep. AEC, Oak Ridge, 1967—69, chief constrn. br. budget divsn. Albuquerque, 1969—70, quality assurance engr., 1970—72, planning specialist planning divsn., 1972—74; chief weapons evaluation br. Dept. of Energy, Albuquerque, 1974—83, dep. dir. quality divsn., 1983—84, strategic planner, 1984—86, dep. dir. Office Strategic Planning, from 1986. Bd. dirs. Hogares, Inc. Mem. budget com. United Way, Albuquerque, 1977—79; judge N.Mex Sci. Fair, 1976—85; bd. dirs. Family Counseling Svc. With USAF, 1950—54. Recipient N.Mex Disting. Pub. Svc. award, 1986. Mem.: Delta Sigma Pi. Republican. Home: Albuquerque, N.Mex. Died Apr. 7, 2007.

DEVIN, RONALD BOYD, theatre educator; b. Heppner, Oreg., Mar. 13, 1933; s. Harlan Justus Devin and Lorah Irene (Hiatt) VanSchoiack; m. Carroll Jeanne Ferguson, Mar. 16, 1957; children: Hillary Jeanne, Scott Ferguson. BS, U. Oreg., 1959, MS, 1961; EdD, Wash. State U., 1971. Instr. Everett (Wash.) Jr. Coll., 1960-69; from asst. prof. to prof. Eastern Wash. U., Cheney, from 1969, chmn. dept. theatre, 1970-77, 83-86. Dir. over 120 plays and musicals. Staff sgt. USAF, 1952-56. Named one of Outstanding Educators of Am., 1973-74, for Dept. of Def. Best Play on Tour, 1971, 84. Mem. NEA, Phi Delta Kappa. Democrat. Episcopalian. Avocations: travel, photography, restoration of automobiles. Home: Mesa, Ariz. Died Nov. 10, 2006.

DEVINE, BING (VAUGHAN PALLMORE DEVINE), retired professional sports team executive; b. Mar. 1, 1917; m. Mary Anderson; children: Joanne (Mrs. Schaumburg), Janice, Jane. Grad., Washington U. Asst. pub. relations dept. St. Louis Cardinals, MLB, 1939-41, mgr. bus. Cardinals farm system teams Johnson City, Tenn., 1941-42, Fresno, Calif., 1942, Decatur, Ill., 1942, mgr. farm system team Columbus, Ga., 1946-49, gen. mgr. farm system team Rochester, 1949-55, exec. asst. to gen. mgr. parent orgn., 1955-57, gen. mgr., 1957—64, 1968—78, exec. v.p., 1973-78, spl. scout & adv. to gen. mgr., 1999—2007; pres., gen. mgr. NY Mets, MLB, 1965-67; pres., COO St. Louis Cardinals, NFL, 1981—86. Served with USNR, 1943-46, PTO. Recipient Major League Exec. of Year, 1963, 64 Died Jan. 27, 2007.

DEVINE, VAUGHAN PALLMORE See DEVINE, BING

DEVONS, SAMUEL, retired physicist; b. Bangor, N.Wales, U.K., Sept. 30, 1914; came to U.S., 1959; s. David Isaac and Edith (Edlestein) D.; m. Celia Ruth Toubkin, Sept. 7, 1938; children— Susan Danielle, Judith Rosalind, Amanda Jane, Cathryn Ann Julie. BA, Trinity Coll., Cambridge U., Eng., 1935, MA, PhD (Exhbn. 1851 scholar), 1939; M.Sc., Manchester U., Eng., 1959. Sr. sci. officer Air Ministry, Ministry Supply, U.K., 1939-45; fellow, dir. studies, lectr. physics Trinity Coll., 1946-49; prof. physics Imperial Coll., London, Eng., 1950-55; Langworthy prof. physics, dir. phys. labs. U. Manchester, 1955-60; prof. physics Columbia U., 1960-84, prof. emeritus, spl. rsch. scientist, 1985—2006, chmn. dept., 1963-67. Royal Soc.-Leverhulme vis. prof., Andhra, India, 1967-68; Racah vis. prof. physics Hebrew U., Jerusalem, 1973; Balfour vis. prof. history of sci. Weizmann Inst., Israel, 1974, bd. govs.; Royal Soc. Rutherford Meml. Lectr., Australia, 1989; mem. Tech. Assistance-UNESCO Team of UN to S. Am., 1957 Author: Excited States of Nuclei, 1949; Editor: Biology and the Physical Sciences, 1969, High Energy Physics and Nuclear Structure, 1970. Served with RAF, 1944-45. Recipient Rutherford medal and prize Inst. Physics, U.K., 1970 Fellow: Phi Beta Kappa, The Joseph Priestley Assn. (founder, convenor from 1986), N.Y. Acad. Scis., Am. Phys. Soc., Royal Soc. London. Home: Irvington, NY. Died Dec. 6, 2006.

DEWALD, GRETTA MOLL, county official; b. Kutztown, Pa., Oct. 26, 1929; d. Lloyd A. and Olga (Wuchter) M.; m. Charles Frederick Dewald, Dec. 20, 1951; children: Michael S., Jonathon G., Henry L., Janie P., Joseph C. BA, Agnes Scott Coll., 1950. Tchr. secondary schs. Eastman City Schs., Ga., 1950-51, Bass High Sch., Atlanta, 1951-52; project exec. sec. Appalachian project Day Care and Child Devel. Coun. Am., Atlanta, 1971-73; researcher Ga. Senate, Atlanta, 1973-74; aide to commr. DeKalb Bd. Commrs., 1974-77; community rels. officer Met. Atlanta Rapid Transit Authority, 1976-77, bd. dirs., 1977; dir. women's div. Democratic Nat. Com., Washington, 1977-80; exec. asst. to chief exec. officer and bd. commrs. DeKalb County, Decatur, Ga., 1981-89; coord. DeKalb County Pretrial Svcs., 1989—. Mem. Ga. Commn. on Volunteerism, 1970-74, Ga. Women's Adv. Com., 1972-74, Nat. Adv. Com. of Women, 1977-80. Chmn., DeKalb County Dem. Com., 1972-74, 4th Congl. Dist. Ga. Com., 1974-77; campaigner, Peanut Brigade, N.H., Vt., Md., Ohio, Wi., Fla., Pa., 1976; del. Dem. Nat. Conv., 1972, 74, 76, 80; mem. adv. bd. Ga. Women's Polit. Caucus, 1983-86; So. regional coord. Dem. Task Force, Nat. Women's Polit. Caucus, 1983-85; organizer, mem. adv. bd. DeKalb Women's Network, 1983-86; bd. dirs. DeKalb Libr. System, 1983-89; bd. dirs. DeKalb Humane Soc., 1985—; bd. dirs. Our House, Inc., 1987-89; mem. Women's Resource Ctr. DeKalb, 1986-88. Mem. Nat. Assn. County Adminstrs., Ga. Coun. County Adminstrs. and Mgrs. (v.p. 1986-87, pres. 1987-88), Nat. Assn. Counties (steering com. intergovtl. rels. 1981-89, mem. women ofcls. chpt.), Women's Coun. Nat. Assn. Counties, Assn. County Commrs. Ga. (bd. dirs. 1986-88), Abigails (organizer), 1984—. Presbyterian. Home: Stone Mountain, Ga. Died Oct. 30, 2006.

DEWAR, HELEN, reporter; b. Stockton, Calif., 1936; BA in Polit. Sci., Stanford U. Reporter The Northern Virginia Sun, Arlington, Va., 1959—61; metro reporter The Washington Post, Washington, 1961-77, nat. staff reporter, 1977—2004. Named to Va. Communications Hall of Fame, 2006; recipient Everett McKinley Dirksen award for Disting. Reporting of Congress, Nat. Press Found., 1984, Lifetime Achievement award, Wash. Press Club Found., 2006. Died Nov. 4, 2006.

DEWITT, SANDRA LOU, finance and insurance company executive; b. Bremerton, Wash., Feb. 2, 1944; d. Miles Eugene and Billie Elizabeth (McLean) Hurley; student public schs., Garden Grove, Calif.; m. William Albert DeWitt, Dec. 30, 1961; children— Rebecca Sue, William Albert. Sec., claims examiner RIMCO, Dallas, 1972-73; casualty claims supr. Am. PetroFina Co. of Tex., Dallas, 1973-77; dir. ins. and risk mgmt. Ramada Inns, Inc., Phoenix, 1977—. Bd. dirs., sec. Ramada Inn Employee Credit Union, 1980—. Mem. Risk and Ins. Mgmt. Soc. (chpt. v.p. 1981-82, pres. 1982—), Am. Bus. Women's Assn., Am. Soc. Profl. and Exec. Women, Nat. Assn. Female Execs., Ariz. Assn. Ins. Adjusters. Republican. Methodist. Club: Order Eastern Star. Home: Phoenix, Ariz. Died July 21, 2006.

DEYOUNG, LILLIAN JEANETTE, nurse, retired educational administrator; b. Ogden, Utah, July 26, 1926; d. Peter and Gertrude (Dallinga) DeY. R.N., Dee Meml. Sch. Nursing, Utah, 1947; BS in Nursing Edn., U. Utah, 1950, MS in Ednl. Adminstrn., 1955, PhD in Ednl. Adminstrn, 1975. Assoc. dir. nursing edn. Latter Day Saints Hosp., Salt Lake City, 1954-55; dir. Sch. of Nursing, instr. St. Luke's Hosp. Sch. of Nursing, Denver, 1955-72; assoc. prof., curriculum coordinator Intercollegiate Center for Nursing Edn., Spokane, Wash., 1972-73; asst. dir. nursing service U. Utah Med. Center, Salt Lake City, 1973-75; prof., dean Coll. of Nursing, U. Akron, Ohio, 1975-88, ret. Ohio, 1988. Cons. Duquesne U. Sch. Nursing, 1980, Youngstown State U. Dept. of Nursing, 1979; mem. State of Ohio Bd. of Nursing Edn. and Nurse Registration, 1979-83, v.p., 1980-82, pres., 1982-83. Author: Dynamics of Nursing, 4th edit., 1981, 5th edit., 1985. Active ARC; mem. exec. com. bd. trustee Akron Gen. Med. Ctr., exec. bd. Huntington Nat. Bd., 1986. Isobel Robb scholar, 1974-75; recipient pearl pin Am. Nurses Assn., 1972, Mentor award Sigma Theta Tau Delta, 1988; named Colo. Nurse of Yr., 1965; research award and scholarship named in her honor, 1988. Mem. Ohio League for Nursing, Ohio Nurses Assn. (dir. 1977-81), Am. Assn. Collegiate Nursing (by— laws com. 1980—) Mem. Lds Ch. Died Feb. 19, 2007.

DICK, ELLIOT COLTER, virologist, epidemiologist, educator; b. Miami, Fla., June 30, 1926; s. Elliot C. Dick and Helen Jean Cribb; m. Claire Rebecca Blumer, Sept. 23, 1967; children: Emily Diane, Elliot Mayhew, Frederic Krichton, Catherine Virginia. BA in Bacteriology, U. Minn., 1950, MS in Bacteriology, 1953, PhD in Bacteriology, 1955. Asst. prof. Bacteriology U. Kans., Lawrence, 1955-59; asst. prof. medicine Tulane U., New Orleans, 1959-61; asst. prof. Preventive Medicine U. Wis., Madison, 1961-64, assoc. prof., 1964-72, prof., 1972-96. Cons. Kans. State Bd. Health, Topeka, 1955-59; mem. collaborative com. rhinoviruses WHO, 1966—; vis. scientist Delta Regional Primate Ctr., Tulane U., Covington, La., 1967-72; Sigrid Juselius Found. lectr., Turku, Finland, 1991. Contbr. articles, abstracts to profl. jours. including Jour. Infectious Diseases, Jour. Allergy and Clinical Immunology, Jour. Clinical Investigation, chpts. to books; patentee in field. With U.S. Army, 1944-46, ETO. Recipient Antarctic medal U.S., 1979; grantee U. Kans., 1956-59, Kans. State Bd. Health, 1957-58, USPHS, 1959-70, 71-73, 76, 79, 82, 85, 88, S.C. Johnson, 1966-67, 70-79, Smith, Kline & French, 1966-71, 74, 75, NASA, 1967-82, NSF, 1976-88, Kimberly-Clark, 1981-96, Hoffmann-LaRoche, 1986-96, Sterling Drug, 1989-96. Fellow Am. Acad. Microbiology (diplomat clin. microbiology), Infectious Disease Soc., Explorers Club; mem. AAAS, Am. Soc. Virology (founder), Am. Soc. Microbiology (Wis. legis. rep. 1970-96), Soc. Exptl. Biology and Medicine, N.Y. Acad. Scis., Phi Sigma, Sigma Xi. Mem. Unitarian Ch. Avocations: sailing, tennis, economics, history. Home: Madison, Wis. Died Sept. 13, 2006.

DICKENSON, HENRY BOYD, mechanical engineer, corporate executive; b. Bristol, Va., Sept. 2, 1924; s. Charlie Ellington and Verna Hazel (Jessee) D.; m. Mary Ann Hubbard, Aug. 3, 1951; children: Lawrence Boyd, Ann Marie, Charles David, Roger Conley, Edward Allen, Mary Elizabeth. Student, Tex. A&M U., 1943-44; BSME, MIT, 1949. Registered profl. engr., Ohio, Tenn., S.C., Va., Miss., Del., N.Y., Mo., Minn., N.C., Fla., D.C., Ky., Ga., La., Md., Ala., N.J. Estimator, asst. mgr. S & M Engring. Corp., Roanoke, Va., 1949-50; asst. project mgr. Hayes, Seay, Mattern & Mattern, Inc., Radford, Va., 1951-52, successively chief engr., assoc., sr. assoc., chief assoc., 1952-60, ptnr. to mng. ptnr., 1960-88, chmn., chief exec. officer, from 1988. Pres. Palmer & Baker Engring., Inc. Mem. ASME, Am. Cons. Engr. Coun. (nat. bd. dirs.), Va. Soc. Profl. Engrs. (pres. Roanoke chpt.), Hidden Valley Country Club, Shenandoah Club, Sigma Nu. Methodist. Avocations: tennis, golf, gardening. Died June 11, 2006.

DICKINSON, JAMES MILLARD, metallurgy researcher; b. Waterloo, Iowa, July 31, 1923; s. Emery Elmer and LaTosca Marie (Prugh) D.; m. Ada E. Holmes, Mar. 23, 1947; children— Judy Ann, Patricia Sue, Barbara Kay. B.S., Iowa State U., 1949, Ph.D., 1953. Jr. scientist Ames Lab., AEC, 1947-53; mem. staff metallurgy Los Alamos Lab., 1953-74, asst. group leader, 1974-80, dep. group leader, 1980-81, group leader, 1981—. Contbr. articles to profl. jours. Patentee in field. Served with USMCR, 1942-46. Mem. Am. Soc. Metals (chpt. chmn. 1976-77), AIME, Am. Def. Preparedness Assn. Republican. Methodist. Home: Livingston, Tex. Died Jan. 25, 2006.

DICKINSON, RICHARD RAYMOND, retired oil company executive; b. Orange, Calif., Jan. 28, 1931; s. Raymond Russel and Florence Marie (Jacobson) D.; m. Barbara Jean Morrison, June 16, 1957; children: Roderick, Christine. BS, Calif. Inst. Tech., 1952; MS, U. So. Calif., 1960. Chem. engr. L.A. Refinery Texaco, 1952-68, gen. mgr. supply and distbn. London, 1968-76, plant mgr. Eagle Point plant Westville, NJ, 1976-79, gen. mgr. alternate energy group White Plains, NY, 1979, v.p. strategic planning, 1979-82; sr. v.p. U.S. refining, mktg., supply and transp. Texaco U.S.A., Houston, 1982-87; v.p. tech. Texaco, Inc., White Plains, NY, 1988-94. Served with USNR, 1955-58. Home: Mc Kinney, Tex. Died Apr. 3, 2006.

DICKMAN, JOHN W., sales executive; b. Milw., June 18, 1930; m. Alvina Rae Henrich, Feb. 19, 1955; children: Jeffrey, Steven, Mary Beth, Michael, James, Bradley. BSc., Loyola U., Chgo., 1951. Salesman Kendall Co., Chgo., 1953-56; territory salesman The Gillette Co., Toledo, 1956-57, sales supr. Chgo., 1957-59, dist. mgr. Detroit, 1959-61, The Gillette Co, Chgo., 1961-63; sales promotion mgr. The Gillette Co., Chgo., 1963-66, mgr. western region LA, 1966-68, v.p. sales Boston, 1968-84; pres. Braun Inc. (Div. Gillette), Lynnfield, Mass., from 1984. With U.S. Army 1951-53. Avocations: boating, golf, tennis. Home: Manchester, Mass. Died Oct. 14, 2006.

DIEMER, FERDINAND PETER, government official; b. N.Y.C., Oct. 16, 1920; s. Ferdinand Francis and Cunigunda Marie (Kolm) D.; B.S.E.E., Cooper Union U., 1948; M.S.E.E., N.Y.U., 1950; m. Maureen Margaret Davoren, May 8, 1952; children— Margretta, Jeanne Marie, Ferdinand, Dolores, Peter, Mary, Maribeth, Paul, Leon. Dir. spl. projects, asst. dir. engring. Martin Marietta Corp., Balt., 1961-66; mgr. command, control, communications systems TRW, Inc., McLean, Va., 1966-71; phys. sci. adminstr. Navy Oceanographic Sci., Office Naval Research, Arlington, Va., 1971-80; energy info. adminstr., dir. systems engring. U.S. Dept. Energy, Washington, 1980—; cons. dept. indsl. engring. Columbia U., Nat. Oceans Com., U. Miami, 1965-71; grad. lectr. applied sci. and engring. U. So. Calif., Am. U., 1959-71; dep. dir. Agard Internat. Tech. Conf., 1978; dir. Primars Sci. Internat. Conf., U. Manchester (Eng.), 1979. Active various community drives. Served with Signal Corps, U.S. Army, 1944-46; ETO, PTO. Recipient Outstanding Performance award USN, 1978. Mem. IEEE (life, chmn. computer soc.), AAAS, Am. Soc. Photogrammetry, Assn. Computing Machinery, Instrument Soc. Am., Soc. Indsl. and Applied Math., Engring. Soc. Balt., N.Y. Acad. Scis., Armed Forces Electronic Communication Assn. Author: Advanced Concepts in Ocean Measurements, 1978; Processes in Marine Remote Sensing, 1982. Home: Luthvle Timon, Md. Died Dec. 24, 2006.

DIETZ, JOHN RAPHAEL, engineering executive, consultant; b. Carbondale, Pa., Jan. 31, 1912; s. John A. and Bridget (Barrett) D.; m. Elizabeth Harding Bezilla, Mar. 15, 1983; children by previous marriage: Robert J., Elizabeth Dietz Brown. BS in Civil Engring., Drexel U., Phila., 1934. Registered profl. engr., Pa. Contract estimator J.A. Dietz Co., 1934-35; designer Pa. Dept. Hwys., 1935-38; designer, resident engr. Pa. Turnpike Commn., 1938-40; san. engr. for J.E. Greiner Co., Camp Meade, Md., 1940; designer Caribbean Architect-Engrs., 1941-42; chief designer for Gannett Eastman & Fleming, Inc., Andrews Air Field, Washington, 1942-43; civilian with U.S. Engr. Corps on study Potomac River Basin flood control, 1943-44; with Gannett Fleming Corddry and Carpenter, Inc., cons. engrs., from 1942, dir. hwy. div., then pres. Harrisburg, Pa., 1950-76, chmn. bd., 1970-83, chmn. emeritus, from 1983. Dir. CCNB Bank (N.A.) Trustee Drexel U. Bd.; dirs. Holy Spirit Hosp., Camp Hill, Pa., 1965—, pres., 1983; bd. dirs. Villa Teresa Nursing Home, Harrisburg, Pa., 1973—, pres., 1973-75. Recipient A.J. Drexel Paul award Drexel U., 1973; named Knight of St. Gregory, Pope John Paul II, 1983; selected in 100 Most Outstanding Men Drexel U. Alumni, 1992. Life fellow ASCE (past pres. Central Pa. chpt.); mem. Am. Council Cons. Engrs., Nat. Soc. Profl. Engrs., Am. Road and Transp. Builders Assn. (past dir.), Pa. Hwy. Info. Assn. (past pres.), Pa. Soc. Profl. Engrs. (Profl. Engrs. Disting. Service award Harrisburg chpt. 1965) Roman Catholic. Died Dec. 27, 2005.

DIETZ, WILLIAM, retired aeronautics engineer, consultant; b. Chgo., Apr. 17, 1919; BS, Aeronaut Inst., 1940. V.p. F16 engring. Gen. Dynamics Corp., 1972-78, v.p. Tomahawk Missile, 1979-82, v.p. spl. projects, 1982-90, v.p. divsn., sr. tech. staff, 1990-93; cons. Lockheed Corp., Ft. Worth, 1993-99; ret. Mem. NAE, AIAA (Sylvanus Reed award). Home: Fort Worth, Tex. Died July 31, 2006.

DIETZE, GOTTFRIED, political science professor; b. Kemberg, Germany, Nov. 11, 1922; came to U.S., 1949; s. Paul and Susanne (Pechstein) D. Dr.Jur., U. Heidelberg, Germany, 1949; PhD, Princeton U., 1952; SJD, U. Va., 1961. Instr. polit. sci. Dickinson Coll., 1952-54; mem. faculty Johns Hopkins U., Balt., from 1954, prof. polit. sci., 1962—2006. Vis. prof. U. Heidelberg, 1956, 58-60, Brookings Instn., 1960-61, 67. Author: Ueber Formulierung der Menschenrechte, 1956, The Federalist, 1960, In Defense of Property, 1963, Magna Carta and Property, 1965, America's Political Dilemma, 1968, Youth, University and Democracy, 1970, Bedeutungswandel der Menschenrechte, 1971, Academic Truths and Frauds, 1972, Two Concepts of the Rule of Law, 1973, Deutschland-Wo Bist Du?, 1980, Kant und der Rechtsstaat, 1981, Kandidaten, 1982, El Gobierno Constitucional, 1983, Liberalism Proper and Proper Liberalism, 1984, Reiner Liberalismus, 1985, Konservativer Liberalismus in Amerika, 1987, Liberaler Kommentar zur Amerikanischen Verfassung, 1988, Amerikanische Demokratie, 1988, Politik-Wissenschaft, 1989, Der Hitler-Komplex, 1990, Liberale Demokratie, 1992, American Democracy, 1993, Problematik der Menschenrechte, 1995, Briefe aus Amerika, 1995, Begriff des Rechts, 1997, Deutschland 1999, 1999, Deutschland: besser und schöner, 2001, Amerikas Schuldgefuehl, 2005, Schuld und Schulden, 2006; editor: Essays on the American Constitution, 1964. Mem.: Acad. Human Rights, Phi Beta Kappa. Lutheran. Died May 19, 2006.

DIGNAM, WILLIAM JOSEPH, retired obstetrician; b. Manchester, NH, Aug. 11, 1920; s. Walter Joseph and Margaret Veronica (Lowe) D.; m. Winifred Kennedy, June 7, 1947; children— Mary Brett, Kevan Jean, Erin Margaret, Meighan Ann AB, Dartmouth Coll., 1941; MD, Harvard U., 1943. Intern Boston City Hosp., 1944; resident in ob-gyn U. Kans. Med. Ctr., Kansas City, 1947-50; instr. U. Calif., San Francisco, 1950—53; asst. prof. obstetrics & gynecology UCLA, 1953—59, assoc. prof., 1959—66, prof., 1966—91, prof. emeritus, 1991—2006. Affiliated with UCLA Med. Ctr., Cedars-Sinai Med. Ctr., Harbor-UCLA Med. Ctr. Roman Catholic. Home: Pacific Palisades, Calif. Died Dec. 5, 2006.

DILAURA, EUGENE LEWIS, JR., accounting consultant; b. Albion, NY, Nov. 4, 1911; s. Giovanni and Euegenia (Belli) DiL.; m. Jean Marie D'Orazio, May 28, 1938; children: John, David, Paul. Student in acctg. and banking. With Nat. Bank of Detroit, 1933-42; with gen. acctg. staff Bunding Tubing Co., Detroit, 1942-44, supr. cost dept., 1944-60, supr. salary and payroll, benefits adminstr., 1960-70, divisional acct. Mt. Clemens, Mich., 1971-76; cons. East Detroit, Mich., from 1976. Mem. Nat. Assn. Tax Preparers. Clubs: Fathers (pres.); Royal Wing (Detroit) (treas. 1948-56). Roman Catholic. Avocations: golf, reading. Home: East Detroit, Mich. Died Oct. 11, 2006.

DILL, CHARLES WILLIAM, food science educator, researcher; b. Greenville, SC, June 1, 1932; s. William Ralph and Eunice (Few) D.; m. Shirley Lee Roberts; children: Charles Jr., Kevin, Susan. BS, Berea Coll., Ky., 1954; MS, N.C. State U., 1957, PhD, 1962. Instr. N.C. State U., Raleigh, 1959-62; asst. prof. U. Nebr., Lincoln, 1962-66; from assoc. prof. to prof. food sci. Tex. A&M U., College Station, from 1966. Grantee Nat. Inst. Child Health and Human Devel. Presbyterian. Avocation: woodworking. Home: Bryan, Tex. Died Apr. 11, 2007.

DILLEY, JOSEPH WILLIAM, educator; b. Pocatello, Idaho, Nov. 14, 1939; s. Joseph Campbell and Agnes Cynthia (George) D.; m. Barbara Grace Walsh, Apr. 6, 1974; children— Barbara Corlin, Joseph Campbell, George Charles Clyde. B.S., Coll. of Idaho, 1963; cert. in spl. edn. U. Oreg., 1965; postgrad. U. Guam, U. Idaho, U. Mont., U. Alaska, 1965-83. Cert. secondary sch. tchr., Alaska; spl. edn. tchr., Oreg. Constrn. worker Morrison Knudsen, Hells Canyon, Oreg., 1960-61; tchr. sci. Nampa (Idaho) Pub. Schs., 1963-65; tchr. spl. edn. Ontario (Oreg.) Pub. Schs., 1965-69; tchr. spl. edn. and sci., adminstrv. asst. dept. edn. Govt. of Guam, Agana, 1969-75; dist.-wide work study coord. spl. edn., tchr. sci. and ceramics, dir. student activities Soldotna (Alaska) High Sch., 1980-90; tchr. earth, phys. sci., sci. dept. chmn. Skyview High Sch., Soldotna, 1990—, Kenai Peninsula Borough Sch. Dist., 1974—; prin. Alaska Recreational Rentals, Soldotna. Bd. dirs. Kenai Peninsula Mental Health Clinic, 1979-80, Frontier Tng. Ctr., Soldotna, 1991—. Served with Army N.G., 1957-63. Mem. Am. Fedn. Tchrs. (del. nat. conv. 1980), Kenai Peninsula Fedn. Tchrs. (pres. 1990-92), Am. Pers. and Guidance Assn. Republican. Lutheran. Lodge: Elks. Co-author ednl. curriculum for handicapped young adults Kenai Peninsula Borough Sch. Dist., 1975-76; community coll. curriculum for Treasure Valley Community Coll., Ontario, 1966. Home: Soldotna, Alaska. Died Oct. 25, 2006.

DILLIN, S. HUGH, federal judge; b. Petersburg, Ind., June 9, 1914; s. Samuel E. and Maude (Harrell) D.; m. Mary Eloise Humphreys, Nov. 24, 1940; 1 child, Patricia Wright. AB in Govt, Ind. U., 1936, LLB, 1938, LLD, 1992; D of Civil Law (hon.), Ind. State U., 1990. Bar: Ind. 1938. Ptnr. Dillin & Dillin, Petersburg, 1938-61; U.S. dist. judge So. Dist. Ind., from 1961, chief judge, 1982-84. Mem. Jud. Conf. U.S., 1979-82, mem. exec. com., 1980-82, mem. Jud. Conf. Com. on Ct. Adminstrn., 1983-89, chmn. subcom. on fed.-state rels., 1983-89; mem. Jud. Panel on Multidist. Litigation, 1983-92; sec. Pub. Svc. Commn. Ind., 1942; mem. Interstate Oil Compact Commn., 1949-52, 61. Mem. Ind. Ho. of Reps. from Pike and Knox Counties, 1937, 39, 41, 51, floor leader, 1951; mem. Ind. Senate from Pike and Gibson Counties, 1959-61, pres. pro tem, 1961. Capt. AUS, 1943-46. Recipient Disting. Alumnus award Ind. U. Coll. Arts and Scis., 1985, Ind. U. Sch. Law, 1987, 2001 Am. Inns of Ct. Professionalism award in the 7th Cir. Mem. Am. Bar Assn., Ind. State Bar Assn., Fed. Bar Assn., 7th Cir. Judges Assn. (pres. 1977-79), Am. Judicature Soc., Delta Tau Delta, Phi Delta Phi. Clubs: Indianapolis Athletic. Democrat. Presbyterian. Home: Cambridge, Mass. Died Mar. 13, 2006.

DINOSO, VICENTE PESCADOR, JR., physician, educator; b. San Marcelino, Philippines, Oct. 17, 1936; came to U.S., 1961, naturalized, 1973; s. Vicente Dinoso and Eugenia Corpus (Pescador) D.; m. Alice M. Dinoso, June 19, 1965; children: Vincent, David. BS, U. Philippines, 1955, MD, 1960. Intern Mt. Sinai Hosp., Hartford, Conn., 1961-62; resident St. Mary's Hosp., Waterbury, Conn., 1962-64, Lahey Clinic Found., Boston, 1964-65; research fellow Temple U. Sch. Medicine, Phila., 1965-66, 68-69, instr. medicine, 1969-72, asst. prof., 1972-74; assoc. prof. medicine Hahnemann U. Sch. Medicine, Phila., 1974-78, prof. medicine, assoc. prof. physiology, 1978—93. Practice medicine specializing in gastroenterology, 1969—93 Co-editor: Gastrointestinal Emergencies, 1976; contbr. articles to med. jours. Mem. Am. Gastroenterol. Assn., Am. Physiol. Soc., Am. Fedn. for Clin. Research, AAAS, Sigma Xi. Republican. Home: Blue Bell, Pa. Died Jan. 13, 2007.

DIOTTE, ALFRED PETER, investment executive, consultant; b. Newport, NH, Apr. 16, 1925; s. J. Alfred and Mary Ellen (Perry) D.; m. Helen M. Foote, June 12, 1948; children: Cathy, Cere, Peter. BS, Marquette U., 1950; JD, U. Wis., 1953, MBA, 1979; postgrad., Harvard U., 1961. Bar: Wis. 1953. Ptnr. Fett, Murphy & Diotte, Janesville, 1953-54; with Parker Pen Co., Janesville, 1954-86, asst. sec., asst. to exec. v.p., 1957-59, asst. sec., gen. counsel, 1959-62, corp. sec., gen. counsel, 1962-68, v.p. adminstrn., sec., 1968-77, exec. v.p. adminstrn., 1977-83, sr. v.p. adminstrn., 1983-86, ret., 1986; pres. DOTT Assocs., Janesville, from 1986. Bd. dirs. M&I Bank, Janesville. With U.S. Navy Air Corps, 1943-47. Mem. ABA, Wis. Bar Assn., Rock County Bar Assn. Died Dec. 18, 2005.

DI SALVO, NICHOLAS ARMAND, dental educator, orthodontist; b. NYC, Nov. 2, 1920; s. Frank and Mary (Ruberto) DiS.; m. Pauline Rose Pluta, June 2, 1945; children— Allan, Donald BS, CCNY, 1942; D.D.S., Columbia U., 1945, PhD in Physiology, 1952, cert. in orthodontics, 1957. Diplomate Am. Bd. Orthodontics. Fellow Inst. Dental Research, Columbia U., 1950-52; instr. physiology Coll. Physicians and Surgeons, Columbia U., 1948-51, asst. prof. physiology, 1952-57, assoc., 1957-58, prof. dentistry, 1958-87, dir. orthodontics, 1957-87, prof. emeritus dentistry, from 1987; attending dentist Presbyterian Hosp., NYC, 1975-87, cons. emeritus dentistry, from 1987. Cons. N.Y. State Dept. Health, 1970—, VA, N.Y.C., 1975, Project/HOPE/Egypt, Alexandria and Cairo, 1976, Nat. Def. Med. Ctr., Taipei, Taiwan, 1982 Contbg. editor book chpts. Contbr. articles to profl. jours. Pres., Hartsdale-Fels Civic Assn., 1960-66. Served to lt. USNR, 1945-50 Recipient Disting. Service award Orthodontic Alumni Soc. Columbia U., 1973; fellow 8th Inst. Advanced Edn. in Dental Research Mem. Am. Assn. Orthodontists (del. 1970-76), Northeastern Soc. Orthodontists (pres. 1974-75, Disting. Svc. award 1995), Angle Soc. of Orthodontists (pres. 1977-79), Internat. Soc. Craniofacial Biology (pres. 1965-66). Republican. Roman Catholic. Died June 8, 2007.

DITTERT, J. LEE, JR., lawyer; b. Houston, Sept. 22, 1931; s. J. Lee and Hazel Lenore (Young) D.; m. Dinah Lee VanSandt, July 10, 1955; children: Theresa Ann, Diana Lynn, Christopher Lee, Johanna Marie. BA, U. Tex., 1952, LL.B., 1957. Bar: Tex. 1957. Since practiced in, Bellville; co-owner, mng. ptnr. radio Sta. KACO, Bellville, Tex., 1974-90; Land title examiner Bellville (Tex.) Abstract Co., Stewart Title Co., from 1959, Chgo. Title Co., 1974-86; Lawyers Title Ins. Corp., 1986; county judge Austin County, Bellville, 1967-74, 89-94; chmn. Austin County Juvenile Bd., 1989-94. County atty. Austin County, 1979-81 Pres. Silver Spurs Svc. Orgn., U. Tex., 1955-56, Bellville Indsl. Found., 1961-71, 78—; pres. Bellville Little League, 1970, mgr., 1971-77; mem. exec. com. Houston-Galveston Area Coun., projects rev. chmn., 1972, 91, sec., treas., 1973, 92, v.p., 1993, pres. 1994; state del. to Dem. Conv., 1968; trustee Bellville Hosp. Authority, 1975-81, chmn., 1980. Served to lt. comdr. USNR, 1954-66, Korea. Named Citizen of Yr., Bellville Lions Club, 1989. Mem. ABA, Austin County Bar Assn. (pres. 1970-71, sec. 1977-78, 91-92), State Bar of Tex. (grievance com. 1986-88), AC Farm Bur., Ex-Students Assn. UT at Austin, Bellville C. of C., VFW, Am. Legion, Phi Delta Phi, Lions, Golf Club, Lions (pres., v.p., sec., dir., tail twister Bellville Club, Bellville Citizen of Yr 1990, Melvin Jones fellow 1993, chair zone III-A 1995-96, region III 1996-97, tail twister dist. 2-S5 mid winter confs., Columbus and Brenham, dist. convention, Seguin; named King of Tail Twisters 1995). Episcopalian (mem. diocesan constn., canons com. 1965-70, layreader, vestryman, sr. warden, treas. Diocese conf. del.). Died Nov. 3, 2006.

DITTMANN, ALBERT STEPHEN, JR., lawyer; b. New Orleans, June 4, 1941; s. Albert Stephen (dec.) and Dorothy Anna (Duclos) D.; m. Marilyn I. Vidacovich, Aug. 1, 1964; children: Todd Albert, Scott Stephen. BA, Loyola U., New Orleans, 1963, JD, 1966. Bar: La. 1966, U.S. Dist. Ct. (ea. dist.) La. 1966, (mid. and we. dists.) La. 1988, U.S. Supreme Ct. 1980. Atty. Landrieu, Calogero & Kronlage and Kronlage and Dittmann), New Orleans, 1966-81; pvt. practice Albert S. Dittmann, Jr., P.C., New Orleans, 1981; assoc Adams and Reese, New Orleans, 1982-85, ptnr., from 1985. Rep. United Way, New Orleans, 1970; elected mem. Orleans Parish Dem. Com., New Orleans, 1972-76; pres., bd. dirs. Goodwill Industries, New Orleans, 1977-78. Capt. USAR, 1969. Mem. ABA, La. State Bar Assn., New Orleans Bar Assn., La. Def. Attys. Assn., Jesuit High Sch. Alumni Assn. (pres. 1988-89), Valencia, Inc. Club (pres., bd. trustees 1985). Roman Catholic. Home: New Orleans, La. Died Dec. 25, 2006.

DITTMAR, ROBERT L., state senator, retired army officer; b. Fayette County, W.Va., Dec. 18, 1931; m. Mary Dittmar; children: Robb, Demetria. Student, W.Va. Inst. Tech. Mem. W.Va. Senate, Charleston, from 1989. Mem. agr. com., banking and ins. com., judiciary com., mil. com., natural resources com., transp. com. Bd. dirs. Jackson Gen. Hosp.; mem. Jackson County Devel. Authority; mem. Ravenswood (W.Va.) City Coun.; recorder City of Ravenswood, mayor. Named Ky. col. Mem. VFW, NRA, American Legion, Masons, Shriners. Democrat. Methodist. Died May 25, 2006.

DIXON, FITZ EUGENE, JR., professional sports team executive; b. Winter Harbor, Maine, Aug. 14, 1923; s. Fitz Eugene and Eleanor Elkins (Widener) D.; m. Edith B. Robb, June 5, 1952; children: George Widener, Edith Eleanor. Student, Harvard U., 1942-43; LHD (hon.), Pa. Mil. Coll., Lafayette Coll., Hahnemann Med. Coll., Cabrini Coll., Pa. Coll. Podiatric Medicine; LLD (hon.), Widener Coll., Chestnut Hill Coll.; DPub Service (hon.), Temple U.; ScD (hon.), Spring Garden Coll.; LLD (hon.), U. Pa.; LittD (hon.), Drexel U. Ptnr. Phila. Phillies Baseball Team. Life trustee Phila. Free Library, 1974-2006; former pres. Fairmount Park Commn.; trustee Abington (Pa.) Meml. Hosp., 1944-2006, sec. bd., 1947-53, v.p., 1953-68, chmn. bd., 1968-74; chmn. bd. govs. State System Higher Edn.; bd. dirs. Devon Horse Show; trustee Ellis Fund Adv. Com., Newtown, Pa., Episcopal Acad., Merion, Pa., 1961-2006, chmn. bd., 1972-75; trustee Maine Coast Meml. Hosp., Ellsworth, 1951-2006, chmn. bd., 1971-75, hon. chmn. bd., 1975-2006; trustee Phila. Mus. Art, 1979-2006; trustee emeritus Woodlynde Sch.; mgr. emeritus Germantown Hosp. and Med. Ctr.; pres. Soc. of Four Arts, Palm Beach, Fla., Widener Meml. Found. in Aid of Handicapped Children; hon. life trustee Temple U.; chmn. bd. govs. Temple U. Hosp., 1975-77; chmn. bd. Widener U., 1972-2006; co-chmn. American Gold Cup, 1973-2006; hon. trustee Winter Harbor Pub. Library, Nat. Mus. Racing; mem. Phila. Internat. City Coordinating Com., 1979-2006; hon. life dir. U.S. Equestrian Team. Mem. Nat. Steeplechase Assn. (life, past pres.), Am. Horse Show Assn. (life), U.S. Dressage Fedn., Am. Grand Prix Assn. (dir.), Phila. Soc. Promotion Agr., Pa. Hist. Soc., Soc. War of 1812, Phila. Hist. Preservation Corp., Soc. Colonial Wars, Swedish Colonial Soc., Navy League U.S., Maine Maritime Mus., Nat. Trust Hist. Preservation, Pa. Horse Breeders Assn., Inc., Pa. Soc., Thoroughbred Owners and Breeders Assn.,

Winterthur Mus. and Gardens, Hosp. Assn. Pa., Palm Beach Civic Assn., Preservation Found. Palm Beach, Am. Mus. Britain, Henry Morrison Flagler Mus. Clubs: Athenaeum, Phila., Corinthian Yacht, Phila., Phila. Racquet, Union League (Phila.), Gov.'s of the Palm Beaches; Palm Beach (Fla.) Everglades, Palm Beach Polo & Country, Bath and Tennis, Jockey, Key Largo (Fla.) Anglers, Sunnybrook Golf, Whitemarsh Valley Country, Winter Harbor Yacht (treas. 1948-2006), Bal Harbour (Fla.), Delray Beach Yacht (Fla.), Farmers of Pa., N.Y. Yacht, Marquis Soc. of Lafayette Coll., St. James's Club (London), Pyramid Club (bd. govs.). Episcopalian. Home: Lafayette Hill, Pa. Died Aug. 2, 2006.*

D'LAURO, FRANK ANDREW, JR., real estate development executive; b. Phila., Nov. 11, 1940; s. Frank Andrew and Dorothy (Adams) D'L. BA, Washington and Lee U., 1962; MArch, U. Pa., 1965. Architect FKWP, Phila., 1967-68; project mgr., exec. v.p., pres. Frank A. D'Lauro Co., Phila., from 1968; pres. D'Lauro Devel. Corp., Phila., from 1974, D'Lauro Corp., Phila., from 1979. Chmn. Montgomery County Young Rep. Fedn., 1970-72; mem. Montgomery County Rep. Fin. Com., 1972—; chmn. Worcester Twp. Planning Commn., 1990—; bd. dirs. Young Reps. of Pa., 1972-74; chmn. Montgomery County Housing Authority, 1976-92; bd. dirs., v.p. Big Bros. Assn. Phila., pres., 1972—; bd. dirs. Sacred Heart Hosp., 1980-94. Capt. U.S. Army, 1965-67, Vietnam. Decorated Bronze Star with oak leaf cluster, Soldiers medal; recipient award of merit Big Bros. Phila., 1972. Mem. Pa. Soc. Sons Revolution, Sigma Nu. Clubs: Union League, Racquet Philadelphia Cricket (Phila.). Home: Fairview Vlg, Pa. Died Feb. 10, 2007.

DOBBINS, GEORGE, JR., maintenance and pest control company executive; b. Hernando, Miss., Aug. 14, 1940; s. George and Eddye Joy (William) D.; m. Jean E. Gordon, Aug. 13, 1966; children— Alondas, Ashley. B.S., Miss. Indsl. Coll., 1965; postgrad. U. Tenn. Head football coach Hernando High Sch. (Miss.), 1965-70; stock broker Investor Diversified Co., 1970-73; spl. account rep. 3M Co., 1973-80; pres. Dobbins & Co., Memphis, 1980—. Mem. Memphis and Shelby County Planning Commn., 1974-79, chmn., 1978; cons. City Beautiful Commn., Memphis, 1982; mem. polit. selection com. Shelby County Republican Com., 1979—; mem. Shelby County Port Commn., Memphis, 1983. Named Sales Person of South Region, IDS Brokers, 1972. Mem. Nat. Maintenance Assn., C. of C., New South Media (bd. dirs.), Nat. Assn. Security Dirs. Baptist. Club: Kiwanis. Home: Memphis, Tenn. Died Oct. 13, 2006.

DODGE, CLEVELAND EARL, JR., retired manufacturing executive, director; b. NYC, Mar. 7, 1922; s. Cleveland Earl and Pauline (Morgan) D.; m. Phyllis Boushall, Dec. 19, 1942 (dec. Jan. 2004); children: Alice Berkeley, Sally Mole, Cleveland Earl III. BS in Mech. Engring., Princeton U., 1943; D in Humanics, Springfield Coll., 1996. With DeLaval Steam Turbine Co., 1942, GE, 1946-51; v.p., dir. Warren Wire Co., Pownal, Vt., 1951-55; pres., dir. Dodge Industries, Inc., Hoosick Falls, NY, 1955-67; v.p., dir. Engineered Yarns, Inc., 1962-68; pres., dir. Circuit Materials Corp., 1962-68; pres., treas., dir. Internat. Dodge, Inc., 1968—2005; pres., dir. Dodge Machine Co., 1968—2005; pres., bd. dirs. Alta Energy Corp., 1980-89, Amex Plastics Inc., 1972-74, Am. Hydride Corp., 1991—2005; ret., 2005. Bd. dirs. Display Sys., Inc., Imetrix Corp., Internat. Dodge, Inc., Cleeland Corp., Am. Hydride Corp., Dodge Machine Co., Inc., Wild Goose Island Corp., Imetrix, Inc.; bd. dirs. emeritus Phelps Dodge Corp., Atlantic Mut. Ins., Key Bank. Patentee in field. Chmn., bd. dirs. Cleveland H. Dodge Found.; vice chmn. emeritus YMCA Retirement Fund; bd. dirs. emeritus Springfield Coll., Bennington Mus., Antique Boat Mus., Brisbee Coun. on Arts and Humanities, Silver City Mus., YMCA Retirement Fund. Lt. USNR, 1943-45. Mem. Princeton Engring. Assn., Princeton Rowing Assn., Laurentian Lodge (Shawbridge, Que., Can.), Taconic Golf Club (Williamstown, Mass.), Kiwanis. Congregationalist. Avocations: skiing, golf, travel. Home: Pownal, Vt. Died Jan. 28, 2007.

DODGE, EARL FARWELL, foundation administrator; b. Malden, Mass., Dec. 24, 1932; s. Earl Farwell Dodge and Dorothy Mae (Harris) Hook; m. Barbara V. Dodge, July 20, 1951; children: Earl F., Barbara F., Allen C., Faith D., Karen J., Calvin G., Michael R. Student pub. schs., Malden; grad., Narcotic Edn. Inst., Evanston, Ill. Nat. chmn. Prohibition Nat. Com., Denver, 1957—63; exec. dir. Colo. Alcohol Drug Edn. Inc., Denver. Sec.-treas. Nat. Prohibition Found., Denver; treas. Nat. Temperance and Prohibition Coun., Denver Editor: Nat. Statesman, The Colo. Challenge, Dodge Family Jour. Mem. Community Relations Bd., Kalamazoo, Mich., 1968-71; sec.-treas. Right to Life Edn. Fund, Denver; pres. Nat. Civic League Inc., Denver; candidate for various offices on Prohibition ticket, including pres. of U.S., 1984, 88, 92; deacon Arvada Bapt. Ch. Recipient Good Govt. award Good Govt. Assn. Kalamazoo, 1971, 78; Friend of Life award Colo. Right to Life Com., Denver, 1981. Mem. SAR (pres. Colo. soc. 1987-88). Mem. Prohibition Party. Avocation: collecting polit. memorabilia. Home: Lakewood, Colo. Died Nov. 7, 2007.*

DOENGES, BYRON FREDERICK, former government official, finance educator; b. Ft. Wayne, Ind., June 18, 1922; s. Arthur Philip and Elsie (Mesing) D.; m. Elaine Aiken, June 15, 1947. Diploma, Internat. Bus. Coll., 1941; student, DePauw U., 1943—44; AB, Franklin Coll., Ind., 1946; MBA, Ind. U., 1948, PhD, 1962; LittD (hon.), Franklin Coll. of Ind., 1985. Instr., headmaster boarding dept. Punahou Sr. Acad., Honolulu, 1948-50; dir. scholarships and loans Ind. U., Bloomington, 1951-56, asst. dean Coll. Arts and Scis., 1955-65; prof. econs., dean Coll. Liberal Arts Willamette U., 1965-71; econ. cons. Gov. Oreg., 1971-72; dep. asst. dir. ACDA, Washington, 1972-73, chief econs. and spl. studies divsn., 1973-76; sr. econs. advisor U.S. Arms Control and Disarmament Agy., 1976-93; ind. writer and internat. econ. cons., from 1993. Program devel. head Title II NDEA, U.S. Office Edn., Washington, 1958-59; assoc. dir. Salzburg (Austria) Seminar Am. Studies, 1962-64; mem. Higher Commn. N.W. Assn. Secondary and Higher Schs., 1968-71; mem. exec. bd. N.W. Assn. Pvt. Colls. and Univs., 1969-70; chmn. planning com. Navy V-12 Nat. Colloquium, 1989; conduct spl. rsch. on internat. capital movements, econs. higher edn., econs. arms control, Soviet and successor states to former Soviet Union economies, econ. impact of def. spending. Editor: Accountability, 1973, World Military Expenditures and Arms Transfers, 1981-84, Arms Control Ann. Report, 1981-91, Arms Control Impact Statement for the Congress, 1991; contbr. articles to profl. jours. Lt. comdr. USNR, 1943-46, PTO. Recipient alumni citation Franklin Coll., 1977. Mem. Am. Econ. Assn., Cosmos Club (Washington), Lambda Chi Alpha (mem. nat. fellowship bd. 1965-2000, Meritorious Svc. award 1984), Pi Gamma Mu, Omicron Delta Kappa. Home: Pittsboro, NC. Died May 26, 2006.

DOHERTY, ALFRED EDWARD, engineer, consultant; b. Shaker Heights, Ohio, Nov. 11, 1929; s. Alfred Edward and Florence (Pylick) D.; m. Jeannette Smith, Dec. 31, 1931 (dec. Feb. 1981); children: James Edward, Thomas Vincent, George Michael; m. Virginia Dolores Meza. BS, Calif. Coast U., 1987. Registered profl. engr.; cert. mech. engr. Methods devel. Douglas Aircraft Co., Torrance, Calif., 1954-59; mgr. advanced materials Aerojet Gen. Corp., Downey, Calif., 1959-69; v.p. Electro-Form, Inc., Ft. Worth, 1969-78; pres. A&T Engring., A&T Mfg., Ft. Worth, 1978-84; plant mgr. Leland Southwest, Ft. Worth, 1984-87; v.p. and gen. mgr. formed products Explosive Fabricators, Inc., Louisville, Colo., from 1987. Contbr. technical papers to profl. jours.; patentee in field. Sgt. U.S. Army, 1948-54, Korea. Mem. Soc. Mech. Engrs., Elks. Lutheran. Avocations: golf, fishing, woodworking. Home: Fort Worth, Tex. Died June 20, 2006.

DOHERTY, THOMAS ANTHONY, banker; b. Bklyn., Jan. 20, 1938; s. Joseph William and Gertrude Mary (Haggerty) D.; m. Marianne T. Hoffman, July 20, 1960; children— Arlene, Karen, Bryan, Linda BS in Fin., Fordham U., 1959; postgrad. in bus., NYU, 1962-63. Exec. trainee Chase Manhattan Bank, NYC, 1960-64; v.p. Franklin Nat. Bank, Franklin Square, N.Y., 1964-71; pres., chief exec. officer, dir. Bank Suffolk County, Hauppauge, N.Y., 1971-81, Norstar Bank L.I., Garden City, N.Y., 1982-87, pres., chmn., chief exec. officer, from 1987. Dir., chmn. transp. com. L.I. Assocs., Commack, N.Y. Bd. dirs. Arthritis Found. Recipient Disting. Citizens award Suffolk County council Boy Scouts Am., Man of Yr. award Am. Cancer Soc., 2d annual award Episcopal Health Services, 1988. Mem. Soc. of Friendly Sons of St. Patrick Clubs: Nissequoque Country (St. James, N.Y.). Roman Catholic. Avocations: golf; tennis. Home: Cold Spring Harbor, NY. Died Apr. 7, 2007.

DOLAN, RONALD VINCENT, insurance company executive; b. Charleroi, Pa., Aug. 27, 1942; s. James L. and Kathryn (Stopp) D.; m. MaryJane Tousignant, 1978; children: Gina, Ronalee, Mark, Craig, Samantha. BA, St. Vincent Coll., Latrobe, Pa., 1964. Mgr. El Bent Supply, Pa., 1964-67; actuarial assoc. Penn Mut. Ins., Phila., 1967-72; pres., chief exec. officer First Colony Life, Lynchburg, Va., from 1973, also bd. dirs. Bd. dirs. Ctrl. Fidelity Bank, Richmond, Va., Am. Mayflower Life, N.Y., Ethyl Corp., 1st Colony Corp. Chmn. Ctrl. Va. C.C. Found.; bd. dirs. Randolph Macon Women's Coll., United Way of Ctrl. Va. Mem. Soc. Actuaries (assoc.), Am. Acad. Actuaries. Home: Wingina, Va. Died Nov. 14, 2005.

DOLAN, WILLIAM MARK, retired newspaper executive; b. Ely, Nev., Apr. 2, 1923; s. Mark and Muriel (Fletcher) D.; m. Dorothy Fendrich, Nov. 5, 1945; children: Susan Jeanne, Lowrey Trent. BA in Journalism, U. Nev., 1950. Prin. Cherry Creek (Nev.) Sch., 1950-54; reporter, photo editor Nev. Appeal, Carson City, 1957-60, advt. mgr., 1962-66; editor Nev. Graphic Mag., Carson City, 1965-69, Carson Chronicle, 1970-85. Bus. editor Nev. Appeal, 1976-86, entertainment editor, 1970-85. Mem. Carson City Fourth of July Com., 1978-85, Nev. 125th Anniversary Commn., 1989-91; bd. dirs. Nev. Day Com., Carson City, 1970-91. With AUS, 1942-45, ETO; pres. Nev. Landmarks Soc., Carson City, 1990-92. Mem. Nat. Press Assn. (Silver Rule award 1987), Lions (pres. 1960-62, editor and pub. dist. 4-N newspaper 1989-93), Elks, Toastmasters (area gov. 1959-61), Sigma Delta Chi. Home: Carson City, Nev. Died Oct. 12, 2006.

DOMBAR, BENJAMIN, architect; b. North Vernon, Ind., Sept. 3, 1916; s. Joseph and Ida (Tobis) D.; m. Shirley Sloam, Aug. 23, 1942; children: Taaron Dombar Makrauer, Rockell Dombar Meese, Janisan Dombar Slaughter. Designer, draftsmen Carl A. Strauss AIA, Cin., 1945-48; prin. Benjamin Dombar AIA & Assocs., Cin., from 1948. Asst. editor Ohio Architect mag., 1955-58; prin. works exhibited including Cin. Modern Art Soc. (Good Citizenship award 1969), Contemporary Art Soc. (Best Lighted Room award N.Am. Illuminating Engrs. Soc. 1958), Clifton Town Meeting, Warren County Hist. Soc. Arbitrator Am. Arbitration Assn., Cin., 1969—; past pres. Cin. Archtl. Soc., 1950-52. Tech. sgt. U.S. Army 1942-45. Frank Llyod Wright Taliesin fellow 1934-41. Mem. AIA (pres. Cin. chpt. 1950-52), Architects Soc. Ohio, Nat. Counc. Architect Registration Bd., Guild for Religious Architecture. Home: Cincinnati, Ohio. Died Oct. 3, 2006.

DONALDSON, ROBERT BRUCE, oil company executive; b. Balt., Mar. 27, 1932; s. Lennox Bruce and Gladys Sydelle (Durham) D.; m. Betty Ellen Roy, June 10, 1955; children— Debborah Leigh Cantrell, Grant Bruce. B.B.A., U. Ga., 1957. Warehouse mgr. Ofcl. Products Co., Atlanta, 1955-57; account exec. mktg. Gulf Oil Corp., Houston, 1959-85, Gulf Products div. BP Oil, Inc., Cleve., 1985—; vital source speaker Gulf Oil Corp., Birmingham, Ala., 1979-82; mem. speakers bur. Ala. Petroleum Council, Birmingham, 1979-82. Advisor Vulcan Dist. Boy Scouts Am., 1975. Served to 1st lt. U.S. Army, 1957-59. Republican. Baptist. Club: Civitan (Birmingham) (pres. 1973-74, lt. gov. 1974). Avocations: swimming; fishing; painting. Home: Hattiesburg, Miss. Died Feb. 8, 2007.

DONALDSON, WILLIAM FIELDING, JR., orthopedic surgeon; b. May 12, 1921; s. William Fielding and Isabel (McGranahan) D.; m. Jean Marguerite Waechter, Jan. 21, 1946; children— Susan, Anne, William Fielding, Nancy BS, U. Pitts., 1942, MD, 1943. Diplomate Am. Bd. Orthopedic Surgery. Intern St. Francis Gen. Hosp., Pitts., 1944; resident orthopaedic surgery VA Hosp., Anspinwall, Pa., 1946-49, Children's Hosp., Pitts., 1949-50; Gibney fellow in scoliosis Hosp. Spl. Surgery, NYC, 1952-53; sr. staff mem. emeritus Presbyn.-Univ. Hosp., Pitts., from 1951; sr. staff mem., med. dir. Children's Hosp. Pitts., 1951-93, emeritus, 1994, bd. trustees, from 1981; sr. staff mem. emeritus St. Margaret Meml. Hosp., Pitts., 1964-70; attending cons. VA Hosp., Pitts., from 1970; mem. countesy staff St. Francis Gen. Hosp., 1961-86, mem. emeritus staff, 1990; mem. countesy staff Shadyside Hosp., from 1961; practice medicine specializing in orthopedic surgery Pitts.; prof. emeritus. Clin. instr. U. Pitts., 1951-58, asst. prof., 1958-62, clin. assoc. prof., 1962-67, clin. prof., 1967—, bd. trustees, 1981-87, trustee emeritus, 1989—; mem. Coordinating Council Med. Edn., 1978-80; cons. grad. med. edn. Nat. Adv. Com. to Sec. HEW, 1975-80; pres. Adv. Council for Orthopedic Resident Edn.; mem. Nat. Commn. on Arthritis and Related Musculoskeletal Diseases, 1975-77; orthopaedic adv. bd. chmn. Shriners Hosp. Crippled Children, 1981-93, chmn. emeritus 1993—; mem. adv. com. Allegheny County chpt. Nat. Found. Mar. of Dimes, 1968; mem. search com. for dir. Allegheny County health Dept., 1969; mem. health adv. council Community Action Pitts., 1965; bd. dirs. Western Pa. Comprehensive Health Planning Agy., 1960-77; 2d vice chmn. Hosp. Council Western Pa., 1974-77; bd. dirs. Hosp. Utilization Project, 1970, many others Contbr. articles to profl. jours. Served with USN, 1944-46 Recipient Frederick M. Jacob Physician's Merit award Allegheny County Med. Soc., 1976, Man of Yr. award Pitts. Acad. Medicine, 1977 Mem. ABA (com. on med. profl. liability 1976-80), Council Med. Splty. Socs. (rep. of ACS), Am. Acad. Orthopedic Surgeons (dir. 1970-79, pres. 1975-76), ACS (bd. regents 1976-85, v.p.-elect, v.p. 1986-87), AMA, Am. Orthopedic Assn., Am. Rheumatism Assn., Pan Pacific Surg. Assn. (v.p. 1975), Rocky Mountain Traumatologic Soc. (pres. 1986), Pa. Med. Soc. (ho. of dels. 1964-70, pres. 1987-88), Pa. Orthopedic Soc. (pres. 1961-62), Allegheny County Med. Soc. (pres. 1970), Am. Assn. Surgery of Trauma, Assn. Bone and Joint Surgeons (hon.), Can. Orthopedic Assn., Central Surg. Assn., New Eng. Orthopedic Soc., N.Y. Acad. Sci., Pediatric Soc., Scoliosis Research Soc., Soc. Research in Hydrocephalus and Spina Bifida, S.C. Orthopedic Soc. (hon.), Pitts. Acad. Medicine, Pitts. Pediatric Soc., Pitts. Surg. Soc., Pitts. Rheumatism Assn. Republican. Presbyterian. Died Nov. 22, 2006.

DONAVAN, GEORGE EDGAR, retired banker; b. Jackson, Miss., Feb. 23, 1916; s. George Edgar and Annie Mivian (Nelson) D.; m. Katie Bell Holmes, Dec. 3, 1938; children— George Edgar III, Carl Howard. Student, Miss. State U., 1933-34; BSc, U. Miss., 1937. With Lamar Life Ins. Co., Jackson, 1937-42, Scharff & Jones, Inc. (investments), 1946-60; with 1st Nat. Bank, Jackson, 1960-74; v.p. Unifirst Fed Savs. & Loan Assn., Jackson, 1974-85, Unifirst Bank for Savs., Jackson, 1974-85; ret., 1985. Served with USNR, 1943-46. Mem. Omicron Delta Kappa, Pi Kappa Alpha. Clubs: Rotary (pres. Jackson 1972-73), Capital City, Petroleum, Jackson Country, University. Home: Jackson, Miss. Died Apr. 14, 2007.

DONEHUE, JOHN DOUGLAS, interdenominational ministries executive; b. Cramerton, NC, July 5, 1928; s. John Sidney and Annie (Shepherd) D.; m. Mary Phelps, Jan. 9, 1952 (dec. 1964); children: Teresa Jean, Marilyn Phelps; m. Sylvia Louise McKenzie, Feb. 11, 1966 (dec. Nov. 1971); children: Hayden Shepherd, John Douglas; m. Virginia Kirkland, June 28, 1975; children: Anne Mikell, Robertson Carr. Student, Am. Press Inst., Columbia U., 1965, 71-73; LHD (hon.), Charleston So. U., 1985. Sports editor Orangeburg Times and Dem., SC, 1948-50; polit reporter Montgomery Advertiser, Ala., 1954-55; sports editor Charleston News and Courier, SC, 1956, copy editor SC, 1958, state editor SC, 1959-62, city editor SC, 1962-68, mng. editor SC, 1968-71, promotion dir. SC, 1971-75, v.p. for corp. pub. rels. SC, 1975-96; v.p. corp. comm., adminstr. The Post and Courier Found., 1996—2006, pres., 2006—07; bd. dirs. Star Gospel Mission, Charleston, 1962-80, chmn. bd. dirs., 1980-96, exec. dir., 1996—2007. Faculty advisor Student Newspaper, Charleston So. U.; lectr.; spl. adviser comdt. 7th USCG dist. for establishment of dist.-wide pub. info. program, 1960-61; journalism lectr. Charleston So. U.; sec. 1st bd. founders, 1969. Author: Charleston on the Air, A History of Radio Broadcasting in Charleston, 2000; compiler: News and Courier Style Books, 1969; guest commentator Nat. Pub. Radio. Chmn. adv. bd. Salvation Army; chmn. regional adv. coun. S.C. Dept. Youth Svc.; chmn. planning bd. United Way; pres. Palmetto Safety Coun.; chmn. bd. Charleston County Libr. Found.; lay reader, vestryman, sr. warden Episc. Ch.; bd. dirs. Charleston Mus., S.C. Tricentennial Parade Com., 1972, S.C. Humanities Coun. With S.C., N.G., 1948—50 USAF, 1950—54 USMCR, 1955—56 USAR, 1956—59 USCGR, 1959—66, with USNR, 1966—75. Recipient Freedoms Found. award, 1969, S.C. Family of Yr. award, Am. Advt. Fedn., Silver Medal award, 1987, VA citation for meritorious svc., 1971, La Societe Francaise de Bienfaisance Humanitati medal of Honor, 2001, S.C. Order of the Palmetto, 1996, S.C. Gov.'s award for the humanities, 2005, Disting. Svc. award, S.C. Press Assn., 2006. Mem. John Ancrum Soc. of Soc. Prevention Cruelty to Animals, Carolina Art Assn., Internat. Newspaper Promotion Assn., S.C. Press Assn. (pres. 1985), Air Force Assn. (dir. Charleston coun.), Naval Civilian Mgrs. Assn., Navy league (v.p. Charleston coun.), Charleston Trident C. of C. (pres. 1983), Toastmasters Internat. (charter mem. Okinawa club), Okinawa Soc., Downtown Athletic Club, Pacific Stars and Stripes Alumni Assn. (bd. dirs.), Rotary Club (pres. 1974-75, Service Above Self award 2002). Achievements include only person to serve in all 5 branches of armed forces per Defence Department records. Home: Charleston, SC. Died Oct. 11, 2006.

DONLEY, JOHN P., state legislator, lawyer; b. Evergreen Park, Ill., Mar. 10, 1939; s. John and Dorothy Donley; m. Sandra Kay Smith, 1961; children: John, Amy, Matt, Grant. AA, George Washington U., 1957, BA, 1961; postgrad., Kans. U., 1961—63; JD, U. Colo., 1966. Counsel United Agrl. Products, Inc.; co-owner Greeley Recycling Inc.; asst. county atty. Weld County, Colo.; asst. mcpl. judge; asst. city prosecutor, mem. Colo. State Senate, from 1982. Mem.: Ducks Unlimited, Rotary, Omicron Delta Kappa, Sigma Xi. Republican. Presbyn. Died Feb. 10, 2007.

DONNELLY, JOHN JOSEPH, JR., other: health services; b. NYC, Feb. 12, 1927; s. John Joseph and Lillian Mary (Frazer) Donnelly; m. Margaret Mary Bollerman, Oct. 17, 1953; 1 child: John Jeffrey. BS, Rider Coll., 1950; cert. in acctg., NYU, 1956. Acctg. mgr. Statistic, Inc., Englewood, NJ, 1950—53; staff asst. to corp. controller Curtiss Wright Corp., Woodridge, NJ, 1953—63, gen. mgr. Cleve., 1963—66; group v.p., adminstr. Aeronca, Inc., Middletown, Ohio, 1966—72; v.p. fin. Am. Seating Co., Grand Rapids, Mich., 1972—80; v.p. corporate devel. Care Corp., Grand Rapids, from 1908. Pres. Thorn Apple River Assn., from 1984. Served USAF, 1945—46. Mem. Fin. Execs. Inst, Cascade Hills Country Club (dir. 1983-). Roman Catholic. Home: Sedona, Ariz. Died July 17, 2007.

DONNELLY, JOHN PATRICK, judge; b. Chelsea, Mass., Feb. 8, 1919; s. Stephen J. and Margaret M. (Gavin) D.; m. Hazel M. Fiske, Apr. 13, 1941; children— Dennis M., John Patrick, Margaret. Student Boston U., 1938-39; J.D., Suffolk U., 1943. Bar: Mass. 1943, U.S. Dist. Ct. Mass. 1946, U.S. Supreme Ct. 1948, U.S. Mil. Ct. Appeals 1952. Practice law, Malden, Mass., 1946-80; city solicitor, City of Malden, 1980; justice Commonwealth of Mass. Dist. Ct., Malden, 1980—; gen. counsel Mass. Mayors Assn., 1965-74. Alderman, City of Malden, 1955-57, mayor, 1959-60; trustee Malden Pub. Library, 1983—. Mem. Middlesex County Bar Assn. (pres. 1975, treas. 1975-80), Mass. Bar Assn. (bd. dels. 1974-75). Home: Malden, Mass. Died Mar. 15, 2007.

DONNEM, ROLAND WILLIAM, retired lawyer, real estate developer, health facility administrator; b. Seattle, Nov. 8, 1929; s. William Roland and Mary Louise (Hughes) D.; m. Sarah Brandon Lund, Feb. 18, 1961; children: Elizabeth Donnem Sigety, Sarah Madison. BA, Yale U., 1952; JD magna cum laude, Harvard U., 1957. Bar: NY 1958, U.S. Dist. Ct. (ea. and so. dists.) NY 1959, U.S. Ct. Appeals (2d cir.) 1959, U.S. Ct. Claims 1960, U.S. Tax Ct. 1960, U.S. Supreme Ct. 1963, U.S. Ct. Appeals (3d cir.) 1969, DC 1970, U.S. Ct. Appeals (DC cir.) 1970, Ohio 1976, U.S. Dist. Ct. (no. dist.) Ohio 1980, U.S. Ct. Appeals (7th cir.) 1980, U.S. Ct. Appeals (6th cir.) 1984. With Davis Polk & Wardwell, NYC, 1957-63, 64-69; law sec. appellate divsn. NY Supreme Ct., NYC, 1963-64; dir. policy planning antitrust divsn. Justice Dept., Washington, 1969-71; v.p., sec., gen. counsel Std. Brands Inc., NYC, 1971-76; from v.p. law to sr. v.p. law and casualty prevention Chessie Sys., Cleve., 1976-86; ptnr. Meta Ptnrs., real estate devel., 1984—2002, mng. ptnr., 1989—2002, registered security rep., 1985-90; gen. counsel Acorn Properties, Inc., Cleve., 1985—2002, pres., 1989—2002; gen. counsel Meta Devel. Corp., Cleve., 1985—2002, pres., 1989—2002; gen. counsel Meta Properties, Inc., Cleve., 1988—2002, pres., 1989—2002. Founding mem., bd. dirs. Assn. Sheraton Franchisees N.Am., 1997—2002. Mem. editl. bd. Harvard Law Rev., 1955-57. Bd. dirs., fin. v.p. Presbyn. Home for Aged Women, NYC, 1972-76; bd. dirs., treas. James Lenox Ho., Inc., 1972-76; trustee Food and Drug Law Inst., 1974-76; trustee, sec. Brick Presbyn. Ch., NYC, 1974-76; sec. class of 1952, Yale U., 1992-97; bd. dirs. Yale Alumni Fund, 1990-95; chmn. Cleve. Area Yale Campaign, 1991-97. Lt. (j.g.) USNR, 1952-54. Fellow Timothy Dwight Coll., Yale U., 1987-2007 Mem. Am. Law Inst. (life), Am. Arbitration Assn. (nat. panel arbitrators), Def. Orientation Conf. Assn. (bd. dirs. 1996-99), Yale U. Alumni Assn. Cleve. (treas. 1982-84, del. 1984-87, trustee 1984-93, adv. coun. 1993-2002), Yale U. Alumni Assn. (bd. govs. 1987-90), Union Club (NYC and Cleve.), Washington Chevy Chase Club, Cleve. Racquet Club, Kirtland Country Club (Cleve.), Met. Club (Washington), Carolina Yacht Club, The Country Club of Charleston, Mory's Assn. (New Haven), Phi Beta Kappa. Republican. Presbyterian. Home: Charleston, SC. Died Oct. 4, 2006.

DONOVAN, DAVID GERARD, librarian; b. Boston, May 27, 1921; s. David Joseph and Margaret Elizabeth (Sullivan) D.; m. Katharine E. Hickey, Mar. 16, 1951; 1 dau., Jane Elizabeth. AB, Boston U., 1949; MA, Simmons Coll., Boston, 1951. Librarian U.S. Govt., 1951-61, Gen. Electric Co., Croton-on-Hudson, N.Y., 1961-62; cultural affairs officer USIA, New Delhi, India, 1962-65; field dir. Library of Congress, Karachi, Pakistan, 1965-67; dir. internat. relations ALA, Washington, 1967-72; assoc. dir. libraries U. Notre Dame, 1972-76; tech. info. officer AID, Washington, 1976-82, cons., from 1982. Adviser UNESCO and UNDP, 1978-79; adminstr. Ford and Rockefeller found. grants to ALA for library devel. abroad, 1967-72; mem. Govt. Adv. Com. Internat. Book and Library Programs; cons. in field. Contbr. to profl. publs. Bd. dirs. Karachi Am. Sch., 1965-67, Music Soc. Pakistan, 1965-67, York County, Va. Pub. Libr., 1988—. Mem. ALA, Indian Libary Assn. (life mem.), Phi Beta Kappa, Delta Phi Alpha. Home: Leesburg, Va. Died Feb. 9, 2007.

DONOVAN, GERALD ALTON, retired academic administrator, dean; b. Hartford, Conn., Feb. 10, 1925; s. Gerald Joseph and Alice Gertrude (Gleason) D.; m. Barbara Ann Hue, Feb. 1, 1948; children: Deborah E., Clayton H., Bruce G. BA, U. Conn., 1950, MS, 1952; PhD, Iowa State U., 1955. Poultry nutritionist Charles Pfizer & Co., Inc., Terre Haute, Ind., 1955-60; prof., chmn. poultry sci. dept. U. Vt., 1960-66; asso. dir. U. Vt. (Vt. Agrl. Expt. Sta.); asso. dean Coll. Agr. and Home Econs., U. Vt., 1966-73; dean Coll. Resource Devel., U. R.I., Kingston, 1973-89, dir. Internat. Ctr. Marine Resource Devel., 1975-89, ret., from 1989; exec. dir. Northeastern Region Aquaculture Ctr., Southeastern Mass. U., 1988-90, ret., 1990. Mem. U.S. AID/BIFAD Joint Research Council, 1979-83. Contbr. articles to profl. jours. Bd. dirs. Vt. C.C., 1970-73, Operation Clean Govt., 1997—; tech. specialist AARP-Tax Aide Program, 1993-2001; chairperson Narragansett Rep. Com., 1991-93; vol. tax cons. to the elderly. With USN, 1943-46. Mem. Am. Inst. Nutrition, Agrl. Research Inst., Assn. Agrl. Expt. Sta. Dirs., Sigma Xi, Alpha Zeta, Alpha Gamma Rho. Died July 5, 2006.

DONOVAN, WILLIAM CLINTON, JR., state agency administrator, consultant; b. Providence, Nov. 12, 1943; s. William Clinton and Elizabeth Helen (Mullen) Donovan; m. Karen Connelly, Aug. 29, 1970; children: Robert Michael, Kathryn Elizabeth. BA, Providence Coll., 1967; MEd, Boston U., 1972. Child devel. supr. J. Arthur Trudeau Ctr., Warwick, R.I., 1970—72, asst. exec. dir., 1972—73; adminstr. cmty. svcs. State of R.I., Cranston, 1973—77; exec. dir. Ariz. Gov.'s Coun. on Devel. Disabilities, Phoenix, from 1977. Cons. spl. edn. dept. U. Mass., R.I. Coll., U. Denver, HHS. Contbr. articles to profl. jours. Co-chmn. Jamestown Cancer Drive, RI, 1976; me. coun., bd. dirs. SW Regional Lab., Los Alamitos, Calif., from 1980. With US Army, 1968—69. Decorated D.S.M. U.S. Army. Mem.: Nat. Assn. Devel. Disabilities Coun. (v.p. from 1982), Nat. Assn. Retarded Citizens, Am. Assn. Mental Deficiency. Democrat. Roman Catholic. Died May 16, 2007.

DORAN, CHARLES EDWARD, textile manufacturing executive; b. Hartford, Conn., Mar. 31, 1928; s. Charles Edward and Josephine Catherine (Maher) D.; m. Anne Marie McGovern, May 18, 1957; children: Charles Francis, John Francis, Pamela Anne. BA, Hamilton Coll., 1951; MA, Yale U., 1952. Trainee Gen. Elec. Co., 1953-56, financial mgmt. positions, 1956-65; asst. treas. Collins & Aikman Corp., NYC, 1965-71, treas., 1971-88. Mem. adv. bd. Arkwright-Boston Ins. Co., 1981-87. Served with USNR, 1946-48. Mem. Fin. Execs. Inst., Nat. Assn. Corp. Treasurers, Yale Club, Union League Club (N.Y.C.), Phi Beta Kappa, Chi Psi. Republican. Roman Catholic. Home: Somers, NY. Died Feb. 1, 2006.

DORFMAN, MARK STANLEY, educator; b. Chgo., Apr. 14, 1945; s. Daniel B. and Mildred (Trilling) D.; m. Marcia Tuckey, June 8, 1968; children: Matthew, Michael. BA, Northwestern U., Evanston, Ill., 1966; MA, U. Ill., Urbana, 1967, PhD, 1970. Prof. Miami U., Oxford, Ohio, 1970-86; Whitbeck-Beyer chair U. Ark., Little Rock, from 1986. Pres. Am. Risk & Ins. Assn., Madison, Wis., 1984-85. Author: Dow Jones Guide to Life Insurance, 1988, Introduction to Insurance, 5th edit., 1994, Life Insurance, 2d edit., 1992. Christian Scientist. Avocations: swimming, history, rose growing. Home: Charlotte, NC. Died Dec. 22, 2006.

DORSCH, BERNARD JEROME, surety company executive; b. Chgo., Oct. 27, 1927; s. Bernard Peter and Ann (Jalloway) D.; m. Marilyn McSweeney, Sept. 9, 1950; children— Debra Lynn, Christine Marie, Mary Beth. BA, Loyola U., Chgo., 1951. With Seaboard Surety Co., Chgo., 1952-65, mgr. to, 1965; v.p., dir. Capitol Transamerica Corp., Madison, Wis., 1965-68; with Fidelity & Deposit Co. of Md., Balt., from 1968, exec. v.p., chief operating officer, dir., from 1979. Chmn. United Way Central Md., 1978. Served with U.S. Navy, 1944-46. Decorated Purple Heart. Mem. Am. Ins. Assn. (dir.), Surety Assn. Am. Clubs: Center, Balt. Country, Maryland. Republican. Roman Catholic. Home: Phoenix, Md. Died July 19, 2006.

DOUGHERTY, RUSSELL ELLIOTT, lawyer, retired military officer; b. Glasgow, Ky., Nov. 15, 1920; s. Ewell Walter and Bess (House) D.; m. m Geralee Shaaber, Apr. 26, 1943 (dec. Jan. 1978); children: Diane Ellen, Mark Elliott, William Bryant (dec. 1990); m. Barbara Brooks Lake, Sept. 1978. AB, Western Ky. U., 1941; JD, U. Louisville, 1948; grad., Nat. War Coll., 1960; LLD, U. Akron, 1975, U. Nebr., 1976, U. Louisville, 1977; DSc, Westminster Coll., 1976, Embry-Riddle Aeronautical U., 1986, Bellevue Coll., 1989. Bar: Ky. 1948, U.S. Supreme Ct. 1953. Commd. 2d. lt. USAF, 1943, advanced through grades to gen., 1972; various staff and command assignments in Far East Air Forces, SAC, U.S. European Command, World War II; dir. European region Office of Sec. of Def., 1965-67; dep. chief of staff for plans & ops. USAF, 1970; comdr. 2d Air Force (Strategic Air Command), 1971; chief of staff Supreme Hdqrs. Allied Powers Europe, 1972-74; comdr.-in-chief Strategic Air Command, dir. U.S. Strategic Target Planning, 1974-77; exec. dir. Air Force Assn., 1980-86; corp. atty. McGuire, Woods, Battle and Boothe, 1987—2000. Bd. dirs. DynCorp Inc., Reston, Va.; former bd. dirs. ENRON Corp.; vice chmn. bd. trustees Aerospace Corp.; mem. Def. Sci. Bd.; trustee Inst. Def. Analysis; planned operation Powerflight Misson, 1957; U.S. planner Stanleyville (Republic of Congo) Rescue Operation, 1964. Bd. dirs. Atlantic Coun. of U.S., Falcon Found., Air Force Assn.; mem. Va. War Meml. Bd., 1990. Decorated D.S.M. USAF (3), D.S.M. Dept. Def. (2), Legion of Merit (2), Bronze Star (2); recipient Outstanding Alumnus award Western Ky. U., 1976, David Sarnoff award Armed Forces Communications and Electronics Assn., 1980, Gen. Thomas D. White Nat. Def. award U.S. Air Force Acad., 1983; named Man of Yr. Nat. Jewish Hosp., 1976, Man of Yr. L.A. Philanthropic Soc., 1976, Disting. Grad., Louisville Law Sch., 1984, Outstanding Alumnus, U. Louisville, 1991, Outstanding Alumnus of Ky., Gov. and Ky. Advocates, 1987, Disting. Civilian Svc. award Dept. Def., 1990, Nat. Aviation Club (Cliff Henderson award 1992). Mem. Ky. Bar Assn., Va. Bar Assn., Omicron Delta Kappa, Phi Alpha Delta, Lambda Chi Alpha. Home: Arlington, Va. Died Sept. 7, 2007.

DOUGHTY, FREDERIC CONE, manufacturing executive; b. Phila., July 22, 1929; s. Dennis Roland and Dorothy May (Bolton) Doughty; m. Barbara Jean Shea, Aug. 16, 1952; children: Denise Rolana, Frederic Cone Jr. BSE, Widener U., Chester, Pa., 1969. Test equipment technician Radio Condenser, Camden, NJ, 1952—54; radar technician RCA, Moorestown, NJ, 1954—55; engr. Burroughs Corp., Paoli, Pa., 1955—71; mgr. engring. ELCO Safelite, Warrington, Pa., 1971—72; pres. Acme Gear & Machine, Phila., from 1972. Contbr.: articles to profl. jours. Served USAF, 1948—52. Mem.: NAM, Sci. Rsch. Soc. (assoc.), U.S. Power Squad (electronics tchr. and tng. aids chmn.), Aircraft Owners and Pilots Assn. Republican. Achievements include patents in field. Avocations: tennis, bridge, amateur radio, aircraft pilot, yacht capt. Home: Valley Forge, Pa. Died Mar. 30, 2007.

DOUGLAS, JAMES NATHANIEL, astronomer, educator; b. Dallas, Tex., Aug. 14, 1935; s. Loyd and Nell (Curtis) D.; m. Charlotte Cummings, Aug. 30, 1956 (div. 1980); children— Neva Jean, James Loyd, Alan Nevins.; m. Elizabeth Gunn; 1 dau., Eleanore. BS, Yale U., 1956, MS, 1958, PhD, 1961. Instr. Yale U., 1960-61, asst. prof., 1961-65; asso. prof. astronomy U. Tex., Austin, 1965-71, prof., from 1971; dir. U. Tex. (Radio Astronomy Obs.); mem. adv. panel for astronomy NSF, 1971-74. Contbr. articles to profl. jours. NSF fellow, 1959-60 Mem. Am. Astron. Soc., Internat. Astron. Union, Phi Beta Kappa. Home: Austin, Tex. Died Aug. 20, 2006.

DOUGLAS, JAMES WALTER, pharmaceutical auditing company executive, consultant pharmacist; b. Clarendon, Tex., Feb. 10, 1929; s. Clyde James and Dorinda (Tatum) D.; m. Mary Sanders, July 21, 1961. B.S. in Pharmacy, U. Tex., 1949. Registered pharmcist, Tex. Owner, operator Douglas Pharmacy, Irving, Tex., 1961-69; pres. Family RX Systems, Irving, 1970-74, PAS, Irving, 1982—; v.p. Meyers & Rosser Pharmacies, Dallas, 1975-82. Served with USN, 1950-54; Korea. Mem. Dallas County Pharm. Soc., Tex. Pharm. Assn., Am. Pharm. Assn. Republican. Lodge: Optimist. Avocations: fly fishing; quail hunting; tennis. Home: Irving, Tex. Died Mar. 23, 2006.

DOW, GEORGE FARRINGTON, director agricultural experimental station; b. South Portland, Maine, July 22, 1905; s. J. Henry and Abbie Louise (Farrington) D.; m. Myrtle Walker, June 11, 1930; children— Margaret, Barbara, Elizabeth. B.S., U. Maine, 1927, M.S., 1929, D.Sc. (hon.), 1969; Ph.D., Cornell U., 1938. Asst. agrl. economist Maine Agr. Exptl. Sta., Orono, 1927-29, assoc. agrl. economist, 1929-43, agrl. economist, 1943-47, asst. dir., 1947-51, assoc. dir., 1951-57, dir., 1957-69; chmn. Class I Milk Price Com., Boston, 1947-58. Contbr. articles to profl. jours. Mem. budget and adv. com. Town of Nobleboro, Maine, 1972-74; historian Town of Nobleboro, 1976—. Recipient Pine Tree award U. Maine Alumni Assn., 1964, Disting. Service to Youth YMCA, 1968. Mem. Northeast Agrl. Econ. (life), New Eng. Agrl. Econ. Council (life). Republican. Baptist. Avocations: gardening; local history; tennis. Home: Nobleboro, Maine. Died June 9, 2006.

DOWNER, WILLIAM JOHN, JR., retired health facility administrator; b. Springfield, Ill., Sept. 29, 1932; s. William John and Geraldine (Foster) D.; m. Wanda M. Parson, Oct. 3, 1953; children: William E., Lawrence R. BA, Mich. State U., 1954; MHA, U. Mich., 1961. Various mgmt. positions Blodgett Meml. Med. Ctr., Grand Rapids, Mich., 1961-74, pres., CEO, 1974-84; pres., chief exec. officer Columbus Hosp., Great Falls, Mont., 1985-95, sr. cons., 1995-96. Contbr. articles to profl. jours. City commr. City of Gt. Falls, 1996—99; hosp. divsn. chmn. United Way Kent County, Grand Rapids, 1969; mem. cmty. adv. bd. N.W. Mont. for Horizon Air, 1990—97; bd. dirs. No. Rockies Easter Seals/Goodwill, 1995—2000; bd. dirs. Big Sky chpt. ARC, 1986—92, 1996—97; commr. 211th Gen. Assembly Presbyn. Ch. USA, 1999—2000; elder Westminster Presbyn. Ch., Grand Rapids, 1968—85, 1st Presbyn. Ch., Gt. Falls, 1985—2000, Oceanside, Calif., from 2001; mem. com. on ministry Glacier Presbytery, 1996—2000, moderator, 1997. Lt. col. AUS, ret. Fellow Am. Coll. Healthcare Execs. (life, regent for Mich. 1978-84, regent for Mont. 1986-89, Regent's award 1996); mem. Am. Hosp. Assn. (life, mem. governing coun. sect. for met. hosps. 1991-94), Mont. Hosp. Assn. (bd. dirs. 1987-90, chmn. 1989), Mich. Hosp. Assn. (bd. dirs. 1973-82, chmn. 1980-81, Homminga award 1982), Great Falls C. of C. (mem. exec. com. 1988, chmn. 1991-92, mil. affairs exec. com. 1995-99, vice chmn. 1998, chmn. 1999), Rotary, Phi Kappa Phi, Beta Gamma Sigma. Avocations: civil war history, golf, travel. Home: Oceanside, Calif. Died June 15, 2007.

DOWNING, WAYNE ALLAN, retired military officer; b. Peoria, Ill., May 10, 1940; s. F. Wayne and Eileen M. D.; m. Linda Chester, July 21, 1962 (div. Dec. 1980); children: Elizabeth, Laura; m. Kathryn Bickerman, May 6, 1996. BS, U.S. Mil. Acad., 1962; MBA, Tulane U., 1971. Commd. 2d lt. US Army, 1962, advanced through grades to gen., 1993, ret., 1996; student basic airborne course Jumpmaster Sch., Ft. Benning, Ga., 1962; student Ranger Sch., Ft. Benning, Ga., 1963; student Brit. jungle warfare course Kota Tingii, Malaya, 1963; rifle platoon leader Co. C, 2d Airborne Battle Group 503d Inf. Combat Team, Okinawa, 1963-64, asst. ops. officer (S3) 1st Bn. (Airborne, 1964; aide-de-camp to commdg. gen. 173d Airborne Brigade, Okinawa, S. Vietnam, 1964-65; intelligence officer (S2) 1st Bn. (Airborne) 503d Inf., S. Vietnam, 1965-66; instr. The Inf. Sch., Ft. Benning, Ga., 1966-67; student Pathfinder Sch., Ft. Benning, 1967; comdr. Co. E, 3d Bn., 1st Brigade U.S. Army Tng. Ctr., Ft. Benning, 1967-68; student inf. officers advanced course Ft. Benning, 1968; comdr. Co. A, 2d Bn., 14th Inf. 25th Inf. Div., S. Vietnam, 1968-69, ops. office (S3), 2d Brigade, 1969; student Armed Forces Staff Coll., Norfolk, Va., 1972; staff analyst S.E. Asia Div. Office Dep. Asst. Sec. Def., Washington, 1972-73, staff analyst spl. regional studies div., 1973-75; student Jungle Warfare Sch., Panama, 1876, 77, 79; ops. officer (S3) 1st Bn. (Ranger) 75th Inf., Ft. Stewart, Ga., 1975-76, exec. officer, 1976; comdr. 24th Inf. Div. Task Force, Ft. Stewart, 1976; comdr. 2d bn. 75th Inf., Ft. Lewis, Wash., 1977-79; student Air War Coll., Maxwell AFB, Ala., 1980; sec. joint staff Hdqrs. U.S. European Comman, Stuttgart-Vaihingen, Germany, 1980-82; comdr. 3d Brigade 1st Armored Div., Bamberg, Germany, 1982-84; comdr. 75th Inf., Ft. Benning, 1984-85; spl. asst. to commdg. gen U.S. Army Inf., Ft. Benning, 1985; dep. commdg. gen. 1st Spl. Ops. Command, Ft. Bragg, N.C., 1985-87; dir. Washington Office U.S. Spl. Ops. Commandat MacDill AFB, Fla., 1987-88; dep. chief of staff for tng. U.S. Army Tng. and Doctrine Command, Ft. Monroe, Va., 1988-89; comdr. Joint Spl. Ops. Command, Ft. Bragg, 1988-91, US Army Spl. Ops. Command, Ft. Bragg, 1991-93, US Spl. Ops. Command (USSOCOM), MacDill AFB, Fla., 1993—96; dep. asst. to Pres., nat. dir., dep. nat. security adv. for combating terrorism The White House, 2001—02; Disting. Chair Combatting Terrorism Ctr., US Mil. Acad. Mem. Nat. Commn. on Terrorism (The Bremer Commn.), 1999—2000. Contbr. articles to profl. jours. Decorated D.S.M. with oak leaf cluster, Silver Star with oak leaf cluster, French legion of Honor, Def. Disting. Svc. Medal with oak leaf cluster, Def. Superior Svc. medal, Legion of Merit with three oak leaf cluters, D.F.C. with oak leaf cluter, Soldier's medal, Bronze star with V Devise and five oak leaf clusters, Purple Heart, Def. meritorious Svc. medal, Meritorious Svc. medal with three oak leaf clusters, Air medal with V Device and 35 oak leaf clusters, Army commendation medal with V Device and three oak leaf clusters, Nat. Def. Svc. medal with one bronze star, Vietnamese Gallantry Cross with three silver stars, Free Fall Jumpmaster Badge, Vietnamese Parachutist Badge with palm, Polish Parachutist Badge, French Parachutist Badge, Thai Parachutist

Badge, Taiwan Parachutist Badge, Israeli Free Fall Badge, Indonesian Free Fall Badge; recipient Kraus award Young Men's Bus. Club Greater New Orleans, 1970; recipient Disting. Grad. award, US Mil. Acad., 2006 Mem. Assn. U.S. Army, Ranger Assn., 173d Airborne Assn., VFW, Beta Gamma Sigma, Omicron Delta Kappa. Home: Peoria, Ill. Died June 18, 2007.

DOYLE, DONALD VINCENT, retired state legislator, lawyer; b. Sioux City, Iowa, Jan. 13, 1925; s. William E. and Nelsine E. (Sparby) D.; m. Jant E. Holtz, Aug. 9, 1963; 1 child, Dawn Renee. BS, Morningside Coll., Sioux City, 1951; JD, U. S.D., 1953. Bar: S.D. 1953, Iowa 1953, U.S. Supreme Ct. 1976. Pvt. practice, Sioux City, 1953—2006; mem. Iowa Ho. of Reps., 1956-80, Iowa Senate, 1981-93, chmn. judiciary com., 1982-90. Mem. law and justice com. Nat. Conf. State Legis., 1987-89, chmn., 1988-89; chmn. Iowa Boundary Commn., 1991, 92; mem. Commn. Accreditation Law Enforcement Agys., Inc., 1988-95. With USAF, 1943—46. Recipient award Woodbury County Peace Officers, 1974, Restoration Club Sioux City, 1964, Outstanding Elected Ofcl. award Iowa Corrections Assn., 1979. Mem. Iowa Bar Assn., S.D. Bar Assn. (50-Yr. plaque 2003), Woodbury County Bar Assn., CBI Vets. Assn. (past nat. judge adv., Iowa comdr. 1965), Am. Legion, VFW (comdr. post 1997-2001), DAV, 40 and 8 (chef de gare 1999-2001). Home: Sioux City, Iowa. Died June 4, 2007.

DOYLE, JOSEPH THEOBALD, physician, educator; b. Providence, June 11, 1918; s. Joseph Donald and Gertrude Harriet (Theobald) D.; m. Elizabeth Thompson, Dec. 26, 1944 (dec.); children: Shelagh Thompson, Michael Kedian; m. Joan Gleason Mastrianni, Dec. 30, 1976. AB, Harvard U., 1939, MD, 1943. Successively intern, asst. resident, chief resident in medicine Harvard Med. Service, Boston City Hosp., 1943-44, 47-49; Whitehead fellow in physiology, asst. in medicine and physiology Emory U. Med. Sch., 1950-52; assoc. in medicine Duke U. Med. Sch., 1952; mem. faculty Albany (N.Y.) Med. Coll., from 1952, prof. medicine, from 1961, head div. cardiology, 1961-84, dir. cardiovascular health center, 1952-90, head pvt. diagnostic clinic, 1957-82. Cons. Albany VA Med. Center, 1962-1991. Author papers in field. Served as 1st lt. M.C. AUS, 1944-45. Fellow A.C.P., Am. Coll. Cardiology; mem. AMA, Am. Heart Assn. (chmn. council epidemiology 1969-71), Assn. Univ. Cardiologists, N.Y. Heart Assembly (pres. 1968-69), Med. Soc. County of Albany (pres. 1971-72) Clubs: Ft. Orange, Schuyler Meadows. Presbyterian. Home: Albany, NY. Died June 18, 2007.

DOYLE, RICHARD LEE, architect, engineer; b. Franklin Park, Ill., May 1, 1919; s. Richard Earl and Mildred Cleone Doyle; m. Donna Alberta Draland; children: Rebecca Ann, Mary Agnes. BA, U. Ill., 1949. Registered architect, Ill. Clk. of the works Lankton Zeigele Architects, Peoria, Ill., 1950-54; architect, engineer Doyle Assocs. Architects/Engrs., Peoria, from 1955. Planning cons. Peoria Heights Planning Commn., 1965—, cons. Peoria Public Sch. 1990—. Prin. works include Pleasant Valley Schs., Peoria High Rehab., also designed various high schs., churches, public works, libraries. Served with U.S. Army, 1939-45, PTO. Mem. AIA, Am. Arbitration Soc. (sr., arbiter), Am. Architects Soc. (arbiter), Ill. Sch. Bds. Assn. (service assoc.), Constrn. Coordinating Council (chmn. 1968-69). Lodges: Kiwanis (pres. Peoria 1985). Home: Peoria, Ill. Died July 15, 2006.

DRAKE, ARNOLD JACK, freelance writer, producer; b. N.Y.C., Mar. 1, 1924; s. Max and Pearl (Cohn) Druckman; m. Lillian Rachel Levy, June 15, 1951; 1 child, Pamela Delano. Student elec. engring. U. Mo., 1943-44, Pace U., 1941, NYU, 1948-50. Freelance writer 1948—; film producer Vulcan Prodns., N.Y.C., 1960-70; nat. exec. dir. Vets. Bedside Network, N.Y.C., 1981-88; media cons. VA, 1982—. Author: (novels) The Steel Noose, 1954, This One Will Kill You, 1956; (plays) Smart Alec (Alexander Graham Bel), You'll Never Get It Off the Ground (The Wright Brothers), G & S (Gilbert and Sullivan). Writer (films) Who Killed Teddy Bear, 1965, 20,000 B.C., 1966, Thirty Claws, 1969; writer, producer (film) The Flesh Eaters, 1963; animated cartoons and comics inc. Batman, Plastic Man, Little Lulu, Bugs Bunny; creater "Deadman", "The Doom Patrol"; producer, dir. VA Nat. Music Fesitval, 1982-86. Vol. Vets. Bedside Network, N.Y.C., 1973—. Served to sgt. U.S. Army, 1942-46, ETO. Mem. Writers Guild Am., East, Internat. Radio and TV Soc. Avocations: 19th century U.S. and European history, photography, travel. Home: New York, NY. Died Mar. 12, 2007.

DRECHSEL, EDWIN JARED, retired magazine editor; b. Bremen, Germany, Apr. 17, 1914; came to U.S., 1924, naturalized, 1935; s. William A. and Estelle Laura D.; m. Ilona Bolya, Aug. 12, 1972; children: John M., Barbara A. Grad., Dartmouth Coll., Amos Tuck Sch. Bus. Adminstrn., 1936. With Standard Oil Co., N.J., 1936-43; with U.S. News and World Report, 1943-79, regional editor, editorial ombudsman San Francisco, 1976-79. Author shipping company histories and fleet lists, catalogs of ship mail postal markings, including A Century of German Ship Posts, 1886-1986, 1987, Norddeutscher Lloyd, Bremen 1857-1970, vol. 1, 1994, vol. 2, 1995. Former chmn. Reed Sch. Bd., Marin County, Calif.; lay reader, former vestryman St. Stephen's Episcopal Ch., Belvedere, Calif., former mayor, City of Belvedere. Mem.: San Francisco Press. Home: Point Roberts, Wash. Died Mar. 27, 2006.

DRERUP, JOHN WILLIAM, shoe company executive; b. Brookfield, Mo., May 22, 1922; s. Alphonse Lawrence and Mary (Killion) D.; B.S., Murray State U., 1947; postgrad. U. S.D., 1943, Washington U. Law Sch., 1946-47; m. Margaret Burrus, Oct. 9, 1948; children— Patricia, John William. Salesman Bay Bee Shoe Co., Inc., Dresden, Tenn., 1949-51, sales mgr., v.p., 1951-62, pres., 1962-78, chmn. bd., 1978—; pres. First Realty Co., 1969—; partner Venture Investment Co.; dir. First Am. Bank, Jackson and Union City, DCM Co. Mem. U. Tenn. Devel. Council, U.S. Jaycees (past nat. dir.). Served with Signal Corps, U.S. Army, 1943-46. Named Young Man of Year, Jr. C. of C., 1956, Civitan award for outstanding work in community, 1978. Mem. Shoe Travlers Assn., Am. Legion. Roman Catholic. Lodges: Rotary, Moose. Home: Union City, Tenn. Died Aug. 10, 2006.

DRESSLER, ROBERT CLAY, cosmetics executive; b. Glen Ridge, NJ, July 22, 1943; s. JohnClay and Maxine Lillian (McLeod) Dressler. BS in Chemistry, Columbia U., 1964. Chemist Max Factor & Co., Hollywood, Calif., 1966, Revlon Co., NYC, 1967—69; dir. product devel. Elizabeth Arden, NYC, 1970—73; v.p. R&D Merle Norman Cosmetics, LA, 1973—79, mem. exec. com., from 1976, sr. v.p., 1979—83, exec. v.p., from 1983, dir., from 1980. Mem. Presdl. Regulatory Commn. Mem.: Cosmetics, Toiletries and Fragrance Assn. (sci. adv. com., exec. com., chmn. color additive com.), Soc. Cosmetic Chemists, Am. Chem. Soc. Home: Tustin, Calif. Died Dec. 15, 2005.

DREWRY, JOE SAMUEL, JR., design engineer executive; b. Boykins, Va., Feb. 16, 1921; s. Joe Samuel and Lucy Lavern (Moore) D.; m. Ann Hunter Crutchfield, Oct. 5, 1946 (div. July 1947); m. Virginia Daniel Pearson, June 12, 1948; children: Christoper Morris, Martha Kay. BS, Va. Mil. Inst., 1942. Profl. engr., multiple states. From engr. to asst. chief engr. Va.-Carolina Chem. Corp., Richmond, Va., 1946-62; chief engr. Armour Agrl. Chem. Corp., Atlanta, 1962-66; v.p. engring. Kiernan-Gregory Corp., Atlanta, St. Louis, 1966-82; pres. Drewry & Assocs., Inc., Atlanta, from 1982. Dir. Fertilizer Industry Roundtable, Balt., 1962-92; bd. dirs. Tri-State Plant Food Corp., Dothan, Ala. Vol. Boy Scouts Am., Atlanta, 1962—; vol. staff Atlanta Olympic Com., 1996; pres. PTA, Atlanta, 1985-87. Col. U.S. Army, 1942-73, ETO, ret. Decorated Legion of Merit, Bronze Star medal, Purple Heart medal; recipient Bishop's award of merit for work with Boy Scouts, United Methodist Ch., Atlanta, 1989. Mem. Am. Soc. Civil Engrs. Avocations: golf, music, computer operations, travel. Died Oct. 17, 2006.

DROEGE, THOMAS ARTHUR, theology educator; b. Seymour, Ind., Apr. 10, 1931; s. Walter Henry and Minna Lydia (Strasen) D.; m. Esther K. Kuehn, Jan. 29, 1956; children: Donna, Paula, Karla. BA, Concordia Sem., St. Louis, 1953, MST in Theology, 1956; MA in Theology, U. Chgo., 1963, PhD in Theology, 1965. Ordained to ministry Luth. Ch.-Mo. Synod, 1956. Pastor Redeemer Luth. Ch., Oneida, N.Y., 1956-60; instr. in theology Valparaiso (Ind.) U., 1964-65, asst. prof., 1966-67, assoc. prof., 1968-77, prof., from 1978, chairperson dept. theology, 1978-91, Univ. rsch. prof., 1988-89. Study dir. Med. Mission Conf., India, 1966-67. Author: That Thy Saving Health May Be Known, 1968, Self-Realization and Faith: Beginning and Becoming in Relation to God, 1978, Theological Roots of Wholistic Health Care, 1979, Ministry to the Whole Person: Eight Models of Healing Ministry in Lutheran Congregations, 1982, Faith Passages and Patterns, 1983, Guided Grief Imagery: Exercises in Guided Imagery for Death Education and Grief Ministry, 1987, The Faith Factor in Healing, 1991; also articles; (with others) The Church and Pastoral Care, 1988, Death Imagery, 1991. Recipient O. P. Kretzmann Rsch. award Valparaiso U., 1978, 81, 84, 88, Disting. Teaching award, 1986-87; Lilly faculty fellow, 1981-82. Mem. Am. Assn. Pastoral Counselors. Home: Atlanta, Ga. Died Apr. 5, 2007.

DROHAN, THOMAS ANTHONY, public relations executive; b. Winchester, Mass., June 12, 1933; s. Edward William and Rose (Condrey) D.; m. Judith Smith, Oct. 24, 1960 (div. July 1964); children: Kathleen and Karen (twins); m. Linda Drohan, Nov. 24, 1968. BSBA, Boston Coll. Reporter Boston Post, 1952-58; sportswriter Boston Herald Traveler, 1960-62; pub. relations mgr. Allied Chem. Co., NYC, 1962-68, Pepsi-Cola Co., NYC, 1968; v.p. pub. relations Inmont Corp., NYC, 1968-82, United Technologies, Hartford, Conn., 1982-87. Served with U.S. Army, 1959-60. Mem.: Hartford (Conn.) (bd. dirs. 1986-88). Democrat. Roman Catholic. Avocations: golf, writing. Home: Old Saybrook, Conn. Died Jan. 1, 2007.

DROLLINGER, HOWARD BLAINE, II, real estate developer; b. Los Angeles, June 16, 1922; s. Howard and Ella Margaret (Lewin) Drollinger; m. Jewel Eisenhower, Oct. 27, 1950 (dec. 1996); children: Karen Joy Dial, Howard James. BS, U. So. Calif., 1945—47. Broker Frank H. Ayres and Son, LA, 1947—52; mng. ptnr. Ella L. Drollinger Co., LA, from 1952; pres. H.B. Drollinger Co., 1952—2006. Founder Fox Hills Savs. and Loan, 1962; founder, dir. Gateway Nat. Bank, 1963—70, Wedbush, Noble, Cooke, Inc., 1975—81. Dir., treas. Westchester YMCA, 1958-62; mem. LA Bd. Zoning Appeals, 1960-61; mem. Mayor's Com. Capital Improvements, 1963, 65, adv. bd. Daniel Freeman Marina Hosp., 1980-, Calif. C. of C. Served, AUS, 1943-45. Decorated D.F.C., Air medal, Purple Heart. Mem. Commerce Assn. U. So. Calif., U. So. Calif. Alumni Assn., Religious Science Ch., Wesport Beach Club, Rotary. Died Aug. 13, 2006.

DROOZ, DANIEL BERNARD, trading company executive; b. Wilmington, Del., Mar. 27, 1945; s. Herbert E. and Florence (Zubres) D.; m. Angela Klenter, Jan. 31, 1977; 1 child, Andrei. BA, Antioch Coll., 1967; MA in Communications, U. Mich., 1969. Editor ABC News Radio, Washington; reporter Chgo. Sun Times, Jerusalem, CBC, Jerusalem, Time/Life, Jerusalem; correspondent Chgo. Sun Times/Daily News, Johannesburg, Republic of South Africa; chief executive officer Commerce Internat., Wilmington, Del., from 1984. Cons. fgn. risk, Indpls., 1978-86. Author columns Balt. Evening Sun, 1978—; contbr. numerous investigative features to various mags. Recipient Nat. Newspaper award Canadian Press Assn., 1976. Mem. Overseas Press Club. Avocations: kayaking, fishing. Home: Newark, Del. Died Dec. 24, 2006.

DRVOTA, MOJMIR, retired cinema educator, author; b. Prague, Czechoslovakia, Jan. 13, 1923; came to U.S., 1958, naturalized, 1963; s. Jan and Zdenka (Krejcikova) D.; m. Jana Kratochvilova, May 18, 1957; 1 child, Monica. Student, Charles U., 1945-48; PhD, Palacky U., 1953; MS, Columbia U., 1961. Stage dir. state theaters, Czechoslovakia, 1952-56; libr. Bklyn. Pub. Libr., 1958-62; asst. prof. dramatic arts Columbia U., NYC, 1962-69; assoc. prof. cinema NYU, NYC, 1969-72; prof. cinema Ohio State U., Columbus, 1972-92, prof. emeritus, from 1992; ret., 1992. Script writer Czechoslovak State Film, Prague, 1948-52; author: Short Stories, 1946, Boarding House for Artists, 1947, Solitaire, 1974, Triptych, 1980, Solitaire, Triptych in Czech, 1993; The Constituents of Film Theory, 1973, in Czech, 1994, How Many ANgels Can Dance on the Tip of a Needle?, in Czech, 2002. Mem. Univ. Film Assn., AAUP, Phi Kappa Phi. Home: Columbus, Ohio. Died Apr. 27, 2006.

DRYDEN, MARTIN FRANCIS, JR., retired gas company executive; b. Baton Rouge, July 21, 1915; s. Martin Francis and Elizabeth (Mulvery) D.; m. Mary Mildren Franques, Mar. 9, 1941; children: Mary Frances, Ann Elizabeth. BA, La. State U. Auditor Gen. Gas Corp., Baton Rouge, v.p., gen. mgr.; pres. Gas & Chems., Inc., Lafayette, La. and Memphis, 1962-69; sr. v.p. Empire Gas Corp., Lebanon, Mo., 1969, pres., pres. emeritus, ret. Lebanon, Mo., 1989. Maj., Q.M.C. U.S. Army, 1940-46. Recipient Jefferson award Mem. Nat. LP Gas Assn. (nat. dir. 1977—), Western LP Gas Assn. (dir. 1975—), Lebanon Area C. of C. (pres. 1981) Republican. Roman Catholic. Home: Lebanon, Mo. Died July 10, 2006.

DUBES, GEORGE RICHARD, geneticist, educator; b. Sioux City, Iowa, Oct. 12, 1926; s. George Wesley and Regina Eleanor (Kelleher) D.; m. Margaret Joanne Tumberger, July 25, 1964; children: George Richard, David Frank, Deanna Marie, Kenneth Wesley, Deborah Joanne, Keith Timothy. BS, Iowa State U., 1949; PhD, Calif. Inst. Tech., 1953. Predoctoral fellow U.S. AEC, Pasadena, Calif., 1951-52; McCallum fellow div. biology Calif. Inst. Tech., Pasadena, 1951-52; rsch. assoc. McCollum-Pratt Inst. for Rsch. in Micronutrient Elements, Johns Hopkins U., 1953-54; rsch. assoc. sect. virus rsch. dept. pediatrics U. Kans. Sch. Medicine, Kansas City, 1954-56, asst. prof., 1956-60, assoc. prof., 1960-64; head viral genetics Eppley Cancer Inst.-U. Nebr. Med. Ctr., Omaha, 1964-68, assoc. prof. dept. med. microbiology (now dept. pathology and microbiology), 1964-81, prof., 1981—96, prof. emeritus, from 1996. Vis. lectr. U. Baghdad, Iraq, 1977, U. Mosul, Iraq, 1977; cons. Viva Labs., Council Bluffs, Iowa, 1972-75. Author: Methods for Transfecting Cells with Nucleic Acids of Animal Viruses: A Review, 1971; contbr. chpt. to 2 books; contbr. over 50 articles to sci. jours. Co-pres. Adams Sch. PTA, Omaha, 1976-77; mem. citizens adv. com. Omaha Pub. Schs., 1977-80. With AUS, 1945-46. Grantee Nat. Inst. Allergy and Infectious Diseases, 1966-69; gen. rsch. support grantee NIH, 1964-72. Mem. Am. Assn. Cancer Rsch., AAAS, Am. Genetic Assn., Am. Inst. Biol. Scis., Am. Soc. Microbiology (pres. Missouri Valley br. 1983-84), Biometric Soc., Genetics Soc. Am., Nebr. Acad. Scis. (co-chmn. biol. and med. scis. sect. 1983-85), N.Y. Acad. Scis., Sigma Xi Achievements include discovery of transfection enhancement by insoluble facilitators, of viral RNA inactivation by catecholamines and copper, of trophozoite production of excystment inhibitors, and of cold-adapted genetic variants of poliovirues; development of theory proposing role of asbestos-mediated oncogene transfer between cells in asbestos carcinogenesis. Home: Omaha, Nebr. Died Nov. 13, 2005.

DUBLIN, THOMAS DAVID, retired preventive medicine physician; b. NYC, Jan. 18, 1912; s. Louis I. and Augusta (Salik) D.; m. Christina Macdonald Carlyle, June 3, 1939 (dec. Sept. 1997); children: Sarah Carlyle Dublin Slenczka, Barbara Dublin Van Cleve. AB, Dartmouth Coll., 1932; MD, Harvard U., 1936; MPH., Johns Hopkins U., 1940, DPH, 1941. Diplomate Nat Bd. Med. Examiners, Am. Bd. Preventive Medicine (dir. 1961-71, vice. chmn. for gen. preventive medicine 1965-71). Intern 2d Harvard med. svc. Boston City Hosp., 1936—38; asst. resident physician Hosp. Rockefeller Inst. for Med. Rsch., NYC, 1938—39; epidemiologist-in-tng. N.Y. State Dept. Health, 1939—40, asst. dist. health officer, 1940, epidemiologist, 1941—42; instr. preventive medicine Johns Hopkins U. Med. Sch., 1940—41; instr. preventive medicine and public health Albany Med. Coll., 1942; lectr. epidemiology DeLamar Inst. Pub. Health, Coll. Physicians and Surgeons, Columbia U., 1942—45, assoc. prof., 1942—43; prof., exec. officer dept. preventive medicine/cmty. health L.I. Coll. Medicine, Bklyn., 1943—48; epidemiologist Kingston Ave. Hosp., Bklyn., 1943—48; exec. dir. Nat. Health Coun., 1948—53; med. cons. Nat. Found. for Infantile Paralysis, 1953—55; med. dir. USPHS, 1955—76, Cmty. Svcs. Programs, Office of Dir., NIH, Bethesda, Md., 1955—60; chief epidemiology and biometry br. Nat. Inst. Arthritis and Metabolic Diseases, Bethesda, 1960—66; rsch. adviser, health svc. Office Tech. Coop. and Rsch., AID, 1966—68; dir. Office Health Manpower, HEW, 1968—70; program planning officer Bur. Health Manpower, Health Resources Adminstrn., 1970—72, spl. asst. dep. dir. bur., 1972—76; cons. health manpower supply and edn., 1976—78; cons. divsn. med. edn. AMA and Coordinating Coun. on Med. Edn., 1976—78; cons. R&D Ednl. Commn. for Fgn. Med. Grads., 1978—86. Expert adv. panel pub. health adminstrn. WHO, 1954-80; mem. Nat. Adv. Com. Epidemiology and Biometry, 1956-60; chmn. com. on cert. Am. Bd. Med. Specialists, 1972-77 Contbr. articles to profl. jours. Fellow Am. Pub. Health Assn. (governing coun. 1954-60, chmn. rsch. policy com. 1957-60), Am. Coll. Preventive Medicine (regent 1973-76), N.Y. Acad. Medicine; mem. AMA, AAAS, Am. Epidemiol. Soc., Assn. Tchrs. Preventive Medicine (sec. 1944-48), Internat. Epidemiol. Assn., Delta Omega. Home: Washington, DC. Died May 3, 2007.

DUEWER, RAYMOND, horticulturist; b. Ill., Mar. 28, 1926; s. John William and Mattie Elizabeth Duewer; m. Elizabeth Ann Hubbard Duewer, Aug. 31, 1963; children: John Robert (dec.), Mary Elizabeth, Julia Ann. BS, U. Ill., Urbana, 1961; MS, 1962; PhD, U. Ariz., Tucson, 1969. Asst. prof. U. Wis., Platteville, 1969-75, assoc. prof., 1975-84, prof., 1984-95, prof. emeritus, from 1995. Coach U. Wis. Pi Alpha Xi Nat. Collegiate Flower Judging Contest, 1980, 82-95. Merit badge leader Boy Scouts Am., Platteville, Wis., 1977-80; project leader Platteville City Doers 4H Club, Platteville, Wis., 1979-96. Recipient Scholarly Activity Improvement Fund award, U. Wis., Great Britain, 1988, Platteville, 1992-93, 4-H Meritorious Svc. award Grant County, Wis., 1996. Mem. Am. Soc. for Horticultural Sci., Am. Horticultural Soc., The Nature Conservancy, Sigma Xi. United Methodist. Avocations: gardening, reading. Home: Platteville, Wis. Died Sept. 10, 2006.

DUFFY, ESTHER RODGERS (MRS. ROGER FRANCIS DUFFY), librarian; b. Pitts., Aug. 14, 1911; d. Arthur Gregory and Charlotte Catherine (Nagle) Rodgers; B. Music and B.S. in Music Edn., Seton Hill Coll., 1932; postgrad. U. Pitts., 1933, Carnegie Inst., 1935, Simmons Coll., 1941-42; m. Roger Francis Duffy, Nov. 14, 1945; children— Katherine, Mary Anne, Roger. Instr. music Coll. Misericordia, Dallas, Pa., 1932-37; music librarian Cornell U., Ithaca, N.Y., 1937-41; asst. music librarian Columbia U., N.Y.C., 1942-43; research librarian OSS, State Dept., 1943-44, Balkans outpost rep. Office War Info., 1944-46, Balkans regional rep. USIS, 1946; asst. to pres. Juilliard Sch. Music, N.Y.C., 1947-49; asst. to mng. dir. U.S. Internat. Book Assn., N.Y.C., 1945-47; librarian fine arts Greenwich (Conn.) Library, 1961-81. Mem. adv. com. Greenwich Sr. Center. Mem. Greenwich Arts Council, AAUW, Kappa Gamma Pi. Home: Riverside, Conn. Died Jan. 10, 2007.

DUGAN, CHARLES CLARK, retired physician, surgeon; b. Penn Yan, NY, Jan. 24, 1921; s. Charles Emanual and Wilhemia May (Clark) D.; m. Eugenie Alice Pounds, Aug. 12, 1944 (div. 1963); children: Charles Clark II, Douglas Craig, Timothy Gene; m. Ruth Louise Fugh, Dec. 3, 1965 (dec. 1983); adopted children: Dain Walters, Carl Jay. AA, Wentworth Mil. Jr. Coll., 1940; AB, Cornell U., 1942; MD, Jefferson Med. Coll., 1946; MPH, Naval Med. Sch. and Johns Hopkins U., 1956. Diplomate Am. Bd. Dermatology, Am. Bd. Allergy and Immunology, Spl. Bd. Dermatopathology, Am. Bd. Cosmetic Plastic Surgery, Am. Bd. Preventive Medicine, Aviation Medicine and Pub. Health, Nat. Bd. Med. Examiners. Resident in psychiatry Pa. Psychiat. Hosp., Phila., 1945-46; rotating intern extended in gen. surgery Harrisburg (Pa.) Gen. Hosp., 1946-47; resident in dermatology U. Colo. Med. Ctr., Denver, 1956-57; resident in dermatology and allergy Henry Ford Hosp., Detroit, 1957-59; pvt. practice dermatology, allergy, immunology, cosmetic plastic surgery West Palm Beach, Fla., 1959—2004; ret., 2004. Physician mem. bd. Palm Beach County Environ. Control Hearing Bd., West Palm Beach, 1981-94; active staff Palm Beach Gardens (Fla.) Cmty. Hosp., Good Samaritan Hosp., West Palm Beach, St. Mary's Hosp., West Palm Beach; mem. Wellington Regional Med. Ctr., West Palm Beach. Contbr. articles to profl. jours. Lt. col., pilot/flight surgeon USAF, 1947—56. Recipient Cert. of Svc., Am. Cancer Soc., West Palm Beach, 1961, numerous other awards; named Surgeon of Yr., Fla. Soc. Dematol. Surgeons, 1997. Fellow AMA, Fla. Med. Assn., Palm Beach County Med. Soc., Am. Acad. Dermatology, Am. Coll. Preventive Medicine, Am. Coll. Allergy, Asthma and Immunology, Am. Acad. Allergy, Asthma and Immunology, Internat. Acad. Cosmetic Surgery, Am. Acad. Facial Plastic and Reconstructive Surgery, Am. Acad. Cosmetic Surgery, Am. Soc. for Dermatol. Surgery (bd. dirs. 1980-83), Am. Soc. Dematopathology, Am. Soc. Cryosurgeons, Am. Soc. Cert. Allergists, Internat. Soc. Dematopathology, Fla. Soc. Dermatology (pres. 1973-74, Practitioner of Yr. award 1993), Am. Soc. Dermatol. Surgery (coun. 1980-83) Fla. Soc. Dermatol. Surgery (Lifetime Achievement award, 2005), numerous others; mem. Noah Worcester Dermatologic Soc. Republican. Presbyterian. Achievements include development of vaccine for herpes simplex and herpes immune virus; first person to describe correct pathophysiology of cerebral concussion correctly. Avocations: swimming, scuba diving, tennis, stamp collecting/philately, coin collecting/numismatics. Home: West Palm Beach, Fla. Died July 22, 2007.

DUGAS, LOUIS, JR., lawyer; b. Beaumont, Tex., Dec. 12, 1928; s. Louis and Loney (Duron) D.; m. Frances Elizabeth Tuley, Feb. 3, 1956; children: Mary Hester Dugas Koch, Kerry Beth Dugas Davidson, Louis Claiborne, Evin Garner, Reagan Taylor. AA, Lamar Jr. Coll., 1950; BBA in Banking and Fin., U. Tex., 1956, LLB, 1960. Bar: Tex. 1960, U.S. Ct. Appeals (5th cir.) 1972, U.S. Ct. Appeals (11th cir.) 1984, U.S. Supreme Ct. 1967. Pvt. practice, from 1960. Mem. Tex. Ho. of Reps., 1954-60; justice of the peace, Orange County, Tex., 1963; spl. counsel D.C. com. U.S. Ho. of Reps., 1967; dist. and county atty., Orange County, 1968-72; former tchr. Tex. history and govt., Lamar U. Former columnist The Opportunity Valley News; columnist Orange County Record, 1993—. Regent Nat. Criminal Def. Coll., Mercer Law Sch., Macon, Ga.; explorer leader Boy Scouts Am., 1963; comdr. Am. Legion Post, 1967; mem. Bd. Adjustments, City of Orange, 1967; founder "Les Acadiens du Texas"; pres. Orange County Hist. Soc., 1974-76; active Orange Art League; bd. dirs. Orange Cmty. Players, 1977-82; tchr. Cajun French Orange City Parks and Recreation Dept., 1980-81; nominee Rep. Party for 2d Congl. Dist., Tex., 1984; pres. Lamar U. Friends of Arts, 1985-86; mem. adminstrv. bd. 1st United Meth. Ch., Orange, 1983, 84, 85, also trustee; pres. S.E. Tex. Vets. Coalition, 1999—. Sgt. USMC, 1950-52, Korea. Mem. Tex. Bar Assn. (sec. criminal law sect. 1969, 72), Orange County Bar Assn. (pres. 1979), Nat. Assn. Criminal Def. Lawyers (bd. dirs. 1982-88), Tex. Criminal Def. Lawyers Assn. (bd. dirs. 1976-88, pres. 1985-86, contbr. to pub. The Voice), Tex. Criminal Def. Lawyers Inst. (pres. 1986), Tex. Assn. Bd. Cert. Specialists in Criminal Law (pres. 1983), Tex. Criminal Def. Lawyers (sec.-treas. 1981), Nat. Acad. Elder Law Attys., VFW, Gulf Coast Leathernecks (founder 1995), Optimists Club, Phi Alpha Delta Avocations: historical research, bird watching, photography, conchology, writing. Home: Beaumont, Tex. Died Dec. 15, 2005.

DULING, ROBERT WEBSTER, judge; b. Richmond, Va., Nov. 13, 1928; s. Daniel Webster and Minnie Belle (Schools) D.; m. Barbara Brause, Oct. 25, 1980. B.S., U. Richmond, 1950, J.D., 1963. Bar: Va. 1963, U.S. Supreme Ct. 1971. Ptnr. Wicker, Baker & Goddin, Richmond, 1963-65, Wicker, Goddin & Duling, 1965-70, Duling, Guill & Mann, Richmond, 1970-77; asst. commonwealth atty., Richmond, 1970-75; judge Richmond Gen. Dist. Ct., 1977-85; judge Cir. Ct., City of Richmond, 1985—. Served with USMC, 1948-56. Mem. Am. Judges Assn., Richmond Bar Assn., Va. Bar Assn., Richmond Criminal Bar Assn. (past pres.). Baptist. Home: Richmond, Va. Died Aug. 30, 2006.

DUMAS, RHETAUGH ETHELDRA GRAVES, retired academic administrator; b. Natchez, Miss., Nov. 26, 1928; d. Rhetaugh Graves and Josephine (Clemmons) Graves Bell; m. A.W. Dumas, Jr., Dec. 25, 1950; 1 child, Adrienne. BS in Nursing, Dillard U., 1951; MS in Psychiat. Nursing, Yale U., 1961; PhD in Social Psychology, Union Inst. and Univ., 1975; D Pub. Svc. (hon.), Simmons Coll., 1976, U. Cin., 1981; LHD (hon.), Yale U., 1989; LLD (hon.), Dillard U., 1990; LHD (hon.), U. San Diego, 1993, Georgetown U., 1996; D Pub. Svc. (hon.), Fla. Internat. U., Miami, 1996; DSc (hon.), Ind. U., Gary, 1996; LHD (hon.), U. Mass, 1997; JD (hon.), Bethune-Cookman Coll., 1997; LHD (hon.), Regis Coll., 2002. Instr. Dillard U., 1957-59, 61; research asst., instr. Sch. Nursing Yale U., 1962-65, from asst. prof. nursing to assoc. prof., 1965-72, chmn. dept. psychiat. nursing, 1972; dir. nursing Conn. Mental Health Ctr., Yale-New Haven Med. Ctr., 1966-72; chief psychiat. nursing edn. br. Div. Manpower and Tng. Programs, NIMH, Rockville, Md., 1972-76; dep. dir. Div. Manpower and Tng. Programs NIMH, 1976-79, dep. dir. alcohol, drug abuse and mental health adminstrn., 1979-81; dean, prof. U. Mich. Sch. Nursing, 1981-94; vice provost health affairs U. Mich., 1994-97, Lucille Cole prof. sch. nursing, from 1994, vice provost emerita, 1997—2007, dean emerita, 1997—2007. Dir. Group Rels. Confs. in Tavistock Model; cons., speaker, panelist in field; fellow Helen Hadley Hall, Yale U., 1972, Branford Coll., 1972; dir. Community Health Care Ctr. Plan, New Haven, 1969-72; mem. U.S. Assessment Team, cons. to Fed. Ministry Health, Nigeria, 1982; mem. adv. com. Health Policy Agenda for the Am. People, AMA, 1983-86; cons. NIH Task Force on Nursing Rsch., 1984; mem. Nat. Commn. on Unemployment and Mental Health, Nat. Mental Health Assn., 1984-85; mem. com. to plan maj. study of nat. long-term care policy Inst. Medicine, 1985; mem. adv. com. to dir. NIH, 1986-87; mem. Sec.'s Nat. Commn. on Future Structure of VA Health Care System, 1990-91; mem. coun. on grad. med. edn. Nat. Adv. Coun. on Nurse Edn. and Practice Workgroup on Primary Care Workforce Projection, Divsn. Nursing, 1994; mem. com. to rev. breast cancer rsch. program U.S. Army Med. Rsch. and Material Command, Inst. of Medicine, 1996-97; mem. Pres.'s Nat. Bioethics Adv. Commn., 1996-2007. Author profl. monographs; contbr. over 40 articles to profl. publs.; mem. editorial bd. Community Mental Health Rev., 1977-79, Jour. Personality and Social Systems, 1978-81, Advances in Psychiat. Mental Health Nursing, 1981. Bd. dirs. Afro Am. Ctr., Yale U., 1968-72; mem. New Haven Bd. Edn., 1968-71, New Haven City Demonstrations Agy., 1968-70, Human Rels. Coun. New Haven, 1961-63, Nat. Neural Circuitry Database Com., Inst. Medicine, Nat. Acad. Scis., mem. bd. scientific advisors, 1985-2007; mem. commn. on future structure of vets. health care U.S. Dept. Vets. Affairs, 1990; mem. Pres. Clinton's Nat. Bioethics Adv. Commn., 1996-01. Named Disting. Alumna, Dillard U., 1966; recipient various awards, including cert. Honor NAACP, 1970, Disting. Alumnae award Yale U. Sch. Nursing, 1976, award for outstanding achievement and service in field mental health D.C. chpt. Assn. Black Psychologists, 1980, Pres. 21st Century award The Nat. Women's Hall of Fame, 1994, Lifetime Achievement award, nat. Black Nurses Assn., 2000-07. Fellow A.K. Rice Inst., Am. Coll. Mental Health Adminstrs. (founding), Am. Acad. Nursing (charter, pres. 1987-89); mem. Inst. Medicine NAS, Am. Nurses Assn., Nat. Black Nurses Assn., Am. Assn. Colls. Nursing (govtl. affairs com. 1990-93), Am. Pub. Health Assn., Nat. League Nursing (pres. 1997-99), Nat. Bioethics Adv. Commn., Sigma Theta Tau Internat. (mentor award 1989), Delta Sigma Theta. Home: Houston, Tex. Died July 22, 2007.

DUNAVIN, LEONARD SYPRET, agronomist, researcher; b. Algood, Tenn., Dec. 17, 1930; s. Leonard Sypret and Odell (Cornwell) D.; m. Willie Mae Payne, Dec. 22, 1962; children— Sheri Patricia, Juliana Kathleen. B.S., Tenn. Tech. U., 1952; M.S. in Agr., U. Fla., 1954, Ph.D., 1959. Asst. agronomist West Fla. Expt. Sta., Jay, 1959-67; assoc. prof. agronomy Agr. Research and Edn. Ctr., U. Fla., Jay, 1967—. Contbr. articles to profl. jours. Served with U.S. Army, 1954-56. Mem. Am. Soc. Agronomy, Crop Sci. Soc. Am., Soil and Crop Sci. Soc. Fla., Am. Forage and Grassland Council, Gamma Sigma Delta. Methodist. Avocation: hunting. Home: Milton, Fla. Died Oct. 2, 2006.

DUNBAR, BYRON HERBERT, lawyer, educator; b. Three Forks, Mont., June 8, 1927; s. Bryon B. and Georgette (Walsh) D.; m. Margaret Jo Lovelace, Dec. 23, 1948; children: Lynn Dunbar Ryerson, Michael, Patrick, Lisa. JD, U. Mont., 1952. Bar: Mont. 1952. Spl. agt. FBI, 1952-79; pros. atty. Bozeman, Mont., 1979-80; legal cons. Mont. Law Enforcement Acad., 1980-81; U.S. atty. Billings, Mont., from 1981. Chief legal instr. Mont. Law Enforcement Acad., 1966-79; legal instr. Mont. Supreme Ct., Helena, 1980— Served to lt. U.S. Mcht. Marine, 1944-47. Mem. Mont. Bar Assn., Gallatin County Bar Assn., Yellowstone County Bar Assn. Lodges: Elks; Bozeman Rotary. Home: Billings, Mont. Died Apr. 21, 2007.

DUNCAN, CYNTHIA BERYL, university library administrator; b. Madison, Pa., Apr. 26, 1932; d. Andrew and Harriet (Morris) D. BS, California State Coll., Pa., 1953; M.Litt., U. Pitts., 1958; MS, Fla. State U., 1965; PhD (fellow), Ind. U., 1973. Tchr., Gateway Union Sch., Monroeville, Pa., 1953-64; instr. Fla. State U., 1965, spl. librarian, 1966, acting librarian, 1967; asso. prof. library sci., head of reference Mansfield (Pa.) State Coll., 1966-67, Winthrop Coll., Rock Hill, S.C., 1967-70; adj. prof. library sci. Ind. State U., 1972; prof. library sci., dir. Sandel Library, N.E. La. U., 1973-76; dean library services Old Dominion U., Norfolk, Va., from 1976. Adj. lectr. library sci. Cath. U. Am., 1979-80; dir. SOLINET, 1982-85; mem. OCLC Users Council, 1979-81, 85-86 Mem. ALA (chmn. ULS 1984, chmn. sect. rev. com. 1985-86), La. Library Assn., Va. Library Assn. (chmn. coll./univ. sect. 1980-81), Assn. Am. Library Schs. Died June 4, 2007.

DUNCAN, STARKEY DAVIS, JR., behavioral sciences educator; b. San Antonio, Aug. 24, 1935; s. Starkey Davis and Catherine (Poulson) D.; m. Susan Morton, June 30, 1960; children: Arne, Sarah, Owen BA, Vanderbilt U., 1957; PhD, U. Chgo., 1965. Postdoctoral fellow U. Chgo., 1965-67, asst. prof. behavioral scis., 1967-74, assoc. prof., 1974-81, prof., 1981-89, prof. psychology, 1989—2007. Author: (with others) Face-to-Face Interaction, 1977, (with others) Interaction Structure and Strategy, 1985; contbr. articles to profl. jours. Served to lt. (j.g.) USNR, 1957-59 Grantee, NSF, 1972, 75, 80, NIMH, 1978, 83, 88. Fellow Am. Psychol. Soc.; mem. AAAS, Soc. for Research in Child Devel. Died May 15, 2007.

DUNCAN, VIRGINIA IRWIN, lawyer; b. Parker Dam, Calif., May 7, 1949; d. George Gothic and Virginia E. (Dick) Irwin; m. Richard Vaughn Duncan, Jan. 25, 1971; 1 dau., Jessica Von. BS in Spl. Edn., No. Ariz. U., 1972, BS in Elem. Edn., 1972, MA in Spl. Edn., 1978; JD, U. Ariz., 1983. Cert. tchr. elem. edn., spl. edn., learning disabled, gifted, mentally retarded, blind, Ariz.; bar: Ariz. 1983. Dir., instr. spl. edn. program Beaver Creek Sch. Dist., Rimrock, Ariz., 1975-78; instr. Yavapai Community Coll., Verde Campus, Ariz., 1977-78; tchr. Verde Valley Sch., Sedona, Ariz., 1978, Beaver Creek Sch., Rimrock, 1972-79; assoc. Joyce & Frankel, P.A., Sedona, 1983-87; ptnr. Joyce, Levin & Duncan, P.A., 1988-91, ptnr. Duncan & Kazraqis, 1991—; bd. dirs. Sedona Acad., Ariz. Bar Estate and Trust Adv. Commn.; mem. exec. coun. Probate and Trust sect. Ariz. State Bar. Recipient Am. Jurisprudence award Lawyers Coop. Pub. Co. and Bancroft-Whitney Co., 1982, Samuel M. Fegtly award U. Ariz., 1982; Am. Field Service fgn. exchange student, 1966. Mem. ABA, Ariz. Bar Assn., Phi Kappa Phi, Phi Delta Phi. Democrat. Home: Cottonwood, Ariz. Died Apr. 28, 2006.

DUNHILL, JOHN STOKES, banker; b. Toronto, Ont., Can., Jan. 25, 1920; s. Reginald O. and Dorothy (McCune) D. BA, Princeton U., 1941. With Harris Trust & Savs. Bank, Chgo., 1941-80, sr. v.p., 1975-80. Served to 1st lt. AUS, 1942-46. Mem.: University (Chgo.). Home: Chicago, Ill. Died May 15, 2006.

DUNLOP, GEORGE RODGERS, retired surgeon; b. St. Peter, Minn., Mar. 31, 1906; s. George Crawford and Pearl (Rodgers) D.; m. Barbara Wallace, Apr. 3, 1939; children: Susan Dunlop Roberts, Madora Howell. BS, U. Cin., 1927; MD, Harvard U., 1931. Diplomate Am. Bd. Surgery. Intern Cin. Gen. Hosp., 1931-32; asst. resident in surgery N.Y. Hosp.-Cornell Med. Ctr., 1932-35; resident in surgery Worcester (Mass.) City Hosp., 1935-36; practice medicine specializing in surgery, 1935-82; sr. surgeon, past chief surgery Worcester Meml. Hosp. Prof. surgery emeritus U. Mass. Med. Sch.; dir., past chmn. Mass. Blue Shield; bd. dirs., past chmn. bd. Nat. Assn. Blue Shield Plans; past dir. Med. Indemnity Am.; bd. commrs. Joint Commn. Accreditation Hosps., chmn. bd. coms.; mem. Pres.'s Commn. for Study of Ethical Problems in Medicine and Biomed. and Behavioral Rsch. Bd. dirs. Meml. Hosp. Found.; bd. dirs., past chmn. Mass. divsn. Am. Cancer Soc., also, Worcester Found. Exptl. Biology; bd. dirs. U. Mass. Med. Sch. Found., Meml. Health Care Found.; past bd. dirs. Bancroft Sch., Worcester Boys' Club, Cmty. Chest. Served to lt. comdr. M.C. USNR, 1942-45. Fellow ACS (past pres.), Royal Australasian Coll. Surgeons (hon.); mem. AMA, New Eng. Surg. Soc. (past pres.), New Eng. Cancer Soc., Northwestern Med. Soc. (past pres.), Am. Surg. Assn., Boston Surg. Soc., Soc. Surgery Alimentary Tract (founder), Pan Am. Med. Assn. Clubs: Worcester. Home: Worcester, Mass. Died Mar. 11, 2007.

DUNN, JENNIFER BLACKBURN, former congresswoman; b. Seattle, July 29, 1941; d. John Charles and Helen (Gorton) Blackburn; m. Dennis Dunn (div. 1977); children: Bryant, Reagan; m. Keith Thomson, 2004 Student, U. Wash., 1960-62; BA in English Lit., Stanford U., 1963. Sys. engr. IBM, 1964-69; with King County Dept. of Assessments, 1979-80; chmn. Wash. State Rep. Party, 1981-92; mem. US Congress from 8th Wash. dist., Washington, 1993—2005. Bd. dirs. Nat. Endowment Democracy; mem. ways and means com., homeland sec. com., econ. com.; mem. adv. bd. Internat. Rep. Inst.; participant Preparatory Commn. World Conf. Status of Women, Nairobi, 1985, World Econ. Forum, Davos, Switzerland, 2000. Del. Rep. Nat. Conv., 1980, 84, 88; presdl. apptd. adv. coun. Historic Preservation, adv. coun. volunteerism SBA; apptd. presdl. commn. on debates; N.W. Regional Dir. Met. Operal Regional Auditions; mem. Jr. League of Seattle Named one of 25 Smartest Women in Am., Mirabella mag., one of 10 Most Powerful Women in Wash., Washington Law and Politics mag. Mem. Internat. Women's Forum (Wash. chpt.), Gamma Phi Beta. Republican. Died Sept. 5, 2007.

DUNN, WESLEY ASBURY, clinical and child psychologist; b. Winchester, Ind., Dec. 20, 1922; s. Francis W. and Florence (Goodrich) D.; m. Elsie Ann Locke, Apr. 5, 1952 (div. Jan. 1968); children— George, Stephanie, Francis, Elizabeth; m. Sandra L. Toneman, Oct. 13, 1973; children— J. Todd Aschleman, Jane Ann Aschleman. A.B., Harvard U., 1946, M.S., Purdue U., 1947; postgrad. Columbia U., 1948-50; Ph.D., Purdue U., 1951. Diplomate Am. Bd. Profl. Psychology. Asst. dir. Marion County Child Guidance Clinic, Indpls., 1951-62; cons. Marion County Juvenile Ct., 1958-74; pvt. practice psychology, 1960-74, Punta Gorda, Fla., 1980—. Bd. dirs. NAACP, Indpls., 1958-62, Ind. Civil Liberties Union, 1963-71. Served to 1st lt. USAF, 1944-47, Japan. Mem. Am. Psychol. Assn., Fla. Psychol. Assn., Ind. Psychol. Assn. (bd. dirs.). Avocations: sailing, golf, tennis, scuba diving. Died Aug. 1, 2006.

DUNNAHOO, TERRY (MRS. THOMAS WILLIAM DUNNAHOO), editor, author; b. Fall River, Mass., Dec. 8, 1927; d. Joseph Alfred and Emma Marie (Dolbec) Janson; m. Thomas William Dunnahoo, Sept. 18, 1954; children: Kim, Sean, Kelly. Student, Fall River Bus. Inst., 1948-49. Sec. Fall River Bus. Inst., 1949-51, Edwin Macy Esq., Fall River, 1951-52; land title researcher U.S. Navy, Guam, 1952-54; escrow officer S.W. Escrow Co., Inglewood, Calif., 1954-55; instr. Pasadena (Calif.) City Coll., 1971, 73, Pepperdine U., Los Angeles, 1971, So. Mass. U., Dartmouth, 1973, UCLA, from 1976; children's book editor, book reviewer W. Coast Rev. Books, 1977-92; book reviewer Los Angeles Herald-Examiner, 1980-85. Story cons. Asselin Prodns., Inc., Walt Disney Ednl. Media Co., 1987—; mem. mentor adv. bd. UCLA, 1987. Author: Nellie Bly, 1970, Annie Sullivan, 1970, Emily Dunning, 1970, Before the Supreme Court: The Story of Belva Ann Lockwood, 1974 (So. Calif. Council on Lit. for Children and Young People award 1975), Who Cares About Espie Sanchez?, 1975, This Is Espie Sanchez, 1976, Who Needs Espie Sanchez?, 1977, (pseudonym Margaret Terry) Last of April, 1982, Love For Tomorrow, 1983, Breakdancing, 1985, How to Write Children's Books, 1985, Alaska!, 1987, U.S. Territories, 1988, How to Win a School Election, 1989, The Lost Parrots of America, 1989, Pearl Harbor: America Enters The War, 1991, How To Survive High

School, 1993, Baseball Hall of Fame, 1993, Basketball Hall of Fame, 1993, Football Hall of Fame, 1993, Boston's Freedom Trail, 1994, Plimoth Plantation, 1995, Sacramento, 1997, The United States Mint, 1999. Mem. So. Calif. Coun. Lit. for Children and Young People (exec. bd. 1990—, Dorothy C. McKenzie award 1988). Mem. Authors Guild Am., Calif. Writers Guild (membership com. 1973-74, dir. 1974-78), PEN (exec. bd. 1972-77, pres. Los Angeles Center 1975-77), Book Publicists So. Calif., Women in Film, Soc. Children's Book Writers, Friends of Children and Librs. (exec. bd. dirs. 1979—). Home: Portland, Oreg. Died Nov. 21, 2006.

DUPLANTIER, ADRIAN GUY, federal judge; b. New Orleans, Mar. 5, 1929; s. F. Robert and Amelie (Rivet) D.; m. Sally Thomas, July 15, 1951; children: Adrian G., David L., Thomas, Jeanne M., Louise M., John C. JD cum laude, Loyola U., New Orleans, 1949; LLD, Loyola U., 1993; LLM, U. Va., 1988. Bar: La. 1950, U.S. Supreme Ct. 1954. Pvt. practice law, New Orleans, 1950-74; judge Civil Dist. Ct. Parish of Orleans, 1974-78, U.S. Dist. Ct., New Orleans, 1978-94, sr. judge, from 1994. Part-time prof. code of civil procedure Loyola U., 1951—, lectr. dental jurisprudence, 1960-67, lectr. English dept., 1948-50, chmn. law sch. vis. com., 1995-97, adj. prof. law, 1952—; prof. summer sch. abroad Tulane Law Sch., Rhodes, Greece, 1992, Cambridge, England, 1993, Loyola Law Sch., Vienna, Austria, 1996; mem. La. State Senate, 1960-74; 1st asst. dist. atty. New Orleans, 1954-56; mem. Jud. Conf. of U.S. Bankruptcy Rules Adv. Com., 1994-96, chmn. 1997—; elected La. State Senate, 1960-74; 5th cir. dist. judge rep. Jud. Conf. U.S., 1993-94, com. bicentennial of constn., 1986-91; chmn. Bill of Rights Bicentennial Conf. Fed. Judges, 1991. Editorial bd.: Loyola Law Rev, 1947-48; editor-in-chief, 1948-49. Del. Democratic Nat. Conv., 1964; pres. Associated Cath. Charities New Orleans, Social Welfare Planning Council Greater New Orleans; mem. adv. bd. St. Mary's Dominican Coll., 1970-71, Ursuline Acad., 1968-73, Mt. Carmel Acad., 1965-69; chmn. pres.'s adv. coun. Jesuit H.S., 1980-81, mem., 1976—; chmn. bd. dirs. Boys Hope, 1980—, nat. bd. dirs., 1982-92, coun., 1992—; active Assn. Retarded Children. Recipient Meritorious award New Orleans Assn. Retarded Children, 1965, Gov.'s Cert. of Merit, 1970, Outstanding Alumnus award Loyola U., 1985, Vol. Activist award Outstanding Vol. Svc., 1986. Mem. ABA (award 1960), La. Bar Assn., New Orleans Bar Assn., Loyola Law Sch. Vis. Com. (chmn. 1993-96), Jud. Conf. of U.S., Loyola Law Sch. Alumni Assn. (St. Ives award 1998), U.S. Adv. Com. (jud. conf. on bankruptcy rules 1993—, chmn. 1996—), Order of Coif, Alpha Sigma Nu. Died Aug. 15, 2007.

DURBIN, JAMES EDWARD, lawyer; b. Racine, Wis., Dec. 9, 1944; BS, USAF Acad., 1967; MBA, U. So. Calif., 1970; JD cum laude, Loyola Marymount U., 1973. Bar: Calif. 1973. Mem. Arter, Hadden, Lawler, Felix & Hall, LA. Articles editor Loyola Marymount Law Review, 1972-73. Capt. USAF, 1963-71. Mem. State Bar Calif., St. Thomas More Law Soc. Died Dec. 2006.

DURFEE, N. BARRY, JR., b. Fall River, Mass., Dec. 23, 1932; s. N. Barry and Ruth (Brayton) D.; m. Florence Wykoff, Aug. 20, 1965; children— John, Marjorie, Elizabeth, N. Barry III BA, Yale U., 1955. Salesman Ziff-Davis Pub. Co., from 1963, advt. dir., assoc. pub.; v.p., pub. CBS Mags., NYC, from 1985. Served to capt. USAF, 1956-59 Mem.: Country of New Canan (Conn.); Johns Island (Vero Beach, Fla.). Avocations: flying; golf; skiing. Home: Vero Beach, Fla. Died July 27, 2006.

DURKEE, JACKSON LELAND, civil engineer; b. Tatanagar, India, Sept. 20, 1922; s. E. Leland and Bernice J. (Jackson) D.; m. Marian H. Carty, Feb. 20, 1943; children: Janice M. Parry, Judith A. Durkee, Christine P. Simpson. BSCE, Worcester Poly. Inst., Mass., 1943, CE, 1951; MCE, Cornell U., Ithaca, NY, 1947. Registered profl. engr., Calif., Conn., N.Y., Pa.; chartered engr., U.K. Designer Douglas Aircraft Co., 1943-44; various engring. positions Fabricated Steel Constrn. div. Bethlehem Steel Corp., 1947-65, chief bridge engr., 1965-76; vis. prof. structural engring. Cornell U., 1976; ptnr. Modjeski and Masters, cons. engrs., Harrisburg, Pa., 1977-78; cons. structural engr. Bethlehem, Pa., 1978—2007. Contbr. chapters to books, articles on bridge and structural engring. to profl. jours. Served to lt. USNR, 1944-46, PTO. Recipient constrn. industry citation Engring. News-Record, 1968, Robert H. Goddard award Worcester Poly. Inst., 1998, John A. Roebling medal Engrs. Soc. Western Pa., 2002. Fellow ASCE (Ernest E. Howard award 1982, hon. mem. 1996), Instn. Civil Engrs. (U.K.), Instn. Structural Engrs. (U.K.); mem. Am. Inst. Econ. Rsch. (voting mem. corp. 2006-07), Nat. Soc. Profl. Engrs., Am. Ry. Engring. and Maintenance-of-Way Assn., Am. Welding Soc., Structural Stability Rsch. Coun., Internat. Assn. Bridge and Structural Engring., Nat. Acad. Engring. (cited for origination and devel. of innovations in fabrication and erection engring. of longspan bridges), Tau Beta Pi, Sigma Xi. Republican. Mem. Moravian Ch. Clubs: Silver Creek Country (Hellertown, Pa.); Cosmos (Washington); St. Andrews Golf, New Golf (St. Andrews, Scotland). Achievements include patents for shop-fabricated parallel-wire-strand method for construction of suspension bridge cables, and for pipe-assembly anchorage method and plastic-type weather protection system for such cables. Died June 14, 2007.

DURNBAUGH, DONALD FLOYD, church history educator, researcher; b. Detroit, Nov. 16, 1927; s. Floyd Devon and Ruth Elsie (Tombaugh) D.; m. Hedwig Therese Raschka, July 10, 1952; children: Paul D., Christopher S., Renate E. BA, Manchester Coll., Ind., 1949, LHD (hon.), 1980; MA, U. Mich., 1953; PhD, U. Pa., 1960; LHD (hon.), Juniata Coll., Pa., 2003. Dir. program Brethren Svc. Commn., Austria, 1953-56; asst. prof. history Juniata Coll., Huntingdon, Pa., 1958-62, J. Omar Good disting. prof. evang. Christianity, 1988-89, archivist, from 1992; assoc. prof. ch. history Bethany Theol. Sem., Oak Brook, Ill., 1962-69, prof. ch. history, 1970-88; dir. in Europe Brethren Colls. Abroad, France, Germany, 1964-65; Carl W. Zeigler prof. religion and history Elizabethtown (Pa.) Coll., 1989-93. Cons. Brethren Hist. Com., Elgin, Ill., 1982—; moderator Ch. of the Brethren, 1985-86 Author: European Origins of the Brethren, 1958, 4th edit., 1986, The Brethren in Colonial America, 1967, 3rd edit., 1996, Guide to Research in Brethren History, 1968, The Believers' Church: The History and Character of Radical Protestantism, 1968, 2nd edit., 1985, Every Need Supplied: Mutual Aid and Christian Community in the Free Churches, 1525-1675, 1974, Pragmatic Prophet: The Life of M.R. Zigler, 1989, Brethren Beginnings: The Origin of the Church of the Brethren in Early Eighteenth-Century Europe, 1992, Fruit of the Vine: A History of the Brethren, 1708-1995, 1997; editor: Die Kirche der Brueder: Vergangenheit und Gegenwart, 1971, The Church of the Brethren: Past and Present, 1971, To Serve the Present Age: The Brethren Service Story, 1975, On Earth Peace: Discussion on War/Peace Issues Between Friends, Mennonites, Brethren and European Churches, 1935-1975, 1978, Church of the Brethren: Yesterday and Today, 1986; editor-in-chief The Brethren Ency., Inc., 1978-84; contbr. articles, book revs. to scholarly jours., periodicals. Alternative svc. as conscientious objector, 1953-56. U. Pa. Scholar, 1956-57, fellow, 1957-58; NEH sr. fellow, 1976-77; fellow Assn. Theol. Schs., 1986-87; recipient Alumni award Manchester Coll., 1978. Fellow Young Ctr. for Study of Anabaptist and Pietist Groups; assoc. Inst. of Mennonite Studies; mem. Am. Soc. Ch. History, Brethren Jour. Assn., Soc. German Am. Studies, Communal Studies Assn., Pa. German Soc. Mem. Ch. Of The Brethren. Home: James Creek, Pa. Died Aug. 27, 2005.

DUROSS, WILLIAM JAMES, JR., mortician; b. Detroit, Nov. 6, 1935; s. William James and Mary Augusta (Rotarius) D.; m. Nancy Marie Gipperich, Sept. 28, 1968; children— William James III, Amy Marie. Student, U. Detroit, 1953-54; cert. mortuary sci. Wayne State U.-Detroit, 1956. Lic. mortician, Mich. Resident tng. Weitenberner Funeral Home, Detroit, 1952-56 owner, pres., treas., dir., 1983—; with William R. Hamilton Co., Detroit, 1957, DeSantis Funeral Home, Detroit, 1957-65, owner, pres., treas., dir. Wm. J. Duross Funeral Home, Warren, Mich., 1966—. Mem. Nat. Funeral Dirs. Assn., Mich. Funeral Dirs. Assn., Warren Symphony Assn., Kolping Soc. Roman Catholic. Clubs: Elks, Kiwanis, Optimist, Lions. Died Mar. 20, 2007.

DU SAULT, PHILIP AMES, federal agency administrator; b. Spokane, Wash., June 19, 1937; s. Philemon Edward and Helen Violet (Ames) Du S.; m. Deborah Elizabeth Sullivan, Sept. 30, 1967; children: William Ames, Anne Sullivan. BA, Harvard U., 1961. Program officer Peace Corps, Washington, 1962-66; budget examiner for internat. affairs Office Mgmt. and Budget, Washington, 1966-75, br. chief internat. econ. affairs, 1975-80, div. chief internat. affairs, from 1980. Sgt. USAR, 1965-67. Recipient Meritorious Exec. Svc. award Office Pers. Mgmt., 1985, Presdl. Disting. Svc. award White House, 1987. Mem. Harvard Club. Episcopalian. Home: Washington, DC. Died Aug. 30, 2006.

DUVAL, MERLIN KEARFOTT, health consultant, former dean; b. Montclair, NJ, Oct. 12, 1922; married 1944; 3 children. AB, Dartmouth Coll., 1943; MD, Cornell U., 1946; DSc, NJ Coll. Medicine & Dentistry, Dartmouth Coll., Med. Coll. Wis., Coll. Osteo. Medicine; LHD, Ohio Coll. Podiatric Medicine. Founding dean coll. medicine U. Ariz., 1964-79; asst. sec. for health US Dept. Health, Edn. & Welfare, Washington, 1971-73; pres., CEO Nat. Ctr. for Health Edn., 1979-82, Am. Healthcare Inst., 1982-88; health cons., 1990—2006. Mem. AMA, ACS, Am. Surg. Assn., Soc. Med. Adminstrs. Home: Phoenix, Ariz. Died Dec. 5, 2006.

DVORAK, ROGER GRAN, health facility executive; b. St. Paul, Aug. 30, 1934; s. William Anthony and Evelyn Carolyn (Gran) D.; m. Gail Ann Peterson, Dec. 30, 1960; children: Karen, Mark. BBA, U. Minn., 1955, MHA, 1957. Asst. adminstr. Glenwood Hills Hosp., Mpls., 1958-61; asst. hosp. adminstrv. svcs. dir. Phila. Gen. Hosp., 1961-65; asst. dir. Presbyn. U. Pa. Med. Ctr., Phila., 1965-67, assoc. dir., 1967-72; adminstr. Symmes Hosp., Arlington, Mass., 1972-78; exec. dir. Lawrence Hosp., Bronxville, N.Y., 1978-86, pres., 1986-2000; ret., 2000. Fellow Am. Coll. Healthcare Execs. Presbyterian. Avocations: painting, music. Home: Woodbury, Minn. Died Jan. 9, 2007.

DWIGHT, JAMES SCUTT, JR., state agency official; b. Pasadena, Calif., Mar. 9, 1934; s. James Scutt and Natalie (Phelps) D.; m. Elsa Fae Hardy, Dec. 27, 1953; children: Catherine, Janet, Dianne, James Scutt III. Student, Pomona Coll., 1951-53; BS, U. So. Calif., 1956. C.P.A., Calif., D.C. With Deloitte Haskins & Sells (C.P.A.'s), Los Angeles, 1955-59; controller Sunkist Growers, Inc., Los Angeles, 1959-66; chief dep. dir. fin. State of Calif., 1966-72; assoc. dir. Office Mgmt. and Budget, Exec. Office Pres., Washington, 1972-73; adminstr. Social and Rehab. Service, HEW, 1973-75; dep. dir. Calif. State Dept. Fish and Game; chief dep. dir. Calif. State Dept. Fin., Sacramento, from 1990; ptnr. Deloitte Touche (CPAs), Washington, 1975-90, ret., 1990. Dir. Calif. Pub. Employees Retirement System, 1967-72, Calif. State Tchrs. Retirement System, 1967-72; alt. mem. Calif. Franchise Tax Bd., 1967-72, Calif. State Lands Commn., 1967-72, 90—, Calif. Toll Bridge Authority, 1967-72; alt. dir. San Francisco Port Authority, 1970-72; lectr. Fed. Exec. Inst., Charlottesville, Va., 1972-78, MFOA Career Devel. Center, 1979-81; chmn. Calif Commn. on State Mandates, 1990—; dir. Calif. State Bond Coms., 1990. Bd. dirs., v.p. Los Angeles Jr. C. of C., 1962-66; bd. dirs. Red. Shield Youth Center, 1963-66, United Black Fund D.C., 1977-85; mem. D.C. Mayor's Adv. Panel, 1977; bd. dirs. Nat. Inst. Public Mgmt., 1981; chmn. Pres.'s Commn. on Hostage Compensation, 1981; mem. transition team on budget Office of Pres.-elect, 1981; bd. govs. govt. relations com. United Way of Am., 1981-85; trustee, treas. Meridian House, 1982-89; mem. Cabinet Council Work Group on Federalism, 1982; pvt. citizen mem. Adv. Commn. on Intergovtl. Relations, 1983-89. Recipient Outstanding Young Man award U.S. Jaycees, 1966 Mem. AICPA (fed. govt. exec. com.), Washington Golf and Country Club, Arden Hills Country Club (Sacramento). Home: Sacramento, Calif. Died Apr. 16, 2006.

DWINGER, PHILIP, educator, university dean; b. The Hague, The Netherlands, Sept. 25, 1914; came to U.S., 1956; s. Aron and Geline (van Dam) D. PhD in Math, U. Leiden, The Netherlands, 1938. Tchr. Lyceum, The Netherlands, 1937-52; prof. math., head dept. U. Indonesia, 1952-56; prof. Purdue U., 1956-62, Tech. U. Delft, The Netherlands, 1962-65, U. Ill. at Chgo. Circle, from 1965, head dept. math., 1975-79; dean U. Ill. at Chgo. Coll. Liberal Arts and Scis., 1979-85, dean, prof. emeritus, from 1985. Vis. prof. U. Hamburg, W. Germany, 1960, Calif. Inst. Tech., 1971, U. Amsterdam, Netherlands, 1972, Technol. U., Darmstadt, West Germany, summer 1974; vis. mathematician Math. Assn. Am., 1966— Author: Introduction to Boolean Algebras, 1961, (with R. Balbes) Distributive Lattices, 1974; also research papers in lattice theory and universal algebra. Mem. Math. Assn. Am., Am. Math. Soc., Royal Netherlands Acad. Scis. and Letters (corr.), Math. Assn. The Netherlands, Sigma Xi., Phi Kappa Phi Died Nov. 2, 2006.

DWYER, TERRY TAYLOR, editor; b. Alexander, ND, Apr. 4, 1922; s. James William and Grace Isabel (Taylor) Dwyer; m. Marie Gustafson, May 17, 1941; children: VerNel Carver, Colleen Lulf, Maureen Downey, Kelly, Sean. Reporter Ind.-Record, Helena, Mont., 1946—53, Tribune, Gt. Falls, Mont., 1953—65, city editor, 1965—74, mng. editor, from 1974, corp. v.p., mng. editor, from 1984. Recipient Disting. Reporter of Pub. Affairs award, Am. Polit. Sci. Assn., 1962. Mem.: Sigma Delta Chi. Home: Great Falls, Mont. Died Mar. 11, 2007.

DYER, GEORGE LEWIS, JR., lawyer; b. Detroit, Dec. 30, 1931; s. George Lewis and Florence Coote (Rock) D.; m. Dolores Lei Eaton, Nov. 8, 1957; children— Matthew E., Jennifer F.P., Mary F. B.A., Cornell U., 1955; LL.B. cum laude, Harvard U., 1961. Bar: Hawaii 1961. Assoc. Goodsill Anderson & Quinn, Honolulu, 1961-66, ptnr., 1967-80; pvt. practice Honolulu, 1981-87; pres. George L. Dyer, Jr., Law Corp., Honolulu, 1981-87; house counsel Ludlow Maintainance Commn., Port Ludlow, Wash., 1988—; lectr. U. Hawaii, Hawaii Inst. Continuing Legal Edn. Mem. rules com., del. Republican Nat. Conv., 1972, 76; 4th vice chmn. Rep. Party Hawaii, 1971-73; chmn. Rep. State Conv., 1972; chmn. Hawaii Lawyers Com. to Re-elect the Pres., 1972; chmn. rules com. Rep. Party Hawaii, 1970-73, 83-87; mem. State of Hawaii ofcl. observers primary and gen. elections, 1974, chmn., 1976, 78; mem. State of Hawaii Lt. Gov.'s election adv. com. 1974-76, chmn., 1976-78; mem. Hawaii Bicentennial Commn., 1986-87; bd. dirs. Legal Aid Soc. Hawaii 1969-72, Friends of Hawaii Pub. TV, 1977-79, Arts Coun. Hawaii, 1980-83, Small Bus. Hawaii, 1983-87. Served to lt. (j.g.) USNR, 1955-58. Mem. ABA, Hawaii Bar Assn. (bd. dirs. 1972). Editor, Hawaii Bar Jour., 1965-66. Home: Gig Harbor, Wash. Died May 12, 2006.

DYKEMAN, WILMA, writer, educator; b. Asheville, NC, May 20, 1920; d. Willard J. and Bonnie (Cole) Dykeman; m. James R. Stokely Jr., Oct. 12, 1940 (dec. 1977); children: Dykeman Cole, James R. III. BS inSpeech, Northwestern U., 1940; LittD, Maryville Coll., 1974; LHD, Tenn. Wesleyan Coll., 1978; DHL (hon.), U. N.C., Asheville, 1997. Lectr. English dept. U. Tenn., Knoxville, 1975-95, adj. prof., 1985-95; now writer, lectr. Columnist Knoxville News-Sentinel, 1962-99; historian State of Tenn., 1980-2006; nat. lectr. in field. Author: The French Broad: A Rivers of America Volume, 1955, The Tall Woman, 1962, Seeds of Southern Change: The Life of Will Alexander, 1962, The Far Family, 1966, Prophet of Plenty: The First Ninety Years of W.D. Weatherford, 1966, Look to This Day, 1968, Return the Innocent Earth, 1973, Too Many People, Too Little Love: Edna Rankin McKinnon, Pioneer for Birth Control, 1974, Tennessee: A Bicentennial History, 1975, Tennessee Women: Past and Present, 1977, Explorations, A Collection of Essays, 1984, Tennessee Women: An Infinite Variety, 1993; co-author: (with James R. Stokely) Neither Black Nor White (Sidney Hillman award), 1957, The Border States: Kentucky, North Carolina, Tennessee, Virginia, West Virginia, 1968, Highland Home: The People of the Great Smokies, 1978; (with Dykeman Stokely) Applachin Mountains, 1980; contbr. articles to nat. mags. and Ency. Brit. Trustee Berea Coll., 1971-95, Phelps Stokes Fund, 1981-91, U. N.C.-Asheville, 1985-91; active Friends of Great Smokies Nat. Park. Guggenheim fellow, 1956-57, NEH fellow, 1976-77; recipient North Carolina award for Lit, 1985, Disting. So. Writers award So. Festival of Books, 1989; N.C. Gold medal for Contbn. to Am. letters, 1985. Mem. PEN, Authors Guild, So. Hist. Assn., Cosmos Club, Phi Beta Kappa, Delta Kappa Gamma. Home: Newport, Tenn. Died Dec. 22, 2006.

DZURIK, JOHN GERARD, lawyer; b. Bridgeport, Conn., May 2, 1950; s. John Joseph and Mary Ann (Orlovski) D. Grad., Sch. Fgn. Service, Georgetown U., 1972; JD, Georgetown U., 1975. Bar: Conn. 1975, U.S. Dist. Ct. Conn. 1975, Wash. 1987. Assoc. Goldstein & Peck, P.C., Bridgeport, 1975-81, now ptnr.; corp. counsel Gen. Electric. Credit Corp., Stamford, Conn., 1981-82; assoc. Gamm & Gamm, P.C., Hamden, Conn., 1982-83; of counsel Harlow Knott & Adams, Stratford, Conn., 1983-85; former ptnr. Chaplowe Dzurik & Jaekle, Stratford, from 1986. Mem. ABA (state membership chmn. 1984—, dist. del. young lawyers div. 1981-83), Conn. Bar Assn. (ho. of dels. 1986—), Bridgeport Bar Assn., Georgetown U. Alumni Assn. (bd. dirs. 1981—), Delta Phi Epsilon. Home: Bridgeport, Conn. Died Aug. 12, 2007.

EARLE, RICHARD ALAN, lawyer; b. NYC, Apr. 30, 1941; s. Edward William and Ruth Henrietta (Quinn) E.; m. Nancy Ann Nikkinen; children: Jonathan, Karen, Geoffrey. BBA, U. Mich., 1963, MBA, 1964, JD, 1968. Bar: Mich. 1968, U.S. Supreme Ct. 1968, D.C. 1969. Ptnr. Patton Boggs, L.L.P., Washington, from 1968. Served to lt. USN, 1963-66. Mem. Am. Soc. Internat. Law, Washington Fgn. Law Soc. Avocation: sailing. Home: Galesville, Md. Died Feb. 13, 2006.

EBRIGHT, GEORGE WATSON, health care company executive; b. Chadds Ford, Pa., Mar. 27, 1938; s. George Grant and Letitia Myrtle (McKee) E.; m. Catherine Edna Sharp, Sept. 30, 1961; children— Bradford, Katherine BA, Franklin and Marshall Coll., 1960; MBA, U. Del., 1965. Salesman Atlantic Refining Co., Phila., 1960-61; various mgmt. positions Sun Olin, Claymont, Del., 1961-63, Smith Kline Beckman Corp., Phila., 1963-89; pres., chief operating officer SmithKline Beckman Corp., Phila., 1989; chmn., pres., chief exec. officer Cytogen Corp., from 1989. With U.S. Army, 1960-66 Mem.: Merion Golf, Merion Cricket (Ardmore, Pa.), Sunday Breakfast, Masons. Home: Chesapeake City, Md. Died Apr. 24, 2006.

EDEL, ABRAHAM, philosophy educator; b. Pitts., Dec. 6, 1908; s. Simon and Fannie (Malamud) E.; m. May Mandelbaum, Jan. 30, 1934 (dec. May 1964); children: Matthew (dec.), Deborah; m. Elizabeth Flower, May 11, 1973 (dec. June 1995); m. Sima Szaluta, Apr. 20, 1997. BA, McGill U., 1927, MA, 1928; BA, Oxford U., 1930; PhD, Columbia U., 1934. Mem. faculty dept. philosophy CCNY, 1931-73, prof., 1962-73, prof. emeritus, from 1973; Disting. prof. Grad. Sch. CUNY, 1970-73; emeritus City U. N.Y. Grad. Sch., from 1973; rsch. prof. philosophy U. Pa., 1974—2001, rsch. prof. emeritus, from 2001. Vis. appointments instns. including Columbia U., U. Calif., Berkeley, Swarthmore Coll., U. Pa., Case Western Res. U., SUNY, Downstate Med. Ctr., others. Author: The Theory and Practice of Philosophy, 1946, Ethical Judgment, 1955, 2d edit. with new intro., 1995, Science and the Structure of Ethics, 1961, 2nd edit., 1998, with new intro., Method in Ethical Theory, 1963, with new intro., 1994, Aristotle, 1967; co-author: (with May Edel) Anthropology and Ethics, 1959, rev. edit., 1971, 2000, Analyzing Concepts in Social Science, 1979, Exploring Fact and Value, 1980, Aristotle and His Philosophy, 1982, with new intro., 1996, Interpreting Education, 1985, (with Elizabeth Flower and Finbarr O'Connor) Morality, Philosophy and Practice, 1988, Relating Humanities and Social Thought, 1990, The Struggle for Academic Democracy, 1990, In Search of the Ethical, 1993, (with others) Critique of Applied Ethics, 1994; (with Yervant H. Krikorian) Contemporary Philosophic Problems, 1959; editor: (with May M. Edel) The Chiga of Uganda, 1996, Ethical Theory and Social Change: The Evolution of John Dewey's Ethics, 1908-32, 2001. Assoc. Nat. Humanities Ctr., 1978-79; sr. fellow Ctr. for Dewey Studies, 1981-82. Recipient Butler Silver medal Columbia U., 1959; Guggenheim fellow, 1944-45; Grantee, Rockefeller Found., 1952-53, NSF, 1959-60. Mem. Am. Philos. Assn. (v.p. Ea. div. 1972), Metaphys. Soc., Am. Soc. Polit. and Legal Philosophy, Am. Soc. Value Inquiry (pres. 1984), Internat. Assn. Philosophy Law and Social Philosophy (v.p. Am. sect. 1971-73, pres. 1973-75, hon. pres. 1997), Philosophy Edn. Soc., Soc. for Advancement Am. Philosophy. Home: Philadelphia, Pa. Died June 22, 2007.

EDMONDSON, HAZEL MARIE, plumbing and heating supply company executive; b. Mercer County, Ky., June 24, 1929; d. Harlan and Jennie (Chapman) Parker; m. Henry Nathan Edmondson, May 27, 1950; 1 child, Nathan Alan. Grad. high sch., Harrodsburg, Ky. Pres., bookkeeper, office mgr. Edmondson Plumbing and Heating Supply, Inc., Lawrenceburg, Ky., 1975—. Democrat. Methodist. Avocations: china painting; ceramics. Home: Lawrenceburg, Ky. Died Jan. 29, 2006.

EDMONSON, JAMES HOWARD, history educator, minister; b. Sylacanga, Ala., May 19, 1931; s. Cecil Howard Edmonson and Flora Belle (Owings) Coleman: m. Frances Tucker, Nov. 23, 1954; children: Betty Faith Edmonson Porter, Deborah Lynn Edmonson Thoni, James David. BA, Samford U., 1957; MDiv, So. Bapt. Theol. Sem., 1961; MA, La. State U., Baton Rouge, 1963, PhD, 1971; postgrad., U.S. Army War Coll., 1978-80, London Poly. Inst., 1987. Prof. history Union U., Jackson, Tenn., from 1965, chmn. history dept., from 1971, 1971-89. Adj. instr. U. Tenn., Martin, 1972—; pastor Woodlawn Bapt. Ch., Nutbush, Tenn., 1973—. Del. Ltd. Constl. Conv., Nashville, 1971; mem. com. State Exec. Dem. Com., Tenn., 1972-86; elector Presdl. Electoral Coll., Tenn., 1976; commr. Tenn. Hist. Commn., Nashville, 1976-85, Bd. Commrs., Madison County, Tenn., 1978-82. Col., chaplain USAR, lt. col. Tenn. Def. Forces, 1990—. Mem. Am. Hist. Assn., Tenn. Hist. Soc., West Tenn. Hist. Soc. (v.p. 1979—, Cert. award 1982), So. Hist. Assn., Orgn. Am. Historians. Clubs: Jackson Exchange (mem. exec. bd. 1979-83, Cert. Appreciation 1976). Democrat. Baptist. Avocation: football. Home: Jackson, Tenn. Died Feb. 3, 2006.

EDMUNDS, JANE CLARA, media consultant; d. John Carson and Clara (Kummerow) Carrigan; m. William T. Dean, Aug. 30, 1947 (div. 1953; dec. July 1984); 1 son, John Charles; Edmund S. Kopacz, Sept. 24, 1955 (div. 1973); children: Christine Ellen, Jan Carson. Student in chemistry and math., Northwestern U. Chemist Mars Inc., Oak Park, Ill., 1942-47; with Cons. Engr. Mag., Maujer Pub. Co., St. Joseph, Mich., 1953-58, 69-74; sr. editor Cons. Engr. Mag. Tech. Pub. Co., Barrington, Ill., 1975-77, exec. editor, 1977-82, editorial dir., 1983-86; asst. editor women's pages rewrite desk News-Palladium, Benton Harbor, Mich., 1967-68; freelance journalist St. Joseph, 1959-68; communications cons. Schaumburg, Ill., from 1987. Chmn. Berrien County (Mich.) Nat. Found. March of Dimes, 1968; mem. campaign com. Rep. Party, 1954. Recipient award Bausch & Lomb, 1940, award Nat. Found. Service, 1969, Silver Hat award Constrn. Writers Assn., 1986, honor mem. 2000, Chmn.'s award Profl. Engrs. in Pvt. Practice div. NSPE, 1987; grantee AID, 1979 Assoc. fellow Soc. Tech. Communication (chmn. St. Joseph chpt. 1972 Disting. Tech. Communication awards); mem. Am. Soc. Bus. Press Editors (past bd. mem.), Constrn. Writers Assn., Smithsonian Instn., Chgo. Art Inst. Assocs., Field Mus. Assocs. Republican. Episcopalian. Home: Hoffman Est, Ill. Died Aug. 24, 2007.

EDWARDS, ALFRED LEROY, economist; b. Key West, Fla., Aug. 9, 1920; s. Eddie E. and Kathleen L. E.; m. Willie Mae Lewis, June 4, 1949; children— Beryl L., Alfred Leroy. BS, Livingstone Coll., Salisbury, NC, 1948; MA, U. Mich., 1949; PhD, U. Iowa, 1957. Spl. asst. to commnr. Consumer Product Safety Commn., Washington, 1973-74; dep. asst. sec. agr., 1963-74; asst. prof. econs. Mich. State U., East Lansing, 1957-60, prof., from 1974; dir. research Mich. State U. (Grad. Sch. Bus. Adminstrn.), from 1974; prof. emeritus bus. adminstrn. U. Mich., from 1991. Econ. advisor to, Nigeria, 1960-62; mem. adv. com. equal opportunity Dept. Agr., 1979; dir. Security Bankcorp., Southgate, Mich.; cons. in field. Trustee Western Mich. U. Served with USAAF, 1943-46. Postdoctoral fellow Ford Found., 1957; Postdoctoral fellow U. Mich., 1958; Danforth Faculty fellow, 1956 Mem. Am. Econs. Assn., Nat. Econs. Assn. Presbyterian. Home: Ann Arbor, Mich. Died Jan. 26, 2007.

EDWARDS, CHARLES HAYDEN, former railroad executive; b. Louisville, June 24, 1924; s. James P. and Margaret (Wathen) E.; m. Sara Hulette Cummins, June 7, 1958; children— Richard Wathen, Cecilia Barber. AB, Harvard, 1948; LL.B., U. Va., 1951. Bar: Ky. 1951. Asst. city atty., Louisville, 1952-57; pvt. practice law, 1957-58; with L. & N. R.R., from 1958, sec., gen. atty., 1965-66, sec., treas., from 1967, v.p., from 1972; also v.p. and corp. sec. all corps. comprising The Family Lines Rail System.; now ret. Trustee Aquinas Prep. Sch., 1965-67; campaign chmn. Louisville Fund for Arts, 1973, pres., 1974; pres. Filson Club Hist. Soc., 1987—. Mem. ABA, Ky. Bar Assn., Louisville Bar Assn., Assn. Am. R.R. (chmn. treasury div.). Clubs: Louisville Country, Tavern (pres. 1970), River Valley (Louisville) (pres. 1973-74); Harmony Landing Country (Goshen, Ky.). Democrat. Roman Catholic. Home: Louisville, Ky. Died Mar. 25, 2006.

EDWARDS, CHARLES RICHARD, retired printing equipment and supplies company executive; b. South Bend, Ind., July 16, 1931; s. Bernard Stuart and Mary Irene (Chamberlaine) Edwards; m. Joanne Wood, Dec. 15, 1950; children: Timothy Stuart, Terry Lynne, David Bryan. Pressman Toastmasters Internat., Santa Ana, Calif., 1954—60; with 3M Co., 1960—66, salesman Western U.S. tech. svc. and nat. market mgr. St. Paul, 1966—69; CEO, sec., CFO, co-owner Graphic Arts Supplies, Inc., Orange, Calif., 1969—86; owner, operator Edwards Bus. Svcs., 1987—91; bu.s and trade cons., 1986—91; instr., cons. in field. Bd. dirs., treas. #1 Network, Inc., Chgo., 1982—86. With USAF, 1950—54, Korea. Mem.: Nat. Assn. Printing House Craftsmen (past chpt. pres., regional officer), Nat. Assn. Lithographic Clubs (chpt. co-founder, officer, dir.), Hobo Golf Assn. (pres. from 1985), Toastmasters Club. Republican. Home: Westminster, Calif. Died Oct. 31, 2006.

EELLS, WILLIAM HASTINGS, retired automobile company executive; b. Princeton, Mar. 30, 1924; s. Hastings and Amy (Titus) E.; 1 child, Jonathan William. BA, Ohio Wesleyan U., 1946; MA, Ohio State U., 1950; DHL (hon.), Kent State U., 1983; D of Pub. Svc., Bowling Green State U., 1983; D of Cmty. Leadership (hon.), Franklin U., 2005. Asst. to dir. Inst. Practical Politics Ohio Wesleyan U., 1948-50, dir., 1953-57, instr. dept. polit. sci., 1952-59; instr. polit. sci. Mt. Union Coll., 1950-51; mem. Ohio Gov.'s Cabinet, 1957-59; coord. Atomic Devel. Activities State of Ohio, 1957-59; Midwest regional mgr. civic and govtl. affairs Ford Motor Co., Columbus, 1959-87. Author: Your Ohio Government, 1953 (6 edits.); contbr. articles to profl. jours Mem. Nat. Coun. on Arts, NEA, 1976-82; chmn. bd. Blue Cross of Northeast Ohio, 1963-72, Blossom Music Ctr., Cleve., 1968—; chmn. bd. govs. Gov.'s Coun. on Rehab., 1966-68; mem. exec. com. Met. Opera's Nat. Coun., 1967-81; pres. Nat. Coun. High Blood Pressure Rsch., 1974-79; chmn. Ohio Pub. Expenditure Coun., 1981-84, Gov.'s Task Force on State Ops., 1984-85; vice chmn. Ohio Northwest Bicentennial Com., 1986-87; bd. dirs. Am. Heart Assn., 1974-79, Columbus Mus. Art, 1982-88, Opera/Columbus, 1984-86, Columbus Ballet, 1985-86, Nat. Coun. French Am. Scholarship Found., 1985-87; trustee Cleve. Orch., 1964—, Hist. Morven Found., Princeton, N.J., 1988-96, Ednl. TV, Cleve., 1965-75, Cleve. Playhouse, 1965-82, Cleve. Ballet, Cleve. Zoo, 1965-76, Ohio Arts Coun., Columbus Symphony, Cleve. Luth. Hosp., 1966-76, Mt. Union Coll., 1984—, Ohio Wesleyan U., 1988—; trustee Franklin U., 1987—, Columbus Assn. Performing Arts, 1978—, Ohio Found. Ind. Colls., 1986—, Grady Meml. Hosp., 1987-94, Riverside Hosp. Found., 1990-96; hon. chmn. Del. Arts Ctr., 1989—; life trustee Fairview Health Cleve., 1980—; trustee, v.p. Oak Grove Cemetery, 1983—; chmn. Ohio Commn. for Son of Heaven Imperial Arts of China, 1988; mem. Ohio Humanities Coun., 1993-95; patron Morgan Libr., N.Y.C., 1995—; trustee Del. County Dist. Libr. Bd., 1994—; mem. Ohio Bicentennial Commn., 1997-2002; trustee Columbus Zoo Assn., 1998—; mem. Friends Princeton U. Libr., 1997- Recipient USCG Disting. award, 1965, Silver medal Royal Life Saving Soc., Ohio State U. Devel. award, 1967, award for disting. svc. Am. Heart Assn., 1979, Ohio Arts Coun. award, 1979, Ohio Theatre Alliance award, 1981, Gov. award, 1985, Alumni Achievement award Ohio State U., 1987, Silver medal Japanese Red Cross Soc Mem.: Rock & Roll Hall of Fame (charter mem. from 1995), Blossom Bd. Overseers (life). Republican. Presbyterian (elder). Home: Delaware, Ohio. Died May 11, 2007.

EGAN, WILLIAM EUGENE, labor union administrator; b. Hawthorne, Calif., Aug. 23, 1936; s. Eugene and Charlotte (Baldwin) Egan; m. Marlene R. McEwen, Sept. 30, 1956; children: Edward, Richard, James, Pamela. Lic. electrician various states. With Anaconda Co., Butte, 1952—54, Victor Chem., Butte, 1955—56, Tierney Bros., Butte, 1957—60; operating engr. F & S Constrn., Butte, 1960—62; electrician Elec. Industries, various locations, 1962—76; bus. mgr. fin. sec. Internat. Brotherhood Elec. Workers, Local #122, Gt. Falls, Mont., from 1976; v.p. Mont. State Bldg. and Constrn. Trades, Helena, from 1976. Pres. Mont. Conf. Elec. Workers, Cascade County Trades and Labor Assembly; mem. exec. bd. Mont. Elec. Constrn. Labor and Mgmt. Coop. Com.; bd. dirs. Mont. Elec. Joint Apprenticeship Tng., Helena, from 1976; advisor trustee 8th Dist. Elec. Pension Trust, Denver, from 1976. Bd. dirs. Western Environ. Trade Assn., Helena, from 1977, Gt. Falls Econ. Growth Coun., 1981—83; adv. bd. Pacific N.W. Power Planning Coun., from 1980; advisor Butte VoTech Ednl. Ctr., from 1974. Mem.: Internat. Found. Employment Benefit Plans, Mont. Mining Assn. (pres. 1968—71). Democrat. Methodist. Home: Great Falls, Mont. Died July 15, 2006.

EICHFELD, TIMOTHY JOSEPH, manufacturing executive; b. Camden, NJ, Sept. 22, 1946; s. Paul A. and Loretta A. (Henwood) E.; m. Kathleen Patricia Struzinski, June 7, 1969 (div. Mar. 1990); children: Timothy Joseph 2d, Joseph Brian, Damian James, David John. AAS, Camden County Coll., 1974; BBA cum laude, U. Pa., 1977. V.p., gen. mgr. Van Wood Mfg. Co., Inc., Cherry Hill, NJ, 1966—77; pres., chmn. bd. Disstim Corp., Deptford, NJ, from 1977. Guest spkr. Wharton Sch., U. Pa., 1978—79. Active Runnemede Youth Assn. Served US Army, 1967—69. Decorated Bronze Star, Purple Heart, Air medal; cert. in practical machining prins. Mem. Am. Mgmt. Assns., VFW, DAV, Sigma Kappa Phi, KC Club (3d deg.). Democrat. Roman Catholic. Achievements include patents in Work Hold-down for Machine Tool having Table and Column, Folding Stepladder, Adjustable Flow Coolant Nozzle, Fishing Poke Mounting Device. Home: Stratford, NJ. Died June 10, 2007.

EICHOLD, SAMUEL, internal medicine educator, curator; b. Mobile, Ala., May 27, 1916; s. Bernard H. and Myra (Solomon) E.; m. Charlotte Hartsig, Feb. 26, 1943; children: Beth, Alice, Bert. BS, Tulane U., 1937, MD, 1940; LLD (hon.), Spring Hill Coll., 1991. Intern Touro Infimary, 1941; resident in internal medicine City Hosp. Mobile, 1941; pvt. practice medicine specializing in internal medicine Mobile, 1946-72; prof. medicine dept. internal medicine U. South Ala., Mobile, 1973-84, prof. emeritus, from 1984; hon. prof. Universidad Francisco Marroquin, from 1985; dir. continuing edn. U. South Ala., Mobile, 1975-82, perceptor history of medicine, 1976, perceptor rural and tropical medicine in developing nation, from 1976; med. dir. Central Plaza Towers Med. Ctr., 1981-98, Allen Meml. Home, 1973—2002, Cogburn Nursing Home, 1975-81, Hillhaven-Mobile, 1980-85, Mercy Med. Hosp., 1985-94; med. advisor Ala. Dept. Corrections, from 1987. Bd. dirs. Mercy Med., 1989-98, vice chmn. Old Mobile Restoration; bd. trustees Spring Hill Coll., 1991-2000, emeritus, 2001; pres. Mobile Revolving Fund for Hist. Properties, 1992-96. Author: Without Malice-100 Year History of Comic Cowboys of Mobile; mem. editorial bd. ADA Forecast mag., 1987-91, Ala. Treasure Forest Gulf Coast Hist. rev.; contbr. articles to profl. jours. Asst. county health officer Mobile County; bd dir. Preventable Disease, 1974-75; active Josiah C. Nott Found., 1980; founder, curator Heustis Med. Mus.; established Camp Seale Harris for Diabetic Children, 1947; sec./treas. Mobile Imfirmary, 1967-68; officer Mobile Tree Commn., 1968-73, chmn., 1973; bd. dirs. Mobile Symphony, Mobile Chamber Music Soc., Inc., 1952-75, Mobile Opera Assn., Hist. Mobile Preservation, 1977-84, Mobile chpt. ARC, 1951, Fine Arts Mus. of South, 1975-81, Mobile Mus., 1975-81, Mobile Hist. Mus., 1994—, Mobile Mus. Art, 1995—, Cmty. Found. S.W. Ala., 1998—, Friends Magnolia Cemetery, 1999—; active adv. bd. Ala. Hist. Commn., 1974—; pres. Mobile Hist. Devel. Found., 1973-75, bd. dirs., 1973-76; mem. council, chmn. regents Spring Hill Coll., 1984, trustee, 1991—. With USNR, 1941-69, comdr. ret. Recipient M.O. Beale Scroll of Merit award, 1951, 56, 59, Doc E award ADA, 1975, Ruth E. Hanson award 1978, Dept. Internal Medicine Faculty award, 1979, Comic Cowboy of Yr. award, 1982, Joe Treadwell award Ala. affiliate ADA, 1990; named Hon. Fellow Mobile Coll., 1977, Lifetime Achievement award Ala. Hist. Commn, 2004; named Mobilian of Yr. Mobile Civitan Club, 1989. Mem. AMA, ACP, Am. Assn. Diabetes Educators, Med. Soc. Mobile County (recognition award 1975), So. Med. Assn., Am. Diabetes Assn. (citation Mobile chpt. 1980, Becton Dickinson award 1981), Am. Soc. Internal Medicine, Ala. Diabetes Assn., Mobile County Physicians, Franklin Soc. (pres. 1975), Mobile Area C. of C. Clubs: Country of Mobile, Mobile Yacht. Lodges: Masons, Shriners, Kiwanis. Republican. Jewish. Home: Mobile, Ala. Died May 25, 2006.

EICKELBERG, JOHN EDWIN, retired process control company executive; b. Fairmont, Minn., Oct. 31, 1944; s. Elmer W. and Emma H. (Hansen) E.; m. Sue Ellen Keller, June 29, 1968; children: Janeen Ellen. BS in Engring., Case Inst. Tech., 1966, MS in Engring., 1968. Control engr. Indsl. Nucleonics, Columbus, Ohio, 1970-71, control systems mgr., 1971-72, systems engring. mgr., 1973-74, mktg. mgr., 1975-76, dir. Latin Am., 1977-78; dir. quality Accuray Corp., Columbus, 1979, v.p. N.Am., 1979-84, v.p. internat., 1984-86, Combustion Engring., Columbus, 1987-89, sr. v.p. internat., 1989-90; v.p. internat. Asea Brown Boveri, Columbus, 1990-93. Bd. dirs. Upper Arlington (Ohio) Civic Assn., 1977-78; v.p. Case Alumni Assn. of Cen. Ohio, Columbus, 1977-84. Case Engring. fellow, 1967-68. Mem. Tech. Assn. Pulp and Paper Industry (vice chmn. process control com. 1974-76). Clubs: Hoover Yacht, Brookside Country Club, Mercedes-Benz of N.Am. (Columbus). Republican. Methodist. Avocations: sailing, automobiles, music. Home: Columbus, Ohio. Died Apr. 13, 2007.

EINSEL, DAVID WILLIAM, JR., retired military officer; b. Tiffin, Ohio, Nov. 4, 1928; s. David William and Naomi Dorothy (Williams) E.; m. Elva yates Aylor, June 16, 1956; children: Susan Vagnier, Mary Kost. BA, MA in Chemistry, Ohio State U., 1950; MSc, U. Va., 1956. Commd. 2d lt. U.S. Army, 1950, advanced through grades to maj. gen., 1980, ret., 1985; staff officer Orgn. of the Joint Chiefs of Staff, Washington, 1968-70; comdr. Harry Diamond Labs., Adelphi, Md., 1970-75; chief nuclear-chem. officer hdqrs. Dept. of the Army, Washington, 1975-76; dep. commanding gen. U.S. Army Armament R&D Command Picatinny (N.J.) Arsenal, 1976-80; asst. to sec. US Dept. Def., Washington, 1980-85; officer Nat. Intelligence Coun., Washington, 1985-89; cons. Tiffin, Ohio, 1989—2006. Author: International Military Encyclopedia, 1991; contbr. article to Jour. Analytical Chemistry. Decorated Silver Star, Bronze Star for Valor with oak leaf cluster for meritorious svc., Purple Heart; named to U.S. Army Chem. Corps Hall of Fame, 1993; recipient Profl. Achievement award, Ohio State U., 1998, Disting. Citizenship award, Tiffin (Ohio) Area C. of C., 2004, Intelligence medal of Merit, Def. & Army Disting. Svc. medals, Legion of Merit, Army Commendation medal, Meritorious Svc. medal. Mem. AAAS, Assn. U.S. Army, Am. Def. Preparedness Assn., Kiwanis, Masons (33d degree), Phi Beta Kappa, Sigma Xi. Republican. Methodist. Achievements include patent in automatic electrolytic apparatus for determining acid prodn. rates. Died Oct. 30, 2006.

EISERER, LEONARD ALBERT CARL, publishing executive; b. Polar, Wis., June 3, 1916; s. Herman Frederick and Anna Elizabeth (Schnieder) E.; m. Lorraine Elizabeth Hickey, June 28, 1941; children: Carol Jean, Elaine Roberta, Leonard Arnold, Beverly Arlene. BA, Roosevelt U., Chgo., 1937; MS in Journalism, Northwestern U., 1939. Editor Am. Aviation Publs., Inc., Washington, 1939—42, v.p., gen. mgr., 1946—57, exec. v.p., sec., 1958-62; pres., pub. Sports Age, Inc., Washington, 1962-63; chmn., CEO Bus. Pubs., Inc., Silver Spring, Md., from 1963. Chmn. Carol Jean Cancer Found., Inc.; bd. dirs. U. N.C. at Greensboro Excellence Found.; pres., dir. Eiserer-Hickey Found., Inc.; dir. Univ. Club of Washington Found. Lt. USN, 1942-46. Named to Hall of Fame Newsletter Pubs. Found.,

1994, Man of Yr. Univ. Club of Washington, 1995; inductee Hall of Achievement, Northwestern U. Medill Sch. Journalism, 1997. Mem.: Air and Waste Mgmt. Assn., Water Environ. Fedn., Soc. Profl. Journalists, Newsletter Pubs. Assn., Nat. Press Club, Univ. Club. Home: Silver Spring, Md. Died May 21, 2007.

EISNER, MURRAY RICHARD, writing instrument and paper company executive; b. NYC, July 26, 1919; s. Frank and Anna Eisner; m. Harriet Zaban; children— Jolie, Dean, Alan BA in Bus., Ohio State U., 1941. Vice pres. Mead Corp., Dayton, Ohio, 1966-69, pres. ednl. services, 1969-74; pres. Baker & Taylor, W. R. Grace, NYC, 1974-76; v.p. mktg. Sheaffer Eaton Textron, Pittsfield, Mass., 1977-81, pres., from 1981. Instr., cons. U. Mass., Amherst, 1979-80; corporator Bershire County Savs. Bank, Pittsfield Contbr. articles to profl. jours. Mem. bus. adv. council U. Mass., 1981—; corporator Berkshire Med. Ctr. Served to capt. inf. U.S. Army, 1942-46 Recipient gold medal N.Y. Art Dirs. Mem. Writing Instrument Mfrs. Assn. Republican. Avocations: sailing; tennis; hiking; art. Home: Atlanta, Ga. Died Feb. 27, 2007.

EKBERG, CARL EDWIN, JR., civil engineering educator; b. Mpls., Oct. 28, 1920; s. Carl Edwin and Ruth Elizabeth (Olin) E.; m. Dorothy Heley, May 25, 1944; children: Carl Edwin III, Gretchen Heley Brommelhoff, Janet Heley, Thomas William. BCE, U. Minn., 1943, MS, 1947, PhD, 1954. Instr. math. and mechanics U. Minn., 1946-51; structural engr. M., St. P. & S.Ste.M. R.R., summers, 1948-51; asst. prof. civil engring. N.D. State U., 1951-53; asst. prof., assoc. prof. civil engring. Lehigh U., 1953-59; prof. civil engring. Iowa State U., 1959-88, head dept., 1959-85, prof. emeritus, from 1988. Author articles in field. Served as lt. (j.g.) USNR, 1943-46. Fellow ASCE, Am. Concrete Inst. (hon.); mem. NSPE (life), Iowa Engring. Soc. (hon. life), Am. Soc. Engring. Edn. (life), Am. Ry. Engring. Assn. (life), Rotary, Sigma Xi (emeritus mem.), Tau Beta Pi, Chi Epsilon, Phi Kappa Phi (emeritus life). Home: Ames, Iowa. Died May 30, 2007.

EKELMAN, DANIEL LOUIS, lawyer; b. Cleve., May 1, 1926; s. William Harry and Edna Mae (James) E.; m. Ann Jane Farnacy, Aug. 5, 1950 (dec. June 1993); children: Sally, Karen, Barbara, Beth; m. Phyllis E. Patton, Oct. 18, 1997. BA, Ohio Wesleyan U., 1950; LLB, Case Western Res. U., 1952. Bar: Ohio 1952, U.S. Dist. Ct. (no. dist.) Ohio 1953, U.S. Tax Ct. 1955. Assoc. Calfee, Halter & Griswold, Cleve., 1952-59, ptnr., 1959-77, mng. ptnr., 1977-85, sr. ptnr., 1985-95; ret., 1996. Gen. ptnr. Sawmill Creek Resort, Huron, Ohio, 1968-80. Trustee Brentwood Hosp., Cleve., 1960-94, Greater Cleve. Hosp. Assn., 1975-78 (Outstanding Trustee award 1992), Case Western Res. Law Sch., 1984-87, Meridia South Pointe Hosp., 1995, Brentwood Found., 1995-99. With USN, 1944-46, PTO. Fellow ABA; mem. Ohio Bar Assn., Cleve. Bar Assn., Soc. Benchers, Order of the Coif, The Country Club (Pepper Pike, Ohio, trustee 1988-91), Union Club, Jupiter Hills Club (Jupiter, Fla.). Republican. Home: Shaker Heights, Ohio. Died Oct. 2006.

ELDER, MARK LEE, retired university research administrator, writer; b. Littlefield, Tex., May 3, 1935; s. Mark Gray and Ethel Ruby (Hill) E.; m. Elizabeth Ellen Lovejoy, Dec. 19, 1992; 1 child, Staci Lee. BA in Journalism, U. Okla., 1965, MA in Comm., 1973; MBA, Newport U., 1996. Tech. writer/editor rsch. inst. U. Okla., Norman, 1962-64, asst. dir., then dir. info. svcs. dept., rsch. inst., 1964-73, assoc. dir., sponsored programs adminstr./dep. dir., dir. office rsch. adminstrn., 1973-84, security supr., 1977-83; tech. writer/editor Los Alamos (N.Mex.) Sci. Lab., 1964-66; presentations writer/editor Martin-Marietta Corp., Orlando, Fla., 1966-67, Collins Radio Co., Richardson, Tex., 1967-68; dir. office rsch. devel. and adminstrn. Ariz. State U., Tempe, 1984-85; univ. patent/copyright officer, dir. sponsored projects U. North Tex., Denton, 1986-97, asst. v.p. rsch., 1987-97; dep. dir., exec. v.p. North Tex. Rsch. Inst., 1989-96. U. North Tex. primary rep. Tex. consortium participants, chair preaward issues subgroup, Tex. state issues task force, mem. nat. state issues com. Fed. Demonstration Project, 1988—; dep. dir., corp. sec. North Tex. Rsch. Inst., 1989—; cons. to pres. U. Tex., San Antonio, 1991; mem. various coms. U. Okla., Ariz. State U., U. North Tex.; speaker in field. Author: Jedcrow, 1974; (with R. Martin) Handbook for Effective Writing, 1975; Wolf Hunt, 1976, Swedish edit., 1977, Italian edit., 1978, The Prometheus Operation, 1980, Brit. edit., 1981; (with others) Research Administration and Technology Transfer, 1988; tech. editor: Energy Alternatives: A Comparative Analysis (D. Kash., et al.), 1975, Energy From the West: A Progress Report of a Technology Assessment of Western Energy Resource Development (I. White, et al.), 1977. With U.S. Army, 1954-56. Mem. Nat. Coun. Univ. Rsch. Adminstrs. (chair nat. publs. com., 1980-81, v.p. 1981-82, pres. 1982-83, exec. com. 1986-88, co-chair regional congress 1988, mem. various coms., editor newsletter, 1986-87, Past Pres.'s award 1983, Spl. Citation region V 1984, Spl. Citation newsletter editor 1987), Assn. Univ. Tech. Mgrs., Tex. Tech. Transfer Assn. (charter, co-founder 1988—, interim sec.-treas. 1988, v.p., pres.-elect 1988-89, pres. 1989-90, bd. dirs. 1990-91, Bob G. Davis award 1991). Home: Essex Junction, Vt. Died May 20, 2007.

ELDER, WILLIAM HANNA, zoology educator; b. Oak Park, Ill., Dec. 24, 1913; s. Robert A. and Margaret (Hanna) E.; m. Nina Leopold, Sept. 20, 1941; children— Nina, Patricia; m. Glennis Martin, Mar. 31, 1973. BS, U. Wis., 1936, Ph.M., 1938, PhD, 1942. Game technician Ill. Natural History Survey, 1941-43; toxicologist Nat. Def. Research Com., U. Chgo., 1943-45; asst. prof. zoology U. Mo., Columbia, 1945-47, asso. prof., 1948-51, prof., 1952-54, chmn. dept. zoology, 1950-53, William Rucker prof., 1954-84, prof. emeritus, from 1984; Sabbatical year study in Europe, 1953. Guggenheim Found. fellow for research in Hawaii, 1956-57; Fulbright fellow for research Rhodesia, 1965-66; NSF grantee for elephant research Zambia, 1967-68 Mem. Nature Conservancy (pres. Mo. 1959, 68), Soc. Mammalogists, Wildlife Soc., Wilson Ornithol. Soc., Phi Beta Kappa, Sigma Xi, Gamma Alpha. Home: Columbia, Mo. Died Aug. 14, 2006.

ELDRIDGE, CARL WALLACE, real estate consultant; b. Seattle, Aug. 24, 1923; s. Clark Henry and Eleanor (Niles) E.; m. Norma Jeanette Zabriskie; children from previous marriage: Susan Carol (Mrs. Harry J. Repstad), George Earl. Student, U. Wash., 1941. Purchasing agt. Met. Constrn. Co., Seattle, 1946-47; gen. mgr. mortgage loan and real estate investment dept. Prudential Ins. Co. of Am., Seattle, Portland, Oreg., Newark and Los Angeles, 1947-64; sr. v.p., trustee Wash. Mut. Savs. Bank, Seattle, 1964-72, exec. v.p., 1972, pres., from 1973, chmn., from 1981. Served with USNR, 1943-46, PTO. Mem. Seattle Mortgage Bankers Assn. (past pres.), Mortgage Bankers Assn. Am., Nat. Assn. Mut. Savs. Banks. Clubs: Rainier (Seattle). Republican. Presbyterian. Home: Bellevue, Wash. Died Dec. 28, 2005.

ELDRIDGE, DOUGLAS HILTON, economist; b. Lewistown, Mont., Apr. 12, 1916; s. Harry Hilton and Elsie (Hobensack) E.; m. Clara E. Young, June 8, 1940; children— Douglas Alan, Maurice Paul. BA, U. Wash., 1937, MBA, 1941; MA, U. Chgo., 1948, PhD, 1949. Research asst. Wash. State Tax Commn., Olympia, 1939-41; fiscal economist U.S. Dept. Treasury, Washington, 1949-62, chief tax analysis staff, 1957-62; prof. public fin. Claremont (Calif.) Men's Colls. and Claremont Grad. Sch., 1962-65; v.p., exec. sec. Nat. Bur. Econ. Research, NYC, 1965-78; economist Scarborough, N.Y., from 1978. Cons. in field. Contbr. articles to profl. jours. Served to lt. USNR, 1942-46. Social Sci. Research Council fellow, 1947-49 Mem. Am. Econ. Assn., Nat. Assn. Bus. Economists, Nat. Tax Assn., Tax Inst. Am., Phi Beta Kappa, Beta Gamma Sigma. Home: Briarcliff Manor, NY. Died July 19, 2007.

ELLIOTT, EDWARD, investment executive, financial planner; b. Madison, Wis., Jan. 11, 1915; s. Edward C. and Elizabeth (Nowland) Elliott; m. Letitia Ord, Feb. 20, 1943 (div. Aug. 1955); children: Emily, Ord; m. Melita Uihlein, Jan. 1, 1958 (dec.); 1 child, Deborah; m. Sally Dodds Combs, Jan. 5, 2002. BS in Mech. Engring, Purdue U., 1936. Engr. Gen. Electric Co., Schenectady, 1936—37; with. Pressed Steel Tank Co., Milw., 1937-41, 46-58; v.p. sales Cambridge Co. div. Carrier Corp., Lowell, Mass., 1958-59; mgr. indsl. and med. sales Liquid Carbonic div. Gen. Dynamics Corp., Chgo., 1959-61; v.p. Haywood Pub. Co., Chgo., 1961-63; pres. Omnibus, Inc., Chgo., 1963-67; gen. sales mgr. Resistoflex Corp., Roseland, NJ, 1967-68; investment exec. Shearson, Hammill & Co., Inc., Chgo., 1968-74; v.p. McCormick & Co., Inc., 1974-75, Paine Webber, Inc., Naples, Fla., 1975-91, ret., 1991. Mem. pres.' coun. Purdue U. Lt. col. USAAF, 1941-46. Decorated officer Order Brit. Empire; inducted Indiana Basketball Hall of Fame. Mem.: ASME, Air Force Assn., Rotary, Family Club (San Francisco), Naples Yacht Club, Royal Poinciana Golf Club, Hole-in-Wall Golf Club, Naples Athletic Club, Phi Delta Theta. Episcopalian. Home: Naples, Fla. Died Oct. 17, 2007.

ELLIOTT, ELEANOR THOMAS, foundation executive, volunteer; b. NYC, Apr. 26, 1926; d. James A. and Dorothy Q. (Read) Thomas; m. John Elliott, Jr., July 27, 1956 (dec. 2005). BA, Barnard Coll., 1948; DHL (hon.), Duke U., 2002. Assoc. editor Vogue mag., 1948-52; asst. dir. research and speech writing div. N.Y. State Republican Com., 1952; social sec. to Sec. of State and Mrs. John Foster Dulles, 1952-55; dir. James Weldon Johnson Community Centers, NYC, 1955-60; bd. dirs. Celanese Corp., 1974-87, CIT Fin. Corp., 1978-81, INA Life Ins. Co. of N.Y., 1983-1998. Author: Glamour Magazine Party Book, 1966. Trustee Barnard Coll., 1959—2006, chmn. bd., 1973-76; bd. dirs. Maternity Center Assn., 1960-70, pres., 1965-69; bd. govs. N.Y. Hosp., 1972-2006, v.p., 1979—2006; bd. dirs. Found. for Child Devel., N.Y.C., 1969—2006, chmn., 1972-79, 1973—2006; bd. dirs. United Way Greater N.Y., 1977-86, NOW Legal Def. and Edn. Fund, 1983-90, Catalyst Inc., 1978-83, Am. Women's Econ. Devel. Corp., 1980-86, Woodrow Wilson Nat. Fellowship Found, 1983-2006, chmn. 1993-1999, co-chair, Nat. Adv. Coun., 2000-06, Edna McConnell Clark Found., 1984-93, Coun. on Women's Studies, Duke U.; overseer Cornell U. Med. Coll., 1995-2006. Recipient Alumni medal, Columbia U., 1977, medal of distinction, Barnard Coll., 1979, Red Cross Humanitarian award, 1986, Extraordinary Woman of Achievement award, NCCJ, 1978, Disting. Trustee award, United Hosp. Fund., 1991, Disting. Cmty. Svc. award, 1994, award for disting. svc. to City of New York, St. Nicholas Soc., 2002. Mem.: Colony Club of N.Y.C. Episcopalian. Home: New York, NY. Died Dec. 3, 2006.

ELLIOTT, MAX CARTER, bank executive; b. Provo, Utah, Sept. 7, 1920; s. Earl Lamond and LaRelle (Carter) Elliott; m. Norma Edith Holley, Jan. 12, 1943; children: Sue Ann Call, Jeri Lea. Attended, Brigham Young U., 1938—43; grad., Pacific Coast Banking Sch. U. Wash., 1961. Loan officer 1st Security Bank Utah, Ogden, 1947—50; bank examiner, auditor 1st Security Corp., Ogden, 1950—53; asst. v.p., asst. mgr. 1st Security Bank, Provo, 1953—56, v.p. and asst. mgr., 1956—67, v.p. and mgr., 1967—84, v.p., from 1984. Pres. Utah County Bankers, 1957-58, United Fund Utah County, 1967, Utah Valley Indsl. Devel. Assn., 1968; adv. bd. Brigham Young U. Continuing Edn., 1972; fin. adv. com. Provo City, Provo City Sch. Dist., 1983; chmn. Ctrl. Utah County Cancer Soc., 1955; trustee Ctrl. Utah Health Care Found.; chmn. investment com. Orem Cmty. Hosp., Utah Valley and Am. Fork Hosp.; gen. adv. com. Utah Tech. Coll., 1977-78; trustee Provo City Libr., 1983-; mem. Provo C. of C. (pres. 1957). Named Outstanding Businessman of Yr., Brigham Young U. Coll. Bus., 1969; recipient honor to light the Y, Brigham Young Stadium, 1978, Banker Advocate of Yr., State of Utah, 1984. Mem.: Mountainland Assn. Govts. (chmn. comprehensive health coun. 1973—75), Rotary Club (pres. 1982—83), Cougar Internat. Club (dir. 1976—79), Kiwanis (v.p. 1968—69). Home: Orem, Utah. Died June 25, 2007.

ELLIOTT, THERON PAUL, visual design educator, advertising designer; b. Grand Rapids, Mich., Dec. 13, 1945; s. Albert Cole and Nevah Washburn (Koontz) E. BS, Grand Valley State U., Allendale, Mich., 1976; MA, Mich. State U., 1984. Owner, mgr. Theron Elliott Graphic Design, Grand Rapids, 1969-70; v.p., creative dir. Archer Assocs., Inc., Grand Rapids, 1970-72; dir. graphic design Steketee Van Huis, Inc., Holland, Mich., 1972-75; mem. adjunct faculty advt. dept. Grand Valley State U., 1975-77; instr. advt. Kendall Coll. Art and Design, Grand Rapids, 1976-81, asst. prof. visual communication, 1981-86, assoc. prof., chmn. design studies, 1986-92; owner, pres. Elliott & Assocs., Grand Rapids, from 1969. Ptnr. Parkbench Pub. Grand Rapids. Creator, producer, dir. exptl. film A Mouse in a Box, 1975 (Vicci award), Academy Leader, 1976 (Vicci award). Mem. NARAS, NATAS, Broadcast Designers Assn. Avocations: model countrying, landreth. Home: San Francisco, Calif. Died Nov. 13, 2006.

ELLIS, ALBERT, clinical psychologist, educator, author; b. Pitts., Sept. 27, 1913; s. Henry Oscar and Hettie (Hanigbaum) E. BBA, CCNY, 1934; MA, Columbia U., 1943, PhD, 1947. Diplomate: Am. Bd. Profl. Psychology; in clin. hypnosis Am. Bd. Psychol. Hypnosis; Am. Bd. Med. Psychotherapists, Am. Bd. Sexology. Free-lance writer, 1934-38; personnel mgr. Distinctive Creations, 1938-48; sr. clin. psychologist N.J. State Hosp., Greystone Park, 1948-49; instr. psychology Rutgers U., 1948-49, adj. prof., 1971-83; instr. psychology N.Y. U., 1949; adj. prof. Union Grad. Sch., 1971-77, U.S. Internat. U., 1974-80, Pittsburg State U., from 1978; chief psychologist N.J. State Diagnostic Center, Menlo Park, 1949-50, N.J. Dept. Instns. and Agys., Trenton, 1950-52; pvt. practice psychotherapy and marriage and family therapy NYC, 1943-68; exec. dir. Albert Ellis Inst. for Rational Emotive Behavior Therapy, NYC, 1959-89, pres., 1989—2007. Cons. clin. psychology VA, 1961-67 Author: An Introduction to the Principles of Scientific Psychoanalysis, 1950, The Folklore of Sex, 1951, (with A.P. Pillay) Sex, Society and the Individual, 1953, The American Sexual Tragedy, 1954, Sex Life of the American Woman and the Kinsey Report, 1954, New Approaches to Psychotherapy Techniques, 1955, (with Ralph Brancale) The Psychology of Sex Offenders, 1956, How to Live With a Neurotic, 1957, Sex Without Guilt, 1958, What Is Psychotherapy, 1959, The Place of Values in the Practice of Psychotherapy, 1959, The Art and Science of Love, 1960, (with Robert A. Harper) A Guide to Successful Marriage, 1961, (with R.A. Harper) A Guide to Rational Living, 1961, (with Albert Abarbanel) The Encyclopedia of Sexual Behavior, 1961, Reason and Emotion in Psychotherapy, 1962, The Intelligent Woman's Guide to Manhunting, 1963, If This Be Sexual Heresy, 1963, Sex and the Single Man, 1963, The Origins and the Development of the Incest Taboo, 1963, Nymphomania, A Study of the Over-Sexed Woman, 1964, Homosexuality, 1965, Suppressed: Seven Key Essays Publishers Dared Not Print, 1965, The Case for Sexual Liberty, 1965, The Search for Sexual Enjoyment, 1966, (with others) How to Raise an Emotionally Healthy, Happy Child, 1966, (with Roger O. Conway) The Art of Erotic Seduction, 1967, Is Objectivism a Religion, 1968, (with John M. Gullo) Murder and Assassination, 1971, (with others) Growth Through Reason, 1971, Executive Leadership: A Rational Approach, 1972, The Civilized Couple's Guide to Extramarital Adventure, 1972, How to Master Your Fear of Flying, 1972, The Sensuous Person: Critique and Corrections, 1972, (with others) Sex and Sex Education: A Bibliography, 1972, Humanistic Psychotherapy: The Rational-Emotive Approach, 1973, (with Robert A. Harper) A New Guide to Rational Living, 1975, Sex and the Liberated Man, 1976, Anger How to Live With and Without It, 1977, (with Russell Grieger) Handbook of Rational-Emotive Therapy, 1977, (with W. Knaus) Overcoming Procrastination, 1977, (with E. Abrahms) Brief Psychotherapy in Medical and Health Practice, 1978, (with J.M. Whiteley) Theoretical and Empirical Foundations of Rational-Emotive Therapy, 1979, The Intelligent Woman's Guide to Dating and Mating, 1979, (with I. Becker) A Guide to Personal Happiness, 1982, (with M. Bernard) Rational-Emotive Approaches to the Problems of Childhood, 1983, (with M. Bernard) Clinical Applications of Rational-Emotive Therapy, 1985, Overcoming Resistance, 1985, (with Russell Grieger) Handbook of Rational-Emotive Therapy, Vol. 2, 1986, (with Windy Dryden) The Practice of Rational-Emotive Therapy, 1987, (with others) Rational-Emotive Treatment of Alcoholism and Substance Abuse, 1988, How To Stubbornly Refuse to Make Yourself Miserable About Anything-Yes Anything!, 1988, (with others) Rational-Emotive Couples Therapy, 1989, (with R. Yeager) Why Some Therapies Don't Work: The Dangers of Transpersonal Psychology, 1989, (with Windy Dryden) The Essential Albert Ellis, 1990, (with Patricia Hunter) Why Am I Always Broke: How to Be Sane about Money, 1991, (with Windy Dryden) A Dialogue with Albert Ellis: Against Dogma, 1991, (with Emmett Velten) What To do When AA Doesn't Work For You: Rational Steps to Quitting Alcohol, 1992, (with Lidia Dengelegi and Michael Abrams) The Art and Science of Rational Eating, 1992, (with Arthur Lange) How to Keep People from Pushing Your Buttons, 1994, (with Michael Abrams) How to Cope with a Fatal Illness, 1994, Reason and Emotion in Psychotherapy Revised, 1994, Better, Deeper and More Enduring Brief Therapy, 1996, (with Jack Gordon, Michael Neenan and Stephen Palmer) Stress Counseling: A Rational Creative Behavior Therapy Approach, 1996, (with R.A. Harper) A Guide To Rational Living, 1997, (with R.C. Tafrate) How to Control Your Anger Before It Controls You, 1997, (with Catherine MacLaren) Rational Emotive Behavior Therapy: A Therapist's Guide, 1998, How to Control Your Anxiety Before It Controls You, 1998, (with Shawn Blau) The Albert Ellis Reader, 1998, (with Emmett Velten) Optimal Aging: How to Get Over Growing Older, 1998, How to Make Yourself Happy and Remarkably Less Disturbable, 1999, (with Marcia Grad Powers) The Secret of Coping With Verbal Abuse, 2000, (with S.L. Nielsen and Brad Johnson) Counseling and Psychotherapy With Religious Persons: A Rational Emotive Behavior Therapy Approach, 2001, Feeling Better, Getting Better, Staying Better, 2001, Overcoming Destructive Beliefs, Feelings, and Behaviors, 2001, (with Ted Crawford) Intimate Connections, 2001, (with Robert A. Harper) Dating, Mating, and Relating: How To Build a Healthy Relationship, 2001, (with Jerry Wilde) Case Studies in Rational Emotive Behavior Therapy with Children and Adolescents, 2001, (with Stevan Nielsen and W. Brad Johnson) Counseling and Psychotherapy with Religious Persons: A Rational Emotive Behavior Therapy Approach, 2001, Overcoming Resistance: A Rational Emotive Behavior Therapy Integrative Approach, 2002, (with Ira L. Reiss) From The Dawn of The Sex Revolution, 2002, Anger: How To Live With and Without It, 2003, Ask Albert Ellis, 2003, Sex Without Guilt in the Twenty-First Century, 2003, (with W. Dryden) Albert Ellis, Live!, 2004, Rational Emotive Behavior Therapy: It Works for Me, It Can Work for You, 2004, The Road To Tolerance, 2004, The Myth of

Self-Esteem, 2005. Fellow APA (pres. divsn. cons. psychology 1961-62, exec. com. divsn. psychotherapy 1969-73, coun. reps. 1963-64, 72-74), AAAS, Am. Assn. Marriage and Family Therapists (exec. com. 1957-59), Soc. Sci. Study Sex (exec. com. 1957-58, pres. 1958-60), Am. Orthopsychiat. Assn., Am. Sociol. Assn., Am. Assn. Applied Anthropology; mem. ACA, Am. Assn. Sex Educators, Counselors and Therapists (bd. dirs. 1981-82), Nat. Acad. Practice, Soc. Psychotherapy Rsch., N.Y. Assn. Clin. Psychologists in Pvt. Practice (chmn. 1952-54), N.Y. Joint Coun. Psychologists on Legislation (exec. com. 1951-53), Am. Group Psychotherapy Assn., Am. Acad. Psychotherapists (exec. com. 1954-64, v.p. 1962-64), Mensa, Am. Assn. Advancement Psychotherapy, N.Y. State Psychol. Assn., Soc. Exptl. and Clin. Hypnosis. Home: New York, NY. Died July 23, 2007.

ELLIS, EDWARD GENDALL, oil company executive, consultant; b. NYC, May 19, 1934; s. William Arthur and Freda (Bergmeister) E.; m. Geraldine Agnes Sebring, Aug. 17, 1957; children: Loretta, Valerie, Matthew, John, Steven. BSCE, Cooper Union, NYC, 1956; MBA, Rutgers U., Newark, NJ, 1960. Mgr. U.S. sales Exxon Rsch. & Engring., Florham Park, N.J., 1956-94; pres. World Resource Cons., Sparta, N.J., from 1994. Bd. mgmt. YMCA, Newton, N.J., 1995; chmn. assoc. mems. Sparta (N.J.) Ambulance Corp, 1995; mem. Sparta Kiwanis, 1995. Avocations: sailing, health conditioning, hiking, motorcycling. Home: Sparta, NJ. Died Mar. 22, 2006.

ELLIS, GEORGE EDWIN, JR., chemical engineer; b. Beaumont, Tex., Apr. 14, 1921; s. George Edwin and Julia (Ryan) E. BSChemE, U. Tex., 1948; MS, U. So. Calif., 1958, MBA, 1965, MS in Mech. Engring., 1968, MS in Mgmt. Sci., 1971, Engr. in Indsl. and Systems Engring., 1979. Rsch. chem. engr. Tex. Co., Port Arthur, 1948-51, Houston and Long Beach, Calif., 1952-53, Space and Info. Divsn., N.Am. Aviation Co., Downey, Calif., 1959-61, Magna Corp., Anaheim, Calif., 1961-62; chem. process engr. AiResearch Mfg. Co., LA, 1953-57, 57-59; chem. engr. Petroleum Combustion & Engring. Co., Santa Monica, Calif., 1957, Jacobs Engring. Co., Pasadena, Calif., 1957, Sesler & Assocs., LA, 1959; rsch. specialist Marquardt Corp., Van Nuys, Calif., 1962-67; sr. project engr. Conductron Corp., Northridge, Calif., 1967-68; info. systems asst. LA Dept. Water and Power, 1969-92. Instr. thermodynamics U. So. Calif., LA, 1957. With USAAF, 1943-45. Mem. ASTM, ASME, AIChE, Inst. Supply Mgmt., Nat. Contract Mgmt. Assn., Am. Inst. Profl. Bookkeepers, Am. Soc. Safety Engrs., Am. Chem. Soc., Am. Soc. Materials, Am. Electroplaters and Surface Finishers Soc., Nat. Assn. Corrosion Engrs., Inst. Indsl. Engrs., Am. Prodn. and Inventory Control Soc., Am. Soc. Quality, Soc. for Protective Coatings, Soc. Plastics Engrs., Inst. Mgmt. Accts., Soc. Mfg. Engrs., Fedn. Socs. for Coatings Tech., Assn. Finishing Processes, Soc. Tribologists and Lubrication Engrs., Soc. Human Resources Mgmt., Soc. Engring. and Mgmt. Systems, Nat. Fire Protection Assn., Assn. for Facilities Engring., Pi Tau Sigma, Phi Lambda Upsilon, Alpha Pi Mu. Died Mar. 31, 2007.

ELLIS, GROVER, JR., retired banking educator; b. Dallas, Oct. 3, 1920; s. Grover and Lula (Hewett) E.; m. Mineth Rowland, Dec. 5, 1942; children: Grover III, David Rowland. BS in Petroleum Engring., U. Okla., 1942; MBA with high distinction, Harvard U., 1947; grad Sch. Banking, Rutgers U., 1955. Asst. to pres. Frazier Oil Co., Houston, 1947-49; with First City Nat. Bank, Houston, 1949-85, exec. v.p., 1975-81, vice chmn., 1981-85, also adv. dir.; adj. prof. banking Rice U., Houston, 1986-90. Pres. Florence Crittendon Home, Houston, 1962-64; treas. ARC, Houston, 1970-76; pres. Houston Ballet Found., 1979-81. Lt. USNR, 1942-46, PTO. Mem. Robert Morris Assocs. (pres. 1954-55), Houston Clearing House Assn. (pres. 1972-73), Tex. Bankers Assn. (bd. dirs. 1975-77), Houston Country Club, Rotary (pres. Houston chpt. 1968-69). Presbyterian. Avocations: tennis, golf, birdwatching. Home: Houston, Tex. Died Dec. 22, 2005.

ELLSWORTH, DAVID G., lawyer; b. LA, Jan. 20, 1941; s. Kennedy and Catherine C. (Carroll) Ellsworth; children: Brett, Erin. BS, U. So. Calif., 1962, JD, 1965. Bar: Calif. 1966, U.S. Ct. Appeals 1982. Law clk. to judge U.S. Dist. Ct. (cen. dist.) Calif.; assoc. Meserve, Mumper & Hughes, LA, 1966—70, ptnr., 1970—80, Memel, Jacobs & Ellsworth, LA, 1980—87. Head dept. real estate U. So. Calif., guest lectr. on land devel. law, spring, 1980; mem. bd. commrs. Housing Authority of County of LA, 1977—78, chmn. bd. commrs., 1978—81; mem. LA County Beach Adv. Commn., from 1981; chmn. LA County Housing Commn., 1982—84, LA County Commn. Disposal of Hazardous Waste, from 1984. Contbr. articles to profl. publs.; assoc. editor: Land Devel. Law Reporter, Resort Timesharing Law Reporter. Mem.: Nat. Assn. Corp. Real Estate Execs., Pacific Area Travel Assn. (devel. authority), Nat. Timesharing Coun. (dir., chmn. com. on internat. affairs), Am. Land Devel. Assn. (dir., chmn. internat. coun.), Indian Wells Country Club, The Vintage (Indian Wells, Calif.). Died June 18, 2006.

ELMORE, JAMES WALTER, architect, educator, retired dean; b. Lincoln, Nebr., Sept. 5, 1917; s. Harry Douglas and Marie Clare (Minor) E.; m. Mary Ann Davidson, Sept. 6, 1947; children: James Davidson, Margaret Kay. AB, U. Nebr., 1938; MS in Architecture, Columbia U., 1948. Mem. faculty Ariz. State U., 1949-86, prof. architecture, 1959-86, founding dean Coll. of Architecture, 1964-74. Cons. architect, 1956— Trustee Heard Museum, Phoenix, 1968-79; bd. dirs. Valley Forward Assn., 1969-89, pres., 1985; bd. dirs. Central Ariz. chpt. Ariz. Hist. Soc., 1973-89; bd. dirs. Ariz. Architects Found., 1978-86, Rio Salado Devel. Dist., 1980-87. Served to col., C.E. U.S. Army, 1940-46. Decorated Bronze Star. Fellow AIA; mem. Ariz. Acad. Home: Phoenix, Ariz. Died Apr. 19, 2007.

ELSTER, SAMUEL KASE, college dean, medical educator, physician; b. NYC, Dec. 6, 1922; s. Morris and Rebecca (Post) E.; m. Maxine Lefkowitz, June 17, 1945; 1 child, Charles BS, CCNY, 1942; MD, NYU, 1946. Diplomate Am. Bd. Internal Medicine, Cardiovascular Diseases. Intern Mt. Sinai Hosp., 1946-47, resident, 1950-52; asst. in pathology NYU Sch. Medicine, NYC, 1947-48; instr. medicine Columbia U. Coll. Physicians and Surgeons, NYC, 1959-66; clin. prof. medicine Mount Sinai Sch. Medicine, CUNY, NYC, 1974-97, clin. prof. emeritus medicine, from 1997, dean Page and William Black Postgrad. Sch. of Medicine NYC, 1976-85, dean emeritus and from 1985, dean emeritus for continuous edn., from 1985. Contbr. articles in field to profl. jours. Mem., pres. bd. edn., Tenafly, N.J., 1968-73. Served to capt., M.C. U.S. Army, 1948-50. Fellow Am. Coll. Cardiology, ACP, N.Y. Acad. Medicine; mem. Am. Heart Assn. (mem. council in clin. cardiology), Assn. Am. Med. Colls. Democrat. Jewish. Died July 19, 2006.

ELY, CHARLES AUBREY, anatomist; b. Washington, Pa., Dec. 11, 1913; s. Charles A. and Lida M. (Iams) E. AB, Washington and Jefferson Coll., Pa., 1936; MS, U. Hawaii, 1940; PhD, U. Wis., 1948. Mem. faculty Columbia U. Coll. Physicians and Surgeons, from 1948, prof. anatomy, 1975-81; ret., 1981. Grantee Damon Runyon Fund, NIH, Am. Cancer Soc. Mem. Am. Physiol. Soc., Endocrine Soc., Am. Assn. Cancer Research, Soc. Study Exptl. Biology and Medicine, Am. Assn. Anatomists, AAAS, N.Y. Acad. Sci., Harvey Soc., Sigma Xi. Home: New York, NY. Died Mar. 11, 2006.

EMERY, JOHN COLVIN, JR., investment company executive; b. Madison, Wis., July 14, 1924; s. John Colvin and Janet (Millar) E.; m. Frances Toomy, May 28, 1960; children: John Colvin III, Susan Farlow, Ann Louise, Michael William, Patricia Millar. Student, Dartmouth Coll., 1942-43. With United Airlines, 1944-45, Nat. Airlines, 1945-46; with Emery Air Freight Corp., Wilton, Conn., 1946-87, v.p. sales, 1956-62, exec. v.p., 1963-68, pres., from 1968, chief exec. officer, 1975-88, chmn. bd., 1979-88, chmn. exec. com., 1988-89, also dir.; ret., 1987; pres. Emery Enterprises, Stamford. Founder, former chmn. Bank of Darien, Conn.; vice chmn. Robbins Co., Attleboro, Mass.; bd. dirs. Gen. Housewares, Stamford, Conn., Pitney Bowes, Inc., Stamford. Chmn. White House Conf., Stamford, 1988-89; mem. vestry St. Lukes Episc. Ch. Served with A.C. USNR, 1943-44. Mem. Sales Execs. Club N.Y. (pres. 1967-69, dir. 1963—), Nat. Def. Transp. Assn. (life), Wee Burn Country Club (Darien, Conn.), Wings Club (N.Y.C., pres. 1980-81), Landmark Club (Stamford, bd. dirs.). Episcopalian (vestry). Clubs: Wee Burn Country (Darien, Conn.); Wings (N.Y.C.) (pres. 1980-81). Died Apr. 19, 2007.

EMMERICH, ANDRÉ, art dealer, writer; b. Frankfurt, Germany, Oct. 11, 1924; came to U.S., 1940; s. Hugo and Lily (Marx) E.; m. Constance R. Marantz, Aug. 25, 1958; children: Adam Oliver, Tobias David Hugo, Noah Nicholas; m. Susanne Bross, Jul. 21, 1994. BA, Oberlin Coll., 1944. Writer, editor Time-Life Internat., NYC, N.Y. Herald Tribune, NYC, Realites Mag., Paris, 1944-53; with Andre Emmerich Gallery, Inc., NYC, 1954-98. Art adv. panel of Commr. Internal Revenue, 1986-89; mem. vis. com. Allen Meml. Art Mus., Oberlin Coll., Ohio. Author: Art Before Columbus, 1963, Sweat of the Sun and Tears of the Moon- Gold and Silver in Pre-Columbian Art, 1965. Mem. Century Assn., Art Dealers Assn. Am. (pres. 1972-74, 91-94). Home: New York, NY. Died Sept. 25, 2007.

EMMETT, MARTIN FREDERICK CHEERE, investment banker; b. Johannesburg, Aug. 30, 1934; s. Cecil Frederick Cheere and Thelma Marie (Ford) E.; m. Alice Ellen Lavers, Aug. 18, 1956; children: Karen Ann, Robert Martin Cheere, Susan Marie. BSME, U. Witwatersrand, Johannesburg, 1957; MBA, Queens U., Kingston, Ont., Can., 1962. V.p. consumer products Alcan Aluminum Co., Montreal, Que., Can., 1962-72; pres., chief exec. officer Standard Brands Ltd., Montreal, 1972-76, NYC, 1980-81; pres. Internat. Standard Brands Ltd., NYC, 1976-79; sr. exec. v.p., bd. dirs. Nabisco Brands, Inc., NYC, 1981-83; chmn., chief exec. officer Internat. Nabisco Brands, 1981-83; vice chmn. Nabisco Brands, Ltd., Toronto, Ont., Can., 1985, Burns, Fry and Timmins, Inc., NYC, 1983-85, chmn., 1985-89; chief exec. officer Tambrands Inc., 1989-93. Bd. dirs. Fry Ltd., Toronto. Mem. Assn. Profl. Engrs. Ont. Clubs: Econ.; Brook. Home: Greenwich, Conn. Died Feb. 28, 2006.

ENGLAND, DONALD LINKLATER, physician; b. Westimber, Oreg., Mar. 27, 1924; s. David Charles and Lillian Linklater (Gorrie) E.; m. Katherine Mowat Sutherland, Sept. 14, 1946; children: Janet Mowat, Barbara Joan, James David, John Mark. BA, U. Oreg., 1945, MD, 1997. Diplomate Am. Bd. Internal Medicine, added qualifications for geriatrics. Rotating intern St. Francis Hosp., Pitts., 1947-48; med. resident Md. Gen. Hosp., Balt., 1948-49, U.S. VA Hosp., Portland, Oreg., 1951-53; med. staff physician Eugene (Oreg.) Hosp. & Clinic, 1953-95; physician Peace Health Med. Group, Eugene, from 1995. Bd. mem. Oreg. State Bd. Med. Examiners, Portland, 1977-85; Oreg. rep. Fedn. State Med. Bds. Flex Test Com., Phila., 1978-86. Capt. U.S. Army, 1949-51. Fellow ACP; mem. AMA, Oreg. Med. Assn., Lane County Med. Soc. (pres. 1972). Presbyterian. Avocations: personal computer, bread baking, photo printing, sewing, jogging. Home: Eugene, Oreg. Died Apr. 18, 2007.

ENGLER, ROBERT, political science professor; b. NYC, July 12, 1922; s. Isidore and Esther (Haber) E.; m. Rosalind Elowitz, May 16, 1946 (div. June 1960); children: Richard J., Elise P.; m. Inea Bushnaq, Sept. 5, 1968; 1 dau., Nadya Kate. BSS., CCNY, 1942; MA, U. Wis., 1946, PhD, 1947. Mem. faculty U. Wis., 1946-47, Syracuse U., 1947-50, Columbia U., 1959-63; prof. polit. sci. Queens Coll., CUNY, 1964-69, Grad. Sch. and Bklyn. Coll., CUNY, 1969-91, prof. emeritus, 1991—2007; prof. polit. sci. Sarah Lawrence Coll., 1951-71; mem. faculty New Sch. Social Research, 1961-64; chair, vis. prof. world politics of peace and war Princeton U., 1988-89. Vis. prof. U. P.R., 1961, U. Sask., 1973, Ctr. for Rsch. in Rural and Indsl. Devel., India, 1992, 2001, U. Havana, 1987, 92-93; disting. vis. scholar Indian Coun. Social Sci. Rsch., 2001-02; disting. vis. prof. Am. U., Cairo, 1978; assoc. fellow Inst. for Policy Studies, Washington, 1979-80. Author: The Politics of Oil: Private Power and Democratic Directions, 1961, The Brotherhood of Oil: Energy Policy and the Public Interest, 1977 (Notable Book of Yr., NY Times); editor: America's Energy: Reports From the Nation on 100 Years of Struggle for the Democratic Control of Our Resources, 1980; contbr. chpts. to books; contbr. articles to profl. jours. Asst. to pres. Nat. Farmers Union, Washington, 1950-51; dir. Encampment for Citizenship, N.Y.C., 1961, 63. Served with AUS, 1943-46, ETO. Recipient Sidney Hillman Found. prize award polit. writing, 1955. Home: New York, NY. Died Feb. 23, 2007.

ENO, CHARLES FRANKLIN, soil science educator; b. Atwater, Ohio, May 21, 1920; s. Clarence and Alice (Rhoads) E.; m. Fern A. Imler, Sept. 8, 1948; children: Charles Franklin, Mark Imler. BS, Ohio State U., 1942, MS, 1948; PhD, Purdue U., 1951. Asst. prof., assoc. prof., prof. soil microbiology U. Fla., Gainesville, 1950-65, prof., chmn. soil sci. dept., 1965-82, asst. dir. internat. programs, from 1982. Served to lt. col. AUS, 1942-46, 51-52. Decorated Bronze Star. Fellow Am. Soc. Agronomy (pres. 1983), Soil Sci. Soc. Am. (pres. 1975); mem. Council for Agrl. Sci. and Tech., Fla. Hort. Soc., Soil and Crop Sci. Soc. Fla. (pres. 1965), Sigma Xi, Gamma Sigma Delta. Clubs: Gainesville Golf and Country. Republican. Methodist. Home: Gainesville, Fla. Died June 6, 2007.

ENSIGN, RICHARD PAPWORTH, transportation executive; b. Salt Lake City, Jan. 20, 1919; s. Louis Osborne and Florence May (Papworth) E.; m. Margaret Anne Hinckley, Sept. 5, 1942; children: Judith Ensign Lantz, Mary Jane Ensign Hofmeister, Richard L., James R., Margaret. BS, U. Utah, 1941. With Western Air Lines, 1941-70, v.p. in-flight service, 1963-70, v.p. passenger service, 1970, Pan Am. World Airways, 1971, sr. v.p. field mgmt., 1972-74, sr. v.p. mktg., 1974-75; exec. v.p. Western Airlines, 1975-82; pres. R.P. Ensign & Assocs., 1982—2007; spl. asst. to pres. Marriott-Host, Marriott Corp., 1990-91; spl. asst. to chmn. Caterair Internat. Corp., 1991-96. Chmn. Utah Nat. Adv. Coun., 1984-86; bd. dirs. Western Airlines, 1980-81, Pacific Area Travel Assocs., 1976-81, Marriott Airport Svc. Co., Osaka, Japan, 1986-92; resident dir. Marriott Internat. Corp., Seoul, People's Republic of Korea. Patentee in field. Nat. fund raising chmn. U. Utah, 1982-83, 83-84. Recipient Disting. Service award Fla. Internat. U., 1973; named Disting. Alumnus U. Utah, 1976, 86, recipient merit award of honor, 1985. Mem. Nat. Aeros. Assn. Clubs: Lochinvar. Republican. Mem. Lds Ch. Home: Malibu, Calif. Died May 1, 2007.

EPSTEIN, JEREMIAH FAIN, anthropologist, educator; b. NYC, Feb. 14, 1924; s. Joseph and Carol (Fain) E.; divorced; children: Anne, Louise, Suzanne. BS in Agr., U. Ill., 1949, MA in Anthropology, 1951; PhD, U. Pa., 1957. Lectr. Hunter Coll., NYC, 1954-58; rsch. scientist anthropology U. Tex., Austin, 1958-60, mem. faculty, from 1958, prof. anthropology, 1970—97, prof. emeritus, from 1973. Fieldwork in, Mex., Belize, Honduras, France, U.S. Contbr. articles to profl. jours. Served with AUS, 1942-45. Decorated Purple Heart; grantee NSF, 1963, 64; grantee Wenner Gren Found., 1961; grantee U. Tex. Inst. Latin Am. Studies, 1963, 75; grantee U. Tex., 1988; Fulbright-Hays fellow, 1964; Mellon Found. fellow in Latin Am. studies, 1988; U. Tex. faculty rsch. assignment, 1988. Mem. AAAS, Am. Anthrop. Assn., Soc. Am. Archaeology, Soc. Mexicana Anthropologia. Home: Austin, Tex. Died Dec. 15, 2005.

EPSTEIN, KENNETH ROBERT, retail company executive; b. Washington, Nov. 19, 1942; s. Seymour and Libby (Appel) E.; m. Tamara Vandenberg, Aug. 7, 1982; 1 child, Shayna BBA, Hofstra U., 1964; MBA, NYU, 1966; PhD, Columbia, 1967. Personnel mgr. R.H. Macy's, NYC, 1964-66; dir. personnel Curtiss Wright Corp., Woodridge, N.J., 1966-68; v.p. ops. Elder Beerman Stores Corp., Dayton, Ohio, 1968-72, v.p. human resources, 1972-80, sr. v.p. human resources, 1980-84, sr. v.p. adminstrn., from 1984, exec. v.p., from 1991. Chmn. SEEK (summer employment), Dayton, 1985; co-chmn. Pvt. Industry Council, 1984—. Served with Army N.G., 1963-64 Home: Burbank, Calif. Died Aug. 10, 2006.

EPSTEIN, LEON DAVID, political science educator; b. Milw., May 29, 1919; s. Harry Aaron and Anna (LeKachman) E.; m. Shirley Galewitz, Jan. 12, 1947. BA, U. Wis., 1940, MA, 1941; PhD, U. Chgo., 1948; D.Litt. (hon.), U. Warwick, Eng., 1980. Jr., also asst. economist Nat. Resources Planning Bd., 1941-42; asst. prof. polit. sci. U. Oreg., 1947-48; faculty U. Wis., Madison, 1948-88, prof. polit. sci., 1954-88, Bascom prof., 1973-80, Hilldale prof., 1980-88, prof. emeritus, from 1988. Chmn. dept., 1960-63; dean Coll. Letters and Sci., 1965-69; fellow Center for Advanced Study in Behavioral Scis., 1970-71 Author: Britain-Uneasy Ally, 1954, Politics in Wisconsin, 1958, British Politics in the Suez Crisis, 1964, Political Parties in Western Democracies, 1967, 2d edit. 1980, 3d edit. 1993, Governing the University, 1974, Political Parties in the American Mold, 1986; contbr. articles to profl. jours. Served to capt. AUS, 1942-46. Guggenheim fellow, 1979-80. Fellow Am. Acad. Arts and Scis.; mem. Am. Polit. Sci. Assn. (pres. 1978-79), Midwest Polit. Sci. Assn. (pres. 1971-72) Home: Middleton, Wis. Died Aug. 1, 2006.

ERDMAN, PAUL EMIL, author; b. Stratford, Ont., Can., May 19, 1932; (parents Am. citizens); s. Horace Herman and Helen E.; m. Helly Elizabeth Boeglin, Sept. 11, 1954; children: Constance Anne Catherine, Jennifer Michele. Student, Concordia Coll., Ft. Wayne, Ind., 1950-51, Concordia Sem., St. Louis, 1952-53; BA, Concordia Coll., St. Louis, 1954; BS, Georgetown U., 1956; MA, PhD, U. Basel, Switzerland, 1958. Econ. cons. European Coal and Steel Community, Luxembourg, Luxembourg, 1958; internat. economist Stanford Research Inst., Menlo Park, Calif., 1958-61; exec. v.p. Electronics Internat. Capital Ltd., Hamilton, Bermuda, 1962-64; vice chmn. United California Bank in Basel A.G., 1965-70. Cons. RAI Corp., TV corp., Italy.; host Moneytalk Sta. KGO, ABC, San Francisco, 1983-86, commentator, 1987-2007; adv. bd. Sch. Bus. and Econs. Sonoma State U., Ronerd Pk., Calif., 2001-07. Author: Swiss-American Economic Relations, 1959, Die Europaeische Wirtschaftsgemeinschaft und die Drittlaender, 1960, The Billion Dollar Sure Thing, 1973 (Edgar award, Mystery Writers Am., 1974), The Silver Bears, 1974, The Crash of '79, 1976, The Last Days of America, 1981, Paul Erdman's Money Book: An Investor's Guide to Economics and Finance, 1984, The Panic of '89, 1987, The Palace, 1988, What Next? 1988, The Swiss Account, 1991, Warning to the Yen, 1992, Zero Coupon, 1993, Tug of War, 1996, The Set-Up, 1997; contbg. editor, columnist M Inc. mag.,

1987-92; columnist The Nikon Keizai Shimbun, 1987-88, The Japan Post, 1989-2007, CBS Market Watch, 1998-2007; contbr. articles, revs. to popular mags. Mem. bd. advisors program in internat. bus. diplomacy, Georgetown U. Sch. Fgn. Svc., Washington, 1980—2007, faculty mem. Georgetown leadership seminar, 1982—2007. Recipient Champion Media award for econ. understanding Amos Tuck Sch. Bus. Administrn., Dartmouth Coll., 1984 Mem. Authors Guild, Mysters Writers Am., PEN Am. Ctr., Commonwealth Club Calif. (adv. bd. 2005). Lutheran. Died Apr. 23, 2007.

ERICH, DOROTHY BEATRICE, nurse; b. Chillicoth, Ohio, Oct. 4, 1915; d. Oliver Gustave and Daisy Mae (Orr) Erich. RN, Bethesda Hosp., 1941; BTh, Olivet Nazarene U., 1953. Nurse Ft. Hamilton Hosp., Hamilton, Ohio, 1953—55, Chillicothe Hosp., 1955—62; orthopedic nurse Mt. Logan Sanitorium, Chillicothe, 1962—70; nurse surgery Greenfield Hosp., Ohio, 1970—73; nursing cons. Gospel Light Nursing Home, Kingston, Ohio, 1980—84; pres. Kingston Care Ctr. Part-time preacher in youth work; pres. sr. citizens group, 1989; active vol. various sr. citizen orgns. Mem.: Am. Nurses Assn. Republican. Mem. Ch. Of Christ In Christian Union Ch. Home: Kingston, Ohio. Died Sept. 6, 2006.

ERICKSON, RALPH D., retired physical education educator, small business owner, consultant; b. Beresford, SD, June 25, 1922; s. John Henning and Ester Christina (Lofgren) E.; m. Nancy Erickson, Sept. 1949 (div. 1961); m. Patricia Erickson, Apr. 1973 (div. 1975); m. Karen Ann Erickson, June 1, 1989; 1 child, Karina Ann. BS in Phys. Edn., Northwestern U., 1949, MA in Edn., 1953. Swim instr., coach Chgo. Park Dist., 1946-54; social studies tchr., swim coach Elmwood Park (Ill.) High Sch., 1954-65; swimming, water polo coach Loyola Univ., Chgo., 1965-87, assoc. prof. phys. edn., 1971-87; salesman Alexander Hamilton Inst., Chgo., 1966-69; tchr. Chgo. Bd. Edn., 1969-70. Bd. dirs. Capital Investments & Ventures Corp., Santa Ana, Calif., 1983-93, Cosmopolitan Comm., Santa Ana, 1991-93; vice chmn. Internat. Profl. Assn. Diving Inst., Santa Ana, 1966-93. Author: Under Pressure, 1961, Discover the Under Water World, 1971, V/W Navigation, 1972, Search and Recovery, 1973. Sgt US Army, 1942-45 Recipient Reach Out award Diving Equipment Mfg. Assn., Our World Underwater award; named to Ill. H.S. Swimming Coaches Hall of Fame, 1982, Athletic Hall of Fame Loyola U. Chgo., 1986, Internat. Divers Hall of Fame, 2007. Mem. Profl. Assn. Diving Instrs. (co-founder). Died May 26, 2006.

ERON, LEONARD DAVID, retired psychology professor; b. Newark, Apr. 22, 1920; s. Joseph I. and Sarah (Hilfman) E.; m. Madeline Marcus, May 21, 1950; children: Joan Hobson, Don, Barbara Christensen. BS, CCNY, 1941; MA, Columbia U., NYC, 1946; PhD, U. Wis., Madison, 1949. Diplomate Am. Bd. Profl. Psychology. Asst. prof. psychology and psychiatry Yale U., New Haven, 1948-55; rsch. assoc. prof. Yale U. Sch. Medicine, New Haven, 1955—69; dir. rsch. Rip Van Winkle Found., 1955-62; prof. psychology U. Iowa, Iowa City, 1962-69, dir. grad. tng. clin. psychology; rsch. prof. U. Ill.-Chgo., 1969-89, emeritus rsch. prof. of the social sci. in psychology, 1989—2007; rsch. scientist, prof. psychology Inst. for Social Rsch., U. Mich., Ann Arbor, 1992—2003; assoc. dean rsch. Sch. Social Work U. Mich., Ann Arbor, 2001—03. Cons. Chgo. Bd. Edn., 1981—89. Author 8 books; editor Jour. Abnormal Psychology, 1973-80; assoc. editor Am. Psychologist, 1986-90; mem. editl. bd. Guggenheim Found. Rev. on Violence and Aggression, 1996-2003; contbr. numerous articles to profl. jours. Served to 1st lt. US Army, 1942—45. Fulbright lectr., Free U. Amsterdam, 1967-68; recipient Fulbright Sr. Scholar award, Queensland U., Australia, 1976-77, James McKeen Cattell Sabbatical award, U. Rome, 1984-85. Fellow AAAS, APA (chair commn. violence and youth 1991-93, Disting. Contbns. to Knowledge award 1980, Gold medal award for Life Contbn. to Psychology in the Pub. Interest 1995, Lifetime Contbn. to Media Psychology award 2003), Am. Orthopsychiat. Assn.; mem. NIMH, Midwestern Psychol. Assn. (pres. 1985-86), Internat. Soc. for Rsch. in Aggression (pres. 1989-90), Nat. Rsch. Coun. (panel understanding and control violent behavior, 1987-1992), Commn. Social Scis. and Humanities, Am. Coun. Learned Socs. Home: Lindenhurst, Ill. Died May 3, 2007.

ERTEGUN, AHMET MUNIR, record company executive; b. Istanbul, Turkey, July 31, 1923; s. M. Munir and Hayrunisa Rustem (Temel) E.; m. Ioana Maria Banu, Apr. 6, 1961. BA, St. John's Coll., Annapolis, Md., 1944; postgrad., Georgetown U., 1944-46; MusD (hon.), Berklee Coll. Music, 1991; DHL (hon.), N.Y. Inst. Tech. Co-founder Atlantic Records, NYC, 1947, co-chmn. bd., co-chief exec. officer, 1947—96, co-chmn. bd., 1996—2006; co-founder Cosmos Soccer Club, NYC, 1971, pres., 1971-83. Chmn. Am. Turkish Soc., Rock and Roll Hall Fame Found., Am. br. Nordoff-Robbins Music Therapy Ctr.; trustee Parrish Art Mus.; mem. adv. council Dept. Near Eastern Studies Princeton U. Producer various Grammy-Award-winning records; writer various award-winning songs. Recipient Humanitarian award Conf. Personal Mgrs., 1977, Humanitarian of Yr. award T.J. Martell Found. Leukemia Research, 1978, Humanitarian award Nat. Conf. Christians and Jews, 1987, TTV Turkish Presl. award, 1987, Golden Plate Am. Acad. award, 1988, Arts and Tech. award N.Y. Inst. Tech./Young Audiences of N.Y.; named Man of Yr. United Jewish Appeal, 1970, Turkish Am. Yr., Am. by Choice, 1986; inductee Rock and Roll Hall Fame, 1987, Best Dressed Hall Fame, 1987. Mem. ASCAP, Rec. Industry Assn. Am. (dir.), Black Music Assn. (dir.), Nat. Assn. Record Merchandisers (Presdl. award 1977), Nat. Acad. Rec. Arts and Scis. (Trustee award 1992-93), Broadcast Music Industry. Died Dec. 14, 2006.

ERWIN, RICHARD CANNON, SR., federal judge; b. McDowell County, NC, Aug. 23, 1923; s. John Adam and Flora (Cannon) E.; m. Demerice Whitley, Aug. 25, 1946; children: Richard Cannon, Jr., Aurelia Whitley. BA, Johnson C. Smith U., 1947; LLB, Howard U., 1951; LLD, Pfeiffer Coll., 1980, Johnson C. Smith U., 1981. Bar: N.C. 1951, U.S. Supreme Ct. 1974. Practice law, Winston-Salem, N.C., 1951-77; judge N.C. Ct. Appeals, 1978, U.S. Dist. Ct. (mid. dist.) N.C., 1980-88, chief judge, 1988-92, sr. judge, from 1992. Rep. N.C. Gen. Assembly, chmn. hwy. safety com.; mem. law bd. vis. Wake Forest U., 1984—. Trustee Forsyth County Legal Aid Soc., Amos Cottage, Inc.; chmn. bd. trustees Bennett Coll.; bd. dirs. N.C. 4-H Devel. Fund, Inc.; bd. visitors Div. Sch., Duke U.; trustee Children's Home, Winston-Salem; mem. steering com. Winston-Salem Found.; bd. dirs. United Fund; bd. dirs., pres. Citizens Coalition Forsyth County and Anderson High Sch., PTA; mem. N.C. Bd. Edn., 1971-77, N.C. State Library Bd. Trustees, 1968-69; mem., chmn. personnel com. Winston-Salem/Forsyth County Sch. Bd.; chmn. bd. trustees St. Paul United Methodist Ch. Mem. N.C. Bar Assn. (v.p. 1983-84), N.C. Assn. Black Lawyers, Forsyth County Bar Assn. (pres.), N.C. State Bar. Home: Winston Salem, NC. Died Nov. 7, 2006.

ESCHBACH, JESSE ERNEST, former judge; b. Warsaw, Ind., Oct. 26, 1920; s. Jesse Ernest and Mary W. (Stout) Eschbach; m. Sara Ann Walker, Mar. 15, 1947; children: Jesse Ernest III, Virginia. BS, Ind. U., 1943, JD with distinction, 1949, LLD (hon.), 1986. Bar: Ind. 1949. Ptnr. Graham, Rasor, Eschbach & Harris, Warsaw, 1949—62; city atty. Warsaw, 1952—53; dep. pros. atty. 54th Jud. Circuit Ct. Ind., 1952—54; judge U.S. Dist. Ct. Ind., 1962—81, chief judge, 1974—81; judge U.S. Ct. Appeals (7th cir.), W. Palm Beach, Fla., 1981—85, sr. judge, 1985—2000. Pres. Endicott Church Furniture, Inc., 1960—62; sec., gen. counsel Dalton Foundries, Inc., 1957—62. Mem. editl. staff: Ind. Law Jour., 1947—49. Trustee Ind. U., 1965—70. With USNR, 1943—46. Recipient U.S. Law Week award, 1949; scholar Hastings scholar, 1949. Mem.: FBA, ABA, Am. Judicature Soc., Ind. Bar Assn. (bd. mgrs. 1953—54), Ind. Mfrs. Assn. (dir. 1962, ho. dels. 1950—60), Nat. Assn. Furniture Mfrs. (dir. 1962), Warsaw C. of C. (pres. 1955—56), U.S. C. of C. (labor rels. com. 1960—62), Rotary (pres. Warsaw 1956—57), Order of Coif. Presbyterian. Died Oct. 25, 2005.

ESCHBACH, JOSEPH WETHERILL, nephrology educator; b. Detroit, Jan. 21, 1933; s. Joseph William and Marguerite (Wetherill) E.; m. Mary Ann Charles, June 16, 1956; children: Cheryl Louise, Ann Elizabeth, Joseph Charles. BA, BS, Otterbein Coll., 1955; MD, Jefferson Med. Coll., 1959. Practitioner nephrology and internal medicine Minor and James Med., Seattle, 1965—2003; dir. home dialysis U. Wash., Seattle, 1965-72, clin. asst. prof. div. nephrology, 1967-70, clin. assoc. prof. div. nephrology, 1970-75, clin. prof. div. nephrology, 1975-85, clin. prof. divs. nephrology and hematology, 1985—2003. Cons. Ortho Pharm., Raritan, N.J., 1987-88, Amgen, Thousasnd Oaks, Calif., 1985-91. Co-editor: Erythropoietin: Molecular, Cellular and Clinical Biology, 1991; contbr. articles to jours. in field, chpts. to textbooks. Trustee First Ave. Svc. Ctr., 1976-86; pres. bd. trustees Northwest Kidney Ctr., Seattle, 1985-87 (Haviland award 1991). Recipient Disting. Svc. award Seattle Jaycees, 1979, Alumni Achievement award Otterbein Coll., 1991. Fellow: ACP; mem.: AMA, Washington Assn. Biomed. Rsch. (pres. 1999—2001), King County Med. Soc. (pres. 1987), Internat. Soc. Nephrology, Am. Soc. Nephrology, Inst. Medicine of NAS. Presbyterian. Avocations: squash, woodworking, singing. Home: Bellevue, Wash. Died Sept. 7, 2007.

ESON, MORRIS ESRIEL, psychology educator; b. Montreal, Que., Can., Apr. 18, 1921; came to U.S. 1937, naturalized, 1945; s. Max and Rose (Grusby) Isenberg; m. Joy Platt, Mar. 21, 1943; children— Charles, Elizabeth Eson Vigoda, Marc L., Jud. B.S., Ill. Inst. Tech., 1942; A.M., U. Chgo., 1944, Ph.D., 1951. Prof. psychology SUNY-Albany, 1951—; adj. prof., Albany Med. Coll., 1963—, prof. emeritus, 1993. Author: Psychological Foundations of Education, 1972. Contbr. articles to profl. jours. Served to capt. chaplain corps, U.S. Army, 1945-47. Fellow Am. Psychol. Assn.; mem. Am. Ednl. Research Assn., Nat. Soc. Study of Edn. Home: Albany, NY. Died Dec. 26, 2006.

ESPALDON, ERNESTO MERCADER, plastic surgeon, former senator; b. Sulu, Philippines, Nov. 11, 1926; arrived in Guam, 1963; s. Cipriano Acuna Espaldon and Claudia (Cadag) Mercader); m. Leticia Legaspi Virata, May 31, 1952; children: Arlene Espaldon Ramos, Vivian Espaldon Wolff, James, Diane, Karl, Ernesto Jr. AA, U. Philippines, Manila, 1949; MD, U. Santo tomas, Manila, 1954; postgrad., U. Okla., 1959, Washington U., St. Louis, 1961. Diplomate Am. Bd. Plastic Surgery. Plastic surgeon Guam Meml. Hosp., Agana, 1963—2006, chief surgery, 1965-69; pres., plastic surgeon Espaldon Clinic, Agana, 1969—2006; senator Guam Legislature, Agana, 1974-80, 86-92, chmn. Com. on Health, Welfare and Ecology and Com. on Ethics and Standards, 1974-80. Vis. prof. Bicol Med. and Edn. Ctr., Legaspi City, The Philippines; cons. plastic surgery U.S. Naval Hosp., Guam, 1972-76; chmn. com. on advance health care Assn. Pacific Islands Legislators, 1988-92, Coll. Assurance Plan Pre-Need Ednl. Plan, Guam; bd. dirs. Coll. Assurance Plan Pension, Philippines, Coll. Assurance Plan, Philippines. Author: With The Bravest, 1996. Pres., founder Guam Balikbayan Med. Mission, Agana; organizer, co-founder Aloha Med., Mission, Honolulu; Guerrilla comdr. Sulu (Philippines) Area Command, 1943-46, 2d lt. Philippine Army, 1946-47. Recipient Thomas Jefferson award for pub. svc. Am. Inst. Pub. Svc., Washington, and Honolulu Advertiser, 1983, Raja Baguinda award for humanitarian svc. 6th Centennial Celebration of Islam in The Philippines, 1980; named Most Outstanding Filipino Overseas Philippine Govt. and Philippine Jaycees for Pub. Svc., 1982, Most Outstanding Cmty. Filipino Leader of Guam Philippine-Am. Cmty., 1979, Man of Yr. and Disting. Svc. award Inst. Philippine Am. Affairs, Hawaii, 1983; named Most Outstanding Alumni Achiever for Humanitarian Svc., U. Santo Tomas, 1981, Ernesto M. Espaldon profl. chairship in plastic and reconstructive surgery U. Santo Tomas, 1995. Fellow ACS, Philippine Coll. Surgeons; mem. AMA, Pan Pacific Surg. Assn., Guam Med. Soc. (pres. 1970-72, chief del. to AMA 1973-76), KC. Republican. Roman Catholic. Home: Hagatna, Guam. Died Aug. 4, 2006.

ESTES, GERALD WALTER, newspaper executive; b. Memphis, Apr. 21, 1928; s. Edward Leon and Grace Virginia (Knight) E.; m. Mary Charlene Owen, Nov. 7, 1953 (div. July 1975); children: Patricia Estes Tischler, Charles, Susan, Jacqueline; m. Bernice Pendleton O'Mery, Mar. 20, 1976 (div. Nov. 1984); m. Mary Owen Estes, Nov. 17, 1984 Student, Memphis State U., 1949-50. Research asst. Washington Star, 1954-56, asst. prodn. mgr., 1956-68; prodn. mgr. Richmond (Va.) Newspapers, 1968-69; v.p., gen. mgr. SE Media, Inc., Richmond, 1969-73; v.p. newspaper div. Media Gen., Inc., Richmond, 1974-77, sr. v.p., 1977-89; pres. ESC Restaurants, Inc., from 1993. Chmn. LBE, Inc., 1993—. Served with USAF, 1946-49. Mem. Brandermill Country Club, Foundry Golf Club, Bull and Bear Club. Clubs: Bull and Bear, Willow Oaks Country. Republican. Methodist. Home: Midlothian, Va. Died Dec. 6, 2006.

ETGES, FRANK JOSEPH, parasitology educator; b. Chgo., June 18, 1924; s. Joseph Peter and Anna Marie (Foss) E.; m. Ruth Camille Storkan, Sept. 20, 1948 (div. June 1984); children: Robert J., William J., Anne C., David J., Thomas J.; m. Lesta Judith Cooper-Freytag, July 6, 1985. AB, U. Ill., 1948, MS, 1949; PhD, NYU, 1953. Asst. prof. U. Ark., Fayetteville, 1953-54, U. Cin., 1954-59, assoc. prof., 1959-66, prof. parasitology, 1966-95; prof. emeritus, from 1995. Rsch. assoc. U.S. Army Tropical Rsch. Med. Lab., San Juan, P.R., 1961-62; guest investigator London Sch. Tropical Medicine and Hygiene, 1971-72. Sgt. U.S. Army, 1943-46, ETO, PTO. NSF rsch. grantee, 1959-65; La. State U. Med. Sch. rsch. fellow, Santo Domingo, P.R., 1961-62, 64, 65, 67, 69; postdoctoral fellow NIH, London, 1971-72, WHO, Egypt, Sudan, Rhodesia, 1975. Mem. Am. Soc. Parasitologists (editorial com.), Am. Soc. Tropical Medicine and Hygiene, Am. Microscopical Soc. (v.p. 1970), Royal Soc. Tropical Medicine and Hygiene, Australian Soc. Parasitology, Soc. Protozoologists, Midwestern Parastiologists (pres. 1969), Helminthol. Soc. Washington, Sigma Xi. Avocations: travel, golf. Home: Maineville, Ohio. Died Dec. 6, 2006.

EVANS, COOPER, congressman; b. Cedar Rapids, Iowa, May 26, 1924; s. Thomas and Ora E.; m. Jean Marie Ruppelt, June 20, 1948; children: Jim, Charles. BS, Iowa State U., 1949, MS, 1955. Registered profl. engr., Iowa. With C.E. U.S. Army, 1949-65; dir. advanced manned lunar missions NASA, Washington, 1963-65; farmer, mng. ptnr. nr. Grundy Center, Iowa, from 1965; mem. Iowa Ho. of Reps., Des Moines, 1974-79, 98th Congress from 3d Iowa Dist. Served to lt. col., inf. U.S. Army, 1943-46. Decorated Army Commendation medal Mem. Am. Legion Lodges: Rotary. Republican. Methodist. Died Dec. 22, 2005.

EVANS, DAVID A., plant geneticist; b. Apr. 9, 1952; m. Kitty Ann Reninger, Dec. 19, 1978. BSc in Plant Genetics, Ohio State U., 1973, MSc in Plant Genetics, 1975, PhD, 1977; MA in Mgmt. Devel., Harvard U., 1987. Rockefeller Found. postdoctoral fellow NRC/Prairie Regional Lab., Sask., Can., 1977-78; asst. prof. dept. biol. scis. SUNY, Binghamton, 1978-80; mgr. cellular genetics Campbell Inst. for Rsch. and Tech., Cinnaminson, N.J., 1981; v.p. tech. and prodn. devel. DNA Plant Tech. Corp., Cinnaminson, 1981-89, v.p. mktg., from 1989. Adj. prof. divsn. biology grad. program plant scis. Rutgers U., New Brunswick, N.J., 1980—, bd. mgrs., 1992—; mem. bd. advisors coll. agriculture Ohoi State U., 1988—; mem. departmental vis. com. dept. botany U. Tex., 1989—. Co-author: Handbook of Plant Cell Culture, Vols. 1-6, 1983-89, Biotechnology of Plants and Microorganisms, 1986; contbr. articles to sci. jours. Home: Orinda, Calif. Died June 1, 2006.

EVANS, FRANKLIN BACHELDER, finance educator, consultant; b. Chgo., Feb. 9, 1922; s. Franklin B. and Arline (Brown) E.; m. Barbara V. Both, Sept. 16, 1943; children: Mary A., Amy B., Geoffrey B., Christopher G. AA, U. Chgo., 1941, AB, 1943, MBA, 1954, PhD, 1959. Asst. prof. mktg. U. Chgo., 1957-64; prof. mktg. U. Hawaii, 1964-69; prof. advt. Northwestern U., 1969-80, prof. emeritus, 1981. Cons. to bus. and industry; researcher on consumer motivation. Contbr. articles to profl. jours. Served with U.S. Army, 1943-45. Decorated Bronze Star. Home: Nashville, Tenn. Died Aug. 6, 2006.

EVANS, FREDERICK JOHN, psychologist; b. Wollongong, Australia, Nov. 17, 1937; came to U.S., 1963; s. Frederick John and Phyllis Lurline (Wiffen) E.; m. Barbara Joan Marcelo, June 8, 1968 (div. 1990); children: Christopher Arthur, David Troy, Mark Fredrick (dec.), Diana Joy; m. Patricia E. Burns, Nov. 26, 1993; children: Mariefred Joy, Ellen Blessing. BA Honors Class I, U. Sydney, Australia, 1959, PhD, 1966. Tchg. fellow U. Sydney, 1959-63; rsch. psychologist Mass. Mental Health Center, 1963-64; from instr. psychology in psychiatry U. Pa. Sch. Medicine, Phila., 1965-66, to assoc. prof. psychiatry, 1972-81, assoc. prof. psychology, 1974-79; sr. rsch. psychologist Unit for Exptl. Psychiatry Inst. of Pa. Hosp., Phila., 1964-79; cons. psychologist pain mgmt. ctr. Med. Ctr. Princeton, NJ, from 1998; mem. cons. staff dept. psychiatry Princeton House, from 1998; cons. psychologist Pain Care Inst., Phila., from 1999, Arthritis Osteoporosis Ctr., West Reading, Pa. Vis. fellow psychology Yale U., 1970-71; trustee Inst. Exptl. Psychiatry, Boston, 1970-79; adj. prof. U. Medicine and Dentistry N.J.-Robert Wood Johnson Med. Sch., 1979-88; dir. rsch. divsn. Carrier Found., Belle Mead, N.J., 1979-88; v.p. Tex. Inst. Behavioral Medicine and Neurosci., 1989-96; pres. Pathfinders, Cons. in Human Behavior; dir. Pain Mgmt. Behavioral Medicine Svcs., Reading, Pa.; consulting psychologist The Elms Nursing Home, 1995—, The Back Rehab. Inst., Cranbury, N.J., Hamilton, N.J., 1997—; dir. psychol. svcs. Pain Mgmt. Ctr. The Med. Ctr. at Princeton, 1998—. Adv. editor: Internat. Jour. Clin. and Exptl. Hypnosis, 1968-69, assoc. editor, 1969—; assoc. editor: Am. Jour. Clin. Hypnosis, 1986-91, 95—; cons. editor: Jour. Abnormal Psychology, 1979-87, assoc. editor, 1989-91; co-editor: Functional Disorders of Memory, 1979, Springer Series in Behavior Modification and Behavioral Medicine, 1980-86; contbr. chpts. to textbooks, articles to profl. jours. Mem. Montgomery County Sch. Bd., 1983-89. Served to capt. Australian Army, 1961-63. Fulbright grantee, 1963-66 Fellow AAAS, APA (divsn. 30 program chmn. 1972, sec-treas. 1973-75, pres. 1978-79), Am. Soc. Clin. Hypnosis (chmn. liaison com. 1975-77, 88-89, cert. cons. 1993—), N.J. Psychol. Soc., Pa. Psychol. Soc., Soc. Clin. and Exptl. Hypnosis (co-chmn. sci. program 1970, 99, chmn. rsch. workshop, 1971, 76, 79, 80, 87-90, 97-2000, sec. 1973-86, co-chmn. publs. com. 1975-77, v.p. 1979-81, pres. 1981-83, chmn. budget com. 1987-89); mem. Am. Pain Soc. (founding dir. 1977-80), Internat. Soc. Hypnosis (sec.-treas. 1973-79, co-chmn. 7th Internat. Congress Hypnosis

1976, vice chmn. bd. dirs. organizing com. 10th Internat. Congress 1985, pres.-elect 1986-88, pres. 1987-91, immediate past pres. 1991-94, chair nominations and election com. 1991-94), Nat. Pain Found. (pres. 1989-92), Royal Soc. Medicine, Internat. Soc. Inner Mental Tng. (v.p. 1993-96). Died Feb. 23, 2006.

EVANS, RICHARD JESSE, lumber company executive; b. East St. Louis, Ill., Aug. 17, 1913; s. Elmer D. and Elizabeth (Rogers) E.; m. Lucille H. Tiefenauer, May 21, 1939; children: Joyce Carol, Sharon Gail. Student, Wash. U., 1938-41. Constrn. and engrng. supr. S.W. Bell Telephone Co., St. Louis, 1938-64; pres., chief exec. officer United Lumber Co., Inc., Anchorage, from 1964. Republican. Baptist. Home: Anchorage, Alaska. Died May 19, 2007.

EVANS, RICHARD VIRDIN, business administration educator; b. Balt., Mar. 29, 1930; s. George Heberton and Elinor (Virdin) E.; m. Elizabeth Morgan Eaton, June 28, 1958; children— Dorothy Eaton, Sally Morgan, Margaret Canby, Richard Virdin. AB, Princeton, 1951; D.Eng., Johns Hopkins, 1959. Instr. U. Mich., 1958-59, asst. prof., 1959-62, U. Calif., Los Angeles, 1962-65; assoc. prof. Case Western Res. U., 1965-69; prof. bus. adminstrn. U. Ill., Urbana, from 1969, acting head dept., 1969-70. Contbr. articles to profl. jours. Served to 2d lt. AUS, 1951-54. Lord Baltimore Press fellow, 1956-58 Mem. Ops. Research Soc. Am. (asso. editor jour. 1965-74), Inst. Mgmt. Sci., Inst. Math. Statistics, Royal Statis. Soc., Assn. Computing Machinery, Soc. Indsl and Applied Math. Home: Champaign, Ill. Died Jan. 28, 2007.

EVANS, ROBERT L., restaurant executive; b. Sugar Ridge, Ohio, May 30, 1918; s. Stan and Elizabeth E.; m. Jewell Waters, 1940; children: Stanley, Robin, Gwen, Debbie, Steve, Bobbie. Grad., Ohio State U. Engaged in restaurant bus., from 1944; now pres. Bob Evans Farms, Inc., Columbus, Ohio. Mem. Vet. Medicine Adv. Com. Ohio, Dept. Agr. Meat Adv. Bd.; dir. council Food Industries Ctr. Fund raising chmn. Ohio Soc. Prevention Blindness, 1977; hon. chmn. Heart Fund Drive, 1979; state chmn. Easter Seal Campaign; mem. exec. bd. Rio Grande Coll.; sponsor Ohio 4-H Conservation Camp; trustee Ohio Forestry Assn. Served with AUS, 1944-45. Named Ohio Soil Conservationist of Year, 1969, Ohio Wildlife Habitat Conservationist of Year, 1972, 80; named Ohio Ambassador Natural Resources, 1981; named to Hall of Fame Ohio State Fair, 1976, Hall of Fame Ohio 4-H, 1982; recipient Bus. Tourism award, 1973, Gov. Ohio award, 1978, Meritorious Service award Ohio State U. Coll. Agr., 1978, Ohio Conservation Achievement award, 1978, Wildlife Council Service award, 1978, 79, Meritorius Service award Ohio State U. Coll. Agr. Alumni, 1983, Hon. award Furture Farmers Am., Disting. Service award Gallia County Soil and Water Conservation Dist., Nat. Charolais Congress Breeders award Mem. Am. Charolais Assn. (past dir.), 4-H Club (adv. bd. Ohio), Ohio Charolais Assn. (dir.), Ohio Wildlife Council, Ohio C. of C. (dir.); mem. Spanish-Barb Mustang Breeders Assn. (founding mem.) Died June 21, 2007.

EVANS, ROBERT VAN ORMAN, lawyer; b. Cleve., Jan. 15, 1920; s. Miles Erland and Edna E.; m. Virginia Michael, June 15, 1945; children: Amanda, Miles, David, Alison. BA, Dartmouth Coll., 1941; LL.B., U. Mich., 1948. With CBS, from 1950, gen. counsel, v.p., 1968-76. Served with USNR, 1942-45. Fellow Am. Bar Found.; mem. Am. Bar Assn., Assn. Bar City N.Y. Republican. Home: San Francisco, Calif. Died July 25, 2007.

EVANS, WILLIAM JAMES, lawyer; b. Balt., Nov. 9, 1928; s. John L. and Florence (Redding) E.; m. Georgia Johnson, May 10, 1952; children: Patricia, Olivia, John. AB, Johns Hopkins U., 1952; LLB, U. Md., Balt., 1956. Bar: Md., U.S. Dist. Ct. Md. 1956, U.S. Ct. Appeals (4th cir.) 1956, U.S. Supreme Ct. 1967. Asst. U.S. atty. U.S. Dept. Justice, Balt., 1956-60; atty. Lord, Whip, Coughlan & Green, Balt., 1960-64, Miles & Stockbridge, Balt., from 1964, ptnr., from 1967. Author: Robert's Rules of Order Newly Revised, 1970, 2d rev. edit., 1990. Chmn. Bd. Suprs. Elections, Balt., Md. State Ethics Commn. With U.S. Army. Mem. ABA (ho. dels. 1972-77), Md. State Bar Assn. (sec. 1971-77), Nat. Assn. Parliamentarians (pres. 1979-81, parliamentarian), Miles White Soc. (bd. dirs., treas. 1969—). Republican. Mem. Soc. Of Friends. Avocation: welsh language. Home: Baltimore, Md. Died July 20, 2007.

EVANSON, ROBERT VERNE, pharmacy educator; b. Hammond, Ind., Nov. 3, 1920; s. Evan and Dorothy (Gordon) E.; m. Helen Louise Wolber, June 29, 1947; children: Yvonne Louise Evanson Nash, Karen Denice Evanson Ivanson. BS in Pharmacy, Purdue U., 1947, MS in Indsl. Pharmacy, 1949, PhD in Pharmacy Adminstrn., 1953. Apprentice pharmacist Physician's Supply Co., Hammond, 1946; grad. asst. pharmacy Sch. Pharmacy, Purdue U., 1947-48, mem. faculty, from 1948, prof. pharm. adminstrn., 1963-86, head dept., 1966-72; assoc. head dept. pharmacy practice, 1982-86; prof. emeritus, from 1986. Cons. in field. Contbr. articles to profl. jours.; contbg. author: Central Pharm. Jour., 1964-72. Served with AUS, 1943-46. Recipient Lederle Faculty award, 1964; award for excellence in pharmacy adminstrn. Nat. Assn. Retail Druggists, 1985; Robert V. Evanson Walgreen scholarship, 1986—. Fellow Am. Found. Pharm. Edn., Am. Pharm. Assn.; mem. Ind. Pharm. Assn., Am. Assn. Coll. Pharmacy (dir., Disting. Educator award 1982), Am. Assn. Coll. Pharmacy Council Faculties (chmn. 1985-86), Acad. Pharm. Scis., Acad. Pharmacy Practice, Soc. Preservation and Encouragement Barbershop Quartet Singing in Am., Sigma Xi. Mem. Fed. Ch. W. Lafayette. Home: West Lafayette, Ind. Died Apr. 7, 2007.

EVERHART, DAVID LESLIE, hospital administrator; b. Granville, Ohio, May 24, 1928; s. William Alfred and Mary Elder (Lough) E.; m. Margaret Weber, June 23, 1951; children: John David, Barbara Weber, Margaret Leslie. BA, Denison U., 1950; MS in Hosp. Adminstrn., Columbia U., 1953. Adminstrv. intern Ohio State U. Hosp., Columbus, 1950-51; adminstrv. resident Henry Ford Hosp., Detroit, 1952-53, adminstrv. asst., 1953-55, asst. dir., 1955-61, assoc. dir., 1961-63; adminstr., adminstrv. v.p. John Hopkins Hosp., Balt., 1963-70; exec. dir. New Eng. Med. Ctr. Hosp., Boston, 1970-75; pres. Northwestern Meml. Hosp., Chgo., 1976-85, Northwestern Meml. Group, from 1985. Mem. Am. Hosp. Assn., Am. Coll. Hosp. Adminstrs., Assn. Am. Med. Colls., Soc. Health Service Adminstrs., Am. Pub. Health Assn., Ill. Hosp. Assn. (trustee 1976-82), Inst. Medicine, Phi Gamma Delta, Blue Key Presbyterian. Died Jan. 1, 2006.

EXTER, JOHN, monetary consultant; b. Chgo., Sept. 17, 1910; s. Joseph and Edith (Gray) E.; m. Marion Fitch, Dec. 18, 1937; children— John Kempton, Janet Exter Butler, Nancy Exter Downs, George Fitch. B.A., Coll. Wooster, 1932; M.A., Fletcher Sch. Law and Diplomacy, 1934; postgrad. Harvard U., 1939-43. Far East econ., acting chief bd. govs. Fed. Res. System, Washington, 1945-50; gov. Central Bank Ceylon, Colombo, Sri Lanka, 1950-53; chief Middle East div. Internat. Bank for Reconstrn. and Devel., Washington, 1953-54; v.p. Fed. Res. Bank N.Y., N.Y.C., 1954-59; sr. v.p., internat. monetary adviser for internat. banking group First Nat. City Bank (now Citibank), N.Y.C., 1959-72; cons. domestic and internat. money, Mountain Lakes, N.J., 1972—. Contbr. articles to profl. jours. Trustee China Found. Promotion Edn. and Culture, 1973—. Recipient Disting. Alumni award Coll. of Wooster (Ohio), 1981. Mem. Council Fgn. Relations, Com. Monetary Research and Edn. (dir. 1973—), Monetary Peleoin Soc., Phi Beta Kappa. Republican. Mem. United Ch. of Christ. Club: University. Died Feb. 28, 2006.

FAILING, GEORGE EDGAR, editor, clergyman, educator; b. Kingston, Ont., Can., Nov. 25, 1912; s. Roy Augustus and Nellie (Richardson) F.; m. Phyllis Ogden, Apr. 12, 1939; children: Bunnie Jean, Alice Joy, Lynn Odgen. BA magna cum laude, Houghton Coll., 1940, Litt.D., 1960; MA, Duke U., 1947; D.D., So. Wesleyan U., 1996. Ordained to ministry Wesleyan Meth. Ch., 1938. Pastor in, Fillmore, NY, 1935-41, Louisville, 1941-44, Marion, Ind., 1953-56; prof. Cen. S.C. Wesleyan Coll., 1944-47; prof. theology Houghton (N.Y.) Coll., 1947-53, dir. pub. rels., 1947-53; editor Sunday sch. lit., pastor Wesleyan Meth. Ch., Marion, Ind., 1956—59; editor Wesleyan Meth., 1959-68; chancellor Satellite Christian Inst., San Diego, 1968-73; prof. Greek and N.T. United Wesleyan Coll., Allentown, Pa., 1973; gen. editor Wesleyan Advocate, Marion, 1973-84. Author: 1 Corinthians, 1963, The Way of Holiness, 1970, Presence, 1977, Secure and Rejoicing, 1980, Did Christ Die for All?, 1980; contbg. author: Ency. World Methodism, 1974; contbg. author, editor: And They Shall Prophesy, 1978, With Open Face, 1983, Way of Wonder, 1983, History of the Wesleyan Ch., 1991, Death Has No Dominion, 1991. Mem. gen. bd. trustees Wesleyan Meth. Ch. Am., 1959-68, 74-84; pres. Presence, Inc., 1979-2007. Recipient Spl. Alumnus award United Wesleyan Coll., 1969, Houghton Coll., 1983. Mem. Soc. Bibl. Lit. and Exegesis, Evang. Press Assn. (pres. 1965-67), Am. Schs. Oriental Rsch. Avocations: photography, travel. Home: Easley, SC. Died Feb. 26, 2007.

FAIRBURN, SANDRA JEAN, nursing educator; b. Fairfield, Ala., June 20, 1942; d. Thomas William and Eddress Kathleen (Johnson) F.; m. David Edward Henderson, Jan. 27, 1984. BS in Nursing, U. Ala., Tuscaloosa, 1964; M in Nursing, U. Wash., Seattle, 1973. RN, Ala., Fla.; cert. nursing adminstr., clin. specialist in community health nursing. Instr. nursing Ariz. State U., Tempe, 1976-83; coord. Family Advocacy Ctr. USN, San Miguel Base, Philippines, 1984-85; maternity nursing cons. Ariz. Dept. Health Svcs., Phoenix, 1985-87; coord. family health svcs. Nev. Health Div., Carson City, 1987-88, chief community health svcs., 1988-95; instr. nursing Daytona Beach C.C., from 1995. Advisor State Student Nurses' Assn.; mem. competency adv. com. Nev. State Bd. Nursing. Col. USAF Res., 1965-95, ret. 1995. Mem. adv. com. family & consumer scis. Flagler County Coop. Extension; vol. Flagler County Coun. on Aging; mem. bd. dirs. Flagler County Habitat for Humanity, AAUW of Flagler County. Mem. APHA, ANA (chair nominating com. coun.), AAUW (bd. dirs. Flagler County chpt.), Ariz. Nurses Assn. (chair), Am. Orgn. Nurse Execs., Nat. Assn. Sch. Nurses, Sigma Theta Tau. Home: Reno, Nev. Died Jan. 28, 2006.

FAIRCHILD, JAMES DELANO, broadcasting executive; b. Buffalo, Mar. 26, 1942; s. George C. and Harriett L. (Kepley) F.; m. Pamella Ann Tutton, July 22, 1962; children: Patricia, Tamara, Thomas James. Student, SUNY, 1962. News reporter radio and TV, 1966-69; C. of C. exec., 1969-87; pres. Providence C. of C., 1981-87; owner, pres. Sta. KTLG Radio and Fairchild Communications Inc., Gilmer, Tex., from 1987. Bd. dirs. Nat. Religious Broadcasters, S.W. region. Mem. Am. C. of C. Execs., New Eng. C. of C. Execs. (chmn.), Young Life (chmn.). Home: Shorewood, Ill. Died July 20, 2007.

FAIRCHILD, THOMAS EDWARD, federal judge, former state supreme court justice; b. Milw., Dec. 25, 1912; s. Edward Thomas and Helen (Edwards) Fairchild; m. Eleanor E. Dahl, July 24, 1937 (dec. 2005); children: Edward, Susan, Jennifer, Andrew. Student, Princeton, 1931—33; AB, Cornell U., 1934; LLB, U. Wis., 1938. Bar: Wis. 1938. Practiced, Portage, Wis., 1938—41, Milw., 1945—48, 1953—56; atty. OPA, Chgo., Milw., 1941—45; hearing commr. Chgo. Region, 1945; atty. gen. State of Wis., Madison, 1948—51; cons. Office of Price Stabilization, 1951; U.S. atty. (we. dist.) Wis. US Dept. Justice, 1951—52; justice Wis. Supreme Ct., 1957—66; judge US Ct. Appeals (7th Cir), 1966—81, chief judge, 1975—81, sr. judge, 1981—2007. Dem. candidate Senator from Wis., 1950, 1952. Mem.: KP, FBA, ABA, Am. Law Inst., Am. Judicature Soc., Dane County Bar Assn., 7th Cir. Bar Assn., Milw. Bar Assn., Wis. Bar Assn., Phi Delta Phi. Democrat. Mem. United Church Of Christ. Died Feb. 12, 2007.

FAIRLEY, EDWARD LEE, retired diplomat; b. Hannibal, N.Y., Dec. 4, 1917; s. Edward James and Helen (Hewitt) F.; m. Katherine Marie Spradlin, Apr. 30, 1944 (dec. Apr. 1956); children: Alan, Carol; m. Gisela Elsa Hensel, Mar. 30, 1957 (dec. 2001); 1 child, Helen. Mus. B., Eastman Sch. Music, 1939, Mus. M., 1941. Asst. reference librarian Library of Congress, Washington, 1941-48; music specialist Dept. State, Washington, 1948-53; fgn. affairs info. officer USIA, Paris, 1952-54, Bonn, 1955-57, Kampala, 1960-65, Rabat, 1966-69, Washington, 1969-75; dir. internat. affairs Am. Pub. Works Assn., Washington, 1976-79; fgn. affairs cons., McLean, Va., 1979-2007; program annotator Nat. Symphony Orchestra, Washington, 1942-52; former treas. Kindler Found. Inc. Author of essays. Editor Jour. Notes, 1946-52. Pres. Potomac Hills Civic Assn., McLean, 1984-86. Mem. Am. Fgn. Service Assn., Am. Music Library Assn., Am. Musicological Soc. Democrat. Presbyterian. Clubs: Dacor, Friday Morning Music (Washington). Avocations: reading, travelling, playing chamber music. Died May 19, 2007.

FAIRLEY, RICHARD L., university administrator; b. Washington, July 16, 1933; s. Richmond Alvin and Gladys (Wilkinson) F.; m. Wilma King Holmes, Aug. 25, 1955 (div. Jan. 1980); children: Ricki Louise, Sharon Renee; m. Charlestine Dawson Hickson, Mar. 25, 1989. BA, Dartmouth Coll., 1935; MA, Stanford U., 1969; EdD, U. Mass., 1974; DHL, Rust Coll., Holly Springs, Miss., 1988, St. Pauls Coll., Laurenceville, Va., 1989. Tchr. D.C. Pub. Sch. Systems, Washington, 1955-61; mem. faculty Eastern Tng. Ctr., Dept. Def. Staff Coll., Bklyn., 1961-64; ednl. specialist U.S. Office of Edn., Washington, 1964-65, regional dir., 1965-68, chief so. br., 1968-70, dep. commr., 1970-80, dpe. asst. sec., dir., 1980-90; exec. v.p. U. D.C., Washington, from 1990. Mem. faculty Nova U., Ft. Lauderdale, Fla., 1987—, Nat. Coll. Edn., McLean, Va., 1989—. Author numerous articles and govt. publs. U.s. Office of Edn. fellow, 1966, Nat. Inst. Pub. Affairs fellow, 1968. Mem. NEA, NAACP, Am. Coun. on Edn., Nat. Urban League, Nat. Assn. for Ednl. Opportunity, Kappa Phi Kappa. Avocation: boating. Home: Annapolis, Md. Died July 24, 2006.

FALETTI, RICHARD JOSEPH, lawyer; b. Spring Valley, Ill., Nov. 15, 1922; s. Michael Joseph and Alfonsa M. (Delo) F.; m. Barbara Louise Shaft, Aug. 11, 1947; children: Martha DeWitt Keilman, Joan Delo Scottberg, Carol Louise Wolfe, Michael John, Margaret Mary Anderson. BS, U. Ill., 1947, JD, 1948. Bar: Ill. 1949, Ariz. 1987. Assoc. Arrington & Healy, Chgo., 1948-50; asst. prof. law U. Ill., Urbana, 1950-55; assoc. Winston & Strawn, Chgo., 1955-58, ptnr., 1958-91. Chmn. exec. com., dir. Bank of Clarendon Hills, Ill., 1959-84, chmn. bd., 1984-88; sec. Carus Corp., LaSalle, Ill., 1956-89; bd. dirs. Ill. Regional Bancorp., 1987-88; sec. Internat. Coun. Shopping Ctrs., 1957-74. Governing life mem. Art Inst. Chgo., 1975—; trustee, sec. Mus. African Art, N.Y.C.,1989—, Ctr. Italian Culture, Phoenix, 1988-91; trustee Heard Mus., Phoenix, 1991—, Samaritan Charitable Trust, Phoenix, 1991-92; mem. U. Ill. Found.,1 979—; chmn. fin. com., village trustee Village of Clarendon Hills, 1960-64. 1st lt. USAAF, 1944-46. Decorated Air medal with 3 oak leaf clusters. Mem. ABA, Ill. Bar Assn., Ariz. Bar Assn., Chgo. Bar Assn., Law Club Chgo., Am. Judicature Soc., Mid-Day Club (Chgo.), Hinsdale (Ill.) Golf Club, Plaza Club, Order of Coif, Beta Gamma Sigma. Republican. Roman Catholic. Home: Clarendon Hills, Ill. Died Dec. 25, 2006.

FALK, HARRY (CHARLES H. FALK), stock exchange executive; b. 1940; m. Joan Falk; 5 children. With Czarnikow-Rionda, 1958—82, Richco Sugar, 1982—84; chmn. Coffee, Sugar & Cocoa Clearing Assn., 1983—91; with Louis Dreyfus Corp., from 1984; bd. mgrs. Coffee, Sugar & Cocoa Exch., Inc., 1989—90, vice chmn., 1990, chmn., 1991—95; vice chmn. NY Bd. Trade, LI, 2000, chmn., 2000—03, acting pres., CEO, 2002—03, pres., CEO, 2003—06. Died Jan. 3, 2006.

FALK, LAWRENCE CLASTER, publisher, editor, public official; b. Birmingham, Ala., Oct. 6, 1942; s. August Lawrence and Mildred (Claster) F.; student U. Ala. Law Sch., 1963-64, BA, U. Ala., 1978, postgrad., 1978-79; m. Willo Ella Niebow, Mar. 16, 1974; children: Wendy Rebecca, Laura Davida. Reporter, Birmingham Post-Herald, 1964-65; newsman UPI, Raleigh, N.C., 1965-67, mgr., Charlotte, N.C., 1967-68, Birmingham, 1968-70, nat. editor, Chgo., 1970-74; news bur. editor AMA, Chgo., 1973-74; news mgr. Northwestern U., 1974-75; dir. info. services U. Ala., Tuscaloosa, 1975-78; asst. v.p. U. Louisville, 1978-82; pres., chief exec. officer Falsoft, Inc., 1981—; pub., editor Rainbow mag., 1981—, PCM mag., 1982—; pub. ScoreCARD mag., 1983—; pub. Soft Sector mag., 1984-87, Rainbow Books, 1983—; pub. VCR Mag., 1985—, Voice Newspaper, 1986-87, Louisville Skyline Newspaper, 1986-87, New Pilot mag., 1986-90; pub. Software Shopper, 1990—, Power User Newsletter, 1991—; pres., chief exec. officer FPSS, Ag., 1963—; chief exec. officer, chmn. Posh Travel Assistance, Inc., 1985—; pres. Falsoft Video Prodns., 1988—; instr. pub. rels., 1979—; cons. Gadsden Community Coll.; speaker, seminar leader Coun. for Advancement and Support Edn.; mem. City Coun., Prospect, Ky., 1992-93; mayor Prospect, 1994—; pres. Jefferson County League Cities, 1994—; mem. Jefferson County Governance Steering Com., 1994—, Ohio River Corridor Study Commn., 1994—. Recipient Louisville Creative Competition award, 1980, 81, Council for Advancement and Support of Edn. award, 1980, 81, citation Ala. Legislature, 1971. Mem. Pub. Rels. Soc. Am., U. Louisville Assocs. (v.p. 1989—), Sigma Delta Chi (Investigative Reporting award 1970). Jewish. Lodge: B'nai B'rith (Outstanding Adv. to Youth citation 1971) Club: Jewish Community Center, The Temple, Jefferson, Hunting Creek Country, Harrod's Landing Yacht Club, Churchill Downs Turf Club. Home: Prospect, Ky. Died June 9, 2006.

FALWELL, JERRY LAMON, minister, academic administrator; b. Lynchburg, Va., Aug. 11, 1933; s. Carey H. and Helen V. (Beasley) Falwell; m. Macel Pate, Apr. 12, 1958; children: Jerry L., Jeannie, Jonathan. BA, Bapt. Bible Coll., Springfield, Mo., 1956; DD (hon.), Tenn. Temple U.; LLD (hon.), Calif. Grad. Sch. Theology, Cen. U., Seoul, Korea. Founder, pastor Thomas Rd. Bapt. Ch., Lynchburg, Va., 1956—2007; founder Liberty U. (formerly Lynchburg Baptist Coll.), 1971, chancellor, 1971—2007; founder Moral Majority Inc., 1979—89; founder, nat. chmn. Moral Majority Coalition, 2004—07. Host TV show Old Time Gospel Hour; lectr in field. Author: Listen, America!, 1980, The Fundamentalist Phenomenon, 1981, Finding Inner Peace and Strength, 1982, When It Hurts Too Much to Cry, 1984, Wisdom for Living, 1984, Stepping Out on Faith, 1984, Champions for God, 1985, If I Should Die Before I Wake, 1986, Strength For the Journey, 1987, New American Family, 1992,

Falwell: A Autobiography, 1997, Fasting Can Change Your Life, 1998, The How To Book: God's Principles for Mending Broken Lives, 1999, Disarming the Powers of Darkness: Personal Victory in the Spiritual World, 2002, Building Churches of Dynamic Faith: A Five-Session Study Guide, 2005; co-author: Church Afflame, 1971, Capturing a Town for Christ, 1973. Named Christian Humanitarian of Yr., Food for the Hungry Internat., Number One Most Admired Conservative Man Not in Congress, Conservative Digest, 1983, Most Influential Ctrl. Virginian of 20th Century, News and Advance, Lynchburg, Va., 1999; named one of Most Influential People in Am., U.S. News & World Report, 1983, 10 Most Admired Men, Good Housekeeping, 1982, 1984, 1986; named to Hall of Fame, Nat. Religious Broadcasters, 1985; recipient Clergyman of Yr. award, Religious Heritage Am., 1979, Jabotinsky Centennial medal, 1980, Two Hungers award, Food for the Hungry Internat., 1981. Mem.: Nat. Assn. Religious Broadcasters (bd. dirs.). Baptist. Died May 15, 2007.

FAMILO, EDWARD DOUGLAS, lawyer; b. Detroit, July 15, 1921; s. Joseph and Josephine (Ostrum) F.; m. Gloria Blessing, Apr. 8, 1943; children— Nancy Familo Hamilton, Timothy E. A.B., Adelbert Coll., Western Reserve U., 1943, LL.B., 1948; Bar: Ohio 1948, U.S. Dist. Ohio 1948. Assoc. Grossman, Schlesinger, & Carter, Cleve., 1948-53, ptnr., 1953-64; ptnr. Grossman, Familo, Cavitch, Kempf & Durkin, Cleve., 1964-69, Grossman, Stotter, Familo & Cavitch, Cleve., 1969-70, Stotter, Familo, Cavitch, Elden & Durkin, Cleve., 1970-77, Cavitch, Familo & Durkin, Cleve., 1978—, pres. Served to capt. USMC, 1942-50. Mem. Greater Cleve. Bar (exec. com. 1959-62), Ohio State Bar Assn. ABA. Methodist. Clubs: Westwood Country (Rocky River, Ohio), Cleve. Yachting (past commodore 1964), Mid-Day of Cleve. (pres. 1978-85—). Home: Cleveland, Ohio. Died Nov. 22, 2006.

FANTE, RONALD LOUIS, engineer; b. Phila., Oct. 27, 1936; s. Frank Louis and Jeanne Gloria (Bossone) F.; m. Clara Connie Patalano, Apr. 23, 1961; children: Robert, Richard, Karen. BS, U. Pa., 1958; MS, MIT, 1960; PhD, Princeton U., 1964. Sr. scientist AVCO Corp., Wilmington, Mass., 1964-71, Air Force Cambridge Rsch. Labs., Bedford, Mass., 1971-80; asst. v.p. Textron Def. Systems, Wilmington, 1980-87; corp. fellow The MITRE Corp., Bedford, from 1988. Author: Signal Analysis and Estimation, 1988; contbr. numerous articles to jours. in field; mem. editl. bd. Waves in Random Media. Recipient Atwater Kent prize U. Pa., 1958, Dept. Labs. Achievement award USAF, 1974, Marcus O'Day prize USAF, 1975, I Migliori award Pirandello Lyceum, 1989, MITRE Corp. Best Paper prize, 1992, 2002, IEEE Disting. Lectr., 1995, 96. Fellow IEEE (editor in chief Transactions 1983-86, Third Millennium medal 2000, Scheklunoff prize 2002), Optical Soc. Am., Inst. Physics; mem. Electromagnetics Acad., Internat. Union Radio Sci. Roman Catholic. Home: Reading, Mass. Died 2006.

FARIA, EDWARD CYRINO, health care administrator; b. Peabody, Mass., Aug. 12, 1924; s. Celestino and Laura (Lucio) F.; student U. S.C., 1948-50, 1956-60, U.S. Armed Forces Inst., 1957-58, So. Ill. U., 1961-65; certificate USAF Sch. Aviation Medicine Air U., 1955; m. Gloria Jewel Harrison, Jan. 15, 1944; children— Gloria Dawn, Evelyn Celeste, Elizabeth Vermel. Served as enlisted man USAAF, 1942-46, USAF, 1950-67, advanced through grades to chief master sgt. USAF, 1960; med. adminstrv. specialist USAAF, 1942-46; chief storekeeper VA Regional Office, S.C., 1946-50; med. adminstrv. supt. Lawson AFB Hosp., Ga., 12th Air Force Surgeons' Office, Wiesbaden, Germany, Spangdahlem Air Base, Toul-Rosier Air Base, France, 1950-67; adjutant Spandahlem Air Base, 1951-54; exec. officer Mil. Air Transport Service, Scott AFB, Ill., 1961-62, chief adminstrv. services, 1965-66; asst. adminstr. Myrtle Beach (S.C.) AFB Hosp., 1966-67; sr. instr. med. adminstr. USAF Med. Service, USAF Med. Sch., Gunter AFB, Ala., 1954-60; ret., 1967; loan guarantee analyst VA Regional Office, Columbia, S.C., 1967; personnel statistician U.S. Army Hosp., Ft. Jackson Hosp., S.C., 1967-68; adminstr. Columbia (S.C.) Area Mental Health Center, 1968—; cons. in community mental health; instr. healthcare adminstrn., psychiat. residency Hall Psychiat. Inst., Columbia. Chmn. deacons Seventh Day Adventist Ch., Montgomery, Ala., 1957-58, supt. Sabbath Sch., Columbia, 1966-67, asst. supt. Sabbath Sch., Orangeburg, S.C., 1975-76, ednl. sec., 1975-76. Fellow Am. Acad. Med. Adminstrs.; mem. Adminstrv. Mgmt. Soc., Assn. Mental Health Adminstrs., Soc. Personnel Adminstrn., USAF Assn., S.C., Am. hosp. assns., Am. Cancer Soc., Heart and Lung Assn., Southeastern Statisticians, Smithsonian Inst. Assos. Clubs: Armed Forces, Am. Legion, DAV, VFW, Elks (hon.), Optimists (v.p. internat. 1971-72). Author: Medical Services Financial Management, 1959; Base Level Medical Checklist for Self Inspection, 1954, 3d rev. edit., 1956. Home: Saint Matthews, SC. Died Apr. 5, 2006.

FARLEY, JAMES BERNARD, retired financial services company executive; b. Pitts., Nov. 1, 1930; s. James and Marie (Wallace) F.; m. Mary W. Williams, Feb. 14, 1951; children— James J., Michele M., Constance M., J. Scott BBA, Duquesne U., 1953; MBA, Case Western Res. U., 1961. Indsl. engr. U.S. Steel Co., Pitts., 1952-60; supt. Newburgh & So. Shore Ry. Co., Cleve., 1960-63; v.p. Booz, Allen & Hamilton, NYC, 1963-73, pres., CEO, 1973-76, chmn. bd., CEO, 1976-85, sr. chmn. bd., 1985-88; pres., COO Mut. of N.Y., NYC, 1988-89, chmn., pres., CEO, 1989-91, chmn., CEO, 1991-94. Bd. dirs. Promus Cos., Inc., Memphis, Ashland Oil Inc., Ky., Conf. Bd., N.Y.C., Mut. of N.Y., 1988-2003 Mem.: Links, Sky (N.Y.C.); Gulf Stream Golf (Delray Beach, Fla.); Baltusrol Golf (Springfield, N.J.) (bd. govs. 1978-84). Home: Delray Beach, Fla. Died Jan. 20, 2007.

FARLOW, CARL PEARSON, JR., iron and steel manufacturing executive; b. Albertville, Ala., May 21, 1921; s. Carl Pearson and Margaret (Hood) F.; m. Mary Ann Nance, Sept. 2, 1943; children: Sam, Margaret Farlow Lee. BSM.E., U. Ala., 1943; BA, B.Arch., U. Minn., 1960. Registered profl. engr., Ala. Engr. Am. Cast Iron Pipe Co. (Acipco), Birmingham, Ala., 1939-43, 46-47, sales engr., 1948-51, NYC, 1952, design engr. Birmingham, Ala., 1953-55, chief engr., 1956-63, v.p. engring., 1963-76, exec. v.p., 1976-78, pres., from 1978, dir. various subs. Dir. First Ala. Bank of Birmingham Bd. govs. Brookwood Med. Ctr., Birmingham; bd. visitors Berry Coll.; mem. pres.'s council U. Ala.; bd. dirs. Community Chest, Jr. Achievement, Warrior-Tombigbee Devel. Assn., Birmingham Area Alliance of Bus., Met. Devel. Bd. Birmingham, Operation New Birmingham, ARC; mem. adv. bd. Salvation Army. Served with USN, 1943-46. Mem. ASME (past dir.), Assn. Iron and Steel Engrs. (dir., past dist. chmn.), Nat. Mgmt. Assn. Clubs: Birmingham, The Club, Downtown, Shoal Creek, Kiwanis. Methodist. Home: Birmingham, Ala. Died Jan. 31, 2006.

FARNHAM, HARRY JUD, lawyer; b. Lincoln, Nebr., Sept. 20, 1925; s. Harry C. and Grace M. (Binfield) F.; LL.D., U. Colo., 1949; m. Sally Link, June 10, 1946; children— Jeff, Dan, Amy. Admitted to Nebr. bar, 1949, since practiced in Omaha and Elkhorn, Nebr. Mem. Nebr. State Racing Commn., 1961—, chmn., 1963—; pres. Nat. Assn. State Racing Commrs., 1969. Mem. legacy com. Morris Animal Found.; sr. warden St. Augustine Episc. Ch., 1981-85. Served with USMCR, 1943-45. Recipient Racing Man of Year award Jockeys' Guild, 1970; Disting. Service award Am. Horse Council, 1972; Man of Year award Horseman's Benevolent Protective Assn., 1970; named to Nebr. Racing Hall of Fame, 1971, Gt. Plains Amateur Boxing Assn. Hall of Fame, 1975; Horsemans Nat. Hall of Fame, 1987. Fellow Am. Acad. Matrimonial Lawyers; mem. Am., Nebr., Omaha bar assns. Democrat. Mason (33 deg.). Died May 24, 2007.

FARRER, WILLIAM CAMERON, lawyer; b. Cleve., Apr. 27, 1922; s. William M. and Jean (Cameron) F.; m. Constance Webb, July 25, 1953; children: William W., Cameron W., Jonathan S., Webb M. AB, UCLA, 1943; JD, Duke U., 1949. Bar: Calif. 1950. Pvt. practice, LA, from 1950; atty. Hill, Farrer & Burrill, from 1950, ptnr., from 1958. Del. Calif. Bar Conf., 1952-71; chmn. bd. First Fed. Savs. & Loan Assn. San Gabriel Valley, 1990—. Mem. Calif. Coordinating Coun. on Higher Edn., 1970; bd. dirs. Greater L.A. Zoo Assn., 1968-71; regent U. Calif., 1970-71; mem. adv. bd. Orthopaedic Hosp., 1974-78; trustee UCLA Found., 1970-74; bd. counsellors U. So. Calif. Law Ctr., 1972-77; bd. dirs. Dunn Sch., 1977-80; mem. legal com. L.A. Music Ctr., 1982-92. Capt. inf. AUS, 1943-46. Decorated Bronze Star medal; named one of Best Lawyers of Am. Woodward-White, 1991-92. Fellow Am. Bar Found. (life); mem. Am. Bar Assn. (ho. of dels. 1957-80, mem. council sect. internat. law 1964-72, bd. govs. 1973-76), UCLA Alumni Assn. (pres. 1969-71), Am. Counsel Assn. (bd. dirs. 1989-90), Am. Law Inst., Am. Judicature Soc. (dir. 1972-75), Duke Law Alumni Council, Newcomen Soc. N.Am., Bel Air Assn (dir. 1981), Phi Gamma Delta, Phi Alpha Delta. Clubs: Beach (dir. 1972-73), Lincoln, Chancery (pres. 1973-74), Chevaliers du Tastevin; Balboa (Mex.). Home: Los Angeles, Calif. Died Mar. 8, 2006.

FASCIA, REMO MARIO, aviation consultant, airplane company executive; b. Buenos Aires, Oct. 5, 1922; came to U.S., 1956; s. Remo Raul and Maria Juana (Dematteis) F. BSEE, Otto Krause Indsl. Sch., Buenos Aires, 1941; MS in Aero. Enging., U. La Plata, 1948. Quality control engr. Def. Dept., Argentina, 1942-48; flight test engr. Argentine Air Force, 1949-54; faculty mem. aerodynamics and aircraft structures Air Force Inst., Buenos Aires, 1950-53; chief procurement testing engr. Techint-Dalmine, Argentina, 1955-56; sr. design engr. Convair Corp., San Diego, 1956-60; asst. project engr. Ford Motor Co., Buenos Aires, 1960; structural engr. Lockheed Aircraft Corp., Burbank, Calif., 1960; sr. structural engr. Norair Aircraft div. Northrop Corp., Hawthorne, Calif., 1961-62, sec. chief engr., 1966-70; sr. design engr. N.Am. Aviation Corp., Downey, Calif., 1962-63; scientist specialist Douglas Aircraft Corp., Long Beach, Calif., 1963-66; dir. Fascia Aviation Cons., St. Louis, from 1965; configuration synthesis engr. specialist McDonnel Douglas Co., St. Louis, 1970-88; mgr. S.Am. Mktg. Cons., St. Louis, from 1970; ptnr. Profl. Profile, Leadership and Creativity Evaluation Services, St. Louis, from 1975. Guest lectr. profl. creativity vs. graphoanalysis, 1975—; instr., lectr. numerous colls. and bus. including St. Louis C.C., N.W. Earth Inst., St. Louis. Hon. rep. City of St. Louis mayor-St. Louis Ambassadors, 1975—; treas. McCarthy for Pres. campaign, mo., 1976; state advisor U.S. Congl. Adv. Bd., Washington, 1982—; arbitrator St. Louis Better Bus. Bur., 1983—; with Disaster Action Team, St. Louis chpt. ARC, 1991—; mem. Republican Inner Circle State of Mo., 2000—; mem.-at-large Citizen com. for Environment, Chesterfield, Mo., 2000—. Mem. AIAA, Internat. Graphoanalysis Soc., Soc. Aero. Weight Engrs., Internat. Platform Assn., St. Louis Council World Affairs, Citizen for Modern Transit. Clubs: Marriot Swim and Tennis (St. Louis); Gaslight (Chgo.). Roman Catholic. Died June 7, 2007.

FAULKNER, AVERY COONLEY, architect; b. Bronxville, NY, Jan. 23, 1929; s. Waldron and Elizabeth (Coonley) F.; m. Alice Watson, June 7, 1951 (dec. 2006); children: Sara, Waldron, Lydia. BA, Yale U., 1951, BArch, 1954, MArch, 1955. Desinger Faulkner, Kingsbury and Stenhouse, Washington, 1958-64; ptnr. Faulkner, Stenhouse, Fryer and Faulkner, Washington, 1964-68; sr. ptnr. Faulkner, Fryer and Vanderpool, Washington, 1968-82; pres. Cannon/Faulkner, Washington, 1982-91; pvt. practice architecture and planning, 1991—2007. Treas. Coonley Found., Washington, 1982-2007; chmn. bd. trustees Potomac Sch., McLean, Va., 1976-78; presdl. apptd. mem. Adv. Coun. Hist. Preservation, Washington, 1987-92. Decorated Air Force medal, 1958. Fellow AIA (chmn. octagon com. 1974-80, v.p. AIA Found. 1975-79, pres. Washington chpt. AIA 1980-81, Regional Honor award 1969, Nat. Honor award 1970), Chevy Chase Club, Metropolitan Club (Washington), Hillsboro Club (bd. dirs.). Avocations: tennis, horseback riding, golf. Home: Delaplane, Va. Died Feb. 21, 2007.

FAUST, JAMES E., religious organization administrator; Second counselor LDS Ch., Salt Lake City, 1995—2007. Served in US Army. Mem.: Utah Bar Assn. (pres. 1962—63). Died Aug. 10, 2007.

FAVORITE, FELIX, oceanographer; b. Quincy, Mass., Mar. 18, 1925; s. Felix Christian and Irene Vibert (Doyle) F.; m. Betty Lou Donnelly, Nov. 2, 1951; children: Lee H., Kim C., Kit C., Felix Scott. BS, Mass. Maritime Acad., 1950; postgrad., Boston U., 1949-50; BS, U. Wash., 1956, MS, 1966; PhD, Oreg. State U., 1968. Research oceanographer U. Wash., 1957; dir. oceanographic research Bur. Comml. Fisheries Biol. Lab., Seattle, 1957-70; program mgr. oceanography Nat. Marine Fisheries Service, Seattle, 1971-75, resource ecology studies coordinator, 1977-80. Prin. investigator Outer Continental Shelf Environ. Assessment Program, 1976-78; expert in oceanography Internat. No. Pacific Fisheries Commn., 1959-72; oceanographic cons., 1981—. Served to lt. comdr. USNR, 1947-48, 50-53. Recipient Silver medal Dept. Commerce, 1973 Mem. Sigma Xi. Clubs: Sheridan Beach Community of Seattle (trustee 1960-61). Home: Lk Forest Park, Wash. Died Feb. 15, 2007.

FAWCETT, HENRY MITCHELL, b. Canton, Ohio, Nov. 30, 1919; s. John Andrew and Pauline (Heingartner) F.; m. Mary Ellen Bloch, Mar. 27, 1943; children— Mary Ellen Fawcett Tobin, Jane M. Fawcett Comunale, Julie Ann Fawcett Deane. BA, Colgate U., 1941; BA indsl. adminstrn. degree, Harvard, 1943. Various sales positions Mohawk Rubber Co., Akron, Ohio, 1946-51, asst. pres., 1951-56, pres., chief exec. officer, 1956-81, chmn., chief exec. officer Hudson, Ohio, from 1981, also dir. Dir. Twin Coach Co., Buffalo, 1st Nat. Bank Akron, Pfleuger Corp., Akron. Trustee Boy Scouts Am., YMCA, Salvation Army, Children's Hosp. Akron, Akron City Hosp.; bd. dirs. Assos. Harvard Bus. Sch.; bd. govs. Mass. Gen. Hosp., Boston. Served as lt. USNR, 1942-45. Mem. Akron C. of C. (trustee), Harvard Bus. Sch. Alumni Assn., Newcomen Soc., Sigma Nu. Clubs: Portage Country. Home: Akron, Ohio. Died Dec. 8, 2006.

FAY, LEO CHARLES, language education educator; b. St. Paul, Feb. 27, 1920; s. Leo and Marie Ulricka (Miller) F.; m. Elsa Jean Schwantes, Nov. 27, 1943; children: Dan, Wendie, Jon. BS, U. Minn., 1942, MA, 1947, PhD, 1948. Tchr. pub. schs., Richfield, Minn., 1941-43; asst. prof. SUNY, Cortland, 1948-50, prof., 1950-52; assoc. prof. edn. Ind. U., Bloomington, 1952-56, prof. edn., from 1956, chair lang. edn., 1965-90, prof. emeritus, from 1990. Vis. prof. Sri Nakarm Wrirot U., Bangkok, 1956-58; mem. adv. bd. Compton's Ency., Chgo., 1968-80; mem. editorial adv. bd. Reading Rsch. Quar., Newark, Del., 1965-75; bd. dirs. Internat. Reading Assn. Found., Newark, 1985-93. Author textbooks for Rand McNally Reading Program, 1972, revised, 1981; author textbooks for Riverside Reading Program, 1986, revised, 1989; editor: Compton's Dictionary of Natural Sciences, 1968; author articles. Mem. Gov.'s Com. to Improve Participation in Post Secondary Edn., Indpls., 1986-91; mem. standing com. Campus Ministry/Luth. Coun. U.S.A., 1968-72, chair, 1971-72. Served to sgt. USAAC, 1943-45. Named to Reading Hall of Fame, 1982, pres. 1985-86. Mem. Internat. Reading Assn. (bd. dirs. 1963-66, pres. 1968-69, William S. Gray citation of merit 1985), Nat. Coun. Tchrs. English, Nat. Conf. on Rsch. in English, Ind. State Reading Coun., Phi Delta Kappa. Avocations: travel, gardening, volunteer activities. Home: Bloomington, Ind. Died Feb. 26, 2006.

FEE, DOROTHEA LILLIAN, nurse; b. Wheeling, W.Va., Aug. 17, 1929; d. Harvey Gorrell and Elva (Borck) F. Diploma, Wheeling Hosp., 1950. BS in Nursing Edn., Franciscan U., 1954; MA in Nursing Adminstrn., U. Pitts., 1961. RN; cert. nurse adminstr. Dir. nursing Meml. Hosp., Charleston, W.Va. 1963-71, Northwestern Meml. Hosp., Chgo., 1971-73; asst. v.p. Children's Meml. Hosp., Chgo., 1973-75; v.p. nursing Jewish Hosp., Cin., 1975-81; v.p. nursing High Plains Bapt. Hosp., Amarillo, Tex., 1982-93, ret. 1993. R.N. mgmt. cons., 1995— Col. USAR, 1989, ret. Mem. Am. Nurses Assn., Tex. Orgn Nursing Execs., Sigma Theta Tau (mentor award 1991, pres award in oncology nursing 1993). Methodist. Home: Amarillo Tex. Died May 19, 2007.

FEENEY, ROBERT EARL, research biochemist; b. Oak Park Ill., Aug. 30, 1913; s. Bernard Cyril and Loreda (McKee) F.; m Mary Alice Waller, Dec. 3, 1954; children: Jane, Elizabeth Student, Rochester Jr. Coll., Minn., 1932-33; BS in Chemistry Northwestern U., 1938; MS in Biochemistry, U. Wis., 1939 PhD in Biochemistry, 1942. Diplomate Am. Bd. Nutrition. Rsch assoc. Harvard U. Med. Sch., Boston, 1942-43; rsch. biochemist USDA Lab., Albany, Calif., 1946-53; prof. chemistry U. Nebr. Lincoln, 1953-60; prof. dept. food sci. and tech. U. Calif., Davis 1960-84, prof. emeritus, rsch. biochemist, from 1984, interim dir. protein structure lab., 1990-91. Bd. dirs. Creative Chemistry Cons., Davis. Author: (with Richard Allison) Evolutionary Biochemistry of Proteins, 1969, (with Gary Means) Chemical Modification of Proteins, 1971, Professor On the Ice, 1974 Polar Journeys, 1998, The Role of Food and Nutrition in Early Exploration, 1998; editor: (with John Whitaker) Protein Tailoring for Food and Medical Uses, 1986. Capt. wound rsch. team M.C., U.S. Army, 1943-46. Recipient Superior Svc. award USDA, 1953,; Feeney Peak, Antarctica named in his honor U.S. Bd. on Geog. Names, 1968. Mem. Am. Chem. Soc. (chmn. div. agrl. and food chemistry, 1978-79, award for disting. svc. in agrl. and food chemistry, 1978), Am. Soc. for Biochemistry and Molecular Biology, Inst. of Food Technologists, Explorers Club Democrat. Avocations: polar science, polar exploration writing Home: Davis, Calif. Died Sept. 21, 2006.

FELDMAN, AVNER IRWIN, neurosurgeon; b. N.Y.C., Mar. 9 1927; s. Joseph O. and Lillian (Markowitz) F.; B.S., NYU, 1947 M.D., State U. Coll. Medicine, N.Y.C., 1950; m. Helene West July 21, 1975; children by previous marriage— Sheri, David Intern, Beth Israel Hosp., N.Y.C., 1950-51; asst. resident in gen. surgery Maimonides Hosp., Bklyn., 1951-52, in neurology Mt. Sinai Hosp., N.Y.C., 1952; resident neurosurgery Beth Israel Hosp., 1953, Bronx Municipal Hosp., N.Y.C., 1955-56; resident Montefiore Hosp., N.Y.C., 1956-57, chief resident, 1957-58; pvt. practice specializing in neurosurgery, Inglewood, Calif 1959—; assoc. clin. prof. neurol. surgery UCLA Med. Center Served with USAF, 1953-55. Diplomate Nat. Bd. Med. Examiners, Am. Bd. Neurosurgery. Recipient William S. Linder Surg prize, 1950. Fellow A.C.S.; mem. Am. Assn. Neurol. Surgeons Congress Neurol. Surgeons, So. Calif. Neurosurg. Soc., Los Angeles Soc. Neurology and Psychiatry, Calif., Los Angeles County med. assns., Alpha Omega Alpha. Home: Beverly Hills Calif. Died July 10, 2007.

FELDMAN, MYER (MIKE FELDMAN), lawyer, former federal official; b. Phila., June 22, 1917; s. Israel and Bella (Kurland) F.; m. Adrienne Arsht, Sept. 28, 1980; children by previous marriage: Jane Margaret, James Alan. Student, Girard Coll., Phila., 1922-31; BS in Econs., U. Pa., 1935, LL.B. (fellow 1938-39), 1938. Bar: Pa. 1938, D.C. 1965, U.S. Supreme Ct. 1965. Pvt. practice, Phila. and D.C., 1939—42, 1965—2007; spl. counsel, exec. asst. to chmn. SEC, 1946-54; mem. counsel armed svcs. com. US Senate, 1954-55, mem. counsel banking and currency commn., 1955-57, legis. asst. to Senator John F. Kennedy, 1958-61; dep. spl. counsel to Pres. The White House, 1961-64, counsel to Pres. Washington, 1964-65; founder, ptnr. Ginsburg Feldman & Bress, Washington, 1965-98; pres. Ardman Broadcasting Corp., 1992—2007. Pres. S.W. Fla. Broadcasting, KEFCO Apparel Corp.; lectr. law U. Pa., 1941-42; prof. law Am. U., 1955-56; pres. Radio Assocs., Inc., 1959-81; dir. Music Fair Group, Inc.; chmn. bd. Fin. Satellite Corp.; partner Key Stas., 1960-79; chmn. bd. Speer Publs., 1972-77, Capital Gazette Press, Inc., 1972-77, Bay Publs., 1972-77; bd. dirs. Nat. Savs. & Trust Co., Flame Hope, Inc., Media and Art Svcs., Inc., WSSH, Inc., Internat. Fusion Energy Systems Co., Inc., WLLH Broadcasters, WLAM Broadcasters, Capitol Broadcasting Inc., Lazare Kaplan, Inc., Trade Nat. Bank; chmn. bd., CEO Totalbank Corp.; pres. Les Amis Constrn., 1997; v.p. Crystal Galleria LLC, 2000-07; chmn. bd. Neogenix, 2004-07. Author: Standard Pennsylvania Practice, 4 vols., 1958; prodr. various broadway musicals and plays; prodr. Am. Forum TV show; contbr. articles to profl. jours. Pres. N.Y. Art Festival, Inc., 1972-80; del. Democratic Nat. Conv., 1968; pres. McGovern for Pres. Com., 1971-72; vice chmn. Congl. Leadership for Future, 1970; fin. chmn. Bayh for Pres. Com., 1975-76; bd. dirs. Weitzman Inst., 1963-84; chmn. exec. com. Spl. Olympics, Inc.; trustee Eleanor Roosevelt Meml. Found., 1963-2007, Jewish Publ. Soc., 1966-78, Declaration of Independence, House and Library, 1965-75; bd. dirs. Henry M. Jackson Found., 1984-92, trustee; mem. exec. com. Hollings for Pres. Com., 1984; bd. dirs. John F. Kennedy Library, 1983—2007; bd. overseers V.I. U., 1962-2007; dir. U. Minn. Freeman Ctr., 1991-2007 Served with USAAF, 1942-46. Mem. U. Pa. Law Alumni Assn. Washington (pres. 1952-58), Potomac Tennis Club, Tau Epsilon Rho (pres. 1938) Died Mar. 1, 2007.

FELDMAN, SAMUEL MITCHELL, neuroscientist, educator; b. Phila., Sept. 26, 1933; s. Boris and Fanya B. (Shrager) F.; children— Lee Stephen, David Saul. BA, U. Pa., 1954; MA, Northwestern U., 1955; PhD, McGill U., 1959. Fellow in physiology U. Wash., Seattle, 1958-60; from instr. to asso. prof. physiology Albert Einstein Coll. Medicine, 1960-71; prof. psychology N.Y. U., from 1971, head dept., 1972-76, prof. neuroscience, from 1988, dir. grad. studies neural sci., from 1989; mem. psychol. sci. study sect. NIMH, 1968-72, chmn., 1970-72, mem. biol. sci. tng. grant rev. com., 1977-83. Cons. in field. Contbr. articles to profl. jours. Fellow USPHS, 1958-60; recipient Career award, 1969-71, research grantee, 1963— Mem. Am. Physiol. Soc., Soc. Neurosci., Sigma Xi. Home: New York, NY. Died Dec. 18, 2006.

FELL, JAMES FREDERICK, lawyer; b. Toledo, Nov. 18, 1944; s. George H. Fell and Bibianne C. (Hebert) Franklin; children from a previous marriage: Jennifer A., Brian F.; m. Betty L. Wenzel, May 23, 1981. BA, U. Notre Dame, 1966; JD, Ohio State U., 1969. Bar: N.Y. 1970, Calif. 1972, Idaho 1978, Wash. 1981, Oreg. 1984, U.S. Ct. Appeals (9th cir.) 1983, U.S. Dist. Ct. Idaho 1978. Assoc. Breed, Abbott & Morgan, NYC, 1969-72; ptnr. McKenna & Fitting, LA, 1972-78; atty. Office Atty. Gen., State of Idaho, Boise, 1978-79; dir. policy and administrn. Idaho Pub. Utilities Commn., Boise, 1979-81; gen. counsel, dep. dir. Northwest Power Planning Coun., Portland, Oreg., 1981-84; ptnr. Stoel Rives LLP, Portland, from 1984. Mem. ABA (pub. utility law sect.), Oreg. State Bar (pub. utility law sect.). Home: Portland, Oreg. Died Aug. 2006.

FELTON, JULE WIMBERLY, JR., lawyer; b. Macon, Ga., July 22, 1932; s. Jule Wimberly and Mary Julia (Sasnett) F.; m. Kate Gillis, May 15, 1965; children— Jule Wimberly III, Mary Katherine, Laura Borden Student, Emory U., Atlanta, 1949-50; AB, U. Ga., Athens, 1954, LL.B, 1955. Bar: Ga. 1954. Assoc. Hansell & Post, Atlanta, 1955-59, mng. ptnr., 1959-89; sr. of counsel Jones Day Reavis & Pogue, Atlanta, 1989-92; ptnr. Ford & Felton, 1993-95, Proctor, Felton & Atkinson, Atlanta, 1995-96, Proctor, Felton & Chambers, Atlanta, 1996-99. Bd. dirs. dept. cmty. affairs Ga. State, chair, from 2003. Mem. Ga. Gen. Assembly, Atlanta, 1969-72; mem. ofcl. bd. dirs. Northside United Meth. Ch., Atlanta, 1974-85, 88; mem. U. Ga. Bd. Visitors, 1986, 87, 91, chmn., 1987-88, 93-94; bd. dirs. Ga. Dept. Cmty. Affairs Bd., 1999-2003, chair, 2002-03. 1st lt. JAGC, U.S. Army, 1955-56. Recipient Disting. Svc. award, U. Ga. Law Sch. Fellow Am. Bar Found.; mem. ABA, Ga. Bar Assn. (pres. 1973-74), Nat. Conf. Bar Pres., Am. Coll. Trial Lawyers, Ga. Bar Found., Am. Judicature Soc., U. Ga. Law Sch. Assn. (pres. 1984-85), Lawyers Club Atlanta, Old War Horse Lawyers Club (pres. Atlanta chpt. 1983), Piedmont Driving Club, Capital City Club. Avocations: piano, golf, boating. Home: Atlanta, Ga. Died Jan. 17, 2007.

FELZER, LIONEL HERBERT, other: health services; b. Phila., July 18, 1923; s. Philip and Esther (Willig) F.; m. Doris Felzer, Nov. 22, 1953; children: Stuart, Jordan, Benjamin. BS in Econs., U. Pa., 1949. CPA Pa. Staff acct. Jack Felzer & Co, CPA, Phila., 1949—53, ptnr., 1953—69; controller R.H. Med. Svcs., Elkins Park, Pa., 1969—72, v.p. fin., treas., 1972—81, bd. dirs., 1969—81; v.p. fin., treas. MEDIQ Inc., Pennsauken, N.J., 1981—84, sr. v.p. fin., 1984—88, sr. v.p., treas., bd. dirs., 1988—92. V.p., dir. HMG Property Investors, Miami, 1972—85. With US Army, 1943—46, ETO, CBI. Mem.: Fedn. Am. Hosps. (bd. dirs. 1975—80). Home: Boynton Beach, Fla. Died Mar. 23, 2006.

FENDLER, JANOS HUGO, chemistry professor; b. Budapest, Hungary, Aug. 12, 1937; came to U.S., 1964; s. Janos and Vilma (Csiky) F.; m. Eleanor Johnson, june 15, 1965 (div. 1975); children: Michael, Lisa; m. Ann Fendler, Feb. 15, 1976 (div. 1997); children: Peter, Monika; m. Eliza Hutter, Sept. 15, 1997; children: Veronika Isabelle, David Viktor. BSc, U. Leicester, Eng., 1960; Diploma in Radiochemistry, Leicester Coll. Tech., 1961; PhD, U. London, 1964, DSc, 1978; DSc (hon.), U. Szeged, Hungary, 1999. Postdoctoral fellow U. Calif., Santa Barbara, 1965-66; fellow Mellon Inst., Pitts., 1966-70; assoc. prof. chemistry Tex. A&M U., College Station, 1970-75, prof., 1975-81; prof. chemistry Clarkson Coll., Potsdam, NY, 1982-85; disting. prof. chemistry, dir. Ctr. Membrane Engring. & Sci. Syracuse U., 1985-97; disting. Camp prof. chemistry Clarkson U., from 1997. Adj. prof. U. Montreal, 1967—94; indsl. cons., vis. prof., Japan, 1975, Switzerland, 79, Sweden, 81, France, 85, Germany, 92, Israel, 97, Paris, from 2001. Author: Catalysts in Micellar and Macromolecular Systems, 1975, Membrane Mimetic Chemistry, 1982, Membrane Mimetic Approach to Advanced Materials, 1994; rsch., numerous publs. in field; N.Am. editor Colloid and Polymer Sci.; mem. editl. bd. Jour. Organic Chemistry, 1978-82, jour. Colloid and Interface Sci., 1981-87, Langmuir, 1985-87, Bull. Chem. Soc. France, 1986-92, Magyar Kèmiai Folyoirat, 1992—, Advanced Materials, 1994—, Chemistry of Materials, 1997—. Recipient Sr. Humboldt Rsch. award, 1992. Mem. Am. Chem. Soc. (Kendall award 1982), Royal Chem. Soc., Internat. Assn. Colloid and Interface Scientists. Home: Potsdam, NY. Died July 12, 2007.

FENDLEY, WILLIAM RAY, JR., university administrator, educator; b. Tuscaloosa, June 24, 1941; s. William Ray Sr. and Minnie Lee (Moore) F.; m. Carolyn Kay DeLon, June 12, 1965; 1 child, Howell DeLon. BA, U. Tenn., 1963, MS, 1968; PhD, Fla. State U., 1977. Asst. to dean U. Tenn., Knoxville, 1963-68, dir. student info., 1968-73; rsch. asst. Bd. Regents State Univ. System, Tallahassee, 1973-74; rsch. assoc. U. Tenn., 1974-79; asst. dir. Instnl. Rsch. U. Va., Charlottesville, 1979-81, assoc. dir. Instnl. Rsch., 1981-94; dir. Instnl. Rsch. U. Ala., Tuscaloosa, from 1994. Adj. faculty Piedmont Va. C.C., Charlottesville, 1987-94; working group Nat. Ctr. for Edn. Stat., Washington, 1993-95, nat. postsecondary edn. consortium, 1995—. Editor: Reference Sources: An Annotated Bibliography, 1993. Mem. adv. bd. Charlottesville Tennis Patrons Assn., Charlottesville, 1985-90, Soccer Orgn. Albemarle County, Charlottesville, 1980-85; cert. referee U.S. Tennis Assn. Umpires Coun., N.Y., 1987-89. Recipient Pres.'s award Va. Assn. for Mgmt., Analysis and Planning, 1983. Mem. Assn. Instnl. Rsch. (advancement and devel. taskforce 1991-93, taskforce for student right to know 1993-95, forum chair 1994-95, Forum Chair award 1995), So. Assn. Instnl. Rsch. (treas., program chair, pres. 1989-94, Pres.'s award 1994, Svc. award 1996), Ala. Assn. Instnl. Rsch., Soc. Coll. and Univ. Planning, Rotary, Nat. Postsecondary Edn. Consortium. Episcopalian. Avocations: furniture refinishing, tennis, travel. Home: Tuscaloosa, Ala. Died Mar. 26, 2007.

FENSTER, LAURA, jewelry manufacturer's representative; b. N.Y.C., Aug. 14, 1932; d. Irving Israel and Fannie (Rosenbaum) Sternberg; m. Bernard Fenster, June 14, 1952; children— Frederic, Kenneth, Ivan. Mgr. order dept. Norman M. Morris Corp., N.Y.C., 1950-54; mgr. sales, buying Lipson Potter, Ltd., Highland Park, Ill., 1970-83; prin. Laura Fenster Enterprises, Higland Park, Ill., 1984—; rep. manufacturers of fine jewelry Eshel Jewelry Co., N.Y.C., 1984—, Sandy Baker Jewelry Co., N.Y.C., 1984—. Fundraiser Democratic Party, Highland Park, 1968-72. Jewish. Club: Women's Am. Ort. Lodge: Ctr. for Enriched Living. Avocations: boating; swimming; tennis; racquetball; aerobics. Died Mar. 15, 2006.

FERGUSON, JOHN LEWIS, state historian; b. Nashville, Ark., Mar. 1, 1926; s. Clarence Walter and Nannye Nell (McCrary) F.; m. Oris Brandon, June 9, 1956; children— Clay Walt, Ora Lee. B.A., Henderson State Tchrs. Coll., 1950; M.A., U. Ark., 1952; Ph.D., Tulane U., 1960. Head dept. social studies Conway Bapt. Coll., Ark., 1952-58; asst. prof. history Ark. Poly. Coll., Russellville, 1958-60; state historian Ark. History Commn., Little Rock, 1960—. Editor: Arkansas and the Civil War, 1965; author: Arkansas Lives, 1965; co-author: Historic Arkansas, 1966. Baptist. Home: Little Rock, Ark. Died Mar. 25, 2006.

FERGUSON, NEIL TAYLOR, savings and loan executive; b. Alameda, Calif., Mar. 15, 1922; s. Hector Donald and Erna (Taylor) F. BA, San Jose State Coll., 1944. Mgr. Fields Store, Campbell, Calif., 1946-48; partner Paul C. Rudolph & Co., San Jose, Calif., 1948-51; pres., dir. Mut. Fund Assos., Inc., San Rafael, Calif., 1951-71; v.p., dir. Putnam Mgmt. Co., 1961-68; chmn., dir. Putnam Fin. Services, Inc., 1972-74, Western Travelers Life Ins. Co., Inc., 1972-74; pres., dir. Funded Investors, Inc., 1971-74; chmn. bd. Centennial Savs. and Loan Assn., 1976-84, vice chmn., 1984-85. Pres. Union R.R. Oreg., 1978-87; ptnr. Jamestown Hotel (R.R. Consultants); chmn. Sierra Western Rail Corp., 1980—; dir. Forestville Park Devel. Inc. Mem. Forestville Citizens Adv. Com.; v.p. Forestville Sch. Facilities Corp.; bd. dirs. Big Bros. and Sisters of Sonoma County, 1978-79, Clear Water Ranch Childrens House, Inc., Russian River Region Inc., Sonoma State U. Pres.'s Assocs.; adv. Prime Timers, Forestville, 1978—; adv. bd. Ret. Sr. Vol. Program, Santa Rosa, Calif., 1979—; mem. adv. bd. Sonoma State U., 1984—; bd. dirs. Community Found. Sonoma County, 1985; adv. bd. Clear Water Ranch, 1985—. Served to lt. USNR, 1942-49. Mem. Marin County C. of C. (dir. 1971-74), Forestville C. of C. (v.p., dir. 1965-85), Nat. Assn. Securities Dealers (vice chmn. dist. bus. conduct com. 1972-75), Am. Assn. Pvt. Railroad Car Owners (v.p. 1980), UN Orgn., Native Sons Golden West, Forestville Grange. Clubs: Optimists, Commonwealth (San Francisco). Home: Lewisville, Tex. Died Mar. 15, 2006.

FERGUSON, PAUL SANDERS, JR., real estate executive; b. Chester, SC, Oct. 30, 1923; s. Paul Sanders and Floris (Chambers) F.; m. Sarah Frances Wilkes, Sept. 27, 1947; children: Paul III, Francis Eric. Sec., controller J.A. Jones Constrn., Charlotte, 1976-77, v.p., sec., 1978-86, Jones Group, Inc., Charlotte, 1984-86; chmn. bd. Queens Properties, Inc., Charlotte, from 1986; pres. Mark III, Inc., Atlanta, 1983-86. Capt. Oasis Temple Patrol, Charlotte. Served with U.S. Army, 1943-46. Decorated Purple Heart. Mem. Am. Mgmt. Assn. Baptist. Home: Charlotte, NC. Died May 13, 2007.

FERGUSON, ROBERT WILLIAM, telephone company executive; b. Newark, Feb. 1, 1923; s. Elbert W. and Henriette (Schaefer) F.; B.S., Rutgers U., 1947; postgrad. Indsl. Relations, Princeton U., 1952; postgrad. Inst. Humanistic Studies for Execs., U. Pa., 1956; m. Jeanne Kathleen Schroth, Apr. 22, 1950; children— Robert William, John William, Thomas William, Bruce William, Jeanne Marie, Elizabeth Marie, Emily Marie, Kathleen Marie, Frank William, Christine Marie. With AT&T Co., 1947—, asst. traffic engr. N.J. Bell Telephone Co., 1947-50, with Bell Telephone Co. Pa., 1950-55, 56-68, gen. traffic engr., 1957-59, div. plant supt., Pitts., 1959-60, gen. comml. mgr., 1960-64, gen. ops. mgr., 1964-66, v.p. staff, 1966-67, v.p., gen. mgr., 1967-68, also v.p., gen. mgr. Diamond State Telephone Co. (Del.), 1967-68, asst. v.p. ops. traffic, AT&T, N.Y.C., 1968-73, v.p. ops., dir., mem. exec. com. Wis. Telephone Co., Milw., 1973-76, v.p. ops., dir., mem. exec. com. Southwestern Bell Telephone Co., St. Louis, 1976-77; asst. v.p. AT&T Antitrust Activities and Computer Inquiry II, 1978; chief exec. officer designate Yellow Pages, 1982; v.p. Western Electric Co., 1983; v.p. AT&T Techs., Inc., Basking Ridge, N.J., 1984-85; pres. Robert W. Ferguson and Assocs. Inc., Delray Beach, Fla., 1985-87; chmn. bd. Metal Products Co., Inc. Fla., 1987, Ferguson-Olderman Mgmt. Group, Inc., 1987—; dir. Merc. Bancorp., St. Louis, Merc. Trust Co., St. Louis, Marine Corp., Milw. Vice chmn. suburban cos., bus. and industry div. United Fund, 1969; chmn. orgn. and extension Gen. Wayne dist., Valley Forge council Boy Scouts Am., troop dir., Newton Square, Pa.; bd. dirs. Ams. Competitive Enterprise System, Delaware Valley Council, Family and Children's Service, Negro Emergency Ednl. Fund, Pa. Council Crime and Delinquency; trustee St. Elizabeth Coll. Served with AUS, World War II; PTO. Recipient Meritorious Service award Bell System; named Business Man of Day. Pitts. C. of C. (dir.). Clubs: Aronimink Golf (Newtown Square); (Phila.); Seaview Country (Absecon, N.J.); Canoe Brook Country (Summit, N.J.); Delray Beach (Fla.) Country; Citrus (Orlando, Fla.), Rotary. Died Mar. 23, 2007.

FERNANDES, JOSEPH EDWARD, small business owner; b. Maderias, Portugal, Mar. 12, 1923; came to U.S., 1924; s. Jose and Rosa (Teixerira) F.; m. Annabelle Watson, Apr. 24, 1954; children: Joseph, Marcia, Donna Maria. BS in Bus. Adminstrn., Boston U., 1947; D in Comml. Sci. (hon.), Stonehill Coll., 1964. With Fernandes Super Mkts., Inc., Norton, Mass., from 1948, pres., treas., from 1952, chmn. bd. until 1979. Treas. Fernandes Realty Corp., Brockton East Shopping Plaza, Inc., Fernandes Twin-City Realty Corp.; pres. Portuguese Times Newspaper, 1980—, Portuguese Cable TV Network, 1981—, Sta. WRCB, Providence, 1982—; dir. Fall River Line Pier, Mass.; cons. Alliance for Progress, Uruguay, 1962. Pres. Annawon council Boy Scouts Am., 1974—, regional NE Dir., 1971—, also bd. dirs.; former chmn. Portuguese Am. Fedn. U.S. and Can.; bd. dirs. Mass. Blue Sheild, Mass. Easter Seals, U.S.S. Mass. Meml. Com., R.I. Philharm. Orch.; trustees council U. Mass., 1973; former trustee Salve Regina Coll., Newport, R.I.; former pres. Portuguese Cultural Found.; pres. Bristol County Devel. Council, 1980—. Served with AUS, 1943-45. Decorated knight St. Gregory the Great; Order Prince Henry the Navigator (Portugal); recipient Peter Francisco award Portuguese Continental Union, 1966, Silver Beaver, Silver Antelope awards Boy Scouts Am., 1977; named Man of Yr. NCCJ. Mem. Internat. Assn. Chain Stores (pres. 1968-71), Portugal-U.S. C. of C. (dir.). Home: Norton, Mass. Died Aug. 19, 2007.

FERNANDEZ, GUILLERMO J., ophthalmologist, medical-paralegal consultant; b. San Juan, Dec. 25, 1928; s. Guillermo and Margarita (Marti) F.; m. Casilda Sanchez Toro. MD, U. Madrid, 1958; postgrad. in ophthalmology, NYU, 1959-60. Diplomate P.R. Bd. Med. Examiners. Intern Presbyn. Hosp., San Juan, P.R., 1958-59; preceptor in ophthalmology Eye Inst. P.R., San Juan, 1960-63; pvt. practice ophthalmologist San Juan, from 1963. Chief of surgery Eye Inst. P.R., 1972-76, 83-90, bd. dirs., 1963-90. Chmn. Orlando (Fla.) Civil Svc. Bd., 1994—. Fellow ACS, Am. Acad. Ophthalmology; mem. AMA, Fla. Med. Assn., Fla. Soc. Ophthalmology, P.R. Med. Soc. Avocations: travel, exercise. Home: Maitland, Fla. Died May 7, 2006.

FERST, BARTON E., lawyer; b. Phila., Jan. 23, 1920; s. Abe and Helen (Kaufman) F. BS in Econs., U. Pa., 1940, LL.B., 1944; MA in Govt., La. State U., 1941. Bar: Pa. 1944. Assoc. Herman H. Krekstein, Phila., 1944-52, firm Blank & Rudenko, Phila., 1952-55; ptnr. Blank, Rome, Comisky & McCauley, Phila., from 1955. Lectr. in field. Co-author: Basic Accounting for Lawyers, 1976. Vice pres. Fedn. Jewish Agys. of Greater Phila., 1973-76; bd. dirs. United Way, Phila., 1974-79; chmn. bd. overseers Gratz Coll., 1978-83. Mem. Pa., Phila. bar assns., Order of Coif. Died July 30, 2006.

FETT, WILLIAM FREDERICK, plant pathologist; b. Hinsdale, Ill., Oct. 30, 1952; s. Walter William and Francis Henrietta F.; m. Maria Iracy Da Silva, Nov. 24, 1977; children— Andrew, Melanie. B.S., U. Ill., 1974; M.S., U. Wis.-Madison, 1977, Ph.D., 1979 NRC postdoctoral research assoc. Eastern Regional Research Ctr., Agrl. Research Service, USDA, Phila., 1979-80, research plant pathologist, 1980—2006. Assoc. editor Jour. of Phytopathology, 1993-2006; contbr. articles to profl. jours. Recipient Spl. Achievement award U.S. Dept. Agr. Agrl. Research Service, 1983, Cert. of Merit, 1985; Edmund J. James scholar U. Ill., Champaign-Urbana, 1970-74. Mem. Soc. for Indsl. Microbiology, Am. Phytopath. Soc. (bacteriology com. 1983-85, biochemistry, physiology, molecular biology com., 1987-89), Am. Soc. Microbiology. Avocations: tennis; golf. Home: Blue Bell, Pa. Died May 17, 2006.

FETTERMAN, JOHN HENRY, JR., naval officer; b. Ashland, Pa., Aug. 4, 1932; s. John Henry and Mary (Horvath) F. BA, Albright Coll., 1954; grad., Naval War Coll., 1964-65; postgrad., Harvard U., 1981. Commd. ensign U.S. Navy, 1955, advanced through grades to rear adm., 1981; comdg. officer USS Roosevelt, Carrier Air Wing 8, USS Nimitz, 1975-76, USS LaSalle, 1977-78, Naval Base, Guantanamo Bay, Cuba, 1979-81, Tactical Wings Atlantic NAS Oceana, Va., 1981-83; comdr. tng. U.S. Atlantic Fleet, Norfolk, Va., from 1983. Decorated Legion of Merit (3); decorated Meritorious Service medal Mem.: Elk. Home: Virginia Beach, Va. Died Mar. 24, 2006.

FETTERS, BILL, insurance agent; b. Pierce City, Mo., Dec. 2, 1937; s. Simon B. and Velma H. (Reynolds) F.; m. Mona A. McConnell, Feb. 14, 1960 (div. Dec. 1978); children: James, Phillip, Patricia, Myra; m. Catherine L. Long, July 7, 1979; children: Christopher, Dustin. AA, S.W. Bapt. Coll., 1962. Sales mgr. Model Laundry Co., Rogers, Ark., 1967—70; tchr. McDonald County HS, Anderson, Mo., 1970—73; ins. agt. Hartley Agy., Inc., Baxter Springs, Kans., from 1980. Pres., bd. dirs. C. of C., Baxter Springs, from 1983; blood chmn. ARC, Baxter Springs, from 1980, chmn. blood svcs. com. Springfield, Mo., 1985, 1986; county chmn. Am. Heart Assn., Cherokee County, Kans., 1982—83; parade chmn. Jessie James Days, Pineville, Mo., 1971—73; pastor Bapt. chs., various states, from 1960; bd. dirs. ARC, Springfield, Mo., from 1982. Sgt. US Army, 1955—60. Recipient Citizen of Month, Baxter Springs C. of C., 1981. Mem.: Ind. Ins. Agts. Am., Lions (v.p. Riverton, Kans. 1984). Republican. Baptist. Home: Riverton, Kans. Died July 29, 2006.

FIASCO, CAROLYN LEE, counselor; b. Wayne, Mich., Oct. 16, 1944; d. Manuel Maurice and Virginia Lee (Tapp) Graddy; B.S., Murray (Ky.) State U., 1966; M.A. in Communications, Purdue U., 1969, Ed.S. in Counseling and Personnel, 1971; m. John Mirrell Fiasco, May 1, 1981; children: John Christopher, Mark Brenton. Family living editor, agrl. info. dept. Purdue U., 1969-72; tech. assoc. Center Vocat. and Tech. Edn., Ohio State U., Columbus, 1972, residence complex dir., 1972-74; dir. residence life Capital U., Columbus, 1975-78; counselor, faculty mem. Manatee Community Coll., Bradenton, Fla., 1978—, also mem. exec. bd.; workshop dir., cons. in field. Mem. Circle 12, Palma Sola Presbyterian Ch., Bradenton, 1982-83. Assoc. editor Fla. Speech Communication Jour. Contbr. articles to profl. jours. Mem. Am. Personnel and Guidance Assn., Am. Coll. Personnel Assn., Nat. Assn. Student Personnel Adminstrs., Nat. Assn. Women Deans, Adminstrs. and Counselors, Speech Communication Assn., Fla. Community Coll. Press Assn. (past pres.), Fla. Community Coll. Activities Assn. (exec. com.), Alphecca, Alpha Omicron Pi, Chi Delta Phi, Lambda Iota Tau. Died July 19, 2006.

FIDDLER, THOMAS ROBERT, retail executive; b. NYC, Mar. 24, 1921; s. Earl Thomas and Margaret (Martsolf) F.; m. Jane Carol Sundlof, Sept. 12, 1942; children: Martha J., Thomas N. (dec.), Kathryn A. AB, Princeton U., 1942. With Marshall Field and Co., Chgo., 1945-51, buyer, 1950-54; with Rich's Inc., Atlanta, 1954-60, gen. mgr. Tenn., 1955-60; with Frederick Atkins, NYC, 1960-67, pres., 1963-67; with D.H. Holmes Co. Ltd., New Orleans, from 1967, pres., 1972-86, chmn., from 1986. Dir. Hibernia Nat. Bank, Delchamps, Inc.; tchr. mktg. U. Ga., evenings 1952-54; bd. dirs. Internat. Trade Mart, 1983—; mem. council advisers Tulane U. Grad. Sch. Bus. Bd. dirs., exec. com. New Orleans Econ. Devel. Council, 1974—; chmn. maj. gifts United Way, 1974-75; sr. v.p. Council for a Better La., 1983; bd. dirs. New Orleans Met. Area Com., 1970—, New Orleans Symphony, 1974, 79; bd. dirs. New Orleans Tourist Commn., 1969—, pres., 1977-78, chmn., 1979; trustee King Sch., Stamford, Conn., 1962-66, Low Heywood Sch., Stamford, 1964-67, Xavier U., 1979; bd. dirs., exec. mgmt. com. La. World Expn., 1980—, also v.p.; mem. Pres.'s council Tulane U., 1983—; v.p. Los Angeles World Expn., 1980-83; trustee Gulf South Research Inst., Ochsner Found. Hosp. Served to lt. comdr. USNR, 1942-45. Recipient Weiss Brotherhood award NCCJ, 1985. Mem. Nat. Retail Mchts. Assn. (dir. 1974—), Am. Retail Fedn. (dir. 1981—), New Orleans Retail Mchts. Council (pres. 1972-73), New Orleans C. of C. (dir., exec. com.), World Trade Ctr. (dir., exec. com.) Clubs: Univ. (N.Y.C.); New Orleans Country (New Orleans), Boston (New Orleans), Plimsoll (New Orleans); Pass Christian Golf (Miss.), Pass Christian Yacht (Miss.); Diamondhead. Republican. Episcopalian. Home: Ponte Vedra Beach, Fla. Died June 27, 2007.

FIELD, ELOIS RACHEL, nurse, educator; b. Farnum, Nebr., Apr. 19, 1921; d. Joseph Walter and Mary Jane (Johnston) F. AA, Jr. Coll. S.E. Colo., 1940; R.N., Baylor U., 1943; BA, Wheaton Coll., 1945; M. Nursing, U. Wash., 1949; PhD, U. Chgo., 1961. Supr. polio epidemic ARC, N.W. Tex. Hosp., Amarillo, 1943; pvt. duty nurse, 1943-44; supr. medicine, surgery, 1945; instr. sch. nursing, 1945-46, 50-51; instr. St. Luke's Hosp. Sch. Nursing, Denver, 1946, Baylor Sch. Nursing, Dallas, 1947-48, 54-57, asst. dean, 1951-53; lectr. U. Calif., 1959-60; dir. baccalaureate programs Emory U. Sch. Nursing, Atlanta, 1962-64; dean Sch. of Nursing, U. Ark. Med. Center, 1964-78; prof. U. Tex., Arlington, from 1979. Author articles profl. jours. Mem. Am. Nurses Assn., Nat. League Nursing, Am. Ednl. Research Assn., Sigma Theta Tau, Pi Lambda Theta Baptist. Died Feb. 4, 2007.

FINCH, DONALD GEORGE, poet; b. Peoria, Ill., June 30, 1937; s. Lloyd Lindo and Jean Alberta Harsy; student Bradley U., 1955—. With Peoria Post Office. Works include: On Strawberry Eve, 1972; She Waits for Me, 1972; A Dandelion is Not a Rose, 1973; Georgia, 1976; We Are All the Children of God Through Jesus, 1977, Commanders of the Universe, 1988. Served with USAF, 1957-60. Mem. Peoria Poetry Club (v.p.), United Amateur Press, Am. Biog. Inst., Intercontinental Biog. Assn., DAV. Methodist. Died Nov. 22, 2006.

FINESILVER, SHERMAN GLENN, retired federal judge; b. Denver, Oct. 1, 1927; s. Harry M. and Rebecca M. (Balaban) F.; m. Annette Warren, July 23, 1954; children: Jay Mark, Steven Brad, Susan Saunders. BA, U. Colo., 1949; LLB, U. Denver, 1952; cert., Northwestern U. Traffic Inst., 1956; LLD (hon.), Gallaudet Coll., Washington, 1970, Met. State Coll., Denver, 1981, N.Y. Law Sch., NYC, 1983, U. Colo., 1988. Bar: Colo. 1952, U.S. Ct. of Appeals (10th cir.) 1952, U.S. Supreme Ct. 1952. Legal asst. Denver City Atty.'s Office, 1949-52; asst. Denver city atty., 1952-55; judge Denver County Ct., 1955-62, Denver Dist. Ct., 2d Jud. Dist., 1962-71, presiding judge domestic relations div., 1963, 67, 68; judge U.S. Dist. Ct., Denver, from 1971, elevated to chief judge, 1982-94; ret., from 1995; spl. counsel Popham Haik Schnobrich & Kaufman, Attys. at Law, Denver, from 1995. Adj. prof. U. Denver Coll. Law and Arts and Sci. Sch., 1955—, Met. State Coll., 1989—; mem. faculty Nat. Coll. Judiciary, Reno, 1967-84, Atty. Gen.'s Advocacy Inst., Washington, 1974—, seminars for new fed. judges, 1974—; elected to Jud. Conf. U.S., 1985-88; mem. Jud. Conf. Com. on Rules for Admission to Practice in Fed. Cts., 1976-79, Com. on Adminstrn. Probation System, 1983-87, Adv. Com. on Criminal Rules, 1984-87, Com. on Bicentennial of Constn., 1985-87, Com. on Criminal Law and Probation Adminstrn., 1988—. Contbr. chpt. to Epilepsy Rehabilitation, 1974; contbr. articles and publs. on law, medicine, legal rights of deaf, aging, physically impaired and many others, 1974-94. Mem. task force White House Conf. on Aging, 1972, presdl. commn., 1980-84; mem. Probation Com., U.S. Cts., 1985-88, Nat. Com. to Study Qualifications to Practice in Fed. Cts., 1976-82, bd. visitors Brigham Young U., 1977-80, Nat. Commn. Against Drunk Driving, 1982-86. Decorated Inspector Gen. 33d degree; recipient numerous awards including medallion for outstanding service by a non-handicapped person to physically disabled Nat. Paraplegia Found., 1972, cert. of commendation Sec. Transp., 1974, Norlin award for outstanding alumni U. Colo., 1988, numerous others. Fellow Am. Coll. Legal Medicine (Chgo., hon. fellow); mem. ABA (nat. chmn. Am. citizenship com. 1968, award of merit Law Day 1968), Colo. Bar Assn. (chmn. Law Day 1964, chmn. Am. citizenship com. 1963, bd. govs. 1982-94), Denver Bar Assn. (chmn. Law Day 1964), Am. Judicature Soc., Am. Amateur Radio, B'nai B'rith, Masons, Shriners, Phi Sigma Delta (trustee 1960-66, Nat. Man of Yr. Zeta Beta Tau chpt. 1989). Home: Denver, Colo. Died Oct. 12, 2006.

FINLEY, ALLEN BROWN, religious organization administrator; b. Albermarle, Va., Nov. 11, 1929; s. William Walter and Melissa (Hoover) Finley; m. Ruth Ann Goodwin, Aug. 14, 1953; children: Ruth Naomi, Catherine Ann, Gayla Melissa. BA, Bob Jones U., Greenville, SC, 1952; MA, Calif. Grad. Sch. Theology, 1981. Ordained to ministry Evang. Ch. Alliance, 1952. Pastor Setzer's Gap Presbyn. Ch., Lenoir, NC, 1950—52, Beattie Meml. Presbyn. Ch., Lenoir, 1950—52; missionary Gospel Fellowship Assn., 1952—53; office dir. Internat. Students, Inc., Phila., 1953—54, West Coast dir., 1954—60; gen. dir. Christian Nat. Evangelism Commn., San Jose, Calif., 1960—76, internat. pres., from 1976. Internat. bd. dir. Christian Nat. Evang. Commn.; bd. dir. Christian Nat. Evang. Commn. Coun., Sydney, Green Pastures, Inc., Mountain View, Calif.; dir. Fellowship Bible Inst. Commn., Evang. Ch. Alliance; del. World Congress Evangelism, Berlin, 1966, Lausanne Com. for World Evangelization, 1974, Thailand, 80, Internat. Conf. Itinerant Evangelists, Amsterdam, 1983; cons. U.S. Ctr. World Mission, Pasadena, Calif. Author: Assisting Third World Church Ministries, vol. II, no. 3, 1980, Mission: A World-Family Affair, 1981, Is Supporting Nationals Biblical?, 1982, The Family Tie, 1983; editor: CNEC Communique, 1960—72, World Report, 1960—72. Elder Berkeley (Calif.) First Presbyn. Ch., 1957—60, Westminster Presbyn. Ch., San Jose, from 1968; mem. Council Advisors Presbyn. United for Mission Advance (No. Calif. chpt.); bd. dir. ENI Mission, Sinoe, Liberia, 1972—80, Evang. Ch. Alliance, Ill., from 1955; mem. N.Am. bd. reference Nairobi Evang. Grad. Sch. Theology; mem. bd. reference Chinese for Christ Theol. Sem. Home: Matthews, NC. Died Oct. 30, 2006.

FIORE, ROBERT JAMES, advertising executive; b. NYC, Oct. 21, 1934; s. Louis Robert and Marie (Baletti) F.; m. Barbara Marie Renner, July 9, 1960; children: Christina, John. Student, N.Y.C. Community Coll. Sr. v.p. Papert Koenig Lois, NYC, 1961-66; pres. Chappel Fiore Endelman, NYC, 1967-72; exec. v.p. Gaynor & Ducas, NYC, 1972-74; ptnr. Acme Communications, NYC, 1974-76; exec. v.p. Kenyon & Eckhardt, NYC, 1976-84; pres. Warwick, Baker & Fiore, NYC, from 1885. Mem. hon. com. Cannes Film Festival, N.Y.C., 1990—. With USAR, 1957-63. Roman Catholic. Mem. N.Y. Advt. Club (mem. blue ribbon judging panel 1992—), Hempstead Golf Club (L.I.). Died July 9, 2006.

FIROR, JOHN WILLIAM, physicist, research center director; b. Athens, Ga., Oct. 18, 1927; s. John William and Mary Valentine (Moss) F.; m. Carolyn Merle Jenkins, Sept. 17, 1950 (dec. 1979); children: Daniel William, Katherine Eleanor, James Leonhard, Susan Elizabeth; m. Judith Eva Jacobsen, Oct. 15, 1983 (dec. 2004) BS with honors, Ga. Inst. Tech., 1949; PhD in Physics, U. Chgo., 1954. Mem. staff, dept. terrestrial magnetism Carnegie Instn., Washington, 1953—61; dir. high altitude obs. Nat. Ctr. for Atmospheric Rsch., Boulder, Colo., 1961—68, dir., 1968—74, exec. dir., 1974—80, dir. advanced study program, 1980—96, sr. rsch. assoc., 1996—2007. Sr. Wirth fellow U. Colo., Denver, 1996-98; vis. prof. Calif. Inst. Tech., 1963; Barnaby lectr. Nat. Soaring Mus., 1982 Author: The Changing Atmosphere: A Global Challenge, 1990; co-author (with wife Judith Jacobsen): The Crowded Greenhouse: Population, Climate Change, and Creating a Sustainable World. Trustee Boulder YMCA, pres. bd., 1972-75; trustee to hon. trustee Environ. Def. Fund, 1973—2007, chmn., 1976-80, vice-chmn., 1980-86; trustee Internat. Fedn. of Insts. Advanced Study, 1981-89; trustee, pres. Colo. Music Festival, 1981-83; trustee, founding bd. dir., mem. exec. com. World Resources Inst., 1982-99, vice chair, 1996-99. Served with C.E. U.S. Army, 1946. Mem. AAAS (v.p. astronomy 1968, chair atmospheric hydrol. sci. 1995), Am. Geophys. Union, Am. Meteorol. Soc., Internat. Astron. Union, Am. Astron. Soc. (chmn. solar physics divsn. 1970, vis. prof. 1960-61), Soaring Soc. Am. Died Nov. 5, 2007.*

FISCHER, AARON JACK, accountant; b. Chgo., Feb. 6, 1947; s. Ralph Hyman and Florence Idel (Kaufman) F.; m. Robin Gail Cole, Jan. 23, 1972; children: Amy Lauren, Michael Kenneth. BS in Commerce, DePaul U., 1969. CPA, Ill.; diplomate Am. Bd. Forensic Accts., Am. Bd. Forensic Examiners. Staff acct. BDO Seidman, Chgo., 1969-79, ptnr., 1979-86, tech. dir. acctg., auditing sec midwest regional, 1986-89; ptnr. Drobny and Fischer CPA (now Adler Drobny Fischer LLC), Crystal Lake, Ill., from 1990. Bd. dirs. Young Men's Jewish Coun., 1978-79. Mem. AICPA, Ill. Soc. CPA (acctg. principles com. 1978-80, ethics com. 1980-82), Am. Coll. Forensic Examiners, Twin Orchard Country Club. Home: Highland Park, Ill. Died Dec. 2, 2005.

FISCHER, BEN, labor relations educator; b. Hoboken, NJ, Nov. 26, 1913; s. Herman and Selma (Metzger) F.; m. Edwin Loeb, July 1, 1954 (dec. July 1979); children: Frederick, Susan Wynne, Mark (dec. 1987), Elise, Kari Uman; m. Sylvia Felser, Oct. 25, 1980. Student, Rand Sch. Social Sci., NYC, 1934-35. Research dir. Aluminum Workers Am., CIO, Pitts., from 1944; head contract adminstrn. dept. United Steelworkers Am., Pitts., from 1948, asst. to pres., 1978; dir. Ctr. Labor Studies Carnegie Mellon U., Pitts., from 1982; dist. pub. service prof. Sch. Urban and Pub. Affairs CMU, Pitts., from 1986. Chmn. Pa. Employment and Tng. Council, Harrisburg, Telecomputer Conf. Am. Productivity Ctr., 1984-85; mem. steering com. Leadership Pitts. Trustee Point Park Coll., Pitts.; pres. bd. Action Housing, Inc., Pitts.; mem. Pa. Labor-Mgmt. Task Force, Pitts., 1987. Named Pitts. Man of Yr. in Labor, Vectors, Pitts., 1984, Top 10 Vols., United Way, Pitts., 1978. Mem. Indsl. Relations Research Assn., Am. Arbitration Assn. (dir.). Democrat. Home: Pittsburgh, Pa. Died Nov. 12, 2006.

FISCHER, ERNST OTTO, chemist, educator; b. Munich, Nov. 10, 1918; s. Karl T. and Valentine (Danzer) Fischer. Diplom, Munich Tech. U., 1949, Dr. rer. nat., 1952, Habilitation, 1954, Dr. rer. nat. h.c., 1972, D.Sc.h.c., 1975, Dr. rer. nat. h.c., 1977, Dr.h.c., 1983. Lectr. Tech. Coll., 1955—57; assoc. prof. inorganic chemistry U. Munich, 1957—59, chair, 1959—64; prof. inorganic chemistry inst. Munich Inst. Tech., from 1964; prof. emeritus Tech. U. Munich, from 1984. Firestone lectr. U. Wis., 1969; vis. prof. U. Fla., Gainesville, 1971; Arthur D. Little vis. prof. MIT, Cambridge, 1973; vis. disting. lectr. U. Rochester, NY; lectr. Inorganic Chemistry Pacific West Coast, 1971. Author: (with H. Werner) Metall-pi-Komplexe mit di- und oligoolefinischen Liganden, 1963; transl. Complexes with di- and oligo-olefinic Ligands, 1966; Contbr. (with H. Werner) numerous articles in field to profl. jours. Recipient ann. prize Göttingen Acad. Scis., 1957, Alfred Stock Meml. prize Soc. German Chemists, 1959, Nobel Prize in Chemistry, 1973; Am. Chem. Soc. Centennial fellow, 1976 Mem. Bavarian Acad. Scis., Soc. German Chemists, German Acad. Scis. Leopoldina, Austrian Acad. Scis. (corr.), Accademia Nazionale dei Lincei, Italy (fgn.), Acad. Scis. Göttingen (corr.), Am. Acad. Arts and Scis. (fgn., hon.), Chem. Soc. (hon.) Achievements include special research in organometallic chemistry: metal pi complexes of arenes, olefins, carbene and carbyne complexes with metals, ferrocene type sandwich compounds, metal carbonyls. Died July 23, 2007.*

FISCHER, JAMES ADRIAN, retired clergyman; b. St. Louis, Oct. 15, 1916; s. John and Agnes (Henke) F. AB, St. Mary's Sem., Perryville, Mo., 1941; S.T.L., Cath. U. Am., 1949; S.S.L., Pontifical Bib. Inst., Rome, Italy, 1951; LL.D. (hon.), Niagara U., 1968. Joined Congregation of Mission, 1936; ordained priest Roman Cath. Ch., 1943; prof. sacred scripture St. John's Sem., San Antonio, 1943-45, St. Mary's Sem., Houston, 1951-56, Perryville, 1958-62; provincial Western province Vincentian Fathers, 1962-71, De Andreis Sem., Lemont, Ill., 1971-81; pres. Kenrick Sem., St. Louis, 1981-86, St. Thomas Sem., Denver, from 1995. Author: The Psalms, 1974, God Created Woman, 1979, How to Read the Bible, 1981, Priests, 1987, Looking for Moral Guidance, 1993, Interpreting the Bible, 1996. Chmn. bd. trustees De Paul U., Chgo., 1962-71. Mem. Cath. Bibl. Assn. (pres. 1976-77) Died Nov. 25, 2005.

FISCHER, JANET JORDAN, retired physician, educator, researcher; b. Pitts., Apr. 28, 1923; d. W. Edward and Jeannette (Kinnear) Jordan; m. Newton D. Fischer, Aug. 7, 1951; children: Amelia Fischer Drake, Jeannette Fischer Stein, Duncan, Helen, Anne. AB, Vassar Coll., 1944; MD, Johns Hopkins U., 1948. Diplomate: Am. Bd. Internal Medicine; lic. physician N.C. Intern John Hopkins Hosp., Balt., 1948-49, fellow in infectious disease, 1950-52; resident Salt Lake Gen. Hosp., Salt Lake City, 1949-50; instr. medicine U. N.C. Meml. Hosp., Chapel Hill, 1953-54, asst. prof., 1954-67, assoc. prof., 1968-73, prof., 1973-93, Sarah Graham Kenan prof., 1981-93. Mem. Durham Orange County Med. Soc., N.C. Med. Soc., Phi Beta Kappa Alpha Omega Alpha Died Feb. 24, 2007.

FISH, DAVID EARL, insurance company executive; b. Port Jervis, NY, Sept. 22, 1936; s. William Earl and Elizabeth Dorthea (Schleer) F.; m. Patricia Ann Reilly, June 14, 1958 (dec.); children: Nancy S., Susan L., Brian D. BSBA, Muhlenberg Coll., 1958. Claims adjuster Liberty Mut. Ins., East Orange N.J., 1961-65, claims supr. Pitts., 1966-68, claims examiner Boston, 1969-70, claims mgr. Buffalo, Syracuse, Balt., Phila. 1971-80, asst. divsn. claims mgr. Phila., 1980-81, asst. v.p Chgo., 1981-86, divsn. claims mgr., asst. v.p., 1986-87, v.p Boston, 1988-94, sr. v.p., from 1994. Bd. dirs. Arbitration Forums, Tampa, Fla., Nat. Ins. Crime Bur., Palos Hills, Ill Avocations: golf, spectator sports. Home: East Sandwich, Mass Died Oct. 25, 2006.

FISHER, CRAIG BECKER, film and television executive; b Manila, Jan. 19, 1932; s. Dale Davis and Francis Mary (Major F.; m. Helen Rossi Ashton, Sept. 5, 1970; children: Christophe Ashton, Wenda Francis; children by previous marriage: Cathleen Anne, Dean Barnett. BA, U. Md., 1954. With Sta. WRC TV, Washington, 1950, Sta. WTOP-TV, Washington, 1952, Sta WMAL-TV, Washington, 1954; successively unit mgr., assoc producer, film dir. CBS News, 1957-60; producer, dir., write NBC News, 1960-70; pres. Osprey Prodns., Inc., NYC, 1970-95, Fund for Arts & Scis. Films, Inc., from 1981, Kingfishe Prodns., from 1996. Adj. assoc. prof. film dept. St. John's U. NYU Film Sch.; dir. MFA Film Program, Rockport Coll.; instr Maine Film & Video Workshops; Master Class instr. Bosto Film and Video Found.; cons. Nat. Commn. Population Growt and the Am. Future; judge D.W. Griffith Film Festival; cons. TV radio and film dept. U. Md.; bd. dirs., treas. Am. Friends of Bri Acad. Film and TV Arts; mem. selection com. NEH; script cons NEA; media cons. Green Peace, Am. Express, Office Pub Responsibility; awards chmn. Sir Peter Ustin Writing Competition. Contbr. articles to profl. jours. and mags. Mem. exec. com Scott Newman Drug Abuse Prevention Award. Served to capt USAF, 1955-57, reserves, 1957-69. Recipient Thomas Alv Edison award, George Foster Peabody award, Freedoms Found award, Wrangler award Western Heritage Ctr., Criss award Golden Eagle award Council Internat. Nontheatrical Events IFPA Cindy award., Best Documentary Script on Current Event award Writers Guild Am., Best Film award Nat. Press Photog raphers Assn., Emmy award, All Am. award Radio-TV Daily, Fame award TV Today and Motion Picture Daily, Blue Ribbon award Am. Film Festival, Silver Oscella La Biennale di Venezia, cert. Venice Film Festival, cert. Adelaide/Auckland (Australia) Internat. Film Festival, Western Writers Am. Spur award. Fellow Explorers Club; mem. AAAS, Writers Guild Am. East (pres. 1977-79, exec. dir. found., del. internat. affiliation, Richard B. Jablow award for disting. svc.), Nat. Acad. TV Arts and Scis. (nat. trustee, chmn. Emmy awards), Internat. Acad. TV Arts and Scis. (assoc., awards chair Sir Peter Ustinov Writing Competition, judge Internat. Emmy awards), Internat. Interactive Comm. Soc., Assn. Am. Mus., Internat. Radio and TV Soc., Air Force Assn. (Charles Lindburgh chpt. v.p. comm.), Maine Film and Video Assn. (founding mem., vice chair), Overseas Press Club, Am. Alpine Club, Omicron Delta Kappa, Sigma Chi. Home: Camden, Maine. Died Sept. 17, 2006.

FISHER, RICHARD FORREST, research scientist, editor-in-chief; b. Champaign, Ill., May 15, 1941; S. Richard Forrest Fisher and Hannah Elizabeth Ponath; m. Karen Dangerfield, Sept. 4, 1959; children: William Forrest, Marilu, Kevin Royden. BS, U. Ill., 1963; MS, Cornell U., 1967, PhD, 1968. Rsch. scientist Can. Forestry Svc., Sault Sainte Marie, Ont., 1968-69; asst. prof. forestry U. Ill., Urbana, 1969-72; assoc. prof. U. Toronto, Ont., 1972-77; prof. U. Fla., Gainesville, 1977-82; prof., head dept. forest resources Utah State U., Logan, 1982-90; prof., head dept. forest sci. Tex. A&M U., 1990-96, prof., 1996-99; dir. rsch. Temple-Inland, Diboll, Tex., from 1999. Author: (with others) Ecology and Management of Forest Soil, 3d edit.; contbr. articles to profl. jours. Fellow Soc. Am. Foresters, Soil Sci. Soc. Am. (co-editor in chief Forest Ecology and Mgmt.); mem. Internat. Soc. Tropical Foresters, Ecol. Soc. Am., Nat. Assn. Profl. Forestry Schs. and Colls. (pres. 1994-96), Internat. Assn. Round Dance Tchrs. (gen. chmn. 1997-99). Democrat. Avocations: round dance cuer, tchr. Home: Lufkin, Tex. Died June 6, 2006.

FISHER, WILL STRATTON, illumination consultant; b. Nashville, June 27, 1922; s. Will Stratton and Estelle (Carr) R.; m. Patricia A. Fesco, Nov. 10, 1945; children: Patricia Jo, Will Stratton, Robert J. BSE.E., Vanderbilt U., 1947. Registered profl. engr., Ohio. With Lighting Bus. Group, Gen. Elec. Co., Cleve., 1947-87, mgr. advanced application engring., 1971-84, mgr. lighting edn., 1985-87; cons. lighting Moreland Hills, Ohio, from 1987. Cons. Lighting Research Inst. Contbr. articles, papers to profl. jours., symposia and internat. profl. meetings. Patentee parabolic wedge louver; developer concepts for utilizing heat from lighting systems to heat bldgs.; designer calorimeter; developer procedure for calculation contbn. of lighting to heating of bldgs. Served to 1st lt. C.E., AUS, 1943-46, Manhattan Project. Fellow Illuminating Engring. Soc. North Am. (pres. 1978-79, Disting. Service award 1980, Louis B. Marks award for exceptional service 1988); mem. SAR, Internat. Commn. Illumination (U.S. expert on tech. com., U.S. rep. to div. 3, interior lighting), ASHRAE, IEEE. Lodges: Kiwanis (pres. 1990-91). Methodist. Died Sept. 11, 2006.

FITCH, STONA JAMES, retired corporate executive; b. Wetumka, Okla., Oct. 20, 1931; s. Stona Lee and Lessie Opal (Tims) F.; m. Barbara Lou Jager, Aug. 26, 1976; children: Valerie, Stona, Michael, Susan, Melissa BA, U. Okla., Norman, 1955. Personnel mgr. Procter & Gamble, Cin., 1963-67, plant mgr. Augusta, Ga., 1968-69, Kansas City, Kans., 1969-72; mgr. mfg. Paper Products div. Procter & Gamble, Cin., 1979-83; mgr. indsl. relations Procter & Gamble, Cin., 1983, v.p. mfg., from 1984. Chmn. Vocat Edn. Adv. Council. Cin., 1983-85; steering com. Leadership Cin., 1984-85; chmn. bd. dirs., past pres. Children's Family House; adv. coun. U. Okla. Sch. Bus. Adminstrn., 1987—; v.p., bd. trustees Cin. Playhouse in the Park, 1987-93, pres. bd. trustees, 1993—. Served with U.S. Army, 1950-52; Korea Mem.: Cin. Country, Camargo Racquet, Queen City (Cin.). Democrat. Episcopalian. Avocations: Tennis; golf; reading. Home: Cincinnati, Ohio. Died Nov. 8, 2005.

FITZGEORGE, HAROLD JAMES, former oil and gas company executive; b. Trenton, NJ, June 15, 1924; s. George T. and Cecilia M. (Jansen) Fitzgeorge; m. Bette M. Weidel, June 23, 1945 (dec. May 1987); children: Barbara Marsh, Virginia Fisher, Patricia Dunning, Elizabeth Brown; m. Roberta Tefft, July 23, 1999. AB in Geology, Princeton U., 1948; MBA, MIT, 1964. Geologist Magnolia Petroleum Co., Oklahoma City, 1948; numerous positions with petroleum cos., 1948-60; with Mobil U.S. Exploration, NYC, 1960-63; v.p. Mobil Exploration Can., 1964-66; mgr. Mobil Fgn. Exploration, NYC, 1966-68; pres. Mobil de Venezuela, 1968-73; gen. mgr. Western U.S. Exploration & Prodn., Mobil Oil, Denver, 1973-77; cons. in field, 1977-78; pres. Pennzoil Exploration and Prodn., Houston, 1978-84, chmn., 1981—84, adv. dir., 1984; now ret. Served with USMC, 1943-46, 50-52. Decorated Purple Heart, Bronze Star Combat V; Sloan fellow, 1963-64 Mem. Am. Assn. Petroleum Geologists, Assn. Profl. Engrs. and Geologists of Alta., Am. Petroleum Inst. Clubs: Princeton (N.Y.); Moorings; Hawksnest (Vero Beach, Fla.), Vero Beach Yacht Club. Republican. Roman Catholic. Home: Vero Beach, Fla. Died June 14, 2007.

FITZGERALD, JOHN EDMUND, retired civil engineering educator; b. Revere, Mass., Sept. 29, 1923; s. John Valentine and Gertrude Margaret Fitzgerald; m. Elaine Louise Ohlson, Feb. 24, 1945; children: Deborah Lee, Christine Louise, David John, John Paul (dec.). Student, Tufts U., 1941-42, 46; MCE, Harvard U., 1947; MS in Math.-Physics, Nat. U. Ireland, Cork, 1970, DSc, 1972. Registered profl. engr., Utah, N.D.; chartered physicist, U.K. Regional constrn. engr. Liberty Mut. Ins. Co., Dallas, 1947-48; assoc. prof. N.D. State U., Fargo, 1948-51; supr. structures and dynamics Armour Rsch. Found., Chgo., 1951-53; mgr. applied mechanics and med. physics Rsch. divsn. Am. Machine & Foundry Corp., Chgo., 1953-56; mgr. applied math. and mechanics Borg-Warner Ctr. Rsch. Labs., Des Plaines, Ill., 1956-59; dir. devel. br. Lockheed Propulsion Co., Redlands, Calif., 1959-66; prof. civil engring., chmn. dept. U. Utah, Salt Lake City, 1966-74, prof., assoc. dean, 1973-74; prof., dir. Sch. Civil Engring. Ga. Inst. Tech., Atlanta, 1975-89, prof. emeritus, 1991—2007, assoc. dean, 1989-91; ret., 1991. Cons. numerous aerospace cos., govt. agys., 1966-2007; guest lectr. Trinity Coll., Dublin, Ireland, U. Bristol, U.K., U. Marseilles, France, NATO Advanced Study Inst., Italy, others., 1968-2007; bd. dirs. EFM Corp., Dublin. Author: Engineering Structural Analysis of Solid Propellants, 1971; editor Structural Integrity Handbook, 1972; contbr. over 100 articles to profl. jours.; 27 patents. Served with submarine service USN, 1942-46, ETO. Recipient U.S. Sr. Scientist award for teaching and research Alexander von Humboldt Found., 1973-74. Fellow Inst. Physics U.K., ASCE, AIAA (assoc., Outstanding Achievement in Solid Propulsion award 1987); mem. Soc. Rheology, Am. Acad. Mechanics, Structural Engring. Inst., Am. Phys. Soc., Irish Sailing Assn. Clubs: Royal Cork Yacht (Crosshaven, Ireland). Roman Catholic. Avocations: swimming, bicycling, sailing. Home: Marietta, Ga. Died Apr. 13, 2007.

FITZGERALD, JOHN WARNER, law educator; b. Grand Ledge, Mich., Nov. 14, 1924; s. Frank Dwight and Queena Maud (Warner) F.; m. Lorabeth Moore, June 6, 1953; children: Frank Moore (dec.), Eric Stiles, Adam Warner. BS, Mich. State U., 1947; JD, U. Mich., 1954. Bar: Mich. 1954. Practiced in Grand Ledge, 1955-64; chief judge pro tem Mich. Ct. Appeals, 1965-73; justice Mich. Supreme Ct., 1974-83, dep. chief justice, 1975-82, chief justice, 1982; prof. law Thomas M. Cooley Law Sch., Lansing, Mich., from 1982. Mem. Mich. Senate from 15th Dist., 1958-64 Served with AUS, 1943-44. Mem. ABA, State Bar Mich. (bd. commrs. 1985-90), Am. Judicature Soc. Died July 7, 2006.

FITZGERALD, RICHARD JOSEPH, JR., lawyer, educator; b. Mpls., Oct. 28, 1930; s. Martin Richard and Irene Catherine (Quealy) FitzG.; m. Nancy Ann Day, June 18, 1952 (div. Mar. 1973); children: Shawne, Kathleen, Sharron, Richard Joseph Jr.; m. Beverly Nan Silverman, Aug. 22, 1974; children: Jaime, Gregg, Cori, Jon, Darcey. BS, U. Minn., 1957, LLB, 1959. Bar: Minn. 1959. Asst. prof., asst. dean Law Sch. U. Minn., Mpls., 1959-61; with Lindquist & Vennum, Mpls., from 1961, now pres. Bd. dirs. Citizens League, Mpls., 1965-75, pres., 1970. With USN, 1951-55, Korea. Mem. Minn. Bar Assn. (bd. dirs. bus. lawyers sect. Mpls. chpt. 1985—, chmn. bus. lawyers sect. 1990—). Home: Minneapolis, Minn. Died Oct. 14, 2006.

FITZGERALD, ROBERT HANNON, JR., orthopedic surgeon; b. Denver, Aug. 25, 1942; s. Robert Hannon and Alyene (Webber) Fitzgerald Anderson; m. Lynda Lee Lang, Apr. 27, 1968 (div. 1984); children: Robert III, Shannon, Dennis, Katherine, Kelly; m. Jamie Kathleen Dent, Mar. 9, 1985; children: Brian, Steven. BS, U. Notre Dame, 1963; MD, U. Kans., 1967; MS, U. Minn., 1974; Magistri Artivum, U. Pa., 1995. Cert. Am. Bd. Othropaedics, 1975, Am. Bd. Othropaedics, 1995. Instr. orthop. surgery Mayo Med. Sch., Rochester, Minn., 1974-77, cons. orthop. surgery, 1974-89, asst. prof., 1977-82, assoc. prof., 1982-86, prof., 1986-89, chief adult reconstructive surgery, 1987-89, dir. orthop. rsch., 1988-89; prof. chmn. dept. orthop. surgery Wayne State U. Sch. Med., 1989-95; chief orthop. surgery Hutzel Hosp., 1989-95, Detroit Receiving Hosp., 1989-95; orthopedist-in-chief Detroit Med. Ctr., 1989-95, chmn. coun., specialist-in-chief, 1993-95; chmn. dept. orthop. surgery U. Pa. Sch. Med., Phila., 1995-99; chief orthop. surgery Hosp. U. Pa., Phila., 1995—2000; P.B. Magnuson prof. bone and joint surgery U. Pa. Sch. Med., Phila., 1996—2001; chief orthop. surgery Phila. Veterans Med. Ctr., Adgors Meml. Hosp. Dir. Pa. Orthop. Inst., U. Pa. Health Sys., 1997—2001; cons. CDC, Atlanta, 1981—2007, NIH, 1987—93, chmn. orthop. study sect., 1989—91; cons. health care financing adminstrn. Ctr. of Excellence Program, 2001; cons. MMS, 2001, CMS, 2002—07; chief orthop. surgery Bell Meml. Hosp., 2001—04, Adams Meml. Hosp., 2004—07. Mem. editl. bd. Jour. Orthop. and Traumatology, from 1978, Jour. Bone Joint Surgery, 1982—88, Clin. Orthop. and Related Rsch., from 1988, Jour. Long Term Results Biomed. Devices, 1990; editor: Seminars in Arthoplasty, from 1993, Am. Acad. of Orthop. Surgery Ortho Knowledge Online, 2000—03; trustee Jour. Bone Joint Surgery, 1987—92, sec., 1988—92. Mem. bd. devel. Mayo Clinic, 1984—86, St. John's Ch., 1988—89; mem. bd. edn. St. John's Grade Sch., Jr. H.S., Rochester, 1983—87; trustee Hutzel Hosp., 1989—95; bd. dirs. Adams County ARC, from 2004, ARC; trustee Lourdes H.S. Devel. Bd., Rochester, 1982—88. Capt. USAF, 1968—70. Decorated Air Commendation medal; Traveling fellow AOA N.Am., 1974, Am. Brit. Can., 1981; recipient Kappa Delta award, 1983. Fellow Am. Acad. Orthop. Surgeons, Phila. Coll. Physicians; mem. AMA, Am. Orthopedic Assn., Rsch. Soc., Assn. Bone and Joint Surgeons, Interurban Ortho Soc., Internat. Soc. Microbiology, Zumbro County Med. Soc., Min-Da-Man Orthop. Soc., Minn. Orthopedic Soc., Am. Soc. Microbiology, NY Acad. Scis., Am. Hip Soc. (Stinchfield award 1985, Charnley award 1986, 95, pres. 1993-94), Internat. Hip Soc., Am. Orthop. Assn. (N.Am. traveling fellow 1974, Am. Brit. Can. traveling fellow, 1981), Surg. Infection Soc. (charter mem.), Clin. Orthop. Soc., Internat. Soc. Orthop. Surgery and Traumatology, Mid-Am. Orthop. Soc. (bd. dirs. 1989-93, 94—, pres. elect 1994, pres. 1996), Detroit Acad. Orthop. Surgery, Mich. Orthop. Soc., Mich. State Med. Soc., Detroit Acad. Med., Pa. Orthop. Soc., Phila. Orthop. Soc. (bd. dirs. 1998-2001), Phila. Acad. Med., Ind. State Med. Assn., Interurban Club, Sigma Xi, Kappa Delta, Alpha Epsilon Delta. Republican. Roman Catholic. Avocation: skiing. Died Jan. 15, 2007.

FITZGERALD, THOMAS JOSEPH, clinical psychologist, consultant; b. St. Louis, Jan. 12, 1924; s. Michael and Alice (Power) F.; m. Margaret June Gretzer, Nov. 8, 1952; children—Thomas Joseph, Mary, Kathy, James. B.S., St. Louis U., 1950, M.S., 1953, Ph.D., 1968. Chief psychologist, exec. dir. Community Out-Patient Clinics, Iowa, 1953-55, exec. dir., Ill., 1964-69; chief service St. Louis City Child Guidance Clinic, 1971-76; coordinator Mo. Children's Mental Health Service, 1976-77; coordinator, cons. Ill. State Dept. Mental Health and Developmental Disabilities, Chester, 1978-82; pvt. practice clin. psychology, St. Louis, 1969—; sr. partner S.W. Ill. Therapy Clinic, O'Fallon, 1980—; asst. prof. Marillac Coll., 1970-74; lectr. So. Ill. U., Edwardsville, 1965—. Past chmn. Jennings Youth Commn.; mem. White House Conf. on Edn.; active St. Louis Mental Health Assn., Childrens Study Home. Served with USMC, 1942-45, USAFR, 1950-68. Mem. AAAS, Am. Psychoo. Assn., Orthopsychiat. Assn., Psychology-Law Assn., Assn. Children with Learning Disabilities, Nat. Soc. Autistic Citizens, Am. Legion, VFW, Ill. Psychol. Assn., Mo. Psychol. Assn., Sigma Xi. Club: Scott AFB Officers. Home: Kirkwood, Mo. Died Aug. 19, 2006.

FITZHUGH, WILLIAM WYVILL, JR., printing company executive; b. Bklyn., June 27, 1914; s. William Wyvill and Portia (Starr) F.; m. Florence Hardy, Dec. 13, 1941; children: William, Priscilla, John, Portia. AB, Dartmouth Coll., 1935; BA, Trinity Coll., Cambridge U., 1937, MA, 1938; M in Philosophy, Columbia U., 1977; JD, Pace U. Law Sch., 1980. Fellow Carnegie Endowment for Internat. Peace, 1938-39; sec. rapporteur Internat. Studies Conf., League of Nations, 1938-39; instr. govt. Columbia U., 1939-42; pres. William W. Fitzhugh, Inc., 1945-99, chmn. bd. dirs.; pres. New Haven Bd. & Carton Co., Inc., 1960-64; ptnr. Dalsemer, Fitzhugh & Catzen, NYC, 1964-66; pres. Newspaper Preprint Corp., NYC, 1966-75. Past chmn. Chappaqua Orchestral Assn. Lt. USNR. Mem. Gravure Tech. Assn. (past pres.), Folding Paper Box Assn Am. (past pres. met. N.Y. group), Label Mfrs. Assn. (past dir.), Bklyn. C. of C. (past dir.), Phi Beta Kappa, Sigma Chi. Republican. Episcopalian. Home: Hanover, NH. Died June 2, 2005.

FITZPATRICK, JOHN J., bishop; b. Trenton, Ont., Can., Oct. 12, 1918; s. James John and Lorena (Pelkey) F. Student, Propaganda Fide Coll., Italy, Our Lady of Angels Sem.; BA, Niagara U., 1941. Ordained priest Roman Catholic Ch., 1942. Titular bishop of Cenae and Aux. of Miami, Fla., 1968—71; bishop of Brownsville, 1971—91; bishop emeritus, 1991—2006. Roman Catholic. Died July 16, 2006.

FITZPATRICK, JOSEPH EDWARD, temporary employment service company executive; b. Auburn, NY, Oct. 14, 1931; s. Joseph E. and Stella (Bannon) F.; m. Jean M. Cuddy, May 1, 1954; children: Michael, Kevin, Brian, Mary Jo. BBA, LeMoyne Coll., 1953. C.P.A., N.Y., Calif. Staff acct. Price Waterhouse & Co., NYC, 1955-58, sr. acct. Rochester, N.Y., 1958-61, audit mgr. Bogota, Colombia, 1961-63, Phila., 1963-64; v.p., controller Saga Corp., Menlo Park, Calif., 1964-79; v.p., treas. Western Temporary Svcs., Inc., Walnut Creek, Calif., from 1979. Served to cpl. AUS, 1953-55. Mem. AICPA, N.Y. State Soc. CPAs. Democrat. Roman Catholic. Home: Bend, Oreg. Died Dec. 2, 2006.

FITZSIMONDS, ROGER LEON, bank holding company executive; b. Milw., May 21, 1938; s. Stephen Henry and Wilhelmine Josephine (Rhine) F.; m. Leona I. Schwegler, July 11, 1958; children: Susan Fitzsimonds Hedrick, Stephen. BBA in Fin., U. Wis., Milw., 1960, MBA in Fin., 1971, D in Comml. Sci. (hon.), 1989. From mgmt. trainee to 1st level officer 1st Wis. Nat. Bank, Milw., 1964-69; pres. 1st Wis. Bank Green Bay, 1970-73, 1st Wis. Mortgage Co., Green Bay, 1974-78; exec. v.p. retail banking and real estate fin. 1st Wis. Nat. Bank, Milw., 1978-84, exec. v.p. comml. fin. group, 1984-86; pres. Firstar, Milw., 1986-87, Firstar Corp., 1987-88, vice- chmn., 1990, chmn., CEO, 1991-98, chmn., from 1998; also bd. dirs. Firstar Bank, Milw. Bd. dirs. Milw. Boys and Girls Club, Columbia Health Sys., Milw., Med. Coll. Wis., 1986—; past pres., dir. Competitive Wis., Inc.; past pres. Bankers Round Table, chmn.; chmn., dir. Met. Milw. Assn. Commerce; dir. Wis. Policy Rsch. Inst.; past pres. Greater Mils. Com.; chmn. adv. coun. Sch. Bus. U. Wis. Capt. U.S. Army, 1960-64. Recipient Alumni of Yr. award U. Wis., Milw., 1983. Mem. Wis. Assn. Mfrs. and Commerce (past chmn., bd. dirs. 1988—), Milw. Country Club. Republican. Lutheran. Avocations: tennis, golf, fishing. Home: Milwaukee, Wis. Died Mar. 19, 2007.

FLANNERY, THOMAS AQUINAS, retired federal judge; b. Washington, May 10, 1918; s. John J. and Mary (Sullivan) C.; m. Rita Sullivan, Mar. 3, 1951 (dec. 2002); children: Thomas Aquinas, Irene M. LL.B., Cath. U., 1940. Bar: D.C. 1940. Practice in, Washington, 1940-42, 45-48; trial atty. US Dept. Justice, Washington, 1948-50, asst. US atty., 1950-62, US atty., 1969-71; ptnr. Hamilton & Hamilton, Washington, 1962-69; judge US Dist. Ct. D.C., 1971-85, sr. judge, 1985—2001. Served as combat intelligence officer USAF, 1942-45, ETO. Fellow Am. Coll. Trial Lawyers; Mem.: ABA, DC Bar Assn., John Carroll Soc. Died Sept. 20, 2007.

FLEISCHMAN, ALEXANDER, national association executive; b. NYC, Feb. 22, 1921; s. Joseph and Ethel (Schuller) F.; m. Georgette Duval, Apr. 14, 1946. Pres. Md. Assn. of Deaf, Ocean City, 1960-64, Am. Athletic Assn. of Deaf, Denver and Hollywood, Calif., 1961-63, Nat. Congress of Jewish Deaf, Greenbelt, Md., 1958-72, exec. dir., from 1972; pres. World Orgn. of Jewish Deaf, Tel Aviv, Israel, 1975-88. Founder, chmn. Am. Athletic Assn. for Deaf Hall of Fame, 1952-55; conv. chmn. Internat. Games of Deaf, Washington, 1965, Nat. Congress Jewish Deaf, Washington, 1982, Md. Assn. Deaf, Ocean City, 1987; dir. workshop Health, Edn. and Welfare USA, Washington, 1970—; chmn. Nat. Congress Jewish Deaf Hall of Fame, 1986—. Former editor various publs. in field. Active United Hearing and Deaf Svc. Agy., Broward County, Fla. Inducted into Am. Athletic Assn. for Deaf Hall of Fame, 1965, Nat. Congress Jewish Deaf Hall of Fame, 1986. Mem. Kappa Gamma. Jewish. Died Mar. 23, 2007.

FLEMING, JAMES GRANT, materials scientist; b. Maui, Hawaii, Nov. 28, 1959; s. John Fredrick and Nancy Ann Fleming; m. Carol Holiman, May 30, 1992; children: Jesse, Keila, Brighid. B of Engring. Sci., Johns Hopkins U., 1982; MS, Stanford U., 1984, PhD, 1986. Prin. mem. tech. staff Sandia Nat. Labs, Albuquerque, from 1988. Office Naval Rsch. fellow, 1982-86, Alexander Von Humboldt fellow, 1986-88. Mem. Am. Vacuum Soc. (symposium coord. 1997-98), Materials Rsch. Soc. Achievements include patents for field emission by fillets for flat panel display, CVP WSiN and bistable micromachined structure; patents pending for MEMS and photonic lattice. Home: Albuquerque, N.Mex. Died Feb. 13, 2007.

FLEMING, THOMAS CRAWLEY, retired physician, medical director, former editor; b. Chgo., June 16, 1921; s. Frederic Sydney and Margaret A. (Moore) F.; m. Katherine Slaughter, Oct. 14, 1949; children— Sandra, Wendy, Margot, Frederic

Student, Calif. Inst. Tech., 1940-42; MD, Columbia U., 1945. Intern St. Luke's Hosp., NYC, 1945-46; instr. physiology. Coll. Physicians and Surgeons, Columbia U., NYC, 1948-50; with dept. clin. research Hoffmann-LaRoche, Nutley, N.J., 1950-55, dir. med. info., 1955-56, product devel. mgr., 1956-57; dir. clin. research Mead Johnson & Co., Evansville, Ind., 1957-58, dir. product devel., 1958-59; med. dir. Warner-Chilcott Labs., Morris Plains, N.J., 1959-60; exec. v.p., med. dir. Robert E. Wilson Inc., NYC, 1960-62; dir. med. edn., chief chronic medicine Bergen Pines County Hosp., Paramus, N.J., 1962-64; med. dir. Sudler & Hennessey, Inc., NYC, 1964-73, sr. v.p., med. dir., 1982-88, med. cons., 1988-97; med. dir. Little Hill-Alina Lodge, Blairstown, N.J., 1974-79, 84-89. Editor-in-chief Postgrad. Medicine, Mpls., 1979-82; contbr. articles to profl. jours. Served to capt. M.C., U.S. Army, 1946-48 Mem. Am. Soc. of Addiction Medicine. Died Mar. 9, 2007.

FLEMMING, BILL (WILLIAM NORMAN FLEMMING), sports commentator; b. Chgo., Sept. 3, 1926; s. Norman Albert and Elizabeth (Morrisson) F.; m. Barbara Alice Forster, Aug. 5, 1950; children: Lindy, William Mason. BA, U. Mich., 1949. Sports dir. WUOM, U. Mich., 1950-53; sports dir. WWJ-TV, Detroit, 1953-59; NCAA football announcer CBS, NYC, 1960-62, NBC, NYC, 1962-64; former sports commentator ABC Sports, NYC; covered Olympics, Mexico City and winter games in Grenoble, France, 1968, Munich and Montreal games, 1972, 76. Pres. Detroit Sports Broadcasters Assn., 1957-58; guest lectr. U. Mich., 1960 State chmn. March of Dimes, 1978. Served with USAAF, 1944-45. Hon. mem. M Club; U. Mich. letter winners; elected to Mich. Media Hall of Fame, 1980 Mem. AFTRA (past dir.), Screen Actors Guild, Nat. Assn. Sportscasters. Clubs: Bloomfield Hills Country, Bloomfield Open Hunt, Little Harbor. Republican. Home: Bloomfield Hills, Mich. Died July 20, 2007.

FLETCHER, NORMAN COLLINGS, architect; b. Providence, Dec. 8, 1917; s. Robert C. and Lily (Wilcock) F.; m. Jean Bodman, Sept. 23, 1944 (dec. Sept. 1965); children: Judith, Jon B., Jeremy B., Mollie H., Rebecca H., Katrina H.; stepchildren: Max Mason Jr., Cynthia Kava, Eliza Mason; m. Betty Mason, Apr. 19, 1986. BFA in Architecture, Yale U., 1940. Designer Skidmore, Owings and Merrill, NYC, 1942-43, Saarinen, Swanson & Assocs., Washington, Birmingham, Mich., 1943-45; prin. The Architects Collaborative Inc., Cambridge, Mass., 1945-95, FHCM Inc. Architects, Boston, from 1995. Instr. architecture Grad. Sch. Design, Harvard, 1949-52; vis. critic Sch. Architecture, Mass. Inst. Tech., 1957-58, Sch. Architecture, Yale U., 1956, U. Tucuman, Argentina, 1954; Thomas Jefferson prof. architecture U. Va., 1977; mem. jury Higher Edn. Facilities Design Award Program, Dept. Health, Edn. and Welfare, 1966; mem. com. Rotch Travelling Scholarship, 1964-68, 73-77, mem. preliminary jury, 1969; mem. architecture com. Boston Arts Festival, 1955-57, Yale Arts Assn., 1965—, pres., 1970; mem. Fed. Res. Bank Archtl. Rev. Panel, 1975-77; sec. Rotch Travelling Scholarship, 1980-87; mem. vis. com. visual and environ. studies Harvard U., 1981-85; archtl. adv. cons. Dept. State Office Fgn. Bldgs. Ops., 1983-86. Recipient numerous awards, including winner nat. competition for 21st Century Ctr. for Agriculture and Renewable Resources, Okla. State U. in Assn. with Frankfurt-Short-Bruza, 1983, citation Progressive Architecture Design awards for Chem. Lab. Tufts U., Medford, Mass., 1963, for IBM fed. systems divsn. Gaithersburg, Md., 1964, 1st prize Nat. House competition, 1945, 1st prize Smith Coll. dormitory competition, 1946; honor award for YMCA, Roxbury, Mass. New Eng. regional coun. AIA, 1966; nat. honor award for dormitory and dining commons Clark U., Worcester, Mass. AIA, 1967; dormitory and dining commons complex 2, cen. Mass. AIA, 1970; for Worcester Found. for Exptl. Biology, Shrewsbury Ctrl. Mass. AIA, 1970, Merit award for Roxbury YMCA HUD, 1968, Architecture and Allied Arts award Tau Sigma Delta, 1970; Alice Kimball travelling fellow Yale U., 1940, Merit award Monmouth County Planning Bd., N.J., Ann. Cmty. Betterment award Middletown Area C. of C., ATEC Bldg. Brookdale Cmty. Coll. Fellow AIA; mem. Nat. Acad. Design (academician), Boston Soc. Architects (pres. 1966-67, Award of Honor 1989), Mass. Assn. Architects (exec. com. 1963-68). Home: Lexington, Mass. Died May 31, 2007.

FLEXNER, KURT FISHER, economist, educator; b. Vienna, Sept. 26, 1915; arrived in U.S., 1928; s. Otto Gerard and Wilhelmine (Fisher) Flexner; m. Josephine Moncure, Dec. 20, 1942; children: Thomas Moncure, Peter Wallace. BS in Econs., Johns Hopkins U., 1946; PhD in Econs., Columbia U., 1954. From asst. prof. to prof. econs. NYU Grad. Sch. Arts and Scis., U. Coll. and Sch. Commerce, 1946-59; chief economist, dep. mgr. The Am. Bankers Assn., 1959-66; adj. prof. banking and fin. NYU, 1965-66, prof., chmn. dept. econs., 1968-78; prof. econs. U. Memphis, 1978-87, prof. emeritus, from 1987. Cons. U.S. Savs. and Loan League, 1955—59, N.Y. State Savs. and Loan League, 1955—59; P. K. Seidman vis. distin. prof. Christian Bros. U., Memphis, 1990—94; lectr. intergenerational seminars Bard Coll., Annandale on the Hudson, NY, from 1987, Ctr. for Life Studies, Marist Coll., Poughkeepsie, NY, from 1995; chief fin. instns. advisor U.S. Agy. for Internat. Devel., Seoul, Republic of Korea, 1966—68; spkr. in field; adv. com. to Chancellor Franz Vranitzky Prime Minsister of Austria, 1991—93; guest lectr. Inst. USA and Can. Acad. Sci., Moscow, 1991—95; advisor to coun. Pres. Mikhail Gorbachev, 1990—91, Pres. Boris Yeltsin, 1991—94. Author: The European Payments Union 1950 to 1954, 1957, The Savings and Loan Associations in the State of New York, 1958, Mortgage Lending by Commercial Banks, 1964, The Enlightened Society: The Economy with a Human Face, 1989, The 21st Century-The Best or the Last, 2005; columnist Memphis Daily News, 1986—90, Comml. Appeal, 1980—87; contbr. articles to profl. jours. Trustee M. L. Seidman Town Hall Meml. Lecture Series, 1968—87; mem. Gov. Alexander's Action Team, 1980—85. With US Army, 1944—45. Mem.: Econ. Club Memphis (exec. dir. 1973—85, pres. 1985—92). Died July 13, 2006.

FLINNER, LYLE PAYSON, religious communications educator; b. New Castle, Pa., Aug. 11, 1918; s. Harry George and Leah Frances (Sweet) F.; m. Beatrice Jeffreys Allayaud, June 27, 1947; children: Donald Allayaud, Carol Jean Flinner Dorough. BA with honors, Geneva Coll., Beaver Falls, Pa., 1949; MDiv with honors, Asbury Theol. Sem., 1952; ME, U. Pitts., 1960, PhD, 1967. Ordained to ministry Ch. of Nazarene, 1952. Adminstr. Jones & Laughlin Steel Corp., Pitts., 1936-46; pastor various congregations Ch. of Nazarene, Pa., 1952-63; mem. faculty Geneva Coll., Beaver Falls, 1960-67; prof. speech communication, psychology, Christian edn., religion dept. So. Nazarene U., Bethany, Okla., 1968-92, grad. coord., 1968-92. Presenter seminars, Christian edn. cons., supply minister, adult tchr., Ch. of Nazarene, various locations, 1968—; adj. prof. Mid-Am. Bible Coll., 1995—. Contbr. articles denominational pubs. Mem. city planning commn., City of Bethany, 1988—. Sgt., U.S. Army, 1942-46, ETO. Home: Bethany, Okla. Died Dec. 2, 2006.

FLIPSE, JOHN EDWARD, naval architect, mechanical engineer; b. Montville, NJ, Feb. 4, 1921; SB, MIT, 1942; MME, NYU, 1948. Registered profl. engr., NY, Va., Tex. Sr. engr., ship stabilization dept. head, marine div. Sperry Gyroscope Co., Great Neck, NY, 1955-57; rsch. engr., dir. rsch., mgr. systems dept., asst. to pres. Newport News (Va.) Shipbuilding and Dry Dock Co., 1957-68; chmn., pres., chief exec. officer Deepsea Ventures, Inc., Gloucester, Va., 1968-77; pres., chief exec. officer Tex. A&M Rsch. Found., College Station, 1983-84; dep. dir. Tex. Engring. Experiment Sta., 1985-88; disting. prof. civil and ocean engring. Tex. A&M U., 1982-92, assoc. dean engring. College Station, 1984-88, assoc. dep. chancellor for engring., 1984-89, Wofford Cain prof. engring., 1988-91, dir. Offshore Tech. Rsch. Ctr., 1988-91, dir. emeritus, 1991—2000. Chmn. Nat. Adv. Com. on Oceans and Atmosphere, 1985-86; mem. marine bd. Nat. Rsch. Coun., 1979-84, chmn., 1982-84; mem. marine facilities panel U.S./Japan Coop. Program in Natural Resources, 1980-96; mem. marine petroleum and minerals adv. com. Dept. Commerce, 1974-75; expert mem. U.S. delegation to Law of the Sea Conf., UN, 1975-76; cons., lectr. in field. Contbr. articles to profl. jours. Mem. dean's adv. coun. Sch. Engring. & Applied Sci., U. Va., 1995-98. Fellow Marine Tech. Soc. (pres. 1985-87), Soc. Naval Architects and Marine Engrs. (past chmn. tech. and rsch. steering com.); mem. Nat. Acad. Engring. (membership policy com. 1987-90, membership com. 1987-90, peer rev. com. 1985-86), Va. Inst. Marine Sci. (vice chmn. bd. dirs. 1968-76). Achievements include patents in field. Died Jan. 24, 2007.

FLOWERS, LANGDON STRONG, food company executive; b. Thomasville, Ga., Feb. 12, 1922; s. William Howard and Flewellyn Evans (Strong) Flowers; m. Margaret Clisby Powell, June 3, 1944 (dec. Nov. 22, 1003); children: Margaret Flowers Rich, Langdon Strong, Elizabeth Powell, Dorothy Howard Flowers Swinson, John Howard. BS, MIT, Boston, 1944, MS, 1947; H.H.D., Presbyn. Coll., Clinton, SC, 1984. Engr., Douglas Aircraft, Los Angeles, 1947; supr. Flowers Baking Co., Thomasville, 1947-50, sales mgr., 1950-58, v.p. sales, 1958-65; pres., chief operating officer Flowers Industries, Inc., Thomasville, 1965-76, vice chmn. bd., chief exec. officer, 1976-80, chmn. bd., 1980-85, ret., 1985. Past pres. Thomasville YMCA, 1958-62; past trustee Presbyn Coll., Clinton, S.C., Archbold Meml. Hosp., Thomasville. Served as lt. (j.g.) USNR, 1943-46. Named Man of Year, Thomas County C. of C., 1974 Mem. Am. Bakers Assn. (exec. com. 1974-75, chmn. 1975-76), So. Bakers Assn. (chmn. bd. 1969-70), NAM (dir., exec. com.), Thomasville C. of C. (pres. 1953-54), Sigma Alpha Epsilon. Presbyterian (chmn. bd. deacons 1952-56, elder 1956—, rep. Gen. Assembly 1966). Club: Rotarian. Home: Thomasville, Ga. Died June 20, 2007.

FLYNN, JAMES LEONARD, manufacturing executive; b. Cleve., Oct. 14, 1934; s. H. Leonard and K. Nadine (Yanney) F.; m. Shirley Ann Mix, July 8, 1967; children— Sharon, Douglas AB, Dartmouth Coll., 1956, MBA, 1957. Mgr. budgeting and acctg. Intertype div. Harris Corp., Bklyn., 1957-61, asst. mgr. material control, 1961-63; asst. contr. Corning Inc., N.Y., 1964-66; asst. to treas. Corning Glass Works, N.Y., 1963-64, prodn. supt. Bradford plant N.Y., 1966-68, dir. corp. planning N.Y., 1968-72, gen. mgr. chem. systems dept. N.Y., 1972-74, asst. treas. to treas. N.Y., 1974-76, treas. N.Y., 1976-81, v.p., treas. N.Y., 1981-85, sr. v.p., treas. N.Y., 1985-86, sr. v.p. fin. N.Y., 1986-89, sr. v.p. N.Y., 1989-94; ret., 1994. Investment counselor, 1994—. With USAF, 1957. Gen. Elec. fellow, 1956-57 Mem. Dartmouth Coll. Alumni Assn. Republican. Methodist. Home: Naples, Fla. Died Dec. 27, 2005.

FLYNT, JOHN JAMES, JR., (JACK FLYNT), retired congressman, lawyer; b. Griffin, Ga., Nov. 8, 1914; s. John James and Susan Winn (Banks) F.; m. Patricia Irby Bradley, Feb. 7, 1942; children: Susan, John James III, Crisp. AB, U. Ga., 1936; postgrad., Emory U., 1937-38; LL.B., George Washington U., 1940; grad., Nat. War Coll., Command and Gen. Staff Sch., Air Corps Advanced Flying Sch., Brooks Field, Tex. Bar: Ga. 1938. Asst. U.S. atty. (no. dist.) Ga. US Dept. Justice, 1939-41, 45-46; mem. Ga. Ho. of Reps., 1947-48; solicitor gen. Griffin Jud. Circuit, 1949-54; mem. US Congress from 4th Ga. Dist., 1954—79, chmn. com. on standards of official conduct, 1975-79, mem. com. on interstate & fgn. commerce, 1954-51, subcoms. on transp. and communications and investigation, com. on Appropriations, 1961-79; ptnr. Smalley Cogburn & Flynt (P.C.), Griffin, 1979-88, Flynt & Flynt, Griffin, 1988—2007. Chmn. bd. visitors USAF Acad.; del. Internat. Geophys. Yr. (Antartica), 1957; U.S. rep. at ceremonies dedicating St. Lawrence Seaway; chmn. bd. dirs. Bank of Spalding County. Author and complier House document - Congl. tributes in memory of life and service of Winston S. Churchill. Chmn. bd. trustees N. Ga. Meth. Children's Home; trustee La Grange Coll., Ga., Woodward Acad. Served in U.S. Army, 1936-37, 41-45, ETO; col. Ret. Decorated Bronze Star medal. Fellow Ga. Bar Found. (charter); Mem. ABA, Ga. Bar Assn. (pres. 1954-55), Am. Legion, V.F.W., Phi Delta Phi, Sigma Alpha Epsilon. Democrat. Methodist (trustee, chmn. bd. stewards). Lodges: Masons; Kiwanis; Shriners. Died June 24, 2007.

FOLKINS, DOROTHEA MADISON, personnel agency executive, consultant; b. Springfield, Mass., Aug. 10, 1928; d. William Albert and Mae Bernardine (Boardway) Madison; m. Wallace Odber Folkins, Jan. 21, 1950; children— William Anthony, Jeffrey George. Student in acctg. Am. Internat. Coll., Springfield, Mass., 1945, student in math., 1973. Acct. for real estate firm, Longmeadow, Mass., 1963-75; field rep. March of Dimes, Springfield, 1975-76; personnel cons. Barker Personnel Service, Springfield, 1976-81, owner, personnel cons., 1981—; resume adviser; small bus. acct. Past treas. and exec. sec. Community Scholarship Clearing House, Springfield; past ofcl. Western Mass. Basketball Ofcls. Assn.; mem. by-law com., vice chmn. elem. sch. bldg. com., sec. town facilities study com., vice chmn. elem. sch. study com. Town of Longmeadow; co-chmn. games com. Longmeadow Bicentennial Com.; first pres., co-chmn. snack bar Longmeadow Baseball Assn. Aux.; chmn. Heart Sunday, Longmeadow, March of Dimes Mother's March, Longmeadow; various chairmanships Longmeadow Maternal Assn.; coffee shop chmn. Wesson Women's Hosp. Aux., Springfield; corporator Bay State Med. Ctr. Aux., Springfield; past pres., bd. dirs., sec., ways and means chmn., nominating chmn. St. Mary's Guild, Longmeadow. Recipient Life Membership award as founder Basketball Hall of Fame, Springfield, 1974. Mem. Nat. Personnel Assocs., Mass. Bus. Assn., Nat. Assn. Female Execs. Republican. Roman Catholic. Avocations: bridge; reading; antique glass collecting; sports. Home: East Longmeadow, Mass. Died June 10, 2006.

FORCE, CHARLES THOMAS, government executive; b. Washington, Ind., Feb. 22, 1935; s. John Thomas and Anna Margaret (McCarty) F.; m. Marilyn Irene Wininger, June 10, 1956; children: Carlos, Gregory, Jeffery, Timothy, Michelle. BS in Aero. Engring., Purdue U., 1957. Mem. tech. staff Sandia Corp., Albuquerque, 1957-61; sr. project engr. Rocket Power Inc., Mesa, Ariz., 1961-63; co-founder, v.p. Space Data Corp., Phoenix, 1963-65; dir. Guam Apollo Sta. NASA, Guam, 1965-72, dir. Quito Tracking Sta. Quito, Ecuador, 1972-74, dep. project mgr. tracking and data relay satellite project Goddard Space Flight Ctr. Greenbelt, Md., 1974-75, assoc. chief network ops. divsn., 1975-78, chief network ops. divsn., 1978-80, mgr. deep space network program Washington, 1982-84, dir. ground networks divsn., 1984-86, dep. assoc. adminstr. for space ops., 1986-89, assoc. adminstr. for space comm., from 1989; dep. dir. Computer Scis. Tech. Assocs., Greenbelt, 1980-81; sr. staff Computer Scis. Corp., Falls Church, Va., 1981-82. Mem. U.S. del. Inter-Agy. Consultative Group for Space Sci., Japan, 1983, Estonia, 1984, Italy, 1986; mem. com. of prins. Nat. Comm. Sys., Washington, 1989—; head U.S. del. on space comm. cooperation Moscow and Crimea, 1989, Moscow and Vladivostok, 1991; dir. Internat. Found. for Telemetering, Woodland Hills, Calif., 1990—; del. World Adminstrv. Radio Conf., Torremolinos, Spain, 1992, Internat. Telecomm. Union Plenipotentiary Conf., Kyoto, Japan, 1994 Recipient Meritorious Honor award Dept. State, 1974, Disting. Exec. award U.S. Govt., 1991, Meritorious Exec. award, 1987, 94. Fellow Am. Astron. Soc.; mem. Am. Inst. Aero. and Astron., Armed Forces Comm. and Electronics Assn. (pres. Marianas chpt. 1969), Masons, Tau Beta Pi, Sigma Gamma Tau. Home: Dunkirk, Md. Died Aug. 9, 2007.

FORD, GERALD RUDOLPH, JR., 38th President of the United States; b. Omaha, July 14, 1913; s. Leslie King, Sr., Gerald R. (Stepfather) and Dorothy Ayer (Gardner) Ford; m. Elizabeth (Betty) Bloomer Warren, Oct. 15, 1948; children: Michael Gerald, John Gardner, Steven Meigs, Susan Elizabeth. BA in Economics, U. Mich., 1935; LL.B., Yale U., 1941; LL.D., Mich. State U., Albion Coll., Aquinas Coll., Spring Arbor Coll. Bar: Mich. 1941. Mem. law firm Buchen & Ford, Grand Rapids, 1941—42, Butterfield, Keeney & Amberg, Grand Rapids, 1946—49; mem. US Congresses from 5th Mich. Dist., 1949-74 minority leader, 1965—73; v.p. US, Washington, 1973-74, pres., 1974-77. Del. Interparliamentary Union, Warsaw, Poland, 1959 Belgium, 1961, Bilderberg Group Conf., 1962; mem. Pres Commn. on the Assassination of Pres. Kennedy (The Warren Commn.), 1963-64, internat. adv. coun. Inst. Internat. Studies permanency chmn., Rep. Nat. Convention, 1968, 1972, hon co-chmn, Nat. Commn. on Fed. Election Reform, 2001. Co-author (with Jack Stiles): Portrait of the Assassin, 1965; author A Time to Heal: The Autobiography of Gerald R. Ford, 1979 Humor and the Presidency, 1987. Served as lt. comdr. USNR 1942-46. Recipient Grand Rapids Jr. C. of C. Disting. Svc award, 1948, Disting. Svc. award as one of ten outstanding young men in US US Jr. C. of C., 1950, Silver Anniversary All-Am. Sports Illustrated, 1959; Disting. Congl. Svc. award Am. Polit. Sci. Assn., 1961, Presdl. Medal of Freedom, 1999 Congl. Gold medal, 1999, Profile in Courage award John F Kennedy Libr. Found., 2001. Mem. ABA, Mich. State Bar Assn. Grand Rapids Bar Assn., Delta Kappa Epsilon, Phi Delta Phi Clubs: University (Kent County), Peninsular (Kent County) Lodges: Masons. Republican. Episcopalian. Died Dec. 26, 2006

FORD, GORDON BUELL, JR., literature educator, writer; b Louisville, Sept. 22, 1937; s. Gordon Buell Sr. and Ruby (Allen) F. AB summa cum laude in Classics, Medieval Latin and Sanskrit, Princeton U., 1959; AM in Classical Philology an Linguistics, Harvard U., 1962, PhD in Linguistics, Slavic an Baltic Langs. and Lits., 1965; postgrad., U. Oslo, 1962-64, U Sofia, Bulgaria, 1963, U. Uppsala, Sweden, 1963-64, U. Stockholm, 1963-64, U. Madrid, 1963. CPA. Yeager, Ford, an Warren Found. Disting. prof. Indo-European, Classical, Slavic and Baltic linguistics, Sanskrit, and Medieval Latin Northwestern U., Evanston, Ill., 1965—2007; Lybrand, Ross Bros., an Montgomery Found. Disting. prof. English and linguistics U No. Iowa, Cedar Falls, 1972—2007; sr. exec. v.p. for real estat acctg. fin. mgmt., bd. dirs. The Southeastern Real Estate Co Inc., Louisville, 1976-93; sr. exec. v.p. reimbursement and rate acctg. fin. mgmt., hosp. acctg. divsn. Humana Inc., The Hosp Co., Louisville, 1976-93; bd. dirs. Southeastern Investmen Trust, Inc., Louisville, 1976-93; rsch. prof. The Southeaster Investment Trust, Inc. Rsch. Found., Louisville, 1976—2007 Vis. prof. Medieval Latin, U. Chgo., 1966-2007; vis. pro linguistics U. Chgo., Downtown Ctr., 1966-2007; prof. Englis evening divs. Northwestern U., Chgo., 1968-69, prof. anthro pology, 1971-72. Author: The Ruodlieb: The First Mediev Epic of Chivalry from Eleventh-Century Germany, 1965, Th Ruodlieb: Linguistic Introduction, Latin Text with a Critic Apparatus, and Glossary, 1966, The Ruodlieb: Facsimile Ed tion, 1965, 3d edit. 1968, Old Lithuanian Texts of the Sixteent and Seventeenth Centuries with a Glossary, 1969, The Ol Lithuanian Catechism of Baltramiejus Vilentas (1579): A Pho nological, Morphological, and Syntactical Investigation, 196 Isidore of Seville's History of the Goths, Vandals, and Suev

1966, 2d edit. 1970, The Letters of Saint Isidore of Seville, 1966, 2d edit. 1970, The Old Lithuanian Catechism of Martynas Mazvydas (1547), 1971, others; translator: A Concise Elementary Grammar of the Sanskrit Language with Exercises, Reading Selections, and a Glossary (Jan Gonda), 1966, The Comparative Method in Historical Linguistics (Antoine Meillet), 1967, A Sanskrit Grammar (Manfred Mayrhofer), 1972; contbr. numerous articles to many scholarly jours. Appointed to Hon. Order Ky. Cols. (life). Mem. Linguistic Soc. Am. (life, Sapir life patron), Internat. Linguistic Assn. (life), Societas Linguistica Europaea (charter, life), Am. Philol. Assn. (life), Classical Assn. of the Atlantic States (life), Classical Assn. of the Middle West and South (life), Classical Assn. of N.Eng. (life), Medieval Acad. of Am. (life), Renaissance Soc. of Am. (life), MLA (life), Am. Assn. Tchrs. Slavic and East European Langs. (life), Am. Assn. Advancement Slavic Studies (life), Am. Coun. Tchrs. Russian (life), Assn. for Advancement Baltic Studies (life), Inst. Lithuanian Studies (life), Tchrs. of English to Speakers of Other Langs. (charter, life), SAR (life), Princeton Club (N.Y.C., Chgo.), Princeton Alumni Assn. (Louisville), Harvard Club (N.Y.C., Chgo., Louisville, Lexington, Ky.), Pres.'s Soc. Bellarmine Coll. (life), Louisville Country Club, KC (life), Phi Beta Kappa (life). Baptist. Home: Louisville, Ky. Died May 6, 2007.

FORD, THOMAS ROBERT, retired sociologist, educator, writer; b. Lake Charles, La., June 24, 1923; s. Gervais w. and Alma (Weil) F.; m. Harriet Lowrey, Aug. 13, 1949; children: Margaret Erin, Janet Patricia, Mark Lowrey, Charlotte Elizabeth. BS, La. State U., 1946, MA, 1948; PhD, Vanderbilt U., 1951. Instr. sociology La. State U., 1948-49; asst. prof. U. Ala., 1950-53; supervisory analytical statistician (demography) USAF Personnel and Tng. Research Center, Maxwell AFB, Ala., 1953-56; faculty U. Ky., Lexington, 1956-90, prof. sociology, 1960-90, chmn. dept., 1966-70; dir. Center Developmental Change, 1975-90. Research dir. So. Appalachian Studies, Inc., 1957-62; Mem. Pres.'s Nat. Adv. Com. on Rural Poverty, 1966-67; sr. adviser Population Council to Colombian Assn. Med. Faculties, Bogota, 1970-72 Author: Man and Land in Peru, 1955, Health and Demography in Kentucky, 1964; Editor: The Southern Appalachian Region: A Survey, 1962, The Revolutionary Theme in Contemporary America, 1965, (with Gordon DeJong) Social Demography, 1970, Rural U.S.A.: Persistence and Change, 1978. Served with USAAF, 1943-45. Decorated Air medal with 6 oak leaf clusters.; Guggenheim fellow, 1962; Fulbright rsch. grant, Costa Rica, 1988-89. Mem. AAAS, Am. Sociol. Assn., Population Assn. Am., Rural Sociol. Assn. (pres. 1972-73), So. Sociol. Assn. (pres. 1976-77), Internat. Rural Sociology Assn. (sec. 1976-80) Home: Lexington, Ky. Died Apr. 27, 2006.

FORDYCE, PHILLIP RANDALL, university administrator; b. Lyons, Ind., May 28, 1928; s. Russell and Agnes (Fulk) F.; m. Lois Marilyn Lamb, Dec. 27, 1947; children— Deborah, Natalie, Marilyn, Kerry, Timothy. BS, Butler U., 1951, MS, 1954. Asst. prof. sci. edn. Fla. State U., Tallahassee, 1963-67, asso. prof., 1967-70, prof., from 1970; asst. dean Fla. State U. (Coll. Edn.), 1965-67, asso. dean, 1967-69, dean, 1969-74, provost, 1974-77, asst. chief exec. officer, 1977-80, assoc. chief exec. officer, 1981-84, spl. asst. to pres. for internat. programs, from 1984. Cons. AID Sci. Edn. in India Program, summer 1964, Ford Found. Sci. Lise, Turkey, 1966 Co-author sci. text.; Contbr. articles to profl. jours. Dir. NSF-U.S. Office Edn. Grant projects, 1963-67. Fellow A.A.A.S. (council 1969-75, sec. edn. sect. 1969-75); mem. Assn. for Edn. Tchrs. in Sci., Nat. Assn. Biology Tchrs. (editor newsletter 1965-68, pres. 1963), Phi Delta Kappa, Kappa Delta Pi, Omicron Delta Kappa. Home: Tallahassee, Fla. Died Feb. 21, 2006.

FORMAN, GEORGE WHITEMAN, mechanical design consultant; b. Salt Lake City, Dec. 9, 1919; s. Frank Shane and Daisy (Taylor) F.; m. Ruth Skaggs, Aug. 9, 1941; children— G.L., John S., Jane Ann Forman Cigard BS in Mech.Engring., U. Ill., 1941; MS in Mech. Engring., U. Kans., 1957. Design engr. Hamilton Standard, East Hartford, Conn., 1941-46; mech. engring. mgr. Marley Co., Kansas City, Mo., 1946-53; research mgr. Butler Mfg. Co., Kansas City, Mo., 1953-55; prof. U. Kans., Lawrence, from 1955; design cons. George W. Forman, P.E., Lawrence, Kans., from 1955. Contbr. articles to profl. jours. Recipient Gould award U. Kans., 1967 Fellow ASME (chmn. Kansas City chpt. 1958); mem. Tau Beta Pi (Disting. Service award 1975), Sigma Xi, Pi Tau Sigma. Lodges: Masons. Avocation: photography. Home: Lawrence, Kans. Died July 19, 2006.

FORST, MARION FRANCIS, bishop; b. St. Louis, Sept. 3, 1910; s. Frank A. J. and Bertha T. (Gulath) F. Grad., Kenrick Sem., Webster Groves, Mo., 1934. Priest Roman Cath. Ch., 1934. Pastor St. Mary's Cathedral, Cape Girardeau, Mo., 1949—60; vicar gen. Diocese of Springfield-Cape Girardeau, 1956—60; bishop Dodge City, Kans., 1960—76; aux. bishop Archdiocese of Kansas City, Kans., 1976—86; ret., 1986. Kans. chaplain KC, from 1964. With Chaplains Corps USNR, WWII. Roman Catholic. Died June 2, 2007.

FORSTER, DENIS, chemistry research scientist; b. Newcastle-on-Tyne, Eng., Feb. 28, 1941; came to U.S., 1965; s. Thomas Reginald and Margaret (Dobson) F.; m. Hazel Frances Onions, Apr. 18, 1964; children: Juliet, Rachel. B.Sc., Imperial Coll., London, 1962, PhD, 1965. Fellow Princeton U., 1965-66; sr. research chemist Monsanto Co., St. Louis, 1966-70, group leader, 1970-75, sci. fellow, 1975-80, sr. sci. fellow, from 1980, disting. fellow, from 1984; dir. chem. scis. Monsanto Corp. Rsch., St. Louis, from 1986. Editor: Homogeneus Catalysis, 1974; contbr. articles to profl. jours.; patentee in field. Mem. Am. Chem. Soc. (Ipatieff prize 1980), Am. Inst. Chemists (Chem. Pioneer award 1980) Clubs: Racquet (St. Louis). Home: Saint Louis, Mo. Died May 11, 2006.

FORSTER, JULIAN, physicist, consultant; b. NYC, Aug. 31, 1918; s. Meyer Kivetz and Rose (Sommer) F.; m. Frieda Bain, July 2, 1941; children: Jeffrey M., Laura Gherman. BS in Physics, CCNY, 1940. Registered nuclear engr., Calif. Sr. physicist US Naval 4th Dist., Phila., 1941-56; sr. nuclear engr. GE, San Jose, Calif., 1956-70, sr. project mgr. nuclear energy dept., 1970-80; sr. mgmt. tech. Quadrex Corp., Campbell, Calif., 1980-85, cons., 1985-96, GE-NE, from 1996. Contbr. articles to profl. jours. Commr. Fine Arts, San Jose, 1987-95. Fellow IEEE (life, emeritus; standards bd. 1970—, computer soc. 1985—, nuclear scis. soc. 1963—, power engring. soc. 1975—, coord. pace divsn. IV 1993-2000, chmn. awards and recognition com. 1986-95, Divsnl. Profl. Achievment award 1994, Standards Bd. Spl. Achievement award 1995, Stds. Dist. Svc. award 2000, 3d Millennium medal of Honor 2000, C.A. Steinmetz Tech. award, 2004); mem. Internat. Electro Tech. Com. (nuclear power com. SC45A 1969—, R.F. Shea Svc. award 1992). Democrat. Jewish. Avocations: music, wine, fine arts, golf. Home: San Jose, Calif. Died May 29, 2007.

FORTNER, JOSEPH GERALD, surgeon, educator; b. Bedford, Ind., May 30, 1921; s. Everett Rex and Lula Alice (Robbins) F.; m. Roberta Olson, Nov. 4, 1948; children: Kathleen Alice Fortner, Joseph Jr. BS, U. Ill., 1944, MD, 1945; MSc in Immunology, Birmingham U., Eng., 1965. Diplomate: Am. Bd. Surgery. Intern St. Luke's Hosp., Chgo., 1945-46; resident in pathology Tulane U., New Orleans, 1948-49; surg. resident Bellevue Hosp., NYC, 1949-51, Meml. Hosp., NYC, 1951—54, clin. asst. surgeon, asst. to clin. dir., 1955-59, asst. attending surgeon, 1958-66, assoc. attending surgeon, 1966-69, attending surgeon, 1969-94, chief transplantation svc. and gastric and mixed tumor svc., 1970-78, chief surg. research service, 1978-91, assoc. chmn. for lab. affairs dept. surgery, 1978-84, chief div. surg. research, 1968-77; chief Gen. Motors Surg. Rsch. Lab., 1977-92; instr. surgery Sloan-Kettering Inst., NYC, 1954-58, asst. prof. clin. surgery, 1958-64; clin. asst. prof. surgery Cornell U. Med. Coll., NYC, 1964-70, assoc. prof. surgery, 1970-72, prof., 1972—2007. Contbr. articles to profl. jours.; editor Accomplishments in Cancer Research. Pres. Gen. Motors Cancer Rsch. Found., 1978-96, pres. emeritus, 1996-2007, trustee mem. awards assembly. Served in US Army, 1946-48. Recipient Alfred P. Sloan award Sloan-Kettering Inst. Cancer Research, 1963 Fellow ACS, Royal Coll. Surgeons Edinburgh (hon.); mem. AAAS, Am. Assn. Cancer Research, Am. Gastroent. Assn., Am. Radium Soc., Am. Soc. Clin. Oncology, European Soc. Exptl. Surgery, Harvey Soc., Soc. Surg. Oncology, N.Y. County, N.Y. State med. socs., Am. Surg. Assn., N.Y. Surg. Soc., Soc. Univ. Surgeons, Hellenic Surg. Soc. (hon.), Chgo. Surg. Soc., Korean Surg. Soc., Am. Soc. Transplant Surgeons, Transplantation Soc., N.Y. Cancer Soc., Econ. Club of N.Y., Explorer Club N.Y., Met. Club N.Y., Madison Beach Club, Sigma Xi, Alpha Omega Alpha. Republican. Home: New York, NY. Died Feb. 18, 2007.

FOSTER, ALAN HERBERT, diversified financial services company executive, educator; b. Somerville, Mass., Nov. 7, 1925; s. Herbert and Margaret J. (Griffin) F.; m. Cynthia Ann Brooks, June 26, 1954; children— Mark Brooks, Andrew Herbert. BS, BA, Boston Coll., 1951; MBA, Harvard U., 1953. With Sylvania Electric Products, Inc., 1953-63; with Am. Motors Corp., 1963-77, corp. dir. financial planning and analysis, 1963-67, treas., 1967-68, v.p., treas., 1968-77; pres. A.H. Foster & Co. (Cons. in Corp. Fin.), Ann Arbor, Mich., from 1977, Fin. Risk Mgmt. Inc., Ann Arbor, from 1983, ret., from 2002. Adj. prof. corp. strategy and internat. bus. Grad. Sch. Bus., U. Mich. Author: Practical Business Management, 1962, Treasurer's Handbook; also articles. Served with USNR, 1945-46. Mem. Commanderie de Bordeaux, Fin. Execs. Inst. (pres. Detroit chpt. 1972-73), Baker Street Irregulars, Speckled Band Boston, Inst. Mgmt. Scis. (past nat. chmn. coll. planning), U. Mexico Club, Samuel Pepys Club, Harvard Club N.Y.C., Harvard Faculty Club. Home: Ann Arbor, Mich. Died Oct. 18, 2006.

FOSTER, CHARLES THOMAS, secondary school educator; b. Fremont, Ohio, Apr. 17, 1921; s. Charles Lincoln and Lucy Elizabeth (Rooney) Foster; m. Evelyn May Foster, Jan. 1, 1942; children: Charles Thomas, Stephanie. BGE, U. Nebr., 1964; MA, Chapman Coll., 1974. Cert. elem., secondary, and coll. tchr. Calif. Asst. to sales mgr. Henkel Clauss Co., Fremont, Ohio, 1945—50; commd. USAF, 1950, advanced through grades to lt. col., 1964; ret., 1967. Tchr. Los Padres Elem. Sch., Lompoc, Calif., 1968—85. Mem. exec. bd. PTA, 1974—75; mem. site com. Calif. Sch. Improvement Program, 1974—75; mem. instructional evaluation panel Curriculum Devel. & Supplemental Materials Commn. of Calif. State Bd. Edn., 1978—79. Served to capt. US Army, 1942—45. Decorated Bronze Star, Army Commendation medal, Air Force Commendation medal with two oak leaf clusters; recipient Hon. Svc. award, PTA. Mem.: PTA, Ret. Officers Assn., Air Force Assn., Thousand Trails Club, Officers Club, Elks Lodge. Republican. Lutheran. Died Mar. 31, 2007.

FOSTER, JOSEPH W., III, industrial engineer; b. Waco, Tex., Feb. 25, 1938; s. Joseph W. F.; m. Lucille Terry, July 15, 1961; children: Nancy Karen, Joseph W. BS in Mech. Engring., So. Meth. U., 1961; MS in Indsl. Engring., Lehigh U., 1965; D.Engring., U. Okla., 1968. Registered profl. engr., Tex., Okla. Prodn. engr. Western Electric Co., Oklahoma City, 1961-63, research engr. Princeton, NJ, 1963-65, sr. computer specialist Oklahoma City, 1965-66; instr. U. Okla., 1966-67, vis. asst. prof., 1968; mem. facutly Tex A&M U, College Station, from 1968; prof. indsl. engring. Tex. A&M U., College Station, from 1975, head indsl. engring., from 1977. Mem. producability assessment space shuttle team Marshall Space Flight Ctr., Huntsville, Ala. Mem. Am. Inst. Indsl. Engrs. (sr.), Am. Soc. Quality Control (sr.), Am. Waters Works Assn. Methodist. Home: Bryan, Tex. Died Dec. 12, 2005.

FOSTER, ROBERT W., state legislator; b. Springfield, Mass., Mar. 6, 1920; m. Mary Ann (dec.); two children; m. Jane, 2001 Student, Northeastern U., 1946-48, U. Mass. Former mktg. mgr. Mobil Oil Corp.; past town trustee; state rep. N.H. Dist. 10. Chmn. emeritus health, human svcs. and elderly affairs com.; mem. rules com. Chmn. N.H. Hosp. Assoc. Trustee Forum, Huggins Hosp., Moultonborough; mem. Moultonborough Acad. Scholar Trust; chmn. Amherst Sch. Bd., 1966-68; selectman Mountainborough, 2000-03 Mem. Bald Peak Colony Club (bd. dirs.), Mason. Home: Georgetown, Mass. Died Jan. 6, 2006.

FOULKE, WILLIAM GREEN, retired banker; b. Whitemarsh, Pa., Nov. 20, 1912; s. Walter Longfellow and Helen (Pardee) F.; m. Louisa Lawrence Wood, Nov. 2, 1934 (dec. 2001); children: Louisa Lawrence Foulke Newlin, Walter Longfellow, William Green. AB, Princeton U., 1934. Asst. treas. Provident Trust Co., Phila., 1940-41, trust officer, 1945-50, v.p., 1950-57; sr. v.p. charge trust divsn. Provident Tradesmens Bank and Trust Co., Phila., 1957-60, exec. v.p., 1960-62, pres., 1962-64, Provident Nat. Bank, Phila., 1964-69, chmn., CEO, 1969-74, Provident Nat. Corp., 1969-73, chmn., 1973-74; ret. Gen. chmn. United Campaign, 1975. Served to lt. comdr. USNR, 1941-45. Mem. Pa. Bankers Assn. (pres. 1970-71) Clubs: Racquet; Ivy (Princeton). Episcopalian. Home: Philadelphia, Pa. Died Mar. 30, 2007.

FOWLER, CONRAD MURPHREE, retired manufacturing company executive; b. Montevallo, Ala., Sept. 17, 1918; s. Luther J. and Elsie (Murphree) F.; m. Virginia Evelyn Mott, June 15, 1945; children: Conrad, Randolph. BS, U. Ala., 1941, JD, 1948. Bar: Ala. 1948. Practiced in, Columbiana, 1948-53; mem. firm Ellis and Fowler, 1948-53; dist. atty. 18th Jud. Circuit Ala., 1953-59; probate judge, chmn. Shelby County Commn. Shelby County Ct., Columbiana, 1959-77; v.p. pub. affairs West Point-Pepperell, Inc., 1977-89, ret., 1989. Mem. Presdl. Adv. Commn. on Intergovtl. Relations, 1970-77 Mem. Ala. Dem. Exec. Com., 1966-77; chmn. Ala. Constl. Commn., 1970-76; bd. dirs. Associated Industries Ala., 1979-87, Pub. Affairs Coun., 1979-89; v.p. Am. Lung Assn., 1980-82, pres., 1982-83; mem. coun. Nat. Mcpl. League, 1976-82; vice chmn. Pub. Affairs Coun., 1987-89; bd. dirs. Ga. Bus. Coun., 1987-89. Col. USMCR, 1941-78. Decorated Silver Star with gold star, Purple Heart (2); named to Ala. Acad. Honor, 1981; recipient William Crawford Gorgas award Ala. Med. Assn., 1985; Rotary Paul Harris fellow, 1997; Kiwanis George F. Hixson fellow, 1999. Mem.: West Ala. Ret. Officers Club (pres. 2000—01), Probate Judges Assn. Ala. (pres. 1968—69), Assn. County Commrs. Ala. (pres. 1970—71), Nat. Assn. Counties (pres. 1969—70), Murphree Geneal. Assn. (pres. 1990—91), U. Ala. Nat. Alumni Assn. (pres. 1969, Alumnus of Yr. 1992), Tuscaloosa Exch. Club. Home: Tuscaloosa, Ala. Died Jan. 1, 2007.

FOWLER, DONALD RAYMOND, retired lawyer, educator; b. Raton, N.Mex., June 2, 1926; s. Homer F. and Grace B. (Honeyfield) F.; m. Anna M. Averyt, Feb. 6, 1960; children: Mark D., Kelly A. BA, U. N.Mex., 1950; JD, 1951; MA, Claremont Grad. Sch., 1979, PhD, 1983. Bar: N.Mex. 1951, Calif. 1964, U.S. Supreme Ct. 1980. Atty. AEC, Los Alamos and Albuquerque, 1951-61, chief counsel Nev. Ops., 1962-63; pvt. practice, Albuquerque, 1961-62; asst., then dep. staff counsel Calif. Inst. Tech., Pasadena, 1963-72, staff counsel, 1972-75, gen. counsel, 1975-90; lectr. exec. mgmt. program Claremont Grad. Sch., Calif., 1981-84. Contbr. articles to profl. publs. Served with USAAF, 1944-46. Recipient NASA Pub. Svc. award, 1981. Mem. Calif. State Bar Assn., Fed. Bar Assn., Nat. Assn. Coll. and Univ. Attys. (exec. bd. 1979-82, 84-90, chmn. publs. com. 1982-84, pres. 1987-88, chmn. nominations com. 1988-89, chmn. honors and awards com. 1989-90, Life Mem. award 1991, Disting. Svc. award 1992), Calif. Assn. for Rsch. in Astronomy (sec. 1985-90). Home: Cambria, Calif. Died May 18, 2007.

FOWLER, H(ORATIO) SEYMOUR, retired science educator; b. Detroit, Mar. 1, 1919; s. Horatio Seymour and Bessie Liona (Ladd) F.; m. Kathleen M. Marshall, Nov. 21, 1945 (dec.); 1 dau., Kathleen Marie Fowler Barto. BS, Cornell U., 1941, MS, 1946, PhD, 1951. Tchr. sci. McLean (N.Y.) Central Sch., 1946-47, Dryden (N.Y.) Freeville Central Sch., 1947-49; asst. prof. sci. edn. So. Oreg. Coll., Ashland, 1951-52; asst. prof. biology U. No. Iowa, Cedar Falls; also dir. Iowa Tchrs. Conservation Camp, 1952-57; prof. edn., dir. Pa. Conservation Lab. for Tchrs., Pa. State U., University Park, 1957-83, chmn. sci. edn. faculty, 1969-83, coordinator div. acad. curriculum and instrn., 1974-76, prof. nature and sci. edn. emeritus, from 1983; dir. Pa. Gov.'s Sch. for Scis., 1978-79. Sci. advisor Nat. Jr. Sci. and Humanities Symposium, Program U.S. Army Research Office, Acad. Applied Sci., 1979—. Author: Secondary School Science Teaching Practices, 1964, Las Ciencias en la Esquelas Secundarias, 1968, Fieldbook of Natural History, 1974; contbr. articles to profl. jours. Served with 9th inf. div. AUS, 1942-45, ETO. Fulbright lectr. Korea, 1968-69; recipient citation Pa. Dept. Edn., 1970, 83, Centre County (Pa.) Conservation award, 1973, Faculty Service award Nat. Univ. Continuing Edn. Assn., 1983, citation Pa. Ho. of Reps., 1983, Service award U.S. Army Office of Research, 1983; Paul Harris fellow Rotary Club, 1983 Fellow AAAS, Iowa Acad. Sci., Explorers Club; mem. Am. Nature Study Soc. (pres. 1967), Nat. Assn. Biology Tchrs. (v.p. 1956, dir. region II 1971-74, hon. mem. 1974), Nat. Assn. Rsch. in Sci. Teaching, Nat. Sci. Tchrs. Assn. (Disting. Svc. citation 1976), Pa. Sci. Tchrs. Assn. (dir. 1971—, v.p. 1975, pres. 1976, meritorious svc. to sci. teaching citation 1975), Korean Sci. Tchrs. Assn., Royal Asiatic Soc., Masons, Shriners, Rotary (1st v.p. 1981, pres. 1982, gov. dist. 735 1988-89), Elks, Sigma Xi, Phi Kappa Phi, Phi Delta Kappa (chpt. v.p. 1973, pres. 1974-75, Leadership award 1983), Beta Beta Beta. Clubs: Masons, Shriners. Home: Petersburg, Pa. Died Feb. 22, 2007.

FOWLER, MAUD MCELVEEN, museum administrative assistant, civic worker; b. Birmingham, Ala., Sept. 26, 1922; d. James Cleveland and Annie Olivia (Gardner) McElveen; m. Ray Benson Fowler, Feb. 14, 1952; 1 child, Leslie Anne. Grad. high sch., Birmingham, Ala. Sec. Prudential Ins. Co., Birmingham, 1940-46, asst. head tax dept., 1946-55, dept. head, 1955-59; tchr. 11th Ave. United Meth. Ch. Kindergarten, Birmingham, 1965-66; receptionist/bookkeeper L.G. Balfour Co., Birmingham, 1968-71; sec. to curator Birmingham Mus. Art, 1971-77, adminstrv. asst. to dir. and mus. bd., 1977-87. Researcher, author: History of 11th Avenue United Methodist Church, 1974, 77. Sec. to pres. Ala. Dental Bd., Birmingham, 1940-44; neighborhood rep. Am. Heart Fund, 1958-81; mem. adv. bd. Ala. Hist. Commn., 1975—; sec. Glen Iris Neighborhood Assn., 1978-80, v.p., 1980-82; mem. citizens adv. bd. Southside Community, 1978-82; vol. tutoring program local elem. sch.; mem. adv. council Southside Community Sch., 1980—; historian ofcl. bd. 11th Ave. United Meth. Ch. Recipient Service certs. USO, Nat. Civilian Def., ARC, Red Cross Nurse Aide Corps U. Hosp.;

inducted Woodlawn High Sch. Hall of Fame, 1988. Mem. Birminham Mus. Art, Ala. Hist. Soc., Birmingham Hist. Soc., Ala. Congress Parents and Tchrs. (hon. life), Ala. Writers Conclave. Home: Wexford, Pa. Died Jan. 20, 2006.

FOX, JOHN DAVID, physicist, educator; b. Huntington, W.Va., Dec. 8, 1929; s. David and Eleanor (Griffin) F.; children: Heidi Roberts Fox, Lise, Peter, Paul, Michelle Fox Lundy; m. Georgiana Fry Vines, Oct. 23, 1993. SB, MIT, 1951; Fulbright fellow, Rijksuniversiteit, Groningen, Netherlands, 1951-52; MS, U. Ill., 1954, PhD, 1960. Asst. physicist Brookhaven Nat. Lab., Upton, NY, 1956-59; asst. prof. physics Fla. State U., Tallahassee, 1959-63, asso. prof., 1963-65, prof., 1965-94, prof. emeritus, from 1994. Adj. prof. U. Tex., El Paso, 1996; guest scientist Max-Planck Inst. für Kernphysik, Heidelberg, Germany, 1968-69, Inst. für Kernphysik U. Köln, 1975; cons. physics divsn. Argonne Nat. Lab., 1982—; guest scientist Oak Ridge Nat. Lab., 1994—, program dir. nuclear physics NSF, 1990-92, 95-97; dir. Branchland Pipe & Supply Co., Huntington, W.Va., 1965-81; mem. MIT Ednl. Coun., 1981-90; cons. physics dept. U. Tenn., Knoxville, 1999—. Co-editor: Isobaric Spin in Nuclear Physics, 1966, Nuclear Analogue States, 1976; Contbr. articles to sci. jours. Mem. Leon County Dem. Com., 1970-74; mem. Dem. Nat. Com.; bd. dirs. LeMoyne Art Found., Tallahassee, 1971-73. NSF Grad. fellow, 1955-56; Sr. postdoctoral fellow, 1968-69; sr. U.S. scientist award Alexander von Humboldt-Stiftung, 1975 Fellow Am. Phys. Soc.; mem. AAAS, ACLU, Fedn. Am. Scientists. Home: Knoxville, Tenn. Died Mar. 11, 2007.

FOX, RAYMOND BERNARD, retired English educator; b. Woodstock, Minn., Feb. 8, 1926; s. Fred Joseph and Esther (Short) F.; m. Gudelia Agnes Utz, Jan. 27, 1950; 1 dau., Jacalyn Ann. BS, Mankato State Coll., 1949; MA, Colo. Coll., 1952; Ed.D., U. Calif.-Berkeley, 1957. Tchr., English and dramatics Springfield High Sch., Minn., 1949-50, Reno Sr. High Sch., Nev., 1950-53; tchr. social studies Pittsburg Sr. High Sch., Calif., 1953-57; asst. prof. edn. St. Cloud State Coll., 1957-59; prof. edn., head edn. dept. No. Ill. U., 1959-65, assoc. dean Coll. Edn., 1965-69, prof. edn., 1969-85; now ret. Dir. Am. Sch. Project, Addis Ababa, Ethiopia. Contbr. articles profl. jours. Served with USNR, 1943-46. Mem. Assn. for Supervision and Curriculum Devel. (bd. dirs.), Ill. Assn. for Supervision and Curriculum Devel. (pres., dir.), Ill. Curriculum Council (exec. bd.), Am. Assn. Colls. for Tchr. Edn. (instl. rep.), Am. Ednl. Research Assn., Nat. Soc. Coll. Tchrs. Edn. Home: Wabasha, Minn. Died Jan. 9, 2006.

FRANCE, BILL, JR., (WILLIAM CLIFTON FRANCE JR.), retired sports association executive; b. Washington, Apr. 4, 1933; s. William and Anne France; m. Betty Jane Zachary; children: Lesa Kennedy, Brian. Student, U. Fla. Pres. NASCAR, Daytona Beach, Fla., 1972—2000, chmn. bd., 2000—03; CEO Internat. Speedway Corp., Daytona Beach, Fla., 1972—2007. Dir. Nat. Motorsports Coun. of ACCUS. Served in USN. Named one of Forbes' Richest Americans, 2006; named to Internat. Motorsports Hall of Fame, 2004. Died June 4, 2007.

FRANCIS, GORDON DEAN, physician; b. Bancroft, Nebr., Dec. 6, 1930; s. Marvyn Bliss and Lillian Grace (Slepicka) F.; m. Harriette Salter, May 27, 1951; children— Michele Francis Stine, Rene F. Hinton, Mark Salter Francis. A.B. U. Nebr., 1952; M.D. U. Nebr.-Omaha, 1955. Diplomate Am. Bd. Family Practice. Intern William Beaumont U.S. Army Gen. Hosp., El Paso, Tex., 1955-56; gen. practice medicine, Bellevue, Nebr., 1958-60, Arapahoe, Nebr., 1960-66, Grand Island, Nebr., 1966—. Served with U.S. Army, 1955-58; to col. USAFR. Decorated Legion of Merit USAF. Fellow Am. Acad. Family Practice, Aerospace Med. Assn. (assoc.); mem. AMA, Nebr. Med. Assn., Hall County Med. Assn. (pres. 1978), Assn. Mil. Surgeons U.S. (life), Lions Club Internat. (dist. gov. dist. 38-I 1995-96), Jaycees (Arapahoe pres. 1964-65, state v.p. 1965-66). Lodges: Lions, Masons. Republican. Presbyterian. Avocations: amateur radio, hunting, fishing. Home: Grand Island, Nebr. Died Aug. 26, 2006.

FRANCIS, TALTON LOE, hospital administrator; b. Arcadia, La., Mar. 17, 1924; s. Raymond Henry and Mary Allie (McClain) F.; m. Bronwen Tyler Francis, July 5, 1944; children: Trefor Lee, Terry Lane, Tanya Lynette, Twoinselle LeBronwen. BS, La. Tech., 1950; postgrad., Centenary Coll.; HADP program, Cornell U., 1970. Adminstr. Beauregard Meml. Bapt. Hosp., DeRidder, La., 1950-60, Parkview Bapt. Hosp., Yuma, Ariz., 1960-62, Scottsdale (Ariz.) Bapt. Hosp., 1962-64, Meml. Gen. Hosp., Las Cruces, N.Mex., 1965-78, Eastwood Hosp., El Paso, Tex., 1978-80, Talley Walker Hosp., Marlow, Okla., 1981-83, Great Plains Med. Ctr., Elk City, Okla., from 1983. Exec. administr. dir. Western Bapt. Hosp. Assn., Scottsdale, 1962-64. Pres. United Fund, Elk City, 1993—. With USN Med. Corps., 1942-45, PTO. Honored Talton L. Francis Day City of Elk City, Mayor's Honor, 1988. Fellow Am. Coll. Healthcare Execs.; mem. Elk City C. of C. (chmn. med. devel. com.), Western Okla. Hist. Soc. (Western Okla. Hall of Fame 1989), Rotary. Avocations: bicycling, freelance writing, fishing, hunting, gardening. Died Dec. 26, 2006.

FRANCISCO, WAYNE, automotive executive; b. June 14, 1943; s. George Lewis and Helen M. (Markland) F.; m. Susan Francisco; children: Diana Lynn, W. Michael. Student, Ohio State U., 1962-63; BS in Mktg. and Acctg., U. Cin., 1967. Unit sales mgr. Procter & Gamble, Cin., 1967-69; mktg. mgr. Nat. Mktg. Inc., Cin., 1969-70; pres. Retail Petroleum Marketers, Inc., Cin., 1970-72, chmn. bd., CEO Phoenix, 1972-85, DMC Industries, Inc., 1985-99. Pres., CEO Cassia Petroleum Corp., Vancouver, B.C., Can., 1980-84; bd. dirs. P.F.K. Enterprises, F.I.C. Inc., Internat. Investment and Fin. Enterprises, Inc., Alpha Realty, Inc. Class agt. 62G Culver Mil. Acad., 1958-62. Mem. Culver Legion, bd. trustees, 1990—; mem. Phoenix Bd. Appeals, 1978-80; v.p. Cuernavaca Homeowners Assn., 1982, pres., 1983-86. Recipient Image Maker award Shell Oil Co., 1979, Top Performer award Phoenix dist. Shell Oil Co., 1979, 80. Mem. Petroleum Retailers Ariz. (pres. 1977-79), Nat. Congress Petroleum Retailers (adv. bd.), Automotive Svc. Excellence (cert.), Studebaker Drivers Club (zone coord. Pacific S.W. 1983, nat. v.p. 1986, 87, 88, nat. pres. 1989-90, Grand Canyon chpt. pres. 1986), Avanti Owners Assn. (nat. bd. dirs. 1975-96, internat. pres. 1986-89), Eugene C. Eppley Club, Optimists (bd. dirs. Paradise Valley club 1984, sec.-treas. 1984). Republican. Home: Paradise Valley, Ariz. Died Nov. 2, 2006.

FRANK, HARVEY, lawyer, writer; b. NYC, Aug. 24, 1930; s. Leon and Hannah (Lehr) F.; m. Judith Ellen Lewis, Nov. 29, 1959; 1 child, David. AB, NYU, 1951, LLM, 1961; JD, Harvard U., 1954. Bar: N.Y. 1954, Md. 1981, Ohio 1982. Ptnr. Hays Feuer Porter & Spanier, NYC, 1963-69, Burns, Summit, Rovins & Feldesman, NYC, 1970-74; prof. law Coll. William and Mary, Williamsburg, Va., 1974-80; adj. prof. Johns Hopkins U., Balt., 1981; ptnr. Benesch Friedlander, Coplan & Aronoff, Cleve., 1982-93; pvt. practice Law Offices Harvey Frank, Phila., from 1993. Sec. Banner Aerospace, 1990-93. Author: The ERC Closely Held Corporation Guide, 1981, 2d edit., 1984; contbr. articles to law jours. Mem. ABA, Am. Law Inst. Died Oct. 25, 2005.

FRANKEL, KENNETH MARK, thoracic surgeon; b. Bklyn., July 29, 1940; s. Clarence Bernard and Ruth (Rutes) F.; m. Felice Cala Oringel, Dec. 10, 1967; children: Matthew David, Michael Jacob. BA, Cornell U., 1961; MD, SUNY, Bkyln., 1965. Diplomate Am. Bd. Surgery, Am. Bd. Thoracic Surgery. Intern in surgery Yale New Haven Hosp., 1965-66; resident in surgery Kings County-SUNY Med. Ctr., Bklyn., 1966-67, 69-71, chief resident in gen. surgery, 1971—72, resident in thoracic surgery, 1972-73, chief resident thoracic and cardiovasc. surgery, 1973-74; sr. attending thoracic surgeon Mercy Hosp., Springfield, Mass., from 1974; attending thoracic surgeon Holyoke (Mass.) Hosp., 1974—2004; pvt. practice medicine specializing in thoracic surgery Springfield, from 1974; chief thoracic surgery Baystate Med. Ctr., Springfield, 1977—2005, mem. hon. staff, from 2006; clin. prof. cardiothoracic surgery Tufts U. Sch. Medicine, from 1978; dir. Baystate Thoracic Surgery Assocs., 2004—06. Cons. Shriners Hosp. for Children, Mary Lane Hosp., Ware, Mass., 1997-2004; bd. dirs. Pioneer Health Care Inc., 1997—, sec. of bd., 1998-2001, v.p. of bd., 2001-04 Contbr. articles to profl. jours. Rep. to Blue Cross/Blue Shield Regional Health Care Improvement Coun., 1995-98. Capt. U.S. Army, 1967-69. Decorated Bronze Star, Gallantry Cross (Republic of Vietnam). Fellow: ACS, Am. Coll. Chest Physicians; mem.: ACLU, AMA, Physicians for Social Responsibility, Hampden Dist. Med. Soc. (exec. com. 1990—96), Mass. Med. Soc. (councilor 1981—83), Springfield Acad. Medicine (past pres.), New Eng. Cancer Soc., Am. Thoracic Soc., Soc. Thoracic Surgeons, Union Concerned Scientists, Internat.Physicians for Prevention Nuc. War, Porsche Club Am., Cornell Club N.Y., Amnesty Internat., Maimonides Med. Club (past pres.). Democrat. Jewish. Home: Longmeadow, Mass. Died June 17, 2007.

FRANKLE, ALLAN HENRY, psychologist; b. Des Moines, Nov. 5, 1921; s. Harry Raymond and Ruth (Cohen) Frankle; m. Esther Alpern, June 22, 1947; children: Katherine, Jonathan. Student, U. Chgo., 1939, PhD, 1953; student, U. Minn., 1943. Diplomate Am. Bd. Profl. Psychology. Dir. Des Moines Child Guidance Ctr., 1947—52; pvt. practice clin. psychology Des Moines, 1952—85; clin. rsch., from 1985. Univ. fellow Drake U., from 1970; vis. clin. assoc. prof. psychology U. Iowa, 1969—70; cons. clin. psychology Broadlawns Polk County Hosp., 1967—81; cons. VA Hosp., Knoxville, Iowa, 1976—81; supervising psychologist N. AM. Mensa, 1966—78. Contbr. articles to profl. jours. With US Army, 1943—45. Decorated Bronze Star. Fellow: Am. Orthopsychiat. Assn.; mem.: Mensa, San Diego Ind. Scholars, Brit. Psychol. Soc. (fgn. mem.), Internat. Neuropsychology Soc., Am. Acad. Psychotherapists, Iowa psychol. Assn. (pres. 1960—61, Disting. Svc. award 1973), Am. Psychol. Assn., Psi Chi, Sigma Xi. Democrat. Jewish. Home: La Jolla, Calif. Died Apr. 11, 2007.

FRANKLIN, KENNETH LINN, astronomer; b. Alameda, Calif., Mar. 25, 1923; s. Myles Arthur and Ruth Linn (Huston) F.; m. Beverly Mattson, Nov. 29, 1949 (dec. Mar. 1956); children: Kathleen (Mrs. James R. Williams), Christine (Mrs. Russell Redding); m. Charlotte Walton, May 18, 1958; 1 adopted dau., Julie (Mrs. A.D. Jones). AA, U. Calif., Berkeley, 1943, AB, 1948, PhD, 1953. Sci. asst. dept. astronomy U. Calif., 1953-54; research fellow dept. terrestrial magnetism Carnegie Instn., 1954-56; asst. astronomer Am. Museum-Hayden Planetarium, NYC, 1956-58, assoc. astronomer, 1958-63, astronomer, 1963-85, astronomer emeritus, 1985—2007, asst. chmn., 1968-72, chmn., 1972-74. Cons. aerospace firms, pubs., news media on astronomy and space sci.; mem. faculty CUNY, NYU, Cooper Union, Rutgers U.; participant Nat. Security Seminar, Army War Coll., 1975; chmn. Mus. Council N.Y.C., 1977, 78; guest lectr. Soc. Expeditions, Lindblad Travel, 1985, 86, Am. Hawaii Cruises, Tahiti, 1986, Am. Mus. Nat. History, 1991. Numerous appearance TV, Radio; astronomy editor: World Almanac, 1968-96, Farmers Almanac, 1981-93; mem. editl. adv. panel: Sci. Digest, 1970-85; weekly columnist N.Y. Times, 1983. Served with AUS, 1943-46. Fellow AAAS, Royal Astron. Soc., Explorers Club; mem. Am. Astron. Soc. (pub. info. rep. 1973-79, soc. vis. prof. 1959-79), Astron. Soc. Pacific, IEEE, N.Y. Acad. Scis., Sigma Xi. Clubs: Trap Door Spiders. Discoverer (with B.F. Burke) radio emissions from Jupiter, 1955; devised a system for lunar-based timekeeping, 1970. Appeared CBS Sputnik Special, 1957; CBS Landing Surveyor I, 1966; NBC Apollo 8, 1968, Apollo 10, 11, 1969; CBS Eclipse Special, 1970; asteroid #2845 named Franklinken in his honor. Home: Estes Park, Colo. Died June 18, 2007.

FRANKLIN, MORTON JEROME, emergency physician; b. Boston, Dec. 25, 1927; s. Jacob and Rose Ann (Borax) F. BA, Harvard U., 1949, MD, 1954. Diplomate Am. Bd. Emergency Medicine. Many positions as emergency physician, various cities and states, 1955-2001. Lt. cmmdr. USN, 1955-57. Died Mar. 10, 2006.

FRANZETTA, BENEDICT C., bishop; b. Liverpool, Ohio, Aug. 1, 1921; Attended, St. Charles Coll., Calonsville, Md., St. Mary Sem., Cleve. Ordained priest Roman Cath. Ch., 1950. Priest Roman Cath. Ch., Youngstown, Ohio, titular bishop Oderzo and aux. bishop, from 1980. Died Sept. 26, 2006.

FRATES, MEX (MRS. CLIFFORD LEROY FRATES), civic worker; b. Moweaqua, Ill., Jan. 15, 1908; d. William James and Gertrude (Gunderson) Rodman; m. Clifford L. Frates, Nov. 15, 1935; children: Rodman A., Kent F. Student, Pine Manor Jr. Coll., 1924; BA, U. Okla., 1929. Mem. bd. ARC, Oklahoma City; dir. Community Fund Bd.; trustee Jane Brooks Sch. Deaf, Okla. Art Center, Okla. Coll. for Women; chmn. adv. bd. Mercy Hosp., also trustee; bd. dirs. Okla. State Library, Library for Blind, dir. Jr. Leagues of Am.; mem. bd. Okla. Heritage Assn., Allied Arts of Oklahoma City, Oklahoma City Symphony, YWCA, Blood Inst., Better Bus. Bur.; mem. Children's Rehab. and Edn. Bd.; drive chmn. Central Vol. Bur.; chmn. women's div. United Fund; chmn. Art Center drive; chmn. Oklahoma City Savs. Bond Com.; chmn. Episcopal Women's Conf. Okla.; div. chmn. for Christian social relations; mem. Episcopal Bishop and Council; mem. vestry All Souls Ch. chmn. Re-act campaign for Oklahoma City Vol. Action Center, 1971. Recipient award NCCJ, Humanitarian award Oklahoma City Pub. Sch. Found., 1986, By-Liners award Women in Comm., 1979, Okla. Gov.'s Arts award, 1985, Mary Baker Rumsey award Jr. League Redlands, award for volunteerism Girl Scouts U.S., Richard Clements award United Appeal, Pathfinder award Oklahoma County Hist. Soc., Dean's award Coll. Medicine for Cmty. Svc.; named to Okla. Hall of Fame, 1969. Home: Oklahoma City, Okla. Died Aug. 30, 2006.

FREDERICKS, WILLIAM JOHN, chemistry professor; b. San Diego, Sept. 18, 1924; s. William and Jenney (Cunnion) F.; m. Lola M. Schneider, Sept. 20, 1942. BS, San Diego State Coll., 1951; PhD, Oreg. State U., 1955. Technician, planner USN, San Diego, 1942-46; electronics technician Waldorf Appliance Co., San Diego, 1946-47; jr. civil engr. Calif. Div. Architecture, San Diego, 1947-51; phys. chemist, solid state mgr. Stanford Research Inst., Menlo Park, Calif., 1956-62; prof. chemistry Oreg. State U., Corvallis, 1962-87, prof. chemistry emeritus, from 1988. Rsch. prof. chemistry and materials sci. U. Ala., Huntsville, 1988-94, ret.; vis. acad. Atomic Research Establishment, Harwell, Eng., 1973-74; sr. vis. fellow U. Western Ont. Ctr. Chem. Physics, 1982; cons. in field; faculty advisor Oreg. State U. Flying Club. Contbr. articles to profl. jours. Chmn. Corvallis Airport Commn., 1979-83. Fulbright fellow 1955-56. Mem. AAAS. Am. Assn. Crystal Growth (mem. exec. bd. West Sect. 1976-86), Am. Chem. Soc. (sect. chmn.), Am. Phys. Soc., Materials Research Soc. Democrat. Avocations: flying, fishing, bonzai, golf. Died July 29, 2007.

FREDRICKSEN, CLEVE LAURANCE, farm owner and alpaca breeder, real estateinvestor; b. Bklyn., Nov. 28, 1941; s Cleve John and Harriet (Johnson) F.; m. Beverly Janice Simon, Dec. 28, 1963; children: Cristi Louise, Cleve Matthew. BBA, Bucknell U., 1963. With comml. lending dept. Bankers Trust NYC, 1964-66, investment advisory dept., 1966-68; acct. exec Kidder Peabody, NYC, 1968-71; owner, mgr. Ore Hill Farm, Spottswood, Va., from 1972. Served to E-5 USCGR, 1963-69 Mem. Alpaca Owners and Breeders Assn., Staunton Racque Club. Avocations: tennis, swimming. Died Aug. 20, 2007.

FREDRICKSEN, JOSEPHINE, bank executive; b. Leechburg, Pa., Sept. 6, 1926; d. Steve George and Catherine (Yansky Strapac; m. Robert Leonard Fredricksen, Oct. 12, 1946; children: Robert, William, Janet. Typist 1st Fed. Savs. & Loan NYC, 1945—46; teller Citibank, NYC, 1946—47; teller, head savs. teller, note teller, platform asst. Citizens Nat. Bank Bergenfield, NJ, 1964—72; asst. mgr. to mgr. Midlantic Nat Bank/Citizens, Bergenfield, from 1972. Treas. Salvation Army from 1970, Bergenfield Libr., from 1982; mem. Rep. Com. Bergenfield. Mem.: Bergenfield C. of C. (pres. from 1983) Home: Bergenfield, NJ. Died June 20, 2006.

FREE, JOHN MARTIN, architectural, engineering and planning company executive; b. Melrose, Minn., Oct. 30, 1923; s John V. and Anne (Geyer) F.; m. Rosemary Buman, June 14 1949; children— Wanda Ann, John George (dec.), Linda Jo, Rit Denise, Mary Ruth, James John, Ruth Ann, Paul Lee. BS i Archtl. Engring, Iowa State U., 1949. Diplomate: Registere profl. engr., Iowa, Utah., Registered architect, Conn., Iowa, Ill Kans., Mass., Minn., Mo., Nebr., N.J., N.D., S.D., Tex., Wis Wyo., Singapore. Architect, engr. Leo A. Daly, Omaha, 1949-53 assoc., 1953-60, v.p., 1960-66, sr. v.p., exec. dir. Omaha office 1966-86, mng. dir. Asia, 1970-82, exec. dir. hdqrs. div., 1982-87 corp. dir. ops., 1987-91; retired, 1991. Cons. in field, 1990— project mgr. USAF Acad. Expansion program, 1964-67; mem Internat. Engring. Commn., vice chmn., 1978-82. Bd. dirs Goodwill Industries Nebr., Met. YMCA, Omaha; chmn. adv coun. Coll. Engring. and Architecture, U. Nebr., 1982—; mem engring. adv. coun. Iowa State U., 1978-91, chmn. 1978-79 pres.'s coun. Creighton U.; chmn. UCS of Midlands Adv. Coun Bus. and Industry; trustee Marian High Sch. Served with AUS 1943-45, ETO. Decorated Bronze Star.; Recipient Engr. citatio Iowa State U., 1974 Fellow Royal Australian Inst. Architects Mem. AIA, Nat. Soc. Profl. Engrs., Nat. Council Archt Registration Bds., Architects Registration Council U.K., Neb Cons. Engrs. Assn., Cons. Engrs. Council U.S., Royal Inst. Bri Architects, Nebr. Assn. Commerce and Industry, Omaha Inds Found., Office of Internat. Fin. (dir. 1978-81), Soc. Am. Mi Engrs., Omaha C. of C. (dir. 1969-71, v.p. transp. counc 1977-81, dir. 1981-88) Lodges: K.C. (Omaha) (4 deg.), Rota (Omaha). Republican. Roman Catholic. Home: Omaha, Neb Died Apr. 1, 2006.

FREEARK, ROBERT JAMES, surgeon, educator, heal facility administrator; b. Chgo., May 14, 1927; s. Ray H. ar Lizette (Stauffer) F.; m. Ruth Nelson, June 24, 1950; childre Kris, Kim. BS, Northwestern U., 1949, MD magna cum laud 1952; grad., Oak Ridge Inst. Nuclear Studies, 1953. Diploma Am. Bd. Surgery (dir. 1980-86), Nat. Bd. Med. Examiner Rotating intern, then resident in gen. surgery Cook Coun Hosp., Chgo., 1952-58, dir. surgery, 1958-68, attending phys cian, 1960-70, hosp. dir., 1968-70; research fellow Jerome Solomon Found. Chgo., 1953-54; mem. faculty Northwestern Med. Sch., 1960-70, prof. surgery, 1968-70; prof. surgery, chm dept. Loyola U.-Stritch Sch. Medicine, Maywood, Ill., 1970-9 Surgeon-in-chief Loyola U.-Foster G. McGaw Hosp., 1970-9 prof. emeritus, 1995—; asst. to pres. Loyola U. Health Sys

1995-2002. Served with USMCR, 1945-46. Recipient Outstanding Clin. Prof. award Stritch Sch. Medicine, 1973, Alumni medal Northwestern U., 1980, Stritch medal Loyola U., 1981; named to Navy Pier Hall of Fame, Alumni Assn./U. Ill., Chgo, 1991. Fellow ACS (Surgeons award Nat. Safety Coun. 1987); mem. Am. Assn. Surgery Trauma (pres. 1982), Am. Surg. Assn. (v.p. 1995), AMA, Am. Trauma Soc. (pres. 1982), Central Surg. Assn. (pres. 1980-81), Soc. Internat. de Chirurgie, Soc. Surgery Alimentary Tract, Soc. Surg. Chmn., Soc. Univ. Surgeons, Western Surg. Assn., Ill. Surg. Soc. (pres. 1983-84), Ill. Med. Soc., Midwest Surg. Soc. (pres. 1970), Chgo. Med. Soc., Inst. Medicine Chgo., Chgo. Surg. Soc. (pres. 1984), Alpha Omega Alpha, Omega Beta Pi. Congregationalist. Home: Riverside, Ill. Died Dec. 12, 2006.

FREEDMAN, ALEXANDER ISRAEL, accountant, coin collector and appraiser; b. Boston, Jan. 2, 1916; s. Zax and Ida Ethel (Steinberg) F.; m. Eleanor Rose Gitelmann, Jan. 10, 1943; children— Zachary Roy, Amy Jo. Student, Bentley Coll., 1936-40. C.P.A., Mass. Prin. acctg. firm, Boston, 1945—; coin collector and appraiser. Served to capt. U.S. Army, 1941-46. Mem. Am. Inst. C.P.A.s. Jewish. Home: Brookline, Mass. Died May 28, 2006.

FREELAND, FRANCES JEANNETTE, alcoholism treatment center executive; b. Danville, Ill., Apr. 11, 1938; d. John Terrence and Marie Amber (Iliff) F.; B.S. in Nursing, Coll. Mt. St. Joseph, Cin., 1960; M.S. in Extension Edn., Purdue U., Indpls., 1978, postgrad. in health adminstrn. Staff nurse in premature and critical care nursery Good Samaritan Hosp., Cin., 1960-61; joined Carmelite order, Roman Catholic Ch., 1961, with Carmelite Contemplative Community, Indpls., 1961-71; staff nurse VA Hosp., Indpsl., 1971-72; med./surg. staff nurse St. Francis Hosp., Beech Grove, Ind., 1972-74; dir. alcoholism detoxification unit Salvation Army, Indpls., 1974-79, program dir. Salvation Army Adult Rehab. Center, 1979-85; administrv. asst. Salvation Army Harbor Light Ctr., 1985—; tchr. alcoholism therapy; mem. Ind. Substance Abuse Task Force; v.p. Ind. Free Standing Addiction Agys. Coalition. Bd. dirs., mem. exec. bd. First Step Inc., half-way house for women, Indpls. Recipient award of appreciation Koala Center, Lebanon, Ind., 1978, Salvation Army Territorial Nurse Yr. award, 1984. Mem. Ind. Nurses Soc. on Alcoholism, Nat. Nurses Soc. on Alcoholism (planning com. 1982 Forum). Democrat. Home: Indianapolis, Ind. Died July 4, 2007.

FREEMAN, CLARENCE CALVIN, retired diversified financial services company executive; b. Lancaster, Pa., July 2, 1923; s. Clarence Calvin and Margaret (Hollinger) F.; m. B. Virginia Miller, Aug. 26, 1944; children: Margaret Ann, Elizabeth Ann, Martha Suzanne. AB cum laude, Franklin and Marshall Coll., 1951. Asst. bookkeeper Battery & Brake Service Co., Lancaster, 1941-42; supr. inventory records and receiving Armstrong Cork Co., Lancaster, 1946-48; accountant Internat. Latex Corp., Dover, Del., 1951-52, Ebasco Services, Inc., Holtwood, Pa., 1952-53; office mgr., accountant A.O. Smith Corp., Leola, Pa., 1953-54; office mgr., plant accountant Sybron-Permutit divsn. Lancaster, 1954-57; divsn. controller BCA divsn. Fed. Mogul Corp., Lancaster, 1957-64, controller Southfield, Mich., 1964-74; v.p., controller Addressograph-Multigraph Corp., Cleve., 1974-78; adminstrv. v.p., controller Irvin Industries, Stamford, Conn., 1978-79; v.p. fin. Technical Tape Inc., New Rochelle, NY, 1979-80; v.p. fin., treas., dir. K-D Mfg. Co., Lancaster, 1980-83; CFO C-F Manbeck, Inc., 1984-86; exec. v.p. Sensenich Corp., Lancaster, 1986-90, also bd. dirs.; sr. v.p. fin., CFO Sensenich Propeller Co., Lancaster, 1991-94; ret. Owner acctg. svc., 1953-64, Dairy Queen, 1956-60; lectr. Franklin and Marshall Coll., 1957-58, adj. faculty, 1983-89; lectr. Wayne State Grad. Sch., 1966-67; guest speaker Nat. Assn. Accts. Mem. Oakland County Planning Commn., 1967-68; adviser Jr. Achievement, 1957-58. Served with AUS, 1943-46, PTO. Mem. Nat. Assn. Accountants, Fin. Execs. Inst., Phi Beta Kappa (v.p. Detroit), Pi Gamma Mu. Republican. Presbyterian (elder, deacon). Club: Conestoga Country. Lodges: Masons, Kiwanis, Elks. Home: Elizabethtown, Pa. Died Feb. 19, 2007.

FREEMAN, MARK PRICE, JR., investment company executive; b. Memphis, Dec. 7, 1930; s. Mark Price and Ernestine (Stalons) F.; m. Martha Gene Nash, Oct. 19, 1956; children: Mark Price III, Dal, David, Wynne. BA, La. State U., 1954; postgrad., Harvard, 1968. Cert. fin. planner. Pitcher N.Y. Yankees (and farm clubs), 1951-58, Kansas City Athletics, 1959, Chgo. Cubs, 1960; dist. mgr. Waddell & Reed Inc., Denver, 1960-62; regional mgr. Westamerica Securitie Inc., Denver, 1963-69, exec. v.p., dir., 1969-72, pres., dir., 1972-78; exec. v.p., nat. dir. mktg. Angeles Realty Corp., 1978-87; v.p. mktg. Am. Funds Distbrs., from 1988. Trustee St. Mary's Acad. 1st lt. inf. AUS, 1954-56. Mem. Inst. Cert. Fin. Planners, Denver Country Club, Denver Bronco Quarterback Club (pres. 1961-68), Colo. Harvard Bus. Sch. Club, Rotary, Sigma Chi, Psi Chi. Home: Denver, Colo. Died Feb. 21, 2006.

FREEMAN, MARY LOUISE, state legislator; b. Willmar, Minn., Oct. 21, 1941; d. James Martin and Luella Anna (Backlund) Hawkinson; children: Mark D., Sara L., Cary D., Maret S. BA, Gustavus Adolphus Coll., 1963. Substitute tchr. Arrowhead Edn. Assn., Storm Lake, Iowa, 1982-93; tchr., cons. Midwest Power, Des Moines, 1991-94; mem. Iowa Senate from 5th dist., Des Moines, from 1994. Mem. Iowa State Bd. Health, 1988-94; mem. early childhood intervention com., 1994—, mem. disaster prevention svcs. com., 1994—. Del. alt. Rep. Nat. Conv., Kansas City, 1976; active Midwest-Can. Relations Co., 1994—. Mem. Am. Legis. Exch. Coun., Nat. Coun. State Govts., Buena Vista County Farm Bur., Storm Lake C. of C., Delta Kappa Gamma. Lutheran. Home: Alta, Iowa. Died Sept. 4, 2006.

FREEMAN, RAYMOND SAVAGEAU, pediatrician; b. Denver, Nov. 17, 1920; s. William Bradly and Gertrude Eda (Savageau) F.; m. Babette Hartzel Stiefel, Apr. 20, 1961; children— William B., Gary Stiefel, Raymond S., Scott Dana, Peter Alexis BA, Yale U., 1943; MD, U. Colo., 1950. Diplomate Am. Bd. Pediatrics. Practice medicine specializing in pediatrics, Denver, 1953-59; practice medicine specializing in pediatrics Salina, Kans., from 1959; pediatrician Mowery Clinic, Salina, 1959-84. Pres. med. staff Asbury Hosp., Salina, 1968; health officer Saline County, 1965-70 Fellow Am. Acad. Pediatrics; mem. Kans. Med. Soc., Saline County Med. Soc. (pres. 1976) Republican. Episcopalian. Died June 4, 2006.

FREESE, ROBERT GERARD, financial executive; b. NYC, Oct. 6, 1929; s. Sylvester V. and Helen (Haverty) F.; m. Joan Anne Walsh, Sept. 6, 1952; children— Bernadette Freese Pavlis, Maryellen, John M. BBA, Manhattan Coll., 1951; MBA, NYU, 1953. Internal auditor Texaco, Inc., NYC, 1951-56; various fin. mgmt. positions Grumman Corp., Bethpage, N.Y., 1956-72, treas., from 1972, v.p., 1974-80, sr. v.p. fin., 1980-86, vice chmn. fin., from 1986, also bd. dirs. Regional dir. The Bank of N.Y.; trustee Roslyn Savs. Bank; chmn. bd. Paumanock Ins. Co.; chmn. bd., pres. Grumman Fgn. Sales Corp.; bd. dirs. Grumman Corp., Grumman Houston Corp., Grumman St. Augustine, Grumman Tech. Svcs., Grumman Allied Industries, Inc., Grumman Emergency Products, Grumman Credit Corp., Grumman Internat., Grumman Ventures, Grumman Aerospace Corp., Grumman Data Systems Corp., Farmhouse Dining Svcs., Inc., Calldata Systems Inc., others. With U.S. Army, 1953-55. Mem. L.I. Assn. Commerce and Industry (dir.), Pocono Farms Country Club, Indian Hills Country Club. Died May 17, 2006.

FREEZE, JAMES DONALD, clergyman, retired academic administrator; b. Balt., Sept. 15, 1932; s. Frank Leo and Helen Angela (Sweeney) F. AB, Boston Coll., 1956, MA, 1957; S.T.L., U. Innsbruck, Austria, 1964. Joined S.J., Roman Catholic Ch., 1950, ordained priest, 1963; mem. faculty dept. philosophy Wheeling (W.Va.) Coll., 1965-70, chmn. dept., 1967-70; asst. dean Coll. Arts and Scis., Georgetown U., Washington, 1971-74, asst. v.p. for acad. affairs, 1974-79, exec. v.p., provost, 1979-91; dir. Loyola Retreat House, Faulkner, Md., 1992-97; v.p., treas. Corp. Roman Cath. Clergyman, Balt., 1997—2002. Trustee Georgetown Prep. Sch., Rockville, Md., 1975-79, chmn. bd., 1978-79; trustee Loyola Coll., Balt., 1982-88, U. Detroit, 1983-90, Fairfield U., 1990-96, Manresa Retreat House, Staten Island, N.Y., 1997-98. Died Dec. 10, 2006.

FREIDSON, ELIOT LAZARUS, sociologist, educator; b. Boston, Feb. 20, 1923; s. Joseph and Grace (Backer) F.; m. Helen Emery Giambruni, Apr. 21, 1976; children by previous marriages— Jane Beatrice, Oliver Eliot (dec.), Matthew Aaron. Student, U. Maine, 1941-42; Ph.B., U. Chgo., 1947, MA, 1950, PhD, 1952; MA, St. John's Coll., (Eng.), 1979. Postdoctoral fellow U. Ill., 1952-54; asst. prof. sociology City Coll. N.Y., 1956-61, assoc. prof. sociology, 1961—64, prof. sociology, 1964—93; mem. faculty N.Y.U., 1961—93, prof. sociology, 1963—93, head dept. sociology, 1975-78; dir. études associé École des Hautes Études en Sci. Sociales, Paris, 1978, 87; Pitt prof. Am. history and instns. Cambridge (Eng.) U., 1979-80. Cons. in field, 1956—2005; Adviser div. research grants NIH, 1963-66; adviser joint research program Social Security Adminstrn. and Social Rehab. Service, HEW, 1968-70; fellow Center Advanced Study in Behavioral Scis., 1974-75; Eastern Sociol. Assn. Falk Fund lectr., 1976; mem. Pres.'s Commn. on Mental Health, 1977-78; mem. Commn. Professionalism ABA, 1985-86 Author: Patient's Views Medical Practice, 1961, Profession of Medicine, 1970, Professional Dominance, 1970, Doctoring Together, 1976, Professional Powers, 1986, Medical Work in America, 1989, also articles.; Editor: Student Government, Student Leaders and American Colleges, 1955, Hospital in Modern Society, 1963, Jour. Health and Social Behavior, 1966-69, The Professions And Their Prospects, 1973; Co-editor: Med. Men and Their Work, 1972. Served with inf. AUS, 1943-46, ETO. Decorated Bronze Star; Guggenheim fellow, 1981-82 Fellow Am. Sociol. Assn. (chmn. med. sociol. sect. 1963-64, Sorokin award 1972), AAAS; mem. Soc. Study Social Problems, Eastern Sociol. Soc. (pres. 1986), AAUP, Internat. Sociol. Assn. (pres. com. research med. sociology 1967-70), Inst. Medicine, Nat. Acad. Sci. Died Dec. 14, 2005.

FREMONT, WALTER GILBERT, university dean; b. Terre Haute, Ind., July 20, 1924; s. Walter G. and Muriel Margarette (Carson) F., Sr.; m. Gertrude M. Reed, Aug. 12, 1947; children— Gail Marlene Fremont Berger, Elaine Marie, Walter G., III. B.S., U. Dayton, 1949; M.S., U. Wis.-Madison, 1950; Ed.D., Pa. State U., 1961; L.H.D. (hon.), Hyles-Anderson Coll., Hammond, Ind., 1977. Prof. edn. Bob Jones U., Greenville, S.C., 1950-53, dean Sch. Edn., 1953-90, dean emeritus, 1990—. Co-author: Formula for Family Unity, 1980; Forming a New Generation, 1990, Preparing the Christian for the 21st Century. Served to lt. U.S. Army, 1943-46, ETO. Mem. exec. bd. Gospel Fellowship Assn., Greenville, 1962—; speaker family seminars, 1964—; bd. dirs. Children's Gospel clubs, Greenville, 1961—, Wilds Camp and Conf., Brevard, N.C., 1969—. Mem. NEA (life), S.C. Assn. Coll. Tchrs. Edn. (pres. 1960-61), S.C. Adv. Council Tchrs. Edn., S.C. Assn. Student Teaching (pres. 1959-60). Republican. Baptist. Home: Greenville, SC. Died Jan. 7, 2007.

FRENCH, JOSEPH FRANK, professional society administrator; b. NYC, July 14, 1925; s. Joseph William and Anna (Vrba) F.; m. Doris Condon. Grad. in bus. sci., Hofstra U. Retired dir. of econ. devel. N.Y. Telephone, NYC; now pres. Bklyn. C. of C. Sr. v.p. Long Beach (N.Y.) Hosp., 1975—; regent St. Francis Coll., Bklyn., 1984—. Bd. dirs. Greater N.Y. YMCA, 1981—. Served with USMC, 1941-45. Mem. Am. Arbitration Assn., Nassau, Suffolk County Mini Pub. Employee Relations Bur. Lodges: Elks. Avocations: golf, fishing. Home: Long Beach, NY. Died Feb. 12, 2007.

FREUDENSTEIN, FERDINAND, mechanical engineering educator; b. Frankfurt, Germany, May 12, 1926; came to U.S., 1942, naturalized, 1945; s. George Gerson and Charlotte (Rosenberg) F.; m. Leah Schwarzschild, July 5, 1959 (dec. May 1970); children: David George, Joan Merle; m. Lydia Gersten, 1980. Student, N.Y.U., 1942-44; MS, Harvard U., 1948; PhD, Columbia U., 1954. Devel. engr. instrument div. Am. Optical Co., 1948-50; mem. tech. staff Bell Telephone Labs., 1954; mem. faculty Columbia U., 1954-96, chmn. dept., 1958-64, prof. mech. engring., from 1959, Stevens prof. mech. engring., from 1981, Eugene Higgins prof. mech. engring., 1985-96, Eugene Higgins prof. emeritus mech. engring., from 1996. Cons. to industry, 1954—. Served inf. AUS, 1944-46. Recipient Gt. Tchr. award Soc. Older Grads., Columbia U., 1966, Applied Mechanisms Conf. award, 1989, Egleston medal for disting. engring. achievement, 1992; Guggenheim fellow, 1961-62, 67-68; guest of honor at conf. Tribute to Work of Ferdinand Freudenstein, Brainard, Minn., 1991. Fellow ASME (hon. life 1992, Jr. award 1955, Machine Design award 1972, Mechanisms com. award 1978, Charles Russ Richards Meml. award 1984), N.Y. Acad. Scis.; mem. Harvard Soc. Engrs. and Scientists, Columbia Engring. Soc., Nat. Acad. Engring., Verein Deutscher Ingenieure (hon.), Sigma Xi. Achievements include research in kinematics, dynamics, mechanisms, engring. design. Home: Bronx, NY. Died Mar. 30, 2006.

FREY, GERARD LOUIS, retired bishop; b. New Orleans, May 10, 1914; s. Andrew and Marie Therese (DeRose) F. DD, St. Joseph's Sem. Coll., St. Benedict, La., 1933; student, Notre Dame Sem., New Orleans. Ordained priest Roman Cath. Ch., 1938; asst. pastor Taft, La., 1938-46; asst. dir. (Confraternity Christian Doctrine, Archdiocese New Orleans); also asst. (St. James Ch.), New Olreans, 1946; dir. (Confraternity Christian Doctrine), Archdiocese New Orleans, 1946-67; also in residence Archdiocese New Orleans (St. Leo the Great Parish), 1946-54; founding pastor (St. Frances Cabrini Ch.), New Orleans, 1952-63; pastor (St. Frances de Sales Parish), Houma, La., 1963-67; clergy rep. 2d Vatican Council, 1964; dir. Diocesan Friendship Corps, New Orleans, 1966; bishop of Savannah Ga., 1967-72; bishop of Lafayette La., 1972-89; retired, from 1989. Episcopal moderator Theresians Am., 1968—. Recipient Bishop Tracy Vocation award St. Joseph's Sem. Alumni Assn., 1959. Home: Carencro, La. Died Aug. 16, 2007.

FRICKE, EDWIN FRANCIS, nuclear engineer; b. Mackay, Idaho, July 25, 1910; s. William Henry and Blache Myrtle (Ewing) F.; B.S., U. Idaho, 1935; M.A., U. Calif. at Los Angeles, 1937, Ph.D., 1940; m. Harriet Harmon Gronbeck, Dec. 26, 1942; children— Kathleen, William, Robert, Karen, Edwin, Jr., Kathleen (Mrs. Clifford Wainman), Karen (Mrs. Allen Penrod). Design engr. Stone & Webster, Boston, 1940-43; engr. Manhattan project, N.Y.C., 1943-45; physicist Republic Aviation Corp., Farmingdale, N.Y., 1946-49, sr. devel. engr., chief nuclear analysis, 1959-65; sr. scientist Argonne (Ill.) Nat. Lab., 1950-56; sr. nuclear physicist ACF Industries, Washington; research scientist Bell Aerosystems, Buffalo, 1965-66; sr. engr. Sanders Assocs., Nashua, N.H., 1967-68; prin. engr. Jackson Moreland, Boston, 1968-70; engr. Stone & Webster Boston, 1973-78, now ret. Instr. physics St. Francis Coll., Biddeford, Me., 1970-71. Pres. Downers Grove (Ill.) Orch. Soc., 1954-55. Will Rogers fellow. U. Calif. at Los Angeles, 1939-40. Registered profl. engr., Mass., N.H. Mem. Am. Nuclear Soc., Am. Chem. Soc., AAAS, Ill. Acad. Sci., N.Y. Acad. Sci., Research Soc. Am., Sigma Xi, Phi Delta Chi. Contbr. articles to profl. jours. Home: Merrimack, NH. Died Sept. 7, 2006.

FRIDLEY, ROBERT BRUCE, agricultural engineer, educator; b. Burns, Oreg., June 6, 1934; s. Gerald Wayne and Gladys Winona (Smith) Fridley; m. Jean Marie Griggs, June 12, 1955; children: James Lee, Michael Wayne, Kenneth Jon. BSME, U. Calif., Berkeley, 1956; MS in Agrl. Engring., U. Calif., Davis, 1960; PhD in Agrl. Engring., Mich. State U., East Lansing, 1973; D (hon.), U. Poly., Madrid, 1988. Asst. specialist U. Calif., Davis, 1956-60, prof. agrl. engring., 1961-78, 1985—94, prof. emeritus, from 1994, acting assoc. dean engring., 1972, chmn. dept. agrl. engring., 1974-76, dir. aquaculture and fisheries program, 1985-89, exec. assoc. dean agrl. and environ. scis., 1989-94; dept. mgr. R & D Weyerhaeuser Co., Tacoma, 1977-85. Vis. prof. Mich. State U., East Lansing, 1970—71; NATO vis. prof. U. Bologna, 1975; bd. agrl. and natural resources NRC, 2000—02. Co-author: (book) Principles and Practices for Harvesting and Handling Fruits and Nuts, 1973; contbr. articles to profl. jours. Recipient Charles G. Woodbury award, Am. Soc. Hort. Sci., 1966, Alumni citation, Calif. Aggie Alumni Assn., 1990, 2005. Fellow: Am. Soc. Agrl. Engrs. (v.p. Found. 1989—93, pres. Found. 1993—96, pres. 1997—98, Young Rschrs. award 1971, Concept of the Yr. award 1976, Outstanding Paper award 1966, 1968, 1969, 1976, 1986, Disting. Svc. award 1988, 1997, 1999); mem.: NAE. Achievements include patents in field. Home: El Macero, Calif. Died Mar. 19, 2006.

FRIEDENBERG, DAVID, banker; b. Balt., June 15, 1934; s. Charles and Rose (Selenkow) F.; m. Georgeanne Lindquist, May 24, 1969 BS, Pa. State U., 1956; MBA, NYU, 1970. Vice pres. Mfrs. Hanover Trust Co., NYC, 1963-73; sr. v.p., mgr. Seafirst Bank, Seattle, from 1973. Dir. Seattle Pub. TV Bd. dirs. Northwest Kidney Ctr., Seattle, Seattle Symphony, Seattle Art Mus., Bob Hope Heart Inst., Seattle; bd. dirs., past pres. Poncho Mem. Robert Morris Assocs. Home: Bellevue, Wash. Died May 26, 2007.

FRIEDLANDER, SHELDON KAY, chemical engineering professor; b. NYC, Nov. 17, 1927; s. Irving and Rose (Katzewitz) F.; m. Marjorie Ellen Robbins, Apr. 16, 1934; children: Eva Kay, Amelie Elise, Antonia Zoe, Josiah. BS, Columbia U., 1949; SM, MIT, 1951; PhD, U. Ill., 1954. Asst. prof. chem. engring. Columbia U., NYC, 1954-57, Johns Hopkins U., Balt., 1957-59, assoc. prof. chem. engring., 1959-62, prof. chem. engring., 1962-64; prof. chem. engring., environ. health engring. Calif. Inst. Tech., Pasadena, 1964-78; prof. chem. engring. UCLA, 1978—2007, Parsons prof., 1982—2007, chmn. dept. chem. engring., 1984-88, chmn. steering com. Ctr. for Clean Tech., 1989-92. Chmn. EPA Clean Air Sci. Adv. Com., 1978-82. Author: Smoke, Dust, and Haze: Fundamentals of Aerosol Dynamics, 2nd edit., 2000. Served with U.S. Army, 1946-47. Recipient Sr. Humboldt prize Fed. Republic of Germany, 1985, Internat. prize Am. Assn. for Aerosol Rsch./Gesellschaft für Aerosolforschung/Japan Assn. for Aerosol Sci. and Tech., Fuchs Meml. award, 1990, Christian Junge award European Aerosol Assn., 2000, Aurel Stodola medal Swiss Fed. Inst. Tech., Zurich, 2004; Fulbright scholar, 1960-61; Guggenheim fellow, 1969-70. Mem.: AIChE (Colburn award 1959, Alpha Chi Sigma award 1974, Walker award 1979, Lawrence K. Cecil award in environ. chem. engring. 1995, Particle Tech. Forum Lifetime Achievement award 2001), NAE, Am. Assn. for Aerosol Rsch. (pres. 1984—86). Home: Pacific Palisades, Calif. Died Feb. 9, 2007.

FRIEDMAN, ALBERT BARRON, retired literature and language professor; b. Kansas City, Mo., Aug. 16, 1920; s. Jay and Edith (Barron) F. BA, U. Mo., 1941; MA, Harvard U., 1942, PhD, 1952. Instr. Harvard U., 1952-55, asst. prof., 1955-60; assoc. prof. Claremont (Calif.) Grad. Sch., 1960-62, prof., 1962-69, W.S. Rosecrans prof., 1969—88, prof. emeritus, 1988—2006. Rsch. assoc. Folklore and Mythology Ctr., UCLA. Author: Folk Ballads, 1956, The Ballad Revival, 1961, Ywain and Gawain, 1964, Creativity in Graduate Education, 1964, The Usable Myth, 1970, Myth and Ideology, 1976; Asso. editor: Jour. Am. Folklore, 1958-63; editor: Western Folklore, 1966-70, Pacific Coast Philology, 1983-86; contbr. articles to profl. jours. Served to capt. AUS, 1942-46. Decorated Legion of Merit, Silver Star, Order of George I, Order of Phoenix Greece, Kaisar-i-Hind India; recipient Internat. Folklore Soc. 1st prize, 1961; Guggenheim fellow, 1957-58, 65-66; Nat. Endowment Sr. fellow, 1971 Fellow Am. Folklore Soc. (life), mem., Mediaeval Acad. Am., Mediaeval Assn. (v.p.), English Inst. (supr. 1964-67), Calif. Folklore Soc. (v.p. 1965, 73), Modern Lang. Assn. (chmn. comparative lit. 1960, 68, Arthurian lit. 1971, Medieval lit. 1972), Philol. Soc. (pres. 1982-83) Home: Los Angeles, Calif. Died Nov. 11, 2006.

FRIEDMAN, ALVIN EDWARD, brokerage house executive; b. NYC, Aug. 8, 1919; s. Harry and Frances (Levin) F.; m. Pesselle Rothenberg, Feb. 2, 1943; children: Jeffrey F., Joan M. BBA, CCNY, 1942; MBA, NYU, 1949. Ptnr. Kuhn Loeb & Co., NYC, 1951-78; sr. mng. dir. Lehmann Bros. Kuhn Loeb, NYC, 1978-84; dir. Dillon Read & Co., NYC, 1984-86, sr. advisor, from 1986. Bd. dirs. Dreyfus Corp., Avnet, Inc. Pres. Hebrew Arts Sch., N.Y. Served to 1st lt. USAAF, 1943-46, PTO. Home: New York, NY. Died Oct. 15, 2005.

FRIEDMAN, SYLVAN HAROLD, author, publisher; b. Chgo., July 9, 1918; s. Meyer and Rebecca Beatrice (Finkel) F.; m. Sara Robbin, June 18, 1939 (dec. Aug. 1964); children: David, Robert, Barbara; m. Mary Marjorie Peck Steinberg, July 31, 1966; stepchildren: Michael, Martha. Grad. high sch., Chgo. Gen. mgr. Leterstone Sales Co., Chgo., 1936-47; owner, operator Am. Bearing Co., Chgo., 1947-49, Mpls., 1953-66; sales mgr. Am. Ball Bearing Corp., Bklyn., 1949-50, United Bearing Co., Mpls., 1950-53; owner, operator Interchange Inc., St. Louis Park, Minn., from 1966, also bd. dirs. Cons. in field, Mpls., 1966-74. Author/pub. (cross-reference guides) Internat. Bearing Interchange, 1966, Internat. Seal Interchange, 1975, Internat. Drive Belt Interchange, 1979, Internat. Drive Line Interchange, 1986, Internat. Filter Interchange, 1989, Internat. Drum & Rotor Interchange, 1989. Bd. dirs. Big Bros. Inc., Mpls., 1951-65; vol. Amicus, Mpls., 1966-74; pres. Crossroads, Mpls., 1984. Served with USAR, 1944-46. Democrat. Jewish. Avocations: travel, photo albums, radio and tv talk shows. Home: Minneapolis, Minn. Died Jan. 12, 2006.

FRIEDMANN, E(MERICH) IMRE, biologist, educator; b. Budapest, Hungary, Dec. 20, 1921; arrived in U.S., 1965; s. Hugo and Gisella (Singer) Friedmann; m. Roseli Ocampo, July 22, 1974; 1 child, Daphna. BS Sch. Agriculture, Hungary, 1943, MS Sch. Agriculture, 1944, postgrad. U. Debrecen, 1948; PhD in Botany, Zoology, U. Vienna, 1951. Instr., lectr. Hebrew U., Jerusalem, 1952-66; assoc. prof. Queens U., Kingston, Ont., Canada, 1967-68, Fla. State U., Tallahassee, 1968-76, prof., 1976—2001, Robert Lawton Disting. prof., 1991—2001, dir. Polar Desert Rsch. Ctr., 1985—2001; sr. NRC rsch. fellow NASA Ames Rsch. Ctr., Moffett Field, Calif., from 2001; vis. prof. U. Wash., Seattle, from 2005. Concurrent prof. Nanjing U., People's Republic of China, 1987—; vis. prof. Fla. State U., Tallahassee, 1966-67, U. Vienna, 1975, U. Wash., 2005-; disting. sr. vis. scientist Jet Propulsion Lab., 1999-2000. Editor Antarctic Microbiology, 1993; contbr. articles to profl. jours. Recipient Congl. Antarctic Svc. medal NSF, 1979, Alexander von Humboldt award, 1987, resolution of commendation Gov. of Fla., 1978, Bergey's medal Bergey's Manual Trust, 2001. Fellow: AAAS, Am. Acad. Microbiology, Am. Soc. Microbiology (Procter and Gamble award in environ. microbiology 1998), Royal Microsci. Soc., Linnean Soc. London, Exploreres Club; mem.: Internat. Soc. Study of Origins of Life, Soc. Phycol. France, Hungarian Algological Soc. (hon.), Internat. Phycol. Soc., Am. Phycol. Soc. (award of Excellence 2002), Indian Phycol. Soc., Brit. Phycol. Soc., Hungarian Acad. Scis. (fgn.). Jewish. Achievements include co-discovery of micro-organisms (cryptoendolithic lichens) living in Antarctic rocks, 1976; discovery of fossil bacteria in the Martian meteorite ALH 84001, 2001. Home: Kirkland, Wash. Died June 11, 2007.

FRIEND, ROBERT NATHAN, financial counselor, economist, market technician; b. Chgo., Feb. 2, 1930; s. Karl D. and Marion (Wollenberger) Friend; m. Lee Baer, Aug. 12, 1979; children: Karen, Alan. AB, Grinnell Coll., 1951; MS, Ill. Inst. Tech., 1953. Cert. fin. counselor. With K. Friend & Co., Chgo., from 1953, v.p., from early 60s, 1st v.p., from 1964, dir. merger activities with Standard Oil Co. Ind., from 1958, trustee employee's benefit trust, from 1968. Active Friend Fin. Svcs.; admissions cons. Grinnell Coll., Ill. Inst. Tech., Chgo., 1968—70. Dir. State Astor Lake Shore Assn.; bd. dirs. Nat. Anorexia Nervosa and Associated Disorders Assn. Fellow: AIC (life), Acad. Polit. Sci., Market Technicians Assn., Ea. Fin. Assn., Am. Econ. Assn., Acad. Internat. Bus., Am. Acad. Polit. and Social Sci., Southwestern Fin. Assn., So. Finance Assn., Chgo. Coun. Fgn. Rels., Am. Assn. Individual Investors, Phi Kappa Phi; mem.: Sarah Siddons Soc., Seed Savers Exch., Renaissance Soc., Vintage Soc., Yale Club, Carlton Club. Died May 8, 2006.

FRIENDLY, ED, television producer; b. NYC, Apr. 8, 1922; s. Edwin S. and Henrietta (Steinmeier) F.; m. Natalie Coulson Brooks, Jan. 31, 1952 (dec. May 9, 2002); children: Brooke Friendly, Edwin S. III; m. Paula Reddish Zinnemann, Nov. 27, 2003. Grad., Manlius Sch., 1941. Radio exec., dir. BBD&O, NYC, 1946-49; sales exec. ABC-TV, NYC, 1949-53; ind. prodr. & packager NYC, 1953-56; prodr., program exec. CBS-TV, NYC, 1956-59; v.p. spl. programs NBC-TV, NYC, 1959-67; pres., founding mem. Ed Friendly Prodns., Los Angeles, 1967—2007. Co-chmn. steering com. Caucus for Producers, Writers and Dirs. Exec. prodr.: (TV series) Laugh-In, 1968—73, NBC Little House on the Prairie, 1974—83; prodr.: (films) Peter Lundy and the Medicine Hat Stallion (Emmy nomination), Young Pioneers, (miniseries) Backstairs at the White House (11 Emmy nominations), (motion pictures and TV spls.); exec. prodr./prodr. Barbara Cartland's The Flame is Love, 2005. Served to capt., U.S. Army, 1942-45, PTO. Recipient Spl. award Internat. Film and TV Festival N.Y., 1967; Emmy award for Laugh-In, 1968; Producer of Yr. award Producers Guild of Am., 1968; Golden Globe award Hollywood Fgn. Press, 1968; Gold medal of honor Internat. Radio and TV Soc., 1970; Christopher award for motion picture, 1975; Western Heritage award Nat. Cowboy Hall of Fame and Western Heritage Center, for Little House on the Prairie, 1975, for Peter Lundy and the Medicine Hat Stallion, 1978; Scout awards for best weekly series and show of yr. for Laugh-In, 1969 Mem. Calif. Horsemen's Benevolent and Protective Assn. (pres. 1994, former mem. bd. dirs.), Thoroughbred Owners Calif. (founder, pres., chmn. 1993-96, chmn. 1996-97, bd. dirs. 1993-2000), Nat. Thoroughbred Assn. (vice chmn., bd. dirs. 1996-98, founding mem.), Nat. Thoroughbred Racing Assn. (bd. dirs. 1997-99). Home: Rancho Santa Fe, Calif. Died June 17, 2007.

FRITZ, JOHN WAYNE, government executive, lawyer; b. Winston-Salem, NC, Aug. 27, 1948; s. Eugene and Ethel Jennette (Snow) F.; m. Mary Kristine Hansen, May 31, 1969 (div. 1981); m. Carolyn Jane Woodcock, Sept. 11, 1982. BS, S.D. State U., 1970; JD, U. Minn., 1973. Bar: Minn. 1973, U.S. Dist. Ct. Minn. 1975. Atty. 3M Co., St. Paul, 1973-76, div. atty., 1976-81, sr. atty., 1981; dep. asst. sec. Dept. Interior, Washington, 1981-85, cons. to undersec., from 1985. Dir. Minn. Bd. Law Examinters, 1978-84, Minn. Bd. Adv. Com., 1979-84 Bd. dirs. A. Indian Lawyer Tng. Program, Oakland, Calif. Served to 1st lt. U.S. Army, 1973. Am. Indian Law Ctr. scholar, 1970-73 Mem. ABA, Minn. Bar Assn., Am. Legion, Assn. Old Crows Clubs: St. Paul Pool and Yacht (Lilydale, Minn.). Republican. Presbyterian. Home: Wayzata, Minn. Died Mar. 29, 2006.

FROMM, PAUL OLIVER, physiology educator; b. Ramsey, Ill., Dec. 2, 1923; s. August Moltke and Edith Marie (Wollerman) F.; m. Mary Magdalene Shaw, June 15, 1947; children: David, Emily. BS, U. Ill., 1949, MS, 1951, PhD, 1954. Instr. dept. physiology Mich. State U., East Lansing, 1954-58, asst. prof., 1958-62, assoc. prof., 1962-65, prof., 1965-87, prof. emeritus, from 1987. Cons. U.S.-Can. Great Lakes Commn., Windsor, Ont., Can., 1981, Nat. Research Council Can., 1983 Contbr. articles to profl. jours. Served with USMC, 1943-46 Fulbright rsch. scholar Musée Oceanographique Monaco, 1963-64. Mem. N.Am. Benthological Soc. (pres. 1958), Am. Soc. Zoologists, Am. Physiol. Soc., Soc. Exptl. Biology and Medicine Died Feb. 16, 2007.

FROWICK, ROBERT HOLMES, retired diplomat; b. Des Moines, Iowa, Dec. 12, 1929; s. James E. and Hallie M. (Holmes) F.; children: R. Bren, George, Lesley, Brook; m. Ann Louise Powell, Aug. 18, 1975; stepchildren: Kristen, Kirk. BA, Ind. U., 1953, MA, 1957, Yale U., 1959. Vice consul, Montreal, Que., Can., 1960-62; 2d sec. Am. Embassy, Bucharest, Romania, 1964-66, 1st sec. Paris, 1969-73, dep. chief of mission Prague, Czechoslavakia, 1976-79, charge d'affaires, 1978-79, polit. counselor Rome, 1979-82; polit advisor U.S. Mission to NATO, Brussels, 1982-86; amb., dep. chmn. U.S. del. to Vienna meeting of Conf. on Security and Cooperation in Europe (CSCE), 1986-89, amb., dep. chmn. U.S. del. to negotiations on confidence and security bldg. measures Vienna, 1989; amb., exec. sec. N.Y. ministerial meeting to prepare Paris summit Conf. on Security and Cooperation in Europe, 1990, del. to Paris Summit, 1990; amb., head of CSCE Monitor Mission to Macedonia, 1992; exec. sec. Search for Common Ground in Macedonia, 1993-94; amb., head of U.S. del. to CSCE seminar on Early Warning Warsaw, Poland, 1994; amb. head of OSCE Mission to Bosnia and Herzogonia, from 1995; amb. head of U.S. del. to OSCE seminar on the human dimension Warsaw, 1998; amb. Dept. of State coord.for NATO 50th Anniversary Summit, 1998-99; amb. Charge d'Affaires Am. Embassey Tirana, 1999; amb. deputy special advisor to President and Secretary of State for Dayton implementation, 1999-2000; amb. personal rep. of OSCE chmn-in-office for situation Macedonia, 2001. Vis. scholar Stanford U., 1989-95; mem. adv. bd. Dean of Coll. of Arts and Scis. Ind. U., 1993—. Contbr. articles on fgn. affairs to jours. Trustee St. Steven's Sch., Rome, 1979-82; chmn. sch. bd. Internat. Sch. of Prague, 1976-79. Served to 1st lt. USAF, 1953-56, to capt. USAFR. Recipient Nat. Def. Svc. medal, 1956, Superior Honor award Dept. State, 1963, 68, 75, 86, 89, Masaryk award Czechoslovak Nat. Coun. of Am., 1988, Disting. Alumni Svc. award Ind. U., 1998; Disting. Citizen fellow Ind. U. Inst. Advanced Study, 1993, Order of Njegos Pres. Plavsic, Republic Srpska, 1997. Home: Santa Rosa, Calif. Died Jan. 17, 2007.

FRUTON, JOSEPH STEWART, retired biochemist; b. Czestochowa, Poland, May 14, 1912; s. Charles and Ella (Eisenstadt) F.; m. Sofia Simmonds, Jan. 29, 1936. BA, Columbia U., 1931, PhD, 1934; MA (hon.), Yale U., 1950; D.Sc. (hon.), Rockefeller U., 1976. Asst. in chemistry Rockefeller Inst. for Med. Research, 1934-38, assoc., 1938-45; faculty Yale U., from 1945, successively assoc. prof. physiol. chemistry, prof. biochemistry, 1951-57, Eugene Higgins prof. biochemistry, 1957-82, prof. emeritus, from 1982, prof. history of medicine, 1980-82, prof. emeritus, from 1982, chmn. dept. biochemistry, 1951-67, dir. div. sci., 1959- 62. Spl. fellow Rockefeller Found., 1948, Commonwealth Fund, 1962-63, Guggenheim Found., 1983-84; mem. div. chemistry and chem. tech. NRC, 1950-52, chem. biol. coordination center, 1946-51, fellowship bd., 1951-53, 55-58, panel on enzymes, chmn. com. on growth, 1946-49, exec. com., div. med. scis., 1961-64; sci. advisor NIH, 1951-52, Anna Fuller Fund, 1951-72; vis. prof. Rockefeller U., 1969 Author: Molecules and Life, 1972, Selected Bibliography of Biographical Data for the History of Biochemistry Since 1800, 1974, 2d edit., 1977, A Bio-Bibliography for the History of the Biochemical Sciences, 1982, supplement, 1985, 2d edit. 1995, Contrasts in Scientific Style, 1990, A Skeptical Biochemist, 1992, Eighty Years, 1994; co-author: (with S. Simmonds) General Biochemistry, 1953, 2d edit., 1958; Mem. editorial bd.: Jour. Biol. Chemistry, 1948-58, Biochemistry, 1962-72. Exec. sec. presdl. search com. Yale U., 1985-86 Recipient Lilly Award in biol. chemistry, 1944; Benjamin Franklin fellow Royal Soc. Arts. Fellow AAAS; mem. Internat. Commn. Biochem. Nomenclature, Am. Soc. Biol. Chems. (mem. council 1959-62), Am. Chem. Soc. (Dexter award 1993), Chem. Soc. Gt. Britain, Biochem. Soc. (Gt. Britain), Harvey Soc., N.Y. Acad. Sci., History Sci. Soc. (council 1951-54, Pfizer award 1973, Sarton lectr. 1976), Am. Philos. Soc. (council 1972-74, 78-81, John Frederick Lewis award 1990), Nat. Acad. Sci., Am. Acad. Arts and Sci., Sigma Xi, Phi Beta Kappa. Home: New Haven, Conn. Died July 29, 2007.

FRY, DORIS HENDRICKS, museum curator; b. Bristol, Pa., Jan. 20, 1918; d. John Reading and Mary Cordelia (Mariner) Hendricks; m. Wayne Franklin Fry, Aug. 30, 1944; children: Christine Mariner Bode, David Whiteley, Janet Margaret. Student, Temple U. Sch. Music, 1936-40. Cert. tchr. Hist. Soc. Early Am. Decoration, Inc. Art tchr. home studio, Delmar, N.Y., from 1957; art tchr. The Arts Ctr., Albany, N.Y., 1972-76, Albany Inst. History and Art, 1972-76; tchr. Mus. Hist. Soc. Early Am. Decoration, Albany, 1982-90, dir., curator, 1981-88; trustee Hist. Soc. Early Am. Decoration, Albany, 1976-86; dir. Sch. Mus. Hist. Soc. Early Am. Decoration, Albany, 1979-81, chmn. tchr. cert. com., 1979-80. Class coordinator Albany Inst. History and Art, 1972-76; lectr. Hitchcock Mus., Conn., Conn. Valley Mus., Mass., 1981-82, N.Y. State Mus. Contbr. articles to profl. jours. and popular mags. Recipient awards Hist. Soc. Early Am. Decoration, including Disting. Service award, 1986, Pres.'s award, 1989. Mem. PEO. Died Nov. 29, 2005.

FRY, HARRY WELLMAN, tool company executive; b. Bozeman, Mont., Mar. 22, 1932; s. William Everett and Naida Olive (Wellman) F.; m. Keige Allaire Mosby, Sept. 11, 1954; children: Ronald S., Valerie N. Student, U. Mont., 1953; BS in Indsl. Engring., Mont. State U., 1955. Engr. phys. distbn. Dow Chem Co., Midland, Mich., 1955-62, div. mgr. distbn. and traffic Cleve., 1962-65; mgr. distbn. ctr. Mattel Toy Co., Holmdel, N.J., 1965; dir. phys. distbn. Snap-On Tools Corp., Ottawa, Ill. 1966-70, dir. phys. distbn. and info. services Kenosha, Wis., 1970-73, v.p. phys. distbn. and info. services, 1973-79, v.p. adminstrn., 1980-81, sr. v.p. adminstrn., 1981-90; ret., 1990. Bd. dirs. 1st Fin. Assn., Inc., Kenosha, 1st Nat. Bank, Kenosha; bd. bus. advisors U. Wis., Parkside. Pres., v.p., bd. dirs. United Way Kenosha, 1973-80; bd. dirs. Pvt. Industry Coun. Southeastern Wis., Kenosha, 1983-90, chmn., 1990, chmn. exec. com. 1982-90; pres., chmn. exec. com., bd. dirs. Kenosha Area Devel Corp., 1987-92; mem. County Blue Ribbon com., county wide assessment, County Task Force Econ. Devel.; mem. South Por Lakeshore Devel. Com.; chmn. Great Lakes Composites Consortium Inc., 1989-90; chmn. response com. Navy Ctr. Excellence For Composites Mfg. Tech., 1989-90; bd. dirs. Wis. Acad Scis. Arts and Letters, 1991-92. Mem.: Kenosha Country (bd dirs. 1984-86), "306" Club, Rotary (bd. dirs. Kenosha club 1975 Paul Harris fellow). Home: Kalispell, Mont. Died July 16, 2007

FRY, MALCOLM CRAIG, retired clergyman; b. Detroit, June 6, 1928; s. Dwight Malcolm and Adrienne (Craig) F.; m. Myrtle Mae Downing, June 5, 1948 (dec.); children: Pamela Mae Malcolm Craig Jr., Rebecca Fry Gwartney, Matthew Dwight Student, Bible Bapt. Sem., 1950; Th.B., Am. Div. Sch., Chgo. 1959; student, McNeese State Coll., Lake Charles, La., 1958-61 BS, Austin Peay State Coll., 1962; M.Ed., U. Ariz., 1969; D Laws and Letters (hon.), Clarksville Sch. Theology, 1974 D.Ministry, Luther Rice Sem., 1978. Ordained to ministry Free Will Bapt. Ch., 1955. Asst. jewelery store mgr. Sonne Bros. Norwich, N.Y., 1948-50; pastor in Lake Charles, La., 1955-58 59-61, Bryan, Tex., 1958-59, Ashland City, Tenn., 1961-62; ass pastor in Royal Oak, Mich., 1962-64; pastor First Free Wi Bapt. Ch., Tucson, 1964-71; dir. curriculum and rsch. Bd. Ch Tng. Svc. Nat. Assn. Free Will Baptists, Nashville, 1971-72 gen. dir., treas. Bd. Ch. Tng. Svc., 1972-78; dir. Nat. Yout Conf., 1972-83, asst. dir. Bd. Sunday Sch. and Ch. Tng 1978-83; pastor Unity Free Will Bapt. Ch., Smithfield, N.C 1983-89, Goodlettsville Free Will Bapt. Ch., Goodlettsville Tenn., 1991-96; asst. dir. Randall House Publs., 1989—96; ret 1996. Program writer, teen tng. mgr. Nat. Assn. Free Will Bapts 1963-78, clk., 1965-67, chmn. stewardship commn., 1962-67 editor in chief bd. Sunday Sch. and Ch. Tng., 1989-95. Autho Total Involvement, 1964, Why Worry?, 1967, Precepts fo Practice, 1971, Discipling and Developing, 1971, The Teacher in-Training, 1972, Contemporary Topical Studies, 1973, re edit., 1991, The Ministry of Music, 1974, Balancing Christia Education, 1977, Leader's Guide Discipling and Developing 1979, Leader's Guide the Ministry of Ushering, 1980. Serve with AUS, 1946-48; with USAF, 1951-57, Korea. Mem. Evang Philos. Soc., Kiwanis, Civitan, Phi Delta Kappa. Home: Locus Grove, Okla. Died Aug. 24, 2007.

FRY, WILLIAM JAMES, surgeon, educator; b. Ann Arbo Mich., Mar. 21, 1928; s. Lynn W. and Inez (Hayes) F.; m. Marth Earl, June 18, 1949; children: Richard E., William R. MD, U Mich., 1952. Diplomate: Am. Bd. Surgery (examiner 1974-7 dir. 1976-82, chmn. 1980-82). Intern, U. Minn. Hosp., 1952-5 resident U. Mich. Hosp., 1953-54, 56-59; instr. surgery U. Mic Med. Sch., Ann Arbor, 1959-61, asst. prof. surgery, 1961-6 assoc. prof., 1964-67, prof., 1967-76, head sect. gen. surge dept. surgery, 1967-74, F.A. Coller prof. surgery, 1974-7 attending physician Ann Arbor VA Hosp., 1960-61, chief surgery, 1961-64, cons., 1964-76, Wayne County (Mich.) Ge Hosp., Eloise, 1967-76; chmn. dept. surgery Southwestern Me Sch., Dallas, from 1976, Lee Hudson-Robert Penn prof. surge from 1976; sr. active med. staff Parkland Meml. Hosp., fro 1976. Cons. VA Hosp., Dallas, 1976—, Baylor U. Med. Cente 1976—, St. Paul Hosp., 1977—; dir. Am. Bd. Surgery, 1974-8 chmn., 1980-82 Contbr. articles on surgery and vasular diseas to book chpts. and profl. jours. Served with USNR, 1954-5 Fellow A.C.S. (pres. Mich. chpt. 1970-71); mem. Soc. Cli Vascular Surgery, Soc. Univ. Surgeons, Soc. for Surgery Alimentary Tract, Am., Western surg. assns., Internat. Soc. Surgery, Assn. for Acad. Surgery, Soc. Vascular Surgery, Inte nat. Cardiovascular Soc. (pres. 1983), Frederick A. Coller Su Soc. (pres. 1977-78), Central Surg. Assn. (pres. 1974-7 Collegium Internat. Chirurgiae Digestivae, So. Assn. Vascul Surgery, Dallas Soc. Gen. Surgeons. Home: Ann Arbor, Mic Died May 28, 2007.

FUDIM, ALLAN, lawyer; b. NYC, Jan. 21, 1945; BS, JD, St. Louis U., 1969; postgrad., U. Barcelona. Bar: N.Y. 1972, Calif. 1972. Ptnr. Lester, Schwab, Katz & Dwyer, NYC. Mem. N.Y. State Bar Assn. (drug and cosmetics, tort and ins. practice sects.), State Bar Calif., Def. Rsch. Inst., Phi Delta Phi. Died May 7, 2007.

FULKS, SARAH JANE See WYMAN, JANE

FULLAGAR, PAUL RICHARD, medical association administrator; b. Ocean City, NJ, Aug. 26, 1936; s. George E. and Muriel M. (McCarty) F.; m. Barbara Kay Watkins, Apr. 19, 1959 (div. June 1962); 1 child, Mark R.; m. Carol Lee Rice, Nov. 13, 1971; 1 child, Jill Anne. AA, Fullerton Jr. Coll., 1961; BS, U. Wash., 1967, MS, 1969. Electronic technician Autonetics, Fullerton, Calif., 1959-61; electronic sys. technician Boeing, Seattle, 1961-67; mem. promotions staff RCA Records, Seattle, 1962-69; cons. United Rsch. Co., South Orange, N.J., 1970-75; med. adminstr. Thomas Jefferson U. Hosp., Phila., 1975-80, assoc. exec. dir., 1980-86; exec. dir. Am. Roentgen Ray Soc., Reston, Va., from 1986; asst. exec. dir. Am. Coll. Radiology, Reston, from 1986. Author: Consultancy in Non-Profit Organizations, 1985; contbr. articles to profl. publs. Mem. Save the Whale Found. Staff sgt. USAF, 1955-59. Mem. Am. Soc. Assn. Execs., Soc. Rsch. Adminstrs., Am. Acad. Med. Adminstrn., Sierra Club, Alpha Gamma Sigma (pres. 1960-61). Avocations: photography, fishing. Home: Camano Island, Wash. Died Dec. 18, 2005.

FULLER, ALBERT, musician, educator; b. Washington, July 21, 1926; Student, Georgetown U.; studies organ with Paul Callaway; student, Peabody Conservatory; BS, Johns Hopkins U., 1950; MusM, Yale U., 1954. Organist, harpsichordist, improvisor of the basso continuo; mem. faculty The Juilliard Sch., NYC, 1964—2007; assoc. prof. music Yale U., New Haven, 1977-80. Co-founder, artistic dir. Aston Magna Found., 1972-83; mem. vis. com. to Music Dept. Harvard U., Cambridge, Mass., 1977-83; founder, pres., artistic dir. The Helicon Found., 1985-2007; participant recitals, chamber music programs throughout U.S. and Europe; artist Cambridge, Decca and Nonesuch Recording Cos. Contbr. editions of works of Gaspard le Roux, Francois Couperin to profl. publs.; writer critical musicological reviews. Died Sept. 22, 2007.

FULLER, GERALD RALPH, retired veterinarian; b. Chandler, Ariz., Sept. 8, 1919; s. Horace Ralph and Hortense (McClellan) F.; student Ariz. State U., 1937-39; B.S. in Dairy Husbandry, U. Ariz., 1941; M.S. in Dairy Mfg., Tex. A. and M. U., 1943, D.V.M., 1954; m. Glenda Richardson, June 6, 1941; children— Gerald Ralph, Gilbert R., Barbara Ann (Mrs. Melvin Doyle Shurtz), Glen R., Gordon R., Gene R., Grant R. Instr. agrl. sci. Ariz. State U., Tempe, 1946-50; fed. veterinarian U.S. Dept. Agr., Animal and Plant Health Inspection Service-Meat and Poultry Inspection Program Tex., Ark., Okla., 1953-82. Served to 1st lt. AUS, 1943-46, lt. col. Vet. Corps, Res. Mem. Nat. Assn. Fed. Veterinarians (pres. Okla. chpt. 1974-82), Ariz. Aggie Club (pres. coll. chpt. 1940-41), Ariz. State Future Farmers Am. (pres. 1936-37), Alpha Zeta, Lambda Delta Sigma. Democrat. Mem. Ch. of Jesus Christ of Latter Day Saints. Author: Hoop(e)s Genealogy Book, Vol. 1, 1979, Vols. 2 and 3, 1983. Adamic Lineage, 1968; Ancestors and Descendants of Andrew Lee Allen, 1952. Home: Grand Junction, Colo. Died Feb. 7, 2006.

FULLER, PERRY LUCIAN, lawyer; b. Central City, Nebr., Oct. 26, 1922; s. Perry L. and Ruth (Howorth) F.; m. Alice Moorman, Mar. 6, 1948; 1 child, Leslie Ann Fuller. Student, U. Chgo. Law Sch., 1946-47; AB, U. Nebr., 1947, JD, 1949. Bar: Ill. 1950, U.S. Supreme Ct. Mem. staff Chgo. Crime Commn., 1949; sr. ptnr. Hinshaw & Culbertson and predecessors, Chgo., from 1956. Lectr. in law U. Chgo., 1970-76, mem. vis. com., 1991-93. Vice chmn. exec. com. Law in Am. Soc. Found., 1966, chmn., 1967—69, pres., 1969—95; chmn. Cook County CSC, 1967—69; mem. Ill. Law Enforcement Commn., 1971—72; v.p. Fed. Defender, Inc., 1964; trustee Village of Winnetka, 1992—96; bd. dir. Winnetka Cmty. Chest, Ill., 1966—69, Ill. Humane Soc., from 1978, pres., 1986. 1st lt. USMC, 1942—46, Capt. USMC, 1952—53. Decorated Air medal. Fellow Am. Coll. Trial Lawyers (state chmn. 1972-74), Am. Bar Found., Ill. Bar Found.; mem. ABA (chmn. pub. relations com. 1968-69, gavel awards com. 1974-77, chmn. 1976-78), Ill, Fed., 7th Cir. Chgo. (bd. mgrs. 1967-69) bar assns., Am. Law Inst., Am. Judicature Soc., Internat. Assn. Def. Counsel (chmn. Continuing Legal Edn. bd. 1982-86, exec. com. 1983-86), Soc. Trial Lawyers Ill. (bd. dirs. 1967-68, 73-74, sec. 1975-76, pres. 1977-78), Def. Rsch. Inst. (chmn. insts. com. 1986-90), Scribes, Legal Club, Law Club (pres. 1987-88). Republican. Home: Winnetka, Ill. Died May 10, 2007.

FULLER, WALLACE HAMILTON, research scientist, educator; b. Old Hamilton, Alaska, Apr. 15, 1915; s. Henry Ray and Bessie (Gaines) F.; m. Winifred Elizabeth Dow, Dec. 23, 1939; 1 dau., Pamela Elizabeth. BS, Wash. State U., 1937, MS, 1939; PhD, Iowa State U., 1942. Research asst. Wash. State U., Pullman, 1937-39; soil surveyor U.S. Dept. Agr., Lancaster, Wis., Neosho, Mo., 1939-40, bacteriologist Beltsville, Md., 1945-47, soil scientist, 1947-48; research asso. Iowa State U., Ames, 1940-45; asso. prof., biochemist U. Ariz., Tucson, 1948-56, prof., biochemist, head dept. agrl. chemistry and soils, 1956-72, prof., biochemist soils, water and engring. dept., from 1972, prof. soil and water sci. dept., from 1985, prof. emeritus. Cons. in field; adj. prof., poet-in-residence Ariz. State Hist. Soc., 1986—. Fellow Am. Soc. Agronomy and Soil Sci., AAAS, N.Y. Acad. Sci.; mem. Am. Chem. Soc., Am. Soc. Biol. Sci., Am. Soc. Plant Physiologists, Sigma Xi, Phi Kappa Phi, Phi Lambda Upsilon, Gamma Sigma Delta, Alpha Zeta. Presbyterian. Home: Tucson, Ariz. Died Aug. 21, 2006.

FULLMER, HAROLD MILTON, dentist, educator; b. Gary, Ind., July 9, 1918; s. Howard and Rachel Eva (Tiedge) F.; m. Marjorie Lucile Engel, Dec. 31, 1942 (dec. Apr. 1983); children: Angela Sue, Pamela Rose; m. Shirley Ford Davis, Mar. 28, 1987. BS, Ind. U., 1942, DDS, 1944; doctorate (hon.), U. Athens, Greece, 1981. Diplomate: Am. Bd. Oral Pathology. Intern Charity Hosp., New Orleans, 1946-47, resident, 1947-48, vis. dental surgeon, 1948-53; instr. Loyola U., New Orleans, 1948-49, asst. prof., 1949-50, assoc. prof. gen. and oral pathology, 1949-53; cons. pathology VA hosps., Biloxi and Gulfport, Miss., 1950-53; asst. dental surgeon Nat. Inst. Dental Research, NIH, Bethesda, Md., 1953-54, dental surgeon, 1954-56, sr. dental surgeon, 1956-60, dental dir., 1960-70; chief sect. histochemistry Nat. Inst. Dental Research, 1967-70, chief exptl. pathology, 1969-70, cons. to dir., 1971-72; mem. dental caries program adv. com. HEW, 1975-79, chmn., 1976-79; dir. Inst. Dental Research; prof. pathology, prof. dentistry, assoc. dean Sch. Dentistry, U. Ala. Med. Center, Birmingham, 1970-87; prof. emeritus, from 1987; sr. scientist cancer research and tng. program, sci. adv. com. Sch. Dentistry, U. Ala. Med. Center (Diabetes Research and Tng. Center), 1977-87. Mem. med. rsch. career devel. com. VA, 1977-81; mem. com. grants and allocations Am. Fund for Dental Health, 1977-83. Editor: (with R.D. Lillie) Histopathologic Technic and Practical Histochemistry, 1976; editor in chief, founder Jour. Oral Pathology, 1972-90, Tissue Reactions, 1976-88; assoc. editor Jour. Cutaneous Pathology, 1973-83, Oral Surgery, Oral Medicine, Oral Pathology, 1970. Served to capt. AUS, 1944-46. Recipient Isaac Schour award for outstanding research and teaching in anat. scis. Internat. Assn. Dental Research, 1973, Disting. Alumnus of Yr. award Ind. U. Sch. Dentistry, 1978; Disting. Alumnus of Yr. award, Ind. U., 1981; Disting. Faculty Lectr. award, U. Ala. Med. Ctr., Birmingham, 1989—, Disting. Scientist award Am. Assn. Dental Rsch, 1990. Fellow Am. Coll. Dentists, Am. Acad. Oral Pathology (v.p. 1984-85, pres.-elect 1985-86, pres. 1986-87), AAAS (chmn. sect. 1976-78, sec. sect. 1979-87); mem. ADA (cons. Coun. Dental Rsch. 1973-74), Internat. Assn. Dental Rsch. (v.p. 1974-75, pres. 1976-77, pres. Exptl. Pathology Group 1985-86), Am. Assn. Dental Rsch. (pres. 1976-77), Internat. Assn. Pathologists, Histochem. Soc., Nat. Soc. Med. Rsch. (dir. 1977-79), Biol. Stain Commn. (trustee 1977—), Commd. Officers Assn., Internat. Assn. Oral Pathologists (co-founder, 1st pres. 1979-81, 1st editor 1971-89), Brit. Soc. Oral Pathologists (hon.), Exchange Club (Birmingham, pres. New Orleans 1952-53). Home: Birmingham, Ala. Died Jan. 20, 2007.

FURMAN, MARTIN WILLIAM, automotive parts co. exec. b. Balt., June 16, 1930; s. Max B. and Ruth (Marowitz) F.; m. Norma Rejas, July 15, 1969; children— Ronald C., Laurie A., Kenneth E., Jennifer L. BS, Franklin and Marshall Coll., 1952; postgrad., U. Balt. Law Sch., 1952-54. With RPS Products, Inc., Balt., from 1953, pres., 1968-74, chmn. bd., chief exec. officer, from 1974. Home: Pikesville, Md. Died Sept. 24, 2006.

FURNAS, HOWARD EARL, recreational facility executive, retired federal official; b. Battle Creek, Mich., Jan. 29, 1919; s. Howard Earl and Dorothy Anna (Collings) F.; m. Gail Abbott, May 14, 1942; children: Howard Earl III, Paul Abbott, Christopher Collings. AB, Hillsdale Coll., Mich., 1940; postgrad., Harvard U., Cambridge, Mass., 1945-47. Joined Fgn. Svc. Dept. State, 1947; assigned to embassy, New Delhi, 1948—49; asst. to spl. asst. to sec. state for intelligence, 1949-52, 54-57; assigned to U.S. mission to NATO, Paris, 1952—54; mem. policy planning staff, also alternate Dept. State rep. to plannning bd. NSC, 1957-61; dep. spl. asst. to sec. state for atomic energy and outer space, 1961-62; dept. exec. sec. Dept. State, 1962-63; del. 2d Nat. Conf. Peaceful Uses Space, Seattle, 1962; dep. spl. asst. to sec. state for multilateral force negotiations, 1963-64; spl. asst. to sec. state, 1964-65; mem. VIII sr. seminar in fgn. policy, 1965-66; assigned Office Undersec. State Polit. Affairs, 1966-69; spl. asst. to dir. ACDA, 1969-71, spl. adviser to chmn. gen. adv. com. on arms control and disarmament, 1969-71; prof. internat. rels. Windham Coll., Putney, Vt., 1971-76, also trustee; pres. Unipro Tennis Svcs., Howard Furnas Assocs., Windsor, Vt., from 1974, Chuckle Hill, Ltd., 1975-76. Pres. The Vermont Group, Internat. Cons., 1989-90. Contbr. articles to profl. jours. and newspaper columns. Bd. dirs. Montgomery County Scholarship Fund, Md., 1954-60; trustee Woodstock Country Sch., Vt., 1973-75; vestryman St. James Ch., Woodstock, Vt.; justice of peace West Windsor, Vt., 1986-95, U.S. joint chief of staff, Washington, DC, 1945. Maj. USAAF, 1942-45, ETO. Recipient Alumni Achievement award Hillsdale Coll., 1957. Mem. Kenwood Golf and Country Club (Washington), Woodstock Country Club, Twin States Valley Club, The Round Table, Delta Tau Delta. Episcopalian. Died Feb. 18, 2007.

FURST, EDWARD JOSEPH, educator; b. Chgo., Dec. 23, 1919; s. Joseph and Elizabeth (Pratscher) F.; m. Helene Mae Rowe, Aug. 26, 1951; children— Linda Ann, Donald Edward, Kenneth Lee. A.B., U. Chgo., 1941, M.A., 1947, Ph.D., 1948. Asst. chief to chief evaluation and exams div. U. Mich., Ann Arbor, 1948-56; assoc. prof. psychology U. Idaho, Moscow, 1956-61; assoc. prof. psychology Ohio State U., Columbus, 1961-66, co-dir. cooperative research project, 1963-66; prof., program coordinator U. Ark., Fayetteville, 1966—; cons. editor Jour. of Experimental Edn., 1967—; research editor Jour. of Staff Program and Orgn. Devel., 1983—. Author: Constructing Evaluation Instruments, 1958. Co-author: Taxonomy of Educational Objectives, 1956, Development of Economics Curricular Materials, 1966. Served to capt. U.S. Army, 1942-46. Fellow Am. Psychol. Assn.; mem. Am. Ednl. Research Assn., Mid-S. Ednl. Research Assn., Evaluation Network, Southwestern Philosophy of Edn. Soc. Avocations: travel; hiking. Home: Fayetteville, Ark. Died Mar. 6, 2007.

FUSFELD, DANIEL ROLAND, economist; b. Washington, May 23, 1922; s. Irving Sidney and Cecile (Leban) F.; m. Harriet Miller, Aug. 30, 1947; children: Robert, Sarah, Yaakov Sadeh. BA, George Washington U., 1941; MA, Columbia U., 1947, PhD, 1953. Instr. Hofstra Coll., Hempstead, N.Y., 1947-53, asst. prof., 1953-56, Mich. State U., East Lansing, 1956-60; assoc. prof. U. Mich., Ann Arbor, 1960-64, prof., 1964-87, prof. emeritus, from 1987. Lectr. USAF Inst. Tech., Dayton, Ohio, 1958-59; vis. assoc. prof. Columbia U., N.Y.C., 1960; bd. dirs. Spectrum Human Svcs., 1992-98, Avalon Housing, Inc. Author: Economic Thought of Franklin D. Roosevelt, 1956, The Age of the Economist, 1966, 9th edit. 2001, Economics, 1972, The Basic Economics of the Urban-Racial Crisis, 1973, Rise and Repression of Radical Labor, 1877-1918, 1985; co-author: The Political Economy of the Urban Ghetto, 1984; co-editor: The Soviet Economy, 1962; also articles. With US Army, 1943—46. Mem. Am. Econ. Assn., Assn. for Evolutionary Econs. (v.p. 1970, pres. 1971), Internat. Network for Econ. Method (chmn. 1989-92), Hist. Econ. Soc. Home: Ann Arbor, Mich. Died Aug. 11, 2007.

GABERMAN, HARRY, retired lawyer; b. Springfield, Mass., May 6, 1913; s. Nathan and Elizabeth (Binder) G.; m. Ingeborg Luise Gruda, Sept. 24, 1953; children: Claudia, Natalie Razzook, Victor Lucius. JD, George Washington U., 1941; LLM, Cath. U. Am., 1954. Bar: D.C. 1942. Priorities analyst War Prodn. Bd., 1942, asst. indsl. and indsl. analyst, 1943-45; asst. chief industry control sect., legal and intercorp. rels. analyst U.S. Mil. Govt. and U.S. High Commn. for Germany, Berlin, Frankfurt, Bonn; atty.-investigator, atty-advisor; indsl. specialist, bus. economist U.S. Mil. Govt. and U.S. High Commn. for Germany, Berlin, Frankfurt, Bonn, 1945—53; asst. legal advisor, attache, dep. U.S. agt. Italian-U.S. Conciliation Commn., Am. Embassy, Rome, 1953; pvt. practice Washington, 1953-55; intelligence analyst Army Transp. Intelligence Agy., Gravelly Point, Va., 1955-56; supervisory atty.-advisor, atty.-advisor Air Force Sys. Command, Andrews AFB, Md., 1956-75; ret. Asst. to U.S. mem. Four-power liquidation of German War Potential Com., Berlin, 1946; chief deconcentration br. U.S. High Commn., Frankfurt, 1949; acting dep. U.S. mem. law com. Allied Kommandatura, Berlin, 1951; U.S. mem. 3-power Film Reorgn. Com., Bonn, 1949-50. Contbr. articles to profl. jours. Recipient Profl. Achievement award George Washington U. Law Assn., 1983. Mem. Fed. Bar Assn. (dep. coun. and com. coord. 1982, coun. and com. coord. 14 substantive law couns. containing 83 constituent coms. 1983, chmn. coun. on govt. contracts 1970-75, 80-81, chmn. internat. procurement com. 1977-79, dep. chmn. sect. on internat. law and its newsletter editor 1984-97, dep. chmn. sect. on internat. law and its newsletter contbg. editor 1998-99, found. advisor 1996-2000; numerous Disting. Svc. and other awards), D.C. Bar Assn. (chmn. govt. contracts com. 1964-66), Diplomatic and Consular Officers Ret. (charter mem., DACOR House), Am. Fgn. Svcs. Assn., Air Force Assn. Avocations: walking, reading, listening to classic and semi-classic music. Died Apr. 16, 2006.

GAGE, AVERY ODELL, former corporate executive; b. South Wayne, Wis., Mar. 29, 1919; s. John R. and Lela M. (Stites) G.; m. Helen Evans, Aug. 22, 1942 (dec.); children: John, Mary (Mrs. Robert Miller); m. Jean Body, Sept. 1, 1984 BA, Beloit Coll., 1939. Field rep. Browns Bus. Coll., Rockford, Ill., 1940-41; office mgr. mechanics univ. joint div. Borg-Warner, Rockford, 1941-53; with J.L. Clark Mfg. Co., Rockford, 1953-79, asst. sec., 1961-62, sec., 1962-79; ret., 1979. Trustee, chmn. Swedish Am. Hosp., Rockford, 1966—, Clark Found., 1962-79; dir., chmn. Swedish Am. Med. Found., Rockford, 1981—. Served to capt. USAAF, 1942-44. Decorated D.F.C., Air medal with 3 oak leaf clusters. Mem. C. of C. (pres., bd. dirs. 1973—) Clubs: University. Lodges: Elks. Home: Rockford, Ill. Died Apr. 21, 2006.

GAINES, MIRAH, management theory and marketing educator; b. Jersey City, Mar. 25, 1917; d. Morris and Ruth (Goldstein) G.; B.A., U. Chgo., 1935, M.B.A., 1937. Supr. R.R. Donnelley, Chgo., 1937-42; personnel dir. Wm. Shanhouse & Sons, Rockford, Ill., 1943-44; personnel mgr. 20th Century Glove and Safety Mfrs., 1944-46; asst. plant supr. Hoosier Factories, Michigan City, Ind., 1946-48; comptroller Proebsting-Taylor Ad Agency, 1956-61; ops. mgr. Associated Shops, Inc., 1967—; prof. bus. Richard J. Daley City Coll., Chgo., 1967—, acting acad. dean, 1972-73; instr., lectr. Elmhurst Coll., Ill., 1976—. Contbr. articles to profl. jours. Republican. Avocations: art, ballet, opera, writing. Home: Hinsdale, Ill. Died July 4, 2006.

GALE, DANIEL BAILEY, architect; b. St. Louis, Nov. 6, 1933; s. Leone Caryll and Gladys (Wotowa); m. Nancy Susan Miller, June 15, 1957; children: Caroline Hamilton, Rebecca Fletcher, Daniel Bailey. Student, Brown U., 1951—53; Ecole Des Beaux Arts, Paris, 1954—55; BArch, Washington U., 1957. With Gale & Cannon, Architects and Planners, Helmut, Obata & Kassabaum, Inc., Architects, St. Louis; exec. v.p. corp. devel., dir. HOK, Inc., St. Louis, 1961—79; ptnr. Henegan and Gale, Aspen, Colo., 1967—69; pres., CEO Gale Kober Assocs., San Francisco, 1979—83; pvt. practice Belvedere, Calif., from 1984; pres. Program Mgmt. Inc., Belvedere, 1984. Named Citizen of Yr., Belvedere, Calif., 2004; recipient Henry Adams prize, Washington U., 1957. Mem.: AIA, Singapore Inst. Architects, Union Club San Francisco. Died Mar. 4, 2006.

GALL, LAWRENCE HOWARD, lawyer, consultant; b. Leesville, SC, Dec. 17, 1917; s. John J. and Bertha (Smyer) G.; m. Winifred Belle Nelson, Dec. 18, 1948; children: Sally Patricia, Linda, Constance. AB, U. S.C., 1939, LL.B., 1941. Bar: S.C. 1941, D.C. 1948, U.S. Supreme Ct. 1952, Tex. 1966. Mem. legal dept. E.I. duPont de Nemours & Co., Inc.; asst. to gen. counsel Remington Arms Co., Bridgeport, Conn., 1941-43; assoc., then ptnr. Disney & Gall, Washington, 1946-52; research dir., gen. counsel Ind. Natural Gas Assn. Am., Washington, 1952-61, exec. dir., 1961-65; v.p., gen. counsel Transcontinental Gas Pipe Line Corp., 1965-74; v.p., gen. atty. Transco Energy Co., 1974-80, v.p. govtl. affairs, 1980-83, legal cons., from 1983. Houston Met. dir. Nat. Alliance Businessmen, 1971; bd. dirs. Tex. Mfrs. Assn., 1971-73, Tex. Research League, 1975-83. Served to lt. (s.g.) USNR, 1943-46. Mem. Am. Fed. Energy, Tex., Houston Bar Assns. Home: Houston, Tex. Died July 10, 2006.

GALLAGHER, GEORGE R., retired judge; b. New Haven, Conn., Apr. 10, 1915; m. Judith Kuertz; children: Christopher R., Mary Elizabeth. Grad., George Washington U.; JD, Catholic U. Atty., criminal divsn. US Dept. Justice, 1938—41, 1946—48, spl. asst. to atty. gen., 1948—52; gen. counsel Subversive Activities Control Bd., 1952—59; pvt. law practice, 1959—68; judge D.C. Ct. Appeals, 1968—81, sr. judge, 1981—2001. Served in US Army, 1941—45. Mem.: Lawyers Club. Wash., John Birch Soc., Congl. Country Club. Died Feb. 4, 2007.

GALLAGHER, PHIL C., insurance executive; b. Miami, Fla., Nov. 10, 1926; s. Phil J. and Blonda (Burrow) G.; children: Pamela Robertson, Vivien Elizabeth. BBA, U. Miami, 1949. With D.R. Mead & Co., Miami, 1949-72, exec. v.p., 1958-72; pres. Gallagher-Cole Assocs., Miami, 1972—; dir. Skylake State Bank, North Miami Beach, Fla.; underwriting mem. Lloyd's of London; former instr. Lindsey Hopkins Edn. Center. Bd. dirs. Grand Jury Assn. Fla., J. Edwin Larson Found. for Ins. Edn. Served with USNR, 1944-46. Mem. Ind. Ins. Agts. Am. (past nat. dir., past chmn. agy. mgmt. com.), Nat. Assn. Ins. Brokers, Am. Risk and Ins. Assn., Nat. Assn. Casualty and Surety Agts., Fla. Surplus Lines Assn., Nat., Fla., Miami assns. life underwriters, Fla. Assn. Ins. Agts. (past pres.), Ind. Ins. Agts. Dade County (past pres.), Assn. Internat. Ins. Agts. (intersure, past dir.), Profl. Ins. Agts., Profl. Ins. Agts. Fla. and Caribbean, Profl. Ins. Agts. Dade County, Greater Miami C. of C., Econ. Soc. South Fla., Rod & Reel Club, Miami Club, La Gorce Country Club, Bath Club, Surf Club. Home: Miami, Fla. Died June 1, 2006.

GALLENT, MARTIN, lawyer, city planner; b. Bklyn., Feb. 1, 1931; s. Joseph and Selma (Rykus) G.; m. Aline J. Isaacs, June 13, 1954; children— Amy Beth, Judith Monique, Gregory Adam. B.S., N.Y. State Coll. Forestry, 1953; LL.B., NYU, 1960. Bar: N.Y. bar 1960, U.S. Ct. Appeals (2d cir.) 1960, U.S. Dist. Ct. (ea. and so. dists.) N.Y. 1961. Credit reporter Dun & Bradstreet, N.Y.C., 1955-57, sales rep., 1957-60; ptnr. Kagan & Gallent, Jackson Heights, N.Y., 1960-69; sole practice, Jackson Heights, 1969—2006; adj. prof. Queens Coll., mem. N.Y. City Planning Commn., 1969-86, vice chmn., 1973-86. Contbr. articles to various publs. Vice pres., sec. N.Y. chpt. Am. Jewish Com., 1974—2006; mem. adv. council field study office Coll. Human Ecology, Cornell U., 1981—2006; mem. adv. council Sch. Architecture and Urban Planning, Princeton U., 1977-83; mem. regional bd. Anti-Defamation League; bd. dirs. Green Guerillas. Served with U.S. Army, 1954-56. Mem. Am. Planning Assn. (v.p. Met. chpt. 1982-84), Am. Inst. Cert. Planners (founding mem.), Am. Arbitration Assn. (arbitrator), Comml. Law League Am., Queens Bar Assn. Jewish. Home: Jackson Hts, NY. Died July 16, 2006.

GALLO, ERNEST, vintner; b. Jackson, Calif., Mar. 18, 1909; s. Giuseppe (Joseph) and Assunta (Susie) (Bianco) Gallo; m. Amelia Gallo (dec. 1993); children: Joseph, David(dec.). Co-owner (with Julio Gallo), chmn. bd. dirs. E & J Gallo Winery, Modesto, Calif., 1933—2007. Named one of Forbes Richest Americans, 2006. Died Mar. 6, 2007.

GALLOWAY, THOMAS D., dean; b. Bakersfield, Calif., Oct. 23, 1939; B.A., Westmont Coll., Santa Barbara, 1962; M.U.P., U. of Washington, 1969, PhD, 1972. Rsch. assoc., Ctr. for Rsch. U. Kans., 1972, asst. prof., Sch. Architecture & Urban Design, 1971—74, assoc. dir. & sr. rsch. assoc., Inst. for Soc. & Environ. Studies, 1973—75, assoc. prof., Sch. Architecture & Urban Design, 1975—80, dir. grad. prog. in urban planning, 1974—80, assoc. dean, Sch. Architecture & Urban Design, 1979—80; dir., prof. Grad. Sch. of Community Planning & Urban Affairs, U. of Rhode Island, 1980—85; dir. Design Research Inst., Iowa State U., 1985—92; dean, prof. College of Design, Iowa State U., 1985—92; dean Coll. Architecture Ga. Inst. Tech., Atlanta, 1992—2007. Died Mar. 11, 2007.

GALOVICH, STEVEN PHILIP, mathematics educator; b. Sacramento, Feb. 13, 1945; s. Steve P. and Helen (Vukelich) G.; m. Jennifer Ruth Hunter, June 12, 1971 (div. Aug. 1985); children: Alexandra, Anna Catharine; m. Elizabeth Ann Culver, July 16, 1988. BA, BS, U. Calif., Davis, 1966; PhD, Brown U., 1972. Asst. prof. math. Carleton Coll., Northfield, Minn., 1971-77, assoc. prof., 1977-78, 79-83, prof., from 1983, assoc. dean, from 1990. Vis. assoc. prof. U. Calif., Davis, 1978-79; vis. scholar U. Calif., Berkeley, 1979-80, 84-85; dir. NSF Regional Confs. in Math., 1975, 81. Author: Introduction to Mathematical Structures, 1989, Doing Mathematics, 1993; contbr. articles to math. jours. Grantee Vaughn Found. Fund, 1980, 84. Mem. Am. Math. Soc., Math. Assn. Am. (sec. North Cen. sect. 1977-78, pres. 1990-91, Carl B. Allendoerfer award 1988), Phi Beta Kappa, Sigma Xi. Achievements include research in the areas of algebraic number theory and combinatorial group theory, with respect to the study of class groups of finite groups, units and class groups of algebraic number fields over finite fields, and the theory of splittings of finite and infinite groups. Home: Lake Forest, Ill. Died Dec. 15, 2006.

GAMBLE, THOMAS ELLSWORTH, academic administrator; b. Chgo., Nov. 14, 1941; s. Slade LeBlount and Anna Marie VanDuzer G.; m. Donna Kay Dersch, Nov. 3, 1973; children: Brendan, Shari, Oscar, Rebecca, Slade, Aubrey, David, Donna. BA in Biology, Northwestern U., 1964; MEd in Ednl. Psychology, U. Ill., 1970, PhD in Higher Ednl. Adminstrn., 1973. Asst. to dean student pers. U. Ill., Urbana-Champaign, 1968-71, asst. prof. edn., 1972, asst. dean Coll. Medicine, 1972—76, assoc. prof. Coll. Medicine Chgo., 1976—83; exec. asst. to chancellor U. Ill. Med. Ctr., Chgo., 1976-78, asst. chancellor, 1976—83; dean intercampus affairs Ill. Ea. C.C., Olney, 1983-84; dean of instrn. Wabash Valley Coll., Mt. Carmel, Ill., 1984—89, dean of coll., 1989-90; pres. Dodge City (Kans.) C.C., 1990-95, Joliet (Ill.) Jr. Coll., 1995-98, Brevard C.C., Cocoa, Fla., from 1999. Asst. prof. U. Ill. Coll. Edn., 1972-77; assoc. prof. U. Ill. Coll. Medicine, 1982-83; pres. Kans. Jayhawk C.C. Athletic Conf., 1993-94, Ill. N4C C.C. Athletic Conf., 1996-97. Contbr. articles to profl. jours. Bd. dirs. Kans. Newman Coll., Wichita, 1994-96, U.S. Naval Inst., 1968—, Jr. Achievement East Ctrl. Fla., Econ. Devel. Com. Fla. Space Coast, Brevard County Workforce Devel. Bd., Brevard C.C. Found.; chmn. Fla. Coun. Pres., 2003-04; mem. Am. Coun. on Edn., Commn. on Life Long Learning, 2002-05; mem. policy adv. bd. Fla. Solar Energy Ctr.; mem. First Bapt. Ch. Merritt Island, Fla. Capt. USNR, 1964-87, ret. Mem. VFW (life), Am. Assn. Cmty. Colls. (commn. on econ. and workforce and econ. devel. 2005—), Am. Coun. Edn., Fla. Assn. Colls. and Univs., Fla. Assn. C.C.'s, Fla. Space Rsch. Inst., Fla. Sterling Coun., Inc. (bd. dirs.), U. Ill. Coll. Edn. Alumni Assn. (life, sr. advisor, pres. 1988-90), Rotary, Beta Beta Beta, Chi Gamma Iota, Kappa Delta Pi, Phi Delta Kappa, Phi Kappa Phi. Avocations: non-fiction reading, children, classical music, naval science. Home: Merritt Island, Fla. Died 2006.

GAMBRELL, RICHARD DONALD, JR., endocrinologist, educator; b. St. George, SC, Oct. 28, 1931; s. Richard Donald and Nettie Anzo (Ellenburg) G.; m. Mary Caroline Stone, Dec. 22, 1956; children: Deborah Christina, Juliet Denise. BS, Furman U., 1953; MD, Med. U. SC, 1957. Diplomate Am. Bd. Obstetrics and Gynecology, Diplomate Div. Reproductive Endocrinology. Intern Greenville Gen. Hosp., S.C., 1957-58, resident S.C., 1961-64; commd. USAF, 1958, advanced through grades to col., chmn. dept. ob-gyn, cons. to surgeon gen. USAF Hosp. Wiesbaden, Germany, 1966-69, chief gynecologic endocrinology Wilford Hall USAF Med. Ctr. Lackland AFB, Tex., 1971-78, ret., 1978; clin. prof. ob-gyn and endocrinology Med. Coll. Ga., Augusta, 1978—2001; practice medicine specializing in reproductive endocrinology Augusta, from 1978. Fellow in endocrinology Med. Coll. Ga., 1969-71; mem. staff Westlawn Bapt. Mission Med. Clinic, San Antonio, 1972-78; assoc. clin. prof. U. Tex. Health Sci. Ctr., San Antonio, 1971-78; internat. lectr.; mem. ob-gyn. adv. panel U.S. Pharmacopeial Conv., 1986-90; mem. sci. adv. bd. Nat. Osteoporosis Found., 1988-91. Co-author: The Menopause: Indications for Estrogen Therapy, 1979, Sex Steroid Hormones and Cancer, 1984, Unwanted Hair: Its Cause and Treatment, 1985, Estrogen Replacement Therapy, 1987, Hormone Replacement Therapy, 3rd edit., 1992, 6th edit., 2005, Estrogen Replacement Therapy Users Guide, 1989, 2d edit., 1997; mem. editl. bd. Jour. Reproductive Medicine, 1982-85, Maturitas, 1982-99, The Female Patient, 1992-2007, Menopause: Jour. of the N.Am. Menopause Soc., 1995-2007; mem. editl. bd. Internat. Jour. Fertility, 1986-91, assoc. editor, 1988-91; contbr. articles to med. jours., chpts. to books. Deacon, Sunday sch. tchr. Baptist Ch., 1971-2007; mem. sci. adv. bd. Nat. Osteoporosis Found., 1988-91. Recipient Chmn.'s Best Paper in Clin. Rsch. from Tchg. Hosp. award Armed Forces Dist. Am. Coll. Ob-Gyn., 1972, 88, Host award, 1977, Chmn.'s award, 1978, Purdue-Frederick award, 1979, Outstanding Exhibit award Am. Fertility Soc., 1983, Am. Coll. Obstetricians and Gynecologists award, 1983, Thesis award South Atlantic Assn. Ob-Gyn., Winthrop award Internat. Soc. Reproductive Medicine, 1985, Chmn.'s Best Paper award Pan Am. Soc. for Fertility, 1986, Outstanding Sci. exhibit award Am. Acad. Family Physicians, 1986, 87, 92, Boston, 1994, New Orleans, 1996, Merit award ACS, 1994, Cert. of Appreciation for Sci. Exhibit, 1995, Best Doctors for Women award Good Housekeeping, 1997; named to Hall of Fame, Lloyd Meml. H.S., Erlanger, Ky., 1996. Fellow ACOG (mem. subcom. on endocrinology and infertility 1983-86, Kermit Krantz award 2000); mem. Pacific N.W. Ob-Gyn Soc. (hon.), So. Med. Assn. (2nd place Sci. Exhibit award 1992), Am. Fertility Soc., Ga. Obstetric and Gynecologic Soc., Tex. Assn. Ob-Gyn., Augusta Obstetric and Gynecologic Soc., San Antonio Ob-Gyn. Soc. (v.p. 1975-76), Chilean Soc. Ob-Gyn. (hon.), South Atlantic Assn. Obstetricians and Gynecologists (v.p. 1997-98, pres.-elect 1998-99, pres. 1999-00), Soc. Obstetricians and Gynecologists of Can. (hon.), Internat. Family Planning Rsch. Assn., Internat. Menopause Soc. (mem. exec. com. 1981-84), Internat. Soc. for Reproductive Medicine (program chmn. 1980, pres. 1986-88), Am. Assn. of Pro-Life Obs. and Gyn. (exec. bd. 1995-2007), Christian Med. and Dental Assn., Am. Geriat. Soc. (mem. editl. bd. 1981-83), N.Am. Menopause Soc. (Ortho-McNeil Pharm. Rsch. award 2001), Nat. Geog. Soc., Phi Chi, Alpha Epsilon Delta. Home: Augusta, Ga. Died June 20, 2007.

GANDER, RODERICK MACLEAN, former state senator, retired academic administrator; b. Bronxville, NY, Dec. 26, 1930; s. MacLean and Helen (Hadley) G.; m. Isabelle Salamone, Dec. 20, 1954; children: Maclean Charles, James Thomas, Elizabeth Gander Pierce. BA in Lit. and Polit. Sci., Hamilton Coll., 1952, LLD (hon.), 1989. Reporter, writer Newsweek Mag., NYC, 1954-59, asst. to the editor, 1960-65, news editor, 1965-67, chief of corrs., 1967-81; pres. Marlboro (Vt.) Coll., 1981—96, interim pres., 2003; mem. Vt. State Senate, 2003—07. Died Sept. 24, 2007.

GARBERS, DAVID LORN, biochemist; b. La Crosse, Wisc., Mar. 17, 1944; BSc, U Wisconsin, Madison, 1966; MSc, 1970, PhD, biochemistry, 1972. Assoc. physiologist Vanderbilt U., Nashville, Tenn., 1972-74; asst. prof., 1974-76; assoc. prof., from 1977; investigator Howard Hughes Med. Inst., Nashville, Tenn., from 1976; visiting prof. Johns Hopkins Med. Sch., Baltimore, Md., 1984-85; NIH, 1984-87. Recipient Max-Plank-Forschungs-Preis, Alexander von Humboldt-Stiftung, 1994. Mem., Am. Soc. Biol. Chemists. Achievements include research in the molecular biology of fertilization. Died Sept. 5, 2006.

GARCIA, ALEX R., career military officer; b. Albuquerque, June 17, 1941; s. Samuel M. Garcia and Isabel Zimmerman; m. Dolores Lucero, May 13, 1961; children: Alex Jr., Delia, Sammy, Steven. Grad., N.Mex. Mil. Acad., U.S. Army Command Coll., 1978, Nat. Def. Univ., 1985; BSBA, Nat. Coll., 1992. Enlisted N.Mex. Nat. Guard, 1958-63, commd., from 1963, advanced through ranks to brigadier gen., from 1963, dep. adjutant gen., chief of staff, from 1992. Bd. dirs. POUNDERS Internat. Decorated meritorious svc. medal with oak leaf cluster, army commendation medal with oak leaf cluster, N.Mex. disting. svc. medal, others. Mem. Nat. Guard Assn. U.S., N.Mex. Nat. Guard Officers Assn. (past pres.), Assn. U.S. Army (past pres. Albuquerque chpt.), Air Def. Artillery Assn., Res. Officers Assn., N.Mex. Law Enforcement Officers Assn. Democrat. Roman Catholic. Avocations: music, golf, jogging, walking. Home: Albuquerque, N.Mex. Died June 22, 2006.

GARDINE, JUANITA CONSTANTIA FORBES, educator; b. St. Croix, V.I., Aug. 6, 1912; d. Alphonso Sebastian and Petrina (Actien) Forbes; B.A., Hunter Coll., 1934; M.A., Columbia U., 1940; postgrad. U. Chgo., 1949, NYU, 1960-66, Cheyney Coll., 1967; M.Ed., U. Ill.-Chgo., summer 19865; postgrad., U. Miami, 1988-90; m. Cyprian A. Gardine, Apr. 23, 1942; children— Cyprian A., Vicki Maria Camilla, Letitia Theresa, Richard Whittington. Tchr. elementary schs., 1934-35; tchr. math. high sch., 1935-41, 48-49; acting asst. high sch. prin., 1941; jr. high sch. prin., 1941-47; substitute tchr. English, math., physics, Montclair, N.J., 1947-48; asst. supt. edn., 1949-55; assoc. dean Community Colls., supr. elem. schs., 1955-57; high sch. prin., 1957-58; supr. ednl. stats., 1958-62; social worker Dept. Welfare, 1962-63; prin. Christiansted (St. Croix) Pub. Grammar Sch., 1963-74; tchr. math. evening session extension classes Cath. U. P.R., 1960-61; asst. dir. and tutor St. Croix Tutorial Sch., 1974-82; part-time instr. math. Coll. V.I., 1974-75, 80-81. Past sec. bd. dirs. St. Croix Fed. chpt. ARC; mem. bd., chmn. supervisory com. St. Croix Fed. Credit Union; past sec. St. Croix Sch. Health Com., Girl Scout Com., Fredericksted Hosp. Aux.; past mem. and pres. St. Croix (V.I.) Mental Health Assn. Pres., Tchrs. Assn., 1940, Municipal Employees Assn., 1942. Sch. named in her honor, 1974; honoree P.R. Friendship Day Com., 1979, St. John's Ch., 1981. Mem. Am. Statis. Assn., NAESP, V.I. Fedn. Bus. and Profl. Women's Clubs (past sec.), Episcopal Ch. Women of V.I. (past chmn. world affairs com.), Christiansted Bus. and Profl. Women's Club (past pres.; Woman of Year 1966), Daus. King (sec.), Christiansted Bus. and Profl. Club (past parliamentarian, past pres., also asst. treas., treas., v.p.). Episcopalian (past pres. women's group). Died Oct. 29, 2006.

GARDNER, ALVIN FREDERICK, oral pathologist, government official; b. Chgo., Mar. 22, 1920; s. Leon William and Sarah (Kanter) G.; m. Ruth Myra Moskovitz, May 2, 1982; 1 dau., Ava Lee. AA, U. Fla., 1940; D.D.S., Emory U., 1943; postgrad. certificate, U. Kansas City, 1946; postgrad. (NIH fellow), State U. Ia., 1954-55; MS (NIH fellow), U. Ill., 1957; PhD (NIH fellow), Georgetown U., 1959. Diplomate: Internat. Bd. Applied Nutrition. Staff dentist AEC, Richland, Wash., 1944-45; chief dental staff Stockton (Calif.) State Hosp., 1945-46; pvt. practice dentistry, 1946-54; resident in oral pathology, mem. dental staff Armed Forces Inst. Pathology, Walter Reed Army Med. Center, Washington, 1957-59, mem. research staff, from 1954; asso. prof. pathology U. Md., Balt., 1959-63; dental officer Bur. of Medicine, FDA, HEW, from 1963. Vis. scientist Nat. Bur. Standards, 1957-59; cons. in oral pathology Stedmans Med. Dict., USPHS, VA. Author: Oral Pathology, Oral Roentgenology and Periodontics, 1963, Pathology in Dentistry, 1968 Differential Oral Diagnosis in Systemic Disease, 1970, Pathology of Oral Manifestations of Systemic Diseases, 1971, Dental Examination Review Book, 1983; also monographs, numerous articles in profl. jours.; Editor: American Lectures in Dentistry 1968, Dental Postgraduate Handbook Series, 1976, Allied Health Handbook Series, 1983, Nursing Monograph Series 1983; corr. editor: El Salvador Dental Jour; sci. editor: Jour. of Conn. Dental Assn. Served to capt., Dental Corps AUS Res. 1942-51. Grantee U.S. Army Research and Devel. Command Surg. Gen.'s Office, 1962-63; Grantee NIH, USPHS, 1961-64 Grantee Sigma Xi, New Haven, 1962-63; Grantee Md. div. Am Cancer Soc., 1962-63; recipient 3d prize Am. Soc. Oral Surgeons, 1962, Schering essay award, 1957 Fellow AAAS, Internat. Assn. Anesthesiologists, Internat. Coll. Applied Nutrition Internat. Coll. Dentists, Am. Soc. Advancement Gen. Anesthesia in Dentistry, Am. Pub. Health Assn., Am. Med. Writer's Assn. mem. A.M.A. (asso.), Am. Dental Assn., Md. Dental Assn. (asso. editor Jour. 1977), Calif. (hon. mem.), Conn. Dental Assns., So. Md. Dental Soc., Am. Assn. Dental Editors, Am Acad. Oral Pathology, Am. Acad. Dental Medicine, Internat Assn. Dental Research, Fedn. Dentaire Internationale, Am Nutrition Soc., Am. Assn. Endodontists, Royal Soc. Health (Eng.), Am. Soc. Cytology, N.Y. Acad. Arts and Scis., Georgetown U., U. Ill., Emory U. alumni assns., Sigma Xi. Home Silver Spring, Md. Died Oct. 2, 2005.

GARDNER, LENANN MCGOOKEY, management consultant; d. James Lester McGookey; m. Ken Reidy, Mar. 24, 200[illegible] 1 child, Lindsay Erica McGookey Gunther. MBA, Harvard U 1976. V.p. mktg. MNC Fin., Balt., 1990—91; pres. LM Gardner Mgmt. Consulting, Inc., Albuquerque, from 1992. Dir. of mktg advt. and strategic planning Blue Cross Blue Shield, Balt 1988—89. Chair devel. com., bd. dirs. Cuidando Los Ninos Albuquerque, 2003—04; leader, faith care ministries Faith Luth Ch., Albuquerque, from 2006. Mem.: Am. Mktg. Assn. (Prof Svcs. Marketer of the Yr. 1996), Harvard Club. Home: Albuquerque, N.Mex. Died 2007.

GARGETT, GEORGE GRANT, insurance company executive; b. Alma, Mich., Sept. 28, 1917; s. Ford William and Emil[illegible] (Slocum) G.; m. Josephine Besancon, Nov. 25, 1944; children Frederick Ford, John Besancon, Mark George. BA, Mich. Sta Coll., 1940. Diplomate: registered health underwriter. Asst. gen. mgr. Mut. of Omaha Ins. Co., Indpls., 1957-60, dir. mark research Omaha, 1960-63, gen. mgr. Seattle, 1963-72, dir. agy west Los Angeles, 1972-73; v.p. div. office sales Mut. OmahaIns. Co., Omaha, 1973-81; sr. exec. v.p. mktg. Mut. Omaha Ins. Co., Omaha, from 1981. Active Boy Scouts Am Omaha, 1958—; mem. Com. on Fgn. Relations, 1980—. Republican. Home: Omaha, Nebr. Died Mar. 4, 2006.

GARLAND, PHYLLIS TWYLA (PHYL GARLAND), retired journalism educator; b. McKeesport, Pa., Oct. 27, 1935; Percy Andrew and Hazel Barbara Maxine (Hill) G. BS Northwestern U., 1957. Writer, feature editor Pitts. Courie 1958-65; asst., then asso. editor Ebony mag., 1965-69, N. editor, 1969-71, contbg. editor, 1971-77, Stereo Rev. mag., fro 1977; music commentator Sta. WNET-TV, 1978-80; asst. pro Black studies SUNY at New Paltz, 1971-73, acting chmn. Blac Studies dept., 1973; asst. prof. journalism Grad. Sch. Journa ism, Columbia U., 1973-79, assoc. prof., 1979—89, pro 1989—2004; Ralph Metcalfe prof. Marquette U., spring 198 Author: The Sound of Soul: The Story of Black Music, 196 Contbr. articles to books, mags. Mem. adv. bd. Columb Journalism Rev.; mem. jazz panel Nat. Endowment for Ar 1977-80. Recipient Golden Quill award for feature writi Western Pa., 1962, award for pub. service reporting N.Y. ch Pub. Relations Soc. Am., 1974; Disting. scholar United Neg Coll. Fund, 1985-86. Mem. Women in Communications (N Headliner award 1971), Delta Sigma Theta (commn. on arts a letters) Home: New York, NY. Died Nov. 7, 2006.

GARLAND, SYLVIA DILLOF, lawyer; b. NYC, June 4, 19[illegible] d. Morris and Frieda (Gassner) Dillof; m. Albert Garland, M 4, 1942; children: Margaret Garland, Paul B. BA, Bklyn. Co 1939; JD cum laude, N.Y. Law Sch., 1960. Bar: N.Y. 1960, U.

Ct. Appeals (2d cir.) 1965, U.S. Ct. Claims 1965, U.S. Supreme Ct. 1967, U.S. Customs Ct. 1972, U.S. Ct. Appeals (5th cir.), 1979. Assoc. Borden, Skidell, Fleck and Steindler, Jamaica, NY, 1960-61, Fields, Zimmerman, Skodnick & Segall, Jamaica, 1961-65, Marshall, Brater, Greene, Allison & Tucker, NYC, 1965-68; law sec. to N.Y. Supreme Ct. justice Suffolk County, 1968-70; ptnr. Hofheimer, Gartlir & Gross, NYC, from 1970. Asst. adj. prof. N.Y. Law Sch., 1974-79; mem. com. on character and fitness N.Y. State Supreme Ct., 1st Jud. Dept., 1985—, vice chmn., 1991—. Author: Workman's Compensation, 1957, Labor Law, 1959, Wills, 1962; contbg. author: Guardians and Custodians, 1970; editor-in-chief Law Rev. Jour., N.Y. Law Forum, 1959-60 (svc. award 1960); contbr. articles to mag. Trustee N.Y. Law Sch., 1979-90, trustee emeritus, 1991—; pres. Oakland chpt. B'nai Brith, Bayside, N.Y., 1955-57. Recipient Disting. Alumnus award N.Y. Law Sch., 1978, Judge Charles W. Froessel award N.Y. Law Sch., 1997. Mem. ABA (litigation sect., family law sect.), N.Y. State Bar Assn. (family law sect.), Queen's County Bar Assn. (sec. civil practice 1960-79), N.Y. Law Sch. Alumni Assn. (pres. 1976-77), N.Y. Law Forum Alumni Assn. (pres. 1963-65). Jewish. Home: New York, NY. Died June 16, 2007.

GARMENDIA, FRANCISCO, bishop; b. Lozcano, Spain, Nov. 6, 1924; came to U.S., 1964, naturalized. Ordained priest Roman Cath. Ch., 1947. Ordained titular bishop Limisa and aux. bishop., NYC, from 1977; Episcopal vicar of the South Bronx N.Y. Archdiocese, Bronx. Died Nov. 15, 2005.

GARNER, HAROLD JOSEPH, art dealer, retail book company executive, investor; b. Tuscaloosa, Ala., June 5, 1930; s. Henry Calvin and Flora Hester (Winter) G.; m. Judith Beatriz Leon Smith, Sept. 1, 1953 (div. July 1972); children— Paul Marvin, David Leon. B.A., U. Ala.-Tuscaloosa, 1952, M.A., 1954; postdoctoral studies U. Tex., 1954-55, 57-58, 60-61. Teaching asst. in Spanish, U. Ala., Tuscaloosa, 1952-54, U. Tex., Austin, 1954-55, 57-58; instr. Spanish, U. Okla., Norman, 1955-58; dir. Centro Colombo-Americano, U.S. State Dept., Manizales, Colombia, S.Am., 1958-60, prof. catedratico U. Caldas, Manizales, 1959; spl. instr. English phonetics and methods of research U. Tex., Austin, 1961-62; ptnr. Garner & Smith Bookstores, Austin, 1962—; dir., ptnr. Garner & Smith Art Gallery, Austin, 1969—. Trustee Sta. KMFA-FM, Austin, 1975—. Mem. Am. Booksellers Assn. Democrat. Avocations: gardening; classical music; books, art, antiques collector. Home: Smithville, Tex. Died May 3, 2006.

GARRETT, DONALD EVERETT, research and development company executive; b. Long Beach, Calif., July 5, 1923; s. Walter E. and Dorothy M. Marriam; m. JoAnne Brown, Sept. 17, 1946 (div. 1973); children— Mark Calvert, DiAnn, Carolyn Anne, David Donald. BS in Chemistry, U. Calif., Berkeley, 1947; MS in Chem. Engring, Ohio State U., 1948, PhD in Chem. Engring, 1950. Research and devel. engr., group leader Dow Chem. Co., Pittsburg, Calif., 1950-52; with Union Oil Co., Brea, Calif., 1952-55; mgr. research Am. Potash & Chem. Co., Trona, Calif., 1955-60; pres. Garrett R&D Co., LaVerne, Calif., 1960-75; exec. v.p. research, engring. and devel. Occidental Petroleum Corp., Los Angeles, 1968-75; pres. Garrett Energy R&D Engring., Inc., Ojai, Calif., from 1975, Saline Processors, Inc., from 1975, Liquid Chem. Corp., Hanford, Calif., from 1979. Mem. gen. tech. adv. com. Fossil Fuel div. ERDA, 1969-78; engring. adv. council U. Calif., 1970-85 Recipient Distinguished Alumni award Ohio State U., 1971; Lamme medal, 1976; Kirkpatrick Chem. Engr. achievement awards, 1963, 71; personal achievement award in chem. engring., 1976 Mem. Am. Inst. Chem. Engrs. (pres. Mojave Desert sect. 1957, Engr. of Year Los Angeles sect. 1964), Am. Chem. Soc., Sigma Xi, Tau Beta Pi. Home: Ojai, Calif. Died Dec. 14, 2006.

GARST, DAVID, agricultural company sales manager, consultant; b. Des Moines, Sept. 10, 1926; s. Roswell and Elizabeth Francis (Henak) G.; m. Georganne Orenstein (dec.); children— Samuel David, Sally Marilyn Haerr, James Morton; m. Marily Ann Shinn. B.A., Stanford U., 1950. Ptnr., operator, Garst Co. Farms, Coon Rapids, Iowa, 1941-56; sales mgr. Garst Seed Co., Coon Rapids, 1956—; mem. presdl. mission for agrl. devel. to Central Am., Carribean, 1980. Mem. Nat. Agrl. Mktg. Assn. (named AgriMarketer of Yr. 1987), Am. Seed Trade Assn., U.S. Feed Grain Council, Am. Soc. Agrl. Cons. Served with U.S. Army, 1944-45. Democrat. Helped develop Acra-Plant planting concept; helped open trade with Eastern Europe, 1955-59. Home: Coon Rapids, Iowa. Died Jan. 9, 2006.

GARVEY, JOHN CHARLES, violist, conductor, retired music educator; b. Canonsburg, Pa., Mar. 17, 1921; s. Frank Sherwood and Esther (Gegenheimer) G.; m. Evelyn Ficarra, Mar. 13, 1947; children: Deborah, Frank, Deirdre. Student, Temple U., 1940-43. Prof. music Sch. Music, U. Ill., Urbana, 1948-91. Violinist, violist Jan. Savitt and Jerry Wald Jazz orchs., 1943-45; prin. violist Columbus Philharm. Orch., 1945-48, Aspen Festival Orch., 1964; condr. NIRTV Chamber Orch., Iran, 1973; founder, dir. Jazz Band, 1959, Chamber Orch., 1964, Russian Folk Orch., 1974; violist Walden Quartet, 1948-69, State Dept. Jazz Tours, 1968-69; condr. Harry Partch Ensemble, 1959-63 (Wihner Nat. Coll. Jazz Band champaionships 1967-69, Russian Ctr. grantee for study balalaika in Moscow 1970, 72, Ctr. for Advanced Studies grantee for study ethnic music 1972-73, recipient Ill. Gov.'s award in arts 1980); dir. U. Ill. Jazz Band tour of USSR, 1990; guest condr. Belarus State Jazz Band, Minsk, 1992; condr. New Ill. Jazz Band, 1995-96. Balinese Gamelan study grantee S.O.K.A.R., Bali, 1979, 87; grantee for study of Catalan Sardana music, Barcelona, 1986. Mem. Am. Fedn. Musicians (local 196), Soc. for Ethno-musicology, Internat. Assn. Jazz Educators, Balalaika and Domra Assn. Am. Home: Silver Spring, Md. Died July 18, 2006.

GARWICK, ROBERT WIATT, petroleum geologist; b. St. Louis, May 17, 1921; s. Walter Cleveland and Ruth Beryl (Wiatt) G.; m. Catherine Augusta Okeefe, Aug. 15, 1942; children— Erin, Kenneth, Lydia, Lorin, Carrie, Gael, Guy, Matthew. B.A., Dartmouth Coll., 1942; M.A., Columbia U., 1947. Geologist, Nfld. Geol. Survey, 1946; stratigrapher Sinclair Ethiopia, 1947; geologist Gen. Crude Oil Co., 1948-53; ind. cons., Houston, 1953-64; cons. geologist Butler, Miller & Lents, Houston, 1964-70; pres. Kaygar Corp., Houston, 1970—. Served with USAF, 1942-45. Decorated Air medal with twelve oak leaf clusters. Mem. Am. Assn. Petroleum Geologists. Died Apr. 18, 2007.

GARWOOD, JOHN DELVERT, former college administrator; b. Carroll, Nebr., Mar. 20, 1915; s. Harvey and Forrest (Hill) G.; m. Kathleen Marie Schnoor, Aug. 6, 1943; children: Jan Dierks, Shelley Hill. AB, Wayne State Coll., Nebr., 1936; Ph.M., U. Wis., 1940; postgrad., U. La., 1940-41, U. So. Calif., 1947; PhD in Econs, U. Colo., 1951. Supt. schs., Lindsay, Nebr., 1936-38; teaching fellow U. La., 1940-41, U. Colo., 1949-51; instr. Morningside Coll., Sioux City, 1941- 42; prof. econs. Ft. Hays (Kans.) State U., 1947- 49, 51-62, dean faculty, 1962-79, v.p. for acad. affairs, 1979-80. Author: Back to the Basics, 1978, Values, A New Frontier for the 21st Century, 2001. Mem. exec. com. Kans. Council Econ. Edn., 1961—; pres. Smoky Hill Pub. TV Corp., 1977-79, Danforth asso., 1957—. Served with AUS, 1942-46. Recipient Disting. Service award Ft. Hays State U., 1982 Mem. NEA, Kans. Tchrs. Assn. (pres. 1969-70), Am. Econ. Assn., Sons of Am. Revolution, Phi Kappa Phi, Sigma Phi Sigma, Pi Gamma Mu, Phi Delta Kappa, Lambda Delta Lambda, Kappa Mu Epsilon. Lutheran. Home: Mesa, Ariz. Died Nov. 27, 2006.

GASSER, WILBERT, JR., (WILBERT WARNER GASSER JR.), retired banker; b. Marquette, Mich., Apr. 5, 1923; s. Wilbert Warner and Mildred (Carpenter) G.; m. Mary C. Kratz, Dec. 6, 1952; 1 child, Wilbert Warner III. Student, Purdue U., 1941-42; BS in Bus., Ind. U., 1948. With Gary (Ind.) Nat. Bank (name changed later to Gainer Bank), 1948-92, v.p., 1953-63, chmn. bd., 1964-92, ret. Pres. Gary YMCA, 1960-62; treas. Gary Urban League, 1960-65, N.W. Ind. Heart Assn., 1961-64; bd. dirs., treas. Meth. Hosp., Gary. With USAAF, 1943-46. Mem. Gary C. of C. (v.p. 1961), Kiwanis (treas. Gary club 1963—). Presbyterian. Home: Ogden Dunes, Ind. Died Oct. 1, 2006.

GAUBATZ, JOHN THOMAS, law educator; b. Denver, Apr. 21, 1942; s. Philipp and Dorothy Amelia Gaubatz; m. Kathryn Susan Bell, Jan. 13, 1986; 1 child, Daniel B. At, Colo. Coll., 1960—61; BS, Colo. State U., 1964; JD, U. Chgo., 1967. Bar: Colo. 1967, U.S. Dist. Ct. Colo. 1967, U.S. Ct. Appeals (10th cir.) 1970. Assoc. Dawson, Nagel, Sherman & Howard, Denver, 1967—71; asst. prof. Case Western Res. U., 1971—73, assoc. prof., 1973—76, assoc. dean, 1973—76; vis. prof. law U. Miami, 1976—77, prof. law Coral Gables, 1977—2007, assoc. dean, 1977—80; cons. Isham, Lincoln & Beale, Chgo., 1979—80; dir. Philip E. Heckerling Inst. on Estate Planning, 1980—2007. Author: The Moot Ct. Book, 1979, Estates, Trusts and Taxes, 1983; contbr. numerous articles to profl. jours. Capt. US Army, 1968—69. Mem.: ABA. Republican. Presbyn. Home: Miami, Fla. Died June 13, 2007.

GAUDINO, MARIO, physician, pharmaceutical company executive, scientist; b. Buenos Aires, May 22, 1918; came to the U.S., 1945, naturalized, 1966; s. Nicolas M. and Maria Teresa (Ferrari) G.; m. Ann Murray, Sept. 24, 1947 (div. Jan. 1983); children: David, Brian; m. Judith A. Jenkins, May 19, 1984. BA, U. Buenos Aires, 1934, MD with hons., 1944; PhD in Physiology, NYU, 1950; student in Radioisotope Techniques, Oak Ridge Inst. Nuc. Studies, 1952. Lic. physician N.J., 1979, N.Y., 1981. Asst. Inst. Histology and Embryology, U. Buenos Aires, 1936; asst., rsch. asst. Inst. Physiology, 1937-42, chief lab. biol. physics, 1944; resident, chief resident Ramos Mejia Hosp., Buenos Aires, 1941-44; Millet and Roux fellow Argentine Assn. for Advancement Sci., 1943; asst., attending physician Inst. Semiology, Nat. Clin. Hosp., Buenos Aires, 1944-46; fellow Argentine Nat. Cultural Commn., 1945; Sauberan fellow Argentine Assn. Advancement Sci., 1946; physiol. rsch. fellow NYU, U.S. State Dept., Dazian Found. Med. Rsch., 1946-49; asst. prof. Tex. U., 1949; chmn. dept. biol. physics U. La Plata Med. Sch., Argentina, 1950-51; attending physician Ctrl. Inst. Cardiology, Buenos Aires, 1950-51; assoc. dir. med. writing and advt. Lederle Labs. divsn. Am. Cyanamid Co., NYC, 1951-52; rsch. assoc., prof. dept. surgery NYU, 1952-55, adj. assoc. prof. surgery, rsch., 1955-57; established investigator Am. Heart Assn., NYC, 1954-57; med. dir. Abbott Labs Internat. Co., Abbott Universal Ltd., Chgo., 1957-61; assoc. prof. dept. medicine Northwestern U., 1959-61; assoc. med. dir. Pfizer Internat. Inc., NYC, 1962-67; assoc. dir. advanced clin. rsch. Internat. Merck Sharp & Dohme Rsch. Labs., Rahway, N.J., 1967-70, dir., 1970-71, sr. dir. clin. rsch. internat. med. affairs area, 1971-74; dir. med. compliance drug regulatory affairs CIBA-GEIGY Pharms., Summit, NJ, 1974-80, assoc. dir. med. svcs. med. affairs dept., 1980—89, dir. med. cons. svcs., 1989—96, ind. expert, from 1997. Clin. asst. prof. medicine Cornell U., N.Y.C., 1971-77. Fellow N.Y. Acad. Scis.; mem. AMA, Internat. Soc. Nephrology, Am. Fedn. Clin. Rsch., Am. Soc. Nephrology, Am. Soc. Clin. Pharmacology and Therapeutics, Am. Physiol. Soc., Am. Acad. Clin. Toxicology, Acad. Medicine N.J., Summit Med. Soc., Soc. for Exptl. Biology and Medicine, Microcirculatory Soc., Jockey Club, Argentine Yacht Club, Univ. Club, Buenos Aires Rowing Club. Died Apr. 1, 2006.

GAUNT, ABBOT STOTT, zoology educator; b. Lawrence, Mass., July 4, 1936; s. Ernest Abbot and Kathleen Mary (Stott) G.; m. Sandra Louise Lovett, Aug. 17, 1963. BA, Amherst Coll., Mass., 1958; PhD, U. Kans., 1963. Instr. Middlebury (Vt.) Coll., 1963-66, asst. prof., 1966-67, U. Vt., Burlington, summer 1967, SUNY, Buffalo, 1968-69, Ohio State U., Columbus, 1969-74, assoc. prof., 1974-86, prof., 1986-95, prof. emeritus, from 1995. Cons. USN, San Diego, 1979; mem. adv. bd. Hubbs Marine Inst., San Diego, 1979-82; chair rev. panel bd. regents State of La., Baton Rouge, 1983. Assoc. editor: Biology of the Reptiles, Vol. 19, 1998; contbr. articles to profl. jours., chpts. to books. NSF grantee, 1973-75, 80-82, 83, N.Y. state postdoctoral fellow, SUNY, Buffalo, 1967. Fellow AAAS, Am. Ornithologists Union; mem. Wilson Ornithological Soc. (pres. 1981-83). Achievements include study of flow in avian respiratory vocal system, electromyography of syfinx; discovery that almost all avian musculture has the in-series fiber architecture. Home: Columbus, Ohio. Died Mar. 30, 2006.

GAWTHROP, DAPHNE WOOD, performing company executive; b. Houston, July 22, 1940; Dir. programs and devel. Houston Mus. Natural Sci., 1987-89; dir. Inst. Mus. Svcs., Washington, 1989-91; dir. spl. projects Houston Grand Opera, 1991-92; dep. chmn. (pub. partnership) Nat. Endowment for the Arts, Washington, 1991-92; interim dir. Fotofest Ctr. for Photography, Houston, 1992; exec. dir. Sacramento Ballet, from 1994. Mem. Pres. Com. Arts and Humanities, Arts in Embassies coun. U.S. Dept. of State; adv. Arts Indemnity Program U.S. Info. Agy.; trustee Houston Ballet, Mus. of Fine Arts, Houston, Contemporary Arts Mus., Alley Theater. Recipient Nat. Devel. award Am. Assn. Museums; citation of Highest Achievement Nat. Endowment Arts. Home: Houston, Tex. Died Nov. 12, 2005.

GAYLORD, NORMAN GRANT (NORMAN GRANT GOLDSTEIN), chemical and polymer consultant; b. Bklyn., Feb. 16, 1923; s. Irving M. and Tillie (Horowitz) G.; m. Marilyn Einhorn, June 24, 1945; children— Lori Gaylord Wright Gagliardi, Kathy Gaylord Fleegler, Richard, Cory Gaylord-Ross BS, CCNY, 1943; MS, Poly. Inst. Bklyn., 1949, PhD in Polymer Chemistry, 1950. Chemist Elko Chem. Works, Pittstown, N.J., 1943-44; chemist Pa. Salt Mfg. Co., Pittstown, 1945, Merck & Co., Rahway, N.J., 1946-48; research chemist E.I. duPont de Nemours & Co., Buffalo, 1950-54; group leader Interchem. Corp., NYC, 1955-56, asst. dept. dir., 1957-59; v.p. Western Petrochem. Corp., Newark, 1959-61; pres. Gaylord Research Inst., New Providence, NJ, 1961-87, Gaylord Assocs., New Providence, 1987—2007; fellow Rsch. Inst. for Scientists Emeritus, Drew U., Madison, NJ, 1987. Adj. prof. polymer chemistry Canisius Coll., Buffalo, 1951-54, Poly. Inst. Bklyn., 1955-62, U. Lowell, Mass., 1981—. Author: Reduction with Complex Metal Hydrides, 1956, Linear and Stereoregular Addition Polymers, 1959, Polyalkylene Sulfides and Other Polythioethers, 1962, Polyalkylene Oxides and Other Polyethers, 1963; mem. editorial adv. bd. Jour. Macromolecular Sci.-Chemistry, 1968—, Macromolecular Syntheses, 1963—, Jour. Polymer Sci., 1959-80, Jour. Applied Polymer Sci., 1959-74, Ency. of Polymer Sci. and Tech., 1964-72, Soc. Plastics Engrs. Transactions, 1963-64, Polymer Engring. and Sci., 1965-66, Revs. in Macromolecular Chemistry, 1968-73, Macromolecular Reports, 1991; contbr. numerous articles to profl. publs.; patentee in field Recipient Honor Scroll, N.J. Inst. Chemists, 1984, Founders' award Am. Acad. Optometry, 1985. Fellow Soc. Plastics Engrs.; mem. TAPPI, Am. Chem. Soc., Soc. Plastics Engrs., Sigma Xi. Achievements include developed a rigid material, siloxane-methacrylate, that was both permeable and suited to the production of lenses; patents in field. Died Sept. 18, 2007.

GEANAKOPLOS, DENO JOHN, retired history professor; b. Mpls., Aug. 11, 1916; s. John Christ and Helen (Economou) G.; m. Effie Vranos, Aug. 23, 1953 (dec. 2001); children: John, Constance. Diploma in violin, Juilliard Sch. Music, 1939; BA, U. Minn., 1941, MA, 1946; Litt.D., U. Pisa, Italy, 1946; PhD, Harvard U., 1953; MA (hon.), Yale U., 1967; D.Litt. (hon.), Hellenic Coll. Violinist, Mpls. Symphony Orch., 1939-42, 46; teaching fellow Harvard U., 1951-53; fellow Dumbarton Oaks, Washington, 1949-50; instr. history Brandeis U., 1953-54; prof. Greek Theol. Sch., Boston, 1953-54; from asst. prof. to prof. Western medieval and Renaissance history U. Ill., Urbana, 1954-67; prof. history and religious studies Yale U., 1967—87, prof. emeritus, 1987—2007; teaching Byzantine and Renaissance history, history Eastern Orthodox Ch., from 1967, Bradford Durfee prof. history, from 1986. Lectr. univs., Athens, Greece, 1961, Paris, 1964, Salonika, Greece, 1964, Rome, 1964, Oxford, Eng., 1967; U. Ill., Chgo., 1967, Cini Found., Venice, Italy, 1962-68; lectr. on Orthodoxy, Rosary Coll., Chgo., 1959; speaker Brit. Eccles. History Soc., Oxford, 1976, Cambridge U., 1973; attended Vatican II Council, 1964, Council of Chalcedon conf. World Council Chs., Geneva, 1969, Greek Orthodox-Jewish Colloquium, N.Y.C., 1972; ann. lectr. Inst. Balkan Studies, Salonika; mem. U.S. Com. Byzantine Studies. Author: Emperor Michael Palaeologus and the West, 1959 (Greek edit. 1967, Italian edit. 1985), Erasmus and the Aldine Academy, 1960, Greek Scholars in Venice in the Renaissance, 1962 (repub. as Byzantium and the Renaissance, 1975), Byzantine East and Latin West, 1966, Bisanzio e il Rinascimento, 1967, Western Civilization, 1975, (with others) Byzantium, in Perspectives on the Past, 1971, Byzantium and the Later Crusades, in a History of the Crusades, 1975, Interaction of the Sibling Byzantine and Western Cultures in Middle Ages and Italian Renaissance, 1976 (Greek edit. 1986), Medieval Western Civilization and the Byzantine and Islamic Worlds, 1979 (Greek transl. 1994), Byzantium: Church, Society and Civilization Seen through Contemporary Eyes, 1984, Constantinople and the West: Essays on the Late Byzantine (Palaeologan) and the Italian Renaissances and the Byzantine and Roman Churches, 1989; editor: Jour. Greek Roman and Byzantine Studies, 1962-79; editorial bd.: Greek Orthodox Theol. Rev.; contbr. articles, revs. to profl. jours. Trustee Hellenic Coll. Served to capt. Q.M.C., AUS, 1942-46. Recipient award Am. Council Learned Socs., 1960, 61, 68, 72; Griswold award, 1978, 79, 86, award Hellenic Coll.; decorated gold cross Order King George (Greece), 1966; named to Order St. Andrew by Patriarch Constantinople; title Archon Didaskalos tou Genous, 1972; Fulbright scholar, 1960-61; Guggenheim fellow, 1964; grantee Am. Philos. Soc., 1962, 66, 72; Yale concilium, 1973; Nat. Humanities Inst., summer 1974; named Hon. Citizen Heraklion, Crete, 1965. Fellow Medieval Acad. Am.; mem. Am. Hist. Assn., Ch. History Soc. (exec. com. 1967-72, pres.-elect 1983-84), Renaissance Soc. Am. (exec. com. 1979), Cretan Hist. Soc., Soc. Byzantine Studies (Athens), Soc. Macedonian Studies (Salonika), Modern Greek Studies Assn., Greek Hist. Soc., Orthodox Theol. Soc. Am. Died Oct. 4, 2007.

GEBHARDT, ROBERT FRANK, architect, professional planner; b. North Bergen, N.J., Mar. 19, 1925; s. William Fred and Elizabeth Mary (Hillenbrand) G.; m. Kathryn Mary Jester, Oct. 5, 1957. B.Arch., Cooper Union, 1952. Registered architect, profl. planner N.J. Ptnr., Martin, Gebhardt & DiPaola, Saddle

Brook, N.J., 1953-78, Martin & Gebhardt Assocs., Saddle Brook, 1979-83; prin. Robert F. gebhardt Assocs., Saddle Brook, 1984—. Served with U.S. Army, 1943-45; France and Germany. Recipient award of merit for residential bldg. House & Home Mag., 1956. Mem. AIA, Am. Inst. Planners, N.J. Soc. Architects (dir. 1969-73), Architects League No. N.J. (pres. 1971, Vegliante Meml. award 1970). Republican. Roman Catholic. Home: Ocala, Fla. Died Oct. 16, 2006.

GEBHART, CARL GRANT, security broker; b. Santa Monica, Calif., Jan. 24, 1926; s. Carl V. and Hazel (Grant) G.; m. Margaret Mary del Bondio, Nov. 29, 1952 (dec. Feb. 1989); children: Elizabeth G. Gebhart-Hardin, Peggy G. McFarland, Julia Ann Seamon. BA in Journalism, U. So. Calif., 1947; MBA in Fin, Harvard U., 1949. Registered rep. Mitchum, Jones & Templeton, Inc., Los Angeles, 1949-56, gen. partner, 1956-62, sr. v.p., sec., dir., 1962-73; v.p. investments Paine Webber, Los Angeles, from 1973; financial reporter radio sta. KABC, Los Angeles, 1968-73. Mem. L.A. Soc. Fin. Analysts (v.p. 1959), Spring St. Forum (pres. 1962), Petroleum Club (L.A.), Univ. Club L.A., Univ. Assocs. U. So. Calif. (life), Tennis Patrons Santa Monica (life), Beach Club (Santa Monica), Phi Beta Kappa, Phi Kappa Phi, Phi Eta Sigma, Chi Phi, Sigma Delta Chi. Republican. Presbyterian. Home: Pacific Palisades, Calif. Died Jan. 10, 2007.

GEE, DAVID ALAN, hospital administrator; b. Cambridge, Mass., Apr. 17, 1928; s. Harold F. and Thelma A. (Gilbert) G.; m. Lois Jean Ellis, Dec. 26, 1949 (dec. May 1969); children— Thomas H., John M., William M., Kimberley E.; m. Mary E. Kemp, Aug. 26, 1988. A.B., DePauw U., 1949; M.H.A., Washington U., St. Louis, 1951. Asst. dir. Jewish Hosp., St. Louis, 1951-63, pres., 1963—; mem. faculty Washington U. Sch. Medicine, 1957—. Contbr. chpts. to books, articles to profl. jours. Recipient Goldstein award Jewish Fedn. St. Louis, 1977; Disting. Service award Vaad Hoeir, 1978. Fellow Am. Coll. Hosp. Adminstrs. (regent 1977-80); mem. Am. Hosp. Assn. (bd. dirs. 1983—), Mo. Hosp. Assn. (chmn. 1976-78), Hosp. Assn. Met. St. Louis (chmn. 1966-68). Republican. Clubs: University, Washington U. Faculty (St. Louis). Home: Chesterfield, Mo. Died Dec. 5, 2006.

GEEHERN, JOSEPH JOHN, lawyer; b. Westfield, Mass., Aug. 25, 1919; s. Joseph F. and Alice L. (Caldon) Geehern; m. Marguerite T. Gorman, Apr. 22, 1950; children: Joseph J., Christopher P. AB in Govt., Harvard U., 1940, LLB, 1949. Bar: Mass. 1949. Assoc. then jr. ptnr. Nutter, McClennen & Fish, Boston, 1949—59; with Stanhome, Inc., Westfield, Mass., from 1959, former v.p., gen. counsel and sec. To 1st lt. US Army, 1942—46, ETO. Mem.: ABA, Westfield Bar Assn., Mass. Bar Assn., Am. Soc. Corp. Secs., Tax Execs. Inst. Died May 27, 2006.

GEEN, WILLIAM JOHN, lawyer; b. Harrisburg, Pa., May 30, 1930; s. William John and Annie (Jones) G.; m. Ruth Brinton Parker, Oct. 22, 1955; children: Barbara Lemaster, David, Elizabeth, Robert, Christopher. BBA, Drexel U., 1951; LLB, U. Pa., 1959. Bar: N.Y. 1960, U.S. Ct. Appeals (3d cir.) 1964, U.S. Tax Ct., 1962. Assoc. atty. Shearman & Sterling, NYC, 1959-66; asst. dir. taxation Celanese Corp., NYC, 1966-69; assoc. atty. Chadbourne & Parke, NYC, 1969-71, ptnr., from 1971. Presbyterian. Avocations: skiing, sailing, music. Home: Easton, Md. Died Apr. 1, 2006.

GEERTZ, CLIFFORD JAMES, anthropology educator; b. San Francisco, Aug. 23, 1926; s. Clifford James and Lois (Brieger) G.; m. Hildred Storey, Oct. 30, 1948 (div. 1981); children: Erika, Benjamin; m. Karen Blu, 1987. AB, Antioch Coll., 1950; PhD, Harvard U., 1956, LL.D. (hon.), 1974; L.H.D. (hon.), No. Mich. U., 1975, U. Chgo., 1979, Bates Coll., 1980, Knox Coll., 1982, Brandeis U., 1984, Swarthmore Coll., 1984, New Sch. for Social Research, Yale U., 1987, Williams Coll., 1991, Princeton U., 1995, Cambridge U., Eng., 1997; L.H.D. (hon.), Colby Coll., 2003. From asst. prof. to prof. dept. anthropology U. Chgo., 1960-70; prof. dept. social sci. Inst. for Advanced Study, Princeton, NJ, from 1970, Harold F. Linder prof. social sci., 1982-2000, prof. emeritus, 2000—06; Eastman prof. Oxford U., 1978-79. Author: The Religion of Java, 1960, Agricultural Involution, 1963, Peddlers and Princes, 1963, The Social History of an Indonesian Town, 1965, Islam Observed, 1968, The Interpretation of Cultures, 1973, (with H. Geertz) Kinship in Bali, 1975, (with L. Rosen and H. Geertz) Meaning and Order in Moroccan Society, 1979, Negara: The Theatre State in Nineteenth-Century Bali, 1980, Local Knowledge: Further Essays in Interpretive Anthropology, 1983, Works and Lives: The Anthropologist as Author (Nat. Book Critics Circle award), 1988, After the Fact: Two Countries, Four Decades, One Anthropologist, 1995, Available Light, 2000. Served with USNR, 1943-45. Recipient Asian Cultural prize, Fukuoka, Japan, 1992, Bintang Jasa Utama, Govt. of Indonesia, 2002; Nat. Acad. Scis. fellow, 1973. Fellow AAAS, Am. Philos. Soc., Am. Acad. Arts and Scis., Brit. Acad. (corr.); mem. Am. Anthrop. Assn., Assn. for Asian Studies, Middle East Studies Assn. Home: Princeton, NJ. Died Oct. 30, 2006.

GELSHENEN, ROSEMARY ROBINSON, marketing executive; b. Queens, N.Y., Feb. 24, 1950; d. John Joseph and Ann (Doyle) Gelshenen; m. Dennis Berkholtz, Oct. 27, 1973 (div. 1980). B.A., Marquette U., 1972. Receptionist Atlanta Conv. Bur., 1974; sales mgr. Rodeway Inns, Atlanta, 1974; pub. relations dir. McDonald's Corp., Atlanta, 1975, McDonald & Little, Atlanta, 1976; dir. mktg. Ga. World Congress Center, Atlanta, 1976—. Banquet chmn. Beastly Feast, Zool. Soc., Atlanta, 1983, 84. Mem. Sales & Mktg. Execs. (dir.), Nat. Assn. Exposition Mgrs., Hotel Sales Mgmt. Assn., Profl. Conv. Mgmt. Assn., European Soc. Assn. Execs. (allied), Greater Washington Soc. Assn. Execs. (allied), Meeting Planners Internat. Roman Catholic. Died Jan. 18, 2006.

GENDRON, EDWARD CHARLES, steel company executive; b. Uxbridge, Mass., July 1, 1928; s. Charles L. and Grace E. (Wilmot) G.; m. May P. Gagnon, Sept. 6, 1948; children— Judy, Jay. Student, Coll. of Holy Cross, 1945-47; BBA, U. Detroit, 1959. Mgr. mktg. adminstrn. RCA, Needham, Mass., 1962-64; pres., treas. AcraMation, Inc., North Adams, Mass., 1964; plant controller Internat. Tel. & Tel. Corp., Clinton, Mass., 1965-66, divisional controller Morton Grove, Ill., 1966; v.p. Crucible Steel Co., Pitts., 1967-68; pres. Crucible Steel Co. (Crucible Stainless Steel div.), 1968-69, Midland Ross Corp., Cleve., from 1969, now vice-chmn., also bd. dirs. Home: Boynton Beach, Fla. Died June 1, 2007.

GENOVESE, THOMAS LEONARDO, lawyer; b. Flushing, NY, Feb. 28, 1936; s. Robert Pasquale Sisto and Jean Laura (Lundari) G.; m. Linda Luella Le Maire, Nov. 30, 1980; children: Torene Lucia, Andrea Lisa, Richard Michael. AB, U. Va., 1957; JD, Fordham U., 1960. Bar: N.Y. 1961. Atty. FAA, Jamaica, N.Y., 1961-65, NBC, NYC, 1965-66, Grumman A/C Engring. Co., Bethpage, N.Y., 1966-70; gen. counsel Grumann Data Systems Co., Bethpage, N.Y., 1970-73, Grumman Corp., Bethpage, N.Y., from 1979, v.p., from 1981. Dir., v.p., sec. Grumair Ltd., Hamilton, Bermuda; adj. prof. SUNY-Stony Brook, 1976-78; mem. civil case flow com. U.S. Dist. Ct. for Eastern Dist. N.Y. Contbr.: legal articles to Fordham Law Rev. Chmn. United Way Grumman corp., 1983. Mem. ABA, Am. Corp. Counsel Assn., N.Y. State Bus. Coun. (mem. gen. counsel's com.), U.S. C. of C. (govt. and regulatory affairs). Episcopalian. Home: Hilton Head Island, SC. Died Feb. 20, 2007.

GENTRY, JOANNE MOSBAUGH, educator; b. Noblesville, Ind., Dec. 16, 1924; d. Harry and Lois (Tice) Mosbaugh; m. Neil R. Gentry, Sept. 25, 1943 (div.); children— John Michael, Sheryl Lynn. B.S., Ball State U., 1962, M.A., 1968; Ed.D., Ind. U., 1978. Tchr., elem., secondary, coll. and continuing edn. for adults, 1962-78; curriculum coordinator Wayne Twp. Elem. schs., Indpls., 1979—; cons. in field. Republican Precinct committeewoman, 1978-82. Recipient Delta Pi Epsilon Reward for Outstanding Research, Ball State U., 1968. Mem. Nat. Council Tchrs. Math., Internat. Reading Assn. (council treas.), Ind. U. Profl. Women, Ind. Assn. Supervision and Curriculum Devel.; Delta Pi Epsilon, Pi Lambda Theta, Phi Delta Kappa, Delta Theta Tau. Mem. Refuge Christian Ch. Contbr. articles to profl. jours. Home: Indianapolis, Ind. Died Nov. 28, 2006.

GEORGE, ALEXANDER LAWRENCE, political scientist, educator; b. Chgo., May 31, 1920; s. John and Mary (Sargis) G.; m. Juliette Lombard, Apr. 20, 1948; children: Lee Lawrence, Mary Lombard. AM, U. Chgo., 1941, PhD, 1958; DHL (hon.), U. San Diego, 1987; PhD (hon.), U. Lund, Sweden, 1994. Rsch. analyst OSS, 1944-45; dep. chief rsch. br. Info. Control divsn. Office Mil. Govt. for Germany, 1945-48; specialist study of decision-making and internat. rels. RAND Corp., Santa Monica, Calif., 1948-68, head dept. social sci., 1961-63; prof. polit. sci. and internat. rels. Stanford U., Calif., 1968. Lectr. U. Chgo., 1950, Am. U., 1952—56; chmn. com. on Conflict Rrsolution NRC/NAS, 1995—2000. Author: (with Juliette L. George) Woodrow Wilson and Colonel House: A Personality Study, 1956, Propaganda Analysis, 1959, The Chinese Communist Army in Action, 1967; (with others) The Limits of Coercive Diplomacy, 1971; (with Richard Smoke) Deterrence in American Foreign Policy: Theory and Practice, 1974 (Bancroft prize for Deterrence in Am. Fgn. Policy 1975), Towards A More Soundly Based Foreign Policy: Making Better Use of Information, 1976, Presidential Decisionmaking in Foreign Policy, 1980, Managing U.S.-Soviet Rivalry, 1983; (with Gordon Craig) Force and Statecraft, 1983, 3rd edit., 1995; editor: (with others) U.S.-Soviet Security Cooperation: Achievements, Failures, Lessons, 1988, Avoiding War: Problems of Crisis Management, 1991, Forceful Persuasion, 1992, Bridging the Gap: Theory and Practice of Foreign Policy, 1993; (with William E. Simons) The Limits of Coercive Diplomacy, 2d. edit., 1994; (with Juliette L. George) Presidential Personality and Performance, 1998, (with Andrew Bennett) Case Studies and Theory Development in the Social Sciences, 2005, On Foreign Policy: Unfinished Business, 2006. Mem. Carnegie Commn. on Preventing Deadly Conflict, 1993-97. Fellow Ctr. Advanced Study Behavioral Scis., 1956-57, 76-77, NIMH, 1972-73, MacArthur Prize, 1983-88, Disting. fellow U. S. Inst. Peace, 1990-91, 91-92; Founds. Fund for Rsch. in Psychiatry grantee, 1960, NSF rsch. grantee, 1971-73, 75-77; recipient award for behavioral rsch. relevant to prevention of nuclear war NAS, 1997, Johan Skytte prize in polit. sci., Uppsala U., Swden, 1998; Carnegie Corp. grantee, 1999. Mem. Am. Acad. Arts and Scis., Coun. on Fgn. Rels., Am. Polit. Sci. Assn., Internat. Studies Assn. (pres. 1973-74), Am. Philos. Soc., Phi Beta Kappa. Died Aug. 16, 2006.

GERBER, CARL JOSEPH, hospital administrator, psychiatrist; b. Detroit, Feb. 15, 1934; s. William J. and Signe (Wallin) G.; m. LaVora R. Sartain, Oct. 28, 1932. BS, U. Detroit, 1956; PhD, Washington U., St. Louis, 1960; MD, Duke U., 1967. Diplomate Am. Bd. Psychiatry and Neurology. Assoc. prof. med. Duke U., Durham, N.C., 1961-72; chief consultation, liaison psychiatrist Wash. U., Seattle, 1972-74; chief of staff V.A. Med. Ctr., Tacoma, Washington, 1974-82, Des Moines, 1982-86, dir. Ft. Meade, S.D., from 1986. Prof. psychiatry U. S.D., 1988—. Contbr. sci. articles to profl. jours. Lt. col. USAR, 1986—. Mem. Am. Psychiat. Assn., Am. Coll. Physician Execs. Avocations: golf, bowling. Home: Mountain Home, Tenn. Died Mar. 7, 2007.

GERBER, STEVEN HIRAM, investment company executive; b. NYC, Apr. 2, 1938; s. Newcom Lifton and Dorothy (Horowitz) G.; m. Susan Marr, Nov. 26, 1981 (div. Oct. 1985). ABA, Nichols Coll., 1959; BS, Syracuse U., 1961; postgrad., CUNY, 1965. Registered investment advisor. Sales mgr. Xerox Corp., NYC, 1962-68; dir. mktg. Fox & Carskadon Corp., Menlo Park, Calif., 1969-73; sr. v.p. Robert A. McNeil Corp., Los Angeles, 1974-83; pres. Tandam Capital Funding Corp., Los Angeles, from 1985-. Mem. adv. bd. City Savs. & Loan, Westlake Village, Calif., 1983--. Bd. dirs. Thalians, Cedars-Sinai Hosp., Los Angeles. Recipient Top Fund Raiser award Cedars-Sinai Hosp., 1980. Mem. Nat. Assn. Fin. Wholesalers (found, pres. 1983-86), Internat. Assn. Fin. Planners (bd. dirs.), President's Club, Cellar Club (pres.), Vikings, Racquet Club Palm Springs (pres. 1979--). Avocations: tennis, sailing, deep sea fishing. Home: Los Angeles, Calif. Died Mar. 15, 2007.

GERBIE, ALBERT BERNARD, obstetrician, gynecologist, educator; b. Toledo, Nov. 20, 1927; s. Louis and Fay (Green) G.; m. Barbara Hirsch, June 29, 1952; children: Gail Diane, Stephen Ralph. MD, George Washington U., 1951. Intern Michael Reese Hosp., Chgo., 1951-52; preceptorship in ob-gyn. under Drs. R.A. Reis, J.L. Baer, E.J. DeCosta, Chgo., 1952-55; practice medicine specializing in ob-gyn. Chgo., from 1955; mem. faculty Northwestern U. Med. Sch., Chgo., 1952—2007, prof. ob-gyn., 1972—2007, prof. emeritus, 2007, dir. continuing grad. edn., 1975—2007. Mem. staff Northwestern Meml. Hosp., 1955-2007; chief divsn. ob-gyn. Children's Meml. Hosp.; bd. dirs. Am. Bd. Ob-Gyn, 1976-2007, v.p., 1978-81, asst. to dir. evaluation, 1982-89, 1996-98, chmn. 1988-90, 1994-96, pres. 1990-94, historian, 1998-2000; chmn. liaison com. for ob-gyn., 1989; rep. Am. Bd. Med. Specialties; bd. dirs. Chgo. Maternity Ctr., Found. for Excellence in Women's Health Care. Author textbooks; assoc. editor Surgery, Gynecology, and Obstetrics, Am. Jour. Ob-Gyn.; editor ACOG Current Jour. Rev.; contbr. chpts. to books, articles to profl. jours. Served with U.S. Army, 1946-47. Mem. ACS (bd. govs.), ACOG (chmn. learning resources commn.), AMA, Am. Gynecol. Soc., Am. Assn. Obstetricians and Gynecologists, Am. Gynecol. and Obstet. Soc., Am. Bd. Med. Specialties, Am. Coll. Sports Medicine, Ctrl. Assn. Ob-Gyn, Soc. Human Genetics, Southwestern Ob-Gyn. Soc. Chgo. Gynecol. Assn. (pres. 1977-78), Skokie Valley Figure Skating Club, (pres. 2003). Home: Highland Park, Ill. Died Oct 15, 2007.

GERHART, JAMES BASIL, physics professor; b. Pasadena Calif., Dec. 15, 1928; s. Ray and Marion (van Deusen) G.; m Genevra Joy Thomesen, June 21, 1958; children: James Edward Sara Elizabeth. BS, Calif. Inst. Tech., 1950; MA, Princeton 1952, PhD, 1954. Instr. physics Princeton, 1954-56; asst. prof physics U. Wash., Seattle, 1956-61, assoc. prof., 1961-65, prof. 1965-98, prof. emeritus, 1998—2007. Exec. officer Pacifi Northwest Assn. for Coll. Physics, 1972-94, bd. dirs., 1965-99 chmn., 1970-72; governing bd. Am. Inst. Physics, 1973-76 78-81. Recipient Disting. Teaching award U. Wash. Regents an Alumni Assn., 1982, Ann. Gerhart lectr., 1997. Fellow Am Phys. Soc, AAAS; mem. Am. Assn. Physics Tchrs. (sec. 1971 77, v.p. 1977, pres.-elect 1978, pres. 1979, Millikan meda 1985). Home: Seattle, Wash. Died Feb. 24, 2007.

GERMANN, RICHARD P(AUL), pharmaceutical compan chemist, chemicals executive; b. Ithaca, NY, Apr. 3, 1918; s Frank E.E. and Martha Minna Marie (Knechtel) G.; m. Malind Jane Plietz, Dec. 11, 1942 (dec. Dec. 2005); 1 child, Cherann Lee (dec.). Student, U. N.Mex., 1938-39; BA, U. Colo., 1939 postgrad., 1940-41, Western Res. U., 1941-43, Brown U., 1954 Chief analytical chemist Taylor Refining Co., Corpus Christ 1943-44; rsch. devel. chemist Calco Chem. divsn. Am. Cyana mid Co., 1944-52; devel. chemist charge pilot plant Alros Chem. Co. divsn. Geigy Chem. Corp., 1952-55; new produc devel. chemist, rsch. divsn. W.R. Grace & Co., Clarksville, Md 1955-60; chief chemist soap-cosmetic divsn. G.H. Packwoo Mfg. Co., St. Louis, 1960-61; coord., promoter chem. produc devel. Abbott Labs., North Chicago, Ill., 1961-71; interna chem. cons. to mgmt., 1971-73; pres. Germann Internat. Ltd 1973-82, Ramtek Internat. Ltd., 1973-2000. Real estate broke 1972-90; cons. major Japanese chem. cos., 1971-85; cons. dep chemistry Bowling Green (Ohio) State U., 1988. Author: Th Technical Man of the Sea of Change, 1965, Decontamination Plant Wastes--An Overview, 1969, Science's Ultima Challenge--The Re-evaluation of Ancient Occult Knowledg 1978, Science and Innovation, 1993; patentee in U.S. and fg countries on sulfonamides, vitamins, detergent-softeners ar biocides. Rep. Am. Inst. Chemists to Joint Com. on Employme Practices, 1969-72; vestryman St. Paul's Episc. Ch., Norwal Ohio, 1978-81, chmn. adminstrn. and long-range plannir commn., 1980-81, The Ch. of Light; sec. Friends of the Norwa Pub. Libr., 1996, pres., 1997-99, 2006—; trustee Svcs. for th Aging, Inc., 1982-94, treas., 1992-93, pres., 1994; mem. nut tional coun. Ohio Dist. Five Area Agy. on Aging, 1983-84; adv. Ohio Assn. Ctrs. for Sr. Citizens, Inc., 1982-90; bd. dir Christie Lane Industries, 1981—2005, chmn., 1988-94; mer com., sec. Huron County Disaster Svcs. Agy., 1987-89. Fello AAAS, Am. Inst. Chemists (chmn. com. employment rel 1969-72), Chem. Soc. (London); mem. Am. Chem. Soc. (cou cilor 1971-73, chmn. membership com. chem. mktg. and ecor divsn. 1966-68, chmn. program com. 1968-69, del. at large f local sects. 1970-71, chmn. 1972-73, chmn. Chgo. progra com. 1966-67, chmn. Chgo. endowment com. 1967-68, d Chgo. sect. 1968-72, chmn. awards com. 1972-73, sec. cher mktg. and econs. group Chgo. sect. 1964-66, chmn. 1967-68 Am. Numastic Soc., Internat. Sci. Found., Sci. Rsch. Soc. Am Comml. Chem. Devel. Assn. (chmn. program com. Chgo. con 1966, mem. fin. com. 1966-67, ad hoc com. of Comml. Che Devel. Assn. and Chem. Market Rsch. Assn. 1968-69, co-chm pub. rels. Denver conv. 1968, chmn. membership com. 1969-7 mem. directory com. 1967-68, employment com. 1969-70), N Security Indsl. Assn. (com. rep. ocean sci. tech. com., main nance adv. com., tng. ad. com. 1962-70), Midwest Planni Assn., Am. Assn. Textile Chemists and Colorists, Am. Phar Assn., Midwest Chem. Mktg. Assn., Am. Mgmt. Assn., N. Acad. Scis., Internat. Platform Assn., Am. Meteorol. Soc., Wa Pollution Control Fedn., Lake County Bd. Realtors, Wor Future Soc., Midwest Planning Assn., Am. Fedn. Astrologe Washington Astrological Assn. (v.p. 1959-60), Ancient Ast naut Soc., Am. Philatelic Soc., Am. Numismatic Assn., A Rose Soc., AARP (pres. Huron county Firelands chpt. #41 1986-88, chmn. legis. com. 1988-90, active project vote, pr 1997-98, bd. dirs. 1998—), Friends Norwalk Pub. Libr. (s 1997-98, pres. 1998-2000), Chemists Club (N.Y.C., Chgo Torch Club, Toastmasters, Lions (sec. Allview, Md. 1956-5 Kiwanis, Masons, (32nd degree, Knights Templar, Rota Gamma Delta (pres. Cleve. chapt. 1941-42), Sigma Xi, Alp Chi Sigma (chmn. profl. activities com. 1968-70, pres. Chg chpt. 1968-70). Died Jan. 15, 2007.

GEROW, ROBERT KENT, former construction equipm distribution company executive, consultant; b. Bay City, Mic Nov. 23, 1919; s. Lyman Claire and Alice Marie (Kent) G.; Betty Marie Cardenas, Jan. 9, 1942; children— Ronald David R., James D. Student Rose-Hulman Inst. Tech., 1937- Ind. U., 1939-40. Draftsman, designer J.D. Adams Mfg. C

Indpls., 1938-40, Victor div. RCA, Indpls., 1940-44; sales rep. Minn.-Honeywell, Indpls., 1946-47; v.p., gen. mgr. Reid Holcomb Co., Indpls., 1947-80. Bd. dirs. Angus-Scientech Edn. Found., Indpls., 1968—. Served with USN, 1944-46. Mem. Ind. Equipment Distbrs. Assn. (pres. 1968-69), Assn. Equipment Distbrs. (lt. dir. 1968-69, indsl. relations com. 1970). Presbyterian. Club: Scientech (pres. 1978). Lodge: Masons (pres. shrine chanters 1960). Avocations: woodworking; music; genealogy. Home: Indianapolis, Ind. Died Dec. 26, 2006.

GERSHON, FRANCES WANG, toy company executive; b. Bklyn., June 18, 1923; d. Philip and Sarah (Eckstein) Wang; B.S. with high honors, U. Ill., 1945; m. Elvin B. Klein, June 23, 1943 (div. 1983); children: Michael, Bari Klein Freiden, Philip; m. Jerald Gershon, May 1988. Pre-sch. tchr. Kansas City (Mo.) Co-op. Pre-Sch., 1952-59; co-founder U.S. Toy Co., Inc., Kansas City, Mo., 1952, exec. v.p., 1952—, founder Constructive Playthings div., 1954; guest lectr. at tchr.-tng. instns., 1959—; mem. adv. council, spl. edn. dept. Shawnee-Mission Sch. Dist., 1972. Named Woman of Distinction, United Jewish Appeal. Mem. Mo. (state sec. 1967-68), Kansas City (v.p. 1956-57) assns. for edn. young children, Johnson County Assn. Children with Learning Disabilities (v.p. 1970-71), Council Jewish Women, Phi Sigma Sigma. Jewish. Clubs: Hadassah, Altrusa (dir.) (Kansas City, Mo.). Home: Shawnee Mission, Kans. Died Aug. 28, 2007.

GERWICK, BEN CLIFFORD, JR., civil engineer, consultant; b. Berkeley, Calif., Feb. 22, 1919; s. Ben Clifford and Bernice (Coultrap) Gerwick; m. Martelle Louise Beverly, July 28, 1941 (dec. Jan. 1995); children: Beverly Brian, Virginia Wallace, Ben Clifford III, William; m. Ellen Chaney Lynch, May 18, 1996. BS, U. Calif., 1940. With Ben C. Gerwick, Inc., San Francisco, from 1946, pres., 1952—88, chmn., 1988—2000, hon. chmn., sr. tech. cons., 2000—06; exec. v.p. Santa Fe-Pomeroy, Inc., 1968—71; prof. civil engring. U. Calif., Berkeley, 1971—89, prof. emeritus, 1989—2006. Sponsoring mgr. Richmond-San Rafael Bridge substructure, 1953—56, San Mateo-Hayward Bridge, 1964—66; lectr. constrn. engring. Stanford U., 1962—68; cons. major bridge and marine constrn. projects; cons. engr. ocean structures and overwater bridges, also offshore structures. U.S., North Sea, Arctic Ocean, Japan, Australia, Indonesia, Arabian Gulf, China, Europe, Can., S.E. Asia, S.Am.; mem. Arctic Rsch. Commn., 1990—95. Author: (book) Russian-English Dictionary of Prestressed Concrete and Concrete Construction, 1966, Construction of Prestressed Concrete Structures, 1971, 2d edit., 1996, Construction and Engineering Marketing for Major Project Services, 1981, Construction of Marine and Offshore Structures, 1986, 2d edit., 2000, The Bridge Beyond, 2006; contbr. articles to profl. jours. Chmn. marine bd. NRC, 1978—80. With USN, 1940—46, comdr. USNR, ret. Named one of Top Engrs. in Past 125 Yrs., Engring. News Record, 2000; recipient Golden Beaver award, Beavers Constrn. Soc., 1974, Mörsch medal, Deutsche Beton Verein, Weisbaden, Germany, 1978, Blakely Smith Ocean Engring. medal, Soc. Naval Archs. and Marine Engrs., 1981, Lockheed Ocean Engring. award, Marine Tech. Soc., 1982, Berkeley citation, U. Calif., Berkeley, 1989, Internat. award, Japan Soc. Civil Engring., 2001, award, Swedish Concrete Soc., 1986. Fellow: ASCE (hon. Karp award 1976, G. Brooks Earnest award 1980, Peurifoy award 1989, Pres.'s award 1989, Disting. Constructor award 2000, Ralph B. Peck Lectr. award 2001, Outstanding Lifetime Achievement award 2001), Norwegian Concrete Soc. (Holand award 2002, Ivar Holand award 2002), Am. Segmental Bridge Inst., Nat. Acad. Constrn., Deep Founds. Inst. Disting. Svc. award 1996), Internat. Assn. Bridge and Structural Engrs., Am. Concrete Inst. (hon.; dir. 1960, Turner award 1974, Corbetta award 1981, Franklin Inst. Brown award 1984, Offshore Tech. Rsch.Ctr. Honors award 1992, Ocean Tech. Pioneer award 2004); mem.: NAE, Nat. Acad. Engrs., Prestressed Concrete Inst. (hon.; pres. 1957—58, Titan award 2004), Fédn. Internat. Procontrainte (hon.; pres. 1974—78, Freyssinet medal 1982), Claremont Country Club (Oakland), Bohemian Club San Francisco). Congregationalist. Home: Oakland, Calif. Died Dec. 25, 2006.

GETZELS, MORTIMER, judge; b. N.Y.C., Nov. 3, 1917; s. Saul and Nettie (Rosenblum) G.; m. Ruth Suzanne Herz, Jan. 3, 1954; 1 son, Paul David. B.A., CCNY, 1938; LL.B., NYU, 1943. Bar: N.Y. 1943, U.S. Dist. Ct. (so. dist.) N.Y. 1948, U.S. Dist. Ct. (ea. dist.) N.Y. 1972. Staff atty., adminstrv. atty. Legal Aid Soc., N.Y.C., 1947-78; judge Family Ct. State of N.Y., N.Y.C., 1978—. Served with U.S. Army, 1943-46. Mem. ABA, N.Y. County Lawyers Assn., Am. Judicature Soc. Died Sept. 14, 2006.

GEUMEI, AIDA M., physician; b. Alexandria, Egypt, Dec. 26, 1930; d. Mohamed Geumei and Amina (Bassuni) G.; m. Ahmed M. Khalifa, Sept. 22, 1955; children: Soumaya, Amina, Anwar. MB, ChB, U. Alexandria, 1955, diploma in physiology, 1957, diploma in pharmacology, 1959, diploma in medicine, 1960, PhD in Pharm, 1965. Instr., lectr. U. Alexandria, 1956-69; asst. prof. internal medicine Southwestern Med. Sch., Dallas, 1969-71; fellow in cardiovasc. divsn. Meth. Hosp.-U. Tex., Dallas, 1971-73, fellow in pulmonary divsn., 1973-75; asst. prof. internal medicine U. Tex., Dallas, 1975-77, clin. asst. prof. internal medicine, from 1978; med. dir. pulmonary clin. rsch. Meth. Hsop., Dallas, 1976-79; dir. pulmonary divsn. Henderson (Tex.) Meml. Hosp., Dallas, from 1978. Author: Chron. Obst. Pulm. Disease, 1978, Vasoactive Intes. Pept., 1982. Fellow ACP, Am. Coll. Chest Physicians; mem. Am. Thoracic Soc., Tex. Med. Soc., Rusk County Med. Soc. Died Feb. 23, 2007.

GIBALDI, MILO, dean; b. NYC, Dec. 17, 1938; s. Ignatius and Angela G.; m. Florence D'Amato, Dec. 26, 1960; 1 child, Ann Elizabeth. BS, Coll. Pharmacy, Columbia U., 1960, PhD, 1963. Asst. prof. pharmacy Columbia U., NYC, 1963-66; asst. prof. pharmaceutics SUNY, Buffalo, 1966-67, assoc. prof., 1967-70, prof., 1970-78, chmn. dept., 1970-78; prof. pharmaceutics U. Wash., Seattle, from 1978; dean U. Wash. Sch. Pharmacy, Seattle, 1978-95, dean emeritus, from 1995. Cons. Bur. Drugs, FDA, 1970-72, VA, Washington, 1971-72; vis. prof. U. Rochester, 1972-74; program dir. clin. pharmacokinetics and biopharmaceutics NIH, 1973-78, pharmacology study sect., 1976-80; sci. adv. bd. G.D. Searle & Co., 1978—. Author: (with Donald Perrier) Pharmacokinetics, 1976; contbr. articles to profl. jours. Fellow Acad. Pharm. Scis., AAAS; mem. Am. Chem. Soc., Am. Pharm. Assn., Acad. Soc. Clin. Pharmacology, Am. Soc. Pharmacology and Exptl. Therapeutics, N.Y. Acad. Scis., Am. Assn. Colls. Pharmacy, Nat. Acad. Scis. (mem. Inst. Medicine 1986), Health Scis. U. Wash. (assoc. v.p. 1983), Sigma Xi, Rho Chi. Home: Edmonds, Wash. Died Jan. 13, 2006.

GIBB, ARTHUR, Vt. state senator; b. Bklyn., Apr. 16, 1908; s. Henry Elmer and Grace Dwight G.; A.B., Yale U., 1930; m. Barbara Lowrie, 1932; children— John Dwight, Arthur Lowrie, Barbara Grace, Henry F. Mem. Vt. Ho. of Reps., 1963-70, vice-chmn. com. on ways and means, 1965, chmn., 1969, chmn. Com. on Natural Resources, 1966, 67, 69; mem. Vt. State Senate, 1970—; chmn. Agr. Com., 1973-74, Natural Resources Com., 1975-76, Fin. Com., 1977-83. Chmn. Gov.'s Commn. on Environ. Control, 1969. Served with USNR, 1942-45. Decorated Bronze Star. Mem. Nat. Pilots Assn., Farm Bur. Congregationalist. Home: Middlebury, Vt. Died Nov. 1, 2005.

GIBBS, MARTIN, biologist, educator; b. Phila., Nov. 11, 1922; s. Samuel and Rose (Sugarman) G.; m. Svanhild Karen Kvale, Oct. 11, 1950; children: Janet Helene, Laura Jean, Steven Joseph, Michael Seland, Robert Kvale. BS, Phila. Coll. Pharmacy, 1943; PhD, U. Ill., 1947. Scientist Brookhaven Nat. Lab., 1947-56; prof. biochemistry Cornell U., 1957-64; Abraham S. and Gertrude Berg prof. biology, chmn. dept. Brandeis U., Waltham, Mass., 1965-93. Cons. NSF, 1961-64, 69-72, NIH, 1966-69, Cosmos Club, 1984; mem. corp. Marine Biol. Lab., Woods Hole, Mass., 1970, RESA lectr., 1969; NATO cons. fellowship bd., 1968-70; mem. Coun. Internat. Exch. of Scholars, 1976-82; chmn. adv. com. selection Fulbright Scholars for Eastern Europe; adj. prof. Bot. Inst., U. Munster, Fed. Republic of Germany, 1978, 80, 87; adj. prof. dept. botany U. Calif., Riverside, 1979-89. Author: Structure and Function of Chloroplasts, 1970, Crop Productivity-Research Imperatives, 1975, Crassulacean Acid Metabolism, 1982, Crassulacean Acid Biosynthesis and Function of Plant Lipids, 1983, Crop Productivity-Research Imperative, Revisited, 1985, Hungarian-USA Binational Symposium on Photosynthesis, 1986; editor-in-chief: Plant Physiology, 1963—92, assoc. editor: Physiologie Vegetale, 1966—76, Ann. Rev. Plant Physiology, 1966—71. Recipient Charles Reid Barnes award, 1984, Adolph E. Gude award, 1993, Martin Gibbs medal, 1993, U. Ill. Achievement award, 1996, Gold medal Bulgarian Acad. Scis.; Alexander von Humboldt fellow, 1987. Mem. NAS, AAUP, Am. Soc. Plant Physiologists (Barnes, Gude, Gibbs medal), Russian Soc. Plant Physiologists (hon. life mem.), Am. Acad. Arts and Scis., Am. Soc. Biochem. Molecular Biology, Can. Soc. Plant Physiologists (hon. life), Acad. Scis. France. Home: Lexington, Mass. Died July 24, 2006.

GIBSON, CHARLES ALFRED, bank executive; b. Newcastle, Ont., Can., Jan. 5, 1927; s. Alfred Luck and Edith Roberta (O'Brien) G. BA, Hobart Coll., 1952. Asst. nat. bank examiner Comptroller of Currency, NYC, 1852-56; sr.v.p., trust officer First Nat. Bank of Cortlant, N.Y., from 1956, trust cons., 1989-1995. Bd. dirs., Cortland Rural Cemetery, Cortland meml. Found., 1890 House Mus., Cortland, 1987—. Staff sgt. U.S. Army, 1945-47, Japan. Mem. Cortland Country Club, Cortland Exchange Club, University Club, Cortland Elks, Masons. Home: Cortland, NY. Died Aug. 25, 2006.

GIBSON, CURTIS A., aircraft systems engineer; b. Springfield, Ohio, Nov. 5, 1929; s. Frank Z. and Helen W. (Cox) G.; Chem.E., U. Cin., 1952; Ph.D. in Religion, D.D. (hon.), Universal Life Ch., 1979. Chem. engr. Sylvania Elec. Products Co., Emporium, Pa., 1952-54; chem. engr. U.S. Air Force, Wright-Patterson AFB, Ohio, 1956-59, mech. engr., 1959-70, life support systems engr., 1970-79, aircraft systems engr., 1979—. Active Boy Scouts Am. Recipient Silver Beaver award Boy Scouts Am., 1973. Mem. Am. Def. Preparedness Assn., Air Force Assn., Internat. Acad. Profl. Bus. Execs. Home: Springfield, Ohio. Died Nov. 2, 2006.

GIBSON, PAUL RAYMOND, international trade and investment development company executive; b. Cathay, Calif., Apr. 10, 1924; s. Otto and Louella (Vestal) G.; m. Janice Elizabeth Carter, dec. 19, 1952; children: Scott C., Paula S. BS in Fgn. Svc., Georgetown U., 1956. With U.S. Govt., Heidelberg, Germany, 1948—52; export mgr. Asia, Philip Morris Co., San Francisco, 1952-54; founder, v.p., gen. mgr. McGregor and Werner Internat. Corp., Washington, 1954-62; v.p., dir. McGregor and Werner Corp., 1955-62; v.p. fin. Parsons & Whittemore, Inc., NYC, 1962-65; founder, pres. Paul R. Gibson & Assocs., Washington, 1965-70; mng. dir. Black Clawson Pacific Co., Sydney, Australia, 1970-72; pres. Envirotech Asia Pacific, Sydney, 1972-75, Envirotech Internat., Menlo Park, Calif., 1975-80; founder, pres. INTERACT, San Francisco, 1980-91; pres. Manchester Group, Ltd., Washington, 1987—89; pres., mng. assoc. Projects Internat. Assocs., Inc., Washington, 1991—95; pres. Projects Internat., Inc., from 1996, Sustainable Project Mgmt. USA, from 1994. Mem. Pacific Basin Econ. Coun., 1975-2007, vice chmn. policy and planning U.S. sect., 1976-91, chmn. Vietnam Task Force, 1998-2000; mem., trustee San Francisco World Affairs Coun., 1980-91; mem. World Affairs Coun., Washington, 1998-2002. Served to sgt. USMC, 1941-45, PTO. Mem. Am. C. of C. Sydney (chmn. Asia-Pacific coun. Am. C. of C. 1973-74, adv. com. 1975-2007), Dirs. Cir., Rural Health Internat. (co-chmn. 2002-07), Am. Nat. Club (Sydney), Washington Met. Club. Home: Naples, Fla. Died June 15, 2007.

GIBSON, ROBERT VALENTINE, lawyer; b. Indpls., Feb. 7, 1921; s. Nathaniel Alexander and Emily Pauline (Boos) G.; m. Maxine Cathrine Henkle, Oct. 12, 1944; children: Gail Valerie Gibson Vandagriff, Gregory Valentine, Beth von Henkle Haglund. Student, Wayne U., 1938-41; BA, Stanford U., 1949; LLB, U. San Francisco, 1950. Bar: Calif. 1950. Assoc. Bailie, Turner and Lake, LA, 1951-54; ptnr. Newell, Chester and Gibson, LA, 1954-60; pvt. practice Newport Beach, Calif., from 1973; ptnr. Gibson and Haglund, LA, 1990. Bd. dirs. Presley Cos., Newport Beach, Calif., Am. Telecommunications Corp., El Monte, Calif., Moran Properties, Inc., Alhambra, Calif., Raymar Book Corp., Monrovia, Calif., GB Foods Corp., Amaliens, Calif.; lectr. Am. Mgmt. Assn., 1967; mem. adv. com. Internat. Monetary Conf., Claremont (Calif.) Coll., 1969, observer, 1980 conf. Bd. dirs., mem. exec. com., v.p Opera Pacific. Lt. USNR, PTO. Mem. Calif. Bar Assn., L.A. Bar Assn. Mem. LDS Church. Home: Newport Beach, Calif. Died Oct. 15, 2006.

GIEDT, WARREN HARDING, mechanical engineer, educator; b. Leola, SD, Nov. 1, 1920; s. William John Peter and Julia Emelia (Klauss) G.; m. Leta McCarty, June 24, 1950. Student, U. Chgo., 1938-40; BS, U. Calif.-Berkeley, 1944, MS, 1946, PhD, 1950. Asst. prof. Air Force Inst. Tech., Wright Field, Ohio, 1946-47; instr. dept. mech. engring. U. Calif., Berkeley, 1947-50, asst. prof., 1950-56, assoc. prof., 1956-61, prof., 1961-65, Davis, 1965— 83; prof. emeritus U. Calif, Davis, from 1983; chmn. dept. mech. engring. U. Calif., 1965-69; assoc. dean grad. studies U. Calif. (Coll. Engring.), 1972-80; research engr. Detroit Controls div. Am. Standard, 1952-60; cons. Am. Standard (Advanced Tech. Labs. div.), 1961-65, Monolith Portland Midwest, 1962-63, NASA, 1964-67, Boeing Co., 1962-66, Lawrence Livermore Nat. Lab., from 1960, Sandia Nat. Labs., from 1984. Fulbright prof. U. Tokyo, 1963 Author: Principles of Engineering Heat Transfer, 1957, Thermophysics, 1971; editor: Jour. Heat Transfer, 1967-72, Procs. Heat Transfer and Fluid Mechanics Inst, 1964. Served with USAAF, 1943-47. Recipient Assoc. Students Outstanding Tchrs. award U. Calif., 1966, Thermal Engring. mem. award Japan Soc. Mech. Engrs., 1990. Fellow ASME (Heat transfer meml. award 1976, James Harry Potter Gold medal 1985), Japan Soc. Promotion of Sci. (fellow 1980); mem. Am. Soc. Engring. Edn. (Western Electric award 1971, G. Edwin Burks award 1974), Am. Welding Soc. (Charles Jennings award 1971, Hobart Meml. medal award 1991), Order of Golden Bear, Phi Beta Kappa, Sigma Xi, Tau Beta Pi, Pi Tau Sigma. Home: San Jose, Calif. Died Mar. 23, 2007.

GIFFORD, ERNEST MILTON, retired biologist, educator; b. Riverside, Calif., Jan. 17, 1920; s. Ernest Milton and Mildred Wade (Campbell) G.; m. Jean Duncan, July 15, 1942; 1 child, Jeanette AB, U. Calif., Berkeley, 1942, PhD, 1950; grad., U.S. Army Command and Gen. Staff Sch., 1965. Asst. prof. botany, asst. botanist expt. sta. U. Calif.-Davis, 1950-56, assoc. prof. botany, assoc. botanist, 1957-61, prof. botany, botanist, 1962-87, prof. emeritus, from 1988, chmn. dept. botany and agrl. botany, 1963-67, 74-78. Author: (with A. S. Foster) Morphology and Evolution of Vascular Plants, 3d edit., 1989, (with T. L. Rost) Mechanisms and control of Cell Division, 1977; editor in chief Am. Jour. Botany, 1975-79; advisor to editor Ency. Brit.; contbr. articles on anatomy, ultrastructure and morphogenesis of higher plants to profl. jours. Served to maj. U.S. Army, 1942-46; ETO; to col. USAR, 1946-73. Decorated Bronze Star medal; named disting. contbr. Ency. Brit., 1964; NRC fellow Harvard U., 1956; Fulbright research scholar, France, 1966; John Simon Guggenheim Found. fellow, France, 1966; NATO sr. postdoctoral fellow, France, 1974; recipient Acad. Senate Disting. Teaching award U. Calif.-Davis, 1986. Mem. Bot. Soc. Am. (v.p. 1981, pres. 1982, merit award 1981), Internat. Soc. Plant Morphologists (v.p. 1980-84), Am. Inst. Biol. Scis., Sigma Xi. Home: Davis, Calif. Died June 14, 2006.

GIFFORD, FRANKLIN ANDREW, JR., meteorologist, consultant; b. Union City, NJ, May 7, 1922; s. F.A. and Hazel (Sheehan) G.; m. Eleanor Mary Frith, Aug. 7, 1943; children: Michael J., Robert K. BS, NYU, 1947; MS, Pa. State U., 1954, PhD, 1955. Area chief meteorologist Northwest Airlines, NYC, 1945-50; rsch. meteorologist U.S. Weather Bur. (NOAA), Washington, 1950-55; dir. Atmospheric Turbulence Diffusion Lab. NOAA, Oak Ridge, Tenn., 1955-80. Cons. Los Alamos Nat. Lab., 1980—, U.S. NRC Adv. Com. on Reactor Safety, Washington, 1958-82; cons. Internat. Atomic Energy Agy., Vienna, 1966-82; mem. U.S.-USSR Bilateral Working Group on Air Pollution, 1974-75. Author: Meteorology and Atomic Energy, 1968; contbr. over 140 articles to profl. jours. Capt. USAF, 1943-45, ETO. Recipient Gold medal U.S. Dept. Commerce, 1963. Fellow AAAS, Am. Meteorol. Soc. (Contbn. to Applied Meteorology award 1990). Home: Mc Lean, Va. Died Feb. 18, 2007.

GIFFORD, HARRY CORTLAND FREY, health educator; b. NYC, Sept. 21, 1919; s. Frank Dean and Hazel (Frey) G.; m. Catherine Huber, Sept. 14, 1946; children— Linda Gifford Reece, Frank Dean. Grad., Kent Sch., Conn., 1938; BA in History, Yale, 1942; MS in Hosp. Adminstrn, Columbia, 1947. Adminstrv. resident Greenwich (Conn.) Hosp., 1947; asst. supt. Hackensack (N.J.) Hosp., 1948-49; adminstr. Community Hosp., Glen Cove, N.Y., 1949-61; exec. dir. Springfield (Mass.) Hosp. Med. Center, 1961-67, exec. v.p., dir., 1967-74; pres. Baystate Med. Center, Springfield, 1974-81; asst. prof. U. Mass., Amherst, 1981-86. Vis. lectr. hosp. adminstrn. Columbia, 1961-81, preceptor hosp. adminstrn. residency, 1953-60; preceptor hosp. adminstrn. residency Yale U., 1973; prof. Bryant Coll., Providence, 1985—. Contbr. articles to profl. jours. Mem. Springfield Mental Health Bd., 1965-67; mem. gov.'s com. Health and Ednl. Facilities Authority, 1970-73; Corporator Springfield Tech. Community Coll. Served to 1st lt. Med. Services AUS, 1942-45. Decorated Bronze Star with palm. Fellow Am. Coll. Hosp. Adminstrs. (regents council 1970-71); mem. Am. Hosp. Assn. (trustee 1973-75, 77-80, del.-at-large 1971-73, del. 1967-70, 76-80, chmn. regional adv. bd. 1969-70, 77-80), Mass. Hosp. Assn. (pres. 1967-68) Lodges: Rotary. Died Mar. 8, 2006.

GILBRIDE, JOHN THOMAS, retired shipyard executive; b. Bklyn., May 29, 1916; s. Francis Joseph and Mary (Figueira) G.; m. Rosemary Shelare, Sept. 7, 1940; children: Francis Joseph, John Thomas, Gary George. BA, U. Pa., 1938; postgrad., Bklyn. Poly. Inst., Pratt Inst. With Bklyn. divsn. Todd Shipyards Corp., 1932-46, asst. gen. mgr. L.A. divsn., 1946, gen. mgr. L.A. divsn., 1946-58, pres., 1958-75, chmn., 1975-86; trustee Paget Disease Found. Dir. Emigrant Savs. Bank. Trustee United Seaman's Service; bd. dirs. Oceanic Ednl. Found. Fellow Soc. Naval Architects and Marine Engrs. (hon. v.p.); mem. U.S. Naval Inst. (assoc.), Am. Australian Assn., Am. European Community Assn., Am. Soc. Naval Engrs., Maritime Assn. Port of N.Y., Am. Welding Soc., Nat. Def. Transp. Assn., Navy League U.S., N.E. Coast Instn. Engrs. and Shipbuilders (Eng.), Life

Saving Benevolent Assn. N.Y., Newcomen Soc. N.Am., New Orleans C. of C., Marine Hist. Soc., Phi Sigma Kappa. Clubs: Whitehall Luncheon (past pres., bd. govs.), India House, Chiselers, N.Y. Yacht (N.Y.C.); Nantucket Yacht. Lodges: Knights of Malta. Roman Catholic. Home: Stamford, Conn. Died Mar. 17, 2007.

GILES, NORMAN HENRY, geneticist, science educator; b. Atlanta, Aug. 6, 1915; s. Norman Henry and Alice (Guerard) G.; m. Dorothy Lunsford, Aug. 26, 1939 (dec. Jan. 1967); children: Annette Guerard, David Lunsford; m. Doris Vos Weaver, Aug. 1, 1969 (dec. Aug. 2004); stepchildren: Gayle Weaver (dec.), Alix Weaver. AB, Emory U., 1937, ScD (hon.), 1980; MA, Harvard U., 1938, PhD, 1940; MA (hon.), Yale U., 1951. Instr. botany Yale U., New Haven, 1941-45, asst. prof., 1945-46, assoc. prof., 1946-51, prof., 1951-61, Eugene Higgins prof. genetics, 1961-72; Fuller E. Callaway prof. genetics U. Ga., 1972-86, emeritus, from 1986. Prin. biologist Oak Ridge Nat. Lab., 1947-50; cons. AEC, 1954-64; mem. genetics study sect. NIH, 1960-64, genetics tng. com., 1966-70; ednl. adv. bd. John Simon Guggenheim Meml. Found., 1977-86. Mem. editorial bd. Radiation Research, 1953-58, Am. Naturalist, 1961-64, Devel. Genetics, 1979-86. Bd. dirs. U. Ga. Research Found., 1979-85. Parker fellow Harvard U., 1940-41, Fulbright and Guggenheim fellow Genetics Inst., U. Copenhagen, 1959-60, Guggenheim fellow Australian Nat. U., Canberra, 1966; recipient Bicentennial Silver medallion U. Ga., 1984, Lamar Dodd award for rsch. U. Ga., 1985, Thomas Hunt Morgan medal Genetics Soc. Am., 1988. Fellow Am. Acad. Arts and Scis., AAAS; mem. Nat. Acad. Scis. (chmn. genetics sect. 1976-79), Genetics Soc. Am. (treas. 1954-56, pres. 1970), Bot. Soc. Am., Am. Soc. Naturalists (pres. 1977), Am. Inst. Biol. Scis., Genetics Soc. Japan (hon.), Royal Danish Acad. Scis. and Letters (fgn.), Am. Ornithologists Union, Phi Beta Kappa, Sigma Xi. Died Oct. 16, 2006.

GILLETTE, EDWARD LEROY, radiation oncology educator; b. Coffeyville, Kans., May 21, 1932; s. Harold R. and Laura Belle (McLaughlin) G.; m. Carol J. Peterson, June 2, 1956 (div. Oct. 1981); children: William R., Jeffrey S., Timothy E., Jennifer L.; m. Sharon L. McChesney, Nov. 26, 1988. BS, DVM, Kans. State U., 1956; MS, Colo. State U., 1961, PhD, 1965. From instr. to prof. radiology and radiation biology Colo. State U., Ft. Collins, 1959-72, prof., 1972-2000, prof., chmn. emeritus, from 2000, dir. comparative oncology, 1974-98, chmn. dept. radiol. health scis., 1989-98, assoc. dean rsch. Coll. Vet. Medicine and Biomed. Sci., 1997-98; adj. clin. prof. dept. radiation oncology UCLA Med. Sch., from 1998. Adj. prof. dept. radiation oncology Duke U. Med. Coll., Durham, N.C.; bd. dirs. The Children's Hosp. Kempe Rsch. Ctr., Denver, 1984-90; vis. scientist M.D. Anderson Cancer Ctr. U. Tex., 1988. Assoc. editor Radiation Rsch., 1979-82, 86-90; assoc. editor, Internat. Jour. of Radiation Oncology Biology and Physics, 1990-95, mem. editl. bd., 1995—; contbr. articles to profl. jours. Bd. dirs. Colo. State Sci. Fair, 1984-90. 1st lt. U.S. Army, 1956-58. Recipient Outstanding Svc. to the Vet. Profession award Am. Animal Hosp. Assn., 1984, Ralston-Purina rsch. award, 1988, Kans. State U. Alumni Assn. Medallion award, 1999; U. Tex. fellow, 1968-69. Mem. AVMA, Am. Coll. Vet. Radiology (cert., pres. 1973-74), Am. Coll. Vet. Internal Medicine, Oncology (cert.), Am. Cancer Soc. (mem. exec. com. Colo. divsn. 1978-82, bd. dirs. Colo. divsn. 1984-90, pres. Larimer County chpt. 1977-81), Vet. Cancer Soc. (pres. 1982-84), Radiation Rsch. Soc. (councilor 1988-91), Am. Soc. Therapeutic Radiology and Oncology, Am. Assn. Cancer Rsch., Colo. State U. Alumni Assn. (Honor Alumnus award 1985), Rotary. Republican. Avocation: reading. Home: Fort Collins, Colo. Died Nov. 17, 2006.

GILLETTE, HYDE, retired brokerage house executive; b. Chgo., June 23, 1906; s. Edwin Fraser and Mabel (Hyde) G.; m. Marie Clarke Smith, Sept. 7, 1932 (dec. Sept. 28, 1994); 1 child, Marie Clarke Gerald. Grad., Exeter Acad., 1924; AB cum laude, Princeton U., 1928; MBA with distinction, Harvard U., 1930. With Glore, Forgan & Co., 1930-53, ptnr., 1950-53; dep. asst. & dep. under sec. USAF, 1953-57; asst. postmaster gen., bur. finance U.S. Post Office Dept., Washington, 1957-61; ptnr. Auchincloss Parker & Redpath, 1961-70; regional v.p. Thomson & McKinnon Auchincloss, Inc., Washington, 1970-73; v.p. Thomson McKinnon Securities, 1973-89, Prudential Securities, 1989-91. Exec. bd. Chgo. Area Project, 1936-53, chmn., 1948-53; bd. dirs., v.p. Nat. Capital area council Boy Scouts Am.; regent Nat. Eagle Scout Assn.; dir., vice chmn. budget com. Community Fund of Chgo., 1942; chmn. exec. com. Chgo. Opera Theatre, 1947; adv. bd. Dept. Public Welfare Ill., 1949-53; pres. Barrington Country Day Sch., 1941; v.p. Washington Heart Assn., 1961; bd. dirs. Am. Heart Assn., 1960-63. Served as lt. comdr. USNR, 1943-46. Recipient Exceptional Civilian Svc. award USAF, 1956; Disting. Svc. award U.S. Post Office Dept., 1960; disting. Eagle Scout Nat. award. Mem. Mayflower Descs., Soc. Colonial Wars, English Speaking Union (dir. 1977-86), Barrington Countryside Assn. (pres. 1949-50), Quadrangle Club (Princeton), Chevy Chase Club (Washington), Met. Club (Washington), Beverly Yacht Club (Marion, Mass.), Phi Beta Kappa. Episcopalian. Home: Westwood, Mass. Died June 16, 2007.

GILLETTE, JOHN WILLIAM, marketing executive; b. Oct. 16, 1923; BA in Polit. Sci. and History, Wittenberg U., 1947; postgrad., Princeton U., 1947-50. Sales corr. plastics sales divsn. Rohm & Haas Co., Phila., 1950-55; sales technician Delta Products divsn., Air Accessories, Ft. Worth, Tex., 1955-60; nat. v.p., southeastern dist. mgr., br. mgr. Comml. Plastics and Supply Corp., Atlanta, 1960-76; asst. adjutant gen. Army Ga. Dept. Def., Atlanta, 1976-83; security mgr. Royal Creek Apts., Stone Mountain, Ga., 1983-86; spl. projects mgr. Borg-Warner Security Corp., Atlanta, 1996; gen. mgr. Bartronics divsn. Barton Protective Svcs., Inc., Atlanta, 1996-97; product mgr. additives group Mayzo, Inc., Norcross, Ga., 1990-95, sr. v.p., from 1997. Home: Austin, Tex. Died May 18, 2006.

GILLILAND, CHARLES HERBERT, SR., physician; b. Melrose, Iowa, Sept. 26, 1911; s. Herbert Roy and Maggie Jane (Clark) G.; m. Marion Charlotte Spjut, Mar. 6, 1942; children—Charles Herbert, Marion Charlotte, Patricia Ann, Normal Paul, Cynthia Eileen. BS, U. Fla., 1935, postgrad., 1936-37; MD, U. Iowa, 1941. Diplomate: Am. Bd. Obstetrics and Gynecology. Epidemiologist U. Iowa Hosps., 1940-41, intern, 1941-42; commd. lt. j.g. M.C. U.S. Navy, 1942, designated flight surgeon, 1943, resigned, 1954; resident obstetrics-gynecology U.S. Naval Hosp., Bethesda, Md., 1948-51; practice medicine, specializing in obstetrics-gynecology Gainesville, Fla., from 1954; clin. prof. dept. obstetrics and gynecology U. Fla., from 1975; mem. staff Alachua Gen., N. Fla. Regional hosps., both Gainesville; ret. Dir. Fla. Nat. Bank, Gainesville Trustee N. Fla. Regional Hosp. Served to capt. USNR. Fellow A.C.S., Am. Coll. Obstetricians and Gynecologists (chmn. Fla. sect. 1975, dist. chmn. 1979-82); mem. South Atlantic Assn. Obstetricians and Gynecologists (v.p. 1976), Fla. Obstetric and Gynecologic Soc. (pres. 1972-73), AMA, So. Med. Assn., Fla. Med. Assn., Alachua County Med. Soc., Explorers Club, Phi Kappa Phi, Alpha Kappa Kappa, Rho Chi, Phi Sigma. Lodges: Kiwanis (pres. 1979-80). Home: Gainesville, Fla. Died Mar. 4, 2007.

GILLIS, ROBERT ELLIOT, food company executive; b. Lincoln, Maine, June 7, 1938; s. Hugh Allen and Helen (Bucknell) G.; m. Shirley Diane Smith, June 21, 1958; children: Jeffry Todd, Michael Darron, Lauren Ashley. BA, Pacific U., 1961; postgrad., Grad. Sch. Internat. Relations and Law-U. Conn., 1961. Adminstrv. asst. United Fruit Co., Boston, 1961-62, mgr. export, 1962-63, mgr. sales adminstrn., 1963-65, dir. mktg., 1966-68; pres. Intermarket Internat. Inc., Boston, 1965-66, Concept Foods Corp., Chgo., 1968-70; mgmt. cons.-investor Stowe, Vt., 1970-76, Dallas, 1970-76; gen. mgr. food service group Central Soya Co. Inc., Ft. Wayne, Ind., 1976-77, gen. mgr. food div., 1977, v.p., 1977-80, group v.p., 1980-83, exec. v.p., pres. food group, from 1983; chmn. bd. J.H. Filbert Inc. subs. Central Soya Co., from 1979, Butcher Boy Food Products Inc., subs., from 1982, Fred's Frozen Foods Inc., subs., from 1982. Bd. govs. Med. Ctr. Hosp., Burlington, Vt., 1974—; trustee Pacific U., Forest Grove, Oreg., 1978—. Mem. Internat. Food service Mfg. Assn. (dir. 1978—, chmn. bd. 1983), Nat. Restaurant Assn. (action com. 1973-75) Republican. Home: Fort Wayne, Ind. Died Feb. 5, 2007.

GILLMOR, PAUL EUGENE, congressman, lawyer; b. Tiffin, Ohio, Feb. 1, 1939; s. Paul Marshall and Lucy Jeannette (Fry) Gillmor; m. Karen Lee Lako, Dec. 10, 1983; children: Linda Dianne, Julie Ellen, Paul Michael, Connor Sheldon, Adam William BA, Ohio Wesleyan U., Delaware, 1961; JD, U. Mich. Law Sch., 1964; LLD (hon.), Tiffin U., Ohio, 1985; degree (hon.), Defiance Coll., Ohio U., Rio Grande Coll. Bar: Ohio 1965. Mem. Ohio State Senate, 1967-89, minority leader, 1978—81, 1983—85, pres., 1981—83, 1985—88; mem. US Congress from 5th Ohio dist., 1989—2007, mem. fin. svcs. com., ranking mem. subcommittee on fin. instns. and consumer credit, dep. minority whip. Assoc. firm Tomb and Hering, Tiffin, 1967-88; bd. dirs. Old Fort Banking Co., Ohio; chmn. econ. and security com. NATO Parliamentary Assembly. Pres. Ohio Electoral Coll., Columbus, 1984. Served to capt. USAF, 1965—66. Recipient Gov.'s award, Ohio, 1980, Phillips medal of Pub. Svc. Ohio U. Coll. Osteopathy, 1981, Exec. Order, Ohio Commodores Assn., 1981, Disting. Citizen award Med. Coll. Ohio, 1982, FT Stone Lab. Partnership award, Ohio State U., 1995, Ground Water Protector award, Nat. Ground Water Assn., 2004; named Legislator of Yr., Ohio VFW, 1994. Mem. ABA, Ohio State Bar Assn., Nat. Rep. Legislators Assn. (named Outstanding Legislator of Yr. 1983). Republican. Methodist. Home: Old Fort, Ohio. Died Sept. 5, 2007.

GILMAN, ALBERT FRANKLIN, III, mathematics educator; b. Chgo., June 25, 1931; s. Albert Franklin and Regina Anna (Raymann) G.; m. Mia Lindsay Peterson, Sept. 5, 1964; children: Albert, Eugenia, Clifford, Patience, Anastasia, Nicholas, Alexandra, Georgia, Henry, Peter. BS, Northwestern U., 1952; MA, U. Mont., 1958, Ind. U., 1962, PhD, 1963. Instr. to asst. prof. math. Bowdoin Coll., Brunswick, Maine, 1963-66; assoc. prof. to prof. math. Coll. of V.I., St. Thomas, 1966-69; prof. math. Western Carolina U., Cullowhee, N.C., from 1969, asst. v.p. acad. affairs Cullowheee, N.C., 1969-72, acting vice chancellor, 1972. Vis. prof. Bulgarian Acad. Scis., 1978. Editor Caribbean Jour. Sci. and Math., 1967-70; contbr. articles to profl. jours. Exec. dir. Rep. steering com. U.S. Ho. of Rep., Washington, 1973-74. Nat. Endowment for Humanities fellow, U. Chgo., 1982. Mem. Math. Assn. Am., Am. Legion, Biltmore Forest Country Club, Rotary (pres. 1981-82), Sigma Xi, Pi Mu Epsilon. Republican. Greek Orthodox Ch. Avocations: politics, theology, byzantine music, sailing, genealogy. Home: Cullowhee, NC. Died Jan. 17, 2006.

GILMAN, COOPER LEE, manufacturing company finance executive; b. Tientsin, China, Oct. 3, 1928; s. Frank Shepard and Clare (Cooper) G.; m. Judith Matthews Partelow, July 29, 1961; children: Scott, Bradley. BS, U.S. Naval Acad., 1951. Indsl. engr. Am. Viscose Corp., Front Royal, Va., 1955-56; fin., engring., mfg. staff and mgmt. positions Gen. Electric Co., Lynn, Mass., 1956-66; asst. controller ITT Semiconductors, West Palm Beach, Fla., 1966-67; controller ITT Gen. Controls, Glendale, Calif., 1967-70; v.p. fin. ITT Aetna, St. Louis, 1970-71; corp. mgr. fin. controls ITT, NYC, 1971-72; v.p., controller Reed Tool Co., Houston, 1972-74; v.p. fin., dir. DeLaval Separator Co., Poughkeepsie, N.Y., 1974-78; v.p. fin. Am. Biltrite Inc., Cambridge, Mass., 1978-79, Caloric Corp., Topton, Pa., 1979-83; group audit mgr. Raytheon Co., Lexington, Mass., 1983-86, mgr. acctg. systems, from 1986. Served to capt. USMC, 1951-55. Decorated D.F.C., Bronze Star, Air medal (8), Purple Heart. Republican. Episcopalian. Home: Sun City Center, Fla. Died Jan. 8, 2006.

GILMAN, RICHARD, drama educator, author; b. NYC, Apr. 30, 1925; s. Jacob and Marion (Wolinsky) G.; m. Esther Morgenstern, 1949 (div.); 1 child, Nicholas; m. Lynn Nesbit, 1966 (div.); children: Priscilla, Claire; m. Yasuko Shiojiri, 1992 BA, U. Wis., 1947; L.H.D., Grinnell Coll., 1967. Free-lance writer, 1950-54; assoc. editor Jubilee mag., 1954-57; drama critic, lit. editor Commonweal, 1961-64; assoc. editor, drama critic Newsweek mag., 1964-67; lit. editor New Republic, 1968-70; prof. drama Yale U., 1967—78, 1979—98. Vis. lectr. English, Columbia U., 1964-65, vis. prof., 1980, 84; vis. prof. drama Stanford U., summer 1967, theater arts CCNY, 1978-79, Boston U., 1984-85, Barnard Coll.; McGraw Disting. lectr. Princeton U., 1990; pres. PEN Am. Center, 1981-83, v.p., 1983-86. Author: The Confusion of Realms, 1970, Common and Uncommon Masks, 1971, The Making of Modern Drama, 1974, Decadence: The Strange Life of an Epithet, 1979, Faith Sex Mystery: A Memoir, 1987, Checkhov's Plays, 1996, The Drama Is Coming Now: The Theater Criticims of Richard Gilman, 1961-1991, 2005; contbg. editor Partisan Rev. Served with USMCR, 1943-46. Recipient George Jean Nathan award for drama criticism, 1971; Morton Dauwen Zabel award Am. Acad. and Inst. Arts and Letters, 1979; fellow N.Y. Inst. for Humanities., 1977-80 Died Oct. 28, 2006.

GILMORE, KENNETH OTTO, editor; b. Providence, Dec. 25, 1930; s. Otto Troly and Mildred (Young) G.; m. Janet Keenan Dunseath, Dec. 22, 1962; children: Lara Troly, Alexandra Bailey BA, Brown U., 1953. Copyboy Washington Post, 1953-54; writer Newspaper Enterprise, Washington, 1954-57, successively assoc. editor and sr. editor Reader's Digest, Washington, 1957-73, asst. mng. editor Pleasantville, N.Y., 1973-75, mng. editor, 1975-82, exec. editor, v.p., 1982-84, editor-in-chief, dir., mem. exec. com., 1984-90. Bd. dirs. Readers' Digest Found., Pleasantville, 1984—; dir. Dewitt Wallace and Lila Wallace Reader's Digest Funds, 1988; mem. adv. bd. Ctr. for Strategic Internat. Studies, Washington, 1984—. Author: (with others) The Great Deception-The Inside Story of How the Kremlin Took Cuba, 1963; editor: A Time to Heal, 1979 KGB-The Secret Work of Soviet Secret Agents, 1973 Trustee Loomis-Chafee Sch., Windsor, Conn., 1978-84; mem. libr. com. Brown U. Mem. Coun. Fgn. Rels., Am. Assn. Mag. Editors Clubs: Cosmos (Washington). Home: Mount Kisco, NY. Died Apr. 15, 2006.

GILMORE, ROBERT CURRIE, railroad company executive b. Vancouver, BC, Can., Aug. 22, 1926; s. Robert H. and Isabe M. (Currie) G.; m. Shelagh M. Rowlette, Mar. 9, 1957; children Katherine, Claudia, Robin, Jennifer. B. Comm., U. B.C., 1954 With Can. Pacific Rail, from 1961, asst. to gen. mgr. and mgr mktg. Montreal, Que., Can., 1961-66, systems mgr. marke planning, 1966-70, regional mgr. mktg. and sales Toronto, Ont Can., 1970-71, gen. mgr. mktg. and sales, 1972-74, asst. v.p mktg. and sales Montreal, Que., Can., 1974-75, 77, v.p. mktg and sales, 1977-84, exec. v.p., 1984-86; pres., chief operatin officer Soo Line Railroad Co., from 1986. Dir. Aroostook Rive R.R. Co., Can. Pacific Steamships Ltd., CanPac Terminals Ltd Houlton Br. R.R. Co., Incan Ships Ltd., Incan Superior Ltd Internat. R.R. Co. of Maine, Soo Line R.R. Co., Thunder Ba Terminals Ltd.; apptd to coal industry adv. bd. Internat. Energ Agy., Paris, 1980 Mem. Nat. Freight Transp. Assn., Montrea Bd. Trade Clubs: Whitlock Golf (Hudson, Que.); Can. Ry Traffic of Montreal. Home: Hudson Heights, Canada. Died Ma 29, 2006.

GINSBERG, DONALD MAURICE, physicist, researcher; b Chgo., Nov. 19, 1933; s. Maurice J. and Zelda Ginsberg; m. Jo D. Lasker, June 10, 1957; children: Mark D., Dana L. BA, U Chgo., 1952, BS, 1955, MS (NSF fellow), 1956; PhD (NS fellow), U. Calif., Berkeley, 1960. Mem. faculty U. Ill., Urbana 1959-97, prof. physics, 1966-97, prof. emeritus, 1997—200 Vis. scientist in physics Am. Assn. Physics Tchrs.-Am. Ins Physics, 1965-71; vis. scientist IBM, 1976; mem. evaluatic com. for Nat. High-Field Magnet Lab., NSF, 1977-79, 85, 9 mem. rev. com. for solid state sci. div. Argonne Nat. Lab 1977-83, chmn., 1980; mem. rev. panel for basic energy sci div. Dept. Energy, 1981 Editor: Physical Properties of Hig Temperature Superconductors, Vols. 1, 2, 3, 4, and 5, 1989, 9 92, 94, 96; contbr. to Ency. Britannica, 1971, 82, 88, 94, 9 Concise Ency. of Magnetic and Superconducting Material 1992. Alfred P. Sloan rsch. fellow, 1960-64, NSF fellow 1966-67; U. Ill. scholar, 1994; recipient Daniel C. Drucke award U. Ill. Engring. Coll., 1992. Fellow Am. Phys. So (winner Oliver E. Buckley Consensed Matter Physics priz 1998); mem. AAAS, Phi Beta Kappa, Sigma Xi. Achievemen include research and publications on low temperature physic superconductivity, cryogenic instrumentation. Home: Urban Ill. Died May 7, 2007.

GITTIS, HOWARD, lawyer; b. Phila., Feb. 16, 1934; Herman and Sonia (Forman) Gittis; m. Sondra Hamberg, Ju 26, 1960; children: Caroline, Hope, Marjorie. BS Econ., U. Pa 1955; LLB, 1958. Bar: Pa. 1958, US Supreme Ct. 1971, Fl 1976. Ptnr. Wolf, Block, Schorr & Solis-Cohen, Phila.; chm MacAndrews & Forbes Holdings Inc. Lectr. in field. Mem.: Ar Law Inst., Am. Coll. Trial Lawyers, Am. Judicature Soc., Ju Conf. of 3rd Cir., Phila. Trial Lawyers Assn., Fla. Bar Assn., P Bar Assn., Phila. Bar Assn., ABA, Fedn. Jewish Agy. of Great Phila., Thomas Jefferson U., Temple U., Mus. Am. Jewi History, Phila. Orch. Assn. Died Sept. 16, 2007.

GIUSTI, GINO PAUL, natural resources company executiv b. New Kensington, Pa., May 31, 1927; s. Peter Paul and Ro (Bonadio) G.; m. Ruth Marie Greblunas, May 4, 1957; childre Paul, Susan, Patricia, John, Christopher. BS in Chem. Engrir U. Pitts., 1949, MS, 1953, PhD in Bus. and Econs, 19 Registered profl. engr., Pa. Texasgulf research fellow Mell Inst. Indsl. Research, Pitts., 1948-57; asst. to pres. Texasgu Inc., Stamford, Conn., 1958-61, mgr. market research, 1962-6 corp. personnel mgr., 1965-71, v.p. employee relations a adminstr., 1972-77, v.p. agrl. chems. div., 1978-79, sr. v.p., 197 pres., COO, 1979-82, pres., CEO, 1982-88, ret., vice chmn., d from 1988; pres. Texasgulf Chems. Co., 1979; vice chmn., d Elf Aquitaine Inc. (parent co.), 1983-88; dir. Northeast Banco Inc. Mem. metals and minerals unit Nat. Def. Exec. Res., De Interior, 1962—. Bd. dirs. Am. Phosphate Found., Stamfo Hosp. Served with USAAF, 1945-46. Mem. AICE, AIME, A Chem. Soc., Am. Econs. Assn., Chem. Market Rsch. Assn., S Mining Engrs. Clubs: Woodway Country, Landmark (bd. dirs Sky. Roman Catholic. Home: Stamford, Conn. Died Mar. 2006.

GJOSTEIN, NORMAN ARTHUR, materials engineer, co sultant, educator; b. Chgo., May 26, 1931; m. 1959; 2 childr BS, Ill. Inst. Tech., 1953, MS, 1954; PhD in Metallurgi Engring., Carnegie-Mellon U., 1958. Rsch. engr. Thmops Ramo-Wooldridge, Inc., 1958-60; sr. rsch. scientist Ford Mo

Co., 1960-61, prin. rsch. scientist assoc., 1961-64, staff scientist, 1964-69, prin. rsch. scientist, 1969-73, mgr. metallurgy dept., 1973-76, mgr. European rsch. liaison, 1976-78, mgr. rsch. planning, 1978-79, dir. long-range and sys. rsch., 1979-81, dir. Sys. Rsch. Lab., 1981-86, dir. power train and materials, 1986-88, dir. Material Rsch. Lab., 1986-96; cons. materials engring. U. Mich., from 1996, clin. prof. engring., from 1996. Fellow ASM Internat. (trustee 1991-93, Shoemaker award 1990, C.S. Barrett Silver medal 1996); mem. NAE, IEEE, The Minerals, Metals and Materials Soc., Engring. Soc. Detroit (bd. dirs. 1991-93), Sigma Xi. Died Apr. 5, 2006.

GLADSTONE, WILLIAM SHELDON, JR., radiologist; b. Des Moines, Dec. 19, 1923; s. William Sheldon and Wanda (Rees) G.; m. Ruth Alice Jensen, June 19, 1944; children— Denise Ann, William Sheldon, Stephen Rees BA, State U. Iowa, 1954, MD, 1947. Diplomate Am. Bd. Radiology. Intern Hurley Hosp., Flint, Mich., 1947-48; gen. practice medicine Iowa Falls, Iowa, 1948-49; asst. dept. pathology State U. Iowa Coll. Medicine, Iowa City, 1949-50; resident in radiology Univ. Hosp., Iowa City, 1950-51, 53-54; practice medicine specializing in radiology Kalamazoo, 1954—84. Exec. v.p. Kalamazoo Radiology; clin. asst. prof. radiology Mich. State U. Coll. Human Medicine; chief radiology Bronson Meth. Hosp., Kalamazoo, 1973-75, 77-79 Bd. dirs. Kalamazoo County Tb Soc., 1955-59, Mich. Children's Aid, 1960-62, Am. Cancer Soc., Kalamazoo, 1964-66. Served with AUS, 1943-46; served to capt. USAF, 1951-53 Fellow Am. Coll. Radiology; mem. Kalamazoo Acad. Medicine, AMA, Mich. Radiologic Soc. (pres. W. Mich. sect. 1976), Mich. State Med. Soc., SW Mich. Surg. Soc., Am. Roentgen Ray Soc., Phi Beta Kappa (pres. SW Mich. chpt. 1963) Clubs: Kalamazoo Country. Lodges: Masons, Shriners. Republican. Episcopalian. Died Mar. 25, 2006.

GLASGOW, JESSE EDWARD, newspaper editor; b. Monroe, NC, Mar. 28, 1923; s. Jesse Edwin and Alma (Brown) G.; m. Beth BonDurant, June 25, 1949; children— Jeffrey David, Charles Christopher. BS, Wake Forest U., 1948. Reporter Kannapolis (N.C.) Ind., 1947, Durham (N.C.) Sun, 1948, Norfolk Virginian-Pilot, 1949-52; reporter Balt. Sun, 1953-59, financial editor, from 1960. Served with AUS, 1943-45. Democrat. Methodist. Home: Glen Arm, Md. Died June 7, 2006.

GLASS, DANIEL, lawyer; b. Apr. 11, 1918; s. Louis and Sarah (Hertzoff) G.; m. Madeleine Michel, Sept. 10, 1961; 1 child, Kenneth. B.S., NYU, 1938; LL.B., Harvard U., 1947. Bar: N.Y. 1947, Fla. 1961. Assoc. Phillips, Nizer, Benjamin & Krim, N.Y.C., 1947-55; gen. counsel Screen Gems, Inc., 1955-60; individual practice law, 1960-66; ptnr. Migdal, Tenney, Glass & Pollack, 1966—. Mem. N.Y.C. Bar Assn., Phi Beta Kappa. Club: Friars. Avocations: reading; tennis. Home: New York, NY. Died Nov. 12, 2006.

GLASS, WENDY DAVIS, art dealer; b. N.Y.C., Aug. 28, 1925; d. Aaron Wise and Helen Miller (Obstler) Davis; B.A., Bard Coll., 1948; children— Robin, Tim. Group worker with children Greenwich House, 1948, Mus. Modern Art, N.Y.C., 1958; owner, dir. Glass Gallery, N.Y.C., 1960—. Campaign worker Democratic candidates. Mem. Antiques Appraisers Assn. (registered), N.Y. Am. Women's Bus. Assn., Ukiyo-e Soc., Japan. Soc., Asia Soc. Jewish. Died Mar. 15, 2006.

GLEISSER, MARCUS DAVID, writer, lawyer, journalist; b. Buenos Aires, Feb. 14, 1923; s. Ben and Riva (Kogan) G.; m. Helga Marianne Rothschild, Oct. 23, 1955; children: Brian Saul, Julia Lynne Wainblat, Hannah Tanya Sharnsky, Ellyn Ruth Klein. BA in Journalism, Case Western Res. U., 1945, MA in Econs., 1949; JD, Cleve. State U., 1958. Bar: Ohio 1958, U.S. Dist. Ct. (no. and ea. dists.) Ohio 1981, U.S. Supreme Ct. 1962. Police reporter Cleve. Press, 1942-44, copy editor, 1944-47; advt. copy writer McDonough-Lewy, Inc., 1947-50; copy editor Cleve. Plain Dealer, 1950-52, gen. assignment reporter, 1952-57, courthouse reporter, 1957-63, real estate editor, 1963-81, fin. writer and investment columnist, from 1981. Instr. journalism, fin., law Cuyahoga C.C., from 2002. Author: The World of Cyrus Eaton, 1965, Juries and Justice, 1968; also articles.; editor in chief: Cleve.-Marshall Law Rev., 1956, 57. Trustee Cleve. Coll. Alumni Assn., 1968, Euclid Mayor's Exec. Council, 1973-76, Euclid Charter Commn., 1975-76. Recipient Nat. Bronze medal Am. Newspaper Pubs. Assn., 1944, Nat. Silver Gavel award ABA, 1958, Bronze medal Nat. Legal Aid and Defender Assn., 1963, Loeb award for disting. bus. and fin. writing U. Conn., 1966; cert. of recognition NCCJ, 1967, Silver Medal award consistently outstanding spl. feature columns Nat. Headliners club, 1969, award Ohio Bar Assn., 1957, 58, 59, 60, 61, 62, award pub. svc. Cleve. Newspaper Guild, 1959, award for best column, 1976, award Nat. Assn. Real Estate Editors, 1965, 71, 72, 73, 80, 91, award Nat. Assn. Real Estate Bds., 1966, 67, 68, 69, 70, 71, 73, award Nat. Assn. Home Builders, 1970, 1st prize Nat. Assn. Realtors, 1980, Bus.-Fin. Writing award Press Club Cleve., 1969, Disting. Merit award Cleve. Assn. Real Estate Brokers, 1976, Excellence in Bus. Journalism award Press Club Cleve., 1983, 85, Fin. Writing award Pannell, Kerr & Forster, 1985, State and Dist. Winner Ohio Journalist Advocate of Yr., U.S. Small Bus. Adminstrn., 2002; runner-up Pulitzer Prize in Journalism for local reporting, 1973; named to N.E. Ohio Apt. Assn. Hall of Fame, 1996. Mem. Am. Newspaper Guild, Soc. Profl. Journalists (Disting. Svc. award Cleve. chpt. 1994), City Club. Clubs: City (Cleve.). Home: Aurora, Ohio. Died Oct. 8, 2005.

GLENN, JOSEPH CHRISTOPHER, broadcast journalist; b. NYC, Mar. 23, 1938; s. Jack and Althea (Hill) G.; m. Dianne West, Mar. 26, 1960; children: Rebecca, Lindsay. BA, U. Colo., 1959. Reporter, producer, anchor WICC Radio News, Bridgeport, Conn., 1963-64; reporter, producer, anchor WNEW Radio News, NYC, 1964-70; mng. editor Metromedia Radio News, Washington, 1970-71; producer, reporter, corr. CBS News, NYC, from 1971; co-anchor CBS News Nightwatch, 1982-84, CBS World News Roundup, from 1985. Reporter, narrator: (TV series) Int the News, from 1971; co-editor: (TV series) 30 Minutes, 1978-82. Served with U.S. Army, 1960-63. Recipient George F. Peabody award, Emmy award, AP award, Action for Children's TV award, ABA award, others. Mem. Am. Fedn. TV and Radio Artists, Writers Guild Am., Mensa, Sigma Delta Chi. Died Oct. 17, 2006.

GLENN, ROLAND DOUGLAS, chemical engineer; b. Somerville, Mass., Mar. 22, 1912; s. Charles Rathford and Anna Amanda (Card) G.; m. Eleanor Norwood Greene, June 19, 1939; children: Meg Mary Eleanor Glenn-Albiez, Nancy Anne Hansen, Sara Elisabeth Baker, Rolene Douglas Ramsey. BSChemE, MIT, 1933, MSChemE, 1934, postgrad. Registered profl. engr., N.Y., Conn., Va. Prodn. supr. Union Carbide Corp., South Charleston, W.Va., devel. group leader, plant mgr., 1934-56, div. v.p. NYC, 1957-68; v.p. Pope, Evans & Robbins, NYC, Alexandria, Va., 1969-71; pres. Combustion Processes, Inc., NYC, 1972-90, Darien, Conn., 1991-93. Editor: (directory) Consulting Services, 1978-88; contbr. numerous reports and papers to profl. jours. Sloan fellow MIT, 1939. Mem. Am. Inst. Chem. Engrs., Am. Chem. Soc., Assn. Cons. Chemists & Chem. Engrs. (dir. 1974-92). Home: Arlington, Va. Died June 7, 2006.

GLENN, TERRY KIMBALL, retired brokerage house executive; b. Pitts., Sept. 22, 1940; s. Theodore N. and Elizabeth Hope (Glenn) G.; m. Eileen Joyce Reider, June 8, 1969; children: Erin Hope, Brooke Katherine BA, Coll. William & Mary, Va., 1963; JD, U. Pa., Phila., 1967. Bar: N.Y., Mass., D.C. Assoc. Hall, McNicol, Marett & Hamilton, NYC, 1967-69; sec., legal counsel Keystone Custodian Funds Inc., Boston, 1969-80; pres., CEO Carnegie Capital Mgmt. Co., Cleve., 1980-83; exec. v.p. Merrill Lynch Asset Mgmt. Co., Princeton, 1983—2004. Dir. Merrill Lynch Inst., Govtl. Fund, Instl. Tax Exempt Fund ML Convertible Securities, Inc., Boston; chmn. US Fed. Securities Fund, Luxembourg; dir., pres. Merrill Lynch Series Fund, Princeton; pres., bd. dirs. First Convertible Securities Fund, Multi-Currency Bond Portfolio, Luxembourg. Served with U.S. Army, 1963-64 Home: Bryn Athyn, Pa. Died Mar. 8, 2007.

GOBRECHT, ROBERT WILLIAM, retired retail toy store executive; b. Waukegan, Ill., July 8, 1923; s. Edwin Rudolph and Ruth Martha (Parmenter) G.; m. Betty Barbara Cazel, Apr. 15, 1944; children: Janet Claire, Robert Edwin, Carol Ruth. BS, U. So. Calif. Underwriter Firemans Fund Ins. Co., Los Angeles, 1946-48; with exec. tng. program Sears Roebuck & Co., Calif., 1948-60, operating supt. Calif., 1959-60; founder, owner, pres. Macabob Toys Co., Inc., Pasadena, Calif., 1961-87. Cons. to toy cos. and factories throughout U.S. and Far East. Dep. sheriff Los Angeles County; former pres. Los Angeles County Sheriff Rhythm Posse, 1973-75. Served with USAAF, 1942-45, USAF, 1951-54. Named to Hon. Order Ky. Cols. Mem. Family Motor Coach Assn. (nat. exec. bd., nat. treas.). Clubs: U. So. Calif. Trojans. Lodges: Masons, Maestros. Republican. Presbyterian. Avocation: tuba player. Home: Pasadena, Calif. Died June 22, 2006.

GODDARD, SAMUEL PEARSON, JR., lawyer, former governor; b. Clayton, Mo., Aug. 8, 1919; s. Samuel Pearson and Florence Hilton (Denham) G.; m. Julia Hatch, July 1, 1944; children: Samuel Pearson III, Pascal Hatch, William Denham. AB, Harvard, 1941; LL.B., U. Ariz., 1949. Bar: Ariz. 1949. Practiced in, Tucson, 1949-64, Phoenix, from 1964; sr. ptnr. Goddard & Goddard (and predecessor firms), 1960—2006; gov. State of Ariz., Phoenix, 1965-67. Co-chmn. Tucson Civic and Conv. Center Study Com., 1958-59; chmn. Tucson Youth Study Com., 1959; mem. White House Conf. Com. Children and Youth, 1959; Campaign chmn. United Fund, 1959; pres. Leffingwell Forest Preserve, 1960-61; Chmn. Democratic Party of Ariz., 1960-62, 78—2006; Bd. dirs. Ariz. Acad., 1963-64, Catalina council Boy Scouts of Am., 1963-64; pres. United Fund, 1960-62, Western Conf. Community Chests, United Funds and Councils Am., 1961-63; mem. exec. com. United Community Funds and Councils Am., 1966-69; task force chmn. United Way Am., bd. govs., 1972-78; bd. dirs., chmn. nominating com. overseers and dirs. Associated Harvard Alumni, 1970-71, v.p., 1971-74; mem. Tucson Hosp. Co-ordinating Com., 1964; Dem. nat. committeeman for Ariz., 1972-78 mem. exec. sect. charter commn., 1972-76; chmn. Nat. Acad. Volunteerism, 1973-75; chmn. blue ribbon study com. on U.S.O.s, 1974-75; an organizer Tucson Civic Chorus, Tucson Festival Soc., Tucson Watercolor Guild; Bd. dirs. Phoenix Symphony Assn., Govt. Relations Com., Transition Zone Horticultural Zone; trustee Nat. Rowing Found., Nat. Council on Philanthropy, 1979—2006; Served to maj. USAAF, 1941-46, to col. USAFR. Named Tucson Man of Yr., 1959 Mem. Am., Ariz., Pima County, Maricopa County bar assns., Res. Officers Assn., VFW, Air Force Assn., Am. Legion, Phi Alpha Delta. Clubs: Harvard Varsity, Old Pueblo. Unitarian Universalist. Home: Phoenix, Ariz. Died Feb. 1, 2006.

GOEHRING, KENNETH, artist; b. Evansville, Wis., Jan. 8, 1919; s. Walter A. and Ruth I. (Rossman) G.; m. Margretta M. MacNicol, Dec. 1, 1945. Student, Cass Tech. Inst., 1933-35, Meinzinger Sch. Applied Art, 1945-46, Colorado Springs Fine Arts Ctr., 1947-50. Works have appeared in over 100 exhibitions in 17 states and 20 museums; 17 one-man shows; Terry Inst., Miami, Symphony Hall, Boston, de Cordova Mus., Fitchburg Mus., Mass., Farnsworth Mus., Maine, Corcoran, Washington, Joslyn Meml. Mus., Nebr., Detroit Inst. Arts, Nebr. Galleries, Stanford U. Galleries, Calif, De Young Mus., San Francisco, Denver Art Mus., Okla. Art Ctr., La Jolla Art Ctr., Calif., Colorado Springs Fine Arts Ctr., 1998, 99, Boulder Mus. Avant Garde Art, 1999, others; represented in permanent collections, Sheldon Art Ctr., Lincoln, Nebr., Colorado Springs Fine Arts Ctr., Foothills Gallery, Golden Colo., Canon City Fine Arts Ctr., Colo., Washburn U. Gallery, Wichita, Kans., Swedish Consulate, Washington, El Pomar Found., Colo. Springs, in many pvt. collections Purchase awards include Colorado Springs Fine Arts Ctr., 1958; Washburn U., 1957; Am. Acad. Design, 1977. Died June 27, 2007.

GOETZ, JOHN BULLOCK, graphic designer; b. Natchez, Miss., July 8, 1920; s. Charles Clifton and Katie G. (Meath) G.; m. Lorette Graves McClatchy, Feb. 17, 1945 (div. May 1980); children— Charles, Christopher, Karen, Stephen. AB, Spring Hill Coll., Ala., 1941; postgrad., Pratt Inst., 1946-48. Reporter Mobile (Ala.) Press-Register, 1941-42; prodn. editor Henry Holt & Co., NYC, 1946-48; book designer Am. Book Co., NYC, 1948-49; mgr. prodn. and design U. Calif. Press, Berkeley, 1950-58; mgr. prodn. U. Chgo. Press, 1958-62, asst. dir., 1963-65; mng. editor ADA, Chgo., 1966-84; pres. Design & Prodn. Services Co., Chgo., 1984-94. Lectr. publ. design U. Chgo. Downtown Center, 1959-60; lectr. dental editors seminar Ohio State U., 1967-73, Mich. State U., 1974-80 Contbr. articles to profl. jours. Served to lt. USNR, 1942-46, PTO. Decorated Bronze Star; recipient Bronze medal for book design Leipzig (Germany) Book Fair, 1963, Gold medal for book design Sao Paulo (Brazil) Biennial, 1964, Disting. Service award for journalism Am. Coll. Dentists, 1974, Disting. Service award Am. Assn. Dental Editors, 1978, award of Merit Internat. Coll. Dentists, 1984. Mem. Am. Inst. Graphic Arts, Chgo. Book Clinic (pres. 1965), Am. Soc. Dentistry for Children (award of recognition 1991). Clubs: Caxton, Chicago. Roman Catholic. Home: Chicago, Ill. Died Oct. 1, 2006.

GOLBITZ, PATRICIA CUNNINGHAM, book publishing executive, editor; b. Wexford, Pa., Feb. 27, 1927; d. Hugh James and Anna Marie (Evans) Cunningham; m. Milton Jay Salamon, Sept. 15, 1950 (div. 1958); 1 child, Michael Hugh; m. Kenneth Golbitz, Feb. 25, 1961 (dec. Mar. 1970); 1 child, Jacob John. BA, U. Pitts., 1950. Sr. editor Pyramid Publs., NYC, 1970-72, Warner Books, NYC, 1972-75, Pocket Books, NYC, 1975-77; sr. editor, v.p. William Morrow & Co., NYC, from 1977. Guest speaker NYU, 1976, New Sch. Social Rsch, N.Y.C., 1976, UCLA, 1979, 80, 81; guest staff mem. Emory U., Atlanta, 1978. Editor: A Walk Across America, 1979 (Peter Jenkins), The Walk West (P. Jenkins), (how-to books) The One-Minute Manager (Kenneth H. Blanchard and Spencer Johnson), 1982 and Callanetics (Callan Pinckney), 1984, (nonfiction) With a Daughter's Eye (Catherine Bateson, N.Y. Times 10 Best Books Yr.), 1984, A Lesser Life (Sylvia Hewlett), 1986, The White-boned Demon (Ross Terrill), 1984, The Life of Kenneth Tynan (Kathleen Tynan), 1987 (Time mag. 10 Best Books Yr.), (novel) The Dancer from the Dance (Andrew Holleran), 1978, books by Ken Follett, The Key to Rebecca, 1980, The Man from St. Petersburg, 1982, On the Wings of Eagles, 1983, Lie Down with Lions, 1986, The Pillars of the Earth, 1989. Democrat. Home: New Hope, Pa. Died Feb. 25, 2006.

GOLD, RAYMOND L., sociologist, educator; b. Chgo., Nov. 15, 1921; s. Samuel and Shirley (Katz) G.; m. Marjorie Doris McClelland, Dec. 23, 1948 (dec. Oct. 1986); 1 child, Karen Joan; m. Alice W. Sterling, Aug. 7, 1987. Student, Wilson Jr. Coll., Chgo., 1946-47; MA, U. Chgo., 1950, PhD, 1954. Asst. prof. sociology U. Ala., 1953-57; from asst. prof. to prof. sociology U. Mont., from 1957, now prof. emeritus. Dir. Social Research and Applications, Missoula; sociol. cons. bus. and govt. Author: Ranching, Mining, and the Human Impact of Natural Resource Development, 1985; contbr. articles to profl. jours. and books. Served with AUS, 1942-46. Fellow Am. Sociol. Assn. Mem. Unitarian-Universalist Ch. (pres. Missoula fellowship 1970-71, 82-83). Home: Missoula, Mont. Died Jan. 6, 2007.

GOLDBERG, DAVID, lawyer, educator; b. NYC, Dec. 31, 1934; s. Philip and Esther (Dobbs) G.; m. Emily Ruth Messing, Aug. 17, 1958; children: Sara, Ari. BA, CUNY, 1956; LLB, Yale U., 1959. Bar: N.Y. 1960. Law clerk to judge US Dist. Ct., NYC, 1960-62; assoc. Kaye, Scholer, Fierman, Hays and Handler, NYC, 1962-68, ptnr., 1969-83, Cowan, Liebowitz and Latman, NYC, from 1983, sr. counsel. Adj. prof. law NYU, 1976-96. Contbr. articles on copyright and trademark law to N.Y. Law Jour., other profl. jours. Pres. Hillcrest Jewish Ctr., Jamaica Estates, N.Y., 1987-89. Served as sgt. U.S. Army, 1959-60. Mem. ABA (fin. officer sect. intellectual property law 1986-89, spkr. on copyright devels. 1984, 85, 87, 90, 2000), Copright Soc. USA (pres. 1978-80, hon. trustee 1980—, spkr. on copyright devels. annually 1984-2003), U.S. Trademark Assn. (spkr. on trademarks and copyright overlap 1987). Democrat. Avocation: fishing. Home: Floral Park, NY. Died Dec. 20, 2006.

GOLDBERGER, BLANCHE RUBIN, sculptor, jeweler; b. N.Y.C., Feb. 2, 1914; d. David and Sarah (Israel) Rubin; m. Emanuel Goldberger, June 28, 1942 (dec. 1994); children— Richard N., Ary Louis. B.A., Hunter Coll., N.Y.C., 1934; M.A., Columbia U., 1936; Certificat d'Etudes, Sorbonne, Paris, 1936; postgrad. Westchester Arts Workshop Sculpture and Jewelry, White Plains, 1961-70, Silvermine Coll. Arts, 1962, Nat. Acad. Arts, N.Y.C., 1968. Tchr. French and Hebrew, N.Y.C. High Sch. System, Scarsdale Jr. and Sr. High Schs. One-woman shows include: Bloomingdale's, Eastchester, N.Y., 1975, Scarsdale Pub. Library, N.Y., 1976, Temple Israel, White Plains, N.Y., 1975, Greenwich Art Barn, Conn., 1972 Westlake Gallery, White Plains, N.Y., 1981; exhibited in group shows at Hudson River Mus., Yonkers, N.Y., 1978, Silvermine-New Eng. Ann., Silvermine, Conn., 1979; represented in permanent collection at Scarsdale High Sch. Library, N.Y.; sculpture commn. Jewish Community Ctr. White Plains, N.Y., 1988; commn. Manchester, Vt.; also pvt. collections. Recipient award Beaux Arts of Westchester, White Plains, N.Y., 1967, First Prize, White Plains Art Show, Holocaust Meml. Bronze Plaque for Synagogue Congregation Israel, Manchester, Vt.; various commns. for calli collis calligraphic collages. Mem. Nat. Assn. Women Artists, Nat. Assn. Tchrs. French, Scarsdale Art Assn. (bd. dirs.; first prizes for sculpture). Jewish. Avocations: lecturing on sculpture, reading contemporary lit. in Hebrew, the violin, classical music concerts, callicollies. Home: Rye Brook, NY. Died Mar. 5, 2007.

GOLDEN, HARVEY L., lawyer; b. Bklyn., Oct. 15, 1929; AB, U. S.C., 1953, JD, 1954. Bar: S.C. 1954. Editor-in-chief S.C. law quarterly, 1954; guest lectr. U. S.C. Law Ctr., 1973-82, U. S.C., 1978, Luth. So. Theol. Sem., 1977, Atlanta Bar Assn. Continuing Legal Edn., 1982, Wis. Bar Assn., 1983, W Va. Bar Assn., 1984, Fla. Bar Assn., 1986, Tex. Bar Assn., 1987, Md. Bar Assn., 1987, Conn. Bar Assn., 1987, Ill. Bar Assn., 1988; coord., moderator first divorce law seminar U. S.C. Law Ctr., 1975, family law faculty lectr. and participant Am. Acad. of Matrimonial Lawyers; spl. judge Richland County Juvenile-Domestic Rels Ct., 1962, Family Ct., 1963, 67, 72, Civil Ct., Jury Trials, 1975, 76, Criminal Ct., Jury Trials, 1976. Mem. S.C.

Supreme Ct. Family Law Specialization Adv. Bd., 1982. Recipient Top 43 Divorce Lawyers in Am. Nat. Law Jour., 1987. Fellow Am. Acad. of Matimonial Lawyers, Internat. Acad. of Martrimonial Lawyers; mem. ABA (cert. Outstanding Contbn. to ABA Family Law Sect. 1976, sect. on individual rights and responsibilities econ. law practice, state membership chmn. 1976, 87, regional vice-chmn. mid-south 1976, 77, chmn. paternity and illegitimacy com. 1978-81, nat. coun. 1981-83, chmn. Ad Hoc com. on model adoption act 1982-83, nat. chmn. family law sect. 1987-88, nat. inst. and conventions), Richland County Bar Assn. (chmn. sect. of personal injury 1974-74, vice-chmn. com. on adminstrn. justice 1974-76), S.C. Bar (chmn. family law sect 1982), Assn. of Trial Lawyers of Am., S.C. Trial Lawyers Assn. (chmn. famil law sect. 1981-83), Died Sept. 15, 2006.

GOLDEN, WILLIAM THEODORE, trustee, corporate director; b. NYC, Oct. 25, 1909; s. S. Herbert and Rebecca (Harris) Golden; m. Sibyl Levy, May 2, 1938 (dec. 1983); children: Sibyl Rebecca, Pamela Prudence; m. Jean E. Taylor, July 8, 2001 (div. Aug. 3, 2005); m. Catherine Morrison, Feb. 3, 2007. AB, U. Pa., 1930, LLD (hon.), 1979; postgrad. bus. adminstrn., Harvard U., 1930-31; DSc (hon.), Poly. Inst. N.Y., 1975, Bard Coll., 1988; MA, Columbia U., 1979, LLD (hon.), 1986, Hamilton Coll., 1987; DHL (hon.), CUNY, 1997, Mt. Sinai Sch. Medicine, NYU, 2000. Lic. amateur radio operator, 1922-2007, station 2AEN. Asst. to pres. Cornell, Linder & Co., NYC, 1931-34; with Carl M. Loeb & Co., Carl M. Loeb, Rhoades & Co., 1934-41; dir. Woodward Iron Co., 1940-68; asst. to commr. AEC, Washington, 1946-50, cons., 1950-58; chmn. bd. Nat. U.S. Radiator Co. (and successor cos.), 1952-74; dir. Pitts. Railways Co., 1952-63, United Carbon Co., 1957-63, Crowell-Collier and Macmillan, Inc., 1964-71, Paribas Corp., 1965-69; trustee Mitre Corp., 1958-72, 76-85, System Devel. Corp., 1957-66, chmn. bd. trustees, 1961-66. Spl. cons. on rev. govt. sci. activities Pres. Truman, Washington, 1950-51; advisor on NSF to dir. Bur. Budget, 1950-51; mem. mil. procurement task force Commn. on Orgn. Exec. Br. Govt., Hoover Commn., 1954-55; adv. com. on pvt. enterprise in fgn. aid US Dept. State, 1964-65; pub. mem. Hudson Inst., 1964-94; mem. commn. on delivery personal health svcs. Mayor's Piel Commn., 1966-68; adv. coun. Sch. Gen. Studies, Columbia U., NYC, 1966-2001, emeritus, 2001; vis. com. on astronomy Princeton U., NJ, 1969-2007, chmn., 1976-89; vis. com. on engring. and applied physics and on medicine and dental medicine Harvard U., Cambridge, Mass., 1969-77, vis. com. on astronomy, 1976-90; vis. com. Assn. Univs. for Research in Astronomy, 1973-76, dir. at large, 1988-91, Disting. advisor, 1991-2007; mem. vis. com. Space Telescope Sci. Inst., 1982-87; adv. panel on space transp. ops. NASA, 1976-77; adv. panel U.S. Postal Svc., 1981-83; vice chmn. Mayor's Commn. on Sci. and Tech., 1983-91, hon. chair, 1992-2007, Commn. Coll. Retirement, 1984-88, Scientists Inst. Pub. Info., 1985-94; co-chmn. Carnegie Commn. on Sci., Tech. and Govt., 1988-96; bd. dirs. Verde Exploration, Ltd., Inc., Block Drug Co., Inc.; founder Carnegie Group of Ministers of Sci. and Sci. Advisors to Heads of G8 countries, Russia and European Union, 1991-2007 Editor, co-author: Science Advice to the President, 1980, 2d rev. edit., 1993, Science and Technology Advice to the President, Congress and Judiciary, 1988, 2d rev. edit., 1993, Worldwide Science and Technology Advice to the Highest Levels of Governments, 1991; contbr. articles to profl. jours. Trustee Hebrew Free Loan Soc., 1935—2007, treas., 1985—2000, United Neighborhood Hos., 1952—61, Associated Hosp. Svc. NY, 1959—74, Univ. Corp. for Atmospheric Rsch., 1965—74, Riverside Rsch. Inst., 1967—76, NYC-Rand Inst., 1969—75, Ctr. for Advanced Study Behavioral Scis., 1970—76, Bennington Coll., 1971—76, Haskins Labs., 1971—92, SIAM Inst. Math. and Soc., 1973—91, Columbia U. Press, 1974—77, John Simon Guggenheim Meml. Found., 1978—81, Nat. Humanities Ctr., 1978—90, emeritus, 1990—2007; trustee Population Coun., 1979—89, Catskill Ctr. for Conservation and Devel., from 1981, U. Pa. Press, from 1985; mem. Marine Biology Lab., Woods Hole, Mass., from 1968, trustee, 1968—87, trustee emeritus, 1987; trustee Mt. Sinai Hosp., NYC, from 1955, vice chmn., from 1977; governing coun. Courant Inst. Math. Scis., NYU, 1962—91, vice chmn., 1962—86, chmn., 1986—91; trustee Mt. Sinai Med. Sch., from 1963, vice chmn., from 1977; trustee NY Found., 1963—84, treas., 1974—78; chmn. bd. trustees City Univ. Constrn. Fund, 1967—71; exec. com. Health Rsch. Coun., NYC, 1968—75; trustee Am. Mus. Natural History, from 1968, v.p., 1971—88, vice chmn., 1988—89, chmn., 1989—94, chmn. emeritus, from 1994; trustee Carnegie Instn. Washington, from 1969, sec., 1971—99, sr. trustee, from 2000; trustee Barnard Coll., from 1973, vice chmn., 1975—79, 1986—92, treas., 1980—83, hon. vice chmn., 1992—98, emeritus, from 1998; trustee NY Coun. for Humanities, 1975—78, chmn., 1976—78; bd. overseers Sch. Arts and Scis., U. Pa., Phila., 1976—97, emeritus, from 1997; coun. mem. Rockefeller U., from 1978; bd. visitors Grad. Sch. and Univ Ctr., CUNY, 1979—96, bd. dirs. Grad. Ctr. Found., from 1996; trustee Am. Trust for Brit. Libr., 1980—92, from 1998, vice chmn., 1985—92, co-chmn., treas., from 1998; trustee Neurosci. Rsch. Found., 1981—99, chmn., 1981—87, Black Rock Forest Consortium, from 1988; adv. bd. Johns Hopkins Sch. Hygiene and Pub. Health, 1995—98; trustee After Sch. Corp., 1999—2007; bd. dirs. Grad Sch. Arts and Sci. Alumni Assn., Columbia U., 1984—93, vice chmn., 1984—91; bd. dirs. Internat. Univ. Exch., Inc., 1996—2007. Lt. comdr. USNR, 1941—45. Recipient Letters of Commendation with ribbon Sec. of Navy and chief Bur. Ordnance for invention of naval gunfire device used in WWII, Pub. Svc. award Mus. City of N.Y., 1981, Disting. Pub. Svc. award NSF, 1982, Tribute of Appreciation, Nat. Sci. Bd., 1991, Pub. Welfare medal NAS, 1996, medal of distinction Barnard Coll., Columbia U., 1999, Dean's award for disting. achievement Grad. Sch. A&S, Conservation Citizen award Ctr. Environ. Rsch. and Conservation, 2003. Fellow AAAS (treas., bd. dirs. 1969-2000, treas. emeritus 2000, Lifetime Achievement award 2001), N.Y. Acad. Scis. (hon. life; mem. bd. govs. 1977-2007, pres. 1988, chmn. 1989, life gov. 1991), Am. Acad. Arts and Scis. (Scholar-Patriot award 2001), Assn. Women in Sci., N.Y. Acad. Medicine; mem. Nat. Acad. Pub. Adminstrn., Am. Philos. Soc. (mem. coun. 1985-91, v.p. 1992-2007, Benjamin Franklin award for disting. pub. svc. 1995), History of Sci. Soc., Coun. Fgn. Rels., Army and Navy Club, Cosmos Club (Washington), Century Assn. Home: New York, NY. Died Oct. 7, 2007.

GOLDENBERG, ARTHUR PAUL, financial consultant; b. Phila., July 19, 1932; s. Benjamin and Ruth (Gruenberg) G.; m. Carole Gruskin, Dec. 1965 (div. 1967); m. Mary Elizabeth Bralow, Nov. 23, 1975. BS in Indsl. Engring., Lehigh U., 1953; MBA, Harvard Bus. Sch., 1957. Planning mgr. Luria Bros. & Co., Inc., Shaker Heights, Ohio, 1966-69; mgr. strategic planning IU Internat. Mgmt. Corp., Phila., 1969-72; v.p. Gotaas-Larsen Shipping Co., N.Y.C., 1972-77; sr. v.p. fin. Namolco, Inc., Willow Grove, Pa., 1977-84; exec. v.p. C Brewer Terminals Inc., Willow Grove, 1984-86; pres. Fincom Inc., Jenkintown, Pa., 1986-2006. Bd. dirs. Rydal Meadowbrook Civic Assn., 1980-84, pres., 1985-2006. Mem. Fin. Execs. Inst. (com. chmn. 1983-85), Am. Inst. Indsl. Engrs. Republican. Jewish. Clubs: Harvard (N.Y.C.); Philmont Country (Pa.). Avocations: tennis, golf, theater, computers. Home: Jenkintown, Pa. Died Apr. 3, 2006.

GOLDMAN, BERNARD MARVIN, art history educator; b. Toronto, Ont., Can., May 30, 1922; came to U.S., 1925, naturalized, 1943; m. Norma Wynick, Aug. 1, 1944; 1 son, Mark. PhD, U. Mich., 1959. Prof. art history Wayne State U., Detroit, from 1966; dir. Wayne State U. Press, 1974-85. Author: Sacred Portal, 1966, Reading and Writing in the Arts, 1972, rev. edit., 1978; editor: Hopkins, Discovery of Dura-Europos, Bull. of Asia Inst. Served with USAAF, 1943-45. Fellow Am. Council Learned Socs. Home: Bloomfield Hills, Mich. Died Mar. 22, 2006.

GOLDSMITH, CLAUDE ORVILLE, petroleum company executive; b. Robinson, Ill., Aug. 10, 1932; s. Alonzo Fremont and Ona Cleo (Bean) G.; m. Shirley Ann Moore, Aug. 29, 1954; children— Christopher Kent, Gretchen Claudette. BS in Bus. Adminstrn, Ohio State U., 1954, JD, 1956. Bar: Ohio bar 1956. Accountant Marathon Oil Co., Findlay, Ohio, also Tripoli, Libya, 1956-58, auditor, 1958-59, supr. acctg., 1960, chief accountant, 1961-62, tax specialist, 1962-65; with Atlantic Richfield Co., 1965-86, mgr. fin. reporting Phila., 1965-66, controller internat. div. Los Angeles, 1966-68, asst. treas. finance NYC, 1969-71, treas., 1971-75, v.p. financing and tax, 1975-80, sr. v.p., chief fin. officer, 1980-84, sr. v.p. acquisition and divestments, 1984-86. Bd. dirs. Mfrs. Bank. Mem. Beta Gamma Sigma, Delta Theta Phi, Sigma Pi. Republican. Mem. Disciples of Christ Ch. Club: Bear Creek Golf, Petroleum of Los Angeles. Home: Pasadena, Calif. Died Mar. 28, 2006.

GOLDSTEIN, NORMAN GRANT See GAYLORD, NORMAN

GOLLOBIN, LEONARD PAUL, chemical engineer; b. NYC, July 2, 1928; s. Morris and Jennie (Levine) G.; m. Charlotte Weissman, Jan. 21, 1951; children: Michael L., Susan D. Brown. BSChemE, CUNY, 1951; MS, Kans. State U., 1952; grad. mgmt. program, Harvard U., 1975. Design engr. Foster Wheeler Corp., NYC, 1952-55; mfg. engr. Gen. Electric Co., Waterford, NY, 1955-58; program dir. ORI, Inc., Silver Spring, Md., 1958-63; chmn., chief exec. Presearch, Inc., Fairfax, Va., 1963—2004; dir., mgr. Level II Sys., Longboat Key, Fla., from 2004; chief scientist, engr. Hicks and Assocs., Sci. Applications Internat. Corp., McLean, Va., from 2004. U.S. del. NATO Indsl. Avd. Group, 1989, chmn., 1992-93, chmn. emeritus, 1994-95; bd. visitors Nat. Def. U., Washington, 1989-98. Bd. dirs. Cultural Alliance Greater Washington, 1980-88, northern Va. bd. Va. Opera, 2000-01; trustee Washington Opera, 1988-90. Recipient NSIA Adrm. Charles Weakley award, 1986, Meritorious Pub. Svc. award U.S. Dept. Navy, 1987, U.S. Marine Corps, 1989. Mem. Nat. Security Indsl. Assn. (exec. com. 1986—, chmn. antisubmarine warfare com. 1981-84, chmn. amphibious warfare com. 1986-89, chmn. environ. com. 1990-92, chmn. internat. com. 1991-93, vice chmn. exec. com. 1993, chmn. 1994, chmn. bd. trustees 1994-95), Nat. Def. Indsl. Assn. (chmn. fin. com. 1998—, mem. exec. com., chmn. energy security com. 2006-), Am. Chem. Soc., Naval Undersea Warfare Found. Mus., Loudon Golf and Country Club (Purcellville, Va.), Lougboat Key Club. Home: Longboat Key, Fla. Died Aug. 11, 2007.

GOLTER, HARRY, lawyer; b. Chgo., Dec. 5, 1924; s. David and Eva (Woloshin) G.; m. Gretl Philippi, Sept. 9, 1951; children: Barbara Lynn Golter Heller, Jay Warren. Grad., Wilson Jr. Coll., 1942-46, U. Chgo., 1949, JD, 1952. Bar: Ill. 1952, U.S. Dist. Ct. (no. dist) Ill. 1956, U.S. Ct. Appeals (7th cir.) 1958, U.S. Supreme Ct. 1967. Adminstrv. asst. dept. fin. State of Ill., Springfield, 1952-53; assoc. Fink & Coff, Chgo., 1954-63; ptnr. Overton, Schwartz & Fritts, Chgo., 1963-81, Wildman, Harold, Allen & Dixon, Chgo., 1981-87, Hamblet, Casey, Oremus & Vacin, Chgo., from 1987. Revision author: Fletcher Cyclopedia Corporations vol. 19. Chmn. Com. on Ill. Govt., Chgo., 1962; vol. atty. ACLU, Chgo.; bd. dirs Adv. for the Handicapped, Chgo., 1980-85. Served with USAAF, 1943-46. Mem. ABA, Ill. Bar Assn., Chgo. Bar Assn., Chgo. Council of Lawyers. Democrat. Jewish. Home: Arlington, Va. Died Feb. 8, 2006.

GOMEZ, MANUEL RODRIGUEZ, physician; b. Minaya, Spain, July 4, 1928; came to U.S., 1952, naturalized, 1961; s. Argimiro Rodriguez Herguedas and Isabel Gomez Torrente; m. Joan A. Stormer, Sept. 25, 1954; children: Christopher, Gregory, Douglas, Timothy. MD, U. Havana, Cuba, 1952; MS in Anatomy, U. Mich., 1956. Intern Michael Reese Hosp., 1952-53, asst. resident in pediatrics, 1953-54; resident in neurology U. Mich., 1954-56; fellow in pediatric neurology U. Chgo. Med. Sch., 1956-57; instr. neurology U. Buffalo Med. Sch., 1957-58, 59-60; clin. clk. neurology Inst. Neurology, U. London, 1958-59; asst. prof., then assoc. prof. neurology Wayne State U. Med. Sch., 1960-64; mem. faculty Mayo Med. Sch., Rochester, Minn., from 1964, prof. pediatric neurology, from 1975, emeritus prof. pediatric neurology Rochester, Minn., from 1994. Cons. pediatric neurology, head sect. Mayo Clinic, 1964-84, sr. cons. 1992—; vis. prof. King Faisal Hosp., Riyjadh, Saudia Arabia, 1994, Children's Hosp. Miami, 1995, Seville, Spain, 1995. Author: Tuberous Sclerosis, 1979, 2nd edit., 1988, 3d edit., 1999, Neurocutaneous Diseases, 1987; co-editor: Tuberous Sclerosis and Allied Disorders, 1991, Neurologia y Neuropsicologia Pediatrica, 1996; adv. bd. Brain and Devel., Pedriatrika. Recipient Ramón y Cajal award Academia Iberoamericana de Neuropediatría, 1995. Mem. Am. Acad. Neurology, Am. Neurol. Assn., Child Neurology Assn. (founder, former pres., Hower award 1989), N.Y. Acad. Scis., Philippine Pediatric Soc. (hon.), Sociedad Española de Neurologia (hon.), Sociedad Española de Neuropediatria (hon.), Assn. Research Nervous and Mental Disease, Orton-Dyslexia Soc. (adv. bd.), Am. Epilepsy Soc., Internat. Child Neurology Soc. (founder), Cen. Soc. Neurol. Research, Nat. Tuberous Sclerosis Assn. (hon. profl. advisor, Leadership award 1994), Sociedad Centroamericana de Neurologia y Neurociugia, Colombian Neurologic Soc. (hon.), Soc. Psiquiatría y Neurologia de Infancia y Adolescencia Chile (hon.), Costarican Neurol. Sci. Soc. (hon.), soc. Argentina de Neurologia Infantil (hon.). Home: Rochester, Minn. Died Jan. 21, 2006.

GONG, HENRY, JR., internist, researcher, educator; b. Tulare, Calif., May 23, 1947; s. Henry and Choy (Low) Gong; m. Janice Wong; children: Gregory, Jaimee. BA, U. of the Pacific, 1969; MD, U. Calif., Davis, 1973. Diplomate Am. Bd. Internal Medicine, 1977, Am. Bd. Pulmonary Disease, 1980. Resident in medicine Boston U., 1973-75; fellow in pulmonary medicine UCLA Med. Ctr., 1975-77; asst. prof., then assoc. prof. Sch. Medicine UCLA, 1977-89, prof. medicine, 1989-93; assoc. chief pulmonary div. UCLA Med. Ctr., 1985-92; chief Environ. Health Svc. Rancho Los Amigos Med. Ctr., from 1993; prof. medicine U. So. Calif., 1993—2007, prof. preventive medicine, 1997—2007. Dir. Environ. Exposure Lab. UCLA, 1988—93; chmn. dept. medicine Rancho Los Amigos Med. Ctr., from 1996; mem. pub. health and socio-econs. task force S. Coast Air Quality Mgmt. Dist., El Monte, Calif., 1989—90, Calif. Air Resources Bd., from 2004. Contbr. articles to profl. jours., chapters to books; mem. editl. bd. Jour. Clin. Pharmacology, 1983—2002, Am. Jour. Critical Care, 1999—2001, Arch Environ. Health, 2000—05, Inhalation Toxicology, from 2005. Elder session Pacific Palisades Presbyn. Ch., 1984—86, 1989—91, 2003. Recipient Clean Air award, Am. Lung Assn., 2000, Environ. Achievement award, EPA, 2004. Fellow: Am. Coll. Clin. Pharmacology, Am. Coll. Chest Physicians (pres. Calif. chpt. 1991—92); mem.: Western Soc. Clin. Investigation, Am. Fedn. Clin. Rsch., Am. Thoracic Soc., Phi Eta Sigma. Avocation: travel. Home: Pacific Palisades, Calif. Died Aug. 17, 2007.

GONIA, CHARLES, electronics executive; b. Benton Harbor, Mich., Aug. 28, 1925; s. Eli Hubert and Marie Catherine (Fuchs) G.; m. Luize Esther Politis, June 11, 1953; 1 child, Elizabeth Mara. BSE, U.S. Naval Acad., 1947. Commd. ensign USN, 1947, served to lt., retired, 1954; mgr. advanced applications Librascope div. Gen. Precision, Inc., Glendale, Calif., 1954-64, sec.-treas., mem. tech. staff Ocean Tech., Inc., Burbank, Calif., 1964-66, v.p., 1966-85, exec. v.p., 1985-86, pres., 1986-88, bd dirs., from 1986; mgmt. cons., from 1988. Republican. Home: Encino, Calif. Died July 15, 2007.

GOODALL, HARRY ALONZO, air force officer; b. Follansbee, W.Va., Oct. 29, 1932; s. Alonzo C. and Lena Flo G.; m. Frances Sue Kee, Feb. 2, 1952; children— Randal Keith, Rhonda Kay Goodall White, Richard Kenneth Grad., Squadron Officers Sch., 1959; BS, U. Nebr.-Omaha, 1965; grad., Air Command and Staff Coll., 1967; MBA, George Washington U., 1967; MS in Pub. Adminstrn., Auburn U., 1974; disting. grad. Air War Coll., 1974. Served as enlisted man U.S. Air Force 1949-57, commd. first sgt., 1957, advanced through grades to lt. gen., 1984; pilot 405 Tactical Fighter Wing, Clark AFB, Philippines, 1967-69; chief fighter br. Directorate of Ops., Hdqrs. U.S. Air Force, Washington, 1969-73; comdr. 8th Tactical Fighter Wing, Ubon Royal Thai Air Base, Thailand, 1974-75; also comdr. 56 Spl. Ops. Wing, Nakhon Phanom Royal Thai Air Base, Thailand, %; vice comdr. Alaskan Air Command, Anchorage, 1975-77; also dep. comdr. Alaskan N.Am. Def. Command Region, Anchorage, 1975-77; and comdr. Air Force Forces Anchorage, %; mil. asst. to under sec. U.S. Air Force, Washington, 1977-78; dep. dir. plans and policy for internat. negotiations Joint Chiefs of Staff, Washington, 1978-80; dep. dir. plans Hdqrs. U.S. Air Force, Washington, 1980-81; chief of staff 4th Allied Tactical Air Force, NATO, Heidelberg, Fed. Republic Germany, 1981-82; comdr. 17th Air Force, Sembach Air Base Fed. Republic Germany, 1982-84, Allied Tactical Ops. Ctr NATO, Allied Air Def. Sector III, Nato, Boerfink, Fed. Republic Germany; dep. comdr. in chief U.S. Readiness Command MacDill AFB, Fla., from 1984; also vice dir. Joint Deployment Agy., MacDill AFB, Fla., %. Dep. U.S. commr. U.S.-Soviet SALT Standing Consultative Commn., Washington and Geneva 1978-80 Mem. adminstrv. bd. deacons Bayshore Baptist Ch. Decorated Legion of Merit with 2 oak leaf clusters, D.F.C. Bronze Star medal, Meritorious Service medal, Air medal with 12 oak leaf clusters; Cross of Gallantry with palm (Republic Vietnam); Flying Wings of German Luftwaffe; Def. Disting. Service medal, Def. Superior Service medal; recipient George Washington Honor medal Freedom Found., 1981, Humanitarian Service medal (2) 7th Air Force, 1975. Mem. Air Force Assn. Daedalians (flight capt. Billy Mitchell flight 1983-84), Air Force Hist. Soc., Greenland Assn. Avocations: fishing; golf; tennis; racquetball; antique automobiles. Home: Tampa, Fla. Died Sept. 2, 2006.

GOODFRIEND, HERBERT JAY, lawyer; b. NYC, Sept. [illegible] 1926; s. Sidney and Blanche (Prager) G.; m. Barbara Gottlieb Oct. 12, 1952; children: Sandra, Beth Ann. AB, NYU, 194[illegible] LLB, 1950, LLM in Taxation, 1953. Bar: N.Y. 1950, U.S. Dist. Ct. (so. dist.) N.Y. 1951, U.S. Dist. Ct. (ea. dist.) N.Y. 1952, U.S. Ct. Appeals (2nd cir.) 1953, U.S. Tax Ct. 1954. Assoc. Otte[illegible]bourg, Steindler Houston & Rosen, NYC, 1950—55, ptnr. 1955—86; counsel Summit, Solomon & Feldesman, 1986-9[illegible] NYC, Philips, Nizer, from 1993. Counsel N.Y. Bd. Trade N.Y.C., 1981-87, bd. dirs., 1982-88; spl. master Supreme Ct. New York County, N.Y.C., 1977-79; vice chmn., bd. dirs. Jones Apparel Group, Inc., 1990-98., sec., 1990-2001. Columnist N.Y. Law Jour., 1977-79, treas. 2001-04. Treas., dir. N.Y.C. Alliance Against Sexual Abuse, 2001—; dir. Cmty. Health Charities N.Y. 2004—. With U.S. Army, 1945-46. Fellow Am. Bar Found. Coll. Law Practice Mgmt.; mem. ABA (chmn. econs. la[illegible] practice sect. 1984-85, ho. of dels. 1994-97), N.Y. State Bar Assn. (chmn. com. on law office econ. and mgmt. 1983-85), N.Y. County Lawyers Assn. (com. on arbitration 1974-87), NYU Club (v.p. exec. com. 1976-80), Adelphi U. Inst. for Paralegal Tng. (adv. bd. 1976-96), Am. Apparel Mfg. Assn. (fin. mgmt. com. 1980-2001), Tau Delta Phi (nat. pres. 1952-57). Avocations: golf, computers. Home: New York, NY. Died Aug. 10, 2007.

GOODLOE, ROBERT KENNETH, osteopathic physician; b. Kurthwood, La., Oct. 4, 1937; s. Rufus Kemp and Avis (Martin) G.; m. Dianna Kay Scott, Nov. 7, 1964; children— Jeffrey Michael, Mark Alan. B.S. in Pharmacy, Southwestern Okla. U., 1959; D.O., Kans. City Coll. Health Scis., 1964. Intern, Hillcrest Hosp., Oklahoma City, 1964-65, chmn. dept. gen. practice, 1969-71; gen. practice osteo. medicine, Mustang, Okla., 1964—. Republican. Home: Mustang, Okla. Died Apr. 11, 2007.

GOODMAN, DONALD JOSEPH, dentist; b. Cleve., Aug. 14, 1922; s. Joseph Henry and Henrietta Inez (Mandel) G.; BS, Adelbert Coll., 1943; DMD, Case-Western Reserve U., 1945; m. Dora May Hirsh, Sept. 18, 1947; children: Lynda (Mrs. Barry Allen Levin), Keith, Bruce; m. Ruth Jeanette Weber, May 1, 1974. Pvt. practice dentistry, Cleve., 1949-86; lectr. in field. With Dental Corps, USNR, 1946-48. Mem. Am. Acad. Gen. Dentistry, ADA Ohio State Dental Assn., Cleve. Dental Soc., Fedn. Dentaire Internationale, Cleve. Council on World Affairs, Greater Cleve. Growth Assn., Council of Smaller Enterprises, Phi Sigma Delta, Zeta Beta Tau, Alpha Omega. Clubs: Masons (32 deg.), Shriners, Travelers' Century (Gold award, special award), Circumnavigators. Home: Pepper Pike, Ohio. Died Mar. 3, 2007.

GOODMAN, ELLIOT RAYMOND, political scientist, educator; b. Indpls., Sept. 3, 1923; s. Lazure L. and Esther (Miller) G.; m. Norma B., Mar. 1, 1947; children— Laura Goodman Humphrey, Jordan, Roger. AB, Dartmouth Coll., 1948; MA and cert. Russian Inst., Columbia U., 1951, PhD, 1957; MA (hon.), Brown U., 1960. Ford teaching intern Brown U., Providence, 1955-56, instr., 1956-58, asst. prof., 1958-60, asso. prof., 1960-70, prof. polit. sci., 1970-87, prof. emeritus, from 1987. Author: The Soviet Design for a World State, 1960, The Fate of the Atlantic Community, 1975; contbr. numerous articles to profl. jours. Served with U.S. Army, 1943-46. Guggenheim fellow, 1962-63; NATO research fellow, 1962-63 Mem. Internat. Inst. Strategic Studies (London), Atlantic Council U.S. (politico-mil. com. 1971-74, acad. assoc. 1985—), New Eng. Polit. Sci. Assn., Am. Polit. Sci. Assn., Am. Assn. Advancement of Slavic Studies, Com. Atlantic Studies (N. Am. sect.) Home: Cranston, RI. Died Nov. 27, 2005.

GOODMAN, JOHN WILLIAM, materials and structures engineer; b. Paterson, NJ, June 5, 1934; s. Alfred Henry and Celeste Alberta (Langdon) G.; m. Marjorie Ellen Race, June 9, 1956; children: Terry Sue, Thomas David, Patricia Gail. BSME, Rutgers U., 1955; MS in Engring. Mechanics, Pa. State U., 1957; PhD in Materials Sci. with distinction, UCLA, 1970. Structures engr. TRW Space, El Segundo, Calif., 1960-64, materials engr. Redondo Beach, Calif., 1965-70; structures engr. USAF Aeronautical Systems Ctr., Wright-Patterson AFB, Ohio, 1972, chief fatigue & fracture br., 1973-75, structures specialist, 1976-86; sr. staff materials engr. TRW Space, Redondo Beach, from 1987; chief engr. Tensiodyne Scientific Corp., LA, from 1993. Speaker in field. Editor: Advanced Aluminum and Titanium Structures, 1981. Scoutmaster Troop 81 Boy Scouts Am., Kettering, Ohio, 1984-87. 1st lt. USAF, 1957-59. Rutgers U. scholar, 1951-55, Postdoctoral scholar Materials Dept. UCLA, 1971. Fellow ASME (chair aerospace divsn. 1991-93, chair aerospace structures & materials com. 1987-88, Shuttle Flag award 1991); mem. AIAA, Am. Soc. Metals, Soc. Advancement Material and Process Engring. Achievements include directing the damage tolerance assessment of the USAF A-10 aircraft; devising a graphic method for leak before burst analysis of pressure vessels; testing pressure vessel alloys in biaxial stress states; testing early advanced composite tubular columns for spacecraft. Home: Redondo Beach, Calif. Died Mar. 6, 2007.

GOODRICH, HERBERT FUNK, JR., lawyer; b. Phila., Dec. 4, 1942; s. Herbert Funk and Mary (Dern) G.; m. Virginia Page, Sept. 10, 1966; children: Cynthia Dern, Matthew Page, Steven Withington. AB, Dartmouth Coll., 1964; LLB, Harvard U., 1967. Bar: Pa. 1967, U.S. Dist. Ct. (ea. dist.) Pa. 1967. Assoc. Dechert Price & Rhoads, Phila., 1967-74, resident ptnr. Brussels, 1974-78, ptnr. Phila., 1978—2007. Vis. lectr. Villanova (Pa.) U.; faculty participant Pa. Bar Inst., Harrisburg Bd. dirs. Episc. Cmty. Svcs., Phila.; trustee Chestnut Hill Healthcare Corp., Phila., vice chmn., 1995-2000, former chmn. Mem. ABA, Phila. Bar Assn., Pa. Bar Assn., Am. Law Inst. Republican. Home: Wyndmoor, Pa. Died Mar. 16, 2007.

GOODWIN, RICHARD HALE, retired botany educator; b. Brookline, Mass., Dec. 14, 1910; s. Harry Manley and Mary Blanchard (Linder) G.; m. Esther Bemis, Oct. 12, 1936; children: Mary G. Wetzel, Richard H. Jr. AB, Harvard U., 1933, MA, 1934, PhD, 1937. Fellow Am.-Scandinavian Found., U. Copenhagen, 1937-38; instr. botany U. Rochester, NY, 1938-41, asst. prof., 1941-44; prof. Conn. Coll., New London, 1944-76, prof. emeritus, 1976—2007. Dir. Conn. Arboretum, New London, 1944-65, 67-68; pres. Conservation and Rsch. Found., Boston, 1953-94; treas. Inst. Ecology, Washington, 1975-77. Co-author: Inland Wetlands of the U.S. Fellow AAAS, Am. Acad. Arts and Scis.; mem. Nat. Com. Plant Sci. Socs. (coord. 1961-62), Am. Inst. Biol. Scis. (governing bd. 1967-71), Nature Conservancy (pres. 1956-58, 64-66), Conservation and Rsch. Found. (pres. 1953-94), Am. Soc. Plant Biology, Ecol. Soc. Am., New Eng. Bot. Soc., Bot. Soc. Am., Torrey Bot. Club. Democrat. Unitarian-Universalist. Achievements include research in plant morphogenesis, growth inhibitors, fluorescent constituents of plants, long range vegetation studies, effects of prescribed burning. Home: Salem, Conn. Died July 6, 2007.

GORALSKI, PATRICIA JEAN, retired lawyer; b. Paynesville, Minn., June 16, 1923; d. Arthur and Lillian Constance (Hanson) Schwarz; m. Edwin Anthony Goralski, Sept. 4, 1947. BS, U. Minn., 1947, MA, 1956, PhD, 1964, JD, 1981. Bar: Minn. 1982, U.S. Dist. Ct. Minn. 1982, U.S. Ct. Appeals (8th cir.) 1983. Cert. elem. and secondary sch. tchr., cert. secondary sch. prin., Minn., Ill. Engring. aide U.S. Govt., 1943-45; with Maple Lake State Bank, Minn., 1941-42; teller First Nat. Bank Mpls., 1942; collateral evaluator Mdse. Nat. Bank, Chgo., 1951-52; tchr. Whittier Jr. High Sch., Lincoln, Nebr., 1948-51, Blackhawk Jr. High Sch., Park Forest, Ill., 1954-55, Stillwater Sr. High Sch., Minn., 1962-66; instr., supr. off campus student tchrs., coord. off campus student tchrs. U. Minn. Coll. Edn., Mpls., 1955-62; developer, presenter workshops for various coll. faculty, state personnel, 1968-77; rsch. coord. Mpls. Pub. Schs., 1966-68; personnel adminstr. R.R. Donnelley and Sons Co., Chgo., 1953-54; dir. Professions Devel. Sect. Minn. State Dept. Edn., St. Paul, 1968-77; sole practice law, St. Paul, 198-88—. Author: Handbook for Student Teachers, Handbook for Supervising Teachers. Contbr. articles to profl. jours. Mem. ABA, Minn. State Bar Assn., Ramsey County Bar Assn., Minn. Trial Lawyers Assn., Phi Beta Kappa, Phi Kappa Phi, Pi Lambda Theta. Died Jan. 21, 2007.

GORDON, HOWARD, accountant, educator; b. Chgo., July 19, 1938; s. Maurice J. and Doris (Smutok) Gordon; m. Gerda Halbreich, July 10, 1960; children: Renee, Jeffrey. BSBA, Roosevelt U., Chgo., 1960. CPA Ill., Calif. Contr. Joseph Stern & Co., Northbrook, Ill., 1959—72; tax ptnr. Maryanov, Madsen, Gordon & Campbell, Palm Springs, Calif., from 1972. Mem faculty U. Calif., Riverside Ext. Bd. dirs. Palm Springs SR. Citizens Ctr., 1978, Lyceum of the Desert, 1979—82, City of Palm Springs Pks., Open Space and Trails, Arthritis Found, Palm Springs, 1977—81; mem. devel. authority Agua Caliente; mem. planning com. Eisenhower Hosp., Rancho Mirage, Calif., 1977—80. Mem.: AMA, AICPA, Inst. Cert. Fin. Planners, Desert Estate Planning Coun. (charter pres. 1990—91), Calif. Soc. CPA's. Home: Palm Springs, Calif. Died July 10, 2007.

GORDON, IRVING, physician, educator; b. Cleveland, June 20, 1914; s. N. Beryl and Minna (Singer) G.; m. Toini Lefren, June 16, 1939 (dec. May 1967); children— James Norrby, Elizabeth Britt (Mrs. Michael Ascher), Thomas Rolf; m. Francis Maxwell Hawkes, Oct. 18, 1968. MD, U. Mich., 1937. Diplomate Am. Bd. Pathology, Am. Bd. Microbiology, Nat. Bd. Med. Examiners. Intern L.I. Coll. Med. Sch. Hosp., 1937-38, resident, 1938-39; fellow Rockefeller Found., 1941; profl. assoc. commn. acute respiratory disease Army Epidemiological Bd., Ft. Bragg, N.C., 1943-46; staff mem. div. labs. and research N.Y. State Health Dept., 1946-55, asst. dir., 1952-55; assoc. prof. medicine and bacteriology Albany (N.Y.) Med. Coll.; also assoc. attending physician Albany Hosp., 1949-55; prof. dept. microbiology U. So. Calif. Med. Sch., 1955-85, prof. emeritus, from 1985, chmn., 1955-81, assoc. dean, 1963-65; sr. attending physician U. So. Calif. Med. Ctr., 1956-87. Mem. coms. NIH, Armed Forces Epidemiological Bd., WHO. Author research contbns. to virology and infectious deseases; contbr. to med. microbiol. textbooks; mem. editorial bd. sci. jours. Mem. Am. Cancer Soc. (research coms.), Nat. Lung Assn. Home: Pasadena, Calif. Died Sept. 24, 2005.

GORDON, JACK LEONARD, construction company executive; b. Cedar Rapids, Iowa, Aug. 17, 1928; s. W. Ward and Agnes (Knox) G.; m. Zahava; children: Gaile A., Scott W., Timothy R., Asaf, Anat. Student, U. Calif., Berkeley; grad., Advanced Mgmt. Program, Harvard, 1975. Adjuster Comml. Credit Corp., Stockton, Calif., 1949-50; salesman U.S. Gypsum Co., Sacramento, 1950-54, Calaveras Cement Co. div. Flintkote Co., San Francisco, 1954-64, asst. sales mgr., 1957-59, mgr. sales, 1959-64; gen. mgr. Standard Materials Co. subsidiary Flintkote Co., Modesto, Calif., 1964, pres., 1964-68, Western Aggregate Products div. Flintkote Co., Los Angeles, 1968-70; group corporate v.p. stone products The Flintkote Co., White Plains, N.Y., 1970-74, sr. v.p., also dir., 1974-76; pres., chief exec. officer Centex Homes Corp. subs. Centex Corp., 1976-79, Atlantic Cement Co., Inc. subs. Newmont Mining Corp., Stamford, Conn., 1979-85; v.p. Newmont Mining Corp., NYC, 1985-88; pres. J.L. Gordon and Assocs., New Canaan, Conn., 1988-89; pres., chief exec. officer CDN-USA, Boston, from 1989. With U.S. Army, 1945-48. Mem. Winged Foot Golf Club, Harvard Bus. Sch., Landmark (Stamford). Home: New Canaan, Conn. Died May 26, 2007.

GORDON, NORMAN BOTNICK, psychologist, educator; b. NYC, Feb. 12, 1921; s. Moses and Molvine (Botnick) G.; m. Diana Jean Drews, July 27, 1974; children: Jane Ellen, Judith Ann, Marc Daniel, Aaron Drew. BA, Bklyn. Coll., 1942; MA, New Sch. Social Rsch., 1951; PhD, NYU, 1957. Research psychologist U.S. Naval Tng. Device Ctr., Port Washington, N.Y., 1951-58; assoc. prof. psychology Yeshiva U., NYC, 1959-68, prof., 1968-74; guest investigator Rockefeller U., NYC, 1964-77; prin. rsch. scientist N.Y. State Office of Drug Abuse Svcs., 1974-77; prof. SUNYCO-Oswego, from 1977, chmn. dept. psychology, 1977-86, prof. emeritus, from 1988. Adj. prof. SUNY-Oswego, 1988-97, rsch. assoc., 1997—. Served with U.S. Army, 1942-46. Grantee USPHS, 1966-74, 64-67 Mem. APA, Eastern Psychol. Assn., Sigma Xi. Home: Oswego, NY. Died Aug. 9, 2007.

GORNER, PETER, journalist; b. Chgo., Aug. 4, 1942; children: Jeremy, Peter David. Grad., Northwestern U.; student in music criticism, U. S.C. Feature writer, critic, editor Chgo. Tribune. Recipient (with Jeffrey Lyon) Pulitzer prize for explanatory journalism, 1987. Recipient Pulitzer Prize, Explanatory Journalism, 1987. Died June 27, 2007.

GORSKI, JACK, biochemistry educator; b. Green Bay, Wis., Mar. 14, 1931; s. John R. and Martha (Kenney) G.; m. Harriet M. Fischer, Sept. 9, 1955; children: Michael, Jo Anne. Student, Calif. Poly. Coll., 1949-50; BS, U. Wis., 1953; postgrad., U. Utah, 1957; MS, Wash. State U., 1956, PhD, 1958. NIH postdoctoral fellow U. Wis., 1958-61; asst. prof., asso. prof. physiology U. Ill., Urbana, 1961-66, prof. physiology, 1967—73, prof. biochemistry, 1969—73; prof. biochemistry and animal scis. U. Wis., Madison, 1973—97, Wis. Alumni Research Found. prof., 1985, now prof. emeritus. NSF research fellow Princeton, 1966-67; mem. endocrinology study sect. NIH, 1966-70, molecular biology study sect., 1977-81; mem. biochemistry adv. com. Am. Cancer Soc., 1973-76, mem. personnel for research com., 1983— Contbr. articles to profl. jours. Recipient NIH Merit award, 1986. Fellow Am. Acad. Arts and Sci.; mem. NAS, Am. Soc. Biol. Chemists, Endocrine Soc. (Oppenheimer award 1971, Disting. Leadership award 1987, pres. 1990-91, F.C. Koch award 1995). Democrat. Unitarian Universalist. Died Aug. 31, 2006.

GORSLINE, SAMUEL GILBERT, JR., school administrator; b. San Jose, Calif., Oct. 20, 1921; s. Samuel Gilbert Sr. and Gladys Zeiters (Wolf) G.; m. Barbara Jeanne Clifton, Mar. 22, 1946 (div. 1969); children: Samuel Gilbert III, John Clifton, James Scott; m. Ann Moyes Todd, Sept. 3, 1969; children: Carroll Ann, Robert Todd. BS, U.S. Naval Acad., 1944. Commd. ensign USN, 1944, advanced through grades to capt., 1965, naval aviator Korea, 1949-74, commanded fleet oiler Vietnam, 1968-69, commanded attack carrier USS Coral Sea, 1969-70, ops. officer U.S. Atlantic fleet, 1971-72, commdr. naval tng. ctr. Great Lakes, Ill., 1972-73, ret., 1974; owner, operator Panmure Arms Hotel, Edzell, Scotland, 1974-81; adminstr.v.p. Army and Navy Acad., Carlsbad, Calif., 1986-90. Troop com. chmn. Boy Scouts Am., Fallbrook, Calif., 1987-88; steering com. Fallbrook Incorp. Coalition, 1986-88; elder Fallbrook Presbyn. Ch., 1989-92. Decorated 3 legions of merit, disting. flying cross, 5 air medals; honored Sam Gorsline Day, Battle Creek, Mich., 1972. Mem. Mil. Order World Wars, Naval Acad. Alumni Assn. Lodges: Rotary, Masons (sr. warden 1979-81). Avocations: tennis, swimming. Home: Escondido, Calif. Died Mar. 2, 2006.

GOSS, WILBUR HUMMON, physicist, researcher; b. Tacoma, Wash., June 16, 1911; s. Virgil Dow and Iva May (Hummon) G.; m. Mildred Carolyn Wallin, Jan. 1, 1938; children: Barry D., Carolyn M., Barbara S. BS, U. Puget Sound, 1932; PhD, U. Wash., 1939. Lectr. U. B.C., Vancouver, Can., 1939-40; asst. prof. N.Mex. State U., Las Cruces, 1940-42; rsch. physicist Applied Physics Lab Johns Hopkins U., Silver Spring, Md., 1942-50, asst. dir. Applied Physics Lab, 1950-67. Part-time cons., 1967-76; part-time cons. Gen. Motors Corp., Santa Barbara, Calif., 1967-76; v.p. SeaTek Corp., Santa Barbara, 1976-86. Patentee ramjet engine for Talos missile. Recipient U.S. Presdl. cert. of merit, 1948, Disting. Pub. Svc. award USN, 1961, Howard N. Potts medal Franklin Inst., 1962. Fellow Am. Phys. Soc. Republican. Home: Santa Barbara, Calif. Died May 8, 2006.

GOTTHILF, DANIEL LAWRENCE, accountant; b. N.Y.C., Jan. 7, 1924; s. Morris Harris and Rose (Gold) G.; B.B.A., U. Mich., 1948; postgrad. Mgmt. Inst., N.Y.U., 1968. CPA, N.Y.; 1 dau., Marcy. Pvt. practice pub. acctg., N.Y.C., 1948-57; asst. to pres. The Mautner Co., N.Y.C., 1957-62; treas., controller Tech. Tape Corp., Yonkers, N.Y., 1962-65; sr. v.p. fin. Savin Corp., Valhalla, N.Y., 1965-83, also dir.; pres. Columbia Bus. Systems, Inc., 1983-87; pvt. practice acctg., 1987—; mem. Westchester County adv. bd. Chem. Bank; lectr. Am. Mgmt. Assn. Served with USAF, 1942-45. Mem. Am. Inst. C.P.A.s, N.Y. State Soc. C.P.A.s, Nat. Assn. Accts., Fin. Execs. Inst., Beta Gamma Sigma, Phi Eta Sigma. Republican. Clubs: Princeton, Michigan, Lotos. Author: Treasurers and Controllers Desk Book, 1977; Financial Analysis for Decision Making, 1979. Home: Ridgefield, Conn. Died Sept. 3, 2006.

GOTTLIEB, ANITA BOBROW, blouse manufacturing company executive; b. N.Y.C., June 7, 1930; d. Max and Sylvia Estelle (Adlerstein) Bobrow; m. Merle Gottlieb, Jan. 12, 1969. Student UCLA, 1950; B.B.A., CCNY, 1951. Mem. exec. tng. program Kirby Block, 1949-50, asst. buyer, 1953-55; trainee to dept. mgr. Saks Fifth Ave, N.Y.C., 1950-51; fashion coordinator Donnybrook Coat and Suit Mfrs., 1951; asst. buyer Aaron Schwab, Los Angeles, 1951-53; assoc. buyer Frederick Atkins, 1955-67; operator June Bradlee, 1967-69; asst. to designer Alice Stuart, N.Y.C., from 1969, later sales and prodn. exec., asst. to pres., exec. v.p., now pres.; instr. seminars Fashion Inst. Tech. Mem. Nat. Blouse Assn. (gov.). Democrat. Jewish. Home: New York, NY. Died Mar. 22, 2006.

GOTTLIEB, JOSEPH ABRAHAM **See BISHOP, JOEY**

GOTTLIEB, LEONARD SOLOMON, pathology educator; b. Boston, May 26, 1927; s. Julius and Jeanette (Miller) G.; m. Dorothy Helen Apt, Mar. 23, 1952; children: Julie Ann, William Apt, Andrew Richard. AB cum laude, Bowdoin Coll., 1946; MD, Tufts U., 1950; MPH, Harvard U., 1969. Diplomate Am. Bd. Anatomic Pathology. Intern in surgery Boston City Hosp., 1950-51, resident Mallory Inst. Pathology, 1951-55; assoc. pathologist Mallory Inst. Pathology, Boston, 1957-66, assoc. dir., 1966-72, dir., 1972—2003; asst. chief pathology U.S. Naval Hosp., Chelsea, Mass., 1955-57; chief pathology dept. Boston U. Med. Ctr. Hosp., 1973-96; prof. pathology Tufts U. Sch. Medicine, 1967—71; prof. pathology and lab. medicine Sch. Medicine Boston U., from 1971, chmn. dept., 1980—2003, chmn. emeritus, 2003—06; dir. Mallory Inst. Pathology Found., 1980—2003; pathologist-in-chief divsn. pathology Boston City Hosp., 1994-96; pathologist-in-chief, divsn. pathology Boston Med. Ctr., 1996—2003. Lectr. Harvard Med. Sch., 1963-98; dir. student faculty exch. program Boston U. and Hebrew U., Hadassah Med. Sch., 1988—. Gen. editor Biopsy Pathology Series, Chapman and Hall, 1981-93, editor emeritus, 1993—; mem. editl. bd. Am. Jour. Surg. Pathology, 1981-00, Judeo Med. Jour., 2002-; author or co-author approximately 185 publs. and abstracts and 14 book chpts. dealing primarily with exptl. and human diseases of the liver and gastrointestinal tract. Assoc. mem. bd. govs. Hebrew U. Jerusalem, 1991-95, mem. bd. govs., 1995-2006, mem. exec. com., 2001-06; pres. New Eng. region Am. Friends of Hebrew U., 1989-97, 2000-06, coun. trustees, 1992-2006, founder, 1991, trustee, 1994, guardian, 2000, mem. grants com., 1997-, mem. nat. bd. dirs., 2005-06; mem. sci. adv. bd. Boston chpt. Israel Cancer Rsch. Fund, 1991-92; co-chair and chair Physicians divsn. Greater Boston chpt. State of Israel Bonds Cabinet, 1991-98; pres. Am. Physicians Fellowship for Medicine in Israel, 1990-93; class sec. 1977 Program for Health Sys. Mgmt., Harvard Bus. Sch., 1995-97; dir. Hillel House Programs, Boston U. Sch. Medicine, 2004-06, faculty dir. Maimonides Soc., 2004-06; mem. Am. Coun. Trustees and

Alumni, 2002-06. Lt. M.C. USNR, 1955-57, lt. comdr. res. ret. 1963. Recipient Stanley L. Robbins award for excellence in tchg. Boston U. Sch. Medicine Students, 1986, Jerusalem City of Peace award Boston chpt. State of Israel Bonds, 1992, Disting. Bowdoin Educator award, 1995, Torch of Learning award Am. Friends of The Hebrew U., 1997, Lion of Judah award State of Israel Bonds, 1998, Lifetime Achievement award The Hebrew U., 2000, Lewis H. Millender Cmty. Excellence award Combined Jewish Philanthropies, 2005; named hon. mem. faculty medicine Hebrew U., 1987; James Bowdoin scholar, 1945, Bingham scholar, 1944-50; hon. fellow, Wall of Life, Hebrew U. Jerusalem, 2001; Leonard and Dorothy Gottlieb Hebrew U. Med. Student Scholarship Fund established in their honor, 2004, Leonard S. Gottlieb student prize in pathology established at Boston U. Sch. Medicine, 2005. Mem. AAAS, Am. Soc. for Investigative Pathology, Am. Assn. for Study of Liver Diseases, U.S.-Can. Acad. Pathology, Coll. Am. Pathologists, Am. Soc. Cell Biology, Am. Gastroenterol. Assn., Am. Soc. for Clin. Pathology, Am. Coll. Physician Execs., Coll. Am. Pathologists, New Eng. Soc. Pathologists (pres. 1968-69), Mass. Med. Soc., Charles River Med. Soc., Am. Coun. Trustees and Alumni, Assn. Pathology Chairs (Lifetime Achievement award 2003), N.Y. Acad. Sci., Chester S. Keefer Soc. (charter), Torch of Jerusalem Soc. (founding mem.), Crohn's and Colitis Found. Am., Am. Friends Hebrew U., Alpha Omega Alpha (faculty mem.). Home: Brookline, Mass. Died Dec. 7, 2006.

GOULD, ARTHUR IRWIN, lawyer; b. Chgo., July 31, 1929; s. Gerson M. and Molly (Sitron) G.; m. Barbara Young, Jan. 7, 1961; Jonathan, Thomas, David. BS, U. Ill., 1951; JD, Northwestern U., 1956. Bar: Ill. 1956, U.S. Supreme Ct. 1961, numerous cts. of appeals, U.S. Dist. Ct. (no dist.) Ill. 1963, U.S. Tax Ct. 1963, U.S. Claims Ct. 1959; C.P.A., Ill. Trial atty. Tax Div., Dept. Justice, Washington, 1956-63; assoc. Winston & Strawn, Chgo., 1963-68, ptnr., chmn. tax dept., 1968-87, also chmn. tax dept. Lectr. tax insts. and seminars Contbr. articles to legal jours. Mem. Winnetka Design Rev. Bd. and Winnetka Plan Commn., Ill.; chmn. pub. affairs com. Winnetka Caucus, 1976-77. Served to 1st lt. USAF, 1951-53. Participant Program for Honor Law Grads. Dept. of Justice, 1956 Fellow Am. Coll. Tax Counsel; mem. ABA, Chgo. Bar Assn., Ill. Bar Assn., Internat. Fiscal Assn. (exec. com.), Chgo. Fed. Tax Forum (past chmn.) Clubs: Mid-Day (Chgo.); Old Willow (Northfield, Ill.) (dir.). Home: Winnetka, Ill. Died Nov. 21, 2006.

GOULET, DENIS ANDRÉ, development ethicist; b. Fall River, Mass., May 27, 1931; s. Fernand Joseph and Lumena (Bouchard) G.; m. Ana Maria Reynaldo, Nov. 21, 1964; children: Andrea, Sinane. BA in Philosophy, St. Paul's Coll., Washington, 1954, MA in Philosophy, 1956; MA in Social Planning, Institut de Recherche et de Formation en Vue du Développement, Paris, 1960; PhD in Polit. Sci., U. São Paulo, Brazil, 1963. Laborer, France, Spain, Algeria, 1956-59; planning advisor AID, Recife, Brazil, 1964-65; vis. prof. U. Sask., Regina, Canada, 1965-66; assoc. prof. Ind. U., Bloomington, 1966-68; vis. fellow Ctr. for Study of Dem. Instns., Santa Barbara, Calif., 1969; vis. prof. U. Calif., San Diego, 1969-70; sr. fellow Ctr. for Study Devel. and Social Change, Cambridge, Mass., 1970-74; vis. fellow Overseas Devel. Coun./OAS, Washington, 1974-76; sr. fellow Overseas Devel. Coun., Washington, 1976-79; O'Neill chair in edn. for justice, dept. econs. U. Notre Dame, Ind., 1979—2002, O'Neill chair emeritus Ind., from 2002; faculty fellow Kellogg Inst. for Internat. Study, Kroc Inst. for Internat. Peace Studies. Vis. prof. U. Warsaw, Poland, 1989-90. Author: The Cruel Choice, 1971, The Uncertain Promise, 1977, Mexico: Development Strategies for the Future, 1983, Incentives for Development: The Key to Equity, 1989, Development Ethics: A Guide to Theory and Practice, 1995. Editl. bd. Jour. of Health and Population in Developing Countries; internat. adv. coun. TODA Inst. for Global Peace and Policy Rsch.; internat. adv. bd. Internat. Centre for Islamic Political Economy. Decorated chevalier Odre Nat. du Cèdre (Lebanon), 1960; OAS grantee, 1961-62, Fulbright grantee, 1986; recipient Reinhold Niebuhr award U. Notre Dame, 1988. Democrat. Roman Catholic. Avocation: piano. Home: South Bend, Ind. Died Dec. 26, 2006.

GOULET, ROBERT GERARD, entertainer; b. Lawrence, Mass., Nov. 26, 1933; s. Joseph and Jeannette (Gauthier) G.; m. Louise Longmore, 1956 (div. 1963); 1 child, Nicolette; m. Carol Lawrence, 1963 (div. 1981); children: Christopher, Michael; m. Vera Chochrovska Novak, 1982. Student, Royal Conservatory Music, U. Toronto; studied with George Lambert and Ernesto Vinci. Actor (Broadway debut): Camelot, 1960, (plays): Thunder Rock 1951, Sunshine Town 1951, Visit To a Small Planet 1951, Spring Thaw, 1955-57, Carousel, 1955, 60, 79, The Pajama Game, 1956, 57-58, Gentlemen Prefer Blondes, 1956, Finian's Rainbow, 1956, South Pacific, 1956, 86-89, 2002, The Optimist, 1957, The Beggars Opera, 1958, Bells Are Ringin, 1959, Dream Girls, 1959, Meet Me in St. Louis, 1960, Camelot, 1960-62, 75, 92-94, The Happy Time, 1967-68 (Tony award for best actor), I Do, I Do, 1970-71, On a Clear Day, 1980-81, Kiss Me Kate, 1981, The Fantasticks, 1990, Moon Over Buffalo, 1996, Man of La Mancha, 1996-97, La Cage aux Folles, 2005, (films): Honeymoon Hotel, 1964, I'd Rather Be Rich, 1964, I Deal in Danger, 1966, Underground, 1970, Atlantic City, 1980, Beetlejuice, 1988, Naked Gun II 1/2: The Smell of Fear, 1991, Mr. Wrong, 1996, Toy Story 2, 1999, The Last Producer, 2000, G-Men From Hell, 2000; (TV films): The Enchanted Nutcracker, 1961, Brigadoon, 1966, Carousel, 1967, Kiss Me Kate, 1968, The Couple Takes a Wife, 1972, The Dream Merchants, 1980, Acting Sheriff, 1991, Based on an Untrue Story, 1993; guest appearance (TV series): Howdy Doody, 1954, The Patty Duke Show, 1965, Blue Light, 1966, The Jackie Gleason Show, 1967-69, The Big Valley, 1967, Mission Impossible, 1972, The Tonigh Show Starring Johnny Carson, 1973, Police Woman, 1975, The Love Boat, 1978, Fantasy Island, 1980-83, Matt Houston, 1983, Murder, She Wrote, 1985, Finder of Lost Loves, 1985, In the Heat of the Night, 1992, Burke's Law, 1995, Recess 1998-2000; singer (albums): Always You, 1962, Two of Us, 1962, Sincerely Yours, 1962, The Wonderful World of Love, 1963, (with Doris Day) Annie Get Your Gun, 1963, In Person, 1963, This Christmas I Spend with You, 1963, Without You, 1964, Manhattan Tower, 1964, My Love, Forgive Me, 1964, Summer Sounds, 1965, On Broadway, 1965, vol. 2, 1967, I Remember You, 1966, Travelin' On Tour, 1966, Hollywood Mon Amour, 1967, Woman, Woman, 1968, Both Sides Now, 1968, Come Back To Sorrento, 1969, Today's Greatest Hits, 1970, Robert Goulet's Wonderful World of Christmas, 1968, I Never Did as I Was Told, 1971, After All Is Said And Done, 1976, Close to You, 1982, and several others. Recipient numerous awards including World Theatre award, Tony award, Grammy award Best New Artist, 1962, Grammy award Gold Album for My Love Forgive Me, 1964. Fellow (hon.) Toronto Royal Conservatory Music. Fellow Royal Conservatory Music (hon.). Died Oct. 30, 2007.*

GOVE, ROGER MADDEN, physician; b. Mechanicsburg, Ohio, Nov. 30, 1914; s. Thurman Harrison and Leah Marie (Madden) G.; m. Eleaner Jane Rooney, June 15, 1938; children— Jon Duane, Janet Marie (Mrs. David Dye), Joann Leah (Mrs. Jerry Webb) and Judith Lynn (twins). BA, Ohio State U., 1937, MD, 1941. Intern White Cross Hosp., Columbus, Ohio, 1941-42; resident psychiatry Columbus State Hosp., 1942, 45-46; Commonwealth Fund fellow child psychiatry Children's Service Center Wyoming Valley, Wilkes Barre, Pa., 1946-47; dir. Upper Miami Valley Guidance Center, Piqua, Ohio, 1947-50; supt. Columbus State Sch., 1950-54, 58-66; asst. commr. Ohio Div. Mental Hygiene, 1966-70, commr., 1970-74; chief Bur. Mental Retardation, 1954, 66—; med. dir. mental retardation unit Athens Mental Health and Mental Retardation Center, Athens, Ohio, 1977-78; practice medicine specializing in psychiatry, from 1978; supt. Juvenile Diagnostic Center, Columbus, 1954-58. Clin. asst. prof. psychiatry and prof. pediatrics Ohio State U. Coll. Medicine, 1951—; Chmn. Task Force Mental Retardation Planning Ohio, 1963-65; mem. com. long term care United Cerebral Palsy Assn., 1963— Trustee Urbana (Ohio) Coll., 1964-71. Served to capt. M.C. USAAF, 1942-45. Fellow Am. Assn. Mental Retardation (chmn. exam. bd. 1963-67); mem. Am. Psychiat. Assn., Ohio Psychiat. Assn. (pres. 1961), Epilepsy Assn. Ohio (v.p. 1979) Died Nov. 12, 2006.

GOWARD, RUSSELL, former state legislator; b. St. Louis, Aug. 25, 1935; s. William and Zenobia (Askew) G.; m. Dolores Jean Thornton, 1957; children: Russell II, Monika. Cert., Hubbard's Bus. Coll., 1959; student, Harris Tchrs. Coll. Divsn. leader 21st Ward Dem. Orgn., Mo., 1963-65; rep. Mo. State Ho. Reps. Dist. 60, 1967-97; pres., treas. Goward's & Assocs., Inc., 1967-99; ret. Active Boy Scouts Am. Decorated Nat. Def. Svc. Ribbon, European Occupl. medal. Mem. Masons. Home: Florissant, Mo. Died July 27, 2007.

GOYAN, JERE EDWIN, pharmaceutical executive, former dean; b. Oakland, Calif., Aug. 3, 1930; s. Gerald H. and Lucille (Johnson) G.; m. Patricia B. Mesirow, Aug. 24, 1952 (div.); children: Pamela, Terrence H., Andrea; m. Linda Lloyd Hart, Mar. 25, 1988. BS, U. Calif. Sch. Pharmacy, 1952, PhD, 1957. Asst. prof. pharmacy U. Mich., 1956-61, assoc. prof., 1961-63; assoc. prof. pharmacy and pharm. chemistry U. Calif. at San Francisco, 1963-65, prof., 1965-79, 81-92, assoc. dean Sch. Pharmacy, 1966-67, dean, 1967-79, 81-92; commr. FDA, US Dept. Health & Human Services, Washington, 1979—81; pres., COO Alteon, Inc., Ramsey, NJ, 1993-99; pres. Goyan & Hart Assocs., from 1999. Fellow AAAS; mem. Inst. Medicine of NAS, N.Y. Acad. Scis., Am. Pharm. Assn., Acad. Pharm. Scis., Am. Assn. Pharm. Scientists (pres. 1990), Calif. Pharm. Assn., Am. Assn. Colls. Pharmacy (pres. 1978-79), Sigma Xi, Rho Chi, Phi Lambda Upsilon. Died Jan. 17, 2007.

GRACE, DONALD J., engineering researcher; b. Oklahoma City, Feb. 21, 1926; m. 1949; 2 children. BSEE, Ohio State U., 1948, MSEE, 1949; PhD, Stanford U., 1962. Lectr. Ohio State U., 1948-49; rsch. engr. Airborne Instruments Lab., 1959-61; rsch. assoc. Stanford U., 1962-63; sr. rsch. assoc. Systs & Techniques Lab., 1963-66, assoc. prof. elec. engring., 1963-67, dir., 1966-67, assoc. dean engring., 1967-69; dir. rsch. Kentron Hawaii Ltd., 1969-73; dir. ctr. engring. rsch. U. Hawaii, 1973-76; dir. engring. exp. sta. Ga. Inst. Tech., from 1976. Mem. panel FORECAST USAF, 1963, mem. reconnaissance adv. bd., 1964-65; tech. adv. bd. U.S. Army Sec. Agy., 1965-66; dir. Stanford U. Instuctional TV Network, 1967-69; asst. sec. Ga. Tech. Rsch. Inst., rep. Pub. Svc. Sattelite Consortium, 1977—; univ. adv. panel Nat Solar Energy Rsch. Inst., 1978-79; mem. forum nat. sec. affairs Pentagon, 1980. Mem. IEEE, AAAS, Sigma Xi. Avocations: microwave components and subsystems, defense electronics, alternate energy, instructional television, rsch. adminstrn., mgmt. and planning. Died Mar. 15, 2007.

GRACE, JOHN ROBERT, manufacturing executive; b. Dallas, Dec. 11, 1926; s. Joe William and Luola (Floyd) Grace; m. Diane Dickey, Feb. 28, 1953; children: John Robert Jr., Kevin Dickey, Cynthia Ruth. BS in Mech. Engring., Tex. A&M U., 1950. Registered profl. engr., Tex. Engring. trainee Hughes Tool Co., Houston, 1950—51; project engr. A-1 Bit & Tool Co., Houston, 1952—54; salesman Frank Holister Co., Houston, 1955—58, plant mgr., 1959—65; prs. Spring Engrs., Inc., Houston, from 1966. Chmn. bd. Spring Engrs. of Houston and Dallas, from 1966, Spring Engrs., Memphis, from 1976, Gotco Internat., Inc., Houston, from 1981; dir. Commonwealth Bank, Bellaire, Tex., from 1975. With AUS, 0945—1946. Mem.: Spring Mfrs. Inst. (dir. 1980—83, v.p. from 1983), Raveneaux Country (Houston), Houston Racquet. Republican. Episcopalian. Home: Houston, Tex. Died Oct. 19, 2006.

GRAHAM, ANNE, government official; b. Annapolis, Md., Dec. 28, 1949. Grad., Bradford Coll.; postgrad., Columbia U. Spl. asst. to dep. dir. for communications Republican Nat. Com., Washington, 1971; with White House News Summary Office, Washington, 1973, Office of Sec. of Treasury, 1974-75; press sec. to Senator Harrison Schmitt, Washington, 1976-79; asst. press sec. Reagan-Bush Campaign, 1980-81; dep. spl. asst. to Pres. for communications, Washington, 1981; asst. sec for legislation and pub. affairs Dept. Edn., Washington, 1981-85; mem. Consumer Product Safety Commn., 1985—. Died Dec. 26, 2005.

GRAHAM, COLIN, performing company executive; b. Hove, Sussex, Eng., Sept. 22, 1931; s. Frederick Eaton and Diana Alexandra (Finlay) G. Diploma, Royal Acad. Dramatic Art, 1953; D Arts (hon.), Webster U., 1988, U. Mo., 1992. ordained to ministry Ind. Christian Evang. Ch., 1987. Dir. prodns. English Opera Group, 1963-75; artistic dir. Aldeburgh Festival, 1969-90, v.p., from 1990; artistic dir., founding dir. English Music Theatre, from 1975; dir. of prodns. English Nat. Opera, London, 1968-83; assoc. artistic dir., dir. prodns. Opera Theatre of St. Louis, 1978-85; artistic dir. Banff Festival Opera, 1984-91, Opera Theatre of St. Louis, 1985—2007. Dir. prodns. for Met. Opera, N.Y.C., N.Y.C. Opera, Santa Fe Opera, San Francisco Opera, Chgo. Lyric Opera, Glyndebourne Opera, Royal Opera Covent Garden, others. Lighting and set designer; librettist: Penny for a Song (Bennett), 1967, Golden Vanity (Britten), 1967, Postman Always Rings Twice (Paulus), 1982, Joruri (Miki), 1985, The Woodlanders (Paulus), 1986, Oberon (Weber), 1988, others. Recipient Art and Edn. award for Personal Achievement in the Arts, 1993, Orpheus award for War and Peace, 1973, Opera Am. award for prodn., 1988; Winston Churchill fellow, 1974; nominated Best Opera Prodn., Royal Opera Ho., 1992. Mem. Brit. Actors Equity, Can. Actors Equity Am. Guild Mus. Artists. Died Apr. 6, 2007.

GRAHAM, DELLAS, business executive; b. White County Ill., Feb. 10, 1934; s. Clyde and Edith G. (Pollard) G.; m. Norma J. Tait, Nov. 7, 1957; children: Deborah, Brenda, Gregory. BS in Engring., Evansville Coll., Ind., 1957, MBA, 1982. Prodn planner Keller-Crescent Co., Evansville, 1960-65, bindery supr. 1965-68, asst. prodn. mgr., 1968-69, prodn. mgr., 1969-73, v.p. 1973-81, exec. v.p., 1981-92, sr. exec. v.p., from 1992. Bd. dirs Epi-Hab, Evansville, 1980—; trustee Oakland City (Ind.) City Coll., 1984—. 1st lt. USAF, 1957-60, Japan. Home: Evansville Ind. Died Jan. 13, 2007.

GRAHAM, ERWIN HERMAN, ret. automobile co. exec. b Detroit, Jan. 28, 1921; s. Jacob and Marie Pauline (Schulz) G. m. Ellen Marie Eliasen, Sept. 12, 1944; children— Leigh Ellen Michael Randall. Grad. in acctg., Bus. Inst., 1943. C.P.A., Mich Cost acct. Parke, Davis & Co., 1939-43; pub. acct. Ernest & Ernst, 1945-51; comptroller's staff Chrysler Corp., 1951-54 comptroller, 1958-67, DeSoto div., Detroit, 1954-58, corp. v.p 1964-80. Bd. dirs. YMCA Met. Detroit, 1964-85; trustee Detroit Inst. Tech., 1970-80. Served to 1st lt. USAAF, 1943-45. Mem Am. Inst. C.P.A.s, Mich. Assn. C.P.A.s (life), Fin. Execs. Inst Clubs: Detroit Athletic, Detroit Golf. Home: Grosse Pointe Mich. Died Sept. 25, 2006.

GRAHAM, GEORGE GORDON, physician, educator; b Hackensack, NJ, Oct. 4, 1923; s. Charles Stewart and Angelic (Gomez de la Torre) G.; m. Simone H. Custer, Mar. 3, 1949 children— Marianne, Alexander, Monica, Carol. AB, U. Pa 1941, MD, 1945. Diplomate: Am. Bd. Pediatrics, Am. Bd Nutrition. Intern, resident Brit. Am. Hosp., Lima, Peru, 1946-48 staff pediatrics, 1948-50, 52-55, dir. research, 1960-71, Institut de Investigacion Nutricional, Lima, Peru, 1971-83, pres., 1987 89; rsch. U. Pa. Hosp., 1951; resident pediatrics Balt. Cit Hosp., 1955-56, asso. chief pediatrician, 1965-68; assoc. prof pediatrics Johns Hopkins U., 1965-78, prof., from 1978, pro human nutrition, 1968-91, prof. emeritus, from 1992, di nutrition program, 1976-85; staff pediatrician Cleve. Clinic 1957-59. Mem. com. amino acids Food and Nutrition Bd. c NRC, 1966-71, com. internat. nutrition programs, 1978-79 mem. Food and Nutrition Bd., 1981-84; cons. nutrition AID GAO, NIH; mem. nutrition study sect. NIH, USPHS, 1971-75 chmn., 1973-75, mem. cancer control intervention program re com., 1985-86; mem. Pres.'s Commn. on Food Assistanc 1983-84. Mem. editorial bd. Jour. Nutrition, 1968-73, Am. Jou Clin. Nutrition, 1969-74. Decorated Orden al Merito Agrico Peru; Orden Hipolito Unanue; recipient Joseph Goldberge award AMA, 1972; Borden award Am. Acad. Pediatrics, 197 Fellow Am. Inst. Nutrition; mem. Am. Soc. Clin. Nutritic (coun. 1980-84), Soc. Pediatric Rsch., Am. Pediatric So Achievements include rsch. on infantile malnutrition, its long term effects, its prevention by new protein sources. Died Jan. 1 2007.

GRAHAM, GEORGE J., JR., political scientist, educator; Dayton, Ohio, Nov. 12, 1938; s. George J. and Mary Elizabe (McBride) G.; m. Scarlett Gower, Sept. 10, 1966 (div. 1991); child, Carmen Michelle. BA in History, Wabash Coll., 196 PhD, Ind. U., 1965. Instr. Vanderbilt U., Nashville, 1963-6 asst. prof., 1965-71, assoc. prof., 1971-77, prof. polit. sc 1977—2006, assoc. dean, 1986-88, 97-00, chair dept. polit. sc 1988-92. Series editor Chatham (N.J.) House Pub., 1978-200 Fulbright John Marshall chair Budapest U. of Econ. Studie 1995-96. Author: Methodological Foundations, 1971; autho editor: Post-Behavioral Era, 1972, Founding Principles, 197 contbr. articles to profl. jours. Chair Mt. Juliet (Tenn.) Sew Commn., 1985-86; sec. Zoning Commn., Mt. Juliet, 1988-8 Guggenheim fellow, 1973-74, NEH fellow New Haven Na Humanities Inst., 1976-77; Fulbright John Marshall chair Budapest, Hungary, 1995-96. Mem. Am. Polit. Sci. Ass (founder Found. Polit. Theory sect. 1975-2006), So. Polit. S Assn. (mem. coun. 1987-90), Midwest Polit. Sci. Assn., Interna Polit. Sci. Assn., Com. Conceptual Analysis (chair). Avocation painting, guitar, travel, bicycling. Home: Nashville, Tenn. Di Nov. 30, 2006.

GRAHAM, JAMES BERNARD, state government official; Fairfield, Ky., Dec. 24, 1923; s. Bruce Alexander and Bess (Caldwell) G. m. Lorena Pauley, June 7, 1952; children: Dia Gail, Janet Marie. AB, William Jewell Coll., 1945; MA, Kans., 1947; PhD, U. Ky., 1956. Supt. schs. Nelson Coun Bardstown, Ky., 1954-68, Ashland, Ky., 1968-70, Bowli Green, Ky., 1970-75; supt. pub. instrn. Commonwealth K Frankfort, 1976-79; auditor pub. accounts State of Ky., fr 1979. Vice chmn. Study of Minimum Found. Program of K 1966; mem. Ky. Crime Commn., Coun. Pub. Higher Edn., K Authority Ednl. TV. Trustee Ky. Tchrs. Retirement Syste Oneida (Ky.) Inst.; sec. Ky. Textbook Commn.; pres. bd. truste Stephen Foster Drama Assn., 1957-65. Named Ky. Col.; Kello Found. grantee, 1956. Mem. NEA, Am. Assn. Sch. Adminstr Ky. Assn. Sch. Adminstrs. (past pres.), Ky. Sch. Bds. Ass Century Club, Masons, Kiwanis (past pres. Bardstown clu Kappa Delta Pi, Phi Delta Kappa. Democrat. Baptist. Hon Bowling Green, Ky. Died June 22, 2007.

GRAHAM, ROBERT C., management consultant; b. Mpls., June 7, 1925; s. Samuel A. and Sybil F. (Fleming) G.; m. Elizabeth Needham, Nov. 26, 1946; children: Christopher, Peter; m. Janice Tellefsen, Aug. 1983. BS in Engring., U. Mich., 1945, MS, 1948. Aero. research scientist Cleve. Flight Propulsion Lab., NASA, 1948-52; with Ford Motor Co., 1954-86; pres., dir. Ford Brasil (S.A.), São Paulo, 1977-80; v.p. automotive ops. parent co. Latin Am., Dearborn, Mich., 1980-86; v.p. diversified products Ford Motor Co.; pres. RCG Assocs., Inc., Harbor Springs, Mich., from 1986, Brighton Graham Engring., Inc., from 1987. Mem. Soc. Automotive Engrs. Died Apr. 17, 2006.

GRAHAM, WILLIAM PATTON, III, plastic surgeon, educator; b. Plainfield, NJ, Apr. 30, 1934; s. William Patton and Mary Alice (Bucher) G.; children: Susan Patton, Elizabeth Ames. AB, Princeton U., 1955; MD, U. Pa., 1959. Diplomate Am. Bd. Surgery, Am. Bd. Plastic Surgery (chmn. 1985-86). Intern U. Colo. Med. Ctr., Denver, 1959-60; resident in surgery VA Hosp., Denver, 1960-61, U. Calif., San Francisco, 1961-64, chief resident in surgery, 1964-65; resident and instr. plastic surgery U. Pa., Phila., 1965-67, asst. prof. surgery, 1967-70; assoc. prof. surgery Pa. State U., Hershey, 1971-74, prof. surgery, 1974-85, chmn. divsn. plastic surgery, 1971-85 and from 1996, clin. prof. surgery, 1985-96; prof. surgery U. Colo., from 1994. Chmn. Plastic Surgery Research Council, Hershey, 1979-80 Co-author: The Hand-Surgical and Non-Surgical Management, 1977, Practical Points in Plastic Surgery, 1980. Trustee Harrisburg Acad., 1980-85. Maj. USAR, 1960-73. USPHS research grantee, 1974-76; advanced clin. fellow Am. Cancer Soc. Phila., 1969-70. Fellow ACS; mem. Am. Surg. Assn., Am. Assn. Plastic Surgeons (trustee 1983-86, 91-94), Am. Soc. Surgery of Hand (mem. coun. 1989-92), Soc. Head and Neck Surgeons, Am. Soc. Aesthetic Plastic Surgery (pres. 1992-93), Northeastern Soc. Plastic Surgeons (pres. 1988-89, Newport R.I.), Robert H. Ivy Soc. (pres. Hershey 1974-75), Sigma Xi (full), Alpha Omega Alpha, Nu Sigma Nu, Tower Club (Princeton, N.J.). Republican. Home: Thomasville, Pa. Died Oct. 8, 2006.

GRAMLICH, EDWARD MARTIN, public policy educator, former federal official; b. Rochester, NY, June 18, 1939; s. Jacob Edward and Harriet (Williams) G.; m. Ruth Brown, Aug. 29, 1964; children: Sarah, Robert. BA in economics, Williams Coll., 1961; MA in economics, Yale U., 1962, PhD in economics, 1965. Mem. staff Fed. Res. Bd., 1965-70; dir. policy rsch. divsn. Office Econ. Opportunity, 1971—73; sr. fellow The Brookings Instn., 1973-76; prof. economics and pub. policy U. Mich., 1976—97, dir. Inst. Pub. Policy Studies, 1979-83, 1991—95, chmn. economics dept., 1983—86, dean Sch. Public Policy, 1995—97, interim provost & exec. v.p. acad. affairs, 2005—06, Richard A. Musgrave Collegiate Prof. Pub. Policy, 2005—06, prof. emeritus, 2006—07; mem. bd. govs. Fed. Res. Sys., 1997—2005; Richard B. Fisher Sr. Fellow The Urban Inst., Washington, 2006—07. Vis. lectr. Monash U., Australia, 1970, Stockholm U., 1979; adj. prof. George Washington U., 1974-75; vis. prof. Cornell U., 1975-76; cons. Res. Bank of Australia, 1970, Nat. Inst. Edn., 1973-75, US Dept. Labor, 1973-75, Health Edn. & Welfare, 1974—, Congl. Budget Office, 1975-78, Senate of Puerto Rico, 1975, Collier's Encyclopedia, 1975-79, Indsl. Research Inst., Sweden, 1979-81, Abt Assocs., 1979-80, Minimum Wage Study Commn., 1981, Fed. Res. Bd. Acad. Cons., 1981. Author: Savings Deposits, Mortgages and Housing in the FRB-Mit-Penn Econometric Model, 1972, Educational Performance Contracting: An Evaluation of an Experiment, 1975, Setting National Priorities: The 1975 Budget, 1974, Setting National Priorities: The 1976 Budget, 1975, Benefit-Cost Analysis of Governmental Programs, 1981, Tax Reform: There Must Be A Better Way, 1982. Editorial bd. National Tax Jour., 1970-73, Jour. Policy Analysis and Mgmt., 1980, Evaluation Review, 1980-83, Jour. Econ. Lit., 1981-2007. Contbr. articles to profl. jours. Mem. Brookings Panel on Economic Activity, 1973—, Brookings Panel on Social Experimentation, 1973-74, White House Summit Conf., 1974, Econ. Adv. Panel Nat. Inst. of Edn., 1973-74, Edn. Grants Panel, Nat. Inst. Edn., 1973-74, Edn. and Human Resources Adv. Bd., Rand Corp., 1975-78, Com. on Evaluation Research, Social Sci. Research Council, 1977-79, N.Y. State Productivity Commn., 1977-79, Assn. for Pub. Policy and Mgmt. (policy council 1979-84, v.p. 1979-80, program chmn. 1981), Nat. Acad. of Scis. Edn. Research Found., 1980-2007, State of Mich. Com. on Prof. and Occupational Licensure, 1981-82, Sime-Dime Rev. Panel, US Dept. Health & Human Services, 1980-81, Vis. Com. Albion Coll. Pub. Policy Sch., 1981—, Truman Scholarship Selection Panel, Michigan-Ohio, 1982-2007, Review Com., Md. Econs. Dept., 1993-2007, Chmn., Nat. Inst. of Edn. Policy Study Group, 1983. Home: Ann Arbor, Mich. Died Sept. 5, 2007.*

GRANT, DAVID JAMES WILLIAM, pharmacy educator; b. Walsall, Eng., Mar. 26, 1937; came to U.S., 1988; s. James and Attie Hilda May (Stringer) G. BA in Chemistry with 1st class honors, Oxford U., Eng., 1961, MA, DPhil in Phys. Chemistry, 1963, DSc in Phys. Sci., 1990. Lectr. chemistry U. Coll. of Sierra Leone, Freetown, 1963-65; lectr. then sr. lectr. pharm. chemistry U. Nottingham, Eng., 1965-81; prof. phys. pharmacy Sch. Pharmacy, U. Toronto, Ont., Can., 1981-88, assoc. dean grad. studies and rsch. Ont., 1984-87; endowed prof. pharmaceutics Coll. Pharmacy, U. Minn., Mpls., from 1988. Bd. dirs. Hosokawa Micron Internat., Inc., 1998-2001; mem. grants com. for pharm. sci. Med. Rsch. Coun. Can., Ottawa, 1983-87; mem. com. on health rsch. Ont. Univs., Toronto, 1985-87; vis. prof. Med. Rsch. Coun. Can.; mem. stds. expert com. for excipients: test methods for U.S. Pharmacopeia, 1991—; cons. to numerous chem. and pharm. cos. Co-author: Physical Chemistry for Students of Pharmacy and Biology, 1977, Solubility Behavior of Organic Compounds, 1990; mem. editl. bd. Jour. Pharm. Scis., 1990-93, assoc. editor, 1994—; mem. editl. adv. bd. Pharm. Devel. and Tech., 1995—, Kona, 1996—, AAPS Pharm. Sci., 1999—; contbr. more than 200 articles to sci. jours. Lt. Brit. Army, 1955-57. Recipient Rsch. award Leverhulme Found., U.K., 1969, Pharmaceutics award of excellence PhRMA Found., 1999, award European Soc. Applied Phys. Chemistry, 2004, Mettler Toledo award N. Am. Thermal Analysis Soc., 2005; grantee rsch. couns. and indsl. cos., U.K., Can., U.S. Fellow AAAS, Royal Soc. Chemistry, Am. Assn. Pharm. Scientists (sustaining charter mem. 1986—, Dale E. Wurster award 2004), Internat. Union Pure and Applied Chemistry; mem. Am. Inst. Chem. Engrs., Am. Crystallographic Assn., Am. Chem. Soc. Achievements include showing how small amounts of additives or impurities modify the physical properties of crystalline drugs and excipients; development of crystal engineering of pharmaceutical substances. Home: Minneapolis, Minn. Died Dec. 9, 2005.

GRANT, GAIL GROVER, real estate broker; b. Painesville, Ohio, Nov. 9, 1921; s. Gail Grover and Gladys Felton (Beadle) Grant Gilliland; m. Dinah Tilling, Dec. 31, 1951 (div. Apr. 1960); children— Gail Grover III, Lorna Melanie; m. Elizabeth Clarke Browne, May 17, 1973. B.A., Dartmouth Coll., 1942, M.B.A., Tuck Sch., 1943. Pres. Gail G. Grant Co., Painesville, 1937-58; sales mgr. Service Awning Co., Miami, Fla., 1958-60; salesman Allen Morris Co., Miami, 1960-63; island sales mgr. McPherson & Brown, Freeport, Bahamas, 1963-71; pres. Ocean One Realty Inc., Boca Raton, Fla., 1978—, Royal Palm Properties Corp., Boca Raton, 1971—. Trustee Concord Twp., Ohio, 1953-58. Served as lt. USNR, 1943-45, ETO, PTO. Mem. Nat. Assn. Realtors (cert. comml. investment mem.), Nat. Assn. Realtors, Internat. Real Estate Fedn., Theta Delta Chi. Republican. Methodist. Club: Boca Raton Hotel and Country. Lodge: Elks. Avocations: hunting, fishing, sailing, swimming. Home: Pompano Beach, Fla. Died Feb. 16, 2007.

GRANT, JOHN ROBERT, management consultant; b. Chgo., Oct. 7, 1932; s. John F. and Ann T. (Murchan) G.; m. Diane Margaret Donovan, Oct. 22, 1960; children: Deirdre, Patrice, Marilynn, Marijane, Jennifer, John, Diane. BSc, DePaul U., 1955; grad., U. Dayton. Cert. Mgmt. Cons. Inst. Mgmt. Cons. With Standard Oil Co., Ind., 1956-60, Internat. Packers, Chgo., 1960-63, Internat. Harvester, Chgo., Springfield, Ill., 1963-70, Hay Assocs., Chgo., Kansas City, 1970-78, A.T. Kearny Inc., Chgo., 1978-80, Modern Mgmt. Inc., Lake Bluff, Ill., from 1980. Author (with A.E. Cameron) Credit Union Salary Administration, 1992; contbr. chpts. to books. Capt. USMCR, 1951-62. Recipient Literature award Am. Soc. Healthcare Human Resource Adminstrn., Chgo., 1992. Mem. Inst. Mgmt. Cons., Am. Compensation Assn., Adminstrv. Mgmt. Soc., Soc. Human Resource Mgmt., Am. Soc. Healthcare Human Resources Adminstrn. (author handbook), Chgo. Compensation Assn., Soc. Human Resource Profls., Royal Soc. Health (London). Roman Catholic. Avocations: golf, reading. Home: Lake Bluff, Ill. Died Jan. 14, 2007.

GRANT, VERNE EDWIN, biology professor; b. San Francisco, Oct. 17, 1917; s. Edwin and Bessie (Swallow) G.; m. Alva Day, June 12, 1946 (div. Aug. 1959); children: Joyce Grant Mixon, Brian, Brenda; m. Karen Alt, Nov. 3, 1960. AB, U. Calif., Berkeley, 1940, PhD, 1949. Teaching asst. botany U. Calif., Berkeley, 1946-49; NRC fellow Carnegie Inst., Stanford, Calif., 1949-50; geneticist Rancho Santa Ana Bot. Garden, Claremont, Calif., 1950-67; asst. prof. Claremont Grad. Sch., 1951-53, assoc. prof., 1953-57, prof., 1957-67; prof. biology Inst. Life Sci., Tex. A&M U., College Station, 1967-68; prof., dir. Boyce Thompson Southwestern Arboretum U. Ariz., Superior, 1968-70; prof. botany U. Tex., Austin, 1970-87, prof. emeritus, from 1987. Author: Natural History of the Phlox Family, 1959, The Origin of Adaptations, 1963, The Architecture of the Germplasm, 1964, (with Karen Grant) Flower Pollination in the Phlox Family, 1965, (with Karen Grant) Hummingbirds and Their Flowers, 1968, Plant Speciation, 1971, 2d edit., 1981, Genetics of Flowering Plants, 1975, Organismic Evolution, 1977, The Evolutionary Process, 1985, 2d edit., 1991, The Edward Grant Family and Related Families in Massachusteets, Rhode Island, Pennsylvania, and California, 1997; mem. editl. bd. Ency. Americana, 1955-64, Brittonia, 1957-62, Evolution, 1960-62, Am. Naturalist, 1964-67, Biologisches Zentralblatt, 1974-97; contbr. articles to profl. jours. Recipient Sci. award Phi Beta Kappa, 1964 Fellow Am. Acad. Arts and Scis.; mem. NAS, Soc. for Study of Evolution (pres. 1968), Bot. Soc. Am. (cert. of merit 1971), Internat. Soc. Plant Taxonomists, Am. Soc. Plant Taxonomists, Acad. Medicine, Engring. and Sci. of Tex. Home: Austin, Tex. Died May 29, 2007.

GRANT, WILLIAM ROBERT, investment banker; b. NYC, Jan. 9, 1925; s. William Vincent and Adelaide (Marshall) G.; m. Dorothy Annetta Corbin, June 29, 1951 (dec. Aug. 1994); children: Deborah, Byron, Melissa, Elise; m. Adele T. Reilly, Mar. 23, 1996. BS in Chemistry, Union Coll., Schenectady, 1949. Trainee Gen. Electric Co., 1949-50; with Smith, Barney, Harris Upham & Co., Inc., 1950-77, vice chmn., 1976-77, also bd. dirs.; vice chmn. Endowment Mgmt. Corp., 1977-78; chmn. MacKay Shields Co., 1979-87, N.Y. Life Internat., 1987-89, Galen Assocs., from 1989. Bd. dirs. Witco Chem. Co., Fluor Corp., Smith Kline Beecham Corp., N.Y. Life Ins. Co., Seagull Energy Co., Allergan Inc., Datamedic Inc., Fountain Head Water Co. Trustee Union Coll., Elfun Trust, Cary Trust. Mem. Fin. Analysts Fedn., Nat. Assn. Bus. Economists, Delta Upsilon. Clubs: University, Knickerbocker, Links (N.Y.C.); Nat. Golf, Maidstone (L.I.). Roman Catholic. Home: New York, NY. Died Apr. 15, 2007.

GRAY, DAVID LAWRENCE, retired air force officer; b. Portland, Oreg., Aug. 19, 1930; s. Thomas Graham and Helen Lee (Brown) G.; m. Nelda Joyce Ryan, Nov. 17, 1951 (dec. June 1987); children: David Scott, Vicki Lynn, Steven Mark; m. Patricia F. Umstead, Mar. 22, 1991. BS, U. Colo., 1958; MBA, George Washington U., 1962. Registered rep. United Services Planning Assn. & Ind. Research Agy., Montgomery, Ala., 1982-83, dist. agt. Charleston, SC, 1983-86; exec. dir. Air Force Assn., Arlington, Va., 1986-87. Host: TV talk show Def. Issues, 1982-83 Exec. dir. Air War Coll. Found., 1982-94. Maj. gen. USAF, 1951-82; Korea, Vietnam. Mem. Air Force Assn. (pres. Charleston chpt. 1985-86, nat. exec. dir. 1986-87), Daedallians. Republican. Avocations: golf, boating. Home: Melbourne, Fla. Died May 12, 2006.

GRAY, E. ARTHUR, funeral director; b. Port Jervis, NY, Feb. 28, 1925; s. Arthur Aloysius and Elizabeth Agnes (Brown) G.; m. Helen Agnes Hart; children: Gerald E., Brigid Elizabeth. BA, U. Colo., 1947. Pres. Gray Funeral Home, Inc., Port Jervis, from 1948, E. Arthur Gray Memls., Inc., Port Jervis, from 1948. Mayor City of Port Jervis, 1977-87. Served to lt. (j.g.) USN, 1943-47. Mem. Nat. League Cities (bd. dirs. 1987-88). Democrat. Roman Catholic. Avocations: reading, golf, other sports. Home: Port Jervis, NY. Died Apr. 10, 2007.

GRAY, MARIE TERESA, nursing administrator; b. Butte, Mont., Nov. 20, 1945; d. Robert Sam and Teresa Rose (Brusati) Vukmanovich; children: Robert, Misti; m. Gary E. Gray. Diploma, St. James Hosp. Sch. Nursing, Butte, Mont., 1966. Lic. nursing home administrator. Pediatric staff nurse, relief supr. St. James Hosp., Butte, Mont., 1966-87; sales assoc., dist. coord. AFLAC, Butte, Mont., 1986-88; staff nurse Butte (Mont.) Park Royal, 1988-89, staff devel. coord., 1989-91; dir. nurses Crest Nursing Home, Butte, Mont., from 1991. Died July 20, 2007.

GRAY, WALTER P., III, historian, archivist, consultant; b. San Francisco, Aug. 8, 1952; s. Walter Paton II and Elsie Josephine (Stroop) G.; m. Mary Amanda Helmich, May 23, 1980. BA in History, Calif. State U., Sacramento, 1976. Rschr. Calif. State R.R. Mus., Sacramento, 1977-80, curator, 1980-81, 85-90, archivist, 1981-85, mus. dir., 1990-98; Calif. state archivist, 1998—2004; state hist. records coord., 1999—2004; chief archeology, history and museums divsn. Calif. State Parks, from 2004. Trustee Golden State Mus., 2003-04; cons. in field, 1976—. Contbr. articles to profl. jours. Buddhist. Avocations: woodworking, antique automobiles, photography. Home: Sacramento, Calif. Died May 8, 2007.

GRAYDON, AUGUSTUS TOMPKINS, lawyer; b. Columbia, SC, July 14, 1916; s. Clinton Tompkins and Raven VanderHorst (Simkins) G.; m. Marion Hunt, Dec. 3, 1952 (dec. Jan. 1984); children: Raven Simkins, Augustus Tompkins (dec.), Jefferson Hunt; m. Ann Ruggles, Jan. 10, 1985. BA in English and History, U. of the South, 1937; MS in Journalism, Columbia U., 1938; LLB, U. S.C., 1948, JD, 1960. Bar: S.C. Mem. news staff, editor Columbia Record, 1938-41; ptnr. Graydon & Suber, Columbia, from 1948. Pres. State-Record Co. Found. Bldg.; bd. dirs. State-Record Co. Author: (with Bishop Thomas) History of the Episcopal Church in South Carolina 1830-1957, Tales of Columbia, 1965; (with Nell S. Graydon) Eliza of Wappoo, 1968, (with others) The Governor's Mansion of the Palmetto State, 1978; (reprint) The Philadelphia Blue Book of Furniture, 1977. Chmn. Richland County Pub. Library, 1947-52, ARC drive, 1950; mem. Gov.'s Mansion Commn., 1971—; founder Hist. Columbia Found., Endowment Fund, Found. award, 1978; active in saving of Boylston House and Garden, 1963-78, Order of Palmetto, 1977, Columbia Mus. Art, Nat. Trust; dir. tours for Antiques mag. Maj. USAAF, 1941-46. Mem. ABA, Am. Law Inst., S.C. Bar Assn. (chmn. exec. com. 1961-62), Richland County Bar Assn. (pres. 1962), English-Speaking Union, Forest Lake Club, Palmetto Club, Pine Tree Hunt Club, Phi Beta Kappa. Home: Columbia, SC. Died June 15, 2007.

GREADY, THOMAS GERALD, JR., obstetrician-gynecologist; b. Palestine, Tex., Mar. 25, 1911; s. Tom and Emma Gready; m. Mary Jean Gready; children: Thomas III, Robert M., Connie. BA, Rice U., 1933; MD, U. Tex., 1937. Intern U. Iowa Hosp., 1937-38; resident Chgo. Lying-In Hosp., 1939-42; chief of staff Hermann Hosps., Houston, 1960—75. Asst. prof. emeritus Baylor U. Mem. AMA, Am. Coll. Surgeons, Am. Coll. Ob-gyn., Ctrl. Assn. Ob-gyn. Home: Waller, Tex. Died July 23, 2007.

GREELEY, BURNHAM H., lawyer; b. Mapleton, Minn., Feb. 13, 1934; BA, Grinnell Coll., 1956; LLB, Harvard U., 1959. Bar: Hawaii 1960. Ptnr. Greeley Walker & Kowen, Honolulu. Bd. dir. Kuakini Medical Ctr.; mem. Hawaii Federal Jud. Selection comm. Fellow Am. Bar Found.; mem. ABA (ho. of dels. 1989-91, bd. gov. 2003-2006, chmn. Coalition for Justice comm.), Hawaii State Bar Assn. (pres. 1987), Am. Inn of Ct. IV Hawaii chptr., Am. Judicature Soc. Hawaii chptr. (dir., chmn. Civil Justice comm.). Died Jan. 26, 2006.

GREEN, ARTHUR GEORGE, electric utility executive; b. Columbus, Ohio, Dec. 14, 1911; s. George Jacob and Clara Pauline (Moeffert) G.; m. Josephine Virginia Courtright, Sept. 24, 1938; children— George Frederick, Sarajo Courtright. BS in Bus. Adminstrn, Ohio State U., 1933. With Columbus & So. Ohio Electric Co., 1934-76, pres., 1971-76, chmn. bd., 1973-76, now dir. Former pres. Jr. Achievemnt of Columbus; pres. Central Ohio Council Boy Scouts Am., 1973—; Bd. dirs. Met. YMCA, Columbus, 1972—, Childrens Hosp., 1974-87, Center of Sci. and Industry, 1974-87. Mem. Nat. Assn. Accountants (past pres. Columbus), Fin. Execs. Inst. (past pres. Columbus), Columbus C. of C. (dir. 1972-76) Presbyterian (elder, treas., past commr.). Clubs: Controllers, Columbus Country, Masons. Home: Columbus, Ohio. Died May 8, 2006.

GREEN, CLIFFORD SCOTT, federal judge; b. Phila., Apr. 2, 1923; s. Robert Lewis and Alice (Robinson) G.; m. Mabel Louise Green (dec.), 1 child David Scott (dec.); m. Carole Chew Williams Green, 1 child Terri; 3 stepchildren: Lisa Dawn, Anthony, Clifford Kelly BS, Temple U., 1948, JD, 1951. Bar: Pa. 1952. Pvt. practice law, Phila., 1952-64; dep. atty. gen. State of Pa., 1954; judge County Ct., Phila., 1964-68, Ct. Common Pleas, 1968-71, US Dist. Ct. (ea. dist.) Pa., Phila., 1971-88, sr. judge, 1988—2007. Former lectr. in law Temple U. Former bd. dirs. Children's Aid Soc. of Pa.; former bd. mgrs. Children's Hosp., Phila.; trustee Temple U. Served with USAAF, 1943-46. Recipient Judge William Hastie award NAACP Legal Def. Fund, 1985, awards for cmty. service Women's Christian Alliance, Health and Welfare Council, awards for cmty. service Opportunities Industrialization Ctr., J. Austin Norris Barrister's award, 1988, Temple Law Alumni Assn. award 1994, Justice Thurgood Marshall Meml. award Nat. Bar Assn., 1994, gen. alumni award Temple U., 1999, Spirit of Excellence award ABA, 2002 Mem. Sigma Pi Phi. Presbyterian. Home: Philadelphia, Pa. Died May 31, 2007.

GREEN, DALE MONTE, retired judge; b. Outlook, Wash., Apr. 27, 1922; s. Carey W. and Minnie M. (Gunness) G.; m. Maxine Spencer, June 30, 1946; children— Judith Louise, Frederick William. BA in Econs. and Bus, U. Wash., 1948, BS in Law, 1949, JD, 1950. Bar: Wash. 1950. Pvt. practice,

Spokane, 1950-54; asst. U.S. dist. atty. Eastern Dist. Wash., 1954-56; trial atty. civil div. Dept. Justice, Washington, 1956-58; U.S. dist. atty. Eastern Dist. Wash., 1958—61; mem. firm Sherwood, Tugman & Green, Walla Walla, Wash., 1960-69; judge Wash. Ct. Appeals Div. III, Spokane, 1969-91, chief judge, 1972-74, 78-80, 84-86, 90-91; presiding chief judge Wash. Ct. Appeals, 1985. Chmn. state adv. com. on judicial ethics; mem. Wash. Pattern Jury Instrn. Com., 1971-86, State Adv. Bd. Jud. Edn., 1974-77, Wash. State Jud. Council, 1972-75 Editorial bd.: Wash. Law Rev, 1949-50. Served with AUS, 1943-46. Mem. ABA, Fed. Bar Assn., Wash. Bar Assn., Am. Judicature Soc., Rotary. United Methodist. Home: Spokane, Wash. Died June 11, 2007.

GREEN, DAVID THOMAS, retired surgical company research and development executive, inventor; b. Biggleswade, Eng., Aug. 5, 1925; came to U.S., 1961; s. George and Elizabeth (Course) G.; m. Jeanne Mary Todd, June 30, 1951; children: Lawrence, Lynn, Peter. Cert., Luton Inst. Tech., Eng., 1945. Engr. apprentice Weatherly Oil Gear, Biggleswade, 1941-45, design engr., 1948-52; group leader spl. purpose machines Orenda Aircraft Group, Malton, Ont., Can., 1952-61; mgr. design automotive emission controls Am. Machine and Foundry, LA, 1961-65; sr. v.p. R&D U.S. Surg. Corp., Norwalk, Conn., 1966-94. Holder 129 patents in surg. stapling and clip devices. Sgt. Brit. Army, 1945-48. Recipient Inventor of Yr. award N.Y. Patent, Trademark and Copyright Law Assn., Inc., 1991. Avocations: boating, fishing, travel. Home: Gulf Stream, Fla. Died Jan. 10, 2006.

GREEN, HARVEY EUGENE, engineering executive; b. Lava Hot Springs, Dec. 19, 1932; s. Harvey Gerald and Donna (Stephenson) G.; m. Ramona E. Wiles; (div.) children: Harvey E., Steven R., Richard A., Sheryl; m. Mary-Jane Seeley, Feb. 11, 1983; children: Britany L., Charla F. BSCE, U. Wash., 1966; MBA, Seattle U., 1971. Registered profl. engr. Plant planner The Boeing Co., Seattle, 1957-59, engr./facilities analyst, 1959-70, mgr., facilities constrn., 1970-71; dir. engring. U.S. Postal Svc., San Francisco, 1971-73; pres. Resources Conservation Co., Seattle, 1974-78; v.p. BOECON (Boeing subs.), Seattle, 1978-82; pres., CEO, Boeing Engring. & Constrn., Seattle, 1982-84; pres., CEO Interserv, Inc., Tulsa, 1984-85; chmn., CEO EDECO, Inc., Tulsa, 1985-95; pres., CEO ECMS Inc., Tulsa, from 1995. Bd. dirs. Emerald Airlines, Tulsa; corp. gen. ptnr. Ltd. Partnership, Tulsa; ptnr. Winter-Green Partnership, Tulsa. Bd. dirs., pres. Engrs. Soc. of Tulsa, 1988-94; sponsor Nat. China Trade Corp., Tulsa, 1987-88. Mem. Okla. Soc. Profl. Engrs., NSPE, Growing Co. Counsel, Tau Beta Pi (past pres. 1965-66), Beta Gamma Sigma. Avocations: golf, skiing, tennis. Home: Tulsa, Okla. Died May 2, 2006.

GREEN, JACK PETER, pharmacologist, educator; b. NYC, Oct. 4, 1925; s. Maurice and Tillie (Herman) G.; m. Arlyne Genevieve Frank, Oct. 25, 1958. BS, Pa. State U., 1947, MS, 1949; PhD, Yale, 1951, MD, 1957; postgrad., Poly. Inst., Copenhagen, 1953-55, Inst. de Biologie Physico-Chimique, Paris, 1964-65. Vis. scientist Poly. Inst., Copenhagen, 1953-55, Inst. de Biologie Physico-Chimique, Paris, 1964-65; asst. prof. Yale, 1957-61, asso. prof., 1961-66, Cornell U. Med. Coll., 1966-68; prof., chmn. dept. pharmacology Mt. Sinai Sch. Medicine, 1968—98. Mem. research grant rev. com. USPHS; mem. N.Y.C. Health Research Council, Dysautonomia Found., Irma T. Hirsch Trust. Contbr. articles profl. jours.; mem. editl. bds. profl. jours. Recipient Claude Bernard Vis. Professorship U. Montreal, 1966 Mem. AAAS, N.Y. Acad. Sci., Am. Chem. Soc., Am. Soc. Biol. Chemists, Soc. Drug Rsch., N.Y. Acad. Medicine, Harvey Soc.,Am. Soc. Pharmacology and Exptl. Therapeutics, Internat. Soc. Quantum Biology, Am. Coll. Neuropsychopharmacology, Am. Soc. Neurochemistry, Soc. for Neurosci., Sigma Xi, Alpha Omega Alpha, Phi Lambda Upsilon, Gamma Sigma Delta. Home: New York, NY. Died Feb. 7, 2007.

GREEN, JOYCE, book publishing company executive; b. Taylorville, Ill., Oct. 22, 1928; d. Lynn and Vivian Coke (Richardson) Reinerd; m. Warren H. Green, Oct. 8, 1960. AA, Christian Coll., 1946; BS, MacMurray Coll., 1948. Pres. Warren H. Green, Inc., St. Louis, from 1992, Affirmative Action Register, from 1977, InterContinental Industries, Inc., from 1980; chief exec. officer Pubs. Svc. Ctr.; pres. Epoch Press, from 2004. Mem. St. Louis C. of C., Jr. League Club, Media Club, Mo. Athletic Club. Died Dec. 19, 2005.

GREEN, RAYMOND ARTHUR, county official; b. Gary, Ind., Aug. 18, 1944; s. Harold and Clara (Taylor) G.; m. Lucile McConnell, June 18, 1971; children— Caleb, Adam. B.A. in Indsl. Engring., Ind. State U.-Terre Haute, 1966; B.A., U. Chgo.; postgrad. in law Cornell U. Engr., United Cons. Engrs., Indpls., 1979-81; asst. engr. Lake County Commr., 1981-85; chief dep. recorder County of Lake, Crown Point, Ind., 1985—; owner, trainer U.S. Trotting Assn., Columbus, Ohio. Democrat. Home: Gary, Ind. Died July 7, 2006.

GREEN, RAYMOND BERT, lawyer; b. Hartford, Conn., July 12, 1929; s. William Gottlieb and Mayme Pauline (Judatz) G.; m. Barbara Louise Miller, Jan. 31, 1955; children: Elizabeth Hollister, William Goodrich. BA, Yale U., 1951, LLB, 1954. Bar: Conn. 1954, U.S. Dist. Ct. Conn. 1959, U.S. Dist. Ct. (so. and ea. dists.) N.Y. 1976, U.S. Ct. Mil. Appeals 1974, U.S. Ct. Appeals (2d cir.) 1966, U.S. Ct. Appeals (3d cir.) 1989, U.S. Supreme Ct. 1962. Counsel Fed. Grievance Com. Dist. Ct.; assoc. Camp, Williams & Richardson, New Britain, Conn., 1954-55, Day, Berry & Howard, Hartford, Conn., 1958-65, ptnr., from 1966. Dir. New Britain Herald; trustee Collinsville Savs. Soc. (Conn.); judge of probate Dist. of Canton, Conn., 1963—. Bd. editors Conn. Probate Law Jour. Bd. dirs. Am. Friends of Coll. Cevenol (France), pres., 1970-90; bd. dirs. YMCA Met. Hartford, 1963-84, 86—; sec., bd. trustees Children's Mus. Hartford, 1977-85, Sci. Mus. of Conn., 1985-86. With USNR, 1955-58; comdr. JAGC, Res., 1958-79. Mem. ABA, ATLA, Hartford County Bar Assn., Conn. Bar Assn. (chmn. ins. com. 1978-85, ethics com. 1987—), Judge Advs. Assn., Def. Rsch. Inst., Conn. Def. Lawyers (bd. dirs. 1985-87), Nat. Coll. Probate Judges, Officers of Conn. Club, Naval Res. Officer Luncheon Club, Assn. Ex-Mems. Squadron A Club, Phi Beta Kappa, Phi Delta Phi. Republican. Congregationalist. Home: Wallingford, Conn. Died June 28, 2006.

GREEN, RICHARD MORRIS, construction executive, consultant; b. Haty, Colo., Dec. 30, 1933; s. William Clarence and Patresa Nell (Hicks) Green; m. Dawen Marlene Reasbeck, Nov. 25, 1956; children: Joy, Christopher, Jennifer. BS in Elec. Engring. and Bus. Mgmt., U. Colo., 1961. Cert. constrn. estimator. Quality control mgr. Denver Divsn. Martin Marietta Aerospace, 1961—63; cost engr., asst. mgr. cost estimating dept. Denver Equipment Co., 1963—65; constrn. engr. Espro, Denver, 1965—66; pres. Assoc. Constrn. Cons., Inc., Aurora, Colo., from 1966. With USN, 1953—57. Mem.: Am. Assn. Cost. Engrs. Constrn. Specifications Inst., Am. Soc. Profl. Estimators (pres. Denver chpt. 1969, 1970, 1971, 1976, Nat. Constrn. Estimator of Yr. 1974—75). Home: Boulder, Colo. Died Aug. 17, 2007.

GREEN, SAUL, biochemist; b. NYC, Jan. 8, 1925; s. Isidore and Rose (Margiloff) G. BS, CCNY, 1948; MS, U. Iowa, 1950, PhD, 1952. Predoctoral tchr. U. Iowa, 1950-52; instr. biochemistry U. Va. Med. Sch., Charlottesville, 1952-54; dir. clin. chemistry U. Va. Hosp., Charlottesville, 1952-54; rsch. assoc. dept. medicine Cornell U. Med. Sch., NYC, 1954-59; rsch. assoc. biochemistry Sloan Kettering Inst., NYC, 1959-63, asst. mem., 1963-70, assoc. mem., 1970-81; assoc. prof. Cornell U. Grad. Sch., NYC, 1973-81; sci. dir. Emprise, Inc., Washington, from 1987. Pres. ZOL Cons., N.Y.C., 1982—; dir. R&D Phil. Biologics, Phila., 1984-86. Contbr. articles to profl. jours. Cpl. inf. U.S. Army, 1944-46, ETO, PTO. Recipient award Damon Runyon Found., 1968-70, career devel. award NIH, 1963-68, ACS, 1968-70, 75-77, Nat. Cancer Inst., 1977-80. Mem. Am. Assn. for Cancer Rsch., Am. Soc. Biol. Chemists, Sigma Xi (mem.-at.-large), Phi Lambda Upsilon. Jewish. Avocations: fishing, tennis, scuba diving, swimming. Died July 1, 2007.

GREENE, LEONARD MICHAEL, manufacturing executive, aerospace transportation executive; b. NYC, June 8, 1918; s. Max and Lyn (Furman) G.; m. Beverly Kaufman, June 27, 1943 (div. 1957); children: Randall Ashley, Bonnie LeVar, Laurie Baldwin; m. Phyllis Saks, June 8, 1958 (dec. Oct. 1965); children: Douglas, Charles, Donald (dec.), Stephen, Terry; m. Joyce Teck, Jan. 2, 1967; stepchildren: Jeffrey Meller, William Meller, Gary Meller, Amy Meller Gerbe. BS in Engring., CCNY, 1937, MS in Engring., 1939; postgrad., Guggenheim Sch. Aeronautics, NYU; D in Civil Law (hon.), Pace U., 1977. Rsch. chemist Rubber & Asbestos Corp., NJ, 1938-41; aerodynamicist, engring. test pilot Grumman Aircraft Corp., LI, NY, 1941-45; hon. chmn. Safe Flight Instrument Corp., White Plains, NY, 1946—2006. Pres., founder SoundTitles, Inc., 1989; bd. dirs. Nationwide Ins. Author: Free Enterprise Without Poverty, 1981, The National Tax Rebate: A New America With Less Government, 1998, Inventorship: The Art of Innovation, 2001, (monographs) A Plan for a Nat. Demogrant Fianced by a Value-Added Tax, The Medical Costs Recovery Program. Mem. adv. bd. Martha's Vineyard Hosp.; pres., founder Inst. for SocioEcon. Studies, 1970; v.p., co-founder Corp. Angel Network, White Plains, 1981—; mem. spl. com. on income maintenance and council on trends and perspectives U.S. C. of C., 1975-76; bd. dirs. Blythedale Children's Hosp., Urban League Westchester Inc., Nationwide Ins.; chmn. Income Assistance/Community Devel. Program of Westchester Council of Social Agys.; pres., founder Fair Share Found., Inc.; mem. income maintenance com. Community Svc. Soc.; mem. work group on welfare reform Task Force on N.Y.C. Fiscal Crisis; mem. Westchester Coordinating Coun. on Handicapped; mem. Conf. Bd.'s Econ. Forum, 1979. Recipient Air Safety award Flight Safety Found., 1949, 81, Pilot Safety award Nat. Bus. Aircraft Assn., 1961, Employer Merit award Pres.'s Com. on Employment of Handicapped, Albert Gallatin award for Civic Leadership, Flight Safety Found award for Meritorious Svc., Disting. Svc. award Human Rights Commn. of White Plains, 1976, Medallion award Found. for Westchester C.C., 1988, U.S. EPA, Region I Spl. Act award, 1989, Meritorious Svc. to Aviation award Nat. Bus. Aircraft Assn., 1996, AlliedSignal Bendix trophy for aviation safety Flight Safety Found., 1999, Carrels award Outstanding Achievement Elecs. Aviation Week & Space Tech., 1999, Laureate award for lifetime achievement as a pioneer in flight safety, performance and innovation Aviation Week & Space Tech., 2001, Contbn. to Am. Innovation award U.S. Patent and Trademark Office, 2002; nominated N.Y. State Employer of Yr; cited by N.Y. Gov.'s Com. to Employ Handicapped, 1966; commendation from sec. dept. HEW, private sector initiative commendation Pres. of U.S.; inducted into Nat. Inventors Hall of Fame, 1991. Fellow AIAA (assoc.); mem. Soc. Exptl. Test Pilots (life), Nat. Aviation Assn., Internat. 12 Meter Assn. (voting), Edgartown Yacht Club, N.Y. Yacht Club, Sheldrake Yacht Club (Mamaroneck, N.Y.), Royal Hamilton Amateur Dinghy Club (Bermuda), Quaker Ridge Golf Club (Scarsdale, N.Y.), Alpha Beta Gamma. Achievements include co-founding Courageous Sailing Ctr., Inc., Boston, to which donated 12-meter yacht Courageous IV, winner America's Cup, 1974, 77. Home: Mamaroneck, NY. Died Nov. 30, 2006.

GREENE, RICHARD EFRAIM, data processing executive; b. NYC, Feb. 2, 1938; s. Jack and Helen (Cohn) G.; m. Karen Sandra Stein, July 1, 1962 (div. May 1980); children: Barry, Lauren; m. Arlene Catherine Tarinelli, Aug. 15, 1986; children: Bryan, Kevin. BS, U. Houston, 1958; LLD (hons.), Sacred Heart U., 1983. Sales exec. IBM, NYC, 1963-69, mktg. mgr. Westport, Conn., 1969-71, NYC, 1971-74; corp. exec. T-Bar, Wilton, Conn., 1974-76; pres. chmn. bd. Data Switch Corp., Shelton, Conn., 1976-85, chmn. bd. founder, 1985-94; pres., CEO Consertech Learning Syss.Corp., Sarasota, Fla., from 1995. Guest lectr. Duke U., Durham, N.C., 1986-89. Mem. Fair Rent Commn., Assn. Venture Founders. Jewish. Avocations: flying, tennis. Home: Bradenton Beach, Fla. Died Aug. 27, 2006.

GREENE, THEODORE PHINNEY, retired history professor; b. NYC, May 20, 1921; children: 3. BA, Amherst Coll., 1943; MA, Columbia U., 1948. Lectr. Am. history Columbia U., 1950-52; from asst. prof. to assoc. prof. history Amherst Coll., Mass., 1952-57; prof. history Amherst Coll., Mass., 1973-88, Winthrop H. Smith prof. history Mass., prof. emeritus Mass., 1988—2007. Editor: American Imperialism in 1898, 1955, Wilson at Versailles and Roger Williams and the Massachusetts Magistrates, 1962; author: American Heroes: The Changing Models of Success in American Magazines, 1970. Mem. Am. Hist. Assn., Am. Studies Assn. Died Jan. 15, 2007.

GREENFIELD, SEYMOUR STEPHEN, mechanical engineer; b. Bklyn., July 9, 1922; s. Herman and Yetta (Silfen) G.; m. Eleanor Levy, Oct. 30, 1949 (dec. 1987); children: Meryl Joy, Bruce Howard; m. Judith A. Abrams, 1990. Student, N.Y. U., 1939-40; B.Mech. Engring., Poly. Inst. N.Y., 1943. Registered profl. engr., Calif., Conn., Mass., N.J., N.Y., La., Tex., Ohio. Engr. Percival R. Moses Assos., NYC, 1946-47; sr. engr. and assoc. Parsons, Brinckerhoff, Quade & Douglas, NYC, 1947-64, ptnr., from 1964, chmn. bd., 1979-90, chmn. emeritus, from 1990. Adviser Manhattan Coll., NYC, from 1974; mem. devel. coun. Tex. A&M Sch. Architecture, 1981; chmn. coun. on transp. Ctr. for Transp. Policy and Mgmt., NYU. Bd. dirs. N.Y. chpt. March of Dimes, 1989. Served to lt. USNR, 1944-46. Recipient Engring. News Record Citation for Outstanding Contbns. to Constrn. Industry, 1982, Moles award, 1993, Golden Eagle award Soc. Am. Mil. Engrs., 1997; named Transp. Man of Yr., March of Dimes, 1982. Fellow Poltechnic Univ. of N.Y.; mem. Soc. Am. Mil. Engrs. (nat. pres. 1977, dir. 1975—, pres N.Y.C. post 1974-75), Nat. Acad. Engring. Bldg. Research (mem. adv. bd. 1972—), N.Y. C. of C. and Industry (vice chmn Transp. Council 1973—), N.Y. State Soc. Profl. Engrs., ASME, Am. Soc. Heating, Refrigerating and Air Conditioning Engrs., Moles (pres. 1986, trustee, chmn. coun. on transportation N.Y.C.). Home: Fort Lee, NJ. Died Nov. 17, 2006.

GREENLEAF, THOMAS R., retired motor carrier company executive; b. July 2, 1927; m. Jane Chivers, 1951; children Ford, Peter, Adam, John. Grad., Duke U. With Chem. Leaman Tank Lines Inc., Lionville, Pa., 1951, v.p., exec. v.p., pres., COO and mem. exec. com., 1971, pres., CEO and mem. exec. com. also dir. Avocation: tennis. Died May 31, 2007.

GREENOUGH, Mrs. PETER B. See SILLS, BEVERLY

GREENSTADT, MELVIN, investor, retired educator; b. NYC Jan. 18, 1918; s. Sol Max and Sadie (Rosenberg) G.; m. Hele Levy, June 22, 1941; children: Laurie Greenstadt Brow Kenneth, Olivia Greenstadt Parker. BS, Coll. City N.Y., 1938 AB, U. So. Calif., 1948, AM, 1949; PhD, 1956. Chemist Littaue Pneumonia Rsch. Fund, N.Y. U. Coll. Medicine, NYC, 1938-4 War Dept., Radford, Va., 1941-42; tchr. chemistry and math Fairfax H.S., LA, 1950-66, 69-80; real estate and securitie investor, from 1980; assoc. prof. chemistry Calif. State U., Lon Beach, 1966-69. Cons. sci. and math. edn. Co-author: CHEM Study Text, 1960, SMSG Math. Text, 1963. Lt. comdr. USNR 1942-46. Recipient award Com. for Advanced Sci. Tng., 1962 Western Regional award in high sch. chemistry tchg. Am. Chem Soc., 1972; James Bryant Conant award h.s. chemistry tchg. 1973; award for chemistry tchg. So. Calif. sect., 1974, 77, 78 79; H.S. Chemistry Tchr. Regional award Mfg. Chemists Assn 1978; other awards including Los Angeles County Bd. Suprs 1978 Died June 13, 2006.

GREENWALD, EDWARD HARRIS, mining company executive, mining consultant, researcher; b. Pitts., Mar. 30, 1920; s. Harold Putnam and Sophia (Jones) G.; m. Betty Jean Pelter (div. Apr. 1960); children: Edward H., Jr., Catherine D. Greenwal Perry; m. Charlotte Ann Tomlinson, Apr. 25, 1964. B.S. cu laude, U. Pitts, 1942. Registered profl. engr. Pa., W.Va., Ky. La Mining engr. Boone County Coal Corp., Sharples, W.Va 1942-45, chief engr., 1945-47, asst. to v.p., 1947-52, gen. mgr chief operating officer, 1952-56; ptnr. Eavenson, Auchmuty & Greenwald Cons., Pitts., 1956-57, owner 1967—, chmn Coraopolis, Pa., 1978—; pres., dir., CEO Washington Energ Processing, Inc., Coraopolis, 1984—; dir., v.p. La. Coal Services, La. Energy Services, U.S. Energy Services, Lafayette La., 1978-82; dir., exec. v.p. Miller Coal Systems, Housto 1980-81; pres. Resource engring. and Mgmt., Pitts., 1974-78 v.p., treas. dir. Spruce River Coal Co., Pitts., 1962-70, Aquitair of Pa., Inc., Pitts., 1973-78, Kanawha Coal Operators Assn Charleston, W.Va., 1952-56. Contbr. articles to profl. jour Patentee in field. Mem. Commn. on Mine Safety, State of Pa 1963-64; bd. dirs. Logan County chpt. ARC, 1952-56, Loga County Tax Payers Assn., 1952-56; v.p. Chief Corn Sto council Boy Scouts Am., Logan, 1954-56. Named Engring Alumnus of Yr., U. Pitts., 1975; recipient Pa. Gov.'s Energ award, 1991, Energy Innovation award, U.S. Dept. Energ 1992. Mem. Am. Inst. Mining and Metall. Engrs. (Legion of Honor 1994), Am. Mining Congress, Coal Mining Inst. Am Nat. Mine Rescue Assn., W. Va. Coal Mining Inst., Nat. De Preparedness Assn., Am. Inst. Mining Engrs. (vice chm Central Appalachian sect. 1955-56), Coal River Mining Ins (pres. 1950). Home: Lawrence, Pa. Died Aug. 23, 2006.

GREER, ROBERT STEPHENSON, retired insurance company executive; b. Apr. 2, 1920; s. Fred Jones and Nann (Stephenson) G.; m. Patrica Pettry, Oct. 1, 1944; childre Robert S., John P. BS, La. State U., 1941. Ins. agt. Union Na Life Ins. Co., Baton Rouge, 1941-42, dist. mgr., 1945-48, v.p 1948-56, exec. v.p., 1956-70, pres., CEO, 1970-85, chmn. bd CEO, 1985-90; pres., CEO Union Nat. Fire Ins. Co., Bat Rouge, 1970-85, chmn. bd., CEO, 1985-90. Dir. Premier Regional Bank. Chmn. United Way, 1977, pres., 1980-81; bd. dir Salvation Army, Our Lady of the Lake Found., Hospice Foun NCCJ, Pennington Biomed. Rsch. Ctr., Woman's Hosp., Bat Rouge, 1976-80, Baton Rouge Area Found., 1978-82, 87– chmn. bd. trustees 1st United Meth. Ch., 1970—; past bd. dir past pres. YMCA. Lt. USN, WWII. Named Alumni Endow Chair of Bus. Adminstrn., La. State U., 1989, Disting. Citizen Yr., Boy Scouts Am., 1989, Alumnus of Yr., La. State U. Alum Assn., 1990; recipient YMCA Lifetime Achievement awa 1999. Mem. Baton Rouge C. of C. (past pres.), BBB Bat Rouge (past pres.), La. State U. Coll. Bus. Alumni (past pres La. State U. Alumni Fedn. (past pres., Hall of Distinction 198 Life Insurers Conf. (past chmn. Disting. Svc. award 1991), L Insurers Conf., Coun. for a Better La. (past pres.), Country Cl (past pres.), City Club (bd. dirs. 1968-70), Rotary (past pres., Free Enterpriser of Yr. 1985, Exec. of Yr. 1986), Kappa Sigma (Disting. Alumnus award 1996), Beta Gamma Sigma. Home: Baton Rouge, La. Died July 24, 2006.

GREGG, JAMES CALVIN, lawyer; b. Ebensburg, Pa., Dec. 26, 1924; s. Oliver E. and Sophia G.; m. Dora Osterstock, June 9, 1951; children: Gregory Michael, Watson W. Student, Ind. State Tchrs. Coll., 1946-47; LL.B., George Washington U., 1950. Bar: D.C. 1950, Va. 1953. Partner firm Gregg & Tait, Washington, 1950-57, MacLeay, Lynch, Bernhard & Gregg, Washington, from 1957. Served with USAAF, 1943-46. Mem. Bar Assn. D.C., Va. State Bar, Va. Assn. Def. Attys., D.C. Def. Lawyers Assn., The Counselors, Defense Research Inst., Phi Delta Phi. Home: Arlington, Va. Died June 5, 2007.

GREIG, WILLIAM TABER, II, publishing company executive; b. Mpls., Apr. 16, 1924; s. William Taber and Margaret Naomi (Buckbee) G.; m. Doris Jane Walters, June 23, 1951; children: Kathryn Ann Greig Rowland, William Taber, III, Gary Stanley, Doris Jane. B.Arch., U. Minn., 1945. Jr. exec. Bur. Engraving, Mpls., 1946-48; partner, mgr. Praise Book Publns., Mound, Minn., 1948-50; v.p., exec. v.p., gen. mgr. Gospel Light Publs., 1950-76, pres., owner Ventura, Calif., 1972—2006, chmn., 1989—2006. Bd. dirs. Lighthouse Ptnrs. Bookstores; founder, chmn., Gospel Light Worldwide, 2000-2006; founder, chmn. bd. Credo Pub., St. Petersburg, Russia. Ruling elder Presbyn. Ch. (U.S.A.); co-founder Minn. Sunday Sch. Assn., 1953; bd. dirs., chmn. Joy of Living Bible Studies, 1978-2006; trustee Concerts of Prayer Internat., 1988—; chmn. bd. dirs. John M. Perkins Found. for Christian Cmty. Devel., Jackson, Miss. Lt. (j.g.) USNR, 1943-46. Mem. Evang. Christian Pubs. Assn. (co-founder 1974, bd. dirs., pres. 1981-83) Clubs: Tower. Republican. Home: Ventura, Calif. Died Feb. 15, 2006.

GREIMANN, JANE, state representative, elementary school educator; b. Mason City, Iowa, Jan. 25, 1942; m. Lowell Greimann; children: Amy, Blair, Chad. BA, Iowa State U., 1964. Cert. tchr. Iowa. Tchr. Nevada, Iowa Mid. Sch., 1982—97; supr. student tchrs. Iowa State U., 1998—99; state rep. dist. 45 Iowa Ho. of Reps., from 2000; mem. edn. com.; mem. environment com.; mem. human svcs. appropriations com.; mem. natural resources com. Bd. hawk-i, 1996—99, CPTF Steering Com.; bd. dirs. Mid. Iowa Cmty. Action, 2001—02. Mem.: Family and Consumer Sci. Profl. Orgn., League Women Voters. Democrat. Presbyterian. Died Feb. 4, 2006.

GREINER, GORDON GARY, lawyer; b. Harvey, Ill., Sept. 7, 1934; s. Gordon E. and Mable (Davis) G.; m. Jean E. McFadden, June 15, 1958 (div. Jan. 1970); children: David E., Gail E.; m. Kathleen C. Rolby, Nov. 10, 1978. BSBA, Northwestern U., 1956, JD, 1959. Bar: Colo. 1959. Assoc. Holland & Hart, Denver, 1959-66, ptnr., from 1966. Bd. dirs. NAACP Legal Def. and Ednl. Fund, Inc., N.Y.C., 1987—. Recipient Whitehead award ACLU Colo., 1972. Mem. ABA, Colo. Bar Assn., Denver Bar Assn. Democrat. Avocations: scuba diving, fly fishing. Home: Deer Harbor, Wash. Died Aug. 24, 2006.

GREISEN, KENNETH INGVARD, retired physicist; b. Perth Amboy, NJ, Jan. 24, 1918; s. Ingvard C. and Signa (Nielsen) G.; m. Elizabeth C. Chase, Apr. 12, 1941 (dec.); children: Eric Winslow, Kathryn Elise; m. Helen A. Leeds, Mar. 27, 1976 (dec. 1996). Student, Wagner Coll., 1934-35; BS, Franklin and Marshall Coll., 1938; PhD, Cornell U., 1942. Instr. Cornell U., 1942-43, asst. prof., 1946-48, assoc. prof., 1948-50, prof. physics, 1950-84, prof. emeritus, 1984—2007, chmn. dept. astronomy, 1976-79, univ. ombudsman, 1975-77, dean faculty, 1978-83; scientist Manhattan Project, Los Alamos, 1943-46. Fellow Am Phys. Soc.; mem. Am. Astron. Soc., Internat. Astron. Union, Nat. Acad. Sci., AAUP. Rsch. cosmic rays. Home: Ithaca, NY. Died Mar. 17, 2007.

GRENGA, HELEN EVA, chemical engineering educator; b. Newnan, Ga., Apr. 11, 1938; d. Angelo and Eva Jane (Kelley) G. AB, Shorter Coll., 1960; PhD in Chemistry, U. Va., 1967. Postdoctoral fellow Ga. Inst. Tech., Atlanta, 1967, asst. prof. chem. engring., 1968-72, assoc. prof., 1972-77, prof., from 1977, assoc. dean, 1978-82, asst. v.p., 1985-89, assoc. v.p., dean grad. studies, from 1989. Contbr. articles to profl. jours. Grantee NSF, 1969-70, 71-79, Office Edn., 1978—. Mem. AIME, Am. Soc. Metals, Soc. Women Engrs. (coun. sect. reps. 1975-76, nat. chmn. career info. ctr. and indsl. support 1976-77, exec. com. 1977-79, nat. student activities chmn. 1977-78, nat. sec. 1978-79, nat. 1st v.p. 1980-81, nat. pres. 1981-82), Am. Soc. Engring. Edn., Sigma Xi (pres. 1978-79), Alpha Delta Kappa. Baptist. Home: Newnan, Ga. Died Apr. 12, 2006.

GREULICH, RICHARD CURTICE, retired anatomist, gerontologist; b. Denver, Mar. 22, 1928; s. William Walter and Mildred Almena (Libby) G.; m. Betty Brent Mitchell, Dec. 19, 1948 (div. 1955); children: Christopher, Robert; m. Leonora Faye Colleasure, Dec. 27, 1958 (dec. 1993); children: Jeffrey, Hilary; m. Bertha Margaret Voelker, Aug. 12, 1994. AB, Stanford U., 1949; PhD (AEC fellow), McGill U., Canada, 1953. Instr. Sch. Medicine, UCLA, 1953-55, asst. prof. anatomy, 1955-61, asso. prof. anatomy, 1961-64, prof. anatomy, 1961-66, asso. prof. oral biology Sch. Dentistry, 1961-64, prof. oral biology, 1964-66; sci. dir. Nat. Inst. Dental Research, NIH, Bethesda, Md., 1966-74; acting dir. Nat. Inst. Aging, Bethesda, 1975-76; dir. Gerontology Research Center and sci. dir. Nat. Inst. Aging, Balt., 1976-88; exec. officer Am. Assn. Anatomists, 1994-95. Staff dir. U.S. Pres.'s Biomed. Research Panel, 1974-75; vis. investigator Karolinska Inst., Stockholm, 1955-57, U. London, 1962-63, McGill U., 1963; vis. prof. anatomy U. Va., 1966-73 Served with F.A., U.S. Army, 1946-48. Recipient award for basic research in oral sci. Internat. Assn. Dental Research, 1963, Superior Service award HEW, 1971; Bank of Am.-Giannini Found. fellow, 1955-57; USPHS spl. fellow, 1962-63 Mem. AAAS, Am. Assn. Anatomists, Gerontol. Soc., Am. Inst. Biol. Scis., Am. Soc. Cell Biology, Cosmos Club (Washington), Sigma Xi. Achievements include rsch., publs. on growth, differentiation and aging at cellular and organismic level. Home: Ocean Pines, Md. Died Jan. 27, 2007.

GREY, JAMES T., JR., chemist; b. Newstead, N.Y., May 27, 1914; s. James T. and Clara (Jochum) G.; m. Grace Whitelock, Aug. 9, 1941; children— James T. III, Linda G., Bruce W. (dec.). BA cum laude, U. Buffalo, 1936, PhD, 1940; Diploma in Isotopes, Oak Ridge Inst., 1951. Chemist, Durez Plastics and Chems., North Tonawanda, N.Y., 1939-43; sect. head Cornell Aero. Lab., Buffalo, 1943-57; sci. advisor USAF Hdqrs., Washington, 1957-59; dir. research and devel. Thiokol Corp., Newtown, Pa., 1959-82. Author: Handbook for the Margaree, 1975, 2d edit., 1981, 3d edit., 1987; Salmon Rivers of Cape Breton Island, 1985. Active Boy Scouts Am. Recipient Patriotic Civilian Service award U.S. Army, 1946. Mem. Am. Chem. Soc., AIAA (sect. pres.), Combustion Inst. Club: Cosmos. Lodge: Masons. Avocations: Hunting; fishing; stamp collecting. Died Dec. 22, 2006.

GRIER, WILLIAM ROBERT, patent corporation executive; b. Elmira, N.Y., July 10, 1920; s. Glen L. and Mina Marie (Root) G.; engring. student Chamberlin Aircraft Tng. Div., Inc., Newark, 1939-42; student Am. law and procedure LaSalle U. Extension, Chgo., 1948-51; m. Gladys Eleanor Tuttle, June 30, 1945; children— Lynn Dian Grier Willis, Dale Elizabeth Grier McCoy. Engine lathe operator, machinist, insp. naval ordnance Crucible Steel Co. Am., 1940-42; VA trainee with William S. Gubelmann, Convent, N.J., 1945-48; patent office mgr., machine designer, inventor Realty and Indsl. Corp., Morristown, N.J., 1948-80; v.p., sec., engring. and patent mgr. R&I Patent Corp. (subs. Realty and Indsl. Corp.), Morristown, 1974—. Deacon, Presbyn. Ch., New Vernon, N.J., mem. choir, 1935—. Served with USAF, 1942-45. Recipient commendations, 1943. Mem. Soc. Am. Inventors (life), Am. Soc. Inventors. Republican. Clubs: Florham Park (N.J.) Country, Antique Automobile Club Am. (Lehigh Valley region, hon. life mem. N.J. region). Chief designer, specification and claims writer patents and patents pending relating to calculators and intelligent typewriters, U.S., Canada, Great Britain, Fed. Republic Germany, Japan. Died July 27, 2007.

GRIFFIN, CLAYTON HOUSTOUN, retired electric power industry executive; b. Atlanta, June 14, 1925; s. George Clayton and Eugenia (Johnston) G.; m. Gloria Giegel Handley; 1 child, Clayton Houstoun; m. Lela Lounsbery Griffin, June 6, 1953; children: Lela Griffin Lofgren, George Duncan Bryan, Phillips Lounsbery B.E.E., Ga. Inst. Tech., 1945, MS in E.E., 1950. Registered profl. engr., Ga. Tester Ga. Power Co., Atlanta, 1949-51, test engr., 1953-58, protection engr., 1958-63, chief protection engr., 1963-79, mgr. system protection and control, 1979-89. Contbr. tech. papers to profl. publs. Trustee Ga. Tech Nat. Alumni Assn., Atlanta, 1977-80. Served to lt. comdr. USNR, 1943-47, 51-53 Named Engr. of Yr., Ga. Power Engring. Soc., Atlanta, 1966, Ga. Soc. Profl. Engrs., Atlanta, 1984; named to Sch. of Engring. Hall of Fame, Ga. Inst. Tech., 2002. Fellow IEEE (chmn. Atlanta chpt. 1974, chmn. stds. com. on dispersed generation 1982-89, chmn. power sys. relaying com. 1987-89, Disting. Svc. award power sys. relaying com. 1990, Charles Proteus Steinmetz Major Contbns. to Devel. Elec. Engring. Stds. award 1994). Clubs: Cherokee Town and Country (Atlanta). Republican. Episcopalian. Avocations: stamp collecting/philately, golf. Home: Atlanta, Ga. Died June 16, 2006.

GRIFFIN, LELAND MILBURN, speech educator; b. Kansas City, Kans., Apr. 9, 1920; s. Herbert Lester and Cliffe (Connell) G.; m. Dorothy M. Schlotzhauer, July 4, 1943; children: Dorothy Lee, Charles James Grant, Andrew Dion Crispin. AB, U. Mo., 1941, MA, 1942; PhD, Cornell U., 1950. Asst. prof. speech Washington U., St. Louis, 1950-54; asso. prof., chmn. dept. speech Boston U., 1954-56; asso. prof. speech Northwestern U., Evanston, Ill., 1956-64, prof. speech, 1964-89, Van Zelst research prof. in communication, 1982-83, prof. emeritus, from 1989; prof. speech Garrett Theol. Sem., 1958-68. Assoc. editor: Quar. Jour. Speech, 1954-59, 69-71, Central States Speech Jour, 1950-52, 64-66, Bicentennial Monograph Series, 1972-78; Contbr. articles to profl. jours. Bd. dirs. Rhetoric Soc. Am., 1972-74. Served to lt (j.g.) USNR, 1943-46. Recipient Citation of Merit award U. Mo., 1971, Lifetime Achievement award Kenneth Burke Soc., 1990. Mem. Am., Central States speech assns., AAUP, Rhetoric Soc. Am., Internat. Soc. History Rhetoric, Phi Kappa Phi. Republican. Episcopalian. Died June 23, 2006.

GRIFFIN, MERV EDWARD, television producer; b. San Mateo, Calif., July 6, 1925; s. Mervyn Edward and Rita (Robinson) G.; m. Julann Elizabeth Wright, May 18, 1958 (div. June 1976); 1 son, Anthony Patrick. Student, San Mateo Coll., 1942-44; L.H.D., Emerson Coll., 1981. Owner Teleview Racing Patrol Inc., Miami, Fla., Video Racing Patrol Inc., Seattle, Beverly Hilton Hotel, Beverly Hills, Calif., 1987—2003, The Scottsdale (Ariz.) Hilton, Wickenburg (Ariz.) Inn; chmn. bd. Griffin Group, Inc., Beverly Hills, from 1987, Givenchy Hotel and Spa, Palm Springs, Calif., Blue Moon Hotel, So. Beach, Miami Beach, Fla.; owner Merv Griffin Entertainment, Beverly Hills, 1996—2007, Cleran's Manor Ho., Galway, Ireland. Performer Merv Griffin Show radio sta. KFRC, San Francisco, 1945-48, vocalist Freddy Martin's Orch., 1948-52; contract player, star So This is Love, Warner Bros., 1953-55; TV master ceremonies, 1958-2007, Merv Griffin Show, NBC-TV, 1962-63, Westinghouse Broadcasting Co., 1965-69, CBS-TV, 1969-72, syndication, 1972-86; currently exec. producing: Wheel of Fortune, Jeopardy; Autobiography: Merv: Making the Good Life Last. Recipient 17 Emmys including a Lifetime Achievement Emmy, 2005. Mem.: Bohemian (San Francisco). Achievements include donates $10 million Wickenburg Inn & Dude Ranch in Arizona to Childhelp USA, now Merv Griffin Village, a model center for healing abused children, 2000. Died Aug. 12, 2007.

GRIFFIN, WILLIAM MARTIN, credit union executive; b. Steubenville, Ohio, Feb. 24, 1943; s. John Joseph and Anna Mary (Burke) Griffin; m. Mary Laura Muse, Sept. 9, 1967; children: John, Amy, Eileen. BA, U. Steubenville, 1965; MBA, Loyola Coll., Balt., 1971; postgrad. Grad. Sch. Savs. and Loan, 1975. With Martin-Marietta Corp., 1965—67, Fairchild Industries, 1967—70; spl. asst. to dir. Office of Exams. and Supervision Fed. Home Loan Bank Bd., Washington, 1971—73; exec. v.p. Ctrl. Pa. Savs. Assn., Shamokin, Pa., 1973—80; CEO Cecil Fed. Savs. & Loan Assn., Elkton, Pa., 1980—82; pres Mcpl. Employees Credit Union of Balt., Inc., from 1982. Chmn. bd., dir. Fin. Acctg. Services, Inc., Pitts., 1978—83; past adj. faculty Susquehanna U., Howard County Coll. Mem.: Nat. Credit Union Roundtable, Credit Union Execs. Soc. (legis. and personnel policies coms.), Md. Credit Union League. Home: Ruxton, Md. Died Nov. 18, 2006.

GRIGGS, KATHERINE EILEEN, educator, meeting consultant; b. Chico, Calif., Oct. 31, 1924; d. Thomas Mervyn and Nancy Fay (Orendorff) Kaney; m. David B. Morrison, July 3, 1945 (dec. 1954); children: Patricia E., John T., D. Paul; m. Charles V. Griggs, Nov. 19, 1960. BA in Psychology, San Jose State U., 1945. Cert. meeting profl., Conv. Liaison Council. Owner, mgr. K&M Personnel, Sacramento, 1959-65; dir. personnel Mercy Hosps., Sacramento, 1965-75; dir. edn. and tng. Sutter Community Hosps., Sacramento, 1975-82, community health educator, 1982-85, trustee educator, 1985—; meeting plan cons. Griggs Assocs., Sacramento, 1984—. Contbr. articles to profl. jours. Active health com. Sacramento C. of C., 1983—. Recipient cert. of achievement Sta. KVIE TV, 1984; Outstanding Contbr. award Vocat. Indsl. Clubs Am., 1985. Mem. Sacramento Soc. Assn. Execs., Meeting Planners Internat., Sacramento Women's Network. Republican. Roman Catholic. Avocations: golf, camping, handcrafts, bridge, spectator sports. Died Mar. 20, 2006.

GRILLO, HERMES CONRAD, surgeon; b. Boston, Oct. 2, 1923; s. Giacomo and Rose G.; children: Andrea York, Hermes Conrad, Paula, Amy. AB, Brown U., 1943; MD, Harvard U., 1947. Diplomate Am. Bd. Surgery, Am. Bd. Thoracic Surgery (dir. 1979-84). Intern Mass. Gen. Hosp., Boston, 1947-48, resident, 1948-51, 53-55, mem. surg. staff, from 1955, chief gen. thoracic surgery, 1969-94; pvt. practice medicine specializing in thoracic surgery Boston, from 1955. Prof. surgery Harvard U. Med. Sch., from 1973. Author: Surgery of Trachea and Bronchi, 2004; editor 3 books; mem. editl. bd. Jour. Thoracic and Cardiovasc. Surgery, 1975-82; contbr. over 350 sci. articles to profl. jours. Served with USMC, 1951-52; with USN, 1952-53. Decorated Commendation medal with Combat V, Cavaliere dell'Ordine al Merito della Repubblica Italiana, Order Civil Merit (Korea), Korean campaign ribbon with 3 battle stars; Hermes C. Grillo Professorship Thoracic Surgery endowment Harvard Med. Sch., 2002. Mem. ACS, Am. Assn. Thoracic Surgery, Soc. Thoracic Surgeons (pres. 1987-88, Bakken Sci. Achievement award 2002), Am. Surg. Assn., Am. Coll. Chest Physicians (Medallist 1994), Am. Thoracic Soc., Thoracic Surgery Dirs. Assn. (pres. 1983-85), Am. Broncho-Esophagological Assn. (hon.), Belgian Surg. Soc. (hon.), Can. Soc. Cardiovasc. and Thoracic Surgeons (hon.), European Soc. Thoracic Surgeons (hon.), French Surg. Assn. (hon.), Italian Thoracic Surg. Soc. (hon.), Italian Surg. Soc. (hon.), Japanese Assn. for Chest Surgery (hon.), Korean Med. Assn. (hon.), Soc. Thoracic and Cardiovasc. Surgeons Gt. Britain and Ireland (hon.), Assn. Thoracic Surgeons Asia (hon.), Boston Surg. Soc. (pres. 1997, Bigelow medal 2003), Mass. Thoracic Soc. (Chadwick medal 1996), N.E. Surg. Soc. (Nathan Smith award 2000), World Soc. Cardiothoracic Surgery (hon.). Home: Cambridge, Mass. Died Oct. 14, 2006.

GRINSTEAD, ROBERT RUSSELL, chemist, researcher; b. Sacramento, Apr. 15, 1923; s. Allen Ray and Emilie Roberta (Poppe) Grinstead; m. Helen Janney Stabler, Oct. 29, 1949; children: James Russell, Charles Miller, Catherine Roberta. BS, U. Calif., Berkeley, 1946; PhD in Chemistry, Calif. Inst. Tech., 1950. Rsch. chemist Dow Chem. U.S.A., from 1949, assoc. scientist Walnut Creek, Calif., from 1968. Mem. editl. bd. Hydrometallurgy. Contbr. articles to profl. jours. Chmn. Friends Com. Legislation Calif., 1959—67; mem. Concord Pub. Safety Commn., Calif., 1959. With US Army, 1943—46. Mem.: AIME, AAAS, Am. Chem. Soc. (exec. com. Calif. sect. 1960—69, from 1972). Democrat. Mem. Soc. Of Friends. Home: Walnut Creek, Calif. Died Aug. 7, 2007.

GRISWOLD, EARL WILLIAM, other: insurance; b. LA, Dec. 31, 1926; s. Earl William and Aimee Loretta (Nordensauld) Griswold; m. Marlene White, July 1, 1958 (div. 1970); children: Steven, Glenn, Gregg, Laura; m. Kay Kokubo, Feb. 23, 1946. BA, LA City Coll., 1946; MBA, Loyola U., LA, 1948, PhD, 1956. Registered health underwriter Nat. Assn. Health Underwriters, 1981. Owner The Griswold Group, LA, from 1952; ins. cons. Nichols Inst. and Found., San Juan Capistrano, Calif., from 1970, Estell-Doheny Eye Med. Clin., LA, from 1980; ins. cons., chief fin. officer Calif. Cancer Found., LA, from 1983. Tchr., moderator Disability Ins. Tng. Coun., 1983—84, Life Ins. Tng. Coun., Washington, 1983—84. Editor (pub.): Point Mag., 1948—50; editor: Campus Mag., 1950; author: Corporate Split Dollar for Medical Corporation, 1982; contbr. articles in various publs. Mem. bd. Harbor U. Calif. LA Med. Ctr., from 1983; v.p., program chmn. Long Beach Symphony, from 1982; mem. bd. Calif. Cancer Found., from 1983; v.p., program chmn. Sunset Young Reps., West LA, 1958—62. Mem.: LA Life Underwriters Assn. (bd. dirs. from 1983), Citizens for Am. (LA). Home: Palos Verdes Peninsula, Calif. Died Sept. 19, 2006.

GRISWOLD, KENNETH WALTER, educator; b. Joliet, Ill., Nov. 2, 1937; s. Robert P. and Louise A. (Kaatz) G.; BS, Ill. State U., 1961; MS, No. Ill. U., 1965; EdD, No. Ill. U., 1986; m. Carole Rockwood, Feb. 3, 1962; children— Stephen R., Kent R. Tchr., coach Reed-Custer High Sch., Braidwood, Ill., 1961-64; counselor Lockport (Ill.) Central High Sch., 1964-66, Santa Ana (Calif.) Unified and Jr. Coll. Dist., 1966-67; prof. Rock Valley Coll., Rockford, Ill., 1967—. Mem. Am. Assn. Counseling and Devel., Am. Psychol. Assn., Am. Coll. Personnel Assn., Internat. Soc. Sport Psychology. Republican. Episcopalian. Contbr. articles in field to profl. jours. Home: Rockford, Ill. Died Oct. 31, 2006.

GRIZZARD, GEORGE, actor; b. Roanoke Rapids, NC, Apr. 1, 1928; s. George Cooper and Mary Winifred (Albritton) G. BA, U. N.C., 1949. Appeared at Arena Stage, Washington, 1950, 52-54; Broadway appearances include The Desperate Hours, 1955, The Happiest Millionaire, 1956-57, The Disenchanted,

1958-59 (nominee Tony award), Face of a Hero, 1960, Big Fish, Little Fish, 1961 (nominee Tony award), Mary, Mary, 1962, Who's Afraid of Virginia Woolf?, 1962, The Glass Menagerie, 1965, You Know I Can't Hear You When the Water's Running, 1967, Sweet Potato, 1968, The Gingham Dog, 1969, Inquest, 1970, The Country Girl, 1972, The Creation of the World and Other Business, 1972, Crown Matrimonial, 1973, The Royal Family, 1975, California Suite, 1976, Man and Superman, 1978, A Delicate Balance, 1996 (Best Leading Actor Tony award 1996), Judgement At Nuremberg, 2001, Seascape, 2005; also appeared with Assn. of Producing Artists, N.Y.C., 1961-62, Tyrone Guthrie Theatre, Mpls., 1963-65, Show Boat, Toronto, 1995, London, 1998, Regrets Only, Manhattan Theater Club, 2006; (films) From the Terrace, 1960, Advise and Consent, 1961, Warning Shot, 1967, Happy Birthday, Wanda June, 1971, Comes a Horseman, 1978, Firepower, 1979, Seems Like Old Times, 1980, Wrong is Right, 1981, Bachelor Party, 1983, The Wonder Boys, 2000, Small Time Crooks, 2000, Flags of Our Fathers, 2006; TV appearances include Twilight Zone, The Adams Chronicles (nominated Emmy award), 1976, The Oldest Living Graduate (recipient Emmy award 1980), Caroline?, 1988, Simple Justice, 1993, Breaking the Silence, 1993, Queen, 1993, Scarlett, 1994, Suspicion of Innocence, 1997. Named to Theater Hall of Fame. Mem. Kappa Alpha. Died Oct. 2, 2007.

GRIZZLE, MARY R., state senator; b. Lawrence County, Ohio, Aug. 19, 1921; ed. Portsmouth Interstate Bus. Coll.; m. Ben F. Grizzle (dec.); children— Henry, Polley, Lorena, Mary Alice, Betty, Jeanne; m. Charles H. Pearson. Mem. Fla. Ho. of Reps., 1963-78; mem. Fla. Senate, 1978—, chmn. Exec. Bus. Com., vice chmn. Natural Resources and Conservation Com., Appropriations Com. Past chmn. Fla. Commn. on Status of Women; govt. rep. Nat. Conf. Women Community Leaders for Hwy. Safety; active P.T.A.; mem. Pinellas County (Fla.) Civil Service Com., Pinellas County Planning Com. Former town commr.; past pres. Women's Rep. Com. Named One of Ten Outstanding Women, St. Petersburg Times, 1966; recipient Achievement award Fla. Rehab. Assn., 1979; hon. life mem. Pinellas County Sch. Food Services, 1979; Largo Jr. Women's Club Woman of Year, 1980. Mem. League Women Voters, Largo Bus. and Profl. Womens Club, Altrusa, Woman's Club, Nat. Soc. Arts and Letters, Delta Kappa Gamma (hon. Alpha Phi chpt.). Episcopalian. Author: (with others) Thimbleful of History. Home: Indian Rocks Beach, Fla. Died Nov. 9, 2006.

GROBERG, JAMES JAY, information technology executive; b. Bklyn., May 29, 1928; s. David and Anna (Gross) G.; m. Marcia J. Black, June 25, 1950 (div. June 1986); children: Neil H., Richard L., Eric L.; m. Carol Ann De Barros, Sept. 4, 1986. BS in Econs., U. Pa., 1951. Asst. v.p. Economy Fin. Corp., Indpls., 1959-62; v.p. Rosenthal & Rosenthal, Inc., NYC, 1962-68, Brandon Applied Systems, Inc., NYC, 1970-71; fin. v.p. Telco Mktg. Svcs., Inc., Chgo., 1971-73; exec. v.p. Volt Info. Scis., Inc., NYC, 1973-81, sr. v.p., CFO, from 1985, bd. dirs.; chmn., CEO Multivest, Inc., Ft. Lauderdale, Fla., 1981-82, Mego Corp., NYC, 1982-85, also bd. dirs. Chmn. bd. dirs. Am. Community Pubs. Inc., 1989-91; bd. dirs. Autologic Info. Internat., Inc. Capt. USAFR, 1950-66. Mem. Fin. Execs. Inst. Home: New York, NY. Died Apr. 21, 2006.

GROISS, FRED GEORGE, lawyer; b. Glen Cove, NY, Mar. 12, 1936; s. Frederick F.W. and Dorothy C. (Roberts) G.; m. Jacqueline C. Grosse; children— Frederick C., Katherine E., Jennifer L. AB, Cornell U., 1958, LL.B., 1961. Bar: N.Y. 1961, Wis. 1963, U.S. Dist. Ct. (ea. dist.) Wis., 1963, U.S. Ct. Appeals (7th cir.) 1965. Assoc. Sage, Gray, Todd & Sims, NYC, 1961-63; assoc. Porter, Quale, Porter & Zirbel, Milw., 1963-65, Brady, Tyrrell, Cotter & Cutler, Milw., 1965-70; ptnr. Quarles & Brady, Milw., 1970-2000; ret. Mem. Gov.'s Commn. on Civil Service Reform, Madison, Wis., 1977—78. Mem.: Wis. Bar Assn. (bd. dirs. labor law sect. 1975—77), Greencroft ACAC Club. Republican. Avocation: sports. Home: Charlottesville, Va. Died July 26, 2006.

GROSS, JAMES DEHNERT, pathologist; b. Harvey, Ill., Nov. 15, 1929; s. Max A. and Marion (Dehnert) G.; m. Marilyn Agnes Robertson, Jan. 9, 1960; children: Kathleen Ann, Terrence Michael, Brian Andrew, Kevin Matthew. BS in Biology, U. Chattanooga, 1951; MD, Vanderbilt U., 1955. Diplomate Am. Bd. Pathology, Am. Bd. Med. Mgmt. Rotating intern U.S. Naval Hosp., St. Albans, NY, 1955-56; resident in anatomic and clin. pathology Nat. Naval Med. Ctr., Bethesda, Md., 1956-59; dir. labs. U.S. Naval Hosp., Memphis, 1959-62, St. Mary's Hosp., Streator, Ill., 1962-93, pres. med. staff, 1972-73. Instr. pathology and microbiology U. Tenn. Med. Sch., 1960-62; bd. dirs. La Salle County bd. Am. Cancer Soc., 1966-68 Mem. parish council St. Anthony's Roman Catholic Ch., Streator, 1969-72. Served to lt. comdr. M.C., USNR, 1955-68 Fellow Am. Soc. Clin. Pathologists, Coll. Am. Pathologists, Assn. Clin. Scientists (founder); mem. AMA, Ill. Med. Soc., Sigma Chi, Alpha Kappa Kappa Lodges: K.C., Rotary (past bd. dirs.). Republican. Died Jan. 12, 2007.

GROSSMAN, JACK, advertising agency executive; b. NYC, Mar. 22, 1925; s. Benjamin Robert and Sarah Dora (Bender) G.; m. Esther Arline Goldman, Nov. 23, 1949; children— Barbara Ruth, Neil David. B.Sc., NYU, 1950, MBA, 1952. With Biow Co., Inc., NYC, 1952-56, mgr. sales research, 1954-56; with William Esty Co., Inc., NYC, 1956-87, mgr. research dept., then v.p. research, 1964-73, sr. v.p., dir. research, 1973-87; pres. MBN Research Assocs., NYC, from 1987. Adj. asso. prof. mktg. Pace U., 1962-74, adj. prof., 1988; adj. prof. mktg. Parsons Sch. Design, 1988; lectr. Baruch Coll., CUNY, 1990. Bd. dirs. L.I. Cons. Center, 1979—. Served with AUS, 1943-47. Decorated Bronze Star with oak leaf cluster, Purple Heart. Jewish. Home: New York, NY. Died Oct. 8, 2005.

GROSSMAN, MAURICE (MIKE GROSSMAN), home improvement products retail stores executive; b. Quincy, Mass., Jan. 11, 1922; s. Reuben A. Grossman; m. Marilyn Silverston, Apr. 2, 1943; children: JoAnne Grossman Pearlman, Robert, Nancy, James. BA, Pa. State U., 1943; MBA, Boston U., 1947. Pres. Vets. Surplus Sales, Boston, 1948-50; v.p. merchandising Grossman's Inc., Braintree, Mass., 1958-69, former pres., chmn., now chmn., pres., chief exec. officer; exec. v.p. Evans Products Co., Portland, Oreg., from 1969. With USAAF, 1943-46. Recipient Silver Jubilee Prime Minister's medal State of Israel, 1972. Jewish. Died Dec. 14, 2005.

GROVE, KALVIN M(YRON), lawyer; b. Chgo., Aug. 27, 1937; s. Jacob S. and Hazel (Levitetz) G.; m. Eileen Dobbs, June 22, 1965; children— Pamela, Jonathan BA, U. Mich., 1958; JD, DePaul U., 1961. Bar: Ill. 1961, Fla. 1961, U.S. Dist. Ct. (no. dist.) Ill., U.S. Ct. Appeals (D.C. cir.), U.S. Ct. Appeals (1st cir.), U.S. Ct. Appeals (2d cir.), U.S. Ct. Appeals (3d cir.), U.S. Ct. Appeals (4th cir.), U.S. Ct. Appeals (5th cir.), U.S. Ct. Appeals (6th cir.), U.S. Ct. Appeals (7th cir.), U.S. Ct. Appeals (8th cir.), U.S. Ct. Appeals (9th cir.), U.S. Ct. Appeals (10th cir.), U.S. Ct. Appeals (11th cir.), U.S. Supreme Ct. 1971. Atty. NLRB, 1962-65; mem. adv. com. on manpower Gov. of Ill., 1962-65; mem. Fed. Mediation and Conciliation Service, from 1970; ptnr. Fox and Grove, Chartered, from 1974. Arbitrator Am. Arbitration Soc., 1967—; guest lectr. labor law DePaul U., Stetson U. Contbr. articles to legal jours. Mem. ABA, Ill. State Bar Assn., The Fla. Bar. Died Mar. 23, 2006.

GROVE, WILLIAM JOHNSON, physician, surgery educator; b. Ottawa, Ill., Mar. 23, 1920; s. Joseph Roy and Florence (Johnson) G.; m. Betty Pedigo, Mar. 23, 1944; children: William Johnson, Pamela J., Holly Lynn. BS, U. Ill., 1941, MD, 1943, MS in Surgery, 1949. Intern U. Ill. Research and Ednl. Hosps., 1944, asst. resident surgery, 1949-50, chief resident surgery, 1951-52; asst. resident surgery Hines VA Hosp., 1950-51; mem. faculty U. Ill. Coll. Medicine, from 1951, prof. surgery, 1964-81, prof. emeritus, from 1981, dean, 1968-70, exec. dean, 1970-76; vice chancellor for acad. affairs U. Ill. Coll. Medicine (U. Ill. Med. Center), 1976-80, vice chancellor emeritus, from 1981; acting dir. U. Ill. Coll. Medicine (Center for Study of Patient Care), 1980-81. Attending surgeon U. Ill. Hosp.; cons. W.K. Kellogg Found., 1981-86; prof. med. edn. U. Ill., Chgo., 1981-86. Author numerous articles in field. Served to capt. AUS, 1944-46. Fellow ACS; mem. Assn. Am. Med. Colls., Central, Chgo. Surg. Socs., Soc. Univ. Surgeons, Warren H. Cole Soc., Soc. Clin. Surgery, Am. Surg. Assn., Sigma Xi, Alpha Omega Alpha, Phi Delta Epsilon. Home: Naples, Fla. Died Jan. 15, 2006.

GRUBB, DONALD HARTMAN, paper industry company executive; b. West Chester, Pa., Oct. 22, 1924; s. Donald C. and Bessie (Hanthorne) G.; m. Jean Louise Flounders, Sept. 7, 1946; children: Donna Jean (Mrs. Robert Kanich), Deborah Anne (Mrs. James R. Jackson), Donald Philip. BA, U. Pa., 1949; MA, Am. U., 1954; postgrad., NYU, 1963-64. With U.S. Treasury Dept., Washington, 1949-57, recruitment officer, 1951-53, dir. personnel, 1953-57; mgr. personnel Westvaco Corp., NYC, 1957-59, regional adminstrv. mgr. Hoboken, NJ, 1959-61, mgr. sales, 1961-64; asst. to v.p. Huyck Corp., Stamford, Conn., 1964, v.p. adminstrn. and mktg., 1969-70, exec. v.p., 1970-73, pres., dir., chief exec. officer, 1973-81; chmn. BTR Paper Group, 1981-82; pres. Gedon Enterprises, from 1982; v.p., gen. mgr. Formex Co. of Can., Kentville, N.S., 1965-67; also dir.; v.p., gen. mgr. Huyck Formex Co. of U.S., Greeneville, Tenn., 1967-69. Mgr. Grubb Assocs., LLC dba Fasteners Supply of Goldsboro; retired dir. various cos. in U.S. and U.K. Bd. dirs. Blanchard-Fraser Meml. Hosp., Kentville, N.S., Can., 1966-67, Wake County Hosp. System, Raleigh, 1983-87, N.C. State U. Pulp and Paper Found.; mem. N.C. State U. Sch. Engring. Foun., N.C. State U. Sch. Humanities Found. Served with AUS, 1943-46. Mem. Raleigh C. of C. (dir. 1976-78), Phi Beta Kappa. Presbyterian. Died Oct. 13, 2006.

GRUBB, SHIRLEY MCCLURE, corporation executive; b. Belmont, N.C., Sept. 24, 1935; d. Woodrow D. and Emma (Austin) Ferguson; m. Donald Reid Grubb, July 31, 1954; children— Edwin Brian, Joy Donee. Grad. Sacred Heart Coll., Belmont, N.C., 1953. Tech. adminstr. Western Electric Co., Winston-Salem, 1958-62; adminstrv. asst. R.J. Reynolds Tobacco Co., Winston-Salem, 1964-66; adminstrv. asst. Admiral Hamilton Howe, Winston-Salem, 1966-69; adminstrv. asst. Smith Bagley, Winston-Salem and Washington, 1969-80; v.p. Musgrove Plantation, St. Simons Island, Ga., 1980—. Appointed mem. Lady Bird Johnson's Beautification Com., Washington; vol. Davidson County Democratic Party, Lexington, N.C., 1984. Mem. Am. Bus. Womens Assn. (sec. treas. 1969-72), N.C. Garden Club (dist. sec. 1965-67), Am. Found. Research in Medicine (pres. 1972-85). Methodist. Club: Village Garden (pres. 1964-65). Avocations: swimming; dancing; hydroponic gardening; flutist. Home: Welcome, NC. Died Apr. 21, 2007.

GRUBBS, FRANK LESLIE, JR., history educator; b. Lynchburg, Va., June 21, 1931; s. Frank Leslie and Grace Louise (Smith) G.; m. Carolyn Barrington, July 31, 1965; children— Thomas Ashby, Robert Barrington. B.A. in English, Lynchburg Coll., 1959; M.A. in History, U. Va., 1960, Ph.D. in History, 1963. Mem. quality control staff Mead Paper Products, Lynchburg, 1949-59; asst. instr. Grad. Sch., U. Va., Charlottesville, 1961-62, instr., 1962-63; prof. history Meredith Coll., Raleigh, N.C., 1963—. Author: Struggle for Labor Loyalty, 1968 (Choice award 1970); Protecting Labor's Standards, 1982. Contbr. articles to profl. jours. Lectr. Episcopal Ch., Raleigh and Cary, N.C., 1965—; instr. Occaneechi council Boy Scouts Am., 1975-86; mem. dept. records and history N.C. Diocese Episcopal Ch., Raleigh (histoniographer, 1987—), 1984—; mem. Commn. on Ch., Episcopal Ch., Raleigh, 1985—. Served to sgt. U.S. Army, 1952-54; Korea. Nat. Humanities grantee, 1968; named outstanding Tchr., Meredity Coll., 1975; recipient Perry award in research Meredith Coll., 1985. Mem. Smithsonian Assocs., So. Hist. Assn., Torch Internat. (pres. Raleigh chpt. 1970-80, N.C. charter corp., 1987—), Phi Alpha Theta. Avocations: painting; historical travel. Home: Raleigh, NC. Died July 16, 2006.

GRUEBEL, BARBARA JANE, retired internist, pulmonologist; b. Honolulu, May 12, 1950; d. Robert William and Elenor Jane (Perry) G. BS, Stephen F. Austin State U., 1977; MD, Baylor Coll. Medicine, 1974. Diplomate Nat. Bd. Med. Examiners. Intern in internal medicine U. Rochester, 1974-75, resident in internal medicine, 1975-77; pulmonary fellow U. Mich., 1977-79; mem. med. staff Anthony L. Jordan Health Center, Rochester, N.Y., 1976-77, Univ. Health Service, Ann Arbor, Mich., 1978-79; med. dir. progressive respiratory care unit Meth. Med. Ctr., 1979-80; asst. prof. medicine U. Tex. Health Sci. Center, Dallas, 1979-80; cons. in pulmonary disease Dallas, 1980-93; pvt. practice of pulmonary medicine, 1993—99, Nacogdoches, Tex., from 1999. Clin. asst. prof. medicine U. Tex. Health Sci. Center, 1980-97; nat. affiliate faculty Am. Heart Assn.; mem. faculty First Internat. Conf. Women's Health, Beijing, 1993; lectr. in field. Mem. TEXPAC. Recipient award for gen. excellence in pediatrics, 1974, Stanley W. Olson award for acad. excellence, 1974, John Richard Fox award, 1974, Stuart A. Wallace award in pathology, 1974; named one of Am.'s Top Physicians, Consumers Rsch. Coun. Am., 2004-05; Welch Found. grantee, 1970; Am. Lung Assn. tng. fellow, 1977-79; Robert Wood Johnson Found. scholar; Coll. Women's Club scholar. Fellow Am. Coll. Chest Physicians (named Young Pulmonary Physicians of Future 1979); mem. Am. Med. Women's Assn. (scholastic excellence award 1974), Am. Thoracic Soc., Am. Lung Assn., AMA, Am. Coll. Physicians, Dallas County Med. Soc., Tex. Med. Soc., Dallas Internist Assocs., Dallas Acad. Internal Medicine, Am. Cancer Soc., Dallas C. of C., Dallas Mayors Outstanding Women of Dallas, Oak Cliff C. of C., Alpha Omega Alpha, Beta Beta Beta. Home: Nacogdoches, Tex. Died Aug. 31, 2006.

GUBLER, CLARK JOHNSON, biochemist, educator; b. LaVerkin, Utah, July 14, 1913; s. Henry W. Gubler and (Pickett) Susanna; m. Maurine Kjar, Sept. 21, 1938; children: David Clark, Kathleen, Ann, Ronald Kjar. BS, Brigham Young U., 1939; MS, Utah State U., 1941; PhD, U. Calif., Berkeley, 1945. Rsch. assoc. medicine U. Utah, Salt Lake City, 1946—56; spl. rsch. fellow U. Wis., Madison, 1956—58; assoc. prof. Brigham Young U., Provo, Utah, 1958—60, prof. biochemistry, 1960—82; vis. prof. Kuwait U., 1982—86. Editor (with others): Thiamin, 1976, Thiamin 20 Years Progress, 1982. Spl. Rsch. fellow, USPHS, 1971—72, Rsch. fellow, Am. Heart Assn., 1958—60, established investigator, 1961—66. Mem.: N.Y. Acad. Scis., Am. Inst. Nutrition, Am. Soc. Biol. Chemists, Am. Chem. Soc. (chpt. pres. 1980—82), Kiwanis, Sigma Xi. Republican. Mem. Lds Ch. Home: Orem, Utah. Died Jan. 27, 2007.

GUDE, GILBERT, former congressman; b. Washington, Mar. 9, 1923; s. Adolph Elbert and Inez Elinor (Gilbert) G.; m. Jane Wheeler Callaghan, June 19, 1948; children: Sharon, Gilbert Jr., Gregory, Daniel, Adrienne. BS, Cornell U., 1948; MA, George Washington U., 1958; DSc (hon.), Georgetown U., 1977. Mem. Md. Gen. Assembly, Annapolis, 1953-58, Md. State Senate, 1962-66, US Congress from Md. dist., 1967—77; dir. Congl rsch. svc. Library of Congress, Washington, 1977-86; ind. cons. Bethesda, Md., 1987—2007. Mem., past chmn. consultative com. Ctr. Parliamentary Documentation Inter-Parliamentary Union, Geneva, 1984-89; mem. exec. com. Environ. and Energy Study Inst., Washington, 1986-89; exec. dir. Potomac River Basin Consortium, Bethesda. Author: Where the Potomac Begins, 1984, Small Town Destiny, 1989; contbr. articles on rsch. and info. systems in support of legis. bodies to various publs. Trustee Montgomery County Hist. Soc., Rockville, Md., Md. Hist. Trust; bd. dirs. Pks. & History Assn.; With U.S. Army 1943-46, PTO. Mem. Nat. Acad. Pub. Adminstrn., Chevy Chase Club, Capitol Hill Club. Republican. Roman Catholic. Died June 7, 2007.

GUDGER, ROBERT H., retired printing company executive b. Mamaroneck, NY, Nov. 17, 1927; married Sept. 11, 1955 children: Margot T., Gail T., Robin H. BA Polit. Sci., U Redlands, 1953; MA Psychology, Columbia U., 1958; JD, N.Y Law Sch., 1961. Adminstrv. asst. dept. conf. svcs. UN, NYC 1954-55; rehab. counselor State N.Y., White Plains, 1955-59 assoc. dir. Urban League Westchester, White Plains, N.Y. 1959-62; exec. dir. Urban League, Rochester, N.Y., 1965-66 mgmt. devel. coord. TRW System, Redondo Beach, Calif. 1966-67; adminstr. personnel rels. affirmative action program Am. Airlines, NYC, 1962-65, asst. to. vice. chmn. bd., 1970-71 labor rels. arbitrator, 1967-71; mgr. Corp. Affirmative Action Employee Rels., 1971-82; mgr. corp. responsibility, v.p. Xerox Found. Xerox Corp., Stamford, Conn., 1982-93; retired, 1993 Bd. dirs. Ctr. Devel. and Populatin Activities, Easter Seal Rehab Ctr., Neighborhood Housing Svcs., New Neighborhoods Inc. Nat. Neurofibromatosis Found., U.CApetown, Nat. Community AIDS Ptnrship., David Winfield Found., World Learning Inc Mem. Polit. Sci. Assn., Omicron Delta Kappa, Phi Delta Phi Home: Danbury, Conn. Died Mar. 24, 2006.

GUENDEL, THOMAS JOSEPH, machinery manufacturing company executive; b. NYC, July 1, 1927; s. Cornelius Herma and Helen Rose (Sommer) G.; m. Ann Marino, May 26, 1951 children: Douglas, Richard, Stephen. BS in Mech. Engring, Pra Inst., 1950; MBA, NYU, 1960. Sales engr. sales, mgmt. cons service Gen. Electric Co., NYC, 1950-62; mgr. distbn. Westinghouse Air Brake Co., Peoria, Ill., 1962-65, v.p. internat. div 1965-69; v.p. constrn. equipment div. J.I. Case Co., Racine Wis., 1969-72, pres., 1972-79, chmn., 1979-80, chief exec officer, 1972-79; chmn., chief exec. officer Portec, Inc., Oa Brook, Ill., from 1980, now also pres., chief operating office also bd. dirs. Dir. Modine Mfg. Co., Ceco Corp. Mem. adv council U. Ill., 1981—; mem. Pres.'s Adv. Council; Bd. dir Nat. Chamber Found.; vice chmn. Spl. Com. for U.S. Exports Served with USNR, 1945-46. Mem. NAM (dir., exec. com. Chgo. Council Fgn. Relations, Traffic Club Detroit Clubs: Chgo Golf, Mid-Am; Somerset (Racine). Roman Catholic. Home Hinsdale, Ill. Died Mar. 18, 2006.

GUENTHER, ARTHUR HENRY, research scientist, educator b. Hoboken, NJ, Apr. 20, 1931; s. George Gregory and Florenc B. (Roberts) G.; m. Joan Roth, Nov. 21, 1954; children: Traci Katherine, Wendy Katherine. BS in Chemistry, Rutgers U 1953; PhD in Chemistry-Physics, Pa. State U., 1957; DS (hon.), U. Albuquerque, 1973. Dir. pulse power lab. Kirtland AFB, Albuquerque, 1959-62, dir. material dynamics lab., 1962-65, sci. advisor, chief simulation and pulsed power group 1965-66, chief sci. support group, sci. advisor, 1966-69, chie tech. div. Air Force Weapons Lab., 1969-70, sci. dir. tech. div

1970-74, chief scientist Air Force Weapons Lab., 1974-88; chief scientist for advanced def. tech. Los Alamos (N.Mex.) Nat. Lab., 1988-91; sci. advisor lab. devel. Sandia Nat. Labs., 1991-97; sci. advisor to Gov. of N.Mex., 1988-94; chmn. sci. and tech. commercialization com. N.Mex.; prof. Ctr. for High Tech. Materials U. N.Mex., from 1997. Vice chmn., chmn. Gordon Rsch. Conf., 1970-71; chmn. permanent sci. com. Internat Symposium on Discharges and Elec. Insulation in Vacuum; chmn. internat. steering com. Internat. Conf. on Phenomena in Ionized Gases, 1991—; founder, co-chmn. bd. dirs., pres. ann. Symposium on Optical Materials for High Power Lasers, 1969—; chair SPIE OE Laser, 1992; mem. adv. com. several NATO advanced study insts., sci. dir NATO Advanced Study Inst. on High Brightness Accelerators, Pitlochery, Scotland, 1986; mem. European Study Group on Laser-Produced Plasmas; mem. NAS-NRC Rev. Bd., 1974; chmn. PILOT Adv. Com.; vice chmn. Fgn. Applied Sci. Assessment Ctr. Study on Macroelectronics, 1985; apptd. by Gov. of N.Mex. to Energy R&D Rev. Com., 1975-78; mem. nat. steering com. on nuclear tech. Coun. Math. and Sci. Edn., 1975; adj. prof. U. N.Mex., Tex. Tech. U., Air Force Inst. Tech.; external reader U. Salford, Eng., Indian Inst. Sci., Bangalore; chmn. Optics Tech. Transger Strategic Def. Initiative office, 1989—; chair confs. in field. Editor Advances in Pulse Power Tech., Symposium on Optical Materials for High Power Lasers, High Brightness Accelerators, NATO Brightness Accelerators; assoc. editor Jour. Lasers and Particles Beams, Laser Interaction and Related Plasma Phenomena; mem. editl. adv. bd. Lasers and Optronics, Photonics Tech Briefs, O.E. mag.; patentee in field; contbr. more than 350 articles to tech. jours. Mem. Gov.'s Com. on Tech. Excellence, Task Force on Higher Edn. Reform, 1987, U. N.Mex. Joint Ctr. Materials Sci.; bd. dirs., past chmn., mem. Ctr. for Occupational R&D Edn. Coun., 1989-98, trustee CORD Found.; vice chmn. sci. and tech. adv. com. State of N.Mex., 1984-86; bd. dirs. N.Mex. Math. Engring. Scientists. 1st lt. USAF, 1957-59. Recipient Disting. Pub. Svc. award State of N.Mex., 1982, 2001; Meritorious Presdl. award Pres. of U.S., 1983, Disting. Exec. Rank award, 1985. Fellow IEEE (pres. U.S., editor numerous spl. edits., chmn. standards activities, Harry Diamond award 1971, Peter Haas award 1989, Ben Dasher award), Laser Inst. Am. (bd. dirs. pres., Arthur L. Schawlow medal 1983), Optical Soc. Am. (bd. dirs., chmn. adv. com., chmn. fellows com. 1980, fin. com. 1982, edn. coun. 1989—, Eastman Lectr.); mem. IEEE Laser Electro-Optic Soc. (adv. com., chmn. fellows com. 1986, ad com. 1983, chmn. govt. rels. com.), Am. Chem. Soc., N.Mex. Acad. Sci. (Disting. Scientist of Yr. 1977), Russian Acad. Sci. (fgn. mem.), Forum for Mil. Applications of Directed Energy (dir.), Directed Energy Profl. Soc. (organizer 1999), AMBA (pres.), Sigma Xi, Phi Lambda Upsilon. Avocations: woodworking, the outdoors, music, bowling. Home: Albuquerque, N.Mex. Died Apr. 21, 2007.

GUERIN, JOHN WILLIAM, artist; b. Houghton, Mich., Aug. 29, 1920; s. Omer Francis and Mildred Montague (Miller) G.; m. Anne Walden Dewey, Dec. 28, 1948 (dec. 1979); m. Martha McAshan, Apr. 10, 1982. Student, Am. Acad. Art, Chgo., Art Students League, NYC, Escuela de Bellas Artes, San Miguel, Mexico. Prof. art U. Tex., 1953-80, prof. emeritus, 1980—2006. Artist in residence, Skowhegan (Maine) Sch. Painting and Sculpture, 1960; one-man shows, Kraushaar Galleries, N.Y.C., 1960, 63, 68, Ft. Worth Art Center, 1956, 64, 65, Marion Kooglar McNay Art Inst., San Antonio, 1961, 65, Centennial Mus., Corpus Christi, Tex., 1963, Carlin Galleries, Ft. Worth, 1962, 64, 67, 70, 77, 81, 87, Nat. Acad. Design, N.Y.C., 1987; one-man retrospective show, Nave Mus., Victoria, Tex., 1982, group exhbns. include, Met. Mus. Art, Whitney Mus. Art, Art Inst. Chgo., Corcoran Mus. Art, Carnegie Inst.; represented in permanent collections, Chrysler Mus., Provincetown, Mass., Joslyn Mus., Omaha, New Britain (Conn.) Mus., Houston Mus., Dallas Mus., U. Notre Dame Art Gallery, Colorado Springs (Colo.) Fine Art Center., Archives Am. Art, Smithsonian Instn., Washington. Served with USAAF, 1942-45. Grantee Am. Acad Arts, Nat. Inst. Arts & Letters, 1960, Ford Found., 1978; recipient Henry Ward Ranger Fund Purchase prize NAD, 1958; Research Inst. grant U. Tex., 1960, 66 Mem. Art Students League N.Y.C. (life), Nat. Acad. Design (academician). Episcopalian. Died Dec. 5, 2006.

GUGAS, CHRIS, SR., criminologist, consultant; b. Omaha, Nebr., Aug. 12, 1921; s. Nicholas and Vera (Henas) Gugas; m. Anne Claudia Setaro, June 27, 1942; children: Chris, Steven Edward, Carol Ann Gugas Hawker. DDiv, Ch. Living Sci., 1968; BA, U. Beverly Hills, 1977, MA in Pub. Adminstrn., 1977, PhD in Behavioral Psychology, 1983. Asst. dir. security L.A. Bd. Edn., 1948—49; spl. agt. CIA, Washington, 1950—54; criminol. cons. LA, 1955—61; pub. safety dir. Omaha, 1962—65; dir. polygraph svcs. Profl. Security Cons., LA, 1966—93; exec. dir. Calif. Acad. Polygraph Scis., 1974—76, The Truthseekers. Cons. U.S. Police, Greece, 1949, Turkey, 51; instr. Gormac Polygraph Sch., LA, 1972—73, L.A. Inst. Polygraph; chief instr. Las Vegas Acad. Polygraph Sci., 1982—83; chmn. Polygraph Legal Def. Fund; columnist L.A. Daily Jour., Security World mag., The Truthseekers. Author: The Silent Witness: A Polygraphist's Casebook, 1979; co-author: The National Corruptors, Pre-Employment Polygraph, 1984, The Polygraphist in Court, The Truthseekers, Our National Rebellion, 1982; contbr. articles to profl. jours. Founder (with others) Toys for Tots, 1948; tech. advisor Pres. MIA/POW Commn., 1986; sec. and mem. adv. bd. Calif. Dept. Consumer Affairs, 1971—76. With USMC, 1940—45, with USMC, 1947—49. Fellow: Acad. Cert. Polygraphists; mem.: Am. Soc. Indsl. Security, Nat. Polygraph Assn. (pres. from 1989), Am. Polygraph Assn. (pres. 1971, exec. dir. 1972—73), Security Officers Assn. (pres. 1968), Nat. Bd. Polygraph Examiners (pres. 1958), Marine Corps Combat Corr.'s Assn. (pres. L.A. chpt. 1975—77), Marine Corps League (comdr. 1946), L.A. Press Club. Home: Burke, Va. Died Oct. 20, 2007.

GUIDO, MICHAEL ANTHONY, mayor; b. Detroit, July 3, 1954; s. Emilio and Elena Maria (Tosto) G.; m. Kari Dee Arvanigian, Aug. 25, 1984; children: Michael A. Jr., Anthony E. BA, Wayne State U., 1982; Dr. Laws (hon.), Detroit Coll. Bus., 1990. City councilman City of Dearborn, Mich., 1978-85, mayor, 1986—2006. Pres. US Conf. Mayors, 2006. Hon. chmn. Dearborn Goodfellows, 1986—. Named Outstanding Young Man Mich., Mich. Jaycees, 1981; recipient Disting. Svc. award Detroit Coll. Bus., 1987. Mem. Mich. Assn. Mayors (bd. dirs. 1990—, pres. 1993-94), U.S. Conf. of Mayors (subcom. chair 1990—), Rotary (Paul Harris Fellow 1990), Exch. Club of Dearborn (bd. dirs. 1985-90, Disting. Svc. award 1984, 89), Centurions (hon.). Roman Catholic. Avocations: golf, hunting. Home: Dearborn, Mich. Died Dec. 5, 2006.

GUIGUI, EFRAIN, conductor; b. Buenos Aires, Argentina, Sept. 19, 1935. Student Music Conservatory, Buenos Aires, 1954; B.A., Boston U., 1959. Assoc. condr. Am. Ballet Theatre, 1966-68; condr. Music in our Time, Town Hall, N.Y.C., 1966-68; condr., music dir. Composers Conf., Wellesley, Mass., 1966; prin. guest condr. P.R. Symphony, San Juan, 1968-74; condr. Vt. Symphony Orch., Burlington, 1974-89; Mem. Vt. Council Arts, Am. Symphony League. Died June 18, 2007.

GUILLÉN, CLAUDIO, comparative literature educator; b. Paris, Sept. 2, 1924; s. Jorge and Germaine (Cahen) G. BA, Williams Coll., 1943; MA, Harvard U., 1947, PhD in Comparative Lit., 1953. Teaching fellow Harvard U., Cambridge, Mass., 1948-50, 1952-53, instr. summr sch., 1967, prof. comparative lit. and Romance Langs., from 1978, chmn. dept. comparative lit., from 1979, chmn. lit. maj., from 1981; instr. Spanish Cologne, 1950-52; asst. prof. Spanish Princeton U., 1953-60, assoc. prof.Spanish, 1960-65, dir. program in comparative lit., 1963-65; prof. comparative lit. U. Calif.-San Diego, 1965-76, dir. Center for Iberian and Latin Am. Studies, 1975-76; vis. prof. Bryn Mawr, 1956-57, Johns Hopkins U., 1964-65, Ecole Normale d'Auteuil, 1954, Malaga, 1977-78, Barcelona, 1982-83, 87; instr. summer schs. Middlebury, 1953, 1955, 1957, Malaga, 1975, 1980, Salamanca, 1976, Santander, 1978, 1979; dir. Calif. Edn. Abroad Program, Madrid, 1972-74; mem. Com. on Comparative History of Lit. in European Langs., from 1980; dir. Clasicos Alfaguara, Madrid, from 1974; editorial council mem. PMLA, Princeton Series in European and Comparative Lit. Author: Lazarillo de Tormes and El Abencerraje, 1966, Literature as System: Essays Toward the Theory of Literary History, 1974, Entre Lo Uno y Lo Diverso, 1985, The Anatomies of Roguery, 1985, El primer Siglo de Oro, 1988; essays, reprinted in anthologies, Germany, Spain, Italy; contbr. articles to pubs. in field. Served with Free Franch Forces, Worl War II. Mem. MLA (exec. council 1970-74), Internat. Comparative Lit. Assn. (exec. com. 1973-79), Am. Comparative Lit. Assn. (exec. com. 1966-72), Spanish Soc. Comparative Lit. (pres. 1983), Am. Acad. Arts and Scis. Died Jan. 27, 2007.

GUMERSON, JEAN GILDERHUS, health foundation executive; b. Hayfield, Minn., Mar. 19, 1923; d. Nordeen Palmer and Mable Jeannette (Scharberg) Gilderhus; m. William Dow Gumerson Sr., Mar. 5, 1943 (dec. Jan. 1978); children: William Dow Jr., Ted Lee, Jon David. Student, U. Minn., 1941-42, U. Okla., 1961-62. Adminstrv. asst. to Rep. state party chmn., Oklahoma City, 1976-77; campaign coord. 1st dist. Paula Unruh for Congress, Tulsa, 1978; dir. pub. rels. C.R. Anthony Co., Oklahoma City, 1979-87; dir. human rels. Wilson Agy., Mass. Mut. Ins. Co., Oklahoma City, 1987; adminstrv. dir. Okla. Art Ctr., Oklahoma City, 1988-89; exec. dir. Children's Med. Rsch., Inc., Oklahoma City, from 1989; exec. dir., then pres. Presbyn. Health Found., Oklahoma City, 1989—2002, pres. emeritus, from 2002. Active exec. com. Pres.'s Com. on Mental Retardation, Washington, 1986-91; So. Govs. Conf. on Infant Mortality, Washington, 1987-92; chmn. City-County Health Dept. Bd., Oklahoma City, 1980-93; gov. appointee steering com. Healthy Futures, Oklahoma City, 1988-92; bd. dirs. Children's Med. Rsch. Inc., Okla. City 1982—; nat. bd. Contact U.S.A., Okla. City, 1992—. Recipient Gov.'s Arts award for community svc. Okla. Arts Coun., Woman of Yr. award Okla. Mental Health Assn., Humanitarian award Opportunities Indsl. Ctr., Outstanding Vol. Fund Raiser award Okla. chpt. Nat. Soc. Fund Raising Execs., 1988, Humanitarian award Nat. Conf. for Comty. and Justice, 1999; inducted to Okla. Hall of Fame, 1999; Jean Gumerson Endowed Chair in Pediat. Psychology established in his honor, 1999. Mem. AIA (hon.), Exec. Women in Govt., Charter 35, Econ. Club. Okla., Oklahoma City C. of C., Theta Sigma Phi. Presbyterian. Home: Oklahoma City, Okla. Died 2006.

GUPTA, KULDIP CHAND (KC), retired electrical and computer engineering educator, researcher; b. Risalpur, India, Oct. 6, 1940; arrived in US, 1982; s. Chiranjiva Lal and Gauran (Agarwal) G.; m. Usha Agarwal, Apr. 4, 1971; children: Parul, Sandeep, Anjula. BSc, Punjab U., Chandigarh, India, 1958; BE, Indian Inst. Sci., Bangalore, India, 1961, ME, 1962; PhD, Birla Inst. Tech. Sci., Pilani, India, 1969. Asst. prof. Punjab Engring. Coll., Chandigarh, 1964-65, Birla Inst. Tech. and Sci., Pilani, 1968-69; asst. prof., then prof. Indian Inst. Tech., Kanpur, India, 1969-84; prof. U. Colo., Boulder, 1983—2004. Vis. assoc. prof. U. Waterloo, Ont., 1975-76; vis. prof. Swiss Fed. Tech. Inst., Lausanne, 1976, Zurich, 1979, Tech. I. Denmark, Lynby, 1976-77, U. Kans., Lawrence, 1982-83, Indian Inst. Sci., 1993-94; advisor, cons. UN Devel. Programme, People's Republic of China, 1987, India, 1990, 94-95; cons. UNIDO project, India, 1993, Indian Telephone Industries, 1993-94. Author: CAD of Microwave Circuits, 1981, Chinese transl., 1986, Russian transl., 1987, Microstrip Lines and Slotlines, 1979, 2d edit., 1996, Microwaves, 1979, Spanish transl., 1983; editor, author: Microwave Integrated Circuits, 1974, Microstrip Antenna Design, 1988, Analysis and Design of Planar Microwave Components, 1994; founding editor Internat. Jour. Microwave Millimeter-Wave Computer Aided Engring., 1991—; contbr. articles to profl. jours. and chpts. to books; patentee in field. Bd. dirs. Hindu U. of Am. Fellow IEEE (guest editor spl. issue IEEE Transactions on Microwave Theory and Tech. 1988), Instn. Electronics and Telecommunication Engrs. India (guest editor jour. July 1982) Hindu. Home: Orlando, Fla. Died Feb. 7, 2007.

GURD, FRANK ROSS NEWMAN, biochemist, educator; b. Montreal, Que., Can., Jan. 20, 1924; came to U.S., 1946, naturalized, 1954; s. Fraser Baillie and Jessie (Newman) G.; m. Ruth Sights, June 12, 1956; children: Fraser, Kathleen, Martha, Charles. Grad. cum laude, Phillips Exeter Acad., 1941; BS, McGill U., 1945, MS, 1946; PhD, Harvard, 1949. Asst. dir. Bur. Med. Research, Equitable Life Assurance Soc., NYC, 1955-59; asst. prof. clin. biochemistry Med. Coll. Cornell U., 1955-60; prof. biochemistry Sch. Medicine, Ind. U., 1960-66, prof. chemistry, 1965-79, disting. prof. biochemistry and chemistry, 1979-86, prof. emeritus, from 1986. Chmn. biophysics and biophys. chemistry B study sect. NIH, 1968-70 Author: Chemical Specificity in Biological Interactions, 1954, (with D.J. Hanahan) Chemistry of the Lipides, 1960; Editorial bd.: Jour. Biol. Chemistry, 1966-72, 76-81. John Simon Guggenheim and Helen Hay Whitney fellow dept. biochemistry Sch. Medicine, Washington U., 1954-55 Mem. Am. Soc. Biol. Chemists, Am. Chem. Soc., Biophys. Soc., N.Y. Acad. Scis., A.A.A.S., Sigma Xi. Research, publs. on lipoprotein isolated from blood; combination of proteins with certain metal salts; identification of sites of binding and effects on conformation; modes of combination of metal ions with peptides; chem. modification of proteins to correlate structure in solution with that in crystalline state, Sequence determinations on myoglobins of different Species; Specific enrichment proteins with carbon-13 for nuclear magnetic resonance studies, semisynthesis of proteins; interactions of carbon dioxide with peptides and proteins; analysis of electrostatic effects and internal motions in proteins. Home: Albuquerque, N.Mex. Died June 17, 2007.

GURSKI, WALTER STEPHEN, podistrist; b. Newark, July 22, 1946; s. Walter Stephen and Alice Katherine (Bell) G.; m. Joekie van Bavel, Dec. 6, 1976; children: Stephen Walter, Nicole Joekie. BS in Biology, U. Charleston, 1970; D Podiatric Medicine, Ill. Coll. Podiatric Medicine, 1974. Podiatrist Danbury (Conn.) Podiatry Assocs., from 1974, Norwalk (Conn.) Podiatry Assocs., from 1976; CEO Podiatric Ind. Physicians Assn., Danbury, from 1994. Lectr. in radiowave surgery in podiatry, 1990—; mgmt. cons., 1988—; podiatric cons. to med. product cos., 1989—. Contbr. articles to profl. publs. Chmn. bd. dirs. Mid Fairfield Coun. Campfire Girls, Danbury, 1982-84; mem. pres.'s club. Nat. Rep. Com. Mem. Am. Assn. Podiatric Physicians and Surgeons. Unitarian Universalist. Avocations: travel, skiing. Died May 27, 2006.

GURSKY, HERBERT, retired astrophysicist; b. Bronx, NY, May 27, 1930; s. Joseph Mayer and Sonia Pauline (Balen) G.; m. Flora Pauline Aronson, Sept. 13, 1958; children: David Meyer, Robert Aaron. BS, U. Fla., 1951; MS, Vanderbilt U., 1953; PhD, Princeton U., 1959. Staff scientist Am. Sci. and Engring. Inc., Cambridge, Mass., 1961-68; v.p., 1968-73; supr. astrophysics Smithsonian Astrophys. Obs., Cambridge, Mass., 1973-81; prof. astronomy Harvard U., Cambridge, 1974-81; assoc. dir. Harvard/Smithsonian Center for Astrophysics, Cambridge, 1976-81; former supt. space sci. div., chief sci. E.O. Hulburt Center for Space Research, Naval Research Lab. Author: (with R. Ruffini) Neutron Stars, Black Holes and Super Nova, 1976, (with R. Giacoconi) X-Ray Astronomy, 1974; contbr. numerous articles to profl. jours. Fellow Am. Phys. Soc., AAAS, Am. Astron. Soc. Home: Great Falls, Va. Died Dec. 1, 2006.

GUSHEE, RICHARD BORDLEY, lawyer; b. Detroit, Aug. 25, 1926; s. Edward Tisdale and Norine Amelia (Bordley) G.; m. Marilyn Lucy Flynn, June 9, 1951; children: Jacqueline Lowe (dec. 1977), Peter Hale. BA, Williams Coll., 1947; JD, U. Mich., 1950. Bar: Mich. 1951, U.S. Supreme Ct. 1961. Assoc. Miller, Canfield, Paddock and Stone, Detroit, 1950-58, ptnr., 1959-93, of counsel, from 1994. Chmn. Tri-county Hearing Panel #18 of Atty. Discipline Bd. Former trustee United Community Svcs.; former chancellor Episc. Diocese Mich. With USAF, 1945. Mem. ABA. Home: Detroit, Mich. Died May 15, 2006.

GUSTAFSON, GEORGE ROBERT, association executive; b. Austin, Tex., May 19, 1928; s. Fred W. and Nell V. (Wheless) G.; student U. Tex., Austin, 1948-51, 59; m. Norma June Windsor, July 22, 1950; children: Cynthia Ann, Deborah Kay, Tami Lynn. With Tex. Dept. Public Safety, 1949-50; with Tex. Safety Assn., Austin, 1950-90, now pres. V.p. Nat. Safety Coun., 1989—; mem. Citizens Traffic Safety Commn.; mem. adv. com. Tex. Transp. Inst. Corp. charter mem. Boys Club of Austin. Recipient citation for disting. service to safety Nat. Safety Coun., 1980. Mem. Am. Soc. Assn. Execs. (pres.), Assn. Safety Council Execs. (cert.), Tex. Soc. Assn. Execs. (chmn. 1989-90), Austin Civitan Club (pres. 1967-68). Home: Georgetown, Tex. Died Aug. 5, 2006.

GUSTAFSON, LEIF VALENTINE, structural engineer, consultant; b. Gothenburg, Sweden, Dec. 31, 1911; s. Oscar Gustaf and Olga Alida (Anderson) Gustafson; m. Joan Miller, Nov. 15, 1969; children: Glenn Nordhal, Linda Margaret. BS in Civil and Structural Engring., Chalmers Inst. Tech., Sweden, 1934; post grad. in bus. adminstrn., Alexander Hamilton Inst., 1969. Registered profl. engr., engring. contractor. Chief structural engr. Elec. Bond & Share Co., NYC, 1947—52; supervising engr. Bechtel Corp., LA, Calif., 1952—61; pres. and owner Leif Engring. & Constrn. Corp., Studio City, 1961—67; mgr. engring. Western Precipitation, LA, 1967—69; pres. and gen. mgr. Esco Internat., Guam, Saipan, 1969—74; dep. dir. pub. works Govt. Am. Samoa, Pago Pago, 1974—76. Cons. ballistics and space sys. divsn. USAF, 1962—65; bd. Project 75 Dept. Def. Contbr. articles to profl. jours. With US Army, 1943—45. Republican. Achievements include design of minute man and atlas missile launching systems; invention of hydrolaunch system; sonic electrostatic precipitator; acid applications electrostatic precipitator; knob conveyor; research in missile launching designs. Home: West Hills, Calif. Died Oct. 22, 2006.

GUTFELD, NORMAN E., lawyer; b. Pitts., Dec. 8, 1911; s. Adolph and Fannie (Haupt) G.; m. Evelyn Kirtz, Aug. 9, 1938 (dec. Jan. 1989); children: Nancy Gutfeld Brown, Howard, Charles, Joan Gutfeld Miller, Rose Gutfeld Edwards, Steven. BA, Case-Western Res. U., 1933, LL.B., 1935. Bar: Ohio 1935. Individual practice law, Cleve., 1935-43; atty. U.S. Regional War Labor Bd., Cleve., 1944; assoc. firm Benesch, Friedlander & Morris, Cleve., 1944-53; treas. Builders Structural Steel Corp., Cleve., 1953-59; partner Garber, Gutfeld & Jaffe, Cleve., 1959-73, Simon, Haiman, Gutfeld, Friedman and Jacobs, Cleve., 1973-80; of counsel Hertz Kates Friedman & Kammer, Cleve., 1981-93; pvt. practice Cleve., 1993-95; retired, 1995. Mem. Cleveland Heights-University Heights Bd. Edn., 1956-63, pres., 1958-59; treas. Bur. Jewish Edn. Cleve., 1974-79; trustee Cleve.

Jewish Community Fedn., 1976-77. Mem. Bar Assn. Greater Cleve., Ohio State Bar Assn., Citizen's League Cleve. Clubs: Cleve. City. Home: Columbus, Ohio. Died Nov. 14, 2006.

GUTHRIE, ROBERT VAL, retired psychologist and educator; b. Chgo., Feb. 14, 1930; s. Paul Lawrence and Lerlene Yvette (Cartwright) G.; m. Elodia S. Guthrie, Sept. 15, 1952; children: Robert S., Paul L., Michael V., Ricardo A., Sheila E., Mario A. BS, Fla. A&M U., 1955; MA, U. Ky., 1960; PhD, U.S. Internat. U., 1970. Tchr. San Diego City Schs., 1960-63; instr. psychology San Diego Mesa Coll., 1963-68, chmn. dept., 1968-70; assoc. prof. U. Pitts., 1971-73; sr. research psychologist Nat. Inst. Edn., Washington, 1973-74; asso. dir. orgnl. effectiveness and psychol. scis. Office Naval Research, Arlington, Va., 1975; supervising research psychologist Naval Pers., R & D Center, San Diego, 1975-82; pvt. practice psychology, San Diego, 1982-90; prof. psychology So. Ill. U., Carbondale, 1991-95; ret., 1995. Adj. assoc. prof. George Washington U., Washington, 1975; lectr. Georgetown U., 1975; adj. assoc. prof. U. Pitts., 1977, adj. prof. San Diego State U., 1989. Author: Psychology in the World Today, 1968, 2d edit., 1971, Encounter, 1970, Black Perspectives, 1970, Man and Society, 1972, Psychology and Psychologists, 1975, Even the Rat Was White, 1976. Served with USAF, 1950-59, Korea. Mem. AAAS, Am., Western, Calif. psychol. assns., Fedn. Am. Scientists, Am. Acad. Polit. and Social Scis., Kappa Alpha Psi. Achievements include research on social psychology, organizational and personnel psychology variables in small groups. Home: San Diego, Calif. Died Nov. 6, 2005.

GUTTMAN, CHARLES, lawyer; b. Landsberg, Germany, Mar. 11, 1948; BS in Chemistry, MIT, 1969; PhD in Chemistry, U. Chicago, 1974; JD cum laude, Brooklyn Law Sch., 1978. Bar: NY 1979, US Dist. Ct., NY, Eastern & Southern Dist. 1979, US Ct. of Appeals, Federal Circuit 1986, US Ct. of Appeals, Second Circuit 1994, registered: US Patent and Trademark Off. (Patent Atty.). Ptnr. Proskauer Rose LLP, NYC, co-chair, intellectual property group. Mem.: ABA (sci. and techn. com.), Am. Technion Soc., NYC Bar Assn., NY Intellectual Property Assn. Died Feb. 26, 2007.

GUY, JOHN MARTIN, lawyer; b. Detroit, July 16, 1929; s. Alvin W. and Ann G. (Martin) G.; B.S., Butler U., 1958; JD, Ind. U., 1961; children: Janice Lynn, Robert John. Bar: Ind. 1962. Practice law, Monticello, 1962—; atty. firm Guy, Christopher, Loy, 1962—; mem. Ind. Ho. of Reps., 1971-74, house majority leader, 1973-74; mem. Ind. Senate, 1977-84, majority leader, 1979-80; Pros. atty. 39th Jud. Circuit, 1963-67. Pres. White County Mental Health Assn., 1965-68. Trustee Monticello-Union Twp. Library Bd., pres., 1970-71. With USAF, 1951-55. Named Outstanding Republican Freshman Ind. Ho. of Reps., 1971, Ind. Senate, 1977. Mem. Ind., Monticello Bar Assns., Monticello C. of C. (pres. 1975-76), Am. Legion, Masons, Shriners, Moose. Home: Monticello, Ind. Died Mar. 31, 2006.

GUY, ROBERT DEAN, lawyer, soft drink company executive; b. Muncie, Ind., Jan. 22, 1934; s. Fred F. and Mary (Wiltrout) G.; m. Carol V. Fry, Apr. 5, 1955; children: Dani-Sue, Robin, Kristin, James, Stacy. AB in Econs. with distinction and honors, U. Mich., 1955, JD with distinction, 1957. Bar: Mich. 1958, N.C. 1961. Assoc. firm Kennedy, Covington, Lobdell & Hickman, Charlotte, N.C., 1960-64; tax atty. Am. Oil Co., Chgo., 1964-66; tax mgr. Amoco Chem. Corp., Chgo., 1966-72; v.p. taxes Quaker Oats Co., Chgo., 1972-78; v.p., gen. tax counsel Coca-Cola Co., Atlanta, from 1978. Mem. adv. bd. Tax Mgmt. Inc. Served to capt. USAF, 1957-60. Mem. ABA, Tax Execs. Inst., Nat. Fgn. Trade Council, Internat. Fiscal Assn., Arnold Air Soc., Order of Coif., Phi Beta Kappa, Phi Kappa Phi Home: Atlanta, Ga. Died June 6, 2006.

GWIAZDA, STANLEY JOHN, retired university dean; b. Phila., Feb. 14, 1922; s. Nicholas and Pauline (Stanczak) G.; m. Regina R. Grzeskowiak, Nov. 26, 1944; 1 dau., Marianne C. BS in Mech. Engring., Drexel Inst. Tech., 1944, MS, 1952. Mem. faculty Drexel U., 1946-87, assoc. prof. mech. engring., 1952-87, dean evening coll., 1963-87, assoc. prof. emeritus mech. engring., dean emeritus evening coll., 1987—97; ret., 1997. Bd. dirs. Phila. Govt. Tng. Inst.; mem. pres.'s coun. Holy Family Coll., 1984-89, acad. affairs com., 1989-2002. Author: (with J. H. Billings) Advanced Machine Design, 1958. Lt. (j.g.) USNR, 1944-46, PTO; lt. comdr. Res. ret. Stanley Gwiazda Professorship named in his honor Drexel U.; recipient Vol. Svc. award Holy Family Coll., 1994. Mem. Assn. Univ. Evening Colls. (chmn. com. on faculty devel. 1971-72), Am. Soc. Engring. Edn., Assn. Continuing Higher Edn. (dir. 1976-79, chmn. ethics com. 1979-83, pres. 1985-86, chmn. adv. com. 1986-87, Educator of Yr. award Region IV 1991), Res. Officers Assn. (pres. N.J. dept. 1973-74), Naval Res. Assn., Ret. Officers Assn., Cross Keys, Pi Tau Sigma, Alpha Sigma Lambda (assoc. dir. adult edn. found. 1984-90, bd. dirs. 1990-2002, Alpha Sigma Lambda Leadership award in Adult Edn. 1986). Roman Catholic. Home: Vincent, Ohio. Died Sept. 12, 2006.

HAAG, EVERETT KEITH, architect; b. Cuyahoga Falls, Ohio, Jan. 27, 1928; s. Arnold and Lois (Martz) H.; m. Eleanor Jean Baker, Nov. 1, 1961; children— Kurt, Paula, Pamela. BS in Architecture, Kent State U., 1951; B.Arch., Western Res. U., 1953. Founder, prin. firm Keith Haag & Assos. (architects), Cuyahoga Falls, 1955-72; founder, pres. Keith Haag Assos. Inc. (architecture-engring.-planning), Cuyahoga Falls, 1972-81; archtl. and planning cons. Cuyahoga Falls, from 1981. Instr. Kent State U., 1952-54 Pres. Tri-County Planning Commn., 1960-61; chmn. Urban Renewal Review Commn., Cuyahoga Falls, 1971—, Regional Planning Group, Northampton Twp., 1970—; mem. Akron Regional Devel. Bd.; bd. dirs. Goodwill Industries, chmn. strategic planning com., 1988—, Akron, Stan Hywet Hall Found., Inc. (pres. 1991-92); chmn. Historic Bldgs. Com., 1988—; mem. alumni bd. Kent State U., 1970-72, co-developer Polymer Housing system, 1989. Recipient 46 archtl. design awards. Fellow AIA (past pres. Akron chpt., nat. com. on office practice); mem. Architects Soc. Ohio (exec. com., sec. 1975-76, v.p. 1977-78, pres. 1979, Gold medal 1986), Northampton C. of C. (pres. 1972), Summit County Hist. Soc. (dir. 1974—) Clubs: President's (Kent State U.), Hilltoppers (Akron U.). Home: Cuyahoga Falls, Ohio. Died Apr. 19, 2007.

HAAS, GEORGE AARON, lawyer; b. NYC, July 6, 1919; s. Herman Joseph and Violet (Cowen) H.; m. Miriam Durkin, Aug. 1942; children— Thomas Leonard, Karen Ann (Mrs. Michael Davenport), James G.D. AB, Princeton U., 1940; LL.B., Yale U., 1947. Bar: Ga. 1947. Since practiced in, Atlanta; partner Haas, Bridges & Kane (and predecessor firms), from 1947. Sec., dir. Lucerne Corp., East Freeway Corp., Crescent View Corp., Mountain View Corp., Lake Placid Corp. Mem. hosp. and health div. Atlanta Community Council, 1962-68; mem. tech. assistance com., del. White House Conf. on Children and Youth, 1970; state trustee from Ga. Nat. Easter Seal Soc. for Crippled Children and Adults, 1959-65, mem. exec. com., 1961-65, v.p., 1963-65, 1st v.p., 1965-66, mem. ho. of dels., 1965-73, pres. 1971-73; bd. dirs. 1965-73, chmn. formula rev. bd., mem. relations and standards rev. com., 1967-69, pres., 1969-71; trustee Ga. Easter Seal Soc. for Crippled Children and Adults, 1955-65, 78—, sec., 1957-58, pres., 1959-61, chmn. ho. of dels., 1967-69; Bd. dirs. Fulton-DeKalb chpt. Nat. Found.; mem. med. adv. bd. Ga. chpt. Am. Phys. Therapy Assn. Served to capt. F.A. AUS, World War II. Mem. ABA, Ga. Bar Assn., Atlanta Bar Assn. Clubs: Standard (Atlanta) (past sec., dir.). Lodges: Kiwanis. Died Jan. 2, 2007.

HAAYEN, RICHARD JAN, academic administrator, insurance company executive; b. Bklyn., June 30, 1924; s. Cornelius Marius and Cornelia Florence (Muskus) H.; m. Marilyn Jean Messner, Aug. 30, 1946; children— Richard Jan, Peter Wyckoff, James Carell. BS, Ohio State U., 1948; D in Pub. Svc. (hon.), Nat. Coll. Edn., Evanston, Ill. With Allstate Ins. Co., from 1950, v.p. underwriting, 1969-75, exec. v.p. Northbrook, Ill., 1975-80, pres., 1980-86, chmn., chief exec. officer, 1986-89; exec.-in-residence So. Meth. U., Dallas, from 1989. Bd. dirs. Guaranty Fed. Savs. Bank, Dallas. Bd. dirs. Communities-in-Schs., Dallas. Mem. Am. Arbitration Assn. (arbitrator), Phi Delta Theta. Republican. Home: Dallas, Tex. Died Apr. 26, 2006.

HACKER, HAROLD SCHWORM, librarian; b. Buffalo, July 9, 1916; s. Joseph Frederick and Henrietta Catherine (Schworm) H.; A.B., Canisius Coll., 1937, L.H.D., 1976; B.L.S., U. Buffalo, 1941. Dir. pub. rels. Grosvenor Libr., Buffalo, 1941-44, Buffalo Pub. Libr. and Grosvenor Libr., 1945-46; adminstrv. asst. Grosvenor Libr., 1946-47, dir., 1952-53; first. dep. dir. Erie County Pub. Libr., 1948-52; dir. Rochester (N.Y.) Pub. Libr. and Monroe County Libr. System, 1954-78; mem. Gov. Dewey's Com. on Libr. Aid, 1949, reference and rsch. resources com. Commr. Edn., 1960-62; vice chmn. commr. of Edn. Com. on Pub. Libr. Svc., 1956-58; chmn., commr. Edn.'s Com. Libr. Devel., 1967-70; mem. Gov.'s Com. on Librs., 1965-66. Trustee St. John Fisher Coll., 1960-83, now hon. trustee; bd. dirs. John F. Wegman Found., 1959—, pres., 1972-74; pres. Rochester Area Ednl. Television Assn., 1961-67, now mem. adv. coun.; pres. Reynolds Libr.; trustee Rochester Regional Libr. Council. Recipient Rochester Civic Medal award Rochester Mus. and Sci. Ctr., 1977, Bd. Regents Medal of excellence, 1984. Fellow Rochester Mus. Arts and Scis.; mem. ALA, N.Y. Libr. Assn. (pres. 1947, Outstanding Advocate of Librs. award 1989). Club: Philosophers. Died Oct. 22, 2006.

HACKNEY, WILLIAM PENDLETON, lawyer; b. Uniontown, Pa., June 5, 1924; s. Henry Eastman and Elisabeth Moore (Pendleton) H.; m. Doris M. Fast, June 28 1947 (dec. Nov. 1988); children: W. Penn, Peter E., Jeanne S. Hackney Kingsland; m. Myrna Solomon-Kline Schwalb, July 1, 1989. AB, Princeton U., 1946; LLB, Harvard U., 1951. Bar: Pa. 1951. Assoc. Reed Smith Shaw & McClay, Pitts., 1951-64, ptnr., 1964-91, of counsel, from 1992. Author: Pennsylvania Corporations Law Practice, 1966; contbr. articles to profl. jours. Elder, former clk. session, former trustee Centennial Fund, former pres. bd. trustees E. Liberty Presbyn. Ch.; former mem. Fin. Acctg. Standards Adv. Coun., 1988-91; former trustee Pitts. Presbytery; pres. Arts and Crafts Ctr., 1972-73. With USAAF, 1943-46. Mem. ABA (past chmn. com. law and acctg., mem. com. legal opinions), Pa. Bar Assn., (past chmn. sect. corp., banking and bus. law, past chmn. corp. law com., title 15 task force), Allegheny County Bar Assn. (past chmn. corp. law sect.), Am. Law Inst., Assn. Bar City N.Y., Duquesne Club, Pitts. Golf Club, HYP-Pgh. Club. Republican. Home: Pittsburgh, Pa. Died July 31, 2006.

HADDAD, DELORRE SALEM, orthodontist; b. Canton, Ohio, Jan. 22, 1935; s. Tofy and Sumia (Rahal) H.; m. Lily Jean Baker, Mar. 18, 1956; children— Ellen Sue, David Delorre. Student Kent State U., 1953-56; D.D.S., Ohio State U., 1960, M.S., 1969. Practice dentistry specializing in orthodontics, Medina, Ohio, 1969—; del. China Am. Sci. and Tech. Exchange Group, 1984. Served to capt. USAF, 1960-62. Mem. ADA, Am. Assn. Orthodontists, Great Lakes Orthodontic Assn., Great Lakes Soc. Orthodontists (gen. chmn. 1987—), Cleve. Orthodontic Assn., Cleve. Dental Soc., Akron Dental Soc., Medina County Dental Soc., EICO Study Club (sec. 1984—), Rocky Mountain Study Club. Republican. Methodist. Club: Ohio State U. Pres's. Avocations: golf; interior design; office planning. Home: Westfield Center, Ohio. Died Mar. 26, 2007.

HADDOX, BENJAMIN EDWARD, emeritus sociology educator; b. Orlando, Fla., Dec. 11, 1923; s. James Henry and Lily (Caldwell) H.; m. Geraldine Hayes, Sept. 14, 1942; children: Benjamin Edward, Cheryl Ann, John Stephen. AB magna cum laude, Stetson U., 1945; B.D., So. Bapt. Theol. Sem., 1950; MA, U. Fla., 1960, PhD, 1962. Ordained to ministry Baptist Ch., 1945; minister in Fla., 1950-62; asst. prof. sociology Miss. State U., 1962-64; asst. prof., acting chmn. dept. sociology Stetson U., 1964-66; prof., head dept. sociology Butler U., Indpls., 1966-87, prof., dept. head emeritus, from 1988; rsch. in Bogota Colombia, 1961. Author: Sociedad y Religión en Colombia, 1965, Joint Decision Making Patterns and Related Factors Among Low Income Families, 1965; also articles. Miss. rep. regional research project low income families, 1962-64. U.S. Steel Found. fellow, 1960-62 Mem. AAUP (pres. Butler U. chpt. 1968-69), AAAS, Am. Sociol. Assn., North Central Midwest, So. sociol. socs., Latin Am. Studies Assn., Nat. Council on Family Relations, Council on Religion in Internat. Affairs, N.Y. Acad. Sci., Soc. Sci. Study of Religion, Population Inst., Population Reference Bur., Union Concerned Scientists, Phi Beta Kappa, Phi Kappa Phi (pres. Butler chpt. 1971-72). Democrat. Presbyterian. Home: Townsend, Tenn. Died Mar. 5, 2006.

HADERLEIN, THOMAS M., retired lawyer; b. Chgo., Sept. 2, 1935; BSC, DePaul U., 1957; JD, Georgetown U., 1960, LLM, 1962. Bar: Ill. 1960, D.C. 1960. With Baker & McKenzie, Washington, 1959-64, ptnr. Chgo., ret., 2000. Died Aug. 22, 2007.

HADLEY, JERRY, opera singer; b. Princeton, Ill., June 16, 1952; s. Jerry Tilman and Loretta M. (Seghetti) H.; m. Cheryl Drake, Oct. 2, 1976 (div.); children: Nathan, Ryan BME, Bradley U., 1974; MusM, U. Ill., 1977. Instr. U. Conn., Storrs, 1977—79. Prin. artist N.Y.C. Opera, 1979, Washington Opera at Kennedy Ctr., 1980, Vienna State Opera, 1982, Bavarian State Opera, Munich, Fed. Republic Germany, 1983, Glyndebourne Festival, England, 1983, Edinburgh Festival, Scotland, 1983, Netherlands Opera, Amsterdam, 1983, Royal Opera Covent Garden, London, 1984, Carnegie Hall Recital Debut, N.Y., 1984, Hamburg State Opera, Fed. Republic. Germany, 1986, Lyric Opera Chgo., 1986, Met. Opera, N.Y.C., 1987, Teatro Communale, Florence, Italy, 1987, Geneva Opera, 1987, Berlin Opera, 1988, San Francisco Opera, 1988; solo recordings Beethoven Symphony #9, 1985, Mozart Requiem, 1986, 88, Donizetti Anna Bolena, 1986, Verdi Requiem, 1987, as Freddie in My Fair lady, 1987, as Rodolfo in La Boheme, 1987, Showboat, 1988, Kurt Weill's Street Scene, 1989, Broadway Favorites, Mozart's Cosi Fan Tutte, Gounod's Faust, In the Real World, Golden Days. Grantee Nat. Opera Inst., 1978, Richard Tucker Found., 1982. Mem. Am. Guild Musical Artists, Phi Mu Alpha (sustaining alumnus). Lutheran. Died July 18, 2007.

HADLEY, PAUL ERVIN, international relations educator; b. South Ovid, Mich., July 17, 1914; s. Ervin C. and Viola M. (Barnes) H.; m. Virginia Faye Last, May 15, 1945; 1 dau., Deborah Faye. AB, Occidental Coll., Los Angeles, 1934; A.M., U. So. Calif., 1946, PhD in Comparative Lit, 1955; L.H.D., Nat. U., 1980. Tchr. El Monte (Calif.) Union High Sch., 1935-42; exec. sec. Centro Cultural Paraguayo Americano, Asunción, Paraguay, 1943-44; head Cultural Insts. unit U.S. Dept. State, Washington, 1945; instr. internat. relations U. So. Calif., Los Angeles, 1945-47, asst. prof., 1947-55, assoc. prof., 1955-64, prof., 1964-81, prof. emeritus, 1981—2007, disting. emeritus prof., 1992. Dean summer session, 1960-73; dean Coll. of Continuing Edn., 1966-73, assoc. v.p. acad. adminstrn., 1973-77, interim acad. v.p., 1975-77, acad. v.p., 1977-81, dir. emeriti ctr., 1997-2001; exec. sec. Inst. World Affairs, 1948-73, chmn. Pacific Coast Council Latin Am. Studies, 1956-57; mem. Woodrow Wilson Fellowship selection com. Region XV, 1960-67; fgn. leader and specialist program Am. Council on Edn., 1960-62; mem. State Com. on Continuing Edn., 1966-76; mem. adv. com. Servicemembers Opportunity Colls., 1978-81; chmn. edn. sect. Town Hall of Calif., 1965-68, chmn. internat. relations sect., 1969-71; trustee Latin Am. Scholarship Program Am. Univs., 1972-74; trustee So. Calif. Presbyn. Homes(chmn. 1988-89). Pres. Assn. Retirement Orgns. in Higher Edn., 2001-03. Mem. Assn. Univ. Summer Sessions (pres. 1970-71), Inst. Internat. Edn. (adv. bd. West Coast region), Nat. U. Extension Assn. (chmn. region VI 1970-71, pres. 1976-77), Adult Educators Greater Los Angeles (chmn. 1970-71), Phi Beta Kappa, Pi Sigma Alpha, Sigma Alpha Epsilon, Phi Kappa Phi. Presbyn. (elder, stated clk. Presbytery 1983-87). Home: Glendale, Calif. Died Apr. 10, 2007.

HAGAN, WILLIS COBB, JR., aircraft company executive; b. Birmingham, Ala., Sept. 19, 1925; s. Willis Cobb and Elizabeth (Gueard) H.; student Howard Coll., 1946; LL.B., U. Ala., 1950; m. Jane Jeffers, Apr. 25, 1952; children— Jane Jeffers, Willis Cobb. With Hayes Internat. Corp., Birmingham, Ala., 1951—, corp. sec., 1957-64, v.p. orgn., systems and indsl. relations, 1964-67, v.p. mfg., 1967, exec. v.p., 1967-69, pres., chief exec. officer, 1969—; dir. Guaranty Savs. & Loan Assn., Hayes Internat. Corp. Served with USAAF, 1943-45. Mem. Assoc. Industries Ala., Air Force Assn., U.S. C. of C., Nat. Aerospace Services Assn., Ala. Bar Assn., Birmingham Bar Assn., Ala. Zool. Soc., Ala. C. of C., Birmingham C. of C. Episcopalian. Clubs: Birmingham Country, Downtown, The Club, Relay House, Mountain Brook Country, SAR. Home: Birmingham, Ala. Died Sept. 19, 2006.

HAGEDORN, DONALD JAMES, plant pathologist, educator, agricultural consultant; b. Moscow, Idaho, May 18, 1919; s. Frederick William and Elizabeth Viola (Scheyer) H.; m. Eloise Tierney, July 18, 1943; 1 child, James William BS, U. Idaho, 1941, DSc (hon.), 1979; MS, U. Wis., 1943, PhD, 1948. Prof. agronomy and plant pathology U. Wis., Madison, 1948-64, prof. plant pathology, from 1964. Courtesy prof. plant pathology Oreg. State U., Covallis, 1972-73; vis. scientist DSIR Lincoln Rsch. Ctr., Christchurch, N.Z., 1980-81; cons. Asgrow Seed Co., 1987-93; affiliate prof. plant pathology U. Idaho, 1991—. Contbr. chpts. to books, articles to profl. jours. With USAAF, 1943-46. Recipient Campbell award AAAS, 1961, CIBA-Geigy award, 1974, Meritorious Svc. award Nat. Pea Improvement Assn., 1979, Bean Improvement Coop., 1979, Forty-Niners award, 1983, Citation for Outstanding Sci. Achievement, Wis. Acad. Letters, Arts and Scis., 1986; NSF sr. fellow, 1957; named Disting. Centennial Alumnus, U. Idaho, 1989; named to U. Idaho Alumni Hall of Fame, 1990. Fellow Am. Phytopath, Soc.; mem. Kiwanis, Sigma Xi, Gamma Sigma Delta, Alpha Zeta. Methodist. Home: Madison, Wis. Died Apr. 11, 2007.

HAGEMAN, JAMES C., rancher; b. Douglas, Wyo., Mar. 2 1930; s. Fred August and Ruth (Shaw) H.; m. Marion Malvin, May 19, 1956; children: Julia Newman, James P., Rachel Rubino, Hugh, Harriet Dewey, Ted Yellowwolf. Owner, operator ranch, Ft. Laramie, Wyo., from 1961. Chair edn. com. Wyo. Ho. of Reps., Cheyenne, 1990—; chmn. sch. bd. exec. com. Wyo. tockgrows, Torrington. Republican. Home: Fort Laramie, Wyo. Died Aug. 23, 2006.

HAGEMAN, JOSEPH CHARLES, surgical nurse; b. Point Pleasant, NJ, Jan. 20, 1951; s. Raymond Ellsworth and June Marie (Riker) Hageman; m. Regina Marie Newland, June 8

1974 (div. May, 1991); children: Jennifer Louise, Michele Lisette; m. Susan Claire Horner, Apr. 25, 1992. BSN, Trenton State Coll., 1974. CEN, N.C.; RN, N.J., Wyo., N.C.; EMT, Wyo. Staff nurse emergency dept. Burlington County Hosp., Mt. Holly, N.J., 1974-76; emergency dept. supr. Carbon County Hosp., Rawlins, Wyo., 1976-77; emergency dept./operating rm./ICU supr. Pungo Dist. Hosp., Belhaven, N.C., 1977-78; emergency dept. supr. Craven County Hosp., New Bern, N.C., 1978-82; DON New Bern Outpatient Surgery Ctr., from 1982. Mem. Atlantic Coastal Constrn. Assn., New Bern, 1993—, Bird Island Preservation Soc., Sunset Beach, N.C., 1993—. Recipient Outstanding Young Man of Am. award U.S. Jaycees, 1976. Republican. Methodist. Avocations: fishing, hunting, travel, camping. Home: New Bern, NC. Died May 28, 2006.

HAGER, ORVAL O., retired lawyer, consultant; b. Lincoln, Nebr., Nov. 18, 1918; s. Ora Orval and Marie Katherine (Schafer) H.; m. Margaret Anne Ambrose, Nov. 21, 1984; 1 dau., Nancy Ellen (dec.). B.S., U. Nebr., 1940; J.D. cum laude, Willamette U., 1949. Bar: Oreg. 1949, U.S. Dist. Ct. Oreg. 1949. Assoc. Miller, Nash, Wiener, Hager & Carlsen, Portland, Oreg., 1949-53, ptnr., 1953-92. Bd. dirs. First Am. Title Ins. Co. Oreg. Past bd dirs. YMCA of Columbia-Willamette; life trustee Willamette U.; regent U. Portland; past pres. Oreg. Heart Assn., 1968. Served to lt. col. USAR, 1940-67. Republican. Clubs: Arlington (dir., past pres.), Waverley Country (dir., past pres.); Portland Golf (dir., past pres.), Multnomah Athletic, Rotary (dir., past pres. Portland club). Died Nov. 28, 2005.

HAGGARD, FORREST DELOSS, minister; b. Trumbull, Nebr., Apr. 21, 1925; s. Arthur McClellan and Grace (Hadley) H.; m. Eleanor V. Evans, June 13, 1946; children— Warren A., William D., James A., Katherine A. AB, Phillips U., 1948; M.Div., 1953, D.D. (hon.), 1967; MA, U. Mo., 1960. Ordained to ministry Christian Ch., 1948; minister Overland Park (Kans.) Christian Ch., from 1953; pres. Kansas City Area Ministers Assn., 1959, Kans. Christian Ministers Assn., 1960; mem. adminstrn. com., gen. bd. Christian Ch., 1968-72; pres. World Conv. Chs. of Christ (Christian/Disciples of Christ), from 1975. Chmn. Grad. Sem. Council, Enid, Okla., 1970; pres. Nat. Evangelistic Assn., 1972; pres. bd. dirs. Midwest Counseling Ctr., Kansas City, 1987—. Author: The Clergy and the Craft, 1970, also articles. Pres. Johnson County (Kans.) Mental Health Assn., 1962-63; mem. coun. Boy Scouts Am., 1964-69; bd. dirs. Kans. Home for Aged, 1960-65, Knas. Children's Svc. League, 1964-69, Johnson County Mental Health Ctr., 1991—; pres. bd. dirs. Kans. Masonic Home, 1974-75; bd. dirs. Kans. Masonic Found., 1970—; trustee Nat. Properties Christian Ch., 1987—. Mem. Masons (grand master Kans. chpt., chaplain gen. Grand chpt. Royal Arch Internat. 1975—, Grand Cross Supreme coun. 33d degree 1989, Disting. Svc. medal 1991). Mem. Masons (grand master Kans., chaplain gen. Grand chpt. Royal Arch Internat. 1975—, Grand Cross Supreme Coun. 33rd degree 1989, pres. Philolethes Soc. 1994—). Home: Shawnee Mission, Kans. Died Aug. 10, 2007.

HAGGLUND, CLARANCE EDWARD, lawyer, publishing executive; b. Omaha, Feb. 17, 1927; s. Clarance Andrew and Esther May (Kelle) H.; m. Dorothy Souser, Mar. 27, 1953 (div. Aug. 1972); children: Laura, Bret, Katherine; m. Merle Patricia Hagglund, Oct. 28, 1972. BA, U. S.D., 1949; JD, William Mitchell Coll. Law, 1953. Bar: Minn. 1955, U.S. Ct. Appeals (8th cir.) 1974, U.S. Supreme Ct. 1963; diplomate Am. Bd. Profl. Liability Attys. Ptnr. Hagglund & Johnson and predecessor firms, Mpls., from 1973; mem. Hagglund, Weimer and Speidel, PA; publ., pres. Common Law Publishing Inc., Golden Valley, Minn., from 1991; mem. Blackwell Igbanogo Attys., Mpls., 2004; with Hagglund Law Offices, from 2004. Pres. Internat. Control Sys., Inc., Mpls., 1979—, Hill River Corp., Mpls., 1976—; gen. counsel Minn. Assn. Profl. Ins. Agts., Inc., Mpls., 1965-86; CFO, Pro-Trac, software for profl. liability ins. industry. Contbr. articles to profl. jours. Served to lt. comdr. USNR, 1945-46, 50-69. Fellow Internat. Soc. Barristers; mem. Lawyers Pilots Bar Assn., U.S. Maritime Law Assn. (proctor), Acad. Cert. Trial Lawyers Minn. (dean 1983-85), Nat. Bd. Trial Advocacy (cert. in civil trial law, bd. dirs.), Douglas Amdahl Inns of Ct. (pres.), Ill. Athletic Club (Chgo.), Edina Country Club (Minn.), Calhoun Beach Club (Mpls.). Roman Catholic. Avocation: flying. Died Mar. 5, 2007.

HAIGH, GEORGE WHYLDEN, banker; b. Toledo, Aug. 4, 1931; s. Frederick Dwight and Annette (Lipe) H.; m. Joan DuBois, Oct. 15, 1954; children— Constance, Stephen. BA, Dartmouth Coll., 1953; postgrad., Fgn. Service Sch., Georgetown U., 1953-54. With DeVilbiss Co., Toledo, 1956-76, pres., 1972-76, Trustcorp Bank, Ohio, from 1976, Trustcorp., Inc., 1976-77, pres., chief exec. officer, 1977-89, chmn., 1985-89. Dir. Champion Spark Plug Co., Therma-Tru Corp., Inc.; bd. dirs. Internat. Fin. Conf., chmn., 1983-84 Pres. Family Services Greater Toledo, 1971-73; chmn. Toledo Economic Planning Council, 1977-83, chmn. Com. 100; pres. bd. trustees Toledo Mus. Art; trustee Toledo Hosp., 1985-87; trustee U. Toledo; bd. dirs. Toledo-Lucas County Port Authority. Served with Signal Corps, U.S. Army, 1954-56. Mem. Toledo C. of C. (pres. 1977-78) Clubs: Toledo Country, Toledo, Inverness (Toledo); Carranor Hunt and Polo (Perrysburg, Ohio); Georgetown (Washington); Golf (Columbus); Pine Valley (N.J.); Quail Creek (Naples), Vineyards of Naples. Republican. Episcopalian. Home: Toledo, Ohio. Died Feb. 1, 2006.

HAIZLIP, HENRY HARDIN, JR., real estate broker, consultant, retired bank executive; b. Pine Bluff, Ark., Dec. 18, 1913; s. Henry Hardin and Rebecca (Porter) H.; m. Emily Williamson, Feb. 15, 1947; children: Henry Hardin III, Wilson, Jean Hunter, Selden. Student, Tulane U., 1932-33. With W.N. Ballou Cotton Co., Memphis, 1933-36; with First Nat. Bank Memphis, 1936-73, exec. v.p., 1968-70, chmn. exec. com., 1970-73; pres. First Memphis Realty Trust, 1970-73, chmn., 1973-76; pres. First Tenn. Corp., 1973-78; real estate cons. Haizlip/Lovitt, Memphis, 1979—2002. Dir. Mid South Title Co., Union Service Industries Inc.; vice chmn. First Tenn. Nat. Corp., until 1979; ret.; instr. in mortgage financing La. State U., Ohio State U. Pres. Memphis Cotton Carnival Assn., 1966, bd. dirs., 1967—; vice chmn. Shelby United Good Neighbors, 1967-68; mem. Chickasaw coun. Boy Scouts Am.; pres. Future Memphis, Inc., 1974-77; bd. dirs. Memphis and Shelby County unit Am. Cancer Soc., 1967-68; trustee Comty. Found. Greater Memphis, chmn., 1978; mem. pres.'s coun. Tulane U., New Orleans, Rhodes Coll., Memphis; vice-chmn. The Trezevant Manor Episcopal Home. Capt. AUS, 1941-46. Mem. Am. Bankers Assn., Downtown Assn. Memphis (chmn. bd.), Kappa Alpha. Clubs: Memphis Country; Menasha Hunting and Fishing (Turrell, Ark.); Memphis Hunt and Polo. Episcopalian. Home: Memphis, Tenn. Died Nov. 27, 2005.

HAKEEM, MICHAEL, sociologist, educator; b. Fall River, Mass., Sept. 5, 1916; s. Joseph and Sophia (Daghir) H.; m. Helen Louise Cook, June 8, 1949. BS, Ohio State U., 1942, MA, 1945, PhD, 1950. Sociologist Ill. Div. Criminology, 1943-46; instr. State U. Iowa, 1946-47; instr., then asst. prof. Ohio State U., 1948-52; mem. faculty U. Wis., Madison, from 1952, prof. sociology, 1962-83, prof. emeritus, from 1983. Spl. advisor on correctional adminstrn.; research cons. on crime and mental health Ohio Div. Mental Hygiene, 1948-52. Contbr. articles to profl. jours. Fellow Am. Sociol. Assn.; mem. Am. Acad. Polit. and Social Sci., Soc. Study Social Problems (exec. com. 1961-64), Am. Soc. Criminology, Nat. Conf. Delinquency and Crime, AAUP, Coun. Dem. and Secular Humanism, Nat. Coun. Family Rels. Home: Madison, Wis. Died Nov. 2, 2006.

HAKIMI, S. LOUIS, electrical and computer engineering educator; b. Meshed, Iran, Dec. 16, 1932; came to U.S., 1952, naturalized, 1967; s. A. Moshe and Miriam (Nabavian) H.; m. Mary Yomtob, Aug. 22, 1965; children: Alan, Carol, Diane. BS in Elec. Engring., U. Ill., Urbana, 1955, MS in Elec. Engring., 1957, PhD in Elec. Engring., 1959. Asst. prof. elec. engring. U. Ill., 1959-61; assoc. prof. Northwestern U., Evanston, Ill., 1961-66, prof., 1966-86, chmn. dept. elec. engring., 1972-77; prof. U. Calif., Davis, 1986—2001, chmn. elec. and computer engring., 1986-96, prof. emeritus, from 2001. Assoc. editor Networks, 1975-90, adv. editor, 1990—; assoc. editor IEEE Transactions on Circuits and Systems, 1975-77; bd. adv. editors Transp. Sci., 1985—. Fellow IEEE (life); mem. Soc. Indsl. and Applied Math., Sigma Xi, Tau Beta Pi, Phi Kappa Phi. Home: El Macero, Calif. Died June 23, 2006.

HAKIMOGLU, AYHAN, electronics executive; b. Erbaa, Turkey, Aug. 19, 1928; came to U.S., 1955; s. Mekki and Mediha H.; children by previous marriage: Zeynep B., Incigul R. O'Brien, Deborah A. Cueto, Leyla P.; m. Rachida Elmir, July 12, 1997; 1 child, Ayhan, Jr. BSEE, Robert Coll., Istanbul, 1949; MSEE, U. Cin., 1950. Founder, pres., chmn. bd. Dynaplex Corp., Princeton, NJ, 1962-67; gen. mgr. Teledyne Telemetry Co., Los Angeles, 1966-67; founder, chmn. bd., pres. Aydin Corp., Horsham, Pa., 1967-96. Cons. Aydin Corp., Plymouth Meeting, Pa.; investor. Served to lt. Turkish Army, 1951-52. Named Turkish Am. of Yr. Assembly Turkish Am. Assn., 1985; recipient Outstanding Pub. Svc. award, Assembly Turkish Am. Assns., 1988, 89, Disting. Alumni award U. Cin., 1991. Muslim. Home: Narberth, Pa. Died Aug. 22, 2007.

HALBERSTAM, DAVID, journalist, writer; b. NYC, Apr. 10, 1934; s. Charles A. and Blanche (Levy) H.; m. Elzbieta Tchizevska, June 13, 1965 (div. 1977); m. Jean Sandness Butler, June 29, 1979; 1 dau., Julia Sandness. AB, Harvard U., 1955; degree (hon.), CCNY, Colby Coll., Colorado State Columbia Tchrs. Coll., NYC, Columbia Coll., Chgo., Dartmouth Coll., Drew Univ., Elizabethtown Coll., Ithaca Coll., Knox Coll., Lake Forest Coll., Lawrence Coll., Mercy Coll., Univ. Mich., Ann Arbor; degree, Nazareth Coll., Rochester, NY; degree (hon.), Univ. New Haven, Niagara Coll., Tufts Univ., Tulane Univ., Univ. South, Sewanee, Univ. South Carolina, Spartanburg, Wesleyan Univ. Reporter West Point Daily Times Leader, Miss., 1955—56, Nashville Tennessean, 1956—60; mem. staff N.Y. Times, 1960—67, corr. Democratic Republic of Congo, 1961—62, Vietnam, 1962—63, 1964—65, Warsaw, 1965—66; contbg. editor Harper's mag., 1967—71. Author: The Noblest Roman, 1961, The Making of a Quagmire: America and Vietnam During the Kennedy Era, 1965, One Very Hot Day, 1968, The Unfinished Odyssey of Robert Kennedy, 1969, Ho (Ho Chi Minh), 1971, The Best and the Brightest, 1972, The Powers That Be, 1979, The Breaks of the Game, 1981, The Amateurs: The Story of Four Young Men and Their Quest for an Olympic Gold Medal, 1985, The Reckoning, 1986, Summer of '49, 1989, The Next Century, 1991, The Fifties, 1993, October 1964, 1994, (intro for a requiem) The Photographs of the Photographers Who Died in the Vietnam War, 1997, Playing for Keeps: Michael Jordan and The World He Made, 1998, The Children, 1998, War in a Time of Peace: Bush, Clinton, and the Generals, 2001, Firehouse, 2002, The Teammates: A Portrait of a Friendship, 2003, Bill Belichick: The Education of a Coach, 2005, The Coldest Winter: America and the Korean War (published posthumously), 2007, (foreword) The Gigantic Book of Fishing Stories, 2007; co-editor: (with Glenn Stout) The Best American Sports Writing, 1991; editor: (with Glenn Stout) The Best American Sports Writing of the Century, 1999. Trustee The Brearley Sch., 1993. Recipient Pulitzer prize for internat. reporting, 1964, George Polk Meml. award, 1964, Louis Lyons award, 1964, Page One award for Congo reporting, 1962, Overseas Press Club award, 1973, Elijah Lovejoy award Colby Coll., 1997, Bob Considine award St. Bonaventure Coll., 1999, Robert Kennedy Book award, 1999, Christopher award, 1999, Frederick Melcher Book award Unitarian Ch., 1999, All for the Children Pres. award, Trinity Coll., Jean Mayer Award, Tufts Univ., 1999. Mem. Soc. Am. Historians. Died Apr. 23, 2007.

HALE, BRUCE DONALD, retired marketing professional; b. Oak Park, Ill., Dec. 21, 1933; s. Edward Garden and Mildred Lillian (Pelc) H.; m. Nancy Ann Novotny, July 2, 1955 (div. 1976); children: Jeffrey Bruce, Karen Jill Hale; m. Connie Luella Green Gunderson, Apr. 21, 1979. BA in Econs., Wesleyan U., Middletown, Conn., 1955. Trainee Caterpillar Tractor Co., Peoria, Ill., 1955-56, dealer tng. rep., 1956-59, dist. rep. Albuquerque, 1959-62; asst. sales mgr. Rust Tractor Co., Albuquerque, 1962-65, gen. sales mgr. Albuquerque, 1965-71, v.p. sales, 1971-81, v.p. mktg., 1981-96; ret., 1996. Mem. Am. Mining Congress, Soc. Mining Engrs., Associated Contractors N.Mex., Associated Equipment Distbrs., Rocky Mountain Coal Mining Inst., N.Mex. Mining Assn., Albuquerque Country Club. Avocations: golf, fishing, music, classic cars. Home: Albuquerque, N.Mex. Died Feb. 24, 2007.

HALL, ERNST PAUL, retired federal agency administrator, chemical engineer; b. Clarksburg, W. Va., Aug. 23, 1925; s. Herbert Paul and Nola (Simmons) H.; m. Mary Louise Hepler, Apr. 2, 1948 (div.); children: Ernst Paul, Barbara Ann, Sandra Lee, Robert P.; m. Suzette Solon, Feb. 14, 1986. BS in Chem. Engring., W. Va. U., 1947; MS, U. Pitts., 1954. Devel. engr. Pennwalt Corp., Natrona, Pa., 1947-48; asst. tech. div. Celina Stearic Acid Co. (Ohio), 1948-51; fellow Mellon Inst., Pitts., 1951-54; sr. engr. Dewey and Almy div. W.R. Grace Co., Lockport, N.Y., 1954-55; product engr. Gen. Electric Co., Coshocton, Ohio, 1955-57; rsch. cons. Consol. Coal Co., Pitts., 1957-66; chief. metals industry br. U.S. EPA, Washington, 1966-91. Contbr. articles to profl. jours. Recipient Bronze medal for commendable service U.S. EPA, 1973, 89; S.A. Braley award Coal Industry Adv. Com., 1974; Silver medal for superior service U.S. EPA, 1975, 76, 82. Mem. Am. Chem. Soc., Am. Inst. Chem. Engrs., ASME, AIME, Nat. Soc. Profl. Engrs., Pa. Soc. Profl. Engrs. Home: Arlington, Va. Died Oct. 31, 2006.

HALL, NEWMAN A., retired mechanical engineer; b. Uniontown, Pa., June 14, 1913; s. Homer) Maxwell and Susan (Newman) H.; m. Eileen Creevey, Aug. 14, 1938; children: James Creevey, Elizabeth Arnold. AB, Marietta Coll., Ohio, 1934, D.Sc. (hon.), 1959; PhD, Calif. Inst. Tech., 1938; MA, Yale, 1956. Registered profl. engr., Conn. Instr. in math. Queens Coll., Flushing, N.Y., 1938-41; engr. Chance Vought div. United Aircraft Corp., Stratford, Conn., 1941-42, supr. engring. personnel, 1942-43; research engr. United Aircraft Corp., Hartford, 1944-47, head analysis sect., research div., 1946-47; prof. mech. engring. and head heat power div., mech. engring. dept. U. Minn., 1947-55; prof. mech. engring., asst. dean charge Grad. Div. Coll. Engring., N.Y. U., 1955-56; Strathcona prof., chmn. dept. mech. engring. Yale, 1956-64; cons. on ednl. facilities and adminstrn.; cons. engr. in thermodynamics, fluid dynamics, combustion; author, lectr. genealogy and local history. Exec. Commn. Engring. Edn., 1962-71; sci. adviser AID, Korea, 1972-73, Korea Ministry Sci. and Tech., 1974-76; ednl. cons., from 1976. Dir. div. engring. scis. Office of Ordnance Research, U.S. Army, 1952-53 Sr. author: Engineering Thermodynamics, 1960. Fellow ASME (chmn. bd. edn. 1959-61); mem. Soc. Automotive Engrs., Am. Soc. Engring. Edn. (v.p. 1960-62), Internat. Combustion Inst. (hon. dir.), Order of Founders and Patriots Am. (registrar gen.), Soc. Mayflower Desc., Nat. Geneal. Soc., Arnold Family Assn. South (pres. 1977-81), Phi Beta Kappa, Sigma Xi, Tau Beta Pi. Condr. rsch. in thermodynamics, fluid mechanics, aerodynamics, heat transfer, anthropology, demography, genealogy. Died Mar. 23, 2006.

HALLIGAN, DWIGHT EUGENE, optometrist; b. Iona, S.D., June 2, 1931; s. Eugene and Mary Nora (Speckles) H.; m. Barbara Jean Kunert, Aug. 13, 1955. B.S., Ill. Coll. Optometry, 1958, O.D., 1959. Gen. practice optometry, Eau Claire, Wis., 1959—; examiner U.S. Army, Eau Claire, 1968-69, Soc. Security Adminstrn., Eau Claire, 1980—, Served with USCG, 1952-55. Mem. Indianhead Optometric Soc. (pres. 1962-64), Wis. Optometric Assn. (bd. dirs. 1964-70), Am. Optometric Assn. (charter mem. contact lens sect.), U.S. Coast Guard Aux. (flotilla edn. officer 1980—). Lodges: Masons, Shriners. Avocations: pilot; renovating log cabin. Home: Sun Lakes, Ariz. Died Jan. 13, 2007.

HAM, ANITA SUE, systems engineer, nursing administrator; b. Kewanee, Ill., May 31, 1949; d. Virgil and Mary Lou (Ogle) Ham. BSN, U. Md., Balt., 1971; MBA with honors, City Coll., Seattle, 1979. RN Md., Wash., Calif. Commd. 1st lt. U.S. Army, 1971, advanced through grades to maj., 1983; stationed Madigan Army Med. Ctr., Tacoma, 1972—73; head nurse drug and alcohol rehab. and psychiat. unit U.S. Army Hosp., Waurzburg, Germany, 1974—76; chief adult day care svc., dept. psychiatry Fitzsimmons Army Med. Ctr., Denver, 1976—77; ret., 1977; asst. dir. Seattle City Coll., 1978—80; mgmt. analyst Wash. Dept. Transp., Olympia, 1980; mgr. med. support svcs. Western State Hosp., Ft. Stelacoom, Wash., 1980—81; sr. engr. ops., database mgmt. Martin Marietta Corp., Vandenburg AFB, Calif., from 1981. Cons. U.S. Army Dept. Nursing. Mem.: NAFE, Assn. MBAs. Died Apr. 7, 2006.

HAMBRO, LEONID, pianist; b. Chgo., June 26, 1920; s. Simeon and Dora (Levitan) H.; m. Crystal Cooper, Apr. 1946 (annulled 1951); m. Barbara Schnapp, July 25, 1952; children— Aralee, Simeon Grad., Julliard Grad. Sch. Music, 1941. Pianist for Joseph Szigeti and Felix Salmond, 1946; staff pianist Sta. WQXR, NYC, 1947—64; ofcl. pianist NY Philharm. Symphony Orch.; assoc. in concerts and TV with Victor Borge, 1961—70; performing artist, faculty mem. New Coll. Summer Music Festival, 1965; concert pianist, rec. artist Columbia and Victor records; mem. faculty Julliard Inst. Mus. Art, 1949-52, Calif. Inst. Arts, 1970—87. Served with USNR, 1942-45 Recipient Naumburg Found. award, 1946. Mem. Am. Guild Musical Artists, Bohemians Died Oct. 23, 2006.

HAMILTON, ANN STANLEY, marketing executive; b. Phila., Mar. 25, 1960; d. Russell and Helen Marcia (Brown) H. B.A. in Psychology, Temple U., 1982. Customer service rep. Continental Bank, Phila., 1977-82; mgr. pub. div. Hay Assocs., Phila., 1983-84; pres. Hamilton Assocs. mktg. cons., Phila., 1985—. Rep. Senatorial Inner Circle, Washington, 1986. Mem. Alliance Française de Philadelphie, Christian Endeavor, Nat. Assn. Female Execs. Republican. Presbyterian. Avocations: travel; reading; foreign cultures and languages. Home: Philadelphia, Pa. Died Apr. 30, 2006.

HAMILTON, BOBBY, professional race car driver; b. Nashville, May 29, 1957; m. Debbie Hamilton (div.); 1 child, Bobby Jr.; m. Lori Hamilton. Recipient NASCAR Winston Cup Series Rookie of Yr. award, 1991, Talladega winner Nextel Cup, 2001, NASCAR Craftsman Truck Series Champion, 2004. Achievements include former Nashville Speedway track champion; NASCAR Winston Cup Series debut 1991; winner Dura-Lube

5000, Phoenix, 1996; 1997 season includes winner Rockingham, AC Delco 400; 1998 season includes winner Goody's 500, 2 top-5s, 8 top-10s, top 15 in points; winner Talladega 500, 2001; winner, Craftsman Truck Series, 2004. Died Jan. 7, 2007.

HAMILTON, DONALD BENGTSSON, author; b. Uppsala, Sweden, Mar. 24, 1916; s. Bengt L.K. and Elise (Neovius) H.; m. Kathleen Stick, 1941 (dec. Oct. 28, 1989); children: Hugo, Elise, Gordon, Victoria. BS, U. Chgo., 1938. Writer and photographer, from 1946. Creator Matt Helm series; author books including Death of a Citizen, 1960, The Wrecking Crew, 1960, The Removers, 1961, The Silencers, 1962, Murderer's Row, 1962, The Ambushers, 1963, The Ravagers, 1963, The Shadowers, 1964, The Devastators, 1965, The Betrayers, 1966, The Menacers, 1968, The Interlopers, 1969, The Intriguers, 1972, The Intimidators, 1974, The Terminators, 1975, The Terrorizers, 1977, The Retaliators, 1976, The Poisoners, 1971, Cruises with Kathleen, 1980, The Mona Intercept, 1980, The Revengers, 1982, The Annihilators, 1983, The Infiltrators, 1984, The Detonators, 1985, The Vanishers, 1986, The Demolishers, 1987, The Frighteners, 1989, The Threateners, 1992, The Damagers, 1993; contbr. articles on hunting, yachting, and photography to mags. Mem. Mystery Writers Am., Western Writers Am., Outdoor Writers Assn. Am. Died Nov. 20, 2006.

HAMILTON, JOSEPH HEBERLING, textile company executive; b. Iowa City, Aug. 8, 1920; s. Clair E. and Prudence M. (Heberling) H.; m. Joan Van Gonsic, Oct. 8, 1952; children— Holly Heberling, Joseph Jeffrey. B.A., Harvard U., 1946, M.B.A., 1948. Asst. to chmn. bd. Burlington Industries, Greensboro, N.C., 1948-55; pres. Burlington Throwing Co., High Point, N.C., 1955-60; v.p. Madison Throwing Co., N.C., 1960-63; founder Textured Fibres, Inc. (name changed to Texfi Industries Inc. 1969), Greensboro, 1963, now chmn., chief exec. officer. Served to lt. USNR, 1942-45. Episcopalian. Home: Greensboro, NC. Died Aug. 18, 2006.

HAMILTON, RHODA LILLIAN ROSÉN, retired guidance counselor, language educator, consultant; b. Chgo., May 8, 1915; d. Reinhold August and Olga (Peterson) Rosén; m. Douglas Edward Hamilton, Jan. 23, 1936 (div. Feb. 1952); remarried, Aug. 1995 (dec. 1997); children: Perry Douglas, John Richard Hamilton. Grad., Moser Coll., Chgo., 1932-33; BS in Edn., U. Wis., 1953, postgrad., 1976; MAT, Rollins Coll., 1967; postgrad., Ohio State U., 1959-60; postgrad. in clin. psychology, Mich. State U., 1971, 76, 79, 80; postgrad., Yale U., 1972, Loma Linda U., 1972; postgrad. in computer mgmt. sys., U. Okla., 1976; postgrad. in edn., U. Calif., Berkeley, 1980. Exec. sect. to pres. Ansul Chem. Co., Marinette, Wis., 1934-36; pers. counselor Burneice Larson's Med. Bur., Chgo., 1954-56; adminstrv. asst. to Ernst C. Schmidt Lake Geneva, Wis., 1956-58; assoc. prof. fin. aid Ohio State U., 1958-60; tchr. English to spkrs. of other langs. Istanbul, Turkey, 1960-65; counselor Groveland (Fla.) H.S., 1965-68; guidance counselor, psychol. cons. early childhood edn. Dept. Def. Overseas Dependents Sch., Okinawa, 1968-85; instr./lectr. early childhood Lake Sumter Jr. Coll., Leesburg, Fla., 1986-88; pres. Hamilton Assocs., Groveland, Fla., 1986; ret. Vis. lectr. Okla. State U., 1980; co-owner plumbing, heating bus., Marinette, 1943-49; journalist Rockford (Ill.) Morning Star, 1956-58, Istanbul AP, 1960; lectr. Lake Sumter C.C., 1989, Lake Sumter Jr. Coll., 1989. Author poetry on Middle East, 1959-64; Career Awareness, 1978; Listen Up, 1997-98. Vol. instr. U.S. citizenship classes, Okinawa, 1971-72; judge Gold Scholarships Okinawa Christian Schs., 1983, 84. Mem. Am. Fedn. Govt. Employees, Fla. Retired Educators, Order Ea. Star (organist; life mem. Shuri One in Okinawa and Trillium 208 in Wis.), Marinette Woman's Club (Wis., pres. 1949-51), Groveland Woman's Club (Fla.), Phi Delta Gamma. Episcopalian. Home: Brunswick, Md. Died May 2, 2006.

HAMLIN, DONALD LEWIS, civil engr.; b. Binghamton, N.Y., Feb. 10, 1932; s. Lewis P. and Juanita (Krager) H.; student U.S. Naval Acad.; m. Margaret Mary Allison, Feb. 14, 1953; children— Geoffrey, Richard. Chief survey, soil and design engr., resident engr. interstate hwy. system in N.Y., Md., Vt. and N.J., McFarland & Johnson, Inc., Binghamton, 1953-64; founder Donald L. Hamlin Cons. Engrs., Inc., Essex Junction, Vt., 1965, pres., 1965—. Regional dir. Nat. Ski Patrol, 1948-78; mem. Junction Planning Commn., 1966-74; mem. Chittenden County Regional Planning Commn., 1966-74, 79—, chmn., 1972-74; mem. State Vt. Emergency Med. Adv. Bd., 1978-80; mem. Essex Junction Rescue Squad, 1971-78; vice chmn. No. Vt. chpt. ARC, 1982-84. Served with USNR, 1947-48, USMC, 1949-52. Mem. Nat. Soc. Profl. Engrs., Soc. Am. Mil. Engrs., ASCE, Vt. Soc. Surveyors (pres. 1982-83), Am. Cons. Engrs. Council (pres. Vt. 1982) Am. Congress Surveying and Mapping, Am. Water Works Assn., Vt. Soc. Engrs. Clubs: Essex Junction Rotary, Ethan Allen of Burlington, Masons. Home: Essex Junction, Vt. Died May 11, 2006.

HAMMOCK, JOSEPH CULVER, psychologist, educator; b. Holly Pond, Ala., Sept. 20, 1926; s. Joseph Emmett and Katie Bell (Taylor) H.; m. Edna Hill Haynes, Sept. 10, 1947; children: Joseph Culver Jr., Baxter Haynes, Margaret Anne. Student, Birmingham So. Coll., 1944; BS, U. S.C., 1948, MA, 1950; PhD, U. Tenn., 1953. Instr. U. S.C., 1949-50; psychometrician U. Tenn., 1951-52; research psychologist Human Resources Rsch. Office, George Washington U., Washington, 1952-55; dir. research Air Def. Human Resources Rsch. Office, U.S. Army, 1956-59; research psychologist Bell Telephone Labs., Inc., Murray Hill, N.J., 1959-62; mem. faculty U. Ga., from 1955, prof. psychology, from 1962, head dept., 1962-69, dir. instructional research and devel., 1969-72; vice-chancellor for acad. devel. Univ. System Ga., 1974-76, cons. organizationsl and human resources devel. Served with USNR, 1944-47. Mem. Am. Psychol. Assn. (rep. to council), Southeastern Psychol. Assn. (pres., exec. com.), Ga. Psychol. Assn. (pres., bd. dirs.), Sigma Xi, Psi Chi, Sigma Alpha Epsilon, Omicron Delta Kappa. United Methodist. Lodge: Kiwanis. Home: Athens, Ga. Died July 10, 2007.

HAMMOND, GEORGE SIMMS, chemist, consultant; b. Auburn, Maine, May 22, 1921; s. Oswald Kenric and Marjorie (Thomas) Hammond; m. Marian Reese, June 8, 1945 (div. 1977); children: Kenric, Janet, Steven, Barbara, Jeremy; m. Eva L. Menger, May 22, 1977; stepchildren: Kirsten Menger-Anderson, Lenore Menger-Anderson. BS, Bates Coll., 1943; MS, PhD, Harvard U., 1947; DSc (hon.), Wittenberg U., 1972, Bates Coll., 1973; DHC (hon.), U. Ghent, 1973, Georgetown U., 1985, Bowling Green State U., 1990, Weizman Inst. Sci., 1993. Postdoctoral fellow UCLA, 1947—48; mem. faculty Iowa State Coll., 1948—58, prof. chemistry, 1956—58; prof. organic chemistry Calif. Inst. Tech., Pasadena, 1958—72, chmn. divsn. chemistry and chem. engring., 1968—72; Arthur Amos Noyes prof. chemistry; vice chancellor natural scis. U. Calif., Santa Cruz, 1972—74, prof. chemistry, 1972—78; exec. dir. for biosci., metals and ceramics Allied Corp., Morristown, NJ, 1978—88; cons., from 1988. Vis. assoc. prof. U. Ill., 1953; mem. chem. adv. panel NSF, 1962—65; fgn. sec. NAS, 1974—78. Author (with J.s. Fritz): Quantitative Organic Analysis, 1956; author: (with D.J. Cram) Organic Chemistry, 1958; author: (with J. Osteryoung, T. Crawford and H. Gray) Models in Chemical Science, 1971; co-editor: Advances in Photochemistry, 1961; editl. bd. Jour. Am. Chem. Soc., from 1967. Recipient James Flack Norris award, 1968, Nat. medal of sci., 1994, Othmer Gold medal, Chem. Heritage Found., 2003. Mem.: NAS (fgn. sec.), European Photochem. Soc., Inter-Am. Photochem. Soc., Materials Rsch. Soc., Am. Acad. Arts and Scis., Am. Chem. Soc. (award in petroleum chemistry 1960, Priestly medal 1976, Nat. medal of Sci. 1994, Seaborg medal 1994), Sigma Xi, Phi Beta Kappa. Home: Portland, Oreg. Died Oct. 5, 2005.

HAMON, GERARD YVES, publishing company executive; b. Caen, Calvados, France, July 26, 1943; s. Louis and Suzanne H.; m. Lana Elizabeth Taras, Sept. 5, 1970; children— Nathaniel, Christopher, Emmanuel License es Lettres, U. de Caen, 1965; Diplome, Inst. d'Etudes Politiques de Paris, 1969; MA in Polit. Sci., U. Pitts., 1970. Sales exec. Henry M. Snyder & Co., NYC, 1970-71; export sales mgr. Hachette, Paris, 1971-81; sus. rights mgr. Larousse, Paris, 1981-82; pres. Larousse & Co., NYC, from 1982, Gerard Hamon, Inc. books and periodicals. Soccer coach Larchmont Jr. Soccer League, N.Y., 1983-85 Travel grantee Fulbright Found., 1967; teaching fellow U. Pitts., 1967-68 Mem. French-Am. C. of C. (N.Y. chpt., bd. dirs. 1985), Alumni Assn. of Inst. Polit. Studies of Paris (N.Y.C. chpt., treas. 1985) Clubs: Larchmont Shore. Avocations: sailing; tennis. Home: Larchmont, NY. Died Mar. 21, 2007.

HAMPEL, ROBERT EDWARD, advertising executive; b. Cin., Apr. 29, 1941; s. John Edward and Ruth Elizabeth (Pister) H.; m. Nanci Jean Nau, Aug. 24, 1963; 1 child, Jeffrey Braam. BBA, U. Cin., 1964; MBA, U. Evansville, 1980. Asst. account mgr. Procter and Gamble, Balt., 1965, corp. forecaster Cin., 1966-68; asst. contr. Keller-Crescent Co., Evansville, Ind., 1968-71; dir. mgmt. info. svcs. Keller-Crescent div. Am. Standards, Evansville, 1971-76, exec. v.p. fin., 1976-85, sr. exec. v.p., 1985-86; sr. exec. v.p., sec., treas., CFO Keller-Crescent Co., Inc., Evansville, from 1987, bd. dirs. Bd. dirs. Hahn, Inc. Pres. Jr. Achievement of S.W. Ind., Evansville, 1976-77, Evansville Philharm., 1981-82; pres. United Way of S.W. Ind., 1988-89; bd. dirs. Evansville Mus. Arts and Scis., 1988-95, treas., 1987-88; treas. Evansville Regional Econ. Devel. Corp., 1994—. Mem. Nat. Assn. Accts. (pres. Evansville chpt. 1980-81, nat. bd. dirs. 1984-85, nat. com. 1985-87). Home: Naples, Fla. Died Mar. 18, 2007.

HAMPTON, WILLIAM WADE, III, lawyer, magistrate, consultant; b. Gainesville, Fla., Oct. 24, 1915; s. William Wade and Mae Romaine (McMillan) H.; m. Carol Dorothy Maples, Dec. 17, 1942; children— Dorothy Mae Hampton Loggins, Margaret Hampton Kauffman, William Wade, John Thomas. B.S.B.A., U. Fla., 1937, J.D., 1939. Bar: Fla. 1939. Assoc. Knight & Knight, Jacksonville, Fla., 1940; assoc. Jordan Lazonby & Dell, Gainesville, 1941, 46-50; sole practice, Gainesville, 1951—; judge Mcpl. Ct. Gainesville, 1954-73; magistrate judge U.S. Dist. Ct. No. Dist. Fla., 1974-93; v.p. Employers Service Corp., 1954, pres., to 1980; cons. to ins. service firm. Served to capt. U.S. Army, 1941-46. Decorated Bronze Star. Mem. 8th Jud. bar Assn., Fla. Bar, ABA, Am. Judicature Soc. Democrat. Episcopalian. Clubs: Rotary (Gainesville); Elks, Masons, Shriners. Home: Gainesville, Fla. Died May 2, 2006.

HAND, CADET HAMMOND, JR., retired marine biologist; b. Patchogue, NY, Apr. 23, 1920; s. Cadet Hammond and Myra (Wells) H.; m. Winifred Werdelin, June 6, 1942; children: Cadet Hammond III, Gary Alan. BS, U. Conn., 1946; MA, U. Calif., Berkeley, 1948, PhD, 1951. Instr. Mills Coll., 1948-50, asst. prof., 1950-51; rsch. biologist Scripps Inst. Oceanography, 1951-53; mem. faculty U. Calif. at Berkeley, 1953—2003, prof. zoology, 1963-85, prof. emeritus, 1985—2006; dir. Bodega Marine Lab., 1961-85; Cons. NIH, 1964-66, NSF, 1964-69; mem. atomic safety and licensing bd. panel Nuc. Regulatory Commn., 1971-92, adminstrv. judge atomic safety and licensing bd. panel, 1980-92; rsch. Bodega Marine-Lab., 1992—2003; ret., 2003. NSF sr. postdoctoral fellow, 1959-60; Guggenheim fellow, 1967-68 Contbr. articles to profl. jours. Fellow Calif. Acad. Scis.; mem. No. Calif. Malacozool. Soc. (pres. 1963-87), Soc. Systematic Zoology, Ecol. Soc. Am., Ray Soc. (Gt. Britain), Am. Soc. Zoologists (chmn. div. invertebrate zoology 1977-78), Am. Soc. Limnology and Oceanography. Home: Bodega Bay, Calif. Died Nov. 29, 2006.

HANGEN, JOHN, JR., former paper manufacturing company executive; b. Dayton, Ohio, Feb. 23, 1924; s. Cleo John and Glenna (Welsh) H.; m. Eleanor Mae Krauss, Mar. 2, 1946 (div. June 1976); children— Diane, Ronald; m. Beverly Arlene Hawn, May 7, 1977. Grad., Internat. Accountants Soc., 1950. With NCR Corp., Dayton, 1941-78, controller, 1961-64, v.p. finance, 1964-72, v.p. corp. affairs, 1972-75, sr. v.p. corp. affairs, 1975-77, sr. v.p. media products group Appleton, Wis., 1977-78; also dir.; chmn. bd., chief exec. officer Appleton Papers Inc. subs. BAT Industries, 1978-84. Bd. dirs. Standard Oil Co. Ohio Home: Troy, Ohio. Died Feb. 5, 2006.

HANKS, CARL THOMAS, oral pathology educator, researcher; b. Cushing, Okla., Aug. 10, 1939; s. John Carl and Ruby Jewel (Bias) H.; m. Judith Melinda Sharp, Dec. 30, 1961; children: Stephanie Brett, John Conrad. BS, Phillips U., 1961; DDS, Washington U., St. Louis, 1964; PhD, SUNY, Buffalo, 1970. Diplomate Am. Bd. Pathology. Asst. prof. oral pathology SUNY, Buffalo, 1969-70; with Sch. of Dentistry U. Mich., Ann Arbor, from 1970, assoc. prof. Sch. of Medicine, from 1978, prof. oral pathology Sch. of Dentistry, from 1979. Contbr. articles to profl. jours. Fogarty Found. Internat. Fellow, 1976. Mem. Internat. Assn. for Dental Rsch. (pres. sect. 1989—), Am. Acad. Oral Pathology, Nat. Tissue Culture Assn., AAAS, Pulp Biology Group. Democrat. Home: Ann Arbor, Mich. Died Sept. 14, 2006.

HANLINE, ALAN LEROY, public relations executive; b. Brigham City, Utah, June 13, 1933; s. Harry Leroy and Gladys (Hansen) Hanline; m. Mary Kirk Hanline, Feb. 4, 1955; children: Jeffrey Alan, Brian Dwight, Melinda Louise, Steven Robert. AS, Weber State Coll., 1959, BS, 1968; MEd, Brigham Young U., 1980. Mgr. pub. rels. Thiokol Chem. Corp., Brigham City, 1957—66; adminstr. program support Clearfield Job Corps, Utah, 1966—72; mgr. pub. rels. Amalgamated Sugar Co., Ogden, Utah, 1972—77; supr. vocat. tng. Weber State Coll. Ctr., Ogden, 1977—80; dir. pub. affairs Westminster Coll., Salt Lake City, from 1980; tng. cons. Am. Profl. Seminars, Salt Lake City, from 1983. Asst. prof. Westminster Coll., Brigham Young U., from 1980. Author: Little League Football Coaches Manual, 1966; contbr.: articles to profl. jours. Coach, dir. Little League Football/Baseball, Brigham City, 1956—59; bd. dirs. Utah Diabetes Found., from 1976, Sugar House C. of C., from 1983. Served with USN, 1952—56. Named Coach of Yr., Little League Football, 1962, 1965. Mem.: Internat. Assn. Bus. Communicators, Pub. Rels. Soc. Am. (accredited, 1st v.p. 1984), Phi Kappa Phi. Lds Ch. Home: Ogden, Utah. Died Mar. 9, 2007.

HANNUM, JOHN BERNE, retired federal judge; b. Chester, Pa., Mar. 19, 1915; s. John Berne and Helen (Weaver) H.; m. Nancy Penn Smith, Dec. 21, 1940; children: John Berne, Richard P.S., Carol A. (Mrs. Bruce O. Davidson). Grad., Lawrenceville Sch., 1934; student, Princeton U., 1934-37, Franklin and Marshall Coll., 1937-38; LLB, Dickinson Sch. Law, 1941; LLD (hon.), Widener U., 1976, Lincoln U., 1978, Dickinson Sch. Law, 1987. Bar: Pa. 1942. Ptnr., trial lawyer firm Pepper, Hamilton & Scheetz, Phila., 1955-69; judge Superior Ct. Pa., 1968-69, US Dist. Ct. (ea. dist.) Pa., 1969—84, sr. judge, 1984—2007. Mem. com. on adminstrn. fed. magistrates system Jud. Conf. U.S., 1975-81. Mem. commissary, past ch. advocate Episcopal Diocese Pa.; past mem. sch. bd., chmn. exec. com. Unionville-Chadds Ford Dist., Chester County, Pa., 1947-68; mem. Electoral Coll., 1956; chmn. Chester County (Pa.) Republican Com., 1962-64; mem. Pa. Republican Exec. Com., 1962-64; del. Pa. Constl. Conv., 1967-68, Rep. Nat. Conv., 1960; trustee Dickinson Sch. Law, Chester County Hosp., Widener U.; mem. regional panel White House Fellows. Served to lt. USN, 1941-45. Mem. ABA, Pa. Bar Assn., Justinian Soc. (hon.), State Soc. Cincinnati Pa. (hon.), Am. Judicature Soc. Episcopalian (vestry). Club: Abraham Lincoln Assn. (bd. dirs. 1987). Lodge: Masons. Died Apr. 23, 2007.

HANSEN, KATHRYN GERTRUDE, editor, retired state official; b. Gardner, Ill., May 24, 1912; d. Harry J. and Marguerite (Gaston) Hansen. BS with honors, U. Ill., 1934, MS, 1936. Sec. U. N.C., Chapel Hill, 1936—37; sec. Univ. H.S. U. Ill., Urbana, 1937—44, pers. asst., 1944—46, supr. tng. and activities, 1946—47, pers. officer, instr. psychology, 1947—52; exec. sec. U. Civil Svc. Sys., Ill., also sec. for merit bd. Ill., 1952—61, adminstrv. officer, sec. merit bd. Ill., 1961—68, dir. sys. Ill., 1968—72; law asst. Webber, Balbach, Theis and Follmer, P.C., Urbana, 1972—74. Author: (with others) A Plan of Position Classification for Colleges and Universities: A Classification Plan for Staff Positions at Colleges and Universities, Grundy-Corners, 1982, Sarah, A Documentary of Her Life and Times, 1984, Ninety Years with Fortnightly, Vols. I and II, an historical compilation, 1986, Vol. III, 1995, Whispers of Yesterday, 1989, Through the Years with the Champaign-Urbana Business and Professional Women's Club, 1912-33, 1993, My Heritage, 1995, Presbyterian Women of First Presbyterian Church, Champaign, Illinois, An Historical Documentary, 1870-1995, 1996, (with Patricia Phillips) Fifty Golden Years, Altrusa International of Champaign-Urbana, Illinois, 1950-2000, 2001, Heritage, Vision and Mission: The First Prebyterian Church, Champaign, Illinois, 1850-2000, 2005; editor: The Illini Worker, 1946-52, Campus Pathways, 1952-61, This is Your Civil Service Handbook, 1960-67; author, cons., editor publs. on personnel practices. Bd. dirs. U. YWCA, 1952-55, chmn., 1954-55; bd. dirs. Champaign-Urbana Symphony, 1978-81; mem., sec. Presbyn. Women 1st Presbyn Ch., Champaign, 1986-90, mem. coordinating team, 1986-91, hon. life mem., 1999. Mem. Coll. and Univ. Pers. Assn. for Human Resources (hon., life, editor jour. 1955-73, newsletter, internat. pres. 1967-68, nat. publs. award named in her honor 1987, Ill. State award 1996), Annuitants Assn. State Univs. Retirement Sys. Ill. (state sec.-treas. 1974-75), U. Ill. Found., Pres.'s Coun. (life), Laureate Cir., U. Ill. Alumni Assn. (life), Friends of U. Ill. Libr. (bd. dirs. 1987-91), Nat. League Am. Pen Women, AAUW (state 1st v.p. 1958-60, hon., life), Secretariat U. Ill. (life, named scholarship 1972—), Grundy County Hist. Soc. (life), Altrusa Internat., Fortnightly Club (Champaign-Urbana), Eastern Star, Delta Kappa Gamma (state pres. 1961-63), Phi Mu (life), Kappa Delta Pi, Kappa Tau Alpha Home: Champaign, Ill. Died July 26, 2006.

HANSEN, PER BRINCH, computer scientist, researcher; b. Copenhagen, Nov. 13, 1938; came to U.S., 1970, naturalized, 1992; s. Jorgen Brinch and Elsebeth (Ring) H.; m. Milena Marija Hrastar, Mar. 27, 1965; children: Mette, Thomas. MS, Tech. U. Denmark, Copenhagen, 1963, Dr.techn., 1978. Sys. programmer Regnecentralen, Copenhagen, 1963-70, mgr. software devel., 1967-70; rsch. assoc. Carnegie-Mellon U., Pitts. 1970-72; assoc. prof. Calif. Inst. Tech., Pasadena, 1972-76, chmn. dept. computer sci. U. So. Calif., LA, 1976-77, prof. 1976-84, Henry Salvatori prof., 1982-84; prof. U. Copenhagen 1984-87; disting. prof. Syracuse (N.Y.) U., from 1987. Cons Burroughs, Honeywell, IBM, JPL, Mostek, TRW, others. Author: Operating System Principles, 1973, The Architecture of Concurrent Programs, 1977, Programming a Personal Computer, 1982, On Pascal Compilers, 1985, Studies in Computational Science, 1995, The Search for Simplicity, 1996, Programming for Everyone, 1999, Classic Operating Systems, 2001, The Origin of Concurrent Programming, 2002, A Programmer's Story, 2005; mem. editl. bd. Acta Informatica, Annals of the History of Computing, Concurrency, Software, Lecture Notes in Computer Sci.; contbr. articles to profl. jours.; inventor programming langs. Concurrent Pascal, Edison, Joyce, SuperPascal. Recipient Chancellor's medal Syracuse U., 1989; grantee NSF, Army Rsch. Office, Office Naval Rsch., Rome Air Devel. Ctr. Fellow IEEE (life; Computer Pioneer award 2002). Avocations: history, photography, jazz. Home: Fayetteville, NY. Died July 31, 2007.

HANSEN, STEPHEN CHRISTIAN, banker; b. NYC, July 3, 1940; s. Norbert C. and Harriet C. H.; m. Ethel Olmsted, June 12, 1971; 1 son, Lee Christian. AB, Princeton U., 1962; LL.B., U. Va., 1966; postgrad., Brown U. Grad. Sch. Banking. Bar: N.Y. 1966. Assoc. Alexander & Green, NYC, 1966-68; mem. N.Y. State Legis., 1968-70; spl. asst. to under sec. US Dept. Housing & Urban Devel., Washington, 1970-73; spl. asst. to chmn. FDIC, Washington, 1973-76; sr. v.p. Dollar Bank FSB, Pitts., 1976-78, pres., 1978—82, pres., CEO, 1982—2007, chmn. emeritus, 2007. Chmn. Regional Indsl. Devel. Corp.; bd. dirs. Am. Respiratory Alliance, World Affairs Coun. Active Regional Air Svc. Partnership; trustee Carnegie Inst.; bd. dirs. Carnegie Sci. Ctr.; bd. dir. Cleve. Dist. Pitts. Fed. Res. Mem.: Regional Investors Coun., NY State Bar Assn., Allegheny Conf. on Cmty. Devel. Home: Pittsburgh, Pa. Died Aug. 21, 2007.

HANSON, DONALD NORMAN, retired engineering educator; b. Minooka, Ill., Aug. 3, 1918; s. Charles M. and Nellie K. (Pope) H.; m. Sarah L. Hartman, Nov. 6, 1943; children: Charles Hartman, David Frederick, Kristin Ann. BS, U. Ill., 1940; MS, U. Wis., 1941, PhD, 1943. Mem. faculty U. Wis., 1943-44, Kans. State U., 1946; engr. Shell Devel. Co., 1944-46; mem. faculty U. Calif., Berkeley, 1947—87, prof. chem. engring., 1958—87, prof. emeritus, 1987—2007, chmn. dept., 1963-67. Vis. prof. U. Philippines, 1956-58 Author: (with others) Computation of Multistage Separation Processes, 1961. Recipient Disting. Teaching award, U. Calif Berkeley, 1986. Mem. Am. Inst. Chem. Engrs., Am. Chem. Soc., Sigma Xi, Delta Sigma Phi, Alpha Chi Sigma, Tau Beta Pi. Home: Orinda, Calif. Died Jan. 11, 2007.

HANSON, DORIS J., state legislator; b. Oct. 24, 1925; Student, U. Wis. Former bus. mgr., now v.p. real estate co.; mem. from dist. 48 Wis. State Assembly, Madison, 1992-98; exec. dir. Teach Wis., Madison, from 1998. Former sec., now pres. Village of McFarland, Wis.; former chairwoman Dane County Regional Airport Commn. Home: Monona, Wis. Died Nov. 8, 2006.

HANSON, JOHN BERNARD, retired botanist, agronomy and plant biology educator; b. Denver, Mar. 24, 1918; BA, U. Colo., 1948; MS, State Coll. Wash., 1950, PhD in Botany, 1952. Asst. State Coll. Wash., 1948-51; NRC fellow Calif. Inst. Tech., 1952-53; from asst. prof. to prof. U. Ill., Urbana, 1953-85, head dept. botany, 1967-77, prof. emeritus agronomy and plant biology, from 1985. Fulbright Rsch. scholar Waite Agr. Experimental Sta., Australia, 1959-60; NATO sr. fellow U. East Anglia, Eng., 1968. Mem. Am. Soc. Plant Physiologists (Adolph E. Gude Jr. award 1989). Home: Urbana, Ill. Died Oct. 23, 2006.

HANSON, ROBERT DELOLLE, retired lawyer; b. Harrisburg, Pa., Dec. 13, 1916; s. Henry W. A. and Elizabeth (Painter) H.; m. Barbara Esmer, Apr. 22, 1949 (dec. Mar. 2000). BA, Gettysburg Coll., 1939; LLB, Dickinson Law Sch., 1942. Bar: Pa. 1942. Pvt. practice, Harrisburg, 1946-98; solicitor Dauphin County, 1958-76, Dauphin County Redevel. Authority, 1959-98; et. Pres. coun. of congregation Luth. Ch., 1953-55, 57-59; pres. Family and Children's Svc. of Harrisburg, 1956-57; mem. Harrisburg Sch. Bd., 1952-57, Dauphin County Housing Authority, 1960-98; gen. chmn. Tri-County United Fund, 1969, pres., 1971-72; trustee Gettysburg Coll., 1974—, sec., 1980, vice chmn., 1983-86; pres. Keystone area coun. Boy Scouts Am., 1980-82. Maj. inf. AUS, 1942-46, ETO. Decorated Bronze Star, Purple Heart; recipient Silver Beaver award Boy Scouts Am., 1980, Eagle award Boy Scouts Am., 1990, Alexis de Tocqueville award United Way of Am., 1991, Others award Salvation Army, 1992, Lavern Brenneman award Gettysburg Coll., 1996, Wisdom award of honor The Wisdom Soc. for the Advancement of Knowledge, Learning and Rsch. in Edn., 1999. Mem. ABA, Pa. Bar Assn. (sec., treas. taxation sect. 1948-59), Dauphin County Bar Assn. (dir. 1958-59), Gettysburg Coll. Alumni Assn. (treas. 1958-59, v.p. 1968-71, pres. 1971-72), Masons (33d degree, past master, pres. bd. trustees 1982-85), Execs. Club (pres. 1953), Harrisburg Rotary (pres. 1979). Lutheran. Home: Harrisburg, Pa. Died Apr. 2006.

HANSON, ROBERT JOHN, educator; b. Dubuque, Iowa, Oct. 10, 1918; s. Peter John and Esther Anna (Flynn) H.; m. Josephine Corpstein, June 30, 1943; children— Robert John, David J., Peter T., Christina A. B.S.E.E., U.S. Naval Acad., 1941; M.B.A., U. So. Calif., 1967; postgrad. George Washington U., 1959, U. Va., 1962, UCLA, 1963-64. Commd. ensign U.S. Navy, 1941, advanced through grades to capt., 1963, ret., 1968; with McDonnell Douglas, Huntington Beach, Calif., 1968-70; faculty Los Angeles Harbor Coll., 1970—, prof. acctg., 1974—; prof. naval sci. U. So. Calif., Los Angeles, 1964-67. Mem. Assn. Naval Aviation, Ret. Officers Assn., Naval Acad. Alumni Assn., Skull and Dagger Soc. Roman Catholic. Clubs: So. Calif. Golf Assn., K.C. Home: Palos Verdes Peninsula, Calif. Died Feb. 7, 2006.

HARA, ERNEST HIDEO, architect; b. Honolulu, Nov. 15, 1909; s. Kaichi and Maki (Yamane) H.; m. Claire Hanako Nishigawa, Nov. 27, 1937; children— John Masayuki, Ann Misayo, Michael Takao B.Arch., U. So. Calif., 1935. Registered architect. Architect Ernest H. Hara, Honolulu, 1941-56; pres. Ernest H. Hara & Assocs., Inc., Honolulu, from 1957. Trustee Punahou Sch., Honolulu, 1969-85, Honolulu Acad. Arts, Honolulu, 1967-81, Found. for Study in Hawaii and Abroad, Honolulu, 1969; mem. Japan-Hawaii Econ. Council, Honolulu, 1971— Recipient Fourth Class Order of the Rising Sun, Japanese Govt., 1984. Fellow AIA Clubs: Waialae Country, Pacific (Honolulu). Died Nov. 19, 2006.

HARBIN, OTIS LEE, county official; b. Toccoa, Ga., May 2, 1932; s. Claude Lee and Ruth (Thompson) H.; student pub. schs.; divorced. Enlisted in U.S. Army, 1950, advanced through ranks to staff sgt., 1968; service in Korea, W. Ger., Thailand and Vietnam; ret., 1971; instr. welding Airco Tech. Inst., Cleve., 1972, tng. supr., Balt., 1972-75, tng. dir., Pitts., 1976-77, edn. dir., 1978-79; with Dept. Lands and Bldgs., Allegheny County San. Authority, 1980-94, ret., 1994. Decorated Army Commendation medal. Mem. Am. Welding Soc., Indsl. Arts Assn. Allegheny County, Am. Legion, Nat. Rifle Assn., AMVETS. Baptist. Club: Masons. Home: Grayson, Ga. Died Apr. 21, 2007.

HARDER, VIRGIL EUGENE, business administration educator; b. Ness City, Kans., July 19, 1923; s. Walter J. and Fern B. (Pausch) H.; m. Dona Maurine Dobson, Feb. 4, 1951; children— Christine Elaine, Donald Walter. BS, MA, U. Iowa, 1950; PhD, U. Ill., 1958. Instr. bus. adminstrn. U. Ill., Urbana, 1950-55; asst. prof. U. Wash., Seattle, 1955-59, assoc. prof., 1959-67, prof., 1967-86, prof. emeritus, from 1986, asso. dean sch. bus. adminstrn., 1966-74; dir. Inst. Fin. Edn. Sch. for Exec. Devel., Seattle, 1974-83. With AUS, 1943—45. Fellow: Am. Bus. Communications Assn. (pres. 1965); mem.: Trail Blazers Club. Died Nov. 15, 2006.

HARDESTY, EGBERT RAILEY, retired engineering firm executive; b. Kansas City, Mo., July 25, 1915; s. Shortridge and Adelia V. (Ferrell) H.; m. Martha Elizabeth Josi, Oct. 11, 1940; children— Christopher, Pamela Hardesty Van Horn. B.C.E., Rensselaer Poly. Inst., 1940. Designer Waddell & Hardesty, NYC, 1940-42, Hardesty & Hanover, NYC, 1945-51, assoc. engr., 1953-58, ptnr., 1958-85, ret., 1986, cons., from 1986. Mem. Town of Mamaroneck (N.Y.) Bd. Zoning, Appeals., 1972-85; Vestryman St. John's Episcopal Ch., Larchmont, N.Y., 1972-75. Served to lt. Civil Engr. Corps USNR, 1942-45; to lt. comdr. 1951-53. Fellow ASCE (life mem., pres. met. sect. 1981-82, com. on sects. and dist. councils 1982-85, The John Fritz medal bd. of award 1982—), Am. Cons. Engrs. Council; mem. Am. Rd. Transp. Builders Assn. (life, dir. 1976-80, pres. planning and design div. 1976-77, Guy Kelcy award 1985) N.Y. Soc. Profl. Engrs. (life mem.), Internat. Bridge Tunnel Turnpike Assn., Am. Ry. Engring. Assn., Sigma Xi, Tau Beta Pi, Chi Epsilon Clubs: Larchmont Yacht. Home: Larchmont, NY. Died Jan. 30, 2006.

HARDING, CAROL GIBB, psychologist, educator; b. Mercer, Pa., July 2, 1943; d. Raymond E. and Edith Elizabeth (Martin) Gibb; m. L. Arthur Safer; children: Julie, Chris, Alan, Elizabeth, Mark. BS Edn., Indiana U. Pa., 1965, MS, 1966; PhD, U. Del., 1981. Tchr. pub. schs. Pa., N.Y., Del., 1965-80; prof. Loyola U., Chgo., from 1980, dir. Rsch. Ctr. for Children & Families, from 1987. Editor: Moral Dilemmas, 1987; contbr. articles to profl. jours. Home: Sarasota, Fla. Died Sept. 4, 2006.

HARDING, HURSHEL RUDOLPH, lawyer; b. Texico, N.Mex., Oct. 22, 1929; s. Nathan Robert and Ethel (McQuatters) H.; m. Joyce Yvonne Hart, Nov. 10, 1954; children: Deborah Joyce, David Randolph. Student, Tex. Tech U., 1948-51; JD, Baylor U., 1954. Bar: Tex. 1954. County atty., Palmer County, Tex., 1957-75; ptnr. Aldridge, Harding, Aycock & Atkinson, Farwell, Tex., from 1961. Contbr. articles to profl. jours. 1st lt. USAF, 1954-56. Mem. Tex. Bar Assn., 154th Jud. Dist. Bar Assn., Farwell C. of C. (pres. 1961-63, bd. dirs. 1963-66), Baylor Law Aluni Assn. (bd. dirs. 1974-76), Am. Rifle Assn., Masons, Lions (local pres. 1959-60), Phi Alpha Delta Democrat. Home: Brownwood, Tex. Died Feb. 25, 2006.

HARDING, JOHN CHARLES, III, manufacturing executive; b. Fall River, Mass., Feb. 28, 1937; s. John Charles and Alice (Wallace) H.; m. Elizabeth Katherine Donovan, Sept. 3, 1960; children: John Christopher, Elizabeth Ann, Daniel Joseph, Katherine Patricia, Margaret Mary, Richard Daniel, Christina Ann, Jennifer Kathleen, Laura Christine. BS, Lehigh U., 1959, MBA, 1961. With Price Waterhouse & Co., Boston, 1961—64, Plimpton Press div. McCall Corp., Norwood, Mass., 1964—66; asst. controller Dyson-Kissner Corp., 1966, v.p., controller, 1967—72; pres., CEO, bd. dirs. Bickford's Family Fare, Inc., Brighton, Mass., from 1972. Bd. dirs. Kearney Nat., Inc., NYC. Trustee Francis Ouimet Caddie Scholarship Fund, Weston, Mass., from 1977. Mem.: Nat. Restaurant Assn., Am. Inst. CPAs, Algonquin Club, Charles River Country Club, Kittansett Club, Beta Alpha Psi, Pi Gamma Mu, Beta Gamma Sigma. Republican. Roman Catholic. Home: Weston, Mass. Died Mar. 29, 2006.

HARDMAN, JOHN MALEY, pathologist; b. Matheson, Colo., Jan. 15, 1933; s. John Maley and Agness Scott (Hill) H.; m. Margaret V. Nesom, Feb. 27, 1978; children by previous marriage— John S., Shari L. BS, U. Colo., 1954, MD, 1958; MS, Baylor U., Waco, Tex., 1965. Commd. 1st lt. M.C. U.S. Army, 1958, advanced through grades to col., 1973; rotating intern (Walter Reed Army Med. Center), 1958-59; gen. pathology resident (Brooke Army Med. Center), 1959-63; neuropathology tng. (Armed Forces Inst. Pathology), 1965-69; service in Korea, 1963-64; chief dept. pathology (Walter Reed Army Med. Center), Washington, 1975-77; ret., 1977; prof. pathology, chmn. dept. John A. Burns Sch. Medicine, U. Hawaii, Manoa, from 1977, dir. residency program univ. integrated pathology residency program, 1978-85; dir. labs. Kapiolani-Children's Med. Center, Honolulu, from 1978. Cons. neuropathology St. Francis Hosp., Straub Clinic and Hosp., Kapiolani Med. Ctr., Tripler Army Med. Center; dir.-at-large Hawaii div. Am. Cancer Soc., 1971-75; hosp. coordinator Tripler Army Med. Center, 1974; adv. com. Pacific S.W. Regional Med. Library Service, 1978—; chmn. Western Regional Assn. Pathology Chmn., 1979-80; chmn. med. adv. com. Hawaii chpt. Multiple Sclerosis Soc., 1979— Editor: Compendium of Tests Available in HBS Clinical and Veterinary Laboratories, Vol. 5, 1976; contbr. articles med. to publs. Chmn. carnival com. Ft. Shafter Area Youth Activities Council, 1973; pres. Ft. Shafter-Tripler Dolphin Swim Club, 1972-73. Decorated Legion of Merit, Army Commendation medal, Army Meritorious Service medal; recipient Sir Henry Wellcome medal, 1968 Mem. Internat. Acad. Pathology, Coll. Am. Pathologists, Assn. Mil. Surgeons U.S., Am. Assn. Neuropathologists, Am. Assn. Pathologists and Bacteriologists, Am. Assn. Pathologists, Assn. Pathology Chmn., Hawaii Soc. Pathologists, Sigma Xi, Alpha Omega Alpha, Alpha Epsilon Delta, Rho Chi, Nu Sigma Nu. Clubs: Viking. Episcopalian. Home: Honolulu, Hawaii. Died May 17, 2006.

HARKIN, JAMES C., pathologist, educator; b. Fayette, Miss., Dec. 9, 1926; s. James C. and Ethel M. (Jones) H.; m. Gerda Van Leeuwen, Jan 27, 1962; 1 child, Graham K. Student, U. Colo., 1943-45, 47; MD cum laude, U. Nebr., 1951. Diplomate Am. Bd. Pathology. Intern, then resident U. Hosps., Cleve., 1951-55; fellow in neuropathology Montefiore Hosp., NYC, 1956; instr. asst. prof. Washington U., St. Louis, Mo., 1955-59; asst. prof. Cornell U., NYC, 1959-62; from assoc. prof. to prof. pathology Tulane U., New Orleans, from 1962. Vis. scientist U. Oxford, Eng., 1965; mem. pathology study sect. USPHS, Bethesda, Md., 1973; prof. Internat. Ctr. Med. Rsch. and Tng. U. del Valle, Cali, Colombia, 1969-75; vis. prof. Univ. del Zulia, Maracaibo, Venezuela, 1986; invited vis. lectr. in 9 univs. in the U.S., Eng. and Colombia. Author: Tumors of the Peripheral Nervous System, 1969; mem. editorial bd. USAF Inst. Pathology, Washington, 1966-67; contbr. 52 sci. papers. Pres. People to People Internat., New Orleans, 1965-66. Sgt. U.S Army, 1945-46. Rsch. grantee Nat. Multiple Sclerosis Soc., 1963-66. Fellow Coll. Am. Pathologists; mem. Am. Assn. Neuropathologists, Am. Assn. Pathologists, New Orleans Neurol. Soc. (pres. 1967-68), La. Soc. Electron Microscopy (pres. 1966-67). Avocation: painting. Home: Covington, La. Died Dec. 8, 2006.

HARKINS, JAMES CLARKEN, state official; b. Wilmington, Del., May 11, 1925; s. James F. and Ann Marie (Clarken) H.; m. Margaret Anne Ward, July 17, 1948; children— Suzanne Ward, Joseph Thomas. Student, U. Del., 1945-48. Supr. stores E.I. duPont de Nemours & Co., Wilmington, Del., 1948-63; sec.-treas., owner Wrecking & Resale Distbrs., Wilmington, 1963-68; bridge supt. Delaware River & Bay Authority, New Castle, 1968-82; gen. mgr. Del. Meml. Bridge, New Castle, 1982—; dir. Del. Safety Council, 1984—; trustee N.J. Safety Council, Newark, 1982—. Commr., Del. Alcoholic Beverage Control Comm., 1965-75; chmn. Internat. Com. to Study A.B.C. Laws, Washington, 1972; pres. Nat. Conf. State Liquor Adminstrs., 1974-75; dir. Internat. Bridge, Toll and Tunnel Assn., 1982—. Served with U.S. Army, 1943-45; ETO. Democrat. Roman Catholic. Clubs: University, Whist. Home: Wilmington, Del. Died Sept. 14, 2006.

HARLAN, RIDGE LATIMER, corporate executive; b. Pilot Grove, Mo., Feb. 25, 1917; s. George B. and Dale (Latimer) H.; m. Barbara Hawley, Oct. 7, 1939 (div.); children: Brooke, Holly Ann, Robert Ridge; m. Marjory Folinsbee, June 4, 1976. BJ, U. Mo., 1939; postgrad., Harvard U., 1943, Colo. U., 1945—46, Stanford U., 1965. Pres. Barnes-Hind Pharms., Inc., 1972—76; prin. Harlan & Clucas, Inc., San Francisco, 1968—82; pres. Charila Found., 1969—73; chmn. bd., pres. Flores de las Americas, 1979—81; chmn. Millenium Systems, Inc., 1978—82; pres. Velo-Bind, Inc., 1983—85, chmn., CEO, 1985—87, chmn., bd. dirs., 1987—88. Chmn. Harlan Comm., from 1983; bd. dirs. Impulflor de Mex., Velo-Bind Inc., Bishop, Inc. Lt. (j.g.) USNR, 1943—46. Mem.: Assn. Corp. Growth (bd. dir.), Nat. Investor Rels. Inst. (bd. dir.), Boulders Club Ariz., Family Club San Francisco, Olympic Club, Kappa Tau Alpha, Alpha Delta Sigma. Home: Ennis, Mont. Died Jan. 3, 2006.

HARLAN, ROSS EDGAR, retired utility company executive, writer, lecturer, consultant; b. Poteau, Okla., July 11, 1919; s. Edgar Leslie and Leola (Carter) H.; m. Margaret Burns, May 31, 1942; children: Raymond Carter, Rosemary, Marvin Allen, Scott Lee. Student, Southeastern Okla. State U., 1937-38, Eastern Okla. State Coll., 1938-39; BSBA, Okla. State U., 1941; postgrad., Harvard U., 1942. Mem. faculty, coach Poteau High Sch., 1945-46, Poteau Jr. Coll., 1945-46; with Okla. Gas & Electric Co., Oklahoma City, 1946-85, mgr. rates and contracts dept., 1954-64, v.p., 1964-78, sr. v.p. div. mgmt., 1978-80, sr. v.p. adminstrn. & pub. affairs, 1980-85; ind. cons., writer Oklahoma City, 1985—2007. Cons. spl. books div. Reader's Digest, 1985—. Author: Strikes, 1946, Frontier Oklahoma-The Twin Territories, 1994. Pres. Okla. Council on Econ. Edn., 1977-79; pres. alumni bd. Ea. Okla. State Coll., 2000-03; bd. govs. Nat. Wrestling Hall of Fame, 1977-85; pres. adv. bd. Okla. State U. Coll. Bus. Assos.; adv. bd. Okla. State U. Tech. Inst.; bd. govs. Okla. State U. Found., bd. govs. Ea. Okla. State Coll. Devel. Found. With Army N.G., 1937-38; to lt. col. USAAF, 1941-46, Res. 1946-79. Named to Okla. State U. Coll. Bus. Hall of Fame, 1980, Ea. Okla. State Coll. Hall of Fame, 1992; recipient George Washington Honor medal Freedoms Found. Am., 1970, 2002, Disting. Alumnus award Okla. State U., 1979; named Boss of Yr., Nat. Secs. Assn., 1977; charter mem. Poteau (Okla.) Athletic Hall of Fame. Mem. Oklahoma City C. of C., Ea. Okla. State Coll. Alumni Assn. (pres. 2001-03), Toastmasters Internat. (comm. and leadership award 1985), Am. Legion, VFW, Mil. Order of World Wars (Silver Patrick Henry medallion 2000), Disabled Am. Vets Methodist. Died May 21, 2007.

HARLEY, ROBISON DOOLING, ophthalmologist, educator; b. Pleasantville, NJ, Feb. 27, 1911; s. Halvor L. and Alice (Robison) H.; children: Robison Dooling, Ardee R., Heather L., Halvor L. II, William W. B.Sc., Rutgers U., 1932; MD, U. Pa., 1936; PhD, U. Minn., 1949. Diplomate Am. Bd. Ophthalmology. Intern Phila. Gen. Hosp., 1936-38; fellowship Mayo Clinic, Rochester, Minn., 1938-41, jr. staff cons., 1941-42; pvt. practice as ophthalmologist and ophthalmic surgeon Atlantic City and Phila., 1947-67; attending surgeon, dir. ophthalmology St. Christopher's Hosp. for Children, Phila., 1958-70; chief surgeon Atlantic City Hosp., 1950-67; cons. Shore Meml. Hosp., Somers Point, 1958-67; attending surgeon Temple U. Hosp., Phila., 1947-87, Wills Eye Hosp. and Rsch. Inst. Cons. Betty Bacharach Home for Children; cons. surgeon Wills Eye Hosp.; attending surgeon, dir. dept. pediatrics and motility; formerly prof., chmn. ophthalmology, prof. pediatrics Temple U. Health Sci. Ctr., Phila.; now prof. emeritus; dir. Overseas Eye Programs: Project Hope, Care-Medico, Internat. Eye Surgeons, Project Orbis; adj.

prof. Thomas Jefferson U.; A.L. Morgan lectr., Toronto, 1972, Antonio Navas lectr., P.R., 1979, Frank Costenbader lectr., Washington., 1979; vol. over 20 countries Author 152 med. publs. indluding book chpts. and 4 textbooks; contbg. author: Textbook of Pediatrics, 1975, 77, 79, 98; contbr. chpt. Pediatric Ophthalmological Surgery; editor: Pediatric Ophthalmology, 1975, Pediatric Opthalmology textbook, 2 vols., 1983, 5th edit., 2005; contbr. articles to profl. jours., chpts. to books; mem. editorial bd.: Jour. Pediatric Ophthalmology and Strabismus. Mem. exec. bd. Atlantic area coun. Boy Scouts Am., 1949—; mem. Fight for Sight Inc., NYC, Retinitis Pigmentosa Found. Served to lt. col. AUS, 1942-47. Decorated Legion of Merit from Panama (Vasco Nunez de Balboa); recipient Outstanding Humanitarian award Am. Acad. Ophthalmology, Dallas, 2000, Hero of Medicine, Pride of the Profession award AMA, 2001; honoree Robison D. Harley MD, PhD Endowed Chair Pediat. Ophthalmology Alfred I. duPont Hosp. Children, 2006. Fellow ACS (gov. 1959-62), Am. Acad. Ophthalmology (assoc. sec. continuing edn., Outstanding Humanitarian award 2000); mem. Assn. Rsch. Ophthalmology, Pan-Am. Congress Ophthalmology, Am. Ophthal. Soc., Del. Assn. Blind. (pres.), Phi Beta Kappa, Sigma Xi. Clubs: Explorers N.Y.C., Brigantine (N.J.) Yacht (commodore); Union League (Phila.); Corinthian Yacht (Cape May, N.J.). Home: Wilmington, Del. Died Jan. 3, 2007.

HARLOW, ROBERT PALMER, management consultant, educator; b. Somerville, Mass., Dec. 29, 1935; s. Frank Webster and Alice Irene (Jenks) Harlow; m. Marcia Elizabeth Galvin, Mar. 10, 1962; 1 child, Robert Bradford. BSEE, The Citadel, 1957; MSEE, U. Pitts., 1963; MBA, U. Utah, 1976; grad., Indsl. Coll. Armed Forces, 1966. Field engr. Sperry Gyroscope, New Hyde Park, NY, 1957—62; systems analyst Def. Atomic Support Agy., Dept. Def., Albuquerque, 1963—66; div. mgr. contract mgmt. div. USAF, Avco Corp., Wilmington, Mass., 1966—69; commd. 2d lt., advanced through grades to maj. USAF, 1957—68; systems analyst Air Force Systems Command, USAF, 1969—72; comdr. 1801st Support Squadron Air Force Comm. Svc., Belton, Mo., 1972—74; dir. ops., program control ECA, Weisbaden, Germany, 1974—76; ret., 1976; prin. Westford Assocs., Harvard, Mass., from 1976. Mgmt. cons. Colonial Gas Credit Union; prof. fin. Salem State Coll.; dir. Harlow Ins. Agy., Milford, Conn. Columnist: The Weekly Investor in Beacon Publs., 1976—78. Regional dir. Gov.'s Coun. Info. Svcs., Boston, 1977—79; bd. dirs. Sgt. William Harlow Family Assn. Decorated Meritorious Svc. medal; recipient Kirschner Meml. award, New Haven, 1953. Mem.: IEEE, Am. Mgmt. Assn., Tau Beta Pi. Congregationalist. Home: West Palm Bch, Fla. Died June 15, 2007.

HARMS, LOUISE IVIE, librarian; b. Birmingham, Ala., June 25, 1924; d. Henry J. and Lola Bell (Hicks) Ivie; m. Willard D. Harms, Oct. 17, 1955 (dec.); children: Dennis Leon, Danial Lee (dec.), Willard Daniel. BS, U. Ala., 1944; BS in Libr. Sci., George Peabody Coll. for Tchrs., 1946. Asst. librarian Coll. of Edn. Libr., U. Ala., 1944-45; ref. asst. George Peabody Coll. for Tchrs., 1945-46; cataloguer Allegheny Coll., Meadville, Pa., 1946-47; 1st asst. cataloger U. Ark., Fayetteville, 1947; head cataloger Coll. of Edn., U. Ala., 1948-51; spl. svcs. librarian U.S. Army-Europe, 1951-55, 58-63; tchr. English Sweetwater High Sch. (Tenn.), 1963-64; asst. librarian Tenn. Wesleyan Coll., Athens, 1964-65, head librarian, 1965-87; cons. Olin Corp., Charleston, Tenn. Named Tchr. of Yr., U. Ala., 1950. Mem. Am. Libr. Assn., Southeastern Libr. Assn., Tenn. Libr. Assn., VFW Ladies Aux., Kappa Delta Pi, Alpha Beta Alpha. Democrat. Presbyterian. Home: Sweetwater, Tenn. Died Nov. 21, 2006.

HARNAPP, HARLAN LUCINE, minister; b. Columbus, Nebr., July 3, 1932; s. Oscar Henry and Ida Wilhelmina (Behrens) H.; m. Darleen Ann Graning, June 23, 1957; children: Debra, Brian, Heidi. Student, St. Paul's Coll., 1950-51; AA, St. John's Coll., 1952; BA, Theology diploma, Concordia Sem., St. Louis, 1957, MDiv, 1986. Ordained to ministry Luth. Ch.-Mo. Synod, 1957. Min. Luth. Ch, B.C., Can., 1957-59, S.D., 1959-65, Our Redeemer Ch., North Platte, Nebr., 1965-80, Beautiful Savior Ch., Broomfield, Colo., from 1980. Dist. steward Arapahoe Cir. So. Nebr., 1965-68; pastoral adviser Luth. Layman's League, S.D. Dist., 1960-62, Nebr. Dist., 1967-71, 2d v.p. Nebr., 1971-74, 3d v.p., 1974-75, 2d v.p., 1975-78, 1st v.p., 1978-80, Luth. Ch.-Mo. Synod Synodical Commn. on Appeals, 1983—; mem. 125th Anniversary of Synod Com., Nebr. Dist., 1972; chaplain S.D. Senate, 1964-65. Home: Broomfield, Colo. Died Apr. 30, 2006.

HARNETT, JAMES FRANCIS, contrabassist; b. Royal Oak, Mich., Apr. 18, 1921; s. Francis Timothy and Mary Ellen (Bethel) H.; m. Marie Frances Wecker, June 30, 1961; children: Andrew T., Benjamin T. Student, New Eng. Conservatory Music, 1939-41. Mem. Nat. Symphony Orch., summer 1947, Indpls. Symphony, 1947-49, N.C. Symphony, 1949-50, Cleve. Orch., 1950-55, Boston Pops, 1960, others; prin. Seattle Symphony, 1957-87, Seattle Opera, 1962-87; assn. prin. Seattle Sympnhony and Opera, 1988-91, Chautauqua Symphony, 1974-77; instr. U. Wash., Seattle, 1957-71, 74-77, Chautauqua Inst., 1974-77; author: (method & hist. survey of double bass) The New Virtuoso Technique, 2 Vols. Died Jan. 18, 2006.

HARPER, DONALD ASENDORF, lawyer; b. Andrews, SC, Sept. 10, 1946; s. Samuel Montgomery and Ann (Asendorf) H.; m. Marsha Miller, Feb. 20, 1971; children: Kathryn Croft, Miller Montgomery. BS in Econs., Clemson U., 1968; JD, U. S.C., 1971. Bar: S.C. 1971, U.S. Dist. Ct. S.C. 1974, U.S. Ct. Appeals (4th cir.) 1974. Minority counsel U.S. Senate Judiciary Com., Washington, 1972-73; exec. asst. U.S. Senator Strom Thurmond, Washington, 1973-74; asst. U.S. atty. U.S. Dept. Justice, Greenville, S.C., 1974-77; ptnr. Haynsworth, Marion, McKay & Guerard, Greenville, from 1977. Capt. USAF, 1971-72. Avocation: golf. Home: Greenville, SC. Died Mar. 1, 2007.

HARPER, JOHN EVERETT, JR., accountant; b. Warrenton, Ga., Apr. 16, 1943; s. John Everett and Sara Rebecca (Seymour) Harper; m. Judy Ann Stephens, Jan. 15, 1983; 1 child, John E. III; children: Jennifer Kathryn, John Richard. Student acctg., Bolen's Bus. U., 1965. CPA Ga. Acct. Bedingfield & McCutcheon, Augusta, 1962—75; controller Knox Mortgage Co., Augusta, 1975—76; acct. pvt. practice pub. acctg., Newnan, Ga., from 1976; v.p. fin., treas. Flex-On, Inc., Senoia, Ga., from 1980. Mem. Newnan C. of C. Mem.: Nat. Assn. Accts., Ga. Soc. CPAs, Am. Inst. CPAs, Eufaula Sailing Club, Masons, Elks, Rotary. Home: Newnan, Ga. Died May 28, 2007.

HARRELL, ROY G., JR., lawyer; b. Norfolk, Va., Sept. 14, 1944; s. Roy G. and Winifred B. H. BS with honors, The Citadel; LLB cum laude, Washington & Lee. Bar: Fla.; cert. in real property. Assoc. Jennings, Watts, Clarke & Hamilton, Jacksonville, Fla., 1971-75, Greene, Mann, Rowe, Stanton, Mastry & Burton, St. Petersburg, Fla., 1975-76, ptnr., 1976-83; founding ptnr. Baynard, Harrell, Ostow & Ulrich (formerly Baynard, Harrell, Mascara & Ostow), St. Petersburg, 1983-94; of counsel Carlton, Fields, Ward, Emmanuel, Smith & Cutler, P.A., St. Petersburg, 1994-98; ptnr. Holland & Knight LLP, St. Petersburg, from 1998. Coun. Am. Lawyer's Auxiliary, 1992-93. Notes editor Washington & Lee Law Review. Past chmn. governing bd. S.W. Fla. Water Mgmt. Dist., 1985-98; past co-chair Pinellas Anclote River Basin Bd.; former mem. policy com. Tampa Bay Nat. Estuary Program; former mem. Tampa Bay Water Coordinating Coun.; pres. United Way, Pinella County, 1986; grad. leadership St. Petersburg, 1976, Leadership Tampa Bay; past chmn. campus adv. bd. U. South Fla. Bayboro Campus; former bd. dirs. Bayfront Ctr. Found.; mem. Citizens Vision 2000; former bd. dirs. 1000 Friends of Fla.; immediate past chmn. bd. dirs. St. Anthony's Devel. Found.; former mem. bd. dirs. ARC, Tampa. Capt. U.S. Army, 1969-71. Recipient Leadership award Leadership St. Pete, 1986, Leadership award Nat. Assn. Leadership Orgn., 1986, PACE award Pinellas Emergency Mental Health Svcs. 1986, Human Svcs. award, 1987. Mem. ABA (mem. various coms.), Am. Coll. Mortgage Attys., Va. Bar Assn., Fla. Bar, St. Petersburg Bar Assn., Greater St. Petersburg C. of C. (Mem. of Yr. award 1981, pres. 1986-87), Leadership St. Pete Alumni Assn. (former chair bd. dirs.), Dragon Club, St. Petersburg Yacht Club, Suncoasters, Suncoast Tiger Bay Club, Anthonians (former pres.), Phi Sigma Alpha, Phi Alpha Delta. Died Jan. 25, 2006.

HARRINGTON, WILLIAM DAVID, utility executive; b. Medford, Mass., July 19, 1930; s. William David and Ann Emily (Raeke) H.; m. Mary Glenn Cardinal, Apr. 19, 1954; children— Kathleen, Carol, David, Gerard A in Elec. Engring., Northeastern U., 1959, BS in Engring. and Mgmt., 1961, MBA, 1978; PMD 17, Harvard U. Div. head Boston Edison Co., 1965-74, dept. head, 1974-79, v.p., 1979-82, sr. v.p., from 1982. Mem. council Northeastern U., Boston. Served as sgt. U.S. Army, 1952-54 Mem.: Beacon Soc. (Boston) (1st v.p.); Bear Hill Golf (Stoneham, Mass.). Republican. Roman Catholic. Avocations: tennis; sailing. Home: Naples, Fla. Died Feb. 10, 2007.

HARRIS, BILL J., utilities executive; b. Mill Creek, Okla., Oct. 17, 1924; s. John M. and Irene W. (Penner) H.; m. Margarett Maxine Howard, July 25, 1947; children: Deborah, Gerald. BS in Biol. Sci. and Physics, East Central State Coll., 1947; MS in Secondary Edn., Okla. State U., 1952. With Pub. Service Co. of Okla., 1955-76; area mgr. McAlester, 1962-72; v.p. adminstrn. Tulsa, 1972-75; v.p. fuel, 1975-76; pres. Transok Pipe Line Co., 1975-76; pres., chief operating officer Central & South West Corp., Dallas, from 1976, now vice chmn., dir., from 1987, also bd. dirs. Served with USAAF, 1943-45. Mem. Edison Electric Inst. (dir., com. on research) Clubs: Bent Tree Country, Tower, Chaparral, Gleneagles Country (Dallas). Lodges: Masons (32 degree). Democrat. Methodist. Home: Dallas, Tex. Died Oct. 7, 2006.

HARRIS, EDWIN FRIEDMAN, retail executive; b. St. Paul, Minn., Oct. 9, 1913; s. Barney and Clara (Friedman) Harris; m. Margery Zimmerman, July 1, 1976; children: Jon, Harris. BA, Macalester Coll., 1936. Pres. Harris Industries, Mpls., from 1938. Chmn. bd. Northwest Standard Products Co., Mpls., from 1954. Trustee Mt. Sinai Hosp., Mpls., from 1979, Macalester Coll., 1964; pres. Temple Israel, Mpls., 1974—75. Lt. comdr. USNR, 1943—46, PTO. Named to Athletic Hall of Fame, Macalester Coll., 1983; recipient Friends of Israel award, Jewish Nat. Fund, 1983. Mem.: Nat. Remodelers Assn. Minn. (pres. 1960—64, Man of Yr. 1977), Nat. Remodelers Assn. Am. (nat. v.p. 1960—64), Oak Ridge Country Club, Shriners, Masons. Home: Minneapolis, Minn. Died Sept. 4, 2006.

HARRIS, ELLEN STERN, foundation administrator, public policy educator, writer; b. LA, Nov. 2, 1929; d. Herman Jastro Stern and Geraldine (Rosenberg) Wayne; children: Tom, Jane. Instr. pub. affairs workshop Comm. Workers Am., LA, 1977—78; instr., program coord., moderator, guest lectr. UCLA; exec. dir. Pub. Access Prodrs. Acad., Beverly Hills, Calif.; consumer advocate columnist L.A. Times, 1971—78; consumer advisor Times Mirror Satellite Cable/Apple Prodns., 1981; prodr., host TV program Who's In Charge, Sta. KPFK-TV, 1979—80, Consumer Connection Sta. KCRW-TV, 1979; co-host consumer edn. TV series NBC, 1975. Trustee Sta. WETA-TV-AM, Washington, 1975-78; coord. Calif. Friends of Pub. Broadcasting, 1976-80; exec. sec. Coun. for Planning and Conservation, 1967-73, Friends of Santa Monica Mountains Parks, 1965-66; exec. dir. Fund for Environment, 1970-2006; asst. founder Ctr. for Study Dem. Insts., 1964; bd. dirs. Bay Inst. San Francisco, 1982-86, Friends of Beverly Hills Pub. Libr., 1982-83; mem. cable adv. com. Beverly Hills City coun., 1986, Mayor's adv. com. on Beverly Hills Water, 1986; adv. bd. Calif. Tomorrow, 1967-83, Urban Environ. Found., 1977-79, Town Hall of Calif. 1976-, L.A. Conservancy, 1978-; mem. AIA Land Use Task Force, 1972-74; bd. dirs. Met. Water Dist. So. Calif., 1978-81; chmn. Mayor's adv. com. on cable TV, City of Beverly Hills, 1982-83, 85; vice chmn. Calif. Coastal Zone Conservation Commn., 1972-76; mem. spl. com. access conveners City of L.A., 1990-; mem. EMF consensus group Calif. Pub. Utilities Commn., 1991-92; mem. recreation and pks. commn. City of Beverly Hills, 1991-96, vice chair, 1991-92, chair, 1992-93; com. mem. dept. tech., 1996-; mem. electromagnetic fields sci. adv. cons. Calif. Dept. Health Svcs., 1994-; mem. Fed. Coastal Zone Mgmt. Adv. Com., 1973-75, L.A. County Environ. Quality Control Com., 1970-73, L.A. County Beach Adv. Com., 1970-73, L.A.-Ventura Regional Water Quality Control Bd., 1966-70, Dist. Atty.'s Cmty. Adv. Coun. for L.A. County, 1976-82, Calif. Atty. Gen.'s Environ. Task Force, 1970-79, others. Named Woman of Yr. L.A. Times, 1969, Voorhis Disting. Visitor Claremont Colls. and Calif. Poly., 1991; honored by Sierra Club, 1969, Audubon Soc., 1969, Clarence Darrow Found., 1978; recipient Am. Motors Conservation award, 1970, World Comm. award UN Assn., 1983. Died Jan. 2, 2006.

HARRIS, HENRY WOOD, cable television executive; b. Raleigh, NC, June 11, 1938; s. Henry W. and Charlotte Louise (Allen) H.; m. Mary Margaret Durham, June 10, 1960; children— Stephen Gregory, Charlotte Durham. BS in Bus. Adminstrn, U. N.C., 1960, MBA, 1964. Loan officer Trust Co. Bank, Atlanta, 1964-66; operating v.p. Cox Cable Communications Co., Atlanta, 1966-69, pres., 1969-79; exec. v.p. Cox Broadcasting Corp., Atlanta, 1977-79; pres. Metrovision, Inc., Atlanta, 1979-95; divsn. pres. Time Warner Cable, Atlanta, from 1995. Mem. lay adv. bd. Marist Sch.; deacon Peachtree Presbyterian Ch. Served with USMCR, 1960-63. Mem. Phi Beta Kappa, Phi Eta Sigma. Clubs: Capital City. Home: Atlanta, Ga. Died July 29, 2006.

HARRIS, JOHN WILLIAM, hematologist, educator; b. Boston, Mar. 30, 1920; s. Ulysses Sylvester and Lillian (Dennett) H.; m. Stephanie Jean Bunting, Apr. 7, 1951; children: Wendy Alexandra, Alison Dennett, Stephen Bunting. BS, Trinity Coll., Hartford, Conn., 1941; MD, Harvard, 1944. Intern Boston City Hosp., 1944-45, resident, 1947-48; research fellow medicine Thorndike Meml. Lab., Harvard Med. Sch., 1948-51, research assoc., 1951-52; sr. instr. medicine Western Res. U., Cleve., 1952-54, asst. prof., 1954-57, assoc. prof., 1957-62, prof., 1962-99, prof. emeritus, from 1999. Hematologist, vis. physician Cleve. Met. Gen. Hosp., 1952-99, assoc. dir. dept. medicine, 1967-81; attending physician VA Hosp., Cleve., 1953-58, sr. attending physician hematology, 1959-99; cons. staff Lutheran Hosp., 1965-99; mem. hematology study sect. NIH, 1962-66, chmn., 1983-85, mem. hematology tng. grants com., 1969-73; mem. com. blood and transfusion Nat. Acad. Scis.-NRC, 1963-65; chmn. Merit Rev. Bd. in Hematology, Med. Research Service, VA, 1977-80 Served to capt. U.S. Army, 1945-47. Recipient USPHS Research Career award, 1962, Martin Luther King, Jr. award for outstanding research in sickle cell anemia, 1972; Alfred Stengel Research fellow ACP, 1951-52; Markle scholar in medicine, 1955-60; named to Cleve. Med. Hall of Fame, 1998. Fellow ACP, Internat. Soc. Hematology (nat. counselor, Interam. div. 1986); mem. AAAS, Am. Fedn. Clin. Research, Am. Soc. Clin. Investigation (past v.p.), Central Soc. Clin. Research, Soc. Exptl. Biology and Medicine, Am. Soc. Hematology (pres. 1981-82), Acad. Medicine Cleve., Assn. Am. Physicians, Phi Beta Kappa, Alpha Omega Alpha. Home: Cleveland, Ohio. Died May 3, 2006.

HARRIS, MARK, writer, retired literature educator; b. Mt. Vernon, NY, Nov. 19, 1922; s. Carlyle and Ruth (Klausner) Finkelstein; m. Josephine Horen, Mar. 17, 1946; children: Hester Jill, Anthony Wynn, Henry Adam. BA, U. Denver, 1950, MA, 1951; PhD, U. Minn., 1956; L.H.D. (hon.), Ill. Wesleyan U., 1974. Reporter Port Chester (N.Y.) Item, 1944, PM, NYC, 1945, I.N.S., St. Louis, 1945-46; prof. English San Francisco State Coll., 1954-68, Purdue U., 1967-70; mem. faculty Calif. Inst. Arts, Valencia, 1970-73, Immaculate Heart Coll., Los Angeles, 1973-74, U. So. Calif., 1973-75, U. Pitts., 1975-80; prof. English Ariz. State U., Tempe, 1980—2002. Vis. prof. Brandeis U., 1963 Author: (novels) Trumpet to the World, 1946, City of Discontent, 1952, The Southpaw, 1953, Bang the Drum Slowly, 1956, Something About a Soldier, 1957, A Ticket for a Seamstitch, 1957, Wake Up, Stupid, 1959, The Goy, 1970, Killing Everybody, 1973, It Looked Like For Ever, 1979, Lying in Bed, 1984, Speed, 1990, The Tale Maker, 1994; (non-fiction) Mark the Glove Boy, 1964, Twentyone Twice: A Journal, 1966, (autobiography) Best Father Ever Invented, 1976, Short Work of It: Selected Writing, 1979; Saul Bellow: Drumlin Woodchuck, 1980; editor abridged version of six vols. of Boswell's papers: The Heart of Boswell, 1981, Diamond, 1994; (plays) Friedman & Son, 1963; also screen plays, essays, reviews, articles, stories; subject of Norman Lavers book Mark Harris, 1978 Mem. San Francisco Art Commn., 1961-64. Served with AUS, 1943-44. Recipient award Nat. Inst. Arts and Letters, 1961, Profl. Achievement award U. Denver Alumni Assn., 1984; Fulbright prof. Japan, 1957; Ford Found. grantee, 1960; Guggenheim Found. fellow, 1965, 74; Nat. Endowment Arts grantee, 1966; numerous other invitations and awards. Died May 30, 2007.

HARRIS, ROBERT L., welding engineer; b. Plattsburgh, N.Y. May 1, 1927; s. Platt John and Nora Mary (Trombley) H.; m. Nannette Ellen Hollister, Sept. 26, 1948; children— Nancy Elaine, Alan Robert, David Paul. Student, Rutgers U.; grad. Modern Welding Sch., Schenectady, N.Y., 1948. Welder, Alco Products Inc., Schenectady, 1948-52, Hi-Grade Welding, Amsterdam, N.Y., 1952-53; welding technician Gen. Electric Co. Schenectady, 1953-57, metallurgy specialist, 1962-64, welding devel. engr. Alco Products Inc., Schenectady, 1957-62; welding engr. Electric Boat div. Gen. Dynamics, Groton, Conn., 1964-65; supr. Combustion Engring. Inc., Chattanooga, Tenn., 1965-69; mgr. welding dept. Badenhausen Corp. div. Riley Stoker Corp., Cornwells Heights, Pa., 1969-70; staff materials engr TVA, Knoxville, 1970-75, supr. welding engring. staff, 1975-81 mgr. nuclear quality assurance Bristol Steel & Iron Works, Va. 1975; lead welding engr. Butler Services Group Inc., Midland Mich., 1982-83; welding quality engr. Piping Design Services Moscow, Ohio, 1983-84; lead welding engr. So. Calif. Edison Co., San Onofre Nuclear Generating Sta., 1984-86. Served to cpl. U.S. Army, 1945-46. Recipient numerous awards for profl excellence. Mem. ASME, Am. Welding Soc. (cert. welding inspector, Dist. Meritorious award 1982), Am. Soc. Metals Republican. Presbyterian. Club: Deane Hill Country (Knoxville). Avocations: golf; bowling. Died Oct. 26, 2006.

HARRIS, STANLEY GALE, JR., banker; b. Chgo., June 19 1918; s. Stanley Gale and Muriel (Bent) H.; children: John Trumbull, Thomas Bartlett; m. Alice Harwood, Nov. 4, 1972 Student, Yale, 1936-38; certificate in indsl. adminstrn, Harvard Grad. Sch. Bus. Adminstrn., 1943. With Nat. Bank Commerce Seattle, 1939-41, Carnegie-Ill. Steel Corp., 1943-44; with Harri Trust & Savs. Bank, Chgo., from 1944; formerly chmn. bd., nov dir.; Harris Bankcorp Inc., now dir. Life trustee Rush-Presbyn.-St. Luke's Med. Center, Ill. Children's Home and Aid Soc.; trustee U. Chgo. Mem.: Chicago (Chgo.), Commercial (Chgo.), Casino (Chgo.), Little Wheels (Chgo.), Tavern (Chgo.), Yale (Chgo.); Skokie Country. Home: Chicago, Ill. Died Oct. 17, 2005.

HARRISON, MAURICE R., JR., construction company executive; b. Des Moines, Iowa, Aug. 1, 1918; s. Maurice Rowlen and Helen (Cowles) H.; m. Mae McDonald; children: Maurice R., Michael J., Peter R. BS in Archtl. Engring., Civil Engring., Iowa State U., 1940. Registered profl. engr. Engr. M.R. Harrison Constrn. Corp., Miami, Fla., 1940-55, pres., 1955-72, chmn. bd., chief exec. officer, from 1972. Mem. Profl. Engrs. Assn. S.E. Fla. (pres. 1955-56), Young Pres.'s Orgn. (pres. 1960), Am. Auto. Assn. (chmn. 1977-78), Associated Gen. Contractors (pres. 1952-53), Execs. Assn. Clubs: Rotary (pres. 1959), Miami, Bath. Democrat. Presbyterian. Home: Delray Beach, Fla. Died Aug. 12, 2007.

HARRISON, PAUL MANSFIELD, educator, minister; b. Phila., May 7, 1923; s. Robert Leslie and Ruth (Boyd) H.; m. Nancy Jane Romig, Sept. 11, 1948; children— Cynthia Lee, John Robert. B.A., Pa. State U., 1949; B.D., Colgate-Rochester Div. Sch., 1952; Ph.D., Yale, 1958. Ordained to ministry Am. Baptist Conv., 1952. Instr., then asst. prof. religion Princeton U., 1956-63; vis. lectr. Union Theol. Sem., N.Y.C., 1961-62; lectr. Inst. Religious and Social Studies, Jewish Theol. Sem. Am., 1961-66; mem. faculty Pa. State U., 1963-88, prof. sociology of religion and religious ethics, 1971-88, prof. emeritus, 1988—; rsch. dir. study theol. edn. United Ch. Christ, 1966-67. Author: Authority and Power in the Free Church Tradition, 2d edit., 1971. Melcancthon W. Jacobus instr. Princeton, 1958-60; Proctor Gamble fellow, 1961-62; Enoch Pond lectr. Bangor (Maine) Theol. Sem., 1969. Mem. Am. Sociol. Assn., Soc. Sci. Study Religion, Am. Soc. Christian Social Ethics Profs., New Haven Theol. Discussion Group, N. Central Assn. Colls. and Secondary Schs. Died July 26, 2007.

HARRISON, TERENCE, animation director, animator, educator; b. Peterborough, Eng., Mar. 19, 1931; came to U.S., 1968; Student, Cambridge U., Eng., 1950-52; tchr.'s credential, Avery Hill Coll. Edn., London, 1973. Animator Halas & Batchelor Animation Ltd., London, 1955-67; studio animation dir. Trillium Prodns. Ltd., Toronto, 1967-68; animator Hanna-Barbera, Hollywood, Calif., 1968-69; directing animator Nat. Film Bd. Can., Montreal, 1970-71; unit dir. Halas & Batchelor Animation Ltd., London, 1972-73; animator Potterton Prodns., Montreal, 1974; animation/storyboard artist Melendez Prodns., London, 1975; feature animator Nepenthe Prodns., London, 1976; animator, animation director Hanna-Barbera, Hollywood, 1977-79, studio animation supr. San Francisco, 1980, animation dir. Hollywood, 1981; feature animator Walt Disney Prodns., Burbank, Calif., 1982-86; animation dir. Walt Disney TV Animation, Burbank, from 1986. Animation dir. (TV series) Winnie the Pooh, 1989-90 (Emmy award). Died Feb. 28, 2007.

HARSANYI, JANICE, retired soprano, educator; b. Arlington, Mass., July 15, 1929; d. Edward and Thelma (Jacobs) Morris; m. Nicholas Harsanyi, Apr. 19, 1952; 1 son, Peter Michael. BMus, Westminster Choir Coll., 1951; postgrad., Phila. Acad. Vocal Arts, 1952-54. Voice tchr. Westminster Choir Coll., Princeton, NJ, 1951-63, chmn. voice dept., 1963-65; lectr. music Princeton Theol. Sem., 1956-63; voice tchr. summer sessions U. Mich., 1965-70; artist-in-residence Interlochen Arts Acad., 1967-70; voice tchr. N.C. Sch. Arts, Winston-Salem, 1971-78; music faculty Salem Coll., 1973-76; condr. voice master classes, choral clinics various colls., from 1954; prof. voice Fla. State U., Tallahassee, from 1978, chmn. dept., 1979-83; ret., 2005. Concert singer, 1954—, debut, Phila. Orch., 1958; appearances with, Am., Detroit, Houston, Minn., Nat., Symphony of Air orchs., Bach Aria Group, 1967-68, maj. music festivals, U.S., 1960—; toured with, Piedmont Chamber Orch., 1971-78, concerts and recitals, in major U.S. cities, also in Belgium, Eng., Ger., Italy, Switzerland and Sweden; rec. artist, Columbia, Decca, CRI records. Mem. Nat. Assn. Tchrs. Singing, Music Tchrs. Nat. Assn., Coll. Music Soc., Riemenschneider Bach Inst., Sigma Alpha Iota, Pi Kappa Lambda. Home: Tallahassee, Fla. Died Mar. 21, 2007.

HART, JACK, lawyer; b. NYC, Jan. 13, 1909; s. Harry and Clara (Mersack) H.; m. Rose Ratner, Aug. 15, 1937; children-William, Jane. BA, Coll. City N.Y., 1930; LL.B., Columbia, 1933. Bar: N.Y. bar 1934. Practice in, NYC, 1933—; assoc. George Z. Medalie, 1933-38; pvt. practice, 1938-50; ptnr. Hart & Hume and predecessor firms, from 1950. Mem. ABA, Internat. Assn. Ins. Counsel, Princeton Club. Home: New York, NY. Died July 24, 2006.

HART, JOHNNY (JOHN LEWIS HART), cartoonist; b. Endicott, NY, Feb. 18, 1931; s. Irwin James and Grace Ann (Brown) H.; m. Bobby Jane Hatcher, Apr. 26, 1952; children: Patti Sue, Perri Ann. Student pub. schs. Free-lance cartoonist, 1954-58; commerical artist GE, Johnson City, NY, 1957-58; syndicated cartoonist, 1958—2007. Comic strip, B.C., nationally syndicated, 1958-2007, (with Brant Parker) The Wizard of Id, 1964-2007; collections include: Hey B.C., 1958, Hurray for B.C., 1958, Back to B.C., 1959, B.C. Strikes Back, 1961, What's New B.C., 1962, B.C.- Big Wheel, 1963, B.C. is Alive and Well, 1964, The King is a Fink, 1964, Take a Bow, B.C., 1965, The Wonderous Wizard of Id, 1965, B.C. on the Rocks, 1966, The Peasants are Revolting, 1966, B.C. Right On, 1967, B.C Cave In, 1967, Remember the Golden Rule, 1967, There's A Fly in My Swill, 1967, The Wizard's Back, 1968, B.C., 1972, B.C. Cartoon Book, 1973. Served with USAF, 1950-53, Korea. Recipient Yellow Kid award, 1970; Internat. Congress Comics for best cartoonist, Lucca, Italy; Best Humor Strip award, French Comics Council, 1971; Public Service Award, NASA, 1972. Mem. Nat. Comics Council, Nat. Cartoonists Soc. (Best Humor Strip awards, 1967-71, Outstanding Cartoonist of Year (Reuben Award), 1968) Achievements include premiering nationally pub. cartoon in Sat. Eve. Post, 1954. Died Apr. 7, 2007.

HART, KITTY CARLISLE, performing arts association administrator; b. New Orleans, Sept. 3, 1910; d. Joseph and Hortense (Holtzman) Conn; m. Moss Hart, Aug. 10, 1946 (dec. Dec. 20, 1961); children: Christopher, Cathy. Student, London Sch. Econs., Royal Acad. Dramatic Arts; DFA (hon.), Coll. New Rochelle; DHL (hon.), Hartwick Coll.; LHD (hon.), Manhattan Coll., Amherst Coll., Curtis Inst. Music. Chmn. NY State Council on the Arts, 1976—96. Actress: (films) Murder at the Vanities, 1934, She Loves Me Not, 1934, Here Is My Heart, 1934, A Night at the Opera, 1936, Larceny With Music, 1943, Radio Days, 1987, Six Degrees of Separation, 1993; Broadway theatre appearance French Without Tears, 1938, The Night of January 16th, 1939, Walk With Music, 1940, The Merry Widow, 1943, Design For Living, 1943, There's Always Juliet, 1943, The Rape of Lucretia, 1948, The Man Who Came to Dinner, 1949, Anniversary Waltz, 1954, Die Fledermaus, 1966, On Your Toes, 1983-84; singer, Met. Opera; one woman show on Great Performances My Broadway Memories, 1999; panelist (TV game show) To Tell the Truth, 1956-67; author: (autobiography) Kitty, 1988; contbr. book revs. to jours. Assoc. fellow Timothy Dwight Coll. of Yale U., NYU, Skidmore Coll.; bd. dirs. Empire State Coll.; formerly spl. cons. to N.Y. Gov. on women's opportunities; mem. vis. com. for the arts MIT Recipient Nat. Medal Arts from Pres. George H. W. Bush, 1991. Died Apr. 18, 2007.

HARTLEY, WILLIAM DOUGLAS, art educator; b. Indpls., Nov. 24, 1921; s. James Worth and Bertha Sophia (Beuke) H.; m. Marucha del Socorro Trevino, Aug. 19, 1951; children—Gretel, Hetzal, Litzi. B.S., Ind. U., 1948, M.F.A., 1949; M.F.A., Kansas City Art Inst., 1951; Ph.D., NYU, 1971. Dir. art Pueblo High Sch., Colo., 1951-54; mem. faculty Ill. State U., Normal, 1954—, prof. art history, 1967—; art cons., 1959—. Author: The Search for Henry Cross, 1966; Things Invisible to See, 1979. Editor Alumni Bull., 1984—. Contbr. articles to profl. jours. Commd. sculptures include Arvin Inustries, Columbus, Ind., St. Matthew's Episcopal Ch., Bloomington, Ill., Adlai Stevenson Lecture Commn., Bloomington, Christ the King Episcopal Ch., Normal, Ill. Fellow Internat. Inst. Arts and Letters; mem. Midwestern Art History Soc. Republican. Episcopalian. Avocations: watercoloring painting; music; fiction writing. Home: Normal, Ill. Died Apr. 12, 2006.

HARTMAN, JOHN WHEELER, publisher; b. Detroit, June 3, 1922; s. Hubert Ezra and Margaret Mary (Martin) H.; m. Esther Kelly Bill, Nov. 8, 1947; children: Kelly Bill, Raymond Bill. Student, Colgate U., 1939; BA, Duke U., 1944. Pub. U.S. Navy News, 1945-46; area corr. United Press., 1946; partner, founder Bacon, Hartman & Vollbrecht, Inc. (advt. agy.), Jacksonville, Fla., 1946-69; dir. sales Sales Mgmt. Mag., NYC, 1951-57; exec. v.p. Bill Communications, Inc., NYC, 1955-57, pres., 1957-65, chmn. bd., 1966-89, chmn. emeritus, 1989-91; columnist Ocean Reef Free Press Fla. and Bus. Mktg. Chmn. bd. Hartman Communications, Inc. Bd. dirs. Duke U., People-to-People Sports Com., Inc., Fla. Land & Sea Trust; Lt. j.g. USNR, 1943-45, ETO. Mem. Young Pres.' Orgn. (internat. pres. 1963-64, past bd. dirs.), Chief Execs. Orgn. (forum chmn. 1980), World Pres.' Orgn., Am. Bus. Conf., Black Hall Club, Univ. Club, Old Lyme Country Club, Card Sound Golf Club, Ocean Reef Yacht Club, Key Largo Anglers Club, Racquet Club (past pres.). Home: Key Largo, Fla. Died Apr. 5, 2007.

HARTMANN, ROBERT CARL, retired physician, educator; b. Everett, Wash., July 23, 1919; s. Rudolf and Eugenie (Kaiser) H.; m. Margaretta O'Sullivan, Mar. 16, 1946 (div. Aug. 1975); children— Kathleen, Robert Carl, David, Richard, Margaret, Ellen; m. Joyce S. Anton, Sept. 4, 1977. AB, Johns Hopkins U., 1941, MD, 1944. Rotating intern Pa. Hosp., 1944-45, resident medicine, 1945-46; fellow medicine Johns Hopkins Sch. Medicine, 1948-49, 50-52, resident in medicine, 1949-50; faculty Vanderbilt U. Sch. Medicine, Nashville, 1952-74, prof. medicine, 1963-74, dir. div. hematology, 1952-74; prof. medicine U. South Fla. Coll. Medicine, 1974-89, retired, chief sect. hematology/oncology, 1974-79, mem. staff div. hematology, 1979-89; part-time cons. J.A. Haley Vets. Hosp., from 1989. Cons. nat. nutrition survey USPHS; anemia and nutrition survey Inst. Nutrition for Central Am. and Panama, Guatemala, 1965-68; mem. hematology study sect., sub-com. platelet-glass-adhesion Internat. Commn. Haemostasis and Thrombosis, 1967-71; adv. com. blood disease and blood resources NIH, 1980-84 Mem. editorial staff Am. Jour. Hematology, 1985—; contbr. papers to profl. jours. Served with AUS, 1946-48. Mem. So. Soc. Clin. Research, Am. Soc. Clin. Investigation, Am. Soc. Clin. Oncology, Am., Internat. Socs. Hematology, Am. Fedn. Clin. Research, Am. Assn. Physicians, Johns Hopkins Alumni Assn. (pres. Tenn. chpt. 1967) Home: Tampa, Fla. Died Apr. 30, 2006.

HARTUNG, THOMAS FREDERICK, state legislator; b. Eugene, Oreg., June 11, 1927; m. Beverly Hartung; 5 children. BS in Agr. Econs., Oreg. State U., 1950; postgrad., U. Oreg. Agrl. cons.; owner Hartung Meat Co.; mem. Oreg. Legislature, Salem, 1967—2003, chair edn. com., mem. rev. com., mem. subcom. on edn.; pres. Oreg. Senate. Past chair Beaverton Sch. Bd.; co-founder Beaverton Edn. Found.; past chair Oreg. Ethics Commn. Republican. Protestant. Home: Portland, Oreg. Died Nov. 14, 2005.

HARTZLER, ALFRED JAMES, government official, scientist; b. Manhattan, Kans., Apr. 17, 1922; s. Melvin Earnest and Zora Frances (Harris) H.; m. Mary Peterson, Feb. 17, 1950; 1 son, Peter Harris. S.B., U. Chgo., 1943, S.M., 1944, Ph.D., 1951. With research lab. Gen. Electric Co., Schenectady, N.Y., 1945-46; research assoc. Carnegie Inst. Tech., 1950-55; analyst to div. dir. ops. evaluation group, MIT, 1955-65; div. chief U.S. ACDA, Washington, 1965—. Served with AUS, 1942-43. U. Chgo. honor scholar, 1940-43; Ency. Brit. fellow, 1944-45; AEC predoctoral fellow, 1946-50; recipient Superior Honor award ACDA, 1968, Meritorious honor award, 1980. Mem. Am. Phys. Soc., AAAS, Ops. Research Soc. Am., Philos. Soc. Am., Sigma Xi. Home: Alexandria, Va. Died Feb. 1, 2007.

HARVEY, IRWIN M., carpet mill executive; b. Chgo., Apr. 24, 1931; s. Herman and Clara (Pomerantz) Harvey Smith; m. Marilyn G. Greenspahn, June 7, 1952; children: Beth I. Dorfman, Jill F. Harvey Stein, Gail L. BS, Roosevelt U., 1952. Sales rep. Pinksy Floor Covering Co., Chgo., 1954-58; sales agt. Hyams & Harvey, Chgo., 1958-63; v.p., regional mgr. Evans & Black Carpet Mills, Elk Grove Village, Ill., 1963-67, v.p., dir. mktg. Dallas, 1967-68; chmn.-pres. Galaxy Carpet Mills Inc., Elk Grove Village, Ill., and Chatsworth, Ga., 1968-83, chmn., chief exec. officer, from 1984; bd. dirs., exec. com. Floor Covering Industry Found., Chgo., from 1980. Mem. adv. bd. Acad. Design Sch., Chgo., 1978-83, Dallas Trade Mart, 1983—Served with U.S. Army, 1952-54. Named Man of Year Floor Covering Industry Found., 1983 Mem. Carpet and Rug Inst. (dir. 1971—, exec. com. 1973-82, 1978-80), Chgo. Floor Covering Assn. Jewish. Home: Highland Park, Ill. Died June 25, 2006.

HARVEY, WATKINS PROCTOR, physician, educator; b. Lynchburg, Va., Apr. 19, 1918; s. William Cochran and Caroline (Proctor) H.; m. Irma M. Burns, Apr. 30, 1949; children: Watkins Proctor, Jr. (dec.), Janet Carolyn, Blair Burns (dec.). AB, Lynchburg Coll., 1939; MD, Duke, 1943; Sc.D. (hon.), Georgetown U., 1979. Intern medicine Peter Bent Brigham Hosp., Boston, 1943-44, sr. asst. resident medicine, 1948-49, chief resident medicine, 1949-50; fellow medicine Harvard Med. Sch., 1946-48; faculty Georgetown U. Sch. Medicine, 1950—2007, prof. medicine, 1960—2007. Staff div. cardiology Georgetown U. Hosp., 1950—2007; cons. Walter Reed Army, VA, U.S. Naval, hosps., US Dept. State, NIH. Co-author: Clinical Auscultation of the Heart, rev. edit, 1959; Co-editor: Year Book Series on Cardiology, 1962—2007; editor emeritus: Current Problems in Cardiology. Master A.C.P. (Disting. Tchr. award 1985), Am. Coll. Cardiology (Disting. Tchr. award 1972); mem. Am. Heart Assn. (pres. 1969-70, fellow council clin. cardiology, chmn. 1969-70, Gold Heart award 1972, James Herrick award 1978), Washington Heart Assn. (pres. 1962-64), Assn. Univ. Cardiologists (sec.-treas. 1967-69, v.p. 1969-70, pres. 1970-71), Assn. Am. Physicians, Clin. and Climatol. Assn., Am. Fedn. Clin. Research, AMA, D.C. Med. Soc., So. Soc. Clin. Research, Clinico-Path. Soc. D.C., Alpha Omega Alpha. Died Sept. 26, 2007.

HARVIN, WILLIAM CHARLES, lawyer; b. San Francisco, Feb. 15, 1919; s. William Charles and Irma Beth (Hawkins) H.; m. Ruth Helen Beck, Nov. 30, 1942; children: David Tarleton, Susan Elizabeth Harvin Lawhon, Andrew Richard. BA, U. Tex., 1940, LL.B., 1947. Bar: Tex. 1946. Ptnr. Baker & Botts LLP, 1956—84, mng. ptnr., chmn. exec. com., 1972-84. Bd. dirs. Tex. Commerce Bancshares, Inc., 1975-91; chmn. U.S. Circuit Judge Nominating Commn. 5th Circuit, 1977-80. Chmn. bd. dirs. Houston C. of C., Tex. Med. Center; bd. dirs. U. Tex. Health Scis. Ctr. Houston, San Jacinto History Mus.; vice chmn. bd. dirs. St. Luke's Episcopal Hosp.; trustee St. John's Sch., Houston, Episc. Theol. Sem. of S.W., Austin; chmn. bd. trustees Kelsey-Seybold Found.; pres. Greater Houston Community Found.; chmn. bd. govs. The Houston Forum. Served with USN, 1941-45. Recipient Brotherhood award Nat. Conf. Christians and Jews, 1985, Disting. Alumnus award U. Tex., 1987, Inst. of Religion award for significant svc. to Tex. Med. Ctr, 1988, Leon Jaworski award of Houston Bar Assn. for svc. to the community, 1991. Fellow Am. Coll. Trial Lawyers, Am. Bar Found., Tex. Bar Found.; mem. ABA, Coun. on Fgn. Rels., Philos. Soc. Tex., Am. Law Inst., Fedn. Ins. and Corp. Counsel (pres. 1969-70), Def. Rsch. Inst. (dir. 1969-72), Ramada-Tejas Club, Phi Delta Theta, Phi Delta Phi. Episcopalian (vestry). Clubs: Houston Country, Ramada, Eldorado Country, Old Baldy. Died July 14, 2007.

HARWOOD, JOHN HENRY, retired corporate executive; b. Milw., Apr. 3, 1919; s. Paisley B. and Sylvia (Rehm) H.; m. Betty Ann Cattell, Feb. 10, 1942; children— John C., Nevin R., James C., Christopher R. BS, U. Mich., 1941, MBA, 1942. Sales rep. Metal Goods Corp., St. Louis, 1947-51, personnel dir., 1951-59, sec.-treas., 1959-68, v.p. finance, 1968-69, dir., 1960-69; asst. to pres. Debron Corp. (formerly Mississippi Valley Structural Steel Co.), Chgo., 1969-70, v.p. finance and adminstrn., 1970-74, also dir., 1973-77; pres. John H. Harwood & Co., cons. to mgmt., 1974-78; corp. valuations officer A.G. Edwards & Sons, Inc., 1978-80, v.p., 1980-84; ret., 1984. Dir. Intertherm, Inc., 1975-78 Mem. Fin. Execs. Inst. Home: Sarasota, Fla. Died June 18, 2006.

HASEN, BURTON STANLEY, painter; b. NYC, Dec. 19, 1921; s. Herman Harold and Mina (Leibowitz) H. Student, Art Students League, 1940-42, 46, H. Hoffmann Sch. Fine Arts, 1947-48, Acad. dela Grande-Chaumiere, Paris, 1948-50, Acad. delle Belle-Arti, Rome, 1959-60. Tchr. Sch. Visual Arts, NYC, 1953-2000, Mpls. Sch. Art and Design, 1966 One-man shows include Galerie 8, Paris, 1950, Grand Ctrl. Moderns, NYC, 1958-61, DArcy Gallery, NYC, 1964, Landmark Gallery, NYC, 1976, T'Pandje Gallerie, Belgium, 1981, Anita Shapolsky Gallery, 1987, 1992, 94, Gallery 1100-Niagara, Buffalo, 1993, Staller Ctr. for Arts, SUNY, Stony Brook, 1995, Hamilton Coll., Clinton, NY, 1996, Hugode Pagano gallery, NYC, 1997, Nat. Jewish Mus., Washington, 1997, Islip Art Mus., NY, 2003, Retrospective Southeast Mo. State Regional Mus., Cape Girardeau, 2005; group shows include Mus. Modern Art, Paris, 1951, Whitney Mus. Am. Art, NYC, 1964, Corcoran Gallery Art, Washington, 1959, Kresge Art Center, U. So. Ill., 1961, Krannert Art Mus.-U. Ill., Urbana, Am. Acad. Arts and Letters, NYC, 1965, Berlin Acad. Arts, 1956, W.G. Picker Gallery, 1969, Colgate U., Hamilton, NY, 1969, Mus. Modern Art, NYC, 1966, Met. Mus. Art, N.Y.C., 1952, Worcester (Mass.) Art Mus., 1968, Walker Art Center, Mpls., 1966, Bklyn. Mus., 1954, Artist Choice Mus., NYC, NAD, NYC, 1985, Anita Shapolsky Gallery, 1989, 90, 92, 2000, Neo Persona Gallery, 1989, 90, Rider Coll., 1992, Albright-Knox Mus., 1992, Islip Art Mus., 1992, Cleve. Inst. Art, 1993, Swiss Cultural Inst., 1993, David Anderson Gallery, Buffalo, 1993, Henry St. Settlement, NYC, 1993, Sordoni Art Gallery, Wilkes-Barre, Pa., 1994, Nat. Acad., 1995, 96, 97, 99, 00, 01, 03, 05, Alysia Duckler Gallery, Portland, 1996, Pagano Gallery, NYC, 1997, 98, Studio 18 Gallery NYC, 2002, 04, Studio 18 Gallery Graphics Show, Sheldon Meml. Art Gallery, U. Nebr., Lincoln, 2003, Brooms Street Gallery, NYC, Denise Bibro Gallery, NY, Lohin Geduld Gallery, NY, 2005, NY Soc. Etchers, Studio 12N, NYC, NAD, NYC, Terrain Gallery, NYC, Artist's Equity Gallery, NYC, Hunterdon Art Ctr., Clinton, NJ, 2007; represented in permanent collections Walker Art Center, Worcester Art Mus., Hampton Inst., CIBA-GEIGY Co., Bibliotheque Nationale, Paris, NY Pub. Library, Princeton U., Columbia U., Mus. Fine Art, Portland, Maine, NY Crestview Coll., Muhlenberg, Fine Prints Dept., SUNY, Buffalo, 1989, CCNY, Rider U., Lawrenceville, NJ, 1993, Islip Mus., East Islip, NY, Hamilton Coll., Clinton, NY, Nat. Jewish Mus., Washington, Southeast Mo. State U., Cape Giradeau, Mo., Birmingham So. Coll., Ala., Hudgens Ctr. Arts, Duluth, Ga., High Mus., Miami, Fla., Newberger Mus. Art, Purchase, NY, Libr. Congress, Fine Print Collection, Smithsonian, Washington, Jules Sherman Collection, NY, Robert Blackburn Collection, Elizabeth Found., NY, The Lowe Art Mus., U. Miami, U. Chgo.; illustrator books, 1959-89, Beyond the Furies, 1985, Franklin Mint, Phila., 1991, The Flame Charts, 2002; archives include Smithsonian Mus. Am. Art, Centre Georges Pompidou, Musée d'Art Moderne, Paris. With AUS, 1942—46. Recipient Emily Lowe Found. Purchase prize, 1955; grantee Fulbright Found., 1959-60, NY Found. Arts, 1990, Richard Florsheim Art Fund, 1993, 96, 97, Nat. Acad. Design, 2001; Pollack Krasner fellow 1995-96, 1999-2000, 2003, 04, Am. Acad. Arts & Letters, 2000, 01, 02, 03. Mem.: NY Artists Equity (hon. pres. 2005), Nat. Acad. Design, Fulbright Alumni Assn. Home: New York, NY. Died Sept. 7, 2007.

HASIJA, VIJAY KUMAR, civil engr.; b. India, June 5, 1939; came to U.S., 1964, naturalized, 1978; s. Rishikesh and Shakuntla H.; B.E., U. Jabalpur, 1960; M.E., Indian Inst. Sci., 1962; M.S., U. Minn., 1965; Ph.D., U. Pitts., 1972; m. Joyce Jordan, Dec. 12, 1970; children— Manisha, Anjali. Figld engr. Cementation Co. Ltd., India, 1962-64; design engr. Richardson Gordon Assos., Pitts., 1965-68; chief engr. Reliance Steel Products Co., McKeesport, Pa., 1969-72, v.p. engring., 1972-78; gen. mgr. Dynamic Products Corp., Middletown, Pa., 1979—. Mem. ASCE. Home: Camp Hill, Pa. Died Feb. 14, 2007.

HASKELL, HELEN BEAUMONT PARK (MRS. WILLIAM PECKHAM HASKELL), real estate executive; b. N.Y.C., Feb. 3, 1916; d. Halford Woodward and Helen Irene (Curtis) Park; B.A., Wellesley Coll., 1939; M.S., Mass. Inst. Tech., 1941; m. William Peckham Haskell, May 12, 1945; children— William Beaumont, Halford Whittier, Helen Hilton. With research and devel. Inst. Optics, U. Rochester, 1941-45; tchr. math. Rosemary Hall, Greenwich, Conn., 1947-61; owner Helen Park Haskell, Realtor, West Chop, Mass., 1968—. Trustee, Rosemary Hall Found., Inc., 1956-62. Mem. U.S. Field Hockey Assn., U.S. Women's LaCrosse Assn., Sigma Xi (asso.). Home: Cambridge, Mass. Died Mar. 8, 2006.

HASTINGS, BAIRD, conductor, music educator, writer; b. NYC, May 14, 1919; s. Albert Baird and Margaret (Johnson) H.; m. Louise Laurent, Dec. 22, 1945. BA, Harvard U., 1939; diploma (hon.), Paris Conservatory, 1946, Tanglewood Sch., Mass., 1957, Mozarteum, Salzburg, Austria, 1961; MA, Oueens Coll., 1966; PhD, Sussex Coll., Hayward Heath, Eng., 1976. Founder, condr. Mozart Festival Orch., NYC, from 1961; dir. instrumental music Trinity Coll., Hartford, Conn., 1965-70; asst. music critic Hartford Times, 1966-70; orch. adminstr., libr., music advisor dance dept. Juilliard Sch. Music, NYC, 1973-85. Condr. premieres works of Virgil Thomson and many re-auditions; guest condr. numerous groups including N.Y. State Theater, Hartford Symphony, Queens Philharm., Am. Symphony, Westport Cmty. Chorus, Dessoff Chorus; music advisor Sch. Am. Ballet, 1973-85, Eqlevsky Ballet, 1965-80; cons. Royal Acad. Music, London; lectr. Harvard U., Tufts U., MIT, NYU, N.Y. Pub. Libr., Hofstra U., numerous other instns. Author: Christian Berard, 1950, Sonata Form in Classical Orchestra, 1966, Choreographer and Composer, 1983, Mozart, 1989; editor: Mozart's Practical Elements of Thorough bas, 1976, and 6 other books; producer numerous radio programs on the arts; arranger numerous art exhbns.; program annotator at Carnegie Hall, N.Y.C., Fisher Hall, Tully Hall; arts commentator N.Y. Observer, N.Y. Times. Trustee Boston Arts Festival, 1959-61. Staff sgt. in mil. intelligence, U.S. Army, 1942-46, ETO. Fulbright fellow, France, 1949-50. Mem. Am. Fedn. Musicians. Clubs: Bohemian (N.Y.C.). Democrat. Presbyterian. Avocations: collecting prints, tennis, travel, languages. Died May 16, 2007.

HATCH, CALVIN SHIPLEY, retired home products executive; b. Heber City, Utah, Feb. 23, 1921; s. Edwin D. and Vernico B. (Burton) H.; m. JeNeal Nebeker, Dec. 23, 1945; children: Marcia Ann, Julie Lynne. BS in Fin., U. Utah, 1943. Salesman, N.Y. Life Ins. Co., Salt Lake City, 1946-47; with Procter & Gamble Co., 1947-71, sales merchandising mgr. Cin., 1966-68, mgr. cen. div. Cin., 1968-71; v.p. sales Clorox Co., Oakland, Calif., 1971-73, group v.p., 1973-76, exec. v.p., 1977-81, pres., chief exec. officer, 1981-82, chmn., chief exec. officer, 1982-86; dir. Interstate Bank Calif. Bd. dirs. Am. Pres. Cos. Active fund raising Salvation Army, Better Bus. Bur. Served to capt. F.A., AUS, 1942-45. Mem. Assn. Nat. Advertisers (dir. 1976-82) Home: Lafayette, Calif. Died Oct. 1, 2006.

HATCH, HAROLD ARTHUR, retired military officer; b. Avon, Ill., Dec. 29, 1924; s. Walter Samuel and Marie (Fennessy) H.; m. Mildred Jean Gehrig, Aug. 18, 1950; children: Sue, Sara, Sallie. BS, Coll. William and Mary, 1962. Commd. 2d lt. U.S. Marine Corps, 1949, advanced through grades to lt. gen., 1981; divsn. asst. chief staff for logistics (3d Marine Divsn.), Okinawa, 1970-71; dep. chief staff Fleet Marine Force Pacific, Hawaii, 1971-74; dep. chief staff for installations and logistics Hdqrs. U.S. Marine Corps, Washington, 1977-84; ret. Decorated Legion of Merit, Bronze Star, Air Medal, Meritorious Service medal, Disting. Service medal Republican. Presbyterian. Home: Vienna, Va. Died Feb. 19, 2006.

HATCHER, WILLIAM JULIAN, JR., chemical engineer, educator; b. Augusta, Ga., July 21, 1935; s. William Julian and Norvell (Kelley) H.; m. Katherine Wyant Mullis, Dec. 14, 1985; children: Jeffrey Craig, Rebecca Lynn, Michael William. BChemE with honors, Ga. Inst. Tech., 1957; MChemE, La. State U., 1964, PhD, 1968. Rsch. engr. Esso Rsch. Labs., Baton Rouge, 1960-66; rsch. asso. La. State U., Baton Rouge, 1966-68, sr. rsch. engr., 1968-69; asst., assoc. prof. chem. engring. U. Ala., 1969-73, dept. head chem. and metall. engr., 1973-81, acting dean engring., 1981-83, rsch. prof., from 1983, acting head chem. engring., 1988, interim head aerospace engring., 1990, acting head computer sci. dept. Tuscaloosa, 1990-91, acting head elec. engring., 1991-92, dept. head chem. engring., from 1992. Cons. U.S. Bur. Mines, 1972—; mem. adj. faculty USMC Command and Staff Coll., 1978-84; Mem. Ala. Hazardous Wastes Adv. Com., 1978-84; rsch. in petroleum processes, 1960-66, air pollution control, 1968-69, catalysis, 1970, reactionkinetics, 1979—. Contbg. author: Environmental Engineering Handbook, 1973, Computer Programs for Chemical Engineering Education, Vols. II and IV, 1972, Handbook for Heat and Mass Transfer, 1986. Served to lt. USMC, 1957-60. NSF research grantee, 1970-72, 77-80 Fellow Am. Inst. Chem. Engrs., Am. Soc. Engring. Edn., AAAS; mem. Phi Kappa Phi, Tau Beta Pi, Phi Eta Sigma, Omega Chi Epsilon, Phi Lambda Upsilon. Presbyterian. Home: Tuscaloosa, Ala. Died June 1, 2006.

HAUGHEY, JAMES MCCREA, lawyer, artist; b. Courtland, Kans., July 8, 1914; s. Leo Eugene and Elizabeth (Stephens) H.; m. Katherine Hurd, Sept. 8, 1938; children: Katherine (Mrs. Lester B. Loo), Bruce Stephens, John Caldwell. Student, Deep Springs Coll., Dyer, Calif., 1930-31; LLB, U. Kans., Lawrence, 1939. Bar: Kans. 1939, Mont. 1943. Landman Carter Oil Co., 1939-43; practice in Billings, Mont., 1943-98; ptnr. Crowley, Haughey, Hanson, Toole & Dietrich, 1950-86, counsel, 1986-98; ret. dir. Mont.-Dakota Resources Group Inc., 1998. One-man shows include, U. Kans., U. Mont., Mont. State U., Concordia Coll., Nebr., C.M. Russell Mus., Great Falls, Mont., Boise Mus. Art, Mont. State Mus., Helena, Sandzen Gallery, Bethany Coll., Lindsborg, Kans., Yellowstone Art Mus., Billings, Mont., also numerous group shows. Pres. Rocky Mountain Mineral Law Found., 1957-58, trustee, 1955—2007; pres. Mont. Inst. Arts Found., 1965-67; pres. Yellowstone Art Center Found., 1969-71, trustee, 1964-81; mem. Mont. Ho. of Reps., 1960-64, Mont. Senate, 1966-70, minority leader, 1969-70. Recipient Gov.'s award Arts, 1981 Fellow Mont. Inst. Arts (Permanent Collection award 1960), Am. Artists Profl. League; mem. ABA, Am. Coll. Real Estate Lawyers, Yellowstone County Bar Assn. (pres. 1960-61), U. Kans. Law Soc. (bd. govs. 1989-92), Am. Watercolor Soc. (Midwest v.p. 1978-82), N.W. Watercolor Soc. (life), Midwest Watercolor Soc., Kans. Watercolor Soc. (hon.), Mont. Watercolor Soc. (hon.), Yellowstone Art Mus. (Pres.'s award svc. to Arts, 2005, Philanthropist of Yr.), Phi Delta Theta, Phi Delta Phi. Republican. Episcopalian. Home: Billings, Mont. Died Sept. 11, 2007.

HAUPIN, WARREN EMERSON, molten salts scientist; b. Youngsville, Pa., Apr. 4, 1920; s. Orrie Bert and Edna Earl (Donaldson) H.; m. Edna Hazel Oyler, Sept. 3, 1949; children— Barbara Haupin La Veck, Ronald (dec.), Laura Haupin Kappler, Carol Haupin Blair. B.S. in Electrochem. Engring., Pa. State U., 1942. Registered profl. engr., Pa. Research engr. Alcoa Labs., New Kensington, Pa., 1943-59, electrochem. sect. head, 1959-61, sr. scientist, 1961-65, sci. assoc., 1965-81, fellow, Alcoa Center, Pa., 1981-84, sr. fellow, 1984-85; cons. Molten Salts and Electrochem. Engring., 1986—; adj. instr. Pa. State U.-New Kensington, evenings 1961-66, Carnegie Mellon U., Pitts., 1977-79, Chatham Coll., Pitts., 1979-80; vis. scientist Norwegian Inst. Tech., Trondheim, 1981. Contbr. articles to profl. jours., chpts. to books. Patentee in field. Recipient Francis C. Frary award Aluminum Co. Am., 1984, Wasserman award Am. Welding Soc., 1971. Mem. Metall. Soc. of AIME (vice chmn. Pitts. sect. 1984-85, Light Metals award 1985), Instrument Soc. Am., Electrochem. Soc., Am. Inst. Chem. Engrs., Sigma Xi, Eta Kappa Nu, Sigma Tau. Republican. Methodist. Club: Toastmasters (pres. 1975) (Alcoa Center). Avocations: camping; photography. Died June 20, 2007.

HAUPTFLEISCH, LOUIS ALOIS, investment company executive; b. Waterloo, Ill., July 17, 1918; s. Herman E. and Amanda L. (Koenigsmark) H.; m. Margaret Jane Hall, Oct. 31, 1942; 1 son, David L.; m. Pamela Wilson Mitchell, Sept. 6, 1974; children— Melinda, Gayle, Lauren, Hillary. BS, U. Ill., 1940. Vice pres. Halsey, Stuart & Co., Inc., NYC, 1946-60, exec. v.p., dir., 1968-72; 1st v.p. Smith Barney, Harris Upham & Co. Inc., NYC, 1973-83; v.p. Goldman, Sachs & Co., NYC, 1961-68. Served with AUS, 1942-45. Decorated Bronze Star medal, Purple Heart. Mem. Municipal Bond Club N.Y. (pres. 1976-77) Clubs: Univ. (N.Y.C.); Morris County Golf (Convent, N.J.). Home: Summit, NJ. Died Dec. 14, 2006.

HAVERTY, RAWSON, retail furniture company executive; b. Atlanta, Nov. 26, 1920; s. Clarence and Elizabeth (Rawson) H.; m. Margaret Middleton Munnerlyn, Aug. 25, 1951; children: Margaret Elizabeth, Jane Middleton, James Rawson, Mary Elizabeth, Ben Munnerlyn. BA, U. Ga., 1941. With Haverty Furniture Co., Atlanta, 1941 and from 46, sec., v.p., treas., pres., CEO, 1955-84, chmn. bd., mem. exec. com., from 1984. Instr. credit and collection So. Retail Furniture Assn. Sch. for Execs., U. N.C., 1960, instr. credits, collections and market analyses, 1951; instr. br. stores Nat. Retail Furniture Sch. for Execs., U. Chgo., 1957—; chmn. bd. dirs. Bank South Corp., 1977-90. Former chmn. Met. Atlanta Rapid Transit Authority; former chmn. bd. trustees St. Joseph's Hosp.; pres. U. Ga. Alumni Soc., 1973-75, mem. exec. com., 1975—, chmn. loyalty fund, 1969-70, 70-71; past chmn. bd. trustees St. Joseph's Village; trustee Atlanta Arts Alliance, Westminster Sch., Atlanta, U. Ga. Found.; past pres. bd. sponsors Atlanta Art Sch.; life trustee High Mus. Art; life trustee High Point U., N.C.; former mem. Fulton Indsl. Authority; bd. dirs. Nat. Retail Fedn., Washington, Aquinas Ctr. of Theology at Emory U., Create Your Dream of Atlanta. Maj. AUS, 1942-46. Decorated Bronze Star medal, Order of Leopold, Croix de Guerre with palms (Belgium); named All Am. Mcht. in retail furniture industry, 1958, knight comdr. Order of St. Gregory the Great, 1990. Mem. Atlanta Retail Mchts. Assn. (past pres., dir.), Nat. Home Furnishings Assn. (past v.p., dir., Retailer of Yr. award 1980), Nat. Furniture Mfrs. Assn. (Johnny Shillngs award 1990), Nat. Retail Furniture Assn. (divsn. 1952-69), Am. Retail Fedn., Atlanta Jr. C. of C. (hon. life), Assn. U.S. Army (past pres., adv. bd.), Atlanta C. of C., Piedmont Driving Club, Capital City Club, Ponte Vedra Club, Kiwanis, Sigma Alpha Epsilon. Roman Catholic. Home: Atlanta, Ga. Died Jan. 26, 2007.

HAVLICEK, FRANKLIN J., communications executive; b. NYC, July 18, 1947; s. Raymond Joseph and Rosalia Maria (Zona) H.; m. Louise Sferrazza, Dec. 21, 1980. BA, Columbia U., 1968, JD, 1973, MA, 1977, MPhil, 1980; cert., Internat. Inst. Human Rights, Strasbourg, France, 1972. Bar: N.Y. 1974, U.S. Dist. Ct. (so. and ea. dists.) N.Y. 1974, U.S. Ct. Appeals (2d cir.) 1975, U.S. Supreme Ct. 1979, D.C. 1990. Atty. Battle & Fowler, NYC, 1973-78; spl. advisor to Mayor of N.Y.C., 1978-82; ptnr. Seham, Klein, Zelman, NYC, 1982-84; dir. labor rels. NBC, NYC, 1984-88; v.p. personnel, indsl. rels. and environ. svcs. Washington Post, 1988-97; pres. stratagem adv. svcs. Washington, 1997-98; with Internat. Monetary Fund, Washington, from 1998. Adj. prof. internat. & pub. affairs Columbia U., N.Y.C., 1978-88, Sch. Pub. Affairs & Sch. Internat. Svc., Am. U., Washington, 1999—. Editor: Collective Bargaining, 1979, Presidential Selection, 1982, Election Communications, 1984; contbr. numerous articles on law, govt., communications to mags., newspapers. Exec. com. N.Y. Gov.'s Task Force in Schs. and Bus., 1986-88; counsel Vietnam Vets. Meml. Commn., 1982-85, State Commn. on Dioxin, 1983-85; candidate for U.S. Senate in N.Y., 1986; mem. U.S. U.S.S.R. Emerging Leaders Summit, 1988, 90; bd. dirs. World Affairs Coun., 1991-97, Washington Performing Arts Soc., 1995-97, Internat. Peace Acad., 1989-90, World Media Colloquium UNESCO, 1989; U.S. Tech. expert ILO, 1990; cons. to UN High Commr. for Human Rights in Bosnia, 1992; study grant on media and communications European Cmty., 1994; cons. Cath. Relief Svcs., Kosovo, 1999. With U.S. Army, 1968-70. Ford Found. fellow, 1977; study grantee on media and comms. European Cmty., 1994. Mem. ABA, Assn. of Bar of City of N.Y., Am. Polit. Sci. Assn., Am. Acad. Polit. Sci., N.Y. Acad. Scis. Clubs: City N.Y. (trustee 1985-87). Roman Catholic. Avocations: tennis, running, climbing, films, architecture. Home: Chevy Chase, Md. Died Aug. 4, 2006.

HAWK, NORMAN RAY, academic administrator, retired; b. Butte Falls, Oreg., Apr. 14, 1918; s. Norman Lee and Inez (Pullen) H.; m. Phyllis Virginia Porter, July 1, 1939; children: Kenneth Alan, William Lee, Ronald Dean. BS in History, U. Oreg., 1947, MS in History, 1948, EdD, 1949. Dir. tchr. tng. So. Oreg. Coll., Ashland, 1949; dean of men U. Oreg., Eugene, 1950-57, 59-63, asst. to pres., 1963-69, acting pres., 1969, v.p. adminstrn. and fin., 1969-82; Carnegie Postdoctoral Fellow U. Mich., Ann Arbor, 1958-59. Col. USAF, 1942-46, Africa, France. Named Eugene First Citizen, 1995. Mem. Eugene Town Club. Avocations: travel, photography, gardening, fishing, reading. Home: Eugene, Oreg. Died May 28, 2006.

HAWKINS, ARMIS EUGENE, former state supreme court chief justice; b. Natchez, Miss., Nov. 11, 1920; s. Charles Mayfield and Lela (Hill) H.; m. Patricia Burrow, Aug. 20, 1948; children: Janice Hawkins Shrewsbury, Jean Ann, James Charles. Student, Wood Jr. Coll., 1938-39, Millsaps Coll., 1943; LL.B., U. Miss., 1947. Bar: Miss. 1947. Pvt. practice law, Houston, Miss., 1947-51; dist. atty. 3d Cir. Ct. Dist. Miss., 1951-59; assoc. justice Miss. Supreme Ct., 1981-88, presiding justice, 1988-92, now chief justice, 1993-95. Served with USMC, 1942-46, PTO. Mem. ABA, Am. Judicature Soc., Miss. Trial Lawyers Assn., Miss. State Bar. Baptist. Home: Houston, Miss. Died Feb. 28, 2006.

HAWKINS, AUGUSTUS FREEMAN, retired congressman; b. Shreveport, La., Aug. 31, 1907; s. Nyanza and Hattie H. (Freeman) H.; m. Pegga A. Smith, Aug. 28, 1945 (dec. Aug. 1966); m. Elsie Taylor, June 30, 1977 (dec. 2007) AB in Econs., UCLA, 1931. Engaged in real estate and retail bus., Los Angeles, from 1945—; mem. Calif. Assembly, Los Angeles County, 1935-62, chmn. rules com., 1961-62; mem. US Congress from 29th Calif. dist. (formerly 21st Calif. dist.), 1963-91, chmn. edn. & labor com., 1973—79. Chmn. House Edn. and Labor Com.; chmn. Subcom. on Elem., Secondary and Vocational Edn. Mem.: Masons. Democrat. Methodist. Died Nov. 11, 2007.*

HAWKINS, PHILLIP LEE, Christian Science practitioner; b. Oklahoma City, Feb. 16, 1926; s. Charles Bartow and Norma Gladys (Thompson) H.; m. Cora May Nickell, May 29, 1965; children— Valerye Kirsten, Allyson Kelly, Phillip Lee II. With various oil cos., Tulsa, 1949-62; asst. supr. travel Cities Service, Tulsa, 1962-68; mgr. corp. travel, meetings coordination Conoco, Inc., Houston, 1968-85; cons. Hawkins and Assocs., Houston, 1985-86; cons. Harper Travel Internat., Houston, 1985-86, Internat. Tours., Inc., Tulsa, 1985-86; practitioner Christian Science, 1987—; cons. Lynda's Travel, Siloam Springs, Ark., 1994. Active Assn. Retarded Citizens, 1979—. Mem. Tex. Passenger Traffic Assn. (life), Nat. Passenger Traffic Assn. (hon.), Nat. Passenger Traffic Assn. (bd. dirs. 1979-83), Conn. Westchester Passenger Traffic Assn. (pres., chmn. 1974-77), Del. Inst. Travel Mgrs., Internat. Bus. Travel Assn., Soc. Co. Meeting Planners. Christian Scientist. Died Jan. 5, 2006.

HAY, ELIZABETH DEXTER, embryologist, educator; b. St. Augustine, Fla., Apr. 2, 1927; d. Isaac Morris and Lucille Elizabeth (Lynn) H. AB, Smith Coll., 1948; MA (hon.), Harvard U., 1964; ScD (hon.), Smith Coll., 1973, Trinity Coll., 1989; MD, Johns Hopkins U., 1952, LHD (hon.), 1990. Intern in internal medicine Johns Hopkins Hosp., Balt., 1952-53; instr. anatomy Johns Hopkins U. Med. Sch., Balt., 1953-56, asst. prof., 1956-57, Cornell U. Med. Sch., NYC, 1957-60, Harvard Med. Sch., Boston, 1960-64, Louise Foote Pfeiffer assoc. prof., 1964-69, Louise Foote Pfeiffer prof. embryology, from 1969, chmn. dept. anatomy and cellular biology, 1975-93, prof. dept. cell biology, 1993—2007. Cons. cell biology sect. NIH, 1965-69; mem. adv. coun. Nat. Inst. Gen. Med. Sci., NIH, 1978-81; mem. sci. adv. bd. Whitney Marine Lab., U. Fla., 1982-86; mem. adv. coun. Johns Hopkins Sch. Medicine, 1982-96; chairperson bd. sci. counselors Nat. Inst. Dental Rsch., NIH, 1984-86; mem. bd. sci. counselors Nat. Inst. Environ. Health Sci., NIH, 1990-93. Author: Regeneration, 1966; (with J.P. Revel) Fine Structure of the Developing Avian Cornea, 1969; editor: Cell Biology of Extracellular Matrix, 1981, 2d edit., 1991; editor-in-chief Developmental Biology Jour., 1971-75; contbr. articles to profl. jours. Mem. Scientists Task Force of Congressman Barney Frank, Massach, 1982-92. Recipient Disting. Achievement award N.Y. Hosp.-Cornell Med. Ctrl. Alumni Coun., 1985, award for vision rsch. Alcon, 1988, Excellence in Sci. award Fedn. Am. Socs. Exptl. Biology. Mem. Soc. Devel. Biology (pres. 1973-74, E.G. Conklin award 1997), Am. Soc. Cell Biology (pres. 1976-77, legis. alert com. 1982-2007, E.B. Wilson award 1989, chair 40th anniversary 2000), Am. Assn. Anatomists (pres. 1981-82, legis. alert com. 1982-2007, Centennial award 1987, Henry Gray award 1992), Am. Acad. Arts and Scis., Johns Hopkins Soc. Scholars, Nat. Acad. Sci., Inst. Medicine, Internat. Soc. Devel. Biologists (exec. bd. 1977, keynote spkr. 1st Australian EMT conf. 2003), Boston Mycol. Club. Home: Weston, Mass. Died Aug. 20, 2007.

HAY, RICHARD LE ROY, geology educator; b. Goshen, Ind., Apr. 29, 1926; s. Edward Le Roy and Angela H.; m. Barbara J. Herbert, Dec. 13, 1956; 1 child, Randall E.; m. Lynn Simonds, July 14, 1973. BS, Northwestern U., 1946, MS, 1948; PhD, Princeton U., 1952. Asst. prof. geology La. State U., Baton Rouge, 1955-57; asst. prof. to prof. geology and geophysics U. Calif., Berkeley, 1957-83; Ralph E. Grim prof. geology U. Ill., Urbana-Champaign, 1983-97. Geologist U.S. Geol. Survey, intermittently 1948-84; adj. prof. U. Ariz., 1999—. Author: Geology of the Olduvai Gorge, 1976. Recipient Arnold Guyot award, Nat. Geog. Soc., 1978, Leakey prize, L.S.B. Leakey Found., 2001. Fellow AAAS, Geol. Soc. Am. (Kirk Bryan award 1978, Rip Rapp award 2000), Mineral. Soc. Am., Calif. Acad. Sci. Home: Tucson, Ariz. Died Feb. 10, 2006.

HAY, ROBERT DEAN, retired management educator; b. LaPorte, Ind., Nov. 17, 1921; s. Carl Roy and Almetta (Diedrich) H.; m. Margaret B. Appelman, 1944; children— Sue Ann, Carol Lynn, Taj Margaret. BS, U. Okla., 1949, MBA, 1950; PhD, Ohio State U., 1954. Mem. faculty U. Ark., Fayetteville, 1949-90, mem. emeritus, from 1990, prof. mgmt., 1959-86, Univ. prof., 1986-90. Author: (with F. Broyles) Athletic Administration, 1979, (with Ed Gray and Paul Smith) Business and Society, 1989, Strategic Management in Non-Profit Organizations, 1990; also 10 other books. Served with USAAF, 1942-47. Mem. Am. Bus. Communications Assn., Acad. Mgmt., Case Rsch. Assn., other profl. orgns. Home: Fayetteville, Ark. Died Dec. 28, 2006.

HAYASHI, YOSHIMI, state supreme court justice; b. Honolulu, Nov. 2, 1922; s. Shigeo and Yuki H.; m. Eleanor Hayashi, Aug. 8, 1953; 1 child, Scott K. BA, U. Hawaii, 1950; LL.B., George Washington U., 1958. Bar: Hawaii 1958. Pvt. practice law, Lihue, Kauai, Hawaii, 1958-61; asst. U.S. atty., 1961-67; U.S. atty. for Hawaii, 1967-69; judge U.S. Dist. Ct. (1st dist.) Hawaii, 1974-80; chief judge Hawaii Intermediate Ct. Appeals, 1980-82; assoc. justice Hawaii Supreme Ct., Honolulu, from 1982. Served to sgt. U.S. Army, 1943-46. Democrat. Buddhist. Died Apr. 23, 2006.

HAYES, CHARLES AMOS, JR., mathematics educator; b. Winnipeg, Manitoba, Apr. 9, 1916; arrived in U.S., 1923, naturalized, 1940; s. Charles Amos and Amy (Noblett) Hayes; m. Lola Thelma Valente, June 21, 1942; children: Rodney Charles, Laura Louise. BA, U. Calif.-Berkeley, 1937, MA, 1938, PhD, 1942. Instr. U. Calif.-Berkeley, 1946—47; asst. prof. U. Calif.-Davis, 1947—53, assoc. prof., 1953—59, prof., 1953—78, prof. emeritus, from 1978. Author: Concepts Real Analysis, 1964; author: (with C.Y. Pauc) Derivation and Martingales, 1970; contbr. articles pub. to Profl. jours. Served to 1st lt. USAAF, 1942—46, World War II. Mem.: Pi Mu Epsilon, Sigma Xi, Phi Beta Kappa. Home: Davis, Calif. Died Aug. 26, 2007.

HAYES, COY DENVERT, packaging company executive; b. Middlesboro, Ky., Aug. 23, 1928; s. Samuel and Rutha Edward (Drummonds) H.; m. Wanda Joyce McBee, May 24, 1947; 1 child, Arlene Nancy Hayes Willis. B.B.A., East Mich. U., 1967. Quality control supr. Consol. Paper Co., Monroe, Mich., 1964-65; paper mill chemist Union Camp Corp., Monroe, 1966-68; plant mgr. Sonoco Products Co., Rockton, Ill., 1968-72, midwest region mgr., 1972-73, so. region mgr., Hartsville, S.C., 1973-76, dir. mfg. services, Hartsville, 1976-81; prodn. mgr. Jefferson Smurfit Corp. formerly Alton Packaging Corp., Ill., 1981-84, gen. mgr., 1984—. Mem. TAPPI, Paper Industry Mgmt. Assn. Republican. Avocations: photography, golf, woodworking. Home: Jacksonville, Fla. Died Dec. 3, 2006.

HAYES, EDWARD D(ENNIS), judge; b. Rochester, N.Y., June 21, 1921; s. Archibald D. and Olivia M. (Sherlock) H.; m. Elizabeth J. Wojciechowski; children: Richard, Michael, Stephen, Kathleen. Student U. Rochester, 1940-41, 50-52; J.D., Albany Law Sch., 1955. Bar: N.Y. 1955, U.S. Dist. Ct. (we. dist.) N.Y. 1955. Assoc. McFarlin Harris, Rochester, 1955-56; claims adjuster Allstate Ins. Co., Rochester, 1956; atty. adv. Rochester Ordinance Dist., 1956-59; ptnr. Thompson & Hayes, Rochester, 1959-65; sole practice, Rochester, 1965-74; bankruptcy judge U.S. Bankruptcy Ct. We. Dist. N.Y., 1974—. Bd. dirs. Rochester Housing Authority, 1963-72. With U.S. Army, 1942-46. Mem. ABA, Nat. Conf. Bankruptcy Judges. Roman Catholic. Died May 18, 2006.

HAYES, JAMES EDWARD, retired insurance executive; b. Mound City, Mo., June 7, 1928; s. Edward Perry and Gladys Marie (Plummer) H.; m. Edith Louise Beckett, June 15, 1951 (dec.). BS, U. Mo., 1951. Vice pres. mortgage and real estate Equitable Life Assurance Soc., NYC, 1970-74, v.p. bond investments, 1974-76, sr. v.p. investment affairs, 1976-79, sr. v.p. fin. ops. area, 1979-80; exec. v.p. Equitable Life Assurance Soc. of U.S.; exec. v.p. and chief ops. officer Equitable Life Holding Corp., 1980-83. Chmn. bd., chief exec. officer Equico Lessors, Inc., 1982-83; chmn. bd., dir. Equico Capital Corp., Inc., to 1983, Equico Securities, Inc., to 1983. Served with U.S. Army, 1946-47, 51-53. Mem. Am. Inst. Real Estate Appraisers. Home: Moraga, Calif. Died Dec. 20, 2006.

HAYGOOD, JOHN WARREN, retired lawyer; b. Richmond, Tex., Sept. 16, 1924; s. Claude Culberson and Jessie (Scott) H.; m. Mary Forea McGill, Aug. 25, 1946 (div. 1979); children: Scott McGill, Reid Alexander (dec.), Holly Mary. BA, Centenary Coll., 1947; JD, Tulane U., 1950. Bar: La. 1950, U.S. Dist. Ct. (we. dist.) La. 1952, U.S. Ct. Mil. Appeals 1956, U.S. Supreme Ct. 1959, U.S. Ct. Appeals (5th cir.) 1960, U.S. Dist. Ct. (ea. dist.) La. 1966, U.S. Dist. Ct. (mid. dist.) La. 1966, U.S. Dist. Ct. (so. dist.) Miss. 1968. Pvt. practice, Shreveport, La., 1950; assoc. Brown & Fleniken, Shreveport, 1952-53; atty. Ark. Fuel Oil Corp., Shreveport, 1953-58; ptnr. Stagg, Cady, Haygood & Beard, Shreveport, 1958-65, Jones, Walker, Waechter, Poitevent, Carrere & Denegre, New Orleans, 1965-87; ret., 1987. Instr. trial practice Tulane U. Law Sch., 1974 Named Outstanding Class Agt. Tulane Alumni Fund, 1980. Mem.: La. Bar Assn., P-51 Mustang Pilots Assn., P-40 Warhawk Pilot Assn., Phi Delta Phi, Kappa Alpha Order, Omicron Delta Kappa. Home: Metairie, La. Died Nov. 20, 2006.

HAYNES, CARL WILLIAM, finance company executive; b. Oceanside, NY, July 28, 1938; s. Carl William and Mary Edna (Higgins) Haynes; m. Linda Louise Higgins, July 20, 1960; children: Michael, Timothy, Carl III, Kerri, Diane, Catherine. BBA, Fairfield U., 1960. C.P.A. N.Y. Acct. Price Waterhouse, NYC, 1960—67; sr. fin. analyst ITT Corp, NYC, 1967—69; asst. comptr. ITT Ednl. Services, Indpls., 1969—71, comptr., treas., 1974—81; mgr. corp. acctg. ITT Grinnell, Providence, 1971—74; v.p., treas. ITT Pub., Providence, 1981—85, dir. operational audits, from 1985. Mem. Wilton Vol. Ambulance Corps. Mem.: Am. Inst. C.P.A.s, N.Y. Health and Racquet. Republican. Roman Cath. Home: Denver, Colo. Died May 13, 2007.

HAYNES, DOUGLAS MARTIN, obstetrician, gynecologist, educator; b. NYC, Jan. 25, 1922; s. Daniel Hagood and Courtenay (Collins) H.; m. Elizabeth B. Johnson, June 17, 1961; children: Douglas Marshall, Lewis Daniel. BA, BS, So. Meth. U., 1943; MD, Southwestern Med. Coll., 1946; MA, Louisville Presby. Theol. Sem., 1989, ThM, 1994. Diplomate Am. Bd. Obstetrics and Gynecology (assoc. examiner). Intern in pathology Parkland Meml. Hosp., Dallas, 1946-47, resident obstetrics and gynecology, 1949-52; asst. prof. obstetrics and gynecology U. Tex. Southwestern Med Sch., 1952-55; assoc. prof. obstetrics and gynecology U. Louisville Sch. Medicine, 1955-57, prof., 1957-87, prof. emeritus, from 1987, chmn. dept., 1957-69; interim dean U. Louisville Sch. Medicine (Sch. of Medicine), 1969-70, dean, 1970-72. Author: Medical Complications During Pregnancy, 1969; Contbr. articles to profl. jours. Served to capt., M. C. AUS, 1947-49. Fellow Am. Gynec. and Obstet. Soc.; mem. ACOG, A.C.S., Central Assn. Obstetricians and Gynecologists (v.p. 1977-78), So. Med. Assn., Phi Beta Kappa, Phi Chi, Delta Chi, Alpha Omega Alpha, Phi Kappa Phi. Democrat. Episcopalian. Home: Louisville, Ky. Died July 25, 2007.

HAZEL, DAVID WILLIAM, coll. dean; b. Boston, May 15, 1920; s. Francis Putnam and Bessie (Coleman) H.; m. Ruth Naomi Rivers, Dec. 26, 1946; children— Cheryl (Mrs. Russell Roberts), Daryl, David, Kim. AB, Tufts U., 1943; M.Ed., Boston U., 1946; PhD, U. Mich., 1957. Asst. prof. sociology and polit. sci. Tuskegee (Ala.) Inst., 1946-47, 49-52; asst prof. econ. Prairie View (Tex.) A. and M. Coll., 1953-57; asso. prof. polit. sci. So. Univ., Baton Rouge, 1957-58; prof. polit. sci. Central State U., Wilberforce, Ohio, 1958-65, chmn. dept., 1966-71; dean Central State U. (Coll. Arts and Scis.), 1971-85. Vis. prof. Miami U. Ohio, Central Mich. U. Treas. Mental Health Assn. Greene County, 1971-72; mem. sub-com. community planning, comdg. gen.'s com. Wright-Patterson AFB, 1971; Bd. dirs. Faith Community Methodist Housing Authority, Xenia, Ohio. Served with USAAF, 1942-43. Gen. Edn. Bd. fellow, 1947-49; So. Fellowship Fund fellow, 1956-57 Mem. Am. Polit Sci. Assn. (ethics com.) Democrat. Episcopalian. Home: Xenia, Ohio. Died Oct. 24, 2006.

HAZEL, JOSEPH ERNEST, geology educator, stratigrapher; b. Caruthersville, Mo., July 7, 1933; s. Joseph and Pearl Irene (Hall) H.; m. Marilyn Mae Pate, Aug. 11, 1956; children: Joseph, James, Jonathan. BA, U. Mo., 1956, MA, 1960; PhD, La. State U., 1963. NRC postdoctoral fellow Harvard U., 1963-64; rsch. geologist U.S. Geol. Survey, Washington, 1964-83, chief paleontologist, 1973-78; rsch. assoc. Amoco Prodn. Co., Tulsa, 1983-86; Campanile prof. geology La. State U., Baton Rouge, from 1986, chmn. dept. geology and geophysics, 1990-94. Chmn. Internat. Rsch. Group, Ostracoda, 1985-88; cons. Govt. Japan, 1985. Co-editor: Biostratigraphy, 1977; contbr. numerous articles to profl. jours., book chpts. Lt. U.S. Army, 1956-58. Recipient Meritorious Svc. award Dept. Interior, 1980; Humble Oil fellow, 1961-63. Mem. Soc. Econ. Paleontologists and Mineralists, Paleontol. Soc. Am., Geol. Soc. Am., Internat. Paleontol. Union, Brit. Micropaleontol. Assn. Avocation: genealogy. Home: Tulsa, Okla. Died Feb. 9, 2006.

HAZLETT, JAMES STEPHEN, university administrator; b. Kansas City, Mo., Feb. 27, 1940; married; 2 children. Student, Inst. Polit. Studies, Paris, 1960-61; BA, Yale U., 1962; MA, Harvard U., 1963; PhD, U. Chgo., 1968. Instr. edn. U. Chgo., 1967-68, asst. prof., 1968-71; asst. prof. cultural founds. edn. U. Tex., Austin, 1971-74, assoc. prof., 1975-80; prof. ednl. adminstrn., supervision and founds., assoc. dean Coll. Edn., U. Nebr., Omaha, 1980-83; dean Sch. Edn., Ind. State U., Terre Haute, 1983-90; v.p. for acad. affairs U. S.D., Vermillion, from 1990. Ind. Assn. Colls. for Tchr. Edn. (pres. 1988-89), Tchr. Edn. Coun. of State Colls. and Univs. (pres.-elect 1989), Am. Assn. Colls. for Tchr. Edn. (bd. dirs. 1989-92). Home: Vermillion, SD. Died Mar. 14, 2006.

HEADLAND, EDWIN HARVEY, military officer, educator; b. Litchville, ND, Nov. 15, 1911; s. Edwin Henry and Olga (Strand) Headland; m. Margaret McGinnis, Feb. 12, 1942. Student, U. Chgo., 1929—31; BS, U.S. Naval Acad., 1935; postgrad., Nat. War Coll., 1945; MBA, U. Puget Sound, 1963, U. Wash., 1968. Commd. ensign U.S. Navy, 1935, advanced through grades to capt., 1954, comdr. ships during World War II, ret., 1961; lectr. econs. and bus. U. Puget Sound, 1963—67, U. Md. Overseas, 1968—79, Pierce Coll., Tacoma, from 1980. Decorated for combat. Mem.: AAUP, Gyro, Lions, Mil. Officers, Tacoma Country, Psi Upsilon. Republican. Episcopalian. Died Apr. 8, 2006.

HEALD, MILTON TIDD, educator, geologist; b. Woburn, Mass., Feb. 19, 1919; s. Walter Milton and Susan Edgell (Tidd) H.; m. Doris Shirley Ethier, June 15, 1941; children— Sandra (Mrs. Robert G. Simmons), Cynthia (Mrs. Stephen B. Patton), Marcia (Mrs. Michael M. McGlothlin). BA, Wesleyan U., Middletown, Conn., 1940; MA, Harvard, 1947, PhD, 1949. Mem. faculty W.Va. U., Morgantown, from 1948, asso. prof. geology, 1955-60, prof., 1960-84, prof. emeritus, from 1984. Cons. to industry. Cooperating geologist W.Va. Geol. Survey, 1970— Contbr. articles to profl. jours. Served to lt. (j.g.) USNR, 1943-46. Fellow Geol. Soc. Am.; mem. Am. Assn. Petroleum Geologists, Soc. Econ. Paleontologists and Mineralogists, Nat. Assn. Geology Tchrs. (v.p. 1958), W.Va. Acad. Scis., Sigma Xi, Phi Beta Kappa. Home: Roanoke, Va. Died Feb. 22, 2007.

HEALY, HAROLD HARRIS, JR., lawyer; b. Denver, Aug. 27, 1921; s. Harold Harris and Lorena (Isom) H.; m. Elizabeth A. Debevoise, May 24, 1952; 1 son, Harold Harris III. AB, Yale U., 1943, LL.B., 1949. Bar: NY 1949, U.S. Supreme Ct. 1957. Exec. asst. to atty. gen. US Dept. Justice, Washington, 1957-59; mem. Debevoise & Plimpton, NYC, 1959-89, resident ptnr. Paris, 1964-67, of counsel NYC, 1989-92. Mem. Am. adv. council Ditchley Found., 1972-99; bd. dirs. Legal Aid Soc., 1968-89, chmn., 1975-79, pres.'s coun., 1989-2007 Bd. dirs. Met. Opera Guild, 1975-2000, Acad. Am. Poets, 1993-94; nat. coun. Glimmerglass Opera, 1992-2004; adv. dir. Met. Opera Assn., 1986-95; trustee Vassar Coll., 1977-86. Capt. F.A., AUS, 1943-46, ETO. Decorated Bronze Star medal. Mem. ABA (mem. coun. sect. of internat. law and practice 1987-90), N.Y. State Bar Assn., Assn. Bar City of N.Y. (sec. 1959-61), Am. Law Inst., Order of Coif, Am. Soc. Internat. Law (mem. exec. coun. 1977-80), Internat. Law Assn., Internat. Bar Assn., Union Internationale des Avocats (pres. 1979-81), Am. Coll. Investment Counsel, Coun. Fgn. Rels., Pilgrims U.S., Yale Law Sch. Assn. (exec. com. 1974-82, v.p. 1980-82), Century Assn., Univ. Club, Met. Club, Phi Beta Kappa, Zeta Psi, Phi Delta Phi, Chevalier de la Legion d'Honneur. Republican. Episcopalian. Home: New York, NY. Died Mar. 4, 2007.

HEALY, THOMAS P., lawyer; b. Rochester, NY, June 14, 1926; BA, U. Mich., 1949; LLB, Harvard U., 1952. Bar: Ill. 1952. Counsel Lord, Bissell & Brook, Chgo. Mem. ABA. Died Oct. 9, 2006.

HEATH, JOHN LAWRENCE, candy company executive; b. Robinson, Ill., Dec. 30, 1935; s. Vernon Lawrence and Beatrice (Kane) H.; m. Sheila Carole Owens, June 8, 1958; children: Lawrence A., Kerry L., April J., David O. Student, U. Ill., 1953-55; BS in Social Sci., Eastern Ill. U., 1958. Program dir., sta. mgr. Radio Sta. WEIC, Charleston, Ill., 1960-62; with L.S. Heath & Sons Inc., Robinson, Ill., from 1962, advt. merchandising and promotions mgr., 1962-64, gen. mgr. fund raising div., 1964-69, sr. v.p., 1969-71, chmn., from 1971. Dir. 1st Nat. Bank Robinson, 1970-87, vice chmn., 1976-85; dir. Central Ill. Pub. Service Co., Springfield, 1977— Mem. adminstrv. bd. 1st United Meth. Ch., Robinson, 1968—, chmn. adminstrv. bd., 1982-84, lay leader, 1972-75; trustee Wesley Found., So. Ill. U., Carbondale, 1980-87; mem. Nat. Bd. Ch. and Society, United Meth. Ch., 1984—, lay del. So. Ill. Ann. Conf., 1980-87; mem. Ill. Bldg. Authority, 1971-74; county fund raising chmn. Blackhawk dist. Wabash Valley Council Boy Scouts Am., 1970-71; bd. dirs. Embarras Regional Health Planning Council, Olney, Ill., 1975-78, chmn., 1975-76; trustee U. Ill. YMCA, Champaign, 1970-75; bd. dirs. Ill. 4-H Found. Campaign, 1973-75; mem. Eastern Ill. U. Found., Charleston, 1980—, bd. dirs., 1985—, v.p., 1987-88; bd. dirs. Crawford County Hosp. Dist., 1974-85, 1st vice chmn., 1975-76, 79, chmn., 1977-78, 80; bd. dirs., pres. Robinson High Sch. Acad. Found., 1984-85. Served with AUS, 1958-60. Mem. Nat. Confectioners Assn. (dir. 1974-79, v.p. 1981-83, co-chmn. nat. conv. 1974, gen. chmn. nat. conv. 1980, publicity com. 1970-72, 82-85), Nat. Candy Wholesalers Assn. (hon. dean 1978), Chocolate Mfrs. Assn. U.S. (dir. 1977-80, 85-87), Robinson C. of C. (dir. 1968-71), U.S. C. of C., Ill. C. of C. (dir. 1976-82, v.p. 1978-80), Eastern Ill. U. Alumni Assn. (dir. 1980-83, v.p. 1981-82, pres. 1982-83, chmn. alumni giving campaign 1981-82, Disting. Alumnus award 1984), Alpha Tau Omega Clubs: Quail Creek Country (Robinson) (trustee 1974-78), Union League (Chgo.), Mo. Athletic (St. Louis). Lodges: Kiwanis (Robinson) (pres. 1967), Elks, Moose. Died Jan. 9, 2006.

HECHT, JAIME SELIG, utility exec. b. NYC, Apr. 23, 1929; s. Samuel T. and Kate (Reisman) H.; m. Suzanne Goldemberg, June 8, 1952; children— Rachel, Joseph, David. BA, Columbia U., 1950; LL.B., 1953. Bar: N.Y. State bar 1954. Labor relations specialist Gen. Electric Co., Conneaut, Ohio, Louisville, 1953-61; atty. N.Y. State Electric & Gas Corp., Binghamton, 1961-63, Ithaca, 1963-67, asst. sec., 1967-70, sec., from 1970. Mem. Tompkins County Bar Assn., Am. Soc. Corp. Secs. Home: Ithaca, NY. Died Apr. 19, 2006.

HECHT, MANFRED H., psychologist, psychoanalyst; b. Vienna, Dec. 6, 1918; came to U.S., 1938; naturalized, 1943; s. Maximilian and Ada C. (Spiro) H.; m. Marie L. Engel, Aug. 25, 1941; 1 stepchild, Andrew M. (dec.). Cert., Med. Sch., U. Vienna, 1938; PhD, Columbia U., 1958; Psychoanalytic cert., Postgrad. Ctr. Mental Health, NYC, 1962. Leading bariton N.Y.C. Opera, 1948-52; psychology intern VA, 1955-58; fellow Postgrad. Ctr. Mental Health, NYC, 1958-62; pvt. practice psychotherapy and psychoanalysis NYC, from 1960; assoc. dir. dept. cmty. svsc. and edn., dir. pastoral counseling, 1964-80; sr. supr., tng. analyst, from 1978; affil. profl. staff Berkshire Med. Ctr., Pittsfield, Mass., 1989-99. Supr., cons. Religious Cons. Ctr., Roman Catholic Diocese of Bklyn., 1970-80; mem. adv. bds. various agencies and publs. Author various pubs. Cantor Congregation B'nai Jeshurun, Newark, 1948-58. Served with M.I. U.S. Army, 1943-45. Fellow Coun. Psychoanalytic Soc. (past pres.), N.Y. State Psychol. Assn. Home: Lenox, Mass. Died Feb. 4, 2006.

HEER, DAVID MACALPINE, sociology educator; b. Chapel Hill, NC, Apr. 15, 1930; s. Clarence and Jean Douglas (MacAlpine) H.; m. Nancy Whittier, June 29, 1957 (div. 1980); m. Kaye S. Heymann, Dec. 11, 1980 (dec. Apr. 2000); children: Douglas (dec.), Laura, Catherine. AB magna cum laude, Harvard U., 1950, MA, 1954, PhD, 1958. Statistician population div. U.S. Bur. Census, Washington, 1957-61; lectr., asst. research sociologist U. Calif., Berkeley, 1961-64; asst. prof. demography Harvard U. Sch. Public Health, Boston, 1964-68, assoc. prof., 1968-72; dir. Population Rsch. Lab., U. So. Calif., LA, 1995—2000, prof. sociology, 1972—2000, prof. sociology emeritus, from 2000; sr. fellow Ctr. Comparative Immigration Studies, U. Calif. San Diego, from 2000. Mem. population research study sect. NIH, 1971-73 Author: After Nuc. Attack: A Demographic Inquiry, 1965, Soc. and Population, 1968; author: (with Pini Herman) A Human Mosaic: An Atlas of Ethnicity in Los Angeles County, 1980—86, 1990, Undocumented Mexicans in the United States, 1990, Immigration in America's Future: Social Sci. Findings and the Policy Debate, 1996, Kingsley Davis: A Biography and Selections from his Writings, 2005; editor: Readings on Population, 1968, Social Stats. and the City, 1968. Mem. Population Assn. Am. (dir. 1970-73), Internat. Union Sci. Study Population. Home: San Diego, Calif. Died Mar. 13, 2007.

HEFFERN, GORDON EMORY, banker; b. Utica, Pa., Feb. 19, 1924; s. Cluade E. and Lillian A. (McKay) H.; m. Neva Lepley, Sept. 19, 1946 (dec.); children: Mary Heffern Maddex, John, Robert, Richard; m. Margaret. Student, Stevens Inst. Tech., 1944, U. Va., 1949. Asst. to pres., security analyst Peoples Nat. Bank of Charlottesville, Va., 1949-51; v.p. Nat. City Bank of Cleve., 1951-62, First Nat. City Bank of Alliance, Ohio, 1962-63; pres., chief exec. officer Goodyear Bank, Akron, 1963-74; pres., dir. Society Nat. Bank, Cleve., 1974-83, chmn., 1983-87; pres., chief exec. officer, dir. Society Corp., Cleve., 1975, chmn., 1983-87. Goodyear exec. prof. Coll. of Bus. Kent State U., 1988-90, mem. adv. bd. Bus. Sch.; mem. Pioneer-Standard Electronics, Inc., Scripps Howard Broadcasting Co., Biskind Devel. Co., A. Schulman, Inc. Mem. Fairmount Presbyterian Ch.; trustee U., Knight Found., Miami, Fla., Cleve. Clinic Found.; pres., chief exec. officer Akron Community Found., 1990-92. With USNR, 1942-46. Fellow Christian Athletes. Clubs: Akron City, Pepper Pike, Portage Country, Union; 50 (Cleve.), Congress Lake. Republican. Home: Bratenahl, Ohio. Died Aug. 20, 2007.

HEFFERNAN, NATHAN STEWART, retired state supreme court chief justice; b. Frederic, Wis., Aug. 6, 1920; s. Jesse Eugene and Pearl Eva (Kaump) H.; m. Dorothy Hillemann, Apr. 27, 1946; children: Katie (Mrs. Howard Thomas), Michael, Thomas. BA, U. Wis., 1942, LLB, 1948, LLD, 1999; postgrad., Harvard U. Sch. Bus. Adminstrn., 1943-44; LLD, Lakeland Coll., 1995. Bar: Wis. 1948, U.S. Dist. Ct. (we. dist.) Wis. 1948, U.S. Dist. Ct. (ea. dist.) Wis. 1950, U.S. Ct. Appeals (7th cir.) 1960, U.S. Supreme Ct. 1960. Assoc. firm Schubring, Ryan, Peterson & Sutherland, Madison, Wis., 1948-49; practice in Sheboygan, Wis., 1949-59; partner firm Buchen & Heffernan, 1951-59; counsel Wis. League Municipalities, 1949; research asst. to Gov. State of Wis., Madison, 1949; asst. dist. atty. Sheboygan County, 1951-53; city atty. City of Sheboygan, 1953-59; dep. atty. gen. State of Wis., 1959-62; U.S. atty. (we. dist.,) Wis. US Dept. Justice, 1962-64; justice Wis. Supreme Ct., 1964—95, chief justice, 1983-95. Lectr. mcpl. corps., 1961-64, appellate procedure and practice U. Wis. Law Sch., 1971-83; faculty Appellate Judges Seminar, Inst. Jud. Adminstrn., NYU, 1972-87; former mem. Nat. Council State Ct. Reps., chmn., 1976-77; ex-officio dir. Nat. Ctr. State Cts., 1976-77, mem. adv. bd. appellate justice project; former mem. Wis. Jud. Planning Com.; chmn. Wis. Appellate Practice and Procedure Com., 1975-76; mem. exec. com. Wis. Jud. Conf., 1978-95, chmn., 1983; pres. City Attys. Assn., 1958-59; chair Citizens Panel on Election Reform; co-chair Equal Justice Coalition. Wis. chmn. NCCJ, 1966-67; past exec. bd. Four Lakes Coun., Boy Scouts Am.; gen. chmn. Wis. Dem. Conv., 1960, 61; mem. Wis. Found.; bd. dirs. Inst. Jud. Adminstrn.; visitors U. Wis. Law Sch., 1970-83, chmn., 1973-76; past mem. corp. bd. Meth. Hosp.; former curator Wis. Hist. Soc., curator emeritus, 1990; trustee Wis. Meml. Union, Wis. State Libr., emeritus, William Freeman Vilas Trust Estate; v.p. U. Wis. Meml. Union Bldg. Assn.; former deacon Conglist. Ch. Lt. (s.g.) USNR, 1942-46, ETO, PTO. Recipient Disting. Svc. award NCCJ, 1968, Ann. Disting. Svc. award Wis. Mediation Assn., 1995, Lifetime Achievement award Milw. Bar Assn., 1995, Disting. Svc. award Dem. Party Sheboygan County, 1995; Disting. Jud. fellow Marquette U. Law Sch., 1996. Fellow Am. Bar Found. (life), Inst. for Jud. Adminstrn. (hon., bd. dirs., mem. faculty seminar), Wis. Bar Assn. (chmn. Wis. bar com. study on legal edn. 1995-96, hon. chmn. Equal Justice Coalition 1997—, Goldberg award for disting. svc.), Wis. Bar Found.; mem. ABA (past mem. spl. com. on adminstrn. criminal justice, mem. com. fed.-state delineation of jurisdiction, jud. adminstrn. com. on appellate ct., com. appellate time standards), Am. Law Inst. (life, adv. com. on complex litigation), Dane County Bar Assn., Sheboygan County Bar Assn., Am. Judicature Soc. (dir. 1977-80, chmn. program com. 1979-81), Wis. Law Alumni Assn. (bd. dirs., Disting. Alumni Svc. award 1989), Nat. Conf. Chief Justices (bd. dirs.), Nat. Assn. Ct. Mgmt., Wis. Rivers Alliance (bd. dirs.), Order of Coif, Iron Cross, U. Club (Madison, Wis.), Phi Kappa Phi, Phi Delta Phi. Clubs: Madison Lit. (pres. 1979-80); Harvard (Milw.); Harvard Bus. Sch. (Wis.). Home: Madison, Wis. Died Apr. 13, 2007.

HEGGLAND, RADOY WITT, energy company executive, consultant; b. Chgo., July 15, 1928; s. Thurlow Martin and Alice Marie (Witt) H.; m. Nancy Elizabeth Redd, June 12, 1949 (dec. Aug. 1983); children: Sherry, Sally; m. Shirley M. Agnew, Apr. 12, 1985. BS, Calif. Inst. Tech., 1949; MS (Sloan fellow), Mass. Inst. Tech., 1965. Mem. geol. dept. staff Conoco (formerly Continental Oil Co.), Wichita Falls, Tex., Roswell, N.Mex., New Orleans, Houston, 1949-62, divs. exploration mgr. Lafayette, La., 1962-64, chief geologist internat. NYC, 1965-67, mgr. exploration for N. Am. Houston, 1967-69; v.p. Conoco (Western Hemisphere exploration), 1970-76; exec. v.p. minerals Conoco (formerly Continental Oil co.), Denver, 1976-83, energy cons., from 1983. Mem. Am. Assn. Petroleum Geologists, Am. Mining Congress., Soc. Mining Engrs. Clubs: Hiwan Golf. Died Sept. 21, 2006.

HEGYI, JULIUS, conductor, musician; b. NYC, Feb. 2, 1923; s. Francois and Rose (Konye) H.; m. Charlotte Ann Barrier, Aug. 27, 1953; 1 child, Lisa. BA, Juilliard Sch. Music, 1943; pupil violin, Sascha Jacobsen, Jacques Gordon, Eddy Brown; pupil composition, Vittorio Giannini; pupil conducting, Dimitri Mitropoulos. With music faculty Williams Coll., from 1965, lectr. music, condr. and violinist in residence, from 1971; resident condr. Fla. Philharmonic, from 1991. Spl. cons. Nat. Endowment for Arts, Washington, 1979— Condr. Wagner Coll. Symphony, 1941-43, asso. condr., San Antonio Symphony, 1948-51, condr., San Antonio Little Orch., 1949-51, Abilene (Tex.) Symphony, 1952-55, Southwestern Symphony Center, 1951-56, Chattanooga Symphony, 1955-65, founder-dir., Sewanee Summer Music Center, 1958, founder-condr., Carlatti Orch., 1964, debut violinist, Town Hall, N.Y., 1945, chamber music concerts, solo recitals, U.S., Mexico; founder, Hegyi and Amati string quartets, 1941, Music in the Round series, 1951, mem., Gordon, Am. string quartets, N.Y. Philharmonic, City Center Ballet, RCA Victor Symphony, N.Y. Little Orch. Soc.; performer complete Beethoven String Quartet cycle, Bershire Quartet, 1970; mem., Williams Trio, dir. chamber music activities, music dir., condr., Albany (N.Y.) Symphony, 1966—, Berkshire Symphony, 1966—, Beijing Philharm., Shanghai Symphony, 1985; resident condr. Fla. Philharm. Orch., 1991. Recipient Frank Damrosch Scholarship, 1941, Alice Ditson award for service, 1957, nat. condr. recognition award Am. Symphony League, 1959; award for artistic excellence Albany League Arts, 1977; Alice M. Ditson Condrs. award Columbia U., 1983 Home: Fountain Hls, Ariz. Died Jan. 1, 2007.

HEILBRON, LOUIS HENRY, lawyer; b. Newark, May 12, 1907; s. Simon L. and Flora (Karp) H.; m. Delphine Rosenblatt, Oct. 30, 1929 (dec. 1993); children: John L., David M. AB, U. Calif., Berkeley, 1928, LLB, 1931, LLD, 1961, Golden Gate Coll., 1970; DHL, San Francisco State U., 1988. Bar: Calif. 1931. Assoc. Heller, Ehrman, White & McAuliffe, San Francisco, 1934-48, ptnr., from 1948. Sec., spl. cons. Dept. Social Welfare, State of Calif., 1932, asst. relief adminstr.,Calif., 1933, spl. cons. Dept. Relief Adminstrn., 1934-41; prin. atty. Bd. Econ. Warfare, 1942-43. Mem. Calif. Bd. Edn., 1959-61, pres., 1960-61; mem. Calif. Coordinating Council Higher Edn., 1961-69; chmn. bd. trustees Calif. State Colls., 1960-63, chmn. ednl. policy com. and faculty staff com., 1963-69; mem. Nat. Commn. on Acad. Tenure, 1971-73, Select Com. to Rev. Calif. Master Higher Edn. Plan, 1971-72, Fedn. Regional Accrediting Commns. Higher Edn., Council Post Secondary Edn., 1972-86; pres. San Francisco Jewish Community Ctr., 1949-52, San Francisco Pub. Edn. Soc., 1950-52; chmn. San Francisco Com. Fgn. Relations, 1977-79; trustee, exec. com. World Affairs Council No. Calif., pres., 1965-67; trustee Sta. KQED, 1966-72, v.p., 1971-72; trustee Golden Gate U., chmn., 1979-81; trustee Newhouse Found., 1956-76, U. Calif. Internat. House, 1953-77, U.C. Found., 1973-79; trustee Calif. Hist. Soc., v.p., 1981-83, pres., 1983-85; mem. San Francisco Human Rights Commn., 1969-75; chmn. adv. com. San Francisco State Coll., 1970-76. Served to maj. AUS, 1944-46, ETO. Decorated Bronze Star. Mem. ABA, Labor Law Com., Phi Beta Kappa (pres. No. Calif. 1972-73), Zeta Beta Tau. Jewish (pres. congregation 1954-57). Home: San Francisco, Calif. Died Dec. 20, 2006.

HEIMAN, GROVER GEORGE, JR., editor, writer; b. Galveston, Tex., July 26, 1920; s. Grover George and Rose Mary (Ulch) H.; m. Virginia D. Williamson, Feb. 14, 1942 (dec.); children: Virginia, Grover, Deborah, Richard. Student, Lee Coll., 1937-40, U. Tex., 1940-41; BS in Commerce cum laude, U. So. Calif., 1959. With USAAF, 1941-45; News reporter Corsicana (Tex.) Daily Sun, 1945-47; commd. 2d lt. USAAC, 1942; advanced through grades to col. USAF, 1963; spl. asst. to USAF Chief of Staff, Pentagon, Washington, 1959-63; chief of info. Allied Air Forces So. Europe, Naples, Italy, 1963-66; chief mags. and books divsn. Dept. Def., Pentagon, 1966-68; ret., 1968; mng. editor Armed Forces Mgmt. mag., Washington, 1968-70; assoc. editor Nation's Business mag., Washington, 1970-76, industry editor, 1976-78, mng. editor, 1978-80, editor, 1980-82, editor emeritus, 1982-99. Chmn. Naples Dependent Schs. bd., 1964-65. Author: (with Rutherford Montgomery) Jet Navigator, 1959, Jet Tanker, 1961, Jet Pioneers, 1963, (with Virginia Myers) Careers For Women In Uniform, 1971, Aerial Photography, 1973. Decorated DFC, Legion of Merit. Mem. Nat. Press Club, Beta Gamma Sigma. Roman Catholic. Home: Fairfax, Va. Died Oct. 12, 2006.

HEINEMAN, JACKLYN KAY, real estate consultant, relocation specialist; b. St. Louis, Apr. 18, 1939; d. E. Carleton and Nelle L. (Wilson) Spinney; m. Mason Scott Thomas, 1958 (div. 1968); 1 child, Toy Michelle Thomas Evans; m. G. Wendel Heineman, Oct. 1989. Student U. Denver, 1962, 1967-68. Credit mgr. Info. Handling Svcs., Denver, 1964-66; real estate agt., Denver, 1966-68; chpt. dir. Am. Express Club Continental, Denver, 1968-70; relocation dir. Koelbel & Co., Denver, 1977-80; dir. HomeSearch, Van Relco, Inc., Denver, 1980-84; East Coast mktg. cons. VanRelco Relocation Mgmt., 1984-85; founder, pres. The Deaton Group, 1986—. Active Am. Med. Ctr. Mem. Urban Land Inst., Nat. Assn. Corp. Real Estate Execs., Am. Soc. Home Inspectors, Am. Econ. Developers Coun., Am. Mensa. Clubs: English Speaking Union, Rocky Mountain Jaguar, Toastmasters Internat. Home: Bel Air, Md. Died Jan. 4, 2007.

HEINTZ, ROGER LEWIS, biochemist, educator, researcher; b. Jackson Center, Ohio, Mar. 15, 1937; s. Claude O. and Ruth A. (Thompson) H.; m. Judith A. Fisher, Aug. 11, 1962; children— Claude R., Robert A., James S., Steven G. BS, Ohio No. U., 1959; MS, Ohio State U., 1961; PhD, U. Wis.-Madison, 1964. NIH postdoctoral fellow U. Ky., Lexington, 1964-66, Am. Heart Assn. research fellow, 1966-68; asst. prof. Iowa State U., Ames, 1968-75; prof. biochemistry, biophysics SUNY-Plattsburgh, from 1975, chmn. biochemistry, biophysics sect., from 1978, chmn. dept. biol. sci., 1986-94. Bd. dirs. Plattsburgh Little Theatre, 1978-83; coach Babe Ruth baseball Grantee NIH, 1967-82, SUNY Research Found., 1976-82 Mem. AAAS, Am. Soc. for Biochemistry and Molecular Biology, Am. Chem. Soc., Sigma Xi, Phi Lambda Upsilon Democrat. Avocation: amateur ornithology. Home: Plattsburgh, NY. Died Feb. 10, 2007.

HEISERMAN, RICHARD DEAN, financial executive; b. Portland, Oreg., May 29, 1938; s. Ord J. and Lillian Irene (Poyser) H.; m. Patricia Ann Boyd, Mar. 19, 1960; children— Richard Scott, James Todd, Judith Ann, Pamela Sue. BS in Bus. Adminstrn, U. Denver, 1960; grad. diploma, Savs. & Loan Inst., 1966; postgrad., U. Ind., 1976. Mgmt. trainee Capitol Fed. Savs. & Loan Assn., Denver, 1960; sr. v.p. Capitol Fed. Savs. & Loan Assn. (constrn./comml. loan dept.), 1976-78, Capitol Fed. Savs. & Loan Assn. (mortgage loan div.), 1978, chmn. bd., pres., dir., from 1978; pres., chmn. bd. 1st Capitol Corp., from 1971, Columbine Title Co., 1974-80, C & H Investment Co., 1975-80; chmn. bd. First Capitol Mortgage, 1978-80. Mem. Denver U. adv. bd. real estate and constrn. mgmt., 1981; bd. dirs. Schlessman br. YMCA, 1962-64, Colo. Apt. Assn., 1972-75, Home Builders of Met. Denver, 1975. Mem. Denver C. of C. (chmn. econ. devel. council 1980-81), Mountain States Alumni Assn. of SAE (pres. 1966), U.S. League Savs. Assn. (mem. legis. com. 1979-80), Savs. & Loan League of Colo. (legis. steering com. 1980, pres., dir. 1980-81) Clubs: Masons (Shriner), Rotary (program chmn.). Republican. Methodist. Home: Englewood, Colo. Died Aug. 29, 2006.

HEIZER, PATRICIA HUDSON, insurance company official; b. Dallas, July 31, 1927; d. Daryl Jack and Mary Lila (Hale) Hudson; m. E.C. Webb, Sept. 8, 1950 (div. 1952); m. Bobby V. Heizer, July 29, 1966; 1 dau., Mary Patricia. B.A., So. Meth. U., 1948. Gen. clk. Travelers Ins. Co., Dallas, 1948-51; tchr. Dallas Pub. Schs., 1952-56; clk. thru underwriter U.S.-Ins. Group, Dallas, 1956-76, trainer, 1976—, sr. tng. assoc. of underwriting, 1976—. Mem. Ins. Women Dallas (dir., chmn., pres.), Am. Soc. Tng. and Devel., Nat. Assn. Ins. Women (cert.; Ins. Woman of Yr. 1981; dir. Dallas). Methodist. Lodge: Eastern Star. Home: Grapevine, Tex. Died Mar. 19, 2006.

HELLER, CHARLES ANDREW, JR., electric utilities company executive; b. Teaneck, NJ, Mar. 18, 1929; s. Charles Andrew and Lillian Laura (Reuter) H.; m. Helen Johansen, July 19, 1952; children: Charles Andrew, Janice Maria, Richard Craig. BA, Rutgers U., 1951; MBA, U. Pa., 1956; MS (Alfred P. Sloan fellow), M.I.T., 1966. With Am. Electric Power Service Corp., NYC, 1956-63; with Ohio Power Co., Canton, 1963-68, 70—, v.p., 1974-76, exec. v.p., 1976-81, chief operating officer, from 1976, pres., from 1981. Exec. asst. Wheeling Electric Co., W.Va., 1968-70; former exec. v.p., dir. Ohio Electric Co.; v.p., dir. Cardinal Operating Co., Central Coal Co., Central Ohio Coal Co., Central Operating Co., So. Ohio Coal Co., Windsor Power House Coal Co., from 1976; v.p. Beech Bottom Power Co., Inc., Franklin Real Estate Co., from 1976, Ind. Franklin Realty, Inc., from 1976; dir. Ohio Electric Utility Inst., from 1976, pres., from 1978; dir. Central Trust Co. Northeastern Ohio, from 1975 Mem. Council for Reorganization of Ohio State Govt., 1967; dir. Canton Welfare Found., 1975-78; mem. Malone Coll. Adv. Bd., from 1976. Served to capt. USAF, 1951-53. Mem.: Canton, Brookside Country, Columbus Athletic, Elks, Rotary. Republican. Lutheran. Home: Canton, Ohio. Died Sept. 26, 2006.

HELLER, DANIEL ROBERT, investment banker, portfolio manager; b. Washington, Mar. 23, 1950; s. Lester Harry and Adele (Ravsky) H. BA, U. Md., 1972; MA, Catholic U. Am., 1976. Project mgr. Nat. Dist. Atty.'s Assn., Washington, 1973-75; theatre mgr. Catholic U., Washington, 1975-82; dir. devel. Provincetown (Mass.) Playhouse, 1982-84; computer mgr. Tandy Corp., Washington, 1984-91; investment advisor Prudential Securities, Washington, 1992-95; CFO Computer Ctr. Electronics, Kensington, Md., 1995-98; sr. v.p. investment bankingm sr, portfolio mgr. Strategic Assets, Inc., 1997-98; sr. v.p., CFO, dir. rsch. Bethesda Ptnrs., L.P., from 1998. Investment advisor Summer Opera Theatre Co., Washington, 1993—; bd. dirs. Br. Am. Bus. Coun., Washington. Author: Structure and Efficiency Models for District Attorney Offices, 1973, 2d edit., 1974, 3d edit., 1975; photographer (book) 1915, The Cultural Moment, 1991. Bd. dirs. Project SHARE, Washington, 1993—, Summer Opera Theatre Co., Washington, 1993—, Am. Opera Scholarship Soc. Mem. Am. Opera Scholarship Soc. (bd. dirs.), Internat. Brotherhood Knights of the Vine, City Tavern Club. Republican. Roman Catholic. Avocations: theater, opera, antiques, sailing, yachting. Home: Silver Spring, Md. Died Jan. 5, 2006.

HELLMAN, HENRY MARTIN, chemistry educator; b. Norrfors, Sweden, July 4, 1920; came to U.S., 1927, naturalized, 1942; s. Karl Johan and Mathilda (Karlsson) H.; m. Isabel Julia Paul, Dec. 21, 1951. BS, Ind. U., 1943; MS, Purdue U., 1945, PhD, 1947. Instr. N.Y.U., 1947-50, asst. prof. chemistry, 1950-55, asso prof., 1955-69, prof. organic chemistry, from 1969, chmn. chemistry dept., 1964-70. Contbr. articles profl. jours. Hon. fellow Am.-Scandinavian Found.; mem. Am. Chem. Soc., Chem. Soc. London, Sigma Xi, Phi Lambda Upsilon. Home: New York, NY. Died Nov. 3, 2005.

HELMBOLD, NANCY PEARCE, classical languages educator; b. Abilene, Tex., Dec. 16, 1918; d. George Alfred and Bess (Hall) Pearce; m. William Clark Helmbold, July 27, 1958 (dec. 1969); 1 child, Alexandra Katherine AB, U. Tex.-Austin, 1939; MA, U. Calif.-Berkeley, 1953, PhD, 1957. Asst. prof. Mt. Holyoke Coll., South Hadley, Mass., 1957-59; vis. asst. prof. U. Oreg., Eugene, 1961-63; asst. prof. U. Chgo., 1963-70, assoc. prof., 1970-83, prof., 1983—89. Mem. editl. bd. Classical Philology, 1966—. Served to lt. (j.g.) USN, 1943-46 Mem. Am. Philol. Assn. Clubs: Chgo. Classical (pres. 1981-83). Democrat. Home: Chicago, Ill. Died Oct. 27, 2007.

HELMSLEY, LEONA MINDY, hotel executive; b. NYC, July 4, 1920; m. Leo E. Panzirer (div. 1952); children: Jay Robert (dec. 1982); m. Joseph Lubin 1953 (div. 1960); m. Harry B. Helmsley, Apr. 8, 1972 (dec. Jan., 1997). Former model; vice pres. Pease & Elliman, NYC, 1962-69; pres. Sutton & Towne Residential, NYC, 1967-70; sr. v.p. Helmsley Spear, NYC, 1970-72, Brown, Harris, Stevens, NYC, 1970-72; pres., CEO, chmn. bd. Helmsley Hotels, Inc., NYC, 1980—2007. On Dec. 30, 1989, was sentenced to four years in prison and fined $7.1 million for tax fraud; started and served the prison sentence for tax fraud, 1992—93; was released from home confinement, 1994. Was the subject (TV film) Leona Helmsley: The Queen of Mean, 1990, and (books) The Queen of Mean by Ransdell Pierson, Palace Coup by Michael Moss, Unreal Estate: the Rise and Fall of Harry & Leona Helmsley by Richard Hammer. Contributed monies to NY-Presbyn. Hosp., Hurricane Katrina relief efforts, help the families of firefighters after 9/11, & help rebuild African-American churches that had been burned down in the South. Named Woman of Yr. N.Y. Council Civic Affairs, 1970; named Woman of Yr. Town & Country Condos & Coops., 1981; named one of Forbes' Richest Americans, 2006; recipient Service award Ort Sch. Engring., 1981, Profl. Excellence award Les Dames d'Escoffier, 1981, Spl. Achievement award Sales Execs. Club N.Y., 1981, Woman of Yr. award Internat. Hotel Industry, 1982. Died Aug. 20, 2007.

HELSLEY, GROVER CLEVELAND, pharmaceutical company executive; b. Strasburg, Va., Sept. 26, 1926; s. Grover Clevel and Vallie Mae (Putnam) H.; m. Betty Jean Midkiff, Oct. 30, 1949; children— Grover Cleveland, Linda Suzanne, Robert Christopher. BS with honors, Shepherd Coll., 1954; MS, U. Va., 1956, PhD (Philip Francis duPont fellow), 1958. Research chemist E.I. duPont de Nemours & Co., Inc., Richmond, Va., 1958-62; research chemist A.H. Robins Co., Richmond, 1962-64, group leader, 1964-68, asso. dir. chem. research, 1968-70; dir. research Hoechst-Roussel Pharms. Inc., Somerville, N.J., 1970-72, v.p. pharm. research, from 1972, sr. v.p. pharm. research, from 1987. Contbr. sci. articles to profl. jours. Served with USAAF, 1945-47. Mem. Am. Chem. Soc., Pharm. Mfrs. Assn. (editorial adv. bd. drug devel. research 1980), Indsl. Research Inst. Mem. Christian Ch. (Disciples Of Christ). Patentee in field. Died Apr. 13, 2006.

HEMBARSKY, IRENE P. DRAGANOSKY, nurse; b. Freeland, Pa., Jan. 13, 1936; d. Joseph and Helen (Yencho) Draganosky; m. Myron Hembarsky, Aug. 2 1958 (div.); 1 child, Mark. Diploma in Nursing, Allentown Hosp., Pa., 1956; BA in Sociology cum laude, La Salle coll., 1980, MBA in Healthcare Adminstrn., 1985. Cert. profl. healthcare quality nurse, Pa., N.J. Charge nurse Albert Einstein Med. Ctr., Phila., 1969-77, quality assurance nurse coord., 1982-86; coord., dept. head quality assurance program St. Joseph Hosp., Phila., 1977-82; clin. svcs. nurse coord. Spectrum Health Svcs., Phila., 1986; UR nurse coord. Grad. Hosp., Phila., 1988; P.I. coord. Our Lady of Lourdes, Camden, N.J., 1988-94. Cons. in nursing, Tech. Adv. Svc. to Attys., Ft. Washington, Pa.; nursing cons. quality assurance, Phila., 1987-89, Greater Atlantic Health Svcs., Phila., 1995. Reviewer books in field; contbr. articles to profl. publs. Chair Youth Aid Panel, Phila., 1988-91; mem. com. Walnut St. Theatre, Phila.; vol. Betsy Ross House, Walnut St. Vol. Troups, PCT Co., Wilma Theatre, Parish Pastoral Coun.; tour guide Holy Trinity Ch. Mem. ANA, Pa. Nurses Assn., Hosp. Assn. of Pa., Nat. Assn. Healthcare Quality, Am. Soc. Healthcare Risk Mgmt., Allentown Hosp. Sch. Nursing Alumni (bd. dirs. 1957). Avocation: volunteer work. Home: Philadelphia, Pa. Died Apr. 25, 2007.

HEMPSTONE, SMITH, JR., journalist, former ambassador; b. Washington, Feb. 1, 1929; s. Smith and Elizabeth (Noyes) H.; m. Kathaleen Fishback, Jan. 30, 1954; 1 dau. Student, George Washington U., 1946-47; BA with honors, U. of South, 1950, LittD (hon.), 1969; Nieman fellow, Harvard U., 1964-65. Rewrite man AP, Charlotte, NC; 1952; with Nat. Geog. mag., Washington, 1954; reporter Louisville Times, 1953, Evening Star, Washington, 1955-56; fgn. corr. Africa, Asia, Europe and Latin Am. for Chgo. Daily News, 1960-66, Washington Evening Star, 1966-69, assoc. editor, 1970-75; exec. editor Washington Times, 1982-84, editor-in-chief, 1984-85; nationally syndicated newspaper columnist, 1970-89; US amb. to Kenya US Dept. State, Nairobi, 1989-93; diplomat in residence U. South, Sewanee, Tenn., 1993, Va. Mil. Inst., Lexington, 1994. Fellow Inst. Current World Affairs, 1956-60 Author: (non-fiction) Africa, Angry Young Giant, 1961, Rebels, Mercenaries and Dividends-The Katanga Story, 1962, Rogue Ambassador, 1997; (novels) A Tract of Time, 1966, In the Midst of Lions, 1968; mem. editl. bd. Nieman Reports, 1965-73. Alumni trustee U. South, 1974-78; bd. govs. Inst. Current World Affairs, 1974-78. Recipient Fgn. Corr. award Sigma Delta Chi and Overseas Press Club. Mem. Chevy Chase Club (Md.), Met. Club (Washington). Episcopalian. Died Nov. 19, 2006.

HEMRY, JEROME ELDON, lawyer; b. Kirksville, Mo., July 22, 1905; s. U.S.G. and Rose M. (Plumb) H.; m. Martha L. Langston, Aug. 1, 1934; children: Jerome Louis, Kenneth Marshall. AB, Oklahoma City U., 1926; JD, U. Okla., 1928; LL.M., Harvard U., 1929. Bar: Okla. 1928. Partner Hemry & Hemry, Oklahoma City, 1931-82, of counsel, from 1983; prof. law Central Okla. Sch. Law, 1931-41; dean, prof. law Langston U., 1948-49; dir., counsel Am. Gen. Life Ins. Co. Okla., 1959-79. Pres., gen. counsel Gen. Constrn. Corp., 1941-45; legislative counsel Okla. Chain Store Assn., 1941-44; Mem. Bd. Conf. Claimant's Okla. Ann. Conf.; treas. Oklahoma City S. Dist. Contbr. articles legal jours. Bd. dirs. Family and Children's Service, 1939-56. Mem. Okla. Assn. Mcpl. Attys. (pres. 1956-57), Am., Okla. bar assns., Order of Coif, Phi Delta Phi, Lambda Chi Alpha. Methodist (pres., counsel trustees). Clubs: Lions (Oklahoma City), Men's Dinner (Oklahoma City). Home: Oklahoma City, Okla. Died Dec. 30, 2006.

HENDERSON, DONALD MUNRO, geology educator; b. Boston, Nov. 8, 1920; s. William Davis and Margaret (Fessenden) H.; m. Margaret R. Foster, 1948; children: Donald M., Robert W., Peter F., Margaret A., Alexander M. AB, Brown U., 1943; PhD, Harvard U., 1950. Faculty U. Ill., Urbana-Champaign, from 1948, prof. geology specializing in mineralogy, from 1969. Home: Urbana, Ill. Died Oct. 21, 2006.

HENDERSON, DONALD WAYNE, air force officer, aeronautic engineer; b. Roanoke, Va., Feb. 26, 1938; s. Grover Q. and Margaret H. (Bolton) H.; m. Dawn E. BeMent, Aug. 25, 1962; children— Scott A., Gary W. BS in Aero. Engring., U. Va., Charlottesville, 1960; MS in Instrumentation Engring., U. Mich., Ann Arbor, 1962; MS in Systems Mgmt., U. So. Calif., Los Angeles; Cert. program mgmt. devel., Harvard U., Boston. Commd. 2d lt. U.S. Air Force, 1962, advanced through ranks to maj. gen., 1985, flight test engr. Holloman AFB, N.Mex., 1962-66, aerospace research pilot sch. Edwards AFB, Calif., 1966-69, asst./sr. officer mgmt. HQ A FSC Andrews AFB, Md., 1969-71; dep. dir./program control SRAM Program Office WPAFB, Ohio, 1971-73; exec. to DCS/Systems HQ AFSC Andrews AFB, Md., 1973-75; program mgr. SD Los Angeles AFB, Calif., 1975-82; comdr. SAMTO Vandenberg AFB, Calif., 1982-86; v.p. engring. and tech. Burlington No. R.R., Overland Park, Kans., from 1986. Recipient Gen. Bernard A. Schriever award Calif. Air Force Assn., 1985, Man of Yr., 1985; Thomas D. White Space trophy Nat. Geographic Soc., 1985. Home: Marco Island, Fla. Died July 29, 2006.

HENDERSON, GWENDOLYN WITHERSPOON, education educator; b. Charleston, S.C., Sept. 11, 1931; d. James William and Myrtle Louise (Ruff) Witherspoon; A.B., Fisk U., Nashville, 1951; M.S., Oreg. State U., 1974, Ph.D., 1976; divorced; children: Valton D., Alan C. Researcher, Sloan-Kettering Inst., N.Y.C., 1951-53; tchr. sci., chmn. dept. W.A. Perry Jr. High Sch., Columbia, S.C., 1956-62; tchr. math. and chemistry, div. chmn. Tolleston High Sch., Gary, Ind., 1962-68; tchr. phys. scis., chemistry, chmn. sci. dept. Lower Richland High Sch., Columbia, 1968-73; instr. sci. edn. Oreg. State U., 1973-76, EOP dir., acad. coordinator 1974-79; assoc. dir. govt. contract leadership/mgmt. tng. Atlanta U., 1979-80; prof., coordinator math. and sci. dept. edn. U. N.C., Asheville, 1980—; past pres. Richland County Edn. Assn. Exec. bd., exec. com., chmn. budget com. United Way Benton County (Oreg.), 1974-79; exec. bd., exec. com. Consumer Credit Counseling Service, Asheville, 1980-84; pres. Corvallis NAACP, 1976-79; mem. exec. bd. LWV, Columbia, 1968-73; mem. Oreg. Gov.'s Commn., 1976-78; exec. bd. YWCA, Asheville, 1982-84; exec. bd., chmn. planning and programs com., vice-chair UNC Faculty Assembly. Recipient award N.C. Sci. Edn. Assn., Feldman award UNCA Minorities, 1989; grantee Carnegie Corp., 1954-55, NSF, 1957, 59-60, 71-73, Oreg. State U. Found., 1973, 75, 77, 83; N.C. State Dept. Public Instrn. grantee, 1986; F. Smith Reynolds grantee. Mem. Nat. Sci. Tchrs. Assn. (bd. dirs. 1990-91, tchr. edn. com. 1990-91, Task Forces on Articulation and Non-Confs., chmn. nominations com. Task Force on U.S. Sci. Standards), Nat. Assn. Women Deans, Adminstrs. and Counselors, Assn. Edn. Tchrs. of Sci. (bd. dirs. 1984-91, pres.-elect 1989-90, pres. 1990-91), Am. Chem. Soc. (membership com. 1987-90, western N.C. long-range com.), N.C. Sci. Tchrs. Assn. (award 1985, chair long range planning com. 1988-90, chmn. multicultural com. 1992—), Urban League (exec. bd. Columbia 1970-73), Phi Delta Kappa, Delta Sigma Theta (chpt. community relations com. chmn. 1949, service cert. 1981, v.p. 1982-87, pres. 1987-91), Delta Kappa Gamma (profl. relations chmn., v.p. 1988-90). Methodist. Club: Altrusa (v.p., chmn. internat. relations com. Corvallis, Oreg. 1977-79, Asheville, 1980-85). Author articles in field. Home: Fletcher, NC. Died July 25, 2006.

HENDERSON, ROBERT EARL, mechanical engineer, educator, consultant; b. Olean, NY, Nov. 1, 1935; s. Kenneth Peter and Marion (Nichols) H.; m. E. Annalee Rosenwie, Aug. 10, 1957 (dec. July 1994); children: Gregory Dwight, Michael Edwin, Lori Elizabeth; m. Mary J. Ball, Dec. 28, 1996. BS, Pa. State U., 1958, MS, 1962; PhD, Cambridge U., Eng., 1973. Aerodynamicist McDonnel Applied Rsch. Lab., Pa. State U., 1959-73, assoc. prof. mech. engring., 1973-79, prof., 1979-91, prof. emeritus, from 1991. Cons., 1991-95; chief sci. Noesis, Inc., 1995—; assoc. dir. Garfield Thomas Water Tunnel, 1980-82, head dept. fluid dynamics and turbomachinery, 1983-89, asst. dir. applied sci. div., 1990-91. Contbr. articles to profl. jours. Recipient Disting. Performance award Applied Rsch. Lab., Pa. State U., 1981. Fellow ASME, AIAA (assoc.); mem. Sigma Xi, Pi Mu Epsilon. Died Sept. 22, 2006.

HENDL, WALTER, conductor, composer, musician; b. West New York, NJ, Jan. 12, 1917; s. William and Ella (Wittig) H.; m. Barbara Heisley; 1 dau by previous marriage, Susan. Pvt. study piano with, David Saperton; student, Clarence Adler, 1934-37; pvt. study conducting with, Fritz Reiner; faculty, Sarah Lawrence Coll., 1939-41, Curtis Inst. Music, 1937-41; MusD (hon.), Cin. Coll. Music, 1954; LHD (hon.), Edinboro U. Pa., 1990. Dir. Eastman Sch. Music, Rochester, NY, 1964-72; prof. conducting D'Angelo Sch. Music Mercy Hurst Coll., Erie, Pa., 1990-94. Active as condr. and pianist, Berkshire Music Center, 1941-42, asst. condr., pianist, N.Y. Philharmonic 1945-49, mus. dir., Dallas Symphony, 1949-58, Chautauqua (N.Y.) Symphony Orch., 1953-74, assoc. condr., Chgo. Symphony Orch., 1958-64, mus. dir., Ravinia (Ill.) Festival, 1959-63; orchestral dir., Erie (Pa.) Philharm., 1976-89, condr. emeritus, 1989-2007; guest condr. in Europe, USSR, S. Am., Japan, Asia; also recs.; composer: Broadway prodn. Dark of the Moon, 1945, A Village Where They Ring No Bells, Loneliness (recipient Alice M. Ditson award, Columbia 1953). Home: Erie, Pa. Died Apr. 10, 2007.

HENDREN, GARY E., retail executive; b. Muskogee, Okla., Apr. 9, 1943; s. Conley L. and Millie M. (Olson) H.; m. Cecelia L. Ryser, June 16, 1962 (div. Feb. 1996); children: Tracy E., Jeffrey S.; m. Nancy J. James, June 7, 1996. BS in Pharmacy, U. Okla., 1965; student, U. Kansas City, Mo., 1960-63. Registered pharmacist, Okla., Mo., Ind. Pharmacist Kirk's Drug Shop, Muskogee, 1965-66; successively regional v.p., v.p. ops., v.p. mktg., pres. Super X Drugs, Cin., 1966-90; retail cons. Cin., 1990-91; exec. v.p. Fred's, Inc., Memphis, 1991-94; retail consultant Memphis, from 1994. Mem. adv. bd. U. Cin. Coll. Pharmacy, 1986-91, U. Ga. Coll. Pharmacy, 1985-90, U. Ky. Coll. Pharmacy, Drug Store News, N.Y.C., 1985-90. Bd. dirs. Boys Hope-Cin., 1987-91; chmn. bd. trustees Ursuline Acad., Cin., 1988-91. Mem. Kenwood Country Club, Chickasaw Country Club. Republican. Methodist. Avocations: golf, tennis, model railroads. Died July 1, 2006.

HENDRICKSON, LOUISE, retired association executive, retired social worker; b. Lansdowne, Pa., Sept. 14, 1916; d. Norman and Gertrude (Powers) H. AA, Long Beach Jr. Coll., 1936; BA, U. Calif., Berkeley, 1938, gen. secondary tchr.'s cert., 1939; MS in Social Work, Columbia U., 1952. Cert. secondary tchr., Calif.; registered social worker, Calif. Dir. young adult program YWCA, Oakland, Calif., 1944-48, dir. group work and informal edn. svcs. Bklyn., 1948-53, exec. dir. Spokane, Wash., 1953-58; field cons. Nat. Bd. YWCA, Chgo., 1958-63, assoc. exec. community divsn. NYC, 1963-66, exec. community divsn., 1966-71, dir. orgn. devel., 1971-74, dep. exec. dir., 1974-82, ret., 1982. Contbr. articles to profl. jours. Pres. Cmty. Welfare Coun., Spokane, 1956-57; mem. majority coun. Emily's List, Washington; mem. Common Cause, LWV. Mem. NASW (charter 1958-62). Home: Newtown, Pa. Died Jan. 7, 2007.

HENKIN, LEON ALBERT, mathematician, educator; b. Bklyn., Apr. 19, 1921; s. Ascher and Rose (Goldberg) H.; m. Ginette Potvin, Sept. 8, 1950; children: Paul Jacques, Julian David. AB, Columbia U., 1941; MA, Princeton U., 1942, PhD, 1947; DS (hon.), U. Ill., Chgo., 1995. Mathematician Manhattan Project, 1942-46; Henry B. Fine instr., Frank Jewett postdoctoral fellow Princeton U., 1947-49; from asst. prof. to asso. prof. math. U. So. Calif., 1949-53; mem. faculty U. Calif.-Berkeley, 1953-91, prof. math., 1958-91, prof. emeritus, 1991—2006, chmn. dept., 1966-68, 83-85, assoc. dir. Lawrence Hall Sci., 1973—75. Vis. prof. Dartmouth Coll., 1960-61; Fulbright rsch. scholar, Amsterdam, The Netherlands, 1954-55, Technion, Haifa, Israel, spring 1979; Guggenheim fellow, mem. Inst. Advanced Study, Princeton, 1961-62; vis. fellow All Souls Coll., Oxford (Eng.) U., 1968-69; vis. scholar U. Colo., 1975, U. de Paris VII, 1987; Disting. vis. prof. Mills Coll., 1990-95. Author: La Structure Algebrique des theories Mathématique, 1955, (with others) Retracing Elementary Mathematics, 1962, Cylindric Algebras, Part I, 1971, Part II, 1985, Cylindric Set Algebras, 1981 also articles. Mem. U.S. Commn. on Math. Instrn., 1978-83, chmn., 1981-82. Recipient Lester R. Ford award, 1972, Berkeley Citation, U. Calif-Berkeley, 1991, Leon Henkin Citation for Disting. Svc., 2000. Fellow AAAS (coun. del. for math. sect.); mem. Nat. Coun. Tchrs. Math., Assn. Symbolic Logic (pres. 1962-64), Am. Math. Soc. (coun. 1962-64), Math. Assn. Am. (Chauvenet prize 1964, Yueh-Gin Gung and Dr. Charles Y. Hu award for Disting. Svc. to Mathematics, 1990), Can. Math. Soc., Assn. for Women in Math., Nat. Assn. Math., ACLU (bd. dirs. Berkeley chpt. 1964-66), Phi Beta Kappa (vis. lectr. 1993-94), Sigma Xi. Home: Oakland, Calif. Died Nov. 1, 2006.

HENLE, PETER, retired economist, arbitrator; b. NYC, Feb. 12, 1919; s. James and Marjorie (Jacobson) H.; m. Theda W. Ostrander, Aug. 25, 1941 (dec. 2005); children: Michael G., James M., Paul J. BA, Swarthmore Coll., 1940; MA, Am. U., 1947. Mem. rsch. staff, asst. dir. rsch. Am. Fed. Labor, Washington, 1946-55; asst. dir. rsch. AFL-CIO, Washington, 1955-61; chief economist Bur. Labor Stats. US Dept. Labor, Washington, 1961-71, dep. asst. sec. for planning & evaluation rsch., 1977-79; sr. specialist Labor Congl. Research Service, Library of Congress, Washington, 1972-77; vis. economist Brookings Instn.; econ. cons., arbitrator Arlington, Va., 1979-92. Contbr. articles to profl. jours. Chmn. Arlington County (Va.) Manpower Planning Coun., 1975-77; trustee Arlington County Employees Retirement System, 1985-89. With AUS, 1941-42; served to maj. USAAF, 1942-45. Recipient Disting. Achievement award US Dept. Labor, 1968; Brookings Instn. fed. exec. fellow, 1971-72 Mem. Nat. Acad. Arbitrators, Indsl. Rels. Rsch. Assn. Died Feb. 20, 2007.

HENLEY, EARLE BURR, JR., retired manufacturing company executive; b. Oakland, Calif., Apr. 16, 1915; s. Earle Burr and Pauline (Mathews) H.; m. Grace H. Jones, 1940; children: Matthew O., Peter J. BS, Cornell U., 1937, LL.B., 1940. Bar: N.Y. 1940, also U.S. Supreme Ct. 1946. With firm Mudge, Stern, Williams & Tucker, NYC, 1940-43, Mudge, Stern, Baldwin & Todd, 1946-55; sec. Gen. Equipment Precision Corp., Tarrytown, N.Y., 1955-68; asst. sec. Singer Co., NYC, 1968-85. Mem., chmn. New Castle (N.Y.) Town Planning Bd., 1958-80. Served to 1st lt. AUS, 1943-46. Mem.: Church (N.Y.C.). Republican. Home: Chappaqua, NY. Died Oct. 3, 2006.

HENNECY, BOBBIE BOBO, former English language educator; b. Tignall, Ga., Aug. 11, 1922; d. John Ebb and Lois Helen (Gulledge) Bobo; m. James Howell Hennecy, Dec. 28, 1963; 1 child, Erin. Student, Wesleyan Conservatory, 1943-44; AB summa cum laude, Mercer U., Macon, Ga., 1950; postgrad. English-Speaking Union scholar, Oxford U., Eng., 1961; MA, Emory U., 1962; postgrad., Cambridge U., Eng., 1987. Sec. Tattnall Sq. Bapt. Ch., 1943-48; sec., adminstrv. asst. to pres., instr. Mercer U., 1950-61, instr. English, 1961-76, asst. prof., 1976-89, emeritus assoc. prof. and adj. prof., from 1989. Founder Tattnall Sq. Acad., Macon, 1968, sec. acad. corp., 1968-73, dir., 1968-78. Author numerous poems printed in anthologies Nat. Libr. Poetry. Bobbie Bobo Hennecy scholarship named in her hon. Tattnall Sq. Acad., Mercer U.; NDEA fellow Emory U., 1962; recipient plaque for thirty yrs. svc. as advisor to Psi Gamma Chi Omega, 1983, named outstanding Psi Gamma Chi Omega, 1995; recipient award for Poetry by U.D.C., 1995, Editors Choice awards for Oustanding Achievement in Poetry, Nat. Libr. Poetry, 1995, 96, 97, 98; named to Internat. Poetry Hall of Fame, 1997. Mem. AAUW (chpt. v.p. 1959, pres. 1964), AAUP, MLA, Nat. Libr. Poetry, S. Atlantic MLA, LWV, UDC (pres. 1994-96, award for poetry 1995), DAR (registrar 1980-82), YWCA (life), So. Comparative Lit. Assn., Am. Comparative Lit. Assn., Internat. Soc. Poetry (disting. mem. 1997), Internat. Comparative Lit. Assn., Nat. Assn. Tchrs. English, Ga. Assn. Tchrs. English, English Speaking Union, Collegiate Press (adv. bd.), Am. Acad. Poets, Soc. Am. Poets, Pres. Club of Mercer U., Mid. Ga. Art Assn., Hereditary Register, Soc. Genealogists London, Nat. Soc. So. Dames, Nat. Soc. Magna Charta, Daus. of 1812, Descendants, Colonial Clergy, Daus. of Am. Colonists, Jamestowne Soc., Colonial Dames XVII Century (chpt. 1st v.p. 1988-91), Colonial Order of the Crown (descendants of Charlemagne), Ams. of Royal Descent, Mid. Ga. Hist. Soc., Coosa County Ala. Hist. Soc., Marion County S.C. Mus., Friends of the Cannonball House, Cardinal Key, Sigma Tau Delta, Sigma Mu (pres., v.p., sec.-treas.), Phi Delta (advisor), Phi Kappa Phi, Alpha Psi Omega, Chi Omega (alumnae pres. 1953, advisor 1953-83). Baptist. Home: Forsyth, Ga. Died Feb. 19, 2006.

HENNESSEY, EDWARD FRANCIS, retired state supreme court justice; b. Boston, Apr. 20, 1919; s. Thomas M. and Winifred C. (Tracey) H.; m. Elizabeth Ann O'Toole, Oct. 15, 1945; 1 dau., Beth Ann. BS cum laude, Northeastern U., 1941, LL.D., 1976; LL.B. cum laude, Boston U., 1949, LL.D., 1976, Suffolk U., 1974, New Eng. Sch. Law, 1974. Bar: Mass. 1949. Partner firm Martin Magnuson & Hennessey, Boston, 1950-66; judge Mass. Superior Ct., 1967-71; asso. justice Supreme Jud.

Ct. of Mass., 1971-76, chief justice, 1976-89. Lectr. on trial practice Boston U., 1956-64 Author: (with Martin) Trial Practice, 2 vols, 1954. Served to capt. U.S. Army, 1941-45. Decorated Bronze Star; recipient Distinguished Pub. Service award Boston U., 1975, St. Thomas More Pub. Service award Diocese of Worcester, 1975 Fellow Am. Bar Assn.; mem. Boston Bar Assn., Mass. Bar Assn., Nat. Conf. of Chief Justices (pres. 1985-86), Nat. Ctr. for State Cts. (pres. 1985-86). Home: Needham, Mass. Died Mar. 8, 2007.

HENNIN, PATRICIA KANE, construction and real estate company executive, consultant; b. Rockville Center, N.Y., June 17, 1943; d. Daniel H. and Helen (Shirkey) Kane; m. Patrice Marcel Hennin, Dec. 28, 1965; children: Raoul François, Gaius Clayton, Blueberry Alice. BA, Tufts U., 1965; postgrad. U. N.H., 1967-69. Lic. real estate broker. Founder, dir. Shelter Inst. Realty, Bath, Maine, 1974—; owner Woodbatcher Tools, Bath, Maine, 1978—; bd. dirs. Bath Meml. Hosp., 1988—, corporator Mid Coast Health Svcs., 1988—, Bath/Brunswick Daycare. Contbr. articles to profl. jours. V.p. Portland (Maine) LWV, 1970-74; mem. exec. bd. Natural Resources council, Augusta, Maine, 1981, bd. dirs., 1982; mem. housing commn. HUD, 1978-79; appropriate tech. rep., NSF, 1979. Mem. Bath C. of C. (exec. v.p. 1983, bd. dirs. 1984-86). Home: Woolwich, Maine. Died Nov. 3, 2006.

HENNING, JOHN FREDERICK, JR., publishing company executive; b. San Francisco, Nov. 28, 1923; s. John Frederick and Mary Ellen (Bashore) H.; m. Frances R. Sorensen, Jan. 4, 1947; children: John Frederick III, Robert Turner. BA with distinction, Stanford U., 1947. In promotion and gen. assignment positions San Francisco Examiner, 1947-51; with Lane Pub. Co., Menlo Park, Calif., from 1951, v.p., 1963-82, asst. pub., 1967-72, assoc. pub., 1972-74, v.p., gen. mgr., 1974-82, pres., assoc. pub., 1982-90, vice chmn., from 1990, also bd. dirs. Served to lt. (j.g.) USNR, 1943-45. Mem. Am. Soc. Travel Agts., Advt. Club San Francisco, Mag. Pubs. Assn., Wine and Food Soc. San Francisco. Clubs: The Family, World Trade, Stanford Golf. Presbyterian. Home: La Quinta, Calif. Died Mar. 6, 2006.

HENSHEL, HARRY BULOVA, watch manufacturer; b. NYC, Feb. 5, 1919; s. Harry D. and Emily (Bulova) H.; m. Joy Altman, Nov. 4, 1948; children— Dale, Patti, Diane, Judith. AB, Brown U., 1940; grad., U.S. Army Command and Gen. Staff Sch., 1945; MBA, Harvard U., 1951. With Bulova Watch Co., Inc., Flushing, NY, 1938—2007, asst. sec., 1950, sec., 1951, v.p. finance, 1957, exec. v.p., 1958, pres., 1959-74, chmn., 1973-96, vice-chmn., 1996—2007. Bd. dirs. Ampal Corp., mem. audit com., Universal Holdings Corp., mem. audit com.; chmn. bd. dirs. Bulova Internat., Ltd., 11961-81; chmn. Atlantic Time Products Corp., 1991-2007; chmn. chief execs. coun. The Omega Group, 1991; chmn. Bulova Watch Co., 1973-96, vice chmn., 1991-2007. Vice chmn., trustee Adelphi U., 1955-88, emeritus trustee, 1989-2007; bd. overseers Parsons Sch. Design; bd. dirs. U.S. Com. for UNICEF, 1979-87, Fedn. Employment and Guidance Svcs., Westchester Philharm. Orch., 1990; mem. bus. coun. UN Bus. Adv. Com., policy study com. Heller Inst., 1979-85; mem. adv. bd. N.Y.C. chpt. Am. Cancer Soc., N.Y. State Bus. Venture Partnership. Mem. Amateur Athletic Union U.S. (timing com.), N.Y. C. of C. (dir.), Am. Ordnance Assn (life), Newcomen Soc. N.Am., UN Assn. U.S. (dir.), Thoroughbred Owners and Breeders Assn., Sigma Chi (Significant Sig medal) Clubs: Harvard Business School, Sales Executives, New York (dir.), Brown Univ, Harmonie, Economic; Army and Navy (Washington); Old Oaks Country (Purchase, N.Y.); Turf and Field; Town (Scarsdale). Republican. Home: Scarsdale, NY. Died June 29, 2007.

HENTEL, NAT HERBERT, former state supreme court judge, former prosecutor; b. Bronx, N.Y., Mar. 29, 1919; s. Morris M. and Sarah (Schechtman) H.; B.S. in Social Sci., CCNY, 1939; J.D., NYU, 1946; grad. Nat. Jud. Coll., U. Nev., 1971; m. Diana Klebanow, Nov. 14, 1942; children: Elayne Rae Hentel Leshtz, Susan Hentel Michel. Admitted to N.Y. bar, 1947, U.S. Supreme Ct. bar, 1956; law asst. to Queens (N.Y.) Surrogate, 1949-54; ptnr. firm Karow and Hentel, N.Y.C., 1954-65; dist. atty. Queens County, Yr., 1966; counsel to firm Fields, Zimmerman & Segall, Jamaica, N.Y., 1967-69; judge Civil Ct. City N.Y., 1969-87; justice Supreme Ct. N.Y. 11th Jud. Dist., 1988-92; judge pro tem Ariz. Superior Ct., Pima County, 1993-2007; acting justice Supreme Ct. N.Y. 2d and 11th Jud. Dists., 1977-82; arbitrator N.Y. State Bd. Mediation, 1964-69; pres. Bd. Civil Ct. Judges City N.Y., 1974-76; bd. sponsors Inst. Trial Judges, NYU Law Ctr., 1973-92; mem. faculty Nat. Jud. Coll., U. Nev., 1973-93; adj. prof. Sch. Gen. Studies, Queens Coll., City U. N.Y., 1976-92, chmn., hon. chmn. paralegal studies program adv. bd. Chmn. Queens adv. coun. N.Y. State Div. Human Rights, 1959-65, 67-69, chmn. N.Y.C. adv. coun., 1969; mem. N.Y. Gov.'s Com. on Human Rights, 1967-68; vice chmn. and acting chmn. Queens Legal Svcs. Corp., 1967-69; former v.p. United Cerebral Palsy of Queens; v.p., dir. Queensboro Soc. Prevention Cruelty to Children, 1968-69; pres. Queens Speech and Hearing Service Center, 1960-61, Queens Coll., City U. N.Y.; bd. dirs. Queens region NCCJ, 1963-69. Served to capt. F.A., AUS, 1941-46. Named Man of Yr., South Queens Boys Club, 1966; recipient award of honor United Cerebral Palsy of Queens, 1966, Queens Speech and Hearing Service Center, 1962, Queens Child Guidance Center, 1966; recipient numerous awards charitable orgns. Mem. ABA (mem. several coms., chmn. com. on cts. and the community 1985-87), Queens County Bar Assn. (pres. 1963-64, bd. mgrs. 1956-66, chmn. numerous coms.), N.Y. State Bar Assn. (chmn. com. profl. econs. 1967-68, chmn. com. Am. citizenship 1964-65, chmn. com. cts. and the community 1982-85, chmn. jud. sect. 1981-82), Assn. Bar City N.Y. (mem. council on jud. admn., 1982-85), Am. Arbitration Assn. (arbitration panel), N.Y. State Dist. Attys. Assn., Jewish War Vets., NYU Law Alumni Assn. (pres. 1963), Brandeis Assn. Queens County (chmn. bd. dirs. 1974-76), Phi Delta Phi. Home: Tucson, Ariz. Died Jan. 31, 2007.

HENTON, WILLIS RYAN, retired bishop; b. McCook, Nebr., July 5, 1925; s. Burr Milton and Clara Vaire (Godown) H.; m. Martha Somerville Bishop, June 7, 1952; 1 son, David Vasser. BA, U. Nebr., 1949; S.T.B., Gen. Theol. Sem., NYC, 1952, D.S.T., 1972; D.D., U. of South, Sewanee, Tenn., 1972. Ordained priest Episcopal Ch., 1953; missionary St. Benedicts Mission, Besao, Mountain Province, Philippines, 1952-57; mem. staff St. Lukes Chapel, NYC, 1957-58; rector Christ Ch., Mansfield, La., 1958-61, St. Augustine's Ch., Baton Rouge, 1961-64; archdeacon Diocese of La., 1964-71; bishop coadjutor Diocese N.W. Tex., 1971-72; bishop N.W. Tex. Lubbock, 1972—80; bishop Western La., 1980—90; ret., 1990. Pres. Tex. Conf. Chs., 1978-80; pres. La. Inter-Ch. Conf., 1985-86. Served with inf. AUS, 1944-46. Decorated Bronze Star. Episcopalian. Home: New Iberia, La. Died Feb. 15, 2006.

HERBERT, DONALD JEFFREY (MR. WIZARD), film and television producer, performer; b. Waconia, Minn., July 10, 1917; s. Herbert Geoffrey and Lydia (Peopple) Kemske; m. Norma Kasell, 1972. BS, LaCrosse State Tchrs. Coll., 1940. Pres. Prism Prodns. Inc., Canoga Park, Calif. Actor stage mgr. Minn. Stock Co., Mpls., 1940- 41, N.Y.C., 1941-42, radio actor, writer, Chgo., 1945-47, radio dir. Community Fund, Chgo., 1948-49; co-producer, interviewer radio show It's Your Life, Cong. Indsl. Health Assn., 1949-50; creator and star radio show Mr. Wizard TV show, NBC Network, 1951-65; TV progress reporter radio show Gen. Electric Co, CBS Network, 1954-62; exec. producer radio show Experiment: The Story of a Scientific Search, 1963-66, Science Close Up; ednl. film series, 1964; producer video series for schools Assignment: Science; star Mr. Wizard TV Show, 1970-71; producer, host film Nuclear Power Questions and Answers, 1974; producer, star film Mr. Wizard Close-Ups, 1976; exec. producer, on-camera reporter sci. and engring. oriented TV news reports How About, 1979-86; creator, star Mr. Wizard's World for Nickleodean Cable Network, 1983; author: Mr. Wizard's Science Secrets, 1952, Mr. Wizard's Experiments for Young Scientists, 1959, Beginning Science with Mr. Wizard, 1960, (with Fulvio Bardossi) Kilauea, Case History of a Volcano, 1968, Secret in the White Cell, 1969; sci. kits Mr. Wizard's Experiments in Chemistry, 1970, Ecology, Crystal Growing, Mr. Wizard's Mystery Garden; Mr. Wizard's Supermarket Science. Served from pvt. to capt. USAAF, 1942-45. Recipient D.F.C., Air Medal with 3 oak leaf clusters, Sch. Broadcast award, 1951, N.J. Sci. Tchrs. award, 1951, Chgo. Federated Advt. Club award, 1951, Peabody award, 1953, 1st award Inst. Radio and TV Broadcasting, Ohio State U., 1952-53; 1st award Inst. for Edn. by Radio-TV, Ohio State U., 1953, 54, 55, 57; Spl. award Mfg. Chemists Assn., 1957, 58; Thomas Alva Edison Found. Nat. Mass Media awards, 1955, 63 Mem. Nat. Acad. Television Arts and Scis. (gov. 1963-64) Died June 12, 2007.

HERBURGER, EVELYN RENKE, interior designer, nurse; b. Hanna, Alta., Can., Dec. 3, 1921; d. David Martin and Helena (Jurczweskey) Renke; m. Robert Darrell Herburger, June 18, 1944 (div.); children: James, Carol Pollard, Sylvia McKittrick, Cindy Hetzler. RN, St. Alexius Sch. Nursing, 1940; AA in Psychology, Dickinson State Coll., 1937. Employment counselor Associated Placement Svc. and Western Girl Inc., Boise, Idaho, 1964—66; doctor's asst. Van de Vlugt Med. Ctr. and Hosp., John Day, Oreg., 1950—64; profl. rels. rep. Office Profl. Svcs., Blue Shield, Portland, Oreg., 1967—69; rehab. specialist Oreg. Worker's Compensation Dept., 1975—81; dir. indsl. rels. D.R. Johnson Lumber Co., Riddle, Oreg., 1981—83; self-employed interior decorator Salem, Oreg., from 1983. Mem. exec. bd. dirs. Oreg. Gov.'s Com. Employment of Handicapped, 1977—80; mem. Gov.'s steering com. for Handicapped Legis. sub-com., 1981. Mem.: Am. Soc. Safety Engr., Altrusa Internat. Roseburg C. of C. (legis. com.), Nat. Disability Evaluation Assn., Nat. Job Developers Assn., Nat. Rehab. Assn. Republican. Episcopalian. Died Dec. 3, 2006.

HERD, HAROLD SHIELDS, state supreme court justice; b. Coldwater, Kans., June 3, 1918; BA, Washburn U., 1941, JD, 1942. Bar: Kans. 1943. Partner firm Rich and Herd, Coldwater, 1946-53; individual practice law Coldwater, 1953-79; justice Kans. Supreme Ct., 1979-93; ret., 1993; disting. jurist in residence Washburn Law Sch., Topeka, from 1993. Mayor, Coldwater, 1949-53, county atty., Comanche County, Kans., 1954-58; mem. Kans. Senate, 1965-73, minority floor leader, 1969-73. Bd. govs. Washburn Law Sch., 1974-78, disting. jurist in residence, 1993-94; mem. Kans. Com. for Humanities, 1975-80, chmn. 1980, Hall Ctr. for Humanities, adv. coun. Kans. U. Mem. S.W. Bar Assn. (pres. 1977), Kans. Bar Assn. (exec. council 1973-80). Died Apr. 23, 2007.

HERMACH, FRANCIS LEWIS, consulting engineer; b. Bridgeport, Conn., Jan. 8, 1917; s. Frank and Barbara (Dauenheimer) H.; m. Frances M. Roberts, June 22, 1940 (dec. Feb. 1996); children: George, William (dec. 1972); m. Friede Groen, Oct. 11, 1998. B.E.E., George Washington U., 1943. Sci. aid Nat. Bur. Standards, Washington, 1939-42; elec. engr., 1942-63; chief elec. instruments sect., 1963-72; dep. chief electricity div., 1970-72; cons., 1972-76; cons. engr. Elec. Measurements, Silver Spring, Md., 1976—82. Contbr. articles on elec. measurements to profl. jours. Served with USNR, 1945-46. Recipient Disting. service award US Dept. Commerce, 1954; Morris E. Leeds award IEEE, 1976, Centennial medal, 1984; Engr. Alumni Achievement award George Washington U., 1985 Fellow IEEE, Instrument Soc. Am., Washington Acad. Scis.; mem. Precision Measurements Soc., Philos. Soc. Washington. Methodist. Achievements include patents in field. Home: Silver Spring, Md. Died May 11, 2007.

HERMAN, ROGER ELIOT, professional speaker, consultant, futurist, writer; b. San Francisco, Dec. 11, 1943; s. Carlton Martin and Estelle (Nadler) H.; m. Janet I. Meyer, June 22, 1969 (div. Feb. 1974); 1 child, Scott Philip; m. Sandra Jean Steckel, May 2, 1974 (div. Sept. 1997); Jennifer; m. Joyce L. Gioia, Dec. 27, 1997. BA in Sociology, Hiram Coll., 1969; MA in Pub. Adminstrn., Ohio State U., 1977. Cert. mgmt. cons.; cert. speaking profl. Mgr. Rayco, Inc., Kent, Ohio, 1970-72; pvt. practice sales Stow, Ohio, 1972-76; pub. service dir. City Hilliard, Ohio, 1976-78; city mgr. City Rittman, Ohio, 1978-80; pres. The Herman Group, Greensboro, N.C., from 1980. Author: Disaster Planning for Local Government, 1982, Emergency Operations Plan, 1983, The Process of Excelling, 1988, Keeping Good People, 1990, 99, Turbulence!, 1995, Lean & Meaningful, 1998, Signs of the Times, 1999, Workforce Stability, 2000, How to Become an Employer of Choice, 2000, How to Choose Your Next Employer, 2000, Impending Crisis, 2002; contbg. editor: Workforce and Workplace Trends, The Futurist mag.; contbr. mag. columns, articles to profl. jours. Commr. Ohio Boy Scouts Am., 1970, scoutmaster Texas (Ohio) Boy Scouts Am., 1966-70; mem. bd. visitors Hiram (Ohio) Coll., 2002--. Served with U.S. Army, 1965-68. Named Most Interesting Person In Northeast Ohio, Cleve. mag., 1981, named one of Outstanding Young Men Am., 1976, 77, 78, 79; recipient Arrowhead award Boy Scouts Am., Ohio, 1969. Fellow Inst. Mgmt. Cons. (cert. mgmt. cons., pres. Ohio chpt. 1991-95, nat. bd. dirs. 1996-2000, vice chair 1999-2000); mem. ASTD (chmn. profl. devel. 1987-88, program chmn. 1985-86, newsletter editor N.E. Ohio chpt. 1985-86), Nat. Spkrs. Assn. (cert. speaking profl.), World Future Soc., Assn. Profl. Futurists (charter mem.), Ohio Jaycees (Hilliard pres. 1976-77, Blue Chip Disting. Svc. award 1977), Toastmasters (dist. lt. gov. Texas, Ohio 1965-80, Able Toastmaster award 1969). Republican. Jewish. Avocations: writing, travel. Home: Greensboro, NC. Died Nov. 6, 2006.

HERMANN, PAUL DAVID, retired association executive; b. Chgo., Feb. 1, 1925; s. Edgar Paul and Marjory (Alexander) H.; m. Joan Louise Mullin, Nov. 10, 1948; children: Bruce Phillip, Susan Marie. Student, Lawrence U., 1942-45; BS in Bus. Adminstrn, Northwestern U., 1948. Cert. assn. exec. Asst. dir. news bur. Ill. Inst. Tech., Chgo., 1945-48; editor Constrn. Equipment News, Chgo., 1948-49; exec. v.p. Assn. Equipment Distbrs., Oak Brook, Ill., 1950-90; pres. AED Research & Services Corp., 1974-90. Contbr. articles on assn. mgmt. to various jours. Mem. Am. Soc. Assn. Execs. (hon., pres. 1974, Key award 1985), Chgo. Soc. Assn. Execs. (life, pres. 1969), U.S. C. of C. (dir. 1980-82, chmn. assn. com. 1981-86, small bus. council 1976-82), Nat. Chamber Alliance for Politics (adv. council 1978-82), Inst. Orgn. Mgmt. (mem. bd. regents 1969-72), Delta Tau Delta (Alumni Achievement award 1982) Home: Galena, Ill. Died Dec. 31, 2005.

HEROY, WILLIAM BAYARD, JR., geology educator; b. Washington, Aug. 13, 1915; s. William Bayard and Jessie Minerva (Page) H.; m. Dorothy M. Meincke, June 16, 1937; children: Bayard Page, David Bassett, June Catherine, Barbara Ann. AB, Dartmouth Coll., 1937; PhD, Princeton U., 1941. Geologist Texaco, 1941-45; geologist Geotech. Corp., Garland, Tex., 1945-47, supr., 1947-52, v.p., dir., 1952-65, pres., 1960-65; group exec. Teledyne, 1965-68, asst. to pres., 1968-70; v.p., treas. So. Meth. U., 1970-77, prof. geol. sci., 1977-81, prof. emeritus, from 1981. Pres. Inst. Study Earth and Man. Trustee Hockaday Sch., 1981, Ft. Burgwin Rsch. Ctr., Yellowstone Bighorn Rsch. Assn., Am. Geol. Inst. Found., 1984-87; bd. dirs. Meml. Hosp. Garland, Circle 10 council Boy Scouts Am., Space Applications Bd. NASA, 1971-77. Fellow AAAS, Geol. Soc. Am. (councilor 1967-70, treas. 1976-82, Disting. Svc. award, trustee Geol. Soc. Am. Found. 1989—); mem. Am. Assn. Petroleum Geologists (treas. 1970-72), Am. Geol. Inst. (fin. v.p. 1966-69, pres. 1969, Ian Campbell award 1986), Am. Inst. Profl. Geologists (cert.), Soc. of Econ. Geologists, Dallas Geophys. Soc. (hon., life), Dallas Geog. Soc. (hon., life), Cosmos Club (Washington), Phi Beta Kappa. Republican. Unitarian Universalist. Home: Durham, NC. Died Sept. 25, 2006.

HERPICH, WILLIAM ARTHUR, metal company executive; b. Mansfield, Ohio, May 17, 1922; s. Arthur Matthew and Francis Elizabeth (Waters) H.; m. Phyllis Elaine Bottomley, Dec. 23, 1943; children: Kay Herpich Goldsmith, William M., Roc E. Student, Coll. Wooster, U. Iowa. With svc. inspection and engring. depts., mgr. mfg. Galion (Ohio) Allsteel Body Co., until 1955; chief engr. Dempster Bros., Inc., Knoxville, Tenn., 1955-59; v.p., dir. engrs. Hercules Galion Corp., 1959-65; exec. v.p. R&D Peabody Galion Corp., from 1965. Holder numerous patents. With USNR, 1942-45. Mem. Truck Body Equipment Distbrs. Assn., Nat. Solid Waste Mgmt. Assn., Am. Pub. Works Assn., Truck Body Equipment Assn., Detachable Container Assn. Home: Galion, Ohio. Died Sept. 15, 2006.

HERRICK, JOHN BERNE, veterinarian, consultant; b. Sheffield, Iowa, Dec. 18, 1919; s. Joseph and Mary (Lamb) H.; m. Joan Stubbelfield, Aug. 28, 1965 BS, Iowa State U., 1940, DVM, 1946, MS, 1950. From asst. prof. to prof. Iowa State U., Ames, 1948-84; cons. Paradise Valley, Ariz., from 1984. Contbr. 100 articles to profl. jours. Recipient award AVMA, USDA, Am. Assn. Bovine Practitioners Mem. Gamma Sigma Delta. Roman Catholic. Died May 17, 2007.

HERRMANN, GEORGE, mechanical engineering educator; b. USSR, Apr. 19, 1921; Diploma in Civil Engring., Swiss Fed. Inst. Tech., 1945, PhD in Mechanics, 1949. Assoc. prof. civil engring. Columbia U., 1951—62; prof. civil engring. Northwestern U., 1962-69; prof. applied mechanics Stanford U., 1969—84, chmn. applied mechanics dept., 1970—75, prof. emeritus, 1984—2007. Cons. SRI Internat., 1970-80 Contbr. 260 articles to profl. jours.; editl. bd. numerous jours. Fellow ASME (hon. mem. 1990, Centennial medal 1980); mem. ASCE (Th. v. Karman medal 1981), Nat. Acad. Engring., AIAA (emeritus). Died Jan. 7, 2007.

HESS, JOHN, JR., physician; b. Hospers, Iowa, Dec. 20, 1916; s. John and Emma (Ehlenfeldt) H.; m. Veronica Ann Lindsey, June 21, 1942; children— John, Michael, Ann, Patrick. B.S., U. Iowa, 1939, M.D., 1941. Diplomate Am. Bd. Family Practice. Intern, Broadlawns Polk County Hosp., Des Moines, 1941-42, resident, 45; practice medicine, Des Moines, 1946-75; mem. staff Meth., Mercy, Luth. and Broadlawns hosps., asst. prof. family medicine U. Iowa, Iowa City, 1975—. Bd. dirs. Iowa Found. for Med. Care, 1977—. Served to maj. U.S. Army, 1942-46. Fellow Am. Acad. Family Physicians; mem. AMA, Iowa Acad. Family Physicians, Iowa Med. Soc., Polk County Med. Soc. Home: Des Moines, Iowa. Died Aug. 10, 2006.

HESTER, LAWRENCE LAMAR, JR., medical educator; b. Anderson, SC, May 23, 1920; s. Lawrence Lamar and Carrie Rose (McCelvey) H.; m. Ruth Elizabeth Catling, July 12, 1947; children: Barrie, Lawrence Lamar, Elizabeth Porcher, Frances Stuart. BS, The Citadel, 1941, D.Sc., 1980; MD, Med. U. S.C., 1944. Intern Roper Hosp., Charleston, S.C., 1944-45, resident,

1945-46, 48-50; instr. Med U. S.C., Charleston, 1950-52, asst. prof., 1954-56, prof., chmn. dept. obstetrics and gynecology, 1956-85, J. Marion Sims prof. emeritus, from 1984. Served to capt. USAF, 1946-48. Fellow South Atlantic Assn. Obstetricians and Gynecologists, Am. Coll. Obstetricians and Gynecologists, Am. Gnecol. and Obstet. Soc.; mem. S.C. Obstet. and Gynecol. Soc. (pres. 1959), Am. Gynecol. Club (pres. 1980-81) Episcopalian. Home: Highlands, NC. Died May 10, 2006.

HESTON, WILLIAM MAY, educational administrator; b. Toledo, Nov. 2, 1922; s. William May and Helen Marie (Lippstrew) H.; m. Marian Cannon Watt, June 17, 1950; children— Mary, Elizabeth, Katherine, Richard. B.Sc. cum laude with highest honors in Chemistry, Ohio State U., 1943; MA, Princeton U., 1948, PhD in Chemistry (LeRoy Wiley McKay advanced fellow in phys. chemistry 1949), 1949. With E.I. duPont de Nemours & Co., Inc., 1949-59; dir. office research Western Res. U., 1959-63, asso. chemistry, 1959-67, v.p. research, 1963-64, v.p. student svcs., 1964-66, vice provost, assoc. dean Faculty Arts and Scis., 1966-67; v.p. plans and programs Case Western Res. U., 1967-69; exec. dir. Mental Devel. Center, cons. for spl. programs, 1969; v.p. Hofstra U., 1969-73; exec. dir. Nassau Higher Edn. Consortium, 1973-75, L.I. Regional Adv. Council on Higher Edn., 1975-76, ind. cons., from 1976; assoc. provost N.Y. Inst. Tech., 1977-78; dir., dean Center for Natural Scis., 1978-88, prof. life scis., 1981-90, chmn. grad. program in clin. nutrition, 1983-90. Chmn. Cleve. Regional Com. Comprehensive Mental Health Planning Report, 1964-66; mem. adv. council Ohio Dept. Mental Hygiene and Correction, 1966-69; cons. grad. chemistry research facilities br. NSF, 1965-68, cons. sci. devel. program br., 1968-70; tech. cons. chemistry AID Govt. India, 1965; mem. program project com. Nat. Inst. Dental Research, NIH, 1964-68; spl. cons. Dental Research Inst. program, 1968-70; mem. Dental Research Inst. and spl. program adv. com., 1970-74; cons. to pharmacology-toxicology research program com. Nat. Inst. Gen. Med. Sci., NIH, 1976-81; mem. clin. cancer program project rev. subcom. Nat. Cancer Inst., 1981-88; cons. Engrng. Research Group, Stanford Research Inst. Internat., 1981-84 Vice pres. Cleve. chpt. UNICEF, 1968-69; mem. 12th grade sci. adv. com. Cleve. Bd. Edn., 1967-69; mem. adv. council Natural Sci. Mus., Cleve., 1967-69; mem. health goals com. Cleve. Welfare Fedn., mem. community planning and devel. com., 1965-69, chmn. mental health planning com., 1966-69; mem. sci. adv. com. Nassau County Police Dept., 1969-72; edn. adv. com. Garden City Pub. Sch. System, 1974-75; mem. Garden City Bd. Edn., 1975-87, v.p., 1978-83, pres., 1983-87; research adv. group Nassau-Suffolk Regional Med. Program, 1974-75, pres. 1983-87; mem. Nassau County Manpower Adv. Council, 1974-75; sec. bd. trustees N.Y. Ocean Sci. Lab., 1969-72, vice chmn. trustees, 1972-74; trustee Cleve. Center Alcoholism, 1961-64, Mental Health Rehab. and Research, 1963-69, Vocat. Guidance and Rehab. Services, 1963-69, Laurel Sch., Cleve., 1967-69; chmn. bd. dirs. Nassau-Suffolk Community Health Edn. System, 1973-76; bd. dirs. Central Garden City Property Owners Assn., 1973-75; trustee L.I. Library Resources Council, 1975-78, AMD Research Found., 1977-78; bd. advs. Academic Financier; v.p. Garden City Hist. Soc., 1976-78, trustee, 1978-79; pres. Unitarian Universalist Ch. Cen. Nassau, 1989-91, pres. emeritus, 1991-92, treas., 1992—; trustee Metro N.Y. Dist. Unitarian-Universalist Assn., 1991-94; dir. Toll Lodge Preservation Assn., 1994—; Served with USNR, 1944-46. Fellow AAAS, Explorers Club; mem. N.Y. Acad. Pub. Edn., Hempstead C. of C. (participating dir. 1974-76), Phi Beta Kappa, Sigma Xi, Phi Lambda Upsilon, Phi Eta Sigma. Clubs: Cleveland Skating; Chapoquoit Yacht (West Falmouth, Mass.) (sec. 1969); Rowfant (Cleve.). Home: Garden City, NY. Died Mar. 9, 2006.

HETHERINGTON, JOHN ALAN CRAWFORD, legal educator; b. St. Catharines, Ont., Can., Sept. 26, 1928; m.; 3 children BA, Dartmouth Coll., 1950; LL.B., Cornell U., 1953, LL.M., 1956. Bar: N.Y. 1956. Law clk. U.S. Ct. Appeals (9th cir.), 1956-57; assoc. Lundgren, Lincoln & McDaniel, NYC, 1957-58, Mudge, Stern, Baldwin & Todd, NYC, 1958-60; Asst. prof. law U. Wis., Madison, 1960-62, assoc. prof., 1962-66, prof., 1966-71, asst. dean, 1966-67; prof. law U. Va., Charlottesville, from 1971, David A. Harrison prof. Vis. prof. U. Calif., Berkeley, 1971, Stanford U., 1975-76; Marshall P. Madison prof. U. San Francisco Sch. Law, 1985 Contbr. articles to profl. jours. Died Dec. 10, 2006.

HEUSSER, CALVIN JOHN, biology educator, researcher; b. North Bergen, NJ, Sept. 10, 1924; BS, Rutgers U., 1947, MS, 1949; PhD, Oreg. State U., 1952. Am. Geog. Soc., NYC, 1952-67; MS NYU, 1967-91, prof. emeritus, from 1991; mem. Heusser & Heusser, cons., Tuxedo, N.Y., from 1991. Author: Late Pleistocene Environments, 1960, Pollen and Spores of Chile, 1971. Pfc. U.S. Army, 1944-45, ETO. Recipient David Livingstone medal Am. Geog. Soc., 1987; Guggenheim Found. fellow, 1963, Fulbright Commn. fellow, 1963, Clare Hall U. Cambridge (Eng.) fellow, 1985. Mem. Am. Quaternary Assn., Am. Assn. Stratigraphic Palynologists, Torrey Bot. Club (pres. 1975-76) Avocations: classical music, art. Home: Tuxedo Park, NY. Died Nov. 11, 2006.

HEYMANN, HENRY LEWIS, conservationist; b. Phila., June 27, 1920; s. Roy Arthur and Edna (Eliel) H.; B.A., Princeton, 1943; postgrad. Cornell U., 1955-56; m. Renate Burchardi, Aug. 8, 1959. With Fgn. Ser., State Dept., 1950-75, chief Visa Sect., Hamburg, Germany, 1950-53, chief Protection-Welfare Sect., Naples, Italy, 1953-55, polit. officer Djakarta, Indonesia, 1956-58, 61-65, intelligence research analyst, Washington, 1959-60, prin. officer, Surabaja, Indonesia, 1965-66, internat. relations officer, Washington, 1966-75; HLH. Served as capt. U.S. Army, 1943-46. Decorated Soldiers medal. Mem. Animal Welfare Inst., Zero Population Growth, Population-Environ. Balance, World Wildlife Fund, Sierra Club, Environ. Def. Fund., Internat. Primate Protection League. Clubs: Farmington Country (Charlottesville, Va.); University (Washington); Coral Beach and Tennis (Bermuda). Home: Washington, DC. Died Feb. 8, 2007.

HEYMANN, STEPHEN, marketing management consultant; b. NYC, Dec. 7, 1940; s. Harold Joseph and Estelle Olga H.; m. Elaine Puciat, June 24, 1962; children: Elizabeth Jill, Michael Carroll, Andrew Harold. BS, Wharton Sch., U. Pa., 1962. Div. mgr., mdse. mgr. Sears, Roebuck & Co., Phila., 1962-65; brand mgr. Household Products div. Procter & Gamble Co., Cin., 1965-69; pres., dir., mgmt. cons. Glendinning Assos., Westport, Conn., 1969-81; founder, pres. New Eng. Cons. Group, 1981-90, Tech. Transfer Assocs., Wilton, Conn., 1990-96; pres., COO Netalk, Internet Svcs., Los Gatos, Calif., 1996-97; pres., prin. Paladin Cons. Group, Los Altos, Calif., from 1997. Founder, pres. Paladin Consulting Group, 1992-98; dir. Penniman Chems. Inc., Glenco Enterprises Ltd., Glendinning Cos. Inc., Aficionado. Author: More People on Skis, 1972, Like, series of children's books, 1972-74. Mem. ASTM, Am. Mgmt. Assn., Am. Mktg. Assn., Young Pres. Orgn., Assn. Nat. Advertisers. Clubs: Stratton Mountain, Wharton, Lotos. Died July 31, 2006.

HIBBS, RICHARD GUYTHAL, anatomy educator; b. Winner, SD, Feb. 17, 1922; s. George G. and Verna (Smith) H.; m. Dorothy H. Taggart, Aug. 19, 1946; children— Richard Gene, Linda Marie, Mary Jo. Student, Loyola U., Chgo., 1947-49; BA, U. S.D., 1950; PhD, U. Minn., 1955. Instr. anatomy U. Minn. Med. Sch., 1954-55; mem. faculty Tulane U. Med. Sch., New Orleans, 1955-75, asso. prof. anatomy, 1963-66, prof. anatomy, 1966-75; prof. anatomy, head dept. La. State U. Sch. Medicine, Shreveport, from 1975. Served with USMC, 1940-46. Recipient gold award original research Am. Acad. Dermatology and Syphology, 1958, Career Devel. award USPHS, 1960-65, 65-70 Mem. Am. Assn. Anatomists, Am. Physiol. Soc., La. Soc. Electron Microscopy, So. Soc. Anatomists, Sigma Xi. Spl. research electron microscopy of skin and appendages, electron microscopy and histochemistry cardiovascular system. Home: Shreveport, La. Died Feb. 26, 2007.

HICHENS, WALTER WILSON, state senator; b. Lynn, Mass., Mar. 8, 1917; s. Walter Grimes and Mary Eleanor (Norton) H.; grad. Essex Agrl. & Tech. Inst., 1937; m. Elmira A. Ballard, Nov. 8, 1941; children: Walter, Mary, Jared, Janice, Judith, Myra (dec.), Kathy, Laurie Jo (dec.), Bethany. Vegetable gardener, poultryman, Eliot, Maine, 1937-72; selectman Town of Eliot (Maine), 1949-52; dir. Water Dist., Eliot, 1952-55; toll collector N.H.-Maine Interstate Bridge Authority, 1956-72; state rep. Maine, 1967-71, 91-92; mem. Maine Senate, 1971-88; chmn. Agrl. Commn., Maine, 1974-83, vice chmn. chmn. agrl.-natural resources com. Nat. Council State Legislatures, 1982-83. Maine corr. Georgetown U. Health Center, 1977-78; exec. bd. NE Canadian-Am. Health Council, 1979-83; chmn. state legis. commn. AARP, 1989, state adv. bd. the elder's commn., 1994-95. Recipient certs. of commendation Maine Right to Life Assn., 1975, Maine Spl. Olympics, 1978, 83; award Christian Civic League, Maine State Grange. Mem. Assn. Blind (life), Assn. Deaf (life), Gideons Internat. (past pres. Maine). Republican. Baptist. Author: (poetry) Holy Land Reflections, 1970, Footsteps of Jesus, 1973, Homespinnings, 1976, Inspirations, 1978, Echoes of Happiness, 1983, Seal Island Memories, 1985, Memories, 1995; (nonfiction) Island Trek, 1982, Back to My Father & Home, 1987, Light in the Darkness, 1993. Home: Eliot, Maine. Died July 22, 2007.

HICKS, BOBBY GENE, state legislator; b. Washington County, Tenn., Dec. 27, 1938; married; 3 children. Mem. Tenn. State Legis. Republican. Baptist. Died Jan. 7, 2007.

HIEBERT, PAUL GORDON, anthropology teacher; b. Shamshabad, India, Nov. 13, 1932; (parents Am. citizens); s. John Nicholas Christian and Anna Luetta (Jungas) H.; m. Frances Flaming, Dec. 28, 1954; children: Eloise, Barbara, John. BA, Tabor Coll., 1954; MA, Mennonite Brethern Sem., 1956, U. Minn., 1959, PhD, 1967. Missionary Mennonite Brethern Ch., Shamshabad, 1960-66; asst. prof. Kans. State U., Manhattan, 1966-71, assoc. prof., 1971-72, U. Wash., Seattle, 1972-77; prof. anthropology Fuller Sem., Pasadena, Calif., 1977-90; prof. anthropology and South Asian studies Trinity Evang. Divinity Sch., Deerfield, Ill., from 1990. Research cons. Mennonite Brethern Bd. of Missionary Service, Winnapeg, Man., Can., 1969—; Fulbright prof. Osmania U., Hyderabad, India, 1974-75. Author: Konduru, 1971, Cultural Anthropology, 1977, Anthropological Insights, 1985, Case Studies in Missions, 1987, Anthropological Reflections, 1994; contbr. articles to profl. jours. Named Alumnus of Yr., Tabor Coll., 1983. Fellow Am. Anthropol. Assn.; mem. Assn. Asian Studies, Soc. of S. Indian Studies, Assn. of Profs. of Missions. Democrat. Home: Highland Park, Ill. Died Mar. 11, 2007.

HIGGINS, GEORGE EDWARD, sculptor; b. Gaffney, SC, Nov. 13, 1930; BA, U. N.C. Instr. sculpture Parsons Sch. Design, NYC, 1961-62. Vis. prof. Cornell U., 1968, U. Wis., 1968-69, U. Ky., 1969-70, Sch. Visual Arts, N.Y.C., 1964-72 One man shows, Leo Castelli Gallery, N.Y.C., 1960, 63, 66, Richard Feigen Gallery, Chgo., 1964, Mpls. Inst. Art, 1964, exhibited group shows Art, USA, 1959, Detroit Inst. Art, 1959-60, Carnegie Inst., 1961, Mus. Modern Art, N.Y.C., 1961, 63, Martha Jackson Gallery, N.Y.C., 1960, Andrew Dickson White Gallery, 1960, Bernard Gallery, Paris, France, 1960, Whitney Mus., N.Y.C., 1964, 66, Documenta, Kassel, Germany, 1968, Art Inst. Chgo., Brandeis U., Tate Gallery, London, Phila. Mus. Arts, New Sch. Art Center, N.Y.C., Smithsonian Instn., numerous others; represented in permanent collections, Whitney Mus., N.Y.C., Guggenheim Mus., N.Y.C., Albright-Knox Gallery, Buffalo, Houston Mus. Fine Arts, Mus. Modern Art, N.Y.C., Albright Art Gallery, Chase Manhattan Bank, N.Y.C., others. Died Mar. 4, 2006.

HILEMAN, LINDA CAROL, elementary school educator; b. Aliquippa, Pa., Mar. 29, 1947; d. Charles Allen and Aurelia (Oprean) Cunningham; m. Hazen E. Hileman, June 11, 1971. BS, Clarion State U., Pa., 1969, MEd, 1970; EdS, U. Wyo., 1977. Sci. tchr. Center Area Schs., Monaca, Pa., 1970-71; intermediate tchr. Purchase Line Schs., Commodore, Pa., 1971-72; tchr. 5th grade Carbon County #2 Schs., Medicine Bow, Wyo., 1972-73, team tchr. Saratoga, Wyo., 1973-80, prin. middle sch., 1980-83, tchr. math. and sci., from 1983. Adj. instr. U. Wyo., Laramie, 1988—; participant Marine Resource Inst., Key Largo, Fla., 1990, Nat. Radio Astronomy Obs., Green Bank, W.Va., 1992.; presenter in field. Co-author: First Women of Wyoming, 1990, Trek of the Mammoth II, 1993. Dir. Bible Sch. First Presbyn. Ch., Saratoga, 1985-87; moderator Presbyn. Women, Saratoga, 1988-92, vice moderator, 1992—; mem. Wyo. Commn. for Women, 1975-92. Named Tchr. of Yr., Saratoga Edn. Assn., 1977, Educator of Yr., Vets. Orgn., Saratoga, 1990, Wyo. Elem. Sci. Tchr. of Yr., Wyo. Sci. Tchrs. Assn., 1991; recipient Presdl. Award for Elem. Sci. Teaching, 1992, Predl. Award for Excellence in Teaching, 1993. Mem. Delta Kappa Gamma (pres. chpt. 1984-86). Republican. Avocations: hunting, hiking, bird watching, astronomy, observing nature. Home: Saratoga, Wyo. Died Dec. 27, 2006.

HILFINGER, DEAN FARRAR, architect; b. Winfield, Kans., Aug. 10, 1912; s. Roy Morton and Faye (Farrar) H.; m. Avis E. Elmendorf, May 27, 1943; children— DeAnne, Sharmon BA, S.W. Coll., 1932; BS Archtl. Engrng. with honors, U. Ill., 1935; DSc (hon.), Southwestern Coll., 1985. Registered architect, Ill. and 40 other states; registered profl. engr., Ill. Archtl. draftsman George E. Ramey and Co., Champaign, Ill., 1935-57; archtl. draftsman Lundeen and Roozen, Bloomington, Ill., 1937-38; prin. Lundeen and Hilfinger, Bloomington, Ill., 1938-64, Lundeen, Hilfinger and Asbury, Bloomington, Ill., 1965-73, Hilfinger, Asbury, Cufaude and Abels, Bloomington, Ill., 1974-88, Hilfinger, Asbury, Abels & Assocs., Bloomington, from 1989. Vis. lctr. U. Ill., 1973 Author: Reducing Liability in your Architectural Practice, 1987, Reducing Liability in your Engineering Practice, 1987; contbr. chpts. to handbooks in field. Pres., bus. mgr., exec. com. Bloomington Normal Symphony Soc., 1951-85; pres., bd. dirs. Bloomington Library Bd., 1952-74 Ill. Sr. Olympic tennis winner, 1982-84, 87-89; nat. Sr. Olympics Bronze medaliist for tennis doubles, 1989, 91. Fellow AIA (treas. 1967-69, Edward C. Kemper award 1984, Cert. Exceptional Svc. award 1981); mem. ASTM, Constrn. Specifications Inst. (cert. constrn. specifier), Am. Concrete Inst., Internat. Union Architects (dep. v.p. 1970-72, AIA del. 1965, 69, 72, 75, MASTERSPEC archtl. rev. com. 1989—), Rotary (bd. dirs. 1977-80), Young Men's Club (pres. 1971-72). Republican. Avocations: chamber music; tennis. Home: Bloomington, Ill. Died Jan. 20, 2006.

HILKEMEYER, RENILDA ESTELLA, nurse; b. Martinsburg, Mo., July 29, 1915; d. Henry Gerard and Anna Marie (Bertels) Hilkemeyer. Diploma in nursing, St. Mary's Hosp., St. Louis U., 1936; BS in Nursing Edn., George Peabody Coll. for Tchrs., Nashville, 1947; postgrad., U. Minn., 1950, U. Tex. Sch. Nursing, 1981; D of Pub. Svc. (hon.), St. Louis U., 1988. Staff nurse o.r. St. Mary's Hosp., Jefferson City, Mo., 1936—37; dist. pub. health nurse Mo. Divsn. Health, Jefferson City, 1937—40, 1950—55; asst. dir. nursing Gen. Hosp. No. 1, Kansas City, Mo., 1947—49; asst. exec. sec. Mo. Nurses Assn., Jefferson City, 1949—50; dir. nursing U. Tex. Sys. Cancer Ctr., Houston, 1955—77, asst. to pres. nursing resources, 1977—79, staff asst. to pres., prof. oncology nursing, 1979—84. Mem. grant rev. com. NIH Nat. Cancer Inst., 1979—83, program rev. com., 1975—77, cons., 1982—2006, NIH Nat. Heart, Blood and Lung Inst., 1983—2006, Worker's Inst. Safety, Health, 1983—2006; chmn., mem. scholarship and professorship com. Cancer Soc., 1980—2006, mem. nursing adv. com., 1963—80, 1985—2006, profl. edn. com., 1984—2006, emeritus mem., 1996—2006; chmn. nursing adv. com., mem. adminstrv. bd. Renilda Hilkemeyer Child Care Ctr., U. Tex. Med. Ctr., 1969—2006. Book reviewer Am. Jour. Nursing, 1982; contbr. articles to profl. jours., chapters to books. Pres. Braes Interfaith Ministries, 1991, 1994, 1995, 1998, bd. dirs. emeritus, 2002—06. Named Vol. of the Yr., Braes Interfaith Ministries, 1997; recipient Outstanding Profl. Women's award, Tex. Fedn. Houston Profl. Women, 1983, Outstanding Contbns. award, NCI, 1983, Disting. Svc. award, Am. Cancer Soc., 1981, Nurse of the Yr. award, Houston Area League Nursing, 1973, Matrix award, Theta Sigma Phi, Houston, 1963, Disting. Merit award, Internat. Soc. Nurses in Cancer Care, 1986, new child care ctr. named in her honor, U. Tex. Med. Ctr., 1981, 1st Nat. Nursing Leadership award, Am. Cancer Soc., 1989; grantee, HEW, 1974—77, Am. Cancer Soc., 1974—75, Tex. Fedn. Profl. Women's Clubs, 1977—83. Mem.: ANA, Am. Med. Writers Assn. (Houston-Galveston sect. 1983—84), Tex. Nursing Assn. (pres. 1962—64, bd. dirs. 1964—66, 1971—75, Dist. 9 Svc. award 1970, Nurse of Yr. award 1979), Oncology Nursing Soc. (founding mem. 1991, Lifetime Achievement award 2002), Altrusa Club (pres. Houston chpt. 1983—84, emeritus mem. 2002—), Sigma Theta Tau. Home: Houston, Tex. Died June 10, 2006.

HILL, ALVIN, digital equipment company executive; b. Moultrie, Ga., Feb. 3, 1940; s. Berry and Elizabeth H.; m. Maude E. Simmons, Apr. 14, 1979. Student Phila. Wireless Tech. Inst., 1962-64, U. Pa., 1966, Rider Coll., 1975. Customs engr. IBM, Phila., 1963-67; field engr. RCA, Riverton, N.J., 1967-70, Control Data Corp., Phila., 1970-72; product support mgr. Digital Equipment Corp., Rolling Meadows, Ill., 1972-83, br. mgr., Schaumburg, Ill., 1983—. Served with USN, 1957-62. Mem. Am. Mgmt. Assn., Assn. Field Service Mgrs. Democrat. Baptist. Lodge: Masons. Home: Schaumburg, Ill. Died Mar. 22, 2006.

HILL, ARTHUR, actor; b. Melfort, Sask., Can., Aug. 1, 1922; s. Olin Drake and Edith (Spence) H.; m. Peggy Hassard; children: Douglas, Jennifer. BA, U. B.C. Profl. stage debut in Home of the Brave, London, 1948; Broadway debut in The Matchmaker, 1955; other theatre appearances include The Way Back (prodr.) 1949, The Male Animal, Man and Superman, 1951, The Country Girl, 1952, Look Homeward Angel, 1957, The Gang's All Here, 1959, All the Way Home, 1960, Who's Afraid of Virginia Woolf?, 1962-63 (Tony award 1963, Drama desk Critics award 1963), Something More! 1964, The Porcelain Year, 1965, More Stately Mansions, 1967, Terra Nova, 1977; appeared in motion pictures The Body Said No!, 1950, The Undefeated, 1951, Scarlet Thread, 1951, Miss Pilgrim's Progress, 1952, Paul Temple Returns, 1952, Salute the Toffi, 1952, A Day To Remember, 1953, Family Affair, 1954, The Deep Blue Sea, 1955, Raising a Riot, 1957, The Young Doctors, 1961, In the Cool of the Day, 1963, The Ugly American, 1963, Harper, 1966, Moment to Moment, 1966, Petulia, 1968, The Chairman, 1969, Don't Let the Angels Fall, 1969, Rabbit, Run, 1970, The Andromeda Strain, 1971, The Pursuit of Happiness, 1971, The Killer Elite, 1975, Futureworld, 1976, A Bridge Too Far, 1977, Butch and Sundance: The Early Days, 1979, The

Champ, 1979, A Little Romance, 1979, Dirty Tricks, 1981, The Amateur, 1982, Making Love, 1982, Simething Wicked This Way Comes, 1983, One Magic Christmas, 1985; TV films include Born Yesterday, 1956, The Sacco-Vanzetti Story, 1960, Focus, 1962, The Desperate Hours, 1967, The Other Man, 1970, Vanished, 1971, Owen Marshall: A Pattern of Morality (pilot) 1971, Ordeal, 1973, Death Be Not Proud, 1975, The Rivalry, 1975, Judge Horton and the Scottsboro Boys, 1976, Tell Me My Name, 1977, The Ordeal of Dr. Mudd, 1980, The Revenge of the Stepford Wives, 1980, The Return of Frank Cannon, 1980, Angel Dusted, 1981, Churchill and the Generals, 1981, Tomorrows Child, 1982, Intimate Agony, 1983, Prototype, 1983, The Guardian, 1984, Murder in Space, 1985, Christmas Eve, 1986, Perry Mason: The Case of the notorious Nun, 1986, Love Leads the Way, 1986; star TV series Owen Marshall, Counselor-at-Law, 1971-74, Hagen, 1980, Glitter, 1984. Served with RCAF, 1942-45. Recipient Tony award, Drama Critics award as best actor, 1962-63 Died Oct. 22, 2006.

HILL, FRANK WHITNEY, JR., insurance company executive; b. Topeka, Aug. 4, 1914; s. Frank Whitney and Blanche (Scott) H.; m. Mary Louise Booth, May 18, 1940; children— Frank Whitney III, Marilyn Louise, Barbara Jane. Student, U. Kans., Kansas City Sch. Law. With Equitable Life Assurance Soc. U.S., from 1946, field asst. Peoria, Ill., asst. agy. mgr., dist. mgr. Bloomington, Ill., agy. mgr. Albany, N.Y., 1946-58, field v.p. NYC, 1958-61; v.p. agy. affairs Equitable Life Assurance Soc. U.S. (N.Y. met. dept.), 1961-61, agy. mgr. Pitts., from 1962. Former mem. nat. bd. Gen. Agts. and Mgrs. Conf.; 1st v.p. Equitables So. Calif. Retirees Assn. Chmn. life div. Greater Alegehny United Fund; gen. chmn. Greater Albany Community Chest Fund, 1957-8. Mem. Albany Gen. Agts. and Mgrs. Assn. (past pres.), Pitts. Gen. Agts. and Mgrs. Assn. (pres.), Pitts. Life Underwriters Assn. Clubs: Duquesne, Stoneridge Country. Home: San Diego, Calif. Died Nov. 8, 2005.

HILL, JAMES ROWLAND, real estate developer, architect; b. Oneida, Tenn., July 12, 1935; s. Ransom Powell and Isabella O. Hill B.A., Columbia U., 1954; M.A., U. Colo., 1980; M.A. in Architecture, Columbia Pacific U., 1982. Lic. gen. contractor, real estate developer, Colo. Gen. mgr. Am. Savs. and Loan, 1964-65; sales mgr. Witkin Homes Inc., Denver, 1966-67; exec. v.p. Golden Key Bldg. Corp., Denver, 1968-71; pres. Regency Homes Inc., Englewood, Colo., 1971—. Served with USAR, 1958-67. Mem. Nat. Assn. Home Builders, SAR. Republican. Presbyterian. Clubs: Heather Ridge Country, Aspen Flying, Sports Car Am., Vail Athletic. Home: Englewood, Colo. Died July 21, 2007.

HILL, RALPH HAROLD, wholesale grocery company executive; b. Miller, Mo., Dec. 22, 1914; s. Richard Henry and Geneva Gertrude (Woodard) H.; m. Velma Lee Friar, Sept. 20, 1937; children: James Ralph, Richard Lee, Janice Louise. Student pubs. schs. With San Diego div. Alfred M. Lewis, Inc., Riverside, Calif., from 1935, mgr. dept. frozen food, 1953-56, mgr. Ariz. div. Phoenix, 1956-63, pres., chief exec. officer Riverside, 1963-82, 83-86, chmn. bd., from 1980; v.p., bd. dirs. Orange Empire Fin. Inc., Riverside; pres. Alfred M. Lewis Properties, Inc., Riverside; pres., chief exec. officer Lewis Retail Foods, Inc., Riverside, from 1988. Dir. M&M, L.A., Riverside. Served with USNR, 1943-45. Mem. So. Calif. Grocers Assn., Pres. Assn., Am. Mgmt. Assn., Riverside C. of C. (bd. dirs. 1970-76, pres. 1974-75) Lodges: Rotary (pres. 1972-73). Home: Riverside, Calif. Died Jan. 19, 2006.

HILL, ROBERT DRAPER, investment company executive; b. Lexington, Ky., Jan. 12, 1920; s. George D. and Margaret (Trimble) Hill; m. Lorraine Wright, Oct. 31, 1953; children: Robert D., Melissa W., Elizabeth P. BS, Harvard U. Ptnr. Newborg & Co., NYC, 1946—64; sr. v.p. Clark Dodg & Co., NYC, 1964—74, Chem. Bank, NYC, 1974—83; exec. v.p. Favia Hill & Assocs., NYC, from 1983. Dir. Flo-Sun Corp., Palm Beach, Fla. Served to comdr. USN, 1942—64. Mem.: Wee Burn (Darien, Conn.). Republican. Episcopalian. Home: Darien, Conn. Died Feb. 22, 2006.

HILL, ROBERT GEORGE, JR., horticulturist; b. Silver Spring, Md., Jan. 11, 1922; BS, U. Md., 1943, MS, 1948, PhD in Horticulture, 1950. Asst. prof. Ohio State U., from 1950, prof., 1960-83, assoc. dept. chmn. horticulture, 1970-83, prof. emeritus, from 1983. Fellow Am. Soc. Horticulture Sci.; mem. Am. Soc. Plant Physiology, Weed Sci. Soc. Am. Died June 10, 2007.

HILL, W(ILLIAM) SPEED, English literature educator; b. Louisville, Jan. 19, 1935; s. Eugene Dubose and Lila (Robinson) H.; m. Emita Brady, July 23, 1960 (div. Oct. 1982); children: Julie Beck, Christopher Eugene, Madeleine Vedel; m. Linda Mandelbaum, Sept. 7, 1984. AB with honors, Princeton U., 1957; AM, Harvard U., 1959, PhD, 1964; DHL (hon.), Seabury-Western Theol. Sem., 1993; LittD (hon.), U. of South, 1995. Asst. prof. English Western Res. U., Cleve., 1964-69, Univ. Coll., NYU, NYC, 1969-73; assoc. prof. English Lehman Coll., CUNY, NYC, 1973-78, prof. English, from 1978, Grad. Ctr., CUNY, NYC, from 1980. Cons. panelist NEH, 1977, 78, 79, 82, 83, 86; mem. adv. bd. Anatomy of Melancholy, The Theological Works of William Tyndale. Author: Richard Hooker: A Descriptive Bibliography of the Early Editions, 1593-1724, 1970; editor: (with Egil Grislis) Richard Hooker: A Selected Bibliography, 1971, Studies in Richard Hooker: Essays Preliminary to an Edition of His Works, 1972, New Ways of Looking at Old Texts: Papers of the Renaissance English Text Society, 1985-91, 1992; gen. editor: The Folger Library Edition of the Works of Richard Hooker, 8 vols., 1977-98. Fellow Woodrow Wilson Found., 1957-58, Am. Coun. Learned Socs., 1973-74, NEH, 1981-82. Mem. MLA (com. on scholarly edits. 1981-84, chmn. 1984-88, mem. divsn. exec. com., methods of lit. scholarship com. 1990-94), Renaissance English Text Soc. (coun. 1985—, pres. 1980-84), Soc. for Textual Studies (steering com. 1981-83, 88—, treas. 1984-86, co-editor TEXT 1981—, sr. editor TEXT, 1997—, co-chmn. conf. 1987), Assn. for Documentary Editors, Internat. Assn. Profs. English (internat. com.), Bibliog. Soc., Bibliog. Assn. Am., Phi Beta Kappa. Democrat. Home: Bronx, NY. Died May 8, 2007.

HILLIER, JAMES, retired technology management executive, researcher; b. Brantford, Ont., Can., Aug. 22, 1915; came to U.S., 1940; s. James Sr. and Ethel Anne (Cooke) H.; m. Florence Marjory Bell, Oct. 24, 1936 (dec. 1992); children: James Robert, William Wynship (dec.). BA, U. Toronto, 1937, MA, 1938, PhD, 1941, DSc (hon.), 1978, N.J. Inst. Tech., 1981; LLD (hon.), Wilfrid Laurier U., 2002. Rsch. asst. Banting Inst. U. Toronto Med. Sch., 1938-40; head electron microscope rsch. RCA Labs., Camden and Princeton, NJ, 1940-53; adminstrv. engr. corp. rsch. and engrng. RCA Corp., Princeton, 1954-55, chief engr. comml. electronic products Camden, 1955-57, gen. mgr. labs. Princeton, 1957-58, v.p. labs., 1958-68, v.p. corp. rsch. and engrng. NYC, 1968-69, exec. v.p. rsch. and engrng., 1969-76, exec. v.p., sr. scientist, 1976-77, ret., 1977; dir. corp. rsch. Westinghouse Air Brake Co., Pitts. and Alexandria, Va., 1953-54. Mem. higher edn. study com. Gov.'s Office, State of N.J., 1963-64; mem. commerce tech. adv. bd. U.S. Dept. Commerce, Washington, 1964-70; chmn. adv. coun. dept. elect. engrng. Princeton U., 1963-65; mem. adv. coun. Coll. Engrng., Cornell U., Ithaca, N.Y., 1966-99; mem. joint consultative com. U.S. AID/Egyptian Acad. Sci. Rsch. and Tech., Cairo, 1978-84. Co-author: Electron Optics and the Electron Microscope, 1945; co-contbr.: Medical Physics, 1944, vol. II, 1950, Colloidal Chemistry, vol. VI, 1946; contbr. Ency. Britannica, 1948. Pres., founder James Hillier Found., Inc., 1996—. Decorated officer Order of Can; inducted into Nat. Inventors Hall of Fame, 1980, N.J. Inventors Hall of Fame, 1992; recipient James Loudon Gold medal U. Toronto, 1937, Albert Lasker award APHA, 1960, Commonwealth award, 1980, Presdl. award Microbeam Analysis Soc., 1989; mem. Can. Sci. and Engrng. Hall of Fame, 02. Fellow AAAS (chmn. nomination com. sect. M 1965), IEEE (David Sarnoff award 1967, Founders medal 1981), Am. Phys. Soc. (mem. at large, governing bd. 1964-65); mem. Microscope Soc. Am. (pres. 1944, Disting. Scientist award 1977), Indsl. Rsch. Inst. (bd. dirs. 1960-65, pres. 1964, Inst. medal 1975), Nat. Inventors Hall of Fame Found., Inc. (bd. dirs. 1992—, Lifetime Achievement award 2002), Nat. Acad. Engrng. (coun. 1971), Rotary (bd. dirs. 1988-91), Nassau Club, Sigma Xi. Achievements include 41 patents in field; co-design of first successful electron microscope in North America, of first commercially available electron microscope in North America; discovery of principle of Stigmator for correcting astigmatism of electron microscope objective lenses; invention of electron microprobe microanalyser; first to picture tobacco mosaic virus, bacterial viruses and ultra-thin section of a single bacterium. Home: Princeton, NJ. Died Jan. 15, 2007.

HILLMAN, DOUGLAS WOODRUFF, retired federal judge; b. Grand Rapids, Mich., Feb. 15, 1922; s. Lemuel Serrell and Dorothy (Woodruff) H.; m. Sally Jones, Sept. 13, 1944; children: Drusilla W., Clayton D. (dec.). Student, Phillips Exeter Acad., 1941; AB, U. Mich., 1946, LL.B., 1948. Bar: Mich. 1948, U.S. Supreme Ct. 1967. Assoc. Lilly, Luyendyk & Snyder, Grand Rapids, 1948-53; partner Luyendyk, Hainer, Hillman, Karr & Dutcher, Grand Rapids, 1953-65, Hillman, Baxter & Hammond, 1965-79; judge US Dist. Ct (we. dist.) Mich., Grand Rapids, 1979—91, chief judge, 1986-91, sr. judge, 1991—2002; ret., 2002. Instr. Nat. Inst. Trial Adv., Boulder, Colo; dir. Fed. Judges Assn.; mem. jud. conf. com. on Adminstrn. of Magistrate Judges Sys., 1993-99; chair 6th Circuit Standing Com. on Jud. Conf. Planning; mem. exec. com. ABA jud. adminstrn. divsn. Nat. Conf. Fed. Trial Judges, 1995-98. Co-author articles in legal publs. Chmn. Grand Rapids Human Relations Commn., 1963-66; chmn. bd. trustees Fountain St. Ch., 1970-72; pres. Family Service Assn., 1967. Served as pilot USAAF, 1943-45. Decorated Air medal DFC; named One of 25 Most Respected Judges, Mich. Laywers Weekly, Grand Rapids Med. Hall Fame, 2001; recipient Ann. Civil Liberties award, ACLU, 1970, Disting. Alumni award, Ctrl. High Sch., 1986, Raymond Fox Advocacy award, 1989, Champion of Justice award, State Bar Mich., 1990, Profl. & Cmty. Svc. award, Young Lawyers Sect., 1996, Svc. to Profession award, Fed. Bar Assn., 1991; grantee Paul Harris fellow, Rotary Internat. Fellow Am. Bar Found.; mem. ABA, Mich. Bar Assn. (chmn. client security fund), Grand Rapids Bar Assn. (pres. 1963), Am. Coll. Trial Lawyers (Mich. chmn. 1979, com. on teaching trial and appellate adv.), 6th Circuit Jud. Conf. (life), Internat. Acad. Trial Lawyers, Fedn. Ins. Counsel, Internat. Assn. Ins. Counsel, Internat. Soc. Barristers (pres 1977-78, chair annual Hillman Trial Adv. Seminar), M Club of U. Mich. (com. visitors U. Mich. Law Sch.), Univ. Club (Grand Rapids), Torch Club. Home: Montague, Mich. Died Feb. 1, 2007.

HILLSMITH, FANNIE L., artist; b. Boston, Mar. 13, 1911; d. Clarence and Clara (Huston) H. Student, Sch. Boston Mus. Fine Arts, 1930-34, Art Students League, 1935-36, Alalier 17, 1946-50. Instr. Black Mountain Coll., N.C., 1945; vis. critic Cornell U., Ithaca, N.Y., 1963-64. One-woman exhbns. include Norlyst Gallery, N.Y., 1943, Egan Gallery, N.Y., 1949, 50, 54, Frameshop Gallery, Boston, 1949, Swetzoff Gallery, Boston, 1949-50, 52, 54, 57, 63, Santa Barbara (Calif.) Mus. Art, 1950, Milton (Mass.) Acad., 1952, Currier Gallery Art, Manchester, N.H., 1953, DeCordova and Dana Mus. and Park, Lincoln, Mass., 1953, 58, The Dayton (Ohio) Art Inst., 1954, Inst. Contemporary Art, Boston, 1954, Am. Acad. Arts and Letter, N.Y.C., 1957, Peridot Gallery, N.Y.C., 1957-58, 62, 65, Cornell U., 1963, Bristol (R.I.) Art Mus., 1972, So. Vt. Art Ctr., Manchester, 1978, Currier Gallery Art, N.H., 1987, Susan Teller Gallery, N.Y.C., 1994; group exhbns. include Art of this Century, N.Y.C., 1943-44, 45, Mus. Modern Art, N.Y.C., 1946-51, Riverside Mus., N.Y., 1946-58, Art Inst. Chgo., 1947-48, 54-55, Va. Mus. Fine Arts, Richmond, 1948, Whitney Mus. Am. Art, N.Y.C., 1949-51, 55, New Gallery, N.Y.C., 1951, Currier Gallery Art, 1952-58, 60, 78, 80, Walker Art Ctr., Mpls., 1953-54, Inst. Contemporary Art, Boston, 1954, Solomon R. Guggenheim Mus., N.Y.C., 1954, Springfield (Mass.) Mus. Fine Arts, 1954, Bklyn. Mus., 1955, Corcoran Gallery Art, Washington, 1955, 57, The Phillips Gallery, Washington, 1955, Phila. Print Club, 1955, Mus. Fine Arts, Boston, 1977, Washburn Gallery, N.Y.C., 1981, Graham Gallery, N.Y.C., 1987, Susan Teller Gallery, N.Y., 1993; permanent collections include Addison Gallery Am. Art, Andover, Mass., Currier Gallery Art, Fitchburg (Mass.) Art Mus., Fogg Art Mus., Cambridge, Mass., Met. Mus. Art, N.Y.C., Mus. Fine Arts, Boston, Mus. Modern Art, N.Y.C., N.J. State Mus., Trenton, N.Y. Pub. Libr., Newark Mus., Phila. Mus. Art. Alumni Travelling scholar Mus. Fine Arts, Boston, 1958; recipient The Currier Art Gallery award, 1952, 54, Pioneer Valley Art Exhbn. award Pioneer Valley Art Gallery, 1953, Boston and Maine Railroad First award The Berkshire Mus., 1956, Boston Arts Festival First award, 1957, 63, Second award, 1957. Portland Summer Festival award Portland (Oreg.) Art Mus., 1957. Died July 27, 2007.

HILLYER, IRA BARTHOLOMY, financial consultant; b. New London, Conn., July 19, 1932; s. Ira A. and Amy (Bartholomy) H.; student U. Md., 1952; m. Patricia Baldwin, Feb. 14, 1953; children— David, Michael, Mary, Margaret, Kathryn, Stephen, Joseph, Martha, Dennis, Paula, Ira C., Amy, Anne, Nathaniel, John. With Savs. Bank of New London, 1952-62; gen. mgr. Community Service Credit Union, Inc. (formerly Submarine Base Credit Union, Inc.), Groton, Conn., 1962-80, chief exec. officer, 1980-82, treas., 1972-82, also dir.; pres. H. G. Co., 1983-85; pres. Hillyer Assocs. Inc., 1985—. owner Swiss Chalet, 1983-85. Chmn., Zoning Bd. Appeals, North Stonington, Conn., 1977-79, mem., 1979-82; justice of peace Town of North Stonington, 1979-85. Mem. Credit Union Execs. Soc., Nat. Assn. Credit Union Mgmt. Assn., New London County Homebuilders Assn., Electronic Banking Economists Soc., Am. Mgmt. Assn., Chimney Hill Assn. (dir. 1979—, v.p., treas. 1980-82, pres. 1982-84, past pres. 1984-86). Republican. Roman Catholic. Club: Lions (pres. 1978-79, dir.). Home: North Stonington, Conn. Died Feb. 16, 2007.

HILTON, RONALD, language educator; b. Torquay, Eng., July 31, 1911; came to U.S., 1937, naturalized, 1946; s. Robert and Elizabeth Alice (Taylor) H.; m. Mary Bowie, May 1, 1939; 1 child, Mary Alice Taylor. BA, Oxford U., Eng., 1933, MA, 1936; student, Sorbonne, Paris, 1933-34, U. Madrid, 1934-35, U. Perugia, Italy, 1935-36. Dir. Comité Hispano-Inglés Library, Madrid, 1936; asst. prof. modern langs. U. B.C., 1939-41; assoc. prof. Romanic langs. Stanford U., 1942-49, prof., 1949-75, prof. emeritus humanities and scis., 1975—2007. Dir. Inst. Hispanic Am. and Luso-Brazilian studies; hon. prof. U. de San Marcos, Lima, Peru; vis. prof. U. Brazil, 1949; cultural dir. U. of Air, KGEI, San Francisco.; founder, pres. World Assn. Internat. Studies; vis. fellow Hoover Instn., 1973-2007. Author: Campoamor, Spain and the World, 1940, Handbook of Hispanic Source Materials in the U.S, 1942, 2d edit., 1956, Four Studies in Franco-Spanish Relations, 1943, La America Latina de Ayer y de Hoy, 1970, The Scientific Institutions of Latin America, 1970, The Latin Americans, Their Heritage and Their Destiny, 1973; assoc. editor: Who's Who in America; editor: The Life of Joaquim Nabuco, 1950, The Movement Toward Latin American Unity, 1969, World Affairs Report, 1970-2007, Spain. From Monarchy to Civil War, 1990, La Legende Noir, 1995. Decorated officer Cruzeiro do Sul (Brazil); Commonwealth Fund fellow U. Calif., 1937-39. Mem. Am. Assn. Tchrs. Spanish and Portuguese, Hispanic Soc. of Am., Am. Acad. Franciscan History. Home: Stanford, Calif. Died Feb. 20, 2007.

HILTY, WILLIAM JACOB, retired association executive; b. Bucyrus, Ohio, Dec. 1, 1921; s. Harold Eugene and Gladys Marie (Heinlen) H.; m. Davelyn Lawrence, July 15, 1942; children: Harold Lawrence, Amanda Sue, Melissa Kay, Laura Ann. Advt. mgr. Flexible Bus. Co., Loudonville, Ohio, 1948-51; account exec. Fuller, Smith & Ross, Cleve., 1951-59; dir. communications Am. Soc. Metals, Metals Park, Ohio, 1969-71, IEEE, NYC, 1971; mng. dir. expositions and publs. Soc. Mfg. Engrs., Dearborn, Mich., 1971-81, exec. v.p., gen. mgr., 1981-86. Served to maj. USAF, 1941-45, ETO. Mem. Nat. Assn. Exposition Mgrs. (pres. 1970) Died Dec. 6, 2005.

HIMES, JANE ANN, public relations executive; b. Johnstown, Pa., June 20, 1923; d. Joseph George and Anna (Berg) Dupin; m. William E. Himes, Dec. 29, 1943 (div. Mar. 1977); children: Douglas D., Gregory T. Student, Memphis State U., 1977-86. Sec. Nat. Radiator Co., Johnstown, 1940-44; student loan officer lst Nat. Bank Mercer County, Sharon, Pa., 1970-76; adminstrv. asst. trust div. Nat. Bank Commerce, Memphis, 1976-78; adminstrv. asst. to chmn. bd. Buckman Labs. Internat., Inc., Memphis, 1978-79, dir. pub. rels., from 1979, editor Bu-Lines/By-Lines, from 1980. Mem. profl. adv. bd. Sch. Journalism, Memphis State U., 1986—. Mem. adv. bd. Adopt-A-Sch., Memphis, 1983-86, 88—; chmn. bd. dirs. Crime Stoppers Memphis, 1987-88, 89—; mem. adv. bd. arts in schs. Memphis Arts Coun., 1989—; v.p. bd. dirs. Home Health Care Found., Memphis, 1989—; bd. dirs. communications chmn. Tenn. chpt. Am. Heart Assn., Memphis and Nashville; elder Prsbyn. Ch., Memphis; mem. adv. bd. Porter Leath Children's Ctr. Recipient Vol. of Yr. award Am. Heart Assn., Memphis, l985. Mem. Pub. Rels. Soc. Am. (bd. dirs. Memphis l985—, pres. l988, Profl. of Yr. award l988, nat. presdl. citation l988), Optimists, Rotary. Republican. Avocations: swimming, gardening, arts, reading, cooking. Home: Memphis, Tenn. Died Oct. 10, 2006.

HIMSL, MATHIAS ALFRED, state senator; b. Bethune, Sask., Can., Sept. 17, 1912; s. Victor S. and Clara C. (Engels) H.; came to U.S., 1913; B.A., St. John's U., Collegeville, Minn., 1934; M.A., U. Mont., 1940; m. Lois Louise Wohlwend, July 18, 1940; children— Allen, Marilyn Himsl Olson, Louise Himsl Robinson, Kathleen, Judith Himsl Choury. Tchr., supt. schs., Broadus, Mont., 1934-45; sec. Himsl Wohlwend Motors, Inc., Kalispell, Mont., 1945-68; pres. Skyline Broadcasters, Inc., radio sta. KGEZ, Kalispell, 1958-95; part-time instr. Flathead Valley Community Coll., 1969-72; mem. Mont. Ho. of Reps. from Flathead County, 1966-72, Mont. Senate from 3d dist., 1972-91; Senate pres. pro tempore, 1989. Chmn. Flathead County Republican Com., 1952-64; del. Rep. Nat. Conv., 1964; bd. govs. ARC, 1956-59. Roman Catholic. Club: Elks. Home: Kalispell, Mont. Died Dec. 30, 2006.

HINDERAKER, IVAN, retired political science professor; b. Hendricks, Minn., Apr. 29, 1916; s. Theodore and Clara (Hanson) H.; m. Evelyn Birkholz, June 7, 1941 (dec. June 17, 2004); 1 child, Mark (dec. Feb. 23, 2004). BA, St. Olaf Coll., 1938; MA, U. Minn., 1942, PhD, 1949. Mem. faculty UCLA, 1948—2007, prof. polit. sci., 1956—2007, chmn. dept., 1960-62; vice chancellor acad. affairs U. Calif.-Irvine, 1962-64; chancellor U. Calif.-Riverside, 1964-79, chancellor emeritus,

1979—2007. Mem. Minn. Ho. of Reps., 1941-43; mem. Calif. Transp. Commn., 1978-84, chmn., 1982. Served to 1st lt. USAAF, 1943-46. Home: Irvine, Calif. Died Sept. 23, 2007.

HINES, EDWARD FRANCIS, JR., lawyer; b. Norfolk, Va., Sept. 5, 1945; m. Elaine Geneva Carroll, Aug. 21, 1971; children: Jonathan Edward, Carolyn Adele. AB, Boston Coll., 1966; JD, Harvard U., 1969. Bar: Mass. 1969. Assoc. Choate Hall & Stewart, Boston, 1969-77, ptnr., 1977-2001, mng. ptnr., 1983—87; ptnr. Hines & Corley LLC, Lexington, Mass., 2001—07. Bd. dirs. Boston Coll. HS, Boston Med. Ctr., Boston Med. Ctr. Ins. Co., Cayman Islands, Chase Corp., Investors Fin. Svcs. Corp.; trustee Merrimac Fund Complex, 1996—2003. Trustee, treas. World Heart Fedn., Geneva, from 2003; trustee Social Law Libr., 1993—98; bd. dirs. Cath. Charities, from 2002, Assoc. Industries Mass., from 1990, chmn., 1996—98; bd. dirs. Am. Heart Assn., Dallas, 1984—86, 1991—2000, chmn., 1998—99; bd. dirs. Mass. Taxpayers Found., 1987—93, Boston Coll. H.S., from 2005, Carroll Ctr. for the Blind, 1983—89, 1990—96, chmn., 1994—96. With USAR, 1969—75. Recipient Boston Coll. H.S. St. Ignatius award, 1998, Gold Heart award, Am. Heart Assn., 2003. Fellow: Am. Coll. Trust and Estate Counsel; mem.: Mass. CLE (pres. 1985—87), Accion Internat. (bd. dirs. 1999—2005), Supreme Jud. Ct. Hist. Soc. (trustee 1989—96), Am. Coll. Greece (Athens bd. dirs., vice chmn. 1988—97), Boston Bar Found. (pres. 1995—97), Boston Bar Assn. (pres. 1988—89), Allen Harbor Yacht Club, Boston Coll. Club, North Andover Country Club. Home: Andover, Mass. Died Aug. 14, 2006.

HINRICHS, JAMES VICTOR, psychology educator, researcher; b. Harlan, Iowa, May 19, 1941; s. James Victor Hinrichs and Leona Gladys (Vander Stoep) Hinrichs Levinson; m. Charlene Ruth Becker, Dec. 29, 1964; children: Susan Elaine, Kristine Ann. BA, U. Iowa, 1963; AM, Stanford U., 1964, PhD, 1967. Asst. prof. U. Iowa, Iowa City, 1967-70, assoc. prof., 1970-78, prof., from 1978. Rsch. assoc. U. Minn., Mpls., 1974-75; vis. prof. Ind. U., Shah Alam, Malaysia, 1988-89; chmn. dept. psychol. U. Iowa, 1989—. Contbr. various articles to profl. jours., 1964—. James McKee Cattell fellow, 1974-75. Fellow Am. Psychol. Assn., Am. Psychol. Soc.; mem. Psychonomic Soc., Phi Beta Kappa, Sigma Xi. Home: Iowa City, Iowa. Died Jan. 18, 2006.

HIRSCH, BARRY, lawyer; b. NYC, Mar. 19, 1933; s. Emanuel M. and Minnie (Levenson) H.; m. Myra Seiden, June 13, 1963; children: Victor Terry II, Neil Charles Seiden, Nancy Elizabeth. BSBA, U. Mo., 1954; JD, U. Mich., 1959; LL.M., N.Y. U., 1964. Bar: N.Y. bar 1960. Assoc., then partner firm Seligson & Morris, NYC, 1960-69; v.p., sec., gen. counsel dir. B.T.B. Corp., 1969-71; v.p., sec., gen. counsel Loews Corp. (and subsidiaries), 1971-86, sr. v.p., sec., gen. counsel, 1986—2003. Bds. dirs. Neuberger Berman Funds. Served to 1st lt. AUS, 1954-56. Mem. ABA, Assn. of Bar of City of N.Y., N.Y. State Bar Assn., Zeta Beta Tau, Phi Delta Phi. Home: New York, NY. Died July 27, 2006.

HIRSCHBERG, VERA HILDA, writer; b. NYC, Sept. 19, 1929; d. Bernard and Minnie (Margolis) Lieberman; m. Peter Hirschberg, Aug. 21, 1949 (dec. 2002); children: Karen Hirschberg Reses, Paul. BA, Hunter Coll., 1950. Staff writer Pacific Stars and Stripes, Tokyo, 1956-64; corr. Newsweek, Guatemala, 1964-65; transp. staff writer N.Y. Jour. Commerce, Washington, 1969-70; transp. editor Nat. Jour. Mag., Washington, 1970-72; dir. women's programs, presdl. speechwriter The White House, Washington, 1972-74; dir. tech. transfer HUD, Washington, 1974-75; dep. spl. asst. to Sec. Pub. Affairs Dept. Treasury, Washington, 1975-77; press. sec. U.S. Sen. William Roth, Jr., Washington, Jan. to Dec. 1977; editorial cons. various govt. and non-govt. clients, 1977-78; pub. affairs dir. The White House Conf. on Libr. & Info. Svcs., Washington, 1978-80; sr. writer, adminstr.'s speechwriter NASA, Washington, 1980-92; cons. in field., 1992—2007. Author numerous newspaper and mag. articles. Art info. vol. Nat. Gallery of Art. Recipient Outstanding Svc. citation The White House, 1973, Meritorious Svc. award Dept. Treasury, 1977, Exceptional Performance award NASA, 1982, Exceptional Svc. medal, 1988. Mem. Exec. Women in Govt. (founding mem. 1973), Zionist Orgn. Am., Wash. Concert Opera Soc. Mem. Wash. Hebrew Congregation. Avocations: gourmet cooking, foreign travel, reading, museums, art collecting. Home: Washington, DC. Died Oct. 29, 2007.*

HITCHENS, CHARLES NORWOOD, JR., artist; b. Strafford, Pa., Oct. 29, 1926; s. Charles Norwood and Corrie Anderson (Dawkins) H.; student U. Ill., 1947, 56, Pa. Acad. Fine and Applied Arts, 1958-62. One man shows include: Lynn Kottler Gallery, N.Y.C., 1964, Galerie de Mouffe, Paris, 1973, Galerie Vallombreus, Biarritz, France, 1974; group shows include: Lynn Kottler Gallery, Wayne (Pa.) Art Center, 1963; paintings include: Imagination No 10, Man's Dream, Bubbles, Fish and Flowers, Red Streaming, Avonwood Farm in Strafford, Washington's Headquarters, One in A Million. Home and Died Nov. 4, 2006.

HO, DON (DONALD TAI LOY HO), entertainer, singer; b. Honolulu, Aug. 13, 1930; s. James A. Y. and Emily L. (Silva) H.; m. Melvamay Kolokea Wong, Nov. 22, 1951 (dec. 1999); children: Donald Jr., Donalei, Dayna, Dondi, Dori, Dwight; m. Patricia Swallie Choy; children: Hoku, Kea, Kaimana; m. Dayna Ho Student, Springfield Coll., 1950; BS, U. Hawaii, 1954. Entertainer Honey's, Kaneohe, Hawaii, 1959-61, Flamingo Hotel, Las Vegas, Nev., 1964-72, Duke Kahanamoku's, Honolulu, 1964-70, Polynesian Palace, Honolulu, 1970-81, Don Ho's, Waikiki, 1981-82, Hilton Hawaiian Village, Honolulu, 1982-90, Hula Hut, Honolulu, 1991-92, Outrigger's Polynesian Palace, Honolulu, from 1992, Waikiki Beachcomber Hotel/Don Ho Supper Club, 1994—2007. With Alii's, Midway Island, 1964, Barabosa Club, San Francisco, 1965, Coconut Grove, Ambassador Hotel, L.A., 1965-68, 1967 Tour U.S./Can., Royal Box, Americana Hotel, N.Y.C., 1968, Empire Rm., Chgo., 1968; with Variety Club, Ambassador of Variety Club, Honolulu, 1978-87. Rec. with Reprise Co., Los Angeles, 1963-65 (Mainland, Can. tour Sept.-Dec. 1980); host, The Don Hon Show, 1976-77; actor (films) Joe's Apartment, 1996, First Daughter, 1997; (TV appearances) Hawaiian Eye, 1963, McCloud, 1974, Served to 1st lt. USAF, 1954-59. Died Apr. 14, 2007.

HOAGLAND, PETER JACKSON, lawyer, former congressman; b. Omaha, Nov. 17, 1941; s. Laurance and Naomi (Carpenter) H.; m. Barbara Joan Erickson, Sept. 1, 1973; children: Elizabeth, Kate, Christopher and David (twins), Nick. AB with Great Distinction, Stanford U., 1963; LLB, Yale U., 1968. Bar: Nebr. 1968, D.C. 1968. Assoc. Wald, Harkrader & Ross, Washington, 1968-69; law clk. to Hon. Oliver Gasch US Dist. Ct. D.C., Washington, 1969-70; trial atty. Pub. Defender Service, Washington, 1970-73; pvt. practice Omaha, 1974-89; mem. Nebr. State Senate, Lincoln, 1979-86, chmn. judiciary com. and rules com.; atty. Hoagland & Gerdes, 1985—89; mem. US Congress from 2d Nebr. Dist., 1989-95, mem. House Ways and Means Com.; ptnr. Arent Fox Kintner Plotkin & Kahn, Washington, 1995—2007. Served to 1st lt. U.S. Army, 1963-65. Recipient numerous awards in connection with public service career. Mem. K.S. Assn. Former Mems. Congress (bd. mem.), Yale Law Sch. Alumni Assn. Democrat. Episcopalian. Home: Chevy Chase, Md. Died Oct. 30, 2007.*

HOBBS, EDWARD HENRY, political science educator; b. Selma, Ala., Jan. 14, 1921; s. Edward Henry and Mary Olivia (Dannelly) H.; m. Marleah Marguerite Kaufman, Dec. 23, 1943; children: Milton Dannelly, Miriam Kaufman, Edward Henry, Vivian Blair. AB in Am. History, U. N.C., 1943; MA in Polit. Sci, U. Ala., 1947; So. Regional Tng. Program in Pub. Adminstrn. advanced scholar, 1947-48; MA, Harvard, 1949, PhD, 1951. Instr. U. Ala., 1946-47; faculty U. Miss., 1949-67, prof. polit. sci., 1957-67, acting chmn. dept. research in bus. and pub. adminstrn., 1957-59, chmn. dept. research in bus. and pub. adminstrn., 1959-61, chmn. dept. research in bus. and govt., 1961-67; dean Sch. Arts and Scis. Auburn U., 1967-87, dean emeritus Sch. Arts and Scis., from 1986, prof. emeritus, from 1986. Corr. So. Regional Tng. Program in Pub. Adminstrn., 1955—; mem. Auburn U. delegation to Hunan U. and Ubei U., Peoples Republic China, 1986. Author: Behind the President: A Study of Executive Office Agencies, 1954, Yesterday's Constitution Today: An Analysis of the Mississippi Constitution of 1890, 1960, Legislative Apportionment in Mississippi, 1956, Executive Reorganization in the National Government, 1953, A Manual of Mississippi Municipal Government, 1962, (with others) Mississippi in Maps-Industry, Resources and Agriculture, 1959, A Directory of Mississippi Municipalities, 3d edit, 1962, Money for Miles in Mississippi: A Highway Finance Report, 1962, also articles.; Co-author: (with others) A Compendium of Selected Information on Mississippi Municipalities, 1966, Power in American State Legislatures, 1967; Co-compiler: (with others) Annotated Bibliography on Mississippi Economy, Business, Industry and Government, 1950-1963, 1964; project dir., co-author: (with others) Arts and Sciences Council Report to Alabama Commn. on Higher Edn, 1972; Editor: (with others) Mississippi's Workmen's Compensation: Selected Cases, 1964, U.S.A. and the World's Three Biggest Economic Myths, 1965; Contbr. (with others) numerous articles in acad. and profl. jours. Chmn. Oxford (Miss.) Planning Commn., 1959-67, Oxford Council Aging, 1959, Council of Deans of Arts and Scis. Ala. Commn. on Higher Edn., 1983—; cons. Miss. Council Aging, 1957; pres. Miss. Research Clearing House, 1957-58; bd. dirs. Miss. Planning Conf., 1959-64, Citizens' Com. for Constl. Conv., 1977, Miss. Heart Assn., Ala. Med. Ctr. Found., 1986; chmn. campaign dist. II Miss. Mental Health Assn., 1960; corr. Nat. Municipal League, 1955-67, Conf. Met. Area Problems, 1958—; co-chmn. univ. relations com. Citizens' Conf. on Ala. State Govts., 1973; moderator Conf. on Pres. Truman's Orgn. and Adminstrn. of Presidency, Kansas City, Mo., 1977; mem. Auburn City Planning Commn., 1987. Served to lt. USNR, World War II; capt. in Res. Nat. fellow to 2d Summer Inst. in Social Gerontology U. Calif. at Berkeley, 1959; recipient Howard and Robert Strong award, 1982, Presdl. Citation for Meritorious Service, 1981, Golden Eagle Trophy, Army ROTC, 1985. Mem. So. Polit. Sci. Assn., So. Pub. Adminstrn. Research Council, Am. Soc. Pub. Adminstrn. (nat. adv. com. 1957—), Am. Polit. Sci. Assn., Oxford-Lafayette County C. of C., Pi Sigma Alpha (nat. exec. com. 1958—, Disting. Service award 1986), Delta Kappa Epsilon, Omicron Delta Kappa (honoris causa 1955), Phi Kappa Phi (chpt. pres.), Alpha Epsilon Delta, Pi Delta Phi. Presbyn. (elder). Club: Rotarian. Home: Auburn, Ala. Died June 25, 2006.

HOCH, FRANK WILLIAM, banker; b. White Plains, NY, May 14, 1921; s. Herman and Hanny (von Salis) H.; m. Lisina de Schulthess, Aug. 14, 1951; children: Steven George, Alix Monica, Daphne Lisina, Roland Eric. Student, Kantonales Gymnasium, Zurich, Switzerland; LL.D., U. Geneva, Zurich U., Switzerland Law Sch., 1947. With Brown Bros. Harriman & Co., NYC, from 1947, partner, from 1960. Mem. adv. bd. Lehndorff Properties (USA) Ltd. Mem. nat. bd. Smithsonian Assocs. Mem. Council on Fgn. Relations. Home: Irvington, NY. Died Apr. 12, 2007.

HODAPP, LEROY CHARLES, bishop; b. Seymour, Ind., Nov. 11, 1923; s. Linden Charles and Mary Marguerite (Miller) H.; m. Polly Anne Martin, June 12, 1947; children: Anne Lynn Hodapp Gates, Nancy Ellen Hodapp Wichman. AB, U. Evansville, Ind., 1944, DD (hon.), 1961; BD, Drew Theol. Sem., Madison, NJ, 1947; LHD (hon.), Ill. Wesleyan U., 1977; DD (hon.), McKendree Coll., 1978; D.D., Wiley Coll., 1980. Ordained to ministry Methodist Ch., 1947; pastor chs. in Ind., 1947-65; supt. Bloomington (Ind.) Dist. Meth. Ch., 1965-67, supt. Indpls. West Dist., 1967-68, supt. Indpls. N.E. Dist., 1968-70; dir. S. Ind. Conf. Council, 1970-76; bishop Ill. area United Meth. Ch., Springfield, 1976-84, Ind. area United Meth. Ch., Indpls., from 1984; pres. United Meth. Gen. Bd. Ch. and Soc., 1980-84, United Meth. Coun. Bishops, 1990-91. Coeditor: Change in the Small Community, 1967. Democrat. Died May 26, 2006.

HODGE, MARY HARRISON, county official; b. Morristown, Tenn., Mar. 27, 1918; d. Baldwin Harle and Julia Elizabeth (Skeen) Harrison; m. Hubert leach Hodge Aug. 28, 1945 (dec. 1975); children— Nancy Elizabeth Hodge McGuire, Susan Janet Hodge Greene, Mary Hugh, Ruthelen. Student Morristown Sch. of Bus., 1977. Clk. and bookkeeper Dick's 5 & 10, Morristown, 1937-43; elementary tchr. Hamblen county, Tenn., 1943-45; bookkeeper and gen. office worker So. Furniture, Morristown, 1945-47; West Elem. Sch., Morristown, 1966-67; dep. clk. Register of Deeds, Morristown, 1960-66; bookkeeper and computer operator Bob Bales Ford, Morristown, 1967-76; register of deeds Hamblen County, 1978— (first woman elected to county-wide office in Hamblen County). Active Hamblen County Women's Democratic Club, First Bapt. Ch. Mem. Woman's Missionary Union. Home: Morristown, Tenn. Died Dec. 24, 2006.

HODGSON, JANE ELIZABETH, obstetrician, gynecologist, consultant; b. Crookston, Minn., Jan. 23, 1915; d. Herbert and Adelaide (Marin) H.; m. Frank Walter Quattlebaum, Feb. 22, 1940 (dec. Mar. 2004); children: Gretchen, Nancy. BS, Carleton Coll., 1934, DSc (hon.), 1994; MD, U. Minn., 1939, MS in Ob-gyn., 1947. Diplomate Am. Bd. Ob-gyn. Fellow Mayo Clinic, Rochester, Minn., 1941-44; pvt. practice in ob-gyn. St. Paul, 1947-72; med. dir. Preterm Clinic, Washington, 1972-74; med. dir. fertility control clinic St. Paul Ramsey Med. Ctr., 1974-79; med. dir. Planned Parenthood Minn., St. Paul, 1980-82, Midwest Health Ctr. Women, Mpls., 1981-83, Women's Health Ctr., Duluth, Minn., 1981-84, mem. staff, 1986—2006; ostetrician/gynecologist Project Hope, Grenada, West Indies, 1984; vis. prof. ob-gyn. project hope Zheijiang Med. Sch., Hangzhou, China, 1985-86; clin. assoc. prof. ob-gyn. U. Minn., Mpls., 1986—2006. Vis. med. educator Project Hope, Cairo, 1979—80; vis. prof. dept. ob-gyn. U. Calif., San Francisco, 1983. Editor: Abortion & Sterilization, 1981; contbr. numerous articles to profl. jours. Bd. dirs. Genesis II Women, Mpls., 1988—, Pro Choice Resources, Mpls., 1991—, Wellstone Alliance, Mpls., 1992—; bd dirs. Ctr. for Reproductive Rights, N.Y.C., 1995-2004, hon. trustee, 2004—. Recipient Ann. Humanitarian award Nat. Abortion Fedn., 1981, Woman Physician of Yr. award Med. Women Minn. Med. Assn., 1983, Ann. Jane Hodgson Reproductive Freedom award Nat. Abortion Rights Action League, 1989, Hanah G. Solomon award Nat. Coun. Jewish Women, 1990, Margaret Sanger award Planned Parenthood Fedn. of Am., 1995, Harold Swanberg award Am. Med. Writer's Assn., 1996. Fellow Am. Coll. Ob-Gyn. (founding); mem. Am. Med. Women's Assn. (E. Blackwell award 1992, Reproductive Health award 1994), Minn. Ob-Gyn. Soc. (pres. 1967), Minn. Med. Assn. (So. Minn. Med. award 1952), Minn. Women's Polit. Caucus (16th Ann. Founding Feminist award 1988), Mayo Clinic Alumni Assn. Died Oct. 23, 2006.

HODGSON, MATTHEW MARSHALL NEIL, publishing company executive; b. Washington, June 28, 1926; s. Hal King and Georgia Frances (Gregory) H.; m. Patricia Kindelan, Jan. 8, 1967; children: Laura Ann, Edward Telfair. AB, U. N.C., 1949. With Appleton-Century-Crofts, Inc., 1949-55; sr. editor Houghton Mifflin Co., Boston, 1955-68; developmental editor U. Press of Ky., Lexington, 1968-70; dir. U. N.C. Press, Chapel Hill, from 1971. Bd. dirs. Assn. Am. U. Presses, 1973-74, pres., 1978-79; bd. dirs. N.C. Art Soc. Served with USNR, 1944-45. Mem. Phi Gamma Delta. Clubs: Century Assn. (N.Y.C.); Long Hope Trout (N.C.). Athenaeum (London). Home: Chapel Hill, NC. Died June 16, 2006.

HODGSON, PETER JOHN, author, composer, lecturer; b. Birmingham, Eng., Apr. 6, 1929; came to U.S., 1965, naturalized, 1974; s. Eric Christopher and Dorothy (Price) H.; m. Mary Thatcher, 1958; 1 son, Michael. MusB, U. London, 1964; MusM, Royal Coll. Music, 1965; PhD in Music (Univ. fellow), U. Colo., 1970. Resident music master Univ. Sch., Victoria, B.C., Can., 1952-55; mem. faculty, adminstr. Mt. Royal Coll., Calgary, Alta., Can., 1955-65; mem. faculty Banff (Alta.) Sch. Fine Arts, 1960-66; mem. faculty, adminstr. Sch. of Music, Ball State U., Muncie, Ind., 1968-78; dean New Eng. Conservatory of Music, 1978-83; prof. music, chmn. dept. music Tex. Christian U., Ft. Worth, 1983-87; dean faculty Principia Coll., Elsah, Ill., 1987-94, prof. music, 1987-96; ind. scholar, from 1996. Author: Music of Herbert Howells, 1971, Toward an Understanding of Renaissance Musical Structure, 1972, Benjamin Britten: A Composer Resource Manual, 1996; composer: 39 pieces for piano and/or organ, 1996, 10 vocal solos, 1996-98. Served with Brit. Army, 1947-49. Recipient award Brit. Council, 1964 Home: Grass Valley, Calif. Died Aug. 9, 2007.

HOECKER, WAYNE H., lawyer; b. Ames, Iowa, Nov. 27, 1939; s. Wesley H. and Grace (Semon) H.; m. Sara Shipp; children: Carolyn S., Anne E. BS in Bus. Adminstrn., U. Mo., 1961, JD, 1967. Bar: Mo., U.S. Dist. Ct. (we. dist.) Mo., U.S. Ct. Appeals (2d and 8th cirs.). Asst. atty. gen. State of Mo., Jefferson City, 1969-71; ptnr. Gage & Tucker, Kansas City, Mo., from 1971; gen. counsel Mid-Am. Dairymen, Springfield, Mo., from 1984, MFA, Inc., Columbia, Mo., 1982-93. Lt. USN, 1961-64, PTO. Republican. Home: Kansas City, Mo. Died July 31, 2006.

HOERNER, EARL FRANKLIN, physician; b. Harrisburg, Pa., Feb. 23, 1922; s. Earl F. and Kathryn Mae (Raybuck) H.; m. Rhea Joy Smith (dec.); children: Thomas Earl, Kenneth Todd, Jeffrey Scott. Student, Carnegie Inst. of Tech., 1942-44; MD, Hahnemann Med. Coll., 1949; M of Pub. Health, U. Pitts., 1952. Intern U.S. Marine Hosp., SI, N.Y., 1949-50; resident NYU-Bellevue Med. Ctr., NYC, 1950-54; clin. dir. Kessler Inst. for Rehab., West Orange, N.J., 1954-57, N.J. Orthopedic Hosp., West Orange, 1957-74; prof. rehab. medicine N.J. Coll. of Medicine, 1957-76; prof. Tufts Univ., Boston, 1976-80, Univ. Conn. Med. and Grad. Schs., Storrs, 1981-87; dir./med. officer Biomotions/BioMed, West Haven, Conn., from 1987; med. dir. Kinematic Cons., N.J., Mass. and Conn., from 1990. Chair safety and protective equipment USA Hockey, 1976. Editor Am. Jour. of Clin. Assessment, 1987—. Chmn. of bd. Livingston YMCA, 1956-64; bd. dirs. Internat. Health Evaluation, 1970—, Am. Ptnrs., 1994—. Named Man of Yr. ASTM, 1993, Internat. Man of the Yr. Internat. Conf. on Comparative Biophys. Edn., 1977, Man of Valor U.S. Olympic Team, Am. Bicycle League, 1972; recipient Safety in Sports award Am. Alliance of Health, Phys. Edn. and Recreation, 1976. Fellow IEEE, Internat. Coll. of Surgeons; mem. AMA, APHA, Am. Congress of Occupational

Medicine, Am. Biomechanics Soc., Internat. Biomechanics Soc., Am. Assn. of Automotive Engrs., Forensic Soc. Avocation: sports safety risk analysis. Home: North Andover, Mass. Died June 10, 2006.

HOFF, JULIAN THEODORE, neurosurgeon, educator; b. Boise, Idaho, Sept. 22, 1936; s. Harvey Orval and Helen Marie (Boraas) H.; m. Diane Shanks, June 3, 1962; children— Paul, Allison, Julia. BA, Stanford U., Calif., 1958; MD, Cornell U., NYC, 1962. Diplomate Am. Bd. Neurol. Surgery. Intern N.Y. Hosp., NYC, 1962-63, resident in surgery, 1963-64, resident in neurosurgery, 1966-70; asst. prof. neurosurgery U. Calif., San Francisco, assoc. prof. neurosurgery, 1974-78, prof. neurosurgery, 1978-81, U. Mich., Ann Arbor, from 1981, head sect. neurosurgery, 1981—90, chair dept. neurosurgery, 1990—96. Sec. Am. Bd. Neurol-Surgery, 1987-91, chmn., 1991-92; mem. bd. sci. councillors Nat. Inst. Neurol. Diseases and Stroke-NIH, 1993-97, nat. adv. coun., 1999—. Editor: Practice of Neurosurgery, 1979-85; Current Surgical Management of Neurological Diseases, 1980; Neurosurgery: Diagnostic and Management Principles, 1992, Mild to Moderate Head Injury, 1989; co-editor: Neurosurgery: Scientific Basis of Clinical Practice, 1985, 3rd edit., 1999; contbr. articles to profl. jours. Served to capt. US Army, 1964-66. Recipient Tchr.-Investigator award, NIH, 1972—77, Javits Neurosci. Investigator award, 1985—99, Macy Faculty scholar, London, 1979. Fellow: ACS (2d v.p.-elect 1998—99); mem.: Soc. Neurol. Surgeons (pres. 1999—2000, Grass prize 2001), Cen. Neurosurg. Soc. (pres. 1985—86), Am. Acad. Neurosurgeons (treas. 1989—92, sec. from 1992, pres. from 1996), Congress Neurol. Surgeons (v.p. 1982—83, Honored Guest 2003), Am. Surg. Assn., Am. Assn. Neurol. Surgeons (v.p. 1991—93, pres. 1993—94, Cushing medal 2001), Inst. Medicine NAS. Republican. Presbyterian. Home: Ann Arbor, Mich. Died Apr. 16, 2007.

HOFFER, PAUL B., nuclear medicine physician, educator; b. NYC, Apr. 9, 1939; m. Vicki Kornbluth; children: Marjorie, Joanne, Ilene, Suzanne, Alexandra. Student, Union Coll., 1956-59; MD, U. Chgo., 1963; MS, Yale U., 1977. Diplomate: Am. Bd. Radiology, Am. Bd. Nuclear Medicine. Resident in radiology U. Chgo., 1966-69, radiologist, 1969-70, dir. nuclear medicine, 1970-74; prof., dir. nuclear medicine U. Calif.-San Francisco, 1974-77, Yale U., New Haven, 1977-96, prof., from 1996. Mem. NIH Diagnostic Radiology Study Sect., 1984-86. Editor: Gallium 67 Imaging, 1978, Yearbook of Nuclear Medicine, 1981—, Diagnostic Nuclear Medicine, 1988; inventor radiation camera system, 1973. Served to lt. comdr. USN, 1964-66. Recipient Meml. medal Assn. Univ. Radiologists, 1968; James Picker Found. scholar, 1969-72 Mem. Soc. Nuclear Medicine (v.p. 1980-81), Am. Coll. Radiology, Am. Coll. Nuclear Physicians, Radiol. Soc. N.Am., AAAS Jewish. Home: New Haven, Conn. Died May 9, 2006.

HOFFER, THOMAS WILLIAM, communications educator, educator; b. Toledo, Iowa, May 31, 1938; s. Martin Herbert and Margaret Kathryn (Plum) H. BA in Speech and Drama, U. Iowa, 1960; MA in Communication Arts, U. Wis., 1969, PhD in Communication Arts, 1972. Instr. photography-cinema U. Wis., Madison, 1965-68; prof. comm. Fla. State U., Tallahasse, from 1972. Pres. Dunecrest, Eastpoint, Fla., 1987; pubr. Franklin County Chronicle, 1991. Author: Animation: A Reference Guide, 1981, contbr. to books, monographs, jours.; producer, dir., film editor for sci. and instructional films. Served to lt. comdr. USNR, 1961-71, Vietnam. Mem. Broadcast Edn. Assn. Democrat. Methodist. Avocations: collecting rare books, photography, travel. Died Dec. 9, 2006.

HOFFMAN, ALFRED JOHN, retired mutual fund executive; b. Amarillo, Tex., Apr. 16, 1917; s. Kurt John and Mabel (Beven) H.; m. Falice Mae Pittinger, Jan. 5, 1946 (dec. Feb. 1990); children: Peter Kurt (dec.), Susan Terry, John; m. Frances Ward, Sept. 15, 1990. JD, U. Mo., 1942. Atty. Prudential Ins. Co. Am., 1946-50, Kansas City Fire & Marine Ins. Co., 1950-59; CEO, founder Jones & Babson, Inc., Kansas City, 1959-85, vice chmn., 1985-93; pres., dir. Babson and UMB Mut. Funds, 1959-85, dir., 1985-93. Naval aviator USN, 1942-46. Mem. ABA, Mo. Bar Assn., Kansas City Golf Assn. (past pres., bd. dirs.), Kansas City Golf Found. (founder, chmn., bd. dirs.), Kansas City Srs. Golf Assn. (past pres., bd. dirs.), U.S. Golf Assn. (com.), Western Golf Assn. (past dir.). Died Mar. 27, 2007.

HOFFMAN, BARBARA ANN, English language educator; b. Rochester, NY, Dec. 19, 1941; d. Joseph George and Lucy Rose (Voelkl) H. Student, Nazareth Coll., Rochester, NY, 1959-62; BA, D'Youville Coll., 1963; MA, Cath. U. Am., 1965; postgrad., Duquesne U., 1966-69. Instr. English Marywood Coll., Scranton, Pa., 1969-72, asst. prof., 1972-90, prof., from 1990. Catechist U. Scranton, 1987-92. Author (poetry) Cliffs of Fall, 1979; contbr. poetry to various publs. Student of Japanese Tea Ceremony. Recipient Excellence in Teaching award Sears Roebuck and Co., 1990; Marywood Scholarship named in her honor, 1991. Mem. AAUP, Urasenke Chanoyu Soc. Democrat. Roman Catholic. Home: Scranton, Pa. Died Apr. 29, 2007.

HOFFMAN, DONALD BROOKS, former county official, business executive; b. Franklin, Pa., Nov. 20, 1911; s. Camilla C. and Hazel (Brooks) H.; m. Margaret Jane Gruber, July 27, 1935; children— Margaret J. (Mrs. Harry Adams), Donald Brooks, Edwin P., William G. Ph.B., Muhlenberg Coll., 1932; M.A., Lehigh U., 1963; LL.D., Otterbein Coll., 1964. Claims mgr. Liberty Mut. Ins. Co., 1934-45; bus. mgr. Phoebe Floral Co., Allentown, Pa., 1945-52; county treas. Lehigh County, Pa., 1952-55, 64-67; with firm Yarnall, Biddle & Co., Allentown, 1955-75; v.p. investments Janney Montgomery Scott, Allentown, 1975—. Chmn. bd. commrs. Lehigh County, 1968-75. Trustee Muhlenberg Coll., 1963—. Mem. Orgn. Am. Historians, Am. Hist. Assn., So. Hist. Assn., Western Hist. Assn., County Treas. Assn. Pa. (sec., treas. 1954-71), Pa. Assn. Elected County Ofcls. (sec., treas. 1954-71), Assn. Coll. Honor Socs. (sec.-treas. 1965-75, pres. 1977-79), Pa. Dist. Exchange Clubs (pres. 1977-78, nat. dir. 1979-80), Phi Alpha Theta (exec. sec.-treas. 1937—). Republican. Mem. United Ch. of Christ. Clubs: Masons, Odd Fellows, Exchange. Home: Allentown, Pa. Died Jan. 19, 2006.

HOFFMANN, PHILIP, pharmacology educator; b. Evanston, Ill., June 18, 1936; s. Robert Charles and Dorothy Elizabeth (Shaw) H. BS in Biochemistry, U. Chgo., 1957, PhD in Pharmacology, 1962. NSF postdoctoral fellow Pharmacology Inst., U. Marburg, Germany, 1962-63; postdoctoral fellow Kungl Högskolan, Stockholm, 1963-64; from instr. to assoc. prof. U. Chgo., 1964-81, prof. pharmacology, from 1981. Mem. Am. Soc. Pharmacology and Exptl. Therapeutics, Soc. for Neuroscience. Democrat. Home: Chicago, Ill. Died July 21, 2006.

HOFMAN, ELAINE D., state legislator; b. Sacramento, Sept. 20, 1937; d. Willard Davis and Venna (Gray) Smart; m. Cornelius Adrianus Hofman, Dec. 14, 1956; children: Catharina, John, Casie, Cornelius. BA, Idaho State U., 1974. Tchr. music edn. Sch. Dist. 25, Pocatello, Idaho, 1977-84; spl. asst. to Gov. Evans State of Idaho, Pocatello, 1984-87; field rep. to Congressman Stallings 2d Dist. Congressional Office, Pocatello, 1987-89; mem. Idaho Ho. of Reps., Pocatello, 1990-96. Recipient Elect Lady award Lambda Delta Sigma, 1991; named Idaho Mother of Yr., Am. Mother's Assn., 1992, S.E. Idaho Family of the Yr., 1980. Democrat. Mem. Ch. of Jesus Christ of Latter-day Saints. Avocations: prof. vocalist. Home: Pocatello, Idaho. Died Mar. 28, 2007.

HOFMANN, HANS, theology educator, author; b. Basel, Switzerland, Aug. 12, 1923; came to U.S., 1951, naturalized, 1956; s. Oscar and Henriette (Burbiel) H.; m. Emilie Scott Welles, Oct. 15, 1955; children— Elizabeth Scott, Mark Lawrence, David Hans, Scott Cluett. AB, Thurg. Kantonsschule, 1943; B.D., U. Basel, 1948; Th.D., U. Zurich, 1953. Mem. faculty Princeton Theol. Sem., 1953-57, asso. prof., 1956-57; mem. faculty Harvard Div. Sch., 1957-62, prof. theology, 1961-62, Ingersoll lectr. at univ., 1956-57. Leader Danforth seminar religion and bus. ethics Grad. Sch. Bus. Adminstrn., 1958, dir. project religion and mental health at univ., 1957-61; inaugural Thorp lectr. Cornell U., 1955-56; exec. dir. Center Study Personality and Culture, Inc., Cambridge, Mass., 1964-66; pres. Inst. for Human Devel., Cambridge, 1966—; ordained to ministry United Ch. Christ, 1957; cons. dept. internat. affairs Nat. Council Chs. Author: The Theology of Reinhold Niebuhr, 1955, Religion and Mental Health, 1961, Incorporating Sex, 1967, Breakthrough to Life, 1969, Discovering Freedom, 1969; Editor: Making the Ministry Relevant, 1960, The Ministry and Mental Health, 1960, Sex Incorporated, 1967. Mem. bd. overseers Shady Hill Sch., Cambridge. Mem. Internat. Platform Assn., Nat. Cum Laude Soc. (hon. mem.), Nat. Inst. Arts and Letters, English-Speaking Union, Soc. Sci. Study Religion, Am. Soc. Christian Social Ethics, Fedn. Am. Scientists, AAUP, Signet Soc. Home: Sedona, Ariz. Died July 2, 2007.

HOGAN, WILLIAM JOHN, physicist; b. Omaha, Oct. 8, 1940; s. William J. and Hazel E. (Johnson) H.; m. Sharon Lynn Hodson, June 30, 1962; children— Scot E., Kevin A., Heather L. B.S., Calif. Inst. Tech., 1962; Ph.D., Princeton U., 1966. Physicist Naval Weapons Lab., Corona, Calif., 1960-61, Princeton U., 1962-66, Lawrence Livermore Nat. Lab., Livermore, Calif., 1966—. Contbr. articles to profl. jours. Patentee in field. Chmn. Community Concerns Com., Pleasanton, Calif., 1968-75; scoutmaster San Francisco Bay Area council Boy Scouts Am., 1975-83; mem. Sci. adv. bd. U.S. Air Force, 1972-78. Mem. Am. Phys. Soc., AAAS, Am. Nuclear Soc., Sigma Xi. Democrat. Home: Livermore, Calif. Died Oct. 19, 2006.

HOGBERG, CARL GUSTAV, retired metal products executive; b. Escanaba, Mich., July 19, 1913; s. Claus Emil and Anna C. (Franson) H.; m. June Loraine Evans, June 10, 1935 (dec. Aug. 1991); children: David K., Janet H. (Mrs. Nicholas A. Matwiyoff). BS in Metall. Engring., Mich. Coll. Mining and Tech., 1935; DEng (hon.), Mich. Tech. U., 1968. Blast-furnace apprentice South Chgo. works Carnegie-Ill. Steel Corp., 1935, various operating positions blast-furnace dept., 1935—38, sec. blast-furnace and coke-oven com. Pitts., 1939—41; asst. chmn. blast-furnace com. U.S. Steel Corp., Pitts., 1942—54; asst. to v.p. Mich. Limestone divsn., Detroit, 1955, asst. v.p., 1956, v.p., 1957—60, pres., 1960—63, v.p. raw materials svc., parent co., 1964; pres. Orinoco Mining Co. subs., Caracas, Venezuela, 1965—70; v.p. internat. U.S. Steel Corp., 1970—73; ret., 1973. Contbr. tech. articles to trade publs. Mem. AIME (J.E. Johnson, Jr. award 1945), Assn. Iron and Steel Inst., Ea. Western States Blast Furnace and Coke Assns. Home: Cranberry Township, Pa. Died July 12, 2007.

HOGGARD, LARA GULDMAR, conductor, educator; b. Kingston, Okla., Feb. 9, 1915; s. Calvin Peter and Eva Lillian (Smith) H.; m. Mildred Mae Teeter, Sept. 11, 1943; 1 dau., Susan. BA, Southea. Tchrs. Coll., 1934; MA, Columbia U., 1940, EdD, 1947. Supr. music Durant (Okla.) Pub. Schs., 1934-39; dir. choral activities, opera and oratorio U. Okla., 1940-43; assoc. founder, prin. instr. Waring Summer Choral Workshops, 1948-52; co-editor Shawnee Press, Del. Water Gap, Pa., 1946-52; dir. music and music edn. rsch. Indian Springs Sch., Ala. Edn. Found., Birmingham, 1955-60; founder Nat. Young Artist Competition, Midland-Odessa, from 1962; William Rand Kenan prof. music U. N.C., Chapel Hill, 1967-80, founder Carolina Choir, from 1967; founder N.C. Collegiate Choral Festival, from 1969; Fuller E. Callaway prof. music Columbus Coll., U. Ga., 1981-82. Condr. NBC-USN Navy Hour, 1945, assoc. condr. Waring's Pennsylvanians, 1946—52, condr., dir. (nat. touring concert group) Civic Music and Nat. Concert Artists Corp., Festival of Song, 1952—53; dir.: N.C. Summer Insts. in Choral Art, 1953—83; founder, condr., musical dir. Midland-Odessa (Tex.) Symphony Orch. and Chorale, 1962—67, condr. numerous music festivals, Am., Europe, artistic dir., prin. condr. Festival of Three Cities, Vienna-Budapest-Prague, 1973, Internat. Jugendmusikfest in Wien, 1973, 1974, guest lectr. and condr. univs. and conservatories in Am. and Europe, condr. several musical premieres, including Behold the Glory (Talmage Dean) with Louisville Orch., 1964, Light in the Wilderness (Dave Brubeck), Chapel Hill, 1968, new edit. Ein deutsches Requiem (Brahms) with N.C. Symphony, 1986, numerous others; author: Improving Music Reading, 1947, Exploring Music, 1967; editor: an oratorio Light in the Wilderness (Dave Brubeck), 1968; composer, arranger, editor 37 choral publs.; editor: new English transl. and corr. orch. score and parts Ein deutsches Requiem (Brahms), 1983—89; composer: Le Jongleur, 1951. Served to lt. (j.g.) USN, 1943-45, PTO. Recipient award for outstanding svc. to music in Ala., Ala. Fine Arts Festival, 1958, citation for outstanding svc. to fine arts in Tex., Tex. Senate and Gov., West Texan award, 1967, Tanner award U. N.C., 1972, Ten Best Profs. award, 1978, Order Long Leaf Pine Gov. N.C., 1980, Disting. Alumnus award Southeastern Okla. State U., 1981, Lara G. Hoggard endowed professorship named in his honor U. N.C., 1993. Mem. Music Educators Nat. Conf. (life; Master Builder), Am. Choral Dirs. Assn. (life, award for contbn. to music in N.C. 1976, citation for contbn. to music in Am., divsn. 5, 1986, award for excellence and lifelong commitment So. divsn. 1998), AAUP, N.C. Music Educators Assn. (hon. life), N.C. Lit. Soc. (life), Rotary, Phi Mu Alpha Sinfonia (nat. hon. life). Democrat. Presbyterian. Home: Durham, NC. Died Mar. 16, 2007.

HOGIN, PHILIP EDWARD, manufacturing executive; b. Oak Park, Ill., May 4, 1920; s. Ralph M. and Loretta (Murphy) H.; m. Betty Jane Harrison, Nov. 5, 1949; children: Harrison David, Christen Evangeline, Lauretta Joann, Sarah Elizabeth. BS in Engring, Cornell U., 1942; MS in Indsl. Mgmt. (Alfred P. Sloan fellow), Mass. Inst. Tech., 1954. Registered profl. engr., N.Y., N.J., Ill., Conn. With Western Electric Co., 1942-48, 50—, gen. mgr. service div., central region, 1963-64, v.p. staff, mfg. div., 1964-65, v.p. pub. relations, 1965-66, v.p. mfg., 1966-67, exec. v.p., dir., from 1967. Mem. tech. staff Bell Telephone Labs., 1948-50; dir. Teletype Corp., Phoenix Mut. Life Ins. Co., Sandia Nat. Labs. Served to lt. (j.g.) USNR, 1944-46. Mem. Soc. Sloan Fellows, Phi Kappa Sigma, Kappa Tau Chi. Clubs: Field of Greenwich (Conn.). Died Dec. 26, 2005.

HOGNESS, JOHN RUSTEN, internist, educator, academic administrator; b. Oakland, Calif., June 27, 1922; s. Thorfin R. and Phoebe (Swenson) Hogness. Student, Haverford Coll., Pa., 1939—42, DSc (hon.), 1973; BS, U. Chgo., 1943, MD, 1946; DSc (hon.), Med. Coll. Ohio at Toledo, 1972; LLD, George Washington U., Washington, DC, 1973; DLitt, Thomas Jefferson U., Phila., 1980. Diplomate Am. Bd. Internal Medicine. Intern Presbyn. Hosp., NYC, 1946—47, asst. resident, 1949—50; chief resident King County Hosp., Seattle, 1950—51; asst. U. Wash. Sch. Medicine, 1950—52, Am. Heart Assn. research fellow, 1951—52, mem. faculty, 1954—64, prof. medicine, 1964—71, med. dir. univ. hosp., 1958—63, dean, chmn. bd. health scis., 1964—69, exec. v.p., 1969—70; dir. Health Scis. Ctr., 1970—71; pres. Inst. Medicine, Nat. Acad. Scis., 1971—74; prof. medicine George Washington U., 1972—74; pres. U. Wash., Seattle, 1974—79, pres. emeritus, 1979—2007, prof. medicine, 1974—79; pres. Assn. Acad. Health Ctrs., 1979—88. Disting. professorial lectr. dept. medicine Georgetown U., 1983—88; prof. U. Wash. Sch. Pub. Health, 1989—92; provost Hahnemann U., 1992—93; commr.'s adv. com. on exempt orgns. IRS, 1969—71; adv. com. for environ. scis. NSF, 1970—71; adv. com. to dir. NIH, 1970—71; mem. Nat. Cancer Adv. Bd., 1972—76, Nat. Sci. Bd., 1976—82; selection com. for Rockefeller pub. svc. awards Princeton U., 1976—82; chmn. med. injury compensation study steering com. Inst. Medicine NAS, chmn. com. to evaluate the artificial heart, 1990—91; council for biol. scis. U. Chgo. Pritzker Sch. Medicine, 1977—89; chmn. adv. panel on cost-effectiveness of med. techs. Office Tech. Assessment, U.S. Congress, 1978—80; chmn. study sect. for health care tech. assessment Nat. Ctr. for Health Svcs. Rsch. and Health Care Tech. Assessment, 1985—88; pres. Sun Valley Forum on Nat. Health, 1986—94; dir. Inst. for Health Policy Edn. and Rsch., U. Tex. Health Sci. Ctr., Houston, 1988; council health care tech. HEW; adv. panel for study fin. grad. med. edn. Dept. Health and Human Svcs., 1980—87. Contbr. articles to profl. jours. Trustee Case Western Res. U., 1972—73. With US Army, 1947—49. Recipient Disting. Svc. award, Med. Alumni Assn. U. Chgo., 1966, Profl. Achievement award, Alumni Assn. U. Chgo., 1973, Convocation medal, Am. Coll. Cardiology, 1973, Cartwright medal, Columbia U. Coll. Physicians and Surgeons, 1978, Carel C. Koch Meml. award, Am. Acad. Optometry, 1986; Centennial scholar, Johns Hopkins U., 1976. Master: ACP (regent 1987—2000); fellow: AAAS, Am. Acad. Arts and Scis. (v.p. 2001—04); mem.: Assn. Am. Med. Colls., Assn. Am. Physicians, Assn. Am. Med. Colls. (chmn.-elect coun. of deans 1968—69, exec. coun.), Assn. Am. Physicians, Inst. Medicine NAS, Alpha Omega Alpha. Home: Seattle, Wash. Died July 2, 2007.

HOGUE, JAMES LAWRENCE, clergyman; b. Wellsburgh, W.Va., June 9, 1923; s. Dewey Talmadge and Mary Inez (Lawrence) H.; m. Ethel Florence Park, Sept. 15, 1945; children: James Lawrence, Kelsey Graham, Kerrilee, Janiel Louise. B.D., Louisville Presbyn. Sem., 1951; BS in Bus. Adminstrn. (Bank of Maryville Econ. award 1948), Maryville Coll., Tenn., 1948. Ordained to ministry United Presbyn. Ch., 1951; pastor chs. in Ind., 1951-52, 60-64; dir. Washington County Student Tng. Parish, Salem, Ind., 1953-59; field adminstr. Synod Colo.; Bd. Nat. Missions United Presbyn. Ch., 1964-68; exec. dir. Synod of Sierra, Sacramento, 1968-72; dir. Council Adminstrv. Services, NYC, 1972-80; v.p. Hogue and Assos. (accountants), Steamboat Springs, Colo., from 1980. Moderator Synod Rocky Mountains, 1984-86; interim pastor Delta (Colo.) Presbyn. Ch., 1984; interim sr. pastor Immanuel Presbyn. Ch., Albuquerque, 1985-87; interim exec. presbyter Presbytery of Wabash Valley, 1987-88; interim minister Westminster Presbyn. Ch., Cin., 1988—. Served as aviator USNR, 1942-46. Mem. Am. Mgmt. Assn., Am. Philatelic Soc., Aircraft Owners and Pilots Assn. Clubs: Rotary (charter dir. Salem), Masons, Odd Fellows. Republican. Home: Cincinnati, Ohio. Died Apr. 5, 2007.

HOHNHORST, JOHN CHARLES, judge; b. Jerome, Idaho, Dec. 25, 1952; m. Raelene Casper; children: Jennifer, Rachel, John. BS in Polit. Sci./Pub. Adminstrn., U. Idaho, 1975, JD cum laude, 1978. Bar: Idaho 1978, U.S. Dist. Ct. Idaho 1978, U.S. Ct. Appeals (9th cir.) 1980, U.S. Ct. Claims 1983, U.S. Supreme Ct. 1987. Adminstrv. asst. to Sen. John M. Barker Idaho State

Senate, 1975; ptnr. Hepworth, Lezamiz & Hohnhorst, Twin Falls, Idaho, 1978—2001; dist. judge 5th Jud. Dist. Ct., Twin Falls County, Idaho, from 2001. Contbr. articles to profl. jours. Mem. planning & zoning commn. City of Twin Falls, 1987-90. Mem. ABA, ATLA, Idaho State Bar (commr. 1990-93, pres. 1993), Am. Coll. Trial Lawyers, Idaho Trial Lawyers Assn. (regional dir. 1985-86), 5th Dist. Bar Assn. (treas. 1987-88, v.p. 1988-89, pres. 1989-90), Am. Acad. Appellate Lawyers, Greater Twin Falls C. of C. (chmn. magic valley leadership program 1988-89, bd. dirs. 1989-92), Phi Kappa Tau (Beta Gamma chpt., Phi award 1988). Died Feb. 4, 2007.

HOHNSTEDT, LEO FRANK, retired chemist, educator; b. Alton, Ill., June 12, 1924; s. Leo Thomas and Esther (Paris) H.; m. Margaret Mary Gorman, Aug. 13, 1960. BS in Chemistry, St. Louis U., 1949; PhD, U. Chgo., 1955. Instr. chemistry St. Louis U., 1954-55, asst. prof., 1955-60, assoc prof., 1963-69, prof., 1969-83, chmn. chemistry dept., 1966-77. Assoc. prof. Poly. Inst. Bklyn., 1960-61; weapon systems analyst Weapon Systems Evaluation Div., Inst. for Def. Analysis, Washington, 1961-63 Served with AUS, 1943-46. Named Alumni Chemist of Yr. St. Louis U. Alumni Chemists, 1970 Fellow Am. Inst. Chemists; mem. Inst. for Theol. Encounter with Sci. and Tech., VFW, Sigma Xi, Phi Lambda Upsilon, Pi Mu Epsilon, Alpha Chi Sigma. Roman Catholic. Home: Godfrey, Ill. Died June 6, 2007.

HOIE, CLAUS, artist; b. Stavanger, Norway, Nov. 3, 1911; came to U.S., 1924, naturalized, 1942; s. Claus and Marie (Foss) H.; m. Helen Hunt Bencker, Nov. 17, 1956. Student, Pratt Inst., 1930-33, Ecole des Beaux Arts, Paris, 1945. Art dir., designer, illustrator various advt. and pub. firms in, N.Y.C., 1933-41, 46-62, painter, graphic artist, 1962—; exhibited in one man shows at Denver Art Mus., 1943, Saltpeter Gallery, N.Y.C., 1962, 63, Monmouth (N.J.) Art Ctr., 1970, Benson Gallery, Bridgehampton, N.Y., 1972, 77, 80, 86, Southampton Coll., 1972, Guild Hall Mus., East Hampton, N.Y., 1973, Norwegian-Am. Mus., 1975, U. Minn. Galleries, Mpls., 1976, Akershus Mus., Oslo, 1982, Vered Gallery, 1987, 88, East Hampton, 1984, 85, 86, 89; group shows at Chgo. Art Inst., 1946, NAD, 11 shows 1956-89, Am. Water Color Soc., 1960-80, 82, 89, L.I. Painters, 1972, 75, Nat. Inst. Arts and Letters, 1975, Am. Watercolor Soc., 1985, 88, Mexico City Mus. Watercolor, 1989, numerous others; represented in permanent collections Bklyn. Mus., Norfolk Mus., Okla. Mus. Art, Butler Inst., East Hampton Guild Hall Mus., Akershus Mus., Oslo, U. Minn., Centre Coll. Ky., Norwegian-Am. Mus., Brigham Young U. Contbr. articles to profl. jours. Served with AUS, 1942-45, ETO. Decorated Bronze Star medal; recipient Nat. Inst. Arts and Letters award for painting, 1975, Adolph and Clara Obrig prize NAD, 1985, John Pike Meml. award NAD, 1989, Audubon Artists Ann. Exhbn. award, 1990, Marine Environ. Wildlife award, Mystic Seaport Mus., 1998. Mem. N.A.D., Soc. Illustrators, Am. Watercolor Soc. (v.p. 1960-62, Gold medal of honor 1962) Clubs: Devon Yacht (East Hampton). Episcopalian. Died July 29, 2007.

HOJNACKI, MICHAEL JOHN, advertising agency executive; b. Chgo., May 13, 1950; s. Matthew F. and Genevieve (Blaszak) H.; m. Marisue Scafidi, Aug. 14, 1971. B.F.A., Sch. of Art Inst. Chgo., 1973; student U. Ill., 1968-70. Owner, The Natural Union, Union Pier, Mich., 1975, Rainbow Gardens, Bridgman, Mich., 1976; v.p., corp. mgr. Sawyer Products (Mich.), 1977; pres. Artistic Energy Group/Madmoney, Union Pier, 1979—. Mem. Soc. Mfg. Engrs., Harbor County C. of C. Democrat. Roman Catholic. Died Jan. 5, 2007.

HOLBIK, KAREL, economics professor; b. Czech Republic, Sept. 9, 1920; came to U.S., 1948, naturalized, 1952; s. Karel and Catherine (Krouzel) H.; m. Olga Rehackova, Sept. 10, 1956; 1 son, Thomas. JD, Charles U., Prague, 1947; MBA, U. Detroit, 1949; PhD, U. Wis., 1956. Researcher Bank of Am., San Francisco, 1951-53; teaching asst. in banking U. Wis., 1953-55; asst. prof. econs. Lafayette Coll., Easton, Pa., 1955-58; prof. econs. Boston U., 1958-86, prof. econs. emeritus, from 1986. Cons. U.S. Naval War Coll., Newport, R.I., 1963-64, lectr., 1964-73; vis. prof. U. Brussels, 1969-70; vis. faculty Harvard U., 1981-98; chief sect. for devel. fin. instns. UN, 1976-80; Fulbright sr. scholar U. Tunis, 1983-84; internat. fin. cons., 1986—. Author: Italy in International Cooperation, 1959, Postwar Trade in Divided Germany, 1964, The United States, The Soviet Union and the Third World, 1968, West German Foreign Aid 1956-1966, 1968, American-East European Trade, 1969, Contemporary American Economic Problems, 1970, Trade and Industrialization in the Central American Common Market, 1972, Monetary Policy in Twelve Industrial Countries, 1973, Industrialization and Employment in Puerto Rico, 1975; others. Mem. Am. Econ. Assn., Am. Fin. Assn. Home: Newton, Mass. Died July 1, 2006.

HOLCOMB, ELIZABETH CARGILL, real estate broker; b. Orlando, Fla., Mar. 8, 1928; s. Theodore Ira Parrott and Lucy (Stimpson) Parrott Cargill; m. Edgar D. Holcomb, Jr., Dec. 9, 1946; children— Jane Elizabeth Purdy, Leslie Sherwood Bell, Melanie Ardath George, E. David III. Student Fla. State U., 1945-46, Avon Park Jr. Coll., 1966, U. Fla., 1970; grad. Realtors Inst. Salesperson Ed Schlitt Real Estate Agy., Vero Beach, Fla., 1970-71, F. Rickman Real Estate, Stuart, Fla., 1971-73; real estate broker, pres. Accent Realty, Inc., Stuart, 1973—; owner, buyer, mgr. Gingerbread House, Stuart, 1978—; agt. CP Chem. Sales, 1985—. Co-founder Holcomb Scholarship award U. Fla., 1972. Mem. Fla. State Hort. Soc., Fruit Crops Alumni and Friends U. Fla., Martin County and Fla. Farm Bur., Kappa Alpha Theta. Died Apr. 7, 2006.

HOLDEN, RAYMOND THOMAS, retired obstetrician; b. Washington, Apr. 11, 1904; s. Raymond Thomas and Celeste Selma (Moritz) H.; m. Mary Lightle, Oct. 9, 1958; 1 dau., Mary Elliott. Student, U. Notre Dame, 1922-24; MD, Georgetown U., 1928, D.Sc. (hon.), 1980. Diplomate: Am. Bd. Obstetrics and Gynecology. Intern Providence Hosp., Washington, 1928-29, assoc., then attending obstetrician and gynecologist, 1932-56, cons., 1956-60; resident Columbia Hosp. for Women, Washington, 1929-30, asst., assoc., attending staff, 1933, chief med. staff, 1952-54, 62-64, acting adminstr., 1958-59; preceptorship Dr. R.Y. Sullivan Georgetown U. Sch. Medicine, 1930-32; assoc., attending obstetrics and gynecology D.C. Gen Hosp., 1932-47; asst., assoc., also attending obstetrics and gynecology Georgetown U. Hosp., 1933—; from clin. instr. to clin. prof. obstetrics and gynecology Georgetown U. Sch. Medicine, 1933-85, assoc. chmn. dept. ob/gyn, 1977-85, emeritus clin. prof., 1985—2007; cons. obstetrics and gynecology U.S. Naval Hosp., Bethesda, Md., 1948-68. Bd. dirs., exec. com. TB Assn. D.C., 1947-49; bd. dirs., exec. com. D.C. divsn. Am. Cancer Soc., 1950-56; mem. Health Facilities Planning Coun., Washington, 1964-70; bd. dirs. D.C. chpt. ARC, mem. exec. com., 1975-86; trustee Columbia Hosp. for Women. Served to Capt., M.C. USNR, 1942-46; rear adm. Res. Fellow ACS, Am. Coll. Obstetricians and Gynecologists; mem. AMA (D.C. mem. Ho. Dels. 1952-68, chmn. com. on human reproduction 1964-68, trustee 1968-77, vice chmn. 1974-75, chmn. 1975-77, Disting. Svc. award 1987), D.C. Med. Soc. (chmn. exec. bd. 1951-52, pres. 1946-47), Washington Gynecology Soc. (sec. 1950-54, pres. 1956), So. Med. Assn., Assn. Profs. Gynecology and Obstetrics, Am. Legion, Alpha Omega Alpha. Clubs: Fifty Year of Am. Medicine (pres. 1979-80), Chevy Chase, Metropolitan. Home: Washington, DC. Died Mar. 14, 2007.

HOLL, WALTER JOHN, retired architect, interior designer; s. John and Rose Holl; m. Eleanor Mary Triervieler (dec. 2006); children: Mark Walter (dec. 2001), Michael John, Randolph Gregory, Linda Michelle, Timothy James, John Walter Student, Internat. Corr. Schs., 1946-47, 59; student in interior design, U. Nebr., 1976; student, Clarke Coll., 1981, student in photography, 1981. Licensed arch., Calif., interior designer, Ill.; cert. Nat. Coun. for Interior Design Qualifications. Steel detailer, estimator E.J. Voggenthaler Co., Dubuque, Iowa, 1941-42; engr., also methods developer Marinship Corp., Sausalito, Calif., 1942-44; ptnr. Holl & Everly, Dubuque, Iowa, 1946-47; prin. Holl Designing Co., also W. Holl & Assocs., Dubuque, San Francisco, 1947-87, Walter J. Holl, Arch., Burlingame, Calif., 1987, 89, San Diego, Calif., from 1989. Cons. Clarke Coll. Art Students, Dubuque, 1953-61; commd. arch., interior designer, constructor renovations and hist. preservation Dubuque County Courthouse, 1978-85; mem. convoy USCG Ofcl. Presdl. Security Patrol, 1979; oral exam commr. Calif. Bd. Archtl. Examiners, 1994-96; cert. mem. Calif. State Office Emergency Svc.; participant The Brit. Coun.-Archs. Study Tour, Belfast, No. Ireland, 1995; juror Nat. Coun. for Interior Design Qualification, 1996, 98. Chmn. Dubuque Housing Rehab. Commn., 1976-77. With AUS, 1944-46, ETO. Decorated 2 bronze stars; recipient Nat. Bldg. Design awards, 1968, 69, 73, 94. Mem. AIA (bd. dirs. 1993-99, pres.-elect north county sect. San Diego chpt. 1995, pres. 1996, bldg. codes and stds. com. San Diego chpt. 1998-99), USCG Aux. (comdr. 1975-78), Am. Soc. Interior Designers (profl.), Am. Arbitration Assn. (panel arbitrators), Inst. Bus. Designers (profl. Chgo. chpt.), Dubuque Golf and Country Club (bldg. commn. 1953-54), Julien Dubuque Yacht Club (commodore 1974-75), Mchts. and Mfrs. Club (Chgo.). Roman Catholic. Achievements include patent for castered pallet. Died June 30, 2007.

HOLLAND, KENNETH JOHN, retired editor; b. Mpls., July 19, 1918; s. John Olaf and Olga Marie (Dahlberg) H.; m. Maurine M. Strom, Aug. 15, 1948; children: Laurence, Wesley. BA in Religion, Union Coll., Lincoln, Nebr., 1949; postgrad., Vanderbilt U. Div. Sch., 1964-69. Chemist Capitol Flour Mills, St. Paul, 1937-40; copy editor So. Pub. Assn., Nashville, 1949-51; asso. editor These Times, 1952-56, editor, from 1957, These Times (merged with Rev. and Herald Pub. Assn.), Washington, from 1981, Signs of the Times (merged with These Times), Boise, Idaho, 1984-93. Ordained to ministry Seventh-day Adventist Ch., 1958; condr. editorial councils overseas, writers workshops, U.S. Author: books, the most recent being The Choice, 1977. Served with U.S. Army, 1941-43; with USAAF, 1943-45. Recipient Am. In God We Trust Family medal Family Found. Am., 1980, Disting. Service award Union Coll., Lincoln, 1984, Silver Angel award Religion in Media, 1986, 87, 88, 1990. Mem. Assoc. Ch. Press (award of merit 1976, 77, 78, 80, 85, 87, 89, Citation of Honor 1990), Ams. United for Separation Ch. and State, Religious Public Relations Council, Internat. Platform Assn. Clubs: Wexford Country, Hilton Head Island, S.C. Republican. Died July 19, 2007.

HOLLAND, ROBERT CAMPBELL, anatomist, educator; b. Bushnell, Ill., Aug. 16, 1923; s. Harvey Howard and Lois Sarah (Campbell) H.; m. Hilda P. Burgi, Sept. 26, 1946 (dec. 1980); children: Jonathan Robert, Heather, Judith Ashley. BS, U. Wis., 1948, MS, 1949, PhD, 1955. Instr. Dental Sch. Northwestern U., 1949-51; asst. prof. anatomy Sch. Medicine U. N.D., 1955-60; assoc. prof. Sch. Medicine U. Ark., 1960-66; prof. chmn. dept. anatomy Mahidol U., Bangkok, 1966-76; prof., chmn. dept. anatomy Morehouse Sch. Medicine, Atlanta, 1976-90, prof. emeritus dept. anatomy, from 1990. Mem. staff Rockefeller Found., 1966-76; vis. prof. UCLA Sch. Medicine, 1976. Author research pubs. on the brain. With M.C., U.S. Army, 1943-46. Fellow Wis. Alumni Rsch. Found., 1951-54, Nat. Found. Infantile Paralysis, 1957-58; grantee NIH, 1959-88. Mem. Am. Assn. Anatomists, Am. Acad. Neurology, Soc. Exptl. Biology and Medicine, Soc. Neurosci., Sigma Xi Home: Kennesaw, Ga. Died Feb. 4, 2007.

HOLLAND, ROSETTA CLARE, dietitian; b. Flandrenau, S.D., Nov. 11, 1919; d. Stephen Elton and Josephine (Johnson) Perley; m. George Alfred Holland, June 24, 1950 (dec. 1980). BS in Dietetics, U. Minn., 1940; postgrad. U. Calif., Berkeley, 1947-48, George Pepperdine Coll., 1952, Utah State U., 1970. Cert. tchr., dietitian. State supr. Sch. Lunch Program, S.D., 1940-43; dietitian VA, Gulfport, Miss., 1943-44, Cutter Lab., Berkeley, Calif., 1945-47; homemaking tchr. Elk Grove Sch. Dist., Calif., 1947-48; editor Western Home Econs., San Francisco, 1948-49; nutritionist Calif. State Dept. Edn., Berkeley, 1949-52; dir. food services San Jose Unified Sch. Dist., Calif., 1961—. Contbg. editor California School Lunch Guide and newsletters. Research grantee Calif. Dept. Edn., 1976-79, 79-82, U.S. Office Edn., 1982-87. Mem. Nat. Sch. Food Service Assn., Calif. Sch. Food Service Assn., No. Calif. Sch. Food Service Assn. (hon. life and pres.), Calif. Liaison Council Home Econs. (vice chmn., program dir.), Calif. Assn. Urban Food Services Dirs. (pres.), Home Econs. Assn., AAUW, Nutrition Edn. Assn. Republican. Lutheran. Clubs: Quota (San Jose); League of Friends of Santa Clara Council Commn. on Status of Women. Avocations: piano; photography; reading; gardening; stamp collecting. Home: Coquille, Oreg. Died Oct. 2, 2006.

HOLLEB, ARTHUR IRVING, retired surgeon; b. NYC, Apr. 1, 1921; s. Simon and Kate (Liss) H.; m. Carolyn R. Oglesby, June 16, 1951; children: Susan Jane and David Gene (twins). AB, Brown U., 1941; MD, NYU, 1944. Diplomate: Am. Bd. Surgery. Intern Queens Gen. Hosp., Jamaica, N.Y., 1944-45; resident tumor surgery and pathology Meadowbrook Hosp., Hempstead, N.Y., 1945-46, chief resident gen. surgery, 1948-50, asst. dir. tumor svc., 1954-56; mem. staff Meml. Hosp., NYC, 1950-67, assoc. chief med. officer, 1966-67, cons. breast svc. surgery dept., 1968-95; assoc. vis. surgeon James Ewing Hosp., NYC, 1966-67; mem. rsch. staff M.D. Anderson Hosp. and Tumor Inst., Houston, 1967-68, cons. breast cancer study sect., 1968-88; sr. v.p. med. affairs and rsch., chief med. officer Am. Cancer Soc., NYC, 1968-88. From instr. to clin. assoc. prof. surgery Med. Coll. Cornell U., 1965-67; assoc. clinician Sloan-Kettering Inst., 1961-67; assoc. prof. surgery U. Tex. M.D. Anderson Hosp. and Tumor Inst., 1967-68, assoc. dir. edn., 1967-68; James Ewing Meml. lectr. Soc. Surg. Oncology, 1980; Wendell Scott Meml. lectr. Am. Coll. Radiology, 1978; mem. evaluation panel, sr. clin. traineeships in surgery, cancer control br. USPHS, 1965-68; mem. cancer control adv. com. diagnostic rsch. adv. group and therapy com. Nat. Cancer Inst., NIH, 1972-82. Author: You Can Fight Cancer and Win, 1977; Editor in chief: Jour. CA; editorial adv. bd. Am. Jour. Preventive Medicine. With USNR, 1946-48. Recipient W.W. Keen Disting. Svc. award Brown U., 1977, Disting. Alumnus award Meml. Sloan Kettering Cancer Ctr., 1989. Mem. ACS, AMA, Am. Assn. Cancer Edn., Am. Assn. Cancer Rsch., Am. Cancer Soc. (bd. dirs. N.Y.C. chpt. 1964-67), Am. Radium Soc. (v.p. 1969-70), Assn. Am. Med. Colls., Assn. Hosp. Dirs. Med. Edn. (chmn. surg. edn. com. 1965-67), Harris County Med. Soc., Am. Soc. Clin. Oncology, James Ewing Soc. (pres. 1972-73), N.Y. Acad. Medicine, N.Y. County Med. Soc., N.Y. Acad. Scis., N.Y. Cancer Soc. (pres. 1971), N.Y. Surg. Soc., Brown U. Club. Died Oct. 19, 2006.

HOLLEN, SALLY GENE, gemology shop owner; b. San Jose, Calif., July 24, 1927; d. George Edward and Arlyne Florence (O'Malia) Hallett; m. Merritt (Mike) Leroy Hollen, Apr. 26, 1950; children— Theresa Mills, Suzanne, Sharon. Student U. Calif., Coll. San Mateo, Gemological Inst. Am. Newspaper reporter Los Angeles Times, 1946-47, Santa Ana (Calif.) Register, 1948; reporter Mineral County News, Hawthorne, Nev., 1949; legal sec. Moyle & Moyle Attys., Salt Lake City, 1950-57; sec. Steinhart, Goldberg, Feigenbaum & Ladar, attys., San Francisco, 1957-59, Chester A. Lebsack, atty., Redwood City, Calif., 1961-63, John Lyons, Conciliation Counsellor, Redwood City, Calif., 1964-66, U.S. Rubber Co., Salt Lake City, 1953-57; part-time sec. Vacu-Blast, Belmont, Calif., 1967-69; owner, pres. Hollen's Broc Shop, Lapidary, San Carlos, Calif., 1982-84. Mem. San Carlos Fine Arts Assn., 1982-83; sec. exec. bd. Bayside Intermediate Sch. PTA, San Mateo, Calif., 1959-61; leader Girl Scouts U.S., San Mateo, 1958-60; mgr. Bobby Sox Softball, San Mateo, 1973-75. Mem. Sequoia Gem and Mineral Soc., Gem and Mineral Soc. San Mateo County, Ye Old Times Mineral Club, Nat. Assn. Female Execs., San Carlos C. of C. Republican. Episcopalian. Clubs: Eastern Star (past matron San Mateo), Daus. of Nile (San Francisco). Home: Lake Havasu City, Ariz. Died May 10, 2006.

HOLLIES, LINDA HALL, pastor, pastoral counsel, educator, author, publisher; b. Gary, Ind., Mar. 29, 1943; d. James Donald and Doretha Robinson (Mosley) Adams; m. Charles H. Hollies, Oct. 14, 1972; children: Gregory Raymond, Grelon Renard, Grian Eunyke. BS in Adminstrn., Ind. U., 1975; M.Div., Garrett-Evang. Theol. Sem., 1986—; D of Ministry United Theol. Sem., Dayton, Ohio, 1996. Tchr. Hammond Public Schs., Ind., 1975-77; supr. Gen. Motors Corp., Willow Springs, Ill., 1977-79; gen. supr. Ford Motor Co., East Chicago Heights, Ill., 1979-82; coord. Women in Ministry, Evang. Theol. Sem., Evanston, Ill., 1984-86; clin. pastoral edn. intern supr., 1986-88; pastor Richards St. United Meth. Ch., 1988-92; pastor 1st Ch., Arlington Heights, Ill, 1992-94, Southlawn United Meth. Ch., 1994-96; assoc. coun. dir. W. Mich. ann. conf. United Meth. Ch., 1997—; founder, dir., cons. Woman Space, Inc., 2002, sr. pastor Mt. Hope United Meth. Ch., Lansing, Mich. Ford fellow, 1975, Benjamin E. Mays fellow, 1984; Crusade scholar United Meth. Ch., 1984; Lucy Ryder Myer scholar, 1985-86, Dr. Martin L. King scholar. Recipient Kilgore prize for creative ministry Claremont Sch. Theol., 1996. Mem. Zonta Profl. Women's Assn., Nat. Assn. Pastoral Educators, Internat. Toastmasters (pres. 1976-77). Author: Innner Healing for Broken Vessels, 1990, Womanist Rumblings, 1991, Womanistcare: Tending the Souls of Women, 1992, A Trumpet for Zion: Liturgical Resources for Year A, 1995, Taking Back My Yesterday, 1997, Jesus and Those Bodacious Women, 1997. Democrat. Avocations: reading, preaching, creative writing. Home: Grand Rapids, Mich. Died Aug. 19, 2007.

HOLLINGER, MANNFRED ALAN, pharmacologist, toxicologist, educator; b. Chgo., June 28, 1939; BS, North Park Coll., Chgo., 1961; PhD, Loyola U., Chgo., 1967. Postdoctoral fellow Stanford U., Palo Alto, Calif., 1967-69; prof. U. Calif., Davis, from 1969, chmn. dept. med. pharmacology and toxicology, from 1990. Author: Respiratory Pharmacology and Toxicology, 1985, Yearbook of Pharmacology, 1990, 91, 92; asst. editor, field editor Jour. Pharm. Exptl. Therapy, 1978—; cons. editor CRC Press, Boca Raton, Fla., 1989—. Mem. Yolo County Grand Jury, Woodland, Calif.; bd. dirs. Davis Little League. Burroughs-Wellcome fellow Southampton U., U.K., 1986; Fogarty sr. fellow NIH, Heidelberg (Germany) U., 1988. Died Apr. 19, 2007.

HOLLIS, LUTHER RAY, training instructor, consultant; b. River Rouge, Mich., Dec. 30, 1949; s. Luther and Adel (Jones) H.; m. Debra Fay Devold, Aug. 27, 1969; children— Anthony, Felicia, Cassandra. Student Wayne State U., 1980-82; Assoc. B.A., Highland Park Community Coll., 19—; B. Gen. Studies, Oakland U., 1978. Supr. Fisher Body Fleetwood, Detroit,

1974-75, gen. supr., 1976-77; gen. supr. Fisher Body Pontiac, Mich., 1977-80, supr., Detroit, 1980-83; tng. program instr. assembly div. Gen. Motors, Orion, Pontiac, 1983—; chief cons. D&L Research Mktg., Southfield, Mich., 1983—. Author supr. tng. manual, 1975. Served with USN, 1969-73. Mem. Econ. Club Detroit. Democrat. Baptist. Home: Southfield, Mich. Died Apr. 28, 2007.

HOLLISTER, WILLIAM GRAY, retired psychiatrist; b. Lincoln, Nebr., July 21, 1915; s. Vernon Leo and Lela Gretchen (Pilcher) H.; m. Frances Flora Scudder, Mar. 23, 1940; children— David W., Robert Michael, Alan Scudder, Frances Virginia. AB in Anthropology, U. Nebr., 1937, BS in Psychology, 1940, MD, 1941; M.P.H. (Rockefeller fellow), Johns Hopkins U., 1947; postgrad., Washington Psychoanalytic Inst., 1958-65. Diplomate Am. Bd. Psychiatry and Neurology, Am. Bd. Preventive Medicine. Intern Grady Hosp., Atlanta, 1941-42; resident in psychiatry Bishop Clarkson Meml. Hosp., Omaha, 1942-43, USPHS Hosp., Fort Worth, 1947-49; supr. venereal disease control Miss. Bd. Health, Jackson, 1943-46; psychiat. cons. Region IV USPHS, Atlanta, 1949-56; nat. sch. mental health cons. NIMH, Bethesda, Md., 1956-61, chief br. community research and services, 1962-65; prof. psychiatry, dir. comty. psychiatry U. N.C., Chapel Hill, 1965-86, prof. emeritus, 1988, ret., 1988. Cons. in occupational psychiatry IBM, Research Triangle Park, N.C., 1965-85; nat. mental health chmn. Nat. Congress PTA, 1958-62, 65-69 Author: Experiences in Rural Mental Health, 1974, Alternative Services in Community Mental Health: Programs and Processes, 1985; (with E. M. Bower) Behavior Science Frontiers of Education, 1967; composer, librettist (opera) Inca's Chosen Bride, 1997. Served with NIMH, 1943-65. Fellow Am. Psychiat. Assn., Am. Public Health Assn. (Disting. Service medal 1964); mem. AMA. Home: Chapel Hill, NC. Died Oct. 12, 2005.

HOLLOWAY, JEROME KNIGHT, publisher, retired foreign services officer, former military strategy educator; b. Phila., May 8, 1923; s. Jerome Knight and Emily Margaret (Ennis) H.; m. Gertrud Harms, Apr. 16, 1953 (dec. Jan. 1976); children— Jerome Knight III, Karen M., Nicholas H. AB, Cath. U., 1947; MA, U. Mich., 1959; lang. student, Tokyo, Japan, 1958-60; fellow, Harvard, 1968-69. Joined U.S. Fgn. Service, 1947, ret., 1975; 3d sec. Rangoon, Burma, 1947-49; vice-consul Shanghai, China, 1949-50, Bremen, Germany, 1950-52; consul Hong Kong, 1952-57; 2d sec. Tokyo, 1960-61; assigned State Dept., Washington, 1961-64, 69-70; 1st sec. Stockholm, Sweden, 1964-65; counselor, 1965-68; consul gen. Osaka-Kobe, Japan, 1970-74; state dept. adviser to pres. U.S. Naval War Coll., Newport, R.I., 1974-75, prof. strategy, 1976-90; pub. Hanlin Press, Newport, R.I., from 1990. Served to lt. (j.g.) USNR, 1942-46. Mem. U.S. Naval Inst., Assn. Asian Studies. Home: Newport, RI. Died Oct. 2, 2006.

HOLLOWAY, WILLIAM JIMMERSON, retired education educator; b. Smithfield, Va., May 6, 1917; s. Arnett Jimmerson and Lucy Pernell (White) H.; m. Julia Naomi Edmundson, June 17, 1944; children: Wendell, Arnett, Lynn. BS with honors, Hampton Inst., 1940; MA, U. Mich., 1946; EdD, U. Ill., 1961; postgrad., Harvard U., 1950. Prin. Union Sch., Hampton, Va., 1946-47; dean students Savannah State Coll., 1947-55; prin. Ligon High Sch., Raleigh, NC, 1956-57; counselor N.C. Central U., Durham, 1959-61; supt. Va. State Sch., Hampton, 1961-65; edn. program officer U.S. Office Edn. Washington, 1965-70; vice provost Ohio State U., Columbus, 1970-78, prof. edn., 1970-82, prof. emeritus, 1982—2006; dir. Nigerian edn. program, Ohio State U., 1980-82; pres. Internat. Ednl. and Service Inst., Inc., Raleigh, NC, 1981-88; disting. prof. edn. St. Augustine's Coll., Raleigh, 1983-87. Author: The Education of Blacks in Virginia Before the Civil War, 1619-1860, 1993, The Odyssey of a North American Educator, 2001; mem. editl. bd. The Negro Educational Review, 1972, editor-in-chief, 1995; editor-in-chief emeritus, 1999; chief cons. Insight Enterprises African Am. Disability Program, 1998. Trustee Freedoms Found., 1974, St. Augustines Coll., 1968-77. Recipient Freedoms Found. medal, 1954, Superior Accomplishment award HEW, 1968, Disting. Alumni award Hampton Inst., 1970, award Nat. Press Inst., 1972, Outstanding Citizen award Ohio Gen. Assembly, 1978, Outstanding Achievement award Ohio State U., 1978, Disting. Service award Ohio State U., 1984, Community Leadership award Capital U., 1978, Nat. Disting. Service award United Negro Coll. Fund, 1979, Excellence in Internat. Edn. award Govt. of Nigeria, Disting. Career award Negro Ednl. Rev., 1984, Outstanding Achievement award U. Mich., 1987, Negro Ednl. Rev. Golden Anniversary Disting. Svc. award, 2000; Harvard Far Eastern Studies fellow, 1956, Disting. Svc. award Insight Enterprises Emmet H. Scott, 1998.; named to Ohio State U. Coll. Edn. Hall of Fame, 2002. Mem. Am. Assn. Higher Edn., Am. Personnel and Guidance Assn., Alpha Kappa Delta, Phi Delta Kappa, Kappa Delta Pi. Democrat. Presbyterian (elder). Clubs: Lions (pres. 1975); Cosmos (Washington). Avocations: duplicate bridge, saltwater fishing. Died Nov. 12, 2006.

HOLMES, CHARLES HARVEY, retired insurance company executive; b. Rochester, NY, Apr. 5, 1918; s. William Harvey and Lillian L. (Popp) H.; m. Mary Celestine Phelan, Nov. 3, 1943; children— Jane Elizabeth Jones, Mary Ann, Peter Charles, William Harvey. BA, U. Toronto, 1940, MA, 1946. With Phoenix Mut. Life Ins. Co., Hartford, Conn., 1947-84, controller, 1966-84, 2d v.p., 1979-84; ret., 1984. Treas. Phoenix Equity Planning Corp., 1968-84, Phoenix Fund, Inc., 1970-78; Phoenix Capital Fund, Inc., 1970-78 Treas. Phoenix Fed. Credit Union, 1957-66, St. Mary's Fed. Credit Union, Simsbury, Conn., 1956—. Served to capt. USAAF, 1941-46; lt. col. Res. ret. Fellow Life Mgmt. Inst. Clubs: K.C. Home: Simsbury, Conn. Died May 29, 2007.

HOLMES, JAMES GORDON, retired vascular surgeon, medical educator; b. Salt Lake City, Jan. 14, 1924; s. Ernest Samuel and Ida (Eldredge) H.; m. Jeanette Taggart, June 3, 1943 (div. 1985); children: James, Jeffrey, John, Alexander, Elizabeth; m. Marilyn Louise Ullman. AB, Stanford U., 1944, MD, 1947; MPH, U. Calif., 1984. Diplomate Am. Bd. Surgery. Intern Stanford Lane Hosp., San Francisco, 1948; resident in Gen. Surgery Ft. Miley VA Hosp., San Francisco, 1950-54; pvt. practice vascular surgery Berkeley, Calif., 1954-70; instr. Surgery Stanford U., 1954-57, assoc. in Surgery, 1957-70; dir. surg. intern tng. Herrick Meml. Hosp., Berkeley, 1961-67, chief of surgery, 1963-67, pres. med. staff, 1966-67, chief of staff, 1968-70; chief of surgery Alta Bates Hosp., Berkeley, 1973-76; prof. Health Scis., Med. Edn., Surgery U. Calif., Berkeley and San Francisco, from 1973. Cons. Highland, Alameda County Hosp., Oakland, Calif., 1955-75, Tom Dooley Hosp., Ban Nam Yao, Thailand, 1981,; vis. prof. Vishnevsky Inst. Vascular Surgery, U. Moscow, 1971; examiner certifying examination Am. Bd. Surgery, 1981; presenter in field. Founding mem. Movement to Incorporate, Lafayette, Calif., 1968; mem. city coun., City of Lafayette, 1968, mayor, 1969, treas., 1970-85; mem. mayors' conf. Contra Costa County, Calif., 1969; chmn. Bay Area rapid transit com., Lafayette, 1970; cons. Assembly com. on health, State of Calif., 1984; mem. search com. Stanford Med. Sch., 1984. Capt. USAF, 1948-50. Fellow Am. Coll. Surgeons, Internat. Coll. Surgeons; mem. AMA, Calif. Med. Assn., Pacific Coast Surgical Assn., Pan Pacific Surgical Soc., Royal Soc. Medicine, Contra Costa County Med. Assn., San Francisco Surgical Soc., Alameda Med. Assn.,East Bay Surgical Soc., Stanford U. Sch. Medicine Alumni Soc., (alumni rep. to acad. senate 1979-85, bd. govs. 1978-84, pres. 1984-85). Republican. Mem. Lds Ch. Home: Lafayette, Calif. Died July 30, 2007.

HOLMES, MELVIN ALMONT, insurance company executive; b. West New York, NJ, Jan. 2, 1919; s. Edward L. and Sarah J. (Brown) H.; m. Clare G. White, May 30, 1943; children: Clare Ann, Karen, Joan, Patricia, Catherine, Donald, Jacqueline. Student in bus. adminstrn., NYU; L.H.D. (hon.), Coll. of Ins., 1976. C.P.C.U., 1955. With Frank B. Hall & Co., Inc., Briarcliff Manor, N.Y., 1937-84, asst. mgr. liability dept., 1945-52, asst. v.p., 1952-56, v.p., 1956-68, chief exec. officer, pres., 1968-73, vice chmn., 1973-79, cons., dir., 1979-84. Chmn. bd. trustees Coll. of Ins., 1974-76 Hon. trustee Valley Hosp., Ridgewood, N.J. Served to capt. C.E., U.S. Army, 1941-46. Recipient Good Scout award Boy Scouts Am., 1975; Free Enterprise award Ins. Fedn. N.Y., 1975 Mem. Nat. Assn. Ins. Brokers (past pres.), Ins. Soc. N.Y., Soc. CPCUs (Eugene A. Toale Meml. award 1976), Ins. Inst. Am., Am. Inst. Property and Liability Underwriters Inc. (past trustee), Ins. Fedn. N.Y. (past pres.), Tequesta Country Club. Home: Juno Beach, Fla. Died Jan. 23, 2007.

HOLOUBEK, JOE, physician; b. Clarkson, Nebr., Sept. 9, 1915; s. Joe and Marie (Kucera) H.; m. Alice Baker, July 18, 1939; children: Mary Josephine, Brian, Robert, Martha Alice. BS, U. Nebr., 1937, MD, 1938. Diplomate Am. Bd. Internal Medicine. Intern Univ. Hosp., Omaha, 1938-39; fellow dept. medicine La. State U. Sch. Medicine, New Orleans, 1939-41, clin. assoc. prof. medicine Shreveport, 1958-68, 68-72, clin. prof. medicine, 1972-90, clin. prof. emeritus, from 1990. Del. task force on aging State of La. from Diocese of Shreveport, 1986-88; mem. com. on aging La. Interfaith Conf., 1988—. Assoc. editor: The Linacre Quarterly, 1967-78. Maj. U.S. Army med. corps, 1941-46. Recipient Diocesan medal of honor Bishop William B. Friend, 1995; appt. to Knight Comdr. of Order of St. Gregory the Great by Pope John XXIII, 1962, Knight of the Equestrian Order of the Holy Sepulchre of Jerusalem by Pope Paul VI, 1978, Knight Comdr. of the Order by Pope John Paul II, 1983, Knight Commander with Star, 1988, Knight of the Grand Cross of the Order, 1993, Knight Commander with Star of Order of St. Gregory the Great, Pope John Paul II, 1999. Fellow Am. Coll. Cardiology, Am. Coll. Physicians Laureate award 1987), Coun. Clin. Cardiology, N.Y. Acad. Scis.; mem. AMA, AHA (bd. dirs. 1955-58, Disting. Achievement award 1970), So. Med. Assn., La. Heart Assn. bd. dirs. 1950-70, pres. 1956), Shreveport Med. Soc. (Disting. Svc. award 1967), La. State Med. Assn., Nat. Fedn. Cath. Physicians Guilds (del. 1952-65, 70—, 2d v.p. 1957-59, v.p. 1959-61, pres. 1961-63), Am. Fedn. Clin. Rsch. (sr. mem.), So. Soc. Geriatric Medicine (founding mem.), Knights of St. Gregory the Great (pres. La. Conf. 1989-90), Cath. Acad. of Scis. of U.S. of Am. (academician 1990—), Nu Sigma Nu, others. Home: Shreveport, La. Died May 17, 2007.

HOLSEN, JAMES NOBLE, JR., retired chemical engineer; b. Palo Alto, Calif., June 20, 1924; s. James N. and Esther (Giltrud) H.; m. Nancy Schwankhaus, Feb. 24, 1950 (div.); children— James Noble III, David Edwards; m. Margot Meyer Best, Nov. 11, 1977; stepchildren— Victoria, Christopher, John. BS, Princeton U., 1948; D.Sc., Washington U., St. Louis, 1954. Registered profl. engr., Mo. Chem. engr. Olin Mathieson Chem. Corp., 1954-55; asst. prof. chem. engring. Washington U., 1955-58, assoc. prof., 1958-61, prof., 1961-73; prof. chem. engring. U. Mo.-Rolla, 1973-74, vis. prof. engring. mgmt., 1974-75; program mgr. McDonnell Douglas Corp., St. Louis, 1977-92; ret., 1992. Cons. chem. engring. and aerospace scis.; vis. prof. engring. Kabul U., Afghanistan, 1963-64, 69-73; mem. U.S. Engring. Team, Kabul, 1963-64, 69-73 Served with AUS, 1942-46 Fellow AIAA (assoc.); mem. Am. Inst. Chem. Engrs. (chmn. St. Louis sect. 1962), Am. Chem. Soc., Am. Soc. Engring. Edn., AAAS, Ethical Soc. Sigma Xi, Tau Beta Pi Clubs: Princeton Quadrangle. Achievements include research on gas phase reaction kinetics, gaseous transport properties, materials processing in space, satellite components and structure, thermodynamics. Active in environmental affairs with St. Louis Audubon Soc. Home: Kirkwood, Mo. Died Mar. 12, 2007.

HOLT, JOSEPH WILLIAM, reinsurance company executive; b. Apr. 16, 1930; s. Joseph W. and Helen G. Holt; m. Irina von der Launitz, July 19, 1952; children: Lise MArgaret Bradley, Helen Alexandra Lizotte. BA, Mayrville Coll., 1950; MA, U. Pa., 1954. Mgr. Parker & Co. Internat., Phila., 1952—54; with Price Forbes, London, 1955, Interocean Agy., NYC, 1956—67; co-founder, exec. v.p., dir. Duncanson & Holt, Inc., from 1967; pres. RA Fulton & Co., Inc., from 1968; v.p. Reed & Brown, from 1974. V.p. Aerospace Mgrs., from 1974, D & H Tech. Svcs., Inc., from 1974; exec. v.p. ERG Mgmt. Corp., from 1975; exec. dir., dir. Rochdale Ins. Co., from 1976; pres., dir. United Ams. Ins. Co., from 1978, Holt Corp., from 1981; chmn., pres., CEO Federated Reins Corp., from 1982; mgr. Pinehurst Accident Reins Group, from 1982; bd. dirs. First Manhattan Intermediaries Inc., RMS, Inc., CIU, Inc.; chmn. bd. dirs. Nat. Marine Underwriters, from 1983; chmn. John Hewitt and Assocs., from 1986, Nat. Marine Ins. Co., from 1987, Mgmt. and Facilities Corp., from 1987. Mem.: World Trade Club, Union Club. Home: Wayne, NJ. Died Feb. 7, 2007.

HOLZ, HAROLD A., chemical and plastics manufacturing company executive; b. NYC, June 26, 1925; s. Herman A. and Genevieve (Murphy) H.; m. Joanne Axtell, Oct. 3, 1953; children: Gretchen, Timothy. BS, Stevens Inst. Tech., 1946, ME, 1947. Tech. rep. Union Carbide Corp., NYC, 1947-49, Hartford, Conn., 1949-52, St. Louis, 1952-58, asst. regional mgr. Chgo., 1958-64, regional mgr., 1964-65, acct. exec. NYC, 1965-85; v.p. sales, new product devel. Marval Industries, Inc., 1986-97; cons. Old Lyme, Conn., from 1997. Nat. bd. govs. Nat. Plastics Ctr. and Mus., Leominster, Mass., 1995—. Served to lt. (j.g.) USNR, 1943-50. Named to Plastics Hall of Fame, 2000; recipient Stevens Honor award Stevens Tech., Hoboken, NJ, 2001 Mem. The Plastics Acad. (bd. dirs. 1996—, adminstr. Plastics Hall of Fame), Soc. Plastics Engrs. (disting. mem., pres. 1975-76), Plastics Pioneers Assn. (bd. govs. 1981-85, pres. 1993-95), Plastics Inst. Am. (trustee 1995—), Union Carbide Retiree Corps. (pres. Lower Westchester County chpt. 1996-97), Old Guard Club of Stevens Tech. (pres. 2002—). Died Dec. 23, 2005.

HOMJAK, JOHN, JR., hospital administrator; b. Ambridge, Pa., Dec. 5, 1933; s. John and Helen (Panek) H.; m. Dale Marea Carter, June 9, 1966; children: Kara Marie, Kendra Lee. BS in Pharmacy, Duquesne U., 1958; M.H.A., St. Louis U., 1960; LL.B., LaSalle Extension U., Chgo., 1966. Asst. hosp. adminstr. Aramco Med. Dept., Dhahran, Saudi Arabia, 1962-69; exec. adminstr. Burde Rehab. Ctr., White Plains, N.Y., 1969-70; assoc. adminstr. Timken Mercy Med. Ctr., Canton, Ohio, 1970-74; assoc. exec. adminstr. King Faisal Spl. Hosp., Riyadh, Saudi Arabia, 1974-75; pres., chief exec. officer Hawkes Hosp. of Mt. Carmel, Columbus, Ohio, 1975-83; mem. chief exec. officers council Holy Cross Health System, South Bend, Ind., 1979-83; mem. appeals com. Blue Cross, Columbus, 1981-82, chmn. dist. council, 1982-83; chmn. adminstrv. council Coalition for Cost Effective Health Care, Columbus, from 1983. Author: The Organization of Hospital Administration Based on Manpower by Function, 1986 Mem. Ohio Health and Med. Leaders People-to-People Del. to Peoples Repub. China Ohio State Health Dept. Served with AUS, 1954-55. Mem. Am. Coll. Health Care Execs. Home: Scottsdale, Ariz. Died Aug. 3, 2007.

HONEY, MARGARET C., association executive; b. Newark, Sept. 13, 1915; d. Edgar Thomas and and Edna Margaret (Armitage) H. BA, State Tchrs. Coll., Montclair, NJ, 1938; MA, Columbia U., 1947. Tchr. Buxton Country Day Sch., Short Hills, N.J., 1938-39; bus. and indsl. program dir. YWCA, Elmira, N.Y., 1940-43, indsl. program dir. Germantown, Pa., 1943-45, met. young adult dir. LA, 1945-48, exec. dir. Ridgewood, N.J., 1948-62, br. dir. Westside, N.Y., 1962-65, dir. Womens Job Corps Ctr. Jersey City, 1967-73, exec. dir., 1973-75; asst. exec. coll. and univ. divsn. Nat. Bd. YWCA of U.S.A., NYC, 1965-67, field cons., 1975-80. Part-time cons. Rsch. & Action, N.Y.C., 1980-81; interim exec. YWCA, Summit, N.J., 1981-82, Passiac, N.J., 1982-83. Bd. dirs. YWCA, Greensburg, Pa., 1988-94; v.p. Pa. State Coun. YWCA, 1989-93; mem. pub. policy com. State Coun YWCAs, 1990—; mem. Act 101 adv. bd. Seton Hill Coll., Greensburg, Pa., 1988—. Internat. fellow Ford Found., 1953-54; recipient Village Com. on Youth citation, 1962, Essie W. Mayer Leadership award YWCA, 1963, Nat. Bd. YWCA U.S.A. citation, 1980. Mem. AAUW, Friday Club. Avocations: tennis, travel, theater, reading, volunteering. Home: Greensburg, Pa. Died Dec. 13, 2006.

HONNING, BENGT EUGENE, chiropractic physician, consultant, biochemist; b. Sundsvall, Sweden, Sept. 8, 1927; came to U.S., 1931; s. Walfrid Eugen and Julia Margareta (Vestine) H.; m. Mary Lou Neely, Feb. 7, 1948; children: Sharon Ann, Dale Eldred. BS, Calif. State U., 1964; MS, Wm. Darren U., 1965, PhD in Biochemistry, 1967; LLB, Blackstone Sch. Law, 1978; DC, L.A. Coll. Chiropractic, 1969. Diplomate Nat. Bd. Chiropractic Examiners; lic. clin. lab. scientist, Calif. Biochemist Am. Med. Labs., LA, 1956-69; chiropractor, neurologist Long Beach, Calif., from 1969. Biochemist Biochem. Consultants, Long Beach, 1967-88; prof. biochemistry L.A. Coll. Chiropractic, 1967-69. Author: Self Winding Clock Company, 1980; contbr. articles to profl. jours. Chief libr. Self Winding Clock Assn., Long Beach, 1979—. Served with USN, 1945-47. Mem. Am. Chem. Soc., Calif. Assn. of Med. Technologists, Am. Astron. Soc., Nat. Assn. of Watch and Clock Collectors (cert. of merit 1993, chpt. 4 pres. 1980-84). Lutheran. Avocations: clockmaking, scientific and medical photography. Home: Long Beach, Calif. Died Nov. 8, 2006.

HOOD, DOROTHY HUSTON, accountant; b. Louisville, May 17, 1924; d. Elijah Northcutt and Vida Fern (Carpenter) Huston; B.S.B.A., U. Louisville, 1981; m. James Clifton Hood, Jan. 4, 1940; children— Gloria Hood Costanzo, Barbara Hood Kidd, James Clifton. Mgr. classification, control and research IRS, Louisville, 1951-61, conferee, 1961-66, tax auditor, 1966-73, internal revenue agt., 1973—; exec. v.p., nat. treas. Employee Union chpt. 25, Louisville, 1981. Sec.-treas. Louisville and Jefferson County Youth Orch., 1958-61. Recipient Superior Performance awards IRS, 1965, 80, Spl. Service award, 1974. Mem. Am. Soc. Women Accts. Methodist. Died Jan. 10, 2006.

HOOD, LOUISE B., former state legislator; b. Windsor, Vt., Aug. 27, 1916; d. Albert E., Sr., and Gladys H. (Robinson) Buckman; student schs. Windsor; m. Lee B. Hood, Sept. 4, 1938 (dec.); children: L. Robert, Bonnie Lee, David John. Sec. to attys., payroll clk. Goodyear Tire and Rubber, Windsor, 1947-50; bookkeeper, sec., asst. town clk., justice of peace, notary public, Town of Windsor, 1950-68, treas., 1968-78; mem. Vt. Gen. Assembly, rep. from Dist. 3, 1979-89, ret. Trustee, Windsor Library; trustee, sec. Davis Home; sec. Salvation Army, 1975—; vice chmn. Rep. Town Com.; bd. dirs. Windsor Cemetery Assn., 1982—. Methodist. Home: Windsor, Vt. Died Oct. 25, 2006.

HOOPES, MARIA SEGURA, librarian; b. Cananea, Mex., Jan. 16, 1945; came to U.S., 1954; d. Juan Segura Zabalza and Elvira (Garcia) Segura; m. F. Lance Hoopes, Dec. 26, 1964;

children— Lance Patrick, Claire, Thomas. B.A., U. Ariz., 1975, M.L.S., 1978. Unit asst. Ariz. Health Sci. Ctr., Tucson, 1976-78; spl. agt. trainee FBI, Washington, 1980; librarian Donaldson Sch., Tucson, 1980-82; reference librarian U. Ariz. Tucson, 1982—; chmn. affirmative action com. Library Faculty Assembly, Tucson, 1983—. Mem. ALA, Ariz. State Library Assn., Reforma, Sigma Delta Pi. Democrat. Roman Catholic. Home: Sonoita, Ariz. Died Nov. 27, 2006.

HOPKINS, GEORGE MATHEWS MARKS, retired lawyer, engineering executive; b. Houston, June 9, 1923; s. C. Allen and Agnes Cary (Marks) H.; m. Betty Miller McLean, Aug. 21, 1954; children: Laura Hopkins Corrigan, Edith Hopkins Collins. Student, Ga. Inst. Tech., 1943-44; BSChemE, Ala. Poly. Inst., 1944; LLB, JD, U. Ala., 1949; postgrad., George Washington U., 1949-50. Bar: Ala. 1949, Ga. 1954; registered patent lawyer, U.S.; registered profl. engr., Ga.; Can. qualified deep-sea diver. Instr. math. U. Ala., 1947-49; assoc. A. Yates Dowell, Washington, 1949-50, Edward T. Newton, Atlanta, 1950-62; ptnr. Newton, Hopkins and Ormsby (and predecessor), Atlanta, 1962-87; sr. ptnr. Hunt, Richardson, Garner, Todd & Cadenhead, Atlanta, 1987-91; ptnr. Hopkins & Thomas, 1991-95; ret., 1996; spl. asst. atty. gen. State of Ga., 1978; chmn. bd. Southeastern Carpet Mills, Inc., Chatsworth, Ga., 1962-77, Thomas-Daniel & Assocs., Inc., 1981-85, Ea. Carpet Mills, Inc., 1983-87; CEO, Airamar Chem. Engring., Inc., Doraville, Ga., from 1997. Asst. dir. rsch., legal counsel Auburn (Ala.) Rsch. Found., 1954-55; spl. asst. atty. gen. State of Ga., 1978; chmn. bd. S.E. Carpet Mills, Inc., Chatsworth, Ga., 1962-77, Thomas-Daniel & Assocs., Inc., 1981-85, Ea. Carpet Mills, Inc.; dir. Xepol Inc. Served as lt., navigator, Submarine Service USNR, 1944-46, 50-51. Mem. ABA, Ga. Bar Assn. (chmn. sect. patents 1970-71), Atlanta Bar Assn., Am. Intellectual Property Law Assn., Am. Soc. Profl. Engrs., Submarine Vets. World War II (pres. Ga. chpt. 1977-78), Phi Delta Phi, Sigma Alpha Epsilon, Atlanta Lawyers Club, Phoenix Soc., Cherokee Town and Country Club, AtlantaSoc. Episcopalian. Died July 14, 2006.

HOPPE, PETER CHRISTIAN, biologist, geneticist; b. Long Beach, Calif., Feb. 16, 1942; s. John Calvin and Venetia Bodell (Mortensen) H.; m. Linda Lee Peters, June 14, 1963; children— Tina Christine, Kirk Christian, Todd Christopher. BS, Calif. State Poly. U., 1964; MS, Kans. State U., 1966, PhD, 1968. Asso. staff scientist The Jackson Lab., Bar Harbor, Maine, 1970-73, staff scientist, 1973-81, sr. staff scientist, 1981-95, emeritus, from 1995. Vis. prof. U. Geneva, 1979-80 Contbr. articles to profl. jours. Named Disting. Alumnus Calif. State Poly. U., 1981; Am. Cancer Soc. Eleanor Roosevelt fellow, 1979-80 Home: Bar Harbor, Maine. Died Feb. 2, 2006.

HOPPER, ELLEN MARIE, editor; b. Elgin, Ill., Apr. 26, 1946; d. Edward Charles and Leona Joyce (Smith) Hubbard; stepdau. Robert Eugene and Joyce (Smith) Musall; m. Eugene Hopper, Oct. 22, 1969 (div. Dec. 1980). Writer, Daily Citizen, Cushing, Okla., 1976-78; society editor Derrick & Jour., Drumright, Okla., 1978-80, news editor, 1982—. Contbg. author: Cimarron Family Legends, 1978. Mem. Okla. Press Assn., Drumright C. of C. Democrat. Lutheran. Home: Drumright, Okla. Died Feb. 14, 2006.

HOPPONEN, RAYMOND ELLWOOD, retired pharmacist, university dean; b. New York Mills, Minn., July 6, 1921; s. Victor William and Hilma Lydia (Ruonakoski) H.; m. Mary Helen Robinson, Sept. 4, 1955; children— Lisa, Andrew, Susan. BS, U. Minn., 1943, PhD, 1950; postgrad., U. Wis., 1962-63. Asst. prof., asso. prof., prof. U. Kans., 1950-64, asst. dean, 1964-66; dean pharmacy S.D. State U., Brookings, 1966-86; ret., 1986. Contbr. to Handbook of Non-Prescription Drugs, 1st-7th edits, 1967-86. Mem. Brookings Area Betterment Com., 1975-77, 79—; bd. dirs. Dakota affiliate Am. Heart Assn. Served with M.C. AUS, 1943-46. Recipient hon. mention Ebert prize in pharm. research, 1953; NIH Career Devel. fellow, 1962 Mem. Am. Pharm. Assn., Acad. Pharm. Scis., Am. Assn. Colls Pharmacy (exec. com., sec. council of deans), S.D. Pharm. Assn., Rho Chi (nat. pres. 1972-74) Lodges: Kiwanis. Democrat. Methodist. Died Dec. 1, 2005.

HORN, CHARLES LILLEY, lawyer; b. Mpls., May 12, 1927; s. Charles Lilley and Louise Eugenie (Brace) H.; m. Nancy Lou Taylor, Oct. 17, 1959 (dec. Feb. 1977); children: David Andrew, Louise Alicia; m. Barbara Allinson Teachout, Jan. 28, 1978 BA, Princeton U., NJ, 1950; JD, U. Minn., Mpls., 1953. Bar: Minn. 1953. Assoc. Faegre & Benson, Mpls., 1953-65, ptnr., from 1965. Author: The Iron Ore Industry of Minnesota and Problems of Depleted Reserves, 1950 (Wolf Ballieson Meml. prize). Trustee, sec. Minn. Chpt. of Nature Conservancy, Mpls., 1972-87. Served with U.S. Army, 1945-47 Recipient Oak Leaf award The Nature Conservancy, 1978 Mem. Minn. State Bar Assn. Clubs: Minikahda, Mpls. Athletic. Lodges: Masons. Republican. Episcopalian. Avocations: birding; golf. Home: Minneapolis, Minn. Died Aug. 18, 2006.

HORNE, BLANCHE COBB GREENWAY, small business owner; b. Charleston, S.C., Mar. 3, 1937; d. John H. and Patsy P. (Pullin) Cobb; m. Jesse T. Greenway, Sr., Aug. 25, 1953 (div. Dec. 1970); children— Jesse Thomas, Kathleen Ann Greenway Davis, Sondra Leigh Greenway Sikes; m. Carey Wilson Horne, Jr., June 23, 1974. Grad. high sch. with honors. Cashier, Adler's Dept. Store, Savannah, Ga., 1953-56; cashier, stock clk. Fine's, Inc., Savannah, 1956-67; office mgr., bookkeeper Hillcrest Meml. Park, Savannah, 1967-82; owner, operator salesperson Gravel Hill Monument Co., Bloomingdale, Ga., 1982—; mgr., salesperson Meml. Gardens Cemetery, Bloomingdale, 1985—; sec. Pooler Athletic Assn., Ga., 1972. Mem. Nat. Bus. Women Assn., Ga. Bus. Women's Assn., Pooler Bus. Assn., Am. Legion Aux. Methodist. Avocations: family; helping others. Died May 18, 2007.

HOROWITZ, MORRIS A., retired economics professor; b. Newark, Nov. 19, 1919; s. Samuel and Anna (Litwin) H.; m. Jean Ginsburg, July 12, 1941; children— Ruth, Joel. BA in Econs., NYU, 1940; PhD in Econs., Harvard U., 1954. Mem. faculty Northeastern U., Boston, from 1956, prof. econs., chmn. dept., 1959-90, prof. emeritus, from 1992. Vice-chmn. Mass. Joint Labor-Mgmt. Com. for Mcpl. Police and Fire, 1980—; ad hoc labor arbitrator, manpower cons. Home: Lexington, Mass. Died July 20, 2007.

HORROCKS, LLOYD ALLEN, medical biochemistry educator; b. Cin., July 13, 1932; s. Robert and Martha (Keeler) H.; m. Marjorie Lee Werstler, June 30, 1956; children: Richard A., Rebecca A. Horrocks Haxe. BA in Chemistry with honors, Ohio Wesleyan U., 1953; MS in Physiol. Chemistry, Ohio State U., 1955, PhD in Physiol. Chemistry, 1960. Research assoc. neurochemistry lab. Cleve. Psychiat. Inst., 1960-68; sr. clin. instr. neurosurgery Case Western Res. U., Cleve., 1965-66; from asst. prof to prof. physiol. chemistry Ohio State U., from 1968. Mem. project rev. com. NIH Neurol. Disorders Program, 1981-85; vis. prof. NATO, Nat. Research Council of Italy, 1986; chmn. numerous coms. on profl., ednl., adminstrv., and acad. policies; lectr. on biochemistry Ohio State U. Editor: (with others) Phospholipids in the Nervous System, Volume I: Metabolism, 1982, Volume II: Physiological Roles, 1985, Phospholipid Research and the Nervous System: Biochemical and Molecular Pharmacology, 1986, Biochemical and Molecular Pathology, 1988, Neuromethods, vol. 7, Lipids and Compounds, 1988, Phospholipids and Signal Transmission, 1993, Trophic Factors and the Nervous System, 1990; (jour.) Neurochem. Pathology, 1982—, Molecular and Chem. Neuropathology, 1989—; assoc. editor Lipids, 1985—; mem. editorial bd. Jour. Lipid Research, 1976-83; mem. editorial bd. Jour. Neurochemistry, 1978-85, advisory bd., 1976-77. Lt. USAF, 1955-58. Grantee NIH, 1961—, Spinal Cord Rsch. Found., 1986-87; NIH spl. fellow U. Birmingham, 1964; Macy Faculty scholar U. Louis Pasteur, Strasbourg, 1974. Mem. Internat. Soc. for Neurochemistry (mem. spl. coms. 1978-79, 79-81, 85-87, co-organizer Satellite Symposia, 1980-81, 82-83, 84-85, 86-87, mem. Council 1981-85), Internat. Soc. for Devel. Neurosci., European Soc. for Neurochemistry, AAAS, AAUP, Am. Soc. Biol. Chemists, Am. Soc. for Neurochemistry (local chmn. 1973, program chmn. 1987-88), Soc. for Neurosci. (cen. Ohio chpt. sec., treas. 1972-73, chmn. 1973-74, 76-78), Biochem. Soc., Royal Acad. Scis. (fgn. corr.), Omicron Delta Kappa, Phi Lambda Upsilon, Sigma Xi. Home: Columbus, Ohio. Died Aug. 18, 2007.

HOSOKAWA, WILLIAM K., newspaper columnist, author; b. Seattle, Jan. 30, 1915; s. Setsugo and Kimiyo (Omura) H.; m. Alice Tokuko Miyake, Aug. 28, 1938 (dec. 1998); children: Michael, Susan Hosokawa Boatright, Peter, Christie Hosokawa Harveson. BA, U. Wash., 1937; LHD (hon.), U. Denver, 1990. Mng. editor Singapore Herald, 1939-40; writer Far Eastern Rev., Shanghai, China, 1940-41; editor Heart Mountain Sentinel, Wyo., 1942-43; copy editor Des Moines Register, 1943-46; with Denver Post, 1946-83, war corr., 1950; editor Empire mag., 1950-57, exec. news editor, 1957-58, asst. mng. editor, 1958-60, Sunday editor, 1960-62, assoc. editor, 1963-77, editor editorial page, 1977-83, columnist, 1983-84, Rocky Mountain News, 1985-92. Pulitzer prize journalism juror, 1969, 70, 75, 76, 81; lectr. journalism U. No. Colo., 1973-75, U. Colo., 1974, 76, U. Wyo., 1985; lectr. Asian affairs U. Denver, 1986-2007 Author: Nisei: The Quiet Americans, 1969, The Two Worlds of Jim Yoshida, 1972, Thunder in the Rockies, 1976, 35 Years in the Frying Pan, 1978, (with Robert W. Wilson) East to America, 1980, JACL in Quest of Justice, 1982; (with Mike Masaoka) They Call Me Moses Masaoka, 1987, Old Man Thunder: Father of the Bullet Train, 1997, Out of the Frying Pan, 1998, Colorado's Japanese Americans, 1886 to the Present, 2005. Del. Japanese-Am. Assembly, 1972, Japanese-Am. Bilateral Meeting, Internat. Press Inst., 1972, 73, 75, 79, 81; bd. dirs. Iliff Sch. of Theology, 1985-91. Decorated Japanese Order of the Rising Sun, gold rays with neck ribbon, 1987; recipient Disting. Achievement award Japanese Am. Citizens League, 1952, Nisei of Biennium, 1958, Western Heritage award Cowboy Hall of Fame, 1966, Outstanding Colo. Journalist award U. Colo., 1967, Outstanding Journalist award Colo. Soc. Profl. Journalists, 1976, Outstanding Colo. Communicator award Denver Press Club, 1985, Lowell Thomas award Colo.Soc. Profl. Journalists, 1990, World Citizen award Inst. Internat. Edn., Denver, 1991; hon. consul-gen. Japan for Colo., 1975-99. Mem. Colo. Freedom of Info. Coun. (pres. 1988-91), Japan Am. Soc. Colo. (sr. v.p. 1992-2007). Home: Lakewood, Colo. Died Nov. 9, 2007.*

HOTCHKISS, SALLY MCMURDO, psychology educator, university official and dean; b. Leominster, Mass., Sept. 13, 1929; d. Montagu Henry and Mary Frances (Fisher) McMurdo; m. Sanford Norman Hotchkiss, Feb. 13, 1954; children: Charles Montagu, Douglas Logan. AB, Randolph-Macon Woman's Coll., 1949; MA, U. Minn., 1950, PhD, 1959. Lic. psychologist, Ohio. Instr., chmn. dept. psychology Rockford (Ill.) Coll., 1953-54; study dir. U. Pitts., 1961-66; asst. prof. psychology Youngstown (Ohio) State U., 1968-74, assoc. prof., 1974-78, prof., from 1978, assoc. provost, dean grad. studies, from 1982, acting provost. Mem., sec., examiner, pres. Ohio Bd. Psychology, Columbus, 1978-83. Editor: Survey of American Pathologists, 1966; contbr. articles to profl. jours. Bd. dirs., pres. Mahoning County Diagnostic and Evaluation Clinic, 1977-81; bd. dirs. Hospice of Youngstown, 1978-87, Goodwill Industries, Youngstown,1988—. Mem. Am. Psychol. Assn., Midwestern Psychol. Assn., Ohio Psychol. Assn., Phi Beta Kappa, Phi Kappa Phi (chpt. pres.), Delta Kappa Gamma (chpt. pres.). Republican. Episcopalian. Avocations: travel, reading. Home: Youngstown, Ohio. Died Feb. 4, 2006.

HOTCHKISS, WESLEY AKIN, clergyman, educator; b. Spooner, Wis., Jan. 26, 1919; s. Fay W. and Codie L. (Akin) H.; m. Mary Ellen Fink, Sept. 16, 1941; 1 child, Tannia Hotchkiss. BA, Northland Coll., Wis., 1944, Th.D., 1958; MS, U. Chgo., 1948, PhD, 1950; D.D., Yankton Coll., 1956; LL.D., Pacific U., 1965; L.H.D., Ill. Coll., 1979, Talladega Coll., 1981; LL.D., Hawaii Loa, 1983; Litt.D., Ripon Coll., 1982. Ordained to ministry, Congl. ch., 1944. Research asso. Chgo. Theol. Sem., 1947-49; research dir. Greater Cin. Council Chs., 1949-50, United Ch. Bd., 1950-55, sec., 1955-58, gen. sec. for higher edn., 1958-82; ret., 1982. Trustee Affiliate Artists, Inc. Served as chaplain AUS, 1945-47. Fellow Assn. Am. Geographers; mem. Nautical Research Guild, Internat. Soc. Folk Harpers and Craftsman, Nature Conservancy, People for the Am. Way. Home: Summerland Key, Fla. Died Jan. 7, 2007.

HOUCHIN, LLOYD KENNETH, air force officer; b. Osceola, Ark., Nov. 14, 1935; s. Lloyd Stanley and Edna Lucy (Sielbeck) H.; m. Mary Kathryn Mitchell, May 25, 1956; children: Ramona Lynne, Mitchell Lloyd. BS in Edn., So. Ill. U., 1956; MS in Pub. Adminstrn., George Washington U., 1968. Cert. fin. planner. Commd. to lt. U.S. Air Force, 1956, advanced through grades to col., from 1973, jet fighter pilot, 1956-71, curriculum mgr. Air Force Air Command and Staff Coll. Maxwell AFB, Ala., 1971-75, sr. controller HDQ Strategic Air Command Offutt AFB, Nebr., 1975-78, ops. dir., vice comdr. Strategic Missele Wing Whiteman AFB, Mo., 1978-82; prof. aerospace studies U. Ill., Urbana, 1982-85; fin. planner, investment broker A.G. Edwards & Sons, Belleville, Ill., from 1985. Dir. Computerized System to Teach Planning of Air Force Ops., Fast Stick II, 1975 Research dir., editor: Battle for the Skies Over North Vietnam, 1976. Republican. Home: Belleville, Ill. Died July 18, 2007.

HOUGHTON, RAYMOND CARL, JR., education educator; b. Greenfield, Mass., May 26, 1947; s. Raymond Carl and Phyllis Irene (Richason) H.; m. Jan Marie Laws, Sept. 22, 1973; children: Raymond James, April Monica, Amy Rose BS Math., Norwich U., 1969; MS Computer Sci., George Washington U., 1975; MSEE, Johns Hopkins U., 1980; PhD Computer Sci., Duke U., 1991. Computer operator Norwich U., Northfield, Vt., 1967—69; specialist programmer power transformer dept. GE Co., Pittsfield, Mass., 1969—70, mathematician armament dept. Burlington, Vt., 1972—73; mem. tech. staff Computer Scis. Corp., Silver Spring, Md., 1974—75; data systems analyst computer security applications divsn. Nat. Security Agy., Ft. Meade, Md., 1975—78; computer scientist Inst. Computer Scis. and Tech./Nat. Bur. Stds., Gaithersburg, Md., 1978—83; instrnl. rsch. asst. dept. computer sci. Duke U., Durham, NC, 1984—91; assoc. prof. dept. math. and computer sci. Augusta State U., Ga., 1987—93; lectr. Skidmore Coll., NY, 1993—95; owner Cyber Haus, Delmar, NY, from 1995. Bd. advisers, columnist Software Engring: Tools, Techniques, Practice, 1990-94, info. sys. del., Peoples Rep. China, 2000; adj. prof. SUNY Sch. Bus., Albany, 1997-2000; mission in understanding del. People to People Amb. Programs, Vietnam, 2002; spkr. in field Contbr. articles to profl. jours.; author history-based travel books. Town historian Bethlehem, N.Y., 2005—. 1st lt. U.S. Army, 1971-72, Vietnam Decorated Purple Heart; recipient Certs. Recognition, U.S. Dept. Commerce, 1981, 83, cert. appreciation IEEE Computer Soc., 1985 Mem.: IEEE, Assn. Computing Machinery, 101st Airborne Divsn. Assn., People to People Internat. Lutheran. Home: Delmar, NY. Died May 30, 2007.

HOUSER, ROBERT NORMAN, insurance company executive; b. Bloomfield, Iowa, Sept. 21, 1919; s. Charles B. and Venna C. (Bartholomew) H.; m. Doris V. Miller, Dec. 18, 1943; children: Theodore Alan, Judith Eileen, James Robert. BA summa cum laude, U. Iowa, 1947. With Bankers Life Co., 1936-38, 40-43, 47—, asst. actuary, 1953-60, asso. actuary, 1960-63, 2d v.p., actuary, 1963-68, v.p., actuary, 1968-71, v.p., chief actuary, 1971-72, sr. v.p., chief actuary, 1972-73, pres., 1973-75, pres., chief exec. officer, from 1975, now chmn., chief exec. officer. Chmn. bd., pres. BLC Growth & Income Funds, BLC Fund, Inc.; chmn. bd. BLC Equity Mgmt. Co., BLC Equity Services Corp.; dir. BLC Ins. Co. Bd. dirs. Drake U., Mercy Hosp., United Way Greater Des Moines; bd. govs. Iowa Coll. Found. Served to 1st lt. USAAF, 1943-45; Served to 1st lt. USAF, 1951-52. Decorated D.F.C., Air medals. Fellow Soc. Actuaries; mem. Greater Des Moines C. of C. (dir.), Am. Council Life Ins. (dir.), Health Ins. Assn. Am. (dir.) Home: Des Moines, Iowa. Died Mar. 2, 2007.

HOUSKA, ROBERT BARON, educational consultant; b. Chamberlain, SD, Sept. 14, 1933; s. Raymond L. and Hazel E. (Potter) Houska; m. Beverly Florence Ponto, Feb. 13, 1960; children: Derrick, Cerise, Carina. Attended, S.D. Sch. Mines, 1951—53; BS, U. S.D., 1959; MEd, U. N.D., 1961; EdD, N.Mex. State U., 1969. Dir. guidance Juneau-Douglas Schs., Juneau, Alaska, 1961—65; dormitory mgr. N.Mex. State U., 1965—69; cons. Minn. Higher Edn. Coordinating Commn., St. Paul, 1969—70; asst. acad. dean Nat. Coll. Bus., Rapid City, S.D., 1970—74; v.p. svc. area devel. Colo. Northwestern Cmty. Coll., 1974—84; register agt. Equitable Life Assurance Soc., 1984—88; sch. prin. Genoa-Hugo Schs., Hugo, Colo., from 1988. Pub. rels. coord. Am. Sch. Counselor Assn., 1964—65. Bd. dirs. Craig C. of C., Colo., 1981—83; mem. Craig Planning and Zoning Commn., 1982—86; candidate for county commr. Moffat County, Colo., 1982. Recipient Nat. Educator of Yr. award, Outstanding Educators Am., 1972; NSF scholar, 1960, NDEA scholar, 1960—61. Mem.: Am. Vocat. Assn., Colo. Assn. Sch. Execs., ASCD, Elks Club (Craig), Lions Club, Masons, VFW, Shriners, Phi Kappa Phi, Phi Delta Kappa, Psi Chi. Mem. Ch. Of Christ. Home: Parachute, Colo. Died Mar. 10, 2006.

HOVNANIAN, ARMEN, retail chain and direct mail executive; b. Akron, Ohio, Feb. 6, 1930; s. Aram and Marmar (Avedisian) H.; m. Suzanne C. Roberts, May 18, 1973; 1 son, Michael. BS in Pharmacy, Detroit Inst. Tech., 1951. With Cunningham Drug Stores, Inc., Detroit, 1948-78, store mgr., 1954-63, dist. mgr., 1963-67, dir. store ops. Mich., 1967-69, v.p. store ops., v.p. corp. store ops., 1969-70, dir., 1970-78, sr. v.p. corp. ops., 1971-77, sr. v.p. mktg., 1977-78; exec. v.p., ptnr. Living Distbrs., Inc., Walled Lake, Mich., 1978-82; exec. v.p., gen. mgr. Citrin Corp., Romulus, Mich., from 1983. Dir. Jackson Nat. Life Ins. Co. Served with AUS, 1951-53. Mem. Kappa Psi. Mem. Armenian Apostolic Ch. (trustee). Home: Farmington Hills, Mich. Died June 2, 2006.

HOWARD, GEORGE, JR., federal judge; b. Pine Bluff, Ark., May 13, 1924; Student, Lincoln U., 1951; BS, U. Ark., JD, 1954; LL.D., 1976. Bar: Ark. bar 1953, U.S. Supreme Ct. bar 1959. Pvt. practice law, Pine Bluff, 1953-77; spl. assoc. justice Ark. Supreme Ct., 1976, assoc. justice, 1977; justice U.S. Ct. Appeals, Ark., 1979-80; U.S. dist. judge, Eastern dist. Little Rock, from 1980. Mem. Ark. Claims Commn., 1969-77; chmn. Ark. adv. com. Civil Rights Commn. Recipient citation in recognition of faithful and disting. svc. as mem. Supreme Ct. Com. of Profl. Conduct, 1980, disting. jurist award Jud. Coun. Nat. Bar Assn., 1980, Wiley A. Branton Issues Symposium award, 1990; voted outstanding trial judge 1984-85 Ark. Trial

Lawyers Assn.; inducted Ark.'s Black Hall of Fame, 1994; recipient keepers of the spirit award Univ. Ark., Pine Bluff, 1995, quality svc. award Ark. Dem. Black Caucus, 1995, Drum Major award, Ark. Martin Luther King, Jr., Commn., 2003. Mem. ABA, Ark. Bar Assn. (Disting. Svc. Pursuit Justice award 2003), Jefferson County Bar Assn. (pres.) Baptist. Home: Pine Bluff, Ark. Died Apr. 21, 2007.

HOWARD, WALTER BURKE, chemical engineer; b. Corpus Christi, Tex., Jan. 22, 1916; s. Clement and Nell (Smith) H.; m. Virginia Kentucky Freeman, Feb. 14, 1942; children— Thomas Clement, Virginia Ann. BA, U. Tex., 1937, BS in Chem. Engring, 1938, MS, 1940, PhD, 1943. Registered profl. engr., Tex.; chartered engr., U.K. From asst. to sr. chem. engr. Bur. Indsl. Chemistry, U. Tex., Austin, 1939-52; from sr. engr. to scientist Monsanto Chem. Co., Texas City, Tex., 1952-64; mgr. process safety, sci. fellow to disting. fellow Monsanto Co., St. Louis, 1965-81; process safety tech. cons., from 1981. Contbr. chapters to books, articles to profl. jours.; patentee in field. V.p. Texas City Sch. Bd., 1963-64; chmn. bd. dirs. Mainland Opportunity Sch., 1958-61; mem. area coun. Boy Scouts Am., 1958-60; active P.T.A.; trustee Austin Presbyn. Theol. Sem., 1961-64. Fellow Brit. Instn. Chem. Engrs., Am. Inst. Chem. Engrs. (dir., Walton/Miller award 1987, Ann. Inst. lectr. 1987), Am. Chem. Soc., Combustion Inst. Internat., Nat. Fire Protection Assn. (Disting. Svc. award 1984), Austin Engrs. Club (past dir.), Phi Beta Kappa, Sigma Xi, Phi Lambda Upsilon. Presbyterian (elder). Died Oct. 30, 2006.

HOWARD, WINSTON STANLEY, lawyer; b. Des Moines, Oct. 15, 1907; s. William Shadrick and Amanda (Sandstrom) H.; m. Marguerite Blair, June 7, 1933; children— Alan Blair, Joan. Student, U. Nebr., 1925-26; JD cum laude, U. Wyo., 1930. Bar: Wyo. bar 1930, Colo. bar 1935. Practice in, Big Horn County, Wyo., 1931-35, Denver, 1935—; partner firm Sherman & Howard, 1939—. Co-organizer, former chmn. bd. Continental Nat. Bank, Englewood, Colo.; co-organizer Boulevard Nat. Bank, Denver; dir. various bus. corps. Mem. nat. council, Denver adv. bd. Salvation Army; chmn. Colo. Women's Coll.; bd. dirs. Denver Symphony Assn., Nat. Western Stock Show Assn.; former chmn. trustees Swedish Med. Center. Served from lt. to lt. comdr. USNR, 1944-46. Recipient Others award Salvation Army, 1962, 73, Distinguished Alumni award U. Wyo., 1967 Mem. ABA, Colo. Bar Assn. (past gov.), Denver Bar Assn., Denver C. of C., Englewood C. of C., Sigma Nu, Delta Sigma Rho. Republican. Episcopalian (former vestryman, warden). Clubs: Denver (Denver), Kiwanis (Denver) (past pres.), Mile High (Denver); Garden of the Gods (Colorado Springs, Colo.). Died Mar. 15, 2006.

HOWELL, SIDNEY CHARLES, manufacturing corporation executive; b. Elizabeth, NJ, Apr. 6, 1923; s. William Charles and Mabel Irene (Schmidt) H.; m. Aileen Read, June 9, 1945; 1 dau., Wendy. BS, MIT, 1949; M.Indsl. Mgmt., NYU, 1956. With Weatherhead Co., Cleve., 1956-66, 69-78, v.p. sales, 1962-66, sr. v.p. ops., 1969-74, exec. v.p., 1975-76, pres., 1976-78, also dir.; v.p. automotive mktg. Cummins Engine Co., Columbus, Ind., 1966-69; group v.p. Dana Corp., Toledo, 1978-80, sr. v.p., 1980-81, exec. v.p., from 1981. Dir. Blue Cross Northwestern Ohio Mem. adv. bd. Case Western Res U., Cleve., 1977-82. Served to 1st lt. USAAF, 1943-45, ETO. Decorated D.F.C.; decorated Air medal; Teagle Found. scholar, 1946-49 Mem. Soc. Automotive Engrs., Ohio C. of C. Clubs: Inverness Country; Belmont Country (Toledo). Presbyterian. Died Mar. 8, 2006.

HOWES, MARSHALL FREDERICK, manufacturing executive; b. Pittsfield, Mass., Apr. 28, 1937; s. Maurice Warren and Carrie Mae (Thomas) Howes; m. Barbara Jean Thurston, May 24, 1974; children: Valerie Jean, William Thomas, Linda Michelle, Steven Mitchell, Jeffrey Scott, Charles Larry, Jane Jeanette. BS in Acctg., Bryant Coll., 1958. Asst. controller Phillips Petroleum Co., Idaho Falls, 1958—66; controller, asst. treas. Aerojet Nuc. Co., Idaho Falls, 1971—76, chmn. retirement/investment com.; controller, asst. sec.-treas. Cordova Chem. Co., Sacramento, 1976—78; dir. fin. planning Aerojet Gen. Corp., El Monte, Calif., 1978—80, group controller, 1980—83; dir., CFO Nimbus, Inc., Carmichael, Calif., 1982—83, pres., dir., CEO, 1983—87; chmn., pres., CEO Hybrid Products, Inc., Rancho Cordova, Calif., from 1987. Chmn. bd. trustees Idaho Nuc. Ednl. Trust Fund; chmn. co. campaign United Way of Idaho Falls; adviser Jr. Achievement. Mem.: Am. Mgmt. Assn., Nat. Assn. Accts., Elks Club. Republican. Episcopalian. Home: Carmichael, Calif. Died Nov. 11, 2006.

HOWLAND, RICHARD HUBBARD, architectural historian; b. Providence, Aug. 23, 1910; S. Carl Badger and Cora Augusta (Hubbard) H. AB, Brown U., 1931, also hon. doctor's degree; A.M., Harvard U., 1933; PhD, Johns Hopkins U., 1946. Fellow Agora excavations, Athens, Greece, 1936-38; instr. Wellesley Coll., 1939-42; chief pictorial records sect. OSS, 1943-44; founder dept. history art Johns Hopkins, 1947, chmn. dept., 1947-56; pres. Nat. Trust for Historic Preservation, 1956-60; chmn. dept. civil history Smithsonian Instn., Washington, 1960-67, spl. asst. to sec., 1968-85. Trustee Am. Sch. Classical Studies, Athens; founding mem. Am. Com. Internat. Commn. Historic Sites and Monuments. Author: (with Eleanor Spencer) Architecture of Baltimore, 1954, Greek Lamps and Their Survivals, 1958. Trustee Irish Georgian Soc., Evergreen Found. Decorated Order Brit. Empire, Order George I (Greece), U.S. Order St. John of Jerusalem. Fellow Royal Soc. of the Arts; mem. Soc. Archtl. Historians (founding mem.), English Speaking Union, Soc. Cincinnati (hon.), Md. Soc. Colonial Wars, Victorian Soc. in Am. (former pres.), Century Assn., Knickerbocker Club, 14 West Hamilton St. Club, Cosmos Club, Arts Club, Dacor-Bacon Club, City Tavern Club, Phi Gamma Delta. Home: Washington, DC. Died Oct. 26, 2006.

HOYT, DANIEL REXFORD, management educator; b. Joplin, Mo., May 20, 1943; s. Rexford P. and Oletha Bell (Mills) H.; m. Sara Lou Payne, Dec. 16, 1967; children— Judith Danielle, Audrey Elizabeth. A.A., Mo. So. State Coll., 1963; B.A., U. Mo., 1965; M.B.A., Memphis State U., 1969; Ph.D., U. Nebr., 1976. Teaching asst. Memphis State U., Tenn., 1968-69; asst. prof. bus., Mo. Western State U., St. Joseph, 1969-76; prof. mgmt., dir. transp. mgmt. program Ark. State U., Jonesboro, 1976—; dir. Am. Soc. for Personnel Adminstrn. Found., Alexandria, Va., 1985—. Author: (with others) Personnel, HRM, Instructors Manual, 1984. Mem. Am. Soc. for Personnel Adminstrn. (bd. dirs. 1985-87, v.p. personnel research 1985—, pres. 1988), Acad. Mgmt., Northeast Ark. Transp. Club (pres. 1983), Indsl. Relations Research Assn., Soc. Nonprofit Mgmt., Northeast Ark. Personnel Mgrs. Assn. (pres. 1981). Lodge: Lions. Avocations: reading; travel; fishing. Home: Jonesboro, Ark. Died Apr. 19, 2007.

HSU, IMMANUEL CHUNG YUEH, history professor; b. Shanghai, May 6, 1923; came to U.S., 1949, naturalized, 1962; s. Thomas K.S. and Mary (Loh) H.; m. Dolores Menstell, Apr. 14, 1962; 1 child, Vadim Menstell. BA, Yenching U., China, 1946; MA, U. Minn., 1950; PhD (Harvard-Yenching fellow), Harvard U., 1954. Postdoctoral research fellow Harvard U., 1955-58; vis. asso. prof. history, vis. prof. Harvard Summer Sch., 1961, 64, 68, 75; asst. prof. history U. Calif. at Santa Barbara, 1959-60, asso. prof., 1960-65, prof., 1965-91, chmn. history dept., 1970-72. Faculty rsch. lectr., 1971; mem. del. to Chinese Acad. Scis., Beijing, spring 1979, 80; vis. prof. Hamburg U., Germany, spring 1973, Stockholm U., 1990, Leningrad (St. Petersburg) U., 1991; Fulbright lectr., 1973; vis. Wei Lun prof. The Chinese U. Hong Kong, 1998. Author: Intellectual Trends in the Ch'ing Period, 1959, China's Entrance into the Family of Nations, 1960, The Ili Crisis: A Study of Sino-Russian Diplomacy, 1871-1881, 1965, The Rise of Modern China, 1970, 2d edit., 1975, internat. edit., 1975-76, 3d edit., 1983, 4th edit., 1990, 5th edit., 1995 (Commonwealth Lit. priz of Calif. 1971), 6th edit., 2000, Chinese trans., 2001-02; editor: Readings in Modern Chinese History, 1971, Late Ch'ing Foreign Relations, 1866-1905, in The Cambridge History of China, Vol. 11, 1980, China Without Mao, 1983, 2d edit., 1990. Guggenheim fellow, 1962-63; Nat. Acad. Scis. disting. scholar to China, spring 1983 Mem. Am., Pacific hist. assns., Assn. Asian Studies, Assn. Ch'ing Studies. Home: Santa Barbara, Calif. Died Oct. 24, 2005.

HUBBELL, JOHN HOWARD, radiation physicist; b. Ann Arbor, Mich., Apr. 9, 1925; s. Howard Adams Hubbell and Mildred Jeanetta (Lipe) Hubbell Dyson; m. Jean Garber Norford, June 11, 1955; children: Anne Virginia Hubbell Cooper, Shelton Eric, Wendy Jean Hubbell Carballo. BS in Engring. Physics, U. Mich., 1949, MS in Physics, 1950; dr. honoris causa, U. Cordoba, Argentina, 1996. Rschr. x-ray crystal diffraction group Nat. Bur. Stds. (name now Nat. Inst. Stds. & Tech.), Washington, 1950-51, rschr. thermodynamics sect., 1951, rschr. radiation theory group, 1951-62, dir. x-ray and ionizing radiation data ctr. Washington & Gaithersburg, Md., 1963-81, rschr. Ctr. for Radiation Rsch. Gaithersburg, 1982-88, rschr., cons. Photon and Charged Particle Data Ctr., 1988—2007. Mem. cross sect. evaluation working group Brookhaven (N.Y.) Nat. Lab., 1965—88; cons. Lawrence Livermore (Calif.) Nat. Lab., 1966—2007, Lawrence Berkeley (Calif.) Nat. Lab., 1966—2007, Internat. Atomic Energy Agy., Vienna, 1987—2007, WHO, Geneva, 1989—2007; sec. task force on x-ray absorption coefficients Internat. Union Crystallography, 1979—2007; lectr. USSR Acad. Scis., 1979, People's Republic of China State Bur. Metrology, 1987, 93, India under Indo-U.S. Spl. Fgn. Currency Program, 1972, 74, 90; invited lectr. Japanese Soc. Radiol. Tech., Nagoya Ann. Conf., Kyoto, Osaka, 1995; vis. prof. U. Cordoba, Argentina, 1996. Author: Photon Cross Sections, Attenuation Coefficients and Energy Absorption Coefficients, 1969; editor: Jour. Applied Radiation and Isotopes, 1988—92; editor-in-chief: Radiation Physics and Chemistry, 1992—2001, cons. editor:, from 2002; contbr. articles to profl. jours. and encys., chapters to books. Scoutmaster, Boy Scouts Am., Washington, 1953-60; ch. sch. tchr. Foundry United Methodist Ch., Washington, 1963-78. With U.S. Army, 1943-45, ETO. Decorated Bronze Star; recipient Faculty medal Tech. U. Prague, 1982; named Outstanding Alumnus U. Mich. Nuc. Engring. Dept., 1995. Fellow Am. Nuc. Soc. (Radiation Industry award 1985, Profl. Excellence award 1990), Health Physics Soc. (chmn. gen. radiation protection sect., stds. com. 1984-90, Disting. Sci. Achievement award 2001), Am. Phys. Soc.; mem. Soc. Nuc. Medicine (Paul C. Aebersold award 1985), Internat. Radiation Physics Soc. (pres. 1994-97, sec. to adv. bd. 2000-07), Radiation Rsch. Soc., Hubbell Family Hist. Soc., Internat. Higher Edn. Acad. Scis. (Moscow). Achievements include development of computationally tractable solutions for the now called Hubbell rectangular source integral and Epstein-Hubbell generalized elliptic-type integral. Avocations: eclipse chasing, playing harmonica. Home: Gaithersburg, Md. Died Mar. 31, 2007.

HUBER, GORDON FLOYD, franchise food service executive; b. Victoria, Ill., Jan. 19, 1921; s. Floyd Benjamin and Edna (Moak) H.; m. Betty Louise Terpening, Feb. 27, 1944; children: James Clay, Elizabeth Ann Huber Webster, Jay Gordon. BA, Monmouth Coll., Ill., 1943; mgmt. course, Am. Mgmt. Assn., 1969-70. Local mgr. Intra.-State Telephone Co., Galesburg, Ill., 1947-52; mgr. Capitol Dairy Queen, Inc., Galesburg, 1953-56; gen. mgr. Illini Dairy Queen, Inc., Springfield, Ill., 1957-62; exec. v.p. Internat. Dairy Queen, Inc., Mpls., from 1962; pres. Dairy Queen of Utah, Inc., Minnetonka, Minn., from 1980. Dir. Dairy Queen of Japan Co., Ltd., Tokyo Served to lt. (j.g.) USNR, 1942-46, PTO. Mem.: Wayzata Country (Minn.) (v.p. 1976). Republican. Congregationalist. Home: Excelsior, Minn. Died Dec. 25, 2005.

HUDSON, ROBERT FRANKLIN, JR., lawyer; b. Miami, Fla., Sept. 20, 1946; s. Robert Franklin and Jane Ann (Reed) Hudson; m. Edith Mueller, June 19, 1971; children: Daniel Warren, Patrick Alexander. BSBA in Econs., U. Fla., 1968, JD, 1971; cert., U. London, 1970; LLM in Taxation, NYU, 1972. Bar: Fla. 1971, N.Y. 1975. Law clk. to judge Don N. Laramore U.S. Ct. Claims, Washington, 1972-73; assoc. Wender, Murase & White, NYC, 1973-77; ptnr. Arky, Freed, Stearns et al, Miami, 1977-86, Baker & McKenzie LLP, Miami, from 1986; mem. policy com. Baker & McKenzie, Miami, 1990-93, mem. client credit com., 1992-99, mng. ptnr. Miami office, 1996-98; N. Am. Tax Practice Group Mgmt. com., 2000—03. Mem. adv. bd. Tax Mgmt., Inc., Washington, from 1986, Fgn. Investment N.Am., London, 1990—96; legal counsel to her majesty's Britanic Counsel, Miami, 1988—94. Author: Federal Taxation of Foreign Investment in U.S. Real Estate, 1986; contbr. articles to profl. jours. Bd. dirs. Camillus House, from 2003, Concert Assn. Fla., from 1992, exec. com., from 1993, vice chmn., 1994—98, 2003—05, chmn., from 2005; bd. dirs. Performing Arts Ctr. Found., from 1994, vice chmn., from 2000; bd. dirs. Fla. Philharm., 1996—97, Internat. Wine and Food Soc., from 2002, v.p., from 2005. Mem.: ABA, Internat. Trust Adv. Bd Fiduciary Trust, World Trade Ctr. (bd. dirs. 1992—94), Coll. Tax Lawyers, Internat. Tax Planning Assn., Internat. Bar Assn., Inter-Am. Bar Assn., Internat. Fiscal Assn. (v.p. S.E. region U.S. br. 1985—92, mem. exec. coun. from 1987), Fla. Bar Assn. (chmn. tax sect. 1989—90, Oustanding Spkr. 1995), Fla. Internat. Bankers Assn. (bd. dirs. from 2002), Japan Soc. S. Fla. (chmn. pub. affiars com. 1991—93, bd. dirs. 1993—2000, treas. 1995—96, pres. 1996—99), S.E./U.S. Japan Assn. Democrat. Methodist. Avocations: skiing, boating, photography, travel, hiking. Home: Miami, Fla. Died May 29, 2006.

HUFFAKER, CRAIG JACKSON, communications company financial executive; b. Knoxville, Aug. 5, 1945; s. William Jackson and Reva (Smith) H.; m. Nancy Leigh Reagan, July 14, 1973; 1 son, Aaron. B.S., Tenn. Tech. U., 1968; J.D., John Marshall Law Sch., 1981. Bar: Ga., 1981. C.P.A., Ga., Tenn. Auditor, Deloitte Haskins & Sells, C.P.A.s, Atlanta, 1968-69, 71-72; sr. acct. Joseph Decosimo & Co., Chattanooga, 1972-73; controller Scottish Inns of Am., Kingston, Tenn., 1973; v.p. Quick Foods Inc., Tucker, Ga., 1973-76; v.p. fin., dir. Digital Communications Assocs., Inc., Norcross, Ga., 1977—. Served to 1st lt. U.S. Army, 1969-71. Mem. Ga. Bar Assn., ABA, Ga. Soc. C.P.A.s, Tenn. Soc. C.P.A.s, Am. Inst. C.P.A.s. Home: Atherton, Calif. Died May 2, 2007.

HUGEL, MAX, retired communications executive, former federal agency administrator; b. Bronx, N.Y., May 23, 1925; s. Max and Theresa (Sturman) H.; m. Shirley Lorraine Feig, June 7, 1953; children: Susan Jill Hugel Selbst, David, Richard. B.A., U. Mich., 1953. pres., CEO Brother Internat. Corp., Piscataway, N.J., 1954-75; exec. v.p., COO, Centronics Computer Corp., Hudson, N.J., 1975-80; spl. asst. to dir., dep. dir. for adminstrn., dep. dir. for ops. CIA, Washington, 1981; chmn. bd. InterDigital, Inc., Princeton, N.J., Rockingham Park, Salem, N.H.; pres. Internat. Syndications, Inc., Washington, Advanced Broadcast Media, Washington, Carmen, Carmen & Hugel Inc.; with Newslink, Inc., Washington. Nat. chmn. Project '88: Americans for the Reagan Agenda; Contbr. articles on politics, nat. security, bus. to mags. and newspapers. Founder, Mt. Sinai Hosp., Miami, Fla., nat. dir. voter groups Reagan-Bush Campaign 80, Washington; mem. Reagan-Bush Adv. Com., Washington, 1984; mem. Conservative Caucus; mem. Reagan Nat. Com. Served as 1st lt. Intelligence, U.S. Army, 1943-47. Recipient Martin Luther King award Ams. Progressing Together, 1969; named Man of Yr., City of Hope, 1982. Mem. Assn. Former Intelligence Officers. Jewish. Clubs: Friar's, N.H. Jockey. Lodges: Masons, Knights of Malta. Home: Bal Harbour, Fla. Died Feb. 19, 2007.

HUGHES, HENRY MERVIN, II, management consultant; b. Atlanta, Jan. 4, 1930; s. Henry Mervin and Uldine (Sullivan) H.; m. Virginia B. Biggart, Dec. 29, 1956; children— Sherrie, Cindy, Henry. A.B., Mercer U., 1952; M.A., U. Houston, 1979; Ph.D., Kensington U., 1983. Sr. mgmt. analyst NASA Johnson Space Center, 1961-83; pres., chief fin. officer CCC Inc. of Tex., 1983—; mgmt. cons., Houston. Author: Productivity and Creativity in the Knowledge Worker, 1984. Served to 1st lt. USAF, 1952-56. Patron Boy Scouts Am.; mem. dedication com. U. Houston, Clear Lake City; chmn. pub. relations com. Houston Fed. Exec. Bd. Mem. AIAA, Am. Soc. for Tng. and Devel., Nat. Contract Mgmt. Assn., Am. Soc. for Pub. Adminstrn. (past v.p.), Am. Mgmt. Assn., Acad. Polit. Sci., Nat. Assn. Self Employed, Clear Lake Personnel Assn., DAV, VFW, Ret. Officers Assn., Friends of Freeman Meml. Library, Air Force Assn. Sigma Iota Epsilon. Lodges: Rotary Internat. (perfect attendance award 1983), Elks: Bay Area Lions. Died Nov. 25, 2006.

HUGHES, WILLIAM LEWIS, retired dean, electrical engineer; b. Rapid City, SD, Dec. 2, 1926; s. Clarence William and Newell (Chase) H.; m. Stella Marie Platt, June 9, 1950; children: Elizabeth Helen, James Edward, Judith Lee, Michael George. BS in Elec. Engring, S.D. Sch. Mines and Tech., 1949; MS, Iowa State U., 1950, PhD, 1952; DSc (hon.), S.D. Sch. Mines and Tech., 2000. Broadcast and TV engr., 1946-49; mem. faculty Iowa State U., 1949-60; prof. elec. engring., 1959-60; prof. elec. engring., head Sch. Elec. Engring., Okla. State U., Stillwater, 1960-76, Clark A. Dunn prof. engring., 1976-86, dir. Engring. Energy Lab., 1976-86; pres. InEn Corp, 1972-88; v.p. S.D. Sch. Mines and Tech., Rapid City, 1988-93; pres. Dakota Alpha Inc., 1994. Chmn. ad hoc com. NAS, 1976, 79, mem. bd. sci. and tech. in devel., 1983; chmn. NAS/Philippine Govt. del. to Philippines, 1978, Indonesia, 1979, India, 1979, 85, 89, Thailand, 1990, 93; cons. industry and govt.; mem. indsl. com. TV frequency allocation studies FCC, 1957-59. Author: Nonlinear electrical Networks, 1960; also articles; co-author: Lines, Waves and Antennas, 1961, 2d edit., 1973; contbr. sects. to 6 engring. handbooks. Served with USNR, World War II. Named S.D. Profl. Engr. of Yr., S.D. Engring. Soc., 1995, Disting. Alumnus, SD Sch. Mines and Tech., 2006. Fellow IEEE; mem. NSPE (life, Disting. Svc. award 1997), Sigma Xi, Sigma Tau, Tau Beta pi, Eta Kappa Nu, Pi Mu Epsilon. Achievements include patented nonlinear systems, color TV systems, direct energy conversions systems. Home: Rapid City, SD. Died Feb. 21, 2007.

HUIE, IRVING RAYMOND, construction company executive; b. Catskill, NY, Sept. 30, 1928; s. Irving V.A. and Irene G. (Gartl) H.; m. Patricia Cronin, Mar. 27, 1955; children— Michael, Barbara, Terence, Peter, James, Eileen, Patricia, Kevin. BCE, Rensselaer Poly. Inst., Troy, NY, 1950; postgrad., Northwestern U. From engr. to v.p. Perini Corp., Framingham, Mass., 1959-81, sr. v.p. heavy constrn., from 1981, also bd. dirs., now ret. Served with C.E., AUS, 1950-53. Recipient Outstanding Achievement in Constrn. award The Moles, 1990 Mem. ASCE, Am. Soc. Mil. Engrs. Democrat. Roman Catholic. Died Aug. 6, 2007.

HULL, ARTHUR NILES, marine meteorologist; b. Troy, NY, Oct. 26, 1926; s. Alson Joy and Fannie (Niles) Hull; m. Dawn Harriet Harwood, Dec. 11, 1948; 1 child, Kathleen Pillsbury Rutledge. BS, U.S. Naval Acad., 1947; BS in Meteorology, US Naval Postgrad. Sch., 1952, MS in Meteorology, 1961; PhD in Meteorology, U. Hawaii, 1973. Commd. ensign, advanced through grades to lt. USN, 1947; comm. officer, forecaster U.S. Navy Fleet Weather Ctrl., Port Lyautey, French Morocco, 1952—55; asst. staff meteorologist Operation Deepfreeze I, Antarctica, 1955—56; instr. U.S. Naval Postgrad. Sch., Monterey, Calif., 1959—61; rsch. meteorologist Extended Forecast Bur., Wash., 1961—62, Weather Bur. Rsch. Facility, Las Vegas, 1962—66; techniques devel. meteorologist Nat. Weather Svc. Pacific Region Hdqrs., Honolulu, 1966—73; meteorologist-in-charge, Nev. State mgr. Nat. Weather Svc. Forecast Office, Reno, 1974—76, meteorologist-in-charge, Wash. State mgr. Seattle, 1976—82; marine svcs. mgr. Global Weather Dynamics, Inc., Monterey, 1982—84; pres. Art Hull Marine Weather, Carmel, Calif., from 1984. Mem. Sea Use Coun., Seattle, 1976—82. Contbr. articles to profl. jours. Mem. Wash. State Mt. St. Helens Adv. Com., Olympia, 1980—82. NOAA scholar in oceanography, 1968—69. Mem.: Nat. Weather Assn. (councillor 1976—78, marine com. from 1984), Am. Meteorol. Soc. (cert. cons. meteorologist). Home: Carmel, Calif. Died Feb. 7, 2007.

HULL, GORDON FERRIE, physicist; b. Hanover, NH, May 23, 1912; s. Gordon Ferrie and Wilhelmine (Brandt) H.; m. Mona Jerusha Cutler, June 24, 1937; children: Gordon, Mona, David, Jonathan, Berney. AB, Dartmouth Coll., 1933, MA, 1934; PhD, Yale U., 1937. Rsch. physicist Bell Telephone Labs., Murray Hill, N.J., 1937-44; prof. physics Dartmouth Coll., Hanover, N.H., 1944-55; sci. officer Office Naval Rsch., London and Washington, 1949-51; sci. attaché Am. Embassy, Bern, Switzerland, 1951-52; pres. Hull Assocs., Sci. Cons. to Industry and Ednl. Insts., Concord and Rockport, Mass., from 1955. Contbr. over 50 articles to profl. publs. Chmn. Rockport Planning Bd., 1975-90. Fellow AAAS, Am. Phys. Soc. Achievements include microwave and optical analogies. Home: Rockport, Mass. Died July 17, 2006.

HULSE, JOHN EDWARD, former telephone company executive; b. Hannibal, Mo., June 11, 1933; s. Giles and Edythe (Watt) Hulse; m. Mary Jean Pfeiffer, Aug. 21, 1954; children: Celine, Michelle, Christi, Mary Pat, Michael. BS, U.S.D., 1955. Gen. comml. and mktg. mgr. Northwestern Bell Tele. Co., Omaha, 1968—72; dir. mktg. sales project AT&T, NYC, 1972—74, v.p., CEO Sioux Falls, SD, 1974—75, Mpls., 1975—79, sr. v.p Omaha, 1979—81; exec. v.p., CFO Pacific Telesis Group (formerly Pacific Tel. & Tel.), San Francisco, 1981—82, vice-chmn. bd.,CFO, 1983—92. Trustee San Francisco Ballet Assn. Mem.: Pvt. Sector Coun., World Affairs Coun. No. Calif., San Francisco C. of C. (dir., treas.), Telephone Pioneers Am. (sr. v.p. 1990, pres. 1991), Fin. Execs. Inst. (pres. San Francisco chpt. 1986, dir. western area 1987-90), 1987—90), Blackhawk Country, Commonwealth, San Francisco Bankers. Home: La Quinta, Calif. Died Dec. 24, 2005.

HUMBARD, REX EMANUEL, evangelist; b. Little Rock, Aug. 13, 1919; s. Alpha Emanuel and Martha Bell (Childers) H.; m. Maude Aimee Jones, Aug. 2, 1942; children— Rex Emanuel, Don Raymond, Aimee Elizabeth, Charles Raymond. D.D. (hon.), Trinity Coll., Dunedin, Fla., 1970; L.H.D. (hon.), Oral Roberts U., Tulsa, 1973. Ordained to ministry Evang. Ch., 1943; evangelistic radio ministry, 1933—; founder, pastor Cathedral of Tomorrow, Akron, Ohio, 1952-83, chmn. bd. dirs.; worldwide evangelistic TV ministry, 1952—82; chmn. bd. Rex Humbard Ministry in Can.; del. Congress on Evangelism, Lausanne, Switzerland, 1974; pub. Rex Humbard Prophecy Bible, 1984. Author: Put God on Main Street, 1970, Miracles in My Life, 1971, The Third Dimension, 1972, Personal Promises from God, 1984, To Tell the World, 1984, also numerous spiritual periodicals, tracts and recordings. Home: Boynton Beach, Fla. Died Feb. 21, 2007.

HUMPHREY, WILLIAM ROLAND, aerospace company executive; b. Wilcoe, W.Va., Dec. 2, 1917; s. Church Gordon and Clarice (Booth) H.; student Harvard, 1937, Am. Mgmt. Assn., 1962-63; BS cum laude, U. Hartford, 1968, MBA magna cum laude, 1978; postgrad. Indsl. Coll. of Armed Forces, 1968-69; m. Alice E. Waters, June 30, 1956; children by previous marriage: Clarice Hilda, Margaret Helena, Stephen William. With N.Y., N.H. & H. R.R., 1937-50, traffic rep., Hartford, Conn., 1944-50; asst. traffic mgr. Billings & Spencer Co., Hartford, 1950-52; traffic mgr. Mattatuck Mfg. Co., Waterbury, Conn., 1952-56; traffic rep. Clipper Carloading Co., Chgo., 1957; traffic mgr. Kaman Aerospace Corp., Bloomfield, Conn., 1957—, dir. traffic, 1989—. Asst. dir. carrier agy. coordination and liaison Office Emergency Transp., 1964—; mem. Nat. Def. Exec. Res., 1954—; asst. dir. for resource mgmt. U.S. Dept. Transp., 1971—; adj. prof. dept. mktg. Austin Dunham Barney Sch. Bus. and Pub. Adminstrn., U. Hartford, 1974—; mem. DOD/NASA Traffic Logistics Interface Com., 1989—. Trustee East Hartford Inter-Ch. Housing Adminstrn., v.p., 1971—. Served with USCGR, 1940-44. Mem. Aerospace Industries Assn. (nat. vice chmn. traffic com. 1962-63), Nat. Indsl. Transp. League, New Eng. Shipper-Carrier Council, New Eng. Shippers Adv. Bd., Am. Soc. Traffic and Transp., Conn. Internat. Trade Assn., U.S. Naval Inst. Nat. Def. Transp. Assn., Am. Soc. Internat. Execs., Greater Hartford C. of C., Capitol Region Transp. Assn., Nat. Wildlife Fedn., Am. Mktg. Assn., Nat. Assn. Purchasing Mgmt. (life cert. purchasing mgr.), Charter Oak Shippers Assn., Am. Security Council (com. strikes in transp.), Internat. Platform Assn., Travelers' Century Club, Transp. Club, Conn. Quarter-century Traffic Club, City Club, Kiwanis, Delta Nu Alpha. Methodist (pres. ofcl. bd. 1965—, pres. bd. trustees). Home: East Hartford, Conn. Died June 3, 2006.

HUMPHRY, JAMES, III, retired librarian, publishing executive, educator; b. Springfield, Mass., July 21, 1916; s. James and Elizabeth Lucy (Ames) H.; m. Priscilla Eaton, Dec. 26, 1942; children: Susan H. Zolnier, Elizabeth Ames Schnabel. AB, Harvard U., 1939; MS, Columbia U., 1941. Reference asst. N.Y. Pub. Library, 1939-41, 46, chief map divsn., 1946; librarian, prof. bibliography Colby Coll.; bus. mgr. Colby Coll. Press, 1947-57; chief librarian Met. Mus. Art, 1957-68; v.p. H.W. Wilson Co., Bronx, 1968-82, pres., dir. found., 1995-2000, also bd. dirs., from 1968; prof. Pratt Inst., Bklyn., 1982-98. Lectr. Columbia Sch. Libr. Svc., 1967-68; vis. assoc. prof. Grad. Sch. Libr. Studies, U. Hawaii, 1983; libr. cons. Am. Heritage, 1965-68, John Wiley & Sons, 1966-69, Coun. Advancement Small Colls., 1956, Gossage Regan Assocs., N.Y.C., 1988-96; coord. Maine Libr. Assn. for ALA sponsored Library Services bill, 1948-49, 55-57; nat. bd. Libr. Presdl. Papers, 1967-69; adminstr. grants-in-aid program N.Y. State Council Arts, 1967-68 Compiler, Library of Edwin Arlington Robinson, 1950; Editor: (with Carl J. Weber) Fitzgerald's Rubaiyat, 1959; Contbr. articles to mags. and jours. Trustee, chmn. adv. com. Archives Am. Art, 1967-88; mem. fine arts vis. com. Harvard U., 1967-73; mem. adv. council St. John's U. Congress for Librarians, 1963-67; bd. dirs. Huguenot YMCA; trustee N.Y. Met. Reference and Research Library Agy., 1967-77, Westchester Library System, 1974-83, New Rochelle Pub. Libr., 1977-87, Thomas Paine Nat. Hist. Assn., 1980-96; pres. Westchester Libr. System. 1980-82, New Rochelle Pub. Library 1979-80, 82, New Rochelle Pub. Libr. Found., 1994-96. With AUS, 1942-46, maj. U.S. Army, 1951-54; lt. col. USAR. Mem. ALA (councilor 1959-63, 67-69, chmn. com. on Wilson index reference services div. 1959-65, mem. subscription books com. 1963-66), Met. Mus. Art Employees Assn. (pres. 1961-63, gov. 1958-66), Maine Library Assn. (pres. 1955-56), Am. Assn. Museums (chmn. library group), Archons of Colophon (convener 1963-65), N.Y. Library Assn. (cons.), Spl. Libraries Assn. (chpt. vice chmn., chmn. mus. group 1962-64, N.Y. conf. chmn. 1967), Assn. Coll. and Research Libraries (pres., dir. 1966-69), Internat. Council Museums (corr.) Clubs: Grolier, N.Y. Library (council 1959-67, pres. 1965-66), Harvard (N.Y.C.). Home: Bethlehem, Pa. Died Jan. 11, 2007.

HUNGATE, WILLIAM LEONARD, retired federal judge, former congressman; b. Benton, Ill., Dec. 14, 1922; s. Leonard Wathen and Maude Irene (Williams) H.; m. Dorothy N. Wilson, Apr. 13, 1944; children: William David, Margie Kay (Mrs. Branson L. Wood III). AB, U. Mo., 1943; LL.B., Harvard U., 1948; LL.D. (hon.), Culver-Stockton Coll., Canton, Mo., 1968; JD (hon.), Central Meth. Coll., Fayette, Mo., 1975. Bar: Mo. 1948, Ill. 1949, U.S. Supreme Ct 1960, D.C. 1967. Practiced law, Troy, Mo., 1948-68, St. Louis, 1977-79; sr. ptnr. Hungate & Grewach LLP, 1956-68; ptnr. Thompson & Mitchell, St. Louis, 1977-79; judge U.S. Dist. Ct. (ea. dist.) Mo., 1979-92; pros. atty. Lincoln County, Mo., 1951-55; spl. asst. atty. gen. State of Mo., 1958-64. Rsch. adminstrn. criminal justice in U.S. Am. Bar Found., 1956; mem. 88th-94th congresses, 9th Dist. Mo.; mem. judiciary com., chmn. subcom. criminal justice, select com. on small bus., chmn. subcom. on activities of regulatory agys.; vis. prof. polit. sci. U. Mo., St. Louis, 1977-79. Author: It Wasn't Funny at the Time, 1994. Chmn. small bus. adv. com. Treasury Dept., 1977; chmn. Mo. Gov.'s Commn. on Campaign Reform and Ofcl. Conduct, 1978-79; mem. Adv. Com. on Criminal Rules, 1977-86. Mem. ABA (nat. conf. of fed. trial judges exec. com. 1980-86, chmn. 1985-86), FBA, ASCAP, Ill. Bar Assn., Mo. Bar Assn., Harvard Law Sch. Assn. Mo. (pres. 1962-64, 83-84, coun. mem.), Mo. Squires, Jud. Conf. U.S. (com. on jud. br. 1987-90), 8th Cir. Dist. Judges Assn. (pres. 1984-86). Mem. Troy Christian Ch. (chmn. bd. 1964). Club: Kiwanian (Troy) (pres. 1951, lt. gov. 1959). Home: Saint Louis, Mo. Died June 22, 2007.

HUNT, JOHN MAURICE, foundation administrator; b. Mpls., Sept. 23, 1944; s. Maurice Glenn and Mary Alice (James) Hunt. Attended, St. Michael's Coll., 1962—64; BA, Mt. Angel Sem. Coll., 1966, postgrad., 1966—68. Coord. activities therapy Nazareth Hosp., Albuquerque, 1969—74; adminstr. arthritis project, divsn. regional med. programs U. N.Mex. Sch. Medicine, 1974—76; exec. dir. Arthritis Found., Albuquerque, from 1975, mem. nat. rsch. com., 1978. Instr. U. N.Mex. Cmty. Coll., 1979, 80; cons. to consultation edn. dept. Bernalillo County Mental Health/Mental Retardation Ctr., 1980, 81. Chmn. Nat. Health Agencies Coordinating Com., 1976-77; mem. human rsch. com. Presbyn. Hosp. Ctr., 1976-; profl. adv. bd. Share Your Care/Sr. Daily Living program, 1977-; exec. com. Hosp. Home Health Care/St. Joseph's Presbyn. Hosps., 1978, profl. adv. group mem., 1976-, chmn., 1978; bd. dirs. N.Mex. Assn. Home Health Agencies, 1975-77. Mem.: Profl. Staff Assn. Arthritis Found. Democrat. Home: Albuquerque, N.Mex. Died Oct. 2, 2006.

HUNT, JOHNNIE BRYAN, trucking company executive; b. Heber Springs, Ark., Feb. 28, 1927; m. Johnelle DeBusk, 1952; children: Bryan, Jane. With Superior Forwarding Co., 1945-61; chmn. J.B. Hunt Transport Inc., Towell, Ark., 1961—95, sr. chmn., 1995—2004. Died Dec. 7, 2006.

HUNT, LAMAR, professional football team executive; b. El Dorado, Ark., Aug. 2, 1932; s. H.L. and Lyda (Bunker) H.; m. Rosemary Carr (div.); m. Norma Hunt; children: Lamar Jr., Sharron, Clark, Daniel. BS, So. Meth. U., 1956. Founder, owner Kans. City Chiefs (formerly Dallas Texans), 1959—2006, pres., 1959-76, chmn., 1977-78; founder, pres. Am. Football League (became Am. Football Conf.-NFL 1970), 1960—69; pres. Am. Football Conf., 1970—2006. Co-founder N. Am. Soccer League, 1967—84. Bd. dirs. Profl. Football Hall of Fame, Canton, Ohio. Named Salesman of Yr., Kansas City Advt. and Sales Execs. Club, 1963, Southwesterner of Yr., Tex. Sportswriters Assn., 1959; recipient Medal of Honor Nat. Soccer Hall of Fame, 1999 inducted into the Pro Football Hall of Fame, 1972, Nat. Soccer Hall of Fame, 1982, Tex. Sports Hall of Fame, 1984, Internat. Tennis Hall of Fame, 1993. Died Dec. 13, 2006.

HUNT, RAYMOND GEORGE, management educator; b. Buffalo, July 1, 1928; s. William Raymond and Florence (Elkington) H.; m. Viola Carolyn Wannenwetsch, June 3, 1949; children— Gregory William, Karen Susan. B.A. magna cum laude, U. Buffalo, 1952, Ph.D., 1958. Asst. prof. Washington U., St. Louis, 1958-61; assoc. prof. SUNY-Buffalo, 1961-64, prof., 1965—, chmn. Sch. Mgmt., 1978—, assoc. dir. China M.B.A. Program, 1984-87; sr. fellow, dir. research William O. Douglas Inst., Seattle, 1975—; bd. dirs. China Trade Ctr. Co-author, editor: Current Perspectives in Social Psychology, 1963-76; Classic Contributions to Social Psychology, 1972, Impacts of Racism on White Americans, 1981. Author: Strategies for Management, 1974. Served with U.S. Army, 1946-48. Recipient DeRoy award Soc. Study of Social Problems, 1963. Fellow Am. Psychol. Assn. (mem. various coms.); mem. Acad. Mgmt. (mem. various coms.), Internat. Assn. Applied Psychology, Phi Beta Kappa, Sigma Xi, Beta Gamma Sigma. Democrat. Home: Buffalo, NY. Died Apr. 29, 2006.

HUNTER, HARRY LAYMOND, physician, pharmaceutical company executive; b. Girard, Kans., Mar. 7, 1923; s. Adolphus Osborne and Mary Elizabeth (White) H.; m. Louise R. Leone, Aug. 19, 1949 (dec. July 1982); children— John Patrick, Mary Anne; m. Emily F. Esau, Oct. 19, 1985. A.B., U. Ill., Urbana, 1944; B.S., U. Ill.-Chgo., 1944, M.D., 1946. Diplomate: Am. Bd. Internal Medicine. Intern Gorgas Hosp., C.Z., 1946-47, resident in internal medicine, 1947-48; resident Ill. Central Hosp., Chgo., 1949-50, U. Mich., Ann Arbor, 1950-51; assoc. chief medicine Blanchard Valley Hosp., Findlay, Ohio, 1951-52; dir. exec. health Ill. Central Hosp., Chgo., 1953-57, assoc. chief medicine, 1957-64, chief med. officer, 1968-74; clin. assoc. prof. medicine U. Ill. Coll. Medicine, Chgo., 1953-76; assoc. dir. clin. pharmacology Abbott Labs., North Chicago, Ill., 1965-67, med. dir., 1975-76; dir. clin. studies Mead Johnson & Co., Evansville, Ind., 1976-83, dir. med. services, 1984-88. Contbr. numerous articles to profl. jours.; patentee med. devices. Bd. dirs. Ill. Council on Alcoholism, Chgo., 1970-74, Am. Cancer Soc., Evansville, 1978-80. Served to capt. U.S. Army, 1946-49; Panama. Fellow ACP, Am. Soc. Clin. Oncology, Chgo. Soc. Internal Medicine, Chgo. Inst. Medicine; mem. AMA. Died Feb. 24, 2006.

HUNTER, JOE (JOSEPH EDWARD HUNTER), musician; b. Jackson, Tenn., Nov. 19, 1927; s. John G. and Vada Idona (Dreke) H.; m. Mable Daisy Miller, June 15, 1957 (div.); children— Joseph Jr., Michelle Dana. Student Lane Coll., U. Detroit, Detroit Inst. Tech. Profl. pianist, 1956-59; pianist, arranger, band leader Motown Record Corp., Detroit, 1959-61; band leader with Jackie Wilson, 1961; musical dir. Pied Piper records, 1967-68; musical dir. cons. Brohun Pub., 1968—2007; cons. various chs., rec. artists and firms. Served with USAF, 1946-49. Recipient awards Grammy Lifetime Achievement award, 2004, Black Music Found., Upper Room, Mother Waddles' Perpetual Mission. Mem. Nat. Com. for Rec. Arts, Detroit Fedn. Musicians. Lodge: Masons. Composer numerous published songs. Home: Detroit, Mich. Died Feb. 2, 2007.

HURD, JAMES BRADDOCK, retired physician; b. Chgo., Mar. 29, 1921; s. Max Harold and Eunice (Braddock) H.; m. Jean Wescott, June 12, 1943; children: Barbara Wescott, Ann Braddock, Janet Darrow; m. Clare Lutes, July 6, 1974. AB, Amherst Coll., 1942; MD, Northwestern U., 1946; M.Sc. in Pathology, 1950. Intern Evanston (Ill.) Hosp., 1945-46; fellow in pathology Cook County Hosp., Chgo., 1948-49, resident in medicine, 1950-51; fellow in medicine New Eng. Deaconess Hosp., Boston, 1949-50; pvt. practice Chgo., from 1951; mem. sr. attending staff Chgo. Wesley Meml. Hosp. (name changed to Northwestern Meml. Hosp.), from 1957, chief med. service D, 1961-74, sec. staff, 1961-64, vice chief staff, 1964-66, chief staff, 1966-68; mem. faculty Northwestern U. Med. Sch., from 1951, asst. prof. internal medicine, 1965-71, asso. prof., from 1971. Served to capt. M.C. AUS, 1946-48. Mem. Am. Diabetes Assn. (dir. 1961—, chmn. com. affiliates 1963—, chmn. assembly affiliate dels. and state govs. 1961-63, v.p. 1968, pres. 1970-71), Diabetes Assn. Greater Chgo. (dir. 1952—, pres. 1959-61, chmn. camp. com. 1952—), A.M.A., Joslin Soc. Clubs: Glen View (Golf, Ill.). Republican. Home: Barrington, Ill. Died June 9, 2006.

HURLBUT, ROY BROWN, business executive; b. Havana, Cuba, Oct. 23, 1927; s. Roy Cole and Emma Lou (Brown) H. (parents Am. citizens); B.S., Heald Coll., 1962; M.B.A., U. San Francisco, 1968; m. Candis Carol Smyk, July 16, 1967; 1 dau. by previous marriage, Ellayne Margaret. Asst. engr. Pacific Gas & Electric Co., San Francisco, 1949-66, forecast engr., 1970-71; systems planning engr. Lockheed Missile & Space Co., Sunnyvale, Calif., 1966-68; sr. budget analyst U. Calif., Berkeley, 1968-69; utility engr., pub. utility commr. State of Oreg., Salem, 1972-74; sr. coordinator, cost and scheduling Alyeska Pipeline Service Co., Kenmore, Wash., 1975-77; sr. cost engr. Alyeska Pipeline Service Co., Anchorage, 1977-78; sr. ops. analytical engr. Atlantic Richfield Co., Anchorage, 1978-80; commr. Anchorage Mcpl. Light & Power, 1980; N.W. power mgr. Anaconda Industries, Vancouver, Wash., 1980-82; chief elec. engr. Dallah Establishment, Riyadh, Saudi Arabia, 1983—. Mem. Nat. Assn. Bus. Economists, IEEE. Clubs: Masons (32 deg.), Shriners. Home: Vancouver, Wash. Died Dec. 9, 2006.

HURN, RAYMOND WALTER, minister, religious order administrator; b. Ontario, Oreg., June 27, 1921; s. Walter H. and Bertha Sultana (Gray) H.; m. Madelyn Lenore Kirkpatrick, Dec. 30, 1941; children: Constance Isbell, Jacqueline Oliver. BA, So. Nazarene U., 1943; DD (hon.), So. Nazarene U, 1967; postgrad., U. Tulsa, 1946-47, Fuller Sem., Pasadena, Calif., 1978-81. Ordained to ministry Ch. of Nazarene, 1943. Pastor Ch. of Nazarene chs., Kans., Okla., Ga., Oreg., 1943-59; dist. supt. Ch. of Nazarene, West Tex. dist., Tex., 1959-68; dir. home missions and ch. extension Internat. Hdqrs. Ch. of Nazarene, Kansas City, Mo., 1968-85, gen. supt., 1985-93. Author: Mission Possible, 1973, Black Evangelism, Which Way from Here, 1973, Spiritual Gifts Workshop, 1977, Finding Your Ministry, 1980, Mission Action Sourcebook, 1980, Unleashing the Lay Potential in the Sunday School, 1986, The Rising Tide: New Churches for the New Millenium, 1997. Recipient Exec. award Am. Inst. Ch. Growth, 1980, B award Bethany So. Nazarene Univ., 1982, Heritage award So. Nazarene U., 1993, Lifetime Achievement award Assn. of Nazarene Bldg. Prof., 1993, Multicultural Fellowship award, 1993; named Gen. Supt. Emeritus, 23rd Gen. Assembly of the Ch. of the Nazarene, 1993. Home: Olathe, Kans. Died Jan. 20, 2007.

HURST, VERNON JAMES, geologist, educator; b. Glenmore, Ga., July 18, 1923; s. Lonnie T. and Essie (Arnold) H.; m. Julia Corneil Wells, Nov. 5, 1950; children: Marc V., Karen Anne. Student, U. S.D., 1943; S.D., State Coll., 1944; BS, U. Ga., 1951; MS, Emory U., 1952; PhD, Johns Hopkins, 1954. Geol. cons., bldg. contractor, Alaska, 1946-50; geologist N.J. Zinc Co., 1951; geologist, chief mineralogist Ga. Dept. Mines, Mining and Geology, 1956-61; prof., head dept. geology U. Ga., Athens, 1961-69, chmn. phys. scis. div., 1966-69, research prof. geology, from 1969. Cons. geologist, Alaska, Colombia, Panama, P.R., Honduras; pres Research Analysis, Inc.; Past mem. Environmental Scis. Panel, NSF; mem. marine resources adv com. Coastal Plains Regional Commn.; Trustee Coastal Plains Center for Marine Devel. Services; past chmn. bd. govs. Center for Research in Coll. Instrn. of Sci. and Math. Served with USAAF, 1943-46, ETO; Served with USAAF, PTO. Fellow Geol. Soc. Am. (past chmn. S.E. sect.), Mineral. Soc. Am.; mem. Ga. Acad. Sci. (past pres.), Soc. Econ. Geologists, Ga. Geol. Soc. (pres.), Clay Minerals Soc., Fine Particle Soc., Societe Francaise de Mineralogie et Cristallographie, Southeastern Assn. Spectrographers, Sigma Xi. Clubs: Kiwanian. Democrat. Presbyterian. Home: Athens, Ga. Died July 28, 2006.

HUTCHINGS, GEORGE HENRY, food company executive; b. Fort Worth, June 23, 1922; s. George H. and Emma (Harder) H.; m. Edith Van Gils, Mar. 23, 1946 (dec.); children: Mark Dennis Lisa Ellen; m. Elizabeth T. Storey, Apr. 10, 1968 (dec.). Student, Tex. A&M, 1940-42. Analyst mktg. research Frito Food Mfg., Dallas, 1946, mgr. mktg. research Los Angeles, 1946-57, div. sales mgr. San Mateo, Calif., 1958-60, div. gen. mgr., 1961, v.p., 1961-62; v.p. for ops. Western zone, from 1962; pres. Nalley's, Inc., Tacoma, 1964, Nalley's div. W.R. Grace & Co., from 1966, ret. Tacoma, 1972-81; pres. Wash. Beverages, Inc., Tacoma, 1972-81. Dir., mem. exec. com. Puget Sound Nat. Bank, Tacoma; cons. 1964-83; dir. mem. examining com. Key Bank of Wash., Tacoma, 1993-94, ret., 1994. Served to capt. USAAF, 1942-46. Decorated D.F.C., Air medal with 7 clusters. Mem. Masons. Baptist. Home: Tacoma, Wash. Died July 21, 2007.

HUTCHINSON, DUANE DOUGLAS, storyteller, writer, clergyman; b. Elgin, Nebr., June 16, 1929; s. William Clyde and Eva Susan (Martin) H.; m. Marilyn Ann Burton, Sept. 3, 1950; children— Stephen Kent, James Wesley. B.A. in Edn., Kearney State Coll., 1953; Th.M., Perkins Sch. Theology, So. Meth. U., 1956; postgrad. U. Chgo., 1956-57; M.A. in English, U. Nebr., 1979. Ordained to ministry United Methodist Ch., 1954; cert. pub. sch. tchr., Nebr. Pastor, Chester and Hubbell, Nebr., 1957-61; teaching fellow Centennial Coll., U. Nebr., 1979-81; campus minister U. Nebr., 1961-79; travelling storyteller Nebr. Arts Coun., S.D. Arts Coun. and Iowa Arts Coun., 1979—; condr. writing and storytelling workshops. Author: Doc Graham: Sandhills Doctor, 1970; Exon: Biography of a Governor, 1973; Images of Mary, 1971; Savidge Brothers: Sandhills Aviators, 1982; Storytelling Tips: How to Love, Learn and Relate a Story, 1983, A Storyteller's Ghost Stories, 1987, A Storyteller's Hometown, 1989; Grotto Father, Artist-Priest of the West Bend Grotto, 1989, A Storyteller's Ghost Stories Book 2, 1990, Book 3, 1992; The Gunny Wolf and Other Fairy Tales, 1992; Bily Brothers, Wood Carvers and Clock Makers, 1993, Matt: The Story of Lewis Edward Mattingly, 1995, Sister Augusta: Teacher from Fancy Farm, 1995, The History of the Lincoln Mutual Life Insurance Company, 1996. County del. Democratic party; past pres. local chpt. UN Assn. Mem. Nat. Assn. Preservation and Perpetuation of Storytelling, Nebr. Library Assn. (Mari Sandoz award 1996), Nat. Council Tchrs. English. Home: Lincoln, Nebr. Died Mar. 5, 2007.

HUTCHISON, DORRIS JEANNETTE, retired microbiologist, educator; b. Carrsville, Ky., Oct. 31, 1918; d. John W. and Maud (Short) H. BS, Western Ky. U., 1940; MS, U. Ky., 1943; PhD, Rutgers U., 1949. Instr. Russell Sage Coll., 1942-44, Vassar Coll., 1944-46; research asst. Rutgers U., 1946-48, research assoc., 1948-49; instr. Wellesley Coll., 1949-51; asst. Sloan-Kettering Inst., NYC, 1951-56, assoc., 1956-60, assoc. mem., 1960-69, mem., 1969-90, mem. emeritus, 1990—2007, sect. head, 1956-90, acting chief div. exptl. chemotherapy, 1965-66, div. chief drug resistance, 1967-72, co-head lab. exptl. tumor therapy, 1973-74, lab. head drug resistance and cytoregulation, 1973-84, coordinator field edn., 1975-81. Instr. Sloan-Kettering div. Cornell U. Grad. Sch. Med. Sci., N.Y.C., 1952-53, rsch. assoc., 1953-54, asst. prof., 1954-58, assoc. prof., 1958-70, prof. microbiology, 1970-90, prof. emeritus, 1990-2007, chmn. biology unit, 1968-74, assoc. dir., 1974-87; assoc. dean Cornell U. Grad. Sch. Med. Sci., 1978-87, asst. dean Cornell U., Ithaca, 1978-87; mem. Meml. Sloan-Kettering Cancer Ctr., 1984-90, mem. emeritus, 1990-2007; del. dir. Am. Cancer Soc., Inc., 1986-90. Bd. dirs. Westchester div. Am. Cancer Soc., 1976-90, exec. com., 1976-91; project chmn. Target 5, 1977-80, v.p., 1979-81, pres., 1981-83, sec., 1983-87, charter mem. So. Westchester Unit, 1984, pres., 1984-86. Named to Order of Ky. Cols., 1988; recipient Disting. Alumna, Western Ky. U., 2003; faculty fellow, Vassar Coll., 1946, USPHS fellow, 1951—53, Phillippe Found. fellow, Paris, 1959, Dorris J. Hutchison fellowship established in her honor, 1999. Fellow N.Y. Acad. Sci., Am. Acad. Microbiology (charter), N.Y. Acad. Medicine (assoc.); mem. AAAS, Am. Assn. for Cancer Edn., Am. Assn. Cancer Research (emeritus), Harvey Soc., Genetics Soc. Am., Am. Inst. Nutrition, Am. Soc. for Microbiology (hon., councilor N.Y.C. br. 1954-58, pres. N.Y.C. br. 1958-60, nat. councilor 1961-63, chmn. nat. meeting 1967, mem. pres.'s fellowship com. 1973-76, chmn. 1975-76), Soc. for Cryobiology (hon. mem.), Am. Genetic Assn., Internat. Soc. Biochem. Pharmacology, N.Y. Soc. Ky. Women (pres. 1988-2007), N.Y. Found. Ky. Women (pres. 1990-2000), Bronxville Field Club, Elizabeth Hamilton Cullem Svc. Club, 2000-07. Achievements include numerous publs. antibiotics and chems. effective in treatment of Tb and leukemia, reports on mechanisms explaining how leukemic cells become resistant to treatment; searches for more effective antileukemia drugs. Home: Mystic, Conn. Died May 9, 2007.

HUTCHISON, WILLIAM ROBERT, history educator; b. San Francisco, May 21, 1930; s. Ralph Cooper and Harriet (Thompson) H.; m. Virginia Quay, Aug. 16, 1952; children: Joseph Cooper, Catherine Eaton, Margaret Sidney, Elizabeth Quay. BA, Hamilton Coll., 1951, DHL (hon.), 1991; BA (Fulbright scholar), Oxford U., 1953, MA, 1957; PhD, Yale U., 1956; MA (hon.), Harvard U., 1968. Instr. history Hunter Coll., 1956-58; assoc. prof. Am. studies Am. U., 1958-64, prof. history and Am. studies, 1964-68; Charles Warren prof. history of religion in Am. Harvard U., 1968—2000; master Winthrop House, 1974-79; Charles Warren rsch. prof., from 2000. Vis. assoc. prof. history U. Wis., 1963-64 Author: The Transcendentalist Ministers: Church Reform in the New England Renaissance, 1959, The Modernist Impulse in American Protestantism, 1976, Errand to the World: American Protestant Thought and Foreign Missions, 1987; Religious Pluralism in America: The Contentious History of a Founding Ideal, 2003; editor: American Protestant Thought, the Liberal Era, 1968; co-editor and joint author: Missionary Ideologies in the Imperialist Era, 1982; editor and joint author: Between the Times: The Travail of the Protestant Establishment in America, 1900-1960, 1989; co-editor and joint author: Many are Chosen: Divine Election and Western Nationalism, 1994; contbr. articles to profl. jours. Recipient Brewer prize Am. Soc. Ch. History, 1957; Am. Religious Book award, 1976; Guggenheim fellow, 1960-61; fellow Charles Warren Ctr. for Studies in Am. History, Harvard, 1966-67; Fulbright Sr. Research scholar Free U., Berlin, 1976; Fulbright Disting. lectr. in Am. history India, summer 1981, USIA lectr. East Asia and Pacific, 1983; Fulbright Western European Regional Research grantee, 1987; Fulbright Disting. lectr. in Am. hist. and rel., Indonesia, 1993; Olaus Petri lectr., Uppsala U. (Sw.), 1996. Mem. Am. Hist. Assn., Orgn. Am. Historians, Am. Studies Assn., Am. Soc. Ch. History (pres. 1981), Unitarian Universalist Hist. Soc., Mass. Hist. Soc., Phi Beta Kappa. Democrat. Mem. Soc. Of Friends. Home: Cambridge, Mass. Died Dec. 16, 2005.

HUTTON, HERBERT J., federal judge; b. Phila., Nov. 26, 1937; m. Valerie Russell, 1961 (div. 1991); children: Brandon, Jeffrey, Debbie. AB, Lincoln U., 1959; JD, Temple U., 1962. With Housing and Home Fin. Agy., 1962-64; mem. firm Norris Brown & Hall, 1964-69, Norris, Wells & Neal, 1969-72, Norris & Wells, 1972-76, Simpkins & Tucker, 1977-88; hearing officer Bd. Revision Taxes, Phila., 1982-88; judge US Dist. Ct. (ea. dist.) Pa., Phila., 1988—2003, sr. judge, 2003—07. Recipient Bd. Dirs. City Trusts' award, 1988. Mem. Phila Bar Assn. (Medal of Svc. 1982), Phila. Bar Found. (trustee), Fed. Judges Assn. Died Apr. 6, 2007.

HYDE, HERBERT LEE, lawyer; b. Bryson City, NC, Dec. 12, 1925; s. Ervin M. and Alice (Medlin) H.; m. Kathryn Long, Dec. 25, 1949; children: Deborah, Lynn, Karen, Benjamin, Jane, William. AB, W. Carolina U., 1951; JD, NYU, 1954. Bar: N.C. 1954, U.S. Dist. Ct. (we. dist.) N.C. 1954, U.S. Ct. Appeals (4th cir.) 1957, U.S. Supreme Ct. 1962, U.S. Dist. Ct. (mid. dist.) N.C. 1975, U.S. Dist. Ct. (ea. dist.) N.C. 1980. Ptnr. Van Winkle, Buck, Wall, Starnes & Hyde, Asheville, NC, 1954-79; sole practice Asheville, from 1979. Sec. N.C. Dept. Crime Control and Pub. Safety, Raleigh, 1979. Author: Genuine Hyde, 1976, My Home is in the Smoky Mountains, 1998, Of Truth and Freedom, 2001, Living and Learning, Just Natural, 2001, Mountain Speaking, 2002; writer (song) The Cold Icy Waters of Swain. Senator N.C. Senate, Raleigh, 1964-66, 1990-94; mem. N.C. Ho. of Reps., Raleigh, 1972-76; chmn. Dem. Exec. Com. of Buncombe County, Asheville, 1988—; chmn. Dem. Congl. Dist. 11, 1988-90, N.C. State Dems., 1990—, chmn., 1993. Named N.C. Bar Assn. Gen. Practice Hall of Fame, 1999. Mem.: Am. Coll. Trial Lawyers. Democrat. Home: Candler, NC. Died Oct. 15, 2006.

HYTCHE, WILLIAM PERCY, academic administrator; b. Porter, Okla., Nov. 28, 1927; s. Goldman and Bartha L. (Wallace) H.; m. Deloris Juanita Cole, Dec. 27, 1952; children— Pamelia Renee, Jaqueta Anita, William Percy Jr. BS, Langston U., 1950; MS, Okla. State U., 1958, EdD, 1967; LHD (hon.), Fisk U., 1995, Washington Coll., Md., 1995, U. Md., 1996; LLD (hon.), Tuskegee U., 1997. Tchr. math., Ponca City, Okla., 1952-60; asst. prof. math. Md. State Coll., Princess Anne, 1960-66, dean student affairs, 1968-70, Md. State Coll. (name changed to U. Md. Eastern Shore), 1970, assoc. prof. math., 1970-71; head dept. math. and computer sci., dir. Md. State Coll. (13 Coll. Curriculum Program), 1971-73, acting chmn. div. liberal studies, 1973-74, chmn. divsn. liberal studies, 1974-75, chancellor, pres., 1975-97, pres. emeritus, 1997—2007. Lectr. in field. Author: Step by Step to the Top: The Saga of a President of a Historically Black University, 1999; contbr. chpts. in books and articles to profl. jours. Mem. Somerset County Econ. Devel. Commn., Greater Salisbury Com., Joint Com. Agrl. R&D; mem. Pres.'s Bd. Advisors on Historically Black Colls. and Univs., 1988-92; adv. bd. Nat. Aquarium; bd. trustees Peninsula Regional Med. Ctr., 1978-94. NSF grantee, 1957-58, 60; recipient Thurgood Marshall Ednl. Achievement award Johnson Pub. Co., 1992; named to Hall of Fame, Okla. State U. Alumni Assn., 1993, George Washington Carver Pub. Svc. Hall of Fame Tuskegee U., 1994. Fellow Acad. Arts and Scis. (Okla. State U. 1978); mem. Nat. Assn. State Univs. and Land-Grant Colls. (exec. bd. 1988-91), Am. Coun. on Edn. (bd. dirs. 1988-90), Nat. Assn. Equal Opportunity Higher Edn. (bd. dirs. 1975-90), Phi Sigma, Phi Delta Kappa, Alpha Phi Alpha, Phi Kappa Phi. Methodist. Home: Princess Anne, Md. Died July 15, 2007.

IACONO, JAMES MICHAEL, research and development company executive, nutrition educator; b. Chgo., Dec. 11, 1925; s. Joseph and Angelina (Cutaia) I.; children: Lynn, Joseph, Michael, Rosemary. BS, Loyola U., Chgo., 1950; MS, U. Ill., 1952, PhD, 1954. With U.S. Army Nutrition Ctr., Letterman Army Hosp., Denver, 1954—58; assoc. prof. biochemistry and exptl. medicine U. Cin. Sch. Medicine, 1958—70; chief Lipid Nutrition Lab. Nutrition Inst. Agrl. Rsch. Svc. USDA, Beltsville, Md., 1970-75, dep. asst. adminstrv. nat. program staff Washington, 1975-77, assoc. adminstr. office human nutrition, 1978-82, dir. Western Human Nutrition Rsch. Ctr. San Francisco, 1982-94. Prof. nutrition Sch. Pub. Health UCLA, from 1987. Author over 100 rsch./tech. publs. and chpts. in books relating to nutrition and biochemistry and lipids. With US Army, 1944—46. Recipient Rsch. Career Devel. award NIH, 1964-70. Fellow Am Heart Assn. (coun. on arteriosclerosis and thrombosis), Am. Inst. Chemists; mem. Am. Inst. Nutrition, Am. Soc. Clin. Nutrition, Am. Oil Chemists Soc. Home: Cincinnati, Ohio. Died Dec. 10, 2006.

ICHBIAH, JEAN DAVID, software designer; b. Mar. 25, 1940; Mem. programming rsch. divsn. CII Honeywell Bull, Louveciennes, France; founder Alsys Corp. (Ada Language Systems), 1980—91; owner, head of Textware, 1991. Recipient Cert. Disting. Svc., Dept. Def. Mem.: French Acad. Sciences, French Legion of Honor. Achievements include design of of the Ada programming language form 1977-1983; virtual keyboard Fitaly; invention of instant text. Died Jan. 26, 2007.

IDLEMAN, LEE HILLIS, investment company executive; b. Washington, June 13, 1933; s. Holland Beecher and Marion (Cox) I.; m. Sue Ann O'Connor, May 7, 1960; children: Douglas Lee, Christopher Holland, Scott Clark. BS in Commerce and Fin., Bucknell U., 1954. Chartered financial analyst. V.p., research analyst Merrill Lynch, Pierce, Fenner & Smith, NYC, 1957-69; exec. v.p., dir. research Dean Witter Reynolds, NYC, 1969-84; ptnr., dir. rsch. pension fund portfolio mgr. Neuberger and Berman, NYC, from 1984. Guest appearances on Today Show, Wall Street Week, Fin. News Network, CBS Radio, others. Contbr. articles to profl. jours. and newspapers. Trustee Bucknell U., 1980—, chmn. fin. com., 1986-88, vice-chmn. bd. trustees, 1988-90, chmn., 1990—; trustee Kappa Delta Rho Found., 1989-95. With U.S. Army, 1954-56. Named One of Top Five Wall St. Research Dirs., Instl. Investor, 1984. Mem. N.Y. Soc. Security Analysts, Inst. Chartered Fin. Analysts, N.Y. Stock Exchange (allied), Delta Mu Delta, Kappa Delta Rho (ordo hon.). Clubs: Williams (N.Y.C.); Noe Pond (Chatham, N.J.); Bison (Lewisburg, Pa.) (exec. com. 1988—). Republican. Unitarian Universalist. Avocations: travel, bridge, reading, civil war history. Home: Madison, NJ. Died June 26, 2006.

IHARA, GRACE REIKO, speech pathologist; b. Newell, Calif., Nov. 17, 1943; d. Tamotsu and Betsy Shizue (Ito) I. BA, U. Hawaii, 1965; MS, U. Oreg., 1966. Staff speech pathologist Syracuse (N.Y.) VA Hosp., 1966; dir. adult speech and lang. program Mt. Diablo Therapy Ctr., Pleasant Hill, Calif., 1967-70; chief speech pathology Pacific Inst. Rehab. Medicine, Honolulu, 1970-72; pvt. practice as speech pathology cons. Honolulu, from 1972. Bd. dirs. Spl. Edn. Ctr. of Oahu; cons. Dept. Social Services, Hawaii Ear, Nose & Throat Group, Kuakini Med. Ctr., Castle Hosp., 15 skilled nursing and intermediary care facilities; lectr. Honolulu Community Coll., 1985—; guest lectr. KMC Gerontology series; tchr. Kaimuki Adult Edn.; commr. State Bd. Speech Pathology and Audiology; faculty and guest lectr. Hawaii Stroke Seminar. Mem. stroke com. Hawaii Heart Assn., 1976—. Recipient Community Service award Hawaii Heart Assn., 1976-84; grantee Vocat. Rehab. Adminstrn. Mem. Am. Speech and Hearing Assn. (cert.), Council Exceptional Children, Hawaii Assn. Retarded Children, Phi Beta. Clubs: Quota (charter, pres.). Home: Honolulu, Hawaii. Died Apr. 6, 2006.

IMHOFF, JOHN CLAWSON, hospital administrator; b. Lorain, Ohio, Nov. 5, 1925; s. Grover Cleveland and Sadie I.; B.Sc., Ohio State U., 1949; postgrad. Baldwin Wallace Coll., 1949-50; M.B.A., U. Chgo., 1952; postgrad. Cleveland Marshall Law Sch., 1953-54; m. Vera Louise Chance, July 19, 1952; children— Jeffrey C., Judson C., Jane C. Adminstrv. resident Cleve. City Hosp., 1951-52, asst. adminstr., 1952-54; adminstr. Polyclinic Hosp., Cleve., 1954-62; adminstr. Shadyside Hosp., Pitts., 1962-67; exec. v.p. Mountainside Hosp., Montclair, N.J., 1967-78; pres., chief exec. officer Galion (Ohio) Community Hosp., 1978—; chmn. Hosp. Council Western Pa., 1964-65; bd. dirs. Ohio Health Systems Agy.; dir. Scranton-Averell, Inc. Mem. Olmsted Falls (Ohio) Council, 1958-61, pres., 1960-61; pres. Community Ch., Olmsted Falls., 1960-61; pres. Galion Betterment Commn.; pres. Community Improvement Corp., Galion; trustee Bishop Brown Fund; mem. adv. com. N. Central Tech. Coll.; bd. dirs. Crawford County Shared Health Services; sec.-treas. Tri-Hosp Home Health Care, Inc. Served with USMC, 1944-46. Recipient citation for public service Alumni Assn. U. Chgo., 1962. Mem. Am. Hosp. Assn. (life), Ohio Hosp. Assn. (dir. polit. action com., trustee, chmn. fin. com., chmn.-elect Central dist.), N.J. Hosp. Assn. (trustee), Am. Coll. Hosp. Adminstrs., Am. Occupational Therapy Assn., Ohio PSRO (dir.). Presbyterian. Clubs: Elks, Rotary, Kiwanis (pres. club 1961-62) (Olmsted Falls). Home: Galion, Ohio. Died Mar. 26, 2006.

INGHAM, RICHARD GERALD, lawyer; b. Oklahoma City, Mar. 10, 1948; s. Kermit William and Mary Louise (Bosworth) I.; m. Susan Frances Holt, May 16, 1971; children: Katherine, Daniel, Mary Coleman. BA, Okla. State U., 1970; MA, U. Okla., 1972; JD, So. Meth. U., 1977. Bar: Okla. 1978, U.S. Tax Ct. 1978. Legal svcs. developer Aging Svcs. Divsn. Okla. Dept. Human Svcs., Oklahoma City, from 1977. Bd. dirs. Carpenter Square Theater, Oklahoma City, 1986-94, Okla. Mental Health Coun., Oklahoma City, 1988, Ronald McDonald House, 1991—. 1st lt. U.S. Army, 1972-74. Democrat. Unitarian Universalist. Avocation: running. Home: Edmond, Okla. Died Dec. 22, 2005.

INGLESON, LEWIS, architect; b. LA, Apr. 18, 1932; s. Samuel and Pearl (Goldberg) Ingleson; m. Michele Marbach, Aug. 21, 1954 (div. 1972); children: Adam, Kim; m. Donna Mae Vaughn, Dec. 20, 1980. BArch, U. So. Calif., 1957. Registered architect, Hawaii. Designer Chapman/McCorkell, Beverly Hills, Calif., 1957—58, Buff, Straub & Hensman, LA, 1958—59; instr. architecture U. Hawaii, Honolulu, 1959—64; v.p. Design Assocs., Ltd., Honolulu, 1964—67; pres. L. Ingleson & Assocs., Honolulu, 1967—82; prin. Ingleson & Meyers, Honolulu, 1982—85, Lewis Ingleson, AIA, from 1985. Mem. Oahu Devel. Conf., Honolulu, from 1967; commr. City Planning Commn., Honolulu, 1969; chmn. Housing Coalition, Honolulu, 1982—83; mem. Acad. Arts, Honolulu, from 1984, Honolulu C. of C. Mem.: AIA (v.p. 1982, pres. 1983, Honor award 1973, 1974, 1975, Merit award 1984), Bldg. Industry Assn. (dir. from 1983), Hawaii Yacht Club (Honolulu). Jewish. Died May 16, 2007.

INMAN, STUART K., retired professional sports team executive; m. Elinor Inman; children: Nancy, Sandy, Janice, Carol, David. BS, San Jose State U., 1950. Basketball coach San Jose State U., Calif., 1957-66; head coach Portland (Oreg.) Trailblazers, NBA, 1971—72, gen. mgr., v.p., 1981—86. Died Jan. 30, 2007.

INNES-BROWN, GEORGETTE MEYER, real estate broker, insurance broker; b. Wilmington, Del., Mar. 20, 1918; d. George and Flora Sue (Saunders) Meyer; m. Andrew T. Innes, Jr., Nov. 26, 1947 (dec.); m. Roy Glen Brown, Jr., Mar. 6, 1991. Grad. Real Estate Law, theory, Conveyancing and Practice, Phila. Bd. Realtors Sch., 1945; grad. Fire, Marine, Casualty Ins., North Phila. Realty Bd. Sch., 1946; cert. appraiser, Villanova Coll., 1974. Lic. realtor, Pa., ins. broker and appraiser, Phila. Ins. broker, realtor, Phila., from 1945; ins. broker, from 1946; also appraiser. Residential and single family home builder, Bucks County, Pa., Princeton, N.J., 1955-61. Mem., spkr. Juniata Pk. Civic Assn., Phila., 1984. Recipient Knights Legion award Italian-Am. Press, 1971. Mem. Nat. Assn. Realtors (sec.-treas. and v.p. chpt. 1975-80), Am. Bus. Women's Assn. (chpt. v.p. 1971, Businesswoman of Yr. 1971), Phila. Women's Realty Assn. (pres. bd. govs. 1949-85, pres. 1949-51, Woman of Yr. 1972-73), Phila. Bd. Realtors (v.p. residential divsn. 1975), North Phila. Realty Bd. (v.p. 1975, 76, pres. 1977, Gustav A. Wick award 1979), Del. Coun. Realty Bds. (sec. 1974), Real Estate Multiple Listing Burs. (treas. 1972-76), Sigma Lambda Soc. (chpt. pres. 1948). Avocations: golf, dance, gardening, cooking, embroidery. Home: Boca Raton, Fla. Died June 25, 2007.

INNIS, PAULINE, writer, publishing company executive; b. Devon, England, Dec. 8, 1917; came to U.S., 1954; m. Walter Deane Innis, Aug. 1, 1959 (dec. 1991). Student, U. Manchester, U. London. Author: Hurricane Fighters, 1962, Ernestine or the Pig in the Potting Shed, 1963, The Wild Swans Fly, 1964, The Ice Bird, 1965, Wind of the Pampas, 1967, Fire from the Fountains, 1968, Astronumerology, 1971, Gold in the Blue Ridge, 1973, My Trails (transl. from French), 1975, Prayer and Power in the Capital, 1982, The Secret Gardens of Watergate, 1987, Attention: A Quick Guide to Armed Services, 1988, Desert Storm Dairy, 1991, The Nursing Home Companion, 1993, Bridge Across the Seas, 1995, The Gospel of Joseph, 1998, I've Smashed the Devil's Window, 1999; co-author: Protocol: The Complete Handbook of Diplomatic, Official and Social Usage, 1977. Bd. dirs. Washington Goodwill Industries Guild, 1962-66; membership chmn. Welcome to Washington Club, 1961-64; co-chmn. Internat. Workshop Capital Spkr.'s Club, 1961-64; pres. Children's Book Guild, 1967-68; dir. Ednl. Commn., bd. dirs. Internat. Conf. Women Writers and Journalists, Nat. Arboretum, 1992-96; criminal justice com. D.C. Commn. on Status of Women; founder vol. program D.C. Women's Detention Ctr.; chmn. women's com. Washington Opera, 1977-79; mem. Liaison Com. Med. Edn., 1979-85; nat. trustee Med. Coll. Pa., 1980—; mem. Edn. Commn. for Fgn. Med. Grads., 1986-97. Named Hoosier Woman of Yr., 1966. Mem. Soc. Women Geographers, Authors League, Smithsonian Assocs. (women's bd.), English-Speaking Union, Spanish-Portuguese Group D.C. (pres. 1965-66), Br. Inst. U.S., Am. Newspaper Women's Club (pres. 1971-73), Internat. Soc. Poets (disting.), Internat. Clubs (co-chair 1997), Venerable Order St. John Jerusalem (comdr.), Internat. Neighbors Club. Home: Washington, DC. Died Aug. 18, 2007.

INVERNIZZI, FREDERICK WILLIAM, retired judge; b. Somerville, Mass., Dec. 11, 1910; s. Mathew A. and Cesira M. (Casassa) I.; m. Virginia Budd Taylor, Sept. 2, 1938; children—Ellen Budd Invernizzi Andersen, Marcia Ann Invernizzi Gallahue. B.A., U. Md.-College Park, 1932; LL.B., U. Md.-Balt., 1935. Bar: Md. 1935, U.S. Dist. Ct. Md. 1936, U.S. Ct. Appeals (4th cir.) 1936, U.S. Supreme Ct. 1972. Law clk. U.S. Dist. Ct. Md., Balt., 1935-36; practice law, Balt., 1937-55; dir. Adminstrv. Office, Cts. of Md., 1955-73; assoc. judge Dist. Ct. Md., Balt., 1973-77, qualified ret. assoc. judge, 1977—; instr. law U. Md., 1937-38, asst. prof. law, 1938-40, assoc. prof., 1940-46, prof., 1946-55, lectr., 1955-69; reporter standing com. on rules of practice and procedure Ct. Appeals of Md., 1947-73, mem. rule com., 1973-86; sec. State Bd. Law Examiners, 1969-73. Contbr. articles to legal jours. Mem. Gov.'s Commn. on Uniform Comml. Code, 1964-65. Served to lt. comdr. USNR, 1942-46. Mem. Md. State Bar Assn., Balt. Bar Assn., Am. Law Inst., Inst. Jud. Adminstrn., Gamma Eta Gamma, Phi Delta Theta. Democrat. Presbyterian. Home: Charlottesvle, Va. Died Feb. 6, 2006.

IRVIN, CHARLES LESLIE, lawyer; b. Corpus Christi, Tex., Mar. 2, 1935; s. Joseph and Louise (Frelon) I.; m. Shirley Jean Smith, Feb. 8, 1964; children— Kimberley Antoinette, Jonathan Charles. B.A., Tex. So. U., 1961, LL.B., 1964. Bar: Tex. 1964, U.S. Dist. Ct. (so. dist.) Tex. 1973, U.S. Dist. Ct. (ea. dist.) Tex. 1973, U.S. Supreme Ct. 1971, U.S. Ct. Appeals (9th cir.) 1982. Atty. U.S. Dept. Labor, Kansas City, Mo., 1964-67, Chgo., 1964-73; atty. Texaco, Inc., Chgo., 1973-74, Houston, 1974-79, Harrison, N.Y., 1979-81, sr. atty., Houston, 1981-88; divsn. atty., Midland, Tex., 1988, Denver, 1989-93, regional atty., mng. atty. adminstrn., Harrison, 1993-94, pvt. practice, Conroe, Tex., 1994—. Sgt. U.S. Army, 1955-58. Mem. Tex. Bar Assn., Tex. Bar Found., Houston Lawyers Assn. Congregationalist. Died Apr. 29, 2006.

IRVINE, FRANCIS SPRAGUE, lawyer; b. Okmulgee, Okla., May 27, 1923; s. Francis Sprague and Hazel (Beckett) I.; m. Betty Lee Sullivan, Sept. 3, 1949; children: Marilee, Robyn. BA, Okla. State U., 1948; LL.B., Okla. U., 1950. Bar: Okla. 1950, U.S. Dist. Ct. (no., ea., we. dists.) Okla., U.C. Ct. Appeals (10th cir.). Sole practice, Oklahoma City, 1950-57; ptnr. Kerr, Conn and Davis, Oklahoma City, 1958-60; mng. ptnr. Kerr, Irvine, Rhodes & Ables, Oklahoma City, 1981-90; of counsel Kerr, Irvine & Rhodes, Oklahoma City, from 1990. Mem. Spl. Commn. to Study Jud. Sys., Oklahoma City, 1985-86; bd. dirs. Lyric Theatre of Okla., Inc., 1968-73. Served to 1st lt. AUS, 1943-46. Mem. ABA, Okla. Bar Assn., Okla. Co. Bar Assn., Mineral Lawyers Group (past pres.), Title Lawyers Assn. (pres.). Clubs: Petroleum (Oklahoma City). Democrat. Christian Scientist. Home: Oklahoma City, Okla. Died Nov. 8, 2005.

ISAAC, MARGRETHE GLORIA, retired music educator; b. Chgo., May 6, 1927; d. Merle J. and Margrethe D. (Lehmann) Isaac. BEd, Chgo. Tchrs. Coll., 1947; MA, Northwestern U., 1950, PhD, 1962. Tchr. Chgo. Pub. Schs., 1947—58; instr. TV Tchrs. Coll., Sta. WGN-TV, Chgo., 1958—59; asst. prof. Chgo. Tchrs. Coll., 1959—61; assoc. prof. Northeastern Ill. U., Chgo., 1961—94, assoc. chmn. dept. early childhood edn., 1968—71, 1973—80, chmn., 1980—83; ret., 1994. Vis. faculty Northwestern U., 1964. Book reviewer: Ill. Reading Svc., 1971—76. Mem. exec. com. Elem. Sch. sect. Nat. Safety Coun., 1972—81, vice-chmn., 1975—76, chmn., 1976—77, mem. exec. com. Sch. and Coll. divsn., 1976—81, bd. dirs., 1977—80; mem. adv. com. Child Safety Club, from 1977. Recipient Outstanding Svc. award, 1977. Mem.: AAUW, AAUP, NEA, Am. String Tchrs. Assn., Music Educators Nat. Conf., Nat. Assn. Edn. Young Children, Assn. Tchr. Educators, Assn. Childhood Edn. Internat. (chmn. various coms. from 1954, v.p. Chgo. area br. 1973—77), Ill. Assn. Higher Edn. (pres. 1968—69), Ill. Edn. Assn. (pres. Chgo. divsn. 1964—66, Disting. Svc. award 1967), Kindergarten-Primary Assn. (pres. 1954—56), Chgo. Pub. Schs., Kappa Delta Pi, Phi Delta Kappa (chpt. historian 1977—79), Delta Kappa Gamma (music chmn. Ill. Gamma Alpha chpt. 1972—76, pres. Ill. Alpha Chi chpt. 1988—90), Pi Lambda Theta (rec. sec. Alpha Zeta chpt. 1965—67, corr. sec. Chgo. area chpt. 1973—77, pres. Chgo. area chpt. 1977—81), Alpha Delta Kappa (pres. Ill. Alpha Epsilon chpt. 1957—59, Ill. historian 1958—60, Ill. rec. sec. 1964—66). Home: Des Plaines, Ill. Died Aug. 14, 2007.

ISAACS, JOHN H., obstetrician-gynecologist, educator; b. Alton, Ill., Sept. 2, 1922; m. Patricia Agnes; 5 children. Student, St. Louis U., 1940-43, MD, 1946. Diplomate Am. Bd. Ob-Gyn (oral examiner 1975, bd. dirs. 1980-86, treas. 1984—), Am. Bd. Gynecologic Oncology. Intern Mercy Hosp., Loyola U. Clinics, Chgo., 1946-47; resident ob-gyn Mercy Hosp., Loyola U. Clinics, Lewis Meml. Maternity Hosp., 1947-52; exec. resident Loyola U., Lewis Meml. Maternity Hosp., 1952-53; clin. fellow Mercy Inst. Radiation Therapy, Am. Cancer Soc., Chgo., 1953-54; clin. asst. ob-gyn Stritch Sch. Medicine, Loyola U., Chgo., 1952-56, clin. instr., 1956-60, assoc. clin. prof., 1962-68, clin. prof., 1968-79, prof., from 1979, chmn. dept., from 1986, dir. div. gynecologic oncology, from 1979. Mem. attending staff St. Francis Hosp., Evanston, Ill., 1956—, chmn. dept. ob-gyn, 1962-86; attending staff gynecology and gynecologic tumor svc. Cook County Hosp., Chgo., 1967-71; attending staff Loyola U. Med. Ctr., Maywood, Ill., 1968, dir. div. gynecologic oncology, 1979, chmn. dept. ob-gyn, 1986—; lectr. Cook County Grad. Sch. Medicine, 1965—; cons. Resurrection Hosp., Chgo., 1976, cancer info. svc. comprehensive cancer program Ill. Cancer Coun., 1977—; vis. prof., cons. Ind. U. Med. Ctr., Indpls., 1971-73; vis. prof. dept. surgery Westminster Sch. Medicine, London, Mar.-May, 1983; speaker profl. meetings. Author: (with others) Manual of Procedures for the Seminar on Clinical Enzymology, 1976, Gynecology & Obstetrics, Vol. 1, 1977, rev., 1984, 85, The Pelvic Surgeon, Vol. 1, 1981, Your Patient and Cancer, Vol. 2, 1982, Reid's Controversy in Obstetrics Gyencology III, 1983, Clinical Problems, Injuries and Complications of Gynecologic Surgery, 1983, rev., 1986, 2d. edit., 1988, Current Therapy in Surgical Gynecology, 1987, Obstetrics and Gynecology Clinics of North America, Vol. 14, 1987, Current Concepts in Gynecologic Surgery, Advances in Clinical Obstetrics and Gynceology, Vol. 3, 1987; contbr. numerous articles to profl. jours.; author, participant in med. films, Video Jour. Ob-Gyn and audio tapes. With U.S. Army, 1948-50. Rsch. grantee G.D. Searle Co., 1969-71, 71-73, Lederle Labs., 1971, 72. Mem. AMA (residency rev. com. 1976-81), Ill. State Med. Soc., Chgo. Med. Soc., Am. Coll. Obstetricians and Gynecologists (various coms. 1972-81), ACS (bd. regents 1980—, exec. com. 1985—), Chgo. Gynecol. Soc. (pres. 1970-71), Inst. Medicine Chgo., Cen. Assn. Obstetricians and Gynecologists, Assn. Profs. Ob-Gyn, Am. Cancer Soc. (bd. dirs. N.Shore br. 1969-81), Barren Found. Chgo. (pres. 1970), Continental Gynecol. Soc., Soc. Gynecologic Oncologists (charter), Ill. Obstet. Soc. (hon.), Pitts. Ob-Gyn Soc. (hon.), Wash. State Obstet. Soc. (hon.), Soc. Surg. Oncology, Am. Gynecol. Obstet. Soc., Soc. Pelvic Surgeons, Chgo. Assn. Gynecologic Oncologists, Gynecologic Soc. Study of Breast Disease, Am. Soc. Clin. Oncology, Am. Bd. Med. Spltys., Soc. Gynecologic Surgeons, Cen. Assn. Travel Club, Mid-Ea. Obstet. and Gynecol. Travel Club, Alpha Omega Alpha. Home: Wilmette, Ill. Died July 29, 2007.

ISENBERG, HENRY DAVID, microbiology educator; b. Giessen, Germany, Mar. 9, 1922; came to U.S., 1937, naturalized, 1943; s. Gerson and Flora (Gruenebaum) I.; m. Lila S. Grossman, Feb. 15, 1948; children: Ina Pepi Isenberg Stein, Gerald Alan. BS, CCNY, 1947; MA, Bklyn. Coll., 1951; PhD, St. Johns U., 1959. Diplomate Am. Bd. Med. Microbiology (chmn. 1976-79, Disting. Svc. award 1994). Asst. dir. Angrist Labs., 1947-54; chief microbiology L.I. Jewish Med. Ctr., New Hyde Park, NY, 1954-97, chief emeritus, cons., 1997—2002, chief emeritus microbiology (pathology), dir. infection control (medicine), 2002—05, chief emeritus, from 2005; cons. clin. microbiology Mt. Sinai Med. Ctr., 1997—2001; cons. Univs. Space Rsch. Assn., from 1998; asst. clin. prof. orthopedic surgery SUNY Downstate Med. Ctr., Bklyn., 1963-68, assoc. clin. prof. orthopedic surgery, 1968-71, professorial lectr. orthopedic surgery, 1971-89. Prof. clin. pathology SUNY Health Sci. Ctr., Stony Brook, 1970-89; clin. prof. microbiology and immunology U. South Fla. Sch. Medicine, 1982-87; prof. lab. medicine Albert Einstein Coll. Medicine, 1989-96, prof. pathology, 1996-05, prof. emeritus, 2005—; cons. in microbiology NASA, 1990—; lectr. pathology Mt. Sinai Sch. Medicine, 1998-2001 Editor Jour. Clin. Microbiology, 1974-79, editor-in-chief, 1979-89; editor CRC Critical Revs. in Microbiology, 1978-81; editor in chief: CRC Forum in Bacteriology; sect. editor Manual of Clin. Microbiology, 4th edit.; editor: Manual of Clinical Microbiology, 5th edit.; editor-in-chief Clinical Microbiology Procedures Handbook, 1991-2002, 2d edit. 2002-04, Essential Procedures in Clinical Microbiology, 1997-2002; mem. editl. bd. Applied Microbiology, 1969-74; contbr. numerous articles to profl. jours. and books; patentee in field. Served with U.S. Army, 1943-45. Named Microbiologist of Yr. Lab World Mag., 1978; recipient Kimble awrd, 1980; Profl. Recognition award Am. Bd. Microbiology/Am. Acad. Microbiology, 1994. Fellow Am. Acad. Microbiology (bd. govs.), N.Y. Acad. Scis., Am. Inst. Chemists, Infectious Disease Soc. Am., N.Y. Acad. Medicine; mem AAAS, Am. Soc. Microbiology (Becton-Dickinson award 1979, Alexander C. Sonnenwirth Meml. Lectr. award 1989, Disting. Svc. award N.Y. br. 1991, nat. 1996, hon. mem. 1999), Harvey Soc., Sigma Xi. Jewish. Home: Floral Park, NY. Died Dec. 15, 2006.

ISHIZAKA, JIRO, banker; b. Shanghai, Dec. 22, 1927; s. Rokuro and Ayako I.; m. Masako Hirayama, Apr. 11, 1954. Grad., Faculty of Law, U. Tokyo, 1951. With Bank of Tokyo, from 1951, dir., 1977, mng. dir., 1980; chmn. bd. Bank of Tokyo Trust Co., 1980-84; dir. Calif. First Bank, 1982-84; resident mng. dir. N.Y. Regional Exec. Americas, 1980-84; adv. to pres. Nippon Life Ins. Co., 1984-89, Bank of Tokyo, 1989; chmn. bd. Union Bank, LA, from 1989. Trustee Calif. Inst. Arts, Jr. Achievement, L.A., Japanese Am. Nat. Mus.; bd. govs. Music Ctr., L.A.; bd. dirs. Japan Am. Soc., L.A. World Affairs Coun., L.A. Chamber Orch., Japan Am. Cultural and Com. Ctr.; bd. overseers Huntington Libr. and Bot. Gardens; bd. dirs. internat. Sta. KCET. Mem. L.A. C. of C. (bd. dirs.), Nippon Kogyo Club (Tokyo), Met. Club (N.Y.C.), Jonathan Club (L.A.), Sagami Country Club (Tokyo). Died Jan. 29, 2006.

ISKENDERIAN, ARMENAG, marketing executive; b. Istanbul, Turkey, Feb. 10, 1943; came to U.S., 1965; naturalized, 1974; s. Philip and Veron (Der Mesropian) I.; m. Shakeh Kurkjian, Dec. 3, 1966; children— Saro Philip; Laura Aline. B.S. in Mech. Engring., Robert Coll., Turkey, 1965; M.S. in Indsl. Engring., Northeastern U., Boston, 1968. Mgr. dist. sales Tex. Instruments, Clark, N.J., 1972-75, mgr. area sales, Chgo., 1975-76; mgr. mktg. Polymetallurgical Corp., North Attleboro, Mass., 1976-82, v.p. mktg., 1982-86, exec. v.p. 1986—; pres. Omnimet Corp., North Attleboro, 1979—; dir. Polymetallurgical Corp., Omnimet Corp. Registrar Westwood Youth Soccer Club, 1983—; chmn. bazaar com. St. James Ch., 1984; mem. parish council St. Thomas Armenian Ch., 1974-75. Lodge: Lions. Avocations: soccer; tennis; skiing; software development; photography. Home: Watertown, Mass. Died Jan. 12, 2006.

ISTRABADI, RASOUL MAHMOOD, civil engineer; b. Baghdad, Iraq, Oct. 5, 1927; s. Mahmood H. and Bebeya A. (Kutub) I.; m. Amel A. Istrabadi, Apr. 18, 1953; children— Zaineb, Feisal. B.S. in C.E., Baghdad U., Iraq, 1949; M.S. in E.C., La. State U., 1951; postgrad. U. Mich.-Ann Arbor, 1954. Dist. engr. Iraqi Railways, Baghdad, 1954-59; instr. N.C. State U., Raleigh, 1959-62; bridge engr. Transp. Cons., Washington, 1962-64; instr. Inst. Tech., Baghdad, 1964-68, Va. Poly. Inst., Blacksburg, 1971-72; chmn. civil engring. dept. Inst. Tech., Baghdad, 1968-69; city engr. City Bloomington, Ind., 1972-75; pres. Mideast-Midwest Cons., Bloomington, 1975-76; environ. engr. West Central Ind., Terre Haute, 1976-78; engr. expert Abu Dhabi Fund, Abu Dhabi, United Arab Emirates, 1979—. Avocations: music; sports; reading. Home: Bloomington, Ind. Died May 18, 2006.

ITZLER, RONALD STEPHEN, lawyer; b. Bronx, NY, Apr. 17, 1937; s. David Henry and Caroline (Spielberg) I.; m. Ronnie Lubell, Dec. 4, 1969; children— Jason Lubell, Jane Lubell. BS, N.Y. U., 1957; MBA, Cornell U., 1959, LL.B., 1960. Bar: N.Y. bar 1961. Since practiced in N.Y.C. specializing in debtor rehab.; partner firm Ballon, Stoll & Itzler, from 1967. Lectr. Cornell U. Law Sch., N.Y. U. Law Sch.; sec., dir. Bakers Equipment/Winkler, Inc. Mem. Mayor Fort Lee (N.J.) Adv. Com., 1976; bd. govs., treas. Ned B. Frank Philanthropic League. Served with USAF, 1961. Named Man of Year sportswear div. Am. Jewish Com., 1976 Mem. Assn. Bar City N.Y., Bankruptcy Lawyers Bar Assn. (gov.) Clubs: Montammy (Alpine, N.J.) (exec. com., gov., v.p.); Friars, Le Club, Friars (N.Y.C.) (bd. govs., scribe). Home: Cliffside Park, NJ. Died Feb. 12, 2006.

IVER, WILLIAM HENRY, dentist; b. Port Chester, N.Y., June 22, 1917; s. Alex R. and Beulah (Levy) E.; student U. Wis., 1936-38; D.D.S. cum laude, Georgetown U., 1942; m. Ruth Levin, Nov. 29, 1981; children— Robert Drew, Randolph, Lawrence. Pvt. practice dentistry, Miami Beach, Fla., 1945—; dir. Lincoln Small Bus. Investment Corp., Ka-Line Mfg. div. Sun Engring. Corp. Served to lt. comdr. USNR, 1942-45. Mem. ADA, Fla., East Coast, Miami Beach dental assns. Clubs: Cricket, Jockey, Carriage. Died Apr. 11, 2007.

JACKSON, ARTHUR GREGG, lawyer, director; b. Phila., June 19, 1921; s. Arthur and Anna M. (Gregg) J.; m. Dorothy Kempton Hollis, June 26, 1943; children: Gail, Laura, Nancy, Sarah. BS, Yale U., 1943; JD, Harvard U., 1950. Bar: Pa. bar 1951. Asso. firm Mancill, Cooney, Semans & Hedges, Phila., 1953-60; partner MacCoy, Evans & Lewis, Phila., 1961-75, Montgomery, McCracken, Walker & Rhoads, Phila., 1976-79; v.p., gen. counsel, sec. SPS Technologies, Inc., Jenkintown, Pa., 1979-86; of counsel Montgomery, McCracken, Walker & Rhoads, Phila., from 1986. Dir. Mutual Fire Marine & Inland Ins. Co., Phila., 1979—, UMI Group, Inc., Phila., 1979— Pres. Merion (Pa.) Community Assn., 1974-80, Merion (Pa.) Civic Assn., 1972-73; dir. Merion (Pa.) Bot. Soc., 1964—; trustee Friends Central Sch., 1972-80. Served with Signal Corps U.S. Army, 1943-46, 51-52. Mem. Am. Pa., Phila. bar assns., Soc. Friends. Clubs: Union League Phila. Republican. Home: Merion Station, Pa. Died June 10, 2007.

JACKSON, DANIEL FRANCIS, engineering scientist, educator; b. Pitts., June 11, 1925; s. Daniel F. and Edna (Marzolf) J.; m. Bettina Bush, Dec. 15, 1951. BS, U. Pitts., 1949, MS, 1950; PhD, State U. N.Y. Coll. Forestry at Syracuse U., 1957. Lectr. U. Pitts., 1949-51; asst. prof. Coll. Steubenville, Ohio, 1951-52; engr. C.E. U.S. Army, Pitts. dist., 1952-53; asst. prof., then asso. prof. Western Mich. U., 1955-59; asso. prof. U. Louisville, 1959-63; prof. civil engring. Syracuse U., 1963-73; dir., prof. div. environ. and urban systems Sch. Tech., Fla. Internat. U., Miami, 1973-78; prof., dir. Inst. Environ. Studies La. State U., Baton Rouge, 1982-86; dir. research Jim Rodgers Pools, Inc., 1978-82; enivron. editor Civil Engring. News, 1988-92. Dir. C.C. Adams Center Ecol. Study, 1955-59; asso. dir. Potamological Inst., 1960-63; dir. 1st NATO sponsored Advanced Study Inst., U.S., summer 1962 Author: Algae and Man, 1963, Some

Aquatic Resources of Onondaga County, 1964, Some Aspects of Mexomixis, 1967, Algae, Man, and Environment, 1968, Some Endangered and Exotic Species, 1978; filmstrip sets Environmental Pollution, 1969, Man in the Biosphere, 1971; also articles. Pres. Ky. Soc. Natural History, 1961-63; Bd. dirs. Mich. Conservation Clubs, 1955-57. Served with AUS, 1943-46, ETO. Recipient Rotary Internat. award as outstanding tchr. in Ky., 1962; Outstanding Community Leader award for environ. improvement Onondaga County, 1969 Mem. Internat. Limnological Soc., Freshwater Assn. Brit. Empire, Water Pollution Control Fedn., Air Pollution Control Assn., Ecol. Soc. Am., Brit. Ecol. Soc., Limnology and Oceanography Soc., Sigma Xi, Phi Sigma, Nu Sigma Nu, Beta Beta Beta. Home: Naples, Fla. Died June 18, 2007.

JACKSON, JAMES CORNELIUS, dean; b. Fountain Hill, Pa., Mar. 10, 1949; s. Robert Clinton and Eva (Cornelius) Jackson; m. Susan Palmer, June 14, 1975. BA, Wagner Coll., 1971; postgrad., Drew U., 1971—72; MA, Columbia U., 1975; postgrad., U. So. Calif.-L.A., 1976—80. Coord. internat. studies Wagner Coll., SI, NY, 1971—75, asst. dir. admissions, 1971—75; asst. dean Calif. Luth. Coll., Thousand Oaks, Calif., 1975—79, dean grad. studies, continuing edn., from 1979. Mem. North Lynn Ranch Homeowners Assn., Thousand Oaks; bd. dirs. Westlake Hosp.; adv. com. Wildwood Homeowners Assn., Thousand Oaks, 1979—80, Westlake Village, Calif., 1981—83. Mem.: Western Assn. Summer Sch. Adminstrs., Coun. for Advanced Exptl. Learning, Assn. for Study of Higher Edn., Am. Assn. for Adult and Continuing Edn., Am. Assn. Higher Edn., Phi Sigma Kappa. Methodist. Died May 24, 2006.

JACKSON, ROBERT LAWRENCE, pediatrician, educator; b. Clare, Mich., Nov. 30, 1909; s. Lawrence W. and Josephine L. (Cour) J.; m. Sara Elizabeth Soisson, Sept. 6, 1937; children—Ann, Mary, Sara, Kathryn, Margaret, Martha, Robert. BS, U. Notre Dame, 1930; MD, U. Mich., 1934. Intern U. Iowa, 1934-35, resident, 1935-37, instr., 1937-41, assoc., 1941-43, asst. prof., 1943-46, asso. prof., 1946-51, prof. pediatrics, 1951-54; resident U. Rochester, 1936-37; prof., chmn. dept. pediatrics U. Mo., Columbia, 1954-79, prof. emeritus, from 1979; prof. pediatrics U. Kansas City, Kans., from 1980. Guest lectr. Internat. Pediatric Congress, Zurich, Switzerland, 1950, Pan Am. Pediatric Congress, Sao Paulo, Brazil, 1954; vis. prof. pediatrics Am. U. Beirut, 1962-63; mem. NRC; cons. NIH. Mem. Am. Council Rheumatic Fever, Am. Diabetes Assn. (Banting medal 1969), AMA, Am. Pediatric Soc., Soc. Pediatric Research, Am. Acad. Pediatrics, Central Soc. Clin. Research. Am. Inst. Nutrition, Sigma Xi, Alpha Omega Alpha. Home: Shawnee Mission, Kans. Died May 5, 2007.

JACKSON, WILLIAM CLARK, JR., computer information industry executive; b. Whittier, Calif., July 2, 1932; s. William Clark Sr. and Mabel Kathryn (Plummer) J.; children: Victoria, Kimberly, William III, Robert, Shannon; m. Kathleen Pankow Jennings. AA, Fullerton Jr. Coll., 1953; BS in Econs., Whittier Coll., 1955. Various exec. positions IBM Corp., Armonk, N.Y., 1960-76; exec. v.p. Teletext Corp., NYC, 1976-78; v.p. planning and program mgmt. office products div. Xerox Corp., Dallas, 1979, v.p. bus. ops., 1979-80, v.p., gen. mgr. electronic typing products, 1980-82, pres., chief exec. officer office products div., 1982-84; pres., chief exec. Genra Group Inc., Dallas, 1984; chmn., chief exec. officer Software Corp. Am., NYC, 1985; exec. v.p., pres. info. mgmt. group Bell and Howell Corp., Chgo., from 1985; chmn., chief exec. officer Bell and Howell Publication Systems Co., from 1989. Bd. dirs. records mgmt. co. Bell and Howell, Los Angeles, NB Jackets De P.R., Caguas; chmn., chief exec. officer Bell and Howell Netherlands B.V. Mem. Dallas Citizens Council, Dallas, 1982-84; trustee Bishop Coll., Dallas, 1982-84, Dean Sch., Dallas, 1982-84; bd. dirs. Dallas Opera Co., 1982-84. Served as 1st lt. USMC, 1955-57. Recipient Disting. Alumni award Whittier Coll., 1986; William C. Jackson Jr. Computer Lab. named in his honor Dallas Acad., 1986. Mem. Assn. for Info. and Image Mgmt., Internat. Mgmt. Congress. (bd. dirs. 1985-88), Computers-Bus. Equipment Mfrs. Assn. (bd. dirs.), Sunset Ridge Country Club (Northbrook, Ill.) Republican. Avocations: golf, tennis, music. Home: Dallas, Tex. Died Sept. 20, 2006.

JACOBS, ALAN MARTIN, physicist, researcher; b. NYC, Nov. 14, 1932; s. Samuel J. and Amelia M. (Ziegler) J.; m. Evelyn Lee Banner, Aug. 7, 1955 (dec. Jan. 1977); children: Frederick Ethen, Heidi Joelle; m. Sharon Lynn Auerbach, Oct. 14, 1978; children: Aaron Michael, Seth Joseph. B.Engring. Physics (John McMullen scholar, LeVerne Noyes scholar, Clevite scholar), Cornell U., Ithaca, NY, 1955; postgrad., Oak Ridge Sch. Reactor Tech., 1955-56; MS, in Physics, Pa. State U., 1958, PhD, 1963. Research asso. nuclear reactor facility Pa. State U., 1956-63, mem. faculty, from 1963, prof. nuclear engring., 1968-80; prof. U. Fla., Gainesville, from 1980, chmn. dept. nuclear engring. scis., 1980-82; chief scientist Future Tech, Inc., Gainesville, 1986-87. Cons. to industry. Co-author: Basic Principles of Nuclear Science and Reactors, 1960; patentee dynamic radiography, control of radiation beams by vibrating media, multichannel radiograph, digital x-ray imaging system, snapshot backscatter x-ray imaging system, radiography by selection detection scatter field components. NSF sci. faculty fellow, 1960-61; recipient Glenn Murphy award for nuclear sci. edn. ASEE, 1994. Mem.: Tau Beta Pi, Sigma Xi, Pi Mu Epsilon. Home: Gainesville, Fla. Died Aug. 3, 2007.

JACOBS, RICHARD LEWIS, wholesale distribution executive; b. Georgetown, Ky., Nov. 10, 1950; s. George Alexander Jacobs and Ellida (Sadler) Fri. B.A., Whittier Coll., 1972; student Internat. Study Program, U. Oslo, 1971; M.B.A., Vanderbilt U., 1981. Asst. to v.p. Whittier Coll. (Calif.), 1973-74, dir. of devel., 1974-76; v.p. River Oil Co., Memphis, 1976-81; pres. River Oil Co. of Jackson, Tenn., 1981—; bd. dirs. Compro, Inc., River Oil Co., Memphis, Touchstone Ry. and Supply Co., Jackson, Rail Research, Jackson; mem. Nat. Oil Jobbers Council Planning Com. Past chmn. Tenn. Young Republican Fedn.; commr. Tenn. Civil Service Commn., 1981-87; mem. Nat. Young Rep. Exec. Com.; vice chmn. Madison County Rep. Party; mem. Commitment Memphis; mem. adv. bd. Pub. Service Commn.; chmn. Nat. Young Rep. Fedn.; del. Nat. Rep. Conv., 1984; bd. dirs. Am. Council Young Polit. Leaders; mem. Tenn. Reps. State Exec. Com., 1986—. Mem. Tenn. Oil Marketers Assn. (pres.), Jackson C. of C. (chmn. legis. com. 1981-84, bd. dirs. 1984—), Jackson Area C. of C. Mem. Christian Ch. (Disciples of Christ). Home: Jackson, Tenn. Died July 21, 2006.

JACOBSEN, LAWRENCE E., state legislator; b. Gardnerville, Nev., July 1, 1921; m. Betty Lundergreen; children: Bruce, Gary, Susan, Tim. Mem. Nev. Assembly, 1963-77, spkr. pro tempore, 1969; mem. Nev. Senate, Western Nev., Carson City, from 1978; pres. pro tempore Nev. Senate, 1987-90, 93-95, mem. fin. com., mem. transp. com., vice chair natural resources com. Mem. Legis. Commn., 1963-93. With USN. Mem. Am. Legion (comdr. Carson Valley Post 110, Minden Rotary Club, Douglas County Engine Co., C. of C., Gardnerville Gun Club, Douglas County Emergency Response Commn., Sierra Front Wildlife Cooperators, Nev. State Rep. Ctrl. Com., Douglas-County Edn. Found., State 4-H Camp Adv. Coun., Navy League, Douglas County Rep. Ctrl. Com. Republican. Died July 26, 2006.

JALILI, MAHIR, lawyer; b. Mosul, Iraq, Nov. 22, 1944; s. Ahmad and Khadija Jalili. BS, Leeds U., 1967; MEng., Colo. Sch. Mines, 1971; JD, Loyola U.-Chgo., 1976; LLM, Univ. Coll., London. Bar: Ill. 1977, Calif. 1993, Colo. 1994, Eng. 1999. Assoc. Kenyon & Kenyon, NYC, 1977, Graham & James, London, 1977-83; ptnr. Whitman & Ransom, London, 1983-92, Whitman Breed Abbott & Morgan, L.A., 1993-94; pvt. practise Oak Brook, Ill., from 1994. Numerous publ. and lectures in U.S., U.K. Contbr. articles to various prof. journs. Mem. Panel of Arbitrators, ICC Nat. Com. U.S.,Chgo.Internat. Dispute Resolution Assn.(CIDRA), Euro-Arab Arbitration Sys., World Intellectual Property Orgn. (WIPO), mem. ATLA, Internat. Arbitration Club, Soc. of Construction Law, Soc. of English and Am. Lawyers. Died Aug. 24, 2006.

JAMESON, PAULA ANN, retired lawyer, consultant; b. New Orleans, Feb. 19, 1945; d. Paul Henry and Virginia Lee (Powell) Bailey; children: Paul Andrew, Peter Carver. BA, La. State U., 1966; JD, U. Tex., 1969. Bar: Tex. 1969, D.C. 1970, U.S. Dist. Ct. D.C. 1970, U.S. Ct. Appeals (D.C. cir.) 1972, Va. 1973, U.S. Supreme Ct. 1973, U.S. Dist. Ct. (ea. dist.) Va. 1976, U.S. Ct. Appeals (4th cir.) 1976, N.Y. 1978, U.S. Ct. Appeals (5th cir.) 1978, U.S. Ct. Appeals (2d cir.) 1985. Asst. corp. counsel D.C. Corp. Counsel's Office, 1970-73; sr. asst. county atty. Fairfax County Atty.'s Office, Fairfax, Va., 1973-77; atty. Dow Jones & Co., Inc., NYC, 1977-79, ho. counsel, 1979-81, asst. to chmn. bd., 1981-83, ho. counsel, dir. legal dept., 1983-86; sr. v.p., gen. counsel, corp. sec. PBS, Alexandria, Va., 1986-98; ptnr. Arter & Hadden, Washington, 1998-2000; v.p., gen. counsel Gibson Guitar Corp., Nashville, 2000-01; pres. Jameson Legal & Cons. Svcs., McLean, Va., 2000—03; exec. v.p., COO Children's Def. Fund., Washington, 2003—04; ret., 2004. Mem.: D.C. Bar Assn., Fed. Comms. Bar Assn. Democrat. Roman Catholic. Home: Arlington, Va. Died June 8, 2007.

JAQUA, FREDERICK WILLIAM, lawyer; b. Muncie, Ind., Sept. 26, 1921; s. John Clayton and Matilda Lindsley (Over) J. AB, Cornell U., 1942; MBA, Harvard U., 1943; LLB, Yale U., 1949. Bar: N.Y. 1949. Lawyer Cravath, Swaine & Moore, NYC, 1949-56, GE, NYC, 1956-58, Am. Standard Inc., NYC, 1958-61 and from 65, v.p., gen. counsel, sec., from 1989; lawyer The Equity Corp., NYC, 1961-65. Capt., U.S. Army, 1943-46, PTO, ATO. Republican. Home: Blooming Grove, NY. Died July 19, 2007.

JARBOE, EVERETT ESTEL, retired teacher educator; b. Henryville, Ind., Aug. 16, 1918; s. William Andrew and Edith Hazel (Gabbert) J.; m. Betty M. McCoy, July 22, 1944; 1 child, John Andrew (dec.). B.S., Evansville Coll., 1940; M.S., Ind. U., 1948, Ed.D., 1949. Asst. prof. edn. North Tex. State U., Denton, 1949-52, assoc. prof., 1952-55; prof. edn. D.C. Tchrs. Coll., Washington, 1956-65; prof. edn. Ind. U., Bloomington, 1965-84, emeritus prof. edn., 1984—; lic. commr. Ind. State Dept. Edn., 1971-79; dir. div. of edn. Ind. U.-Purdue, Indpls., 1969-76. Served with M.C., U.S. Army, 1942-46, ETO. Mem. Ind. State Bd. Edn. Methodist. Lodges: Masons. Shriners. Home: Bloomington, Ind. Died Apr. 20, 2006.

JARVIS, JAMES HOWARD, II, judge; b. Knoxville, Tenn., Feb. 28, 1937; s. Howard F. and Eleanor B. J.; m. Martha Stapleton, June 1957 (div. Feb. 1962); children: James Howard III, Leslie; m. Pamela K. Duncan, Aug. 23, 1964 (div. Apr. 1991); children: Ann, Kathryn, Louise; m. Gail Stone, Sept. 4, 1992. BA, U. Tenn., 1958, JD, 1960. Bar: Tenn. 1961, U.S. Dist. Ct. (ea. dist.) Tenn. 1961, U.S. Ct. Appeals (6th cir.) 1965. Assoc. O'Neil, Jarvis, Parker & Williamson, Knoxville, Tenn., 1960-68, mem., 1968-70, Meares, Dungan, Jarvis, Knoxville, Tenn., 1970-72; judge Law & Equity Ct., Blount County, Tenn., 1972-77, 30th Jud. Ct., Blount County, Tenn., 1977-84, U.S. Dist. Ct. (ea. dist.) Tenn., Knoxville, from 1984, chief judge, 1991-98. Bd. dirs. Maryville (Tenn.) Coll., 1991-98; past chmn. fin. com. St. Andrews Episc. Ch.; past bd. dirs. Detoxification Rehab. Inst. Knoxville; past com. codes of conduct Jud. Conf. U.S. Named Trial Judge of Yr., Am. Bd. Trial Advs., 2004. Mem. Tenn. Bar Assn. (bd. govs. 1983-84), Am. Judicature Soc., Tenn. Trial Judges Assn. (pres. exec. com.), Tenn. Jud. Conf. (pres. 1983-84), Blount County Bar Assn., Knoxville Bar Assn. (Judicial Excellence award 2002), Great Smoky Mountains Conservation Assn., Phi Delta Phi, Sigma Chi (significant Sigma Chi). Republican. Home: Knoxville, Tenn. Died June 6, 2007.

JARVIS, WILLIAM DAVID, pharmacologist, researcher; s. Floyd Eldridge and Pauline Lemon Jarvis. BA in English in Biology, U. Va., Charlottesville, 1984, PhD in Neurosci., 1991; post doctoral, Massey Cancer Ctr. Postdoctoral fellow U. Va., Charlottesville, Va.; rsch. assoc cancer biology Massey Cancer Ctr., Richmond, Va., 1996—99; asst. prof., then assoc prof. integrative biology and pharmacology U. Tex. Health Sci. Ctr., Houston, 1999—2003; chief tech. officer Dominion Diagnostics, Inc., North Kingstown, RI, from 2003. Author over 70 reports, revs., chpts., articles in field. Recipient Howard Temin Rsch. Scientist Devel. award, NIH/Nat. Cancer Inst., from 1999; Individual Nat. Rsch. Svc. fellow, 1993—95, Specialized Program of Excellence in Cancer Rsch. grantee, from 2004. Mem.: Endocrine Soc., Soc. Neuroscience, Am. Soc. Biochemistry and Molecular Biology, Am. Soc. Pharmacology and Exptl. Therapeutics, Am. Cancer Soc. Episcopalian. Achievements include research in pharmaceutical development and mechanistic investigations of multiple anti-neoplastic drugs; discovery of delineation of the ceramide signaling pathway for initiating cell death in human cancers; development of effective drug interactions for more powerful and innovative anti-cancer treatments (Leukemia, Lymphoma); discovery of multiple protective signaling systems that allow cancers to thwart various modern treatment strategies; research in complex and interrelated signaling networks that centrally regulate tumor cell survival. Avocations: historical / architectural rennovation, collecting antiques, rare books, ephemera, travel, writing, photography. Home: Newport, RI. Died Sept. 17, 2006.

JASEN, MATTHEW JOSEPH, lawyer, retired judge; b. Buffalo, Dec. 13, 1915; s. Joseph John and Celina (Perlinski) Jasinski; m. Anastasia Gawinski, Oct. 4, 1943 (dec. Aug. 1970); children: Peter M., Mark M., Christine, Carol Ann; m. Gertrude O'Connor Travers, Mar. 25, 1972 (dec. Nov. 1972); m. Grace Yungbluth Frauenheim, Aug. 31, 1973 (dec. Nov. 13, 2003). BA, Canisius Coll., 1937; LLB, U. Buffalo, 1939; postgrad., Harvard U., 1944; LLD (hon.), Union U., 1980, N.Y. Law Sch., 1981. Bar: N.Y. 1940. Ptnr. firm Beyer, Jasen & Boland, Buffalo, 1940-43; pres. U.S. Security Rev. Bd., Wurttemberg-Baden, Germany, 1945-46; judge U.S. Mil. Govt. Ct., Heidelberg, Germany, 1946-49; sr. ptnr. firm Jasen, Manz, Johnson & Bayger, Buffalo, 1949-57; justice N.Y. Supreme Ct. (8th jud. dist.), 1957-67; judge N.Y. Ct. Appeals, 1968-85; U.S. Supreme Ct. spl. master S.C. v. U.S., 1987-88; spl. master Ill. vs. Ky. U.S. Supreme Ct., 1989-95; of counsel Moot & Sprague, Buffalo, 1986-90; counsel Jasen, Jasen & Sampson, P.C., Buffalo, 1990-99, Jasen & Jasen, P.C., Buffalo, from 1999. Mem. N.Y. State Jud. Screening Com., 1996—. Contbr. articles to profl. jours. Mem. council U. Buffalo, 1963-66; trustee Canisius Coll. Chair of Polish Culture, also, Nottingham Acad. Served to capt. AUS, 1943-46, ETO. Fellow Hilbert Coll.; recipient Disting. Alumnus award SUNY-Buffalo Sch. Law, 1969, Disting. Alumnus award Alumni Assn., 1976, Disting. Alumnus award Canisius Coll., 1978, Edwin F. Jaeckle award SUNY-Buffalo Sch. Law, 1982. Mem. Nat. Conf. Appellate Judges, State U. N.Y. at Buffalo Law Sch. Alumni Assn. (pres. 1964-65), Am., N.Y. State, Erie County bar assns., Am. Law Inst., Am. Judicature Soc., Lawyers Club Buffalo (pres. 1961-62), Nat. Advocates Club, Profl. Businessmen's Assn. Western N.Y. (pres. 1952), Phi Alpha Delta, DiGamma Soc. Roman Catholic (mem. Bishop's Bd. Govs., Buffalo diocese 1951—). Clubs: K.C. (4 deg.). Home: Orchard Park, NY. Died Feb. 4, 2006.

JASKOT, JOHN JOSEPH, retired insurance company executive; b. Allentown, Pa., Dec. 5, 1921; s. George W. and Anna (Kuzma) J.; m. Joyce Ranck, May 25, 1946; children: Lisa Anne, Philip Ross. Student, Muhlenberg Coll., Allentown, 1947-49; JD with honors, George Washington U., 1951, LL.M., 1953. Bar: D.C. 1951. Exec. v.p., gen. counsel, corp. sec. United Svcs. Life Ins. Co., Washington, 1953-88; v.p., legal counsel United Svcs. Gen. Life Co., 1968-87; v.p. Bankers Security Life Ins. Soc., 1985-88, also bd. dirs.; sec. Provident Life Ins. Co., 1983-86, United Olympic Life Ins. Co., 1984-86; sec., sr. v.p. USLICO Corp., 1984-88; ret., 1988. With USCGR, 1942-46, PTO. Mem. Am. Arbitration Assn. (arbitrator 1988—). Died Mar. 9, 2006.

JAYE, DAVID ROBERT, JR., retired health facility administrator; b. Chgo., Aug. 15, 1930; s. David R. and Gertrude (Gibfried) J.; m. Mary Ann Scanlan, June 6, 1953; children—David, Jeffery, Kathleen. BS, Loyola U. at Chgo., 1952; M.H.A., Northwestern U., 1954. Adminstrv. asst. Chgo. Wesley Meml. Hosp., 1953-54; asst. adminstr. Sharon (Pa.) Gen. Hosp., 1957-60, St. Joseph Hosp., Joliet, Ill., 1960-65; adminstr. Sacred Heart Hosp., Allentown, Pa., 1965-69; pres., chief exec. officer St. Joseph's Hosp., Marshfield, Wis., 1969-90; cons. Marshfield, from 1990. Regional v.p. Sisters of Sorrowful Mother Ministry Corp., Milw., 1989-91; cons., Marshfield, Wis., 1991—. Past pres. North Central Wis. Hosp. Coun.; mem. Wis. State Health Policy Council; bd. dirs. Wis. Blue Cross, Marshfield Devel Corp., Health Care Ministry, Manitowoc, Wis., 1992-2004. Served as lt., Med. Service Corps USAF, 1954-57. Fellow Am. Coll. Hosp. Adminstrs. (coun. regents); mem. Am. Hosp. Assn. (coun. fed. rels., ho. of dels.), Cath. Hosp. Assn. (past trustee), Wis. Hosp. Assn. (past chmn. bd. trustees), Rotary, Elks, KC. Died Apr. 15, 2006.

JEBE, WALTER GEORGE, shop owner, photographer; b. San Francisco, Aug. 15, 1924; s. Henry Herman and Eleanore M (Weigman) Jebe; m. Vivian A. Ferrera, Jan. 25, 1952; children Vivian Ann, Walter George II. Attended, Pa. State Coll., 1943 Founder, owner Jebe's Camera Shop, San Francisco, from 1946. Jebe & Assocs. Photography, San Francisco, from 1960; columnist San Francisco Progress, 1963. Formulator, tchr. first course photo product retailing for city and fed. govt. San Francisco Pub Schs., 1962, lectr. San Francisco history; tchr. photography classes, from 1962. Commr. Boy Scouts Am., 1965—70, scoutmaster, 1955—60; mem. Delinquency Prevention Commn. 1975; mem. com. Golden Gate Park Centennial, 1969, Youth Devel. Ctr., 1967; pres. John McLaren Soc., 1969—70, 1976 San Francisco Pub. Libr. Commn., 1982, San Francisco Ar Commn., 1982; mem. Mayor's Com. for Africa Week, 1961 chmn. Dems. for Nixon for Gov., 1962. With USAF, 1943—46 with USAF, 1951—52. Named Citizen of the Week, Sta. KABL 1966; recipient Civic Svc. award, Silver Beaver award, Boy Scouts Am., 1971. Mem.: San Francisco Coun. Dist. Mchts Assn. (pres. 1975), Master Photo Dealers and Finishers Assn (territorial v.p. 1963, area pres. 1962), Lions Club (pres. 1966) Home: San Francisco, Calif. Died Feb. 25, 2006.

JELASKO, MICHAEL JOSEPH, insurance company executive; b. Derby, Conn., Dec. 30, 1949; s. Michael J. and Helen Lena (Telep) J.; m. Lois Agnes Haggerty, Apr. 26, 1975 children: Deborah E., Lisa M., Karl E., Elizabeth M. Student South Conn. State U., 1967-68; ABAS, South Cen. Community

Coll., New Haven, Conn., 1968-70. CLU Am. Coll., Bryn Mawr, Pa., 1987; chartered fin. cons. Am. Coll., 1987. Spl. agt. John Hancock Cos., Hamden, Conn., 1974-76, sales supr., 1976-80, sales mgr., 1980-83; v.p. Coordinated Benefits, Inc., Madison, Conn., 1983-85, pres., treas. Milford, Conn., from 1985. V.p. Karl, Inc., 1985-89, pres., treas., 1989—. Mem. Dem. Town com., Orange, Conn. Staff sgt. USAR, 1970-78. Recipient Pres.'s Cabinet award John Hancock Cos., 1984, 86, 88, Pres. Hon. Club award John Hancock Cos., 1979, 80, 83, 85, 87, Pres.' Honor Coun. award Prin. Mut. Life 1986, 87, 88. Mem. New Haven Life Underwriters Assn. (bd. dirs.), New Haven County Sheriff's Assn., New Haven CLUs Assn. (bd. dirs.), Million Dollar Round Table (life and qualifying mem.), Quinnipiak Club (New Haven), Milford Yacht Club, Racebrook Country Club (Orange), Pres's. Honor Club (Boston), Pres. Club. Democrat. Roman Catholic. Home: Milford, Conn. Died Aug. 3, 2007.

JENCKS, WILLIAM PLATT, biochemist, educator; b. Bar Harbor, Maine, Aug. 15, 1927; s. Gardner and Elinor (Melcher) J.; m. Miriam Ehrlich, June 3, 1950; children: Helen Esther, David Alan. Grad., St. Paul's Sch., Balt., 1944; MD, Harvard U., 1951. Intern Peter Bent Brigham Hosp., Boston, 1951-52; postdoctoral fellow Mass. Gen. Hosp., Boston, 1952-53, 55-56; postdoctoral fellow chemistry Harvard U., 1956-57; mem. faculty Brandeis U., Waltham, Mass., from 1957, prof. biochemistry, from 1963. Served as 1st lt., M.C. AUS, 1953-55. Recipient ASBMB-Merck award Am. Soc. Biochem. and Molecular Biology, 1992. Fellow Royal Soc.; mem. NAS, AAAS, Am. Chem. Soc. (award in biol. chemistry 1962, James Flack Norris award in phys.-organic chemistry 1995, Repligen award 1996), Am. Philos. Soc., Am. Soc. Biol. Chemists, Am. Acad. Arts and Scis., Alpha Omega Alpha. Home: Lexington, Mass. Died Jan. 3, 2007.

JENKINS, CHARLES RILEY, aerospace company executive; b. Coffee Springs, Ala., Apr. 5, 1926; s. Charlie Morrell and Lessi Belle Jenkins; M.A., Midwestern U., 1973, Ph.D. (hon.), 1974; children— Charles Michael, Treasa Louise Friend. Buyer, Bomarc program, Boeing Co., Eglin AFB, Fla., 1959-60; buyer-supr. Minuteman missile, Cape Canaveral, Fla., 1961-65, Saturn program Kennedy Space Center, Fla., 1965-71; contracts adminstr. Boeing Services Internat., Inc., Kennedy Space Center, 1971-77, contracts mgr., 1977-81, contracts mgr. U.S. Army Nat. Tng. Center, Ft. Irwin, Calif., 1981-82. Served with U.S. Army, 1944-46; now col. Res. Mem. Res. Officers Assn. (pres.), Nat. Contract Mgmt. Assn., Nat. Guard Assn. U.S. Democrat. Baptist. Club: Masons. Home: Santa Maria, Calif. Died Mar. 12, 2006.

JENKINS, GEORGE, stage designer, film art director; b. Balt., Nov. 19, 1908; s. Benjamin Wheeler and Jane (Clarke) J.; m. Phyllis Adams, May 6, 1955 (dec. 2004); 1 dau by previous marriage, Jane Jenkins Dumais; 1 stepdau., Alexandra Kirkland Marsh (dec.). Student architecture, U. Pa., 1931. Cons. theatre U. Pa., Anenberg Theatre. Vis. prof. motion picture design UCLA, 1985-87, 88. Set designer Broadway prodns. including I Remember Mamma, 1944, Dark of the Moon, 1945, Lost in the Stars, 1949, Bell, Book and Candle, 1950, The Bad Seed, 1954, Happiest Millionaire, 1956, Miracle Worker, 1959, Wait Until Dark, 1966, Only Game in Town, 1968, Night Watch, 1972, Sly Fox, 1976; art dir. (films) Best Years of Our Lives, 1946, Secret Life of Walter Mitty, 1948, Bishop's Wife, 1947, A Song Is Born, 1948, Enchantment, 1948, Roseanna McCoy, 1948, At War with the Army, 1950, The Miracle Worker, 1962, Up the Down Staircase, 1966, Wait Until Dark, 1967, No Way to Treat a Lady, 1967, The Subject Was Roses, 1968, Me, Natalie, 1968, The Pursuit of Happiness, 1971, Klute, 1971, Seventeen Seventy-Six, 1972; production designer: (films) The San Francisco Story, 1952, Mickey One, 1965, The Angel Levine, 1970, Seventeen Seventy-Six, 1972, The Paper Chase, 1973, Parallax View, 1974, Funny Lady, 1975, All the President's Men, 1976 (Acad. award for Art Direction, 1977), Comes A Horseman, 1978, The China Syndrome, 1978, Starting Over, 1979, The Postman Always Rings Twice, 1981, Roll Over, 1981, Sophie's Choice, 1982, Dream Lover, 1984, Orphans, 1987, See You in the Morning, 1989, Presumed Innocent, 1990; (TV movies) including Annie Get Your Gun, NBC TV, 1957, The Dollmaker, 1983; art dir. in charge color, CBS-TV, 1953-54. Recipient Donaldson award for I Remember Mama, Billboard Publs., 1946 Mem. Delta Phi. Died Apr. 6, 2007.

JENKINS, LEROY, violinist, composer; b. Chgo., Mar. 11, 1932; m. Linda Harris; 1 child, Chantille Kwintana. Student with, Walter Dyett, Chgo.; BA, Fla. A&M U., 1961. Mem. Assn. for Advancement of Creative Musicians, Chgo., 1965-69. Composer-in-residence, Assessore Cultura, Italy. Formed trio with Anthony Braxton and Leo Smith, 1968; also played with Albert Ayler, Archie Shepp, Alice Coltrane, Cecil Taylor; formed Revolutionary Ensemble, 1971-77; performed solo violin concerts; formed trio with Muhal Richard Abrams and Andrew Cyrille; also performed duets with Oliver Lake; artistic dir. Composers Forum, 1986-2007; mem. adv. bd., co-founder Meet the Composer; appeared in jazz festivals including Ann Arbor, 1973, Newport Jazz Festival, 1974, numerous others; performed at Carnegie Hall, 1985, Kennedy Ctr., 1986; albums and CD's include Space Minds, New Worlds Survival of America, Vietnam 1 & 2, Manhattan Cycles, The People's Republic, Creative Construction Company, Urban Blues, For Players Only, Mixed Quintet, Ei Glatson, Swift are the Winds of Life, Leroy Jenkins Live!, Monkey on the Dragon for Violin and Chamber Ensemble, Dream of Dreams for Home for Baritone, Flute, and Viola, Psyche, The Revolutionary Ensemble, 2004; compostions include Themes and Improvisations on the Blues, 1985, Out of the Mist, String Quartet, Concerto for Improvised Violin and Chamber Orchestra, 1983; opera and theater pieces Mother of Three Sons, 1991, Off-Duty Dryad, 1991, Fresh Faust, The Negroes Burial Ground, The Three Willies, 1997, among others; recording with Cleve. Chamber Symphony: "Wonderlust", 1998, other solo concerts, 1998; commd. for baritone and piano for N.Y.C. performance, Equal Interest Tours, 1999, Spolletto Festival at Chgo. Cultural Ctr., pieces for trio: violin, trumpet and piano, string quarter, others; solo violin tour in Fla. and La. Recipient Downbeat poll award, 1974-83, Lila Wallace/Meet the Composer award; NEA grantee, 1973, 74, 78, 83, 86, N.Y. Found. for the Arts, The Rockefeller Found.; Guggenheim fellow, 2004, Fromm Found. fellow, 2004. Mem. Assn. for the Advancement of Creative Musicians. Died Feb. 23, 2007.

JENKINS, ORVILLE WESLEY, retired religious administrator; b. Hico, Tex., Apr. 29, 1913; s. Daniel Wesley and Eva (Caldwell) J.; m. Louise Cantrell, June 29, 1939; children— Orville Wesley, Jan (Mrs. John Calhoun), Jeanne (Mrs. David Hubbs). Student, Tex. Tech U., 1929-34; BA, Pt. Loma Nazarene Coll., 1938; student, Nazarene Theol. Sem., 1946-47; D.D., So. Nazarene U., 1957. Ordained to ministry Ch. of Nazarene, 1939; pastor Dinuba, Calif., 1938-42, Fresno, Calif., 1942-45, Topeka, 1945-47, Salem, Oreg., 1947-50, Kansas City, Mo., 1959-61; supt. West Tex. Dist. Ch. of Nazarene, 1950-59, Kansas City Dist., 1961-64; exec. sec. dept. home missions Ch. of Nazarene, Kansas City, 1964-68, gen. supt., 1968-85. Author: The Church Winning Sunday Nights, 1961; contbr. articles to ch. publs. Former trustee So. Nazarene U. Home: Olathe, Kans. Died Feb. 5, 2007.

JENKINS, THOMAS DAVID, petroleum company executive; b. Watervalley, Miss., Feb. 22, 1927; s. David Smith and Mattie Rozelle (Brooks) J.; m. Roberta Xandra Williams, Dec. 23, 1951; children: Robin Murray, Thomas David. BBA, U. Miss., 1950, LL.B., 1951, JD, 1968. Bar: Miss. 1951. Landman California Co., 1951-54; v.p. Cactus Petroleum Inc., Houston, 1954-60; vice president Permian Corp., Houston, 1960-70, pres., 1970-83; pres., chief operating officer Occidental Oil & Gas Co., Houston, 1975-83, chmn., from 1983. Exec. v.p. Occidental Petroleum Corp., Los Angeles, from 1972; now chmn., chief exec. officer Can. Occidental Petroleum Ltd.; dir. S.W. Bancshares, Inc. Served with USMC, 1944-47. Mem. Am. Petroleum Inst. Clubs: Houston, Riverbend Country, University. Died Apr. 14, 2007.

JENKINS, THOMAS LLEWELLYN, physics professor; b. Cambridge, Mass., July 16, 1927; s. Francis A. and Henrietta (Smith) J.; m. Glen Pierce, July 8, 1951; children: Gale F., Phillip P., Matthew A., Sarah E. BA, Pomona Coll., 1950; PhD, Cornell U., 1956. Physicist Lawrence Radiation Lab., Livermore, Calif., 1955-60; faculty Case Western Res. U., Cleve., from 1960, prof. physics, 1968-94, prof. emeritus physics, from 1994. Sci. and Engring. Research Council fellow Southampton U., (Eng.), 1983 Mem. Am. Phys. Soc., AAAS, Phi Beta Kappa, Sigma Xi. Home: Chagrin Falls, Ohio. Died Mar. 19, 2007.

JENKINS, WILLIAM MAXWELL, banker; b. Sultan, Wash., Apr. 19, 1919; s. Warren M. and Louise (Black) Jenkins; m. Elisabeth Taber, Oct. 11, 1945 (div. 1976); children: Elisabeth Cordua Beckstead, Ann Hathaway Rohrbacher, William Morris, Karen Louise Olanna, Peter Taber, David Maxwell, Barbara Fessenden Sanchez; m. Ann Ramsay, Jan. 31, 1987. BA, U. Wash., 1941; MBA, Harvard U., 1943. Asst. cashier, asst. v.p. Seattle-1st Nat. Bank, 1945—53; v.p., exec. v.p., pres. First Nat. Bank of Everett, 1953—61; exec. v.p., mgr. Everett divsn. Seattle-1st Nat. Bank, 1962, chmn., CEO, 1962—82. Chmn. Everett Trust & Savs. Bank, 1956—61, Seafirst Corp., Seattle, 1974—82; former dir. United Air Lines, UAL, Inc., Scott Paper Co., SAFECO Corp. Incorporator, mem. exec. com. Fifth Ave. Theatre Assn.; mem. adv. com. Grad. Sch. Bus. Adminstrn., U. Wash. Lt. (j.g.) USN, 1944—45. Decorated Navy Cross, Croix de Guerre with palm. Mem.: Assn. Res. City Bankers (pres. 1973—74), Bohemian Club, Univ. Club (Seattle), Rainier Club, Seattle Tennis Club, Bainbridge Racquet Club, The Reading Room (Maine). Republican. Presbyterian. Home: Bainbridge Is, Wash. Died June 27, 2007.

JENNI, DONALD MARTIN, composer, music educator; b. Milw., Oct. 4, 1937; MusB, DePaul U., 1958; MA, U. Chgo., 1962; D of Mus. Arts, Stanford U., 1966. Prof. U. Iowa, Iowa City, from 1974, head composition and theory, from 1988; dir. music La Compagnie de Danse Jo Lechay, Montreal, Que., Can., 1975-82. Composer-in-residence Ford Found., Ann Arbor, Mich., 1960. Compositions: Axis, 1968, Asphodel, 1969, Eulalia's Rounds, 1972, Musica dell'autunno, 1975, Long Hill May, 1976, Crux Christi ave!, 1977, Canticum Beatae Virginis, 1979, Pharos, 1980, Ballfall, 1981, Sam mbira, 1985, Romanza, 1987, Gales, 1989, Per Elysios, 1990, Figura Circulorum, 1993; (albums) Musique Printaniere, 1967, Cucumber Music, 1969; author: Cum novo cantico: A Primer of Biblical and Medieval Latin, 1983. Recipient Broadcast Music, Inc. award 1953, 55, 56, Stanford Humanities award in the Craeative Arts, 1965, 66; grantee Ill. Sesquicentennial Commn., 1968, Nat. Endowment for the Arts, 1982. Mem. Am. Composers Alliance. Died June 21, 2006.

JENNINGS, FRANK LAMONT, pathologist, educator; b. Mpls., Apr. 25, 1921; s. Frank L. and Helen (Germond) J.; m. Beverly K. Carlson, Dec. 15, 1948; children— Frank Lamont III, Kathryn Eleanor, Paul Ernest, Mark Oliver. AB, Ind. U., 1942, MD, 1947. Fellow U. Chgo. Hosps., 1947-51, intern, 1951-52; instr., then asst. prof. U. Chgo. Clinics, 1954-60; mem. faculty U. Tex. Med. Br., Galveston, 1960-77, prof. pathology, chmn. dept., 1963-75; prof., chmn. dept. pathology Wright State Sch. Medicine, 1977-87. Sec. Gulf Coast Waste Disposal Authority, 1970-77 Bd. dirs. Tex. div. Am. Cancer Soc. Served with M.C. AUS, 1955-57. Mem. AMA, Am. Soc. Clin. Pathologists, Coll. Am. Pathology (bd. govs. 1975-81), Am. Assn. Pathologists Bacteriologists, Internat. Acad. Pathology, Am. Soc. Exptl. Pathology, Am. Assn. Cancer Edn., Radiation Research Soc. Home: Galveston, Tex. Died July 15, 2006.

JENSEN, DOROTHY LOU WYLIE, librarian, educator; b. Wenatchee, Wash., Feb. 27, 1933; d. Clifford Todd and Beatrice Dorothy (Masden) Wylie; m. Richard Franklin Jensen, June 15, 1952; children: Richard Todd, Susan Dorothy Purcell, Catherine Beth. BE, San Jose State U., 1966; MA in Librarianship, U. Wash., 1972. Libr. asst. Hoover Instn., Stanford, Calif., 1962—64; libr. Los Altos HS, Calif., 1966—73, Atwalt HS, Mountain View, 1973—81; tchr. Mountain View HS, 1981—83; libr. Los Altos HS, from 1983. Mem.: NEA, Calif. Media and Libr. Educators Assn., Calif. Tchrs. Assn. (treas. 1972—73, chpt. pres. 1981—83, state coun. rep. 1978—80), ALA, Commonwealth Club (Calif.), Beta Phi Mu. Republican. Lutheran. Home: Los Altos, Calif. Died Sept. 8, 2006.

JENSEN, ERIC FINN, lawyer; b. NYC, Oct. 17, 1927; s. Olaf and Sigrid (Anderson) J.; m. Janet Stirling Clark, Aug. 26, 1950; children— Mari Nelms, Deborah Bowne, Eric David. BS, Cornell U., 1951; LL.B., Bklyn. Law Sch., 1956; grad., Advanced Mgmt. Program Harvard, 1968. Bar: N.Y. 1956, Conn. 1987. Law practice, White Plains, N.Y.; arbitration atty. Bethlehem Steel Corp., 1956-61; mgr. labor relations ACF Industries, Inc., NYC, 1961-64, dir. indsl. relations, 1964-65, v.p. indsl. relations, 1965-79, v.p. govt. and labor relations, 1979-85; of counsel Epstein, Becker & Green, P.C., Stamford, Conn., 1986-94, Keane & Beane, White Plains, N.Y., from 1994. Adj. prof. law Pace U. Law Sch., dept. mgmt. Stevens Inst., exec. MBA program U. New Haven; chmn. adv. coun. Cornell U. Sch. Indsl. and Labor rels., 1970-78; Nat. Ctr. on Occupational Readjustment, 1983-89. With AUS, 1945-47. Mem. ABA, N.Y. State Bar Assn., Westchester County Bar Assn., Am. Arbitration Assn., N.Y. Indsl. Rels. Assn., Cornell Club N.Y.C. Home: Sleepy Hollow, NY. Died Jan. 3, 2007.

JENSEN, HARRY ARTHUR, manufacturing executive; b. Council Bluffs, Iowa, July 17, 1918; s. Arthur J. and Bess (Crowl) Jensen; m. Lydia Cole, July 30, 1941 (dec. Dec. 1979); children: Stephen, Kristie, Eric; m. Abby C. Koehler, May 10, 1980. AB, Grinnell Coll., 1940. With Armstrong World Industries, Inc. (formerly Armstrong Cork Co.), Lancaster, Pa., from 1940, successively floor div. salesman Chgo., asst. dist. mgr., dist. mgr. Lancaster, mktg. mgr, 1940—61, gen. sales mgr. fl. div., 1961—62, v.p., gen. mgr. floor and indsl. ops., 1962—68, exec. v.p., 1968—78, pres., CEO, 1978—83, also bd. dirs. Bd. dirs. Pa. Power & Light Co. Served as lt. (j.g.) USNR, 1943—46. Mem.: Hamilton (Lancaster), Lancaster Country. Presbyn. Home: Lancaster, Pa. Died Nov. 14, 2005.

JENSEN, ROLAND JENS, utility company executive; b. Hayti, SD, Oct. 19, 1929; s. Chris Nels and Cicely Elizabeth (Wahala) J.; m. Deloris Edna Mangels, Aug. 10, 1958; children: Georgiann Jensen-Bohn, Roland Chris. BS, S.D. State U., 1959; MS, U. Minn., 1963. Nuclear engr. No. States Power Co., Mpls., 1960-75, dir. planning, 1975-81, sr. v.p., from 1981; chief exec. officer Norenco, Mpls., from 1987, also chmn. bd. dirs.; chief exec. officer NRG Group, Inc., Mpls., 1990-95; pres., CEO La. Energy, from 1996. Bd. dirs. City Conv. Ctr., Mpls., 1986—. Served as staff sgt. USAF, 1952-56. Named Disting. Engr. S.D. State U., 1983. Mem. Am. Nuclear Soc. (bd. dirs. 1970-73), Mensa. Lutheran. Home: Minneapolis, Minn. Died Feb. 15, 2006.

JESSUP, JOHN BAKER, lawyer; b. NYC, July 30, 1921; s. Henry Herbert and Eugenia Griffin (Baker) J.; m. LaVerle J. Jessen, July 29, 1989; 1 child from previous marriage, John M. BA, Yale U., 1942, LLB, 1948. Bar: N.Y. 1948, Conn. 1955. Assoc. Winthrop Stimson Putnam & Roberts, NYC, 1948-58, ptnr., 1959-93; counsel, from 1994. Mem. Zoning and Planning Commn., Ridgefield, Conn., 1958-65. Lt. USN, 1942-46, PTO. Mem. N.Y. State Bar Assn., Conn. Bar Assn., Down Town Assn., N.Y. Yacht Club. Republican. Episcopalian. Avocation: sailing. Home: North Salem, NY. Died Apr. 26, 2006.

JINDRAK, KAREL FRANCIS, pathologist, researcher, educator; b. Merin, Czechoslovakia, Mar. 29, 1926; came to U.S., 1967; s. Frantisek and Marie (Vetik) J.; m. Heda Kult, Jan. 6, 1951; 1 child, Heda. MD, Charles U. Med. Sch., Prague, Czechoslovakia, 1950, PhD, 1963. Diplomate Am. Bd. Anatomic and Clinical Pathology. Asst. prof. pathology Charles U. Med. Sch., 1956-65; pathologist Rsch. Inst. for Pharmacy and Biochemistry, Prague, 1965-67; researcher U. Hawaii, Honolulu, 1967-68; resident in pathology Mt. Sinai Hosp., NYC, 1969-71; attending pathologist Meth. Hosp., Bklyn., from 1971. Dir. dept. pathology Czechoslovakian Hosp., Vietnam, 1957-60; clin. asst. prof. pathology SUNY, Bklyn., 1973— Co-author: (with Alicata J.E. Jindrak) Angiostrongylosis in the Pacific and Southeast Asia, 1970, (with H. Jindrak) Sing, Clean Your Brain, and Stay Sound and Sane, 1986. Capt. M.C., Czechoslovakian Army, 1951-56. Recipient Spl. award Czechoslovakian Ministry Health, 1951. Fellow Am. Coll. Pathologists. Achievements include research in auxiliary mechanisms of intracerebral diffusion. Home: Forest Hills, NY. Died Oct. 12, 2005.

JOBSON, THOMAS WOOTTEN, retired editor; b. Montvale, NJ, Feb. 26, 1925; s. C. Drew and Margaret Alice (Wemple) J.; m. Helyn Louise Burrows, June 12, 1949 (dec. Feb. 2007); children: Gary Alan, James Drew, Ginger BS in Journalism, Mich. State U., 1949. Reporter Westwood News, 1950-51; editor Lakewood Daily Times, NJ, 1951-52; reporter Asbury Park Press, Toms River, NJ, 1952—57, bur. chief Asbury Park, NJ, 1957—58, copy editor, 1958—59, night editor, 1959—61, mng. editor, 1961—87. Adj. prof. Monmouth Coll., West Long Branch, N.J., 1962-87. Recipient Aumnus of Yr. award, Mich. State U., 1986. Mem. N.J. Press Assn. (chmn. news editorial com. 1970-71), N.J. Assn. Press Mng. Editors (pres. 1965), AP Mng. Editors (com. chmn. 1981-85), Am. Soc. News Editors, Sigma Delta Chi Clubs: Beachwood Yacht (commodore 1961-62), Toms River Yacht (bd. govs.); Miles River Yacht (St. Michaels, Md.). Episcopalian. Avocations: sailing; travel; history; baking; gardening. Home: Saint Michaels, Md. Died May 22, 2007.

JOHANOS, DONALD, conductor; b. Cedar Rapids, Iowa, Feb. 10, 1928; s. Gregory Hedges and Doris (Nelson) J.; m. Thelma Trimble, Aug. 27, 1950; children: Jennifer Claire, Thea Christine, Gregory Bruce (dec.), Andrew Mark, Eve Marie; m. Corinne Rutledge, Sept. 28, 1985 (dec. 2001); m. Jane Johanos Mus.B., Eastman Sch. Music, 1950, Mus.M., 1952; D.F.A. (hon.), Coe Coll., 1962. Tchr. Pa. State U., 1953-55, So. Meth. U., 1958-62, Hockaday Sch., 1962-65. Mus. dir., Altoona (Pa.) Symphony, 1953-56, Johnstown (Pa.) Symphony, 1955-56, asso. condr., Dallas Symphony Orch., 1957-61, resident condr., 1961-62, mus. dir., 1962-70, assoc. condr., Pitts. Symphony, 1970-79, mus. dir., Honolulu Symphony Orch., 1979-95, artistic dir., Hawaii Opera Theater, 1979-83, guest condr., Phila. Orch.,

Amsterdam Concertgebouw Orch., Pitts. Symphony, Rochester Philharm., New Orleans Philharm., Denver Symphony, Vancouver Symphony, Chgo. Symphony, San Francisco Symphony, Netherlands Radio Philharm., Swiss Radio Orch., Mpls. Symphony, Paris Opera, Boston Symphony, San Antonio Symphony, Orchestre Nat. de Lyon, others; recordings for Marco Polo, Naxos, Turnabout, Candide, others. Advanced study grantee Am. Symphony Orch. League and Rockefeller Found., 1955-58 Mem. Am. Fedn. Musicians Internat. Congress of Strings (dir.) Died May 29, 2007.

JOHNPOLL, BERNARD KEITH, communications educator; b. NYC, June 3, 1918; s. Israel Joseph and Ray (Elkin) J.; m. Lillian Kirtzman, Feb. 14, 1944; children: Janet Johnpoll Greenlee, Phyllis. AB magna cum laude, Boston U., 1959; A.M., Rutgers U., 1963; PhD, SUNY, 1966. Reporter, rewriter Post-Gazette, Pitts., 1946-51; copy editor news editor Boston Record Am., 1951-61; asst. prof. polit. sci. Hartwick Coll., 1963-65; vis. asst. prof. U. Sask., 1965-66; prof. polit. sci. SUNY-Albany, 1966-82; prof. communications Fla. Atlantic U., Boca Raton, from 1982. Writer-producer: ednl. TV series Prologue, Berkshire Prodns.; TV program American Diary, A Year to Remember; author: The Politics of Futility, 1967, Pacifist's Progress, 1970, The Impossible Dream, 1981; editor, contbr.: Polit. Sci., 1977—. NDEA, 1960-63; Nat. Council Jewish Culture fellow, 1963-65 Mem. Am. Polit. Sci. Assn., Soc. Propagation Judaism (trustee 1971-85), Pi Sigma Alpha. Clubs: Workmen's Circle (Albany, N.Y.). Democrat. Jewish. Home: Boca Raton, Fla. Died Oct. 19, 2006.

JOHNSON, BETTY JEAN, state educational administrator; b. Indpls., July 16, 1944; d. Hezekiah and Easter Gertrude (Lewis) Hill; m. William George Ryder, July 17, 1965 (div. Mar. 1974); 1 son, Mark Oliver; m. Steven Maurice Johnson, Nov. 2, 1977. B.Ed., Butler U., 1965, M.Ed., 1969. Tchr., Indpls. pub. schs., 1965-69, reading tchr., 1969-71, elem. cons., 1972-73; reading cons. Ind. Pub. Instrn. Dept., Indpls., 1973-77; assoc. prof. edn. Ind. U.-Purdue U.-Indpls., 1974-76; asst. dir. div. reading effectiveness Ind. Dept. Pub. Instrn., Indpls., 1977-78, dir. div. reading effectiveness, 1978—. Bd. dirs. Operation PUSH, 1977-82, 500 Festival Assocs.; state vice-chmn. Am. Cancer Soc., 1976-77; state vice-chmn. Black Republicans, 1975-77. Mem. Internat. Reading Assn., Nat. Tchrs. Council English, Nat. Alliance Black Educators, Nat. Assn. State English and Reading Specialists, NAACP (edn. chmn. 1980), Alpha Kappa Alpha. Republican. Club: Jack and Jill of Am. Home: Daytona Beach, Fla. Died Feb. 3, 2007.

JOHNSON, DAVID LINCOLN, lawyer, insurance company executive; b. Boston, May 21, 1929; m. Agnes M. D'Aguiar, Oct. 8, 1967; children: David, Burr, Chris, Ture, Jennifer. BA, U. Conn., 1950; LL.B., Boston U., 1954; LL.M., Northeastern U., 1956. Bar: Mass. 1954. Supr. group underwriting John Hancock Mut. Life Ins. Co., Boston, 1953-56; sr. assoc., counsel George B. Buck, NYC, 1956-65; asst. gen. counsel Factory Mut. System, Providence, 1965-71; gen. counsel Allendale Mut. Ins. Co., Johnston, R.I., 1971-77, v.p., gen. counsel, 1977-81, v.p., sec., gen. counsel, 1981-90, sr. v.p., sec., gen. counsel, from 1990. Mem. Bd. of Reps., Stamford, Conn., 1960-63, minority leader, 1960-63; mem. Rep. Town com., Barrington, R.I., 1968-84, mem. Bd. Tax Appeals and Bd. Assessors, 1972-75; trustee R.I. Coun. on Econ. Edn., Providence, 1983-85, 92—. Mem. Fedn. Ins. and Corp. Counsel, ABA, Greater Providence C. of C., Gov.'s Ins. Coun. Clubs: R.I. Country. Home: Barrington, RI. Died Oct. 24, 2006.

JOHNSON, DENNIS WAYNE, professional basketball coach, retired professional basketball player; b. San Pedro, Calif., Sept. 18, 1954; m. Donna Johnson; children: Dwayne, Denise, Daniel. Student, Los Angeles Harbor Jr. Coll.; Grad., Pepperdine U., 1976. Profl. basketball player Seattle Supersonics, 1976-80, Phoenix Suns, 1981-83, Boston Celtics, 1983—90, asst. coach, 1993—97; head coach LaCrosse Bobcats, Continental Basketball Assn., 1999—2000; asst. coach LA Clippers, 2000—03, interim head coach, 2003; advance scout Portland Trail Blazers, 2003; head coach Fla. Flame, NBA Developmental League, 2004—05, Austin Toros, 2005—07. Named to NBA All-Star Game, 1979-82, 1985; named NBA Finals MVP, 1979, All-NBA First Team, 1981, All-Defensive First Team, 1979-83, 1987; mem. NBA Championship Teams, 1979, 84, 86. Died Feb. 22, 2007.

JOHNSON, EUGENE MANFRED, marketing educator; b. Milford, Del., Oct. 21, 1940; s. Willis Moore and Elizabeth (Duling) J.; m. Carolyn Passwaters, July 7, 1962; children: Laura, Greta. BS, U. Del., Newark, 1962; MBA, U. Del., 1964; DBA, Wash. U., 1969. Asst. prof. U. Del., Newark, 1968-71; assoc. dean U. R.I., Kingston, 1971-76, acting dean, 1976-77, assoc. dean, 1977-79, prof. mktg., 1979-84 and from 85. Cons. R.I. Hosp. Trust Nat. Bank, Providence, 1979-80; v.p. mktg. DVC Ind., Bay Shore, N.Y., 1984. Author: Sales Management, 1986, 94, Profitable Service Marketing, 1986, Managing Your Sales Team, 1986, Successful Marketing for Service Organizations, 1986, Strategic Marketing Planning, 1989, Fundamentals of Marketing, 1990, 96, Motivating Salespeople through Incentives and Compensation, 1996. Mem. Am. Mktg. Assn., AAUP. Mem. United Ch. of Christ. Lodge: Lions (pres. 1985). Avocations: travel, golf. Home: Narragansett, RI. Died Oct. 4, 2006.

JOHNSON, GEORGE, JR., physician, educator; b. Wilmington, NC, Apr. 6, 1926; s. George W. and Evelyn (Hill) J.; m. Marian Patterson Ritchie, July 1, 1950; children: Sally Hope, George William, David Ritchie, Robert Hill. BS, U. N.C., 1949, certificate medicine, 1950; MD, Cornell U., 1952. Intern, resident surgery N.Y. Hosp., 1952-59; pvt. surg. practice, 1959-62; asst. prof. to prof. U. N.C., from 1961, chief gen. surgery svcs., 1969-93; vice-chmn. dept. surgery, from 1969; Roscoe B.G. Cowper disting. prof. in surgery U. N.C., from 1973. Mem. adv. com. N.C. Emergency Med. Svcs., chmn., 1973—, N.C. Gov.'s Hwy. Safety Com., 1977-89. Mem. editorial bd. Jour. of Trauma, 1980—, Jour. Vascular Surgery, 1983—; contbr. chpts. to books, articles to profl. jours. Served to 1st lt. inf. AUS, 1944-46. Mem. AMA (rep. to ho. of dels. from SCVS 1994), Univ. Assn. Emergency Med. Svcs. (pres. 1973), Am. Soc. Surg. Assns., N.C. Bd. Med. Examiners, Internat. Cardiovascular Soc. (v.p. 1989-93), Internat. Soc. Cardiovascular Surgery (pres. 1985-86), ACS (pres. N.C. chpt., gov. 1977-83, 91-96, trauma com. 1974-81, exec. bd. trauma com. 1977-81), So. Univ. Surgeons, So. Assn. Vascular Surgery (sec.-treas. 1981-85, pres.-elect 1986, pres. 1987), Durham-Orange County Med. Soc. (pres. 1971), Halsted Soc., Am. Venous Forum (pres. 1992). Clubs: Rotary. Home: Chapel Hill, NC. Died May 15, 2007.

JOHNSON, GERALD HUGH, engineering and construction company financial executive; b. San Bernardino, Calif., Feb. 27, 1945; s. Odin J. Johnson and Irene P. (Breit) Johnson Hilliard; m. Jacquelyn Ann Stevenson, Sept. 25, 1944; children— Stacey Michelle, Craig Michael. B.B.A., U. Houston, 1968. C.P.A., Tex. Acct. Price Waterhouse, Houston, 1968-75; v.p.-controller Tex. Internat. Co., Oklahoma City, 1975-79; v.p.-fin. Raymond Internat. Inc., Houston, 1979—. Mem. Am. Inst. C.P.A.s, Tex. Soc. C.P.A.s, Tex. Soc. C.P.A.s (Houston chpt.), Fin. Execs. Inst. Republican. Baptist. Clubs: University (Houston); Memorial NW (Spring, Tex.). Home: Spring, Tex. Died May 15, 2006.

JOHNSON, GLENN STEWART, gift manufacturing company executive; b. Milw., June 18, 1932; s. Sverre Christian and Lorraine Ethel (Bergner) J.; B.S. in Journalism, U. Wis., 1954; postgrad. U. Chgo., 1966-70; D.Min., Meadville Sem., U. Chgo., 1970; m. Beth Leona Hosier, July 17, 1954; children— Aleen, David. Mgr. advt. Warner Electric, Beloit, Wis., 1962-66; minister First Parish, Unitarian Ch., Wayland, Mass., 1970-74; v.p. mktg. Lance Internat., Hudson, Mass., 1974—; dir. Caithness Glass, Inc., Perth, Scotland. Pres. Beloit Club, 1964-65; chmn. Wayland Youth Adv. Com., 1970-74. Served to 1st lt., U.S. Army, 1954-56. Recipient Carleton Prize in Philosophy of Sci., U. Chgo., 1968. Mem. Assn. Unitarian Ministers, Mensa. Democrat. Author: Sebastian Miniatures Collectors Guide, 1980, 82; The Caithness Collection 1981. Home: Vlg Nagog Wds, Mass. Died Feb. 22, 2006.

JOHNSON, HALLMAN TROY, engineering photographer; b. Gadsden, Ala., Jan. 30, 1925; s. Johnnie Jackson and Mabel Oyester (Story) J.; m. Lorena Elizabeth Cassenta, Feb. 7, 1953. Grad. high sch., Gadsden, 1943. Photographer, Gadsden Studio, 1941-42, P.C. Smith Studio, Gadsden, 1942-43; foreman and photographer Gadsden Photo, 1946-49; self-employed photographer Ala. Studio, Gadsden, 1949-60; engring. photographer Nat. Aeronautic and Space Adminstrn., Marshall Space Flight Ctr., Ala., 1960—; shop steward Am. Fedn. Gov't. Employees, Huntsville, Ala., 1982—. Developer of a method to accomplish better photographic results on motion pictures, 1977 (Outstanding Performance award 1977). State dept. chaplain Am. Legion of Ala., Montgomery, 1958-60; ordained deacon Bapt. Ch., 1949; dir. Mt. Zion Baptist Sunday Sch., Huntsville, 1975—. Served to sgt. USAF, 1943-46, ETO. Democrat. Club: Internat. Civitan (sec. 1949-60). Lodge: Masons. Avocations: religious work, gardening, flowers. Home: Madison, Ala. Died May 23, 2006.

JOHNSON, JAMES ROBERT, county agricultural official, educator; b. Pittsfield, Mass., Feb. 13, 1950; s. George Edwin and Geraldine Lucille (Thomas) J.; m. Diana Lee Welch, Jan. 15, 1972; children: Benjamin, Rebecca, Caroline, David. A in Liberal Arts, Berkshire C.C., Pittsfield, 1971; BS, U. Mass., Amherst, 1973; MS, U. Mass., 1976. Grad. rsch. asst. U. Mass., Amherst, 1974-76; lectr. Stockbridge Sch., U. Mass., Amherst, 1976-77, Sch. Continuing Edn., U. Mass., Amherst, 1977; county ext. agt. agr. Sullivan County, N.H., 1977-82, coord. cooperative ext. svc. N.H., 1978-80, 82; county agrl. agt. III Cumberland County, N.J., 1982-88, county agrl. agt. II N.J., 1988-92, county agrl. agt. III N.J., from 1992. Active Cumberland County Bd. Agr., 1984—, Farm Bur. Nursery Adv. Com., 1987, FCI-Fairton Agrl. Edn. Adv. Com., 1993—; presenter in field. Author booklets; contbr. articles to profl. jours. Mem. horticulture adv. com. Cumberland County Coll. Agr., 1983—. Grantee N.J. Assn. Nurserymen, 1982-87, Vermiculite Ltd., 1983, Centerton Nursery, 1986, Cumberland County Bd. Agr., 1986, N.J. Agrl. Experiment Sta., 1986, 87, 88, Plant Food Chem. Co., 1987, Sierra Chem., 1988, 89, Ctrl. Controlled Environ. Agr., 1990, Plantco., 1992, Hort. Rsch. Inst., 1992, Cumberland County Utilities Authority, 1993, 94. Mem. N.J. Nursery and Landscape Assn. (cert. nursery profl. com.), N.J. Agri-bus. Assn., Internat. Plant Propagators' Soc. (mem. long range planning com. 1986-88, mem. rsch. com. 1990-92, chair 1992, mem. local site com. 1993-94, chair tour com., mem. program com. 1993-94), Agrl. Agts. Assn. N.J. (mem. profl. tng. com. 1983-89, mem. pub. rels. com. 1987, state chair recognitions and awards com. 1987—, mem. constn. and by-laws com. 1994—, bd. dirs. 1994—), Nat. Assn. County Agrl. Agts. (chair nat. meeting spl. meals com. 1986-89, vice chair recognition and awards com. 1991-93, Rohm & Haas State Merit cert. for pub. info. newsletter 1978, Scotts Hort. Comm. Program State award 1981, Search for Excellence Farm Income State award 1986, 89, Ciba-Geigy Crop Prodn. State award 1986, 88, 89, Ciba-Geigy Crop Prodn. Northeast Regional award 1990, Disting. Svc. award 1990, Ciba-Geigy Crop Prodn. Nat. award Agrl. Tour Switzerland 1991), Epsilon Sigma Phi (mem. Alpha Xi awards com. 1989). Baptist. Avocations: bicycling, hiking. Home: Bridgeton, NJ. Died June 14, 2007.

JOHNSON, JAMES WAYNE, lawyer; b. Tucson, Ariz., May 26, 1945; s. Wayne Shepherd and Marjorie (Smith) J.; m. Barbara Ann Booher, Sept. 11, 1976; children: Jason Powell, Paige Elizabeth. BA with high hons., U. Ariz., 1967, JD with high hons., 1970. Bar: Ariz. 1970, U.S. Dist. Ct. Ariz. 1970, U.S. Ct. Appeals (9th cir.) 1982, U.S. Supreme Ct. 1973. Pvt. practice, Phoenix, from 1970. Chmn. Fennemore Craig, Natural Resources and Environmental Law, Phoenix, 1986—, Gov.'s Exec. Com. on Cen. Ariz. Project, Phoenix, 1978-84, Gov.'s Task Force on Cen. Ariz. Project Issues, Phoenix, 1992-93, Water Resources Task Force Nat. Assn. Mfrs., Phoenix, 1978-85; mem. Western Govs.' Adv. Group on Interstate Compacts, Phoenix, 1984. Contbr. articles to profl. jours. Sgt. USANG, 1968-70. Fellow Ariz. Bar Found.; mem. Rocky Mtn. Mineral Law Inst. (reporter newsletter 1982-94, chmn. water law sec. 1981, grants com. 1987-95), ABA (subcom. fiduciary environ. problems 1992), State Bar Ariz. Home: Phoenix, Ariz. Died Jan. 21, 2007.

JOHNSON, LADY BIRD (MRS. CLAUDIA ALTA TAYLOR JOHNSON), former First Lady of the United States; b. Karnack, Tex., Dec. 22, 1912; d. Thomas Jefferson and Minnie (Pattillo) Taylor; m. Lyndon Baines Johnson (36th Pres. US), Nov. 17, 1934 (dec. Jan. 22, 1973); children: Lynda Bird, Luci Baines. BA in History, U. Tex., 1933, BJ, 1934, LittD (hon.), 1964; LLD (hon.), Tex. Women's U., 1964; LittD (hon.), Middlebury Coll., 1967; LHD (hon.), Williams Coll., 1967, U. Ala., 1975; HHD (hon.), Southwestern U., 1967; LHD (hon.), Southwest Tex. State U., 1983, Washington Coll., Md., 1983; D Pub. Svc. (hon.), George Washington U., 1986; LHD (hon.), Johns Hopkins U., 1990, SUNY, 1990, Southern Meth. U., 1996, St. Edwards U., 1998, Boston U., 1998. Mgr., husband's Congl. office US Ho. of Reps., Washington, 1941—42; owner, operator KTBC radio-TV sta., Austin, Tex., 1942—63; owner, cattle ranches Tex., 1943—2007; First Lady of the US, 1963—68. Author: A White House Diary, 1970; co-author (with Carlton Lees): Wildflowers Across America, 1988. Trustee Am. Conservation Assn.; trustee emeritus Nat. Geog. Soc.; founder Nat. Wildflower Rsch. Ctr., Austin, Tex., 1982; trustee Jackson Hole Preserve; hon. mem. LBJ Meml. Grove on the Potomac, Washington; hon. chair Nat. Headstart Program, 1963—68, Town Lake Beautification Project; bd. regents U. Tex. 1971—77, mem. internat. conference steering com., 1969 Recipient Togetherness award, Marge Champion, 1958, Humanitarian award, B'nai B'rith, 1961, Businesswoman's award Bus. and Profl. Women's Club, 1961, Theta Sigma Phi citation 1962, Disting. Achievement award, Washington Heart Assn. 1962, Industry citation, Am. Women in Radio and TV, 1963 Humanitarian citation, Vols. of Am., 1963, Peabody award fo Whit House TV visit, 1966, Eleanor Roosevelt Golden Candlestick award, Women's Nat. Press Club, 1968, Damon Woods Meml. award, Indsl. Designers Soc. Am., 1972, Conservatior Svc. award, Dept. Interior, 1974, Disting. award, Am. Legion 1975, Woman of Yr. award, Ladies Home Jour., 1975, Medal o Freedom, 1977, Nat. Achievement award, Am. Hort. Soc., 1984 Texan of Yr., State of Tex., 1985, Congl. Gold Medal, 1988 Gold Seal award, disting. svc. & achievement, Nat. Coun. State Garden Clubs, 1990, Charles Leonard Weddle Meml. award Native Plant Soc., 1994, Lifetime Achievement award, Nature Conservancy of Tex., 1994, Motorola Earth Day award, 1995 Golden Plate award, Am. Acad. of Achievement, 1995, Laurance Spelman Rockefeller Conservation award, disting. svc., 1996 Lifetime Achievement award, Native Plant Conservation Initiative, 1999, Cornerstone award, Tex. Soc. Architects, 2000 Theodore Roosevelt Nat. Park Medal of Honor, Nat. Par Found., 2000, Medal of Honor, DAR, 2003, Edwin P. Hubbl award, Edwin P. Hubble Soc., 2004, History Making Texan, Th Tex. State History Mus. Found., 2005, Nat. Conservatio Achievement award, conservationist of Yr., Nat. Wildlife Fedn. 2005, Lindy Boggs award, Stennis Ctr. for Pub. Svc., 2005 Fellow: Weizmann Inst. Sci. (hon.); mem.: Ex-Student Assn. U Tex. (life). Democrat. Episcopalian. Died July 11, 2007.

JOHNSON, RICHARD AUGUST, literature and languag professor; b. Washington, Apr. 18, 1937; s. Cecil August an Esther Marie (Nelson) J.; m. Michaela Ann Memelsdorff, Aug 20, 1960; children— Nicholas, Patrick, Hong, Loeun. BA Swarthmore Coll., 1959; PhD, Cornell U., 1965. Instr. Englis U. Va., Charlottesville, 1963-65; asst. prof. Mt. Holyoke Coll South Hadley, Mass., 1965-71, assoc. prof., 1971-74, prof chmn. dept., 1974-80, 1988-91, prof. Alumnae Found., 1980-86 Lucia, Ruth and Elizabeth MacGregor prof. English 1986—2004, emeritus prof., from 2004. Vis. prof. Amhers Coll., 1979, 84-88. Author: Man's Place: An Essay on Auden 1973; co-author: Common Ground: Personal Writing and Publi Discourse, 1992, Finding Common Ground, 1996; contbr. articles to profl. jours. Mem. MLA, AAUP, Phi Beta Kapp Democrat. Episcopalian. Home: Silver Spring, Md. Died Ma 27, 2006.

JOHNSON, ROBERT HERSEL, journalist; b. Colorado Cit Tex., May 28, 1923; s. Robert Hersel and Leah (Sikes) J.; m Luise Putcamp, Jr., Feb. 24, 1945; children: Robert Hersel, II Luise Robin, Jan Leah, Stephanie Neale, Jennifer Anne, An Tapia. BS in Journalism, So. Methodist U., 1947. Reporte Phoenix Gazette, Ariz., 1940-42; asst. sports editor Ariz. Re public, Phoenix, 1942-43; newscast writer Sta. KOY, Phoenix 1943; reporter Dallas Times-Herald, 1946; with AP, 1946-8 UT/ID bur. chief, 1954-59, Ind. bur. chief, 1959-62, Tex. bu chief, 1962-69, gen. sports editor, 1969-73, mng. editor, 197 77, asst. gen. mgr., spl. asst. to pres., 1977-84, N.Mex. bur. chie 1984-88; prof. journalism N.Mex. State U., Las Cruces, N.Mex 1988, U. N.Mex., Albuquerque, 1989; exec. dir. N.Mex. Foun. for Open Govt., Albuquerque, 1989—2007. Mem. Newspape Readership Coun., 1977-82. Mem. N. Mex. Hist. Records Ad Bd., 1993-2002. Capt. USMCR, 1943-46, 51-52. Named N.Mex. Press Hall of Fame, 2000, Heroes of the 50 States: Th Open Govt. Hall of Fame, 2003; recipient Liberty Bell awar Albuquerque Bar Assn., 2002, Working for the Best in Gov award, Common Cause N.Mex., 2004. Home: Albuquerqu N.Mex. Died Aug. 25, 2007.

JOHNSON, ROBERT MERLE, lawyer; b. Denver, Sept. 1 1917; s. George Elmer Clarence and Helen Gertrude (Wearn J.; m. Jean Turton Nevius; children— Randolph Marcus, Que tin Byron BA, Yale U., 1940; JD cum laude, U. Denver, 194 Bar: Colo., U.S. Dist. Ct., 1947. Assoc. Edward L. Woo Denver, 1946-47; assoc. Pershing, Bosworth, Dick & Dawso Denver, 1947-52, ptnr., 1952-56, Dawson, Nagel, S&H, Denve 1956-80, Sherman & Howard, Denver, 1980-87, of couns from 1987. Tchr. Denver U. Coll. of Law; faculty Agy. ar Partnership 1947-48 Served to capt. U.S. Army, 1942-46 Mer ABA (mem. house of del. 1966-68, chmn. local gov. law se 1963-64, hon. mem. council urban state and local gov. law se 1969—), Phi Delta Phi, Omicron Delta Kappa Clubs: U. Denv Republican. Episcopalian. Avocations: bridge; fishing; footba Home: Denver, Colo. Died Jan. 2, 2007.

JOHNSON, ROBERT MILTON, insurance broker; b. Salt Lake City, Utah, Jan. 20, 1945; s. Milton Ross and Virginia Aleen (Giles) J.; m. Peggy Lorainne Growton, June 13, 1969; children— Angela, Matthew, Michael, Marcus, Amanda, Ashley. B.S., U. Utah, 1970. Registered health underwriter. Group sales supr. Pacific Mutual Co., Salt Lake, Utah, 1976-78; prin. RMJ & Assocs., Salt Lake City, 1978-82; mktg. dir. Ins. Exchange, Salt Lake City, 1983—; sec. TDM Corp., Salt Lake City, 1983—; bd. dirs. Med. Rev. Inst. Am., Salt Lake City, 1984—. State del. Utah Republican Com., 1980, 82; coach Utah Youth Soccer Assn., Magna, 1978—, Community Youth Baseball, Magna, 1984—; mem. Magna stake high council Ch. of Jesus Christ of Latter-day Saints, 1983-84. Mem. Nat. Assn. Life Underwriters. Republican. Home: Magna, Utah. Died Nov. 11, 2006.

JOHNSON, RUSSELL, architect; b. Briar Creek, Pa., Sept. 14, 1923; s. Frederick Russell and Reba (Davenport) J. B.Arch., Yale U., 1951. Theatre cons., New Haven, 1949-54; tech. dir. Bolt, Beranek & Newman, Cambridge, Mass., 1954-69; pres., founder Artec Cons., Inc., N.Y.C., 1970—2007; acoustics designer Clowes Hall, Indpls., 1960, The Shed, Tanglewood, Mass., 1957, Meyerson Symphony Ctr., Dallas, 1982. Mem. U.S. Inst. Theatre Tech. (v.p. 1967-68), Acoustical Soc. Am. Avocation: sailing. Home: New York, NY. Died Aug. 7, 2007.

JOHNSON, THOMAS HAROLD, radiologist; b. El Dorado, Ark., Dec. 11, 1933; MD, U. Ark., 1957. Diplomate Am. Bd. Radiology. Intern Washington U./City Hosp., St. Louis, 1957-58; resident in internal medicine Washington U./VA Hosp., St. Louis, 1958-59; resident Baylor Hosp., Houston, 1959-60; resident in radiology Cin. Gen. Hosp., 1960-63; radiologist Okla. Meml. Hosp., Oklahoma City; prof. radiol. scis. U. Okla. Health Sci. Ctr., Oklahoma City. Mem. AMA, Am. Coll. Radiology, Radiol. Soc. N.Am. Died Apr. 3, 2007.

JOHNSON, WARREN DONALD, retired pharmaceutical executive, retired military officer; b. Blackwell, Okla., Sept. 2, 1922; s. Charles Leon and Vera Ruth (Tucker) J.; m. Vivian Tolley Johnson (div.); 1 child, Richard Johnson; m. Frances Johnson (div.); children: Patricia Suzanne Johnson Peak, Lindabeth Johnson Brown; m. Judy Luken-Johnson; 1 child, Ross Anthony. Student, Oklahoma City U., 1940-41. Served to 1st lt. U.S. Army, 1942-45; commd. 1st lt. USAAF, 1945; advanced through grades to lt. gen. USAF; chief of staff Strategic Air Command, Offutt AFB, Nebr., 1971-73; dep. dir. then dir Def. Nuclear Agy., Washington, 1973-77; ret., 1977; corp. v.p. Baxter Internat. Inc., Deerfield, Ill., 1977-91. Cons., tchr. Lake Forest Grad. Sch. Mgmt., 1991-99; ptnr. Cort & Assoc. Aircraft Sales and Charter. Decorated D.S.M., Legion of Merit with 2 oak leaf clusters, Joint Commendation medal. Died Jan. 23, 2007.

JOHNSON, WAYNE RICHARD, utility environmental engineer; b. Kansas City, Kans., Sept. 3, 1921; s. Willis Richard and Pearl May (White) J.; m. Marguerite Elinor Hunzicker, Aug. 14, 1943; children— Steven Wayne, Jerry Wayne. B.S., U. Kans., 1948. Registered profl. engr., Mo. Engr., Kans. City Power & Light Co., Kansas City, 1948-57, project engr., 1957-59, supt. stores, 1959-60, mgr. internal services, 1960-61, engr., 1961-64, maintenance supr., 1964-67, staff engr., 1967-70, supt. Hawthorn Sta., 1970-71, mgr. prodn., 1971-78, asst. to pres., chief environmental engr., 1978—. Served to lt., USNR, 1942-45. Mem. ASME, Air Pollution Control Assn. Republican. Lodge: Mason (Shriner). Club: Kansas City. Home: Shawnee Mission, Kans. Died Feb. 12, 2006.

JOHNSON, WILLARD LYON, JR., humanities educator; b. Des Moines, May 30, 1939; s. Willard Lyon and Margerie Elta (Hackenberg) J. BA, Oberlin Coll., 1961, postgrad., 1963-64; MA, U. Wis., 1966, PhD in Indian Langs. and Lit., 1972. Tutor English and philosophy Am. Coll. and Lady Doak Coll., Madurai, India, 1961-63; lectr. religious studies, lit., Calif. State U.-Long Beach, 1970-76, acting dir. program religious studies, 1972-73; lectr. philosophy, U. Calif.-San Diego, 1971-79; assoc. prof. religious studies, San Diego State U., 1988—, U. Humanistic Studies, Del Mar, 1979-88; asst. prof. religion Oberlin Coll., Ohio, 1980-81; vis. prof. religion U. Fla., Gainesville, 1983. Author: (with Robinson) The Buddhist Religion 1977, 3d rev. edit. 1983; Riding the Ox Home, 1982, 86, Glossary of Technical Terms for the Academic Study of Religion, 1982; (book) Poetry and Speculation of the Rg Veda, 1980; producer cassette tape series Introduction to Eastern Religions, 1978; also articles and revs. Bd. dirs. Cuyamungue Inst., Santa Fe; Woodrow Wilson fellow, 1964-66; grantee NDEA. Home: Pauma Valley, Calif. Died Dec. 29, 2006.

JOHNSON, WILLIAM BRUCE, business educator; b. Denver, Feb. 13, 1948; s. William Bruce and Evelyn Alice (Jones) J.; m. Candy Jean Cameron, Mar. 21, 1970 (div. July 1979); 1 child, Cory Elizabeth; m. Diane Helen Ramsey, Nov. 28, 1981. BA, U. Oreg., 1970; MA, Ohio State U., 1973, PhD, 1975. Asst. prof. U. Wis., Madison, 1975-81, Northwestern U., Evanston, Ill., 1980-87; assoc. prof. U. Iowa, Iowa City, 1987-92, prof., from 1993. Vis. asst. prof. U. Chgo., 1986-87; dir. McGladrey Inst. for Acctg. Rsch., U. Iowa, 1988-90; pres., founder ValueMetrics Group; presenter in field. Editorial bd.: Acctg Rev., 1979-82; contbr. articles to profl. jours., books; referee numerous jours. in field. Named Phillips Outstanding Prof., U. Iowa, 1988, Arthur Andersen Prof., 1992, others; recipient Standard Oil scholarship, 1969-70. Mem. Am. Acctg. Assn., Fin. Execs. Inst., Am. Inst. for Decision Scis. (nat. mtg. program chmn. acctg. 1983), Beta Gamma Sigma, Beta Alpha Psi. Avocations: jazz performance, fly fishing, travel. Home: Cedar Rapids, Iowa. Died June 1, 2006.

JOHNSON, WILLIAM EARL, textile company executive; b. Aiken, SC, Sept. 13, 1933; s. William Earl and Mary Butler (Crawford) J.; m. Mary Jane Snapp, Sept. 17, 1955; children: Laura Ann, Virginia Lynn Johnson Rhoden. BA in Econs., Clemson U., 1955; cert. Grad. Sch. Credit & Fin. Mgmt., Dartmouth Coll., 1966. With pub. relations dept. Ford Motor Co., 1957, The Mich. Bank, 1958-59; bus. devel. officer C&S Bank, 1960-62; v.p. adminstrn. Graniteville (S.C.) Co., from 1963. Pres. Augusta (Ga.) Kiwanis, 1974, Augusta Advt. Club, 1977; exec. com. Univ. Health Care Found. Univ. Hosp., Augusta, 1986. Mem. S.C. Textile Mfrs. Assn. (chmn. pub. relations div. 1977). Avocations: golf, running. Home: Augusta, Ga. Died July 15, 2006.

JOHNSON, WILLIAM HOWARD, JR., sales executive; b. Chgo., Jan. 24, 1943; s. William H. and Lois C. (Banks) J.; m. Joan C. Cervantes, Dec. 22, 1972 (div. Jan. 1985); children— Kevin L., Marvin E. B.S., Bradley U., 1965. Tchr. pub. schs., Evanston, Ill., 1965; design engr. Conveyor Systems, Inc., Morton Grove, Ill., 1965-67; with IBM Corp., 1967—, dist. sales mgr., Rolling Meadows, Ill., 1984—; dir. edn. tech. div. Nexus, Chgo., 1985—; com. mem. CC&Q, Atlanta, 1985; cons. computer game America Us, 1985. Mem. com. United Negro Coll. Fund, N.Y.C. Recipient Black Achiever award YMCA, Boston, 1979. Mem. Cell Found. Democrat. Methodist. Avocation: tennis. Home: Chicago, Ill. Died Dec. 2, 2005.

JOHNSON, WILLIAM RICHARD, JR., computer company executive, electrical engineer; b. Lewistown, Pa., May 29, 1942; s. William R. and Vivien (Ferguson) J.; children— Steven, Kevin, Glenn BSE.E., Pa. State U., 1963; MSE.E., Northeastern U., Boston, 1967, MBA, 1971. Registered profl. engr., Mass. Diagnostic Digital Equip. Corp., Maynard, Mass., 1973-77, tech. dir. office of devel., 1977-79, software engring., 1979-81, v.p. engring. systems and communications, 1981-82, v.p. engring. systems and clusters, 1982-84, v.p. engring., mktg. distributed systems, 1984-89; v.p. telecommunications and networks bus., 1989-91; v.p. corp. mktg., from 1991. Mem. exec. com. Mass. High Tech. Council, Boston, 1985—; indsl. advisor Wang Inst., 1984. Contbr. articles on testing of complex logic boards to profl. publs. Past mem. exec. com. Home Prayers, N.H.; mem. computer engring. commn. Northeastern U., Boston, 1983; mem. engring. adv. group Pa. State U., 1984 Avocations: photography; travel; food. Home: New York, NY. Died Aug. 26, 2007.

JOHNSON, ZANE QUENTIN, retired petroleum company executive; b. Bristow, Okla., Mar. 5, 1924; s. Sylvester B. and Meta B. (Biggs) J.; m. Nila Jean Caylor, June 4, 1949; children: Zane Quentin, Mark Caylor, Janis Lyn. BS in Chem. Engring, U. Okla., 1947. With Gulf Oil Corp. (and subs. cos.), from 1947; pres., chief operating officer Gen. Atomic, Inc., San Diego, 1969-70; exec. v.p. Gulf Oil Corp., Pitts., 1970-75; pres. Gulf Sci. & Tech. Co., Pitts., from 1975, now ret. Faculty Sch. Chem. Engring., U. Okla. Mayor, Port Arthur, Tex., 1957-58; bd. dirs. United Community Services of San Diego County, 1969-70, Boy Scouts Am., Duquesne U.; trustee Shadyside Hosp. Served to 1st lt. USAAF, PTO. Decorated Air medal with three oak leaf clusters; recipient U. Okla. Coll. Engring. Hall of Fame award. Mem. AIChE, Am. Petroleum Inst., Port Royal Club, Royal Poinciana Golf Club, Hound Ears Golf Club (Blowing Rock, N.C.). Republican. Presbyterian. Died May 19, 2006.

JOHNSTON, DAVID WHITE, JR., textile manufacturing company executive; b. Atlanta, Mar. 31, 1921; s. David White and Annie Kate (Johnston); m. Sally Onie Ingram, July 30, 1949; children: Elizabeth, David. BS in Indsl. Mgmt, Ga. Inst. Tech., 1942; postgrad., U. Western Ont., U. N.C. Plant mgr. Dominion Textile Co., Ltd., Drummondville, Que., Can., 1952-60, v.p. mfg., 1963-68; div. v.p. Deering Milliken Co., Spartanburg, S.C., 1960-64; v.p. mfg. Bibb Mfg. Co., Macon, Ga., 1968-70; chmn. bd., chief exec. officer Dan River Inc., Danville, Va., 1970-87, also bd. dir., chmn. exec. com., 1987-89; ret., 1989. Bd. dirs. Dibrrell Bros. Bd. dirs. Roman Eagle Nursing Home, Danville,; adv. bd. Duke U. Hosp., Durham, N.C. Lt. USNR, 1942-46. Mem. Danville C. of C. (bd. dir.) Clubs: Danville Golf. Presbyterian. Home: Danville, Va. Died June 12, 2006.

JOHNSTON, JEAN VANCE, retired chemistry educator, civic worker; b. Shippensburg, Pa., Feb. 17, 1912; d. William Rankin and Jean Moodey (Beattie) J. AB cum laude, Smith Coll., 1934; PhD, Yale U., 1938. Teaching and research asst. Smith Coll., Northampton, Mass., 1939; asst. prof. Furman U., Greenville, S.C., 1940-42; asst. prof. chemistry Conn. Coll., New London, 1942-45, assoc. prof., 1945-75, assoc. prof. emeritus, 1975—; assoc. prof. Shippensburg U., Pa., summers 1976-77. Sec. Gen. Fedn. Women's Clubs, Shippensburg, 1976-77, 1st v.p., 1977-78, pres., 1978-79, chmn. pub. affairs com., 1979—; trustee Shippensburg Presbyn. Ch., 1977-79; corr. sec. Cumberland County Fedn. Women's Clubs, 1977-79; ruling elder, commr. to Presbytery, Shippensburg Presbyn. Ch., 1981-84, commr. to synod, 1984, pres. United Presbyn. Women, 1982-84; bd. dirs., mem. exec. com., sec. Community Services, Inc., Shippensburg, 1980-87; mem. distbn. com. Alexander Stewart Found., Phila. Research fellow Pa. State U., 1960, 69-70. Mem. Am. Chem. Soc. (treas. Conn. Valley sect. 1949-60), U.S. daus. 1812, Kittochtinny Hist. Soc., Shippensburg Hist. Soc. Republican. Avocation: gardening. Home: Shippensburg, Pa. Died Mar. 4, 2006.

JOHNSTON, ROBERT ELLIOTT, former steel company executive; b. Johnstown, Pa., June 29, 1921; s. David Blair and Anna (Stephenson) J.; m. Nancy Jane Pyle, June 19, 1943; children: Michael, Lawrence, Susan (Mrs. Ronald Lindbeck), Martha (Mrs. Raymond Suarez). BS, U. Pitts., 1942; postgrad., Harvard Sch. Bus. Adminstrn., 1973. Research engr. Bethlehem Steel Corp., Lackawanna, N.Y., 1942-51, plant indsl. engr. Steelton, Pa., 1951-56, asst. gen. mgr. Sparrows Point, Md., 1956-72, v.p. manufactured products, steel ops. Bethlehem, Pa., 1972-74, v.p. prodn., 1974-77, v.p. steel ops., 1977-82. Served with AUS, 1943-44. Mem. Am. Iron and Steel Inst., Assn. Iron and Steel Engrs., U.S. Power Squadron, Sigma Chi. Clubs: Talbot Country, Sparrow Point Country, Miles River Yacht. Republican. Presbyterian. Home: Easton, Md. Died Nov. 20, 2006.

JONES, ALAN ANTHONY, chemistry educator; b. Jamestown, NY, Nov. 15, 1944; s. Elliot Jones and Lois (Patterson) Purcell; m. Eunice Li, Mar. 1, 1972. BA, Colgate U., 1966; PhD, U. Wis., 1972. Research instr. Dartmouth Coll., Hanover, N.H., 1972-74; asst. prof. Clark U., Worcester, Mass., 1974-78, assoc. prof., 1978-82, prof., from 1983, dept. chmn., 1980-84, 85-87, acting provost, 1987-88. Vis. prof. U. Wis., Madison, 1984. Contbr. articles to profl. jours. Mem. Conservation Commn., Worcester, 1981-82. Grantee NSF, 1976-86. Mem. Am. Chem. Soc., Am. Phys. Soc., Phi Beta Kappa. Avocations: skiing, waterskiing, windsurfing. Home: North Brookfield, Mass. Died May 23, 2006.

JONES, ARTHUR EDWIN, JR., library director, literature educator; b. Orange, NJ, Mar. 20, 1918; s. Arthur Edwin and Lucy Mabel (Alpaugh) J.; m. Rachel Evelyn Mumbulo, Apr. 24, 1943; 1 child, Carol Rae Jones Jacobus BA, U. Rochester, 1939; MA, Syracuse U., 1941, PhD in English, 1950; MLS, Rutgers U., 1964. Instr. English Syracuse U., N.Y., 1946-49, Drew U., Madison, N.J., 1949-52, asst. prof., 1952-55, assoc. prof., 1955-60, prof. English and Am. lit., 1960-86, dir. libraries, 1956-85, prof., libr. emeritus, from 1986. Evaluator Middle States Assn. Colls., Phila., 1955-85. Author: Darwinism and American Realism, 1951; contbr. articles to profl. jours.; book reviewer Library Jour., 1956-75, Choice, 1969— Trustee Madison Pub. Library, N.J., 1958-79, pres., 1976-79. Served to 1st lt. U.S. Army, 1941-46 Named to U. Rochester Athletic Hall of Fame, 1997; Lilly Endowment scholar Am. Theol. Libr. Assn., 1963-64 Mem. MLA, Nat. Coun. Tchr. of Eng., ALA (councillor 1970-71), Am. Theol. Libr. Assn. (pres. 1967-68), AAUP, Lions Club, Habitat for Humanity. Democrat. Home: Davidson, NC. Died Mar. 23, 2007.

JONES, DONALD LEE, construction engineer; b. Buffalo, Dec. 26, 1932; m. Joan Dimenstien, Feb. 19, 1961; children— Helaine V., LeAnn A., Paula R., David L. A.A.S., NYU, 1953; B. Bldg. Constrn., U. Fla., Gainesville, 1959; M. Indsl. Engring., Pacific Western U., 1979, Ph.D. in Bus. Adminstrn., 1980. Lic. plumber, N.Y. Estimator, field engr. housing contractors, Buffalo, 1955-56; field engr. Turner Constrn. Co., Chgo., 1959; field engr., supt. Raymond Concrete Pile Co. div. Raymond Internat., Inc., Chgo., 1959, office mgr., N.Y.C., 1960, supt., engr., Jamaica, W.I., 1961, asst. mgr. N.Y. dist., 1962, dist. mgr., design and constrn. engr., Houston, 1962-64, regional mgr., Atlanta 1964-66, dist. mgr., Boston, 1966-71; founder D.L. Jones Subsurface Inv., JEM Mgmt. Corp., Boston, 1972-78; mgr., ptnr. Civil Engring., Inc., Boston, Universal Testing, Inc., Hill Internat., Inc., 1979—, Jocaro Trading, U.S.A., Boston; bd. dirs. Dept. Profl. Regulations. Served with USNR, 1949-60. Mem. Am. Arbitration Assn., Gargoyle, Am. Legion, Alpha Phi Omega. Home: Valrico, Fla. Died Jan. 15, 2006.

JONES, EDWARD WITKER, bishop; b. Toledo, Mar. 25, 1929; BA, William Coll., 1951; BD, Va. Theol. Sem., 1954, DD, 1978. Rector Christ Ch., Oberlin, Ohio, 1957-68; exec. asst. to bishop and planning officer Diocese of Ohio, Cleve., 1968-71; rector St. James' Ch., Lancaster, Pa., 1971-77; bishop Episc. Diocese of Indpls., from 1977. Home: Indianapolis, Ind. Died July 28, 2007.

JONES, ELMER EVERETT, chemistry educator; b. Hinsdale, Ill., Sept. 2, 1926; s. Elmer E. and Laura Anna (Klein) J.; m. F. Alice Williamson, Aug. 25, 1956; 1 child, Laura Alice. Ph.B., U. Chgo., 1948, B.S., 1950; Ph.D., Washington U., 1957. Research assoc. Boston Dispensary, Tufts Med. Sch., 1955-58; asst. prof. Northeastern U., Boston, 1958-62, assoc. prof. chemistry, 1962—. Author/editor various books. Com. mem. Weston Democratic Town Com., Mass., 1980—; trustee Weston Forest and Trail Assn.; speaker Northeastern sect. Am. Chem. Soc. Served with USN, 1944-45. Mem. AAAS, Am. Chem. Soc., Nat. Assn. Advisors for Health Professions, Nat. Sci. Tchrs. Assn., New Eng. Assn. Chemistry Tchrs., Sigma Xi. Democrat. Avocations: naturalist; walking. Home: Weston, Mass. Died May 24, 2006.

JONES, ELVIS CALVIN, psychologist, educator, journalist; b. Oct. 26, 1937;, Calif. State U., Sacramento. Adj. instr. Mgmt. Devel. Ctr., State of Md., 1986—; reporter Cumberland (Md.) Tiimes-News, 1987—. With USAF, 1957-61. Home: Sacramento, Calif. Died July 4, 2006.

JONES, ERNEST OLIN, educator, radiation physicist; b. Atlanta, Feb. 1, 1923; s. Ernest and Annie Jane (Bryan) J.; m. Dorothy Irene Berg, May 20, 1946; children: Michael Bruce, Jacquelyn Ann (Mrs. Robert H. Hanks). BA, Emory U., 1948, MA (Research Corp. fellow), 1949; MS, U.S. Naval Postgrad. Sch., 1959; PhD, N.C. State U., 1964. Diplomate in radiol. physics Am. Bd. Radiology. Commd. 2d lt. U.S. Army, 1950, advanced through grades to lt. col., 1965; dep. dir. div. nuclear medicine WRAIR, 1964-67, dir. div. biometrics, 1967-68; ret., 1968; asso. prof. radiology U. Nebr., Omaha, 1968-72, prof., from 1972. Cons. in field. Decorated Legion of Merit. Fellow Am. Coll Radiology; mem. Am. Assn. Phys. Medicine (pres. Missouri River Valley chpt. 1972-73), Midlands Soc. Therapeutic Radiologists (pres. 1983-84), Nebr. Radiol. Soc., Assn. Mil. Surgeons, Am. Coll. Nuclear Physicians, Am. Coll. Med. Physics. Research minority carrier lifetimes in silicon radiation detectors, 1961-64, dosimetry of neutrons in modified research reactor, 1964-67, dosimetry of moving radiation sources, 1985-87. Home: Pagosa Springs, Colo. Died Nov. 25, 2006.

JONES, HENRY VINTON, insurance company executive; b. McKeesport, Pa., July 10, 1938; s. Robert Evan and Norma Winifred (Vinton) J.; m. Carol Anne Stelter, July 23, 1966; children: Bruce Vinton, Stephanie Ruth. AS, Tampa Coll., 1977; BS magna cum laude, Jones Coll., 1979; student Ashland Coll., 1982-84, Bradley U., 1988. Casualty underwriter Nat. Union Ins. Co., Pitts., 1960-62; spl. agt. CNA, Erie, Pa., 1962-65; multi-line underwriter Ohio Casualty Co., St. Petersburg, Fla., 1965-75; mgr. Aetna Ins. Co., Columbia, S.C., 1975-81; asst. v.p., dir. casualty underwriting Lumbermen's Mut. Ins. Co., Mansfield, Ohio, 1981-84, sr. mgr. CNA, Chgo., 1984-86; v.p., chief underwriting officer Gt. Cen. Ins., Co., Peoria, Ill., 1986—. Mem. expansion fund com. Mansfield Gen. Hosp., 1982, bd. edn. Concordia Sch. With AUS, 1956-60. Mem. Soc. Ins. Rsch., Internat. Brotherhood of Magicians, Nat. Coun. on Compensation Ins. (underwriting com.), Responsible Beverage Svcs. Council (charter). Republican. Lutheran. Home: Bel Air, Md. Died June 16, 2006.

JONES, JOE CHESTER, aerospace company executive; b. Birmingham, Ala., Sept. 18, 1922; s. James Marion and Cynthia (Byram) J.; B.S. in Aero. Engring., Auburn (Ala.) U., 1943; S.M. in Indsl. Mgmt. (Sloan fellow), M.I.T., 1957; m. Mary Emma Bowdon, Aug. 17, 1940; children— Cynthia Louise Jones Wertz, Cheri Lynn Jones Hall, James Marion, Joe Chester. With Dept. Air Force, 1947-73, dep. asst. sec. research and devel., 1966-73; asst. to chmn. bd. Northrop Corp., Los Angeles, 1974-79, v.p., asst. to chief exec. officer for aero. systems, 1979—; mem. research and tech. adv. com. aeros. NASA, 1968-70. Served to capt. USAF, 1943-46. Recipient Air Force Exceptional Civilian Service award, 1965, 69, 73, Dept. Def. Disting. Service award, 1972. Mem. Air Force Assn., Soc. Sloan Fellows, Sigma Nu. Republican. Home: Beaverton, Oreg. Died July 30, 2007.

JONES, MARY VIRGINIA WALTERS, newspaper editor; b. Dothan, Ala., Apr. 10, 1923; d. Thomas Jackson and Rachel Irell (Etheridge) Walters; B.A., in Journalism, U. Bridgeport, 1973; postgrad. in pub. communications Fordham U., 1975, U. Bridgeport, 1976-77; m. Raymond C. Jones, Dec. 3, 1943; children— Virginia Ann, Thomas Christopher, Edward William. Airways radio operator CAA, 1942-44; reporter, bur. chief Bridgeport Post-Telegram, 1960-73; editor Fairfield (Conn.) Citizen News, 1973-76, Westchester-Rockland Newspapers, White Plains, N.Y., 1976-77, Fairfield County Morning News, Trumbull, Conn., 1977—, Pensacola (Fla.) News Jour., 1978—. Instr. journalism U. Bridgeport, 1974-78. Rep. Trumbull Town Council, 1955-59; vice chmn. Trumbull Democratic Town Com., 1959-61. Recipient editorial award New Eng. Press Assn., 1976. Mem. Women in Communications, Inc., Deadline Club N.Y.C., Soc. Profl. Journalists. Episcopalian. Club: Nat. Press (Washington). Home: Crestview, Fla. Died Apr. 13, 2007.

JONES, NONA MAE, office manager; b. Kissimmee, Fla., Nov. 27, 1919; d. Arthur Eugene and Nina Mae (Sharpe) Jones; nursing home adminstr. licensure St. Petersburg Jr. Coll., 1972; 1 adopted dau., Sandra Jane Jones Dempsey. Bookkeeper, sales clk. H.B. Allen Firestone Store, Kissimmee, 1945-53; bookkeeper, key punch operator Tupperware Home Parties, Orlando, Fla., 1953-60; bookkeeper, office mgr. Cinderella Internat., Orlando, 1960-62; NCR operator/key punch Corporate Group Services, Orlando, 1963-68; bookkeeper, asst. adminstr. John Milton Nursing Home, Inc., Kissimmee, 1967-78, adminstr., 1978-80; office mgr./bookkeeper Robert L. Larson Contracting, Inc., Kissimmee, 1982—. Bd. dirs. Osceola County Mental Health Dept. Mem. Fla. Health Care Assn. (treas. dist. 3), C. of C. Osceola County. Mem. Christian Ch. (Disciples of Christ). Democrat. Home: Kissimmee, Fla. Died Mar. 22, 2006.

JONES, RAYMOND BOLIN, ceramic engineering consultant; b. Vicksburg, Miss., May 4, 1920; s. Alva Lewis and Flora Belle (Bolin) J.; m. Roberta Ownby, June 22, 1947; children— Raymond B. Jr., Karin Sue, Robert L., Elizabeth Ann. B.S. in Ceramic Engring., Mo. Sch. Mines, 1946. Vice pres., treas. Ceramo Co., Jackson, Mo., 1946-52; v.p. mfg. Nat. Tile Co., Anderson, Ind., 1952-62; ops. mgr. color div. Ferro Corp., Cleve., 1962-72, mgr. electronic materials, 1972-80, bus. devel. mgr. color div., 1980-82; cons. ceramic engring., Bay Village, Ohio, 1982—; cons. Glass Beads Co., Latrobe, Pa., 1982—. Contbr. articles to profl. jours. Patentee in field. Fellow Am. Ceramic Soc. Republican. Methodist. Died June 26, 2006.

JONES, RAYMOND EDWARD, JR., brewing executive; b. New Bern, NC, Jan. 27, 1927; s. Raymond Edward and Ellen LaVerne (Mallard) J.; children: Leslie Anne, Raymond Edward III. BS, U. Md., 1953; LLB, U. Balt., 1962. Bar: Md. 1962. Office mgr. Hopkins Furniture Co., Annapolis, Md., 1953-55; sr. v.p. legal, sec. Nat. Brewing Co., Balt., 1956-75; (merged with Carling Brewing Co. 1975); sr. v.p. legal and indsl. relations, dir. Carling Nat. Breweries, Inc., 1975-78; sec., assoc. gen. counsel Miller Brewing Co., 1978-84, v.p., gen. counsel, sec., 1984-89. House counsel and/or officer Divex, Inc., Laco Products, Inc., Laco Corp., C.W. Abbott, Inc., Pompeian, Inc., Interhost Corp., Solarine Co., Balt. Baseball Club, Inc., 1967-75 Bd. dirs. Soc. Preservation Md. Antiquities, 1969-71. Served with USNR, 1942-45. Mem. ABA, Md. Bar Assn., Balt. Bar Assn., Sigma Chi, Sigma Delta Chi. Presbyterian. Home: Saint Michaels, Md. Died Nov. 9, 2006.

JONES, ROBERT ALFRED, retired clergyman; b. Buffalo, July 19, 1930; s. Ralph A. and Edna Mae (Carver) J.; m. Helen T. Webster, July 20, 1957; children: Marc E., Paul R., Nancy L. BA, Houghton Coll., 1953; MA, Alfred U., 1959. Ordained to ministry United Meth. Ch., 1959. Assoc. pastor University United Meth. Ch., Buffalo, 1959-63; campus min. SUNY, Buffalo, 1963-67; pastor Woodside United Meth. Ch., Buffalo, 1967-74; sr. pastor Baker Meml. United Meth. Ch., East Aurora, NY, 1974-80; supr. Rochester dist United Meth. Ch., 1980-86; sr. pastor Ctrl. Park United Meth. Ch., 1986-89; asst. to bishop N.Y. west area United Meth. Ch., Syracuse, 1989-91; sr. pastor Williamsville (N.Y.) United Meth. Ch., 1991—99. Home: Williamsville, NY. Died Feb. 7, 2006.

JONES, SHERMAN JARVIS, state senator; b. Winton, NC, Feb. 10, 1935; s. Starkie Sherman and Gladys (Cherry) J.; m. Amelia Collins Buchanan, Dec. 16, 1956; children: Sheila C., Shelly C., Shelton C. Student, Kansas City C.C., 1976-77. Profl. baseball player, NYC, Cin., S Francisco, 1953-65; police officer Kansas City (Kans.) Police Dept., 1965-88; state rep. Kans. Legislature, 1988-92, senator, 1993-00. Named one of Outstanding Young Men Am., 1970. Mem. Nat. Conf. State Legislators, Kans. Legis. Black Caucus (chmn. 1991—), Optimists (v.p. 1982-83), Masons. Democrat. Home: Kansas City, Kans. Died Feb. 21, 2007.

JONES, TOM, track and field coach; m. Sandy Jones; children: Sean, Chris. B.Phys. Edn., UCLA, 1969; M.Phys. Edn., U. Wash., 1971. Tchr., coach Metter (Ga.) H.S., 1971-72, Forest Park (Ga.) Sr. H.S., 1972-74, Mainland Sr. H.S., Daytona Beach, Fla., 1974-75, Chamberlain Sr. H.S., Tampa, Fla., 1975-76; asst. coach U. Ala., 1976-78; head coach N.C. State U., 1978-84, U. Tex., El Paso, 1984-88, Ariz. State U., 1988-92; head coach track and field U. Fla., Gainesville, 1992—2007. Mem. USA Track & Field's exec. com., bd. dirs., 1988-2007; U.S. head men's coach 1988 U.S. vs. Gt. Britain meet; head coach U.S. Olympic Festival South team, 1985, 87. With U.S. Army. Named NCAA Men's Coach of the Yr. (Dist. 3), 1984, Indoor Coach of the Yr. (Dist. 7), 1986, Women's Coach of the Yr. (Dist. 8), 1990, Divsn. I Women's Indoor Coach of the Yr., 1997, Divsn. I Women's Outdoor Coach of the Yr., 1997, Dist. 3 Coach of the Yr., 1997, numerous SEC awards; inductee Helms Athletic Hall of Fame. Died Mar. 21, 2007.

JONES, WARREN DAVID, landscape architect, landscape architecture educator; b. Pasadena, Calif., July 3, 1914; s. Morris Shelly and Dorothy Grace (Brokaw) J.; m. Patricia Ruth Duffey, Oct. 27, 1941 (dec. Feb. 1966); children: David Morris, Scott Catterlyn, Stephen Duffey; m. Ruth Carol Cowley, Aug. 7, 1967. BS in Landscape Architecture, Oreg. State U., 1937; postgrad., U. Oreg., 1937-39. Registered landscape architect, Ariz., Calif. Landscape insp. Fed. Pub. Housing Authority, So. Calif., 1946-48; pvt. practice landscape architecture La Habra Heights, Calif., 1948-67; archtl. cons. Tucson, 1967—; prof. landscape architecture Sch. Renewable Natural Resources, Coll. Agriculture, U. Ariz., Tucson, 1967-86, prof. emeritus, from 1986. Mem. U. Ariz. landscape design team King Faisal Specialist Hosp., landscape cons.; numerous projects U.S. in Mexico, Saudi Arabia, Kuwait, Sudan, etc.; adv. bd. Boyce Thompson Arboretum, Ariz. Sonoran Desert Mus. Author: (with M.R. Duffield) Plants for Dry Climates, rev. edit., 1992, (with Dr. Charles Sacamano) Desert Trees and Shrubs for Landscape Use in the Desert Southwest, 1995; contbr. New Western Garden Book, Sunset Mag., articles to profl. jours., chpts. to books. Fellow Am. Soc. Lanscape Architects (Ariz. chpt., past trustee for Ariz.); mem. Ariz. Sonoran Desert Mus., Am. Assn. Bot. Gardens and Arboreta, Tucson Bot. Soc., Ariz. Native Plant Soc. (Tucson chpt.), Mex. Soc. Landscape Architecture (hon.) Home: Tucson, Ariz. Died Apr. 7, 2007.

JONISH, ARLEY DUANE, retired bibliographer; b. Walker, Minn., June 18, 1927; s. Howard Florian and Mabel Pauline (Rinde) J.; m. Thelma O. Ofstedal, Aug. 13, 1955 (dec. May 1988); children— Eleanor Ann, David Paul BS, Bemidji State U., 1949; MA, U. Minn., 1962. Tchr., librarian Pub. Schs., Red Lake Falls, Minn., 1949-55, Mahnomen, Minn., 1955-60; instr. libr. sci. U. No. Iowa, Cedar Falls, 1960-62; circulation librarian U. N. Mex., Albuquerque, 1962-63; reference librarian Western Oreg. Coll., Monmouth, 1963-66; dir. Penrose Meml. Libr. Whitman Coll., Walla Walla, Wash., 1966-87, bibliographer, 1987-89; ret., 1989; libr. cons. Walla Walla, 1990—2007. Mem. Wash. Govs. Conf. on Libraries and Info. Sci., Olympia, 1977-80, Wash. State Adv. Council on Libraries, Olympia, 1975-80 Precinct committeeman Republican Party, Walla Walla County, 1980-82. Served with USN, 1945-46, PTO Mem. ABA, Wash. Library Assn., Pacific Northwest Library Assn., AAUP, NEA, Northwest Assn. Pvt. Colls. and Univs. (chmn. library sect. 1970, 80), Assn. Coll. and Research Libraries (pres. Wash. state chapter 1987), Elks (life). Avocations: gardening; history of printing. Home: Walla Walla, Wash. Died Aug. 6, 2007.

JONTZ, JIM (JAMES PRATHER JONTZ), former congressman; b. Indpls., Dec. 18, 1951; s. Leland Dale and Pauline (Prather) J. AB, Ind. U., 1973. Program dir. Lake Mich. Fedn., Chgo.; exec. dir. Ind. Conservation Council, Indpls., 1972-74; mem. Ind. Ho. Reps., Indpls., 1974-84, Ind. State Senate, Indpls., 1984-86, US Congress from 5th Ind. dist., Washington, 1987—93. Pres. American for Democratic Action, 1998—2002. Democrat. Methodist. Home: Monticello, Ind. Died Apr. 14, 2007.

JORDAN, JACQUELYN, health agency executive, rancher; b. Hamilton, Ohio, Feb. 11, 1935; d. Harry Adolph and Kathryn Marie (Baird) Herman; m. Nov. 21, 1953 (div. Feb. 1977); children— Steve, Diana, Jeff. Student Miami U., 1953-54, U. Ill., 1955-56, Tarrant County Jr. Coll., 1973-76. Sec., Bookkeeper North Central Tex. Home Health Agy., Inc., Fort Worth, 1970-73, asst. bus. mgr., 1973-75, bus. mgr., 1975-80, pres., 1980—; rancher registered Santa Gertrudis cattle. Mem. Tarrant County Health Planning Council; charter mem. Ft. Worth Boot Brigade, 1985. Mem. Tex. Assn. Home Health Agys. Inc. (Named Tex. Chairperson of Yr. 1985), Nat. Assn. Home Care Inc., Bus. and Profl. Women's Orgn., Nat. Assn. Women Bus. Owners, Ft. Worth C. of C., Women Entrepreneur, Inc., Santa Gertrudis Breeders Internat. Democrat. Mem. Ch. of Christ. Avocations: outside activities; handicrafts. Home: Weatherford, Tex. Died Aug. 25, 2006.

JORDAN, ROBERT See RIGNEY, JAMES JR.

JORDAN, WINTHROP DONALDSON, historian, educator; b. Worcester, Mass., Nov. 11, 1931; s. Henry Donaldson and Lucretia Mott (Churchill) J.; m. Phyllis Henry, Aug. 30, 1952 (div. 1979); children: Joshua H., J. Mott, W. Eliot; m. Cora Miner Reilly, Feb. 27, 1982. AB, Harvard U., 1953; MA, Clark U., 1957; PhD, Brown U., 1960. Instr. history Phillips Exeter (N.H.) Acad., 1955-56; lectr. in history Brown U., Providence, 1959-61; fellow Inst. Early Am. History and Culture, Williamsburg, Va., 1961-63; from asst. prof. to prof. history U. Calif., Berkeley, 1963-82, assoc. dean for minority group affairs Grad. div., 1968-70; vis. prof. history and black studies U. Miss., Oxford, 1981, prof. history & Afro-Am. studies, 1982—2004, prof. emeritus, 2004—07. Vis. asst. prof. history U. Mich., Ann Arbor, 1966; vis. prof. history U. Calif., Berkeley, 1989; William F. Winter prof. history and prof. Afro-Am. studies, U. Miss., 1993-2004, F.A.P. Barnard Disting. prof., 1998—; vis. prof. history U. Zimbabwe, 1994. Author: White Over Black: American Attitudes Toward the Negro, 1550-1812, 1968, Tumult and Silence at Second Creek: An Inquiry Into a Civil War Slave Conspiracy, 1993; co-author: The United States, 1979, The Americans, 1982, The American People, 1986; mem. editorial bd. various scholarly jours. Council mem. Inst. Early Am. History and Culture, 1977-79. Recipient Ralph Waldo Emerson award Phi Beta Kappa, 1968, Parkman prize Soc. Am. Historians, 1969, Nat. Book award for History and Biography Am. Book Pubs., 1969, Bancroft prize Columbia U., 1969, 94, Landry award LSU Press, 1992, Eugene M. Kayden award, 1994, Disting. Alumnus citation Brown U. Grad. Sch., 1993, B.L.C. Wailesaward Miss. Hist. Soc., 2007; fellow Charles Warren Ctr. for Study Am. History Harvard U., 1965, Social Sci. Rsch. Coun., 1966, Guggenheim Found., 1967, Ctr. for Advanced Study Behavioral Scis., Palo Alto, 1975-76; grantee NIMH, 1970-73. Mem. Am. Antiquarian Soc. (elected), Am. Hist. Assn., Orgn. Am. Historians, So. Hist. Assn., Mass. Hist. Soc. (elected), Miss. Hist. Soc., Krokodiloes Club. Home: Oxford, Miss. Died Feb. 23, 2007.

JORGENSEN, GORDON DAVID, retired engineering company executive; b. Chgo., Apr. 29, 1921; s. Jacob and Marie (Jensen) J.; m. Nadina Anita Peters, Dec. 17, 1948 (div. Aug. 1971); children: Karen Ann, David William, Susan Marie; m. Barbara Noel, Feb. 10, 1972 (div. July 1976); m. Ruth Barnes Chalmers, June 15, 1990. BSEE, U. Wash., 1948, postgrad. in bus. and mgmt., 1956-59. Registered profl. engr., Alaska, Ariz., Calif., Colo., Nev., N.Mex., N.D., Utah, Wash., Wyo. With R.W. Beck & Assocs., Cons. Engrs., Phoenix, from 1948, ptnr., 1954-86; pres. Beck Internat., Phoenix, from 1971; ret. Project mgr. for mgmt., operation studies and reorgn. study Honduras power sys., 1969-70. Served to lt. (j.g.) U.S. Maritime Svc., 1942-45. Recipient Outstanding Svc. award Phoenix Tennis Assn., 1967, Commendation, Govt. Honduras, 1970. Mem. IEEE (chmn. Wash.-Alaska sect. 1959-60), NSPE, Am. Soc. Appraisers (sr. mem.), Ariz. Cons. Engrs. Assn., Ariz. Soc. Profl. Engrs., Internat. Assn. Assessing Officers, Southwestern Tennis Assn. (past pres.), U.S. Tennis Assn. (pres. 1987-88, chmn. U.S. Open com.), chmn. U.S. Davis Cup com., chmn. Internat. Tennis Fed., Davis Cup com.). Presbyterian (elder). Home: Indian Wells, Calif. Died June 10, 2007.

JORGENSEN, JAMES DOUGLAS, research physicist; b. Salina, Utah, Mar. 23, 1948; m. Ramona Gurr, June 6, 1970; children: Lynn Neilson, Michael Neilson, Kristeen Stenblik, Kathryn Brimball, Karen Russell, Scott Neilson. BS in Physics, Brigham Young U., 1970, PhD in Physics, 1975. Postdoctoral rsch. asst. Argonne (Ill.) Nat. Lab., 1974-77, asst. physicist solid state div., 1977-80, physicist material sci. div., 1980-89, sr. physicist, from 1989, group leader, from 1988. Mem. U.S. Nat. Com. for Crystallography, 1990-92, 94-97. Mem. editl. adv. bd. Jour. Solid State Chemistry, 1990—; contbr. over 300 articles to profl. jours. Bishop LDS Ch., Woodridge, Ill., 1984-89, stake pres., Naperville, Ill., 1998—. Recipient award for disting. performance at Argonne Nat. Lab., 1983, Barrett award, 1997; co-recipient Pacesetter award Argonne Nat. Lab., 1986, Dir.'s award, 1988; materials scis. rsch. competition award for outstanding sci. accomplishments in solid state physics U.S. Dept Energy, 1987, 91; named honored alumnus Brigham Young U., 1992. Fellow Am. Phys. Soc.; mem. Materials Rsch. Soc., Am Crystallographic Assn. (B.E. Warren Diffraction Physics award 1991). Home: Downers Grove, Ill. Died Sept. 7, 2006.

JOSEPH, EDNA WHITEHEAD (MRS. LAWRENCE J. JOSEPH), tax financial consultant, former banker; b. Everett Mass., Feb. 4, 1924; d. Alfred Edward and Mary Kathleen (Butler) Whitehead; attended Winthrop Schs., Boston U., Am Inst. Banking, Lee Real Estate Inst.; m. Lawrence James Joseph May 30, 1958. With Shawmut Bank of Boston, N.A. (now Flee Fin. Group), 1941-55, 57-84, asst. tax officer, 1965-69, tax officer, 1969-79, sr. trust officer, 1979-84; owner The Old Looking Glass, antiques; income tax mgr. Sam C. Charlson Manhattan, Kans., 1955-57. Bd. dirs. Found. of Hope, Boston mem. Republican Nat. Com., Women's Rep. Club Essex County, Nat. Fedn. Rep. Women. Mem. Fiduciary Tax Assos. Mass. Bankers Assn. (vice chmn. taxation com. 1971-72, chmn 1972-73, tax cons. com. 1975-84), Nat. Assn. Bank Women Am. Inst. Banking, Nat. Early Am. Glass Club (founders chpt.) North Shore Antique Assn., Soc. Preservation New Eng. Antiquities, Friends of Sandwich Mus., Woman 76 (Boston organizing com.), Soc. Jesus in New Eng. (liaison com. 1974-75, exec com. 1975-76), Mus. Fine Arts, Bostonian Soc., Victorian Soc. Essex Inst., Peabody Mus., Lynn Hist. Soc., Jones Gallery Glass and Ceramics. Home: Lynnfield, Mass. Died May 9, 2007.

JOYCE, DAVID, government administrator; b. Providence Aug. 17, 1919; s. Charles E. and Mary A. (Silva) J.; m. Mary A Costello, June 28, 1944; children— David Jr., Michael K., Pau B., Kevin W., Anne K., Charles C., Mary E. B. Philosophy Providence Coll., 1942. Probation counselor State of R.I 1944-48; sr. social worker State R.I., 1948-49; exec. dir. Famil Relocation Service City Providence, 1949-67, dir., Div. Minimum Standards, 1967-70, exec. dir. Housing Authority, 1970-78; adminstr. Dept. Mental Health State R.I., 1978—; cons. Sch Environ. Studies U. Pa., 1966-68. Author: Social Functioning o the Dislodged Elderly, 1968. Mem. fund raising com. Providence Council Boy Scouts Am., Providence, 1951; charter mem Friends for People, R.I., 1967. Served with USN, 1943. Recipient Citation Gov. J. Joseph Garrahy, R.I., 1977, Citation R.I Gen. Assembly, 1977, Proclamation Mayor Providence, 1977 Mem. Nat. Assn. Housing and Redevel. Officials (regional pres 1970-72, nat. bd. govs. 1970-74). Democrat. Roman Catholic Avocations: Reading; hiking. Home: Cranston, RI. Died Apr. 2(2007.

JOYNER, CLAUDE REUBEN, JR., cardiologist, educator; b Winston-Salem, NC, Dec. 4, 1925; s. Claude R. and Lytl (Mackie) J.; m. Nina Glenn Michael, Sept. 21, 1950; children Emily Glenn, Claude Courtney. BS, U. N.C., 1947; MD, U. Pa 1949. Intern Hosp. U. Pa., 1949-50; resident Bowman Gre Med. Sch., 1950, U. Pa., 1954-55, fellow in cardiology; Na Heart Inst. trainee, 1952-53; asst. instr. medicine Hosp. U. Pa Phila., 1951-53, instr., 1953-56, assoc. medicine, 1956-59, ass prof., 1959-64, assoc. prof., 1964-72; prof. medicine U. Pitts 1972-87, Med. Coll. Pa., 1987-96, vice dean, 1989-96; chie medicine Allegheny Gen. Hosp., Pitts., 1972-96. Contbr. article to profl. jours. Served to lt. M.C. USNR, 1950-52. Fellow Am Coll. Cardiology, ACP, Councils on Circulation, Arterioscleros and Cardiovascular Radiology of Am. Heart Assn.; men AAAS, Am. Heart Assn., Am. Clin. and Climatol. Soc. Home Sewickley, Pa. Died Nov. 17, 2006.

JUDD, BURKE HAYCOCK, geneticist; b. Kanab, Utah, Sep 5, 1927; s. Zadok Ray and Elva (Haycock) J.; m. Barbara An Gaddy, Mar. 21, 1953; children: Sean Michael, Evan Patric

Timothy Burke. BS, U. Utah, 1950, MS, 1951; PhD, Calif. Inst. Tech., 1954. Postdoctoral fellow Am. Cancer Soc. U. Tex., Austin, 1954-56, from instr. to prof., 1956-79, dir. Genetics Inst., 1977-79; geneticist Atomic Energy Commn., Germantown, Md., 1968-69; chief lab. genetics Nat. Inst. Environ. Health Sci., Research Triangle Park, NC, 1979-95. Vis. asst. prof. Stanford U., Palo Alto, Calif., 1960; Gosney vis. prof. Calif. Inst. Tech., Pasadena, 1975-76; adj. prof. U. N.C., Chapel Hill, 1979-99, Duke U., Durham, 1980-2002; mem. panel genetic biology NSF, Washington, 1969-73, genetics study sect. NIH, Washington, 1974, 77, 79, 88, com. on germplasm resources NAS, Washington, 1976-77; chmn. human genome initiative rev. panel Dept. of Energy, Washington, 1988. Author: Introduction to Modern Genetics, 1980; editor: Molecular and Gen. Genetics, 1986-95; assoc. editor Genetics, 1973-78; contbr. articles to profl. jours. With U.S. Army, 1946-47. Fellow AAAS; mem. Am. Soc. Naturalists (sec. 1968-70), Genetics Soc. Am. (sec. 1974-76, v.p., pres. 1979-80). Avocations: travel, poetry, fiction. Home: Chapel Hill, NC. Died June 11, 2007.

JUDGE, JEAN FRANCES, newspaper editor; b. Fall River, Mass., Mar. 18, 1930; d. James Edward and Dolores Veronica (Dunn) J.; B.A. magna cum laude in English Lit., Salve Regina Coll., Newport, R.I., 1951. Mem. staff Fall River Herald News, 1951—, editor woman's page, 1972-80, lifestyle editor, 1980—. Named Woman of Achievement Greater Fall River Bus. and Profl. Women's Club, 1982. Home: Fall River, Mass. Died Dec. 23, 2006.

JUDSON, PHILIP LIVINGSTON, retired lawyer, consultant; b. Palo Alto, Calif., Oct. 25, 1941; s. Philip MacGregor and Elizabeth Stuart (Peck) Judson; m. Dorothy Louisa Lebohner, Sept. 6, 1963 (div. Jan. 1996); children: Wendy Patricia, Philip Lebohner, Michael Lee; m. Danielle DuPuis Kane, May 18, 1996. BA, Stanford U., 1963; JD, U. Calif., Hastings, 1969. Bar: Calif. 1970, Tex. 1999, U.S. Dist. Ct. (no. dist.) Calif. 1970, U.S. Ct. Appeals (9th cir.) 1970, U.S. Dist. Ct. (ctrl. dist.) Calif. 1984, U.S. Dist. Ct. (ea. dist.) Calif. 1985, U.S. Supreme Ct. 1987, DC 1988, U.S. Dist. Ct. (so. dist.) Calif. 1989, Tex. 1999, U.S. Dist. Ct. (no. and we. dists.) Tex. 2000, U.S. Dist. Ct. (ea. dist.) Tex. 2002. Assoc. Pillsbury, Madison & Sutro, San Francisco, 1969-76, ptnr., 1977-99, Skjerven Morrill MacPherson, LLP, San Jose, Calif., 1999, Austin, Tex., 1999—2002; shareholder Winstead Sechrest & Minick, P.C., Austin, 2002—04, ret., 2004; cons. in field. Lectr. Practicing Law Inst., U. Tex. Advanced Intellectual Property Law Inst., Inst. Am. and Internat. Law Intellectual Property Law Program. Founding mem. trustee St. Mark's Sch., San Rafael, 1980—86, pres., 1983—85; trustee Marin Acad., San Rafael, 1985—91. 1st lt. US Army, 1963—65. Mem.: ABA (mem. antitrust and litig. sects.), Austin Bar Assn., Austin Intellectual Property Law Assn., Am. Judicature Soc., San Francisco Bar Assn., Order of Coif, Phi Delta Theta. Republican. Episcopalian. Home: Highlands Ranch, Colo. Died Aug. 11, 2007.

JUNG, EDMUND DIXON, physician; b. Hanford, Calif., June 29, 1914; s. Ming Stanley and Mabel (Wye) J.; m. Haw Chan, Jan. 28, 1950. AB, Stanford U., 1938; MS, U. Calif., San Francisco, 1941, MD, 1944. Diplomate Am. Bd. Internal Medicine. Staff physician, chief allergy sect. VA Med. Ctr., Oakland, Martinez, Calif., 1951-82; assoc. clin. prof. medicine U. Calif., San Francisco, from 1983. Cons. allergy VA Regional Office, San Francisco, 1961-66; asst. clin. prof. U. Calif., San Francisco, 1974-83, assoc. clin. prof., 1983—. Bd. dirs. Chinese Hist. Soc. Am., San Francisco, 1986-90. Capt. M.C. U.S. Army, 1945-47, PTO. Fellow ACP; mem. Am. Acad. Allergy and Clin. Immunology, Am. Soc. Clin. Hypnosis. Home: Oakland, Calif. Died Oct. 28, 2006.

JUNGMAN, YOUNG FRANK, real estate broker; b. Houston, Mar. 18, 1929; s. J. Frank and Thelma Katherine (Young) J.; B.B.A., U. Tex., 1948, J.D., 1950; postgrad. U. Houston, Wichita State U., U. Ga., So. Methodist U.; m. Marilyn Virginia Skipwith, June 7, 1952; children: Robert Frank, John Skipwith. Sec.-treas., dir. Paul E. Wise Co., Inc., and affiliated cos., 1954-61; real estate broker, appraiser, cons., investor, Houston, 1961—; moderator/arbitrator, Houston, 1991—. Admitted to Tex. bar, 1950, U.S. Supreme Ct. bar, 1954; instr. real estate U. Houston, 1970-73. Mem. Harris County Flood Control Task Force, 1975-77; mem. Harris County Democratic Exec. Com., 1978-80, del. to GOP Senatorial Dist. Conv., 1988, 90, precinct fl. chmn. 1988. Mem. Houston City Library Bd., 1965-76, v.p., 1973-76; mem. vestry Trinity Episcopal Ch., 1979-82, 87-90, sr. warden, 1989-90; trustee St. James House, 1986-89. Served to 1st lt. USAF, 1951-53. Mem. Nat., Tex., Houston assns. realtors, Am. Arbitration Assn., Tex., Houston bar assns., Pi Kappa Alpha, Phi Alpha Delta. Mason. Home: Houston, Tex. Died Apr. 30, 2006.

KACHMAR, LILLIAN SANDRA, lawyer, author; b. Phila., Jan. 13, 1954; d. Michael and Lillian (Corwonski) Kachmarchik; m. John F. Steele, Mar. 10, 1979; 1 dau., Barbara Courtney. B.A. in History maxima cum laude, LaSalle Coll., 1975; J.D., U. Villanova, 1978. Bar: Pa. 1978, Fla. 1979, U.S. Dist. Ct. (so. dist.) Fla. 1979, U.S. Ct. Appeals (5th cir.) 1979, Assoc. firm Ruden, Barnett, McClosky, Schuster & Russell, Ft. Lauderdale, Fla., 1978-80; counsel spl. project Control Fluidics, Inc., F/K/A I.W.S.S. Corp., N.Y.C., 1980; asst. counsel Reliance Ins. Co., Phila., 1980-81; sole practice law, Villanova, Pa., 1981—. Author: (novel) Zeus: The Cronus File, 1983. Mem. ABA, Fla. Bar Assn., Pa. Bar Assn. Republican. Roman Catholic. Home: Villanova, Pa. Died Apr. 13, 2007.

KADRMAS, EDWIN E., publishing company executive; b. Dickinson, N.D., Feb. 18, 1934; s. William J. and Emilie A. Kadrmas; B.S., N.D. State U., 1956; postgrad. Mont. State U.; m. Melda Pfenning, Aug. 16, 1955; children— Ronald L., Robert R., Russell W., Roger J. Instr. bus. Rosebud (Mont.) High Sch., 1956-58, Dawson County (Mont.) High Sch., 1958-59, Dawson County Jr. Coll., Glendive, Mont., 1958-59; coll. and gen. rep. South-Western Pub. Co., 1959-67, asst. regional mgr., West Chicago, Ill., 1967-78, regional v.p., 1979—. Chmn., West Chicago Crusade of Mercy, 1974-75; pres. United Way of West Chicago, 1975-77; pres. Suburban Mgmt. Assn., 1974, top mgmt. adv. com., 1975—; div. v.p. Internat. Mgmt. Council, 1974-76. Cert. profl. mgr. Mem. Ill. State C. of C., Ill. Bus. Edn. Assn., Am. Vocat. Assn., Nat. Bus. Edn. Assn., Chgo. Bus. Edn. Assn. Republican. Club: Rotary (gov.'s rep. 1977—, dist. gov. 1982-83). Died Apr. 16, 2006.

KAHL, RICHARD C., lawyer; b. Vandergrift, Pa., Apr. 19, 1924; s. John C. and Margaret M. (Gagen) K.; m. Beverley Rogers, Dec. 11, 1943; children— David R., Leslie R. BA, Alleheny Coll., Meadville, Pa., 1948; JD, U. Buffalo, 1953. Bar: NY, U.S. Dist. Ct. (we. dist.) NY Assoc., ptnr. Hille & Kahl, Niagara Falls, NY, 1954-81; sole practice, Lewiston, 1981—; atty. Lewiston Porter Central Sch., Youngstown, Village of Youngstown. Served to 1st lt. USAF, 1943-46; served to major NY N.G.; aircraft comdr., PTO. Decorated Air medal; named Outstanding Cadet in Pilot Tng. Mem. Niagara Falls Bar Assn., Niagara County Bar Assn. Republican. Clubs: Youngstown Yacht (commodore 1983), Niagara (pres. 1964), Niagara Falls Country. Home: Youngstown, NY. Died May 24, 2007.

KAHN, DONALD JAY, retired energy company executive; b. Balt., Aug. 10, 1930; s. Louis Julian and Ruth (Brager) K.; B.A., Princeton U., 1952; Ph.D., U. Chgo., 1957; m. Ruth Revzen, May 29, 1960; children: Jonathan, Robert, Ariel. Researcher, mgr. Exxon Research & Engring. Co., N.J., 1957-67; aviation tech. div. mgr. Exxon Internat., N.Y.C., 1967-71; sr. adv. environ. affairs Exxon Corp., N.Y.C., 1971-76, sr. adv. African affairs, 1977, sr. tech. adv., 1981-84, planning cons., 1984-86, ret., 1986; gen. mgr. Exxon Enterprises, N.Y.C., also chief exec. Solar Power Corp., Boston, 1978-81; bd. dir. Societe des Applications de l'Helioenergie, Paris, 1979-80. Mem. Metuchen (N.J.) Bd. Health, 1965-73, pres., 1973; bd. dirs. Neve Shalom Synagogue, Metuchen, 1967-74; environ. commr., Metuchen, 1973-77, chmn., 1973-77; mem. Metuchen Drug Abuse Coun., 1980-85, Metuchen Planning Bd., 1987—. Mem. Am. Chem. Soc., Internat. Solar Energy Soc., Sigma Xi. Jewish. Patentee in field. Home: Metuchen, NJ. Died Apr. 27, 2006.

KAINLAURI, EINO OLAVI, architect; b. Lahti, Finland, June 13, 1922; came to U.S., 1947, naturalized, 1954; s. William and Eva K.; m. Genevieve Marjorie Mobley, Aug. 20, 1949; children: John Stanford, William Eino, Mary Ann. Student, Finland Inst. Tech., 1945-47; B.Arch., U. Mich., 1950, M.Arch., 1959, PhD, 1975. Draftsman U. Mich. Architect's Office, Ann Arbor, 1951-55; dealer systems planner Ford div. Ford Motor Co., Livonia, Mich., 1955-56; ptnr., gen. mgr. Davis, Kainlauri & MacMullan (architects, engrs., planners), Ann Arbor, 1956-59; pres. KMM Assocs. (architects, engrs., planners), Ann Arbor, 1959-75; prof. architecture Iowa State U., Ames, 1975-92, prof. emeritus, from 1992. Works include Finnish Cultural Ctr., Farmington, Mich., also schs. and chs.; author: Multinational Cooperation in Regional Planning for Lapland, 1976; editor proc. internat. symposia and confs.; contbr. numerous articles to profl. jours. Served to 1st lt. Finnish Army, World War II. Decorated cross and medal of Liberty; Fulbright Hayes sr. scholar, 1973-74; Fulbright rsch. scholar, 1983-84; recipient Knighthood of the Order of White Rose, 1st Class, Finland, 1993. Fellow AIA (design com., Architects in Edn.); mem. ASTM, ASHRAE (disting. svc. awrad 1995), Soc. Bldg. Sci. Educators, Nat. Trust Historic Preservation, Am. Solar Energy Soc., Internat. Solar Energy Soc., Am.-Scandinavian Found., Finnish-Am. Soc., Intelligent Bldgs. Inst., Finland Soc. Clubs: Optimist (life), Lions. Lutheran. Home: Ames, Iowa. Died Jan. 11, 2006.

KAISER, ELSA CAROL, association management specialist, craft designer; b. Lancaster, Pa., Aug. 31, 1953; d. Gunter Peter and Grace (Helsel) K.; m. Roger Ernst Landauer, Sept. 10, 1982. B.S.B.A., U. Denver, 1974; postgrad. U. Colo., Denver, 1976-77. Vice pres. Peggy Jones & Co., Denver, 1975-77; exec. dir. Assn. of AV Tech., Denver, 1977-78; owner Elcole Mgmt. Inc., Denver, 1978—. Mem. Inst. of Assn. Mgmt. (dir. 1983—), Am. Soc. Assn. Execs., Colo. Soc. Assn. Execs., Nat. Assn. Exhibit Mgrs., Sigma Pi Eta. Home: Golden, Colo. Died Dec. 1, 2006.

KAISER, PHILIP MAYER (P.M. KAISER), retired ambassador; b. Bklyn., July 12, 1913; s. Morris and Temma (Sloven) K.; m. Hannah Greeley, June 16, 1939; children: Robert Greeley, David Elmore, Charles Roger. AB, U. Wis., 1935; BA, MA (Rhodes scholar), Balliol Coll., Oxford U., Eng., 1939. Economist, bd. govs. Fed. Res. System, 1939-42; chief project ops. staff, also chief planning staff enemy br. Bd. Econ. Warfare and Fgn. Econ. Adminstrn., 1942-46; expert on internat. orgn. affairs US Dept. State, 1946, exec. asst. to asst. sec. internat. labor affairs, 1946-47; dir. Office Internat. Affairs, US Dept. Labor, 1947-49, asst. sec. labor for internat. affairs, 1949-53; labor adv. Com. for Free Europe, 1954; spl. asst. to Gov. W. Averell Harriman State of NY, Albany, 1955-58; prof. internat. rels. Sch. Internat. Svc. Am. U., 1958-61; U.S. ambassador to Senegal & Mauritania US Dept. State, 1961-64; minister Am. Embassy, London, Eng., 1964-69; chmn. Ency. Brit. Internat. Ltd., London, 1969-75; dir. Guinness Mahon Holdings, Ltd., 1975-77; US amb. to Hungary US Dept. State, Budapest, 1977-80, US amb. to Austria Vienna, 1980-81; professorial lectr. Johns Hopkins Sch. Advanced Internat. Studies, 1981—83, Woodrow Wilson vis. fellow, 1984; sr. cons. SRI Internat., 1981-97. Mem. interdept. com. to develop programs under Marshall Plan, 1947—48, interdept. com. to develop programs for Greek-Turkish aid and Point 4 Tech. Assistance, 1947—49, Internat. del. to Hungary's Parliamentary elections, 1990; spl. amb. for Pres. Kennedy to Rwanda for its ind. day, 62. Author: Journeying Far and Wide: A Political and Diplomatic Memoir, 1993. Bd. dirs. Am. Ditchley Found., Ptnrs. for Dem. Change, Coun. Am. Ambs., Assn. Diplomatic Studies, Am. Acad. Diplomacy. Decorated knight comdr. Austrian Govt., Cross of Order of Merit of Republic of Hungary. Mem. Am. Assn. Rhodes Scholars, Coun. Fgn. Rels., Washington Inst. for Fgn. Affairs, Phi Beta Kappa. Home: Washington, DC. Died May 24, 2007.

KAKOL, STANLEY JOSEPH, engineering test pilot; b. Olean, N.Y., Nov. 28, 1926; m. Dowling H. Maxim, June 5, 1950 (div. 1972); m. Sandra L. Ehnis, Feb. 14, 1981; 1 child, Stanley J. Student, U. Rochester, 1944-45, Hobart Coll., 1945-46, U. Pa., 1946, U. Buffalo, 1950-52. Chief exptl. test pilot Bell Aerospace, Niagara Falls, N.Y., 1964-68; test pilot FAA, N.Y., 1973-74; captain Zantop Internat. Airlines, Ypsilanti, Mich., 1978-82; engring. test pilot Gen. Electric Co., Lynn, Mass., 1982—. Served to capt. USNR, 1943-49, 52-54. Piloted first flight of X-ZZA, Bell Aerospace, 1966. Fellow Soc. Exptl. Test Pilots (assoc.). Roman Catholic. Club: Navy League. Avocations: golf; tennis; chess; bridge. Home: Petoskey, Mich. Died Dec. 1, 2006.

KALBFLEISCH, GEORGE RANDOLPH, physicist, researcher; b. Long Beach, Calif., Mar. 14, 1931; s. Carl Friedrich and Hildegard (Fuchs) K.; m. Ruth Ann Adams, Oct. 23, 1954; children: Karen Ruth, George Randolph, Julie Marie, Carl William. BS in Chemistry, Loyola U., LA, 1952; PhD in Physics, U. Calif., Berkeley, 1961. Quality control supr. Hunt Foods, Inc., Hayward, Calif., 1952-56; analytical chemist, spectroscopist Hales Testing Labs., Oakland, Calif., 1956-57; technician Lawrence Radiation Lab., Berkeley, 1957-59, grad. rsch. asst., 1959-61, physicist, 1961-64; assoc. physicist Brookhaven Nat. Lab., Upton, L.I., 1964-66, physicist, 1966-76, Fermi Nat. Accelerator Lab., Batavia, Ill., 1976-79; prof. physics U. Okla., Norman, from 1979. Cons. Anamet Labs., Oakland, 1962-64; bd. dirs. Univ. Rsch. Assn., Washington, 1989-95. Contbr. articles to profl. jours. Dept. Energy grantee, 1980—. Fellow Am. Phys. Soc. Lutheran. Avocations: family, genealogy. Home: Norman, Okla. Died Sept. 12, 2006.

KALODNER, ALFRED LEONARD, gynecologist, obstetrician; b. Phila., Dec. 25, 1924; s. Edwin Jacob and Reba (Hoffman) K.; m. Corinne Feinberg, June 24, 1945; children: John David, Ellen Hope Isdaner. Grad., Temple U., 1944, MD, 1947, MSc in ob-gyn, 1954. Diplomate Am. Bd. Ob-Gyn. Practice medicine specializing in ob-gyn, Phila., from 1955; instr. ob-gyn Temple U., Phila., 1955-60, assoc., 1960-61, asst. prof., 1961-64, assoc. prof., 1964-67, clin. prof., from 1967. Cons. Maternity Child Health, City of Phila., 1957-80; chmn. dept. Ob-Gyn Jeanes Hosp., Phila, 1981—. Fellow Am. Pub. Health Assn. Republican. Jewish. Home: Blue Bell, Pa. Died July 18, 2007.

KANE, CECELIA DRAPEAU, state legislator, registered nurse; b. Concord, NH, Oct. 12, 1915; d. Esdras and Marguerite Elizabeth (Carter) Drapeau; m. Thomas J. Kane, Jan. 23, 1986 (dec.); children: Maureen, Cheryl, Charlene, Thomas D. (dec.). Diploma, Sch. Nursing, 1938; postgrad., 1939. Legislature N.H. House of Reps., Portsmouth, N.H., from 1988. Mem. Cath. Daughters Am., Portsmouth, 1987, Dem. State Com., 1942—, N.H. OWLS, 1990—; bd. registrars Supr. of Checklist, Portsmouth, 1987—; bd. dirs. Betty's Dream, Portsmouth, 1990—. Democrat. Roman Catholic. Avocations: knitting, crochetting. Home: Portsmouth, NH. Died Dec. 8, 2005.

KANE, HARRY JOSEPH, financial executive; b. Spokane, Wash., Jan. 5, 1923; s. Harry Joseph and Ann Elizabeth (Hartmeier) K. m. Antoinette Marie Van Parys, Oct. 28, 1944; 1 child, Thomas Robert. BS, U. Wash., 1948. CPA, Wash., Oreg. Mgr. indsl. audits Arthur Andersen & Co., Seattle, 1948-55; with Ga. Pacific Corp., Portland, Oreg., 1955-83, exec. v.p. fin., bd. dirs., 1966-83, mem. exec. com, 1973-83; chmn. Fin. Mgmt. Group, Portland, from 1983. Bd. dirs. Portland Gen. Svcs., Inc. Chmn. bd. Oreg. Ind. Coll. Found.; trustee Com. Econ. Devel.; bd. dirs. NCCJ, Oreg. Investment Coun. With USMRC, 1941-44. Mem. AICPA, Wash., Oreg. socs. CPAs, Fin. Execs. Inst., Waverley Country Club, Alington Club, Multnomah Athletic Club. Republican. Roman Catholic. Home: Portland, Oreg. Died Nov. 15, 2005.

KANE, MARGARET BRASSLER, sculptor; b. East Orange, NJ, May 25, 1909; d. Hans and Mathilde (Trumpler) Brassler; m. Arthur Ferris Kane, June 11, 1930; children: Jay Brassler, Gregory Ferris. Student, Packer Collegiate Inst., 1920—26, Syracuse U., 1927, Art Students League, 1927—29, N.Y. Coll. Music, 1928—29, John Hovannes Studio, 1932—34; PhD (hon.), Colo. State Christian Coll., 1973. Head craftsman sculpture, arts and skills unit ARC, Halloran Gen. Hosp., NY, 1942—43; jury mem. Bklyn. Mus., 1948, Am. Machine & Foundry Co., 1957; com. mem. An Am. Group, Inc. Exhibitions include, Phila. Mus., Chgo. Art Inst., Am. Fedn. Arts, NY Bot. Garden, 1981, 60th Anniversary Exhbn. Lever House, 1987—98, Sculptors Guild 50th Anniversary Exhbn., Lever House, 1987—96, 1st Bi-Coastal exhibits San Francisco, Collection Donald Trump, 1988, Collection Rene Anselmo, 1991, Shidoni Galleries, Santa Fe, N.Mex., 1989, Am. Sculpture, Hofstra Mus., 1990, exhibitions include nat. tour Am. sculpture by EducArt Projects Inc., 1992, exhibitions include, Stamford Mus. and Nature Ctr., 1996, Zimmerli Art Mus. Historical Exhibit, 1999—2000, Treasures from the Smithsonian Am. Art Mus., 2000—02, numerous others, Represented in permanent collections, Zimmerli Art Mus., Rutgers U., NJ, 1992, Nat. Mus. Am. Art, Smithsonian Instn., Washington, 1993, 2000, Bruce Mus., Greenwich, Conn., 1996, Packer Collegiate Inst., Bklyn., 2003, one-woman shows include sculpture, Friends Greenwich (Conn.) Library, 1962, prin. works include 18 foot carving in limewood, 2002, prin. works include six foot carving Reaching the Galaxies, from 2002, prin. works include plaque Burro Monument, Fair Play, Colo., prin. works include bronze panels Earthbound, cast by Tallix Art Foundry Beacon, NY, 2005, Symbols, 2005, Micro-macrocosm, 2005, Five episodes in human history, bronze works placed against a cosmic background, 2006; reprodns. Contemporary Stone Sculpture, 1970, Contemporary Am. Sculptures, Am. References, Chgo.; CD-ROM, Smithsonian Nat. Mus. Am. Art, Washington, 1995; contbr. articles to mags. Recipient Hyatt Huntington award, 1942, Am. Artist Profl. League and Monclair Art Assn. awards, 1943, 1st Henry O. Avery prize, 1944, Sculpture prize, Bklyn. Soc. Artists, Bklyn. Mus., 1946, John Rogers award, 1951, Lawrence Hyder prize, 1952, 1954, David H. Zell Meml. award, 1954, 1963, Hon. Mention, U.S. Maritime Commn., 1941, A.C.A. Gallery Competition, 1944, medal of Honor for Sculpture, Nat. Acad. Galleries, N.Y., prize for carved sculpture, 1955, prize for animal sculpture, 1956, 1st award for sculpture, Ann. New Eng. Exhbns., Silvermine, Conn. Fellow: Internat. Inst. Arts and Letters (life); mem.: Nat. Trust Hist. Preservation, silvermine Guild Artists, Internat. Soc. Artists (charter), Internat.

Sculpture Ctr., Greenwich Soc. Artists (mem. coun.), Bklyn. Soc. Artists, Artists Coun. U.S.A., Pen and Brush (emeritus 1992), Nat. League Am. Pen Women, Inc. (OWL award for the Arts 1991), Nat. Assn. Women Artists (2d v.p. 1943—44), Sculptors Guild, Inc. (life; sec. to exec. bd. 1942—45, chmn. exhbn. com. 1942, 1944). Died Apr. 10, 2006.

KANE, STANLEY PHILLIP, insurance company executive; b. St. Paul, Oct. 3, 1930; s. Bernard J. and Bertha (Pusin) K.; m. Judith Zaikaner, July 1, 1952; children: Brian, Debra, Elizabeth, David. Student, Beck Radio Sch., Mpls., 1948-49. V.p. Arlan Agys., Inc., Mpls., 1950-57; pres. BOMA Inc., Mpls., 1957-68, North Central Life, St. Paul, 1972-76; exec. v.p. North Central Cos., St. Paul, 1968-76; chmn. bd., pres., chief exec. officer Early Am. Life Ins. Co., St. Paul, 1976-90; cons., from 1990; cons. ins. asset mgmt. Radio announcer, writer, WJMC, Rice Lake, Wis., 1949-50. Scoutmaster Boy Scouts Am., 1967-69, dist. chmn., 1971-74; Bd. dirs., v.p. Jewish Family Service, 1975-81; chmn. bd. Alfred Adler Inst. of Minn., 1980-84; pres.-elect Mt. Zion Temple, St. Paul, 1987-89, pres., 1989-91. With M.C. AUS, 1952-54. Mem. Life Underwriters Assn., Presidents Assn. Jewish (bd. dir. temple 1960-64, 75-79, pres. men's club 1960-64), Am. Council Life Ins. (chmn. exec. roundtable 1985-87, bd. dirs. 1989-91) Died Dec. 3, 2006.

KANNER, BERNICE, columnist, writer; b. NYC, Jan. 21, 1949; d. Al and Lillian Kanner; m. David B. Cuming, Oct. 10, 1982; children: Elisabeth, Andrew. BA, Harpur Coll., Binghamton, NY, 1969; MA in English Lit., SUNY, Binghamton, 1972. Account exec. J. Walter Thompson, NYC, 1974-77; sr. editor, reporter Advt. Age Mag., NYC, 1977-81; columnist Daily News, NYC, 1980-81; sr. editor, columnist N.Y. Mag., 1981-94; columnist Bloomberg Bus. News, NYC, from 1994, Screaming-Media, NYC; editor-in-chief WomensBiz.US, NYC, 2002—06. Author: Are You Normal?: Do You Behave Like Everyone Else?, 1995, Lies My Parents Told Me: The Hilarious, Outrageous and Outright Incredible Things We Grow up Believing, 1996, The 100 Best TV Commercials And Why They Worked, 1999, Are You Normal About Money?: Do You Behave Like Everyone Else?, 2001, The Super Bowl of Advertising: How the Commercials Won the Game, 2003, Are You Normal About Sex, Love and Relationships, 2004, Pocketbook Power: Marketing to Women in the 21st Century, 2004, When It Comes To Guys, What's Normal?, 2005. Mem.: exec. com., Women's Bus. Coun. for Peace. Home: New York, NY. Died Oct. 24, 2006.

KAPLAN, HAROLD IRVING, lawyer; b. Boston, Jan. 6, 1921; s. Bernard A. and Florence R. (Stone) K.; m. Eleanor G. Moranz, Jan. 1, 1949; children— Joanne Sue, Bart Alan. BS in Mech. Engring, U. Maine, 1942; JD, Harvard, 1948; LL.M., George Washington U., 1950. Bar: Mass. 1948, N.Y. 1951, U.S. Supreme Ct. 1964. Patent examiner U.S. Patent Office, Washington, 1948-50; patent atty. NYC, from 1950; with firm Blum, Kaplan, NYC, from 1960, mng. partner, from 1971. Mem. Nat. Panel Arbitrators, Am. Assn. Arbitrators, 1967— Served to capt. USAAF, 1942-46, ETO. Mem. Assn. Bar City N.Y., N.Y., N.J., Am. patent law assns., ABA Clubs: Harvard of N.Y. Home: Palm Beach, Fla. Died Oct. 28, 2005.

KAPLAN, PETER ROBERT, cardiologist; b. Peterson, NJ, June 10, 1939; BA, Princeton U., 1960; MD cum laude, U. Pa., 1964. Diplomate Nat. Bd. Med. Examiners, Am. Bd. Internal Medicine. Intern U. Va. Hosp., 1964-65, jr. asst. resident medicine, 1967-68, sr. asst. resident medicine, 1968-69, clin. fellow cardiovascular disease, 1969-71, chief resident, asst. attending physician, 1971-72; cardiologist St. Thomas Cardiology Group, Nashville, from 1972; chief cardiology St. Thomas Hosp., Nashville, from 1995, pres. med. staff, 1995-97. Capt. Med. Corps U.S. Army, 1965-67. Mem. Tenn. Med. Assn., Albermarle County Med. Soc., Davidson Med. Soc., Seton Soc., Phi Beta Kappa. Died Mar. 2, 2006.

KAPSON, JORDAN, automotive executive; b. 1923; Chmn. Jordan Motors, Inc. dba Jordan Ford, Mishawaka, Ind., from 1947, Jordan Toyota dba Jordan Volvo, Jordan KIA, from 1981, Jordan Motors, Inc. Died Feb. 22, 2006.

KARAKASH, JOHN J., engineering educator; b. Istanbul, Turkey, June 14, 1914; came to U.S., 1936, naturalized, 1948; s. Joachim Theodore and Irene (Georges) K.; m. Marjorie Rutherford, June 21, 1945; 1 child, John Thomas. Student, Robert Coll., Istanbul, 1932-35; BS, Duke U., 1937; MS (Moore fellow), U. Pa., 1938; D Engring. (hon.), Lehigh U., 1971. Registered profl. engr., Pa. Instr. U. Pa., 1938-40; project engr. Moore Sch. Elec. Engring., 1944-46; rsch. engr. Am. TV Labs., Chgo., 1940-42; edn. dir. 6th Svc. Command Signal Corps Radar Sch., Chgo., 1942-44; from asst. prof. to assoc. prof. elec. engring. Lehigh U., 1946-55, prof., head dept., 1955-58, disting. prof., 1962-81; dean Lehigh U. Coll. Engring., 1965-81; project engr. UHF filters Lehigh U., 1950-54; project dir. active networks Signal Corps., 1954-60. Cons. Bell Telephone Labs., Murray Hill, N.J., 1950-56, Dept. Edn. Commonwealth P.R., 1972, IBM, 1980-93; bd. dirs. Komline & Sanderson Engring. Corp. Author: Transmission Line and Filter Networks, 1950, also articles. Mem. Gen. State Authority Commonwealth of Pa., 1974-81. Recipient Alfred Nobel Robinson award for svc. to univ., 1948, Hillman award for disting. svc. Lehigh, 1962, 81, Outstanding Tchr. award, 1968, Outstanding Prof. award Lehigh U. Alumni Assn., 1990, Pa. Profl. Engring. award for distinction, 1965; rebuilt north wing Packard Lab. dedicated in his honor, 1981. Fellow IEEE (life, co-founder Lehigh Valley chpt. 1963, Centennial medal award 1984); mem. Am. Soc. Engring. Edn. (life), Engring. Coun. for Profl. Devel. (nat. accreditation com. for engring.), Franklin Inst., Pergamon Inst. (hon. adv. bd.), Phi Beta Kappa, Sigma Xi, Phi Beta Delta, Tau Beta Pi, Omicron Delta Kappa, Eta Kappa Nu, Iota Gamma Pi. Home: Bethlehem, Pa. Died Mar. 22, 2006.

KARANIKAS, ALEXANDER, language educator; b. Manchester, NH, Oct. 5, 1916; s. Stephen and Vaia (Olgas) K.; m. Helen J. Karagianes, Jan. 2, 1949; children: Marianthe Vaia, Diana Christine, Cynthia Maria. Student, U. N.H., 1934-36; AB cum laude, Harvard, 1939; MA, Northwestern U., 1950, PhD in English, 1953. With N.H. Writers Project, 1940-41; editor Allegheny-Kiski Valley Edit. The CIO News, 1941-42; radio news commentator Sta. WMUR, Manchester, 1946; grad. asst. Northwestern U., Evanston, Ill., 1950-52; instr. Kendall Coll., Evanston, Ill., 1952-53, Northwestern U., Evanston, 1953-54, 57-58; mem. faculty U. Ill. at Chgo., from 1954, prof. English, 1974-82, prof. emeritus, from 1982; owner Deerhaven Orchard, 1974-96. Cons. in field. Author: When a Youth Gets Poetic, 1934, In Praise of Heroes, 1945, Tillers of a Myth: The Southern Agrarians as Social and Literary Critics, 1966 (Friends of Lit. award 1967), (with Helen Karanikas) Elias Venezis, 1969, Hellenes and Hellions: Modern Greek Characters in American Literature, 1981; (musical) Nashville Dreams, 1991; (screenplay) Marika (Neptune award Moondance Film Festival 2003); (poetry) Stepping Stones, 1994. Mem. nat. cabinet Am. Youth Congress, 1937-39; exec. sec. Mass. Youth Coun., 1939-40; co-chmn. Nat. Bicentennial Symposium on the Greek Experience in Am., 1976; Publicity dir. N.H. Ind. Voters, 1946; sec. Manchester Vets. Council, 1946; Candidate for Congress, 1948; exec. com. United Hellenic Am. Congress, 1983—; exec. sec. Am. Coun. for Dem. Greece, 1947. With USAAF, 1942-45, Alaska corr. YANK, 1943-45. Named to Goffstown (NH) H.S. Hall of Fame, 2004. Mem. Hellenic Profl. Soc. Ill., Modern Greek Studies Assn., Screen Actors Guild, Friends of Lit., Harvard Club Chgo., Phi Eta Sigma, Order Ahepa (dist. sec. 1946). Mem. Greek Orthodox Ch. Home: Oak Park, Ill. Died Nov. 30, 2006.

KARDON, ROBERT, mortgage company executive; b. Phila., Mar. 8, 1922; s. Morris and Sophie (Winkleman) K.; m. Janet Stolker, Nov. 19, 1949; children— Roy, Nina, Ross. Student, U. Miami, Fla., 1940-42, Shriveham Am. U., Swindon, Eng., 1945-46. Chmn. bd. B.T. Babbitt Co., Inc., 1964-66, Pitts. Mortgage Corp., 1964-72, Murphree Mortgage Co., Nashville, 1966-72, Kardon Investment Co., 1945-75, Peoples Bond & Mortgage Co., Phila., 1950-72. Chmn. bd., v.p. United Container Co., Phila., 1938-75; pres., chief exec. officer Kardon Industries, Inc., 1974—, also chmn. Trustee Phila. Mus. Art. Served with AUS, 1942-46. Mem. Young Pres. Orgn., World Bus. Council. Home: New York, NY. Died Mar. 23, 2007.

KARL, MICHAEL M., endocrinology professor; b. Milw., Jan. 30, 1915; BS, U. Wis., 1936; MD, U. Louisville, 1938. Am. Bd. Internal Med., 1946. Intern St. Louis City Hosp., 1938-42, resident Internal Med., 1940-42; pvt. practive St. Louis, 1942-87; dir. clinical affairs, dept. Medicine St. Louis City Hosp., 1987-93; prof. Clinical Medicine Wash. U. Sch. Med., St. Louis, from 1972. Dir. third yr. medicine clerkship St. Louis City Hosp., 1942-44 and Dept. Med. Jewish Hosp., St. Louis, 1963-64; med. dir. Red Cross Mobile Blood Unit, 1942-44; bd. dirs. Munic Nursing Bd., St. Louis; cons. USAF, 1962-64; co-organizer Jeff-Vander-Lou Med. Clinic, 1967-72; pres. Faculty Ctr., Wash. U., 1969; exec. faculty mem. Sch. Med., 1975-76, 85-86; chmn. Com. Svc. to Elderly, Nat. Coun. Jewish Fedns., 1976-81; mem. White House conf. Families, 1978-80; mem. Accreditation Coun. Continuing Med. Edn., 1987—, chmn. 1991; mem. prog. com. Inst. Med. Nat. Acad. Sci., 1988-90; Irene & Michael Karl prof. endocrinology. Recipient Laureate award Am. Col. Physicians, 1988, Ralph O. Claypoole Sr. Meml. award Am. Col. Physicians, 1990. Mem. AMA, Inst. Med. Nat. Acad. Sci., Am. Col. Physicians (fellow and master), Ctr. Soc. Clin. Rsch., Am. Assn. Study Liver Disease, Am. Soc. Internal Med. Died Nov. 22, 2006.

KAROW, ARMAND M., medical facility executive; b. New Orleans, Nov. 11, 1941; s. Armand M. and Eunice Louise (Durham) K.; m. Ramona Evelyn McClelland, Sept. 5, 1964; children: Christopher A., Jonathan C. BA, Duke U., 1962; PhD, U. Miss., 1968. Lic. clin. lab. dir. Asst. prof. Med. Coll. Ga., Augusta, 1968-70, assoc. prof., 1970-75, prof., 1975-97, prof. emeritus, from 1998; pres., founder Xytex Corp., Augusta, from 1975. Bd. dirs. Human Gamete Lab. LLC, Xytex Tissue Svc., Inc.; rsch. on tissue cryopreservation led to the establishment of Xytex Corp. as one of the first clin. sperm banks, 1975; cons. on tissue preservation, U.S. Govt./NIH; cons. FDA. Editor: Organ Preservation for Transplantation, 1974, 2nd edit. 1981, Biophysics of Organ Cryopreservation, 1987, Reproductive Tissue Banking, Scientific Principle, 1997; contbr. articles to profl. jours. Recipient Silver medal for meritorious svc. Am. Heart Assn., Ga. Affiliate, Atlanta, 1978, Disting. Faculty award Med. Coll. Ga., 1983; fellow NEH, Washington, 1980, Sr. Internat. fellow Fogarty Ctr., NIH, Washington, 1981. Fellow AAAS; mem. Am. Soc. Pharmacology and Exptl. Therapeutics, Am. Assn. Tissue Banks (bd. govs. 1998-2000), Am. Soc. for Reproductive Medicine, Biotech. Industry Orgn. (bd. dirs. emerging cos. sect. 1993-94), European Soc. for Human Reproduction and Embryology, Soc. for Cryobiology (editl. bd. 1976—, bd. govs. 1977-80, 92-97), Sigma Xi. Methodist. Avocation: aviation/piloting. Home: Augusta, Ga. Died Feb. 6, 2007.

KARPEN, MARIAN JOAN, financial executive; b. June 16, 1944; d. Cass John and Mary (Jagiello) Karpen. BA, Vassar Coll.; postgrad., Sorbonne, Paris, NYU, 1974—77. New England corr. Women's Wear Daily, 1966—68; Paris fashion editor Capital Cities Network, 1966—69; syndicated newspaper columnist, photojournalist Queen Features Syndicate, NYC, 1971—73; acct. exec. Blyth Eastman Dillon (merged into Paine Webber), 1973—75, Oppenheimer, NYC, 1975—76; v.p. mcpl. bond coord. Faulkner Dawkins & Sullivan (merged into Shearson Hayden Stone Smith Barney et al), 1976—77; mgr. retail mcpl. bond dept. Warburg Paribas Becker-A.G. Becker (merged into Merrill Lynch), sr. v.p., prin., 1977—84; sr. v.p., ltg. ptnr. Bear Stearns & Co., 1984—87, assoc. dir., 1987—90; pres., prin., CEO EuroEast® Group, Inc., NYC, 1990—92; writer, creator newsletter Ea. European News; founder, pres., CEO WorkTalk®, Forum WorkTalk®, Inc., NYC, from 1992; website creator, writer newsletter WorkTalk® Times; pres., founder, CEO, counselor Career Renewal Ctr.®, Inc. Past bus. adv. coun. U.S. Senate; lectr., presenter in field. Contbr. articles and photographs to newspapers and mags.; author: Career Crossroads: Ideas and Inspiration for Your Work/Life Journey. Mem. benefit com. March of Dimes, 1983; mem. Torchlight Ball com. Internat. Games for Disabled, 1984; vol. Whitney Mus. Am. Art. Named New Yorker of Week, Channel One, 1996. Mem.: Vassar Club NY (bd. dirs., exec. com., ex-officio chmn. corp. devel. com., chmn. benefit holiday open house 1989, chmn. major scholarship benefit 1991, chmn. scholarship fundraising raffle benefit 1992). Home: New York, NY. Died Oct. 22, 2005.

KARR, JOHN F., sports executive; b. Detroit, Apr. 13, 1929; s. Eino E. and Helen K.; married; children: John E., Karen, Christopher, Susan. BS, Wayne State U., 1952; MBA, Ind. U., 1953. Formerly with Burroughs Corp., Trane Co., Arthur D. Little, Inc., Goodyear Tire & Rubber Co.; with Cole Nat. Corp., Cleve., 1968-78, v.p. fin. and adminstrn., dir., to, 1978; pres., dir. Northstar Met Center Mgmt. Corp., Bloomington, Minn., from 1978, now vice chmn. Served in U.S. Army, 1946-48. Died Mar. 13, 2007.

KARST, GARY GENE, retired architect; b. Barton County, Kans., Sept. 2, 1936; s. Emil and Clara (Nuss) K.; m. Loretta Marie Staub, Nov. 30, 1957; children: Kevin Gene, Sheri Lynn, Stacey Marie. BArch, Kans. State U., 1960. Registered profl. arch., Kans., Nat. Coun. Archl. Registration Bds., cert. NCARB. Staff architect Horst & Terrill Architects, Topeka, 1960—64; ptnr. Horst, Terrill & Karst Architects, Topeka, 1965—2001, dir. design, 1965—2001, sec., 1973—78, v.p., treas., 1978—92, v.p., 1992—99; pres., 1999—2001; ret., 2001; design architect Ruhnau, Evans, Brown & Steinman Architects, Riverside, Calif., 1964—65. Mem. Capital City Redevel. Agy., Topeka, 1978-86; mem. adv. bd. dept. architecture Kans. State U., Manhattan, 1986-87. Prin. works include Emporia (Kans.) H.S., 1972, (Kans. Soc. Architects award 1975), S.W. Bell Telephone Co. Equipment Bldg., 1974 (Bell Sys. award 1976), Durland Hall-Univ. Engring. Bldg., 1981 (Kans. Soc. Architects award 1983), Kans. State Prison Medium Security Facility, 1983 (Kans. Soc. Architects award 1985), Lansing H.S., 1988 (William W. Caudill citation Am. Sch. and Univ. Mag.), Leavenworth H.S., 1990 (citation Am. Sch. and Univ. Mag.), Plant Scis. Bldg., Kans. State U., 1994, Tomanek Hall, Ft. Hays State U., 1995; featured in publs. including Archtl. Record. Mem. Future Heritage Topeka, Capitol City Redevelopment Agy., Topeka, 1978—86. Recipient citation Am. Sch. and Univ. Mag.; Bales Organ Recital Hall, U. Kans., 1995, Weigel scholar Kans. State U., 1958-60; over 80 recognitions for design excellence. Mem. AIA (Henry W, Schirmer Disting. Svc. award 2001), Kans. Soc. Architects (pres. 1981-82), Optimists Internat. (pres. Topeka breakfast club 1970-71, lt. gov. Kans. dist. 1981-82). Republican. Lutheran. Avocations: woodworking, photography, sculpting. Home: Topeka, Kans. Died July 29, 2007.

KASANIN, MARK OWEN, lawyer; b. Boston, June 28, 1929; s. Jacob Sergei and Elizabeth Owen (Knight) K.; m. Anne Camilla Wimbish, Dec. 18, 1960; children: Marc S., James W. BA, Stanford U., 1951; LL.B., Yale U., 1954. Bar: Calif. Assoc. McCutchen, San Francisco, 1957-62, 63-67; ptnr. Brigham McCutchen, San Francisco, from 1967. Mem. planning commn. City of Belvedere, Calif., 1974-76; chair tech. adv. com. San Francisco Bay Area Water Transit Authority, 2001-. Served with USNR, 1955-2005. Named one of Best Lawyers in Am., Woodward/White, 1995—2006. Fellow Am. Coll. Trial Lawyers; mem. Maritime Law Assn. U.S. (exec. com. 1984-87), Jud. Conf. U.S. (mem. fed. civil rules adv. com. 1992-2002). Home: Belvedere Tiburon, Calif. Died May 18, 2007.

KASKEY, GILBERT, mathematician, former dean; b. Phila., Apr. 24, 1924; m. Sylvia Slotkin, Feb. 3, 1945; children: Karen Jay BA in Math., U. Pa., 1946, PhD in Statistics, 1954; MA in Math., U. Del., 1948. With Sperry Univac, Blue Bell, Pa. 1970—87, v.p. human resources Info. Systems Group, 1981-85 sr. v.p. human resources, 1985—87; dean Am. Coll., Bryn Mawr, Pa., 1987—2003. Home: Blue Bell, Pa. Died Mar. 18 2007.

KATCHATAG, STANTON OSWALD, civic and politica worker; b. Unalakleet, Alaska, Nov. 9, 1917; s. Joseph H. and Helga (Muktuk) K.; m. Irene Unal Benjamin, Sept. 27, 1940 children: Pearl, Shirley, Sheldon, Vernita, Virgil, Helga, Paul Student pub. schs., Unalakleet. Various positions U.S. Postal Svc., until 1970, mail carrier, 1970-75; journeyman carpenter 1975-86. Pres. Native Village Unalakleet; chmn. bd. Kawerak Inc., Bering Straits Native Assn.; mem., former chmn. Western Alaska Tribal Coun.; mem. Eskimo Walrus Commn.; bd. dirs Norton Sound Health Corp., Rural Alaska Cmty. Action Program; mem. exec. bd. dirs., co-founder Alaska Inter-Tribal Coun.; mem. dels. from Alaska to Inuit Circumpolar Conf. With U.S. Army, 1945-46. Recipient recognition of esteemed elde Unalakleet Native Corp., 1973; Elder of Yr. award Kawerak Inc., Nome, Alaska, 1987, Bd. Mem. of Yr. award, 1993; Citize of Yr. award City of Unalakleet, 1992. Democrat. Home Unalakleet, Alaska. Died Jan. 6, 2007.

KATZ, MURRAY L., food products executive; b. Liberty, NY Sept. 25, 1932; s. Joseph N. and Shirley (Weidman) K.; m Harriet Lasker, June 17, 1956; children: Steve, Alan, Jocelyn Student, U. Miami. Pres. Empire Kosher Poultry Co., Mif flintown, Pa., from 1961. Dir. Pa. C. of C., 1986. Served as cp U.S. Army, 1953-55. Mem.: Rotary, Masons. Jewish. Avocations: boating, travel. Home: Jupiter, Fla. Died Oct. 7, 2005.

KAUFFMAN, DANIEL ERB, college official; b. Hesston Kans., June 19, 1922; s. James A. and Mable (Erb) K.; m. Edit L. Yoder, May 27, 1944; children: Daniel Eric, Deborah An (Mrs. Maurice Miller), Salome Elaine (Mrs. Joe Green), Jame David. BA, Goshen Coll., 1946; MA, Columbia, 1957. Bus mgr. Hesston Coll., 1946-61; dir. stewardship Mennonite Ch Scottdale, Pa., 1961-66; assoc. supt. Southmoreland (Pa.) Schs 1966-71; dir. coll. relations Goshen Coll., Ind., 1971-86. Sec dir. Goodville Mut. Casualty Co., New Holland, Pa., 1973– Mem. Hesston City Council, 1955-61; Vice chmn. bd. Prairi View Hosp., Newton, Kans., 1956-61; chmn. bd. Kiowa Count Hosp., Greensburg, Kans., 1954-61; pres. bd. Schowalte Found., Newton, 1970-85; bd. dirs. Greencroft Retiremen Home, Goshen, Ind., 1980—. Mem.: Lions, Exchange. Mennonite. Home: Goshen, Ind. Died Nov. 7, 2006.

KAUFFMAN, STANLEY CHESTER, retired financial consultant, public utility executive; b. Cleve., Apr. 13, 1924; m Violet Jean Miller, Aug. 31, 1946; children— Jeff Kauffman

Linda Kauffman Peterson, Corinne Kauffman Garvey, Lori Kauffman Faison, Tad BS in Bus. Adminstrn., Ohio State U., 1948. Audit mgr. Arthur Andersen & Co., Columbus, Ohio, 1948-72; v.p. Columbia Gas System, Wilmington, Del., 1972-80, v.p., gen. auditor, 1980-82, v.p., treas., 1982-88, sr. v.p., 1988-90; pvt. investor, fin. cons. Wilmington, from 1990. Served with U.S. Army, 1943-46 Mem. Am. Gas Assn. (acctg. adv. council 1982-88), Am. Inst. C.P.A.s, Ohio Soc. C.P.A.s, Beta Alpha Psi, Beta Gamma Sigma Republican. Lutheran. Avocations: water sports; golf; skating; woodworking; bridge. Home: Columbus, Ohio. Died Oct. 18, 2005.

KAUFMAN, CHARLES EDWARD, university administrator; b. Kendallville, Ind., Jan. 22, 1926; s. Edward Ernest and Marguerite Albert (Smith) K.; m. Joyce Elaine Friar, Aug. 6, 1950; children— Kim Edward, Gregory Lawrence, Richard Charles. B.S., Ball State U., 1950, M.S., 1954; postgrad. St. Francis Coll., 1962-63, Ind. U., 1964-65. Cert. guidance counselor, prin., Ind. Tchr., coach Bluffton Community Schs. (Ind.), 1950-56; counselor, tchr. Culver Mil. Acad. (Ind.), 1956-60; dir. guidance Huntington Community Schs. (Ind.), 1960-66; dir. pre-admission services Ball State U., Muncie, Ind., 1966—; cons. in field. Dist. adminstr. Circle K, 1977-80; sec. Ind. Kiwanis Found., 1980. Served with USN, 1944-46; PTO. Recipient WASSON achievement award Kiwanis Internat., 1979. Mem. Ind. Assn. Coll. Admissions Counselors, Nat. Assn. Coll. Admissions Counselors, Ind. Assn. Registrars and Admissions Officers, Nat. Assn. Registrars and Admissions Officers, Ind. Sch. Adminstrs. Assn., Ind. State Tchrs. Assn., Phi Delta Kappa. Republican. Methodist. Lodge: Kiwanis (lt. gov. 1983-84). Author: Academic Planning for High School & College and How to Pay the Bills, 1983. Died Apr. 25, 2007.

KAUFMAN, IAN JAY, lawyer; b. NYC, May 23, 1940; BA, NYU, 1962, JD, 1965; doctorate, U. Paris, 1966. Bar: N.Y. 1967. Mem. Ladas & Parry, NYC. Mem. Internat. Bar Assn. Died Oct. 3, 2005.

KAVANAGH, AIDAN JOSEPH, priest, university educator; b. Mexia, Tex., Apr. 20, 1929; s. Joseph Gerard and Guarrel Dee (Mullens) K. AB, St. Meinrad Sem., Ind., 1957; STL, U. Ottawa, Ont., Can., 1958; STD, Theologische Fakultat, Trier, Germany, 1963; MA (hon.), Yale U., 1974. Ordained priest Roman Cath. Ch., 1957. Asst. prof. St. Meinrad Sem., 1962-66; assoc. prof. U. Notre Dame, Ind., 1966-71, prof. Ind., 1971-74, Yale U. Div. Sch., New Haven, Conn., 1974-94, prof. emeritus, from 1994, acting dean, 1989-90. Founding mem. N.Am. Acad. Liturgy, 1975; lectr. schs. and colls. Author: The Shape of Baptism, 1978, Elements of Rite, 1982, On Liturgical Theology, 1984, Confirmation: Origins and Reform, 1988, also articles; assoc. editor Worship, 1968-87. Fellow Woodrow Wilson Internat. Ctr. Scholars, 1981. Mem. Liturgical Conf. (dir. 1964-68), N.Am. Acad. Liturgy, Societas Liturgica, Yale Club (N.Y.C.). Home: Hamden, Conn. Died July 9, 2006.

KAYE, ALAN STEWART, linguistics educator; b. Los Angeles, Mar. 2, 1941; s. Sam and Ray Kaye; m. Susan Marianne Mazur, Aug. 27, 1972 (div.); children: Jennifer Danielle, Jeremy Daniel. Teaching assoc. U. Calif., Berkeley, 1967-69; asst. prof. linguistics U. Colo., Boulder, 1969-71; asst. prof. Calif. State U., Fullerton, Calif., 1971-74, dir. phonetics lab., 1971—2007, assoc. prof., 1974-78, prof., 1978—2007. Author: Chadian and Sudanese Arabic, 1976 (UCI Libr. award 1977), A Dictionary of Nigerian Arabic, 1982 (UCI Libr. award 1983), Nigerian Arabic-English Dictionary, 1986 (UCI Libr. award 1986); editor: Semitic Studies, 2 vols., 1991 (UCI Libr. award 19920; contbr. articles to profl. jours. Bd. trustees Yorba Linda (Calif.) Library Dist., 1979; bd. trustees N. Orange Coutny Community Coll. Dist., Fullerton, 1979-83. Grantee NSF, 1969-70, NEH, 1973-74, Am. Phil. Soc., 1973-74, 75-76, Fulbright, 1978-79, Werner-Gren Found., 1985-86; recipient: Disting. Faculty award, Cal. State U. Fullerton Coll. Humanities & Social Sciences, 1998 Mem. Linguistic Soc. Am., Am. Oriental Soc. (bd. dis.), Can. Linguistics Assn. Republican. Roman Catholic. Avocations: chess, bridge, athletics. Home: Orange, Calif. Died May 31, 2007.

KAYE, DIANE LYNN, lawyer; b. Detroit, Dec. 25, 1950; d. Charles and Mildred Kaye BA, U. Mich., 1972, JD, 1975. Bar: Mich. 1975, U.S. Dist. Ct. (ea. dist.) Mich. 1975. Atty. Gen. Motors Corp., Detroit, 1975-84, sec., 1983-86, sr. counsel, from 1984; gen. counsel Delco Electronics Corp., from 1986. Mem. ABA, Mich. State Bar Assn. Died July 23, 2007.

KAYE, RICHARD LEON, broadcasting company executive; b. Boston, Apr. 15, 1925; s. Abraham Isaac and Pearl Loretta (Simon) K.; m. Muriel Elaine Shea, June 14, 1949; children: Hannah Sarah Kaye Gross, Miriam Eve, Bennett Nathan, Ava Rebecca. AB cum laude, Harvard Coll., 1944, MA, 1945. Music dir., sta. mgr., exec. v.p., pres., chmn./treas. subs. Sta. WCRB, Charles River Broadcasting Co., Waltham, Mass., from 1950. Overseer Boston Symphony Orch.; bd. dirs. New Eng. Jewish Music Forum, Boston. Mem. IEEE, Mem. Audio Engring. Soc. (sr.), Soc. Broadcast Engrs. (charter), Am. Symphony Orch. League (assoc.). Jewish. Avocations: music, computers, photography, model trains, stamps and coins. Home: Waban, Mass. Died Nov. 29, 2006.

KAYE, STEPHEN RACKOW, lawyer; b. Nyack, NY, May 4, 1931; s. Edward and Florence (Karp) K.; m. Judith Smith, Feb. 1, 1964; children: Luisa Marian, Jonathan Mackey, Gordon Bernard. AB, Cornell U., 1952, LL.B. with honors, 1956. Bar: N.Y. 1956, U.S. Supreme Ct. 1961. Assoc. Sullivan & Cromwell, NYC, 1956-63, Proskauer Rose Goetz & Mendelsohn, NYC, 1964-68, ptnr., past chair, co-chmn. lit. dept., 1968; optional svc. ptnr. Proskauer Rose. Mem. Judicial Inst. on Professionalism in the Law, 1999-2006. Author treatise texts on trials and appeals of comml. cases; mng. editor Cornell Law Quar.; contbr. to profl. publs. Served to 1st lt. AUS, 1952-54, Korea. Mem. ABA, N.Y. State Bar Assn., Assn. of Bar of City of N.Y. (past chmn. com. on profl. and jud. ethics, chmn. com. on profl. discipline), N.Y. County Lawyers Assn. (past vice chmn. com. on Supreme Ct.), 1st Dept. Disciplinary Commn. (hearing panel chair, policy com. 1991-96, 1999-2002), Order of Coif, Phi Kappa Phi. Home: New York, NY. Died Oct. 30, 2006.

KAYE, WILBUR IRVING, chemist, researcher; b. Pelham Manor, N.Y., Jan. 28, 1922; s. Roy George and Edith Adele (Dusenberry) K.; m. Virginia Agett, Feb. 7, 1944; children— Roy Arthur, Elsa Campbell. B.S., J.B. Stetson U., 1942; Ph.D., U. Ill.-Urbana, 1945. Grad. asst. U. Ill., Urbana, 1942-45; research chemist Tenn. Eastman Co., Kingsport, 1945-49, sr. research chemist, 1949-55; research dir. Beckman Instruments Inc., Fullerton, Calif., 1956-73, sr. scientist, Irvine, Calif., 1973-80, prin. staff scientist, Irvine, 1980-87; cons. 1987—. Patentee (23); mem. editorial bd. advisor Applied Spectroscopy Jour., 1970-73, Analytical Chemistry Jour., 1980-83; contbr. articles to profl. jours. Beckman Instruments fellow, 1982, 83—. Fellow AAAS; mem. Optical Soc. Am. (local pres. 1957), Soc. Applied Spectroscopy, Am. Chem. Soc., ASTM. Republican. Presbyterian. Died Nov. 27, 2006.

KAZDA, LOUIS FRANK, electrical and computer engineering educator, consultant, researcher; b. Dayton, Ohio, Sept. 21, 1916; s. Ludwig Augustus and Elizabeth Theresa (Novak) K.; m. Jane Elizabeth Glover, Aug. 24, 1940; children— Judith Ann Kazda Burd, Sally Louise Kazda Stites, Joan Elizabeth E.E., U. Cin., 1940, MSE., 1943; PhD, Syracuse U., 1962. Research engr. Bendix Corp., Teterboro, N.J., 1943-45; mem. elec. and computer engring. faculty U. Mich., Ann Arbor, from 1946, prof., dir. power systems lab., 1979-84, prof. emeritus, from 1984; prof. N.Mex. State U., Las Cruces, from 1985. Cons. Willow Run Labs., U. Mich., Ypsilanti, 1953-72; cons. summer study Nat. Acad. Sci., Falmouth, Mass., 1973; co-chmn. NSF Workshop, Ann Arbor, 1972; chmn. Joint Automatic Control Conf., Ann Arbor, 1968 Author: (with others) Optimal and Self Optimizing Control, 1966; contbr. articles to profl. jours. Recipient Prize Paper award Am. Inst. Elec. Engrs., N.Y.C., 1960; named Disting. Alumnus U. Cin., 1981 Fellow IEEE (Centennial medal 1984, Disting. mem. Control System Soc.); mem. U. Cin. Alumni Assn., Syracuse U. Alumni Assn., U. Mich. Alumni Assn., Sigma Xi, Eta Kappa Nu, Tau Beta Pi. Republican. Presbyterian. Avocations: swimming; horseback riding. Home: Las Cruces, N.Mex. Died Jan. 15, 2006.

KEANE, EDMUND J., JR., banker; b. Syracuse, NY, June 29, 1933; s. Edmund J. and Elizabeth (Byrne) K.; m. Suzanne M. Lamica; children— Edmund J. III, Sean T., Catharine A., Timothy C., Michael P. BS in Bus. Adminstrn., Holy Cross Coll., 1955. Asst. bank examiner Fed. Res. Bank N.Y., 1958-61; asst. to pres. Gramatan Nat. Bank, Bronxville, N.Y., 1961-62; asst. v.p. Scarsdale Nat. Bank, N.Y., 1962-67; v.p. Key Bank of No. N.Y., N.A., Watertown, 1967-69, sr. v.p., sr. loan officer, 1969-75, exec. v.p., sr. loan officer, 1975-80, pres., 1980, pres., chief exec. officer, 1981-88, Key Bank of Idaho, Boise, from 1988. Bd. dirs. Samaritan Keep Home, United Way of Ada County, Bishop Kelly Found., Bronco Athletic Assn., BSU Found.; chmn. scholarship com. BSU; mem. Robert Morris Assocs. Served to capt. USAF, 1955-58. Avocations: skiing; reading; personal computers; travel. Died June 14, 2006.

KEARNS, WARREN KENNETH, manufacturing executive, director; b. Wilmington, Ohio, July 15, 1929; s. Roy William and Marie (Kay) K. BS in Civil Engring., Case Western Res. U., 1951. Registered profl. engr., Ohio, Pa. Supr. Pa. R.R. Co., 1951-56; exec. v.p. Pitts. & W.Va. Rwy. Co., 1956-64; mgr. mfg. services Wheeling Steel Corp., W.Va., 1964-67; v.p. L. B. Foster Co., Pitts., 1967-70, pres., 1979-85; v.p. Sharon Steel Co., Pa., 1970-73; pres. Ogden Steel Co., Cleve., 1973-79, Warren Kearns Assocs., from 1985. Bd. dirs. N.W. Pipe & Casing Co., Portland, Oreg., Erie (Pa.) Forge & Steel Co. Mem.: Sigma Xi, Tau Beta Pi. Avocation: music. Home: Hudson, Ohio. Died Mar. 24, 2007.

KEELEY, ARTHUR JAMES, insurance company executive; b. Stamford, Conn., Feb. 13, 1930; s. William Carroll and Esther Wilcox (Harris) K.; A.B., Yale U., 1952; M.B.A., U. Pa., 1954; m. Diann Munson, Aug. 15, 1959; 1 dau., Lynn M. Budget dir., supr. corp. acctg. CBS Inc., 1958-62; mgr. budgets and fin. analysis Westvaco, N.Y.C., 1962-67; dir. corp. acctg. Avon Products, N.Y.C., 1967-70; v.p. fin. cons. Devel. Assocs., Westport, Conn., 1971; controller Depository Trust Co., N.Y.C., 1972-75; v.p. fin. Ins. Services Office, Inc., N.Y.C., 1975—. Mem. Planning Execs. Inst. (pres. N.Y. chpt. 1968-69), Fin. Execs. Inst., Am. Mgmt. Assn., Assn. Yale Alumni (rep. 1975-78). Republican. Clubs: University; Yale (pres. 1972-74, chmn. fin. com. 1976—) (N.Y.C.). Home: New York, NY. Died Jan. 22, 2007.

KEENAN, JACK ALLEN, oil and ice company executive, securities dealer; b. Paris, Ill., Dec. 1, 1915; s. Zollie O. and Ethel (Mosher) K.; m. Eleanor K. Kennedy, Dec. 13, 1968; children— by previous marriage— James, Thomas. B.S., U. Calif.-Berkeley, 1937; M.B.A., U. So. Calif., 1951. Registered profl. engr., Calif. Engr., Standard Oil of Calif., San Francisco, 1937-40, Wilshire Oil Co., Norwalk, Calif., 1940-42; project engr., mgr. Gen. Tire & Rubber, Pasadena, 1946-48, The Ralph M. Parsons Co., Los Angeles, 1948-53; sec. Green River Steel Corp., Ownesboro, Ky., 1953-57; pres. Tonawanda Share Corp., Buffalo, 1982—; chmn. bd. S.C. Parker & Co., Inc., Buffalo, 1982—; pres. Connohio, Inc., Buffalo, 1957—. Served to maj. U.S. Army, 1942-46. Mem. ASME, ASCE, Am. Nat. Def. Assn. Republican. Club: Bond of Buffalo. Home: Buffalo, NY. Died Jan. 23, 2007.

KEETON, ROBERT ERNEST, retired federal judge; b. Clarksville, Tex., Dec. 16, 1919; s. William Robert and Ernestine (Tuten) K.; m. Elizabeth E. Baker, May 28, 1941; children: Katherine, William Robert. BBA, U. Tex., 1940, LLB, 1941; SJD, Harvard U., 1956; LLD (hon.), William Mitchell Coll., 1983, Lewis and Clark Coll., 1988. Bar: Tex. 1941, Mass. 1955. Assoc. firm Baker, Botts, Andrews & Wharton (and successors), Houston, 1941-42, 45-51; assoc. prof. law So. Meth. U., 1951-54; Thayer teaching fellow Harvard U., 1953-54, asst. prof., 1954-56; prof. law Harvard Law Sch., 1956-73, Langdell prof., 1973-79, assoc. dean, 1975-79; judge US Dist. Ct. Mass., Boston, 1979—2003, sr. judge, 2003—06. Commr. on Uniform State Laws from Mass., 1971-79; trustee Flaschner Jud. Inst., 1979-86; exec. dir. Nat. Inst. Trial Advocacy, 1973-76; ednl. cons., 1976-79; mem. com. on ct. adminstrn. U.S. Jud. Conf., 1985-87, mem. standing com. on rules, 1987-90, chmn., 1990-93. Author: Trial Tactics and Methods, 1954, 2d edit., 1973, Cases and Materials on the Law of Insurance, 1960, 2d edit., 1977, Legal Cause in the Law of Torts, 1963, Venturing To Do Justice, 1969, (with Jeffrey O'Connell) Basic Protection for the Traffic Victim: A Blueprint for Reforming Automobile Insurance, 1965, After Cars Crash: The Need for Legal and Insurance Reform, 1967, (with Page Keeton) Cases and Materials on the Law of Torts, 1971, 2d edit., 1977, Basic Text on Insurance Law, 1971, (with others) Tort and Accident Law, 1983, 2d edit., 1989, (with others) Prosser & Keeton, Torts, 5th edit., 1984, Pocket Part, 1988, (with Alan Widiss) Insurance Law, 1988, Judging, 1990, Judging the American Legal System, 1999, Guidelines for Drafting, Editing, and Interpreting, 2002; also articles. Served to lt. comdr. USNR, 1942-45, PTO, 1945-56. Recipient Wm. B. Jones award Nat. Inst. Trial Advocacy, 1980; recipient Leon Green award U. Tex. Law Rev., 1981, Francis Rawle award Am. Law Inst.-ABA, 1983, Samuel E. Gates litigation award Am. Coll. Trial Lawyers, 1984 Fellow Am. Bar Found., mem., Am. Acad. Arts and Scis., Am. Bar Assn., Mass. Bar Assn., State Bar Tex., Am. Law Inst., Am. Risk and Ins. Assn., Chancellors, Friars, Order of Coif, Beta Gamma Sigma, Beta Alpha Psi, Phi Delta Phi, Phi Eta Sigma. Died July 2, 2007.

KEITH, ROBERT ALLEN, psychology educator; b. Brea, Calif., Mar. 16, 1924; s. Albert Henry Keith and Delphene Ruth (Morgan) Parker;m. Nanette Hardesty, Sept. 1, 1949; children: Leslie Susan Keith Berclaz, Claudia Lynn Keith Lorenzana. BA, U. Calif., LA, 1948, MA, 1951, PhD, 1953. Lic. psychologist, Calif.; diplomate in clin. psychology. Clin. psychology intern L.A. Psychiat. Svcs., 1950-53; dir. counseling svcs. Claremont (Calif.) Coll., 1953-59; from asst. to assoc. prof. psychology Claremont Grad. Sch., 1953-89. Dir. rsch. div. Casa Colina Hosp., Pomona, Calif., 1968—. Contbr. articles related to med. rehab. to profl. jours. Lt. USNR, 1943-46, PTO. Harvard U. fellow, 1960-61; Rehab. Psychol. fellow, 1984, World Rehab. Fund of London fellow, 1987. Fellow Am. Psych. Assn., Am. Assn. U. Profs., Am. Congress Rehab. Medicine, Assn. for Health Svcs. Rsch., Am. Pub. Health Assn. Home: Claremont, Calif. Died Mar. 5, 2006.

KELLER, FRANCES RICHARDSON, history educator; b. Lowville, N.Y., Aug. 14, 1914; d. Stephen Brown and Sarah Eliza (Bell) Richardson; m. Chauncey A.R. Keller, June 20, 1936 (div. 1964); children: Reynolds, Stephen, Julia, William; m. William P. Rhetta, May 10, 1969. BA, Sarah Lawrence Coll.; MA, U. Toledo; PhD, U. Chgo., 1973. Lectr., U. Ind.-Gary, 1966-67, U. Ill.-Chgo., 1967-68, Chgo. City Coll., 1968-70, Centre Inter. Universitaire, Paris, 1970-71, U. Calif.-Berkeley Extension, 1972-74, San Jose (Calif.) State U., 1974-78; adj. prof. history San Francisco State U., 1978—; panelist, reader NEH, 1978, 79, 81. Author: An American Crusade: The Life of Charles Waddell Chesnutt, 1978; editor, contbr.: Women in Western Tradition; translator, editor, author interpretive essay in Slavery and the French Revolutionists (Anna Julia Cooper), 1988. Mem. Nat. Women's Studies Assn. (chair publicity and pub. relations, founding conv. 1976, ofcl. historian 1978), Western Assn. Women Historians (program chair 1979, pres. 1981-83), Am. Hist. Assn. (nominating com. 1983—), Orgn. Am. Historians, Women in Hist. Profession (pres. coordinating com. 1985-88), Western Soc. French History. Died June 25, 2007.

KELLER, THOMAS WHITNEY, retired building supply company executive; b. Hinsdale, Ill., July 26, 1921; s. Raymond L. and Mildred (Whitney) K.; B.A., Duke, 1946; m. Marcia E. Marland, Sept. 6, 1951; children— Peter J., Mark T., Marcia E. II, Scott R. With E.A. Keller Co., La Grange, Ill., 1946-71, sec., 1949-71; pres. TriCounty Land Corp., Lemont, Ill.; owner Keller Plantations, Holland, Mich., 1971—; dir. adv. bd. La Grange State Bank, 1979; past dir. Edgewood Bank, La Grange. Mem. Village of La Grange Parking Commn., 1957-77; former mem. asso. bd. La Grange Community Meml. Gen. Hosp.; former bd. dirs. West Suburban YMCA. Served with AUS, 1942-45. Mem. Am. Legion, Sigma Chi. Methodist. Clubs: Spring Lake Country, Masons, Kiwanis. Home: Spring Lake, Mich. Died Feb. 12, 2006.

KELLEY, EUGENE JOHN, retired business educator; b. NYC, July 8, 1922; s. Eugene Lawrence and Agnes Regina (Meskill) K.; m. Dorothy W. Kane, Aug. 3, 1946; 1 child, Sharon A.; m. Linda S. Phillips, Sept. 30, 1992. BS, U. Conn., 1945; MBA, Boston U., 1949, MEd, 1948; PhD, NYU, 1955. Instr. mktg. Babson Inst., 1947-49; dir. divsn. bus. adminstrn. Clark U., 1949-56, asst. prof., 1949-54, assoc. prof., 1954-56; vis. lectr. Harvard U. Bus. Sch., 1956-57; asst. prof. Mich. State U., East Lansing, 1957-58, assoc. prof., 1958-59; prof. mktg., asst. dean Grad. Sch. Bus. Adminstrn. NYU, NYC, 1959-60, prof., assoc. dean, 1960-64; rsch. prof. bus. adminstrn. Coll. Bus. Adminstrn. Pa. State U., 1963-88, dean, 1973-88; dean and rsch. prof. emeritus Pa. State U., 1988; disting. prof. mktg. Fla. Atlantic U., Boca Raton, from 1989, dir. Ctr. for Svcs. Mktg. and Mgmt., Coll. Bus., from 1990. Regional dir. Mellon Bank Central; mem. nat. adv. Council SBA; mem. Commn. on Edn. for Bus. Professions of Nat. Assn. State Univs. and Land Grant Colls.; cons. GAO, N.J. Bd. Higher Edn. Author: Marketing Planning and Competitive Strategy, 1972, Managerial Marketing: Policies, Strategies and Decisions, 1973, Social Marketing: Perspectives and Viewpoints, 1973; Editor: Jour. Mktg, 1967-73. Served with USAAF, 1942-43. Mem. Am. Mktg. Assn. (pres. 1982-83, dir., mem. disting. mktg. educator com.), Acad. Mgmt., Am. Assembly Collegiate Schs. of Bus. Home: State College, Pa. Died Feb. 10, 2007.

KELLEY, HENRY PAUL, academic administrator, psychology educator; b. Cleburne, Tex., July 4, 1928; s. Henry Rowell and Jane Frances (Wynn) K.; m. Lucerle DeCourcy Scott, Aug. 18, 1949; children: Roger Wynn, Scott Franklin, Gordon Henry. BA in Pure Math., U. Tex., 1949, MA in Ednl. Psychology, 1951; AM, PhD in Psychology, Princeton U., 1954. Cert. and lic.

psychologist, Tex. Psychometric fellow Ednl. Testing Svc., Princeton, N.J., 1951-54; pers. mgmt. and evaluation psychologist pers. and tng. rsch. ctr. USAF, San Antonio, 1954; aviation exptl. psychologist U.S. Naval Sch. Aviation Medicine, Pensacola, Fla., 1955-57; coord. measurement svcs., testing and counseling ctr., from asst. to assoc. prof. ednl. psychology U. Tex. Austin, 1958-64, lectr., 1964-67, dir. measurement and evaluation ctr., prof. ednl. psychology, 1967—99, prof. emeritus ednl. psychology, from 1999; regional dir. southwestern office Coll. Entrance Exam. Bd., Austin, 1964-67. Regional coord. Project TALENT, Austin, 1959-61; mem. southwestern regional adv. com. Coll. Entrance Exam. Bd., Austin, 1968-73, vice-chmn. com. rsch. and devel., N.Y.C., 1970-73, chmn., 1973-76, mem. adv. panel econ. implications recognizing prior learning, 1979-80; vis. faculty mem. ann. inst. coll. entrance, acad. placement and student fin. assistance Coll. Entrance Exam. Bd. and U. N.C., Chapel Hill, 1975-94; tech. reviewer, panel mem. rsch. projects br., bur. edn. handicapped, office edn. HEW, Washington, 1977; asst. hearing officer minimum competency study Nat. Inst. Edn., 1980-81; mem. gen. faculty U. Tex. Austin, 1960-64, 67-99, sec., 1981-87, mem. faculty senate, 1972-74, 81-95, sec., 1975-79, adminstrv. adviser ednl. policy com., 1968-99; reviewer comprehensive program fund improvement secondary edn. U.S. Dept. Edn., 1983; mem. rsch. adv. panel, manpower and pers. divsn. Air Force Human Resources Lab., Brooks AFB, San Antonio, 1984-86; mem. com. testing, coordinating bd. Tex. Coll. and Univ. Sys., Austin, 1985-86, mem. adv. com. basic skills testing, coordinating bd., 1987; mem. basic skills test rev. panel Tex. Edn. Agy., Austin, 1987; mem. Tex. acad. skills coun. Tex. Higher Edn. Coord. Bd., 1987-93, chmn. adv. com. tests and measurements Tex. acad. skills coun., 1987-93; mem. planning com. Ann. Tex. Testing Conf., 1987-94; cons., spkr. in field. Author: (with Bruce Walker) Self-Audit of CLEP Policies and Procedures: A Guide to Policy Decisions for Colleges and Universities, 1981; contbr. articles to profl. jours. and publs. Lt. USNR. Recipient Edward S. Noyes award Coll. Bd., 1976, Advanced Placement Spl. Recognition award, 1985; recipient numerous grants in field. Fellow APA, Am. Psychol. Soc.; mem. Am. Assn. Applied and Preventive Psychology, Am. Ednl. Rsch. Assn., Nat. Coun. Measurement Edn., Nat. Soc. Study Edn., Am. Assn. Higher Edn., Am. Evaluation Assn., Measurement Svcs. Assn., Nat. Coll. Testing Assn., Psychometric Soc., Phi Beta Kappa, Phi Delta Kappa, Phi Eta Sigma, Phi Kappa Phi, Sigma Xi. Methodist. Avocations: reading, bridge. Home: Austin, Tex. Died Mar. 31, 2007.

KELLEY, TIMOTHY MICHAEL, environmental engineer, consultant; b. Batesville, Ind., Apr. 21, 1952; s. Robert Leo and Bernice Elizabeth (Gonder) K.; m. Darcy Kay Pierce, Aug. 2, 1975; children— Jessica, Courtney. B.S. in Environ. Sci., Ind. State U., 1974. Health insp. City of Madison, Wis., 1973; sanitarian NIH, USPHS, Bethesda, Md., 1974; sanitarian hazardous waste sect. Ind. State Bd. Health, Indpls., 1977-81; environ. engr. Roll Coater, Inc., Greenfield, Ind., 1981—. Mem. South Deanery Indpls. Bd. Cath. Edn., 1984, St. Roch Cath. Sch. Bd. Edn., Indpls., 1985. Mem. Nat. Coil Coaters Assn. (environ. chmn. 1982—, asst. tech. sec. 1984—), Air Pollution Control Assn., Ind. Water Pollution Control Assn. Roman Catholic. Avocations: scuba diving; hunting; fishing. Home: Indianapolis, Ind. Died Feb. 15, 2006.

KELLY, DOUGLAS, JR., retired agricultural chemical company executive, consultant; b. Huntsville, Ala., Jan. 25, 1915; s. Douglas and Roberta (Bradford) K.; m. Francenia Irwin, June 18, 1937; children: Douglas, III, William Laird. BBA, Tulane U., 1936; postgrad., U. Pa., 1947. Sales rep. Allied Chem. Corp., 1936-49; dist. mgr. Monsanto Co., 1949-67; v.p. Riverside Industries, Marks, Miss., 1967-72; pres. Riverside Chem. Co., Memphis, from 1972; v.p. Cook Industries, Memphis, from 1972, Terra Chem. Internat., Inc., from 1979, cons., from 1981; chmn. bd. Riverside Chem. Co., 1979-81. Cons. Cook Internat. (Palm Beach), Fla. Active local Boy Scouts Am. Served to lt. USNR, 1943-47. Mem. Natl. Agrl. Chems. Assn. (dir.), Southeastern Agrl. Chems. Assn. (dir.) Clubs: Chickasaw Country, Summit, Rotary. Methodist. Home: Covington, La. Died Jan. 23, 2007.

KELLY, GARY MICHAEL, career military officer; b. Utica, NY, Oct. 1, 1948; s. Raymond H. and Arline M. (Zilliou) K.; m. Patricia Christine Gillis, Oct. 30, 1980; 1 child, Scott. BS, Syracuse U., 1970, N.Y. State Coll. Forestry, 1970; MBA, U. Alaska, 1975. Commd. 2d lt. USAF, 1970, advanced through grades to col., 1991, maintenance officer F-100 and A-7D England AFB, La., 1971-73, officer in charge orgnl. maintenance, field maintenance officer Alaska, 1973-75, field maintenance squadron comdr., maintenance control officer 354th Tactical Fighter Wing Myrtle Beach AFB, S.C., 1975-77, aircraft maintenance inspector Office of the Inspector Gen. Tactical Air Command Langley AFB, Va., 1978-80, comdr. maintenance squadron F-117A Stealth Fighter 4450th Tactical Group Tonopah, Nev., 1980-83, logistics and aircraft maintenance advisor to Royal Saudi Air Force U.S. Ctrl. Command Dhahran, Saudi Arabia, 1984-86, dep. program mgr. for logistics F-117A Sys. Program Office Wright-Patterson AFB, Ohio, 1986-89, dir. logistics F-22 Advanced Tactical Fighter, 1990-92, dir. support sys. integrated product team F-22 Sys. Program Office, 1992, dir. F-22 air vehicle integrated product team, 1992-93, dir. C-17 sys. support mgmt. directorate San Antonio Air Logistics Ctr. Kelly AFB, Tex., 1993-95, dir. aerospace equipment mgmt. directorate San Antonio Air Logistics Ctr., from 1995. Mem. Air Force Assn. Avocations: racquetball, hunting, fishing. Died Oct. 15, 2006.

KELLY, JOHN FRANKLIN, physician, psychoanalysis educator; b. Dallas, Sept. 22, 1931; s. John Franklin and Evelyn Eugenia (Poe) K. M.D., U. Tex.-Dallas, 1955; Diplomate Am. Bd. Psychiatry and Neurology; cert. in psychoanalysis. Intern USPHS Hosp., S.I., N.Y., 1955-56; resident in U. Colo. Med. Ctr., 1959-62; psychoanalytic tng., Denver Inst. Psychoanalysis., 1969-74; dir. psychiatric inpatient services U. Colo. Med. Ctr. Denver, 1968-74; gen. practice psychoanalysis, Denver, 1974—; tng. and supr. analyst Denver Inst. Psychoanalysis, Denver, 1984—. Served to sr. asst. surgeon USPHS, 1955-58. Fellow Am. Psychiat. Assn. Home: Denver, Colo. Died June 19, 2006.

KELLY, JOSEPH BURNS, law educator; b. Fort Smith, July 31, 1923; s. John Joseph and Mary Margaret (Farrell) K.; m. Jeanne Mary Garties, July 23, 1949; children: Douglas, Lawrence, Jeffrey, Roger, Paul, Christopher. BS, Xavier U., 1947; JD, U. Cin., 1949; LLM, Georgetown U., 1959, MA, 1960. Bar: Ohio 1949, Pa. 1980. Assoc. Schmidt, Effron, Josselson & Weber, Cin., 1949-50; commd. 1st lt. U.S. Army, 1950, advanced through grades to lt. col., 1963, judge advocate officer U.S., Germany, Korea, 1950-69, ret., 1969; prof. law Dickinson Sch. Law, Carlisle, Pa., from 1969. Vis. prof. law U.S. Mil. Acad., 1992-93. Author: International Law (vol. 2), 1963, Family Law in Pennsylvania, 1991; contbr. articles to legal jours. Lt. field arty., U.S. Army, 1943-46, CBI. Mem. ABA, Am. Soc. Internat. Law, Officers Club. Avocation: civil war re-enactments. Home: Carlisle, Pa. Died Apr. 16, 2006.

KELMAN, STEPHEN JAY, chiropractor; b. Louisville, Feb. 11, 1944; s. Ben and Billie Ethel (Hark) K.; m. Delores Sue Callaway, Feb. 11, 1968; children: Jason David, Rachel Leah. AA, U. Louisville, 1968; D of Chiropractic magna cum laude, Palmer Coll. Chiropractic, 1971. Dir. Chiropractic Arts Ctr., Ft. Wayne, Ind., 1971-72; owner Kelman Chiropractic Ctr., Ft. Wayne, 1972—; guest examiner, Ind. State Bd. Chiropractic Examiners, 1985—; mem. faculty, lectr. practice cons. Found. for Advancement Chiropractic Edn., 1986—. Bd. dirs. Allen County chpt. Am. Cancer Soc., 1976-79; rep. Ft. Wayne Jewish Fedn., 1975-79, 80-81, 87—, chmn. leadership devel. com., 1987—; bd. dirs. N.E. Subarea adv. council No. Ind. Health Systems Agy., 1977-82; bd. dirs. B'nai Jacob Synagogue, 1973-76, 78-79, 80-82, 84—, pres. Men's Club, 1978-79. v.p. 1989—; advisor B'nai B'rith Youth Orgn., 1972-79. Served with U.S. Army, 1964-66. Recipient Service award B'nai Jacob Synagogue, 1980, Merit award B'nai B'rith Youth Orgn., 1981; named Hon. Ky. Col. Mem. Am. Chiropractic Assn. (alt. state del. 1977-83), Ky. Assn. Chiropractors, Ky. Chiropractic Soc., Ind. State Chiropractic Assn., Inc. (bd. dirs. 1973-81, 2d v.p. 1977-78, 1st v.p. 1978-79, pres. 1979-80, sec. 1982-83, chmn. council on ins. 1981-84, peer rev. chmn. 1981-86, legal com. chmn. 1983—, Service award, 1974, 75, 81, Chiropractor of Yr. award 1982), Allen County Chiropractic Soc. (pres. 1973-75), Palmer Coll. Alumni Assn. Ind. (pres. 1984-87), Delta Delta Pi, Pi Tau Delta. Lodge: B'nai B'rith. Died Oct. 5, 2006.

KEMP, RENE D., state legislator; b. July 15, 1935; Attended, Ga. Mil. Coll.; JD, U. Ga. Atty.; mem. Ga. Senate, from 1977; vice chair judiciary com.; mem. def. and vets. affairs; mem. natural resources and transp. coms. Home: Hinesville, Ga. Died Feb. 4, 2006.

KEMPIN, VAN A., printing company executive; b. Leavenworth, Kans., Apr. 15, 1932; s. Walter and Illa F. (Barnett) K.; m. Donna L. Lidikay, Aug. 11, 1956; children— Sara L., Shari L., Donald A., Vance T. B.A., Baker U., 1956; M.B.A., U. Kans., 1964. C.P.A., Kans. Audit sr. Arthur Andersen & Co., Kansas City, Mo., 1957-60; regional controller Avon Products, Inc., Cin., 1960-73; group controller Times-Mirror Co., Los Angeles, 1973-77; bus. mgr. The World Co., Lawrence, Kans., 1977-79; pres. Lawrence Printing Service, Inc., 1979-84. Served with U.S. Army, 1953-55. Mem. Am. Inst. C.P.A.s, Calif. Soc. C.P.A.s, Kans. Soc. C.P.A.s. Club: Alvamar Country (Lawrence). Lodges: Kiwanis (pres. 1965), Masons. Home: Lawrence, Kans. Died Mar. 18, 2006.

KEMPTER, CHARLES PRENTISS, chemist, materials scientist; b. Burlington, Vt., Feb. 12, 1925; s. Rudolph Harbison and Marjorie A. (Prentiss) K.; m. Anke Margreeth Smit, Apr. 10, 1953 (div.); children— Colin, Eric, Reid; m. Judith Anne Hardison, Aug. 16, 1977. Student, U. Vt., 1942-43, 46-48, U. N.H., 1943-44; BS, Stanford U., 1949, MS, 1950, PhD, 1956. Cert. profl. chemist, 1965. Teaching asst. phys. scis. Stanford U., 1949-50; Owens-Ill. research fellow chem. dept. Stanford, 1953-56; physiochemist research and devel. Dow Chem. Co., Pittsburg, Calif., 1950-53; staff mem. nuclear propulsion div. Los Alamos Sci. Lab., U. Calif. at Los Alamos, 1956-63, 64-71; participant Kiwi-A test, Project Rover, 1958-59, sci. cons., 1971-73; tech. dir. Kempter-Rossman Internat., Washington, 1973-75, sci. advisor, from 1975. Thesis adviser Los Alamos Grad. Center, U. N.Mex., 1959-71; adviser N.Mex. State Crime Lab., 1971-73; vis. scientist Inst. Phys. Chemistry, U. Vienna, Austria, 1963-64 Contbr. numerous articles on solid state sci. and high temperature materials in sci. to profl. publs.; contbg. author: Plutonium, 1960. Served with AUS, 1943-46, ETO; res. col. NG, 1971-85. Recipient Scroll of Honor U.S. Holocaust Meml. Council, 1981 Life fellow, hon. fellow Am. Inst. Chemists (adviser to pres. 1969-72, mem. new activities com. 1962-64, nat. membership com. 1962-68, hon. membership com. 1969-71, long range planning com. 1971-72); mem. Internationale Planseegesellschaft für Pulvermetallurgie, N.Mex. Inst. Chemists (councillor 1969-72), Am. Chem. Soc., AAAS, Union Concerned Scientists, Ret. Officers Assn., DAV, Res. Officers Assn., Sigma Xi, Sigma Phi. Clubs: Stanford of San Diego, Admiral Kidd. Patentee in field. Died Dec. 18, 2006.

KENAN, RICHARD PEARSON, physicist, educator; b. Waycross, Ga., Dec. 25, 1931; s. Owen Thomas and Iwononia Rebecca (Pearson) K.; m. Jane Anne Dodge, May 25, 1968; children: Jeffrey Clark Timmons, Diane Leigh Timmons Vincent, Richard Arthur. BS in Physics, Ga. Inst. Tech., 1955; PhD in Physics, Ohio State U., 1962. Rsch. physicist Battelle Meml. Inst., Columbus, Ohio, 1962-86; prof. of elec. enging. Ga. Inst. of Tech., Atlanta, from 1986. Inventor: 10 patents 1962-86; contbr. numerous articles to profl. jours. Mem. IEEE (sr. mem.), Am. Physical Soc., Optical Soc. of Am. Avocations: music, shop, reading, square dance. Home: Atlanta, Ga. Died Mar. 18, 2007.

KENDE, HANS JANOS, plant physiology educator; b. Szekesfehervar, Hungary, Jan. 18, 1937; came to U.S., 1965, naturalized, 1970; s. Istvan and Katalin (Grosz) K.; m. Gabriele F. Guggenheim, May 15, 1960; children: Benjamin R., Michael, Judith N. Nat. PhD, U. Zurich, Switzerland, 1960; DSc (hon.), U. Fribourg, Switzerland, 1995. Research Council fellow, Ottawa, Can., 1960-61; research fellow Calif. Inst. Tech., Pasadena, 1961-63; plant physiologist Negev Inst. of Arid Zone Research, Beersheva, Israel, 1963-65; assoc. prof. Mich. State U.-Dept. Energy Plant Research Lab., East Lansing, 1965-69, prof., from 1969; dir. Dept. Energy Plant Research Lab. Mich. State U., 1985-88; program mgr. for plant growth and devel. USDA, Washington, 1992. Vis. prof. Swiss Fed. Inst. Tech., Zurich, 1972-73, 79-80; vis. scientist Friedrich Miescher Institut, Basel, Switzerland, 1991. Mem. editorial bd. Plant Physiology, 1969-84, Biochemie und Physiologie der Pflanzen, 1975-93, Plant Molecular Biology, 1981-83, Planta, 1982-97; (editorial bd.) Jour. Plant Growth Regulation, 1982-84, Sci. 1997-2000, Plant Jour., 1998—; contbr. articles to profl. jours. Mem. adv. panel for devel. biology NSF, 1974-77. Guggenheim fellow, 1972-73 Fellow AAAS; mem. NAS, Am. Soc. Plant Biologists (Stephen Hales prize 1998), Leopoldina German Acad. Natural Scis. Home: East Lansing, Mich. Died Sept. 26 2006.

KENDRICK, RONALD H., banker; b. San Diego, Sept. 17 1941; s. Wesley Samuel and Ruth Helen (Hunter) K.; m. Cheryl Donofrio Ayers, June 10, 1989; 1 child by previous marriage Kirsten Dawn; stepchildren: Joshua Ayers, Benjamin Ayers. AB in Econs., San Diego State U., 1964, MBA in Fin., 1975; grad investment mgmt. workshop, Harvard U., 1974, grad. strategic mktg. mgmt., 1993; grad., Pacific Coast Banking Sch. U. Wash. 1981. Chartered fin. analyst. Exec. v.p. Union Bank, San Diego from 1959. Lectr. San Diego State U., 1975-81; faculty Pacific Coast Banking Sch., Seattle, 1983-85; regent Fin. Analysts Seminar, Rockford, Ill., 1975-78; bd. dirs. Union Bank Found. Union Bank PAC, Old Globe, Pacific Bankers Mgmt. Inst.; bus and econ. devel. counsel to Mayor of San Diego, 1995; chmn bd. dirs. San Diego State U. Coll. Bus., 2000—. Treas. Bo Scouts Am. San Diego coun., 1984-85, bd. dirs. 1977-94; mem adv. com. North County Campus San Diego State U., 1984-89 mem. adv. com. Calif. State U., San Marcos, 1989-93; truste Hall Sci. and Reuben H. Fleet Space Theater, San Diego 1984-91, pres., 1988-90; bd. dirs. ARC, SanDiego, 1983-90 chmn., 1985-87; bd. dirs. Symphony Assn., San Diego, 1983-86 San Diegan's Inc., San Diego, 1984-89, United Way San Diego 1988-94, chmn. United Way San Diego campaign, 1995-96, San Diego County YMCA, 1992-2000, Old Globe Theatre, 1995-2000; bd. dirs. Lead, Inc., 1985-86, 87-93, pres., 1990-91; b dirs. Children's Hosp. Found., 1988-98, chmn., 1992-93; bd dirs. Children's Hosp., 1998—; mem. task force to study inds element San Diego gen. plan, 1977; mem. bus. and econ. deve coun. Mayor of San Diego, 1995. Recipient Disting. Alumnu award Coll. Bus. San Diego State U.,1984, Silver Beaver award Humanitarian of Yr. Boy Scouts Am., 1991, Disting. Eagl award Boy Scouts Am., 1993; named Alumnus of Yr., Lead Inc 1992. Mem. Fin. Analysts Soc. (pres. 1978-79), Calif. Banker Assn. (bd. dirs.), Greater San Diego C. of C. (exec. com. 1989 Zool. Soc. San Francisco, Indian Wells C. of C., La Joll Country Club (bd. dirs. 1997-00), Century Club (bd. dirs 1996-2000), Rotary. Republican. Avocations: tennis, golf, wood working, skiing. Home: San Diego, Calif. Died June 1, 2007.

KENNEDY, BERNARD JOSEPH, retired utilities executive b. Niagara Falls, NY, Aug. 16, 1931; s. Edward J. and France (Coyle) K.; m. Geraldine Drexelius, Sept. 20, 1958; childre Mary Kathleen, Maureen Jean, Patricia, Colleen, Joseph B. BA Niagara U., 1953; LL.B., U. Mich., 1958. Bar: N.Y. 1960. Leg asst. Nat. Fuel Gas Distbn. Corp., Buffalo, 1958-63, gen. atty 1963-67, sec., gen. counsel, 1967-75, v.p., gen. counsel, 197 77, sr. v.p., 1977-87, pres., 1987; chief exec. officer Nat. Fu Gas Co., Buffalo, from 1988, chmn. bd., from 1989; pres. Na Fuel Gas Supply Corp., 1978-89, Penn-York Energy Corp 1978-89, Seneca Resources Corp., 1983-89, Empire Explora tion, 1983-89; chmn. Inst. of Gas Tech., Chgo., from 1989; CE Nat. Fuel Gas Co., Buffalo, 1989—2002. Chmn. Lloyd's Sy dicate 1225; bd. dirs. Associated Electric & Gas Ins. Svc. Lt Past chmn. Greater Buffalo Partnership; past chmn., bd. regent past chmn. coun. Bus. Sch. of Canisius Coll.; past trust Niagara U.; past chmn. bd. dirs. Erie County chpt. ARC; chm Cath. Charities Appeal, 1981; bd. dirs. Nat. Petroleum Cour 1990-2004. 1st lt. U.S. Army, 1953-55. Mem. ABA (past vi chmn. gas com.), N.Y. State Bar Assn. (chmn. pub. utilities co 1973), Fed. Energy Bar Assn., Erie County Bar Assn. (past dir Am. Gas Assn., Buffalo Club, Buffalo Canoe Club, Count Club of Buffalo, Sitzmarker Ski Club, Cherry Hill Club (Fo Erie, Ont.). Home: Williamsville, NY. Died Mar. 6, 2007.

KENNEDY, BRUCE ROGER, retired air transportation e ecutive; b. Denver, Oct. 11, 1938; s. Roger W. and Je (Converse) K.; m. Karleen Isaacson, Nov. 21, 1965; childre Kevin, Karin. BBS, U. Alaska, 1963. Corp. sec. Alaska Con nental Devel. Corp., Fairbanks, 1959-64, v.p., 1964,-67, pre 1967-72, chmn., 1972; dir. Alaska Airlines, Inc., Seattle, 197 sr. v.p. properties, 1973-78, pres., COO, 1978-79, chmn., pre CEO, 1979—91; chmn. Quest Aircraft Co. Bd. dirs. Alas Airlines, Inc. Served to 1st lt. U.S. Army, 1965-67. Mem. A Transport Assn. (dir.) Republican. Presbyterian. Home: Seatt Wash. Died June 29, 2007.

KENNEDY, EUGENE RICHARD, microbiologist, universi dean; b. Scranton, Pa., July 3, 1919; s. Thomas A. and Marga (Culkin) K.; m. Marjorie Giblin, July 24, 1945 (dec. 199 children: Anne, Michael, Christine. BS, U. Scranton, 1941; M Cath. U., 1943; PhD, Brown U., 1949. Diplomate Am. B Microbiology. Serologist Walter Reed Army Med. Center, Was ington, 1942; instr. bacteriology and immunology R.I. Hos Sch. of Nursing, Providence, 1946-48, Brown U., Providen 1946-48; instr. Cath. U. Am., Washington, 1949-51, asst. pr microbiology, 1951-55, assoc. prof., 1956-66, prof. emerit 1985—2006, dean Sch. Arts and Scis., 1973-85. Contbr. artic to profl. jours. Served to capt. Med. Service Corps U.S. Arm 1943-46. Mem. Am. Soc. for Microbiology, AAAS, Sigma Phi Beta Kappa. Home: Silver Spring, Md. Died Dec. 11, 20

KENNEDY, JAY, editor-in-chief; b. Toledo, Ohio; s. Jean M. Kennedy; m. Sarah Jewler (dec. 2005). BA in Sociology, U. Wis. Cartoon editor Esquire mag., 1983—88; comics editor King Features Hearst Corp., 1988—97, editor-in-chief, 1997—2007. Died Mar. 15, 2007.

KENNEDY, KEN, computer science educator; b. Washington, Aug. 12, 1945; s. Kenneth Wade and Audrey Ruth K.; m. Carol Quillen; 1 stepdaughter, Caitlin Lohrenz BA in Math. summa cum laude, Rice U., 1967; MS in Math., NYU, 1969, PhD in Computer Sci., 1971. Asst. prof. dept. math. scis. Rice U., Houston, 1971-76, assoc. prof., 1976-80, prof., 1980-84, Noah Harding prof. dept. computer sci., 1985-97, chmn. computer sci. program com., 1982-85, chmn. dept. computer sci., 1984-88, 90-92, dir. Computer and Info. Tech. Inst., 1986-92, dir. Ctr. for Rsch. on Parallel Computation, 1989—2007, Ann and John Doerr prof. comp. engring., 1997—2007; adjunct prof., computer sci. dept. U. Houston, 1997—98, dist. adjunct prof., computer sci., 1998—2007. Vis. prof. computer sci. dept. Stanford U., 1985-86; v.p. R.M. Thrall & Assocs., Inc., 1974-81, pres., 1981-93; mem. programming langs. and implementation sub-area panel computer sci. and engring. rsch. Div. Computer Rsch. NSF, 1975-77, mem. adv. com. for computer rsch., 1984-88, chmn., 1985-87, adv. commn. computer and info. sci. and engring., 1995-2007; vis. scientist Space Shuttle Program Lead Office NASA, 1975, Dept. Computer Sci. IBM Thomas J. Watson Rsch. Ctr., Yorktown Heights, N.Y., 1978-79, cons., 1979-2007, Lawrence Livermore Nat. Lab., 1985-2007; vis. staff mem. computer div. Los Alamos Sci. Lab., 1977-2007; mem. exec. com. CSNET, 1984-86, computer sci. and telecom. bd., NRC, 1992-94, mem. commn. phys. scis., math. and applications, 1995-97; co-chair adv. com. high performance computin gand comm. Indo. Tech. and Next Generation Internet, 1997-2007; presenter numerous prof. meetings; dir. numerous masters theses, PhD dissertations; mem. program com., PPoPP, 1998; chmn. awards com., Supercomputing, 1999. Mem. editorial bd. Jour. Parallel and Distributed Computing, 1988-2007, Concurrency: Practice and Experience, ACM Transactions on Software Engring. and Methodology, 1989-2007; sect. editor langs. and programming Jour. Supercomputing, 1986-93; contbr. numerous chpts. to books, articles to profl. jours. Bd. dirs. Houston Soc. Performing Arts, 1986-2007, v.p. artistic adv., 1987-1997. Grantee NSF, 1973-2007, IBM, 1979-94, DARPA, 1987, W.M. Keck Found., 1990-92, Office of Gov. State of Tex., 1990-95, Office Naval Rsch., 1993-96, NASA, 1993-96; Woodrow Wilson Nat. fellow, 1967-68; NSF grad. fellow, 1968-71; recipient NYU Founders Day award for Acad. Achievement, 1972. Fellow IEEE (W. Wallace McDowell award 1995), AAAS, ACM (program com. SIGPLAN nat. conf. 1982, 84, chmn. program com. principles of programming langs. confs. 1983, software sys. award com. 1983-85, chmn. 1984, chmn. program com. Supercomputing 1992); mem. Soc. Indsl. and Applied Math., Nat. Acad. Engring., Phi Beta Kappa, Sigma Xi. Home: Houston, Tex. Died Feb. 7, 2007.

KENNEDY, THOMAS JAMES, JR., association executive; b. Washington, June 24, 1920; s. Thomas James and Ruth Elizabeth (Norris) K.; m. F. Elaine Godtfring, Sept. 30, 1950; children— Thomas James III, Ann Elizabeth, Joan Frances, Paul Edward, Christopher Alan. BS, Cath. U. Am., 1940; MD, Johns Hopkins, 1943. Diplomate Am. Bd. Internal Medicine. Intern med. service Peter Bent Brigham Hosp., Boston, 1944; research fellow, research service 3d med. div. Goldwater Meml. Hosp., NYC, 1945-47, resident physician, research service 1st med. div., 1947-50; research fellow NYU Coll. Medicine, 1945-47; asst. medicine Columbia Coll. Phys. and Surg., 1948-50; joined USPHS, 1950, served to asst. surgeon gen.; assoc. medicine George Washington U. Sch. Medicine, 1951-65; investigator lab. kidney and electrolyte metabolism Nat. Heart Inst., 1950-60, attending physician, responsible physician, 1953-60; asst. to dir. labs. and clinics Office Dir., NIH, 1960-62, spl. asst. to dir. for sci. communications, 1962-65, dir. div. research facilities and resources, 1965-68, asso. dir. for program planning and evaluation, office of dir., 1968-74; exec. dir. Assembly Life Scis., NRC-Nat. Acad. Scis., 1974-76; dir. dept. planning and policy devel. Assn. Am. Med. Colls., Washington, 1976-87, assoc. v.p., 1987-90. Served to capt. AUS, 1944-47. Mem. Am. Fedn. Clin. Research, Am. Physiol. Soc. Home: Garrett Park, Md. Died Nov. 19, 2006.

KENNEDY, WILLIAM BEAN, theology educator; b. Spartanburg, SC, Oct. 18, 1926; s. Leland McDuffie and Elizabeth Fleming (Bean) K.; m. Frances Barron Harris, July 9, 1952; children: Katharine Fleming, William Bean, Jane Harris, Emily Pou. BA, Wofford Coll., 1947, LL.D. (hon.), 1970; MA, Duke U., 1948; B.D., Union Theol. Sem., Richmond, Va., 1954; PhD, Yale U., 1957; LittD (hon.), The Jewish Theol. Sem. of Am., 1995. Ordained to ministry Presbyn. Ch. U.S., 1954. Tchr. Spartanburg High Sch., 1948-49; instr. Emory U. at Oxford, 1949-51; minister of edn. First Congl. Ch., West Haven, Conn., 1954-57; asst. prof. Christian edn. Union Theol. Sem., Richmond, 1957-59, assoc. prof., 1959-65; sec. edn. Bd. Christian Edn., Presbyn. Ch. U.S., Richmond, 1965-69; dir. office edn. World Council Chs., Geneva, 1969-75; dir. Atlanta Assn. Internat. Edn., 1976-79; prof. religion and edn. Union Theol. Sem., NYC, 1979-81, Skinner and McAlpin prof. practical theology, 1981-94, prof. emeritus, from 1994. Mem. task force on world hunger Presbyn. Ch. U.S., Atlanta, 1976-82; cons. hunger program Nat. Council Chs., N.Y.C., 1981; cons. pilot immersion project for globalization of theol. edn., Plowshares Inst., 1988-93. Author: Into Covenant Life, 1963, Shaping of Protestant Education, 1965; author, editor: (with others) Pedagogies for the Non-Poor, 1987; contbr. numerous articles, revs. to profl. jours. Pres. Buncombe County Sr. Dems., 1995—; alderman Town of Black Mountain, N.C., 1997—. With USN, 1945-46. Moore fellow, 1954; recipient research grant Assn. Theol. Schs., 1963, 73. Mem. Nat. Council Chs. (pres., profs. and research sect. 1961-62, div. edn. and ministry unit com.), Religious Edn. Assn. (bd. dirs. 1981-89, chmn. bd. dirs. 1984-89), Assn. Profs. and Researchers in Religious Edn. (bd. dirs. 1983-85, pres. 1990-91), Am. Acad. of Religion, Soc. for the Scientific Study of Religion, Phi Beta Kappa. Home: Black Mountain, NC. Died Oct. 12, 2006.

KENNEDY, WILLIAM JESSE, III, insurance company executive; b. Durham, NC, Oct. 24, 1922; s. William Jesse and Margaret (Spaulding) K.; m. Alice C. Copeland, Jan. 29, 1949; 1 child, William Jesse IV. BS, Va. State Coll., 1942; MBA, U. Pa., 1946, NYU, 1948, postgrad., 1948-50; LLD (hon.), N.C. Cen. U., 1986. Adminstrv. asst. N.C. Mut. Life Ins. Co., Durham, 1950-52, asst. to contr., 1952-56, asst. v.p., 1956-59, contr., 1959-61, asst. sec.-contr., 1961-65, asst. fin. v.p., contr., 1965-66, fin. v.p., bd. dirs., 1966-69, sr. v.p., 1969-72, pres., 1972-75, vice chmn. bd., pres., chief exec. officer, 1975-79, chmn., pres., chief exec. officer, from 1979. Bd. dirs. UNC Ventures, Inc., Boston (chmn.), Mechanics & Farmers Bank, Durham, Pfizer, Inc., N.Y.C., Jones Group, Inc., Charlotte, N.C., Mobil Corp., N.Y.C., Quaker Oats Co., Chgo., Investors Title Co., Chapel Hill, N.C. Bd. dirs. Durham Tech. Community Coll. Found., Inc.,, Rsch. Triangle Found. of N.C., N.C. Citizens Assn., John Avery Boy's Club, Durham; past chmn. Durham's War on Drug and Alcohol Abuse; S.E. regional adv. coun. Boy Scouts Am.; chmn.'s adv. coun. United Student Aid Funds, Indpls., others.; bd. visitors N.C. Cen. U.; trustee White Rock Baptist Ch. Lt. U.S. Army, 1943-45. Recipient Ann. award for profl. achievement Tribune Charities, 1974, Ann. award in fin. Black Enterprise Mag., 1975, Pathfinder award Opportunities Industrialization Ctrs. Am., 1976, C.C. Spaulding Ins. award Nat. Bus. League, 1976, The Twenty First Century Found. Achievement award, 1977, Alumnus of Yr. award Va. State Coll., 1977, Achievement award NYU Grad. Sch. Bus. Adminstrn. Alumni Assn., 1980-81, Am. Black Achievement award Ebony Mag., 1985, J.E. Walker Humanitarian award Nat. Bus. League, 1987; inducted into Nat. Minority Bus. Hall of Fame, 1977. Mem. N.C. Soc. Fin. Analyst (charter), The Conf. Bd. (sr.), Omega Psi Phi (Beta Phi chpt.). Democrat. Home: Durham, NC. Died May 23, 2007.

KENNERLY, STEPHEN LYNN, architect; b. Houston, Oct. 11, 1941; s. Seward Joshua and Jeannette Lee (Bishop) K.; m. Marlene Bell, Sept. 28, 1979; children— Ronnie, Robby, Jon. B.S. in Arch., U. Houston, 1966. Registered architect, N.J., Pa. Assoc. W. R. Jenkins Architects, Houston, 1968-71; pres. various cos., Bucks County, Pa., 1971-77; sr. assoc. The Kling Partnership, Phila., 1977-80, Wallace Roberts & Todd, Phila, 1981-82; ptnr. The Kling Partnership, Phila., 1982-84; prin. Environ. Design Corp., Phila., 1984—. Contbr. articles to profl. jours. T. J. Bettes scholar, 1964. Mem. AIA, Soc. for Mktg. Profl. Services (dir. 1982-84), Nat. Assn. Office and Indsl. Parks, Nat. Assn. Corp. Real Estate Execs. Republican. Home: Cherry Hill, NJ. Died Dec. 10, 2006.

KENNETT, JOHN HOLLIDAY, JR., lawyer; b. Atlanta, June 28, 1929; s. John Holliday and Alice Bruyere (Work) K.; m. Barbara Miller, Aug. 13, 1965; children— Elizabeth B., Leigh H. B.S. in Acctg., Va. Poly. Inst., 1951; LL.B., U. Va., 1954. Bar: Va. 1953, U.S. Supreme Ct. 1960. With Kennett & Kennett, C.P.A.s, 1954; assoc. with Holman Willis, Jr., Roanoke, 1954-61; sole practice, Roanoke, 1961—; instr. comml. law Va. So. Coll., Roanoke, 1961-67; dir. various corps. Named Boss of Yr., Roanoke Valley Legal Secs. Assn., 1980. Mem. ABA, Va. Bar Assn., Roanoke Bar Assn., Roanoke Estate Planning Council (pres. 1961). Presbyterian. Club: Roanoke Country. Died July 11, 2006.

KENT, ROSALIE HELEN, transportation executive, columnist, educator; b. Detroit, July 10, 1939; d. Harold J. and Anna Bernadine (McGlone) K. Cert. instr. internat. trade. Rate analyst USAC Transport Co., Detroit, 1960-64; asst. mgr. marine ins. dept. Security Storage Co., Washington, 1964-70; export coordinator Wilkerson Corp., Denver, 1970-73; ops. mgr. Samaras Internat., Denver, 1973-76; ptnr. World Cargo Ltd., Denver, 1976-79; dist. mgr. Schenkers Internat. Forwarders, Inc., Denver, 1979—; instr. internat. trade Community Coll. Denver; instr. internat. transp. and cargo movement Rocky Mountain Inst. Fgn. Trade and Fin., 1984—. Mem. Internat. Trade Assn. Colo. (dir. 1980-82, newsletter editor 1978-80), Traffic Club Denver (monthly publ. columnist), Delta Nu Alpha. Republican. Roman Catholic. Home: Broomfield, Colo. Died Apr. 25, 2007.

KENWORTHY, WILLIAM P., lawyer; b. Memphis, Nov. 20, 1947; BA, So. Meth. U., 1969; JD, Memphis State U., 1974. Bar: Tenn. 1975. Ptnr. Heiskell, Donelson, Bearman, Adams, Williams & Kirsch, P.C., Memphis. Lt. USNR, 1969-72. Mem. ABA (com. employee benefits, sect. on taxation 1984), So. Employee Benefits Conf., Tenn. Bar Assn., Memphis Bar Assn., Delta Theta Phi. Died Mar. 12, 2007.

KERNOCHAN, JOHN MARSHALL, lawyer, educator; b. NYC, Aug. 3, 1919; s. Marshall Rutgers and Caroline (Hatch) K. BA, Harvard U., 1942; JD, Columbia U., 1948. Bar: N.Y. 1949. Asst. dir. Legis. Drafting Research Fund Columbia U., NYC, 1950-51, acting dir., 1951-52, dir., 1952-69, lectr. law, 1951-52, assoc. prof., 1952-55, prof., 1955-77, Nash prof. law, 1977-89, Nash prof. law emeritus, 1990—2007; spl. lectr., 1991—2000. Cons. Temporary State Commn. to Study Orgnl. Structure of Govt. N.Y.C., 1953; exec. dir. Coun. for Atomic Age Studies, 1956—59, co-chmn., 1960—62; chmn. bd. Galaxy Music Corp., 1956—89; bd. dirs. E.C. Schirmer Music Co., Inc.; pres. Gaudia Music & Arts, Inc., 1987—2004. Author: The Legislative Process, 1980; co-author: Legal Method Cases and Materials, 1980; contbr. articles to profl. jour. Mem. civil and polit. rights com. President's Commn. on Status of Women, 1962-63; dir. emeritus Vol. Lawyers for the Arts; mem. legal and legis. com. Internat. Confedn. Soc. Authors and Composers. Mem. Assn. Bar City of N.Y. Internat. Lit. and Artistic Assn. (mem. d'honneur, internat. exec. com., mem. U.S.A. group), Copyright Soc. U.S.A. (exec. com. 1986-89), Assn. Tchrs. and Rschrs. in Intellectual Property. Home: Jamaica Plain, Mass. Died Oct. 29, 2007.*

KERR, DEBORAH JANE, actress; b. Helensburgh, Scotland, Sept. 30, 1921; came to U.S., 1947; d. Arthur Kerr-Trimmer; m. Anthony C. Bartley, Nov. 28, 1945 (div. 1959); children: Melanie, Francesca; m. Peter Viertel, July 23, 1960. Student, Helensburgh schs., Northumberland House Sch., Bristol. Actress: (films) Contraband, 1940, Major Barbara, 1940 Love on the Dole, 1941, Penn of Pennsylvania, 1942, Hatter's Castle, 1942, The Avengers, 1942, The Life and Death of Colonel Blimp, 1943, Perfect Strangers, 1945, I See a Dark Stranger, 1946, Black Narcissus, 1947 (N.Y. Critics award for Best Actress, 1947), The Hucksters, 1947, If Winter Comes, 1947, Edward, My Son, 1949, Please Believe Me, 1950, King Solomon's Mines, 1950, Quo Vadis, 1951, Thunder in the East, 1952, Prisoner of Zenda, 1952, Julius Caesar, 1953, Dream Wife, 1953, Young Bess, 1953, From Here to Eternity, 1953, The End of the Affair, 1955, Proud and Profane, 1956, The King and I, 1956 (Golden Globe award for Best Actress, Hollywood Fgn. Press, 1957), Tea and Sympathy, 1956, Heaven Knows Mr. Alison, 1956 (N.Y. Critics award for Best Actress, 1957), An Affair to Remember, 1957, Kiss Them for Me, 1957, Bonjour Tristesse, 1958, Separate Tables, 1958, Count Your Blessings, 1959, The Journey, 1959, Beloved Infidel, 1959, The Grass is Greener, 1960, The Sundowners, 1960 (N.Y. Critics award for Best Actress, 1960), The Naked Edge, 1961, The Innocents, 1961, Chalk Garden, 1964, The Night of the Iguana, 1964, Marriage on the Rocks, 1965, Eye of the Devil, 1966, Casino Royale, 1967, Prudence and the Pill, 1968, The Gypsy Moths, The Arrangement, 1969, The Assam Garden, 1985; (TV movies): Witness for the Prosecution, 1982, Reunion at Fairborough, 1985, Hold the Dream, 1986; (TV mini-series) A Woman of Substance, 1985; appeared on stage in Heartbreak House, 1943, Gaslight (for Brit. troops in Europe), 1945, Tea and Sympathy, 1954-55, The Day After the Fair, London, 1972-73; appeared in: U.S. tour of Seascape, 1975, Long Day's Journey into Night, Los Angeles, 1977, Candida, London, 1977, The Last of Mrs. Cheney, US and Can., 1978-79, The Day After the Fair, Australia, 1979; appeared on London stage in Overheard, 1981 (Recipient Sarah Siddons award as Chgo. actress of the year.) Named a Honorary Knight Comdr. of the Most Excellent Order of the British Empire, Her Majesty Queen Elizabeth II, 1998; recipient BAFTA Spl. award, 1991, Hon. Academy award, Acad. Motion Pictures Arts & Sciences, 1993. Home: Klosters, Switzerland. Died Oct. 17, 2007.

KERR, ROBERT MARK, state legislator, farmer, stockman; b. Jackson County, Okla., May 20, 1932; s. Mark C. and Frances Elizabeth Kerr; married. BS in Agr., Okla. State U. Farmer and stockman; real estate developer; mem. Okla. State Senate, from 1987. Mem. Agr. and Rural Devel., Appropriations, Edn., Rules, Tourism and Recreation, Transp., Vets., Mil. Affairs and Pub. Safety coms. Okla. State Senate. Co-chair Okla. Dem. Party; mem. Okla. Hwy. Commn.; mem. Okla. State Bd. Agr., 10 yrs., served as commr. of agr. Mem. Okla. Wheat Growers (past pres.), Okla. Cattlemen's Assn., Okla. Plant Food Ednl. Soc., C. of C., Masons, Kiwanis. Democrat. Methodist. Avocations: boating, water-skiing, antique cars. Home: Altus, Okla. Died Jan. 25, 2006.

KERSLAKE, KENNETH ALVIN, artist, printmaker, art educator; b. Mt. Vernon, NY, Mar. 8, 1930; s. Archibald and Cecilia Fox (Gotterson) K.; m. Sarah Jane Allen, Aug. 25, 1956; children: Scott Paul, Katherine Rachel. Student, Pratt Inst., 1950-53; BFA, U. Ill., 1955, MFA, 1957. Grad. asst. U. Ill.-Champaign, 1955-57; interim instr. U. Ill., Champaign, 1957-58; instr. U. Fla., Gainesville, 1958-60, asst. prof. art, 1961-68, assoc. prof., 1969-74, prof., 1974-91, Disting. Svc. prof., 1991-96, Disting. svc. prof. emeritus, 1996—2007. Workshop lectr. U. Alaska-Fairbanks, 1982, Frogman's Print & Paper Workshop, Vermillion, S.D., 2000, Penland (N.C.) Sch. Crafts, 2000; artist-in-residence U. Mo.-Columbia, 1980, Frans Masereel Print Ctr., Kasterlee, Belgium, 1986, U. Tex., Austin; invited faculty U. Ga. Studies Abroad Program, Cortona, Italy, 1982; juror Fla. Printmakers 3rd Ann. Exhbn., 1989, Honolulu Printmakers 62nd Ann. Exhbn., 1990, Pacific States Nat. Print Exhbn., U. Hawaii, Hilo, 1992, Nat. Print Exhbn., U. Tex., Tyler, 1999, Regional Print Exhbn., Alma (Mich.) Coll., 2000, 1st Internat. Print Exhbn., Art & Culture Ctr., Hollywood, Fla., 2000, Juried Traveling Show, So. Graphics Coun., 2000—; exch. prof. Coll. of Art, Edinburgh, Scotland, 1995. Exhibitions include Impressions of Forty Years: The Prints of Kenneth A. Kerslake, Samuel P. HArn Mus. Art, U. Fla., Fla. Ctr. Arts, Gainesville and Vero Beach, Fla., 1997, LeMoyne Art Found., Tallahassee, Fla., 1998, U. Hawaii, Hilo, 1999, Webster U., Ga. Coll. and State U., St. Louis and Atlanta, Pacific Rim Internat. Exhbn., 2001 (Purchase award, 2001), 28th Bradley Nat. Print and Drawing Exhbn., Bradley U., Peoria, Ill. (Dean's Purchase award), The Boston Printmasters, 2001 (N.Am. Print prize, 2001), Herron Sch. Art, Indpls., 2003, featured in publs. including, Forty American Contemporary Printmakers. Recipient Joseph Pennell award Library of Congress, 1975, Assoc. Am. Artist award Associated Am. Artist Gallery, 1979, Disting. Faculty award Fla. Blue Key-U. Fla., 1979, Tchr. Improvement Program award, 1993, Purchase award Pacific Rim Internat. Print Exhbn. U. Hawaii, Hilo, 2001, Purchase award 28th Bradley Nat. Print and Drawing Exhbn. Bradley U., Peoria, Ill., Exhbn. award Boston Printmakers North Am. Print Exhbn., 2001; named Tchr. of Yr., Coll. Fine Arts, U. Fla., 1987; grantee Tamarind Found. Inc., 1964. Mem. Soc. Am. Graphic Artists, Fla. Printmakers Soc., Samuel P. Harn Mus. Art Alliance, Boston Printmakers, Print Club Phila., So. Graphics Coun. (organized 15th ann. conf., pres. 1990-92, newsletter editor), Am. Print Alliance (exec. bd., exec. com. 1992-93). Democrat. Episcopalian. Home: Gainesville, Fla. Died Jan. 7, 2007.

KERTZ, HUBERT LEONARD, telephone company executive; b. San Francisco, July 11, 1910; s. Hubert J. and Laura V. (Seavey) K.; m. Paula Schmoranzer, Mar. 22, 1991; children: Brenda L., Pamela. AB, Stanford, 1934, E.E., 1936. With Pacific Tel. & Tel. Co., 1926-42, 46-61, asst. v.p., 1953-58, v.p., 1958-61; asst. v.p. AT&T, 1961-64, v.p., 1964-75; pres., mng. dir. Am. Bell Internat. Inc., 1975-79; cons., from 1980. Bd. dirs. Teltone Corp., Coasteom Corp. Served from lt. (j.g.) to comdr. USNR, 1942-46, PTO. Decorated Bronze Star. Fellow IEEE; mem. Soc. Calif. Pioneers, Met. Club N.Y. Died Apr. 17, 2007.

KESSLER, A. D., business, financial, investment and real estate advisor, consultant, educator, lecturer, author; b. N.Y.C., May 1, 1923; s. Morris William and Belle Miriam (Pastor) K.; m. Ruth Schwartz, Nov. 20, 1944 (div. 1974); children: Brian Lloyd, Judd Stuart, Earl Vaughn; m. Jaclyn Jeanne Sprague. Student U. Newark, 1940-41, Rutgers U., 1941-42, 46, Albright Coll., 1942, Newark Coll. Engring., 1946; PhD in Pub. Adminstrn. U. Fla.,

1972; MBA, Kensington U., 1976, PhD in Mgmt. and Behavioral Psychology, 1977. Sr. cert. rev. appraiser; cert. bus. counselor; cert. exchanger; registered mortgage underwriter; registered investment advisor. Pvt. practice real estate, ins. and bus. brokerage, N.J., Pa., Fla., N.Y., Nev., Calif., Hong Kong, 1946—; pres. Armor Corp., 1947-68; pres. Folding Carton Corp., Am., N.Y.C., 1958-68; exec. v.p. Henry Schindall Assocs., N.Y.C., 1966-67; tax rep. Calif. State Bd. Equalization, 1968-69; aviation cons. transp. div. Calif., Dept. Aeros., also pub. info. officer; 1969-71; FAA Gen. Aviation Safety Counselor; broker, mgr. La Costa (Calif.) Sales Corp., 1971-75; chmn. bd. Profl. Ednl. Found., 1975—, Timeshare Resorts Internat., 1975—, Interex, Leucadia, Calif., 1975-82, The Kessler Orgn., Rancho Santa Fe, Calif., 1975—, The Kessler Fin. Group, Fin. Ind. Inst., 1977—; pres. Ednl. Video Inst., 1978—, Fin. Planning Inst., 1975—, Rancho Santa Fe Real Estate & Land, Inc., 1975—; treas., exec. bd. dirs. Nat. Challenge Com. on Disability, 1983-90; dir. Practice Mgmt. Cons. Abacus Data Systems, 1984—; broker mgr. Rancho Sante Fe Acreage & Homes, Inc., 1987-89; mktg. dir. Commercial Real Estate Services, Rancho Santa Fe, 1987—; cons. broker Glenct. Properties Ptnrs., 1989-90; dir. U.S. Advisors, 1989—; founder Creative Real Estate Movement, 1946—; pub., editor in chief Creative Real Estate Mag., 1975—; pub. Creative Real Estate Mag. of Australia and New Zealand; founder, editor Moderator of Tape of the Month Club; founder, producer, chmn. Internat. Real Estate Expo; chmn. bd. The Brain Trust, Rancho Santa Fe, Calif., 1977—; fin. lectr. for Internat. Cruise Ships, Cunard Line, Norwegian Am. Cruises, P&O, Princess, others; lectr. life enrichment and stress mgmt. Internat. Cruise Ships; Calif. adj. faculty, prof. fin. Clayton U., St. Louis; developer, operator Barnegat Baywood Seaplane Base, Barnegat Bay, N.J.; owner, operator Skyline Airport, Hunterdon County, N.J. Scoutmaster Orange Mountain coun. Boy Scouts Am., 1955-62; harbor master N.J. Marine Patrol, 1958-67; dep. sheriff, Essex County, N.J., 1951-65; mem. pres.' adv. bd. Seton Hall U., 1961-64; chmn. Stop Smoking, 1990, Quick Study, 1990; feature broadcaster/producer Kalaidascope Radio Mag., Am. Radio Network, 1990—. Served with USAF, 1942-45. Decorated D.F.C., Air medal, Purple Heart; named to French Legion of Honor, Order of Lafayette; named a flying col, a.d.c., Gov. of Ga., 1957. Mem. Am. Soc. Editors and Pubs., Author's Guild, Internat. Platform Assn., Nat. Speakers Assn., Nat. Press Photographers Assn., Guild Assn. Airport Execs., Aviation and Space Writers Assn., Nat. Assn. of Real Estate Editors, Internat. Exchangors Assn. (founder), Air Force Assn. (dep. comdr. N.J. chpt. 1955-57). Clubs: Nat. Press, Overseas Press, La Costa Country, Cuyamaca, Rancho Santa Fe Country, Passport. Lodges: Masons, Shriners. Author: A Fortune At Your Feet, 1981, How You Can Get Rich, Stay Rich and Enjoy Being Rich, 1981, Financial Independence, 1987, The Profit, 1987, A Fortune at Your Feet in the '90s, 1994, The Midas Touch, Turning Paper Into Gold, 1994; author, instr. Your Key to Success seminar, 1988, Your Key to Creative Real Estate Success tng. program, 1996; The A to Z of Lease Purchase and 11 Other Options Training Prog.; editor: The Real Estate News Observer, 1975—; fin. editor API, 1978—; fin. columnist Money Matters, 1986—; syndicated columnist, radio and TV host of "Money Making Ideas," 1977—; songwriter: Only You, 1939, If I'm Not HomeFor Christmas, 1940, Franny, 1940, Flajaloppa, 1940, They've Nothing More Dear Only They've Got It Here, 1941, The Summer of Life, 1956; producer (movies) The Flight of the Cobra, Rena, We Have Your Daughters, Music Row; speaker for radio and TV as The Real Estate Answerman, 1975—; host (radio and TV show) Ask Mr. Money; conceptualist, exec. prodr. (TV show) The Trading Game, 1994; exec. prodr., moderator (TV show) A.D. Kessler's Real Estate Roundtable, 1993—. Inventor swivel seat, siptop, inflatumbrella. Home: Rancho Santa Fe, Calif. Died Mar. 31, 2007.

KIEFT, LESTER, chemist, educator; b. Grand Haven, Mich., Sept. 18, 1912; s. Martin and Dena (Rossien) K.; m. Norma Elaine Richenbacher, June 28, 1941; children: John Martin, Richard, James. AB, Hope Coll., 1934; MS, Pa. State Coll., 1936, PhD, 1939. Asst. Pa. State Coll., 1934-37; asst. prof. chemistry Pa. State Jr. Coll., 1937-42, Bucknell U., 1942-44, prof. and head chemistry dept., 1944-81, prof. emeritus, from 1981; summer lectr., engring. (sci. and mgmt. war tng. program), 1941; dir. Inst. High Sch. Sci. Tchrs., Bucknell U., from 1957, Inst. for High Ability Secondary Students. Eastern Pa. tng. specialist Tah-Aide program Am. Assn. Ret. Persons, 1989—. Pres. Lewisburgh Borough Council, 1962-65; In charge Lewisburg (Pa.) Youth Activities, 1944-51; pres. Eastern Union County United Fund. Recipient Disting. Svc. award Jr. C. of C., 1977, Good Citizenship award SAR, 1979, Coun. of Honor, POSA, 1989. Mem. Am. Chem. Soc. (analytical subcom. on exams. and tests for soc. coop. chemistry test, vice chmn. central Pa. sect. 1954, chmn. 1955, chmn. Susquehanna Valley sect. 1958-59), AAAS, Pa. Sci. Tchrs. (dir. 1958—), Nat. Sci. Tchrs. Assn., Blue Key, Sigma Xi, Alpha Chi Sigma, Phi Eta Sigma, Sigma Xi, Phi Lambda Upsilon. Republican. Mem. United Ch. Christ (ch. coun. 1944—). Club: Lions (dist. gov. 1956-57, chmn. Sight Conservation and Eye Research Found. 1957—, Internat. Pres. award 1985, Ambassador of Good Will award, 1986, Melvins Jones fellow 1987). Home: Lewisburg, Pa. Died Apr. 14, 2006.

KIEL, FREDERICK ORIN, lawyer; b. Columbus, Ohio, Feb. 22, 1942; s. Fred and Helen Kiel; m. Vivian Lee Naff, June 2, 1963; 1 child, Aileen Vivian. AB magna cum laude, Wilmington Coll., 1963; JD, Harvard U., 1966. Bar: Ohio 1966, U.S. Supreme Ct. 1972. Assoc. Peck, Shaffer & Williams, Cin., 1966—71, ptnr., 1971—80, Taft, Stettinius & Hollister, Cin., 1980—89; pvt. practice law Cin., from 1990. Co-founder Bond Attys.' Workshop, 1976. Editor: Bond Lawyer, 1982, Nat. Assn. Bond Lawyers Quarterly Newsletter, 1982, Bond Lawyers and Bond Law: An Oral History, 1993, Bondletter, 1991—, Anderson Insights, 1992—; contbr. articles to profl. jours. Arbitrator Mcpl. Securities Rulemaking Bd., 1985-92; sec. Anderson Twp. Greenspace Adv. Com., 1990—; rep. precinct exec. Precinct H Anderson Twp., 1991-92, 94-2001, Precinct X Anderson Twp., 2001—; twp. atty. Anderson Twp., 1997-2003; twp. law dir., 2003—. Mem. Ohio State Bar Assn., Cin. Bar Assn., Nat. Assn. Bond Lawyers (life, co-founder 1979, dir. 1979-84, pres. 1982-83, hon. dir. 1984—, bond attys. workshop steering com. 1976, 83, 85, scrivener com. stds. practice 1987-89, Disting. Svc. award 2002, 04). Home: Cincinnati, Ohio. Died Aug. 4, 2007.

KIESEL, ILMAR OTTO, retired radiologist; b. Tiflis, Caucasus, Russia, Oct. 14, 1912; came to U.S., 1949; MD, U. Tartu, Estonia, 1938. Cert. in radiology. Intern U. Tartu, 1937-38, resident in roentgenology, 1938-42; resident U. Minn. Hosp., 1957-60, Mpls. VA Hosp., 1957-60; prof. emeritus Oreg. Health Scis. U. Mem. AMA, Am. Coll. Radiology, Radiol. Soc. N.Am. Home: Beaverton, Oreg. Died Aug. 10, 2006.

KILBOURNE, DEANE EARLE, geologist; b. Leslie, Mich., Feb. 6, 1918; s. Hubert Lynn and Dorothy May (Mudge) K.; m. Jeanne Louise Bridges, Feb. 27, 1954. B.S., Mich. State U., 1941, M.S., 1947; Ph.D., U. Ariz., 1967. Geologist, Texaco, Inc., Casper, Wyo., 1947-62, Enserch Exploration, Midland, Tex., 1975-76; dist. geologist Am. Trading & Prodn. Corp., Midland, 1978—. Contbr. articles to profl. jours. Served as cpl. USAF, 1942-45, ETO. Mem. Am. Assn. Petroleum Geologists, Sigma Xi. Republican. Avocation: golfing. Home: Midland, Tex. Died Dec. 29, 2006.

KILIAN, WALTER DANIEL, personnel consultant; b. N.Y.C., Dec. 22, 1935; s. Daniel C. and Isabelle (Walter) K.; B.Marine Engring., N.Y. State Maritime Coll., 1957; M.Occupational Edn., U. N.H., 1977; m. Cynthia Ann Carter, June 15, 1957; children— David, Elizabeth, Jonathan. With shipbldg. div. Bethlehem Steel Co., Quincy, Mass., 1957-64; project engr. Ingersoll-Rand Co., N.H., 1964-66; mfg. engr., then sales engr. Hitchiner Mfg. Co., Milford, N.H., 1966-68; pres. availABILITY of N.H., Inc., Bedford, 1968—; guest lectr. colls. Past chmn. dist. adv. council SBA; mem. N.H. Adv. Com. Tech. Insts. and Vocat. Tech. Colls., 1975—. Moderator, Mont Vernon (N.H.) Sch. Dist. and Town; chmn. Hillsborough County (N.H.) Republican Com., 1976-80; bd. dirs., v.p. N.H. Assn. for Blind, 1982-87, pres., 1987-88. Served to capt. USNR, 1957-87. Cert. personnel cons., Nat. Asn. Personnel Cons. Mem. Bus. and Industry Assn. N.H. (past v.p.-treas.), N.H. Pvt. Employment Assn. (charter pres.), Nat. Personnel Cons. (v.p., dir.). Home: Mont Vernon, NH. Died May 28, 2007.

KILLAM, EVA KING, pharmacologist; b. NYC, Nov. 16, 1921; d. Charles H. and Louise C. (Richter) King; m. Keith F. Killam, Jr., May 12, 1955; children: Anne Louise, Paul Fenton, Melissa Helen. AB, Sarah Lawrence Coll., 1942; AM, Mt. Holyoke Coll., 1944; PhD in Pharmacology, U. Ill., 1953. Pharmacologist Army Chem. Center, Md., 1948-51; jr. rsch. pharmacologist, then assoc. rsch. pharmacologist UCLA Med. Sch., 1953-59; research asso. Stanford U. Med. Sch., 1959-68; prof. physiology U. Calif., Davis, 1968-72, prof. pharmacology, 1972-91, prof. emeritus, from 1991; epilepsy adv. com. NIH, 1976-80; study sect. preclin. pharmacology NIMH, 1972-76. Co-editor: Handbook of Electroencephalography, Vol. 7, 1977; editor-in-chief: Jour. Pharmacology and Exptl. Therapeutics, 1978-91; edit. bd.: Soc. Exptl. Biology and Medicine, 1957-58, Internat. Jour. Neuropharmacology, 1962-68, Exptl. Neurology, 1980-83; contbr. articles to sci. jours. Fellow Am. Coll. Neuropsychopharmacology (counselor 1980-84, pres. 1988); mem. AAAS, Am. Soc. Pharmacology and Exptl. Therapeutics (counselor 1972-75, pres.-elect 1988, pres. 1989-90, Abel award 1954), Western Pharmacology Soc. (Council 1980-83, pres. 1984), Epilepsy Soc., Bd. Sci. Counselors, Nat. Inst. for Neurological and Communicature Disorders and Stroke, Sigma Xi. Home: Glendale, Calif. Died July 30, 2006.

KILLEBREW, JAMES ROBERT, architectural engineering firm executive; b. Okmulgee, Okla., Dec. 10, 1918; s. Robert Herman and Edith (Tyler) K.; m. Emma Herrington, Feb. 24, 1989; 1 child by previous marriage, Laura Janice. BS in Archtl. Engring., U. Tex., 1948. Registered architect, Tex. registered profl. engr., Tex. Prin. James R. Killebrew, FAIA, PE, architect, cons. engr., Granbury, Tex.; sr. structural engr. DFW Internat. Airport, from 1991. Sr. cons. architect engr. Yandell-Hiller, 1989-90, Dallas-Ft. Worth Airport/Am. Airlines; sr. structural engr. Dallas-Ft. Worth Internat. Airport Bd. Prin. archtl. works include Gen. Hosp. Plainview, Tex., Vernon (Tex.) Hosp., Vernon Geriatrics Psychiat. Hosp., Wichita Gen. Hosp., Gen. Hosp. Nocona (Tex.), Sci. Bldg., Phys. Edn. Bldg., Midwestern State U., Teenage Drug Addiction Center, Vernon, Fine Arts Bldg. at Midwestern State U., AC Spark Plug Ceramics Complex-Gen. Motors Corp., Parker Sq. Savs. and Loan, Union Sq., Four Story Savs. & Loan Bldg., Wichita Falls, Sprague Electric Co., Howmet Turbine, Wichita Clutch Corp., G.H. Foster Plant, Family YMCA, SW Nat. Bank Tower; coord. measuring machine for Gen. Motors-CPC plant, Arlington, Tex. Elder Christian Ch., 1979-81. Lt. comdr. USN, 1940-45, PTO; capt. Res. (ret.). Fellow AIA (pres. Wichita Falls chpt. 1966-67, 81); mem. Nat. Soc. Profl. Engrs., Tex. Soc. Profl. Engrs. (pres. N. Tex. chpt. 1960-61), Am. Soc. Archtl. Engrs. (charter mem.), ASHRAE, Wichita Falls C. of C. (chmn. various coms.), Navy League (pres. 1967-68), Fine Art Soc. Tex. (pres. 1970, chmn. bd. 1973). Mem. Christian Ch. Club: Rotary (pres. 1983-84). Achievements include inspection for expansion of terminals, multi-story parking facilities, aircraft rescue fire fighting training facility, hangar addition, FAA technical facility and five story parking garage, DFW runway 16/34 East UPS Hdqs., Terminal 3E-B code inspection, American Airlines new 3-EA terminal 5 story parking garage, new consol. rent-a-car parking facility, airport expansion, others. Home: Grapevine, Tex. Died Dec. 30, 2005.

KILLEN, BUDDY (WILLIAM D. KILLEN), recording industry executive; b. Florence, Ala., Nov. 13, 1932; s. Willie Lee and Minnie Jane (Sharp) K.; m. Carolyn Nelson, 1986; children: Linda, Robin. Grad., high sch. Joined Tree Pub. Co., Nashville, 1953, exec. v.p., co-owner, 1957—80, pres., CEO, 1980—89; founder Killen Music Group, 1990—2006. Bd. dirs. 1st Am. Nat. Bank. Bass player, Grand Ole Opry, traveled with country artists, 1950-53; active songwriter and producer for numerous artists.; Songs include Ain't Goinna Bump No More. Chmn., co-host Easter Seal Telethon, Nashville; bd. dirs. Am. Inst. for Pub. Service, Washington; mem. Met. Tourist Commn., Tenn. Film and Tape Commn., Nashville Symphony; dir. W.O. Smith Community Music Sch.; dir. WPLN Radio Ednl. Found. Recipient gold and platinum records for artists produced various labels; award Broadcast Music Inc.; first inductee in non-performing category, Ala. Hall of Fam., 1985. Mem. NATAS (chpt. pres. 1969), ASCAP (bd. dirs.), Country Music Assn. (v.p. 1977, treas. 1983-84), Nashville Songwriters Assn., Nashville Music Assn., Nat. Music Pubs. Assn. (bd. dirs.), Acad. Country Music, Gospel Music Assn., Fedn. Internat. Country Air Personalities, Better Bus. Bur., Nashville Area C. of C. (bd. dirs. 1983-84), Metro Tourism Commn. Clubs: Nashville City. Baptist. Home: Franklin, Tenn. Died Nov. 1, 2006.

KIM, JAI SOO, retired physicist; b. Taegu, Korea, Nov. 1, 1925; came to U.S., 1958, naturalized, 1963; s. Wan Sup and Chanam (Whang) K.; m. Hai Kyou Kim, Nov. 2, 1952; children: Kami, Tomi, Kihyun, Himi. BSc in Physics, Seoul Nat. U., Korea, 1949; MS in Physics, U. Sask., Can., 1957, PhD, 1958. Asst. prof. physics Clarkson U., Potsdam, NY, 1958-59, U. Idaho, Moscow, 1959-62, assoc. prof., 1962-65, prof., 1965-67; prof. atmospheric sci. and physics SUNY, Albany, 1967-95, chmn. dept. atmospheric sci., 1969-76; emeritus prof., from 1995; rep. Univ. Corp. for Atmospheric Research SUNY, Albany, 1970-76, cons. Korean Studies Program Stony Brook, 1983-85. Vis. prof. Advanced Inst. Sci. and Tech., Seoul, Korea, 1983; cons. U.S. Army Research Office, 1978-79, Battelle Meml. Inst., 1978-81, Environ. One Corp., 1978-84, N.Y. State Environ. Conservation Dept., 1976-82, Norlite Corp., 1982-84, Korean Antarctic Program, 1988—. Contbr. articles to profl. jours. Mem. Am. Inst. Physics, Am. Geophys. Union, Sigma Xi. Home: Slingerlands, NY. Died Sept. 5, 2006.

KIMBROUGH, WILLIAM JOSEPH, librarian; b. Bowling Green, Ky., Apr. 21, 1930; s. William Joseph and Mary Alice (Sexton) K.; m. Ann Cecil Cornett, Nov. 25, 1954; children: Charles Madison, Howard David. AB, Western Ky. U., 1952; MA, Ind. U., 1956. Reference asst. Grosse Pointe (Mich.) Pub. Library, 1956-58; head librarian Sturgis (Mich.) Pub. Library, 1958-60; supr. adult services Lansing (Mich.) Pub. Library, 1960-65, chief librarian, 1965-69; asst. librarian, dir. pub service Denver Pub. Library, 1970-75; dir. Mpls. Pub. Library and Information Center, from 1975. Editor: (with others) Requiem for the Card Catalog, 1979. Served to 1st lt. AUS, 1952-54. Mem. ALA (past pres. library adminstrn. div.), Mich Library Assn. (past pres.), Minn. Library Assn. (past pres.) Minn. Assn. Continuing and Adult Edn. (past pres.) Died Aug 15, 2007.

KINDEL, JAMES HORACE, JR., lawyer; b. LA, Nov. 8 1913; s. James Horace and Philipina (Butte) K.; m. Lupe Hernandez Kindel; children: William, Mary, Robert, John. AB UCLA, 1934; LLB, Loyola U., Los Angeles, 1940. Bar: Calif 1941; CPA, Calif., 1942. Founding ptnr. Kindel & Anderson LA, 1945—96. Mem. ABA, L.A. Bar Assn., Orange County Ba Assn., State Bar Calif., AICPA, Chancery Club, Calif. Club, Ph Delta Phi, Theta Xi. Home: Los Angeles, Calif. Died Mar. 29 2007.

KINDS, HERBERT E(UGENE), secondary education educator; b. Cleve., Feb. 25, 1933; s. Levander and Esther (Johnson K. BS (Tyng scholar), Williams Coll., 1951-55; postgrad Harvard U., 1955-58, Case Western Res. U., 1972, 80-81, LHI (hon.) Natchez Jr. Coll., 1968. Instr. Natchez (Miss.) Jr. Coll 1958-68, registrar, 1967, dean, 1968; tchr. Cleve. Pub. Schs. 1968—; owner Kinds Tutorial Svc., 1972—; instr. med. sci Cuyahoga Community Coll., 1975-81, instr. chemistry. Deaco Mt. Herodon Bapt. Ch.; mem. Cleve. City Club, 1968, Comdr.' Club for Disabled Am. Vets.; nat. assoc. Smithsonian Instn Named one of Outstanding Young Men of Am., 1967. Mem Math. Assn. Am., Am. Chem. Soc., Am. Fedn. Tchrs., Cleve Mus. Art, Mus. Natural History, Internat. Platform Assn., Th World of Poetry, Case Western Reserve U. (fellow), William Club of N.Y., Williams Club of Northeastern Ohio, Phi Bet Kappa (pres. kinds ednl. svcs.). Home: Cleveland, Ohio. Die Jan. 24, 2006.

KINERSON, KENDALL SCOTT, mathematics and physic educator; b. Peacham, Vt., Mar. 8, 1921; s. Charles Raymon and Elizabeth (Scott) K.; m. Shirley Laighton, May 25, 194 children— Nancy Kinerson Dwyer, Linda Kinerson Saunders Margaret Louise Kinerson Robertson, Katherine Scott Kinerso Renzo BS, U. N.H., 1943; MS, Rensselaer Poly. Inst., 195 PhD, Mich. State U., 1957. Instr. physics U. Mass., Ft. Devens 1946-48; instr. physics and math. to prof. physics and math chmn. dept. math. Russell Sage Coll., Troy, N.Y., 1948-8 Cons. N.Y. State Dept. Edn., Bur. Secondary Curriculum Devel Div. Evaluation of Higher Edn., Rensselaer Poly, Inst. Autho (with Parsegian, Meltzer and Luchins) Introduction to Natur Science, 1968, Laboratory and Mathematics Supplement t Introduction to Natural Science, 1968. Served to capt. AU 1943-46. Danforth tchr., 1955 Mem. Am. Assn. Physics Tchrs Math. Assn. Am., AAUP. Presbyn. (elder, trustee). Lodge Mason (32 deg., Shriner). Home: Troy, NY. Died Jan. 16, 200

KING, ANGELA E.V., retired international organization offi cial; b. Kingston, Jamaica; m. Wilton James (div.); 1 chil Richard A. BA in History, U. Coll. West Indies; MA Edn Sociology & Adminstrn., U. London; LLD (hon.), U. We Indies. With UN, 1966—2004, dir. recruitment & placement, d staff adminstrn. & training, dep. to asst. sec. gen. for huma resources mgmt., dir. operational services divsn., chief Observ Mission in South Africa Johannesburg, 1992—94, dir. Advance ment of Women divsn., Dept. Econ. & Social Affairs, 1996—9 spl. adv. to sec. gen. on gender issues & advancement of wome 1997—2004. Died Feb. 6, 2007.

KING, BARRINGTON, diplomat; b. Knoxville, Tenn., Sep 25, 1930; s. Barrington and Madeline (Peacock) K.; m. Sara Minka Tinius, Dec. 23, 1953; children— Sarah Sevilla, Ba rington IV B.F.A., U. Ga., 1952. Polit. officer Dept. State, Cair Egypt, 1957-59; chief econ. sect. Am. embassy, Nicosia, Cypru 1964-67, polit. officer Athens, Greece, 1967-72, dep. chi mission Tunis, Tunisia, 1975-79, Karachi, Pakistan, 1979-8 ambassador Brunei, 1984-87. Recipient Meritorious Hon award U.S. Dept. State, 1966; Superior Honor award U.S. Dept. State, 1975, Woodrow Wilson fellow Princeton U., 1972-73 Mem.: Royal Brunei Polo. Died Mar. 28, 2006.

KING, GEORGE SMITH, JR., university athletic director; b. Charleston, W.Va., Aug. 16, 1928; s. George Smith and Margret F. (Nichols) K.; m. Jeanne Greider, June 18, 1949; children— George, Kristy (Mrs. Gary Danielson), Kathy (Mrs. Drew Hirsty), Kerry (Mrs. Paul Rzeznik), Gordon. BS, Morris Harvey Coll., 1950; MA, W.Va. U., 1958. Basketball coach Morris Harvey Coll., 1955, W.Va. U., 1958-65; basketball coach Purdue U., 1965-71, dir. athletics, from 1971. Named to W.Va. Hall of Fame. Home: Naples, Fla. Died Oct. 5, 2006.

KING, JAMES FORREST, JR., lawyer; b. Salina, Kans., Jan. 9, 1949; s. James Forrest Sr. and Carolyn (Prout) K.; m. Mary Lou A. Goodwin, May 18, 1985; 1 child, James Forrest King III. BA, U. Md., 1970; JD with honors, George Washington U., 1974. Bar: D.C. 1975, U.S. Dist. Ct. D.C. 1976, U.S. Ct. Appeals (D.C. cir.) 1977, U.S. Supreme Ct. 1979, Md. 1982, U.S. Ct. Appeals (4th cir.) 1985. Atty. Law Offices of Washington, 1975-76; ptnr. Reuss, McConville & King, Washington, 1976-80, Reuss, Herndon, McConville & King, Washington, 1980-85; of counsel Herndon, McConville, Brown, Teller & Hessler, Washington, 1986-87; ptnr. Law Offices of James Forrest King, Washington, from 1987. Mem., bd. dirs. Family Ct. Trial Lawyers Assn., Dist. Col. Superior Ct., from 2001. Commr. D.C. Commn. Human Rights, 1984-90. Mem. Am. Arbitration Assn. (panel mem.), ABA (econs. law practice sect.), Superior Ct. Trial Lawyers Assn. (bd. dirs. 1997—), DC Bar Assn. (co-chmn. divsn. 6, 1981-84, arbitration bd. 1981-83, employment discrimination panel, 1977-80). Home: Washington, DC. Died Oct. 28, 2006.

KING, JOHN FRANCIS, lawyer; b. Waynesboro, Pa., Apr. 23, 1925; s. Thomas Henry and Victoria Walker (Beaver) K.; m. Nancy Lee Packard, Aug. 14, 1954 (div. June 1974); children: John. F. Jr., Anne Lee, Margaret Packard; m. Linda Louden Meding, June 10, 1977. BA, Dickinson Coll., 1949; JD, Georgetown U., 1951. Bar: Md. 1952. Ptnr. Anderson, Coe & King, Balt., from 1957. Vis. faculty Harvard U. Law Sch., Cambridge, Mass., 1982; faculty Md. Inst. for Continuing Legal Edn., Balt., 1980-85; instr. comml. law McCoy Coll. Johns Hopkins U., Balt., 1954-74. Contbr. articles to profl. jours. Pres. Md. chpt. Arthritis Found., 1967-69; bd. dirs. Lawyers' Com. for Civil Rights, Balt., 1963-70, Md. Conf. Social Welfare, Balt., 1970-75, Md. chpt. ACLU, Balt., 1971-80; mem. City-County Dem. Club, 1963, Med.-Legal Found. Md., 1968—. Fellow Am. Coll. Trial Lawyers, Md. Bar Found.; mem. ABA, Md. Bar Assn., Balt. City Bar Assn. (treas. 1962-65, sec. 1965-66), Am. Judicature Soc., AMA, Wig & Pen Club, Wednesday Law Club, Johns Hopkins Faculty Club, Elkridge Club, L'Hirondelle Club. Home: Baltimore, Md. Died July 4, 2007.

KING, ROBERT JOHN, real estate executive; b. Holyoke, Mass., Oct. 20, 1935; s. John Steven and Doris H. (Gosselin) K.; m. Anita Louise Cunningham, Sept. 24, 1960; children: Robin Ann, Robert John. BA, Amherst Coll., 1957; MBA, Fordham U., 1975. Mgr. N.Y. Telephone Co., NYC, 1957-60; dir. adminstrv. services Reader's Digest Assn., Pleasantville, N.Y., 1960-71; v.p. adminstrn. Griswold, Heckel & Kelly Assos., NYC, 1971-76; sr. v.p. adminstrn. J. Walter Thompson Co., NYC, 1976-83; adminstrv. v.p. Marine Midland Bank, NYC, 1983-86; v.p., dir. corp. real estate The Continental Corp., NYC, from 1986. Bd. dirs. Mt. Kisco (N.Y.) Boys Club, 1970—. Mem. Nat. Assn. Corp. Real Estate Execs., Real Estate Bd. N.Y., Westchester County Assn., Mt. Kisco C. of C. (past bd. dirs.), Downtown-Lower Manhattan Assn. (dir.), Mt. Kisco Country Club. Republican. Roman Catholic. Home: Mount Kisco, NY. Died Feb. 1, 2007.

KINGSLEY, ELLEN, publishing executive; b. NYC, Oct. 1, 1951; d. Theodore Kingsley and Judith Kingsley-Fitting; m. Robert M.A. Hirschfeld, Jan. 21, 1984; children: Theodore, Andrew. BA, Sarah Lawrence Coll., 1973; MA, NYU, 1977. Speech writer for Elinor Guggenheimer, NYC; speech writer for commr. consumer affairs, 1974—76; speech writer for John Sawhill, (pres. NYU), 1976—77; consumer affairs reporter, anchor WJZ-TV, Balt., 1977—80; consumer affairs reporter WUSA-TV, Washington, 1980—90; pres. Kingsley Comm., 1990—97; editor, pub. ADDitude Mag., 1998—2004. Contbr. articles to newspapers, mags. Recipient six Emmy awards, Media award, World Hunger Yr., 1983, Best Documentary award, UPI, 1984, Consumer Journalism award, Nat. Press Club, 1984, Media award, Consumer Fedn. Am., 1985. Home: Houston, Tex. Died Mar. 8, 2007.

KINGSLEY, LEONARD EDWARD, financial services executive; b. June 26, 1929; s. Samuel J. and Esther B. Kingsley. BA, Hamilton Coll., Clinton, NY, 1951; MBA, Harvard U., 1955. Chmn. bd. Montgomery Capital Corp., 1964-94; ptnr. Kingsley, Schreck, Wells & Reichling. Chmn. Aviva Sport Inc., 1989-91; dir. Sports Lab. Inc., Wild Planet Toys; faculty San Francisco State U., 1976-78; guest lectr. 1980 Western Conf. of Fulbright Scholars. Past chmn. San Francisco Human Rights Commn.; pres. bd. trustees The Fine Arts Mus. of San Francisco; trustee San Francisco Symphony Assn., Hamilton Coll.; chmn. San Francisco Found.; pres. San Francisco Planning and Urban Rsch. Assn.; bd. dirs. Big Bros. of Am.; past pres. Big Bros. of San Francisco (Big Bro. of the Yr. 1966); adv. coun. Sch. Bus., San Francisco State U.; mem. San Francisco Mayor's Fiscal Adv. Com. Recipient Coun. for Civic Unity Man of the Yr. award, 1972, Chevalier de la Legion d'Honneur, Republic of France. Died Aug. 11, 2007.

KINGSTON, ROBERT CHARLES, retired military officer; b. Brookline, Mass., July 16, 1928; s. John James and Mary (Shehan) K.; m. Josephine Rae, Aug. 14, 1956 (dec. 1992); stepchildren: George R. Cody, Leslie C. Reiman. BA, U. Omaha, 1965; MA, George Washington U., 1969; postgrad., Armed Forces Staff Coll., 1966, Nat. War Coll., 1969, Advanced Mgmt. Program, U. Pitts., 1972. Commd. 2d lt. US Army, 1949, advanced through grades to gen., 1984, ret., 1985; comdr. 1st and 3d brigades, 1st Cavalry div. 1st and 3d brigades, 1st Cavalry divsn., Vietnam, 1969-70; dep. sec. gen. staff, Office Chief of Staff US Army, 1970-72, dep. commdg. gen., Second Regional Assistance Command, dep. sr. adv. II Corps & Mil. Region Vietnam, 1972—73, comdr. Joint Casualty Resolution Ctr. Thailand, 1973; asst. divsn. comdr. 1st Inf. divsn., Ft. Riley, Kans., 1974-75; comdr. US Army Inst. for Mil. Assistance, Fort Bragg, 1975—77; chief of staff UN Command, Seoul, Republic of Korea, 1977-79; comdr. 2d Inf. Divsn., 1979-81, Rapid Deployment Joint Task Force, MacDill AFB, Fla., 1981—83, US Ctrl. Command, 1983—85. Decorated D.S.C., D.S.M. with oak leaf cluster, Dept. Def. Disting. Service medal, Silver Star with oak leaf cluster, Bronze Star, others. Mem. Co. Mil. Historians, Assn. U.S. Army, Spl. Forces Assn. (hon.), Uniformed Services Benefit Assn. (bd. govs.), Airlift Assn. (dir.), Am. Legion, VFW. Roman Catholic. Died Feb. 28, 2007.

KINNEY, HARRY EDWIN, mechanical engineer; b. Trinidad, Colo., June 7, 1924; s. Oliver Earl and Opal (Sanger) K.; m. Carol N. Roberts, Aug. 30, 1970; children: Charlotte Jean, Donald Bruce. BS in Mech. Engring., U. N.Mex., 1945; degree in pub. adminstrn. (hon.), U. Albuquerque, 1985. Staff mem. Sandia Labs., 1956-73; commr. City of Albuquerque, 1966-73, vice chmn. City Commn., 1970-71, chmn., 1971-73, mayor, 1974-77, 81-85; gen. contractor, residential constrn., 1977-81; bldg. contractor, dir. bus. devel. Jacobs Engring. Group, Inc., Albuquerque, 1987-88; pvt. bldg. contractor Albuquerque, from 1988. Commr. Bernalillo County, N.Mex., 1956-58, 61-65; mem. adv. panel on infrastructure to U.S. Senate budget com., 1985-86; mem. mgmt. adv. group for constrn. grants EPA, 1982-86. Chmn. Middle Rio Grande Council Govts. of N.Mex., 1970-72; mem. U.S. Adv. Commn. on Intergovtl. Relations, 1975-77; mem. adv. bd. U.S. Conf. Mayors, 1975-77, 82-85, chmn., 1977; Pres. Albuquerque-Bernalillo County Econ. Opportunity Bd., 1964-66; pres. N.Mex. Council Social Welfare, 1965-67; chmn. City-County Joint Alcoholism Bd., 1969-72; pres. Ams. for Rational Energy Alternatives, 1980-84, 85—; v.p. Chapparal council Girl Scouts U.S.A., 1978-81; bd. dirs. Met. YMCA, 1977-81; bd. dirs. Lovelace Med. Ctr. Health Plan, 1985-89; spl. asst. to U.S. senator, 1973-74. Served with USNR, 1943-46, 50-52. Mem. ASME (Pub. Service award Region VIII, 1977, 84), Naval Res. Assn., Kappa Sigma. Episcopalian. Died May 9, 2006.

KIP, HERBERT WEBSTER, village manager; b. N.Y.C., Oct. 27, 1915; s. Charles Jay and Lillian Annie (Webb) K.; m. Alice Marie Kreher, June 15, 1942; children— Sandra Diane Murphy, Linda Carol Hatt; m. Gloria Mary Unico, Feb. 3, 1967. Student Rutgers U., 1934-36. With Standard Oil Co. N.J. (now Exxon Corp.), N.Y.C., 1934-51, bus. history researcher, 1947-51; v.p. Floyd L. Carlisle Co., N.Y.C., 1951-57; city coordinator, city mgr., dir. parks and recreation City of West Palm Beach (Fla.), 1957-66; town mgr. Springfield (Vt.), 1967-70; bus. adminstr. City of Bridgeton (N.J.), 1970-73; city mgr. Garfield (N.J.), 1973-74, Northlake (Ill.), 1974-75; village mgr. Vernon Hills (Ill.), 1976—. Served with USAF, 1942-45. Mem. Internat. City Mgmt. Assn., Am. Pub. Works Assn., Ill. City Mgmt. Assn., Metro Mgrs. Assn. (dir.). Died Feb. 11, 2006.

KIRCHMAN, KENNETH PAUL, computer software services company executive; b. Belle Glade, Fla., Feb. 24, 1935; s. Paul and Ruth (Sundby) Kirchman; children: Kim, Kevin, Karen. BS in Math., John B. Stetson U., 1958. Sales rep Sperry Rand Corp., Dayton, 1959—65, regional sales mgr., 1964—65; nat. sales mgr. Nat. Cash Register Co., Dayton, 1965—67; exec. v.p. mktg. Gen. Computer Services, Inc., Huntsville, Ala., 1967—68; pres., chmn. bd., dir. Fla. Software Services, Inc., Orlando, from 1968. Contbr. articles on softward to profl. publs. Mem. mayor's Mgmt. and Efficiency Adv. Commn., Orlando, Fla., 1975—76, Gov.'s Edn. Means Bus. Com., 1983; vice chmn. bd. trustees Stetson U.; trustee Fla. Ind. Coll. Fund; bd. dirs. Tangerine Bowl Assn., Channel 24, Orlando; trustee Florida House. Served to 1st lt. US Army, 1958. Mem.: Presidents Assn., Data Processing Mgmt. Assn., Soc. of Indsl. and Applied Math., Assn. of Computing Machinery, Am. Mgmt. Assn. (info. systems and tech. coun, pres.'s assn.), Delta Sigma Phi (award, pres. alumni control bd. 1975). Died Mar. 13, 2007.

KIRK, ALEXANDER, artist; b. Tucson, Sept. 30, 1948; s. Edward B. and Nadia Kirk. Student, Sch. Visual Arts, 1969-70, SUNY, from 1982. Pres., dir. Art-O-Rama Gallery, New Rochelle, 1968-72; prodn. mgr., photographer, color pressman Web Co. Press, Mt. Vernon, N.Y., 1971-77; dir. Kirk Studio, Eastchester, N.Y., 1972-76; printer, artist, art dealer Kirk's Art Gallery, NYC, 1977-79; dir. Kirk Merchandising Svc., Patterson, N.Y., 1977-79, Art-Vall Gallery, New Rochelle, N.Y., from 1979. Tchr., master martial arts. Democrat. Episcopalian. Died Aug. 21, 2006.

KIRKSEY, ROBERT EDWARD, naval officer; b. Atlanta, Aug. 5, 1930; s. Lester Lynn and Florence Ester (Bearden) K.; m. Viola Marie Kaikkonen, July 7, 1953; children: Jennifer Lynn, Robert Edward, Gregg Alan, Andrew Jon. BA, U.S. Naval Postgrad. Sch., 1966; MS, George Washington U., 1970. Commd. ensign, naval aviator U.S. Navy, 1953, advanced through grades to vice adm., 1976; dir. carrier programs div. Navy Dept., Washington, 1976-78; comdr. Carrier Group Three, Alameda, Calif., 1978-79, Carrier Group Five, Cubi Point, Philippines, 1979-81; dir. strategy, plans and policy div. Dept. Navy, Washington, 1981-83; dir. plans and policy Comdr. Pacific, Camp Smith, Hawaii, 1983-84; dir. space, command and control Dept. Navy, Washington, 1984-86; v.p. Northrop Corp., from 1987. Decorated D.S.M., Silver Star, Legion of Merit, D.F.C., Air medal. Mem. Assn. Naval Aviators, Tailhook Assn. Naval Aviators, Lambda Chi Alpha. Home: Arlington, Va. Died Dec. 16, 2006.

KIRSCHNER, LEONARD, lawyer; b. Cin., Feb. 3, 1928; s. Saul and Dorothy Sylvia (Chodash) K.; m. Yolanda Dorothy Negin, Aug. 28, 1960; children— Mark, Steven, Tami, Mindy, Debra, Barry. B.A., U. Cin., 1948, J.D., 1949. Bar: Ohio 1950, U.S. Dist. Ct. (so. and no. dists.) Ohio, U.S. Ct. Appeals (6th cir.) 1950, U.S. Supreme Ct. 1953. Sole practice, Cin., 1950—; asst. pros. atty. Criminal div. Hamilton County, Ohio, 1951-66, chief asst. pros. atty. Appellate div., 1966—; spl. prosecuter Village of Evendale, Ohio, 1974—, solicitor, 1980—; lectr. in field. Mem. ABA, Ohio State Bar Assn., Cin. Bar Assn., Fed. Bar Assn., Am. Judicature Soc., Nat. Assn. Dist. Attys., Ohio Assn. Pros. Attys. (Outstanding Asst. Pros. Atty. award 1979-80). Republican. Jewish. Clubs: B'nai B'rith, Masons. Died Mar. 14, 2006.

KIRSHEN, EDWARD JEROME, obstetrician, gynecologist; b. Syracuse, N.Y., Oct. 30, 1944; s. Gerald Bernard and Corrine (Markson) K.; B.A., Syracuse U., 1962-65; M.D., SUNY, Syracuse, 1969. Intern, then resident in ob-gyn U. Calif. Med. Center, San Diego, 1969-73; fellow in reproductive endocrinology Boston Hosp. Women, also instr. Harvard U. Med. Sch., 1973-74; practice medicine specializing in ob-gyn, San Diego, 1974-86; dir. Ob-Gyn Emergency Services Sharp Meml. Hosp., 1986—; mem. staff Donald Sharp Hosp., Mission Bay Hosp.; mem. exec. med. bd. Sharp Meml. Hosp., 1980—, chief ob-gyn, 1983—; clin. instr. U. Calif. Med. Sch., San Diego. Mem. Am. Coll. Ob-Gyn, Am. Fertility Soc., Am. Assn. Gynecol. Laparoscopy, Pacific Coast Fertility Soc., Calif. Med. Assn., San Diego County Med. Soc. Died Dec. 9, 2006.

KIRSHENBAUM, ISIDOR, chemist, consultant; b. N.Y.C., June 22, 1917; s. Samuel and Kate (Smithkin) K.; BS, CCNY, 1938; MA, Columbia U., 1939, PhD, 1942; m. Lucy Gutstein, June 1, 1947; children— Howard, Steven, Barbara, Kenneth. Teaching fellow Columbia U. and CCNY, 1938-42; research scientist Manhattan Project, AEC, Columbia U., 1942-45; with Exxon Research and Engring. Co., Linden, N.J., 1945-85, sci. advisor, head info. research and analysis unit, 1977-85; cons. AEC, 1947-55. Recipient Inventors Hall of Fame Bicentennial medallion, 1976. Mem. Am. Inst. Chemists (chmn. chpt. 1961-65), AAAS, Am. Chem. Soc., Phi Beta Kappa, Sigma Xi. Author: Physical Properties and Analysis of Heavy Water, 1951; Isobutylene in Vinyl and Diene Monomers, Vol. 3, 1971; contbr. articles to encys., tech. jours. Patentee in field. Died Sept. 24, 2006.

KIRVEN, PEYTON EDWARD, architect; b. Dallas, Feb. 28, 1924; s. Percy Edward and Mildred (Powers) K.; m. Perpetua Anne Deak, Jan. 12, 1952; children: Lawrence Edward, Kimberly Anne. BArch, U. Tex., 1948. Registered architect, Calif. Designer, draftsman Bennett and Bennett Architects, Pasadena, Calif., 1948-52; draftsman, specifications writer A.C. Martin and Assocs., Los Angeles, 1954-58; designer, draftsman Allison & Rible Architects, Los Angeles, 1958-65; assoc. Allison, Rible, Robinson and Ziegler Architects, Los Angeles, 1965-74; prin. The Raymond Ziegler Partnership, Los Angeles, 1974-78, Ziegler Kirven Parrish Architects, Los Angeles, 1978-89; pvt. practice Westlake Village, Calif., from 1989. Author: (chpt.) Emerging Techniques in Architecture, 1976. Served to lt. USNR, 1943-46, PTO, 1952-54, Korea. Fellow AIA, Am. Arbitration Assn. Republican. Avocations: travel, photography. Died Feb. 1, 2007.

KISER, KENNETH KING, wax manufacturing company executive, safety consultant; b. Concord, N.C., July 5, 1930; s. Lawrence King and Margaret (Hudson) K.; children— Kenneth K., Jr., Susan Kiser Bradford, Charles; m. Margaret Ellen Jones, Aug. 28, 1976; children— Karen Ellen, Margaret Carol. B.S., Appalachian State U., 1951. Indsl. engr. trainee Cannon Mills, Concord, N.C., 1951-53; indsl. engr. Am. Efird Mills, Albemarle and Whitnel, N.C., 1953-56; plant mgr. Kohler and Campbell Piano Co., Granite Falls, N.C., 1956-65; tax supr. Caldwell County, Lenoir, N.C., 1965-67; pres., owner Wax-Crafters, Inc., Concord, N.C., 1967—; mem. N.C. Ho. of Reps., 1973-74; chmn. N.C. OSHA Review Bd., Raleigh, 1973-79, 85—; safety cons. Electrical Service Co., Hickory, N.C., Guy Frye & Sons, Inc., Hickory. Inventor: round-square hole wax disc for textile industry, 1981. Pres. Western Piedmont Safety Council, Lenoir, N.C., 1962-63; campaign chmn. Holshouser for Gov. Ga., 1972; Rep. chmn. Caldwell County, 1975-77; campaign chmn. Martin for Gov. N.C., 1984, Reagan-Bush re-election com., Cabarrus County, N.C., 1984; chmn. Cabarrus County Bd. Elections, 1985—. Recipient Presidential invitation Pres's. Conf. Occupational Safety, 1962, 500 Club Placque N.C. Rep. Party, 1973. Mem. Am. Soc. Safety Engrs., Am. Inst. Indsl. Engrs., Appalachian State U. Alumni Council, Piedmont Personnel Assn. (pres. 1954-55). Methodist. Lodge: Lions. Avocations: boating; hunting; fishing. Died May 14, 2007.

KISHI, TOYOHISA, banker; b. Kanonji, Kagawa Prefecture, Japan, June 3, 1929; came to U.S., 1977; s. Toru and Mieko (Yokoyama) K.; m. Yoko, Nov. 9, 1957; children: Hitoshi, Tetsuro. Edn., Kyoto U., Japan. Dep. gen. mgr. Fuji Bank, Ltd., Tokyo, 1973-76, dep. chief mgr. internat. div., 1976-77; pres. Fuji Bank and Trust Co., NYC, 1977-81, chmn., from 1981; dir., gen. mgr. Fuji Bank, Ltd., NYC, from 1981. Died May 5, 2007.

KISSEL, WILLIAM THORN, JR., sculptor; b. Feb. 6, 1920; s. William Thorn and Frances A. (Dallett) K.; m. Barbara Eldred Case, June 17, 1943 (dec. June 1978); children: William Thorn III (dec.), Michael C. Grad., Choate Sch., 1939; BA, Harvard U., 1944; postgrad., Pa. Acad. Fine Arts, 1951-53; grad., Barnes Found., 1953, Rinehart Grad. Sch. Sculpture, Balt., 1958; BFA (hon.), Md. Inst. Coll. Art, 1996. T. Exhibited sculpture Lever House, N.Y.C., N.A.D., N.Y.C., Balt. Sculptor's Exhibit, York, Pa., Beverly, Mass., Gloucester, Woodmere Gallery, Germantown, Pa.; represented in pvt. collections, U.S.; executed large granite meml., Montclair, N.J.; also many animal sculpture studies and commns. Pilot, lt. (j.g.) USNR, 1943-45. Recipient Mass. Sculptor's award Regional Exhibit, 1958, Speyer award NAD, 1966, 68, Am. Artists Profl. League award, 1966; fellow Pa. Acad. Fine Arts, 1951-53. Fellow Am. Artists Profl. League, Nat. Sculpture Soc. Republican. Episcopalian. Home: Towson, Md. Died Feb. 10, 2006.

KITCHELL, SAMUEL FARRAND, construction company executive; b. Hingham, Mass., Nov. 6, 1921; s. Francis R. and Jeanette (Abbott) K.; m. Betty Heimark, June 17, 1943; children: Kaaren, Jane Kitchell LaPrade, Jonathan Abbott, Ann Kitchell Denk, Susan Kitchell Edwards. BA, Amherst Coll., 1943, LL.D., 1983. Field engr. Anchorage Homes, Inc., Westfield, Mass., 1946-48; chief insp., specification writer E.L.

Varney Assocs., Phoenix, 1948-49; estimator J.R. Porter Constrn. Co., Phoenix, 1949-50; founder/ptnr. Kitchell-Phillips Contractors, Inc., Phoenix, 1950-54; chmn. Kitchell Corp., Phoenix, from 1954. Bd. dirs. Security Pacific Bank Ariz.; guest speaker constrn. mgmt. seminars Active Phoenix Art Mus., Phoenix Symphony Assn., Internat. Heart Found.; founding pres., bd. dirs. Ariz. Kidney Found., Phoenix, 1963-69; trustee, pres. St. Luke's Hosp. Med. Ctr., Phoenix, 1962-77; trustee Heard Mus. Anthropology, Phoenix, 1975—, pres., 1985-87; trustee, pres. Scottsdale (Ariz.) Sch. Bd., 1966-71; bd. dirs. Ariz. Acad.; trustee Amherst (Mass.) Coll., 1983-89. Lt. (j.g.) USN, 1943-46, ATO, PTO. Recipient award for community leadership, real estate and devel. Valley Leadership Alumni Assn., 1987, Ariz. Entrepreneur of Yr. award Arthur Young & Co. and Inc. mag., 1989; honoree for contbn. to Am. enterprise and society-at-large Newcomen Soc. of U.S., 1991; named to Ariz. Bus. Hall of Fame, 1992. Mem. Assoc. Gen. Contractors Am. (past pres., past bd. dirs. Ariz. bldg. chpt.), Phoenix C. of C. (past bd. dirs. and officer) Clubs: Thunderbirds (Phoenix, life mem). Republican. Home: Scottsdale, Ariz. Died Sept. 11, 2006.

KIZER, BERNICE LICHTY PARKER, judge; b. Ft. Smith, Ark., Aug. 14, 1915; d. Ernest and Opal C. Lichty; m. Harlan D. Kizer; children— J. Mayne, Shirley Parker Wilhite, Karolyn Parker Sparkman, Mary K. Holt. Student Ft. Smith Jr. Coll., 1932-33, Stephens Coll., 1934-35; J.D., U. Ark., 1947. Judge 12th Jud. Dist. Chancery and Probate Cts., Ft. Smith, Van Buren and Greenwood, Ark., 1975-87; dir. City Nat. Bank of Ft. Smith. Mem. Ark. Ho. of Reps., 1961-74; chmn. women's div. United Fund; mem. Gov.'s Commn. for Aging, Chancery Ct.; state chmn. Library Week, Christmas Seals for Tb, Mental Health Assn.; bd. dirs. Western Ark. Counseling and Guidance Center, Cottey Coll., Nevada, Mo., Western Ark. Planning and Devel. Dist. Inc. Recipient Woman Achiever award Southwest Times Record, 1969; named Outstanding Alumnae, Sch. of Law, U. Ark.; Horizons-100 Ark. Women of Achievement, 1980. Mem. AAUW, Bus. and Profl. Women's Club, PEO, LWV. Home: Little Rock, Ark. Died Jan. 16, 2006.

KLEIMAN, BERNARD, lawyer; b. Chgo., Jan. 26, 1928; s. Isidore and Pearl (Wikoff) Kleiman; m. Gloria Baime, Nov. 15, 1986; children: Leslie, David. BS, Purdue U., 1951; JD, Northwestern U., 1954. Bar: Ill. 1954. Practice law in assn. with Abraham W. Brussell, 1957-60; dist. counsel United Steel Workers Am., 1960-65, gen. counsel, 1965-97, spl. counsel, 1997—2006; ptnr. Kleiman, Cornfield & Feldman, Chgo., 1960-75; prin. B. Kleiman (P.C.), 1976-77, Kleiman, Whitney, Wolfe & Elfenbaum, P.C., 1978-99. Mem. collective bargaining coms. for nat. labor negotiations in basic steel, tire mfg., and shipbuilding industries. Contbr. articles to legal jours. With US Army, 1946—48. Mem.: ABA, Allegheny County Bar Assn. Home: Pittsburgh, Pa. Died Dec. 13, 2006.

KLEIN, CHARLES HENLE, lithographing company executive; b. Cin., Oct. 5, 1908; s. Benjamin Franklin and Flora (Henle) K.; student Purdue U., 1926-27, U. Cin., 1927-28; m. Ruth Becker, Sept. 23, 1938 (dec. 1997); children— Betsy (Mrs. Marvin H. Schwartz), Charles H., Carla (Mrs. George Fee III). Pres., Progress Lithographing Co., Cin., 1934-59, Novelart Mfg. Co., Cin., 1960—; dir. R.A. Taylor Corp. Founding mem. Chief Execs. Orgn., Losantiville Country Club, Queen City Club, Bankers Club. Home: Cincinnati, Ohio. Died Apr. 16, 2006.

KLEIN, GERALD S., lawyer; b. Washington, Aug. 27, 1941; s. Herbert M. and Mary (Olschansky) K.; m. Ellen F. Klein, Sept. 10, 1967. LL.B., U. Balt., 1963; LL.M., U. Chgo., 1965. Bar: Md., Sup., U.S. Ct. Apls. (4th cir.), U.S. Dist. Ct. Md. Atty., Singer Co., N.Y.C., 1966-67; sole practice, Balt., 1967—; asst. solicitor City of Balt., 1967-75. Served with USNR. Mem. ABA, Md. Bar Assn., Balt. City Bar Assn. Democrat. Jewish. Died Oct. 10, 2006.

KLEIN, RICHARD DEAN, banker; b. Elkhart, Ind., Mar. 11, 1932; s. Wilbert Joseph and Mary Katherine (Elsasser) K.; m. Marian Garfield, Aug. 2, 1958; children— James Garfield, Allen Harwood, Robert Howlett BA, Kalamazoo Coll.; postgrad., Mich. State U., 1954; postgrad. Grad. Sch. Banking, U. Wis., 1958. Vice chmn. First of Am. Bank Corp., Kalamazoo. Dir. numerous banks in Mich., Ill., Ind. Chmn. Mich. Higher Edn. Commn., 1973-77, Mich. Higher Edn. Facilities Commn., 1973-77 Mem. Am. Bankers Assn., Mich. Bankers Assn., Kalamazoo Country Club, Park Club (Kalamazoo), Chgo. Club, Bonita Bay Club (Fla.). Republican. Presbyterian. Home: Kalamazoo, Mich. Died Dec. 4, 2005.

KLEMENS, THOMAS A., insurance company executive; b. 1951; Degree, Calif. Polytechnic U. CPA. From v.p. to CFO First American Corp., Santa Ana, Calif., 1985—93, CFO, 1993—2006, sr. exec. v.p., 2003—06. Bd. dir. First American Title Ins. Co. Mem.: AICPA, Nat. Assn. Accts., Calif. Soc. CPAs. Died Jan. 3, 2006.

KLEPPA, OLE J., chemistry professor; b. Oslo, Feb. 4, 1920; m. Abbie Joy Stodder, June 26, 1948; 2 children. MS, Norwegian Inst. Tech., 1946, DS, 1956. Union Carbon and Carbide postdoctoral fellow, instr. U. Chgo. Inst. Study of Metals, 1948-50; rsch. supr. divsn. chemistry and metallurgy Norwegian Def. Rsch. Establishment, 1950-51; asst. prof. U. Chgo., 1952-57, assoc. prof., 1958-62, prof. dept. chemistry, 1962-90, prof. dept. geophys. scis., 1968-90, prof. emeritus, 1990—2007, assoc. dir. James Franck Inst., 1968-71, dir., 1971-77, dir. materials rsch. lab., 1984-87. Cons. Argonne Nat. Lab., 1959-71; dir. The Calorimetry Conf., 1963-69, chmn., 1966-67; vis. prof. Japan Soc. Promotion of Sci., 1975, U. Paris, Orsay, 1977; presenter confs. in field. Bd. editors Jour. Chem. Physics, 1965-67, Jour. Chem. Thermodynamics, 1981-87, Jour. Phase Equilibria, 1995—; contbr. articles to profl. jours. Recipient Huffman Meml. award, 1982, U.S. Sr. Sci. Humboldt award, 1983-84. Fellow AAAS, Am. Soc. Metals; mem. Am. Chem. Soc., Am. Ceramic Soc., Soc. Norwegian Engrs., Royal Norwegian Soc. Sci. and Letters, Norwegian Acad. Tech. Scis., Minerals, Metals, and Materials Soc. (Hume-Rothery award 1994). Achievements include pioneering development of new technique of high-temperature oxide melt solution calorimetry; being the first person to extensively apply the Calvét-type twin microcalorimeter in high temperature thermochemistry; originator of a novel high-temperature reaction calorimeter suitable for continuous use at temperatures up to about 1500K; applying new calorimeter in extensive studies of binary alloys of transition metals and rare earth metals with Group VIII transition metals and with noble metals. Died May 27, 2007.

KLICKSTEIN, GILBERT DAVID, surgeon; b. Stoneham, Mass., May 16, 1930; MD, Tufts Univ., 1955. Intern Bellevue Medical Ctr., NYC, 1955-56; resident surgery Bellevue Hosp. Ctr., NYC, 1956-57; resident Triboro Hosp., Jamaica, 1958; resident surgery Knickerbokcer Hosp., NYC, 1958-50; staff Cen. Mich. Cmty. Hosp., Mt. Pleasant, Mich. Fellow Am. Coll. Surgeons; mem. AMA., Assn. Military Surgeons of U.S. Home: Mount Pleasant, Mich. Died Aug. 24, 2006.

KLINE, LEE B., retired architect; b. Renton, Wash., Feb. 2, 1914; s. Abraham McCubbin and Pearl Kline; m. Martha Myers, Aug. 29, 1936 (div. Oct. 1995); children— Patricia, Joanne Louise Kline Kresse; m. Marilyn Gibson, May 7, 1997. B.Arch., U. So. Calif., 1937. Draftsman, designer, 1937-43; pvt. archtl. practice Los Angeles, 1943-2001; ret., 2001. Instr. engring. extension U. Calif., 1947-53; mem. panel arbitrators Am. Arbitration Assn., 1964— Pres. LaCanada Irrigation Dist., 1966-96, dir., 1963-96; bd. dirs. Foothill Mcpl. Water Dist., 1980-96, LaCanada br. ARC, 1959-81. Recipient Disting. Service citation Calif. council AIA, 1960, honor awards AIA, 1957, 59, Sch. of Month awards Nation's Schools, 1964, 71 Fellow AIA (pres. Pasadena chpt. 1957, pres. Calif. council 1959) Home: Arcadia, Calif. Died June 1, 2007.

KLINSKY, JOSEPH WESLEY, industrial hygienist; b. Cedar Rapids, Iowa, July 17, 1921; s. Joseph and Zora Vera (Bezdek) K.; B.S. in Chem. Engring., Iowa State U., 1943; postgrad. Akron U., U. Iowa; m. Marianne Trejtnar, Sept. 3, 1943; children— J. Dennis, R. Gary, Pammela S. Chief chemist Cryovac Corp., Cedar Rapids, 1951-55; indsl. hygienist U. Iowa, Iowa City, 1955-74, 77—; coordinator occupational health Kirkwood Community Coll., Cedar Rapids, 1975-77. Mem. exec. com. Ames Patriotic Council, 1979—. Cert. Am. Bd. Indsl. Hygiene. Mem. Am. Indsl. Hygiene Assn., Am. Acad. Indsl. Hygiene, Am. Conf. Govt. Indsl. Hygienists, Am. Soc. Safety Engrs. (cert. safety profl.), Am. Inst. Chem. Engrs. Republican. Methodist. Club: Ames Lions (dir.). Home: Ames, Iowa. Died Mar. 12, 2007.

KLOS, JEROME JOHN, lawyer, director; b. La Crosse, Wis., Jan. 17, 1927; s. Charles and Edna S. (Wagner) K.; m. Mary M. Hamilton, July 26, 1958; children— Bryant H., Geoffrey W. BS, U. Wis., 1948, JD, 1950. Bar: Wis. 1950. Pres. Klos, Flynn and Papenfuss, La Crosse, from 1950. Bd. dirs. Union State Bank, West Salem, Wis. Mem. LaCrosse County Bd., 1957-74, vice chmn., 1972-74; pub. adminstr. La Crosse County, 1962-73; bd. dirs. West Salem Area Growth, Inc., La Crosse Area Growth, Inc.; trustee Sander and McKinly Scholarship Funds of West Salem Sch. Dist. Fellow Am. Coll. Real Estate Lawyers, Am. Coll. Probate Counsel, Wis. Law Found.; mem. Wis. Bar Assn., Elks, KC. Home: West Salem, Wis. Died Nov. 5, 2006.

KLOTZ, FLORENCE, costume designer; b. NYC, Oct. 28, 1920; d. Philip K. and Hannah Kraus. Student, Parsons Sch. Design, 1941. Designer: Broadway shows Take Her She's Mine, 1960, Never Too Late, 1962, Nobody Loves An Albatross, 1963, On An Open Roof, 1963, Owl and the Pussycat, 1964, One by One, 1964, Mating Dance, 1965, The Best Laid Plans, 1966, Superman, 1966, Paris Is Out, 1970, Norman Is That You, 1970, Legends, Follies, 1971 (Drama Desk award, Tony award), A Little Night Music, 1973 (Drama Desk award, Tony award), Side By Side Sondheim, 1975, Pacific Overtures, 1976 (Drama Desk award, Tony award, Los Angeles Critic Circle award), On the 20th Century, 1978 (Drama Desk award), Broadway Broadway, Dancin' In The Streets, 1982, Grind, 1984 (Tony award), Jerry's Girls, 1985; (ballet-jazz opus) Antique Epagraph, N.Y.C.; Broadway musicals Rags, 1986, Roza, 1987; Ctr. prodns. Carousel, 1956, Oklahoma, 1956, Annie Get Your Gun, 1958, 4 Baggatelle; movies Something for Everyone, 1969, A Little Night Music, 1976 (Oscar nomination, Los Angeles Critic Circle award); ice shows John Curry's Ice Dancing, 1979; Broadway musical A Doll's Life; ballet 8 Lines, 1986, I'm Old Fashioned (Jerome Robbins), Ives Songs (Jerome Robbins), City of Angels, 1989 (Tony award nomination, Outer Critics Circle award), Kiss of the Spider Woman, 1989 (Tony award 1989, Drama Desk award 1989), Show Boat, Toronto, Can., 1993, Broadway, 1994-95 (N.Y. Outer Critics Cirlce award 1995, Drama Desk award 1995, Tony award 1995, Theatre L.A. Ovation award 1997, Jessie award 1996), Whistle Down the Wind, 1996. Recipient Life Achievement award Theatre Crafts Internat., 1994, L.A. Ovation award, 1997, award NAACP, 1997, Dramalogue, 1997, L.A. Drama Desk, 1997; inducted into Theatre Hall of Fame, 1997, Patricia Zipprodt award, Fashion Inst. of Techn., 2002, Irene Sharaff award, 2005. Democrat. Home: New York, NY. Died Nov. 1, 2006.

KNEELAND, MUNROE HAZEN, osteopathic physician; b. St. Albans, Vt., Jan. 23, 1919; s. Guy Franklin and Althea Diantha (Reynolds) K.; m. Dorothy Violet Robinson, June 28, 1942; 1 dau., Betty Guyleen Galvan. Student N.E. Mo. State U., 1937; D.O., Kirksville Coll. Osteo Medicine, 1941. Diplomate Am. Bd. Med. Examiners. Physician, Liberal Community Clinic, Mo., 1944-85; cons. physician Barton County Hosp., Lamar, Mo., Oak Hill Hosp., Joplin, Mo. Bd. dirs. Water and Light Dept., Liberal, Mo., 1955-78, city physician water analysis, 1955-85; bd. dirs. Farmers State Bank, Liberal, 1970-85. 25 Yr. Sch. Physician Service award, Liberal, Mo. PTA, 1976. Mem. Am. Osteo. Assn., Am. Acad. Osteopathy, Am. Acad. Family Physicians, Civil Aviation Med. Assn., Am. Coll. Gen Practictioners Osteo. Med and Surgery, Mo. Pilots Assn., Republican. Congregationalist, Methodist. Club: South West Mo. Pilots. Lodges: Lions, Masons. Avocations: aviation; forestry; wildlife conservationist. Home: Liberal, Mo. Died Feb. 9, 2007.

KNEVEL, ADELBERT MICHAEL, pharmacy educator; b. St. Joseph, Minn., Oct. 20, 1922; s. Henry John and Angeline Marie (Terwey) K.; m. Lillian Margaret Zent, June 19, 1950; children: Kenneth, Laura, Christi, Robert, Lisa. Student, St. Johns U., Collegeville, Minn., 1940-41, 48-49; BS, N.D. State U., 1952, MS, 1953; PhD, Purdue U., 1957. Instr. N.D. State U., 1953-54; instr. pharmacy Purdue U., West Lafayette, Ind., 1954-57, asst. prof., 1957-61, assoc. prof., 1961-65, prof., 1965-91, prof. emeritus, from 1991; asst. dean Purdue U. (Sch. Pharmacy), 1969-75, assoc. dean, 1975-88; retired, 1991. Treas. Tippecanoe County Mental Health Assn., 1960-61. Author: (with F.E. DiGangi, S. R. Byrn) Quantitative Pharmaceutical Chemistry, 1977; Contbr.: chpt. to Remington's Pharmaceutical Sciences, 1985; articles to sci. publs. Served with USN, 1942-48. Sagamore of Wabash Ind. Fellow Am. Assn. Pharm. Sci., Am. Chem. Soc. (chmn. Purdue sect. 1963-64), Sigma Xi, Phi Lambda Upsilon, Phi Kappa Phi, Rho Chi. Roman Catholic. Home: Lafayette, Ind. Died Dec. 11, 2006.

KNIGHTON, JAMES BUNDERSON, data processing executive, consultant; b. Tremonton, Utah, Mar. 24, 1948; s. James Barker and Nona (Bunderson) K.; m. Patricia Jene Gibson, Oct. 20, 1979; children— David, Derek, Rebecca. B.Sc. in Computer Sci., Weber State Coll., 1973. Systems engr. Electronic Data Systems, Dallas, 1973-78; mgr. mgmt. adv. services Deloitte Haskins & Sells, Salt Lake City, 1978-83; dir. data processing div. Utah State Tax Commn., Salt Lake City, 1983—; cons. Idaho State Tax Commn., Boise, Hawaii Dept. Revenue, Honolulu, Kans. Dept. Revenue, Topeka, Utah State Tax Commn., Salt Lake City, 1978-83. Mem. Nat. Assn. Tax Adminstrs., Western States Assn. Tax Adminstrs. Mormon. Home: Salt Lake City, Utah. Died Jan. 26, 2007.

KNOX, JAMES LESTER, electrical engineer; b. Youngstown Ohio, July 30, 1919; s. Lester Wirt and Alma Freda (Johnson) K.; m. Elizabeth Jane Williams, Mar. 19 1946 (dec. Dec. 1982) children: Susan Louise, Patricia Ellen, Linda Anne, Thomas Lester, Stephen Williams; m. Anna Wilcox Goins, June 5, 1993 B.E.E., U. Tenn., 1942; MS, U. Mich., 1954; PhD, Ohio State U., 1962. Instr. U. Tenn., 1942-43; engr. Gen. Elec. Co. Schenectady and Syracuse, N.Y., 1943-46; with Am. Baptis Fgn. Mission Soc., 1947-65; assignments U. Shanghai, 1947-48 asst. prof. Central Philippine Coll., 1948-50; tech. dir. Sta DYSR, Dumaguete City, P.I., 1950-51; asst. prof. Centra Philippine U., 1951-53, asso. prof., 1954-60, prof., dean, 1962-65; research asso. Ohio State U. Research Found., Columbus 1960-62; prof. U. Petrol and Min., Dhahran, Saudi Arabia 1973-75, 76-78, 81-87; prof. elec. engring. Mont. State U. Bozeman, 1965-82, ret., 1982. Cons. elec. engring., communit acoustics. Served with USNG, 1934-37. Mem. IEEE, Am. Soc Engring. Edn., Instrument Soc. Am., Sigma Xi, Tau Beta Pi, Ph Kappa Phi. Baptist. Home: Bozeman, Mont. Died Jan. 17, 2007

KNUDSON, HARRY EDWARD, JR., retired electrical manu facturing company executive; b. NYC, Dec. 30, 1921; s. Harr Edward and Helen (Jones) K.; m. Anne Howland, Sept. 21 1944; children— Anne, Erik. BS in Elec. Engring, Bucknell U 1947. Cadet engr. Phila. Electric Co., 1947; with Fed. Pacifi Electric Co., Newark, 1947-80, exec. v.p., 1970-76, pres 1976-80; also dir., corp. v.p. parent co. Reliance Electric Co 1979-80; v.p; gen. mgr. distbn. and control GTE Products Corp Danvers, Mass., 1980-84, ret. Bd. dirs. Trenton Psychiat. Hosp 1995-98, 99—. Served with USNR, 1943-46. Mem. Nat. Elec Mfrs. Assn. (chmn. bd. govs., mem. officers com.), Elec. Mfrs Club, Phi Kappa Psi, Kappa Eta Nu. Methodist. Home Watchung, NJ. Died Aug. 24, 2006.

KNUTSON, HOWARD ARTHUR, state senator, lawyer; b Grand Forks, N.D., May 16, 1929; s. Arthur K. and Ella M (Kamplin) K.; m. Jerroldine M. Sundby, Oct. 5, 1958; children David, Douglas, Eric, Annette, Amy. Student Wabash Coll 1947-49; AB, Luther Coll., 1951; JD, William Mitchell Col Law, 1959. Bar: Minn. 1959, U.S. Dist. Ct. Minn. 1959. Claim mgr. Federated Ins., 1953-60; ptnr. Bergman, Knutson, Street Ulmen, Mpls., 1959-79; mem. Minn. Ho. of Reps., 1967-7 mem. Minn. Senate, 1972-90; ptnr. Knutson, Stier, Ilstrup Knutson, Burnsville, Minn., 1988—. Bd. dirs. Fairview Com munity Hosp.; chmn. Fairview-Ridge Hosp.; mem. adv. bd. St WCAL Radio, Northfield, Minn. Served with U.S. Arm 1951-53. Recipient Disting. Service award Minn. Social Se vices Assn., 1974; Pub. Service award Met. State U. Alum Assn., 1984. Mem. Dakota County Bar Assn., Minn. Bar Assn ABA, Nat. Conf. State Legislators. Republican. Luthera Home: Burnsville, Minn. Died Oct. 1, 2006.

KOELZER, GEORGE JOSEPH, lawyer; b. Orange, NJ, Ma 21, 1938; s. George Joseph and Albertina Florence (Grau Koelzer; m. Patricia Ann Kilian, Apr. 8, 1967; 1 child, Jam Patrick. AB, Rutgers U., 1962, LLB, 1964. Bar: N.J. 1964, D 1978, N.Y. 1980, Calif. 1993, registered: Eng. (fin. lawye 2001. Assoc. Louis R. Lombardino, Livingston, NJ, 1964-6 Lum Biunno & Tompkins, Newark, 1971-73, Giordano, Hall ran & McOmber, Middletown, NJ, 1973-74; asst. U.S. atty. f N.J. US Dept. Justice, 1966-71; ptnr. Evans, Koelzer, Osborne Kreizman, NYC and Red Bank, N.J., 1974-86, Ober, Kale Grimes & Shriver, NYC, 1986-92, Lane Powell Spears Lube sky, LA, 1993-97, Hancock, Rothert & Bunshoft, LA, 199 2000, Coudert Bros., L.A., London, 2000—05, Archer Norri LA, 2006—07. Adj. prof. Seton Hall U. Sch. Law, 1989—9 mem. lawyers adv. com. U.S. Ct. Appeals (3d cir.), 1985—8 vice chmn., 1986, chmn., 87; mem. lawyers adv. com. U.S. Di Ct. N.J., 1984—92; permanent mem. Jud. Conf. U.S. C Appeals (3d cir.); del. jud. conf. U.S. Ct. Appeals (2d cir 1987—89. Recipient Atty. Gen.'s award, 1970. Fellow: Am. B Found.; mem.: ABA (co-chmn. com. admiralty and maritin litig. 1979—82, mem. nominating com. 1982, dir. divsn. procedural coms. 1982—85, chmn. 9th ann. meeting sect. liti 1984, mem. nominating com. 1984, mem. coun. sect. liti 1985—88, advisor standing com. lawyer competen 1986—2001, mem. nominating com. 1987, dir. divsn. I admi strn. 1988—89, co-chmn. com. admiralty and maritime liti 1989—90, sect. litig.), Assn. Bus. Trial Lawyers, Assn. Avera Adjusters U.S., Assn. Average Adjusters Gt. Britain, Comm Bar Assn. (London), Fed. Bar Coun., DC Bar Assn., Assn. B

City of N.Y. (mem. admiralty com. 1987—90), N.Y. State Bar Assn. (chmn. admiralty com., comml. and fed. litig. sect. 1989—92), State Bar Calif., Maritime Law Assn. U.S. (vice chmn. com. maritime fraud and crime 1989—94, chmn. 1994—98, bd. dirs. 1998—2001, mem. ABA rels. com., mem. fed. procedure com.), Civil Justice Inst., L.A. World Affairs Coun., Jonathan Club (L.A.), Mid-Ocean Club (Bermuda). Republican. Roman Catholic. Home: Pasadena, Calif. Died May 14, 2007.

KOESTNER, ADALBERT, pathology educator; b. Hatzfeld, Romania, Sept. 10, 1920; came to U.S., 1955; s. Johann and Gertrud (Gruber) K.; m. Adelaide Wacker, Jan. 20, 1951; children: George A., Rosemarie K. D.V.M., U. Munich, W. Ger., 1951; MS, Ohio State U., 1957, PhD, 1958. Diplomate: Am. Bd. Vet. Pathology. Practice vet. medicine (Untergriesbach), Bavaria, W. Ger., 1951-55; faculty mem. Ohio State U., Columbus, 1955-81, prof. vet. pathology, 1964-81, chmn. dept., 1972-81, prof. emeritus, from 1991; prof. pathology, chmn. dept. Mich. State U. Colls. Human, Osteo. and Vet. Medicine, East Lansing, 1981-90; prof. vet. pathobiology Ohio State U., Columbus, 1990-91, prof. and chmn. emeritus, from 1991. Treas. Am. Bd. Toxicology, Washington, 1979-83; mem. sci. adv. bd. Nat. Ctr. Toxicol. Research, Jefferson, Ark., 1981-86 Author: Diseases of Swine, 1975; contbr. chpt. to books, 150 articles to profl. jours.; editorial bd.: Internat. Jour. Anticancer Research, 1981—, Vet. Pathology, 1988—. Spl. vis. scientist Max Planck Inst. Brain Rsch., Cologne, Fed. Republic Germany, 1970, 73, 75; neuro-oncology grantee Nat. Cancer Inst., 1968—, grantee Internat. Life Sci. Inst., 1991—; recipient Disting. Alumnus award Ohio State U., 1985, Hon. Vet. Alumnus award Mich. State U., 1991. Mem. AVMA (chmn. adv. bd. vet. spltys. 1982 Gaines award), Am. Assn. Neuropathologists (Weil award 1971), Am. Assn. Pathologists, Internat. Acad. Pathology, Soc. Neurosics., Am. Assn. Cancer Research Roman Catholic. Home: Columbus, Ohio. Died Aug. 2, 2006.

KOFMEHL, PAUL JACOB, retired business machines company executive; b. Cin., June 3, 1928; s. Paul and Emma (Zingg) K.; m. Dorothy Frickman, June 14, 1952 (dec. Feb. 1970); children: Sharon Leslie, Sandra Lynne; m. Linda De Stefanis, Feb. 24, 1971. BS, MA, U. Cin.; postgrad. in mgmt., Harvard U.; LLD (hon.), Lincoln U., 1984; HHD (hon.), Mo. Western State Coll., 1987. Economist Cin. Gas & Electric Co., 1950-55; various mgmt. positions IBM, Armonk, N.Y., 1955-88; including v.p. and group exec. IBM World Trade Ams. Group, Armonk, N.Y., 1955-88. Bd. dirs. Howe Richardson Soc., Am. Coll. in Paris Found. Mem. exec. com. Bus. Coun. Internat. Understanding; exec. dir. Mayor's Pvt. Sector Survey, N.Y.C. Died Feb. 17, 2007.

KOHLER, GEORGE OSCAR, research chemist, consultant; b. Milw., Apr. 9, 1913; s. Oscar Charles and Thora (Zachariasen) K.; m. Christine Gilchrist, Oct. 5, 1940; children— Cynthia Ann Castner, Sylvia Luftig, William Mark Kohler. B.S., U. Wis., 1934, M.S., 1936, Ph.D., 1938. Postdoctoral research fellow U. Wis., Madison, 1938-39; lab. dir., v.p. research Cerophyl Labs., Inc., Kansas City, Mo., 1939-55, owner, pres., 1955-56; lab. chief Western Regional Research Ctr., Dept. Agr., Albany, Calif., 1956-81; pres., cons. G. O. Kohler & Assocs., Inverness, Calif., 1981—; cons. France Luzerne, Chalons-Sur-Marne, France, 1972—, Gen. Electric Co., Valley Forge, Pa., 1981-82, NASA, Moffet Field, Calif., 1983, Hokuto Koki Engring. Co., Sapporo, Japan, 1980-82; U.S. del. OECD, Paris, 1979-81, UN-FAO Working Group, Rome, 1976, Brazil Conf. on Leaf Protein-Nat. Acad. Sci., 1978; mem. U.S.-Japan Coop. Program on Natural Resources, Tokyo, 1979-81; charter mem. Sr. Exec. Service, U.S. Dept. Agr., 1979-81. Contbr. articles to tech. jours., chpts. to books on forages, oilseeds and agrl. processing. Patentee processing of agrl. commodities. Recipient Superior Service award Dept. Agr., 1962, award of merit, 1970; award of merit Am. Dehydrators Assn., 1962. Mem. Am. Chem. Soc., Am. Assn. Cereal Chemists, Am. Poultry Sci. Assn., Am. Inst. Nutrition, Inst. Food Tech., Am. Soc. Animal Sci., Sigma Xi, Phi Beta Kappa, Phi Lambda Upsilon, Gamma Alpha. Lutheran. Lodge: Masons. Died Apr. 15, 2006.

KOLATCH, ALFRED JACOB, publisher; b. Seattle, Jan. 2, 1916; s. Sander and Yetta (Jacobs) K.; m. Thelma Rubin, June 5, 1940; children: Jonathan, David. BA, Yeshiva U., 1937; rabbi, Jewish Theol. Sem., 1941. Ordained rabbi, 1941; rabbi Columbia, S.C., 1941-43, Kew Gardens, N.Y., 1946-48; founder, pres. Jonathan David Pubs., Middle Village, N.Y., from 1949. Author: These Are the Names, 1948, Who's Who in the Talmud, 1964, The Name Dictionary, 1967, Jewish Information Quiz Book, 1967, The Family Seder, 1968, Names for Pets, 1971, JD Dictionary of First Names, 1980, Jewish Book of Why, 1981, Complete Dictionary of English and Hebrew First Names, 1984, The Second Jewish Book of Why, 1985, Today's Best Baby Names, 1986, This Is the Torah, 1987, The New Name Dictionary, 1989, The Jewish Home Advisor, 1990, The Jewish Child's First Book of Why, 1992, The Jewish Mourner's Book of Why, 1992, Classic Bible Stories for Jewish Children, 1994, The Jewish Heritage Quiz Book, 1995, Great Jewish Quotations, 1996, Let's Celebrate Our Jewish Holidays, 1997, A Child's First Book of Jewish Holidays, 1997, Best Baby Names for Jewish Children, 1998, What Jews Say About God, 1999, The Presidents of the United States and the Jews, 2000, The Masters of the Talmud, 2003, (paperback edit.) The Jewish Book of Why: The Torah, 2004, The Jewish Books of Why Library, 2004, The Comprehensive Dictionary of English and Hebrew First Names, 2004, Inside Judaism: The Customs, Concepts, and Celebrations of the Jewish People, 2006. Served as chaplain U.S. Army, 1943-46. Mem. Rabbinical Assembly, Assn. Jewish Chaplains (past pres.), Mil. Chaplains Assn. (past v.p.) Home: Forest Hills, NY. Died Feb. 7, 2007.

KOLB, NATHANIEL KEY, JR., architect; b. Sherman, Tex., Aug. 17, 1933; s. Nathaniel Key and Nelcine (Dial) K.; m. Catherine Conner, Nov. 24, 1958; children: Nathaniel Key, Mary Catherine, Amy Monica, Peter Paul, John Conner, Elizabeth Dial. BArch, Tex. A&M U., 1957; MArch, U. Pa., 1960. Registered architect, Tex. With CRSS, Houston, 1955-58, Vincent G. Kling, Phila., 1958-61, William B. Tabler, NYC, 1961-63; chmn. bd., pres. Omniplan, Inc., Dallas, 1963-99. Instr. Tex. A&M Univ., Coll. Station, 1957-58; adj. asst. prof. Columbia U., N.Y.C., 1961-62; bd. dirs. Fidelity Bank, Dallas, 1985-98; mem., chmn. Urban Design Task Force, Dallas, 1974-83; dir., mem. exec. com. Greater Dallas Planning Coun., 1982-85; mem. adv. coun. Ryan Real Estate Coun., U. Tex., Arlington, 1985-88; bd. dirs. Peacock Alley, 1998—. Chmn. Hist. Landmarks Com., Dallas, 1977-79; pres., dir. Dallas Ballet, 1982-87. Recipient Outstanding Alumni award, Coll. Architecture, A&M U./ Tex., 2003, Disting. Alumni award, Sherman HS, 2002. Fellow AIA; mem. Tex. Soc. Architects, Dallas chpt. AIA (dir. 1976-80, pres. 1979), Dallas Club (pres., dir. 1980-86) Home: Dallas, Tex. Died 2006.

KOLE, JACK (JOHN WILLIAM KOLE), writer; b. Zeeland, Mich., Jan. 27, 1934; s. John Henry and Una (Messer) K.; m. Betty Lou Zuege, Sept. 15, 1956; children: Linda Sue, Leslie Ann, James David, Sara Louise, Susan Margaret. BA, Mich. State U., 1955; MS, Northwestern U., 1956. Reporter Milw. Jour., 1956-64, (Washington bur.), 1964-70, chief, 1970-89; sr. writer Rep. David R. Obey, Washington, 1989-95; comm. dir. Dem. Staff, House Appropriations Com., 1995—97. Nieman fellow Harvard U., 1962-63; recipient awards Am. Polit. Sci. Assn., 1961, awards Milw. Press Club, 1960-63, 72. Mem. Soc. Profl. Journalists, Gridiron Club (pres. 1985). Home: Arlington, Va. Died Sept. 15, 2007.

KOLLER, WILLIAM CARL, neurologist, educator; b. Milw., July 12, 1945; m. Vicki Royse Koller; children: Todd, Chad, Kyle. BS, Marquette U., 1968; MS, Northwestern U., Chgo., 1971, PhD, 1974, MD, 1976. Diplomate Am. Bd. Psychiatry and Neurology, 1982. Instr. Northwestern Med. Sch., Chgo., 1975-77, Rush Med. Coll., Chgo., 1976-80; asst. prof. Neurology U. Ill., Chgo., 1980-82; staff neurologist VA Med. Ctr., Chgo., Ill., 1980-82; assoc. prof. Neurology Loyola U. Stritch Sch. of Medicine, Chgo., Ill., 1982-86; staff neurologist VA Med. Ctr., Hines, Ill., 1982-87; prof. Neurology Loyola U. Stritch Sch. of Medicine, Chgo., 1986-87; prof., chmn. U. Kans. Med. Ctr., Kansas City, 1987-99; prof. U. Miami, from 1999; dir. Nat. Parkinson Found., Miami, from 1999. Cons. Merrill-Marion Dow Pharm., Kansas City, 1991—; dir. Am. Parkinson Disease Assn., Kansas City, 1987—; chmn. Internat. Tremor Found., 1988—; mem. Med. Adv. Bd. DuPont, Wilmington, 1991—. Author: Tremor, 1990; editor: Handbook of Parkinson's Disease, 1987, 92. Fellow NIH Predoctoral, Nat. Inst. Health, 1968-74, Pillsbury Co., 1979-80. Mem.Am. Acad. Neurology, Am. Neurol. Assn., Soc. for Neuroscience, Kans. Neurol. Soc., Cen. Soc. Neurology, Am. Soc. for Neurologic Investigation, Behavioral Neurology Soc., Internat. Med. Soc. Motor Disturbances, Assn. U. Prof. Neurology, So. Clin. Neurol. Soc. Home: Miami, Fla. Died Oct. 4, 2005.

KOLLROS, JERRY JOHN, educator emeritus, zoologist; b. Vienna, Dec. 29, 1917; came to U.S., 1920, naturalized, 1926; s. Jacob and Theresa (Hruby) K.; m. Catharine Zenker Lutherman, Sept. 19, 1942; children— James Carl, Peter Richard. S.B., U. Chgo., 1938, PhD, 1942. Research asst. neurosurgery U. Chgo., 1943-45, research asso. toxicity lab., 1945, instr. zoology, 1945-46; asso. U. Iowa, 1946-47, asst. prof., 1947-50, asso. prof., 1950-57, prof., 1957-88, chmn. dept. zoology, 1955-77, prof. emeritus, 1988. Vis. asst. prof. UCLA, summer 1950; cons. zoology Am. Coll. Dictionary, Random House Dictionary of the English Language.; Mem. cell biology study sect. NIH, 1960-64; mem. biol. scis. tng. rev. com. Nat. Inst. Mental Health, 1967-71; chmn. Commn. Undergrad. Edn. in Biol. Scis., 1969-71 Contbr. articles to profl. jours. Fellow A.A.A.S. (regional cons. sci. teaching improvement program 1956-57), Iowa Acad Sci. (Disting. Fellow award 1988); mem. Am. Assn. U. Profs., Am. Assn. Anatomists (mem. exec. com. 1962-66), Am. Soc. Zoologists (exec. com., past treas.), Internat. Inst. Embryologists, Soc. Exptl. Biology and Medicine, Soc. Developmental Biology, Am. Soc. Cell Biology, Phi Beta Kappa, Sigma Xi. Home: Iowa City, Iowa. Died June 8, 2007.

KOLVENBACH, DONALD M., consumer products company executive; b. Milw., Dec. 23, 1934; m. Marilyn A. Yach, May 28, 1960; 1 child, Jeffrey Donald. Student, Milw. Sch. English, 1955. Grocery mgr. Roundy's Inc., Milw., 1955-79; dir. purchasing mdse. Louis Lehrman & Sons, Harrisburg, Pa., 1979-81, Affiliated of Fla., Tampa, 1981-85, 1st v.p., 1985-87, gen. mgr., 1987-88, pres., chief exec. officer, from 1988. Pres. Store Devel. Inc., Affiliated Mil. Sales, Mchts. Ins. Inc., Tampa, 1988—; dir. Supermarket Ins. Inc., Tampa, 1988—. With U.S. Army, 1957-59. Mem. Nat. Grocers Assn. (dir.), ROFDA (dir.). Republican. Roman Catholic. Home: Valrico, Fla. Died May 1, 2006.

KOMPKOFF, GARY PHILLIP, chief of native village, fisherman; b. Tatitlek, AK, July 21, 1954; s. Carroll Mike and Mabel Seena (Allen) K.; m. Carolyn Marie Selanoff Kompkoff, Sept. 1, 1973; children: Katherine, Kristi, Kelly, Nanci, Kerry, Caroline. Grad. high sch., Cordova, AK, 1972. Chief, pres. Tatitlek (AK) Village IRA Coun., 1978-79 and from 80. Chmn. bd. dirs. The Tatitlek Corp., Cordova, AK, 1978-80, 86-92 (shareholder of the yr. 1992); bd. dirs. Chugachmiut, Anchorage, AK; vice chmn. Chugach Regional Resources Commn., Anchorage, AK, 1986—; mem. The North Pacific Rim Housing Authority Bd. Commr., Anchorage, AK, 1980—; adminstr. Fishing Vessels Alyeska/SERVS Oil Spill Response, Valdez, AK, 1990—. Bd. dirs. Prince William Sound Sci. Ctr., Cordova, AK; chmn. Tatitlek Ednl. Adv. Com., 1986-88, 90-92; mem. Prince William Sound Econ. Devel. Coun., Valdez, AK, 1991— (innovative econ. devel. award 1994), Prince William Sound Regional Citizen's Adv. Coun., Anchorage, AK, 1993—, Citizen's Oversight Coun. on Oil & Other Hazardous Substances, 1991—, South Ctrl. AK Subsistence Regional Adv. Coun., 1992-94; pres. The Copper Mountain Fdn., Anchorage, AK, 1991—, Chugach Environ. Protection Consortium, 1992—; dir. Tatitlek Emergency Med. Svcs., 1984-93; starosta St. Nicholas Orthodox Church, Tatitlek, 1988—. Russian Orthodox. Home: Tatitlek, Alaska. Died Feb. 20, 2007.

KONOPKA, MARY ANN STEPHANY, container manufacturing company executive; b. Chgo., Jan. 30, 1933; d. Thomas Stephen and Mary Irene (Plucinski) Poltorak; m. Louis Steven Konopka, Nov. 22, 1964 (dec. 1976); stepchildren: Linda Marie Konopka Orseno, Lorraine Louise Konopka Capra. With Continental Container Systems, West Chicago, Ill., 1952—, project control supr., 1978-83, supr. inventory control, 1983—. Mem. Am. Inventory and Prodn. Soc., Nat. Assn. Female Execs., Am. Soc. Profl. and Exec. Women, U.S. CB Radio Assn. Democrat. Roman Catholic. Club: Northwest Internat. Trade. Home: Lombard, Ill. Died Nov. 30, 2006.

KOOKEN, JOHN FREDERICK, retired bank holding company executive; b. Denver, Nov. 1, 1931; s. Duff A. and Frances C. K.; m. Emily Howe, Sept. 18, 1954; children: Diane, Carolyn. MS, Stanford U., 1954, PhD, 1961. With Security Pacific Nat. Bank-Security Pacific Corp., LA, 1960-92; exec. v.p. Security Pacific Corp., LA, 1981-87, CFO, 1984-92, vice chmn. Los Angeles, 1987-92; ret., 1992. Bd. dirs. Golden State Bancorp., 1992-2002, ACE Ltd., 1985-91 Centris Group, 1986-99, Pacific Gulf Properties, 1994-2001, East West Bancorp, 2002-; lectr. Grad. Sch. Bus. U. So. Calif., 1962-67; chmn. Bank Adminstrn. Inst., 1989-90. Pres. bd. dirs. Children's Bur., L.A., 1981-84; bd. dirs. United Way, L.A., 1982-89, Huntington Meml. Hosp., Pasadena, 1985—, chmn., 1999—2002; bd. dirs. So. Calif. Healthcare Systems, 1993—2005, chmn. 2001—2005. Lt. (j.g.) USNR, 1954-57. Mem.: Fin. Execs. Inst. (pres. LA chpt. 1979—80, dir. 1981—84). Home: San Marino, Calif. Died May 1, 2007.

KOPP, HARRIET GREEN, communication specialist; b. NYC, June 18, 1917; m. George A. Kopp, 1948 (dec. 1968); m. Kurt Friedrich, 1972 (dec. 1996). MA, Bklyn. Coll., 1939; diploma in edn. of deaf, Columbia U., 1939, PhD, 1962. Scientist Bell Telephone Labs., 1943-46; mem. faculty Eastern Mich. U., 1946-48; adj. prof. Wayne State U., Detroit, 1948-70; dir. communication clinics Rehab. Inst. Met. Detroit, 1955-59; dir. programs deaf and aphasic Detroit Bd. Edn., 1959-70; prof., chmn. communication disorders San Diego State U., 1970-80; acting dean Coll. Human Svcs., 1980-83; prof. emerita San Diego State U., from 1983. Mem. Nat. Adv. Com. on Deaf, 1965-72, chmn., 1970-72; mem. Nat. Adv. Com. on Handicapped, 1972-73; adv., rev. panels Bur. Educationally Handicapped, HEW, 1963-83. Author: (with R. Potter, G.A. Kopp) Visible Speech, 1948, 68, Some Applications of Phonetic Principles, 1948, 65, 62, 68, 70, 78, 85, 86; editor: Curriculum, Cognition and Content, 1968, 75, Reading: Cognitive Input and Output, 49th Claremont Reading Conf. Yearbook, 1982, Bilingual Problems of the Hispanic Deaf, 1984 Chair quality of life bd. City of San Diego, 1978-92. Recipient Outstanding Faculty award San Diego State U., 1983. Fellow Am. Speech and Hearing Assn.; mem. AAAS, A.G. Bell Assn. (dir. 1964-68, chmn. edit. bd. 1966-75), Calif. Speech and Hearing Assn., Phi Kappa Phi. Died Feb. 11, 2007.

KOPP, ROBERT WALTER, lawyer; b. Boston, Feb. 21, 1935; s. Robert A. and Marie (Powers) K.; m. Carol A. Rosenberger, Aug. 22, 1959; children: Robert A., Christopher F., J. Brian, David W., Karen A. BS in Physics, Holy Cross Coll., 1957; LLB, Georgetown U., 1963. Bar: N.Y. 1963. Sr. ptnr. Bond, Schoeneck & King, Syracuse, N.Y., from 1963; gen. counsel Pay Bd. Econ. Stabilization Program Phase II, Washington, 1972-73. Lt. (j.g.) USN, 1957-62. Fellow Am. Bar Found., Coll. Labor and Employment Law (founding); mem. ABA (coun. sect. labor and employment law 1980-88, sect. governance liaison 1989-90, 94-2000, sect. del. to ho. of dels. 1990-93), N.Y. State Bar Assn. Roman Catholic. Home: Syracuse, NY. Died Jan. 24, 2006.

KOPS, VICTOR BARRY, psychologist; b. Phila., Aug. 2, 1945; s. Samuel Harry and Sarah Helene (Press) Kops; m. Sheila Helene Gross, Oct. 7, 1975 (div. May 1983); 1 child, Brett Ari. BA, Yeshiva U., 1966; MA, Miami U., 1967; PhD in Clin. Psychology, U. Tenn., 1972. Lic. clin. psychologist. Tng. supr. U. Tenn., Knoxville, 1967—70, supr. grad. students, 1968—69; VA trainee V.A. Hosp., New Orleans, 1968, Gulfport, Miss., 1969; group therapist Eastern State Hosp., Knoxville, 1968—69; asst. clin. psychologist Regoinal Mental Health, Oak Ridge, Tenn., 1971—72; clin. psychologist Sacramento County, Calif., 1973—75, Garrard Ctr. Psychotherapy, La Mesa, Calif., 1976—79; dir., clin. psychologist San Diego Ctr. Psychotherapy, from 1979. Clin. coord. Ctr. Psychology and Edn., Citrus Heights, Calif., 1973—76. Pub. and editor: newsletter Psychotherapy Digest, 1976—83, contbr.: articles to profl. jours. Chmn. Ctrl. City Assn.-Task Force, San Diego, from 1981; com. mem. Mil. Liaison Com., San Diego, from 1982, Women's Task Force, San Diego, from 1982. Mem.: Calif. State Psychol. Assn., Assn. Advancement Psychology, Acad. San Diego Psychologists, APA, Optimist Club (bd. dirs. from 1981), Psi Chi. Democrat. Home: San Diego, Calif. Died June 12, 2007.

KORNBERG, ARTHUR, biochemist, educator; b. Bklyn., Mar. 3, 1918; s. Joseph and Lena (Katz) Kornberg; m. Sylvy R. Levy, Nov. 21, 1943 (dec. 1986); children: Roger David, Thomas Bill, Kenneth Andrew; m. Charlene Walsh Levering, 1988 (dec. 1995); m. Carolyn Frey Dixon, 1998. BS, CCNY, 1937, LLD (hon.), 1960; MD, U. Rochester, 1941, DSc (hon.), 1962, U. Pa., U. Notre Dame, 1965, Washington U., 1968, Princeton U., 1970, Colby Coll., 1970; LHD (hon.), Yeshiva U., 1963; MD honoris causa, U. Barcelona, Spain, 1970. Intern in medicine Strong Meml. Hosp., Rochester, NY, 1941—42; commd. officer USPHS, 1942, advanced through grades to med. dir., 1951; mem. staff NIH, Bethesda, Md., 1942—52, nutrition sect., div. physiology, 1942—45; chief sect. enzymes and metabolism Nat. Inst. Arthritis and Metabolic Diseases, 1947—52; guest research worker depts. chemistry and pharmacology coll. medicine NYU, 1946; dept. biol. chemistry med. sch. Washington U., 1947, prof., head dept. microbiology, med. sch. St. Louis, 1953—59; dept. plant biochemistry U. Calif., 1951; prof. biochemistry Stanford U. Sch. Medicine, 1959—88, chmn. dept., 1959—69, prof. emeritus dept. biochemistry, 1988—2007. Mem. sci. adv. bd. Mass. Gen. Hosp., 1964—67, Regeneron Pharmaceuticals Inc., Maxygen, XOMA Corp.; bd. govs. Weizmann Inst., Israel; founder DNAX. Author: For the Love of Enzymes, 1989, The Golden Helix: Inside Biotech Ventures, 1995; contbr. sci. articles to profl. jours. Lt. (j.g.), med. officer USCGR, 1942. Co-recipient Nobel prize in Physiology or Medicine, Nobel Found., 1959; named Arthur Kornberg Med.

Rsch. Bldg. at U. Rochester in his honor, 1999; recipient Paul-Lewis award in enzyme chemistry, 1951, Max Berg award prolonging human life, 1968, Sci. Achievement award, AMA, 1968, Lucy Wortham James award, James Ewing Soc., 1968, Borden award, Am. Assn. Med. Colls., 1968, Nat. medal of sci., 1979, Gairdner Found. Internat. Awards, 1995. Mem.: NAS, Am. Philos. Soc., Am. Acad. Arts and Scis., Royal Soc., Harvey Soc., Am. Chem. Soc., Am. Soc. Biol. Chemists (pres. 1965), The Japan Soc. (hon.), Alpha Omega Alpha, Sigma Xi, Phi Beta Kappa. Died Oct. 26, 2007.*

KORNFELD, ROSALIND HAUK, research biochemist; b. Dallas, Aug. 2, 1935; d. Walter L. and Margaret (Wallace) Hauk; m. Stuart A. Kornfeld, June 11, 1959; children: Katherine, Stephen Kerry, Carolyn. BS, George Washington U., 1957; PhD, Washington U., 1961. Post-doctoral rsch. fellow dept. biol. chemistry Washington U., St. Louis, 1961-63; staff fellow NIH, Bethesda, Md., 1963-65; rsch. instr. dept. medicine Washington U., St. Louis, 1965-69, rsch. asst. prof., 1969-71, rsch. assoc. prof., 1971-78, assoc. prof. biochemistry and medicine, 1978-81, prof. medicine and biol. chemistry, from 1981. Mem. com. on cancer immunobiology Nat. Cancer Inst., Bethesda, 1975-78, physiol. chemistry study sect. NIH, Bethesda, 1980-83. Editorial bd. Jour. of Biol. Chemistry, 1981-86; contbr. articles to profl. jours. Named scholar of the Leukemia Soc. Am., Washington U. Sch. Medicine, 1971-76. Mem. Am. Soc. Biochemistry and Molecular Biology, Am. Soc. Hematology, The Soc. for Glycobiology, Clayton Twp. (Mo.) Dem. Club (pres. 1974-76), Phi Beta Kappa. Democrat. Died Aug. 10, 2007.

KORNGOLD, ALVIN LEONARD, broadcasting company executive; b. NYC, Nov. 28, 1924; s. Samuel and Sadelle (Samisch) K.; m. Joyce Singer, Jan. 10, 1954; children: Susan Korngold Osherow, Wendy Ellen Korngold Roseman, Ben Alan. AB, NYU, 1943, JD, 1948; certificate, U. Cambridge, Eng., 1946. Bar: N.Y. 1948, U.S. Dist. Ct. (so. dist.) N.Y. 1948, U.S. Ct. Appeals (2nd cir.) 1950, U.S. Dist. Ct. Conn. 1953, U.S. Supreme Ct. 1956, U.S. Dist. Ct. (ea. dist.) N.Y. 1964, Ariz. 1967, U.S. Ct. Appeals (D.C. cir.) 1968, U.S. Ct. Dist. Ct. Ariz. 1970. Practiced in, NYC, 1948-65; spl. asst. dist. atty. Queens County, N.Y., 1951-52; spl. dep. atty. gen. N.Y. State, 1952; pres. Sta. KEVT, Tucson Radio, Inc., 1966-81, All Spanish Network, Tucson, 1972-78; licensee, owner Sta. KAMX, Albuquerque, 1971-78, Sta. KWFM, Tucson, 1970-81, Sta. KLAV, Frontier Broadcasting Inc., Las Vegas, 1976-83, Sta. WWAM, Savannah, Ga., 1983; chmn. Caribbean Broadcast Systems Ltd. Chmn. stas. ZHIT-FM, ZWAVE-FM, ZGOLD-FM, Tortola, Brit. Virgin Islands; dir. Gold Medal Motion Picture Studios, N.Y.C., 1954-59, New Haven Clock & Watch Corp., 1964-66. Contbr. articles to profl. jours. Co-chmn. Vets. for Truman, 1948; dir. Dem. N.Y. Lawyers for Kennedy, 1960; Rep. candidate for County Atty. Tucson, 1968; col., a.d.c. Gov. N.Mex., 1978. Served to cpl. U.S. Army, 1943-46, ETO. Mem. ABA, N.Y. Bar Assn., Tau Kappa Alpha. Home: Road Town, Tortola, British Virgin Islands. Died Oct. 21, 2006.

KORNREICH, MORTON ALAN, insurance brokerage company executive; b. N.Y.C., Dec. 4, 1924; s. Saul and Gertrude Kornreich; B.A. cum laude, U. Pa., 1949; m. Jo Anne Colnes, Nov. 26, 1950 (dec. 2001); children— James, Thomas, Nancy. Asst. to v.p. sales promotion Allied Stores, N.Y., 1949; with S. Kornreich & Sons, Inc., N.Y.C., 1950—2007, v.p., 1960, chmn. bd., 1973—; pres. Kornreich Life Assos., N.Y.C., 1972—2007, Kornreich Internat., N.Y.C., 1974—2007; dir. N.Y. State Motor Vehicle Accident Indemnity Corp. N.Y. State fin. chmn. Udall for Pres. Campaign, 1975; v.p. Westchester Jewish Community Council; Greater N.Y. chmn. United Jewish Appeal-Fedn. Joint Campaign, 1988-90, chmn. steering com. Greater N.Y., 1983-84; bd. overseers U. Pa.; bd. dirs. N.Y. Conv. Ctr.; pres. Congregation Emanu El, Westchester, 1982; v.p. Westchester chpt. Am. Jewish Com., 1982; pres. United Jewish Appeal Greater N.Y., 1985-86; vice chmn. Nat. United Jewish Appeal, 1984; former nat. chmn., United Jewish Appeal, N.Y.C., now chmn. bd. trustees. Served with USAAF, 1943-46; C.L.U. Mem. Top of Table-Million Dollar Round Table (life). Democrat. Clubs: Brae Burn Country (past pres.) (Purchase, N.Y.); Harmonie (N.Y.C.). Died Mar. 27, 2007.

KOSHLAND, DANIEL EDWARD, JR., biochemist; b. NYC, Mar. 30, 1920; s. Daniel Edward and Eleanor (Haas) Koshland; m. Marian Elliott, May 25, 1945 (dec. 1997); children: Ellen, Phyllis, James, Gail, Douglas; m. Yvonne Cyr, Aug. 27, 2000. BS, U. Calif., Berkeley, 1941; PhD, U. Chgo., 1949; PhD (hon.), Weizmann Inst. Sci., 1984, U. Mass., 1992, Ohio State U., 1995, Brandeis U., 2000, Scripps Inst., 2003; ScD (hon.), Carnegie Mellon U., 1985; LLD (hon.), Simon Fraser U., 1986; LHD (hon.), Mt. Sinai U.; LLD (hon.), U. Chgo., 1992; PhD (hon.), Cold Spring Harbor, 2004, Ben Gurion U., 2004. Chemist Shell Chem. Co., Martinez, 1941—42; rsch. assoc. Manhattan Dist. U. Chgo., 1942—44; group leader Oak Ridge Nat. Labs., 1944—46; postdoctoral fellow Harvard, 1949—51; staff mem. Brookhaven Nat. Lab., Upton, NY, 1951—65; affiliate Rockefeller Inst., NYC, 1958—65; prof. biochemistry U. Calif., Berkeley, 1965—97, prof. molecular biology, 1997—2007, chmn. dept., 1973—78. Fellow All Souls Oxford U., 1972; Phi Beta Kappa lectr., 76; John Edsall lectr. Harvard U., 1980, Robert Woodward vis. prof., 86; William H. Stein lectr. Rockefeller U., 1985; G. N. Lewis lectr.U U. Calif., Berkeley. Author: Bacterial Chemotaxis as a Model Behavioral System, 1980; mem. editl. bd. jours.: Accounts Chem. Rsch., Jour. Chemistry, Jour. Biochemistry, editor-in-chief: Sci. Mag., 1985—95. Founder Marian Koshland Sci. Mus., NAS. Recipient T. Duckett Jones award, Helen Hay Whitney Found., 1977, Nat. Medal of Sci., NSF, 1990, Merck award, Am. Soc. Biochemistry and Molecular Biology, 1991, Clark Kerr award, U. Calif., 1994, Lasker Found. award, 1998, Westheimer award, Harvard U., 2002, Welch Chemistry award, Welch Found., 2006; fellow Guggenheim Found., 1972. Mem.: NAS (editor-in-chief Jour. Procs. 1980—85), Acad. Forum (chmn.), Am. Acad. Arts and Scis. (coun.), Am. Philos. Soc., Am. Chem. Soc. (Edgar Fahs Smith award 1979, Pauling award 1979, Rosentiel award 1984, Waterford prize 1984, Seaborg medal 2000), Royal Swedish Acad. Scis. (hon.), Japanese Biochem. Soc. (hon.), Am. Soc. Biol. Chemists (pres.), Alpha Omega Alpha (hon.). Home: Lafayette, Calif. Died July 23, 2007.

KOSKI, DORIS JEAN, advertising executive; b. Ft. Smith, Ark., May 26, 1923; d. Stanley C. and Ruberta (Brumbelow) Speer; student Ohio State U., 1940-43, 78-79; B.A., Franklin U., 1944; student Oglethorpe U., 1940; m. Edward Zacharias Koski, July 29, 1943; children— Ellen Irene, Edward Greg, Diana Lee. Owner, mgr. Ohio China Co., Columbus, 1955-63; buyer The Fashion and F & R Lazarus, Columbus, 1963-65; exec. sec. Otterbein Coll., 1965-67; pres. Stan Speer Inc., Marion, Ohio, 1967-78, exec. v.p. client liaison, 1978-86, exec. cons. advt., 1987—. Precinct judge, Westerville, Ohio, 1962-67. Mem. Specialty Advt. Assn. (mem. conventions com.), Advt. Splty. Ladies, Ad Club, Internat. Platform Assn., Marion C. of C., Kappa Delta. Republican. Episcopalian. Died Sept. 23, 2006.

KOSSEFF, WILLIAM, agribusiness executive; b. N.Y.C., May 29, 1923; s. Benjamin and Mae (Mauss) K.; m. Helen Frances Rubin, Dec. 19, 1943 (div. 1974); children— Alexandra Mae Rubin Martin, Robert Alan; m. 2d Beatrice Pearl Krupit, May 12, 1974. B.B.A., Pace U., 1953; M.S., Columbia U., 1956. With Namolco, Inc., Willow Grove, Pa., 1953-85, v.p., 1983; mgr. trading Cargill, Inc., 1983—. Contbr. articles to profl. jours. Served to capt. USAAF, 1941-45; ETO. Democrat. Jewish. Avocations: photography; flying. Home: Hatboro, Pa. Died Oct. 7, 2006.

KOSTEM, CELAL NIZAMETTIN, civil engineer, educator; b. Ankara, Turkey, Feb. 8, 1939; came to U.S., 1963; s. Halil Naki and Habibe Suada K.; m. Katy Michele Nieuwenhuis, Aug. 30, 1966. Diploma Engr.-MS in, C.E., Istanbul Tech. U., 1961; PhD, U. Ariz., 1966. Engr. Istanbul Harbor Constrn., 1960-61; postdoctoral research assoc. Lehigh U., Bethlehem, Pa., 1966-68, asst. prof., 1968-72, assoc. prof., 1972-78, chmn. Computer Systems Group Fritz Engring. Lab., from 1978, co-dir. Computer-Aided Engring. Lab., 1982-84, prof. civil engring., from 1978. Structural cons., 1966—, shelter analyst, multiprotection designer; bd. dirs. Def. Design Inst., 1968—, Transp. Research Bd., 1970— Editor: Computer-Aided Design in Civil Engineering, 1984; contbr. numerous articles to profl. jours.; structural designer bridges and bldgs. Served to 1st lt. C.E. Turkish Land Forces, 1961-63; served to 1st lt. C.E. Turkish Res., 1963—. Fulbright fellow, 1963, 64, 65; UN Agy. for Internat. fellow, 1979; grantee State of Pa., 1972— Mem. ASCE (past pres. Lehigh Valley sect., Outstanding Civil Engr. of Yr. award 1985), Am. Concrete Inst., Earthquake Engring. Research Inst., Internat. Assn. Bridge and Structural Engring., Assn. For Shell and Spatial Structures, Sigma Xi, Chi Epsilon Home: Bethlehem, Pa. Died Feb. 9, 2006.

KOSTYO, JACK LAWRENCE, physiology educator; b. Elyria, Ohio, Oct. 1, 1931; s. Louis and Matilda (Thomasko) K.; m. Shirlianne Guth, June 10, 1953; children: Cecile A., Louis C. AB, Oberlin Coll., 1953; PhD, Cornell U., 1957; MD (hon.), U. Göteborg, 1978. NRC fellow Harvard Med. Sch., Boston, 1957-59; asst. prof., then prof. physiology Duke U., 1959-68; prof., chmn. dept. physiology Emory U., Atlanta, 1968-79; prof. physiology U. Mich. Med. Sch., Ann Arbor, 1979-94, chmn. dept. physiology, 1979-85, active prof. emeritus in internal medicine, from 1995; assoc. dir. Mich. Diabetes Rsch. and Tng. Ctr., Ann Arbor, 1986-97, dir. grants program, from 1997. Mem. endocrinology study sect. NIH/USPHS, 1967-71, internat. and coop. projects study sect., 1992-96; mem. physiology test com. Nat. Bd. Med. Examiners, 1974-77, mem. comprehensive part II com., 1986-91, U.S. Med. Licensure Examination Step 2 Com., 1990-91. Editor in chief Endocrinology, 1978-82; sect. editor Ann. Rev. Physiology, 1982-86; mem. editorial bd. Growth Regulation, 1990-97; contbr. articles to profl. jours. Mem. adv. bd. Searle Scholars, 1982-85. Recipient Lederle Med. Faculty award, 1961, Ernst Oppenheimer Meml. award Endocrine Soc., 1969 Mem. Endocrine Soc. (editl. bd., coun., chmn. awards com.), Am. Physiol. Soc. (editl. bd., coun., chmn. standing com. on edn., mem. coun. of endocrinology and metabolism sect., chmn. endocrinology and metabolism sect. 1990-91, rep. to Coun. Acad. Socs. of Assn. Am. Med. Colls., mem. AAAS sect. on med. scis., editor Handbook of Physiology sect. 7, Endocrinology, vol. 5), Soc. for Exptl. Biology and Medicine (editl. bd.), Internat. Union Physiol. Scis. (commn. on med. edn.), Assn. Chmn. Depts. Physiology (pres. 1979, coun.), Am. Diabetes Assn., Coun. Acad. Socs. (adminstrv. bd. 1983-86), Sigma Xi. Died Apr. 4, 2007.

KOVÁCS, LÁSZLÓ, cinematographer; b. Budapest, Hungary, May 14, 1933; came to U.S., 1957, naturalized, 1963; s. Imre and Julia K.; m. Audrey, children: Julianna, Nadia MA, Acad. Drama and Motion Picture Arts of Budapest, Hungary, 1956. Lectr. at univs., film schs. Dir. photography (films) The Incredibly Strange Creatures Who Stopped Living and Became Mixed-Up Zombies!!?, 1964, Kiss Me Quick!, 1965, The Notorious Daughter of Fanny Hill, 1966, A Smell of Honey, a Swallow of Brine, 1966, Mondo Mod, 1967, Hell's Angels on Wheels, 1967, A Man Called Dagger, 1968, Mantis in Lace, 1968, Psych-Out, 1968, The Savage Seven, 1968, Single Room Furnished, 1968, Targets, 1968, The Savage Seven, 1968, Single Room Furnished, 1968, A Day with the Boys, 1969, That Cold Day in the Park, 1969, Blood of Dracula's Castle, 1969, Easy Rider, 1969, Hell's Bloody Devils, 1970, Alex in Wonderland, 1970, Getting Straight, 1970, Five Easy Pieces, 1970, The Last Movie, 1971, The Marriage of a Young Stockbroker, 1971, The King of Marvin Gardens, 1972, Pocket Money, 1972, Slither, 1972, Steelyard Blues, 1972, What's Up Doc?, 1972, Huckleberry Finn, 1973, Paper Moon, 1973, A Reflection of Fear, 1973, Freebie and the Bean, 1974, For Pete's Sake, 1974, At Long Last Love, 1975, Shampoo, 1975, Harry and Walter Go to New York, 1976, Baby Blue Marine, 1976, Nickelodeon, 1976, New York, New York, 1977, The Last Waltz, 1978, Paradise Alley, 1978, F.I.S.T., 1978, Heart Beat, 1979, The Runner Stumbles, 1979, Butch and Sundance: The Early Days, 1979, Inside Moves, 1980, The Legend of the Lone Ranger, 1981, Frances, 1982, The Toy, 1982, Crackers, 1982, Ghostbusters, 1983, Mask, 1985, Legal Eagles, 1986, Little Nikita, 1988, Say Anything, 1989, Shattered, 1991, Radio Flyer, 1992, Ruby Cairo, 1992, The Next Karate Kid, 1993, The Scout, 1993, Free Willy 2: The Adventure Home, 1994, Copycat, 1994, Multiplicity, 1995, My Best Friends Wedding, 1996, Jack Frost, 1998, Return To Me, 2000, Miss Congeniality, 2000, Two Weeks Notice, 2002; (TV movies) Los Angeles: Where It's At, 1969, Making of the President, 1969; (TV series) Time-Life Specials: The March of Time, 1965 Recipient Lumanaria award for Lifetime Achievement, Santa Fe Film Festival, 2006. Mem. Acad. Motion Picture Arts and Scis., Am. Soc. Cinematographers. Died July 22, 2007.

KRAAR, LOUIS, journalist; b. Charlotte, NC, July 26, 1934; s. Herbert and Ruth (Miller) K. BA, U. N.C., 1956. Staff reporter Wall St. Jour., NYC, 1956-58, Pentagon reporter Washington, 1958-62; Pentagon corr. Time mag., Washington, 1962-63, bur. chief New Delhi, India, 1963-65, Bangkok, Thailand, 1965-68, Asia corr. Singapore, 1969-74; bd. editors Fortune mag., NYC, from 1975, Asian editor Hong Kong, 1983-88. Fellow Coun. Fgn. Relations. Home: New York, NY. Died Mar. 10, 2006.

KRAEMER, JEAN ANN, legislative agent; b. Elizabeth, N.J., Oct. 23, 1940; d. Benson and Edith Carolyn (Krouse) Rosenberg; m. Waldron Kraemer, June 17, 1962; children— Adam, Elise. B.A., Wellesley Coll., Mass., 1962. Research chemist Merck & Co., Rahway, N.J., 1962-65; dir. govtl. affairs Home Health Agy. Assembly of N.J., Princeton, 1978—. Co-chmn. Columbia High Sch. Fgn. Exchange Com., Maplewood, N.J., 1982-86; bd. dirs. LWV, Maplewood, 1982-83; mem. nat. domestic affairs com. Am. Jewish Com., N.Y.C., 1974-84, co-chmn. annual dinner, 1975-77; bd. dirs. family advocacy com. Jewish Counseling and Service Agy., 1979-83; alumna rep. Wellesley Coll., 1980—; organizer Maplewood Anti-Vandalism Campaign, 1975; v.p. South Orange-Maplewood Pub. Edn. Com., 1975-76; pres. Jefferson Sch. PTA, 1974-75; coordinator events Del Tufo for Gov. Campaign, 1984, Degnan for Gov. Campaign, 1981; Maplewood chmn. Shapiro for County Exec., 1978; dir. of speakers Bureau Essex County Byrne for Gov., 1977; fund raising coordinator state staff, Jordon for Gov., 1977; Democratic candidate for Maplewood Township Com., 1976. Jewish. Avocations: travel; sailing; swimming. Died Feb. 5, 2006.

KRAEMER, PAUL WILLIAM, computer and consulting company executive; b. Newark, Jan. 2, 1930; s. Herman David and Olive (Baker) K.; B.S., N.Y. U., 1951, M.B.A., 1952; m. Phyllis Elaine Ferster, Dec. 25, 1952; children— David, Beth, Samuel. Pvt. practice acctg., Newark and N.Y.C., 1956-60; partner Mattersdorf & Kraemer, C.P.A.s, N.Y.C., 1960-72; pres. A 02 Medical, Dania, Fla., 1972-82, Jacksonville, Fla., 1975-83; pres. Automated Med. Billings, Inc., Pacific Palisades, Calif., 1979-81, fin. v.p., 1981-83, chmn. bd., 1979-83; pres. MBA Corp., Pacific Palisades, Calif., 1982-83; v.p. planning and devel. AMBI Mgmt Systems, Inc., 1983-84, v.p. AMBI/McKesson, Santa Monica, Calif., 1984—; instr. Seton Hall U., 1955-59, Upsala Coll., 1959-61, Bernard M. Baruch Sch. Bus. and Public Adminstrn. CCNY, 1961-72; community prof. Fla. Internat. U., 1972-73; cons. McKesson Drug Co. Formost-McKesson, 1980-83, cons. profl. devel. Am. Inst. C.P.A.s, 1959-72. Columnist, Home Care Advisor, Home Care Mag. Mem. Republican Com. Essex County (N.J.), 1973; bd. dirs. Jewish Fedn. South Broward (Fla.), 1970-72; chief fin. officer Nat. Inst. for Jewish Hospice, 1986—. Served with AUS, 1952-54. C.P.A., N.J., N.Y. Mem. Am. Inst. C.P.A.s, N.J. Soc. C.P.A.s, Am. Acctg. Assn., Nat. Affiliation Durable Med. Equipment Cos. (dir. 1973-75, v.p. 1975-76), Assn. Ind. Suppliers Med. Equipment (pres. 1977-78, dir. 1979-82), Nat. Affiliation Med. Equipment Suppliers (dir. 1982-84). Jewish. Home: Pacific Palisades, Calif. Died May 5, 2006.

KRAKOFF, ROBERT LEONARD, publishing executive; b. Pitts., May 4, 1935; s. Frank and Della (Zionts) Krakoff; m. Sandra Gusky, June 22, 1958; children: Roger, Hope, Reed. BS with honors, Pa. State U., 1957; MBA, Harvard U., 1959. Sta[illegible] v.p. mktg. planning TWA, NYC, 1963—70; v.p., contr. consumer product div. Singer, NYC, 1970—71; staff v.p. strategic planning RCA, NYC, 1971—72; pres. Am. Internat. Travel Svc. Boston, 1972—73, Cahners Travel Group, NYC, 1973—7[illegible] Cahners Expn. Group, NYC, 1974—86; exec. v.p., COO Reed Pub. U.S.A., Newton, Mass., 1986—89, pres., COO, 1989—9[illegible] chmn., CEO, 1991—96, Advanstar, Inc. (formerly Advanstar Holdings, Inc.), Boston, 1996—2003, 2004, Blantyre Ptnrs. Boston, 2004—06; pres., CEO VNU Bus. Media, Inc., NYC, 2006—07. Bd. dirs. Freedom Comms., Inc., 1996—200[illegible] Trustee Beth Israel Deaconess Med. Ctr., 2004—07. With USAR, 1957—63. Died Mar. 22, 2007.

KRAMER, CECILE EDITH, retired medical librarian; [illegible] NYC, Jan. 6, 1927; d. Marcus and Henrietta (Marks) K. B[illegible] CCNY, 1956; MS in L.S., Columbia U., 1960. Reference ass[illegible] Columbia U. Health Scis. Library, NYC, 1957-61, asst. librar-ian, 1961-75; dir. Health Scis. Libr. Northwestern U., Chgo., 1975-91, asst. prof. edn., 1975-91, prof. emeritus, from 199[illegible] Instr. library and info. sci. Rosary Coll., 1981-85; cons. Francis A. Countway Library Medicine, Harvard U., 1974. Pres. Friends of Libr., Fla. Atlantic U., Boca Raton. Fellow Med. Libr. Assn. (chmn. med. sch. librs. group 1975-76, editor newsletter 197[illegible]-77, instr. continuing edn. 1966-75, mem. panel cons. editors Bull. 1987-90, disting. mem. Acad. Health Info. Profls. 1993—, mem. Biomed. Comm. Network (chmn. 1979-80). Home: Boca Raton, Fla. Died Jan. 25, 2007.

KRAMER, GEORGE P., lawyer; b. Holyoke, Mass., Feb. 2[illegible] 1927; m. Elizabeth M. Truax, Oct. 13, 1973; children: Alice Truax, R. Hawley Truax, Charles W. Truax. AB, Harvard U., 1950, LL.B., 1953; Cert., Sorbonne, 1948. Bar: N.Y. 195[illegible] Assoc. Watson Leavenworth Kelton & Taggart, NYC, 1953-5[illegible] partner, 1960-65, Conboy, Hewitt, O'Brien & Boardman, NYC, 1965-86, Hunton & Williams (merger Conboy, Hewitt, O'Brien & Boardman), NYC, from 1986. Lectr. Practising Law Inst.; bd. dirs. Burleson Corp.; mem. vis. com. Peabody Mus. of Harvard U., 1974-80; mem. N.Y. Cotton Exch., N.Y. Bd. Trade. Author: Misleading Trademarks and Consumer Protection. Trustee Hancock Shaker Village, 1982—; trustee Harvard U. Law Sch. Assn. of N.Y., 1985-87, v.p. 1987-89. Served to lt. USNR, 1945-[illegible] Recipient Congl. Antarctic medal, 1977 Mem. ABA, Internat. Bar Assn., Assn. Bar City N.Y. (sec. 1963-65, exec. com. 1970-74, chmn. various coms.), Am. Law Inst., Internat. Trademark Assn. (dir. 1975-78), Assn. Internationale pour la Protection de la Propriete Industrielle, Harvard U. Alumni Assn. ([illegible] dirs. 1983-89), Mass. Speleological Soc. (pres.), Antarctic

Soc., Am. Polar Soc., Century Assn., Harvard Club (sec. 1972-83, 88-90, bd. mgrs. 1983-86), Harvard Faculty Club. Home: New York, NY. Died Apr. 27, 2007.

KRAMER, STEVEN G., ophthalmologist, educator; b. Chgo., Feb. 28, 1941; s. Paul and Maria Kramer; m. Anne Crystal Kramer, Dec. 26, 1961 (div.); children: Janice Lynn, Kenneth David; m. Bernadette E. Coatar, June 30, 1974 (div.); children: Daniel Steven, Susan Mary; m. Susan E. Garrett, Jan. 17, 1997. BA in Biology, U. Chgo., 1967; MD, Case Western Res. U., 1965; PhD, U. Chgo., 1971. Cert. assoc. examiner Am. Bd. Ophthalmology; lic. ophthalmologist, Calif., Wash. Instr. ophthalmology U. Chgo., 1968-71; chief of ophthalmology Madigan Army Med. Ctr., Tacoma, 1971-73; chief of ophathlmology VA Med. Ctr., San Francisco, 1973-75; prof. ophthalmology, chmn. U. Calif., San Francisco, from 1975, dir. Beckman Vision Ctr., from 1988. Mem. various coms. VA Hosp., San Francisco, 1973—; mem. exec. med. bd. sch. medicine U. Calif., 1975—, mem./chmn. various coms., 1975—, mem. clin. dept. chmn. group, 1975—, mem. governing bd. continuing med. edn. program, 1984-85, mem. clin. rev. working group, 1985-86, pres.-elect med. staff, 1985, pres., 1986-88, mem. chancellor's governance group, 1986—, mem. adv. group devel. spine svcs., 1992—; v.p. That Man May See, Inc., 1975—, bd. trustees, 1975—, campaign cabinet mem. for Vision Rsch. Ctr., 1983—; sec., bd. govs. Francis Proctor Found. for Rsch. in Opthalmology, 1975—; mem. Rsch. to Prevent Blindness, Inc., N.Y., 1976—, ad hoc adv. com., 1976-77; NIH mem. vision rsch. program com. NEI, 1978-82, chmn., 1980-82; site visit chmn. U. Wash., Seattle, 1979, Mass. Eye and Ear Infirmary, Boston, 1980, dept. neurobiology Harvard Med. Sch., Boston, 1980; mem. joint program and planning bd. sch. medicine U. Calif./Mt. Zion, 1985-88; mem. courtesy staff San Francisco Gen. Hosp.; lectr. in field. Editor, editl. bd. therapeutics rev. sect. Survey of Ophthalmology, 1977-84, diagnostic and surg. techniques sect., 1984—; sci. referee Am. Jour. Ophthalmology, 1967-81, editl. bd., 1981—; editl. bd. Ophthalmic Soc.; sci. referee Life Scis.; editor CMA Ophthalmology Epitomes, Western Jour. Medicine, 1976-77; med. adv. bd. Nat. Soc. to Prevent Blindness, 1979—; editor sect. cornea and sclera Yearbook of Ophthalmology, 1982. Mem. legis. com. for State of Calif., 1977; bd. dirs. Found. for Glaucoma Rsch., 1980—. Maj. U.S. Army, 1971-73. USPHS Spl. fellow in ophthalmologic rsch., 1970; VA Hosp. Rsch. Program grantee; NIH grantee, That Man May See grantee. Mem. AMA, ACS, Am. Acad. Ophthalmology, Am. Intra-Ocular Implant Soc., Assn. for Rsch. in Vision and Ophthalmology, Pacific Coast Oto-Ophthalmology Soc., Frederick C. Cordes Eye Soc., Calif. Med. Assn. (sci. adv. panel 1974—, adv. panel on ophthalmology subcom. for accreditation 1976-77, 78), Calif. Assn. Ophthalmology (adv. cons.), Assn. Univ. Profs. Ophthalmology (chmn. resident placement svc. com., mem. ophthalmology resident and fellowship edn. com.), No. Calif. Soc. To Prevent Blindness (med. adv. bd.), Pan Am. Assn. Ophthalmology, Am. Congress, San Francisco Ophthal. Round Table, Rsch. to Prevent Blindness, Retinitis Pigmentosa Internat. Soc. (founding mem., sci. adv. bd.), Castroviejo Corneal Soc., Internat. Cornea Soc., Internat. Soc. Refractive Keratoplasty, Calif. Cornea Club, Ophthalmologic Hon. Soc. of Am. Ophthal. Soc., Phi Beta Kappa, Sigma Xi, Alpha Omega Alpha. Achievements include patents on surgical instrument tray; multi-compartmentalized bottle; instrument for cataract extraction through small incision; bottle closure; reminder closure; surg. instrument; internally sterile pulsatile irrigator, others. Home: Pacifica, Calif. Died Dec. 24, 2005.

KRAMER, YALE, business appraiser, broker; b. St. Louis, Oct. 1, 1944; s. Paul and Evelyn (Reiss) K.; m. Mary Helene Miller, Feb. 17, 1968; children— Christopher, Paul, Jonathon. B.A., Drake U., 1967, J.D., 1969, M.B.A., 1971; student law Washington U., St. Louis, 1966-68. C.P.A., Iowa. Sr. tax specialist Peat Marwick Mitchell, Des Moines, 1970-72; v.p. R.G. Dickinson Co., Des Moines, 1972-78; pres. Iowa Capital Corp., Des Moines, 1978-80; pres. Reiss Corp., Des Moines, 1980—, V R Bus. Brokers, Des Moines, 1982—. Fellow Des Moines Soc. Fin. Analysts; mem. Am. Soc. Appraisers (sr. mem.; mem. bus. valuation com. 1981—), Am. Inst. C.P.A.s (mem. bus. law com. 1983—), Iowa Soc. C.P.A.s (bd. dirs. 1980-83). Home: Des Moines, Iowa. Died Nov. 13, 2006.

KRANTZ, JOHN FRANKLIN, recreation company executive; b. Des Moines, Sept. 1, 1929; s. Walter Michael and Nettie (Piper) K.; m. Mary Jan Krantz; children— Kathleen, John M., Laura, Mary Beth, Matthew, Molly, Michael. Pres., Custom Built Homes, Inc., Des Moines, 1960-84, Empire Investment Corp., Des Moines, 1969-84, Adventure Land of Am., Inc., Des Moines, 1971—. Mem. Internat. Assn. Amusement Parks and Attractions (v.p. 1983—). Republican. Lodge: Masons (32 deg.). Died Jan. 7, 2006.

KRANTZ, KERMIT EDWARD, obstetrician, department chairman; b. Oak Park, Ill., June 4, 1923; s. Andrew Stanley and Beatrice H. (Cibrowski) K.; m. Doris Cole Krantz, Sep. 7, 1946; children: Pamela (Mrs. Richard Huffstutter), Sarah Elizabeth, Kermit Tripler. BS, Northwestern U., 1945, BM, 1947, MS in Anatomy, 1947, MD, 1948; LittD (hon.), William Woods Coll., 1971. Diplomate Am. Bd. Ob-Gyn. Intern ob-gyn. N.Y. Lying-In Hosp., 1947-48; asst. resident, asst. ob-gyn. Cornell U. Med. Coll., N.Y. Lying-In Hosp., N.Y. Hosp., 1948-50; fellow, resident in ob-gyn Mary Fletcher Hosp., Burlington, Vt., 1950-51; Durfee Clinic, 1952-55; instr., then asst. prof. U. Vt. Coll. Medicine, 1951-55; asst. prof. U. Ark. Med. Sch., 1955-59; prof., chmn. dept. ob-gyn. U. Kans. Med. Ctr., 1959-90, obstetrician and gynecologist in chief, 1959-90, lectr. history medicine, from 1959, prof. anatomy, from 1963, dean clin. affairs, 1972-74, chief staff, 1972-74, assoc. to exec. vice chancellor for facilities devel., 1974-83, Univ. Disting. prof., 1990—92; univ. disting. prof. emeritus ob/gyn. and anatomy U. Kans., from 1994. Cons. in field. Author numerous articles in field. Mem. Nat. Adv. Child Health and Human Devel. Council, NIH, 1974-76. Named Outstanding Prof. in Coll. of Medicine Nu Sigma Nu, 1955, Charles A. Durham Meml. lectr., Ann. Session Tex. Med. Assn., 1978; recipient Found. award, South Atlantic Assn. Obstetricians and Gynecologists, 1950, Am. Assn. Obstetricians and Gynecologists, 1950, Wyeth-Ayerst Pub. Recognition award, 1st Am. Assn. Prof. of Gynecology and Obstetrics, 1988, Robert A. Ross lectureship award, Armed Forces Dist. meeting Am. Coll. Obstetricians and Gynecologists, 1972, Outstanding Civilian Svc. medal, U.S. Army-Dept. Def., 1985; Bowen-Brooks fellow, N.Y. Acad. Medicine, 1948—50, Markle scholar med. sci., 1957—62, Kermit E. Krantz Soc. established at U. Kans. Med. Ctr., 1982, Arey-Krantz Mus. Anatomy established at Northwestern U. Sch. Medicine, 2004. Founding fellow Am. Coll. Obstetricians and Gynecologists (Kermit E. Krantz Lectureship award established 1973, Outstanding Dist. Services award 1978, 82); fellow ACS, Am. Coll. Ob-Gyn (life); mem. Am. Assn. Anatomists, Am. Fedn. Clin. Research, AMA, Am. Med. Writers Assn., Am. Fertility Soc., AAUP, Soc. Exptl. Biology and Medicine, Aerosopace Med. Assn., Endocrine Soc., Soc. Gynecologic Investigation, Central Assn. Obstetricians and Gynecologists, N.Y. Acad. Medicine, N.Y. Acad. Sci., Kans. Med. Soc., Assn. Mil. Surgeons U.S. (sustaining), Kans. Obstet. Soc., Arey-Krantz Mus. Anatomy Northwestern U. Sch. Medicine, Sigma Xi, Alpha Omega Alpha. Died July 30, 2007.

KRANTZ, STEVE (STEPHEN FALK KRANTZ), film producer; b. NYC, May 20, 1923; s. Philip and Rose (Scharf) K.; m. Judith Tarcher, Feb. 19, 1954; children: Nicholas, Anthony. BA, Columbia Coll., 1943. Licensed pvt. pilot. Dir. program devel. Columbia Pictures TV, 1954-56; v.p. charge world sales and prodn., 1956-58; pres. Steve Krantz Prodns. Prodr.: The Tonight Show and Kate Smith Show, 1950-52; program dir., NBC, 1953-54; prodr.: (films) Fritz the Cat, 1973, Heavy Traffic, 1974, The Nine Lives of Fritz the Cat, 1974, Cooley High, 1975, Ruby, 1977, Which Way Is Up?, 1977, Jennifer, 1978, Swap Meet, 1979; (TV movies) Princess Daisy, 1983, Dadah Is Death, 1988, Deadly Matrimony, 1992, Torch Song, 1993, House of Secrets, 1993, Jack reed: Badge of Honor, 1993, Children of the Dark, 1994, Jack Reed: A Search for Justice, 1994, Dazzle, 1995, Jack Reed: One of Our Own, 1995, Jack Reed: Death and Vengeance, 1997; (TV mini-series) Mistral's Daughter, 1984, Sins, 1986, Till We Meet Again, 1989; (TV series) The Marvel Superheroes, 1966, Rocket Robin Hood, 1966, Max the 2000-Year Old Mouse, 1967, Spider-Man, 1967; author: Laurel Canyon, 1979 Served to 2d lt. USAAF, World War II, PTO. Mem. Ind. Producers Assn. (pres. 1951-52), Motion Picture Acad. Arts and Scis. Died Jan. 4, 2007.

KREAGER, EILEEN DAVIS, financial consultant; b. Caldwell, Ohio, Mar. 2, 1924; d. Fred Raymond and Esther (Farson) Davis. BBA, Ohio State U., 1945. With accounts receivable dept. M & R Dietetic, Columbus, Ohio, 1945—50; complete charge bookkeeper Magic Seal Paper Products, Columbus, 1950—53, A. Walt Runglin Co., LA, 1953—54; office mgr. Roy C. Haddox and Son, Columbus, 1954—60; bursar Meth. Theol. Sch. Ohio, Delaware, 1961—86; adminstrv. cons. Fin. Ltd., from 1986. Ptnr. Coll. Administrv. Sci., Ohio State U., 1975-80; seminar participant Paperwork Systems and Computer Sci., 1965, Computer Systems, 1964, Griffith Found. Seminar Working Women, 1975; pres. Altrusa Club of Delaware, Ohio, 1972-73. Del. Altrusa Internat., Montreal, 1972, Altrusa Regional, Greenbrier, 1973. Fellow Am. Biog. Inst. (life); mem. AAUW, Assoc. Am. Inst. Mgmt. (exec. coun. of Inst. 1979), Am. Soc. Profl. Cons., Internat. Platform Assn., Ohio State U. Alumna Assn., Columbus Computer Soc., Air Force Assn., Fraternal Order of Police Ohio, Motts Mil. Mus., Innovation Alliance, Toastmasters Internat., Ohio State U. Faculty Club, Univ. Club Columbus, Capital Club, Delaware Country Club, Columbus Met. Club, Friends Hist. Costume & Textile Collection Ohio State U., Internat. Order Police Ohio, Inc., Kappa Delta Methodist. Died June 20, 2007.

KREBS, MAX VANCE, retired foreign service officer, educator; b. Cin., June 26, 1916; s. August Leonidas and Katherine Louise (Vance) K.; m. Esther Willard Winn, Aug. 8, 1942; children: Marlynn Vance Clayton, Timothy Winn. AB, Princeton U., 1937; postgrad., U. Cin., 1938-39, U. Calif., 1946-47. Asst. to purchasing agt. Strietmann Biscuit Co., Mariemont, Ohio, 1937-38, asst. credit mgr., 1938-41; asst. export mgr. Gantner & Mattern Co., San Francisco, 1946-47; 3d sec., vice consul Am. Embassy, Montevideo, 1947-49, 2d sec., vice consul Bogota, 1950-52; consul Am. Consulate Gen., Antwerp, 1952-55; tng. assignments officer Office of Personnel, Dept. of State, 1955-57, spl. asst. to U.S. undersec. state, 1957-59, spl. asst. to U.S. sec. state, 1959-60; polit. counselor Manila, 1961-64, Rio de Janeiro, 1964-67; dep. chief mission Guatemala, 1967-70; polit. adviser to comdr.-in-chief U.S. So. Command, C.Z., 1970-71; dep. chief mission (minister-counselor) Buenos Aires, 1971-74; ambassador to Guyana, 1974-76; vis. fellow Woodrow Wilson Nat. Fellowship Found., 1976-84; instr. Sandhills C.C., Pinehurst, 1976—96. Mem. Gov.'s Advocacy Coun. for Persons with Disabilites, 1992-99, N.C. Symphony Found., 1996-99. Served as capt. AUS, 1941-46. Golden Eagle lifetime achievement award honoree Walnut Hills H.S., Cin., 1998. Mem.: Rotary. Presbyterian. Home: Southern Pines, NC. Died Apr. 22, 2006.

KREIDER, THOMAS MCROBERTS, English language educator; b. Wadsworth, Ohio, Mar. 2, 1922; s. Paul Vernon and Mildred (McRoberts) K.; m. Janet Elizabeth Callahan, June 9, 1952; children: Anne Whitaker, Carol Latham Kreider Lisensky. AB in History, U. Cin., 1946, MA in English, 1949, PhD, 1952; MA in History, Harvard U., 1947; cert. theol. studies, Pacific Sch. Religion, 1968; postdoctorate, Oxford U., Eng., 1949, Union Theol. Sem., NYC, 1954. Mem. faculty dept. English, Berea (Ky.) Coll., from 1952, assoc. prof., 1956-61, prof., from 1961, Chester D. Tripp prof. humanities, from 1976, prof. emeritus, from 1987, chmn. dept., 1971-84. Fulbright prof. U. Karachi, Pakistan, 1959-60; vis. prof. U. Cinn., 1961; vis. scholar in residence No. Ariz. U., 1984-85; dir. Columbia U. sect. Harvard-Yale-Columbia Intensive Summer Studies Program, summer, 1967; participant Danforth Conf., Colorado Springs, summer, 1968; cons. museums and hist. orgns. program NEH, 1976—, also coll. English curricula, 1979—. Author: Aristocratic Tradition in Southern Literature, in Venture, 1960. Vice pres. bd. dirs. Berea Coll. Outdoor Drama Assn.; bd. dirs. Greater Berea Human Rights Commn., 1969-71, Project Opportunity Ky., 1968-75; bd. dirs. Ky. Humanities Council, 1972-79, pres., 1974-78; examiner So. Assn. Colls. and Schs., 1971—. Served with AUS, 1943-46, PTO. Taft fellow, 1948-52; Charles Shedd fellow, 1967-68; Danforth grantee, 1954; NSF grantee, 1965; Lilly grantee, 1961-63; NEH grantee, 1975; recipient Seabury award for excellence in teaching, 1971 Mem. MLA, AAUP, Hemingway Soc., Phi Beta Kappa, Omicron Delta Kappa. Episcopalian. Home: Cincinnati, Ohio. Died July 28, 2006.

KREIPKE, SVEN AXEL, engineering company executive; b. Taarbaek, Denmark, Oct. 13, 1926; arrived in U.S., 1953, naturalized, 1965; s. Bendt and Oda (Valborg) Kreipke; m. Jytte Engel, May 4, 1964; children: Per E., Anette E., Niels E. MSMechE, Royal Tech. U. Copenhagen, 1951. Project engr. E.I. duPont Co., Charleston, W.Va., 1953—57; project mgr. The Lummus Co., 1957—67; mgr. ops. Lummus Nederland, The Hague, 1967—71, dir., 1971—75; v.p. European ops. The Lummus Co., NJ, 1975—78, exec. v.p. ops., 1978—80, pres., 1980—81; pres. and CEO Lummus Crest, Inc., Bloomfield, from 1981; v.p. Combustion Engring., Inc., Stamford, Conn., from 1981. Bd. overseers N.J. Inst. Tech. With Danish Army, 1951—52. Mem.: N.J. C. of C. (bd. dirs.), Netherlands Royal Inst. Engrs., Danish Soc. Engrs., Am. Inst. Chem. Engrs., ASME (Outstanding Leadership award 1984). Home: Boca Raton, Fla. Died Mar. 30, 2007.

KREIS, WILLI, physician; b. Switzerland, Nov. 3, 1924; came to U.S., 1961; naturalized citizen, 1992; s. Alfred and Lina (Kuratli) K.; m. Emily Lowndes, Dec. 8, 1962; children: Elizabeth, Katherine, Christopher, Rebecca. MD, U. Zurich, Switzerland, 1954; PhD, U. Basel, Switzerland, 1957. Rsch. mem. Sandoz, Ltd., Basel, 1958-61; rsch. assoc. Sloan-Kettering Inst., Rye, N.Y., 1961-64, assoc., 1964-69, assoc., head lab., 1969-81; assoc. prof. biochemistry Grad. Sch. Med. Scis., Cornell U., 1970-81, assoc. prof. pharmacology and exptl. therapeutics, 1980-81; assoc. rsch. prof. Med. Coll., Cornell U., NYC, 1982-92, rsch. prof., from 1992; assoc. attending North Shore Univ. Hosp., Manhasset, N.Y., 1982-95, attending physician, from 1995. Rsch. prof. NYU Sch. Medicine, 1997—. Contbr. numerous articles to profl. jours. Grantee NCI, ACS, Don Monti Meml. Rsch. Found., ICI Pharm., Merck Sharp Dohme, Janssen Rsch. Found. Mem. Am. Assn. for Cancer Rsch., Am. Soc. for Clin. Oncology, Am. Soc. for Clin. Pharmacology and Therapeutics, Am. Soc. Biol. Chemists, N.Y. Acad. Scis. Home: Stamford, Conn. Died Dec. 26, 2005.

KRESHOVER, SEYMOUR JACOB, biomedical researcher, educator; b. NYC, June 22, 1912; s. Jacob Siegfried and Rose (Herzenstein) K.; m. Jacqueline Baxter, Dec. 21, 1946; children: Karen, Douglas, Janis, Lauren. BA, NYU, 1934; DDS, U. Pa., 1938; PhD, Yale U., 1942; MD, NYU, 1949; DSc (hon.), SUNY, Buffalo, 1961, U. Pa., 1967, Boston U., 1969; D of Odont., U. Goteborg, Sweden, 1973; DSc. (hon.), U. Mich., 1975. Diplomate Am. Bd. Oral Medicine. Univ. fellow U. Ill. Grad. Sch. Medicine, Chgo., 1938; asst. resident in pathology Grace New Haven (Conn.) Hosp. Yale U., 1939-41; tchg. fellow in anatomy NYU, NYC, 1946-48; prof. oral pathology to dir. dental residency program Va. Med. Coll., Richmond, 1949-56; sci. dir. to dir., asst. surgeon gen. NIDR-NIH NIH, Bethesda, Md., 1956-75; asst. surgeon gen. USPHS, Bethesda, 1970-75. Assoc. trustee bd. medicine, U. Pa., Phila., 1956-60; chmn. commn. dental rsch. Fedn. Dental Intern., Geneva, 1961-67; pres. Internat. Assn. Dental Rsch., Washington, 1962; sec., fellow AAAS, Washington, 1963-66; vis. prof. pathology Med. Coll. Va., Richmond, 1966-70, vis. prof. dentistry SUNY, Buffalo, 1975-76; regent Am. Coll. Dentists, Washington, 1968-72. Editor: Environmental Variables in Oral Disease, 1966. With U.S. Army, 1942-45, PTO; rear adm., USPHS, 1966. Carnegie fellow Yale U. Grad. Sch. Medicine, 1939-41, Calhoun scholar, 1941-42; recipient award Leadership in Oral Pathology, Tufts. U., 1960, Alumni Rsch. Award medal Columbia U., 1965, Alfred C. Fones Meml. award Conn. Dental Assn., 1970, Henry Spenadel award N.Y. Dental Soc., 1970, Pierre Fauchard medal Fauchard Acad., 1972, Kreshover Lecture ann. award NIH. Unitarian Universalist. Avocations: sailing, carpentry. Home: Winter Park, Fla. Died Jan. 23, 2006.

KRESS, ELEANOR LADD, educator; b. N.S., Can., Sept. 14, 1919; came to U.S., 1925, naturalized, 1937; d. Philip Putnam and Katherine Fraser (MacKay) Murphy; B.S., Ind. U., 1950, M.S., 1953; Ed.D., Fla. State U., 1960; m. Roy Alfred Kress, Dec. 4, 1969; children— Alexander Ladd, Lisa Ladd Kidder. Classroom tchr., then asst. supt. instrn. Pinellas County (Fla.) schs., 1950-67; assoc. prof. U. Ga., 1967-70, psychology of reading dept. Temple U., Phila., 1970-78; prof. U. S.C., Spartanburg, 1978—; tchr. NDEA seminars, Japan, 1966, Switzerland, 1967. Fellow Linguistics Inst., U. Calif., Berkeley, 1967; Fulbright sr. research fellow, Pakistan, 1983. Mem. Internat. Reading Assn. (dir. 1978-81, pres. Fla. chpt. 1960-61), AAUW (pres. Clearwater chpt. 1964-65), Assn. Childhood Edn. Internat. (pres. Fla. chpt. 1963-64), AAUP, Assn. Supervision and Curriculum Devel., Am. Ednl. Research Assn. Democrat. Club: Altrusa. Author articles in field. Home: Kutztown, Pa. Died May 31, 2006.

KRESTON, MARTIN HOWARD, advertising, marketing, public relations, and publishing executive; b. NYC, May 27, 1931; s. Henry and Frances (Stoll) Kreizvogel; m. Audrey Elizabeth Muir, Aug. 20, 1960 (dec. Jan., 1992); children: Mark Bradley, Rebecca Sarah; m. Judith Kate Stern, Dec. 15, 1996. BS in Econs, Wharton Sch., U. Pa., 1953; postgrad., N.Y. U., Northwestern U. Asst. dept. mgr. R.H. Macy & Co., NYC, 1953-54; mktg. supr., account exec. Edward H. Weiss & Co., Chgo., 1956-60; with Doyle Dane Bernbach Inc., NYC, 1960-86, v.p., mgmt. supr., 1970-72, sr. v.p., mgmt. supr., 1972, group sr. v.p., 1972-86, exec. v.p., 1984-86, cons., 1986-88; exec. v.p. England & Co. Pub. Rels., 1988-89; pres., chief exec. officer Caggiano, Kreston & Siebel, NYC, 1989-90; dir. mktg. optical group Jobson Pub. Corp., NYC, 1990; N.E. sales dir. USA Today, NYC, 1991-98; ret. With U.S. Army, 1954-56. Mem. Univ. Club Republican. Jewish. Home: New York, NY. Died Jan. 5, 2007.

KRISHER, RALPH EDWARD, JR., lawyer; b. Dayton, Ohio, Jan. 7, 1938; m. Barbara Jean Ziegler, Aug. 19, 1961; children: Ralph, Reed. M.E., U. Cin., 1962; JD, George Washington U., 1966. Bar: D.C. 1966, Ind. 1968. Patent examiner U.S. Patent Office, Washington, 1962-66; patent atty. GE, Ft. Wayne, Ind.,

1966-67; patent counsel, 1969-98. Asst. corp. patent counsel CTS Corp., Elkhart, Ind., 1967-69. Organizer, mem. governing council Pepsi Youth Soccer League, Ft. Wayne, 1977-89. Mem. D.C. Bar Assn., Ind. Bar Assn., Allen County Bar Assn. Republican. Presbyterian. Home: Fort Wayne, Ind. Died Apr. 1, 2006.

KRITCHEVSKY, DAVID, retired chemistry professor; b. Kharkov, Russia, Jan. 25, 1920; arrived in U.S., 1923, naturalized, 1929; s. Jacob and Leah (Kritchevsky) K.; m. Evelyn Sholtes, Dec. 21, 1947; children: Barbara Ann, Janice Eileen, Stephen Bennett. BS, U. Chgo., 1939, MS, 1942; PhD, Northwestern U., 1948. Chemist Ninol Labs., Chgo., 1939-46; postdoctoral fellow Fed. Inst. Tech., Zurich, Switzerland, 1948-49; biochemist Radiation Lab., U. Calif., Berkeley, 1950-52, Lederle Lab., Pearl River, NY, 1952-57, Wistar Inst., Phila., 1957—2006; prof. biochemistry Sch. Vet. Medicine U. Pa., Phila., 1965—92, prof. emeritus, 1992—2006, prof. biochemistry Sch. Medicine, 1970—81, chmn. grad. group molecular biology, 1972-84. Mem. USPHS study sect. Nat. Heart Inst., 1964-68, 72-76; chmn. rsch. com. Spl. Dairy Industry Bd., 1963-70; food and nutrition bd. NAS, 1976-82. Author: Cholesterol, 1958; Western Hemisphere editor Atherosclerosis, 1978-90, cons. editor, 1990-2006; contbr. articles to profl. jours. Recipient Rsch. Career award Nat. Heart Inst., 1962, Herman award Am. Soc. Clin. Nutrition, 1992, Disting. Svc. award U. N.C. Inst. Nutrition, 1993, Auenbrugger medal U. Graz, Austria, 1994, SUPELCO/AOCS award, 1996, Lifetime Achievement award Am. Inst. for Cancer Rsch., 1996; first recipient David Kritchevsky Nutrition Excellence award, Am. Soc. Nutrition, 2006; Caspar Wistar scholar, 1992. Fellow: AAAS, Am. Soc. Oil Chemists (chmn. methods com. 1963—64), Am. Coll. Nutrition (award 1978), Am. Inst. Nutrition (pres. 1979, Borden award 1974), Am. Oil Chemists Soc.; mem.: Am. Oil Chemistry Soc., Internat. Soc. Fat Rsch., Am. Heart Assn. (spl. recognition coun. on atherosclerosis 1993), Arteriosclerosis Coun., Soc. Exptl. Biology and Medicine (pres. 1985—87), Am. Chem. Soc. (award Phila. sect. 1977), Am. Soc. Biol. Chemists. Achievements include research on role vehicle when cholesterol and fat produces atherosclerosis in rabbits, effects of saturated and unsaturated fat, deposition of orally administered cholesterol in aorta of man and rabbit, caloric restriction and cancer. Home: Bryn Mawr, Pa. Died Nov. 20, 2006.

KRONBERGER, ROBERT SAMUEL, naval officer; b. Boston, Dec. 17, 1917; s. Samuel and Barbara (Bock) K.; m. Marion Alberta McLaughlin, Nov. 23, 1978; children— David Walter, Jessie Marie. Student, U.S. Armed Forces Inst. Commd. U.S. Navy, 1935, advanced through grades to comdr., ret., 1970; project engr. ILS Analists, Litton Industries, Culver City, 1970-72; ILS mgr. Probabilistic Software Inc., Montrose, Calif., 1972-74; engr., sr. project mgr. Hughes Aircraft Co., Los Angeles, 1974-80; ret.; cons. in field, 1980—. Contbr. articles to profl. jours. Decorated numerous medals, U.S. Navy. Mem. Am. Soc. Naval Engrs., Ret. Officers Assn., Fleet Res. Assn., U.S. Naval Inst. V.F.W., Am. Legion, Amvets, Pearl Harbor Survivors Assn. (pres. 1975-76), Palm Springs Ret. Officers Assn. Republican. Presbyterian. Club: Jesters of Desert Club. Lodges: Elks, Masons, Shriner, Nat. Sojourners, Heros of 76, Order of Quetzacoatal, Royal Order Jesters. Died Oct. 5, 2006.

KRONFELD, DAVID SCHULTZ, veterinarian, educator; b. Auckland, New Zealand, Nov. 5, 1928; came to U.S., 1957; s. Samuel Tonga and Clara Louisa (Schultz) K.; m. Susan Donoghue, Apr. 8, 1986. B.V.Sc., U. Queensland, Brisbane, Australia, 1952, M.V.Sc., 1957, D.Sc. in Biochemistry, 1972; PhD in Physiology, U. Calif., Davis, 1959; MA, U. Pa., 1971. Demonstrator U. Queensland, 1953-54, lectr., 1954-57, U. Calif., Davis, 1957-59, asst. prof., 1959-60, U. Pa., Phila., 1960-63, assoc. prof., 1963-67, prof., 1967-81, Elizabeth Clark prof., 1981-88; Paul Mellon prof. Virginia Poly. Inst., Blacksburg, from 1988. Author: Vitamin and Mineral Supplementation for Dogs and Cats, 1989; editor: Canine Nutrition, 1972; patentee in field. Recipient Outstanding Achievement medal N.Y. Farmers, 1983, medal City of Blagnac, France, 1990; King George VI Meml. fellow English Speaking Union, 1957. Mem. Am. Coll. Vet. Internal Medicine (diplomate), Am. Coll. Vet. Nutrition (diplomate, chmn. 1988-89), Am. Acad. Vet. Nutrition (pres. 1973-75), Royal Coll. Vet. Surgeons (U.K.). Avocations: biking, hiking. Home: Pembroke, Va. Died Dec. 17, 2006.

KRONICK, DAVID A., librarian; b. Connelsville, Pa., Oct. 5, 1917; s. Barnett L. and Rose (Miller) K.; m. Marilyn Abramson, Oct. 25, 1959; children— Steven Leonard, Leah BA, Adelbert Coll., 1939; BS in Library Sci., Western Reserve U., 1940; PhD, U. Chgo., 1956. Librarian Western Reserve U. Sch. of Medicine, Cleve., 1946-49; librarian U. Mich. Med. Libr., Ann Arbor, 1955-59; dir. Cleve. Med. Library, Cleve., 1959-64; chief reference dir. Nat. Library of Medicine, Bethesda, Md., 1964-65; dir. U. Tex. Health Sci. Ctr. Lib., San Antonio, 1965-84. Bus. mgr. Med. Library Assn., Chgo., 1958-59, mem. bd., 1967-68; pres. Tex. Council Health Sci. Libraries, 1968-69; mem. rev. com. Nat. Library Medicine, 1969-73 Author: History of Scientific Periodicals, 2d edit., 1976, Literature of the Life Sciences, 1985; contbr. articles to profl. jours. Vice pres. South Tex. Health Edn. Ctr., San Antonio, 1970-80; pres. San Antonio Chamber Music Soc., 1976-79. Served to capt. U.S. Army, 1944-46 Fellow AAAS, 1964, Council on Library Resources, 1972 Fellow Med. Library Assn.; mem. Hist. Sci. Soc., Am. Assn. for History of Medicine Jewish. Avocations: chamber music; gardening. Home: San Antonio, Tex. Died Feb. 12, 2006.

KROTINGER, SHEILA, secondary school educator; m. Nathan J. Krotinger, Mar. 7, 1949; children: Eve, Michelle. AA summa cum laude, East Los Angeles Coll., 1956; BA magna cum laude, Calif. State U., Fullerton, 1966. Cert. life credential Calif. Tchr. Norwalk-La Mirada Unified Sch. Dist., Calif., from 1968. Contbr. articles to profl. jours.; editor, prodr.: (cable TV shows). Publicity dir. La Mirada Friends of Theatre, from 1982; chmn. City of La Mirada Hist. Heritage Commn., 1991—94; founder Heritage Coalition of South Calif., chmn., emeritus bd. dirs.; v.p. La Mirada Dem. Club; mem. initiative com. Californians for Non-Smokers Rights, 1980; founder Temple Beth Shalom, Whittier, Calif., 1952, Temple Beth Ohr, La Mirada, 1960; bd. dirs. La Mirada Festival of Arts, 1981—82, publicity dir., from 1982; bd. dirs. Friends of McNally Ranch, La Mirada, 1984; mem. by-laws com., co-chmn. Hist. Com. Friends of La Mirada Civic Theatre, 1983; bd. dirs. Sr. Net Learning Ctr., La Mirada. Recipient Excellence Sr. Innovation award, Vols. in Action, 1998, Lifetime Achievement award, 2004. Home: La Mirada, Calif. Died Mar. 4, 2006.

KRUECKEBERG, DONALD ALLEN, urban planning educator; b. Ft. Wayne, Ind., Aug. 31, 1938; s. Ferdinand H. and Ruth M. (Vollmer) K.; m. Lenore J. Spengler, Sept. 4, 1961; 1 child, John Christian. BS cum laude, Mich. State U., 1960; M of City Planning, U. Pa., 1962, PhD, 1966. Asst. prof. Mich. State U., East Lansing, 1965-67, Rutgers U., New Brunswick, N.J., 1967-70, assoc. prof., 1970-75, prof. I, 1975-84, prof. II, from 1984, acting dean faculty of planning, from 1986. Author: Urban Planning Analysis, 1974, Local Population, 1978, Introduction to Planning History, 1983, The American Planner, 1983; editor: Jour. Am. Inst. Planners, 1976-78. Chair Zoning Bd., Highland Park, N.J., 1978-80; bd. dirs. Camden (N.J.) Luth. Housing Corp., 1986—, Alliance for Affordable Housing, 1987—. Recipient Outstanding Service award Am. Inst. Planners, 1978. Mem. Am. Planning Assn. (Disting. Service award 1984), Planning History Group (exec. com. 1982-84), Soc. Am. City and Regional Planning History (v.p. 1987—), Assn. Collegiate Schs. Planning (pres. 1987—). Clubs: Raritan Yacht (Perth Amboy, N.J.) (vice commodore 1988). Home: New Brunswick, NJ. Died Dec. 15, 2006.

KRUGER, ARTHUR NEWMAN, speech communication educator, author; b. Boston, Feb. 4, 1916; s. Samuel and Minnie (Meline) K.; m. Eleanor Weisbrot, Dec. 28, 1941; children— Robert Samuel, Marylin Jane. Student, CCNY, 1932-34; AB, U. Ala., 1936, postgrad., 1937-38; PhD, La. State U., 1941. Instr. Essex Jr. Coll., Newark, 1940-41, N.C. State U., Raleigh, 1941-42; v.p. Empco, Atlantic City, 1946-47; asst. prof. Wilkes Coll., Wilkes-Barre, Pa., 1947-54, asso. prof., 1954-59, prof., 1959-62, dir. forensics, 1948-62; prof., dir. forensics, chmn. dept. speech communication C.W. Post Coll., Greenvale, N.Y., 1962-84, prof. emeritus, from 1984. Author: Modern Debate: Its Logic and Strategy, 1960; author or co-author: Championship Debating, 1961, Argumentation and Debate: A Classified Bibliography, 1964, rev. edit., 1975, Championship Debating, Vol. II, 1967, Counterpoint: Debates About Debate, 1968, Essentials of Logic, 1968, rev. edit., 1976, Workbook for Essentials of Logic, 1968, Effective Speaking: A Complete Course, 1970; Contbr. to: Rhetoric of Our Times, 1969, The Comparative Advantage Case, 1970, Ventures in Research, 1974, also to publs. in field. Bd. dirs. Eastern Debate Inst., Greenvale, N.Y., 1965—. Served to 1st lt. AUS, SIS and OSS, 1942-46. Recipient Presdl. Unit citation, Four Battle Stars. Mem. A.A.U.P., Speech Communication Assn. Am., Am. Forensic Assn., Speech Assn. Eastern States, Rhetoric Soc. Am., Eastern Forensic Assn., Phi Delta Kappa, Delta Sigma Rho, Tau Kappa Alpha. Clubs: University (L.I.). Home: Wynnewood, Pa. Died Dec. 24, 2005.

KRUSELL, CHARLES ROBERT, business executive; b. Virginia, Minn., July 14, 1924; s. Charles Emil and Helga Louise (Hoilein) K.; m. Virginia Mary Eaton, Apr. 10, 1946; children: Sally Virginia, Patricia Eaton, Barbara Louise, Charlene Roberta, Margaret Jean. Student, Va. Jr. Coll., 1942-43; BBA, U. Minn., 1949. Office mgr. dept. taxation div. income tax State of Minn., 1949-55; asst. exec. dir. Mpls. Housing and Redevel. Authority, 1955-56, exec. dir., 1966-70, Greater Mpls. Met. Housing Corp., from 1970; exec. v.p. Greater Mpls. C. of C., 1973-80; pres. Industry Square Pen. Co., Mpls., from 1981. Bd. dirs. Minn. Housing Fin. Agy.; cons. dept. housing and urban devel. Nat. Capital Housing Authority; lectr. dept. urban affairs U. Minn. Chmn. conv. and tourism commn., City of Mpls.; commr. Met. Sports Facilities Commn. With U.S. Army, 1943-46. Mem. Nat. Assn. Housing and Redevel. Ofcls. (dir.), Mpls. Club, Alumni Club, Edina Country Club. Presbyterian. Home: Saint Paul, Minn. Died Dec. 12, 2006.

KRUSKAL, MARTIN DAVID, mathematical physicist, astrophysicist, educator; b. NYC, Sept. 28, 1925; m. Laura Lashinsky, 1950; children: Karen, Kerry, Clyde. BS, U. Chgo., 1945; MS, NYU, 1948, PhD in Math., 1952; DSc (hon.), Herlot-Watt U., 2000. Rsch. scientist Plasma Phys. Lab., Princeton U., 1951—61, prof. astrophys. sci., 1961—2006, prof. math., 1981—89, prof. emeritus, 1989—2006; David Hilbert prof. math. Rutgers U., New Brunswick, NJ, 1989—2006. Trustee Soc. for Indsl. & Applied Math., 1985—91, Math. Scis. Edn. Bd. of NRC, 1986—89; Ext. Adv. Com. Ctr. for Nonlinear Studies, Los Alamos Nat. Lab., 1980—2006. Co-recipient Leroy P. Steele prize for Seminal Contribution to Rsch., Am. Math. Soc., 2006; recipient Dannie Heineman Math. Phys. prize, 1983, Potts Gold medal, Franklin Inst., 1986, Nat. Medal Sci., NSF, 1993, John von Neumann Prize, Soc. Indsl. and Applied Math., 1994, James Clerk Maxwell Prize, Internat. Congress on Indsl. and Applied Math., 2003; fellow Japan Soc. Promotion Sci., 1979; sr. fellow, NSF, 1959—60, Weizmann Inst. Sci., 1973—74. Fellow: Am. Phys. Soc., Royal Soc. Edinburgh (hon.); mem.: NAS (chmn. sect. of applied math. scis. 1990—93, award in Applied Math. and Numerical Analysis 1989), AAAS, Russian Acad. Nat. Scis. (fgn.), Royal Soc. London (fgn.) (fgn.), Math. Assn. Am., Am. Math. Soc. (Gibbs lectr. 1979). Home: Arroyo Seco, N.Mex. Died Dec. 26, 2006.

KUBIAK, TIMOTHY JAMES, geography educator; b. Toledo, Nov. 22, 1942; s. Benedict J. and Alice T. (Hintz) K.; m. Lavinia Nancy Harvey, Jan. 1, 1982; m. Sandra Sue Schlosser, June 6, 1964 (div. 1976); children: Alex, Sarah. BA, U. Toledo, 1965; MA, Mich. State U., 1967, PhD, 1973. Instr. Wright State U., Dayton, Ohio, 1967-71; prof. Eastern Ky. U., Richmond, from 1973. Research asst. USDA Econ. Resource Service, East Lansing, 1971-73; planning cons. City Richmond, 1975-76, City Berea, 1983, City Corbin, 1987. Author: Soup Line, 1973, Companion Guide to Portugal, 1989; contbr. articles to profl. jours. Chmn. adv. bd. Child Devel. Ctrs. of Bluegrass, Richmond, 1987-88. Named to Hon. Order Ky. Cols., 1979; Fulbright scholar, 1984; NASA fellow, 1975. Mem. Travel and Tourism Rsch. Assn., Am. Planning Assn., Flubright Alumni Assn., Am. Inst. Cert. Planning, Polish Inst. Arts and Scis. Am., Rotary (bd. dirs. 1987, v.p. 1989, pres. 1990). Lodges: Rotary (bd. dirs. 1987). Democrat. Roman Catholic. Avocation: travel. Home: Atlantic Bch, Fla. Died June 24, 2007.

KUHL, FREDERICK WILLIAM, English language and journalism educator; b. Camrose, Alta., Can., Mar. 8, 1923; parents Am. citizens; s. Edward and Frances Leopoltine (Roth) K.; m. Beverly Jean Allen, May 5, 1950; children: Katherine A-F., William E., Suzanne J. BS, U. Oreg., 1947, MS, 1961; EdD, Nova U., 1981. Cert. jr. coll. tchr., community coll. supr.; cert. naval intelligence profl. Asst. dir. pub. info. Aluminum Co. Am., Vancouver, Wash., 1947-51; dir. pub. info. Housing Authority-Urban Redevel., Portland, Oreg., 1951-52; reporter, columnist, city editor Enterprise-Courier, Oregon City, Oreg., 1952-56; corr. The Portland Oregonian, Oregon City, 1953-56, 60-61; tchr. English and journalism Clackamas High Sch., Milwaukie, Oreg., 1957-59; pub. info. dir. English and journalism Willamette U., Salem, Oreg., 1960-61; tchr. English and journalism David Douglas High Sch., Portland, 1961-65; dir. pub. info., prof. English and journalism American River Coll., Sacramento, 1965-88, emeritus, from 1988. Editorial cons. Goodyear Pub. Co., L.A., 1975-76, Wadsworth Pub. Co., Belmont, Calif., 1976-77, Peek Pub. Co., Palo Alto, Calif., 1989-91; staff instr. Unit Pub. Affairs Sch., Calif. N.G., Sacramento, 1982-90. Contbr. chpts. to books. Chair bd. edn. Faith Luth. Ch. and Sch., Fair Oaks, Calif., 1972-74, 89-91; mem. adv. com. Martin Manor, Sacramento, 1985—; editorial advisor Calif. N.G. mag. Grizzly, 1982—. Lt. (j.g.) U.S. Navy, 1943-46, PTO, lt. comdr. USNR ret. Recipient Commendation medal, medal of Merit Mil. Dept., State of Calif., 1992, Pres.'s award Vancouver Jaycees, 1950; named Man of Yr., Optimist Internat., 1955 Mem. Assn. for Edn. in Journalism and Mass Communication, Soc. Profl. Journalists, C.C. Journalism Assn., Naval Intelligence Profls., Naval Res. Assn. (life), The Res. Officers Assn. (life), Kappa Tau Alpha. Democrat. Lutheran. Avocations: reading, golf, travel. Home: Gold River, Calif. Died Apr. 9, 2007.

KUHN, BOWIE KENT, lawyer, former major league baseball commissioner; b. Takoma Park, Md., Oct. 28, 1926; s. Louis & Alice Kuhn; m. Luisa Hegeler; children: Stephen, Alix; step children: Paul, George BA, Princeton, 1947; LL.B., U. Va. 1950. Bar: N.Y. 1951, U.S. Supreme Ct. 1972. With Willkie Farr & Gallagher LLP, 1950-69; commr. pro tempore MLB 1969, commr., 1969-84; of counsel Willkie, Farr & Gallagher LLP, 1984-87; ptnr. Myerson & Kuhn LLP, NYC, 1988-89; pres The Kent Group Inc., Ponte Vedra Beach, Fla., 1990—2007 Sports Franchises, Inc., Milford, Conn., 1992—2007. Bd. mem Ave Maria Found.; chmn. adv. bd. Thomas Moore Law Ct Co-author: (with Martin Appel) Hardball: The Education of Baseball Commissioner, 1987. Achievements include being th youngest person to be named commissioner of major leagu basebal, 42 years old. Died Mar. 15, 2007.

KUHN, DENIS GLEN, architectural firm executive; BArch Pratt Inst., 1964. Registered arch., N.Y.; cert. Nat. Coun. Archt Registration Bds. Arch., draftsperson Giorgio Cavaglieri, Arch 1964-68, assoc., 1968-74, sr. assoc., 1974-79; assoc. Ehrenkrantz & Eckstut Archs., P.C., 1979-84, sr. assoc., 1984-87 prin., 1987—2007. Adj. prof. architecture N.Y. Inst. Tech Westbury, N.Y., 1976-88. Prin. works include Bklyn. Club, N.Y Shakespeare Festival, Blackwell Farm House, Roosevelt Island N.Y., Mid Manhattan Libr., Old 83d Precinct Sta. House, Bklyn Soldiers and Sailors Monument, Pitts., Mcpl. Bldg., N.Y.C Carnegie Lab. Bldg. at Stevens Inst. Tech., Hoboken, N.J., Tow Hall, N.Y.C., Balt. Gas & Electric Co. Bldg., Bethesda Ter., Ct Park, N.Y.C., Fulton Hall at Mcht. Marine Acad., Kings Poin N.Y., Sealand Industries, Elizabeth, N.J., One Church S Nashville, CUNY Law Sch., N.Y., Temple Rodef Shalom, Pitts Equitable Bldg., N.Y.C., The Dakota, N.Y.C., War Mem Trenton, N.J., The Lafayette Restaurant at Drake Swiss Hote N.Y.C., The Jockey Club, N.Y.C., Smithsonian Inst. Nat. Mu Am. Indian, Washington, Alexander Hamilton U.S. Custo House, Bowling Green, N.Y., many others. Mem. AIA (N.Y chpt., chmn. hist. bldg. com. 1972-75, 92-94, editor Ocul 1976-79, dir. archs.-in-tng. program 1986-88, 1st v.p. 1988-8 pres. 1989-90, chmn. Oculus com. 1994). Died May 10, 200

KULAKOWSKI, BOHDAN TADEUSZ, mechanical eng neering educator; b. Piotrkow Trybunalski, Poland, June 2 1942; came to U.S., 1979; s. Tadeusz and Krystyna (Kolacinsk K.; m. Barbara Elzbieta Gluszkiewicz, Oct. 29, 1964; childre Dorota Anna Smith, Dominik. MS in Engring., Warsaw Tech., Poland, 1966; PhD, Polish Acad. Scis., Warsaw, 197 Rsch. asst., rsch. assoc., then head rsch. group Inst. Glass a Ceramics, Warsaw, 1965-74; head process control div. Comput Ctr. for Bldg. Industry, Warsaw, 1975-79; prof. mech. engrin Pa. State U., University Park, 1979-91, prof., from 1991, dir. P Transp. Inst., from 1992. Bd. dirs. Transp. Safety Rsch. Allian Pitts., 1992—; cons. Micromation Sys. Inc., Airline Pilots Ass ins. cos.; univ. liaison Transp. Rsch. Bd., Washington, 1994— Author: (with J.L. Shearer) Dynamic Modeling and Control Engineering Systems, 1990; editor: Vehicle-Road Interacti 1994; contbr. articles to profl. jours. Recipient premiere tc award Pa. State U. Engring. Soc., 1994; UN Econ. Commn. Europe fellow U. York, Eng., 1974; Fulbright scholar, 19 Mem. ASME, ASHRAE, Am. Soc. for Engring. Edn., S Automotive Engrs., Pi Tau Sigma (hon.). Achievements inclu design of Pennsylvania Transportation Institute drag sled tes to measure slip resistance of walking surfaces. Died Mar. 2006.

KULZICK, KEN STAFFORD, retired lawyer, writer; Milw., July 20, 1927; s. Earl Joseph and Claire Agnes (Bla K.; m. Patricia Louise Siekert, June 19, 1949; 1 child, K Kulzick Stafford. PhB, Marquette U., Milw., 1950; JD, UCL 1956. Bar: Calif. 1956, U.S. Dist. Ct. (no. and cen. dists.) Ca 1956, U.S. Ct. Appeals (9th cir.) 1956. Tchg. asst., rschr. UCL 1953—56; asst. U.S. atty. (honor grad program) Dept. Justi L.A., San Francisco, 1956-58; ptnr. Lillick, McHose & Charl LA, 1958-86, Liebig & Kulzick, LA, 1987-91, Gipson, Hoffm & Pancione, LA, 1991-94; copyright lawyer, past pres. L Copyright Soc. Media cons. specializing in dramatic docum taries, 1958—; media advisor League of Women Voters, L.

1986, 90; lectr. UCLA, 1987—. Contbr. articles to L.A. Lawyer mag., EMMY mag., Entertainment Law Reporter, others; bd. editors UCLA Law Rev., 1954-56. Served to lt. USN, 1950-53; Korea Died June 30, 2007.

KUNZLER, JOHN EUGENE, physicist; b. Willard, Utah, Apr. 25, 1923; s. John Jacob and Freida (Meier) K.; m. Lois McDonald, Dec. 29, 1950; children: Carol Kunzler Blaine, Marilyn Kunzler Barker, Bonnie Kunzler Stein, Kim Kunzler Tomeo. BS in Chem. Engring, U. Utah; PhD, U. Calif., Berkeley. With AT & T Bell Labs., Murray Hill, NJ, from 1952, dir. electronic materials lab., 1969-73, dir. electronic materials and device lab., 1973-79, dir. electronic materials, processes and devices lab., 1979-83, dir. magnetic bubble subsystems and common tech. support lab., 1983-85, dir. future devices study ctr., 1985-86; retired, 1986. Contbr. articles to profl. jours.; patentee in field. Recipient John Price Wetherill medal Franklin Inst., 1964; Internat. prize for new materials Am. Phys. Soc., 1979; Kamerlingh Onnes medal, 1979 Fellow Am. Phys. Soc.; mem. Am. Chem. Soc., Nat. Acad. Engring., Sigma Xi, Tau Beta Pi, Alpha Chi Sigma. Home: Port Murray, NJ. Died Jan. 11, 2006.

KUPPERMAN, ROBERT HARRIS, former federal official; b. NYC, May 12, 1935; s. Nathan Greenspan and Rose (Winnick) K.; m. Helen Slotnick, Dec. 23, 1967; 1 child, Tamara; m. Barbara Norris BA, NYU, 1956, PhD (fellow), 1962. Prin. mathematician Republic Aviation Co., Farmingdale, N.Y., 1959-60; sr. researcher Calif. Inst. Tech., 1960-62; exec. adv. Douglas Aircraft, Santa Monica, Calif., 1962-64; sr. staff mem. Inst. Def. Analyses, Arlington, Va., 1964-67; asst. dir. Office Emergency Preparedness, Washington, 1967-73; dep. exec. dir. Pres.'s Property Rev., 1971-73; adv. counter-terrorism Nat. Security Council; mem. Cabinet Com. to Combat Terrorism; chmn. Interagy. Com. Mass. Destruction and Terrorism, 1976-78; vis. prof. U. Md., 1974-76; dep. asst. dir. mil. and econ. affairs ACDA, Washington, 1973-75, chief scientist, 1975-79; exec. dir. Ctr. for Strategic and Internat. Studies, 1979-83, sr. adv., 1983—2006; pres. Robert H. Kupperman and Assocs., from 1979, RGD Trading Ltd., 1983-85; mem. Army Sci. Bd., 1979-86; cons. to chief of staff U.S. Army, 1979-83; cons. to dep. sec. US Dept. Transp., 1980-83; cons. to under sec. US Dept. Def., 1980-83, cons. to dir., US Secret Svc., 1980-83; prin., treas. Mobern Electric Corp., 1984-88. Mem. math. dept. faculty NYU, 1956-59; lectr. econs. U. Md., 1965-66; cons. Army Security Agy., 1965, CSC, 1965, Rand Corp., 1979-84, Sandia Nat. Labs., 1980-81, ABC News, 1980-81, NBC News, 1985-86; sr. fellow Los Alamos Sci. Lab.; adv. bd. Fed. Emergency Mgmt. Agy., 1985-93. Author: (with H.A. Smith) Mathematical Foundations of Systems Analysis, 1969, The Potential for Energy Conservation; The Potential for Energy Conservation: Substitution for Scarce Fuels, 1973, Facing Tomorrow's Terrorist Incident Today, 1977; (with D.M. Trent) Terrorism, Threat, Reality, Response, 1979; (with J. Garn and D. Innouye) Opportunities for Crisis Control in a Nuclear Age, 1985, Combating Terrorism: A Matter of Leverage, 1986; (with W. J. Taylor, Jr.) Strategic Requirements for the Army to the Year 2000; (with Taylor and Williamson) Low Intensity Conflict; (with J. Garn and D. Boren) Realistic Arms Control Today: New Directions in Nuclear Weapons Policy; (with Jeff Kamen) Final Warning, 1989; contbr. articles to profl. jours. Mem. Council on Foreign Relations. Recipient Founder's Day award N.Y. U., 1962; Outstanding Service award Exec. Office of Pres., 1968, 69, 70, 71; Disting. Service award, 1973; Order Paul Revere Patriots State Mass., 1970; Presdl. citation, 1971, 73; Superior Honor award ACDA, 1977 Fellow Ops. Rsch. Soc., N.Y. Acad. Scis.; mem. AAAS, Am. Math. Soc., Washington Ops. Rsch. Coun., Soc. Indsl. and Applied Math., Internat. Inst. Strategic Studies, Internat. Club (Washington), Univ. Club, Sigma Xi, Zeta Beta Tau. Home: Washington, DC. Died Nov. 14, 2006.

KUSAR, DANIEL DUSAN, aluminum manufacturing company executive; b. Ljubljana, Yugoslavia, May 9, 1928; came to U.S., 1950, naturalized, 1953; s. Savo A. and Angelica Setina K.; M.B.A., U. Chgo., 1957; m. Rosanne M. Egelske, Sept. 24, 1960; children— Angelica, Jennifer. Asst. to pres. Calumet Steel div. Borg Warner Corp., 1957-61; pres. Kusar Investment Corp., 1961-67; corp. fin. asso. Hornblower-Weeks, Hemphill, Noyes, 1967-71; chmn., pres. Darfield Industries, Inc., Sun Valley, Calif., 1971—; chmn. Sun Valley Archtl. Co., Sun Valley Products, Inc. Served with U.S. Army, 1951-53. Republican. Roman Catholic. Clubs: University, Economics, Jonathan. Died Sept. 8, 2006.

KUYKENDALL, JANICE HAVILAND, marine supply company executive; b. Houston, June 17, 1944; d. John Thompson and Doris Evelyn (Brock) Rector; m. Dean Kings Haviland, May 12, 1962 (div. Fed. 1981); children— Carol, Shelby; m. 2d, Herbert Brent Kuykendall, Jan. 1, 1984. Student U. Tex., 1962-64, Tex. A&M U., 1964-65. Far East regional mgr. Grolier Internat. Corp., Tokyo, 1967-72; dir. Tech. Ctr., Inc., Houston, 1972-74; sr. sales counselor Snelling & Snelling, Houston, 1974-78; v.p. Blue Water Marine Supply, Houston, 1978-84; pres. AIMS, marine supply co., Houston, 1984—. Mem. Marine Services Assn. Tex. (dir.), Tex. Safety Assn., Nat. Assn. Female Execs., Propeller Club Houston. Republican. Home: Corpus Christi, Tex. Died Aug. 29, 2006.

KUZELA, DENNIS MICHAEL, lawyer; b. Lorain, Ohio, Sept. 16, 1944; s. Peter Michael and Mary (Puskas) K.; m. Elizabeth Kay Davies, June 26, 1971; children— Darren, Denise. B.S., Kent State U., 1967, B.S. summa cum laude in Math, 1968; J.D. with honors, Cleve. State U., 1972. Bar: Ohio, U.S. Dist. Ct. (no. dist.) Ohio. Tchr., Lorain City Schs., 1969-73; asst. prosecutor Lorain County, Elyria, 1973-81; sole practice law, Lorain. Mem. Lorain City Council, 1972-73; bd. dirs. Mayor's Youth Council, Lorain, 1972-73; treas. Young Democrats, Lorain, 1974-75; Bd. dirs., mem. exec. com. Lorain County Urban League, Elyria, 1984. Mem. Ohio Bar Assn., Lorain County Bar Assn., Nat. Dist. Attys. Assn. Democrat. Roman Catholic. Home: Lorain, Ohio. Died Aug. 17, 2006.

KYLE, JANET HINKLE, modeling school administrator; b. Portland, Oreg., Aug. 14, 1918; d. Walter Berkeley and Minnie (Naylor) Hinkle; m. David M. Kyle, May 4, 1940 (dec. 1980); children— Michaele Kyle Leitch, Kris Kyle Ross, David M. III. B.S.S., Oreg. State U., 1939. Lic. irrigation contractor; lic. psychologist, Fla. Founder, owner, operator Turnabout Modeling Sch., and Agy. Stuart, Fla., 1970—, Vero Beach, Fla., 1973-85, owner, operator St. Lucie Pump and Water Supply, Stuart, 1980-84; owner, mgr. Kyle Ctr., Stuart, 1980-85; Columnist, Mil. Press, Hawaii, 1962-65. Fashion editor Indian River Life, 1979-81. Author, editor: Save Your Blushes, 1938. Mem. Stuart C. of C., Internat. Talent/Modeling Schs. Assn. (sec. 1983-84, v.p. 1984-85, bd. dirs. 1978-85), Internat. Modeling Assn. (adv. bd.), Internat. Modeling and Talent Assn., Alpha Chi Omega Panhellenic. Republican. Avocations: reading; travel; writing. Died Apr. 14, 2007.

LABARRE, CARL ANTHONY, retired federal agency administrator; b. Sherwood, ND, July 16, 1918; s. William Paul and Josephine K. LaB.; m. Persis Wester, Sept. 9, 1941; 1 son, William Paul, II. Student, U. Mont., 1936-40; postgrad., Naval Acad. Postgrad. Sch., 1945-46; grad., Naval War Coll., 1958-59, Advanced Mgmt. Program, Harvard U. Commd. ensign U.S. Navy, 1941, advanced through grades to capt., 1971; served in various fin., inventory control systems and purchasing assignments, to 1971; insp. gen. (Naval Supply Systems Command), to 1971; ret., 1971; dep. dir. materials mgmt. service GPO, Washington, 1971-75, dir. materials mgmt. service, 1975, asst. public printer, supt. documents, 1975-82. Decorated Navy Commendation medal with V, Joint Service commendation medal, Legion of Merit with gold star; recipient Public Printers Disting. Service award, 1977, 81 Mem.: Harvard Bus. Sch. (Washington). Home: Alexandria, Va. Died June 28, 2007.

LA BLANC, CHARLES WESLEY, JR., financial consultant; b. Bayshore, L.I., N.Y., June 4, 1925; s. Charles Wesley and Anne (Dobson) LaB.; m. Marie Dolan, Oct. 26, 1963 (dec. Jan. 1985); children: Charles Wesley III, Gregory, Suzanne; m. Joan H. Trapp, Dec. 29, 1993. BS, Tufts Coll., 1949; MBA, NYU, 1952, PhD, 1956. Securities portfolio mgr. Manhattan Life Ins. Co., NYC, 1952-57; asst. to pres. Magnavox Co., Ft. Wayne, Ind., 1957-60; security analyst C.W. LaBlanc & Assos., NYC, 1960-62; treas. Macke Co., Cheverly, Md., 1962-74, dir., 1974-80; exec. v.p., sec.-treas., dir. After Six, Inc., Phila., 1972-84; pres. Bert Paley Ltd., Inc. subs., 1976-77; chmn. bd. dirs. Cymaticolor, 1983-84; CFO Std. Telecom. Sys. Inc., South Hackensack, N.J., 1983-87, also bd. dirs. Pres. Std. Profit Sharing Fund, 1987—; bd. dirs. Acad. of Vocal Arts. Pres. Queens County Young Reps., 1955-57; bd. dirs. adv. council Temple U. With AC USNR, 1943-46. Fellow N.Y. Soc. Security Analysts; mem. Washington Soc. Investment Analysts, Fin. Analysts Phila., Fin. Execs. Inst., Am. Acctg. Assn., Am. Soc. Ins. Mgmt., Pub. Rels. Soc. Am., Nat. Assn. Bus. Economists, Nat. Investor Rels. Inst., Nat. Assn. Corp. Dirs., Phila. Securities Assn. (pres. 1991, bd. dirs.), Am. Stock Exch. Club, Union League, The Bond Club. Died Mar. 25, 2006.

LABOUISSE, HENRY RICHARDSON, former ambassador; b. New Orleans, Feb. 11, 1904; s. Henry Richardson and Frances Devereux (Huger) L.; m. Elizabeth Scriven Clark, June 29, 1935 (dec. 1945); 1 dau., Anne (Mrs. Martin Peretz); m. Eve Curie, Nov. 19, 1954. AB, Princeton U., 1926, LL.D.; LL.B., Harvard U., 1929; LL.D., U. Bridgeport, Lafayette Coll., Tulane U.; L.H.D., Hartwick Coll., Brandeis U. Bar: N.Y. 1930. Practice with firm of Taylor, Blanc, Capron and Marsh (and successor), NYC, 1929-40; mem. firm Mitchell, Taylor, Capron and Marsh, 1940-41; with State Dept., 1941-51, chief div. def. materials, 1943, chief Eastern Hemisphere div., 1944; minister econ. affairs Am. embassy, Paris, 1944-45; spl. rep. in France FEA, 1944-45; spl. asst. to under sec. for econ. affairs Washington, 1945-46; spl. asst. and econ. advisor to dir. Office European Affairs, 1946-48; head U.S. del. Econ. Commn. Europe, 1948; coordinator fgn. aid and assistance, 1948-49; dir. Office Brit. Commonwealth and No. European Affairs, 1949-51; chief ECA (Marshall Plan) mission to France, 1951-52; chief MSA spl. mission to France, 1953-54; dir. UN Relief and Works Agy. for Palestine Refugees, 1954-58; cons. IBRD., 1959-61; dir. ICA, 1961; U.S. ambassador to Greece, 1962-65; exec. dir. UNICEF (orgn. won Nobel Peace prize 1965), 1965-79. Bd. dirs. Farmers' Museum, Bassett Hosp., Cooperstown, N.Y., Internat. Inst. for Environment and Devel., Washington; trustee Clark Found., N.Y.; chmn. Am. Farm Sch., Thessoloniki, Greece. Mem. N.Y. State Hist. Assn. (dir.), Council Fgn. Relations. Clubs: Metropolitan (Washington), Chevy Chase (Washington); Century Assn. (N.Y.C.). Episcopalian. Home: New York, NY. Died May 25, 1987; interred New Orleans, La.*

LACHNER, BERNARD JOSEPH, hospital administrator; b. Rock Island, Ill., Oct. 13, 1927; s. Bernard Joseph and Anne Lenore (Canty) L.; m. Berneice Groen, Aug. 16, 1952; children: Bernard Joseph, Thomas Frederick, James Timothy. Student, U. Notre Dame, 1945-46, student, 1947-48; BS, Creighton U., 1950; MBA, U. Chgo., 1952; D.MS (hon.), Med. Coll. Ohio, Toledo, 1981. Adminstrv. intern to adminstrv. asst. Iowa Methodist Hosp., Des Moines, 1950-54, asst. adminstr., 1954-58; assoc. adminstr. Ohio State U. Hosps., Columbus, 1958-62, adminstr., 1962-71; asst. dean Ohio State U. Coll. Medicine, Columbus, 1961-71, asst. v.p. med. affairs, 1971, v.p. adminstrv. ops., 1971-72, prof. grad. program hosp. and health services adminstrn., 1967-72; pres., chief exec. officer Evanston (Ill.) Hosp. Corp., 1972-88, vice chmn., chief exec. officer, from 1988; prof. Grad. Sch. Mgmt., Northwestern U., from 1972. Chmn. Hosp. Rsch. and Devel. Inst., 1989, Nat. Com. for Quality Healthcare, 1989—; treas. Internat. Hosp. Fedn., 1983-89. Contbr. articles to profl. jours. Rep. Coordinating Council on Med. Edn., 1977—; bd. dirs. McGaw Med. Ctr., Northwestern U., 1972—, chmn. adminstrv. com., 1974-77; nat. adv. com. Sangamon State U., Springfield, Ill., 1973—; adv. com. citizens com. U. Ill., 1973—. Served with U.S. Army, 1946-47. Recipient Creighton U. Alumni Merit award, 1977; recipient Disting. Service award Ohio State U. Hosp. and Health Services Adminstrn., 1978 Fellow Am. Coll. Healthcare Execs. (regent 1970-71, gov. 1976-80, Gold medal 1984); mem. Am. Assn. Med. Colls. (exec. com., coun. teaching hosps.), Am. Hosp. Assn. (trustee 1978-82, chmn. 1981), Ill. Hosp. Assn. (exec. com. 1975-78, chmn. 1976-77), Ohio Hosp. Assn. (pres. 1969-70), Assn. Univs. for Rsch. and Astronomy (dir. 1971-72), U. Chgo. Hosp. Adminstrn. Alumni Assn. (pres. 1967-68), Chgo. Coun. Fgn. Rels., Kiwanis (trustee 1969-70). Home: Winnetka, Ill. Died Nov. 4, 2005.

LAESSIG, ROBERT H., artist; b. West NY, NJ, Nov. 15, 1913; s. Ernest and Martha (Weigert) L.; m. Isolde Helene Grosser, June 6, 1942 (dec. 1995); children: Thomas, Constance; m. Sandra Guerrera-Studio, June 1998. B.F.A., Textile Sch., Pauen, Germany; postgrad., Art Students League, NYC. Sr. art cons. Am. Greetings, Inc.; painting represented in collections Norfolk Mus. Art, Cleve. Mus. Art, Springfield Inst. Fine Art, Denver Mus. Art; designer personal Christmas cards Pres. Lyndon B. Johnson, 1964-66, Gov. Celeste, Ohio, 1983-90; works exhibited 100th anniversary Met. Mus., NYC; combat artist 13th Air Force; illustrator From the Fijis Through the Philippines; instr. condr. seminars. Pub. of prints Art Beats, Salt Lake City; assoc. with Gallery One, Mentor, Ohio. Served with USAAF, 1942-46. Recipient award Am. Watercolor Soc., 1979, 81, 82, 83, award Ky. Watercolor Soc., 1984, Adirondack Nat. Show, Old Forge, N.Y., 1982, 83, Ohio Watercolor Soc., 1979-85, Pitts Watercolor Soc., 1981, award Mainstreams Marietta, Ohio, 1983, Lifetime Achievement award, Fairmount Ctr., Ohio, 2003. Mem. NAD (assoc. 1964-94, academician, 1994-)., Am. Watercolor Soc., Ohio Watercolor Soc. (Gold medal 1987, 88, other awards 1979-87), Dolphin Club. Lutheran. Home: Chagrin Falls, Ohio. Died Dec. 2005.

LAFOREST, JAMES JOHN, retired electrical engineer; b. Tupper Lake, NY, Feb. 28, 1927; s. George Hector and Florence Alice (Trudel) L. BSE.E., Union Coll., 1957; M.E.E., Rensselaer Poly. Inst., 1964. Registered profl. engr., N.Y., Mass., Wyo., Colo. Engr. Gen. Electric Co., Pittsfield, Mass., 1951-58, research engr., 1959-69, application engr. Schenectady, 1970-77, sr. application engr., 1978-87, ret. Author: (with others) EHV Transmission Line Reference Book, 1968; editor-co-author: Transmission Line Reference Book, 1982 Bd. dirs., sec. Mohawk Opportunities in Mental Health, Schenectady, 1985. Fellow IEEE; mem. Sigma Xi Democrat. Roman Catholic. Avocations: alpine skiing, fishing, carpentry, travel, golf. Home: Indian Lake, NY. Died July 5, 2006.

LAINE, FRANKIE (PAUL LOVECCHIO), singer; b. Chgo., Mar. 30, 1913; s. John Philip and Anna Concetta (Salerno) LoVecctio; m. Eschol Loleet Miller, July 25, 1921; children: Pamela Westropp Donner, Jan Anna Westrope Steiger; m. Marcia Ann Kline, 1999 Entertainer, singer; composer, music publisher. Singer: (songs) That's My Desire, 1946, Mule Train, 1949, Jezebel, 1950, On Sunny Side Of The Street, 1951, I Believe, 1953, Moonlight Gambler, 1957; co-author (with Joseph F. Laredo): That Lucky Old Son: The Autobiography of Frankie Lane, 1993. Roman Catholic. Home: San Diego, Calif. Died Feb. 6, 2007.

LAMBETH, VICTOR NEAL, horticulturist, researcher; b. Sarcoxie, Mo., July 5, 1920; s. Odus Houston and Carrie (Woods) L.; m. Sarah Katherine Smarr, May 24, 1946; children: Victoria Kay, Debra Jean. BS, U. Mo., 1942, MA, 1948, PhD, 1950. Asst. prof. U. Mo., Columbia, 1950-51, assoc. prof., 1951-59, prof. dept. horticulture, 1959-91, prof. emeritus, from 1991. Cons. horticulture to Thailand, Taiwan, Liberia; judge All-Am. Vegetable Trials, 1985-92. Inventor plant growth media, 1979; plant breeder tomato lines and cultivars; contbr. articles to profl. jours. Mem. Fin. Com. City of Columbia, Mo., 1970, mem. Bd. Zoning Adjustment, 1973-76, mem. Bd. Spl. Appeals, 1975-77. Served to lt. USN, 1943-46, PTO. Recipient Hort. award Mo. Hort. Soc., 1942; recipient Alumni Faculty award U. Mo. Alumni Assn., 1974; NSF grantee, 1982 Fellow Am. Soc. Hort. Sci. (grad. teaching award 1978); mem. Am. Soc. Plant Physiologists, Internat. Soc. Hort. Sci., Sigma Xi, Gamma Sigma Delta (pres. Mo. chpt. 1959-60) Methodist. Home: Columbia, Mo. Died Jan. 25, 2006.

LANA, ROBERT EDWARD, retired psychology professor; b. Hoboken, NJ, Aug. 9, 1932; s. Edward Vincent and Daisy (Taborelli) L.; m. Mary Jean Harris, June 16, 1965; 1 child, Renata BA, Rutgers U., 1954; MA, U. Md., 1956, PhD, 1958. Asst. prof. Am. U., 1958-61; asso. prof. Alfred U., NY, 1962-65; sr. Fulbright lectr. U. Rome, Italy, 1965-66; mem. faculty Temple U., 1966—2005, prof. psychology, chmn. dept., 1969-80, dean, Grad. Sch., 1981-86. Cons. NSF, 1966-67 Author: Assumptions of Social Psychology, 1969, The Foundations of Social Psychology, 1976. Fellow Am. Psychol. Assn. Home: Narberth, Pa. Died Oct. 17, 2006.

LANDAU, BERNARD ROBERT, biochemist, educator, internist; b. Newark, June 24, 1926; s. Morris Harry and Estelle (Kirsch) L.; m. Lucille Slosberg, Jan. 11, 1956 (dec. 2004); children: Steven Brian, Deborah Louise (dec.), Rodger Martin. S.B., MIT, 1947; PhD, Harvard U., 1950, MD, 1954; MD (hon.), Karolinska Inst., 1993. Diplomate: Am. Bd. Internal Medicine. Intern Peter Bent Brigham Hosp., Boston, 1954-55; clin. assoc. Nat. Cancer Inst., Bethesda, Md., 1955-57; fellow in biochemistry Harvard U., 1957-58; sr. resident Peter Bent Brigham Hosp., 1958-59; asst. prof. medicine & pharmacology Case Western Res. U., 1959-62, assoc. prof., 1962-67, prof., 1969—2007, prof. biochemistry, 1979—2007, physician Univ. Hosps., 1969—2007. Dir. dept. biochemistry Merck and Co., Rahway, N.J., 1967-69 Contbr. articles to profl. jours. Fellow Commonwealth fund, 1965-66, Fogarty Sr. Internat. fellow 1986-87, 93-94, Nobel fellow Karolinska Inst., 1996-97; grantee Am. Heart Assn., 1959-64; recipient William B. Peck Postgrad. Research award, 1961 Fellow AAAS; mem. Am. Fedn. Clin. Research, Am. Soc. Clin. Investigation, Assn. Am. Physicians, Am. soc. Biol. Chemists, Am. Physiol. Soc., Endocrine Soc., Central Soc. Clin. Research, Am. Diabetes Assn., Sigma Xi, Alpha Omega Alpha Home: Cleveland, Ohio. Died Mar. 24, 2007.

LANDAU, SIEGFRIED, conductor; b. Berlin, Sept. 4, 1921; came to U.S., 1940, naturalized, 1946; s. Ezekiel and Helen (Grynberg) L.; m. Irene Gabriel, May 2, 1954; children— Robert, Peter. Student, Stern Conservatory, Klindworth-

Scharwenka Conservatory, Berlin; L.G.S.M., Guildhall Sch. Music and Drama, London, Eng., 1939-40; condrs. degree, Mannes Coll., NYC, 1942. Condr. Bklyn. Philharmonia, 1954-71, Music for Westchester Symphony Orch. (now White Plains Symphony Orch.), 1961-81, Chattanooga Opera Assn., 1960-73; gen. music dir., chief condr. Westphalian Symphony Orch., West Germany, 1973-75. Works include opera The Sons of Aaron, 1959; symphonic poem ballets, orchestral and choral scores. Recipient award Music Tchrs. Assn. outstanding contbn. music edn., 1963 Fellow Jewish Acad. Arts and Scis.; mem. Societa Mici Della Music Jesi (hon.), Nat. Jewish Music Council, ASCAP, Am. Musicol. Soc., Assn. Am. Condrs. and Composers. Home: Brushton, NY. Died Feb. 19, 2007.

LANDIS, SARA MARGARET SHEPPARD, editorial consultant; b. Badin, NC, May 20, 1920; d. Thomas Coates and Ouida (Watson) Sheppard; m. Williard Griffith Landis, Dec. 7, 1945; children: Susan Sheppard, Timothy Joseph, Margaret Carol. Student, Flora MacDonald Coll. Women, 1937-38, Rice Bus. Coll., 1939; AB in Journalism, U. N.C., 1942. Editorial asst. Redbook Mag., NYC, 1942-43; with Doubleday and Co., NYC, 1944-46, Eagle Pencil Co., NYC, 1953-54; mgr. personnel Workman Service, NYC, 1955-56, Clay Adams Co., NYC, 1957-58; job analyst Bigelow Carpet Co., NYC, 1959-60; asst. to guidance dir. Childrens Village, Dobbs Ferry, N.Y., 1960-61; dir. promotions, advt. Oceans Publs., Dobbs Ferry, 1961-66; mgr. promotions Reinhold Pub. Co., NYC, 1967-68, Watson Guptil Pub. Co., NYC, 1968, Chilton Book Co., Phila., 1968-69; cons. editorial, promotions Sheppard-Landis Ink, NYC, from 1969. Cons. Parker, Rebel Without Rights, Millbrook, 1996, George Washington Series, Millbrook, Alexander Hamilton, 1996-98. Collaborator: (with Tereso Pregnall) Treasured Recipes from the Charleston Cake Lady, 1996; abridgement editor Kente Books on Tape, 1996. Mem. St. George Episc. Ch. Mem. English Speaking Union (head book discussion group 1989-92), Friends Ephiphany chpt. N.Y. Pub. Library, United Daughters Confederacy, Squadron A Club. Died June 24, 2006.

LANDO, ROBERT N., franchise company executive; b. Pitts., Nov. 5, 1915; m. Patti B. Lando, Dec. 19, 1946; children— Sandi, Mark B. in Journalism, U.Mo., 1938. Pres. Lando Advt. Agy., Inc., Pitts., 1946-75; chmn. bd. Athlete's Foot Mktg. Assocs., Inc., Atlanta, 1975-93; pres. Pioneer Supply Co. Inc. Pitts., from 1988. Home: Pittsburgh, Pa. Died Nov. 4, 2005.

LANE, ALVIN S., lawyer; b. Englewood, NJ, June 17, 1918; s. Martin Lane and Nettie (Gans) Daniels; m. Terese P. Lyons, Apr. 24, 1949; children: Mary-Jo, Judith Lyons. Ph.B., U. Wis., 1940; LL.B., Harvard U., 1943. Bar: N.Y. 1947. Sr. ptnr. Wien, Lane & Malkin, 1954-83; chmn. Rapidata, Inc., 1967-82; Mem. adv. bd. to N.Y. atty. gen. on art legis., 1966-71. Contbr. articles to art publs. and legal jours. Mem. bd. mgmt. Henry Ittleson Rsch. Ctr. Disturbed Children, Riverdale, N.Y., 1961-70; fellow Brandeis U., nat. adv. coun. 20th Century Art Soc. High Mus. of Art, 1986-95; sec., trustee Aldrich Mus. Contemporary Art, Inc., 1969-76; trustee Lexington Sch. Deaf, 1971; v.p., trustee Soho Ctr. Visual Artists, Inc., 1974-83; dir. Creative Artists Pub. Svc. Program, Inc., 1982-84; mem. drawing com. Whitney Mus. Am Art, 1991-93; mem. The Elvehjem Mus. Art Coun. Served as lt. USNR, 1942-46. Mem. Assn. of Bar of City of N.Y. (chmn. com. art 1963-65), N.Y. Artists Equity Assn. (dir. 1982-84) Clubs: Harvard (N.Y.C.), Riverdale Yacht. Died Sept. 13, 2007.

LANE, EUGENE NUMA, classics educator; b. Washington, Aug. 13, 1936; s. George Sherman and Colette (Resweber) L.; m. Carol Downes Gault, Aug. 22, 1964; children: Michael, Helen. AB, Princeton U., 1958; MA, Yale U., 1960, PhD, 1962. Asst. prof. U. Va., Charlottesville, 1962-66; assoc. prof. U. Mo., Columbia, 1966-76, prof., from 1976, chmn. classics dept., 1981-84. Author: Corpus Monumentorum Religionis Dei Menis, 4 vols., 1971-79; Corpus Cultus Iovis Sabazii II-III, 1984-89; co-editor: (with Ramsay Mac Mullen) Paganism and Christianity 100-425 C.E., A Sourcebook, 1992. Active Columbians Against Throwaways, Columbia, Mo., 1977-88. Grantee Am. Council Learned Socs., 1972-73, 1976, 86-87; grantee Am. Philos. Soc., 1972-73, 86-87, NEH, 1979 Mem. Am. Philol. Assn., Archaeol. Inst. Am., Classical Assn. of Middle West and South Episcopalian. Home: Columbia, Mo. Died Jan. 1, 2007.

LANE, MELVIN BELL, former publishing company executive; b. Des Moines, May 11, 1922; s. Laurence William and Ruth (Bell) L.; m. Joan Fletcher, Feb. 15, 1953; children: Whitney Miller, Julie Lane Gay. BA, Stanford U., 1944; LLD (hon.), Pomona Coll., 1976. Production asst. Lane Pub. Co., Menlo Park, Calif., 1946-51, bus. mgr., 1952-59, pres., 1974-85, also chmn. bd. dirs.; pub. Sunset Mag. and Books, Menlo Park. Adv. council SRI Internat., Menlo Park, 1975-89; bd. dirs. Lucky Stores, Dublin, Calif., 1980-88, PG&E, San Francisco, 1986. Chmn. Calif. Coastal Commn., 1972-77; chmn. exec. com. Conservation Found./World Wildlife Fund, Washington, 1985; trustee Stanford U., 1981-91, adv. council grad. sch. bus., 1986-89. Served to lt. USNR, 1943-46. Mem. Advt. Coun. (bd. dirs. 1985-89), Calif. Environ. Trust (chmn. 1985), Calif. Nature Conservancy (bd. dirs. 1977). Clubs: Bohemian, Pacific Union (San Francisco). Home: Atherton, Calif. Died July 28, 2007.

LANGERAK, ESLEY OREN, retired research chemist; b. Pella, Iowa, Oct. 28, 1920; s. William Henry and Grace Dena (Vander Linden) L.; m. Elizabeth Jane Rhodes (dec.), Nov. 18, 1944; children— Kristin, Lisbeth, Peter; m. Marian Sawin Stauffer, May 22, 1999. BS in Chemistry, Central Coll., Iowa, 1941; MS, U. Del., 1947, PhD in Organic Chemistry, 1949. High sch. tchr. Garden Grove Consol. Sch., Iowa, 1941-42; research chemist, supr., lab mgr. DuPont Co., Wilmington, Del., 1949-81, compensation mgr. chems. and pigments dept., 1981-85; ret., 1985. Contbr. articles to profl. jours.; patentee in field (3). Served with Ordnance, U.S. Army, 1942-46, PTO. Mem.: DuPont Country. Republican. Presbyterian. Home: Wilmington, Del. Died Feb. 23, 2006.

LANGFORD, CHARLES DOUGLAS, lawyer, retired state legislator; b. Montgomery, Ala., Dec. 9, 1922; s. Nathan G. and Lucy B. (Brown) Langford. BS, Tenn. State U., 1948; LLB, Cath. U. Am., 1952, JD, 1967. Bar: Ala. 1953, U.S. Dist. Ct. (mid. dist.) Ala. 1954, U.S. Ct. Appeals (5th cir.) 1969, U.S. Supreme Ct. 1976, U.S. Ct. Appeals (11th cir.) 1982. Ptnr. Gray, Langford, Sapp, McGowan, Gray & Nathanson, Montgomery, Ala., 1968—2007; mem. Ala. State Senate, Montgomery, 1983—2002. Officer St. John A.ME. Ch. With US Army, 1943—46. Mem.: Elks (past exalter ruler So. Pride lodge), Alpha Phi Alpha. Democrat. Home: Montgomery, Ala. Died Feb. 11, 2007.

LANGFORD, IRVIN JAMES, lawyer; b. Mobile, Apr. 28, 1927; s. Irvin Cobb and Wesley Blacksher (Coffin) L.; m. Marylyn Judith Cleland, Sept. 17, 1954; children: Debra Lynne, Kimberly Anne, David Wesley. BS, U. Ala., 1949, LL.B., 1951. Bar: Ala. 1951. Since practiced in Mobile; ptnr. firm Howell, Johnston, Langford & Watters, from 1958; spl. judge Probate Ct. Mobile County, 1970. Served with USNR, 1945-46. Mem. Am., Ala., Mobile bar assns., Ala. Trial Lawyers Assn., Farrah Order Jurisprudence, Sigma Chi, Phi Alpha Delta. Clubs: Mason (Mobile) (Shriner), Athelstan (Mobile), Internat. Trade (Mobile). Democrat. Presbyterian. Home: Mobile, Ala. Died Aug. 7, 2006.

LANGLAND, JOSEPH THOMAS, author, emeritus educator; b. Spring Grove, Minn., Feb. 16, 1917; s. Charles M. and Clara Elizabeth (Hille) L.; m. Judith Gail Wood, June 26, 1943; children— Joseph Thomas, Elizabeth Langland, Paul. BA, U. Iowa, 1940; MA, 1941; DLitt (hon.), Luther Coll., 1974. Instr. in English Dana Coll., Blair, Nebr., 1941-42; part-time instr. U. Iowa, 1946-48; asst. prof., then asso. prof. U. Wyo., 1948-59; mem. faculty U. Mass., Amherst, 1959-79, prof. English, 1964-79, prof. emeritus, from 1979. Dir. program for MFA in writing, 1964-70, 78-79; vis. lectr. U. B.C., U. Wash., Seattle, San Francisco State U.; guest reader, Republic of Madedonia, 1995. Author: poems For Harold, 1945, The Green Town, 1956, The Wheel of Summer, 1963, 2d edit., 1966, An Interview and Fourteen Poems, 1973, The Sacrifice Poems, 1975, Any Body's Song (Nat. Poetry Series), 1980, (poem with etchings) A Dream of Love, 1986, Twelve: Preludes & Postludes, 1988, Selected Poems, 1991, 2d edit., 1992; co-editor: poems Poet's Choice, 1962, 83, The Short Story, 1956; co-translator: poems Poetry From the Russian Underground, 1973. Served to capt., inf. AUS, 1942-46, ETO. Ford fellow in humanities Harvard-Columbia U. 1953-54; Amy Lowell Poetry fellow, 1955-56; Arts and Humanities fellow in poetry, 1966-67; recipient Melville Cane prize poetry Poetry Soc. Am., 1964; named Living Art Treasure in Lit., New Eng. Arts Biennial, 1985 Democrat. Home: Amherst, Mass. Died Apr. 9, 2007.

LANGSTAFF, ELLIOT KENNEDY, management consultant; b. NYC, Feb. 1, 1923; s. B. Meredith and Esther Knox (Boardman) L.; m. Percy Lee, Dec. 20, 1952; children— David Hamilton, Lee Meredith, Maxim Kennedy. AB, Harvard U., 1947, MBA, 1949. Asst. to dir. Fgn. Trade Adminstrn., Athens, Greece, 1949-52; asst. to spl. adviser, U.S. rep. to regional orgns. FOA, Paris, 1953-55; asst. sec. Am. Overseas Fin. Corp., NYC, 1955-59, asst. v.p., 1959-62, v.p., 1962-65; regional mgr. Africa, Asia, Middle East Arbor Acres Farm, Inc. (subs. Internat. Basic Economy Corp.), Glastonbury, Conn., 1964-66; sec., dir. pers. Internat. Basic Economy Corp., NYC, 1967-71, v.p. pers., 1969-72; ptnr., dir., sec. Ward Howell Internat., Inc., NYC, 1972-89, ptnr., 1989-91. Bd. dirs. Internat. Instl. Svcs.; cons. Ward Howell Internat. Inc., 1991-92, Internat. Exec. Sr. Corps, 1992—. Trustee Am. Farm Sch., Thessaloniki, Greece, The N.Y. Revels, Inc. (dir.). Served to 1st lt., inf. AUS, 1943-46. Decorated Army Commendation medal. Mem.: Harvard of N.Y.C. Episcopalian. Died Mar. 11, 2006.

LANTZ, ROBERT, literary and talent agent; b. Berlin, July 20, 1914; s. Adolf and Ella (Schloessingk) L.; m. Sherlee Lantz, 1950; 1 child, Anthony; came to U.S., 1948, naturalized Brit. citizen, 1946; student U. Berlin, 1931-32; m. Feb. 1950; 1 child, Anthony Robin. Story editor Am. film cos., London, 1936-46; talent and lit. agt., N.Y.C., 1948-2007; pres. The Lantz Office, N.Y.C., 1973-2007; pres. TARA, N.Y. Mem. British P.E.N. Plays include L'Inconnue de la Seine, Voegelchen, others. Home: New York, NY. Died Oct. 18, 2007.

LANZONI, VINCENT, medical school dean; b. Kingston, Mass., Feb. 23, 1928; s. Vincent and Caroline (Melloni) L.; m. Phoebe Krey, June 12, 1960; children: Karen, Susan, Margaret. BS, Tufts U., 1949, PhD, 1953; MD, Boston U., 1960. USPHS fellow Tufts U., 1953-54; intern in medicine Boston City Hosp., 1960-61, resident and fellow in medicine, 1961-65; asst. prof. pharmacology Boston U., 1964-67, assoc. prof. medicine and pharmacology, 1967-73, prof., 1973-75; assoc. dean Sch. Medicine, 1969-75; prof. U. Medicine and Dentistry N.J., Newark, from 1975, dean N.J. Med. Sch., 1975-87, interim dean Grad. Sch. Biomed. Scis., from 1987. Bd. dirs., sec.-treas. Postgrad. Med. Inst., 1972-75; bd. dirs. Mass. Health Research Inst., Mass. Registration in Nursing, Roxbury Neighborhood Clinic. Served to 1st lt. USAF, 1954-56. Researcher cardiovascular pharmacology, hypertension. Home: Millburn, NJ. Died June 28, 2007.

LA PAZ, IRENE MCGOVERN, city official; b. Havana, Cuba, Sept. 9, 1932; came to U.S., 1960; d. Francis and Irene (Diaz) McGovern; m. George La Paz, June 8, 1954; children: Mayra, Marlen, George. Student U. Tampa, 1977, U. South Fla., 1977. With City of Tampa Sanitation Dept., 1961—, sanitation asst. dir., 1973-83, adminstrv. and fiscal mgr., 1983—. Mem. Govtl. Refuse Collection and Disposal Assn. (past chpt. pres.), Am. Pub. Works Assn. (past br. chmn. West Coast). Democrat. Roman Catholic. Home: Clearwater, Fla. Died July 18, 2006.

LAPRADE, CARTER, lawyer; b. Richmond, Va., Nov. 21, 1942; s. Edmund Moseley and Page (Walker) LaP.; m. Suzanne Williams, June 7, 1967; children: Suzanne, Carter, Burch. BA, Yale U., 1965; LLB, Columbia U., 1968. Bar: N.Y. 1968, Conn. 1973, U.S. Dist. Ct. Conn. 1974, U.S. Ct. Appeals (2d cir.) 1974. Asst. U.S. atty. So. Dist. N.Y., 1971-73, Dist. of Vt., Rutland, 1973; ptnr. Thompson, Weir & Barclay, New Haven, 1973-82, Tyler, Cooper & Alcorn, New Haven, 1982-94; retired, 1994. Chmn. bd. Gaylord Hosp., Wallingford, Conn., 1985-87; pres. Conn. Soc. to Prevent Blindness, Madison, 1982-84; trustee Quinnipiac Coll., Hamden, Conn., 1987-97. Capt. USMC, 1968-71. Fellow Am. Bar Found.; mem. ABA (Profl. Merit award 1969), Conn. Bar Assn., New Haven County Bar Assn. (pres. 1988), Lawyer-Pilots Bar Assn., Yale Club New Haven (pres. 1989-91). Avocations: scuba diving, running. Home: Irvington, Va. Died Aug. 26, 2006.

LARDNER, HENRY PETERSEN (PETER LARDNER), insurance company executive; b. Davenport, Iowa, Apr. 5, 1932; s. James Francis and Mary Catharine (Decker) L.; m. Marion Cleaveland White, Dec. 28, 1954; children: Elisabeth, Emily, David, Peter, Sarah (dec.). BSE. (Indsl. Engring.), U. Mich., 1954; MA, Augustana Coll., 1982. C.P.C.U. Indsl. engr. Cutler-Hammer, Milw., 1954; Agt. H.H. Cleaveland Agy., Rock Island, Ill., 1956-60; with Bituminous Ins. Cos., Rock Island, 1960—2001, exec. v.p., 1968-72, pres., 1972-95, chmn. and CEO, 1984-2000, chmn., 2000—01; pres. Bitco Corp., Rock Island, 1973-95, chmn. bd. dirs., 1973—2001. Bd. dirs. Old Republic Internat., 1985—; trustee Underwriters Lab., Inc., 1997-2004. Bd. govs. State Colls. and Univs., 1971-80; trustee Black Hawk Coll., 1964-72; mem. Ill. Bd. Higher Edn., 1976-77; chmn. Ill. State Scholarship, 1982-85. Served with AUS, 1954-56. Home: Rock Island, Ill. Died Aug. 14, 2007.

LARKIN, MICHAEL JOSEPH, retail food executive; b. NYC, June 6, 1941; s. John Thomas and Mary (Finnerty) L.; m. Sandra L. Pagano, July 15, 1978; 1 child, Lisa. BBA, Iona Coll., 1963; postgrad., Cornell U., 1970. Supermarket mgr. Grand Union Co., NYC, 1963-69, dist. mgr. Syracuse, N.Y., 1969-71, dir. ops., 1971-75, div. v.p. Mt. Kisco, N.Y., 1975-78, regional v.p. Elmwood Park, N.J., 1978-84; ops. v.p. Gt. Atlantic and Pacific Tea Co., Montvale, N.J., 1984-85, group v.p., 1985-87, sr. v.p. ops., 1987-89, exec. v.p. ops., 1989-95, COO, 1991-95; owner, pres. Gemini Food Mkts., L.P., Morristown, N.J., from 1995. Pres. Daitch Shopwell Co., N.Y.C., 1986-95. With USMC, 1960-65. Named Man of Yr. Cath. Inst. of Food Industry, N.Y.C., 1986, Boys Town of Italy, 1993; recipient award of merit Deborah Hosp., Browns Mill, N.J., 1988. Republican. Roman Catholic. Home: Coral Springs, Fla. Died Nov. 8, 2005.

LARROWE, CHARLES PATRICK, economist, educator; b. Portland, Oreg., May 1, 1916; s. Albertus and Helen (Maginnis) L.; 1 child, Peter (dec.). BA, U. Wash., Seattle, 1946, MA, 1948; PhD, Yale U., 1952. Asst. instr. econs. U. Wash., 1946-49, Yale U., 1949-52; assoc. prof. U. Utah, 1952-56; mem. faculty Mich State U., East Lansing, 1956-89, prof. econs., 1961-89, faculty grievance ofcl., 1976-80, 88-89. Cons. to govt. Author: Shape-Up and Hiring Hall, 1955, Harry Bridges, 2d edit., 1977, Lashing Out, 1982. Served with Am. Field Service, 1942-43; Served with AUS, 1943-45. Decorated Silver Star, Purple Heart with oak leaf cluster, Combat Infantryman's badge; grantee Rabinowitz Found., 1962 Mem. ACLU, NAACP, Amnesty Internat., Rolls-Royce Owners' Club. Democrat. Home: East Lansing, Mich. Died July 7, 2006.

LARSEN, TOM LEONARD, other: manufacturing; b. Lincoln, Nebr., Sept. 30, 1932; s. Leonard Peter and Hazel Ione Larsen; m. Jane Rosamond Bergquist, Sept. 11, 1954; children Laurie Sue, Leslie Jane (twins), Lisa Anne. BSBA, U. Nebr 1954, postgrad. in econs., 1957—59. Mem. econs. faculty Grad Sch. U. Nebr., Lincoln, 1957—59; coord. mktg., asst. to pres Valley Nat. Bank, Phoenix, 1959—69; pres. Palo Alto Edn Systems, Phoenix, 1969—77, chmn. bd., 1977—83; pres. Phoenix Investment Co., Holt County, Nebr., from 1976, Lincoln Equipment Co., from 1976, JBL, Inc., Holt County, from 1981 v.p. Phoenix Farms, Inc., Holt County, from 1976. Mem Scottsdale (Ariz.) Bd. Edn., 1967—72, pres., 1967—72; bd govs. Wesleyan U., 1980—81, Lincoln Found., from 1980 trustee Doane Coll., from 1980, Nebr. Found., from 1980; mem Nebr. Bd. Ind. Colls.; bd. dirs. Millicent Rogers Mus., Taos N.Mex., 1981—82. 1st lt. USAF, 1954—57. Mem.: Plaza Clu (Phoenix), Paradise Valley Country Club, Univ. Club (Lincoln) Lincoln Country Club. Republican. Presbyterian. Home: Lincoln, Nebr. Died July 11, 2006.

LARSON, CHARLES LESTER, television writer, produce author; b. Portland, Oreg., Oct. 23, 1922; s. Charles Oscar an Ina May (Couture) L.; m. Alice Mae Dovey, Aug. 25, 1966; stepson, Wyn Donavan Malotte. Student, U. Oreg., 194 Contract writer MGM Studios, Culver City, Calif., 1943-4 freelance mag. writer, 1941-51. Assoc. producer: TV progra Twelve O'Clock High, 1964; producer: TV program The FB 1965-68, The Interns, 1970-71, Cades County, 1971-72; exe producer: TV program Nakia, 1974; producer: TV movie Crim Club, 1973; co-creator: TV series Hagen, 1979-80; author: Th Chinese Game, 1969, Someone's Death, 1973, Matthew's Han 1974, Muir's Blood, 1976, The Portland Murders, 1983. Mem Writers Guild Am. West, Producers Guild, Mystery Writers Am (spl. award 1974), Authors League Am. Democrat. Hom Portland, Oreg. Died Sept. 21, 2006.

LARSON, DOYLE EUGENE, retired air force officer, con sultant; b. Madelia, Minn., Oct. 2, 1930; s. Edgar Louis an Gyneth Mae (Weldy) L.; m. Lois James, May 29, 1953; childre James, Nancy, Mary, Mark. Student, Macalester Coll., 1948-5 BA, Hardin-Simmons U., 1962; postgrad., Armed Forces Sta Coll., 1965, Air War Coll., 1971; MS in Polit. Sci., Auburn U 1971. Enlisted USAF, 1951, commd. 2d lt., 1953, advance through grades to maj. gen., 1977; sr. mil. rep. Nat. Securi Agy., Pentagon, 1971-72; asst. for joint matters, asst. chief sta for intelligence Hdqrs. USAF, 1972-73, dir. policy and resour mgmt., dep. chief staff for intelligence, 1973-74; dir. intelligen Hdqrs. Pacific Command, Camp H.M. Smith, Hawaii, 1974-7 dep. chief staff for intelligence Hdqrs. SAC, Offutt AF Omaha, 1977-79; comdg. gen. Security Svc., 1979-83; com Electronic Security Command, San Antonio, 1979-83; dir. Joi Electronic Warfare Ctr., San Antonio, 1980-83; ret., 198 Trustee Macalester Coll. Decorated DSM, Legion of Merit wi 2 oak leaf clusters, Air medal with 3 oak leaf clusters; named Order of the Sword. Mem. Air Force Assn. Lutheran. Hom Burnsville, Minn. Died Aug. 13, 2007.

LARSON, RICHARD FRANCIS, sociology educator; Yakima, Wash., Apr. 2, 1931; s. Renus Matthew and Helen Ma (Snyder) L.; m. Celine M. Krupka, Apr. 6, 1968. B.A., Seat

U., 1957; M.A., U. Wash., 1958; Ph.D., U. Notre Dame, 1961. Asst. prof. sociology U. Ala., 1961-62, U. R.I., 1962-64; assoc. prof. sociology Okla. State U., 1964-67, U. Mo.-St. Louis, 1967-68; prof. sociology U. Fla., 1968-73; prof., chmn. dept. sociology Calif. State U.-Hayward, 1973-78; prof. sociology, head sociology dept. Clemson U. (S.C.), 1978—. Served with USN, 1950-54. Mem. AAUP, Am. Sociol. Assn., Soc. for Study of Social Problems, Soc. for Sci. Study Religion. Roman Catholic. Co-author: Introductory Sociology, 1973, 3d edit., 1980; Statistics— A Tool for the Social Sciences, 1974, 4th edit., 1987; Readings for Introducing Sociology, 1982; The Sociology of Social Problems, 9th edit., 1988. Home: Greendale, Wis. Died Jan. 31, 2006.

LARSON, RUSSELL EDWARD, university provost emeritus, agriculturist, consultant; b. Mpls., Jan. 2, 1917; s. Karl Sam and Belle (Wing) L.; m. Margaret Agnes Johnson, Aug. 19, 1939; children: Gayle Margaret, Beverly Jean, Russell Troy. BS, U. Minn., 1939, MS, 1940, PhD, 1942; DSc (hon.), Delaware Valley Coll. Sci. and Agr., 1966. Asst. prof. U. R.I., Kingston, 1941-44, Pa. State U., University Park, 1944-45, assoc. prof., 1945-47, prof., 1947-77, head dept. horticulture, 1952-62, dean Coll. Agriculture, 1963-72, provost, 1972-77. Sci. advisor Am. Cocoa Rsch. Inst., McLean, Va., 1975-87; cons. Agriculture R & D, State Coll. Pa., 1977—. Contbr. 46 tech. articles on plant sci. to profl. jours. Recipient Outstanding Alumnus award U. Minn., 1961. Fellow AAAS, Am. Soc. Hort. Sci. (pres. 1963-64, L.H. Vaughan award 1948); mem. Am. Genetic Assn., Am. Inst. Biol. Sci., Sigma Xi. Republican. Lutheran. Avocations: gardening, golf, fishing. Home: State College, Pa. Died Nov. 30, 2005.

LARSON, SWEN, former mayor; b. Sweden, Oct. 3, 1924; m. Helen Larson; children: Ruth Ann, Jack. Mem. city coun. City of Redlands, Calif., 1989—93, mayor, 1993—97. Steering com. Inland Empire Legislative Caucus; chmn. bd. dirs. Home Again; bd. dirs. Youth Accountability, Omni, Sanbag. Bd. dirs. Congrl. Ch.; past v.p. League Calif. Cities, Redlands C. of C.; past pres. House Neighborly Svc., Redlands Optimist Club, San Bernardino Internat. Airport Authority; mem. Redlands Planning Commn., 1977-85, Redlands Cmty. Hosp. Bd. Served in US Army. Named Man of Yr. Redlands Svc. Orgn. and C. of C., 1994, Disting. Citizen award Boy Scouts by Inland Empire Coun., 1994; recipient Civic Achievement award LWV. Mem. Automobile Club (adv. bd. So. Calif.). Home: Redlands, Calif. Died May 1, 2007.

LARUSSA, JOSEPH ANTHONY, optical company executive; b. NYC, May 10, 1925; s. Ignacio and Jennie (Bellone) LaR.; m. Stella M.A. Braconnier, July 2, 1946; children— Joseph, Raymond Paul, Debra Marie. BME, CCNY, 1949; MS, Columbia U., 1955, postgrad. math., mechanics, 1955-59; postgrad. math., physics, NYU, 1959-62; diploma in Infrared Tech, U. Mich. Registered profl. engr., N.Y. V.p. charge advanced engring. Farrand Optical Co., Inc., Valhalla, N.Y., 1952, sr. v.p., tech. dir., 1952-88; pres., chief oper. officer Tech. Innovation Group Inc, Pleasantville, N.Y., 1988-90, Electro Visual Engring. Inc., Yorktown Heights, N.Y., from 1991. Designed Mercury, Gemini, Apollo LM visual spaceflight simulators for NASA; designed space shuttle Aft and Ohd visual simulators for NASA, others for USAF. Patentee in fields of simulation, optics, holography and medical devices; contbr. articles profl. publs. Served with inf. AUS, World War II, ETO. Recipient NASA Lifetime Achievement award, 1998. Mem. AIAA (DeFlorez award 1968), Tau Beta Pi, Pi Tau Sigma. Died June 4, 2007.

LASUCHIN, MICHAEL S., artist, retired art educator; b. Kramatorsk, Russia, July 24, 1923; came to U.S. 1951; s. Sergei and Agafia I. (Okolelova) L.; m. Dorothy L. Roschen, Aug. 6, 1988. BFA, Phila. Coll. Art, 1970; MFA, Temple U., 1972. Prof. art U. Arts, Phila., 1972-90; ret., 1990. Author/pub.; Interpolated Voids, 1970; one-man shows include Capital Air Ctr. Gallery, Taichung, Taiwan, 1989, U. of the Arts, Phila., 1991; permanent collections include Phila. Mus. Art, Bklyn. Art Mus., Mus. Modern Art, N.Y., Mus. Modern Art, Barcelona, Spain, Libr. Nat., Paris, Berlin Mus. of Art, Russian State Mus., Tretjakow Gallery, Moscow, Pushkin Mus., Moscow, Victoria Albert Mus., London; traveling group exhibit, "A Legacy of Excellence: Artistic Achievements of Older Pennsylvanians," 2004. Recipient Gold medal, Color Print Soc. Am., 2005. Mem. Watercolor USA Honor Soc., Nat. Watercolor Soc., Color Print Soc., Soc. Am. Graphic Artists, Phila. Print Club, Boston Printmakers, NAD (academician, 1994-). Avocations: music, books, travel. Home: Philadelphia, Pa. Died Nov. 23, 2006.

LATTIMER, JOHN KINGSLEY, physician, educator; b. Mt. Clemens, Mich., Oct. 14, 1914; s. Eugene and Gladys Soulier (Lenfestey) L.; m. Jamie Elizabeth Hill, Jan. 1948; children: Evan, Jon, Gary. AB, Columbia U., 1935, MD, 1938, ScD, 1943; student, Balliol Coll., Eng., 1944, Med. Field Svc. Sch., Paris, 1945. Diplomate Am. Bd. Urology. Surg. intern Meth.-Episcopal Hosp., NYC, 1938-40; urol. resident Squier Urol. Clinic Presbyn. Hosp., NYC, 1940-43, dir. Squier Urol. Clinic, 1955-80, dir. urol. svc., 1955-80, also dir. urology Sch. Nursing. Staff asst., instr. urology Columbia Coll. Physicians and Surgeons, 1940-53, asst. prof. clin. urology, 1953-55, prof. urology, chmn. dept. urology, 1955-80; vis. prof. Med. Coll. S.C., Med. Coll. Va., Mayo Clinic Med. Sch., Rochester, Minn., 1977, Boston U., Tufts U., U. Oreg., Ind. U., UCLA, Leeds Med. Sch. Witwatersrand, South Africa; guest lectr. Akron City Hosp., 1977, Reno Surg. Soc., 1977; chief urology Babies Hosp., Vanderbilt Clinic, Frances Delafield Hosp., N.Y.C., 1955; cons. urology VA, N.Y.C., 1947-80, USPHS Hosp., S.I., N.Y.C., Meth. Hosp., Bklyn., Englewood (N.J.), Yonkers (N.Y.) gen. hosps., Harlem, Roosevelt, St. Lukes hosps. (all N.Y.C.); mem. com. surgery in Tb, genito-urinary Tb, VA; med. cons. Time mag.; cons. to com. on therapy Nat. Tb Assn.; mem. expert adv. panel biology human reprodn. WHO; mem. N.Y. Supreme Ct. Med. Arbitration Panel, 1975; Am. Urol. Assn. rep. to NRC-Nat. Acad. Scis.; mem. tng. grants com. NIH, 1968-72; lectr. in field. Contbr. over 350 articles on urology and history to various publs., also chpts. in books; guest author New Eng. Jour. Medicine; rschr., writer, speaker on assassinations of Pres. Lincoln and Kennedy, and Nuremberg Trials. Trustee Presbyn. Hosp., 1974-78; mem. vis. com. Ft. Ticonderoga Mus.; mem. vis. com. sect. arms and armour Met. Mus. Art, 1978, Abraham Lincoln U., Harrogate, Tenn.; chmn. book com. Englewood Hist. Soc.; mem. Dallas Coun. World Affairs, Phila. Coun. World Affairs; ofcl. historian City of Englewood, N.J. Maj. M.C., AUS, 1943-46; med. officer at Nuremberg Trials, 1945-46. Decorated Croix de Guerre (France and Belgium); recipient Joseph Mather Smith prize for kidney disease rsch. Columbia U., 1943, honor award for meritorious work in field Tb, Am. Acad. Tb Physicians, also prizes for sci. exhibits, gold medal Coll. Physicians and Surgeons Alumni Assn., 1971, Disting. Svc. award, 1993, Hugh Young medal for outstanding work in infectious diseases, 1973, Belfield medal Chgo. Urol. Soc., Burpeau medal N.J. Acad. Medicine, Edward Henderson gold medal Am. Geriat. Soc., 1978, Gt. medal City of Paris, 1979, Normandy Liberation medal Soc. French War Vets., Paris Liberation medal French Govt., medal Nat. Kidney Fedn., 1987, Am. Acad. Pediatric Urology, 1987, Chevalier French Legion Hon., 2004,; named a Knight of French Legion, 2005. Fellow ACS (chmn. adv. com. urology 1962-64, gov. 1966-79, com. on undergrad. tng. 1967-80, chmn. nominating com. 1976-77, com. to study size and composition of bd. govs.), AMA (prize rsch. kidney Tb 1953), Am. Acad. Pediatrics (chmn. com. on pediatric urology, pres. sect. urology 1973-79); mem. AAAS, Am. Assn. Clin. Urologists, Assn. Am. Med. Colls., Clin. Soc. Genito-Urinary Surgeons (pres. 1984), N.Y. Acad. Sci. (trustee), N.Y. Acad. Medicine (chmn. genito-urinary surg. sect. 1956-57, trustee 1978-84, v.p. 1986-87, chmn. bldg. com. 1982-87), Am. Assn. Genito-Urinary Surgeons (pres. 1982), Am. Urol. Assn. (pres. 1975-76, chmn. com. on pediatric urology, pres. N.Y. sect. 1966, exec. com. 1967-80, com. on surgery, rev. and long range planning com., editorial bd. Jour. Urology 1965-68, chmn. com. to gather info. about urology, chmn. coordinating coun. for urology, chmn. nominating com. 1976-77, 1st prize for clin. rsch. 1950, 60, Ramon Guiterez medal 1980, Keyes medal 1996), Am. Thoracic Soc., AAUP, Soc. U. Urologists (pres. 1969), Nat. Inst. Social Scis., St. Nicholas Soc., Assn. Mil. Surgeons Harvey Soc., Nat. Tb Assn., N.Y. State Pediatrics Soc., N.Y. Med. Socs., New York County Med. Soc., Soc. Pediatric Urology (pres. 1961-62), Brit. Assn. Urol. Surgeons (corr.), N.Y. Soc. Surgeons, N.Y. Soc. Professions, Internationale Société d'Urology (v.p. 1967-73, pres.1973-79), Assn. Pediatric Urology (pres. 1961), Spanish Urol. Assn. (hon.), Paleopathology Assn., Charles A. Lindbergh Soc. (ofcl. historian City of Englewood 1990), Dallas Surgical Soc., Japanese Urol. Assn. (hon.), Italian Urol. Assn. (hon.), SAR, Assn. Mil. Historians, Soc. War 1812, Mil. Order Fgn. Wars U.S., Order of Founders and Patriots, Arms and Armour Soc. N.Y., Arms and Armour Soc. Eng., Arms and Armour Soc. Gueurnsey, Soc. Colonial Wars, Englewood Hist. Soc., Manuscript Soc., Revolutionary War Round Table of N.Y., Abraham Lincoln Soc., Lincoln Soc. N.Y., Wis., Ill., Fla., Washington, Civil War Surgeons (hon.), Am. Legion, 82d Airborne Div. Assn., 101st Airborne Div. Assn., Res. Officers Assn., Metropolitan Club, Sigma Xi. Achievements include In 1972, the family of President Kennedy chose him to be the first non-governmental medical specialist to review evidence in the assassination. Died May 10, 2007.

LAUBACH, ROGER ALVIN, accountant; b. Riegelsville, NJ, July 3, 1922; s. Harry and Daisy (Cyphers) L. Diploma in bus. adminstrn., Churchman Bus. Coll., Easton, Pa., 1941; BS cum laude in Acctg., Rider U., 1949. CPA NY, NJ. Acct. Coopers & Lybrand, CPAs, NYC, 1949-60; asst. to treas. Coca-Cola Bottling Co. N.Y., NYC, 1960-63; mgr. audits and systems Atlantic Rsch. Corp., Alexandria, Va., 1964-65; contr. Ely-Cruisksbank Co., Inc., Realtors, NYC, 1965-66, asst. treas., 1966-67, treas., dir., 1967-71; dir. N.Y. Fed. Savs. & Loan Assn., 1970-71; dir. Phila. Acctg. Ctr. Ogden Food Svc. Corp., 1971-72, treas., 1972-77; dir. corp. auditing Ogden Corp., NYC, 1977-79; contr. Burlington County Cmty. Action Program, Burlington, NJ, 1981-84. With US Army, 1942—46, ETO. Decorated Bronze Star, N.J. Disting. Svc. medal, 1998; recipient Cold War cert. recognition, 2000, Burlington County Mil. Svc. medal, 2001, Thank You Am. cert. for participation in liberation of France during World War II, Embassy of France. Mem. AICPA, ARC (vol. bloodmobile 1986—), Inst. Internal Auditors, N.Y. State Soc. CPAs, N.J. Soc. CPAs, Real Estate Bd. N.Y., SAR (registrar, geneal. 1995-2001, War Svc. medal, Liberty medal with 3 bronze oak leaf clusters, cert. of disting. svc.), VFW (life), Am. Legion (life), 100th Inf. Divsn. Assn., Soc. Colonial Wars (life), Laubach Family Assn. (book com. 1989-93), Nat. Trust for Hist. Preservation, Bucks County (Pa.) Hist. Soc., Warren County (N.J.) His. Soc., Delta Sigma Pi (life). Lutheran. Home: Marlton, NJ. Died Nov. 10, 2006.

LAUGHERY, JACK ARNOLD, restaurant chain executive; b. Guthrie Center, Iowa, Feb. 25, 1935; s. Gerald Reve and Mildred Eva (Ansberry) L.; m. Helen Herboth, Sept. 14, 1968; children: Brenda, Kelly, Christine, Sarah. B.C.S., U. Iowa, 1957; grad. exec. program, U. N.C., Chapel Hill, 1976. Salesman Conn. Gen. Ins. Co., 1957-62; with Sandy's Systems, 1962-72, pres., 1969-72, chief operating officer, 1970-72, chief exec. officer, 1971-72; exec. v.p. Hardee's Food Systems, Inc., Rocky Mount, N.C., 1972-73, pres., from 1973, chief operating officer, 1973-75, chief exec. officer, 1975-89, chmn. bd., from 1983; chmn. bd., pres., chief exec. officer Imasco, USA, Rocky Mount, from 1983. Dir. First Union Nat. Bank, Charlotte, N.C. Bd. dirs. Wesleyan Coll., Rocky Mount, Mary Frances Ctr., Tarboro, N.C., N.C. Zool. Soc. Served with AUS, 1957-60. Mem. Nat. Restaurant Assn., N.C. Restaurant Assn., Rocky Mount C. of C. (dir. 1976—, pres. 1985), Am. Mgmt. Assn. Republican. Episcopalian. Home: Rocky Mount, NC. Died Aug. 20, 2006.

LAUGHLIN, CHARLES WILLIAM, agriculture educator, research administrator; b. Iowa City, Iowa, Dec. 9, 1939; s. Ralph Minard and Geraldine (O'Neill) L.; m. Barbara Waln, Dec. 17, 1966; children: Shannon Morris, Charles Tudor, Debra Ann. BS, Iowa State U., 1963; MS, U. Md., 1966; PhD, Va. Tech., 1969. Asst. extension nematologist U. Fla., Gainesville, 1968-69; asst. prof., extension nematologist Mich. State U., East Lansing, 1969-73, assoc. prof., asst. dir. acad. and student affairs, 1973-78, prof., asst. dean, dir. acad. and student affairs, 1978-80; prof., dept. head plant pathology and weed sci. Miss. State U., Starkville, 1980-83; prof., assoc. dir. Ga. Agrl. Expt. Sta. U. Ga., Athens, 1983-92; dir. co., Agrl. Expt. Sta. Colo. State U., Ft. Collins, 1992-96; dean coll. tropical agriculture and human resources U. Hawaii, Honolulu, 1996-99; adminstr. USDA/Coop. State Rsch., Edn., and Ext. Svc., Washington, from 1999. Cons. Brazilian Ministry of Edn. and Culture, Brasilin, Brazil, 1975-77, Brazilian Nat. Agrl. Rsch. Agy., 1978, W.K. Kellogg Found., Battle Creek, Mich., 1983—, Latin Am. Inst. of Creativity, Sáo Paulo, Brazil, 1991. Recipient Colleague award Creative Edn. Found., 1988. Mem. Soc. Nematologists, Am. Phytopathological Soc., Brazilian Soc. Nematologists. Avocations: creative problem solving, outdoors recreation. Died Apr. 27, 2006.

LAVELLE, JOHN W., state legislator; s. Mary Lavelle; m. Susan Lavelle; children: John, Christopher, Danny. Apptd. N.Y. State Charter Commn. for City of Staten Island, 1993; mem. NY State Assembly from 61st dist., 2001—07. Chair Staten Island Continuum of Edn., Silver Lake Area Com. of Cmty. Bd. One, Bd. of Verts. Action Coalition. Serves on Edn., Mental Health, Govt. Employees, Social Svcs., Transp. and Vets. Affairs; vice chair Camelot Counseling Ctrs. Bd. of Dirs.; cmty. adv. bd. Sisters of Charity Health Care Sys.; chmn. adv. bd. St. Vincent's Med. Ctr. Mem.: Brighton Kiwanis Club. Died Jan. 24, 2007.

LAVENDER, ARDIS RAY, health care company executive; b. Bedford, Ind., July 2, 1927; s. Hayden and Genevieve (Hendricks) L.; m. Andrea M. Sabol, Dec. 7, 1968; children: Michael, Teresa, Curtis, Kara, Marc. Student Purdue U., 1944-45, Ind. U., 1947-48; MD, Ind. U., 1953. Assoc. prof. medicine U. Chgo., 1954-68; prof. medicine Loyola U., Maywood, Ill., 1968-75; chief nephrology Hines VA Hosp., Maywood, 1968-75; dir. Kidney & Hypertension Inst., Scranton, Pa., 1975-80; cons. Revlon Health Care, Tuckahoe, N.Y., 1980-82, v.p. med. devices, 1982-87; cons. med. devices, 1988—; cons., lectr. in field; staff U. Chgo., 1953-68, Loyola U. McGaw Hosp., 1968-75, Martha Washington Hosp., Chgo., 1975, Moses Taylor Hosp., Scranton, Pa., 1975-79, Mercy Hosp., Scranton, 1975-79, Community Med. Ctr., Scranton, 1975-79, Scranton State Hosp., 1975-79, Mid-Valley Hosp., Peckville, Pa., 1977-79, St. Joseph's Hosp., Carbondale, Pa., 1977-79, Carbondale Gen. Hosp., Pa., 1977-79. Contbr. articles to profl. jours. Editor Pakistanian Jour. Medicine, 1972. Reviewer, Jour. Lab. and Clin. Medicine, Jour. of AMA, Archives of Internal Medicine, Kidney Internat., Jour. Applied Physiology. USPHS Research Career Devel. awardee, 1965-68; recipient Presdl. citation White House, 1970. Mem. Am. Fedn. Clin. Research, AAAS, Am. Heart Assn., N.Y. Acad. Scis., Central Soc. Clin. Research, Internat. Soc. Nephrology, Chgo. Soc. Internal Medicine, Am. Soc. Nephrology, Am. Soc. Artificial Internal Organs, European Dialysis and Transplant Assn., Am. Assn. for Advancement of Med. Instrumentation, AMA, Lackawanna Med. Soc., Pa. Med. Soc., Internat. Soc. Artificial Internal Organs, Am. Soc. Inventors, Am. Fedn. Clin. Research (pres. 1965-66), Alpha Omega Alpha. Died July 28, 2006.

LAVERNE, MICHEL MARIE-JACQUES, international relations consultant; b. Paris, June 1, 1928; s. Charles Henri Andre and Anne Marie Henriette (Bour) L.; m. Genevieve Laverne Pierès, June 29, 1963; children: Beatrice, Thierry, Loic Heaulme, Christophe, Matthieu. MBA, Ecole des Hautes Etudes Commerciales, 1953; postgrad., Centre de Perfectionnement dans l'Adminstrn. des Affaires, 1960. Various mktg., adminstrn. and fin. positions Shell Group Cos., internat. locations, 1954-73; account exec. Union d'Etudes et Investissements (subs. Credit Agricole), Paris, 1973-76; v.p. fin. Salmon et Cie, Paris, 1976-81; chief exec. officer Cartonneries de St. Germain, 1977-79, Papeteries Maunoury, 1979-80; exec. Generale Biscuit, Athis-Mons, France, 1981-83, former chmn. bd. Italy; pres., CEO Mother's Cookies, Oakland, Calif., 1983-91, Mother's Cookies/Gen. Biscuit Am., 1990-91; assoc. MLG Plus Cons., Oakland, from 1991, Eurosite, Oakland, from 1992. Commr. Internat. Trade and Fgn. Investment Commn., City of Oakland. Mem. Conseiller du Commerce Exterieur de la France (pres. U.S.A. N.W. sect.). Roman Catholic. Avocations: sailing, skiing, photography, hunting. Died May 3, 2006.

LAVIN, BERNICE E., retired cosmetics executive; b. Chgo., Nov. 6, 1925; m. Leonard H. Lavin, Oct. 30, 1947; children: Scott Jay (dec.), Carol Marie, Karen Sue. Student, Northwestern U. Vice chairperson, sec.- treas. Alberto-Culver Co., 1955—2003; dir., v.p., sec.- treas. Alberto-Culver U.S.A., Inc. Sec.-treas., dir. Alberto-Culver Internat., Inc.; sec.-treas. Sally Beauty Co., Inc. Died Oct. 29, 2007.*

LAW, THOMAS HART, lawyer; b. Austin, Tex., July 6, 1918; s. Robert Adger and Elizabeth (Manigault) L.; m. Terese Tarlton, June 11, 1943 (div. Apr. 1956); m. Jo Ann Nelson, Dec. 17, 1960; children: Thomas Hart Jr., Debra Ann. AB, U. Tex., 1939, JD, 1942. Bar: Tex. 1942, U.S. Supreme Ct. 1950. Assoc. White, Taylor & Chandler, Austin, 1942; assoc. Thompson, Walker, Smith & Shannon, Ft. Worth, 1946-50; ptnr. Tilley, Hyder & Law, Ft. Worth, 1950-67, Stone, Tilley, Parker, Snakard, Law & Brown, Ft. Worth, 1967-71; pres. Law, Snakard, Brown & Gambill, P.C., Ft. Worth, 1971-90; of counsel Law, Snakard & Gambill, P.C., Ft. Worth, from 1990. Gen. counsel Gearhart Industries, Inc., Ft. Worth, 1960-88, Tarrant County Coll. Chmn. Leadership Ft. Worth, 1974-90; bd. regents U. Tex. System, 1975-81, vice chmn., 1979-81. Lt. USNR, 1942-46. Recipient Nat. Humanitarian award Nat. Jewish Hosp./Nat. Asthma Ctr., 1983; named Outstanding Young Man, City of Ft. Worth, 1950, Outstanding Alumnus, Coll. of Humanities, U. Tex., 1977, Outstanding Citizen, City of Ft. Worth, 1984, Bus. Exec. of Yr., City of Ft. Worth, 1987, Blackstone award for contbns. field of law Ft. Worth Bar Assn., 1990, Disting. Alumnus U. Tex., 1992. Fellow Am. Bar Found., Tex. Bar Found., Am. Coll. Probate Counsel, Tarrant County Bar Found. (founding chmn.); mem. Ft. Worth C. of C. (pres. 1972), Mortar Bd., Phi Beta Kappa, Omicron Delta Kappa, Pi Sigma Alpha, Delta Sigma Rho, Phi Eta Sigma, Delta Tau Delta. Clubs: Ft. Worth (bd. govs. 1984-90), Century II (bd. govs. to 1985), River Crest Country, Exchange (pres. 1972), Steeplechase. Lodges: Rotary (local club pres. 1960). Democrat. Presbyterian. Avocation: coin collecting/numismatics. Home: Fort Worth, Tex. Died Sept. 2, 2006.

LAWRENCE, EDWARD J., state legislator; b. Everett, Mass., Sept. 14, 1931; m. Marjorie Lawrence; children: James, Nancy, Catherine. Student, Brown U. Ins. broker, cons. Warwick (R.I.) Ins. Agy., Inc., Lawrence Assocs.; senator dist. 15 R.I. State Senate, Providence. Mem. corporations and labor coms., joint com. on vets. affairs, R.I. State Senate. Mem. Profl. Ins. Assn., R.I. Ins. Agts. Assn., Warwick Regular Firearms Assn., Ancient & Honorable Assn., Elks. Died Nov. 9, 2006.

LAWRENCE, WILLIAM JOSEPH, JR., retired corporate executive; b. Kalamazoo, Feb. 1, 1918; s. William J. and Borgia M. (Wheeler) L.; m. Doris Luella Fitzgerald, Aug. 19, 1955; children: Aaron Frances, Cleve Moren, Julie Anne, William III. AB, Kalamazoo Coll., 1941. Engaged in personal investments; dir. emeritus Superior Pine Products Co.; dir. LPI. Trustee emeritus Kalamazoo Found.; trustee emeritus Kalamazoo Coll., Borgess Med. Ctr. With AUS, 1942-46. Mem. Kalamazoo C. of C., Kiwanis, Com. of Twenty-Five (Palm Springs, Calif.), O'Donnell Golf Club (Palm Springs), Gull Lake Country Club, Park Club. Roman Catholic. Home: Richland, Mich. Died Oct. 9, 2006.

LAWSON, DAVID JERALD, retired bishop; b. Princeton, Ind., Mar. 26, 1930; s. David Jonathon and Bonnetta A. (White) L.; m. Martha Ellen Pegram, July 16, 1950; children: John Mark, Karen Sue Lawson Eynon. A.B., U. Evansville, 1955; M.Div., Garrett Theol. Sem., 1959; D.D., U. Evansville, 1977. Ordained to ministry United Methodist Ch. Bishop United Meth. Ch., Wis., 1984-92, Ill., 1992-96, bishop in residence, Perkins Sch. Theology, So. Methodist U., 1996-2007; trustee Ill. Wesleyan Coll., McKendree Coll., MacMurray Coll., Meth. Health Svcs., Peoria, No. Ctrl. Coll., Naperville, Ill., 1984-92; pres. United Meth. Bd. Disciplineship, also chairperson; mem. com. theol. edn. World Meth. Coun., also mem. exec. com.; mem. originating steering com. New Africa U.; mem. Ill. Conf. of Churches, Coun. of Bishop's to Study the Ministry. Author monograph: Administrative Spirituality; contbr. articles to profl. jours. Home: Springfield, Ill. Died May 31, 2007.

LAWSON, NEILS VINTON, retired grocery store chain executive; b. Glenwood, Iowa, Mar. 4, 1922; s. Fred Neils and Mary Alice (Ellingwood) L.; m. L. Lea Bachler, Jan. 3, 1943 Student, U. Nebr., 1946-51; BBA, John F. Kennedy U., 1976. Bookkeeper Safeway Stores, Inc., Omaha, 1945-51, gen. ledger bookkeeper Wichita, Kans., 1951-53, office mgr., 1953-55, systems acct. Oakland, Calif., 1955-57, controller Kansas City, Mo., 1957-61, NYC, 1961-62, staff acct. Oakland, 1962-64, controller S.W. region, 1964-65, mgr. retail acctg. div., 1965-71, mgr. acctg. and data processing orgn., v.p., mgr. mgmt. info. and services group, 1971-83, exec. officer, 1979-84, sr. v.p., 1982-84, dir. corp. strategic systems, 1983-84, ret., 1984. Served with USAF, 1943-45 Mem.: Diablo Country (pres. 1986-87, dir., sec.-treas.) (Calif.). Republican. Presbyterian. Avocations: golf; bowling; art. Home: Lake Quivira, Kans. Died Apr. 2, 2007.

LAWSON, ROBERT BERNARD, psychology professor; b. NYC, June 20, 1940; s. Robert Bernard Sr. and Isabella Theresa (McPeake) L.; children: Christina Megan, Steven Robert, Jennifer Erin. BA in Psychology, Monmouth U., 1961; MA in Psychology, U. Del., 1963, PhD in Psychology, 1965. Mem. faculty U. Vt., Burlington, from 1966, asst. prof. psychology, 1966-69, assoc. prof., 1969-74, prof., from 1974, assoc. v.p. acad. affairs, 1978, assoc. v.p. rsch., dean Grad. Coll., 1978-86, dir. gen. exptl. psychology, 1988-90, chmn. dept. pub. adminstrn., 1990-95, acting dir. MPA program, 1998-99, dir. MPA program, 1999—2002, chmn. dept. psychology, 2002—06. Presenter, worker in China, Russia, and Italy; cons. Mgmt. Sys., 1986—; vis. scholar Stanford U., 1986-87; pres. Alliance Mgmt. Cons. Group, Burlington, 1987—, N.E. Assn. Grad. Schs., Princeton, N.J., 1983-86; bd. dirs. Grad. Record Exams-ETS, Princeton, 1984-88. Author: (with S.G. Goldstein and R.E. Musty) Principles and Methods of Psychology, 1975; (with W.L. Gulick) Human Stereopsis: A Psychophysical Approach, 1976; (with Zheng Shen) Organizational Psychology: Foundations and Applications, 1998; (with Jean E. Graham and Kristin M. Baker) A History of Psychology: Globalization, Ideas, and Applications, 2007. Mem. bd. govs. Univ. Press New England, 1978-86, bd. dirs., 1979-80. Recipient George V. Kidder Disting. Faculty award U. Vt., 2003; numerous grants NIH, NSF, USDA, numerous awards from Nat. Eye Inst. Mem. AAAS, APA, Psychonomic Soc., Coun. Grad. Schs., N.Y. Acad. Scis., Ea. Psychol. Assn. Home: Williston, Vt. Died May 2, 2007.

LAWTON, NANCY, artist; b. Gilroy, Calif., Feb. 28, 1950; d. Edward Henry and Marilyn Kelly (Boyd) L.; m. Richard Enemark, Aug. 4, 1984; children: Faith Lawton, Forrest Lawton. BA in Fine Art, Calif. State U., San Jose, 1971; MFA, Mass. Coll. Art, Boston, 1980. Artist-in-residence Villa Montalvo Ctr. Arts, Los Gatos, Calif., 1971, Noble & Greenough Sch., Dedham, Mass., 1990. One-woman shows include The Bklyn. Mus., 1983, Victoria Munroe Gallery, N.Y.C., 1993, Hirschl & Adler Galleries, N.Y.C., 2002-05; group shows include San Francisco Mus. Modern Art, 1973, The Bklyn. Mus., 1980, 83, Staempfli Gallery, N.Y.C., 1984, The Ark. Art Ctr. Mus., Little Rock, 1984, 88, 92, 93, Victoria Munroe Gallery, 1985, 87, 88, 92, Butler Inst. Am. Art, Ohio, 1988, Smith Coll. Mus. Art, 1988, NAD, N.Y.C., 1988, Reynolds Gallery, Richmond, 1994, Nancy Solomon Gallery, Atlanta, 1995, Arnot Art Mus., Elmira, N.Y., 2001-03, Hunt Inst. for Bot. Documentation, Carnegie Mellon U., Pitts., 2001-02, Hirschl and Adler Galleries, N.Y.C., 2002-06, John Pence Galleries, San Francisco, 2004, Vose Galleries, Boston, 2004, Telfair Mus. Art, Savannah, 2006; pub. collections include The Ark. Art Ctr. Mus., Art Inst. Chgo., Bklyn. Mus., Met. Mus. Art, Smithsonian Am. Art Mus., Washington. Scholar Mellon Found., 1982; N.Y. State Creative Artists grantee, 1983, N.Y. State Arts Devel. Fund grantee, 1989. Died May 5, 2007.

LAY, DONALD POMEROY, retired federal judge; s. Hardy W. and Ruth (Cushing) L.; m. Miriam Elaine Gustafson; children: Stephen Pomeroy(dec.), Catherine Sue, Cynthia Lynn, Elizabeth Ann, Deborah Jean, Susan Elaine. Student, U.S. Naval Acad., 1945—46; BA, U. Iowa, 1948, JD, 1951; LLD (hon.) (hon.), Mitchell Coll. Law, 1985. Bar: Nebr. 1951, Iowa 1951, Wis. 1953. Assoc. Kennedy, Holland, DeLacy & Svoboda, Omaha, 1951—53, Quarles, Spence & Quarles, Milw., 1953—54, Eisenstatt, Lay, Higgins & Miller, 1954—66; judge US Ct. Appeals (8th Cir.), 1966—92, chief judge, 1980—92, sr. judge, 1992—2006. Faculty mem. on evidence Nat. Coll. Trial Judges, 1964—65, U. Minn. Law Sch., William Mitchell Law Sch.; mem. U.S. Jud. Conf., 1980—92. Mem. editl. bd.: Iowa Law Rev., 1950—51; contbr. articles to legal jours. With USNR, 1944—46. Recipient Hancher-Finkbine medal, U. Iowa, 1980, Disting. Alumni award, 2000. Mem.: ATLA (bd. govs. 1963—65, Jud. Achievement award), ABA, Am. Judicature Soc., Wis. Bar Assn., Iowa Bar Assn., Nebr. Bar Assn., Internat. Acad. Trial Lawyers, Order of Coif, Sigma Chi, Phi Delta Phi, Delta Sigma Rho (Significant Sig award 1986, Herbert Harley award 1988). Presbyterian. Died Apr. 29, 2007.

LAY, WILLIAM EDWARD, JR., holding company executive; b. May 11, 1926; s. William E. and Mildred (Woodford) Lay; m. Elizabeth Miller, Aug. 15, 1949; children: Susan, John, Robert, Jane, Anne. BA, Furman U., 1949; postgrad., U. N.C., 1976. With Liberty Life Ins., Greenville, SC, from 1949, sr. v.p., 1978—81; v.p. adminstrn. Liberty Corp., Greenville, SC, from 1974, also dir. Campaign chmn. United Way Greenville County, 1972—73; vice chmn. bd. dirs. Goodwill Industries S.C., 1975—77; chmn. accountancy adv. bd. Greenville Tech. Coll. With USN, 1942—45. Mem.: Adminstrv. Mgmt. Soc. (pres. 1962—63, nat. bd. dirs. 1965—66), Life Office Mgmt. Assn., Am. Mgmt. Assn. Methodist. Home: Greenville, SC. Died Aug. 20, 2006.

LAYBOURNE, EVERETT BROADSTONE, lawyer; b. Springfield, Ohio, Oct. 26, 1911; s. Lawrence Everett and Jean (Broadstone) L.; m. Dorrise Barclay, Sept. 19, 1936 (dec. Nov. 1973); m. Ottilie Kruger, July 31, 1974. BA, Ohio State U., 1932; JD, Harvard, 1935. Bar: Calif. bar 1936. Mem. firms Macdonald, Schultheis & Pettit, 1936-40, Schultheis & Laybourne, 1940-54, Schultheis, Laybourne & Dowds, 1954-68, Laybourne, Keeley & MacMahon, 1968-69; sr. partner Macdonald, Halsted & Laybourne, Los Angeles, 1969-88; of counsel Baker & McKenzie, Los Angeles, 1988-93. Dir. Viking Industries, Pacific Energy Corp., McBain Instruments, Coldwater Investment Co., Brouse-Whited Packaging Co., Calif. Energy Co. Trustee Brite-Lite Corp. Calif.; Calif. chmn. UN Day, 1960; regional vice chmn. U.S. Com. for UN, 1961-64; mem. adv. council Stamp Out Smog, 1963-75; mem. spl. rev. com. Los Angeles Air Pollution Control Dist., 1964-65; Bd. dirs. Fedn. Hillside, Canyon Assos., Los Angeles, 1952-59, chmn. bd., 1957-59; bd. dirs. WAIF, Inc., 1977—, chmn. bd., 1978—; bd. dirs. UN Assn. U.S.A., 1964-65; bd. dirs. Ralph M. Parsons Found., 1977—, v.p., 1978—; trustee, sec. Beta Theta Pi Scholastic Found. So. Calif., 1947-58. Served as lt. USNR, 1944-46. Recipient Commendation Los Angeles City Council, 1957, Ohio State U. Alumni Centennial award, 1970, Alumni Citizenship award, 1988. Mem. Big Ten Univs. Club So. Calif. (pres. 1941-42, Man of Yr. 1997), L.A. Bar Assn. (exec. com. internat. law sect. 1968-74), World Affairs Coun., Selden Soc., Roscomare Valley Assn. (pres. 1952-54), Calif. Club, Bel-Air Country Club, Phi Beta Kappa. Republican. Episcopalian (sr. warden 1966-67). Home: Los Angeles, Calif. Died Dec. 25, 2005.

LAYZER, ARTHUR JAMES, physicist, educator, composer; b. Cleve., Sept. 21, 1927; s. Hilary and Rhea Volk L.; B.S., Case Western Res. U., 1950; Ph.D., Columbia U., 1960; m. Judith Mushabac, 1964; 1 dau., Varese. Research scientist Courant Inst. Math. Scis., 1960-63; asst. prof. physics Stevens Inst. Tech., Hoboken, N.J., from 1964, now asso. prof.; resident visitor Acoustics and Behavioral Research Center, Bell Labs., Murray Hill, N.J., 1967-83. Served with AUS, 1946-48. Brookhaven Nat. Lab. summer research fellow, 1966; U.S. Dept. Edn. grantee, 1978-80. Mem. AAAS, Am. Ednl. Research Assn. Pioneer in print display mode of word replication and its effectiveness for deaf readers, also magnetically-linked pairing mechanism for superfluid state of liquid Helium 3 and supercondrs.; created Morning Elevator, 1st combined computer-generated music and text display and computer-adapted score. Home: New York, NY. Died May 28, 2006.

LEA, ALBERT ROBERT, manufacturing executive; b. Melrose, Mass., May 27, 1921; s. Robert Wentworth and Lillian (Ryan) L.; m. Joyce Winona Padgett, May 17, 1943 (div.); children: Patricia, Jennifer, Anne, Melissa Lea; m. Helen Clay Jones, May 12, 1961; children: Albert Robert, Robbert Wentworth II. AB, Amherst Coll., 1943; student Harvard Grad. Sch. Bus. Adminstrn., 1943. Exec. v.p. Ashcraft Inc., Kansas City, 1957-67, 83-86, pres., 1967-83, also dir.; pres. The Lea Co., 1986—. Trustee Westminster Coll., Fulton, Mo., 1983-88. Lt. Supply Corps, USNR, 1943-46. Mem. Mission Hills Country Club, University Club, Met. Club, Phi Gamma Delta. Home: Kansas City, Mo. Died May 22, 2006.

LEADABRAND, RAY L., engineering executive, defense industry consultant; b. Pasadena, Calif., Oct. 12, 1927; s. Russell Lewis and Monica Laurel (Irwin) L.; m. Mildren Helen Armbruster, Apr. 2, 1955; 1 child, Paul Lewis. AA, Visalia Jr. Coll., 1948; BS, San Jose State U., 1950; MSEE, Stanford U., 1955. Project leader SRI Internat., Menlo Park, Calif., 1955-62, dir., 1962-69, exec. dir., 1969-77, v.p., 1977-79, sr. v.p., 1979-86, Sci. Applications Internat. Corp., Los Altos, Calif., 1986-89. Past mem. Naval Studies Bd. Nat. Rsch. Coun., Washington, adv. com. Def. Intelligence Agy., Washington, 1983-92. Contbr. articles to profl. jours. Served with USN, 1945-46. Fellow IEEE; mem. AIAA (sr.), Am. Geophys. Union, Armed Forces Comm. and Electronics Assn., Assn. Unmanned Vehicle Systems, Am. Bonanza Soc. (bd. dirs.), Assn. Old Crows. Clubs: Cosmos (Washington). Avocation: private pilot. Home: Boise, Idaho. Died Feb. 2, 2006.

LEADERS, FLOYD EDWIN, JR., pharmacologist; b. Denison, Iowa, Dec. 11, 1931; s. Floyd E. and Jessie (Ransom) L.; m. Madeline C. Mullins Van Hoose, Aug. 1, 1975; 1 child, Terra Leaders Singletary. BS in Pharmacy, Drake U., 1955; MS in Pharmacology, State U. of Iowa, 1960, PhD in Pharmacology, 1962. Registered pharmacist, Iowa, Kans., Tex. Instr., then asst. prof. pharmacology U. Kans. Med. Ctr., Kansas City, Mo., 1962-67; head pharmacologic rsch. Alcor Labs., Ft. Worth, 1967-72; dir. rsch. svcs. Plough divsn. Schering-Plough, Memphis, 1972-73; dir. R&D labs. Rennwalt Pharms., Rochester, N.Y., 1973-78; pres. Tech. Evaluation and Mgmt. Sys., Inc., Dallas, 1977-91, Tech. Evaluation and Mgmt. Svcs., Inc., Dallas, 1983-91, The Leaders Group, Inc., Rockville, Md., from 1992. Cons., FDA liaison Office Alternative Medicine, NIH, Bethesda, Md., 1993-95; affiliate prof. dept. pharmacy and toxicology Sch. Pharmacy Purdue U., West Lafayette, Ind., 1978-87; adj. asst. prof. dept. pharmacy Southwestern Med. Sch., Dallas, 1970-72; adj. asst. prof. dept. biology Tex. Christian U., Fort Worth, 1970-72; co-chair DIA workshop on alternative medicine on botanicals. Contbg. author: Pharmacology in Medicines, Principals and Practices, 1986; also author abstracts, reports and articles in field. Founding bd. dirs. Family Gateway, Dallas, 1985-88. With USN, 1951-53. Grantee US-PHS, 1963-67, Am. Cancer soc., 1964-67, NASA, 1965-67. Mem. Am. Soc. Pharmacol. and Exptl. Therapists, Drug Info. Assn., Regulatory Affairs Profl. Soc., Assn. Clin. Pharmacology. Achievements include research in new drug status for three traditional Chinese medicine herbal products and one homeopathic product for pilot studies. Home: Gaithersburg, Md. Died Feb. 26, 2006.

LEAF, BORIS, physicist, researcher; b. Yokohama, Japan, Mar. 4, 1919; came to U.S., 1922, naturalized, 1936; s. Aron L. and Dora (Guralsky) L.; m. Genevieve Lukman, Aug. 28, 1947; children: Evelyn Marie, David Alexander, Michael Leon. BS summa cum laude, U. Wash., 1939; PhD, U. Ill., 1942. Research asst. NDRC, U. Ill., 1942-43; faculty U. Ill., 1943-44; assoc. chemist metall. lab. U. Chgo., 1944-45; Frank B. Jewett fellow Yale, 1945-46; faculty Kans. State U., 1946-65; prof. SUNY, Cortland, 1965-89, chmn. dept. physics, 1965-82, prof. emeritus, 1989, prof. Binghamton, 1968-71; faculty scis. Free U. Brussels, 1958-60; research physicist U.S. Naval Radiol. Def. Lab., San Francisco, 1963, 64, 66; vis. prof. Cornell U. 1973-74. Faculty exchange scholar SUNY, 1974—, to Moscow 1981 Assoc. editor Am. Jour. Physics, 1976-79. Fellow Am Phys. Soc. (exec. com. N.Y. State sect. 1971-73), AAAS; mem AAUP (nat. council 1963-66, nat. com. C 1965-71), N.Y. Acad Sci., Am. Assn. Physics Tchrs., Phi Beta Kappa, Sigma Xi Mem. Phi Kappa Phi; mem. Pi Mu Epsilon, Sigma Pi Sigma, Ph Lambda Upsilon. Achievements include research in statis. mechanics, thermodynamics and quantum mechanics. Home: Seattle, Wash. Died Apr. 25, 2007.

LEBAMOFF, IVAN ARGIRE, lawyer; b. Ft. Wayne, Ind., July 20, 1932; s. Argire V. and Helen A. (Kachandov) L.; m Katherine S. Lebamoff, June 9, 1963; children— Damian I Jordan I., Justin A. AB in History, Ind. U., 1954, JD, 1957. Bar Ind. 1957, U.S. Ct. Dist. Ct. (no. and so. dists.) 1958, U.S Supreme Ct. 1963. Sole practice, Ft. Wayne, Ind., 1957-68; ptn Lebamoff, Ver Wiebe & Snow, Ft. Wayne, Ind., 1968-71; mayo City of Ft. Wayne, 1972-75; sole practice Lebamoff Law Offices Ft. Wayne, from 1975. U.S. commr. No. Dist. Ind., 1957-62; fgr service officer USIA Dept. Commerce, Bulgaria, 1964; vis. prof dept. urban affairs Ind. U.-Purdue, Ft. Wayne, 1976-77 Chmn Allen County Democratic Com., 1968-75, Ft. Wayne Dep Parks and Recreation, 1984-88; nat. pres. Macedonian Patrioti Orgn. of U.S. and Can., 1983-94. Served with USAF, 1958-6 Mem. ABA, Allen County Bar Assn., Ind. Bar Assn., Am. Tria Lawyers Assn., Ind. Trial Lawyers Assn. Lodges: Kiwanis Eastern Orthodox. Home: Fort Wayne, Ind. Died May 18, 2006

LEBECK, WARREN WELLS, commodities consultant; b Chgo., Mar. 13, 1921; s. Emil and Hazel (Wells) L.; m. Doroth Lester, Feb. 1, 1943; children: Sara Beth, Kenneth, Clayton A Frederick E. BA, North Central Coll., Naperville, Ill., 194 With Montgomery Ward & Co., Chgo., 1941-42, 46-54; wit Chgo. Bd. Trade, 1954-79, sec., then exec. v.p., 1957-73, pres 1973-77, sr. exec. v.p., 1977-79; pvt. practice cons. Chgo., fro 1979. Past dir. Bank of Hinsdale, Ill.; past chmn. bd., pres. Sout Loop Improvement Project; mem. U.S. Agrl. Policy Adv. Com 1976-87; trustee Nat. Agrl. Forum, 1983-86; bd. dirs., exe com. U.S. Feed Grains Coun., 1978-90, Agrl. Coun. Am 1980-90; bd. dirs., exec. com. Nat. Grain Trade Coun., 1968-9 chmn., 1988-89; mem. founding com., bd. dirs., exec. com. Na Futures Assn., 1982—. Former mem. bd. edn. Downers Grov (Ill.) Twp. High Sch. Served with USNR, 1942-45. Died Fe 14, 2007.

LEBLANC, RUFUS JOSEPH, SR., geology educator, co sultant, researcher; b. Erath, La., Oct. 12, 1917; s. Aladain ar Orore (Nunez) LeB.; m. Alva Mae Broussard, Mar. 10, 194 children: Rufus Jr., Paul, Lucille. BS in Geology, La. State U 1939, MS in Geology, 1941. Chief geologist Mississippi Riv Commn., Baton Rouge, 1941-48; rsch. geologist, then mgr. ge rsch. Shell Oil Co., Shell Devel. Co., Houston, 1948-86; pri Rufe LeBlanc Sch. Sediments, Houston, from 1986. Cont numerous articles to profl. jours. Fellow Geol. Soc. Am. (sr. hon. life mem. Am. Assn. Petroleum Geologists (Best Pap award 1974, assoc. editor jour. 1975-81, Sidney Powers Men award 1988), Soc. for Sedimentary Geology, Gulf Coast Ass Geol. Socs., Houston Geol. Soc. Republican. Roman Catholi Avocation: music collector. Died June 19, 2007.

LE CLAIR, CHARLES GEORGE, artist, retired dean; Columbia, Mo., May 23, 1914; s. Carl Amie and Marie (Fes LeC.; m. Margaret Foster, May 30, 1945 (dec. Nov. 1991). B MS, U. Wis., 1935; posgrad., Acad. Ranson, Paris, 193 Columbia U., 1940-41. Instr. art U. Ala., 1935-36, asst. pro head dept., 1937-42; asst. prof. art, head dept. Albion Co 1942-43; tchr. painting and design Albright Art Sch., Buffa 1943-46; assoc. prof., head dept. Chatham Coll., 1946-52, pro 1952-60; dean Tyler Sch. Art, Temple U., Phila., 1960-74, de emeritus, 1981—2007, prof. painting, 1974-81, chmn. painti and sculpture dept., 1979-81. Founder Tyler Sch. Art, Rom Italy, 1966. Author: The Art of Watercolor, 1985, rev. ed. 1994, expanded edit., 1999, Color in Contemporary Paintin 1991; contbg. author: Everything You Ever Wanted to Kno About Oil Painting, 1994; works exhibited at Pa. Acad. M Mus. Art, Carnegie Inst., Whitney Mus., Corcoran Mus., Chg Art Inst., Richmond Mus., Butler Mus. Art, Am. Waterco

Soc., Bklyn. Mus.; one-man shows include Carnegie Inst., 1954, Salpeter Gallery, N.Y.C., 1956, 59, 65, Rochester Inst. Tech., 1958, Phila. Art Alliance, 1962, 73, 2000, Franklin and Marshall Coll., 1969, Galleria 89, Rome, 1970, Left Bank Gallery, Wellfleet, 1983, 87, 96, Temple U., 1978, Visual Images, Wellfleet, 1978-80, Gross-McCleaf Gallery, Phila., 1979, 81, 96, 98, 2002, 04, More Gallery Phila., 1983, 87, 89, Villanova U., 1998, Carspecken-Scott Gallery, Wilmington, Del., 1999, Susquehanna Mus. Art, Harrisburg, Pa., 2003. Named Pitts. Artist of Yr., 1957; recipient Pennell medal Pa. Acad. Fine Arts, 1965, Achievement award Am. Artist mag., 1995, Lifetime Achievement award Watercolor Honor Soc., 1997; fellow Fund for Advancement Edn. Ford Found., 1952-53. Achievements include being subject of Elizabeth Leonard's book Painting Flowers, 1986, cover story Watercolor mag., 1999. Home: Philadelphia, Pa. Died Apr. 2, 2007.

LECLERCQ, JACQUES JEAN, retail grocery exexcutive; b. Brussels, Aug. 15, 1929; came to U.S., 1981; s. Jean Louis and Marguerite (Francois) LeC.; m. Therese Blaton, Sept. 12, 1954 (div. 1983); 1 child, Sophie; m. Winnie Mae Chandler, Mar. 16, 1983; 1 child, Sophie. BSBA, U. Antwerp, 1951. With La Couverture, Alost, Belgium, 1954-57, Dehaize The Lion Am., Inc., Atlanta, from 1957; dir. Food Lion, Inc., Salisbury, N.C., from 1974, Johnson Wax/Belgium, Brussels, Le Lion/Belgium; pres. Delhaize/Am., Atlanta, from 1981. Site cons. Wakefern Food Corp., Edison, N.J., 1987—. Res. lt. Belgian Army, 1952-54. Decorated Order of Merit French Govt., Order of Merit Belgian Govt., Order of Merit Italian Govt. Mem. Food Mktg. Inst., Internat. Assn. Chain Stores, World Trade Club, Tastevin Club, Cherokee Club. Republican. Roman Catholic. Avocations: swimming, travel. Home: Atlanta, Ga. Died July 17, 2006.

LE CORGNE, RICHARD KENNETH, insurance and investment company executive, consultant; b. New Orleans, Nov. 2, 1943; s. Earl Raymond and Isabelle Marie (de los Reyes) Le C.; m. Mary Ellen Smyer, Dec. 17, 1966; children— Richard Kenneth, Michelle Elizabeth. B.A., U. New Orleans, 1965. Vice pres. Tele Tector of La., New Orleans, 1969-71; trainer, agt. Mut. of N.Y., New Orleans, 1971-77; sales mgr. Life of Va., New Orleans, 1977-79; unit supr. Provident Mut. Life Ins. Co., New Orleans, 1979-80; agy. supr. Conn. Mut. Life Ins. Co., New Orleans, 1981-84; owner The LeCorgne Fin. Group, 1984—; gen. agt. CM Alliance, New Orleans, 1984—. Contbr. articles to profl. jours. Ambassador Life Underwriters Polit. Action Com., 1983-86; bd. dirs. Lafreniere Park Found., Metairie, La., 1985-86; pres. Friends of Lafreniere Park, Metairie, 1985-86. Mem. New Orleans Life Underwriters Assn. (dir. 1983-88), New Orleans Gen. Agts. and Mgrs. Assn. (sec., bd. dirs. 1985-87), Assn. C.L.U.s (bd. dirs. New Orleans chpt. 1985-88), New Orleans Life Underwriters Assn. (chmn. legis. com. 1983—), New Orleans Health Underwriters Assn. Democrat. Roman Catholic. Avocations: tennis; the arts; fishing; photography; art. Home: Metairie, La. Died Feb. 22, 2007.

LE COUNT, VIRGINIA G., communications company executive; b. L.I. City, NY, Nov. 22, 1917; d. Clifford R. and Luella (Meier) LeCount. BA, Barnard Coll., 1937; MA, Columbia U., 1940. Tchr. pub. schs., P.R., 1937-38; supr. HOLC, NYC, 1938-40; translator Guildhall Publs., NYC, 1940-41; office mgr. Sperry Gyroscope Co., Garden City, Lake Success, Bklyn. (all NY), 1941-45; billing mgr. McCann Erickson, Inc., NYC, 1945-56; v.p., bus. mgr., bd. dirs. Infoplan Internat, Inc., NYC, 1956-69; v.p., bus. mgr. Communications Affiliates Ltd., Communications Affiliates (Bahamas) Ltd., NYC, 1964-69; bus. mgr. Jack Tinker & Ptnrs., Inc., NYC, 1969-70; mgr. office services Interpublic Group of Cos., Inc., NYC, 1971-72, corp. records mgr., 1972-83, mktg. intelligence data mgr., 1975-83. Mem. Alumnae Barnard Coll., N.Y. Health and Racquet Club Spa. Mem. Marble Collegiate Ch. Home: University Park, Fla. Died Mar. 12, 2006.

LEDDY, SUSAN KUN, retired nursing educator; b. NJ, Feb. 3, 1939; d. Bert B. and Helen (Neumann) Kun; children: Deborah, Erin. BS, Skidmore Coll., 1960; MS, Boston U., 1965; PhD, NYU, 1973; cert., Harvard U., 1985. Chair dept. nursing Mercy Coll., Debbs Ferry, N.Y.; dean sch. nursing U. Wyo., Laramie, dean coll. health scis.; prof. Widener U. Sch. Nursing, Chester, Pa., 1988—2006, prof. emeritus, from 2006, dean, 1988-93. Author: (with M. Pepper) Conceptual Bases of Professional Nursing, 1985, 4th edit., 1998, (with L. Hood), Leddy and Pepper's Conceptual Bases of Professional Nursing, 2003, Integrative Hearth Promotion, 2003. Bd. dirs. Springfield Hosp., 1992-94. Postdoctoral fellow U. Pa., 1994-96. Mem. NLN (bd. dirs. and 1st v.p. 1985-87), Soc. Rogerian Scholars (bd. dirs. 2001-03). Avocations: travel, watercolor painting, knitting, quilting, weaving. Home: Aston, Pa. Died Feb. 23, 2007.

LEDERLE, JOHN WILLIAM, political science professor, former academic administrator; b. Royal Oak, Mich., May 26, 1912; s. Emil John and Minnie Louise (Shore) L.; m. Angie Pamela King, Apr. 16, 1938; children: Pamela Jean, Thomas Paine. AB, U. Mich., 1933, A.M., 1934, LL.B., 1936, PhD, 1942; Litt.D., Amherst Coll., 1963, Holy Cross, 1963, Boston U., 1965; LL.D., Hokkaido U., Japan, 1963, U. Mass., 1970; D.Pub. Adminstrn., Northeastern U., 1964; D.Sc. in Edn, Lowell State Coll., 1970. Bar: Mich. bar 1936, U.S. Supreme Ct. bar 1947. With firm Lucking, Van Auken & Sprague, Detroit, 1936-40; staff atty. Mich. Municipal League, 1945-48, gen. counsel, 1948-51; instr. polit. sci. Brown U., 1941-44, asst. prof., 1944, asst. to dean coll., 1942-44, asst. dean coll., 1944; asst. prof. polit. sci. U. Mich., 1944-48, assoc. prof., 1948-50, prof., 1950-60, on leave, 1953-54; sec. Inst. Pub. Adminstrn., 1947-48, dir. curriculum, 1948-50, dir., 1950-60; pres. U. Mass., 1960-70, Joseph B. Ely prof. govt., 1970-82. Controller State of Mich., 1953-54; sec. State Adminstrv. Bd., 1953-54; mem. Mich. State Bldg. Commn., 1953-54; chmn. Mich. Commn. on Interstate Cooperation, 1953-54; mem. exec. com. Flint Coll., U. Mich., 1958-59, Dearborn Center, U. Mich., 1959-60; cons. to U.S. Senate spl. campaign expenditures coms. of, 1944 and 1946, to U.S. Ho. of Reps. spl. campaign expenditures com. of, 1950; cons. sub-com. on privileges and elections U.S. Sen. Com. Rules and Adminstrn., 1952; cons. Mut. Security Agy., 1952; ..., adviser Inst. Pub. Adminstrn., U. Philippines, 1952-53; collaborator U.S. Forest Service; cons. Com. on Govt. and Higher Edn., 1958-59 Bd. editors: Pub. Adminstrn. Rev, 1954-56; Contbr. articles to profl. jours. Mem. Mass. Bd. Ednl. Assistance, 1960-65; mem. New Eng. Bd. Higher Edn., 1961-73, Mass. adv. bd. Higher Edn. Policy, 1962-65; Mass. Bd. Regional Community Colls., 1960-70; Mem. state com. YMCA Mich., 1957-60; chmn. Mass. Gov.'s Spl. Com. on Local Govt. Mgmt. Capacity, 1976-78; Trustee Hampshire Coll., 1965-70, Clarke Sch. for Deaf, 1975-86. Recipient Univ. medal for outstanding service U. Mass., 1982; Sesquicentennial Disting. Service award U. Mich., 1967 Mem. Am. Soc. Pub. Adminstrn. (chmn. conf. of dirs. bur. govt. research 1958-61), Assn. State Univ. and Land Grant Colls. (exec. com. 1967-70), Am. Polit. Sci. Assn., Mich. Municipal Attys. Assn. (sec.-treas. 1947-48), Mich. Union, Mich. Municipal League (hon. life) Home: Amherst, Mass. Died Feb. 13, 2007.

LEE, HARRY REES, civil engineer; b. Des Moines, July 21, 1929; s. Harry Rees and Evelyn Marie (Croxen) L.; B.S. in Civil Engring., U. Wash., 1953, M.S. in Civil Engring., 1954; m. Mary Ann Penty, Nov. 12, 1955; children— Mark, Marica, Michael. Materials engr. Naval Civil Engring. and Research Lab., Port Hueneme, Calif., 1954-56; pres. Alaska Testlab, Anchorage, 1956-78; partner Dowl Engrs., Anchorage, 1973-78; pres. H4M Corp., Anchorage, 1979—; chmn. bd. Denali Drilling Co. Chmn. sch. budget advisory com. Municipality of Anchorage, 1979-84, mem. geotech. com., 1977-83, chmn. geotech. com., 1977, chmn. mcpl. budget com., 1966-77, chmn. economic devel. com., 1972-75. Served with USNR, 1950-51. Decorated Air medal. Fellow ASCE; mem. Nat. Soc. Profl. Engrs., Alaska Soc. Profl. Engrs. (pres. 1963), ASTM, AAAS. Home: Anchorage, Alaska. Died Feb. 15, 2007.

LEFEVRE, PERRY DEYO, minister, theologian, educator; b. Kingston, NY, July 12, 1921; s. Johannes and Faye (McFerran) LeF.; m. Carol Baumann, Sept. 14, 1946; children: Susan Faye, Judith Ann, Peter Gerret. AB, Harvard U., 1943; BD, Chgo. Theol. Sem., 1946, DD, 1992; PhD, U. Chgo., 1951. Ordained to ministry Congl. Ch. (now United Ch. of Christ), 1946. Instr. religion Franklin and Marshall Coll., 1948-49; asst., then assoc. prof. religion Knox Coll., 1949-53, Fed. Theol. Sem., U. Chgo., 1953-61; prof. constructive theology Chgo. Theol. Sem., 1961-92, dean of faculty, 1961-81, acting dean, 1990-91. Author: The Prayers of Kierkegaard, 1956, The Christian Teacher, 1958, Introduction to Religious Existentialism, 1963, Understandings of Man, 1966, Philosophical Resources for Christian Thought, 1968, Conflict in a Voluntary Association, 1975, Understandings of Prayer, 1981, Radical Prayer, 1982; editor: Aging and the Human Spirit, 1981, Paul Tillich: The Meaning of Health, 1984, Spiritual Nurture and Congregational Development, 1984, Daniel Day Williams Essays in Process Theology, 1985, Pastoral Care and Liberation Praxis, 1986, Bernard Meland Essays in Constructive Theology, 1988, Creative Ministries in Contemporary Christianity, 1991, Modern Theologies of Prayer, 1995, Challenge and Response, 1999. Mem. Phi Beta Kappa. Died Aug. 20, 2006.

LEFKOWITZ, HOWARD N., lawyer; b. Utica, NY, Oct. 28, 1936; s. Samuel I. and Sarah Lefkowitz; m. Martha Yelon, June 16, 1958; children: Sarah, David. BA, Cornell U., 1958; LLB, Columbia U., 1963. Bar: N.Y. 1963. Ptnr. Proskauer Rose LLP, NYC, from 1963. Cons. in field. Co-author: New York LLC and LLP Forms and Practice Manual, Data Trace, rev. edit. 2003; co-author: Transactional Lawyers Deskbook: Advising Business Entities West, 2001; editor Columbia Law Rev., 1963; contbg. editor Encyclopedia of Private and Venture Capital. Lt. (j.g.) USN, 1958-61. Kent scholar, Columbia U. Law Sch. Mem.: Tri Bar Opinion Com., N.Y. Pvt. Investment Funds Forum (chmn. 2004), N.Y. County Lawyers Assn. (chmn. com. on comm. entertainment and arts-related law 1983—86), Assn. Bar City of N.Y. (chmn. com. on corp. law 1990—93, com. on corp. law 1997—2000), ABA (mem. partnership and uninc. bus. orgns. from 1993, legal opionions from 1995). Home: New York, NY. Died Mar. 12, 2007.

LEIBOWITT, SOL DAVID, lawyer; b. Bklyn., Feb. 18, 1912; s. Morris and Bella (Small) Leibowitt; m. Ethel Leibowitt, June 18, 1950 (dec. Aug. 1985); m. Babs Lee, Dec. 28, 1986 (dec. June 2000). BA, Lehigh U., Bethlehem, Pa., 1933; JD, Harvard U., Cambridge, Mass., 1936. CPA; bar: NY 1937, Conn. 1970. Pvt. practice, NYC, 1937-84, Stamford, Conn., 1970-78, Milford, Conn., 1978-79; gen. counsel New Haven Clock and Watch Co., 1955-59, pres., 1958-59, Diagnon Corp., 1981-83, vice chmn., 1983-86. Chmn. Card Tech. Corp., 1983-85; Phi Beta Kappa 1977-79. Author: (folk poetry) Wit and Whimsy, A Lawyer's Adventures on the Road to Success, 2005. Pres. Ethel and David Leibowitt Found.; dir. Am. Com. for Weizmann Inst. Sci.; mediator family law Supreme Ct. State Fla. 15th Jud. Ct., 1990—; arbitrator Am. Arbitration Assn., Fla.; chmn. Israel Cancer Assn. USA; dir. Am. Assocs., Ben-Gurion U., 1999. Recipient Human Rels. award Anti-Defamation League, 1969, Ethel Leibowitt Fund Johns Hopkins U. Sch. Medcine Meml. award Anti-Defamation League, 1971, Tikvah award Israel Cancer Assn., 1995. Mem.: ABA, Am. Soc. for Technion U. (bd. dirs., v.p., Conn. pres., life trustee), Anti-Defamation League (commr.), NY State Bar Assn., Assn. Bar NYC, Harvard Club (NYC), Lotos Club. Died July 31, 2006.

LEIGHTON, FRANCES SPATZ, writer, journalist; b. Geauga County, Ohio; m. Kendall King Hoyt, Feb. 1, 1984 (dec. Aug. 2001). Student, Ohio State U. Washington corr. Am. Weekly, Internat. News Svc.; corr. and Washington editor This Week Mag.; Washington corr. Met. Group Sunday Mags.; contbg. editor Family Weekly; freelance journalist Metro Sunday Group, Washington. Lectr. summer confs. Dellbrook-Shenandoah Coll., Georgetown U., Washington. Author over 30 books on hist. figures, celebrities, Hollywood, psychiatry, the White House and Capitol Hill, 1957—; co-author (with Louise Pfister) I Married a Psychiatrist, 1961, (with Francois Rysovy) A Treasury of White House Cooking, 1968; (with Frank S. Caprio) How to Avoid a Nervous Breakdown, 1969; (with Mary B. Gallagher) My Life with Jacqueline Kennedy, 1969; (with Traphes Bryant) Dog Days at the White House, 1975; (with William Fishbait Miller) Fishbait— the Memoirs of the Congressional Doorkeeper, 1977; (with Lillian Rogers Parks) My 30 Years Backstairs at the White House, 1979, The Roosevelts, a Family in Turmoil, 1981; (with Hugh Carter) Cousin Beedie, Cousin Hot--, My Life with the Carter Family of Plains, Georgia, 1978; (with Jerry Cammarata) The Fun Book of Fatherhood-or How the Animal Kingdom is Helping to Raise the Wild Kids at Our House, 1978; (with Natalie Golos) Coping with Your Allergies, 1979; (with Ken Hoyt) Drunk Before Noon— The Behind the Scenes Story of the Washington Press Corps, 1979; (with Louis Hurst) The Sweetest Little Club in the World, The Memoirs of the Senate Restaurateur, 1980; (with John M. Szostak) In the Footsteps of Pope John Paul II, 1980; (with June Allyson) June Allyson, 1982; (with Beverly Slater) Stranger in My Bed, 1985, The Search for the Real Nancy Reagan, 1987; (with Oscar Collier) How To Write and Sell Your First Nonfiction Book, 1990, How to Write and Sell Your First Novel, 1986; (with Stephen M. Bauer) At Ease at the White House, 1991; contbg. author: Katherine Graham's Washington, 2002; contbr. numerous feature stories on polit., social and govtl. personalities to various publs. Bd. dirs. Nat. Found., 1963-2007. Recipient Edgar award, 1961. Mem. AAUW, Senate Periodical Corr. Assn., White House Corr. Assn., Am. News Women's Club, The Writers Club, Nat. Press Club, Writers League of Washington (pres.), Washington League Am. Pen Women (pres.), Washington Ind. Writers, Smithsonian Assocs., Nat. Trust Hist. Preservation, Lake Barcroft Women's Club, Delta Phi Delta, Sigma Delta Chi. Unitarian Universalist. Died Apr. 6, 2007.

LEIGHTON, THOMAS GIBBONS, management consultant; b. Mpls., Mar. 13, 1925; s. William Henry and Anna Marie (Jensen) L.; B.A. cum laude, U. Minn., 1948; grad. study, U. Wis.; m. Mary Miller, July 20, 1963; children— Pamela Ann, Thomas Jensen. Reporter, columnist Mpls. Daily Times, 1942-48; officer savs. bonds div. U.S. Treasury Dept., Washington, 1948-50; dir. info. U.S. Displaced Persons Commn., Washington, 1951-52; advisor to majority policy com. U.S. Senate Washington, 1953-56; dir. pub. relations Nat. Cultural Center for Performing Arts, Washington, 1956-60; sr. v.p., dir., dir. mgmt. counseling div. Dudley-Anderson-Yutzy Pub. Relations and Pub. Affairs, Inc., N.Y.C., 1960-77; pres. Thomas G. Leighton & Co., mgmt. cons., 1977—; cons. to W. K. Kellogg Co., Northeast Utilities, Kaiser Aluminum & Chem. Corp., Westinghouse Corp., McKinsey & Co., Inc., 1977—. Mem. Pub. Relations Soc. Am. (counselors sect., recipient Silver Anvil award 1975). Unitarian. Home: Winchester, Va. Died July 25, 2007.

LEMERT, JAMES BOLTON, retired journalist, educator; b. Sangerfield, NY, Nov. 5, 1935; s. Jesse Raymond and Caroline Elizabeth (Brown) L.; m. Rosalie Martha Bassett, Mar. 23, 1972. AB, U. Calif., Berkeley, 1957, M in Journalism, 1959; PhD, Mich. State U., 1964. Newspaper reporter Oakland (Calif.) Tribune, 1955-56, Chico (Calif.) Enterprise-Record, 1957, 58-60; asst. prof. journalism So. Ill. U., Carbondale, 1964-67; asst. prof. U. Oreg., Eugene, 1967-69, assoc. prof., 1969-76, prof. sch. journalism/comm., 1976-98, dir. divsn. comm. rsch., 1967-94, dir. grad. program Sch. Journalism, 1983-86, 88-93. Chairperson task force to revise faculty governance U. Oreg., 1983-84, mem. senate, 1981-83, 86-88, 93-94, mem. pres.'s adv. coun., 1990-91, chairperson pres.'s adv. coun., 1991-92, mem. grad. coun., 1984-86, 89-90, 94-96, chairperson grad. coun., 1993-94, chairperson task force on rsch. and grad. edn., 1990-91. Prodr., on-air host Old Grooves show Sta. KWAX-FM, 1977-80, 82-84; author: Does Mass Communication Change Public Opinion After All? A New Approach to Effects Analysis, 1981, Criticizing the Media: Empirical Approaches, 1989, News Verdicts, The Debates and Presidential Campaigns, 1991, Politics of Disenchantment: Bush, Clinton, Perot and the Press, 1996; editor Daily Californian, 1957; contbr. articles to profl. jours., newspapers and mags., chpts. to books. Mem. Oreg. Alcohol and Drug Edn. Adv. Com., 1968-69; pres. South Hills Neighborhood Assn., 1976-77, bd. dirs., 1982-84, 86-88; bd. dirs. Traditional Jazz Soc. Oreg., 1981-83, 87; v.p. Met. Cable Access Corp., 1983-84; mem. exec. bd. AAUP, 1975-76, 91-94; mem. state exec. com., head chpt. Assn. Oreg. Faculties, 1981-83, 85-87, state v.p., 1987-89, del. to Oreg. Faculties Polit. Action Com., 1986-89. Recipient Outstanding Journalist award Sigma Delta Chi, 1957, Donald M. McGammon Communication Rsch. Ctr. critical rsch. grantee, 1988-89, Allen Family Found. grantee; NSF fellow, 1963, 64; Calif. Newspaper Pubs. fellow, 1957; Butte County Alumni scholar, 1953-54 Mem. Assn. Edn. in Journalism and Mass Comm. (vice chairperson civic journalism interest group 1995-96), Am. Assn. Pub. Opinion Rsch., Am. Polit. Sci. Assn., Phi Beta Kappa (membership chmn. 1985-86, v.p., pres. 1989-91). Home: Waldport, Oreg. Died Dec. 13, 2005.

LEMESSURIER, WILLIAM JAMES, JR., structural engineer; b. Pontiac, Mich., June 12, 1926; s. William James and Bertha Emma (Sherman) LeM.; m. Dorothy Wright Judd, June 20, 1953; children: Claire Elizabeth, Irene Louise, Peter Wright. AB cum laude, Harvard U., 1947, postgrad., 1948; SM, MIT, 1953. Registered profl. engr., Mass., D.C., N.Y., Tenn., Colo. Ptnr. Goldberg, LeMessurier Assocs., Boston, 1952-61; pres. LeMessurier Assocs. Inc., Boston and Cambridge, 1961-73; chmn. Sippican Cons. Internat. Inc., Cambridge, 1973-85, LeMessurier Cons. Inc., Cambridge, 1985—2007. Instr. dept. bldg. constrn. and engring. MIT, 1951-52, asst. prof., 1952-56, assoc. prof. dept. architecture, 1964-67, sr. lectr. dept. civil engring., 1976-77, lectr., 1983-86; assoc. prof. grad. sch. design Harvard U., 1956-61, adj. prof., 1973; vis. lectr. Yale U., U. Mich., U. Ill., Chgo., Rice U., Washington U., St. Louis, Northeastern U., R.I. Sch. Design, Cornell U., U. Pa., Roger Williams Coll., U. Calif., Berkeley, U. Tex., Austin; speaker Assn. Collegiate Schs. of Architecture Constrn. Materials and Tech. Inst., Harvard U.; mem. sci. adv. com. Nat. Ctr. Earthquake Engring. Research. Co-author: Structural Engineering Handbook, 1968, 2d edit., 1979; prin. works include New Boston City Hall, Shawmut Bank Boston, 1st Nat. Bank Boston, Fed. Res. Bank Boston, Citicorp Ctr., N.Y.C., Dallas-Ft. Worth Airport Terminal Bldgs., Ralston Purina Hdqrs., St. Louis, Nat. Air and Space Mus., Washington, AIA hdqrs., Washington, One Post Office Sq., Boston, Bank Southwest Tower, Houston, InterFirst Plaza Dallas Main Ctr., Treasury Bldg., Singapore, King Khalid Mil. City, Al Batin, Saudi Arabia, TVA Hdqrs., Chattanooga, Lafayette Place Hotel, Boston, acad. bldgs. at

Harvard U., Princeton U., Amherst Coll., Bowdoin Coll., Williams Coll., U. Mass., U. Wis., U. Ill., Colby Coll., U. N.H., Northea. U., Kirkland Coll., Cornell U. Mem. Cambridge Experimentation Rev. Bd., 1977; juror Capitol area archtl. and planning bd. State Capitol Bldg. Extension, St. Paul, 1977, Progressive Architecutre mag., Portland Cement Assn. Awards, 1986, Fazlur Rahman Kahn Internat. Fellowship, N.Y.C., 1987; tech. advisor to jury Boston Archtl. Ctr. Competition. Recipient Profl. Svc. award Engring. News-Record, 1978, Prestressed Concrete Inst. award, 1984. Fellow ASCE (hon.), Am. Concrete Inst., AIA (hon., juror regional awards program No. Vt. 1980, Allied Professions medal 1968); mem. NAE, Boston Soc. Archs. (hon.), Boston Soc. Civil Engrs. (hon.), Boston Assn. Structural Engrs. (past pres.), Am. Inst. Steel Constrn. (specifications adv. com. 1961—, Award of Excellence 1962, 66, 70, 77, 79, Spl. award 1972), VA (adv. bd. div. constrn.), Nat. Com. on Housing Tech., Structural Clay Products Inst. (bldg. code com.), Seismic Safety Coun. (task com.), Bldg. Code Com., Internat. Masonry Inst. (rsch. coun.), Tau Beta Pi. Clubs: Met. (N.Y.C.), St. Botolph, Boston. Episcopalian. Achievements include developing Mah-LeMessurier high-rise housing system; conceived and developed Staggered Truss System for use in high-rise steel structures; conceived, developed and applied Tuned Mass Damper System to reduce tall bldg. motion. Home: Casco, Maine. Died June 14, 2007.

LENDER, HERMAN JOSEPH, reinsurance company executive; b. Irvington, NJ, Sept. 2, 1923; s. Herman Joseph and Monica (Martesteck) L.; m. Janet Harriet Van Wert, June 15, 1945; children: Mark, Jonathan, David, Paul. Student, NYU, 1941-43, Rutgers U., 1943-45. Underwriter, br. office Am. Surety Co., Newark, 1940-49; supervising underwriter Fidelity & Casualty Co., NYC, 1949-58; v.p. bonding Excess and Treaty Mgmt. Co., NYC, 1958-67; v.p. mktg. Gen. Reins. Corp., Greenwich, Conn., 1967-85; reins. cons., from 1986. Instr. Coll. Ins., N.Y.C., 1949-55 Pres., trustee Mt. Tabor Free Library Assn., N.J., 1962-71; lay leader United Meth. Ch., 1955-71, chmn. edn. com., New Canaan, 1971-85; chmn. council of ministries United Meth. Ch., Mt. Tabor, N.J. Mem. Soc. C.P-.C.U.s (chmn. edn. com. H.Y. chpt. 1951-53) Died Oct. 1, 2005.

L'ENGLE, MADELEINE (MRS. HUGH FRANKLIN), writer; b. NYC, Nov. 29, 1918; d. Charles Wadsworth and Madeleine (Barnett) Camp; m. Hugh Franklin, Jan. 26, 1946 (dec., 1986); children: Josephine Franklin Jones, Maria Franklin Rooney (adopted), Bion (dec. 1999). AB, Smith Coll., 1941; postgrad., New Sch., 1941-42, Columbia U., 1960-61; holder 19 hon. degrees. Tchr. St. Hilda's and St. Hugh's Sch., from 1960; mem. faculty U. Ind., 1965-66, 71; writer-in-residence Ohio State U., 1970, U. Rochester, 1972, Wheaton Coll., 1976—2007, Cathedral St. John the Divine, NYC, 1965—2007. Author: The Small Rain, 1945, Ilsa, 1946, Camilla Dickinson, 1951, A Winter's Love, 1957, And Both Were Young, 1949, Meet the Austins, 1960, A Wrinkle in Time, 1962, The Moon by Night, 1963, The 24 Days Before Christmas, 1964, The Arm of the Starfish, 1965, The Love Letters, 1966, The Journey with Jonah, 1968, The Young Unicorns, 1968, Dance in the Desert, 1969, Lines Scribbled on an Envelope, 1969, The Other Side of the Sun, 1971, A Circle of Quiet, 1972, A Wind in the Door, 1973, The Summer of the Great-Grandmother, 1974, Dragons in the Waters, 1976, The Irrational Season, 1977, A Swiftly Tilting Planet, 1978, The Weather of the Heart, 1978, Ladder of Angels, 1980, A Ring of Endless Light, 1980, Walking on Water, 1980, A Severed Wasp, 1982, And It Was Good, 1983, A House Like a Lotus, 1984, Trailing Clouds of Glory, 1985, A Stone for a Pillow, 1986, Many Waters, 1986, Two-Part Invention, 1988, A Cry Like a Bell, 1987, Sole Into Egypt, 1989, From This Day Forward, 1988, An Acceptable Time, 1989, The Glorious Impossible, 1990, Certain Women, 1992, The Rock That Is Higher: Story As Truth, 1993, Anytime Prayers, 1994, Troubling a Star, 1994, Penguins and Golden Calves, 1996, A Live Coal in the Sea, 1996, Glimpses of Grace, 1996, Wintersong, 1996, Mothers and Daughters, 1997, Friends for the Journey, 1997, Bright Evening Star: Mystery of the Incarnation, 1997, The Other Dog, 2001, Madeleine L'Engle Herself: Reflections on a Writing Life (with Carole Chase), 2001 Pres. Crosswicks Found. Recipient Newbery medal, 1963, Sequoyah award, 1965, runner-up Hans Christian Andersen Internat. award, 1964, Lewis Carroll Shelf award, 1965, Austrian State Lit. award, 1969, Bishop's Cross, 1970, U. South Miss. medal, 1978, Regina medal, 1985, Alan award Nat. Coun. Tchrs. English, 1986, Kerlan award, 1990, Margaret Edwards award, 1998; collection of papers at Wheaton Coll. Mem. Authors Guild (mem. council), Authors League (mem. council), Writers Guild Am. Episcopalian. Home: New York, NY. Died Sept. 7, 2007.

LEON, DONALD FRANCIS, university dean, medical educator; b. Washington, Aug. 19, 1932; s. Frank A. and Madeline (Wildman) L.; children: Anne, James, John, Sharon. AB, Georgetown U., 1953, MD, 1957. Diplomate Am. Bd. Internal Medicine, Subspeciality Bds. in Cardiovascular Diseases. Instr. medicine U. Pitts., 1965-67, asst. prof. medicine, 1967-70, assoc. prof., 1971-75, vice chmn. medicine, 1971-75, assoc. prof., 1975-77, exec. assoc. dean, 1975-79, prof. medicine, from 1977, pres. Univ. Health Ctr., 1979-83, dean Sch. Medicine, 1979-84; dean clin. affairs Georgetown U. Hosp., Washington, 1989-94, prof. medicine divsn. cardiology, 1994-99, disting. prof. medicine and cardiology, from 1999. Bd. dirs. Blue Cross Western Pa. Co-editor: Pericardial Disease, 1982, Am. Heart Assn. Monograph, 1975. Served to capt. USAF, 1961-63. Am. Heart Assn. scholar, 1968-73 Fellow ACP, Am. Heart Assn. (coun. on clin. cardiology, coun. on circulation, Am. Coll. Cardiology (master; bd. dirs.); mem. Am. Fedn. for Med. Rsch., Cen. Soc. for Clin. Rsch. Home: Potomac, Md. Died June 21, 2006.

LEONARD, JOHN HARRY, advertising executive; b. NYC, June 28, 1922; s. Frederick H. and Florence (Kiechlin) L.; m. Marjorie Jane Haslun, Oct. 19, 1946; children— John Kiechlin, Janet Ann. BS, N.Y. U., 1942, MBA, 1951. Advt. mgr. Autographic Register Co., 1946-47; promotion mgr. Macfadden Pub. Co., 1947-50; successively copywriter, account exec., v.p. and account supr. Batten, Barton, Durstine & Osborn, 1950-64; with DDB Needham Worldwide (formerly Doyle Dane Bernbach, Inc.), NYC, 1964-87, group sr. v.p., 1972-87. Lectr. Grad. Sch. Bus., N.Y. U., 1959-61 Bd. dirs., past exec. com. Am. Bible Soc.; past chmn. bd. dirs. Wartburg Home, Mt. Vernon, N.Y.; trustee NYU, 1978-84. With USAF, 1943—46. Recipient Alumni Meritorious Service award N.Y. U., 1969 Mem. NYU Grad. Sch. Bus. Alumni Assn. (pres.), NYU Commerce Alumni Assn. (pres. 1979-80), Alpha Delta Sigma. Home: Southbury, Conn. Died Mar. 4, 2006.

LEONORA, JOHN, physiologist, educator; b. Milw., Jan. 30, 1928; s. Joseph and Carmela (Folise) L.; m. Johanna Mae Zwemer, Sept. 14, 1952; children: Carmela Marie, Andrea Sue. BS, U. Wis., 1949, MS, 1954, PhD, 1957. Instr. Loma Linda U., Calif., 1959-62, asst. prof. physiology Calif., 1962-65, assoc. prof. Calif., 1965-68, prof. Calif., from 1968. Recipient Teaching and Research MacPherson Soc.; grantee Don Baxter Found., 1968-80, NIH, 1981— Mem. Endocrine Soc., AAAS, N.Y. Acad. Sci., Sigma Xi Home: Yucaipa, Calif. Died Feb. 17, 2006.

LEOPOLD, RICHARD WILLIAM, retired history professor; b. NYC, Jan. 6, 1912; s. Harry and Ethel A. (Kimmelstiel) L. AB with highest honors, Princeton U., 1933; A.M., Harvard U., 1934, PhD, 1938. Instr. history Harvard U., 1937-40, asst. prof., 1940-48; assoc. prof. history Northwestern U., 1948-53, prof., 1953-63, William Smith Mason prof. Am. history, 1963-80, prof. emeritus, 1980—2006, acting chmn. dept., 1954, 62, chmn., 1966-69. Albert Shaw lectr. Johns Hopkins, 1963, Taft lectr. U. Cin., 1964, James M. Callahan lectr. W.Va. U., 1983; mem. Inst. Advanced Study, Princeton, 1960-61; mem. hist. adv. com. Dept. Army, Dept. State, Navy Dept., AEC, Library of Congress, Nat. Archives Adv. Council, U.S. Marine Corps. Author: Robert Dale Owen: A Biography, 1940, Elihu Root and the Conservative Tradition, 1954, The Growth of American Foreign Policy: A History, 1962; Editor and contbr.: (with Arthur S. Link) Problems in American History, 3d edit, 1966, 4th edit., 1972; contbg. author: Change and Continuity in Twentieth-Century America, 1964, Interpreting American History, 1970; Pearl Harbor as History, 1973, The Future of History, 1977, The Korean War: A 25-Year Perspective, 1977, The Wilson Era, 1991; also articles in profl. jours. Bd. dirs. Harry S. Truman Library Inst. Served from ensign to lt. USNR, 1942-46. Predoctoral field fellow Social Sci. Research Council, 1935-36; recipient John H. Dunning prize Am. Hist. Assn., 1940, Graebner prize Historians Am. Fgn. Rels., 1990. Fellow Soc. Am. Archivists; mem. Am. Hist. Assn., Mass. Hist. Soc. (corr. mem.), Orgn. Am. Historians (pres. 1976-77), Soc. for Historians of Am. Fgn. Relations (pres. 1970), Social Sci. Research Council, Phi Beta Kappa. Home: Evanston, Ill. Died Nov. 23, 2006.

LERCH, RICHARD HEAPHY, retired lawyer; b. Balt., Oct. 8, 1924; s. Charles Sebastian and Marguerite Mary (Mullen) L.; m. Marie Therese Logan, Feb. 11, 1950; children— Marie L., Elizabeth L., Ellen C. AB magna cum laude, Loyola Coll., Balt., 1947; LL.B., U. Md., 1949. Bar: Md. bar 1948. Since practiced in, Balt.; partner Lerch & Huesman, 1959-96; ret., 1996. Pres. Jr. Bar Assn., 1960 Served with AUS, 1944-46, 51-52. Mem. Am., Md., Balt. bar assns., Internat. Assn. Ins. Counsel. Democrat. Roman Catholic. Home: Baltimore, Md. Died Nov. 2, 2005.

LERNER, AARON BUNSEN, dermatologist, biochemist, educator; b. Mpls., Sept. 21, 1920; m. Marguerite Rush, 1945 (dec. 1987); children: Ethan, Michael, Peter, Harry; m. Mildred Lerner. BA, U. Minn., 1941, MS, 1942; M of Medicine, PhD in Physiology Chem., 1945, MD, 1945. Diplomate Am. Bd. Dermatologists. Asst. physiol chemist U. Minn., 1941—45; asst. prof. dermatology U. Mich. Med. Sch., 1952—59; assoc. prof. U. Oreg., 1952—55; assoc. prof. dermatology and biochemistry Yale U. Med. Sch., 1955—57, prof. dept. dermatology, 1958—95, prof. emeritus, 1995—2007. Chmn. dermatology dept. Yale U. Sch. Med., 1958—85. Named Dome Lectr., 1980; recipient Myron-Gordon award, 1969, Stephen Rothman award, 1971, Li Annenberg Hazen award, 1981. Died Feb. 3, 2007.

LESHER, JOHN LEE, JR., consulting services company executive; b. Harrisburg, Pa., Feb. 7, 1934; s. John Lee and Mary Alice (Watkeys) L.; m. Nancy Smith, July 11, 1970; children by previous marriage: John David, James Elam, Andrew Gwynne. BA cum laude, Williams Coll., 1956; MBA, Harvard U., 1958. Budget dir., asst. sec. The Barden Corp., Danbury, Conn., 1958-61; cons. Booz, Allen & Hamilton Inc., NYC, 1961-64, assoc., 1964-66, v.p., 1966-76, pres., 1976-85, Mars & Co. Cons. Inc., Greenwich, Conn., 1985-87, Home Group Fin. Services, NYC, 1987-88; v.p. Cresap, McCormick & Paget, NYC, 1988-89; mng. dir. Korn/Ferry Internat., NYC, 1989-93; pres. Jack Lesher & Assocs., Greenwich, Conn., from 1993. Mem.: Harvard Bus. Sch., Watch Hill Yacht, Misquamicut (Watch Hill, R.I.), Round Hill (Greenwich, Conn.), River (N.Y.C.), Coral Beach (Bermuda). Died Aug. 8, 2006.

LESLIE, ROBERT CAMPBELL, clergyman, counseling educator, writer; b. Concord, Mass., Oct. 20, 1917; s. Elmer Archibald and Helen Fay (Noon) L.; m. Paula Frances Eddy, June 14, 1941; children— William, Heather. A.B., DePauw U., 1939; S.T.B., Boston U., 1942, Ph.D., 1948. Lic. psychologist, Calif. Ordained to ministry United Methodist Ch., 1941; pastor The Methodist Ch., Peabody, Mass., 1941-43; chaplain Boston State Hosp., 1948-56; clin. assoc. Sch. Theology Boston U., 1948-56; prof. pastoral psychology Pacific Sch. Religion, Berkeley, Calif., 1956-82, prof. emeritus, 1983—,dean, 1979-80. Author: Jesus and Logotherapy, 1965; Sharing Groups in the Church, 1971; Man's Search for a Meaningful Faith, 1968, Health, Healing and Holiness, 1971; (with Wilhelm Wuellner) The Surprising Gospel, 1984; (with Margaret Alter) Sustaining Intimacy, 1978; (with Chiu Siok Hui) Between Person and Person, 1981; mem. editorial bd. Jour. Pastoral Care, 1965-82, Pastoral Psychology, 1959-67, Internat. Forum for Logotherapy, 1978—. Bd. dirs. Fred Finch Youth Ctr., Oakland, Calif., 1955—, pres., 1969. Served to maj. U.S. Army, 1943-46. Am. Assn. Theol. Schs. fellow, 1960; NIMH fellow, 1968. Fellow Am. Psychol. Assn., Inst. Logotherapy; mem. Am. Assn. Pastoral Counselors (Diplomate, Disting. Contbr. award 1983). Democrat. Home: Napa, Calif. Died June 14, 2006.

LESTER, BARNETT BENJAMIN, retired foreign affairs officer; b. Toronto, Can., Aug. 7, 1912; came to U.S., 1917; s. Louis and Lena (Rubenstein) L.; m. Rita Constance Hatcher, May 31, 1943 (dec.); m. Claudette Yvonne Gionet, Apr. 19, 1970. Student, Cleve. Coll., Western Res. U., 1933; AB (Miller Scholar), Oberlin Coll., 1934, postgrad., 1934-35, Fletcher Sch. Law and Diplomacy, 1935-36; student, Fgn. Service Inst., 1952-56. Mem. staff, corr. Cleve. Plain Dealer and Cleve. News, 1928-33; feature writer Boston Sunday Post, 1935-38; mng. editor, later editor Exclusive Features Syndicate, Boston, 1936-38; asso. editor The Writer mag., Boston, 1936-38; info. officer Dept. Justice, 1938-41; asst. dir. feature div. Office Inter-Am. Affairs, 1941-45; info. publicist Dept. State, 1945; pub. relations exec. Al Paul Lefton Co., Inc., Phila., 1945-46; info. specialist, chief motion pictures, acting chief audio-visual sect. USPHS, Office Surgeon Gen., 1947-48; info. specialist Fed. Security Agy., 1948-49; chief editorial and prodn. sect. Nat. Heart Inst. (info. specialist, sci. reports br. NIH), 1949-52; pub. info. chief NIH, 1950; review officer Dept. State, 1952-61, supervisory publs. editor, 1961-63, editor-writer, 1963-73, pub. info. officer, 1973-85; assoc. editor Newsletter, 1977-81, State Mag., 1981-86, sr. editor, 1986-89, on contract, 1989; pub. affairs specialist, 1985-89. Fgn. svc. res. officer, 1965-73, assigned to policy and pub. info. affairs program, 1962-67; assigned to policy and pub. info affairs program Newsletter and Info. Office, Office Dir. Gen. Fgn. Svc., 1967-81, Office Pub. Affairs and State Mag., Office Dir. Gen. Fgn. Svc., 1981-89, Career counselor Oberlin Coll., 1940—, pub. affairs officer Inter-Am. Air Pilot Program, sponsored by War Dept. and Office of Inter-Am. Affairs, 1942-44; rep. Office Surg. Gen., USPHS, on Interdepartmental com. med. tng. aids, 1947-48; invited participant U.S. Commr. Edn. Conf Audio-Visual Aids to Edn., 1948; mem. info. staff Pres.'s Midcentury White House Conf. on Children and Youth, 1950 mem. spl. survey audio-visual tchg. and tng. aids Nat. Heart Inst., USPHS and Assn. Am. Med. Colls., 1951; invited participant symposium The White House: The First 200 Yrs., White House Hist. Assn., 1992; invited participant, symposium Two Hundred Years at the White House: Actors and Observers, White House Hist. Assn., 2000; invited participant, symposium The West Wing-Workshop of Democracy, White House Hist. Assn. 2002. Author: (with others) The Writer's Handbook, 1936 Recipient War Service award Coord. Inter-Am. Affairs, 1945 Meritorious Honor Group award Dept. State, 1967, 40 Yea Service award, 1979, Spl. Achievement award, 1979, Superio Honor award, 1983, Superior Honor Group award, 1984; Loy W Henderson—Joseph C. Satterthwaite award for pub. service 1987; Bicentennial award Am. Revolution Bicentennial Admin strn., 1977; award for excellence Soc. Tech. Communications 1982; award for achievement Soc. Tech. Communication, 1985 50 Yr. Pin, Fletcher Sch. Law and Diplomacy, 1986; 50 Yr. Svc award, bronze plaque for 51 yrs. U.S. Govt. Svc., 1989; Joh Jacob Rogers award for outstanding career achievement, Dep State, 1989; cert. commendation Dept. State, 1989. Mem. Am Fgn. Svc. Assn., Am. Polit. Sci. Assn., Acad. Polit. Sci Diplomatic and Consular Officers Ret., Fed. Editors Assn. (Blu Pencil award 1975), Nat. Assn. Govt. Communicators (Blu Pencil Publs. award 1983), Marquis Libr. Assn. (adv. mem.) U.S. Diplomatic Courier Assn. (hon., Silver Diplomatic Courie medal and cert. appreciation 1990), Nat. Press Found. (charter) Nat. Trust for Hist. Preservation, White House Hist. Assn (charter), U.S. Capitol Hist. Soc., Assn. for Diplomatic Studie and Tng., Fgn. Affairs Retirees of No. Va., Internat. Clu (charter, honored as founding mem.), Nat. Press Club, Silve Owls Club, Am. Fgn. Svc., Diplomatic and Consular Officer Ret. Achievements include having two suggestions adopted b U.S. Postal Service resulted in issuing Treaty of Paris stamp an Great Seal of U.S. embossed stamped envelope. Home: Arlington, Va. Died Feb. 27, 2007.

LESTER, JAMES DUDLEY, classicist, educator; b. Fo Smith, Ark., Mar. 5, 1935; s. Kenneth R. and Essie Fae (Bailey L.; m. Martha B. Lester, 1958; children: Jim, Mark. BA, Eas Cen. Okla. State U., 1957; MA, Okla. State U., 1963; PhD, Tuls U., 1970. Dir. pub. rels. East Cen. Okla. U., Ada, 1957; aide t Sen. Robert S. Kerr U.S. Senate, Washington, 1958-59; tch Fort Smith (Ark.) High Sch., 1959-63; from instr. to asst. pro Emporia (Kans.) State U., 1963-67; grad. asst. Tulsa U 1967-70; from asst. prof. to prof. Austin Peay State U., Clarks ville, Tenn., from 1970. Pub., editor: Cumberland Mag., 197 80, Tenn. Monthly, 1980-82. F.B. Parriott scholar U. Tuls 1969-70. Mem. MLA, South Ctrl. MLA, Nat. Coun. Tchr English, Conf. Coll. Comm. and Composition. Democrat. Meth odist. Home: Clarksville, Tenn. Died Jan. 10, 2006.

LEV, DANIEL SAUL, political scientist, educator; b. Young stown, Ohio, Oct. 23, 1933; s. Louis and Bessie (Gessen) L.; r Arlene C. Offenhender, Mar. 22, 1958; children— Claire Elle Louis Benjamin George. BA, Miami U., Oxford, Ohio, 195 PhD, Cornell U., 1964. Asst. prof. polit. sci. U. Calif. Berkeley, 1965-70; asso. prof. U. Wash., Seattle, 1970-73, pro from 1974. Author: The Transition to Guided Democracy Indonesia, 1966, Islamic Courts in Indonesia, 1972. Mem. Ar Polit. Sci. Assn., Assn. Asian Studies. Home: Seattle, Was Died July 29, 2006.

LEVA, JAMES ROBERT, retired electric utility compar executive; b. Boonton, NJ, May 10, 1932; s. James and Ro (Cocci) L.; m. Marie Marinaro, Dec. 19, 1950; children: Jame Daniel, Linda, Michael, Christopher. BSEE magna cum laud Fairleigh Dickinson U., 1960; JD, Seton Hall Law Sch., 198 Lineman Jersey Ctrl. Power and Light Co., Morristown, N. 1952-60, elec. engring. and oper. depts., 1960-62, pers. re 1962-68, mgr. employee rels., 1968-69, v.p. pers. and svc 1969-79, v.p. consumer affairs, 1979-82, dir., 1976-82; pre COO, dir. Pa. Electric Co., Johnstown, 1982-86; pres., CC Jersey Ctrl. Power & Light Co., Morristown, 1986-92; chm CEO, bd. dirs. Gen. Pub. Utilities, 1992-97, ret., 1997. Chm pres., CEO, bd. dirs. GPU Svc. Corp., Parsippany, N.J.; chm bd. dirs. GPU Nuc. Corp., Parsippany, N.J.; chmn. CEO, b dirs. Met. Edison Co., Reading, Pa., Pa. Electric Co., Johnstow Pa., Utilities Mut. Ins. Co., N.J. Utilities Assn.; chmn. St. Clar Health Care Found.; trustee Tri-County Scholarship Fur Fairleigh Dickinson U.; chmn. Sch. Planning & Pub. Poli

Rutgers U. Served with USMC, 1949-51, Korea. Mem. N.J. Bar Assn., Mendham Golf and Tennis Club, Naples Nat. Golf Club. Roman Catholic. Home: Marco Island, Fla. Died Oct. 10, 2006.

LEVCHUK, GEORGE, mechanical-aeronautical consulting engineer; b. Poland, Nov. 27, 1907; s. Ioan Basili and Nadia Kornilia (Ferencewich) L.; came to U.S., 1949, naturalized, 1952. M.E., Warsaw (Poland) Inst. Tech., 1938, M.S., 1969; Ph.D., Kensington U., 1982. Polish State aircraft factory designer, 1932-38; engr. Polish Airlines, 1938-39; d essinatuer Leo-45 bomber, Argenteuil, France, 1940; interim prototype shop mgr. Turkish Air League, 1941-48; impact extrusion engr. Victor Metal Industries, Bklyn., 1949-50; engr. Chase Aircraft Co., Trenton, N.J., 1950-53; designer N.Am. Aviation Corp., 1953-60; mathematician-designer U.S. Steel Corp., 1960-61; re-entry flow engr. Hughes Aircraft Corp., 1962-63; aerodynamicist Aeronutronics-Ford subs. Aeronutronic, Newport Beach, Calif., 1965-66; research scientist Calif. Inst. Tech., Pasadena, 1967-70; B-1 structures engr. Rockwell Corp., Inglewood, Calif., 1970-72, shuttle stress engr., 1973-77; stress engr. McDonnell Douglas Corp., St. Louis, 1978-81, Bell Helicopter Textron, 1985-86; mech.-aero. cons. engr., Downey, Calif., 1982—. Served to lt. Polish Air Force, 1940-41, Eng. Mem. AIAA. Home: Downey, Calif. Died June 11, 2007.

LEVERE, RICHARD DAVID, internist, educator; b. Bklyn., Dec. 13, 1931; s. Samuel and Mae (Fain) L.; m. Diane L. Gonchar, Jan. 15, 1978; children: Elyssa C., Corinne G., Scott M. Student, NYU, 1949-52; MD, SUNY, NYC, 1956. Intern Bellevue Hosp., NYC, 1956-57, resident, 1957-58, Kings County Hosp., 1960-61; asst. prof. medicine SUNY Downstate Med. Center, 1965-69, assoc. prof., 1969-73, prof., 1973-77, vice-chmn. dept. medicine, 1975-77, chief hematology/oncology div., 1970-77; asst. prof. Rockefeller U., 1964-65; prof., chmn. dept. medicine N.Y. Med. Coll., 1977-93, vice dean, 1991-93; med. dir. Westchester County Med. Ctr., 1991-92; v.p. med. affairs St. Agnes Hosp., 1991-93; sr. v.p. Bklyn. Hosp. Ctr., 1994-98; assoc. dean NYU Sch. Medicine, 1994-99, prof. medicine, 1994-2000, adj. prof., from 2000; v.p. med. affairs Westchester Med. Ctr.-St. Agnes Hosp. Mgmt. Corp., 2002—03. Adj. prof. Rockefeller U., 1973—98, 2002—07, vis. prof., 1998—2000; pres. Cantigny Rsch. Found., 1986—2007; dep. dir. Lang Rsch. Ctr., N.Y. Hosp., Queens, 1999—2001; clin. prof. medicine Weill Cornell Sch. Medicine, NYC, 2001—02, NY Med. Coll., 2002—07; chmn. bd. dirs. The Wellness Cmty., Atlanta, 2005—07. Contbr. articles to profl. jours. Trustee Our Lady of Mercy Med. Ctr., 1993—96; exec. dir. Resurgens Charitable Found., 2005—07; bd. dirs. Leukemia Soc. Am., 1970—85, Am. Heart Assn., 1978—94, Wellness Cmty., Atlanta, 2004—07, chmn. bd. dirs., 2005. NIH grantee, 1971-76, 65-86. Master ACP (gov. N.Y. State 1990-94, pres. N.Y. State chpt. 1992-93, Physician Recognition award 1986, Cmty. Svc. award Ga. state chpt., 2006); fellow N.Y. Acad. Medicine; mem. Harvey Soc., Am. Soc. Clin. Investigation, Soc. Study of Blood (pres. 1973-74), Soc. Devel. Biology, Am. Soc. Pharm. Exptl. Therapeutics (William Dock Teaching award, Tinsley Harrison Rsch. award), Den Tiroler Adler-Ordern of Austria, Alpha Omega Alpha. Home: Marietta, Ga. Died Apr. 23, 2007.

LEVIN, ALAN M., television journalist; b. Bklyn., Feb. 28, 1926; s. Herman and Shirley (Levinstein) L.; m. Hannah Alexander, Oct. 30, 1948; children: Marc, Nicole, Danielle, Juliet. BA, Wesleyan U., Middletown, Conn., 1946. Reporter, columnist Plainfield (N.J.) Courier News, 1957-60; statehouse corr. AP, Trenton, N.J., 1960-61; writer N.Y. Post, 1961-63; press sec. Sen. Harrison Williams, Washington, 1963-64; news producer, writer WABC-TV, NYC, 1965-67; owner Levin Mediaworks Inc., producers documentaries for comml. and pub. TV, NYC; sr. prodr. Blowback Prodns. Documentary film maker, NET, N.Y.C., 1968-69, documentary film maker, pub. affairs, news writer, dir., producer, WNET-TV, N.Y.C., 1969-82 Served with AUS, 1944-46. Recipient numerous awards including George Polk Meml. award, Dupont Columbia award, Emmy awards. Home: Maplewood, NJ. Died Feb. 13, 2006.

LEVIN, IRA, writer, playwright; b. NYC, Aug. 27, 1929; s. Charles and Beatrice (Schlansky) L.; m. Gabrielle Aronsohn, Aug. 20, 1960 (div. 1968); children: Adam, Jared, Nicholas; m. Phyllis Finkel, Aug. 26, 1979 (div. 1982). Student, Drake U., Des Moines, 1946-48; AB, N.Y. U., 1950. Freelance writer, 1950—2007; author: (novels) A Kiss Before Dying, 1953 (Edgar Allan Poe award for Best First Novel, 1953), Rosemary's Baby, 1967, This Perfect Day, 1970, The Stepford Wives, 1972, The Boys from Brazil, 1976, Sliver, 1991, Son of Rosemary, 1997; (plays) No Time for Sergeants, 1955, Interlock, 1958, Critic's Choice, 1962, General Seeger, 1962, Drat! the Cat, 1965, Dr. Cook's Garden, 1967, Veronica's Room, 1973, Deathtrap, 1978 (Edgar Allan Poe award, 1980), Break a Leg, 1979, Cantorial, 1989, Sliver, 1991, Son of Rosemary: The Sequel to Rosemary's Baby, 1997. Served with U.S. Army, 1953-55. Recipient Bram Stoker award, 1997; named a Grand Master award, Mystery Writers of Am., 2003. Mem. Dramatists Guild (council mem. 1980). Died Nov. 12, 2007.*

LEVINE, GEOFFREY, pharmacist; b. Sept. 2, 1942; BS in Pharmacy, Temple U., 1965, MS in Radiol. Health, 1967; PhD in Environ. Health Engring., Northwestern U., 1978. Bd. cert. in nuclear pharmacy; lic. pharmacist, Pa. Pharmacist Profl. Practice-Community Peoples Drug Stores, 1965-67; radioisotope chemist Abbott Labs., Chgo., 1966-68; dir. radiopharmaceutical svcs. U. Pitts. Health Ctr., 1972-93; asst. prof. radiology U. Pitts. Sch. Medicine, 1972-83, assoc. prof., 1983-95; nuclear pharmacist Presbyn.-Univ. Hosp., 1972-95; dir. nuclear pharmacy Cen. Imaging Svcs., Inc., 1985-93; assoc. mem. Pitts. Cancer Inst., 1987-89, 89-95, clin. dir. Monoclonal Antibody Ctr., 1993-95, full mem. Mem. adj. faculty U. Pitts. Sch. Pharmacy, 1981; clin. prof. Allegheny County C.C., 1984-90; mem. Radiation Safety Com. U. Pitts. Med. Ctr., Radioactive Drug Rsch. Com. and Human Use Subcom. Radioactive Materials, 1972—; cons. U. Pitts. Med. Ctr., dir., pres. 900 comm., 1995—. Contbr. some 150 articles to profl. jours. and publs. Recipient AEC-AUA-ANL fellowship, USPHS traineeship, teaching assistantship, W.P. Murphy fellowship; recipient Founder's Award Plaque, Am. Pharm. Assn., 1978. Mem. AAAS, Am. Pharm. Assn., Health Physics soc., Soc. Nuclear Medicine, Pa. Coll. Nuclear Medicine and Nuclear Physicians, Sigma Xi, Rho Chi. Home: Pittsburgh, Pa. Died Dec. 12, 2006.

LEVINE, JEROME PAUL, mathematician, educator; b. NYC, May 4, 1937; s. Stanley H. and Jeanette (Kirschbaum) L.; m. Sandra Joy Bardfeld, July 3, 1958; children: Laura Ellen, Michael Richard, Jeffrey Robert. BS, MIT, 1958; PhD, Princeton U., 1962. Instr. MIT, Cambridge, 1961-63; asst. prof. U. Calif., Berkeley, 1964-65, assoc. prof., 1965-66, Brandeis U., Waltham, Mass., 1966-69, prof., from 1969, chmn. math. dept., 1974-76, 88-90. Vis. prof. U. Geneva, 1977. Contbr. articles to profl. publs. Recipient Humboldt Sr. U.S. Scientist award Humboldt Found., Federal Republic of Germany, 1989; postdoctoral fellow NSF, Cambridge, Eng., 1963-64, Sloan Found. fellow, Waltham, 1966-68; Sci. Rsch. Coun. grantee, Oxford, Eng., 1972-73, vis. scholar, 1972-73. Mem. Am. Math. Soc. Home: Newton, Mass. Died Apr. 8, 2006.

LEVINE, LAWRENCE WILLIAM, retired history professor; b. NYC, Feb. 27, 1933; s. Abraham and Anne (Schmookler) L.; m. Cornelia Roettcher, May 29, 1964; children: Joshua, Issac; 1 stepson, Alexander Pimentel. BA, CCNY, 1955; MA, Columbia U., 1957, PhD, 1962. Lectr. CCNY, 1959-61; instr. Princeton U., 1961-62; asst. prof. U. Calif.-Berkeley, 1962-67, assoc. prof., 1967-70, prof. dept. history, 1970-84, Margaret Byrne prof., 1984—94; prof. history George Mason U., Fairfax, 1994—2006. Vis. prof. U. East Anglia, Norwich, Eng., 1967-68, Free U., Berlin, W. Ger., 1977; nat. adv. bd. Ctr. Am. Culture Studies Columbia U., 1983-84; delivered the Massey lectrs. in Am. Culture, Harvard U., 1986, Merle Curli lectrs., U. Wis., 1991. Author: Defender of the Faith, 1965, Black Culture and Black Consciousness: Afro-American Folk Thought from Salvery to Freedom, 1977 (Chgo. Folklore prize 1977), High Brow/Low Brow: The Emergence of Cultural Hierarchy in America, 1988, The Unpredictable Past: Explorations in American Cultural History, 1993, The Opening of the American Mind: Canons, Culture and History, 1996; co-author: (with Cornelia Levine) The People and the President: America's Conversation with F.D.R., 2002; co-editor: The Shaping of 20th-Century America, 1964, The National Temper, 1968; assoc. editor Jour. Am. Folklore, 1985-90; editorial bd.: Societas: A Jour. of Social History, 1970-80. Pres. Congregation Beth El, Berkeley, 1979-82. Social Sci. Rsch. Coun. fellow, 1965-66, Regents fellow Nat. Mus. Am. History Smithsonian Instn., 1981-82, Woodrow Wilson fellow Internat. Ctr. for Scholars, 1982-83, MacArthur Found. fellow, 1983-88, fellow Ctr. for Advanced Study in Behavioral Scis., 1990-91. Mem. Am. Acad. Arts and Scis., Am. Studies Assn. (nat. coun. 1980-82), Am. Hist. Assn. (mem. coun. 1987-90), Orgn. Am. Historians (exec. bd. 1984-87, 91-2006, pres. elect 1991-92, pres. 1992-93), Am. Folklore Soc., Am. Film Inst., Soc. of Am. Historians. Jewish. Home: Berkeley, Calif. Died Oct. 23, 2006.

LEVINE, SUMNER NORTON, industrial engineer, educator, editor, writer, financial consultant; b. Boston, Sept. 5, 1923; s. Frank and Lillian (Gold) L.; m. Caroline Gassner, Nov. 27, 1952; 1 dau., Joanne. BS, Brown U., Providence, 1946; PhD, U. Wis., 1949; postgrad., MIT, Cambridge, 1956. Instr. U. Chgo., 1949-50; sr. rsch. fellow Columbia, 1950-54; dir. rsch. labs. VA, East Orange, NJ, 1954-56; adv. scientist comml. atom power div. Westinghouse Electric Co., Pitts., 1956; dir. chemistry Metallurgy and Materials Labs.; also staff adv. engr. Gen. Engring. Labs., Am. Machine & Foundry Co., Greenwich, Conn., 1956-58; sect. head, materials and advanced electronic devices RCA, 1958-61; chmn. materials scis. dept., prof. engring., also prof., dir. grad. program in indsl. adminstrn. SUNY, Stony Brook, 1961-91; dir. urban rsch., vis. prof. CUNY Grad. Ctr., 1967-68; Danforth vis. lectr., 1968-69; vis. prof. Yale Sch. Orgn. and Mgmt., 1976; prof. fin. Coll. Urban and Policy Scis., SUNY, Stony Brook, from 1978. Cons. to industry; editl. adviser Ocean Engring. Author textbooks, profl. articles; editor: Financial Analysts Handbook, 1975, 2d edit., 1987, Investment Manager's Handbook, Dow Jones-Irwin Bus.and Investment Almanac, 1976—, Acquisition Manual, 1990, Turnaround and Bankruptcy Investing, 1991, Handbook of Global Investing, 1992, Internat. Bus. and Investment Almanac, 1992—; editor-in-chief Jour. Biomed. Materials Rsch., 1966-78, Jour. Socio-Econ. Planning Scis., 1966, Advances in Biomed. Engring. and Med. Physics, 1966. Recipient award for disting. contbn. to biomed. materials rsch., 1973. Mem. IEEE, World Conf. Planning Scis., Am. Chem. Soc., Am. Soc. Metals, Electrochem. Soc., Ops. Rsch. Soc. Am., Inst. Mgmt. Scis., NY Acad. Scis. (chmn. conf. materials in biomed. engring. 1966, chmn. colloquia socioecon. planning 1966-68), Soc. for Biomaterials (dir. 1974-76), NY Soc. Security Analysts (chmn. edn. and seminar com., Vols. award 1984), Brown U. Club, Sigma Xi. Died Mar. 20, 2007.

LEVY, CHARLOTTE LOIS, law librarian, educator, lawyer; b. Cin., Aug. 31, 1944; d. Samuel M. and Helen (Lowitz) Levy; m. Herbert Regenstreif, Dec. 11, 1980; 1 child, Cara Rachael Regenstreif. BA, U. Ky., 1966; MS, Columbia U., 1969; JD, No. Ky. U., 1975. Bar: Colo. 1979, NY 1985, Ky. 1985, U.S. Ct. Appeals (6th cir.) 1986. Law libr. No. Ky. U., 1971—75; law libr., assoc. prof. law Pace U., 1975—77; mgr. Fred B. Rothman & Co., Littleton, Colo., 1977—79; law libr., prof. Bklyn. Law Sch., 1979—85; adj. prof. Pratt Inst. Grad. Sch. Libr. and Info. Sci., 1982—85; atty. Cabinet for Human Resources, Frankfurt, Ky., 1985—87; atty., pres. Vantage Info. Cons., Inc., Frankfurt, from 1983. Cons. to various librs., pubs. Author: The Human Body and the Law, 1974 (Am. Jurisprudence Book award in domestic rels., 1974, in trusts, 1975), 2d edit., 1983, Computer-Assisted Litigation Support, 1984; mem. editl. bd.: No. Ky. U. Law Rev., 1974—75. 1st v.p. Ohavay Zion Synagogue; pres. bd. trustees Syncopated, Inc. Mem.: ABA, Fayette County Bar Assn., Ky. Bar Assn., Am. Assn. Law Librs. (cert. law libr.). Democrat. Jewish. Home: Cincinnati, Ohio. Died Aug. 13, 2006.

LEWIN, KLAUS JONATHAN, pathologist, educator; b. Jerusalem, Aug. 10, 1936; came to U.S., 1968; s. Bruno and Charlotte (Nawratzki L.; m. Patricia Coutts Milne, Sept. 25, 1964; children: David, Nicola, Bruno. Attended, King's Coll. U. London, 1954-55; MB, BS, Westminster Med. Sch. London, Eng., 1959; MD, U. London, 1966. Diplomate Am. Bd. Pathology, Royal Coll. Pathologists (London), lic. Calif. Casualty officer Westminster Med. Hosp., 1960; resident Westminster Hosp. Med. Sch., London, 1960-68; pediatric house physician Westminster Hosp. Med. Sch., Westminster Children's Hosp., 1961; house physician St. James Hosp., Balham, London, 1961; asst. prof. pathology Stanford (Calif.) U., 1979-86; assoc. prof. pathology UCLA, LA, 1977-80, vice chmn. dept. pathology, 1970-86; attending physician Dept. Medicine Gastroenterology divsn. UCLA-Wadsworth VA Hosp., from 1978; prof. pathology UCLA Med. Sch., 1980—2002, prof. dept. medicine divsn. gastroenterology, 1986—2002; dir. divsn. surg. pathology UCLA Ctr. Health Scis., 1986-95, mem. diagnostic surg. pathology svc., dir. divsn. liver, pancreas and gastrointestinal pathology, 1996—2002. Resident pathologist clinical chemistry, bacteriology, hematology, blood transfusion, serology, Westminster Hosp. Med. Sch., 1961-62, registrar dept. morbid anatomy, 1962-64, rotating sr. registrar morbid anatomy, Royal Devon, Exeter Hosp., 1964-68; vis. asst. prof. pathology, Stanford U. Med. Sch., 1968-70; vice chmn. pathology UCLA, L.A., 1979-86; pres. L.A. Soc. Pathologists Inc., 1985-86; mem. curriculum com. U. Calif. Riverside, 1977-84; cons. Wadsworth VA Hosp., L.A., carcinoma of esophagus intervention study, Polyp Prevention study, Nat. Cancer Inst., Cancer Preservation Studies br., Bethesda, Md.; chief gastrointestinal liver/pancreas sect. surg. pathology; rschr. structure, function, pathologic disorders of gastrointestinal tract and liver; vis. prof. U. Leeds, Eng., Porto Alegre, Brazil, Nat. Cancer Inst., Washington, 1999. Co-author (Riddel R., Weinstein W.): Gastrointestinal Pathology and Its Clinical Implications, 1992; co-author: (Henry Appelman) Atlas of Tumor Pathology: Tumors of the Esophagus and Stomach, 1997; editl. bd. Human Pathology, from 1986, Am. Jour. Surg. Pathology, from 1990, reviewer Gastroenterology and Archives of Pathology; contbr. 170 papers, 80 abstracts, 26 book chpts., 250 invited lectures. Recipient Chesterfield medal Inst. Dermatology, London, 1966; named Arris and Gale lectr. Royal Coll. Surgeons, London, 1968; Welcome Trust Rsch. grantee, 1968; fellow Found. Promotion Cancer Rsch., Tokyo, 1992. Fellow Royal Coll. Pathologists (Eng.); mem. Pathological Soc. Great Britain, Am. Gastroenterology Soc., Gastrointestinal Pathology Soc. (founder, pres. 1985-86, exec. com., edn. com. 1990-99), U.S. Acad. Pathology, Can. Acad. Pathology, Assn. Clin. Pathologists, Pathological and Bacteriological Soc. Great Britain, Internat. Acad. Pathology, L.A. Pathology Soc. (bd. dirs.), Calif. Soc. Pathology (edn. com. 1983—), So. Calif. Soc. Gastrointestinal Endoscopy, Arthur Purdy Stout Soc., Gastrointestinal Pathology Soc. (pres., by-laws com., chmn. edn. com., exec. com.). Avocations: travel, geographic pathology, hiking, swimming. Home: Pacific Palisades, Calif. Died Oct. 25, 2005.

LEWIN, LEONARD, electrical engineering educator; b. Southend-On-Sea, Eng., July 22, 1919; came to U.S., 1968; s. Abraham and Leza (Roth) L.; m. Daphne Smith, June 26, 1943; children: David Ian, Wendy Patricia. Student, pub. schs., Southend; D.Sc., U. Colo., 1967. Chartered elec. engr., U.K. Sci. officer Brit. Admiralty, Witley, Surrey, Eng., 1941-45; sr. engr. Standard Telecommunication Labs., Harlow, Essex, Eng., 1946-50, head microwave dept., 1950-60, asst. mgr. transmission research, 1960-66, sr. prin. research engr., 1967-68; prof. elec. engring. U. Colo., Boulder, 1968-86, prof. emeritus, from 1987. Cons. Standard Telecommunication Labs., 1968-90, Medion Ltd., London, 1970-90, Nat. Bur. Standards, Boulder, 1978-90, Nuclear Protection Adv. Group, London, 1980-90, MIT Lincoln Labs., 1984-90, NOAA, 1984-93; Nat. Prestige lectr. Inst. Elec. Engring, New Zealand, 1987 Author: Theory of Waveguides, 1975, Polylogarithms and Associated Functions, 1981; editor: Telecommunications in the U.S.: Trends, 1981, Telecommunications: Interdisciplinary, 1985, Structural Properties of Polylogarithms, 1991. Mem. Accountability Com. Boulder Valley Schs., 1979-81; active Colo. Assn. for Gifted and Talented, Boulder, 1976-90. Grantee U.K. Sci. Research Council, 1973, 75; grantee Fulbright Commn., 1981 Fellow IEEE (Microwave award, W.G. Baker 1963, Microwave Career award 1993), Brit. Interplanetary Soc.; mem. Instn. Elec. Engrs. U.K. (Premium award 1952, 60), Internat. Sci. Radio Union (U.S. nat. com.). Home: Boulder, Colo. Died Aug. 13, 2007.

LEWIS, ARTHUR, producer, director; b. NYC, Sept. 15, 1916; s. Albert and Laura (Furst) L.; m. Evelyn Eisner, Apr. 7, 1946; children: James L., Peter N. Student, U. So. Calif., 1934-36, Yale U., 1936-38. Assoc. producer 20th Century-Fox Film Corp., Los Angeles, 1938-40, screenwriter, 1947-49; stage mgr. Cabin in the Sky, NYC, 1940-41; assoc. producer Feuer and Martin Prodns., NYC, 1953-57; ind. producer NBC, NYC, 1957-58; producer Plautus Prodns., NYC, 1958-60, 61-63, also exec. v.p.; producer MGM TV, Culver City, Calif., 1960-61; producer, dir. Dorchester Prodns., London, 1963-64, Bernard Delfont Orgn., London, 1964-70, Performing Arts Ltd., London, 1970-79, also chmn.; producer NBC-Katz Gallin, Los Angeles, 1980-82. Pres. Versailles Prodns., A.L. Prodns.; bd. dirs. Prinmar Ltd., Playbill Ltd.; cons. EMI Ltd. Producer: (stage prodns.) A Tribute to Edwin Lester, Three Wishes for Jamie, (London prodns.) How to Succeed in Business Without Really Trying, Funny Girl, Barefoot in the Park, Little Me, Guys and Dolls, Queenie, Joey Joey, The Solid Gold Cadillac, The Owl and the Pussycat, Golden Boy, Our Man Crichton, A Thousand Clowns, The Odd Couple, (with Mermaid Theatre Trust) The Brig, Rockefeller and the Red Indians, (films) Loot, Baxter, (with Martin Baum) The Killer Elite, Brass Target, (TV shows) Brenner, CBS, The Nurses, CBS, The Asphalt Jungle, ABC, 601 Park, CBS, Charlie Paradise, CBS, The Diary of Anne Frank, NBC, Splendor in the Grass, NBC; producer, dir.: Queenie, Guys and Dolls, (London stage prodns.) Little Me, The Solid Gold Cadillac, Joey Joey, (TV shows) Ring Lardner's You Know Me, Al, NBC, The Paris Story, NBC; dir., assoc. producer: (stage prodns.) Can Can, Silk Stockings, The Boy Friend, Kean; screenwriter (with Albert Lewis) Golden Girl, Oh, You Beautiful Doll, also Conquest of Cochise. Served to 1st lt. U.S. Army, 1941-45. Recipient Evening Standard Drama award, London, 1964, 66. Fellow Royal Soc. Arts London; mem. Brit. Tennis Umpires Assn. (founder), Writers Guild Am., Acad. Motion Picture Arts and Scis. Avocations: tennis, sports. Died June 30, 2006.

LEWIS, JOAN MARIE, executive office leasing company executive; b. Galveston, Tex., June 20, 1944; d. Robert Walter and Fern Elizabeth (Rocket) Snipes; m. Austin Lester Lewis, Jr., Feb. 1, 1963 (div. Nov. 1973); children— Elizabeth, Carrie, Amy. Mgr. Preston Forest Exec. Suites, Dallas, 1973-75; sec. to pres. Mich. Gen. Corp., Dallas, 1975-76; sec. North Park Exec. Suites, Dallas, 1976-79; ptnr. P & L Exec. Suites, Dallas, 1979-82; owner, pres. Joan M. Lewis Co., Inc., also Town Center Exec. Suites, Inc., Dallas, 1982—. Mem. Nat. Assn. Secretarial Services, Dallas-Ft. Worth Exec. Women's Assn. (pres. 1984-85, Woman of Yr. 1984). Republican. Methodist. Home: Richardson, Tex. Died Apr. 16, 2006.

LEWIS, JOHN LEEMAN, JR., obstetrician, gynecologist; b. San Antonio, June 5, 1929; s. John Leeman and Lois Black (Perry) L.; student U. Tex. at Austin, spring, 1948; B.A., Harvard, 1952, M.D. (Frederick Sheldon Traveling fellow 1952-53, Nat. scholar 1953-57), 1957; m. Jane Darling Davis, July 30, 1955 (div. 1976); children— Anne Darling, Elizabeth Perry, Katherine Folsom; m. Susan Vere Paris, Oct. 16, 1976 (div. 1981); m. Patricia Ann Mazzola, May 8, 1984 (div. 1994). Diplomate Am. Bd. Ob-Gyn (dir. 1971—, cert. spl. competence gynecologic oncology). Intern Mass. Gen. Hosp., Boston, 1957-58, resident, 1958-59, 61-62; clin. asso. endocrinology Nat. Cancer Inst., Bethesda, Md., 1959-61; resident Boston Lying-in Hosp., 1962-65, Free Hosp. for Women, Brookline, 1962-65; sr. investigator surgery br. Nat. Cancer Inst., Bethesda, Md., 1965-67; assoc. attending obstetrician and gynecologist Presbyn. Hosp., N.Y.C., July-Dec. 1967, also asso. prof. obstetrics and gynecology Coll. Phys. and Surgs. Columbia; pvt. practice medicine, specializing in obstetrics and gynecology, N.Y.C., 1967—; chief gynecology service Meml. Hosp. for Cancer and Allied Diseases, N.Y.C., 1968-90, attending surgeon, 1990—; chmn. instl. rev. bd., 1984—; assoc. prof. Cornell U. Med. Coll. at N.Y.C., 1968-71, prof., 1971—; assoc. attending obstetrician and gynecology N.Y. Lying-in Hosp., N.Y.C., 1968-71, attending obstetrician and gynecologist, 1971—; mem. Sloan Kettering Inst. Cancer Rsch., 1971—; v.p. Internat. Gynecologic Cancer Soc., 1993—; chmn. Gynecologic Cancer Found., 1994—; mem. editorial bd. Jour. Am. Coll. Surgeons, 1994—. Served with USPHS, 1959-67. Recipient Alumni award Harvard Med. Sch., 1957. Mem. Harvard Med. Alumni Assn. (councilor 1969-70). Democrat. Episcopalian. Clubs: Griffis Faculty (N.Y.C.), Englewood Field Club (N.J.); Harvard (N.Y.C.). Assoc. editor Obstetrical and Gynecological Survey. Contbr. articles to profl. jours. Home: New York, NY. Died Mar. 16, 2006.

LEWIS, MELVIN, psychiatrist, pediatrician, psychotherapist; b. London, May 18, 1926; came to U.S., 1956; s. Abraham George and Kitty (Merrick) L.; m. Dorothy S. Otnow, May 30, 1963; children: Gillian Io, Eric Anthony. M.B., BS, Guy's Hosp. Med. Sch., London, 1950; D.C.H., 1954; MA (hon.), Yale U., 1972. Diplomate Am. Bd. Psychiatry and Neurology, Am. Bd. Child Psychiatry; cert. in psychoanalysis, child and adolescent psychoanalysis. Intern Lambeth Hosp., 1950, Fulham Hosp., 1951 (both Eng); resident in pediatrics Yale U. Sch. Medicine, 1956-57, resident in psychiatry and child psychiatry, 1957-61; from instr. child psychiatry to sr. rsch. sci., prof. child psychiatry and pediats. Yale U. Child Study Ctr., New Haven, 1961—2002, prof. emeritus, sr. rsch. sci., from 2002. Author: Clinical Aspects of Child and Adolescent Development, 1971, 3d edit. (with Fred Volkmar), 1991; editor: Jour. Am. Acad. Child & Adolescent Psychiatry, 1975-87, Child and Adolescent Psychiatry, A Comprehensive Textbook, 2002, 3d edit., 1996; cons. editor: Child and Adolescent Psychiatric Clinics of North America, 1991—. Served with M.C. Royal Army, 1951-53. Fellow: Royal Coll. Psychiatrists, Am. Psychiat. Assn. (disting. life fellow), Am. Acad. Child and Adolescent Psychiatry; mem.: Am. Psychoanalytic Assn., Western New Eng. Psychoanalytic Inst. and Soc., Am. Pediat. Soc. Home: New Haven, Conn. Died Apr. 28, 2007.

LEWIS, MICHAEL JOHN, diversified financial services company executive; b. Long Beach, Calif., Apr. 7, 1944; s. Theodore Edward and May Catherine (McMahan) L.; m. Shirley Kay Reddin, June 24, 1966 (div. Jan. 1983); 1 child, Todd; m. Kathryn Alice Braun, Sept. 24, 1984. CPA, Calif. Staff acct. Price, Waterhouse & Co., Los Angeles, 1967-69; ptnr. Godfrey & Cotton, Garden Grove, Calif., 1969-72; v.p. fin. Coastal Recreation Inc., Irvine, Calif., 1972-75; v.p. fin. and adminstrn. Frontier Mfg. Inc., Costa Mesa, Calif., 1975-78; mgr., cons. Arthur Young & Co., Costa Mesa, 1977-78; v.p. fin. and adminstrn., chief fin. officer, treas. Western Digital Corp., Irvine, 1978-82; exec. v.p. The Vieth Co., Newport Beach, Calif., 1982-85; v.p. fin., treas., chief fin. officer Emulex Corp., Costa Mesa, 1985-88; pres., chief oper. officer August Internat., Inc., Orange, Calif., 1989-90; cons. Newport Beach, 1990-92; CEO Nat. Case Mgmt., Oxnard, Calif., from 1992; dir., chmn. audit and compensation coms. 1st Fiedlity Thrift & Loan, San Diego, 1993-94. Trustee Art Inst. So. Calif., Laguna Beach, 1989—, treas.; chmn., bd. trustees Share Our Selves Corp., 1990—. Mem. AICPA, Calif. Soc. CPAs, Fin. Execs. Inst. (v.p. Orange county chpt. 1979). Clubs: Pacific (Newport Beach). Home: Newport Beach, Calif. Died Aug. 4, 2007.

LEWIS, PHILIP, educational association administrator, consultant; b. Chgo., Oct. 23, 1913; s. Solomon and Fannie (Margolis) L.; m. Geraldine Gisela Lawenda, Sept. 1, 1947; 1 child, Linda Susan. BS, DePaul U., Chgo., 1937, MA, 1939; EdD, Columbia Tchrs. Coll., 1951. Chmn. dept. edn. Chgo. Tchrs. Coll.; also asst. prin., tchr. South Shore High Sch., Chgo., 1940-51; prin. Herman Felsenthal Elementary Sch., Chgo., 1955-57; dir. Bur. Instructional Materials, Chgo. Pub. Schs., 1957-63, Bur. Research Devel. and Spl. Projects, 1963-67; pres. Instructional Dynamics Inc., Chgo., 1967-89, ret., 1989; ednl. and tech. cons., from 1991. Nat. cons. TV and instructional techniques, 1955—; ednl. cons. to accrediting bur. Health Edn. Schs., 1971-89; chmn. adv. com. U.S. Office Edn., Title VII, 1964-67 Author: Educational Television Guidebook for Electronics Industries Association, 1961, also numerous articles.; mem. editorial bd. Nation's Schs. and Colls; multimedia tech. editor: Tech. Horizons in Edn; cons.: Jour. Ednl. Tech. and Communications; producer ednl., multimedia, tng. and mental health and human devel. materials. Served to lt. comdr. USNR, 1942—45. Mem. Soc. Programmed and Automated Learning (pres. 1960-65), NEA (v.p. dept. audiovisual instrn., chmn. commn. on tech. standards dept. audiovisual instrn. 1965-85), Nat. Assn. Ednl. Broadcasters, Am. Legion, Council for Ednl. Facilities Planners (editorial adv. bd. 1972-80) Ill. C. of C. (edn. com. 1970-77), Chgo. Assn. Commerce and Industry (chmn. edn. com. 1970-80), Nat. Audio-Visual Assn. (profl. devel. bd. 1969-76, chmn), Chgo. Press Club, Masons, Shriners, Rotary, Phi Delta Kappa. Died Oct. 15, 2005.

LEWIS, ROBERT TURNER, former psychologist; b. Taft, Calif., June 17, 1923; s. D. Arthur and Amy Belle (Turner) L.; m. Jane Badham, Mar. 23, 1946; children: Jane, William, Richard. BA, U. So. Calif., 1947, MA, 1950; PhD, U. Denver, 1952. Chief psychologist Hollywood Presbyn. Hosp., L.A., 1953-58; dir. psychol. svcs. Salvation Army, Pasadena, Calif., 1958-68; dir. Pasadena Psychol. Ctr., 1964-74; successively asst. prof., assoc. prof. and prof. Calif. State U., LA, 1952-83, prof. emeritus, from 1984. Assoc. dir. Cortical Function Lab., L.A., 1972-84; clin. dir. Diagnostic Clinic, West Covina, Calif., 1983-85; dir. Job Stress Clinic, Santa Ana, Calif., 1985-95. Author: Taking Chances, 1979, A New Look at Growing Older, 1995, Money Hangups, 1995; co-author: Money Madness, 1978, Human Behavior, 1974, The Psychology of Abnormal Behavior, 1961. Lt (j.g.) USNR, 1943-46, PTO. Mem. APA, Calif. State Pscyhol. Assn. Republican. Home: Orange, Calif. Died Apr. 4, 2006.

LEWIS, WILLIAM RAYMOND, city official; b. Elwood, Ind., Apr. 29, 1934; s. Richard Raymond Lewis and Sarah Evelyn (George) Lockridge; m. Shirley Faye Hoover, Mar. 21, 1954; children: Melynda Sloan, William Bradley, Scott Anthony. BS in Aero. Engring., Tri-State Coll., Angola, Ind., 1961. Registered profl. engr., Ind., Miss., Ohio. Mechanic Hoosier Sales & Svc., Tipton, Ind., 1952-53; inspector Delco Radio Div. GMC, Kokomo, Ind., 1953-54; stress engr. Piper Aircraft, Lock Haven, Pa., 1961-63, Allison div. GMC, Indpls., 1963-71; dep. dir. Pub. Works Dept., City Indpls., 1971-78; cons. engr. Presnell & Assocs., Louisville, 1978-80; pub. works dir. City of Jackson, Miss., 1980-89; owner Am. Cons. Engring., Inc. With USN, 1954-56. Mem. Am. Pub. Works Assn. (chpt. pres. 1987—), Am. Water Works Assn., Nat. Soc. Profl. Engrs., Miss. Engring. Soc., Lions Club (dist. gov. 1972-73), Masons, Shriners. Republican. Avocations: golf, hunting. Home: Jackson, Miss. Died Mar. 6, 2007.

LEWY, JOHN EDWIN, pediatric nephrologist; b. Chgo., Apr. 22, 1935; s. Stanley B. and Lucile (Mayer) L.; m. Rosalind Portnoy, June 9, 1963; children— Karen, Steven. BA, U. Mich., 1956; MD, Tulane U., 1960. Diplomate Am. Bd. Pediat. (oral examiner 1985-89, oral exam com. 1987-89, certifying exam. com. on clin. problems 1989-92, com. on rsch. and rev. 1992-98), Am. Bd. Pediatric Nephrology. Intern Michael Reese Hosp. Med. Center, Northwestern U., 1960-61, resident in pediatrics, 1961-62, Michael Reese Hosp. Med. Center, 1963-64, chief resident, 1964, pediatric nephrology fellow, 1965, dir. sect. pediatric nephrology, 1967-70; fellow dept. pediatrics Cornell U. Med. Coll., NYC, 1966, research fellow physiology, 1966-67, asst. prof. pediatrics, 1970-71, assoc. prof., 1971-75, prof., 1975-78, dir. div. pediatric nephrology, 1970-78; Reily prof., chmn. dept. pediat. Tulane U. Sch. Medicine, New Orleans, 1978—2007; physician-in-chief Tulane Hosp. for Children, New Orleans, 1993—2007. Pediatrician La. Handicapped Children's Program; mem. exec. com., sci. adv. com. La. End Stage Renal Disease Coun.; mem. life options adv. bd. Rehab. Digest for Nephrologists, 1999—2007; mem. sci. adv. bd. Nat. Kidney Found., 1979—86, mem. health and sci. affairs com., 1989—95, mem. pub. policy com., 1990—96, chmn. pub. policy com., 1994—96, bd. dirs., 1994—96, mem. task force on early intervention and prevention, 1996—2007; mem. clin. sci. coun. Tulane U., chmn., 1980—90, 1995—2007, mem. exec. com. of clin. sci. coun., 1978—2007, mem. faculty senate, 1987—90; mem. task force on cmty. health care Tulane Sch. Pub. Health and Tropical Medicine, 1993—2007; bd. dirs. Kidney Found. La., 1984—2007, mem. med. adv. bd., 1981—2007, mem. sci. adv. bd., 1982—2007, rep., regional dir., 2000—07, task force early intervention and prevention, 1996—2007. Contbr. over 200 articles and abstracts to profl. jours. Mem. profl. adv. com. Nat. Found. March of Dimes; sci. adv. com. U.S. Renal Data System, HHS, 1990—93; mem. com. on future of pediat. nephrology NIDDK, 1991—2007; spl. com. on ctrs. of excellence in kidney and urology diseases HHS Nat. Kidney and Urology Diseases Adv. Bd., 1994—96. Served with M.C. USAF, 1962—63. Named Intern of Year, Michael Reese Hosp. Med. Ctr., 1961; recipient award, La. Pediatric Soc., 1960, Ronald McDonald Children's Charities Gift of Love award, 1996, Disting. Svc. award, Nat. Kidney Found., 1996, Julio Figueroa Gift of Life award, Nat. Kidney Found. La., 1999, Disting. Svc. award, Tulane U. Med. Alumni Assn., 1999. Mem.: AAAS, APHA, Nat. Assn. Children's Hosps. (liason from comm. on Federal Gov. Affairs 2002), So. Soc. Pediatric Rsch. (Founder's award 2003), Greater New Orleans Pediatric Soc., Orleans Parish Med. Soc. (pub. health com. 1981—2007, media resource panel 1999—2007, Award for excellence in rsch. 2003), Am. Soc. Artificial Internal Organs, Assn. Med. Sch. Pediatric Dept. Chairmen, La. State Med. Soc., Internat. Pediatric Nephrology Assn. (asst. sec. gen. 1977—78), Internat. Pediatric Chairs Assn., N.Y. Acad. Scis., Midwest Soc. Pediatric Research, Internat. Soc. Nephrology, Am. Soc. Nephrology, Am. Soc. Pediatric Nephrology (sec.-treas. 1974—80, pres. 1980—81, pub. policy com. 1991—94, 1996—2000, Founder's award 2000), Am. Pediatric Soc. (co-chair work group on pub. policy), Soc. Pediatric Rsch., Am. Acad. Pediat. (liaison from AMSPDC 1992—95, coun. fed. govt. affairs 1992—2007, task force on access 1999—2007, chmn. 2002, coun. on coms. 2002—07, rsch./edn./orgn. action group 2002—07, Henry L. Barnett award 1999), Am. Soc. Transplant Physics, Inst. Medicine (end stage renal disease com. 1989—91), Salt and Water Club, Alpha Omega Alpha (faculty advisor 1987—92). Home: New Orleans, La. Died Apr. 19, 2007.

LIBET, BENJAMIN, neuroscience educator; b. Chgo., Apr. 12, 1916; s. Morris and Anna L.; m. Fay Rosella Evans, July 1, 1939; children: Julian Mayer, Moreen Lea, Ralph Arnold, Gayla Bea. SB, U. Chgo., 1936, PhD, 1939. Instr. physiology Albany Med. Coll., 1939-40; rsch assoc. Inst. Pa. Hosp., Phila., 1940-43; materials engr. personal equipment lab. USAF, Wright Field, Ohio, 1944-45; instr. physiology sch. medicine U. Pa., Phila., 1943-44; instr. biol. scis. U. Chgo., 1945-47, asst. prof. physiology, 1947-48; dir. rsch. Kabat-Kaiser Inst., Vallejo, Calif., 1948-49; from asst. to assoc. prof. physiology U. Calif., San Francisco, 1949-62, prof. physiology, 1962-84, prof. emeritus, 1984—2007. Author: Neurophysiology of Consciousness, 1993, Mind Time: The Temporal Factor in Consciousness, 2004; contbr. 185 articles to profl. jours. Fellow Lalor Found., 1947-48, Commonwealth Found., 1956-57; scholar in residence Rockefeller Ctr. Study, 1977; vis. scholar Japan Soc. Sci., 1979. Fellow AAAS; mem. Soc. Neurosci., Am. Physiology Soc. Avocations: classical and opera singing, mountain hiking. Home: Davis, Calif. Died July 23, 2007.

LIEBENOW, ROBERT C., trade association executive; b. Aberdeen, SD, Sept. 13, 1922; s. Albert C. and Leta V. (Foot) L. Student, No. State Tchrs. Coll., Aberdeen, 1940-42; JD, U. S.D., 1946. Bar: Ill. bar 1948, D.C. bar 1969. Lawyer First Nat. Bank, Chgo., 1946-52; asst. sec. Bd. Trade, City of Chgo., 1952, sec., 1953-55, exec. sec., 1955, pres., 1956-65, Corn Refiners Assn., Inc., from 1965. Named One of Ten Outstanding Young Men U.S. Jr. C. of C., 1956 Mem. Am. Assn. Cereal Chemists (hon.), Phi Delta Theta Alumni Assn. Clubs: National Press (Washington), Congressional Country (Washington), University (Washington); Union League (Chgo.), Economic (Chgo.). Home: Front Royal, Va. Died Feb. 1, 2006.

LIEF, HAROLD ISAIAH, psychiatrist; b. NYC, Dec. 29, 1917; s. Jacob F. and Mollie (Filler) L.; m. Theodora Cohen, 1946 (div. 1959); children: Polly Lief Goldberg, Jonathan F.; m. Myrtis A. Brumfield, Mar. 3, 1961; children: Caleb B., Frederick V., Oliver F. BA, U. Mich., 1938; MD, NYU, 1942; cert. in psychoanalysis, Columbia Coll. Physicians and Surgeons, 1950; MA (hon.), U. Pa., 1971. Army physician WWII, Africa, Italy, France and Germany; intern Queens Gen. Hosp., Jamaica, NY, 1942-43; resident in psychiatry LI Coll. Medicine, 1946-48; pvt. practice NYC, 1948-51; asst. physician Presbyn. Hosp., NYC, 1949-51; asst. prof. Tulane U., New Orleans, 1951-54, assoc. prof., 1954-60, prof. psychiatry, 1960-67, U. Pa., Phila., 1967-82, prof. emeritus, 1982—2007, dir. div. family study, 1967-81; dir. Marriage Council of Phila., 1969-81, Ctr. for Study of Sex. Edn. in Medicine, 1968-82; mem. staff U. Pa. Hosp., 1967-81, Pa. Hosp., 1981—2007; clin. prof. psychiatry Jefferson Med. U., from 1994. Author: (with Daniel and William Thompson) The Eighth Generation, 1960; Editor: (with Victor and Nina Lief) Psychological Basis of Medical Practice, 1963, Medical Aspects of Human Sexuality, 1976, (with Arno Karlen) Sex Education in Medicine, 1976, Sexual Problems in Medical Practice, 1981, (with Zwi Hoch) Sexology: Sexual Biology, Behavior and Therapy, 1982, (with Zwi Hoch) International Research in Sexology, 1983, Human Sexuality With Respect to AIDS and HIV Infection, 1989; contbr. numerous articles to publ. Mem. La. State Commn. Civil Rights, 1958—67; Bd. dirs., chmn. Ctr. for Sexuality and Religion, 1988—2001; mem. adv. bd. False Memory Syndrome Found., from 1992. Maj. M.C. US Army, 1943—46. Commonwealth Fund fellow, 1963-64; recipient Gold Medal award Mt. Airy Hosp., 1977, Lifetime Achievement award Phila. Psychiat. Soc., 1992, Gold Medal, World Assn. Sexology, 1999; named practitioner of yr. Phila. County Med. Soc., 1998. Fellow Phila. Coll. Physicians, Am. Psychiat. Assn. (50 yr. disting. life), NY Acad. Sci., AAAS, Am. Acad. Psychoanalysis (charter, past pres.), Am. Coll. Psychiatrists (founding), Am. Coll. Psychoanalysts (charter); mem. AMA, Sex Info. and Edn. Coun. US (past pres.), Group Advancement Psychiatry (life), Am. Psychosomatic Soc., Assn. Psychoanalytic Medicine (life), Am. Psychoanalytic Assn. (life), Internat. Psychoanalytic Assn., Internat. Acad. Sex Rsch., Soc. Sci. Study of Sex, Am. Soc. Sex Educators, Counselors and Therapists, Soc. Sex Therapists and Rschr., World Assn. Sexology (past v.p.), Soc. Exploration of Psychotherapy Integration (adv. bd.), Pa. Med. Soc., Phila. Med. Soc., Pa. Psychiat. Soc., Columbia Club, Mich. Club of Greater Phila., Penn Club of NY, Sigma Xi, Alpha Omega Alpha, Phi Eta Sigma, Phi Kappa Phi. Home: Bryn Mawr, Pa. Died Mar. 15, 2007.

LIEF, LEONARD, retired academic administrator; b. NYC June 14, 1924; s. Aaron and Tillie (Newman) L.; m. Ruth Ann Haring, June 21, 1954 (dec. 2003); 1 child, Madelon. AB, N.Y. U., 1946; MA, Columbia U., 1947; PhD, Syracuse U., 1953. Instr. English Syracuse U., 1947-52; instr. Wayne U., 1953-55; Hunter Coll., CUNY, 1955-61, asst. prof., 1961-65, assoc. prof. 1965-67, prof., from 1968, chmn. English dept., 1965-67; provost Hunter-in-the-Bronx, 1967; pres. Herbert H. Lehman Coll., CUNY, 1968-90. Author: (with David Hawke) American Colloquy, 1963, (with Myron Matlaw) Story and Critic, 1963; The New Conservatives, 1967, (with James Light) The Modern Age, 1969, 72, 76, 81. Bd. mgrs. N.Y. Bot. Garden; bd. dirs. Fordham Redevel. Corp., Wave Hill. Served with AUS, 1943-45. Mem. Coun. of Pres.'s City U. N.Y., Assn. Colls. and Univs. of State of N.Y., Century Assn., Phi Beta Kappa. Home: Briarcliff, NY. Died July 30, 2007.

LIGHT, KENNETH B., manufacturing executive; b. NYC, June 2, 1932; s. Max and Mollie (Schein) Lichtenholtz; m. Judith Klein, May 28, 1961; children: Corey, Randi Beth Allison. BS, NYU, 1954, LL.B. cum laude, 1957; MBA, U. Chgo., 1976. Bar: N.Y. 1957. Partner firm Light & Light, Bklyn., 1958-61; asst. sec. Gen. Bronze Corp., Garden City, N.Y., 1961-69; sec., gen. counsel Allied Products Corp., Chgo., 1969-76, v.p., gen. counsel, 1976-79, sr. v.p., 1979-83, exec. v.p., 1983-93, dir. Chgo., from 1993, exec. v.p., CFO, from 1995; pres. Midwest Steel Processing, Inc., 1982-84. Dir. Auror Corp. Ill., Chgo.; vice chmn. Family Res. Ctr., Chgo., 1989-94, chmn., 1994-96; v.p., dir. Verson Corp., Bush Hog Corp. Mem. N.Y.C. Subcontractors Assn. (v.p. 1967-69), Am. Subcontractors Assn. (dir. 1967-68), Chgo. Assn. Commerce and Industry. Home: Lake Forest, Ill. Died Dec. 26, 2005.

LIGHTSEY, HARRY MCKINLEY, JR., academic administrator, lawyer; b. Dec. 27, 1931; BS, Clemson U., 1952; DVM, U. Ga., 1956; JD, U. S.C., 1961; PhD (hon.), Coll. Charleston; LLD (hon.), U. Charleston, Limestone Coll.; DHL (hon.), Winthrop U. Bar: SC 1961. Legal counsel SC Senate, Columbia, 1961—64; gen. counsel SC Pub. Svc. Commn., Columbi

1964—67; ptnr. Berry, Lightsey, Gibbes, & Bowers, Columbia, 1965—72, Barnes, Austin & Lightsey, Columbia, 1972—80; of counsel McNair & Sandford, Columbia, from 1993; prof. U. SC Sch. Law, Columbia, 1972—77, dean, 1980—86; pres. Coll. of Charleston (SC), 1986—92, pres. emeritus, from 1992. Author: A Study of S.C. Medical Organizations, 1970, S.C. Code Pleading, 1974; author: (with Flanagan) S.C. Civil Practice, 1985; author: Gems in a Crown, 1993; editor: S.C. Law Rev., 1961. Chmn. March of Dimes Campaign, Columbia, 1962, S.C. Dem. Party, Columbia, 1970; mem. Commn. Bicentennial U.S. Constitution, S.C. Com. Humanities; chmn. bd. trustees S.C. Govs. Sch. Sci. and Math.; S.C. rep. to So. Regional Edn. Bd., mem. exec. com.; vestryman Trinity Episcopal Cathedral, Columbia, 1970—72. Lt. US Army, 1952. Recipient Sapp Meml. award, 1961, Outstanding Prof. award, U. SC Law Sch., 1973, Outstanding Alumnus award, U. SC, 1992. Mem.: ABA, Coun. of Coll. Pres. of SC (chmn. 1990—91), SC Bar Found., SC Bar Assn. (bd. govs. 1980—86), U.S. Supreme Ct. Bar and Hist. Soc., Forest Lake Club (Columbia), ATE Summit Club. Avocations: fly fishing, golf. Home: West Columbia, SC. Died Jan. 15, 2006.

LIN, EDMUND CHI-CHIEN, microbiology educator; b. Beijing, Oct. 28, 1928; s. Hsin-Kwei and Chen Kwan (Pan) L. AB, U. Rochester, 1952; PhD, Harvard U., 1957. From instr. to asst. prof. Harvard Med. Sch., Boston, 1957-67, assoc. prof., 1968-70, prof. microbiology, from 1970. Chmn. bd sci. advisors Hong Kong Inst. Biotech., 1989— Author: Bacteria, Plasmids, and Phages, 1984; mem. editorial bd. Jour. Bacteriology, 1973-75, 91—, Jour. Biol. Chemistry, 1976-81, Jour. Molecular Evolution, 1983-86. Guggenheim fellow Pasteur Inst. Paris, 1969, Fogarty sr. fellow U. Paris, 1977-78. Mem. AAAS, NIH (microbial genetics study sect. 1991—), Am. Soc. Microbiology, Phi Beta Kappa. Home: Boston, Mass. Died Mar. 7, 2006.

LIN, TUNG HUA, civil engineering educator; b. Chungkin, China, May 26, 1911; s. Yao-Ching and Yue (Kuo) L.; m. Susan Z. Chiang, Mar. 15, 1939; childern: Rita P., Lin Wood, Robert P., James P. BS, Tangshan Coll., Chiaotung U., 1933; S.M., MIT, 1936; D.Sc., U. Mich., 1953. Prof. Tsing Hua U., China, 1937-39; chief engr. Chinese 2d Aircraft Co., Nancheun, Szechuan, 1939-44; prodn. mgr. Mfg. Factory, China, 1940-44; mem. tech. mission in charge of jet aircraft design, 1945-49; prof. aero. engring. U. Detroit, 1949-55; prof. engring. & applied scis. UCLA, 1955-78, prof. emeritus, 1978—2007. Cons.N.Am. Aviation, N.Am. Rockwell, L.A., 1964-74, Atomic Internat., Canoga Park, Calif., 1965-68, ARA Inc., Industry City, Calif., 1964-94. Author: Theory of Inelastic Structure, 1968; contbr. articles to profl. jours.; mem. editorial bd.: Jour. Composite Materials, 1966-75. Named Chinese Nat. fellow, Tsing-Hua U., 1933, prin. investigator, Office Naval Rsch., 1985—93, Air Force Office of Sci. Rsch., 1988—97; recipient medal for design of 1st Chinese twin-engine airplane, 1944, Disting. Svc. award Applied Mechanics Rev., ASME, 1966; grantee NSF, 54-78. Fellow ASME, Am. Acad. Mechanics; mem. ASCE (life, gen. chmn. engring. mechanics conf. 1965, Theodore von Karman award 1988); mem. NAE. Acad.Sinica (China). Achievements include patents in field. Home: Pacific Palisades, Calif. Died June 18, 2007.

LINCOLN, ROBERT ADAMS, retired foreign service officer, foundation executive; b. Walton, NY, Apr. 4, 1921; s. Floyd Hastings and Louise (Adams) L.; m. Viola Roberti, Jan. 15, 1944 (div. 1968); 1 child, Leslie; m. Catherine R. Allen, Feb. 19, 1968; children: Henry Allen, Thomas Adams. AB, Yale U., 1942. Mem. pub. rels. staff AICPA, 1946-47; prin. assoc. Stephen Fitzgerald & Co., NYC, 1950-55; joined USIA, 1955; info. officer U.S. Info. Svc., Damascus, Syria, 1955-56, pub. affairs officer, 1956-58, Colombo, Ceylon, 1958-61; dep. asst. dir. USIA, Washington, 1962-63, asst. dir. charge Nr. East-South Asia area, 1963-64, asst. dir. charge European area, 1964-66; counselor pub. affairs Am. Embassy, Ankara, Turkey, 1966-71; min.-counselor pub. affairs, also dir. joint U.S. Pub. Affairs Office, Am. Embassy, Saigon, Vietnam, 1971-73; ret., 1973; pres. The Pub. Diplomacy Found., Inc., McLean, Va., from 1988. Author: U.S. Direct Investment in the U.K., 1975; non-fiction book reviewer Richmond (Va.) Times-Dispatch, 1984—. Bd. dirs. Va. Cultural Laureate Soc., 1977—, pres., 1978; bd. dirs. Indochinese Refugees Social Svcs., met. D.C. area, 1979-82; mem. Assn. Yale Alumni, rep. Cen. Va. Yale Club, 1977-80. With USAAF, World War II. Recipient Disting. Honor award USIA, 1973. Mem. USIA Alumni Assn. (past v.p., past bd. dir., pres. 1988-89), Downtown Club. Home: Richmond, Va. Died Dec. 19, 2005.

LINDAHL, HERBERT WINFRED, appliance manufacturing executive; b. Malvern, Ark., Nov. 25, 1927; s. Herbert Winfred and Helen Ester (VanDusen) L.; m. Mary Evalyn Nenon, Feb. 27, 1954; children: Evalyn Nenon, Eric VanDusen. BA, Vanderbilt U., 1950. With State Industries, Inc., Nashville, from 1946, v.p., 1955-68, pres., Ashland City, from 1968. Mem.: City, Hillwood (Nashville). Republican. Avocations: tennis, wine, poetry. Home: Nashville, Tenn. Died Jan. 2, 2006.

LINDENBERGER, GEORGE FERDINAND, former insurance executive; b. N.Y.C., Sept. 6, 1924; s. Richard George and Anna (Aulbach) L.; m. Hazel Maude Gueldenapfel, July 25, 1947; 1 child, Linda Marlene Curle. Student public schs. Pearl River, N.Y. With Equitable Life Ins. Co., N.Y.C., 1941-84, asst. v.p., 1980-81, v.p., 1981-84. Mem. Am. Pension Conf., Washington, 1980-81. Developed and installed 1st pvt. national system for direct deposit of pension benefits by electronic fund transfer. Mem. council Good Shepherd Ch., Pearl River, 1967-74, sec., 1971-73. Served with USAAF, 1943-45. Recipient Outstanding Performance award Equitable Ins. Co., 1975. Mem. Life Office Mgmt. Assn. (chmn. program com. 1980-81), Spray Beach (N.J.) Yacht Club, All Am. Photo (Park Ridge, N.J.) (pres. 1983-84). Republican. Lutheran. Avocations: boating, bill fishing (sailfish), golfing, traveling, horticulture. Died Apr. 28, 2007.

LINDER, FRANK WALTER, utility company executive; b. Washington, Ill., Mar. 23, 1918; s. Walter Henry and Louise (Lowell Miller) L.; m. Kathleen Almira Reese, Sept. 10, 1947; children— Jean, Mark, Kay, Greg. B.E.E., U. Ill., 1940. Elec. engr. Rural Electrification Adminstrn., 1940-47; chief elec. engr. Dairyland Power Coop., 1947-73, asst. gen. mgr., 1973-78, gen. mgr., 1978—; dir. Norwest Bank La Crosse, N.A., Inst. Nuclear Power Ops., Chippewa Flambeau Improvement Co. Chmn. Bd. Elec. Examiners, City of La Crosse. Recipient Nikola Tesla award Westinghouse Electric Corp., 1984. Mem. IEEE, Power Engring. Soc. Methodist. Lodge: Kiwanis. Home: La Crosse, Wis. Died Apr. 11, 2006.

LINDLEY, CURTIS PRICE, manufacturing executive; b. Modesto, Calif., Nov. 20, 1924; s. Curtis Mendenhall and Sarah Maude (Price) L.; m. Mary Pryor Black; children— Kathryn Pryor, Jayne Price. BA Engr. at Large, Stanford U., 1948. Engaged in prodn. mgmt. Gen. Mills, Inc., Lodi, Calif., 1948-52; v.p. prodn. Centennial Mills, Portland, Oreg., 1952-67; exec. v.p. manufactured products Univar Corp., Seattle, from 1967. Dir. Timberland Industries, ROCKCOR, Inc., both Redmond, Wash. Served with USNR, 1943-45. Mem. Assn. Operative Millers Internat., Corn Refiners Assn., Seattle C. of C., Northwest Forum. Clubs: Seattle Tennis, Harbor, Rainier, Seattle Rotary, University, Seattle Yacht. Died Feb. 6, 2007.

LINDLEY, MARALEE IRWIN, county official, consultant, speaker; b. Springfield, Ill., June 30, 1925; d. Oramel Blackstone and Rachel Virginia (Elliott) Irwin; m. Joseph Perry Lindley, Sept. 18, 1948; children: Joseph Perry, Richard Fleetwood. BS Psychology, Northwestern U., 1947; MA in Counseling, U. Ill., Springfield, 1973, MA in Comm., 1979. Cert. tchr., Ill. Bookkeeper, acct. Ill. State Bar Assn., Springfield, 1947-48; curriculum coord., tchr. Sch. Dist. 186, Springfield, 1966-80; auditor, trustee Woodside Twp., Springfield, 1977-81; county auditor Sangamon County, Ill., 1980-86, county clk. Ill., from 1986. Dir. Ill. Dept. on Aging, Springfield, 1992-99; co-author/developer Ill. Elem. Gifted Program, 1977-80 (exemplary citation 1978); rep. Internat. Fedn. on Aging of UN; vice chair U.S. Com. for Celebration of UN Internat. Yr. of Older Persons, 1999; chair Nat. Effort for Global Embrace Walk, 1999; adv. com. Nat. Silver Haired Congress; charter mem. Internat. Conf. Intergenerational Programs to Promote Social Change. Mem. Mayor's Commn. on Internat. Visitors, Springfield, 1964—; sec. Sangamon State U. Found., 1984-86, Symphony Guild, Springfield, 1983-86; treas. Springfield Women's Polit. Caucus, 1983-85; pres. Capitol City Rep. Women's Club, Springfield, 1985-87. Recipient hon. Thanks award Land of Lincoln coun. Girl Scouts U.S., 1958, Appreciation award City of Springfield, 1964, Disting. Citizen award Sch. Dist. 1986, Elizabeth Cady Stanton award Springfield Women's Polit. Caucus, 1987; named to Women of Achievement in Govt., Sangamon State U., 1985, One of 5 Rep. County Ofciles. of Yr., 1985. Mem. Ill. Assn. County Auditors (sec. 1982-84, treas. 1984-86, v.p. 1986), Assn. Govt. Accts. (pres. 1984-85), Am. Soc. Pub. Adminstrn., Nat. Assn. Govt. Accts. (regional v.p.), Ill. Women in Govt. (treas.), Women in Mgmt. (Woman of Achievement award 1985), LWV. Lodges: Zonta. Avocations: dulcimer, singing, sports, reading. Home: Springfield, Ill. Died June 7, 2006.

LING, JOSEPH TSO-TI, manufacturing company executive, environmental engineer; b. Peking, China, June 10, 1919; came to U.S., 1948, naturalized, 1963; s. Ping Sun and Chong Hung (Lee) L.; m. Rose Hsu, Feb. 1, 1944; children: Lois Ling Olson, Rosa-Mai Ling Ahlgren, Louis, Lorraine Ling-LaRoy. B.C.E., Hangchow Christian Coll., Shanghai, China, 1944; MS in Civil Engring, U. Minn., 1950, PhD in San. Engring, 1952. Registered profl. engr., Minn., Ala., N.J., Okla., W.Va., N.Y., Ill., Ind., Pa., Mich. Civil engr. Nanking-Shanghai R.R. System, 1944-47; research asst. san. engring. U. Minn., 1948-52; sr. staff san. engr. Gen. Mills, Inc., Mpls., 1953-55; dir. dept. san. engring. research Ministry Municipal Constrn., Peking, 1956-57; prof. civil engring. Bapt. U., Hong Kong, 1958-59; head dept. water and san. engring. Minn. Mining & Mfg. Co., St. Paul, 1960-66, mgr. environ. and civil engring., 1967-70, dir. environ. engring. and pollution control, 1970-74, v.p. environ. engring. and pollution control, 1975-84, community service exec., from 1985. Adv. mem. on air pollution Minn. Bd. Health, 1964-66; mem. Minn. Gov.'s Adv. Com. on Air Resources, 1966-67; mem. adv. panel on environ. pollution U.S. C. of C., 1966-71; mem. chem. indsl. com., adv. to Ohio River Valley Water Sanitation Commn., 1962-76; mem. environ. quality panel Electronic Industries Assn., 1971-80; mem. environ. quality com. NAM, 1965-84; mem. Pres. Nixon's Adv. Bd. on Air Quality, 1974-75; vice chmn. environ. com. U.S. Bus. and Industry Adv. Com. to OECD, 1975-84; mem. adv. subcom. on environ., health and safety regulations Pres. Carter's Domestic Policy Rev. of Indsl. Innovation, 1978-79; adv. panel indsl. innovation and health, safety and environ. regulation Office Tech. Assessment of U.S. Congress, 1978-80; exec. com. engring. assembly NRC, 1977-80; also environ. studies bd. Commn. Natural Resources, 1977-82; mem. staff svcs. subcom. of environ. com. Bus. Roundtable, 1975-84; vice chmn. environ. com. U.S. Coun., Internat. C. of C., 1978-89; adv. com. on rsch. applications policy NSF, 1976-80; mem. Sci. Adv. Bd. EPA, 1984-88, selection com. Pres. Bush's Environment and Conservation Challenge Award, 1991-93. Contbr. articles to profl. jours. Trustee Belwin Outdoor Lab., St. Paul, 1970—; bd. dirs. Fresh Water Found., 1974—, Northwest Area Found., 1970-87, St. Paul Area YMCA, 1974-80, Midwest China Study Center, Minn. Environ. Sci. Found., 1970-78, Nat. Water Alliance, 1983-88, World Environ. Ctr., 1984-99. Woodrow Wilson Sr. fellow, 1975—; recipient numerous awards, including Joan Hodges Queneau award Am. Assn. Engring. Socs., 1990, Outstanding Achievement award Nat. Govt. Taiwan, 1993; named Laureate, Global 500 Honor Role UN Environ. Program, 1999, One of Most Important Engrs. of Past 125 Yrs. Worldwide, Engring. News Record, 1999. Fellow ASCE (life): mem. NAE, Am. Acad. Environ. Engrs. (diplomate, chmn. examination update com. 1981-83), Minn. Assn. Commerce and Industry, Am. Water Works Assn. (life), Air and Waste Mgmt. Assn. (dir.), Chem. Mfg. Assn. Clubs: Rainbow (Mpls.). Died Feb. 22, 2006.

LINK, GEORGE HAMILTON, retired lawyer; b. Sacramento, Calif., Mar. 26, 1939; s. Hoyle and Corrie Elizabeth (Evans) L.; m. Betsy Leland; children— Thomas Hamilton, Christopher Leland. AB, U. Calif., Berkeley, 1961; LLB, Harvard U., 1964. Bar: Calif. 1965, U.S. Dist. Ct. (no., ea., ctrl. and so dists.) Calif. 1965, U.S. Ct. Appeals (9th cir.) 1965. Assoc. Brobeck, Phleger & Harrison, San Francisco, 1964-69, ptnr., 1970—2001, mng. ptnr. LA, 1973-93, mng. ptnr. firmwide, 1993-96; ret., 2001. Chmn. Pacific Rim Adv. Coun., 1992-95. Bd. regents U. Calif., 1971-74; trustee Berkeley Found., Jr. Statesmen Am.; bd. govs. United Way, 1979-81; trustee, v.p. Calif. Hist. Soc., 1987—; bd. dirs. Ancient Egypt Rsch. Assocs. Fellow Am. Bar Found.; mem. ABA, Calif. Bar Assn., L.A. Bar Assn., U. Calif. Alumni Assn. (pres. 1972-75), Calif. Club, Bohemian Club, Jonathan Club. Republican. Methodist. Home: Los Angeles, Calif. Died Dec. 14, 2006.

LINK, MELVIN ROBERT, otolaryngologist; b. Paris, Ky., Aug. 8, 1916; s. Robert and Annie B. (English) L.; m. Margaret Swope, Aug. 15, 1942 (div. Dec. 1970); children— Robert S., Richard M., Jane F.; m. 2d, Evelyne Johnson, Aug. 21, 1976. A.B., Transylvania U., 1938; M.D., U. Louisville, 1942. Diplomate Am. Bd. Otolaryngology. Intern U.S. Naval Hosp., Bethesda, Md., 1942-43; resident in otolaryngology Columbia-Presbyn. Med. Ctr., N.Y.C., 1947-50; practice medicine specializing in otolaryngology, Charlotte, N.C., 1950—; mem. staffs Mercy Hosp., Presbyn. Hosp. Served to lt., M.C., USN, 1942-47. Decorated Bronze Star. Mem. Am. Acad. Bronchoesophagology, AMA, So. Med. Assn., N.C. Med. Assn., Am. Acad. Otolaryngology-Head and Neck Surgery. Republican. Lutheran. Club: Charlotte City. Home: Hilton Head Island, SC. Died May 1, 2007.

LINNELL, ROBERT HARTLEY, editor-in-chief; b. Kalkaska, Mich., Aug. 15, 1922; s. Earl Dean and Constance (Hartley) L.; m. Myrle Elizabeth Talbot, June 17, 1950; children: Charlene LeGro, Lloyd Robert, Randa Ruth, Dean Maxfield. BS, U. N.H., 1944, MS, 1948; PhD, U. Rochester, 1950. Asst. instr. U. N.H., 1942-44, instr., 1947; asst. prof. chemistry Am. U., Beirut, 1950-52, assoc. prof., chmn. chemistry dept., 1952-55; v.p. Tizon Chem. Corp., Flemington, N.J., 1955-58; assoc. prof. chemistry U. Vt., 1958-61; dir. Scott Research Labs., Plumsteadville, Pa., 1961-62; program dir. phys. chemistry NSF, 1962-65, planning assoc., 1965-67, program mgr. departmental sci. devel., 1967-69; dean Coll. Letters, Arts and Scis., U. So. Calif., Los Angeles, 1969-70; dir. Office Instl. Studies U. So. Calif., 1970-82, chmn. safety sci. dept., 1982-85, prof. emeritus, from 1985; pres. Harmony Inst., 1985-92. Cons. Reheis Corp., 1958-61, Coll. Chemistry Cons. Service, 1970-76, EPA, 1971-73, Lake Erie Environment Program, 1971-73 Author: Graduate Student Support and Manpower Resources in Graduate Science Education, 1968, Air Pollution, 1973, Hydrogen Bonding, 1971, Dollars and Scholars, 1982, Meeting The Needs of The Non-Smoking Traveler, 1986, Ignition Interlock Devices: An Assessment of Their Application to Reducing DUI, 1991; editor: my-oped.com, 1999—; contbr. articles to profl. jours. Mem. traffic adv. com. Auto Club So. Calif., 1985-93; treas. Norwich Congl. Ch., 1995-96, chair bus. com. 1996-98; coord. Concord Coalition, Upper Valley, N.H. and Vt., 1995-2000; mem. devel. bd. Upper Valley Tchr. Tng. Program, 1995-97; mem. scholarship com. Upper Valley Cmty. Found., 1996-2005; bd. overseers Dartmouth Hitchcock Med. Ctr., 1997-2002; bd. dirs. Upper Valley Habitat for Humanity, 1993-95; Dem. candidate for Pre. U.S., N.H. Primary, 2004. Recipient Outstanding Achievement award Coll. Tech., U. N.H., 1969 Mem. AAUP, Am. Chem. Soc. (program chmn. Washington 1968, divsn. chem. edn. 1971), Assn. Instl. Rsch., Am. Lung Assn. of Ctrl. Calif. (bd. dirs. 1986-92, pres. 1991-92), Rotary. Achievements include patents in chemistry field. Home: Lebanon, NH. Died Nov. 5, 2006.

LINNEMAN, ROBERT ERNST, retired marketing professor; b. Bloomington, Ill., Dec. 9, 1928; s. William Lewis and Bertha (Ummel) L.; m. L. Annabelle Witt, 1952; children: Robert Daniel, Kurt Ernst. PhB in Bus., Ill. Wesleyan U., 1950; MS in Mktg., U. Ill., 1962, PhD in Mktg., 1964. Prof. mktg. Temple U., Phila., 1964-90, assoc. dean Sch. Bus., 1972—75; dean Temple U., Japan, 1985—86; prof. food mktg. St. Joseph's U., Phila., 1991—2001. Cons., spkr. in field. Author: A Shirt Sleeve Approach to Corporate Planning, 1980; co-author: Making Niche Marketing Work, 1991, Marketing Planning in a Total Quality Environment, 1995, (periodical) Harvard Bus. Rev., 1977; contbr. over 35 articles to profl. publs. Mem. Planning Commn., Bloomington, Ill., 1957-59; mem. Deer Control com., Schuylkill Twp., Pa. Capt. USAF, 1951-55, res., 1958. Recipient Disting. Tchg. award Lindback Found., 1976. Mem. Am. Mktg. Assn. (pres. Phila. chpt. 1971-72, nat. bd. dirs. 1972-74, nat. v.p. bd. dirs. 1980-82). Avocation: sailing. Home: Valley Forge, Pa. Died May 30, 2007.

LINOWES, DAVID FRANCIS, finance educator, corporate financial executive; b. Trenton, NJ, Mar. 16, 1917; m. Dorothy Lee Wolf, Mar. 24, 1946; children: Joanne Linowes Alinsky, Richard Gary, Susan Linowes Allen (dec.), Jonathan Scott. Founder, ptnr. Leopold & Linowes (now BDO Siedman), Washington, 1946-62; cons. sr. ptnr. Leopold & Linowes, Washington, 1962-82; nat. founding ptnr. Laventhol & Horwath, 1965-76; chmn. bd, CEO Mickleberry Comm. Corp., 1970-73; chmn., CEO Perpetual Investment Co., Inc., 1950-88; dir. Horn & Hardart Co., 1971-77, Piper Aircraft, 1972-77, Saturday Rev./World Mag., Inc., 1972-77, Chris Craft Industries, Inc., 1958—2004; prof. polit. economy, pub. policy, bus. adminstrn. U. Ill., Urbana, 1976—2000, Boeschensten prof. emeritus, 1987—2007. Cons. DATA Internat. Assistance Corps., 1962-68, U.S. Dept. State, UN, Sec. HEW, Dept. Interior; chmn. Fed. Privacy Protection Commn., Washington, 1975-77, U.S. Commn. Fair Market Value Policy for Fed. Coal Leasing, 1983-84, Pres.'s Commn. on Fiscal Accountability of Nation's Energy Resources, 1981-82; chmn. Pres.' Commn. on Privatization, 1987-88; mem. Council on Fgn. Relations; cons. panel GAO; adj. prof. mgmt. NYU, 1965-73; Disting. Arthur Young Prof. U. Ill., 1973-74; emeritus chmn. internat. adv. com. Tel Aviv U.; headed U.S. State Dept. Mission to Turkey, 1967, to India, 1970, to Pakistan, 1968, to Greece, 1971; U.S. rep. on privacy to Orgn. Econ. Devel. Intergovtl. Bur. for Informati cs, 1977-81, cons., N.Y.C., 1977-81; U.S. State Dept. mission to Chile, Argentina and Uruguay, July, 1988, Yugoslavia, May, 1991. Author: Managing Growth Through Acquistion, Strategies for Survival, Corporate Conscience; commn. report Personal Privacy in Information Society, Fiscal Accountablility of Nation's Energy Resources; editor: The Impact of the Communication and Computer Revolution on Society, Privacy in

America, 1989, Creating Public Policy, 1998, Living Through 50 Years of Economic Progress with 10 Presidents-The Most Productive Generation in History 1946-1996, 2000; contbr. articles to profl. jours. Trustee Boy's Club Greater Washington, 1955-62, Am. Inst. Found., 1962-68; assoc. YM-YWHA's Greater N.Y., 1970-76; chmn. Charities Adv. Com. of D.C., 1958-62; emeritus bd. dirs. Religion in Am. Life, Inc.; former chmn. U.S. People for UN; chmn. citizens com. Combat Charity Rackets, 1953-58. 1st lt. Signal Corps, AUS, 1942-46. Recipient 1970 Human Relations award Am. Jewish Com., U.S. Pub. Service award, 1982, Alumni Achievement award U. Ill., 1989, CPA Distinguished Pub. Svc. award, Washington, 1989. Mem. AICPA (v.p. 1962-63), U. Ill. Found. (emeritus bd. dirs.), Coun. Fgn. Rels., Cosmos Club, Univ. Club, Phi Kappa Phi (nat. bd. dirs.), Beta Gamma Sigma. Home: Chevy Chase, Md. Died Oct. 29, 2007.

LINSLEY, ROBERT MARTIN, retired geology educator; b. Chgo., Feb. 19, 1930; s. Robert Martin and Mary (Morgan) L.; m. JoAnn Hoehler (div.); children: David, Barbara, Christopher. BS, U. Mich., 1952, MS, 1953, PhD, 1960. Ford teaching intern Colgate U., Hamilton, N.Y., 1954-55, mem. faculty, from 1955, Whitnall prof. geology, chmn. dept. geology, 1955-92, ret., 1992. Contbr. articles to profl. jours. Home: Hamilton, NY. Died July 25, 2006.

LIPSCHULTZ, M. RICHARD, accountant; b. Chgo., July 5, 1913; s. Morris David and Minnie (Moskowitz) L.; student Northwestern U., 1930-35; JD, De Paul U., 1948; m. Evelyn Smolin, May 16, 1945 (dec. 1963); m. Phyllis Siegel, July 11, 1965; children: Howard Elliott, Carl Alvin, Saul Martin. Bar: Ill. 1948; CPA, Ill. Auditor State of Ill., Chgo., 1938-41; conferee IRS, Chgo., 1941-49; tax acct. A.I. Grade & Co., C.P.A.s, Chgo., 1949-50; sr. ptnr. Lipschultz Bros., Levin and Gray and predecessor firms, CPAs, Chgo., 1950-82; fin. v.p., dir. Miller Asso. Industries, Inc., Skokie, 1973-74; dir. Miller Builders, Inc.; dir., chmn. exec. com. Portable Electric Tools, Inc., Geneva, Ill., 1963-67; mem. exec. com. Midland Screw Corp., Chgo., 1958-66; faculty John Marshall Law Sch., 1951-64. Bd. dirs.; pres. bd. dirs. Lipschultz Family Found. With USAAF, 1943-46. Mem. AICPA, ABA, Ill. Soc. CPAs, Fed., Chgo., Ill. bar assns., Decalogue Soc. Lawyers, Am. Legion, Nu Beta-Epsilon. Mem. B'nai B'rith. Clubs: Standard (Chgo.); Ravinia Green Country (Deerfield, Ill.). Contbr. articles to profl. jours. Died Feb. 7, 2007.

LIPSET, SEYMOUR MARTIN, sociologist, political scientist, educator; b. NYC, Mar. 18, 1922; s. Max and Lena (Lippman) L.; m. Elsie Braun, Dec. 26, 1944 (dec. Feb. 1987); children: David, Daniel, Carola; m. Sydnee Guyer, July 29, 1990. BS, CCNY, 1943; PhD, Columbia U., 1949; MA (hon.), Harvard U., 1966; LLD (hon.), Villanova U., 1973, Hebrew U., 1981, U. Buenos Aires, 1987, Free U., Brussels, 1990, U. Judaism, 1991, Hebrew Union Coll., 1993, Boston Hebrew Coll., 1993, U. Guelph, 1996, Georgetown U., 1997, U. Toronto, 1998. Lectr. U. Toronto, 1946-48; asst. prof. U. Calif., Berkeley, 1948-50; asst., then assoc. prof. grad. faculty Columbia U., 1950-56, asst. dir. Bur. Applied Social Rsch., 1954-56; prof. sociology U. Calif., Berkeley, 1956-66, dir. Inst. Internat. Studies, 1962-66; vis. prof. social rels. and govt. Harvard U., 1965-66, prof. govt. and sociology, exec. com. Ctr. Internat. Affairs, 1966-75, George Markham prof. Ctr. Internat. Affairs, 1974-75; sr. fellow Hoover Inst. Stanford U., from 1975, prof. polit. sci. and sociology, 1975-92, Caroline S.G. Munro prof., 1981-92; former Hazel prof. pub. policy George Mason U., Fairfax, Va. Henry Ford vis. rsch. prof. Yale U., 1960-61; Paley lectr. Hebrew U., 1973; Fulbright program 40th Anniversary Disting. lectr., 1987; vis. scholar Russell Sage Found., New York, 1988-89; sr. scholar Woodrow Wilson Ctr.; sr. fellow Progressive Polity Inst. Author: Agrarian Socialism, 1950, (with others) Union Democracy, 1956, (with R. Bendix) Social Mobility in Industrial Society, 1959, expanded edit., 1991, Political Man: The Social Basis of Politics, 1960, expanded edit., 1981, The First New Nation, 1963, expanded edit., 1979, Revolution and Counter Revolution, 1968, expanded edit., 1988, (with Earl Raab) The Politics of Unreason, 1970, expanded edit., 1978, Rebellion in the University, 1972, (with Everett Ladd) Academics and the 1972 Election, 1973, Professors, Unions and American Higher Education, 1973, The Divided Academy, 1975, (with David Riesman) Education and Politics at Harvard, 1975, (with I.L. Horowitz) Dialogues on American Politics, 1978, (with William Schneider) The Confidence Gap, 1983, expanded edit., 1987, Consensus and Conflict, 1987, Continental Divide: The Institutions and Values of the United States and Canada, 1990, The Educational Background of American Jews, 1994; (with Earl Raab) Jews and the New American Scene, 1995, American Exceptionalism: A Double-Edged Sword, 1996, (with Gary Marks) It Didn't Happen Here: Why Socialism Failed in the United States, 2000; co-editor: Class, Status and Power, 1953, Labor and Trade Unionism, 1960, Sociology: The Progress of a Decade, 1961, Culture and Social Character, 1961, The Berkeley Student Revolt, 1965, Class, Status and Power in Comparative Perspective, 1966, Social Structure, Mobility and Economic Development, 1966, Elites in Latin America, 1967, Party Systems and Voter Alignments, 1967, Students in Revolt, 1969, Issues in Politics and Government, 1970, Failure of a Dream? Essays in the History of American Socialism, 1974, rev. edit., 1984, Who's Who in Democracy, 1997, Democracy in Asia and Africa, 1998, Democracy in Europe and the Americas, 1998; co-editor: Democracy in Developing Countries, 3 vols., Africa, Asia and Latin America, 1988, 89, Politics in Developing Countries, 1990, 95, The Encyclopedia of Democracy, 4 vols., 1995; co-editor Public Opinion mag., 1977-89, Internat. Jour. Pub. Opinion Rsch.; editor: Students and Politics, 1967, Politics and Social Science, 1969, Emerging Coalitions in American Politics, 1978, The Third Century, 1979, Party Coalitions in the Eighties, 1981, Unions in Transition, 1986, American Pluralism and the Jewish Community, 1990; adv. editor: various jours. including Sci., Comparative Politics. Mem. Bd. Fgn. Scholarships, 1968-71; bd. dirs. Aurora Found., 1985-95, U.S. Inst. Peace, 1995—; nat. chmn. B'nai B'rith Hillel Found., 1975-79, chmn. nat. exec. com., 1979-84; assoc. pres. Am. Profs. for Peace in the Middle East, 1976-77, nat. pres., 1977-81; co-chmn. exec. com. Internat. Ctr. for Peace in Middle East, 1982-92; co-chmn. Com. for Effective UNESCO, 1976-81; chmn. Com. for UN Integrity, 1981-83; chmn. nat. faculty cabinet United Jewish Appeal, 1981-84; pres. Progressive Found., 1991-95. Recipient Gunyar Myrdal prize, 1970, Townsend Harris medal, 1971, 125th Anniversary alumni medal CCNY, 1963, M.B. Rawson award, 1986, No. Telecom. Gold Medal for Can. Studies, 1987, Marshall Sklare award Assn. Social Sci. Study of Jewry, 1993; fellow Social Sci. Rsch. Coun., 1945-46, Ctr. Advanced Study Behavioral Sci. fellow, 1971-72, Woodrow Wilson Ctr. for Internat. Scholars fellow, 1995-96. Fellow NAS, AAAS (v.p. 1974-78, chmn. sect. on econ. and social sci. 1975-76, 95-96), Nat. Acad. Edn., Am. Sociol. Assn. (coun. 1959-62, MacIver award 1962, pres. 1992-93), Japan Soc.; mem. Sociol. Rsch. Assn. (exec. com. 1981-84, pres. 1985, lifetime career award 2000), Am. Polit. Sci. Assn. (coun. 1975-77, pres. 1981-82, Leon Epstein prize 1989), Internat. Polit. Sci. Assn. (coun. 1981-88, v.p. 1982-88), Internat. Soc. Polit. Psychology (pres. 1979-80), Internat. Sociol. Assn. (chmn. com. polit. sociology 1959-71), World Assn. Pub. Opinion Rsch. (v.p. and pres.-elect 1982-84, pres. 1984-86), Am. Philos. Soc., Finnish Acad. Sci. (hon.), Paul Lazarsfeld Gesellschaft (social rsch. 1994—), Soc. for Comparative Rsch. Home: Arlington, Va. Died Dec. 31, 2006.

LIPSKY, STEPHEN EDWARD, electronics engineer, executive; b. NYC, Jan. 18, 1932; s. Arthur Arnold and Sophie (Malsbrook) Lipsky; m. Laura Roher, May 11, 1958 (div. 1978); children: Janice, Sharon, David; m. Hyla Schaffer, Apr. 7, 1979. B.E.E., NYU, 1953, M.E.E., 1962; PhD in Elec. Engring., Drexel U., 1993. Project engr. Fisher Radio Corp; div. mgr., staff scientist Loral Electronics, Yonkers, NY, 1958-63; corp. v.p. Polarad-Radiometrics, Lake Success, NY, 1963-70; dir. advanced systems Gen. Inst. Corp., Hicksville, NY, 1970-79; chief tech. officer, sr. v.p. Am. Electronic Labs., Lansdale, Pa., 1979-93; founder, chief tech. officer Bynetics Corp., Jenkintown, Pa., from 1993. Adj. univ. prof. Drexel U., Phila.; expert witness RF Comms. Author: (book) Microwave Passive Direction Finding, 1987; contbr. articles to profl. jours. Served to lt. US Army, 1953—55. Decorated Bronze AFCEA medal. Fellow: IEE (assoc.), IEEE (life); mem.: Army Assn., Assn. Old Crows (bd. dirs. 1972—74, Sr. Gold Cert. merit 1990), Navy League, Am. Radio Relay League, Masons. Republican. Achievements include patents in field. Avocations: amateur radio, photography, stamp collecting/philately, antique radios. Home: Barnegat Lgt, NJ. Died May 3, 2007.

LIS, EDWARD FRANCIS, pediatrician, consultant; b. Chgo., Apr. 1, 1918; s. Stephen and Stephanie L.; m. Sonne Nadine Kowalsen, Apr. 3, 1944; children— Jeffrey Warren, James Bryan. Student, DePaul U., 1936-37; BS, MD, U. Ill. Pvt. practice, Park Forest, Ill., 1949-51; faculty U. Ill. Coll. Medicine, 1951-90, prof. pediatrics, also dir. div. services crippled children, 1959-90, prof. emeritus, from 1990. Dir. center handicapped children Univ. Hosp., U. Ill., 1955-90; cons. in field. Contbr. to profl. jours. Chmn. research adv. com. Children's Bur., HEW, 1964-67; mem. Ill. Commn. Children. Served to capt. AUS, 1944-46. Fellow Am. Acad. Pediatrics, Am. Pub. Health Assn.; mem. Sigma Xi. Home: Flossmoor, Ill. Died June 4, 2006.

LIS, LAWRENCE FRANCIS, facsimile company executive; b. Blue Island, Ill., Jan. 27, 1941; s. Anthony C. and Ann Marion (Galazin) L.; student DeVry Inst. Tech., 1958-59; m. Barbara Jean Lisak, Oct. 19, 1963; children— Christ and Connie (twins), David S. With Telautograph Corp., Chgo., 1959-64; regional mgr. Datalog div. Litton Industries, Chgo., 1964-74; regional mgr. Rapicom Inc., Chgo., 1974-78, nat. dir. field service ops., Hillside, Ill., 1978-79, v.p. customer service div., 1979—, v.p. customer service div. Ricoh Corp. and Ricoh Corp. Ltd. subs. Ricoh Ltd., 1980—. dir. Emergency Services and Disaster Agy., Village of Chicago Ridge, 1977-82; mem. Ill. CD Council. Commander Civil Air Patrol, Ill., 1986—. Mem. Assn. Field Service Mgrs. (pres. Chgo. chpt. 1984-85), Armed Forces Communications and Electronics Assn., Suburban Amateur Radio Assn., Mendel High Sch Alumni Assn. Home: Oak Lawn, Ill. Died June 20, 2007.

LISS, JEFFREY FRED, lawyer, educator; b. Balt., June 10, 1951; s. Solomon and Gertrude (Nadich) L.; m. Susan Michelson, July 30, 1972; children: Joanna M., Harrison S. BA, U. Mich., 1972, MA, JD, 1975. Bar: D.C. 1975, Md. 1981. Law clk. Judge Charles R. Richey, U.S. Dist. Ct., Washington, 1975-77; from assoc. to ptnr. Wald, Harkrader & Ross, Washington, 1977-85; ptnr. Piper & Marbury (now DLA Piper US LLP), Washington, 1985—99, COO, 1999—2004, US co-mng. ptnr., 2005—07. Adj. prof. U. Mich. Law Sch., 1996, 2002, 2004, Georgetown Law Sch., 1985-2007, Am. U. Sch. Law, 1978-85; spl. govt. employee, Office of White House Counsel, 1996-97. Co-author: Remedies in Business Torts Litigation, 1992; contbr. articles to profl. jours. Bd. dirs. Washington Lawyers Com. for Civil Rights, Washington, 1992-98; pro bono counsel numerous orgns., Washington, 1977-2007; treas., Friends of Lt. Gov. Kathleen Kennedy Townsend, Md., 1996-2002. Recipient Judge Learned Hand award, Am. Jewish Com., 2003. Fellow Am. Bar Found.; mem. Am. Law Inst., D.C. Cir. Hist. Soc. (bd. dirs.), Balt. Symphony Orch. (exec. com., bd. dirs.). Democrat. Jewish. Avocations: baseball, reading, piano. Died Mar. 17, 2007.

LITES, DAYLE EMORY, city official; b. Many, La., Sept. 4, 1932; s. Joseph G. and Myrtle (Bryant) L.; m. Leona LaFleur, May 7, 1955 (dec. 1969); children— Lynn M., Daniel B.; m. Rene Hand, Mar. 4, 1972; 1 child, Christopher D.; m. Joan E. Johnson, July 23, 1983. B.A., Northeastern Ill. U., 1978; grad. FBI Nat. Acad., 1973. Patrolman, Glenview Police Dept., Ill., 1958-66, sgt., 1966-69, lt., 1969-79, comdr. patrol, 1974-78, comdr. criminal investigations, 1968-73; chief of police, chief adminstr. Roselle Police Dept., Ill., 1979—. Served as sgt. USAF, 1951-55. Mem. Internat. Assn. Chiefs Police, FBI Nat. Acad. Assn., Ill. Police Assn. Avocation: golf. Home: Roselle, Ill. Died Feb. 18, 2006.

LITHGOW, THEODORE T., food company executive; b. Summit Hill, Pa., Mar. 7, 1932; s. Theodore M. and Gertrude (Tracey) L.; m. Lois Spira, Sept. 4, 1978 (div. Mar. 1987); m. Sara Prew, May 9, 1987; children: Theo. D., Lynn Lithgow Tessaglia. BS, Muhlenberg Coll., 1953. Quality control chemist Atlas Chem. Industries, Wilmington, Del., 1953-56; tech. mgr. Aquaness Corp., Houston, 1956-59; prod. mgr. Glyco Chem., Williams Port, Pa., 1959-63; plant mgr. Baird Chem. Ind., Peoria, Ill.; dir mfg. C.J. Patterson Co., Kansas City, Mo., 1968-75; v.p., gen. mgr., 1975-85; pres. Merckens Chocolate div. Nabisco Brands, Mansfield, Mass., from 1986-. Bd. dirs. Nat. 4H Council, Washington, 1976--, Human Resources Ctr. Albertson, N.Y., 1982-- Regional fin. dir. U.S. Olympic Com., 1980-84, bd. dirs. Muhlenberg Coll., Allentown, Pa. 1983--. Mem. Am. Soc. Bakery Engrs., Am. Bakers Assn., Retail Confectioners Assn., Nat. Confectioners Assn. Club: Internat., Wollaston Co. Republican. Avocations: golf, tennis. Home: Mc Donough, Ga. Died Sept. 3, 2006.

LITTELL, WALLACE WILLIAM, retired diplomat; b. Meadville, Pa., Feb. 10, 1922; s. Clair Francis and Lena Augusta (Hamlin) L.; m. Betty Gay Paris, June 4, 1948 (dec. 1984); children: David, Linda, Harriet, Julie, Andrea; m. Helen M. Shaw, June 15, 1985 (dec. 1992); m. Ilda Hall, 2003 BA, Cornell Coll., Mt. Vernon, Iowa, 1947, LLD (hon.), 1978; MA, certificate, Russian Inst., Columbia U., 1949; student, Heidelberg U., Germany, 1949-50, Goettingen U., 1951-52, Columbia, 1955-56. With US Forest Svc., 1944-46, 47, 48, UNRRA, Poland and Greece, 1946; cultural affairs adv. Darmstadt, Germany, 1949, Hanover, Germany, 1950-53; editor Ost-Probleme (USIS publ.), Bonn, Germany, 1953-55; cultural attache Am. embassy, Moscow, 1956-58; fgn. affairs officer USIA, Washington, 1958-59, 60-61; dir. policy & rsch. Am. Nat. Exhbn., Moscow, 1959-60; 1st sec., chief press and cultural sect. embassy Warsaw, 1961-65; dep. asst. dir. Soviet Union and Eastern Europe USIA, 1965-68, asst. dir. Soviet Union and Eastern Europe, 1968-69; counselor embassy for pub. affairs CPAO, Belgrade, Yugoslavia, 1970-74; pub. affairs officer Am. embassy, Berlin, East Germany, 1975-76; assigned to Sr. Seminar in Fgn. Policy, Dept. State, 1976-77; chief Program Evaluation Staff, USIA, 1977-78; counselor embassy for press and culture Am. embassy, Moscow, 1979-83; ret., 1983; pub. affairs adv. Am. del. Budapest Cultural Forum, 1985. Recipient Meritorious Service award USIA, 1958, Meritorious Service award Am. Nat. Exhbn. Moscow, 1959 Mem. Cornell Coll. Iowa Sports Hall of Fame, Phi Beta Kappa. Home: Bethesda, Md. Died May 28, 2007.

LITTLEJOHN, CAMERON BRUCE, retired state chief justice; b. Pacolet, SC, July 22, 1913; s. Cameron and Lady Sara (Warmoth) L.; m. Inell Smith, Feb. 7, 1942 (dec. 1962); children: Inell (Mrs. Dan L. Allen III), Cameron Bruce Jr. AB, Wofford Coll., Spartanburg, SC, 1935; LL.B., U. S.C., 1936, JD, 1970; L.H.D., Converse Coll., 1985; LLD, U. S.C., 1985. Bar: S.C. bar 1936. Practice in, Spartanburg, 1936-43, 46-49; circuit judge, 1949-67; assoc. justice Supreme Ct. S.C., 1967-84, chief justice, 1984-85; LLD Wofford Coll., 1968. Permanent mem. 4th U.S. Ct. Appeals Jud. Conf., 1966— Author: Laugh with the Judge, 1974, Littlejohn's Half Century at the Bench and Bar, 1988, Littlejohn's Political Memoirs, 1990; mem. editorial staff Trial Judges Jour., 1963-67. Mem. S.C. Ho. Reps., 1937-43, 47-49, speaker, 1947-49; del. county, state and nat. Democrat convs.; Trustee North Greenville Jr. Coll., 1962-67; 85— alumni bd. dirs. Wofford Coll., 1966-68. Served to 1st lt. AUS, 1943-46. Recipient Dist. Pub. Service award S.C. Bar Found., 1986, Neville Holcombe Disting. Citizenship award Spartanburg Area C. of C., 1987. Mem. Appellate Judges Conf., Am. Legion, Forty and Eight, V.F.W., Civitan Club, Blue Key, Phi Beta Kappa (hon.). Home: Spartanburg, SC. Died Apr. 21, 2007.

LIVA, EDWARD LOUIS, eye surgeon; b. Lyndhurst, NJ, Aug 30, 1925; s. Paul Francis and Lucy Agnes (Andreozzi) L.; m. Dorothea Lucille Carter, Aug. 29, 1946; children: Edward Jr., Bradford, Douglas, Jeffrey, Elaine. SB, Harvard U., 1946, MD, 1950. Diplomate Am. Bd. Ophthalmology. Intern Med. Coll. Va., Richmond, 1950-51; fellow in eye pathology Mass. Eye and Ear, Boston, 1951; resident Brooklyn Eye and Ear, NY, 1952-53; chief ophthalmic examiner Workman's Compensation Bd. NYC, 1957-63; sr. ophthalmic surgeon Hackensack (N.J.) Med. Ctr., from 1957, Valley Hosp., Ridgewood, NJ, 1963-99; sr. ophthalmic surgeon, resident instr. oculoplastics Manhatten Eye Ear and Throat, NYC, 1957-96, emeritus, from 1996. Pres. Bergen Surg. Ctr., Paramus, N.J., 1991—, Eye Inst. of Paramus 1987—. Author: Advances in Ophthalmic Plastic, 1983. Active Rep. Club, Ridgewood, 1960—. Capt. USAF, 1955-57. Fellow AMA, Am. Acad. Ophthalmology, Internat. Coll. of Surgeons, Am. Soc. of Ophtalmic Plastic and Reconstructive Surgery (chartered). Republican. Roman Catholic. Achievements include development of new lid flaps oculoplastics, prototype of li[illegible] canal laceration repair, major modification of ptosis surgical procedures widely used, disproved Trichromatic theory of colo[illegible] vision in 1952. Died Mar. 3, 2006.

LIVINGSTON, GERALD ALAN, financial executive; b. Tupelo, Miss., Mar. 14, 1939; s. Walter Byron and Francis Eloi[illegible] (Harris) L.; m. Reidun Samuelsen, June 2, 1967; children: Lis[illegible] Anne, Alan David. BBA, U. Miss., 1961. CPA, La. Audito[illegible] Deloitte Haskins and Sells, New Orleans, 1961-68; v.p., controller Avondale Shipyards, Inc., New Orleans, 1968-78; v.p. Ogden Transp. Corp., NYC, 1979-81; v.p. fin. Luria Bros. an[illegible] Co., Inc., Cleve., 1981-85, Avondale Industries, Inc., Cleve. 1985-86, adminstrv. officer materials group, 1986-88; affiliat[illegible] Sr. Cons' Network Co., Inc., Beachwood, Ohio, from 198[illegible] Served with USMCR, 1962-68. Mem. Fin. Execs. Inst. (chmn[illegible] gov. bus. com. 1979-80), Am. Inst. CPA's. Avocations: reading[illegible] family activities. Home: Cincinnati, Ohio. Died June 10, 200[illegible]

LIVINGSTONE, WILLIAM ORR, JR., editor; b. Atlanta[illegible] July 13, 1927; s. William Orr Sr. and Roberta (Weeks) L. AB, U[illegible] N.C., 1947; diploma, U.S. Army Lang. Sch., Monterey, Calif[illegible] 1954, Grad. Sch., U. Copenhagen, 1956. Instr. U. P.R., Ri[illegible] Piedras, 1948-50; staff editor Ency. Americana, NYC, 1956-6[illegible] humanities editor Crowell-Collier Edn. Corp., NYC, 1961-6[illegible] managing editor Stereo Rev., NYC, 1965-78, exec. edito[illegible] 1979-82, editor in chief, 1982-87, editor at large, from 198[illegible] entertainment editor Sound & Image, from 1990. Regula[illegible] panelist Texaco-Met. Opera Quiz, N.Y.C., 1975—; vis. prof. [illegible] criticism U. Tex., Austin, 1979; advisor U.S. Congress Office [illegible]

Tech. Assessment, 1988-89. Contbr. articles on music to various publs. U.S. Dept. State teaching grantee Mexican-Am. Inst. Cultural Relations, Mexico City, 1951; Fulbright scholar U. Copenhagen, 1954-56 Mem. Music Critics Assn., Nat. Acad. Rec. Arts and Scis., Assn. Classical Music, Phi Beta Kappa Home: New York, NY. Died Mar. 5, 2007.

LLORENS, ALFRED SIEBERT, retired obstetrician-gynecologist, educator; b. NYC, Aug. 23, 1931; MD, U. Va., 1956. Cert. in ob-gyn., subspecialty in gynecologic oncology. Intern Grady Meml. Hosp.-Emory U., Atlanta, 1956-57, resident in ob-gyn., 1958-61; fellow in gynecology Roswell Park Hosp., Buffalo, 1967-69; with U. Mo., Columbia, prof. emeritus, 1992. Fellow ACOG; mem. B.C. Med. Soc., Soc. Gynecol. Oncologists, Kansas City Gynecolic Soc. Home: Clemmons, NC. Died May 26, 2006.

LOBITZ, WALTER CHARLES, JR., physician, educator; b. Cin., Dec. 13, 1911; s. Walter Charles and Elsa (Spangenberg) L.; m. Caroline Elizabeth Rockwell, July 11, 1942; children: Walter Charles III, John Rockwell, Susan Hastings. Student, Brown U., 1930-31; B.Sc., U. Cin., 1939, M.B., 1940, MD, 1941; M.Sc., U. Minn., 1945; MA (hon.), Dartmouth, 1958; LL.D., Hokkaido U., 1976. Diplomate Am. Bd. Dermatology (bd. dirs. 1955-64, pres. 1962). Intern Cin. Gen. Hosp., 1940, resident medicine, 1941; fellow Mayo Found., 1942-45; 1st asst. Mayo Clinic, 1945-47; chmn. sect. dermatology Hitchcock Clinic, Hanover, N.H., 1947-59, bd. dirs., 1955; faculty Dartmouth Med. Sch., 1947-59, prof. dermatology, 1957-59; prof. dermatology, head div. U. Oreg. Med. Sch., 1959-69, chmn. dept., 1969-77; prof. Oreg. Health Scis. Univ., until 1980; emeritus prof. U. Oreg. Health Scis. Ctr., from 1980. Area cons. VA, 1949-59; mem. commn. cutaneous diseases Armed Forces Epidemiologic Bd., 1965-75; cons., mem. gen. med. study sect. USPHS, 1961-65; mem. grant rev. com. United Health Found., 1964-65; cons. dermatology tng. grants com. NIAMD, 1966-70; cons. VA Hosp., U. Oreg. Med. Sch., 1959—; civilian cons. to surgeon gen. USAF, 1969-79; U.S. Air Force-Nat. cons. to Surgeon Gen., 1970-80; Dohi Meml. lectr. Japanese Dermatol. Assn., 1964; lectr. U. Copenhagen, Denmark, 1969, 74. Author numerous articles in field.; Co-editor: The Epidermis; editorial bd.: Jour. Investigative Dermatology, 1958-61, Excerpta of Medicine, 1961-78, Clinics in Dermatology, 1982; mem. editorial bd.: Archives Dermatology, 1960-77, chief editor, 1963-68. Trustee Dermatology Found., Med. Research Found. Oreg., 1972, exec. com., 1977-80, v.p., 1975-76, pres., 1977-78; music adv. com. Oreg. Symphony Orch., 1970-73; mem. Oreg. Ballet Council, 1974; bd. govs. Hitchcock Hosp., 1955; trustee Hitchcock Found., 1958-59, exec. com., 1958-59. Recipient Outstanding Achievement award U. Minn., 1964, Disting. Alumni award U. Cin. Coll. Medicine, 1995; dedication of Lobitz-Jillson Libr., Dartmouth-Hitchcock Med. Ctr., 1992; decorated Japanese Order of the Sacred Treasure, Gold Rays with neck ribbon, Emperor of Japan, 1993. Fellow ACP, Am. Acad. Dermatology (hon., bd. dirs. 1958-61, 66-69, pres. 1969, gold medal 1985, Master in Dermatology 1987), Phila. Coll. Physicians (hon.); mem. AMA, AAAS, Am. Dermatol. Assn. (bd. dirs. 1962-67, pres. 1972, hon. 1982), Soc. Investigative Dermatology (hon., v.p. 1952, bd. dirs. 1953-58, pres. 1957, Stephan Rothman medal for disting. achievement 1989), N.H., Multnomah County, Oreg., med. socs., N.Y. Acad. Scis., Pacific N.W. Dermatol. Assn. (pres. 1971), Pacific Dermatol. Assn., Israel Dermatol. Assn. (hon.), N.W. Soc. Clin. Rsch., Oreg. Dermatol. Soc. (pres. 1969), Portland Acad. Medicine, Am. Fedn. Clin. Rsch., Pacific Interurban Clin. Club (councilor 1971), Internat. Soc. Tropical Dermatology, Assn. Univ. Profs. Dermatology (founder, bd. dirs. 1961-66, pres. 1965-66), Soc. Venezolana de Dermatologia & Leprologia (hon.), French Soc. Dermatology, Brit. Assn. Dermatology, Assn. parala Investigacion Dermatologica (Venezuela), Soc. Dermatol. Danicae, Italian, Japan, Hokkaido, Sapporo derm. socs., Sigma Xi, Pi Kappa Epsilon, Alpha Omega Alpha. Presbyterian. Died Apr. 17, 2006.

LOCKLEY, JEANETTE ELAINE, mathematics educator, statistics educator; b. Dallas, Feb. 13, 1933; d. Robert L. and Morita (Williams) Prince; m. Arnold Herbert Lockley, Aug. 5, 1952 (dec. Dec. 1973); 1 child, Geoffrey Lynn Lockley. BS in Math., Wiley Coll., Marshall, Tex., 1953; MS in Math., Tex. So. U., Houston, 1954; MS in Math. Statistics, Stanford U., Calif., PhD in Math. Instr. math. Tex. So. U., Houston, 1954-57; prof. math. Merritt Coll., Oakland, Calif., 1958-76; rsch. assoc. Office of Ednl. Rsch., asst. prof. math. and edn. Macalester Coll., St. Paul, Minn., 1969-70; dept. chmn. math, physics, engrin. and philosophy Merritt Coll., 1972-76, divsn. chmn. math., drafting, electronic, welding, machine shop, aviation adminstrn., pilot technology, avionics, 1976-80; prof. math., dept. chmn. Mountain View Coll., Dallas, from 1976. Pres. and exec. dir. Inst. Ednl. Rsch. & Devel., Inc., Dallas; adj. prof. math. scis. U. Tex., Dallas; panelist NSF, 1977, 78, 79, 80, Dept. Energy, 1979, 80, MISIP Minority Science Improvement Program U.S. Dept. Edn., 1990, 92, 94. Grantee U.S. Dept. Edn., Washington D.C., 1996. Mem. Links, Inc., Girl Friends, Inc. (pres. 1995), Alpha Kappa Alpha. Episcopal. Avocation: bridge. Home: Dallas, Tex. Died Aug. 13, 2007.

LOCKWOOD, RALPH HAROLD, banker; b. Columbus, Ohio, Apr. 17, 1929; s. William L. and Grace Louella (Saville) Hardman; m. Ruth Ellen Buchman, June 24, 1950; children: Kathy Ellen Lockwood Sommerville, Jeffrey Allen. Student, Ohio State U., 1959-61. With Huntington Nat. Bank, Columbus, from 1949, exec. v.p., from 1983; pres., trustee Central Regional Automated Funds Transfer System (CRAFTS Inc.), 1979-81; mem. ops. com. Columbus Clearing House. Mem. adv. bd. Fed. Res. Regional Checking Processing Ctr. Served with USMCR, 1952-53. Mem. Am. Bankers Assn. (exec. com. ops.-automation div. 1975—, chmn. research and planning com. 1975—, co-chmn. nat. ops. and automation conf. 1976), Am. Inst. Banking, Ohio Bankers Assn. (chmn. ops. and automation com. 1975-77) Died Feb. 14, 2007.

LOGAN, JOSEPH GRANVILLE, JR., physicist; b. Washington, June 8, 1920; s. Joseph Granville and Lula (Briggs) L.; m. Esther Taylor, June 30, 1944; children— Joseph Michael, Eileen Cecile. BS, D.C. Tchrs. Coll., 1941; PhD in Physics, U. Buffalo, 1955. Physicist Nat. Bur. Standards, 1944-47, Cornell Aero. Lab., 1947-58; head propulsion research dept. Space Tech. Labs., 1958-61; dir. aerodynamics and propulsion research lab. Aerospace Corp., 1961-67; spl. asst. to dir. research and devel. McDonnell Douglas Astronautics Co., Santa Monica, Calif., 1967-69, mgr. vulnerability and hardening, devel. engring., 1969-74; pres. Applied Energy Scis., Inc., Los Angeles, from 1974. Cons. atomic and molecular modeling; mem. faculty dept. physics Calif. Poly. U., Pomona, 1977-78; bus. devel. specialist Urban U. Center, U. So. Calif., Los Angeles, 1978-79, assoc. dir., 1979-80, dir., 1980-88. Mem. AAAS, AIAA, Am. Phys. Soc., Soc. Info. Display, N.Y. Acad. Scis. Home: Los Angeles, Calif. Died Nov. 30, 2006.

LOGAN, RALPH ANDRE, physicist; b. Cornwall, Ont., Can., Sept. 22, 1926; arrived in U.S., 1948; s. Joseph A. and Lucy T. (Carter) L.; m. Aug. 26, 1950; children: Howard, Mary, Marguerite, Anthony, Enid, Alisa, Ruth, John, Thomas. BSc, McGill U., Montreal, 1947, MSc, 1948; PhD, Columbia U., NYC, 1952. Tech. staff mem. AT&T Bell Labs Research Div., Murray Hill, NJ, 1952-94. Author: numerous tech. pubs.; patentee in field. Fellow IEEE, Am. Physics Soc.; mem. NAE, Optical Soc. Home: Manahawkin, NJ. Died Dec. 1, 2006.

LOH, EUGENE C., physicist, researcher; b. Soochow, China, Oct. 1, 1933; 3 children. BS, Va. Polytech. U., 1955; PhD, MIT, 1961. Rsch. assoc. in physics MIT, Cambridge, Mass., 1961-64, asst. prof., 1964-65; sr. rsch. assoc. in nuc. studies Cornell U., Ithaca, N.Y., 1965-75; assoc. prof physics U. Utah, Salt Lake City, 1975-77, prof., chmn. dept. physics, 1977-90, Disting. prof. physics, 1995, dir. High Energy Astrophysics Inst., 1993-98; program dir. elem. partical physics dept. NSF, Arlington, Va., from 1998. Vis. sci. Stanford Linear Accelerator Ctr., 1980-81. Fellow Am. Physics Soc.; mem. Sigma Xi. Died May 19, 2006.

LOHARA, CHARANJIT SINGH, computer and communications company executive; b. Punjab, India, July 27, 1939; came to U.S., 1957, naturalized, 1970; s. Kartar S. and Gurdial (Dhaliwal) L.; m. Harinder P. Dhaliwal, Apr. 19, 1971; children— Jennajit K., Anoopjit S. B.S. in Chemistry and Physics, Punjab, U., 1957; B.S. in Indsl. Engring., Calif. State Poly. Coll., 1965; postgrad. U. Wash., 1968. Dir. mgmt. services Eastalco, Frederick, Md., 1969-72; dir. planning and ops. analyst Howmet Corp., Greenwich, Conn., 1972-73; exec. v.p., chief fin. officer T.M.I., Russelville, Ark., 1973-76; pres., dir. Arab Aluminum Co., Cairo, Egypt, 1976-79; pres. Compulaser, Inc., Canoga Park, Calif., 1979-80; pres. chmn. bd., chief exec. officer Incomnet, Woodland Hills, Calif., 1980—. Contbr. articles to profl. jours. Bd. dirs. So. Calif. Tech. Exec. Network, Los Angeles, 1983—; mem. indsl. adv. council Sch. Engring., Calif. State Poly. U., Pomona, 1984—. Home: Northridge, Calif. Died Oct. 22, 2006.

LOHMAN, WALTER REARICK, banker; b. Ashland, Ill., Nov. 14, 1917; s. Harry Joseph and Annette (Rearick) L.; m. Carol L. Coultas, June 26, 1948; children: Marian Carol, Roberta Baxter. BS, Ill. Wesleyan U., 1939. Accountant U.S. Dept. Agr., 1939-41; with Pleasant Plains State Bank, Ill., 1941-42, dir., 1951-76; with State Bank of Ashland, Ill., 1946-62, pres. Ill., 1957-62; exec. v.p. 1st Nat. Bank of Springfield, Ill., 1962-67, pres., 1967-81, chmn. bd., 1977-85; pres. First Bank of Ill. Co., Springfield, 1972-83, chmn. bd., 1983-87. Bd. dirs. State Bank of Ashland, 1st Nat. Bank Springfield, First Bank of Ill. Co. and subs., MII Inc., Lincoln, Ill. Pres. Meml. Med. Ctr., 1983, 84, 85; chmn. bd. Meml. Med. Ctr. Found., 1989-91; bd. dirs. Ill. Indsl. Devel. Authority; trustee Ill. Wesleyan U. 1st lt. AUS, 1942-46, PTO. Recipient Distinguished Alumni award Ill. Wesleyan U., 1971; Distinguished Eagle Scout award Boy Scouts Am., 1973 Mem. Assn. for Modern Banking in Ill. (chmn. 1981-83), Ill. C. of C. (v.p., dir.), Springfield C. of C. (pres. 1969, 76-82) Clubs: Mason (Springfield) (Shriner), Illini Country (Springfield), Sangamo (Springfield). Home: Springfield, Ill. Died Jan. 19, 2006.

LOHMANN, GARY BRENT, air force officer, political scientist, geographer, author; b. Farmington, N.Mex., May 26, 1951; s. Edgar Herman and Norma Irene (Evans) L.; m. Carolyn Jean Kluball, June 21, 1975; children: Cameron, Kimberly. BA, U. Northern Colo., 1973; MPA, Southwest Tex. State U., 1979; grad., Air Command and Staff Coll., 1983, Air War Coll., 1988. Adminstrn. officer 38th Organizational Maintenance Squadron, Moody AFB, Ga., 1973-76; exec. officer 3285th Sch. Squadron, Lackland AFB, Rex., 1976-78; chief base adminstrn. 6112th Air Base Wing, Misawa AB, Japan, 1978-81; asst. prof. Calif. State U., Fresno, 1983-86; chief internat. security affairs 5th Air Force, Yokota AB, Japan, 1986-89; chief internat. affairs northeast Asia HQS Pacific Air Forces, Hickam AFB, Hawaii, 1989-93. Decorated Meritorious Svc. medals, Commendation medals; recipient LeMay-Ohio award Air Force Assn., 1984, 85, Outstanding Squadron award Arnold Air Soc., 1984. Republican. Lutheran. Avocations: golf, fencing. Home: Rockledge, Fla. Died Apr. 25, 2007.

LOHR, KENNETH RAYBORNE, pharmacist, drug analyst; b. Quincy, Ill., Dec. 19, 1922; s. Rayborne Peter and Sarah Elizabeth (Houdyshell) L.; m. Eleanor Lucille Hetzler, July 23, 1943; children— Denise, Debra. B.S. in Pharmacy, U. Ill., 1950. Ptnr., mgr. Owl Drug Store, Quincy, 1951-58, Lohr's Prescription Shop, Quincy, 1958—; dir. St. Drug Analysis Service, Quincy. Served with U.S. Army, 1943-45. Recipient A.H. Robbins Bowl of Hygeia award, 1974. Fellow Am. Coll. Apothecaries; mem. Am. Inst. History of Pharmacy, Am. Pharm. Assn., Ill. Pharmacists Assn., Nat. Assn. Retail Druggists, Quincy C. of C. (dir. 1956-59). Republican. Lutheran. Contbr. articles in field to profl. jours. Home: Quincy, Ill. Died June 5, 2006.

LONERGAN, JOYCE, county official; b. Benton County, Iowa, Mar. 5, 1934; d. Robert and Fannie Mary (Duda) Jacobi; student public schs.; m. Paul J. Lonergan (dec.); children— Patrick Joseph, Peter Thomas, Kathleen Ann, Staci Marie. Mem. Iowa Ho. of Reps. from 87th Dist., 1975-86. Mem. Am. Bus. Women's Assn. Democrat. Roman Catholic. Home: Boone, Iowa. Died Jan. 17, 2006.

LONG, FRANCIS MARK, retired electrical engineer; b. Iowa City, Nov. 10, 1929; s. Frank B. and Hilda B. (Rohret) L.; m. Mary Ann Coyne, June 8, 1964 (dec. Apr. 1994); children: Ann Brett, Mary Bronwyn, Thomas Martin Carver, Caitlin Frances. BS, U. Iowa, 1953, MS, 1956; PhD, Iowa State U., 1961. With Collins Radio Co., Cedar Rapids, Iowa, summers 1952, 55, Douglas Aircraft Co., Santa Monica, Calif., summer 1953, USNAMTC, Point Mugu, Calif., summer 1956, Good All Electric Co., Ogallala, Nebr., summer 1957, Lawrence Radiation Lab., Livermore, Calif., summer 1967, Globe Union Co., Milw., summer 1975, Naval Rsch Lab., Washington, 1988, 89, 91; instr. U. Wyo., Laramie, 1956-58, prof. elec. engring., 1960-95, prof. emeritus, from 1995, head elec. engring. dept., 1977-87; instr. Iowa State U., 1958-60. Dir. Wyo. Biotelemetry, Inc., Rocky Mountain Bioengring. Symposium; pres. Alliance for Engring. in Medicine and Biology, 1983, 84, mem. exec. com., 1979-89; conf. chmn., procs. editor 1st, 2d, 3d and 5th Internat. Conf. on Wildlife Biotelemetry; adj. prof. Univ. Denver, 1996—, Colo. Tech. Univ., 1997—, U. Colo., Denver, 1999—. Author: (with E.M. Lonsdale) Introductory Electrical Concepts, 1967, rev. edit., 1977; co-author: (with R.G. Jacquot) Introduction to Engineering Systems, 1988. Trustee St. Paul's Newman Center Parish, 1969-72; mem. City of Laramie Planning Commn., 1970-72. Served CE US Army, 1953—55. Decorated citation Republic of Korea Army C.E.; recipient G.D. Humphrey Outstanding Faculty award U. Wyo., 1973, Western Electric Fund award for engring. teaching, 1978 Mem. IEEE (life, edn. activities com. chmn. Denver sect. 1997), Am. Soc. Engring. Edn. (v.p., dir., 1st Outstanding Biomed. Engring. Educator award biomed. engring. divsn. 1981, chmn. Elec. Engring. divsn. 1986-87), Internat. Soc. for Hybrid Microelectronics (v.p. Rocky Mountain chpt. 1996-97, pres. 1998), Sigma Xi. Republican. Home: Denver, Colo. Died Jan. 16, 2007.

LONG, JOHN PAUL, pharmacologist, educator; b. Albia, Iowa, Oct. 4, 1926; s. John Edward and Bessie May L.; m. Marilyn Joy Stookesberry, June 11, 1950; children: Jeff, John, Jane. BS, U. Iowa, 1950, MS, 1952, PhD, 1954. Research scientist Sterling Winthrop Co., Albany, NY, 1954-56; asst. prof. U. Iowa, Iowa City, 1956-58, assoc. prof., 1958-63, prof. pharmacology, from 1963, head dept., 1970-83. Author 315 research publs. in field. Served with U.S. Army, 1945-46. Recipient Abel award Am. Pharm. Assn., 1958; Ebert award Pharmacology Soc., 1962 Mem. Am. Soc. Pharm. Exptl. Therapy, Soc. Exptl. Biol. Medicine. Republican. Home: Iowa City, Iowa. Died June 10, 2007.

LONG, MARY LOUISE, retired government official; b. Macon, Ga., Aug. 25, 1922; d. Willie and Sarah (Sparks) Tyson; AB, Morris Brown Coll., Atlanta, 1946; m. Samuel F. Long, Apr. 14, 1962 (dec. June 1997). Supervisory procurement clk. Dept. Def., N.Y., 1954-62, purchasing agt. Phila. Procurement Dist., 1962-64, Army Electronic Command, Phila., 1964-66, Med. Directorate, Def. Personnel Support Center, Phila., 1966-75, contracting officer, 1975-80, sect. chief/contracting officer, 1980-83. Active NAACP, YMCA; established Mary Louise Tyson Long Scholarship Fund, Morris Brown Coll., 1986; mem. Phila Inter-alumni coun. United Negro Coll. Fund. Named Alumna of Yr. Morris Brown Coll., 1987, 50th Reunion Cert., 1996. Mem. Beta Omicron, Iota Phi Lambda. Congregationalist. Home: Scottsdale, Ariz. Died Oct. 19, 2006.

LONG, ROBERT, writer, poet, educator; b. NYC, Oct. 15, 1954; BA in English Lit. and Profl. Writing, L.I. U., 1977; MFA in Writing, Norwich U., 1984. Art critic East Hampton (N.Y.) Star, 1983-85; assoc. editor Provincetown Arts, 1990-91; sr. art critic Southampton Press, from 1985. Adj. and asst. prof. L.I. U., Southampton, 1979-89; vis. lectr. Vt. Coll., Norwich U., 1987, 89; adj. asst. prof. English, Suffolk C.C., 1990-90, 92—; instr. Orange County C.C., spring, 1991; asst. prof., writer-in-residence La Salle U., 1991-92; mem. adj. faculty Antioch Coll., 1995-96; reader, condr. workshops New Sch. for Social Rsch., Stony Brook Poetry Ctr., U. Md., La Salle U., Johns Hopkins U., Yeats Soc., Sligo, Ireland, ICA, Boston, Southampton Writers Conf., numerous others; dir. literary program Guild Hall, East Hampton; dir. Southampton Writers Conf., 1981; coodr., dir., adviser various univ. and coll. literary programs and publs. Author: (poem chapbook) Getting Out of Town, 1979, What It Is, 1981, (poems) What Happens, 1989 (Best of Small Presses award Frankfurt Book Fair 1989); editor: (anthologies) Long Island Poets, 1986, For David Ignatow, 1994; contbr. book revs. to Phila. Inquirer, also others; contbr. poetry to New Yorker, Poetry, Partisan Rev., Am. Scholar, Antioch Rev., Kayak, The Nation, Cimarron Rev., Sun & Moon, Crazyhorse, Ind. Rev., Il. Rev., Sycamore Rev., New American Poets of 90s, Anthology of Mag. Verse, N.Y. Gedichte, Sweet Nothings, also others. Home: East Hampton, NY. Died Oct. 13, 2006.

LONG, ROBERT LIVINGSTON, retired photographic equipment executive; b. Abbeville, SC, Jan. 3, 1937; s. Clarance Blakely and Amy (Wolff) L.; m. Phyllis Jo Crews, May 30, 1959; children: J. Blake, Brynn Diane, Brant Wolff. BSCE, U. S.C., 1959; grad. in Indsl. Mgmt. Program, U. Tenn., 1967. Chem. engr. Tenn. div. Eastman Kodak Co., Kingsport, 1959-66, gen. mgmt. staff tech. Tenn. div., 1966-74, mgr. licensing chemicals div., 1974-80, dir. mfg. staff Tenn. div., 1980-83, v.p., dir. planning div., chemicals div., 1983-86, v.p., dir. corp. planning Rochester, N.Y., 1986-92, sr. v.p., 1989; cons., Melbourne Beach, Fla., from 1992. Bd. dirs. Sun Microsystems Inc., Mt. View, Calif., Broadband Comms. Products, Melbourne, Fla., 1995-98. Participant Tenn. Exec. Devel. Program, Knoxville, 1974; multiple adv. bd. City of Kingsport, 1978-86; bd. dirs. Boy's Club Greater Kingsport, 1965-81, chmn., 1973-75; bd. dirs. Holston Valley Hosp. and Med. Ctr., Kingsport, 1983-86, Rochester Gen. Hosp., 1988-92; bd. trustees Fla. Inst. Tech., 1999—. Sgt. U.S. Army N.G., 1955-63. Recipient Medallion, Boys Club Am., 1976, Bronze Keyston award Boys Club Am.,

1985. Mem. Am. Inst. Chem. Engrs., Soc. for Info. Mgmt., Acad. Natural Scis. (bd. dirs. environ. assocs. 1982-85), Rotary (chmn. coms. Kingsport 1975-86), Sigma Alpha Epsilon. Episcopalian. Died May 2, 2006.

LONG, ROLAND JOHN, secondary school principal; b. Chgo., Nov. 15, 1921; s. John and Lillian Catherine (Sigmund) L.; m. Valerie Ann Zawila, Nov. 13, 1954; children: Ronald J., Thomas E. BS, Ill. State Normal U., 1949; MA, Northwestern U., 1951; EdD, Ill. State U., 1972. Instr. of social sci. Ball State U., Muncie, Ind., 1951; comdt. Morgan Park Mil. Acad., Chgo., 1952-54; tchr. history Hyde Park and Amundsen high schs., Chgo., 1955-62; prin. Hubbard Elementary Sch., Chgo., 1962; founder, prin. Hubbard High Sch., Chgo., 1963-85; prin. Chgo. High Sch. for Met. Studies, 1985—; mem. doctoral adv. com. of Ill. State U., 1973-75; panelist Gen. Assembly State of Ill. Sponsored Conf. Ednl. Reform. Author: Dr. Long's Old-Fashioned Basic Report Card and Parent Helper, 1977. Mem. Chgo. Police Dist. 8 steering com., 1974-77; bd. dirs. West Communities YMCA, Chgo., Greater Lawn Mental Health Ctr., Chgo.; mem. Accademia Italia, 1983. Served to 1st lt., inf., U.S. Army, ETO. Decorated Silver Star, Purple Heart, Bronze Star; Ford Found. fellow, 1973; recipient Sch. Mgmt. citation Ill. Gen. Assembly, 1972, Medal of Honor Am. Biog. Inst., 1988. Fellow (hon.) Harry S. Truman Library Inst.,; mem. Ill. Assn. for Supervision and Curriculum Devel., Nat. Assn. of Secondary Sch. Prins., Am. Legion, Phi Delta Kappa (Educator of Yr. aw ard 1980), Pi Gamma Mu, Kappa Delta Pi. Club: Elks. Home: Wheaton, Ill. Died Dec. 29, 2006.

LONG, TERRY LESTER, English and American literature educator; b. Corpus Christi, Tex., Mar. 25, 1936; s. Terry Frank and Ethel Leona (Huebner) L.; m. Lily Mae Rogers, Sept. 1960 (div. 1968); children: Tracy Lee, Herbert Quincy, Nathan Wayne; m. Yvonne B Norrocky, Sept. 10, 1983. BA in English, U. Houston, 1959, MA in English, 1963; PhD, Ohio State U., 1971. Reporter Galveston (Tex.) Tribune, 1959; newspaper reporter Caller-Times, Corpus Christi, 1959-62; instr. Tex. A&M U., College Station, 1963-65, Miami U., Oxford, Ohio, 1966-67; prof. English Ohio State U., Newark, from 1968. Author: Granville Hicks, 1971; contbr. articles to mags. and newspapers. Mem. Bd. Elections of County, Newark, 1988-92. Mem. Am. Folklore Soc., Popular Culture Assn. Democrat. Home: Newark, Ohio. Died Sept. 24, 2006.

LONGUET, JOHN JEFFREY, warehouse executive; b. Houston, July 24, 1944; s. Oscar E. and Billie L. Longuet; student Tex. Tech. U., 1962-66, U. Houston, 1963, S. Tex. Jr. Coll., 1962; m. Cheryl. children— Devin Scott, Traci Lynne, Leslie DeLaine. Adminstrv. account specialist IBM Data Processing div., Houston, 1967-74; warehouse supr. Am. Parts, Houston, 1974-75; warehouse foreman Am. Warehouse Inc., Houston, 1975—, pres., 1980—. Mem. Houston C. of C., Am. Warehousemen's Assn., Asso. Warehouses, Inc., S.W. Warehouse and Transfer Assn., Nat. Council Phys. Distbn. Mgmt. Republican. Mem. Ch. of Christ. Club: Rotary. Home: Houston, Tex. Died June 28, 2006.

LOPEZ, LINDA SINGLETON, mortgage banking administrator; b. Paris, Tex., Sept. 11, 1946; d. Charles Bennett and Floy Evelyn (Ryan) Singleton; m. Phillip D. Lopez de Esquevar, Apr. 19, 1969 (dec. Aug. 1974); 1 child, Charles Robert Thomas. BA, Brigham Young U., 1969; Cert. ct. reporter/paralegal Chapman Ct. Reporting Coll., 1973. Exec. asst. to chief exec. officer Am. Inst. Mortgage, Grand Prairie, Tex., 1974-76; office mgr., cons. The Exception, Dallas, 1976-79; office mgr., bookkeeper Heatilator, Inc., Carrollton, Tex., 1979-80; office mgr., title officer Wood Investments, Houston, 1980-83; escrow adminstr Consol. Capital Co., Emeryville, Calif., 1983-86, title adminstr., sr. paralegal, 1986-87; sr. legal asst., Clorox Co., 1987—; cons. L. Lopez Acctg. Service, Houston, 1980-83, Lopez Enterprises, Novato, Calif., 1985—. Author: Mortgage Banking Terms, 1985; also articles on title and land law. Sec. Daus. of Bilitis, Dallas, 1975-76; founder, pres. N. Dallas chpt. NOW, 1979-80, state del., 1980; social chmn. The Other Side, San Rafael, Calif., 1985-86; vol. acct. Westheimer Art Colony, Houston, 1980-83; vol. clown, entertaining at Spl. Olympics, other events, 1985—. Mem. Mensa (area sec. 1986-87), Bay Area Career Women (vice chair social 1987-88, chair 1988), Alliance Local Orgns. for Women (editor 1985—). Democrat. Avocations: art, astrology, sewing, needlework, volunteer work with children's groups. Home: San Rafael, Calif. Died Jan. 2, 2007.

LOPRESTI, JOSEPH J., lawyer; b. Cleve., Mar. 17, 1947; BBA, U. Notre Dame, 1969; JD, Ohio State U., 1973. Bar: Ohio 1973. Mem. McDonald, Hopkins, Burke & Haber, Cleve. Mem. ABA, Ohio State Bar Assn., Cuyahoga County Bar Assn., Cleve. Bar Assn. Died Mar. 5, 2007.

LORD, HERBERT MAYHEW, lawyer; b. Rockland, Maine, Oct. 9, 1917; s. Kenneth Prince and Helen Elizabeth (Cooper) L.; m. Martha Urquhart, June 14, 1947; children: Herbert, John, Martha, Kenneth. AB, Bowdon Coll., 1939; LLB, Harvard U., 1942. Bar: N.Y., 1942. Assoc. Burlingham, Veeder, Clark & Hupper, NYC, 1942-50, ptnr., 1950-73; sr. ptnr. Burlingham, Underwood & Lord, NYC, 1973-92; ptnr. Curtis, Mallet-Provost, Colt & Mosle, NYC, from 1992. Overseer Bowdoin Coll., 1980-92, overseer emeritus, 1992—. Mem. Maritime Law Assn. U.S. (membership sec. 1958-59, sec. 1959-61, exec. com. 1966-69, pres. 1974-76, del. to ho. of dels. ABA 1974-86); titular mem. Comite Maritime Internat. Home: Greenwich, Conn. Died May 9, 2006.

LORD, WILLIAM GROGAN, financial holding company executive; b. Hearne, Tex., Oct. 21, 1914; s. Otis G. and Erminee G. Lord; m. Dorothy Nell Manning, Dec. 28, 1938 (dec.); children: Roger Griffin, Sharon Lord Caskey; m. Betty Fowler Hendrick, May 24, 1986. L.H.D. (hon.), Southwestern U., Georgetown, Tex., 1967. Sr. chmn. First Tex. Bancorp, Inc., Georgetown, from 1971. Bd. dirs. Frozen Food Express Industries, Inc., Dallas; sr. chmn. bd. 1st Tex. Bancorp, Inc., Georgetown; mem., chmn. State Securities Bd., 1971-83. Trustee, mem. exec. com., vice chmn. bd. Southwestern U., 1958. Served to 1st lt. F.A. AUS, World War II. Decorated Purple Heart, Air medal with 4 oak leaf clusters; named Most Worthy Citizen Georgetown C. of C., 1971 Mem. Nat. Assn. Small Bus. Investment Cos. (past pres.), Regional Assn. Small Bus. Investment Cos, Tex. Research League, Tex. Philosophical Soc. Clubs: River Oaks Country (Houston); (Austin, Tex.), Headliners (Austin, Tex.). Republican. Methodist. Died Jan. 13, 2007.

LORENSEN, RONALD WALTER, lawyer; b. Hamburg, W.Ger., Sept. 16, 1945 (mother Am. citizen); s. Walter Max and Ingeborg Anna (Giese) L.; m. Jacklynne Gail Schutt, Aug. 2, 1969; children— Brian, Carrie. A.B., Dartmouth Coll., 1967, M.B.A., Amos Tuck Sch., 1968; J.D., Albany Law Sch., 1974. Bar: Alaska 1974. Asst. atty. gen. Alaska Dept. of Law, Juneau, 1974-79; ptnr. Josephson, Trickey & Lorensen, Juneau, 1979-80; dep. atty. gen. Alaska Dept. Law, Juneau, 1980—; instr. bus. law U. Alaska/Juneau, fall 1975, 77, 79; mem. Exec. Clemency Review Bd. Alaska, 1985—. Pres. Juneau Teen Home, 1976-79. Served to 1st lt. U.S. Army, 1968-71. Mem. Alaska Bar Assn. (bd. govs., 1982-85, treas. 1982-83, v.p. 1983-84), ABA, Juneau Bar Assn. Home: Juneau, Alaska. Died Mar. 29, 2007.

LOUGHLIN, MARTIN FRANCIS, retired federal judge; b. Manchester, NH, Mar. 11, 1923; m. Margaret M. Gallagher; children: Helen, Margaret, Shane, Mary, Sheila, Martina, Caitlin. AB, St. Anselm's Coll., 1947; LLB, Suffolk U., 1951. Bar: N.H. 1952. Assoc. Conrad Danaid, Esq., Manchester, 1953-58, Broderick & Loughlin, Manchester, 1958-63; judge N.H. Superior Ct., Manchester, 1963-79, chief justice, 1978-79; judge U.S. Dist. Ct. N.H., Concord, from 1979; ret. Instr. St. Anselm's Coll., Franklin Pierce Law Sch. Contbr. articles to legal jours. Mem. ABA, N.H. Bar, Manchester Bar Asssn. Home: Manchester, NH. Died Mar. 7, 2007.

LOUK, SISTER ROSE AGNES, motivational seminars lecturer; b. LaCrosse, Wis., Aug. 17, 1920; d. William Joseph and Mary Agnes (McNamara) L. B.S., Coll. St. Scholastica, 1954; M.S., SUNY, Buffalo, 1973. Joined Franciscan Sisters of Perpetual Adoration, Roman Cath. Ch., 1949; registered record adminstr. Med. record adminstr. St. Anthony Hosp., Carroll, Iowa, 1954-56, 58-62, St. Francis Hosp., LaCrosse, 1962-63, Sacred Heart Hosp., Idaho Falls, Idaho, 1963-69; instr. Viterbo Coll., La Crosse, 1962-63; med. record educator Intermountain RMP, Salt Lake City, 1969-72; assoc. prof. Carroll Coll., Helena, 1973-88. Contbr. articles to profl. jours. Mem. Am. Med. Record Assn. (bd. dirs. 1965-68, exec. bd.). Home: Denver, Colo. Died June 21, 2006.

LOUKS, DAVID JERROLD, manufacturing executive; b. Grand Rapids, Mich., May 13, 1927; s. Harry Benjamin and Marguerite Mary (Lemon) L.; m. Ruth Mae Barthel, July 28, 1950; children: David, Janet, Daniel, Jeffrey. AA, Grand Rapids Jr. Coll., 1948; BBA, U. Mich., 1950. C.P.A., Calif. Internal auditor Rexall Drug Co., Los Angeles, 1953-54; mgr. Alexander Grant & Co. C.P.A.s, Los Angeles, 1954-63; corp. controller Lear Siegler, Inc., Santa Monica, Calif., from 1963, v.p., 1971-85, sr. v.p., from 1985; mem. adv. bd. Allendale Mut. Ins. Co., Los Angeles, from 1982. Served with USNR, 1945-46, 51-52. Mem. Calif. Soc. C.P.A.s, Am. Inst. C.P.A.s, Nat. Assn. Accts., Am. Acctg. Assn., Machinery and Allied Products Inst. (acctg. council) Home: Pacific Palisades, Calif. Died Apr. 7, 2007.

LOVECCHIO, PAUL See LAINE, FRANKIE

LOVEGROVE, ROBERT EMERSON, realtor; b. Bridgeport, Conn., June 30, 1943; s. Robert Emerson and Sylvia (Tyack) L.; m. Martha Robertson, July 25, 1964; children: Lisa Lynn, Brian Scott, Joseph Lee, Carmen Marie. Student, U. N.Mex., 1962; BS in Forestry, U. Mont., 1966; MS in Forestry, Harvard U., 1967; PhD in Econs., Colo. State U., 1971. Asst. prof. Adams State Coll., Alamosa, Colo., 1970-72; research assoc. U. Mont., Missoula, 1972-74; regional economist U.S. Forest Service, Missoula, 1974-78; realtor Lambros Realty, Missoula, 1978-84, broker/owner, from 1991; real estate broker Lovegrove Ltd., Missoula, 1984-85; mayor City of Missoula, 1986-89. Econs. cons. various corps., 1978—. Contbr. articles to profl. jours. Active Boy Scouts Am.; deacon Ch. of Christ. Mem. Nat. Assn. Realtors, Mont. Assn. Realtors, Missoula County Bd. Realtors, Western Mont. Fish and Game Assn. (pres.). Republican. Avocations: hunting, camping, hiking, backpacking, skiing. Home: Missoula, Mont. Died Oct. 23, 2005.

LOVEJOY, LEONARD JAMES, public relations executive; b. Topeka, Apr. 5, 1931; s. Leonard Mark and Margaret Mary (Zeller) L.; Ph.B., Marquette U., 1953; m. Julianne Rolla, May 29, 1954; children— Valerie, Christopher, Kimberly, Leslie, Julianne, Geoffrey. Writer Chgo. chpt. ARC, 1956-58; publicity mgr. U.S. Gypsum Co., Chgo., 1958-62; dir. public relations Holtzman-Kain Advt. Co., Chgo., 1962-64; account supr. Philip Lesly Co., Chgo., 1964-65; account supr. Burson-Marsteller Co., Chgo., 1965-68, client services mgr., 1968, v.p., 1969, group v.p., 1972-76, asst. gen. mgr., 1976, sr. counselor v.p., 1978-83; ptnr. Investor Relations Co., 1983—. Public relations com. Chgo. United Way, 1978—, Drake U., 1974; chmn. fund drive ARC, Westmont, Ill., 1960; agy. chmn. fund drive Girl Scouts U.S.A., Chgo., 1972; bd. dirs. Pop Warner Little Scholars, Inc., 1975—; public relations com. Marquette U., 1970-72. Served with AUS, 1953-56. Mem. Public Relations Soc. Am. (pres. Chgo. chpt. 1981-82, Silver Anvil award, 1972, 73), Publicity Club Chgo. (dir. 1970-74, Golden Trumpet awards 1973, 74, 76, 77, 81). Roman Catholic. Clubs: Headline Chgo., Chgo. Press, Union League (Chgo.); South Haven (Mich.) Country. Died Apr. 9, 2007.

LOVELL, CARL ERWIN, JR., lawyer; b. Riverside, Calif., Apr. 12, 1945; s. Carl Erwin and Hazel (Brown) L.; mchildren: Carl Erwin III, Timothy C., Tishia R., Ashley P., Garrett T., Christopher C. BA, Vanderbilt U., 1966, JD, 1969. Bar: Nev. 1969, D.C. 1971, U.S. Supreme Ct. 1973. Jr. editor Land and Water Law Rev., 1973-89; instr. bus. law U. Nev., Las Vegas, Clark County C.C.; city atty. City of N. Las Vegas, 1970-73; elected city atty. City of Las Vegas, 1973-77; v.p., sec.-treas., legal counsel Circus Circus Hotels, Inc., Las Vegas, 1977-83; sr. ptnr. Lovell, Bilbray & Potter, Las Vegas, 1984-89; pvt. practice Las Vegas, from 1989; ptnr. Lovell & Lovell, 2000—03, Mitchelson & Lovell, Calif., 2001—03; v.p., dir. Air Nev. Airlines, Inc. U.S. rep. to China-U.S. Internat. Trade and Law Talks, Beijing, 1987; arbitrator, AAA, 1989—. Bd. dirs., v.p. BBB, 1983-91; chmn. NCCJ; pres., trustee Nev. Donor Network, Inc., 1992-96. Mem. ABA, ATLA, Nev. State Bar, Nev. Trial Lawyers Assn. Died Sept. 21, 2006.

LOVETT, ROBERT ELIOT, management consultant; b. Washington, Feb. 14, 1926; s. Eliot Callender and Helen Lucetta (Thompson) L.; m. Glenna Beatrice Bartlett, Jan. 26, 1957; children— Sharon, Laura Lee, Robert Eliot. A.B., U. Mich., 1948; M.B.A., N.Y.U., 1950; Ph.D., U. So. Calif., 1965. Fin. rep. Jour. of Commerce, N.Y.C., 1948-49; pub. relations adminstr. N.Y.U., 1949-51; buyer Gladding-McBean, 1951-53; customer service cons., 1953-54; v.p., treas., mktg. dir. Boylhart, Lovett & Dean, Inc., 1954-76; pres. Nat. Research Center, 1966-76; ptnr. BLD Mgmt., 1960-76; pres., dir. Voice in Pasadena, Inc., Los Angeles, 1964-83; pres., chmn. Robert E. Lovett, Inc., Laguna Beach, Calif., 1976—; officer, dir. KRLA, Inc., Los Angeles, 1977-83; dir. Higgins, Marcus & Lovett, Inc., Los Angeles, 1979—; dir. C.W. Driver, Los Angeles, 1970—; dir. workshops on Mng. for Results, 1979—; lectr. mktg. and mgmt. U. So. Calif., UCLA, Pepperdine U., Calif. State U.-Fullerton, 1954—. Past mem. Calif. State Toll Bridge Authority, Orange County Citizens' Direction-Finding Commn.; regular mem. Pasadena Tournament of Roses Assn. Served with U.S. Army, Chem. Corps, USAAF, 1944-46. Mem. Am. Mktg. Assn., Nat. Assn. Realtors, Am. Arbitration Assn. (commercial arbitrator 1986—). Republican. Christian Scientist. Club: Jonathan (Los Angeles). Contbr. articles in field to profl. jours. Home: Laguna Beach, Calif. Died Feb. 20, 2006.

LOVINGER, WARREN CONRAD, emeritus university president; b. Big Sandy, Mont., July 29, 1915; s. Wilbur George and Ruth Katherine (Hokanson) L.; m. Dorothy Blackburn, Aug. 14, 1937; children— Patricia Mae, Jeanie, Warren Conrad. BA, U. Mont., 1942, MA, 1944; EdD, Columbia U., 1947. Tchr., prin. Pub. Schs. Mont., 1937-43; instr. history U. Mont., Missoula 1943-44; pres. No. State U., Aberdeen, SD, 1951-56, Central Mo. State U., Warrensburg, 1956-79, pres. emeritus, from 1979 Exec. sec. Am. Assn. Colls. for Tchr. Edn., 1947-51, nat. pres. 1963-64; nat. pres. Am. Assn. State Colls. and Univs., 1974-75 mem. del. to study effects of Marshall Plan on Western Europe 1950; leader study of tchr. edn. in Fed. Republic of Germany 1964; leader del. People's Republic of China, 1975; mem comparative study tour of Republic of China, 1976 Author General Education in Teachers Colleges, 1948; contbr. articles to profl. jours. Served as lt. USNR, 1944-46, ETO Recipient Silver Beaver award Boys Scouts Am., 1970; Outstanding Civilian Service award Dept. Army, 1979 Mem. Mo. Tchrs. Assn., Am Assn. Sch. Adminstrs., Mo. Assn. Sch. Adminstrs., Columbia U Alumni Assn., Stover C. of C., Am. Legion, Gideons Internat. Phi Kappa Phi, Phi Delta Kappa, Kappa Delta Pi, Lodges Masons, Shriners, Rotary, Lions. Baptist. Avocations: travel writing, fishing, farming. Home: Columbia, Mo. Died July 30 2006.

LOVVIK, DARYL VAUGHN, consulting geologist; b. Eau Claire, Wis., July 26, 1941; s. Oscar W. and Pearl B. (Johnson) L.; m. Sherly Berog; children: Liezel Bayo, Lenie Bayo Welanie Bayo. B.S. in Geology, W. Tex. State U., 1975; MBA U. of Phoenix. Cert. profl. geologist; registered profl. geologist Alaska, Ariz., Ark. Cons. geologist, Golden, Colo., 1975-77 exploration geologist Cotter Corp., Moab, Utah, 1977-79; pres Southwestern Geol. Survey, Mesa, Ariz., 1979-86; water resource dir. Tohono O'Odham Nation, Sells, Ariz., 1986-89, Ariz Dept. Water Resources, 1990-96; pres. Southwestern Geol Tempe, Ariz., 1986—, Pac-Isle Enterprises, Tacloban, Philippines, 1994—, Philippine Connection, Tempe, 1993—. Contbr articles to profl. jours. With USAF, 1960-64. Mem. Am. Inst Profl. Geologists, Geol. Soc. Am., Am. Assn. Petroleum Geologists, Am. C. of C. (The Philippines), Soc. Mining Engrs Republican. Episcopalian. Died July 22, 2006.

LOW, FRANCIS EUGENE, retired physics professor; b NYC, Oct. 27, 1921; s. Bela and Eugenia (Ingerman) L.; m Natalie Sadigur, June 25, 1948 (dec. Feb. 14, 2004); children Julie, Peter, Margaret. BS, Harvard U., 1942; MA, Columbia U 1947, PhD, 1949. Mem. Inst. Advanced Study, 1950-52; asst prof. U. Ill., Urbana, 1952-55, asso. prof., 1955-56; prof. physic MIT, Cambridge, 1957-67, Karl Taylor Compton prof., 1968-85 Inst. prof., 1985-92, Inst. prof. emeritus, 1992—2007, di Center for Theoretical Physics, 1973-76, dir. Lab. for Nuclea Scis., 1979-80, provost, 1980-85. Cons. in field; mem. hig energy physics adv. panel Dept. Energy, 1972-76, chmn., 1987 90. Contbr. articles to profl. jours. Served with USAAF, 1942 43; Served with AUS, 1944-46. Mem. NAS (nat. coun. 1986 89), Am. Phys. Soc. (chmn. divsn. particles and fields 1974 councillor-at-large 1979-82), Fedn. Am. Scientists (nat. cour 1973-77), Am. Acad. Arts and Scis., Internat. Union of Pure an Applied Physics (commn. on particles and fields 1976-82 Home: Rockville, Md. Died Feb. 16, 2007.

LOWDEN, JOHN L., retired manufacturing executive; b Yakima, Wash., Oct. 29, 1921; s. Roy Ruben and Hildegard Annie (Grommesch) L.; m. Janet Katherine Langan, Jan. 2 1961; children: Susan Elizabeth, Jonathan Roy, Andrew Ma thias. BA, U. Nev., 1949. Account supr. Campbell-Ewald Advt 1951-57, Erwin, Wasey Advt., 1957-59; advt. dir. Gen. Dynamics Corp., 1959-61; account supr. Foote, Cone & Belding 1961-63; with ITT Corp., 1963-84, v.p. corp. rels. and advt 1977-84. Author: Silent Wings at War, 1992. Served wi USAAF, 1941-45. Decorated Air medal with oak leaf cluste Presdl. Unit Citation, Bronze Arrowhead of initial assault troop 4th degree Knight Order of William Netherlands. Catholi Home: Wilmington, NC. Died May 18, 2006.

LOWENSTEIN, ALAN VICTOR, lawyer; b. Newark, Au 30, 1913; s. Isaac and Florence (Cohen) L.; m. Amy Lieberma Nov. 23, 1938 (dec. 1999); children: John, Roger, Jane Lowen stein Forsyth. AB, U. Mich., 1933; MA, U. Chgo., 1935; LL Harvard U., 1936. Bar: N.J. 1936. Practiced in Newark an Roseland, 1936—2001; sr. ptnr. Lowenstein, Sandler, PC

1961—2001. Assoc. atty. Temporary Nat. Econ. Com., 1938-39; asst. prof. Rutgers U. Law Sch., 1951-57; chmn. N.J. Corp. Law Revision Commn., 1959-72; spl. hearing officer US Dept. Justice, 1961-65; chmn. bd. United Steel & Aluminum Corp., 1976-96. Pres. Jewish Community Council Essex County, 1950-53, United Way Essex and West Hudson, 1953-55; chmn. Newark Charter Commn., 1953, Newark Citizens Com. Mcpl. Govt., 1954-58, Newark Community Survey, 1959-60; v.p. Council Jewish Fedns., 1965-68, assoc. treas., 1981; pres. N.J. Symphony Orch., 1971-73, chmn. bd., 1973-76; mem. adv. council Rutgers U. Sch. Social Work, 1955-64; vice chmn. Liberty State Park Devel. Corp., 1984—; bd. overseers Rutgers U. Found., 1994-2000. Recipient Brotherhood award Nat. Conf. Christians and Jews, 1972, Trustees award for Disting. Community Service, N.J. Inst. Tech., 1984, Equal Justice award Legal Services N.J./N.J. State Bar Assn., 1988. Mem. ABA, N.J. Bar Assn., Essex County Bar Assn. (Pro-Bono Achievement award 1994), Am. Judicature Soc., Order of Coif, Phi Beta Kappa (v.p. N.J. 1951-52), Phi Kappa Phi, Tau Kappa Alpha. Home: Panton, Vt. Died May 8, 2007.

LOWRY, A. ROBERT, federal government railroad arbitrator; b. Salem, Oreg., Jan. 16, 1919; s. Archie R. and Emaline (Hyland) L.; m. Nancy Jo Srb, May 3, 1975. Student, Albion Normal Coll., Idaho, 1938. With U.P. R.R., 1937-53; local chmn. then asst. to pres. Order R.R. Telegraphers, 1949-64; v.p., then. pres. Transp.-Communications Employees Union, 1964-68; pres. TC div., internat. v.p. Brotherhood Ry. and Airline Clks., 1969-72; supt. ops. Amtrak, 1972-73, dir., top labor rels. officer, 1973-75, asst. v.p., top labor rels. officer, 1975-79; now neutral arbitrator for fed. govt. and R.R. industry San Antonio. Served to lt. col. AUS, 1941-46, USAR, 1946-65, ret. Mem.: Mason, Shriners. Died Oct. 23, 2005.

LUCAS, J. RICHARD, retired mining engineering educator; b. Scottdale, Pa., May 3, 1929; s. J.W. and Mary (Hirka) L.; m. Joan H. Hathaway, Aug. 30, 1952; children: Eric Scott, Jay Hathaway. Student, Pa. State U., 1947-48; BS in Math. and Physics, Waynesburg Coll., 1951; BS in Mining Engring, W.Va. U., 1952; MS in Mining Engring, U. Pitts., 1954; PhD, Columbia, 1965. Registered profl. engr., Va., Ohio, W.Va. Miner Crucible Steel Co., 1947-52; field engr. Joy Mfg. Co., 1952-54; mem. faculty Ohio State U., Columbus, 1954-61; head dept. mining engring. Va. Poly. Inst. and State U., Blacksburg, 1961-71, head div. minerals engring., 1971-76, head dept. mining and minerals engring., 1976-87, Massey prof. mining and minerals engring., 1987-92; dir. mining systems design and ground control Generic Mineral Tech. Ctr.; ret., 1992. Chmn. exec. com. Ann. Inst. on Coal-Mining Health, Safety and Rsch., 1969-87. Mem. Am. Inst. Mining, Metall. and Petroleum Engrs., AAAS, Coal Mining Inst., W.Va. Coal Mining Inst., AAUP, Nat., Va. socs. profl. engrs., Am. Soc. Engring. Edn., Va. Acad. Sci., Soc. Mining Engrs. (bd. dirs., chmn. coal div.) Home: Blacksburg, Va. Died Feb. 15, 2007.

LUCAS, JEANNE HOPKINS, state senator, retired educational administrator; b. Durham, NC, Dec. 25, 1935; m. William Lucas. BA in French and Spanish, N.C. Ctrl. U., 1957, MA in Sch. Adminstrn., 1977. Tchr. French and Spanish, Durham, 1957-75; dir. staff devel., 1977-90; sch. adminstr., 1973-93; dir. pers. and cmty. rels., 1991; ret., 1993; mem. N.C. Senate, Raleigh, from 1993. Vice chmn. appropriations on gen. govt. com., health care com., ways and means com., mem. appropriations/base budget com., edn. and higher edn. com., judiciary I com., chmn. children and human resources com.; mem. black caucus N.C. Legislature; congl. dist. chmn., 1986. Mem. Durham Com. on Affairs Black People; active ARC, Habitat for Humanity; mem. N.C. Dem. Exec. Com.; chmn. Durham County Dem. Exec. Com., 1984; presinct sec., former chmn. Durham Dem. Com.; mem. plan of orgn. Dem. Com. Mem. NEA, N.C. Assn. Educators, Durham County Assn. Educators, NAACP, Links (past pres. Durham chpt.), Delta Sigma Theta. Democrat. Baptist. Died Mar. 9, 2007.

LUCID, ROBERT FRANCIS, language educator; b. Seattle, June 25, 1930; s. Philip Joseph and Nora May (Gorman) L.; m. Joanne K. Tharalson, Sept. 18, 1954; 1 son, John Michael. BA, U. Wash., 1954; MA, U. Chgo., 1955, PhD, 1958. Faculty U. Chgo., 1957-59, Wesleyan U., Middletown, Conn., 1959-64; mem. faculty U. Pa., Phila., from 1964, prof. English, 1975-96, emeritus, from 1996, chmn. dept. English, 1980-85, 90-91, chmn. faculty senate, 1976-77, master Hill Coll. House, 1979-96; master Gregory Coll. House, from 1998. Editor: Journal of Richard Henry Dana, 1968, The Long Patrol, 1971, Norman Mailer, the Man and His Work, 1971. Served with USAF, 1951-53. Recipient Lindback award U. Pa., 1975, Abrams award, 1986; Yaddo fellow, 1970 Mem. MLA, AAUP, PEN (exec. bd. 1987-93), Am. Studies Assn. (exec. sec. 1964-69), Penn Club (N.Y.C.). Home: Philadelphia, Pa. Died Dec. 12, 2006.

LUCKIE, ROBERT ERVIN, JR., advertising executive; b. Clanton, Ala., May 3, 1917; s. Robert Ervin and Eliza (Goodwyn) L.; m. Lois Katherine Drolet, May 15, 1942 (dec. May 1987); children: Katherine (Mrs. Andrew J. Shackelford), Robert Ervin III, Anne Claire Luckie Cobb, Thomas George. AB, Birmingham-So. Coll., 1940, LLD (hon.); HHD (hon.), U. Ala. Reporter-columnist Birmingham (Ala.) News, 1940-41, mem. advt. staff, 1945-48; chmn., ptnr. Tucker Wayne/Luckie & Co., Birmingham, 1958-99. Pres. Nat Advt. Agy. Network, 1960, chmn., Luckie/Birmingham, Inc., 1999-2007; bd. dirs. South Trust Bank. Chmn. for Ala. Radio Free Europe, 1964; co-chmn. Jefferson County United Appeal, 1968; pres. Met. Devel. Bd., 1976; bd. dirs. Blue Cross/Blue Shield, of Ala., Ala. Motorist's Assn.; trustee Birmingham-So. Coll., U. Ala. Birmingham Pres. Coun. Lt. comdr. USNR, 1942-45. Recipient Silver medal award Advt. Fedn. Am. and Printer's Ink, 1963, Disting. Alumni award Birmingham-So. Coll., 1967; named Advt. Man of Yr., Ad Club/Advt. Fedn. Am., 1963; inductee Ala. Acad. of Honor, 1997, Birmingham Bus. Hall of Fame, U. Ala. Comm. Hall of Fame, 1999. Mem. Birmingham-So. Coll. Alumni Assn. (pres. 1966), Kiwanis (pres. 1964), Downtown Club, The Club (Birmingham) (pres. 1980-81), Newcomen Soc., Birmingham Country Club (pres. 1975), Relay House (past pres.), Omicron Delta Kappa, Kappa Alpha. Methodist. Home: Birmingham, Ala. Died Feb. 28, 2007.

LUDINGTON, WILLIAM FLETCHER, packaging and paper company executive; b. NYC, Mar. 5, 1935; s. Francis Henry and Mary Fletcher (Harris) L.; m. Betty Ann Erickson, June 21, 1970; children: William Fletcher Jr., Kristin W., Callaway Ludington Zuccarello, Hoyt. BS, Wesleyan U., Middletown, Conn., 1958. Various positions Chase Packaging Corp., St. Louis, 1961-70, v.p. corp. planning Greenwich, Conn., 1970-72, v.p., div. mgr., 1972-78, exec. v.p., 1978-86, pres., chief oper. officer, 1986-88; pres., chief exec. officer Chase Packaging Corp. subs. Union Camp Corp., Old Greenwich, Conn., from 1988. Bd. dirs. Light House for Blind, St. Louis, 1965-69, Soc. To Prevent Blindness, Middletown, 1991—; chmn. bd. Forum for World Affairs, Stamford, Conn., 1991—; mem. Fairfield County Adv. Bd. of Conn. Nat. Bank. Mem. Flexible Packaging Assn. (bd. dirs. 1987-90), Woodway Country Club (Darien, Conn.), Shenorock Shore Club (Rye, N.Y.), Biltmore Forest Country Club (Asheville, N.C.), Roxbury Club (Stamford), Sea Oaks Tennis Club (Vero Beach, Fla.). Home: Vero Beach, Fla. Died Nov. 27, 2006.

LUDWIG, ARNOLD FRANCIS, candy company executive; b. Toledo, May 30, 1934; s. Clarence J. and Helen D. (Pry) L.; B.S. (scholar), U. Wis., 1956, B.B.A., 1958; M.B.A., U. Ill., 1981; m. Betty Jean Bubolz, Dec. 31, 1958; children— Wendy Lou, Timothy Daniel. Dir. quality control Babcock Dairy Co., Toledo, 1958-60; v.p., co founder Seaway Candy Co., Toledo, 1960-69; pres., founder Ludwig Candy Co., Manteno, Ill., 1969—; co-founder, chief exec. officer Basic Computer Literacy Inc., Manteno, Ill., 1982—; dir. exec. M.B.A. program U. Notre Dame (Ind.), 1984—. also dir. Chmn. music program Manteno Bi-Centennial, 1976. Mem. U. Wis. W Club (dir.), Am. Mgmt. Assn. (pres.), U. Wis. Alumni Assn. (bd. dirs.), U. Ill. Alumni Assn., Wis. Agrl. and Life Scis. Alumni Assn. Roman Catholic. Club: Moose. Home: Manteno, Ill. Died July 25, 2006.

LUECKE, ELEANOR VIRGINIA ROHRBACHER, civic volunteer; b. St. Paul, Mar. 10, 1918; d. Adolph and Bertha (Lehman) Rohrbacher; m. Richard William Luecke, Nov. 1, 1941; children: Glenn Richard, Joan Eleanor Ratliff, Ruth Ann (dec.). Student, Macalester Coll., St. Paul, 1936-38, St. Paul Bus. U., 1938-40. Author lit. candidate and ballot issues, 1970-2003; producer TV local issues, 1981—; contbr. articles to profl. jours. Founder, officer, dir., pres. Liaison for Inter-Neighborhood Coop., Okemos, Mich., 1972—; chair country-wide special edn. millage proposals, 1958, 1969; trustee, v.p., pres. Ingham Intermediate Bd. Edn., 1959-83; sec., dir. Tri-County Cmty. Mental Health Bd., Lansing, 1964-72; founder, treas., pres. Concerned Citizens for Meridian Twp., Okemos, 1970-86; mental health rep. Partners of the Americas, Belize, Brit. Honduras, 1971; trustee Capital Area Comprehensive Health Planning, 1973-76; v.p., dir. Assn. Retarded Citizens Greater Lansing, 1973-83; chair, mem. Cmty. Svcs. for Developmentally Disabled Adv. Coun., 1973-87; dir., founder, treas. Tacoma Hills Homeowners Assn. Bd., 1985-97; facilitator of mergers Lansing Child Guidance Clinic, Clinton and Eaton counties Tri-County Cmty. Mental Health Bd., Lansing Adult Mental Health Clinic, founder; founder, treas., officer Mid-Mich. Land Conservancy, 2002—. Recipient Greater Lansing Cmty. Svcs. Coun. "Oscar," United Way, 1955, state grant Mich. Devel. Disabilities Coun., Lansing, 1983, Disting. award Mich. Assn. Sch. Bds., Lansing, 1983, Pub. Svc. award C.A.R.E.ing, Okemos, 1988, Earth Angel award WKAR-TV 23, Mich. State U., East Lansing, 1990, Cert. for Cmty. Betterment People for Meridian, Okemos, 1990, 2nd pl. video competition East Lansing/Meridian Twp. Cable Comm. Commn., 1990, 1st pl. award video competition, 1992, Outstanding Sr. Citizen award Charter Twp. of Meridian, Okemos, Mich., 2001; Ingham Med. Hosp. Commons Area named in her honor, Lansing, 1971. Mem. Advocacy Orgn. for Patients and Providers (dir. 1994-99). Avocations: reading, interior design, landscaping, gardening. Home: East Lansing, Mich. Died Mar. 10, 2007.

LUKE, JOHN ANDERSON, paper company executive; b. Tyrone, Pa., Nov. 30, 1925; s. David Lincoln and Priscilla Warren (Silver) L.; m. Joy Carter, Dec. 21, 1946; children: John Anderson, Hope S., Jane T., William H. BA, Yale U., 1949. Personnel asst. Westvaco Corp., Charleston, S.C., 1949-51, personnel mgr., 1951-53, asst. mgr. adminstrn., 1953-55, mill mgr. Luke, Md., 1955-60, mgr. fine papers div., 1960-74, v.p. NYC, 1966-74, sr. v.p., 1974-76, exec. v.p., 1976-80, pres., 1980-88, pres., chief exec. officer, 1988-92, dir.; ret. Chmn. Internat. Com. Served with USAAF, 1943-45. Mem. New Canaan Country Club. Died May 7, 2007.

LUNDIN, ROBERT WILLIAM, psychology educator; b. Chgo., Apr. 28, 1920; s. Adolph E. and Agnes (King) L. m. Margaret Waitt, Aug. 8, 1952; children— Sara Jane, Robert King. A.B., DePauw U., 1942; M.A., Ind. U., 1943, Ph.D., 1947. Lic. psychologist, Tenn. Asst. prof. Denison U., Granville, Ohio, 1947-49; assoc. prof. Hamilton Coll., Clinton, N.Y., 1949-64; William R. Kennan, Jr. prof. psychology U. South, Sewanee, Tenn., 1964—; dept. chmn., 1964—. Fellow Am. Psychol. Assn.; mem. S.E. Psychol. Assn., Sigma Xi. Republican. Episcopalian. Club: Ecce Quo Bonum. Author: Personality: An Experimental Approach, 1961; Principles of Psychopathology, 1965; The Study of Behavior, 1965; An Objective Psychology of Music, 1953, rev. edit., 1967, 3d edit., 1985; Personality: A Behavioral Analysis, 1969, rev. edit., 1974, trans. into Portuguese, for Brazilian edit., 1972, 1978; Personality, 1973, trans., 1980; Theories and Systems of Psychology, 1972, rev. edit., 1979, 3d. edit., 1985; contbr. numerous articles to profl. jours.; assoc. editor The Psychological Record. Home: Sewanee, Tenn. Died May 28, 2007.

LUNDY, J. EDWARD (JOSEPH EDWARD LUNDY), retired automobile company executive; b. Iowa, Jan. 6, 1915; s. Vern E. and Mary L. (Chambers) L. BA, U. Iowa, 1936. Fellow Princeton U., 1936-39, mem. econs. faculty, 1940-42, beginning as planning ofcl.; with Ford Motor Co., Dearborn, Mich., 1946-85, successively dir. fin. planning and analysis, gen. asst. contr., 1946-57, treas., 1957-61, v.p., contr., 1961-62, v.p. fin., 1962-67, exec. v.p., 1967-79, vice-chmn. fin. com., 1979-85. Dir. rsch. & analysis Office Statis. Control, Hdqrs. USAAF, 1945; bd. dirs. Ford Motor Co., 1979-85 Served from pvt. to maj. USAAF, 1943-45. Decorated Legion of Merit; named to Automotive Hall of Fame, 2003. Mem. Dearborn Country Club, Phi Beta Kappa, Delta Upsilon. Clubs: Detroit Princeton. Roman Catholic. Home: Dearborn, Mich. Died Oct. 2, 2007.

LUNG, CHANG See RIGNEY, JAMES JR.

LUPKE, WALTER HERMAN, JR., financial planner; b. Ft. Wayne, Ind., Sept. 25, 1922; s. Walter Herman and Lucy Viola (Bell) L.; m. G. Frances McGahey, Aug. 11, 1944; children: Karen Ann McArdle, Hans R. BS in Chem. Engring., Purdue U., 1942. CLU, chartered property casualty underwriter. Underwriter Lupke Ins. Agy., Ft. Wayne, 1946-50, acct., 1950-51, claims mgr., 1951-52, treas., 1946-83, sales exec., 1952-83, chmn. bd., 1970-87; pvt. practice fin. planning, Ft. Wayne, 1987—. Pres. Lupke Found.; bd. dirs. Embassy Found., St. Francis Coll. Found., Kirksville Coll. Medicine Found., Luth. Hosp., Allen Wells chpt. ARC. Served with U.S. Army, 1942-46; ETO. Mem. Ind. Ins. Agts. Assn. U.S.A., Ind. Ind. Ins. Agts. Assn., Ft. Wayne Ind. Ins. Agts., Ft. Wayne C. of C. Republican. Lutheran. Lodge: Kiwanis. Died May 8, 2007.

LUSCOMB, ROBERT CHARLES, JR., automotive executive; b. Lansing, Mich., Apr. 29, 1936; s. Robert Charles and Gertrude Ann Luscomb; m. Karen Marie; children: Mark C., Roberta D., Philip Z., James D., David C. Kipp. BS in Mech. Engring., Gen. Motors Inst., 1958; SM in Mgmt., MIT, 1970. Registered profl. engr., Mich. Supt. press plants Oldsmobile div. Gen. Motors Corp., Lansing, 1970-73, dir. prodn. engring., 1973-76, mgr. mfg. plants Cadillac div., 1976-84, mgr. mfg. engring., 1984-89, program mgr., 1989—. Active Boy Scouts Am., 1945—. Sloan fellow, 1970. Mem. Soc. Automotive Engrs., Soc. Mfg. Engrs. Died Apr. 17, 2007.

LUSSKIN, ROBERT MILLER, chemist; b. NYC, Dec. 14, 1921; s. Abraham and Libby (Miller) L.; m. Ivy M. Lehne, May 1, 1947; children: Marc, Jean. AB in Biochemistry, Harvard U., 1943; MS in Organic Chemistry, NYU, 1947, PhD in Organic Chemistry, 1950. Dir. chem. research and devel. Universal Oil Products, 1947-66; mgr. exploratory research Kimberly-Clark Corp., Neenah, Wis., 1966-75; dir. analytical services Raltech Sci. Services div., Ralston Purina Co., Madison, Wis., 1977-82; dir. central research and devel. Ralston Purina Co., St. Louis, 1982-87. Mem. Am. Chem. Soc., AAAS Home: Saint Louis, Mo. Died Apr. 26, 2007.

LUTES, DONALD HENRY, architect; b. San Diego, Mar. 7, 1926; s. Charles McKinley and Helen (Bjoraker) L.; m. Donnie Wageman, Aug. 14, 1949; children: Laura Jo, Gail Eileen, Dana Charles. BArch, U. Oreg., 2000. Pvt. archtl. practice, Springfield, Oreg., 1956-58; ptnr. John Amundson, Springfield, 1958-70; pres. Lutes & Amundson, Springfield, 1970-72; ptnr. Lutes/Sanetel, 1989—2000. Adj. assoc. prof. architecture U. Oreg., 1964-66, 89-2000; chmn. Springfield Planning Commn., 1954-65, 93-99, Urban Design and Devel. Corp., 1968-70, Eugene Non-Profit Housing, Inc., 1970 Architect: Springfield Pub. Library, 1957, Mt. Hood Community Coll, 1965-79, Shoppers Paradise Expt. in Downtown Revitalization, 1957. Chmn. Springfield United Appeal, 1959. Served to 1st lt. AUS, 1943-46, 51-52. Decorate Bronze Star; named Jr. 1st Citizen, Springfield C. of C., 1957, 1st Citizen, 1968, Disting. Citizen, 1995. Fellow AIA (bd. dirs. 1987-90, v.p. 1991, doc. com. 1993-2000, Northwest & Pacific Region medal hon. 2003); mem. Rotary, Theta Chi. Home: Springfield, Oreg. Died May 21, 2007.

LUZZI, LOUIS ANTHONY, academic administrator; b. Westerly, RI, June 17, 1932; s. Patsy Louis and Mary E. (Meringolo) L.; m. Joyce B. Kaye, 1953; children: Glenda Elise, Patrissa Lou. BS in Pharmacy, U. R.I., 1959, MS in Phys. Pharmacy, 1963, PhD in Phys. Pharmacy, 1966. Asst. prof. U. Ga., Athens, from 1966, then asso. prof., prof., until 1973; dean Coll. Pharmacy, W.Va. U., Morgantown, 1973-80; provost health sci. affairs, dean Coll. Pharmacy, U. R.I., Kingston, from 1980. Served with USCG, 1951-53. Fellow Am. Acad. Sci., Acad. Pharm. Scis.; mem. Am. Pharm. Assn., Am. Assn. Coll. Pharmacy, Council Sects. and Council Deans, Nat. Assn. Retail Druggists, AAAS, R.I. Pharm. Assn., R.I. Health Industries Devel. Coun., Sigma Xi, Rho Chi, Phi Sigma, Phi Kappa Phi. Home: Narragansett, RI. Died May 12, 2007.

LYNESS, ROBERT MARRON, retired retail food chain executive; b. New Orleans, May 21, 1924; s. Robert Fleming and Julia Josephine (Marron) L.; m. Eleanor Ruth Hobart, May 20, 1950; children: Robin Hughes, Anne Lorraine, Stephanie Elizabeth, Cynthia Hobart, Audrey Marron. BS in Civil Engring., U. Calif., Berkeley, 1945; MS in Adminstrn., Stanford U., 1948. Engr., Mcpl. Engrs. Co., San Diego, 1946-47; Engr. Paddock Engring. Co., San Mateo, Calif., 1948-49, F.W. Woolworth Co., San Francisco, 1949-51; with Safeway Stores Inc., Oakland, Calif., 1951-84, v.p., 1969-84; pres. Lyness Enterprises Ltd., from 1984. Guest lectr. constrn. mgmt. U. Calif., Berkeley, Stanford U. Trustee Pacific Sch. Religion, Berkeley, 1970—; bd. dirs. Berkeley Pilgrimage Found., 1979—; mem. U. Calif. Berkeley Found., 1979—. Served to lt. USNR, 1942-46. Mem. ASCE. Republican. Mem. United Ch. Christ. Clubs: Mira Vista Golf and Country, Berkeley Tennis. Died Oct. 2, 2005.

LYNN, JOHN WARREN, retail company executive; b. Bklyn., Mar. 4, 1921; s. Thomas Robert and Olga (Clemens) L.; m. Adele Grant, Feb. 5, 1944; children: Suzanne Lynn Falkenbush, Dianne Lynn Nofi, Robert, Thomas. Student, Syracuse U., 1939-41. Vice pres. Mid-Altantic region F.W. Woolworth Co., NYC, 1965-67, v.p. Northeastern region, 1968, corp. v.p. sales and advt., 1969, v.p. merchandising, 1970-74, sr. v.p. merchandising, 1975-76, exec. v.p., 1977-78, pres. Woolworth/Woolco div., 1978-79, sr. exec. v.p., 1979-80, vice chmn. bd., 1980-82, chmn. bd., 1982-87, dir., from 1970, also chmn. exec. com. Dir. Borden Inc., F.W. Woolworth Co. Ltd., Can., Woolworth Mexicana S.A. de C.V. Served with USAAF, World War II Decorated Purple Heart; decorated Air medal with 8 oak leaf clusters Mem. Newcomen Soc., Boca Raton Resort and Club, Boca West Club. Home: Boca Raton, Fla. Died Oct. 16, 2006.

LYNTON, HAROLD STEPHEN, lawyer; b. NYC, Nov. 2, 1909; widowed, Mar. 12, 1990; children: Stephen Jonathan, Richard David, Andrew Edward; m. Hattie Gruenstein Kalish, Jan. 27, 1991. AB magna cum laude, Yale U., 1929; JD cum laude, Harvard U., 1932. Bar: N.Y. 1933, U.S. Supreme Ct. 1947. Ptnr. Kaufman, Gallop, Gould, Climenko & Lynton, NYC, 1934-51, Lynton & Klein and predecessors, NYC, 1951-80, Shea & Gould, NYC, 1980-91, counsel, 1992-94, Dornbush Schaeffer Strongin & Weinstein, LLP, NYC, from 2004; gen. counsel, trustee, mem. adv. bd. Barron Collier Cos., Naples, Fla., from 1945; also bd. dirs. Barron Collier Cos. and affiliates, Naples, Fla.; counsel Dornbush Mensch Mandelstam & Schaeffer, NYC, 1994—2004. Capt. AUS, 1943-45. Mem. ABA, N.Y. State Bar Assn., Assn. of Bar of City of N.Y., N.Y. County Lawyers Assn., Yale Club N.Y., Sunningdale Country Club, Phi Beta Kappa. Avocations: travel, theater, literature. Home: New York, NY. Died June 11, 2007.

LYON, JAMES TRAVERS, lawyer; b. Butte, Mont., Apr. 30, 1922; s. James Nathaniel and Isabella (Travaas) L.; children: James T. Jr., John G.; m. Jane Harrison Sutherland. AB, U. Chgo., 1947, JD, 1948. Bar: Va. 1987, D.C. 1953, Mont. 1948. Atty., chief counsel IRS, Washington, 1948-52; assoc. Winthrop, Stimson, Putnam & Roberts, NYC, 1952, Dudley, Jones & Ostmann, Washington, 1952-59; asst. to v.p. Balt. and Ohio RR Co., 1959-63; dir. taxes Chessie System, Cleve., 1963-69, asst. v.p. taxes Balt., 1969-79; v.p. taxes Chessie System, Inc., Balt., 1979-80, CSX Corp., Richmond, Va., 1980-86; ptnr. McGuire, Woods, Battle & Boothe, Richmond, 1986-88, ret., 1988. Speaker in tax field. Author: Depreciation and Taxes, 1962. Treas., bd. dirs. Hamlet Condminium Assn., Richmond, 1982-87, Westham Green Assn., 1988—. Sgt. USAF, 1942-46, ETO. Recipient Pres.' award Tax Execs. Inst., 1986. Mem. Order of Coif, Phi Beta Kappa. Republican. Home: Richmond, Va. Died Dec. 22, 2006.

LYONS, JAMES STEPHEN, pharmaceutical company executive; b. Newark, June 17, 1941; s. James Lawrence and Anna Helena (Grimm) L.; m. Frances Pamela Hopkins, Sept. 28, 1963; children: Elizabeth, Kathleen, Eileen, Nancy. BA, St. Peters Coll., 1963; MBA, Seton Hall U., 1968. Treas. Internat. div. Schering-Plough Corp., Kenilworth, N.J., 1973-76; dir. fin. Schering Can., Inc., Pointe Claire, Que., 1976-78, Asia-Pacific Schering Plough Corp., Kenilworth, 1978-80; v.p. fin. Rorer Internat. Corp., Ft. Washington, Pa., 1980-82, Rorer Group, Inc., 1982-86, Seton Co., Chadds Ford, Pa., from 1987, Boots Pharm. Inc., Lincolnshire, Ill., from 1987. Home: Princeton Jct, NJ. Died Jan. 5, 2006.

LYONS, RICHARD CHAPMAN, former urologist; b. Corry, Pa., Nov. 23, 1919; s. Arch C. and Araline (Drought) L.; m. Norma Lydia Wright, Dec. 25, 1945; children: Dorothy A., John C., Sanford D., Timothy R., Valerie A. Grad. U. Pa., 1941; MD, U. Pitts., 1944. Diplomate Am. Bd. Urology. Intern, St. Elizabeth Hosp., Washington, 1945; resident, Mayo Clinic, Rochester, Minn., 1945-46, 48-50; civilian physician U.S. Army, 1946-47; chmn. dept. urology, Hamot Med. Ctr., Erie, Pa., 1955-68, practitioner, surgeon, 1950-86, founder, head urology residency program, 1958-68; hon. mem. med. staffs St. Vincent Health Ctr., Erie, 1951-86; mem. Pa. State Bd. Med. Edn. and Licensure, 1971-85, chmn., 1976-78, 81-85; dir. NW Pa. Corp., Oil City, Mellon-North, Erie; mng. ptnr. Lyons Properties Ltd. Partnership. Trustee Gannon U. Named Disting. Pennsylvanian, Gannon U., 1981. Recipient Integrity award Soc. for Advancement Intergrity in Pub. Life. Fellow ACS (gov. 1975-81); mem. AMA, Pa. Med. Soc., Erie County Med. Soc., Pa. Urologic Assn. (pres. 1974), Mayo Clinic Alumni Assn., Mayo Urol. Alumni Assn. (pres. 1976), Erie Club, Kahkwa Club, Erie Yacht Club, Univ. Club (Pitts.), Elks. Republican. Roman Catholic. Home: Fort Lauderdale, Fla. Died June 15, 2007.

LYONS, THOMAS JAMES, retail company executive; b. San Francisco, Oct. 4, 1928; s. John Michael and Margaret Kathleen (Hanrahan) L.; m. Mary Lou Pilakowski, 1950; children: Kathleen, Pamela, Timothy, Mary Ellen, Erin, Kevin. B.S., U. Santa Clara, 1950. Trainee J.C. Penney Co., Inc., San Jose, Calif., 1950-52, store mgr., Vallejo, Calif., 1960-61, pres. J.C. Penney S.P.A., Milan, Italy, 1970-73, dir. internat. devel., 1973-76, dir. domestic and internat. devel., 1976-78, dir. pub. affairs J.C. Penney Co. Inc., N.Y.C., 1978-79, v.p., dir. spl. bus. ops., 1979-83, exec. v.p. Office of Chmn., 1983—. Mem. adv. bd. Ctr. for Pub. and Corp. Affairs, Drew U., 1982—, NYU Inst. Retail Mgmt., New York, 1983—, U. Santa Clara Retail Mgmt. Inst., Calif. 1983—. Served with U.S. Army, 1950-52. Mem. Nat. Retail Mchts. Assn. (internat. com.). Roman Catholic. Home: Cayucos, Calif. Died July 10, 2007.

LYSAUGHT, J. DONALD, lawyer; b. Kansas City, Kans., Dec. 7, 1923; s. Michael Clarence and Minnie (Hill) L.; m. Jeen Lois Hunter, Dec. 15, 1945; children— Nancy Jeen, J. Donald, Deborah Geralyn, Wendy Lynn, Jeffrey Patrick, Victoria Anne. AB, U. Kans., 1948, LL.B., 1949. Bar: Kans. 1949, U.S. Ct. Appeals (10th cir.) 1962, U.S. Supreme Ct. 1961. Since practiced in, Kansas City; ptnr. Stanley, Schroeder, Weeks, Thomas & Lysaught, 1955-68, Weeks, Thomas & Lysaught (Chartered), from 1969. Served as judge pro tem Dist. Ct. Wyandotte County, Kans., 1953 Served with AUS, World War II. Decorated Army Commendation ribbon with cluster. Mem. Kans. Res. Officers Assn. (judge adv. 1954), Order of Coif, Phi Delta Phi, Alpha Tau Omega. Home: Overland Park, Kans. Died Feb. 9, 2006.

MA, TSU SHENG, chemist, educator, consultant; b. Guangdong, China, Oct. 15, 1911; came to U.S., 1934, naturalized 1956; s. Shao-ching and Sze (Mai) M.; m. Gioh-Fang Dju, Aug. 27, 1942; children: Chopo, Mei-Mei. BS, Tsinghua U., Peking, 1931; PhD, U. Chgo., 1938. Faculty U. Chgo., 1938-46; prof. Peking U., 1946-49; sr. lectr. U. Otago, New Zealand, 1949-51; mem. faculty NYU, 1951-54, CUNY, from 1954, prof. chemistry, from 1958, prof. emeritus, from 1980. Vis. prof. Tsinghua U., 1947, Lingnan, 1949, NYU, 1954-60, Taiwan U., 1961, Chiangmei U., 1968, Singapore U., 1975; hon. prof. Hangzhou Tchrs. Coll., 1998—; specialist Bur. Ednl. and Cultural Affairs State Dept., 1964, Hong Kong, Philippines, Burma, Sri Lanka; Fulbright lectr., 1961-62, 68-69. Author: Small-Scale Experiments in Chemistry, 1962, Organic Functional Group Analysis, 1964, Microscale Manipulations in Chemistry, 1976, Organic Functional Group Analysis by Gas Chromatography, 1976, Quantitative Analysis of Organic Mixtures, 1979, Modern Organic Elemental Analysis, 1979, Organic Analysis Using Ion-Selective Electrodes, 1982, Trace Element Determination in Organic Materials, 1988; editor: Mikrochimica Acta, 1965-89; contbr. articles to profl. jours., chpts. to 10 books. Recipient Benedetti-Pichler award in microchemistry, 1976. Fellow N.Y. Acad. Sci., AAAS, Royal Soc. Chemistry, Am. Inst. Chemists; mem. Am. Chem. Soc., Soc. Applied Spectroscopy, Am. Microchem. Soc., Sigma Xi. Achievements include 1 patent; research in trace element analysis, microchemical investigation of medicinal plants, organic analysis and synthesis in the milligram to microgram range, and the use of small-scale, inexpensive equipment to teach chemistry. Home: Raleigh, NC. Died May 29, 2007.

MACCALLUM, JAMES DUNLOP, surgeon; b. Buffalo, Feb. 16, 1914; s. James Dunlop and Estelle May (Wright) MacC.; m. Joan Elaine Goodchild; children: John, Hugh. MD, SUNY, Buffalo, 1937. Diplomate Am. Bd. Surgery, Am. Bd. Thoracic Surgery. Intern then resident Buffalo Gen. Hosp., 1937-41; asst. resident surgery El Meyer Hosp., Buffalo, 1946-48; chief of surgery Buffalo VA Hosp., 1949-53; attending surgeon Wyo. County Hosp., Warsaw, N.Y., 1953-76; dir. med. services Geneseo (N.Y.) Coll., SUNY, 1978-86; exec. dir. Wyo. Found., Warsaw, 1987-91. Cons. surgeon Erie County Med. Ctr., Buffalo, 1955-76; clin. asst. prof. SUNY, Buffalo, 1955-76. Contbr. articles to profl. jours. Active Library Trustees, Warsaw, 1957-59, Bd. Edn., Warsaw, 1959-70. Served to maj. British Royal Army Med. Corps., 1941-46. Mem. Am. Coll. Surgeons, Alpha Omega Alpha. Democrat. Episcopalian. Avocations: gardening, tennis. Died Apr. 6, 2006.

MACCUTCHEON, EDWARD MACKIE, naval architect, ocean engineer; b. Bridgeport, Conn., Nov. 12, 1915; s. Edward Mackie and Laura (Stout) MacC.; BS, Webb Inst. Naval Arch., N.Y.C., 1937; postgrad. U. Md., 1948-49; M in Engring. Adminstrn., George Washington U., 1958; m. Jean Loeffler, June 20, 1942; children: Barbara Jean MacCutcheon Smith, Maryann MacCutcheon Lucero. Registered profl. engr., Md., D.C. With N.Y. Shipbldg. Co., Camden, N.J., 1937-38, U.S. Coast Guard, Washington, 1938-48, David Taylor Model Basin, Dept. Navy, 1948-49, Bur. Ships, 1949-55, Office of Naval Rsch., Washington, 1955-57; tech. dir. Naval Civil Engring. Lab., Port Hueneme, Calif., 1957-62; chief rsch. and devel. Maritime Adminstrn., Dept. Commerce, Washington, 1962-66; dir. systems devel., Nat. Ocean Survey, NOAA, Rockville, Md., 1966-72; cons. engr., Bethesda, Md., 1973—. Lt. comdr. USCGR, 1943-46. Fellow Soc. Naval Architects and Marine Engrs., Marine Tech. Soc.; mem. Am. Soc. Naval Engrs. Died May 17, 2007.

MACDIARMID, ALAN GRAHAM, metallurgist, educator; b. Masterton, New Zealand, Apr. 14, 1927; m. Marian MacDiarmid, 1954 (dec. 1990); children: Heather, Dawn, Gail, Duncan; m. Gayl Gentile, 2005. BSc, U. New Zealand, 1948, MSc, 1950; MS, U. Wis., 1952, PhD in Chemistry, 1953, Cambridge U., 1955. Asst. lectr. in chemistry St. Andrews U., 1955; from instr. to assoc. prof. U. Pa., Phila., 1955-64, Sloan fellowship, 1959-63, prof. chemistry, 1964—2007, Blanchard prof. chemistry, 1998—2007. Vis. prof. Kyoto Univ., Japan. Recipient Frederic Stanley Kipping award, 1970, Marshall award, 1982, Doolittle award, 1982, Chemical Pioneer award, 1984, Royal Soc. of Chem. Centenary Medal, Francis J. Clamer medal, Franklin Inst., 1993, Nobel Prize in Chemistry, 2000. Mem.: Royal Soc. Chemistry, Am. Chem. Soc. Achievements include preparation and characterization of organosilicon compounds; preparation and charachterization of derivatives of sulfur nitrides and quasi one-dimensional semiconducting and metallic covalent polymers such as polyacetylene and its derivatives. Died Feb. 7, 2007.

MACDONALD, CLIFFORD PALMER, editor, writer; b. Winchester, Mass., Apr. 30, 1919; s. Frederick Cameron and Helen Maud (Palmer) M. Student, Bryant & Stratton Bus. Sch., 1937-38. Chief of publs. Office of Mil. Govt. for Germany, U.S. Army, 1945-46; mgr. Midwest br. Whittemore Assocs., Cleve., 1947-50; asst. dir. fund-raising Am. Bapt. Conv., NYC, 1950-63; writer Marts and Lundy, NYC, 1963-66; editor Am. Bible Soc., NYC, from 1966. Active various bds. and coms. Nat. Council Chs., Religion in Am. Life, Lord's Day Alliance, other religious orgns. Served to capt. U.S. Army, 1941-46, ETO. Current editor, writer one of oldest continuous publs. in U.S., first issue appearing in 1818. Home: Jackson Hts, NY. Died Aug. 31, 2006.

MACDONALD, ROBERT ALAN, language educator; b. Salamanca, NY, Mar. 25, 1927; s. Guy E. and Hildur V. (Helene) MacD. BA, U. Buffalo, 1948; MA, U. Wis., 1949, PhD, 1958. Asst. prof. U. Richmond, Va., 1955-61, assoc. prof., 1961-67, prof. Spanish, 1967-95, prof. emeritus, 1995; ofcl. project reviewer NEH, Washington, 1977-95; mem. Social Sci. and Humanities Rsch. Coun., Ottawa, Ont., Canada, 1981-95. Author: Espéculo, texto juridico atribuido a Alfonso X, 1990, Alfonso X, Libro de las Tahurerias, 1995, Alfonso X, Libro de los Adelantados Mayores, 2000; editor Bull. of Fgn. Lang. Assn. Va., 1962-67, 72-86; contbr. articles to profl. jours. With U.S. Army, 1946-47, 51-53. A.L. Markham traveling fellow U. Wis., 1958-59, Am. Coun. Learned Socs. fellow, 1976; fellow, grantee U. Richmond, 1958-94; named Cultural Laureate of Va., 1977; recipient Disting. Svc. award Fgn. Lang. Assn. Va., 1981. Mem. Acad. Am. Rsch. Historians on Medieval Spain, Am. Assn. Spanish and Portuguese (past pres. state chpt.), AAUP (past pres. local chpt.), Am. Coun. on Tchg. Fgn. Langs., Medieval Acad. Am. MLA, Torch Club (Richmond). Died June 28, 2006.

MACDONALD, ROBERT BRUCE, retired county official; b. Delhi, NY, Dec. 28, 1930; s. Ernest Jamison and Daisy (Beers) MacD.; m. Ferne Huffman, Aug. 17, 1965; 1 child, Robert Bruce II. BS Govt., Pub. Adminstrn., Am. Univ., 1961; postgrad., U. Okla., 1981-83. Enlisted USAF, 1950-59; adminstrv. officer U.S. Govt., Washington, 1961-68; asst. to assoc. adminstr. rsch. and devel. Nat. Hwy. Traffic Safety Adminstrn., Washington, 1968-78; exec. dir. Delaware County Indsl. Devel. Agy., Delhi, N.Y., 1978-96; ret., 1996. Mem. SUNY Bus. & Industry Counsel, So. Tier East Planning and Devel. Bd., Econ. Devel. Com., Kiwanis (pres. Delhi chpt. 1984-85). Home: New Bern, NC. Died Feb. 11, 2006.

MACINTYRE, WILLIAM E., lawyer; b. N.S., Can., July 25, 1924; m. Kathleen T. Kelly, 1949; children— Steven E., Richard J., Donald W. B.A., Bowdoin Coll., 1947; J.D., Harvard U., 1949. Bar: Mass. Law clk., U.S. Ct. Appeals for 1st Circuit, 1949-50; atty. antitrust div. E.I. Du Pont de Nemours & Co., Wilmington, Del., 1950-65, dir. of legal-Europe, Du Pont de Nemours Internat. S.A., 1965-68, sr. atty. gen. legal div. parent co., Wilmington, 1968-70, chief counsel, 1970-75, asst. gen. counsel, 1975—; dir. Desarrolo Quimico Indsl. S.A., 1967-68, Du Pont Overseas Fin. N.V., until 1980. Bd. dirs. Del. Heart Assn., pres., 1975-77, chmn. bd., 1977-78; past v.p., mem. bd. dirs., exec. com. Am. Heart Assn.; mem. St. Joseph's on Brandywine Roman Catholic Ch. Served AC, USN,1943-46, 1953. Mem. Del. C. of C. (exec. com., bd. dirs., chmn. 1985-87), Phi Beta Kappa, Alpha Delta Phi. Club: Wilmington Country. Home: Wilmington, Del. Died June 6, 2007.

MACK, EDWARD GIBSON, retired manufacturing executive; b. Toronto, Ont., Can., Dec. 4, 1917; s. Edward Gibson and Marion Margaret (Ward) M.; m. Ruth Harriet Davies, Aug. 3 1940 (dec.); children: Edward Davies Mack (dec. May 2002) Carol Mack Fuller, Susan Mack Vassel; m. Isolde Maderson Sept. 30, 1978. Grad., Pickering Coll., 1938; student, Syracuse U., 1938-40, U. Pa., 1945-46. Investment analyst trust dept. Syracuse (N.Y.) Trust Co., 1939-43; acct. Hurdman & Cranstoun CPA's, Syracuse, 1943-44; from dist. sales mgr. to dir. mktg. and product research Easy Washing Machine Corp., Syracuse, 1948-55; dir. research Avco Corp., Connersville, Ind., 1955-58; exec sec. planning and policy bd. Aeronca Mfg. Corp., Middletown, Ohio, 1958-60; pres. E.D.I., State College, Pa., 1960-62; pres. dir. Sherman Indsl. Electronics Inc., Eutectics Inc.; exec. Richards Musical Instruments, Inc., Elkhart, Ind., 1962-65; mgr supply and distbn. plastic products Union Carbide Ltd., Lindsay Ont., 1965-68; corp. sec. Dominion Dairies Ltd., Toronto 1968-73, v.p., sec., 1973-81. Sec., dir. Sealtest (Can.) Ltd. 1968-81 Bd. mgmt. Pickering Coll., 1980-88. Served with U.S Army, World War II. Mem. Inst. Chartered Secs. and Adminstrs. Can. Inst. Chartered Secs. (assoc.), Pickering Coll. Alumni Assn (chmn. 1981-86), Am. Legion, Elks, Sigma Chi. Democrat Home: Sacramento, Calif. Died Nov. 11, 2005.

MACKALL, LAIDLER BOWIE, retired lawyer; b. Washington, Aug. 8, 1916; s. Laidler and Evelyn (Bowie) M.; m. Nancy M. Taylor, Aug. 28, 1942; children: Nancy Taylor Mackall Lurton (dec.), Christie Beall Mackall Connard, Susan Somervel Mackall Smythe, Bruce Bowie Mackall McConihe; m. Prudence Robertson Colbert, July 26, 1978. AB, Princeton U., 1938 postgrad., Georgetown U., 1938-40, JD, 1947. Bar: D.C. 1947 Interstate Commerce Commn. 1951, U.S. Supreme Ct. 1958 Law clk. to chief judge of predecessor to D.C. Ct. Appeals 1946-47; assoc. Minor, Gatley & Drury, Washington, 1947-49 Steptoe & Johnson, Washington, 1949-51, ptnr., 1952-86, o counsel, 1986-98; ret., 1998. BAP examiner D.C. Ct. Appeal com. on admissions to D.C. Bar, 1974-78, D.C. Cir. Jud. Conf. 1983, 85, 86; bd. mgrs. Nat. Conf. Bar Examiners, 1974-7 Served to col. USAAF, 1940-46, 51. Decorated Silver Star, D.F.C.s, 5 Air medals, 3 Presdl. unit citations. Fellow Am. Col Trial Lawyers (emeritus); mem. ABA (past vice chmn. standin com. aviation ins. law), D.C. Bar, Bar Assn. D.C. (past chmn com. on negligence, motor vehicle and compensation law) Barristers Club (v.p. 1964), Chevy Chase Country Club, Met Club (Washington), Hawk's Nest Golf Club of Fla. Episcopalian. Home: Vero Beach, Fla. Died June 6, 2007.

MACKANESS, GEORGE BELLAMY, retired pharmaceutical company executive; b. Sydney, Aug. 20, 1922; came to U.S 1965, naturalized, 1978; s. James Vincent and Eleanor France (Bellamy) M.; m. Gwynneth Patterson, May 5, 1945; 1 sor Miles Philip. M.B. BS with honors, U. Sydney, 1945; D.C.P London U., 1949; MA with honors, U. Oxford, 1949, D.Phil 1953. Demonstrator, tutor in pathology Sir William Dunn Sch Pathology, Oxford, 1949-53; sr. fellow Australian Nat. U. 1954-58, asso. prof., 1958-60, professorial fellow, 1960-63 prof. microbiology U. Adelaide, 1963-65; dir. Trudeau Inst. 1965-76; pres. The Squibb Inst. for Med. Research, Princetor N.J., 1976-88. Clin. prof. dept. medicine Coll. of Medicine an Dentistry of N.J.; adj. prof. pathology N.Y. U. Author articles i field. Recipient Paul Ehrlich-Ludwig Darmstaedter prize, 197 Fellow Royal Soc. London. Home: Charleston, SC. Died Mar. 2007.

MACKOWSKI, JOHN JOSEPH, retired insurance compan executive; b. Westport, Mass., Feb. 1, 1926; s. John J. an Victoria K. (Skript) Mieczkowski; m. Ruth Williams, Feb. 1951; children: Martha, John Matthew, Daniel, Joan. AB, Duk U., 1948; student, Harvard Advanced Mgmt. Program, 1970-7 With Ins. Co. of N.Am., Boston, Phila., Chgo., 1948-51; wit Atlantic Mut. Ins. Co., NYC, 1951-88, chmn., CEO, to 198 Bd. dirs. Transatlantic Holdings, Inc. 1st lt. USMCR, 1943-4 Mem. Sawgrass Club (Ponte Vedra Beach, Fla.), Acoax Country Club (Westport Harbor, Mass.), Spindle Rock Yac Club, Sigma Chi, Beta Lambda. Episcopalian. Home: Pon Vedra Beach, Fla. Died Feb. 24, 2007.

MACLEOD, DONALD SHEA, lawyer, paper company exec tive; b. Buffalo, Mar. 16, 1922; s. Alexander D. and Lorrai (Shea) MacLeod; m. Florence Magnuson, July 26, 1952; chi dren: Laura, Scott. AB magna cum laude, U. Rochester, 194 LLB, Harvard U., 1948. CPA Ill.; bar: N.Y. 1949, Ill. 1950, P 1967. Atty. Richards & Coffey, Buffalo, 1949—50; from asso to ptnr. Carney, Cromwell & Leibman (name now Sidley Austin), Chgo., 1950—59; v.p., sec., gen. counsel Am. Phot copy Equipment Co. (name now APECO Corp.), Evanston, Il 1959—65; v.p., gen. counsel N.Am. Rockwell Corp. (former

Rockwell-Std. Corp.), Pitts., 1966—67, v.p., gen. counsel comml. products group, 1967—68, v.p. adminstrn. comml. products group, 1968—69, exec. v.p. comml. products group, 1969—70, v.p., chief adminstrv. officer comml. products group, 1970—71, corp. v.p. adminstrn., 1971—73, corp. v.p. investor rels., 1973—76, v.p., asst. to chmn. bd. dirs. pub. affairs, 1976—79; cons. Rockwell Internat. Corp., 1979—80; pres., CEO Upson Co., Lockport, NY, 1980—86, also bd. dirs., cons., 1987—88; with Domtar Inc., Lockport, from 1988. Served to lt. USNR, 1942—46. Mem.: Allegheny County Bar Assn., Pa. Bar Assn. Died Aug. 10, 2006.

MACLIN, ERNEST, medical products executive; b. NYC, Jan. 25, 1931; s. Samuel and Dora (Sonsky) M.; m. Edith Samuel, Feb. 18, 1956; children: Alan David, Deborah Ellen, Julie Anne. BME, CCNY, 1952, M Engring., 1969. Registered profl. engr., N.Y., N.J. Engr. Reeves Instrument Corp., NYC, 1952-54, Adrian Wilson Assocs., Nagoya, Japan, 1956-57, Ford Instrument Co., LI, NY, 1957-58, Technicon, Tarrytown, NY, 1968-69; engr., unit head Kearfott divsn. Singer Corp., Little Falls, NJ, 1958-68; v.p. R & D, Electro-Nucleonics Inc., Fairfield, NJ, 1969-90; pres. The Product Devel. Group, Paramus, NJ, from 1990. Bd. dirs. Nat. Com. for Clin. Lab. Stds., Villanova, Pa., 1981-87. Contbr. articles to profl. jours.; patentee various instruments. Capt. USAF, 1954-57; mem. USAFR ret. Fellow ASME; mem. Am. Assn. Clin. Chemistry. Jewish. Died July 3, 2006.

MACMAHON, CHARLES HUTCHINS, JR., architect; b. Fort Seward, Alaska, June 6, 1918; s. Charles H. and Charlotte (Currie) MacM.; m. Ethel Hayward Pearce, Nov. 14, 1942; children— Charles H. III, Charlotte (Mrs. Douglas E. Neumann). Student, Bowdoin Coll., 1936-37, U. Pa., 1937-38; B.Arch., U. Mich., 1942. Dist. mgr. U.S. Gypsum Co., Chgo., 1947-52; gen. sales mgr. Spickelmeier Co., Indpls., 1952-55; with Smith, Tarapata, MacMahon, Inc., Birmingham, Mich., 1956-59; pres. Tarapata-MacMahon-Paulsen, Bloomfield Hills, Mich., 1959-73, cons., from 1973; pres. MacMahon-Cajacob Assos., DeLand, Fla., 1978-92; owner Charles MacMahon Architect, DeLand, Fla., from 1992. Mem. Mich. Bd. Registration of Architects, Engrs. and Surveyors, 1964-68; mem. planning bd. City of DeLand, 1978-84. Works include Central Plaza, Canton, O., Gen. Motors Inst, Flint, Mich., Cloisters of DeLand, Fla., Washtenaw Community Coll, Ann Arbor, Mich. Chmn. bd. trustees Bloomfield Twp. Zoning Bd. Appeals, 1968-69; bd. dirs. Brookside Sch., Cranbrook, 1964-68; trustee Inst. for Advanced Pastoral Studies; mem. historic preservation bd. City of DeLand, 1993—. Lt. USNR, 1942-45. Fellow AIA; mem. Sch. Facilities Council (v.p., dir.), Mich. Soc. Architects (pres. 1962-64), Psi Upsilon. Clubs: Lake Beresford Yacht. Episcopalian. Died Feb. 10, 2006.

MACMASTER, DANIEL MILLER, retired museum official; b. Chgo., Feb. 11, 1913; s. Daniel Howard and Charlotte Louise (Miller) MacM.; m. Sylvia Jane Hill, Feb. 22, 1935; children— Daniel Miller, Jane Irene (Mrs. Robert W. Lightell). Student, Lakeside Press Tng. Sch., 1930-31, U. Chgo., 1931-34; L.H.D., Lincoln Coll., 1970; D.H.L., DePaul U., 1978. Mem. staff Mus. Sci. and Industry, Chgo., 1933—, acting dir., 1950, dir., 1951-72, pres., 1968-78, pres. emeritus, from 1978, life trustee, from 1968. Gen. mgr. Chgo. R.R. Fair, 1948-49 Author: (with others) Exploring the Mysteries of Physics and Chemistry, 1938; book reviewer; contbr. to newspapers, mags., encys. Mem. Homewood (Ill.) Bd. Edn., 1945-49, pres., 1948-49; mem. U. Ill. Citizen' Adv. Com., 1945—; sec. Higher Edn. Commn. Ill., 1955-59; dir. Hyde Park Bank and Trust Co., 1965-86; U.S. State Dept. Specialist to Ireland, Germany, Sweden, 1963; dir. Floating Seminar to Greece, 1960; guest mus. cons. Fed. Republic Germany, 1961, Iran, 1973, 74, 76, Hong Kong, 1978, 89, 90, 91, Singapore, Chili and Peru, 1978, Poland, Czechoslovakia and Hungary, 1979, Mexico, 1980, 81, Saudi Arabia, 1981, 82, 84, Columbia, Ecuador and Bolivia, 1983, Taiwan 1986-90, 92, 94; mem. Nat. 4-H Svc. Com.; hon. dir. Chgo. Chamber Orch. Soc., pres., 1969-70; bd. dirs. Sears Roebuck Found., 1970-73, Internat. Coll. Surgeons Hall of Fame; mem. Lincoln Acad. Ill.; hon. trustee U. Chgo. Cancer Rsch. Found.; life trustee Adler Planetarium; dir. emeritus Monmouth Coll.; bd. govs. Chgo. Heart Assn., vice chmn., 1972-73; founder Scotish Heritage Libr., 1999. Decorated Golden Cross Royal Order Phoenix Greece; Officer's Cross Polonia Restituta Poland; Grand Badge of Honor Austria; Grand Badge of Honor of Burgenland Austria; Golden Badge of Honor Vienna; Officer's Cross 1st class Order of Merit Germany; Officer Order of Merit Luxembourg; Order Cultural Merit Poland; Royal Swedish Order North Star; recipient Patriotic Civilian Service award U.S. Army, St. Andrews Soc. Citizen of Yr. award, 1978 Fellow Assn. Sci. and Tech. Centers; mem. Kappa Sigma. Clubs: Tavern, Quadrangle, Commercial. Home: Flossmoor, Ill. Died Dec. 26, 2005.

MAC NAMARA, DONAL EOIN JOSEPH, criminologist, educator; b. NYC, Aug. 13, 1916; s. Daniel Patrick and Rita F.V. (Chambers) Mac N.; m. Margaret Elizabeth Scott, July 30, 1953 (dec. 1990); 1 child, Brian Scott. BS, Columbia U., 1939, M of Phil., 1948; M of Pub. Adminstrn., NYU, 1946; LLD (hon.), August Vollmer U., 1990. Instr. polit. sci. Rutgers U., New Brunswick, N.J., 1948-49; asst. dir. Delinquency Control Inst. L.A., 1949-50; dir. law enforcement program U. So. Calif., 1949-50; vis. prof. U. Louisville, 1950-71, Fla. State U., Tallahassee, 1958, St. Lawrence U., Canton, N.Y., 1954, 56; chmn. Law Enforcement Insts., NYU, 1950-57; coordinator police sci. programs Bklyn. Coll., 1954-57; with N.Y. Inst. Criminology, NYC, 1950-63, assoc. dean, 1955-56, dean, 1956-63; prof. criminology Center Corrections Tng., CUNY, 1966-67; in charge corrections programs John Jay Coll. Criminal Justice, 1965-85, emeritus disting. prof., 1985; dean doctoral programs August Vollmer U., Orange, Calif., from 1987. Dir. summer session CUNY, Ireland, 1970; Disting. vis. prof. U. Melbourne, Australia, 1981; vis. prof. criminology Bar Ilan U., Ramat Gan, Israel, 1982-83; vis. prof. Calif. State U., Spring 1984, U. N.Mex., 1985, U. Tenn., 1986, Calif. State U., 1987-88, Bar Ilan U., Israel, Spring 1989; mng. ptnr. Flath-MacNamara Assocs., N.Y.C., 1958-64; dir. Crime Show Cons., N.Y.C., Traffic Mgmt. Survey Fund, Inc., N.Y.C.; Eastern regional dir. Character Underwriters, Inc., L.A.; vis. mem. faculty Hunter, Queens, Bklyn. colls., 1952-58; vis. lectr. criminology Brandeis U., Waltham, Mass., 1962; lectr. police adminstrn. SUNY, 1966-67; lectr. penology (CCNY), 1965-67; specialist police, correctional adminstrn. grad. program tng. pub. adminstrn., State of N.Y., Albany, 1951-56; criminol. cons. Am. Express Co., 1962-68; cons., Bergen County, N.J., 1967, N.J. Commn. Civil Disorders, 1967-68; vis. prof. criminology U. Utah, Salt Lake City, 1962; pres. League to Abolish Capital Punishment, 1958-70, chmn. bd., 1959-91; col. a.d.c. to commr. Ky. State Police, 1963; external assessor in police and pub. adminstrn. Republic of Ireland, 1975; vis. prof. Inst. Pub. Adminstrn., Dublin, 1974-75. Author: Problems of Sex Behavior, 1968, Perspectives on Correction, 1971, Corrections: Problems of Punishment and Rehabilitation, 1973, Police: Problems and Prospects, 1974, Criminal Justice, 1976, Sex, Crime and the Law, 1977, Incarceration: The Sociology of Imprisonment, 1978, Crime, Criminals and Corrections, 1981, Deviants: Victims or Victimizers, 1984, Deviance, Denigration and Dominance, 1990, also articles.; Am. editor: Excerpta Criminologica, 1965-85; editor-in-chief: Criminology: An Interdisciplinary Jour., 1975-78; asso. editor: Jour. Corrective Psychiatry; editor: UN Crime Conference: Keynote Document Edit., 1981. Exec. v.p. Real Estate Bd., Bronx, N.Y., 1964-65. Served to maj. AUS, 1942-48. Recipient award of honor Internat. Assn. Women Police, 1960, Herbert A. Bloch award Am. Soc. Criminology, 1967, Bruce Smith award Am. Acad. of Criminal Justice Scis., 1990, Lifetime Achievement in Criminal Justice award Am. Soc. for Pub. Adminstrn., 1991; named to Am. Police Hall Fame, 1996. Fellow AAAS (chmn. sci. criminology sect., mem. council 1957-82), Am. Acad. Criminalistics (presiding); mem. Internat. Police Officers Assn. (life), Am. Soc. Criminology (pres. 1960-64), Assn. Psychiat. Treatment Offenders (program coordinator 1954-58), M.P. Assn., Internat. Criminol. Soc., Am. Assn. Criminologists (hon. life), Edn. Research Assn. (exec. dir. 1965-69), Nat. Police Officers Assn. Am. (research dir. 1963-67), Pi Sigma Alpha. Home: Warwick, NY. Died Oct. 18, 2006.

MACPHERSON, WILLIAM ALBERT, physician; b. Detroit, Mar. 12, 1924; MD, Wayne State U., 1954. Diplomate Am. Bd. Ob-Gyn. Intern Huntington Meml. Hosp., Pasadena, Calif., 1954-55; resident in ob-gyn. Detroit City Hosp., 1955-56. Fellow Am. Coll. Ob-Gyn. Home: Arcadia, Calif. Died May 17, 2007.

MACRURY, KING, management consultant; b. Manchester, NH, Oct. 14, 1915; s. Colin H. and Lauretta C. (Shea) MacR.; 1 son, Colin C. AB, Rollins Coll., 1938; postgrad., St. Anselms Coll., L.I. Coll. Medicine, Princeton. Asst. personnel dir. Lily-Tulip Cup Corp., 1939; asst. dir. market research Ward Baking Co., 1940-41; staff mem. Nat. Indsl. Conf. Bd., 1941-43; cons. indsl. relations and orgn. planning McKinsey & Co., 1946-48; internal cons. Oxford Paper Co., 1949-50; installer, dir. indsl. relations Champion Internat. Co., 1950-51; pvt. practice Rye, NH, 1951—2007. Lectr. Indsl. Edn. Inst., 1962-68, Mgmt. Center, Cambridge, 1968-71, Dun & Bradstreet; extension div. U. N.H.; extension program U. Maine; also U. Bridgeport, extension program U. Conn.; coordinator mgmt. edn. extension div. U. Conn., 1964-68, Philippine Council Mgmt., Econ. Devel. Found. Philippines, Am. Metal Stamping Assn.; condr. mgmt. seminars for Asian Assn. Mgmt. Orgns. C.I.O.S., 1972; Mem. Indsl. Devel. Commn. Andover, 1957-58; manpower com. U.S. Dept. Labor Bus. Adv. Council, 1958-61. Author: Developing Your People Potential; Contbr. numerous articles in field to profl. jours. Served to lt. USNR, 1943-46. Mem. N.H. Dental Soc. (hon.), Smaller Bus. Assn. N.E., Res. Officers Assn. Died Apr. 16, 2007.

MADDEN, EDWARD HARRY, philosopher, retired educator; b. Gary, Ind., May 18, 1925; s. Harry Albert and Amelia Dorothy (Schepper) M.; m. Marian Sue Canaday, Sept. 15, 1946; children: Kerry Arthur, Dennis William. AB, Oberlin Coll., 1946, A.M., 1947; PhD, U. Iowa, 1950. Prof. philosophy U. Conn., 1950-59, San Jose State Coll., 1959-64, SUNY, Buffalo, 1964-80, prof. emeritus, 1980, U. Ky., 1982-95, ret., 1995. Vis. prof. Brown U., 1954-55, Amherst Coll., 1962, U. Toronto, 1967, Am. U. Beirut, Lebanon, 1969-70; sr. research fellow Linacre Coll., Oxford U., 1978, Inst. Advanced Study, Princeton, 1980-81, The John Dewey Summer Inst., 2002. Author: Philosophical Problems of Psychology, 1962, Chauncey Wright and the Foundations of Pragmatism, 1963, Evil and the Concept of God, 1968, Civil Disobedience and Moral Law, 1968, The Structure of Scientific Thought, 1960, Causal Powers, 1975, Causing, Perceiving and Believing, 1975, Freedom and Grace, 1982; co-author, editor: Theories of Scientific Method, 1960, Philosophical Perspectives on Punishment, 1968, The Idea of God, 1968; gen. editor: Harvard U. Press Source Books in History Sci.; mem. editl. bd.: The Works of William James, Thoreau Quar., History of Philosophy Quar., Philosophy of Sci., 1960-76; mem. adv. bd.: A Critical Edition of the Correspondence of William James (Am. Coun. Learned Socs.). Served with USNR, 1943-45. Recipient Am. Philos. Soc. research grant, 1961, Fulbright-Hays award, 1969-70, Herbert W. Schneider award Soc. for Advancement Am. Philosophy, 1991. Fellow Asa Mahan Soc.; mem. C.S. Peirce Soc. (pres. 1962-63, sec.-treas., editl. bd. Transactions of Soc.), Am. Coun. Learned Socs. (selection com.), Am. Philos. Assn. (co-chmn. com. publs. 1960-77), Phi Kappa Phi. Home: White River Junction, Vt. Died Nov. 25, 2006.

MADDEN, FRANK AUGUSTUS, JR., lawyer, corporation executive; b. Kansas City, Mo., Dec. 7, 1924; s. Frank Augustus and Helen (Gascon) M.; m. Joan D. Mayne, June 19, 1954; children: Deborah, Pamela, Stephen. BSS, Georgetown U., 1949; JD, N.Y. Law Sch., 1956. Bar: N.Y., U.S. Dist. Ct. (so. and ea. dists.) N.Y., U.S. Supreme Ct.; Lic. real estate broker, N.Y., Conn., N.J., N.C. Spl. agt. FBI, Washington, Chgo., Phila., NYC, 1950-58; atty., mgr. real estate dept. Union Carbide Corp., 1958-62; chief exec. officer Homequity, Inc., Wilton, Conn., 1962-64; chmn., chief exec. officer Holiday Homes Internat., Greenwich, Conn., 1974-78, Executrans, Inc., Northbrook, Ill., 1964-78, Previews, Inc., 1973-78, Exec-Van Systems, Inc., 1972-78; pres. ChemExec. Relocation Systems, Inc., from 1980. Fundraiser Salisbury (Conn.) Sch., Georgetown U.; trustee Camp Sloane YMCA Served with U.S. Army, 1943-45. Mem. Am., Fed. bar assns., Bar Assn. City N.Y., Soc. Former Spl. Agts. FBI, Georgetown Alumni Assn., Nat. Assn. Real Estate Brokers., Bekins Consumer Conf. Bd. Clubs: Woodway Country (Darien, Conn.); Belle Haven (Greenwich). Home: New Canaan, Conn. Died Jan. 11, 2006.

MADDEN, SISTER LORETTO ANNE, nun, administrator; b. Denver, Aug. 21, 1922; d. Edward Joseph and Mary Agnes (Kelly) M. AB, Loretto Heights Coll., 1943; MA, Cath. U. Am., 1955, PhD, 1960. Joined Sisters of Loretto, Roman Cath. Ch., 1946. Tchr. Immaculate Conception High Sch., Las Vegas, N.Mex., 1946-54; from instr. to prof. Loretto Heights Coll., Denver, 1954-73; exec. dir. Colo. Cath. Conf., Denver, from 1974. Chmn. Colo. Social Legis. Com., Denver, 1974-80, legis. liaison, 1984—; chair Caring Connection/Providers' Adv. Com., 1983—; chair Colo. Health Care Campaign, 1989-90, vice chair, 1990-91. Recipient St. Vincent de Paul award St. Thomas Theol. Sem., 1982, Martin Luther King, Jr. Humanitarian award, 1986, Child Health and Welfare award Colo. chpt. Am. Acad. Pediatrics, 1986, Good Citizenship award Colo. Common Cause, 1986, Disting. Svc. award Colo. Civil Rights Commn., 1987, Tribute for Caring award Hospice of Peace, 1988, Florence Sabin award Colo. Pub. Health Assn., 1989; Bonfils scholar Denver Post, 1939, J.K. Mullen scholar, 1955. Home: Nerinx, Ky. Died Oct. 1, 2006.

MADDOX, ROBERT LYTTON, lawyer; b. Middlesboro, Ky., May 18, 1924; s. Robert Lytton and Sybil (Sipher) M.; m. Inez Bentley Pryor, Nov. 23, 1955; children: William Granville, Julie Thornton, Robert Lytton III. AB, Harvard U., 1947, LLB, 1950. Bar: Ky. 1950, U.S. Dist. Ct. (ea. dist.) Ky. 1972, U.S. Dist. Ct. (we. dist.) 1979, U.S. Ct. Appeals (6th cir.) 1974. Assoc. Wyatt, Grafton & Sloss, Louisville, 1950-58, ptnr., 1958-80, Wyatt, Tarrant & Combs, from 1980. Bd. dirs. Whip-Mix Corp., Louisville, Nugent Sand Corp., Louisville, Ky. Tax-Free Income Fund, Lexington, Orr Safety Corp., Louisville. Trustee/treas. Louisville Collegiate Sch., 1976-83, Lees Coll., Jackson, Ky., 1974-86; trustee/pres. Estate Planning Coun., Louisville, 1984-88. With U.S. Army, 1943-45. Decorated Bronze Star medal. Mem. Louisville Country Club, Harmony Landing Country Club, Jefferson Club, Wynn-Stay Club, Rotary. Democrat. Presbyterian. Avocations: golf, bicycling, investing. Died Sept. 18, 2006.

MAECHLING, CHARLES, JR., lawyer, educator, diplomat, writer; b. NYC, Apr. 18, 1920; s. Charles and Eugenie H. M.; m. Janet Leighton, Sept. 2, 1944; children: Philip Leighton and Eugenie Elisabeth (Mrs. David Buchan). Attended, Birch Wathen Sch., NYC, 1924-37; BA with honors, Yale U., 1941; JD, U. Va., 1949. Bar: N.Y. 1949, D.C. 1957. Assoc. Sullivan & Cromwell, NYC, 1949-51; atty. Office Sec. Air Force, 1951-52; counsel Electronics Industries Assn., Washington, 1953-56; founding ptnr. Shaw, Pittman, Washington; dir. for internal def. Dept. State, Washington, 1961-63; staff dir. cabinet level spl. group and spl. asst. to undersec. Averell Harriman, 1963-66; dep. and gen. counsel NSF, 1966-71, spl. asst. to dir., 1972-74; prof. law U. Va., 1974-76; spl. counsel N.Y. law firms, 1976-81; sr. assoc. Carnegie Endowment for Internat. Peace, 1981-85; vis. fellow, mem. law faculty Cambridge U. (Wolfson Coll.), Eng., 1985-88; guest scholar internat. law Brookings Inst., Washington, 1989-93; internat. arbitrator and cons., from 1993. Legal adviser internat. matters NAS, 1970-83, mem. ocean policy com.; mem. law-of-sea and other adv. coms. Dept. State; counsel CIA Propreitaries, 1959-98; adj. prof. Georgetown Univ. Law Sch., Sch. Internat. Svc., Am. U.; mem. adv. bd. Internat. Peace Acad.; lectr. U.S. Def. Schs., also Hague Acad. Internat. Law; arbitrator complex internat. cases Am. Arbitration Assn. Editor-in-chief Va. Law Rev., 1948-49; contbr. articles to N.Y. Times, Internat. Herald Tribune, Boston Globe, L.A. Times, Miami Herald, profl. and lit. jours. Bd. dirs. Coun. for Ocean Law, Washington Inst. Fgn. Affairs; mem. U.S. Com. for IIASA, adv. bd.; outside counsel to CIA, 1957-60. From ensign to lt. comdr. USNR, 1941-47, at sea and secretariat Joint Chiefs Staff, 1943-44, del. 1943 Cairo Conf., UN Law of Sea Conf., 1971-82; asst. naval attache Peru, 1945-47. Mem.: ABA (Ross Essay award 1969), Am. Soc. Internat. Law, Yale Club (NYC), Cosmos Club (Washington), City Tavern Club (Washington). Avocation: European languages. Home: Washington, DC. Died June 23, 2007.

MAESTRONE, FRANK EUSEBIO, diplomat; b. Springfield, Mass., Dec. 20, 1922; s. John Battista and Margaret Carlotta (Villanova) M.; m. Jo Colwell, Jan. 20, 1951; childen: Mark, Anne. BA, Yale U., 1943; grad., Naval War Coll., 1963. With Fgn. Svc., Dept. State, 1948-84; assigned to Vienna and Salzburg, Austria, 1948, 1954, Hamburg, Germany, 1949, Khorramshahr, Iran, 1960; with NATO, Paris, 1963, dep. asst. sec. gen. Brussels, 1968—71; counselor of embassy for polit. affairs Am. Embassy, Manila, 1971-73; Dept. State adviser to pres. Naval War Coll., 1973; min.-counselor Am. Embassy, Cairo, 1974, amb. to Kuwait, 1976-79; diplomat-in-residence U. Calif., San Diego, 1979; spl. rep. of Pres., dir. U.S. Sinai Support Mission, 1980; exec. dir. World Affairs Coun., San Diego, 1984-86; adj. prof. internat. rels., amb.-in-residence U.S. Internat. U., San Diego, 1986-90. Mem. bd. San Diego World Affairs Coun., 2005. With AUS, 1943-46. Decorated chevalier du Merite Agricole (France). Mem. Internat. Inst. Strategic Studies. Died May 22, 2007.

MAGINNIS, GORDON HOBSON, real estate executive, investor; b. New Orleans, Sept. 21, 1928; s. Donald Ambrose and Ruth (Hobson) M. Student U. of South, Sewanee, Tenn., 1947-48, U. Calif.-Berkeley, 1952-54. Co-owner McDougall's Travel Service, Inc., New Orleans, 1961-72; with Parrish Travel Ctr., Ltd., New Orleans, 1973-83; realtor Martha Ann Samuel, Inc., New Orleans, 1980—. Vestryman St. Anna's Episcopal Ch. Served with USN, 1948-52. Mem. Nat. Assn. Realtors, Orleans Parish Bd. Realtors, New Orleans Mus. Art, La. Landmarks Soc., Friends of Cabildo, Preservation Resource Ctr., Nat. Trust for Hist. Preservation, Patio Planters. Republican. Home: New Orleans, La. Died July 15, 2007.

MAGNUSON, NORRIS ALDEN, librarian, history educator; b. Midale, Saskatchewan, Can., June 15, 1932; s. George August and Esther Lydia (Eliason) M.; m. Beverly Sue Carlson, Aug.

17, 1956; children: Douglas, Timothy, Kenneth, Daniel. BA, Bethel Coll., 1954; BD, Bethel Sem., 1958; MA, U. Minn., 1961, PhD, 1968. Instr., asst. libr. Bethel Theol. Sem., St. Paul, 1959-65, asst. prof., asst. libr., 1965-68, assoc. prof., assoc. libr., 1968-72, prof., head libr., 1972-97; archivist Bethel Sem. and Bapt. Gen. Conf., from 1993. Chair hist. com. Bapt. Gen. Conf., Arlington Heights, Ill., 1974—; mem. Conf. on Faith and History. Author: Salvation in the Slums, 1977, 2d edit., 1990, Missionsskolan: The History, 1982; editor: Proclaim the Good News, 1986; author: (with others) American Evangelicalism, 1990, 2d edit., 1996. Mem. Salem Bapt. Ch., chairperson, 1972-73. U. Minn. scholar, 1961-63; Inst. for Advanced Christian Studies fellow, 1968-69. Mem. Am. Theol. Libr. Assn., Minn. Theol. Libr. Assn. (pres. 1974-75, 79-80, 84-85, 88-89). Avocations: tennis, handball, racquetball, travel. Home: Saint Paul, Minn. Died Nov. 8, 2006.

MAGOVERN, JAMES ANTHONY, thoracic surgeon; b. San Antonio, June 8, 1954; MD, U. Pitts., 1980. Diplomate Am. Bd. Thoracic Surgery, Am. Bd. Surgery. Intern Johns Hopkins, Balt., 1980-81, resident in surgery, 1981-82, Pa. State U. Coll. Medicine, Hershey, 1982-89; fellow in rsch. cardiothoracic surgery Milton S. Hershey Med. Ctr., 1985-87; with Allegheny Gen. Hosp., Pitts. Prof. surgery Drexel U. Sch. Med. Mem. Assn. Acad. Surgery, Am. Coll. Cardiology, Am. Coll. Surgeons, Am. Heart Assn., Soc. Thoracic Surgery, Am. Assn. Thoracic Surgery. Died Mar. 17, 2007.

MAGRATH, LAWRENCE KAY, biology educator; b. Garnett, Kans., Mar. 28, 1943; s. Charles Jerome and Ruth (Richardson) M. BS in Edn., Emporia State U., 1967, MS, 1969; PhD, U. Kans., 1973. Asst. instr. biology U. Kans., Lawrence, 1970-72; instr. botany, acting curator herbarium Okla. State U., Stillwater, 1972; prof. biology, curator herbarium U. Sci. and Arts Okla., Chickasha, 1972—; sec., treas. bd. trustees Flora Okla. Inc., Oklahoma City, 1983—. Contbr. articles to profl. jours. Mem. Okla. Rep. Dist. Com., 1983-84, treas. dist. 4, 1984—; mem. Okla. Rep. State Com., 1985—; treas. Grady County Rep. Com., Chickasha, 1984-88. Kans. Acad. Sci. grantee, 1969; U. Sci. and Arts Okla. grantee, 1982, 83. Mem. Internat. Assn. Plant Taxonomists, Am. Soc. Plant Taxonomists, Kans. Acad. Sci., Am. Inst. Biol. Sci., Okla. Native Plant Soc. (bd. dirs. 1987—), Higher Edn. Alumni Council Okla., Bot. Soc. Am., Calif. Bot. Soc., New Eng. Bot Club, Southwestern Assn. Naturalists, Am. Orchid Soc. (chmn. conservation com. S.W. region), Asociacion Mexicana de Orquideologia A.C., Okla. Soc. Med. Tech. Educators, Okla. Acad. Sci. (exec. council 1982-84, rec. sec. 1984), Okla. Orchid Soc. (v.p. Oklahoma City 1983-85), Sigma Xi, Beta Beta Beta, Kappa Delta Pi (v.p. Iota chpt. 1967, faculty sponsor Pi Omega chpt. 1985). Republican. Avocations: book collecting; gardening; landscaping; raising orchids. Home: Chickasha, Okla. Died Feb. 24, 2007.

MAHL, GEORGE FRANKLIN, retired psychologist, educator; b. Akron, Ohio, Nov. 27, 1917; s. Floyd Alexander and Margaret (Strecker) M.; m. Martha Jane Fenn, Jan. 10, 1944; 1 dau., Barbara Jessica. A. B., Oberlin Coll., 1939, MA, 1941; PhD, Yale U., 1948; certificate, Western New Eng. Inst. Psychoanalysis, 1962. Asst. psychology Oberlin Coll., 1939-41; rsch. asst. in psychology Yale U., New Haven, 1941-42, mem. faculty, from 1947, prof. psychiatry and psychology, 1964-88, prof. emeritus, from 1988; tchr. Western New Eng. Inst. Psychoanalysis, 1961-85, pres., 1972-74; ret., 1988. Served to 1st lt. AUS, 1942-46. Fellow AAAS, APA; mem. Ea. Psychol. Assn., Western New Eng. Inst. Psychoanalysis, Western New Eng. Psychoanalytic Soc., Internat. Psychoanalytical Assn., Inst. Psychoanalytic Tng. and Rsch. (N.Y.). Home: North Haven, Conn. Died Mar. 11, 2006.

MAHOOD, WILLIAM H., gastroenterologist; b. Charleston, W.Va., July 28, 1934; m. Perry Mahood; 1 child, Tessa. BA, W.Va. U.; MD, Jefferson Med. Coll., 1960. Diplomate Am. Bd. Internal Medicine, Am. Bd. Gastroenterology. Intern Jefferson Hosp., Phila., 1960-61, resident in internal medicine, 1961-63; resident in gastroenterology Grad. Hosp. Pa., Phila., 1963-64; chief gastroenterology Abington Meml. Hosp., Pa.; pvt. practice. Hosp. staff Holy Redeemer Hosp., Meadowbrook, Pa.; co-chair task force on health Dept. of Health; pres. Digestive Disease Nat. Coalition, Washington. Fellow ACP, Am. Coll. Gastroenterology, Am. Gastroenterol. Assn., Am. Soc. of Gastrointestinal Endoscopy, Am. Soc. Internal Medicine; mem. AMA (bd. trustees 1996, mem. coun. med. svc. 1991, vice chair coun. 1995, mem. task force on credentialing and privileges), Pa. Med. Soc. (com. on health care reform and access, chair coun. med. econs.), Am. Soc. of Gastrointestinal Endoscopy (governing bd.), Pa. Soc. of Gastroenterology (pres.), Montgomery County Med. Soc. (bd. dirs.). Home: Jenkintown, Pa. Died Apr. 22, 2007.

MAI, WILLIAM FREDERICK, plant nematologist, educator; b. Greenwood, Del., July 23, 1916; s. William Frederick and Laurana (Owens) M.; m. Barbara Lee Morrell, June 2, 1941; children: Virginia Mai Abrams, William Howard Mai, Eliabeth Hardy Mai. BS, U. Del., 1939; PhD, Cornell U., 1945. Asst. prof. Cornell U., Ithaca, N.Y., 1946-49, assoc. prof., 1949-52, prof., 1952-81, Liberty Hyde prof. plant pathology, 1981-83, prof. emeritus, from 1983. Cons. Nat. Acad. Scis., Internat. Potato Ctr., Brands Co., AID. Author (with H.H. Lyon), Pictoral Key to Genera of Plant Parasitic Nemtodes, 1960, 5th edit. 1993, Plant Parasitic Nematodes, 1971; editor: Control of Plant Parasitic Nematodes, 1968. Coach Little League Baseball and Football, Ithaca, 1955—60; chmn. Community Orgn., 1960—65. Recipient award of distinction Internat. Plant Protection Conf., 1979; Paul Harris fellow Rotary Found., 1997. Fellow Am. Phytopath. Soc. (pres. Northeastern div. 1968-69 award of merit Northeastern div); mem. AAAS, Soc. Nematologists (pres. 1969 hon. life), Helminthological Soc. Washington, Soc. European Nematologists, Potato Assn. Am. Lodges: Rotary. Home: Ithaca, NY. Died Aug. 15, 2007.

MAICKEL, ROGER PHILIP, pharmacologist, educator; b. Floral Park, NY, Sept. 8, 1933; s. Philip Vincent and Margaret Mary (Rose) M.; m. Lois Louise Pivonka, Sept. 8, 1956; children: Nancy Ellen Maickel Ward, Carolyn Sue Maickel Anderson. BS, Manhattan Coll., 1954; postgrad., Poly. Inst. Bklyn., 1954-55; MS, Georgetown U., 1957, PhD, 1960. Biochemist Nat. Heart Inst., Bethesda, Md., 1955-65; asso. prof. pharmacology Ind. U., 1965-69, prof., from 1969, head sect. pharmacology med. scis. program, 1971-77; prof. pharmacology and toxicology, head dept. Sch. Pharmacy and Pharmacal Scis. Purdue U., West Lafayette, Ind., 1977-83; dir. lab. animal program Purdue U., West Lafayette, 1988-98, emeritus prof., from 1999; acting v.p. product acquisition and devel. BetaMED Pharms., Inc., Indpls., 1983-84. Adv. editor: Pergamon Press, 1970-88; adv. editorial bd.: Neuropharmacology, 1974-88. Bd. dirs. TEAMS, Inc., 1981-87, Am. Coun. on Sci. and Health, 1993-2000; trustee AAALAC, 1992—. Recipient Alumni award in medicine Manhattan Coll., 1972 Fellow: AAAS, Collegium Internat. de Neuro-Psychopharmacologicum, Royal Soc. Chemistry, Am. Coll. Neuropsychopharmacology, Am. Inst. Chemists (bd. dirs. 1989—92, from 2001, pres.-elect 1992—94, pres. 1994—96, chmn. 1996—98); mem.: ASTM, Soc. Toxicology, Soc. Neurosci., N.Y. Acad. Scis., Internat. Soc. Psychoneuroendocrinology, Internat. Assn. Chiefs Police, Soc. Forensic Toxicologists, Am. Soc. Clin. Pharmacology and Therapeutics, Am. Soc. Pharmacology and Exptl. Therapeutics, Am. Chem. Soc., Rho Chi, Sigma Xi. Home: Lafayette, Ind. Died Dec. 26, 2006.

MAIER, JACK C., food products executive; m. Blanche C. Maier. Chmn. Frisch's Restaurants, Inc., Cin. Died Feb. 2, 2005.

MAIER, ROBERT HAWTHORNE, biology educator; b. NYC, Oct. 26, 1927; s. Ernest Henry and Clara Louise M.; m. Jane Hiob, Aug. 31, 1952; children: Pamela, David, Daniel. BS, U. Miami, 1951; MS, U. Ill., 1952, PhD, 1954. Asst. dean Grad. Coll., U. Ariz., 1966-67; asst. chancellor for instrn. and research U. Wis., Green Bay, 1967-69, vice chancellor and dep. chancellor, prof., 1969-75, prof. sci. and environ. change, public and environ. adminstrn., 1975-79; vice chancellor acad. affairs East Carolina U., Greenville, N.C., 1979-83, prof. exptl. surgery, biology, polit. sci., 1983-98, dir. Trace Element Ctr., Sch. Medicine, 1984-98, adj. prof. physics, 1996-98, prof. emeritus biology, polit. sci. and surgrey, from 1998. Pres., chmn. Nat. Investment Advisors, Inc., 1984—; mem. coun. biotech. U. N.C.; reviewer NC Tech. Devel. Authority, 1989-98, NRC, 1990-98. Contbr. articles to profl. jours. Bd. dirs. Lakeland chpt. ARC, 1978-79, Children's Svcs. Ea. N.C., 1987-94, 98—, fin. advisor, 1995—; mem. Edn. Task Force, City of Green Bay, 1977-78, N.C. State Panel Advancement of Women in Adminstrn., 1981-84, Gov.'s Commn. on Future of N.C., 1981-84; treas. Ronald McDonald House, 1987-94, 97—; mem. Vision Task Force, Global Transpark Devel. Commn., Kinston, N.C., 1996-98; bd. dirs. Alexander Performing Arts Series, 1996-99. With U.S. Army, 1954-56. Fellow AAAS, Am. Inst. Chemists, Am. Soc. Agronomy, Soil Sci. Soc. Am.; mem. Am. Chem. Soc., Am. Inst. Biol. Scis. Presbyterian. Home: De Pere, Wis. Died Oct. 24, 2005.

MAILER, NORMAN KINGSLEY, writer, playwright, film director; b. Long Branch, NJ, Jan. 31, 1923; s. Issac Barnett and Fanny (Schneider) M.; m. Beatrice Silverman, 1944 (div. 1952); 1 dau., Susan; m. Adele Morales, 1954 (div. 1962); children: Danielle, Elizabeth; m. Jeanne Campbell, 1962 (div. 1963); 1 dau., Kate; m. Beverly Bentley, 1963 (div. 1980); children: Michael, Steven; m. Carol Stevens, 1980 (div. 1980); 1 dau., Maggie; m. Norris Church, 1980; 1 son, John Buffalo. SB cum laude, Harvard U., 1943; postgrad., Sorbonne, Paris, France, 1947-48. Columnist Village Voice, 1946, Commentary, 1962-63, Esquire, 1962-63; contbg. editor Dissent, 1953-69; co-founding editor Village Voice, 1955. Author: No Percentage, 1941, The Naked and the Dead, 1948, Barbary Shore, 1951, The Deer Park, 1955, The White Negro: Superficial Reflections on the Hipster, 1957, Advertisements for Myself, 1959, Deaths for the Ladies and Other Disasters, 1962, The Presidential Papers, 1963, An American Dream, 1965, Cannibals and Christians, 1966, Why Are We in Vietnam?: A Novel, 1967 (Nat. Book award nomination 1967), The Short Fiction of Norman Mailer, 1967, The Bullfight, 1967, The Armies of the Night: History as a Novel, The Novel as History, 1968 (Pulitzer prize for non-fiction 1969, Nat. Book award, 1969 George Polk award 1969), Miami and the Siege of Chicago: An Informal History of the Republican and Democratic Conventions of 1968, 1968, The Idol and the Octopus, 1968, Of a Fire On The Moon, 1970, King of the Hill, 1971, The Prisoner of Sex, 1971, The Long Patrol, 1971, Existential Errands, 1972, St. George and the Godfather, 1972, Marilyn, 1973, The Faith of Graffiti, 1974, The Fight, 1975, Some Honorable Men, 1975, Genius and Lust, 1976, A Transit to Narcissus, 1978, The Executioner's Song, 1979 (Pulitzer Prize for fiction 1980, Nat. Book Critics Circle award nomination 1979, Am. Book award nomination 1980), Of a Small and Modest Malignancy, Wicked and Bristling with Dots, 1980, Of Women and Their Elegance, 1980, Pieces and Pontifications, 1982, Ancient Evenings, 1983, Tough Guys Don't Dance, 1984, The Last Night, 1984, Harlot's Ghost, 1991, How the Wimp Won the War, 1991, Oswald's Tale: An American Mystery, 1995, Portrait of Picasso as a Young Man, 1995, The Gospel According to the Son, 1997, The Spooky Art: Thoughts on Writing, 2003, The Castle in the Forest, 2007; co-author: (with John Buffalo Mailer) The Big Empty, 2005, (with Michael Lennon) On God: An Uncommon Conversation, 2007; author: (plays) The Deer Park: A Play, 1967, Strawhead, 1985; editor: Genius and Lust: A Journey Through the Major Writings of Henry Miller, 1976; screenwriter: (films) The Executioner's Song, 1982 (Emmy award nomination outstanding adapted screenplay 1983); screenwriter, prodr., dir., actor: (films) Wild 90, 1967, Maidstone: A Mystery, 1971; screenwriter, prodr.: (films) Beyond the Law, 1968; screenwriter, dir.: (films) Tough Guys Don't Dance, 1987; actor: (films) Ragtime, 1981. Served with AUS, 1944-46. Recipient Edward MacDowell medal MacDowell Colony, 1973, Nat. Arts Club Gold medal, 1976, Emerson-Thoreau Medal for lifetime of literary achievement, 1989, Golden Plate award, Acad. Achievement, 2004, Medal for Disting. Contbn. to Am. letters, Nat. Book Found. 2005; Legion of Honor France, 2006; Nat. Inst. and Am. Acad. grantee, 1960; Pappas fellow U. Pa., 1983. Mem. PEN Am. Ctr. (pres. 1984-86), Nat. Inst. Arts and Letters. Died Nov. 10, 2007.*

MAILMAN, VIRGINIA SHEVLIN ADDISON (MRS. NORTON W. MAILMAN), public relations executive; b. Bronxville, N.Y., Apr. 27, 1929; d. Matthew Joseph and Virginia Boyd (McMillan) Shevlin; student U. Colo., 1947-49; B.A., Stanford, m. Norton W. Mailman, June 17, 1965; children—Bruce Addison, Matthew Addison, Christopher. Recruiter with industry A.R.C. Blood Program, Los Angeles, 1951-52; reporter Life mag., N.Y.C., 1952-61; asso. editor, asst. New York Bur. chief Show Bus. Illustrated, 1961-62; formed pub. relations firm Addison, Goldstein & Walsh, Inc., N.Y.C., 1962, v.p., 1962-76; formed Syndicated Airtime, producer 5 minute radio series, 1970; producer James Beard Cook-Along cassette series, 1973; patient relations rep. N. Shore Univ. Hosp., 1977—. Bd. dirs. N.Y. affiliate Nat. Council Alcoholism, 1978—. Club: Piping Rock (Locust Valley, N.Y.). Home: New York, NY. Died May 19, 2007.

MAKRIANES, JAMES KONSTANTIN, JR., management consultant; b. Springfield, Mass., Jan. 15, 1925; s. James K. and Clara (Allen) M.; m. Judith Alden Erdmann, Sept. 30, 1960; children— Mary, James, Susan, Jane, Mahady. BA, Amherst Coll., 1949. V.p., gen. mgr. Nat. Paper Box Co. and Nat. Games, Inc., Springfield, 1949-59; merchandising and acct. exec. Young & Rubicam, Inc., NYC, 1959-63, v.p., acct. supr., 1963-67, sr. v.p., mgmt. supr., 1963-73, exec. v.p., dir., 1973-78; sr. v.p., dir. Haley Assocs., Inc., NYC, 1978-80, pres., from 1980, chief exec. officer, 1985-89; ptnr., dir. Ward & Howell Internat., Inc., NYC, 1989-95; dir. Webb Johnson Assocs., NYC, from 1995. Trustee Boys' Club N.Y., 1976—. With USNR, 1943-46. Mem. Maidstone Club, Racquet and Tennis Club, Links. Home: New York, NY. Died Feb. 10, 2006.

MALAKOFF, JAMES LEONARD, management information executive; b. Phila., June 20, 1933; s. John and Ida Vera (Partman) M.; m. Anne Bronstein Frisch, June 26, 1955; children: Randi Ellen, John Seymour. B in Aerospace Engring., Rensselaer Poly. Inst., 1954, MS, 1955. Structural methods specialist Grumman Aircraft, Bethpage, N.Y., 1955-62; mem. tech. staff Northrop Corp., Hawthorne, Calif., 1962-65; chief, math. analyst Beckman Instruments, Inc., Fullerton, Calif., 1965-68, dir. data processing, 1968-82, v.p. data processing, 1982-85, v.p., mgmt. info., 1985-93, cons. to mgmt., from 1993. Bd. dirs. Little Co. Mary Health Svcs., Little Co. Mary Hosp., San Pedro (Calif.) Peninsula Hosp., Bay Harbor Hosp., Calif.; vis. prof. computer sci. Calif. State U., Fullerton, 1981-82, mem. indsl. adv. coun. Sch. Engring. and Computer Sci. Fellow AIAA (assoc.); mem. IEEE (computer group), U.S. Council Internat. Bus. (bus. and industry adv. com., West Coast com. Internat. Info. and Telecommunications Policy), Assn. Computing Machinery, Data Processing Mgmt. Assn. Home: Palos Verdes Peninsula, Calif. Died July 24, 2007.

MALASANOS, LOIS JULANNE FOSSE, nursing educator; b. LaPorte City, Iowa, Sept. 1, 1928; d. Lewis Reginald and Henrietta Marie Fosse; widowed; 1 child, Toree. BSN, U. Tex., 1948; BA in Gen. Sci., U. Iowa, 1952; MA in Nursing Edn., U. Chgo., 1959; PhD in Physiology, U. Ill., 1973. Assoc. dir. nursing U. Iowa Hosps., Iowa City, 1950-51, staff charge nurse, 1951; instr. operating room Sch. Nursing, Michael Reese Hosp., Chgo., 1951-58; charge nurse, med.-surg. U. Chgo., Billings Hosp., 1952-59; pvt. duty nurse Ill., 1959-63; charge nurse, maternal-infant nursing Weiss Meml. Hosp., Chgo., 1963-66; asst. prof. Loyola U., Chgo., 1966-69; teaching asst. in physiology U. Ill., Chgo., 1969-73, assoc. prof., assoc. head gen. nursing dept. Coll. Nursing, 1973-76, prof., assoc. head gen. nursing dept., 1976-80; prof., dean Coll. Nursing U. Fla., Gainesville, 1980-95, Disting. Svc. prof., 1995—2003. Instr. anatomy and physiology Cook County Hosp., Chgo., 1973; lectr. endocrinology Chgo. Coll. Osteopathic Medicine, 1973-80; active Pres. Clinton's Task Force on Health Care, 1993; cons. Am. Assn. Med. Colls., 1977-78, Am. Heart Assn., 1977-94, Am. Jour. Nursing, 1978-79, Gainesville (Fla.) Vets. Ctr. 1980-95, Lake Butler Receiving Ctr., 1980—; chair Deans and Dirs. of Fla. Colls. Nursing, 1981-89; chair edn. com. State Bd. Nursing, 1983-87, chair probable course com., 1984—; vis. prof. Dokuz Eylul U., Izmir, Turkey, 1995-96; cons., presenter in field. Co-author, editor: Manual of Medical Surgical Nursing, 1983, Translating Comitment to Reality, 1986, Health Assessment, 1977 (Am. Jour. Nursing Book of Yr. award 1977), 4th edit., 1989; editor: Vital Signs, 1981-90, Fla. Cancer Nursing News, 1983-84; co-editor: Fla. Nursing Rev., 1986-90; mem. editl. rev. bd. Image, 1980-96; editl. cons. Nursing, 1982-94; manuscript referee Rsch. in Nursing and Health, 1980-94, Jour. Profl. Nursing, 1985-94, Turkish Jour. Nurse Rshc.; chairperson adv. com. Nursing Outlook, 1986-91, Peer Rev., 1986-94; contbr. more than 100 articles, revs. to profl. jours. Nursing com., scholarship com. and rsch. rev. com. Am. Cancer Soc. Tampa, Fla., 1980-94. Recipient Bronze medal Fla. Heart Assn., 1986, Silver medal Fla. Heart Assn., 1989, 93; named Disting. Alumnus U. Tex. Med. Br., 1985; named to Disting. Faculty, Albany State U., 1988, Hall of Fame, U. Tex. Med. Br., 1992; NEH fellow, 1981; Fulbright awardee to Turkey, 1995-96, 2001-02. Mem. ANA (mem. coun. nurse rschrs.), AACN, AAAS, AAUP, Am. Acad. Nursing (mem. pub. com. 1986-89), Am. Assn. Higher Edn., Am. Assn. Colls. Nursing, Fla. Nurses Assn. (mem. dist. 10), N.Y. Acad. Sci., Fla. League Nursing, Nat. League Nursing (chair, mem. coun. baccalaureate and higher degree program, Dirs. award 1995, site visitor for program rev. 1980—, bd. rev. for accreditation 1993-2002 Outstanding Leadership in Nursing Edn. award 2002), Fla. State Bd. Nursing (probable cause com.), So. Regional Edn. Bd., Sigma Xi, Sigma Theta Tau (Outstanding Leadership award 2003), Phi Kappa Phi (pres. 1987-88). Died Apr. 23, 2007.

MALCOLM, DANIEL DWAYNE, industrial educator; b. Herrin, Ill., Oct. 14, 1942; s. Wayne Edward and Geraldine May (Chitty) M.; m. Nancy Aileen Jones, Aug. 21, 1965; 1 dau., Cara Dyanne. B.S. in Indsl. Arts, Ill. State U., 1965, M.S., 1968; postgrad., 1968—. Cert. vocat. tchr., Ill. Tchr. auto mechanics Irving Crown High Sch., Carpentersville, Ind., 1965-66; tchr. power mechanics Richwoods High Sch., Peoria, Ill., 1966-68; coordinator indsl. edn. Bloomington (Ill.) Area Vocat. Ctr. 1968—; mem. Ill. Indsl. Edn. Assn. Bd., 1971-79. Mem. Am.

Vocat. Assn., Ill. Vocat. Assn., Ill. Indsl. Edn. Assn., Ill. Coordinators Assn., Vocat. Indsl. Clubs Am., Kappa Delta Pi. United Methodist. Died Mar. 22, 2007.

MALECKI, ALFRED, business magazine publisher; b. Leipzig, Germany, May 13, 1921; came to U.S., 1953; s. Gustav David and Dora Leah (Schauber) M.; m. Zenia Berkon, Mar. 6, 1948; 1 child, Sophie. Commissary mgr. M. Hochschild S.A., Oruro, Bolivia, 1941-43; sec. Cia. Boliviana De Fomento, Cochabamba, 1944-46; sr. sales rep. Socony-Vacuum Oil Co., La Paz, Bolivia, 1946-53; sales mgr. Petroleo Ineramericano, NYC, 1954-57; account exec. Advt. Age, NYC, 1957-65; ea. ad mgr. Advt. Age subs. Crain Communications Inc., NYC, 1965-67; dir. advt. Bus. Ins. subs. Crain Communications Inc., NYC, 1967-69, v.p., pub., from 1970. Chmn. fund raising com. Spencer Ednl. Found., N.Y.C., 1986-89. Recipient Ins. Industry Achievement award B'nai Brith Internat., 1987. Jewish. Home: New York, NY. Died July 23, 2006.

MALECKI, HENRY RAYMOND, emeritus administrator, educator; b. Chgo., Mar. 10, 1922; s. Andrew and Maryanne (Baginski) M. BS, No. Ill. U., 1947; MS, Purdue U., 1949, PhD, 1952. Dir. student tchrs. Loyola U., Chgo., 1957-62, dir. tchr. certification and placement, 1962-67, dir. tchr. edn., 1962-67, dir. summer sessions, 1970-77, dean Univ. Coll., 1967-82, prof., 1982-84, prof. emeritus, from 1984. Served with AUS, 1943-46. Fellow AAAS; mem. Am. Personnel and Guidance Assn., Nat. Vocational Guidance Assn., Am. Ednl. Research Assn., Am. Psychol. Assn., Phi Delta Kappa, Kappa Delta Pi. Home: Boynton Beach, Fla. Died Oct. 21, 2006.

MALENG, NORM, prosecutor; b. Acme, Wash., 1938; m. Judy Maleng; 1 child. BS in Econs., U. Wash., 1960, JD, 1966. Bar: Wash. State 1967, U.S. Supreme Ct. 1983, USOC Wash. 1973. Staff atty. U.S. Senate Com. on Commerce; pvt. practice Seattle; chief dep. civil divsn. King County, Seattle, prosecutor, 1978—2007. Chair Gov.'s Task Force on Cmty. Protection, 1989; vice chair Wash. Sentencing Guidelines Commn. Named Outstanding Pub. Ofcl. in King County, Mcpl. League, 1986. Mem. Wash. Assn. Pros. Attys. (pres.), Nat. Dist. Attys. Assn. (v.p., mem. exec. bd.), Wash. Assn. County Ofcls. (pres.). Died May 24, 2007.

MALHOTRA, JAGADISH CHANDRA, psychiatrist; b. Dera Ghazi Khan, Pakistan-India, Mar. 21, 1916; s. Hardasram Malik and Moolobai (Kakar) M.; came to U.S., 1957, naturalized, 1971; student Med. Sch. Hyderabad, Sind, India, 1935-40; license Coll. Physicians and Surgeons Bombay, 1940; diploma in Psychol. Medicine, Grant Med. Coll., Bombay, 1954; licensing exam. Kans. Bd. Healing Arts, 1967; m. Sumitra Devi, Nov. 26, 1941; children: Raj Kumar, Ashok Kumar. Second asst. N.M. Mental Hosp., Thana, Bombay, India, 1948-50; fellow Menninger Sch. Psychiatry, Topeka, 1957-58; resident psychiatrist Topeka State Hosp., 1957-58; clin. dir. Huntington (W.Va.) State Hosp., 1967-69; supt. Spencer (W.Va.) State Hosp., 1969-73; chief mental hygiene clinic VA Hosp., Huntington, 1973; asst. supt. Moccasin Bend Mental Health Inst., Chattanooga, 1973-81; speaker 5th World Congress Psychiatry, Mexico City, 1971, 6th, Honolulu, 1977, participant 7th, Vienna, 1983. Fellow Indian Psychiat. Soc.; mem. Am. Psychiat. Assn. Author articles mental health and Mahatma Gandhi, yoga and mental hygiene. Died June 22, 2007.

MALLETTE, MALCOLM FRANCIS, newspaper editor, educator; b. Syracuse, NY, Jan. 30, 1922; s. Ralph Joseph and Hermia Ruth (Barry) M.; m. Eleanor Christine Ingram, Sept. 21, 1946; children: Gary, Bruce, David. BS magna cum laude, Syracuse U., 1947. Profl. baseball pitcher, Norfolk, Va., Newark, Kansas City, Memphis, Sacramento, Bklyn., Montreal, 1946-52; sports reporter Asheville (N.C.) Times, 1951-54; sports editor Asheville Citizen, 1954-56; sports dir. Winston-Salem (N.C.) Jour. & Sentinel, 1956-59; mng. editor Winston-Salem Jour., 1959-66; assoc. dir. Am. Press Inst., Reston, Va., 1966-69, mng. dir., 1969-75, sec., dir., 1975-79, dir. devel., 1979-87; dir. projects World Press Freedom Com., 1987-96. Guest lectr. Grad. Sch. Journalism, Columbia, 1969-71, Am. Press. Inst., Columbia, 1961-66, U. N.C. Sch. Journalism, 1964; Def. Info. Sch. Ft. Benjamin Harrison, Ind., 1987. Author (with others), editor: Handbook for Journalists of Central and Eastern Europe, 1990, transl. to Polish, Czechoslovakian, Hungarian, Romanian, Bulgarian, Albanian, Russian; author (Seminar) The Story of the American Press Institute, 1992; contbr. articles to various mags. Served to capt. Signal Corps, AC AUS, 1943-46. Named to N.C. Journalism Hall of Fame. Mem. AP Mng. Editors Assn. (dir. 1961-66, regent 1976—), AP News Coun. (pres. N.C. 1964), Assn. Profl. Baseball Players (life) Clubs: Rotarian. Baptist. Home: Durham, NC. Died Nov. 26, 2005.

MALMUTH, NORMAN DAVID, research scientist; b. Bklyn., Jan. 22, 1931; s. Jacob and Selma Malmuth; m. Constance Nelson, 1970; children: Kenneth, Jill. AE, U. Cin., 1953; MA in Aero. Engring., Polytech. Inst. of N.Y., 1956; PhD in Aeronautics, Calif. Inst. Tech., 1962. Rsch. engr. Grumman Aircraft Engring. Corp., 1953-56; preliminary design engr. N.A. Aviation Div., LA, 1956-68; teaching asst. Calif. Inst. Tech., LA, 1961; mem. maths. sci. group Rockwell Internat. Sci. Ctr., 1968-75, project mgr. fluid dynamics rsch., 1975-80, mgr. fluid dynamics group, 1980-82, sr. scientist, project mgr., from 1982. Cons. Aerojet Gen., 1986—89; lectr. UCLA, 1971—72; mem. adv. group for aerospace R&D Fluid Dynamics Panel, 1995; vis. scientist Rensselaer Poly. Inst.; vis. assoc. Calif. Inst. Tech., 2003; chair NATO RTO/AVT meeting, Prague, Czech Republic, 2004. Referee AIAA Jour.; bd. editors Jour. Aircraft; contbr. articles to Jour. of Heat Transfer, Internat. Jour. Heat Mass Transfer, and others. Named Calif. Inst. Tech. fellow; recipient Outstanding Alumnus award Univ. Cin., 1990. Fellow AIAA (Aerodynamics award 1991. lectr. meeting 2005), Am. Phys. Soc.; mem. Am. Acad. Mechanics, Am. Inst. Physics (fluid dynamics divsn.), Soc. Indsl. and Applied Math. Achievements include patent in Methods and Apparatus for Controlling Laser Welding, hypersonic transition delay; pioneering development of high aerodynamic efficiency of hypersonic delta wing body combinations, hypersonic boundary layer stability, transonic wind tunnel interference, plasma aerodynamics, flow control web dynamics, combined asymptotic and numerical methods in fluid dynamics and aerodynamics. Home: Newbury Park, Calif. Died July 3, 2007.

MALONE, DENNIS PHILIP, b. Buffalo, Sept. 3, 1932; s. Robert G. and Mildred (Mitchell) M.; m. Ann Irene Navelle, June 21, 1954; children— Christopher D., Elisabeth Ann. BA, U. Buffalo, 1954; M.Sc., Yale, 1955, PhD, 1960. Research asso. Yale, 1955-60; head modern physics br. Cornell Aero. Labs., Buffalo, 1960-65; asso. prof. engring. and applied sci. State U. N.Y. at Buffalo, 1965-70, prof., chmn. dept. elec. engring., from 1970. Dir. N.Y. Astronautical Corp., Albany. Mem. Am. Phys. Soc., Sigma Xi, Phi Beta Kappa, Pi Mu Epsilon. Research in lasers Research in lasers. Home: Buffalo, NY. Died Aug. 5, 2006.

MALONE, FRANCIS EDWARD, accountant; b. Kempton, Ill., Jan. 18, 1907; s. Frank Mark and Julia Kathern (Walgenback) M.; A.A. in Commerce, Springfield Coll. Ill., 1954; B.S.C., U. Notre Dame, 1956. Mgr., Walgenback-Walker Farm, near Kempton, 1930-42; chief statis. clk. U.S. War Dept., McCook Army Air Field, McCook, Nebr., 1945-46; bookkeeper and office mgr. Tombaugh-Turner Hybrid Corn Co., Pontiac, Ill., 1946-47; safety responsibility evaluator Ill. Div. Hwys., Springfield, 1947-49; agrl. statistician U.S. Dept. Agr. Bur. Agrl. Econs., Springfield, 1949-53; sr. accountant Raymond E. Rickbiel, C.P.A., 1955-61, Ernst & Ernst, Springfield, 1961-62; pvt. practice pub. accounting, Springfield, 1963—. Served to sgt. USAAF, 1942-45. Mem. Am. Accounting Assn., Air Force Assn., Am. Legion (adj. post 1973—), Alumni Assn. U. Notre Dame, Te Deum Internat. (sec.-treas. Ill. chpt. 1962-65), Thomist Assn. (chmn. Ill. chpt. 1957-62), K.C. Died June 7, 2006.

MALONEY, MOIYA JANE, psychiatric social worker, counselor; b. Spokane, Wash., June 28, 1938; d. Justin Close and Geneva Agnes (Walsh) Maloney; B.S., Marylhurst Coll., 1963; M.Ed., St. Lawrence U., 1981; Ed.D., Internat. Grad. Sch., St. Louis, 1983. Cert. counselor, clin. mental health counselor. Tchr., Archdiocese of Portland (Oreg.), 1960-64, Archdiocese of Seattle, 1964-69; psychiat. social worker, counselor N.Y. State Dept. Mental Hygiene, Ogdensburg, 1970—; pvt. practice counseling. Active, Potsdam Hosp. Guild, 1980—. Mem. LVW, Am. Assn. Counseling and Devel., Am. Mental Health Counselors Assn., N.Y. State Mental Health Counselors Assn., No. Zone Assn. Counseling and Devel., Internat. Acad. Behavioral Medicine, Counseling and Psychotherapy. Roman Catholic. Died June 25, 2006.

MALSACK, JAMES THOMAS, retired manufacturing company executive; b. Milw., Apr. 4, 1921; s. Leonard Henry and Florence Alice (Webb) M.; widowed; children: Thomas James, Claudia Irene, Robert Richard, Thomas John, Pamela Joyce. BSBA, Marquette U., 1946; D Pub. Svc. (hon.), No. Mich. U., 1990. Acct. Price Waterhouse & Co., Milw., 1946-51; with Lake Shore, Inc., Iron Mountain, Mich., 1951-88, exec. v.p., 1959-72, pres., chief exec. officer, 1972-84, chmn., 1984-88. Bd. control No. Mich. U., trustee emeritus. With USN, 1942-45. Mem. Masons, Shriners. Republican. Episcopalian. Home: Scottsdale, Ariz. Died Mar. 5, 2006.

MAMATEY, VICTOR SAMUEL, historian, educator; b. North Braddock, Pa., Feb. 19, 1917; s. Albert Paul and Ola (Darnek) Mamatey; m. Denise M. Perronne, Nov. 20, 1945; children: Albert R., Peter V. Student, Wittenberg Coll., 1938-39, U. Chgo., 1939-40; AM, Harvard U., 1941; PhD, U. Paris, 1949. Asst. prof. history Fla. State U., Tallahassee, 1949-55, assoc. prof., 1955-58, prof., 1958-67, chmn. dept. history, 1964-67; rsch. prof. hist. U. Ga., Athens, 1967-82, acting dean Coll. Arts and Scis., 1972-73. Vis. prof. Columbia U., 1961, Tulane U., 1963. Author: The United States and East Central Europe, 1914-18, 1957, Soviet RussianImperialism, 1964, (with Geoffrey Brunn) The World in the Twentieth Century, 1967, The Rise of the Hapsburg Empire, 1526-1815, 1971, (with Radomir Luza) History of the Czechoslovak Republic, 1918-1948, 1973. With U.S. Army, 1942-46. Guggenheim fellow, 1959. Mem. Am. Hist. Assn. (George Louis Beer prize for best book on internat. history 1958), Am. Assn. For Advancement Slavic Studies. Home: Tallahassee, Fla. Died Jan. 16, 2007.

MANDICH, NENAD VOJINOV, chemical industry executive; b. Kos Mitrovica, Serbia, Yugoslavia, Dec. 25, 1944; came to U.S., 1971; s. Vojin P. and Jelica (Zarkovic) M.; m. Olga M. Mamula, 1975; children: Petar, Nikola. Diploma in engring., U. Belgrade, Yugoslavia, 1970; MSc, Roosevelt U., 1990; postgrad., Aston U., Birmingham, UK. cert. electroplater-finisher. Rsch. chemist Coral Chem. Co., Waukegan, Ill., 1971-72; tech. dir. KCI Chem. Co., LaPorte, Ind., 1972-74; sr. process engr. Sunbeam Corp., Chgo., 1974-78; plant mgr. Fed. Tool & Plastics, Evanston, Ill., 1978-79; sr. corp. project engr. Apollo Metals, Bridgeview, Ill., 1979-80; project mgr. Bunker-Ramo, Brodview, Ill., 1981-82; pres., chief exec. officer HBM Electrochem. & Engring. Co., Lansing, Ill., from 1982. Contbr. more than 30 articles to profl. jours. Fellow Inst. Metal Finishing; mem. Am. Electroplating Soc. (chmn. hard chrome plating com. 1990—), Internat. Soc. Electrochemistry, Electrochem. Soc., N.Y. Acad. Sci., Tesla Meml. Soc. (bd. dirs. 1989—). Mem. Eastern Orthodox Serbian Ch. Achievements include 11 patents pending. Home: Homewood, Ill. Died Oct. 7, 2006.

MANDIL, I. HARRY, nuclear engineer; b. Istanbul, Turkey, Dec. 11, 1919; s. Harry Robert and Bertha (Presente) M. (parents Am. citizens); m. Beverly Ericson, June 22, 1946; children: Jean Dale, Eric Robert. BS, U. London, 1939; MS, MIT, 1941; grad., Oak Ridge Sch. Reactor Tech., 1950; DSc (hon.), Thiel Coll., Greenville, Pa., 1960. Devel., design process controls for textile mills and chem. plants Norcross Corp., 1941-42, asst. to pres. charge field engring., 1946-49; asst. to tech. dir. naval reactors br. reactor devel. div. AEC, 1950-54, dir. reactor engring. div. Bur. Ships, Navy Dept. and chief reactor engring. br. Naval Reactors, 1954-64; prin. officer, dir. MPR Assos., Inc. (engrs.), Washington, 1964-85, cons., dir. Alexandria, Va., from 1985. Developer nuclear power for propulsion naval vessels, also for Shippingport Atomic Power Ctrl. Sta.; mem., sec. Energy Adv. Bd., Washington, 1990-93; mem. corp. vis. com. for nuclear engring. dept. MIT, 1984-93; mem. sr. tech. rev. group for plutonium, Amarillo, Tex., 1995-99. Author numerous papers in field. Served with USNR, 1942-46. Recipient Naval Letter of Commendation, 1946, Meritorious Civilian Svc. award Navy Dept., 1952, ASME Prime Movers award, 1956, Disting. Civilian Svc. award, 1959. Mem. Nat. Acad. Engring. Home: Naples, Fla. Died Apr. 27, 2006.

MANFREDI, DOMINICK JAMES, transportation executive; b. NYC, July 26, 1919; s. Francis Paul and Gertrude (DiGiamarco) Manfredi; m. Jocelyn J. Nobile, Aug. 28, 1949; children: Jocelyn, Janice, Joanne, Jennifer, Judith, Jinette, Frank, Jessica, Jeanne. BS in Nautical sci., U.S. Mcht. Marine Acad., 1943; postgrad., U. Madrid, 1949—50, Pro-Deo U. Rome, 1972—76; BS in Fgn. Svc., Georgetown U., 1951. Lic. master steam and motor vessels USCG. Mgr. marine labor rels. Waterfront Commn. N.Y. Harbor, NYC, 1953—56; regional maritime attache Am. Embassy, Paris, 1956—61, Rome, 1961—77; spl. asst. to regional dir. U.S. Maritime Adminstrn., NYC, 1977—78; chmn. Am. West African Freight Conf., NYC, from 1978. Chmn. adv. bd. Marymount Internat. Sch., Rome, 1965—70; chmn. lay coun. Santa Suzanne Roman Cath. Ch., Rome, 1971—77. Capt. USN, 1942—46, ETO, PTO. Recipient Transp. Dept. award, U.S. Coast Guard, 1974, Profl. Achievement award, U.S. Mcht. Marine Acad., 1983; Arthur Godfrey air fellow, Am. U., 1952. Mem.: U.S. Mcht. Marine Alumni Assn., Am. Mens Club Rome, Coun. Am. Master Mariners. Republican. Home: New York, NY. Died Mar. 21, 2007.

MANGANARO, FRANCIS FERDINAND, naval officer; b. Providence, Feb. 27, 1925; s. Ralph and Ada Susanna (Hobden) M.; m. Carol Anne Slater, Sept. 8, 1948; children: Carol Sue, William Francis, John Thomas, Linda Anne, Mary Kathryn. Student, U. R.I., 1943-44; BS in Elec. Engring, U.S. Naval Acad., 1944-47; Post MD, Naval Engr., MIT, 1956; cert., Advanced Mgmt. Program, Harvard U. Sch. Bus., 1971; cert. pub. utilities exec. program, U. Mich., 1984. Registered profl. engr., Conn. Commd. ensign U.S. Navy, 1947, advanced through grades to rear adm., 1975; served in destroyers Atlantic Fleet, 1947-49; served in submarines Pacific Fleet, 1949-53; repair officer, submarines Pearl Harbor Naval Shipyard, 1956-59; design project officer, submarines Bur Ships, 1959-63; inspection and planning officer Office Supr. of Shipbldg. Groton, Conn., 1963-68; prodn. officer Portsmouth Naval Shipyard, 1968-72; comdg. officer Puget Sound Naval Shipyard, 1972-76; chmn. navy claims settlement bd. Naval Material Command, 1976-78; vice comdr. Naval Sea Systems Command Washington, 1978-80; ret. (Naval Sea Systems Command), 1980. V.p., dir. GPU Nuclear Corp., 1980-90; cons. Burns & Roe Utility Mgmt. Cons., 1990-94; cons. Raytheon Engrs. & Constructors, Inc., 1994-96. Decorated DSM, Legion of Merit. Mem. Soc. Naval Architects and Marine Engrs., Am. Soc. Naval Engrs., Sigma Xi, Tau Beta Pi, Beta Psi Alpha. Home: Annapolis, Md. Died Dec. 2006.

MANGELS, DONALD KEITH, banker; b. Durant, Iowa, June 9, 1929; s. Leonard Lester and Evelyn Anna (Ruhser) M.; m. Verlene Mary Dow, Apr. 4, 1953; children— Kristen, Lisa, Eric. B.S. in Commerce, U. Iowa, 1950; M.A. in History, U. Okla., 1966. Trainee, Internat. Harvester, E. Moline, Ill., 1950-52; asst. v.p. First Nat. Bank, Ames, Iowa, 1982—; dir. Ames Found., 1982—; commd. U.S. Air Force, 1952, advanced through grades to col., 1973, ret., 1977. Mem. C. of C. (membership chmn.). Republican. Episcopalian. Advocation: outdoor sports. Home: Ames, Iowa. Died June 2, 2006.

MANION, JERRY ROBERT, hotel chain executive; b. Mt. Vernon, Ill., Feb. 27, 1938; s. Frances Manion; m. Salley Trinkle, Dec. 30, 1964; children: Courtney Elizabeth, Patrick Robert. BBA, U. Ill., 1960; MS in Bus. Mgmt., So. Ill.U., 1962. Sr. v.p., franchise dir. Quality Inns Internat., Inc., Md., 1977-80; sr. v.p., dir. ops. Metro Hotels, Inc., Tex., 1980-83; pres. Economy Motor Inns, Inc., Tex., 1983-85; pres. hotel group Ramada Inc., Phoenix, 1985-89; exec. v.p. Motel 6 Ops., Dallas, 1989-93; exec. v.p. devel. Richfield Hotel Mgmt. Inc., Englewood, Colo., 1993-94. Bd. trustees Ednl. Inst. Adv. Coun., Hotel Sch. No. Ariz. U. Mem. Am. Hotel & Motel Assn. Avocation: tennis. Home: Paradise Vly, Ariz. Died July 16, 2007.

MANN, DELBERT, film director; b. Lawrence, Kans., Jan. 30, 1920; s. Delbert Martin and Ora (Patton) M.; m. Ann Caroline Gillespie, Jan. 13, 1942 (dec. Oct. 10, 2001); children: David Martin, Frederick G., Barbara Susan (dec. 1976), Steven P. BA, Vanderbilt U., 1941; MFA, Yale U.; LLD (hon.), Northland Coll. Dir. Town Theatre, Columbia, SC, 1947-49; stage mgr. Wellesley Summer Theater, 1947-48; floor mgr., asst. dir. NBC-TV, NYC, 1949, dir., 1949-55. Pres. Dirs. Guild Benevolent Found.; former bd. govs. Acad. TV Arts and Scis.; former co-chmn. Tenn. Film, Tape and Music Commn.; former pres. Cinema Circulus; former lectr. Claremont (Calif.) McKenna Coll., U. N.C., Chapel Hill. Dir., Philco-Goodyear TV Playhouse, 1949-55, also Omnibus, Ford Star Jubilee, Playwrights 56, Producers Showcase, DuPont Show of the Month, Playhouse 90; (films) Marty, 1954 (Acad. Award for Best Dir., 1955, Palme d'Or, Cannes Internat. Film Festival, Acad. Award), The Bachelor Party, 1956, Desire Under the Elms, 1957, Separate Tables, 1958, Middle of the Night, 1959, The Dark at the Top of the Stairs, 1960, The Outsider, 1960, Lover Come Back, 1961, That Touch of Mink, 1962, A Gathering of Eagles, 1962, Dear Heart, 1963, Mister Buddwing, 1965, Fitzwilly, 1967, Kidnapped, 1972, Birch Interval, 1976, Night Crossing, 1982; (TV movies) Heidi, 1968, David Copperfield, 1970, Jane Eyre, 1971, The Man Without a Country, 1973, A Girl Named Sooner, 1975, Breaking Up, 1977, Tell Me My Name, 1977, Home To Stay, 1978, All Quiet on the Western Front, 1979, To Find My Son, 1980, All the Way Home, 1981, Bronte, 1982, The Member of the Wedding, 1982, The Gift of Love, 1983, Love Leads the Way, 1984, A Death in California, 1985, The Last Days of Patton, 1986, The Ted Kennedy Jr. Story, 1986, April Morning, 1987, Ironclads, 1991, Against Her Will: An Incident in Baltimore, 1992, Incident in a Small Town, 1993, Lily in Winter, 1994, The Memoirs of Abraham Lincoln, 1996; (plays) A Quiet Place, 1956, Speaking of Murder, 1957, Zelda, 1969, The

Memoirs of Abraham Lincoln, 1996,; opera Wuthering Heights, N.Y.C. Ctr., 1959; author: Looking Back...At Live Television and Other Matters, 1998. Bd. trustees Vanderbilt U., 1962-2007; 1st lt. USAAF, WWII; B-24 pilot and squadron intelligence officer, 1944-45. Robert B. Aldrich Achievement award, Dir. Guil Am., 1997; named hon. life mem., Dir. Guild Am., 2002-07 Mem. Dirs. Guild Am. (past pres. 1967-71) (Dirs. Guild award, 1955), Kappa Alpha. Democrat. Presbyterian. Avocation: reading. Died Nov. 11, 2007.*

MANN, J. KEITH (JOHN KEITH MANN), retired law educator, arbitrator; b. Alexis, Ill., May 28, 1924; s. William Young and Lillian Myrle (Bailey) M.; m. Virginia McKinnon, July 7, 1950; children: William Christopher, Marilyn Keith, John Kevin, Susan Bailey, Andrew Curry. BS, Ind. U., 1948, LLB, 1949; LLD, Monmouth Coll., 1989. Bar: Ind. 1949, D.C. 1951. Law clk. Justice Wiley Rutledge and Justice Sherman Minton, 1949-50; pvt. practice Washington, 1950; with Wage Stblzn. Bd., 1951; asst. prof. U. Wis., 1952, Stanford (Calif.) U. Law Sch., 1952-54, assoc. prof., 1954-58, prof., 1958-88, prof. emeritus, 1988—2006, assoc. dean, 1961-85, acting dean, 1976, 81-82, cons. to provost, 1986-87. Vis. prof. U. Chgo., 1953; mem. Sec. of Labor's Adv. Com., 1955-57; mem. Pres.'s Commn. Airlines Controversy, 1961; mem. COLC Aerospace Spl. Panel, 1973-74; chmn., mem. Presdl. Emergency Bds. or Bds. of Inquiry, 1962-63, 67, 71-72; spl. master U.S. vs. Alaska, U.S. Supreme Ct., 1980-97. Editor book rev. and articles Ind. U. Law Jour., 1948-49. Ensign USNR, 1944-46. Sunderland fellow U. Mich., 1959-60; scholar-in-residence Duke U., 1972. Mem. ABA, AAUP, Nat. Acad. Arbitrators, Indsl. Rels. Rsch. Assn., Acad. Law Alumni Fellows Ind. U., Order of Coif, Tau Kappa Epsilon, Phi Delta Phi. Democrat. Presbyterian. Home: Palo Alto, Calif. Died Nov. 27, 2006.

MANNEL, CHARLES HOWARD, educational administrator; b. Balt., Feb. 5, 1929; s. Charles and Kathleen Agnes (McCrea) M.; B.P.A., U. Md., 1957; B.S. in Edn., U. Minn., 1958, M.A., 1965; m. Rose Janice Schumann, Feb. 26, 1953; children— Charles Howard, Laura Kay, Kurt John. Tchr. Balt. public schs., 1957-58, Duluth (Minn.) public schs., 1959-61; with Investors Diversified, Inc., 1961-62; faculty U. Minn., Duluth, 1962-64; placement dir. U. Minn., Duluth, 1965-67; dir. placement U. Minn., Mpls., 1967-69, asst. dean programs and adminstrn., 1969-73, dir. student services and alumni, 1973-76; dir. career services Am. Grad. Sch. of Internat. Mgmt., Thunderbird campus, Glendale, Ariz., 1976-81, v.p. corp. relations, 1981-86, v.p. external affairs, 1986—; cons. in field; cons. Personnel Decision Inc., 1968—. Active fund raising, YMCA, Boy Scouts Am., Indian Guides; mem. CAP, 1967-76, regional dir. aerospace edn. N.Central Region, 1971-76. Served with USAF, 1950-54, Res., 1955-83. Decorated Air Force Commendation medal, Meritorious Service medal; recipient Outstanding Faculty Staff award U. Minn., 1964, 67; Frank G. Brewer award Nat. Recognition Aerospace Edn., 1975; Frank B. Kokesh award for student service, 1976. Mem. Aircraft Owners and Pilots Assn., Air Force Res. Assn., Council for Advancement and Support of Edn. Republican. Methodist. Lodges: Masons, Kiwanis. Contbr. articles to profl. jours. Home: Sun City, Ariz. Died Feb. 19, 2006.

MANNING, DIANE LOIS, winery executive; b. Bklyn., Dec. 21, 1940; d. William and Louise Margaret (Backer) Pfuhl; m. Thomas Frank Manning, Apr. 9, 1960; children— Craig, Scott, Dawn, Corey. Student Hofstra U. Assoc., Manning and Assocs., San Francisco, 1976-80; controller custom bottling Chateau Diana Cellars, Healdsburg, Calif., 1980-86, owner, controller, 1986—. Home: Healdsburg, Calif. Died May 29, 2006.

MANNING, WILLIAM FREDERICK, retired photographer; b. Gardner, Mass., Aug. 18, 1920; s. Seth Newton and Jennie May (Bennett) M.; m. Yvonne J.C. Winslow, Feb. 29, 1964; children: Pamela Ann, Jeffrey Newton. AA, Boston U., 1950, BS in Comm., 1952. With AP, Boston, 1951-53; photographer UPI, Boston, 1953-88; ret., 1988. Contbr. photos to books, mags., newspapers throughout the world. Served with USN, 1940-46, PTO. Recipient Look 1st Prize All Sports award, 1958; Pictures of the Yr. award U. Mo., 1964, 74; Nat. Headliners Club award for outstanding syndicate photography, 1974. Mem. Boston Press Photographers Assn., Nat. Headliners Club, Delta Kappa Alpha. Congregationalist. Home: Beverly, Mass. Died Sept. 2, 2006.

MANNISTO, RALPH AXEL, violinist, music educator; b. Phoenix, Mich., Mar. 23, 1919; s. Gust and Hilda (Huhta) M.; m. Ruth Edna Siira, Mar. 29, 1948; children— Keith, Dennis, Eliisa, Mark. Diploma U.S. Sch. Music, 1938; pvt. studies in violin, 1931-33; student Detroit Conservatory of Music, 1947-48, Detroit Inst. Mus. Arts, 1949; pvt. studies violin Carl Christensen, Rochester (N.Y.) Symphony, accordion Lloyd Lavaux and Lauri Holzhauer, Edio DiCiantis. Instrumental musician, entertainer, amateur actor Eddie Dowling for Spic and Spam Rev., Eng., 1944; with spl. services shows, World War II. pvt. tchr., 1934-83; with Burroughs Corp., 1947-56; theater projectionist Internat. Alliance of Theatrical Stage Employees and Moving Picture Machine Operators of U.S. and Can.; active in preserving Finnish and Scandinavian music heritage since 1960's; accompanist Internat. Finnish Folk Dance Group; performs for weddings and pvt. parties and Scandinavian festivals; accompanist for singer at sr. citizens homes; active with ethnic folk music group Mannisto Pelimannit; performer Northville (Mich.) Ethnic Festival. Served to cpl., USAAF, 1942-46. Finnish Center Assn. grantee, 1980; recipient 1st prize Farmington (Mich.) Meml. Day Parade, 1976, 2d prize, 1979. Mem. Detroit Fedn. Musicians, Finnish Center Assn., Detroit Finnish Summer Camp Assn. Home: Northville, Mich. Died Aug. 8, 2006.

MANOOGIAN, VARTAN, musician, educator; b. Baghdad, Ieaq, June 5, 1936; arrived in U.S., 1964; s. Ivan Manoogian and Nargis Vartanian; m. Brigitte Gertrude Behm, July 15, 1967; 1 child, Avedis. MusB, Juilliard Sch. Music, 1964, MusM, 1969; chamber music studies, Academia Chigiana, Siena, Italy, 1958. Asst. concert master Lausanne Chamber Orch., Switzerland, 1959—61; concert master Suisse Romande Orch., Geneva, 1961—63, 1963—78; prof. violin U. Wis., Madison, 1980—2007. Faculty artist in residence N.C. Sch. Arts, Winston-Salem, 1970—79; concert master Piedmont Chamber Orch., Winston-Salem, 1973—79; faculty Butler U., Indpls., 1975—85, Ind. U., Bloomington, 1974—77; artistic dir. Madeline Island Chamber Music, LaPoint, Wis., from 1989. Author: Foundations of Violin Technique, 1997. Recipient Cert. of Honor, Pablo Casals Festival, 1974, Mills First Prize Coaching, Coleman Chamber Music Competition, 1975. Mem.: Am. String Tchrs Am., Chamber Music Am. Avocations: photography, reading. Home: Madison, Wis. Died July 12, 2007.

MANULIS, MARTIN ELLYOT, film producer; b. NYC, May 30, 1915; s. Abraham Gustave and Anne (Silverstein) M.; m. Katharine Bard, June 14, 1939 (dec. July 28, 1983); children: Laurie, Karen, John Bard. BA, Columbia, 1935. Mng. dir. Bahamas Playhouse, 1951-52; exec. head TV prodn. Twentieth Century Fox, 1958-60; artistic dir. Ahmanson Theatre, Music Ctr., Los Angeles, 1987-89. Dir. Am. Film Inst. West, 1974-76. Prodr., dir. (with John C. Wilson) Broadway; dir. Private Lives, Laura, Made in Heaven, The Show Off, Westport Country Playhouse, 1946-50; prodr.: (TV series) Crime Photographer, 1951, Studio One, 1952, Playhouse 90, 1956-58, Suspense, 1952-53, Climax!, 1954, Best of Broadway, 1954-55, Playhouse 90, 1956-58, The Many Loves of Dobie Gillis, 1959, Five Fingers, 1959, Adventures in Paradise, 1959, James at 15, 1977; (TV movies) Once Upon an Eastertime, 1954, The Day Christ Died, 1980, The Fighter, 1983, Harem, 1986, Grass Roots, 1992; (films) Days of Wine and Roses, 1962, Dear Heart, 1964, Luv, 1967, Duffy, 1968, Double Solitaire, 1974; (TV miniseries) Chiefs, 1983, James Michener's Space, 1985 Served as lt. USNR, 1942-45. Recipient spl. Svc. award Crusade for Freedom, 1954, Look TV award for Best Dramatic Series, 1955, 56, 57, eleven TV Emmy awards Nat. Acad. TV Arts and Scis., 1956, 57; named to Producers Guild of Am. Hall of Fame for Studio One and Playhouse 90, 1992. Died Sept. 28, 2007.

MARANTZ, PHILIP F., lawyer; b. LA, Feb. 15, 1934; BS in Law, LLB, U. So. Calif., 1957. Founding ptnr. Freshman, Marantz, Orlanski, Comsky & Deutsch, from 1959. Judge pro tem Beverly Hills Mcpl. Ct.; mem. Calif. League Savs. Instns.; lectr. Calif. Real Estate Assn., Nev. Assn. Realtors, CPA's Found. for Edn. and Rsch., Southwestern U., Assn. Corp. Real Estate Execs., Practising Law Inst., Law Sch. U. So. Calif. Alt. mem. bd. govs. NBA; gen. counsel Utah Jazz Basketball Team; mem. sports and the law adv. coun. Constl. Rights Found.; mem. adv. bd. Inst. for Corp. Counsel U. So. Calif.; appointed Century City Mobility Action Com., L.A.; past pres., mem. adv. bd. Maple Ctr., Beverly Hills, Calif. Mem. ABA (real estate com., banking and bus. law com., corp. com., econs. of law practice com., entertainment and sports com.), Am. Land Title Assn., Calif. Bar Assn., L.A. Bar Assn., Beverly Hills Bar Assn., Calif. Land Title Assn. Died Sept. 1, 2006.

MARCH, RALPH BURTON, retired entomology educator; b. Oshkosh, Wis., Aug. 5, 1919; s. Albert Harold and Vanita Ida Cora (Siewert) M.; m. Robinetta Tompkin, Dec. 26, 1942; children: John S., Janice A., Susan E. Student, Oshkosh State Tchrs. Coll., 1937-38; BA, U. Ill., 1941, MA (Grad. scholar 1941-42), 1946, PhD (Grad. fellow 1947-48), 1948. Faculty U. Calif. at Riverside, from 1948, entomologist, from 1957, prof. entomology, 1961-83, prof. entomology emeritus, from 1983, dean grad. div., 1961-68, head div. toxicology and physiology dept. entomology, 1968-72, chmn. dept. entomology, 1978-83. Served with USAAF, 1942-46. Mem. Entomol. Soc. Am., Am. Chem. Soc., AAAS, Phi Beta Kappa, Sigma Xi, Phi Kappa Phi, Phi Sigma. Home: Chapel Hill, NC. Died Aug. 6, 2007.

MARCUCCI, GEORGE FRANCIS, food products executive; b. Chgo., Oct. 6, 1947; s. George D. and Flavis (Trucco) Marcucci; m. Deborah Ann Puralewski, Mar. 31, 1984; 1 child, Elizabeth; children: Michael, Paul. BSBA, Loyola U. Chgo., 1975. CPA Ill. Staff acct. Gonnella Baking Co., Chgo., 1970—74, internal auditor, 1974—80, contr., 1980—84, treas., 1984—2006, pres., 2006. Mem. allocations com. Oak Park/River Forest Cmty. Chest, 1984; team mgr. Elmhurst Baseball Leagues Inc., from 1988. Mem.: AICPA, Bakers Club Chgo. (bd. dirs., 2d v.p. 1986—88, 1st v.p. from 1988), Ill. Soc. CPA, Alpha Kappa Psi. Roman Catholic. Home: Elmhurst, Ill. Died Nov. 28, 2006.

MARIETTA, DON EMMERT, JR., philosophy educator; b. Montgomery, Ala., Nov. 1, 1926; s. Don E. Marietta and Alva E. Shores; m. Carolyn Louise Gordon. AB, Birmingham-So. Coll., 1948; MDiv, Vanderbilt U., 1950, PhD, 1959. Ordained to ministry Episcopal Ch., 1959. Clergyman Diocese of Ala., 1959-61; Episcopal chaplain Auburn (Ala.) U., 1961-65, Fla. Atlantic U., Boca Raton, 1965-68, asst. prof. philosophy, 1968-70, assoc. prof., 1970-76, prof., from 1976, Snyder disting. prof. ethics, 1991-92. Author: For People and the Planet: Holism and Humanism in Environmental Ethics, 1994; contbr. articles on ethics and environ. ethics to profl. jours. Recipient Disting. Tchr. award Fla. Atlantic U., 1981. Mem. Am. Philos. Assn., Am. Soc. for Value Inquiry, So. Soc. for Philosophy and Psychology, Fla. Philos. Assn. (pres. 1980-81), Humanists Fla. (dist. dir. 1985-86, pres. 1985-86, Fla. Humanist of Yr. award 1980). Democrat. Unitarian Universalist. Avocations: birding, canoeing, gardening. Home: Towson, Md. Died Mar. 31, 2006.

MARK, HENRY ALLEN, lawyer; b. Bklyn., May 16, 1909; s. Henry Adam and Mary Clyde (McCarroll) M.; m. Isobel Ross Arnold, June 26, 1940. BA, Williams Coll., 1932; JD, Cornell U., 1935. Bars: N.Y. 1936, Conn. 1981, U.S. Dist. Ct. (so. dist.) N.Y. 1943. Assoc. firm Allin & Tucker, NYC, 1935-40; mng. atty. Indemnity Ins. Co. of N.Am., NYC, 1940-43; assoc. firm Mudge, Stern, Williams & Tucker, NYC, 1943-50, Cadwalder, Wickersham & Taft, NYC, 1950-53; ptnr. Cadwalader, Wickersham & Taft, NYC, 1953-74. Lectr. Practicing Law Inst., N.Y.C., 1955-68. Mem. adv. com. zoning Village of Garden City, N.Y., 1952-54, planning commn., 1957-59, zoning bd. appeals, 1959-61, trustee, 1961-65, mayor, 1965-67; chmn. planning commn. Town of Washington, Conn., 1980-84; trustee The Gunnery Sch., Washington, Conn., 1980-86; mem. adv. com. on continuing care State of Conn., 1996-99. Recipient Disting. Alumnus award Cornell U., 1983. Mem. ABA, N.Y. Bar Assn., Assn. Bar City of N.Y., Conn. Bar Assn., Hartford County Bar Assn., Cornell Law Assn. (pres. 1971-73), Bar Assn. Nassau County (grievance com. 1974-77), St. Andrew's Soc., Masons, Phi Beta Kappa, Sigma Phi, Phi Delta Phi. Republican. Congregationalist. Died Feb. 20, 2006.

MARKGRAF, J(OHN) HODGE, chemist, educator; b. Cin., Mar. 16, 1930; s. Carl A. and Elizabeth (Hodge) M.; m. Nancy Hart, Apr. 4, 1957; children: Carrie G., Sarah T. AB, Williams Coll., 1952; M.Sc., Yale U., 1954, PhD, 1957; postgrad., U. Munich, W. Ger., 1956-57. Research chemist Procter & Gamble Co., Cin., 1958-59; asst. prof. chemistry Williams Coll., Williamstown, Mass., 1959-65, assoc. prof., 1965-69, prof., 1969-98, Ebenezer Fitch prof. chemistry, 1977-85, 94-98, prof. emeritus, from 1998, provost, 1980-83, v.p. for alumni relations and devel., 1985-94, coll. marshal, 1995-98. Vis. prof. U. Calif., Berkeley, 1964—65, 1968—69, 1976—77, Duke U., 1983—84, 2001, U. Houston, 1999, Williams Coll., 2002—04, 2006, Mass. Coll. Liberal Arts, 2005—06. Contbr. articles to profl. jours.; patentee in field. NSF sci. faculty fellow, 1964-65; NSF grantee, 1961-63, Am. Chem. Soc.-Petroleum Rsch. Fund grantee, 1965-68, 70-72, 93-95, Merck & Co. grantee, 1967, Rsch. Corp. grantee, 1963, 75, 90-92, Pfizer Inc. grantee, 1996, 97, 98, Camille and Henry Dreyfus Found. grantee, 2000-01, 04-05 Mem.: Am. Chem. Soc., Phi Beta Kappa, Sigma Xi. Home: Williamstown, Mass. Died Jan. 11, 2007.

MARKWELL, DICK R(OBERT), retired chemist; b. Muskogee, Okla., Feb. 20, 1925; s. Alex J. and May (Albright) M.; m. Virginia Ann Gass, Aug. 28, 1949 (dec. Nov. 2002); children: Steven R., Scot L., Eric R., Cheryl F.; m. Marjorie H. Melville, Feb. 20, 2003. BS, Wichita State U., 1948, MS, 1950; PhD, U. Wis., 1956. Commd. 2d lt. U.S. Army, 1951, ret. lt. col., 1967; with Office Chief Rsch. and Devel.; assoc. prof. chemistry San Antonio Coll., 1967-74; chemist Corpus Christi Dept. Health, 1975-77; supr. chemistry sect. lab. div. San Antonio Met. Health Dist., 1977-87. With USMC, 1942-45. Mem. Am. Chem. Soc. Home: San Antonio, Tex. Died July 29, 2007.

MARLETTE, DOUGLAS NIGEL, editorial cartoonist, comic strip creator; b. Greensboro, NC, Dec. 6, 1949; m. Melinda Hartley; 1 child, Jackson Douglas. Student, Fla. State U. Editorial cartoonist The Charlotte (N.C.) Observer, 1972-87, The Atlanta Constn., 1987-89, NY Newsday, NYC, 1989—2002, Tallahassee Democrat, 2002—06, Tulsa World, 2006—07; syndicated to over 200 newspapers through L.A. Times Syndicate, Inc., 1988—2007. Creator syndicated comic strip Kudzu; works reproduced in Time, Newsweek, Christian Century, Rolling Stone, Der Spiegel, Esquire mags., also textbooks and encys.; author: The Emperor Has No Clothes, If You Can't Say Something Nice, Drawing Blood, Kudzu, 1982, Preacher, The Wit and Wisdom of Will B. Dunn, 1984, Just A Simple Country Preacher, 1985, It's a Dirty Job But Somebody Has To Do It, There's No Business Like Soul Business, 1987, Chocolate is My Life, Shred This Book, I Am Not a Televangelist, Doublewide with a View, 1989, In Your Face, A Cartoonist At Work, 1991; (novels) The Bridge, 2001 (Best Fiction Book of Yr., Southeast Booksellers Assn., 2002), Magic Time, 2006; (children's book) The Before and After Book, Even White Boys Get the Blues, 1992, Gone With the Kudzu, 1995; co-wrote screenplay "EX"; TV appearances include ABC's Nightline, Good Morning Am., Today Show, CBS Morning News, Nat. Pub. Radio's Morning Edition; syndicated animated editorial cartoons NBC Today Show. Nieman fellow, 1st for editorial cartoonist, Harvard U.; recipient Nat. Headliners award 1983, 88, Robert F. Kennedy Meml. award 1984, Sigma Delta Chi Disting. Service award 1986, First Amendment award, 1986, 1st Pl. award John Fischetti Editorial Cartoon Competition, 1986 The Golden Plate Acad. of Achievement award, 1991; named to Register of Men and Women Who Are Changing Am., Esquire Mag., 1984; recipient Pulitzer Prize for editorial cartooning Newsday, 1988; 1st Prize, John Fischetti Editorial Cartoon Competition, 1992. Died July 10, 2007.

MARMORSTEIN, IRWIN, construction company executive; b. Transilvania, Romania, Apr. 29, 1928; came to U.S., 1948, naturalized, 1954; s. Louis and Violet (Geiszt) M.; m. Ruth Marmorstein; children: Daniel, Debra, Amy, Michael. BA, Calif. Western U., 1976. Partner Willow-Shore Builders, Cleve., 1955-67, Multiplex, Inc., Cleve., 1967-69; v.p. Titan Group, Inc. Paramus, N.J., 1969-79; ptnr. F.R.A. Assos., Pitts., 1979-82, Ibis Builders, from 1982. Cons. SAFCO Ins. Co., Titan Group, Inc. Served with U.S. Army, 1950-52. Decorated Purple Heart. Mem. Sullivan County Bd. Realtors, Air Force Assn., DAV, Jewish War Vets. Clubs: B'nai B'rith. Died Dec. 29, 2005.

MARQUARD, WILLIAM ALBERT, retired diversified manufacturing company executive; b. Pitts., Mar. 6, 1920; s. William Albert and Anne (Wild) M.; m. Margaret Thoben, Aug. 13, 1942; children: Pamela, Suzanne, Stephen. BS, U. Pa., 1940 HHD (hon.), U. Puebla, Mex. With Westinghouse Electric Corp., Pitts. and Mexico City, 1940-52; with Mosler Safe Co. Hamilton, Ohio, 1952-67, sr. v.p., 1961-67, pres., 1967-70; sr. exec. v.p. Am. Standard, Inc., NYC, 1970, pres., CEO, 1971-85 chmn., 1971-86. Bd. dirs. Chem. N.Y. Corp., Chem. Bank, N.Y. Life Ins. Co., Shell Oil Co., N.L. Industries, Inc., Allied Stores chmn., bd. dirs. Arkansas Best Corp. Trustee U. Pa., N.Y.C. Citizens Budget Commn., N.Y. Infirmary-Beekman Downtown Hosp., Washington Opera, Found. of U. Ams., Com. Econ. Devel.; bd. overseers Wharton Sch. Bus., Bus. Com. for Arts Brit.-N. Am. Com.; mem. Com. Corp. Support Pvt. Univs.; bd. dirs. Nat. Minority Purchasing Council. Mem. Conf. Bd. (sr. Died Oct. 22, 2006.

MARQUETTE, ANDREW DELBERT, market research executive; b. Oak Park, Ill., Sept. 9, 1946; s. Delbert Webster and Mary Edith (Weith) M.; m. Audrey Jean Walton; children— Emily, Jill. B.S. in Bus. Adminstrn., DePaul U., 1974, M.B.A. 1975. Mktg. cons. Ernst & Whinney, Chgo., 1975-78; market research mgr. Wickes Furniture, Wheeling, Ill., 1978-81; dir. market research DeVry Inc. div. Bell & Howell, Evanston, Ill. 1981—. Bd. dirs. Edison Park Youth Club, Chgo., 1979— Served with U.S. Army, 1966-68, Viet Nam. DePaul U. grad fellow, 1975. Mem. Am. Mktg. Assn. (v.p. edn. div. Chgo. chpt. 1980-82), World Future Soc. Roman Catholic. Avocation: coaching organized youth sports. Home: Chicago, Ill. Died Jan. 12, 2006.

MARRERO, LOUIS JOHN, lawyer; b. Bklyn., May 9, 1936; s. George William and Mamie (Zafonte) M.; m. Maria Louise, June 28, 1958; children: Lisa Anne, Louis Jr. BA in Polit. Sci., CCNY, 1958; LLB, St. John's U., 1963. Bar: N.Y. 1963, U.S. Dist. Ct. (ea., so. dists.) N.Y. 1966, U.S. Supreme Ct. 1967, U.S. Tax Ct. 1973, U.S. Dist. Ct. (so. dist.) N.Y. Sole practice, Bklyn., 1963-90; justice Supreme Ct. N.Y. State, Bklyn., 1991—; law sec. to justice Supreme Ct. Kings County, 1969-72. Mem. N.Y. State Rep. Com. Mem. Bklyn. Bar Assn., Kings County Criminal Bar Assn., N.Y. State Defenders Assn. Roman Catholic. Home: Brooklyn, NY. Died Aug. 26, 2006.

MARRO, CHARLES JOHN, retired bankruptcy judge; b. Rutland, Vt., June 24, 1910; s. Nicola and Albina (Zullo) Marro; m. J. Helen French, May 7, 1948; children: Albina, Charles John, Joseph E. AB, Columbia Coll., 1931; LLB, Fordham Law Sch., 1934. Bar: Vt. 1937, U.S. Dist. Ct. Vt. 1937. Commr. U.S. Dist. Vt., 1940—44; judge U.S. Bankruptcy Ct., Rutland, from 1941; of counsel Timothy N. Maikoff Ltd., Rutland. Mem.: Am. Judicature Soc., Rutland County Bar Assn., Vt. Bar Assn. Home: Rutland, Vt. Died Aug. 4, 2006.

MARTEN, JOHN FRANCIS, investor; b. San Jose, Calif., July 28, 1914; s. John Francis and Mary (Twohy) M.; m. Patricia Boyle, Nov. 9, 1946 (dec. Oct. 1977); children— Maureen, John Francis; m. Nadine Normandin, Apr. 7, 1979. BS, U. Santa Clara, 1936. Title examiner, escrow officer Calif. Pacific Title Ins. Co., 1936-41; v.p. Inglewood Fed. Savs. and Loan Assn., 1946-50; exec. v.p. Am. Savs. and Loan Assn., 1951-55; pres. Gt. Western Savs. and Loan Assn., Los Angeles, 1955-64, Gt. Western Financial Corp., 1955-64; investment banker, securities broker, 1963-85. Bd. dirs. Calprop. Corp./Amex. Bd. dirs. adv. bd. Daniel Freeman Meml. Hosp., Inglewood, pres., 1962-63; bd. dirs. Calif. Mus. Sci. and Industry, pres., 1970-71; regent U. Santa Clara; trustee St. John's Hosp. and Health Center Found., 1976-87. Served from pvt. to lt. col. AUS, 1941-46. Decorated Bronze Star. Mem. Calif. Savs. and Loan League (pres. 1962-63), Sovereign Mil. Order Malta. Clubs: Los Angeles Country, California (Los Angeles). Died Feb. 10, 2006.

MARTIN, ALBERT SIDNEY, JR., retired oil industry executive; b. Edmonson, Tex., Apr. 9, 1930; s. Albert Sidney and Mary Etta (Clift) M.; m. Winona Perkins, June 14, 1952; children— Mary Elizabeth, John, Linda. BA, U. Tex., 1951; postgrad., Ohio State U., 1971-72. C.P.A. Asst. mgr. regulatory gas accounting Sun Oil Co., 1961-67, coordinator prodn. accounting, 1968-69, mgr. corporate projects accounting, 1970-71, controller, 1972-79, gen. auditor, chief control officer, 1979—88. Contbr.: chpt. to Financial Executives Handbook, 1970. Mem. Am., Pa. insts. C.P.A.'s, Fin. Execs. Inst., Am. Petroleum Inst., Inst. Internal Auditors. Home: Villanova, Pa. Died Oct. 26, 2006.

MARTIN, BILLY LEE, lawyer; b. Wetumka, Okla., Apr. 15, 1925; s. Frederick Amon and Della Viola (Hahn) M.; m. Mary Easter Dirickson, June 19, 1943; children— Donna Jean Martin Waddle, Ginger Lee Martin Evans, Kathleen Ann Martin Bradshaw. J.D., Loyola U., New Orleans, 1967. Bar: Okla. 1977, La. 1967, Tex. 1973, U.S. Dist. Ct. (ea. dist.) Okla. 1977. County clk. Okmulgee County, Okla., 1950-56; tax agt. Sunray DX Oil Co., Tulsa, 1956-61; property tax specialist Exxon Co., U.S.A., New Orleans and Houston, 1961-77; sole practice, Okmulgee, 1977-86. Chmn. Okmulgee County Excise-Equalization Bd., 1982-85; judge Temp. Ct. Appeals Div. 105, State of Okla., 1982; precinct chmn. Okmulgee County Dem. party, 1983-85. Served with USN, 1943-46, PTO. Recipient Meritorious Service award Am. Petroleum Inst., 1976. Assoc. mem. Bd. Bar Examiners, Okla. Bar Assn., Okmulgee County Bar Assn. Mem. Disciples of Christ Ch. Lodges: Lions, Gideons Internat. (sec.-treas. 1982-83). Home: Henryetta, Okla. Died Dec. 18, 2006.

MARTIN, CHARLES WALLACE, travel executive, retired university administrator; b. Columbia, SC, Feb. 1, 1916; s. Earle Purkerson and Caroline Louise (Keenan) M.; m. Nancy Miles Chisolm, Sept. 30, 1944; children: Nancy Miles Brown, Charles Wallace, Louise Elizabeth Andrews. BA, U. S.C., 1936. Br. office employee N.Y. Life Ins. Co., Columbia, 1936-38; mgr. Palmetto Theatre Co., Columbia, 1938-42, Reamer Appliance Co., Columbia, 1946-47; local sales mgr. WIS Radio, Columbia, 1947-50; pres., gen. mgr. WMSC Radio, Columbia, 1950-60; dir. devel. U. S.C., Columbia, 1960-66, exec. dir. ednl. found., 1960-77, v.p. for devel., 1966-77, instr. English, 1948-52; retired. Chmn. Carolina V.I.P. Tours, 1977-97; adv. bd. Bankers Trust S.C., Columbia, 1960-78. Chmn. United Way Columbia, 1954; pres. Columbia Philharm. Orch., 1967-68; commr. Columbia Housing Authority, 1971-76, chmn., 1974-76; bd. dirs. Bus. Ptnrs. Found., 1969-77, Providence Hosp. Found., 1977-82; trustee Columbia Mus. Arts and Sci., 1977-80, 88-94, life mem.; co-chmn. S.C. Gov.'s Mansion Found., 1979-83; vestryman Trinity Cathedral, Columbia; chmn. Trinity Found. Lt. USNR, 1942-45. Named Young Man of Year Columbia, 1955; endowed professorship in English established in his name U. S.C., 1977. Mem. Columbia Stage Soc. (dir. 1947-59, 66-69), Greater Columbia C. of C. (pres. 1959), S.C. Broadcasters Assn. (pres. 1954), Am. Coll. Pub. Relations Assn. (dir., treas. Mason-Dixon dist. 1967-72), English-Speaking Union U.S. (pres. Columbia br. 1973-75, nat. dir. 1972-75), Sigma Nu, Omicron Delta Kappa, Pi Gamma Mu. Clubs: Kiwanian (pres. 1957), Forest Lake, Pine Tree Hunt (pres. 1985-86) Centurion Soc., Columbia Ball (pres. 1959), Forum (pres. 1989-90), Palmetto. Episcopalian. Home: Columbia, SC. Died Dec. 10, 2006.

MARTIN, CLINTON G., retired parks director, state representative; b. Bklyn., May 11, 1939; m. Cynthia Taylor; 4 children. BA, Bonaventure U., 1960; MA, NYU, 1968. Pres. Precision Valley Devel. Corp.; dir. pks. and recreation City of Springfield, Vt., ret., 2001; rep. Vt. State Ho. Reps., from 2003. Pres. Windsor County Agr. Fair. Democrat. Home: Springfield, Vt. Died Dec. 17, 2006.

MARTIN, DONALD JAMES, marketing professional; b. Brantford, Ont., Can., May 2, 1928; s. Norman Wilfred and Leeta Maude (Woodley) M.; m. Annette Roselyn Mills, Aug. 25, 1952; children: Paul Stuart, Cheryl Anne. PhB, Northwestern U., 1964; postgrad., U. Chgo., 1965-66. Account rep. J. Walter Thompson, Toronto, Canada, 1951-56, supr. mgmt. Sao Paulo, Brazil, 1956-60, v.p. Chgo., 1960-66; dir. corp. rels. Kraft, Inc., NYC, Chgo., 1966-73; v.p. external affairs Scott Paper, Phila., 1973-76; v.p. com. Conrail, Phila., 1976-79; pres. Rennoc Corp., Vineland, NJ, 1979-84, Martin Broadcasting Inc., Vineland, 1979-84; v.p. internat. paper real estate Hilton Head Island, S.C., 1979-84; pres. Marcom Inc., S.C., from 1989; talk show host Sta. WHHI-TV, from 1992. Instr. internat. mktg. Northwestern U., Evanston, Ill., 1964-66; prof. broadcast mgmt. Mercer (N.J.) Coll., 1980-83; dir. Broadcast Pioneers Am. Mgr. Hilton Head Concert Orch., 1985-89; exec. prodr. summer festival Hilton Head Eastman Sch. Music, 1986-89; bd. dirs. Hilton Head Dance Theater, 1986, 87, Cultural Coun. Hilton Head Island, 1987-90; mem. cmty. adv. bd. Hilton Head Med. Ctr. Clinics, 1995—; actor Hilton Head Playhouse. Recipient Svc. Appreciation award Sunshine Found., 1979, Outstanding Media award United Way, 1998. Mem. Rotary (Svc. Above Self award 1992-93), S. C. Yacht Club. Avocations: tennis, sailing, acting. Died July 18, 2006.

MARTIN, EDWIN PRUITT, lawyer; b. Anderson, SC, Mar. 19, 1938; s. James Roy and Eda Belle (Snoddy) M.; m. Janice Ruth Kay, Sept. 17, 1960; children: Edwin P. Jr., Richard Alan, Brian Crayton, James Michael. BSBA, U. S.C., 1960, JD, 1969. Prodn. planning analyst Owens-Corning Fiberglas, Anderson, S.C., 1964-66; assoc. law Turner, Padget, Graham & Laney, Columbia, S.C., 1969-72, ptnr., from 1972, mng. ptnr., from 1987. Mem. faculty Nat. Inst. Trial Advocacy, Columbia, 1982-84, intensive trial advocacy instr. U. S.C., Columbia, 1988-89; commr. State Bd. on Grievances and Discipline, Columbia, 1983-85. Instr. Adult Literacy Program, Columbia, 1987-89; commr. Richland County Airport Commn., Columbia, 1989—; coun. mem. Nat. Bicentennial Constitution Commn., Columbia, 1987—; vice chmn. Hammond Acad. Bd., Columbia, 1982-88. Fellow S.C. Bar Found.; mem. ABA, S.C. Bar Assn. (ho. of dels. 1983-89, nominating com. 1986-89, CLE com. 1987-89, chmn. law practice mgmt. com. 1989—), Richland County Bar Assn. (exec. com. 1984-89, pres. elect 1987-88, pres. 1988-89), S.C. Def. Trial Attys. Assn., Rotary, Sigma Chi (pres. Columbia chpt. 1959-60). Republican. Methodist. Avocations: photography, videography, piloting, water sports, boating, woodworking. Home: Greenville, SC. Died Apr. 30, 2006.

MARTIN, ERNEST E., church supplies company executive; b. Boston, June 20, 1936; s. Harold E. and Florence (Whitman) M.; m. Virginia Ellen LeNormand, July 27, 1957; children— Bradford, Joanna. B.S. in Pharmacy, Mass. Coll. Pharmacy, 1961; M.B.A., Harvard U., 1963. Portfolio mgr., dir. research funds Keystone Funds, Boston, 1967-75, v.p. adminstrn., 1975-77; pres. Olive Branch, Inc., Norwell, Mass., 1975—, Whittemore's, Needham Heights, Mass., 1980—. Mem. Fin. Analysts Fedn. Home: Norwell, Mass. Died Feb. 28, 2007.

MARTIN, GENE B., geologist, oil company executive; b. Amarillo, Tex., Oct. 31, 1931; s. John Claude and Lydia (Bourland) M.; m. Patsy Lynn Caldwell, Aug. 18, 1952; children— Gene B., Judy Lynn Martin Morro. B.S. in Petroleum Geology, Miss. State U., 1953, M.S. in Gen. Geology, 1954. Instr. geology Miss. U., Starkville, 1954-55; paleontologist Gulf Oil Corp. and Gulf Research, New Orleans, 1957-66; paleontologist Atlantic Richfield Co., Corpus Christi, Tex., 1966-69, sr. paleontologist Corpus Christi and Houston, 1969-76; sr. geol. assoc. Arco Oil & Gas Co., Houston, 1976-81; dir. stratigraphy and paleontology Arco Exploration Co., Houston, 1981-85, mgr. stratigraphy and paleontology, 1985—, sr. advisor geol. support group. Author tech. papers. Served as sgt. U.S. Army, 1955-57. Mem. Am. Assn. Petroleum Geologists, Soc. Econ. Paleontologists and Mineralogists (hon. Gulf Coast sect.), Houston Geol. Soc., Sigma Gamma Epsilon. Republican. Baptist. Club: University (Houston). Avocations: golf; fishing. Home: Laurel, Miss. Died Feb. 14, 2006.

MARTIN, JAMES ALFRED, JR., religious studies educator; b. Lumberton, NC, Mar. 18, 1917; s. James Alfred and Mary (Jones) M.; m. Ann Bradsher, June 1, 1936 (dec. 1982); m. Nell Gifford, Jan. 6, 1984. AB, Wake Forest Coll., 1937, LittD, 1965; MA, Duke U., 1938; PhD, Columbia U., 1944; student, Union Theol. Sem., 1940-43; MA (hon.), Amherst Coll., 1950. Ordained to ministry Bapt. Ch., 1944; asst. pastor Roxboro (N.C.) Ch., 1937-38; instr. philosophy and psychology Wake Forest Coll., 1938-40; asst. philosophy religion Union Theol. Sem., NYC, 1941-44, Danforth prof. religion in higher edn., 1960-67, adj. prof. philosophy religion, 1967-82; prof. religion Columbia U., 1967-82, prof. emeritus, from 1982, chmn. dept., 1968-77; asst. prof. religion Amherst Coll., 1946-47, asso. prof., 1947-50, prof., 1950-54, Marquand and Stone prof., 1954-57, Crosby prof. religion, 1957-60. Ordained deacon P.E. Ch., 1953; vis. prof. Cornell U., summer 1948, Mt. Holyoke Coll., 1949-50, 52-53, 59-60, State U. Iowa, summer 1959, U. N.C., summer 1964; Univ. prof. Wake Forest U., 1984—; vis. prof. religious studies U. Va., 1984; asso. mem. East-West Philosophers Conf., U. Hawaii, 1949 Author: Empirical Philosophies of Religion, 1944, (with J.A. Hutchison) Ways of Faith, 1953, rev., 1960, Fact, Fiction, and Faith, 1960, The New Dialogue between Philosophy and Theology, 1966, Beauty and Holiness, 1990; contbr. articles to profl. jours. and encys., chpts. to books. Chmn. bd. visitors Wake Forest Coll., 1981-83. Served as lt. chaplain USNR, 1944-46, PTO. Recipient Disting. Alumnus award Wake Forest U., 1971, Nat. Faculty award Assn. of Grad. Liberal Studies Programs, 1995. Mem. Soc. Values in Higher Edn. (Kent fellow, pres. 1964-69), Am. Theol. Soc. (v.p. 1981-82, pres. 1982), Soc. Theol. Discussion, Soc. Philosophy of Religion, Phi Beta Kappa, Omicron Delta Kappa, Pi Kappa Alpha. Died Jan. 24, 2007.

MARTIN, JAMES R., lawyer; b. Nov. 14, 1937; BA, Rutgers U., 1959; JD, U. Houston, 1968. Bar: Tex. 1968, Calif. 1969. Law clk. to Hon. John R. Brown U.S. Ct. Appeals (5th cir.), 1968-69; ptnr. Gibson, Dunn & Crutcher, LA. Lectr. law U. Houston, 1967-68. Editor-in-chief Houston Law Review, 1967-68. Mem. ABA (vice-chmn. antitrust sect., intellectual property). Died July 4, 2007.

MARTIN, JERRY C., oil company executive; b. Indpls., May 10, 1932; s. Joel C. and Blanche J. (Traubel) M.; m. Marilyn L. Brock, Sept. 7, 1952 (div. 1976); children: Cathy J., Kiefer, Douglas E.; m. Connie B. Young, May 8, 1979 (div. 1988); m. Rachel M. Fulgieri, Aug. 22, 1990. BS in Acctg., Butler U., 1953. Acct. Allison div. Gen. Motors, Indpls., 1953-57; acctng. and budget mgr. Standard Oil, Indpls., 1957-60; budget dir. Inland Container Corp., Indpls., 1960-71; corp. controller Storm Drilling and Marine Co., Chgo., 1971-75; v.p. Scottsman Norwood, Houston, 1975-76; corp. controller Internat Systems and Controls, Houston, 1976-79; v.p., controller Global Marine Drilling Co., Houston, 1979-85; sr. v.p., chief fin. officer Global Marine, Inc., Houston, from 1985. Bd. dirs. Global Marine Inc., 1993—. Mem. Fin. Execs. Inst., Mensa, Westlake Club, Westside Tennis Club, Houstonian Club. Republican. Avocation: tennis. Home: La Jolla, Calif. Died Nov. 28, 2006.

MARTIN, JOHN HUGH, lawyer, retired; b. Los Angeles, Apr. 19, 1918; s. John Hume and Carrie Suzanne (Hatcher) M.; m. Jean Morrison Park, Sept. 17, 1945; 1 dau., Suzanne L. BS, Monmouth Coll., 1939; JD, U. Chgo., 1942. Bar: Ill. 1943, Calif. 1962. Practice law, Chgo., 1943-52; sec., gen. counsel Am. Community Builders, Park Forest, Ill., 1952-54; dep. counsel Bur. Aero., Dept. Navy, Washington, 1954-57; with Lockheed Aircraft Corp., Burbank, Calif., 1957-79, European counsel, 1960-61, div. counsel, 1961-71, asst. sec., chief counsel, 1971-77, corp. adv., 1977-79; pvt. practice law, 1980-94; retired, 1994. Mem. Am., Fed., Internat., Los Angeles County bar assns., Phi Alpha Delta. Clubs: Legal (Chgo.);. Democrat. Episcopalian. Home: Walla Walla, Wash. Died Mar. 21, 2006.

MARTIN, LESLIE PAUL, food products executive; b. Harrison, Ark., Aug. 31, 1920; s. John Carlyle and Omapearl (Guinne) M.; m. Margie Leverne Thomas, June 1, 1941; children: Paula Kaye, Linda Gaye. Grad. high sch., Harrison, Ark. Clk. Kroger Co., Ft. Smith, Fayetteville and Springdale, Ark., 1939-40, store mgr. Paris, Ark., 1940-51, Ft. Smith, 1951-53; sales mgr. Hale-Halsell Co., Tulsa, 1953-72, 1972-83, sr. v.p. mktg., from 1983, also bd. dirs. Bd. dirs., sec. Git-N-Go Inc., Tulsa; bd. dirs., v.p. Sipes Foodmarkets, Tulsa,, Foodland Inc., H-H Foods Inc., Valu-Fare Inc. Chmn. food div. United Way, Tulsa, 1971-72. Served with USN, 1943-45. Mem. Consistory Club. Democrat. Christian Ch. Lodges: Elks, Lions. Avocation: golf. Home: Tulsa, Okla. Died Dec. 13, 2005.

MARTIN, PAUL ROSS, editor; b. Lancaster, Pa., May 14, 1932; s. Paul Rupp and Amanda (Minnich) M.; m. Julia Ibbotson, June 5, 1954 (div. Apr. 1979); children: Monica Martin Goble, Julia, Paul Jr., Barbara, Drew, Eric. BA, Dartmouth Coll., 1954. Reporter, wire editor Lancaster New Era, Lancaster Newspapers Inc., 1954-60; copyreader, makeup editor Wall St. Jour. divsn. Dow Jones & Co., NYC, 1960-63, copy editor nat. news, 1963-69, editor bus. and fin. column, 1969-72, nat. copydesk chief, 1972-75, page one sr. spl. writer, 1975-90, asst. to mng. editor, 1990-93, asst. mng. editor, 1993—2002. Editor: The Possible Dream, 1978, Retirement Without Fear, 1981, Wall Street Journal Style Book, 1981, 4th edit., 1995, The Wall Street Journal Guide to Business Style and Usage, 2002; co-author, editor: American Dynasties Today, 1983. Bd. dirs. Cmty. Bd. 1, S.I., N.Y., 1976-80. Mem. N.Y. Fin. Writers Assn. (past officer). Avocations: basketball, tennis, travel. Home: Staten Island, NY. Died July 5, 2007.

MARTIN, PAUL SIMEON, lawyer; b. Berlin, Sept. 20, 1914; came to U.S., 1915; s. Simeon and Rochlya (Trifon) M.; m. Claire Bond, Apr. 7, 1940; children— Daniel, George, Lawrence. BS in Engring, Coll. City N.Y., 1935, E.E., 1936; LL.B., JD, George Washington U., 1942. Bar: D.C. bar 1942, N.Y. bar 1948, U.S. Ct. Customs and Patent Appeals 1952. Patent examiner U.S. Patent Office, Washington, 1938-44; mem. staff Columbia U./War Contracts Div., Mineola, N.Y., 1944-46; patent atty. Sylvania Elec. Products, NYC, 1946-54; patent counsel Fed. Pacific Electric Co., Newark, 1954-73, gen. counsel, from 1973. Mem. Bar Assn. D.C., Am., N.Y., N.J. patent law assns. Patentee. Died Feb. 10, 2006.

MARTIN, PRESTON, finance company executive, consultant; b. LA, Dec. 5, 1923; s. Oscar and Gaynell (Horn) M.; 1 child, Pier Preston; m. Genevieve Martin, 2 stepchildren BS in Fin., U. So. Calif., 1947, MBA, 1948; PhD in Monetary Econs., U. Ind., 1952. Prof. fin. Grad. Sch. Bus. Adminstrn. U. So. Calif., 1950-60; prin. in housebldg. firm, 1952-56; cons. mortgage fin. and consumer fin. instns., 1954-57; commr. savs. and loan State of Calif., 1967-69; chmn. Fed. Home Loan Bank Bd., Washington, 1969-72; founder, CEO PMI Mortgage Ins. Co., 1972-80; chmn., CEO Seraco Group subs. Sears, Roebuck & Co., 1980-81; vice chmn. Fed. Res. Sys., Washington, 1982—86; chmn., CEO WestFed Holdings Inc., LA, 1986-92, SoCal Holdings, Inc., LA, 1987-93, H.F. Holdings, Inc., San Francisco, 1986, Honolulu Fed. Bank, Honolulu. Founder Fed. Home Loan Mortgage Corp. (Freddie Mac), 1970; prof. bus. econ. and fin. Inst. Per Lo Studio Orgn. Aziendale, Turin, Italy; bd. dirs., chmn. audit com. ITLA Capital Corp Author: Principles and Practices of Real Estate, 1959; co-author: The Complete Idiot's Guide to the Federal Reserve, 2003. Mem. President's Commn. on Housing, 1980-81; prin. Coun. Excellence in Govt., Washington; bd. dirs. Neighborhood Housing Services Am., Operation Hope Recipient House and Home award, 1969; award Engrng. News Record, 1971; Turntable award Nat. Assn. Home Builders, 1973; Housing Hall of Fame award, Nat. Assn. Home Builders, 2001. Mem. Lambda Chi Alpha. Presbyterian. Home: San Francisco, Calif. Died May 30, 2007.

MARTIN, WILLIAM C., III, lawyer; b. Knoxville, Tenn., Sept. 17, 1942; BS, U. Tenn., 1966; JD with honors, Fla. State U., 1970. Bar: Fla. 1971. Counsel Fla. Hotel and Motel Assn., 1986-87; with Akerman, Senterfitt & Eidson P.A., Orlando, Fla. Assoc. editor Fla. State U. Law Review, 1969-70. Bd. dirs. Jr. Achievement, 1987-92, U. Ctrl. Fla. Found., Econ. Devel.

Commn. Mid.-Fla. Mem. ABA, Fla. Bar (chmn. eighteenth cir. grievance com. 1978-79, atty. realtor joint com. 1983-84), Citrus Club (bd. govs.). Died June 19, 2006.

MARTIN, WILLIAM DISKIN, lawyer, judge; b. Pitts., Mar. 1, 1920; s. Michael J. and Julia M. (Diskin) M.; m. Catherine Martin, Apr. 12, 1958; children— Linda Autore, Maureen E. Martin. B.A., St. Francis Coll., 1942; J.D., Duquesne U., 1952. Asst. dist. atty. Allegheny County, Pitts., 1957-79, solicitor, clk. of cts., 1979-80; dist. judge, Bethel Park, Pa., 1981—. Served to capt. USMC, 1942-46. Democrat. Roman Catholic. Lodge: Elks. Home: Bethel Park, Pa. Died Apr. 24, 2006.

MARTIN, WILLIAM NELSON, state legislator, lawyer; b. Eden, NC, May 25, 1945; s. Thomas W. and Carolyn (Henderson) M.; m. Hazel Broadnax, June 11, 1966 (div. 1975); children: Thomas W. and William N. (twins); m. Patricia A. Yancey, May 28, 1983. BS, N.C. A&T U., Greensboro, 1966; JD, George Washington U., 1973. Bar: D.C. 1974, N.C. 1975. Mgmt. trainee IBM, Bridgeport, Conn., 1966-68; claims adjuster Liberty Mut. Ins. Co., Bridgeport, 1968-70; assoc. Frye, Johnson, Barbee, Breensboro, 1974-76; gen. practice law Breensboro, from 1976; mem. N.C. Senate. Mem. Greensboro Housing Commn., 1979-82; bd. dirs. Triad Sickle Cell Anemia Found., Greensboro, 1978—, Nat. Black Child Devel. Inst., Washington, 1980-82; co-founder, bd. dirs. One Step Further, Greensboro, 1982—, Charlotte Hawkins Brown Hist. Found., Greensboro, 1983—. Recipient Outstanding Leadership award Nat. Assn. Negro Bus. and Profl. Women's Clubs, 1983, Man of Yr. award, 1983; Disting. Svc. award Rutledge Coll., 1983. Mem. N.C. Bar Assn., Greensboro Men's Club, Zeta Phi Beta (award for cmty. svc. and human rels. 1978), Phi Beta Sigma (Outstanding Svc. award 1980). Democrat. Baptist. Home: Greensboro, NC. Died Apr. 7, 2007.

MARTONIK, JOHN F., JR., former federal agency administrator; b. Pitts., 1949; m. Maryanne Martonik; children: Daniel, Rachel, Joanne, Luke. Grad., U. Pitts., MS in Indsl. Engring., 1972. Cert. indsl. hygenist. With Mine Safety & Health Adminstrn. US Dept. Labor, 1972—77, with OSHA, 1977—2004. Recipient Sec.'s Exceptional Achievement award, numerous others. Mem. Am. Conf. Govtl. Indsl. Hygienists (chmn.). Died July 11, 2007.

MARVIN, HELEN RHYNE, state senator; b. Gastonia, N.C., Nov. 30, 1917; d. Dane S. and Tessie (Hastings) Rhyne; B.A. magna cum laude, Furman U., 1938; M.A., La. State U., 1938; postgrad. Winthrop Coll., U. N.C.-Chapel Hill, U. N.C.-Charlotte, U. Colo., U. Vt., U. Oslo; m. Ned Marvin, Nov. 21, 1941; children— Kathryn Nisbet, Richard Morris, David Rhyne. Pres. Gaston County Democratic Women, 1973-75; mem. Gaston County Dem. Exec. Com., 1973-76; mem. N.C. State Dem. Exec. Com., 1973-76; del. Nat. Dem. Conv., 1972, 84; mem. N.C. Senate, 1977—, vice chairperson edn. com., 1979-82, vice-chairperson law enforcement and crime control com., 1981-82, appropriations com., 1981—, chmn. congl. redistricting com., 1981-82, constl. amendment com., 1983-84, 89-92, chmn. legis. study com. on social, econ. and legal needs of women, 1981-86, chmn. pensions and retirement com., 1985-87, vice chmn. children and youth com., 1985-87, chmn. appropriations com. on justice and pub. safety, 1987—, vice chmn. P&R com., 1987—. Bd. dirs. N.C. Equity, Inc., Gaston County Mental Health Assn., Gaston County Family Svcs., Inc., Gaston County Council for Children with Spl. Needs, Gaston County Children's Council, N.C. Coalition on Adolescent Pregnancy, Planned Parenthood, Holy Angels Nursery, With Friends (shelter for runaway children), Carolinas HIV/AIDS Consortium; past mem., sec. So. Piedmont Health Services Agy.; past mem. N.C. State Health Coordinating Council, N.C. State Textbook Commn.; past chairperson N.C. Council on Status of Women, N.C. State Social Services Commn., N.C. Day Care Adv. Council; mem. N.C. Commn. on Yr. 2000; former mem. Gov.'s Advocacy Council on Children and Youth; former mem. N.C. Apprenticeship Council; trustee Vagabond Sch. Drama, Flat Rock Playhouse; former mem. bd. N.C. Child Advocacy Inst.; active N.C. Child Support Council; elder 1st Presbyterian Ch., 1983—. Recipient N.C. Disting. Woman award, 1987, Valand award, 1980, 89, N.C. Mental Health Dir.'s award, 1988, Ham Stevens award for svc. to Pub. Health in N.C., 1988, Ellen Winston award for Social Svcs. Legislation, 1989, Svc. to Pub. Edn. award N.C. Assn. Educators, 1989, N.C. Pediatric award for Svc. to Children, 1990, 1990 Headstart award, 1990, Advocate for Children award N.C. Child Advocacy Inst., 1992, N.C. Assn. for Edn. Young Children award; named Gaston County Outstanding Woman, 1990. Mem. So. Polit. Sci. Assn., N.C. Polit. Sci. Assn. (pres. 1976-77), Altrusa, Delta Kappa Gamma. Home: Gastonia, NC. Died Apr. 11, 2006.

MARWIL, STANLEY JACKSON, chemical engineer, consultant; b. Henderson, Tex., Aug. 13, 1921; s. Mose H. and Stella (Jackson) M.; m. Wilma Estella Cary, Nov. 6, 1949; children— Earl S., Nelson L. B.S. in Chem. Engring., Tex. A&M U., 1943, M.S. in Chem. Engring., 1948. Registered profl. engr., Tex. Sect. supr. Phillips Petroleum Co., Bartlesville, Okla., 1961-84, supr. air sensitive catalyst, 1984-85; mgr. Marco Engring., Bartlesville, 1985—. Patentee in field. Served with U.S. Army, 1943-45; PTO. Recipient Andre Wilkens Meml. award, 1984. Mem. Am. Inst. Chem. Engrs. (past chmn. Bartlesville sect.), Tex. Inst. for the Advancement of Chem. Tech., Com. for Devel. of Downstream Industries, Tau Beta Pi. Republican. Methodist. Lodge: Masons. Home: Bartlesville, Okla. Died Mar. 2, 2006.

MASLOW, WILL, lawyer, legal association administrator; b. Kiev, Russia, Sept. 27, 1907; came to U.S., 1911, naturalized, 1924; s. Saul and Raeesa (Moonves) M.; m. Beatrice Greenfield, Dec. 21, 1933; children: Laura, Catha. AB, Cornell U., 1929; JD, Columbia U., 1931. Bar: N.Y. 1932, U.S. Supreme Ct. 1932. Reporter N.Y. Times, 1929-31; assoc. Arthur Garfield Hays, 1931-34; assoc. counsel Dept. Investigation, NYC, 1934-36; trial atty., trial examiner NLRB, 1937-43; dir. field operations Pres.'s Com. Fair Employment Practice, 1943-45; gen. counsel Am. Jewish Congress, 1945—60, exec. dir., 1960-72. Faculty N.Y. Sch. Social Research, 1948-60; adj. prof. Coll. City N.Y., 1965-84. Editor: Boycott Report, 1977—94, Radical Islamic Fundamentalism Update, 1995—99. Trustee Meml. Found. for Jewish Culture; bd. dirs. Interracial Council for Bus. Opportunity, A. Philip Randolph Inst. Recipient Nat. award Jewish Coun. Pub. Affairs, 1998, award for def. of equal rights NY Bar Assn., 1963. Mem. World Jewish Congress (exec. com.), ACLU (dir. 1963-72), Am. Jewish Congress (Stephen Wise laureate 1972), Phi Beta Kappa. Home: New York, NY. Died Feb. 23, 2007.

MASON, BURTON EUGENE, JR., securities trader; b. St. Albans, NY, Nov. 9, 1942; s. Burton Eugene and Anne (Carlow) Mason; m. Geraldine Lennon, July 24, 1971; children: Joseph, Kathryn, Peter. BS, W.Va. Wesleyan Coll., 1964. Broker fgn. exch. Burton E. Mason, Inc., NYC, 1960—77, v.p., 1967—71, pres., chmn. bd., 1972—77; asst. mgr., broker in charge, assoc. v.p. investments, v.p. investments A.G. Edwards & Sons, 1977—83, assoc. v.p., from 1983. Recipient Eagle Scout award, Boy Scouts Am., 1957. Mem.: Commodity Futures Trading Commn., Fgn. Exch. Brokers Assn. N.Y.C. (past pres.), Shriners, Elks, Masons. Republican. Methodist. Home: Venice, Fla. Died Feb. 22, 2007.

MASON, ROBERT JOSEPH, automotive parts company executive; b. Muskegon, Mich., Nov. 17, 1918; s. Robert J. and Delora (Houle) M.; m. Kathleen Carr, June 24, 1944 (dec. Nov. 1965); children: Marcia (Mrs. Richard Dwyer), Eileen A. (Mrs. Thomas Wilhelm); m. Carol F. Fales, Jan. 31, 1967. MBA, U. Chgo., 1941. Accounting analyst Carnegie-Ill. Steel Corp., Gary, Ind., 1941-45; with Sealed Power Corp., Muskegon, 1945-83, sec.-treas., 1959-70, v.p. finance, 1970-83, dir., 1972-92. Bd. dirs. Muskegon County United Appeal, Muskegon Area C. of C.; adv. bd. Mercy Hosp. Mem. C. of C., Fin. Execs. Inst., Am. Soc. Corp. Secs. Clubs: Century (pres., dir.), Muskegon Country (past bd. dirs.). Home: Fruitport, Mich. Died Nov. 7, 2005.

MASON, STANLEY I., JR., inventor, management consulting executive; b. Trenton, NJ, Aug. 18, 1921; s. Stanley I. Sr. and Anna (Kane) M.; m. Charlotte Creighton Guhr, Aug. 22, 1942; children: Stanley I. III, Douglas C., Mary M. Jager, Richard L. BS in Edn., N.J. State U., 1943; postgrad., Rollings Coll., 1956; cert., Sch. Fine and Indsl. Arts, Trenton. Tech. advt. copywriter Armstron Cork Co., Lancaster, Pa., 1947-48; dir. tech. mktg. Delkote, Inc., Wilmington, Del., 1949-53; mgr. tech. reporting and presentations The Martin Co., Balt. and Orlando, Fla., 1946-49, 53-58; dir. tech. and packaging devel. Hunt Food and Industries (name changed: Norton Simon, Inc.), 1958-67; product devel. v.p. Am. Can Co., 1967-69, v.p. product devel. and tech. and creative svcs., 1967-73; pres., chief exec. officer Simco, Inc., Weston, Conn., from 1973, Simco Tex., Inc., Houston, from 1980. Chmn. Masonware Corp., Newport Beach, Calif., 1978—; pres., chmn. Crisis Communications, Inc., Weston, 1984—, Family Security Systems, Weston, 1986—, Advanced Village Techs., Weston, 1985—; cons. Johnson & Johnson, Health Care Div., Surgikos, Dental Group, Personal Products, Chicopee Am. Hosp. Supply, Kimberly Clark Corp., Internat. Playtes, S.C. Johnson, Velcro Fastening Systems, Procter & Gamble, Neutrogena. Patentee in field; guest lectr. U. Pa., U. Wash., U. Neb., NYU, U. So. Calif., John F. Kennedy U., Fordham U., U. Hawaii, Santa Rosa Jr. Coll., Inventors Can. Symposium, U. Wis., Entrepreneurial Women's Network, Westport Rotary Club. Bd. dirs. Mason Rsch. Found., Honolulu, 1986—. 1st lt. USAF, 1943-46. Mem. Nat. Coun. Indsl. Innovation (trustee 1975), Nat. Congress Inventor Orgn. (bd. dirs. 1975), Inventors Coun. Hawaii, Nat. Def. Exec. Res. Died Dec. 6, 2005.

MASON, THOMAS RICHARD, higher education planner, researcher; b. Trinidad, Colo., Apr. 17, 1930; s. Abraham Gartin and Ethel Arlene (Jackson) M.; m. Margaret Marie Emma Bartram, Aug. 11, 1950 (div. 1979); m. 2d, Mary Lucille Coghlan, Aug. 2, 1980. A.B. magna cum laude, U. Colo., 1952, M.A. (Rotary Found. fellow), 1955; postgrad. London Sch. Econs. and Polit. Sci., 1952-53; Ph.D. (Ford Found. fellow), Harvard U., 1963. News writer, announcer Sta. KBOL, Boulder, Colo., 1948-53; asst. to pres. U. Colo.-Boulder, 1955-56, planning officer, 1959-64; dir. planning U. Rochester, N.Y., 1964-68; dir. instl. research U. Colo.-Boulder, 1968-72, dir. spl. studies, planning, Denver, 1972-74, dir. spl. studies, Boulder, 1975-76; pres. MIRA Inc., Mpls., 1977—. Author: (with others) Higher education Facilities Planning and Management Manuals, 1971; (with Paul L. Dressel & Assocs.) Institutional Research in the University, 1971; editor: Assessing Computer-Based Systems Models, 1976; contbr. numerous papers in field to profl. jours. Mem. Zoning Rev. Com., City of Boulder (Colo.), 1959, Com. on Utility Ownership Study, 1969-70, Com. on Analysis of Growth, 1971-72. Recipient Outstanding Young Men of Am. award, 1965. Mem. Assn. for Instl. Research (pres. 1969-70), Soc. Coll. and Univ. Planning, World Futures Soc., Phi Beta Kappa. Mem. Democratic Farm Labor Party. Roman Catholic. Died July 11, 2007.

MASS, EDWARD RUDOLPH, accountant, finance executive; b. Chgo., Feb. 28, 1926; s. Rudolph and Michelena (Eiben) M.; m. Florence Urso, Sept. 4, 1948; children: MaryChris, Juli, Kurt. BS in Acctg., Northwestern U., 1950. CPA, Ill. Asst. chief acct. Signode Corp., Chgo., 1950-59; asst. treas. Stepan Chem., Northfield, Ill., 1959-67; treas. Mass Feeding Corp., Des Plaines, Ill., 1967-69; corp. controller Nuclear Chicago Corp., Des Plaines, 1969-74; v.p. fin. Cherry Corp., Waukegan, Ill., from 1974. Mem. Am. Inst. CPA's. Roman Catholic. Avocations: sports, reading, investing. Home: Sun Lakes, Ariz. Died Mar. 1, 2006.

MAST, STEWART DALE, retired airport manager; b. Kalamazoo, May 10, 1924; s. Virgil S. and S. Louise (Rippey) M.; m. Judy Jo Bolton; children: Peter S., Frances Ann Mast Adams; m. May 20, 1979. Student, U. Mich., 1942-43; grad., Spartan Sch. Aerospace, Tulsa, 1946, Argubright Bus. Coll., Battle Creek, Mich., 1947. Mgr. Mcpl. Airport, Battle Creek, 1948-60; airport dir. Mitchell Field, Milw., 1961-66; mgr. Tampa (Fla.) Internat. Airport, 1966-89; ret., 1989. Pres. Mich. Assn. Airport Mgrs., 1958. Past mem. aviation coun. Milw. C. of C., Hillsborough County C. of C., Tampa; past mem. bd. rev. Boy Scouts Am., Milw.; bd. dirs. Sun'n Fun Aviation Found., Inc., Lakeland, Fla., 1992—, Sun'n Fun Fly-in, Inc., Lakeland, Fla., 1994—. 1st lt. USAAF, 1943-45. Recipient Cmty. Leadership award Greater Tampa C. of C., 1979. Mem. Am. Assn. Airport Execs. (past bd. dirs., Pres.'s award 1979), Fla. Assn. Airport Mgrs. Avocations: aviation philately, photography. Home: Tampa, Fla. Died Apr. 10, 2007.

MASTROPIERI, FRANCIS JOHN, construction company executive; b. Needham, Mass., Oct. 4, 1925; s. Nicola and Maria Paula (Martini) M.; m. Dorothy Marie Hansen, Nov. 23, 1947; children— Paula, Margo, Lisa BS in Civil Engring. cum laude, Northeastern U., 1946. Field engr. Vappi & Co., Inc., Cambridge, Mass., 1952-54, supt., 1954-64, v.p., 1964-77, Mardian Constrn. Co., Phoenix, 1977-81, pres., 1981-85, chmn., chief exec. officer, from 1985. Bd. dirs. nat. council Northeastern U., 1952— Mem. Assoc. Gen. Contractors (bd. dirs. Mass. 1971-77, nat. bd. dirs. 1972-77, bd. dirs. Ariz. bldg. chpt. 1984—), Tau Beta Pi Clubs: Phoenix Country (house com. 1984-85), Mansion (Phoenix). Republican. Roman Catholic. Home: Saint Petersburg, Fla. Died Mar. 16, 2006.

MATAXIS, THEODORE CHRISTOPHER, consultant, lecturer, writer, retired army officer, educator; b. Seattle, Aug. 17, 1917; s. Chris P. and Edla (Osterdahl) M.; m. Helma Mary Jensen, Aug. 27, 1940; children: Shirley Jeanne (Mrs. J. L. Slack), Theodore Christopher, Kaye Louise (Mrs. Vernon P. Isaacs, Jr.). BA, U. Wash., 1940; student, Def. Services Staff Coll., India, 1950-51, Army War Coll., 1957-58; MA in Internat. Relations, George Washington U., 1965. Commd. 2d lt. U.S. Army, 1940, advanced through grades to brig. gen., 1967; inf. bn. comdr. Europe, World War II; regt. comdr. Korea, 1952-53; mem. Gov. Harriman's Presdl. Mission to Establish Mil. Aid Program India, 1962; mil. asst., speech writer for chmn. Joint Chiefs of Staff, 1962-64; sr. adviser II Vietnamese Army Corps. Pleiku, 1964-65; dep. comdr. 1st Brigade, 101st Airborne Div., 1966; asst. div. comdr. 82d Airborne Div., 1967; chief army sect. Army Mission/MAAG Iran, 1968-70; asst., acting div. comdr. Americal Div. Vietnam, 1970; chief mil. equipment delivery team Cambodia, 1971-72; ret., 1972; ednl. and systems mgmt. cons. Republic of Singapore, 1972-74; asst. supt., comdt. cadets Valley Forge Mil. Acad., Wayne, Pa., 1975-83; dir. AZED Assocs., Ltd., Southern Pines, N.C., from 1983; faculty Am. Mil. U., from 1993. Author: (with Seymour Goldberg) Nuclear Tactics, 1958, (chpt.) International Affairs in South West Asia, 1984, American Military Encyclopedia; also numerous mil. and hist. articles. Mem. adv. council Com. for Free Afghanistan. Decorated D.S.M., Silver Star, D.F.C., Bronze Star with 3 oak leaf clusters with V, Commendation medal with 3 oak leaf clusters and V, Joint Services Commendation medal, Purple Heart with oak leaf cluster, Legion of Merit with 2 oak leaf clusters, Air medal with V and 30 oak leaf clusters, Combat Inf. Badge with 2 stars (U.S.); Nat. Order 5th class; Distinguished Service Order; 4 Gallantry crosses; Honor medal 1st class; Air medal Vietnam; Def. medal Order of Republic Cambodia; Chapel of Four Chaplains-Legion of Honor. Mem. Oral History Assn., Soc. Study Mil. History, U.S. Commn. on Mil. History, Mil. Order World Wars (life), Am. Coun. for Study Islamic Socs., The Federalist Rsch. Inst. (bd. dirs.), Am. Legion, VFW, Airborne Assn. (life), 70th Divsn. Assn. (life), Assn. U.S. Army, Nat. Rifle Assn. (endowment mem.), 82d Airborne Divsn. Life Assn. (life), Am. Security Coun. (spkrs. bur.), Ends of the Earth, Scabbard and Blade (adv. coun. nat. soc.), Freedom Medicine (adv. bd.), Def. Policy Coun., Nat. Policy Forum, Am. Immigration Control (mem. adv. bd.). Clubs: Elks (Southern Pines), Army Navy (Washington); Tanglin (Singapore). Died Mar. 8, 2006.

MATHENY, CHARLES WOODBURN, JR., former army officer, civil engineer, city official; b. Sarasota, Fla., Aug. 7, 1914; s. Charles Woodburn Sr. and Virginia (Yates) M.; m. Jeanne Felkel, July 12, 1942; children: Virginia Ann, Nancy Caroline, Charles Woodburn III. BSCE, U. Fla., 1936; grad., Army Command Gen. Staff Coll., 1944. Registered profl. engr., Ga., 1939; cert. surveyor Ga., 1939, lic. comml. pilot 1952. San. engr. Ga. State Dept. Health, 1937—39; civil engr. Fla. East Coast Rlwy., 1939—41; commd. 2d lt. F.A., USAR through ROTC U. Fla., 1936; 1st lt. F.A., USAR, 1939; vol. active army svc. F.A., US Army, 1941; commissioned 2d lt. F.A., US Army (Regular Army), 1942; advanced through grades to col. F.A. USAR, 1955; comdr. 351st Field Arty. Bn., 1944—45; commr. 33rd Field Arty. Bn., 1st Infantry Divsn., 1946; arty. staff officer 33rd Field Arty. Bn., 1st Inf. Divsn., 1947; gen. staff G-3 Plans Dept. Army, 1948—51; qualified Air Force liaison pilot, 1951; qualified Army aviator airplanes and helicopters, 1952; aviation officer 25th Infantry Divsn., Republic of Korea, 1952—53; sr. Army aviation advisor Korean Army, 1953; first dir. combat devel. dept. first dep. comdt. Army Aviation Sch., Ft. Sill, Okla., 1954—55; dep. dir. rsch., dep. dir. dept. tactics U.S. Army Field Arty. and Missile Sch., Ft. Sill, 1955—57; aviation officer 7th U.S. Army, Germany, 1957—58; Munich sub area comdr. So Area Command, 1958—59; qualified sr. army aviator, 1959; dep. chief of staff for info. So. Area Command, 1960; Mich sector comdr. VI Army Corps., 1961—62, ret., 1962; asst. dir Tampa (Fla.) Dept. Pub. Works, 1963—81, ret., 1981. During World War II, Germany Commd., 351st field arty. Bn. in combat and occupation, 1945, also 33d field arty. bn., 1st Inf. Divsn., in occupation, 1946. Initiator and originator of tactical use of helicopters in Army, 1949, Army warrant officer helicopter aviator program and organization of first five Army Transp Helicopter Co. move combat units battlefield authorized T.O. & E, 55-57, Oct. 24, 1950 by U.S. Army Chief of Staff Gen. J Lawton Collins and establishment of a new U.S. Army pers policy making U.S. Army helicopter pilots warrant officers instead of officers, 1950; 1st to envision army combat units and airphibious army divisions equipped with high performance helicopter mobility capable of land, sea or air warfare operations at 200 mph, 1950; initiated and prepared directive signed by Army chief of staff, Gen. J. Lawton Collins ordering first feasibility tests of Army super-mobile inf. and arty. units equipped with helicopter mobility, 1951; pilot 1st combat observation mission in army helicopter, Korea, 1952; organizer comdr., helicopter pilot 1st Army combat ops. using helicopter mobility to support inf. and engr. front line combat units 25th Inf. Divsn., Korea, 1952 proving feasibility of Army helicopter mobility on the battlefield; 1st to advocate, rsch., prepare orgn plans and design of super-mobile Army combat units equipped with armed and unarmed helicopter mobility, with model designs of helicopters armed with missiles, rockets, etc. to equip proposed combat units, 1955-56; proposed development reconnaisance helicopter 1957 similar to Army O/R Comanche, RAH-66 reconnaissance helicopter later developed by Army; U.S. Army first to exploit and develop helicopter mobility due to Matheny's devotion to its early begining; pilot 100 combat observation missions, Korea, 1952-53; author 1st state legis. to establish profl. sch. civil engring. filed in Fla. Legis. by Sen. Julian Lane, 1974; mem. U.S. Army's Strategic Planning Com., 1950-51. Contbr. articles to profl. jours., popular mags. Troop com. Boy Scouts Am., 1965-73; active various cmty. and ch. activities; patron Tampa Art Mus., 1965-83, Tampa Cmty. Concert Series, 1979-82; bd. dirs. Tampa YMCA, 1967-71, Fla. Easter Seal Soc., 1978, Easter Seal Soc. Hillsborough County, 1971-84, hon. bd. dirs., 1984-95, treas., 1973-76, pres., 1977. Decorated Bronze Star with oak leaf cluster, Air medal with three oak leaf clusters; recipient of the Eagle Scout award, 1928; Letterman football U.F., 1933, 35; named to U. Fla. Student Hall of Fame, 1936. Mem. ASCE (pres. West Coast br., dir. Fla. sect. 1973, Engr. of Yr. award West Coast br. Fla. sect. 1979, life mem. 1980), Am. Soc. Profl. Engrs., Fla. Engring. Soc., Am. Pub. Works Assn. (pres. West Coast br. Fla. chpt. 1972, exec. com. Fla. chpt. 1972-77, v.p. 1977, pres. 1978), Ret. Officers Assn., Army Aviation Assn., SAR, Fla. Blue Key, Alpha Tau Omega, Sigma Tau. Episcopalian. Achievements include research in tactical use of helicopter aerial vehicles. Home: Tampa, Fla. Died Apr. 30, 2007.

MATHER, JEAN PAUL, retired academic administrator; b. Del Norte, Colo., Dec. 15, 1914; s. John Bruce and Leona Hawie (Coe) M.; m. Marie Lorraine Wick, Mar. 1, 1936 (dec.); children— Shirley Jeanne, Barbara Lorraine; m. Harriett R. Pepper, July 7, 1981. Student, U. Colo., 1932-35; BSc, U. Denver, 1937, MBA, 1948; student, U. Chgo., 1939; MA, Princeton, 1951; LL.D., Am. Internat. Coll., 1955, Amherst Coll., 1956, Northeastern U., 1958, U. R.I., 1960, U. Hokkaido, 1963, U. Mass., 1974; D.Sc., Lowell Technol. Inst., 1955; Litt.D., Lesley Coll., 1958. Instr. economics Colo. Sch. Mines, 1938-39, asst. prof., 1939-43; instr. econs. U. Denver, 1946-47, asst. prof. econs. and statistics, dir. curriculum and instrn., 1947-48; lectr. Woodrow Wilson Sch. Pub. and Internat. Affairs, Princeton, 1948-51; research assoc. Princeton Surveys State and Local Govt., 1948-51; staff assoc., asst. treas. Am. Council Edn., Washington, 1951-53; provost U. Mass., Amherst, 1953-54, pres., 1954-60, pres. Coll. Testing Program, 1960-62. Cons. N.J. State Tax Commn., 1948-51, Mass. State Tax Commn., 1949-50, Nat. Found. Consumer Credit, Washington, 1951-52, VA, 1958-61; asst. gen. mgr. Purdue Research Found., Lafayette, Ind., 1962-63, v.p., gen. mgr., 1963-64; exec. v.p. Univ. City Sci. Center, Phila., 1964-67, pres., 1967-69; head dept. mineral economics Colo. Sch. of Mines, Golden, 1969-80, United Bank disting. prof., 1969-80; dir. Fidelity Mut. Growth Fund; cons. Maine Commn. Higher Edn., 1966 Served as lt. USNR, 1943-46. Fellow Am. Acad Arts and Sci.; mem. Beta Gamma Sigma, Phi Eta Sigma, Alpha Kappa Psi, Blue Key. Democrat. Congregationalist. Died June 21, 2007.

MATHERS, THOMAS NESBIT, financial consultant; b. Bloomington, Ind., Apr. 22, 1914; s. Frank Curry and Maud Esther (Bowser) M.; m. Helen M. Curtis, Oct. 23, 1943 (dec.); children: Mary, Abigail. AB, Ind. U., 1936, LL.B., 1939; MBA, Harvard U., 1941. Bar: Ind. 1939. Research asst. No. Trust Co., 1941-43; legal asst. Chgo. Ordnance Dist., 1943-44; employee to ptnr. Woodruff Hays & Co., Chgo., 1944-51; pres. Security Counselors, Inc., Chgo., 1951-62, Mathers & Co., Chgo., 1962-75, chmn. bd., 1975-85, vice chmn., 1985-91. Bd. dirs. Lincoln Income Fund, 1978-2001, Lincoln Convertible Securities Fund, 1986-2001; pres. Mathers Fund, 1965-75, chmn. bd., 1975-85, vice chmn., 1985-91; v.p., bd. dirs. OFC Corp. Meadowood Project, 1991—. Trustee Beloit Coll., 1970-2001, life trustee, 2001—. Recipient Disting. Alumni Service award Ind. U., 1979 Mem. Ind. U. Disting. Alumni Assn. (past pres.). Clubs: Union League, Econ. of Chgo, Westmoreland Country, Mich. Shores, Investment Analysts Chgo. (past pres.). Republican. Presbyterian. Home: Winnetka, Ill. Died Apr. 10, 2007.

MATHEWS, DANIEL MONROE, chemist, educator; b. Paris, Ark., Oct. 18, 1926; s. Marion Daniel and Alice Virginia (LeRoy) M.; m. Charlene Faye Alexander, Aug. 13, 1977; children— Judy Kay Mathews Michaels, Janice Carol Mathews Ray. BS, U. Ark., 1952, MS, 1955, PhD, 1959; postgrad., Ga. Inst. Tech., 1956. Research asso. U. Ark., Little Rock, 1952-55, lectr., 1957-59, asst. prof. chemistry, 1958-62, asso. prof., 1963-72, prof., from 1972, prof. emeritus, 1987; instr. Ga. Inst. Tech., Atlanta, 1956; pres. D.M. Mathews, Inc., from 1979. Cons. radiation safety. Contbr. articles to profl. jours. Served with U.S. Army, 1944-45. Mem. Chem. Soc. (London), Am. Chem. Soc., Health Physics Soc., AAAS, Ark. Acad. Sci., Sigma Xi. Home: North Little Rock, Ark. Died July 2, 2006.

MATHEWS, JUDITH ANN, respiratory therapist; b. Elkhart, Ind., Sept. 2, 1947; d. Earl Clifford Jr. and Virginia Eileen (Kyle) M. AS in Respiratory Therapy, Weber State Coll., 1971; BS in Health Adminstrn., Empire State Coll., 1980. Registered respiratory therapist. Sr. technician St. Joseph's Hosp., Mishawaka, Ind., 1967-68; shift supr. LDS Hosp., Primary Children's, Salt Lake City, 1968-71; asst. chief L.I. Jewish Affiliation, Queens Hosp. Ctr., Jamaica, N.Y., 1971-72; program dir. Bergen Community Coll., Paramus, N.J., 1973-74; dir. Columbia-Presbyn. Med. Ctr., NYC, 1974-80; dir. clin. edn. Kalamazoo (Mich.) Valley Community Coll., 1980-82; dir. Mt. Sinai Svcs. City Hosp. Ctr., Elmhurst, N.Y., 1982-85, King Faisal Specialist Hosp., Riyadh, Saudi Arabia, 1986-87; unit head Aramco, Dhahran, Saudi Arabia, 1988-90; dir. Community Hosp., Bklyn., from 1990. Oral examiner Nat. Bd. Respiratory Care, Lenexa, Kans., 1974-78. Mem. Am. Assn. Respiratory Care (bd. dirs. Greater N.Y.C. chpt. 1977-79), N.Y. State Soc. Respiratory Care (bd. dirs. 1977-79). Mem. Lds Ch. Avocations: computers, gourmet cooking, reading, creative writing. Home: Rego Park, NY. Died July 8, 2006.

MATHEWS, RICHARD ALBERT, communications company executive; b. Trenton, NJ, Apr. 15, 1924; s. Albert Hart and Hazel Eva (Richards) M.; children: JoAnn Mathews Higgins, Linda Jane Mathews Mitchell, Richard Hart, Theodore Morss; m. Barbara Neilson Hilliard, June 14, 1980. B.E.E., Rutgers U., 1948. Registered profl. engr., N.Y. With N.J. Bell Telephone Co., 1948-50; with N.Y. Telephone Co., 1950-59, 59-61, 62-66, 72-81, gen. mgr. Utica, 1959-61, v.p. mktg., 1962-64, v.p. planning, 1964-66, v.p. ops. and engring., 1972-81; planning engr. AT&T, 1959, asst. v.p. mktg., 1961-62, asst. v.p. tng. and edn., 1981-83, corp. v.p. human resources, from 1983. Gen. dir. Bell Telephone Labs., Piscataway, N.J., 1966-72 Mem. Phi Beta Kappa, Tau Beta Pi. Home: Bernardsville, NJ. Died Jan. 17, 2006.

MATSON, WESLEY JENNINGS, educational administrator; b. Svea, Minn., June 25, 1924; s. James and Ettie (Mattson) Matson; m. Doris Cragg. BS with distinction, U. Minn., 1948; MA, U. Calif., Berkeley, 1954; EdD, Columbia U., 1960. High sch. tchr. Santa Barbara County Pub. Schs., Santa Maria, Calif., 1948-50; instr. U. Calif., Berkeley, 1950-54, Columbia U., NYC, 1954-55; lectr. Fordham U., NYC, 1955-56; asst. prof. U. Md., College Park, 1956-59; prof., asst. dean U. Wis., Milw., 1959-72; dean, prof. Winona (Minn.) State U., 1972-88, emeritus, from 1989. Vis. prof. U. P.R., Rio Peidras, We. Wash. U., Bellingham, San Diego State U., U. Minn., Mpls., U. Hawaii; adj. faculty St. Olaf Coll., Northfield, Minn.; cons. U.S. Dept. Edn., Washington, Ill. State U.; bd. regents Wis. Dept. Pub. Instrn.; examiner Nat. Coun. Accreditation Tchr. Edn. North Ctrl. assn., Chgo. Mem. editl. bd. Jour. Instrl. Psychology; contbr. Exec. com. Minn. Alliance of Arts, Mpls.; mem. Minn. com. Certification Stds., St. Paul; cons. ARC; bd. dirs. Ft. Snelling Meml. Chapel Found.; apptd. by Minn. Supreme Ct. to Minn. Bd. CLE. Capt. USAF. Decorated Bronze Star; recipient Disting. Svc. award, Wis. Assn. Tchr. Edn., 1972. Mem.: NEA (life), VFW, Minn. edn. Assn., Assn. Higher Edn., Nat. Assn. Tchr. Educators (exec. com.), Minn. Assn. Colls. for Tchr. Edn. (pres. 1983—85, Hon. life Award of Merit), U. Minn. Alumni Soc. (Outstanding Educator award 1984), Am. Legion, Minn. Hist. Soc., Rotary Club, Alpha Sigma Phi, Kappa Delta Pi, Phi Delta Kappa. Home: Minneapolis, Minn. Died Aug. 12, 2007.

MATTHEWS, DONALD ROWE, political scientist, educator; b. Cin., Sept. 14, 1925; s. William Procter and Janet Burch (Williams) M.; m. Margie C. Richmond, June 28, 1947 (div.); children: Mary, Jonathan; m. Carmen J. Onstad, July 7, 1970 (div.); children: Christopher, Amy. Student, Kenyon Coll., 1943, Purdue U., 1944-45; AB with high honors, Princeton, 1948, MA, 1951, PhD, 1953; Dr. hon. causa, U. Bergen, 1985. Instr. Smith Coll., Northampton, Mass., 1951-53, asst. prof. govt., 1953-57; lectr. polit. sci. U. N.C., Chapel Hill, 1957-58, assoc. prof., 1958-63, prof., 1963-70; research prof. Inst. for Research in Social Sci., 1963-70; sr. fellow in govtl. studies Brookings Instn., Washington, 1970-73; prof. polit. sci. and research assoc. Inst. for Research in Social Sci., U. Mich., Ann Arbor, 1973-76; chmn. dept. polit. sci. U. Wash., Seattle, 1976-83, prof. polit. sci., 1976-94, prof. emeritus, 1995—2007. Guest prof. U. Bergen, Norway, 1980; fellow Ctr. for Advanced Study in the Behavioral Scis., 1964-65; cons. to U.S. Commn. on Civil Rights, 1958-60, NBC News, 1966-68, Ford Found., 1967-68, U.S. Ho. of Reps., 1970-72, others; faculty lectr. U. Wash., 1989. Author: The Social Background of Political Decision-Makers, 1954, U.S. Senators and Their World, 1960, (with James Prothro) Negroes and the New Southern Politics, 1966, Perspectives on Presidential Selection, 1973, (with William Keech) The Party's Choice, 1976, (with James Stimson) Yeas and Nays: A Theory of Decision-Making in the U.S. House of Representatives, 1975, (with Henry Valen) Parliamentary Representation: The Case of the Norwegian Storting, 1999; Contbr. articles to profl. jours. Served with USNR, 1943-46. Recipient Sr. Award for Research in Govtl. Affairs Social Sci. Research Council, 1962; Ford Found. fellow, 1969-70; Guggenheim fellow, 1980-81 Fellow Am. Acad. Arts and Scis.; mem. Am. Polit. Sci. Assn. (treas. 1970-72, v.p. 1985-86), Pacific N.W. Polit. Sci. Assn. (pres. 1977-78), Western Polit. Sci. Assn. (pres. 1979-80), So. Polit. Sci. Assn., Midwestern Polit. Sci. Assn., Inter-Univ. Consortium for Polit. Research (exec. com. 1970-72) Democrat. Home: Seattle, Wash. Died Nov. 3, 2007.*

MATTHEWS, JOHN EDWARD, dentist; b. Indpls., Feb. 17, 1923; s. Edward Michael and Elizabeth (Bethel) M.; m. Willa Jean Trout, June 5, 1948; 1 child, Stepheny. B.S., Ind. U., 1948, D.D.S., 1956. Acct., Eli Lilly Internat. Corp., 1948-52; practice dentistry, Indpls., 1956—. Served with USMC, 1943-46. Mem. ADA, Ind. Dental Assn., Indpls. Dist. Dental Soc., Delta Sigma Delta, Delta Sigma Pi, Alpha Tau Omega. Republican. Roman Catholic. Lodge: K.C. Avocations: fishing; woodworking; bicycling; boating. Home: Indianapolis, Ind. Died Apr. 19, 2007.

MATTISON, JEFFREY RICHARD, consulting engineering company executive, mechanical engineer; b. Springville, N.Y., Apr. 16, 1949; s. Kenneth D. and Beatrice M. (Smock) M.; m. Beverly J. Gerard, Apr. 21, 1972; children: Dawn M., Bradley S. Student Glendale Community Coll., 1967-69, U. Colo., 1969-71. Registered profl. engr., Ariz., Calif. Designer LSW Engring. Co., Phoenix, 1971-78, v.p., project mgr. and design engr., 1982-87; v.p., chief mech. engr. LSW Engring. Co., San Diego, 1987—; dir. computer ops., project mgr. and design engr., 1987—; design engr. Schreiber Engring. Co., Phoenix, 1979-82; com. mem. City of Phoenix Plumbing Code, 1982; com. mem. City of Phoenix Bldg. Safety Adv. Bd., 1986-87. Mem. ASHRAE, Am. Soc. Profl. Engrs., Am. Soc. Plumbing Engrs. (pres. Phoenix chpt. 1981-83). Republican. Roman Catholic. Home: Phoenix, Ariz. Died Feb. 1, 2007.

MATZEN, ROBERT THOMAS, insurance company executive; b. Grand Island, Nebr., May 30, 1924; s. Thomas Adolph and Lois Miriam (Eddy) Matzen; m. Frances Evelyn Udeen, Mar. 1, 1950; children: Mark, Todd, Jan, Jena. BA in Econ., Duke U., 1947. Dist. mgr. western U.S. H.C. Gardner, Inc., 1947—54, asst. v.p. Denver, 1954—63, v.p., 1963—72, pres., 1972—73; v.p. H.C. Gardner. Inc., 1974; pres. Ins. Protectors, Inc., from 1975. Dir. Heritage Fund, Denver, 1973; pres. Colo. Assn. Fire and Casualty Ins. Cos., 1972—74. To ensign USN, 1943—46. Mem.: Denver Athletic Club. Home: Denver, Colo. Died Apr. 8, 2007.

MAURER, WALTER HARDING, educator; b. NYC, July 13, 1921; s. Carl and Frieda (Geib) M.; m. Geraldine Kaufman, Feb. 18, 1961. BA, U. Vt., 1943; postgrad., Princeton U., 1947-48; PhD, U. Pa., 1962. Tchr. classical Greek and German U. Vt., 1946-47; reference librarian South Asia sect. Orientalia div. Library of Congress, Washington, 1950-62; curator South Asia collection East-West Center U. Hawaii, Honolulu, 1962-63; prof. Sanskrit U. Hawaii, from 1962, prof. history, 1964-71, lang. cons. Philosophy East and West, 1967-89, chmn. dept. Indo-Pacific langs., 1971-80. Vis. research fellow Inst. Advanced Studies in Humanities, U. Edinburgh, Scotland, summer 1978 Author: Sugamanvaya Vrtti, 1965, Pinnacles of India's Past, 1986; also articles revs. Served with AUS, 1943-46. Am. Numismatic Soc. grantee, 1948; Fulbright fellow Deccan Coll., Poona, India, 1953-55; Am. Council Learned Socs. area study grantee U. Tübingen, Germany and London, 1968-69; faculty research fellow in Asian and Pacific Studies, 1982-83 Mem. Am. Oriental Soc., Tibet Soc., Royal Asiatic Soc., Sigma Alpha Epsilon, Phi Beta Kappa. Home: Honolulu, Hawaii. Died Aug. 21, 2007.

MAVRIS, NICHOLAS BENNIE, oil industry executive; b. Oklahoma City, Nov. 23, 1923; s. George and Ada Virginia (Diles) Mavris; m. Elizabeth Ann Shaver, July 3, 1943; children: Virginia Ann Mavris Humes, George Samuel, Kathryne Ann Mavris Newton, Nicola Ann. BS in Mech. Engring., Okla. State U., 1948, MS, 1949. Instr. Okla. State U., 1948—49; engr. Interstate Oil Pipeline Co., 1949—51; with Continental Pipe Line Co., Houston, 1951—63; asst. regional mgr. Rocky Mountain region Continental Oil Co., 1963—67, mgr. transp., 1967—68; with Continental Pipe Line Co., Houston, from 1968, pres. and CEO, from 1969. Dir. Continental Pipe Line, Inc., Houston, Platte Pipe Line Co., Explorer Pipeline Co.; pres. Yellowstone Pipe Line Co., 1969—76; chmn. bd. Seadock, Inc., 1972—85, Explorer Pipeline Co., 1979—82; v.p. Seaway, Inc., 1976—84. Bd. dir. Okla. State U. Found., 1976—81, from 1982, trustee, 1975—78. With US Army, 1943—46. Named to Engring. Hall of Fame, Okla. State U., 1979; recipient Disting. Svc. award, 1980. Mem.: Assn. Oil Pipe Lines (exec. com.), Am. Petroleum Inst. (divsn. transp. ctrl. com. from 1968), Rocky Mountain Oil and Gas Assn. (dir.), Houston Petroleum Club, Sugar Creek Country Club, Okla. State U. Alumni Assn. (dir. Houston br. 1973—77). Home: Tulsa, Okla. Died Apr. 21, 2007.

MAXWELL, JOHN CRAWFORD, geology educator; b. Xenia, Ohio, Dec. 28, 1914; s. William and Addie (Crawford) M.; m. Marian Ruth Buchanan, Nov. 4, 1939; children— Judith Margaret, Marilyn Jane. BA, DePauw U., 1936; MA (Thomas F. Andrews fellow), U. Minn., 1937; PhD, Princeton, 1946; DSc (hon.), DePauw U., 1988. Geologist, geophysicist Sun Oil Co., 1938-40; instr. Princeton, 1946-47, asst. prof., 1947-52, assoc. prof., 1952-55, prof. geology, 1955-70, chmn. dept. geol. engring., 1955-66, chmn. dept. geology, 1966-67, chmn. dept. geol. and geophys. scis., 1967-70; Farish chair geol. scis. U. Tex., Austin, 1970-84, prof. emeritus, from 1984. Cons. geologist oil and non-metallic minerals. Chmn. earth sci. div. NRC, 1970-72; chmn. U.S. Nat. Com. for Geodynamics, 1979-84 Served as lt. USNR, 1942-45. Recipient Distinguished Grad. award U. Minn., 1972; NSF sr. post-doctoral fellow Italy, 1961-62 Fellow Geol. Soc. Am. (pres. 1973), Am. Geophys. Union; mem. Am. Geol. Inst. (pres. 1971), Am. Assn. Petroleum Geologists, Yellowstone-Bighorn Research Assn., Societa Geologica Italiana, Sigma Xi (Distinguished lectr. 1967), Phi Beta Kappa. Home: Austin, Tex. Died Jan. 23, 2006.

MAY, BRYCE JON, computer consultant; b. Audubon, Iowa, June 26, 1948; s. Anthony W. and Marie J. (Rasmussen) M. BS, Western Mich. U., 1987. Cert. radiation protection technologist. Congl. aide/counselor Hon. Ron Dellums, Berkeley, Calif., 1973-75; health physics/chemistry engr. Mgmt. Support Svcs., Grand Junction, Mich., 1975-85, pres., from 1985. Treas. Columbia Twp., Van Buren County, Mich., 1995—. With USN, 1968-73. Mem. Bangor Lions (dir. 1992—). Democrat. Avocations: aviation, keyboard music. Died Aug. 12, 2006.

MAYER, FREDERICK RICKARD, oil industry executive; b. Youngstown, Ohio, Jan. 25, 1928; s. Frederick Miller and Mildred Kathryn (Rickard) M.; m. Jan MacCasler Perry, Nov. 1, 1958; children: Frederick MacCasler, Anthony Rickard, Perry Ellen. BA, Yale U., 1950. Founder, pres. Exeter Drilling Co., Dallas and Denver, 1953-70, chmn. bd., chief exec. officer, 1970-80. Chmn. bd., dir. Exeter Drilling No., Inc., Denver, Exeter Drilling So., Inc., New Orleans, until 1982 Chmn. Wallace Village for Children, 1971-74; trustee Graland Country Day Sch., 1973-79; mem. arts adv. com. Phillips Exeter Acad., 1974—, trustee, 1980—; trustee Denver Art Museum, 1970-, v.p., 1971-75, chmn. bd. trustees, 1975-79, interim chmn. bd. trustees, 1980-81; trustee Am. Fedn. Arts, 1977-81, Nat. Gallery, 1983—; founder JFM Foundation, Denver. Served with U.S. Army, 1950-52. Named one of Top 200 Collectors, ARTnews Mag., 2004, 2006. Mem. Ind. Petroleum Assn. Am. (exec. com.), Chief Execs. Forum, Metro Denver Exec. Club, Am. Petroleum Inst. (bd. dirs.), Ind. Petroleum Assn. Mountain States (Rocky Mountain Wildcatter of Yr. award 1983), 25 Yr. Club of Petroleum Industry, Nat. Petroleum Council, Inst. Nautical Archaeology (bd. dirs. 1981-85, chmn. bd. 1985—). Clubs: Cherry Hills Country, Univ. of Denver, Garden of Gods, Castle Pines Golf, Denver and Dallas Petroleum, N.Y. Yacht. Avocation: Collector of Colonial and Latin American art. Home: Denver, Colo. Died Feb. 14, 2007.

MAYERS, EUGENE DAVID, retired philosopher, educator; b. NYC, July 30, 1915; s. Sylvester and Estelle (Weinstein) M.; m. Odette Julia Marguerite Gilchriest, Dec. 30, 1950; children: David Allan, Marilyn Anne, Judith Odette, Peter Michael. AB, Yale U., 1936, LLB, 1940; PhD, Columbia U., 1956. Bar: N.Y. State bar 1941. With Nat. Bur. Econ. Research, NYC, 1941, Office Gen. Counsel, Navy Dept., 1946; mem. faculty Carleton Coll., Northfield, Minn., 1950-61, Columbia, 1959-60, Mills

Coll., Oakland, Calif., 1961-63; prof. philosophy Calif. State U., Hayward, 1963-92, prof. emeritus, from 1992, chmn. dept. philosophy, 1963-73, acting head div. humanities, 1966-67. Adj. prof. Calif. State U., 1996-97. Author: Some Modern Theories of Natural Law, 1957; Contbr. articles to profl. jours. Served to capt. (field artillery) AUS, 1941-46, 51-52; lt. col. judge adv. gen. USAR ret. Fellow Soc. Values in Higher Edn.; mem. AAUP, Am. Philos. Assn. (chmn. conf. dept. chmn. Pacific divsn. 1973-75, Pacific divsn. exec. com. 1976-80, chmn. exec. com. 1978-80), Am. Soc. Polit. and Legal Philosophy, Pacific Coast Theol. Soc. (sec. 1984-86), Internat. Assn. Philosophy Law and Social Philosophy, Am. Acad. Religion, Soc. Advancement Am. Philosophy, Soc. Study Process Philosophies (Pacific Coast rep. 1987-97, jurisprudence 3d internat. Whitehead conf. 1998). Home: Oakland, Calif. Died Feb. 24, 2007.

MAYHEW, MARCE PAUL, advertising agency executive; b. Verwood, Sask., Can., Mar. 17, 1925; came to U.S., 1947; s. George Stevens and Rose Cora (Houle) M.; m. Therese Gagnon, May 13, 1950; children— Marc Vincent, Janine BA, Art Center Coll., Pasadena, Calif., 1950. Art dir. Kudner Co., NYC, 1950-52; art dir. Calkins & Holden, NYC, 1952-55; creative dir. Reach McClinton Co., NYC, 1955-70, Bozell & Jacobs, Inc., NYC, 1970-86, Geer Dubois, NYC, from 1987. Recipient numerous awards for advt. N.Y. Art Dirs. Show, Internat. Film Festival, The Clio, Am. Inst. Graphic Arts, also other internat. shows, 1950— Mem. N.Y. Art Dirs. Club (life) Avocations: art; skiing; golf. Home: Armonk, NY. Died Jan. 1, 2007.

MAYNE, WILEY EDWARD, lawyer, former congressman; b. Sanborn, Iowa, Jan. 19, 1917; s. Earl W. and Gladys (Wiley) M.; m. Elizabeth Dodson, Jan. 5, 1942; children: Martha (Mrs. F.K. Smith), Wiley Edward, John. S.B. cum laude, Harvard, 1938; JD, State U. Iowa, 1941. Bar: Iowa 1941, US Supreme Ct. 1950. Spl. agt. FBI, 1941—43; mem. Shull, Marshall, Mayne, Marks & Vizintos, 1946-66, US Congress from 6th Iowa dist., 1967—75, Mayne & Berenstein, 1975-87, Mayne & Mayne, 1988-99, Mayne, Marks and Madsen, Sioux City, 1999—2007. Mem. judiciary com., agr. com. Commr. from Iowa Nat. Conf. Commrs. Uniform State Laws, 1956-60; chmn. grievance commn. Iowa Supreme Ct., 1964-66; del. FAO, 1973; chmn. Woodbury County Compensation Bd., 1975-80 Chmn. Midwest Rhodes Scholar Selection Com., 1964-66; pres. Sioux City Symphony Orch. Assn., 1947-54, Sioux City Concert Course, 1947-54; vice-chmn. Young Republican Nat. Fedn., 1948-50; bd. dirs. Iowa Bar Found., 1962-68. Lt. (j.g.) USNR, 1943-46. Fellow Am. Coll. Trial Lawyers; mem. ABA (ho. of dels. 1966-68), Iowa Bar Assn. (pres. 1963-64), Sioux City Bar Assn., Internat. Assn. Def. Counsel (exec. com. 1961-64), Harvard Club (N.Y.C.), Sioux City Country Club, Masons (Scottish Rite/33 deg.). Home: Sioux City, Iowa. Died May 27, 2007.

MAYNES, CHARLES WILLIAM, retired foundation administrator, former federal agency administrator; b. Huron, SD, Dec. 8, 1938; s. Charles William and Almira Rose (Summers) M.; m. Gretchen Schiele, July 17, 1965; children: Stacy Kathryn, Charles William. BA, Harvard U., 1960; MA, Oxford U., Eng., 1962. UN polit. affairs ofcl. US Dept. State, Washington, 1962-65; chief monetary economist AID, Laos, 1965-67; econ. officer Am. Embassy, Moscow, 1968-70; sec. Carnegie Endowment Internat. Peace, 1971-76; sr. legis. asst. to Senaator Fred R. Harris US Senate, 1972; mem. issues Sargent Shriver's Vice-Presdl. campaign, 1972; mem. Carter-Mondale Transition team, 1976-77; asst. sec. for internat. orgn. affairs US Dept. State, 1977-80; editor Fgn. Policy mag., 1980-97; mem. Clinton-Gore Transition team, 1992-93, 96-97; pres. Eurasia Found., Washington, 1997—2006. Mem. Coun. Fgn. Rels., Washington Inst. Fgn. Affairs, UN Assn., Nat. Acad. Pub. Adminstrn., Internat. Inst. Strategic Studies. Contbr. articles to profl. jours. Recipient Meritorious Service award Dept. State; congl. fellow Rep. F. Bradford Morse, 1971, Sen. Fred R. Harris, 1971; Rhodes scholar. Mem. Phi Beta Kappa. Democrat. Home: Chevy Chase, Md. Died June 2, 2007.

MAYO, WILLIAM BRUCE, insurance company executive; b. Braddock, Pa., Nov. 2, 1930; s. Joseph G. and Helen (Stanley) M.; m. Rita F. Coyne, June 7; children— William M., Robert J., Diane L., Kathleen R., Daniel D. Student, Rankin Coll., 1948; grad., U. Pitts, 1964. C.L.U. Sales mgr. Met. Life Ins., McKeesport, Pa., 1955-64; sales supr. INA Life Ins. Co., Pitts., 1964-66, mgr. San Francisco, 1967-69, Pitts., 1969-75, v.p. mktg. Phila., 1976-77, sr. v.p. sales., from 1978; instr. Life Underwriting Tng. Council, McKeesport, 1962-64. Served with USN, 1953-55 Recipient Life citation, INA Life Ins. Co. 1974 Mem. Life Underwriters Assn., Am. Soc. C.L.U.s Clubs: Eagle. Lodges: Country. Democrat. Roman Catholic. Avocations: golf; tennis; travel; swimming. Home: Cherry Hill, NJ. Died June 5, 2007.

MAYWALT, WILLIAM D(ONALD), city official, educator; b. Auburn, N.Y., May 18, 1916; s. William Francis Maywalt and Elizabeth Virginia Ringwood; m. Jean Weeks Miller, Feb. 10, 1941; children— Lynn Maywalt Eckert, Christine Maywalt Olp, W. Scott, Thomas, Peter. Assoc. Fire Sci. cum laude, Auburn Community Coll., 1970; A.A. in Liberal Arts, SUNY-Albany, 1973. Firefighter, capt., asst. fire chief Auburn Fire Dept., 1941-65, chief, 1965—; cons. fire sci. curriculum and teaching, Auburn Community Coll., 1971—. Author fire short stories and tech. articles. Treas. Muscular Dystrophy Found. Cayuga County, 1965-69; chmn. health and safety Cayuga County council Boy Scouts Am., 1965—. Served with USN, 1944-46. Recipient Silver Beaver award Boy Scouts Am., 1985. Mem. Internat. Assn. Fire Chiefs, N.Y. State Assn. Fire Chiefs (edn. com. 1965-85, assoc. dir. 1985), Cayuga County Fire Adv. Bd. Democrat. Roman Catholic. Home: Auburn, NY. Died July 18, 2006.

MAZO, EARL, writer; b. Warsaw, July 7, 1919; s. Samuel George and Sonia (Portugal) M.; m. Rita Vane, 1941 (dec. 2003); children: Judith Frances, Mark Elliot; m. Regina Schatz, 2006; 2 stepchildren: Stuart, Nancy Grad., Clemson Coll., 1940. Staff Charleston News and Courier (S.C.), also Greenville News, 1939-41; editor, editorial page Camden Courier Post, N.J., 1945-50; staff N.Y. Herald Tribune, 1950-64; nat. polit. corr.; with New York Times, NYC, 1964-65; with Reader's Digest, 1965-70. Author: Richard Nixon, A Political and Personal Portrait, 1959, The Great Debates, 1961, (with Stephen Hess) Nixon, A Political Portrait, 1968. Served to lt. AUS, World War II; combat corr. European Stars and Stripes. Fellow Woodrow Wilson Internat. Center for Scholars, Smithsonion Instn., 1972; Decorated Air medals, Bronze Star medal, Presidential citations. Mem. Acad. Polit. Sci., Sigma Delta Chi. Clubs: Overseas Press (New York); National Press (Washington). Died Feb. 17, 2007.

MC ARTHUR, JANET WARD, endocrinologist, educator; b. Bellingham, Wash., June 25, 1914; d. Hyland Donald and Alice Maria (Frost) McA. AB, U. Wash., 1935, MS, 1937; M.B., Northwestern U., 1941, MD, 1942; ScD (hon.), Mt. Holyoke Coll., 1962. Diplomate: Am. Bd. Internal Medicine. Intern Cin. Gen. Hosp., 1941-42, asst. resident in medicine, 1942-43; asst. resident, rsch. fellow in medicine H.P. Walcott fellow clin. medicine Mass. Gen. Hosp., Boston, 1943-47, assoc. physician, 1959-84, assoc. children's svc., 1968-84; instr. Harvard U., 1955-57, asst. prof., 1960-64, assoc. prof., 1964-73, prof., 1973-84, prof. emerita, 1984—2006; clin. prof. medicine Boston U. Sch. Medicine, 1984—2006. Adj. prof. Sargent Coll. Allied Health Scis. Boston U., 1982-2006; mem. reproductive biology study sect. NIH, 1974-78, Com. on Population Studies, 1980-84; co-dir. Vincent Meml. Rsch. Lab., 1977-79; sr. scientist U. London, 1985-86. Author: (with others) Functional Endocrinology from Birth Through Adolescence, 1952; editor: (with Theodore Colton) Statistics in Endocrinology, 1970; contbr. articles to profl. jours. Fellow ACP; mem. AMA, AAAS, Endocrine Soc., Am. Soc. Reproductive Medicine, Boston Obstetrical Soc., Phi Beta Kappa, Sigma Xi, Alpha Omega Alpha. Home: Needham, Mass. Died Oct. 6, 2006.

MCATEE, PATRICIA ANNE ROONEY, medical educator; b. Denver, Apr. 20, 1931; d. Jerry F. and Edna E. (Hansen) Rooney; m. Darrell McAtee, Sept. 4, 1954; 1 son, Kevin Paul. BS, Loretto Heights Coll., 1953; MS, U. Colo., 1961; PhD, Union of Univs., 1976. Supr. St. Anthony Hosp., Denver, 1952-55; pub. health nurse, edn. dir. Tri-County Health Dept., Colo., 1956-58; adminstr. sch. health program Littleton (Colo.) Pub. Schs., 1958-60; asst. prof. community health, acad. adminstr. continuing edn. U. Colo., 1968-70; project dir. Western Interstate Commn. for Higher Edn., 1972-74; asst. prof. pediatrics, project co-dir. Sch. Medicine U. Colo., from 1975; mem. profl. svcs. staff Mead Johnson & Co., from 1981. Cons. Colo. Safety Coun.; treas. Vista Nueva Assocs. Editor: Pediatric Nursing, 1975-77. Chmn. bd. dirs. Found. for Urban and Neighborhood Devel.; mem. Arapahoe Health Planning Coun. Mem. NAS, APHA, Inst. Medicine, Nat. Bd. Pediatric Nurse Practitioners and Assocs. (pres.), Nat. Assn. Pediatric Nurse Practitioners (v.p.), Am. Acad. Polit. and Social Scientist, Nat. League Nursing, Western Soc. Rsch., Am. Sch. Health Assn., Sigma Theta Tau. Home: Littleton, Colo. Died June 18, 2007.

MC AULIFFE, MICHAEL F., retired bishop; b. Kansas City, Mo., Nov. 22, 1920; Student, St. Louis Prep. Sem., Cath. U. Ordained priest Roman Cath. Ch., 1945, consecrated bishop, 1969, bishop diocese of Jefferson City Mo., 1969-97. Died Jan. 9, 2006.

MCBRIDE, DOUGLAS LADSON, JR., oil company executive; b. Wichita Falls, Tex., Sept. 19, 1926; s. Douglas Ladson McBride and Beulah Irene (Tanner) McBride Hanson; children— Sue Hanson McBride Rose, Julie McBride Roach, Douglas Ladson III; m. Barbara Joyce Anson, Oct. 16, 1978. B.A., N.Mex. Mil. Inst., 1946. B.S., Tex. Tech U., 1951. Regis. profl. geologist, Calif. Geologist Hanson Oil Co., Roswell, N.Mex., 1951-54, pres., owner, 1973—; ind. cons. geologist, Luling, Tex., 1954-73; pres., owner Ladson Operating Co., Luling, 1969-73, Ladson Oil Corp., Roswell, 1980—, Hanlad Oil Corp., Roswell, 1973—, Hanson Operating Co., Roswell, 1982—, White Mountain Devel. Co., Ruidoso, N.Mex., 1973—; gen. ptnr. Hanson-McBride Petroleum Co., Roswell, 1981—. Served to lt. gen. USNG, 1977-83. Decorated DSM, Legion of Merit; Bronze Star, others.; named to Inf. Hall of Fame, Ft. Benning, Ga., Hall of Fame, N.Mex. Mil. Inst. Mem. Am. Assn. Petroleum Geologists, Soc. Am. Mil. Engrs., Res. Officers Assn., Am. Petroleum Inst., Ret. Officers Assn., N.G. Assn., Assn. U.S. Army, Soc. Ind. Profl. Earth Scientists, Am. Legion. Republican. Baptist. Lodges: Masons (32d degree), Shriners. Home: Roswell, N.Mex. Died Jan. 8, 2007.

MCBRIDE, ROBERT LAWRENCE, judge; b. Dayton, Ohio, Mar. 11, 1910; s. Mark and Mary (Hemler) McB.; m. Evelyn Lewis, Feb. 22, 1937 (dec. 1960); m. Noreen O'Leary, Oct. 14, 1961; children: Robert Lewis, Andrew. AB, U. Dayton, 1932, JD, 1934. Bar: Ohio 1934, U.S. Dist. Ct. (so. dist.) Ohio 1934. Judge Dayton Mcpl. Ct., 1946-53, Ct. Common Pleas, Montgomery County, 1953-75; judge 2d Dist. Ct. Appeals of Ohio, Dayton, 1975-81, ret., 1981, on assignment, 1981-96; chmn. Ohio Jud. Conf., 1962-65. Author: Art of Instructing the Jury, 1969; chmn. Ohio Jury Instructions, 4 vols., 1959-74. Active Boy Scouts Am., 1929-60, Cath. Youth Orgn., 1935-57; bd. visitors U. Dayton Law Sch., 1978-81. Served with USN, 1943-46. Recipient Founder's award Ohio Jud. Conf., 1983, Ritter award Ohio State Bar Found., 1984. Mem. Ohio State Bar Assn., Montgomery County Bar Assn., Common Pleas Judges Assn. (pres. 1959), Mcpl. Judges Assn. (v.p. 1949). Home: Dayton, Ohio. Died Apr. 23, 2007.

MC CABE, ELIZABETH GAILEY, banker; b. Troy, N.Y., Nov. 5, 1928; d. William and Jean (McKay) Gailey; grad. Rochester (N.Y.) Inst. Tech., 1949; m. Raymond J. McCabe, Sept. 30, 1960. Club teller Troy Savs. Bank, 1951-53, paying and receiving teller, 1953-58, gen. ledger bookkeeper, 1958-62, acct., 1962-66, asst. auditor, 1966-67, auditor, 1967—, v.p., 1982—. Cert. internal auditor Inst. Internal Auditors. Mem. Savs. Bank Auditors and Controllers of N.Y. State, Eastern N.Y. chpt. Bank Adminstrs. Inst., Nat. Assn. Bank Women, Am. Inst. Banking (life), Nat. Assn. Mut. Savs. Banks. Home: Daytona Beach, Fla. Died July 1, 2006.

MCCABE, LAURENCE JEROME, transportation company executive; b. Decorah, Iowa, Aug. 10, 1930; s. Anthony A. and Loretta (Mullaney) McC.; m. Jane Moore, Mar. 27, 1954; children— David, Cathy, Philip, Elizabeth, Carrie. BA, Loras Coll., 1951. C.P.A., Tex. With Western Electric Corp., Chgo., 1951-52, Deloitte Haskins & Sells, Dallas, 1952-61; treas. Aero Test Equipment Co., Dallas, 1961-65; asst. treas. TCO Industries, Inc., Dallas, 1965-74, treas., 1974-79; v.p., treas. Trailways, Inc., Dallas, 1979-87, Greyhound Lines Inc., from 1987. Mem. Am. Inst. C.P.A.'s, Tex. Soc. C.P.A.'s, Fin. Execs. Inst. Republican. Roman Catholic. Home: Mabank, Tex. Died Dec. 30, 2006.

MCCANN, SAMUEL MCDONALD, physiologist, educator; b. Houston, Sept. 8, 1925; s. Samuel Glenn and Margaret (Brokaw) McC.; m. Barbara Lorraine Richardson; children: Samuel Donald, Margaret, Karen Elizabeth. Student, Rice U., Houston, 1942-44; MD, U. Pa., 1948. Intern in internal medicine Mass. Gen. Hosp., Boston, 1948-49, resident, 1949-50; mem. faculty U. Pa. Sch. Medicine, 1952-65, prof. physiology, 1964-65, acting chmn. dept., 1963-64; prof., chmn. physiology U. Tex. Southwestern Med. Sch., Dallas, 1965-85, dir. neuropeptide div., 1985-95, prof. internal medicine, 1995; endowed prof. Pennington Biomed. Rsch. Ctr. La. State U., Baton Rouge, from 1995. Cons. Schering Corp., Bloomfield, N.J., 1958; mem. gen. medicine B study sect. NIH, 1965-67, endocrinology study sect., 1967-69, population research com., 1974-76, reproductive biology study sect., 1978-82, chmn. reproductive biology study sect., 1980-82, neurology study sect., 1985-86. Mem. editl. bd. Endocrinology, 1963-68, 72-77, Neuroendocrinology, 1967-76, editor, 1985-92; mem. editl. bd. Ann. Rev. Physiology, 1974-79, Soc. Exptl. Biology and Medicine, 1976-85, 91-96, Am. Jour. Physiology, 1980-85; editor: Endocrine Physiology, Pioneers in Neuroendocrinology; co-editor Neuroimmuno Modulation, 1993—; contbr. articles to profl. jours., chpts. to books. Recipient Spencer Morris prize U. Pa. Med. Sch., 1948, Lindback award for distinguished teaching, 1965, Oppenheimer award for research in endocrinology, 1966, Hartman award Soc. Study of Reproduction, 1986. Mem. Endocrine Soc. (exec. council 1985-88, Fred Conrad Koch award 1979), Am. Physiol. Soc. (council 1979-81), Soc. for Exptl. Biology and Medicine (coun. 1979-83, pres. 1995—), Soc. Clin. Investigation, N.Y. Acad. Scis., Nat. Acad. Scis., Am. Acad. Arts and Scis., Neuroendocrine Discussion Group (chmn. 1965), Internat. Neuroendocrine Soc. (council 1972-79, pres. 1984-88), Internat. Soc. Neuroimmunomodulation (sec. gen. 1990-96, pres. 1996—). Home: Dallas, Tex. Died Mar. 16, 2007.

MCCARTHY, JOHN CHARLES, lawyer; b. Chgo., Nov. 14, 1923; s. Thomas James and Margaret Mary (Schollmeyer) McC.; m. Lorraine Mary Donovan; children— Michael, Mary Pat, Sheila. Student Miami U., Oxford, Ohio, 1942-44; B.S. in Bus., U. So. Calif., 1947; J.D., UCLA, 1952. Bar: Calif. 1953, U.S. Dist. Ct. (cen. dist.) Calif. 1953, U.S. Ct. Appeals (9th cir.) 1973, U.S. Supreme Ct. 1964. Ptnr., Young, Henrie & McCarthy, Claremont, Calif., 1954-63, 66-75; sole practice, Claremont, 1975—; dir. Peace Corps, Thailand, 1963-66. Author: Successful Techniques in Handling Bad Faith Cases, 1973; Punitive Damages in Bad Faith Cases, 1976, 4th edit., 1987; Punitive Damages in Wrongful Discharge Cases, 1985. Named Alumnus of Yr., UCLA Law Sch., 1973. Mem. Masters Trial Practice (Bad Faith chpt.). Home: Claremont, Calif. Died June 27, 2007.

MCCARTHY, JOHN RUSSELL, photographic company executive; b. Nyack, NY, Jan. 28, 1931; s. Russell Chester and Daisy (Lillie) McC.; m. Joanna Steinkamp, June 20, 1953; children— Laura Ann, Kathy, Molly, Amy, Ellen BS, Cornell U., 1953. Mem. employment staff Eastman Kodak Co., Rochester, N.Y., 1953-62, personnel dir., 1962-75, dir. indsl. relations, 1975-82, sr. v.p. corp. relations, from 1982. Bd. dirs. Monroe Savs. Bank, Eastman Kodak. Bd. dirs. Monroe Community Coll., Rochester, 1982—; mem. Indsl. Mgmt. Council, Rochester, 1970—; bd. dirs. Family Service of Am., N.Y.C., 1984—, Exec. Service Corp., Rochester, 1985, Rochester Jobs Inc., 1983—. Served to 1st lt. Med. Service Corps., U.S. Army, 1953-55. Mem.: Monroe Golf (Pittsford, N.Y.). Republican. Presbyterian. Avocations: golf; gardening; reading. Home: Pittsford, NY. Died Dec. 14, 2006.

MCCARTHY, LEO TARCISIUS, former lieutenant governor, former state legislator; b. Auckland, N.Z., Aug. 15, 1930; came to U.S., 1934, naturalized, 1942; s. Daniel and Nora Teresa (Roche) McC.; m. Jacqueline Lee Burke, Dec. 17, 1955; children: Sharon, Conna, Adam, Niall. BS, U. San Francisco, 1955; JD, San Francisco Law Sch., 1961. Bar: Calif. 1963. Supr. Bd. of Supr., San Francisco, 1964-68; assemblyman Calif. State Legislature, Sacramento, 1969-82, speaker, 1974-80; lt. gov. State of Calif., Sacramento, 1983—95; Democratic nominee US Senate, 1988; founder The Daniel Group, 1995—2007. Founder Leo T. McCarthy Ctr. for Pub. Svc. and the Common Good, U. San Francisco, 2002. Chmn. Econ. Devel. Commn. of Calif.; chmn. State Lands Commn.; regent U. Calif.; trustee State Coll. and Univ. System, Calif.; mem. Dem. State Cen. Com.; With USAF, 1951-52. Roman Catholic. Died Feb. 5, 2007.

MCCARTHY, PAUL EUGENE, English educator, writer; b. Des Moines, Apr. 18, 1921; s. Frank Eugene and Vera Glee (Newell) McC.; m. Phyllis Elaine Niemann, Aug. 29, 1948; children: Patricia, Susan, James, Thomas, Marybeth. BA, U. Iowa, 1948, MFA, 1951; PhD, U. Tex., 1962. Instr. Iowa State U., Ames, 1951-53, U. Tex., Austin, 1955-58, U. Idaho, Moscow, 1958-60, U. N.D., Grand Forks, 1960-62; from asst. prof. to assoc. prof. U. Ala., Tuscaloosa, 1962-67; from assoc. prof. to prof. Kans. State U., Manhattan, 1967-91, prof. emeritus, from 1991. Author: John Steinbeck, 1980, The Twisted Mind: Madness in Herman Melville's Fiction, 1990; editor: Long fiction of the American Renaissance, 1974; contbr. articles to profl. jours. 2d lt. Signal Corps, U.S. Army, 1942-45, PTO. Mem. AAUP, VFW, MLA, Melville Soc. Avocations: fishing, hunting, reading, writing, travel. Home: Manhattan, Kans. Died Feb. 9, 2007.

MCCARTNEY, CHARLES PRICE, retired obstetrician, retired gynecologist; b. Barnesville, Ohio, Aug. 18, 1912; s. Jesse Thomas and Carrie (Price) McC.; m. Phyllis Helen Graybill,

Sept. 27, 1940; children— Marilyn B., Ann E. BS, U. Chgo., 1942, MD, 1943. Diplomate: Am. Bd. Obstetricians and Gynecologists. Intern U. Chgo. Clinics, 1943-44, resident, 1947-50; mem. faculty U. Chgo. Med. Sch., 1950-71, prof. obstetrics and gynecology, 1960-71, Mary Campeau Ryerson prof., 1967-71; clin. prof. obstetrics and gynecology U. Ill., 1971-80, prof. emeritus, 1980—2006. Attending gynecologist and obstetrician Chgo. Lying-In Hosp., 1950—2006 Mem. Cook County Com. Maternal Welfare, 1965—2006; Served to maj., M.C. AUS, 1944-46. Fellow Am. Gynecol. Soc.; mem. Am. Gynecol. and Obstet. Soc., Chgo. Gynecol. Soc. (pres. 1967), Chgo. Med. Soc. (councillor 1960-2006, pres. 1973, chmn. bd. trustees 1973), Am. Coll. Obstetricians and Gynecologists (chmn. Ill. sect. 1965-2006), Cen. Assn. Obstetricians and Gynecologists. Died Oct. 8, 2006.

MC CARTNEY, RALPH FARNHAM, lawyer; b. Charles City, Iowa, Dec. 11, 1924; s. Ralph C. and Helen (Farnham) McC.; m. Rhoda Mae Huxsol, June 25, 1950; children: Ralph, Julia, David. JD, U. Mich., 1950; BSc, Iowa State U., 1972. Bar: Iowa 1950. Mem. firm Miller, Heuber & Miller, Des Moines, 1950-52, Frye & McCartney, Charles City, 1952-73, McCartney & Erb, Charles City, 1973-78; judge Dist. Ct. Iowa, Charles City, 1978-87; chief judge 2d Judicial Dist., 1987-92; sr. judge Ct. Appeals, from 1992. Mem. jud. coordinating com. Iowa Supreme Ct. Chmn. Supreme Ct. Adv. Com. on Adminstrn. of Clks. Offices; mem. Iowa Ho. of Reps., 1967-70, majority floor leader, 1969-70; mem. Iowa Senate, 1973-74. Bd. regents U. Iowa, Iowa State U., U. No. Iowa, Iowa Sch. for Deaf, Iowa Braille and Sight Saving Sch. Served with AUS, 1942-45. Mem.: Iowa Judges Assn. Home: Charles City, Iowa. Died Mar. 10, 2007.

MCCAULEY, ELFRIEDA BABNEY, media educator; b. Milw., Aug. 11, 1915; d. Rudolph Babney and Louise (Hetzel) Babney; m. Leon McCauley, June 10, 1938; children— Brian, Christopher, Kevin, Matthew. B.S.Ed., U. Wis.-Milw., 1948; M.S., Columbia U., 1965, D. Library Sci., 1971. Librarian Milw. Pub. Library, 1935-40; reporter Religious News Service, N.Y.C., 1941-43; freelance pub. relations, N.Y.C., 1943-46; sec.-treas. McCauley Enterprises, Greenwich, 1961-65; librarian Greenwich Pub. Schs., 1965-69, coordinator media services, 1969—. vis. lectr. Columbia U., N.Y.C., 1972-73; assoc. prof. Pratt Inst., Bklyn., 1975-76, Fairfield U. (Conn.), 1977-78; del. White House Commn. on Libraries and Info. Services, 1979-80; cons. Ednl. Mission to Teheran, 1975; mem. doctoral com. Columbia U. Sch. Library Sci., 1972-74; mem. library/media suprs. group State Dept. Edn., 1981—, mem. adv. council on computers in edn., 1982—. Author: Book of Prayers, 1955; Treasury of Faith, 1957; Mill Girl Libraries of New England, 1971; Reading for Young People: New England, 1985. Recipient Sch. Library Program of Yr. award Am. Assn. Sch. Librarians/Britannica, Inc., 1979, Rheta Clark award Conn. Ednl. Media Assn., 1982. Mem. Ednl. Film Library Assn. (bd. dirs. 1981-83), ALA (John Cotton Dana award 1970, 75), Assn. Ednl. Data Systems, Am. Assn. Sch. Librarians (chmn. suprs. sect. 1982), Phi Delta Kappa, Beta Phi Mu Contbr. articles to profl. jours. Died Feb. 26, 2007.

MCCLENDON, EDWIN JAMES, health science educator; b. Troy, Okla., Dec. 3, 1921; s. Charles Wesley and Mattie (Reed) McClendon; m. Ruby Wynona Scott, May 5, 1950 (dec. Apr. 8, 2001); children: Edwin James Jr., Melody Jan, Joy Renee. BS, Okla. East Ctrl. State U., 1946; MEd, U. Okla., 1954; EdD, Wayne State U., 1964; hon. DrPH, Seoul Nat. U., 1989. Instr. U. Okla., Norman, 1946-47; head speech dept., tchr. Wewoka High Sch., Okla., 1947-49; assoc. dir. Tb Control, Oklahoma City, 1949-51; dir. sch health project Okla. Dept. Health and Edn., Oklahoma City, 1951-54; assoc. dir. Tb Control, Wayne County, Mich., 1954-56; dir. sch. health Wayne County, Mich., 1956-63; dir. secondary edn. Wayne County Intermediate Sch., Detroit, 1963-67; supt. schs. Highland Park, Mich., 1967-68; v.p. Highland Park Coll., Mich., 1968-69; asst. supt. health Mich. Dept. Edn., Lansing, 1969-71; prof., chmn. health edn. U. Mich., Ann Arbor, 1971-88, prof. health behavior and pub. health, 1971-88, prof. emeritus, from 1988; cons. pub. health care WHO, from 1985. Cons. WHO, 1978-89, dir. field study for Western Pacific, 1981; health field study of Arabic states, 1979-80; cons., Papua, New Guinea, Japan, Korea, Philippines, 1983-84, Fiji and Malaysia, 1987-88; vis. prof. U. Okla., 1965, Okla U. Liberal Arts, 1966, U. Wis., Madison, Kent U., Ohio, Wayne State U., Mich. State U., U. Mich., Flint and Dearborn, 1979-97. Author: Drug Education-A Teacher's Guide, 1969, Maxi Minds in Mini Cages, The Gifted, 1972, Healthful Living for Today and Tomorrow, 1981, Health and Wellness, 1987, Evaluation Study of Growing Healthy, 1993; contbg. author: Practical Stress Management, 2000; editor: Michigan Tenth Largest, A History of Plymouth-Canton Schools, 1986; contbr. 60 articles to profl. publs. Chmn. bd. dirs. Am. Cancer Soc., Detroit, 1977-78, mem. nat. pub. edn. com., 1969-83, hon. life mem., 1980—; mem. adv. coun. alcohol abuse NIH, 1976-80; pres. Plymouth-Canton Sch. Bd., 1974-78, 82-91; Tax Rev. Bd., Plymouth, Mich., 1980-85; chmn. Jr. Red Cross S.E. Mich., 1969-73; chmn., cons. Polio Plus immunization campaign, WHO, Rotary Internat; bd. dirs. ARC S.E. Mich., 1992-98, exec. com., 1993—, mem. health, safety, youth and internat. coms, chair HIV/AIDS com.; Choctaw Tribal rep. Served with USN, 1942-46. Decorated Bronze Star with V for Valor, others; recipient Disting. Health Edn. award Cen. Mich. U., 1978; adminstrn. bldg. Plymouth-Canton (Mich.) schs. dedicated E.J. McClendon Edn. Ctr., 1992, Inductee Hon. Hall of Fame Plymouth Culture Ctr., 2002. Fellow APHA, Am. Sch. Health Assn. (pres. 1970-71, Disting. Service award 1962, William A. Howe award 1976), Am. Cancer Soc. (hon. life mem., bd. dirs.), Am. Social Health Assn. (dir. 1978-86), Royal Soc. Health (London); mem. NEA (hon. life), AAUP, VFW (life), Mich. Sch. Health Assn. (hon. life mem., Disting. service award 1967, Golden Anniversary award 1985), Nat. Assn. Curriculum and Devel., Am. Venereal Disease Assn., Alliance Advancement Health Edn., Soc. Pub. Health Edn., Soc. Sex Educators and Counselors, Nat. Coun. for Internat. Health, Am. Assn. for WHO, Tcgh. Prof. Alumni Wewoka and Seminole (life, disting. svc. award, 50 Yr. Svc. award), Soc. Native Am. Indians, Rotary (pres. 1989-91, chair dist. polio plus campaign, elected to Plymouth Hall of Fame), Phi Delta Kappa. Democrat. Methodist. Home: Hackettstown, NJ. Died Jan. 21, 2006.

MCCLUSKEY, ROBERT TIMMONS, physician; b. New Haven, Jan. 16, 1923; s. Charles Ayling and Lora (Timmons) McC.; m. Jean Ann White, Dec. 28, 1957; children: Ann, James. AB, Yale U., 1944; MD, NYU, 1947. Intern Kings County Hosp., Bklyn., 1947-49; resident Bellevue Hosp., NYC, 1950-52; assoc. prof. pathology NYU, 1956-62, prof., 1962-68; prof., chmn. dept. pathology SUNY, Buffalo, 1968-71; S. Burt Wolbach prof. pathology Harvard U., 1971-75, Mallinckrodt prof. pathology, 1975-82, Benjamin Castleman prof. pathology, 1982-93, emeritus, from 1993. Pathologist in chief Children's Hosp. Med. Ctr., Boston, 1971-74; chief pathology Mass. Gen. Hosp., Boston, 1974-91; mem. allery and immunology study sect. NIH, 1969-72, 72-88, pathology study sect., NIH, 1965-68. Editor: (with H. Fudenberg) Clinical Immunology and Immunopathology Board, 1988-94, (with Stanley Cohen) Series on Basic and Clinical Immunology; mem. editorial bd. Archives of Pathology, 1970-80, Kidney Internat., 1971-75, Am. Jour. Pathology, 1982-93. With AUS, 1953-55. Mem. Am. Assn. Immunologists, Am. Assn. Pathologists and Bacteriologists, AMA, Am. Soc. Exptl. Pathology, Harvey Soc., Alpha Omega Alpha, Internat. Soc. Nephrology, N.Y. Acad. of Sci., Transplantion Soc. Home: Brookline, Mass. Died June 29, 2006.

MC COLOUGH, C. PETER (CHARLES PETER MC COLOUGH), retired printing company executive; b. Halifax, NS, Can., Aug. 1, 1922; came to U.S., 1951, naturalized, 1956; s. Reginald Walker and Barbara Theresa (Martin) McC.; m. Mary Virginia White, Apr. 25, 1953; children: Andrew, Ian, Virginia Student, Dalhousie U., 1943, LL.B., 1947, LL.D., 1970; student, Osgoode Hall Law Sch., Toronto, 1945-46; MBA, Harvard, 1949. V.p. sales Lehigh Coal Navigation Co., Phila., 1951-54; with Xerox Corp. (formerly Habloid Co.), 1954—82; v.p. sales Xerox Corp., 1960-63, exec. v.p. ops., 1963-66, pres., 1966-71, CEO, 1968—82, chmn., 1971—82. Bd. dirs. Union Carbide Corp., NY Stock Exch., Knight Ridder Newspapers, Rank Xerox Ltd., London, Eng., Fuji-Xerox Co. Ltd., Citicorp., N.Y., Citibank (N.A.) Former chmn. Pres.'s Commn. Pension Policy; trustee U. Rochester; mem. corp. Greenwich Hosp. Assn., treas. Dem. Nat. Com., 1974-76 Mem. Council Fgn. Relations (bd. dirs.), Bus. Council, Bus. Com. for Arts Clubs: Harvard, River (N.Y.C.); Belle Haven, Greenwich Country (Greenwich, Conn.). Roman Catholic. Died Dec. 13, 2006.

MCCOMB, KARLA JOANN, educational curriculum and instruction administrator, consultant; b. Tacoma, July 23, 1937; d. John Frank and Lorraine Beatrice (Winters) Bohac; m. Russell Marshall McComb, Nov. 27, 1959 (div.); children: Marsha McComb Hayes, Kathleen McComb Bridge. Cert. instr. French, U. Paris, 1958; BA, Calif. State U., Sacramento, 1960; MS, Nova U., 1984. Cert. secondary tchr., Nev. Tchr. French and music Sacramento Waldorf Sch., 1960-62; tchr. French Red Bluff H.S., 1967-68; tchr. French and music Pocatello (Idaho) Schs., 1969-71; tchr., chairperson dept. Clark County Sch. Dist., 1971-76; curriculum cons. social sci., fgn. lang., profl. growth Las Vegas, 1976-84; cons. staff devel. and profl. growth, 1984-91; dir. staff devel., multicultural edn., substance abuse edn., from 1993. Cons. Taft Inst. Govt., Salt Lake City, 1977—, Tchr. Inservice, Follett Pub. Co., 1980-81. Author: A Cultural Celebration, 1980, Project MCE: Multicultural Education in the Clark County School District, 1992; editor The Nevada Holocaust Curriculum, 1987; author, prodr. Nevada Curriculum on the Holocaust, 1997. Coord. N ev. Close-Up Program, 1980-88; mem. Sacramento Symphony Orch., 1954-66, Nev. Humanities Com.; co-chair, pres. Nev. commn. Holocaust, 1996—; pres., bd. dirs. Ctr. Ind. Living, 1995—; v.p. Nev. Assn. Handicapped, 1994—, pres., 1996; bd. dirs. Love All People Youth Group, supt. Love All People Sch., 1983-93, prodr. staff devel. films, 1986—; mem. Nev. Work Force Devel. bd., 1997—, Gov. Workforce adv. bd., 1996—. Mem. Clark County Fgn. Lang. Tchrs. Assn. (pres.), Nat. Coun. Social Studies, Social Studies Suprs. Assn., Nev. Fgn. Lang. Tchrs. Assn. (pres. Outstanding Humanities Nevadan 1994), AAUW, Vegas Valley Dog Obedience Club (pres.), Jackpot Obedience Assn. (pres.). Democrat. Home: Las Vegas, Nev. Died June 13, 2006.

MCCOY, CHARLES WALLACE, retired banker; b. Marietta, Ohio, Feb. 5, 1920; s. John H. and Florence (Buchanan) McC.; m. Ruth Zimmerman, July 20, 1946; children: Melissa McCoy Waguespack, C. Brent, Shelley McCoy Walker. BA, Marietta Coll., 1942; MBA, Stanford U., 1944; cert., Rutgers U., 1947. V.p. City Nat. Bank (now Banc One), Columbus, Ohio, 1944-59; chmn. bd. La. Nat. Bank, Baton Rouge, 1961-86; now ret. chmn. bd. Premier Bancorp, Inc., Baton Rouge; ret. Bd. dirs. Jefferson-Pilot Corp., Greensboro, N.C., Jefferson-Pilot Life Ins. Co., Premier Bank Regional Bd., La. Seed Capital Corp. Vice chmn. bd. trustees Marietta Coll., 1985—; bd. dirs. Pennington Biomed. Rsch. Ctr., Found. for Mid-South, Our Lady of the Lake Regional Med. Found., Woman's Hosp. Found. Recipient Brotherhood award NCCJ, 1983; named Exec. of Yr., Greater Baton Rouge Bus. Report mag., 1984, Disting. Citizen of Yr., 1987. Mem. Am. Bankers Assn. (bd. dirs. 1985-88), La. Bankers Assn. (pres. 1981-82), La. C. of C. (pres. CHAMPAC 1982-89, named Man of Yr. 1985), Country Club of La., Baton Rouge Country Club, Camelot Club, Rotary, Delta Upsilon. Republican. Episcopalian. Avocations: golf, tennis. Home: Baton Rouge, La. Died Jan. 17, 2007.

MCCOY, FREDERICK LOUIS, financial executive; b. Washington, June 16, 1942; s. Frederick L. and Elizabeth Anne (Crowley) M.; m. Lois Diane Reid, Oct. 7, 1967; 1 son, Eric Scott. B.S., U. Md., 1967, M.A., 1971, postgrad., 1971-80. Sr. economist Ops. Research Inc., Silver Springs, Md., 1967-71; sr. cons. Ernst & Whinney, Washington, 1971-72, supr., 1972-75, mgr., 1975-80, prin., 1980—; mem. fiscal adv. com. Washington Bd. of Trade, 1973-76; chmn. econs. dept. Washington Saturday Coll., 1971-76; assoc. prof. Washington Internat. Coll., 1976-80. Author position paper Nat. Govs. Conf., 1976, Ernst & Whinney Marginal Cost Estimating Methodology, 1978. Bd. dirs. Assn. for Community Edn., Washington, 1973-75. Served to sgt. Army N.G., 1964-70. Md. Senatorial scholar Md. State Senate, 1960. Mem. Ops. Research Soc., Am. Econs. Assn., Am. Stats. Assn., Inst. Mgmt. Sci., Artists Blacksmiths Assn., Am. Bladesmiths Soc. Democrat. Avocations: blacksmithing; decorative metal work; knife making. Home: Silver Spring, Md. Died Mar. 22, 2006.

MCCRARY, MIKE, insurance company executive; b. Nacogdoches, Tex., July 19, 1926; s. Rex T. and Katherine Louise (Gillespie) McC.; m. Evelynn Welch, June 7, 1947; children: Jeri Lynn Ziglar, Kathy Lee Bickham. BA, UCLA, 1949. Sales mgr. Transport Indemnity Co., 1947-55; gen. mgr. Carriers Ins. Co., Des Moines, 1955-70; chmn., chief exec. officer Transport Ins. Co., Dallas, from 1970; chmn., chief officer TICO Ins. Co., Dallas, from 1970; chmn., officer exec. officer Am. Commonwealth Devel. Co., Dallas, from 1972. Dir. Mercantile Nat. Bank, Dallas Served to lt. (j.g.) USN, 1943-47, PTO. Republican. Home: Dallas, Tex. Died Feb. 26, 2007.

MCCREARY, DUSTIN CAMPBELL, lawyer, arbitrator; b. Cleve., July 19, 1928; s. Robert G. and Helen (Galvin) McC.; m. Jean Doyle, June 1, 1957 (div. Mar. 1973); m. Rosalie Ogden, Sept. 29, 1973; children: William D., Patricia Helen. BA, Hobart Coll., 1952; LLB, Western Res. U., 1955. Bar: Ohio 1955, Wash. 1958. Assoc. Wilmot Baskin Lausche & Kelley, Cleve., 1955-56; trial atty. Nat. Labor Rels. Bd., Washington and Seattle, 1956-62; assoc. Bogle Bogle & Gates, Seattle, 1962-71; ptnr. Bogle & Gates and precedessor firms, Seattle, 1971-89; mem. Wash. State Publ. Employment Rels. Commn., 1991-95. Co-founder Ann. Pacific Coast Labor Law Conf., Seattle; labor arbitrator, 1990—. With U.S. Army, 1946-48. Mem. ABA (co-chmn. various subcoms., labor law sect., employee benefit com. 1977-88), Wash. State Bar Assn. (specialization bd. 1986-87), San Juan County Bar Assn., Am. Inns of Ct., Am. Arbitration Assn., Seattle Yacht Club, Wash. Athletic Club, San Juan Island Yacht Club, Phi Delta Phi, Sigma Phi. Democrat. Home: Shoreline, Wash. Died June 25, 2006.

MCCRORY, JOHN PAUL, marketing executive; b. Anderson, Ind., Nov. 23, 1923; s. Ralph and Lola Ethel (Ashby) McCrory; m. Rosemary Atkinson, June 29, 1946; children: Linda Sue McCrory Coleson, Michael David, James Lee. At, Northwestern U., Harvard U., Ind U., FBI Acad. From clk. to staff capt. Ind. State Police, Indpls., 1942—62; factory rep. Best Lock Corp., 1962—72, v.p. mktg., from 1972. V.p. Best Locking Sys., Denver, LA, NYC, Blsystems, Portland, Oreg., Blystems, Pitts.; inventor in field. Trustee Owosso Coll., Mich., 1956—58; mem. Va. dist. bd. Wesleyan Ch., 1970—72, local bd. Rockville, Md., 1970—72, gen. bd., 1970—72; mem. local bd. Ch. of Nazarene, Inpls., 1982. With USAAF, 1943—45, PTO. Named a Sagamore of Wabash, Gov. of Ind., 1956, Hon. Citizen of Tenn., 1958, Boss of Yr., Am. Bus. Women's Assn. (Indpls. chpt.), 1960. Mem.: Am. Soc. Indsl. Security, Harvard Assn. Police Sci., FBI Nat. Acad. Grads., Pioneers Ind. State Police, Brookshire Golf Club. Republican. Home: Carmel, Ind. Died Jan. 29, 2006.

MCCUTCHEON, JAMES MILLER, history and American studies educator; b. NYC, Oct. 31, 1932; s. James Cochrane and Katharine (Miller) McC.; m. Elizabeth Douglas North, Apr. 4, 1959; children: Ian North, Eric James. BA summa cum laude, Hobart Coll., Geneva, NY, 1954; MS, U. Wis., 1955, PhD, 1959. Grad. asst. U. Wis., Madison, 1954-59; Fulbright fellow U. London, 1959-60; asst. prof. history Simpson Coll., Indianola, Iowa, 1960-61; asst. prof. history and Am. studies U. Hawaii Manoa, Honolulu, 1961-66, assoc. prof., 1966-72, prof., from 1972, chair Am. studies, 1984-88; sr. Fulbright fellow Beijing Fgn. Studies U., 1981-82. Spl. asst. pres. U. Hawaii Manoa, Honolulu, 1979, program coord. coll. opportunity, 1971-72; mem. selection com. Community Scholarships, Honolulu, 1973-85; prin. scholar Hawaii Commn. for Humanities, Honolulu, 1973—. Author: China and America: Bibliography, 1972. Recipient Clopton Community Svc. award U. Hawaii Manoa, Honolulu, 1978. Mem. Am. Hist. Assn., Orgn. Am. Historians, Am. Studies Assn., Urban Studies Assn., World History Assn., Phi Beta Kappa. Episcopalian. Avocations: walking, swimming. Home: Honolulu, Hawaii. Died Feb. 7, 2006.

MCDANIEL, AUGUSTUS C., manufacturing executive; b. Cleve., May 19, 1922; s. Augustus C. McDaniel and Florence Osborne; m. Helena Prescott, Jan. 24, 1948; children: Marion, Meredith, Nina. At, Cornell U. Corp. sec. Hill Acme Co., Cleve., 1968—74, v.p., 1974—78, pres., from 1978; v.p. Sherwood-Selpac Corp., Lockport, NY, from 1973. To 2d lt. USAAF, 1942—45. Home: Willoughby, Ohio. Died Nov. 8, 2006.

MC DANIEL, GLEN, business executive, lawyer; b. Seymour, Tex., Mar. 21, 1912; s. Otho and Mary Burnet (Kerr) McD.; m. Marilyn Ballentine, Apr. 15, 1965; children: Laurie McDaniel Norwood, Scott Kerr. AB, So. Meth. U., 1932, A.M., 1933; LL.B., Columbia U., 1936. Atty. Sullivan & Cromwell, NYC, 1936-42; v.p., gen. atty. R.C.A. Communications, Inc., NYC, 1946-48; v.p. RCA, 1948-51; partner Lundgren & McDaniel, NYC, 1951-65; cons. Litton Industries, Inc. Chmn., St. John's Hosp. and Health Ctr. Found., Santa Monica, Calif. Served from lt. (j.g.) to lt. comdr. USNR, 1942-45; chmn. Navy Bd. Contract Appeals 1945-46. Mem. Electronics Industries Assn. (pres. 1951-55) Presbyterian. Died June 7, 2007.

MCDARRAH, FRED WILLIAM, photographer, editor, writer; b. Bklyn., Nov. 5, 1926; s. Howard Arthur and Elizabeth (Swahn) McD.; m. Gloria Schoffel, Nov. 5, 1960; children: Timothy Swann, Patrick James. BA in Journalism, NYU, 1954. Mem. staff Village Voice Newspaper, NYC, from 1959, picture editor, from 1971; book reviewer ASMP Infinity Mag., 1972-73, Photo Dist. News, 1985-88, The Picture Profl., 1990—2002. Exhibited in Soho Photo Gallery, 1973, Whitney Mus., 1974, 76-77, Dallas Mus. Art, 1974, San Francisco Mus. Art, 1975, Wadsworth Atheneum, 1975, Sidney Janis Gallery, 1976, Basel (Switzerland) Art Fair, 1976, Alfred Stieglitz Gallery, 1976, Empire State Mus., Albany, NY, 1978, Lightworks Gallery, Syracuse, NY, 1981, Cape Cod Gallery, Provincetown Mass., 1982, Galleria di Franca Mancini, Pesaro, Italy, 1983, Musée du Quebec, 1987, Anita Shapolsky Gallery, NYC, 1988, Hartnett Gallery U. Rochester, NY, 1989, G. Ray Hawkins Gallery, LA, 1989, Read Gallery Antioch Coll., Ohio, 1989, Mus. Art/Sci./Industry, Bridgeport, Conn., 1989, NYC Gallery Queens Mus., 1989, Ctr. Photography, Woodstock, 1989, Frumkin/Adams Gallery, 1990, Musée d'Art Moderne De La Ville de Paris, 1990, Musée d'Art Contemporain, Montreal, 1990, Pollack-Krasner Mus., East Hampton, NY, 1990, Found. Cartier, Paris, 1990, Marty Carey Pictures Gallery, Woodstock,

NY, 1992, Galerie Gilles Ringuet, Belfort, France, 1992, Galerie Contre Jour, Belfort, France, 1992, Galleria La Pescheria, Cesena, Italy, 1994, Whitney Mus. Am. Art, 1995-2007, Nat. Portrait Gallery, 1996, Candice Perich Gallery, 1996; exhbns. include Jack Kerouac Visions of the Road, Les Rencontres D'Arles, Arles, France, 1991, Jack Kerouac Travelling Writers, Saint-Malo (France) Internat. Festival, 1991, 97, Images of Greenwich Village NY Camera Club, 1992, Walker Art Ctr., Mpls., 1996, M.H. de Young Meml. Mus., San Francisco, 1996, Whitney Mus. Am. Art, 1997-98, New York Stories, Chiostro del Bramante, Rome, 1999, Detroit Inst. Arts, 2000, Great Modern Pictures, NY, 2000, MOCA, Wexner Ctr., Parrish Mus., 2000, Mus. Nat. Modern Art 2001, Gallerie Comunale d'Arte Moderna, Rome, 2001, Mus. City of NY, 2001, Centre Pompidou, Paris, 2001, Albright-Knox Art Gallery, 2002, Mus. Contemporary Art, LA, 2002, Fahey/Klein Gallery, L.A., 2002, Grimaldi Forum, Monaco, 2003, Snap Galleries, Birmingham, Eng., 2004, Castello di Rivoli, Turin, 2004, Triennale di Milano, 2004, Provd Galleries, 2005, Steven Kasher Gallery, NYC, 2007, Shooting Gallery, Hollywood, Calif., 2007; represented in permanent collections: J. Paul Getty Mus., Nat. Portrait Gallery; author: The Beat Scene, 1960, The Artist's World in Pictures, 1961, rev. edit. 1988, Greenwich Village, 1963, NYC, 1964, Sculpture in Environment, 1967, Museums in New York, 1973, French edit., 1979, 5th edit., 1990, Photography Marketplace, 2d edit., 1977, Stock Photo and Assignment Source Book, 1977, 2d edit., 1984, Gay Pride: Photographs from Stonewall to Today, 1994, Frommer's Virginia Guide, 2d edit., 1994, Fodor's Cancun, Cozumel, Yucatan Peninsula, 1996, Kerouac and Friends: A Beat Generation Album, 1984, Japanese edit, 1990, 2nd edit, 2002, Frommer's Atlantic City and Cape May, 4th edit., 1991, 5th edit., 1993, New York Stories, 2001, Anarchy, Protest & Rebellion & the Counter Culture that Changed America, 2003; co-author: The New Bohemia, 1967, 2d edit., 1990, Guide for Ecumenical Discussion, 1970, Greenwich Village Guide, 1992, Frommer's Virginia, 1992, 2d edit. 1994; author: (with Timothy S: LA Pop Art Negli Anni '60 Chiostro del Bram Ante, 1999; author: (with Gloria S. McDarrah) Beat Generation: Glory Days in Greenwich Village, 1998; The Beat Generation: Glory Days in Greenwich Village, editor, 1996; editor: (with Gloria S. McDarrah and Timothy S. McDarrah) The Photography Encyclopedia, 1999; author: (with Gloria S. McDarrah) The Artist's World in Pictures, 2d edit., 1988; Saturday Rev. Executive Desk Diary, 1962-64; photographer: Personality Posters, Fotofolio (post cards) (polit. and social figures); contbr. articles, picture features to various publs. including NY Mag., Vanity Fair. Paratrooper US Army, 1944-47. Recipient numerous photography awards including 1st place spot news photo award. NY Press Assn. 1964, 68, 1st place feature photo award 1967, 1st place picture story award 1969, 2nd place spot news photo award 1967, 70, 3d place spot news photo award 1965, 3d place feature photo award 1965, 3d place picture story award 1970, 1st place Best Pictorial Series Nat. Newspaper Assn., 1966, Page One award Newspaper Guild NY, 1971, 80; Guggenheim fellow in photography, 1972. Mem. N.Y. Press Photographers Assn., Authors Guild, N.Y. Press Club, Am. Soc. Picture Profls. Home: New York, NY. Died Nov. 6, 2007.*

MC DEVITT, JOSEPH BRYAN, retired university administrator, retired naval officer; b. McGehee, Ark., Dec. 22, 1918; s. John and Mary Ann (Zimmer) McD.; m. Kathleen Rita Vaughan, 1943 (dec. 1961), m. Catherine Irene Beatty, Jan. 30, 1965 (dec. 1980); m. Ernestine Moody Minshew, Oct. 9, 1982; children: Jeffrey Bryan, Paul Killian, Rodney Peter, Rita Elizabeth, John Stephen, David Andrew, Joseph Bryan, Richard Vincent, Eugena Rose, Edward Francis, Gerald Christopher, Lisa Ernestine. Student, So. Ill. U., 1936-38; BA, U. Ill., 1940, JD, 1942. Bar: Ill. 1952. Commd. ensign U.S. Navy, 1943, advanced through grades to rear adm., 1968; boat group comdr. U.S.S. Leon, 1944-46; with legal office 8th Naval Dist. New Orleans, 1950; legal officer to comdr. Amphibious Force, Atlantic Fleet, 1952; mem. mil. justice div. Office Judge Adv. Gen., 1954; naval liaison officer to U.S. Senate, 1956; staff legal officer Marine Corps. Schs. Quantico, Va., 1958; student Naval War Coll., 1958-59; assigned Joint Chiefs Staff, 1959-61; dir. internat. law div. Office Judge Adv. Gen., 1962-65; legal affairs officer to comdr. in chief Pacific, 1965-68; judge adv. gen. of navy, 1968-72; ret., 1972. Chief exec. officer People to People Programs Inc., Washington, 1972-73; v.p. exec. affairs, univ. counsel, sec. bd. trustees Clemson U., S.C., 1973-85, ret., 1985. Decorated Purple Heart, Legion of Merit, D.S.M. Mem. Am., Ill., Fed., Inter-Am. bar assns., Judge Advs. Assn., Am. Soc. Internat. Law. Roman Catholic. Died Feb. 26, 2006.

MCDEVITT, MARY ELIZABETH, judge; b. Detroit, May 9, 1930; d. James Edward and Mildred Loretta (Wines) McD. Student U. Detroit, 1947-48, Wayne U., 1949-51; LL.B., Detroit Coll. Law, 1954, J.D., 1968. Bar: Mich., 1954, U.S. Supreme Ct. 1958. With legal dept. Lawyers Title Co., Detroit, 1954-55; aide juvenile div., Macomb County Probate Ct., 1955-56; sole practice, Roseville, Mich., 1956-69; justice of peace Erin Twp., Mich., 1957-58; mcpl. judge City of Roseville, 1958-68; judge 39th Dist., Roseville and Fraser, Mich., 1969—. Formerly active Democratic Party. Mem. ABA, Am. Judges Assn., Am. Judicature Soc., Mich. Dist. Judges Assn., State Bar Mich., Macomb County Bar Assn. (past dir.), Women Lawyers Assn. Macomb County, Macomb County Dist. Judges Assn. (sec. treas. 1982, pres. 1983-85). Died Mar. 25, 2007.

MCDONALD, ALAN ANGUS, federal judge; b. Harrah, Wash., Dec. 13, 1927; s. Angus and Nell (Britt) McD.; m. Ruby K., Aug. 22, 1949; children: Janelle Jo, Saralee Sue, Stacy. BS, U. Wash., 1950, LLB, 1952. Dep. pros. atty. Yakima County, Wash., 1952—54; ptnr. Halverson, Applegate & McDonald, Yakima, 1954—85; judge U.S. Dist. Ct. (ea. dist.) Wash., Yakima, 1985—95, sr. judge, from 1995. Fellow Am. Coll. Trial Lawyers; mem. Yakima Country Club, Royal Duck Club (Yakima). Died July 26, 2007.

MCDONALD, DANIEL, actor; b. July 30, 1960; s. James and Patricia McDonald; m. Mujah McDonald, 1999; children: Fosco, Ondina. Appeared in Broadway play Steel Pier (Tony award nominee 1997), High Society, Mamma Mia!; (off-Broadway) First Night, All My Sons, Heartbeats, The Beautiful Lady, others; (Nat. Tour) Contact; actor (films) Where the Boys Are '84, 1984, The Falcon and the Snowman, 1985, Million Dollar Mystery, 1987, Bound by Honor, 1993, What's Love Go to Do With It, 1993, At Risk, 1994, Let It Be Me, 1995, Jaded, 1996, The Ice Storm, 1997; (TV movie) Thompson's Last Run, 1986, The Betty Ford Story, 1987, Home Fires, 1987, Colombo: No Time to Die, 1992, As Good as Dead, 1995, Tempting Adam, 2004; (TV appearances) The Fall Guy, 1985, Call to Glory, 1985, Cagney & Lacey, 1985, Shadow Chasers, 1985, Freddy's Nightmares, 1988, Murder, She Wrote, 1989, Herman's Head, 1992, New York Undercover, 1994, Law & Order, 1998, Sex and the City, 1999, D.C., 2000, Madigan Men, 2000, Law & Order: Special Victims Unit, 2001, CSI: Miami, 2004 writer, solo performer Chesterfield. Died Feb. 15, 2007.

MCDONALD, ROGER WILSON, insurance company executive; b. Boise, Idaho, Sept. 18, 1925; s. Gedion L. and Annette (Connel) McD.; m. Joan Clark, Sept. 2, 1948; children— Patrick J., Stuart John, Roger Scott, Molly Ann. B.S., U. Denver, 1948, M.B.A., 1950. Lic. broker, Wash. Chief acct. Idaho State Ins. Fund, Boise, 1946-48; underwriting mgr. Liberty Nat. Ins. Co., Boise, 1950-55; regional v.p. Safeco Ins. Cos., Seattle, 1955-86, ret.; pres. Idaho Surveying and Rating Burs., 1973-74. Mem. Wash. Gov.'s Com. on Hwy. Safety; bd. dirs. Seattle Better Bus. Bur. Served to 1st lt. USAAF, 1943-46. Decorated Air medal, D.F.C. Mem. Nat. Assn. Security Dealers, Seattle C. of C., Risk and Ins. Mgmt. Soc., Ins. Inst. Am. (assoc. in risk mgmt.), Kappa Sigma. Clubs: Wash. Athletic, Overlake Golf and Country. Home: Bellevue, Wash. Died July 14, 2007.

MCDONALD, WILLIAM G(ERALD), economist, government official; b. Providence, June 2, 1919; s. William Leo and Catherine Theresa (White) McD.; m. Agnes G. Sellman, Apr. 28, 1944; children: William G., Francis L., M. Brian, Catherine T. BA in Econs., U. Tulsa, 1949; postgrad., Georgetown U., 1950, Columbia U., 1951-54, grad. exec. mgt. program, 1957; grad, Command and Gen. Staff Coll., Armed Forces Staff Coll. Served as enlisted man U.S. Army Air Force, 1942, commd. officer advanced through grades to col., 1959; asst. prof. U.S. Mil. Acad., 1952-56; prof. polit. sci. USAF Acad., 1961-62; spl. asst. chief staff USAF Office Sec. Def., 1962-68; ret. USAF, 1970; with Office Mgmt. and Budget, Washington, 1970-72; dir. plans and schedules AEC NRC, Washington, 1972-77; exec. dir. FERC, Dept. Energy, Washington, from 1977. Active Assn. for Retarded Children. Decorated Legion of Merit; decorated Air Force Commendation medal; recipient Presdl. commendation for work on Presdl. Commn. on Causes and Prevention Violence, 1972, Presdl. commendation for work on Presdl. Budget, 1972, Disting. Serviceaward NRC Roman Catholic. Home: Bethesda, Md. Died Apr. 21, 2006.

MC DONOUGH, JOHN RICHARD, lawyer; b. St. Paul, May 16, 1919; s. John Richard and Gena (Olson) McD.; m. Margaret Poot, Sept. 10, 1944; children— Jana Margaret, John Jacobus. Student, U. Wash., 1937-40; LLB, Columbia U., 1946. Bar: Calif. 1949. Asst. prof. law Stanford U., 1946-49, prof., 1952-69; assoc. firm Brobeck, Phleger & Harrison, San Francisco, 1949-52; asst. dep. atty. gen. U.S. Dept. Justice, Washington, 1967-68, assoc. dep. atty. gen., 1968; of counsel and ptnr. firm Keatinge & Sterling, LA, 1969-70; ptnr. Ball, Hunt, Hart, Brown and Baerwitz, LA, 1970-90, Carlsmith Ball Wichman Case & Ichiki, LA, 1990-96, of counsel, 1996-98, Carlsmith Ball, LA, 1998—2002. Exec. sec. Calif. Law Revision Commn., 1954-59, mem. commn., 1959-67, vice chmn., 1960-64, chmn., 1964-65. With US Army, 1942—46. Mem.: Am. Coll. Trial Lawyers. Democrat. Home: Cupertino, Calif. Died Nov. 11, 2005.

MCDONOUGH, PAUL JOSEPH, construction company executive, market consultant; b. Geneva, NY, July 9, 1925; s. Thomas Francis and Anna (Fitzsimons) McD.; m. Therese Margaret Boland, Apr. 20, 1955; children: Michael Sean, Moira Anna, Patrick Timothy, Siobhan Marie, Keelin Heather, Brigid Maureen. BSF.S., Georgetown U., 1951; BA, Hobart Coll., 1949. Area engr. Metcalf & Eddy, Greenland, 1953-56; dir. internat. programs Daniel, Mann, Johnson & Mendenhall, Los Angeles, 1956-73; dir. internat. ops. Ebasco Services, NYC, 1973-77; v.p. ITT Teleplant, Montvale, N.J., 1977-80; v.p., dir. Canatom Ltd., Montreal, Que., Can., 1980-81; sr. v.p. George A. Fuller Co., NYC, from 1981; dir. George A. Fuller Internat. Ltd., Lagos, Nigeria, Sunley Fuller Mgmt. Ltd., London. Contbr. articles to profl jours. Served to cpl. U.S. Army, 1943-45, ETO. Mem. Assoc. Gen. Contractors, Soc. Am. Mil. Engrs., C. of C. Montreal Clubs: Georgetown U. Alumni (Washington); Hobart (N.Y.C.). Roman Catholic. Died Jan. 5, 2007.

MCDOWELL, JOHN EUGENE, lawyer; b. Toledo, Nov. 22, 1927; s. Glenn Hugh and Evelyn (Millspaugh) McD.; m. Jean Ann Hepler, June 18, 1950; children: Jane Lynn McDowell Thummel, Sheila Lorraine McDowell Laing. BS, Miami U., Oxford, Ohio, 1949; JD, U. Mich., 1952. Bar: Ohio 1952. Assoc. Dinsmore & Shohl, Cin., 1952-59, ptnr., 1959-97, of counsel, from 1997. Mem. solicitation coms. United Appeal, Cin., NCCJ, Cin., Boy Scouts Am., Cin. Mem. ABA, Ohio Bar Assn., Cin. Bar Assn., Cin. Country Club, Queen City Club, Order of Coif. Democrat. Episcopalian. Home: Cincinnati, Ohio. Died Dec. 16, 2005.

MCELLHINEY, ROBERT ROSS, agricultural engineer, educator; b. Princeton, Ind., Sept. 22, 1927; s. Ross Annuel and Myrtle Clementine (Staser) McE.; m. Theresa Philomena Hessig, Feb. 23, 1952; children: Karen Paris, Mona McGregor, Ross, Loretta. BS in Agriculture, Purdue U., 1952; MBA, Ind. U., 1953. Gen. prodn. mgr. milling div. Carnation Co., LA, 1953-75; dir. prodn. and engring. ConAgra, Inc., Omaha, 1975-79; prof. Kans. State U., Manhattan, 1979-93, prof. emeritus, from 1993. Pres. Valhaven, Inc., Princeton, Ind., 1982—, F.M.T. Cons., Inc., Manhattan, 1982—. Editor, author: Truck Management, 1982, Feed Manufacturing Technology III, 1985, IV, 1994; author: Kansas-A-View from the Flinthills, 1989; contbr. 263 articles to profl. jours. Assoc. guardian Job's Daus., Playa del Rey, Calif., 1967-70; jurisdiction dir. Order of DeMolay, Nebr., 1977-79. With U.S. Army, 1946-48, Japan. Inducted into Feed Mfg. Hall of Fame, 1997. Mem. Am. Soc. Agrl. Engrs., Nat. Assn. Colls. and Tchrs. Agr., Am. Feed Industry Assn. (chmn. prodn. com. 1968-69, Disting. Svc. award 1992), Masons, Scottish Rite, Shriners, Order Ea. Star (worthy patron 1986, 90), Am. Legion. Republican. Methodist. Avocations: essay writing, poetry, photography, travel. Home: Manhattan, Kans. Died Apr. 28, 2006.

MCELLIGOTT, JAMES GEORGE, pharmacology educator; b. NYC, June 20, 1938; s. James Patrick and Mildred C. McElligott; m. Sandra Fitzpatrick; children: Seamus, Sean. BS, Fordham Coll., 1960; MA, Columbia U., 1963; PhD, McGill U., 1967. NIH postdoctoral fellow dept. anatomy Brain Rsch. Inst. UCLA, 1967-68, asst. rsch. anatomist, 1968-71; asst. prof. pharmacology Temple U. Med. Sch., Phila., 1971-77, assoc. prof. pharmacology, 1977-87, prof. pharmacology, 1987—2007. Mem. Am. Soc. for Pharmacology and Exptl. Therapeutics, Soc. for Neurosci., N.Y. Acad. Scis., Sigma Xi. Home: Media, Pa. Died Feb. 20, 2007.

MCELROY, ROBERT ASHMAN, telecommunications and data processing executive; b. Oyster Bay, NY, Jan. 21, 1932; s. H. Nelson McE. and Marjorie (Ashman) Pettingill; m. Marjorie R. Roe, Oct. 18, 1953; children: R. Scott, Stephen, Amy. BA, Union Coll., 1953. Pres. IDR, Tampa, Fla., 1971-73; exec. v.p. La Salle Extension U., Chgo., 1973-77; cons. Mgmt. Resources, Chgo., 1978-79; v.p. GTE Data Services, Tampa, 1979-81, GTE Corp., Stamford, Conn., from 1981. Served with U.S. Army, 1953-55. Home: Stamford, Conn. Died Oct. 1, 2005.

MCELWAIN, WILLIAM E., public relations consultant; b. Terre Haute, Ind., Apr. 13, 1921; s. William E. and Anna May (Kenan) McE.; m. Mercedes Perrino, Nov. 3, 1945; children: William Eric, Jeanine Shirley. BA, U. Pitts., 1941. Sportswriter Pitts. Press, 1941-42, reporter, 1946; asst. dean men U. Pitts., 1946-48; copy reader Pitts. Sun-Telegraph, 1948-50, rewrite and gen. assignment, 1951-54; editorial staff Rome (Italy) Daily Am., 1950-51; with Ketchum, MacLeod & Grove, Pitts., Houston, 1954-78, pub. relations account supr. Pitts., 1960-65, v.p., dir. pub. relations Houston, 1965-76, v.p. collateral services, 1976-78; sr. pub. relations counsellor Dale Henderson, Inc., Houston, 1978-80, v.p., 1981-86; pub. relations cons., from 1986. City councilman, El Lago, Tex., 1978-81, 84-86, mayor, 1986—; bd. dirs. Zool. Soc. Houston, 1976-78; chmn. Clear Lake Area Coun. Cities, 1988-89; mem. exec. com. Armand Bayou Nature Ctr., 1984-88, 90—, sec. 1986-87, 89-90, 2d v.p., 1991, 1st v.p., 1992; sec.-treas. Harris County Mayors and Councils Assn., 1991, 2d v.p., 1992. Served with AUS, 1942-45. Mem. Pub. Relations Soc. Am. (dir. 1966-71, 77-80, v.p. 1978, pres. 1979), Omicron Delta Kappa. Died Nov. 9, 2006.

MC EMBER, ROBERT ROLAND, association executive, musician; b. Ludington, Mich., Feb. 26, 1919; s. Francis Roland and Lillian Laurentine (Hansen) McE.; B.A., John B. Stetson U., 1946, B.M., 1946, M.A., 1951; m. Elizabeth Anderson Futch, Dec. 15, 1942; children— Sharon Leigh, Elizabeth Anne. Critic tchr. Western Mich. U., 1950-55; asst. prof. Purdue U., 1955-63; asso. prof. U. Wis., 1964-67; mgr. flight tng. aids and tech. writing Am. Airlines, 1967-69; mgr. flight tng. program devel. Eastern Airlines, Miami, Fla., 1970—; guest lectr.; leader workshops and seminars on instrnl. tech.; mus. dir., condr. Ludington Civic Symphony Orch., 1948-50; condr. Central Wis. Symphony Orch., 1964-67. Served with USAAF, 1942-45; col. Res., 1945-72. Recipient cert. of appreciation U.S. Air Force, 1972. Mem. Nat. Acad. Rec. Arts and Scis., Nat. Soc. Scabbard and Blade, Mil. Order World Wars, Daedalian Soc., Am. Soc. Tng. and Devel., Internat. TV Assn. (pres. 1974-75, dir., chmn. bd. 1976-77), Res. Officers Assn. U.S., Audio Visual Mgmt. Assn., Am. Fedn. Musicians, Phi Delta Kappa. Republican Lutheran. Author: C-124 Aircraft Homestudy, 1970; (with others) Communication Security for AF Personnel, 1972, Principles and Practices of Occupational Safety and Health, 1975; editorial adv. bd. Am. Soc. Tng. and Devel. Jour., 1979-82; editor Flight Line (Flight Safety Found. Publs. award 1980), 1957-81; contbr. articles to ednl. jours.; composer: All-American Bands, 1958; several works for symphony orch. Home: Leesburg, Fla. Died Mar. 22, 2007.

MC FADDEN, SYBILL MARTIN, museum curator; b. Pitts., Mar. 22, 1918; d. Alfred Nicholas and Rachel (Church) Martin; B.A. in Journalism, Pa. State U., 1941; m. William Patrick McFadden, Aug. 19, 1942; children— Suzanne Sybill, William Patrick, Gary J. Public relations dir. advt. ARC, Eastern Area Hdqrs., Alexandria, Va., 1941-46; owner, curator Mus. Antique Dolls and Toys, Lakewood, N.Y., 1960—; artist, one-woman shows, N.Y. and Fla.; writer, photographer nat. doll and toy mags., antiques mag.; writer, columnist Hobbies Mag. Mem. United Fedn. Doll Clubs, Inc., Western N.Y. Doll Club, Fla. West Coast Doll Collectors, Doll Study Club Jamestown (founder), Doll Collectors of America. Author: Portraits in Porcelain. Died June 23, 2006.

MCFEELY, CLARENCE EDWARD, consultant; b. Oak Park, Ill., May 12, 1929; s. Clarence Edward and Ann (Minarik) McF.; m. Margaret Scott, June 13, 1953; children: Thomas E., Scott G., Elizabeth A. Susan C., Carolyn G. BS, Bradley U., 1951. Pers. supr. Campbell Soup Co., Chgo., 1953-55; employee rels. mgr. The Budd Co., Newark, Del., 1955-59; rep. Dansk Designs Inc., Miami, Fla., 1959-60; prin. A.T. Kearney & Co., Chgo., 1960-69; ptnr. William H. Clark & Assoc., Chgo., 1969, McFeely Wackerle Shulman, Chgo., from 1969. Pres. AESC, 1980-82. 1st lt. USMC, 1951-53. Republican. Methodist. Avocations: golf, travel, history, theater, classical music. Home: Barrington, Ill. Died June 22, 2007.

MCGAFFIGAN, EDWARD, JR., commissioner; b. Boston, Dec. 8, 1948; s. Edward McGaffigan and Margaret (O'Brien); m. Peggy Weeks, 1982 (dec. 2000); children: Edward Francis, Margaret Ruth. AB in Physics summa cum laude, Harvard U., 1970; MS in Physics, Calif. Inst. Tech., 1974; M in Pub. Policy, Harvard Kennedy Sch. Govt., 1976. Cons. RAND Corp, 1974—75; with Arms Control and Disarmament Agy., Washington, 1975; fgn. svc. officer US Dept. State, 1976—83; sci. attache US Embassy, Moscow, 1978-80; sr. policy analyst, asst. dir. Office Sci. and Tech. Policy The White House, Washington, 1981-83; staff mem. NSC, Washington, 1982-83; legis. asst. to Senator Jeff Bingman, US Senate, Washington, 1983—88, legis.

dir., 1989—92, sr. policy adv., 1993—96; commr. US Nuclear Regulatory Commn., Rockville, 1996—2005, 2005—07. Recipient NM Medal of Merit, 1986, Eagle award, Nat. Guard Bur., 1996, Disting. Svc. award, Nuclear Regulatory Commn., 2006, Henry DeWolf Smyth Nuclear Statesman award, Am. Nuclear Soc./Nuclear Energy Inst., 2007, Disting. Pub. Svc. award, Am. Nuc. Soc., 2007; fellowship, NFS, Millikan, Woodrow Wilson Found., Sheldon Traveling fellowship, Nat. Grad. fellowship, Harvard U., Undergraduate Nat. scholar. Mem.: Am. Phys. Soc. Democrat. Roman Catholic. Achievements include being the only commisioner in United States Nuclear Regulatory Commision's history to serve three terms. Avocation: marathon running. Home: Arlington, Va. Died Sept. 2, 2007.

MC GARA, HOMER JOSEPH, manufacturing executive; b. Trafford, Pa., May 13, 1913; s. Austin J. and Minerva (Young) McG.; m. Esther L. Skelding, Dec. 25, 1945; children: Jane A., John S. ME, Wayne U., 1942. Engr. Motor Products Corp., Detroit, 1936-49, plant supt., 1949-54; mgr. Macon Arms Inc., Decatur, Ill., 1954-58; pres. Sheridan Mfg. Co. div. Sheller Globe Corp., Wauseon, Ohio, 1958-71, group v.p., 1969-71; exec. v.p. Globe Wernicke Co., Cin., 1961-63; sr. group v.p. Sheller Globe Corp., Toledo, 1971-74, sr. v.p., 1974-76, exec. v.p., 1976-80, also bd. dirs. Pres. Wauseon Community Chest, 1971—. Capt. CE, AUS, 1942-46. Mem. C. of C., Masons, Elks, Rotary (pres. local chpt. 1971—). Republican. Presbyterian. Home: Toledo, Ohio. Died Nov. 16, 2005.

MC GARR, PAUL ROWLAND, textile company executive; b. Webster County, Miss., Nov. 11, 1933; s. Willie B. and Nina Mae (Rowl) McG.; m. Elizabeth Ann Smith, May 1, 1955; children— Paul Rushton, Lee-anne. BS, Miss. State U., 1955. C.P.A., Miss. Indsl. engr., cost accountant ITT, Corinth, Miss. and Raleigh, N.C., 1958-62; treas., exec. v.p. So. Gen. Factors, Inc., High Point, N.C., 1962-66; sr. v.p. fin., bd. dirs. Guilford Mills, Inc., Greensboro, N.C., from 1966. With USN, 1955-57. Mem. Masons. Republican. Lutheran. Home: Greensboro, NC. Died Oct. 31, 2006.

MCGEARY, ROBERT WILLIAM, corporation executive; b. Atlantic City, June 3, 1931; s. Expedit William and Esther (Feeney) McG.; m. Patricia Ann Langan, Sept. 2, 1950; children— Kathleen A., Robert W., Maureen P., Kevin J., William S., John P. AB, U. Ala., 1953; MA (Rockefeller scholar), U. Pa., 1954. Mgmt. analyst Navy Dept., Washington, 1954-56; asst. to pres. Leahy & Co., NYC, 1956-58; mgr. systems planning Am. Standard Corp., NYC, 1958-60; v.p. Leahy & Co., NYC, 1960-62; project dir. Logistics Mgmt. Inst., Washington, 1962-63; dir. mgmt. information services Lever Bros., NYC, 1963-65, asst. comptroller, 1965-67, comptroller, 1967-68; pres. Lever Data Processing Services, Inc., 1968-72; dir. data processing marketing div. Reuben H. Donelley Corp., 1972-76; v.p. Donnelley Mktg., 1976-82; v.p., gen. mgr. data processing ops. Donelley Mktg., from 1982. Contbr. articles to profl. jours. Vice pres. Elmsford (N.Y.) Ednl. Assn., 1964-65. Served with USMCR, 1951. Home: White Plains, NY. Died Nov. 28, 2006.

MCGEHEE, FRANK SUTTON, paper company executive; b. Aug. 15, 1928; s. Clifford G. and Ray (Sutton) McGehee; m. Ann Whitehurst, Mar. 18, 1949; children: Frank Sutton, David Searcy, Ann Lynwood Riley. BA in Econs., U. Ala., 1950. V.p. Jacksonville Paper Co. (now UNIJAX), Fla., 1950-64; dir. Flagship Banks of Jacksonville, Fla.; co-founder, co-chmn. bd. Mac Paper Converters, Inc., Jacksonville, Fla., from 1990, chmn. bd., CEO, 1990. Trustee, mem. exec. com. Bolles Sch.; past pres., dir. Wolfson Childrens Hosp.; past pres., pres. bd. Ga. Christian Sch. and Home, North Fla. Coun. Boy Scouts Am.; past chmn. Weyerhaeuser Mcht. Coun., Kimberly Clark Mcht. Coun.; active San Jose Ch. of Christ. Mem. Nat. Paper Trade Assn. (dir.), Jacksonville Businessmen Club (sec., dir.), Tournament Players Club (founder), River Club, San Jose Country Club, Sawgrass Country Club, Plantation Country Club. Home: Jacksonville, Fla. Died July 12, 2006.

MCGILVRAY, JOAN BAILEY, stockbroker; b. Monrovia, Calif., Nov. 4, 1926; d. William James and Helen Jane (Davis) Bailey; student Stanford U., 1944-47; divorced; children: Alexander Crane, Jr., Mark Rankin, Lynn. Assoc. v.p. Dean Witter & Co., Pasadena, Calif., 1966-76; 1st v.p. Bateman Eichler Hill Richards, Los Angeles, 1976-84; pres. McGilvray & Assocs., Carlsbad, Calif., 1984—. Mem. Nat. Options Soc. (founding dir.), So. Calif. Options Soc. (pres. 1978). Republican. Club: Live Oak Tennis. Home: Aliso Viejo, Calif. Died July 20, 2006.

MCGINNIS, GLENN EDWARD, small business owner; b. Abilene, Kans., July 25, 1939; s. Edward Day and Hannah Andrena (Wang) McG.; m. Crystal Ann Gandy, Dec. 19, 1964; children— Michelle Lee, Craig Alan. Student Kans. State U., 1957-61. Inside salesman Capitol Pipe and Steel Co., Houston, 1960-61, sales rep., 1962-64, dist. mgr., Los Angeles, 1964-67, asst. v.p. mktg., Phila., 1967-70, div. v.p., Houston, 1970-81; owner, operator The Dove's Nest, Kerrville, Tex., 1981—. Vice pres. U.S. Jaycees, Turnersville, N.J., 1969-70; dir. Hill Country Arts Found., Ingram, Tex., 1984—, ARC, Kerrville, 1984—. Served to petty officer USCG, 1961-69. Mem. Christian Booksellers Assn., Kerrville Area C. of C. (bd. dirs. 1982-83, 85—). Republican. Methodist. Lodge: Rotary. Avocations: golfing; jogging; reading; traveling. Home: Kerrville, Tex. Died Sept. 16, 2006.

MCGINTY, THOMAS EDWARD, management consultant; b. Holyoke, Mass., Aug. 20, 1929; s. Patrick John and Alice May (Hill) McG.; m. June Theresa Coutu, Jan. 27, 1951; children: Thomas, Michael, Matthew. BS in Econs. and Commerce, U. Vt., 1951; MBA, NYU, 1957. Chartered fin. analyst. Sr. fin. analyst Moody's Investor Service, 1955-59, Model, Roland and Stone, NYC, 1959-62; with Cleve.-Cliffs Iron Co., 1962-83, v.p. fin., 1971-75, sr. v.p., 1975-83; pres. Belvoir Cons., Inc., from 1983. Bd. dirs. Park Ohio Industries. Author: Project Organization and Finance, 1981. Bd. advisers Notre Dame Coll. Served with U.S. Army, 1951-55, Korea. Decorated Bronze Star. Mem. Assn. Investment Mgmt. and Rsch., Cleve. Skating Club, Wilderness Country Club (Naples, Fla.). Roman Catholic. Home: Cleveland, Ohio. Died Feb. 13, 2007.

MCGLINCHEY, ALEXANDER HERBERT, federal judge; b. Ft. Worth, Aug. 11, 1930; s. Alexander H. and Hilda (Cornelison) McG.; m. Nelda L. Anderson, Dec. 28, 1961; children: Alexander Harold, Finlay Parnell, Zan Edward, Patrick Jonathan Andrew. BA, Tex. Christian U., 1951; postgrad, Georgetown U., 1951-52; JD, So. Meth. U., 1954, LLM, 1965. Bar: Tex. 1954, U.S. Supreme Ct. 1975, U.S. Dist. Ct. (no. dist.) Tex. 1961. Trust adminstr. 1st Nat. Bank, Ft. Worth, 1958-60; ptnr. Pepper, Markward & McGlinchey, Ft. Worth, 1961-65; pvt. practice Ft. Worth, 1965-66; asst. U.S. Atty., criminal chief U.S. Atty.'s Office, Ft. Worth, 1966-75; judge U.S. Magistrate, Ft. Worth, from 1975. Lt. (j.g.) USNR, 1954-57. Mem. State Bar Tex., Tarrant County Bar Assn. Home: Fort Worth, Tex. Died Apr. 2, 2006.

MCGORRILL, BRUCE COURTNEY, retired broadcasting executive; b. Portland, Maine, June 22, 1931; s. Virgil C. and Bernice B. (Butler) McG.; m. Donna Evangeline Tilton, Oct. 17, 1958; children: Melanie, Christopher, Jonathan, Evangeline. Announcer, Sta.-WCSH-TV, Portland, Maine, 1954-56, nat. salesman, 1956-60, gen. sales mgr., 1960-75, sta. mgr., 1975-79, gen. mgr., 1979-81, sr. v.p., 1981-83, exec. v.p., chief exec. officer, 1981-94; ret., 1997; vice chmn. NBC-TV Affiliate Bd., TV Bur. Advt. Bd. Producer (humor records) Saturday Night in Dover-Foxcroft, 1964, Goodnight Phaebe, 1966. Bd. dirs. Maine affiliate Am. Heart Assn. Mem. Nat. Assn. Broadcasters (bd. dirs. 1991-95, Maine Broadcaster of Yr. 1990), Cumberland Club (Portland), Rotary. Died Mar. 28, 2006.

MCGOVERN, JOHN PHILLIP (JACK MCGOVERN), physician, educator; b. Washington, June 2, 1921; s. Francis and Lottie (Brown) McG.; m. Kathrine Dunbar Galbreath, 1961. BS, Duke U., 1945; MD, 1945; postgrad., London and Paris, 1949; degree (hon.), Ricker Coll., Union Coll., Kent State U., U. Nebr., Ill. Coll. Podiatric Medicine, Lincoln Coll., Emerson Coll. Diplomate Nat. Bd. Med. Examiners, Am. Bd. Pediats., subspecialty pediat. alleryg Am. Bd. Allergy and Immunology. Intern in peidats Yale-New Haven (Conn.) Gen. Hosp., 1945-46; resident peidats. Duke U. Hosp., Durham, N.C., 1948; resident Guy Hosp., London, 1949; chief resident Children's Hosp., Houston, 1949-50; chief out-patient dept., 1950-51; John and Mary R. Markle scholar med. sci. George Washington U. Sch. Medicine, 1950-54; asst. prof. pediats., 1950-54; chief George Washington U. pediat. divsn. D.C. Gen. Hosp., 1951-54; assoc. prof. pediats. Tulane U., New Orleans, 1954-56; pvt. practice medicine specializing in allergy/immunology Houston, 1956-58; chief allergy svc. Tex. Children's Hosp., Houston, 1957-74; founder McGovern Allergy Clinic, 1956; clin. prof. pediats. (allergy); prof., chmn. dept. history of medicine U. Tex. Grad. Sch. Biomed. Sci., 1970-81; prof. history & philosophy of biol. sci., 1981—2007. Vis. physician Charity Hosp., New Orleans; adj. prof. dept. microbiology Baylor Coll. Medicine, Houston, M.D. Anderson Hosp. and Tumor Inst., 1976—, dpet. environ. sci. sch. Pub. Health U. Tex., 1978-2007; fellow Green coll. Oxford (Eng.) U.; disting. adj. prof. health and safety edn. Kent (Ohio) State U., 1972-2007 Author: (with Mandel) Bibliography of Sarcoidosis (1876-1963), 1964, (with James Knight) Allergy and Human Emotions, 1967, (with Charles Roland), Wm. Osler: The Continuing Education, 1969, (with Gordon Stewart) Penicillin Alelrgy: Clincial and Immunolgical Aspects, 1970, (with Chester Burns) Humanism in Medicine, 1974, (with Glenn Knotts) Sch. Health Problems, 1975, (with Earl Nation and Charles Roland) An Annotated Checklist of Osleriana, 1976, (with Michael Smolensky and Alain Reinberg) Chronobiology in Allergy and Immunology, 1977, (with others) Recent Advances in the Chronobiology of Allergy and Immunology, 1980; editor: A Way of Life (Osler), 1969, Davison Memorial Addresses, 1976, (with E.F. Nation) Student and Chief: The Osler-Camac Correspondence, 1980, (wth J. Arena) Davison of Duke - His Reminiscences, 1980, (with C. Roland and J. Barondess) The Persisting Osler, 1985, (with C. Roland) The Collected Essays of sir William Osler, Vols. I, II, III, 1985, (with J. Vay Eys) The Doctor as a Person, 1988, (with P.L. Starck) The Hidden Dimension of Illness: Human Suffering, 1992, Am. Lecture Series in Allergy and Immunology); assoc. editor: Annals of allergy, 1965-80, Jour. Sch. Health, 1977-80, Jour. Asthma Rsch.; mem. editl. bd.: Psychosomatics, Headache, Internat. Corr. Soc. Allergists, Acad. Achievement, 1967-75, Geriatrics, 1974-78, numerous others; mem. editl. adv. bd.: Forum on Medicine, 1978-81, The Classics of Medicine Library, 1978—. Pres., bd. dirs. John. P. McGovern Found., 1986-2007; bd. dirs. allergy Found. Am., 1962-74, McGovern Fund for Behavioral scis., 1988-2007; bd. regents nat. Liber. Medicine, 1970-74, cons., 1975-2007; mem. Nat. Adv. Coun. on alcohol Abuse and Alcoholism, 1987-2007; Capt. M.C., AUS, 1946-48. Recipient numerous awards including Disting. Alumni award Duke U. Sch. Medicine, 1976, John P. McGovern award TEx. sch. Health assn., 1977, Pres.'s citation Pres. Reagan, 1985, Royal Medallion of the Polar Star (Sweden), 1988, l'Ordre Nat. merite (France), 1988, Pres.'s Medal U. Tex. Health Sci. Ctr., Houston, 1987, Meritorious Svc. award AMA, 1988, Surgeon Gen.'s Medallion (Koop), 1989. Fellow Am. Coll. Allergy and Immunology (pres. 1968-69), Am. Acad. alelrgy and Immunology, Am. Acad. Pediats., Am. Coll. Chest Physicians (Tex. chpt. pres. 1966-67), Am. Assn. Study Headache (pres. 1963-64); mem. AMA, ACP, Am. Assn. Immologists, Soc. Exptl. Biology and Medicine, Am. Med. Writers Assn., Assn. for Rsch.in Nervous and Metal Diseases, Am. Assn.Hist. Medicine, So. Med. Assn. (life), Tex. Pediat. Soc., Assn. convalescent Homes and Hosps. for Asthmatic Children (pres. Tex. chpt. 1969-70), Duke U. Med. Alumni Assn. (pres. 1968-69), Am. Assn. Cert. Allergists (pres. 1972-73), Am. Osler Soc. (pres. 1973-74), am. Sch.health Assn., Soc. Alergia y Ciencias Afines (Mex., hon.), Soc. Mexicana Alergia e Inmunologia (hon.), Westchester Allergy Soc. (hon.), Candadian allergy Soc. (hon.), Asociacion Argentina Alergia e Inmunologia (hon.), Royal Coll. Physicians (London, hon.), Cosmos, Army-Navy Country (Washington), Osler (London), Vintage (Calif.), Phi Beta Kappa, Alpha Omega Alpha, Sigma Xi (mem. com. on membership-at-large, editor newsletter 1970-71, dir. 1872-73), Sigma Pi Sigma, Pi Kappa Alpha. Died May 31, 2007.

MCGRATH, JOSEPH EDWARD, psychology educator; b. DuBois, Pa., July 17, 1927; s. John Bernard and Winifred Amelia (Senard) McG.; m. Marion Freitag, Sept. 5, 1952; children— Robert E., William D., James G., Janet W. BS, U. Md., 1950, MA, 1951; PhD, U. Mich., 1955. Research scientist Psychol. Research Assocs., Arlington, Va., 1955-57; v.p., sr. research scientist, dir. research office Human Scis. Research, Inc., Clarendon, Va., 1957-60; research asst. prof., assoc. dir. Group Effectiveness Lab., U. Ill., Champaign, 1960-62; asst. prof. psychology U. Ill., Champaign, 1962-64, assoc. prof., 1964-66, prof., from 1966, head psychology dept., 1971-76. Author: Social Psychology: A Brief Introduction, 1964 (with Irwin Altman) Small Group Research: A Synthesis and Critique of the Field, 1966, (with Philip J. Runkel) Studying Human Behavior, 1972, Groups: Interaction and Performance, 1984, (with David Brinberg) Validity and the Research Process, 1985, (with Janice R. Kelly) Time and Human Interaction, 1986, On Time and Method, 1988, (with Andrea Hollingshead) Groups Interacting with Computers, 1993; editor: Social and Psychological Factors in Stress, The Social Psychology of Time, 1988. Served with AUS, 1945-46. Fellow Am. Psychol. Assn., Am. Psychol. Soc.; mem. Midwestern Psychol. Assn., Soc. Psychol. Study Social Issues (past pres.), Internat. Soc. for the Study of Time, Soc. Exptl. Social Psychologists, AAUP, Sigma Xi, Phi Eta Sigma, Psi Chi. Home: Urbana, Ill. Died Apr. 1, 2007.

MCGRIMLEY, THOMAS JOSEPH, judge; b. Boston, Feb. 15, 1921; s. George W. and Annie (Gallagher) McG.; m. Mary Rita O'Hara, Sept. 6, 1948; children— Thomas, John, Kathleen, Patricia. B.S., Boston U., 1948; M.Ed., Boston Coll., 1951; J.D., Suffolk Law Sch., 1956. Bar: Mass. 1957, D.C. 1971. Chmn. Boston Retirement Bd., 1969-79; judge Social Security Adminstrn., Boston, 1979—. Served to col. USAAF, 1943-46; PTO. Home: Quincy, Mass. Died Jan. 1, 2006.

MC ILHENNY, JAMES HARRISON, association executive; b. Cleve., Nov. 9, 1927; s. Edward Lott and Noreen Isobel (Spence) McI.; m. Dorothy Dean Johnson, Aug. 11, 1951 (div.); 1 child, Claire B.; m. Candace Von Salzen, Sept. 14, 1990. Student, USCG Acad., 1945-47; BA in Econs, U. Mich., 1950. Pres. I. Miller & Sons, Inc., 1962-65; dir., v.p. Hickok Mfg. Co., Rochester, N.Y., 1965-68; sr. v.p. Macmillan, Inc., NYC, 1968-72, exec. v.p., 1972-80, U.S. News & World Report, Washington, 1980-81, pres., 1981-85, chief exec. officer, 1981-85; pres. Diversified Printing, Atglen, Pa., 1985-87; pres., CEO Coun. Better Bus. Burs., from 1987. Bd. dirs. Manhattan Life Ins. Corp. Served with USCG, 1945-47. Mem. Sigma Nu. Home: Alexandria, Va. Died Nov. 3, 2006.

MCILRAITH, KENNETH JAMES, banker; b. Buffalo, Jan. 22, 1927; s. Earle Frazer and Hazel Ena (Conner) McI.; m. Dorothy Mae Tousey, Apr. 2, 1955; children— Glenn, Janet, Anne BS in Econs., U. Pa., 1949, MBA, 1950. Vice pres. Moog, Inc., East Aurora, N.Y., 1953-61, also dir.; pres. S.B.I.C. of N.Y., NYC, 1961-64; exec. v.p. Liberty Nat. Bank, Buffalo, 1964-66; pres., dir. Scott Aviation Co., Lancaster, N.Y., 1966-69, Essexbank, Peabody, Mass., 1969-83; pres., chief exec. officer Conifer Group, Worcester, Mass., from 1983; vice chmn. Bank of New England Corp., Boston, from 1987. Chmn. bd. trustees Salem State Coll., Mass., 1980—. Served with USNR Recipient Silver Beaver award North Bay council Boy Scouts Am., 1979; Good Scout award North Bay council Boy Scouts Am., Danvers, Mass., 1982 Mem. Am. Bankers Assn. (bd. dirs.), Mass. Bankers Assn. (chmn. bd. 1978-79) Clubs: Salem Country (Peabody); Worcester. Republican. Episcopalian. Home: Gloucester, Mass. Died Nov. 30, 2005.

MCINTYRE, ROBERT DONALD, publishing executive, consultant; b. Davenport, Iowa, Aug. 9, 1932; s. Horace Francis and Leah Naomi (Synder) McI.; m. Mary Hoke, 1957 (div. 1979); children: Robert, Michael, Laura Lee; m. Judith Ann Sheridan McNamara, Dec. 4, 1982; children: Scott, John Bradley, Lawrence. BA, Dickinson Coll., 1954. Sales rep., then sales promotion mgr. Westminster Press., Phila., 1956-66, pub., 1979-88; sales mgr. dept. religious books and bibles, trade div. J.B. Lippincott, Phila., 1967-70, gen. sales mgr., 1970-75, v.p. sales, 1975-79; pub. Presbyn. Pub. House, Westminster/John Knox Press, Louisville, from 1989. Pub. cons. Barra Found., Phila., 1980-90; founder Phila. Pubs. Group, 1982. With U.S. Army, 1954-56. Mem. Am. Assn. Pubs., So. Pubs. Assn., Coop. Pub. Assn. (bd. dirs.), Protestant Owned Pubs. Assn. (bd. dirs.), Louisville C. of C. Democrat. Presbyterian. Home: New Bern, NC. Died Jan. 19, 2007.

MCISAAC, JOHN L., utility executive; b. Chgo., Dec. 12, 1929; s. Leslie A. and Katherine M. (Collins) McI.; m. Patricia A. Tunney, Dec. 2, 1950; children: Michael, Mary, Martin. Student, Fournier Inst., Lemont, Ill., 1945-49. Svc. and sales Peoples Gas Light and Coke Co., Chgo., 1949-59; indsl. sales engr. Wis. gas Co., Milw., 1960, commercial sales mgr., 1961-62, mgr. customer service, 1963-68, mgr. ops., 1969-74, v.p. ops., 1974-84, sr. v.p. ops., from 1985. Recipient Disting. Service award Milw. Fire Dept., 1971, Hon. Membership award, 1985. Mem. Am. Gas. Assn. (service award 1979), Midwest gas Assn. (com. chmn. 1969-73, bd. dirs. 1982-85). Clubs: Milw. Athletic. Roman Catholic. Avocations: fishing, theater, travel. Home: Milwaukee, Wis. Died Apr. 24, 2006.

MCKAIN, WALTER CECIL, retired educator; b. Columbiana, Ohio, Oct. 12, 1912; s. Walter Cecil and Grace F. (Van Kirk) McK.; m. Elizabeth F. Seckerson, Sept. 30, 1939; children— Richard, Nancy, Walter, Douglas, Susan. AB magna cum laude, Harvard, 1934, PhD, 1947. With Dept. Agr., Upper Darby, Pa., 1938-41, Berkeley, Calif., 1941-47; prof. U. Conn. Coll. Agr., Storrs, 1947-73. Author: Ribbon of Hope, 1965, Retirement Marriage, 1969, Dignity for the Living, 1975; columnist: Nestor's Nuggets. Mem. Conn. Commn. Aging, 1963-65, Cultural Exchange Program, USSR, 1965, 68, 72, 76, Vt. Aging Adv. Bd., 1984—. Mem. AAAS, Sociol. Assn., Gerontology Soc. Home: Northfield, Vt. Died July 2, 2007.

MCKEE, EDITH MERRITT, geologist; b. Oak Park, Ill., Oct. 9, 1918; d. Eustis Ewart and Edith (Frame) McK. BS, Northwestern U., 1946. Geologist, U.S. Geol. Survey, 1943-45, Shell

Oil Co., 1947-49, Arabian Am. Oil Co., 1949-54, Underground Gas Storage Co. Ill., 1956-58; ind. cons. geologist, Winnetka, Ill., 1958—; mem. environ. adv. com. Fed. Energy Adminstrn., 1974; mem. Nat. Adv. Com. Oceans and Atmosphere, 1975; speaker, cons. in field. Commr., Winnetka Park Bd., 1976-79. Fellow Marine Tech. Soc., Geol. Soc. Am.; mem. Am. Geol. Inst., Am. Inst. Profl. Geologists (cert., charter), Assn. Engring. Geologists, Ill. Geol. Soc., Am. Oceanic Orgn. Research on shore erosion, mapping of Gt. Lakes basins and deep ocean basins, global econ. devel. programs and mineral exploration, oil spill containment and retrieval, 3-D current studies lakes and oceans. Died Aug. 3, 2006.

MCKELLAR, LOUIS ALONZO, high technology company executive; b. Los Angeles, July 6, 1933; s. Louis Winston and Frances Carolyn (Field) M.; m. Janet Reid Gresham, Apr. 12, 1958; children— Martha Field, Louis Gresham, James Reid, John Davis. B.S.M.E., Stanford U., 1956, M.S.M.E., 1964. Research engr. Lockheed Palo Alto Research Labs, Palo Alto, Calif., 1959-65; supr., mgr., materials engr. Lockheed Missiles & Space Co., Inc., Sunnyvale, Calif., 1965-69; v.p. Tano Corp., New Orleans, 1969-73; mgr. mfg. Sierra Electronics, Menlo Park, Calif., 1974-75; gen. mgr., then pres. Raytek Inc., Mountain View, Calif., 1976-80; exec. v.p. Thoratec Labs. Corp., Berkeley, Calif., 1980—; pres. Thoratec Med. Inc. subs. Thoratec Labs. Corp., 1984—; pres., dir. Biotex Industries (formerly Thoratec Products, Inc), Berkeley, 1982-84; sec., dir. Thoratec Labs. Corp., 1981—; 83—. Contbr. tech. articles on materials and heat transfer to jours., books. Vice pres. Alliance for Good Govt., New Orleans, 1972, mem., 1971-73; chmn. Awalt High Sch. Community Adv. Council, Los Altos, Calif., 1975-76; chmn. dir. Calif. Coast Opera (formerly Scholar Opera Inc.), Palo Alto, Calif., 1976-85; bd. dirs. Mountain View and Los Altos Edn. Found., 1984. Served to lt. j.g. USN, 1956-59. General Electric Co. thermodynamic fellow Stanford U., 1963. Mem. Aerospace Industries Assn. (panel on thermophys. properties 1962-65), ASTM (exec. com. space simulation 1964-66), AIAA, (vice chmn. thermophysics com. 1965-66). Republican. Roman Catholic. Home: Los Altos, Calif. Died May 5, 2006.

MC KNIGHT, WILLIAM WARREN, JR., retired publisher; b. Normal, Ill., June 9, 1913; s. William Warren and Isabel Alida (Travis) McK.; m. Alice McGuire, Oct. 30, 1937; children: William Warren, III, Michael Joe, John James. BS in Bus. Adminstrn., Northwestern U., 1938. With McKnight Pub. Co., Bloomington, Ill., 1938-83, sec.-treas., 1949-56, pres., 1956-67, chmn. bd., 1968-79. Bd. dirs. Gen. Telephone Co. Ill., Champion Fed. Savs. & Loan Assn., chmn. bd. Pres. Bloomington Rotary Club, 1952, Bloomington C. of C., 1954; mem. Ill. Commn. Higher Edn., 1956-60; chmn. Bloomington-Normal Airport Authority, 1965-70, CETA Pvt. Industry Council Ill. Balance of State, 1979-81. Served with USNR, 1942-46. Recipient Disting. Service award Bloomington Kiwanis Club, 1963, Disting. Service award Normal C. of C., 1973; Good Govt. award Bloomington Jaycees, 1970; Edn. Constrn. award Edn. Council Graphic Arts Industry, 1974; Disting. Alumni award Ill. State U., 1978; Disting. Service award Spirit of McLean County, 1982; Disting. Service citation Epsilon Pi Tau, 1983; award of Merit Am. Vocat. Assn., 1990; disting. assoc. award Coun. on Tech. Tchr. Edn., 1995. Mem. Graphic Arts Edn. Assn., Internat. Tech. Edn. Assn., Nat. Assn. Indsl. and Tech. Tchrs. Educators, Ill. C. of C. (dir. 1964-69), Ill. Mfrs. Assn. (dir. 1954-62) Clubs: Coll. Alumni, Bloomington Country. Republican. Presbyterian. Home: Scottsdale, Ariz. Died May 23, 2006.

MCLAUGHLIN, GLEN HENRY, professional society administrator; b. Abilene, Tex., Feb. 3, 1914; s. John Henry and Clara Elizabeth (Priddy) McL.; B.A., Hardin-Simmons U., 1935, postgrad. 1938-39; student Central State U. Okla., 1933-34; postgrad. U. Tex., Austin, 1937-38; m. Mary Evelyn Ivy, Nov. 19, 1939; 1 dau., Suzanne McLaughlin Rowden. Tchr. sci. Lewisville (Tex.) High Sch., 1935-36, Gatesville (Tex.) High Sch., 1936-37; instr. dept. physics Hardin-Simmons U., 1937; bacteriologist Tex. State Health Dept., Austin, 1937-38; meteorologist U.S. Weather Bur., Abilene, Tex., 1938-39; instr. dept. chemistry, Hardin-Simmons U., summer, 1939; chemist, toxicologist and lab. supr. Tex. Dept. Public Safety, Austin, 1939-45, chief identification and criminal records and dir. labs., 1945-57, chief personnel and staff services, 1957-73, chief adminstrn., 1973-77; exec. sec. Tex. Police Assn., Austin, 1977—; lectr. in field. Chmn. Tex. Commn. on Law Enforcement Officers Standards and Edn., 1965-73; mem. Gov.'s com. for devel. of position classification plan for state govt., Tex., 1953-54; div. dir. United Fund, 1958-59. Recipient citation, Tex. State Legislature, 1948, Tex. Law Enforcement Found., 1956; named Tex. Public Employee of the Yr., 1971; named Public Adminstr. of the Yr. Austin Soc. Public Adminstrn., 1972; Wallace Beasley award for outstanding contribution to law enforcement edn. in Tex., 1976. Fellow Am. Acad. Forensic Sci.; mem. Internat. Assn. for Identification (pres. 1950), Internat. Assn. Automobile Theft (pres. 1961), Harvard Assos. in Police Sci., Internat. Assn. Chiefs of Police, Sheriff's Assn. Tex., Austin Soc. for Public Adminstrn., Tex. Police Assn., Tex. Public Employees Assn. (dir.). Baptist. Clubs: Country of Austin, Austin Knife and Fork (pres. 1973). Asso. editor Tex. Police Jour., 1960—; contbr. articles to profl. jours. Home: Austin, Tex. Died Mar. 22, 2007.

MCLAUGHLIN, ROSEMARY, horse trainer, state representative; b. Royalton, Vt., July 15, 1952; m. Tom Wells; 1 child, Katie. Student, Vt. Tech. Coll., 1969—70, Reed Coll., 1971—73. Prin., owner Hitching Post Farm, Royalton, Vt., from 1973; rep. Vt. State Ho. Reps., from 2003. Mem. Royalton (Vt.) Selectboard, Royalton (Vt.) Sch. Bd., 1990—96. Democrat. Home: South Royalton, Vt. Died Oct. 30, 2006.

MCLEAN, MARGARET STONER, researcher; b. Victoria, Tex., June 5, 1915; d. Thomas Royal and Mame Victoria Stoner; A.A., Victoria Jr. Coll., 1936; B.S., U. Tex., 1939; m. Malcolm Dallas McLean, Feb. 11, 1939; 1 son, John Robertson. Receptionist, postmaster San Jacinto Mus. History, Houston, 1939-41; microfilm camera operator Library of Congress, Washington, 1942; bibliog. researcher, 1947-53; tchr. elem. sch., Fayetteville, Ark., 1954-55; elem. tchr. Am. Sch., Tegucigalpa, Honduras, 1957-58; tchr. English, U.S. Bi-national Center and Am. High Sch., Guayaquil, Ecuador, 1959-61; newspaper microfilm archivist Amon Carter Mus. Western Art, Ft. Worth, 1963-73; microfilm research specialist Spanish Tex. Microfilm Center, Presidio La Bahia, Goliad, Tex., 1973-74; researcher, editorial asst. Papers Concerning Robertson's Colony in Tex., Ft. Worth, 1975—; bibliog. researcher Jenkins Garrett Library, U. Tex., Arlington, 1981-82. Mem. Chancellor's Council U. Tex. System, 1984—. Clubs: U. Tex. at Arlington Woman's; Texas Christian U. Woman's (Ft. Worth). Contbr. articles to profl. jours. Died July 12, 2007.

MCMAHON, GEORGE JOSEPH, academic administrator; b. NYC, June 20, 1923; s. Martin Joseph and Mary (O'Connor) McM. AB, Woodstock Coll., 1946, Philosophy licentiate, 1947, MA, 1948, STL, 1954; MA, Fordham U., 1951; PhD, Laval U., 1959. Joined S.J., 1940, ordained priest Roman Cath. Ch., 1953. Instr. physics and Latin Regis H.S., NYC, 1947-49; instr. philosophy St. Peter's Coll., Jersey City, 1958-60, asst. dean, dir. Sch. Bus. Adminstrn., 1961-62; instr. philosophy Loyola Sem., Shrub Oak, N.Y., 1960-61; dean Fordham Coll., Fordham U., Bronx, N.Y., 1962-74; v.p. adminstrn. Fordham U., 1974-87, v.p. Lincoln Ctr. campus NYC, 1987-94, chaplain, from 1994. Author: The Order of Procedure in the Philosophy of Nature, 1958, The Proemium to the Physics of Aristotle, 1957. V.p. Friends of U. Laval, Que., Can.; trustee Marymount Sch. N.Y. Home: Bronx, NY. Died Nov. 30, 2005.

MCMAHON, JOHN MICHAEL, physicist, research executive; b. St. Paul, May 13, 1941; s. John Hale and Cecilia Geraldine (Mullin) McM.; m. Mary Roarty, Sept. 11, 1965; children— John Joseph, Patrick Rogan. B.S. in Physics, Boston Coll., 1963; M.A. in Physics, Dartmouth Coll., 1965. Physicist, Naval Research Lab., Washington, 1965-69, supr., research physicist, 1969-73, sect. head, 1973-81, assoc. div. supt., 1981—; lectr. laser course George Washington U., Washington, 1971-75, course coordinator, 1974-75. Reviewer Applied Optics Jour., 1969—, Jour. Quantum Electronics, 1971—. Contbr. articles on lasers to profl. jours. Chmn. Local Evaluation Commn., Sch. Bd. Montgomery County, Md., 1977, mem. rev. com., 1979-80; treas. Barry Klein for Sch. Bd. Campaign, Montgomery, 1982; troop com. mem. Troop 30, Boy Scouts Am., Montgomery, 1977-82. Mem. Am. Phys. Soc., Sigma Xi. Democrat. Roman Catholic. Avocation: golf; history. Home: Locust Grove, Va. Died July 1, 2006.

MCMAHON, JOHN PATRICK, retired lawyer; b. Monroeville, Ohio, Feb. 8, 1919; s. George James and Eleanor Helene (Ruffing) McM.; m. Patricia Patterson McDanel, May 6, 1950 (dec. July 1983); children: Colleen, Kevin, Patricia, Brian, Barry, Michael; m. Mary Echard, Mar. 7, 1987. BA cum laude, Ohio State U., 1940, JD summa cum laude, 1942. Bar: Ohio 1942, U.S. Supreme Ct. 1949, U.S. Dist. Ct. Ohio 1949, U.S. Ct. Appeals (6th cir.) 1959, U.S. Ct. Appeals (D.C. cir.) 1975. Ptnr. George, Greek, King, McMahon, Columbus, Ohio, 1954-79, Baker & Hostetler, Columbus, 1979-85, ret.; with nat. coun. Ohio State U. Coll. Law, from 1980. Capt. USAAF, 1943-46, PTO. Mem. ABA, Ohio Bar Assn., Columbus Bar Assn., Transp. Lawyers Assn., Pres.' Club of Ohio State U. (Columbus), Athletic Club (Columbus), Home: Columbus, Ohio. Died May 24, 2006.

MCMAHON, THOMAS RAYMOND, physicist; b. Pittsfield, Mass., Nov. 2, 1948; s. George Joseph and Alice Louise (Griffin) McM.; m. Paula C. McDonald, Aug. 24, 1974. B.S., Christian Bros. Coll., Memphis, 1970; Ph.D. in Physics, U. So. Calif., 1978. Research asst. Center for Laser Studies, U. So. Calif., 1975-78; sr. physicist Sperry Support Services, Huntsville, Ala., 1978-79; sr. scientist Neutral Beam Physics Group, Gen. Atomic Co., San Diego, 1979-83; sr. scientist research and devel. Cooper Vision Diagnostics, San Diego, 1983—. Contbr. articles to profl. jours. Served with U.S. Army, 1970-72. Mem. Optical Soc. Am., IEEE, Quantum Electronics Soc., Laser Inst. Am., Sigma Xi. Roman Catholic. Home: San Diego, Calif. Died Aug. 26, 2006.

MCMANUS, WALTER LEONARD, brokerage house executive; b. NYC, Apr. 27, 1918; s. Charles E. and Eva M. (Olt) McM.; m. Lillian Ziegler, June 21, 1941; children: Walter Leonard, Peter David, Susan. Student, Harvard Bus. Sch.; BS in Fin. Sci., Georgetown U., 1940. With Crown Cork & Seal Co., Inc., Balt., 1940-60, became sec., 1945, v.p., 1949, sec.-treas., 1958-60. Pres., dir. Cem Securities Corp.; assoc. Castlewood Realty Co.; dir. Hospice of Martin County, Fla. Bd. dirs. Vols. of Medicine. Mem. Vols. in Medicine, Halifax River Yacht Club, Lighthouse Point Yacht Club, Cocoanut Point Yacht Club, Internat. Order of Blue Gavel. Home: Stuart, Fla. Died Dec. 22, 2006.

MCMICHEN, ROBERT SIDNEY, retired labor union executive; b. Coral Gables, Fla., Dec. 21, 1925; s. Harlie Jackson and Lois Virginia (Teal) McM.; m. Mildred Payne, Dec. 31, 1949; children: Robert Michael, Beverly Lynn, Brenda Kay, Lori Virginia, Patrick Keith. Student public schs., Atlanta. Printer Internat. Typog. Union, Colorado Springs, Colo., 1945-57, successively pres, internat. rep., mem. exec. council, 2d v.p., 1st v.p., pres., v.p. local br. Atlanta, 1955-57; pres. printing, pub. & media workers, v.p. Communications Workers of Am., Washington, 1987-89. Trustee negotiated pension plans, Internat. Typog. Union, Can., 1974-90. With USAAF, 1943-45; served to maj. USAR, 1949-76. Mem. Internat. Found. Employee Benefit Plans. Clubs: Masons, Shriners. Democrat. Baptist. Home: Colorado Springs, Colo. Died July 1, 2006.

MCMURRAY, WILLIAM, consultant, retired electrical engineer; b. Los Angeles, Aug. 15, 1929; s. William Arthur and Genevieve Leona (Arnold) McM.; m. Marion Elizabeth Schnipp, Oct. 22, 1955; children: William B., Shirley A., Robert C., Barbara C. BSc in Engring. with first class honors, Battersea Poly., London, 1950; MS, Union Coll., 1956; LLD (hon.), Concordia U., Montreal, Que., Can., 1986. Test engr. Gen. Electric, Pittsfield, Mass., 1950-51, elec. engr. corp. rsch. and devel. Schenectady, N.Y., 1953-88; cons., from 1989. Author: Theory and Design of Cycloconverters, 1972; contbg. author: Principles of Inverter Circuits, 1964; patentee in field; contbr. 28 articles to profl. jours. Chmn. troop 31 Boy Scouts Am., Schenectady, 1973. Served as pvt. U.S. Army, 1951-53. Recipient William Newell award Power Electronics Specialists Conf., 1978. Fellow IEEE (Magnetics Soc., chmn. static power converter com. Industry Applications Soc. 1982-83, Centennial medal 1984, Lamme medal 1984), Instn. Elec. Engrs. (assoc.). Republican. Avocations: canoeing, archaeology. Home: Niskayuna, NY. Died Dec. 25, 2006.

MCNAMARA, EDWARD HOWARD, county official, former mayor; b. Detroit, Sept. 21, 1926; s. Andrew Kursina and Ellen Gertrude (Bennett) McN.; m. Lucille Yvonne Martin, June 26, 1948; children— Colleen, Michael, Nancy, Kevin, Terence Ph.B., U. Detroit, 1959; PhD (hon.), Madonna Coll., 1982. Mgr. Mich. Bell Telephone Co., Detroit, 1948-70; mayor City of Livonia, Mich., 1970-86; county exec. Wayne County, Detroit, from 1987. Served with USN, 1944-46 Democrat. Roman Catholic. Home: Livonia, Mich. Died Feb. 19, 2006.

MCNEEL, VAN LOUIS, chemical company executive; b. Laurel, Miss., July 4, 1925; s. George Louis and Pauline (Webb) McN.; m. Betty Tarwater, July 6, 1959 (div. 1966); 1 child, Clayton Webb; m. Diane Kidd, Dec. 30, 1971 (div. 1994); 1 child, Ian Edward. Student, Sanford U. (formerly Howard Coll.); LLB, U. Ala., 1949. Project mgr. Reynolds Metals, Jacksonville, Fla., NYC, 1949-51; div. mgr. Olin Mathieson Chem. Corp., Atlanta, 1951-60, dir. internat. ops., 1960-63; pres. Polymer Internat. Corp., Tampa, 1964-89; chmn., chief exec. officer McNeel Internat Corp, Tampa, Fla., from 1989. Bd. dirs. Tampa chpt ARC; mem. Golden Triangle Civic Assn., Tampa Bay Area Trade Coun. Fgn. Rels. Mem. Am. Mgmt. Assn., Soc. Plastic Engrs. Clubs: Palma Ceia Golf and Country, Tampa Yacht and Country, Ctr. Club, University (Tampa). Home: Tampa, Fla. Died Oct. 4, 2006.

MC NEIL, JOSEPH DENNIS, lawyer; b. Los Angeles, Mar. 30, 1930; s. Joseph Dennis and Ellen Josephine (Redding) McN.; m. Janet R. Timmons, June 7, 1980; children by previous marriage: Timothy Joseph, Patrick Michael. BS, UCLA, 1953, JD, 1956. Bar: Calif. 1957. With Zahradka, Glines & McNeil, Los Angeles, 1957-68, Broderick, McNeil & Spencer, Calif., 1968-1973; mng. ptnr. Bonne, Jones, Bridges, Mueller & O'Keefe, Santa Ana, Calif., from 1974. Served with U.S. Army, 1950-51. Mem. Am. Bar Assn., Calif. Bar Assn., Los Angeles County Bar Assn., Orange County Bar Assn., Am. Bd. Trial Advs. (nat. bd. dirs.). Republican. Roman Catholic. Home: Irvine, Calif. Died Apr. 23, 2006.

MCNESBY, JAMES ROBERT, b. Bayonne, NJ, Apr. 16, 1922; s. James Aloysius and Margaret Cecilia (O'Connor) McN.; m. Helen Louise Rittenhouse, Dec. 27, 1949; children— Kevin Lynn, James Robert, Shawn. BS, Ohio U., 1943; MS, NYU, 1946, PhD, 1951. Research chemist Nat. Bur. Standards, Washington, 1957-63, chief photochemistry sect., 1963-68, chief phys. chemistry div., 1968-71, chief office air-water measurement, 1971-76; prof., chmn. chem. dept. U. Md., College Park, 1976-82, prof. chemistry, 1982-85, prof. emeritus, from 1985. Contbr. articles to profl. jours. Served with U.S. Army, 1944-45. Recipient Rockefeller Pub. Service award, Princeton U., 1958. Fellow AAAS; mem. Am. Chem. Soc., Internat. Photochemistry Conf. (chmn. 1983-85), Phi Beta Kappa. Democrat. Home: Rockville, Md. Died Dec. 12, 2006.

MC QUADE, HENRY FORD, state justice; b. Pocatello, Idaho, Oct. 11, 1915; s. M. Joseph and Mary E. (Farnan) McQ.; m. Mary E. Downing, Apr. 11, 1942; children— Sharon McQuade Grisham, Michael, Frances McQuade Munning, Robert, Joseph, Peter, William. AB, U. Idaho, 1940, LL.B., 1943. Bar: Idaho 1946. Practice in, Pocatello, 1946-51; pros. atty. Bannock County, Idaho, 1946-50; judge 5th Jud. Dist., Idaho, 1951-56; justice Idaho Supreme Ct., 1957-76, chief justice, 1972-75; dep. adminstr. Law Enforcement Assistance Adminstrn., U.S. Dept. Justice, Washington, 1976; adminstrv. law judge Occupational Safety and Health Rev. Commn., Washington, 1976-81. Mem. Nat. Commn. on Criminal Justice Standards and Goals, 1971-73, Nat. Commn. Hwy. Traffic Safety, 1971-74. Chmn. Idaho Gov.'s Com. Traffic Safety, 1958-59, Idaho YMCA Youth Legislature, 1958-69, Boise chpt. ARC, 1970-71. Mem. Am. Bar Assn., Am. Judicature Soc., Idaho State Bar. Home: Boise, Idaho. Died Dec. 13, 2006.

MCQUARRIE, DONALD GRAY, surgeon, educator; b. Richfield, Utah, Apr. 17, 1931; s. John Gray and LoRetta McQ.; m. Dolores Jean Dietrich, July 16, 1956; children: William Gray, Michelle Dolores Colton. BS, U. Utah, 1952, MD, 1956; PhD, U. Minn., 1964. Diplomate Am. Bd. Surgery, Am. Bd. Thoracic and Cardiovascular Surgery. Intern U. Minn. Hosps., 1956—57; resident in surgery U. Minn., Mpls., 1957—59, resident, 1961—65, asst. prof. surgery, 1964—68, assoc. prof. surgery, 1968—72, prof. surgery, 1972—2001, prof. emeritus, from 2002, vice chmn. dept. surgery, 1993—99; mem. surg. staff Mpls. VA Hosp., 1964—99, chief surg. svc., 1993—99, resident in thoracic surgery, 1965—66, dir. surg. rsch. lab., 1964—78. Vis. prof. U. Tex.-San Antonio, 1974, U. Ind. and Indpls. VA, 1977, affiliated program U. Ariz., Phoenix, 1982, Case Western Res. U., 1986. Editor, contbg. author: Head and Neck Cancer, 1986, Reoperations in General Surgery, 1991, 2d edit., 1996; contbr. articles on surg. and basic med. scis. to profl. publs. 1955— Served to lt. M.C., USN, 1959-61 USPHS postdoctoral fellow, 1962-65 Fellow ACS (commn. on cancer 1980-89, exec council commn. on operating room environ. 1985-91, pres. Minn. chpt. 1983-84, liaison to Assn. Oper. Rm. Nurses 1985-97, gov. 1990-96); mem. Minn. Surg. Soc. (pres. 1980-81), Assn. Acad. Surgery, Mpls. Surg. Soc. (pres. 1978-79), Soc. Head and Neck Surgeons, Central Surg. Assn., Western Surg. Soc., Soc. Univ. Surgeons, Société Internationale de Chirurgie, Am. Surg. Assn., Royal Soc. Medicine, Assn. VA Surgeons (pres. 1987), Soc. Surg. Oncology, Hennepin County Med. Soc., Minn. Med. Assn., Am. Soc. Clin. Oncology, Phi Beta Kappa, Phi Kappa Phi Clubs: Minneapolis, Interlachen Country (Mpls.) Avocations: computer applications to medicine, jewelry design, lapidary work. Home: Minneapolis, Minn. Died June 19, 2007.

MCQUEENEY, HENRY MARTIN, SR., publisher; b. NYC, Oct. 29, 1938; s. John Henry and Catherine Mary (Quigg) McQ.; m. Elizabeth Bernino, May 14, 1960; children: Mary E., Henry M. Jr., John P., Matthew S. BBA, St. Johns U., 1961; postgrad., U. Rochester, 1965-67. Advt. sales Curtis Circulation div. Curtis Pub. Co., 1960-62, asst. mgr. NYC, 1962-63, field mgr. Rochester, NY, 1964-67, dept. mgr., account exec. Phila., 1968-74; v.p. sales, exec. v.p. mktg. Manor Books, Inc., NYC, 1974-79; pres. Scott Mag. Dist. Corp., NYC, 1979—93, Kearny Pub., Inc., NYC, 1993-96, Princeton Pub., Inc., NYC, 1996-98; v.p. Irish Connections Mag., NYC, from 2000, Iron Cross, Ltd., NYC, from 1998, Koolhouse Pub. Inc., from 2003, The Irish Examiner USA Newspaper, from 2006. Rep. Western N.Y. Pubs.; cons. Bipad Ednl. Program. Pres. parish bd. Roman Cath. Ch., 1965, editor newspaper, Spencerport, N.Y., 1965, diocesan leader, mem. lay bd., Rochester, 1964-67; certified as tchr. Confraternity Christian Doctrine, Diocese of Rochester, 1964. Served with USAFR, 1956-64. Mem. Am. Legion, Ancient Order of Hiberninas. Home: Centerport, NY. Died Nov. 18, 2006.

MCRUER, DUANE TORRANCE, aerospace engineering executive; b. Bakersfield, Calif., Oct. 25, 1925; s. John Torrance and Ruth Inez (Bartlett) McR.; m. Betty June Mechura, Oct. 5, 1955; 1 child, Lara McRuer; 1 stepson, Stephen Harsey. BS in Engring., Calif. Inst. Tech., 1945, MEE, 1948. Registered profl. engr., Calif. Tech. chief, flight controls Northrop Aircraft Inc., Hawthorne, Calif., 1948-54; pres. Controls Specialists Inc., Inglewood, Calif., 1954-57; pres., tech. dir. Sys. Tech. Inc., Hawthorne, Calif., 1957-92, chmn., from 1992. Regents lectr. U. Calif., Santa Barbara, 1976; Hunsaker prof. MIT, 1992-93; mem. NRC Aero. and Space Engring. Bd., Washington, 1987-95, NASA Adv. Coun., 1990—, NASA Aero. Adv. Com., Washington, 1978-88, Am. Automatic Control Coun. (pres. 1969-73). Author: Analysis of Nonlinear Control Systems, 1961, Aircraft Dynamics and Automatic Control, 1974; author more than 150 tech. papers, 1948—; patentee in field. Lt. (j.g.) USNR, 1943-53. Recipient Louis Levy medal Franklin Inst., Phila., 1960, Disting. Alumnus award Calif. Inst. Tech., 1983. Fellow AIAA (Mechanics and Control of Flight award 1970), IEEE, AAAS, NAE, Soc. Automotive Engrs., Human Factors and Ergonomics Soc. (A.W. Williams award 1976), Caltech Assocs., Am. Alpine Club (N.Y.C.), Sierra Club. Episcopalian. Avocation: mountain climbing. Home: Manhattan Beach, Calif. Died Jan. 24, 2007.

MCWILLIAMS, RALPH DAVID, mathematics educator; b. Ft. Myers, Fla., Nov. 5, 1930; s. Ralph Leonard and Alma Louise (Jenny) McW.; m. Kathleen Dodge, May 23, 1959; children—Linda Louise, Martha Kay. BS, Fla. State U., 1951, MS, 1953; PhD, U. Tenn., 1957. Teaching asst. Fla. State U., 1951-53, asst. prof., 1959-63, assoc. prof., 1963-69, prof., from 1969, assoc. chmn. dept. math., 1969-84, chmn., 1984-90; teaching asst. U. Tenn., 1953-54; NSF fellow, 1954-56; instr. U. Tenn., 1956-57, Princeton, 1957-59; Mathematician Aberdeen Proving Ground, summers 1953-54. Contbr. articles to profl. jours. Mem. Am. Math. Soc., Math. Assn. Am., AAAS, AAUP, Phi Beta Kappa, Sigma Xi, Phi Kappa Phi, Delta Tau Delta. Baptist. Home: Tallahassee, Fla. Died May 13, 2006.

MEAD, GILBERT DUNBAR, retired geophysicist; b. Madison, Wis., May 31, 1930; s. Stanton Witter and Dorothy Elizabeth (Williams) M.; m. Marilyn Kroll (div.); 1 child Robert (dec. 2002); m. Jaylee Montague, Nov. 18, 1968; children: Elizabeth, Diana, Stanton. BS, Yale U., 1952; PhD in Physics, U. Calif., Berkeley, 1962; JD, U. Md., 1991. Physicist theoretical div. NASA Goddard Space Flight Ctr., Greenbelt, Md., 1962-74, head geophysics br., 1974-79, geophysicist crustal dynamics project, 1979-87. Bd. dirs., mem. nominating com. Consolidated Papers, Inc., Wisconsin Rapids, Wis., 1974— Editor: (with W. Hess) Introduction to Space Science, 1968; contbr. numerous articles to profl. jours. Trustee Beloit Coll., 1976-87, Mead Family Found., Arena Stage, Washington, Levine Sch. Music, Washington, Washington Chamber Symphony. Recipient Outstanding Svc. award Goddard Space Flight Ctr., 1978, Washington Post award for disting. cmty. svc., 1996. Mem. Md. Bar, D.C. Bar. Home: Washington, DC. Died May 29, 2007.

MEAD, RONALD H., bank executive; b. Seattle, May 19, 1939; s. Tilson K. and Margaret T. (Peterson) M.; m. Mary Catherine Brown, Aug. 8, 1969; 1 child, Michael BBA, U. Wash., 1961. CPA, Wash. Acct., mgr. Deloitte & Touche (formerly Deloitte, Haskins & Sells), Seattle, 1964-72; sec.-treas. Security Pacific Bancorp. N.W. (formerly Rainier Bancorp.), Seattle, 1972-73, v.p., 1973-78, sr. v.p., treas., from 1978. Dir. Rainier Mortgage Co., Seattle Trustee Acctg. Devel. Fund, U. Wash.; mem. adv. panel U. Wash. Sch. Acctg. Served to 1st lt. U.S. Army, 1961-63 Mem. AICPA, Wash. Soc. CPAs, Fin. Execs. Inst. (pres. Seattle chpt. 1981-82, nat. bd. dirs. 1983—, western area v.p. 1986-87, exec. com. 1986—, vice chmn. bd. 1987-88, chmn. bd. 1988-89, chmn. nominating com. 1989-90, chmn. audit com. 1990—), Theta Chi, Beta Alpha Psi. Clubs: Rainier, Washington Athletic, Seattle Tennis (Seattle); Overlake Golf and Country (Bellevue, Wash.). Died Oct. 14, 2005.

MEANEY, THOMAS FRANCIS, radiologist; b. Washington, Dec. 4, 1927; s. Thomas James and Alice Lorraine (Andrews) M.; m. Mary R. McCallum, Aug. 25, 1951; children: Michael, Patricia, Thomas, Sean, Matthew, Daniel, Maura, Bridget. BS, Georgetown U., 1949; MD, George Washington U., 1953. Diplomate Am. Bd. Radiology (trustee). Intern Providence Hosp., Washington, 1953-54; resident in radiology Cleve. Clinic, 1954-57; chmn. div. radiology Cleve. Clinic Found., from 1966. Contbr. articles on radiology to profl. jours. With USN, 1946-48. Fellow Am. Coll. Radiology (Gold medal 1991), Am. Coll. Chest Physicians; mem. AMA, Ohio Med. Assn., Ohio. Radiol. Soc., Ea. Radiol. Soc., Cleve. Acad. Medicine, Radiol. Soc. N.Am., Am. Roentgen Ray Soc., Am. Soc. Clinic Radiologists, Am. Heart Assn., Soc. Cardiovascular Radiology, Cleve. Radiol. Soc., Alpha Omega Alpha. Died June 6, 2006.

MECREDY, JAMES R., management consultant; b. Roanoke, Va., Sept. 24, 1918; s. James Roderick and Rosalie Digges (Miller) M.; m. Alice Chatfield, April 8, 1944; children: Robert Clark, Thomas Randolph, Russell Edwards. BSME, Purdue U., 1941; attended, Case Inst. Tech., 1946-48, Alexander Hamilton Inst., 1941-43. Student engr. Gen. Motors Corp., Anderson, Ind., 1941-43; foundry foreman Delco-Remy-G.M., Bedford, Ind., 1943-45; foundry engr., trouble shooter Nat. Bronze and Aluminum Foundry Co., Cleve., 1945-46; machine designer Motch & Merryweather Machinery Co., Cleve., 1946-47; engr. Cleve. Range Co., 1947-54, chief engr., 1954-71, v.p. ops., 1971-74; mgmt. cons., 1974-75. Tchr. shop, math. Delco-Remy Foundary, Bedford, Ind., 1943-44, blue print reading, 1943-44. Author: (manual) Instrn. and Maintenance Manual, 1973, District Boy Scouts, 1959; patentee. Dir., coach swimming Anderson YMCA, 1941-42; coach Little League Baseball, Lakewood, Ohio, 1950; precinct committeeman Rep. Com., 1945-46; chmn. dist. fund raising Boy Scouts Am., 1975, scoutmaster, 1955-77, chmn. protestant com., 1974-94. Recipient Scouting Wood badge, 1964, Silver Beaver award Boy Scouts Am., 1968, Nat. Hornaday award N.Y. Zool. Body, 1977, St. Georges award Cleve. Cath. Diocese, 1982, God and Svc. award Presbyn. Western Res., 1991, Nat. Eagle Scout Scoutmaster award, 1990. Mem. Nat. Assn. Presbyn. Scouters (trustee, deacon 1957-66, regional v.p. 1992-95), Kiwanis (pres. 1982-83). Avocations: photography, travel, camping, canoeing, wood carving. Home: Cleveland, Ohio. Died Mar. 26, 2007.

MEDEARIS, KENNETH GORDON, engineering research consultant, educator; b. Peoria, Ill., Aug. 5, 1930; s. Harold Oscar and Ferol Mae (Rowlett) M.; m. Mary Genevieve Barlow, June 28, 1953; children: Mark Allen, Mary Lynne, Terry Gordon. BS, U. Ill., 1952, MS, 1953; PhD, Stanford U., 1962. Registered profl. engr., Calif., Colo., N.Mex., Pa. Stress analyst Sandia Corp., Albuquerque, 1957-58; asst. prof. civil engring. U. N.Mex., 1958-62; assoc. prof. engring. Ariz. State U., 1962-63; engr., computer cons. Sunnyvale, Calif., 1963-66; dir. computer ctr., prof. civil engring. Colo. State U., Ft. Collins, 1966-69, adj. prof. civil and mech. engring., 1969—2007. Lectr. N.Mex. State U., 1982-2007; cons. Kenneth Medearis Assoc., Ft. Collins, 1969-2007; structural dynamics and vibration engring. cons., Ft. Collins, 1969-2007; evaluation cons. UN. Contbr. articles to profl. jours. Mem. Stanford Regional Cabinet. Served to 1st lt. USAF, 1953-56. Recipient Outstanding Engring. Achievement award No. Colo. Profl. Engrs., 1974, Outstanding Engring. Achievement award Profl. Engrs. Colo., 1974, Disting. Engring. Alumnus award U. Ill., 1988, Recipient of The Maurice Simpson Outstanding Tech. Paper award, Inst. of Environ. Scis., 1996. Mem. Colo. Earthquake Rsch. Soc. (v.p.), Univs. Coun. for Earthquake Engring., Internat. Orgn. for Standardization, U N Tech. Evaluation Team, ASCE, SEismol. Soc. Am., Larimer County Computer Soc. (chmn. 1974-2007), Aircraft Owners and Pilots Assn., Rotary, Sigma Xi, Phi Sigma Kappa, Chi Epsilon, Sigma Tau, Tau Beta Pi. Methodist. Home: Fort Collins, Colo. Died Feb. 15, 2007.

MEDLEY, DONALD MATTHIAS, retired education educator; b. Faulkton, SD, Feb. 18, 1917; s. Thomas Arnot and Cecilia Agnes (Kellen) M.; m. Betty Ann Robertsen, Aug. 23, 1948; 1 child, Timothy Laurence. BS, Coll. of St. Thomas, St. Paul, 1938; MA, U. Minn., 1950, PhD, 1954. Tchr. Am. Sch. Guadalajara, Mex., 1941-42, Floodwood (Minn.) Pub. Schs., 1946-48; instr. English, Coll. of St. Thomas, 1948-50; asst. prof. CUNY, 1954-59, assoc. prof., 1959-64, prof., 1964-65; sr. rsch. psychologist Ednl. Testing Svc., Princeton, N.J., 1965-70; disting. prof. U. Va., Charlottesville, 1970-87, prof. emeritus, 1987—2005, ret., 2005. Mem. exec. bd. Consortium for the Improvement of Tchr. Evaluation, Atlanta, 1985-87. Author: (with others) Measurement-Based Evaluation of Teacher Performance, 1984, Handbook of Research on Teaching, 1963, The Teather's Handbook, 1971, Research on Teaching, Concepts, Findings, and Implications, 1979, Ency. of Educational Research, 5th edit., 1982, 6th edit., 1992, Developing Skills for Instructional Supervision, 1984, Measurement-Based Evaluation of Teacher Performance, 1984, Advances in Teacher Education, 1984, International Ency. of Education: Research and Studies, 1984, 2d edit., 1994, Assessment of Teaching: Purposes, Practices, and Implications for the Profession, 1999; contbr. articles to profl. jours. Staff Sgt. U.S. Army, 1942-46. Fellow APA; mem. Am. Ednl. Rsch. Assn. (divsn. sec. 1962), Nat. Coun. on Measurement in Edn., Assn. Tchr. Educators. Independent. Roman Catholic. Avocation: travel. Died Feb. 19, 2007.

MEDWIN, HERMAN, acoustics consultant; b. Springfield, Mass., Apr. 9, 1920; s. Saul and Celia Medwin; m. Eileen Huber, June 3, 1945. BS in Physics, Worcester Poly. Inst., Mass., 1941; MS in Applied Physics, UCLA, 1948, PhD in Physics, 1954; ScD (hon.), Worcester Poly. Inst., 1992. Inspector Navy materials USN at Pratt & Whitney Aircraft and Aircooled Motors Corp., 1941-42; instr. physics L.A. City Coll., 1948-53; rsch. asst. in physics UCLA, 1948-53, rsch. assoc., 1954; cons. in acoustics Bolt, Beranek and Newman, Inc., Cambridge, Mass., 1954-55; assoc. prof. physics Naval Postgrad. Sch., Monterey, Calif., 1955-60, prof. physics, 1960-80, emeritus prof., from 1980; founder Ocean Acoustics Assocs., Pebble Beach, Calif., from 1980. Cons. in archtl. acoustics and noise control, 1955—; cons. Human Resources Rsch. Orgn. of George Washington U., 1955-62; mem. com. on undersea warfare Nat. Acad. Sci./NRC, summer 1957; cons. Stanford Rsch. Inst., 1958; liaison scientist U.S. Office Naval Rsch., London, 1961-62; cons. Hudson Labs. of Columbia U., Dobbs Ferry, N.Y., 1964-65; vis. scientist Imperial Coll., London, 1965-66, Royal Australian Naval Rsch. Lab., Sydney, 1972-73; vis. scientist SACLANT ASW Rsch. Ctr., La Spezia, Italy, summer 1980, Nat. Def. Acad. of Japan, Yokosuka, May 1981, Woods Hole (Mass.) Oceanographic Instn., summer 1985, Academia Sinica, Peoples' Republic China, 1985, Nordic Coun., Gotland, Sweden, 1995. Co-author: (with C.S. Clay) Acoustical Oceanography, 1977, Fundamentals of Acoustical Oceanography, 1997; editor: European Scientific Notes, 1962; contbr. over 100 articles to profl. jours. including Jour. Acoustical Soc. Am., Jour. Geophys. Rsch. Violinist, Worcester Philharmonic Orch., 1937-41; mem. UCLA Symphony Orch., L.A. Civic Orch., 1948-53, Arlington (Mass.) Symphony Orch., 1954-55, Monterey County Symphony Orch., 1955-72, bd. dirs., 1955-60; treas., pres. Chamber Music Soc. of Monterey Peninsula, 1968-72. Sgt. USAAF, 1943-46; ETO. Recipient Goddard Alumni award for outstanding profl. achievement Worcester Poly. Inst., 1991. Fellow Acoustical Soc. Am. (v.p. and chmn. tech. coun. 1987-88, founder tech. speciality group on acoustical oceanography 1989, chmn. 1989-91, chmn. tech. com. on acoustical oceanography 1991, pres. 1992-93, Silver medal 1997); mem. AAUP, Amateur Chamber Music Players, Am. Geophys. Union, Inst. Noise Control Engring. (chmn. internat. com.), Catgut Acoustical Soc., Sigma Xi. Achievements include 5 USN patents. Died Jan. 9, 2006.

MEEKS, CURTIS LEO, financial holding company executive; b. Dallas, Mar. 10, 1913; s. Walter Tucker and Myrtle Elizabeth (Gantz) M.; m. Janie Marie Shirey, Nov. 25, 1939; children—Janis Shirey, Claudia Jill. AA in Acctg, John Tarleton Coll., Stephenville, Tex., 1936; postgrad., U. Tex. Law Sch. With Sears, Roebuck & Co., 1939-75; operating mgr. Sears, Roebuck & Co. (Central Fla. region), Orlando, 1958-75; co-founder, sr. v.p. fin./adminstrn., sec., dir., mem. exec. com. Southland Equity Corp., Orlando, from 1975; cons. Comml. Real Estate Investments, Orlando, from 1979; developer Holiday Inn motels, from 1958. Past pres. C. of C., United Appeal. Served to lt. comdr. A.C. USNR, World War II. Mem. Internat. Auditors Assn., Realtors Assn. Orlando, Winter Park Bd. Realtors. Clubs: Orlando Country, Citrus, Orlando Lions (past sec.); Rotary (Greenville, Miss.) (pres. 1956). Democrat. Methodist. Home: Orlando, Fla. Died Mar. 12, 2006.

MEGAN, THOMAS IGNATIUS, retired judge; b. Chgo., Dec. 24, 1913; s. Charles P. and May M. (Magan) M.; m. Lucyanne Flaherty, Apr. 17, 1948; children: Anne, Thomas, Jane, Sarah, William, Molly. AB, U. Ill., 1935; JD, U. Chgo., 1938. Bar: Ill. 1939, N.Y. 1941. Mem. firm Pruitt & Grealis, Chgo., 1939-40, Pruitt, Hale & MacIntyre, NYC, 1941; atty. U.S. Ordnance Dept., Chgo., 1941-42, Chgo., Rock Island and Pacific R.R. Co., Chgo., 1945-70, v.p., gen. counsel, 1970-74, v.p. law, 1974-75; adminstrv. law judge ICC, Washington, 1975-81, HHS, Washington, 1981, FERC, Washington, 1981-96; ret., 1996. Served to maj. AUS, 1942-45. Mem. ABA, Soc. Trial Lawyers Chgo., Chgo. Law Club, Phi Kappa Tau, Phi Delta Phi. Clubs: Union League (Chgo.). Home: Rockville, Md. Died Dec. 29, 2006.

MEIER, LOUIS LEONARD, JR., lawyer; b. Hawthorne, Calif., Oct. 12, 1918; s. Louis Leonard and Celestine Helen (Gabriel) M.; m. Donna Eleonora Tomacelli-Filomarino, June 5, 1954; children: Renée, Sharon Clark, Catherine Gallo, Marina. BS, U.S. Naval Acad., 1942; LL.B., Georgetown U., 1951; grad., U.S. Naval War Coll., 1963. Bar: Va. 1951, U.S. Supreme Ct. 1970, D.C. 1973. Legal and legis. asst. to Chmn. Joint Chiefs of Staff, Washington, 1965-67; comdr. Guided Missile Destroyer Squadron 18, Atlantic Fleet, U.S. Navy, 1967-69; mem policy planning staff Office Sec. State, Washington, 1969-72; Washington counsel ASCE, 1972-82, exec. dir., 1982-83; sole practice Washington, from 1983. Served to capt. USN, 1941-72. Decorated Legion Merit; recipient U.S.S. Gherardi Battle Efficiency award, 1951, U.S.S. John S. McCain Battle Efficiency award, 1954, Pres. award for svc. to country ASCE, 1996. Mem. ABA, Nat. Inst. Bldg. Scis., Conf. Fedn. Environ. Engrs., Met. Club, Chevy Chase Country Club, N.Y. Yacht Club, Spouting Rock Beach Assn. Republican. Roman Catholic. Died Feb. 11, 2006.

MEIER, RICHARD LOUIS, futurist, planner, behavioral scientist; b. Kendallville, Ind., May 16, 1920; s. Walter A. and Mary (Lottman) M.; m. Gitta Unger, May 20, 1944 (dec.); children: Karen Reeds, Andrea Meier Whitmore, Alan; m. Robin Standish, Apr. 21, 1992. Student, No. Ill. State Tchrs. Coll., 1936-39; BS, U. Ill., 1940; MA, UCLA, 1942, PhD, 1944. With Calif. Research Corp., 1943-47; exec. sec. Fedn. Am. Scis., 1947-48; with Petrocarbon, Ltd., 1949-50; Fulbright scholar Manchester U., Eng., 1949-50; asst. prof. program of edn. and research in planning U. Chgo., 1950-56; research social scientist Mental Health Research Inst., U. Mich., Ann Arbor, from 1957, asso. prof. conservation, 1960-65, prof., 1965-67; prof. environ. design U. Calif., Berkeley, 1967-90, prof. emeritus, 1990—2007. Vis. lectr. Harvard U., 1959-60; vis. prof. Grad. Sch. Ekistics, Athens, 1962, U. Calif., Berkeley, 1966; cons. on social planning and resources planning Joint Ctr. for Urban Studies, MIT and Harvard U., in Venezuela, 1963-65. Author: Science and Economic Development, 1956, Modern Science and the Human Fertility Problem, 1959, A Communications Theory of Urban Growth, 1962, Developmental Planning, 1965, Resource-Conserving Urbanism for South Asia, 1968, Planning for an Urban World, 1974, Urban Futures Observed: In the Asian Third World, 1980; contbr. numerous articles to profl. jours. Mem. AAAS, Am. Planning Assn., Am. Chem. Soc., Soc. for Gen. Sys. Rsch., Fedn. Am. Scis., Holis-Soc. for Sustainable Future. Home: Berkeley, Calif. Died Feb. 26, 2007.

MELBY, JAMES CHRISTIAN, physician, educator; b. Duluth, Minn., Feb. 14, 1928; s. Leonard and Frances (Sullivan) M.; m. Mary E. O'Brien, June 25, 1955; children: Christian Leonard, Elizabeth Anne. BS, U. Minn., 1951, MD, 1953. Diplomate: Am. Bd. Internal Medicine. Intern dept. medicine U. Minn. Hosps., Mpls., 1953-54, resident, 1955-58; part-time practice medicine specializing in internal medicine, endocrinology and metabolism Univ. Hosp., Boston, from 1962; instr. U. Minn., 1958-59; asst. prof. U. Ark., 1959-62, assoc. prof., 1961-62; assoc. prof. medicine Boston U., 1962-69, prof., from 1969. Head sect. endocrinology and metabolism Univ. Hosp., Boston U. Med. Center; vis. physician Boston City Hosp., Univ. Hosp.; mem. VA merit rev. bd. in endocrinology. Mem. editorial bd.: Jour. Clin. Endocrinology and Metabolism; cons. editor: Am. Jour. Medicine; editor: Jour. Steroid Biochemistry; contbr. articles to profl. jours. Served with AUS, 1946-48. Mem. AMA, Assn. Am. Physicians, Am. Diabetes Assn., Am. Soc. Clin. Investigation, Endocrine Soc., Am. Fedn. Clin. Research, Central Soc. Clin. Research, AAAS, Am. Coll. Clin. Pharmacology, AAUP, Sigma Xi, Alpha Omega Alpha. Home: Milton, Mass. Died Aug. 18, 2007.

MELCHER, GEORGE W., JR., physician, educator; b. Portsmouth, Va., Aug. 24, 1922; s. George W. and Estelle (Rea) M.; children: Merrick, Paula, Ellen, Laura, George, John G. BA, Colo. Coll., 1943; MD, Columbia U., 1946. Diplomate: Am. Bd. Internal Medicine. Practice medicine specializing in internal medicine, NYC; formerly instr. Columbia U. Sch. Pub. Health, now assoc. clin. prof. internal medicine; assoc. attending physician Presbyn. Hosp., NYC. Dir. Nat. Genetics Found. Contbr. articles to med. jours. Served to capt. AUS, 1947-49. Fellow N.Y. Acad. Medicine; mem. ACP, N.Y. County Med. Soc., N.Y. Med. Soc. (del.), AMA. Clubs: N.Y. Athletic (N.Y.C.). Home: New York, NY. Died Feb. 26, 2007.

MELDRUM, ALAN HAYWARD, chemist, educator; b. Lethbridge, Alta., Can., May 24, 1913; s. William and Phyllis (Hayward) M.; m. Erma Goodwin, May 31, 1947. B.Sc., U. Alta., 1938; BS, U. Okla., 1946, MS, 1947; PhD, Pa. State U., 1954. Registered profl. engr., N.D. Coke oven chemist Algoma Steel Corp., Sault Ste. Marie, Ont., Can., 1938-44; refinery chemist Brit. Am. Oil Refining Co., Clarkson, Ont., 1944-45; rsch. assoc. Pa. State U., 1947-54; mem. faculty U. N.D., Grand Forks, from 1954, prof. petroleum engring., 1959-62, prof. indsl. engring., 1962-80, prof. emeritus, from 1980, chmn. dept., 1967-80. Mem. N.D. Soc. Profl. Engrs. (life mem.; pres. 1972), Nat. Soc. Profl. Engrs. (life mem.). Clubs: Toastmasters. Lodges: Masons, Shriners, Elks, Lions. Episcopalian. Home: Grand Forks, ND. Died July 14, 2007.

MELOY, HARRIETT CRUTTENDEN, historian, librarian; b. Inkster, ND, June 23, 1916; d. Coran Henry and Muriel Gladys (Jones) Cruttenden; m. Peter George Meloy, July 23, 1941; children: Peter Michael, Timothy John, Steven Henry, Kerry Meloy Massucco, Mark Kingsley. BA, Jamestown Coll., 1937; LLD (hon.), Carroll Coll., 1986. Rschr., libr. Mont. Hist. Soc., Helena, 1957—77. Mem. Mont. Bd. Pub. Edn., 1970—85, chair, 1975—77, 1978—79, 1983—84. Bd. dirs. LWV, Helena, from 1950; rev. panelist U.S. Dept. Edn. Elem. Sch. Recognition Program, 1985—86; v.p. Mont. Dem. Women, 1959—60; state rep. Nat. Com. Support Pub. Schs., 1965—77; mem. City County Comprehensive Planning Bd., from 1987; bd. dirs., trustees Rocky Mountain Coll., Billings, Mont., 1986—91, Jamestown (N.D.) Coll., 1987—90. Recipient Golden Apple award, Mont. Edn. Assn., 1975, Cliff Worthen award, Phi Delta Kappa, 1978, Silver Apple award, Helena Edn. Assn., 1972, Am.'s Women of Distinction award, Soroptimist Internat., 1986. Mem.: AAUW (state div. pres. 1972—74), Nat. Assn. State Bds. Edn., Mont. Libr. Assn., Delta Kappa Gamma (hon.). Home: Helena, Mont. Died Apr. 29, 2006.

MELROY, LUELLA ELIZABETH, insurance agency executive; b. Churchs Ferry, ND, May 22, 1920; d. Roy Arthur and Grace Alma (Dingman) Noltimier; m. Richard Melroy, May 25, 1957. Student, Dakota Bus. Coll., 1938-39. With various ins. offices, Fargo, N.D., 1939-51; with various ins. offices Mpls. and St. Paul, 1951-53, Toledo, 1953-61; with Manhattan Ins. Svc., Inc., Toledo, from 1961, pres., owner, from 1971. Bd. dirs. Toledo YWCA, 1963-76, pres., 1973-75; bd. dirs., treas. Girls Club of Toledo, 1981-82; chmn. Community Planning Council Com. on Battered Women; bd. dirs., treas. Rescue-Crisis Bd., 1979-81. Named Woman of Yr., Toledo chpt. Nat. Mgmt. Assn., 1975; Bus. Woman of Yr., Dist. 2 Bus. and Profl. Women, 1978; Ins. Woman of Yr., Toledo Assn. Ind. Ins. Agts., 1967. Mem. Ohio Assn. Profl. Ins. Agts. (dir. 1980-83, membership chmn. 1981-83), Toledo Assn. Ind. Ins. Agts. (pres. 1980-81, dir. 1973-82), Nat. Assn. Ins. Women (v.p. 1978-79, regional dir. 1976-77), Women Bus. Owners, Nat. Mgmt. Assn. (nat. dir. 1982—, vice chmn. midwest area 1984—), Women Involved in Toledo. Republican. Home: Toledo, Ohio. Died Dec. 2, 2006.

MELTZER, BERNARD DAVID, law educator; b. Phila., Nov. 21, 1914; s. Julius and Rose (Welkov) M.; m. Jean Sulzberger, Jan. 17, 1947; children: Joan, Daniel, Susan. AB, U. Chgo., 1935, JD, 1937; LL.M., Harvard U., 1938. Bar: Ill. 1938. Atty., spl. asst. to chmn. SEC, 1938-40; assoc. firm Mayer, Meyer, Austrian & Platt, Chgo., 1940; spl. asst. to asst. sec. state, also acting chief fgn. funds control div. State, 1941—43; asst. trial counsel U.S. prosecution Internat. Nuremberg War Trials, 1945-46; profl. lectr. to disting. svc. prof. law emeritus U. Chgo. Law Sch., 1946—2007; counsel Vedder, Price, Kaufman & Kammholz, Chgo., 1954-55, Sidley & Austin LLP, Chgo., 1987-89. Hearing commr. NPA, 1952-53; labor arbitrator; spl. master US Ct. Appeals (D.C. Cir.), 1963-64; bd. publs. U. Chgo., 1965-67, chmn., 1967-68; mem. Gov. Ill. Adv. Commn. Labor-Mgmt. Policy for Pub. Employees in Ill., 1966-67, Ill. Civil Service Commn., 1968-69; cons. U.S. Dept. Labor, 1969-70 Author: Supplementary Materials on International Organizations, 1948, (with W.G. Katz) Cases and Materials on Business Corporations, 1949, Labor Law Cases, Materials and Problems, 1970, supplement, 1972, 75, 2d edit., 1977, supplements, 1980, 82 (with S. Henderson), 3d edit. (with S. Henderson), 1985, supplement, 1988; also articles. Bd. dirs. Hyde Park Community Conf., 1954-56, S.E. Chgo. Commn., 1956-57. Served to lt. (j.g.) USNR, 1943-46. Mem. ABA (co-chmn. com. devel. law under NLRA 1959-60, mem. spl. com. transp. strikes), Ill. Bar Assn., Chgo. Bar Assn. (bd. mgrs. 1972-73), Am. Law Inst., Coll. Labor and Employment Lawyers, Am. Acad. Arts and Scis., Order of Coif, Phi Beta Kappa Home: Chicago, Ill. Died Jan. 4, 2007.

MELVIN, RONALD MCKNIGHT, retired museum director; b. Regina, Sask., Can., Oct. 25, 1927; came to U.S., 1953; s. M. Gordon and Mary Gillespie (McKnight) M.; m. Gwen Ellis, Apr. 30, 1955; children: Mary Fleming, Catharine Melvin. Student, U. B.C., 1945-49. Various positions Powell River Co. Ltd., Vancouver, B.C., Canada, 1947-56; asst. to pres. Trans Union Corp., Chgo., 1956-58; mng. dir. Procor Ltd. subs. Trans Union Corp., Toronto, Ont., Canada, 1958-64; ptnr. Blunt Ellis & Simmons, Chgo., 1964-71, pres., 1971-78; vice chmn. Blunt Ellis & Loew, Chgo., 1978-80; founding dir. Terra Mus. Am. Art, Evanston, Ill., 1980-84. Dir. Chef Pierre, Traverse City, Mich., 1972-77, Lawter Internat., Chgo., 1977-84. Author, organizer: (art exhbns.) Important Western Art from Chicago Collections, 1980 Five American Masters of Watercolor, 1981, American Naive Paintings From National Gallery of Art, 1982, Solitude--Inner Visions in American Art, 1982, Woman, 1984. Avocation: collecting worcester porcelain. Home: Southfield, Mass. Died Dec. 18, 2006.

MEMEL, SHERWIN LEONARD, lawyer; b. Buffalo, Mar. 28, 1930; s. Maurice and Nellie (Munshen) M.; children: Jana Sue, Steven Keith, David Scott, Mara Jean. BA, UCLA, 1951, JD with honors, 1954. Bar: Calif. 1955, U.S. Ct. Appeals (9th cir.) 1955, U.S. Dist. Ct. (cen. dist.) Calif. 1959, U.S. Supreme Ct. 1963, D.C. 1979. Sr. ptnr. healthcare industry practice group Manatt, Phelps & Phillips, LA, from 1987. Former chmn. bd. Pac. Pub. Radio Sta. KKJZ; adv. bd., adj. prof. health law U. So. Calif. Sch. Policy, Planning and Devel.; cons. and lectr. in field. Co-author: (with R. Barak) Real Estate Issues in the Health Care Industry, 1996; contbr. articles to profl. jours. Chmn. LA Arts Coun., 1985—87; past pres. Calif. Bd. Med. Quality Assurance; chmn. health adv. bd. U. So. Calif. Sch. Policy, Planning and Devel., bd. councilor; vice-chmn. Dem. Bus. Coun., Washington, 1985—86; bd. dirs., chmn. emeritus Jazz Bakery non-profit pub. performance space. Recipient Disting. Service award Fedn. Am. Hosps., 1970. Mem.: ABA (com. health law), LA County Bar Assn., DC Bar Assn., Calif. Bar Assn., Am. Health Lawyers Assn., Calif. Soc. Healthcare Attys. (life; pres. 1983), Am. Hosp. Assn. (life award of honor 1971). Died May 25, 2007.

MENARD, CHARLES WALTER, JR., envelope company executive; b. Chgo., Apr. 15, 1929; s. Charles Walter and Hazel (Froehde) M.; m. Helen Bernice Ligas, May 14, 1955; children— Charles, Christopher, Juliette, C. Timothy, Jennifer. B.S. in Commerce, DePaul U., 1954. Various positions to controller St. Joseph Hosp., Chgo., 1962-64; controller, sec. Continental Envelope Corp., Chgo., 1965—. Sec. Dist. 231 Bd. Edn., Evergreen Park, Ill.; treas., bd. dirs. Evergreen Park AquaPark; treas. scholarship bd. Evergreen Park Community High Sch. Democrat. Roman Catholic. Lodge: Lions (from dir. to pres. Evergreen Park). Home: Evergreen Park, Ill. Died Jan. 15, 2007.

MENOTTI, GIAN CARLO, composer; b. Cadegliano, Italy, July 7, 1911; came to U.S., 1928; s. Alfonso and Ines (Pellini) M. Grad. in composition, Curtis Inst. Music, 1933, Mus.B. (hon.), 1945. Tchr. Curtis Inst. Music, 1941-45. Writer chamber music, songs and operas; composer: (operas) Amelia al ballo, 1936, The Old Maid and the Thief, 1939, The Island God, 1942, The Medium, 1945 (Pulitzer Prize for music 1950), The Telephone, 1947, The Consul, 1949; Amahl and the Night Visitors, 1951, The Saint of Bleecker Street, 1954 (Pulitzer Prize for music 1955, Drama Critics' Circle Award 1955, New York Music Critics' Award 1955), Maria Golovin, 1958, The Last Savage, 1963, Labyrinth, 1963, Martin's Lie, 1964, Help, Help, the Globolinks, 1968, The Most Important Man, 1971, Arrival, 1973, Tamu-Tamu, 1973, The Egg, 1976, The Hero, 1976, The Trial of the Gypsy, 1978, Chip and His Dog, 1979, La loca, 1979, The Mad Woman, 1979, St. Teresa, 1982, A Bride from Pluto, 1982, The Boy Who Grew Too Fast, 1982, Goya, 1986, Giorino di Nozze, 1988; (symphonies/orchestral) Pastorale and Dance, 1934, (from Amelia al ballo) Prelude, 1937, (from The Old Maid and the Thief) Prelude, 1939, (from The Island God) Two Interludes, 1942, Piano Concert in F, 1945, Sebastian, 1945, Apocalypse, 1951, Introduction, March Shepherds' Dance, 1951, Violin Concerto, 1952, Triple Concerto a tre, 1970, Fantasia, 1975, Symphony No. 1: The Halcyon, 1976, Double Bass Concerto, 1983; (chamber/instrumental) Variations on a Theme of Schumann, 1931, Six Compositions, 1934, Four Pieces, 1936, Trio for a House-Warming Party, 1936, Poemetti per Maria Rosa, 1937, Ricercare e toccata, 1949, Suite, 1973, Cantilena scherzo, 1977; (vocal/choral) Baba's Aria, 1946, The Black Swan, 1946, Monica's Waltz, 1946, Lucy's Aria, 1947, Magda's Aria, 1950, Shepherd's Chorus, 1951, The Hero, 1952, The Death of the Bishop of Brindisi, 1963, Canti della lontananza, 1967, Landscapes and Remembrances, 1976, Missa o pulchritudo, 1979, Four Songs, 1981, Notturno, 1982, Muero porque no muero, 1982; (ballets) Sebastian, 1944, Errand in the Maze, 1947, The Unicorn, the Gorgon and the Manticore, or The Three Sundays of a Poet, 1956; writer own libretti.; Founder: Festival of Two Worlds, Spoleto, Italy, 1958; composer, artistic dir. Spoleto Festival USA, Charleston, S.C. Recipient Guggenheim award, 1946, 47; Honorary associate, Nat'l Inst. for Arts and Letters, 1953, Kennedy Ctr. award, 1984, N.Y.C. Mayor's Liberty award, 1986; George Peabody Medal, Johns Hopkins U., 1987; named Musician of Yr., Musical Am., 1991. Mem. ASCAP. Died Feb. 1, 2007.

MENSENDIEK, CHARLES WILLIAM, missionary educator; b. Ft. Madison, Iowa, July 2, 1925; s. Richard August and Anna Marie (Kruckemeyer) M.; m. Barbara Kathryn Dunn, June 27, 1959; children— Jeffrey, Martha, Kathryn. B.A., Elmhurst Coll., 1945; B.D., Eden Theol. Sem., 1948; Ph.D., Columbia Joint Union, 1957; D.D. (hon.), Eden Sem., 1975. Ordained to ministry Evang. and Reformed Ch., 1948. Missionary, Evang. and Reformed Ch., Sendai, Japan, 1948-51; pastor Salem Evang. and Reformed Ch., Rochester, N.Y., 1955-60, Plymouth Congregation, Buffalo, 1960-63; missionary tchr., prof., United Ch. Christ Christian Studies, Tohoku Gakuin U., Sendai, 1963-91; prof. Tohoku Gakun U., 1991—, ret., 1993; asst. Shiogama United Ch., Japan, 1976—. Author: A Man For His Times, 1972, Not Without A Struggle, 1985, With Uncommon Kindness, 1990, To Japan with Love, 1991. Trustee Tohoku Gakuin U., Sendai, 1977-91. Mem. Theol. Assn. Japan. Democrat. Home: Sendai, Japan. Died Feb. 13, 2006.

MENTZ, HENRY ALVAN, JR., retired federal judge; b. New Orleans, Nov. 10, 1920; s. Henry Alvan and Lulla (Bridewell) M.; m. Ann Lamantia, June 23, 1956; children: Ann, Carli, Hal, Frederick, George BA, Tulane U., 1941; JD, La. State U., 1943. Bar: La. 1943, U.S. Dist. Ct. (ea. dist.) La. 1944. With legal dept. Shell Oil, New Orleans, 1947-48; pvt. practice Hammond, 1948-82; judge U.S. Dist. Ct. (ea. dist.) La., New Orleans, 1982—2001, sr. judge, 1992—2001, ret. Editor: Combined Gospels, 1976 Pres. La. Soc. Music and Performing Arts, 1994-97, L.A. Civil Svc. League, 1979-81; bd. dirs. Southea. La. U. Found., Salvation Army; chmn. Tulane U. 50th Anniversary Reunion for 1991. Decorated 2 Battle Stars, Bronze Star; recipient Disting. Svc. award AMVETS, 1950. Mem. SAR, Royal Soc. St. George (pres.), Boston Club New Orleans, Delta Tau Delta. Republican. Episcopalian. Home: New Orleans, La. Died Jan. 23, 2005.

MERCER, WILLIAM CRAWFORD, retired telecommunications industry executive; b. Phila., Jan. 13, 1919; s. Herbert C. and Wilhelmina (Manz) M.; A.B., Dartmouth, 1940; S.M. (Sloan fellow), Mass. Inst. Tech., 1956; m. Ramona Wells, Sept 4, 1955; children: Lee William, Ray A., John G., Robert T. Salesman, IBM Corp., 1940-46; with Western Electric Co., 1947-58, works comptroller, North Andover, Mass., 1956-58; with New Eng. Tel. & Tel. Co., 1958-62, 71-82, gen. mgr., N.H., 1959-60, v.p. pers., Boston, 1960-62, pres. 1971-82, chmn. bd., 1982, ret., 1982; v.p. ops. Ind. Bell Telephone Co., 1962-64; asst. v.p. pers. Am. Tel. & Tel. Co., N.Y.C., 1964-65, v.p. marketing, 1965-67, v.p. pers., 1967-71; dir. John Hancock Ins. Co.; hon. dir. First Nat. Bank Boston, Bank of Boston Corp. Bd. dirs. United Way Mass.; trustee Colby-Sawyer Coll., Boston Mus. Sci. Served to capt. USAAF, 1941-45. Clubs: Dartmouth (Charles River); Braeburn Country, Comml. of Boston, Hamilton Trust. Home: Westwood, Mass. Died June 6, 2007.

MEREDITH, WILLIAM MORRIS, poet, English language educator; b. NYC, Jan. 9, 1919; s. William Morris and Nelley Atkin (Keyser) M. AB magna cum laude, Princeton U., 1940, Woodrow Wilson fellow, 1946-47. Copy boy, reporter N.Y. Times, 1940-41; instr. English Princeton U., 1946, 47-48, 49-50; asst. prof. English U. Hawaii, 1950-51; assoc. prof. Conn. Coll., 1955-65, prof. English, 1965-83. Opera critic Hudson Rev., 1955-56; instr. Bread Loaf Sch. English, Middlebury Coll., 1958-62; dir. humanities Upward Bound program, Conn. Coll., 1964-68; poetry cons. Library of Congress, 1978-80; chancellor Acad. Am. Poets; mem. Conn. Commn. Arts, 1963-65. Author: (poetry) Love Letter from an Impossible Land, 1944 (Yale Series of Younger Poets award 1943), Ships and Other Figures, 1948, The Open Sea and Other Poems, 1958, The Wreck of the Thresher and Other Poems, 1964, Winter Verse, 1964, Year End Accounts, 1965, Two Pages from a Colorado Journal, 1967, Earth Walk: New and Selected Poems, 1970, Hazard, The Painter, 1975, The Cheer, 1980, Partial Accounts: New and Selected Poems, 1987 (Pulitzer Prize for Poetry, 1988), Effort at Speech, 1997 (Nat. Book Award); (prose) Reasons for Poetry and the Reason for Criticism, 1982, Poems Are Hard to Read, 1991; (libretto) The Bottle Imp, 1958; editor: Shelley, 1962, University and College Poetry Prizes, 1960-66, 1966, (with Mackie L. Jarrell) Eighteenth-Century Minor Poets, 1968, Poets of Bulgaria, 1985, Windows on the Black Sea: Bulgarian Poetry in Translation, 1992; translator: Guillaume Apollinaire's Alcools: Poems, 1898-1913, 1964; recs. include Selected Poems, 1977. Served with USAAF, 1941-42; to lt. USNR, 1942-46, PTO; to lt. comdr. USNR, Korea. Decorated Air medal with oak leaf cluster; recipient Harriet Monroe Meml. prize, 1944, Oscar Blumenthal prize, 1953, Loines prize Nat. Inst. Arts and Letters, 1966, Van Wyck Brooks award, 1971, Internat. Nicola Vaptsarov prize in lit., Sofia, Bulgaria, 1979, L.A. Times prize, 1987; Rockefeller grantee, 1948, 68; Hudson Rev. fellow, 1956; National Inst. of Arts and Letters grantee, 1958; Ford Found. fellow, 1959-60; Nat. Endowment for the Arts grantee, 1972, fellow, 1984; Guggenheim fellow, 1975-76; Acad. Am. Poets fellow, 1990. Mem. Nat. Inst. Arts and Letters. Home: Washington, DC. Died May 30, 2007.

MERIWETHER, JAMES BABCOCK, retired English language educator; b. Columbia, SC, May 8, 1928; s. Robert Lee and Margaret (Babcock) M.; m. Nancy Anderson Callcott, July 29, 1955 (div. May 1992); children: Rebecca, Robert, George, Nicholas, Margaret; m. Anne M. Blythe, Nov. 14, 1992. BA, U. S.C., 1949; MA, Princeton U., 1952, PhD, 1958. Asst. prof. English U. Tex., Austin, 1958-59, U. N.C., Chapel Hill, 1959-62, assoc. prof., 1962-64; prof. U. S.C., Columbia, 1964-70, McClintock prof. So. letters, 1970-90, dir. So. studies program, 1974-80, disting. prof. emeritus, from 1990, William Gilmore Simms rsch. prof., 1999, 2000. Appointed Bd. Fgn. Scholarships, Washington, 1982, 86, vice chmn., 1984, chmn. 1984-87; Fulbright prof. U. Paris, 1970-71, U. Bonn, 1980, Chinese U. Hong Kong, 1993. Author: The Literary Career of William Faulkner, 1961, others; editor: Essays, Speeches and Public Letters of William Faulkner, others; contbr. articles to profl. jours. Served with U.S. Army, 1953-56. Fellow Am. Coun. Learned Socs., 1960-61, Guggenheim Found., 1963-64, Earhart Found., 1989-90. Mem. MLA, Bibliographical Soc. Am., Am. Studies Assn., South Atlantic Modern Lang. Assn., Phi Beta Kappa. Home: Columbia, SC. Died Mar. 18, 2007.

MERKLING, FRANK, writer, music and arts critic, editor; b. Washington, Jan. 20, 1924; s. Frank and Marie (Judd) M.; m. Erica Perl, Nov. 8, 1952; children: Melissa, Maria, Christian. BA cum laude, Harvard U., 1949; studied composition and theory with Walter Piston, Randall Thompson and Irving Fine. Free-lance writer, 1949-54; assoc. editor Opera News, 1954-57, editor, 1957-74; music and arts critic Danbury (Conn.) News-Times, from 1978. Author: English libretto of Carmen for Met. Opera Co, 1951; co-author: The Golden Horseshoe, 1965; contbr.: New Grove Dictionary of Music in the United States, 1986; editor: The Opera News Books of Figaro and Traviata, 1967; Contbr. articles to profl. jours. Chmn. New Milford (Conn.) Commn. Arts, 1977-87. Served with USAAF, 1943-46. Home: New Milford, Conn. Died Mar. 4, 2006.

MERRELL, STANLEY WILSON, manufacturing executive; b. Cin., Jan. 25, 1929; s. Thurston and Helen Theodate (Dresser) M.; m. Lyda Lynn Stuart, June 15, 1956; children: Stanley Wilson III, Caroline Clark, Louise Theodate, Katherine Stuart AB, Princeton U., 1951; MBA, Harvard U., 1957. With TRW Inc., Cleve., 1957-67, Rockwell Internat., Pitts., 1967-70; v.p. J.P. Morgan & Co. Inc., NYC, 1970-73; v.p. planning and devel. Gen. Instrument Corp., NYC, 1973-76; v.p. corp. devel. Bausch & Lomb Inc., Rochester, N.Y., 1976-81, sr. v.p. adminstrn. 1981-88, sr. v.p., asst. to chmn. and pres., from 1988. Bd. govs. Genesee Hosp.; past pres., trustee Allendale Columbia Sch., Rochester; trustee Ctr. Govt. Research; dir. United Way of Greater Rochester, Rochester Downtown Devel. Corp. Served to lt. (j.g.) USN, 1951-53. Baker scholar Harvard U., 1957. Mem. Country of Rochester, Genesee Valley (Rochester). Republican. Episcopalian. Home: Rochester, NY. Died Feb. 14, 2006.

MERRIFIELD, LEWIS BIEHL, III, lawyer, retail corporation executive; b. Phila., Oct. 22, 1939; s. Lewis Biehl Jr. and Nannette (Belina) M. BS with highest distinction, UCLA, 1962; JD, U. So. Calif., 1966. Law clk. William O. Douglas, U.S. Supreme Ct., Washington, 1966-67; asst. prof. law U. So. Calif.

Los Angeles, 1967-69; sole practice Los Angeles, from 1969; chmn. bd. Pic 'N' Save Corp., Los Angeles, 1985-86, elected pres. and chief exec. officer, 1986. Dir. Bishop Graphics, Inc., Westlake Village, Calif.; lectr. Contbr. articles on securities and corp. fin. to profl. jours. Mem. ABA (ann. rev. fed. regulation of securities subcom. 1983—), Am. Fin. Assn., Am. Econ. Assn., Am. Mgmt. Assn., Nat. Retail Mchts. Assn. Republican. Roman Catholic. Died July 14, 2007.

MERRITT, RICHARD LAWRENCE, political scientist, educator; b. Portland, Oreg., Aug. 8, 1933; s. Raymond Arlie and Sarah Elizabeth (Cook) M.; m. Anna Johanna Gode-von Aesch, Aug. 9, 1958; children— Christopher Eugene, Geoffrey Andreas, Theodore Aleyn. BA, U. So. Calif., 1955; MA, U. Va., 1956; postgrad., Free U. Berlin, 1956-57; PhD, Yale U., 1962. Instr. polit. sci. Yale U., 1962-63, asst. prof., 1963-67; asso. prof. polit. sci., research asso. prof. communications U. Ill., Urbana, 1967-69, prof. polit. sci., research prof. communications, from 1969, head dept. polit. sci., 1978-84; Fulbright rsch. prof. Free U. Berlin, Berlin, Germany, 1969-70, vis. prof. internat. rels., 1976; vis. scholar Sci. Center Berlin, 1976-83; Fulbright rsch. prof. Humboldt U., Berlin, 1962-63. Cons. UN, USIA, Fed. Republic Germany; vis. prof. internat. rels., Rhodes U., Grahamstown, Republic of South Africa, 1991. Author: Symbols of American Community, 1735-1775, 1966, Comparing Nations, 1966, Systematic Approaches to Comparative Politics, 1970, Public Opinion in Occupied Germany, 1970, Public Opinion in Semisovereign Germany, 1980, From National Development to Global Community, 1981, Innovation in the Public Sector, 1985, Living with the Wall, 1985, Berlin between Two Worlds, 1986, Communication and Interaction in Global Politics, 1987, Science, Politics, and International Conferences, 1989, International Event-Data Developments: DDIR Phase II, 1993, Democracy Imposed: U.S. Occupation Policy and the German Public, 1945-1949, 1995; editor books and series in field. Recipient Wakefield award for outstanding service U. Ill., Urbana, 1975 Mem. Internat. Polit. Sci. Assn. (program chmn. 1976-79, v.p. 1979-82, book series editor 1980-91), Am. Polit. Sci. Assn. (program chmn. 1970, council mem. 1969-70), Internat. Studies Assn. (program chmn. 1973, v.p. 1980-81, pres. Midwest sect. 1984-85), Peace Sci. Soc., Conf. Group on German Politics (pres. 1986-88). Democrat. Home: Urbana, Ill. Died Nov. 19, 2005.

MERWIN, CHARLES LEWIS, retired economist; b. East Palestine, Ohio, June 30, 1912; s. Charles Lewis and Estella (Meek) M.; m. Elizabeth Jane Quay, Sept. 6, 1939 (dec. 2001); 1 son, Grier Humphrey. BA cum laude, Ohio Wesleyan U., 1934; MA, U. Pa., 1936, PhD, 1942. Instr. Muhlenberg Coll., 1936-37; economist Dept. Commerce, 1938-42, Nat. Bur. Econ. Research, 1938, 40-41, Mission for Econ. Affairs, Am. embassy, London, 1943-46; with IMF, Washington, 1946-77, successively sr. economist, asst. chief Balance of Payments div. Research dept., 1946-52, chief Western European div., asst. dir. European dept., 1952-64, dep. dir. African dept., 1964-77; adj. prof. Am. U., 1947-53, 77-80; faculty Madeira Sch., 1980. Mem. ECA Mission to France, 1948; working party rapporteur Atlantic Council, 1982-83; pres. Miles Merwin Family Assn., 1963—97, IMF Retirees Assn., 1980—97 Author: Financing Small Corporations in Five Manufacturing Industries, 1942. Mem. Am. Econ. Assn., Royal Econ. Soc., Phi Beta Kappa. Clubs: Cosmos (Washington). Methodist. Home: Bethesda, Md. Died Oct. 26, 2007.

MERZ, STUART OSCAR HAROLD, retired lawyer; b. South Orange, NJ, Feb. 6, 1930; s. Harold Oscar Merz and Mildred (Cyphers) M.; m. Joan LeCount Ahlgren, Dec. 27, 1952; children: Jeffrey Stuart, Melinda Joan Merz Gabarik, Wendy Carolyn Merz. BS, Cornell U., 1952, LL.B., 1957. Bar: Ohio 1958. Assoc. Jones, Day, Reavis & Pogue, Cleve., 1957-65, ptnr., 1965-91. Served to lst lt. U.S. Army, 1952-54. Mem. ABA, Bar Assn. Greater Cleve., Cornell Law Assn. Clubs: Mayfield Country (South Euclid, Ohio). Republican. Presbyterian. Home: Cleveland, Ohio. Died Jan. 16, 2007.

MESCHER, WILLIAM CLARENCE, state legislator, management consultant; b. Belknap, Ill., Sept. 5, 1927; s. Clarence H. and Jane (Richards) M.; m. Sallie Kitty Stanley, Feb. 15, 1986; children: Barbara, Kathy, Reed, Karen. BSEE, U. Ill., 1953; MBA, Northwestern U., 1966. Registered profl. engr., Ill., S.C. Past pres. and CEO, Santee Cooper, PSA; pres. William Mescher & Assocs. Mgmt. Cons., Monks Corner, SC, 1976—89; mem. S.C. Senate, Columbia, from 1993. Chmn. gen. com., mem. edn. com., judiciary com., labor, commerce and industry com.; chmn. Demand Reduction Sys. S.C.; adj. prof. U.S.C.; bd. dirs. S.C. Nat. Bank, Moncks Corner; former mem. Utility Tech. Mgmt. Del. to China, S.C. Gov.'s S.W.-Korea Internat. Trad Commn., U.S.-Japan Internat. Commn., World Energy Conf. Bird bander U.S. Dept. Interior; chmn. Berkeley County Mus.; past mem. bd. dirs. Coastal Carolina coun. Boy Scouts Am.; mem. S.C. Coun. on Econ. Edn., Charleston-Trident Devel. Bd.; bd. dirs. Charleston Symphony Orch. Staff sgt. U.S. Army, Korea. Recipient Silver Beaver award Boy Scouts Am. Mem. ASME (adv. bd.), Am. Pub. Power Assn. (past pres.), Tri-County C. of C. (bd. dirs.), Charleston-Trident C. of C., VFW (life), Am. Legion, Greater U. S.C. Alumni Assn. (life), Tau Beta Pi. Republican. Methodist. Home: Pinopolis, SC. Died Apr. 8, 2007.

MESKILL, THOMAS JOSEPH, JR., federal judge, former governor, former congressman; b. New Britain, Conn., Jan. 30, 1928; s. Thomas J.M. Meskill; m. Mary T. Grady; children: Maureen Meskill Heneghan, John Peter, Eileen Meskill Gallupe, Thomas. BS, Trinity Coll., Hartford, Conn., 1950, LL.D., 1972; JD, U. Conn., 1956; postgrad., Sch. Law, NYU; LL.D., U. Bridgeport, 1971, U. New Haven, 1974. Bar: Conn. 1956, DC 1957, US Ct. Appeals (2d cir.) 1975, US Supreme Ct. 1971. Ptnr. Meskill, Dorsey, Sledzik & Walsh, New Britain, 1956—60; asst. corp. counsel City of New Britain, 1960—62, corp. counsel, 1965—66, mayor, 1962—64; mem. US Congress from 6th Conn. Dist., 1967—71; gov. State of Conn., Hartford, 1971-75; judge US Ct. Appeals (2nd Cir.), New Britain, Conn., 1975—93, chief judge, 1992-93, sr. judge, 1993—2007. Pres. New Britain Council Social Agys.; mem. Constl. Conv., Hartford, 1965. Served to 1st lt. USAF, 1950-53. Recipient Disting. Svc. award Jr. C. of C., 1964, Jud. Achievement award ATLA, 1983, Learned Hand medal for Excellence in Fed. Juridprudence, Fed. Bar Coun., 1994. Mem. Conn. Bar Assn. (Henry J. Naruk Jud. award 1994), Hartford County Bar Assn., New Britain Bar Assn., KC. Republican. Died Oct. 29, 2007.

MESSNER, EDWARD, psychiatrist; b. NYC, May 21, 1928; m. Marie M. Blais, Aug. 20, 1961; children: William C., Ellen J., Margaret R. AB, Harvard u., 1949, MD, 1954. Intern Stanford U. Svc., San Francisco City and County Hosp., 1954-55; resident in psychiatry VA Hosp., Boston, 1957-59; fellow in child psychiatry Douglas A. Thom Clnic, Boston, 1950-60; clin. and rsch. fellow in pschiatry Mass. Gen. Hosp., Boston, 1960-62, asst. psychiatrist, 1962-72, assoc. psychiatrist, 1972-80, psychiatrist, from 1981; rsch. fellow in psychiatry Harvard Med. Sch., Boston, 1961-62, asst. in psychiatry, 1962-63, instr. in psychiatry, 1963-69, clin. instr. in psychiatry, 1969-73, asst. clin. prof. psychiatry, 1973-82, assoc. clin. prof. psychiatry, from 1982. Supr. psychiatric residents in practice of psychotherapy Mass. Gen. Hosp., 1960—, leader seminars in field. Contbr. numerous articles to profl. jours. Recipient citation Commonwealth of Mass. Ho. of Reps., 1979. Mem. AMA, AAAS, Am. Psychiat. Assn., Mass. Med. Soc., Mass. Gen. Hosp. Staff Assocs., Suffolk Dist. Med. Soc., Boston Psychoanalytic Soc. Home: Amesbury, Mass. Died June 3, 2006.

MESSNER, KATHRYN HERTZOG, civic worker; b. Glendale, Calif., May 27, 1915; d. Walter Sylvester and Sadie (Dinger) Hertzog; m. Ernest Lincoln, Jan. 1, 1942; children: Ernest Lincoln, Martha Allison Messner Cloran. BA, UCLA, 1936, MA, 1951. Tchr. social studies L.A. schs., 1937-46; mem. L.A. County Grand Jury, 1961. Mem. exec. bd. L.A. Family Svc., 1959-62; dist. atty.'s adv. com., 1965-71, dist. atty.'s adv. coun., 1971-82; mem. San Marino Community Coun.; chmn. San Marino chpt. Am. Cancer Soc.; bd. dirs. Pasadena Rep. Women's Club, 1960-62, San Marino dist. coun. Girl Scouts U.S.A., 1959-68, Am. Field Svc., San Marino, 1983-92; pres. San Marino High Sch. PTA, 1964-65; bd. mem. Pasadena Vol. Placement Bur., 1962-68; mem. adv. bd. Univ. YWCA, 1956-98; co-chmn. Dist. Atty.'s Adv. Bd. Young Citizens Coun., 1968-72; mem. San Marino Red Cross Coun., 1966-86, chmn., 1969-71, vice chmn., 1971-74; mem. atty. gen.'s vol. adv. com., 1971-80; bd. dirs. L.A. Women's Philharm. Com., 1974-89, Beverly Hills-West L.A. YWCA, 1974-85, L.A. YWCA, 1975-84, L.A. Law Affiliates, 1974-89, Pacificulture Art Mus., 1976-80, Reachout Com., Music Center, Vol. Action Center, West L.A., Calif., 1980-85, Stevens House, 1980-98, Pasadena Philharm. Com., 1980-85, Friends Outside, 1983-92, Internat. Christian Scholarship Found., 1984-92; hon. bd. dirs. Pasadena chpt. ARC, 1978-82. Recipient spl. commendation Am. Cancer Soc., 1961; Community Svc. award UCLA, 1981. Contbr. articles to profl. jours. Mem. Pasadena Philharmonic, Las Floristas, Huntington Meml. Clinic Aux., Nat. Charity League, Gold Shield (co-founder), Pi Lambda Theta (sec. 1983-89), Pi Gamma Mu, Mortar Bd., Prytanean Soc. Home: Pasadena, Calif. Died Feb. 8, 2006.

METCALF, JACK, retired congressman; b. Marysville, Wash., Nov. 30, 1927; s. John Read and Eunice (Grannis) M.; m. Norma Jean Grant, Oct. 3, 1948; children: Marta Jean, Gayle Marie, Lea Lynn, Beverlee Ann. Student, U. Wash., 1944-45; BA, BEd, Pacific Luth. U., 1951. Tchr. Elma (Wash.) pub. schs., 1951-52, Everett (Wash.) pub. schs., 1952-81; mem. Wash. State Ho. of Reps., 1960-64, Wash. State Senate, 1966-75, 80-92, US Congress from 2nd Wash. dist., 1995-2001. Chmn. environment and natural resources com., 1988-92; mem. domestic & internat. monetary policy, fin. instns. & consumer credit, aviation, surface transp. coms. Hon. chmn. Innocent Property Owners Protection Initiative. Mem. Coun. State Govts., Wash. Edn. Assn. (bd. dirs.), Wash. Assn. Profl. Educators (state v.p. 1979-81, state pres. 1977-79), Nat. Conf. State Legislatures, Western States Recycling Coalition, South Whidbey Kiwanis. Republican. Home: Langley, Wash. Died Mar. 15, 2007.

METCALF, JOSEPH, III, retired military officer; b. Holyoke, Mass., Dec. 20, 1927; s. Joseph and Alice Folger (Conrad) M.; m. Ruth Daniels, June 13, 1951; children: Joseph, David, Elizabeth. BS, U.S. Naval Acad., 1951, U.S. Naval Postgrad. Sch., 1964; postgrad., U.S. Army War Coll., 1971. Commd. ensign US Navy, 1951, advanced through grades to vice adm., 1983, comdr. Destroyer Squadron 33, 1974-75, comdr. Destroyer Group Mid-Pacific, 1975, asst. chief naval personnel for fin. mgmt. and mgmt. info., 1976-78, dir. total force mgmt. control and analysis div. Office Chief Naval Ops. Washington, 1978-79, comdr. cruiser destroyer group 8, 1979-81, dir. gen. programming and planning office Chief Naval Ops., 1981-83, comdr. 2d Fleet, Strike Fleet Atlantic, 1983-84, dep. chief naval ops. surface warfare, 1984—87; comdr. Grenada relief invasion (Operation Urgent Fury), Oct. 1983. V.p. bd. dirs. Navy Fed. Credit Union, Washington. Decorated Bronze star, Legion of Merit (3), D.S.M. Episcopalian. Died Mar. 2, 2007.

METZ, ROBERT JOHN, endocrinologist; b. Johannesburg, Republic of South Africa, Jan. 23, 1929; came to U.S., 1954; s. Nimy and Nita (Kremler) M.; m. Vera G. Cohen, Jan. 11, 1953; children: Jeremy, Beth, Miriam, Matthew. MB, BCh, U. Witwatersrand, Johannesburg, 1951; MS, Northwestern U., 1959; PhD, U. Toronto, Ont., Can., 1962. Chief Northwestern U. Med. div. Cook County Hosp., Chgo., 1962-65; attending physician Virgina Mason Hosp., Seattle, from 1969; pres. Virgina Mason Rsch. Ctr., 1973-76; head sect. endocrinology Virginia Mason Clinic, 1981-85. Clin. assoc. prof. medicine U. Wash., Seattle, 1977—; attending physician Passavant Meml. Hosp., Chgo., 1966-69 Editor: Blue Book of Endocrinology, 1985, Management and Care of the Diabetic Patient, 1988; contbr. numerous articles to profl. jours. Fellow ACP; mem. Endocrine Soc., Am. Diabetes Assn. Avocations: fly-fishing, bird-watching, golf, sailing. Home: Seattle, Wash. Died Nov. 2, 2006.

METZGER, BRUCE MANNING, clergyman, educator; b. Middletown, Pa., Feb. 9, 1914; s. Maurice Rutt and Anna Mary (Manning) M.; m. Isobel E. Mackay, July 7, 1944; children: John Mackay, James Bruce. AB, Lebanon Valley Coll., 1935, DD, 1951; ThB, Princeton Theol. Sem., 1938, ThM, 1939; AM, Princeton U., 1940, PhD, 1942; LHD (hon.), Findlay U., 1962; DD (hon.), St. Andrews U., Scotland, 1964; DTheol (hon.), Münster U., Fed. Republic Germany, 1970; DLitt (hon.), Potchefstroom U., South Africa, 1985. Ordained to ministry Presbyn. Ch. USA, 1939. Teaching fellow N.T. Princeton Theol. Sem., 1938-40, mem. faculty, 1940—84, prof. N.T. lang. and lit., 1954-64, George L. Collord prof. N.T. lang. and lit., 1964-84, prof. emeritus, 1984—2007. Vis. lectr. Presbyn. Theol. Sem. South, Campinas, Brazil, 1952, Presbyn. Theol. Sem. North, Recife, Brazil, 1952; mem. Inst. for Advanced Study, Princeton, 1964-65, 73-74; scholar-in-residence Tyndale House, Cambridge, 1969; vis. fellow Clare Hall, Cambridge, 1974, Wolfson Coll., Oxford U., 1979, Macquarie U., Sydney, Australia, 1982, Caribbean Grad. Sch. of Theology, Jamaica, 1990, Seminario Internacional Teológico Bautista, Buenos Aires, 1991, Griffith Thomas Lectrs., Dallas Theol. Sem., 1992; mem. mng. com. Am. Sch. Classical Studies, Athens, Greece; mem. Standard Bible com. Nat. Coun. Chs., 1952-2007, chmn., 1975-2007; mem. seminar N.T. studies Columbia U., 1959-80; mem. Kuratorium of Vetus-Latina Inst., Beuron, Germany, 1959-2007; adv. com. Inst. N.T. Text Rsch., U. Münster, 1961-2007, Thesaurus Linguae Graecae, 1972-80; Collected Works of Erasmus, 1977-2007; chmn. Am. com. versions Internat. Greek N.T., 1950-88; participant internat. congresses scholars, Aarhus, Aberdeen, Bangor, Basel, Bonn, Brussels, Budapest, Cairo, Cambridge, Copenhagen, Dublin, Exeter, Frankfurt, Heidelberg, London, Louvain, Manchester, Milan, Munich, Münster, Newcastle, Nottingham, Oxford, Prague, Rome, St. Andrews, Stockholm, Strasbourg, Toronto, Trondheim, Tübingen; mem. Presbytery, N.B. Author: The Saturday and Sunday Lessons from Luke in the Greek Gospel Lectionary, 1944, Lexical Aids for Students of New Testament Greek, 1946, enlarged edit., 1955, A Guide to the Preparation of a Thesis, 1950, An Introduction to the Apocrypha, 1957, Chapters in the History of New Testament Textual Criticism, 1963, The Text of the New Testament, Its Transmission, Corruption, and Restoration, 1964, (with B.D. Ehrman) 4th enlarged edit., 2005, (with H.G. May) The Oxford Annotated Bible with the Apocrypha, 1965, The New Testament, Its Background, Growth, and Content, 1965, 3d edit., 2003, Index to Periodical Literature on Christ and the Gospels, 1966, Historical and Literary Studies, Pagan, Jewish, and Christian, 1968, Index to Periodical Literature on the Apostle Paul, 1960, 2nd edit., 1970, A Textual Commentary on the Greek New Testament, 1971, 2d edit., 1994, The Early Versions of the New Testament, 1977, New Testament Studies, 1980, Manuscripts of the Greek Bible, 1981, The Canon of the New Testament, 1987, (with Roland Murphy) The New Oxford Annotated Bible with the Apocrypha, 1991, (with M.D. Coogan) The Oxford Companion to the Bible, 1993, Breaking the Code-Understanding the Book of Revelation, 1993, Reminiscences of an Octogenarian, 1997, (with Coogan) The Oxford Guide to People & Places of the Bible, 2001, (with Coogan) The Oxford Guide to Ideas and Issues of the Bible, 2001, The Bible in Translation, Ancient and English Versions, 2001; mem. editl. com. Critical Greek New Testament, 1956-84; chmn. Am. com., Internat. Greek New Testament Project, 1970-88; sec. com. translators: Apocrypha (rev. standard version); editor: New Testament Tools and Studies, 34 vols., 1960-2004, Oxford Annotated Apocrypha, 1965, enlarged edit., 1977; Reader's Digest Condensed Bible, 1982; co-editor: United Bible Societies Greek New Testament, 1966, 4th edit., 1993; compiler: Index of Articles on the New Testament and the Early Church Published in Festschriften, 1951, supplement, 1955, Lists of Words Occurring Frequently in the Coptic New Testament (Sahidic Dialect), 1961, Annotated Bibliography of the Textual Criticism of the New Testament, 1955, (with Isobel M. Metzger) Oxford Concise Concordance to the Holy Bible, 1962, (with R.C. Dentan and W. Harrelson), The Making of the New Revised Standard Version of the Bible, 1991; contbr. articles to jours. Chmn. standard bible com. Nat. Coun. Chs., 1977-2000. Recipient cert. Disting. Svc. Nat. Coun. Chs., 1957, Disting. Alumnus award Lebanon Valley Coll. Alumni Assn., 1961, citation of appreciation Laymen's Nat. Bible Assn., 1986, Disting. Alumnus award Princeton Theol. Sem., 1989, lit. competition prize Christian Rsch. Found., 1955, 62, 63, E.T. Thompson award, 1991. Mem. Am. Philos. Soc., Soc. Bibl. Lit. (pres. 1970-71, past del. Am. Coun. Learned Socs.), Am. Bible Soc. (bd. mgrs. 1948-2007, chmn. com. transls. 1964-70), Am. Philol. Assn., Studiorum Novi Testamenti Societas (pres. 1971-72), Cath. Bibl. Assn., N.Am. Patristic Soc. (pres. 1972), Soc. Textual Scholarship (pres. 1995), Am. Soc. Papyrologists; hon. fellow, corr. mem. Higher Inst. Coptic Studies, Cairo; corr. fellow Brit. Acad. (Burkitt medal in Bibl. studies 1994). Republican. Home: Princeton, NJ. Died Feb. 13, 2007.

METZNER, ARTHUR BERTHOLD, chemical engineering educator; b. Can., Apr. 13, 1927; s. Reinhold Berthold and Lillian (Bredis) M.; m. Elisabeth Krieger, May 9, 1948; children: Elisabeth L., Arthur P., Rebecca. BSc, U. Alta., 1948; ScD, MIT, 1951; D.A.Sc. (honoris causa), Katholieke U. te Leuven, Belgium, 1975. With Def. Rsch. Bd., Ottawa, Ont., Can., 1947-48; instr. MIT, 1950-51; with Colgate Palmolive Co., Jersey City, 1951-53; instr. Bklyn. Poly. Inst., 1951-53; mem. faculty U. Del., from 1953, H. Fletcher Brown prof. chem. engring., 1962-91, chmn. dept., 1970-77, prof. emeritus, from 1991. Vis. prof. Stanford U., 1967, U. Cambridge (Eng.), 1968-69; Lacey lectr. Calif Inst. Tech., 1968. Recipient Wilmington Sect. award Am. Chem. Soc., 1958; Guggenheim fellow, 1968. Mem. NAE, Soc. Rheology (Bingham medal 1977), Am. Inst. Chem. Engrs. (Colburn award 1958, Walker award 1970, Lewis award 1977, Founders award 1990). Home: Wilmington, Del. Died May 4, 2006.

MEWISSEN, DIEUDONNE JEAN, radiobiologist, educator; b. Ans, Liege, Belgium, Oct. 25, 1924; came to U.S., 1954; s. Dieudonne Chretien and Renee Jeanne (Groven) M.; m. Marie Renee Breuls, Feb. 10, 1950; children: Evelyn, Mark, Sophie. MD, U. Liege, 1950, PhD, 1961. Resident in surgery U. Liege Cancer Inst., 1950-53; sr. resident Erlanger Hosp., Chattanooga, 1954-55; resident physician Oak Ridge Inst. Nuclear Studies, 1955-56; attending physician U. Liege Cancer Center, 1956-60; mem. faculty U. Chgo. Med. Sch., from 1960, prof. radiology, from 1968; dir. lab. radiobiology Free U. Brussels Med. Sch., from 1960, prof. human radiobiology, from 1970. Author: Radiolesions, Radiocancers and Chemical Radioprotection,

1961; editor: Californum-232 Medical Applications, 1979; co-editor: Exposure of Man to Radiation in Nuclear Warfare, 1963. Served with Belgian Army, 1945-46. Recipient Dag Hammarskjöld Internat. Peace award for sci. achievement, 1980 Mem. Belgian Cancer Soc. (hon. sec.-gen.), Royal Soc. Medicine, Belgian Soc. Radiology, Belgian Soc. Biology, European Soc. Radiobiology, Radiation Research Soc., Belgian Soc. Radiobiology, Am. Assn. Cancer Research. Home: Chicago, Ill. Died Dec. 12, 2006.

MEYER, BURNETT CHANDLER, mathematics educator; b. Denver, Mar. 24, 1921; s. Chandler Otto and Adda Marie (Burnett) M. BA, Pomona Coll., 1943; Sc.M., Brown U., 1945; PhD, Stanford U., 1949. Asst. prof. math. U. Ariz., Tucson, 1949-55, assoc. prof., 1955-57; asst. prof. math. U. Colo., Boulder, 1957-60, assoc. prof., 1960-68, prof., 1968-90, prof. emeritus, from 1990. Author: Introduction to Axiomatic Systems, 1974; contbr. articles to profl. jours. Mem. Am. Math. Soc., Math. Assn. Am., Phi Beta Kappa, Sigma Xi. Home: Denver, Colo. Died Mar. 24, 2006.

MEYER, JEFFERY WILSON, chemical marketing executive; b. San Francisco, June 22, 1923; s. Wilson and Mabel Marian (Wilson) M.; m. Janet Busse, Jan. 28, 1945; children: Pamela Meyer McLaughlin Elizabeth Meyer Helman. BS, U. Calif.-Berkeley, 1948. Lic. ocean operator passenger vessels. With Wilson & George Meyer, San Francisco, 1948—, mgr. coke dept., 1952-56, v.p. agrl. dept., 1956-59, pres., dir., 1959—, chmn. bd., chief exec. officer, 1973—; pres. Hawaii chpt. Sea Genie, Inc., Koua; fish collector for Steinhart Aquarium. Past pres. Norwegian Am. C. of C.; trustee, former chmn. bd. Calif. Acad. Scis.; mem. adv. com. Smithsonian Natural History Mus. Served to 1st lt. AUS, 1942-46, 50-52. Decorated Bronze Star; recipient Order of St. Olav Knight 1st class, Norway. Mem. Bohemian Club, Pacific Union Club, Cercle de l'Union Club, St. Francis Yacht Club (San Francisco), Menlo Country Club (Redwood City). Home: Burlingame, Calif. Died June 24, 2006.

MEYER, SHERMAN WAYNE, physician, surgeon; b. Leedy, Okla., Aug. 17, 1909; s. Murray Clifford and Emma Mae (Cooper) M.; m. Lily Thelmine Rasmusson, Oct. 22, 1932; children: Wayne Leroy, Jon Charles. DO, U. Osteo. Medicine and Health Scis., 1930. Diplomate Am. Bd. Gen. Surgery. Pvt. practice osteo. medicine and surgery, Iowa, N.Mex., Ariz., Tex.; chief of staff Phoenix Gen. Hosp., 1952-59, Parker (Ariz.) Community Hosp., 1974-75. Pres. Parker (Ariz.) C. of C., 1968. Recipient Sir George award Parker C. of C., 1982. Mem. Am. Osteo. Hosp. Assn. (award of merit 1990), Am. Coll. Advancement Medicine, Coll. Osteo. Surgeons, Ariz. Osteo. Med. Assn., Lions, Rotary, Masons, Shriners. Republican. Avocation: ocean fishing. Home: Parker, Ariz. Died Nov. 18, 2006.

MEYER, THERESA MAURINE, nurse, transcutaneous electrical nerve stimulation consultant; b. Blue Earth, MN, June 27, 1939; d. Francis Joseph and Maurine Agnes (Mongeau) Bleess; m. Roger Louis Meyer, Sept. 3, 1960; children— Daniel, Kathleen, David. Grad. St. Mary's Sch. Nursing, Rochester, Minn., 1960. R.N., Minn. Staff nurse in medicine/surgery, Miller Hosp., St. Paul, 1960-61; staff nurse in orthopedics Sharp Hosp., San Diego, Calif., 1979; transcutaneous electrical nerve stimulation consultant PainCare (formerly Midwest Pain Control), Golden Valley, Minn., 1979-85, with sales office, Mpls., 1985—. Contbr. articles to Nursing Magazine. Del., Polit. Convention Fridley, Minn., 1974. Mem. Midwest Pain Soc. Clubs: (Mpls.) (sec. 1984), Sun Harborettes (San Diego) (sec. 1978). Avocations: barbershop singing auxilliary. Home: Eden Prairie, Minn. Died Mar. 29, 2007.

MEYERSON, MARTIN, retired academic administrator, urban planner; b. NYC, Nov. 14, 1922; s. Samuel and Etta (Berger) M.; m. Margy Ellin Lazarus, Dec. 31, 1945; children: Adam, Laura (dec.), Matthew. BA, Columbia U., 1942; MCP, Harvard U., 1949; LLD, U. Pa., 1970, Queen's U., Can., 1968, Shiraz U., Iran, 1973, U. Edinburgh, 1976; PhD honoris causa, Hebrew U., 1987; also 18 other hon. doctorates including ScD, LHD, LittD, DFA, DHum, 1967-98. Mem. staff Michael Reese Hosp., Chgo., 1945-47; asst. prof. coll. and grad. social scis. U. Chgo., 1948-52; assoc. prof., dept. chair city and regional planning U. Pa., 1952-56, prof., 1956-57, pres., 1970-81, pres. emeritus, 1981—2007, chmn. U. Pa. Press, chmn. adv. bd. Inst. Rsch. Higher Edn., Fels Ctr. Govt., 1981—2007, bd dirs. Lauder Inst. Mgmt. and Internat. Studies, co-chmn. Commn. for U. Pa. 250th Anniversary, 1987-90, Univ. prof., 1977—2007; exec. dir. action Am. Coun. to Improve Our Neighborhoods, 1955-56, trustee, 1956-66; Frank Backus Williams prof. city planning and urban rsch. Harvard U., 1957-63, acting dean Grad. Sch. Design, 1963; founding dir. Joint Ctr. for Urban Studies, MIT and Harvard U., 1958-63; dean, prof. urban devel. Coll. Environ. Design, U. Calif., Berkeley, 1963-66; interim chancellor U. Calif., Berkeley, 1965; pres., prof. public policy SUNY, Buffalo, 1966-70; prof. Inst. Urban Rsch. U. Pa.; dir. visitor Inst. for Advanced Study, Princeton, N.J., 1983-84. Dir. Real Estate Rsch. Corp., 1961-67, Marine Midland Bank, 1966-70, 1st Fidelity Bancorp. (now First Union), Scott Paper Co., Penn Mut. Life, Saint Gobain Corp., Certain Teed, Norton, Avatar, Universal Health Svcs.; cons. to govts., pvt. firms U.S. and abroad, UN missions, urban/econ. devel. to, Japan, Indonesia and South Asia, Yugoslavia, 1958-65; sr. adv. urban and regional pub. and pvt. devel. Arthur D. Little, Inc., 1958-66; cons. Sears Roebuck Found., 1958-69; chmn. bd. Western N.Y. Nuclear Rsch. Ctr., 1966-70; adv. coun. NASA, 1960-65; White House presdl. task forces, urban policy, 1960-69; mem. coun. Electric Power Rsch. Inst., 1973-77; mem. U.S. del. UN Conf. on Sci. and Tech. for Less Developed Areas, 1963. Author: (with E. C. Banfield) Politics, Planning and the Public Interest, 1955, Housing, People and Cities, 1962, Face of the Metropolis, 1963, Boston, 1966, Gladly Learn and Gladly Teach, 1978; editor: Conscience of the City, 1970, McGraw-Hill Series on Cmty. Devel.; mem. editorial bd. Ency. Britannica, 1980-98, Daedalus, 1972-90. Mem. Air Conservation Commn., 1962-66; mem. Bay Area Conservation and Devel. Commn., 1965-66; chmn. Assembly Univ. Goals and Governance, 1969-74; commr. N.Y. State Commn. on Post-Secondary Sch. Edn., 1976-77; hon. prof. Nat. U. Asuncion, 1969-2007, Beijing U., 1996-2007; bd. dirs. Phila. Bicentennial Corp., 1970-76, Greater Phila. Partnership, 1973-81, Afro-Am. Film Found., 1966-70, Niagara U., 1968-70, Center for Community Change, 1968-72, Acad. Religion and Mental Health, 1970-78, Center for Ednl. Devel., 1967-70, Phila. Mus. Art, 1974—, Nat. Urban Coalition, 1969-78; trustee, Niagara U., 1968-70, Am. Coll., 1982-92, Curtis Inst. Music, 1987-94, United World Coll.N. Mex., 1984—, Am. Schs. Oriental Rsch., 1985-2007, Tel Aviv U., Coll. Bd., 1986-92, Hebrew U., Internat. House Ctr., Monell Chem. Senses Ctr., chmn., 1993-2007, Fgn. Policy Rsch. Inst., 1981-2007, Panasonic Found., 1982-2007, Ctr. for Visual History, U.S. Com. on the Constl. System; founding dir. Internat. Centre for Study East Asian Devel. Japan; Inst. for Internat. Edn., 1971-2007, chmn., 1981-85; bd. dirs. Internat. Council Ednl. Devel., 1971-94, Am. Council Financial Aid to Edn., 1975-81, Open Univ. Found., U.K., 1979-82; chmn. council pres. Nat. Accelerator Lab., 1972-73; co-chmn. Images (French TV), 1976-79, Salzburg Seminar Bd., 1978-2007, sr. fellow, 1997-2007; co-chmn. Marconi Internat. Fellowship Found., chair exec. com., 1978-96, chmn. bd. dirs., 1996-2007; Internat. gov. Center Environ. Studies, London, 1966-84; mem. sr. exec. council Conf. Bd., 1970-77; trustee Aspen. Inst., 1976-96; chair coun. UN Centre for Regional Devel., Nagoya, Japan, 1983-93; chair internat. selection commn. Phila. Liberty Medal, 1988-2007; bd. overseers Koc Univ., Bosphorus, Turkey, 1994-2007; bd. dirs. Internat. Literacy Inst., 1995-2007. Decorated commendatore Knight-Commdr. (Italy); chevalier de l'Ordre Nat. de Mérite (France); Order of the Rising Sun Emperor of Japan; recipient Einstein medal Am. Technion Soc., 1976, Disting. Achievement award U. Calif. Berkeley, 1984, John Jay award Columbia U., 1982, Disting. Educator award Assn. Collegiate Schs. of Planning, 1996; overseas fellow Churchill Coll. Urban Planning, Cambridge U., 1983; hon. fellow Soc. for Tech. Communication, 1988; Wheelwright fellow Harvard U.; Meyerson Hall named in his honor U. Pa. Grad. Sch. Fine Arts; Martin and Margy Meyerson Professorship named in honor U. Pa., 1995, Philippine Women's U., Manila. Fellow Am. Acad. Arts and Scis., Royal Soc. Arts (Franklin fellow), Buckminster Fuller Inst. of Design Scis. (founder), Am. Philos. Soc. (exec. com.), Nat. Acad. Edn.; mem. Am. Soc. Planning Ofcls. (past dir., aide to exec. dir.), Am. Inst. Planners (past gov., spl. award winner), Internat. Assn. Univs. Paris (Am. dir. 1975—2007, head 1982-85, hon. pres. 1985—2007), Coun. Fgn. Rels., European Acad. Arts, Scis. and Letters (academician), Phi Beta Kappa. Clubs: Philadelphia, Century (N.Y.C.), Cosmos (Washington), U. Pa. (N.Y.C.). Died June 2, 2007.

MICHAELS, JAMES WALKER, retired editor; b. Buffalo, June 17, 1921; s. Dewey and Phyllis (Boasberg) M.; m. Jean A. Briggs, June 1985; children: Robert Matthews, James Walker, Anne Phyllis. BS cum laude, Harvard U., 1942. Ambulance driver Am. Field Service, India and Burma, 1943-44; with USIS, New Delhi, Bangkok, 1944-46; fgn. corr. UP, bur. mgr. New Delhi, 1946-50; with Forbes mag., NYC, 1954—98, mng. editor, 1956-61, editor, 1961—98. Contbr. articles to mags. Home: Rhinebeck, NY. Died Oct. 2, 2007.

MICHALAK, EDWARD M., consultant, retired manufacturing company executive; b. Milw., Oct. 1, 1924; s. Michael and Emily S. (Bulak) M.; m. Rita Y. Glazewski, May 23, 1953; children— Barbara, Mary, Cynthia, Jean. B.S. in Gen. Engring., U.S. Mil. Acad., 1945; B.S.E.E., U. Wis.-Madison, 1952; M.B.A., U. Wis.-Milw., 1976. Registered profl. engr., Wis. Devel. engr. Cutler Hammer & Globe Union, Milw., 1952-57; solid state engr. Allen Bradley Co., Milw., 1958-67, dir. elec. engring., 1967-69, dir. product mgmt., 1969-73, corp. v.p., 1973-86, cons. quality engring., 1987—; engring. advisor Marquette U., Milw., 1980—; mem. engring. adv. com. Milw. Sch. Engring., 1984—. Bd. dirs. Internat. Inst. Milw., 1984—, 1st v.p., 1984-85; mem. Kosciuszko Found., N.Y.C., 1963—. Served with U.S. Army, 1945-49, PTO. Mem. IEEE, Am. Soc. Quality Control, Indsl. Research Inst. (prin. rep. 1978—, program chmn. 1984-85), Wis. Assn. Research Mgmt. (chmn. 1984-85). Avocations: swimming; skiing; photography. Home: Milwaukee, Wis. Died Mar. 16, 2006.

MICHELA, BERNARD JOSEPH, physician; b. Iron Mountain, Mich., Dec. 6, 1924; s. Dominic A. and Anne (Giachino) M.; m. Barbara Trundy, June 24, 1950 (dec. 1982); children— Barton, Douglas, Kathryn, Patrick; m. Lynn Syvertsen, Jan. 23, 1988. Diplomate Am. Bd. Phys. Medicine and Rehab. Cons. phys. medicine and rehab., bur. maternal and child health D.C. Dept. Health, 1955-57; med. dir. Davis Meml. Goodwill Industries Rehab. Center, Washington, 1956-57; asst. dir., chief phys. medicine and rehab. Rehab. Inst. Chgo., 1957-58, dir. inst., 1958-61. Cons. phys. medicine Chgo. Bd. Edn., 1959-60; asst. prof., acting chmn. dept. phys. medicine and rehab. Northwestern U., 1960-61; chief phys. medicine and rehab. Long Beach VA Hosp., 1961-64, cons., 1964—; dir. dept. rehab. Meml. Hosp., Long Beach, 1964-87; corp. med. dir. Casa Colina, Inc., Pomona, Calif., 1987—; asst. prof. phys. medicine U. So. Calif., 1961-65, assoc. prof., 1965-66; asst. prof. phys. medicine and rehab. U. Calif. at Irvine, 1966-68, assoc. prof., 1968-73, prof., 1973—; cons. Desert Hosp., Palm Springs, 1976-81; survey cons. hosp. accreditation program Jount Commn. on Accreditationof Hosps, 1986—. Bd. dirs. Long. Beach Heart Assn., 1967—, pres., 1968; bd. dirs. Calif. HT Assn., pres., 1974; bd. dirs. Long Beach Lung Assn., 1980-84; pres. bd. dirs. Long Beach Stroke Activity Ctr., 1988. Mem. Am. Acad. Phys. Medicine and Rehab., Am. Acad. Med. Dirs., Am. Coll. Physician Execs. Died June 10, 2007.

MICHELFELDER, ELLEN HADEN, hospital administrative executive; b. Richmond, Va., Dec. 8, 1945; d. William H. III and Dorothy (Fowler) Miller; m. Joerg R. Michelfelder, June 10, 1972. BS, Longwood Coll., 1967; MBA, Pepperdine U., 1982. Tchr. Jefferson High Sch., Alexandria, Va., 1967-69, Stuttgart (Germany) High Sch., 1969-73; adminstrv. asst. Sanwa Bank, San Francisco, 1973-74; asst. v.p. Security Pacific Nat. Bank, San Francisco, 1974-78; dir. human resources Nat. Semiconductor, Santa Clara, Calif., 1978-82; exec. dir. human resources Atari, Inc., Sunnyvale, Calif., 1983-84; dir. human resources Fujitsu Am., Inc., San Jose, Calif., 1985; exec. v.p. Bank of Calif., San Francisco, 1985-92; v.p. human resources & support svcs. Lucile Packard Children's Hosp. at Stanford, Palo Alto, Calif., from 1993. Bd. dirs., pres. Alumnae Resources, San Francisco, 1990—. Vol. Am. Cancer Soc., San Francisco, 1991-92. Mem. City Club San Francisco. Home: San Mateo, Calif. Died July 19, 2007.

MICHERO, WILLIAM HENDERSON, retired retail executive; b. Fort Worth, June 19, 1925; s. William Alvin and Lela Belle (Henderson) M.; m. Nan Elaine Henderson, July 9, 1948; children— Jane Elaine Michero Christie, William Sherman, Thomas Edward. BS in Commerce, Tex. Christian U., 1948. Sec. Tandy Corp., Fort Worth, 1960-75, v.p., 1970-75; with Tandycrafts, Inc., Fort Worth, 1975-90, sr. v.p., sec., dir., 1979-83, chmn. bd., 1983-90, ret., 1990. Sec. B.F. Johnston Found., Fort Worth, 1962-90. Bd. dirs David L. Tandy Found., Fort Worth, 1968-99, Oakwood Cemetery Assn., 1979-89, Panther Boys Club, 1974-78, Fort Worth Mus. Sci. and History, 1973-75, pres. 1975, United Way; chmn. Distributive Edn. Council, 1970. Served with U.S. Navy, 1943-46. Mem.: Colonial Country Club, Fort Worth Club. Home: Fort Worth, Tex. Died Dec. 22, 2006.

MIDDENDORF, JOHN HARLAN, English literature educator; b. NYC, Mar. 31, 1922; s. George Arlington and Margaret (Hofmann) M.; m. Beverly Bruner, July 14, 1943 (dec. 1983); children: Cathie Jean Middendorf Hamilton, Peggy Ruth Middendorf Brindisi; m. Maureen L. MacGrogan, Jan. 31, 1986. AB, Dartmouth Coll., 1943; AM, Columbia U., 1947, PhD, 1953. Lectr. English CCNY, 1946, Hunter Coll., 1946-49; faculty Columbia, from 1947, prof. English, 1965-89, prof. emeritus, from 1990, dir. grad. studies, 1971-74, vice-chmn., 1976-80. Chmn. English test com. Coll. Entrance Exam. Bd., 1967—69. Contbr. articles, revs. to profl. jours.; Editor: English Writers of the Eighteenth Century, 1971; asst. editor: Johnsonian News Letter, 1950-58; co-editor, 1958-78, editor, 1978-90; assoc. editor: Yale edit. Works Samuel Johnson, 1962-66; gen. editor, 1966—. Lt. (j.g.) Japanese translator USNR, 1943—45. Faculty fellow Fund Advancement Edn., 1951-52; grantee Coun. Rsch. Humanities, 1958-59, Am. Philos. Soc., 1962, Am. Coun. Learned Socs., 1962, NEH, 1976-88. Mem. Johnsonians (sec.-treas. 1958-68, chmn. 1969, 79), Univ. Seminar on 18th Century European Culture (chmn. 1973-75, 85-87), Oxford Bibliog. Soc., Grolier Club, English Inst. (mem. supervisory com. 1963-66), Modern Lang. Assn., Soc. Sr. Scholars, Am. Soc. 18th Century Studies, Phi Beta Kappa. Home: New York, NY. Died Aug. 14, 2007.

MIDDLETON, DONALD EARL, transportation company executive; b. Phila., Mar. 19, 1930; s. William Joseph and Marian May (Klotz) M.; m. Marilyn Ann Schmit, Feb. 27, 1954; children: David Earl, Donna Lynn, Linda Ann, Gary Lee. Student, Taylor Bus. Coll., Phila., 1948-49; cert. proficiency Accounts and Fins., U. Pa. Wharton Evening Sch., 1957; BBA, Roanoke Coll., 1979. With Norfolk and Western Ry. Co., Roanoke, Va., from 1948, asst. to sec., 1959-67, asst. sec., 1968-71, sec., 1972-82; corp. sec. Norfolk (Va.) So. Corp. (consolidation of Norfolk and Western Ry. with Norfolk So. Ry. Co.), from 1982. Corp. sec. Atlantic Investment Co., Charlotte-So. Hotel Corp., Norfolk So. Found., Norfolk So. Properties, Inc., Rail Investment Co., Richmond-Washington Co.; asst. corp. sec. Norfolk and Western Ry. Co., Norfolk So. Ry. Co., Ctrl. of Ga. R.R. Co., N.Am. Van Linces, Inc., NS Crown Svcs., Inc., Pocahontas Land Corp., Va. Holding Corp., numerous others. Past pres. Fairfield Civic League; bd. dirs., sec. Tidewater chpt. ARC; chmn. adv. com. Virginia Beach Svc., ARC; active ch. affairs Boy Scouts Am., Jr. Achievement. Mem. Am. Soc. Corp. Secs. (past chmn. nat. Jr. Achievement Com.), Va. C. of C., Hampton Roads C. of C., Harbor Club. Republican. Baptist. Home: Virginia Beach, Va. Died June 6, 2006.

MIELE, ALFONSE RALPH, former government official; b. NYC, Jan. 6, 1922; s. Angelo and Alesia (Laudadio) M.; m. Gloria I. Litrento, Nov. 22, 1942 (dec. Dec. 1977); children: Richard Lynn, Barbara Jo, Steven Arnold; m. Ann Carlino Valerio, Mar. 31, 1979 (dec. June 1988); m. Dorothy A. McGowan, July 7, 1990. AB in Litteris Gallicis with honors, Fordham U., 1942; postgrad., U. Nancy, France, 1945; MA, Columbia U., 1947, PhD, 1958. Commd. 2nd lt. U.S. Army, 1942; advanced through grades to col. USAF, 1961; served in 377th Automatic Weapons Bn., 1942-45; ret., brig. gen.; instr. French and pub. speaking Fordham Prep. Sch., NYC, 1946-47; asst. prof. French and Russian U.S. Naval Acad., 1949-52; exec. officer to NATO comdrs., 1953-55; teaching asst. Columbia U., 1955-58; assoc. prof. French USAF Acad., 1958-60, prof., head dept. fgn. langs., 1960-67, assoc. dean, chmn. divsn. humanities, 1967-68; exec. v.p. Loretto Heights Coll., Denver, 1968-70; pres. Coll. St. Rose, Albany, 1970-72; prof. gen. edn. Schenectady County C.C., Schenectady, N.Y., 1972-73; dep. asst. adminstr. internat. aviation affairs FAA, Washington, 1973-75, edn. specialist, from 1976; 1968. Asst. dir. pub. affairs U.S. Dept. Interior, Washington, 1975-76; chief negotiator civil aviation tech. agreement with USSR, 1973-75; project dir. Nat. Aviation Edn. Program for Am. Indians, 1978; asst. dir. Union County (N.J.) Coord. Agy. for Higher Edn., 1979-82; rep. Eckhart Assocs., 1983-88; relocation specialist Bradley/Wildman Co., Monument, Colo., 1989-92. Mem. Westfield (N.J.) Bd. Edn., 1985-88; bd. dirs. Pike's Peak chpt. ARC 1990-93; pres. Colorado Springs World Affairs Coun., 1993-95 bd. dirs. and patron Tri-Lakes Ctr. for the Arts, 1998— Decorated Bronze Star for heroism in ground combat, Legion of Merit (2) with oak leaf cluster, Belgian Fourragère; chevalier Palmes Academiques France; recipient Encaenia award Fordham Coll., 1962 Mem. Monument C. of C. (bd. dirs 1992-94). Home: Monument, Colo. Died July 22, 2007.

MIELKE, DONALD CRAIG, energy company executive; b. Wampum, Pa., Jan. 4, 1943; s. Frank and Nellie (Truby) M.; m. Carol Lee Hoover, June 26, 1964; children: Julie Lynn, Kristin Lee. BS in Acctg., Pa. State U. With Diamond Shamrock Corp. Dallas, 1964, asst. treas., 1973-76, treas., 1976-84, v.p., treas. 1984-86; sr. v.p. fin. and adminstrn. Maxus Energy Corp (formerly Diamond Shamrock Corp.), Dallas, 1987-89, sr. v.p. chief fin. officer, treas., from 1989. Served with USNG, 1966 Methodist. Home: Dallas, Tex. Died Sept. 11, 2006.

MIESBAUER, DONALD THOMAS, financial executive, accountant; b. Milw., May 28, 1926; s. Peter Andrew and Ethel Ellen (Kuechenmeister) M.; m. Janice Ardell Wilcox, Dec. 27, 1952; children— Laura Ellen Miesbauer Christensen, Diane Marie Miesbauer Howarth, Gail Elizabeth Miesbauer Sherman. Student Lawrence Coll., 1944-45; B.B.A., U. Wis.-Madison, 1949; postgrad. U. Wis.-Milw., 1958-67. C.P.A., Wis. Various positions in sales and acctg., 1949-66; asst. dir. bus. affairs U. Wis.-Milw., 1966-67; pres., chief exec. officer Wis. Savs. and Loan, Milw., 1967-77; v.p. 1st Wis. Nat. Bank, Milw., 1977-79; v.p. 1st Savs., Milw., 1979-85. Pres. 1st Savs. Found., Milw., 1979-85; treas. Richard Schilffarth & Assocs. Ltd., 1985—; pres. Congl. Home, Inc., Brookfield, Wis., 1981—; exec. com. Citizen's Environ. and Ecol. Com., Wauwatosa, Wis., 1972-79; bd. govs. Am. Heart Assn., Milw., 1978-88. Served to comdr. USN, 1944-68. Mem. Am. Inst. C.P.A.s, Wis. Inst. C.P.A.s (chmn. com. C.P.A.s in Industry 1980-81). Republican. Home: Milwaukee, Wis. Died Feb. 16, 2006.

MIGDOL, KENNETH M., labor relations consultant, industrial psychologist; b. Bklyn., Apr. 30, 1947; s. Lester and Sylvia (Schutzer) M.; m. Judith Strent; children: Michael, Melanie, Marissa. BA, Hofstra U., 1970; MA in Indsl. Psychology, New Sch., 1972, PhD in Indsl./Orgnl. Psychology, 1974; JD in Labor Law, Southland U., 1978. Cert. labor arbitrator. Mediator form labor rels. Electrophonics, Stamford, Conn., 1969-72; prin., pres. Ramm Assocs., from 1972; v.p. human resources IPCO Corp., LI, NY, 1975, corp. bd. dirs., educator academics and co. tng., from 1978. Mem. ASTD, Am. Arbitration Assn., Adminstrv. Mgmt. Soc., Am. Compensation Assn. Home: Jupiter, Fla. Died Nov. 6, 2006.

MIHOK, ANDREW FRANCIS, JR., theatrical production manager; b. Phila., May 8, 1934; s. Andrew Francis and Lucille Anna (Byers) M.; m. Katherine Hermes Lurker, Mar. 14, 1960; children— Bryan, Charles. BA, Antioch Coll., 1956. Tech. dir. Antioch Shakespeare Festival, 1956; stage mgr. Phoenix Theater, 1959-61; tech. dir. N.Y. Shakespeare Festival, NYC, 1965-70, prodn. mgr., 1970-92; ret. Served with U.S. Army, 1956-59. Home: New York, NY. Died Aug. 3, 2006.

MIKITA, JOSEPH KARL, broadcast executive; b. Va., Oct. 3, 1918; s. John and Catherine (Wargofcak) M.; m. Mary Therese Benya, Nov. 26, 1942; children: Patty-Jane Mikita McGlynn, Michael, M. Noël Mikita Garagiola. BS, Fordham U., 1939; MS, Columbia U., 1940. Treas., controller Capital Cities Broadcasting Co., Albany, NY, 1955-58; controller Westinghouse Broadcasting Co., Inc., NYC, 1958-60, v.p. fin., 1960-64, v.p. fin. and adminstrn., 1964-65, sr. v.p., 1965-69, from 1975; also dir., exec. v.p. Westinghouse Electric Corp. for Broadcasting, Learning and Leisure Activities, NYC, 1969-75. Dir. Sutro Tower, Inc.; ptnr. Emerald Bay Resort Co., Exuma, Bahamas Author: (with others) The Business of Broadcasting, 1964. Bd. dirs. Fordham U. Council, Albany County Workshop, Albany County Heart Assn., Citizens For Reasonable Growth, Boca Raton; chmn. bd. Instructional TV. Served to maj. AUS, 1940-45, ETO. Recipient Order of Merit (Silver), Westinghouse Electric Corp., Disting. Service Alumni award Fordham U., 1969. Mem. AICPA, Internat. Radio and TV Soc., N.Y. Soc. CPAs, Fin. Execs. Inst. (dir., past pres. Manhattan chpt.), Inst. Broadcasting Fin. Mgmt. (past dir.), Town Club, Westchester Country Club, Boca Raton Club, M.G.A., JDM Country Club, Royal Palm Yacht and Country Club, Palm Beach County Golf Assn., Golden Harbour Yacht Club (commodore), Rotary (1st v.p. N.Y.). Home: Boca Raton, Fla. Died Apr. 22, 2006.

MIKOLAJCZYK, HENRY LOUIS, architect, educator; b. Chgo., July 24, 1917; s. Michael F. and Katherine W. (Kowalska) M. BS in Architecture, Armour Inst. Tech., Chgo., 1939; MA in Architecture (J.V. Horn fellow 1940), U. Pa., 1940. Registered profl. engr., Ill. registered architect, Ill. Archtl. draftsman Nat. Youth Adminstrn., 1940, Chgo. San. Dist., 1940-42; engr. Curtiss-Wright Corp., 1942-43, Douglas Aircraft Co., Inc., 1943-45; architect, cons. U. Ill., Chgo., 1945-65, mem. faculty, from 1949, prof. architecture, from 1962. Designer prefabricated bldg. components Protex Corp., Chgo., 1950-60; architect, cons. Code Engring. Co., Inc., 1975-80; v.p. Archtl. Cons., 1980—; mem. architects exam. bd., City of Chgo., 1957-58 Mem. Ill. Civil Def. and Disaster Com., 1958-60. Mem. AIA, Ill. Soc. Architects, Polish-Am. Engrs. Assn., Am. Soc. Advancement Engring. Edn., ASTM, AAUP. Roman Catholic. Home: Deerfield, Ill. Died Dec. 18, 2006.

MILAM, EVELYN LOUISE, college president; b. Memphis, Tex., Feb. 12, 1921; d. John K. and Bessie Lee (Harper) M. BA, West Tex. State U., 1942; MA, Tex. Tech. U., 1951; PhD, U. Wyo., 1968. Cert. psychologist; cert. Tex. State Bd. Examiners of Psychologists. With U.S. Civil Service Censorship, San Antonio, 1942-43; high sch. tchr. Hereford (Tex.) Ind. Sch. Dist., 1943-46, Perryton (Tex.) Ind. Sch. Dist., 1946-47; registrar, counselor, coordinator of guidance Pampa (Tex.) Ind. Sch. Dist., 1947-62; admissions counselor, dir. admissions and fin. aid Austin Coll., Sherman, Tex., 1962-68, assoc. prof. edn. and psychology, 1968-74, prof., 1974; pres. Cottey Coll., Nevada, Mo., from 1974. Moderator Am. Council on Edn. nat. identification program for advancement of women in higher edn., 1981 Recipient Disting. Alumnus award West Tex. State U., 1980, U. Wyo., 1981; Nevada-Vernon County C. of C. Edn. Pacesetter award, 1984; Friend of Coll. award Cottey Coll. Alumnae Assn. Mem. Nat. Assn. Ind. Jr. Colls, NOW, Am. Psychol. Assn., Am. Assn. Counseling and Devel., AAUW, Nevada-Vernon County C. of C. (dir. 1976-78), Delta Kappa Gamma (M. Margaret Stroh Internat. scholar 1967-68), Phi Kappa Phi. Died Dec. 7, 2005.

MILBANK, JEREMIAH, retired foundation administrator; b. NYC, Mar. 24, 1920; s. Jeremiah and Katharine (Schulze) M.; m. Andrea Hunter, July 19, 1947 (dec. Oct. 1982); children: Jeremiah III, Victoria Milbank Whitney, Elizabeth Milbank Archer, Joseph H.; m. Carolyn Amory (div.); m. Rose Jackson Sheppard, May 4, 1991 (dec. Feb. 1998); m. Mary G. Rockefeller, Jan. 25, 1999. BA, Yale U., 1942; MBA, Harvard U., 1948; L.H.D. (hon.), Ithaca Coll., NY, 1976, Sacred Heart U., Conn.; LL.D., Manhattan Coll. With J.M. Found., NYC, former pres. Former pres. Turkey Hill Corp. Author: First Century of Flight in America, 1942. Chmn. emeritus Boys and Girls Clubs Am.; hon. pres. Internat. Ctr. for the Disabled; fin. chmn. Rep. Nat. Com., 1969-72, 75-77. Lt. USNR, 1943-46. Mem. River Club (N.Y.C.), Round Hill Club (Greenwich), Yale Club. Republican. Home: Charlottesvle, Va. Died Aug. 7, 2007.

MILDON, MARIE ROBERTA, legal association executive; b. Pittsburg, Calif., Apr. 18, 1935; d. Samuel Ward and Roberta Alice (Trumpower) Wilson; m. James Lee Mildon, Sept. 17, 1958; 1 dau., Laura Marie. B.S., U. Nev.-Reno, 1983. News editor Seaside News Sentinel (Calif.), 1956-58; adminstrv. asst. for corp. devel. Crown Zellerbach, San Francisco, 1959-64; assoc. dir. Nat. Council Juvenile and Family Ct. Judges, Reno, Nev., 1969—; tng. dir. Nat. Coll. Juvenile Justice, Reno, 1971-72; apptd. cons. to task force on abused and neglected children Mo. Supreme Ct. Alt. trustee John Shaw Field Found., Reno, 1979-85; trustee Cystems, Inc., Juris/Amicus, Inc. Coauthor: Model Statute for Termination of Parental Rights, 1976; Model Statute on Juvenile and Family Court Records, 1981; My World To Share, 1982. Editor: Judicial Concern for Children in Trouble, 1974; Juvenile and Family Law Jour., 1985—; prodn. editor Juvenile and Family Law Digest, 1986-88; mem. bd. cons. editors Jour. Emotional and Behavioral Problems, 1991—. Home: Reno, Nev. Died Oct. 12, 2006.

MILES, ARTHUR J., financial planner, consultant; b. NYC, Sept. 2, 1920; s. Levi and Rachel Goldsworthy (Hiscock) M.; m. Pearl Cooper, Nov. 27, 1947; children: Beverly Miles Kerns, Douglas Robert. BBA, Pace U., 1958; MBA, NYU, 1963; postgrad., Dartmouth Coll., 1966, Brown U., 1970-71. Instr. Brown U., Providence, 1970-71; with Dime Savs. Bank, NYC, 1938-81, exec. v.p., treas., 1975-78, sr. exec. v.p., treas., 1978-81; pres. AJM Assocs., Floral Park, NY, then Sarasota, Fla., 1981—2007. Newscaster Sta. WUSF-FM, Tampa, Fla.; bd. dirs. Cultural Instns. Retirement System, N.Y.C., 1968—89; fin. cons. Bklyn. Inst. Arts and Scis., 1972—89. Trustee, nat. treas. Alcoholics Anonymous, N.Y.C., 1970-79; tech. adviser N.Y.C. Fin. Liason Com., 1975-76. Served to sgt., inf. U.S. Army, 1942-45, Philippines. Fellow Fedn. Fin. Analysts; mem. Nat. Assn. Bus. Economists, Internat. Assn. Fin. Planners, Broadcast Pioneers, NYU Club, Marco Polo Club (N.Y.C.), Tournament Players Club. Republican. Died Feb. 24, 2007.

MILLARD, HAROLD RAY, mortgage banker, management consultant; b. Chattanooga, May 4, 1931; s. William M. and Mable D. Millard; m. Betty Ann Letz, Apr. 8, 1955; children— Stephen. B.B.A., Memphis State U., 1958. C.P.A., Tex. Ptnr., Peat, Marwick, Mitchell & Co., Houston, 1958-80; pres. Larmar Fin. Corp., Austin, 1981; owner, pres. LFS Financial Services, Houston, 1982—. Served with USAF, 1950-54. Mem. Tex. Soc. C.P.A.s, Tex. Savs. and Loan League, Am. Inst. C.P.A.s. Episcopalian. Clubs: Houston, Golfcrest Country. Contbr. articles to profl. jours. Home: Houston, Tex. Died Aug. 8, 2006.

MILLENDER-MCDONALD, JUANITA, congresswoman; b. Birmingham, Ala., Sept. 7, 1938; d. Shelly and Everlina (Dortch) M.; m. James McDonald III, July 26, 1955; children: Valeria, Angela, Sherryll, Michael, Roderick. BS, U. Redlands, Calif., 1980; MS in Edn., Calif. State U., LA, 1986; postgrad., U. So. Calif. Tchr., sch. adminstr., 1981—90; mem. city coun. City of Carson, Calif., 1990—92, mayor pro tempore Calif., 1991—92; manuscript editor Calif. State Dept. Edn., Sacramento; dir. gender equity programs L.A. Unified Sch. Dist.; mem. Calif. State Assembly from 55th dist., 1993—96, US Congress from 37th Calif dist., Washington, 1996—2007, small bus. com., transp. & infrastructure com., 1997, adminstrn. com., chmn., 2007; mem. congl. black caucus. Bd. dirs. S.C.L.C. Pvt. Industry Coun. Policy Bd., West Basin Mcpl. Water Dist., Cities Legis. League (vice chmn.; mem. Nat. Women's Polit. Caucus; mem. adv. bd. Comparative Ethnic Tng. U. So. Calif.; founder, exec. dir. Young Advocates So. Calif. Recipient Most Influential Black Americans, Ebony mag., 2006. Mem. NAACP, NEA, Nat. Assn. Minority Polit. Women, NAFE, Nat. Fedn. Bus. and Profl. Women, Assn. Calif. Sch. Adminstrs., Am. Mgmt. Assn., League African Women, L.A. World Affairs Coun., Nat. Female Execs., Nat. Coun. Jewish Women, Carson C. of C., Phi Delta Kappa. Democrat. Baptist. Died Apr. 22, 2007.

MILLER, BLANCHE RUTH, insurance agency executive; b. Perth Amboy, N.J., Mar. 18, 1920; d. Arthur and Regina (Klein) Berkowitz; m. Leonard D. Miller, May 13, 1952; children— Henry, Cary S., Eric R., Ilene C. A.B., N.J. Coll. Women, 1940. Fin. analyst Lefkowits-Elias Corp., New Brunswick, N.J., 1940-41, U.S. Govt. War Dept., Washington, 1941-42; office mgr. Otten, Liskey & Rhodes, Washington, 1942-44; advt. mgr. Nat. Indsl. Stores Assocs., Washington, 1944-46; office mgr. Tobacco Jobber Publs., N.Y.C., 1946-52; ins. mgr., agt. Miller Ins. Agy., Highland Park, N.J., 1952—. Mem. Middlesex County Ins. Women (treas. 1979-80). Democrat. Jewish. Home: Monroe Township, NJ. Died Apr. 1, 2006.

MILLER, CHARLES A., lawyer; b. Oakland, Calif., Feb. 7, 1935; s. Frank and Janice (Greene) M.; m. Jeanette Segal, Sept. 27, 1964; children: Jennifer Fay Haight, Charlotte Irene Marvin, Ira David. AB, U. Calif., Berkeley, 1955, LLB, 1958. Law clk. to assoc. justice U.S. Supreme Ct., Washington, 1958-59; assoc. Covington & Burling, Washington, 1959-67, ptnr., from 1967, chmn. mgmt. com., 1991-95. Mem. criminal justice coordinating bd., Washington, 1977-78; chmn. hearing com. Bd. on Profl. Responsibility, Washington, 1980-86. Pres. U. Calif. Alumni Club, Washington, 1962-70; mem. various coms. and adv. bds. Washington Pub. Sch. System, 1972-79; chmn. lawyers com. Washington Performing Arts Soc., 1984-86; bd. dirs. Dumbarton Concert Series, Washington, 1986—, chmn., 1990—; trustee U. Calif. Berkeley Found., 2001—, Fed. City Coun.; chair D.C. Citizens Welfare Transformation Com., 1996-97; co-chair Task Force on D.C. Governance, 1996-98; mem. Mayor's Commn. on Juvenile Justice, Washington, 2001-02. Mem. ABA, D.C. Bar Assn., U. Calif. Alumni Assn. (trustee 1989-92), Burning Tree Club (Bethesda, Md.). Democrat. Jewish. Died Mar. 14, 2007.

MILLER, DONALD SPENCER, geologist, educator; b. Ventura, Calif., June 12, 1932; s. Spencer Jacob and Marquerite Rachael (Williams) M.; m. Carolyn Margaret Losee, June 12, 1954; children: Sandra Louise, Kenneth Donald, Christopher Spencer. BA, Occidental Coll., 1954; MA, Columbia U., 1956, PhD, 1960. Asst. prof. Rensselaer Poly. Inst., Troy, N.Y., 1960-64, assoc. prof., 1964-69, prof., 1969-94, prof. emeritus, from 1994. Research assoc. geology Columbia U., 1960-63; research fellow geochemistry Calif. Inst. Tech., Pasadena, summer 1963; NSF Sci. Faculty fellow U. Bern, Switzerland, 1966-67; sci. guest prof. Max-Planck Inst. Nuclear Physics, Heidelberg, Fed. Republic Germany, 1977-78, vis. prof., summer 1979, guest scientist, Aug. 1979, 80, 81, 82; vis. prof. Isotope Geology Lab., U. Berne, summer 1979; participant NATO exchange program Demokritos Inst., Athens, Greece, Sept. 1983, 85; vis. rsch. fellow U. Melbourne, Australia, summer 1988; mem. nat. screening com. Inst. Internat. Edn., 1988-91. Pres., treas. Troy Rehab. and Improvement, Inc., 1968-74; mem. Troy Zoning Bd. Appeals, 1970-85 Fellow Geol. Soc. Am.; mem. Am. Geophys. Union, Geochem. Soc., Nat. Assn. Geol. Tchrs., Sigma Xi, Sigma Pi Sigma. Home: Delmar, NY. Died Dec. 26, 2005.

MILLER, EDWARD BOONE, lawyer, former federal official; b. Milw., Mar. 26, 1922; s. Edward A. and Myra (Munsert) M.; m. Anne Harmon Chase Phillips, Feb. 14, 1969 (dec. Dec. 2001); children by previous marriage: Barbara Miller Anderson, Ellen Miller Gerkens, Elizabeth Miller Lawhun, Thomas; stepchildren: T. Christopher Phillips, Sarah Phillips Parkhill. BA, U. Wis., 1942, LL.B., 1947; student, Harvard Bus. Sch., 1942-43. Bar: Wis. 1947, Ill. 1948. With firm Pope, Ballard, Shepard & Fowle, Chgo., 1947-51, 52-70, ptnr., 1953-70, 75-93, mng. partner, 1979-82, chmn. labor and employment law dept., 1975-76, 87-88, 90-91; of counsel Seyfarth Shaw, Chgo., 1994—2004; arbitrator and mediator Glenview, Ill., 2004—06. Mem. adv. com. Ctr. for Labor Mgmt. Dispute Resolution, Stetson U., 1984-2003, Inst. Indsl. Rels., Loyola U., 1987-91, Kent Pub. Employee Labor Rels. Conf., 1988-2006, Ill. Ednl. Labor Rels. Bd., 1988—; exec. asst. to industry mems. Regional Wage Stblzn. Bd., Chgo., 1951-52, industry mem., 1952; chmn. NLRB, Washington, 1970-74; mem. panel of labor law experts Commerce Clearing House, 1987-2006; dir. Chgo. Wheel & Mfg. Co., 1965-70, 75-88, Andes Candies, Inc., 1965-68, 75-80 Mem. Gov. Ill. Commn. Labor-Mgmt. Policies for Pub. Employees, 1966-67; chmn. Midwest Pension Conf., 1960-61; mem. labor relations com. Ill. C. of C., 1953-70; bd. dirs. Am. Found. Continuing Edn., 1960-69. Served to lt. USNR, 1943-46. Mem. ABA (NLRB practice and procedures com., internat. labor law com.), Ill. Bar Assn., Wis. Bar Assn., Chgo. Assn. Commerce and Industry (chmn. labor relations com. 1980-86, bd. dirs. 1987-97), Am. Employment Law Coun. (mem. adv. bd. 1995-2006), Coll. Labor and Employment Lawyers (emeritus mem.), Order of Coif. Clubs: Legal (Chgo.), Law (Chgo.), Cliff Dwellers ctr. (Chgo.), 1939-03. Republican. Congregationalist. Home: Zionsville, Pa. Died Nov. 10, 2006.

MILLER, FRANCIS MARION, chemist, educator; b. Central City, Ky., Dec. 28, 1925; s. David Green and Mary (Griffin) M.; m. Marjorie Rickman, Mar. 22, 1947; children: Daniel, Jennifer, John; m. Clara Whang, Feb. 26, 1971. BS, Western Ky. State Coll., 1946; PhD, Northwestern U., 1949; postdoctoral fellow, Harvard, 1948-49. Mem. faculty U. Md., College Park, 1949-68, prof., chmn. dept. pharm. chemistry, 1961-68; prof., chmn. dept. chemistry No. Ill. U., DeKalb, 1968-77, prof., 1977-91, prof. emeritus, from 1991, dir. univ. honors program, 1986-91. Guest research prof. Chemische Inst., Heldelberg, Germany, 1958-59; vis. prof. U. Baghdad, Iraq, 1963; vis. scholar U. Va., 1977; cons. to govt. and industry, 1955— Author: (with Ward C. Sumpter) Heterocyclic Compounds with Indole and Carbazole Systems, 1954, Chemistry: Structure and Dynamics, 1984. Mem. Am. Chem. Soc. (chmn. Md. sect. 1966), Sigma Xi. Unitarian Universalist. Patentee local anesthetic. Home: Silver Spring, Md. Died Feb. 20, 2006.

MILLER, FRANK WILLIAM, legal educator; b. Appleton, Wis., May 15, 1921; s. Frank Paul and Ruth Margaret (Arft) M.; m. Lucille Gloria Rinnan, Sept. 8, 1945; children: Deborah Lynn, Patrica Elizabeth. BA, U. Wis., 1946, LLB, 1948, SJD, 1954. Bar: Wis. 1948. Mem. faculty Washington U., St. Louis, 1948-91, Coles prof. criminal law and adminstrn., 1962-64, James Carr prof. criminal jurisprudence, 1964-91, prof. emeritus, from 1991; Dan Hopson Disting. prof. So. Ill. U., Carbondale, 1992. Summer vis. prof. law U. Ark., 1952, 54, 56, Stetson U., 1955, U. Wis., 1957, U. Tex., 1975, 85; vis. prof. law So. Ill. U. at Carbondale, 1973-74, summers 1976-81; chmn. round table council criminal law Assn. Am. Law Schs., 1961; chmn. Pub. Defender Adv. Com. St. Louis County, 1962 Author: (with A.C. Becht) Factual Causation in Negligence and Strict Liability Cases, 1961, Prosecution: The Decision to Charge a Suspect with a Crime, 1969; editor: (with R.O. Dawson, George E. Dix, Raymond I. Parnas) Criminal Justice Adminstration, 1976, 4th edit., 1991, (with Dawson, Dix, Parnas) The Police Function, 1982, 5th edit., 1991, Sentencing and The Correctional Process, 1976, The Juvenile Justice Process, 1976, 3d edit., 1985, The Mental Health Process, 1976, Prosecution and Adjudication, 1982, 4th edit., 1991. Served with AUS, 1942-45. Recipient citation for outstanding teaching Washington U. Alumni Fedn., 1965, Washington U. Law Alumni Assn., 1991. Mem. ABA, Am. Law Inst. (Guttmacher award 1977), Order of Coif. Democrat. Home: Saint Louis, Mo. Died Mar. 11, 2006.

MILLER, HAROLD WAYNE, information services specialist; b. Van Wert County, Ohio, Feb. 25, 1941; s. Dillon Eber and Lois Otto (Pollock) M. BA, Bowling Green State U., 1963; MA, U. Ky., 1964; MLS, Columbia U., 1967. Library asst. Equitable Life Assurance Soc., NYC, 1966-67; chief librarian Touche Ross & Co., NYC, 1967-82, head cen. files, 1975-82, mgr. info. services, from 1982. Mem. Spl. Libraries Assn. (various coms. 1981-88, dir. N.Y. chpt. 1984-86). Republican. Episcopalian. Avocation: english coronation history. Died July 3, 2007.

MILLER, ISABEL MOUNT, architect; b. Denton County, Tex., Mar. 27, 1916; d. Jess Wallace and Ellen Nancy (Donald) Mount; m. Tom Polk Miller, Aug. 10, 1947; children— Crispin Mount, Abigail Mount. B.A. with distinction, Rice Inst., 1936, B.S. in Architecture, 1937. Registered architect, Tex., Calif. Draftsman for various firms, 1937-49; pvt. practice as architect,

Calif., 1952-53; architect Mount-Miller, Denton, Tex., 1953—; mem. Tex. Solar Adv. Commn., Austin, 1980. Mem. editorial bd. The Voice, jour., 1971-73; advt. mgr., contbg. author Arkwork Rev., 1979-83; publs. designer LWV of Tex., 1981-83. Hdqrs. designer Denton County Democrats, 1956, 60, 64; pres. Denton Unitarian Fellowship, 1966-67. Recipient Community Arts Recognition award Greater Denton Arts Council, 1982; Mary Alice Elliott travel grantee Rice Archtl. Faculty, 1940. Mem. Tex. Solar Energy Soc. (bd. dirs. 1981-85), Am. Solar Energy Soc., Soc. Archtl. Historians, Nat. Trust for Hist. Preservation, ACLU, Denton LWV (pres. 1975-76), Fellowship of Reconciliation. Democrat. Avocations: crafts; gardening. Died Jan. 13, 2007.

MILLER, IVAN LAWRENCE, lawyer; b. Cleve., Feb. 2, 1914; s. Ralph and Sarah (Kichler) M. BA, Case Western Res. U., 1936, LL.B., JD, 1938; postgrad., Grad. Sch. Bus. Adminstrn., Harvard U., 1943, Inns of Ct., London, Eng., 1945. Bar: Ohio 1938, U.S. Supreme Ct. 1960. Pvt. practice, Cleve., from 1938; with Ziegler, Metzger & Miller, from 1968. Hon. consul of Belgium, Ohio, 1962—; legal adviser Brit. Consulate Gen., 1947-92, Can. Consulate Gen. and Trade Commn., 1964—; v.p., trustee, legal counsel Maison Francaise. Mem. bd. overseers Case Western Res. U., 1973-76. Maj. (QM) US Army, 1941-45. Decorated Bronze Star; Belgian Mil. Cross 1st Class, Knight Order Crown (Belgium); Civic medal First Class (Belgium); officer Order of Brit. Empire; Knight Order of Leopold (Belgium); chevalier dans l'Ordre des Palmes Academiques (France); chevalier dans l'Ordre Nat. du Merite (France); named Consul of Yr. in U.S., 1974; recipient Law Alumni Assn. award, 1986, Disting. Alumni award Case Western Res. U., 1990. Fellow Ohio State Bar Found. (life); mem. ABA, Fed. Bar Assn. (pres. Cleve. 1974-75), Ohio Bar Assn., Cleve. Bar Assn. (past trustee), English Speaking Union (Cleve. past pres., nat. bd. dirs.), Sch. of Law Alumni Assn. (past pres.), Nat. Alumni Coun. Case Western Res. U. (past pres.), Cleve. World Trade Assn., Soc. Benchers (chmn.), Union Club, Wig and Pen Club (Eng.), Link (Eng.), Rotary (Internat. award 1987), No. Ohio Golf Assn. (emeritus legal counsel 1988—). Home: Cleveland, Ohio. Died June 1, 2007.

MILLER, JACQUELINE K. THOMSON, educational consultant; b. Flora, Inc., March 5, 1940; d. Jack O. and Betty L. (Tolen) T.; children: Elizabeth Ann Miller-Frederick, Victoria Lynne. AS, Mankato State U., 1978; BA, Metro State U., St. Paul, 1980; MA, St. Mary's Coll., 1982. Instr. adult edn. Iowa Community Colls. and YMCA, 1970-75; dir. aquatics Faribault Family YMCA and Faribault Community Services, Minn., 1975-78; tech. sales/tng. rep. Ames div. Miles Labs., Mpls., 1978-80; med. lab. instr. Normandale Community Coll., Boomington, Minn., 1978-80; staff edn. coordinator St. Joseph's Hosp., Marshfield, Wis., 1981-84; dir. ednl. services Fairview Ridges Hosp., Burnsville, Minn., 1984-85; owner, prin. J. Miller Assocs., Burnsville, 1979—; presenter various profl. confs. including Nat. Whim Humor Confs., 1986-88. Developer wellness program Life Styling, 1979, mobile fitness test ctr. Health on Wheels, 1982; author-dir. video programs Body Mechanics, 1982. Chmn. Girl Scouts, Kokomo, Ind., 1964-69; vol. swim instr. ARC, Corning, Iowa, 1970-75, Faribault, Minn., 1975-78. Recipient Traveling Art awards Ia. State Lending Library, Des Moines, Iowa, 1973-74; artist in residence Corning Community Schs., Iowa, 1972. Mem. Mpls. C. of C., Burnsville C. of C., Am. Soc. Tng. and Devel. (bd. dirs. Central Wis. 1982-83, mem. career devel. task force So. Minn. 1986, mem. program com. 1985-86, chair conf. com. 1987), Nat. Wellness Assn. (nat. membership chmn. 1983-85), Am. Soc. Health Edn. and Tng., Am. Soc. Med. Technologists, Am. Soc. Clin. Pathologists, Nat. Assn. Female Execs., Delta Kappa Gamma. Episcopalian. Avocations: art; swimming; gardening; sailing. Died Sept. 7, 2006.

MILLER, JAMES CLIFFORD, III, economist; b. Atlanta, June 25, 1942; s. James Clifford and Annie (Moseley) M.; m. Demaris Humphries, Dec. 22, 1961; children: Katrina Demaris, John Felix, Sabrina Louise. BBA, U. Ga., 1964; PhD in Econs., U. Va., 1969; LLD (hon.), U. of Pacific, 1987; PhD (hon.), Kennesaw Coll., 1988. Asst. prof. Ga. State U., Atlanta, 1968-69; economist U.S. Dept. Transp., Washington, 1969-72; assoc. prof. econs. Tex. A&M U., College Station, 1972-74; economist U.S. Coun. Econ. Advs., Washington, 1974-75; asst. dir. U.S. Council Wage and Price Stability, Washington, 1975-77; resident scholar Am. Enterprise Inst., 1977-81; adminstr. Office Info. and Regulatory Affairs, Office Mgmt. and Budget and exec. dir. Presdl. Task Force on Regulatory Relief, Washington, 1981; chmn. FTC, Washington, 1981-85; dir. Office Mgmt. and Budget, Washington, 1985-88; disting. fellow, chmn., counsellor Citizens for a Sound Economy, 1988—2002; disting. fellow Ctr. for Study of Pub. Choice George Mason U., 1988—2002; sr. fellow Hoover Instn., from 1988. Pres., chmn. bd. Econ. Impact Analysts, Inc., 1978-02; chmn. or chmn. emeritus CapAnalysis Group of Howrey, 2002-06; bd. govs. US Postal Svc., 2003-, chmn., 2005-; sr. advisor Blackwell Sanders Peper Martin, 2006-. Author: Why the Draft?: The Case for a Volunteer Army, 1968, Economic Regulation of Domestic Air Transport: Theory and Policy, 1974, Perspectives on Federal Transportation Policy, 1975, Benefit-Cost Analyses of Social Regulation: Case Studies from the Council on Wage and Price Stability, 1979, Reforming Regulation, 1980, The Federal Trade Commission: The Political Economy of Regulation, 1987, The Economist as Reformer, 1989, Fix the U.S. Budget: Urgings of an "Abominable No-Man", 1994, Monopoly Politics, 1999. Candidate for Rep. nomination for U.S. Senate for Va., 1994, 96. Thomas Jefferson fellow, 1965-66, DuPont fellow, 1966-67, Ford Found. fellow, 1967-68. Mem. Am. Econ. Assn., Pub. Choice Soc., So. Econ. Assn. (exec. com. 1980-81, v.p. 1990-91), Adminstrv. Conf. U.S. (vice chmn. 1987-88). Republican. Baptist. Home: Sperryville, Va. Died Jan. 15, 2007.

MILLER, JOHN HENRY, retired clergyman; b. Ridgeway, SC, Dec. 3, 1917; s. Fletcher and Frances Helo (Turner) Miller; m. Bernice Frances Dillard, June 27, 1945; children: George Frederick, John Henry. BA, Livingstone Coll., 1941; MDiv, Hood Theol. Sem., 1945; postgrad., Hartford Theol. Sem. Found., 1954. Ordained to ministry AME Zion Ch., 1940, consecrated bishop 1972. Bishop 10th Dist., 1972—80, 8th Dist., Dallas, 1980—84, 7th Dist., 1984—88, 5th Dist, 1988; ret. Mem. Gov.'s Advocacy Com. on Children and Youth, from 1985; bd. AME Zion Ch. Trustee Livingstone Coll.; former chmn. bd. Lomax-Hannon Jr. Coll.; chmn. bd. Black Reps. N.C., from 1985; chmn. hon. degrees com. L.C. Mem.: NAACP, World Meth. Counc., Elks, Masons, Alpha Phi Alpha. Died May 23, 2006.

MILLER, MAURICE JAMES, lawyer; b. Barron, Wis., May 14, 1926; s. James Martin and Fern (Harvey) M.; m. Marguerite Joyce Mielke, Nov. 1, 1952; children: Maureen J., Mark J. BBA, U. Wis., 1951, JD, 1955. Bar: Ill., Wis. 1955, C.P.A., Wis. Assoc. Sidley & Austin, Chgo., 1955-62, ptnr., 1963-90, counsel, from 1991. Trustee William H. Miner Found., 1994—. With U.S. Army, 1944-46. Mem. ABA, Chgo. Bar Assn., Phi Alpha Delta. Clubs: Chicago, Mid-Day. Republican. Methodist. Home: Deerfield, Ill. Died Jan. 29, 2006.

MILLER, MICHAEL E., reinsurance executive; b. Omaha, July 9, 1936; s. Cornelius Edward and Viginia Ann (Haines) M.; m. Billie Ann Bosch, June 8, 1957; children: Stephen, Ann, Laurie, Elizabeth, Daniel, Margaret, Bryan. LLB, Creighton U., 1960. Claims rep. State Farm Mut. Ins. Co., Omaha, 1960-62; corp. sec. Imperial Casualty Co., Omaha, 1962-68; sr. v.p. Employers Reins., Overland Park, Kans., from 1968. Mem. Nat. Assn. Ind. Insurers (chmn. reins. com. 1979—), Self Ins. Assn. Ill. (bd. dirs. 1987—). Republican. Home: Barrington, Ill. Died Dec. 11, 2005.

MILLER, ROBERT BRANSON, JR., retired newspaper publisher; b. Battle Creek, Mich., Aug. 10, 1935; s. Robert Branson and Jean (Leonard) M.; m. Pattricia E. Miller; children: Melissa Ann, Gregory Allen, Jennifer Lynn, Jeffrey William. Grad., Hotchkiss Sch., Lakeville, Conn., 1953; BA, Mich. State U., 1959. Advt. salesman State Jour., Lansing, Mich., 1959-61, circulation sales rep., 1961-62, reporter, 1962-65, nat. advt. mgr., 1965-66; asst. to pub. Idaho Statesman, Boise, 1966-69, pub., 1969—71, Daily Olympian, Olympia, Wash., Battle Creek Enquirer, 1979-90, pub., chmn., 1980—91. Bd. dirs. Battle Creek chpt. ARC; advisor Big Bros./Big Sisters; sr. advisor United Way; trustee Miller Found., Battle Creek, 1963—. With USNR, 1956-58. Home: Battle Creek, Mich. Died Mar. 5, 2007.

MILLER, ROBERT CARL, retired library director; b. May 9, 1936; m. Jeanne M. Larson. BS in History and Philosophy, Marquette U., 1958; MS in Am. History, U. Wis., 1962; MA in Libr. Sci., U. Chgo., 1966. Head telephone reference Library of Congress, Wash., 1959-60; reference librarian Marquette U., Milw., 1960-62, acquisition librarian, 1962-66; head tech. services/librarian Parsons Coll., Fairfield, Iowa, 1966-68; head acquisitions dept. U. Chgo. Library, 1968-71, assoc. dir (reader services), 1971-73; assoc dir (gen. service) U. Chgo., 1973-75; dir. of libraries U. Mo., St. Louis, 1975-78; dir of libraries U. of Notre Dame, Ind., 1978-97, ret. Ind., 1997. Vis. prof. IBIN-U. Warsaw, Poland, 1992, 93, 97, 2000, 02. Contbr. articles to profl. jours. Fellow Woodrow Wilson Found. (sr.), Coun. on Libr. Resources; mem. ALA, Polish Inst. of Arts and Letters of Am. Roman Catholic. Home: Chisago City, Minn. Died Oct. 8, 2006.

MILLER, ROBERT CLARK, computer company executive; b. NYC, Sept. 23, 1943; s. Samuel A. and Grace (Friedlander) M.; m. Barbara Ann Peer, Jan. 17, 1981; children by previous marriage: Brian, Jonathan, Jeremy. BS in Engring., Bucknel U., 1965; MS, Stanford U., 1966. Registered profl. engr., N.Y. Lab dir. IBM, Armonk, N.Y., 1966-81; v.p. tech. Data General Corp., Westboro, Mass., 1981-82, sr. v.p., from 1982. Dir. Mass. Tech. Park, Boston, 1982— Contbr. articles to profl. jours.; patentee in field. Bd. dirs. Bucknell Sch. Engring. Mem. IEEE (sr.), Mass. Soc. Profl. Engrs. Home: Weston, Mass. Died Aug. 23, 2006.

MILLER, ROBERT H., university extension director; b. Fremont, Wis., Sept. 19, 1933; married, 1957; 3 children. BS, Wis. State U., 1958; MS, U. Minn., 1961, PhD in Soil Microbiology, 1964. From asst. to full prof. agronomy Ohio State U., 1964-81; head and prof. dept. soil sci. N.C. State U., 1982-89; dean coll. of resource devel. U. R.I., Kingston, 1989-95, dir. coop. extension, from 1995. Fulbright lectr., 1974-75. Fellow AAAS, Am. Soc. Agronomy (bd. dirs. 1978-81), Soil Sci. Soc. Am. (bd. dirs. 1978-81); mem. Am. Soc. Microbiology, Sigma Xi. Achievements include research on plant rhizosphere microorganisms and their interactions with plants; ecology and physiology of Rhizobium japonicum; chemistry of soil organic matter; recycling of organic wastes in soil; international development. Died Apr. 7, 2007.

MILLER, ROBERT LEON, public relations consultant; b. Gothenburg, Nebr., Mar. 9, 1942; s. Cleo Robert and Inez Bell (Bullock) M. Student U. Nebr., 1960-61, U. Alaska, 1965, U. Hawaii, 1979. Reporter two newspapers, Nebr., 1961-66; polit. reporter, columnist, editor Anchorage Times, 1966-69; press sec. Alaska Gov. Keith H. Miller, Juneau, 1966-69; supr. pub. relations Alyeska Pileline Service Co., Anchorage, 1970-71, mgr. pub. affairs, 1971-77; communications coordinator for Alaska Lands, Office of Gov. Jay S. Hammond, Juneau, 1979-80; freelance pub. relations cons., Anchorage, 1981—. Active community affairs; chmn. Alaska State Council on Arts; campaign mgr. Stephen C. Cowper for Gov., 1982. Served with U.S. Army, 1964-66. Mem. Pub. Relations Sco. Am. Episcopalian. Died Mar. 29, 2006.

MILLER, ROBERT STEVENS, JR., (STEVE MILLER), automotive company executive; b. Portland, Oreg., Nov. 4, 1941; s. Robert Stevens and Barbara (Weston) Miller; m. Margaret Rose Kyger, Nov. 9, 1966 (dec. Aug. 11, 2006); children: Christopher John, Robert Stevens, Alexander Lamont. AB with distinction, Stanford U., 1963; LLB, Harvard U., 1966; MBA, Stanford U., 1968. Bar: Calif. 1966. Fin. analyst Ford Motor Co., Dearborn, Mich., 1968-71, spl. studies mgr. Mexico City, 1971-73; dir. fin. Ford Asia-Pacific, Inc., Melbourne, Australia, 1974-77, Ford Motor Co., Caracas, Venezuela, 1977-79; v.p., treas. Chrysler Corp., Detroit, 1980-81, exec. v.p. fin., 1981-90, vice chmn., 1990-92; sr. ptnr. James D. Wolfensohn, Inc., NYC, 1992-93; chmn. Morrison Knudsen, 1995—96; chmn., CEO Waste Management, 1997—99, Fed. Mogul Corp., Smithfield, Mich., 1999—2000, 2004—05, non exec. chmn., 2001; chmn., CEO Bethlehem Steel Corp., Pa., 2001—03, Delphi Corp., Troy, Mich., 2005—06, exec. chmn., from 2007. Home: Sunriver, Oreg. Died Aug. 12, 2007.

MILLER, ROGER ERVIN, chemistry professor; b. Kitchener, Ont., Can., July 23, 1952; came to U.S., 1985. BSc, U. Waterloo, Can., 1975, MSc, 1977, PhD, 1980. Tchg. asst. U. Waterloo, 1975-79; rsch. fellow Australian Nat. U., Canberra, 1980-84; assoc. prof. U. N.C., Chapel Hill, 1985-88, prof., from 1988, John B. Carroll prof. chemistry, 1996, vice chair dept. chemistry, 1989-94. Vis. scientist Max-Planck Inst. for Stromungsforschung, Gottingen, Germany, Hahn-Meitner Inst. for Kernforschung, Berlin, 1983; mem. editl. adv. bd. McGraw-Hill Series in Advanced Chemistry. Recipient W.B. Pearson medal in physics, 1981, Kenan Leave award, 1994, William F. Meggers award Optical Soc. Am., 2000; NRC grad. scholar, 1976, Ont. grad. scholar, 1978; Alfred P. Sloan rsch. fellow, 1987, Alexander von Humboldt-Stiftung Rsch. fellow Max Planck Inst. for Stromungsforschung, Gottingen, 1995. Fellow Am. Phys. Soc. (vice chmn. divsn. phys. chemistry 2001, Earle K. Plyler prize for molecular spectroscopy 1997); mem. Am. Chem. Soc., Am. Geophys. Union. Died Nov. 6, 2005.

MILLER, STANLEY LLOYD, chemistry and biochemistry professor; b. Oakland, Calif., Mar. 7, 1930; s. Nathan Harry and Edith (Levy) M. BS, U. Calif., Berkeley, 1951; PhD, U. Chgo., 1954. F.B. Jewett fellow Cal-Tech., Pasadena, Calif., 1954; asst. prof. Coll. Physicians and Surgeons, NYC, 1955-60; from asst. to full prof. U. Calif., San Diego, 1960—2007. Mem. Am. Chem. Soc., Am. Soc. Biol. Chemists, Nat. Acad. Sci., Internat. Soc. Study of the Origin of Life (pres. 1986-89). Home: Livermore, Calif. Died May 20, 2007.

MILLER, THOMAS W., computer company executive; b. Oakland, Calif., Nov. 6, 1934; s. Walter F. and Audrey (O'Brien) M.; m. Jacquelyn Jolley, June 15, 1957; children— Laurie, Sheri BS in Chemistry, U.Calif.-Berkeley. Vice-pres. profl. services Control Data Corp., Mpls., 1976-77, v.p. U.S. mktg. ops., 1977-79, v.p. edn. div., 1979-81, v.p. bus. devel. div., 1981-83, exec. v.p. mktg., 1983-85, pres. tech. support services group, 1985-86, v.p. European ops., from 1986. Dir. ETA Systems, Inc., St. Paul, The Source, McLean, Va. Bd. dirs. Assn. Computing Machinery Found., N.Y.C., 1984—. Served to 1st lt. U.S. Army 1957-60; Germany Mem. Computer and Bus. Equipment Mfrs. Assn. (dir. 1984—), EDUCOM Republican. Methodist. Avocations: motorhomes; boating; photography; fishing. Died Oct. 9, 2006.

MILLER, WILLIAM LEE, JR., minister; b. Mammoth Spring, Ark., Dec. 27, 1926; s. William L. and Janie Katherine (Murrell) M.; m. Marion Evelyn O'Neal, Mar. 23, 1947 (div 1976); children: Georgia Katherine Miller Beach, William Lee III; m. Judith Ann Bell, Nov. 28, 1977 (dec. July 1997); m Delores Bryan, Dec. 27, 1998. AB, Phillips U., 1950, LittD 1968; postgrad., U. Ark., 1951-52, Tex. Christian U., 1958, U. Ky., 1961; BD, Lexington Theol. Sem., 1961, MDiv, 1997 Ordained to ministry Christian Ch. (Disciples of Christ), 1950 Pastor 1st Christian Ch., Rogers, Ark., 1952-59, Rogers Heights Christian Ch., Tulsa, 1961-62; v.p. Bd. Higher Edn., Indpls. 1962-68; pres. Bd. Higher Edn. Christian Ch. (Disciples of Christ), 1968-77; v.p. devel. Nat. City Christian Ch. Corp. Washington, 1977-82; upper Midwest regional min., pres. Christian Ch. (Disciples of Christ), Des Moines, 1982-93; pres. Miller Devel. Assoc. Dir. Christian Ch. Found., Indpls., 1968-77 84-93; trustee Bethany Coll., W.Va., 1972-85, Culver Stockton Coll., 1970-77, 82-94, Tougaloo Coll., Jackson, Miss., 1970-76 Christian Theol. Sem., Indpls., 1987-94. Author: Vision with Passion, A Church history of the Christian Church (Disciples of Christ, 2004. Precinct committeeman Dem. Party, Indpls., 1968 72; mem. Reagan First Inaugural Religious Com.; bd. dris. St Louis Christian Home, 1956-59; chmn. Coop. Coll. Registry Washington, 1963-70; mem. Disciples of Christ Ch., Disciple Soc. for Faith & Reason; bd. dirs., exec. com. Christian Ch D.C., N.C., 1995-98; pres. Friends of Dare County (N.C.) Librs. 1997-99; v.p. North Dare County Ministerial Assn., 1998-99 Mem. Disciples of Christ Hist. Soc., Coun. Christian Unity (exec. com. 1968-77), Nat. Evangelitic Assn. (bd. dirs. 1983 86), Am. Assn. Higher Edn., Masons, KT, NAACP, Sigma Chi Am. Legion, Interfaith Alliance, Amnesty Internat., Sierra Club Mem. Christian Ch. (Disciples Of Christ). Died Feb. 11, 2006

MILLIMET, JOSEPH ALLEN, retired lawyer; b. West Orange, NJ, July 23, 1914; s. Morris and Dorothy (McBlain) M. m. Elizabeth Gray Gingras, Jan. 10, 1942 (dec. 1995); children Madlyn Ann (Mrs. Angus Deming), Lisa Gray, Rebecca Allen Peter Joseph (dec.). AB, Dartmouth Coll., 1936; LLB, Yale U 1939; LLD (hon.), U. N.H., 1992. Bar: N.H. 1939. Pvt. practice Concord and Manchester, N.H.; sr. ptnr. Devine, Millimet, Stahl & Branch, and predecessors (now Devine Millimet & Branch), Manchester, 1947-93, ret., 1993; with FCC, 1941-42. Mem N.H. Bd. Bar Examiners, 1953-61, legislative counsel to, gov N.H., 1963-66; chmn. Commn. to Revise N.H. Constn., 1964 74, 84; mem. Commn. Uniform State Laws, 1965-73. With USCG, 1942-45. Fellow Am. Coll. Trial Lawyers; mem. N.H Bar Assn. (pres. 1962-63), ABA. Democrat. Home: Manchester NH. Died Nov. 3, 2006.

MILLING, MARCUS EUGENE, SR., geologist; b Galveston, Tex., Oct. 8, 1938; s. Robert Richardson and Leonor Mildred (Currey) M.; m. Sandra Ann Dunlay, Sept. 11, 1959; child, Marcus Eugene Jr. BS in Geology, Lamar U., 1961; MS in Geology, U. Iowa, 1964, PhD in Geology, 1968. Cert. petroleum geologist. Rsch. geologist Exxon Prodn. Rsch. Co., Houston 1968-76; prodn. geologist Exxon Co. U.S.A., Kingsville, Tex 1976-78, dist. exptl. geologist New Orleans, 1978-80; mgr. geo rsch. Arco Oil and Gas Co., Plano, Tex., 1980-86, chie geologist Dallas, 1986-87; assoc. dir. Bur. Econ. Geology U Tex., Austin, 1987-92; exec. dir. Am. Geol. Inst., Alexandria Va., from 1992. Vice-chmn. Offshore Tech. Conf., Dalla 1984-87; dir. Geosci. Inst. for Oil and Gas Recovery Rsch Austin, 1988-91. NSF fellow, 1966. Fellow Geol. Soc. Am (councilor 1986-89); mem. Am. Assn. Petroleum Geologists, Soc. Petroleum Engrs., Am. Inst. Profl. Geologists (Ben H. Parker Meml. medal 1997), Blue Key, Sigma Xi. Died Oct. 17, 2006.

MILLS, CAROL MARGARET, public relations executive, consultant; b. Salt Lake City, Aug. 31, 1943; d. Samuel Lawrence and Beth (Neilson) M. BS magna cum laude, U. Utah, 1965. With W.S. Hatch Co., Woods Cross, Utah, 1965-87, corp. sec., 1970-87, traffic mgr., 1969-87, dir. publicity, 1974-87, cons. various orgns., from 1988. Bd. dirs. Intermountain Tariff Bur. Inc., 1978-88, chmn., 1981-82, 1986-87; bd. dirs. Mountainwest Venture Group. Fund raiser March of Dimes, Am. Cancer Soc., Am. Heart Assn.; active senatorial campaign, 1976, gubernatorial campaign, 1984, 88, congl. campaign, 1990, 92, 94, vice chair voting dist., 1988-90, congl. campaign, 1994, chmn. 1990-92, chmn. party caucus legis. dist.; witness transp. com. Utah State Legislature, 1984, 85; apptd. by gov. to bd. trustees Utah Tech. Fin. Corp., 1986—, corp. sec., mem. exec. com., 1988—; mem. expdn. to Antaractica, 1996, Titanic '96 expdn.; mem. Iceland and Greenland expdn., 2001; mem. Pioneer Theatre Guld, 1985--. Recipient Svc. awards W.S. Hatch Co., 1971, 80; VIP chpt. Easter Seal Telethon, 1989, 90, Outstanding Vol. Svc. award Easter Seal Soc. Utah, 1989, 90. Mem. Nat. Tank Truck Carriers, Transp. Club Salt Lake City, Am. Trucking Assn. (mem. pub. rels. coun.), Utah Motor Transport Assn. (bd. dirs. 1982-88), Internat. Platform Assn., Traveler's Century Club, Titanic Internat., Beta Gamma Sigma, Phi Kappa Phi, Phi Chi Theta. Home: Kamiah, Idaho. Died Jan. 21, 2007.

MILLS, RALPH JOSEPH, JR., English language educator, poet; b. Chgo., Dec. 16, 1931; s. Ralph Joseph and Eileen (McGuire) M.; m. Helen Daggett Harvey, Nov. 25, 1959; children: Natalie, Julian, Brett. BA, Lake Forest Coll., 1954; MA, Northwestern U., 1956, PhD, 1963. Tchr. English Am. lit. U., Chgo., 1959-65; prof. English U. Ill. at Chgo., from 1965. Author: Theodore Roethke, 1963, Contemporary American Poetry, 1965, Richard Eberhart, 1966, Edith Sitwell, 1966, Kathleen Raine, 1967, Creation's Very Self, 1969, Door To The Sun-Poems, 1974, Cry of The Human, 1975, A Man to His Shadow: Poems, 1975, Night Road/Poems, 1978, Living with Distance: Poems, 1979, With No Answer: Poems, 1980, March Light (poems), 1983, For a Day (poems), 1985, Each Branch: Poems 1976-1985, 1986, A While (poems), 1989. Editor: On the Poet and His Craft-Selected Prose of Theodore Roethke, 1965, Selected Letters of Theodore Roethke, 1968, The Notebooks of David Ignatow, 1973, Open Between Us: Essays, Reviews and Interviews of David Ignatow, 1980. Recipient prize for poetry Soc. Midland Authors, 1980; awards for poetry Ill. Arts Council, 1979, 83, 84; Carl Sandburg prize for poetry, 1984. English Speaking Union fellow, 1956-57 Mem. Phi Beta Kappa, Phi Kappa Phi. Roman Catholic. Died Aug. 18, 2007.

MILLS, ROBERT GAIL, retired physicist; b. Effingham, Ill., Jan. 20, 1924; s. Gail A. and Helen June (Taylor) M.; m. Mary Addie Steer, May 25, 1946; children: Susan Elizabeth, Robert William. BS in Engring., Princeton U., 1944; MA, U. Mich., 1947; PhD, U. Calif., Berkeley, 1952. Rsch. assoc. U. Mich., Ann Arbor, 1946-47, U. Calif., 1950-52; Rockfeller Found. nat. sch. fellow U. Zurich, Switzerland, 1952-54; instr. elec. engring. Princeton (N.J.) U., 1943-44, rsch. assoc., 1945-46, rsch. assoc., mem. profl. rsch. staff, 1954-74, prof., 1975-87; ret. 1987. Chief petty officer USNR, 1944-45. Fellow IEEE, Am. Nuclear Soc.; mem. Am. Phys. Soc., Plasma and Nuclear Scis. Soc. (Centennial medal 1974, Disting. Svc. award 1975). Home: Princeton, NJ. Died Dec. 5, 2005.

MILLS, ROBERT LEE, retired academic administrator; b. Erlanger, Ky., Nov. 13, 1916; s. John Clifford and Dixie Lee (Morris) M.; m. Mildred Sizer, June 24, 1942 (div.); children: Robert Lee, Dixie Louise, Barbara Jean. AB in Math. and Physics, U. Ky., 1938, MA in Ednl. Adminstrn, 1941, Ed.D., 1951; LLD, William Jewell Coll., 1971. Tchr. Covington (Ky.) pub. schs., 1938-41; head hydraulics br. Air Force Tech. Sch., Lincoln, Nebr., 1942-44; mem. supervisory staff electromagnetic plant Oak Ridge, Tenn., 1944-48; rsch. asst. U. Ky., Lexington, 1948-51, dean admissions, registrar, 1954-57; dir. sch., head bur. adminstrn. and fin. Ky. Dept. Edn., 1951-54; chmn. dept. ednl. adminstrn. U. Tex., Austin, 1957-59; pres. Georgetown (Ky.) Coll., 1959-78, chancellor, 1978-86, ret., 1986, pres. emeritus, from 1987. Exec. sec. Ky. Adv. Commn. Ednl. Policy, 1952-54; v.p. Ky. Assn. Colls. and Secondary Schs., 1962-63, exec. com., 1959-64, pres., 1963-64; chmn. exec. com. Ky. Ind. Coll. Found.; mem. Ky. Commn. on Higher Edn., 1967-70, Ky. Govt. Council, 1968-72; adviser Texas Assn. Sch. Bds., 1957-59 Contbr. articles to profl. jours. Cons. Pres.' Com., White House Conf. Edn., 1955; mem. Ky. Devel. Council, 1961-65, Ky. Constn. Revision Assembly, 1964-66. Recipient Distinguished Alumni award U. Ky., 1963, Centennial award, 1964 Mem. Nat., Ky. edn. assns., Newcomen Soc., So. Assn. Bapt. Colls. (pres. 1965-66), Bapt. World Alliance (mem. exec. com. 1965-70, chmn. men's dept. 1965-67), So. Assn. Colls. and Schs. (commn. on colls. 1971-77), Kappa Delta Pi, Phi Delta Kappa, Phi Kappa Tau. Lodges: Kiwanis. Democrat. Baptist. Home: Cincinnati, Ohio. Died Jan. 16, 2006.

MILTON, ARTHUR, insurance company executive, writer; b. NYC, June 7, 1922; Established Arthur Milton Orgn., 1945. Author: (book) How Your Life Insurance Policies Rob You, Life Insurance Stocks: The Modern Gold Rush, How to Get a Dollar's Value for a Dollar Spent, You Are Worth a Fortune, Will Inflation Destroy America?, A Nation Saved: Thank You President Reagan, numerous other books and articles. Nat. chmn. Citizens' Com. U.S. Mission to UN; mem. Pres.'s Com. Mem.: Life Ins. Agy. Mgmt. Assn. (dir. Atlantic alumni), Gen. Ins. Brokers Assn. (past dir.). Died Mar. 25, 2006.

MINADAKIS, NICHOLAS JOHN, library director; b. Island of Chios, Greece, Jan. 22, 1924; s. John N. and Charikleia (Mavroudis) M.; came to U.S., 1958, naturalized, 1971; Proficiency in English, English Lang. Inst. U. Mich., 1957; B.A., Boston U., 1962; M.L.S., Simmons Coll., 1964; m. Irene Lydelis, 1976; children— John Nicholas, Demetris Nicholas. Sales mgr. United Africa Co. Ltd., Ghana, West Africa, 1953-57; tchr. modern Greek lang., Assumption Sch., Somerville, Mass., 1958-62; library intern Baker Library Harvard, 1962-64; library dir. Hellenic Coll., 1964-68; library dir. Chelsea (Mass.) Pub. Library, 1969—; corporator Atlantic Bank of Chelsea and Revere (Mass.), 1972-78, trustee, 1978-81; dir. Atlantic div. Boston Five Cents Savs. Bank, 1982—, community advisor, 1983—. Served with Greek Armed Forces, 1951-53. Mem. Am., New Eng., Mass. library assns., Men Librarian's Club, Center of Byzantine and Neohellenic Studies of Belmont (Mass.). Mem. Greek Orthodox Ch. Clubs: Hellicon, Pancretan (Boston), Rotary. Contbr. articles to profl. jours. Home: Wells, Maine. Died Nov. 11, 2006.

MINARIK, JON, marketing executive; b. Cleve., Mar. 9, 1947; s. Paul Francis and Alice Mary (Mann) M.; m. Terri Sue Butler, June 30, 1973 (div.); children: Anne, Michael. B.A. in Communications, Ohio U., 1973; postgrad. No. Va. Sch. Law, 1978-80. Dir. congl. affairs Pub. Service Research Council, Vienna, Va., 1976-78; account exec. The Viguerie Co., Falls Church, Va., 1978-79; dir. direct mail Connally for Pres., Arlington, Va., 1979-80; pres. Jon Minarik & Assocs., Oakton, Va., 1980—89, founding ptnr., BrooksMann Inc., 1989-2007; Served with U.S. Army, 1966-68. Mem. Direct Mktg. Assn. Republican. Roman Catholic. Died Apr. 4, 2007.

MINEAR, PAUL SEVIER, minister, religion educator; b. Mt. Pleasant, Iowa, Feb. 17, 1906; s. George L. and Nellie (Sevier) M.; m. Gladys O. Hoffman, June 14, 1929; children: Paul Lawrence, Richard Hoffman, Anita Sue Minear Fahrni. AB, Iowa Wesleyan U., 1927, LL.D., 1942; B.D., Garrett Bibl. Inst., 1930, D.D., 1981; A.M., Northwestern U., 1930; PhD, Yale U., 1932; Th.D., U. Utrecht, 1962; LL.D., U. Notre Dame, 1966; D.D., Aberdeen U., 1974. Asst. prof. Hawaii Sch. Religion, Honolulu, 1933-34; prof. N.T., Garrett Bibl. Inst., 1934-44; ordained to ministry Meth. Ch., 1938, Congl. Christian Ch., 1944; Norris prof. N.T., Andover Newton Theol. Sch., 1944-56; prof. N.T., Yale U. Div. Sch., 1956-71, Winkley prof. Bibl. theology, 1958-71, dir. grad. studies in religion, 1959-61; vice rector Ecumenical Inst. for Advanced Theol. Study, Jerusalem, 1970-72; dir. faith and order World Council Chs., 1961-63; vis. prof. Episcopal Theol. Sch., 1953, Cath. U., 1975, United Theol. Coll., Vancouver, 1976, Princeton Theol. Sem., 1977, Brite Div. Sch., 1979, Emory U. Sch. Theology, 1980, Phillips U., 1986. Hoover lectr. U. Chgo., 1957; Dudleian lectr. Harvard U., 1954; Fulbright lectr. U. Utrecht, 1958-59; Stone lectr. Princeton Theol. Sem., 1967; Shaffer lectr. Yale U., 1974; Gheens lectr. Louisville Bapt. Sem., 1980; Kantonen lectr. Trinity Luth. Theol. Sem., 1982; mem. Faith and Order Commn., 1952-74, chmn., 1963-67; mem. Standard Bible Translation Com., 1960-89. Author: An Introduction to Paul, 1936, And Great Shall Be Your Reward, 1941, Eyes of Faith, 1946, The Choice, 1948, The Kingdom and the Power, 1950, Christian Hope and the Second Coming, 1954, Jesus and His People, 1956, Horizons of Christian Community, 1959, Images of the Church in the New Testament, 1960, The Gospel of Mark, 1962, I Saw a New Earth, 1969, The Obedience of Faith, 1971, Commands of Christ, 1972, I Pledge Allegiance, 1975, To Heal and To Reveal, 1976, To Die and To Live, 1977, New Testament Apocalyptic, 1981, Matthew: The Teacher's Gospel, 1982, John: The Martyr's Gospel, 1984, Death Set to Music, 1987, The God of the Gospels, 1988, Christians and the New Creation, 1994, The Golgotha Earthquake, 1995; co-author: Kierkegaard and the Bible, 1953, Pentecost 2, 1981; editor: Nature of the Unity We Seek, 1957, Faith and Order Findings, 1963. Home: Guilford, Conn. Died Feb. 22, 2007.

MINISCE, RICHARD ANTHONY, real estate corporation officer; b. Rochester, N.Y., Sept. 16, 1942; s. Anthony J. and Albertine C. (Elman) M.; m. Louise J. Schliessman, Aug. 14, 1971 (div. 1986); children— Heather, Holly, Courtney, Anthony. B.S. in Sociology, St. John Fisher Coll., 1964; M.A. in Sociology, Boston Coll., 1968; postgrad. New Sch. for Social Research, 1969-72, Wash. State U., 1978-79. Asst. to area supr. Bur. Recreation, Rochester, N.Y., 1961-64; instr. sociology Kings Coll., Wilkes Barre, Pa., 1965; asst. prof. St. Lawrence U., Canton, N.Y., 1966-68; prof. Suffolk County Community Coll., Selden, N.Y., 1969-81; dean of instrn. Tillamook Bay Community Coll., Bay City, Oreg., 1981—; pres. RAM Assocs., Mgmt. Services, 1983—; chief exec. officer Diversified Ventures Enterprise Group, Inc.; pres. Tillamook Burner Co. Inc.; chief of security, policeman, park ranger. reviewer coll. texts; cons. criminologist, sociologist. Chmn. bd. dirs., Tillamook County Vol. Bur., 1983-84; fireman, mem budget com. Bay City Vol. Fire Dept.; treas. Clatsop-Tillamook Fire Dept. Adv. Group; sr. warden, vestry St. Albans Ch., Tillamook, Oreg., 1983-84; chmn. personnel com. Bay City City Council, 1983—. Named Jaycee of Yr. Canton, N.Y., 1966; recipient Kiwanis Ruby K award, 1982. Mem. Oreg. Council Instructional Adminstrs., Nat. Council Community Services and Continuing Edn., Oreg. Assn. Community Edn. Deans and Dirs., Am. Sociol. Assn., Am. Vocat. Assn., Oreg. Assn. Criminal Justice Educators, Am. Assn. Community and Jr. Colls., Nat. Council Local Adminstrs., Oreg. Community Edn. Assn., On the Green Condominium Bd. (dir. 1989). Club: Tillamook Kiwanis (dir. 1983-84). Home: Bellevue, Wash. Died July 15, 2007.

MINOR, CHARLES LANNCELOT, surgeon; b. Washington, May 19, 1923; s. John and Mildred Angevine (Truslow) M.; m. Lois Beverley Heilner, Jan. 25, 1958; children— Ellen Pierrepont, Charles L. III, Lucy Landon, Alice Angevine. Student, U. Va., 1941-43; M.D., Harvard U., 1947. Diplomate Am. Bd. Surgery; spl. cert. in pediatric surgery. Intern Mass. Meml. Hosps., Boston, 1947-48, resident in surgery, 1948-49; resident in surgery Children's Hosp., Boston, 1950-51, Hosp. U. Pa., Phila., 1954-55; Chief resident in surgery Children's Hosp., Phila., 1955-56; practice medicine specializing in pediatric surgery, Wilmington, Del., 1966—, chief sect. pediatric surgery Med. Ctr. Del., 1966—; St. Francis Hosp., Wilmington, 1967-73. Mem. standing com. Episcopal Diocese Del., 1980-84; mem. choir Immanuel Episc. Ch., Wilmington, 1967—, mem. vestry, 1985—, lay eucharistic minister, 1987—. Served to lt. JGMC, USNR, 1951-52, Korea. Fellow Am. Acad. Pediatrics, ACS; mem. Am. Pediatric Surg. Assn., Brit. Assn. Pediatric Surgeons, AMA, Med. Soc. Del., New Castle County Med. Soc. Republican. Home: Wilmington, Del. Died Feb. 12, 2006.

MINTON, PAUL DIXON, statistical design consultant, retired university administrator, statistics educator; b. Dallas, Aug. 4, 1918; s. William and Evelyn (Croft) M.; m. Mary Frances Hickman, June 5, 1943; children: George Raymond, Roland Bertram. BS, So. Meth. U., 1941, MS, 1948; PhD, N.C. State U., 1957. Asst. prof. math. So. Meth. U., 1952-56, assoc. prof., dir. computing lab., 1957-61, prof. stats., chmn. dept., 1961-72; dean Sch. Arts and Scis. Va. Commonwealth U., 1972-79, prof. math scis., dir. Inst. Stats., 1979-87; pvt. cons. in statis. design, analysis and quality control Va., from 1987. Assoc. prof. Va. Poly. Inst., 1956-57. Contbr. articles to profl. jours. Fellow Am. Statis. Assn. (bd. dirs. 1987-88), Am. Soc. Quality Control, Tex. Acad. Sci. (dir. 1969-71); mem. Inst. Math. Stats., Biometric Soc., Math. Assn. Am., Va. Acad. Sci. Home: Richmond, Va. Died July 10, 2007.

MINZNER, PAMELA BURGY, state supreme court justice; b. Meridian, Miss., Nov. 19, 1943; BA cum laude, Miami U., 1965; LLB, Harvard U., 1968. Bar: Mass. 1968, N.Mex. 1972. Pvt. practice, Mass., 1968—71, Albuquerque, 1971—73; adj. prof. law U. N.Mex., Albuquerque, 1972—73, asst. prof., 1973—77, assoc. prof., 1977—80, prof. law, 1980—84; judge N.Mex. Ct. Appeals, Albuquerque, 1984—94, chief judge, 1993—94; justice N.Mex. Supreme Ct., Santa Fe, 1994—2007, chief justice, 1999—2001. Mem. faculty Inst. Preparativo Legal U., N.Mex. Sch. Law, 1975, 79; participant NEH Summer Seminars for Law Tchrs. Stanford Law Sch., 1982, U. Chgo. Law Sch., 1978. Author (with Robert T. Laurence): A Student's Guide to Estates in Land and Future Interests: Text, Examples, Problems & Answers, 1981, 2d edit., 1993. Mem.: ABA, State Bar N.Mex. (co-editor newsletter 1979—83, bd. dirs. 1978—79, 1983—84, sect. on women's legal rights and obligations), Gamma Phi Beta. Democrat. Avocations: reading, bridge, movies. Died Aug. 31, 2007.

MIRKIN, BERNARD LEO, pharmacologist, pediatrician; b. Bronx, NY, Mar. 31, 1928; s. Max and Esther M.; m. Phyllis Korduner, Aug. 1954 (dec. 1982); children: Lisa Mia, Mara Rebecca; m. Sarah Solotaroff, 1986; stepchildren: Jennifer, Rachel, Jacob. AB, NYU, 1949; PhD, Yale U., 1953; MD, U. Minn., 1964. Asst. prof. pharmacology SUNY, Downstate Med. Center, 1954-60; Ford Found. postdoctoral fellow Karolinska Inst., Stockholm, 1960-61; USPHS post-doctoral fellow Yale U., 1961-62; resident in pediatrics U. Minn. Hosp., Mpls., 1964-66; asst. prof. U. Minn. Med. Sch., Mpls., 1966-67, asso. prof., 1967-72; prof. pediatrics, pharmacology and biol. chemistry, dir. div. clin. pharmacology U. Minn. Health Sci. Ctr., 1972-89; prof. pediatrics and molecular pharmacology Northwestern U. Med. Sch., Chgo., from 1989; head, dir. rsch. Inst. for Edn. and Rsch. Children's Meml. Hosp., Chgo., 1989—99; assoc. dean rsch. Northwestern U. Med. Sch., 1994—96; dir. rsch. emeritus Inst. for Edn. and Rsch. Children's Meml. Hosp., Chgo., from 2000. Cons. Office of Technology Assessment, U.S. Congress, WHO, U.S. Pharmacopeia, PhARMA Found., Nat. Inst. Health; fellow Jesus Coll., Oxford U., 1974; Ford Found. postdoctoral fellow Karolinska Inst. Stockholm 1960-61. Author: Perinatal Pharmacology and Therapeutics, 1976, Clinical Pharmacology: A Pediatric Perspective, 1978. Served with M.C. U.S. Army, 1954-56. Mem. AAAS, Soc. Pediat. Rsch., Am. Assn. Cancer Rsch., Am. Pediat. Soc., Am. Soc. Pharm. Exptl. Therapeutics, Am. Soc. Clin. Pharm. and Therapeutics. Home: Evanston, Ill. Died Aug. 13, 2007.

MISENER, TERRY RICHARD, dean, nursing educator; b. Apr. 11, 1943; BSN, U. Colo., 1966; M in Health Sci., U. Calif., Davis, 1973; PhD, U. Ill., 1981. Ret. lt. col. U.S. Army Nurse Corps, 1964-87; prof., dept. chair nursing sys. U. Portland, Oreg., 1987-98, nursing prof. Oreg., from 1998. Fellow Am. Acad. Nursing. Died May 30, 2007.

MISRA, RAJ PRATAP, engineering educator, electrical engineer; b. Chhaperpur, India, Dec. 23, 1919; came to U.S., 1939; SB, MIT, 1941; MEE, Cornell U., 1945, PhD in Elec. Engring. & Indsl. Mgmt., 1955. Gen. mgr., chief engr. Hamara Radio & Gen. Industries Ltd., Delhi, India, 1947-50; instr. elec. engring. Cornell U., Ithaca, N.Y., 1950-52; mgr. reliability and high frequency Philco Corp., Lansdale, Pa., 1952-58; mgr. reliability rsch. and devel. Tex. Instruments, Dallas, 1958-62; prof. reliability N.J. Inst. Tech., Newark, 1962-90; disting. prof emeritus. Cons. Tex. Instruments, 1962-93, v.p. cons. Soletron Inc., N.Y., Fla., 1966-69, Kertron, Reriera Beach, Fla., 1969-80; cons. reliability Astro Electronics Divsn. Westinghouse, Calif., 1962-65, Autonetics, Calif., 1965-66; vis. prof. U.S. Acad. Sci. to Romanian Acad., 1988-89, vis. prof., Indian Inst. of Tech., New Dehli, 1990, 93., Fulbright scholar; Fulbright fellow Coun. Internat. Exch. Scholars, 1991-92. Fellow Indian Assn. Engrs.; mem. IEEE (chmn. reliability group 1965-68), ASTE (chmn. ref. planar diode task force 1955-59), Sigma Xi. Home: West Caldwell, NJ. Died Aug. 4, 2007.

MITCHELL, BRUCE WALKER, lawyer; b. Carbondale, Ill., Dec. 1, 1950; s. J.C. and Shirley (Walker) M.; m. Sydelle Claire Grossman. BA, So. Ill. U., 1979; JD, U. Tulsa, 1982. Ptnr. Mitchell and Armstrong Ltd., Marion, Ill. Served with USNG, 1969-76. Mem. ABA, Ill. State Bar Assn., Williamson County Bar Assn., Am. Trial Lawyers Assn., Ill. Trial Lawyers Assn. Avocations: philosophy, gardening. Home: Marion, Ill. Died Mar. 24, 2006.

MITCHELL, DOUGLAS FARRELL, trust company executive, lawyer; b. Pleasant Hill, Ill., Oct. 28, 1940; s. Henry C. and Opal V. Mitchell; m. Pamella Locke; children: Michael, Deborah. BS, U. Ill., 1964; JD, DePaul U., 1969; MBA, U. Chgo., 1976. Asst. sec. No. Trust Co., Chgo., 1964-72, 2d v.p., 1972-78, v.p., 1978-86, sr. v.p., from 1986. Bd. dirs. United Charities, Chgo., 1988-92. Mem. Ill. State Bar Assn., Chgo. Bar Assn. Home: Palm Harbor, Fla. Died Aug. 2, 2007.

MITCHELL, EDWARD JOHN, academic administrator; b. Frackville, Pa., Sept. 11, 1942; s. Edward J. and Elizabeth G. (Habel) M.; m. Penelope S. Mullin, Nov. 28, 1964; children: Erin P., Heather E. AB, Wabash Coll., 1964; PhD, U. Pitts., 1972. Instr. chemistry Frostburg (Md.) State Coll., 1972-73; from asst. prof. to assoc. prof. MacMurray Coll., Jacksonville, Ill., 1973-80, prof., from 1980, dean of coll., 1980-86, v.p. academic affairs, 1984-86, pres., from 1986. Alfred P. Sloan scholar, 1960-64; NSF fellow, 1965-72. Mem. Am. Chem. Soc. Home: Jacksonville, Ill. Died Apr. 21, 2007.

MITCHELL, JOHN WESLEY, physicist, researcher; b. Christchurch, New Zealand, Dec. 3, 1913; came to U.S., 1959; s. John Wesley and Lucy Ruth (Snowball) M.; m. Jo Overstreet Long, June 27, 1968 (div. July 1976); 1 stepdaughter, Jody Karen Long.; m. Virginia Jacobs Hill, Aug. 2, 1976 BSc, U. Canterbury, Christchurch, New Zealand, 1933, MSc, 1934; D Phil, U. Oxford, Eng., 1938, DSc, 1960. Lectr. U. Bristol, Eng., 1945-47, reader, 1947-59; prof. U. Va., Charlottesville, 1959-65, William Barton Rogers prof., 1965-79, prof. emeritus, from 1979; sr. rsch. fellow, from 1979; dir. Nat. Chem. Lab., Teddington, Eng., 1963-64. Editor: Fundamental Mechanisms of Photographic Sensitivity, 1951, Defects in Crystalline Solids, 1955, Reactivity of Solids, 1960; contbr. articles to jours. in field. Recipient kultur preis German Photog. Soc., Cologne, 1981, Lieven Gevaert med. Soc. Photog. Sci. Tech., 1983, Lifetime Achievement award Commonwealth of Va., 1993, Progress medal and hon. fellowship Royal Photog. Soc. Gt. Brit., 1995. Fellow Royal Soc. (London), Royal Photog. Soc., Royal Inst. Chemistry, Am. Phys. Soc., Soc. Photog. Sci. Tech., Washington (hon.), Japan (hon.), Athenaeum Club (London), Cosmos Club (Washington). Avocations: foreign languages, travel, color photography. Home: Charlottesville, Va. Died July 12, 2007.

MITCHELL, MICHAEL JOSEPH, JR., business executive; b. Washington, May 24, 1939; s. Michael J. and Ruth (Alexander) M.; student Everett Jr. Coll., 1960-62. Electronic tech. Boeing Co., Seattle, 1959-62, engring. aide, 1962-64; owner-pres. The Mitchell Co. (U.S.) Ltd., Seattle, 1964-81; partner-v.p. Northwest Avionics Co., Renton, Wash., 1964-66; pres. M.J. Mitchell & Assos., Seattle, 1972-81, The Mitchell Co. (Internat.) Ltd., 1973-81, First Internat. Bus. & Fin. Mgmt. Corp., 1977—, First Internat. Pub. Corp., 1979—, First Internat. Fin. Services, Corp., 1980—, Securintel, Ltd., 1981—, First Internat. Corp., 1982—. Served with USNR, 1957-59. Mem. Seattle Fire Buffs Soc., Am. Mgmt. Assn. Democrat. Elk. Home: Seattle, Wash. Died May 8, 2007.

MITCHELL, PARREN JAMES, former congressman; b. Balt., Apr. 29, 1922; s. Clarence Maurice and Elsie (Davis) M. BA, Morgan State Coll., 1950; MA, U. Md., 1952; postgrad., U. Conn., 1960. Instr. sociology Morgan State Coll., 1953-54; prof. sociology, asst. dir. Urban Studies Inst., 1968-70; probation officer, 1954-59; supr. domestic relations div. Supreme Ct. Balt., 1957-63; exec. dir. Md. Commn. on Interracial Problems and Relations, 1963-65, Community Action Agy., Balt., 1965-68; founding mem. Congl. Black Caucus, 1969; mem. US Congress from 7th Md. dist., 1971—87; mem. banking, fin. and urban affairs com., chmn. small bus. com., joint econ. com. Author: Profile of the Domestic Relations Offender, 1958, (with R.G. Murdy) Signal Four-Family Trouble, 1960. Served to 1st lt., inf. AUS, 1943-46. Decorated Purple Heart. Mem. NAACP (life), Nat. Assn. Community Devels., Alpha Kappa Phi. Home: Baltimore, Md. Died May 28, 2007.

MITCHELL, ROBERT ARTHUR, former academic administrator; b. NYC, Jan. 19, 1926; s. George P. and Vera A. (Duffy) M. AB summa cum laude, Woodstock Coll., 1949, AB summa cum laude, 1950; STL magna cum laude, Facultes SJ de Louvain, Belgium, 1957; ThD, U. Strasbourg, France, 1965; degree (hon.), Le Moyne Coll., 1990, Loyola U., 1991, U. Detroit, 1992. Joined S.J., 1943, ordained priest, Roman Cath. Ch., 1956. Instr. in philosophy LeMoyne Coll., 1950-53, asst. prof. theology, 1958-59, acad. dean, 1959-63, assoc. prof. theology, acad. dean, 1965-66; pres. Loyola Coll., Shrub Oak, 1966; provincial N.Y. State Province (S.J.), 1966-72; pres. Jesuit Conf., chmn. Am. Jesuit Provincials, Washington, 1972-76; dir. Woodstock Theol. Ctr., 1976-79; pres. U. Detroit, 1979-90, chancellor, 1990-92; acting pres. Le Moyne Coll., Syracuse, N.Y., 1993-94, pres., 1994—2000; cons. Higher Edn. to Jesuit U.S. Provincials. Bd. dirs. Economic Club of Detroit, 1979-92, Detroit Econ. Growth Corp., 1983-92, Detroit Symphony Orchestra, 1981-89, Woodstock Theological Ctr., 1977-83, Georgetown U., 1976-82, 1983-92; bd. trustees, Loyola Marymount U., 1986, St. Peter's Coll., 1992, U. Detroit, 1979, Sta. WTVS/Channel 56, 1979-86, 1988-92, Michigan Cancer Foundation, 1985-92, New Detroit, Inc., 1979-92, Fordham U., 1966-74, Le Moyne Coll., 1977-83, Boston Coll., 1966-90. Recipient Simon LeMoyne medal, 2005. Died Oct. 5, 2006.

MITCHELL, RUSSELL HARRY, dermatologist; b. Erie, ND, Oct. 19, 1925; s. William John and Anna Lillian (Sögge) M.; m. Judith Lawes Douvarjo, May 24, 1968 (dec. Mar. 2000); children: Kathy Ellen, Gregory Alan, Jill Elaine, Crystal Anne. BS, BA, U. Minn., Mpls., 1947, BM, 1949, MD, 1951; postgrad., U. Pa., 1968-69. Diplomate Am. Bd. Dermatology. Intern Gorgas Hosp., C.Z., 1951-52; commd. lt. (j.g.) M.C. USN, 1953, advanced through grades to capt., 1968, commdg. officer 1st Med. Bn., 1st Marine divsn. Vietnam, ret., 1981; resident in dermatology U.S. Naval Hosp., Phila., 1967-70; asst. chief out-patient dept. Gorgas Hosp., 1955-64; chief med. and surg. wards Ariz. State Hosp., Phoenix, 1965; pvt. practice Leesburg, Va., from 1978. Staff Loudoun Health Ctr., 1975—; dermatologist Nat. Naval Med. Ctr., Bethesda, Md., 1973-81; asst. prof. Georgetown U. Med. Sch., 1975-85. Contbr. articles to profl. jours. Pres. Archaeol. Soc. Panama, 1962-64. Decorated bronze star with combat V; Vietnam Gallantry Cross with Palm and clasp; Condecoration Vasco Nuñez de Balboa in orden de Caballero (Panamá). Fellow: Am. Acad. Physicians (life), Am. Acad. Dermatology (life), Explorers' Club; mem.: Loudoun County Med. Soc., Am. Soc. Contemporary Medicine and Surgery, Assn. Mil. Surgeons, Assn.Mil. Dermatologists (life), Marine Corps League, Ctr. for Study of First Americans, Am. Archeology Soc., Marines' Meml. Club (assoc.), Phi Chi. Died May 17, 2006.

MITCHELL, VIRGIL ALLEN, clergyman; b. Six Mile, SC, Apr. 21, 1914; s. E.A. and Mozelle (Davis) M.; m. Mary Parks, Mar. 24, 1937; children— Walter Allen, Marilyn (Mrs. Alton C. Hollingsworth), Martha Theresa (Mrs. James Funnell). Th.B., Central Wesleyan Coll., SC, 1943; postgrad., High Point Coll., NC, 1946; D.D., Houghton Coll., 1964. Ordained to ministry Wesleyan Methodist Ch., 1939; pastor in Walhalla, S.C., 1937-39, Westminster, S.C., 1937- 40, Oakway, S.C., 1939-40, Cateeche and Central, S.C., 1940-46, Glenwood, S.C., 1946-49; tchr. Bible Central Wesleyan Meth. Coll., 1943-44, 46-48; pres. S.C. conf. Wesleyan Meth. Ch., 1949-57; nat. asst. sec. home missions and ch. extension and evangelism Wesleyan Meth. Ch., 1957-59, nat. sec. ch. extension and evangelism, 1959-63; gen. supt. Wesleyan Meth. Ch. Am., 1963-68, Wesleyan Ch. (merger Wesleyan Methodist and Pilgrim Holiness Chs.), 1968-84, gen. supr., emeritus, bd. pension, from 1984. Ofcl. visitor 9th World Meth. Conf., 1956; mem. S.C. Bd. Christian Action, 1949-57; pres. S.C. Wesleyan Youth Soc., 1943-45, 47-49; pres. So. Area Youth, 1945-47; mem. World Meth. Council, 1968-84; ofcl. visitor 13th Meth. Conf., Dublin, Ireland, 1976 Bd. dirs. Central Wesleyan Coll., 1950-57, 84—, vice chmn., 1954-57; vice chmn. bd. trustees Hephzibah Children's Home, Macon, Ga., 1984—, chmn., 1988—. Mem. Nat. Assn. Evangelicals, Nat. Holiness Assn. (bd. dirs.) Home: Central, SC. Died Oct. 21, 2006.

MITCHENER, CHARLES GILBERT, farm bureau executive; b. Evanston, Ill., Apr. 5, 1925; s. Charles Gilbert and Bertie Irene (Edmonds) M.; m. Leona Elinor Bone, Aug. 16, 1947; children— Jeff, Steve, John, Ted. Student acctg., Bryant and Stratton Bus. Sch., Chgo. Controller Growmark Inc., Chgo., 1946-61; asst. controller Del Webb Corp., Phoenix, 1962-67; v.p. fin., treas. Ind. Farm Bur. Coop. Assn., Inc., Indpls., from 1967. Chmn. info. systems Am. Feed Mfrs., Chgo., 1974-75 Served with USN, 1943-45, PTO Mem. Fin. Execs. Inst. (bd. dirs., treas. Indpls. chpt. 1982-86), Planning Execs. Inst. (pres. Indpls. chpt. 1977, bd. dirs., treas. 1982-85) Lodges: Elks (membership com. Indpls. 1972-75). Republican. Methodist. Avocations: tennis; bridge. Home: Carmel, Ind. Died Aug. 4, 2007.

MITOFSKY, WARREN JAY, organization executive; b. NYC, Sept. 17, 1934; s. Howard Bernard and Elsie (Sonderling) M.; m. Dolores Evelyn Kilgore, Sept. 17, 1956 (div. Sept. 1971); children: Bryan Dean, Elisa Lynn; m. Ronda Shaw Rubinoff, July 22, 1990 (div. Dec. 1993); m. Mia Mather. BS, Guilford Coll., 1957; postgrad., U. N.C., 1957-58, U. Minn., 1958-60, 62-64. Br. chief Census Bur., Washington, 1960-62, 64-67; exec. producer CBS News, NYC, 1967-90; exec. dir. Voter Rsch. & Surveys, NYC, 1990-93; pres. Mitofsky Internat., NYC, 1993—2006. Cons. Coll. Physicians and Surgeons, Columbia U., N.Y.C., Fintec, N.Y.C., Summit (N.J.) Analytics, N.Y. Times, N.Y.C., Washington Post, Opinion Profl., Mexico City; leader, CNN election night decision team, 1996-2002. Editor: Campaign '76, 1977, Campaign '78, 1979, History of American Association for Public Opinion Research, 1992. Recipient Lifetime Achievement award, Am. Assn. for Pub. Opinion Rsch. & the Nat. Coun. on Pub. Polls, 1999. Fellow Am. Statis. Assn.; mem. Am. Assn. Pub. Opinion Rsch. (pres. 1988-89), Nat. Coun. Pub. Polls (pres. 1981-84). Jewish. Achievements include considered the father of exit polls for pioneering the use of exit polls to project winners in U.S. elections beginning in the 1960s. Avocations: tennis, jogging, scuba diving. Home: New York, NY. Died Sept. 1, 2006.

MITOVICH, JOHN, professional society administrator; b. Youngstown, Ohio, Feb. 8, 1927; s. John and Rose (Elieff) M.; m. Rebecca E. Webb, Aug. 1, 1953; children: Jon, Rosemary, Victoria, Janet, Martha, Matthew; m. Mary Lou Brennan, Nov. 27, 1985; m. Nancy Lexow Reichard, July 14, 1990. BS in Journalism, Ohio U., 1951. Advt. and pub. relations specialist GE, Schenectady, 1955-57, Pittsfield, Mass., 1957-58, pub. affairs specialist Lynn, Mass., 1958-62, mgr. cmty. rels. Johnson City, N.Y., 1962-64, cons. cmty. and govt. rels. NYC, 1964-66; exec. v.p. Rockford (Ill.) C. of C., 1966-70; pres. Southwestern Area (Conn.) Assn. Commerce and Industry, 1970-90; pres., chief exec. officer Metropool Ridesharing Corp., 1980-85; vice chmn. Greater Stamford Conv. and Visitors Bur., 1987-90; pres. SACIA/West, Albuquerque, from 1990. Lectr. econ. devel./western style U. Zagreb (Croatia) Sch. of Mgmt., 1991. Mem. bd. selectmen, North Reading, Mass., 1961-62, chmn. indsl. devel. commn., 1960-62; mem. Rockford Mayor's Urban Devel. Adv. Commn., 1966-68, Ill. Gov. Commn. on Urban Area Govt., 1969-70; founder-dir. Winnebago County (Ill.) Opportunities Industrialization Center, 1968-70, Met. Rockford Housing Devel. Corp., Forward Rockford, Inc., 1969-70; mem. Gov.'s Commn. Services and Expenditures, 1971; corp. chmn. N.Mex. Project Uplift, 1992; active N.Mex. Total Quality Mgmt. Coun. Task Force, 1992, Albuquerque Shared Vision Community Devel., 1993. Served with USMC, 1952-54. Recipient Gen. Electric Mgmt. award, 1958, Associated Industries Mass. award, 1958, Freedoms Found. disting. service award, 1965, Rockford Community Leadership award, 1970, Disting. Salesman's award Southwestern Conn. Sales and Mktg. Exec., 1974, Walter H. Wheeler Jr. Bus. Leadership award, 1990; Dwight B. Havens acad. scholar Acad. Orgn. Mgmt., 1976 Mem. Conn. Assn. C. of C. Execs. (v.p. 1979, pres. 1981-82), Greater Albuquerque C. of C. Republican. Methodist. Home: Albuquerque, N.Mex. Died May 29, 2007.

MITRI, SALVATORE CHARLES, lawyer; b. Hackensack, N.J., Sept. 26, 1929; s. Charles and Rose (Miello) M.; m. Gilda Mitri, Dec. 29, 1956; children— Charles D., Michael F., Paul V., Thomas J. B.S. in Chemistry, Wagner Coll., 1955; LL.B., St. John's U., Bklyn., 1963. Bar: N.Y., 1964, U.S. Patent Office, 1965, U.S. Dist. Ct. (ea. dist.) N.Y., 1965, U.S. Dist. Ct. (so. dist.) N.Y., 1965. Asst. div. patent counsel Union Carbide Corp., N.Y.C., 1963-69; assoc. Howard E. Thompson, Jr., N.Y.C., 1969-74; sr. patent atty. CPC Internat., Englewood Cliffs, N.J., 1974-77; patent counsel Gen. Electric Co., Pittsfield, Mass., 1977-80; sr. patent assoc. Merck & Co., Inc., Rahway, N.J., 1980—; cons. tech. mgmt. Served to cpl. USAAC, 1951-53. Mem. ABA, N.Y. Patent Law Assn., N.J. Patent Law Assn. Collaborated with Anthony William Deller in expanding his 4 vol. work, Deller's Walker on Patents, to 9 vols., 1971-73. Died Feb. 4, 2006.

MIZOTE, HISASHI EARL, optometrist; b. Oakland, Calif., Aug. 2, 1914; s. Sojuro and Shiu M.; m. Toye Uchiyama, Apr. 16, 1950; 1 child, Lisa. O.D., Chgo. Coll. Optometry, 1951; Ph.D., Kensington U., 1984. Police officer, Piedmont, Calif., 1934-38; practice optometry, Chgo., 1952—; adminstrv. to state rep. Ill., 1976; with U.S. Post Office, Chgo., 1951-72. Active Boy Scouts Am. Served with inf. U.S. Army, 1941-46, MTO. Named hon. Ky. Col., 1975; recipient commmendation Chgo. Police Dept., 1971. Mem. Ill. Sheriffs' Assn. Democrat. Avocations: research on Oriental history; mechanical experiments. Home: Chicago, Ill. Died Jan. 21, 2006.

MOALLEM, SHA, surgeon, educator; b. Teheran, Iran, Sept. 1, 1933; s. Morteza and Hakimeh (Yahid) M.; m. 1973; children: Theodore, Serena, Andrew. MD with honors, U. Teheran, 1957; postgrad. in thoracic and cardiovascular surgery, U. Tex., 1965-67, N.Y. Med. Coll., 1967-69. Resident in gen. surgery Mt. Sinai Hosp., NYC, 1959-62, Albert Einstein Coll. of Medicine-Bronx Mcpl. Hosp. Ctr., 1962-65; chief thoracic and cardiovascular surgery Cabrini Med. Ctr., NYC, 1984-94; chief thoracic surgery St. Claire's Hosp., NYC, 1985-94; clin. assoc. prof. N.Y. Med. Coll., Valhalla, from 1988. Contbr. articles, papers to profl. jours. Fellow ACS, Am. Coll. Cardiology, Am. Coll. Chest Physicians, Internat. Coll. Surgeons; mem. Internat. Soc. Cardiovascular Surgery, Soc. Thoracic Surgery. Avocations: swimming, boating, chess. Home: Glen Cove, NY. Died Aug. 9, 2007.

MOCK, RICHARD BASIL, artist; b. Long Beach, Calif., Aug. 2, 1944; s. Ralph Raymond Mock and Maxine (Griffiths) Mock Berry; m. Eileen Mazur, June 17, 1969 (div. 1972); m. Patti Elliot Skaff, Oct. 22, 1982. B.S. in Design, U. Mich., 1965; postgrad. N.Y. Studio Sch., 1965-66, U. Okla., 1969-70. Artist, Brooke Alexander Gallery, N.Y.C., 1980-86; Gallery 72, Omaha, 1985—; Rosa Esman Gallery, N.Y.C., 1986—; Gallery 454, Los Angeles, 1986—, numerous others; illustrator opinions and editorials sect. N.Y. Times, N.Y.C., 1980-84; N.Y. Times, 1980—; ofcl. protrait painter 1980 Winter Olympics, Lake Placid, N.Y., NEA fellow, 1973, Roswell Mus. fellow, 1970; one-person ceramics show Bank of Am. Gallery, San Francisco, 1988. Democrat. Avocations: skin diving; hunting; making duck decoys; flying. Died July 28, 2006.

MOEBIUS, HOWARD EDWARD, printing company executive; b. Milw., Sept. 23, 1917; s. Carl William and Erna Agnes (Rudy) M.; m. Rosemary Babbs, Apr. 6, 1968; children— James, Dalana Schwitzer, Eric, Dallas Lillich, Jeffrey, Elisabeth. Student, Northwestern Mil. Acad., 1932-35. With Moebius Printing Co., Milw., 1935-42, 45—, pres., chmn. bd., 1977— Bd. dirs. Milw. Symphony Orch., 1976—, Milw. Zool. Soc., 1976—. Served to 1st lt. USAAF, 1942-45. Decorated Ai Medal, Purple Heart, D.F.C. Republican. Lutheran. Clubs. Town, University, Milwaukee. Lodge: Rotary. Home: Milwaukee, Wis. Died May 10, 2006.

MOFENSON, HOWARD C., pediatrician, toxicologist; b NYC, Jan. 26, 1925; s. Jack L. and Theresa (Cohen) M.; m. Lois Stugart, July 26, 1947; children: Lynne, Jeffrey, Dayna. MD Jefferson Med. Coll., 1951. Intern Nassau County Med. Ctr. 1951-52; resident Bklyn. Hosp., 1952-53, L.I. Coll. Hosp. 1953-54; attending Winthrop U. Hosp., Mineola, N.Y., from 1954, Nassau County Med. Ctr., East Meadow, N.Y., from 1954 prof. pediatrics SUNY, Stony Brook, N.Y., from 1973, prof emergency medicine, from 1990; prof. clin. pharmacy St. John's Sch. Pharmacy, Queens, N.Y., from 1982; prof. of toxicology N.Y. Coll. Osteo., from 1985. Acting dean SUNY. Contbr articles to profl. jours. With U.S. Army, 1942-46. Decorated Purple Heart (2), Bronze Star (2). Mem. Am. Assn. Poison Control (pres.), Am. Acad. Pediatrics, Am. Diabetes Assn., Am Acad. Clin. Toxicology, Am. Coll. Med. Toxicology. Avocations: writing, photography, art. Home: Mineola, NY. Died Apr 7, 2007.

MOGG, DONALD WHITEHEAD, retired chemist; b. La Grange, Ill., Feb. 11, 1924; s. Harold William and Margaret (Whitehead) M. BS, Allegheny Coll., 1944; postgrad., Harvard U., 1946-47. Asst. chemist Gt. Lakes Carbon Corp., Morton Grove, Ill., 1947-48, chemist, 1948-53, rsch. chemist, 1953-56 project supr., 1956-59, sect. head, 1959-63, Gt. Lakes Rsch Corp., Elizabethton, Tenn., 1963-66; rsch. and devel. mgr. bldg products divsn. Grefco, Inc., Torrance, Calif., 1966-68, corp rsch. and devel. mgr., 1968-72, group mgr., 1972-81, sr. rsch assoc., 1981-82. U.S. and fgn. patentee in field of bldg. products Served with U.S. Army, 1944-46. Mem. Am. Chem. Soc AAAS, Phi Beta Kappa, Phi Kappa Psi. Presbyterian. Home San Diego, Calif. Died Aug. 1, 2007.

MOHAMMAD, NOOR, retired law educator; b. Varanasi, U.P. India, Mar. 25, 1928; came to the U.S., 1960; s. Lal and Zainab (Bibi) M.; m. Ramroon-Nissan, June 1945 (dec. Feb. 1960) children: Aun, Shahina Parveen; m. Ishrat Hussain, Apr. 2 1979. B in Commerce, Aligarh Muslim U., Aligarh, India, 1947 LLB, Banaras Hindu U., Varanasi, India, 1949, MA, 1955 LLM, U. Minn., 1961, Yale U., 1961, Juris Sci. Doctorate, 1967 Asst. prof. U. Sask. Sch. Law, Saskatoon, Sask., Can., 1967-69 asst. prof. bus. law U. Conn., Storrs, 1969-70; assoc. prof. law U. Wyo., Laramie, 1970-71, William Mitchell Coll. Law, St Paul, 1970-71; assoc. prof. U. Balt., 1972-75, prof. law, 1976-92. Vis. prof. law King Abdul Aziz U., Macca Campus, 1979-80 Head edn. com. Assn. Indian Muslims, 1991—. Muslim. Avocation: research on islamic affairs. Home: Bethesda, Md. Died Feb. 6, 2006.

MOHAN, JOSEPH CHARLES, JR., chemical engineer; b Phila., Nov. 2, 1921; s. Joseph C. and Margaret V. (McCarthy) M.; m. June I. Daniels, Nov. 29, 1947; children— Kyle S Corey C. B.S. in Chem. Engring., Pa. State U., 1946. Chem engr. Sinclair Co., Marcus Hook, Pa., 1947-48, Pennwalt Co., Whitemarsh, Pa., 1948-57; supr. research and devel. Am. Viscose/FMC, Fredericksburg, Va., 1957-69, Amoco Chems., Naperville, Ill., 1969—. Patentee in field. Served to lt. U.S. Merchant Marines, 1944-46. Mem. Am. Inst. Chem. Engrs. Avocations: golf; swimming; tennis; jogging; bicycling. Home: Naperville, Ill. Died Aug. 10, 2006.

MOLER, EDWIN STANTON, plastic materials company executive; b. West Orange, NJ, Mar. 15, 1931; s. Edwin Stanton Sr. and Bertha Grace (Hula) M.; m. Patti Jean Smith, Jan. 4, 1934; children: Stephen, Cynthia, Lisa. BA in Chemistry, Lehigh U., 1952. V.p. N.Am. ops. Hilmont Inc., Wilmington, Del. Served to lt. USAF, 1953-54. Died Dec. 20, 2006.

MOLITOR, MICHAEL A., entrepreneur, consultant; b. Bklyn., Nov. 7, 1965; s. Henry J. and Janet A. (Monti) M.; m. Michele A. Emery, July 8, 1995; 1 child, Michael. BS, Siena Coll., 1987; MBA, Columbia U., 2000. CFP. Fin, aid counselor Janet's Coll. Tuition Aid, Massapequa Park, N.Y., 1987-92; income tax acct. Michael A. Molitor, Massapequa, N.Y., from 1988; owner, fin. aid counseling svc. Molitor Coll. Aid Counseling, Massapequa, from 1992; money mgr. Molitor Money Mgmt., Massapequa, from 1992. Cons. Alive-To-Thrive, Inc., Westchester, N.Y., 1992—, cons., adv. bd. Orphan's Aid Soc., Douglaston, N.Y., 1994—; cons. in field. Author: You Can Afford A College Education, 1992; contbr. articles to profl. jours., various TV talk shows. Con. to Guidance Dept. Massapequa Sch. Dist., Massapequa, 1995-98, mem. Long Island Assn., Hauppauge, N.Y., 1990-92. Recipient Top Producer-Pres. Club Transamerica Funds, Houston, 1993-94, mem. signature Club Oppenheimer Funds, Denver, 1995. Mem. Internat. Assn. Fin. Planning, N.Y. Fin. Air Adminstr. Assn., NAt. Assn. Fin. Aid Adminstr., BMW Car Club Am., Porsche Club Am. Mem. Christian Ch. Avocations: golf, drumming, track driving. Home: Melville, NY. Died Aug. 20, 2007.

MOLLITT, DANIEL LAWRENCE, pediatric surgeon; b. Cin., Oct. 23, 1948; m. Barbara Yount, 1978; children: Todd Yount, Meredith Ann, Erin Elizabeth, Seth Yount. BS, St. Joseph's Coll., 1970; MD, St. Louis U., 1974. Diplomate Nat. Bd. Med. Examiners, Am. Bd. Surgery, Am. Bd. Surgery in Pediatric Surgery, Am. Bd. Surgery in Critical Care; cert. advanced trauma life support, advanced trauma life support instr., advanced pediatric life support, pediatric advanced life support. Intern in surgery Ind. U., Indianapolis, 1974-75, resident in surgery, 1975-78; resident in pediatric surgery Babies Hosp., Columbia-Presbyn. Med. Ctr., NYC, 1979-81; inst. surgery Ind. U., Indianapolis, 1978-79; asst. prof. surgery U. Ark. Med. Scis., 1981-85, asst. prof. pediatrics, 1982-85; assoc. prof. surgery U. Fla. Coll. Medicine, 1985-92, prof. surgery, from 1992, prof. pediatrics, from 1992. Dir. surg. rsch. U. Fla. Health Sci. Ctr., Jacksonville, 1994; chief childrens surg. svcs., Wolfson childrens Hosp., Jacksonville, chief divsn. pediatric surgery, U. Fla. Health Sci. Ctr., Jacksonville; lectr. in field. Author books and chpts. in books; contbr. over 70 articles to profl. jours. Recipient rsch. grants Am. Cancer Soc., 1978-79, U. Ark. Instl. Biomed. Rsch. Support, 1984, Groh Trust, 1987-88, 88-89, Dean's Intramural, 1989, Nemours Found., 1990, 92. Fellow ACS (Ensminger award 1977, Gatch award 1978), Am. Acad. Pediatrics; mem. Am. Assn. Surgery of Trauma, Am. Pediatric Surg. Assn., Assn. Acad. Surgery, Brit. Assn. Pediatric Surgeons, Duval County Med. Soc. (John A. Beals award 1988), Fla. Assn. Surgery of Trauma, Fla. Assn. Pediatric Surgeons (sec.-treas. 1992—), Fla. Med. Assn., Internat. Assn. Surgery of Trauma and Surg. Intensive Care, Internat. Soc. Surgery, So. Med. Assn., So. Soc. Pediatric Rsch., Southwestern Surg. Congress, N.E. Fla. Pediatric Soc., Pediatric Oncology Group, Shock Soc., Soc. Critical Care Medicine, Surg. Infection Soc. Home: Jacksonville, Fla. Died Feb. 9, 2007.

MOLONEY, LOUIS CAREY, retired librarian; b. Trenton, N.J., Nov. 26, 1920; s. Louis Carey and Florence (Smith) M.; B.S. in Edn., Trenton State Coll., 1942, B.L.S., 1948; postgrad. U. Chgo., 1950-51; M.S., Tex. A. and I. U., 1958; D.L.S., Columbia U., 1970; m. Doris Lee Pettit, Nov. 30, 1944; children— Doris Lee, Evelyn Estabrook, Louis Carey III. Head librarian Bishop Meml. Library, Toms River, N.J., 1947-50, Trenton Jr. Coll., 1951-52; asst. librarian Tex. A. and I. U., Kingsville, 1952-64; Cons. Welder Wildlife Found. Library, Sinton, Tex., 1958-64; asso. librarian Southwest Tex. State U., San Marcos, 1964-65, head librarian, 1965-75, dir. Learning Resources Center, 1975-82, univ. librarian, 1982-86, ret., 1986. Bd. dirs., chmn., sec. Southside Community Center, 1973-79. Served with USAAF, 1942-43, USNR, 1943-45. Mem. ALA, Tex. Library Assn. (past publicity chmn., Dist. III past chmn.), Tex. Council State U. Librarians (past chmn.), Council Research and Acad. Libraries (past pres.), Phi Delta Kappa (treas.). Democrat. Methodist. Club: Lions (pres. 1976-77). Author articles. Home: San Marcos, Tex. Died Sept. 19, 2006.

MOLONY, MICHAEL JANSSENS, JR., lawyer, arbitrator, mediator; b. New Orleans, Sept. 2, 1922; s. Michael Janssens and Marie (Perret)M.; m. Jane Leslie Waguespack, Oct. 21, 1951; children: Michael Janssens III (dec.), Leslie, Megan, Kevin, Sara, Brian, Ian, Duncan. JD, Tulane U., 1950. Bar: La. 1950, D.C. 1979, U.S. Dist. Ct. (ea. and mid. dists.) La. 1951, U.S. Ct. Appeals (5th cir.) 1953, U.S. Supreme Ct. 1972, U.S. Dist. Ct. (we. dist.) La. 1978, U.S. Ct. Appeals (11th and D.C. cirs.) 1981. Ptnr. Molony & Baldwin, New Orleans, 1950; assoc. Jones, Flanders, Waechter & Walker, New Orleans, 1951-56; ptnr. Jones, Walker, Waechter, Poitevent, Carrere & Denegre, New Orleans, 1956-75, Milling, Benson, Woodward, Hillyer, Pierson & Miller, New Orleans, 1975-91, Chaffe, McCall, Phillips, Toler & Sarpy, New Orleans, 1991-92, Sessions & Fishman, New Orleans, 1993-2000, Molony Law Firm, New Orleans, from 2000. Instr., lectr. Med. Sch. and Univ. Coll. Tulane U., 1953-59; mem. Eisenhower Legal Com., 1952. Bd. commrs. Port of New Orleans, 1976-81, pres., 1978; bd. rev. Assoc. Br. Pilots, 1990—2003; bd. dirs. La. World Expn. Inc., 1974-84; bd. dirs., exec. com. New Orleans Tourist and Conv. Commn., 1971-74, 78, chmn.; family attractions com. 1973-75; chmn. La. Gov.'s Task Force on Space Industry, 1971-73; chmn. La. Gov.'s Citizens' Adv. Com. Met. New Orleans Transp. and Planning Location of new Miss. River Bridge, 1971-77; mem. La. Gov.'s Task Force Natural Gas Requirements, 1971-72; mem. La. Gov.'s Proaction Commn. for Higher Edn., 1995; mem. Goals Found. Coun. and ex-officio mem. Goals Found., Met. New Orleans, 1969-73; vice chmn. Port of New Orleans Operation Impact, 1969-70, mem. Met. Area Com.; New Orleans, 1970-84; trustee Pub. Affairs Rsch. Coun. La., 1970-73, mem. exec. com. Bus./Higher Edn. Coun., U. New Orleans, 1980-94, bd. dirs., 1980-2000, dir. emeritus, 2000—, v.p., 1986-88, pres., 1988-90, chmn. Task Force on Pub. Higher Edn. Funding, 1990-95, chmn. govtl. affairs, 1995-2000, Task Force on Edn./Econ. Devel. Alliances, 1993-95; mem. Mayor's Coun. on Internat. Trade and Econ. Devel., 1978; mem. Mayor's Transition Task Force Econ. Devel., 1994; bd. dirs. La. Partnership for Tech. and Innovation, 1989—, Acad. Sacred Heart, 1975-77, Internat. House, 1985-86, adv. coun., 1985—; vis. com. Sch. Bus. Adminstrn., Loyola U., New Orleans, 1981-2001, trustee Loyola U., 1985-91, vice chmn. bd. trustees, 1990-91; deans coun. Tulane U. Law Sch., 1988-96, vice chmn. bldg. com., 1991-95; bd. dirs., exec. com. Internat. Trade Mart, chmn. internat. bus. com., 1983-85; bd. dirs. U. New Orleans Found., 1991-2003, World Trade Ctr.-New Orleans, 1983—, port activity com. 1985-91, transp. com. 1991-95, 2000—, govt. affairs com. 1996-99; chmn. Task Force on Internat. Banking, 1982; mem. Mayor's Task Force on Drug Abuse, 1989-90. With USAAC, 1942-46, PTO; capt. JAGDR, USAF, 1950-. Recipient Leadership award AIAA, 1971, Yenni award Loyola U., New Orleans, 1979, New Orleans Times Picayune Loving Cup, 1986, First Citizen of the Learning Soc. Dean's award UNO Met. Coll., 1992; also various civic contbn. awards; co-recipient Silver Anvil award New Orleans chpt. Pub. Rels. Soc. Am., 1991. Fellow Coll. Labor and Employment Lawyers (5th cir. credentials com. 2004-07); mem. ABA (labor and employment law and litig. sects., com. equal opportunity law, organizer, chmn. regional EEO com. liaison with equal opportunity commn., office fed. contract compliance programs, ABA Comm. EEO Law Spl. award 2006), D.C. Bar Assn., Fed. Bar Assn., La. Bar Assn. (past sec.-treas., bd. govs. 1957-60, editor jour. 1957-59, sec. spl. supreme ct. com. on drafting code jud. ethics), New Orleans Bar Assn. (dir. legal aid bur. 1954, chmn. standing com. legis. 1968, vice chmn. standing com. pub. rels. 1970-71), Am. Judicature Soc., La. Law Inst. (asst. sec.-treas. 1958-70), Am. Arbitration Assn. (bd. dirs. 1995-98, chmn. reg. adv. coun., chmn. reg. adv. coun. employment law cases, mem. panels-employment, employee benefits, large complex employment and comml. arbitration/mediation cases 1990-2004, Whitney North Seymour Sr. award 1991), So. Inst. Mgmt. (founder), AIM, U.S. C. of C. (urban and regional affairs com. 1970-73), La. C. of C. (bd. dirs. 1963-66), New Orleans and River Region C. of C. (v.p. met. devel. and urban affairs 1969, past chmn. labor rels. coun., bd. dirs. 1970-78, pres. 1971, dir., exec. com. 1972, ex officio mem., bd. dirs. 1979—), Mil. Order Fgn. Wars (vice comdr. La. Commandery 2000-02, comdr. 2003-04, Comdr. Gen. Disting. Svc. award 2004), Nat. Arbitration Forum, Panel Arbitrators, Bienville Club, Pickwick Club, Plimsoll Club, Serra Club, So. Yacht Club, Sigma Chi (pres. alumni chpt. 1956). Roman Catholic. Died May 17, 2007.

MONAGHAN, MARVIN DANIEL, optometrist; b. Wichita Falls, Tex., Mar. 14, 1926; s. Marvin Gaines and Lillian Frances (Adair) M.; m. Ruth Carolyn Rice, June 15, 1952. B.A. in Physics, U. Tex., 1948; O.D., No. Ill. Coll. Optometry, 1950. Lic. optometrist, Tex. Assoc. James L. Crawford, Sulphur Springs, Tex., 1950-52; gen. practice optometry, Garland, Tex., 1952—; curator: Southwest R.R. Hist. Soc. Mus., 1965—. Editor Clearance Card Jour., 1974—. Mem. Landmark Mus. Soc., Garland, 1983—; mem. North Central Expressway Task Force Citizens adv. com., Dallas, 1984, 85; Dallas Area Rapid Transit Citizens adv. com., 1984—. Served with USNR, 1944-46. Recipient Southwest R.R. Hist. Soc. award, 1974. Mem. Am. Optometric Assn., North Tex. Optometric Soc. (pres. 1955-56), Tex. Optometric Assn. Methodist. Lodge: Rotary. Avocations: railroad museum restoration; photography; model building; antique automobiles; amateur radio. Home: Garland, Tex. Died Apr. 5, 2006.

MONAGHAN, WILLIAM HENRY, advertising executive; b. NYC, Feb. 28, 1928; s. Frances Michael and Elisabeth Josephine (Scully) M.; m. Honora Mary Larkin, Aug. 23, 1952; children: Therese, Thomas, Mary Elizabeth, Timothy. BS, St. Johns U., 1950. Media buyer Ruthrauff & Ryan Inc., NYC, 1951-54; media dir. John C. Dowd Inc., Boston, 1954-61; account exec. Harold Cabot & Co. Inc., Boston, 1961-74, v.p., 1974-77, exec. v.p., 1977-86, pres., 1986-90, chmn., chief exec. officer, from 1990, also bd. dirs. Served with USN, 1946-48, PTO. Home: Charlestown, Mass. Died Jan. 4, 2006.

MONDELLO, ANTHONY LOUIS, lawyer; b. Albany, NY, Sept. 5, 1919; s. Filadelfo J. and Mary (Frascello) M.; m. Omah H. Perino, Feb. 5, 1948 (dec. 1984); children: Robert J., Stephen A., Juanita O.; m. Ann Willett, 1986; 2 step children: Russell, Julie BSS., CCNY, 1940; LL.B., Columbia, 1948. Bar: N.Y. 1948, D.C. 1953. Atty. frauds sect., civil divsn. US Dept. Justice, 1948-55, asst. chief frauds sect., 1956-59, sr. appellate atty., appellate sect., 1959-61, exec. asst. to asst. atty. gen., 1961-62, dep. dir. civil divsn. Office Alien Property, 1963-66, spl. atty. Office Legal Counsel, 1966-68; gen. counsel US Civil Svc. Commn., Washington, 1968-75; practice law Washington, 1975—2006; cons. firm Wilmer, Cutler & Pickering, 1975-76; counsel Amtrak, 1977-78, asso. gen. counsel, 1978-79, dep. gen. counsel, 1979-83, gen. counsel, 1983-84. Mem. Adminstrv. Conf. U.S., 1971-86. Served to maj. AUS, 1942-46, 51-52. Mem. Am., Fed. bar assns. Home: Washington, DC. Died Dec. 7, 2006.

MONNETT, VICTOR BROWN, geologist, former educator; b. Ithaca, NY, Dec. 6, 1915; s. Victor Elvert and Kathryn (Brown) M.; m. Mary Wayne Gambill, Jan. 8, 1940; children: Connie Cay, Monte Mary. BS in Geology, U. Okla., 1937; postgrad., U. Tex., 1937-38; PhD in Geology, U. Mich., 1947. Geologist Carter Oil Co., 1938-40, Imperial Oil Ltd., 1943-44; prof. geology Okla. State U., Stillwater, 1947-80, head geology dept., 1947-55, head geology and geography dept., 1955-66; assoc. dean Okla. State U. (Coll. Arts and Scis.), 1966-67, acting dean, 1967-68, asso. dean, 1968-80. Cons. to industry, 1950-57 Served to capt., C.E. AUS, 1942-46. Mem. Am. Assn. Petroleum Geologists (Distinguished lectr. 1961), Okla. Acad. Sci. (pres. 1951-52), Phi Beta Kappa, Sigma Xi, Sigma Gamma Epsilon. Home: Stillwater, Okla. Died Apr. 2, 2006.

MONROE, DORIS DRIGGERS, author; b. Mt. Pleasant, Tex., July 11, 1916; d. Samuel Wyatt and Leola (Harris) Driggers; student Mary-Hardin Baylor Coll., 1934-35, William Jewell Coll., 1935-37, Southwestern Bapt. Theol. Sem., 1937-38, So. Bapt. Theol. Sem., 1938-39, 44-45, George Peabody Coll., 1947-50; m. Edwin Ulys Monroe, Aug. 6, 1937; children: Leola Fran (Mrs. Dudley B. Burton), Billie Barbara (Mrs. William F. Hardy, Jr.). Music dir., pastor's asst. Bethany Bapt. Ch., Kansas City, Mo., 1945-47; asso. editor Story Hour Leader, Bapt. Sunday Sch. Bd., Nashville, 1947-50, editor Primary Leader, Every Day with Primaries, 1950-68, cons. Work with Exceptional Persons, 1968—. Mem. Sunday sch. bd. So. Bapt. Conv. Mem. Nat. Assn. for Retarded Children, Am. Camping Assn., Am. Pen Women, Beta Lit. Soc. Author: When Marcia Goes to Church, 1966; The Come-and-Go Village, 1967; A Church Ministry to Retarded Persons, 1971; Reaching and Teaching the Mentally Retarded through the Sunday School, 1980; co-author: The Primary Leadership Manual, 1957; co-author, co-editor Adventures in Christian Living and Learning, Exploring Life Curriculum Series, 1968-72. Died Dec. 31, 2006.

MONSKY, MARK B. VON SOMMER, communications executive; b. NYC, Aug. 28, 1941; s. Leo Clement and Irma (Reinhold) M.; m. Beverly DuBose, May 2, 1965; children: Alexander Reinhold DuBose, Eric Demarest DuBose. Student, Columbia U., 1959-62. Reporter N.Y.C. newspapers, 1961-66; producer, reporter CBS News, NYC, 1966-69; mng. editor WNEW-TV, NYC, 1970-74, news dir., 1975, v.p. news, 1976-82; pres. Ind. TV News Assn., 1980-82, Metromedia News Inc., from 1983. Instr. journalism New Sch. for Social Research, N.Y.C., 1973-74 (Recipient Emmy award, Nat. Acad. TV Arts and Scis. 1973, 1977, 78, 80, 81, 82); Author: Looking Out for Number One, 1975. Co-chmn. com. on TV in cts. Adminstrv. Bd., N.Y. State Supreme Ct., 1973-81. Served with U.S. Army, 1962-63. Merit award Am. Bar Assn., 1977, 78; gold shield award N.Y. Press Club, 1975; gold typewriter, 1976 Mem. Radio and TV News Dirs. Assn., N.Y. Press Club. Chief undercover film operations Knapp Commn. on Police Corruption, NYC, 1971. Died June 16, 2006.

MONTELEONE, JOSEPH PATRICK, chemical company executive; b. Bklyn., Mar. 17, 1929; s. Joseph J. Monteleone and Josephine Oliveri; m. Dolores Marie Van Pelt, June 25, 1955; children: Joseph, Joanne, Jude, Christopher, Patricia. BS in Chem Engring., Cooper Union Inst., 1955. Eastern sales mgr. indsl. div. Stauffer Chem. Co. subs. Chesebrough Pond's Inc., NYC, 1965-67, asst. to exec. v.p., 1967-68, v.p. purchasing, 1968-72, v.p., gen. mgr. splty. div. Westport, Conn., 1972-81, group v.p. internat. ops., 1981-85, pres. internat. div., from 1985. Bd. dirs. Tex. Alkyls, Inc., Am. Natural Soda Ash Corp. Bd. dirs. U.S. Yugoslav Council, Inc., Washington. Served to 2d lt. USMC. Mem. Nat. Agrl. Chems. Assn. (fgn. trade com.), Am. Chem. Soc. (N.Y. sect.), Soc. Chem. Industry. Clubs: Country of Darien (Conn.). Republican. Roman Catholic. Avocation: golf. Home: Wilton, Conn. Died Oct. 7, 2005.

MONTZ, FLORENCE STOLTE, church official; b. Lowden, Iowa, June 7, 1924; d. Emil L. and Emma Marie (Meier) Stolte; m. C. R. Montz, June 15, 1947; children: Jennifer Montz Rechlin, Fredrick John. BS, RN, U. Iowa, 1947; LLD (hon.), Concordia Coll., Bronxville, NY, 1984; LHD (hon.), Concordia Coll., St. Paul, 1988. RN, Iowa. V.p., then pres. N.D. dist. Luth. Women's Missionary, Luth. Ch.-Mo. Synod, Bismarck, 1960-68, 1st v.p. internat., 1967-71, pres., 1971-75; editor Better Health mag. Luth. Ch.-Mo. Synod, Bismarck, 1983-95, also bd. dirs. Parish nurse instr. Trinity Hosp., Minot, S.D., 1995—. Mem. Assn. Lutheran Older Adults (pres. 1996—), Sigma Theta Tau. Home: Bismarck, ND. Died Feb. 7, 2007.

MOONEY, JAMES HUGH, newspaper editor; b. Pitts., Aug. 18, 1929; s. James H. and Kathryn A. (Hall) M.; m. Eileen Jane Casey, July 30, 1960; children: Mark Hall, Sean Francis, Annina Marie, James Matthew, Lorelei Jane, Paul Adam, Kathryn Celeste. BA in Journalism, Duquesne U., Pitts., 1957. With advt. dept., then editorial dept. Pitts. Post-Gazette, 1953—61; writer-editor Nat. Observer, 1961—77, Nat. Geographic, 1977—79; editor Found. News mag., Washington, 1979—81; press sec. Congressman Mickey Edwards of Okla., Washington, 1982; asst. nat. editor Washington Times, 1982—83; editor Status Report, 1983—92; dir. info. resources Ins. Inst. for Hwy. Safety, 1992—93; editor Western Pa. Medicine, Johnstown, 1993—95, Embassy Flash, Aspen Hill, Md., 1995—96; pres. Mooney Comms., 1997—2006. Former mem. editl. adv. bd. Nat. Study Ctr. Trauma and Emergency Med. Sys. Served with AUS, 1951-53. Home: Silver Spring, Md. Died May 21, 2006.

MOONEY, THOMAS T., history educator, geography educator; b. Albany, NY, Sept. 12, 1954; s. Donald J. and Marguerite A. Mooney; m. Deborah Schneider, 1988; 1 child, Leilah; m. Virginia Rhodes (div.); 1 child, Ruairi Rhodes. BA, Antioch Coll., 1973. Cert. comprehensive social studies tchg. cert. Ohio, 1973. Tchr. Cin. Pub. Schs., 1974—79; pres. Cin. Fedn. Tchrs., 1979—2000; v.p. Am. Fedn. Tchrs., Washington, from 1992; pres. Ohio Fedn. Tchrs., Columbus, from 2000. Bd. dirs. Albert Shanker Inst., Washington, from 1998, Holmes Partnership, Waco, 1996—2000, Nat. Bd. Profl. Tchg., Arlington, from 2000. Mem. Cincinnatus Assn., Cin., Gay, Lesbian, Straight Educators Network, Washington. Democrat. Avocations: travel, music, Irish, Latin Am. and Caribbean history. Home: Cincinnati, Ohio. Died Dec. 3, 2006.

MOORE, ARNOLD J., university dean; b. New Albin, Iowa, June 10, 1925; s. Leonard Francis and Josephine (Schauls) M.; m. Mildred Mae Klug, June 1, 1930; children: Michele, Sheri, Jane, Karen, Connie, John. BA, U. No. Iowa, 1949; MA, U. Iowa, 1955, PhD, 1961. Tchr. math. and sci. Pub. Schs., 1949-50, adminstr., 1956-61; prof., head curriculum and instrn. Kans. State U., Manhattan, 1967-73; dean. sch. edn. Youngstown (Ohio) State U., 1973-80; dean coll. edn. Miss. State U.,

Mississippi State, from 1980. Chmn. accreditation teams Nat. Council Accreditation of Tchr. Edn., Washington, 1973—. Pres. Miss. State U. Starkville Symphony Assn., 1985-86. Served as pvt. U.S. Army, 1950-52. Named Fellow-Team Leader Internat. Council Edn. for Teaching, 1986; recipient Fulbright award, 1987. Mem. Am. Assn. Colls. for Tchr. Edn. (bd. dirs. 1978-81, 83-86), Assn. for Supervision and Curriculum Devel. (bd. dirs. 1969-71), Miss. Assn. Colls. for Tchr. Edn. (bd. dirs. 1981—, pres. 1987), So. Assn. Colls. and Schs. (program evaluator 1982—), Tchr. Edn. Council State Colls. and Univs. (pres. 1978-79), So. Council Tchrs. Edn. (sec. 1986—), Oktibbeha County C. of C. (edn. com., univ. relations com. 1982—), Phi Kappa Phi, Phi Delta Kappa. Lodges: Rotary (program chmn. Youngstown club). Roman Catholic. Home: Starkville, Miss. Died June 20, 2006.

MOORE, JAMES THOMAS, meteorology educator; b. Mineola, N.Y., Feb. 9, 1952; s. John Edward and Alice Elizabeth (Zeller) M.; m. Kathryn Esther Knenzin, Aug. 12, 1978. B.S. in Meterology, N.Y. U., 1974; M.S. in Atmospheric Sci., Cornell U., 1976, Ph.D., 1979. Asst. prof. meteorology State Univ. Coll. Oneonta, N.Y., 1978-80; mem. faculty St. Louis U., 1980—, asst. to assoc. prof. meteorology, 1985—. Contbr. articles to various publs. Postdoctoral fellow Nat. Aero. and Space Adminstrn., 1979, 80, Am. Soc. Engring. Edn., 1982; NSF grantee, 1983-85. Mem. Am. Meteorol. Soc., Nat. Weather Assn., Air Pollution Control Assn. Lutheran. Home: Saint Louis, Mo. Died July 25, 2006.

MOORE, JOHN ROBERT, aerospace company executive; b. July 5, 1916; BSME, Washington U., St. Louis, 1937; cert. advanced course in engring., GE, Schenectady, NY, 1940; cert. exec. program, UCLA, 1957. Pres. Autonetics divsn. N.Am. Aviation, Anaheim, Calif., 1955-66, exec. v.p. El Segundo, Calif., 1966-67; pres. N.Am. aviation part N.Am. Rockwell, El Segundo, Calif., 1967-70; v.p., pres. Actron divsn. McDonnell Douglas Corp., Monrovia, Calif., 1971-78; v.p. electronic sys. group Northrop Corp., LA, Calif., 1980-85, corp. v.p., gen. mgr. Electromech divsn. Anaheim, Calif., 1985-89, cons. high tech enterprise, from 1989. Home: Sherman Oaks, Calif. Died July 13, 2007.

MOORE, JOSEPH BURTON, engineering executive; b. Tuscaloosa, Ala., Jan. 19, 1926; s. Albert Burton and Ruby Mason (Myrick) M.; m. Janet E. Berger, May 30, 1957; children: Donna, Robert, Katherine, Albert, Nancy. BS in Aero. Engring., U. Ala., 1948, MS in Engring., 1955. Supr. materials devel. GE, Evendale, Ohio, 1954-57; mgr. metall. devel. Wyman Gordon Co., Grafton, Mass., 1957-60; sr. scientist So. Rsch. Inst., Birmingham, Ala., 1960-61; dir. materials engring. and tech. Pratt & Whitney Aircraft, West Palm Beach, Fla., 1961-87; dir. materials engring. Pratt & Whitney, West Palm Beach, from 1987. Indsl. cons. dept. materials scis., U. Fla., Gainesville, 1979—, indsl cons. to dean engring. U. Santa Barbara (Calif.), 1983—; mem. nat. materials adv. bd. NRC, Washington, 1982. Contbr. articles to profl. jours.; patentee in field. Lt. USN, 1943-46, PTO, 1951-52. Recipient George Mead Gold medal United Techs., Hartford, Conn., 1972; named Disting. Engring. fellow U. Ala., Tuscaloosa, 1988. Mem. NAE. Republican. Methodist. Avocations: travel, reading, music, fishing. Home: Jupiter, Fla. Died Jan. 7, 2006.

MOORE, KENNETH RAY, coal company executive; b. Hopkins County, Ky., May 2, 1937; s. Leslie and Zelma Otha (Hooper) M.; m. Sylvia Ann Gatlin, Oct. 29, 1955; children: Kenneth Ray, Kevin Wade. Grad. high sch. With Peabody Coal Co., from 1955, pit foreman Greenville, Ky., 1956-64, erection foreman, 1964-68, maintenance supt. Columbia, Mo., 1968-71, supt. mining ops. Macon, Mo., 1971-73, gen. supt. Denver, 1973-74; dir. Peabody Coal Co. (West Central div.), Columbia, 1974-78; v.p. Peabody Coal Co., Flagstaff, Ariz., 1978; pres. div. Peabody Coal Co. (Ariz. div.), 1978-86; corp. v.p. Peabody Coal Co. (Western div.), 1979-88, pres. div., 1986-88; exec. v.p. corp. office Peabody Coal Co., Henderson, Ky., from 1988. Mem. pres.'s adv. council No. Ariz. U., Flagstaff, 1981-88; bd. dirs. Mus. No. Ariz., 1984-88, Flagstaff Med. Ctr., 1983—, Malapai Found., 1986-88; v.p. bd. dirs. No. Ariz. U. Found., 1986-88; state bd. dirs. Ariz. 4-H Youth Found., 1984—. Named to Honorable Order of Ky. Cols. Mem.: Rotary, Masons (master). Republican. Home: Henderson, Ky. Died May 29, 2006.

MOORE, ROBERT CHARLES, artist, educator; b. Phila., Aug. 11, 1921; s. Charles A. and Marguerite G. (Trulear) M. BFA, Phila. Coll. Art, 1950; MFA, Temple U., 1958; m. Gloria D. Harris, Nov. 23, 1950; 1 child, Dyane M. Exhibited in numerous mus. and univ. group shows in Del. and Pa.; one-man show Cheyney State Coll., Pa., 1958; 2-man show U. Chgo., 1965; represented in permanent collection Blue Cross/Blue Shield of Del., 1980; art tchr. Wilmington (Del.) Sch. Dist., 1950-74; comml. artist S.J. Brown Studios, King Lettering Svc. and freelance, Phila., Wilmington, 1946-60; tchr. art Adult Evening Class, W. Phila. High Sch., 1961-64; dir. arts/crafts program Jewish Community Ctr. of Del's Summer Day Camp, 1959-65; instr., leader W. Phila. Center of the Sch. Art League of Phila., 1961-74; instr. sculpture Moore Coll. Art, Phila., summer, 1971; supr. art edn. Wilmington (Del.) Sch. Dist. and New Castle County Sch. Dist., Del., 1974-81; assoc. prof. art edn. U. Del., 1980; instr. drawing Pa. Gov.'s Sch. for the Arts, Bucknell U., summer, 1973, 74, 75, 76, 81; supr. instruction Brandywine Sch. Dist., Claymont, Del., 1981-83; ednl. cons. Richland County Dist. One, Columbia, S.C., 1975; chmn. art curriculum planning com. New Castle County Sch. Dist. Del., 1978; adv. council for art edn. U. Del., 1977-78; ednl. cons. Alachua County Sch. Dist., Gainesville, Fla., 1985. Aux. vestry St. Thomas Episcopal Ch., Phila., 1963-64, tenor soloist choir, 1983—; promotion art dir. ACCENT Publ. Co., Devon, Pa., 1986-91; designer, coord. spl. exhbn. Valley Forge Nat. Hist. Park, Pa., 1987; bd. dirs. Phila. Art Tchrs. Assn., 1969-70, treas., 1970-74; trustee Del. Art Mus., 1979-84; bd. dirs. Art Educators Del., 1980-83. With U.S. Army, 1942-45. John Hay fellow, Ford Found., 1964-65; U.S. Office Edn. fellow, 1966, 68; named Artist of the Yr., Christ in Christmas Com., Council Chs. Wilmington and New Castle County, Del., 1970; Tchr. of the Yr., Wilmington, 1971; Temple U. Alumni Order of the Owl award, 1974; named Del. Art Educator of Yr., Nat. Art Edn. Assn., 1983, Del. Order of Excellence, 1983. Mem. Art Educators Del., Nat. Art Edn. Assn., Music Educators Nat. Conf., Kappa Alpha Psi. Episcopalian. Contbr. articles to profl. jours. Home: Yeadon, Pa. Died Dec. 26, 2006.

MOORE, ROBERT ERIC, artist; b. Manchester, NH, Oct. 13, 1927; s. George Anthony and Verna Winona (Blaisdell) M.; m. Margaret Doherty, June 2, 1950; children: Deirdre, Bridget, Michael O'Doherty. Student, New England Sch. Art, 1949-51, U. N.H., 1953. One-man shows include Allerbescht Gallery, Telford, Pa., Bayberry Art Gallery, Southern Pines, N.C., Benbow Gallery, Newport, R.I., Copley Soc., Boston, Doll and Richards, Boston, Frost Gully Gallery, Portland, Maine, The Gallery, Spartenburg, S.C., Guild of Boston Artists, Hancock Coll. Art, Santa Maria, Calif., Hobe Sound Galleries North, Portland, John Black Gallery, Cold Spring Harbor, N.Y., Loft Gallery, Princeton, N.J., Munson Gallery, New Haven, Conn., Ogunquit (Maine) Gallery, and others; exhibited in numerous group shows; represented in several permanent collections. Juror Audubon Artists 49th Annual Exhbn., N.Y.C., 1991, Annual New England Watercolor Exhbn., Boston, 1989, Audubon Artists 47th Annual Exbhn., N.Y.C., 1989, Adirondacks Nat. Exhbn Am. Watercolor, 1988; nat. juror 118th Annual Am. Watercolor Soc. Exhbn., N.Y.C., 1985. Recipient Cavanaugh award Springfield Mus. Art, 1962, Copley prize Copley Soc. Boston, 1967, Yankee Mag. award, 1967, Arches Paper award, 1977, Griffey's TV award Nat. Watercolor Soc., 1978, Watercolor award N.Mex. Art League, 1978, St. Vincent's Hosp. award Watercolor Soc. Ala., 1981, William Kowalsky prize, 1983, High Winds medal 118th Annual Am. Watercolor Exhbn., 1985, Pulsifer award, 1987, Dick Blick award La. Watercolor Soc., 1987, Garnet award Adirondacks Nat. Exhbn. Am. Watercolors, 1991, 1st prize Transparent Watercolor Soc. Am., 2005, and others. Fellow Am. Watercolor Soc. (Winsor and Newton award 1984, Dale Myers Cooper medal 1985, Internat. Waters travel exhbn. award 1991-92); mem. Nat. Acad. Design (assoc. 1991, Adolph and Clara Obrig prize 1991), Allied Artists Am. (David Soloway Meml. award 1989, Dr. Clifford W. Mills award 1986, Orion Nova Ltd. award 1982, Grumbacher Artists Materials Co. silver medal 1982), Audubon Artists (Grumbacher Gold medallion 1987). Avocations: hunting, fishing. Home: Waldoboro, Maine. Died Oct. 10, 2006.

MOORE, STEPHEN GATES, bank executive; b. Burlington, Vt., Sept. 30, 1923; s. Allen Ewert and Dorothy (Gates) M.; m. Rayelen Bruce Prouty, Nov. 25, 1944; children: Stephen Gates, Ronda, Chandler. AB cum laude, Dartmouth Coll., 1947; post-grad., Am. Inst. Banking, 1947-51, Rutgers U., 1953-54, 56. With Hanover Bank, NYC, 1947-55, asst. sec., 1951-55; with Howard Nat. Bank & Trust Co., Burlington, Vt., 1955-71, exec. v.p., 1965-71; also bd. dirs.; sr. v.p. Mchts. Nat. Bank, Burlington, 1971-79; mgr. spl. sales Gardenway Pub., Charlotte, Vt., 1979-81; spl. asst. to chief exec. officer Vt. Fed. Bank, Burlington, 1981-88. Instr. small bus. adminstrn. seminars Champlain Coll., 1967, 68, 73; bd. dirs. Resolution, Inc., Burlington, Baird Ctr., Inc., Burlington, treas. 1984-85, pres. 1986-87. Trustee Converse Home, Inc., Burlington, treas., 1987-88, pres., 1987—, Ethan Allen Homestead Trust, Burlington, 1990—, Vt. Archeol. Soc., Montpelier, 1991—; mem. local county Rep. coms.; active Lake Chaplain Maritime Mus., Basin Harbor, Vt. With USNR, 1943-46. Mem. Twin Oaks Tennis Club, Myhre Golf Club, Sigma Phi (treas. Vt. chpt. 1958-85, pres. 1985—, trustee nat. ednl. found. 1986—, pres. of found. 1989-94). Episcopalian. Died Nov. 18, 2005.

MOORE, STEVEN E., energy executive; b. Sayre, Okla., 1946; m. Nancy Moore; children: Lisa, Scott. BBA, U. Okla., 1968; JD, U. Okla. Sch. Law, 1971. Asst. atty. gen. State of Okla., Oklahoma City, 1971—74; various positions including gen. counsel, v.p., sr. v.p. law & pub. affairs, bd. dirs. OGE Energy Corp., Oklahoma City, 1974—95, v.p. law & pub. affairs, 1986—94, sr. v.p. law & pub. affairs, 1994—95, pres., COO, 1995-96, chmn., pres., CEO, 1996—2007, chmn., CEO, 2007. Bd. dir. BOK Fin. Corp., Integris Health. Served in USAR, 1968—74. Recipient Dan J. Macer Environ. Stewardship award (5), U. Okla. Coll. Health. Home: Oklahoma City, Okla. Died Sept. 22, 2007.

MORAN, JIM (JAMES MARTIN MORAN), automotive sales executive; b. Chgo., Aug. 8, 1918; s. James and Anna Moran; m. Jan Moran; children: Arline, Pat, Jim. Owner Courtesy Motor Sales Inc. (formerly Hudson Motor Franchise Inc.), Chgo., 1947-68; chmn., now hon. chmn. JM Family Enterprises Inc., Deerfield Beach, Fla., 1969—2007. Founder Youth Automotive Training Ctr., 1984—2007. Named one of Forbes' Richest Americans, 2006; named to The Automotive Hall of Fame, 2005; recipient Horatio Alger award, 1995, S Fla. Sun-Sentinel's Excalibur award, 1996. Died Apr. 24, 2007.

MORENO, MANUEL D., retired bishop; b. Placentia, Calif., Nov. 27, 1930; Ordained priest Roman Cath. Ch., 1961, ordained aux. bishop of L.A., titular bishop of Tanagra Roman Cath. Ch., 1977. Educator U. of Calif., LA, St. John's Sem., Camarillo, Calif.; installed as bishop of Tucson, 1982—2003. Died Nov. 17, 2006.

MORGAN, BRUCE RAY, management consultant; b. LA, Oct. 29, 1932; s. Francis Raymond and Rose Hall (Black) M.; m. Bette Jeanne Moore, Oct. 7, 1957; children: Michael John, Brian Leo, Jeanne Anne. AA, Sacramento Jr. Coll., 1952; BS, U. Calif.-Berkeley, 1954, LL.B., 1957. Bar: Calif. 1957. Judge adv. USAF, Saudi Arabia and Morocco, 1958-61; atty. firm Thelen, Marrin, Johnson & Bridges, San Francisco, 1961-67; dep. dir. Peace Corps, Nepal, 1967-68, dir, 1968-70; exec. dir. Center Research and Edn., Denver, 1971-75; dir. U.S. representation to Saudi Arabia-U.S. Joint Commn. on Econ. Coop., Riyadh, 1975-76; pres. Bruce Morgan Assocs., Inc., Washington, 1976—2007. Editor: Calif. State Bar Jour. Legis. Rev, 1957. Served with USAF, 1958-61. Mem. U.S., Calif. bars. Died Oct. 14, 2007.

MORGAN, BURTON, advertising executive; b. NYC, Apr. 26, 1925; s. Michael and Esther (Lemberg) M.; m. Evelyn Lenora Rivkin, June 20, 1948; children— Judd Mitchell, Scott Franklin Mgr. promotion services Celanese Fibers Mktg., NYC, 1967-77; dir. print prodn. Ogilvy & Mather, NYC, 1977-78, v.p., 1978-83, sr. v.p., from 1983. Contbr. articles to profl. jours. Mem. Gravure Advt. Council (chmn.), Am. Assn. Advt. Agys. (chmn. print prodn. com. 1987—), Art Dirs. Club of N.Y. Avocations: sailing, photography, collecting and restoring antique clocks. Home: Massapequa Park, NY. Died July 19, 2006.

MORGAN, CARL ROBERT, educator; b. Dubuque, Iowa, Nov. 25, 1929; s. John B. and Marie E. (Wilkinson) M.; m. Eunice M. Kunz, Aug. 27, 1950; children— Janice, Mark. BA, Wartburg Coll., 1950; MA, U. Nebr., 1952; PhD, U. Minn., 1963. Instr. dept. anatomy U. Minn., 1963-64; asst. prof. dept. anatomy U. Ind., Indpls., 1964-67, asso. prof., 1967-70, prof., 1970-78; chmn. dept. anatomy East Carolina U., Greenville, N.C., from 1978. Contbr. articles to profl. jours. Mem. Am. Assn. Anatomists, Am. Diabetes Assn., AAAS, Am. Assn. Anatomy Chairmen, Soc. Exptl. Biology and Medicine (editorial bd. 1975—) Lutheran. Home: Rochester, Minn. Died Nov. 5, 2006.

MORGAN, ELMO RICH, former university official; b. Liberty, Idaho, Apr. 25, 1913; s. John S. and Ethel (Rich) M.; m. Frances Bennion, June 19, 1937; children: Kent B., Anthony W., Nancy. BS in Civil Engring, Utah State U., 1935; D.Sc. (hon.), U. Utah, 1983. Research asst. Utah Agrl. Expt. Sta., 1932-34, field engr., 1934-35; asst. engr. Utah Engineer's Office, 1935-40; mgr. Zia Co., Los Alamos, 1946-47; asst. mgr. AEC, Los Alamos, 1947-51; coordinator coop. research U. Utah, 1951-53, v.p., 1953-58; dir. hwys. State of Utah, 1958-60; v.p. phys. planning and constrn. U. Calif. at Berkeley, 1960-70, dir. facilities, 1974-77; pres. Elmo R. Morgan and Assos., cons., from 1977. Sr. v.p. John Carl Warnecke and Assos., architects, 1970-74; dep. asst. sec. interior for water pollution control, 1967-68; cons. State Dept. and Ford Found., Am. univs. abroad; mem. adv. rev. panel, space analysis manual western Interstate Commn. Higher Edn.; chmn. facilities and planning and mgmt. com. Nat. Assn. Coll. and Univ. Bus. Officers; mem. Energy Task Force U.S. Higher Edn.; mem. tech. council Nat. Conf. States on Bldg. Codes and Standards, Inc. Trustee emeritus Pierce Coll., Athens, Greece. Served to lt. col. C.E. AUS, 1940-46. Fellow ASCE; mem. Am. Soc. Pub. Adminstrs., Am. Council Edn. (chmn. commn. adminstrv. affairs) Home: Salt Lake Cty, Utah. Died Mar. 13, 2007.

MORGAN, FREDERIC LEE, allied health educator, curriculum consultant; b. Plymouth, Ind., Feb. 9, 1935; s. Charles Edward and Lura L. (Warner) M.; m. Joyce Ann Staldine, Sept. 4, 1955; children— Kimberle Lou, Michael Lee. B.S., Manchester Coll., North Manchester, Ind., 1957; M.A., Ball State U., Muncie, Ind., 1964, Ed.D., 1969. Sci. tchr., coach Richland Twp. Schs., Rochester, Ind., 1957-59; biology tchr., coach Argos Community Schs. (Ind.), 1959-66; doctoral fellow Ball State U., 1966-68; asst. prof. biology, 1968-69; chmn. biol. and health sci. Coll. Lake County, Grayslake, Ill., 1969-77; dir. allied health, assoc. prof. allied health careers and Sch. Medicine, So. Ill. U., Carbondale, 1977—; tchr. curriculum devel., adminstrn. in higher edn. Pres. Avon Schs. Sch. Bd., 1972-77; chair Lake Dist. camping Boy Scouts Am., 1972-77; mem. Comprehensive Health Planning in So. Ill., Inc., 1978—. HEW grantee, 1977-82, State of Ill. grantee, 1980—. Mem. NEA, Am. Soc. Allied Health Professions, Nat. Assn. Biology Tchrs., Ill. Community Coll. Biology Teaching Assn. Died June 8, 2006.

MORGAN, JAMES ALLEN, accounting firm executive; b. Oklahoma City, Feb. 20, 1934; s. Arthur William and Helen (Hornstein) M.; m. Suzanne Norman, Mar. 16, 1952; children: Gregory, Melanie, Melissa, Stephanie. BBA, West Tex. State U., 1956. CPA, Okla, Tex., La., N.Y. With Peat, Marwick, Mitchell & Co., Tulsa, Houston, New Orleans, Baton Rouge NYC, 1959-79, sr. nat. ptnr. Paris, 1979-83, mng. ptnr. Phila., from 1983. Sec., treas., mem. 1st operating com. Peat, Marwick, Mitchell Found., N.Y.C., 1974-79; chmn. U.S. personnel and profl. devel. com., Peat, Marwick, Mitchell & Co., N.Y.C., 1974-79, chmn. internat. personnel com., Paris, 1979-83, mem. continental European firm's ptnrship. bd. and operating com., Paris, 1979-83. Mem. Am. Inst. CPA's, Pa. Economy League. Clubs: Perdido Bay (Fla.) Country, Union League (Phila.), Phila. Country. Avocations: golf, tennis. Home: Naples, Fla. Died Apr. 1, 2007.

MORGAN, JOHN BRUCE, hospital care consultant; b. Youngstown, Ohio, Oct. 25, 1919; s. John Benjamin and Ida May (Lane) M.; m. Marian Frampton, July 11, 1969; children: John B., Carolyn, Leonard, Suzanne (dec.). BS, Miami U., 1941 MBA, Harvard U., 1946. Field rep. Gen. Motors Acceptance Corp., Youngstown, 1941; pres. Asso. Hosp. Service, Inc. Youngstown, 1947-74, Hosp. Care Corp. (Blue Cross), Cin., 1974-83, cons., from 1983; pres. Health Maintenance Plan, Cin. 1974-83, Health Care Mutual, Cin., 1974-83. Chmn. bd. govs. chmn. exec. com. Blue Cross Assn., Chgo., 1981-82; chmn. bd Community Life Ins. Co., Worthington, Ohio, 1979-83; mem joint exec. com. Blue Cross-Blue Shield Assns., mem. joint bds. Chgo.; mem. bus. adv. com. Miami U., Oxford, Ohio. Gen chmn. United Fund campaign, Youngstown, 1965; pres. Cance Soc., 1965; chmn. bd. trustees Ch. of the Palms, 1996. Servec with AUS, 1942-46. Mem. Am. Hosp. Assn. (Justin Forc Kimball award 1983), Ohio Hosp. Assn., Ohio C. of C. (bd dirs.), Youngstown Area C. of C. (pres. 1966-67), Delray Beach Fla. C. of C., Delray Dunes Golf and Country Club (bd. dirs. v.p.), Rotary (bd. dirs. Delray Beach club, pres. 1992, Pau Harris fellow), Masons, Elks, Sigma Alpha Epsilon, Delt Sigma Pi. Mem. United Ch. of Christ. Home: Boynton Beach Fla. Died Dec. 15, 2005.

MORGAN, RALPH, manufacturing executive; b. Elkhart, Ind Feb. 23, 1924; s. Ralph Samuel and Jeanette Rae (Randall) M. m. Doris Kathleen (Hayward), Sept. 2, 1945 (div. Jan. 1974) children: Christopher Alan, Carol Jane; m. Georgia Lou Teach Feb. 9, 1975. Student, Wayne State U., 1942-43, 46-47. Apprentice mouthpiece maker J.J. Babbitt Co., Elkhart, 1935-36; profl woodwind musician various dance bands, Ind., Mich., 1936-52; owner, dir. band Music by Morgan, Detroit, 1943; woodwind technician The Linton Band Instrument Co., Elkhart, 1948-50, The Selmer Co., Elkhart, 1950-52, mgr. SE dist. sales, 1952-68, mgr. nat. band instrument, 1970-74, chief woodwind designer, 1974-80; owner, operator Morgan Music Co., Tampa, 1968-70; prin. Morgan Enterprises, Springfield, Ohio, from 1980; pres., chief exec. officer R&G Morgan Enterprises, Inc. Lectr., clinician U. Ky. Music Sch., Louisville, 1986, 87, Clarfest '85 Duquesne U., Pitts., 1985, U. Pitts. Music Dept., 1985, Ind. State U., Terre Haute, 1983. Author, editor Colonial Currency, 1976; patentee in field. Bd. dirs. COMACS, Inc., Champaign, Ill., 1988—. Served to T/sgt. USAF, 1943-45, 45 combat missions. Mem.: Optimist (v.p. Springfield club 1982-83, pres. 1983-84). Republican. Avocations: stamp collecting/philately, antiques. Died Aug. 23, 2007.

MORGNER, AURELIUS, economist, educator; b. NYC, May 23, 1917; s. Oscar A. and Anna G. (Hoffmeister) M. BS in Bus. Adminstrn., U. Mo., 1938, MA in Econs., 1940; PhD, U. Minn., 1955. Investigator Dept. Labor, 1941; project dir. Employment Stblzn. Research Inst., 1941-42; instr. bus. adminstrn. U. Minn., 1942-46; lectr. Northwestern U., 1946-47; assoc. prof. Tex. A&M U., 1947-56, prof., 1956-58; vis. prof. U. São Paulo, Brazil, 1958-60, dir. grad. social studies, 1959-60; prof. econs. U. So. Calif., LA, from 1960, chmn. dept., 1962-69; prof. internat. econs. Sch. Internat. Relations, from 1960. Pub. panel mem. Chgo. Regional War Labor Bd., 1943-45; pub. rep. minimum wage com. Dept. Labor, 1942,43; cons. Govt. Eucador, 1965-68, Govt. Guyana, 1968, state Nev., 1970, Philippines, 1971-72, Yemen Arab Republic, 1974-75; U.S. State Dept. vis. lectr., Brazil, summer 1966 Co-author: Local Labor Markets, 1948, Problems in Economic Analysis, 1948, Problems in the Theory of Price, 1954 (trans. Spanish 1965, Portuguese 1967). Ford faculty fellow Columbia U., 1954-55 Mem. So. Calif. Econ. Assn. (pres. 1965-66), Am. Econs. Assn., Western Econ. Assn., Am. Arbitration Assn., Internat. Studies Assn. Died Nov. 1, 2006.

MORIN, ROBERT JAMES, retired railroad executive; b. Superior, Wis., Mar. 15, 1927; s. Peter Emil and Violet Alma (Saterstrom) M.; m. Muriel Joan Benson, June 17, 1950; 1 son, Robert Peck. Cert., Duluth (Minn.) Bus. U., 1948; cert. jr. bus. adminstrn. U. Minn.-Duluth, 1956. Stenographer, clk. Duluth Missabe & Iron Range Ry. Co., Duluth, 1948-50, sta. clk., 1952; trainmaster's clk. Gt. No. Ry. Co., Superior, Wis., 1952-58, sec. to v.p., gen. counsel, St. Paul, 1958-65, sec. to pres., 1965-70; with Burlington No. Inc., St. Paul, 1970-84, asst. corp. sec., 1980-84, asst. corp. sec. subs. Burlington No. R.R. Co., St. Paul, 1981-84, corp. sec. subs. Burlington No. Airmotive Inc., St. Paul, 1981-83; corp. sec. BN Fin. Services, Inc., St. Paul, 1983-84, Clarkland, Inc., St. Paul, 1982-84, Clarkland Royalty, Inc., St. Paul, 1982-84, 906 Olive Corp., St. Paul, 1982-84. Served with U.S. Army, 1946-48, 50-52. Republican. Lutheran. Club: Lost Spur Country (St. Paul). Lodges: Masons, Shriners. Home: Saint Paul, Minn. Died Dec. 26, 2006.

MORONE, JAMES ANTHONY, insurance company executive; b. S.I., NY, Nov. 18, 1922; s. Joseph A. and Carabelle (Long) M.; m. Stanislava Spira, Mar. 19, 1949; children—James, Joseph, Peter. Student, Columbia Coll., 1940-43; BS, Columbia, 1947. Exec. posts in Brazil Am. Fgn. Ins. Assn., 1947-60, v.p. charge S.Am., Far East, 1961-68, v.p. charge worldwide ops., 1968-71, exec. v.p. Wayne, N.J., 1973-84; sr. v.p. Cigna Worldwide, from 1984. Served with AUS, 1943-46. Mem. Am. C. of C. (Internat. Ins. Adv. Council), Far East Council Commerce and Industry (dir.), Am. Brazilian Assn. (past pres.) Home: Philadelphia, Pa. Died Dec. 18, 2006.

MORRIS, BEN RANKIN, publishing company executive; b. Gastonia, NC, Nov. 12, 1922; s. Theodore Page and Nancy (Rankin) M.; m. Henriette Dargan Hampton, Dec. 20, 1946; children: Ben Rankin, Wade Hampton, Henriette Dargan, Frank Page. BS, N.C. State U., 1948; L.H.D., Belmont Abbey Coll., 1982. Prodn. dept. head Textiles Inc., Gastonia, 1948-50; with Aldrich Machine Works of Greenwood, S.C., Atlanta, Ga., 1950-70, v.p., dir., 1953-70. Pres. State Record Co. (publishers Columbia Newspapers, Inc.), State and Columbia Record, State Printing Co., Bestway Express, Gulf Pub. Co. Inc. (publishers The Daily Herald), State Telecasting Co. Inc., Charleston, S.C. also, Lubbock, Tex., Roswell, N.Mex., Newberry Pub. Co., N.C.; chmn. bd. dirs. all subs.; dir. C. & S. Nat. Bank.; dir. Seibels Bruce Group, Ticaro Inc., Knight-Ridder, Inc., Miami. Chmn. S.C. Found. for Modern Liquor Regulations and Controls, 1971; mem. Greater Columbia Community Relations Council, 1972, S.C. Commn. on Human Affairs, 1972-74; Mem. bd. dirs., exec. com. S.C. Safety Council; trustee Richland County Pub. Library; bd. dirs. Allen U., Providence Hosp. Found.; mem. adv. bd. dirs. Aurora Center for Blind; mem. Columbia Hist. Preservation Com., 1980—. Served with USAAF, 1943-46. Named to S.C. Bus. Hall of Fame. Mem. S.C. C. of C. (chmn. 1975), Palmetto Bus. Forum. Clubs: Forest Lake (Atlanta), Summit (Atlanta), Palmetto (Atlanta), Capital City (Atlanta), Piedmont Driving Club (Atlanta). Episcopalian. Home: Columbia, SC. Died Oct. 19, 2005.

MORRIS, CARLOSS (WILLIAM MORRIS), lawyer, insurance company executive; b. Galveston, Tex., June 7, 1915; s. William Carloss and Willie (Stewart) M.; m. Doris Poole, Dec. [illegible], 1939; children: Marietta (Mrs. Morgan Maxfield), William Carloss III, Malcolm Stewart, Melinda Louise (Mrs. Glen Ginter). BA with distinction, Rice Inst., 1936; JD with highest honors, U. Tex., 1939. Bar: Tex. 1938. With Stewart Title Guaranty Co., Houston, 1939—2005, pres., 1951-75, chmn. bd. dirs., chief exec. officer, 1975-91; chmn. bd. dirs., co-chief exec. officer Stewart Info. Services Inc., 1975-2000; chmn. exec. com. Stewart Title Guaranty Co., 1975—2005. Stockholder Morris, Lendais, Hollrah and Snowden, Houston. Chmn. Interdisciplinary Commn. on Housing and Urban Growth, 1974-77; chmn. Star Hope Mission, 1951-90, hon., 1991-2005; pres. Tex. Safety Assn., 1950-51; bd. dirs. Goodwill Industries; bd. dirs., mem. exec. com. Billy Graham Evangelistic Assn., 1956-2000, adv. dir., 2000-05; chmn. Baylor Coll. Medicine, 1968, trustee, 1952-2005; trustee, deacon 1st Bapt. Ch., Houston, chmn. bd. deacons, 1987-89; trustee Baylor U., 1952-72, past vice chmn. bd. dirs.; trustee Oldham Little Ch. Found., B.M. Woltman Found. Recipient Book of Golden Deeds award Exch. Club of Houston, 1974, Disting. Svc. awrad Tex. Soc. Sons Am. Revolution, 1988, Gen. Maurice Hirsch award Soc. for Fund Raising Execs., 1988, George Washington Honor medal Freedoms Found. at Valley Forge, 1990; inducted into Tex. Bus. Hall of Fame, 1995. Fellow Am. Bar Found., State Bar Tex. Found.; mem. ABA (past chmn. younger lawyers sect.), Tex. Bar Assn., Tex. Young Lawyers Assn. (past pres.), Chancellors, Order of Coif, Phi Delta Phi, Alpha Tau Omega. Clubs: River Oaks Country, University. Lodges: Kiwanis. Died Nov. 17, 2005.

MORRIS, LEONARD, state legislator, realtor; b. Batesville, Miss., Sept. 15, 1947; m. Belinda Faye Mackey. Student, U. Miss., U. Okla. State legislator Miss. Ho. of Reps., Jackson, from 1993. Vice chmn. enrolled bills coms. Miss. Ho. of Reps., mem. constitution, edn., fees and salaries, and municipalities coms. Former mem. Sch. Bd.; exec. dir. North Delta Planning and Devel. Dist. Mem. Mason, Nat. Assn. of Realtors, Phi Beta Sigma. Democrat. Baptist. Home: Batesville, Miss. Died Jan. 12, 2007.

MORRIS, ROBERT STEVEN, newspaper publisher; b. Princeton, NJ, Nov. 20, 1951; s. Mac Glenn and Janelle (Connevey) M.; 1 child, Manley Wessling. BA, Davidson Coll., 1974. Asst. retail mgr. Kansas City (Mo.) Star, 1974-78; major accounts mgr. N.Y. Daily News, NYC, 1978-81; advt. dir. Denver Post, 1981-85; v.p. advt. Detroit Free Press, 1985-86, Denver Post, 1986-87; pub. L.A. Daily News, from 1987. Inventor inventory print availability technique, 1985; contbr. articles to newspapers. Bd. dirs. Urban League of Denver, 1986-87. Mem. Internat. Newspaper Advt. and Mktg. Execs. (bd. dirs. 1986—, chmn. retail com. 1986—), Young Pres.'s Orgn. Presbyterian. Home: Woodland Hills, Calif. Died Aug. 3, 2006.

MORRIS, SETH IRWIN, architect; b. Madisonville, Tex., Sept. 1, 1914; s. Seth Irwin and Carrie (Holleman) M.; m. Suzanne Kibler, Dec. 29, 1945; children: Mark Peter, Maria, David Kibler, Laura Houston, John Hampson. BA, Rice Inst., 1935. Practice architecture, Houston, 1935-38; ptnr. Wilson & Morris, 1938-46, Wilson, Morris & Crain, 1946-54, Wilson, Morris, Crain & Anderson, 1954-72, S.I. Morris Assocs., 1972-87, cons., from 1988; ptnr. Morris/Aubry Architects, 1980-85, Morris Architects, 1986-87; cons. Jackson & Ryan, from 1989. Prin. works include Harris County Domed Stadium (Astrodome), 1965, Houston Pub. Library, 1975, S.W. Home Office Texaco Inc., 1975, Prudential Ins. Co., 1977, One Houston Center, 1977, Brown and Root, Inc. hdqrs, 1978, Alfred C. Glassell, Jr. Sch. Art, 1979, 1st City Bank Tower, 1981, Wortham Theater Ctr., 1985. Chmn. bd. trustees Houston Mus. Fine Arts, 1961-63, 67-68, pres., 1967-68; chmn. bd. trustees Contemporary Arts Mus., 1988-89; bd. govs. Rice U., Houston.; bd. dirs. ARC Harris County. Served to comdr. USNR, 1942-46. Decorated Legion of Merit; Order Cloud and Banner China; recipient numerous archtl. honor awards Tex. Soc. Architects, numerous archtl. honor awards Houston chpt. AIA; nat. awards AIA, Gold medal Assn. Rice U. Alumni, 1991; named Disting. Alumnus Rice U., 1981 Fellow AIA; mem. Tex. Soc. Architects (Llewellen Pitts award 1992), Assn. Gen. Contractors (master builder award 1994, Rice Design Alliance award for design excellence 1998), Houston C. of C. (dir. 1964-86). Presbyterian (elder). Home: Houston, Tex. Died Aug. 7, 2006.

MORRISON, FRANK BRENNER, JR., state justice; b. McCook, Nebr., Sept. 27, 1937; s. Frank Brenner and Maxine Elizabeth (Hepp) M.; m. Sharon Romaine McDonald, June 28, 1959; children: John Martin, Anne Elizabeth. BS, U. Nebr., 1959; LL.B., JD, U. Denver, 1962. Bar: Nebr., Mont. Assoc. firm McGinley, Lane, Mueller & Shaanahan, Ogallala, Nebr., 1962-64; ptnr. firm Eisenstatt, Higgins, Miller, Kinnamon & Morrison, Omaha, 1964-69, Morrison & Hedman, Whitefish, Mont., 1969-78, Morrison, Jonkel, Kemmis & Rossback, Missoula, Mont., 1978-80; justice Mont. Supreme Ct., from 1981. Mem. part-time faculty Flathead Valley Community Coll., Kalispell, U. Mont. Law Sch. Past pres. Whitefish Community Devel.; past del. Democratic Nat. Conv. Recipient Disting. Service award Student Bar Assn. U. Mont. Law Sch., Disting. Service award Flathead County Bar Assn.; Gold medal award Law Sci. Acad. Am. Fellow Internat. Soc. Barristers; mem. Order St. Ives, Sigma Chi. Clubs: Toastmasters (past club pres., past area gov.), Kiwanis, Mont, Green Meadow Country. Democrat. Episcopalian. Home: Whitefish, Mont. Died Jan. 8, 2006.

MORRISSEY, THOMAS LEO, lawyer; b. Weehawken, NJ, Aug. 30, 1915; s. Leo W. and Florence (Brown) M.; m. Doris J. Pier, Jan. 17, 1948 (dec.); children— Michael T., Eileen M., Steven A.; m. Eleanor K. Felder, Mar. 10, 1981. BA, Rutgers U., 1937; LL.B., Fordham U., 1940; postgrad., N.Y. U. Law Sch., 1953-54. Bar: N.Y. bar 1940, N.J. bar 1942, also U.S. Supreme Ct 1957. Mem. legal staff N.Y. County dist. atty. Thomas E. Dewey, 1940; with firm Carpenter, Bennett & Morrissey, Newark, from 1947, mem. firm, from 1953. Author: Odyssey of Fighting Two; contbg. author: The Developing Labor Law. Trustee Brundage Charitable Found, Sci. and Wildlife Conservation Found., Upton Charitable Found. Served to lt. comdr. USNR, 1942-46, 51-52, PTO, Korea. Fellow Am. Bar Found.; mem. Internat. Bar Assn. (patron), ABA, N.J. Bar Assn., Essex County Bar Assn., Am. Coll. Trial Lawyers, Tau Kappa Alpha. Clubs: Essex (Newark); Morristown. Republican. Roman Catholic. Died May 17, 2006.

MORROW, DAVID AUSTIN, III, veterinary medical educator; b. Arch Spring, Pa., Jan. 14, 1935; s. David Austin and Mary Harnish (Burket) M.; m. Sarah Linda MacDonough, Aug. 28, 1965; children: David Austin IV, Laurie Elizabeth, Melanie MacDonough. BS, Pa. State U., 1956; DVM, Cornell U., 1960, PhD, 1967. Postdoctoral fellow Cornell U., Ithaca, N.Y., 1965-68; assoc. prof. Mich. State U., East Lansing, 1968-81, prof. Coll. Vet. Medicine, 1981-90, prof. emeritus, from 1990; vet. cons., from 1990. Vis. scientist Colo. State U., Ft. Collins, 1975-76. Editor: Current Therapy in Theriogenology, 1980, 2d edit., 1986. Elder Presbyn. Ch.; trustee Pa. State U., 1987-2002, chmn. bd. trustees phys. plant com., 1994-96, presdl. selection com., 1995. Recipient Norden Disting. Teaching award Mich. State U., 1975, Outstanding Teaching award, 1979-80, 84-86, Dairy Sci. Disting. Alumnus award Pa. State U., 1992, Hon. Lion Ambassador award Pa. State U., 1993, Hon. Alumnus award Mich. State U. Coll. Veterinary Medicine, 1993; coach 1st place team SAVMA Nat. Intercollegiate Bovine Reproduction Contest, 1986, 88-90; named Industry Person of Yr. World Dairy Expo, 1997, Alumni fellow Pa. State U., 1998. Mem. AVMA (Borden award 1980, Am. Feed Mfg. award 1992), Am. Coll. Theriogenologists (charter diplomate), Pa. State U. Coll. Agr. Alumni Soc. (pres.-elect 1985-86, pres. 1987-89, past pres. 1989-91), Greek Alumni Interest Group (pres. 1995-2000), Pa. State U. Alumni Coun. (exec. bd. 1983-95, pres.-elect 1989-91, pres. 1991-93, past pres. 1993-95, Lions Paw award 2002), Phi Zeta (pres. 1977-79), Phi Kappa Phi (exec. bd.), Golden Key (hon.), Alpha Zeta (life, bd. dirs., Centennial Honor Roll 1997, chpt. Centennial Disting. Alumnus 1998), Sigma Xi. Republican. Avocations: skiing, gardening. Home: State College, Pa. Died Dec. 22, 2005.

MORSE, DAVID CHISHOLM, hardware distribution executive; b. Bellingham, Wash., June 30, 1913; s. Robert Irvine and Ada Margaret (Chisholm) M.; m. Evelyn Joyce Pfueller, Aug. 31, 1935; children: Patricia Ann, Robert I., David Chisholm, Catherine Ann. Student Western Wash. U., 1930-31; BBA, U. Wash., 1934. With purchasing div. Morse Hardware Co., Bellingham, 1934-36, salesman, 1936-47, v.p., 1948-58, pres., 1958-75, chmn., 1975—; trustee, chmn. Mt. Baker Mut. Savs. Bank, Bellingham, 1957-85; dir. Bellingham Nat. Bank, 1964-86; exec. com. PRO Hardware, Inc., Stamford, Conn., 1972-78. Vice pres. YMCA, Bellingham, 1954-57; exec. United Good Neighbors, 1962. Served to lt. (j.g.) USNR, 1943-46, PTO. Named Merchandiser of Yr., Hardware Merchandiser Mag., 1969; Paul Harris fellow Rotary Club Bellingham, 1977. Mem. Bellingham C. of C. (pres. 1964). Republican. Baptist. Clubs: Rotary, University. Lodges: Masons, Scottish Rite. Home: Bellingham, Wash. Died Feb. 20, 2007.

MORSE, F.D., JR., dentist; b. Glen Lyn, Va., Apr. 5, 1928; s. Frank D. and Ida Estell (Davis) M.; m. Patsy Lee Apple, Feb. 4, 1967; 1 child, Fortis Davis; m. Nancy Zink; 1 child, Pamela Marie. Student, U. Va., 1945; BS, Concord Coll., 1951; DDS, Med. Coll. Va., 1955. Freelance photographer, 1950-56; practice dentistry Pearisburg, Va., from 1958; mem. staff Giles Hosp., Pearisburg, 1958-86. Served from asst. dental surgeon to sr. asst. dental surgeon USPHS, 1955-57; assigned to USCG, 1957-58. Honors scholar U. Va. Mem. AAAS, ADA, S.W. Va. Dental Assn., Assn. Mil. Surgeons, Nat. Assn. Advancement Sci., Fedn. Dentaire Internat., Internat. Platform Assn., W.Va. Collegiate Acad. Sci., Kiwanis, Beta Phi. Achievements include research in dental ceramics and roof coatings. Died Aug. 23, 2006.

MOSER, HUGO WOLFGANG, neurologist; b. Switzerland, Oct. 4, 1924; came to U.S., 1940, naturalized, 1943; s. Hugo L. and Maria (Werner) M.; m. Monti Lou Brigham (div.); children: Tracey, Peter (dec.); m. Ann Boody, Dec. 28, 1963; children: Karen, Lauren. MD, Columbia U., 1948; A.M. in Med. Sci, Harvard U., 1956. Intern Columbia-Presbyn. Med. Center, NYC, 1948-50; asst. in medicine Peter Bent Brigham Hosp., Boston, 1950-52; research fellow dept. biol. chemistry Harvard U., 1955-57; asst. resident, resident in neurology Mass. Gen. Hosp., 1957-59, asst. neurologist, 1960-67, assoc. neurologist, 1967-69, neurologist, 1969-76. Teaching fellow neuropathology Harvard Med. Sch., 1959-60, instr. neurology, 1960-64, assoc. in neurology, 1964-67, asst. prof., 1967-69, asso. prof., 1969-72, prof., 1972-76; dir. research and tng. Walter E. Fernald State Sch., 1963-68, asst. supt., 1968-73, acting supt., 1973-74, supt., 1974-76; dir. Center for Research on Mental Retardation and Related Aspects of Human Devel., Kennedy Krieger Inst., 1976-88, Neurogenetics Rsch. Ctr., 1995-2007, dir. univ. affiliated facilities for mentally retarded, 1965-74; co-dir. Eunice Kennedy Shriver Center for Mental Retardation, Inc., 1969-74; pres. John F. Kennedy Inst., Balt., 1976-88; prof. neurology and pediatrics Johns Hopkins U., 1976-2007. Author: (with others) Mental Retardation: An Atlas of Diseases with Associated Physical Abnormalities, 1972; Contbr. (with others) articles to med. jours. Served with AUS, 1943-44; to capt. U.S. Army, 1952-54. Recipient Hower award Child Neurology Soc., 1994, Becker award German Soc. for Neuropediats., 1999, Frank Ford award Internat. Child Neurology Assn., 2002. Mem. Am. Acad. Neurology, Am. Assn. Mental Deficiency, Am. Assn. Neuropathologists, Am. Neurol. Assn., Internat. Soc. Neurochemistry, Am. Pediatrics Soc., Sigma Xi, Alpha Omega Alpha. Home: Baltimore, Md. Died Jan. 20, 2007.

MOSES, LINCOLN E., statistician, educator; b. Kansas City, Mo., Dec. 21, 1921; s. Edward Walter and Virginia (Holmes) Moses; m. Jean Runnels, Dec. 26, 1942; children: Katherine, James O'D., William C., Margaret, Elizabeth; m. Mary Louise Coale, 1968. AB, Stanford, 1941, PhD, 1950. Asst. prof. edn. Columbia Tchrs. Coll., 1950—52; faculty Stanford U., from 1952, prof. stats., from 1959, exec. head dept., 1964—68; assoc. dean Stanford U. (Sch. Humanities and Scis.), 1965—68, 1985—86, dean grad. studies, 1969—75; faculty Stanford U. (Med. Sch.), from 1952; adminstr. Energy Info. Adminstrn., Dept. of Energy, 1978—80. L.L. Thurstone disting. fellow U. N.C., 1968—69; com. mem., intermittently Am. Friends Svc. Com., from 1954, chmn. No. Calif. chpt., 1972—76, 1984—88. Bd. dirs. Am. Found. for AIDS Rsch., 1992—97. Fellow Guggenheim, 1960—61, Ctr. for Advanced Study in Behavioral Scis., 1975. Fellow: Inst. Math. Stats. (coun. 1969—72), Am. Acad. Arts and Scis.; mem.: Internat. Statis. Inst., Biometric Soc. (pres. Western N.Am. region 1969), Am. Statis. Assn. (coun. 1966—67), Inst. Medicine of NAS. Died Dec. 17, 2006.

MOSLEY, DONALD CRUMPTON, management educator; b. Starkville, Miss., Apr. 17, 1932; s. Thomas Henry and Elizabeth (Crumpton) M.; m. Susan Young Mosley, Apr. 7, 1961; children: Don, Junior. BS, Miss. State U., 1954; MS, U. Tenn., 1958; PhD, U. Ala., 1965. Trainee Pick Hotel Corp., 1957-59; field rep. Charles E. Merrell Pub. Co., Columbus, Ohio, 1959-60; instr. U. Ala., 1960-62; prof. mgmt., chmn. dept. Miss. State U., 1962-68; vis. prof. U. Otago, N.Z., 1969; prof., dean U. South Ala., Mobile, 1973-82, prof. mgmt., 1983—99, prof. emeritus,

1999—2007. Cons. in field; pres. Synergistic Cons. Group, Mobile, 1985—2007 Author: (with D.C. Williams) Analysis and Evaluation of a Community Action and Poverty Program in the Mississippi Delta, 1967, (with Paul Pietri and Leon Megginson) Management: The Art of Working With and Through People, 1973, Management: Concepts and Applications, 1986, 4th edit., 1992, Supervisory Management, 1985, 3d edit., 1992; contbr. articles to profl. jours. Served with AUS, 1954-56. Mem. Acad. Mgmt., So. Mgmt. Assn., The OD Inst., Assn. Psychol. Type, Beta Gamma Sigma, Delta Sigma Phi. Died July 30, 2007.

MOSS, WILLIAM WARNER, III, archivist; b. NYC, May 11, 1935; BA in Polit. Sci., Haverford Coll., 1957; MA in Pub. Law, Govt., Columbia U., 1964. Interviewer oral history program John F. Kennedy Library, Boston, 1969-71, chief oral history program, 1971-73, sr. archivist, 1973-75, then chief archivist; archivist Smithsonian Instn., Washington, from 1984. Contbr. articles to profl. publs. Mem. Soc. Am. Archivists, Oral History Assn. (mem. council 1975-80, pres. 1978-79), New Eng. Archivists, New Eng. Assn. Oral History (Harvey Kantor Meml. award 1978). Died Aug. 1, 2007.

MOSSON, JUDITH, psychotherapist, educational consultant; b. N.Y.C., Sept. 17, 1942; d. Louis and Harriet (Michelson) M. B.S., Cornell U., 1963, M.A., 1964; M.A. in Wholistic Counseling and Edn., Inst. for Wholistic Edn. and Counseling, Beacon Coll., 1980. Cert. practitioner of neuro-linguistic programming; teaching lic., N.Y.C. Tchr. of gifted N.Y.C. Bd. Edn., 1964-80, dir. gifted programs Dist. 2, 1980-82, project dir. ABC's for sex equity Dist. 2, 1980-81, human relations liaison officer Dist. 2, 1980-82, local equal opportunity coordinator, 1980-82, curriculum devel. coordinator, 1980-82; assoc. N.Y. Tng. Inst. for Neuro-Linguistic Programming, N.Y.C., 1980-83; assoc., clin. cons. Assocs. for Bulimia and Related Disorders, N.Y.C., 1981-84; dir. N.Y. Assocs. for Eating Disorders, N.Y.C., 1984—; pvt. practice psychotherapy, N.Y.C., 1981—; leader, cons. workshop. Mem. Soc. for Neuro-Linguistic Programming, United Fedn. Tchrs. (chpt. chmn. 1964-67), Assn. for Humanitisc Psychology, N.Y. Soc. for Ericksonian Psychotherapy and Hypnosis, Sigma Delta Tau. Democrat. Jewish. Club: Cornell Alumni (N.Y.C.). Home: Tamarac, Fla. Died Mar. 5, 2007.

MOUNTAIN, CLIFTON FLETCHER, surgeon, educator; b. Toledo, Apr. 15, 1924; s. Ira Fletcher and Mary (Stone) M.; m. Merel Ann Grey; children: Karen Lockerby, Clifton Fletcher, Jeffrey Richardson. AB, Harvard U., 1946; MD, Boston U., 1954. Diplomate Am. Bd. Surgery. Dir. dept. statis. rsch. Boston U., 1947—50; cons. rsch. analyst Mass. Dept. Pub. Health, 1951—53; intern U. Chgo. Clinics, 1954, resident, 1955—58, instr. surgery, 1958—59; sr. fellow thoracic surgery Houston, 1959. Mem. staff U. Tex. Anderson Cancer Ctr.; asst. prof. thoracic surgery U. Tex., 1960-73, assoc. prof surgery, 1973-76, prof., 1976-94, prof. emeritus, 1995-2007, prof. surgery Sch. Medicine, 1987-2007, chief sect. thoracic surgery, 1970-79, chmn. thoracic oncology, 1979-84, chmn. dept. thoracic surgery, 1980-85, cons. dept. thoracic and cardiovascular surgery, 1996-2007, chmn. program in biomath. and computer sci., 1962-64, Mike Hogg vis. lectr. in S. Am., 1967; prof. surgery U. Calif., San Diego, 1996-2007; pres., chmn. Mountain Found. for Lung Cancer Rsch. and Edn., 1997-2007; mem. sci. mission on cancer USSR, 1970-78, and Japan, 1976-84; com. health, rsch. and edn. facilities Houston Cmty. Coun., 1964-78; cons. Am. Joint Com. on Cancer Staging and End Result Reporting, 1964-74, Tex. Heart Inst., 1994-96; mem. Am. Joint Com. on Cancer, 1974-86, chmn. lung and esophagus task force; working party on lung cancer and chmn. com. on surgery Nat. Clin. Trials Lung Cancer Study Group, NIH, 1971-76; mem. plans and scope com. cancer therapy Nat. Cancer Inst., 1972-75, mem. lung cancer study group, 1977-89, chmn. steering com., 1973-75, mem. bd. sci. counselors divsn. cancer treatment, 1972-75; hon. cons. Shanghai Chest Hosp. and Lung Cancer Ctr., Nat. Cancer Inst. of Brazil; sr. cons. Houston Thorax Inst., 1994-96. Editor The New Physician, 1955-59; mem. editl. bd. Yearbook of Cancer, 1960-88, Internat. Trends in Gen. Thoracic Surgery, 1984-91; contbr. articles to profl. jours., chpts. to textbooks. Chmn. profl. adv. com. Harris County Mental Health Assn.; bd. dirs. Harris County Chpt. Am. Cancer Soc. Lt. USNR, 1942-46. Recipient award Soviet Acad. Sci., 1977, Garcia Meml. medal Philippine Coll. Surgeons, 1982, Disting. Alumni award Boston U., 1988, Disting. Achievement U. Tex. M.D. Anderson Cancer Ctr., 1990, Disting. Svc. award Internat. Assn. for the Study of Lung Cancer, 1991, Disting. Alumnus award Boston U. Sch. of Medicine, 1992, ALCASE Internat. award for excellence, 1997, Rudolf Nissen medal German Soc. Cardiovascular and Thoracic Surgery, 1998, named hon. pres. First Internat. Congress on Thoracic Surgery, 1997; Fellow ACS Am. Coll. Chest Physicians (chmn. com. cancer 1967-75), Am. Assn. Thoracic Surgery, Inst. Environ. Scis., N.Y. Acad. Sci., Assn. Thoracic and Cardiovascular Surgeons of Asia (hon.), Hellenic Cancer Soc. (hon.), Chilean Soc. Respiratory Diseases (hon., hon. pres. 1982). Mem. AAAS, AMA, Am. Assn. Cancer Rsch., So. Med. Assn., Am. Thoracic Soc., Soc. Thoracic Surgeons, Soc. Biomed. Computing, Am. Fedn. Clin. Rsch., Internat. Assn. Study Lung Cancer (pres. 1976-78), Am. Radium Soc., European Soc. Thoracic Surgeons, Pan-Am Med. Assn., Houston Surg. Soc., Soc. Surg. Oncology, James Ewing Soc., Sigma Xi. Achievements include conception and development of program for application of mathematics and computers to the life sciences, of resource for experimental designs, applied statistics and computational support; concept and implementation of multidisciplinary, site specific cancer mgmt. clinics; first clinical use of physiological adhesives in thoracic surgery; demonstration of clinical behavior of undifferentiated small cell lung cancer; first laser resection of lung tissue at thoracotomy; development of international system for staging of lung cancer. Home: La Jolla, Calif. Died Apr. 19, 2007.

MOUSER, GRANT EARL, III, retired foreign service officer; b. Marion, Ohio, July 11, 1923; s. Grant Earl M. and Hilda Kenyon (Gorham) Crenshaw; m. Lena Little, Feb. 12, 1955; 1 son, Grant Earl IV. BA, Washington and Lee U., 1943, JD, 1948; student, Mannix Walker Sch. Fgn. Service, 1949-50, U.S. Naval War Coll., 1966, Fed. Exec. Inst., 1973. Vice consul Am. consulate gen., Hamburg, W. Ger., 1950-53; econ., comml. officer Am. embassy, Tehran, Iran, 1953-56; Iranian desk officer Dept. State, Washington, 1957-60; polit. officer Am. embassy, Bonn, W. Ger., 1960-65; Indian desk officer Dept. State, 1968-70; polit. officer Am. embassy, New Delhi, India, 1970-73; fgn. service insp. Dept. State, worldwide, 1973-76; State Dept. rep. Armed Forces Staff Coll., Norfolk, Va., 1977-80; cons. gen. Am. consulate gen., Hamburg, W. Ger., 1980-85; exchange officer Dept. Def., Washington, 1966-68; ret., 1985; diplomat in residence Old Dominion U., Norfolk, Va., from 1985. Vis. prof. Allegheny Coll., Meadville, Pa., 1976-77; lecturer Old Dominion U., Norfolk, 1985-86, William and Mary, Williamsburg, Va., 1986-93; site interpreter Jamestown Rediscovery, 1994—; dir. colonial capital br., trustee APVA. Bd. dirs. World Affairs Council, Norfolk, 1977-80; vice chmn. James City County Rep. com., 1991; layman Bruton Parish Ch., 1985-93. Served to lt. USNR, 1943-46. Recipient Superior Service award Dept. State, 1977; recipient Meritorious Honor award Dept. State, 1980, Joint Service Commendation medal Dept. Def., 1978. Mem. SAR (pres. 1992), Am. Fgn. Service Assn., U.S. Naval Inst., Phi Gamma Delta. Republican. Epicopalian. Avocations: map collecting, book collection, tennis. Home: Williamsburg, Va. Died Mar. 26, 2006.

MOYSE, HERMANN, JR., banker; b. Baton Rouge, Aug. 3, 1921; s. Hermann and Rosalie (Gottlieb) M.; m. Marie Louise Levy, June 4, 1942; children— Lewis Arthur, Hermann III, Marie Rosalie. BA, La. State U., 1942. With City Nat. Bank of Baton Rouge, from 1946, v.p., 1962-70, exec. v.p., 1970-72, pres., 1972-81, chmn., 1981-94, chmn. emeritus, from 1995, also dir. Pres., dir. Bistineau-Webster Oil Co.; sec., dir. Baton Rouge Realty Co., Ltd., Lottie Land & Devel. Co., Inc., Melrose Devel. Corp.; chmn. bd. First Commerce Corp., 1992—; bd. dirs. Pan Am. Life Ins. Co., Bank of Zachary, 1971-93. Pres. Capital Area United Givers Fund, 1966-67; mem. exec. com. Pub. Affairs Rsch. Coun., 1968-70; exec. com. Perkins Radiation Ctr.; bd. dirs. La. State U. Found. Maj. F.A. AUS, 1942-46. Decorated Bronze Star. Mem. Am. Bankers Assn. (governing coun. 1975-77), La. Bankers Assn. (pres. 1967-68, Baton Rouge Country Club, City Club of Baton Rouge. Home: Baton Rouge, La. Died Aug. 7, 2007.

MUCHMORE, DON MONCRIEF, retired cultural organization administrator, retired museum director, foundation administrator; b. Wichita, Kans., Dec. 26, 1922; s. Floyd Stephen and Ivy Fay (Campbell) Muchmore; m. Virginia Gunn, June 18, 1949 (div. Dec. 1978); children: Melinda, Marcia. BA, Occidental Coll., Los Angeles, 1945; postgrad., U. So. Calif. Law Sch., 1945, UCLA. Intern Nat. Inst. Pub. Affairs, Washington, 1944; exec. asst. to congressman Washington, 1946-48; teaching asst. UCLA, 1949-50; mem. faculty San Diego State U., 1950-51; asst. prof., adminstr. Calif. State U., Long Beach, 1951-56; pres., CEO The Campbell Found., LA, 1956—2002; spl. asst. to supt. pub. instrn. Calif. Dept. Edn., Sacramento, 1956-57; exec. mus. dir. Calif. Mus. Sci. and Industry, LA, 1957-62, 82-89; exec. v.p., chief exec. officer Calif. Mus. Found., LA, 1957-62, 82-89; dep. dir. (on loan from mus.) Calif. Dept. Fin., Sacramento, 1960; exec. vice chancellor Calif. State Colls. and Univs. System, Long Beach, 1962-64; first exec. asst. to chmn. and chief exec. officer Calif. Fed. Savs. and Loan Assn., LA, 1964-66; sr. v.p. Calif. Fed. Savs. and Loan Assn, LA, 1966-82; pres., CEO PE Conservation Svcs., Inc., 1990-94; ret., 2002. Chmn. bd. dirs., CEO Opinion Rsch. of Calif. Opinion Surveyors, The State Poll and Mktg. Surveys, Inc., Long Beach, 1948—71; syndicated by L.A. Times, 1961—70; also M-R Assocs. Campaigns; cons. in pub. opinion mus. mgmt. and fund raising, 1948—71; chmn., CEO, cons. DMM & Assocs., Long Beach, 1961—2002; sec., treas. EVENUP for the Homeless, 1994—97; mem. Inst. Mus. Svcs., 1983—88. Contbr. chapters to books. Participant in pub. opinion work Dem. and Rep. Campaigns, 1954—72; mem., chmn. 4 presdl. commns., 1970—82, Just Say No Internat., 1989—91, Reading is Fundamental, from 1989, The Buckley Sch., 1989—90; cons. overseas traveling sci. exhibit, planning mus., 1984—96; sr. adminstr., advisor, cons. PCS (South Ctrl. L.A.) Sr. Citizens, 1995—96; cons. Long Beach com. Improvement League, 1995—96; lead cons. New Solution to Homeless, 1993—98; prin. officer Peruvians Cultural Exhibit, 1988—96; prin. cons. cultural exhibit Wonders of World, 1992—95, Queensway Bay, Long Beach, 1992—98; bd. dirs. Bus. Tele Network, 1995—97; active Even up for the Homeless, 1996—98; cons. Christian Outreach Agy., 1998—99; pres. Harborplace Tower Home Owners Assn., from 1999; pres. bd. trustees East Village Cmty. Ch., from 1998, pres., 1998—2001. Named Chpt. Advisor of Yr., Sigma Alpha Epsilon, 1999, Pollster of Yr., Newsweek, 1968; recipient Highest Mus. Edn. award, Sigma Alpha Epsilon, 1992, Citizen of Yr. award and numerous other awards from nat., state and local groups; scholar Elks Nat. scholar. Mem.: AAAS, Calif. Mus. Assn. (pres. 1960, bd. dirs. 1982—88), Am. Polit. Sci. Assn., Am. Assn. Pub. Opinion Rsch., Assn. Sci. and Tech. Ctrs. (bd. dirs. 1982—88), Am. Assn. Mus. Died Oct. 12, 2006.

MUCK, GEORGE ARTHUR, food products executive; b. Filmore, Ill., Sept. 28, 1937; s. George O. and Edna M. (Funderburk) M.; m. E. Joanne Inness, June 6, 1959; children: Jane, Dale, Nancy, Lori, Lynn. BS, U. Ill., 1959, MS, 1961, PhD, 1962. With research dept. Dean Foods Co., Rockford, Ill., 1962-67, dir. research, 1967-70, v.p. research and devel., from 1970. Contbr. articles to profl. jours. Patentee in field. Mem. Am. Dairy Sci. Assn. (pres. 1979-80), Am. Cultured Dairy Products Assn. (pres. 1976). Home: Rockford, Ill. Died Sept. 26, 2006.

MUDANO, FRANK ROBERT, architect; b. Winsted, Conn., Dec. 30, 1928; s. Sebastian Anthony and Marian (Bazzano) M.; m. Joan Reid, Nov. 20, 1950 (div. Feb. 1966); children— Michael David, Nina Marie, Thomas Anthony; m. Cornelia Crawford, July 20, 1966; children— Lisa Marian, Amy Elaine B.Arch.,BS, Ga. Inst. Tech., 1952. Registered architect, Fla. Gen. mgr. Southeastern Engring. Co., Clearwater, Fla., 1954-64; pres. Mudano Assocs., Architects, Inc., Clearwater, Fla., from 1964. Sec. Hytennas Corp. Prin. archtl. works include recreation facility, Clearwater, shopping ctrs. Bd. dirs. Upper Pinellas YMCA, Clearwater, 1967—; pres. Fla. Gulf Coast Art Ctr., Belleair, 1971-73; commr. Town of Belleair, 1976-80, Pinellas Planning Council, 1979. Served to 1st lt. U.S. Army, 1952-54 Fellow AIA (regional dir. 1976-78, pres. Fla. central chpt. 1971, Medal of Honor 1974), Fla. Assn. of AIA (pres. 1974, Gold medal 1978), Fla. State Bd. Architecture, Carlouel Club. Republican. Episcopalian. Home: Clearwater, Fla. Died July 29, 2007.

MUECKE, CARL (CHARLES ANDREW MUECKE), retired federal judge; b. NYC, Feb. 20, 1918; s. Charles and Wally (Roeder) M.; m. Claire E. Vasse; children by previous marriage: Carl Marshall, Alfred Jackson, Catherine Calvert. BA, Coll. William and Mary, 1941; LL.B., U. Ariz., 1953. Bar: Ariz. 1953. Rep. AFL, 1947-50; reporter Ariz. Times, Phoenix, 1947-48; ptnr. Parker & Muecke, 1953-59, Muecke, Dushoff & Sacks, 1960-61; US atty. Dist. Ariz US Dept. Justice, 1961-64; judge US Dist. Ct. Ariz, 1964—97, chief judge, 1979—84; sr. judge US Dist. Ct. Ariz., 1984—97. Mem. Phoenix Planning Commn., 1955-61, chmn., 1960; chmn. Maricopa County Dem. Party, 1961-62. Maj. USMC, 1942-45, USMCR, 1945-60. Mem. Fed. Bar Assn., Ariz. Bar Assn., Maricopa Bar Assn., Dist. Judges Assn. Ninth Circuit, Phi Beta Kappa, Phi Alpha Delta, Omicron Delta Kappa. Home: Paradise Valley, Ariz. Died Sept. 21, 2007.

MUEHE, CHARLES EDWARD, radar engineer; b. Seattle, Sept. 27, 1924; s. Charles Edward and Petronella G. (VanWell) M.; m. Alice Mae Welk, June 28, 1954; children— Barbara, Theresa, Martha, Michael, Joan, Regina. B.S.E.E., Seattle U., 1950; M.S.E.E., MIT, 1952. Asst. prof. Seattle U., 1952-56; sr. staff mem. MIT Lincoln Lab., Lexington, Mass., 1956-90, radar cons., 1990—. Contbr. articles to profl. jours. Mem. IEEE (assoc. editor for radar, AES Transactions 1982-89), Am. Inst. Physics., Sigma Xi. Home: Atkinson, NH. Died July 24, 2007.

MUELLER, RAYMOND JAY, software development executive; b. Denver, Nov. 16, 1959; s. Frank Joseph and JoAnn A. (Seib) M.; m. Hiro K. Abeyta; 1 child, Michael Raymond. A in Acctg. and Computer Sci., Metro State Coll., 1981; cert. in computer sci., Denver U., 1984. cert. data processor, 1985—. Data processing mgr. Bailey Co., Denver, 1980-86; pres. MIS, Inc., Lakewood, Colo., from 1986. Cons. to local high schs., 1985-88; speaker in field. Contbr. articles to computer mags.; inventor Touch 2000; patentee in field. Mem. Assn. for Inst. Cert. of Computer Profls., Colo. Adv. Soft Inst., Colo. Soft Assn. (pres.), Greater Denver C. of C. Republican. Roman Catholic. Avocations: tennis, golf, scuba diving, motorcycling, public speaking. Home: Commerce City, Colo. Died June 1, 2007.

MUELLER, RICHARD EDWARD, lawyer; b. Chgo., Mar. 22, 1927; s. Edward and Edith (Burman) M.; divorced; children: Keith, James. BS, Northwestern U., 1949, LL.B., 1951. Bar: Ill. 1951. Ptnr. Lord, Bissell & Brook, Chgo., from 1961; specialist in ins. def. Selected as One of Best Lawyers in Am. Seaview Putman, 1983, One of Best Lawyers in Am. Town and Country, June 1985, One of Best Lawyers in Am. Woodward White, 1987, 89. Mem. Ill. Appellate Lawyers Assn., Ill. State Bar Assn., Chgo. Bar Assn., Ill. Def. Counsel Home: Chicago, Ill. Died Sept. 15, 2006.

MUHLBACH, ARNOLD, corporate financial executive; b. N.Y.C., May 28, 1932; s. Frederick and Helen (Mislitski) M.; m. Lillian Antionette Meoli, Sept. 3, 1955; children— Helene, Peter, Lisa, Yvonne, Lily Ann. B.B.A., Iona Coll., New Rochelle, N.Y., 1957. Auditor, Price Waterhouse, New York, N.Y., 1957-60; various acctg. positions Gen. Foods, White Plains, N.Y., 1960-65; controller, v.p. adminstrn. Dewey Portland Cement, Davenport, Iowa, 1965-67; v.p. fin., treas. Monroe Auto Equipment, Monroe, Mich., 1967-77; v.p. fin. Skill Corp., Chicago, Ill., 1978-80; sr. v.p., fin. and adminstrv. services Thomas Industries Inc., Louisville, 1980—. Mem. Fin. Execs Inst. (chmn. lecture series com. 1983-84), Nat. Assn. Accts. Club: Jefferson (Louisville). Lodge: Rotary (Louisville). Home: Louisville, Ky. Died Feb. 28, 2007.

MUHLENBRUCH, CARL W., civil engineer; b. Decatur, Ill., Nov. 21, 1915; s. Carl William and Clara (Theobald) M.; m. Agnes M. Kringel, Nov. 22, 1939; children: Phyllis Elaine Wallace, Joan Carol Wenk. BCE, U. Ill., 1937, CE, 1945; MCE, Carnegie Inst. Tech., 1943; LLD, Concordia U., River Forest, Ill., 1995. Lic. profl. engr., Ill., Pa. Rsch. engr. Aluminum Rsch Labs., Pitts., 1937-39; cons. engring., 1939-50; mem. faculty Carnegie Inst. Tech., 1939-48; assoc. prof. civil engring. Northwestern U., 1948-54, lectr. in Civil Engring., 1998—2007; pres TEC-SEARCH, Inc. (formerly Ednl. and Tech. Consultants Inc.), 1954-67, chmn. bd., 1967—2007. Pres. Profl. Ctrs. Bldg Corp., 1961-77; lectr. civil engring., 1997-2007 Author: Experimental Mechanics and Properties of Materials, 1944, 2d edit. 1955; contbr. articles to profl. jours. Treas., bd. dir. Concordia Coll. Found.; dir. Mo. Luth. Synod, 1965-77, vice chmn 1977-79. Recipient Stanford E. Thompson award, 1945. Mem Am. Econ. Devel. Coun. (cert. econ. developer), Am. Soc Engring. Edn. (editor Ednl. Aids in Engring.), NSPE, ASCE Univ. Club (Evanston), Rotary (dist. gov. 1980-81, dir. svc projects Ghana and the Bahamas), Sigma Xi, Tau Beta Phi Omicron Delta Kappa. Died Feb. 15, 2007.

MULDAWER, LEONARD, physics professor, researcher, consultant; b. Phila., Aug. 6, 1920; s. Isaac Jacob and Sadi (Kaufman) M.; m. Marcea Rosen, Dec. 17, 1950 (div. 1972) children— Julia L., Richard W., Elizabeth A.; m. Patricia An Mills, Jan. 1, 1983, A.B., Temple U., 1942, A.M., 1944; Ph.D. MIT, 1948. Prof. physics Temple U., Phila., 1948—90; chmn. exec. com. Council Chautauqua Field Ctr. Dirs., 1980-2005 field ctr. dir. Coll. Chautauqua, Phila.; field ctr. dir. NSTA/NS Chautauqua Courses for sci. Tchrs., Phila.; cons. various gov and pvt. agys.; project dir. for research grants 5 govt. depts. Author book chpts. Contbr. articles to profl. jours. Mem. sci adv. com. Sierra Club Southeastern Pa., Phila., 1983-87; mem devel. com. Choral Arts Soc., Phila. Mem. Am. Phys. Soc., Am Assn. Physics Tchrs., Am. Crystallographic Assn., Am. Soc Metals, Sigma Xi. Home: Wynnewood, Pa. Died Mar. 7, 2006

MULHOLLAND, CHARLES BRADLEY, retired water transportation executive; b. LA, May 24, 1941; s. Charles B. an Dolly B. (Holmes) M.; m. Leslie Mulholland; children: Sar Megan, Mark Bradley. BA in Econs., U. So. Calif., 1965 postgrad., Columbia U. Sch. Bus., 1980. Various position mktg., sales Matson Navigation Co., San Francisco, 1965—7 v.p., sr. v.p., 1979-86; pres. Matson Terminals, San Francisco, 1986-87; exec. v.p. Matson Navigation Co., San Francisco, 1987-89, exec. v.p., COO, 1989—90, pres., 1990—2002, CEO, 1992—2002. Chmn. Matson Terminals Inc., San Francisco, Matson Freight Agys. Inc., San Francisco, Matson Svcs. Inc., San Francisco, Matson Leasing Co. Inc., San Francisco. Fund raiser Boy Scout Am., San Francisco, United Way, San Francisco Area. Recipient Admiral of the Ocean Sea award, United Seaman's Svc., 1996. Mem. Bankers Club Calif., Maritime Mus. Assn. (trustee 1989), Pacific Maritime Assn. (bd. dirs. 1989—), Coast Guard Found. Inc. (bd. dirs. 1989). Home: Piedmont, Calif. Died Feb. 20, 2007.

MULLER, ERNEST H., geology educator; b. Tabriz, Iran, Mar. 4, 1923; (parents Am. citizens); s. Hugo Arthur and Laura Barnett (McComb) M.; m. Wanda Custis, Apr. 7, 1951; children: Ruth Anne, David Stewart, Katherine Lee. BA, Wooster Coll., 1947; MS, U. Ill., 1949, PhD, 1952. Geologist U.S. Geol. Survey, Washington, 1947-54; asst. prof. geology Cornell U., Ithaca, N.Y., 1954-59; assoc. prof. Syracuse U., N.Y., 1959-63, prof. N.Y., 1963-89, interim chmn. dept. geology N.Y., 1970-71, 79-81, prof. emeritus N.Y., from 1989. Seasonal geologist N.Y. Geol. Survey, 1956-76; geologist Am. Geog. Soc., Chile, 1959; rsch. assoc. Natural History Mus., Reykjavik, Iceland, 1968-69; vis. prof. Alaska Pacific U., Anchorage, 1979; Erskine vis. prof. U. Canterbury, Christchurch, New Zealand, 1974; mem. Bering Glacier (Alaska) Rsch. Group, 1988—, N.Y. Pleistocene Stratigraphy. Author: Geology of Chautauqua County, New York, 1964, Seaway Trail Rocks and Landscapes, 1987. 1st lt. USAAF, 1943-46. Fellow Geol. Soc. Am. (geomorphology panel 1962-64, 66-68, 75-77, 97-99), AAAS; mem. Am. Quaternary Assn. (counselor 1982-86), Glaciological Soc., Nat. Assn. Geology Tchrs., Sigma Xi. Home: Houston, Tex. Died Oct. 20, 2005.

MULLINS, JOSEPH A., lawyer; b. Monroe, La., Oct. 5, 1946; BA, Tulane U., 1968; LLB, U. Va., 1971. Bar: N.Y. 1972. Mem. Cravath, Swaine & Moore, NYC. Mem. ABA, N.Y. State Bar Assn., Assn. Bar City N.Y. Died Feb. 19, 2007.

MULLINS, OBERA, retired microbiologist; b. Egypt, Miss., Feb. 15, 1927; d. Willie Ree and Maggie Sue (Orr) Gunn; m. Charles Leroy Mullins, Nov. 2, 1952; children: Mary Artavia, Arthur Curtis, Charles Leroy, Charlester Teresa, William Hellman. BS, Chgo. State U., 1974; MS in Health Sci. Edn., Governors State U., 1981. Med. technician, microbiologist Chgo. Health Dept., Chgo., from 1976, now pers. asst. III, to 1999; ret., 1999. Mem. AAUW, Am. Soc. Clin. Pathologists (cert. med. lab. technician), Ill. Soc. Lab. Technicians. Roman Catholic. Home: Chicago, Ill. Died Jan. 22, 2006.

MULQUEEN, ELLEN, educational administrator, consultant; b. Bklyn., Jan. 11, 1941; d. James C. and Jane E. (Jaenike) M.; A.B. in English, Pace U., 1962; M.A. in English, N.Y. U., 1967. Personnel clk. Book-of-the-Month Club, N.Y.C., 1962; activities sec. Pace U., N.Y.C., 1963; adminstrv. asst. Loeb Student Center, N.Y. U., N.Y.C., 1963-65; asst. dean students SUNY, Geneseo, 1965-67; asst. dean students R.I. Coll., Providence, 1967-70; asst. dir. campus center Trinity Coll., Hartford, Conn., 1970-71, asst. dean student services, 1971-72, asso. dean for student services, 1972-74, dean student services, 1974-76; dean student affairs, adj. instr. English, Post Coll., Waterbury, Conn., 1976-80; assoc. dean student support services Rider Coll., Lawrenceville, N.J., 1980-82; pvt. practice career counseling, 1982—; asst. dir. career services Sch. Law, Western New Eng. Coll., Springfield, Mass., 1984—. Mem. exec. com., edn. and info. com. Planned Parenthood League, Waterbury, 1980; mem. exec. com. Planned Parenthood of Mercer County (N.J.), 1980-84; mem. League of Women Voters of the Springfield Area, 1984—, bd. dirs., 1985—, legis. chair, 1985—. Recipient Trustees' award Pace U., 1962. Mem. LWV of Ewing Twp. (dir. 1981-84). Contbr. papers to publs., also nat., regional confs. profl. orgns. in field. Home: Springfield, Mass. Died Mar. 13, 2007.

MUNDT, PHILIP AMOS, oil company executive; b. Sioux Falls, S.D., Oct. 2, 1927; s. John Carl and Marie Dorothy (Jacobson) M.; m. Lorraine Jean Blom, Dec. 27, 1951; children— Alan Philip, Sheryl Ann, Larry Bruce. B.S. in Geol. Engring., S.D. Sch. Mines, 1951; M.A. in Geology, Washington U., 1953; Ph.D. in Geology, Stanford U., 1955. Registered geologist, Calif. Geologist, supr. Mobil Oil Corp., world-wide, 1955-69, mgr. geol. geochem. research, Dallas, 1972-77, exploration mgr., Lagos, Nigeria, Medan, Indonesia, 1977-82, mgr. regional geology, Dallas, 1982—; exploration mgr. U.S. Natural Resources, Menlo Park, Calif., 1969-72. Served with U.S. Army, 1946-48. Standard Oil Calif. fellow, 1954. Mem. Am. Assn. Petroleum Geologists (cert., sec. 1964-65, v.p. 1965), Dallas Geol. Soc., Sigma Xi, Sigma Tau. Club: Lago Vista Country. Avocations: golf; sailing. Home: Leander, Tex. Died May 6, 2007.

MURFIN, MARK, education educator; b. Pendleton, Ind., Aug. 3, 1913; s. William Riley and Addie (Heiney) M.; m. Bettie A. Crawford, Aug. 25, 1938; children— Ross C., Joe C. BS, Ball State U., 1940; MS, Ind. U., 1942; Ed.D., Grenoble U., France, 1952. Tchr. Pendleton City Schs., 1933-38; prin. schs. in Fowlerton, Noblesville, Peru and Richmond, Ind., 1938-49; elem. supr. Ind. U. Lab. Sch., 1949-51, instr., 1951; assoc. prof. edn. Boston U., 1952-56; prof., chmn. dept. elem. edn. U. Miami, Coral Gables, Fla., 1956—78. Author: (with Bazelon) Cross Number Puzzles, Whole Numbers, 1966, Cross Number Puzzles, Fractions, 1967, Cross Number Puzzles, Teacher's Guide and Student Record Book, 1967, Cross Number Puzzles, Decimals and Percent, 1968, Murfin's Learning Box, 1972. Served with AUS, 1943-46, ETO. Mem. Nat., Fla. edn. assns., Fla. Council Elementary Edn., Phi Delta Kappa. Mem. Christian Ch. (Disciples Of Christ). Home: Rogers, Ark. Died Sept. 21, 2006.

MURPHEY, IRENE GUILBERT, educational consultant; b. Camp Verde, Ariz., Oct. 11, 1930; d. Irving Coleman and Amy Elaine (Stock) West; m. Lionel Ward Guilbert, Apr. 12, 1952 (div. May 1985); children: Marion Elizabeth, Lynelle Marie, Marjorie Ann; m. Norman Alan Murphey, 1994. BA in Secondary Edn., U. Ariz., 1952; MEd in Elem. Edn., Ariz. State U., 1982. Cert. elem. and secondary tchr., prin., Ariz. Tchr. pub. schs., Ariz., 1954-78, 81-83; developer, demonstrator nat. diffusion network U.S. Office Edn., Mesa, Ariz., 1978-85, asst. state facilitator, 1983-85; instrnl. specialist Ariz. Dept. Edn., Phoenix, 1985-88; pres. Ednl. Directions, Inc., Glendale, Ariz., 1985-91, prin., 1988-92; ret., 1994; ind. cons., from 1994. Adj. prof. No. Ariz. U., Flagstaff, 1985-88; mem. Nat. Diffusion Network, U.S. Dept. Edn.; cons. on math., lang. arts, mgmt. and motivation, early childhood, integrated learning, classroom mgmt. Author: Big Tee Math Books, 1986, Math Pages, 1987. Community chmn. Girl Scouts U.S.A., 1958-71; pres. PTA, 1957. Mem. ASCD, NAESP, Ariz. Sch. Adminstrs., Federated Woman's Club (pres.), Mensa, Phi Delta Kappa, Pi Lambda Theta, Alpha Delta Kappa (pres., southwestern regional scholar 1980). Republican. Unitarian Universalist. Died Jan. 20, 2006.

MURPHY, ARTHUR THOMAS, systems engineer, consultant; b. Hartford, Conn., Feb. 15, 1929; s. Arthur T. and Mary (Beakey) M.; m. Jane M. Gamble, Aug. 16, 1952; children: Thomas, Patricia, Mary, John, Sheila, Jane, Joseph. BEE, Syracuse U., 1951; MS, Carnegie-Mellon U., 1952, PhD, 1957. Registered profl. engr., Kans. Instr. Carnegie-Mellon U., Pitts., 1952-56; asst., assoc. prof., head. elec. engring. Wichita State U., Kans., 1956-61; vis. assoc. prof. mech. engring. MIT, Cambridge, Mass., 1961-62; prof., dean engring. Widener U., Chester, Pa., 1962-71, v.p., acad. dean, 1971-75; Brown prof., head mech. engring. dept. Carnegie-Mellon U., Pitts., 1975-79; prof. industry, mgr. computer and automated systems, sr. research fellow DuPont de Nemours Co., Camp Hill, Pa., 1979-87, DuPont fellow Wilmington, Del., 1987-96, DuPont fellow emeritus, 1996—2007, cons., 1996—2006; acting pres. Pa. Inst. Tech., Media, 1998. Vis. rsch. fellow Sony Corp. Rsch. Ctr., Yokohama, Japan, 1991-92, Internat. Superconductivity Tech. Ctr., Tokyo, 1993; vis. prof. control engring. U. Manchester, Eng., 1968-69; cons. Boeing Co., Seattle, Wichita and Morton, Pa., 1957-68; adj. prof. Pa. State U., 1983-87; DuPont rep. Chem. Rsch. Coun., 1994-97; cons. sci. adv. com. Parlec, Inc., 2000-06; cons., chair microwave adv. com. Herley Industries., 2002-06. Author: Introduction to System Dynamics, 1967; contbr. articles to profl. jours.; editor: Pergamon Press, 1966-75; patentee thick film filter connector, substrate and ceramic package, connection method for circuit bd. (ball grid array), superconducting mixer antenna array. Former mem. adv. coun. Tex. A&M U., Swarthmore Coll.; program evaluator Accreditation Bd. Engring. and Tech., 1996—. DuPont fellow, 1987—2006; recipient DuPont Spl. Compensation award, 1988, Electronics Mktg. Excellence award DuPont Co., 1990. Fellow: AAAS, IEEE (life; exec. com., treas. computer packaging), Am. Soc. Engring. Edn. (life; v.p. fin. 2001—05, chmn. grad. studies, instrumentation, awards com., corp. mem. coun., We. Elec. Fund award 1966); mem.: ASME (exec. com. control divsn.), Phi Theta Kappa, Tau Beta Pi, Sigma Xi. Avocations: hiking, photography, travel, genealogy. Died July 2, 2007.

MURPHY, CHARLES FRANCIS, JR., architect; b. Chgo., Dec. 17, 1928; s. Charles F. and Josephine (Christiani) M.; children: Elita, Charles III, Marisa Alexandra, Luke Lawson. B.Arch., U. Notre Dame, 1951. Chmn. Murphy/Jahn, Inc., Chgo. Maj. archtl. works include Xerox Ctr.; Maj. archtl. works include: O'Hare Internat. Airport, First Nat. Bank, Chgo. Civic Ctr., State of Ill. Ctr., all Chgo. Mem. Graham Found. for Advanced Studies in Fine Arts, Chgo.; trustee Field Mus. Chgo. Fellow AIA Clubs: Chicago (all Chgo.), Saddle and Cycle (all Chgo.), Economic (all Chgo.), Tavern (all Chgo.), Racquet (all Chgo.). Died Aug. 27, 2006.

MURPHY, EARL FINBAR, law educator; b. Indpls., Nov. 1, 1928; AB, Butler U., 1949, MA, 1954; JD, Ind. U., 1952; LLM, Yale U., 1955, JSD, 1959. Bar: Ind. 1952. Pvt. practice, Indpls., 1952-54; asst. prof. SUNY, Binghamton, 1955-57; Rockefeller fellow U. Wis. Law Sch., Madison, 1957-58; from asst. prof. to assoc. prof. Temple U., Phila., 1958—65, prof. law, 1965-69; prof. Ohio State U., Columbus, 1969-81, C. William O'Neill prof. law and jud. adminstrn., 1981-2000, prof. emeritus, from 2000. Vis. prof. U. Ariz., 1980. Author: Water Purity, 1961, Governing Nature, 1967, Man and His Environment: Law, 1971, Nature, Bureaucracy and the Rules of Property, 1977, Energy and Environmental Balance, 1980, Quantitative Groundwater Law, 1991. Chmn. Ohio Environ. Bd. Rev., 1972—74. Mem.: ABA, World Soc. Ekistics (pres. 1982—84), Am. Soc. Legal History, Fed. Bar Assn., Ind. Bar Assn., Masons. Unitarian. Home: Indianapolis, Ind. Died July 23, 2006.

MURPHY, JOHN P., lawyer; b. Romulus, N.Y., Feb. 27, 1912; s. Joseph F. and Mary A. (Hamilton) M.; children: Peter Hamilton, Sarah Ann. BS, Cornell U., 1938; JD, Georgetown U., 1942. Bar: D.C. 1943, U.S. Patent Office. Patent counsel Am. Cyanamid Co., Washington, 1940-42, Parke Davis & Co., Detroit, 1942-43, Bristol Myers Co., Syracuse, N.Y., 1946-54; pvt. practice, Skaneateles, N.Y., 1954-97, Naples, Fla., 1997—. 1st lt. C.E., U.S. Army, 1944-46, Manhattan Project. Mem. Am. Chem. Soc., Chemist Club N.Y.C., D.C. Bar Assn., Skaneateles Country Club, Kenwood Club. Republican. Roman Catholic. Home: Auburn, NY. Died July 6, 2007.

MURPHY, LEWIS CURTIS, lawyer, former mayor; b. NYC, Nov. 2, 1933; s. Henry Waldo and Elizabeth Wilcox (Curtis) M.; m. Carol Carney, Mar. 10, 1957; children— Grey, Timothy, Elizabeth. BSBA, U. Ariz., 1955, LLB, 1961. Bar: Ariz. 1961. Pvt. practice, Tucson, 1961-66; trust officer So. Ariz. Bank & Trust Co., 1966-70; atty. City of Tucson, 1970-71; mayor, 1971-87; ret., 1987. Mem. Schroeder & Murphy, Tucson, 1978-88; trustee U.S. Conf. Mayors, 1978-87, chmn. transp. com., 1984-87; pub. safety steering com. Nat. League Cities, 1973-87, transp. steering com., 1973-87; v.p. Ctrl. Ariz. Project Assn., 1978-87. Bd. dirs. Cmty. Food Bank, 1987-2000, United Way Greater Tucson, 1988-90. With USAF, 1955-58. Mem. Ariz. Bar Assn., Pima County Bar Assn., Ariz. Acad., Sigma Chi (Significant Sig award). Republican. Presbyterian. Home: Tucson, Ariz. Died Dec. 1, 2005.

MURPHY, MICHAEL J., lawyer; b. NYC, Apr. 4, 1940; s. James and Mary (Greene) M.; m. Patricia A. Hough, May 25, 1963; children: Michael, Patricia Ann, Kathleen. BA, Manhattan Coll., 1961; JD, Fordham Law Sch., 1968. Bar: N.Y., U.S. Dist. Ct. (so. and ea. dists.) Conn., U.S. Ct. Appeals (2d, 5th, and 9th cirs.), U.S. Supreme Ct., 1985. Law clk. to Hon. Thomas F. Murphy U.S. Dist. Ct. (so. dist.) N.Y., NYC, 1968-69; ptnr. Lord Day & Lord, Barrett Smith, NYC, from 1969, Lord, Day, Lord, Barrett & Smith, NYC, 1976-94, Healy & Baillie, NYC, from 1995. Contbr. articles to legal publs. Died Nov. 13, 2005.

MURPHY, MICHAEL JOSEPH, retired bishop; b. Cleve., July 1, 1915; s. William and Mary Bridget (Patton) M. BA in Philosophy, Gregorian U., Rome, 1938; S.T.L., Catholic U. Am., 1942. Ordained priest Roman Catholic Ch., 1942; prof. pro-tem St. Mary Sem., Cleve., 1943-45, prof., 1947-48, vice-rector, 1948-63, rector, 1963-76; Episcopal vicar Chancery Office, Cleve., 1976-78; coadjutor bishop of Erie, Chancery office (Pa.), 1978-82; bishop of Erie, 1982-90. Mem. scripture trans. com. Nat. Conf. Cath. Bishops. Recipient first Ann. Sem. Dept. award Nat. Cath. Ednl. Assn. Roman Catholic. Died Apr. 3, 2007.

MURPHY, SISTER MICHELLE, nun; b. NYC, July 2, 1927; d. Michael A. and Elizabeth A. (Sweeney) M. BA, Marymount Coll., 1949; MA, Laval U., 1950; MBA with distinction, Pace U., 1980. Joined Religious Order of Sacred Heart of Mary, Roman Cath. Ch., 1945; CPA, N.Y.; cert. mgmt. acct. Provincial treas. Religious of Sacred Heart of Mary, NYC and Tarrytown, N.Y., 1964-76; audit staff Peat Marwick Mitchell, NYC, 1980-81; asst. prof. Lubin Sch. Bus. Pace U., Pleasantville, N.Y., 1981-84; v.p. fin., treas. Marymount U., Arlington, Va., from 1984. Trustee Marymount Sch. N.Y., N.Y.C., 1969—, Loyola Marymount U., L.A., 1989—; v.p. Sisters' Coun., Arlington, Va., 1984-90; regent Marymount Sch., Richmond, Va., 1985—; del. Internat. Plan Group, Religious of Sacred Heart of Mary, Rome, 1988, 89. Mem. AICPA, Nat. Assn. Accts., Inst. Cert. Mgmt. Accts., Nat. Assn. Col. and Univ. Bus. Officers, So. Assn. Coll. and Univ. Bus. Officers. Died Feb. 27, 2006.

MURPHY, PATRICK WILLARD, police chief; b. McMinniville, Oreg., Oct. 26, 1951; s. Willard D. and Betty J. (Hale) M.; m. Susan Byers, July 28, 1979; children— Jennifer, Tennille, Muriel, Oliver-Fitzpatrick. A.S., Chemeketa Community Coll., 1972; B.S., Eastern Oreg. State U., 1973; postgrad. Calif. Western U., 1981-82. Cert. police officer, Wash. Police officer Union Police Dept., Oreg., 1972-73, Seaside Police Dept., Oreg., 1974; police lt. Cottage Grove Police Dept., Oreg., 1974-82; chief police Snohomish Police Dept., Wash., 1982—; dir. Snohomish Region Tng. Acad., Wash., 1983—; assessor Commn. on Accreditation for Law Enforcement Agys., Fairfax, Va., 1984—. Actor in movies Animal House, 1977, Twice in a Lifetime, 1984. Chmn. fundraising March of Dimes, Snohomish, 1983, 84; co-chmn. fundraising United Way, Snohomish, 1984; race dir. LO-K Fun Run, Snohomish, 1983, 83, Snohomish C. of C. Fun Run, 1983. Mem. Internat. Assn. Chiefs Police, Nat. Assn. Chiefs Police, Nat. Criminal Justice Assn., Oreg. Assn. Chiefs Police, Wash. Assn. Sheriffs and Chiefs. Club: Snohomish Little Theatre (v.p. 1983). Lodge: Rotary. Home: Snohomish, Wash. Died Feb. 2, 2006.

MURPHY, ROBERT DROWN, communications educator; b. Jericho, Vt., Oct. 9, 1917; s. Harold James and Constance (Chittenden) M.; m. Reta Rose Vanderburgh, Oct. 16, 1943; children: Constance Anne White, Richard Vanderburgh, Gordon Chittenden. AB, Syracuse U., 1938, MA, 1945, PhD, 1951. Reporter Mt. Vernon (Ohio) News, 1939-42; instr. Westminster Coll., New Wilmington, Pa., 1942; editor A.P., 1943-46; from asst. prof. to prof. Syracuse U. Sch. Journalism, 1946-65, chmn. newspaper dept., 1951-65; prof., dir. U. Ky. Sch. Journalism, 1965-66; dir. Sch. Communications, assoc. dean Coll. Arts and Scis., 1966-73; prof. communications U. Ky., from 1973, dir. Sch. Journalism, 1981-83. Cons. in field, 1951—; vis. prof. Stanford, 1949 Author: Reporting Public Problems, 1960, Mass Communication and Human Interaction, 1977; Contbr. articles to profl. jours., chpts to books. Co-pres. Jamesville DeWitt (N.Y.) Jr.-Sr. P.T.A., 1964-65; troop com., leader local Boy Scouts Am., 1960-62, mem. civil def. com., Onondaga County, N.Y., 1949. Mem. Acad. Polit. Sci., Internat. Communication Assn., Am. Acad. Polit. and Social Sci., Sigma Delta Chi, Phi Kappa Phi, Sigma Nu. Methodist. Home: Lexington, Ky. Died Jan. 14, 2007.

MURPHY, TOM, actor; b. Zimbabwe, Jan. 15, 1968; Actor: (films) In Till You Die, 1992, Michael Collins, 1996, The General, 1998, Mystics, 2002, The Abduction Club, 2002, Boxed, 2002, In America, 2002, Intermission, 2003, Adam & Paul, 2004, Man About Dog, 2004, 48 Angels, 2006, Small Engine Repair, 2006; (TV films) The Snapper, 1993, Benedict Arnold: A Question of Honor, 2003; (TV series) Trouble in Paradise, 2007, (TV appearances) Pure Mule, 2005, Taggart, 2005; (Broadway plays) The Beauty Queen of Leenane, 1998 (Tony award, 1998). Died Oct. 6, 2007.

MURPHY, WILLIAM ROBERT, lawyer; b. New Haven, Oct. 6, 1927; s. Michael David and Loretta Dorothy (Murphy) M.; m. Virginia Anne Selfors, July 23, 1960; children: David M., Christopher W. BA, Yale U., 1950, LL.B., 1953. Bar: Conn. 1953, U.S. Dist. Ct. Conn. 1957, U.S. Ct. Appeals (2d cir.) 1966, U.S Supreme Ct. 1956, U.S. Ct. Appeals (Fed. cir.) 1986. Assoc. Tyler Cooper & Alcorn, New Haven, 1957-60, ptnr., from 1960. Exec. editor: Yale Law Jour., 1952-53. Sec. John Brown Cook Found., 1971—; mem. Woodbridge Bd. Edn., Conn., 1969-75, Woodbridge Planning and Zoning Commn., 1967-69.Served to lt (j.g.) USNR, 1945-46, 53-56. James Cooper fellow Conn. Bar Found. Fellow Am. Coll. Trial Lawyers, Am. Bar Found.; mem. ABA, Conn. Bar Assn., New Haven County Bar Assn., Quinnipiack Club, Mory's Assn. Home: Woodbridge, Conn. Died Mar. 25, 2007.

MURRA, JOHN VICTOR, retired anthropology professor; b. Odessa, Ukraine, Aug. 24, 1916; came to U.S., 1934, naturalized, 1950; BA, U. Chgo., 1936, MA, 1942, PhD, 1956; doctorate (hon.), U. Barcelona, 1993. Instr. U. Chgo., 1943-47; asst. prof. U. P.R., 1947-49; from asst. prof. to prof. Vassar Coll.,

1950-61; vis. prof. Yale U., 1961-63; prin. investigator study Andes, NSF, 1963-66; vis. prof. U. San Marcos, Lima, Peru, 1958, 65-66, hon. prof., 1966; prof. anthropology Cornell U., 1968—82. Lewis H. Morgan lectr. U. Rochester, 1969; area specialist UN Secretariat, 1951; founding mem. Inst. de Estudios Peruanos, Inst. Nacional de Antropologia e Historia of Ecuador; past mem. bd. Am. Com. Africa; mem. Inst. for Advanced Study, Princeton, 1974-75; directeur d'études associé Ecole des Hautes Etudes, Paris, 1975-76 Author: The Economic Organization of the Inka State, 1980. Served with Spanish Republican Army, 1937-39. Decorated Gran Cruz of Order of Sun (Perú); Guggenheim fellow, 1984-85. Mem. Am. Soc. Ethnohistory (pres. 1970-71), Am. Ethnol. Soc. (pres. 1972-73), Inst. Andean Research (former pres.) Home: Ithaca, NY. Died Oct. 16, 2006.

MURRAY, ELIZABETH, artist; b. Chgo., 1940; married; 1 child, Dakota Sunseri. B.F.A., Art Inst., Chgo., 1962; M.F.A., Mills Coll., Oakland, Calif., 1964; D (hon.), Art Inst., Chgo., 1992; degree (hon.), RI School Design, 1993; D (hon.), New School U., 2001. Vis. instr. Wayne State U., 1975, Calif. Inst. Arts, 1975-76, Chgo. Art Inst., 1975-76; instr. Bard Coll., Annandale on Hudson, NY, 1974-75, 76-77, Princeton U., 1977, Yale U., 1978-79. One-woman shows, Jacobs Ladder Gallery, Washington, 1974, Paula Cooper Gallery, N.Y.C., 1975, 76, 78, 81, 83, 88, 89, Jared Sable Gallery, 1975, Ohio State U., Columbus, 1978, Phyllis Kind Gallery, Chgo., 1978, Galerie Mukai, Tokyo, 1980, Susanne Hilberry Gallery, Birmingham, Mich., 1980, Smith Coll. Art Gallery, Northampton, Mass., 1982, Daniel Weinberg Gallery, Los Angeles, 1982, Portland Ctr. Visual Arts, Oreg., 1983, Knight Gallery, Charlotte, N.C., 1984, San Francisco Mus. Modern Art, 1988, Mayor Rowen Gallery, London, 1989, Barbara Krakow Gallery, Boston, 1990, Gallery Mukai, Tokyo, 1990, John Berggruen Gallery, San Francisco, 1990, Wexner Center for the Arts, 1991, 92, Jaffe-Friede Strauss Galleries, Hanover, N.H., 2005, Mus. Modern Art, N.Y.C., 2005, Maier Mus. Art, Lynchburg, Va, 2005; group shows include, Whitney Mus. Am. Art, N.Y.C., 1972, 73, 77, 79, 81, 82, 84, John Doyle Gallery Cologne, Ger., 1974, Paula Cooper Gallery, 1974, 76, 77, 78, 79, 81, 82, 83, 84, Michael Walls Gallery, N.Y., 1975, Middlebury (Vt.) Coll., 1976, Gallery of July and August, Brockport, N.Y., 1976, Susanne Hilberry Gallery, Detroit, 1976, Guggenheim Mus., N.Y.C., 1977, Sarah Lawrence Coll. Gallery, Bronxville, N.Y., 1977, Lowe Art Gallery Syracuse U., 1977, Mus. Contemporary Art, Chgo., 1977, Inst. Contemporary Art, U. Pa., 1978, Tampa Bay Art Center, Fla., 1978, Phyllis Kind Gallery, Chgo., 1979, William Patterson Coll., Wayne, N.J., 1979, Susan Caldwell Gallery, N.Y., 1979, U. N.C. Weatherspoon Art Gallery, Greensboro, 1979, Galerie Yvon Lambert, Paris, 1980, Bklyn. Mus., 1980, Dart Gallery, Chgo., 1981, Contemporary Arts Center, Cin., 1981, High Mus. Art, Atlanta, 1981, 82, Galerie Mukai, Tokyo, 1981, Va. Mus., Richmond, 1981, Boston Mus. Fine Arts, 1982, Milw. Art Mus., 1982, Art Inst. Chgo., 1982, Daniel Weinberg Gallery, Los Angeles and San Francisco, 1983, Hirshhorn Mus., Washington, 1983, Hobart and William Smith Colls., Geneva, N.Y., 1983, Mus. Art, Ft. Lauderdale, Fla., 1986, 40th Biennial Exhbn. Comtemp. Am. Paintings Corcoran Gallery of Art, 1988, Mus. Modern Art, 1990, 91, numerous others; artist and curator Elizabeth Murray: Modern Art N.Y., Mus. Modern Art, N.Y., 1995; represented in permanent collections: Whitney Mus. Am. Art, N.Y.C., Guggenheim Mus., Hirshhorn Mus. and Sculpture Garden, Washington, H.H.K. Found., Milw., St. Louis Art Mus., Detroit Inst. Arts, Albright-Knox Art Gallery, Buffalo, N.Y., Allen Meml. Art Mus., Oberlin Coll., Art Inst. Chgo., Baltimore Mus. Art, Carnegie Mus. Art, Pittsburgh, Pa, Cleveland Mus. Art, Dallas Mus. Art, High Mus. Art, Atlanta, Met. Mus. Art, N.Y.C., Nat. Gallery Art, Washington, Mus. Contemporary Art, L.A., Mus. Fine Arts, Boston, Nelson-Atkins Mus. Art, Kansas City, Phila. Mus. Art, Va. Mus. Fine Arts, Walker Center, Minn., Yale U. Art Gallery. Recipient Walter M. Campana award Art Inst. of Chgo., 1982, Am. Academy & Inst. of Arts & Letters award, 1984, Skowhegan prize for painting, 1986, Larry Aldrich prize in contemporary art, 1993, John D. & Catherine T. MacArthur Found. award, 1999, Nat. Artist award Anderson Ranch Art Ctr., 2002; honored by Artists Space, NYC, 2001. Mem. Am. Acad and Inst. of Arts and Letters, 1992, NAD (academician). Died Aug. 12, 2007.

MURRAY, LAWRENCE LEO, JR., social agency executive; b. Pitts., Apr. 28, 1920; s. Lawrence L. and Julia F. (Ford) M.; m. Mary Louise Vath, Feb. 5, 1943; children— Lawrence L. III, Patrick J., Mary Anne, James J. B.A., Duquesne U., 1941. Sales mgr. U.S. Gypsum Co., Pitts., 1939-52; v.p. sales D.J. Kennedy Co., Pitts., 1952-56; v.p. sales mktg. Grand Rapids Gypsum Co., Mich., 1956-74; exec. dir. Area Agy. on Aging, Grand Rapids, 1974—; dir. Mich. Soc. Gerontology, Lansing, 1978—, Nat. Assn. Area Agencies on Aging, Washington, 1984—; natl. chmn. Soc. St. Vincent De Paul Aging Com., St. Louis, 1980—. Served with USAF, 1942-46, PTO. Democrat. Roman Catholic. Clubs: Press, Breakfast (Grand Rapids). Lodge: K.C. Avocations: walking, swimming, reading. Home: Grand Rapids, Mich. Died Apr. 25, 2006.

MURRAY, RICHARD NEWTON, curator, museum director, archivist; b. Bartlesville, Okla., Aug. 7, 1942; s. Claude Robert and Margaret Pilar (Thompson) M.; m. Maricela Young, Dec. 2, 1967; 1 dau., Xiomara Margarita. BA, San Jose State U., 1968; MA, U. Chgo., 1970. Research asst. Nat. Mus. Am. Art, Smithsonian Instn., 1972-74, Bicentennial exhbn. coordinator, 1974-76, asst. to dir., curator of edn., 1976-79; dir. Birmingham Mus. Art, 1979-83; dir. Archives of Am. Art Smithsonian Instn., 1983-87, curator Nat. Mus. Am. Art, from 1987. Served with U.S. Army, 1965-67. Smithsonian Instn. fellow, 1970-72 Mem. Coll. Art Assn., Am. Assn. Museums, Assn. Art Mus. Dirs. Home: Kensington, Md. Died Mar. 12, 2006.

MURRAY, ROBERT WILLIAM, diversified company executive; b. Cooma, New South Wales, Australia, Feb. 13, 1936; came to U.S., 1972; s. Robert Jack and Dulcie (Cavanough) M.; m. Susanne Roberta Green, Jan. 6, 1962; children: Stephen James, Richard Douglas. Charter in Acctg., Sydney Tech. Coll. (Australia). 1957. Chartered acct., Australia. Mgr. fin. Philip Morris Europe, Lausanne, Switzerland, 1970-71; v.p. fin. Philip Morris Internat., N.Y.C., 1972-74; pres. Benson & Hedges Can. Montreal, 1974-76, Philip Morris Europe, Lausanne, 1976-83, Philip Morris Internat., N.Y.C., 1983-87; vice chmn. Philip Morris Cos. Inc., 1987-94, chmn., 1994-95, also bd. dirs. Bd. dirs. Internat. Tennis Hall of Fame; trustee Poly. U., Bklyn., Alvin Ailey Am. Dance Theater, N.Y.C., Am. Mus. Natural History, N.Y.C. Mem. Inst. Chartered Accts. in Australia. Home: Bronxville, NY. Died Feb. 10, 2007.

MURRAY, WILLIAM F., lawyer; b. Birmingham, Ala., Oct. 17, 1948; BA summa cum laude, Birmingham So. Coll., 1970; JD, U. Va., 1973. Bar: Ala. 1973. Mem. Burr & Forman, Birmingham, Ala. Mem. ABA, Ala. State Bar, Birmingham Bar Assn., Omicrom Delta Kappa, Phi Beta Kappa. Died Apr. 14, 2006.

MURRAY, WILLIAM SPARROW, association executive, former government official; b. Wilkes Barre, Pa., July 15, 1926; s. William and Marion (Sparrow) M.; m. Doris Mae Quinnell, Feb. 23, 1952; children— Barbara Elizabeth, Janet Cole. B.S., Juniata Coll., 1950; M.S., U.Md., 1952, Ph.D., 1963. Biologist Dept. Def., Norfolk, Va. and Washington, 1952-65, USPHS, Washington, 1965-69, FDA, Washington, 1969-71; staff dir. hazardous materials adv. com. EPA, 1971-72, div. dir., 1972-78, assoc. dep. asst. adminstr., 1978-79, research mgr., 1979-82; staff exec. Nat. Elec. Mfrs. Assn., Washington, 1982—; scientist cons. U.S. Congress, 1964-65, 67. Contbr. articles to profl. jours. Served with USN, 1944-46, PTO. Recipient Outstanding Performance award Navy Dept., 1964; Quality Increase award EPA, 1974. Mem. AAAS, Am. Inst. Biol. Scis., Washington Acad. Scis., N.Y. Acad. Sci., Phi Kappa Phi. Club: Cosmos (Washington). Avocations: skiing; scuba diving. Home: Rockville, Md. Died Sept. 8, 2006.

MUSCHEL, LOUIS HENRY, immunologist, educator; b. NYC, July 4, 1916; s. Maurice and Betty (Tobey) M.; m. Anne Orzel, Oct. 22, 1946; 1 child, Ruth Josephine. BS, NYU, 1936; MS, Yale U., 1951, PhD, 1953. Joined U.S. Army, 1941, advanced through grades to lt. col., 1961; chief dept. serology (Walter Reed Army Inst. Research), Washington, 1958-62; faculty U. Minn., Mpls., 1962-70, prof. microbiology, 1964-70; prof. bacteriology U. Calif., Berkeley, 1965, 67; with research dept. Am. Cancer Soc., 1970-88. Adj. prof. microbiology Columbia U., 1977-83; adj. prof. pathology NYU, 1983—. Mem. Am. Assn. Immunologists, Brit. Soc. Immunology, N.Y. Acad. Scis., Am. Soc. Microbiology, Soc. Exptl. Biology and Medicine, Am. Assn. for Cancer Research, Phi Beta Kappa, Sigma Xi, Phi Lambda Upsilon. Achievements include research, publs. on bactericidal action of serum and its role in host defs., natural bactericidal and viral neutralizing antibodies, applications of complement fixation technique. Home: Bronx, NY. Died Oct. 8, 2005.

MUSE, MARGARET BRADLEY, city official; b. LaGrange, Ga., June 15, 1942; d. Paul Phillip and Myrtle Muriel (Tomlin) James; m. Paul W. Grosch, Apr. 5, 1960 (div. 1966); children— Paul M., Mark W.; m. 2d, Frank Rogers Muse, Apr. 29, 1983. Student El Centro Coll., 1978, Eastfield Coll., 1979, So. Meth. U., 1980-81. Owner dance sch. and real estate agy., Plano, Tex., 1965-69; customer service mgr. Blue Cross-Blue Shield, Dallas, 1969-79; employee benefits adminstr. City of Dallas, 1979—; dir. Sanus Health Plan Tex., 1983—; lectr. Dallas Pub. Library, 1975-79, also profl. groups. Named Employee of Yr., Personnel dept. City of Dallas, 1982; recipient Outstanding Achievement award City of Dallas, 1983. Mem. Internat. Found. Employee Benefits, Pub. Employee Benefit Adminstrs., Am. Mgmt. Assn., Risk Ins. Mgrs. Soc. Died Aug. 27, 2006.

MUSE, PATRICIA ALICE, writer, educator; b. South Bend, Ind., Nov. 27, 1923; d. Walter L. and Enid (Cockerham) Ashdown; student Columbia U., 1946; B.A., Principia Coll., 1947; postgrad. Seminole CC, 1977, U. Central Fla., 1978-82; m. Kenneth F. Muse, Dec. 2, 1950; children: Patience Eleanor, Walter Scott. Substitute tchr. public schs., Key West, Fla., also Brunswick, Ga., 1962-68; Author: Sound of Rain, 1971, The Belle Claudine, 1971, paperback, 1973, Eight Candles Glowing, 1976; creative writing instr., Valencia CC, 1974-75; instr. various writers confs. Community resource vol. Orange County (Fla.) Sch. Bd. (cert. of appreciation 1975-77); tutor Adult Literacy League, 1983—. Avocations: travel. Died May 11, 2007.

MUSELES, MELVIN, health care professional, retired naval officer; b. Boston, Oct. 24, 1929; s. Philip and Rose (Goldstein) M.; m. Gail Susan Burtman, July 3, 1962; children: Steven Alan, Nikki Cara, Scott Daniel. AB in Chemistry cum laude, Boston U., 1950; MD, Tufts U., 1954. Diplomate Am. Bd. Pediatrics; bd. cert. quality assurance and utilization rev. Commd. lt. (j.g.) U.S. Navy, 1954, advanced through grades to rear adm., 1978; intern U.S. Naval Hosp. Chelsea, Mass., 1954-55; resident in pediatrics U.S. Naval Hosp., 1955-57; asst. chief pediatrics U.S. Naval Hosp., 1959-62; resident in pediatrics Children's Hosp., Boston, 1955-57; chief pediatrics U.S. Naval Hosp., Guantanamo Bay, Cuba, 1957-59, Portsmouth, Va., 1962-67; chmn. dept. pediatrics Nat. Naval Med. Center, Bethesda, Md., 1967-72; comdg. officer Naval Regional Med. Center, Jacksonville, Fla., 1976-78; assoc. dean Uniformed Services U. Med. Sch., 1973-76; asst. chief Bur. Medicine and Surgery for Profl. Devel., Washington, 1979-82; exec. dir. Assn. Mil. Surgeons of U.S., Kensington, Md., 1982-84; med. dir. Eastern Div. Whittaker Health Services, Arlington, Va., 1985-86. Cons. in pediatrics; med. dir. Health Win, 1986, v.p. Health Affairs prin. Health Care, 1987-92; healthcare cons., 1992—. Contbr. articles to pediatric jours. Decorated Meritorious Service medal, Legion of Merit. Fellow ACP, Am. Acad. Pediatrics, Am. Coll. Med. Dirs.; mem. AMA, Md. Pediatric Soc., D.C. Pediatric Soc., Phi Beta Kappa. Home: Herndon, Va. Died Mar. 12, 2007.

MUSGRAVE, RICHARD ABEL, retired economics professor; b. Königstein, Germany, Dec. 14, 1910; came to U.S., 1933, naturalized, 1940; s. Curt Abel and Charlotte (Pruefer) M.; m. Peggy Brewer Richman, May 7, 1964, 3 stepchildren: Pamela, Roger, Thomas Diploma, U. Heidelberg, 1933; MA, Harvard U., 1936, PhD, 1937; LLD (hon.), Allegheny Coll., 1980; Doktor der Wirtschaftswissenschaften honoris causa, U. Heidelberg, Fed. Republic Germany; Doctoris Oeconomiae honoris causa, Cath. U., Milan, 1989; LLD honoris causa, U. Mich., 1991. Tutor, instr. econs. Harvard, 1936-41; research economist Bd. Govs. Fed. Res. System, Washington, 1941-47; lectr. econs. Swarthmore Coll., 1947-48; prof. econs. U. Mich., 1950-59; prof. polit. economy Johns Hopkins U., 1959-62; prof. econs. and pub. affairs Princeton U., 1962-65; H.H. Burbank prof. polit. econ. Harvard U., faculty arts and scis. and Law Sch., 1965-81, prof. emeritus, 1981—2007. Adj. prof. U. Calif., Santa Cruz, 1980-2007; chief economist Internat. Bank Mission to Columbia, 1949; chief ECA Fiscal Mission to Germany, 1951; pres. Colombian Tax Reform Commn., 1968-69; dir. Bolivian Fiscal Reform Mission, 1976-77; at various times cons. bd. govs. Fed. Res. System, Treasury Dept., Council Econ. Advisers, Commn. on Money and Credit. Author: Theory of Public Finance, 1959, Fiscal Systems, 1969, Public Finance in Theory and Practice, 1973; co-author: (with James M. Buchanan) Public Finance and Public Choice: Two Contrasting Visions of the State, 1999; editor Quar. Jour. Econs., 1970-75, Public Finance in a Democratic Soc., 1986; contbr. profl. jours. Recipient Frank E. Seidman award in polit. economy, 1981 Fellow Am. Acad. Arts and Scis.; disting. fellow Am. Econ. Assn. (exec. com. 1956-59, v.p. 1962); hon. mem. Nat. Tax Assn.; mem. NAS, Internat. Seminar in Pub. econs., Internat. Inst. Pub. Fin. (hon. pres. 1978). Home: Santa Cruz, Calif. Died Jan. 15, 2007.

MUTH, JOHN FRASER, economics professor; b. Chgo., Sept. 27, 1930; s. Merlin Arthur and Margaret Fraser (Ferris) M. BSI.E., Washington U., St. Louis, 1952; MS, Carnegie-Mellon U., 1954, PhD, 1962. Research fellow Carnegie-Mellon U., 1956-59, asst. prof. econs., 1959-62, assoc. prof., 1962-64; prof. Mich. State U., 1964-69, Ind. U., 1969-94; ret., 1994. Author: (with others) Planning Production, Inventories, and Work Force, 1960, (with G. K. Groff) Operations Management: Analysis for Decision, 1972; editor: (with G. L. Thompson) Industrial Scheduling, 1963, (with G. K. Groff) Operations Management: Selected Readings, 1969; contbr. articles to profl. jours. Fellow Econometric Soc. Home: Bloomington, Ind. Died Oct. 23, 2005

MYERS, JACK EDGAR, biologist, educator; b. Boyds Mills Pa., July 10, 1913; s. Garry Cleveland and Caroline (Clark) M.; m. Evelyn DeTurck, June 19, 1937; children: Shirley Ann Jacqueline, Linda Caroline, Kathleen. BS, Juniata Coll., 1934 DSc, 1966; MS, Mont. State Coll., 1935; PhD, U. Minn., 1939 NRC fellow Smithsonian Instn., Washington, 1940-41; asst prof. zoology U. Tex., 1941-45, assoc. prof., 1945-48, prof. 1948—80, prof. botany, 1955—80, prof. emeritus, 1980—99 Author: What Makes Popcorn Pop?, 1991, What Happened to the Mammoths?, 2000; co-author: (with F.A. Matsen and N.H Hackerman) Premedical Physical Chemistry, 1947; sci. editor Highlights for Children, 1960-2006; contbg. author: Algal Culture: from Laboratory to Pilot Plant, 1953, proc. of the World Symposium on Applied Solar Energy, 1956; contbr. articles to profl. jours. Guggenheim fellow, 1959; recipient Founders award Am. Soc. Gravitational & Space Biology, 1998 Mem Soc. Gen. Physiologists, Am. Soc. Plant Physiologists, Phycol Soc., AAAS, Nat. Acad. Sci., Tex. Acad. Sci., Am. Soc Photobiology (pres. 1975), Sigma Xi. Home: Austin, Tex. Died Dec. 28, 2006.

MYERS, KENNETH M., lawyer; b. Miami, Fla., Mar. 1[illegible] 1933; s. Stanley C. and Martha (Scheinberg) M.; div. 1973. AB U. N.C. Chapel Hill, 1954; JD, U. Fla., 1957. Bar: Sept. 1957 Colo. 1986, N.Y. 1987. Ptnr. Myers, Kenin Levinson & Richards, Miami, 1957-87, Shea & Gould, NYC, 1987-88, Squire Sanders & Dempsey, Miami, from 1988. Mem. Fla. Ho. Reps 1965-69, mem. Fla. Senate, 1969-80. Trustee U. Miami, 1985— Mem. ABA, Fla. Bar Assn., Colo. Bar Assn., N.Y. State Bar Assn., Am. Law Inst., Nat. Assn. Bond Lawyers, Dade County Bar Assn. Democrat. Jewish. Home: Miami, Fla. Died July 2[illegible] 2007.

MYERS, PHILLIP SAMUEL, mechanical engineering educator; b. Webber, Kans., May 8, 1916; s. Earl Rufus and Sara Katharine (Breon) M.; m. Jean Frances Alford, May 26, 194[illegible] children: Katharine Myers Muirhead, Elizabeth Myers Baird Phyllis Myers Rathbone, John, Mark. BS in Math. and Commerce, McPherson Coll., 1940; BSME, Kans. State Coll., 194[illegible] PhDME, U. Wis., 1947. Registered profl. engr., Wis. Instr. mech engring. Ind. Tech. Coll., Ft. Wayne, summer 1942; instr. U Wis., Madison, 1942-47, asst. prof., 1947-50, assoc. prof 1950-55, prof., 1955-86, emeritus prof., from 1986, chmn. dep mech. engring., 1979-83. Cons. Diesel Engine Mfrs. Assn., U.S Army, various oil and ins. cos. Contbr. articles to profl. jour Chmn. Pine Lake com. We. Wis. Conf. Meth. Ch., 1955-6[illegible] Mem. Village Bd., Shorewood Hills, 1962-67. Recipient B.S Reynolds Teaching award, 1964, McPherson Coll. Alum citation of merit, 1971; Dugald Clerk award, 1971 Fello ASME (Diesel Gas Power award 1971, Soichiro Honda awar 1993), Soc. Automotive Engrs. (Colwell award 1966, 7[illegible] Horning award 1968, nat. pres. 1969, hon. mem.), AAAS; mem NAE, Am. Soc. for Engring. Edn., Blue Key, Sigma Xi, P[illegible] Kappa Phi, Sigma Tau, Pi Tau Sigma (Gold medal 1949), Ta Beta Pi (Ragnar Onstad Svc. to Soc. award 1978). Mem Brethren Ch. Achievements include patents in field. Hom Middleton, Wis. Died Oct. 18, 2006.

NADEAU, ALLAN J., paper company executive; b. Portlan Maine, Mar. 22, 1935; m. Judith Anne Bennis, Feb. 9, 196 children: Charles Scott, Remy Lyn. BS in Chem. Engring., [illegible] Maine, 1958, MA in Pulp and Paper, 1959; Cert. of Bu Adminstrn., U. Chgo., 1962. Project engr. Beloit (Wis.) Ir Works, 1959-67; asst. supt. Internat. Paper Co., Jay, Main 1967-68; sales engr. Mt. Hope Machinery Co., Taunton, Mas 1968-69; v.p. mfg. Penntech Papers, Johnsonburg, Pa., 1967-7 coord. mfg. N.E. div. Ga.-Pacific Corp., Stamford, Con 1975-78, dir. tissue mfg., 1978-81; pres., chief oper. officer G. Inveresk Corp. U.K., Northampton, Eng., 1981-84; pres. pu and paper div. Ga.-Pacific Corp., Atlanta, 1984-88; pres., chi oper. officer Rolland Inc., Montreal, PQ, Can., 1988-91, also b dirs. Bd. dirs. Rolland Fitchburg, Mass., 1990-91. 1st lt. U. Army, 1957-62. Mem. Tappi, Canadian Pulp & Paper Assn., [illegible] Maine Pulp & Paper Found., Weghannet Country Club. Republican. Roman Catholic. Avocations: golf, wood working, collec ing antiques. Home: Mountain Lakes, NJ. Died June 27, 200

NADICH, JUDAH, rabbi; b. Balt., May 13, 1912; s. Isaac and Lena (Nathanson) N.; m. Martha Hadassah Ribalow, Jan. 26, 1947; children: Leah N. (Mrs. Aryeh Meir), Shira A. (Mrs. James L. Levin), Nahma M. Nadich (Mrs. David Belcourt). BA, CCNY, 1932; MA, Columbia U., 1936; rabbi, M.H.L., Jewish Theol. Sem. Am., 1936, D.H.L., 1953, D.D. (hon), 1966. Rabbi Temple Beth David, Buffalo, 1936-40; co-rabbi Anshe Emet Synagogue, Chgo., 1940-42; lecture tour U.S., South Africa and Rhodesia, 1946-47; rabbi Kehillath Israel Congregation, Brookline, Mass., 1947-57, Park Ave. Synagogue, NYC, 1957-87, rabbi emeritus, 1987—2007. Conducted first Bat Mitzvah in People's Republic of China, 1990. Author: Eisenhower and the Jews, 1953, Jewish Legends of the Second Commonwealth, 1983, Legends of the Rabbis, 2 vols., 1994, Rabbi Akiba and His Contemporaries, 1998; editor, translator: (Menachem Ribalow) The Flowering of Modern Hebrew Literature, 1959; editor: (Louis Ginzberg) Al Halakha v'Aggada, 1960. Pres. Rabbinical Assembly, 1972-74; pres. Jewish Book Coun. Am., 1968-72; hon. bd. dirs. Jewish Theol. Sem. Am.; past bd. dirs., mem. exec. com. Nat. Jewish Welfare Bd., Fedn. Jewish Philanthropies N.Y.; former mem. hospice com. Beth Israel Med. Ctr.; past mem. N.Y.C. Holocaust Meml.; hon. v.p. bd. dirs. Jewish Braille Inst.; bd. dirs. Friends of Jewish Hist. Mus., Warsaw; past pres. Assn. Jewish Chaplains Armed Forces; adv. to Gen. Eisenhower on Jewish affairs, ETO, 1945; com. 50th anniversary World War II U.S. Dept. Defense. Lt. col., chaplain AUS, 1942-46, ETO. Assimilated rank of Maj. Gen. South Vietnam, 1971. Decorated Order Brit. Empire, 1943, ETO with battle star medal, 1944, Croix de Guerre (France), 1945, Occupation of Germany medal, 1945, Victory medal, 1945, Ittur Lohamai Hamedinah (Israel), 1975; fellow Herbert Lehman Inst. Talmudic Ethics, 1958; Jewish Theol. Sem. Am. honoree, 1997. Mem. Mil. Chaplains Assn., Phi Beta Kappa. Lodges: Masons. Home: New York, NY. Died Aug. 26, 2007.

NADLER, PAUL STEPHEN, banking educator, columnist; b. NYC, Apr. 2, 1930; s. Marcus and Cecilia (Sachs) N.; m. Beverly Goldsmith, Nov. 4, 1990; children: Julie, Margaret, David, Saul. AB, Brown U., 1951; MA, U. Wis., 1953; PhD, NYU, 1958. Prof. Rutgers U., Newark, 1958-61 and from 69. Author: Commercial Banking in the Economy, 1968-85, Paul Nadler Writes About Banking, 1973, The Banking Jungle, 1985; contbg. editor Am. Banker, 1959—, Banking Monthly, 1963—, Secured Lender, 1970—, Commercial Lending Review, 1975—. Home: Summit, NJ. Died May 4, 2007.

NAEGELE, RAY STEPHENS, chemical company executive, consultant; b. Cleve., May 12, 1922; s. Ray William and Mary (Stephens) N.; m. Rosamonde Fraunfelder, June 7, 1944; children— Ray S. Jr., Deborah Naegele de Snoo, Thomas. B.S. in Chem. Engring., Case-Western Res. U., 1948; A.M.P., Harvard U., 1966. Bus. mgr. Dow Corning Corp., Midland, Mich., 1967-72, exec. v.p., gen. mgr., Tokyo, 1972-75, gen. mgr. 1975-83, pres., 1983-85, cons., 1985—; exec. v.p. Toyay Silicone Ltd., Tokyo, 1975-80; pres. ToHo Inc., Albuquerque, 1985—; dir., chmn. HUB Computer Med. Sys., 1993—. Chmn. Bluff Hosp., Yokohama, Japan, 1979-81. Served to 1st lt. USAF, 1943-46. Mem. Am. Chem. Soc. Republican. Club: Tokyo Am. (Tokyo). Lodge: Elks. Avocations: photography; Aikido. Home: Sparks, Nev. Died Mar. 17, 2006.

NAGAMATSU, HENRY TAKESHI, aeronautical engineering educator, consultant; b. Garden Grove, Calif., Feb. 13, 1916; s. Yachiro and Sumiko (Okuma) Nagamatsu; m. Emily Kiyoko, Apr. 9, 1942; children— Brian Henry, Nancy Lynn Reese. B.S.M.E., Calif. Inst. Tech., 1938, B.S. in Aero. Engring., 1939, M.S., 1940, Ph.D., 1949. Theoretical aerodynamicist Douglas Aircraft Co., Santa Monica, Calif., 1941-42, Curtis Wright Corp., Buffalo, 1942-43, head aero. research, 1943-46; asst. sect. head Jet Propulsion Lab. Calif. Tech., Pasadena, Calif., 1946-49, sr. research fellow, dir. hypersonic lab, 1949-55; research assoc. Gen. Electric Research and Devel., Schenectady, N.Y., 1955-77; active prof. emeritus aero. engring. Rensselaer Poly. Inst., Troy, N.Y., 1978—; cons. U.S. Naval Ordnance Test Sta., Calif., 1949-56, Rand Corp., Santa Monica, 1950-59, Atlas Project Convair, San Diego, 1950-53, Midwest Research Inst., Kansas City, Mo., 1952-55. Contbr. articles to profl. jours. Patentee in field. Recipient NASA Cert. Recognition 1984. Fellow. AIAA (Aeroacoustics award 1981), Am. Phys. Soc.; mem. N.Y. Acad. Sci., AAAS, Sigma Xi, Tau Beta Pi. Avocations: boating; fishing; hiking; swimming; golf. Home: Niskayuna, NY. Died May 15, 2006.

NAGLE, ROBERT OWEN, lawyer; b. Watertown, SD, Feb. 10, 1929; s. John Raymond and Kathleen Margaret (McQuillen) N.; m. Louise Emerson H'Doubler, Mar. 14, 1954; children— Robert Owen Jr., Charles Francis, Margaret Louise. BS in Econs., U. Wis., 1951; LLB, U. Calif., 1957. Bar: Calif. 1957. Asso. firm Morrison, Foerster, Holloway, Clinton and Clark, San Francisco, 1957-62, ptnr., 1962-64; gen. atty. Spreckels Sugar div. Amstar Corp., San Francisco, 1964-66, v.p., 1966-68, exec. v.p., 1968-71, v.p. parent co. NYC, 1971-76; exec. v.p. Am. Sugar div. Amstar Corp., NYC, 1975-76; pres., chief exec. officer Calif. and Hawaiian Sugar Co., San Francisco, 1976-82, also dir.; ptnr. Brobeck, Phleger & Harrison, 1982-86; pvt. investor Piedmont, Calif., from 1986. Bd. dirs. Providence Hosp., Oakland, Calif. Mem. Law Rev. Bd. dirs. San Francisco Bay Area coun. Boy Scouts Am.; trustee U. Calif. Berkeley Found., Wis. Alumni Rsch. Found., Pacific Vascular Rsch. Found., San Francisco. Served to lt. j.g. USN, 1951-54, Korea. Decorated Bronze Star with V, Air medal. Mem. ABA, State Bar Calif., Bar Assn. San Francisco, Order of Coif. Clubs: Claremont Country, Pacific Union. Home: Piedmont, Calif. Died Dec. 12, 2006.

NASH, CHARLES PRESLEY, chemistry professor; b. Sacramento, Calif., Mar. 15, 1932; s. Clarence and Mildred Vida (Johnson) N.; m. Lois Olive Brown, May 29, 1955 (dec. May 1999); children: Nancy Caroline, Sandra Lee, James Roy, m. D.Clinton Congdon, June 3, 2002. BS, U. Calif., Berkeley, 1952; PhD, UCLA, 1958. Instr. chemistry UCLA, 1956-57; from instr. to assoc. prof. U. Calif., Davis, 1957-70, prof., 1970-93, prof. emeritus, from 1993, chmn. acad. senate, 1987-90, chmn. faculty assn., 1993-97; v.p. external rels. Coun. U. Calif. Faculty Assns., from 1997. Vis. sr. lectr. Imperial Coll., London, 1968-69; disting. vis. prof. USAF Acad., Colorado Springs, 1979-80. Contbr. articles to profl. jours. Bd. pres. Explorit Sci. Ctr., 1995-97. Recipient Disting. Teaching award U. Calif. Davis, 1978; named Disting. Alumnus of Yr. Sacramento City Coll., 2000. Mem. Sigma Xi, Phi Lambda Upsilon. Home: Davis, Calif. Died July 15, 2007.

NASH, FRANK ERWIN, lawyer; b. Pendleton, Oreg., Feb. 27, 1916; s. Frank Lee and Gertrude (Walbridge) N.; m. Elizabeth Ann Kibbe, Apr. 20, 1943; children: Thomas K., Robert L., Carl F., Frances L. BS, U. Oreg., 1937, JD, 1939. Bar: Oreg. 1939. Since practiced in, Portland; with firm Miller, Nash (and predecessors), 1939-91, ptnr., 1948-91, ret., 1991. Bd. dirs. Tri-County United Good Neighbors, 1961-66, pres., 1963-64; pres. U. Oreg. Found., 1979-81; bd. dirs. Med. Research Found., pres., 1980-81; bd. dirs. Library Assn. Portland, pres., 1978-81; bd. visitors U. Oreg. Law Sch. Served to lt. col., inf. AUS, 1941-46, PTO. Recipient Pioneer award U. Oreg., 1980, Meritorious Svc. award., 1992. Fellow Am. Bar Found.; mem. ABA, Multnomah Bar Assn. (pres. 1964-65), Oreg. State Bar, Order of Coif, Phi Delta Phi, Phi Delta Theta. Clubs: Arlington (Portland) (dir. 1963-65), Multnomah Amateur Athletic (Portland) (dir. 1963-65, pres. 1965-66), Waverley (Portland) (pres. 1979-80). Republican. Methodist. Home: Eugene, Oreg. Died Nov. 13, 2005.

NASH, RONALD HERMAN, philosophy educator; b. Cleve., May 27, 1936; s. Herman Nash and Viola McAlpin; m. Betty Jane Perry, June 8, 1957; children: Jeffrey A., Jennifer A. BA, Barrington Coll., RI, 1958; MA, Brown U., 1960; PhD, Syracuse U., 1964. Instr. philosophy Barrington Coll., 1958-60, Houghton Coll., NY, 1960-62; prof. philosophy Western Ky. U., Bowling Green, 1964-91; prof. philosophy, religion Ref. Theol. Sem., Orlando, Fla., 1991—2002; prof. philosophy So. Bapt. Theol. Sem., Louisville, from 1998. Mem. adv. bd. CEBA, Lynchburg, Va., 1989-95. Author over 40 books including Poverty and Wealth, 1986, Faith and Reason, 1988, The Closing of the American Heart, 1990, The Gospel and the Greeks, 1992, Beyond Liberation Theology, 1992, World Views in Conflict, 1992, Great Divides, 1992, The Meaning of History, 1998, Life's Ultimate Questions, 1999; contbg. editor: The Freeman, 1993—, Christian Rsch. Jour., 1993—; mem. bd. editors Durell Jour. Money and Banking, 1988-91. Advisor U.S. Civil Rights Commn., Washington, 1988-91. Fellow NEH, 1969. Home: Oviedo, Fla. Died Mar. 10, 2006.

NASHER, RAYMOND D., real estate developer, art collector; b. Boston, Oct. 26, 1921; BA, Duke Univ., 1943; MA, Boston Univ., 1950; LLD (hon.), So. Methodist Univ., 1973. Chmn. Comerica Bank, Tex., Nasher Co., Dallas. Chmn. Nat. Commn. Urban Develop., 1964—65; mem. U.S. Commn. to UNESCO, 1962—65; U.S. delegate to UN Gen. Assembly, 1967—68; mem. Pres. Com. on Arts & Humanities, Pres. Commn. on Urban Housing (Kaiser Commn.), 1967—68, U.S.-German Cooperative Delegation, 1967. Mem. Nat. Council UN Assn. for USA, 1996, bd. dir., 1994—99; trustee V.P.'s Residence Found.; mem. bd. regents Am. Architects Found.; trustee The Am. Assembly; amb. of cultural affairs City of Dallas, 1988—93; bd. mem. World Affairs Council of Greater Dallas, from 1996; mem. Dallas Bus. Com. for the Arts; mem. pres. council Solomon Guggenheim Found.; council chmn. Mus. Modern Art, NYC; trustee emeritus Duke Univ.; bd. dir. Dallas Mus. Art; bd. mem. nat. council Fine Art Mus. San Francisco; mem. internat. council Tate Gallery, London. Named one of Top 200 Collectors, ARTnews Mag., 2004, 2006; recipient Design of the Decade - 1960s, Am. Inst. Architects, Distinguished Svc. to Visual Arts award, No. Tex. Univ., Flora award, 1994. Mem.: Council for Fgn. Rels., Phi Beta Kappa. Avocation: collector of Oceanic, pre-Columbian, modern & contemporary art, especially sculpture. Died Mar. 16, 2007.

NATZLER, OTTO, ceramic artist; b. Vienna, Jan. 31, 1908; came to U.S., 1938, naturalized, 1944; s. Sigmund and Frieda (Loewy) N.; m. Gertrud Amon, June 1938; m. Gail Reynolds, Sept. 7, 1973. Author: (with others) Form and Fire— Natzler Ceramics 1939-72, 1973; one man exhbns. include, Fine Art Gallery, San Diego, 1940, 42, San Francisco Mus. Art, 1943, 63, Los Angeles County Mus. Art, 1944, 66, Art Inst. Chgo., 1946, 63, La Jolla Mus. Art, Calif., 1953, Cin. Art Mus., 1954, 60, Joslyn Art Mus., Omaha, 1955, Springfield Mus., Mo., 1955, Jewish Mus., N.Y.C., 1958, Bezalel Nat. Mus., Jerusalem, 1959, Mus. Modern Art, Haifa, Israel, 1959, Kunstgewerbemuseum, Zurich, Switzerland, 1959, Stedelijk Mus., Amsterdam, Holland, 1959, Tulane U., 1961, St. Paul Art Center, 1963, Mus. Contemporary Crafts, N.Y.C., 1963, Birger Sandzen Meml. Gallery, Lindsborg, Kans., 1964, Palm Springs Mus., Calif., 1968, George Walter Vincent Smith Art Mus., Springfield Mass., 1970, Carleton Coll., Northfield, Minn., 1970, retrospective, M.W. deYoung Meml. Mus., San Francisco, 1971, Renwick Gallery, Smithsonian Instn., Washington, 1973, Contemporary Crafts Gallery, Portland, 1975, Craft and Folk Art Mus., Los Angeles, 1977, Scottsdale Center for Arts, Ariz., 1977, No. Ariz. U., Flagstaff, 1978, Los Angeles County Mus. Art, 1980; retrospective show Am. Craft Mus, 1993, Juedisches Museum der Stadt, Wien, 1994; works represented in permanent collections, Renwick Gallery, Smithsonian Inst., Am. Craft Mus., N.Y.C., Cooper-Hewitt Mus., N.Y.C., Fine Arts Gallery, San Diego, Everson Mus. Art, Syracuse, N.Y., Cin. Art Mus., Los Angeles County Mus. Art, Walker Art Center, Mpls., Art Inst. Chgo., Dallas Mus. Fine Arts, Tucson Art Mus., Joselyn Art Mus., Met. Mus. Art, U. Nebr., San Francisco Mus. Art, Kantonales Gewerbemuseum, Bern, Switzerland, Phoenix Art Mus., Nat. Mus. Design, Smithsonian Instn., E.B. Crocker Art Gallery, Sacramento, Balt. Mus. Art, Detroit Inst. Art, Fort Worth Mus. Art, U. Minn., Cranbrook Acad. Art, Bloomfield Hills, Mich., Kunstgerwebemuseum, Zurich, Calif. State Fair, Sacramento, Springfield Art Mus., St. Paul Art Center, Phila. Mus. Art, Seattle Art Mus., Slater Meml. Mus., Norwich, Conn., Museo Internazionale delle Ceramiche, Faenza, Italy, Portland Mus. Art, Oreg., U. Wis., UCLA, Ariz. State Coll., Houston Mus. Fine Art, Krannert Art Mus. at U. Ill., Northwestern U., Oakland Art Mus., Calif., La Crosse State Coll., Ind., Birger Sandzen Meml. Gallery, Mus. Modern Art, N.Y.C., Mills Coll., Oakland, Palm Springs Desert Mus., Newark Mus. Art, George Walter Vincent Smith Mus., Springfield, Mass., U. Oreg., Eugene, Victoria and Albert Mus., London, Minn. Mus. Art, St. Paul, Nat. Mus. Am. History, Smithsonian Instn., Washington, Des Moines Art Center, Santa Barbara Mus. Art, Calif., Maurice Spertus Mus. Judaica, Chgo., Staatliche Museen Preussischer Kulturbesitz, Kunstgewerbemuseum, Berlin, Utah Mus., U. Utah, Salt Lake City, Jewish Mus., N.Y.C., Contemporary Crafts Gallery, Portland, Honolulu Acad. Art, Oesterreichisches Mus fuer Angewandte Kunst, Vienna, Austria, Mus. Bellerive, Zurich Switzerland, Bklyn. Mus., Nelson-Atkins Mus. Art, Kansas City, Mo., Skirball Mus., Los Angeles, Mus. Fine Arts, Boston, Va. Mus. Fine Arts, Richmond, others. Fellow Am. Craft Coun., Internat. Inst. Arts and Letters. Died Apr. 7, 2007.

NAUERT, PETER WILLIAM, insurance company executive, lawyer; b. Rockford, Ill., May 3, 1943; s. Robert W. and Irene H. (Hippenbecker) N.; B.S., Marquette U., 1965; J.D., George Washington U., 1968. children: Heather, Justin, Jonathan. Bar: D.C. 1968, Ill. 1969, U.S. Ct. Appeals (7th cir.) 1969, U.S. Supreme Ct. 1971. Vice pres. Pioneer Life Ins. Co. of Ill., Rockford, 1968-75, pres., chmn., CEO, 1975—; chmn., CEO Pioneer Fin. Svcs., Inc., chmn. Ceres Group Inc., Strongsville, Ohio; Mem. ABA, Ill. Bar Assn., Winnebago County Bar Assn., Rockford C. of C., Young Pres. Orgn., World Pres. Assn., University Club, Rockford Country Club. Home: N Barrington, Ill. Died Aug. 19, 2007.

NAVALGUND, ASHOK ANANTRAO, anesthesiologist; b. Belgaum, India, May 17, 1943; s. Ananthrao R. and Laxmi A. (Hublikar) N.; m. Sharauati A. Kulkarni, Dec. 21, 1969; children: Yeshvant, Punam. Degree, Karnatak Coll., Dharwad, India, 1961; MD, Karnatak Med. Coll., Hubli, India, 1966. Diplomate Am. Bd. Anesthesiology. Intern, then resident in anesthesiology Presbyn.-St. Lukes Hosp., Chgo., 1979-82; mem. staff Aestique Med. Ctr., Greensburgh, Pa.; pvt. practice, from 1992. Contbr. articles to med. jours. Mem. Am. Soc. Anesthesiologists, Internat. Anesthesia Rsch. Soc. Home: Greensburg, Pa. Died Oct. 18, 2006.

NAVAS, LINDA MOORE, editor; b. Columbus, Ohio, July 19, 1949; m. George Ernest Navas, 1990' 1 child, Michael Anthony. BA in Journalism, Ohio State U., 1973. Prodn. asst. Wanda Kerr Dunbar, Inc., Columbus, 1969-70; newswriter UPI, Columbus, 1972; slot person, copy editor The Balt. Sun, 1973-84; asst. news editor nat. edition The Washington Times, 1984-85; exec. editor ops. Insight Mag., 1985-90, exec. editor, 1990-91; systems analyst FYI Online, Silver Spring, Md., 1994. Democrat. Home: College Park, Md. Died Mar. 25, 2007.

NAWROCKI, RICHARD A., electronics executive; b. Oct. 30, 1948; BBIM, Lawrence Inst. CEO CMI Internat. Died Apr. 20, 2007.

NAZETTE, RICHARD FOLLETT, lawyer; b. Eldora, Iowa, July 27, 1919; s. Hilmer H. and Genevieve A. (Follett) N.; m. Joan Chehak, June 20, 1942; children— Ronald D., Randall A. BA, U. Iowa, 1942, JD with distinction, 1946. Bar: Iowa bar 1946. Practiced in, Cedar Rapids, from 1946; partner firm Nazette, Marner, Wendt, Knoll & Usher, from 1968; asst. atty. Linn County, Iowa, 1951-56; county atty., 1957-63. Dir. United States Bank, Cedar Rapids, 1968-91, State Surety Co., Des Moines, 1966-78 Bd. dirs. Linn County Health Center, 1968-73, chmn., 1968-69; mem. Iowa Bd. Parole, 1981-84. Served with AUS, 1942-44. Fellow Am. Bar Found., Iowa Bar Assn. (bd. govs. 1972-76), Iowa State Bar Found.; mem. Linn County Bar Assn. (pres. 1963), Iowa County Attys. Assn. (pres. 1959), Iowa Acad. Trial Lawyers (pres. 1964), Masons (33rd degree Scottish Rite), Shriners, Jesters, Elks, Optimists (internat. v.p. 1955), Sigma Phi Epsilon. Republican. Presbyterian. Died May 12, 2007.

NEAL, MARGARET (MRS. PETER S. PATRIQUIN NEAL), publishing company executive, editor; b. Springfield, Mass., Aug. 21, 1933; d. Robert Miller and Helen (Smith) N.; ed. Stephens Coll., U. Wis., U. Mo., Tulsa U.; Levintritt fellow in chamber music; student Yale U. Summer Music Sch.; children— Dorcas Alicia Neal, Judith Elaine, Keith Lowell Neal. Profl. musician, 1945-62; advt. copywriter, group head Grey Advt. Inc., 1962-66; freelance advt. copywriter, 1966—, freelance copy editor, 1966-73; asst. v.p. editorial bur. Bus. Practice div. Prentice-Hall, Waterford, Conn., 1973—; mng. editor Fair Employment Practices Guidelines, Exec. Action Series. Past pres. West River Village, Guilford, Conn., 1976-77; past mem. public relations com. Hammonassett Sch. Author: Management and the Metric System, 1975; Executives Desk Guide to Key Legal Problems, 1979, others. Home: Old Lyme, Conn. Died June 6, 2007.

NEAL, Mrs. PETER S. PATRIQUIN See NEAL, MARGARET

NEARING, VIVIENNE WAX, lawyer; b. NYC, Feb. 3, 1926; d. Abraham M. and Edith Eunice (Webster) N. BA, Queens Coll.; MA, JD, Columbia U. Bar: N.Y., D.C., U.S. Dist. Ct. (so. and ea. dists.) N.Y., U.S. Ct. Appeals (2d cir.), U.S. Claims Ct. Ptnr. Stroock & Stroock & Lavan, NYC. Gen. counsel Plays for Living, 1998—2002, gen. co-counsel, 2002—07. Mem. editorial bd. Communications and the Law, 1978-82, adv. bd. 1982-2007; mem. editl. bd. US Trademark Reporter, 1982-86. Bd. dirs. Light Opera of Manhattan, 1981-82, Lyric Opera N.Y., 1984-90, Concert Artists Guild, 1989-91, Plays for Living, 1998-2007. Mem. ABA, Fed. Bar Coun., N.Y. State Bar Assn., U.S. Trademark Assn., Copyright Soc. U.S.A., N.Y. Lawyers for Pub. Interest (bd. dirs. 1983-87), Am. Arbitration Assn., Commn. for Law and Social Justice, Carnegie Coun., Women's City Club, Respect for Law Alliance. Home: New York, NY. Died July 4, 2007.

NEASE, JUDITH ALLGOOD, marriage and family therapist; b. Arlington, Mass., Nov. 15, 1930; d. Dwight Maurice Allgood and Sophie Wolf Allgood Morris; m. Theron Stanford Nease, Sept. 1, 1962; children: Susan Elizabeth, Alison Allgood. Student, Rockford Coll., 1949-50; BA, NYU, 1953, MA, 1954;

MS, Columbia U. Sch. Social Work, 1956. Lic. clin. social worker, marriage and family therapist. Psychiat. social worker Bellevue Psychiat. Hosp., NYC, 1956-59, St. Luke's Hosp., NYC, 1959-62; asst. psychiat. social work supr. N.J. Neuropsychiat. Inst., Princeton, 1962-64; group co-leader Ctr. for Advancement of Personal and Social Growth, Atlanta, 1973-76; asst. dir., social work supr., group co-leader Druid Hills Counseling Ctr., Columbia Theol. Sem., 1973-82; marriage and family therapist Cath. Social Svcs., Atlanta, 1978-87; chief Cmty. Mental Health Svc., Ft. McPherson, Atlanta, 1987-92; master's level clinician Ctr. for Psychiatry, Smyrna, Ga., 1990-92; pvt. practice Grayson, Ga., from 1992. Mem.: Am. Psychotherapy Assn. (diplomate). Democrat. Episcopalian. Died Apr. 5, 2006.

NEBEL, CARL WALTER, pollution control corporation executive; b. Dover, N.J., July 25, 1937; s. Walter G. and Elsa A. (Peter) N.; m. Theresa A. Storck, June 12, 1960; 1 son, Glen C. B.S., Tusculum Coll., 1958; M.S., Cornell U., 1961; Ph.D., U. Del., 1965. Postdoctoral fellow, U. Karlsruhe, W.Ger., 1968; with PCI Ozone, Corp., West Caldwell, N.J., 1976—, exec. v.p., chief operating officer, 1976—, also dir.; cons. to industry on ozone tech. Contbr. numerous tech. articles to profl. jours.; patentee in field. Von Humbolt scholar, U. Karlsruhe, 1969. Mem. Am. Chem. Soc., Internat. Ozone Assn., Am. Waterworks Assn., Water Pollution Control Fedn. Republican. Lutheran. Home: Millington, NJ. Died Dec. 30, 2006.

NECKERMANN, PETER JOSEF, retired insurance company executive; b. Wuertzburg, Fed. Republic Germany, Oct. 26, 1935; came to U.S., 1977; s. Josef and Annemarie (Brueckner) N.; m. Jutta Voelk, Feb. 10, 1960; children: Susanne, Christian. Grad., J.W. Goethe U., Frankfurt, Fed. Republic Germany, MA, 1962; PhD, Ohio State U., 1990. Pres. Neckermann Versand KGaA, Frankfurt, 1962-77; dir. econ. analysis and systems Nationwide Ins. Cos., Columbus, Ohio, 1977-79, v.p. econ. and investment services, 1979-98. CIV Mem. Columbus Assn. Bus. Economists, Columbus Coun. on World Affairs (bd. dirs.), Rotary Club of Columbus. Avocations: tennis, skiing. Home: Hilliard, Ohio. Died Apr. 24, 2006.

NEEDHAM, JAMES JOSEPH, retired stock exchange executive; b. Woodhaven, NY, Aug. 18, 1926; s. James Joseph and Amelia (Pasta) N.; m. Dolores A. Habick, July 1, 1950 (dec. Feb. 1993); children: James, Robert, Ravenna, Michael, Catherine; m. Patricia Henry Campo, May 24, 1995. Student, Cornell U., 1946; BBA, St. John's U., 1951, LLD (hon.), 1972. CPA, N.Y. Acct. Price Waterhouse & Co., NYC, 1947-54; ptnr. R. T. Hyer & Co., Port Washington, N.Y., 1954-57; ptnr., mem. exec. com. A. M. Pullen & Co., NYC, 1957-69; commr. SEC, Washington, 1969-72; chmn., CEO NY Stock Exch., 1972-76; v.p. Internat. Fedn. Stock Exchs., 1973-75, pres., 1990—94; amb. of U.S. com. gen. to EXPO in Japan, 1984—85; councilman Town of Southampton, from 1986. Disting. prof., grad. div. Coll. Bus. Adminstrn., St. John's U., Jamaica, N.Y.; bd. dirs. Mut. of Am. Mut. Funds. Treas. Central Sch. Dist. 4, 1951-52, mem. budget and finance com., 1951, 63, chmn. high sch. planning com., 1947; active local Boy Scouts Am., 1962-65; mem. bishop's com. of laity Catholic Charities, Rockville Center, N.Y., 1960-68; mem. lay adv. bd. Cath. Youth Orgn., 1964-67; bd. advs. Coll. Bus. Adminstrn., St. John's U.; mem. hon. com. Am. Cancer Soc.; N.Y. State co-chmn. fin. Reagan for Pres. Campaign, 1980; Past dir., auditor Plainview (N.Y.) Republican Club.; Bd. govs. Fed. Hall Meml. Assos.; trustee N.Y. Foundling Hosp. Served with USNR, 1944-46. Recipient Disting. Citizen award N.Y. U. Law Sch., Disting. Service award in investment edn. Nat. Assn. Investment Clubs; named Bus. Person of Year Bus. Adminstrn. Soc. St. John's U., 1975; fellow Aspen Inst. for Humanistic Studies. Mem.: AICPA (past mem. coun.), Accts. Club Am., Cath. Accts. Guild (past pres.), N.Y. Credit and Fin. Mgmt. Assn. (Laurel award), N.Y. Soc. CPA's (past dir., treas., past pres. Nassau-Suffolk chpt., recognition award), Downtown-Lower Manhattan Assn. (dir., exec. com.), N.Y. Chamber Commerce and Industry, L.I. Assn., Internat. C. of C. (U.S. coun.), Burning Tree Club, Wheatley Hills Golf Club (past treas.), Cornell Club of Nassau County, Serra Club (Nassau) (past pres.). Home: Southampton, NY. Died Apr. 6, 2007.

NEEDLE, SUSAN JUDITH, business executive, paramedical makeup specialist, consultant; b. Newark, June 18, 1941; d. Joseph J. and Betty (Levinson) N.; m. Robert J. Henderson. BEd, U. Miami (Fla.), 1962; MA in Human Resources and Psychology, U. Houston, 1979. Tchr. pub. schs., Fla., 1963-72, Houston, 1973-77; part-time profl. model, 1974-79; sales mgr. ADF Services, Houston, 1975-80; event mgr. Summit Arena, Houston, 1980-83; pres. Colorific, Inc., Houston, 1976-87, Can. Am. Energy Corp., 1983-87; assoc. prof. Coll. of Mainland, Dickinson, Tex., 1984-87; v.p., sec. Total H.E.L.P., Inc., Houston, 1984-87; behavior edn. counselor Nutri System, Ft. Myers, Fla., 1987; owner, pres. R.J.H. Cosmetic and Skin Care Ctr., Cape Coral, Fla., 1987—, pres. R.J.H. & Assocs., 1987-89; makeup artist, instr. Naples Internat. Studio, 1988-89, assoc. prof. Edison Community Coll. Ft. Myers, Fla., 1987-89; pres. Studio Magic, Inc., Ft. Myers, 1990—; head of makeup, hair and wardrobe Gulf Coast Studios, 1990—; distbr. RCMA Profl. Makeup, Fla., 1988; makeup cons. Walt Disney World and Disney/MGM Studio, 1988—. Fashion and beauty editor Clear Lake Voice. Author: Fashion Impact, 1986. Named Outstanding Educator in Fla., 1968; Vol. Am. Cancer Soc. makeup artist Look Good, Feel Better program. Mem. NAFE (dir.), Exec. Link, Am. Inst. Esthetics, Hotel Sales Mgmt. Assn., Performax, Am. Bus. Women's Assn. (ways and means, hospitality chmn., pres. 1984-85, v.p. 1985-86, Woman of Yr. Bay Area chpt. 1987), Fla. Motion Picture and TV Assn. (exec. v.p. S.W. Fla. chpt. 1989, pres. S.W. chpt. 1990), Profl. Image Cons. Assn. Internat., Women in Film, Nat. Fashion and Image Cons. Assn. (pres. Bay Area chpt.), Profl. Speakers Internat., Internat. Platform Assn., Assn. Bus. and Profl. Women, Phoenix Soc., Zonta, Alpha Epsilon Phi, Alpha Kappa Alpha. Democrat. Jewish. Home: Alva, Fla. Died Feb. 17, 2006.

NEESE, ELBERT HAVEN, retired paper machinery manufacturing executive; b. Chgo., Nov. 8, 1923; s. Elbert Haven and Laura Janvrin (Aldrich) N.; m. Margaret Eda Knorpp, Apr. 22, 1947; children: Laura Ann, Mary Jane, John, Robert, Margaret, Walter. BS in Mech. Engring., Purdue U., 1944. With Beloit Corp.(Wis.), 1946-86, dir., 1952-86, pres., 1974-78, chmn. bd., pres., 1978-84, chmn. bd., chief exec. officer, 1984-86. Dir. Regal-Beloit Corp., First Nat. Bank & Trust Co. Beloit; pres. Syracuse (N.Y.) Pulp and Paper Found., 1981-83 Trustee Beloit Coll.; pres. Beloit Found.; mem. Beloit City Council, 1956-59. Served with AUS, 1944; Served with USNR, 1944-47. Mem. TAPPI. Republican. Home: Phoenix, Ariz. Died Mar. 10, 2006.

NEILSON, ROBERT MCKENZIE, JR., materials scientist, researcher; b. Buffalo, July 1, 1949; s. Robert McKenzie and Jean E. (Feist) N.; m. Georgette P. Mullen, May 22, l971 (div. May l984); 1 child, Robert McKenzie III; m. Laurel Kim Moncur, Dec. 22, l984; l child, Amber. B Engring. Sci., SUNY, Stony Brook, 1971, MS in Materials Sci., 1973, MS in Indsl. Mgmt., 1979. Sci. assoc. Brookhaven Nat. Lab., Upton, N.Y., 1974-82; sr. scientist EG&G Idaho, Inc., Idaho Falls, 1982-88, rsch. and devel. mgr., from 1988. Cons., Idaho Falls, l983—; lectr. ASME, N.Y.C., l978-82; U.S. rep. IAEA, Vienna, Austria, l980. Editor Jour. Nuclear and Chem. Waste, l980-83; contbr. articles to profl. jours.; patentee tritum waste disposal field. Bd. dirs. Bonneville County unit Am. Cancer Soc., l984—; mem. Idaho Innovation Ctr., l988—. Recipient R & D l00 award R & D mag., l988. Mem. Am. Ceramic Soc., Am. Soc. for Metals (bd. dirs. local chpt. l980-82), Am. Nuclear Soc. (standards com. l98l—), ASTM (C-28 com. l986—), U.S. Power Squadron (sec. Patchogue, N.Y. l980-82), Idaho Falls Ski Club, Tau Beta Pi. Republican. Episcopalian. Home: Idaho Falls, Idaho. Died Mar. 11, 2007.

NELSON, BARRY, actor; b. San Francisco, Apr. 16, 1917; s. Trygve and Betsy (Chritophison) Neilsen. BA, U. Calif., Berkeley. Broadway appearances include Light Up the Sky, 1949, The Rat Race, 1950, The Moon is Blue, 1951-53, No Time For Sergents, London, Eng., 1956, Mary-Mary, 1960-61, Cactus Flower, 1965-67, Everything in the Garden, 1967, The Only Game in Town, 1970, Seascape, 1975, The Norman Conquest, 1975, The Act, 1978 (nominated for Tony award); nat. co. 42d Street, 1983-86, Broadway co., 1986-87; motion pictures appearances in Mary-Mary, 1963, Airport, 1970, Pete and Tillie, 1972, The Shining, 1979; TV series The Hunter, 1953, My Favorite Husband, 1954-55. Died Apr. 7, 2007.

NELSON, LAWRENCE EVAN, manufacturing executive, consultant; b. Chgo., Dec. 3, 1932; s. Evan Thomas and Elizabeth Marie (Stettka) N.; m. Jean H. Clayton, July 11, 1953; children: Lori Jean, Lawrence Evan. BS with honors, So. Ill. U., 1959; MBA, U. Chgo., 1969. CPA, Ill. Sr. acct. Price Waterhouse & Co., CPA's, Chgo., 1959-65; sec.-treas. Bradner Cen. Co., Chgo., 1965-73; pres. Protectoseal Co., Bensenville, Ill., 1973-84, Plan Ahead Inc., Palos Park, Ill., from 1984. Author: (book) Personal Financial Planning, 1985. Treas. City of Palos Heights, Ill., 1964-68, alderman, 1970-71; trustee Palos Heights FPD, 1977-1995. Served with USNR, 1952-56. Mem. Am. Inst. CPA's, Ill. Soc. CPA's. Home: Palos Heights, Ill. Died Nov. 10, 2006.

NELSON, RONALD HARVEY, animal science educator, researcher; b. Union Grove, Wis., Aug. 10, 1918; s. Harvey August and Myra Frances (Sheen) N.; m. Elizabeth Jane Lappley, Apr. 13, 1940; children: David Peter, Marjorie Jean, Linda Louise, Ronda Elizabeth. BS, U. Wis., 1939; MS, Okla. A&M U., 1941; PhD, Iowa State U., 1943. Mem. faculty Mich. State U., 1946-85, prof., head, animal sci. dept., 1950-84, prof. emeritus, from 1985; chief of party Mich. State U. tech. assistance project Balcarce, Pcia, Buenos Aires, 1966-68. Recipient Grad. Distinction award Okla State U., 1987, Nat. Saddle and Sirloin Portrait award, 1990. Fellow Am. Soc. Animal Sci. (Internat. Animal Agr. award 1978, Animal Industry award 1984); mem. Am. Angus Assn. (chmn. research advisory com. 1956-60), Mich. Angus Assn. (pres. 1977-78), Animal Sci. Assn., Sigma Xi, Phi Kappa Phi, Alpha Zeta. Home: East Lansing, Mich. Died May 11, 2007.

NELSON, RUBY EVERTON, banker; b. Logan, Utah, Feb. 18, 1923; d. John Elva and Lucy (Waldron) Everton; student Utah State Agrl. Coll.; m. Caril G. Nelson, Jan. 1, 1965; children— Sharilyn, Judy, Vicki; stepchildren— Alan, James. Cost acct. Wickes Engring. & Constrn. Co., Logan, Utah, 1943-45; with A.B. Robbs Trust Co., Phoenix, 1950-64, sec.-treas., 1955-64, mgr. mortgage servicing, 1960-64; with Continental Bank, Phoenix, 1964—, asst. v.p., comptroller, 1966-70, v.p., comptroller, 1970-76, sr. v.p., comptroller, 1976—, supr. mortgage servicing dept., 1960—; dir. Continental Service Corp. Mem. Nat. Assn. Bank Women, Ariz. Bankers Assn. Republican. Mormon. Clubs: Kiva, Moon Valley Country. Home: Phoenix, Ariz. Died Aug. 6, 2006.

NERENBERG, ARLENE IRIS, lawyer, social worker; b. Phila., Nov. 4, 1951; d. Ralph and Ruth (Kellman) Steinman; m. Sheldon Glen Nerenberg, Dec. 24, 1984; 1 child, Bonnie Renee. AA, C.C. of Phila., 1988; BA, Temple U., 1992, JD, 1996. Bar: Pa., N.J. Supr. social workers Commonwealth of Pa., Phila., 1990-97; assoc. Law Offices of Sheldon G. Nerenberg, Phila., from 1993. Mem. Family and Landlord/Tenant Ct., 1994—. Editor newspaper Trumpet, 1994-97. Tchr., mem. adv. bd. Mayor's Commn. on Literacy, Phila., 1990—; chief shop stewar, Phila. chpt. bd. Pa. Social Svc. Union, 1993-97; vol. re-election bd. Dem. Party, Phila., Harrisburg, Pa. and Washington, 1993—; mem. steering com. Frankford/Torresdale Hosp., Phila., 1995—; active Spl. Olympics, 1994—; mem. Holocaust Mus. of Washington, 1994—; diplomate World Jewish Congress, Washington, 1995—. Mem. ABA (contbr. to mag. Phila. Lawyer 1995, mem. family law, criminal law, and employment law sects.), ATLA (mem. constitutional law, family law, and criminal law sects.), U.S. Holocaust Mus. (assoc., charter), Pa. Bar Assn., Phila. Bar Assn., Phila. Paralegal Assn., Pa. Trial Lawyers Am., Women in the Arts, MADD, Phi Theta Kappa. Avocations: volunteer work, reading, music, travel, theater. Home: Philadelphia, Pa. Died July 29, 2007.

NESSEL, MELVIN BARRY, apparel executive; b. Gainsville, Ga., Aug. 24, 1919; s. Maxwell James and Rose Gwendolyn (Feldman) Nessel; m. Barbara Jane Kramer, July 2, 1945; 1 child, John K. Student, Duke U., 1944. Salesman Puritan Chem. Co., Atlanta, 1937—42, H.O. Rondeau Shoe Co., Farmington, NH, 1946—52; owner, pres. Fenton Shoe Corp., Cambridge, Mass., from 1952, Atlas Importing Corp., Cambridge, from 1964. Bd. dirs. Two-Ten Nat. Found., Boston, 1978, v.p., 1981, pres., from 1984. 1st lt. US Army, 1942—45. Mem.: Belmont Country Club (Mass.), Univ. Club (Boston), Algonquin Club. Home: Boston, Mass. Died Feb. 15, 2007.

NESSIM, DAVID JACQUES, industrial instrument company executive; b. Alexandria, Egypt, Apr. 2, 1925; came to U.S., 1959; s. Jacques David and Flora (Beer) N.; m. Gentille Eskenazi, Dec. 6, 1951; children: Cynthia, Patricia, Delia. Student, Alexandria U., 1943-45; BSMechE, Queen Mary Coll., U. London, Eng., 1948. Mgr. indsl. div. Alexandria Engring. Works, 1949-50; project engr. Decker Corp., Bala Cynwyd, Pa., 1959-60; sr. design engr. Daystrom Inc., Poughkeepsie, NY and Archbald, Pa., 1960-63; sr. engr. Fischer & Porter Co., Warminster, Pa., 1963-67, v.p., then sr. v.p. internat. ops., 1967-83, also bd. dirs., pres. internat. ops., 1983-87, exec. v.p., 1987-89, vice chmn. bd., from 1989, also bd. dirs. 16 fgn. subs. Patentee dry chem. feeder and chlorine leak detector. Avocation: tennis. Home: Fort Washington, Pa. Died Dec. 27, 2005.

NETHERCUT, PHILIP EDWIN, honorary consul, retired; b. Indpls., Apr. 3, 1921; s. William Richard and Ruth Salome (Habbe) N.; m. Leah Teresa Diehl, Apr. 9, 1949; children: Bruce Philip, Gail Ellen, Anne Louise. BS, Beloit Coll., 1942; MS, Lawrence Coll., 1944, PhD, 1949. With Watervliet Paper Co., Mich., 1949-50; research mgr. Scott Paper Co., 1951-56; with TAPPI, NYC, now Atlanta, 1957-86, sec.-treas., 1959-60, exec. sec., 1960-75, treas., 1964-75, exec. dir., 1975-82, vice. chmn. bd., 1983-86. Hon. consul for Finland in Ga., 1976-96; trustee Inst. Paper Chemistry, 1979-83, TAPPI Found., 1990-96. Bd. dirs. Met. Atlanta Boys' and Girls' Club, 1979—. Served to lt. (j.g.) USNR, 1944-46. Recipient Distinguished Service citation Beloit Coll., 1967; Clarke award Ga. Soc. Assn. Execs., 1979; decorated Knight Finnish Order of White Rose, 1987; inductee Paper Industry Hall of Fame, 1997. Fellow TAPPI; mem. Am. Soc. Assn. Execs. (CAE award 1968, Key award 1981), Inst. Paper Chemistry Alumni Assn. (chmn. 1960), Council Engring. and Sci. Soc. Execs. (pres. 1968), Finnish-Am. C. of C. S.E., Phi Beta Kappa, Beta Theta Pi. Clubs: Mountain View. Home: Santa Rosa, Calif. Died June 2, 2006.

NEUDECK, GEROLD WALTER, electrical engineering educator; b. Beach, ND, Sept. 25, 1936; s. Adolph John and Helen Annette (Kramer) N.; m. Mariellen Kristine MacDonald, Sept. 1, 1962; children: Philip Gerold, Alexander John. BSEE, U. N.D., 1959, MSEE, 1960; PhD in Elec. Engring., Purdue U., 1969. Asst. prof. U. N.D., Grand Forks, 1960-64; grad. instr. Purdue U., West Lafayette, Ind., 1964-68, asst. prof., 1968-71, assoc. prof., 1971-77, prof. elec. engring., from 1977, asst. dean engring. West Lafayette, 1988-90, assoc. dir. NSF/ERC Engring., 1988-94, dir. Optoelectronics Rsch. Ctr., 1993-96. Cons. in field. Author: Electric Circuit Analysis and Design, 1976, 2d edit., 1987, Junction Diode/Bipolar Transisters, 1983, 2d edit. 1989; author, editor: Modular Series on Solid State Devices, 1983; contbr. over 250 articles to profl. jours.; inventor/14 U.S. patents in field. Bd. dirs. W. Lafayette Devel. Commn., 1990— Greater Lafayette Pub. Transp., 1975-80; pres. Lafayette Tennis 1976-78. Recipient Dow Outstanding Faculty award Am. Soc. Engring. Edn., 1972, Western Elec. Fund award, 1974-75, D.D. Ewing award Purdue U., 1973, A.A. Potter award, 1973 Honeywell Teaching award, 1995, Aristotle award Semicondr Rsch., 2001. Fellow IEEE (Harry S. Nyquist award 1992, edito Transactions on Electron Devices 1994-97); mem. Am. Vacuum Soc., Sigma Xi, Eta Kappa Nu, Sigma Tau, Sigma Pi Sigma Avocations: tennis, backpacking, fishing, woodworking, bread baking. Home: West Lafayette, Ind. Died Apr. 25, 2007.

NEWELL, STERLING, JR., lawyer; b. Cleve., Sept. 1, 1921 s. Sterling Sr. and Evelyn (Walker) N.; m. Frances Hearne Brown, May 29, 1947; children: Evelyn, Peter, David, Margaret Martha. BS, Haverford Coll., 1943; LL.B., N.Y. U., 1948. Bar Ohio 1948. Sr. partner firm Spieth, Bell, McCurdy and Newell spl. asst. to atty. gen. serving as hearing officer in conscientiou objector cases. Mem. Presiding Bishop's Com. on Investment in S. Africa Contbr. articles. Pres. trustees Youth Service, Cleve. 1966-67; sec; pres. trustees Ch. Home, 1956—; sec., truste Christian Residences Found., 1965—; trustee Karamu House Cleve., Cleve Mus. Natural History, Ohio Conservation Found Univ. Sch.; chancellor Episcopal Diocese of Ohio. Served wit USNR, 1943-46. Mem. ABA, Ohio Bar Assn., Cuyahog County Bar Assn., Cleve. Bar Assn. (pres. 1984-85), Phi Delt Phi. Home: Gates Mill, Ohio. Died Aug. 8, 2006.

NEWHALL, DONALD HARWOOD, engineering compan executive, mechanical engineer, researcher; b. Lynn, Mass., Jan 10, 1909; s. Prescott and Mabel Ethelyn (Stackpole) N.; m Priscilla Hawes Chase, Oct. 28, 1937 (dec. Feb. 1966) children— William Chase, Guy Hawes. Student MIT, 1928-3 B.S.E. in Mech. Engring., U. Mich., 1934, M.S.E. in Mech Engring., 1935. Registered profl. engr., Mass.; chartered engr U.K. Engr. in research and devel. The Foxboro Co., Mass 1946-49; pres., owner Harwood Engring.c o., Walpole, Mass 1948—. Contbr. articles in field of extremely high pressure including pressure viscosity, dynamic measurements, enginī mechanics, to profl. jours. Patentee in field. Active local Repub lican com., Norfolk, Mass. Served to capt. AUS, 1939-4 Fellow Brit. Inst. Mech. Engring.; mem. Internat. Assn. Ad vancement High Pressure and Tech., ASME, Am. Acad. Me chanics, Am. Orchid Soc., Mass. Orchid Soc. (treas. 1965-69 Nat. Assn. Watch and Clock Collectors, Sigma Xi. Avocation orchid culture; fixing antique wooden clocks. Home: Norfol Mass. Died Feb. 24, 2007.

NEWHALL, JEFFREY ROBERT, religious organization ad ministrator; b. Washington, July 14, 1946; s. Robert Moody an Shirley Emily (Raw) N.; m. Sarah Elisabeth Studenmund, Sep 25, 1971; children: Sarah E., Jeremiah R. BA, George Washing ton U., 1969; MA, MDiv, Hartford Seminary, 1972; DMin, Andover/Newton, 1975. Assoc. pastor Ctrl. Bapt., Hartford, Conn., 1972-73, First Calvary, Lawrence, Mass., 1974-78; sr. pastor Palisades Cmty. Ch., Washington, 1978-85; pastor Orchard Park (N.Y.) Cmty. Ch., 1985-91; exec. dir. Internat. Coun. Cmty. Chs., Mokena, Ill., 1991—98; pastor Greendale People's Church, Worcester, Mass., 1998—2006. Therapist Samaritan Counseling Ctr., Buffalo, 1985-91; exec. com. Nat. Coun. Chs., N.Y., 1991-2007, Consultation on Ch. Union, Princeton, N.J., 1991-2007; del. U.S. chpt. World Coun. Chs., N.Y. Editor, writer newsletter Christian Cmty., 1991-97. Mem. Am. Assn. Pastoral Counselors. Democrat. Avocations: reading, writing, hiking, gardening. Home: Worcester, Mass. Died May 4, 2007.

NEWHOUSE, WILLIAM ERWIN, SR., beer and wine wholesaler, trucking company exec.; b. Malta, Mont., Jan. 27, 1921; s. William Arthur and Lottie O. (Bakke) N.; student U. Mont., 1940-41; m. Mary Lorann Wells, Nov. 3, 1945; children: Lottie Ann Blades, Stephanie Davis, William Erwin, Karen Kaus, Lisa Dunning. Pres., gen. mgr. Newhouse Grain Co. Inc., Shelby, Mont., 1946-63, Newhouse Inc., Shelby, 1956-64, Newhouse Cattle Co. Inc., Shelby, 1957-68, United Beverage Co., 1972—, United Trucking Co., Miles City, 1972—. Mem. citizens adv. council U. Mont.; dir. Miles City Endowment Bd., Miles Community Coll. Served to capt. USAAF, 1942-45. Decorated Air medal with 4 clusters, D.F.C., Purple Heart. Mem. Mont. Beer Wholesalers Assn. (dir. 1974-77, 79—), Mont. C. of C. (dir.). Home: Billings, Mont. Died Mar. 26, 2006.

NEWMAN, MARJORIE YOSPIN, psychiatrist; b. NYC, July 8, 1945; d. Toby and Audrey (Kreinik) Yospin; children: Eric, David. Student, Smith Coll., 1963-64; AB, Barnard Coll./Columbia U., 1967; MD, Med. Coll. Pa., 1971. Diplomate Am. Bd. Psychiatry and Neurology. Psychiatry intern, resident Albert Einstein Coll. Medicine, NYC, 1971-75; asst. prof. psychiatry U. Tex. Health Sci. Ctr., San Antonio, 1975-77, UCLA Sch. Medicine, 1977-80; dir. residency tng. in psychiatry Harbor-UCLA Med. Ctr., 1977-79; asst. clin. prof. psychiatry UCLA Sch. Medicine, from 1980; pvt. practice Pasadena, Calif., from 1983. Mem. admissions com. UCLA Med. Sch., 1995—. NSF grantee, London, Eng., 1969; Am. Field Svc. Internat. scholar, Argentina, 63. Fellow Am. Psychiat. Assn., Smith Coll. Alumna Assn., Barnard Coll. Alumnae Assn., Columbia U. Alumni Assn., L.A. (Calif.) Acad. Medicine (bd. govs. 2000—, sec. 2002-03, v.p. 2003-04, pres. 2004-05); mem. So. Calif. Psychiat. Soc. (regional coun. 2001-04). Avocations: travel, music, art, swimming, bicycling. Died Oct. 17, 2006.

NEWMAN, MORRIS, mathematician, educator; b. NYC, Feb. 25, 1924; s. Isaac and Sarah (Cohen) N.; m. Mary Aileen Lenk, Sept. 18, 1948; children: Sally Ann, Carl Lenk. AB, N.Y.U., 1945; MA, Columbia U., 1946; PhD, U. Pa., 1952. Mathematician applied math div. Nat. Bur. Standards, Washington, 1951-63, chief numerical analysis sect., 1963-70, sr. rsch. mathematician, 1970-76; prof. math. U. Calif., Santa Barbara, 1976-94, prof. emeritus, from 1994; dir. Inst. Interdisciplinary Applications of Algebra and Combinatorics, 1976-80. Lectr. U. B.C., 1960, U. Calif.-Santa Barbara, 1965, Am. U., Cath. U., U. Md. Author: Matrix Representations of Groups, 1968, Integral Matrices, 1972; editor: Jour. Research Nat. Bur. Standards, 1966-76, Math. of Computation, 1975-86; assoc. editor: Jour. Linear and Multilinear Algebra, 1973—, Letters in Linear Algebra, 1979—; contbr. articles to profl. jours. Recipient Gold medal U.S. Dept. Commerce, 1966 Mem. Am. Math. Soc. (council 1980-86), London Math. Soc., Math. Assn. Am., Washington Acad. Scis., AAAS, sigma Xi Home: Santa Barbara, Calif. Died Jan. 4, 2007.

NEWQUIST, EDWARD W., rancher, real estate investor; b. Lebanon, Ky., Mar. 27, 1923; s. Carl Arthur and Mande (Edwards) N.; m. Jeanne Utterback, June 25, 1948 (div.); children— Donald S., Charles E., Lea Ann, Janice H.; m. Norma Louise Harshman, Dec. 30, 1970; stepchildren— Stephen, James Lee, Christine Werness. A.B., Transylvania U., 1948. Adminstrv. asst. Commonwealth of Ky., Frankfort, 1948-51, buyer, 1951-55; buyer, mgr. IBM, Armonk, N.Y., 1955-72; Buffalo rancher, cancer researcher Fairplay, Colo., 1970-80; pres., gen. mgr. Mony Finders, Colorado Springs, Colo., since 1984—. Chmn. recreation assn. Longmont, Colo., 1969, steering com. to organize YMCA, Longmont, 1971; bd. dirs. YMCA, Boulder, 1971. Mem. Am. Buffalo Assn. (charter mem., chmn. com. to establish registration procedure 1975). Methodist. Club: Lyons (Fairplay, Colo.). Home: Fairplay, Colo. Died June 26, 2007.

NEWTON, EARLE WILLIAMS, editor, museum director, library and museum consultant; b. Cortland, NY, Apr. 10, 1917; s. Earle Williams Sr. and Anna (Moore) N.; m. Josephine A. Lyon, June 20, 1938; children: Earle W. III, Antoinette Lyon. AB magna cum laude, Amherst Coll., 1938; MA, Columbia U., 1939, postgrad., 1939-40, PhD, 1974; diploma in Mus. Adminstrn., Bristol U., Eng., 1956. Dir. hist. research Webster Pub. Co., St. Louis, 1939-41; dir. Vt. Hist. Soc., Montpelier, 1942-50, Old Sturbridge Village, 1950-54, Inst. on Hist. and Archival Mgmt. Radcliffe-Harvard U., 1954-55; founder, editor Vt. Life Mag., 1946-50, Am. Heritage, 1949-54, cons. editor, 1954-55. Sr. rsch. scholar U. London, 1955-56; lectr. U. Uppsala, Sweden, 1956. Author: Before Pearl Harbor, 1942, The Vermont Story, 1949; editor: Growth of Vermont, 1946-50, Old Cities of the New World, 1967, In Search of Gulf Coast History, 1970, Historic Architecture of Pensacola, 1970, Spain and Her Rivals, 1971; mem. editorial bd. Art in America, 1953-56. Dir. Pa. Bur. Museums and Historic Properties, 1956-59, Mus. Art, Sci. and Industry, Bridgeport, Conn., 1959-62; exec. dir. St. Augustine Hist. and Restoration Commn., 1960-68; exec. dir. Historic St. Augustine Pres. Bd., 1989-91; dir.-gen. Nat. Quadricentennial Commn., 1962-66; pres. St. Augustine Restoration, Inc., 1965-83, 1989-94; acting dir. libraries Flagier Coll., St. Augustine, Fla., 1967-68; exec. dir. Pensacola Hist. Restoration and Preservation Commn., 1968-72; cons. U. of West Fla., 1968-72; acting chancellor Mark Hopkins Coll., 1972; mem. acad. bd. Walden U., 1973; chmn. New England Conf. Museums, 1953, Northeast Conf. Museums, v.p., 1957-59; mng. editor History News, 1948-49; exec. sec. Am. Assn. State and Local History, 1947-52, sec. Soc. Am. Historians, 1947-50; exec. dir. Richmondtown Restoration, 1976-78; adj. prof. humanities, asst. to pres. Norwich U., 1979-86, mem. bd. fellows, 198691; dir. Mus. of the Americas, 1986-90; cons. Newton Ctr. for Anglo-Am. Studies, Savannah Coll. Art and Design, 2000—. Lt. (j.g.) USNR, 1944-46. Decorated comdr. Order of Isabella la Catolica; Order of Merit (Spain), Queen's Order of Brit. Empire, 2003; recipient Spl. award of Merit Am. Assn. State and Local History, 1949, editorial awards Am. Inst. Graphic Arts, 1950, 51, 52. Fellow Internat. Inst. Arts and Letters (life); mem. Am. Assn. Museums, Am. Assn. for State and Local History, Am. Hist. Assn., Nat. Trust for Hist. Preservation, Vt. Hist. Soc., Inter-Am. Inst. Fine Arts (pres. 1966-68), British Mus. Assn., Internat. Coun. on Museums, PEN, Newcomen Soc., Rotary, Phi Beta Kappa, Cum Laude Soc., Sigma Delta Chi. Lodges: Rotary. Avocations: maps, paintings. Home: Ponte Vedra, Fla. Died May 24, 2006.

NICHOL, WILLIAM EDISON, lieutenant governor of Nebraska; b. Windsor, Colo., Mar. 12, 1918; s. William Adam and Barbara Marie (Kraning) N.; m. Ruth Arline Ellis, Nov. 29, 1941; children— James Charles, Linda Ruth Nichol Harsch BS in Edn., Nebr. Wesleyan U., 1940, B.F.A. in Music, 1940; postgrad., U. Kans., 1960. Owner, mgr. ins. agy., Scottsbluff, Nebr., 1945-60; owner credit bur., Scottsbluff, Nebr., 1960-75; mem. Unicamer Legislature, Lincoln, Nebr., 1974-86; speaker Nebr. Legislature, Lincoln, 1983-84, 85, 86; lt. gov. State of Nebr., from 1986. Mayor, City of Scottsbluff, 1958-66; Scottsbluff county commr. Mem.: Scottsbluff Country; Nebraska, University (Lincoln), Elks. Republican. Methodist. Home: Scottsbluff, Nebr. Died Nov. 29, 2006.

NICHOLAS, JAMES A., surgeon, consultant, educator; b. Portsmouth, Va., Apr. 15, 1921; s. Harry and Julie N.; m. Kiki Chris, June 14, 1952; children: Philip Duncan, Stephen James, Nicole Hambro. BA, NYU, 1942; MD, Downstate Med. Ctr., 1945. Diplomte Am. Bd. Orthop. Surgery. Resident various hosps., NYC, 1946—52; asst. dir. rsch. Hosp. Spl. Surgery, NYC, 1952—60; dir. dept. orthop. surgery Lenox Hill Hosp., NYC, from 1970, dir. emeritus, from 1995, James A. Nicholas chair in perpetuity, 2003; founding dir. Nicholas Inst. Sports Medicine, NYC, from 1973; dir. Inst. Sports Medicine & Athletic Trauma, NYC, 1973—99, dir. emeritus, 1999—2006; dir. Gulf & We. Corp., NYC, 1983—93, Paramount Comm., Inc., NYC. Orthopaedic cons. NFL, NYC, 1968—97; mem. Presdl. Coun. Phys. Fitness in Sports, Washington, 1979—82, cons., 1993—98; prof. orthopaedic surgery Cornell Med. Coll., NYC, 1970—2001. Editor 15 books including: Injuries to the Spine and Lower Extremity in Sports Medicine, 1986, 2nd edit., 1995, the Upper Extremity in Sports Medicine, 1990, 2nd edit., 1996; patentee manual muscle tester. Trustee ctr. coun. Cornell U. Med. Ctr. N.Y. Hosp., 1986—94; trustee Am. Jour. of Sports Medicine, 1980—2002. Capt. US Army, 1945—46, capt. US Army, 1952—53. Recipient Frank Babbott Disting. Alumnus award, 1985, Royal Order of Phoenix, Greek Govt. Svc., 1970, medal of distinction Lenox Hill Hosp., 1992; David D. Moyer award Ea. Athletic Tng. Assn., 1997; named Health Am. Fitness Leader, Jaycees, 1982; Spingold Found. grantee in sports medicine, 1976—. Fellow ACS, Am. Orthop. Assn.; mem. Orthop. Rsch. Soc. (sec. treas. 1968-69), Am. Orthop. Soc. for Sports Medicine (pres. 1980, named Mr. Sports Medicine 1982, inducted into Hall of Fame, 2003), N.Y. Acad. Medicine (pres. 1974), Acad. Orthop. Soc., Greek Orthodox, Hellenic Univ. Club, Westchester Country Club. Avocations: astronomy, golf, piano, synthesizer. Home: Scarsdale, NY. Died July 15, 2006.

NICHOLS, THEODORE GEORGE, engineer; b. Chgo., July 27, 1927; s. Michael Feodor and Sophia (Lewandowski) N.; Student Wright Jr. Coll., 1950-53, Ill. Inst. Tech., 1956-61: m. Barbara McKillip, Mar. 14, 1975; children by previous marriage— Michael J., Julie Ann, Theodore George. Supt., Paschen Contractors, Ill. and Ind., 1947-56; dir. phys. plant Ill. Inst. Tech. Research Inst., Chgo., 1956-69; dir. engring. Rush Presbyn. St. Luke's Med. Center, Chgo., 1969—. Deacon, sec. council St. Andrews Ch., 1966-68; com. chmn., instl. rep. Chgo. Area Council Boy Scouts Am., 1967-68. Mem. Am. Hosp. Assn., Inst. Plant Maintenance, Western Soc. Engrs., Chgo. Supts. Assn. Supervised constrn. 1st indsl. nuclear reactor, 1955. Home: Glenview, Ill. Died June 15, 2006.

NICHOLS, WILLIAM DEMING, lawyer; b. New Haven, Nov. 12, 1924; s. Malcolm Parrot and Mabel (Turck) N.; m. Nancy Bird; children: Nathaniel, Malcolm, William, Deborah. BA, Amherst Coll., 1951; LLB, Harvard U., 1954. Sr. ptnr. Sullivan & Worcester, Boston, 1962-94, of counsel, from 1995. Sgt. USMC, 1942-45, PTO. Republican. Protestant. Home: Tamworth, NH. Died Nov. 2, 2006.

NICKENS, DARYL G., writer; b. Washington, Jan. 21, 1949; s. Theodore J. Jr. and June Rose (Turney) N.; m. Gwenne E. Freiman, May 30, 1970 (div. 1972); m. Jean V. Billingham, Feb. 16, 1979; 1 child, Matthew D. BA, Wesleyan U., Middletown, Conn., 1971. Freelance TV writer, Los Angeles, 1982-83; staff writer Webster Paramount TV, Los Angeles, 1983-86; co-screenwriter At Your Service Columbia Pictures, 1986; head writer, creative cons. 19th Annual NAACP Image awards Carson Co., Los Angeles, 1987; exec. story editor Bustin' Loose Universal TV, Los Angeles, 1987, co-producer Bustin' Loose, 1988. Mem. CBS-Writers Guild Am. Negotiating Com., Awards Com. Recipient Richard B. Jablow award for devoted svc. to the Guild, Writers Guild Am., East, 2007. Mem. Writers Guild Am. (Morgan Cox Hon. Svc. Award 2007), Acad. TV Arts and Scis. Democrat. Home: Los Angeles, Calif. Died July 10, 2006.

NICKENS, PAULA E., former political organization administrator; b. Washington, 1948; m. Ronnie Edwards. BA, U. D.C., 1975. Chair Dem. State Com., Washington, 1997—2000; civil right program specialist Woodrow Wilson Bridge Project Fed. Highway Adminstrn., 2001; campaign mgr. for Robert C. Bobb, 2006. Mem. Assn. of State Dem. Chairs. Home: Washington, DC. Died Mar. 10, 2007.

NICKLIN, GEORGE LESLIE, JR., psychoanalyst, educator, physician, writer; b. Franklin, Pa., July 25, 1925; s. George Leslie and Emma (Reed) N.; m. Katherine Mildred Aronson, Sept. 30, 1950 BA, Haverford Coll., 1949; MD, Columbia U., 1951; cert. in psychoanalysis, William A. White Inst., NYC, 1962. Diplomate Am. Bd. Psychiatry and Neurology. Resident, then chief resident Bellevue Psychiat. Hosp., NYC, 1953-56; pvt. practice specializing in psychoanalytic psychiatry, from 1956; staff Bellevue Hosp., from 1956; assoc. clin. prof. psychiatry NYU Med. Sch., from 1970; dir. LI Inst. Psychoanalysis, 1978-88, dir. emeritus and from 1988, dir. emeritus. Mem. Com. to Award Martin Luther King Peace Prize. Author: Doctors In Peril, 2000, War Stories, 2005. Mem. Corp. Haverford Coll., 1957-2003; founder, trustee Westbury Friends Sch., 1957-2006; founder Friends World Coll., 1958. With AUS, 1943-46, ETO. Decorated Purple Heart (3) with oak leaf cluster (3), Bronze Star with oak leaf cluster and three battle stars. Fellow Am. Acad. Psychoanalysis, Am. Psychiat. Assn. (disting. life fellow, 2003); mem. AAAS, NAACP, Soc. Med. Psychoanalysts (pres. 1986-87), White Psychoanalytic Soc., Assn. for World Edn. (charter trustee, treas. 1970-78), 9th Inf. Divsn. Assn., Vets. of the Bulge, Mil. Order of the Purple Heart. Clubs: Gardiner's Bay Country (Shelter Island, NY). Mem. Soc. Of Friends. Died June 20, 2007.

NIEKRO, JOE (JOSEPH FRANKLIN NIEKRO), retired professional baseball player; b. Martins Ferry, Ohio, Nov. 7, 1944; Student, West Liberty State Coll., W.Va. Pitcher Chgo. Cubs, 1967-69, San Diego Padres, 1969, Detroit Tigers, 1970-73, Atlanta Braves, 1973-74, Houston Astros, 1975-85, NY Yankees, 1985—87, Minn. Twins, 1987—88. Named to Nat. League All-Star Team, 1979; Named Nat. League Pitcher of Yr. Sporting News, 1979 Died Oct. 27, 2006.

NIEMANN, KURT MAX WALTER, orthopaedic surgeon, educator; b. Bklyn., July 31, 1932; s. Walter and Walburg V. S. N.; m. Linda Charlene Sparks, Apr. 18, 1987; children— Susan, Kurt Max Walter, Rebecca, Eric, Joel. B.S., Trinity Coll., 1954; M.D., Med. Coll. Ala., 1960. Diplomate Am. Bd. Orthopaedic Surgery. Intern, Med. Coll. Va. Hosp., Richmond, 1961; resident U. Pitts., 1962-65, asst. prof. orthopaedic surgery, 1967-69; assoc. prof. orthopaedic surgery U. Ala., Birmingham, 1969-74, prof. and dir. div. orthopaedic surgery, 1974-90, prof., 1990—. Served to 2d lt. USAF, 1954-56. Mem. Am. Acad. Orthopaedic Surgery, Am. Orthopaedic Assn., Am. Orthopaedic Soc. for Sports Medicine, Clin. Orthopaedic Soc. (pres. 1986-87), So. Orthopaedic Assn. (pres. 1986-87). Lutheran. Contbr. chpts. to books, articles to profl. jours. Home: Columbiana, Ala. Died Oct. 4, 2005.

NILES, CHARLES LANNON, JR., insurance company executive; b. Springfield, Mass., Sept. 16, 1924; s. Charles Lannon and Florence Marie (Brine) Niles; m. Mary Murphy, June 4, 1950; children: Karen Niles Parker, Janet B. Mast, Charles L., Alice M., Clare L. BS in Math., Boston Coll., 1951. Actuarial asst. Am. Mut. Co., Wakefield, Mass., 1951—60; from asst. actuary to pres., COO Gen. Accident Ins. Co., Phila., 1960—85. Bd. dirs. Merchants & Bus. Mens Mut. Ins. Co. With USAAF, 1943—47. Fellow: Casualty Actuarial Soc.; mem.: Casualty Actuaries of Middle Atlantic Region, Am. Acad. Actuaries. Roman Catholic. Died Dec. 14, 2006.

NITSCHE, JOHANNES CARL CHRISTIAN, mathematics professor; b. Olbernhau, Germany, Jan. 22, 1925; came to U.S., 1956; s. Ludwig Johannes and Irma (Raecke) N.; m. Carmen Dolores Mercado Delgado, July 1, 1959; children: Carmen Irma, Johannes Marcos and Ludwig Carlos (twins). Diplom für Mathematik, U. Göttingen, 1950; PhD, U. Leipzig, 1951; Privatdozent, Tech. U. Berlin, 1955. Asst. U. Göttingen, 1948-50; rsch. mathematician Max Planck Institut für Strömungsforschung Göttingen, 1950-52; asst. Privatdozent Tech. U., Berlin, 1952-56; vis. assoc. prof. U. Cin., 1956-57; assoc. prof. U. Minn., Mpls., 1957-60, prof. math., 1960—2000, head Sch. Math., 1971-78, prof. emeritus, from 2000. Vis. prof. U. P.R., 1960-61, U. Hamburg, 1965, Tech. Hochschule Vienna, 1968, U. Bonn, 1971, 75, 77, 80, 81, U. Heidelberg, 1979, 82, 83, U. Munich, 1983, U. Florence, 1983, Tech. Hochschule Aachen, 1997, 98, 99, 2001; keynote spkr. Festive Colloquium, U. Ulm, 1986; co-organizer workshop statis. thermodynamics and differential geometry U. Minn., 1991; keynote spkr. Meml. Colloquium Tech. U. Berlin, 1991, spkr. Internat. Workshop on Geometry and Interfaces, Aussois, France, 1990, others. Author: Vorlesungen uber Minimalflachen, Springer-Verlag, 1975, Lectures on Minimal Surfaces, 1989; mem. editorial bd. Archive of Rational Mechanics and Analysis, 1967-91; editor: Analysis, 1980—; assoc. editor: Contemporary Math., 1980-88, Zeitschrift für Analysis und ihre Anwendungen, 1993—; contbr. articles to profl. jours. Mem. Am. del. joint Soviet-Am. Symposium on Partial Differential Equations, Novosibirsk, 1963, U.S.-Japan Seminar on Differential Geometry, Tokyo, 1977; speaker 750th Berlin Anniversary Colloquium, Free U. Berlin, 1987. Recipient Lester R. Ford award for outstanding expository writing, 1975, George Taylor Disting. Svc. award U. Minn. Found., 1980, Humboldt prize for sr. U.S. scientists Alexander von Humboldt Found., 1981; Fulbright rsch. fellow Stanford, 1955-56. Fellow AAAS; mem. Am. Math. Soc., Circolo Matematico di Palermo, Deutsche Mathematiker-Vereinigung, Edinburgh Math. Soc., Gesellschaft für Angewandte Mathematik und Mechanik, Math. Assn. Am., N.Y. Acad. Scis., Österreichische Mathematische Gesellschaft, Soc. Natural Philosophy. Home: Minneapolis, Minn. Died Aug. 9, 2006.

NOALL, ROGER, bank executive; b. Brigham City, Utah, Apr. 1, 1935; s. Albert Edward Noall and Mabel Clayton; m. Judith Ann Stelter, Mar. 16, 1962 (div.); children: Brennan, Tyler; m. Colleen Henrietta Mannion. BS, U. Utah, 1955; LLB, Harvard U., 1958; LLM, NYU, 1959. Legal asst. Donavan, Leisure, Newton & Irvine, NYC, 1959-61; assoc. Olwine, Connelly, Chase, O'Donnell & Weyher, NYC, 1961-65, ptnr., 1965-67; with Bunge Corp., NYC, 1967-85, exec. v.p., 1975-83; pres., chief fin. officer Centran Corp., Cleve., 1985-85; vice chmn., chief adminstrv. officer Soc. Corp., Cleve., from 1985; sr. v.p., chief adminstrv. officer Key Corp., Cleve., from 1994. Served in USNG, 1959. Died Mar. 29, 2007.

NOBLE, JOSEPH VEACH, retired museum director; b. Phila., Apr. 3, 1920; s. Joseph Haderman and Helen Elizabeth (Veach) N.; m. Olive Ashley Mooney, June 21, 1941 (dec. Sept. 1978); children: Josette Gamble, Ashley, Laurence; m. Lois Cook Cartwright, Oct. 27, 1979; stepchildren Alan and Bruce Cartright. Student, U. Pa., 1942. Cameraman, dir. DeFrenes and Co. Studios, Phila., 1939-41; studio mgr. WPTZ, Philco TV Sta., Phila., 1941-42, DeFrenes and Co. Studios, 1946-49; gen. mgr. Murphy-Lillis Prodns., NYC, 1949-50; exec. v.p. Film Counselors, Inc., NYC, 1950-56, dir., 1950-82; operating adminstr. Met. Mus. Art, 1956-67, vice dir. adminstrn., 1967-70; dir. Mus. City NY, 1970-85, dir. emeritus; exec. dir. Soc. Medalists, 1985-95. Photog. salon exhibitor, from 1936; lectr. CCNY, 1949-51 Author: The Techniques of Painted Attic Pottery, 1965, The Historical Murals of Maplewood, 1961, Forgery of the Etruscan Terracotta Warriors, 1961; Contbr.: Ency. Brit, 1970. Trustee Corning Mus. of Glass, 1970-2007; mem. Morrow Meth. Ch., pres. trustees, 1972-77; chmn. NY State Bd. Hist. Preservation 1972-76; co-chmn. Save Venice, Inc., 1972; trustee Brookgreen Gardens, 1971-2007, pres., 1976-90, chmn., 1990-95, chmn. emeritus, 1995-2007. With AUS, 1942-46. Recipient Venice Film Festival medal for photography in sci., 1948, Sigma Xi award 1963, Maple Leaf award Maplewood, NJ, 1966, 87, Gold medal for The Big Apple NY Film Festival, 1979, Disting. Svc. award Maplewood C. of C., 1987. Fellow Soc. Antiquaries London, Am. Numismatic Soc.; mem. NY State Assn. Museums (pres. 1970-72), NAD (medal 1976), Nat. Sculpture Soc. (medal 1978, 91), Artists' Fellowship (medal 1978), Archeol. Inst. Am. (treas. 1963-70), Museums Coun. NYC (chmn. 1965-67), Am. Assn. Museums (pres. 1975-78, Disting. Svc. Awd., 1991, named to Centennial Honor Roll, 2006), Cultural Instns. Group NYC (chmn. 1984-85), Soc. Promotion Hellenic Studies; Am. Watercolor Soc. (medal 1982). Clubs: Maplewood Country; Explorers (NUC), Century Assn. (NYC). Died Sept. 22, 2007.

NOBLES, LEWIS, retired academic administrator; b. Meridian, Miss., Sept. 11, 1925; s. Julius Sidney and Ruby Rae (Roper) N.; m. Joy Ford, Aug. 29, 1948; children— Sandra Jeanne (Mrs. Ben Nash), Glenda Suzanne (dec.). Student, Ursinus Coll., 1944-45; BS in Pharmacy, U. Miss., 1948, MS, 1949; PhD, U. Kans., 1952; NSF postdoctoral fellow, U. Mich., 1958-59. Mem. faculty U. Miss., 1952-68, prof. pharm. chemistry, 1955-68; dean U. Miss. (Grad. Sch.), 1960-68, coordinator univ. research, 1964-68; pres. Miss. Coll., Clinton, 1968—94. Co-author: Physical and Technical Pharmacy; contbr. to books; editorial adv. bd.: Jour. Pharm. Scis, 1965-71. Mem. regional adv. group Miss. Regional Med. Program 1969-76; chmn. 1971-76; mem. nat. adv. council on regional med. programs HEW, 1976-79; bd. grants Am. Found. Pharm. Ed., 1972-80; trustee New Orleans Baptist Theol. Sem., 1976-82. Served to lt. (j.g.) USNR, 1944-46. Am. Found. Pharm. Edn. fellow, 1949; Gustavus A. Pfeiffer Meml. Research fellow, 1955; recipient award for stimulation of research Am. Pharm. Assn. Found., 1966; named one of Top 18 Most Effective Coll. Pres. in U.S. Exxon Ednl. Found., 1986. Fellow AAAS; mem. Am. Chem. Soc., Chem. Soc. Gt. Britain, N.Y. Acad. Sci., Acad. Pharm. Scis. (chmn. medicinal chemistry sect. 1967-68), Am. Pharm. Assn. Internat. Platform Assn., Jackson C. of C., Am. Assn. Pres. Ind. Colls. and Univs. (trustee 1987—), Nat. Assn. Ind. Colls. and Univs. (bd. dirs. 1990-92), So. Assn. of Colls. and Schs. (mem. commn. on colls.), Rotary, Sigma Xi, Rho Chi, Kappa Psi, Phi Eta Sigma, Pi Kappa Pi. Baptist. Home: Clinton, Miss. Died May 25, 2007.

NOE, JERRE DONALD, computer science educator; b. McCloud, Calif., Feb. 1, 1923; s. Charles J. and Mae H. Noe; m. Mary A. Ward, Oct. 20, 1943 (dec.); children: M. Sherill (Mrs. Michael F. Roberts), Jeffrey W., Russell H.; m. Margarete Wöhlert, Sept. 10, 1983. BS, U. Calif., 1943; PhD, Stanford U., 1948. Rsch. assoc. Radio Research Lab. Harvard and Am. Brit. Lab., Malvern, Eng., 1943-45; devel. engr. Hewlett-Packard Co., Palo Alto, Calif., 1946-48; rsch. engr. Stanford Research Inst., Menlo Park, Calif., 1948-53; asst. dir. engring. rsch., 1954-60; exec. dir. info. sci. and engring., 1961-68; prof. computer sci. U. Wash., Seattle, 1968-89, prof. emeritus, from 1990, chmn. dept., 1968-76. Lectr. Stanford U., 1955-68; vis. prof. Vrije Universiteit, Amsterdam, 1976-77; guest rsch. scientist Gesellschaft fur Mathematik und Datenverarbeitung (GMD), Bonn, Fed. Republic Germany, 1986-87; mem. Army Sci. Bd., 1984-90; trustee Internat. Computer Sci. Inst., 1991-93; panelist NRC, 1991-92. Mem. Assn. Computing Machinery, IEEE. (nat. chmn. profl. group electronic computers 1956-57), Sigma Xi, Eta Kappa Nu, Tau Beta Pi. Tech. dir., devel. 1st computer for banking industry Bank Am. ERMA system, 1950-56. Home: Seattle, Wash. Died Nov. 12, 2005.

NOEL, JOHN EDWARD, lawyer; b. Chgo., Aug. 17, 1946; s. Melbourne Anthony and Kathryn (Hoffman) N.; m. Sara Dinkler, Apr. 5, 1975; children— Benjamin, Matthew. A.B., U. Notre Dame, 1968; J.D., Loyola U., Chgo., 1974. Bar: Ill. 1974, U.S. Dist. Ct. (no. dist.) Ill. 1974, U.S. Ct. Appeals (7th cir.) 1974, U.S. Dist. Ct. (so. dist.) Ill. 1975, U.S. Ct. Appeals (fed. cir.) 1982. Asst. atty. gen. Ill. Atty. Gen.'s Office, Chgo., 1974-78, chief antitrust div., 1978-79; assoc. Ross, Hardies, Babcock, et al, Chgo., 1979-80; assoc. Chadwell & Kayser Ltd., Chgo., 1980-82, officer, 1982—. Contbr. articles to law jours. Chmn. Wood Dale Fire Prevention Dist. Bd. Commrs., Ill., 1978—. Mem. ABA, Ill. State Bar Assn. (author Antitrust Sect. Newsletter 1978-80), Chgo. Bar Assn. Republican. Roman Catholic. Clubs: Union League, Medinah Country. Home: Glen Ellyn, Ill. Died Apr. 29, 2006.

NOLAND, ROYCE PAUL, association executive, physical therapist; b. Walla Walla, Wash., Dec. 6, 1928; s. Homer Vernon and Mildred Bessie (Royce) N.; m. April Lynn Hawkes, Feb. 10, 1979; children: Royce Paul, Richard Mitchell BA, Whitman Coll., Walla Walla, Wash., 1951; Cert. in phys. therapy, Stanford U., 1952. Pvt. practice in phys. therapy, Santa Cruz, Calif., 1961-68; exec. dir. Calif. chpt. Am. Phys. Therapy Assn., Santa Cruz, Calif., 1965-69, exec. dir. Washington, D.C., 1969-87; pres., chief exec. officer Inst. Profl. Health Service Adminstrs., Alexandria, 1988-91; exec. dir., CEO Fedn. of State Bds. of Phys. Therapy, Alexandria, Va., 1992-97; CEO. Nat. Phys. Rehab. Networks, Inc., Alexandria, 1997-2000; ret., 2000. Co-inventor phys. therapy device; contbr. articles to profl. publs. Mem. Am. Soc. Assn. Execs. (cert.), Presdl. Commn. Employment of Handicapped, Am. Pub. Health Assn. Clubs: Belle Haven Country (Alexandria). Republican. Avocation: golf. Home: Alexandria, Va. Died Sept. 10, 2007.

NORCOTT, ALFRED A., retired advertising executive; b. Bklyn., July 13, 1918; s. Alex Fred and Isabella (MacLennan) N.; m. Ruth Marie Jackson, May 15, 1943; children— Alfred A., Ellen M. BS, Rutgers U., 1952. With U.S. Lines Co., 1939-42, Gen. Motors Corp., 1946-47; with Kenyon & Eckhardt, Inc., 1947-85, now ret. sr. v.p., sec. Served with USNR, 1935-39, 42-45. Home: Vienna, Va. Died Feb. 17, 2007.

NORCROSS, MARVIN AUGUSTUS, veterinarian, researcher, retired federal official; b. Tansboro, NJ, Feb. 8, 1931; s. Marvin A. and Katherine V. (McGuigan) N.; m. Diane L. Tuttle, Nov. 22, 1956 (div. 1991); children: James, Janet. Student, Rutgers U., 1954-55; VMD, U. Pa., 1959, PhD, 1966. Pathologist Merck Sharp & Dohme Rsch. Labs., Rahway, NJ, 1966-69, dir. clin. research, 1969-72, sr. dir. domestic vet. research, 1972-75; dir. div. vet. med. rsch. Ctr. Vet. Medicine, FDA, Rockville, Md., 1975-78, assoc. dir. for rsch., 1978-82, assoc. dir. for human food safety, 1982-84, assoc. dir. for new animal drug evaluation, 1984-87; asst. dep. adminstr., then dep. adminstr. Sci. and Tech., Food Safety and Inspection Svc. USDA, Washington, 1987-93, exec. asst. to the adminstr., 1993-94; U.S. coord. for Codex Alimentarius USDA, Washington, 1994-96, sr. sci. advisor to adminstr., 1996; cons. vet. medicine and food safety, 1996—2007. Adj. prof. Va.-Md. Regional Coll. Vet. Medicine, Blacksburg, 1980-85 Contbr. articles to profl. jours. Trustee Scotch Plains (NJ) Cmty. Fund, 1969-72. Lt. AUS, 1952-54; col. Res., 1954-83 (ret.) Recipient FDA Merit award, 1978, Meritorious Presdl. Rank award, 1989; named to Artillery OCS Hall of Fame, 2000. Mem. AAAS, Am. Vet. Med. Assn., Assn. Mil. Surgeons US, Civil Affairs Assn., Nat. Assn. Fed. Veterinarians, NJ Acad. Sci., NY Acad. Scis., Res. Officers Assn., Soc. Toxicologic Pathology, Sigma Xi. Died Sept. 11, 2007.

NORLAND, DONALD RICHARD, retired foreign service officer; b. Laurens, Iowa, June 14, 1924; s. Norman and Aletta (Brunsvold) N.; m. Patricia Bamman, Dec. 13, 1952; children: Richard Boyce, David, Patricia D. Student, Iowa State Tchrs. Coll., 1941-43, N.W. Mo. State Tchrs. Coll., 1943-44; BA, U. Minn., 1948, MS, 1950; postgrad., U. Mich., 1951-52, Grenoble U., France, 1948-49. Instr. history and polit. sci. U. No. Iowa, 1949-51; teaching fellow U. Mich., 1951-52; with Fgn. Svc., U.S. Dept. State, 1952-81; posts include Rabat, Morocco, 1952-56, Washington, 1956-58, Abidjan, Ivory Coast, 1958-60; mem. NATO del., Paris, 1961-63, NATO delegation, The Hague, The Netherlands, 1964-69; dep. chief mission Conakry, Guinea, 1970-72; U.S. Dept. State fellow Stanford (Calif.) U., 1969-70; dep. dir. Office Mil. Assistance and Sales, Bur. Politico-Mil. Affairs, Dept. State, Washington, 1972-73, chief polit. officers counseling br. Office Pers., 1973-75; dep. dir. Office Mgmt. Ops., 1975-76; amb. to Botswana, Lesotho and Swaziland, 1976-79; amb. to Chad, 1979-81; ret. Fgn. Svc., U.S. Dept. State, 1981; lectr. African affairs; internat. cons., specialist econ. devel. Chmn. African studies Fgn. Svc. Inst. of U.S. Dept. of State, Washington, 1987-89; program dir. Ctr. for Internat. Pvt. Enterprise affiliate U.S. C. of C., Washington, 1990-91; sr. cons. World Space, Inc., 1995, sr. policy advisor, 1996—. Bd. dirs. Calvert New Africa Fund, 1995. Lt. (j.g.) USNR, 1943-46. Mem. Am. Fgn. Svc. Assn. (v.p. for retirees 1993-95, sec. 1995-97, mem. editl. bd. Fgn. Svc. Jour. 1992-95), World Space Found. (pres. 1997-98). Home: Washington, DC. Died Dec. 30, 2006.

NORRIS, PHILIP, brokerage executive; b. NYC, Oct. 16, 1928; s. Claude Basil and Fannie Inez (Bell) N.; m. Rose Martin, Aug. 24, 1957 (div.); children: Laura Ashley Coats, Susan Martin Bradford, Philip Blair; m. Rebecca Snider, Oct. 1, 1977. BA, Claremont McKenna Coll., 1953. Account exec. Dean Witter & Co., Honolulu, 1960-66; Hawaii area mgr. E.F. Hutton & Co., Honolulu, from 1966; resident mgr. Prudential-Bache Securities, Honolulu, from 1989. Mem. bus. conduct com. Nat. Assn. Securities Dealers, San Francisco, 1972-74 Bd. dirs. Downtown Improvement Assn., Honolulu, 1983—; vice chmn. Met. YMCA, Honolulu, 1985—. Maj. USMC, 1954-60. Mem. Securities Industry Assn. (govt. relations com. 1980-87), Hawaii C. of C. (bd. dirs. 1985-88). Republican. Mem United Ch. Christ. Lodge: Rotary (pres. Honolulu club 1986-87, pres. Waikiki club 1966-67). Home: Naples, Fla. Died Jan. 19, 2007.

NORTHRUP, HERBERT ROOF, economist; b. Irvington, NJ, Mar. 6, 1918; m. Eleanor Pearson, June 3, 1944; children: James Pearson, Nancy Warren, Jonathan Peter, David Oliver, Philip Wilson. AB, Duke U., 1939; A.M., Harvard U., 1941, PhD, 1942. Instr. econs. Cornell U., 1942-43; sr. hearing officer Nat. War Labor Bd., 1943-45; asst. prof. econs. Columbia U., 1945-49; labor economist Nat. Indsl. Conf. Bd., 1949-52; indsl. relations cons. Ebasco Services, 1952-55; v.p. indsl. relations Penn-Texas Corp., NYC, 1955-58; employee relations mgr. Gen. Electric Co., 1958-61; prof. industry Wharton Sch., U. Pa., Phila., 1961-88, prof. emeritus, 1988—2007, chmn. dept. industry, 1964-69, dir. indsl. rsch. unit, 1964-88, chmn. Labor Rels. Coun., 1968-85. Cons. and expert witness on manpower, pers. and labor rels. problems for many cos.; arbitrator in labor rels. disputes. Author: Organized Labor and the Negro, 1944, Unionization of Professional Engineers and Chemists, 1946, Economics of Labor Relations, 1950, 9th edit., 1981, Government and Labor, 1963, Readings in Labor Economics, 1963, Boulwarism: Labor Policies of General Electric Company, 1964, Negro and Employment Opportunity, 1965, Hours of Labor, 1965, Compulsory Arbitration and Government Intervention in Labor Disputes, 1966, Restrictive Labor Practices in Supermarket Industry, 1967, Negro in the Automobile Industry, 1968, Negro in the Aerospace Industry, 1968, Negro in the Rubber Tire Industry, 1969, Negro in Paper Industry, 1969, Negro in the Tobacco Industry, 1970, Negro Employment in Basic Industry, 1970, Negro Employment in Southern Industry, 1970, Negro Employment in Land and Air Transport, 1971, Impact of Government Manpower Programs, 1975, Open Shop Construction, 1975, The Impact of OSHA, 1978, Objective Selection of Supervisors, 1978, Black and Other Minority Participation in the All-Volunteer Navy and Marine Corps, 1979, Manpower in the Retail Pharmacy Industry, 1979, The Impact of the ATT-EEO Consent Decree, 1979, Multinational Collective Bargaining Attempts, 1979, Multinational Union Organizations in the Manufacturing Industries, 1980, Employee Relations and Regulations in the 80s, 1982, Internat. Transport Workers' Federation and Flag of Convenience Shipping, 1983, Open Shop Construction Revisited, 1984, Personnel Policies for Engineers and Scientists, 1985, Doublebreasted Operations and Pre-Hire Agreements in Construction: The Facts and the Law, 1987, The Federal Government as Employer: The Federal Labor Relations Authority and the PATCO Challenge, 1988, The Changing Role of Women in Research and Development, 1988, Government Protection of Employees in Mergers and Acquisitions, 1989, The Railway Labor Act, 1990, Union Corporate Campaigns and Inside Games as a Strike Form, 1994, Union Violence: The Record and the Response by Courts, Legislatures, and the NLRB, rev. edit., 1999, Construction Union Tactics to Regain Jobs and Public Policy, 2007, The Impact of Union-Management Relations on Urban Industrial Employment, 2000; contbr. over 300 articles in field. Mem. Am. Econ. Assn., Indsl. Relations Research Assn., Am. Arbitration Assn., Phi Beta Kappa. Clubs: Harvard (N.Y.C.); Harvard-Radcliffe (Phila.); University (Washington), Faculty (U. Pa.). Died Oct. 22, 2007.

NORWOOD, CHARLIE (CHARLES WHITLOW NORWOOD JR.), congressman; b. Valdosta, Ga., July 27, 1941; s. Charles Whitlow and Marie (Parham) Norwood; m. Gloria Faye Wilkinson, 1962; children: Charles, Carlton. BS in Biology, Ga. So. U., 1964; DDS, Georgetown U., 1967. Pvt. practice, Augusta, Ga., 1969-94; owner Norwood Tree Nursery, from 1984; mem. US Congress from 9th Ga. dist. (formerly 10th), 1995—2007, mem. energy & commerce, edn. & the workforce coms., vchmn. health subcom., chmn. workforce protection com. Capt. US Army, 1967-69, Vietnam. Decorated Combat Medic badge, Bronze Star for Meritorious Svc., Bronze Star for Meritorious Achievement; recipient: Fighting Frosh award US Bus. & Indsl. Coun., 1995, Guardian of Medicare award US Seniors Assn., 1995, Nat. Health Leadership award Am. Assn Nurse Anesthetists, 1998, True Blue award Family Rsch. Coun. 2003, Champion of Property Rights award League of Pvt Property Owners, Cocklin award Assn. US Army,Guardian of Seniors Rights award 60 Polus Assn., Spirit of Enterprise award US C of C, Taxpayers Friend award Nat. Taxpayers Union Found., Taxpayers Hero award Coun. for Citizens Against Govt Waste Mem. Ga. Dental Assn.(pres. 1983) Republican. Methodist. Died Feb. 13, 2007.

NOVICK, MARVIN, investment company executive; b. NYC July 16, 1931; s. Joseph and Anna Novick; m. Margaret A. Blau Apr. 9, 1960; children: Jeffrey, Stuart, Barry. BBA, CCNY 1952; MBA, NYU, 1955, postgrad., 1955-58. CPA N.Y., Mich. La., N.C. Sr. v.p. Mich. Blue Cross/Blue Shield, Detroit 1961-70; v.p., dir. ops. underwriting Meadowbrook Ins., Southfield, Mich., 1970-72; ptnr. Touche Ross and Co., Detroit 1972-84; vice chmn. Dura Corp., Southfield, 1984-87, Wesnovtek Corp., Birmingham, Mich., 1987-91; pres. R&M Resources Inc., Birmingham, from 1991; advisor Meadowbrook Ins. Group, Southfield, from 1995. Trustee Mich. Assn. Emotional Children, from 1965, also past pres.; chmn. pers. com Jewish Welfare Found., 1987—91, assoc. chmn. cultural an edn. fedn. com., 1984—97; chmn. adv. com. Marrow Found. from 1996; trustee, treas. Fin. and Bldg. Com., from 1990 Mariners Inn, 1996—2000, Karmanos Cancer Inst.; menta health ctr. dir. Rose Hill Ctr., from 1995; chmn. Oak Park Huntington Woods-Pleasant Ridge (Mich.) Dem. Orgn 1970—72, 18th Dem. Congl. Dist., 1972—74; trustee, vic chmn. Union Am. Hebrew Congregation, from 1981; chmn. fin com., fin. sec. World Prog. Judaism-Internat., 1985—99; mem com. Jewish Agy. in Isreal, 1987—99; trustee Temple Beth E Birmingham, Mich., from 1968, past pres.; mem. various coms Jewish Welfare Fedn.; trustee Providence Hosp., Southfield 1975—83, past chmn., trustee bldg. bd., 1982—89; vice chmn fin. com., trustee Sinai Hosp., 1988—92, mem. audit com 1995—97; bd. dirs. B'nai B'rith Centennial Lodge, 1970—79 past pres.; trustee, mem. exec. com. Rose Hill Ctr., Inc., from 1992; mem. com. Hillel Ctr., U. Mich. Named one of Outstanding Young Men Am., Outstanding Am. Found., 1968; recipient Honor and Svc. cert., Oak Park Bd. Edn., 1972, Past Pres award, Mich. Assn. Emotionally Disturbed Children, 1986 Mem.: AICPA, N.Y. State Assn. CPAs, Mich. Assn. CPAs Home: Oak Park, Mich. Died Feb. 5, 2006.

NOVICK, ROBERT, physicist, researcher; b. NYC, May 3 1923; s. Abraham and Carolyn (Weisberg) N.; m. Bernic Lehrman, July 2, 1947; children: Beth, Amy, Peter. M.E Stevens Inst. Tech., 1944, MS, 1949; PhD, Columbia, 195 Microwave engr. Wheeler Lab., Inc., Great Neck, L.I., N.Y 1946-47; instr. physics Columbia U., 1952-54, research assoc 1954-57, assoc. prof. physics, dir. radiation lab., 1960-62, prof co-dir. Astrophysics Lab., 1968-77, 86-92, dir. Astrophysic Lab., 1977-86, prof., 1977-93, prof. of physics emeritus, fro 1993, chmn. dept. physics, 1983-88; asst. prof. physics U. Il Urbana, 1957-59, assoc. prof., 1959-60. Cons to labs., researc insts.; chmn. subpanel on atomic and molecular physics Na Acad. Sci., 1964-65; mem. NASA Commn. on Sci. Uses Space Sta., 1984-86. Recipient Exceptional Sci. Achieveme medal NASA, 1980, Honor award Stevens Inst. Tech., 198 A.P. Sloan fellow, 1958-70 Fellow Am. Phys. Soc., IEE AAAS; mem. Am. Astron. Soc. (sec.-treas. high energy astr physics sect. 1975-78), Internat. Astron. Union. Research, publ on atomic physics, atomic collisions, quantum electronic atomic frequency standards, nuclear spins and moments, X-ra astronomy. Home: Bronx, NY. Died May 6, 2007.

NOWAK, EMMY, manufacturing company executive; b. Hamburg, Germany, Nov. 15, 1923; d. Erwin and Elfriede (Muelle Stamm; m. Joseph E. Gorgens, Dec. 26, 1944 (div. 1960); child, Richard; m. Bernard J. Nowak, Feb. 12, 1966. R.N Bridgeport Hosp. Sc. Nursing, Conn., 1945. Registered nurs Conn. With Alloy Engring. Co. Inc., Bridgeport, 1958—, pres chief exec. officer, 1982—. Recipient Salute to Women awa

YMCA, Bridgeport, 1982. Mem. Bridgeport C. of C. (exec. bd. dirs. 1982—), Bridgeport Hosp. Alumnae Assn. Republican. Episcopalian. Home: Easton, Conn. Died Jan. 7, 2006.

NOWICKI, GEORGE LUCIAN, retired chemical company executive; b. Rutherford, NJ, Dec. 4, 1926; s. Justin Nowicki; m. Mary Elisabeth Baker, Aug. 30, 1947; children: Barbara, Peter, Paul, James. BSChemE, CCNY, 1949; MSChemE, NYU, 1956. Registered profl. engr., N.Y., Pa. Chemist Ideal Toy Co., NYC, 1949; chem. engr. Bklyn. Union Gas Co., 1949-50, Sonotone Corp., Elmsford, N.Y., 1950-52; dept. head Burroughs Wellcome Co., Tuckahoe, N.Y., 1952-70; v.p. mfg. Quaker Chem. Corp., Conshohocken, Pa., 1970-79, v.p. domestic ops., 1984-89, ret., 1989; pres. Selby Batersby Co., Phila., 1979-81; mng. dir. Quaker Chem. Holland BV, Uithoorn, The Netherlands, 1981-84. Chmn. bd. Overdale Corp., Alsip, Ill., 1987-89, Quaker Chem. Can. Ltd., Toronto, 1985-89. Pres. Ctrl. Sch. Dist. 7, Hartsdale, N.Y., 1960-69, Westchester County Sch. Bds. Assn., White Plains, N.Y., 1965; bd. dirs. Suburban Gen. Hosp., Norristown, Pa., 1986; mem. governing bd. Vt. Common Cause, 1993-2004; bd. dirs. Martha Canfield Libr., Arlington, Vt., 1994-2000; counselor Svc. Corps Ret. Execs., 1993-95. With USN, 1944—46, WWII. Mem. Am. Inst. Chem. Engrs., Mfrs. Assn. Del. Valley (bd. dirs. 1987-89). Avocations: swimming, skiing, video photography, stamps. Home: Williamstown, Mass. Died Sept. 18, 2006.

NOYES, WARD DAVID, hematologist, medical educator; b. Schenectady, NY, Aug. 25, 1927; s. Ward and Marion (French) N.; m. Nancy Adair, Aug. 10, 1973; children: Patricia, Ward David, Jeffrey, Katherine, John, Elizabeth, Layne. BA, U. Rochester, 1949, MD, 1953. Intern King County Hosp., Seattle, 1953-54, resident, 1954-56; instr. medicine U. Wash., Seattle, 1959-61, asst. prof., 1961-65, assoc. prof., 1965-68, Sch. Medicine, U. Fla., Gainesville, 1968-70, prof., from 1970, chief hematology, from 1968. Cons. in hematology WHO, 1974-75, 78. Contbr. articles to profl. jours. With USAAF, 1946-47. USPHS fellow, 1956-69. Mem. Fla. Med. Assn., Alachua County Med. Soc., Am. Fedn. Clin. Rsch., Am. Soc. Hematology, Internat. Soc. Hematology, So. Soc. Clin. Investigation, Alpha Omega Alpha. Rsch. in iron metabolism. Died May 9, 2007.

NUGENT, DANIEL PAUL, valve and pipe company executive; b. Harrison, NJ, Oct. 7, 1925; s. James Edward and Helen Marie (McDonald) N.; m. Margorie Magnier, June 18, 1949; children: Mary, James, Daniel Paul, Anthony, Catherine, Sheila, Christopher. Alfred Barnes Palmer scholar, Yale U., 1946-49; D.H.L. hon., Providence Coll. Pres., chief exec. officer, dir. ITT Grinnell Corp., Providence, 1974-84; sr. v.p. ITT Corp., NYC, from 1984; chmn. Grinnell de Mex.; pres. Phelps Dodge Brass Co., NYC; v.p., gen. mgr. Crane U.S.A., NYC; corporate v.p., gen. mgr. L.A. Darling Co., Bronson, Mich.; dir. ITT Industries, ITT Ltd. of Can., NTCC Co., Peninsular Supply Co., Kennedy Valve Co., M & M Supply Co., Jones-Newby Co., No. Power Co., ITT Rayonier B.C., ITT Grinnell Valve Co. Inc., P. N. Howard Co., Brighton Valve, Indsl. Piping Co., Meyer Industries. Bd. dirs. Asia Soc., Council of the Americas, Japan Soc., Taiwan Internat. Standard Electronics, Taipei, Transelectronics Ltd., Hong Kong, Standard Tel and Cables Pty. Ltd., Sydney, Australia, ITT Internat. Trading Services Inc., Tokyo, ITT Far East Ltd., Hong Kong, Internat. Standard Electric Ltd., N.Y.C., Key Lock Mfg. Co., Phelps Dodge Industries, Leroy (N.Y.) Industries. Pres. Convent Assn., 1959-62; chmn. com. elections Yale Alumni, St. Elizabeth Coll. Devel. Corp.; bd. dirs., chmn. personnel com. Liberty State Park Devel. Corp.; mem. com. on. degrees Yale U., trustee St. Thomas More Chapel; mem. council, dir. fin. com. Watch Hill (R.I.) Town Council; vice chmn. United Way, 1974; mem. Com. for Yale U., 1977; chmn. Casey Golf Classic of N.J., 1983; R.I. commodore America's Cup, 1983; trustee Morristown Mus., N.Y. U. Grad. Sch. Retailing, 1965-69, Oak Knoll Sch., St. Elizabeth Coll.; mem. Pres.'s Council Providence Coll.; trustee Nat. Head Injury Found., Tri-County Scholarship Found. Served with inf. AUS, 1943-46. Decorated Bronze Star medal., Knight of Malta; recipient Delbarton Humanitarian award Delbarton Sch., 1982, Bastogne Liberation medal 1945-85, Statue of Liberty medal 1986. Mem. Copper Devel. Assn., Copper and Brass Inst., Valve Mfrs. Assn., Am. Supply Assn. Clubs: Yale (N.Y.C.); Mory's Assn, Morris County Golf, Watch Hill Yacht (dir.), Misquamicut Golf, Serra (pres. 1953-56), Yale of N.J. (dir.). Roman Catholic. Home: Morristown, NJ. Died Jan. 19, 2006.

NUSSBAUM, ARNOLD, pediatrician; b. NYC, Dec. 20, 1925; s. Jack and Clara (Gewirtz) N.; m. Helen P. Coble, June 30, 1951; children: Andrea, Jack, Paul, Robert. BS, Bklyn. Coll., 1949; MD, SUNY, Downstate Med. Ctr., Bklyn., 1954. Diplomate Am. Bd. Pediatrics. Intern USPHS, SI, N.Y., 1954-55; resident in pediats. Jewish Hosp. Med. Ctr., Bklyn., 1955-57; pvt. practice Bklyn., 1957-77, Brook Island Pediats. Group, Bklyn., from 1977. With U.S. Navy, 1943-46, PTO. Mem. AMA, Kings County Med. Soc. Democrat. Jewish. Avocation: racing thoroughbred horses. Home: Brooklyn, NY. Died July 1, 2007.

NYQUIST, JOHN DAVIS, retired radio manufacturing company executive; b. Peoria, Ill., May 28, 1918; s. Eliud and Linnea (Widen) N.; m. Alice Schmidt, June 5, 1942; 1 child, Sarah Lynn. BS in Mech. Engring, U. Ill., 1941. With Collins Radio Co., Cedar Rapids, Iowa, from 1941, v.p., gen. mgr. Iowa region, 1965-69, v.p. operations, 1969-70, sr. v.p., 1970-73, also dir.; ret., 1973; cons. Rockwell-Collins. Dir. Norwest Bank Iowa N.A. (formerly Peoples Bank & Trust Co.), Cedar Rapids. Bd. dirs. Am. Cancer Soc., YMCA, St. Lukes Hosp. Recipient award for outstanding achievement Am. Inst. Indsl. Engrs., 1966, Indsl. Engring. award, 1969, Coll. Engring. Alumni Honor award, 1977; both U. Ill.). Mem. Iowa Mfrs. Assn., Am. Mgmt. Assn., Am. Inst. Indsl. Engrs., IEEE, Cedar Rapids C. of C. (dir.) Clubs: Cedar Rapids Country. Home: Cedar Rapids, Iowa. Died Feb. 13, 2006.

OAKES, JAMES LOWELL, retired federal judge; b. Springfield, Ill., Feb. 21, 1924; m. Evelena S. Kenworthy, Dec. 29, 1973 (dec. Oct. 1997); m. Mara A. Williams, Jan. 1, 1999; m. Rosalyn Landon, Oct. 2, 1945; 3 children. AB, Harvard Coll., 1945; LLB, Harvard U. Law Sch., 1947; LLD, New Eng. Coll., 1976, Suffolk U., 1980, Vt. Law Sch., 1995. Bar: Calif. 1949, Vt. 1950. Law clk. to Harry B. Chase US Ct. Appeals (2d cir.), 1947—48, law clk. to Hon. Harry B. Chase, 1949—50; pvt. practice Brattleboro, Vt., 1948—49; spl. counsel Vt. Pub. Svc. Commn., 1959—60; counsel Vt. Statutory Revision Commn., 1957—60; mem. Vt. State Senate, 1961—65; atty. gen. State of Vt., 1967—69; judge US Dist. Ct. Vt., 1970—71, US Ct. Appeals (2d cir.), Brattleboro, 1971—92, chief judge, 1989—92, sr. judge, 1992—2007. Adj. faculty Duke U. Law Sch., 1985—96, Iowa U. Coll. Law, 1993—97. Home: Brattleboro, Vt. Died Oct. 13, 2007.

OAKLEY, ROBERT LOUIS, law librarian, educator; b. NYC, Nov. 6, 1945; s. Bert Tuttle Oakley and Allese (Duffin) Vestigo; m. Madeleine Cohen, Aug. 13, 1971 (div. 2002); children: Esther Shulamit, Daniel Isaac-Meir; m. Barbara DesRosiers, May 1, 2005 BA, Cornell U., 1968; MLS, Syracuse U., 1972; JD, Cornell U., 1976. Bar: N.Y. 1977, U.S. Dist. Ct. (no. dist.) N.Y. 1977. Assoc. dir. law libr. Cornell U., Ithaca, NY, 1976-79; dir. law libr., assoc. prof. Boston U. Law, 1979-82, Georgetown U., Washington, 1982-87, dir. law libr., prof., 1987—2007. Contbr. articles to profl. jours. Mem. Libr. of Congress, Network Adv. Com., 1986-92, 1995-99, copyright office study group on sec. 108 of Copyright Act; adv. nat. commn. on Preservation and Access, 1988-94; bd. dirs. Montgomery County (Md.) Pub. Librs., 1988-92. Mem. ABA, ALA, Am. Assn. Law Librs. (Washington Affairs rep., mem. exec. bd. 1991-94, v.p. 1999-2000, pres. 2000-01), Assn. Am. Law Schs. Avocations: photography, music, amateur radio. Home: Germantown, Md. Died Sept. 29, 2007.

O'BRIEN, CHARLES H., retired lawyer, retired judge; b. Orange, NJ, July 30, 1920; s. Herbert Rodgers and Agnes Sidman (Montanya) O'B.; m. Anna Belle Clement, Nov. 9, 1966; children: Merry Diane, Steven Shawn (dec.), Heather Lynn. LLB, Cumberland U., 1947. Rep. Tenn. Legislature, Memphis, 1963-65, senator, 1965-67; assoc. judge Tenn. Ct. Criminal Appeals, Crossville, 1970-87; assoc. justice Tenn. Supreme Ct., 1987-94, chief justice, 1994-95; ret., 1995; pvt. practice, Crossville, from 1995. Bd. dirs. Lake Tansi Village Property Owners Assn., 1984-89, chmn., 1989. With U.S. Army, 1938-45, ETO, 1950, UN Command, Tokyo. Decorated Bronze Star, Purple Heart with oak leaf cluster. Fellow Tenn. Bar Found.; mem. Tenn. Bar Assn., Cumberland County Bar Assn., Am. Legion, Lake Tansi Village Chowder and Marching Soc. (pres.). Democrat. Avocation: outdoor activities. Home: Crossville, Tenn. Died Jan. 18, 2007.

O'BRIEN, PATRICK WILLIAM, lawyer; b. Chgo., Dec. 5, 1927; s. Maurice Edward and Ellen (Fitzgerald) O'B.; m. Deborah Bissell, July 2, 1955; children: Kathleen, Mariellen, Patrick, James, Patricia. BS in Mech. Engring., Northwestern U., 1947, JD, 1950. Bar: Ill. 1951, U.S. Dist. Ct. (no. dist.) Ill. 1954, U.S. Dist. Ct. (so. dist.)Ill. 1956, U.S. Ct. Appeals (7th cir.) 1955, U.S. Ct. Appeals (8th cir.) 1972, U.S. Supreme Ct. 1970. Assoc. Bell, Boyd, Marshall & Lloyd, Chgo., 1950—51, Mayer, Brown, Rowe & Maw, Chgo., 1953—62, ptnr., 1962—94, sr. counsel, from 1995. Served to capt. USAF, 1951-53. Fellow Am. Coll. Trial Lawyers; mem. ABA, Ill. Bar Assn., Chgo. Bar Assn. Clubs: Chgo., Mid-Day, University, Westmoreland Country, Cliff Dwellers, Dairymen's Country. Republican. Roman Catholic. Home: Evanston, Ill. Died Aug. 11, 2006.

O'BRIEN, ROBERT S., state official; b. Seattle, Sept. 14, 1918; s. Edward R. and Maude (Ransom) O'B.; m. Kathryn E. Arvan, Oct. 18, 1941 (dec. June 1984). Student public schs. With Kaiser Co., 1938-46; restaurant owner, 1946-50; treas. Grant County, Wash., 1950-65, State of Wash., 1965-89; chmn. Wash. State Fin. Com., 1965-89, Wash. Public Deposit Protection Commn., 1969-89, Wash. Public Employees Retirement Bd., 1969-77, Law Enforcement Officers and Firefighters Retirement System, 1971-77, Wash. State Investment Bd., 1981-89; retired, 1989. Mem. Wash. Data Processing Adv. Bd., 1967-73; Gov.'s Exec. Mgmt. and Fiscal Affairs Com., 1978-80, Gov.'s Cabinet Com. on Tax Alternatives, 1978-80; trustee Wash. Tchr.'s Retirement System, 1965-89; bd. dirs. Centennial Bank, Olympia, Wash. Recipient Leadership award Joint Council County and City Employees-Fedn. State Employees, 1970, Eagles Leadership award, 1967 Mem. Nat. Assn. State Auditors, Comptrollers and Treasurers (pres. 1977), Nat. Assn. Mcpl. Fin. Officers, Nat. Assn. State Treasurers, Western State Treasurers Assn. (pres. 1970), Wash. County Treas. Assn. (pres. 1955-56), Wash. Assn. Elected County Ofcls. (pres. 1955-58), Olympia Area C. of C., Soap Lake C. of C. (pres. 1948) Clubs: Elks (hon. life); Moose, Eagles, Lions, Olympia Yacht, Olympia Country and Golf; Empire (Spokane); Wash. Athletic (Seattle). Democrat. Died Oct. 16, 2006.

O'BRIEN, THOMAS JOSEPH, lawyer, retired government official; b. Omaha, Aug. 2, 1928; s. Thomas Joseph and Ruth (Howard) O'B.; m. Catherine Elizabeth O'Keefe, Feb. 6, 1954; children— Thomas, Michael, Daniel, Paul, Hugh BS, Georgetown U., 1951, JD, 1958. Bar: Va. Dep. chief Office Indsl. Security, Office Sec. Def., Washington, 1971-74; dir. security plans and programs Office Sec. Def., Washington, 1974-81; dir. Def. Investigative Service, Dept. Def., Washington, 1981-88, ret. Columnist Pentagon Corner Served to lt. (j.g.) USN, 1951-54 Mem. Am. Soc. Indsl. Security (treas. found. 1985—), Assn. Fed. Investigators (v.p. 1985—), Nat. Classification Mgmt. Soc. (bd. dirs. 1973) Clubs: Bayside Tennis (South Bethany, Del.) (pres. 1982). Republican. Roman Catholic. Avocations: tennis; sailing. Died Dec. 10, 2005.

OCHAL, BETHANY JACQUITA, law library administrator; b. Flint, Mich., Dec. 2, 1917; d. Llewellyn Lane and Idah B. (Stewart) Ziegler; m. Edward Louis Ochal, July 1, 1944 (div.); children— Myrna Irene, Edward Llewellyn. B.A., Wayne State U., 1944, J.D., 1945. Bar: Mich. sup. ct. 1945, U.S. Dist. Ct. (ea. dist.) Mich. 1945, U.S. Ct. Apls. (6th cir.) 1960, U.S. Sup. Ct. 1964. Sole practice, Detroit, 1945-51; reference librarian Detroit Bar Assn., 1951-60, librarian, 1960-61; law librarian Wayne State U., 1961-72, dir. Legal Research program, 1962-67; dir. Orange County (Calif.) Law Library, Santa Ana, 1972—. Mem. State Bar Mich. (chmn. legal pubs. com. 1968-70), Women Lawyers Assn. Mich. (pres. 1966-67), Am. Assn. Law Libraries (chmn. com. membership 1965-67, chmn. com. chapters 1968-70, chmn. com. audio visual 1970-71, 82-83), Ohio Regional Assn. Law Libraries (pres. 1969-70), Internat. Assn. Law Libraries, AAUW. Democrat. Club: Soroptimists Internat. Contbr. in field to profl. jour. Died June 3, 2007.

O'CONNELL, HAROLD PATRICK, JR., banker; b. Chgo., Sept. 11, 1933; s. Harold P. and Charlotte Anne (Woodward) O'C.; m. Geraldine Taylor McLaughlin, 1979; children: Alexandra T. Close, Geraldine S. Kuchman, Peter B. McLaughlin Jr. AB, Dartmouth Coll., 1955; JD, U. Mich., 1958. V.p. Continental Ill. Nat. Bank and Trust Co., Chgo., 1958-83, No. Trust Co., Chgo., 1983-86; dir. Terra Mus. of Am. Art, Chgo., 1987-92. Chmn. exec. com. Mid-Am. Nat. Bank, 1989-92, pres., CEO, dir., 1992-93, chmn. bd., 1993-96. Trustee Better Govt. Assn. Chgo., 1974—, pres., 1979-83; governing mem. Chgo. Symphony Orchestra, 1979—; sustaining fellow Art Inst. Chgo., 1982—; bd. dirs. Rehab. Inst. Chgo., 1980—. Mem. Chgo. Club, Racquet Club, Econ. Club, Casino Club (pres. 1988-91), Onwentsia Club (Lake Forest, Ill.), Shoreacres (Lake Bluff, Ill.), Old Elm Club (Highland Park, Ill.), Cypress Point Club (Pebble Beach, Calif.). Home: Lake Forest, Ill. Died June 26, 2007.

O'CONNOR, FRANCIS PATRICK, former state supreme court justice; b. Boston, Dec. 12, 1927; s. Thomas Lane and Florence Mary (Hagerty) O'C.; m. Ann Elizabeth O'Brien; children: Kathleen, Francis P., Brien T., Maureen T., Ellen M., Ann E., Jane C., Joyce E., Thomas J., Matthew P. AB, Holy Cross Coll., 1950; LLB, Boston Coll., 1953; JD (hon.), Suffolk U., 1983, New Eng. Sch. Law, 1984. Bar: Mass. 1953. Assoc. Friedman, Atherton, Sisson & Kozol, Boston, 1954-57, Mason, Crotty, Dunn & O'Connor, Worcester, Mass., 1957-73, Wolfson, Moynihan, Dodson & O'Connor, Worcester, 1974-75; judge Mass. Superior Ct., 1976-81; assoc. judge Mass. Supreme Ct., 1981-97, ret., 1997. Died Aug. 3, 2007.

O'CONNOR, PETER DAVID, college administrator; b. Yonkers, N.Y., Mar. 20, 1936; s. Eugene A. and Mary C. (Donoghue) O'C.; m. Patricia T. Nichols, May 28, 1960; children— Jeanne Marie, Judith, Alison, Peter Jr., David, Séan. B.S. in Edn., Fordham U., 1958; M.A. in English, Lehigh U., 1962, Ph.D. in English, 1969. English tchr. Hicksville High Sch., N.Y., 1958-59; mem. English faculty SUNY-Oswego, 1962-77, U. P.R., Cayey, 1970-71; v.p. for acad. affairs, acad. dean Incarnate Word Coll., San Antonio, 1977-86; pres. Aquinas Coll., Grand Rapids, Mich., 1986—; facilitator, nat. inst. Council for Advancement of Small Colls., Washington, 1981, mem. task force, 1980-81; coordinator Assn. Tex. Colls. and Univs., San Antonio, 1980. Author: Major American Books, 1967; also articles. Mem. Project Equality— The Coll. Bd., 1981-86; mem. edn. com. United San Antonio, 1980-86; adv. mem. bd. trustees San Antonio Art Inst., 1979-80. Alumni Fund fellow Lehigh U., 1964. Mem. Assn. Tex. Acad. Deans and V.P.s (pres. 1985-86), Acad. Council United Colls. of San Antonio (chmn. 1983-84), Joseph Conrad Soc. (v.p. 1975-77). Democrat. Roman Catholic. Home: Grand Rapids, Mich. Died May 22, 2007.

O'CONNOR, ROBERT EMMET, paper company executive; b. NYC, Mar. 27, 1919; AB, Queen's Coll., Flushing, NY, 1941; LL.B., Columbia, 1948. Exec. v.p. Am. Paper and Pulp Assn., 1957-64; pres. Am. Paper Inst., 1964-67; chmn., gen. mgr. Rising Paper Co., Housatonic, Mass., 1967-88; pres. RobMar Holding Co. Inc., Tequesta, Fla., 1987-88, Lake Wales, Fla., from 1988. Bd. dirs. Am. Viewpoint, Inc.; bd dirs. Ethics Resource Ctr., Inc., former chmn. Mem. Am. Assn. Sovereign Mil. Order Malta. Home: Lake Wales, Fla. Died Nov. 11, 2006.

O'CONNOR, WILLIAM JAMES, tobacco and beer company executive; b. NYC, Jan. 28, 1931; s. William D. and Anne B. (Dollard) O'C.; m. Eileen P. Madden, Jan. 2, 1954; children— Kevin, Jeanne, Carolyn, William, Cathy, Thomas, Christy. BBA, St. John's U., 1952; LL.B., Fordham U., 1958; LL.M., N.Y. U., 1960. Bar: N.Y. bar 1958; C.P.A., N.Y. Jr. acct. S.D. Leidesdorf & Co. (C.P.A.'s), 1951-53; sr. acct. Price Waterhouse (C.P.A.'s), 1955-58; partner firm Conboy Hewitt, O'Brien & Boardman, NYC, 1958-68; with Philip Morris, Inc., NYC, from 1968; v.p. adminstrn. and human resources Philip Morris Cos. Inc., from 1978. Served with U.S. Army, 1953-55. Mem. Am. Bar Assn., N.Y. State Bar Assn. Clubs: Board Room. Roman Catholic. Home: Marco Island, Fla. Died Sept. 17, 2006.

O'CROWLEY, JAMES FRANCIS, JR., management consultant; b. Asheville, NC, May 23, 1923; s. James Francis and Frances (Curry) O'C.; m. Ruth Faubion, June 26, 1948; children— Patrick Kevin, Brian Faubion, James Francis III, Timothy Curry, Christopher John. BS in Liberal Arts, Georgetown U., 1947; MS, N.Y. U., 1949; MBA, Harvard, 1951. Sec.-treas. Wm. Frear Co., Troy, N.Y., 1947-50, 53-55, dir., 1953-55; mdsg. exec. R.H. Macy & Co., NYC, 1951-53; advanced exec. trainee Kroger Co., 1957-58; sec.-treas., controller Munsingwear, Inc., Mpls., 1958-63, 64-67, dir., 1964-67; corp. controller Trans World Airlines, NYC, 1963-64; corp. controller, asst. to chmn. Phila. & Reading Corp., NYC, 1967-68; sr. v.p. Nationwide Industries, Inc., Chgo., 1969, dir., 1969; v.p., cons. Donald R. Booz & Assos., Chgo., 1969-71; also dir.; pres., chief exec. officer, dir. Gateway Sporting Goods Co., Kansas City, Mo., 1971-77; chmn. bd., chief exec. officer Coalter Investment, Overland Park, Kans., from 1977. Dir. Rose Marie Reid, 1964-67 Served as lt. (j.g.) USNR, 1942-46. Mem.: N.Y. Athletic. Home: Shawnee Mission, Kans. Died Nov. 15, 2006.

O'DAY, ANITA BELLE COLTON, entertainer, musician, vocalist; b. Chgo., Dec. 18, 1919; d. James and Gladys (Gill) C. Singer, entertainer various Chgo. music clubs, 1939—41; singer with Gene Krupa's Orch., 1941—45, with Stan Kenton Orch., 1944, with Woody Herman Orch., 1945, Benny Goodman Orch., 1959; singing tours in US and abroad, from 1947; rec. artist Polygram, Capitol, Emily Records, Verve, GNP Crescendo, Columbia, London, Signature, DRG, Pablo. Million-seller songs include Let Me Off Uptown, 1941, And Her Tears Flowed Like Wine, 1944, Boogie Blues, 1945; actress (films) Gene Krupa Story, 1959, Jazz on a Summer's Day, 1960, Zigzag, 1970, Outfit, 1974; (TV appearances) 60 Minutes, 1980, Tonight Show, Dick Cavett Show, Today Show, Big Band Bash, CBS Sunday Morning, CNN Showbiz Today; (documentaries) Indestructable, 2006; Author: High Times, Hard Times, 1981, rev. edit., 1989; performer 50 yr. Anniversary Concert Carnegie Hall, 1985, Avery Fisher Hall, 1989, Tanglewood, 1990, JVC Festival Town Hall, 1993, Rainbow and Stars, 1995, JVC Festival Carnegie Hall, 1996, JVC Festival Avery Fisher Hall, 1999, Hollywood Palladium, 1999, Blue Note, NYC, 2000, Atlas Supper Club, LA, 2000, Fez, NYC, 2001, Plush Room, San Francisco, 2002, Iridium, NYC, 2003-05, Blue Note, NYC, Jazz Alley, Seattle, 2003, Pizza-in-the-Park, London, 2004, New Paltz State Coll, NY, 2005; (albums) Drummer Man, Kenton Era, Anita, Anita Sings The Most, Pick Yourself Up, Lady is a Tramp, An Evening with Anita O'Day, At Mr. Kelly's, Swings Cole Porter, Travelin' Light, All the Sad Young Men, Waiter Make Mine Blues, With the Three Sounds, I Told Ya I Love Ya Now Get Out, Uptown, My Ship, Live in Tokyo, Anita Sings the Winners, Incomparable, Anita 1975, Live at Mingos, Anita O'Day/The Big Band Sessions, Swings Rodgers and Hart, Time for Two, Tea for Two, In a Mellowtone (Grammy nomination 1990), At Vine St. Live, Mello'Day, Live at the City, Angel Eyes, The Night Has a Thousand Eyes, The Rules of the Road, Jazz Masters, Skylark, Swingtime in Hawaii, SS 'Wonderful (Carnegie Hall), Jazz Past Midnight, Compact Jazz, Let Me Off Uptown, The Complete Verve/Cleff Sessions, Ultimate Anita O'Day, After Midnight, Hi-Ho Trailus Bootwhip, Legends of the Swing Era, The Legacy Lives On, Finest Hour, Complete Signature and London Recordings, The Young Anita, Still Swinging, Indestructible, Live at Basin St. West. Jazz Masters fellow Nat. Endowment for Arts, 1997, Nat. Endowment fellowship; inductee Jazz Hall of Fame, Tampa, 1997. Mem. AFTRA, BMI, Screen Actors Guild. Died Nov. 23, 2006.

ODER, FREDERIC CARL EMIL, retired aerospace transportation executive; b. LA, Oct. 23, 1919; s. Emil and Katherine Ellis (Pierce) O.; m. Dorothy Gene Brumfield, July 2, 1941 (dec. Jan. 2004); children: Frederic E., Barbara Oder Debes, Richard W.; m. Doris S. Parrish, Sept. 24, 2005. BS, Calif. Inst. Tech., 1940, MS, 1941; PhD, UCLA, 1952. Commd. 2d lt. U.S. Army Air Force, 1941; advanced through grades to col. U.S. Air Force, 1960; ret., 1960; asst. dir. and program mgr. for research and engring. Apparatus and Optical div. Eastman Kodak Co., Rochester, NY, 1960-66; with Lockheed Missiles & Space Co., Sunnyvale, Calif., 1966-91, v.p., asst. gen. mgr. div. space systems, 1972-73, v.p., gen. mgr. div. space systems, 1973-84, exec. v.p., from 1984; cons., 1985-91. Mem. Def. Intelligence Agy. Sci. Adv. Com., 1972-76, assoc. mem., 1976-78; mem. Air Force Studies Bd., Assembly Engring., NRC, 1975-79, Def. Sci. Bd. Summer Study, 1975, Rev. Panel, 1979, Space Applications Bd., 1985-88. Contbr. articles to profl. jours. Decorated Legion of Merit; recipient Nat. Reconnaissance Pioneer. Fellow AIAA; mem. NAE, Masons, Sigma Xi. Episcopalian. Home: Gloucester, Mass. Died May 11, 2006.

O'DONNELL, THOMAS MICHAEL, former brokerage firm executive; b. Cleve., Apr. 9, 1936; s. John Michael and Mary L. (Hayes) O'D.; m. Nancy A. Dugan, Feb. 4, 1961; children: Christopher, Colleen, Julie BBA, U. Notre Dame, 1959; MBA, U. Pa., 1960. Cert. Chartered Fin. Analyst. Fin. analyst Saunders Stiver & Co., Cleve., 1960-65; rsch. dir. McDonald & Co., Cleve., 1965-66, exec. v.p. corp. fin., 1967-83, gen. ptnr., 1968-83; pres. McDonald & Co. Investments, Inc./McDonald & Co. Securities, Cleve., 1984-88; chmn., chief exec. officer McDonald & Co. Securities, Cleve., 1988-98. Bd. dirs. Seaway Food Town; mem. regional firms adv. com. NY Stock Exch., 1986-92, chmn., 1991-92; dir. C.I.D. Venture Funds. Author: The Why and How of Mergers, 1968 Bd. dirs. Greater Cleve. Growth Assn., Inroads Northeast Ohio, PlayHouse Square Found.; bd. regents St. Ignatius High Sch., Cleve.; steering com. Leadership Cleve. Mem. Cleve. Soc. Security Analysts (cert.), Securities Industry Assn. (dir. 1988-94, chmn. 1993), Union Club, Westwood Country Club, 50 Club Cleve., Pepper Pike Club, Double Eagle Club. Roman Catholic. Avocation: golf. Home: Cleveland, Ohio. Died Dec. 30, 2005.

O'DWYER, THOMAS ALOYSIUS, electric company executive; b. Texarkana, Ark., July 21, 1925; s. Thomas A. and Martha (Ryan) O'D.; B.S. in Engring., Texas A. and M. Coll., 1949; m. Jeanne B. Bird, Aug. 2, 1950; children— Ann, Kay, Tom, George, Bill. Estimator Ling Electric, Dallas, 1949-51, v.p., 1952-57, pres., 1958-61; pres. Ling-Oliver-O'Dwyer Electric, Inc. (now Ling Oliver O'Dwyer Mgmt. Co., Inc.), Richardson, Tex., 1962-73, chmn. bd., pres., chief exec. officer, 1973—, also dir.; dir. Century Papers, Inc., Richardson Heights Bank. Active Boy Scouts Am.; trustee Jesuit Prep. Bd. and High Sch. Found., Cath. Found. Dallas. Served with USNR, 1944-46. Recipient Brotherhood citation NCCJ, 1976; Disting. Alumnus award Tex. A&M U., 1984; Silver Beaver award Boy Scouts Am., Silver Antelope award, Disting. Eagle Scout award. Mem. Constrn. Employers Council (past pres., Young Presidents Orgn. (past chmn.), Nat. Elec. Contractors Assn. (past pres., dir. N.E. Tex. chpt.; fellow Elec. Acad.). Roman Catholic. Clubs: KC (4 deg.), Knights of Malta. Home: Dallas, Tex. Died May 10, 2006.

OELMAN, ROBERT SCHANTZ, retired manufacturing executive; b. Dayton, Ohio, June 9, 1909; s. William Walter and Edith (Schantz) O.; m. Mary Coolidge, Oct. 17, 1936; children: Bradford Coolidge, Robert Schantz, Jr., Kathryn Peirce, Martha Forrer. AB summa cum laude, Dartmouth Coll., 1931, MA, 1963, LL.D. (hon.), 1981; postgrad., U. Vienna, 1931-32; H.H.D. (hon.), U. Dayton, 1959; LL.D. (hon.), Miami U., Oxford, Ohio, 1960, Wright State U., 1976; L.H.D. (hon.), Wilmington Coll., Ohio, 1965. With NCR Corp., Dayton, 1933-80, asst. to pres., 1942-45, v.p., 1946-50, exec. v.p., 1950-57, pres., 1957-62, chmn., pres., 1962-64, chmn., 1962-74, chmn. exec. com., 1974-80, dir., 1948-80; ret., 1980. Trustee Dartmouth Coll., 1961-76; Mem. Bus. Coun.; chmn. bd. trustees Wright State U., 1961-76; bd. dirs. Miami Conservancy, 1967-79, pres., 1975-79; chmn. Air Force Mus. Found., Dayton, 1970-80; trustee C.F. Kettering Med. Center, 1971-80; ind. dir. tournament policy bd. PGA Tour, Ponte Vedra, Fla., 1974-83, chmn., 1978-83. Mem. Country Club of Fla., Ocean Club of Fla., Augusta Nat. Club (Ga.), Delray Beach Yacht Club. Home: Boynton Beach, Fla. Died May 10, 2007.

OERTER, AL (ALFRED OERTER JR.), motivational speaker, Olympic athlete; b. NYC, Sept. 19, 1936; s. Alfred Adolph and Mary (Strup) O.; m. Corinne Benedetto, Oct., 1958 (div. May 1975); m. Cathy Jo Carroll, July 23, 1983; children: Crystiana, Gabrielle. Student, Kans. U., 1954-59. Computer mgr. Grumman Data Sys., Bethpage, N.Y., 1959-84; motivational spkr., 1984—2007. Four-time Olympic gold medalist, 1956, 1960, 1964, 1968; mem. Olympic Hall of Fame, Track Hall of Fame; recipient Olympic Order. Died Oct. 1, 2007.

OGDON, THOMAS HAMMER, recruiting consultant; b. Alexandria, Va., Apr. 16, 1935; s. William Duley and Juanita L. (Hammer) O.; m. Michele Scharf, Oct. 30, 1976; children— David Hekma, William Barry, Kristin Angela. BA, Amherst Coll., 1957. Copy trainee Ted Bates Advt., 1957-58; copywriter Grey Advt., 1958-61; with Benton & Bowles Advt., NYC, 1961-75, sr. v.p., mgmt. supr., 1971-75; sr. v.p., dir. and dir. client service Needham, Harper & Steers Advt. Inc., NYC, 1975-78; v.p., exec. recruiter Russell Reynolds Assocs., NYC, 1979-80; exec. v.p., chief operating officer, dir., exec. recruiter Haley Assocs., NYC, 1980-87; prin., exec. recruiter The Ogdon Ptnrship., NYC, from 1987. Trustee Norwich Devel. Corp., 1967 Bd. dirs. counseling and testing br. Greater N.Y. YMCA. Mem. Psi Upsilon. Clubs: Brook (N.Y.C.), Union (N.Y.C.); Indian Harbor Yacht (Greenwich), Stanwich (Greenwich) (founder); Gipsy Trail. Republican. Home: New York, NY. Died Feb. 15, 2006.

O'HARE, DONALD JAMES, manufacturing executive; b. Hartford, Conn., July 28, 1926; s. James Daniel and Mabel (Larson) O'Hare; m. Lois Madigan, Dec. 27, 1949; children: Michael E., Linda S., Mark C. Student, Trinity Coll., Hartford, Conn., 1944; BS in Engring., Princeton U., 1948; postgrad., Central Conn. State Coll., New Britain, 1970; MBA, U. New Haven, 1979. Tchr., coach Kingswood Sch., West Hartfort, Conn., 1948—51; chief project engr. Hamilton Std.-UTC, Windsor-Locks, Conn., 1951—70; v.p. ops. Gulf & Western-North & Judd, Middletown, Conn., 1970—74; plant mgr. Hitchner, Inc., Milford, NH, 1974—75; engring. mgr. Echlin, Inc., Branford, Conn., 1975—85; dir. ops. Brake Sys., Inc. divsn., Statford, Conn., 1985—86; v.p. Friction Materials, Inc. Divsn., Lawrence, Mass., 1986—87; divsn. mgr. Friction, Inc, divsn. Echlin, Inc., from 1987. Mem.: ASTM, ASME, Am. Soc. Metals, Soc. Mfg. Engrs., Soc. Automotive Engrs., Club 32 (West Hartford) (bd. dirs. from 1964). Roman Catholic. Achievements include patents for blade alignment gage. Home: Simsbury, Conn. Died July 24, 2007.

O'KANE, ROBERT MAXWELL, educator; b. Dover, NH, Sept. 13, 1920; s. Bernard D. and Evelyn (Marcotte) O'K.; children— Robert Sean, Kevin Michael, Richard Casey, Timothy Brooks. BA, U. N.H., 1947; M.Ed., U. Vt., 1952; Ed.D., Harvard U., 1958. Tchr. Dover Pub. Schs., 1948-51, prin., 1952-55; supt. schs. Ipswich, Mass., 1956-59, Glen Cove, N.Y., 1959-63; dir. U.S. Dependents Schs., Europe, Africa, Middle East, 1963-65; prof. edn. Rutgers U., 1965-67; dean Sch. Edn., U. N.C., Greensboro, 1967-74, prof. edn., 1974-85. Cons. Ford Found., 1968, Center for Study Instrn., NEA, 1965-71, Gov.'s Conf. on Edn., N.J., 1966, N.C., 1968; Cons. U.S. Office Edn., 1965-67, sch. dists. in N.Y., N.J., N.C., Conn., 1965-73, Bur. Indian Affairs, 1969; spl. lectr. Nova U., 1974; mem. exec. com. N.C. Adv. Commn. Tchr. Edn., 1968-74 Mem. Transatlantic council Boy Scouts Am., 1963-65; Bd. dirs. Center for Study Human Values, Clemmons, N.C. Served with AUS, World War II. Decorated Purple Heart with oak leaf cluster, Bronze Star, Silver Star with 1 oak leaf cluster U.S.; Croix de Guerre; recipient Sch. Bell award Overseas Edn. Assn., 1964 Mem. NEA, Nat. Soc. for Study Edn., Am. Assn. Higher Edn., European Congress PTA (hon. life), Phi Delta Kappa, Kappa Phi Kappa. Research in area of moral dilemmas-decision making. Home: North Hampton, NH. Died Feb. 15, 2007.

OKE, ROBERT EUGENE, state legislator; b. West Seattle, Sept. 4, 1940; m. Judy Oke; 3 children. With USN; mem. Wash. Senate, Dist. 26, Olympia, from 1990; mem. natural resources, parks and recreation com.; Rep. whip Wash. Senate, Olympia, 1993, 94; mem. transp. com.; mem. labor and workforce devel. com.; mem. senate com. on vets. and mil. affairs; mem. Blue Ribbon panel on ferry safety; mem. organized crime adv. bd.; mem. joint legis. audit and rev. com.; mem. legis. oversight com. Pacific Fisheries Task Force; mem. panel transp. beneficiaries; mem. aquatic nuisance species planning com. Former chmn. South Kitsap Parks and Recreation Commn.; mem. Wash. State Coalition Teaming with Wildlife; mem. cmty. correction steering com. Kitsap County; mem. Kitsay County Law and Justice Coun. Recipient Wash. State Sportsmen's Coun. awatrd, 1991, Nat. Sr. Citizen Hall of Fame award, 1994, Cert. of Appreciation Wash. State Farm Bur., 1995-96, 97-98, Cornerstone award Assn. Wash. Bus., 1997. Mem. Port Orchard C. of C., Kiwanis (Port Orchard), Kitsap Poggie Club. Republican. Died May 14, 2007.

OKSAS, JOAN KAY, economist, educator; b. Chgo., Feb. 21, 1927; d. John Joseph and Antoinette (Pestinick) Kazanauskas; m. Casimir G. Oksas, Nov. 3, 1956; children: Stephen, Mary. BS, Northwestern U., 1944; MS in Edn., Chgo. State U., 1975, Northern Ill. U., 1981; EdD, Loyola U., Chgo., 1986. From instr. to assoc. prof. Chgo. State U., 1976-89, prof., 1989-93; ret., 1993; chair dept. libr. sci. and communication Chgo. State U., 1986-88. Judge Am. Film and Video Festival, N.Y., Chgo., 1980-93, Chicagoland History Fairs, 1986—; mem. vis. com. North Ctrl. Assn. Accreditation, Chgo., 1980-93; cons. Adopt-a-Sch. program, 1984; bd. dirs. Mut. Fedn. Savs. and Loan, Chgo. Contbr. articles, revs. to profl. jours. Recipient Faculty Excellence award Chgo. State U., 1991. Mem. Ill. Libr. Assn., Phi Delta Kappa, Delta Kappa Gamma (Ill. Gamma Alpha chpt.) (bd. dirs. 1982—, pres. 1986-88). Republican. Roman Catholic. Home: Willowbrook, Ill. Died Jan. 7, 2007.

OLDSHUE, JAMES Y., chemical engineering consultant; b. Chgo., Apr. 18, 1925; s. James and Louise (Young) O.; m. Betty Ann Wiersema, June 14, 1947; children: Paul, Richard, Robert. BS in Chem. Engring., Ill. Inst. Tech., 1947, MS, 1949, PhD in Chem. Engring., 1951. Registered engr., N.Y. Chem. engr. Manhattan Project, Los Alamos, N.Mex., 1945-46; With Mixing Equipment Co., Rochester, NY, 1950-92, dir. research, 1960-63, tech. dir., 1963-70, v.p. mixing tech., 1970-92; pres. Oldshue Techs. Internat., Rochester, NY, 1992—2007; tchr. Sarasota (Fla.) Sch. Dist., 1992—2007, OASIS, Rochester Sch. Dist., NY, 1992—2007; pres. Pool Tech., Inc., 1968—2007. Adj. prof. chem. engring. Beijing U. Chem. Tech., from 1992; pres. mfr. Pool Tech. Inc., Sarasota, Fla. Author: Fluid Mixing Technology, 1983; contbr. chpts. and articles to books and jours. Chmn. budget com. Internat. div. YMCA; bd. dirs. Rochester YMCA. Served with AUS, 1945-46. Recipient 1st Disting. Svc. award N.E. YMCA Internat. Com., 1979, J.E. Purkynse medal Czech Republic Acad. Sci.; named Rochester Engr. of Yr., 1980 Fellow AIChE (pres. 1979, treas. 1983-89, chmn. 75th anniversary com. 1983, chmn. internat. activities com. 1989-92 Founders award 1981, Eminent Chem. Engr. award 1983, Svc to Soc. award 1989, F.J. and Dorothy van Antwerpen award for Svc. to the Inst. 1999, centennial com. 2001-07); mem. NAE Am. Assn. Engring. Socs. (chmn. 1985, K.A. Roe award 1987) Am. Chem. Soc., Czech Soc. Chem. Engring. (hon.), Worl Congress Chem. Engrs. (v.p. 1986, pres. 1992-96), N.Am Mixing Forum (chmn. 1990-93, Mixing Achievement rsch award 1992), Interam. Confedn. Chem. Engrs. (sec. gen. 1991-93, v.p. 1993-95, pres. 1995-96), Victor Marquez award 1983) Rochester Engring. Soc. (pres. 1992-93, Rochester Engr. of Yr 1980), UN Assn. of Rochester (pres. 2001-2003). Mem. Reformed Ch. in Am. (gen. program coun.). Achievements includ design and scale-up procedures in field of fluid mixing. Home Sarasota, Fla. Died Jan. 16, 2007.

OLEKSIW, DANIEL PHILIP, consultant, former foreig service officer; b. Wilkes Barre, Pa., Feb. 5, 1921; s. Rev Michael Nicholas and Maria Helena (von Kotzko) O.; m Elizabeth Louise Hyatt, Aug. 21, 1948 (dec. 1990); children Barbara Anne, Daniel Hyatt. Student, Duke U., 1938-39; BA Pa. State U., 1940; student, Duke U.; postgrad., U. Mo Princeton U., 1941-42; grad., Nat. War Coll., 1962. Reporte editor small newspapers, Mo. and Mich.; advt. copywrite Cleve.; info. specialist Civilian Prodn. Adminstrn., Washingtor 1946; dep. chief press br. pub. rels. USAF Hdqrs., Washingtor 1947, 48; pub. advt. newspapers Arlington and Alexandria, Va 1948, 49; pub. rels. officer U.S. Mission for Aid to Turkey 1949-50; attache Am. embassy, USIS, Ankara, 1951; pres attache Am. embassy, Cairo, 1952-55; 1st sec. Am. embassy dep. pub. affairs officer USIS, Tehran, 1956-58; consul, pub affairs officer consulate gen. Bombay, 1958-61; program coord Africa USIA, 1962-63, dep. area dir. Africa, 1963-64, dir. medi content, 1964-65; spl. asst. to permanent rep. U.S. mission t UN, 1966; area dir. for East Asia and Pacific USIA, 1966-70 minister-counselor pub. affairs Am. Embassy, New Delhi, 1970-73; dir. USIS, India; sr. faculty adviser Nat. War Coll., 197 insp. gen. USIA, Washington, 1973-78; dir. ednl. programmin Middle East Svcs., Inc., Washington, 1979-80; dir. Washingto Export Info., Inc., 1980-89; program evaluation cons. Bu Cultural and Ednl. Affairs, USIA, 1984-85; dir. Dan Oleksiw & Assocs., Washington. Cons. program evaluator Brit.-Ar Project Johns Hopkins U. Sch. Advanced Internat. Studie 1986-95, Royal Inst. Internat. Affairs, Coun. for Internat. Deve on Mercy Fund programs in Burkina Faso, Eselen Inst. Sa Francisco, 1988, U.S. Bus Leadership Exchange Prograr USSR, 1988, Washington, 1987, Fgn. Svc. Inst., Dept. Stat 1989-90. 2d lt. inf. AUS, 1942-45. Recipient Disting. Servi award USIA, 1966 Roman Catholic. Home: Washington, D(Died Jan. 1, 2006.

OLIN, JAMES R., former congressman; b. Chicago, IL, Fe 28, 1920; m. Phyllis Avery; children: Richard Davis, Thom Avery, Katherine Price Olin Milliken, James Randolph, Kristir Baker Olin Santry. Grad., Deep Springs Coll., (Calif.), 194 BEE, Cornell U., 1943. With Gen. Electric Co., 1946-82, serv as corp. v.p., gen. mgr. Indsl. Electronics div.; mem. 98th-10 Congresses from 6th Dist. Va., 1983-92. Supr. Town of Rothe dam (N.Y.); mem. Schenectady County (N.Y.) Bd. Suprs., 195 bd. dirs. Burrell Hosp.; active Mental Health Assn., United Wa United Negro College Fund. Served as officer Signal Corp U.S. Army, 1943-46. Mem. C. of C., Va. Mfrs. Assn., Na Alliance Businessmen, Roanoke Symphony Soc. Democr Unitarian Universalist. Home: Charlottesvle, Va. Died July 2 2006.

OLIPHINT, BENJAMIN RAY, retired bishop; b. Hemphi Tex., May 28, 1924; s. John H. and Tressie (Post) O.; m. Nan Brooke Kelley, June 7, 1952; children: Mary Brooke, Stu Ray, John Clayton, Kelley MacLauren. BA, So. Meth. U., 194 BD, Duke U., 1946; S.T.M., Union Theol. Sem., 1947; PhD, Edinburg, 1951. On trial, ordained deacon La. Conf., Unit Meth. Ch., 1946; full connection, elder, 1949. Minister Luke's Meth. Ch., New Orleans, 1947-49; assoc. minister Meth. Ch., Alexandria, La., 1951-52; minister St. Paul's Me Ch., Monroe, La., 1952-65, 1st Meth. Ch., Alexandria, L 1965—84; bishop Tex. Conf. United Meth. Ch., Housto 1984—92. Del. Gen. Conf. United Meth. Ch., 1964; mem. Ge Bd. Edn., 1964, Died July 7, 2007.

OLITSKI, JULES, artist; b. Snovsk, USSR, Mar. 27, 19 came to U.S., 1923, naturalized, 1943; s. Jevel and An (Zarnitsky) Demikovsky; m. Gladys Katz, 1944 (div. 1951); dau., Eve; m. Andrea Hill Pearce, Jan. 21, 1956 (div. 1974) dau., Lauren; m. Kristina Gorby, Feb. 29, 1980. Postgrad., N Acad. Design, NYC, 1939-42, Beaux Arts Inst., 1940-42, Ed Alliance, 1947; student, Academie de la Grande Chaumie Paris, 1949-50; postgrad., Ossip Zadkine Sch. Sculpture, Pa 1949; BA, NYU, 1952, MA, 1954; ArtsD (hon.), U. Hartfo CT, 1997, U New Hampshire, NH, 1998. Assoc. prof. art SUN New Paltz, NY, 1954-55; curator Art Edn. Gallery, NY 1955-56; chmn. fine arts div. C.W. Post Coll. L.I.U., Greenv NY, 1956-63; tchr. Bennington Coll., 1963-67. Exhibited many one-man shows including Galerie Huit, Paris, 1951, Io Gallery, N.Y.C., 1958, French & Co., N.Y.C., 1959-61, Po dexter Gallery, N.Y.C., 1961-68, Bennington (Vt.) Coll., 19

Kasmin, Ltd., London, 1964-75, 89, Galerie Lawrence, Paris, 1964, David Mirvish Gallery, Toronto, Ont., Can., 1964-78, Nicholas Wilder, L.A., 1966, Corcoran Gallery, Washington, 1967, 74, Am. Pavillion, Venice Biennale Art Exhbn., 1966, 88, Andre Emmerich Gallery, N.Y.C., 1966-96, Zurich, Switzerland, 1973-78, Met. Mus. Art, N.Y.C., 1969, Inst. Contemporary Art, U. Pa., 1968, 86, Lawrence Rubin Gallery, N.Y.C., 1969, 71, 72, 73, Knoedler Contemporary Art, 1973-77, 79, 81, 83, 85, 87, Dart Gallery, Chgo., 1975, FIAL, Paris, 1976, Berlinische Galerie, 1977, Downstairs Gallery, Edmonton, Can., 1980, 82, Janus Gallery, L.A., 1981, Gallery One, Toronto, 1980-90, Yares Gallery, Scottsdale, Ariz., 1986-89, Galerie Wentzel, Hamburg and Cologne, Fed. Republic Germany, 1975, 77, 81, 89, Mus. Fine Arts, Boston, 1973, 77, Whitney Mus. Am. Art, 1973, Galleria Dell'Ariete, Italy, 1974, Corcoran Gallery Art, 1974-76, Waddington Gallery, London, 1975, Galerie Templon, Paris, 1984-85, Hirshhorn Mus., Washington, 1977, Edmonton (Alta., Can.) Art Gallery, 1979, Martha White Gallery, Louisville, 1982, Harcus/Krakow Gallery, Boston, 1978, 81, 82, Harcus Gallery, Boston, 1984, 86, Meredith Long, Houston, 1981, 82, 87, 90, (retrospective) Fondation du Chateau de Jau, Perpignon, France, 1984, La Musee de Valence, France, 1985, Hokin Gallery, Palm Beach, Fla., 1988, Associated Am. Artists, N.Y.C., 1989, (retrospective) Buschlen/Mowatt Gallery, Vancouver, B.C., Can., 1990, Salander-O'Reilly Galleries, N.Y.C., 1990, 92, 94, Gallery Camino Real, Boca Raton, Fla., 1987, 88, 90, 92, 94, 95, 96, 97, Thorne-Sagendorph Art Gallery, Keene, N.H., 1993, 96, 99, Long Fine Arts, N.Y.C., 1994, 95, 97, 98, 99, U. Miami, Coral Gables, Fla., 1994, C.S. Schulte Gallery, Milburn, N.J., 1995, 97, Drabinsky Friedland Gallery, Naples, Fla., and Toronto, 1996, 97, 99, Dorthy Blau Gallery, Bay Harbor Island, Fla., 1996, 97, 2001, Hodecker Gallery, Waterville Valley, NH, 1997, Belknap Mills, Laconia, NH, 1997, Butler Institute, Youngstown, OH, 1997, 2000, Portland Museum, ME, 1998, Grimaldis Gallery, Baltimore, MD, 1998, Virginia Lynch Gallery, Tiverton, RI, 1998, 99, 2000, 2001, Gould Academy, Bethel, ME, 1998, Bernard Jacobsen Gallery, London (Paintings 1965-75), 1999, Marianne Friedland Gallery, Naples, FL, 1999, 2000, 02 Galeria Metta, Madrid, 1999, Mary McGowan Fine Art, Concord, NH, 1999, Philharmonic Center for the Arts, Naples, FL, 1999, Annandale Galleries, Sydney, Australia, 2000, 2002, Charles Nodrum Gallery, Melbourne, 2000, The Butler Institute of American Art, Youngstown, OH, 2000, Ameringer-Howard Gallery, N.Y.C., 2000, Bunnington Gallery Notthingham Trent U., UK, 2001, Ameringer-Howard Fine Art, Boca Raton, FL, 2001, The Seventies: Painting and Sculpture, Paul Kasmin Gallery, 2006; exhibited in many group shows including Carnegie Internat., Pitts., 1961, 1965, Washington Gallery Modern Art, 1963, Los Angeles County Mus., 1964, Fogg Art Mus. Harvard, 1965, Pasadena Art Mus., 1965, Mus. Basel, Switzerland, 1965, 74, Whitney Mus. Am. Art, 1972, 73, Musée d'Art Contemporain, Montreal, 1973, Hirshhorn Mus., 1974, Corcoran Gallery Art, 1975, Everson Mus. Art, Syracuse, N.Y., 1976, Bass Mus., Miami, Am. Embassy, Madrid, 1984, Ft. Worth Art Mus., Mus. Art, Ft. Lauderdale, 1986, Joseloff Gallery, Hartford, Conn., 1994, Galerie Piltzer, Paris, 1994, N.Y. Studio Sch., N.Y., 1996, Andre Emmerich Gallery, N.Y.C., 1997, 1998, Suzanne Lemberg Usdan Gallery, Bennington College, VT, 1998, Yares Gallery, Scottsdale, Ariz., 1998, Mus. Fine Arts, Boston, 2000, Portland Mus., Oreg., 2001; represented in permanent collections including Mus. Modern Art, N.Y.C., Art Inst. Chgo., Whitney Mus., Corcoran Art Gallery, Nat. Gallery Can., Met. Mus. Art, N.Y.C., Bklyn. Mus., Hirshhorn Mus., Washington, Everson Mus. Art, Syracuse, N.Y., Mus. Fine Arts, Boston, Norman MacKensie Art Gallery, Regina, Can., Portland Mus., Oreg.;also pvt. collections; subject book Jules Olitski by Kenworth Moffett, 1981, Nat. Acad. Design, N.Y., 1993, illustrator limited edition book, Small Mountains (with W.D. Wetherell), 2000. Recipient 2d prize Carnegie Internat. 1961, 1st prize Corcoran Biennial, Washington, 1967, Award for Distinction in the Arts Univ Union, U. S.C., 1975, The Milton and Sally Avery Visting. Professorship, Bard Coll., 1987; named Assoc. Nat. Academician Nat. Acad. of Design, 1993, named Distinguished Artist, Arkansas Celebration of the Arts, Hot Springs, Arkansas, 1996. Fellow AAAS, Nat. Acad. Arts and Scis. Home: Marlboro, Vt. Died Feb. 4, 2007.

OLIVER, ELIZABETH KIMBALL, historian, writer; b. Saginaw, Mich., May 21, 1918; d. Chester Benjamin and Margaret Eva (Allison) Kimball; m. James Arthur Oliver, May 1941 (div. July 1967); children: Patricia Allison (dec.), Dexter Kimball. BA, U. Mich., 1940. Tchr. Dexter (Mich.) High Sch., 1940-41; libr. Sherman (Conn.) Libr. Assn., 1966-75; pres. Sherman (Conn.) Libr. Assn., 1983-84; writer, historian, from 1976. Reporter Sherman Sentinel, 1965-70; editor newsletter Sherman Hist. Soc., 1977-78; columnist Citizen News, Fairfield County, Conn., 1981-83. Author: History of Staff Wives-AMNH, 1961, Background and History of the Palisades Nature Association, 1964, History and Architecture of Grace United Methodist Church, 1990, Legacy to St. Augustine, 1993, Franklin W. Smith and His Casa Monica Hotel, 2000, Viewpoint of a St. Augustine Columnist, 2004; guest columnist Mandarin News, 1995-97; columnist St. Augustine Record, 1998-2005, Viewpoint of St. Augustine, 2004, Florida Impact--8 Biographical Sketches, 2004. Vol. N.Y. Hist. Soc., N.Y.C., 1961-65; treas. Coburn Cemetery Assn., Sherman, 1976-82; historian Greenbrook-Palisades Nature Assn., Tenafly, N.J., 1962-64; mem. St. Augustine Hist. Soc., Naromi Land Trust (life), Cedar Key Hist. Soc.; adv. bd. IBC (Eng.). Mem. AAUW, Friends of Libr. (life), Inst. Am. Indian Studies, Marjorie Kinnan Rawlings Soc. (charter), St. Augustine Woman's Club (archivist, cert. of appreciation 1990), Sherman Hist. Soc., Mandarin Hist. Soc., Smithsonian Nat. Mus. of the Am. Indian (charter). Republican. Congregationalist. Avocations: reading, piano, botany, dulcimer playing. Home: Saint Augustine, Fla. Died July 28, 2007.

OLIVER, WILLIAM ALBERT, JR., paleontologist, researcher; b. Columbus, Ohio, June 26, 1926; s. William Albert and Mary-Maud (Thompson) O.; m. Johanna L. Kramer, Sept. 1, 1948 (dec.); children: Robert A., James A. BS, U. Ill., 1948; MA, Cornell U., 1950, PhD, 1952. From instr. to asst. prof. geology Brown U., Providence, 1952-57; rsch. geologist-paleontology U.S. Geol. Survey, Washington, 1957—70, research geologist-paleontology, 1971—93, emeritus scientist, from 1993; rsch. prof. geology George Washington U., 1970—71; rsch. assoc. dept. paleobiology U.S. Nat. Mus. Natural History-Smithsonian Instn., Washington, from 1967; mem. U.S. Nat. Com. on Geology, 1975-79, chmn., 1978-79; U.S. rep. Internat. Subcommn. on Devonian Stratigraphy, 1973-92; chmn., 1984-89; rsch. prof. in geology George Washington U., 1970—71. Contbr. articles to profl. jours. Recipient Meritorious Svc. award Interior Dept., 1993. Fellow AAAS (coun. 1971-73), Geol. Soc. Am.; mem. Paleontol. Soc. (councilor 1964-69, 73-76, editor Jour. 1964-69, pres. 1974-75), Palaeontol. Assn. (London), Palaeontol. Rsch. Inst. (trustee 1976-89, pres. 1984-86, Harris award, 1994), Am. Geol. Inst. (dir. 1974-77, v.p. 1975-76, pres. 1976-77), Internat. Assn. for Study of Fossil Cnidaria (coun. 1971-88, pres. 1983-88), Internat. Palaeontological Assn. (sec. gen. 1984-89). Home: Riva, Md. Died Oct. 8, 2005.

OLSEN, TILLIE LERNER, author; b. Omaha, Nebr., Jan. 14, 1912; d. Samuel and Ida (Beber) Lerner; m. Jack Olsen; children: Karla, Julie, Kathie, Laurie. LittD (hon.), U. Nebr., 1979, Knox Coll., 1982, Hobart and William Smith Coll., 1984, Clark U., 1985, Albright Coll., 1986, Wooster Coll., 1991, Mills Coll., 1995, Amherst Coll., 1998. Writer-in-residence Amherst Coll., 1969-70; vis. faculty Stanford U., 1972; Writer-in-residence, vis. faculty English M.I.T., 1973-74, U. Mass., Boston, 1974; internat. vis. scholar Norway, 1980; Hill prof. U. Minn., spring 1986; writer-in-residence Kenyon Coll., 1987—2007. Regents lectr. U. Calif. at San Diego, 1977-2007, UCLA, 1987; commencement spkr. English dept. U. Calif., Berkeley, 1983, Hobart and William Smith Coll., 1984 Bennington Coll., 1986. Author: Tell Me A Riddle, 1961 (title story received First prize O'Henry award 1961), Rebecca Harding Davis: Life in the Iron Mills, 1972, Yonnondio: From the Thirties, 1974, Silences, 1978, The Word Made Flesh, 1984; editor: Mother to Daughter, Daughter to Mother, 1984; Preface Mothers and Daughters, That Special Quality: A Exploration in Photographs, 1987, 95, Essay Afterword: Saxton's Bright Web in the Darkness, 1998; short fiction published in over 200 anthologies; books translated in 11 langs. Pres. women's aux. Calif. CIO, 1941-43, dir. war relief, 1944-45. Recipient Am. Acad. and Nat. Inst. of Arts and Letters award, 1975, Ministry to Women award Unitarian Universalist Fedn., 1980, Brit. Post Office and B.P.W. award, 1980, Mari Sandoz award Nebr. Libr. Assn., 1991, REA award Dungannon Found., 1994, Disting. Achievement award Western Lit. Assn., 1996; Grantee Ford Found., 1959, NEA, 1968; Stanford Univ. Creative Writing fellow, 1962-64, Guggenheim fellow, 1975-76, Bunting Inst. Radcliffe Coll. fellow, 1985; Tillie Olsen Day designated in San Francisco, 1981. Mem. Authors Guild, PEN, Writers Union. Home: Berkeley, Calif. Died Jan. 1, 2007.

OLSHAN, JOSEPH RAYMOND, lawyer; b. Pottsville, Pa., May 28, 1929; s. Joseph and Theda (Warakomski) O.; m. Virginia I. Kuczin, Aug. 30, 1952; children— Gary P., Nancy Olshan Paige, David M., Patricia A. student Boston Coll., 1953; LLB, New Eng. Sch. Law, 1958; postgrad. Grad. Law Sch., Suffolk U., 1959. Bar: Mass. 1958. Teller, Home Savs. Bank, Boston, 1954-55; chief adjuster Sentry Ins. Co., Boston, 1955-65; v.p., gen. counsel, sec. Factory Mut. Engring. Corp., Norwood, Mass., 1968—, Factory Mut. Engring. Assn., 1968—, Factory Mut. Research Corp., 1968— (all affiliates of Factory Mut. System). Mem. Norwood Sch. Com.; mem. Norwood Zoning Bd. Appeal, 1971—; mem. Norwood Democratic Town Com., 1960-70. Served with U.S. Army, 1952-54. Decorated Combat Infantryman's badge, Presdl. Unit citation. Mem. ABA (vice chmn. com. on property law sec. tort and ins. practice), Fedn. Ins. and Corp. Counsel (vice chmn. property ins. com. 1978-79, chmn. 1979-82, v.p. 1982-83, chmn. projects and objectives com. 1982-84, dir. numerous terms), Norwood C. of C., Lions (past pres.). Died Mar. 4, 2006.

OLSON, HAROLD ROY, computer company executive; b. Escanaba, Mich., Apr. 8, 1928; s. Roy A. and Sara Calla Margarita (Carlson) O.; m. Angela Davis Hennessy, Sept. 26, 1959. BA in Journalism and Advt., Mich. State U., 1950. Mail clk. McCann Erickson Co., NYC, 1950, 52-53; book promotion specialist, mgr. mag. promotion McGraw-Hill, NYC, 1953-56; mgr. mag. promotion Reinhold Pub. Co., NYC, 1956-58; space salesman McCall Corp., NYC, 1959-60; pres. Visual Identity, Inc., NYC, 1960-68; mktg. rep. Honeywell Info. Sys., Inc., NYC, 1969-86; pres. Hal Olson's EDGE-BUY Express, Inc., from 1986. With U.S. Army, 1950-52. Republican. Episcopalian. Avocation: sailing. Died July 14, 2006.

OLSON, JANE VIRGINIA, editor; b. Chgo., Dec. 14, 1916; d. Oscar Wilford and Mary (Bowles) O.; m. William M. Gooden, Feb. 16, 1955 (div. 1957). BA, U. N.Mex., 1939. Copy editor Atlantic Monthly mag., Boston, 1942-46; copy editor Vogue mag., NYC, 1946-49; tech. editor Ill. Geol. Survey, Urbana, 1949-55; sci. and social sci. editor Yale U. Press, New Haven, 1958-69; editor Am. Scientist mag., New Haven, 1969-80, sr. cons. editor, 1981. Mem. Peabody Mus. Assocs. Fellow Saybrook Coll., Yale U.; Mem. League Women Voters, Sigma Xi. Home: Hamden, Conn. Died Mar. 6, 2006.

OLSON, ROBERT GOODWIN, philosophy educator; b. Mpls., May 8, 1924; s. Goodwin Carl and Mary Helen (Hutchins) O. BA, U. Minn., 1943; Docteur (French Govt. scholar 1951), U. Paris, 1953; PhD, U. Mich., 1957. Staff editor Grolier Soc., NYC, 1946-48; historian Office Mil. Govt., Berlin, Germany, 1948-49; asst. prof. philosophy Ripon (Wis.) Coll., 1953-56; instr. philosophy U. Mich., 1956-58; asst. prof. Columbia U., 1958-61; asso. prof., chmn. dept. philosophy Rutgers U., 1961-65, prof., chmn. dept. philosophy, 1965-69, L.I. U., Bklyn., 1969-97, prof. emeritus, from 1997. Author: An Introducation to Existentialism, 1962, The Morality of Self-Interest, 1965, A Short Introduction to Philosophy, 1967, Meaning and Argument, 1969, Ethics: A Short Introduction, 1977; Contbr. articles to profl. jours. Served with USAAF, 1943-46. Mem. Am., L.I. philos. assns., AAUP, United Fedn. Coll. Tchrs. Home: New York, NY. Died Jan. 3, 2007.

O'MARA, ARTHUR JAMES, civil engineer; b. Trenton, NJ, Sept. 28, 1920; s. Arthur James and Esther Isabelle (Yeoman) O'M.; m. Lois Marion Johnson, Dec. 26, 1943; children: Thomas R., Michael R., Marc J., Dennis A., Brian K. BA, Dartmouth Coll., 1942, CE, 1943. Registered profl. engr., Md., Va., Del., Pa., W.Va., D.C. Engr. Turner Constrn. Co., Phila., 1946-47, Malcolm Pivnie Engrs., White Plains, N.Y., 1947-48, Robert Sawyer Engrs., Hyattsville, Md., 1948-50; ptnr. Greenhorne & O'Mara, Inc., Hyattsville, Md., 1950-65, chmn., CEO Greenbelt, Md., 1965—2000. Lt. (s.g.) USN, 1943-46, PTO. Home: Silver Spring, Md. Died Nov. 7, 2007.*

O'NEAL, REAGAN See RIGNEY, JAMES JR.

OPPENHEIMER, JACK HANS, internist, scientist, educator; b. Egelsbach, Hesse, Germany, Sept. 14, 1927; came to U.S., 1937; s. Julius and Elsa (Reis) O.; m. Ann Ehrlich, Dec. 20, 1953; children: Mark, Lawrence, Adele Oppenheimer Brown. BA, Princeton U., 1949; MD, Columbia U., 1953. Diplomate Am. Bd. Internal Medicine. Intern Boston City Hosp., 1953-54; fellow Sloan Kettering Inst., NYC, 1954-55, Columbia Presbyn. Hosp., NYC, 1959-60; resident Duke U., 1957-59; asst. prof. to prof. medicine Albert Einstein Coll. Medicine, Bronx, N.Y., 1964-76; prof. medicine U. Minn., Mpls., 1976-97, Cecil J. Watson prof., dir. divsn. endocrinology, 1986-93, emeritus prof., 1997. Staff physician Montefiore Hosp. Med. Ctr., Bronx, 1960-76. Contbr. over 270 articles to profl. jours.; editor 2 books. Capt. U.S. Army, 1955-57. Fellow ACP; mem. Endocrine Soc. (coun. 1974-78, Astwood award 1978), Am. Thyroid Assn. (pres. 1985-86, Van Meter award 1965, Parke-Davis award 1984), Am. Soc. Clin. Investigation, Assn. Am. Physicians. Home: Minnetonka, Minn. Died Apr. 16, 2006.

ORCHARD, ROBERT A., system science educator; b. NYC, Nov. 29, 1938; s. Francis A. and Vestal (Fudge) O.; m. Anna Lauria; children: Judith, Frank, Jeniffer; m. Gudrun Jandt; children: Kjen, Anna. BS in Math., Fairleigh Dickinson U., 1964; MS in Math., Stevens Inst., 1967, PhD, 1978. Mem. tech. staff Bell Labs., Murray Hill, N.J., 1964-67, mgr. R&D, 1972-83; assoc. prof. Fairleigh Dickinson U., Teaneck, N.J., 1967-72; prof. system sci. SUNY, from 1980; prof. CUNY, from 1983. Cons. AT&T, Bellcore, Fortune 500, etc., 1975—; trainer Inst. Advanced Systems, N.J., Germany, 1978—; hypnotherapist various insts., 1978—; corp. entepreneur trainer DEC Knowledge Engring., 1991. Contbr. articles to profl. jours. Fellow Internat. Assn. Neuro-Linguistic Programming; mem. Internat. Soc. Communicative Psychoanalysis and Psychotherapy, Internat. Soc. Systems Sci., Math. Assn. Am. Home: Bremen, Germany. Died Aug. 6, 2007.

O'REILLY, JACKSON See RIGNEY, JAMES JR.

ORME-JOHNSON, WILLIAM HENRY, III, chemist, educator; b. Phoenix, Apr. 23, 1938; s. William Henry and Jean Mary (McGhee) O.; m. Nanette Roberts, May 27, 1957 (div. 1982); m. Carol Chamberlain, Aug. 23, 1983; children: Doris Helen, Ruth David, McGhee Charles, Heather. Student, Rice U., 1955-57; BS, U. Tex., 1959, PhD, 1964. Postdoctoral fellow U. Wis., Enzyme Inst., Madison, 1965-67, asst. prof., 1967-70, U. Wis., Dept. Biochemistry, Madison, 1970-71, assoc. prof., 1971-73, 1973-79, prof., 1973-79, MIT, Dept. Chemistry, Cambridge, Mass., from 1979. Sci. cons. various chem. and biotechs. Contbr. over 150 articles to sci. jours. V.p. The Lyric Stage, Boston, 1990-92. Grantee NIH, 1967—. Fellow AAAS; mem. Am. Chem. Soc., Am. Soc. Biol. Chemists. Unitarian Universalist. Avocations: guitar, cello, choral singing, acting, sailing. Home: Cambridge, Mass. Died Jan. 1, 2007.

ORTENBERG, ELISABETH CLAIBORNE See CLAIBORNE, LIZ

ORTH, HARVEY CLINTON, JR., osteopathic physician; b. Lewistown, Pa., Feb. 22, 1926; s. Harvey Clinton and Mary Marjorie (Brindle) O.; m. Dolores Marie Thibault, Dec. 21, 1949; children— Mary Margaret, James Harvey, Mary Patrice, Jeffrey Clinton, Julie Marie. Student, Gettysburg Coll., Pa., 1943-44, U. So. Calif., 1944-45, Coll. Osteopathic Physicians and Surgeons, Los Angeles, 1944-46; D.O., Kirksville Coll. Osteopathy and Surgery, Mo., 1948. Diplomate Am. Osteopathic Bd. Ob-Gyn. Intern, Detroit Osteo. Hosp., 1948-49, resident, 1949-51; resident Riverside Osteo. Hosp., Trenton, Mich., 1951-52; practice osteo. medicine specializing in ob-gyn, Trenton, 1953-83; assoc. prof. obstetrics and gynecology Ohio U. Coll. Osteo. Medicine, Athens, 1983—. Fellow Am. Coll. Osteo. Obstetricians and Gynecologists (pres. 1979-80). Republican. Lutheran. Clubs: Grosse Ile Golf and Country (Mich.); Athens Country. Avocations: Reading, golf. Home: Athens, Ohio. Died Jan. 17, 2006.

ORTIZ, IRMA, retired university administrator, interpreter; b. Calexico, Calif., May 28, 1922; d. Camilo Enrique and Emelina (Trujillo) O.; 1 adopted child, Kumari Mary Ruth Danda. AA, Imperial Valley Coll., 1942; BBA, Academia Coss y Leon, 1942. Cert. profl. sec., 1966. Stenographer U. Calif. Agrl. Extension, El Centro, 1942, sec., 1943-64; adminstrv. sec. U. Calif. Coop. Extension, El Centro, 1965-79, adminstrv. asst., 1980-86, ret.; speaker various high schs. and colls. Dir. Salvation Army, El Centro, 1968-79; chmn. Imperial Valley Coll. Community review com., Calif., 1977-78; pres. Imperial Valley Community Concert Assn., 1983-86; editor Imperial Arts Council, 1987-88; docent Imperial Valley Pioneers Mus., 1987—; sec. Imperial County Retired Employees Assn., 1988-89. Recipient Red Feather award Community Chest, El Centro, 1953; named Employee of Yr. Imperial County, 1969. Mem. Pilot Club (El Centro charter, sec. western region 1968-69, 1st v.p. El Centro chpt. 1969-70, parliamentian, dist. div. 1991-92), Beta Sigma Phi. Republican. Roman Catholic. Club: Euterpe (Mex.) (pres. 1945). Avocations: travel, reading, music, silvercraft, painting. Died May 16, 2006.

ORTIZ MENA, ANTONIO, retired bank executive, former Mexican government official; b. Parral, Chihuahua, Mexico, Apr. 16, 1907; Grad., Sch. Law, Nat. Autonomous U. Mexico; postgrad., Sch. Fine Arts and Philosophy, Sch. Econs.; Dr. h.c, U. Guadalajara, Mex. Chief legal counsel, then department rep. Mixed Agrarian Commn., Dept. Fed. Dist., Govt. Mexico,

1932-38; dir. Property Nationalization Svc.; then chief legal counsel Office of Atty. Gen., 1940-45; 1st dir. gen. professions Ministry Pub. Edn., 1945-46; dep. dir. gen., trust rep., then chmn. Banco Nacional de Obras y Servicios Públicos, 1947-52; chmn., chief exec. officer Mexican Social Security Inst., 1952-58; chmn. Permanent Inter-Am. Social Security Com., 1955-59; sec. fin. and pub. credit Govt. Mexico, 1958-70; pres. Inter-Am. Devel. Bank, Washington, 1971-88; dir. gen. Banco Nacional de Mex., 1988-91. Mem. Polit. Def. Com. of Am. Continent, World War II; cons. Mexican del. Inter-Am. Conf. to Consider Problems of War and Peace, Chapultepec, Mex., 1945; gov. for Mex. IMF, World Bank, Internat. Devel. Assn., Internat. Finance Corp., 1959-70; founding Mexican gov. Inter-Am. Devel. Bank, 1960-70, chmn. bd. govs., 1966-67; Mexico rep. Inter-Am. Econ. and Social Coun. at Ministerial Level, 1961-70, pres., 1962-63; chmn. bd. dirs. Nacional Financiera, Altos Hornos de Mex., Compañía Mexicana de Luz y Fuerza Motriz, Compañía Nacional de Subsistencias Populares, Industria Petroquimica Nacional, Guanos y Fertilizantes de Mex.; vice chmn. bd. dirs. Petroleos Mexicanos, Ferrocarriles Nacionales de Mex. Author: El Desarrollo Estabilizador, 1969, Finanzas Publicas de Mexico, 1969, Development in Latin-America, 1971-75, 76-80, El Desarrollo Estabilizador: reflexiones sobra una epoca, 1998. Decorated grand cross Order of Crown of Belgium; grand officer Legion of Honor; grand cross Nat. Order of Merit France; grand cross Order of Merit Fed. Republic Germany; Order of Flag with Banner Yugoslavia; grand cross Nat. Order of So. Cross Brazil; grand cross Order Orange-Nassau Netherlands; grand cross Order of Merit Bernardo O'Higgins Chile; others. Mem. Mexican Hwy. Assn. (life), AIM (coun. of presidents). Died Mar. 12, 2007.

ORTNER, DONALD RICHARD, psychology and sociology educator; b. Bay City, Mich., Sept. 2, 1922; s. Richard John and Caroline Dorothea Elisabeth (Deuring) O.; m. Gertrude Martha Stoekli, June 29, 1947; 1 child, Stephen Richard Edward. BA, Northwestern Coll., Watertown, Wis., 1944; BMus, Ill. Wesleyan U., Bloomington, 1946; MA, Eastern Mich. U., Ypsilanti, 1957; Candidatus Reverendi Ministerii, Wis. Evang. Luth. Sem., 1947; PhD, Mich. State U., 1964; MS, Va. Commonwealth U., 1980. Lic. profl. counselor, Va.; ordained to ministry Luth. Ch., 1947. Asst. pastor St. John's Luth. Ch., Toronto, Ont., Can., 1947-49; pastor Ch. of the Redeemer, Winnipeg, Man., Can., 1949-52, Christ Ch., St. Catharines, Ont., 1952-54, St. John's Ch., Waltz, Mich., 1954-57; Latin tchr., guidance counselor Rodney B. Wilson High Sch., St. Johns, Mich., 1957-60; asst. prof., dir. counseling Morningside Coll., Sioux City, Iowa, 1960-61; asst. prof. to prof. emeritus psychology and sociology Hampden Sydney (Va.) Coll., from 1961, dean students, 1963-70, coll. psychologist, from 1970, chmn. dept. psychology, 1964-90. Pastor St. John's Luth. Ch., Farmville, Va., 1961—; sociol. researcher Evangelical-Luth. State Ch. Iceland, 1985—. Mem. com. troop 6516 Boy Scouts Am., 1980—. Mem. APA (assoc.), ACA, Soc. for Sci. Study Religion, So. Soc. Philosophy and Psychology, Sigma Nu. Democrat. Home: Frankenmuth, Mich. Died Mar. 3, 2006.

ORY, EDWARD (BUTLER), business executive; b. Lake Charles, La., Jan. 8, 1926; s. Edwin L. and Mary Andrews (Butler) O.; m. Iris Bianchi, Mar. 14, 1959; children: Astrid, Mary Elise, Edward P. BS, U.S. Mcht. Marine Acad., 1950; postgrad., NYU, 1952. Contr. Grace Line Inc., NYC, 1953-60; pvt. investor, 1960-74; pres. U.S. Banknote Corp., NYC, 1974-76; chmn. bd. Overseas Nat. Airways, NYC, 1977-81, Environ. Testing and Certification, NYC, 1981-84; pres., mng. ptnr. Edward B. Ory & Co., NYC, from 1984. Bd. dirs. various cos. With USN, 1943-46. Mem. N.Y. Soc. Security Analysts, Fin. Execs. Inst. Home: New York, NY. Died Apr. 29, 2007.

OSBORN, GLENN RICHARD, audio engineer; b. Los Angeles, Oct. 25, 1928; s. Glenn Litts and Nellie (Hoffman) O.; BS in Audio Engring., U. Hollywood, 1949; m. Joye Elise Hughes, Feb. 15, 1963 (div. 1984); children: Eric William, John Howard; m. Jean B. Linderman, Feb. 14, 1988. Head transmission engr., 1352 Motion Picture Squadron, Hollywood, 1953-60; head sound dept. Sandia Corp., Albuquerque, 1960-65; supr. sound dept. A-V Service Corp., Seabrook, Tex., 1965-80; owner G.R. Osborn & Co., Audio Engrs., Seabrook, 1975-80, supr. sound dept., Mede Service Corp., pres., CEO, Travel Services, Inc., 1987-93. Served with AUS, 1950-52. Mem. Audio Engring. Soc., Acoustical Soc. Am., Soc. Motion Picture and TV Engrs. Died Apr. 20, 2007.

OSBORN, THOMAS MONTGOMERY, educator, musician; b. NYC, Apr. 21, 1934; s. James Marshall and Marie-Louise (Montgomery) Osborn.; m. Joyce Bockel, Sept. 7, 1957; children— Carolyn L., Dorothy B. AB, Princeton U., 1956; BM, Yale U., 1957, MM, 1958; DMA, U. So. Calif., 1964. Mem. faculty Western Wash. State Coll., Bellingham, 1964-69, U. So. Calif., 1969-71, LA Pierce Coll., 1973-80; music dir., condr., prof. music Pepperdine U., Malibu, Calif., 1980—2002; music dir., condr. Calif. State U. Northridge Youth Orch. Acad., 1977-83; music dir., condr. Downey Symphony, 1987; dir., condr. Concertos With Orchestra, Thousand Oaks. Former pres. San Fernando Valley Arts Council. Mem. Calif. Choral Condrs. Guild (past pres.), Am. Symphony Orch. League (past chmn. Youth Symphony Orch. div., dir.), Calif. Assn. Symphony Orchs., Condrs. Guild. Died July 30, 2006.

OSBORNE, RICHARD HAZELET, anthropologist, geneticist, educator; b. Kennecott, Alaska, June 18, 1920; s. Clarence Edward and Margaret Jerenne (Hazelet) O.; m. Barbara White, Oct. 14, 1944; children: Susan, Richard, David; m. Barbara Teachman, Sept. 1, 1970. Student, U. Alaska, 1939-41; BS, BA, U. Wash., 1949; postgrad., Harvard U., 1949-50; PhD, Columbia, 1956; doctorate in odontology (hon.), U. Oulu, Finland, 1994; DSc (hon.), U. Alaska, Fairbanks, 2001. Research asso. Columbia U., 1953-58; asst. Sloan-Kettering Inst., NYC, 1958-60, asso., 1960-62, asso. mem., head sect. human genetics, 1962-64; prof. anthropology and med. genetics U. Wis., Madison, 1964-86, prof. emeritus, from 1986; rsch. assoc. Quatenary Ctr. U. Alaska, Fairbanks, from 1993. Asso. prof. preventive medicine Cornell Med. Coll., 1962-64; clin. geneticist Meml. Hosp. for Cancer, N.Y.C., 1963-65; vis. scientist Forsyth Dental Center, Boston, 1969-71; cons. human genetics Newington (Conn.) Childrens Hosp., 1971-73; Mem. com. on epidemiology and vets. follow-up studies NRC, 1969-73; mem. perinatal research com. Nat. Inst. Neurol. Diseases and Stroke, NIH, 1970-72; mem. cultural anthropology fellowship and rev. NIMH, 1969-73 Author: Genetic Basis of Morphological Variation, 1959, Biological and Social Meaning of Race, 1971; Editor: Social Biology, 1961-77, 81—99; contbr. articles to profl. jours. Served to maj. USAAF, 1942-46. Decorated D.F.C., Air medal with 3 oak leaf clusters.; Named Health Research Council Career Scientist City N.Y., 1962-64 Fellow Explorers Club; Mem. Am. Assn. Phys. Anthropology (exec. com. 1965-67, v.p. 1968-70), Am. Soc. for Human Genetics (dir. 1960-61, 67-69), Behavior Genetics Assn. (pres. pro-tem 1970-71), Soc. for Study Social Biology (editor Social Biology 1961-99, dir. 1981-83, 86-99), Pioneers of Alaska (life), Sigma Xi. Died Oct. 30, 2005.

OSTERBROCK, DONALD EDWARD, astronomy educator; b. Cin., July 13, 1924; s. William Carl and Elsie (Wettlin) O.; m. Irene L. Hansen, Sept. 19. 1952; children: Carol Ann, William Carl, Laura Jane. PhB, SB, U. Chgo., 1948, SM, 1949, PhD, 1952, DSc (hon.), 1992, Ohio State U., 1986, U. Wis., 1997, Ohio U., 2003, U. Cin., 2004. Postdoctoral fellow, mem. faculty Princeton, 1952-53; mem. faculty Calif. Inst. Tech., 1953-58; faculty U. Wis.-Madison, 1958-73, prof. astronomy, 1961-73, chmn. dept. astronomy, 1966-67, 69-72; prof. astronomy and astrophysics U. Calif., Santa Cruz, 1972-92, prof. emeritus, 1993—2007. Dir. Lick Obs., 1972-81; mem. staff Mt. Wilson Obs., Palomar Obs., 1953-58; vis. prof. U. Chgo., 1963-64, Ohio State U., 1980, 86; Hill Family vis. prof. U. Minn., 1977-78. Author: Astrophysics of Gaseous Nebulae, 1974, James E. Keeler, Pioneer American Astrophysicist and the Early Development of American Astrophysics, 1984, Astrophysics of Gaseous Nebulae and Active Galactic Nuclei, 1989, (with Gary J. Ferland) 2d edit., 2006, Pauper and Prince: Ritchey, Hale and Big American Telescopes, 1993, Yerkes Observatory, 1892-1950: The Birth, Near Death and Resurrection of a Scientific Research Institution, 1997, Walter Baade: A Life in Astrophysics, 2001; co-author: (with John R. Gustafson and W.J. Shiloh Unruh) Eye on the Sky: Lick Observatory's First Century, 1988; editor: (with C.R. O'Dell) Planetary Nebulae, 1968, (with Peter H. Raven) Origins and Extinctions, 1988, (with J.S. Miller) Active Galactic Nuclei, 1989; Stars and Galaxies: Citizens of the Universe, 1990; letters editor Astrophys. Jour., 1971-73. With USAAF, 1943-46. Recipient Profl. Achievement award U. Chgo. Alumni Assn., 1982, Antoinette de Vaucouleurs Meml. lecture and medal U. Tex., Austin, 1994, Hans Lippershey medal Antique Telescope Soc., 1999, Alumni medal U. Chgo. Alumni Assn., 2000; Guggenheim fellow Inst. Advanced Studies, Princeton, N.J., 1960-61, 82-83, Ambrose Monnell Found. fellow, 1989-90, NSF sr. postdoctoral rsch. fellow U. Coll., London, 1968-69. Mem. NAS (chmn. astronomy sect. 1971-74, sec. class math. and phys. sci. 1980-83, chmn. class math and phys. sci. 1983-85, councilor 1985-88), Am. Acad. Arts and Scis., Internat. Astron. Union (pres. commn. 34 1967-70), Royal Astron. Soc. (assoc., Gold medal 1997), Am. Astron. Soc. (councilor 1970-73, v.p. 1975-77, pres. 1988-90, vice chmn. hist. astronomy divsn. 1985-87, chmn. 1987-89, Henry Norris Russell lectr. 1991, LeRoy Doggett prize 2002), Astron. Soc. Pacific (chmn. history com. 1982-86, Catherine Wolfe Bruce medal 1991, bd. dirs. 1992-95), Wis. Acad. Scis. Arts and Letters, Am. Philos. Soc., Nat. Acad. Scis., Am. Acad. Arts and Scis., Wis. Hist. Soc., Mexican Acad. Scis. (corr.). Congregationalist. Home: Santa Cruz, Calif. Died Jan. 11, 2007.

O'SULLIVAN, JOHN EDWARD, business executive; b. Providence, Nov. 29, 1920; s. John E. and Mary (Talbert) O'S.; m. Madeleine Paquet, May 1, 1954; children: Joan, Mary Alice. AB, Brown U., 1942; postgrad., R.I. Sch. Design, Advanced Mgmt. Program, Harvard U., 1962. Budget mgr. Textron, Inc., 1949-51; controller, asst. to pres. Atlantic Parachute Corp., 1951-53; sec.-treas. Indian Head Inc. now TBG Inc., N.V., NYC, 1953-56, v.p., treas., 1956-61, exec. v.p., 1961-72, from 1974, pres. splty. textile group, 1972-74, mem. exec. and fin. coms., also bd. dirs., 1961-75. Dir. Mfrs. Hanover Trust Co. Adv. Bd., 1965 Mem. industry adv. com. U.S. Def. Supply Agy., 1964-67; mem. devel. council Brown U., 1967—; chmn. fin. com. Greenwich Acad., Conn.; trustee St. Michael's Ch.; 2d v.p. parents nat. adv. com. Rollins Coll., Winter Park, Fla. Served to lt (s.g.) USCGR, 1942-46. Mem. Newcomen Soc. N.Am., New Eng. Soc. City N.Y. Clubs: Greenwich Country (gov.); Brown Univ. (N.Y.C.) (gov.); N.Y. Athletic (gov.). Died Nov. 19, 2006.

OSVER, ARTHUR, artist; b. Chgo., July 26, 1912; s. Harry and Yetta (Woodrov) O.; m. Ernestine Betsberg, Aug. 12, 1940. Student, Northwestern U., 1930-31, Art Inst. Chgo., 1931-36, Dartmouth U., 1997. Instr. art Washington U., St. Louis, 1960-83. Works exhbtd., Art Inst. Chgo., Pa. Acad. Art, Carnegie Inst., Whitney Mus., St. Louis Art Mus., Nelson Gallery, Atkins Mus., Corcoran Art Gallery, U. Ill. Ann., Mus. Modern Art, Met. Mus., others, works in permanent collections, Whitney Mus., Toledo Mus., Isaac Delgado Mus., Peabody Mus., Rio de Janeiro Mus.; artist in residence, U. Fla., 1954-55; trustee emeritus Am. Acad Rome, 1993, artist in residence, 1957-58, one man shows, Wilson Gallery, Chgo., 1940, Grand Central Moderns, N.Y.C., 1947, 49, 51, 56, U. Tenn., 1948, Syracuse U., 1949, Hamline U., 1950, U. Fla., 1951, 55, Fairweather-Hardin Gallery, Chgo., 1953, 55, 69, Dartmouth U., Hanover, N.H., 1997, St. Louis Art Mus., 2000, others. Recipient John Barton Paine medal Va. Mus., 1944, purchase prize U. Ill., 1949, Temple gold medal and purchase prize Pa. Acad., Prix de Rome, 1952, 53, J. Henry Schiedt prize Pa. Acad. Fine Arts, award Am. Acad. and Inst. Arts and Letters, 1991, Arts & Edn. Excellence in Painting award, Arts and Edn. Coun. Greater St. Louis, 1994, Andrew Carnegie Painting award, Nat. Acad. Design, 2003; James Nelson Raymond traveling fellow, 1936-38; Guggenheim fellow, 1950-51; sabbatical leave grantee Nat. Endowment Arts. Mem. Audubon Artists, Artists Equity. Died July 21, 2006.

O'TOOLE, ALLAN THOMAS, electric utility executive; b. Waterloo, Iowa, Dec. 22, 1925; s. Delmar C. and Elsie M. (Winkelman) O'T.; m. Barbara Joyce Boyd, Sept. 2, 1947; children: Kathy Lynn, Timothy Allan. BA, Westminster Coll., Fulton, Mo., 1948; postgrad., U. Mich., 1965. With Pub. Svc. Co. Okla., 1953-88, asst. treas., 1967-70, treas., 1970-73, v.p. contr., 1973-76, v.p. adminstrn., 1976-80, v.p. materiel an property mgmt., 1980-85, v.p. corp. svcs., 1985-88; ret., 1988 Bd. dirs., chmn. bd., life mem. Tulsa Area chpt. ARC, 1975— regional chmn. midwestern ops. hdqrs., 1989-92; bd. dirs., pres Tulsa Sr. Svcs., Inc., 1990-96; with Okla. State Svc. Coun. 1995-98. Lt. USNR, 1943-46, 51-53. Mem. Tulsa C. of C. Adminstrv. Mgmt. Soc. (bd. dirs., pres.), Westminster Coll Alumni Assn. (life, pres., bd. trustees), K.C., Cedar Ridg Country Club, Kappa Alpha. Roman Catholic. Home: Tulsa Okla. Died Aug. 14, 2007.

OTTO, MARGARET AMELIA, retired librarian; b. Bostor Oct. 22, 1937; d. Henry Earlen and Mary (McLennan) O children— Christopher, Peter. AB, Boston U., 1960; MS Simmons Coll., 1963, MA, 1970; MA (hon.), Dartmouth Coll 1981. Asst. sci. librarian M.I.T., Cambridge, 1963, Lindgre librarian, 1964-67, acting sci. librarian, 1967-69, asst. dir 1969-75, assoc. dir., 1976-79; librarian of coll. Dartmouth Coll Hanover, NH, 1979—2000. Pres., chmn. bd. Universal Seria and Book Exch., Inc., 1980-81; bd. dirs. Rsch. Libr. Grou trustee Howe Libr., Hanover, former chmn.; mem. Brown Lib Com., rsch. lbirs. adv. com. OCLC, ARL; editl. com. Univ. Pres New Eng. Council on Library Resources fellow, 1974; elected t Collegium of Disting. Alumnus Boston U., 1980 Mem. AL (task force on assn. membership issues, ad hoc working grou on copyright issues), Assn. Rsch. Librs. (chair preservation com 1983-85, bd. dirs. 1985-88, mem. stats. com., chair membershi com.), Coun. on Libr. Resources (proposal rev. com.), Dar mouth Club (N.Y.C.), St. Botolph Club (Boston), Sloane Cl (London). Home: Hanover, NH. Died Dec. 10, 2006.

OUTHWAITE, LUCILLE CONRAD, ballerina, educator; Peoria, Ill., Feb. 26, 1909; d. Frederick ALbert and Del (Cornett) C.; m. Leonard Outhwaite, Mar. 1, 1936 (dec. 1978 children: Ann Outhwaite Maurer, Lynn Outhwaite Pulsife Student, U. Nebr., 1929-30, Mills Coll., 1931-32; student pian Paris, 1933-35, Legat Sch., London, 1934, N.Y.C. Balle 1936-41, Royal Ballet Sch., London, 1957-59. Tchr. ballet Per Mansfield, Steamboat Springs, Colo., 1932; toured with Ar Amb. Ballet, Europe and S.Am., 1933-35; tchr. ballet Ca Playhouse, Dennis, Mass., 1937-41, Jr. League, NYC, 1937-4 King Coit Sch., NYC, 1937-41; owner, tchr. dance sch. Oyst Bay, N.Y., 1949-57. Prodr., choreographer ballets Alice Wonderland, 1951, Pied Piper of Hamlin, 1952. Author: Birds Flight, 1992, Flowers in the Wind, 1994, To the Ends of t Earth, 1997, Night Wind Whispers (A Glimpse Down Memo Lane), 1999, Far Suns and Open Seas, 2001, The Spice of Li 2003. Mem. English Speaking Union, Preservation Soc., Al ance Française, Mill Coll. Club, Spouting Rock Beach Clu Clambake Club, Delta Gamma. Republican. Methodist. Di Dec. 12, 2006.

OVERS, RONALD ROLAND, manufacturing executive; Buffalo, Nov. 18, 1931; s. Victor V. and Beatrice Overs; Barbara Quane, 1969; children: April, Cheryl, Randall, Laure Ronald Roland, Gordon, Ingrid, Audrey. Dist. sales mgr. J. Virden Co., Cleve., 1954—58; pres. Overs Assoc., Inc., Wi iamsville, NY, from 1958, Electro Marine Sys., Inc., E Amherst, NY, from 1970, Electro Marine Sys. Internat., In East Amherst, from 1973. Cons. in field. Recipient Pres. awa J.C. Virden Co., 1956—57. Mem.: IEEE, Smithsonian Inst Fox Hunt Farms Civic Assn., Buffalo Zool. Soc., Exptl. Aircr Assn., Boating Industry Assn., Internat. Yacht Racing Ass Aircraft Owners and Pilots Assn., Buffalo Canoe Club, Buff Yacht Club. Achievements include patents for marine inst ments; design of cardiac med. equipment. Home: East Amhe NY. Died May 22, 2007.

OVERTON, JANE VINCENT HARPER, biology profess b. Chgo., Jan. 17, 1919; d. Paul Vincent and Isabel (Vince Harper; m. George W. Overton, Jr., Sept. 1, 1941; childr Samuel, Peter, Ann. AB, Bryn Mawr Coll., 1941; PhD, Chgo., 1950. Rsch. asst. U. Chgo., 1950-52, mem. facu 1952-89, prof. biology, 1972-89; prof. emeritus, 1989. Aut articles embryology, cell biology; artist exhibitions at Fine A Bldg. Gallery, Chgo., 1992-95 NIH, NSF research grant 1965-87. Avocations: painting, ceramics. Home: Chicago, Died June 3, 2007.

OVERTON, SPENCER MILTON, banker; b. Norfolk, V June 14, 1925; s. Marvin Baron and Audrey Jane (Brazenor) m. Rosemary Louise Relph, June 30, 1950 (dec. 1981); childr Toni Overton-Toft, Katharine Overton Lewis. AB in Eco Coll. William and Mary, 1948; MBA in Finance, U. Pa., 19 With Wachovia Bank & Trust Co., Charlotte, N.C., 1950-70, v.p., 1968-70, United Counties Trust Co., Elizabeth, N 1970-83; now pres., chief exec. officer Eastern Nat. Ba Medford, N.J. Dir. Eastern States Bankcard Assn., Inc. Ch bd. trustees Elizabeth Gen. Hosp.; trustee Tri-Hosp. Fou Elizabeth. Served with USAAF, 1943-46. Mem. Robert Mo Assocs., Mensa. Episcopalian. Died Mar. 13, 2006.

OWEN, STEVEN EARL, educator, consultant; b. San L Obispo, Calif., July 29, 1947; s. Leland Earl and Lucille Na Ann (Varda) O.; m. Janet Gail Smith, Oct. 22, 1976; childr Richard Earl, Shawn Marie. BS, Calif. State Poly. U., 19 postgrad., 1969-70; postgrad. Calif. State U., Stanislaus, 19 72; MA in Edn., Fresno Pacific Coll., 1983. Cert. tchr., C Mem. faculty Rivera Jr. H.S., Merced (Calif.) Sch. D 1970-88, tchr., 1970-79, resource tchr. curriculum devel., 19 88; vice prin. Hoover Jr. H.S., 1988-94, prin., 1995—; m dist. curriculum coun., 1970-85, dist. sci. cons., 1983—; in sci., math. and computers Fresno Pacific Coll., 1983-90; m adv. coun. Calif. Mid. Sch. Demonstration Program, 1995 mem. Mid. Sch. Partnership Coordinating Coun., 1995 founder Merced/Mariposa Counties Math. Conf., 1979, ch 1979-88; mem. program rev. teams Calif. Dept. Edn., 1979- 84-95; partipant Project AIMS, NSF. Fellow Calif. Sch. Le ership Acad. Mem. ASCD, Calif. Math. Coun. (affiliate c Ctrl. sect.), Nat. Sci. Tchrs. Assn., Nat. Biology Tchrs. A Democrat. Baptist. Clubs: Breakfast, Kiwanis (Merced). Aut My Favorite Things; co-author: From Head to Toe, I, 1 co-author Key to Balancing Equations, 1983; editor: Handb of State and Local Government, Merced County, 1984; Am. editor/contbn. editor Delto Pubs. Internat. divsn. Delto Verlag; author profl. publs., choral readings. Home: Merced, Calif. Died Sept. 25, 2006.

OWEN, THOMAS BARRON, aerospace transportation executive, retired military officer; b. Seattle, Mar. 19, 1920; s. Thomas Barron and Ruth (Deane) O.; m. Rosemary Stolz, Dec. 24, 1944; children— Catherine Adams, Thomas Barron, James Rowell, Nancy Deane. BS cum laude, U. Wash., 1940; postgrad., U.S. Naval Postgrad. Sch., 1946-47; PhD in Chemistry, Cornell U., 1950; postgrad., U. Amsterdam, 1950-51, Indsl. Coll. Armed Forces, 1961-62, Harvard Grad. Sch. Bus. Adminstrn., 1964. Commd. ensign U.S. Navy, 1940, advanced through grades to rear adm., 1967, ret., 1970, combat duty with Pacific Fleet, 1940-45; officer distbn. div. Bur. Naval Personnel, 1945-46; with armaments br. and mil. operations br. Office Naval Research, 1951-53; asst. repair supt. (hull) and prodn. analysis supt. Long Beach (Calif.) Naval Shipyard, 1953-57; dir. applied scis. div., dir. research and devel. planning div. Navy Bur. Ships, 1957-61; mil. asst. to dep. dir. def. research and engring. engring. and chemistry, 1962-63; assigned Office Asst. Sec. Navy Research and Devel., 1963; dir. support services Naval Research Lab., 1963-65, dir., 1965-67; chief naval research, 1967-70; asst. dir. nat. and internat. programs NSF, 1970-74; assoc. dean grad. affairs and rsch. Am. U., Washington, 1974-76, asst. provost, 1976-79; asst. adminstr. NOAA, Dept. Commerce, Rockville, Md., 1979-81; mgr. program planning Fairchild Space & Electronics Co., Germantown, Md., 1981-83; sr. dir. systems effectiveness Fairchild Space Co., Germantown, 1983-84, v.p. procurement, 1984-86. Author profl. papers. Decorated D.S.M., Silver Star, Bronze Star. Fellow AAAS; mem. Am. Chem. Soc., U.S. Naval Inst., Philos. Soc. Washington, Sigma Xi, Phi Kappa Phi, Phi Lambda Upsilon, Tau Beta Pi, Chi Psi. Clubs: Cosmos (Washington). Home: Gaithersburg, Md. Died Oct. 14, 2006.

OWEN, THOMAS WALKER, banker, portfolio manager; b. Everett, Wash., June 7, 1925; s. Thomas Walker and Frances (Yantis) O.; m. Barbara May Neils, Oct. 20, 1951; children: Thomas W., Gerhard, Caroline, Jeffrey; m. Ingrid Lundgren, June 7, 1975. BA, U. Wash., 1949, MA in Finance, 1953; postgrad., Pacific Coast Banking Sch., 1956. Adminstrv. trainee Seattle Trust & Savs. Bank, 1949-54, asst. br. mgr., 1954-56, trust investment officer, 1956-57, mgr. investment dept., chmn. investment com., 1957-59; v.p., mgr. investment dept. Nat. Bank Wash., Tacoma, 1959-66, vice chmn., 1967-71; exec. v.p. bank adminstrn. Pacific Nat. Bank Wash., 1971-73; v.p. Reeder, Owen & Co., Inc., 1975-92; pres., chmn. Owen, Reeder, Inc., Merrill Lynch, 1991-92; bd. dirs. West One Bank Wash., Tacoma, 1981-93. Served with AUS, 1943-45. Decorated Bronze Star, Purple Heart. Mem. N.W. Forum, Tacoma Club (past pres.), Tacoma Country and Golf Club, Phi Gamma Delta. Home: Lakewood, Wash. Died Mar. 4, 2007.

OWENS, MARVIN FRANKLIN, JR., oil industry executive, director; b. Oklahoma City, Feb. 20, 1916; s. Marvin Franklin and Levis (Coley) O.; m. Jessie Ruth Hay, June 15, 1941 (dec.); children: Marvin Franklin III, William Earl, Jack Hay. BS, U. Okla., 1937; postgrad., Rutgers U., 1960-62. Petroleum engr. Brit. Am. Oil Producing Co., Oklahoma City, 1937-41; chief petroleum engr. Bay Petroleum Corp., Denver, 1946-54; sr. v.p. Cen. Bank of Denver, 1954-81. Elder Presbyn. Ch., Denver. With U.S. Army, 1941-46; col. Res. ret. Home: Centennial, Colo. Died May 20, 2007.

OWENS, ROBERT PHILLIP, police official; b. Stamford, Conn., Sept. 12, 1931; s. Robert Evan and Ann (Humphreys) Owens; children: Steven, Olga. BS in Police Adminstrn., Calif. State U., LA, 1968; MBA, Pepperdine U., 1973. With Los Angeles County Sheriff's Dept., LA, 1954—67; police chief San Fernando City, Calif., 1967—70, Oxnard (Calif.) Police Dept., from 1970. Cons. U.S. Dept. Justice, 1977—81, Office Criminal Justice Planning Calif., from 1977, Ind. U., 1974—78. With USMC, 1949—53. Named Outstanding Law Enforcement Officer, Calif. Trial Lawyers Assn., 1984; recipient Oxnard trophy, Greater Oxnard C. of C., 1983. Mem.: Nat. Orgn. Victim Assistance (bd. dirs. from 1981), Rotary (pres. 1975—76). Republican. Unitarian. Home: San Antonio, Tex. Died May 14, 2006.

OWENS, WARREN SPENCER, librarian; b. Massena, NY, Dec. 28, 1921; s. Spencer Bacon and Charlotte (Eaton) O.; m. Pauli Hartung, Jan. 20, 1946; children: Christie, Patrick, Martha, Andrew. BA, Kalamazoo Coll., 1943; MA, U. Chgo., 1947; M. in L.S, U. Mich., 1953. Lectr. English Ind. U. Calumet Center, East Chicago, 1947-49; instr. English U. N.D., 1950-52; mem. staff U. Mich. Library, 1952-61, supr. divisional libraries, 1959-61; dir. libraries Temple U., 1961-68, U. Idaho, Moscow, 1968-70, dean library services, 1970-87. Chmn. Moscow United Fund, 1972-73; sec. Ballet Folk of Moscow, Inc., 1974-75, chmn., 1977-78; pres. Friends of KUID, Inc., 1981-84; bd. dirs. Wash.-Idaho Symphony Assn., 1985—, Latah County Hist. Soc., 1985—. Served with AUS, 1943-45. Mem. ALA, Idaho Library Assn., Pacific N.W. Library Assn. (pres. 1973-75), Assn. Coll. and Research Libraries, Phi Kappa Phi (pres. chpt. 1980—) Home: Moscow, Idaho. Died Nov. 17, 2006.

OZOLS, LIA, medical technologist; b. Riga, Latvia, Jan. 4, 1929; came to U.S., 1950, naturalized, 1959; d. Karlis and Olga Rozenfelds; B.S., U. Minn., 1957; postgrad. Metro State U., Minn., 1980; m. Laimons Ozols, Mar. 19, 1956; children— Egemars, Arnis. Med. technologist U. Minn. Hosps., 1957-61; chief adminstrv. technologist Abbott Hosp., Mpls., 1957-77; administrv. lab. dir. Abbott-Northwestern Hosp., 1977-79; dir. Les Soeurs Orgn., Mpls., 1979—. Chair adv. bd. City of Richfield (Minn.) Dept. Health; bd. dirs. South Hennepin Human Services Council, Minn., 1986. Recipient Key to City, Richfield, 1985. Mem. Am. Soc. Clin. Pathologists, Am. Baltic Trade Assn. (govt. liaison 1990—), Am. Soc. Med. Technology, Minn. Microbiologists, Minn. Soc. Med. Technology, Minn. LWV, Women's Equity Action League (v.p. 1981-82), Women's Consortium, Minn. Women's Network, Exec. Females. Club: Selga (pres. 1981-82, 91-92). Home: Minneapolis, Minn. Died May 8, 2007.

PABST, MARK L., human resources executive; b. Berwyn, Ill., Mar. 8, 1946; s. Mark William and Thyra (Lindell) P.; m. Margery Lou Cutsinger, June 20, 1968 BA, Cornell Coll., Mt. Vernon, Iowa, 1968; postgrad., Old Dominion Coll., 1969-73. Personnel officer Va. Nat. Bank, Norfolk, 1972-78, mktg. officer, 1978-79; v.p., mgr. corp. personnel Sun Banks, Inc., Orlando, Fla., 1979-82; mng. dir. human resources SW Bancshares, Houston, 1982-84; sr. v.p., mgr. human resources MCorp, Dallas, 1984-86, mng. dir. human resources, 1986-88; sr. v.p. St. Paul Co. Inc., from 1988. Pres. Minn. Employment Law Coun., 1990—; trustee William Mitchell Coll. Law, 1991. Served to lt. comdr. USNR, 1968-72 Woodrow Wilson fellow, 1968 Mem. Am. Bankers Assn. (chmn. human resources div. 1984-85, mem. operating com. 1984-85, exec. com. human resources div. 1982-85), Am. Compensation Assn., Am. Soc. Personnel Adminstrn., Phi Beta Kappa Home: New Smyrna, Fla. Died May 21, 2006.

PACK, ALLEN S., retired coal company executive; b. Bramwell, W.Va., Dec. 11, 1930; s. Paul Meador and Mable Blanche (Hale) P.; m. Glenna Rae Christian, June 21, 1952; children: Allen Scott Jr., David Christian, Mark Frederick, Andrew Ray. BS, W.Va. U., 1952. Gen. mgr. Island Coal Co., Holden, W.Va., 1969-70, pres., 1970-73, v.p. adminstrn. Lexington, Ky., 1973-75; exec. v.p. Cannelton Holding Co., Charleston, W.Va., 1975-77, pres., chief ops. officer, 1977-80, pres., chief exec. officer, 1980-91; chmn., 1991-93; ret., 1993. Bd. dirs. Bucksin coun. Boy Scouts Am., Charleston, 1976—, pres., 1980, chmn., 1994, 95, 96; bd. dirs. W.Va. Univ. Found., Morgantown, 1978-96; trustee Davis and Elkins Coll., 1981. Capt. USMC, 1952-54. Recipient Silver Beaver award Boy Scouts Am., 1981; inductee W.Va. Coal Hall of Fame, 1998. Presbyterian. Home: Charleston, W.Va. Died Nov. 16, 2005.

PACZYNSKI, BOHDAN, astrophysicist, educator; b. Wilno, Poland, Feb. 8, 1940; came to U.S., 1981; s. Jan and Helena (Milkowska) P.; m. Hanna Adamska, Aug. 25, 1965; children: Agnieszka, Marcin MA in Astronomy, Warsaw U., 1962, PhD in Astronomy, 1964, Docent degree in Astronomy, 1967. Technical asst. Warsaw U. Observatory, 1959—62; asst. Inst. Astronomy, renamed in 1975 N. Copernicus Astron. Ctr. Polish Acad. of Sciences, Warsaw, 1962—64, rsch. assoc., 1964—69, asst. prof., 1969—74, assoc. prof., 1974—79, prof., 1979—82; prof., dept., astrophysical sciences Princeton U., NJ, 1982—89, Lyman Spitzer Jr. prof. astrophysics, dept. astrophysical sciences NJ, 1989—2007. Astron. asst., Lick Observatory, U. Calif.; vis. observer, Beograd Astron. Observatory, Yugoslavia, 1964, Haute Provance Observatory, France, 1965; visitor, Meudon Observatory, France, 1966, Inst. Theoretical Astronomy, Cambridge, Eng., 1970, Internat. Ctr. for Theoretical Physics in Trieste, 1973, Inst. Theoretical Astronomy, Cambridge, Eng., 1977; vis. fellow, JILA, U. Colo., Boulder, Colo., 1968-69: vis. prof., Calif. Inst. of Technology, 1973, Sherman Fairchild Disting. Scholar, 1981-82; vis. scientist, Princeton U. Observatory and the Inst. for Advanced Studies at Princeton, 1974, vis. astronomer, 1976, 1977, 1978, 1980, 1981; Sherman Fairchild Disting. Scholar, Calif. Inst. Tech., 1975-76; vis. prof., dept. astronomy, U. Calif., Berkeley, 1979; vis. prof., Ctr. for Astrophysics, Harvard U., 1989; vis. scientist, Institut d'Astrophysique (CNRS) in Paris, France, 1994, Nat. Observatory in Tokyo, Japan, 1995; approximately 10 short visits to the Astron. Coun., USSR Acad. of Sciences in Moscow, 1967 - 1980; lectureships include K. Schwarzschild Lecture, Astronomische Gesellshaft, Innsbruck, 1981, Morris Loeb Lectures on Physics, Harvard U., 1995, Russel Marker Lecture series, Penn State U., 1996, Antoinette de Vaucouleurs medal and Meml. Lecture, U. Tex., 1998, Sackler Lectureship, U. Calif., Berkeley, 1999, Thomas Gold Lectureship at Cornell U., 1999, Marc Aaronson Memorial Lectureship, U. Ariz., 1999, L. Biermann Lectures, Max Planck Inst. for Astrophysics, Garching, 2000, Merle Kingsley Disting. Visitor, Caltech, 2001, Halley Lecture, Oxford U., 2002, Seyfert Lecture, Vanderbilt U., 2003. Contbr. articles to profl. jours. Recipient State prize in Sci., Govt. of Poland, 1980, Alfred Jurzykowski Found. award, 1982, Medaille de l'Adion, Nice, 1985, prize Found. for Polish Sci., 1996, Mem. NAS (fgn. assoc., Henry Draper medal 1997), Polish Acad. Sci. (corr., 1976-91), Deutsche Academie der NaturforscherLeopoldina, Royal Astron. Soc. (assoc. mem., U.K., Eddington medal 1987, Gold medal 1999), Internat. Astron. Union (invited lectr. 1979), Am. Physical Soc., Polish Astron. Soc., Am. Astron. Soc.(Dannie Heineman prize for astrophysics, 1992, Rossi prize of high energy divsn., 2000, Henry Norris Russell Lectreship, 2006), Polish Physical Soc. Died Apr. 19, 2007.

PADEREWSKI, SIR CLARENCE JOSEPH, architect; b. Cleve., July 23, 1908; BArch, U. Calif., 1932. Chief draftsman Sam W. Hamill, 1939-44; with Heitschmidt-Matcham-Blanchard-Gill & Hamill, 1943; prin. C.J. Paderewski, 1944-48; pres. Paderewski, Mitchell, Dean & Assoc., Inc. (and predecessor), San Diego, 1948-78. Instr. adult edn. San Diego city schs., 1939-44, U. Calif. extension div., 1945, 56; lectr. in field. Prin. works include Charactron Labs, Gen. Dynamics Corp., Convair, S.D., 1954, South Bay Elem. Schs., S.D., 1948-74; additions to El Cortez Hotel; including first exterior passenger glass elevator in the world and New Travolator Motor Hotel, S.D., 1959, Palomar Coll., San Marcos, 1951-80, San Diego County U. Gen. Hosp., San Diego Internat. Airport Terminal Bldgs., Fallbrook Elem. Schs., 1948-74, Silver Strand Elem. Sch., Coronado, Tourmaline Terrace Apt. Bldg., San Diego Salvation Army Office Bldg. Mem. adv. bd. Bayside Social Service Center, 1953-75, San Diego Polonia Newspaper, 1994-2007; mem. San Diego Urban Design Com.; adv. bd. Camp Oliver, 1963-2007, pres., 1975-76; bd. dirs. San Diego Symphony Orch. Assn., 1954-62, San Diego chpt. ARC, 1971-74; bd. dirs., chmn. coms., pres. San Diego Downtown Assn., 1963-2007; bd. dirs. Nat. Council Archtl. Registration Bds., 1958-66, bd. dirs. other offices, 1961-64, pres., 1965-66, chmn. internat. relations com., 1967-68, Salvation Army, vice-chmn., 1989, life mem. adv. bd., 1993-2007, Copernicus Found., 1994-2007; mem. Calif. Bd. Archtl. Examiners, 1949-61, past pres., commr., 1961-2007; mem. Nat. Panel Arbitrators, 1953-2007, Nat. Council on Schoolhouse Constrn.; hon. chmn. Ignacy Jan Paderewski Meml. Com., 1991; adv. bd. S.D. Balboa Park Cmty. Endowment Fund, 1995-2007. Decorated Knight Order Polonia Restituta, Polish govt. in exile, 1982, recipient Commodore cross, 2002; recipient Award of Merit for San Diego County Gen. Hosp., San Diego chpt., AIA, 1961, Honor award for San Diego Internat. Airport Terminal, Honor award Portland Cement Co., Golden Trowel award Plastering Inst., 1958-60, 4 awards Masonry Inst., 1961, award Prestressed Concrete Inst., 1976, Outstanding Community Leadership award San Diego Downtown Assn., 1963-65, 80, Polish Engring. award for outstanding arch. and achievement, 2000, Gold award Engring. Soc., 2000, Outstanding INdividual Polish Am. award Polish Ctr. of L.A., 2001. Fellow AIA (pres. San Diego chpt. 1948, 49, bd. dirs. 1947-53, chmn. several coms., spl. award 1977, Calif. Coun. Spl. award 1979, Calif. Coun. Disting. Svc. award 1982, Lifetime Achievement award 2000); mem. San Diego C. of C. (bd. dirs. 1959-62, 64-67), Am. Arbitration Assn. (San Diego adv. coun. 1969-2007), Sister City Soc. (bd. dirs.), Lions (past pres. Hillcrest Club, Lion of Yr. 1990, fellow internat. found. 1991), Father Serra Club (charter, past pres.), Outboard Boating Club San Diego, Chi Alpha Kappa, Delta Sigma Chi. Died July 9, 2007.

PADGETT, GEORGE ARTHUR, retired lawyer; b. NYC, Feb. 17, 1932; s. Arthur Samuel and Marion Louise (Schramm) P.; m. Ann M. Padgett; children: Ann Linton, James Dunbar. AB, Hamilton Coll., 1954; JD, Georgetown U., 1960. Bar: D.C. 1960, N.J. 1961. Assoc. Covington & Burling, Washington, 1959-60, Pitney, Hardin & Kipp, Newark, 1961-65; asst. sec., corp. counsel Lionel Corp., NYC, 1965-70, sec., corp. counsel Edison, N.J., 1970-82, sr. v.p., counsel, corp. sec., 1983-93, also bd. dirs., ret., 1993. Mem. planning bd. Hopewell Boro, N.J., common coun., 1993-94, mayor, 1994—. Mem. ABA, Am. Corp. Counsel Assn., N.J. Bar Assn., Am. Soc. Corp. Secs. Home: Boynton Beach, Fla. Died Dec. 29, 2005.

PAINTER, EDITH G., academic administrator, retired educator; b. Weymouth, Mass., Sept. 19, 1925; d. Charles E. and Mildred F. Pratt; m. Clyde Andrew Painter, Dec. 27, 1952; children: Scott Douglas, Brett Alan. BS, Tufts U., 1947; MA, Columbia U., 1948; EdD, Colo. U., 1964. Asst. dean of women Meredith Coll., Raleigh, NC, 1948—50; asst. dean students New Paltz (NY) State Coll., 1950—51; asst. svc. club dir. U.S. Civil Svc., Ft. Monmouth, NJ, 1951—52; exec. dir. Campfire Girls, Wollaston, Mass., 1952—58; dean of women Boise (Idaho) Jr. Coll., 1959—61, Youngstown (Ohio) U., 1961—72; v.p. student affairs Russell Sage Coll., Troy, NY, 1972—74; dir. MA program Springfield (Mass.) Coll., 1974—78; supt. Marimor Sch., Lima, Ohio, 1978—81; prof. psychology Bluffton (Ohio) U., 1981—91; ret., 1991. Spkr. in field. Contbr. articles to profl. jours. Recipient Tchg. Excellence award, Sears Found., 1990. Mem.: APA (life), Nat. Assn. Women Deans and Counselors (life). Episcopalian. Home: Burnsville, NC. Died Nov. 1, 2006.

PALANCE, JACK, actor; b. Lattimer, Pa., Feb. 18, 1918; s. John and Anna (Gramiak) Palahnuik; m. Virginia Baker, Apr. 21, 1949 (div. 1969); children: Holly Kathleen, Brook Gabrielle, Cody John (dec. 1998); m. Elaine Rochelle Rogers, May 6, 1987 (div.). Student, U. N.C., Stanford U. Appeared in stage plays The Big Two, 1947, Temporary Island, 1948, The Vigil, A Street Car Named Desire, 1948, The Silver Tassle, 1949, Darkness at Noon, 1950, Julius Caesar, The Tempest, 1955; actor (films) Panic in the Streets, 1950, Halls of Montezuma, Sudden Fear (Acad. award nominee best supporting actor 1952), Shane (Acad. award nominee best supporting actor 1953), Arrowhead, Flight to Tangier, The Silver Chalice, Kiss of Fire, Attack!, Ten Seconds to Hell, The Big Knife, Man in the Attic, Warriors Five, Barabbas, I Died A 1000 Times, The Lonely Man, House of Numbers, Contempt, Torture Garden, Kill a Dragon, They Came to Rob Las Vegas, The Desperadoes, The Mercenary, Justine, Legion of the Damned, A Bullet for Rommel, The McMasters, The Professionals, Chato's Land, Companeros, Che, Oklahoma Crude, Craze, The Four Deuces, The Diamond, Hawk the Slayer, Gor, Bagdad Cafe, Young Guns, The Getaway, The Horsemen, The Shape of Things to Come, Hawk the Slayer, Without Warning, Tango & Cash, Batman 1989, Solar Crisis, 1990, City Slickers, 1991 (Acad. award for Best Supporting Actor 1991, Golden Globe award Best Supporting Actor 1991), Cops and Robbersons, 1994, City Slickers II: The Legend of Curley's Gold, 1994, Natural Born Killers, 1994, (voice) The Swan Princess, 1994, Marco Polo, 1998, Treasure Island, 1999, Prancer Returns, 2001; (TV movies) Requiem for a Heavyweight (Sylvania award), Dr. Jekyll and Mr. Hyde, Dracula, Living With the Dead, 2002, Back When We Were Grownups, 2004 (TV series) Bronk, 1975-76, host, Ripley's Believe It Or Not, (miniseries) Buffalo Girls, 1995, Buffalo Girls, 1995, Ebenezer, 1997, I'll Be Home for Christmas, 1997, Sarah, Plain and Tall: Winter's End, 1999, Living with the Dead, 2002. With USAF, 1942—44. Named Most Prominent Newcomer Theatre World, Best Screen Newcomer Look mag.; recipient Emmy, Best Single Performance by an Actor, Requiem for a Heavyweight, 1956. Died Nov. 10, 2006.

PALEY, GRACE, author, educator; b. NYC, Dec. 11, 1922; d. Isaac and Mary (Ridnyik) Goodside; m. Jess Paley, June 20, 1942; children: Nora, Dan.; m. Robert Nichols, 1972. Student, Hunter Coll., NYU. Formerly tchr. Columbia, Syracuse U.; ret. mem. lit. faculty Sarah Lawrence Coll., Stanford, Johns Hopkins, Dartmouth, CUNY. Author: The Little Disturbances of Man, 1959, Enormous Changes at the Last Minute, 1974, Leaning Forward, 1985, Later the Same Day, 1985, Long Walks and Intimate Talks, 1991, New and Collected Poems, 1992, The Collected Stories, 1994 (Nat. Book award nomination, 1994), Just As I Thought, 1998, Begin Again Collected Poems, 2000; contbr. stories to Atlantic, New Yorker, Ikon, Genesis West, others. Sec. N.Y. Greenwich Village Peace Center. Recipient Literary award for short story writing Nat. Inst. Arts and Letters, 1970, Edith Wharton award N.Y. State, 1988, 89, Rea award for short story, 1993, Vt. Gov.'s award for Excellence in the Arts, 1993, award for contbn. to Jewish culture Nat. Found. Jewish Culture; Guggenheim fellow; apptd. Vt. Poet Laureate, 2003-07. Mem. Am. Acad. and Inst. Arts and Letters, Am. Acad. Arts and Scis. Died Aug. 22, 2007.

PALLIN, IRVING M., anesthesiologist; b. Boston, Feb. 11, 1910; s. Abraham and Lillian (Stoler) P.; m. Ann Gertrude Lear, 1940; children: Samuel Lear, Mary Jane, Carol Sue, Jonathan Jacob. BS, Tufts U., 1932, MD, 1937. Diplomate: Am. Bd. Anesthesiology. Intern W.W. Backus Hosp., 1937-39; resident anesthesiology N.Y. Postgrad. Med. Sch. and Hosp., 1939-41; practice medicine specializing in anesthesiology NYC, 1941-70, Sun City, Ariz., 1970-80. Attending anesthesiologist Jewish Hosp. Bklyn., 1942-54, sec. med. bd., 1951-70, pres. med. bd., 1962-63, dir. dept. anesthesiology, 1954-70; cons. anesthesiologist VA Hosp., Bklyn., 1950-65; dir. anesthesiology Cumberland Hosp., 1948-55; dir. dept. anesthesiology Queens Gen. Hosp., 1955-66; former prof. clin. anesthesiology SUNY Coll. Medicine, Bklyn.; chief anesthesia Boswell Meml. Hosp., Sun City, Ariz., 1970-77; dir. Asso. Hosp. Service (Blue Cross) Greater N.Y.; chmn. advisers of AMA to Am. Assn. Med. Assts., 1968-70 Contbr. articles to profl. publs. Co-chmn. Bklyn. physicians div. United Jewish Appeal, 1953-56; pres. Sun City unit Am. Cancer Soc., 1981-85, bd. dirs. Ariz. div., 1982—; pres. Beth Shalom Congregation of Sun City, 1976-78, Brotherhood, 1980, 81, pres. 1982-83; bd. dirs. Ariz. Endowment of Jewish Welfare, 1982-85. Recipient Heritage award State of Israel Bonds, 1983 Fellow Am. Coll. Anesthesiologists, N.Y. Acad. Medicine, N.Y. Acad. Scis.; mem. AMA (del. 1964—), Kings County Med. Soc. (pres. 1960-61, hon.), N.Y. Med. Soc. (ho. dels. 1952-54, sec. sect. anesthesiology 1952057), Acad. Medicine Bklyn. (pres. 1961), Am. Soc. Anesthesiologists (pres. 1957), N.Y. Soc. Anesthesiologists (pres. 1949-50, chmn. jud. com. 1951-56, hon.), Tam O'Shanter Golf Club (pres. 1960-63, Union Hills Country Club. Home: Sun City, Ariz. Died Oct. 8, 2006.

PALMANTEER, EDDIE ADRIAN, JR., tribal government administrator; b. Okanogan, Wash., July 5, 1932; s. Eddie Adrian and Agnes (Whistocken) P.; m. Edith Oppenheimer, 1958 (div. 1967); children: Loni, Dale, Audrey; m. Mary Ann Quill, Aug. 9, 1968; 1 child, Eddie Adrian III. Student, Wenatchee Valley CC, Wash., 1952-53; AA in Acctg., Merritt-Davis Sch. Commerce, Salem, Oreg., 1960. Supt. Colville Indian Agy., Nespelem, Wash., 1974-78; pres., CEO, CTEC, Nespelem, 1985-87; dir. phys. resources Colville Confederated Tribes, Nespelem, 1979-84, chmn., councilman, from 1987. Troop leader Boy Scouts Am., Nespelem, 1970-71; bd. dirs. Wenatchee Intermediate Sch. Dist., 1971-72; leader Disautel Eagles 4-H Club, Omak, Wash., 1972-74; coach Omak Little League, 1972-73; chmn. parents com. JOM, Omak, 1975, PSIS Sch. Bd., Omak, 1979. With U.S. Army, 1953-55. Mem. Am. Legion, Moose. Democrat. Roman Catholic. Avocations: golf, horseshoes, pool, reading, walking. Home: Omak, Wash. Died Aug. 17, 2007.

PALMER, EDWARD HENRY, consulting and development company executive; b. Chgo., Feb. 12, 1932; s. Brian Charles and Catherine Dorothy P.; m. Davalyn D. Nelson, June 4, 1982. B.A., Hanover Coll., 1955; S.T.M., Yale U., 1958; postgrad. Northwestern U., 1960-62. Asst. rector St. Pauls Ch., New Haven, 1958-60; with Chgo. Housing Authority, Chgo., 1960-62; with Hyde Park Kenwood Community Orgn., Chgo., 1962-64; chmn. Palmer France Assocs. Ltd., Chgo.; pres. House Group, Inc.; lectr. Ill. Inst.Tech., U. Ill.; speaker profl. orgns. Episcopalian. Clubs: Cliff Dwellers, Carlton, Quadrangle (Chgo.). Contbr. articles on housing to profl. jours. Died Feb. 12, 2007.

PALMER, EDWARD LEWIS, banker, director; b. NYC, Aug. 12, 1917; s. William and Cecelia (Tierney) P.; m. Margaret Preston, Jan. 5, 1940; children: Edward Preston, Jane Lewis. AB, Brown U., 1938. With N.Y. Trust Co., 1941-59, v.p., 1952-59; with Citibank, N.A., NYC, 1959-82, sr. v.p., 1962-65, exec. v.p., 1965-70, dir., chmn. exec. com., 1970-82; pres. Mill Neck Group, Inc., 1982. Bd. dirs.SunResorts Ltd., FondElec Group Inc.; dir. emeritus Corning Inc.; trustee emeritus Mut. N.Y. Trustee emeritus Met. Mus. Art, Brown U. Served to lt. comdr. USNR, 1942-46. Mem. Phi Gamma Delta. Home: Greenport, NY. Died May 28, 2006.

PALMER, ROBERT BLUNDEN, newspaper, printing executive; b. Port Huron, Mich., Nov. 25, 1917; s. Joseph Frank and Hazel Quinn (Blunden) P.; m. Mary Bellatti (dec.), Feb. 11, 1946; children: Robert L. Palmer, Frances Lobpries, Barbara Caldwell. Office mgr. Palmer Circulation Co., Midwest, 1937-41; reporter, bus. mgr. Titus County Tribune, Mt. Pleasant, Tex., 1941-42, editor, 1946-57; pub., editor Daily Tribune, Mt. Pleasant, Tex., 1957-88; pres. Palmer Media, Inc., Mt. Pleasant, Tex., from 1972, NorTex Press, Inc., Mt. Pleasant, Tex., from 1973. Owner Palmer Real Estate, 1968—. Capt. U.S. Army, 1942-46, ETO. Presbyterian. Avocations: reading, golf, travel, music. Home: Mount Pleasant, Tex. Died Jan. 14, 2006.

PALMER, ROGER FARLEY, pharmacology educator; b. Albany, NY, Sept. 23, 1931; m. Nelida Santiago, Apr. 1994. BS in Chemistry, St. Louis U., 1953; postgrad., Fla. State U., 1955-56, Woods Hole Marine Biology Lab., 1956; MD, U. Fla., 1960. Intern Johns Hopkins Hosp., 1960-61, resident in medicine, 1961-62; asst. dept. biochemistry U. Fla., Gainesville, 1957; asst. medicine Osler Med. Service, 1960-62; instr. pharmacology and therapeutics U. Fla., 1962, asst. prof. pharmacology, therapeutics and medicine, 1964-67, assoc. prof. pharmacology and medicine, 1967-69, prof. medicine, chief div. clin. pharmacology, 1969-70, 71-82; prof., chmn. dept. pharmacology, prof. medicine U. Miami, Fla., 1970-81, clin. prof. medicine, 1982. Chmn. pharmacology sect. Nat. Bd. Med. Examiners, 1977—81; cons. Nat. Acad. Scis. Editorial bd. Pharmacol. Revs.; assoc. editor Advances in Molecular Pharmacology; ad hoc editor Am. Heart Jour.; editor Horizons in Clinical Pharmacology, 1976; author abstracts; contbr. over 100 articles to profl. jours. Served with USAR. Mosby scholar, 1957-60; Markle scholar in acad. medicine, 1965-70; recipient Basic Sci. Teaching award U. Miami, 1975-76; Meritorious Service medal Am. Heart Assn., 1972; citation for meritorious Service So. Region Am. Heart Assn., 1979; Visitante Distinguido award, Costa Rica, 1979; Outstanding Tchr. award U. Miami, 1982. Mem. Am. Coll. Clin. Pharmacology, Am. Fedn. Clin. Rsch., Am. Therapeutic Soc. (prize essay award 1970), Am. Soc. Pharmacology and Exptl. Therapeutics (emeritus), N.Y. Acad. Scis., So. Soc. Clin. Investigation, U.S. Pharmacopeia Revision Com., Internat. Study Group Rsch. Cardiac Metabolism, Am. Soc. Internal Medicine, Royal Soc. Health, Key Biscayne Yacht Club (bd. govs. 1994-97, fleet surgeon 1999-2000), Sigma Xi. Died July 15, 2007.

PALMER, SAMUEL COPELAND, III, lawyer; b. Phila., June 9, 1934; s. Samuel Copeland Jr. and Vivian Gertrude (Plumb) P.; divorced; children: Samuel C. IV, Sarah Anne, Bryan Douglas. Grad., Harvard Sch., Los Angeles, 1952; student, Yale U., 1953; AB, Stanford U., 1955; JD, Loyola-Marymount U., Marymount, 1958. Bar: Calif. 1959, U.S. Dist. Ct. (cen., ea. and so. dists. Calif.) 1959, U.S. Ct. Appeals (9th cir.) 1970, U.S. Supreme Ct. 1971. Dep. city atty., Los Angeles, 1959-60; assoc. firm Pollock & Deutz, Los Angeles, 1960-63; ptnr. firm Pollock & Palmer, Los Angeles, 1963-70, Palmer & Bartenetti, Los Angeles, 1970-81, Samuel C. Palmer III, P.C., 1981-85; ptnr. Thomas, & Snell, from 1985. Adj. prof. Calif. State U., Fresno, 1993. Trustee Western Ctr. Law and Poverty; bd. dirs. Big Bros./Big Sisters, Fresno, Arte Ams., Lively Arts Found., Nat. Sleep Found., Vols. in Parole; pres., bd. dirs. Poverello House; founder, pres. Fresno Crime Stoppers. Mem. ABA, State Bar Calif. (disciplinary subcom., bar examiners subcom.), Fresno County Bar Assn. (pres., bd. dirs. 1988-93), Pickwick Soc., Am. Bd. Trial Advocates, Chancery Club, Downtown Club, Calif. Club, Fig Garden Tennis Club, Rotary, Delta Upsilon, Phi Delta Phi. Home: Fresno, Calif. Died Feb. 7, 2007.

PALMER, THOMAS FRANKLIN, banker; b. Oak Harbor, Ohio, Mar. 28, 1925; s. Fred Joseph and Luella Margaret (Stack) Palmer; m. Helen Rose Starmol, June 21, 1947; children: Douglas M., Sandra L., Karla E. Student, U. Toledo; cert. in banking, Ohio U., 1959. Laborer Interlake Iron and Sun Oil, Toledo, 1946; trainee teller Commerce Nat. Bank, Toledo, 1946—52; cashier Nat. Bank Oak Harbor, 1952—63, from v.p. to pres., CEO, 1963—88, pres., chmn. bd., from 1988; also. bd. dirs. Adv. bd. St. Charles Hosp., Toldedo, Ohio, 1962, St. Francis Rehab. Hosp., Green Springs, Ohio, 1980. Mayor Village of Oak Harbor, 1968—76, trustee bd. pub. affairs, 1962—67. 2d lt. USMC, 1943—45, 2d lt. USMC, 1950—51. Mem.: Am. Inst. Banking, Aircraft Owner and Pilots Assn., Rotary (pres. Oak Harbor 1960—61), KC (navigator 1978—79). Democrat. Roman Catholic. Home: Oak Harbor, Ohio. Died Feb. 9, 2007.

PALOUMPIS, ANDREAS ATHANASIOS, retired academic administrator; b. Minonk, Ill., Sept. 30, 1925; s. Athanacious A. and Sophia (Christofilis) P.; m. Bessie Jolas, Sept. 3, 1950; children: Athanacious A. (Tom), Evan, Andrea (dec.). Student, U. Ill., 1946-49; BS, Ill. State U., 1950, MA, 1953; PhD, Iowa State U., 1956. Tchr. sci. Mason City (Ill.) High Sch., 1950-53; prof. zoology and fisheries Ill. State U., Normal, 1956-66; founding pres. Winston Churchill Coll., Pontiac, Ill., 1966-69; v.p. acad. affairs Ill. Cen. Coll., East Peoria, 1969-77; pres. Onondaga Community Coll., Syracuse, N.Y., 1977-83, Hillsborough Community Coll., Tampa, Fla., from 1983. Contbr. articles to profl. jours. Mem. NAACP, Greater Tampa C. of C. (bd. govs. 1987—, coun. high tech. 1986—). Greek Orthodox. Avocation: ichthyology. Home: Tampa, Fla. Died Jan. 31, 2006.

PALUMBO, DENNIS JAMES, political scientist, educator; b. Chgo., Nov. 18, 1929; s. Richard Anthony and Nora (Griffin) P.; m. Sachiko Onishi, Apr. 15, 1954; children: Jean, Dennis, Linda. MA in Social Sci., U. Chgo., 1957, MA in Polit. Sci., 1958, PhD of Polit. Sci., 1960. Asst. prof. Mich. State U., East Lansing, 1960-62; asst. prof. dept. polit. sci., asst. rschr. U. Hawaii, Honolulu, 1962-63; asst. prof. polit. sci. U. Pa., Phila., 1963-66; assoc. prof., prof. polit. sci. CUNY, Bklyn. Coll., 1966-76; prof. Pub. and Environ. Affairs Ind. U., Bloomington, 1976-77; prof. polit. sci., exec. dir. Ctr. for Pub. Affairs U. Kans., Lawrence, 1977-83; prof. pub. affairs, dir. Morrison Inst. for Pub. Policy Ariz. State U., Tempe, 1983-86, prof. justice studies, 1986-88, Regents' prof. justice studies, from 1988; acting dir. Sch. of Justice Studies, Ariz. State U., 1988-89. Guest lectr. U. Ga., 1975, SUNY Stony Brook, 1975, U. Ala., 1976; cons. Ford Found. Evaluation of Minority Support Program, 1974, N.Y.C. Police Dept., 1975, Ctr. for Law and Poverty, Indpls., Hamilton-Pabinowitz, Inc., Pub. Mgmt. Svcs., Okla. Crime Commn., Shawnee County Kans. Comprehensive Plan for Cmty. Corrections, 1978-79; cons. Home Arrest in Ariz. Project Intervention, Gang Resistance Edn. and Tng., Project Care, Shock Incarceration, Cmty. Partnership of Phoenix, EMPOWER Welfare Reform in Ariz., cmty. punishment program in Ariz., injury prevention team Ariz. Dept. Health Svcs., Juvenile Risk Assessment in Ariz.; expert witness various law firms in discrimination cases.; presenter papers in field; panelist profl. meetings; participant workshops. Author: Workbook to Accompany Statistics in Political and Behavioral Science, 1969, Statistics in Political and Behavior Science, 1969, 2d edit., 1977, American Politics, 1973, American Politics Instructor's Manual, 1973, Public Policy In America: Government in Action, 1989, 2d edit., 1994, Workbook to Accompany Statistics in Political and Behavioral Science, 1969, (with J. Levine and M. Musheno) Criminal Justice A Public Policy Approach, 1980, Criminal Justice in America: Law in Action, 1986 (with Steven Maynard-Moody) Contemporary Public Administration, 1991; editor: The Politics of Program Evaluation, 1987, Optimizing, Implementing and Evaluating Public Policy, 1980, (with Mike Harder) Implementing Public Policy, 1981, (with Steve Fawcett and Paula Wright) Optimizing and Evaluating Public Policy, 1981, Implementation: What Have We Learned and Still Need to Know, 1987, (with Donald Calista) Implementation and the Policy Process: Opening up the Black Box, 1990; co-editor: Introduction to Social Sciences, 11 vols., 1962, (with George Taylor) Urban Policy, 1979; contbr. chpts. to books, numerous articles to profl. jours.; author monographs; founding editor, editor-in-chief Policy Studies Review, 1981-87, editor with Michael Musheno, 1987-90. Pres. Ariz. Evaluation Network, 1988-89. Grantee Pub. Health Sys. Rsch. Project, 1965-67, Kans. Dept. Revenue, 1979-81, Nat. Inst. Justice, 1981-83, Nat. Highway Traffic and Safety Adminstrn., 1982-84, Ariz. Dept. Corrections, 1989-90. Mem. APHA (health programs evaluation com. 1971-73), Am. Polit. Sci. Assn., Am. Soc. Criminology, Am. Evaluation Assn., Assn. of Mgmt. in Pub. Health, Evaluation Rsch. Soc. (chai awards com. 1981), N.Y. State Polit. Sci. Assn. Avocations hiking, biking. Home: Tempe, Ariz. Died Nov. 16, 2006.

PALUMBO, JOHN CHRISTOPHER, educator; b. Bklyn. Feb. 23, 1931; s. John Joseph and Lucy Agnes (Ranelli) P B.B.A., St. John's U., N.Y., 1954, M.A., 1966, Ph.D., 1972 postgrad. U.S. Army Lang. Sch., 1956-57; m. Seiko Murakam Aug. 20, 1959; children— Joseph Michael, Matthew Aloysius Robert John. Routeman, N.Y. Times, 1948-52, N.Y. Daily News 1953-55; tchr. N.Y.C. Bd. Edn., 1960—, tchr. 1st Japanese lang program, 1983-84, asst. dir., coordinator acad. programs Asia Inst. St. John's U., 1987—, chaperone N.Y.C.-Tokyo high sch student exchange program, coach baseball Port Richard Hig Sch. Dir. baseball Stapleton Athletic Club, 1969-72; chaperon N.Y.C.-Tokyo high sch. exchange program. Served with U.S Army, 1955-58. Recipient SilverDolphin award Outstandin Adj. Prof., Coll. SI, 2005; NDEA fellow, 1962-63; Fulbright Hays grantee, Japan, 1967, 86. Mem. Asian Soc., Assn. Asia Studies, Am. Assn. Tchrs. Chinese, Japan Soc., Archaeol. Soc Am. Democrat. Roman Catholic. Club: Italian of Staten Islan (dir.). Author: Konoe, Fumimaro's Efforts for Peace, 1937-194 1972. Home: Staten Island, NY. Died Aug. 18, 2006.

PANKEY, GEORGE STEPHEN, dentist; b. Durham, N.C Dec. 3, 1922; s. Edwin Wilburn and Julia (Bender) P.; A.B., U N.C., 1948; D.D.S., Emory U., 1954; m. Christina R. Curry, Ja 17, 1959 (div. Feb. 1967); children: Julia Gay, Crista Merry; m 2d, Diane Joy Flaim, Oct. 14, 1967 (dec. Sept. 3, 1982); adopte children: Laura Jean, Julia Ann, George Stephen; m. Christa N Atwell, June 23, 1988. Practice dentistry, Winter Garden, Fla 1954-58, North Miami Beach, Fla., 1958-59, St. Cloud, Fla 1959—; dir. Fla. United Investment, Inc. Served with U.S Army, 1943-46; ETO. Mem. Am. Dental Assn., Fla. State Dent Soc., Cen. Dist. Dental Soc., V.F.W., St. Cloud C. of C. (pre 1961-62), Sigma Chi. Republican. Episcopalian. Masons (wo shipful master 1965), Shriner, Rotary (pres. 1962-63). Hom Saint Cloud, Fla. Died Feb. 22, 2007.

PANOFSKY, WOLFGANG KURT HERMANN, physicis researcher; b. Berlin, Apr. 24, 1919; arrived in U.S., 193 naturalized, 1942; s. Erwin and Dorothea (Mosse) Panofsky; r Adele DuMond, July 21, 1942; children: Richard, Margare Edward, Carol, Steven. AB, Princeton U., 1938; PhD, Calif. Ins Tech., 1942; DSc (hon.), Case Inst. Tech., 1963, U. Sask., 196 Columbia U., 1977, U. Hamburg, Germany, 1984, Princeton U 1983, Yale U., 1985, U. Beijing, 1987, U. Rome, 1988; degr (hon.), Uppsala U., Sweden, 1991. Mem. staff mem. radiati lab. U. Calif., 1945-51, asst. prof., 1946-48, asso. prof., 194 51; prof. physics Stanford U., 1951-62, prof. Stanford Line Accelerator Ctr., 1962-89, prof. emeritus, 1989—2007; d Stanford (High Energy Physics Lab., Stanford Linear Acceler tor Center), 1962-84, dir. emeritus, 1984—2007. Am. del. Cor Cessation Nuclear Tests, Geneva, 1959; mem. Pres.'s Sci. Ad Com., 1960—64; cons. Office Sci. & Tech., Exec. Office of t Pres., 1965—73, U.S. ACDA, 1968—81; mem. gen. adv. co to White House, 1977—81; mem. panel Office Sci. & Tec Exec. Office of the Pres., 1977; with nat. def. rsch. Calif. In Tech. and Los Alamos, 1942—45; mem. JASON, from 196 chmn. bd. overseers Superconducting Supercollider Uni Rsch. Assn., 1984—93; mem. com. to provide interim oversig US Dept. Energy nuclear weapons complex NAS, 1988— mem. panel on nuclear warhead dismantlement and speci materials control US Dept. Energy, 1991—92; mem. Comr on Particles and Fields Internat. Union Pure and Appli Physics, 1985—93. Decorated officier Legion of Honor; nam Calif. Scientist of Yr., 1966; recipient Lawrence prize, AE 1961, Nat. med. of Sci., 1969, Franklin medal, 1970, Ann. P Svc. award, Fedn. Am. Scientists, 1973, Enrico Fermi awa U.S. Dept. Energy, 1979, Shoong Found. award for sci., 19 Hilliard Roderick prize Sci., AAAS, 1991, Matteucei med 1997. Fellow: Am. Phys. Soc. (pres. 1974); mem.: AAAS, N (mem. com. on internat. security and arms control from 19 chmn. com. 1985—93, mem. scis. com. on scholarly com with China 1987—92), Chinese Acad. Scis. (fgn.), Nat. Ac Lincei (Italy), Russian Acad. Scis., French Acad. Scis. (fg Am. Philos. Soc. (pres. 1974—75), Sigma Xi, Phi Beta Kap Died Sept. 24, 2007.

PARCELL, RAYMOND EUNICE, JR., aerospace compa manager; b. Fredericksburg, Va., Sept. 22, 1930; s. Raymo Eunice and Irene (Smith) P.; B.S. in Elec. Engring., Va. P Inst. and State U., 1951; M.B.A. (Harriman scholar), Colum U., 1958; exec. course UCLA, 1984-85; m. Winifred Patri Slaght, Nov. 8, 1974. With Hughes Aircraft Co., Culver C Calif., 1954-59, program mgr. Japan Hughes Internat., 1959- mgr. Hughes Washington Internat. office, 1962-65, mgr. A vanced Programs for Air Def., Hughes Aero. Systems D 1965-68, mktg. mgr. Roland Program, 1968, spl. projects m Hughes Aerospace Groups, 1974-75, corp. mgr. spl. progra Hughes Aircraft Co., Culver City, 1975—; dir. Perry D. Ed Inc., Los Angeles, Raybilron, Inc., Staunton Va. Served w U.S. Army, 1951-53; to col. Res. Tau Beta Pi, Pi Delta Epsil Eta Kappa Nu, Alpha Kappa Psi. Methodist. Clubs: Calif. Ya Interstellar, Icarian Flying, Masons. Home: Redondo Bea Calif. Died May 21, 2006.

PARCELLS, CHARLES ABRAM, JR., investment comp executive; b. Grosse Pointe, Mich., Feb. 17, 1920; s. Cha Abram Parcells and Carolyn (Hubbard) Lucas; m. Fran Heartt Hamilton, Feb. 14, 1948; children— Charles A. Frances A., Elizabeth H., Frederick L., Kathryn H., David B.A. in Math., Yale U., 1940; M.B.A., U. Mich., 1948. P Charles A. Parcells & Co., Detroit, 1953—. Pres. William L Phelps Found., Detroit, 1948—. Mem. Fin. Analysts S Republican. Clubs: Detroit, Country of Detroit, Econ. of Detr Home: Grosse Pointe, Mich. Died Apr. 14, 2006.

PARFET, RAY THEODORE, JR., retired pharmaceuti executive; b. Port Huron, Mich., Nov. 25, 1922; m. Ma Gilmore; children: William, Donald, Sally, Jane. Dir. Upj Co., Kalamazoo, from 1958, v.p., 1958-59, exec. v.p. cha research, legal, fin. and personnel activities, 1960-62, pres., mgr., 1962-69, chmn., CEO, 1969—87. Bd. dirs., Upjohn

1969-94, First Nat. Bank & Trust Co., Gilmore Bros. Dept. Store, Mich. Bell Telephone Co., Union Pump Co., Battle Creek, Aro Corp., Bryan, Ohio, First Am. Bank Corp, ARC.; owner Kalamazoo Wings, Internat. Hockey League, 1974-2000 Trustee Bronson Methodist Hosp. Served in Army Air Corps, World War II. Decorated Air medal with 11 clusters, Disting. Flying Cross. Mem. Pharm. Mfrs. Assn. (past dir., past chmn., past dir. internat. fedn.) Home: Hickory Corners, Mich. Died Nov. 27, 2006.

PARKER, BRANT JULIAN, cartoonist; b. Los Angeles, Aug. 26, 1920; s. Theodore Gulbrantson and Rachael (Deats) P.; m. Mary Louise Sweet; children: James Brant, Julie Anne, Laurie Ellen, Kathie Jean, Jeffrey Theodore. Student, Otis Art Inst., Los Angeles, 1939-42. Advt. art dir. IBM Corp., Washington, 1954-64. Artist, Walt Disney Prodns., 1945-47, editorial cartoonist, Binghamton Press; cartoonist: nat. syndicated comic strips Wizard of Id, 1964—97, Crock, 1975—97, Goosemyer, 1980—97; Author: 13 Wizard of Id books. Lectr., tchr. Youth Program, Lorton Penitentiary.; Bd. dirs. No Greater Love, Am. Kidney Fund. Served with USNR, 1943-45; Served with USN, 1950-54, PTO. Recipient: Distinctive Merit award for advt. dir. 16th Ann. Exhbn., Washington, 1963, Nat. Cartoonist Soc. Humor Comic Strip award, 1971, 1976, 1980, 1982-83, Yellow Kid award Internationale 8th Ann., Luca, Italy, 1972, Reuben award, 1984, Elzie Segar award, 1986 Mem. Nat. Cartoonist Soc., Comics Council, Smithsonian Assos. Clubs: Nat. Press. Died Apr. 15, 2007.

PARKER, GEORGE EARL, lawyer; b. Laurel, Miss., Sept. 12, 1937; s. George Edward and Ruth Lee (Gardner) P.; m. Ruth Nora Holloway, Oct. 23, 1965 (div. 1986); children: Marshall Lee, Allison Victoria, Jonathan Wesley; m. Mojan Jenab, Nov. 26, 1988 BBA, U. Miss., 1960, LL.B., 1962; postgrad., N.Y. U. Grad. Sch. Law, 1969-70. Bar: Miss. 1962. Mem. firm Satterfield, Shell, Williams and Buford, Jackson, Miss., 1966-67; counsel, asst. sec. Schick Electric, Inc., Lancaster, Pa., 1967-68; atty., asst. sec. Manville Corp., Denver, 1969-71, counsel, asst. v.p., 1971-73, v.p., corp. counsel, 1973-76, v.p., gen. counsel, sec., 1976-80, sr. v.p. law and public affairs, sec., 1980-86, v.p., 1986-89; ptnr. Geduldij & Parker, NYC, from 1989. Trustee Denver Symphony Assn. Served with JAGC AUS, 1963-66. Mem. Miss., N.Y. State, Colo., D.C. bar assns., Assn. Corp. Secs., Omicron Delta Kappa, Sigma Nu. Clubs: Denver Country. Republican. Episcopalian. Home: Denver, Colo. Died Mar. 10, 2007.

PARKER, JOHN CLARENCE, biological research consultant; b. Washington, Sept. 13, 1935; s. Marion W. and Katherine L. (Hagan) P.; m. Mary Ann Baker, 1957 (div. 1973); children: John C., Robert C.; m. Norma L. Justmann, 1975; 1 child, Jennifer L. BS in Zoology, U. Md., 1957, MS in Parasitology, 1961, PhD, 1965. With Microbiol. Assocs. Inc.; project dir. Bethesda, Md., 1961-78; dir. clin. diagnostic lab. Microbiol. Assocs. Inc., Bethesda, Md., 1973-85, v.p. ops., Walkersville, Md., 1976-79, pres., chief exec. officer, Bethesda, 1979-87, vice chmn. bd. dirs., 1987-89; biol. rsch. cons., nature photographer William S. Miller, Inc., tech. mgmt. cons., 1988-90; vol. U.S. Fish and Wildlife Svc., U.S. Forest Svc., 2989-92. Bd. dirs. Cabinet Resource Group; cons. Charles River Farms, Wilmington, Mass., 1965-70, Inst. Cancer Rsch., Phila., 1970-79, WHO, 1977-79. Contbr. articles to profl. jours. Trustee Shady Grove Adventist Hosp. Found., Rockville, Md., 1986. Mem. Am. Soc. for Adv. Sci., Am. Assn. Immunologists, Am. Assn. Lab. Animal Sci. (assoc. editor jour. 1976-87, Charles A. Griffin award 1979), Am. Soc. Microbiology, Pan-Am. Group Rapid Viral Diagnosis, Fedn. Am. Soc. Exptl. Biology and Medicine, Tissue Culture Assn. Republican. Avocations: photography, environmental sciences, hiking, scuba diving. Died Nov. 18, 2005.

PARKER, PATRICIA ANN, guidance counselor; b. Atlanta, Feb. 6, 1943; d. Willie Lee and Ella M. (Branch) P. B.A., Glassboro State Coll., 1965, M.A. in Student Personnel, 1976, M.A. in Pub. Sch. Adminstrn., 1985. Elem. tchr., Hammonton, N.J., 1965-78; elem. counselor Magnolia Sch. Dist., N.J., 1978-83; jr. high sch. counselor Lower Camden County Regional High Dist. 1, Atco, N.J., 1983-85, dir. pupil personnel services Kingsway Regional High Sch., 1985—, chair Intro to Vocations Adv. Council, 1984—; mem. Winslow Twp. Desegregation Commn., 1984—. Mem. Community Mothers, Atco, 1984. Recipient Outstanding Citizen award Community Mothers, 1983; Citizens award N.J. Assn. Colored Women's Clubs, 1983. Mem. NAACP, Am. Assn. Counseling and Dvel., NEA, N.J. Edn. Assn., Camden County Edn. Assn. Democrat. Baptist. Home: Sicklerville, NJ. Died Oct. 8, 2006.

PARKER, R(ICHARD) MICHAEL, lawyer; b. Indpls., Jan. 6, 1945; s. Chauncey Charles and Martha Ellen (Huff) P.; m. Carole Lynne Rutledge (div. Jan. 1987); 1 child, Catherine Ellen; m. Marcia Rose Haas, Feb. 6, 1988. BA, Wabash Coll., 1967; JD, So. Meth. U., 1970. Bar: Ind. 1970, U.S. Dist. Ct. (no. dist.) Ind. 1974, U.S. Dist. Ct. (no. dist.) Calif. 1986, U.S. Ct. Appeals (7th cir.) 1981, U.S. Supreme Ct. 1980. Ptnr. Barnes & Thornburg, Elkhart, Ind. Editor Jour. Air Law and Commerce, 1969-70. Fellow Ind. Bar Found.; mem. ABA, Ind. Bar Assn., Elkhart Bar Assn. (trustee Scholarship Found. 1974--), 7th Cir. Bar Assn., Ind. Trial Lawyers Assn., Elkart C. of C. (com. chmn.), Elcona Country Club (counsel 1987--). Republican. Avocations: skiing, golf. Home: Elkhart, Ind. Died Mar. 21, 2006.

PARKES, KENNETH CARROLL, ornithologist; b. Hackensack, NJ, Aug. 8, 1922; s. Walter Carroll and Lillian Carolyn (Capelle) P.; m. Ellen Pierce Stone, Sept. 6, 1953. BS, Cornell U., 1943, MS, 1948, PhD, 1952. Curator birds Cornell U., 1947-52; mem. staff Carnegie Mus. of Natural History, Pitts., from 1953; curator birds Carnegie Mus., 1962-86, chief curator life scis., 1975-85, sr. curator birds, 1986-96, curator emeritus birds, from 1997; research fellow epidemiology and microbiology U. Pitts., 1956, vis. lectr. Pymatuning Field Lab., 1957, adj. mem. grad. faculty, from 1963; mem. adminstrv. bd. Lab. Ornithology, Cornell U., 1962-68, 70-75; bd. trustees Del. Mus. Natural History, 1976-90. Taxonomic editor: Avian Biology, 1971-75; co-editor, 1977-93; cons. on bird art to artists, pubs.; contbr. articles to profl. jours., encys. Judge bird carving competition Ward Found., 1979-90, resident ornithologist, 1991—. Served with AUS, 1943-46. Fellow Am. Ornithologists Union (2d v.p. 1975-76); mem. Audubon Soc. Western Pa. (trustee 1982-91, 98—), Wilson Ornithol. Soc. (pres. 1973-75), numerous other profl. socs. Democrat. Unitarian Universalist. Died July 16, 2007.

PARMALEE, PAUL WOODBURN, museum director, educator; b. Mansfield, Ohio, Oct. 17, 1926; s. Max Woodburn and Marion Isabel (Fox) P.; m. Barbara J. Griswold, Aug. 28, 1949; children: John David, Patrice Ellen. BS, Ohio U., Athens, 1948; MS, U. Ill., Urbana, 1949; PhD, Tex. A&M U., 1952. Asst. prof. biology Stephen F. Austin State U., Nacogdoches, Tex., 1952-53; curator zoology, asst. museum dir. Ill. State Mus., Springfield, 1953-73; prof. zooarchaeology, dir. McClung Mus. U. Tenn., Knoxville, from 1973. Author: (with others) Decoys and Decoy Carvers of Illinois, 1969; contbr. articles to profl. jours. Served with AUS, 1944-46. Grantee NSF, Ill. State Mus. Soc. Mem. Am. Soc. Mammalogists, Am. Ornithologists Union, Wilson Ornithol. Soc., Am. Quarternary Assn., Soc. Am. Archaeology, Soc. Vertebrate Paleontology, Am. Malacological Union, Tenn. Acad. Sci., Sigma Xi. Home: Knoxville, Tenn. Died July 4, 2006.

PARNES, HERBERT SAUL, industrial relations specialist; b. Pitts., Apr. 4, 1919; s. Joseph and Bess (Treelisky) P.; A.B., U. Pitts., 1939, M.A., 1941; Ph.D., Ohio State U., 1950; m. Atha R. Brackemyre, Sept. 20, 1944; children— Jane, Marc L., Gail E. Jones. Instr. econs. U. Pitts., 1946-47; from instr. to prof. econs. Ohio State U., Columbus, 1947-80, chmn. faculty labor and human resources, 1975-80; prof. indsl. relations and human resources Rutgers U., New Brunswick, N.J., 1980-83; cons. OECD, Paris, 1961-62. Chmn., Ohio State Adv. Council Employment Security, 1971-76. Served with field arty. USAAF, 1942-46. Mem. Am. Econ. Assn., Indsl. Relations Research Assn., Phi Beta Kappa. Author: Research on Labor Mobility, 1954; Union Strike Votes, 1956; Forecasting Educational Needs for Economic and Social Development, 1962; (with others) Work and Retirement, 1981; Peoplepower: Elements of Human Resource Policy, 1984; (with others) Retirement Among American Men, 1985. Home: South Harwich, Mass. Died Aug. 5, 2006.

PARRY, ROBERT WALTER, chemistry professor; b. Ogden, Utah, Oct. 1, 1917; s. Walter and Jeanette (Petterson) P.; m. Marjorie J. Nelson, July 6, 1945; children: Robert Bryce, Mark Nelson. BS, Utah State Agr. Coll., 1940; MS, Cornell U., 1942; PhD, U. Ill., 1946; DSc (hon.), Utah State U., 1985, U. Utah, 1997. Rsch. asst. NDRC Munitions Devel. Lab. U. Ill., Urbana, 1943-45, tchg. fellow, 1945-46; mem. faculty U. Mich., Ann Arbor, 1946-69, prof. chemistry, 1958-69; Disting. prof. chemistry U. Utah, Salt Lake City, 1969-97, prof. emeritus, from 1997. Chmn. bd. trustees Gordon Rsch. Conf., 1967-68; cons. in field. Founding editor Inorganic Chemistry, 1960-63. Recipient Mfg. Chemists award for coll. tchg., 1972, Sr. U.S. Scientist award Alexander Von Humboldt-Stiftung, West Germany, 1980, First Govs. medal of Sci., State Utah, 1987. Mem. AAAS (chmn. chemistry sect. 1983), Internat. Union Pure and Applied Chemistry (chmn. U.S. nat. com., chmn. com. tchg. chemistry 1968-74), Am. Chem. Soc. (bd. editors jour. 1969-80, dir. 1973-83, pres.-elect 1981, pres. 1982, Disting. Svc. to Inorganic Chemistry award 1965, Disting. Svc. to Chem. Edn. award 1977, Utah award Utah sect. 1978, Priestly medal 1993), Sigma Xi. Achievements include research in structural problems of inorganic chemistry and incorporation results into theoretical models, chemistry of phosphorus, boron and fluorine. Home: Salt Lake City, Utah. Died Dec. 1, 2006.

PARSONS, BENNY, auto racing commentator, retired professional race car driver; b. North Wilkesboro, NC, July 12, 1941; m. Teri Parsons; children: Kevin, Keith. Auto racer NASCAR cir., 1963-88; NASCAR commentator ESPN, 1989-2000, NBC/WTBS, 2001—07. Analyst Winston Cup Race, Busch Grand Nat. Race. Winner: Automobile Racing Club titles, 1968-69, Daytona 500, 1975, NASCAR series championship (Winston Cup), 1973, Daytona 500, 1975, World 600, 1980; recipient Cable ACE award for best sports analyst, 1989; named one of NASCAR's 50 greatest drivers, 1998; inducted into Internat. Motorsports Hall of Fame, 1994, Nat. Motorsports Assn. Stock Car Racing Hall of Fame, 1995 Home: Port Orange, Fla. Died Jan. 16, 2007.

PARSONS, HARRY GLENWOOD, retired surgeon; b. San Bernardino, Calif., Mar. 5, 1919; s. Harry Glenwood and Evelen May (Peris) P.; m. Rubyann Kattenhorn, Sept. 28, 1986. AB, Stanford U., Calif., 1942, MD, 1946. Diplomate Am. Bd. Surgery, Am. Bd. Thoracic Cardio-Vascular Surgery. Intern Stanford Hosp., San Francisco, 1941-42, Rockor fellow in surg. rsch., 1944-45, asst. resident in surgery, 1945-52, chief resident in surgery, 1952-53, Boyd fellow in thoracic cardiovasc. surgery, 1953-54; asst. clin. prof. surgery Stanford Med. Sch., 1955-65; med. dir., faculty head Weimar (Calif.) Med. Ctr., 1955-72; ret. Capt. M.C. U.S. Army, 1940-44. Fellow ACS; mem. AMA, Western Thoracic Surg. Soc., Placer Nevada County Med. Assn. (pres. 1979), Calif. Med. Assn. (del.), Alpha Omega Alpha. Avocation: flying. Home: Weimar, Calif. Died Jan. 10, 2007.

PARSONS, JOHN THOREN, manufacturing executive; b. Detroit, Oct. 13, 1913; s. Carl Berger and Edith Charlotte (Thorén) Parson; m. Elizabeth Mae Shaw, Apr. 20, 1940; children: Carl A, John T. II, Robert S., Grant W., David C., Meredith W. Student, Wayne U., 1934; D of Engring. (hon.), U. Mich., 1988; LLD (hon.), Lake Superior State U., 1997. With Parsons Corp., Detroit & Traverse City, Mich., 1928-68, owner Traverse City, Mich., 1954-68, pres., 1956-68, Parsons Co., France, 1959-68; pres., owner The John T. Parsons Corp., Traverse City, Mich., from 1968. Invited lectr., Japan, Germany, Brazil. Recipient Nat. Medal of Tech., U.S. Dept. Commerce, 1985, Jules Marie Jacquard award, AIM Tech., 1968, Disting. Service award, Nat. Tooling and Machining Assn., Citation Soc. Am. Value Engrs., inductee Inventors Hall of Fame, 1993. Fellow: Soc. Mfg. Engrs. (charter, internat. dir. 1992—93, citation 1975); mem.: Detroit Athletic Club. Democrat. Lutheran. Achievements include invention of products and mfg. processes. Avocations: music, reading. Home: Traverse City, Mich. Died Apr. 19, 2007.

PARSONS, JUDSON ASPINWALL, JR., lawyer; b. Rochester, NY, Dec. 15, 1929; s. Judson A. and Frances (Holsopple) P.; m. Chesley Kahmann, Aug. 8, 1959; children: Ames, Brockett. BA, Amherst Coll., 1951; LLB, Harvard U., 1954. Bar: N.Y. 1954, N.J. 1973. Asst. U.S. atty. So. Dist. N.Y., NYC, 1954-55; assoc. Dewey, Ballantine, Bushby, Palmer & Wood, NYC, 1958-65, ptnr., 1966-82; pres. Orbiting Clef Prodns., Inc., Summit, NJ, 1982-86; spl. counsel Laughlin, Markensohn, Lagani & Pegg, P.C., Morristown, NJ, 1986-90, Parsons & Pegg, Morristown, 1990-91; sole practice, 1991—2004; ret., 2005. Served to 1st lt. U.S. Army, 1955-58. Home: Summit, NJ. Died July 18, 2006.

PARSONS, ROBERT EUGENE, transportation consultant; b. Cin., Apr. 19, 1931; s. Charles Eugene and Samantha Ellen (Snider) P.; m. Beverly Greenhalgh, Dec. 30, 1949; children: Brian Scott, Barry Lawrence, Robert Stephen, Kimberly Ann. ME, U. Cinn., 1954; MSME, Drexel Inst. Tech., 1959. Registered profl. engr., Calif., Nev., Md., Ohio. Asst. project engr. The Martin Co., Balt., 1956-62, sect. mgr., 1962-64; dep. dir. Supersonic Transp. Office FAA, Washington, 1964-71; dir. rsch. and devel. plans U.S. Dept. Transp., Washington, 1971; assoc. adminstr. Fed. RR Adminstrn., Washington, 1975-80; dir. ctr. field methods Nat. Bur. Standards, Gaithersburg, Md., 1980-81; dir. RR rsch. and devel. program U. Calif., Berkeley, 1981-84; cons. Walnut Creek, Calif., 1986-90; dir. program on advanced technology for hwy. U. Calif. Berkeley, 1984-93; prin. Parsons Transp. Assocs., Midlothian, Va., from 1993. Cons. Assn. Am. R.R.s, Washington, U. Calif., Calif. Dept. Transp., U.S. Dept. Transp., DKS Assocs., Radar Control Sys., Rand, Sys. Control Tech., Intelligent Vehicle Hwy. Soc. Techs., Inc., Lawrence Livermore Nat. Lab., French Inst. Transp. Safety, Intelligent Transp. Soc. Am., chmn. sys. arch. com.; cons. IMRA Am., Inc. JKH & Assocs., Sci. Atlanta, Va. Tech., Va. Dept. Transp., Viggon Corp.; mem. rsch. adv. bd. Nat. ITS Implementation Rsch Ctr. Contbr. articles to profl. jours. Mem. SAE, Intelligent Transp. Soc. Am. (chair interoperability subcom.), Intelligent Transp. Sys. of Va. (bd. dirs., futures group), ITS World (editorial bd.). Methodist. Avocations: computer work, woodworking. Home: Midlothian, Va. Died Oct. 26, 2005.

PARTEE, JOHN CHARLES, economist; b. Defiance, Ohio, Oct. 21, 1927; s. Lauren W. and Florence (Paxton) P.; m. Gail Voegelin, June 17, 1946; children— Eric Douglas, Sharon Brooke, Pamela Erminie BS, Ind. U., 1948, MBA, 1949; postgrad., U. Chgo., 1952-53. Economist Fed. Res. Bank Chgo., 1949-56; assoc. economist, 2d v.p. No. Trust Co., Chgo., 1956-61; with Fed. Res. Bd., Washington, from 1962, adviser, from 1964, dir. research, 1969-73, mng. dir. for research and econ. policy, 1973-75, mem. bd. from Va., 1976-86. Dir. Neighborhood Reinvestment Corp.; chmn. Fed. Fin. Instn. Exam. Council Ind. U. Alumni fellow, 1977. Mem. Conf. Bus. Economists, Beta Gamma Sigma Home: Great Falls, Va. Died Feb. 15, 2007.

PASCHALL, LEE MCQUERTER, retired communications executive; b. Sterling, Colo., Jan. 21, 1922; s. Lee McQuerter and Agnes (Woldridge) P.; m. Bonnie Jean Edwards, Oct. 24, 1942; children: Patricia Ann Grillos, Stephen Lee, David Edward. BA, U. Ala., 1957; MA, George Washington U., 1964. Served with U.S. Army, 1940-46; communications engr. Colo. Air N.G., Denver, 1946-51; commd. maj. U.S. Air Force, 1951, advanced through grades to lt. gen., 1974, ret., 1978; ind. cons. Springfield, Va., 1978-81; pres., chief exec. officer Am. Satellite Co., Rockville, Md., 1981-84, chmn., 1984-85. Dir. Gen. Data Comm. Industries. Contbr. numerous articles to profl. publs. Mem. com. rev. nat. communications system initiatives NRC, 1982-88. Decorated Legion of Merit with oak leaf cluster; decorated disting. service medals; recipient Eascon IEEE, 1979 Mem. Armed Forces Comms.-Electronics Assn. (chpt. pres., nat. bd. dirs. Disting. Svc.), Air Force Assn., Phi Beta Kappa. Mem. Christian Ch. (Disciples Of Christ). Died Dec. 17, 2006.

PASCOE, DONALD MONTE, lawyer; b. Jan. 4, 1935; s. Donald Leslie and Marjorie Lucille (Powers) Pascoe; m. Patricia Hill, Aug. 3, 1957; children: Sarah Lynn, Edward Llewellyn, William Arthur. AB, Dartmouth Coll., 1957; LLB, Stanford U., 1960. Bar: Colo. 1960, Calif. 1961. From assoc. to ptnr. Ireland, Stapleton, Pryor & Pascoe, P.C., Denver, 1960—2006. Exec. dir. Colo. Dept. of Natural Resources, Denver, 1980—83; bd. dirs. G.G. Shaw, Inc. Trustee Webb-Waring Lung Inst., Denver, 1985—91, pres.; commr. Denver Water Bd., 1983—95, pres., 1986—89; chmn. Moffat Tunnel Commn., 1996—98; mem. Rocky Mountain Regional Ctr. Inst. Internat. Edn., 1995—2006, trustee, 1998—2001, Legal Aid Found. Colo., 2003—06, Colo. Sch. Mines, Golden, 1979—81, Iliff Sch. Theology, 2002—05, pres., 2005—06. Mem.: ABA, Am. Judicature Soc., Calif. Bar Assn., Colo. Bar Assn., Cactus Club, Law Club Denver, Rotary. Home: Denver, Colo. Died Mar. 2, 2006.

PATE, FINDLAY MOYE, agriculture educator, university center director; b. Davisboro, Ga., Jan. 24, 1941; s. William Wayne and Valeria Moye P.; m. Vicky Lee Scruggs, Jan. 15, 1961; children: Julie, Celia, Joel, Craig. Student, Abraham Baldwin Agr., Tifton, Ga., 1961-63; BS, U. Ga., 1965, PhD, 1970; MS, Oreg. State U., 1967. From asst. to assoc. prof. Everglades rsch. ctr. U. Fla., Belle Glade, 1970-83, prof., dir. Ona rsch. ctr. Ona, from 1983. Methodist. Achievements include development of a feeding system of adding natural protein to a liquid molasses feed for cattle. Died Mar. 21, 2006.

PATRICK, CARL LLOYD, theatre executive; b. Honaker, Va., Dec. 6, 1918; s. Deward and Virginia Mae (McGraw) P.; m. Frances Estelle Wynn, Feb. 14, 1943; children: Carl Lloyd Jr., Michael Wynn. Gen. mgr. Martin Theatres, Columbus, Ga., 1945-69, pres., 1969-70, Fuqua Industries, Inc., Atlanta, 1970-78, vice chmn., 1978-82; chmn. Carmike Cinemas, Inc., Columbus, from 1982. Bd. dirs. Columbus Bank & Trust Co. Trustee Columbus Mus., 1983—, Ga. Southwestern Coll., Americus,

1984—, Columbus Coll., 1985—; bd. dirs. Columbus Tech. Inst., 1988—. Maj. U.S. Army, 1941-45. Mem. Nat. Assn. Theatre Owners (Sherrill Corwin award 1984, Hassanein Humanitarian award 1986, Exhibitor of the Decade award 1990). Methodist. Avocation: golf. Home: Columbus, Ga. Died July 4, 2007.

PATTE, CHRISTIAN, army officer; b. Geneva, Oct. 25, 1935; came to U.S., 1944, naturalized, 1950; s. Edouard Jean and Aymee Henriette (Patry) P.; m. Rebecca Wilson Price, Dec. 16, 1961; children: Amy, Edward, Christian. BS, Presbyn. Coll., 1956, H.H.D. (hon.), 1982; MS, U. Ala., 1961. Commd. 2d lt. U.S. Army, 1956, advanced through grades to maj. gen., 1986, dir. Logistics & Security Assistance USCENTCOM, from 1986. Decorated Def. Superior Svc. medal, Legion of Merit, French Nat. Order of Merit. Mem. Alpha Sigma Phi. Episcopalian. Home: Tampa, Fla. Died Oct. 14, 2005.

PATTEN, CHARLES ANTHONY, management consultant, retired manufacturing company executive, writer, publisher; b. Allentown, Pa., May 12, 1920; s. Charles Henerie and Mae (Doyle) P.; m. Kathleen Marie Breene, Jan. 6, 1951 (dec. 1999); children: Charles Anthony Jr., Amy Elizabeth Goddard, Nancy Kathleen Hansen. BSM.E., Lehigh U., 1942. With Joy Mfg. Co., 1947-63, works mgr., 1956-63; v.p. mfg. White Motor Corp., 1963-68, Colt Industries, 1968-69; With Dravo Corp., Pitts., 1942-47, 69-85, gen. mgr. engring. works div., 1970-71, corp. v.p., gen. mgr. engring. works div., 1971-75, corp. group v.p., chief exec. officer Dravo Mfg. Group, 1975-81, corp. sr. v.p., mem. corp. policy com., chief exec. officer Dravo Mfg. Group, 1981-83, corp. sr. v.p., asst. to pres. and chief exec. officer, mem. exec. com., 1984-85; pres. C.A. Patten Enterprises, from 1985. Bd. dirs., v.p. Dravo (Can.) Ltd., 1975-85; dir., pres. Dravo-Okura Co. Ltd., 1974-79; dir. Dravo Mfg. (Can.) Ltd., 1975-83, Tru Weld Grating Inc., 1983-85; v.p. Dravo Internat., Inc., 1974-85; adv. com. Nat. Mgmt. Assn., 1973-85; chief devel. officer Western Pa. Model RR. Mus., 2001-, corp. mem., Am. Mgmt. Assn., 1954-85 Seminar spkr. in field, contbr. publs. Trustee Ohio Valley Gen. Hosp., McKees Rocks, Pa., 1975-82, Marietta (Ohio) Coll., 1979-89, emeritus trustee, 1989—; bd. dirs. Vocat. Rehab. Ctr. of Allegheny County, 1972-79, Jr. Achievement of S.W. Pa., 1975-80, Sherwood Oaks Residents Assn., 2003—. Recipient Silver Knight of Mgmt. award Nat. Mgmt. Assn., 1976. Mem. ASME, Neville Island Mfrs. Assn. (pres. 1975-85), Am. Arbitration Assn. (panel of arbitrators, 1989-95), Shipyard Steering Com. of Am. Waterways Operators, Inland Waterways Am. Bur. of Ships. Republican. Roman Catholic. Died Aug. 22, 2007.

PATTERSON, CECIL HOLDEN, educator, writer; b. Lynn, Mass., June 22, 1912; s. Cecil Edwin and Emma Mabel (Banks) P.; m. Frances L. Spano, July 4, 1942; children— Joseph, Francine, Jenifer, Christopher, Thomas, Charles, Mary. A.B., U. Chgo., 1938; M.A., U. Minn., 1945, Ph.D., 1955. Research asst. Fels Research Inst., Yellow Springs, Ohio, 1939-41; psychol. asst. USAAF, San Antonio, 1942-45; clin. psychologist U.S. Army, Philippines, 1945-46; counseling psychologist U.S. VA, St. Paul, 1946-55; prof. ednl. psychology U. Ill., Urbana, 1955-77; adj. disting. prof. U. N.C.-Greensboro, 1984—. Author: Counseling and Psychotherapy, 1959; Theories of Counseling and Psychotherapy, 4th edit. 1986; The Therapeutic Relationship, 1985, others. Served with U.S. Army, 1942-46. Fulbright Hays sr. lectr., 1972-73, 76-77. Fellow Am. Psychol. Assn. (past pres. div. counseling psychology). Home: Asheville, NC. Died May 26, 2006.

PATTERSON, DONIS DEAN, bishop; b. Holmesville, Ohio, Apr. 27, 1930; s. Raymond J. and Louella Faye (Glasgo) P.; m. JoAnne Nida, Dec. 22, 1951; children: Christoper Nida, Andrew Joseph. BS, Ohio State U., 1952; STB, Episcopal Theol. Sch., 1957; M Div, Episcopal Divinity Sch., 1972; DD (hon.), Nashotah House Sem., 1984, U. of South, 1986. Rector St. Andrews Ch., Washington Court House, Ohio, 1957-63, St. Marks Ch., Venice, Fla., 1963-70, All Sts. Ch., Winter Park, Fla., 1970-83; bishop Episcopal Diocese Dallas, 1983-92; asst. bishop Episcopal Diocese of Ctrl. Gulf Coast, 1992-96; assisting bishop Cathedral Ch. of St. Luke, Orlando, Fla., from 1996. Trustee Seabury Western Theol. Sem., Evanston, Ill., 1981-82, U. of South, 1983-92, Episcopal Theol. Sem. S.W., 1983-92. Chmn. Episcopal Ch. House of Bishops Armed Forces Com., 1989-93. Col. AUS, 1952-54, Korea, ret., 1990; col. USAR, 1954-90. Home: Winter Park, Fla. Died Feb. 3, 2006.

PATTERSON, GILBERT EARL, bishop; b. Humboldt, Tenn., Sept. 22, 1939; s. W. A. and Mary Patterson; m. Louise Patterson. Studied at, Detroit Bible Inst., LeMoyne Owen Coll.; ThD (hon.), Oral Roberts U. Ordained elder Ch. of God, 1958. Co-pastor Holy Temple Ch. of God in Christ, Memphis, 1962; founder, pastor Temple of Deliverance, Cathedral of the Bountiful Blessings, Memphis, 1975—2007; presiding bishop Church Of God In Christ, Inc. Pres. Charles H. Mason Bible Coll. of Tenn. Fourth Jurisdiction, Memphis. Author: Here Comes The Judge, 2002; pub. Bountiful Blessings Mag., contbg. writer Spirit Filled Life Bible. Named one of Most Influential Black Americans, Ebony mag., 2006. Died Mar. 20, 2007.

PATTERSON, RICHARD R., state senator, social services administrator; b. Miller, S.D., July 9, 1925; student Roger Williams Coll., R.I. Coll. m. Evelyn B. McKenna (dec. July 11, 1985). Past profl. baseball player Cleve. Indians and farm system; former lt. Providence Police Dept., 1968; exec. dir. Retardation Center; mem. R.I. State Senate, 1978—, pres. pro tem, 1982, vice chmn. HEW com., mem. fin. com., chmn. labor com., chmn. permanent adv. com. early intervention. Mem. Warwick Mayors Adv. Commn. on Handicapped. Served with USN, World War II. Mem. Am. Legion, Ret. Providence Police and Fire Assn. (sec.). Democrat. Clubs: Warwick Rotary; KC (Cranston Council). Home: N Providence, RI. Died May 30, 2007.

PATTERSON, WILLIAM ROBERT, retired lawyer; b. Wathena, Kans., Feb. 25, 1924; s. George Richard and Jessie (Broadbent) P.; m. Lee Rhyne, Aug. 16, 1947; children: Martha, Robert, Elizabeth. Student, U. Rochester, 1943-44; AB, Lenoir-Rhyne Coll., 1947; LL.B. with distinction, Duke U., 1950. Bar: Ga. 1951, D.C. 1962. Asso. firm Sutherland, Asbill & Brennan, Atlanta, 1950-58, partner, from 1958; trustee Ga. Tax Conf., 1980-83, pres., 1980-82. Lectr. in field. Mem. bd. visitors Duke U. Law Sch., 1973-87, chmn., 1977-87, life mem., 1987—; trustee Pace Acad., Atlanta, 1958-89, trustee emeritus, 1989—; mem. devel. bd. Lenoir-Rhyne Coll., 1976-79, trustee, 1980-89; elder Trinity Presbyterian Ch., Atlanta. With USN, 1942-46. Fellow Am. Coll. Mortgage Attys. (bd. regents 1993-99, pres. 1997-98); mem. ABA, Ga. State Bar, Atlanta Bar Assn., D.C. Bar Assn., Am. Coll. Real Estate Lawyers (bd. govs. 1987-90), Am. Law Inst., So. Fed. Tax Inst. (trustee 1957-90, adv. trustee 1990—, pres. 1974-75, chmn. 1975-76), Atlanta Tax Forum (trustee 1977-83, pres. 1981-82), Order of Coif, Cherokee Town and Country Club, Commerce Club, Peachtree Club. Home: Atlanta, Ga. Died Mar. 2, 2007.

PATZKE, RICHARD JOSEPH, energy company executive; b. Chgo., July 20, 1941; s. Robert Kirk and Mary Catherine (Foran) P.; m. Kathleen Gallagher, Aug. 10, 1968; children— Ann, Susan, Michael, Kerry, Eileen BA, St. John's U., 1963; MBA, U. Chgo., 1965. CPA, Ill. Mgr. Arthur Andersen & Co., Chgo., 1965-78; exec. v.p., also bd. dirs. Energen Corp., Birmingham, Ala., 1978-92; pres. Red Mountain Enterprises, Birmingham, from 1992. Bd. dirs. ARC, Birmingham, 1979-92. Mem. Fin. Execs. Inst. (pres. Birmingham chpt. 1985), AICPA, Vestavia Country Club. Roman Catholic. Home: Birmingham, Ala. Died Dec. 16, 2006.

PAUERSTEIN, CARL JOSEPH, obstetrician-gynecologist, educator; b. NYC, May 31, 1932; s. Philip and Carolyn (Meyers) P.; m. Marie Louise Rottet, May 11, 1955; children: Jonathan David, Michael Ira, Joshua Daniel. BA magna cum laude, Lehigh U., 1954; MD, Hahnemann Med. Coll., 1958. Diplomate Am. Bd. Ob-Gyn. Resident in ob-gyn Kings County Hosp., NYC, 1959-63; fellow gynecol. pathology Johns Hopkins Sch. Medicine, Balt., 1965-68, asst. prof. ob-gyn, 1966-68; assoc. prof. to prof. ob-gyn U. Tex. Health Scis. Ctr., San Antonio, 1968-79, prof. physiology, 1974-79, prof., chmn. ob-gyn, from 1979, chief ob-gyn, from 1979. Cons. WHO, Geneva, 1976-79, FDA, 1983-86; chmn. Population Rsch. Com., NIH, 1977-80. Author 2 textbooks, 148 published articles; editor 6 textbooks. Capt. USAF, 1963-65. Recipient Rsch. Career Devel. award NIH, 1971-76; grantee NIH, 1969-92, Ctr. for Reproductive Biology Rsch. NIH, 1997-92, Ctr. for Reproductive Biology Tng. Rockefeller Found., 1978-84. Fellow Am. Gynecol.-Obstet. Soc.; mem. Soc. for Gynecol. Investigation (pres. 1989-90), San Antonio Ob-Gyn Soc. (pres. 1982-83). Jewish. Avocations: opera, impressionist art, reading. Died Nov. 21, 2005.

PAUL, HERMAN LOUIS, JR., manufacturing executive; b. NYC, Dec. 30, 1912; s. Herman Louis and Louise Emilie (Markert) Paul; m. Janath Powers (dec. Jan. 1996); children: Robert E., Charles Thomas, Herman Louis III. Student, Duke U., 1931—32, Lehigh U., 1932—33. Power plant engr. Paul's Machine Shop, NYC, 1935—43, pres., chief engr., 1943—48; v.p., chief engr. Paul Valve Corp., East Orange, NJ, 1948—54; pres., chief engr. P-K Industries, Inc., North Arlington, NJ, 1954—59; v.p., dir. rsch. Gen. Kinetics, Englewood, NJ, 1959—62; pvt. practice NYC, 1962—65; v.p., dir. Hydromatics, Inc., Blomfield, NJ, 1965—67; pres., chief engr. P.J. Hydraulics, Inc., Myerstown, Pa., 1967—80, dir., stockholder, 1980—81; pres. Flomega Industries, Inc., Cornwall, Pa., from 1982. Cons. in field. Vice-chmn. Nat. UN Day Com., 1977—80. Mem.: ASME, Am. Soc. Naval Engrs., Instrument Soc. Am., Naval Inst., Navy League, Quentin Riding Club, Heidelberg Country Club (Bernville, Pa.). Achievements include patents in field. Died Mar. 17, 2006.

PAUL, JOHN JOSEPH, retired bishop; b. La Crosse, Wis., Aug. 17, 1918; s. Roland Philip and Louise (Gilles) P. BA, Loras Coll., Dubuque, Iowa, 1939; STB, St. Mary's Sem., Balt., 1943; MEd, Marquette U., 1956. Ordained priest Roman Cath. Ch., 1943. Prin. Regis H.S., Eau Claire, Wis., 1948—55; rector Holy Cross Sem., La Crosse, Wis., 1955—66, St. Joseph's Cathedral, La Crosse, 1966—77; aux. bishop Diocese of La Crosse, 1977—83, bishop, 1983—95. Died Mar. 5, 2006.

PAUL, JOYCE WERTHMAN, management consultant; b. Detroit, Oct. 31, 1941; d. Alfred J. and Mary L. (Janssen) Werthman; student public schs., Warren, Mich.; m. Robert A. Paul, Sept. 23, 1961; children— Kathleen, Carol, Brian. Sales mgr. Tupperware Home Parties, Detroit, 1964-71; distbr. Act II Jewelry Co., Orlando, Fla., 1974-76; sales mgr. Deco Plants Co., Detroit, 1976-79, nat. sales counselor, St. Louis, 1979-81; mgmt. cons. The Joyce Paul Co., Rochester, Mich., 1981—; motivational speaking specialist. Vol., Mich. Spl. Olympics, 1978-82. Mem. The Direct Selling Assn. Author: The Unit Leaders Growing Guide, 1980, others. Died Apr. 7, 2007.

PAUL, LEONARD GEORGE, medical educator; b. Cleve., Oct. 16, 1924; s. Michael Joseph and Mary Elizabeth (Mandula) P.; m. Gertraud Erivd Johannes, May 2, 1947 (div. 1978); m. Nancy Kay Daubenspeck; children: Michael, Kathy, Stephen. BS, Cleve. State U., 1947; MD summa cum laude, Ohio State U., 1951. Intern Phila. Gen. Hosp., 1951-52; ptnr. Med. Group of Michigan City, Ind., 1952-75; assoc. prof. Ohio State U.-Med. Sch., Columbus, 1975-78; assoc. prof., dep. chmn. U. Calif., Irvine, 1978-82; prof., chmn. U. Tex. Health Sci. Ctr., San Antonio, 1982-95, prof. emeritus, chmn., from 1995. Predoctoral chmn. Ohio State U., Columbus, 1976-78; residency dir. U. Calif. Irvine, 1978-82; chmn. U. Tex. Health Sci. Ctr., San Antonio. With U.S. Army, 1943-46. Mem. AMA, Tex. Acad. Family Practice (dir. Alamo chpt.), Am. Acad. Family Practice, Tex. Med. Assn. (del.), Bexar County Med. Soc. (del. edn.), Alpha Omega Alpha. Avocations: reading, tennis, music, plays. Home: Fair Oaks, Tex. Died Aug. 21, 2007.

PAULSON, BOYD COLTON, JR., civil engineering educator; b. Providence, Mar. 1, 1946; s. Boyd Colton and Barbara (McKinstry) P.; m. Jane Margaret Kingdon, Feb. 12, 1970; children: Jeffrey Boyd, Laura Jane. BS, Stanford U., 1967, MS, 1969, PhD, 1971. Asst. prof. U. Ill., Urbana, 1972—73; asst. prof., assoc. prof. civil engring. Stanford U., Calif., 1974, prof., 1984—89, Ohbayashi prof. engring., 1989—91, Charles Leavell prof. civil engring., from 1991. Mem. civil engring. adv. com. NSF, 1983-84; mem. U.S. Nat. Com. on Tunneling, 1986-89 mem. com. on constrn. superconducting supercollider in Tex., NAS, 1988-89; presenter in field. Author: Computer Applications in Construction, 1995; co-author: Professional Construction Management, 1978, 2d edit., 1984, 3d edit., 1992; also articles. Bd. dirs. Peninsula Habitat for Humanity, 1996—2002 Mid-Peninsula Housing Coalition, from 1999. Fellow Humbold Found., Munich, 1983, Brit. Coun., Glasgow, Scotland, 1990-91, Fulbright fellow, 1990-91. Mem. ASCE (chmn. constrn divsn. 1986-87, Huber Rsch. prize 1980, Constrn. Mgmt. awar 1984, Peurifoy Rsch. award 1993), Am. Soc. for Engring. Edn. Urban Land Inst., Nat. Acad. Constrn. Achievements includ research in human-computer systems for project management, i analytical modeling and simulation of construction operations in tunneling in urban environments, in low-cost housing. Home Menlo Park, Calif. Died Dec. 1, 2005.

PAULSON, PETER JOHN, librarian, publishing executive; b NYC, Jan. 30, 1928; s. Peter John and Lillian Agnes Elain (Neuman) P.; m. Josephine C. Bowen, Dec. 5, 1953 (dec. Jun 2002); children: David (dec. Apr. 1997), Debora. B.Social Scis cum laude, CCNY, 1949; MA in History, Columbia, 1950; M in L.S, SUNY, Albany, 1955. Library asst. N.Y. State Librar Albany, 1952-55, head, gift and exchange sect., 1955-65, hea catalog sect., 1965-66, prin. librarian tech. services, 1966-7 dir., 1972-85; exec. dir. OCLC Forest Press, 1985-98. Adj. ass prof. library sci. State U. N.Y. at Albany, 1960-71; Adv. com Ohio Coll. Library Center, 1970-71; adv. council to pub. printe depository libraries, 1972-77, chmn., 1975-77; com. fed. depository library service N.Y. State, 1960-70, chairperson, 1960-7 bd. dirs. Capital Dist. Libr. Coun., Nat. Info. Standards Orgn N.E. Document Conservation Ctr. Mem. ALA (chmn. com. o legislation 1980-82, pres. state library agy. sect. 1982-83), N. Library Assn. (pres. 1975), Hudson-Mohawk Library Assn. (v. 1964), SUNY-OCLC Network (governing bd. 1980-82), Ph Beta Kappa. Home: Albany, NY. Died Sept. 29, 2006.

PAVAROTTI, LUCIANO, lyric tenor; b. Modena, Italy, Oc 12, 1935; s. Fernando and Adele (Venturi) Pavarotti; m. Adu Veroni, Sept. 30, 1961 (separated 1996); children: Lorenz Cristina, Giuliana; m. Nicoletta Mantovani, Dec. 13, 2003; child, Alice. Diploma magistrale, Istituto Magistrale Carl Sigonio, 1955; studied with Arrigo Pola, studied with Etto Campogalliani, degree. Formerly tchr. elem. schs.; salesman in Singer: (Operas) (debut) as Rodolfo in La Bohème, 1961, (role Edgardo in debut Lucia di Lammermoor, 1963, the Duke debut Rigoletto, 1961, Rodolfo in La Bohème, 1963, Tonio debut The Daughter of the Regiment, 1966, (appeared) Lucia Lammermoor, 1965, (Am. debut) Miami, Fla., 1965; perform (numerous): European performances including Italy, Vien Staatsoper, Paris; performer: with San Francisco Opera, 196 singer: (Operas) (debut) Met. Opera, 1968; appeared (Opera The Daughter of the Regiment, Met. Opera, 1971, Elis d'Amore, 1973, La Bohème, Chgo. Opera, 1973, La Favorit San Francisco Opera, 1973, Il Trovatore, 1975, Bellini I Pur tani, Met. Opera, 1976, Ponchielli La Gioconda, San Francis Opera, 1979, Aida, 1981, Mozart, Idomeneo, Met. Opera, 198 Verdi, Ernani, Met. Opera, 1983, Tosca, Met. Opera, 199 numerous internat. performances La Scala, Milan, Hambur Teatro Colon, Buenos Aires, Australian Opera, Sydney, conce series of Am. and internat. cities Carnegie Hall, 1973, Buen Aires, Moscow, Beijing, Hong Kong, Tokyo, including are concerts Madison Square Garden, 1984, and major cities America, Europe, South America, performance in Central Par NY, 1993, appeared (films) Yes, Giorgio, 1983, establish Opera Co. Philadelphia/Luciano Pavarotti Vocal Competitio 1980, rec. artist (albums) Winner Concorso International Reggio Emilia, 1961, O Solo Mio, 1979, Mamma, 198 Passione, 1985, Tutto Pavarotti, 1989, The Essential Pavarot 1990, Carreras, Domingo, Pavarotti in Concert, 1990, Amor 1992, Ti Amo Puccini's Greatest Love Songs, 1993, Pavaro and Friends, 1993, Pavarotti Plus-Deluxe Edit., 1995, The Thr Tenors in Concert, 1994, Pavarotti and Friends 2, 1995, Pava otti Plus, 1997, Pavarotti Greatest Hits: The Ultimate Collectio 1998, The Three Tenors in Paris, 1998, Arias & Duets Fre Pavarotti, 1998, Donizetti Arias, 1998, Notte d' Amore, 199 Verdi Arias-La donna é mobile, 1999, l tre tenor L'album Natule, 2000, The Three Tenors Arias, 2000, Quarant' anni pe Lirica, 2001, Live Recital, 2001, Nessumdorma Arias & Due 2001, Amore: The Essential Romantic Collection, 2001, T Pavarotti Edit., 2001, Luciano Pavarotti-The Singers, 2002, T Best of the Three Tenors, 2002, Ti Adoro, 2003, The Milleni Collection: The Three Tenors, 2005, appeared (PBS TV spl. T series) (with Placido Domingo & Jose Carreras) The Thr Tenors, 1994; performer: Three Tenors Tour, Worldwide Fa well Celebration Tour, 2004. Established teaching facility f young singing students, Mondena, Italy; created annual char concert, Pavarotti & Friends, from 1993; UN Messenger f Peace. Named Artist of Yr. Gramophone, 1992; named to Itali Am. Hall of Fame in Music, Nat. Italian Am. Found., 200 recipient Grammy award, Best Classical Vocal Soloist Perf mance for Luciano Pavarotti-Hits From Lincoln Ctr., 197 Grammy award, Best Classical Vocal Soloist Performance for Solo Mio-Favorite Neapolitan Songs, 1979, Grammy awa Best Classical Vocal Soloist Performance, Live From Linc Ctr.-Sutherland/Horne/Pavarotti, 1981, Grammy award, B Classical Vocal Soloist Performance for Luciano Pavarotti Concert, 1988, Grammy award, Best Classical Vocal Perf mance for Carreras, Domingo, Pavarotti in Concert, 19 Commendatore Cross and Grand Offical Cross for services the Italian Republic, Nansen award, UN High Commissioner Refugees, 2001, World Social award, Pres. Gorbachev, Vien 2001, John F. Kennedy Ctr. Honor award, 2001, Eisenhow Medallion, People to People Internat., 2004, Freedom of t City of London, Corp. of London, 2005, Red Cross award Services to Humanity, 2005, Excellence in Italian Cult award, Culture Ministry, Italy, 2007. Achievements inclu performance at opening ceremonies of Winter Olympics, Tori 2006. Died Sept. 6, 2007.

PAVONE, MICHAEL PHILLIP, music educator, organist, composer; b. Buffalo, Dec. 11, 1945; s. Anthony Benedict and Mary Grace (Muche) P.; m. Karen Ann Krahling, June 3, 1972. Mus.B., Westminster Choir Coll., 1968, Mus.M., 1976. Instr. music Abraham Clark Sch., Clark, N.J., 1969-72; chmn. music dept. Brooks Sch., North Andover, Mass., 1974-76, Tabor Acad., Marion, Mass., 1976-79; grad. teaching assoc. Ohio U., Athens, 1979-81; asst. prof. music, chmn. dept. Ohio Dominion Coll., Columbus, 1981—; guest organist, guest conductor various music festivals. Composer choral and handbell works. Founder, dir. Clarktown Boys Choir, 1969-72; active Merrimack Valley Arts and Humanities Council, Mass. and N.H., 1974-75; participant Hispanic Awareness Week, Columbus, 1983. 1st Baroque Acad./Aston Magna Found. fellow, 1977; choral scholar Classical Music Seminar, Austria, 1977; recipient commendation N.Y. State Senate, 1977, Bronze medal Internat. Choral Festival, Rome, 1975. Mem. Am. Guild Organists (sub-dean 1977-79), Am. Assn. Choral Dirs., Nat. Pastoral Musicians (program coordinator), Royal Sch. Ch. Music, Coll. Music Soc. Republican. Avocations: poetry; swimming; film; tennis. Died Mar. 21, 2006.

PAYNE, WILLIAM EDWARD, exploration geophysicist; b. Kansas City, Mo., Aug. 6, 1932; s. Reed and LaVena (Wilson) P.; m. George Ann Everline, Dec. 7, 1952; children— Deborah Ann, Michael Reed. B.A. in Geology, Tex. Tech U., 1954. Sr. exploration geophysicist Exxon Co. U.S.A., Midland, Tex., 1954-81; dir. geophysics, no. region Kerr-McGee Corp., Oklahoma City, 1981—. Mem. Soc. Exploration Geophysicists, Am. Assn. Petroleum Geologists. Republican. Avocations: golf; travel. Home: Edmond, Okla. Died Sept. 14, 2006.

PAYTON, CALVIN WORTH, ophthalmologist; b. Lethbridge, Alta., Can., Sept. 28, 1919; came to U.S., 1925; s. Franklin Smith and Lona Odessa (Still) P.; m. Bessie Joyce Ross, Aug. 26, 1950; children— Charlotte, Rene, Sandra, Susan, Sheryl, Calvin. A.B., U. Kans., 1940; M.D., 1943; postgrad. U. Pa., 1947-48, U. Tex.-Galveston, 1949-50. Diplomate Am. Bd. Ophthalmology. Intern, Grasslands Hosp., Valhalla, N.Y.; resident in ophthalmology U. Tex. Med. Branch, Galveston, 1949-54; clin. assoc. prof. ophthalmology U. Tex., Galveston, 1953—; pvt. practice ophthalmology, Longview, Tex., 1953-84. Served to capt. U.S. Army, 1944-46. Fellow ACS; mem. Gregg County Med. Soc., Tex. Med. Soc., Am. Med. Soc. Republican. Methodist. Lodge: Rotary. Home: Longview, Tex. Died May 21, 2007.

PAZIK, GEORGE JAMES, magazine editor, publisher; b. Milw., Apr. 7, 1921; s. Richard Francis and Josephine (Bartosiucek) P.; B.S., U. Wis., 1944; m. Bernice Emily Thiele, June 19, 1943; children— Marjorie Anne (dec.), Carol Sue. Mgr., Pazik's Delicatessen, Milw., 1946-54; owner Kitchens by Pazik, Milw., 1952-59; exec. dir. Upper 3d St. Comml. Assn., Milw., 1959-64; exec. v.p., founder Northtown Planning and Devel. Council, Milw., 1964-74; editor, pub. Fishing Facts mag., Menomonee Falls, Wis., 1970—. Chmn. Milw. County Expwy. and Transp. Commn., 1971-74; chmn. Wis. state com. of U.S. Commn. on Civil Rights, 1970-72. Served with U.S. Army, 1944-46. Recipient Human Relations award Milw. Coun. B'nai B'rith, 1968. Mem. Izaak Walton League, Am. Rivers, Wis. Coun. Sportfishing Orgns. Lutheran. Died Oct. 22, 2005.

PEARSON, HARRY FREDERICK, b. S.I., NY, Oct. 20, 1927; s. Carl and Clara Josephine (Johnson) P.; m. Esther Elaine Chiurco, June 26, 1949; children— Judith Pearson Valentine, Harry Frederick. Student, Walter Hervey Jr. Coll., 1947-49; BS in Bus. Adminstrn, L.I. U., 1951. Product sales mgr. Congoleum Industries, Inc., Kearny, N.J., 1961-63, gen. sales mgr., 1963-67, v.p. sales, 1967-69, pres., from 1969; also dir.; exec. v.p., dir. Bath Industries, from 1972; exec. v.p. Congoleum Corp., from 1972. Trustee Walter Hoving Home, Laymen's Nat. Bible Com. Served with USNR, 1945-46. Recipient Torch of Hope award, 1973 Mem. Am. Mgmt. Assn. (pres., dir.) Home: Bernardsville, N.J. Died Aug. 14, 2006.

PEARSON, HENRY CHARLES, artist; b. Kinston, NC, Oct. 8, 1914; s. A. Louis and Estelle P. BA, U. N.C., 1935; MFA, Yale U., 1938; postgrad., Art Students League, 1953-56. Stage scene designer, 1937-42; instr. art New Sch. Social Research, NYC, 1965—2006, Pa. Acad. Fine Arts, Phila., 1973-88. Exhbns. include Workshop Gallery, N.Y.C., 1958, Stephen Radich Gallery, N.Y.C., 1960-70, The Responsive Eye, Mus. Modern Art, 1965, 29th Biennial Exhbn., Corcoran Gallery Art, Washington, 1965, Retrospective N.C. Mus. Art, Raleigh, N.C., 1968, Drawings USA, Minn. Mus. Art, St. Paul, 1971-73, Betty Parsons Gallery, N.Y.C., 1971-76, Art Students League Centennial, 1975, Truman Gallery, N.Y.C., 1976-79, Marilyn Pearl Gallery, N.Y.C., 1980-2006; retrospective Columbia (S.C.) Mus. Art, 1988, Henry Pearson and Friends Arts Ctr., Kinston, N.C., 1993, Gordon Coll., Wenham, Mass., 1996, 99, Native Son, East Carolina U., Greenville, N.C., 1998, Am. Painting, Yale U. Art Gallery, New Haven, 1998, Looking East, DIALOGUE, Ctrl. Conn. State U., New Britain, 2001, Palmer Mus. Art, Pa. State U., 2001, Alexandre Gallery, N.Y.C., 2003, Met. Mus., N.Y.C., 2003; represented in permanent collections Mus. Modern Art, N.Y.C., Met. Mus. Art, N.Y.C., Whitney Mus. Am. Art, N.Y.C., Albright-Knox Gallery, Buffalo, N.C. Mus. Art, Raleigh; commd. works include List Art Posters, 1965, N.Y. Film Festival poster, 1968; illustrator: Rime of the Ancient Mariner, 1964, Five Psalms, 1969, Seamus Heaney's Sweeney Praises the Trees, 1981, Seamus Heaney's Poems and a Memoir, 1982, Seamus Heaney's Three Short Poems, 1993-94. With AUS, 1942-48, USAF, 1948-53. Ford Found. fellow, 1964; Recipient Gold medal for achievement in the fine arts N.C. Gov., 1970 Mem. Am. Abstract Artists, Century Assn. Home: Kinston, NC. Died Dec. 3, 2006.

PECK, ROBERT A., publishing executive, state legislator; b. Riverton, Wyo., Oct. 7, 1924; s. LeRoy E. and Elvira Eugenia (Rostrom) P.; m. Cordelia S. Peck, Oct. 5, 1949 (dec. Feb. 1996); children: Christopher, George, Steven. BA, U. Wyo., 1949. Pub. The Riverton Ranger, from 1949; mem. Wyo. Senate, Dist. 26, Cheyenne, from 1991. Pres. Central Wyo. Coll. Bd., Riverton, 1966-81; sec. CWC Found., Riverton, 1968—. Staff sgt. U.S. Army, 1943-46, ETO. Mem. Soc. Profl. Journalists, Masons, Phi Beta Kappa. Republican. Methodist. Home: Riverton, Wyo. Died Mar. 6, 2007.

PECKHAM, DONALD EUGENE, retired utilities company executive; b. Willis, Kans., Nov. 28, 1922; s. Rolland Claude and Winona Maude (Lewis) P.; m. Evelynn Darlene Dodson, Dec. 20, 1949 (dec.). BA cum laude in Acctg, Eastern N.Mex. U., 1953; MBA, U. Ariz., 1954. Acct. Ill. Power Co., Decatur, Ill., 1954-57; with Public Service Co. of N.Mex., Albuquerque, from 1957, sec., 1968-70, sec., asst. treas., 1970-74, sec., treas., 1974-79, sec., asst. treas., from 1979; sec. Paragon Resources, Inc., 1972-75, sec., asst. treas., from 1975; sec. Sunbelt Mining Co., Inc., 1980-81, sec., asst. treas., from 1981; sec. Meadows Resources, Inc., from 1981; now ret. Served with USMC, 1943-46. Mem.: Elks. Republican. Home: Albuquerque, N.Mex. Died Nov. 6, 2005.

PECSOK, ROBERT LOUIS, chemist, educator; b. Cleve., Dec. 18, 1918; s. Michael C. and Katherine (Richter) P.; m. Mary Bodell, Oct. 12, 1940 (dec. Apr. 1996); children: Helen Pecsok Wong, Katherine, Jean Pecsok Nagle, Michael, Ruth Pecsok Hughes, Alice Pecsok Tominaga, Sara Pecsok Lima; m. Marcella Beeman, Apr. 23, 1997. SB summa cum laude, Harvard U., 1940, PhD, 1948. Prodn. foreman Procter & Gamble Co., Balt., 1940-43; instr. chemistry Harvard U., 1948; asst. prof. chemistry U. Calif., LA, 1948-55, assoc. prof., 1955-61, prof., 1961-71, vice-chmn. dept., 1965-70; prof., chmn. dept. U. Hawaii, Honolulu, 1971-80, dean natural scis., 1981-90. Sci. adviser FDA, 1966-69. Author: Principles and Practice of Gas Chromatography, 1959, Analytical Methods of Organic and Biochemistry, 1966, Modern Methods of Chemical Analysis, 1968, 2d edit., 1976, Modern Chemical Technology, 1970, rev. edit. 1989, Physicochemical Applications of Gas Chromatography, 1978. Lt. USNR, 1943-46. Recipient Tolman medal, 1971; Guggenheim fellow, 1956-57, Petroleum Rsch. Fund Internat. fellow, 1963-64. Mem. Am. Chem. Soc., Am. Inst. Chemists, Phi Beta Kappa, Alpha Chi Sigma, Phi Lambda Upsilon. Home: San Diego, Calif. Died Aug. 19, 2007.

PEIRCE, JOHN WENTWORTH, architect; b. Boston, Feb. 9, 1912; s. Thomas W. and Gabrielle (Dexter) P.; m. Grace Minot, June 27, 1934; children— Thomas W., Lucy (Mrs. David Scanlon III), John W. AB cum laude, Harvard, 1933; postgrad. Archtl. Sch., 1933-35; M.Arch., MIT, 1947. Individual practice architecture, Boston, 1938-42; assoc. Shepley, Bulfinch, Richardson & Abbott, Boston, 1948-60; ptnr. Peirce & Peirce, Boston, 1960-71, Peirce Pierce & Kramer, 1971-75. Mem. Mass. Bd. Registration for Architects, 1954-59, chmn., 1957; mem. Mass. Insp.-Gen. Council, 1981-85 Prin. archtl. works include Shields Warren Radiation Lab, N.E. Deaconess Hosp., Boston, Trinity Episcopal Ch, Topsfield, Mass., Loeb Marine Lab, Woods Hole, Mass., Art/Music Bldg., St. Mark's Sch., Southboro, Mass. Chmn. Topsfield Conservation Commn., 1965-71; commr. Ipswich River Watershed Dist., 1968—, chmn., 1976-80; bd. dirs. Ipswich River Watershed Assn., 1976-87; trustee Essex County Greenbelt Assn., 1961-71, pres., 1966-77, dir., 1977-80, hon. dir., 1980—; trustee Trustees Pub. Reservations, 1966-83; bd. dirs. Plymouth County Wildlands Trust, 1973-79, 81-84, 87-95, trustee, 1984-87. Served to lt. comdr. USNR, 1942-46. Recipient Ann. Conservation award Mass. Trustees of Reservations, 1975, Open Space award Mass. Conservation Council, 1977, Conservation award Ipswich River Watershed Assn., 1984, Conservation award New Eng. Wildflower Soc., 1988. Fellow AIA; mem. Mass. Assn. Architects (pres. 1968), Boston Soc. Architects (v.p. 1968, pres. 1969) Clubs: Bournes Cove Yacht (Wareham, Mass.) (commodore 1966-68); St. Botolph (Boston). Died Apr. 24, 2006.

PELIO, LENA, ballet educator; b. Akron, Ohio, June 11, 1918; d. Isador and Anna (Rujila) Stein; m. Andrew Pelio, Mar. 1, 1941 (dec. 1985); children— Luana Pelio Hansen, Lisa Pelio Whittaker. Cert. tchr. Cecchetti Method of Ballet. Founder, tchr. Lena Pelio Sch. of Dance, Flint, 1937—; founder, dir. Flint Ballet Theatre, 1960—. Bd. dirs. March of Dimes, Flint, 1975—; tchr. Mott Found. Dance Program, Flint, 1938-50; choreographer Flint Light Opera Co., 1938-41, Fine Arts Festival Program, Flint, 1972-78, Musical Performing Arts Assn., Flint, 1970-75, various Flint community players musicals, high sch. musicals, civic affairs, fashion shows. Recipient plaques of appreciation March of Dimes 1970, 72, 76, 80, Flint Ballet Theatre, 1970; Silver Tray award Flint Ballet Theatre, 1965; Pewter Ballerina award Flint Ballet Theatre, 1985. Mem. Cecchetti Council Am. (bd. dirs. 1972—), Dance Educators Am. Republican. Episcopalian. Avocations: reading; concerts; plays; lectures; musicals. Home: Flint, Mich. Died Feb. 27, 2006.

PELLEGRINI, RAYMOND PAUL, educational administrator; b. Bklyn., Jan. 23, 1950; s. Joseph Charles and Mildred Lucille (Bevilacqua) P.; B.S., State Univ. Coll., Oneonta, N.Y. 1972; M.A., Castleton State Coll., 1986; m. Lucy Carr Bergen, Feb. 15, 1975; children— Christopher Carr, Scott William, Catherine Giovanna. Tchr., Herringswell Manor Sch., Bury St. Edmunds, Eng., 1972-74; tchr. Mt. Abraham Union High Sch., Bristol, Vt., 1974-76, asst. prin., 1976-78, tchr./team leader, 1978-81, dept. head, 1981-83, asst. prin., 1983-84; prin. Monkton Central Sch. (Vt.), 1984—; counselor State Dept. Edn., Montpelier, Vt., 1979-84, area coordinator, 1981-83. Mem. adv. bd. Addison County Vocat. Center, 1976-78, 83-84; co-founder, bd. dirs. Bristol Team Center, 1977-78; mem. Bristol Halloween Com., 1978; mem. planning commn. Village of Bristol, 1979-83, mem. zoning bd. adjustment, 1979—; bd. dirs. Lawrence Meml. Library, 1981-83. Recipient Vt. Outstanding Tchr. award, 1982; Vt. Leadership Acad., 1985; IDEA fellow, Kettering Found., 1976. Mem. New Eng. Assn. Schs. and Colls. (evaluation steering com. 1980-82), Assn. Supervision and Curriculum Devel., Nat. Council Social Studies, Nat. Hist. Soc., Early Am. Soc., Vt. Headmasters Assn., Nat. Assn. Elem. Prins. Episcopalian. Clubs: Bristol Recreation, Lions. Home: Bristol, Vt. Died May 7, 2006.

PENN, JOHN GARRETT, federal judge; b. Pittsfield, Mass., Mar. 19, 1932; s. John and Eugenie Gwendolyn (Heyliger) P.; m. Ann Elizabeth Rollison, May 7, 1966; children: John Garrett II, Karen Renee, David Brandon. BA, U. Mass., 1954; LLB, Boston U., 1957; postgrad., Princeton U., 1967-68. Bar: Mass 1957, D.C. 1970. Trial atty. U.S. Dept. Justice, Washington, 1961-65, atty. tax divsn., 1961-70; reviewer, asst. chief gen. litigation sect., assoc. judge Superior Ct. of D.C., Washington, 1970-79; judge U.S. Dist. Ct. D.C., Washington, 1979—98, chief judge, 1992-97, sr. judge, 1998—2007. Ex-officio dir. day care program D.C. Dept. Recreation, 1978-1998. 1st lt. JAGC, U.S. Army, 1958-61. Nat. Inst. Pub. Affairs fellow, 1967. Mem. Nat. Bar Assn., Mass. Bar Assn., Washington Bar Assn., D.C. Bar Assn., Bar Assn. D.C. (hon.), Am. Judicature Soc., Boston U. Law Sch. Alumni Assn. Episcopalian. Home: Silver Spring, Md. Died Sept. 9, 2007.

PENZA, RALPH, reporter; b. Nov. 22, 1932; m. Lucille Penza; 2 children. BA in Radio and TV, NYU. News dir. and anchor KWWL-TV, Waterloo, Iowa; news dir. and anchor WCOJ, Coatsville, Pa., WSAV, Savannah, Ga.; newswriter ABC Network News Team, NYC, 1960—61; producer WABC -TV, NYC, 1961—63; producer 6 PM news WCBS-TV, NYC; co-anchor WCAU-TV, Phila.; corr., weekend anchor WDVM-TV, Washington; sr. corr., backup anchor WNBC-TV, NYC, 1997—2007. Recipient 6 Emmy awards, Gold Typewriter award, N.Y. Press Club, 1982, 1992, Triscourt award, Tri-state Cath. Com. Radio and TV, 1993. Died Feb. 16, 2007.

PEREZ-MENDEZ, VICTOR, physics educator; b. Guatemala, Aug. 8, 1923; came to U.S., 1946; m. 1949; 2 children MS, Hebrew U., Israel, 1947; PhD, Columbia U., 1951. Rsch. assoc. Columbia U., NYC, 1951-53, staff physicist, 1953-61; sr. scientist Lawrence Berkeley Lab., U. Calif., Berkeley, from 1960. Vis. lectr. Hebrew U., 1959—; prof. physics dept. radiology U. Calif., San Francisco, 1968— Fellow IEEE, AAAS, Am. Phys. Soc., N.Y. Acad. Sci.; mem. Soc. Photo Instrumentation Engrs. Home: Berkeley, Calif. Died Nov. 1, 2005.

PERKINS, DAVID DEXTER, retired geneticist; b. Watertown, NY, May 2, 1919; s. Dexter M. and Loretta F. (Gardiner) P.; m. Dorothy L. Newmeyer, Aug. 1, 1952; 1 dau., Susan J. AB in Biology, U. Rochester, 1941; PhD in Zoology, Columbia U., 1949. Mem. faculty Stanford U., 1949—89, prof. biology, 1961—89, prof. emeritus, 1989—2007; research fellow U. Glasgow, Scotland, 1954-55, Columbia U., 1962-63, Australian Nat. U., Canberra, 1968-69. Vis. scholar univs. Wash., Hawaii and Calif., San Diego, 1975-76; participant India-U.S. Exchange Scientists Program, 1974; mem. genetics tng. com. USPHS, 1961-65; mem. Exec. Bd. Internat. Genetics Fedn., 1978-83. Editor Genetics, 1963-67. Served with USAAF, 1943-45. Recipient Rsch. Career award USPHS, 1964, Merit award NIH, 1987; Guggenheim fellow, 1983-85. Mem. NAS, Genetics Soc. Am. (pres. 1977, Thomas Hunt Morgan medal 1994). Home: Menlo Park, Calif. Died Jan. 2, 2007.

PERKINS, ESTHER ROBERTA, literary agent; b. Elkton, Md., May 10, 1927; d. Clarence Roberts and Esther Crouch (Terrell) P.; student West Chester State Tchrs. Coll., 1945-47, U. Del. Acct., E. I. duPont de Nemours & Co., Inc., Wilmington, Del., 1947-65; records specialist U. Del., 1966-78; partner Holly Press, Hockessin, Del., 1977-83; owner Esther R. Perkins Lit. Agy., Childs, Md., 1979—; author's agt. Mem. Cecil County Arts Council. Mem. Authors Guild, Nat. Writer's Club, DAR, Romance Writers Am., Mystery Writers Am. Author: Backroading Through Cecil County Maryland, 1978; Things I Wish I'd Said, 1979; Canal Town, Historic Chesapeake City, Maryland, 1983. Republican. Methodist. Home: North East, Md. Died June 7, 2006.

PERKINS, JAMES FRANCIS, physicist; b. Hillsdale, Tenn., Jan. 3, 1924; s. Jim D. and Laura Pervis (Goad) Perkins; m. Ida Virginia Phillips, Nov. 23, 1949; 1 child, James F. AB, Vanderbilt U., 1948, MA, 1949, PhD, 1953. Sr. engr. Convair, Ft. Worth, 1953—54; scientist Lockheed Aircraft, Marietta, Ga., 1954—61; physicist Army Missile Command Redstone Arsenal, Huntsville, Ala., 1961—77, cons. physicist, from 1977. Contbr. articles to profl. jours. With USAF, 1943—46. AEC fellow, 1951—52. Mem.: Am. Phys. Soc., Sigma Xi. Home: Madison, Ala. Died Apr. 16, 2006.

PERKINS, MARVIN EARL, psychiatrist, educator; b. Moberly, Mo., June 1, 1920; s. Marvin Earl and Nannie Mae (Walden) P.; A.B., Albion Coll., 1942; M.D., Harvard U., 1946; M.P.H. (USPHS fellow), Johns Hopkins U., 1956; L.H.D., Albion Coll., 1968; grad. U.S. Army Command and Gen. Staff Coll., 1966, U.S. Army War Coll., 1972; m. Mary MacDonald, May 24, 1943 (div.); children: Keith, Sandra, Cynthia, Marvin, Mary, Irene; m. 2d, Sharon Johnstone, May 20, 1978; 1 dau., Sharon. Intern, Henry Ford Hosp., Detroit, 1946-47; post surgeon, hosp. comdg. officer Fort Eustis, Va., 1948; resident physician psychiatry Walter Reed Army Hosp., Washington, 1949-52; chief psychiatry br., psychiatry and neurology cons. div. Office U.S. Army Surgeon Gen., Washington, 1952-53, chief records rev. br., 1953-55; chief psychiat. svcs. div. D.C. Dept. Pub. Health, 1955-58, chief bur. mental health, 1959-60; lectr. Johns Hopkins U., Balt., 1960-65; adj. prof. Columbia U., 1961-67; prof. psychiatry Mt. Sinai Sch. Medicine of CUNY, 1967-72; clin. prof. psychiatry Coll. Physicians and Surgeons, Columbia U., 1972-77; prof. psychiatry N.Y. Coll. Medicine, 1977-78; prof. behavioral medicine and psychiatry U. Va. Sch. Medicine, 1978—; dir. N.Y.C. Community Mental Health Bd., 1960-68, commr. mental health svcs., 1961-68; dir. psychiatry Beth Israel Medical Center, N.Y.C., 1967-72, dir. Morris J. Bernstein Inst., 1968-72; dir. Community Mental Health Svcs. Westchester County, 1972-77; dir. psychiatry Westchester County Med. Center, 1977-78; med. dir. Mental Health Svcs. of Roanoke Valley, 1978-82; med. dir. Roanoke Valley Psychiat. Ctr., 1980-82, pres. med. staff, 1985-86; med. dir., pres. med. staff Catawba Hosp., 1988-91; psychiat., mental hygiene clinic VA Med. Ctr., Salem, Va., 1992-95; cons. psychiatrist Blue Ridge Cmty. Svcs., 1992—; med. dir. partial hospitalization program Alleghany Regional Hosp., Low Moor, Va., 1995-96. With AUS, 1943-46; col. M.C. Res. ret. Diplomate in psychiatry

Am. Bd. Psychiatry and Neurology; certified mental hosp. adminstr. Am. Psychiat. Assn. Fellow Am. Psychiat. Assn. (life), N.Y. Acad. Medicine (life); mem. AMA, Group Advancement Psychiatry, Roanoke Acad. Medicine, N.Y. Psychiat. Soc., Neuropsychiat. Soc. Va., Med. Soc. Va., State Hist. Soc. Mo. (life), Res. Officers Assn. (life) Mil. Order of World Wars (perpetual). Home: Roanoke, Va. Died Mar. 29, 2006.

PERLBERG, JULES MARTIN, lawyer; b. Chgo., Jan. 28, 1931; s. Maurice and Louise Mae (Schonberger) P.; m. Dora Ann Morris, Dec. 22, 1968; children: Julia, Michael. BBA with high distinction, U. Mich., 1952, JD with high distinction, 1957. Bar: Ill. 1958, D.C. 1964; C.P.A., Ill. Acct. Arthur Andersen & Co., Chgo., 1954-55; faculty U. Mich. Law Sch., Ann Arbor, 1957-58; assoc. Sidley & Austin and predecessor firm, Chgo., 1958-65, ptnr., 1966-98, sr. counsel, from 1998. Mem. Glencoe (Ill.) Bd. Edn., 1980-87, pres., 1985-86; bd. dirs. Juvenile Diabetes Found., Chgo., 1981-2001, v.p. 1983-85, treas., 1988-90, 96-98; exec. bd. Am. Jewish Com., Chgo., 1978-88, v.p., 1981-83; trustee New Trier Twp. Schs., 1987-91, pres., 1989-91; class co-chairperson parents com. Duke U., 1992-94. 1st lt. U.S. Army, 1952-54. Recipient Gold medal Ill. Soc. C.P.A.s, 1955 Mem. ABA, Chgo. Bar Assn., Lawyers Club, Mid-Day Club (Chgo.), Std. Club, Legal Club, Longboat Key Club. Died May 5, 2007.

PERLOW, GILBERT JEROME, retired physicist, retired editor; b. NYC, Feb. 10, 1916; s. David and Esther (German) P.; m. Mina Rea Jones (dec. April 2004). AB, Cornell U., 1936, MA, 1937; PhD, U. Chgo., 1940. Instr. physics U. Minn., Mpls., 1940-41; physicist Naval Ordnance Lab., Washington, 1941-42, Naval Rsch. Lab., Washington, 1942-52; rsch. assoc. physics dept. U. Minn., Mpls., 1952-53; assoc. physicist Argonne (Ill.) Nat. Lab., 1953-57, sr. physicist, 1957—2007; editor Jour. Applied Physics Am. Inst. Physics/Argonne Nat. Lab., 1970-73, editor Applied Physics Letters, 1970-90, consulting editor Applied Physics Letters, 1990-2000; ret., 2000. Vis. assoc. prof. physics U. Wash., Seattle, 1957; vis. prof. German univs., Munich, Berlin; exch. physicist AERE Harwell, Berkshire, Eng., 1961. Contbr. over 70 articles to profl. jours., also chpts. to books; author numerous U.S. patents. Recipient Alexander von Humboldt award Alexander von Humboldt Found., Tech. U. Munich, 1972. Fellow Am. Phys. Soc.; mem. Chgo. Corinthian Yacht Club (life mem., commodore 1974). Avocations: sailing, woodworking, painting. Home: Downers Grove, Ill. Died Feb. 17, 2007.

PERREAULT, CHARLES JOSEPH, marketing professional; b. Chgo., May 20, 1934; s. Charles Joseph and Anne Felicia (Winstead) Perreault; m. Rosalie Ann Hoefeyzers, July 31, 1971. BBA, Northwestern U., 1966. Sales and mktg. staff Sunmark Co., St. Louis, 1969—77; v.p. mktg. Leaf Confectionery, Chgo., 1977—81, Ovaltine Products, Inc., Villa Park, Ill., 1981—84, Sandoz Nutrition Corp., 1984—87; pres. Internat. Transp. Network, Inc., 1987—88, Moro Photo of Sanibel, Sanibel Island, Fla., from 1988. Mem.: Delta Mu Delta. Home: Franklin, NC. Died Aug. 2, 2007.

PERRY, CHARLES WAYNE, newspaper executive; b. Beech Grove, Ind., Feb. 24, 1951; s. Paul Wayne and Zoe Eleanor (Powell) P.; m. Jan Margason, Nov. 15, 1975. BA magna cum laude, Ind. State U., 1973. Reporter The Terre Haute (Ind.) Tribune, 1973-74, copy editor, 1974-76, city editor, 1976-78, asst. editor, 1978-79, editor-in-chief, 1979-82; suburban editor The Cin. Post, 1982-84, news editor, 1984-86, asst. mng. editor/features, 1986-87, mng. editor, from 1987. Instr. journalism Am. Legion's Hoosier Boys' State, Terre Haute, 1973-89; guest instr. U. Cin., 1988—, Xavier U., 1988-89 Mem. No. Ky. Heritage League, Covington, 1991—, U. Cin. Communications Bd., 1988-90. Recipient Best Edn. Reporting award Ind. State Tchrs. Assn., 1975, Rotary Internat. Journalism grant, 1976, Best Headline award AP of Ohio, 1992, Best Designer Award Scripps Howard Newspapers, 1992. Mem. Soc. Profl. Journalists (Best Page Design and Best Headline awards 1991), AP Mng. Editors, Ind. State U. Alumni Assn., Mensa, Bankers Club, AP Ohio, Scripps Howard Mng. Editors. Avocations: running, cartography, book collecting. Home: Covington, Ky. Died May 4, 2006.

PERRY, JOHN HOLLIDAY, JR., newspaper executive; b. Seattle, Jan. 2, 1917; s. John Holliday and Dorothy Lilly P.; m. Jeanne See, 1946 (div. 1966); children: John Holliday III, Henry A., Stanton See; m. Mariana Rosati, Nov. 5, 1966 (div. 1985); children: Christiana, Francesca, Alessandra; m. J. Helena Greene, May 5, 1989. AB, Yale U., 1939; postgrad., Harvard Sch. Bus. Adminstrn., 1940. Chmn. bd., pres. Perry Oceanographics, Inc.; Chmn. bd. Perry Offshore, Inc.; pres. Bahama Pubs. Ltd., Bahamas Undersea Research Found., Perry Found., Fiscal Policy Council. Former mem. Pres.'s Commn. on Marine Scis., Engring. and Resources; mem. Am. Bur. Shipping, Caribbean Conservation Corp., Fla. Commn. Marine Scis. and Tech., Sea Space Symposium. Author: The National Dividend (with Christiana P. Perry) Methanol: Bridge to a Renewable Energy Future, 1990. Trustee emeritus Internat. Oceanographic Found. Commd. 1st lt. USAAF, 1942-45. Mem. Inter Am. Press Assn. (dir. 1959-69), Zeta Psi. Clubs: Bath and Tennis (Palm Beach, Fla.), Everglades (Palm Beach, Fla.), Sailfish (Palm Beach, Fla.), Pisces (Washington). Presbyterian. Home: West Palm Beach, Fla. Died May 16, 2006.

PERRY, WILLIAM WADE, music educator; b. Cameron, Tex., Apr. 1, 1931; s. Wilson Wade and Lorene Inola (Hillegeist) P.; m. Alice Louise Field, Dec. 22, 1953; children— Elizabeth, Margaret, Edwin. B.Music Edn., North Tex. State U., Denton, 1952, M.Music Edn., 1957, Ed.D., 1966. Dir. band and orch. pub. sch., Beaumont, Tex., 1952-58; prin. solo flutist Beaumont Symphony Orch., 1953-58; prin. flutist Wichita (Kans.) Music Theatre, 1971-83; piccoloist, flutist Wichita Symphony Orch., 1964-74; prof. music Friends U., Wichita, 1962—; musical dir., condr. Friends U.-Community Symphony Orch., 1962—, Camerata Musica Chamber Orch., Wichita, 1980-81. Bd. dirs. George B. Tack Flute Audition Com. Served with U.S. Army, 1953-55. Mem. AAUP, Kans. Music Educators Assn., Music Educators Nat. Conf., Phi Mu Alpha Sinfonia. Republican. Methodist. Author: The Flute, 1963. Home: Wichita, Kans. Died Dec. 23, 2006.

PERSON, ROBERT JOHN, management consultant; b. Mpls., Mar. 7, 1927; s. Otto Carl and Alice Kathryn (Kasper) P.; m. Jeanette Haines, Mar. 11, 1948; 1 dau., Julie Ann. BBA, U. Minn., 1947; MS, Columbia u., 1953. Financial analyst Equitable Life Assurance Soc. U.S., NYC, 1947-53; asst. v.p. bus. devel. met. banking dept. Bankers Trust Co., NYC, 1953-64; v.p. bus. devel. div. Union Bank, Los Angeles, 1964-67; v.p., dir. mktg. Bank of Calif., San Francisco, 1967-70; sr. v.p. Central Nat. Bank of Chgo., 1970-72, 1st v.p., 1973-76, Central Nat. Chgo. Corp., 1973-76; v.p., regional mgr. Lester B. Knight & Assos., Inc., San Francisco, 1976-77; dir. bank cons. Coopers & Lybrand, San Francisco, 1977-80, partner-in-charge, nat. dir. bank cons. Chgo., 1980-89; exec. v.p. RJP Assocs., Inc., Stockton, Calif., 1989-92. Instr. salesmanship sch. pub. relations N.Y. Bankers Assn., 1960-63; instr. mktg. research Stonier Grad. Sch. Banking, Rutgers U., 1964-65, 73, 75-77, Brown U., 1964; instr. Agrl. Lending Sch., Ill. Bankers Assn., 1973-76, Nat. Comml. Lending Sch., Am. Bankers Assn., 1973-76, Sch. Bank Adminstrn., U. Wis., 1982-85, Nat. Grad. Trust Sch., Northwestern U., 1982-84, Southwestern Grad. Sch. Banking, 1983-84; Vice chmn. mgmt. effectiveness com. Community Fund Chgo. Treas. Sch. Bd., Huntington, N.Y., 1957-59; Bd. dirs. Am. Cancer Soc., Chgo.; chief crusader Crusade of Mercy. Served to lt. comdr. USNR, 1944-46, ret. Recipient Florence McNeil Stanley award Columbia, 1953 Mem. Am. Bankers Assn., Bank Mktg. Assn., Am. Mgmt. Assn. (mktg. planning council), Mgmt. Centre-Europe (fin. mgmt. adv. com. 1971—), Sales and Mktg. Execs. Internat., Stockton Symphony Assn. (bd. dirs. 1989-92), Beta Gamma Sigma. Clubs: Eastward Ho (Cape Cod); Stockton Golf and Country (Calif.). Lodges: Elks. Republican. Presbyterian. Home: Sun City West, Ariz. Died Jan. 10, 2006.

PETERS, DONALD CAMERON, construction company executive; b. Milw., Mar. 25, 1915; s. Simon C. and May (Gnewuch) P.; m. Twila Bingel, Dec. 7, 1940; children: Susan (Mrs. Douglas Ingram), David C., Bruce C., Douglas C. BS in Civil Engring, Marquette U., 1938. Registered profl. engr., Wis., Pa. Engr. Siesel Constrn. Co., Milw., 1938-44; v.p., dir. Crump, Inc., Pitts., 1944-51; pres. Mellon-Stuart Co., Pitts., 1951-73, also bd. dirs., chmn., 1973-81. Mem. 5 man gen. com. rewriting Pitts. Bldg. Code, 1947; mem., chmn. Pa. Registration Bd. Profl. Engrs., 1962-82; chmn. bd. standards and appeals Pitts. Bur. Bldg. Inspection, 1960-72; past pres. Pitts. Builders Exch.; adv. bd. Liberty Mut. Ins., 1968-2000. Chmn. bd. suprs. Pine Twp., Allegheny County, 1953-80; chmn. Constrn. Industry Advancement Program We. Pa., 1975-93; trustee La Roche Coll., Pitts., 1967—, chmn., 1983-84; bd. dirs. North Hills Passavant Hosp., 1963-90, chmn., 1983-84. Fellow ASCE; mem. NSPE (nat. dir. 1954-57, chmn. bd. ethical rev. 1978-79), Pa. Soc. Profl. Engrs. (pres. 1953-54), Assn. Gen. Contractors Am. (nat. dir.), Pitts. C. of C. (chmn., dir. 1973-81), Master Builders Assn. Western Pa. (past pres.), SBA, Triangle, Tau Beta Pi, Alpha Sigma Nu. Clubs: Duquesne (Pitts.). Home: Lancaster, Ohio. Died Aug. 16, 2006.

PETERS, RALPH FREW, investment banker; b. Mineola, NY, Mar. 21, 1929; s. Ralph and Helen Louise (Frew) P.; m. Ann Marie Haberski, Dec. 31, 1997; children from previous marriages: Louise Frew, Jean Reid, Ralph Frew, Melvyn T., Richard Clayton. BA, Princeton U., 1951; postgrad., Rutgers U., 1962. With Corn Exchange Bank & Trust Co., 1947-52; chmn. bd., dir. Discount Corp. N.Y., NYC, 1955-93. Bd. dirs. Van Eck Funds. Served with USNR, 1948-55. Mem. Anglers Club, Leash Club, North Woods Club. Episcopalian. Home: Mc Lean, Va. Died July 20, 2006.

PETERS, TED HOPKINS, insurance company executive; b. Greenville, Tex., Dec. 30, 1943; s. Joe Becton and Teddy Rose (Hopkins) P.; B.B.A., E. Tex. State U., 1965; postgrad. U. Tex., 1965-66; m. Fonda Lynn Carter, June 3, 1966; children— Amy Teigh, Andrew Lathen. Fire rate actuary State Bd. Ins., Austin, Tex., 1966; agency dir. Union Security Life Ins. Co., Greenville, Tex., 1967-72, exec. v.p., dir., 1972—; sec. Greenville Hosp. Dist., 1975-78. Bd. dirs. East Tex. State U. Found., 1977-78; mem. exec. bd. N. Central Tex. Council Govts., 1978-80; foreman Hunt County Grand Jury, 1974; dir. Salvation Army adv. bd., sec. Greenville Indsl. Devel. Fund, 1966-70, pres., 1970—; mem. Nat. Eagle Scout Assn., Nat. Genealogy Soc.; tchr. Bible study class Aldersgate Ch., 1985—; mem. bd. regents East Tex. State U., 1983, bd. dirs. The Selwyn Sch.; mem. Hunt County Juvenile Bd. Recipient Spl. Service award Greenville United Fund, 1971. Mem. Tex. Assn. Life Ins. Ofcls. (pres. 1970-71), Life Ins. Advertisers Assn., Lambda Chi Alpha. Democrat. Author: Peters Family History, 1977. Home: Greenville, Tex. Died Nov. 8, 2006.

PETERS, WILLIAM ERNEST, JR., writer, film producer, film director; b. San Francisco, July 30, 1921; s. William Ernest and Dorothy Louise (Wright) P.; m. Mercy Ann Miller, Oct. 12, 1942 (div. 1968); children: Suzanne Peters Payne, Geoffrey Wright, Jennifer Peters Johnson, Gretchen Peters; m. Helene Louise Yager White, May 31, 1987. BS, Northwestern U., 1947. Account exec. pub. relations J. Walter Thompson Co., Chgo., 1947-51; mem. fiction staff Ladies' Home Jour., 1951-52; article editor Woman's Home Companion, NYC, 1952-53; freelance writer, Pelham, NY, 1953-62; producer CBS Reports, CBS News, NYC, 1962-66; freelance writer, film dir. and TV producer/exec. producer NYC, 1966-82; dir. Yale U. Films, New Haven, 1982-89; freelance writer, film dir., TV producer/exec. producer Guilford, Conn., 1990—2007. Author: American Memorial Hospital--Reims, France: A History, 1955, Passport to Friendship--The Story of the Experiment in International Living, 1957, The Southern Temper, 1959; author: (with Mrs. Medgar Evers) For Us, The Living, 1967; author: A Class Divided, 1971, A More Perfect Union, 1987, A Class Divided: Then and Now, 1987; prodr., writer, dir. (CBS Reports documentaries) Mississippi and the 15th Amendment, 1962, Storm Over the Supreme Court, Parts II and III, 1963 (George F. Peabody award, Golden Gavel award ABA), The Priest and the Politician, 1963, Filibuster--Birth Struggle of a Law, 1964 Segregation: Northern-Style, 1964, co-prodr. After Ten Years The Court and the Schools, 1964 (Nat. Sch. Bell award NEA) (ABC News documentaries) Africa (East Africa), 1967 (Peabody award, NATAS award), Southern Accents--Northern Ghettos, 1967 (nominee for writing achievement Writers Guild Am.) The Eye of the Storm, 1970 (George Foster Peabody award Cine Golden Eagle award, Cath. Broadcasters Assn. Gabrie award, Am. Film Festival Blue Ribbon, Saturday Rev. TV award, hon. mention Monte Carlo TV Festival, Nat. Media awards of the Am. Psychol. Found.), An Echo of Anger, 1976 Suddenly an Eagle, 1976, Death of a Family (Writers Guild Am award), A Bond of Iron, 1982, A Class Divided, 1985 (Emmy award, Sidney Hillman award, Cine Golden Eagle award) others, prodr., dir., writer Bill Moyer's Jour. (PBS), S.C. Edn TV Network; exec. prodr.: Boswell's London Journal, 1984 contbr. over 80 articles to mags., jours. Co-founder North Shore Citizens Com., 1946, bd. dirs., 1946-51; co-founder Pelham Com. Human Relations, 1963, vice chmn., 1963-65, chmn. 1965-66. Served to capt., pilot USAAF, 1942-45, ETO. Decorated D.F.C., Air medal with 2 oak leaf clusters; recipient Benjamin Franklin mag. award, 1954, Peabody TV award, 1963 1970, 1976, Golden Gavel award, ABA, 1963, Sch. Bell award NEA, 1964, Emmy award, Sidney Hillman award, 1985, Lincoln Univ. awards (2), Howard Blakeslee award, Am. Heart Assn., Intergroup Rels. award, Adelphi chpt. B'nai B'rith women and Anti-Defamation League of Phila. Mem. Dirs. Guild Am., Writers Guild Am. Democrat. Home: Guilford, Conn. Died May 20, 2007.

PETERSEN, RAYMOND JOSEPH, publishing company executive; b. West Orange, N.J., May 9, 1919; s. Raymond Ott and Ellen (Bond) P.; Rosalie Iovin, July 22, 1949 (dec. Nov 1970); children— R. Jeffrey, Gregory, Mary Petersen Fros John, Teresa Petersen Bracchita, Cathy Petersen Keller, Jeann Peterson Shephard, Matthew; m. Gayle Malles, Feb. 22, 199 Dr. Journalism (hon.), St. Joseph's Coll., 1966. From adv salesman to pub. and v.p. Good Housekeeping Mag., N.Y.C 1948-67, now publs. dir.; sr. v.p. Hearst Mags., N.Y.C., 1967-6 exec. v.p., 1969—, also bd. dirs.; testamentary trustee Hear Founds., N.Y.C., 1969-87; past mem. bd. dirs. Supermarke Gen. Corp., Woodbridge, N.J., Internat. Capital & Tech. Corp N.Y.C.; past mem. bd. dirs. Brand Names Found., Mag. Adv Bur., Acad. Food Market of St. Joseph's U., Phila., Counc Better Bus. burs., Inc., and Consumer Research Inst. for Grocer Mfrs. Am., Inc.; bd. dirs. Covenant House, N.Y.C., 1987; appt to U.S. Nat. Commn. on Libraries and Info. Sci., Washingto 1987; nat. chmn. Religion in Am. Life, 1986, 87, 88, 89; mem pub. service adv. com. Communications Industries Counci 1968; hon. bd. dirs. N.Y. Advt. Club, 1979; bd. dirs. Co Awards Com., 1980-85; chmn. Nat. Advt. Rev. Council, 198 84. Bd. dirs. USO of Met. N.Y., N.Y.C., 1967—, v.p., 1980— mem. chmn.'s com. United Cerebral Palsy Campaign, N.Y.C 1980—; honoree adviser to bd. dirs. Children of Alcoholi Found., N.Y.C., 1984—; mem. adv. bd. St. Vincent's Hosp Harrison, N.Y., 1981-86; bd. dirs. Am. Friends of Jerusale Mental Health Ctr., N.Y.C., 1982-86, Madison Sq. Boys ar Girls Clubs, N.Y.C., 1983—, Nat. Crime Prevention Counci Washington, 1985—. Named Father of Yr., 1966; recipie Good Scout award Boy Scouts Am., 1973; Silver Beaver awa Boy Scouts Am., 1979; Charles E. Wilson award Religion Am. Life, 1985; inducted Advt. Hall of Fame, 1987. Mem. Ar Advt. Fedn. (bd. dirs. 1971—). Republican. Roman Catholi Home: Newport, RI. Died July 11, 2007.

PETERSEN, ROBERT EINAR, magazine publishing exec tive; b. LA, Sept. 10, 1926; s. Einar and Bertha (Putera) P.; r Margie McNally, Jan. 26, 1963. Founder Petersen Pub. C (pubs. Hot Rod, Motor Trend, Car Craft, Motorcyclist, Photog Skin Diver, Teen, Hunting, Guns & Ammo, Circle Track, D Rider, Los Angeles, 1948-2000; owner, chmn. bd. Peters Properties, LA, 1996—2007. Co-founder benefactor Peters Automotive Mus., LA. Mem. Los Angeles Library Comm 1963-64; Bd. dirs. Boys Club Am., past pres. Hollywood br.; b dirs. Thalians; founder Petersen Automotive Mus., L.A. Serv with USAF. Mem.: So. Calif Safari, Confrerie de la Chaine d Rotisseurs, Chevaliers du Tastevin. Died Mar. 23, 2007.

PETERSON, DONALD ALBERT, radio and publishing e ecutive; b. Youngstown, Ohio, Sept. 18, 1917; s. Albert a Hattie M. (Anderson) P.; m. Josephine Phelps Hoiles, July 2 1940; children— Donald A. Jr., Jill P. McCarty. LittD (hon.), M Union Coll., 1988. Pres. Alliance (Ohio) Brick Corp., 1965-7 pub. Alliance Rev., 1962—; pres. Sta. WFAH/WDJQ, Allianc 1967—; dir. Valley Forge Inc., Glamorgan Park Inc. Chmn. b Mt. Union Coll., 1971-87. Lt. (j.g.) USNR, 1944-46. Recipi United Way Merit award, 1956, Mt. Union Coll. Alumni S award, 1981; named Alliance Boss of Yr., 1968; nominated Hall of Fame Ohio Found. Ind. Coll., 1987. Mem. Oh Broadcasters Assn., Am. Newspaper Pubs. Assn., Am. Legic Sigma Delta Chi. Republican. Methodist. Clubs: Wrangle Filibusters, Alliance Country. Lodges: Kiwanis, Elks (Allianc Home: Alliance, Ohio. Died Aug. 26, 2006.

PETERSON, JAMES LINCOLN, museum executive; b. K wanee, Ill., Nov. 12, 1942; s. Reinold Gustav and Floren Josephine (Kjellgren) P.; m. M. Susan Pepin, Aug. 15, 196 children: Hans C., Erika C. BA, Gustavus Adolphus Coll., 196 PhD, U. Nebr., 1972. Sci. tchr. pub. schs., Ill. and Min 1964-68; research asst. U. Nebr., Lincoln, 1968-72; resea assoc. U. Wis., Madison, 1972-74; staff ecologist Nat. Comm Water Quality, Washington, 1974-75; v.p. research Acad. N Scis., Phila., 1976-84, v.p. devel., 1982-84; pres. Sci. M Minn., St. Paul, from 1984. Bd. dirs. Ea. Pa. chpt. Natu Conservancy, Phila., 1982-84, Downtown Coun., St. Pa 1986-93, Keystone (Colo.) Ctr., 1989-93; mem. St. Paul Riv front Commn., 1987-91; mem. adv. com. U. Minn. Coll. Bi Scis., 1989-95. Mem. Assn. Sci. Mus. Dirs., Assn. Sci. and Te Ctrs. (pres. 1993-95), Sci. Mus. Exhibit Collaborative (pr 1986-89), St. Paul C. of C. (bd. dirs. 1985-89), Informal Cl Home: Minneapolis, Minn. Died July 22, 2007.

PETERSON, JOHN ALBERT, brokerage house executive, consultant; b. Spokane, Wash., May 26, 1931; s. Albert C. and Dorothy Dee (Moore) Peterson; m. Janet Fuller, Apr. 27, 1957; children: Claire, John, Robb. AB, Whitman Coll., 1954; MBA, Harvard U., 1956. V.p. Kidder, Peabody & Co., San Francisco, 1959—67, 1970—77; v.p, dir. William Hutchinson & Co., San Francisco, 1967—70; pres. Peterson Investment Mgmt., Inc., Spokane, from 1977. Trustee Joel E. Ferris Found., Spokane, 1981. 1st lt. US Army, 1956—59. Fellow: Fin. Analysts Fedn.; mem.: San Francisco Analysts Soc. Republican. Home: Spokane, Wash. Died May 9, 2006.

PETROCELLI, ANTHONY JOSEPH, management executive, consultant; b. Bklyn., Sept. 25, 1937; s. Lucio and Carmela (Carrione) P.; m. Antoinette Cassata, May 25, 1963; 1 child, Serena Ann. BS in Mgmt., Fairleigh Dickinson, Madison, NJ, 1969, MBA, 1972. Pres. Met. Consolidated Inc., NYC, 1978-84; pvt. practice mgmt. cons., 1984-88; ptnr., mng. dir. D. George Harris & Assocs., NYC, from 1984, vice chmn., from 1989. Vice chmn. Novacarb, France, 1996—, Salt Union Ltd., U.K., 1992—, Societa Chimica Larderello SpA, Italy, 1993—, Harris Chem. Group, 1993—, Harris Specialty Chemicals, Inc., 1994—, Matthes & Weber GmbH, Germany, 1993, U.S. Silica, 1996—, Penrice Soda Products, Australia, 1996—. Trustee Italian Am. Club, North Brunswick, N.J. With U.S. Army, 1956-58, Germany. Died Dec. 25, 2005.

PETRONE, ROCCO A., aerospace manufacturing executive; b. Amsterdam, NY, Mar. 31, 1926; s. Anthony and Theresa (DeLuca) P.; m. Ruth Holley, Oct. 29, 1955; children— Teresa, Nancy, Kathryn, Michael. BS, U.S. Mil. Acad., 1946; degree in mech. engring., MIT, 1952; D.Sc. (hon.), Rollins Coll., 1969. Devel. officer Redstone Missile Devel., Huntsville, Ala., 1952-55; mem. army gen. staff US Army, Washington, 1956-60; mgr. Apollo program Kennedy Space Center, 1960-66, dir. launch ops., 1966-69; Apollo program dir. NASA, Washington, 1969-73; dir. Marshall Space Flight Center, Huntsville, Ala., 1973-74; assoc. adminstr. NASA, Washington, 1974-75; pres., CEO Nat. Center for Resource Recovery, Washington, 1975-81; exec. v.p. Space Transp. and Systems Group, Rockwell Internat., Downey, Calif., 1981-82, former pres. Decorated D.S.M. with 2 clusters NASA; Commendatore Ordine al Merito (Italy). Fellow Am. Inst. Aeros. and Astronautics; mem. Nat. Acad. Engring., Sigma Xi. Died Aug. 24, 2006.

PETTIT, VINCENT KING, bishop; b. New Brunswick, N.J., Aug. 31, 1924; s. John Mervin and Marion (King) P.; m. Virginia Sorensen, June 17, 1950; children— Joan Anders, Ann, Vincent, C. B.S., Rutgers U., 1950; M.Div., Phila. Div. Sch., 1958; S.T.M., Temple U., 1963, N.Y. Theol. Sch., 1981; D.D. (hon.) Gen. Sem., N.Y.C., 1984. Ordained bishop Episcopal Ch., 1984. Rector St. George's Ch., Pennsville, N.J., 1961-67, St. Mary's Ch., Keyport, N.J., 1967-72, Trinity Ch., Cranford, N.J., 1972-?, Christ Ch., Toms River, N.J., 1981-83; bishop Diocese of N.J., Trenton, 1983—; mem. exec. coun. Episcopal Ch., N.Y.C., 1983-88; chmn. standing liturgical com., 1983—. With U.S. Army, 1942-46. Home: Lakehurst, NJ. Died Mar. 10, 2006.

PETTY, CHARLES SUTHERLAND, pathologist; b. Lewistown, Mont., Apr. 16, 1920; s. Charles Frederic and Mae (Reichert) P.; m. Lois Muriel Swenson, Dec. 14, 1957; children— Heather Ann, Charles Sutherland II; children by previous marriage— Daniel S., Carol L. BS, U. Wash., 1941, MS, 1946; MD, Harvard U., 1950. Intern Mary Imogene Bassett Hosp., Coopertown, N.Y., 1950-52; resident in pathology Peter Bent Brigham Hosp., Children's Med. Center, New Eng. Deaconess Hosp., Boston, 1952-55; instr. pathology La. State U. Sch. Medicine, 1955-56, asst. prof., 1956-58; asst. med. examiner State of Md., 1958-67; asst. prof. forensic pathology U. Md. Sch. Medicine, 1958-64, assoc. prof., 1964-67; lectr., then asso. Johns Hopkins U. Sch. Hygiene and Public Health, 1959-67; adj. prof. police adminstrn. U. Louisville, 1978—91. Dir. Balt. Regional ARC Blood Program, 1959-67; prof. forensic pathology Ind. U. Sch. Medicine, Indpls., 1967-69; dir. lab. Ind. Commn. on Forensic Scis., 1967-69; chief med. examiner Dallas County, 1969-91; prof. forensic scis., pathology U. Tex. Southwestern Med. Sch., Dallas, 1969-91; dir. Southwestern Inst. Forensic Scis., 1969-91 Served from ensign to lt. comdr. USNR, 1941-45. Fellow Coll. Am. Pathologists, Am. Soc. Clin. Pathologists, A.C.P., Am. Acad. Forensic Scis. (pres. 1967-68); mem. Sigma Xi. Episcopalian. Home: Dallas, Tex. Died Jan. 9, 2007.

PEYTON, ROBERT G, oil industry executive; b. Wheeling, W. Va., Mar. 1, 1940; s. Robert L. and Nadine (Kendall) S.; m. Paula Stocking, Oct. 26, 1963; children: Erin, Elise, Wendy. BA in Indsl. Mgmt., W. Va. U., 1963. Salesman Pure Oil Co., Columbus, Ohio, 1963-67, area sales mgr. Palatide, Ill., 1967-1970; reg. sales mgr. Union Oil Co., Palatide, 1970-73; mgr. rail leasing Cushman Corp., Atlanta, 1973-76; asst. br. mgr. W. Williams Co., Pitts., 1976-77, br. mgr., 1977-78, state mgr., 1978-86, v.p. power group Atlanta, 1986-88; pres. Williams Detroit Diesel-Allison, Atlanta, from 1988; W.W. Williams Co., Columbus. Bd. dirs. Ga. Motor Truck Assn., Atlanta, W.W. Williams Co., Columbus; pres. N. Am. Distbr. Coun., U.S., 1989—, chmn. Ga. Equipment Distbrs., Atlanta, 1983—. Mem. De Kalb C. of C. Republican. Methodist. Avocations: golf, fishing. Home: Delaware, Ohio. Died Jan. 22, 2007.

PFAHLERT, THOMAS HOPFNER, advertising and marketing communications agency executive, educator; b. Toledo, Mar. ?, 1938; s. Earl Joseph and Ellen Clarinda (Fettig) P.; m. Sandra Lee Kosuth, June 20, 1964; children— Mark Thomas, Matthew Joseph. Student in design Meinzinger Art Sch., Detroit, 1958-61. Art dir. Chiat/Day Advt., Los Angeles, 1965-69; sr. art dir. D'Arcy, McManus, Masius, Los Angeles, 1969-71; v.p., creative dir. Flournoy & Gibbs, Inc., Toledo, 1971-74; pres. Tom Pfahlert, Cons., Toledo, 1974-76, Mktg. Communications Group, Toledo, 1976—; assoc. prof. Bowling Green (Ohio) State U., 1980—. Served with U.S. Army, 1959-64. Recipient medal Art Dirs. Club N.Y., 1974-75, Art Dirs. Club Chgo., 1975, 76; ?. Addy awards, 1976, 77, 72. Mem. Art Dirs. Club Los Angeles (pres. 1970-71, gold medal 1970), Advt. Club Toledo (dir. 1972-75, gold medal 1972, 74, 75, 76), Toledo C. of C. Home: Maumee, Ohio. Died Aug. 4, 2007.

PFLANZE, OTTO PAUL, history professor; b. Maryville, Tenn., Apr. 2, 1918; s. Otto Paul and Katrine (Mills) P.; m. Hertha Maria Haberlander, Feb. 20, 1951; children: Stephen, Charles, Katrine. BA, Maryville Coll., 1940; MA, Yale U., 1942, PhD, 1950. Historian Dept. State, 1948-49; instr. N.Y. U., 1950-51; asst. prof. U. Mass., 1952-58, U. Ill., 1958-61; prof. history U. Minn., 1961-76, Ind. U., 1977-86, emeritus, 1986; Stevenson Prof. of History Bard Coll., Annandale On Hudson, NY, 1987-92, emeritus, 1992. Chmn. Conf. Group Central European History, 1978; mem. exam. bd., grad. record exam Ednl. Testing Service, 1972-76; mem. Inst. Advanced Study, 1970-71, mem. Historisches Kolleg, Munich, 1980-81. Author: Bismarck and the Development of Germany: Vol. 1.-The Period of Unification, 1815-1871, 1963 (Biennal Book award Phi Alpha Theta), rev. edit., 1990, Vol. 2-The Period of Consolidation, 1871-1880, 1990, Vol. 3-The Period of Fortification, 1880-1898, 1990 (3 vols. collectively named Most Outstanding Book in History, Govt. & Polit. Sci. by Assn. Am. Pubs., 1991); translated as Bd. I-Bismarck, Der Reichsgründer, 1997, Bd II-Bismarck, Der Reichskanzler, 1998 (Einhard prize 1999); co-author: A History of the Western World: Modern Times, 3d edit, 1975; editor: Innenpolitische Probleme des Bismarck-Reiches, 1983; co-editor: Documents on German Foreign Policy, 1918-1945, Vols. I-III, 1949-50; editor Am. Hist. Rev., 1976-85; mem. editl. bd. Jour. Modern History, 1971-73, Central European History, 1972-74. Served to 1st lt. U.S. Army, 1942-46. Fulbright research fellow, 1955-57; fellow Am. Council Learned Socs., 1951-52; fellow Guggenheim Found., 1966-67; fellow Nat. Endowment Humanities, 1975-76; fellow Internat. Research and Exchanges Bd., 1976; fellow Thyssen Stiftung, Essen, 1986; recipient Humanities award McKnight Found., 1962. Mem. Am. Hist. Assn., German Studies Assn. Home: Bloomington, Ind. Died Mar. 3, 2007.

PFLIEGER, LARRY LEONARD, apparel company executive; b. Detroit, Sept. 29, 1923; s. Leonard W. and Irene (Luttermoser) P.; BBA, U. Detroit, 1951, MBA, 1955; m. Alexandra Moulios, Aug. 30, 1975; children: Linda, Larry, Peggy. Controller, Burroughs Corp., Detroit, 1942-70; v.p. fin. Gen. Instrument Corp., N.Y.C., 1970-76; v.p. fin., treas. Warnaco, Inc. Bridgeport, Conn., 1976-84, pres., chief op. officer, 1984-86; dir. Toronto Dominion Bank Trust Co.; mem. adv. bd. Arkwright Boston Ins. Co. With USN, 1943-45. Mem. Fin. Execs. Inst. Home: Stamford, Conn. Died Sept. 27, 2006.

PHELAN, THOMAS, clergyman, academic administrator, educator; b. Albany, NY, Apr. 11, 1925; s. Thomas William and Helen (Rausch) P. AB NY State Regents scholar 1942, President's medal 1945, Coll. Holy Cross, Worcester, Mass., 1945; S.T.L., Catholic U. Am., 1951; postgrad., Oxford U., Eng., 1958-59, 69-70. Ordained priest Roman Cath. Ch., 1951; pastor, tchr., adminstr. Diocese of Albany, 1951-58; resident Cath. chaplain Rensselaer Poly. Inst., Troy, NY, 1959-72, prof. history, from 1972, dean Sch. Humanities and Social Scis., 1972-95, inst. historian, inst. dean, sr. adviser to pres., from 1995. Chmn. architecture and bldg. commn. Diocese Albany, 1968-2003; cons. in field. Author: Hudson Mohawk Gateway, 1985, 2001, Achieving the Impossible, 1995; author monographs, articles, revs. in field. Treas. The Rensselaer Newman Found., 1962-2002; pres. Hudson-Mohawk Indsl. Gateway, 1971-84, bd. dirs. exec. com. 1984—; mem. WMHT Ednl. Telecomm. Bd., 1966-77, 84-90, chmn. 1973-77; chmn. Troy Hist. Dist. and Landmarks Rev. Commn., 1975-86, chmn. hist. adv. com., 1987-2003; v.p. Preservation League N.Y. State, 1979-82, mem. trustees coun., 1982-87, 89—, pres. 1987-89; sec. and bd. dirs. Ptnrs. for Sacred Places, 1989—; bd. dirs. Hall of History Found., 1983-87; trustee Troy Pub. Libr., 1992—. With USN, 1943-46. Recipient Paul J. Hallinan award Nat. Newman Chaplains Assn., 1967, Ann. award Albany Arts League, 1977, Disting. Cmty. Svc. award Rensselaer Poly. Inst., 1979, Edward Fox Demers medal Alumni Assn. Rensselaer Poly. Inst., 1986, Disting. Svc. award Hudson-Mohawk Consortium of Colls. and Univs., 1988; named Acad. Laureate of the SUNY Found. at Albany, 1988; Danforth Found. fellow, 1969-70; grantee Homeland Found., 1958-59, Dorothy Thomas Found., 1969-70. Fellow Soc. Arts, Religion and Contemporary Culture; mem. Ch. Soc. Coll. Work (dir., exec. com. 1970—), Am. Conf. Acad. Deans, Liturgical Conf., Soc. Indsl. Archaeology, Assn. Internat. pour l'Etudes des Religions Prehistoriques et Ethnologiques, Cath. Campus Ministry Assn., Cath. Art Assn., Assn. for Religion and the Intellectual Life (bd. dirs. 1987—), Soc. History of Tech. Clubs: Ft. Orange, Troy Country; Squadron A (N.Y.C.). Home: Albany, NY. Died Mar. 31, 2006.

PHELPS, JOSEPH WILLIAM, banker; b. Richmond, Ky., Jan. 6, 1927; s. Ben and Hannah (Blunschi) P.; m. Mary Margaret Culton, Jan. 2, 1954; children: Melanie Jean, Joseph William. Nat. bank examiner U.S. Treasury Dept., 1950-58; asst. cashier Liberty Nat. Bank & Trust Co., Louisville, 1958-59, asst. v.p., 1959-62, v.p., 1962-67, head corr. bank dept., sec. to bd., exec. com., 1967-68, sr. v.p., 1968-70, exec. v.p., 1971-73, pres., from 1973, also dir.; pres. Liberty-United Bancorp. (now named Liberty Bancorp.), from 1983. Dir. Lincoln Income Life Ins. Co. Mem. exec. bd. Old Ky. Home council Boy Scouts Am.; dir. Ky. Council Econ. Edn., Better Rds. Council Ky., Kidney Found. Ky., Spirit of Louisville Found.; bd. dirs. Ky. div. Am. Cancer Soc., Louisville Med. Research Found., YMCA, Assoc. Industries Ky.; gen. campaign chmn. Metro United Way, 1978; chmn. bd. regents Eastern Ky. U.; mem. Gov.'s Council Econ. Devel., Gov.'s Council Land Use Planning; chmn. Fund for Arts Campaign; mem. vis. com. Sch. Dentistry, U. Louisville; bd. dirs. Louisville Orch. Served with USN, 1945. Mem. Am. Inst. Banking, Am. Bankers Assn., Ky. C. of C. (dir.), Louisville C. of C. (chmn. com. econ. edn.), Res. City Bankers, Filson Club, English Speaking Union, Newcomen Soc. Episcopalian (vestryman). Clubs: Pendennis (Louisville), Louisville Country (Louisville). Home: Louisville, Ky. Died Oct. 31, 2005.

PHILIPSON, HERMAN LOUIS, JR., retired investment banker; b. Dallas, May 14, 1924; s. Herman and Lillian (Adler) P.; m. Sonia Topletz, July 20, 1955; children: Cynthia Ann, Leslie, Nancy, Julie. BS, Tex. A&M U., 1946; postgrad., Harvard Sch. Bus. Adminstrn., 1947-48. Pres. Philipson's, Inc., 1946-56; pres. Nat. Data Processing Corp., 1957-60, chmn. bd., 1960-61, Techno-Growth Capital Corp., 1962-72; pres. Recognition Internat. Inc., Dallas, 1961-73, chmn. exec. com., 1973-76; vice chmn. Recognition Equipment Inc., 1976-83; former pres. Internat. Bus. Devel. Ltd., Dallas. Former mem. Dallas Citizens Coun., also v.p., mem. exec. com.; bd. dirs. Dallas County Camp Fire Girls; trustee So. Meth. U. Found. for Sci. and Engring.; mem. engring. adv. coun. Tex. A&M U. 1st Lt. AUS, 1943-46. Decorated Bronze Star, Purple Heart with cluster; recipient Dallas Exporter of Yr. award, 1970, Ernest Thompson Seton award, 1975; named to Tex. A&M U. Acad. Disting. Mech. Engring. Grads. Mem. Dallas C. of C. (world trade com.), Japan-Tex. Assn. Lodges: Masons, Shriners. Achievements include patents in field. Home: Dallas, Tex. Died Mar. 7, 2006.

PHILLIPS, ARTHUR WILLIAM, JR., biology educator; b. Claremont, NH, Sept. 25, 1915; s. Arthur William and Jane Helen (Daley) P.; m. Mary Catherine Mich, Oct. 21, 1950; children: Marilynn, William (dec.). BS, U. Notre Dame, 1939, MS, 1941; DSc, MIT, 1947. Rsch. asst. Lobund lab. U. Notre Dame, Ind., 1937-41, rsch. scientist Ind., 1943-45; rsch. assoc. MIT, 1947-49; rsch. assoc. prof., head div. bioengring. Lobund lab. U. Notre Dame, Ind., 1949-54; rsch. scientist dept. biology and bioengring. MIT, Cambridge, 1942-43, rsch. fellow dept. food tech., 1945-47, rsch. assoc. dept. food tech., 1947-49; rsch. assoc. prof. dept. bacteriology Syracuse (N.Y.) U., 1954-58, prof. microbiology, 1959-86, prof. emeritus, from 1986, founder, dir. biol. rsch. labs., 1955-65, head radiation and isotope lab., 1956-63, dir. germ-free life rsch. lab., 1956-84. Mem. Internat. Congress on Nutrition, Washington, 1960, Internat. Congress for Microbiology, Montreal, Can., 1962, Moscow, 1966, Internat. Congress for Germ-Free Life Rsch., Nagoya, Japan, 1967; mem. com. on nutrition NAS-NRC, Washington, 1964-66; mem. Conf. on Germ-Free Life and Gnobiotics, Madison, Wis., 1986, Internat. Conf. on Gnotobiology, Versailles, France, 1987; cons. NSF, Washington, Cradle Soc. Inc., Evanston, Ill., GE, Syracuse, Am. Cyanamid, Pearl River, N.Y., Carnation Co., L.A., C.V. Mosby, St. Louis, Can. Dry Corp., Greenwich, Conn., Chocolate Mfrs. Assn., Washington, Continental Can Co., Syracuse. Contbr. articles to profl. jours., chpts. to books. Refrigeration Rsch. Found. fellow, 1945-47; NIH grantee, 1956-80. Mem. Am. Soc. for Microbiology (placement com. 1968-78), Gnotobiotics Assn., Soc. for Gen. Microbiology. Avocations: history, genealogy, hiking. Home: East Poultney, Vt. Died Feb. 17, 2006.

PHILLIPS, CECIL LARRY, accountant; b. Waco, Tex., June 20, 1947; s. Cecil A. and Wilma L. (McCollum) P.; m. Mary Lynn Zigel, Nov. 13, 1971; children— Gretchyn J., Robert Scott Student, U. Okla.-Norman, 1970-71; BBA, Baylor U., 1972. C.P.A., Tex., N. Mex., Ariz. Tax specialist Peat Marwick Mitchell & Co., Albuquerque, 1972-74; controller Invesco, El Paso, Tex., 1975-78; mgr. Moody, Kubiak & Nation, Albuquerque, 1979, ptnr., 1980-82, mng. ptnr. Phoenix, from 1982. Mem. Grand Canyon Nat. Airport Devel. Selection Com. Served with U.S. Army, 1968-70 Decorated Purple Heart Mem. Am. Inst. C.P.A.s, Ariz. Tax Inst., Ariz. Estate Planning Council, Phoenix Met. C. of C. Lodges: Kiwanis. Republican. Baptist. Died Mar. 17, 2006.

PHILLIPS, CHARLES ALAN, accounting firm executive; b. Cin., Aug. 12, 1939; s. Charles Stanley and Mary Lucile (Kirkpatrick) P. BS in Bus. Adminstrn., Northwestern U., 1960, MBA, 1961. Cert. systems profl. Investment adviser Continental Ill. Bank, Chgo., 1960-65; asst. to pres. A.S. Hansen, Chgo., 1965-67; investment adviser Francis I. du Pont, NYC, 1967-70; prof. North Central Coll., Mansfield, Ohio, 1970-73; prin. Peat, Marwick, Mitchell (now KPMG Peat Marwick), Cleve., Tulsa, Houston, 1973-88. Presbyterian. Avocations: classical music, natural history, gardening. Home: Henderson, Nev. Died July 24, 2006.

PHILLIPS, CLIFTON J., retired history professor; b. Olean, NY, Apr. 11, 1919; s. Charles Clifton and Edith (Grey) P.; m. Rachel Jacqueline Martin, July 19, 1952; children: Peter Martin, Elaine Abigail, Alexis Anne, Patience Cecily. BA, Hiram Coll., 1941; Th.B., Starr King Sch. Religious Leadership, 1944; MA, Harvard U., 1950, PhD, 1954. Civil edn. officer US Dept. Def., Kobe, Japan, 1946-49; mem. history faculty De Pauw U., 1954—85, prof., 1965-85, sr. prof., 1985—2007, chmn. dept. history, 1969—72. Lectr. Am. Studies, Korea, 1968-69 Author: Indiana in Transition: The Emergence of an Industrial Commonwealth, 1880-1920, 1968, Protestant America and the Pagan World: The First Half Century of the American Board of Commissioners for Foreign Missions, 1810-1860, 1969, (with others) The Missionary Enterprise in China and America, 1974, Missionary Ideologies in the Imperialist Era, 1880-1920, 1982; DePauw: A Pictorial History, 1987, From Frontier Circuit to Urban Church: The History of Greencastle Methodism, 1989. Served with inf. AUS, 1944-46, PTO. Fulbright-Hays fellow Chinese civilization Taiwan, summer 1962 Mem. Am. Hist. Assn., Assn. Asian Studies, Orgn. Am. Historians, Ind. Hist. Soc., Ind. Assn. Historians (past pres.) Home: Greencastle, Ind. Died Mar. 20, 2007.

PHILLIPS, ELLIS LAURIMORE, JR., foundation executive, former academic administrator; b. NYC, Feb. 26, 1921; s. Ellis Laurimore and Kathryn (Sisson) P.; m. Marion Grumman, June 13, 1942; children: Valerie Phillips Parsegian, Elise Phillips Watts, Ellis Laurimore III, Kathryn Noel Phillips Zimmermann, Cynthia AB, Princeton U., 1942; LLB, Columbia U., 1948; LLD, Keuka Coll., NYC, 1956; LLD (hon.), Adelphi U., 1979; LL.D. (hon.), L.I. U., 1980, Ithaca Coll., 1986. Bar: N.Y. 1948. With firm Burke & Burke, NYC, 1948-53; mem. staff Pres.'s Com. Internat. Info. Activities, 1953; asst. dean Columbia Sch. Law, 1953-61, assoc. prof. law, 1953-56, prof., 1956-70, dir. univ. budget, 1961-64; pres. Ithaca (N.Y.) Coll., 1970-75. Spl. asst. to U.S. amb. to Eng. Ct. St. James, US Dept. State,

1957-58. Author: (with others) Cases and Materials in Accounting for Lawyers, 1964, The Legal Profession, 1970, Information Services for Academic Administration, 1971, Look Back from Forty, 1967, A New Approach to Academic Administration, 1969, Accounting and the Law: Cases and Materials, 1978. Pres. Bd. Edn. Union Free Sch. Dist. 15, Jericho, L.I., 1950-53, Ellis L. Phillips Found., 1959-93, v.p., 1993-2006; pres. Action Com. for L.I., Inc., 1978-81; trustee Inc. Village Brookville, L.I., 1958-64, Bangor Theol. Sem. With AUS, USAF, 1942-45. Republican. Home: Westwood, Mass. Died Sept. 28, 2006.

PICARD, CECIL J., school system administrator; b. Maurice, La., Jan. 1, 1938; s. Roman and Evangeline Picard; m. Gaylen David; children: Tyron, Layne. BA in Upper Elem. Edn., Southwestern La. Inst.; MA in Adminstrn. and Supervision, Sam Houston Tchrs. Coll.; postgrad., La. State U.; HHD (hon.), McNeese State U., 1996. Cert. tchr. elem. edn., secondary edn., prin., city/parish supr., La. Tchr., coach Vermilion Parish Sch. System, 1959-66, h.s. prin., 1966-80; mem. La. Ho. of Reps., 1976-79, La. State Senate, 1979-96, chmn., mem. numerous coms.; supt. of edn. State of La., 1996—2007. Mem. Nat. Conf. of State Legislatures, La. Ednl. TV Authority Bd., La. Ednl. Assessment Testing Commn., So. Regional Edn. Bd., Edn. Commn. of the States, La. Commn. on the Deaf. Bd. trustees Tchrs. Retirement System of La.; bd. dirs. La. Sch. for Math, Sci. and the Arts, Acadiana United Way; mem. St. Alphonse Cath. Ch.; mem. Acadian Heritage and Culture Found., Inc., La. Teenage Pregnancy Commn. Recipient Disting. Legislator award La. Assn. of Educators, 1986, Disting. Svc. award, 1989, Senator of Yr. award La. Fedn. of Tchrs., 1988, Friend of Edn. award, 1996, Legislator of Yr. award La. Assn. of Prins., 1994-95. Mem. La. Farm Bur. and Cattleman's Assn., Vermilion Assn. for Retarded Citizens, Greater Abbeville C. of C., Jaycees, Kiwanis Club, La. H.S. Athletic Assn. (exec. com.). Died Feb. 15, 2007.

PICUS, MARK ANTHONY, broadcasting executive; b. Savannah, Ga., Oct. 1, 1953; s. Lawrence Roy and Phyllis Jane (Ortagus) P.; m. Debra Ann Decker, May 7, 1974 (div. Jan. 1976); m. Kimberly Thomas, Aug. 17, 1984; children: Lawrence, Kristen Michelle Foster. Announcer Sta. WPDQ, Jacksonville, Fla., 1968-75; announcer, gen. mgr. Sta. WKUE, Jacksonville, 1975-79; dir. programing Sta. WQMT, Dalton, Ga., 1979-81; gen. mgr. Sta. WENR, Athens, Tenn., 1981-82; asst. program dir. Sta. KXXY, Oklahoma City, 1982-83; gen. mgr., pres. Sta. WZAZ, Jacksonville, 1983-89; founder, pres., treas., gen. mgr. Picus Broadcasting Corp., Inc., Jacksonville, from 1989. Mem. Nat. Assn. Broadcasters, Fla. Assn. Broadcast. Democrat. Jewish. Died May 18, 2007.

PIEPER, HEINZ PAUL, physiology professor; b. Wuppertal, Germany, Mar. 24, 1920; came to U.S., 1957, naturalized, 1963; s. Heinrich Ludwig and Agnes Marie (Koehler) P.; m. Rose Irmgard Hackl, Apr. 23, 1945. MD, U. Munich, Germany, 1948. Resident 2d Med. Clinic, U. Munich, 1948-50, asst. prof. dept. physiology, 1950-57, Coll. Medicine, Ohio State U., Columbus, 1957-60, assoc. prof., 1960-68, prof., from 1968, chmn. dept. physiology, 1974-85, prof. emeritus, from 1985. Established investigator Am. Heart Assn., 1962-67 Mem. editorial bd.: Am. Jour. Physiology, 1973-82; contbr. articles on cardiovascular physiology to profl. jours. Mem. Am. Physiol. Soc., Ohio Acad. Scis., Sigma Xi. Home: Cape Coral, Fla. Died June 4, 2007.

PIERCE, MARGARET HUNTER, former federal official; b. Weedsport, NY, June 30, 1910; d. Thomas Murray and Ruby (Sanders) Hunter; m. John R. Pierce, Nov. 4, 1950 (div. May 1959); 1 dau., Barbara Hunter Churchill. BA, Mt. Holyoke Coll., 1932; JD, N.Y. U., 1939. Bar: NY 1941, DC 1958. Atty. Office Alien Property Custodian, Washington, 1942-43, 45, Office Solicitor, US Dept. Labor, 1943-45, NLRB, 1946, 47-48; atty.-adv. US Ct. Claims, 1947-48, 48-59, reporter decisions, 1959-68; commr. US Indian Claims Commn., 1968-78; pvt. practice Washington, 1978—2007. V.p. Monday Night Musicales, Inc. Mem. D.C. Bar Assn. (ct. claims com. 1958, mil. law com. 1967), Fed. Bar Assn. (Indian law com.), ABA (sec. adminstrv. law-vets. com., mil. law com., immigration and nationality com.), Women's Bar Assn., Nat. Assn. Women Lawyers, Exec. Women in Govt., Bus. and Profl. Women (Cosmopolitan br.), Am. Women Composers, Zonta (Washington pres. 1977-78), Harvard Club (D.C.), Nat. Press Club Washington. Home: Washington, DC. Died Mar. 17, 2007.

PIERSTORFF, BUCKLEY CHARLES, tech. co. exec.; b. Phila., Apr. 30, 1927; s. Arthur Lewis and Marion Louise (Paddock) P.; B.S., Ohio State U., 1951; m. Bette Smith, July 25, 1948; children— Lyle Ann, Scott Lewis. Research engr. servomechanisms Honeywell Corp., Phila., 1951-56; leader tech. staff RCA, Burlington, Mass., 1956-62; pres. Indatacon Corp., Newton, Mass., 1962-64; tech. staff Calspan Corp., Buffalo, 1964—, asst. head systems evaluation dept., 1967-77, dept. head simulation and tng. dept., 1977-79; div. staff scientist C3 div. Mitre Corp., Bedford, Mass., 1979—; lectr. in field. Mem. safety bd. Village East Aurora (N.Y.) 1974—, planning bd., 1975—. Served with USAAF, 1944-47. Registered profl. engr., Pa., Mass. Mem. IEEE (sr.), AIAA, Assn. Old Crows, Soc. Computer Simulation (sr.), Aircraft Owners and Pilots Assn., Nat. Rifle Assn., Sigma Xi. Republican. Home: Acton, Mass. Died Aug. 5, 2006.

PIEZ, KARL ANTON, biochemist, consultant; b. Newton, Mass., Aug. 30, 1924; s. Karl Anton and Margaret Piez; m. Glades Z. Piez, Apr. 18, 1948 (div. May 1972); children: Janet, Karl, Barbara; m. Janet Rau, June 11, 1972; 1 stepchild, Leslie. BS in Chemistry, Yale U., 1947; PhD in Biochemistry, Northwestern U., 1952. Scientist NIH, Bethesda, Md., 1952-66, scientist emeritus, from 1996; chief lab. biochemistry Nat. Inst. Dental Rsch., Bethesda, 1966-82; v.p. rsch. Collagen Corp., Palo Alto, Calif., 1982-88; v.p. molecular scis. Celtrix Labs., Palo Alto, 1988-91; prof. biochemistry Thomas Jefferson U., Phila., 1991-96; cons. biotech. Bethesda, from 1991. Bd. dirs. Fibro-Gen, San Francisco, Found. Advanced Edn. in Scis., Bethesda; cons. in field; scholar in residence Fogarty Internat. Ctr. NIH, 1991-93. Contbr. 152 articles to profl. jours. Sgt. U.S. Army, 1944-46. Recipient T. Ducket Jones Meml. award Helen Hay Whitney Found., 1970, Disting. Scientist award The Coalition Heritable Disorders Connective Tissue, 1992. Fellow AAAS; mem. Am. Soc. Biochemistry & Molecular Biology, Am. Chem. Soc., The Protein Soc., Internat. Soc. Matrix Biology, Phi Lambda Upsilon, Sigma Xi. Home: Chevy Chase, Md. Died Aug. 25, 2006.

PILE, DONALD LEE ROY, chiropractor, researcher; b. Streator, Ill., Aug. 31, 1922; s. Frank S. and Ruby D. (Redman) P.; m. Doris Irene Johnson, Sept. 5, 1944; children— Forrest Lee, Diana Lorene. Student Eureka Coll., 1940-41; diploma Logan Basic Coll. Chiropractic, 1949. Gen. practice chiropractic medicine, Topeka, Kans., 1950—, researcher, 1960—. Served with AUS, 1942-45. Decorated Bronze Star. Mem. Am. Chiropractic Assn., Kans. Chiropractic Assn., Tau Kappa Epsilon. Lodge: Masons. Patentee in field. Home: Topeka, Kans. Died Mar. 20, 2007.

PINGREE, DAVID EDWIN, ancient languages educator; b. New Haven, Conn., Jan. 2, 1933; s. Daniel and Elizabeth (Maconi) P.; m. Isabelle Sanchirico, June 20, 1963; 1 child, Amanda. AB, Harvard U., 1954, PhD, 1960; LittD (hon.), U. Chgo., 1992. Jr. fellow Harvard U., Cambridge, Mass., 1960-63; from asst. prof. to prof. U. Chgo., 1963-71; prof. history of math. Brown U., Providence, R.I., from 1971. Author: Census of the Exact Sciences in Sanskrit, series A, vols. 1-5, 1970-94, The Latin Picatrix, 1986. Recipient Abhinavavarahamihira award Gov. Uttar Pradesh, 1976. Fellow AAAS; mem. Am. Philos. Soc. Home: Providence, RI. Died Nov. 11, 2005.

PINKERTON, SHELTON, veterinarian; b. Georgiana, Ala., Apr. 1, 1926; s. Clarence Hamilton and Flora Mae (Burkett) P.; m. Dorothy Leona Reeves, Apr. 20, 1951; children: Drew Shelton Pinkerton, Sharon. BS, Auburn U., 1948, DVM, 1954. Pvt. practice, Troy, Ala., 1954-59, Pensacola, Fla., 1960-84, Gulf Beach, Fla., 1984-87. With U.S. Army, 1944-46, ETO. Recipient Centennial medallion N.Y. Vet. Soc., 1990; named to Hon. Order Ky. Cols., 1990. Mem. AVMA (chmn. exec. bd. 1988-89, pres. 1990-91), Fla. Vet. Med. Assn. (pres. 1971-72, Vet. of Yr., 1974, Exec. Disting. svc. award 1990), Rotary (mem. various com. 1979-84), Masons, Shriners. Republican. Episcopalian. Home: Pensacola, Fla. Died Jan. 16, 2007.

PINKNEY, ALPHONSO, sociology educator, writer; b. Fla., Dec. 15, 1928; s. Graham and Althea Margaret (Pinkston) P.; m. Sacha Grocholewska, July 30, 1982 (div. Jan. 1984). AB, Fla. A&M U., 1951; MA, NYU, 1952; PhD, Cornell U., 1961. Prof. sociology Hunter Coll., CUNY, NYC, 1961-69, 75-90, prof. emeritus, from 1990; prof. U. Chgo., 1969-71, Howard U., Washington, 1971-72, U. Calif., Berkeley, 1973-75. Author: Black Americans, 1969, The American Way of Violence, 1972, Red, Black and Green, 1976, The Myth of Black Progress, 1984, Lest We Forget, 1992. Ford Found. fellow, 1960-61, 71. Avocation: tennis. Home: New York, NY. Died Jan. 15, 2006.

PINKSTAFF, CARLIN ADAM, anatomist; b. Louisville, Ill., June 10, 1934; s. Lester D. and Helen Eva (Armstrong) P.; m. Delores Aileen McCallum, Jan. 1, 1958; 1 child, Cheryl Ann. Student, Vincennes U., 1956-58; BS with honors, Eastern Ill. U., 1960; PhD, Emory U., 1964. Instr. anatomy U. Oreg. Dental Sch., Portland, 1964-65, asst. prof., anatomy, 1965-67, W.Va. U., Sch. Medicine, Morgantown, 1967-70, assoc. prof., anatomy, 1970-81, prof. anatomy, from 1981. Vis. prof. U. Ibadan, Nigeria, 1973, Yerkes Regional Primate Ctr., Atlanta, 1973, St. Georgia's U. Sch. Medicine, Grenada, W.I., 1979, 90, 91, Semmelweis U. Medicine, Budapest, Hungary, 1982; cons. in histochemistry, FDA, Div. Pathology, Washington, 1979-80. Editorial bd.: European Jour. of Histochemistry, 1984—, Jour. of Histochemistry and Cytochemistry, 1992-96; contbr. articles to profl. jours., books. With USMC, 1954-56. Mem. Am. Assn. Anatomists, Histochem. Soc., Internat. Fedn. Socs. for Histochemistry and Cytochemistry, N.Y. Acad. Scis., Internat. Assn. Dental Rsch., Am. Assn. Dental Rsch., Am. Assn. Dental Schs., AAAS, Am. Soc. Mammalogists, Fedn. Am. Socs. for Exptl. Biology. Home: Morgantown, W.Va. Died Mar. 22, 2007.

PINNEY, SIDNEY DILLINGHAM, JR., lawyer; b. Hartford, Conn., Nov. 17, 1924; s. Sydney Dillingham and Louisa (Griswold) Wells P.; m. Judith Munch, Sept. 30, 1990; children from previous marriage: William Griswold, David Rees. Student, Amherst Coll., 1941—43, BA cum laude, 1947; student, Brown U., 1943, MIT, 1943—44; LLB, Harvard U., 1950. Bar: Conn. 1950. Pvt. practice, Hartford, 1950; assoc. Shepherd, Murtha and Merritt, Hartford, 1950-53; ptnr. Murtha, Cullina, Richter & Pinney (1967) (name changed to Murtha Cullina LLP 2000), 1953-92; of counsel Murtha Cullina LLP, from 1993. Lectr. on estate planning. Contbr. Estate Planning mag. Bd. dirs. Greater Hartford Area TB and Respiratory Diseases Health Soc., 1956-69, pres., 1966-67; mem. Wethersfield (Conn.) Town Coun., 1958-62; trustee Hartford Conservatory Music, 1967-71, 75-81; trustee, pres. Hist. Wethersfield Found., 1961-81; bd. dirs. Hartford Hosp., 1971-80, adv. bd., 1980—; mem. adv. com. Jefferson House, 1978-82; mem. Mortensen Libr. Bd. Visitors U. Hartford, 1984—; corporator Hartford Pub. Libr., 1969—, Renbrook Sch., West Hartford, Conn., 1970-75. 2d lt. USAAF, 1944-46, 1st lt., 1946. Fellow Am. Coll. Trust and Estate Counsel; mem. ABA, Nat. Acad. Elder Law Attys., Conn. Bar Assn. (com. elder law sect.), Hartford County Bar Assn. Republican. Congregationalist. Home: Avon, Conn. Died Jan. 3, 2007.

PIPER, ALEXANDER ROSS, III, investment banker; b. Bklyn., Mar. 6, 1936; s. Alexander Ross, Jr. and Ruth (Fitch) P.; children— Alexandra, Ross J.; m. Martha Famula, 1982 BA in Econs, Cornell U., 1958. With Paine, Webber, Jackson & Curtis, NYC, from 1959, partner, 1960-80, sr. v.p., dir., 1973-80; partner Neild Cruikshank Co., stock option traders, NYC, from 1980; with Cohen, Cohn and Duffy, Am. Stock Exchange option specialists, NYC, from 1985. Mem. Am. Stock Exchange, 1960-62, N.Y. Stock Exchange, 1961-73; dir., mem. exec. com. Chgo. Bd. Options Exchange, 1977-80 Served as 2d lt. U.S. Army, 1958-59. Mem. Nat. Suffolk Sheep Assn., Bond Club N.Y., Am. Stock Exchange Market Makers Assn. (vice chmn. 1982-85) Clubs: Stock Exchange Luncheon (pres. 1976-79) Madison Sq. Garden (N.Y.C.); Brook, Piping Rock, Wyantenuc Country. Republican. Episcopalian. Home: Mount Washington Mass. Died Sept. 20, 2006.

PIPPIN, JOHN ELDON, electronics engineer, electronic company executive; b. Kinard, Fla., Oct. 7, 1927; s. Festus an Mary Elvie (Scott) P.; m. Barbara A. Pippin, June 15, 195 children: Carol Jean Pippin Franklin, John F., Mary Christin Pippin Mobley. B.E.E., Ga. Inst. Tech., 1951, MSE.E., 195 PhD in Applied Physics, Harvard U., 1958. Research. engr. Ga Inst. Tech. Expt. Sta., Atlanta, 1951-53; head research dep Sperry Microwave Electronics Co., Clearwater, Fla., 1958-64 v.p., dir. research Scientific-Atlanta, Inc., 1964-68; pres. Electromagnetic Scis., Inc., Norcross, Ga., from 1968. Adj. prof. U Fla., 1962-64; cons. Cascade Research Corp., 1953-58 Contb articles to profl. jours. Served in USN, 1945-46. NSF fellow Gen. Commns. fellow. Fellow IEEE (Outstanding Engr. Regio III 1972, Engr. of Yr. 1972); mem. Briarean Soc., Am. Phys Soc., Microwave Theory and Techniques Soc. (adminstr com.), Sigma Xi, Tau Beta Pi, Phi Kappa Phi, Eta Kappa Nu Achievements include research in microwave physics; rada tracking problems. Home: Duluth, Ga. Died July 13, 2007.

PITT, LELDON P., retired surgeon, educator; b. Trinity, Ala 1920; MD, Columbia U., 1945. Diplomate Am. Bd. Surger Intern Meth. Hosp., Bklyn., 1945-46; surg. resident Garfiel Meml. Hosp., Washington, 1948-49; resident in pathology Pa Hosp., Phila., 1949-50, surg. resident, 1950-53; surg. fello Jefferson Med. Coll. Hosp., Phila., 1953; staff surgeon Pa Hosp., Phila., 1955-70, sr. surgeon, 1970-89, chief cardiothoracic surgery, 1973-88, chief emergency medicine svcs., 198 89, honorary surgeon, 1989—2007. Asst. prof. U. Pa. Med. Sc Med. officer U.S. Army, 1946-48, The Philippines and Japa Recipient Orville C. King M.D. Surgical award. Fellow ACS mem. AMA. Home: Malvern, Pa. Died Nov. 7, 2007.*

PIVIK, ROBERT WILLIAM, accounting executive; Renton, Pa., Oct. 29, 1937; s. George and Amelia (Kern) P.; m Yvonne C. Pivik, Aug. 6, 1960; children: Keith, Sharon, Trace BS, Pa. State U., 1959. CPA, D.C. Staff acct. Deloitte Haskins Sells, Pitts., 1959-67, mgr. NYC, 1967-72, ptnr., 1972, variou positions, 1967-83, ptnr.-in-charge Washington, 1983-86, are mng. ptnr. Md., Va. and Washington, 1986-89; group mng. ptr Deloitte and Touche, Md., Va., Pa., Washington, from 1989; als bd. dirs. Deloitte Haskins & Sells; chief fin. officer Deloitte Touche, from 1993. Mem. Greater Washington bd. Trade, 198 tax policy task force, 1985, chmn. mktg. com., 1989-90. Legac com. Md. civ. Am. Cancer Soc., Silver Spring, 1984; adv. cor DeSales Sch. Theology, Washington, 1986; trustee Fed. Ci Coun., 1990—; adv. com. mayor of Washington, 1991, mer subcom. Mgmt. System. & Tech. Mem. AICPA, Columbia Ins CPAs, Washington-Balt. Regional Assn. (bd. dirs.), Econ. Cl Washington, Tournament Players Club, Univ. Club, City Clu Beta Gamma Sigma, Phi Kappa Phi, Alpha Psi. Republica Roman Catholic. Avocation: golf. Died July 25, 2006.

PIVIROTTO, RICHARD ROY, former retail executive; Youngstown, Ohio, May 26, 1930; s. Arthur M. and Ru (Erhardt) P.; m. Mary Burchfield, June 27, 1953; children: Ma B., Richard Roy, Susan W., Nancy P., David H., Jennifer P. A Princeton U., 1952; MBA, Harvard U., 1954. Pres. Jose Horne Co., Pitts., 1954-70; vice chmn. Associated Dry Goo Corp., NYC, 1970-72, pres., 1972-76, chmn. bd., 1976-81, al dir.; pres. Richard Pivirotto, Inc., from 1981; non-exec. chm The Gillette Co., Boston, from 2000. Bd. dirs. CBS Corp., N. Gen. Am. Investors Co., N.Y.C., N.Y. Life Ins. Co., Gille Corp., Immunomedics Inc., Morris Plains, N.J.; dir. Greenwi Bank & Trust Co., Infinity Broadcasting Co., Yale New Hav Health Svc., Inc. Trustee Princeton U., 1977—; trustee Gree wich Hosp.; bd. dirs. Gen. Theol. Sem., N.Y.C. Served w AUS, 1955-56. Mem. Am. Retail Fedn. (dir. 1968-81) Clu Princeton (N.Y.C.); Duquesne, Rolling Rock, Fox Chapel G (Pitts.); Greenwich, Country, Field of Greenwich; Bald Pe Colony (Melvin Village, N.H.). Died Jan. 8, 2007.

PLAMONDON, WILLIAM NELSON, JR., oil compa executive; b. Chgo., Sept. 5, 1924; s. William Nelson a Elisabeth Cecile (Hauck) P.; B.Engring., M.E., Yale U., 194 M.S. in Mgmt. Engring., N.J. Inst. Tech., 1954; m. Ma Elizabeth Heller, Aug. 17, 1946; children— William Nels Jeffrey, Donna Plamondon Scully, Mark. With Caltex Petrole Corp., N.Y.C., 1951-55; with Continental-Emsco Co., N.Y. and Houston, 1956-73, mgr. sales-internat. div., 1967-73; m mktg. Dixilyn Corp., Houston, 1973-76; v.p. sales and contra Zapata Off-Shore Co., Houston, 1976-77; v.p. mktg. Dixily Field Drilling Co., Houston, 1977-80; v.p. market devel. Glo Marine Drilling Co., Houston, 1981-82; v.p. mktg. and sa Houston Offshore Internat., Inc., 1982—; lectr. marine offsh seminars Tex. A. and M. U., 1975, 76, 80. Served to lt. (j. USN, 1943-46; PTO. Mem. Soc. Petroleum Engrs., Intern Assn. Drilling Contractors (dir., past chmn. Houston chpt.), A Petroleum Inst., Nomads (past pres. N.Y. chpt.). Republica Roman Catholic. Clubs: Petroleum of Houston, Petroleum Lafayette, Warwick. Contbr. articles to trade jours. Ho Houston, Tex. Died Jan. 21, 2006.

PLASTERR, NORMA LIVELY, English educator; b. Louis, Nov. 8, 1928; d. Charles Elmer and Beulah Alme (Strawhun) Lively; m. Charles Henderson Plasterr, Nov. 1948; children— Adele, Stephen, Michael. Student U. M 1946-48, Washington U., summer 1948; A.B., U. Charlest 1961; M.A., Marshall U., 1965, postgrad., 1968-78. Tc Chapmanville Pub. Schs. (W.Va.), 1958-67; instr. Engli Marshall U., Logan, W.Va., 1967-71; prof. English, So. W. Community Coll., Logan, 1971—. Recipient Nick Savas O standing Faculty award, 1983. Methodist. Lodge: Eastern S Home: Chapmanville, W.Va. Died Nov. 18, 2006.

PLAVOUKOS, SPENCER, advertising executive; b. NY May 30, 1936; s. George and Elva (Murzi) P.; m. Harriet Ph Gladstone, Jan. 9, 1964; children: Stacy, Matthew. BS, Syrac U., 1961. Account exec. SSC&B, Inc., NYC, 1961-64; acco exec. Grey Advt., 1964-67; exec. v.p., dir. account serv lanoff Advt., NYC, 1967-79; exec. v.p. SSC&B, NYC, 1979; hmn., chief exec. officer Lintas: N.Y. (formerly SSC&B), NYC, ntil 1991; formerly vice chmn. Lintas: USA; pres., Lintas: Worldwide, chmn., Lintas: Americas, from 1991. Mem.: Coun-y of New Canaan, Marco Polo (N.Y.C.), St. James (London). Iome: New Canaan, Conn. Died Oct. 26, 2005.

'LETZ, FRANCIS GREGORY, retired banker; b. Lakefield, Iinn., Aug. 23, 1917; s. John F. and Anna (Pietsch) P.; m. 'irginia E. Connell, Sept. 12, 1942 (dec. 1977); children— 'homas G., John F.; m. Florence B. Haynes, Sept. 29, 1978. AB umma cum laude, Coll. St. Thomas, St. Paul, 1940; MBA with istinction (Arthur Andersen accounting fellow), U. Mich., 942; JD magna cum laude, U. Toledo, 1950; grad., Rutgers U., 956. Bar: Ohio bar 1950. Teller First Nat. Bank, Lakefield, 937-38; research asst. Bur. Bus. Research, U. Mich., 1940-41; ccountant Ernst & Ernst, Detroit, summer 1941; with Toledo 'rust Co., from 1946, sr. v.p., head trust dept., 1968-81, sec., 973-81, ret., 1981. Former dir. Alloy Founders, Inc., Mather 'o. Former trustee Toledo Soc. for Blind, Stranahan Charitable 'ound., St. Vincent Hosp. Served to lt. USNR, 1942-46, ETO. Iem. Ohio, Lucas County, Toledo bar assns., Toledo C. of C., ion. Clubs: Toledo (Toledo), Sylvania Country (Toledo). Iome: Toledo, Ohio. Died Jan. 22, 2006.

'LIMPTON, CALVIN HASTINGS, retired academic admin-strator; b. Boston, Oct. 7, 1918; s. George Arthur and Fanny Iastings) P.; m. Ruth Talbot, Sept. 6, 1941; children: David, homas, George (dec.), Anne, Edward. BA cum laude, Amherst 'oll., 1939; MD cum laude, Harvard, 1943, MA, 1947; Med. ci.D., Columbia, 1951; LL.D., Williams Coll., 1960, Wesleyan '., 1961, Doshisha U., Kyoto, Japan, 1962, St. Lawrence U., 963, Amherst U., 1971; L.H.D., U. Mass., 1962; D.Sc., ockford Coll., 1962, St. Mary's, 1963, Trinity Coll., 1966, rinnell Coll., Iowa, 1967; Litt.D., Am. Internat. Coll., 1965, Iich. State Coll., 1969; DSc, N.Y. Med. Coll., 1986. Diplomate: 'at. Bd. Med. Examiners, Am. Bd. Internal Medicine. Intern, sst. resident, resident medicine Presbyn. Hosp., NYC, 1947-50; sst. attending physician Columbia-Presbyn. Med. Center, 1950-0; asso. medicine (Coll. Phys. and Surg.), 1950-59, asst. prof. lin. medicine, 1959-60; prof. medicine, chmn. dept. Am. U. eirut, Am. U. Hosp., Beirut, 1957-59; pres. Amherst Coll., 960-71, Downstate Med. Center, SUNY, 1971-79, dean med. :h., 1971-74, 76-79, prof. medicine, 1971-82, prof. emeritus, 982—2007; pres. Am. U., Beirut, 1984-87. Vis. prof. Columbia 'esbyn. Med. Ctr., 1976-77. Trustee Am. U., Beirut, 1960-90, ustee emeritus, 1990-2007, chmn. bd., 1965-82; trustee World eace Found., 1962-77, Phillips Exeter Acad., 1963-76, Com-onwealth Fund, 1962-83, Hampshire Coll., 1963-71, U. Mass., 962-70, LI U., 1972-82, NY Law Sch., 1976-84; mem. Harvard d. Overseers, 1969-75. Capt. US Army, 1944-46, ETO. Deco-ated comdr. Order of Cedars Lebanon; recipient award Nat. eog. Soc., award New Eng. Soc., John Phillips award Phillip xeter Acad., Battle Star Ctrl. Europe. Fellow ACP; mem. Am. cad. Arts and Scis., Russian Fedn. Acad. Med. Tech. Scis., oun. Fgn. Rels., Soc. Mayflower Descs., Harvey Soc., Alpha mega Alpha, Sigma Xi. Clubs: Century, Univ. (NYC), Charaka IYC), Riverdale Yacht (NYC), Pilgrims (NYC); Tavern Bos-n. Died Jan. 30, 2007.

LOTNICK, MARK MICHAEL, manufacturing executive; b. amford, Conn., Nov. 24, 1935; s. Samuel and Miriam P.; m. ucille Marie Rotanelli, Dec. 28, 1958; children: Kristi, Mike. A, U. Vt., 1957. With AMF Inc., from 1959; gen. mgr. ops. fg. plant Shelby, Ohio, 1973-77; v.p. ops., 1977; pres. bowling v. internat. Westbury, N.Y., 1979; now pres. Plotnick Assocs. apital Equipment, Lexington, Ohio. Mem. Lexington (Ohio) d. Edn., 1978, 84-88; bd. dirs. Miss Ohio Scholarship Pageant, 988-89. With AUS, 1958-59. Named Father of Year Lexington, 974 Home: Mansfield, Ohio. Died Feb. 26, 2006.

LUCKNETT, DONALD LOVELLE, scientific advisor; b. eWitt, Nebr., Sept. 9, 1931; s. William Donald and Phyllis orrine (Barkey) P.; m. Ida Sue Richards, May 14, 1955; ildren: Karen, Roy, Duane BS, U. Nebr., 1953, MS, 1957; iD, U. Hawaii, 1961. Cert. profl. soil scientist, profl. agrono-ist. Grad. asst. U. Hawaii, Honolulu, 1958-60, instr., 1960-61, st. prof., 1961-65, assoc. prof., 1965-70, prof., 1970-80; Ford ound. sr. agrl. cons. Egypt-Aswan Agrl. Devel., 1965; chief soil d water mgmt. div. Office Agr. AID, 1973-76; dep. exec. dir. d. Internat. Food and Agrl. Devel., Washington, 1978-79; chief rl. and rural devel. div. Asia bur. AID, 1979-80, sci. adv. nsultative group on internat. agrl. research World Bank, 980—93. Cons. in field Author: Common Weeds of the iilippines, 1969, The World's Worst Weeds, 1977, Farming ystems Research at the International Agricultural Research enters, 1978, A Geographic Atlas of World Weeds, 1979, anaging Pastures and Cattle Under Coconuts, 1979, Azolla as Green Manure, 1982, Gene Banks and the World's Food, 987; (free verse) The Roof Only Leaked When It Rained, 1985; itor: Vegetable Farming Systems in China, 1981, Small Scale ocessing and Storage of Tropical Root Crops, 1979; (series) estview Tropical Agricultural, Detecting Mineral Nutrient eficiencies in Tropical and Temperate Crops, 1989; contbr. icles to profl. jours. Served to 1st lt. U.S. Army, 1953-55 cipient: Superior Honor award AID, 1976, Alumni Achieve-ent award, Nebr. Alumni Assn., 2002; named an Illustrious umnus, U. Hawaii, 1997; NSF fellow, 1960 Fellow AAAS, n. Soc. Agronomy, Soil Sci. Soc. Am., Crop Sci. Soc. Am.; em. Internat. Soc. Tropical Root Crops (hon. life, pres. 76-79, 79-83), Asian Pacific Weed Sci. Soc. (sec. 1969-70, -81), Indian Soc. Root Crops, Soc. for Econ. Botany, Hawai-i Acad. Sci. Methodist. Home: Annandale, Va. Died Sept. 3, 07.

.UM, CHARLES WALDEN, retired business executive, ucator; b. Circleville, Ohio, Apr. 13, 1914; s. Horace Walden d Anna Frances (Eaton) P.; m. Margaret E. McCollister, Sept. 39; children: David Walden, Donald Alan (dec.). BS, Ohio ate U., 1936; MBA, Case Western Res. U., 1951; postgrad., dvanced Mgmt. Program, Harvard, 1954. CPA, N.Y., Ohio, x. Sr. accountant Coopers and Lybrand, NYC, 1936-42; supr. ctg. Amertorp Corp., Naval Ordnance Plant, St. Louis, 1942-; various positions including asst. contr., dep. contr., contr. to v.p. acctg. and mgmt. systems Standard Oil Co. (Ohio), Cleve., 1945-78; prof. bus. adminstrn. Tex. A&M U., College Station, 1978-89. Dir., chmn. audit com. Hospitality Motor Inns, Inc., Cleve., 1976-79; sec.-treas., dir., mem. mgmt. com. Am. Assembly Collegiate Schs. Bus., 1977-78; lectr. acctg. Western Res. U., 1946-54; bus. exec. in residence, disting. lectr. Tex. A. and M. U., 1976; Mem. bus. adv. council Kent State U., 1967-77 Mem. AICPA, Fin. Execs. Inst., Am. Petroleum Inst. (chmn. com. on cooperation with AICPA 1955-68), Tex. Soc. CPAs, Sigma Phi Epsilon, Beta Gamma Sigma, Beta Alpha Psi. Home: Allen, Tex. Died Nov. 10, 2006.

PODEWELL, KENNETH ROLAND, organization executive; b. Chgo., May 13, 1915; s. Edwin and Anna (Birkigt) P.; m. Dorothy Margaret Buehler, July 1, 1939; children— Roger, Nancy, Carol, Clifford. Chief ranger Ind. Order of Foresters, Blue Island, Ill., 1960-62, high chief ranger, Chgo., 1966-81, 1981—, supreme councillor Supreme Exec. Council, Toronto, Ont., Can., 1981—. Active Republican. Party campaign for presdl. campaign, 1980, 84. Recipient Grand Cross of Legion of Honor, Ind. Order Foresters, 1977. Mem. Traveler's Protective Assn. (pres. 1982-84), South Side Suburban Real Estate Bd. (pres. 1964), Mem. United Ch. of Christ. Died Mar. 28, 2007.

POE, LOUISE ADELINE See SWEARINGEN, LOUISE ADELINE

POLAKOWSKI, WILLIAM J., municipal official; b. Hamtramck, Mich., Dec. 26, 1933; Student, Wayne State U. Gen. mgr. Detroit-Wayne Joint Bldg. Authority. Bd. commrs. Wayne County Bldg. Authority. With U.S. Navy. Mem. UAW, Polish-Am. Citizens for Equity, Bldg. Owners & Mgmt. Assn. Died Apr. 30, 2007.

POLEDOURIS, BASIL K., composer; b. Kansas City, Mo., Aug. 21, 1945; s. Konstantine John and Helen Poledouris; m. Barbara Renée Godfrey, Aug. 15, 1969; children: Zoë Renée, Alexis Elene. BA in Music and Cinema, U. So. Calif., 1967, postgrad., 1967-69. Intern Am. Film Inst., LA, 1969; freelance composer Hollywood, Calif., from 1970; pres. Basil Poledouris, Inc., Encino, Calif., 1987—2006. Bd. dirs. Blowtorch Flats, Venice, Calif.; mem. adv. bd. Soc. for Preservation Film Music, L.A., 1985-2006. Composer (film music) 90028, 1971, Extreme Close-Up, 1973, Tintorerra, 1977, Big Wednesday, 1979, Defiance, 1979, The Blue Lagoon, 1988, The House of God, 1988, Conan the Barbarian, 1981, Summer Lovers, 1982, Making the Grade, 1984, Conan the Destroyer, 1984, Red Dawn, 1984, Protocol, 1984, Flesh and Blood, 1985, Cherry 2000, 1986, Iron Eagle, 1986, Robocop, 1987 (BMI award 1988), No Man's Land, 1987, Split Decisions, 1988, Spellbinder, 1988, Farewell to the King, 1989, Wired, 1989, Hunt for Red October, 1990 (BMI award 1991), Quigley Down Under, 1990, Flight of the Intruder, 1991, White Fang, 1992, Return to the Blue Lagoon, 1991, Harley Davidson and the Marlboro Man, 1991, Robocop III, 1992, Free Willy, 1992 (BMI award 1994, gold record 1994), Hot Shots! Part Deux, 1993, Serial Mom, 1993, On Deadly Ground, 1994, Lassie, 1994, Jungle Book, 1994, Free Willy II, 1995, Under Seige II, 1995, It's My Party, 1995, Celtic Pride, 1996, Amanda, 1996, The War at Home, 1996, Switchback, 1996, Breakdown, 1997, Starship Troopers, 1997, Les Miserables, 1998, Mickey Blue Eyes, 1999, Amanda, 1999, For Love of the Game, 1999, Cecil B DeMented, 2000, Crocodile Dundee in L.A., 2001, The Touch, 2002, (TV film music) Congratulations It's A Boy, 1973, A Whale for the Killing, 1981, Fire on the Mountain, 1981, Amazons, 1984, Single Women, Single Bars, 1984, Amerika, 1987, Intrigue, 1988, Lonesome Dove, 1989 (Emmy award 1988, BMI award 1989), Nasty Boys, 1989, Lone Justice, 1990, Return to Lonesome Dove, 1993, TV pilots Alfred Hitchcock Presents, 1985, Misfits of Science, 1986, Island Sons, 1987, Murphy's Law, L.A. Takedown, 1989, Life and Times of Ned Blessing, 1991, Zoya, 1995, Tradition of Games Opening Ceremonies, 1996 Olympics, If These Walls Could Talk II, 2000, Dark Targets, 2001, The Legend of Butch and Sundance, 2003. Recipient resolution Calif. Legislature, 1990, Orange County Bd. Suprs., 1990, Key to City, Garden Grove City Coun., 1990, Disting. Artist award Calif. State U., Long Beach, 1992. Mem. NARAS, BMI, Am. Fedn. Musicians, Acad. Motion Picture Arts and Scis., Acad. Television Arts and Scis., Soc. Lyricists and Composers. Avocations: sailing, surfing, tai chi, Qi Gong. Home: Vashon, Wash. Died Nov. 8, 2006.

POLK, ROTHWELL CONWAY, retired medical researcher; b. Lakeland, Fla., Apr. 11, 1921; s. Robert Henry and Roberta (Conway) P.; m. Jacqueline Dew, Aug. 31, 1946; children: Beverly Polk Dieball, Rothwell Conway Jr., Richard Lee, Michael Dew. BA, Emory U., 1942; MD, Ga. Med. Coll., 1945. Diplomate Am. Bd. Surgery. Med. researcher G.D. Searle & Co., Skokie, Ill., 1965-86, ret., 1986. Contbr. articles to profl. jours. Bd. dirs. Ill. div. Am. Cancer Soc., Chgo., 1979—, 400 Ode Condominium Assn., Chgo., 1986—. Capt. U.S. Army, 1946-48. Recipient Disting. Svc. award Am. Cancer Soc., 1986. Fellow ACS, Am. Coll. Gastroenterology. Republican. Episcopalian. Avocations: fishing, electronics, travel. Home: Chicago, Ill. Died Mar. 7, 2006.

POLLARD, WILLIAM SHERMAN, JR., civil engineer, educator; b. Oak Grove, La., Jan. 1, 1925; s. William Sherman and Carrie Lois (Hornor) P.; m. Gloria Louise Ponder, June 29, 1946; children: William Sherman, III, Katherine Lynn. BS in Civil Engring, Purdue U., 1946, MS, 1948. Instr. civil engring. Purdue U., 1948-49; instr. U. Ill., 1949-51, assoc. prof., 1951-55; with Harland Bartholomew & Assos., St. Louis, 1955-71, assoc. partner, chief civil engr., 1956-58, partner Memphis, 1958-71, head ops., 1958-60; head Harland Bartholomew & Assos. (Memphis office), 1960-71; pres. William S. Pollard Cons., Inc., Memphis, 1971-81; prof. civil engring. U. Colo., Denver, from 1981. Adj. prof. urban planning Memphis State U., 1973-81; dir. Ctr. Urban Transp. Studies, U. Colo.; chmn. WKNO-TV, Memphis. Served with USMC, 1942-46. Named Distinguished Engring. Alumnus Purdue U., 1969 Fellow Am. Cons. Engrs. Council, ASCE (state of the art award 1970), Inst. Transp. Engrs.; mem. Am. Rd. Builders Assn., Nat. Soc. Profl. Engrs., Soc. Am. Mil. Engrs., Urban Land Inst., Transp. Research Bd., Lambda Alpha. Lodges: Rotary (pres. 1979-80). Presbyterian. Died June 4, 2007.

POLNAK, JOHN LEONARD, humanities educator, administrator; b. Cohoes, N.Y., July 13, 1952; s. Leon J. Polnak and Joan N. (Bullock) Barard; m. Carol S. Frament, May 31, 1975; 1 child, John. BMus., State U. Coll., Potsdam, 1974, MS, 1978; MAT, George Washington U., 1980. Tchr. Madrid/Waddington Sch., N.Y., 1974-78; dir. edn. Rensselaer County Hist. Soc., Troy, N.Y., 1978-81, Albany Inst. History and Art, N.Y., 1981-84; asst. dir. N.Y. State Capitol Commn., Albany, 1984—; cons. Brookside Mus., N.Y., 1981, Hist. Cherry Hill, Albany, 1979-81, Inst. Mus. Services, Washington, 1981, Russell Sage Coll., Troy, 1982, Rensselaer County Hist. Soc. Bd. dirs. United Way Hudson-Mohawk, Troy, 1981-85, Hudson Mohawk Indsl. Gateway, Troy, 1986—, Rensselaer County Jr. Mus., Troy, 1986—, Scotia-Glenville Children's Mus., 1987—; mem. publs. com. Fedn. Hist. Services, 1986—; mem. program com. Rensselaer County Council of Arts, 1987—. Contbr. articles to profl. jours. Bd. dirs. United Way Hudson-Mohawk, Troy, 1981—; mem. Lansingburgh Sch. Redistricting Task Force, Troy, 1984; mem. cultural affairs com. Troy Sr. Ctr., 1979-84. Mem. Am. Assn. Mus., Am. Assn. for State and Local History, Nat. Hist. Trust, Fedn. Hist. Services. Home: Voorheesville, NY. Died May 7, 2007.

POLSBY, NELSON WOOLF, political science professor; b. Norwich, Conn., Oct. 25, 1934; s. Daniel H and Edythe (Woolf) P.; m. Linda Dale Offenbach, Aug. 3, 1958; children: Lisa, Emily, Daniel R. AB, Johns Hopkins, 1956; MA, Yale U., 1958, PhD, 1961; LittD, U. Liverpool, 1992; MA, Oxford U., Eng., 1997; Dr. h.c. (hon.), Ecole Normale Superieure de Cachan, 2002. Instr. U. Wis., 1960-61; from asst. prof. to prof. Wesleyan U., Middletown, Conn., 1961-68; prof. polit. sci. U. Calif., Berkeley, 1967. Dir. Inst. Govtl. Studies U. Calif., 1989-99; vis. faculty Columbia, 1963, Yale, 1963, 67, 75, Hebrew U., Jerusalem, 1970, Stanford, 1977, Harvard U., 1986-87, Oxford U., 1994, 97-98; com. on pub. engring. policy Nat. Acad. Engring., 1973-76; commn. on behavioral and social scis. and edn. NRC, 1983-89. Author: Community Power and Political Theory, 2d edit, 1980, Congress and the Presidency, 4th edit, 1986, (with Aaron Wildavsky) Presidential Elections, 11th edit, 2004, Congress: An Introduction, 1968, Political Promises, 1974, (with Geoffrey Smith) British Government and its Discontents, 1981, Consequences of Party Reform, 1983, Political Innovation in America, 1984, (with Alan Brinkley and Kathleen Sullivan) New Federalist Papers, 1997, How Congress Evolves, 2004; editor: (with R.A. Dentler and P. Smith) Politics and Social Life, 1963, (with R.L. Peabody) New Perspectives on the House of Representatives, 4th edit, 1993, Congressional Behavior, 1971, Reapportionment in the 1970's, 1971, The Modern Presidency, 1973, (with F.I. Greenstein) Handbook of Political Science, 8 vols., 1975, What If?, 1982, (with G. Orren) Media and Momentum, 1987; book rev. editor: Transaction, 1968-71; mng. editor: Am. Polit. Sci. Rev, 1971-77; editor Ann. Rev. Polit. Sci., 1998-2005, The Forum Online; editorial adv. bd. Polit. Sci. Quar., other jours. Mem. commn. on vice presdl. selection Dem. Nat. Com., 1973-74; mem. Yale U. Coun., 1978-2000, pres., 1986-93. Fellow Social Sci. Research Council, 1959, Brookings Instn., 1959-60, Center Advanced Study Behavioral Scis., 1965-66, 85-86, Ford Found., 1970-71, John Simon Guggenheim Found., 1977-78, 85-86, Roosevelt Ctr., 1982-83; recipient Yale U. Wilbur Cross medal, 1985, Yale medal, 1997. Fellow AAAS; mem. Am. Polit. Sci. Assn. (coun. 1971-77, 88-89), Am. Acad. Arts and Scis. (coun. 1993-96), Am. Sociol. Assn., Nat. Acad. Pub. Adminstrn., Coun. on Fgn. Rels., Phi Beta Kappa. Home: Berkeley, Calif. Died Feb. 6, 2007.

POPE, LEAVITT JOSEPH, broadcast company executive; b. Boston, Apr. 2, 1924; s. Joseph and Charlotte (Leavitt) P.; m. Martha Pascale, Nov. 20, 1948; children: Joseph, Daniel, Patricia, Elizabeth, Nancy, Maria, Joan, Christopher, Virginia, Matthew, Charles. BS, Mass. Inst. Tech., 1947. Adminstrv. asst. N.Y. Daily News, NYC, 1947-51; asst. to gen. mgr. Sta. WPIX-TV, NYC, 1951-56, v.p. ops., 1956-72, Sta. WPIX-FM, NYC, 1956-72; sec. WPIX, Inc., NYC, 1958-75, exec. v.p., 1972-75, pres., CEO, 1975-92. Sec., exec. v.p. Conn. Broadcasting Co., Bridgeport, 1967-75, pres., CEO, dir., 1975-87; dir. N.Y. Daily News, 1975-78, Tribune Co., 1978-81; founder Ind. Network News, 1978-89; chair N.Y.C. TV all industry com., advanced TV sys. com. HDTV; chair copyright com. NAB. Mem. N.Y. State Regents Ednl. TV Adv. Council, 1958; bd. govs. Daytop Village, 1972—2007; trustee Catholic Communications Found., St. Thomas Aquinas Coll., 1968-75, Cardinal Cooke Hosp., 1979-2007, vice chair, 1998-2007, Catholic Healthcare Network, 2001-07; dir. Archdiocese N.Y. Instructional TV com. 1976-2007; trustee St. Patrick's Cathedral, N.Y.C., 1992-2007. Served with Signal Corps U.S. Army, 1942-46. Mem. Assn. Ind. TV Stats. (pres. 1976-78, bd. dirs.), ASME, Internat. Radio and TV Soc., Nat. Assn. Broadcasters (dir. 1982-86), N.Y. State Broadcasters (pres. 1976-78), Sigma Nu, Knight of Malta. Clubs: Univ. (N.Y.C.); Riverbend (Tequesta, Fla.). Home: Scarsdale, NY. Died Apr. 18, 2007.

POPE, REBECCA, special education educator; b. Lexington, Ky., Aug. 7, 1948; d. Charles B. and Vela (Moran) Reid; m. W. David Pope, Aug. 16, 1969 (div. Feb. 1981); children: Mark Andrew David, Michael Charles. BA, Asbury Coll., 1969; cert. supr., East Tex. U., 1984; MEd, Western Ky. U., 1978. Cert. tchr. elem. edn., Ky. Tchr. music Fayette County (Ky.) Sch. Dist., 1969-70, tchr. elem. sch., 1970-72; clin. diagnostician Western Ky. U., Bowling Green, 1977-78; coordinator spl. edn. for most handicapping conditions Richardson (Tex.) Ind. Sch. Dist., 1978-81, spl. edn. tchr. emotionally disturbed, 1981—, cons., 1980; lectr. in field. Group leader Mental Health-Mental Retardation, Austin, Tex., 1976-77; in-hospl program for new parents of handicapped children, Austin, 1976-77. Recipient Outstanding Achievement in Spl. Edn. award Richardson Ind. Sch. Dist., 1983. Mem. NEA, Tex. Edn. Assn., Council for Exceptional Children (state student rep. 1977-78), Council for Children with Behavior Disorders, Phi Delta Kappa. Democrat. Methodist. Club: Asbury Coll. Fine Arts (v.p. 1967-68, pres. 1968-69). Died Apr. 25, 2006.

POPPENHAGEN, RONALD WILLIAM, advertising agency executive; b. Chgo., Feb. 23, 1948; s. Andrew Charles and Elaine Edith (Larson) P.; m. Judy Diane Wagenblast, July 25, 1981. BA. in History and Lit., Augustana Coll., 1970. Reporter Sta. KBUR, Burlington, Iowa, 1970-71, Sta. KROS, Clinton, Iowa, 1971-72, Sta. WDWS, Champaign, Ill., 1972-73, news dir., 1973-77; reporter The Morning Courier, Urbana, Ill., 1977-79; mng. editor The Daily Journal, Wheaton, Ill., 1979-80; met. editor The Southern Illinoisan, Carbondale, Ill., 1980-83; editor Green Bay (Wis.) News Chronicle, 1983-86, editor, gen. mgr., 1986-97; v.p., media dir. Wagenblast-Poppenhagen Comms. and Mktg., Green Bay, from 1997. Recipient Best Editls. award Wis. Newspaper Assn., 1985, 86, 93, UPI, 1983-86, Best Local Column award, 1993. Avocation: railroads. Home: Green Bay, Wis. Died Apr. 24, 2006.

POPPER, ROBERT, lawyer, retired dean; b. NYC, May 22, 1932; s. Walter G. and Dorothy B. (Kluger) P.; m. Mary Ann Schaefer, July 12, 1963; children: Julianne, Robert Gregory. BS, U. Wis., 1953; LLB, Harvard U., 1956; LLM, NYU, 1963. Bar: N.Y. 1957, U.S. Dist. Ct. (so. dist.) N.Y. 1962, U.S. Ct. Appeals (2d cir.) 1962, U.S. Supreme Ct. 1962, U.S. Dist. Ct. (ea. dist.) N.Y. 1969, U.S. Ct. Appeals (7th cir.) 1970, U.S. Ct. Appeals (8th cir.) 1971, Mo. 1971, U.S. Dist. Ct. (we. dist.) Mo. 1973. Trial atty. criminal br. N.Y.C. Legal Aid Soc., 1960-61; asst. dist. atty. N.Y. County, 1961-64; assoc. Seligson & Morris, NYC, 1964-69; mem. faculty School of Law U. Mo, Kansas City, 1969-96, prof., 1973-96, acting dean, 1983-84, dean, 1984-93, dean and prof. emeritus, from 1996. Cons. and lectr. in field. Author: Post Conviction Remedies in a Nutshell, 1978, De-Nationalizing the Bill of Rights, 1979; contbr. articles to profl. jours. Bd. trustees Rsch. Psychiat. Ctr. (HCA Midwest). Fellow ABA; mem. Mo. Bar, Kansas City Met. Bar Assn., Mo. Inst. of Justice. Home: Kansas City, Mo. Died Feb. 9, 2007.

PORTE, JOEL MILES, language educator; b. Bklyn., Nov. 13, 1933; s. Jacob I. and Frances (Derison) P.; m. Ilana D'Ancona, June 17, 1962 (div. 1977); 1 child, Susanna Maria; m. Helene Sophrin, Oct. 18, 1985. AB magna cum laude, CCNY, 1957; A.M., Harvard U., 1958, PhD, 1962. Instr. English Harvard U., Cambridge, Mass., 1962-64, asst. prof., 1964-68, assoc. prof., 1968-69, prof., 1969-82, Bernbaum prof. lit., 1982-87, chmn. dept. English and Am. Lit., 1985-87; Frederic J. Whiton prof. English Cornell U., Ithaca, NY, 1987-89, Ernest I. White prof. Am. Studies and Humane Letters, from 1989. Vis. lectr. Am. Studies Rsch. Ctr., Hyderabad, India, spring 1976. Author: Emerson and Thoreau: Transcendentalists in Conflict, 1966, The Romance in America: Studies in Cooper, Poe, Hawthorne, Melville and James, 1969, Representative Man: Ralph Waldo Emerson in His Time, 1979, In Respect to Egotism: Studies in American Romantic Writing, 1991; editor: Emerson in His Journals, 1982, Emerson: Prospect and Retrospect, 1982, Emerson: Essays and Lectures, 1983, New Essays on Portrait of a Lady, 1990, A Cambridge Companion to Ralph Waldo Emerson (with Saundra Morris), 1999, Emerson's Prose and Poetry: A Norton Critical Edit. (with Saundra Morris), 2001, Consciousness and Culture: Emerson and Thoreau Reviewed, 2004. Scholar in Residence, Rockefeller Found., Bellagio, Italy, 1979; fellow John Simon Guggenheim Found., 1981-82. Mem. Am. Lit. Assn., Phi Beta Kappa. Home: Ithaca, NY. Died June 1, 2006.

PORTER, DANIEL REED, III, museum director; b. Northampton, Mass., July 2, 1930; s. Daniel Reed and Eleanor (Parsons) P.; m. Joan Joyce Dornfeld, Nov. 22, 1958; children: Leslie Marie, Andrew Gregory. BA, U. Mass., 1952; MA, U. Mich., 1956. Asst. to dir. State Hist. Soc. Wis., Madison, 1956-58; dir. Hist. Soc. York County, Pa., 1958-61; asst. dir., dir. Ohio Hist. Soc., Columbus, 1961-74; exec. dir. Preservation Soc. Newport County, R.I., 1974-78; dir., prof. Cooperstown (N.Y.) Grad. Programs, 1978-82; dir. N.Y. State Hist. Assn. Farmer's Mus. Cooperstown, 1982-92. Hist. preservation officer State of Ohio, Columbus, 1967-74. Editor: N.Y. Heritage, 1984-92; contbr. articles to publs. in field. With U.S. Army, 1952-54, Korea. Recipient Spl. award of Merit Ohio Assn. Hist. Socs., 1970. Mem. Am. Assn. Mus. (accreditation commn. 1982-88, councillor-at-large 1981-84), Am. Assn. State and Local History (coun., Nashville 1971-73, councillor 1985-87). Congregationalist. Home: Cooperstown, NY. Died Nov. 21, 2006.

PORTER, FREDERICK STANLEY, JR., physician, pediatrics educator; b. Balt., Sept. 18, 1926; s. Frederick Stanley and Agnes (James) P.; m. Barbara Cunningham, Sept. 8, 1951; children: Priscilla Cunningham, Nancy Chase. BS, Princeton U., 1948; MD, Johns Hopkins U., 1952. Am. Bd. Pediatrics. Intern Harriet Lane Home, Johns Hopkins Hosp., Balt., 1952-53, resident, 1953-55; fellow in pediatric hematology Children's Med. Ctr., Boston, 1955-57; instr. Harvard Med. Sch., 1957-58; asst. prof. pediatrics U. Ark., 1958-62, assoc. prof., 1962-64; assoc. prof. pediatrics Duke U. Sch. Medicine, 1964-71, prof., 1971-75; prof., chmn. pediatrics Eastern Va. Med. Sch., Norfolk, from 1975; v.p. med. affairs Children's Hosp., Norfolk, from 1975. Mem. steering com. Va. Council Health and Med. Service for Handicapped Children, Richmond, 1976—; mem. adv. bd. Va. State Dept. Health Genetic and Metabolic Diseases, Richmond, 1980— Mem. adv. bd. Lee's Friends, Norfolk, 1981—; bd. dirs. Tidewater Regional Hospice, 1982. Mem. Assn. Cancer Edn., Am. Pediatric Soc., Am. Assn. Med. Sch. (chmn. pediatric dept.), Am. Soc. Hematology, Soc. Pediatric Research Episcopalian. Home: Virginia Beach, Va. Died July 15, 2006.

PORTERFIELD, RITA ELAINE, banker; b. Hooker, Okla., July 30, 1947; d. Frank Emery and Elsie Gertrude (Brown) Loveland; m. Marion Arthur Crow, Aug. 8, 1962 (dec. Feb. 1965); 1 child, Roberta Sue Crow Jones; m. Clifford Porterfield, Jr., Nov. 13, 1965 (dec. Oct. 1978); children— Buddy Wayne, Paula Jean; m. Gary Gayle Hix, Feb. 14, 1985 (div. Apr. 1987). Grad. Draughn's Bus. Coll., 1972. Office mgr. Millco Moving Service, Amarillo, Tex., 1973-77; bookkeeper Edwards Tires & Auto, Weatherford, Tex., 1977-78; computer operator Liberty State Bank, Tahlequah, Okla., 1981-83, asst. cashier, 1983-85, asst. v.p., 1985—. Co-chmn. Eastern Okla. March of Dimes, Tahlequah, 1984-86. Mem. Nat. Assn. Bank Women (chmn. edn. and tng. com. 1985-86, sec.-treas. 1987-88), Nat. Assn. Female Execs. Republican. Baptist. Club: Ladies Aux. Lodge: Sertoma. Avocations: boating; camping; bowling. Died Mar. 30, 2007.

POST, RICHARD M., securities executive; b. NYC, Nov. 25, 1935; Ptnr. Herzfeld & Stern-Gruntal & Co., NYC, pres. Post Investment Group div. Home: New York, NY. Died Aug. 22, 2006.

POSTELNEK, STEPHEN A., lawyer; b. NYC, Apr. 24, 1940; BSME, Columbia U., 1961; MSME, Poly. Inst. Bklyn., 1968; JD, St. John's U., 1974. Bar: NY 1975, US Supreme Ct., NY State & Fed. Courts. Design engr. Pratt and Whitney Aircraft Engring. Corp., East Hartford, Conn., Grumman Aerospace Corp., Bethpage, NY; ptnr. Wilson, Elser, Moskowitz, Edelman & Dicker LLP, NYC. Mem.: ABA, NY State Trial Lawyers Assn., Assn. of the Bar of the City of NY, St. Thomas More Inst. Legal Rsch., NY State Bar Assn. Died May 5, 2006.

POSTON, MET RAY, retired mfg. co. exec. b. Chattanooga, Mar. 11, 1920; s. Arthur Julian and Lillian (Smith) P.; m. Francella Redwine, May 21, 1946; children— Frederick, Met Ray, George, Wendy, Shelly. BS, U. Chattanooga, 1942; LL.B., George Washington U., 1951. Bar: D.C. bar 1952, N.C. bar 1962. Research chemist Reilly Tar & Chem. Corp., Indpls., 1942-43; engaged in research Oak Ridge Nat. Lab., 1946-48; patent counsel AEC, 1948-51; with Am. Enka Corp., N.C., 1951-70, sec., 1960-70, gen. counsel, 1962-70; v.p., gen. counsel Akzona Inc., Asheville, N.C., from 1970. Trustee Akzona Found.; mem. bd. adv. Janirve Found., 1985—. Served to lt. USNR, 1943-46, PTO. Mem. Am., N.C. bar assns., Phi Alpha Delta. Clubs: Mason, Asheville Downtown, City, Country of Asheville; University (N.Y.). Methodist. Home: Asheville, NC. Died June 23, 2006.

POSTON, TOM, actor; b. Columbus, Ohio, Oct. 17, 1927; s. George and Margaret P.; m. Jean Sullivan, 1955; m. Kay Hudson, June 8, 1968 (dec. July 11, 1999); children: Francesca, Hudson, Jason; m. Suzanne Pleshette, 2001. First appeared on stage as a tumbler with The Flying Zebleys; acting and Broadway debuts in Cyrano de Bergerac, 1947; appeared on Broadway, regional theaters, and summer stock; stage appearances include: The Insect Comedy, King Lear, Will Success Spoil Rock Hunter?, Goodbye Again, Best of Burlesque, Romanoff and Juliet, Drink to Me Only, Golden Fleecing, The Conquering Hero, Come Blow Your Horn, Mary, Mary, Forty Carats, But Seriously..., A Funny Thing Happened on the Way to the Forum, The Odd Couple, Bye Bye Birdie, Mother Courage, host WABC-TV series Entertainment, 1955; regular on TV show The Steve Allen Show, 1956-58 (Emmy award for best supporting actor in comedy series 1959); host TV show Split Personality, 1959-60; panelist TV show To Tell the Truth; (TV appearances) On the Rocks, 1975-76, We've Got Each Other, 1977, Mork and Mindy, 1978-82, Newhart, 1982-90, Grace Under Fire, 1995-98; actor (films) The Tempest, The City That Never Sleeps, 1953, Zotz, 1962, Soldier in the Rain, 1963, The Old Dark House, 1963, Cold Turkey, 1970, The Happy Hooker, 1975, Rabbit Test, 1978, Up the Academy, 1980, Carbon Copy, 1981, Krippendorf's Tribe, 1998, The Story of Us, 1999, Princess Diaries II, 2004, Christmas with the Kranks, 2004 Served with USAAF, World War II. Died Apr. 30, 2007.

POTE, HAROLD WILLIAM (HAL POTE), banker; b. Phila., Sept. 18, 1946; s. Frank Lafferty and Lucille (Bock) P.; m. Judy Elizabeth Constantine, Oct. 12, 1968. AB, Princeton U., 1968; MBA, Harvard U., 1972. Dir. investor rels. Fidelcor/Fidelity Bank, Phila., 1974-76, v.p., head corp. devel. dept., 1976-78, sr. v.p., head corp. devel. dept., 1978-80, exec. v.p., treas. fin. and planning dept., 1980-83, vice chmn., treas. fin. and planning dept., 1983-84; chmn., CEO Fidelity Bank, Phila., 1984-88; pres., CEO Fidelcor, Inc., 1986-88, First Fidelity Bancorp., Phila., 1988; CEO Spl. Situation Fund, NYC, 1988-93; ptnr. The Beacon Group (acquired by J.P. Morgan), NYC, 1993—2000; head, regional banking J.P. Morgan Chase & Co., 2000—04, vice chmn. retail fin. services, 2004—07. Asst. prof. La Salle Coll., Phila., 1972-79; bd. dirs. Norfolk So. Corp. Trustee Pa. Ballet Assn., Phila., 1976-92; mem. exec. coun. Harvard Bus. Sch. Assn., 1980—. Mem. AICPA, Merion Golf Club, Locust Club. Died June 27, 2007.

POTTER, GEORGE JOHN LUND, stock broker; b. Provo, Utah, May 1, 1923; s. David Brown and Aleath (Lund) P.; m. Dorothy Loeffler, Nov. 17, 1950 (div. 1976); children: Dianna Lee, David John, Denise, Dorothy Anne, Tammy; m. Francine Felt, June 13, 1977. BA, U. Utah, 1944; MBA, Stanford U., 1949. Co-mgr., owner O.P. Skaggs System Stores, Salt Lake City, 1940-49; account exec. Merrill Lynch, Pierce, Fenner, Smith, Ogden, Utah, 1949-51; mng. ptnr. Am. Heritage Investment Co., Salt Lake City, 1951-52; dist. mgr. Fitch Investor's Service, Boston, 1953-54; pres. Potter Investment Co., Salt Lake City, from 1954; pres., chmn. bd. govs. Salt Lake Stock Exchange, Salt Lake City, 1968, 69, 70; bd. govs. Intermountain Stock Exchange, from 1964. Mem. Nat. Assn. Securities Dealers (dist. com. 1980, 81, 82), Utah Securities Dealers Assn. (pres. 1968) Clubs: Fort Douglas Country (Salt Lake City). Republican. Mem. Lds Ch. Home: Salt Lake City, Utah. Died Oct. 20, 2006.

POTTER, GUY DILL, radiologist, educator; b. Greensboro, NC, Jan. 24, 1928; s. Guy Dill and Frances Tanner (Porter) P.; m. Pearl Baer, May 11, 1951. BS, U. Chgo., 1957, MD, 1960. Intern Blodgett Meml. Hosp., Grand Rapids, Mich., 1960-61; resident U. Chgo. Clinics, 1961-64; instr. to prof. radiology Coll. Physicians and Surgeons, Columbia U., NYC, from 1964; asst. to attending radiologist Presbyn. Hosp., NYC, 1964-78; dir. dept. radiology Lenox Hill Hosp., NYC, 1979-81; dep. dir. dept. radiology St. Luke's-Roosevelt Hosp. Ctr., NYC, from 1981. Guest lectr. Royal Australasian Soc. Radiologists, 1979; cons. USPHS, 1966—, VA, 1975 Author: Sectional Anatomy and Tomography of the Head, 1971; co-author: Radiology of the Ear, Nose and Throat, 1982; Author numerous articles on radiology of the ear, sinuses and skull; editor: Radiology of the Ear, 1974, Disorders of the Head and Neck, 3d series, 1985, CT of the Head and Neck, 1984; co-editor: Ear Nose and Throat Radiology, 1980; editorial adv. bd.: Radiology. Served with AUS, 1946-47 Named Hickey Lectr. Mich. Radiol. Soc., 1973 Fellow Am Coll. Radiology (head and neck evaluation com.); mem. Radiol Soc. N. Am. (chmn. audiovisual com.), Am. Soc. Head and Neck Radiology (past pres.), AMA, N.Y. Otol. Soc., N.Y. State Med Soc., N.Y. County Med. Soc., N.Y. Roentgen Soc., Am. Roentgen Soc. Died Jan. 5, 2006.

POTTS, ROBERT ANTHONY, publisher; b. Chester, Pa. Sept. 11, 1927; s. William James and Sara Louise (Watson) P. m. Eva A. Morra, Sept. 8, 1955; children: Mark, Matthew, Amy Abby. BA, Pace Coll., 1952. Vice pres. Cahners Pub. Co., Inc. NYC, 1952-72, Intercontinental Publs., Stamford, Conn., 1972-75; exec. v.p., pub. Dun's Bus. Month mag. Dun & Bradstree Publs., NYC, 1975-88; sr. v.p. Full Life Corp., Westport, Conn. from 1988. Contbr. articles on sales and publ. mgmt. to: Folio Mag. Served with USAAF, 1945-47. Mem.: Wings (N.Y.C.) Home: Essex, Conn. Died Dec. 13, 2006.

POWELL, CARLETON DAVIDSON, federal judge; b. Spartanville, SC, 1939; m. Linda Byrd Powell; children: Catherine Cleveland, Alden Byrd. BA, U. Va., 1961; LLB, U. Richmond 1967. With IRS, 1967—70; trial atty. appellate sect., tax divsn. US Dept. Justice, Washington, 1970—77, sr. trial atty. 1977—80, reviewer, 1980—85; spl. trial judge US Tax Ct Washington, 1985—2007. Commd. officer US Army, 1962—64 Mem.: Commonwealth VA Bar Assn. Died Aug. 23, 2007.

POWELL, CHARLES ARTHUR, III, lawyer; b. Atlanta, Ap 8, 1940; s. Charles Arthur Jr. and Leslie (Sibley) P.; m. Nanc Watson, June 7, 1962 (div. Jan. 1982); children: Charles Arthu IV, Christopher Alan; m. Glenda Ryan, Oct. 19, 1989; stepchildren: Clarence Glen Culp Jr., Belinda Culp Williams. AB Birmingham So. Coll., 1961; LLB, Duke U., 1964. Bar: Ala 1964, US Dist. Ct. (no., mid. and so. dists.) Ala., US Ct. Appeal (4th, 5th, 6th, 8th and 11th cirs.), US Supreme Ct. Assoc. Rives Peterson, Pettus & Conway, Birmingham, 1964-65; from assoc to ptnr. Lange, Simpson, Robinson & Somerville, Birmingham 1965-84; proprietory Powell & Assocs., Birmingham, 1984-88 ptnr. Powell, Tally & Frederick, Birmingham, 1988-94, Powe & Frederick, Birmingham, 1994-95, Johnston, Barton, Procto & Powell, Birmingham, 1995—2006. Contbg. editor: The Developing Labor Law (cumulative supplement 1971-75), 1976 editor: The Developing Labor Law, 2d edit., 1983; assoc. edito The Developing Labor Law (fifth supplement 1982-88), 1989 The Developing Labor Law, 3d edit., 1992. Chmn. bd. mgr World Business Advisors. Fellow Am. Bar Found., Coll. Labo and Employment Lawyers (charter, pres. 1998, bd. gov. 1996- mem. ABA (mgmt. co-chair com. on the devel. of the law unde the nat. labor rels. act 1978-81, mgmt. co-chair insts. an meetings com. 1983-86, coun. mem. sect. of labor and employment law 1985-95, chair-elect sect. of labor and employmer law 1993-94, chair sect. of labor and employment law 1994-9 bd. gov. 2003-2005), Ala. State Bar (state labor law sec 1969—, mem. standing com. on Ala. rules of jud. adminstr 1977-94, com. on lawyer advt. and solicitation 1991-94, character and fitness com. 1992—, Ho. of Dels., bd. govs. 2003— Birmingham Bar Assn., Ea. Mineral Law Found. (truste 1984—), Coun. R.R. and Airline Labor Lawyers, Indsl. Rel Rsch. Assn., Bus. Coun. Ala., Fed. Bar Assn., Am. Employme Law Coun. (founding mem.). Home: Birmingham, Ala. Die Mar. 15, 2006.

POWELL, GEORGE EVERETT, JR., motor freight company executive; b. Kansas City, Mo., June 12, 1926; s. Georg Everett and Hilda (Brown) P.; m. Mary Catherine Kuehn, Au 26, 1947; children: George Everett III, Nicholas K., Richardso K., Peter E. Student, Northwestern U. With Riss & Co., Inc Kansas City, Mo., 1947-52, treas., 1950-52; with Yellow Freig System, Inc., Kansas City, Mo., 1952-96, pres., 1957-96, chm bd., 1968-96; ret., 1966; pres. Yellow Freight Systems, Inc. Del., Overland Park, Kans., 1987-88. Dir. 1st Nat. Chart Corp., Butler Mfg. Co. Trustee, mem. exec. com. Mid-We Research Inst., Kansas City, Mo., from 1961, chmn. bd. trustee from 1968; bd. govs. Kansas City Art Inst., from 1964, chm bd. trustees, 1973-75. Served with USNR, 1944-46. Mer Kansas City C. of C. (bd. dirs. 1964-68) Home: Kansas Cit Mo. Died Apr. 25, 2007.

POWELL, RICHARD GORDON, retired lawyer; b. Roche ter, NY, Jan. 7, 1918; BS, Harvard U., 1938; LL.B., Columb U., 1941. Bar: N.Y. 1941, U.S. Supreme Ct. 1955. Asso Sullivan & Cromwell, NYC, 1941-52, ptnr., 1952-85. Form mem. bd. mgrs. Englewood (N.J.) Community Chest; truste elder 1st Presbyterian Ch. Mem. ABA, Assn. Bar City of N.Y. Am. Law Inst. Home: New York, NY. Died Apr. 13, 2006.

POWER, JOHN JAY, labor union official; b. Chgo., Sept. 1946; s. Joseph Thomas and Mary Elizabeth (Powers) P.; r Janet Lynn Pickett, June 20, 1970 (div. Oct. 1977); 1 chil Bevin Mary; m. Joyce Marie Palermo, June 6, 1981. A Bu Adminstrn., No. Va. C.C., 1968; BSBA, Va. Commonwealth U 1970. Legis. asst. United Brotherhood Carpenters, Washingto 1973-75, dir. legis., 1975-80; legis. rep. AFL-CIO, Washingto from 1980. With U.S. Army, 1970-72. Democrat. Avocatior reading, theater. Home: Washington, DC. Died Oct. 10, 2006

POWERS, BERTRAM ANTHONY, retired labor union administrator; b. Cambridge, Mass., Mar. 8, 1922; s. Bertra Anthony and Susan H. (Diehl) P.; m. Patricia Elizabeth Colvil Dec. 2, 1944 (dec. Jan. 1988); children: Kevin, Patricia, Bria Moya. Union printer, 1942-53; rep. N.Y. Typog. Union No. NYC, 1953-61, pres., 1961-90. Mem. exec. bd. N.Y.C. Ce Labor Coun., E. Corsi Labor-Mgmt. Rels. Inst., Pace U., N.Y.C mem. N.Y.C. Allied Printing Trades Coun., N.Y. State Apprenticeship Coun. Mem. adv. com. graphic arts dept. N.Y. Community Coll.; mem. bus. edn. tech. com. N.Y. State Ed Dept. Recipient Labor award Westchester County Cen. Lab Coun., Westchester, N.Y., 1967. Home: New York, NY. Di Dec. 23, 2006.

POWERS, MALA, actress; b. San Francisco, Dec. 20, 1931; George Evart and M. Dell (Thelen) P.; 1 child, Toren Mich Vanton. Student, UCLA; studied with Michael Chekhov. V

Book Pubs. Enterprises Inc., 1985; internat. lectr. Chekhov Drama Method; entertainer troops USO, Korea, 1951-52; founder, bd. dirs. West Coast Michael Chekhov Drama Group, 1988—; presenter bus. and theater workshops and seminars. Writer, narrator: (sponsored by telephone cos. in various cities) Children's Story, Tele-Story and Dial-A-Story, 1979— (sponsored nationally 1988—); author: Follow the Year, 1985, French edit. 1986; editor: The Secret Seven and the Old Fort Adventure, 1972; rec.: Advent calendar and author book Follow the Star, 1980, Spanish edit., 1981, Italian edit., 1982; actress: (films) Cyrano de Bergerac, 1950, Outrage, Edge of Doom, Yellow Mountain, Bengazi, Tammy, Cheyenne, Daddy's Gone A'Hunting, Six Tickets to Hell, 1975, Hitters, 2003; rec. artist, RCA, records for pre-Christmas, 1977, album Follow the Star; stage prodns. include Absence of a Cello (Broadway), 1964-65; Hogan's Goat, Night of the Iguana, Bus Stop, Far Country, The Rivalry, Mr. Shaw Goes to Hollywood, 2003; also starred in radio and TV prodns. including Medical Story, Ironside, Charlie's Angels; co-star with Anthony Quinn in The Man and the City, 1971-72, Murder She Wrote, 1990. Chmn. So. Calif. Mothers' com. March of Dimes, 1972—; bd. dirs. Layman's Nat. Bible Com., 1981—. Mem. NATAS, Acad. Motion Picture Arts and Scis. (fgn. film com.), ANTA (v.p., exec. com. 1974-75), PEN, Actors Equity Assn.,, Women in Film, Authors Club (London). Mem. Christian Community Ch. Home: Sylmar, Calif. Died June 11, 2007.

POWERS, MARCUS EUGENE, lawyer; b. Cedarville, Ohio, Apr. 7, 1929; s. Frederick Armajo and Elizabeth Isabel (Rumbaugh) P. BA, Ohio Wesleyan U., 1951; JD (Root-Tilden scholar), NYU, 1954, LL.M., 1958. Bar: Ohio 1954, N.Y. 1959, Calif. 1964. Asst. prof. law NYU Sch. Law, 1956-60; atty. Am. Brake Shoe Co., NYC, 1959-63; asst. gen. counsel Dart Industries Inc., Los Angeles, 1963-81; sr. v.p., gen. counsel Nat. Med. Enterprises, Inc., Los Angeles, 1981-93; exec. v.p., sec. Health Care Property Investors Inc., Santa Monica, Calif., 1985-87; cons. Nat. Med. Enterprises, Inc., Los Angeles, from 1993. Served with U.S. Army, 1954-56. Mem. ABA (mem. com. on corp. law depts. 1985-93), Los Angeles County Bar Assn. (past chmn. corp. law depts. sect., Outstanding Corp. Counsel 1990), Inst. Corp. Counsel (bd. dirs. 1979-92, chmn. 1984-86), Assn. Bar City N.Y., Calif. State Coastal Conservancy, Phi Beta Kappa, Omicron Delta Kappa, Phi Delta Theta, Kappa Sigma, Pi Sigma Alpha, Theta Alpha Phi. Home: Malibu, Calif. Died May 1, 2007.

POWERS, NOYES THOMPSON, retired lawyer, former federal official; b. New Orleans, Apr. 29, 1929; m. Mary Lamb Powers; children: David N., William C., Thomas L. BA magnum cum laude, Duke U., 1951; LLB cum laude, Harvard U., 1954. Asst. to under sec. US Dept. Labor, 1961, dep. solicitor, 1962-63, exec. asst. to sec., 1964-65; exec. dir. EEOC, 1965; assoc. Steptoe & Johnson, Washington, 1957—61, ptnr. Washington, Phoenix, 1966-94, mng. ptnr., 1982—84; sr. labor counsel Motorola, Inc., Phoenix, 1994—99. Served in USN, 1954—57. Mem. ABA (chair pub. utility, comm. and transp. sect. 1994-95). Home: Penn Valley, Calif. Died Jan. 29, 2007.

POWERS, PETER GALLAUDET, retired lawyer; b. Portland, ME, 1930; m. Elizabeth Powers (div.); children: Amanda, David; m. Kathryn Kistler; children: Peter, Hiram. Grad., Magdalen Coll.; JD, Harvard U., 1957. Law clk. to J. Skelly Wright US Dist. Ct. (ea. dist.) La.; assoc. Hogan & Hartson LLP; gen. counsel Smithsonian Instn., Washington, 1964—95. Former pres. Internat. Student House Inc. Recipient Joseph Henry medal Smithsonian Instn., 1995. Mem.: Kiwanis Club of Capitol Hill, Metropolitan Club. Home: Washington, DC. Died Oct. 31, 2006.

POWERS, WARREN EARL, lawyer, trust consultant; b. Oak Park, Ill., Feb. 17, 1921; s. Earl Warren and Georgia Helen (Sayler) P.; m. Virginia Marie Wenzel, July 22, 1944; childrenn— Judith, William, Janis, James, Christopher. B.A., U. Ill.; J.D., John Marshall Law Sch., Chgo. Real estate atty. 1st Nat. Bank of Chgo., 1946-54; v.p., trust officer 1st Bank of Evanston, Ill., 1955-78, Community Bank of Edgewater, Chgo., 1978-80; trust cons. Mid-City Nat. Bank, Chgo., 1980-86; sole practice, 1986—. Served to lt. USN, 1943-46, PTO. Mem. Profit Sharing Council Am., Land Trust Council Cook County, Chgo. Bar Assn., Am. Legion (comdr. Arlington Heights post 1959). Club: Kiwanis (pres. Evanston 1969). Died July 30, 2006.

PRATT, DAN EDWIN, chemistry educator; b. High Point, NC, Feb. 7, 1924; s. C. Daniel and Carol Druscilla (Wyatt) P.; m. Mana Clariece Peacock, Aug. 29, 1959; 1 child, Mana Lisa. BS, U. Ga., 1950, MS, 1951; PhD (nuclear sci. fellow 1960), Fla. State U., 1962; postgrad. in food sci., U. Mass. Asst. prof. chemistry U. Ga., 1955-61; assoc. prof., research scientist food sci. and nutrition U. Wis., Madison, 1964-69; research scientist, assoc. prof. Purdue U., West Lafayette, Ind., 1969-76, prof. chemistry, 1976-92, prof. emeritus, from 1992; cons. in lipid chemistry, from 1992. Vis. prof. food law Emory U., 1954; vis. rsch. scientist Natick R & D Command, 1980; vis. lectr. U. Viscosa, Brazil, 1982, Harvard U., 1980; vis. scientist Am. Oil Chemists, Cannes, France, 1985; vis. rsch. scientist in lipid chemistry FDA, Washington, 1987, lectr., 1988; cons. to food industry, Taiwan, 1981, Nat. Poultry Industry, Lipid Chemistry, 1990; rsch. scientist Am. Oil Chemists, 1992; rsch. com., rep. Inst. Food Technologists, 1986-89. Contbr. numerous articles profl. jours. Del. Internat. Congress Food Scientists, Tokyo, 1978. With USMCR, 1942-45. Recipient Disting. Scientist Research award Ind. Inst. Food Sci., 1982. Fellow Am. Inst. Chemists, Inst. Food Sci. and Tech., Inst. Food Technologists; mem. Nat. Inst. Food Scientists, Am. Acad. Scis., N.Y. Acad. Scis., Sigma Xi, Phi Kappa Phi, Pi Mu Epsilon, Phi Tau Sigma (exec. sec. 1969), Gamma Sigma Delta. Clubs: Lafayette Toastmasters (pres. 1975). Died Jan. 7, 2007.

PRECOURT, LYMAN ARTHUR, lawyer; b. Milw., Aug. 30, 1926; s. Bernard Antoine and Blanche Elizabeth (Plaisted) P.; m. Patricia Louise Edlredge, Jan. 20, 1947; children: Susan, Diane, Bruce, Laura. BS, U. Wis., 1950, JD, 1952. Bar: Wis. 1952, Fla. 1974. Assoc. Foley & Lardner, Milw., 1952-61, ptnr., from 1961. Mem. ABA, Fla. Bar Assn., Am. Coll. Real Estate Lawyers, Milw. Country Club. Home: Fort Myers, Fla. Died Oct. 14, 2005.

PREECE, WARREN EVERSLEIGH, retired editor; b. Norwalk, Conn., Apr. 17, 1921; s. Everett Lowe and Ethel (Miles) P.; m. Deborah Weeks, July 12, 1947 (dec. 2002); children: Scott Everett, Mark William, Thayer Evelyn. BA cum laude, Dartmouth Coll., 1943; MA, Columbia U., 1947. Instr. English, U. Chgo., 1947-49; reporter Norwalk Hour, 1949-50, writer, copy editor, 1952-56; campaign aide, publicity dir. to U.S. Senator Dodd, 1956-57; exec. sec. bd. editors Ency. Brit., 1957-64, editor, 1964-65, editor-in-chief, 1965-68, gen. editor, 1968-70, editor, 1970-75, vice chmn. bd. editors, 1974-79. Cons. Center Study Democratic Instns.; Ninth ann. C.N. Williamson lectr. Peabody Coll., Nashville. Author: (with others) The Technological Order, 1962; editor: Encyclopaedia Britannica College Preparatory Series, 1964; bd. editorial advisors Internat. Ency., Tokyo, 1974-88. Bd. dirs., sec. Conn. chpt. ARC, 1955-57; pres. Mass. Protestant Social Svcs. Inc., 1977-78; bd. dirs. Protestant Youth Homes, Baldwinville, Mass., 1976-78; mem. Standing Commn. on Peace with Justice, Episcopal Ch., 1989-94. Served with arty. U.S. Army, 1943-46, 50-52. Mem. Phi Beta Kappa Assos., Phi Beta Kappa, Sigma Nu. Democrat. Episcopalian. Home: Nyack, NY. Died Apr. 11, 2007.

PREISNER, RIO THOMAS, German educator; b. Mukacevo, Czechoslovakia, Nov. 13, 1925; came to U.S., 1969; s. Jan M. and Blanka (Kozsler) P; m. Olga K. Witt; 1 child, Ruth. Ph.D., Charles U., 1950. Asst. Prof. Charles U., Prague, Czechoslovakia, 1949-52; instr. Inst. Fgn. Lang. Instrn., Prague, 1955-64, pvt. scholar, 1964-69; prof., fellow German, Pa. State U., University Park, 1969—. Author: J.N. Nestroy, 1968; Aspekte einer provokativen tschechischen Germanistik, Vol. 1, 2, 1980; Critique of Totalitarianism vol 1, 2, 3, 1987; translator: Broch: The Sleepwalkers, 1966 (Mlada fronta award 1966). Mem. Austrian Pen Club. Died Aug. 2, 2007.

PRELL, ARTHUR ELY, business administration educator; b. Los Angeles, Mar. 2, 1924; s. Maurice F. and Bertha (Frischling) P.; m. Joyce Merle Prelutsky, June 12, 1949 (dec.); children: Michael Gary, Stacy Beth, Melissa Ann; m. Gerry Ettlinger, Apr. 2, 1978. BA, U. Redlands, 1946; BS, U.S. Mcht. Marine Acad., 1942; MA, Washington U., St. Louis, 1949; PhD, U. Minn., 1955. Profl. engr. Waterman Co., Mobile, Ala., Matson Nav. Co., San Francisco, 1946-47; instr. U. N.H., 1949-50, asst. prof. sociology and anthropology, 1953-54; asst. prof. sociology Washington U., 1955-57; cons. St. Louis, 1955-60, 72—; exec. v.p., dir. Compumatix, Inc., St. Louis, 1957-58, French Advt., Inc., St. Louis, 1958-63; mktg. dir. Maritz, Ins., 1962-63; prof. mktg., dir. Bur. Bus. Research, So. Ill. U., Edwardsville, 1963-68, chmn., prof. mktg. and mgmt. sci., 1973-78, prof. mktg., 1973-85; dean Sch. Bus., Calif. State Coll., Long Beach, 1968-73; prof. bus. adminstrn. Lindenwood Coll., St. Charles, Mo., from 1985, chmn. dept., from 1985. Dir. Big 4 Mfg. Co., St. Louis, Melay Corp., St. Louis; pres. The Prell Orgn., 1972— Author: (with David J. Luck) Market Strategy, 1968; Contbr. (with David J. Luck) articles profl. jours. Served to lt. (j.g.) USNR, 1942-45; to lt. 1950-52. Mem. Am. Mktg. Assn. (past v.p.) Lodges: Masons. Home: Saint Louis, Mo. Died Dec. 1, 2005.

PRENTICE, NANCY HUTCHISON, public relations and commercial art company executive; b. Slab Fork, W.Va., Sept. 28, 1940; d. Wayman Joseph and Grace Figgett (Dudley) H.; children— Helen Grace, Adrianne Christine. Student Atlanta Sch. Art, 1958-60. Comml. artist, 1960-67; v.p., creative dir. The Art Factory, 1975-77; pres., creative dir. So. Belle/Nancy Prentice, Atlanta, 1978—; pres., creative dir. So. Belle Print Prodns. Ltd., 1983—. Democrat. Presbyterian. Home: Atlanta, Ga. Died Aug. 28, 2007.

PRESCOTT, LAWRENCE MALCOLM, medical and health science writer; b. Boston, July 31, 1934; s. Benjamin and Lillian (Stein) P.; m. Ellen Gay Kober, Feb. 19, 1961 (dec. Sept. 1981); children: Jennifer Maya, Adam Barrett; m. Sharon Lynn Kirshen, May 16, 1982; children: Gary Leon Kirshen, Marc Paul Prescott. BA, Harvard U., 1957; MSc, George Washington U., 1959, PhD, 1966. Nat. Acad. Scis. postdoctoral fellow U.A. Army Rsch., Ft. Detrick, Md., 1965-66; microbiologist/scientist WHO, India, 1967—70, Indonesia, 1970—72, Thailand, 1972—78; cons. to internat. orgns. San Diego, 1978; with pub. rels. GCI, Hill & Knowlton, Aventis, Astra Zeneza, others, 1984. Author manuals; contbr. articles in diarrheal diseases and lab. scis. to profl. jours., numerous articles, stories, poems to mags., newspapers, including Living in Thailand, Jack and Jill, Strawberry, Bangkok Times, Spring, 1977-81; mng. editor Caduceus, 1981-82; pub., editor: Teenage Scene, 1982-83; pres. Prescott Pub. Co., 1982-83; med. writer numerous jours. including Modern Medicine, Dermatology Times, Drug and Market Devel., P&T, Clinical Cancer Letter, Anesthesiology News, Arzte Zeitung, Australian Doctor, Inpharma Weekly, Chronicle of Cardiovascular and Internal Medicine, Ophthalmology Times, Pharmacy Practice News, Body Positive, AIDS Update, Medical Alert, Infectious Diseases, Urology Times, Genetic Engineering News, Medical Week, Gastroenterology and Endoscopy News; author: Curry Every Sunday, 1984. Died Mar. 21, 2007.

PRESTON, RICHARD ARTHUR, historian; b. Middlesbrough, England, Oct. 4, 1910; s. Frank and Florence Rachel (Carter) P.; m. Marjorie Fishwick, Sept. 2, 1939; children— David Frank, Carol Jane, Peter Eric. BA, Leeds U., 1931, MA, 1932, Dip.Ed., 1933; PhD, Yale U., New Haven, Conn., 1936; LL.D., Royal Mil. Coll. Can., 1977. Mem. faculty U. Toronto, 1936-38, U., Coll. South Wales, 1938-45, U. Toronto, 1945-48; mem. faculty Royal Mil. Coll. Can., Kingston, 1948-65, prof. history, to 1965, Duke U., Durham, N.C., 1965-80, 1st N.K. Boyd prof. history, from 1980, dir. Can. studies, 1973-79. Author: Gorges of Plymouth Fort, 1953, Men in Arms, 1956-91, Royal Fort Frontenac, 1958, Kingston Before the War of 1812, 1958, Canada in World Affairs, 1959-61, 1965, Canada and Imperial Defense, 1967, Canada's R.M.C, 1969, For Friends at Home, 1974, Defence of the Undefended Border, 1977, Perspectives in the History of Military Education and Professionalism, 1980, the Squat Pyramid: Canadian Studies in the U.S, 1980, To Serve Canada, 1991. Served with RAF, 1940-45. Commonwealth Fund fellow, 1933-36; Can. Coun. fellow, 1963-64; Social Sci. Rsch. Coun. fellow, 1963-64; Guggenheim fellow, 1972-73; recipient Achievement award City Kingston, 1959, Can. Confedn. medal, 1967, Queen's Jubilee medal, 1975, Donner medal, 1977, No. Telecom. Internat. Can. Studies award and Gold medal, 1983, Kingston Hist. Soc. Centennial award, 1994. Mem. Can. Hist. Assn. (pres. 1961-62), Assn. Can. Studies U.S. (founding pres. 1971-72), Am. Mil. Inst. Home: Durham, NC. Died Nov. 17, 2006.

PRESTON, ROBERT BRUCE, retired lawyer; b. Cleve., Feb. 24, 1926; s. Robert Bruce and Erma May (Hunter) P.; m. Agnes Ellen Stanley, Jan. 29, 1949; children— Robert B., Patricia Ellen Preston Kiefer, Judith Helen Preston Yanover. AB, Western Res. U., 1950, JD, 1952. Bar: U.S. Dist. Ct. (no. dist.) Ohio 1953, U.S. Ct. Appeals (6th cir.) 1959, U.S. Supreme Ct. 1964. Assoc. Arter & Hadden, Cleve., 1952-63, ptnr., 1964-93; ret., 1994. Dir. Service Stampings Inc., Willoughby, Ohio. Vice pres. Citizens League Cleve., 1965; chmn. Charter Rev. Com., Cleveland Heights, Ohio, 1972; mem. Zoning Bd. Appeals, Cleveland Heights, 1974-76; trustee Women's Philanthropic Union, 1977—. Mem. Ohio Bar Assn., Greater Cleve. Bar Assn. Republican. Presbyterian. Avocations: tennis, fishing, travel. Home: Chagrin Falls, Ohio. Died Jan. 26, 2007.

PRESTON, WILLIAM HUBBARD, consultant to specialty businesses; b. Bklyn., July 24, 1920; s. Russell Jackson and Mary Louise (Yetman) P.; m. Marcia Whitney Emery, Dec. 18, 1943; children: William Hubbard, Craig Ryder. BSM.E. cum laude, Poly. Inst. N.Y., 1942. Asst. supt. Ball & Roller div. SKF Industries, Phila., 1946-51; cons. Booz, Allen & Hamilton, NYC, 1951-53; gen. sales mgr. Joy Mfg. Co., Pitts., 1953-59; exec. v.p. Chase Brass/Kennecott, Waterbury, Conn., 1959-62; pres. Indsl. Group Joy Mfg. Co., Michigan City, Ind., 1962-67, Davis-Standard div., Pawcatuck, Conn., 1967-83; v.p. Crompton & Knowles Corp., NYC, 1967-83; prin. Hubbard Assocs., Hopkinton, Mass., from 1983. Served to lt. (j.g.) USNR, 1943-46. Unitarian Universalist. Home: Hopkinton, Mass. Died Nov. 1, 2006.

PREUSS, ROGER EMIL, artist; b. Waterville, Minn., Jan. 29, 1922; s. Emil W. and Edna (Rosenau) P.; m. MarDee Ann Germundson, Dec. 31, 1954 (dec. Mar. 1981). Student, Mankato Comml. Coll., Mpls. Sch. Art. Emeritus instr. Mpls. Coll. Art and Design; emeritus Mpls. Inst. Arts Speakers Bur.; former judge Goodyear Nat. Conservation Awards Program; founder U.S. Fed. Roger Preuss Waterfowl Prodn. Area, LeSueur County, Minn., 1997; former advisor Wildlife Forever Nat. Fish-Art Contest. One-man shows include St. Paul Fine Art Galleries, 1959, Albert Lea Art Ctr., 1963, Hist. Soc. Mont., Helena, 1964, Brotherhood Fine Arts Ctr., 1965, Le Sueur County Hist. Soc. Mus., Elysian, Minn., 1976, Merrill's Gallery Fine Art, Taos, N.Mex., 1980; exhbns. include Mpls. Inst. Art Msa exhibit, 1946, Midwest Wildlife Conf. Exhbn., Kerr's Beverly Hills, Calif., 1947, Laguna Art Mus., Calif., 1947, Joslyn Meml. Mus., Omaha, 1948, Hollywood Fine Arts Center, 1948, Minn. Centennial, 1949, Federated Chaparral Authors, 1951, Nat. Wildlife Art, 1951-52, N.Am. Wildlife Art, dir. exposition, 1952, Ducks Unltd. Waterfowl exhibit, 1953-54, St. Paul Winter Carnival, 1954, St. Paul Gallery Art Mart, 1954, Harris Fine Arts Ctr., Provo, Utah, 1969, Galerie Internat., N.Y.C., 1972, Holy Land Conservation Fund, N.Y.C., 1976, Faribault Art Ctr., 1981, Wildlife Artists of the World Exhbn., Bend, Oreg., 1984, U. Art Mus., U. Minn., Mpls., 1990, Rochester Art Ctr., 1991, Minn. Hist. Soc.-Hill House, 1992, Bemidji Art Ctr., 1992, Jack London Ctr., Dawson City, Yukon Territory, Can., 1992, Weyerhaeuser Meml. Mus., Little Falls, Minn., 1995, Minn. Valley Nat. Wildlife Refuge Ctr., Bloomington, 1995, Sagebrush Artists Exhbn., Klamath Falls, Oreg., 1995, Smithsonian Inst., Blauvelt Art Mus.; represented in permanent collections: Demarest Meml. Mus., Hackensack, N.J., N.Y. Jour. Commerce, Mont. Hist. Soc., Inland Bird Banding Assn., Minn. Capitol Bldg., Mont. State U., Wildlife Am. Collection, LeSueur Hist. Soc., Voyageurs Nat. Park Interpretive Ctr., Krause-Hartig VFW Post, Mpls., Nat. Wildlife Fedn. Collection, Minn. Ceremonial House, U.S. Wildlife Svc. Fed. Bldg., Fort Snelling, Minn., Crater Lake Nat. Park Visitors Ctr., VA Hosp., Mpls., Luxton Collection, Banff, Alta., Can., Internat. Inst. Arts, Geneva, Mont. Capitol Bldg., People of Century-Goldblatt Collection, Lyons, Ill., Harlem Savings Collection, N.Y.C., Weisman Art Mus., Mpls., Minn. Vets. Home, Mpls., Roger Preuss Art Collection, Augustana Ctr. for Western Studies, Sioux Falls, S.D., Minn. Mus. Am. Art, St. Paul, U. Minn. Art Mus., C.M. Russell Mus., Great Falls, Mont., Le Sueur County Courthouse, Le Center, Minn., others, numerous galleries and pvt. collections; designer: Fed. Duck Stamp, U.S. Dept. Interior, 1949, Commemorative Centennial Pheasant Stamp, 1981, Gold Waterfowl medallion Franklin Mint, 1983, Gold Stamp medallion Wildlife Mint, 1983, 40th Anniverary Commemorative Fed. Duck Stamp etching, 1989; panelist: Sportsman's Roundtable, Sta. WTCN-TV, Mpls. (emeritus), from 1953; author: Is Wildlife Art Recognized Fine Art?, 1986; contbr.: Christmas Echos, 1955, Wing Shooting, Trap & Skeet, 1955, Along the Trout Stream, 1979; contbr. Art Impressions mag., Can., Wildlife Art, U.S.; contbr. illustrations and articles in Nat. Wildlife; assoc. editor emeritus: Out-of-Doors mag.; compiler and artist: Outdoor Horizons, 1957, Twilight over the Wilderness, 1972, 75 limited edition prints Wildlife of America, from 1950; contbr. paintings and text Minnesota Today; creator paintings and text Preuss Wildlife Calendar; inventor: paintings and text Wildlife Am. Calendar; featured artist Art West, 1980-84, Wildlife Art; featured in films Your BFA- Care and Maintenance, Black Ducks Along the Border Former del. Nat. Wildlife Conf.; bd. dirs. emeritus Voyageurs Nat. Park Assn., Deep-Portage Conservation Found.; former bd. dirs. Wetlands for Wildlife U.S.A.; active Wildlife Am.; co-organizer, v.p., bd. dirs. Minn. Conservation Fedn., 1952-54; mem. U.S. Hospitalized Vets. Venison Program, 1957—; trustee Liberty Bell Edn. Found.; Waseca Arts Coun.; founder, dir. Roger Preuss Conservation Preserve for Study of Nature, 1990—; adv. Wildlife Forever. With USNR, WWII. Recipient Stamp Design award U.S. Fish and Wildlife Svc., 1994, Minn. Outdoor award, 1956,

Patron of Conservation award, 1956, award for contbns. conservation Minn. Statehood Centennial Commn., 1958, 1st award Am. Indsl. Devel. Coun., citation of merit VFW, award of merit Mil. Order Cootie, 1963, merit award Minn. Waterfowl Assn., 1976, Silver medal Nat. SAR, 1978, Svcs. to Arts and Environ. award Faribault Art Ctr., 1981, Ptnrs. for Wildlife award U.S. Fish and Wildlife Svc., 1994; named Wildlife Conservationist of the Yr., Sears Found.-Nat. Wildlife Fedn. program, 1966, Am. Bicentennial Wildlife Artist, Am. Heritage Assn., 1976; hon. mem. Ont. Chippewa Nation of Can., 1957; named Knight of Mark Twain for contbns. to Am. art Mark Twain Soc., 1978; named to Water, Woods and Wildlife Hall of Fame, named Dean of Wildfowl Artists, 1981, Hon. Ky. Col.; recipient hon. degree U.S. Vets. Venison program, 1980, Western Am. award significant contbns. to preservation arts and history No. Prairie Plains, Augustana Coll. Ctr. for Western Studies, Sioux Falls, S.D., 1992, Pub. Svc. award U.S. Dept. Interior, 1996, Marshall award 2004; named creator first signed, numbered photolithographic modern print pub. in N.Am., 1959; documented Colorado Springs Fine Arts Ctr., 1993, colleague of Frederick R. Weisman Mus., Mpls., 1994; grantee NEH, 1995, Prairie Lakes Arts Coun., 1995. Fellow Internat. Inst. Arts (life), Nat. Wildlife Fedn. (past nat. wildlife week chmn. Minn.), Minn. Ducks Unltd. (bd. dirs. emeritus), Minn. Artists Assn. (v.p., bd. dirs. 1953-59), Minn. Mycol. Soc. (pres. emeritus, hon. life), Le Sueur County Hist. Soc. (hon. life), Minn. Conservation Fedn. (hon. life), Wildlife Artists World (charter, emeritus internat. v.p., chmn. fine arts bd.), Prairie Chicken Soc. (patron), Mission Oceanic Arctic, Minn. Press Club (emeritus), Silver Lake Sports (hon.), Wildlife Rehab. Ctr. Minn. Home: Minneapolis, Minn. Died May 15, 2007.

PRICE, DONALD ALBERT, veterinarian, consultant; b. Bridgeport, Ohio, Dec. 25, 1919; s. Arthur David and Louise Ann (Knellinger) P.; m. June Loree Fleming, July 16, 1945; children: Karen Price Privett, Benita Price Esposito, Donna Price Rocap. Grad., Elliott Sch. Bus., 1938; DVM, Ohio State U., 1950. Lic. veterinarian, Ohio, Ill., Tex. Adminstrv. asst. Wheeling (W.Va.) Steel Corp., 1938-41; counselor psychol. dept. Ohio State U., Columbus, 1946-48, lab. asst. vet. parasitology dept., 1948-50; mem. rsch. faculty Tex. A&M U., Sonora, 1950-55; ptnr. San Angelo (Tex.) Vet. Hosp., 1955-58; assoc. editor AVMA, Chgo., 1958-59, editor-in-chief, 1959-72, exec. v.p., 1972-85; cons., adj. prof. Tex. A&M U., College Station, from 1985. Capt. USAAF, 1941-46. Recipient Disting. Alumnus award Coll. Vet. Medicine, Ohio State U., 1966. Fellow Am. Med. Writers Assn.; mem. AVMA (Svc. Commendation award 1984, Appreciation award, 1984, CEO 1972-85), Ill. Vet. Med. Assn. (hon. life), Mich. Vet. Med. Assn. (hon. life), Tex. Vet. Med. Assn. (disting. life), Am. Equine Practitioners Assn. (hon.), Am. Assn. Sheep and Goat Practioners (hon.), Am. Animal Hosp. Assn. (hon., Merit award 1983), Bexar County Vet. Med. Assn. (hon.), Masons, Phi Eta Sigma, Phi Zeta, Alpha Psi. Republican. Presbyterian. Avocations: woodworking, ranching. Died Dec. 11, 2005.

PRICE, JOANN, physical education educator; b. Youngstown, Ohio, Oct. 12, 1928; d. Norman Ray and Edith (White) P. B.S. in Edn., Youngstown State U., 1950; M.S., U. Wis., 1955; Ed.D., Ind. U., 1969. Tchr. Canfield Jr. Sr. High Sch., Ohio, 1959-52; instr. Bryn Mawr Coll., Pa., 1952-55; instr. phys. edn. Purdue U., West Lafayette, Ind., 1955-60, asst. prof., 1960-73, assoc. prof., 1973—; cons. Nat. Golf Found., West Palm Beach, Fla., 1966-73; evaluator North Central Assn. Secondary Schs. and Colls., Indpls., Beech Grove, Lagrange, Ind., 1967-83. Contbr. articles to profl. jours. Campaigner YWCA, Lafayette, 1974, 84; hon. rules chmn. Ind. High Sch. Athletic Assn., Lebanon, 1971. Recipient Outstanding Woman in Sports award Lafayette and Purdue Women's Caucus, 1976; named to Athletic Hall of Fame, City of Fort Wayne, Ind., 1975. Mem. Assn. Tchr. Educators, Ind. Assn. for Tchr. Educators, Midwest Assn. Health, Phys. Edn., Recreation and Dance, Nat. Assn. Phys. Edn. in Higher Edn., Ind. Assn. Health, Phys. Edn., Recreation and Dance (treas. 1978-81), Midwest Assn. Coll. Women for Phys. Edn. (v.p. 1970-72), AAHPERD. Republican. Methodist. Ind. women's state golf amateur championship flite, 1973, 74, 79, 83, 85, 86; Ind. women's state sr. golf champion, 1981, 83. Avocations: golf; gardening; watching most sports. Home: West Lafayette, Ind. Died Feb. 1, 2006.

PRICE, ROBERT DIDDAMS, JR., community planner; b. Chgo., Apr. 18, 1943; s. Robert Diddams and Adelheid Marie (Haugan) P.; m. Susan Kay Mundhenk, Dec. 18, 1965; children: Jennifer, Robert III. BS in Community Planning, U. Cin., 1966, MA in Community Planning, 1968, MA in Geography, 1968. Cert. paramedic, Ohio. Sr. planner City-County Planning Commn., Rockford, Ill., 1968-70; chief rsch. Cent. N.Y. Regional Planning and Devel. Bd., Syracuse, 1970-72; exec. dir. Warren County Regional Planning Commn., Lebanon, Ohio, 1972—; mem. exec. com. Ohio Ky.-Ind. Regional Council Govts., 1973—; bd. dirs., treas. needs assessment com. Warren County Rehab., Inc., 1977-88, planning com., 1987-88, pres., 1989—. Mem. Warren County Health Planning Com., 1978—, Warren County Litter Adv. Bd., 1985—; chmn. Warren County New Horizons Fair Housing Task Force, 1980—; bd. dirs. Cert. Devel. Corp. of Warren County, 1981—. Sec., treas. Warren County Conv. and Vis. Bur., 1980—; mem. Clearcreek Twp. Life Squad, 1975—, first lt., 1977, chief, 1978-82, Clearcreek Twp. Fire Dept., 1980—; mem. high adventure com. Dan Beard council Boy Scouts Am.; mem. Springboro Band Boosters, 1984-88, pres., 1985-86, treas. 1986-87; bd. dirs. Western Ohio Emergency Med. Svcs. Council, 1978-85, sec. 1980-84, sec.-treas., 1984-85; chmn. Warren County Emergency Med. Svcs. Council, 1981-82; county employee coordinator Warren County United Way, 1980; mem. council St. Paul Luth. Ch., 1976-78, sec., 1976-77; merit badge counselor Boy Scouts Am., 1982—; mem. Camp Stoneybrook Bldg. Com., Girl Scouts U.S.A., 1981-82; mem. Warren County Classifications and Compensation Adv. bd., 1984—, sec. 1984-85; CPR instr. ARC, 1978—; radiol. def. instr. Def. Civil Preparedness Agy., 1978—. Recipient Community Svc. award Springboro-Clearcreek Twp. Jaycees, 1977; Chmn. award Ohio Jaycees, 1978 Ky. Col. award Commonwealth of Ky., 1978. Mem. Am. Planning Assn., Ohio Planning Conf. (bd. dirs. 1978—, v.p. 1979-80, pres. 1980-82), Warren County Emergency Med. Svcs. Assn., Ohio Twp. Assn. (hon.), Ohio County Planning Dirs. Assn. (exec. com. 1982—, sec.-treas. 1985-88, v.p. 1988—), Clearcreek Math. and Sci. Assn. (trustee 1989—), County Commrs. Assn. Ohio (assoc.), Internat. Assn. Torch Club, Inc. Home: Springboro, Ohio. Died Apr. 11, 2006.

PRINCE, JULIUS S. (BUD PRINCE), retired foreign service reserve officer; b. Yonkers, NY, July 21, 1911; s. Julius and Clara B. (Rich) P.; m. Eleanora Molloy, July 6, 1943; children: Thomas Marc, Tod Ainslee (dec.), Richard M. Johnson. BA, Yale U., 1932; MD, Columbia U., 1938, M.P.H., 1948; Dr.P.H., Harvard, 1957. Intern Sinai Hosp., Balt., 1939-40; asst. resident medicine N.Y. U. div. Goldwater Meml. Hosp., 1941-42; dist. state health officer N.Y. State Dept. Health, Jamestown, 1948-58; chief pub. health div. USAID, Ethiopia, 1958-67; prin. investigator demonstration and evaluation project AID, Ethiopia, 1959-67; chief Africa div. Population and Humanitarian Affairs, Population Office, AID, Washington, 1967-73; dir. Africa Regional Population Office, Accra, Ghana, 1973-74; chief health, population and nutrition projects AID, Ghana, 1974-76; cons. internat. health APHA, 1977-78, Pacific Cons., Inc., 1978-82, RONCO Inc., 1982; pub. health specialist/sr. health advisor One Am., Inc., 1982-87; sr. pub. health and nutrition specialist Internat. Sci. and Tech. Inst. Inc., 1985-94; cons. on internat. health, from 1985. Report on sustainability of AID supported health, population and nutrition programs, Ghana, 1963-85, Ctr. Devel. Info. and Evaluation AID, 1988, Annotated History of AID-Supported Health and Nutrition Rsch.: From Outset to Present, Introduction and Background, AID Office Health, 1991, Compendium of Abstracts, 1985-92, rsch. by historically black colls. and univs. under AID Univ. Ctr./Rsch. and Univ. Devel. Linkages, 1985-92. Contbr. chpt. to book. Served from lt. to maj. M.C. Royal Canadian Army, 1942-46. Recipient Letter of Commendation, Adj. Gen. Can. Army, 1946, Superior honor award AID, 1968, Letter of Commendation, 1977 Fellow APHA (Lifetime Achievement award 1996), Soc. Applied Anthropology, Washington Acad. Scis., Royal Soc. Health, Am. Coll. Preventive Medicine; mem. AMA, N.Y. State Pub. Health Assn. (pres. 1957), Pan Am. Med. Assn., Am. Assn. World Health (emeritus mem. bd. dirs.), Internat. Soc. Hypertension in Blacks, Internat. Union for Sci. Study of Population, Population Assn. Am., Soc. Internat. Devel., Nat. Coun. Internat. Health (award 1992), World Med. Assn., Soc. Prospective Medicine, Can. Soc. Internat. Health. Died Nov. 7, 2005.

PROVINE, JOHN CALHOUN, retired lawyer; b. Asheville, NC, May 15, 1938; s. Robert Calhoun and Harriet Josephine (Thoms) P.; m. Martha Ann Monson, Aug. 26, 1966 (div. Jan. 1975); m. Nancy Frances Lunsford, Apr. 17, 1976 (div. Mar. 1996); children: Robert, Frances, Harriet. AB, Harvard U., 1960; JD, U. Mich., 1966; MBA, NYU, 1972, LLM in Taxation, 1975. Bar: NY, Tenn., US Dist. Ct. (so. and ea. dists.) NY, US Ct. Appeals (2nd and 6th cirs.), US Dist. Ct. (mid. dist.) Tenn., US Supreme Ct. From assoc. to ptnr. White & Case, NYC, 1966—74, ptnr., 1974—82, 1992—94, Jakarta and Ankara, 1982—91; counsel Dearborn & Ewing, Nashville, 1981—82; ret., 1994. Lt. USN, 1960-63. Mem. ABA, NY Bar Assn., Tenn. Bar Assn., Assn. of Bar of City of NY Avocations: bluegrass music, rural activities. Died Apr. 14, 2006.

PRYCE, EDWARD LYONS, landscape architect; b. Lake Charles, La., May 26, 1914; s. George Samuel and Dora (Cook) P.; m. Woodia Bernice Smith, Nov. 2, 1940; children— Marilyn C., Joellen G. BS, Tuskegee Inst., 1937; B.L.A., Ohio State U., 1948; MS in Landscape Architecture, U. Calif., Berkeley, 1953. Head dept. ornamental horticulture Tuskegee Inst., 1948-55, supt. of bldgs. and grounds, 1955-69, prof. dept. architecture, 1969-77; pvt. practice landscape architecture Tuskegee, Ala., from 1948. Chmn. Ala. State Bd. Examiners for Landscape Architects, 1981— Mem. Tuskegee City Planning Commn., 1970-76; mem. Tuskegee Model Cities Commn., 1968-72, Ala. State Outdoor Recreation Planning Bd., 1978—. Recipient Alumni Merit award Tuskegee Inst., 1977, Disting. Alumnus award Ohio State U., 1980 Fellow Am. Soc. Landscape Architects. Baptist. Died Aug. 15, 2007.

PRYOR, JOSEPH EHRMAN, retired chemistry professor; b. Melber, Ky., Mar. 19, 1918; s. Lonnie Ernest and Queetro Desdemona (Rives) P.; m. Bessie Mae Ledbetter, Aug. 16, 1946; children: Beverly Jo, Joseph Byron, Susan Rebecca. BA, BS, Harding Coll., Searcy, Ark., 1937; MA, La. State U., 1939, PhD, 1943; student, U. Minn., summers 1949, 55, U. Chgo., summer 1950. Teaching fellow math. La. State U., 1937-39, teaching fellow chemistry, 1939-41, Charles Edward Coates research fellow chemistry, 1941-42, instr. math., 1942-44; prof. phys. sci. Harding Coll., 1944-89, chmn. phys. sci. dept., 1944-62, dean coll., 1960-83, v.p. acad. affairs, 1973-83, prof. emeritus, 1989—2006. Prof. physics Mid. Tenn. State U., summer 1959, Harding U., Florence, Italy, 1987; yearbook advisor Harding Coll., 1944-87 (29 ACP All-American books, ACP Hall of Fame, 1988); research chemist Lion Oil Co., El Dorado, Ark., summer 1957; mem. com. liberal arts edn. N. Central Assn., 1952-54, coordinator, 1963-69; faculty rep. Ark. Intercollegiate Athletic Conf., 1957-88, pres., 1967-68, 77-78, 87-88; broadcasting and recording engr., 1946-60. Bd. dirs. Camp Wyldewood, Searcy, 1948-51, So. Christian Home, Morrilton, Ark., 1978—, Zambia Christian Sch., 1975—; preacher, elder Ch. of Christ. Recipient Disting. Alumnus award Harding Coll., 1974, Golden Eagle award Am. Yearbook Co., 1969, Disting. Svc. Plaque for 15 yrs. chmn. ad hoc pubs., 1994; elected to Harding U. Athletic Hall of Fame, 1989, Nat. Assn. of Intercollegiate Athletics Hall of Fame, 1990; Harding U. Sci. Bldg. named the Joseph E. Pryor Sci. Ctr., 1989. Fellow AAAS; mem. Am. Chem. Soc. (chmn. central Ark. sect. 1954-55, sect. councilor 1959-65, 50-yr. membership pin award 1991, Disting. Svc. plaque Cen. Ark. sect. 1991), Am. Sci. Affiliation, Ark. Acad. Sci., Nat. Edn. Assn., Ark. (2d v.p. dept. higher edn. 1964-65, pres. dept. 1965-66), Ark. Deans Assn. (past chmn.), Nat. Council Coll. Publs. Advisers (dist. chmn. 1973-75, disting. yearbook adviser award 1973), Assn. Coll. Honor Socs. (exec. com. 1976-80), Searcy C. of C., Alpha Phi Gamma, Sigma Xi, Alpha Chi (nat. council 1959-93, sec.-treas. region II 1959-71, nat. sec.-treas. 1970-83, exec. dir. 1983-93, installed 85 chpts., awarded outstanding svc. plaque 1993), Phi Kappa Phi, Alpha Psi Omega, Sigma Delta Psi, Alpha Chi Sigma, Phi Lambda Upsilon, Kappa Mu Epsilon, Pi Kappa Delta, Delta Mu Delta, Phi Eta Sigma. Home: Searcy, Ark. Died Oct. 27, 2006.

PUCHTLER, HOLDE, histochemist, pathologist, educator; b. Kleinlosnitz, Germany, Jan. 1, 1920; came to U.S., 1955; d. Gottfried and Gunda (Thoma) P. Cand. med., U. Würzburg, 1944; Md, U. Köln, 1949; MD, U. Köln, Germany, 1951. Rsch. assoc. U. Köln, 1949-51, resident in pathology, 1951-55; rsch. fellow Damon Runyon Found., Montreal, Que., Can., 1955-58; rsch. assoc. Med. Coll. Ga., Augusta, 1959-60, asst. rsch. prof., 1960-62, assoc. rsch. prof., 1962-68, prof., 1968-90, prof. emerita, from 1990. Assoc. editor Jour. Histotech., 1982-94; mem. editorial bd. Histochemistry, 1977-90. Honored at Symposium on Connective Tissues in Arterial and Pulmonary Diseases, 1980. Fellow Am. Inst. Chemists, Royal Microscopical Soc.; mem. Royal Soc. Chemistry, Am. Chem. Soc., Histochem. Soc. Gesellschaft Histochemie, Anatomische Gesellschaft, Ga. Soc. Histotech. (hon.). Achievements include development of new techniques for light, polarization, visible and infrared flourescence microscopy based on theoretical and physical chemistry and x-ray diffraction data; demonstration of relations between dye configurations and selective affinity for certain components of human tissues, such as collagens, elastin, myosins, neurofibrils, and amyloids; application of molecular orbital theories to histochemistry. Home: Augusta, Ga. Died Feb. 27, 2006.

PULLING, NATHANIEL H(OSLER), mechanical engineer educator; b. Boston, Jan. 10, 1920; s. Howard Edward and Mildred Hosler P.; A.B., Brown U., 1942; Ph.D., Harvard U. 1951; m. Lillian E. Donnelly, Sept. 9, 1955. Chief optics subsect. U.S. Naval Bur. Ordnance, 1945-46; research fellow Harvard U., 1950-52; devel. engr. GE, Lynn, Mass., 1953-61 product and bus. planner, 1962-66; project dir. automotive safety Liberty Mut. Ins. Co., Hopkinton, Mass., 1967-89; adj. prof mech. engring. Worcester (Mass.) Poly. Inst., 1973-90. Contbr articles to profl. jours.; patentee in field. Lt. comdr. USNR 1942-46. Registered profl. engr., Mass. Mem. ASME, Soc Automotive Engrs., Photog. Resource Center (Boston), Human Factors Soc., Creative Arts Ctr., Provincetown Art Assn. & Mus., Photog. Soc. Am., Boston Camera Club, Rotary, Masons Episcopalian. Home: East Orleans, Mass. Died May 26, 2007.

PURCHASE, FLOYD STACEY, transit company executive b. Newark, Oct. 14, 1928; s. Floyd Stacey and Mae Lucinda (Gilpin) P.; m. Joan J. Jackson, Aug. 28, 1953 (div.), m. Ruth Reed Oct. 6, 1984; children: Barbara Ann, Christine. Student Drakes Bus. Coll., 1949, Rutgers U., 1950; cert. in exper accident investigation Dept. Transp. Div. claims mgr. Pub. Svc Coordinated Transport, Maplewood, N.J., 1948-70; dir. safety Transport of N.J., Maplewood, 1970-72, dir. safety, tng. and employment EEO and pensions, 1972-80; dir. operational tng and safety N.J. Transit, Maplewood, 1980-87, mgr. human resources adminstrn., 1990—; exec. asst. to v.p. human resources N.J. Transit; tchr. Middlesex Coll., U. Ind., U.S. Dept Transp. Safety Inst.; exec. v.p. Instruments of War Records Inc. Instruments of War Pub. Co., 1989—, also bd. dirs.; cons. in field. Contbr. articles to profl. jours. Bd. dirs. Alexian Bros Hosp. Found., Elizabeth, N.J., 1968-70, Love of Jesus Ministries, 1988—. Capt. Signal Corps, U.S. Army, 1948-69. Recipient United Way Community Svc. award, 1981, N.J. Soc Prevention of Blindness cert. of appreciation. Mem. Am. Soc Safety Engrs. (past pres.), Internat. Hazard Control Mgrs. Assn Republican. Home: Roselle Park, NJ. Died July 26, 2007.

PURNELL, CHARLES GILES, lawyer; b. Aug. 16, 1921; s Charles Stewart and Ginevra (Locke) P.; m. Sally Hupp (dec.) children: Mimi, Sarah Elizabeth, Charles H., John W.; m. Jan Carter. Student, Rice Inst., 1938-39; BA, U. Tex., 1941; student Harvard Bus. Sch., 1942; LLB, Yale U., 1947. Bar: Tex. 1948 Ptnr. Locke, Purnell, Boren, Laney & Neely, Dallas, 1947-89 Locke, Purnell, Rain & Harrell, Dallas, 1989-90, of counsel 1990-99, Locke, Liddell & Sapp, Dallas, from 1999. Exec. asst to Gov. of Tex., Austin, 1973-75. Bd. dirs. Trinity River Authority of Tex., 1975-81; vice chmn. Tex. Energy Adv Council, 1974. Served to lt. U.S. Navy, 1942-45; PTO. Mem ABA, Tex. Bar Assn., Tex. Bar Found, Yale Club, Dallas Country Club, Dallas Petroleum Club, La Jolla (Calif.) Beach and Tennis Club. Episcopalian. Home: Dallas, Tex. Died Sept 27, 2006.

PURNELL, CHARLES REA, lawyer; b. Wellington, Kans July 31, 1922; s. George W. and Katherine E. (Rea) P.; m. Jan Christy, Jan. 6, 1945; children: Charles, Bradley, Whitney. AB Stanford U., 1947, LL.B., 1949. Bar: Calif. 1949. Assoc Pillsbury, Madison & Sutro, San Francisco, 1949-58, ptnr., from 1959. Bd. visitors Stanford U. Law Sch., 1974-77, 84-86; mem Stanford Assocs. Served to capt. inf. AUS, 1943-46, ETO, PTO Mem. ABA, San Francisco Bar Assn. Republican. Home Redwood City, Calif. Died Jan. 18, 2007.

PUTNAM, FRANK WILLIAM, biochemistry educator, immunologist, educator; b. New Britain, Conn., Aug. 3, 1917; s Frank and Henrietta (Holzmann) P.; m. Dorothy Alice Linder Nov. 18, 1942; children— Frank William, Beverly Susan. BA Wesleyan U., Middletown, Conn., 1939, MA, 1940; PhD, U Minn., 1942; MA (hon.), Cambridge U., Eng., 1973. Instr research asso. Duke U. Med. Sch., 1942-46; biochemist CWS Camp Detrick, Md., 1946; asst. prof. U. Chgo., then assoc. prof biochemistry, 1947-55; Lasdon research fellow Cambridge U 1952-53; prof. biochemistry, head dept. U. Fla., 1955-65; prof biology, dir. div. biol. scis. Ind. U., Bloomington, 1965-69, prof molecular biology and zoology, 1972-74, disting. prof. molecular biology and biochemistry, 1974-88, prof. emeritus, from 1989. Bd. visitors Duke U. Med. Ctr., 1970-75; chmn. com nomenclature of human immunoglobulins Internat. Union Immunol. Socs., 1971-76; chmn. basic sci. rev. bd. VA, 1972-76 chmn. cancer cause and prevention adv. com. Nat. Cancer Inst 1974-75; sci. adv. com. Papanicolaou Cancer Research Inst 1976-82; rsch. rev. com. ARC, 1973-77; sci. com. Brussels Colloquium on Protides of Biol. Fluids, 1970-90; chmn. virus cancer program adv. com. Nat. Cancer Inst., 1975-77; sr. med adv. group VA, 1976-80; coun. divsn. biol. scis. and Pritzker

Med. Sch., U. Chgo., 1977-87; chmn. Assembly Life Scis. Nat. Acad. Scis., 1977-81; mem. U.S. Nat. Com. Biochemistry, 1973-79; pres. sci. adv. com. G.E.R.M.I., Lyon, France, 1981-87. Co-author, editor: The Plasma Proteins, vol. 1, Isolation, Characterization and Function, 1960, vol. 2, Biosynthesis, Metabolism, Alterations in Disease, 1960, The Plasma Proteins, 2d edit., Structure, Function, and Genetic Control, Vol. 1, 1975. Vol. 2, 1975, Vol. 3, 1977, Vol. 4, 1984, Vol. 5, 1987; mem. editorial bd. Archives of Biochemistry and Biophysics, 1954-59, Science, 1968-82, Immunochemistry, 1972-75, Biomed. News, 1969-73, Fedn. Proc, 1958-63; Author numerous research papers. Trustee Argonne Univs. Assn., 1981-82; bd. govs. U. Chgo. Argonne Nat. Lab., 1983-89, chmn. Sci. and tech. com., 1983-87; bd. dirs. Radiation Rsch. Found., 1981-87. Markle scholar med. scis., 1950-56; Guggenheim fellow, 1970; fellow Churchill Coll., Cambridge U., 1973—; recipient Distinguished award teaching and research Wesleyan U., 1964, Distinguished Service award in medicine U. Chgo., 1968; Outstanding Achievement award U. Minn., 1974 Fellow AAAS, N.Y. Acad. Scis.; mem. Nat. Acad. Scis., Am. Acad. Arts and Scis. (Midwest council 1975-84), Pan-Am. Assn. Biomed. Scis. (sec.-gen. 1975-78), Japan Electrophoresis Soc. (hon.), Am. Inst. Biol. Scis. (life), Am. Soc. Biol. Chemists (sec. 1958-63), Soc. Exptl. Biology and Medicine, Am. Assn. Immunologists, Am. Chem. Soc. (chmn. div. biol. chemistry 1966-67), Soc. Peruana de Patologia (hon.), Fedn. Socs. Exptl. Biology (chmn. secs. com. 1958-63), Protein Soc., Internat. Soc. Thrombosis Haemostasis, Phi Beta Kappa, Sigma Xi, Phi Lambda Upsilon, Delta Sigma Rho. Clubs: Cosmos. Died Nov. 29, 2006.

PUTNAM, FREDERICK WARREN, JR., bishop; b. Red Wing, Minn., June 17, 1917; s. Frederick W. and Margaret (Bunting) P.; m. Helen Kathryn Prouse, Sept. 24, 1942; children: James Douglas, John Frederick, Andrew Warren. BA, U. Minn., 1939; M.Div., Seabury-Western Theol. Sem., 1942, D.D., 1963; postgrad., State U. Iowa, 1946-47, Mpls. Coll. of Art & Design, 1984-97. Ordained to ministry Episcopal Ch. as deacon, priest, 1942. Pastor in, Windom and Worthington, Minn., 1942-43, Iowa City, 1943-47, Evanston, Ill., 1947-59, Wichita, Kans., 1960-63; Episc. chaplain State U. Iowa, 1943-47; suffragan bishop Episcopal Diocese, Okla., 1963-79; bishop Episcopal Ch. in, Navajoland, 1979-83; asst. bishop Diocese of N.C., 1983, Diocese of Minn., 1983-89, 96-99; acting rector St. George's Episcopal, Pearl Harbor, Hawaii, 1984-85, 96, St. Clement's, Honolulu, 1986, St. John's, Kula, Maui, Hawaii, 1988, 98, St. Elizabeth's, Honolulu, 1990; interim rector St. Stephen's Episcopal Ch., Edina, Minn., 1991-92, Trinity Episcopal Ch., Pocatello, Idaho, 1994; vis. bishop Diocese of N.J., 1995. Bd. dirs. Kiyosoto Ednl. Experiment Program, 1954-91, Mobile Outreach Ministry, 1998—, v.p., 1989-91; cons. Oklahoma City Community Relation Commn., 1966-70; Pres. Okla. Conf. Religion and Race, 1963-67; v.p. Greater Oklahoma City Council Chs., 1966-67; nat. chaplain Brotherhood of St. Andrew, 1967-79, mem. brotherhood legion, 1972—; priest assoc. Order Holy Cross, 1942—; exec. com. Conf. Diocesan Execs., 1969-76, pres., 1972-74; mem. Okla. Commn. United Ministries in Higher Edn., 1970-79, pres., 1973-75; mem. nat. com. on Indian work Episc. Ch., 1977-80; chaplain Okla. Assn. Alcoholism and Alcohol Abuse, 1974-78; hon. life mem. Oklahoma City and County Criminal Justice Council, 1978—; Bechtel lectr. U. Denver, 1966. Editor: (pub.) Sharers Mag., 1957-63; contbr. articles to profl. publs. Founder, pres. Oklahoma City Met. Alliance for Safer City, 1971-78; Trustee Seabury-Western Theol. Sem., 1959-65, Episcopal Theol. Sem. Southwest, 1966-69, St. Simeon's Episcopal Home, 1963-79, St. Crispins Episcopal Conf. Ctr., 1963-79, Casady Sch., 1963-79, Holland Hall Sch., 1963-79, Episcopal Soc. Cultural and Racial Unity, 1967-70; trustee Neighborhood Services Orgn., treas., 1969; founder, 1st pres. Friends of Wichita Pub. Libr., 1962; bd. dirs. Minn. Photographic Exbn.; chmn. Mpls.-St. Paul Internat. Photog. Exhbn., 1987, 89; State Bd. Minn. Common Cause, 1989-2007, state chmn., 1993-95; bd. dirs. Minn. Com. for Pub. Edn. Recipient Disting. Service award Evanston Jr. C. of C., 1952; Merit award Photog. Soc. Am. Fellow Coll. Preachers; mem. ACLU, Assoc. Parishes (pres. 1960-64), Mpls. Soc. Fine Arts (mem. photo coun.), Photog. Soc. Am., Am. Com. for KEEP (v.p. 1961-70, 90), Walker Art Ctr., Sierra Club, Met. Sr. Fedn., Audubon Club, Am. Assn. Ret. Persons, Minn. Hort. Soc., Hist. Soc. Episcopal Ch., Archaeol. Conservancy, Ancient Bibl. Manuscripts Ctr., Claremont, Calif., World Future Soc., Photographic Soc. Am. (assoc. 1989—, mem. v.p., 1995-97—), Twin Cities Assn. Camera Clubs (v.p. 1987), U. Minn. Alumni Assn., Minn. Hist. Soc., St. Paul Camera Club, Crosstown Camera Club, N.Am. Rights Fund., People for the Am. Way, Episcopal Peace Fellowship, Amnesty Internat., Greenpeace, Liturgical Conf., Living Ch. Found., Worldwatch Inst., Clan Douglas Soc., Northwest Racquet and Swim Club, Explorers Club, Phi Kappa Psi. Clubs: Normandale Tennis and Swim. Episcopalian. Home: Edina, Minn. Died June 7, 2007.

PYKE, RONALD, mathematics professor; b. Hamilton, Ont., Can., Nov. 24, 1931; s. Harold and Grace Carter (Digby) P.; m. Gladys Mary Davey, Dec. 19, 1953; children: Darlene, Brian, Ronald, Gordon. BA (hon.), McMaster U., 1953; MS, U. Wash., 1955, PhD, 1956. Asst. prof. Stanford U., Calif., 1956-58; asst. prof. Columbia U., NYC, 1958-60; prof. math. U. Wash., Seattle, 1960-98, prof. emeritus, from 1998. Vis. prof. U. Cambridge, Eng., 1964-65, Imperial Coll., London, 1970-71, Colo. State U., Ft. Collins, 1979, Technion, Israel, 1988, 90, 92; pres. Inst. Math. Stats., 1986-87; mem. bd. math. scis. NRC/NAS, 1984-88, chmn. com. applications and theoretical stats., 1985-88. Editor Ann. Prob., 1972-75; contbr. articles to profl. jours. NSF grantee, 1961-91. Fellow Internat. Statis. Inst. (v.p. 1989-91), Am. Statis. Assn., Inst. Math. Stats. (pres. 1986-87); mem. Bernoulli Soc., Statis. Soc. of Can. Home: Woodinville, Wash. Died Oct. 22, 2005.

PYNE, EBEN WRIGHT, retired banker; b. NYC, June 14, 1917; s. Grafton H. and Leta Constance (Wright) P.; m. Hilda Holloway, Dec. 16, 1941; children: Constance Howland Ranges (dec.), Lillian Stokes Pyne-Corbin, Mary Alison McNaughton; m. Nancy Gray Clk. 1st Nat. City Trust Co. (formerly City Bank Farmers Trust Co.), 1939, v.p., asst. to pres., 1952—56, exec. v.p., 1956, pres., dir., 1957—61; asst. cashier Nat. City Bank of N.Y., 1946—50, asst. v.p., 1950—52, v.p., 1952—53, sr. v.p., 1960—82. Vice chmn., bd. dirs. The Home Group Inc.; bd. dirs. U.S. Life Ins. Co. City of N.Y., Home Ins. Co., U.S. Internat. Reins., Inc., Gen. Devel. Corp., Slattery Group, Inc., L.I. Lighting Co. Mem. N.Y. State Met. Transp. Authority, 1965—75; commr. N.Y.C. Transit Authority, 1965—75, Triborough Bride and Tunnel Authority, 1965—75, Manhattan and Bronx Surface Transit Authority, 1965—75, Stewart Airport, 1965—75, S.I. Rapid Transit Operating Authority, 1965—75; trustee Juilliard Sch., St. Luke's Hosp.; mem. exec. com. Pres.'s Pvt. Sector on Cost Control. Maj. AUS, 1940—46. Decorated Bronze Star. Mem. Pilgrims of U.S. (exec. com.), Bklyn. Inst. Arts and Scis. (trustee), N.Y. Zool. Soc. (trustee), Piping Rock Club (Locust Valley, L.I.), Bond Club, Racquet and Tennis Club, River Club N.Y.C., Ivy Club (Princeton, N.J.). Home: Northeast Hbr, Maine. Died Apr. 11, 2007.

QUARLES, RUTH BRETT, retired academic administrator; b. Winton, N.C., Nov. 23, 1914; d. Arthur H. and Julia (Pierce) Brett; A.B. summa cum laude, Shaw U., 1935; M.A., Hartford Sem. Found., 1936; Ed.D., Columbia U., 1945; m. Benjamin A. Quarles, Dec. 21, 1952; 1 dau., Pamela Anne; 1 stepdau., Roberta Quarles Knowles. Asst. to dean Spelman Coll., Atlanta, 1936-38; dean women Dillard U., New Orleans, 1938-42; dean students Bennett Coll., Greensboro, N.C., 1942-44; asso. personnel dir. Tuskegee (Ala.) Inst., 1945-49; staff mem. Student Center, Am. Friends Service Com., U. Munich (W.Ger.), 1949-51; dean students Fisk U., Nashville, 1951-53; dir. Center for Counseling and Acad. Advising, Morgan State U., Balt., 1956-80; ret., 1980; cons. Am. Council on Edn. Mem. Commn. Edn. of Women, 1953-57; mem. instrn. and guidance com. Citizens Sch. Adv. Com., Balt. Public Schs.; chmn. orientation com. Md. Com. High Sch.-Coll. Relations, 1959-61; nat. bd. dirs. YWCA, 1957-60; mem. Md. coordinating com. Internat. Women's Yr., 1977. Fellow Nat. Council of Religion in Higher Edn.; mem. NAACP, LWV, Urban League, Am. Coll. Personnel Assn., Nat. Assn. Women Deans, Adminstrs. and Counselors (exec. bd. 1977-80, citation 1980, Disting. Service award 1982; Ruth Brett Symposium on Minorities in Higher Edn. named in her honor 1982), Kappa Delta Pi, Pi Lambda Theta. Presbyterian. Club: The Philomathians. Home: Baltimore, Md. Died Jan. 16, 2007.

QUIGLEY, LEONARD VINCENT, lawyer; b. Kansas City, Mo., June 21, 1933; s. Joseph Vincent and Rosemary (Cannon) Q.; m. Lynn Mathis Pfohl, May 23, 1964; children: Leonard Matthew, Cannon Louise, Daniel Pfohl, Megan Mathis. AB, Coll. Holy Cross, 1953; LL.B. magna cum laude, Harvard U., 1959; LL.M. in Internat. Law, NYU, 1962. Bar: N.Y. 1960. Assoc. Cravath, Swaine & Moore, NYC, 1959-67; ptnr. Paul, Weiss, Rifkind, Wharton & Garrison, NYC, 1968—2004; gen. counsel Archaeol. Inst. Am., Boston. Served to lt. USN, 1953-56. Mem. ABA, Can. Bar Assn., N.Y. State Bar, Coun. Fgn. Rels., Assn. Bar City N.Y., Harvard Club (N.Y.C.), West Side Tennis Club (Forest Hills, N.Y.). Home: Forest Hills, NY. Died Nov. 14, 2005.

QUIGLEY, THOMAS JOSEPH, lawyer; b. Mt. Carmel, Pa., July 22, 1923; s. James S. and Helen C. (Laughlin) Q.; m. Joan R. Reifke, Aug. 11, 1956; children: Thomas J., Jr., Joan E., James S. AB, Bucknell U., 1947; LLB, Yale U., 1950. Bar: Ohio, US Dist. Ct. Ohio, US Ct. Appeals (6th and D.C. cirs.). With Squire, Sanders & Dempsey, 1950—93, adminstr. labor dept., 1971-80, mng. ptnr., Washington, 1980-85; nat. vice chmn., 1985-86; nat. chmn., 1986-90; pres., Nat. Symphony Orch., 1992-95, nat. trustee Musical Arts Assn. Cleve.; bd. dirs. Belgian Am. C. of C. 1st lt. USAAF, 1942-45. Decorated D.F.C., Air medal with oak leaf cluster, Belgium's Order of the Crown. Mem. ABA, Ohio Bar Assn., D.C. Bar Assn., Cleve. Bar Assn., Fed. City Coun., Yale Law Sch. Alumni. Assn. Roman Catholic. Clubs: Yale (N.Y.C.), Edgartown Yacht (Mass.), Edgartown Reading Room, Chevy Chase, Metropolitan (Wash.). Died July 1, 2007.

QUISENBERRY, NANCY LOU, academic administrator, educator; b. Washington, Ind., Jan. 29, 1938; d. Joseph Franklin and Maud Helen (Fitch) Forbes; m. James D. Quisenberry, Feb. 6, 1960; 1 child, James Paul. BS in Home Econs., Ind. State Tchrs. Coll., 1960, MS in Home Econs., 1962; EdD, Ind. U., 1971. Cert. tchr. Ind. Home economics tchr. Honey Creek High Sch., Terre Haute, Ind., 1961-62; third grade tchr. Indpls. Pub. Sch., 1962-64; sustitute tchr. Dep. of Def., Baumholder, Fed. Republic Germany, 1964-65; first grade tchr. Wayne Twp. Schs., Indpls., 1966-67; assoc. faculty lang. arts Ind. U.-Purdue U., Indpls., spring 1970; prof. curriculum and instruction So. Ill. U., Carbondale, 1971—98, assoc. dean Coll. of Edn., 1976-96, interim dean, 1996-98; exec. dir. Orpheum Children's Sci. Mus., Champaign, Ill., from 2004. Cons. U. N.C., Durham, 1977, Ministry Edn., Bangkok, 1980, Bangkok, 84, DePaul U., 1990, Ill. State U., 2002, U. Miss., 2001, Loyola U., 2002, Gov.'s State U., 2002; dir. tech. and tng. assistance grant Head Stard-OCD, Carbondale, 1972—74, Cameroon project USAID, Carbondale, 1984—86; mem. Ill. State Tchr. Cert. Bd., 1981—84, 1984—87. Co-author: Early Childhood Education Programs: Developmental Objectives and Their Use, 1975, Play as Development, 1978, Educators Healing Racism, 1999, Racism in the Classroom: Case Studies, 2002. Bd. dirs. Jackson County YMCA, 1988; chair candidacy com. Ctrl. So. Ill. Synod Evang. Luth. Ch. Am., Springfield, 1987—90, sec. multisynodical com. Chgo., 1987—90, synod coun., 1992—95; pres. Epiphany Luth. Ch. Coun., Carbondale, 1984—85, 1989—92, 1994—96. Recipient Dare To Be Great award, Ill. Women Adminstrs. and So. Ill. Region, 1989, Woman of Distinction award, So. Ill. U., 1992; grantee, Bur. Educationally Handicapped, 1979—82, 1990—95. Mem.: World Orgn. for Pre-sch. Edn. (U.S. nat. com., treas. 1997—99, chmn. strategic planning commn. 1999—2002, webmaster from 2000), Assn. Tchr. Educators (chair com. racism from a healing perspective 1995—98), Ill. Assn. Colls. for Tchr. Edn. (pres. 1984—86), Am. Assn. Colls. for Tchr. Edn. (bd. dirs. 1986—88, chair adv. coun. state reps. 1987—88, bd. dirs. 1991—94), Nat. Coun. for Accreditation Tchr. Edn. (bd. examiners 1987—98, new profl. tchr. project elem. edn. stds. drafting com. 1996—98, transition team elem. stds. 1998—2000, chair Rubics devel. com. 2001, exec. bd. from 2002, chair Coun. Profl. Preparation of Educators from 2003), Assn. Childhood Edn. Internat. (chair tchr. edn. com. 1989—93, folio rev. coord. elem. edn. 1989—2001, sec.-treas. from 1996, pres.-elect 1998—2000, pres. 2001—03, past pres. 2003—04, folio rev. coord. elem. edn. from 2004), Internat. Coun. on Edn. for Tchg. (N.Am. v.p. 1992—94, pres.-elect 1997—2000, pres. 2000—02, bd. dirs.), Rotary (pres. Urbana chpt. from 2005). Avocations: gardening, flute, sewing, walking, organ. Home: Urbana, Ill. Died Sept. 27, 2006.

QURAISHI, MOHAMMED SAYEED, retired health facility administrator, research scientist; b. Jodhpur, India, June 23, 1924; arrived in US, 1946, naturalized, 1973; s. Mohammed Latif and Akhtar Jahan Q.; m. Akhtar Imtiaz, Nov. 12, 1953; children: Rana, Naveed, Sabah (dec.). B.Sc., St. John's Coll., 1942; M.Sc., Aligarh Muslim U., 1944; PhD, U. Mass., 1948. Sr. mem. UN, WHO Team to Bangladesh, 1949-51; entomologist Malaria Inst. Pakistan, 1951-55; sr. rsch. officer Pakistan Council Sci. and Indsl. Rsch., 1955-60; sr. sci. officer Pakistan AEC, 1960-64; assoc. prof. entomology U. Man., 1964-66, N.D. State U., Fargo, 1966-70, prof., 1970-74; chief scientist biology N.Y. State Sci. Svc., Albany, 1974-75; entomologist, toxicologist, chief pest control and consultation sect. NIH, Bethesda, Md., 1976-84; health scientist adminstr., exec. sec. microbiology and infectious disease rsch. com. Nat. Inst. Allergy and Infectious Diseases, Bethesda, Md., 1984-88, sci. rev. adminstr. spl. revs., 1988-96, sci. rev. adminstr. AIDS clin. epidemiol. rsch. rev. br., 1996-2000; ret., 2000; sr. scientist Inst. Nuclear Sci., CENTO, Tehran, Iran, 1960-64; program mgr. interdepartmental contract Project THEMIS, Dept. Def., 1968-74. Cons. breast cancer rsch. program UIS Dept. Def., 2001; vis. scientist Harvard Sch. Pub. Health, 1995. Author: Biochemical Insect Control: Its Impact on Economy, Environment and Natural Selection, 1977; mem. editorial bd. Jour. Environ. Toxicology and Chemistry, 1981-84; author numerous sci. papers. Chmn. NIH Asian-Am. Cultural Assn., 1980—81; mem. Montgomery County Bd. Social Svcs., 2002. Recipient Sustained High Quality Performance award, 1980, Merit Pay Performance awards, 1984, 86, 87, Recognition and Appreciation of Spl. Achievement award NIH, 1988, Spl. Recognition award for Svcs. to NIH, Asian Am. Cultural Com., 1989, Appreciation in Recognition of Outstanding Support for Combined Fed. Campaign, 1991. Mem. Am. Chem. Soc., Soc. Environ. Toxicology and Chemistry (mem. publs. com. in charge spl. publs. 1982-84), Sigma Xi, Phi Kappa Phi. Home: Gaithersburg, Md. Died Feb. 21, 2007.

RADOMSKI, JACK LONDON, toxicology consultant; b. Milw., Dec. 10, 1920; s. Joseph Elwood and Evelyn (Hansen) R.; m. Margery Dodge, Feb. 1, 1947 (div. Nov. 1970); m. Teresa Pascual, Feb. 19, 1971; children: Mark, Linda, Eric, Janet, Mayte. BS, U. Wis., 1942; PhD, George Washington U., 1950. Chemist Gen. Aniline & Film Corp., Binghampton, N.Y., 1942-44; pharmacologist FDA, Washington, 1944-52, acting chief acute toxicity br., 1952-53; prof. pharmacology U. Miami, Coral Gables, Fla., 1953-82; pres. Covington Tech. Svcs., Andalusia, Ala., 1982-88; pvt. practice cons. in toxicology Hudson, Fla., from 1988. Cons. WHO, IARC, GAO, EPA, HEW, NIOSH. Contbr. articles to profl. jours. Recipient Spl. award Commr. FDA, 1952; diplomate in gen. toxicology Acad. Toxicol. Scis., 1982. Mem. Am. Soc. Pharmacology and Exptl. Therapeutics, Soc. Toxicology, Am. Assn. Cancer Rsch., N.Y. Acad. Scis., Am. Bd. Forensic Examiners. Died Mar. 30, 2006.

RAEMER, HAROLD ROY, electrical engineering educator; b. Chgo., Apr. 26, 1924; s. Leo and Fannie (Marx) R.; m. Paulyne Barkin, Dec. 21, 1947; children: Daniel, Liane, Diane. BS, Northwestern U., 1948, MS, 1949, PhD, 1959. Teaching asst. Northwestern U., 1950-52; physicist Bendix Research Labs., Detroit, 1952-55; staff engr. Cook Research Labs., Chgo., 1955-60; sr. engring. specialist Sylvania Applied Research Lab., Waltham, Mass., 1960-63; assoc. prof. elec. engring. Northeastern U., Boston, 1963-65, prof., from 1965, chmn. dept., 1967—77, acting chmn., 1982-84, Snell prof. engring., 1986-93; prof. emeritus, from 1994. Vis. lectr. Harvard U., 1962, hon. research assoc., 1972-73; vis. scientist MIT, 1984-85; cons. in field Author: Statistical Communication: Theory and Applications, 1969, Radar Systems Principles, 1996; contbr. articles to profl. jours. Served with USAAF, 1943-46. Mem. IEEE (sr.), AAAS, Am. Soc. for Engring. Edn., Sigma Xi, Pi Mu Epsilon, Eta Kappa Nu, Tau Beta Pi Home: Needham, Mass. Died Jan. 20, 2007.

RAGLAND, ALWINE MULHEARN, retired judge; b. Monroe, La., July 28, 1913; m. LeRoy Smith, 1947 (dec.); children—LeRoy, Caroline Smith Christman; m. 2d., L. Percy Ragland (dec.). A.A., Principia Coll., St. Louis; J.D., Tulane U., 1935. Bar: La. 1935. Sole practice, Tallulah, La., 1935-74; mem. firm Mulhearn & Smith, 1972-74; judge 6th Jud. Dist. Ct., Lake Prvidence, La., 1974-90; atty. for inheritance tax collector Madison Parish, La., 1968-74; former city atty., Delta, La.; temporary judge La. Ct. Appeals (2d cir.), 1976; atty., Tallulah, La., 1991; now ret. Charter bd. dirs. Silver Waters council Girl Scouts U.S.A.; past pres. Band Boosters Assn. Tallulah High Sch., Tallulah High Sch. PTA; past dist. dir., past bd. dirs, lay reader 1st Ch. Christ Scientist, Vicksburg, Miss.; past bd. dirs. Delta Christian Sch. Mem. ABA, La. Bar Assn., 6th Jud. Bar Assn., La. Def. Counsel Assn. (jud. assoc. mem.), Am. Judges Assn., La. Judges Assn., Am. Judicature Soc., La. Council Juvenile and Family Ct. Ct. Judges (past pres.), Nat. Council Juvenile Ct. Judges, So. Juvenile Ct. Judges, Assn. Trial Lawyers Am., La. Trial Lawyers Assn., Family Conciliation Cts. and Services, Nat. Juvenile Ct. Service Assn., La. Conf. Social Welfare, Practicing Law Inst., Nat. Assn. Women Judges, La. Assn. Def. Counsel. Home: Tallulah, La. Died Apr. 30, 2006.

RAINEY, CLAUDE GLADWIN, retired healthcare executive; b. Enloe, Tex., Apr. 21, 1923; s. Claude C. and Pauline (Whitlock) R.; m. Peggy Ballard, July 27, 1947; children—Kathy Suzanne, David Claude, Mark Jeffery, Joel Allen, Peggy Jan, Susan Elise Student pub. health and adminstrv. medicine, Columbia U., 1961-62. Med. adminstrv., officer dept. medicine and surgery VA, Temple, Tex., 1946-51, med. adminstrv., officer dept. medicine and surgery Muskogee, Okla., 1951-56; med. adminstr. Fite Clinic, Lakeland Med. Ctr., Muskogee, Okla., 1956-59; hosp. adminstr. M.-K.-T. R.R. Employees Hosp. Assn., Denison, Tex., 1959-62, also sec., treas. trustee; hosp. adminstr., cons. Denison Hosp. Authority, Meml. Hosp., 1962-66; adminstr. Seton Hosp., Austin, Tex., 1966-74; exec. v.p. Fort Worth Osteo. Hosp., 1974-83; pres. Health Care of Tex., Inc., Fort Worth, 1983-88, ret. Pres. North Grayson County chpt. Am. Cancer Soc., 1960-66, bd. dirs., Tex., 1961—. Served with USNR, 1942-46. Fellow Am. Coll. Hosp. Adminstrs., Am. Coll. Osteo. Hosp. Adminstrs. (award of merit 1984); mem. Am. Hosp. Assn., Tex. Hosp. Assn., Am. Osteo. Hosp. Assn. (Disting. Svc. award 1985) Home: Arlington, Tex. Died July 20, 2007.

RAJKI, WALTER ALBERT, manufacturing executive, director; b. Cleve., Sept. 24, 1925; s. Stephen and Julia (Zajac) R.; m. Mary Elizabeth Koch, July 12, 1952; children: William, Carl, Joan. BS, M.I.T., 1951; JD, Cleve. State U., 1958. Bar: Ohio 1958. Engr. Chain Belt Co., Milw., 1951-53; plant mgr., pres. Adalet Mfg. Co., Cleve., 1953-72; group v.p. Scott & Fetzer Co., Cleve., 1972-78, sr. v.p., 1978-88; mng. ptnr. Commvest Co., Ft. Myers, Fla., from 1988. Dir. Highland Farms Inc., Commonwealth Investment Co., Commvest Co. Mem. Ohio Bar Assn., Cleve. Bar Assn. Clubs: Cleve. Yachting, Union. Home: Sterling, Va. Died Dec. 29, 2006.

RAKITA, LOUIS, retired cardiologist; b. Montreal, Que., Can., July 2, 1922; came to U.S., 1951, naturalized, 1962; s. S. and Rose (Weinman) R.; m. G. Blanche Michlin, Dec. 4, 1945; 1 son, Robert M. BA, Sir George Williams Coll., Montreal, 1942; MD, C.M., McGill U., 1949. Diplomate: Am. Bd. Internal Medicine. Intern Montreal Gen. Hosp., 1949-50; resident in medicine Jewish Gen. Hosp., Montreal, 1950-51; fellow in medicine Alton Ochsner Med. Found., New Orleans, 1951-52; chief resident in medicine Cleve. City Hosp., 1952-53, Am. Heart Assn. fellow, 1954-55, Inst. for Med. Research, Cedars of Lebanon Hosp., Los Angeles, 1953-54; practice medicine specializing in internal medicine and cardiology Cleve., 1954—2005; instr. medicine Western Res. U., Cleve., 1954-55, sr. instr., 1955-57, asst. prof., 1957-61, asso. prof., 1961-71; asst. vis. physician Cleve. City Hosp., 1954-57, vis. physician, from 1957; advanced fellow Cleve. Met. Gen. Hosp., 1959-61, dir. cardiology, 1966-87, immediate past dir., div. cardiology, 1987—2005; assoc. div. of research in med. edn. Case Western Res. U., Cleve., 1969-75, prof. medicine, 1971-93, prof. emeritus medicine, 1993; ret., 2005. Chmn. Phase IIA Cardiovascular com. Case Western Res. U., 1965-70, Faculty Senate Subcom. for Devel. and Evaluation of Ednl. Methods, 1969, chmn. Univ. Com. on Ednl. Planning, 1971-73, Faculty Coun. Sch. Medicine, 1979-80, Faculty Coun., chmn. Steering Com. Sch. Medicine, 1979-80, mem. bd. trustees Com. on Univ. Plans, 1971-73, Faculty Senate, Exec. Coun.; cons. in cardiology Luth. Med. Ctr., Cleve., 1970—, Crile VA Hosp., Cleve., 1969—; vis. cardiologist Sunny Acres Hosp., Cleve., 1973—; cardiologist rep. of del. to USSR, 1973. Author: (with M. Broder) Cardiac Arrhythmias, 1970, (with M. Kaplan) Immunological Diseases, 1972; Contbr. (with M. Kaplan) articles on cardiovascular diseases to profl. publs. Served with RCAF, 1942-45. Recipient Research Career Devel. award USPHS, 1962-69, Saltzman award Mt. Sinai Med. Health Found., 1997. Fellow ACP (Laureate award Ohio chpt. 1992), Am. Coll. Cardiology, Royal Coll. Physicians and Surgeons Can. (cert.), Am. Heart Assn. (mem. exec. com. N.E. Ohio chpt. 1972—, trustee 1969—, pres. N.E. Ohio chpt. 1972-74, coun. on clin. cardiology 1972—, chmn. various coms., v.p. North Ctrl. Region 1985-86, bd. dirs. 1985-86, hon. life trustee Northeast Ohio affiliate, vice chmn. task force on product licensing feasibility 1987—, Award of Merit 1987, Gold Heart award 1989); mem. AAUP, Am. Fedn. Clin. Rsch., Ctrl. Soc. Clin. Rsch., Soc. Exptl. Biology and Medicine, Cleve. Med. Libr. Assn. (trustee 1972—), Nat. Bd. Med. Examiners, The Press of Case Western Res. U. (adv. com. 1970), Nat. Heart and Lung Inst., Nat. Insts. Health (left ventricular assist device clin. trial program divsn. extramural affairs, data rev. bd. 1981—, adv. com. med. devices applications program 1971-75), Sigma Xi. Home: Cleveland, Ohio. Died Apr. 2, 2007.

RAMER, JAMES DAVID, retired librarian; b. Metropolis, Ill., July 14, 1927; s. Elmon Randolph and Adaline M. (Fournie) R. Student, U. Mich., 1944-45; AB, Occidental Coll., 1951; MS, Columbia, 1957, D.L.S., 1969. Engring. and phys. sci. librarian U. Md., College Park, 1957-59; head engring. and phys. scis. libraries Columbia, 1959-64; library dir. U. N.C., Charlotte, 1964-68; assoc. prof. Emory U., Atlanta, 1968-71; dean, prof. Grad. Sch. Library Service, U. Ala., 1971—88; ret., 1988. Author: Bibliography on Plasma Physics and Magnetohydrodynamics, 1959; editor: The Alabama Librarian, 1974-77. Served with U.S. Army, 1946-48. Mem. ALA, Southeastern, Ala. Libr. Assn. (Exceptional Svc. citation 1987), Assn. Am. Libr. Schs., Pvt. Librs. Assn., Am. Printing History Assn., World Future Soc., Friends of Earth, Phi Beta Kappa. Died Sept. 27, 2007.

RAMSEY, PAUL WILLARD, metallurgical engineer, welding engineering consultant; b. Wilkinsburg, Pa., Feb. 17, 1919; s. Harry Floyd and Clara Edna (Renfrew) R.; m. Shirley Rae Karper, June 27, 1942; children: Paul, Jr., Susan, Roger. BS, Carnegie-Mellon U., 1940; MS, U. Wis., 1956. Metall. engr. N.J. Zinc Co., Palmerton, Pa., 1940-51; metall. researcher A.O. Smith Corp., Milw., 1951-56, welding researcher, 1956-65, mgr. welding research and devel., 1965-80, mgr. welding and metall. research and devel., 1980-82; exec. dir. Am. Welding Soc., Miami, Fla., 1982-87. Contbr. articles to profl. jours. Troop com. chmn. Boy Scouts Am., 1957-59; group chmn. United Fund, 1973, div. chmn., 1974, alderman, City of Wauwatosa, Wis., 1956-72; pres. Common Council, 1968-70; plan commn. chmn. Comprehensive Plan Commn., 1972-82; Mem. indsl. adv. council U. Wis.-Milw., 1968-82; bd. visitors Coll. Engring., U. Wis.-Madison, 1973-82. Served with USNR, 1944-46. Recipient Disting. Service citation Coll. Engring., U. Wis., 1974 Fellow Am. Soc. Metals, Am. Welding Soc. (dir. 1966-78, pres. 1975-76, S.W. Miller medal 1980, R.D. Thomas award 1993); mem. AIME, Welding Rsch. Coun., Beta Theta Pi, Theta Tau. Patentee in field. Died Mar. 9, 2006.

RAMSTAD, PAUL ELLERTSON, chemistry consultant; b. Mpls., Jan. 30, 1918; s. Otto and Otilia (Ellertson) R.; m. Jean Heffron, Mar. 21, 1941 (dec. Mar. 1987); children: John Richard, Julie Carolin, William Edward, Polly Ellen; m. Loretta K. Porter, June 15, 1988. BS, U. Minn., 1939, PhD, 1942. Research chemist Gen. Mills, Inc., 1942-48; assoc. prof. Cornell U., Ithaca, N.Y., 1948-53; asst. dir. research Oscar Mayer & Co., Madison, Wis., 1953-55; quality control exec. Gen. Mills, Inc., Mpls., 1955-65; v.p., dir. Am. Maize-Products Co., Hammond, Ind., also NYC, 1965-78, pres. Corn processing div., 1968-75, pres., chief operating officer, 1976-78; cons., from 1978. Editor: Cereal Science Today, 1957-62; sci. editor: Cereal Chemistry, 1978-84. Corp. Trustee Nutrition Found., 1976-78. Fellow AAAS; mem. Am. Assoc. Cereal Chemists (past pres.), Inst. Food Technologists, Am. Chem. Soc., Corn Refiners Assn. (chmn. 1977), Sigma Xi, Phi Lambda Upsilon. Clubs: Ithaca Yacht. Patentee in field. Died Oct. 13, 2006.

RANDALL, HOWARD MORGAN, academic dean, educator; b. Rockville Center, NY, May 5, 1936; s. Howard Morgan and Caroline (McIntosh) R.; m. Evelyn Ann Wittmann, July 30, 1962 (div. May 30, 1978), 1 child, Barbara Ann; m. Fran Marilyn Songy, Dec. 23, 1978, (div. July, 1990); 1 child, Christine Ellie. Summer fellow Brookhaven Nat. Labs., Upton, N.Y., 1959; instr. physiology La. State U. Sch. Medicine, New Orleans, 1965-68, asst. prof., 1968-71, assoc. prof., 1971-77, asst. dean student affairs, 1977-82, assoc. dean, from 1982, prof. physiology, from 1983. Contbr. articles to profl. jours. Mem. dads club Jean Gordon Elem. Sch., New Orleans, 1988—. Died May 15, 2006.

RANDOLPH, FRANCIS FITZ, JR., cable television executive; b. NYC, July 13, 1927; s. Francis Fitz and Sarah Tod (Bulkley) R.; m. Catherine Ann Meyers, June 6, 1969. BA, Yale U., 1950; LLB, Columbia U., 1953. Bar: U.S. Ct. Appeals (2d cir.) 1954. Law clk. to presiding judge U.S. Ct. Appeals 2d cir., 1953-54; assoc. Cravath, Swaine & Moore, NYC, 1954-61, ptnr., 1962-81; vice chmn. Cablevisions Systems Corp., Woodbury, N.Y., 1982-94; ret., 1994. Exec. com. NAACP Legal Def. Fund, N.Y., 1968-80; trustee Vassar Coll., 1980-92. With USN, 1946. Mem. N.Y. Bar Assn., Assn. of Bar of City of N.Y., Down Town Assn., Union Club; Silver Spring Country Club (Ridgefield, Conn.). Democrat. Home: New York, NY. Died May 1, 2006.

RAPSON, WILLIAM JAMES, electronics executive; b. Midwest, Wyo., May 30, 1931; s. William J. and Thoedocia R.; m. Betty Bober, Jan. 30, 1981; children: William J., Michael H. BA, Rice U., 1953, BSME, 1954. Sales promotion mgr. Garret Oil Tools, Longview, Tex., 1957—61; gen. mgr. Scott Corp., Houston, 1961—63; pres., dir. Uson Corp., Houston, from 1963. Chmn. bd.,dir. Uson Cos.; dir. Panex Corp., Ameriway Bank Brookhollow, Ameriway Fin. Group; chmn. Exec. Group-Houston. Patentee variious leak detection and leak testing instruments. With US Army, 1954—56. Mem.: ASME, Houstonian Club. Episcopalian. Died June 2, 2007.

RASDALL, JOYCE OLIVER, home economist, educator; b. Simpson County, Ky., Dec. 10, 1944; d. Thomas Franklin and Ruth A. (Heard) Oliver; BS, Western Ky. U., 1965; MS, U. N.C., Greensboro, 1968; PhD, Ohio State U., 1973; m. L. D. Rasdall, Jr., Aug. 15, 1965; children: L. Dow, Rebecca Ruth. Consumer svc. specialist Warren Rural Electric Coop. Corp., Bowling Green, Ky., 1966-68; rsch. assoc. Ohio State U., Columbus, 1970-71; instr., then asst. prof. dept. home econs. Western Ky. U., Bowling Green, 1968-78, assoc. prof. interior design, housing and household equipment, 1978-83, prof., 1983—, sabbatical leave, 1982; TV program Women, Yes, 1966-68; radio program House Call, 1967-68; also lectr. workshops. Trustee, Warren Assn. Bapt. Properties, 1978-82, trustee Campbellsville Coll., 1983—, mem. exec. com., 1984-87; mem. North Warren Bicentennial Events Com., 1976; assn. dir. Ky. Bapt. Young Women, 1978-84; participant Ky. to Kenya Partnership, 1985; founding benefactor, College Heights Found., Pres.' Club of Western Ky. U., Pres.' Club of Campbellsville Coll.; v.p., then pres. N.Warren PTA, 1978-80; organist Smiths Grove Bapt. Ch.; cons. and judge electricity projects 4-H Club. Recipient research award Am. Council on Consumer Interests, 1974, outstanding mem. service award Nat. Rural Electric Coops., 1968, R.C.P. Thomas award Western Ky. U., 1965; faculty research grantee, 1979, 83, 86; faculty devel. grantee, 1983, 85, 86; Am. Home Econs. Assn. fellow Ohio State U., 1970-71. Mem. Am. Home Econs. Assn., Am. Assn. Housing Educators, Ky. Home Econs. Assn. (v.p., mem. various coms.), Elec. Women's Roundtable (nat. chmn. Julia Kiene grad. fellowship and Lyle Mamer grad. scholarship), ASTM (affiliate, standards devel. com.), Ky. Elec. Women's Round Table (v.p., sec.), Coll. Educators in Home Equipment (pres. elect, pres., chmn. ann. meeting, research award 1985), Underwriters' Lab. (mem. consumer adv. council), Internat. Microwave Power Inst., Ky. Youth Electric Adv. Council, Nat. Trust Hist. Preservation, Phi Upsilon Omicron (sponsor univ. chpt., Outstanding Alumnus award Western Ky. U. 1983), Omicron Nu. Clubs: Smiths Grove Woman's (pres.), Ky. Fedn. Women's Clubs (coms.). Author: Information on Consumer Products: A Study of Factors Affecting its Use by Consumers, 1974; Product Information as a Resource: Factors Affecting its Usefulness to Consumers, 1974; The Utility of Product Information as a Resource for Consumer Use, 1977; Consumer Competencies in Household Equipment, 1975; Plan the Light in Your Home, 1970; (with others) Microwave Ovens, 1972; The Energy Dilemma: Some Choices Confronting the American Family, 1978; Energy Productivity and Creativity in the Household (series of slides sets and scripts), 1982; Funds and Instrumentation for Conducting Research with Limited Funds and Heavy Teaching Assignments, 1983; Black Women in Kenya: Roles and Resources, 1986, Comparative Energy Usage Consumer Evaluation and Yield of Turkey Cooked by 6 Treatments, 1985, Selected International Experiences for Home Economics Instruction, 1987, others. Contbr. articles to profl. jours. Home: Smiths Grove, Ky. Died Oct. 23, 2006.

RASKIN, FRED CHARLES, retired transportation and utility holding company executive, educator; b. NYC, Sept. 11, 1948; s. Harry and Isabel Raskin; m. Lorraine Mary Sabourin, Apr. 25, 1974; children: Elizabeth Harris, Alexander Eastwood. BS, Syracuse U., 1970; JD, NYU, 1973. Bar: R.I. 1973, Mass. 1974; CPA, Ohio. Assoc. counsel Fleet Nat. Bank, Providence, 1973-75, Bank of Boston, 1975-78; asst. gen. counsel Eastern Enterprises, Boston, 1978-79, treas., 1979-81, v.p., treas., 1981-84; sr. v.p. fin. Eastern Assoc. Coal Co., Pitts., 1984-87; exec. v.p. Midland Enterprises, Inc., Cin., 1987-90, pres., 1991-98; pres., COO Eastern Enterprises, Weston, Mass., 1998-2000; CEO Woods Hole, Martha's Vineyard and Nantucket Steamship Authority, 2002—04; ret., 2004. Lectr. Boston U., 2001—; adj. prof. Merrimack Coll., 2005-. Trustee Boston Heart Found. Home: Andover, Mass. Died Dec. 15, 2006.

RATANU, TRAIAN P., pediatrician; b. Ploiesti, Romania, Sept. 1, 1942; Intern, pediatrics sect. Med. Socs. of Romania, 1966-69; tng. pediatrician Albert Einstein/Montefiore Hosp., Bronx, N.Y., 1966-69, intern, 1990-91, resident, 1991-93; staff pediatrician William F. Ryan Cmty. Health Ctr., NYC, from 1994. Fellow Am. Assn. Pediatricians, Am. Acad. Pediatrics; mem. AMA. Died Mar. 30, 2006.

RATHBUN, FRED CHARLES, geologist; b. Lewiston, Idaho, Feb. 20, 1928; s. Fred Clark and Edith Myrtle (Weaver) R.; m. Beulah Jean Fry, Feb. 9, 1952 (dec. Apr. 1962); children—Sandra Marie, Carol Louise, Peggy Ann, Charles Steven; m. Shirley Ann Jackson, May 3, 1969. B.S. in Geology, U. Idaho, 1957; M.S. in Geology, U. Tulsa, 1969. Exploration geologist Phillips Oil Co., Colo., Okla., Alaska, 1957-81, exploration supr., Denver, 1982-83, sr. geophys. specialist, 1983—. Contbr. articles on geology and archeology to profl. jours., 1969—. Served to sgt. U.S. Army, 1946-54; Korea. Recipient W.A. TARR award Sigma Gamma Epsilon, 1957. Mem. Geol. Soc. Am., Am. Assn. Petroleum Geologists, Rocky Mountain Assn. Geologists, Anchorage Geol. Soc., Soc. Econ. Paleontologists and Mineralogists, Colo. Archeol. Soc. (pres. Denver chpt. 1978-79), Colo. Geneal. Soc., Phi Beta Kappa. Republican. Home: Littleton, Colo. Died Jan. 26, 2006.

RATLIFF, MATTIE (MARTY) LULA, sales executive; b. Sylvester, Ga., Oct. 16, 1918; d. Smith and Netter Mae (Hawkins) Mathis; m. Olden W. Franklin; children— Joyce Ann, Older Wesley, Gail Grace (dec.); m. Paul Ratliff; 1 child, Mark (dec.) Student Franklin U., 1952, 75, Ohio State U., 1975-76. Mem staff Def. Constrn. Supply Ctr., Columbus, Ohio, 1951-65, Def Personnel Support Ctr., Phila., 1965-73; sales person Horizons Land Cooperation Real Estate, Columbus, 1973-74, ITT Palm Coast Real Estate, Columbus, 1974-75; mem. Coop. Extension Service 4-H for Ohio State U., 1976-81; mem. dept. mental retardaton Capital U., Columbus, 1974-75; sales person Fashion Two Twenty, Columbus, 1967-76, Aubrey Creations, 1981, dir. 1985—. Vice pres. Nat. Council of Negro Women, Columbus 1979—; pres. Organized Martha Circle for Tabernacle Ch. 1982; mem. choir Trinity Ch.; pres. Eleanora Roosevelt Democratic Club and Parliamentarian of Franklin County, Columbus 1981—; vol. court watcher Ch. Women United, Nat. Immunization Program. Recipient Cert. of Service, Mayor of Columbus 1980. Clubs: Internat. Toastmistress (Columbus) (pres. 1974-75), Bus. and Profl. (Columbus) (v.p. 1981); Bexley Toastmistress (organizer, pres. 1979, 82-83); Internat. Tng. in Communications (Livingston) (organizer); Twin Rivers Bus. and Profl (v.p. 1981). Avocations: sewing; reading; tennis; traveling. Died Apr. 25, 2007.

RATNER, LORMAN ALFRED, history professor; b. NYC July 23, 1932; s. Mortimer Ratner and Lillian Becker; m. Nina V. Nutt, June 20, 1953 (dec. Feb. 1989); children: Wendy Ratner MacMullen, Todd, Joseph, Matthew; m. Paula T. Kaufman Sept. 17, 1989. AB, Harvard Coll., 1954; MA, Cornell U., 1958 PhD, 1961. Asst. prof. Ithaca (N.Y.) Coll., 1959-61; from asst prof. to assoc. prof. to prof. Lehman Coll., CUNY, Bronx 1961-70, dept. chair, 1970-72, dean of planning and social scis. 1972-77; vice chancellor U. Wis., Kenosha, 1977-83; chancellor U. Wis. Ctrs., Madison, 1983-86; dean of arts and scis., prof. U Tenn., Knoxville, 1986-96, prof. history, 1996-99, prof. emeritus, 1999; adj. prof. U. Ill., Urbana-Champaign, from 1999 Author: Powderkeg, 1968, James Kirke Paulding, 1993, Andrew Jackson and His Tenn. Lieutenants, 1997, others. Mem., pres Bd. of Edn., N.Y., 1971-76. Home: Champaign, Ill. Died July 14, 2007.

RAU, CALISTA JANE, librarian; b. Ft. Edward, N.Y., Aug. 14 1910; d. Edgar Lewis and Lulu Violet (McCarg) Haff; m Stanley Cortlandt Rau, Aug. 5, 1938; children— Alan Spalding Lois Spalding Rau Thomae, Kathleen Spalding, Ames Spalding Mus.B., Syracuse U., 1933; M.L.S., LIU, 1973. Music tchr. pub schs., East Greenbush, N.Y., 1934-35, Copiague, N.Y., 1935-36 Tarrytown, N.Y., 1937-38; vol. West Islip Pub. Library (N.Y.) 1973-76; reference librarian Copiague Meml. Pub. Library 1976—. Recipient Lucille Calvert Pallen award LIU, 1973 Mem. Center for Study Democratic Instns., ALA, AAUW, DAR Mary P. Myton Lit. Soc. Republican. Club: Amityville Woman's (N.Y.). Lodge: Order Eastern Star (chpt. matron 1963). Home Amityville, NY. Died Jan. 21, 2007.

RAUCH, JOHN HAROLD, banker, economist, real estate developer; b. Vienna, Oct. 23, 1930; came to U.S., 1940 naturalized, 1945; s. Carl Leon and Julie (Buchwald) R.; m Ruth Shuster, June 20, 1954; children: Daniel, Mark. BA in Econs., UCLA, 1954; LL.D., U. So. Calif., 1961. With Bank of Am. in, Los Angeles and Berkeley, 1948-53; with Union Bank Los Angeles, 1957-68, v.p., 1968-74; vice chmn. bd. Beverly Hills Nat. Bank, Calif., 1970-74; pres. Beverly Hills Bancorp vice chmn. bd. Western Diversified Equities, Los Angeles 1968-74; pres. Ray Co. Inc. Cons. economist, real estate developer, 1975— Mem. Am. Jewish Com., 1965—; mem exec. bd. Calif. Job Devel., 1967-72; mem. community rels com. L.A. Jewish Fedn., 1966-71; pres. Calif.-Israel C. of C 1965-69, bd. dirs., 1961-69; del. Prime Minister's Econ. Conf Jerusalem, 1968, 73; bd. dirs. Herzl Schs., L.A., 1975-82; bd visitors U. Judaism, 1979-81; bd. dirs. Am. Friends of Tel Aviv U., Am. Friends Shalom Hartman Inst., Jerusalem, 1987—; bd govs. Tel Aviv U., 1982—; bd. dirs. Brandeis Bardin Inst., L.A 1982—, pres., 1986—. 1st lt. AUS, 1954; capt. USAR. Mem Am. Jewish Hist. Soc. (trustee), Zionist Orgn. Am., Phi Alpha Delta. Republican. Jewish. Home: Beverly Hills, Calif. Died Apr. 9, 2006.

RAUCH, PHILIP, manufacturing executive; b. NYC, Sept. 25, 911; s. Philip and Frances (Zahn) R.; m. Louise Fairchild, June 5, 1949 (dec. 1987); 1 child, Patricia. Student, Lehigh U., 929-32; BS in Bus. Adminstrn, N.Y. U., 1935; LL.D. (hon.), ehigh U., 1979. Pres. Ideal Corp., Bklyn., 1932-71; dir. Parker Iannifin Corp., Cleve., 1972-87, chmn. exec. com., 1974-82, hmn. bd., 1975-77, ret., 1987. Former dir. Citizens Bank of klyn., Fairchild Publs. Chmn. bd. Eye Research Inst., Boston ecipient L-in-Life award Lehigh U., 1976 Mem. Young Pres's. Orgn. (founding; chmn. N.Y.C. chpt. 1951-52), Chief Execs. orum. Clubs: Meadow Brook (Jericho, N.Y.); Pine Tree (Delay Beach, Fla.). Republican. Home: Palm Beach, Fla. Died Nov. 8, 2006.

RAUMA, JOHN GUNNAR, architect, educator; b. Virginia, Minn., Jan. 22, 1926; s. Andrew Nestor and Susan Josephine Kunnari) R.; m. Wanda Ruth McIntire, July 11, 1950; hildren— Ann, Peter, Allan, David BS, Marquette U., 1947; .Arch., U. Minn., 1950; M.Arch., MIT, 1952. Registered rchitect, Minn. Designer Magney Tuler Seiter, Mpls., 1948-50; nstr. architecture U. Calif.-Berkeley, 1952-54; v.p. design Thorhon & Cerny, Mpls., 1954-59, The Cerny Assoc., Mpls., 959-63; prof. U. Minn., Mpls., from 1956, dir. grad. studies in rchitecture, from 1985; pres. Griswold Rauma Egge Olson, rchitects, from 1963. Advisor Capitol Area Archtl. and Planing Bd., State of Minn., St. Paul, 1982—, Minn. State History tr. Design Competition, St. Paul, 1983— Prin. works include h. of Architecture Bldg., U. Minn., Ch. of Risen Savior, Mpls., assenger terminal St. Paul Internat. Airport, auditorium and lassroom bldg. U. Minn. Recipient numerous archtl. awards ellow AIA (com. on aesthetics 1966, pres. Minn. sect. 1970), Mpls. C. of C. (chmn. devel. com. 1965) Avocations: sailing; atercolor painting. Home: Minneapolis, Minn. Died Dec. 15, 005.

RAUSCHER, JOHN HOWARD, JR., investment banker; b. ong Beach, Calif., Dec. 18, 1924; s. John Howard and Eleanor uth (Brasher) R.; m. Mary Josephine McCorkle, Feb. 10, 1979; son, John Howard, III. BBA, U. Tex., 1950. With Rauscher ierce Refsnes, Inc., and predecessors, Dallas, from 1949, pres., 969-74, chmn. bd., 1974-89, ret., 1989; bd. dirs. Southwestern lectric Service Co. Pres. Episcopal Found. of Diocese of allas, 1976-81. Served with AUS, 1943-46, ETO. Mem. ecurities Industry Assn. (gov. 1970-73, dist. chmn. 1970-71), appa Sigma. Clubs: Dallas Country (Dallas), Brook Hollow olf (Dallas), City (Dallas). Home: Dallas, Tex. Died Nov. 11, 006.

RAY, CHARLES JOSEPH, dentist; b. South Sioux City, ebr., June 4, 1911; s. Charles Joseph and Katherine Frances Bridgeford) R.; m. Cecilia Estelle Radlinger, Nov. 22, 1933; hildren: Carole, Margie, Kathy, Jeane, Rita, Charles, Chrystal. E, S.D. Sch. of Mines, 1932; DDS, U. Minn., 1936; postgrad. orsythe Dental Infirmary, Boston, 1936-37, Eastman Dental ispensary, 1937-38. Pvt. practice dentistry, 1938—, with Ray ental Group, Rapid City, S.D., 1953—; mem. S.D. Med. Adv. d., 1958-65, S.D. Dental Legis. Com., 1985—, chmn. 1985-86. ctive USO, 1959, pres. Rapid City chpt. 1952-60; pres. S.D. rippled Children's Assn. Mem. ADA (life), S.D. Dental Assn. Gold Tooth award 1980, pres. 1964), Am. Prosthodontic Soc. res. 1980-81, exec. coun. 1981-82, life mem.), Fedn. Prosthdontic Orgn. (sec. 1976-80), Am. Assn. Hosp. Dentists, Am. oc. Psychosomatic Dentistry and Medicine, Pierre-Fauchard cad. (award 1980), Am. Acad. Periodontology, Acad. Internat. entistry and Medicine, Internat. Coll. Dentistry, Am. Acad. ractice Adminstrn., Am. Acad. Gen. Dentistry, Am. Acad. ental Group Practice, Colo. Prosthodontic Soc., Rapid City ental Soc., Black Hills Dist. Dental Soc., Dental Group Mgmt. ssn., Chgo. Dental Soc. (assoc.), Internat. Coll. Dentists, Rapid ity C. of C., Omicron Kappa Upsilon. Roman Catholic. Clubs: nternational Cosmopolitan (pres. 1972), Rapid City Cosmopolin (pres. 1962; Disting. Service award 1977), Sioux Land tudy, KC, Elks. Home: Rapid City, SD. Died Mar. 3, 2007.

RAY, LEONARD NIXON, JR., physics researcher; b. Altoona, a., Apr. 27, 1926; s. Leonard Nixon and Margaret Lois (Stern) .; m. Joan Leatrice Wolfe, Jan. 31, 1948; children— Alison ay Jones, Leonard N., III, Kenneth S. B.A. in Math., Pa. State .-State College, 1946, B.S. in Chemistry, 1947, M.S., 1950, h.D. in Physical Chemistry, 1953. Research asst. Pa. State U., ate College, 1947-51, research fellow, 1951-52; chemist rmstrong World Industries, Lancaster, Pa., 1952-60, sr. chem-t, 1960, sect. head analytical dept., 1960-62, mgr. chemistry esearch unit, 1962-69, mgr. corp. applications research, 1969-3, gen. mgr. corp. applications research, 1973-78, gen. mgr. arpet research, 1978-81, gen. mgr. physics research, 1981-86, en. mgr. basic research, 1986—; mem. spl. adv. com. Bldg. esearch Adv. Bd., Nat. Acad. Sci.-Nat. Research Council, 955, 58, 59. Contbr. articles to profl. jours. and publs. Patentee field. Western Dist. chmn. Lancaster-Lebanon council Boy couts Am., 1969-71, mem. exec. bd., 1969—. Served to lt. g.) USN, 1944-46. Recipient Silver Beaver award Boy Scouts m., 1979. Mem. Am. Chem. Soc., N.Y. Acad. Sci., Computer raphics Assn., IEEE, Pa. Soc. SAR, Sigma Xi (pres. local chpt. 954), Phi Lambda Upsilon. Republican. Presbyterian. Clubs: ancaster Country, Hamilton. Lodge: Eagles. Avocations: Reading, swimming; gardening; cooking; computers. Died Dec. 10, 006.

RAYMOND, JACK, journalist, public relations executive, oundation administrator; b. Lodz, Poland, Oct. 6, 1918; s. Harry nd Anna (Lange) R.; m. Gertrude Silverman, Oct. 6, 1946; hildren: David Alan, Judith. Student, CCNY, 1939. Sports riter N.Y. World-Telegram, 1934-38; ct. reporter, city editor, olumnist N.Y. Daily North Side News, 1938-40; Corr. N.Y. imes, 1940-66, Berlin, 1946-47, Frankfurt, 1947-49, Bonn, 949-52, Balkans, Belgrade, 1952-56, Moscow, 1956, Pentagon rr. Washington, 1956-66; pub. rels. exec., pres. Thomas J. eegan Co., Washington and NYC, 1966-70; v.p. Bryan Publs., YC, 1970-74; founding pres. Internat. Inst. for Environ. and evel., 1970—73; pres. Dialog divsn. J. Walter Thompson Co., 973-75; pres. Jack Raymond & Co., Inc., NYC, 1975—87, mn., 1987—92; pres. JR Cons. Svc., Inc., 1987-96; acting mm. dir. Commonwealth Fund, 1987. Book reviewer The Villager, N.Y.C., 1970-74; cons. UN Conf. on Human Environment, 1972, Aspen Inst. Humanistic Studies, HABITAT, UN Conf. Human Settlements; adv. com. Ctr. for Environ. Info. UN Assn. U.S., 1975-78; mem. Rumanian-U.S. econ. coun. U.S. C. of C., 1973-75; project dir. 1987 Workshop Internat. Environ. Bur. Internat. C. of C.; cons. INFORM, 1989, Rene Dubos Ctr. for Human Environments, 1989-2000; adv. bd. Volvo Journalists Retreat Duke U., 1992; internat. adv. bd. Ctr. for Social Policy in Mid-East, 1983-91; exec. bd. Ency. of Environment. Author: How to Serve and Get Ahead in the Armed Forces, 1963, reissued as Your Military Obligations and Opportunities, 1964, Power at Pentagon, 1964, Robert O. Anderson: Oil Man/Environmentalist, 1988; co-author: This is Germany, 1950; editor U.S. Army Camp Upton Nooz, 1942-43; combat corr. Stars and Stripes, news editor Naples and Rome edits., mng. editor Marseilles edit.; combat corr., war editor, editor Stars and Stripes mag. Paris edit., combat corr., news editor Frankfurt edit., 1943-45; contbr. articles to profl. jours. Trustee N.Y. Urban League, 1969-72; bd. dirs. Internat. Inst. Environ. Affairs, N.Y.C., 1970-74, pres., 1970-73; bd. dirs. Internat. Inst. Environment and Devel., London, 1974-89, mem. adv. coun., 1978-82, mem. exec. com., 1982-89; bd. dirs. Epoch B. Found., La Jolla, Calif., acting pres., 1977-85; trustee Moroccan-Am. Found., 1982-88; bd. overseers Heller Grad. Sch., Brandeis U., 1981-88; founding assoc. John J. McCloy Internat. Ctr., N.Y.C., 1986, bd. dirs., 1987-99; mem. adv. bd. Ctr. for East-West Dynamics, 1992-95, Volvo JNLSTS Retreat, Williamsburg, Va., 1992; With U.S. Army, 1942-45. Decorated 5 Battle Stars, Bronze Star, Purple Heart. Mem. Coun. on Fgn. Rels. Clubs: Overseas Press Am. (N.Y.C.) (pres. 1972-76), Century Assn. (N.Y.C.), Nat. Press (Washington). Died July 20, 2007.

RE, EDWARD DOMENIC, law educator, retired federal judge; b. Santa Marina, Italy, Oct. 14, 1920; s. Anthony and Marina (Maetta) R.; m. Margaret A. Corcoran, June 3, 1950; children: Mary Ann, Anthony John, Marina, Edward, Victor, Margaret, Matthew, Joseph, Mary Elizabeth, Mary Joan, Mary Ellen, Nancy Madeleine. BS cum laude, St. John's U., 1941, LLB summa cum laude, 1943, LLD (hon.), 1968; JSD, NYU, 1950; DPed (hon.), Aquila, Italy, 1960; LLD (hon.), St. Mary's Coll., Notre Dame, Ind., 1968, Maryville Coll., St. Louis, 1969, N.Y. Law Sch., 1976, Bklyn. Coll., CUNY, 1978, Nova U., 1980, Roger Williams Coll., 1982, Dickinson Sch. Law, 1983, Seton Hall U., 1984, Stetson U., 1990, William Mitchell Coll. Law, 1992, St. Francis Coll., Bklyn., 1993; L.LD (hon.), St. Thomas U., Miami, 2003; LHD (hon.), DePaul U., 1980, Coll. S.I., CUNY, 1981, Pace U., 1985, Am. U. Rome, 1995; DCS (hon.), U. Verona, 1987; JD (hon.), U. Bologna, 1988, U. Urbino, 1994. Bar: N.Y. 1943. Apptd. faculty St. John's U., Jamaica, NY, 1947, prof. law, 1951—69, adj. prof. law, 1969—80, Disting. prof., 1980—2002, Disting. prof. emeritus, 2003—06; vis. prof. Georgetown U. Sch. Law, 1962—67; adj. prof. law N.Y. Law Sch., 1972—82; Martin disting. vis. prof. NYU Law Sch., 1982—90; spl. hearing officer US Dept. Justice, 1956—61; chmn. Fgn. Claims Settlement Commn. of U.S., 1961—68; asst. sec. ednl. & cultural affairs US Dept. State, 1968—69; judge US Ct. Internat. Trade (formerly US Customs Ct.), NYC, 1969—91, chief judge, 1977—91, chief judge emeritus, 1991—2006. Mem. Jud. Conf. U.S., 1986-91, adv. com. on appellate rules, 1976-88, com. on internat. jud. rels., 1994-97; chmn. adv. com. on experimentation in the law Fed. Jud. Ctr., 1978-81; mem. bd. higher edn. City of N.Y., 1958-69, emeritus, 1969-2006; Jackson lectr. Nat. Coll. State Trial Judges, U. Nev., 1970. Author: Foreign Confiscations in Anglo-American Law, 1951, Selected Essays on Equity, 1955, (chpt., freedom in internat. soc.) Concept of Freedom, 1955, Cases and Materials on Equitable Remedies, 1975; co-author (with Joseph R. Re): Cases and Materials on Remedies, 1982, 6th edit., 2005, Law Students' Manual on Legal Writing and Oral Argument, 1991, Brief Writing and Oral Argument,9t edit, 2005, 9th edit., 2005; co-author: (with Lester D. Orfield) Cases and Materials on International Law, 1965; co-author: (with Zechariah Chafee Jr.) Cases and Materials on Equity, 1967; contbr. articles to legal jours. Served with USAAF, 1943-47; col. JAGD, ret. Decorated Grand Cross Order of Merit Italy; recipient Am. Bill of Rights citation; Morgenstern Found. Interfaith award; USAF commendation medal; Distinguished service award Bklyn. Jr. C. of C., 1956 Mem. ABA (ho. of dels. 1976-78, chmn. sect. internat. and comparative law 1965-67), Am. Fgn. Law Assn. (pres. 1971-73), Am. Law Inst., Fed. Bar Coun. (pres. 1973-74), Am. Soc. Comparative Law (pres. 1969-91), Am. Justinian Soc. Jurists (pres. 1974-76), Internat. Assn. Jurists: Italy-USA (pres. 1991-2006), Internat. Assn. Judges (prin. rep. to UN 1993-2006), Scribes Am. Soc. Writers on Legal Subjects (pres. 1978). Died Sept. 17, 2006.

READ, WILLIAM LAWRENCE, business executive, former naval officer; b. Bklyn., July 8, 1926; s. Reginald A. and Martha (Bedell) R.; m. Martha Miller, Nov. 25, 1950; children: Allison, William Lawrence, John Alexander. BS, U.S. Naval Acad., 1949; MS, George Washington U., 1970. Commd. ensign U.S. Navy, 1949, advanced through grades to vice adm., 1977; comdr. U.S.S. Van Voorhis, 1961-63, U.S.S. King, 1966-68, Escort Squadron Ten, 1968-69, Cruiser-Destroyer Flotilla Three, 1972-73; sr. aide to SACEUR, 1970-72; mil. asst. to sec. Def., 1963-66; asst. chief Navy Personnel for officer devel. and distbn., 1973-74; dir. Ship Acquisition Div., Office Chief Naval Ops., 1974-77; comdr. Naval Surface Force, U.S. Atlantic Fleet, 1977-79; v.p. constrn. mgmt. Lone Star Industries, Greenwich, Conn., 1979-83. Bd. dirs. Olin Corp., Meml. Health Sys. Decorated D.S.M., Legion of Merit, Navy Commendation medal with combat V, Navy Disting. Service Order 2d class (Republic of Vietnam). Mem. Surface Navy Assn. (bd. dirs.). Episcopalian. Home: Trevett, Maine. Died Jan. 16, 2007.

REBENACK, JOHN HENRY, retired librarian; b. Wilkinsburg, Pa., Feb. 10, 1918; s. Charles Lewis and Carrie (Fielding) R.; m. Dorothy Merle Treat, Oct. 31, 1942 (dec. Apr. 1971); children: Charles Edwin, Christine (Mrs. Clair N. Hayes III); m. Frances Strabley Krieger, May 6, 1972. AB, U. Pitts., 1942; BS in L.S, Carnegie Library Sch., 1947. Reference asst. Carnegie Library, Pitts., 1947-50; librarian Salem (Ohio) Pub. Library, 1950-53, Elyria (Ohio) Library, 1953-57; asst. librarian Akron (Ohio) Public Library, 1957-65, asso. librarian, 1965-67, librarian-dir., 1967-80. Dir. U.S. Book Exchange, Inc., 1972 Mem. United Community Council, Citizens' Com. Pub. Welfare, 1965-66, chmn. group work and recreation div., 1963-66, v.p., 1967-68, pres. conf. of execs., 1975-76; mem. steering com., planning div. United Way; mem. Akron Mayor's Task Force on Human Relations, 1962; mem. library com. President's Com. on Employment of Handicapped, 1967-80, chmn., 1973-80, mem. sch. library manpower adv. com., 1967-73; mem. coll. adv. com. U. Akron, 1972-85; mem. adv. council on fed. programs State Library of Ohio, 1975-79; Bd. visitors Grad. Sch. Library and Info. Sci., U. Pitts., 1968-74; mem. exec. bd. Gt. Trail council Boy Scouts Am., 1977-80; bd. dirs. Summit County unit Am. Cancer Soc., 1976—, pres., 1979-81; bd. dirs. Ohio div., 1981-91, chmn. pub. info. com., 1989-90, exec. com. 1988-91. With AUS, 1942-45. Recipient Newton D. Baker citation, 1968 Mem. ALA (chmn. personnel adminstrv. sect. 1966-67, chmn. bldgs. and equipment sect. 1971-73, chmn. legislation assembly 1976-77), Ohio Library Assn. (exec. bd. 1957-60, chmn. adult edn. round table 1963, chmn. legis. com. 1965-66, 70-72, 76-80, pres. 1966-67, Librarian of Year 1979, named to Hall of Fame 1989), Ohio Library Found. (privileged mem. 1980, privileged dir. 1988—), Carnegie Library Sch. Assn. (pres. 1961-63), U. Pitts. Grad. Sch. Library and Info. Sci. Alumni Assn. (exec. com. 1978-79, Disting. Alumnus award 1980), Am. Assn. UN (v.p. Akron chpt. 1960), Kiwanis Internat. Found. (Tablet of Honor 1997, George F. Hixson fellow 1998), Torch Club (pres. 1968-69), Kiwanis (pres. Akron 1978-79, Man of Yr. 2004), Beta Phi Mu. Congregationalist. Home: Akron, Ohio. Died Sept. 1, 2006.

REBER, SIDNEY CRAFT, JR., religious organization executive; b. Jackson, Miss., June 12, 1918; s. Sidney Craft and Robbie Edna (Merrill) R.; m. Alwilda Montgomery, Dec. 4, 1943; children: Rebecca Alwilda Reber Washington. BS, Trinity U., San Antonio, 1950; postgrad. Trinity U., 1950-52, Miss. Coll., Clinton, 1952-53, Southwestern Bapt. Theol. Sem., 1967-68. With War Dept., Washington and Atlanta, 1940-43; classification analyst U.S. Civil Svc. Commn., Dallas, 1945-46; personnel officer VA, Dallas, San Antonio, Jackson, Miss., 1946-53; regional tng. officer, taxpayer assistance officer IRS, Dallas, 1953-63; bus. mgr., treas. Malaysia-Singapore Bapt. Mission, So. Bapt. Conv., Fgn. Mission Bd., Singapore, 1963-69; dir. mgmt. svcs. div. So. Bapt. Fgn. Mission Bd., Richmond, Va., 1969-80, v.p. mgmt. svcs., 1980—. Served to 2d lt. USAAF, 1943-45. Mem. Am. Mgmt. Assn., Soc. Advancement Mgmt. Baptist. Lodge: Rotary. Home: London, England. Died Jan. 24, 2006.

REBERS, PAUL ARMAND, chemist; b. Mpls., Jan. 24, 1923; s. Ernest Edward and Verna (Rand) R.; m. E. Louise Burrell, Dec. 14, 1952; children— Michael, John, Joseph. B.S. in Chem. Engring., U. Minn., 1944, M.S. in Chem. Engring., 1946, Ph.D. in Agrl. Biochemistry, 1953. Plant devel. chemist Rohm & Haas, Phila., 1946-48; research chemist Holly Sugar Co., Colorado Springs, Colo., 1953-55; asst. prof. Rutgers U., New Brunswick, N.J., 1955-61; research chemist USDA, Ames, Iowa, 1961—; cons. Continental Baking, Rye, N.Y., 1957-60. Contbr. numerous articles to profl. jours. Patentee mech. hand. Mem. Am. Assn. Immunologists, Am. Chem. Soc., Am. Soc. Microbiologists, Sigma Xi, Phi Kappa Phi, Phi Zeta. Methodist. Club: Toastmasters (Ames, Iowa) (pres. 1985). Lodges: Masons (worshipful master 1974-75), Order Eastern Star (worthy patron 1974—). Home: Nevada, Iowa. Died May 31, 2006.

RECORD, RUSH HAMIL, lawyer, educator; b. Hugo, Okla., Dec. 29, 1917; s. Rush R. and Johnnie Katurah Record; m. Helen Hollingsworth, Dec. 12, 1942; children: James, Anne. LL.B., U. Tex., 1940. With Otis E. Nelson, Wichita Falls, 1940-42; ptnr. Nelson, Montgomery & Rubertson, Wichita Falls, 1946-48, Vinson & Elkins, Houston, 1948—2007. Adj. prof. U. Houston Coll. Law, 1952, 71-73, 82-83, uninc. bus. assns. U. Tex., 1985-86. Bd. dirs. Houston Law Rev., 1973-90. Mem. Hogg Found.'s Commn. on Community Care of the Mentally Ill, 1987-92, citizens' planning adv. com. Tex. Dept. Mental Health and Mental Retardation, 1987-92, Tex. Bd. Mental Health and Mental Retardation, Austin, 1981-85, Gov.'s Task Force Intellectually Handicapped Citizens and Criminal Justice System, 1982; trustee Am. Coll. Investment Counsel, 1981-86, Mental Health Needs Coun., Houston, 1975-81; bd. dirs. Mental Health Assn. Houston and Harris County, 1975-81. Maj. USAAF, 1942-45. Mem. ABA (vice chmn. sr. corp. lawyers com. sr. lawyers divsn. 1986-89, chmn. 1989-92), Tex. Bar Assn., Internat. Bar Assn., Houston Com. Fgn. Rels., Houston Philos. Soc., Tex. Mental Health Assn. (bd. dirs. 1989-92), Mental Health Assn. Tex. (bd. dirs. 1989-92). Presbyterian. Home: Houston, Tex. Died May 25, 2007.

RECTOR, ROBERT WAYMAN, retired mathematics and engineering educator, former association executive; b. San Jose, Calif., Jan. 28, 1916; s. Joseph Jones and Eva (Hembree) R.; m. Margaret Eileen Hayden, Aug. 25, 1940; children: Cleone Rector Black, Robin Rector Krupp, Bruce Hayden. BA, San Jose State U., 1937; MA, Stanford U., 1939; PhD, U. Md., 1956. Instr. Compton (Calif.) Coll., 1939-42; asso. prof. math. U.S. Naval Acad., 1946-56; staff mathematician Space Tech. Labs., Los Angeles, 1956-61; asso. dir. computation center Aerospace Corp., El Segundo, Calif., 1961-65; v.p. Informatics, Inc., Van Nuys, Calif., 1965-70, Cognitive Systems, Inc., Beverly Hills, Calif., 1970-71; asso. dir. continuing edn. engring. and math. UCLA, 1971-73, 81-92; dean Coll. Engring. and Computer Sci. West Cost U., LA, 1992-96. Exec. dir. Am. Fedn. Info. Processing Socs., Montvale, N.J., 1973-79; spl. asst. White House Conf. Library and Info. Services, 1979; v.p. Conf. and Meeting Assistance Corp., East Greenwich, R.I., 1980— Bd. govs. Pacific Jour. Math, 1957-92. Mem. Los Angeles Mayor's Space Adv. Com., 1964-73; mem. aviation and space hist. rsch. com. Calif. Mus. Found., 1984-97; mem. aerospace hist. soc. bd. dirs. Mus. of Flying, Santa Monica, Calif., 1997-2007. Served with USNR, 1942-46. Mem. Math. Assn. Am., Assn. Computing Machinery, Naval Res. Assn., Res. Officers Assn., Ret. Officers Assn., Aerospace Hist. Soc. (sec.-treas. 2002—). Avocations: stamp collecting/philately, travel, ragtime piano. Died June 22, 2007.

REDDITT, HORACE MEUX, insurance company executive; b. Greenwood, Miss., Sept. 26, 1927; s. Horace Meux and Lillian (Childress) Redditt. BA, Vanderbilt U., 1948, LLB, 1950. Bar: Tenn. Claim rep. Reliance Ins. Co., Dallas, 1954—57, claim mgr. Houston, 1957—65, Wash., 1965—72, home office mgr. Phila., 1972—77, v.p., from 1977. Mem.: N.J. Def. Counsel, Fedn. Ins. Counsel, Def. Rsch. Inst., Phila. Bar Assn. (arbitrator from 1980), Pa. Def. Inst. (sec., mem. bd. from 1979). Republican. Presbyterian. Home: Philadelphia, Pa. Died Jan. 17, 2006.

REED, FREDERICK R., lawyer; b. Columbus, Ohio, Apr. 28, 1948; AB, Harvard U., 1970; JD summa cum laude, Ohio State U., 1973. Bar: Ohio 1973. Mem. Vorys, Sater, Seymour and Pease, Cin. Editor-in-chief Ohio State Law Jour., 1972-73. Fellow Am. Coll. Bankruptcy; mem. ABA (corp., banking and bus. law sect., mem. bankruptcy subcom. 1980—), Ohio State Bar Assn., Cin. Bar Assn., Order of Coif, Phi Delta Phi. Died Aug. 27, 2007.

REEDER, OLIVER HOWARD, paint products manufacturing executive; b. Balt., Sept. 19, 1916; s. Charles Howard and Nannie Dryden (Kensett) R.; m. Nancy Hardcastle Fisher, Apr. 18, 1942; children: Nancy Fisher, Ellen Dryden. AB, Princeton U., 1939. With Balt. Copper Paint Co., Balt., 1939—, tech. dir., treas., 1939-47, pres., from 1947, chmn., from 1959; v.p. Balt. Copper Paint div. Glidden-Durkee Div. SCM Corp., from 1969; pres. Jotun-Balt. Copper Paint Co., Inc., 1974-76, v.p., 1976-81. Pres. Hosp. for Consumptives of Md., 1968-84, trustee, 1951-95, trustee emeritus, 1995—; trustee Gilman Sch., Balt., 1948-65, Walters Art Gallery, 1978-83, U.S. Frigate Constellation Found., 1976-89; trustee Johns Hopkins Hosp., 1957-87, trustee emeritus, 1987—, vice chmn. bd., 1986-87; trustee Md. Hosp. Laundry, 1970-89, pres., 1975-84. Fellow Am. Inst. Chemists; mem. Am. Chem. Soc., Soc. Naval Architects and Marine Engrs., Phi Beta Kappa, Sigma Xi. Home: Baltimore, Md. Died Aug. 17, 2006.

REEVES, JAMES LOUIS, dairy executive; b. Springfield, Mo., Nov. 17, 1922; s. James William and Hazel Ona (St. Louis) R.; m. Yvonne Ann Bayliff, Dec. 21, 1949; 1 child, Penelope Anne. BA in Econs., S.W. Mo. State U., 1947; MA, U. Mo., 1949. Sales mgr. Producers Creamery Co., Springfield, 1949-61; treas. Twin City Milk Co., Mpls., 1961-63; dir. procurement Southland Corp., Dallas, 1964-71; v.p. Mid Am. Dairymen, Springfield, 1977-80, Purity Cheese Co., Dallas, 1977-80; exec. v.p. Mid Am. Farms, Springfield, from 1980. Bd. dirs. Nat. Dairy Coun., Whey Products Inst.; mem. U.S. Commn. Fedn. Milk Orders. With AUS, 1940-46, 51-52. Decorated Purple Heart, Silver Star, Bronze Star; recipient Disting. Svc. award Nat. Dairy Coun.; named Dairy Amb. Dairy Soc. Internat., 1969. Mem. Nat. Cheese Inst., Springfield C. of C., Exchange Club, Phi Gamma Mu. Republican. Methodist. Home: Springfield, Mo. Died Apr. 20, 2006.

REEVES, JIMMY HARPER, banker; b. Montezuma, Ga., Apr. 7, 1938; s. Charlie George and Luna Mae (Kirkland) R.; m. Evelyn Cross, May 9, 1959; children: Deborah Denese, Michael Mark. BBA in Mgmt., Ga. State U., 1963, MBA in Fin., 1966; postgrad., La. State U. Sch. Banking of South, 1981—83. Adminstrv. asst. trust dept. Trust Co. Bank, 1963—67; tech. dir. finishing plant Riegel Textile Corp., 1967—70; asst. to v.p. fin. Southwire Co., 1970—77; v.p. West Ga. Nat. Bank, Carrollton, from 1977. Pres. Ctrl. High and Middle Sch. PTA, 1977—78; scoutmaster Boy Scouts Am., 1976—77, dist. camping chmn., 1976; mem. Carroll dist. com. Vigil Honor Order of Arrow, 1975; treas. Carroll County Early Childhood Ctr.; pres. Ctrl. High Athletic Booster Club; mem. Carroll County C. of C. Recipient Silver Beaver award, Boy Scouts Am., 1977. Mem.: Carroll County Cattlemen's Assn., Ga. Bankers Assn., Bank Adminstrn. Inst. (dir. West Ga. chpt.), Carrollton Kiwanis Club (pres. 1977—78, lt. gov. internat. 1981—82). Baptist. Home: Roopville, Ga. Died July 10, 2006.

REGALIA, WENDIE MARTINEZ, freelance/self-employed marketing professional; b. San Francisco, Mar. 17, 1923; d. Dolph and Leora (Greene) Martinez; m. Stephen Paige Regalia, Jr., Apr. 13, 1943 (div. 1959); children: Stephenie, Stephen Paige III, Susan Caprice. BA in Merchandising, U. Calif.-Berkeley, 1958. With Ted Lewis Band, 1936—37; vocalist with various bands including Jan Garber, Robby Sherwood, Bob Crosby, 1938—46; European promotion dir. Rose Marie Reid Swimwear, 1956—63; fashion coord. Macy's Calif., 1963—66; self-employed in pub. rels., 1966—68; dir. pub. rels. Mark Hopkins Hotel, San Francisco, 1968—72; v.p., merchandising dir. Western Internat. Merchandising, San Francisco, 1974—84; pres. Video Cookbook Co., Square One Mktg./Merchandising, from 1984. Hostess radio talk show, San Francisco, 1968—69; with Saxon Enterprises, Inc., Palo Alto; agt. for profl. athletes; broadcast crew San Francisco Giants Baseball Team, 1971—72. Mem. bd. Calif. League for Handicapped, 1967—84, San Francisco Conv. and Visitors Bur., from 1967; vol. pub. rels. counsel San Francisco Police Dept., from 1969; mem. San Francisco C. of C. Democrat. Roman Catholic. Died June 8, 2007.

REGAN, MARTIN DANIEL, geologist, consultant; b. Butte, Mont., Aug. 19, 1933; s. Martin Michael and Mary Elizabeth (Broksle) R.; m. Marjorie C. McQuiston, Aug. 18, 1956 (div. 1974); children— Daniel W., Michael R., Timothy S., Alesia L. B.S. in Geol. Engring., Mont. Coll. Mineral, Sci. and Tech., 1957; M.S. in Mgmt., MIT, 1971. Cert. profl. geologist. Miner, sampler The Anaconda Co., Butte, 1952-56; resident geologist, engr. The Taylor Knapp Co., Philipsburg, Mont., 1956-59; exploration geologist Bear Creek Mining Co., N.Mex., Colo., Utah, 1960-64, sr. geologist, staff sr. geologist, Salt Lake City, 1965-70; exploration-acquisition mgr. Kennecott, Spokane, Wash., Salt Lake City, 1971-83; cons. geol. mgmt., Spokane, 1983-84; pres. M.D. Regan & Assocs., Spokane, 1985—. Student counselor MIT Ednl. Council, Spokane, 1972-75. Sloan fellow, MIT, 1970-71. Mem. Am. Inst. Profl. Geologists (cert.), Soc. Econ. Geologists, Soc. Mining Engrs.-Am. Inst. Mining Engrs., N.W. Mining Assn. (trustee 1974-77), Intermountain Assn. Geologists (sec., treas. 1965-66), Mont. Tech. Alumni Assn., MIT Alumni Assn., Theta Tau. Home: Butte, Mont. Died May 11, 2006.

REGAN, TIMOTHY FRANCIS, JR., manufacturing executive; b. Pittsford, Vt., July 20, 1936; s. Timothy Francis and Rita Mary (Carrigan) R.; m. Ellen Marie Reardon, Aug. 29, 1959; children: Kathleen, Timothy F. III, Sean, Colleen, Mary, David, Erin. BA, Tufts U., 1959; MA grad. asst., U. Mass, 1962; LHD, Handel's Arubaanse Acad., 1968. Asst. dir. MA in tchg. program U. Hartford, 1962—64; asst. dean Coll. Humanities Fla. Atlantic U., 1964—67; v.p. Ednl. Systems Corp., Wash., 1967—72, P.R.T., Inc., St. Petersburg, Fla., 1972—73; prin. A.T. Kearney, Inc., Alexandria, Va., 1973—86, mgr. Southwest region Dallas, 1986; v.p. mktg. Bell Tech. Ops. Corp. div. Textron Corp., Tuscson, from 1986. Cons. HEW, U.S. Dept. Edn.; dir. Benchmark One, Cleve. Contbr. articles to profl. jours., chapters to books Handbook of Modern Marketing. Past pres. PTA, Annandale, Va., Holy Spirit Girls Softball League, Annandale; past coach, bd. dirs. Annandale Little League; bd. dirs. Internat. Found. Gifted Children; mem. Rep. Nat. Com., Statue of Liberty-Ellis Island Found., U.S. Congl. Adv. Bd., Rep. Presdl. Task Force. With USMCR, 1959—64. Recipient cert. for disting. svc., Va. Assn. Bus. Educators, 1982, Presdl. Medal of Merit. Mem. AIAA, Am. Arbitration Assn. (cert. arbitrator), Am. Astronautic Soc., Am. Mgmt. Assn., Inst. Mgmt. Cons. (pres. D.C. chpt.), Soc. Am. Engrs., Am. Legion (Medal of Honor), Navy League, Assn. Old Crows, Alpha Tau Omega, Capitol Yacht Club, KC. Roman Catholic. Home: Tucson, Ariz. Died Nov. 29, 2006.

REGISTER, BILLY DEAN, accountant; b. Tallahassee, July 6, 1934; s. Abbott Drafus and Ivy Grace (Benton) R.; m. Judith Elaine Wilkinson, Nov. 1, 1957; children— Marcus, Matthew, Martha. B.S., Fla. State U., 1961. C.P.A., Fla. Agt., IRS, 1961-74; pvt. practice acctg., Havana, Fla., 1974—. Served with USN, 1952-55. Mem. Am. Inst. C.P.A.s, Fla. Inst. C.P.A.s, Naval Res. Assn., Tallahassee Regional Estate Planning Council, Havana Businessmen's Assn. Republican. Club: Country (Havana, Fla.). Died Nov. 19, 2006.

REGNIER, CLAIRE NEOMIE, marketing, advertising and public relations consultant; b. Fort Riley, Kans., May 2, 1939; d. Eugene Arthur and Claire Janet (Macfarlane) Regnier; B.S. cum laude in Journalism, Trinity U., San Antonio, 1961. Advt. cons., San Antonio, 1961-68; editor Paseo del Rio Showboat newspaper, San Antonio, 1968-81; exec. dir. San Antonio River Assn., San Antonio, 1968-81; pres. Regnier, Valdez & Assoc., San Antonio, 1981—. Chmn. Centro 21 Downtown Revitalization Task Force, San Antonio; rep. San Antonio River Corridor Com.; mem. Fiesta San Antonio Commn., San Antonio Parks and Recreation Adv. Bd.; bd. dirs., chmn. public relations com. San Antonio Area council Girl Scouts U.S.A. Recipient awards of excellence for Showboat, Alamo Bus. Communicators, 1970, 71, 73, 74; Headliner award San Antonio chpt. Women in Communications, 1980. Mem. Internat. Assn. Bus. Communicators (Bronze Quill award 1986, 88), Am. Mktg. Assn. (San Antonio chpt., SAMI award 1988), Women in Communications (Southwest region banner award 1981, Proliner awards 1984-88), Tex. Public Relations Assn., Alamo Bus. Communicators (Communicator of Yr. 1977), San Antonio Mus. Assn., San Antonio Conservation Soc. Home: San Antonio, Tex. Died May 18, 2006.

REHAGE, KENNETH J., retired dean, retired educational association administrator; b. Elgin, Ill., June 21, 1910; BA, U. Wisc., 1932; MA, U. Chgo., 1935, PhD, 1949. Dir. Pakistan Edn. Program U. Chgo., 1963—73, dean students, social sci. divsn., 1972—82; sec., treas., editor Nat. Soc. for the Study of Edn., Chgo., 1975—99. Died Jan. 31, 2007.

REID, CHARLOTTE THOMPSON, retired business consultant, former congresswoman; b. Kankakee, Ill., Sept. 27, 1913; d. Edward Charles and Ethel (Stith) Thompson; m. Frank R. Reid, Jan. 1, 1938 (dec. 1962); children— Patricia, Frank, Edward, Susan. Student Ill. Coll., 1931-32; LL.D. (hon.), John Marshall Law Sch., Ill. Coll., Aurora Coll. Vocalist, NBC, Chgo., 1936-39; mem. US Congress from 15th Ill. dist., Washington, 1962-71; commr., FCC, Washington, 1971-76; dir. Liggett Group, N.Y.C., 1977-80, Midlantic Banks, Inc., Edison, N.Y., 1977-88, Motorola Inc., Schaumburg, Ill., 1978-84. Mem. Presdl. Task Force on Internat. Pvt. Enterprise, 1983-85; mem. com. Def. Adv. Com. on Women in the Services, 1982-85; bd. overseers Hoover Instn., 1984-87. Republican. Club: Capitol Hill (dir. 1968-82). Died Jan. 24, 2007.

REID, ROBERT NEWTON, retired lawyer, mortgage and financial consultant; b. Ottawa, Ill., Mar. 28, 1908; s. Robert Joseph and Mae (Newton) R. Ph.B., U. Chgo., 1929, JD, 1930. Bar: Ill. 1930, U.S. Supreme Ct. 1949, Md. 1961, D.C. 1961. Practiced in, Chgo., 1930-39; with Follansbee, Shorey & Schupp, 1933-39; govt. atty. FCA, Washington, 1939-42; atty., counsel RFC, Fed. Nat. Mortgage Assn., 1942-49; asst. gen. counsel Fed. Nat. Mortgage Assn., 1949-50, gen. counsel, 1950-70, spl. counsel, 1970-73, v.p., 1950-59, 68-73, dir., 1954-59, cons., 1973-95; retired, 1995. Mem. bd. advisors Washington Studio Sch., 1985-95. Served from 2d lt. to lt. col. Judge Adv. Gen. Corps USAR, 1942-46. Decorated Legion of Merit. Mem. ABA (life), Fed. Bar Assn. D.C. Bar Assn. (life), Am. Judicature Soc., Supreme Ct. Hist. Soc., Res. Officers Assn. (life), Am. Legion (life), SAR (life), Ret. Officers Assn. (life), Mil. Order of World Wars (life), Nat. Assn., Uniformed Svcs., English Speaking Union, Delta Sigma Phi (life), Phi Alpha Delta. Clubs: Nat. Lawyers (life), University (life) (Washington). Lodges: Masons (life). Home: Washington, DC. Died June 15, 2006.

REIDENBAUGH, LOWELL HENRY, retired sports editor; b. Lititz, Pa., Sept. 7, 1919; s. Harry Martin and Marian Marie (Nies) R.; m. Ruth Elizabeth Cameron, Nov. 23, 1944; children: Karen Lee (Mrs. William Rogers), Kathy Jean (Mrs. William J. Schuchman). AB, Elizabethtown Coll., Pa., 1941. Gen. reporter Lancaster (Pa.) Intelligencer Jour., 1941-42; sports writer Phila. Inquirer, 1944-47; mem. staff The Sporting News, St. Louis, 1947-89, mng. editor, 1962-79, sr. editor, 1980-83, corp. editor, 1983-89. Author: National League History, 1976, The Super Bowl Book, 1981, Cooperstown, Where Baseball's Legends Live, 1983, Take Me Out to the Ballpark, 1983, The Sporting News, First 100 Years, 1985, The 50 Greatest Games, 1986, History 33d Va. Infantry Regiment, CSA, 1987, 25 Greatest Pennant Races, 1987, 25 Greatest Teams, 1988, History 27th Va Infantry Regiment, CSA, 1993, The Battle of Kernstown, 1997 Served with AUS, 1942-43. Home: Chesterfield, Mo. Died Jan 20, 2007.

REIFSNYDER, CHARLES FRANK, retired lawyer; b. Ottumwa, Iowa, Sept. 6, 1920; s. Charles L. and Lena (Emery) R. A.B., George Washington U., 1944, LL.B., 1946; m. Sally Ann Evans, Dec. 27, 1948 (div.); children: Daniel Alan, Jeremy Evans; m. Nancy Lee Laws, Mar. 4, 1960; 1 child, Frank Laws (dec. 2004). Admitted to D.C. bar, 1945; sec. Judge T. Alan Goldsborough, U.S. Dist. Ct., Washington, 1945; law clk. to Hon. Bolitha J. Laws, U.S. Dist. Ct., 1946-47; asst. U.S. atty. US Dept. Justice, Washington, 1947-51; spl. asst. to atty. gen US Dept. Justice, 1950-51; assoc. Hogan & Hartson, Washington, 1951-58, ptnr., 1959-85; chmn. personnel security rev. bd Energy Rsch. and Devel. Adminstrn. (formerly AEC). Trustee Legal Aid Agy. (now Pub. Defender Svc.), Washington, 1960-67; bd. dirs. Nat. Jud. Coll., Reno, 1968-70. Fellow Inst. Jud Adminstrn., N.Y.C., 1967-68. Fellow Internat. Soc. Barristers Am. Bar Found.; mem. Am. (chmn. spl. com. coordination jud improvements 1971-74, mem. spl. com. atomic energy law 1969-73, chmn. div. jud. adminstrn. 1967-68, del. 1968-69) Fed., Fed. Energy (pres. 1981-82, chmn. com. natural gas 1967-68), D.C. (dir. 1955-56) bar assns., Am. Arbitration Assn. (nat. panel arbitrators), Am. Judicature Soc. (dir. 1972-76), Am Law Inst., Phi Delta Phi, Sigma Nu. Episcopalian. Clubs: Met Barristers, Lawyers (Washington), Gibson Island (Md.) Yacht Squadron, Annapolis (Md.) Yacht, Farmington Country (Charlottesville, Va.). Died June 5, 2007.

REIFSNYDER, WILLIAM EDWARD, meteorologist; b Ridgway, Pa., Mar. 29, 1924; s. Howard William and Madoli (Boyer) R.; m. Marylou Bishop, Dec. 19, 1954 (dec. July 1990) children: Rita, Cheryl, Gawain. BS in Meteorology, NYU, 1944 M.F., U. Calif., Berkeley, 1949; PhD, Yale U., 1954. Cert. cons meteorologist. Meteorologist Pacific S.W. Forest and Range Expt. Sta., 1952-55; mem. faculty Yale U., 1955-90, prof emeritus, from 1990, prof. forest meteorology and biometeorology, 1967-90; chief La Lama VFD, from 1998. Vis. scientist Max Planck Inst. for Meteorology, Hamburg, U. Munich Environ. Rsch. Labs., Nat. Oceanic and Atmospheric Adminstrn.; cons. World Meteorol. Orgn., UN Univ., Internat. Coun Rsch. in Agroforestry. Author: Hut Hopping in the Austrian Alps, Footloose in the Swiss Alps, The High Huts of the White Mountains, Radiant Energy in Relation to Forests, Weathering the Wilderness, Adventuring in the Alps; editor-in-chief Agr and Forest Meteorology; editor: Meteorology and Agroforestry Bd. dirs. Am. Youth Hostels. Service with USAAF, 1943-47 Fellow AAAS, Am. Meteorol. Soc. (Outstanding Achievement in Biometeorology award); mem. Conn. Acad. Sci. and Engring (corr.), Soc. Am. Foresters, Internat. Soc. Biometeorology (v.p.) Home: Questa, N.Mex. Died Nov. 3, 2006.

REILLY, CHARLES NELSON, actor, director; b. NYC, Jan 13, 1931; s. Charles J. and Signe E. Reilly Student, U. Conn Tchr. Herbert Bergoff Sch., N.Y.C., The Faculty, Los Angeles Actor appearing on Broadway, off-Broadway, and TV; mem road co. of 22 prodns. including Annie Get Your Gun; Broadway prodns. include: How to Succeed in Business Without Really Trying (Tony award), Bye Bye Birdie, 1960, Hello, Dolly, 1964 Skyscraper, 1965, God's Favorite, 1974, Charlotte, 1980; di The Belle of Amherst, 1979, Broadway prodn. Break a Leg, The Nerd, 1987; starred in TV series Lidsville; (films) A Face in the Crowd, 1957 Two Tickets to Paris, 1962, The Tiger Makes Out 1967, Cannonball Run II, 1984, Body Slam, 1987, All Dogs Go to Heaven, 1989, Rock-A-Doodle, 1991, Boys Will Be Boys 1997, Babes in Toyland, 1997, An All Dogs Christmas Carol 1998, The First of May, 1999; frequent appearances on Match Game, CBS-TV; performed in concerts at Carnegie Hall, Philharmonic Hall; (TV appearances) The New WKRP in Cincinnati, 1991, Car 54, Where Are You, 1961, Here's Lucy, 1968 B.L. Stryker, 1989, Designing Women, 1986, Family Matters 1989, The X Files, 1993, The Five Mrs. Buchanans, 1994, The Drew Carey Show, 1995, Millennium, 1996, Second Noah 1996. Named Best Actor, Variety Critics Poll, 1962; recipient Tony nomination for Skyscraper, Emmy nomination for Ghost and Mrs. Muir. Died May 25, 2007.

REISER, MORTON FRANCIS, psychiatrist, educator; b Cin., Aug. 22, 1919; s. Sigmund and Mary (Roth) R.; m. Lyn B. Whisnant, Dec. 19, 1976; children: David E., Barbara, Linda BS, U. Cin., 1940, MD, 1943; grad., N.Y. Psychoanalytic Inst 1960. Diplomate Am. Bd. Psychiatry and Neurology. Intern King's County Hosp., Bklyn., 1944; resident Cin. Gen. Hosp 1944-49; practice medicine, specializing in psychiatry Cin 1947-52, Washington, 1954-55, NYC, 1955-69; mem. faculty Cin. Gen. Hosp., also U. Cin. Coll. Medicine, 1949-52, Washington Sch. Psychiatry, 1953-55; faculty Albert Einstein Col Medicine, Yeshiva U., NYC, 1955-69, prof. psychiatry, 1958-69 dir. research dept. psychiatry, 1958-65; chief div. psychiatry Montefiore Hosp. and Med. Center, NYC, 1965-69; chmn. dep psychiatry Yale Med. Sch., from 1969, prof., 1969-78, chmn dept., 1969-86, Charles B.G. Murphy prof., 1978-86, Albert E Kent prof., 1986-90, Albert E. Kent prof. emeritus, from 1990 Cons. Walter Reed Army Inst. Research, 1957-58, WHO, 1963 mem. clin. program projects rev. com. NIMH, 1970—, chmn 1973-74. Author: (with H. Leigh) The Patient: Biological Psychological, and Social Dimensions of Medical Practice 1980, Mind, Brain, Body: Toward a Convergence of Psychoanalysis and Neurobiology, 1984; (with H. Leigh) The Patient 3d edit., 1992; Memory in Mind and Brain: What Dream Imagery Reveals, 1990; editor: American Handbook of Psychiatry, vol. IV, 1975; editor in chief Psychosomatic Medicine 1962-72; mem. editorial bd. AMA Archives of Gen. Psychiatry 1961-71, (with H. Leigh) Psychiatry Medicine and Primary Care, 1978; contbr. articles to profl. jours. and books. Fellow Am. Coll. Psychiatrists, Am. Psychiat. Assn. (Seymour Veste nark award 1986); mem. Am. Soc. Clin. Investigation, Am. 'sychosomatic Soc. (pres. 1960-61), Am. Fedn. Clin. Research, Am. Assn. Chairmen Depts. Psychiatry (exec. com. 1971—, res. 1975-76), Acad. Behavioral Medicine Research (exec. ouncil 1978), Am. Psychoanalytic Assn. (pres.-elect 1980-82, res. 1982-84), Internat. Psycho-Analytical Assn., Assn. Psychophysiol. Study of Sleep, Internat. Coll. Psychosomatic Medicine (pres. 1975), Psychiat. Research Soc., A. Graeme Mitchell Jndergrad. Pediatric Soc., Benjamin Rush Soc., Rapaport-Klein tudy Group, World Psychiat. Assn. (organizing com. sect. sychosomatic medicine 1967), Sigma Xi, Phi Eta Sigma, Pi Kappa Epsilon, Alpha Omega Alpha. Home: Hamden, Conn. Died June 21, 2007.

REISS, ALBERT JOHN, JR., sociology educator; b. Cascade, Wis., Dec. 9, 1922; s. Albert John and Erma Amanda (Schueler) R.; children: Peter C., Paul Wetherington, Amy. Student, Mission House Coll., 1939-42; PhB, Marquette U., 1944; MA, U. Chgo., 1948, PhD, 1949; LLD (hon.), CUNY, 1980; PhD (hon.), J. Montreal, 1985. From instr. sociology to asst. prof. U. Chgo., 947-52; assoc. dir. Chgo. Community Inventory-U. Chgo., 948-51, acting dir., 1951-52; asso. prof. sociology Vanderbilt J., 1952-58, prof., 1954-58, chmn. dept., 1952-58; prof. sociology and dir. Iowa Urban Cmty. Rsch. Ctr.-State U. Iowa, 958-60; prof. sociology, dir. survey research labs. U. Wis., 960-61; prof. sociology, dir. U. Mich. Center for Rsch. on ocial Orgn., Ann Arbor, 1961-70, chmn. dept., 1970; prof. ociology Yale U., from 1970, prof. social sci. Inst. Social and olit. Sci., 1970-87, William Graham Sumner prof., from 1977, hmn. dept., 1972-80, 85-89. Chmn. Census Com. on Enumeration Areas, Chgo., 1950-52, Nashville, 1952-58; mem. tech. adv. om. Chgo. Plan Commn., 1951-52; cons. USAF Human Resources Research Inst., 1952-54 Author: A Survey of Probation Needs and Services in Illinois, 1947, (with Paul K. Hatt) Reader in Urban Sociology, 1951, (with Evelyn R. Kitagawa) Mobility of Chicago Workers, 1951, Social Characteristics of Rural and Urban Communities, 1950 (with Otis Dudley Duncan), 1956, Cities and Society, 1958, Occupational and Social tatus, 1960, The Police and the Public, 1971, (with J. Roth) Understanding and Preventing Violence, 1993. Served as pvt., neteorology program A.C., AUS, 1943-44. Recipient Disting. Alumnus award Lakeland Coll., 1990, Beccaria Gold medal, 990. Fellow Am. Sociol. Assn. (chmn. methodology sect. 1960, oun. and exec. com. 1962-65), Sociol. Rsch. Assn. (pres. 1969), Am. Statis. Assn.; mem. NAS (chmn.), Ohio Valley Sociol. Soc. ores. 1966), Am. Soc. Criminology (pres. 1983-84), Soc. for tudy Social Problems (pres. 1968), Social Rsch. (pres. 1949), nternat. Soc. Criminology (sci. commn. 1982-89, pres. sci. ommn. 1985-89, pres. 1990-95). Home: Hamden, Conn. Died Apr. 27, 2006.

REITEMEIER, RICHARD JOSEPH, physician; b. Pueblo, Colo., Jan. 2, 1923; s. Paul John and Ethel Regina (McCarthy) Reitemeier; m. Patricia Claire Mulligan, July 21, 1951; children: Mary Louise, Paul, Joseph, Susan, Robert, Patrick, Daniel. AB, J. Denver, 1944; MD, U. Colo., 1946; MS in Internal Medicine, J. Minn., 1954. Diplomate Am. Bd. Internal Medicine. Intern Corwin Hosp., Pueblo, 1946—47; resident Henry Ford Hosp., Detroit, 1949—50, Mayo Found., Rochester, Minn., 1950—53; ons. internal medicine and gastroenterology Mayo Clinic, Rochester, 1954—87; chmn. dept. internal medicine Mayo Clinic (Mayo Clinic and Mayo Med. Sch.), 1967—74, prof., 971—2006; bd. govs. Mayo Clinic, 1970—74. Gov. Am. Bd. nternal Medicine, 1971—79, chmn., 1978—79, rep. to Am. Bd. Med. Specialites, 1977—80, 1983—84, accreditation council rad. med. edn., 1979—85, chmn., 1982—83; governing bd. Am. Bd. Med. Specialties, 1983—86; sci. and med. dir. Ludwig nst. Cancer Rsch., 1987—88; cons. Kaiser Family Med. ound., 1989—90; med. dir. Phoenix Alliance Inc., 1990—93. Author (with C.G. Moertel): Advanced Gastrointestinal Cancer, Clinical Management and Chemotherapy, 1969; contbr. articles o profl. jours. Trustee Mayo Found., 1970—74, St. Mary's Hosp., Rochester, 1976—82; mem. governing bd. Sisters of Mercy Hosp., St. Louis, 1988—94. With US Army, 1947—49. Recipient Alumni award, U. Colo. Sch. Medicine, Irving Cutter award, Phi Rho Sigma, 1986, Disting. Alumnus award, Mayo ound., 1997. Master: ACP (regent 1979—82, gov. for Minn. 975—79, pres. 1983—84, Alfred Stengel Meml. award 1990); ellow: AMA, Nat. Bd. Med. Examiners (treas. 1987—89), Am. Assn. Study Liver Disease, Am. Assn. Cancer Rsch., Inst. Medicine, Coun. Med. Splty. Socs., Am. Soc. Clin. Oncology, Am. Fedn. Clin. Rsch., Am. Clin. and Climatol. Assn., Am. Gastroenterol. Assn.; mem.: Alpha Omega Alpha. Republican. Roman Catholic. Died Dec. 18, 2006.

REITH, CARL JOSEPH, apparel industry executive; b. Peoria, Ill., Jan. 11, 1914; s. Joseph and May (Kolb) R.; m. Jennie Habbinga, Apr. 3, 1936; 1 child, Joyce Elaine. Grad. high sch. Office staff sales Peoria Creamery Co., Ill., 1932; with Kroger Co., 1934-60, successively asst. br. acct., office mgr., acct. Terre Haute, Ind., Atlanta; adminstr., coord. tng. and mgmt. devel. programing Kroger Co. (Gen. Offices), Cin.; gen. merchandising mgr. Kroger Co. (St. Louis br.), 1946-50; br. mgr. Kroger Co., ndpls., 1950-55, div. v.p. Cin., 1955-57, regional v.p., 1957-60; pres., chief exec. officer Colonial Stores, Inc., 1960-67; bd. dir., pres. Oxford Industries, 1967-78, now dir. Adv. bd. Salvation Army, Atlanta.; bd. dirs. Atlanta Coll. Art; trustee Robert Woodruff Art Ctr. Mem. Indiana Chain Store Council (pres., v.p. 951-55), Ind. C. of C. (bd. 1954-55), Indpls. C. of C. (bd. 950), Ga. C. of C. (indsl. devel. council), Atlanta C. of C. (v.p., d. dir. 1964-67), Augusta (Ga.) Nat. Golf Club, Piedmont Driving Club, Capital City Club, Peachtree Golf Club, Masons, Shriners, Rotary. Home: Atlanta, Ga. Died Nov. 8, 2005.

REMER, RICHARD POST, insurance executive; b. Paterson, N.J., Oct. 15, 1939; s. Richard F. and Carolyn B. (Post) R.; m. Adrienne A. Kriss, Nov. 18, 1961; 1 child, Richard F. B.S. in ndsl. Mgmt., Carnegie Inst. Tech., 1964. C.P.C.U.; C.L.U.; cert. EDP. Analyst, mgr. Gimbel Brothers, Pitts., 1962-66; sr. cons. ouche, Ross & Co., Chgo., 1967-69; mgr. fin. control Allstate ns. Co., Northbrook, Ill., 1969-72, mgr. claims res., 1972-86, dir. claims res., 1986—. Chmn. planning commn. Village of ary, Ill., 1976, trustee, 1978, bd. dirs., 1982. Republican. Home: Daytona Beach, Fla. Died June 5, 2006.

REMUND, JAMES WILLIAM, judge; b. Waseca, Minn., Feb. 12, 1927; s. Lewis Earl and Lilla Henrietta (Priebe) R.; m. Doris Bell, Aug. 12, 1950; children— Barbara, Martin, Daniel, Lawrence. B.S., U. Minn., 1950, LL.B., 1957. Bar: Minn. 1957. Sole practice, Windom, Minn., 1957-75; county atty. Cottonwood County (Minn.), Windom, 1962-75; judge Cottonwood County Ct., Windom, 1975—. Dir. men's chorus Am. Lutheran Ch., Windom, 1962—. Served as 2d lt. U.S. Army, 1950-52, Korea. Republican. Club: Kiwanis (pres. 1964-65) (Windom). Home: Windom, Minn. Died Apr. 16, 2006.

REPLINGER, JOHN GORDON, architect, retired educator; b. Chgo., Nov. 9, 1923; s. Roy Lodawick and Dorothy Caroline (Thornstrom) R.; m. Dorothy Thiele, June 26, 1945; children: John Gordon Jr., Robert Louis, James Alan. BS in Architecture with highest honors, U. Ill., Urbana, 1949, MS in Architecture, 1952. Registered architect, Ill. Designer-draftsman L. Morgan Yost (Architect), Kenilworth, Ill., 1949-50; instr. U. Ill., 1951-53, asst. prof. architecture, 1953-57, assoc. prof. architecture, 1957-61, prof. architecture, 1961-85, prof. housing research and devel., 1972-85, prof. emeritus, from 1985, assoc. head dept. for acad. affairs, 1970-71; practice architecture Urbana, from 1951. Served as combat pilot USAAF, 1943-45. Decorated Air medal with oak leaf clusters; recipient Sch. medal AIA, 1949, List of Tchrs. Ranked as Excellent by Their Students award U. Ill., 1976, 77, 78, 82, 83; Allerton Am. travelling scholar, 1948. Mem. Nat. Trust Hist. Preservation. Died Mar. 27, 2006.

RESEN, FREDERICK LAWRENCE, editor, publisher; b. NYC, July 17, 1923; s. Fred and Olga (Dowick) R.; m. Margaret Jenkins, Nov. 26, 1952; children: John Frederick, Emily. BS in Chem. Engring, U. Colo., 1950. Chem. engr. Dow Corning Corp., Midland, Mich., 1950-51; refining editor Oil and Gas Jour., Houston, 1951-58, NYC, 1958-59; editor, pub. Chem. Engring. Progress, NYC, 1959-84; staff dir. publs. and tech. services Am. Inst. Chem. Engrs., 1978-84; pres. Larry Resen Assocs., Indsl. Communications, Wilton, Conn., from 1984. Editorial dir. Internat. Chem. Engring., 1964-72; editorial cons.; cons. editor Am. Oxford Ency., 1960; Mem. adv. com. Internat. Exposition of Chem. Industries, 1966-75 Author: Wilton Congregational Church From 1726, 1975; columnist The Chem. Engr. (Eng.), 1985-88. Registered Emergency Med. Tech. (Conn.), mem. Wilton Vol. Ambulance Corps, 1985-88, Greenwich Emergency Med. Svc., 1989-94. Served with USN, 1941-45. Recipient Vol. of Yr. award Greenwich Emergency Med. Svc., 1991. Fellow Am. Inst. Chem. Engrs.; mem. Chem. Pub. Relations Soc. (v.p. 1972-74), Am. Chem. Soc., Am. Soc. Bus. Press Editors, Pi Kappa Alpha, Tau Beta Pi. Republican. Conglist. (Sunday Sch. tchr., trustee 1975). Clubs: Silver Spring Country (Ridgefield, Conn.)(bd. govs. 1989-94, sec. 1992-94); Chemists, Overseas Press (N.Y.C.), St. Joseph's Bay Country (Port St. Joe, Fla.). Home: Wilton, Conn. Died Mar. 25, 2006.

RESNICK, MARTIN I., urologist, educator; b. Bklyn., Jan. 12, 1943; s. Daniel and Bertha (Becker) R.; m. Victoria Klein, July 4, 1965; children: Andrew Howard, Jeffrey Scott. BA, Alfred U., NYC, 1964; MD, Bowman Gray Sch. Medicine, Winston-Salem, NC, 1969; MS, Northwestern U., Evanston, Ill., 1973. Diplomate Am. Bd. Urology. Instr. urology Northwestern U., Chgo., 1974-75, Bowman Gray Sch. Medicine, 1974-77, asst. prof., 1977-79, assoc. prof., 1979-81; prof., chmn. dept. urology Case Western Res. U., Cleve., from 1981, prof. oncology, from 1987. NIH awardee. Mem. Am. Urol. Assn. (pres. 2003-04), Am. Bd. Urology (pres. 2002-03), Alpha Omega Alpha. Jewish. Avocation: running. Home: Cleveland, Ohio. Died June 24, 2007.

REVSINE, LAWRENCE, accounting educator, consultant; b. Chgo., May 29, 1942; s. Victor and Pauline (Berger) R.; m. Barbara Sue Epstein, 1963; children: Pamela, David. BS, Northwestern U., 1963, MBA, 1965, PhD, 1968. C.P.A., Ill. Staff acct. Peat, Marwick, Mitchell & Co., Chgo., 1963-64; asst. prof. U. Ill., Urbana, 1968-70, assoc. prof., 1970-71; assoc. prof. acctg. Northwestern U., 1971-74, prof., 1975-79, Eric L. Kohler prof. acctg., 1979-86, John and Norma Darling disting. prof. fin. acctg., 1986—2007, chmn. dept. acctg. and info. systems, 1985-93. Vis. prof. U. Wis., Madison, 1974-75; cons. in field Author: Replacement Cost Accounting, 1973, Accounting in An Inflationary Enviroment, 1977, (with others) Statement on Accounting Theory and Theory Acceptance, 1977; contbr. articles to profl. jours.; editorial cons.: Acctg. Rev., 1977-80, mem. editorial bd., 1971-74, Jour. Acctg. and Pub. Policy, Jour. Acctg. and Bus. Recipient commendation for teaching excellence Northwestern U. Grad. Mgmt. Assn., 1981, 82, 86, 91; recipient Tchr. of Yr. award Northwestern U. Grad. Mgmt. Assn., 1983; Ford Found. doctoral fellow, 1966-68; Peat, Marwick, Mitchell Found. grantee, 1978, Kellogg Alumni Choice Faculty award, 1995. Mem. AICPAs, Am. Acctg. Assn. (chmn. com. on concepts and standards-external fin. reports 1974-76, disting. overseas lectr. 1991, outstanding educator 1992, chmn. fin. reporting issues conf. com. 1994), Ill. Soc. CPAs (outstanding educator 1993, fin. acctg. standards adv. coun. 1992-95), Beta Alpha Psi, Beta Gamma Sigma. Home: Northbrook, Ill. Died May 7, 2007.

REYNOLDS, HERBERT HAL, retired academic administrator; b. Frankston, Tex., Mar. 20, 1930; s. Herbert Joseph and Ava Nell (Taylor) R.; m. Joy Myrla Copeland, June 17, 1950; children: Kevin Hal, Kent Andrew, Rhonda Sheryl. BS, Trinity U., 1952; MS, Baylor U., 1958, PhD, 1961; ScD (hon.), Seinan Gakuin U., Japan, 1990, Baylor Coll. Dentistry, 1993; PhD (hon.), Yonok Coll., Thailand, 2000. Entered USAF, 1948, advanced through grades to col., 1966; with Aeromed. Lab., Alamogordo, N.Mex., 1961—68, Air Force Human Resources Lab., San Antonio, 1968; ret., 1968; exec. v.p. Baylor U., Waco, Tex., 1969—81, pres., 1981—95, chancellor, 1995—2000, pres. emeritus, 2000—07. Vis. fellow, scholar Cambridge U., 1994-97. Contbr. articles to profl. jours. Mem.: Sigma Xi, Phi Beta Kappa, Omicron Delta Kappa, Alpha Chi. Died May 25, 2007.

REYNOLDS, JOHN CORNELIUS, lawyer, foods company executive; b. Mt. Vernon, NY, Jan. 27, 1923; s. Harry Dare and Marian Elizabeth (Putnam) R.; m. Pamela Stemler, June 6, 1946; children: Nora D. Reynolds Smith, Brian, Diana. Student, Hamilton Coll., 1944; JD, Union U., Albany, NY, 1949; LL.M., NYU, 1953. Bar: N.Y. State bar 1950. With Shell Oil Co., 1949-59; atty. dept. law Amstar Corp., NYC, 1959-68, asst. gen. counsel, 1968-72, gen. counsel, from 1972, v.p., from 1973. Served with AUS, 1943-46. Decorated Bronze Star, Purple Heart; Orange Lanyard (Netherlands); Fourragere (Belgium) Fellow Am. Bar Found.; mem. Assn. Gen. Counsel, Assn. Bar City N.Y., N.Y. State Bar Assn., ABA Home: Mount Kisco, NY. Died Sept. 17, 2006.

REYNOLDS, JOHN NORMANDY, judge; b. New Haven, July 15, 1919; s. Patrick Faughnan and Bessie Mary (Normandy) R. B.S. in Bus. Adminstrn., Providence Coll., 1941; LL.B., Georgetown U., 1950; LL.M. in Taxation, NYU, 1951. Bar: Conn. 1950, D.C. 1950. Sole practice, New Haven, 1950-60; judge Circuit Ct. State of Conn., 1961-74, Ct. Common Pleas State of Conn., 1975-77, Superior Ct. State of Conn., New Haven, 1977—. Alderman City of New Haven, 1952-53, majority leader, 1954-58. Served to lt. USN, 1942-46. Mem. Conn. Bar Assn. Democrat. Roman Catholic. Home: Hamden, Conn. Died Feb. 13, 2006.

REYNOLDS, WILEY RICHARD, banker; b. NYC, Dec. 4, 1917; s. Wiley Richard and Nettie H. (Hood) R.; m. Janet Raymer, June 20, 1942; children: Wiley Richard III, Suzanne Raymer, Judith Underhill, Thomas Hood. Grad., Hotchkiss Sch., 1936; AB, Yale U., 1940. With First Nat. Bank, Palm Beach, Fla., from 1940, dir., from 1941, pres., chmn., 1948-65, exec. dir., 1965-91. Philippine rep. Internat. Exec. Svc. Corps, 1966, Indonesian dir. for corps, 1968, Turkish dir., 1977, Philippine dir., 1978, Taiwan dir., 1979. Pres. Palm Beach Pvt. Sch., 1961-65; mem. bd. Civic Assn. Mem. Seminole Golf Club (former dir.)(Juno Beach, Fla.), Garden of the Gods Club, Cheyenne Mountain Country Club (Colorado Springs, Colo.), River Club, Union Club (Sydney, Australia), Bath and Tennis Club (dir.), Everglades Club (former bd. govs.) (Palm Beach). Episcopal. Home: Palm Beach, Fla. Died Nov. 29, 2005.

RHODES, ALLEN FRANKLIN, engineering executive; b. Estherville, Oct. 3, 1924; m. Carol Haisler, 1962; children: James Fleming, Stephen Haisler. BSME, Villanova U., 1947; ML, U. Houston, 1950. Reg. profl. engr., Tex. Asst. dir. engring. adminstrn. Hughes Tool Co., Houston, 1947-52; pres. McEvoy Co., Houston, 1952-63; v.p. engring. & rsch. Rockwell Mfg. Co., Pitts., 1963-70; v.p. corp. planning & devel. ACF Industries, NYC, 1971-73; pres., CEO McEvoy Oilfield Equipment Co., Houston, 1974-79; exec. v.p., CEO Goldrus Marine Drilling, Houston, 1979-82; pres., CEO Warren Oilfield Svc., Houston, 1981-82, Anglo Energy, NYC, 1983-86, Gripper Inc., Houston, 1987-90; v.p., CFO Hydrotech Sys. Inc., Houston, 1991; cons. Allen F. Rhodes, Bus. Advisor & Consulting Engr., Houston, from 1991, Silver Fox Advisors, from 1986. Chmn. Com. Dept. Transp. Gas Pipelin Safety Std., 1969-73; dir. Keystone Internat., 1980-97, Triten Corp., 1980-2007, Rawson-Koenig, 1986-98, S.W. Rsch. Inst., 1989-2007, Tex. Microsystem, 1989-92, Houston Humane Soc., 1999-2007; adj. prof. mech. engring. U. Houston, 2001-07. Dir. T&B Lehman Animal Shelter, Inc., 2002—07; Dir. Dime Box Hist. Soc., 1988—2003. Lt. USN, 1943—46. Recipient Charles Russ Richards Meml. award, 1987, Howard Conley medal Am. Nat. Std. Inst., 1980. Fellow ASME (past nat. pres., Robert Henry Thurston award 1978), Inst. Mech. Engrs. (Gt. Britain); mem. Nat. Acad. Engring., Soc. Petroleum Engrs., Am. Petroleum Inst. Achievements include holding twenty-two US patents for equipment relating to oilfield drilling and completion. Avocations: sailing, history. Died Aug. 18, 2007.

RHODES, SILAS HARVEY, retired academic administrator; b. Bronx, NY, Sept. 15, 1915; m. Beatrice Rhodes (dec. 2002); children: David, Stephen, Anthony. BA, Long Island U.; MA, PhD, Columbia U. Founder, chmn. Sch. Visual Arts, NYC. Died June 27, 2007.

RICE, DAVID AINSWORTH, law educator; b. Oconomowoc, Wis., May 25, 1940; s. Maurice Ainsworth and Frances Mary (Stellflug) R.; m. Virginia M. Griffin, Sept. 5, 1964. BBA, U. Wis., 1962; LLB, Columbia U., 1965. Bar: N.Y. 1965, Mass. 1972. Law clk. U.S. Ct. Appeals 2d Circuit, 1965-66; asst. prof. law Boston U., 1966-69, assoc. prof., 1969-70, prof., 1970-87, assoc. dean Sch. Law, 1976-81; prof. law Rutgers U. Sch. Law, Newark, N.J., from 1987. Sr. research scholar Yale Law Sch., 1982, vis. lectr., 1973; vis. prof. Ariz. State U., 1977, Rutgers-Newark, 1986-87; cons. FTC, 1980-81, Mass. Exec. Office Environ. Affairs, Office Coastal Zone Mgmt., 1975-78; mem. Commonwealth Mass. Consumers Council, 1972-75. Author: Consumer Transactions, 1975, (with M. Baram and W. Lee) Marine Mining of the Continental Shelf, 1978. Mem. Am. Law Inst., Computer Law Assn. Home: Chestnut Hill, Mass. Died Oct. 19, 2005.

RICE, EDWARD EARL, former government official, author; b. Saginaw, Mich., Feb. 6, 1909; s. William Edward and Katherine Marie (Meyer) R.; m. Mary June Kellogg, Oct. 26, 1942. Student, U. Wis., 1926-28; BS, U. Ill., 1930, postgrad., 1934-35, U. Mex., 1931, Coll. Chinese Studies, also pvt. tutors, Beijing, 1935-37. Joined Fgn. Svc., Dept. State, 1935; lang. attache Beijing, 1935-37; vice consul Canton, China, 1938-40; consul Foochow, China, 1940-42; 2d sec. Am. Embassy, Chungking, China, 1942-45; asst. chief divsn. Chinese affairs Dept. State, 1946-48, asst. chief divsn. Philippine affairs, 1948-49; 1st sec., consul Am. Embassy, Manila, 1949-51; consul gen. Stuttgart, Fed. Republic Germany, 1952-56; fgn. svc. insp. Dept. State, 1956-58, dep. dir. pers., 1959, mem. policy planning coun., 1959-61, dep. asst. sec. of state for Far Ea. affairs, 1962-63; consul gen., min. Hong Kong, 1964-67; diplomat in residence with rank of prof. U. Calif., Berkeley, 1968-69, rsch. assoc. Ctr. for Chinese Studies, from 1969. Vis. prof. Marquette U., 1973; advisor U.S. del. 3d, 4th and 5th sessions Econ. Commn. for Asia Far East, 1948-49. Author: Mao's Way, 1972, Wars of the Third Kind, 1988. Recipient Gold medal for non-fiction Commonwealth Club, 1973. Mem. Beta Gamma Sigma. Home: Belvedere Tiburon, Calif. Died Apr. 13, 2006.

RICE, FRANK H., life insurance company executive; b. Iowa City, June 4, 1928; s. Harry L. and Charlotte M. (Funk) R.; m. virginia Ellen Koenig, Sept. 9, 1950; children: Margaret Ruth, Elaine Marie, Craig Matthew. BA, U. Iowa, 1950, MS, 1951. Asst. mgr. data processing Northwestern Mut. Life Ins. Co., Milw., 1961-63, systems coordinating officer, 1963-68, assoc. dir. adminstrv. services, 1968-74; dir. adminstrv. services Northwestern Mut. Life Ins. Co., Milw., 1974-79; v.p. adminstrv. services Northwestern Mut. Life Ins. Co., Milw., 1979-80, v.p. policy benefits, from 1980. Bd. dirs. Am. Baptist Homes of Midwest, Eden Prairie, Minn., 1982—. Fellow Soc. Actuaries; mem. Am. Acad. Actuaries, Phi Beta Kappa Clubs: Exchange (pres. 1974). Home: Hales Corners, Wis. Died Nov. 25, 2006.

RICE, JULIAN CASAVANT, lawyer; b. Miami, Fla., Dec. 31, 1923; s. Sylvan J. and Maybelle (Casavant) R.; m. Dorothy Mae Haynes, Feb. 14, 1958; children— Scott B., Craig M. (dec.), Julianne C., Linda D., Janette M. Student, U. San Francisco, 1941-43; JD cum laude, Gonzaga U., 1950. Bar: Wash. 1950, Alaska 1959, U.S. Tax Ct. 1988. Pvt. practice law, Spokane, 1950-56, Fairbanks, Alaska, from 1959; prin. Law Office Julian C. Rice (and predecessor firms), Fairbanks, 1959, Salcha, Alaska, 1999. Founder, gen. counsel Mt. McKinley Mut. Savs. Bank, Fairbanks, 1965-99, chmn. bd., 1979-80; v.p., bd. dirs., gen. counsel Skimmers, Inc., Anchorage, 1966-67; gen. counsel Alaska Carriers Assn., Anchorage, 1960-71, Alaska Transp. Conf., 1960-67. Mayor City of Fairbanks, 1970-72. Served to maj. USNG and USAR, 1943-58. Decorated Bronze Star, Combat Infantryman's Badge. Fellow Am. Bar Found. (life); mem. ABA, Wash. State Bar Assn. (50-Yr. mem. award 2000), Alaska Bar Assn., Transp. Lawyers Assn., Alternative Dispute Resolution Com., Am. Arbitration Assn. (mem. transp. comml., transp. panel), Spokane Exch. Club (pres. 1956). Died June 22, 2007.

RICE, WILLIAM DAVID, advertising agency executive; b. Salt Lake City, Jan. 30, 1920; s. William and Elsie (Cohn) R.; m. Adrienne G. Schwartz, Mar. 3, 1957 (dec. May 1964); children— William E., Taylor D.; m. Jo Anne Twelves, Nov. 9, 1966; children— Robert G., James A. BS in Chemistry, U. Utah, 1942. V.p. Cooper & Crowe Advt., Salt Lake City, 1947-53; pres. Demiris, Rice & Assocs. Advt., Salt Lake City, 1953—. Pres., Salt Lake Mental Health Assn., 1961-62, Utah Assn. Mental Health, 1964-66, Utah Traveler's Aid Soc., 1972-73; v.p. communications Nat. Assn. Mental Health, 1973-75; chmn. Utah Mental Health Adv. Coun., 1978-80; bd. dirs. Hospice of Salt Lake City, 1978—, chmn., 1979-86; chmn. Com. for Severely Mentally Impaired, 1979-81, Mental Health Media Devel. Com., 1985—; chmn. Community Nursing Svc., 1986-88; exec. v.p. Utah Mil. Vet. Affairs Com., 1986—. Comdr. USN, 1942-46, ret. 1965. Recipient Disting. Svc. award Utah Med. Assn., 1975, Nat. Assn. Mental Health, 1975. Fellow Am. Inst. Mgmt. (pres.'s coun. 1971-72); mem. Utah Assn. Advt. Agys., Internat. Platform Assn., Salt Lake Advt. Club, Univ. Club (Salt Lake City, pres. 1982-83), Mensa (proctor 1970—), Alta Club. Home: Salt Lake City, Utah. Died Apr. 4, 2007.

RICH, CLAYTON, retired academic administrator, educator; b. NYC, May 21, 1924; s. Clayton Eugene and Leonore (Elliot) R.; m. Mary Bell Hodgkinson, Dec. 19, 1953 (div. May 1974); 1 son, Clayton Greig; m. Rosalind Morgan-Jones, Apr. 6, 1987. Grad., Putney Sch., 1942; student, Swarthmore Coll., 1942-44; MD, Cornell U., 1948. Diplomate Am. Bd. Internal Medicine. Intern Albany Hosp., NY, 1948-49, asst. resident, 1950-51; rsch. asst. Cornell U. Med. Coll., 1949-50; asst. Rockefeller U., 1953-58, asst. prof., 1958-60; asst. prof. medicine U. Wash. Sch. Medicine, 1960-62, assoc. prof., 1962-67, prof., 1967-71, assoc. dean, 1968-71; chief radioisotope service VA Hosp., Seattle, 1960-70, assoc. chief staff, 1962-71, chief of staff, 1968-70; v.p. med. affairs, dean Sch. Medicine; prof. medicine Stanford U., 1971-79, Carl and Elizabeth Naumann prof., 1977-79; chief staff Stanford U. Hosp., 1971-77, CEO, 1977—79. Sr. scholar Inst. Medicine, Nat. Acad. Sci., Washington, 1979-80; Mem. gen. medicine B study sect. NIH, 1969-73, chmn., 1972-73; mem. spl. med. adv. group VA, 1977-81; provost U. Okla. Health Scis. Ctr., Oklahoma City, 1980-92—, v.p. for healh scis., 1983-92; also exec. dean, prof. U. Okla. Coll. Medicine, 1980-83, emeritus Regents prof. and provost U. Okla., 1993—. Editorial bd.: Calcified Tissue Research, 1966-72, Clin. Orthopedics, 1967-72, Jour. Clin. Endocrinology and Metabolism, 1971-72; Contbr. numerous articles to med. jours. Bd. dirs. Children's Hosp. at Stanford, Stanford U. Hosp., 1974-79; chmn. Gordon Research Conf. Chemistry, Physiology and Structure of Bones and Teeth, 1967; bd. dirs. Okla. Med. Research Found.; bd. dirs. Leadership Oklahoma City, 1981-92, v.p., 1985-92; bd. dirs. Okla. Blood Inst., 1982-92, Oklahoma City chpt. ARC, 1983-92. Lt. USNR, 1951-53. Fellow ACP, AAAS; mem. Assn. Am. Physicians, Western Assn. Physicians, Am. Soc. Mineral and Bone Research (adv. bd. 1977-80), Am. Soc. Clin. Investigation, Assn. Am. Med. Colls. (exec. council 1975-79), Inst. of Medicine, Western Soc. Clin. Research (v.p. 1967-68), Endocrine Soc., Assn. Acad. Health Ctrs. (bd. dirs. 1984-88, chmn. 1987-88), Sigma Xi, Alpha Omega Alpha. Home: Kirkland, Wash. Died Feb. 22, 2007.

RICH, FRANCES LUTHER, sculptor; b. Spokane, Wash., Jan. 8, 1910; d. Elvo Elcourt Deffenbaugh and Irene (Luther Deffenbaugh) Rich. BA, Smith Coll., 1931; art student, Paris studios, 1933-35, Boston Mus. Sch. Art, 1935-36, Cranbrook Acad. Art, Bloomfield Hills, Mich., 1937-40, Claremont Coll., Calif., 1946-47, Columbia U., 1946-47; pupil of, Malvina Hoffman, Carl Milles, Alexandre Iacovleff. Dir. pub. relations Smith Coll., 1947-50; with pvt. studios Rome, 1950-52, Paris, 1960-62. Pub. and pvt. marble sculpture include Army-Navy-Air Force Nurses Arlington Nat. Cemetery, Washington, 1938, Terra Cotta, Benedictine Abbey Chapel, Mt. Angel, Oreg., 1954, Bronze Pelican, Earle C. Anthony Bldg., U. Berkeley, Calif., 1958, St. Joseph, Guadelupe Coll., Los Gatos, Calif., 1966; Bronze series St. Francis of Assisi, 4' St. Francis, Little Austria Terrace, Millesgården, Lidingö, Sweden, 1960; 6'7" St. Francis, St. Margaret's Episcopal Ch., Palm Desert, Calif., 1970, 7'6" Pierce-Deree Coll., Mt. Hymettus, Athens, Greece, 1970, 7'6" St. Francis, Pres.'s Garden Smith Coll., Northampton, Mass., 1978, 4'4" bronze Cranbrook Acad. Art Mus., Bloomfield Hills, Mich., 1983, 10' bronze "Our Lady of Combermere" grounds, The Madonna House Lay Apolstolate Tng. Ctr., Combermere, Ont., Can., 1960, 19" bronze "Our Lady of Combermere", Madonna House Chapel, Edmonton, Can., medals of Our Lady of Combermere at Combermere Madonna House Tng. Ctr., and 22" bronze "St. Catherine of Siena" (Santa Catalina Sch., Monterey, Calif.), 1968, 89, " Crucifix, The Madonna Chapel, Grace Cathedral, San Francisco, 1972, 30" bronze crucifix St. Margaret's Episcopal Ch., Palm Desert, Calif., 1990, bronze "The Healer", David L. Reeves Meml. Libr., Cottage Hosp., Santa Barbara, Calif., 1973, 15 bronze "Birds in Flight", Living Desert Reserve, Palm Desert, Calif., 1978; reliefs include: 6 nine ' stone panels Union Bldg., Purdue U., Lafayette, Ind., 1939; bronze 4'x 6' panel "Nunc Dimittis", St. Peter's Episcopal Ch., Redwood City, Calif., 1957; 8' "Our Lady Seat of Wisdom", St. Cecelia Ch., Stanwood, Wash., 1965; 8' bronze "Christ of the Sacred Heart", St. Sebastian's Ch., West Los Angeles, Calif. 1972; portraits include: Margaret Sanger, 1957 and Pres. Herbert Davis, 1950, Nielson Libr., Smith Coll., Northampton, Mass., Prof. Henry Russel Hitchcock, marble bust Alice Stone Blackwell, Boston Pub. Library, 1961; 3'6" terra cotta figure Katharine Hepburn, Shakespeare Mus., 1962 and bronze bust of Hepburn, 1961, both as Cleopatra, at Am. Shakespeare Theatre, Stratford, Conn.; also bronze head Lawrence Langner, Shakespeare Theater Foyer, 1963; bronze head Virgil Thomson, Virgil Thomson Room, NYU, 1977; Smith Coll. Mus. Art collection includes bronze portraits of Katharine Hepburn as Cleopatra, Lotte Lehman, Diego Rivera, 1978, terra cotta portrait of Margaret Sanger, cotta portrait of Lotte Lehman; bronze portrait of Pres. Herbert Davis and bronze bas relief of Laura Scales; marble bust of Alice Stone Blackwell; further sculpture collections Smith Coll. Mus. Art and Cranbrook Acad. Art, 1981; one man shows: Art Ctr., Phoenix, 1954, Santa Barbara Mus. Art, 1955, Calif. Palace Legion of Honor, San Francisco, 1955, Laguna Blanca Sch., Santa Barbara, 1955, Palm Springs Desert Mus., 1969, 77, Smith Coll Mus. Art, 1981, Cranbrook Acad. Art Mus., 1983; group exhbns.: Am. Art Exhibit, World's Fair, N.Y., 1939, First Nat. Biennale Contemporary Religious Art, Set Hall Coll., Pa., 1953, Denver Liturgical Art Show, 1952, De Young Mus., Calif Liturgical Artists, 1952, Grace Cathedral, San Francisco, 1957, Knoedler's Gallery, N.Y.C., 1962, Members Exhibit, Archtl. League, N.Y.C., 1962, Boston Pub. Libr.; 10 bronzes Nat. Liturgical Art Week, Seattle World's Fair, 1962; 8 bronzes "Students of Carl Milles" Exhibit, Millesgården, Lidingö, summer 1986; Milles as Mentor: The Work of Cranbrook Sculptors, 1931-51, 5 bronzes Cranbrook Acad. Art, Bloomfield Hills, Mich., summer, 1990;12 1/2" bronzes of Our Lady of Combermere in each of 27 Madonna House Chapels Lay Apostolates Worldwide, 1989, 4'5" bronze St. Francis of Assisi, Botanic Garden Ctr., Fort Worth. 1990; 15" bronze of St. Margaret of Scotland St. Margaret's Episcopal Ch., Palm Desert, 1990, Canongate Kirk, Edinburgh, 1991; 18" bronze crucifix Canongate Kirk Manse; life size bronze bust Dr. George Bass, underwater archaeologist, 1993; numerous portraits, fountains, small bronzes and silvers for pvt. collectors. Served to lt. comdr. USNR, 1942-46. Mem. Archtl. League N.Y.C., Smith Coll. Alumnae Assn., Cosmopolitan Club (N.Y.C.). Home: Payson, Ariz. Died Oct. 14, 2007.

RICH, ROBERT EDWARD, food company executive; b. Buffalo, July 7, 1913; s. Paul J. and Eleanor (MacKenzie) R.; m. Janet Webb, Feb. 24, 1934; children: Joanne Rich Healy, Robert Edward, David A. BSBA, U. Buffalo, 1935; DHL, D'Youville Coll., 1981; LLD (hon.), SUNY, 1987. Owner Wilber Farms, Buffalo, 1935-60; cons. dairy sect. War Food Adminstrn., 1942; milk order adminstr. for Mich. Detroit, 1943; founder Rich Products Corp., Buffalo, 1944, chmn. bd., 1978—2006. Bd. dirs. Marine Midland Bank-Western, VHC Ltd.; vice chmn., bd. dirs. Gibraltar Steel Corp. Recipient Disting. Svc. award U. Buffalo, Samuel P. Capen award, 1959, Nagiara Frontier Businessman of Yr. award, 1966, named to univ. Athletic Hall of Fame, 1966; recipient Founder award Fronzen Food Industry, 1976, Cult of White Buffalo award, 1980, Western New Yorker of Yr. award, 1981. Mem. Nat. Assn. Advanced Foods (pres.), Buffalo Niagara Sales and Mktg. Execs. (Mktg. Man of Yr. award 1968), New Eng. Frozen Food Inst., So.-Southwestern Frozen Food Assn., Delaware Valley Frozen Food Assn. (hon.), Zerocrats (Disting. mem.), Buffalo Club (Businessman of Yr. award 1966), Buffalo Canoe Club, Buffalo Country Club, Cherry Hill Country Club, Palm Beach Nat. Golf and Country Club, Everglades Club, Beach Club, Sea Island Golf Club, Rotary. Died Feb. 15, 2006.

RICH, ROBERT REGIER, physician, medical educator, immunologist; b. Newton, Kans., Mar. 7, 1941; s. Eldon Stahly and Margaret Joy (Regier) R.; m. Susan Jepsen Solliday, Mar. 22, 1974; children from previous marriage: Kenneth Eldon, Cathryn Louise; 1 stepchild, Lynn Solliday Todorov. AB, Oberlin Coll., 1962; MD, U. Kans., 1966. Diplomate Am. Bd. Internal Medicine (bd. dirs. 1990-93), Am. Bd. Allergy and Immunology (bd. dirs. 1987-93, chmn. 1991); cert. spl. qualification Diagnostic Lab. Immunology. Intern, resident in internal medicine U. Wash., Seattle, 1966-68; clin. asso., chief clin. asso., sr. staff fellow NIH, Bethesda, Md., 1968-71; research asso. Harvard Med. Sch., Boston, 1971-73; asst. in medicine Peter Bent Brigham Hosp., 1972-73; asst. prof., assoc. prof. microbiology, immunology and internal medicine Baylor Coll. Medicine, Houston, 1973-78, prof., 1978-95, Disting. Svc. prof., 1995—2002, head immunology sect., 1978-98, chief clin. immunology, 1979-91, v.p., dean rsch., 1990-98; exec. assoc. dean, prof. medicine & microbiology/immunology Emory U. Sch. Medicine, 1998—2004; sr. v.p. for medicine, dean Sch. Medicine U. Ala., Birmingham, from 2004, prof. medicine and microbiology, from 2004. Investigator Howard Hughes Med. Inst., Bethesda, Md., 1977-91; mem. immunobiology study sect. NIH, 1977-81; mem. transplantation biology and immunology com. Nat. Inst. Allergy and Infectious Disease, 1982-86, chmn., 1984-86; mem. nat. ctr. grants com. Arthritis Found., 1983-86, chmn., 1984-86, nat. rsch. com., 1984-89, chmn., 1986-89, ho. of dels., 1985-91, Blue Ribbon com. on rsch. 2000-01; mem. rsch. adv. com. Nat. Multiple Sclerosis Soc., 1989-94, chmn., 1993-94; adv. panel on rsch. Assn. Am. Med. Coll., 1990—, shared responsibility advocacy com., 1997-98; chmn. ctrs. working group Nat. Inst. Arthritis Musculoskeletal Skin Diseases, 1996-97; mem. nat. human rsch. protections adv. com., dept. health and human svcs., 2000-02; vice chmn. UAB Health Sys., 2004—, bd. dirs.; vice chmn. bd. dirs. Ctr. Infectious Diseases Rsch., Zambia, 2006—. Assoc. editor: Jour. Immunology, 1978-82, sect. editor, 1991-96, deputy editor, 1997-2002, editor-in-chief, 2003—; assoc. editor: Jour. Infectious Diseases, 1984-88; adv. editor: Jour. Exptl. Medicine, 1980-84; mem. editl. bd. Jour. Clin. Immunology, 1989-96, Clin. and Exptl. Immunology, 1995-2000; editor-in-chief Clin. Immunology: Principles and Practice, 1996, 2d edit., 2001; contbr. articles to profl. jours. With USPHS, 1968—70. Recipient Rsch. Career Devel. award, NIH, 1975—77, Merit award, 1987. Fellow ACP, Am. Acad. Allergy, Asthma, and Immunology (chmn. basic and clin. immunology interest sect. 1992-93, chmn. profl. edn. coun. 1996-98, v.p. 2001-2002), Infectious Diseases Soc. Am.; mem. AMA, AAAS, Am. Bd. Internal Medicine (diplomate, bd. dirs. 1990-93), Am. Bd. Allergy and Immunology (diplomate, bd. dirs. 1987-93, chmn. bd. 1992), Assn. Am. Physicians, Am. Soc. Clin. Investigation, Am. Assn. Immunologists (chmn. pub. affairs com. 1994-2000, Disting. Svc. award 1999), Am. Assn. Investigative Pathology, Am. Soc. Microbiologists, Am. Fedn. Med. Rsch., Am. Clin. Climatological Assn. (councillor 2001-05), Fedn. Am. Socs. for Exptl. Biology (bd. dirs. 1998-2003, pres. and chmn. bd. dirs. 2001-02), Clin. Immunology Soc. (coun. 1990-96, pres. 1995), Nat. Assn. Biomed. Rsch. (bd. dirs. 2002-05), Assn. for Assessment and Accreditation of Lab Animal Care Internat. (trustee 2003-05), Alpha Omega Alpha, Sigma Xi. Home: Birmingham, Ala. Died Mar. 7, 2006.

RICHARDS, BETTY JANE, employee relations executive; b. Twinsburg, Ohio, July 9, 1930; d. Albert William and Kathryn Irene (Harding) Reese; m. Paul S. Richards, Sept. 4, 1948; children— Leslie, Dolores, Jane, Carol. Student Kent State U. 1974-76. With Ins. Co. N.Am., Cleve., 1948-49; dental asst. Dr. Hammel, Hudson, Ohio, 1949-50; sec. Tom Moore Tractor Co. Mantua, Ohio, 1960-62; inventory control sec. Carlon Products Co., Aurora, Ohio, 1962-65; exec. sec. to pres. Mantaline Corp. Mantua, 1965-73; employee relations mgr. Eaton Corp., Mantua, 1973—. Mem. Pvt. Industry Council, Portage County, Ohio, 1980-83, trustee, 1983; mem. adv. com. Maplewood Area Vocat. Sch., Ravenna, Ohio, 1980-83. Mem. Am. Soc. Personnel Adminstrn. (pres. 1979). Democrat. Died Apr. 22, 2007.

RICHARDS, GALE LEE, communications educator; b. Long Run, W.Va., July 31, 1918; s. Robert Amaziah and Edna Jane (Scott) R.; m. Barbara Lee Neely, Apr. 19, 1944; children: Robin Lee, Wendell Scott, Jeffrey Marshall. BA (Pixley scholar), U. Akron, O., 1940; MA (C.S. Knight Meml. scholar), U. Ia., 1942; PhD, 1950. Instr. speech U. Akron, 1941-42; asst. prof. speech Drake U., 1947-48; asst. prof. English U. Nev., 1948-52; asst. prof. speech U. Wash., 1952-58; assoc. prof. speech U. So. Calif., 1958-65; prof. communication Ariz. State U., Tempe, from 1965, chmn. dept. speech and theatre, 1965-73. Pub. relations cons. Red Feather campaign United Fund, Los Angeles, 1955-58; mgmt. and tng. cons. various profl. and comml. orgns., 1955— Cons. editor: Western Speech, 1957-61, 62-65, 69-72, Jour. of Communication, 1961-67; Contbr. articles profl. jours. Bd. dirs. Phoenix Little Theatre. Served to lt. USNR, 1942-45, PTO. Recipient Distinguished Alumni award Radio Sta. WSUI, 1942 Mem. We. States Communication Assn. (adminstrv. coun., legis. coun., chair commn. on Am. Parliamentary procedure, 1988, emeritus 1991), Internat. Communication Assn. (adminstrv. coun.), Am. Inst. Parliamentarians, Western States Communication Assn. (2d v.p. 1956, 71, pres. Execs. club 1975, Disting. Svc. award 1989), Ariz. Communication and Drama Assn. (pres. 1967, editor jour. 1984-87), Blue Key, Phi Kappa Phi, Delta Sigma Rho. Democrat. Presbyterian. Home: Tempe, Ariz. Died June 28, 2007.

RICHARDS, HUGH TAYLOR, physics professor; b. Baca County, Colo., Nov. 7, 1918; s. Dean Willard and Kate Bel (Taylor) R.; m. Mildred Elizabeth Paddock, Feb. 11, 1944; children: David Taylor, Thomas Martin, John Willard, Margaret Paddock, Elizabeth Nicholls, Robert Dean. BA, Park Coll. 1939; MA, Rice U., 1940, PhD, 1942. Research assoc. Rice U. Houston, 1942; scientist U. Minn., Mpls., 1942-43, U. Calif. Sci. Labs., Los Alamos, N.Mex., 1943-46; research assoc. U. Wis. Madison, 1946-47, mem. faculty, 1947-52, prof., 1952-88, prof. emeritus, from 1988, physics dept. chairperson, 1960-63, 66-69, 85-88. Assoc. dean Coll. Letters and Sci., U. Wis, 1963-66. Author: Through Los Alamos 1945: Memoirs of a Nuclear Physicist, 1993; contbr. articles to profl. jours. Fellow Am. Phys. Soc.; mem. Am. Assn. Physics Tchrs. Unitarian-Universalist. Achievements include neutron measurements first A-Bomb test fission neutron (and other) spectra by new photo-emulsion techniques; mock fission neutron source; spherical electrostatic analyzer for precise reaction energy measurements; negative ion sources for accelerators (He ALPHATROSS, SNICS); accurate proton, deuteron, and alpha particle scattering and reaction cross sections; systematics mirror nuclei; isospin violations in nuclear reactions. Home: Menomonie, Wis. Died Sept. 29, 2006.

RICHARDS, RILEY HARRY, retired insurance company executive; b. North Judson, Ind., Oct. 6, 1912; s. Harry J. and Chestie (Johnson) R.; m. Eloise Quinn Smith, May 4, 1940; children: Roy, Lynne. AB, U. Calif., Berkeley, 1934; MBA, Harvard U., 1937. Chartered fin. analyst. Fin. analyst Savs. Bank Trust Co. N.Y.C., 1937-40, SEC, Washington, Phila., 1940-45; accountant U.S. Steel Corp., Pitts., 1945-47; with Equitable Life Ins. Co. Iowa, Des Moines, 1947-77, v.p. finance, 1961-73, v.p., sec., treas., 1973-76, sr. v.p., sec.-treas., 1976-77; dir., mem. exec. com. Equitable of Iowa Cos., 1977-84; ret. Pres. Westminster House, Inc., 1989-96; dir. F.M. Hubbell Sons & Co. 1977-85. Mem. Des Moines Plan and Zoning Commn., 1959-70, chmn., 1968-69; mem. bd. pensions U.P. Ch. in U.S.A., 1960-72, chmn. finance com., 1963-72; trustee United Presbyn. Found., 1979-87, vice chmn., 1981-83, chmn., 1983-87; bd. regents Life Officers Investment Seminar, 1969-70; trustee Thompson Trust, 1976—, Frederick M. Hubbell Estate, 1977-85. Mem. Am. Coun. Life Ins. (chmn. fin. sect. 1970), Iowa Soc. Fin. Analysts (pres. 1965-67), Embassy Club, Masons, Rotary, Sigma Alpha Epsilon. Republican. Home: Des Moines, Iowa. Died Jan. 30, 2007.

RICHARDSON, CLYDE MYRON, agronomy extension agent; b. Wiggins, Colo., July 19, 1935; s. Albert Lee and Lucille R.; m. Dorothy Emilo, July 11, 1964; children:Catherine

Robert, Connie, Christy. BS in Agronomy, Colo. State U., 1957, BS in Vocat. Agr., 1962, MEd., 1971. With extension service Colo. State U., 1962—, agt. Golden Plains area extension, Wray, 1979—. Bd. dirs. Cliff Dwellers Acting and Singing Soc., Wray, pres., 1984-85. Served with U.S. Army, 1958-60. Recipient Colo. Gov.'s citation, 1965, Vance Lough Meml. trophy Colo. State Fair, 1969, recognition award Colo. Seed Growers Assn., 1979, Disting. Service award Nat. Assn. County Agrl. Agts. and Colo. Assn. County Agrl. Agts., 1983. Mem. Nat. County Agts. Assn. (winner Western Region Crop Prodn. award 1985), Colo. County Agts. Assn., Epsilon Sigma Phi. Home: Wray, Colo. Died May 23, 2006.

RICHARDSON, ROBERT OWEN, lawyer; b. Gallatin, Mo., Sept. 7, 1922; s. Denver Oscar and Opal (Wellman) R.; m. Carroll Sparks, July 7, 1951 (div.); children— Robert Steven, Linda Colleen; m. 2d, Viola Kapantais Wempe, Dec. 22, 1977. B.S. in Physics, Drury Coll., 1946; LL.B., George Washington U., 1954, J.D., 1968; M.S., Fla. Inst. Tech., 1977. Bar: U.S. Dist. Ct. (D.C.) 1954, U.S. Patent Office 1954, U.S. Ct. Customs and Patent Appeals 1958, Calif. 1958, N.H. 1961, Iowa 1976, U.S. Supreme Ct. 1961, Can. Patent Office, 1962, U.S. Ct. Appeals (fed. cir.) 1982. Patent examiner U.S. Patent Office, Washington, 1949-54; patent atty. Navy Electronics Lab., San Diego, 1954-56, Gen. Dynamics, San Diego, 1956-60; chief patent counsel Sanders Assoc., Nashua, N.H., 1960-62; patent atty. TRW, Canoga Park, Calif., 1963-64, McDonnell Douglas, Santa Monica, Calif., 1964-75; patent counsel U.S. Army Armament Munitions Chem. Command, Rock Island, Ill., 1975-85; patent arbitrator Am. Arbitration Assn., 1984—; judge pro tem Los Angeles Mcpl. Ct., 1967-68. Author: How To Get Your Own Patent, 1981, The Weird and Wondrous World of Patents, 1990. Democratic nominee for Congress from Mo. 6th Dist., 1951. Served to lt. comdr. USNR, 1942-73. Mem. MENSA, Govt. Patent Lawyer's Assn., Am. Patent Law Assn., Patent Law Assn. San Diego, Patent Law Assn. Los Angeles, Patent Law Assn. Boston, Patent Law Assn. Iowa. Lodges: Masons, Shriners. Home: Wheaton, Ill. Died Apr. 7, 2006.

RICHARDSON, RUTH GREENE, social worker; b. Washington, Mar. 30, 1926; d. Arthur Alonzo and Ruth Naomi (Conway) Greene; m. Frederick D. Richardson, June 7, 1968; 1 child, Arthur William Boler. BS, St. Louis U., 1948; MSW, Washington U., St. Louis, 1950. Exec. dir. Anna B. Heldman Cmty. Ctr., Pitts., 1962-64; assoc. dir. Hillhouse Assn., Pitts., 1964-67, Dixwell House; also supr. group work svcs. in cmty. schs. New Haven, 1967-69; exec. dir. Three Rivers Youth Inc., Pitts., 1969-91. Participated in juried nat. art shows: Westmoreland County Mus., 1992, Three Rivers Art, 1992; paintings exhibited in Pitts. region. Bd. dirs. Children's Coun. Western Pa.; adv. coun. Booth Home; bd. dirs. Nat. Assn. Homes for Children, Campfire Boys and Girls, 1988, South Arts, YWCA Greater Pitts. Recipient Social Assistance award, Pitts. region Women's Am. ORT, 1975, Internat. Yr. of Child award region III, HEW, 1979, Juror's award, 1991, Images Show, 1991, Pitts., Black Artists William Pitt Union Gallery, U. Pitts., 1986, Purchase prize, Images III Waterworks, 1st prize in watercolor, South Arts Sr. Citizen Show, Purchase prize, C.C. Show, Ann. Svc. award, Children's Coun. Western Pa., 1990, Best of the Show award, Carnegie Ethnic Art Show, 1993, Merit award, South Hills Art League, 1993, Best Floral award, Pitts. Garden Ctr., 1993, Real Pittsburgher award, Pitts. Mag., 1993, First place award, Native Am. Heritage Com., 1993, Best Overall Artistic Achievement award, Cranberry Area Coun. for the Arts, 1993, Cmty. Svc. award, Pitts. Club, Nat. Assn. Negro Bus. and Profl. Women's Club, Inc., 1993, Best of Show award, West Hills Art League, 1993, Outstanding Artistic Achievement award, Cranberry Two, Juried Art Exhibit, 3rd prize award, Pitts. Progressive Artist Annual Show, 1995, Native Am. Art Competition, 1995, 1st place, Westmoreland Heritage Nats., 1995, Merit award, 1997, 1st place, Schoolhouse Art Ctr., 1995, Best of Show, Bethel Park Art League Annual, 1995, 2nd place, Peoples Art Show, Carnegie, Eat and Park Gold Sable award, West Hills Art League Annual, 1996, 1st place Vol. in Arts award, 1996, Vols. in Arts award, 1996, 1998, One Imperative YWCA Racial Justice award, 1997, 1998, Artist of Yr. and Svc. Recognition, McMurray Art League, 1998, 1st place, School House Arts Show, Best of Show-Koppers Gallery, 1st place, Evangelica Lutheran Church Art Show, 1998, Jurors award, Watercolors Show in West Hills ann., 1999, st place in creation exhbn., 1998, Honorable Mention, North Hills Art Show, award of Excellence, South Arts. Com., Choice award, Native Am. Heritage Show, 2000, 2001. Mem. Child Welfare League Am., Nat. Assn. Social Workers, Pitts. Watercolor Soc. (treas.), Pa. Soc. Watercolor Painters, Pitts. Soc. Artist, Black Adminstrs. in Child Welfare, Creative Lens, Visions (v.p.), South Hills Art League (bd. dirs.). Died Oct. 2006.

RICHARDSON, WALKER SCOTT, retired insurance company executive; b. Chgo., Feb. 4, 1924; s. Lawrence and Dorothy (Fox) R.; m. Gloria Baxter, Jan. 20, 1951; children: Walker S., Jonathan M. AB, Cornell U., 1946; student Advanced Mgmt. Program, Harvard Bus. Sch., Boston, 1974. C.P.C.U. Various underwriting and actuarial positons Liberty Mut. Ins. Co., Boston, 1948-70, asst. v.p. actuarial dept., 1970-74, sr. v.p., mgr. personal lines, 1974-78, sr. v.p., mgr. underwriting, 1978-87; dir. Liberty Mut. and subs. cos. Dir. Am. Mut. Reinsurance Co., Chgo., 1980—, Ins. Services Office, N.Y.C., 1981— Chmn. capital outlay commn. City of Wakefield, Mass., 1963; incorporator Historic Harrisville Inc., N.H., 1972. Served with USN, 1942-45. Mem. Soc. C.P.U.s (pres. Boston chpt. 1955 cert. appreciation), Am. Acad. Actuaries Clubs: Algonquin (Boston); Monadnock Country (Petersboro, N.H.); Keene Country. Lodges: Good Samaritan. Republican. Episcopalian. Home: Harrisville, NH. Died Dec. 29, 2006.

RICHETTE, LISA AVERSA, judge; b. Phila., Sept. 11, 1928; d. Domenico and Maria (Giannini) Aversa; m. Lawrence J. Richette, Apr. 15, 1958 (div. Apr. 1971); 1 child, Lawrence Anthony II. BA summa cum laude, U. Pa., 1949; LLB, Yale U., 1952. Bar: Pa. 1954. Rsch. assoc. Yale U. Law Sch., 1952, instr., 1952-54; asst. dist. atty. Dist. Atty.'s Office, Phila., 1954-64, chief family ct. div., 1956-64; judge Ct. Common Pleas, Phila., 1972—2007. Lectr. Temple U. Law Sch., 1972—, adj. prof. law, 1972—; adj. prof. sociology dept. St. Joseph's U.; clin. prof. law Villanova (Pa.) U. Law Sch., 1970-72. Author: The Throwaway Children, 1969. Co-founder, bd. dirs. Big Sisters, Phila. YWCA, Nat. Commn. Child Abuse; pres. Phila. Health and Welfare Coun., 1958-60. Decorated Star of Solidarity (Italy); recipient Disting. Dau. of Pa. award Commonwealth Pa., 1991, St. Thomas More Lawyer of Yr. award, 1994. Mem. Phila. Bar Assn. (vice chmn. chancellor's commn. on drug abuse 1972-75), Justinian Soc., U. Pa. Women's Alumna Soc. (pres. 1966-70), Mortar Bd., Phi Beta Kappa, Phi Alpha Theta. Home: Philadelphia, Pa. Died Oct. 26, 2007.

RICHEY, HERBERT SOUTHALL, II, coal company executive; b. Cleve., June 26, 1922; s. Francis O. and Helen (Betteridge) R.; m. Martha J. Ewig, June 20, 1944; children: Suzanne, Francis O. II. BS, U. Mich., 1944. With Valley Camp Coal Co., Cleve., from 1946, pres., from 1960, chief exec. officer, from 1964, also bd. dirs.; pres. Richey Coal Co., Hot Springs, Va., from 1979. Dir., mem. exec. com., mem. compensation com. Union Savs. Assn., until 1979, Oglebay Norton Co., Sifco Industries, Inc.; bd. dirs., mem. compensation com., chmn. audit com., Fairchild Corp.; dir. mem. audit com., mem. ethics com. Fairchild Industries; v.p., dir. Washington Energy Processing, Inc., 1982. Bd. dirs., mem. compensation com. Nat. Ctr. for Productivity, Washington, 1976-77. Lt. USNR, 1943-46. Mem. U.S. C. of C. (dir. 1968-82, chmn. 1976-77, chmn. exec. com. 1977-78, mem. sr. coun., budget, exec. U.S.-Can. pub. affairs, pension plan investment coms., investment adv. coun.), Nat. Coal Assn. (dir., chmn. 1971-72), Ohio Coal Assn. (dir.), W.Va. Coal Assn. (dir.), Bituminous Coal Opers. Assn. (exec. com., dir., vice chmn. 1st del. of coal execs. to visti USSR coal mines 1970), Union Club, Va. Hot Spring Golf and Tennis Club. Home: Hot Springs, Va. Died Apr. 28, 2006.

RICHMOND, DAVID WALKER, retired lawyer; b. Silver Hill, W.Va., Apr. 20, 1914; s. David Walker and Louise (Finlaw) Richmond; m. Gladys Evelyn Mallard, Dec. 19, 1936; children: David Walker, Nancy L. LLB, George Washington U., 1937. Bar: DC 1936, Ill. 1946, Md. 1950. Assoc. Miller & Chevalier, 1936—46, ptnr., 1946—81; ret., 1981. Lectr. fed. taxation. Contbr. articles to profl. jours. Served to lt. comdr. USNR, 1942—46. Decorated Bronze Star; recipient Disting. Alumni Achievement award, George Washington U., 1976. Fellow: Am. Coll. Tax Counsel, Am. Bar Found.; mem.: ABA (chmn. taxation sect. 1955—57, ho. of dels. 1958—60), Am. Law Inst., Lawyers Club Washington, Masons. Republican. Methodist. Home: Sarasota, Fla. Died Jan. 23, 2007.

RICHTER, EARL EDWARD, manufacturing executive; b. Twin Lakes, Wis., Oct. 16, 1923; s. John Benjamin and Emma Augusta (Kautz) R.; m. Carlista Mae Dean, Sept. 12, 1943; children: Susan Dianne, Robert Dean. BBA, U. Wis.-Madison, 1948. C.P.A., Wis. With Modine Mfg. Co., Racine, Wis., from 1948, v.p., gen. mgr., 1963-74, pres., from 1974, chief operating officer, 1974, chief exec. officer, from 1974. Dir. M&I Bank of Racine, Portec Inc. Served with USAAF, 1943-45. Mem. Racine Mfrs. Assn. (dir.), Conf. Bd., Am. Mgmt. Assn. Clubs: Racine Country, Milw. Athletic. Lutheran. Home: Racine, Wis. Died Nov. 29, 2006.

RICKETTS, JOHN ADRIAN, retired chemistry professor; b. Lakewood, Ohio, Feb. 29, 1924; s. Edwin Virgil and Florence (Magaw) R.; m. Lucille Reininga, Feb. 5, 1948; children: Thomas Grant, Sarah Margaret. BS, Ind. U., 1948; MS, Western Res. U., 1950, PhD, 1953. Mem. faculty DePauw U., from 1952, prof. chemistry, 1962-89, Simeon Smith prof. chemistry, 1976-89, prof. emeritus, 1989—2007, chmn. dept., 1980-89. Summer vis. prof. Western Res. U., 1961, Ind. U., 1964, Purdue U., 1967; vis. prof. chemistry Univ. Coll., Dublin, 1976; vis. scientist Am. Chem. Soc.; cons. to industry. Contbr. articles in field. Served with AUS, 1943-45. Mem. Am. Chem. Soc., Electrochem. Soc., Faraday Soc., Sigma Xi, Alpha Chi Sigma, Phi Lambda Upsilon, Lambda Chi Alpha. Home: Bloomington, Ind. Died June 29, 2007.

RICKSECKER, RALPH EDWARD, metallurgical consultant; b. Cleve., Sept. 9, 1912; s. George Adolphus and Margaret (Tobold) R.; m. Ruth Arlene Iliff, Aug. 24, 1939; children— Ralph Edward, Ruth Ann. B.S., Case Western Res. U., 1944, M.S., 1950. Successively chem. analyst, chief chem. process metallurgist, chief metallurgist, dir. corp. metallurgy Chase Brass & Copper Co., Cleve., 1930-77; metall. cons., Cleve., 1978—. Contbr. articles on copper and copper alloys to profl. jours. Republican. Mem. Disciples of Christ. Avocations: growing plants from seed; wine making; wood working; reading. Died Aug. 25, 2007.

RIDDLE, RITA SIZEMORE, educator in English; b. Fleming, Ky., Sept. 26, 1941; d. Add and Jailey Lou Emma (Stallard) S.; m. Charlie White, July 11, 1959 (div. July, 1985); children: Henry David, Andrew Edward; m. David Coleman Riddle III, Feb. 12, 1987; 1 stepson, Remington Coleman Riddle. BS in English, E. Tenn. State U., 1963, MA in English, 1966; PhD in English, U. Tenn., Knoxville, 1971. English tchr. Ervinton H.S., Nora, Va., 1963-65, Coeburn (Va.) H.S., 1965-66, John I. Burton H.S., Radford, Va., 1966-68; prof. English Radford (Va.) U., from 1971. Author: (books) Pieces for Emma, 1992, Soot and Sunshine, 1993, Aluminum Balloons and other Poems, 1996; contbg. author to Stitches anthology, 1993. Recipient Writing residency awards, Breadloaf Writers Workshop, 1995, MacDowell Colony, 1998, Vermont Studio Ctr., 1998, Spoleto (Italy) Writers Workshop, 1998. Mem. Appalachin Writers Assn. (James Still award for poetry, 1995, essay award 1997), So. Appalachin Writers Conf., Nat. Assn. Tchrs. of English, Va. Assn. Tchrs. of English. Home: Radford, Va. Died Oct. 27, 2006.

RIDEOUT, WALTER BATES, English educator; b. Lee, Maine, Oct. 21, 1917; s. Walter John and Helen Ruth (Brickett) R.; m. Jeanette Lee Drisko, Aug. 2, 1947; children: Linda Carolyn, Richard Bates, David John. AB, Colby Coll., 1938; MA, Harvard U., 1939, PhD, 1950. Teaching fellow English Harvard U., 1946-49, asst. prof., summer 1954, prof., summer 1969; from instr. to assoc. prof. English Northwestern U., Evanston, Ill., 1949-63, dir. program Bell System execs., 1957-58, 59-61; prof. English U. Wis., Madison, from 1963, Harry Hayden Clark prof. English, from 1972, chmn. dept., 1965-68, sr. vis. prof. Inst. Research in Humanities, 1968-69. Vis. prof. U. Hawaii, summer 1977; Disting. lectr. English Kyoto Am. Studies Summer Seminar, Kyoto, Japan, 1981 Author: The Radical Novel in the United States, 1900-1954, 1956; editor: (with Howard Mumford Jones) Letters of Sherwood Anderson, 1953, (with James K. Robinson) A College Book of Modern Verse, 1958, A College Book of Modern Fiction, 1961, The Experience of Prose, 1960, I. Donnelly-Caesar's Column, 1960, (with G.W. Allen and J.K. Robinson) American Poetry, 1965, Sherwood Anderson: Collection of Critical Essays, 1974. Recipient MidAm. award Soc. for Study of Midwestern Lit., Mich. State U., 1983, Outstanding Educator award, 1993; fellow Newberry Libr., 1951, Guggenheim fellow, 1957; Fulbright grantee to Kyoto, 1981. Mem. ACLU, MLA (mem. nat. exec. council 1970-73), Phi Beta Kappa. Home: Madison, Wis. Died Apr. 8, 2006.

RIEGEL, NORMAN, physician; b. NYC, Jan. 22, 1935; children: Bram, Lisa, Karyn, Daniel; m. Joan Ann Gordon, June 17, 1973. AB, Columbia Coll., 1956; MD, Einstein Coll. Med., 1960. Diplomate Am. Bd. Internal Medicine. Intern U. Chgo., 1960-61; resident Kings County Hosp., Bklyn., N.Y., 1961-62; asst. resident Bellevue Hosp., NYC, 1962-63, GI fellow, 1963-64; pvt. practice Hackensack, N.J., from 1966; clin. assoc. prof. medicine Coll. Medicine and Dentistry of N.J., Newark, from 1977; chief dept. gastroeneterol. Bergen Pines County Hosp., Paramus, N.J., from 1970; dir. dept. medicine Bergen Pine County Hosp., Paramus, 1985-87, 89-96. Editor, Jour. of Med. Soc., 1983-87; contbr. numerous articles to profl jours. Served to capt. USAF, 1964-66. Fellow, Am. Coll. Gastroenterol., Am. Soc. Internal Medicine, Am. Coll. Physicians; mem., Am. Soc. Gastrointestinal Endoscopy, Bergen County Med Soc., N.J. Med. Soc. Home: Woodcliff Lk, NJ. Died Aug. 14, 2006.

RIEGER, CAROL T., lawyer; b. Chgo., Apr. 6, 1941; BA, Northwestern U., 1963, JD cum laude, 1973. Bar: Ill. 1973, Minn. 1984. Mem. Lindquist & Vennum, Mpls. Assoc. prof. law sch. U. Minn., 1983-87. Note and comment editor Jour. Criminal Law and Criminology, 1972-73. Mem. ABA, Order of Coif. Died Sept. 12, 2006.

RIEKE, WILLIAM OLIVER, foundation director, medical educator, former university president; b. Odessa, Wash., Apr. 26, 1931; s. Henry William and Hutoka S. (Smith) R.; m. Joanne Elynor Schief, Aug. 22, 1954; children: Susan Ruth, Stephen Harold, Marcus Henry. BA summa cum laude, Pacific Luth. U., 1953; MD with honors, U. Wash., 1958. Instr. anatomy U. Wash. Sch. Medicine, Seattle, 1958, asst. prof., 1961-64, adminstrv. officer, 1963-66, assoc. prof., 1964-66; prof., head dept. anatomy Coll. Medicine U. Iowa, Iowa City, 1966-71; dean protem Coll. Medicine U. Iowa (Coll. Medicine), 1969-70, chmn. exec. com., 1969-70; vice chancellor for health affairs, prof. anatomy U. Kans. Med. Center, Kansas City, 1971-73, exec. vice chancellor, prof. anatomy, 1973-75; affiliate prof. biol. structure U. Wash. Sch. Medicine, Seattle, 1975-96; pres. Pacific Lutheran U., Parkland, Wash., 1975-92; pres. emeritus, from 1992; exec. dir. Ben B. Cheney Found., from 1992. Mem. interdisciplinary gen. basic sci. test com. Nat. Bd. Med. Examiners, 1968-72, chmn. anatomy test com., 1972-75, mem. at large, 1975-79; spl. cons. NIH, 1970-72; mem. adv. com. Inst. Medicine, Nat. Acad. Scis., 1974-76; mem. Commn. on Colls., NW Assn. Schs. and Colls., 1979-84 Editor: Procs. 3d Ann. Leucocyte Culture Conf, 1969; editorial bd.: Am. Jour. Anatomy, 1968-71. Bd. dirs. Luth. Ednl. Council N. Am., 1980-83, pres., 1982-83; chmn. Wash. Friends Higher Edn., 1983-91. Named one of Most Effective Coll. or Univ. Pres., Bowling Green State U. Rsch. Study, 1986, Disting. Alumnus Pacific Luth. U., 1970, Disting. Alumnus Pi Kappa Delta, 1977, Disting. Alumnus U. of Washington Med. Alumni, 1989; decorated Knight First Class Royal Norwegian Order of Merit, 1989; named to Cashmere H.S. Wall of Fame, 1995. Lutheran (mem. ch. council 1967-70). Home: Tacoma, Wash. Died Apr. 22, 2006.

RIEKER, ANNE ELLORA, judge, humanitarian; b. Elmira, N.Y., Sept. 27, 1923; d. Eric Wendell and Viola Della (Hinkley) Phillips; m. Thomas Henry Rieker, Nov. 6, 1943; children: Constance Anne, Carla Anne, Thomas Eric. AS, Hershey Jr. Coll., 1943; student, Washburn U., 1958-59, U. Nev., 1982, 85. Dir. recreation therapy Extended Care Facility, Andover, N.J., 1967-70; exec. dir. Office on Aging, Sussex County, N.J., 1970-74; surrogate judge County of Sussex, Newton, N.J., 1975-89; mem. N.J. State Juvenile Delinquency/Commn., 1987—, N.J. State and Local Expenditure and Revenue Policy Commn., 1987-89, Local Govt. Policy Com. N.J. Dept. Pers. and Civil Svc., 1987-89. Trustee Knoll Heights Sr. Citizens Housing, Sparta, N.J., 1975-86; chmn. March of Dimes, Morristown, N.J., 1978-79; bd. dirs. Vis. Nurses Assn. Sussex County, Sparta, N.J., 1983—, pres., 1988—; chmn. govt. div., Sussex County United Way, 1985—, mem. allocation com., bd. dirs., 1988—; mem. N.J. Assembly Local Govt. Affairs Adv. Coun., 1988—, Sussex County Communities in Transition Planning Com., 1988—. Named Outstanding Citizen of Yr., VFW, 1975; recipient Vol. award March of Dimes, 1981, 82, 83, 84, 85. Mem. N.J. Assn. County Officers (pres. 1979-81), Nat. Coll. Probate Judges, Nat. Judges Assn., N.J. Assn. Counties (4th v.p. 1985, pres. 1987), N.J. Bar Assn. (assoc.), N.J. Assn. Elected Women Ofcls. (bd. dirs. 1981-83), Soroptomist (internat., v.p. 1985), Newton Country. Democrat. Espsicopanian. Avocations: music, golf, handcrafts, travel. Home: Lecanto, Fla. Died Aug. 8, 2006.

RIESS, JONATHAN BENJAMIN, art history educator, researcher; b. N.Y.C., Aug. 3, 1947; s. Chester Louis and Marion (Glazer) R.; m. Michele Morgan, June 15, 1980; 1 child, Christopher. B.A., Amherst Coll., 1968; M.A., Columbia U., 1970, M. in Philosophy, 1973, Ph.D., 1977. Preceptor, Columbia U., N.Y.C., 1971-73; asst. prof. U. Cin., 1976-81, assoc. prof., 1981—, chmn. dept. art history, 1981-84. Editor Midwest Art History Soc. Newsletter, 1982-83. Author: Political Ideals in Medieval Italian Art, 1981; contbr. articles to profl. jours. Kress Found., fellow, 1970, 72; Fulbright fellow, 1973; Woodbridge fellow Columbia U., 1973; Whiting fellow Columbia U., 1974; Harvard U. fellow Villa I Tatti, Florence, Italy, 1974; Am.

Philos. Soc. grantee. Mem. Midwest Art History Soc. (adv. bd. 1983-84), Coll. Art Assn., Renaissance Soc. Am. Democrat. Jewish. Avocations: hiking; tennis. Home: Cincinnati, Ohio. Died May 19, 2006.

RIGBY, PAUL CRISPIN, artist, cartoonist; b. Melbourne, Australia, Oct. 25, 1924; came to U.S., 1977; s. James Samuel and Violet Irene (Wood) R.; m. Marlene Anne Cockburn, Nov. 16, 1956; children: Nicole, Pia, Peter, Paul, Danielle. Student, Brighton Tech. Sch., Australia, Art Schs., Victoria, Victoria Nat. Gallery, Australia. Free lance artist, 1940-42; illustrator West Australian News, Ltd., 1948-52; editorial cartoonist Daily News Australia, 1952-69; daily cartoonist London Sun and News of the World, 1969-74; editorial cartoonist New York Post, 1977—84, 1993—2000, New York Daily News, 1984-93. Illustrator numerous books; represented in exhbns. of painting in, Australia, Europe and U.S.A.; Contbr. work to numerous publs., U.S., Europe, Asia. With Royal Australian Air Force, 1942-46. Decorated Order of Australia, knight comdr. Order of St. John, Knights of Malta; recipient Walkley award Australia, 1960, 61, 63, 66, 69; N.Y. Press Club award for art, 1981, 83, Page One award for excellence in journalism Newspaper Guild, 1982, 83, 84, 85. Mem.: Rolls Royce Owners, Royal Freshwater Bay Yacht; Friars, Players. Mem. Ch. Eng. Home: Palm Beach Gardens, Fla. Died Nov. 15, 2006.

RIGNEY, JAMES OLIVER, JR., (ROBERT JORDAN, CHANG LUNG, REAGAN O'NEAL, JACKSON O'REILLY), writer; b. Charleston, SC, Oct. 17, 1948; s. James Oliver and Eva May (Grooms) Rigney; m. Harriet Stoney Popham, Mar. 28, 1981; 1 child, William Popham McDougal. BS, The Citadel, 1974. Nuc. engr. U.S. Civil Svc., 1974—78. Author: Conan the Invincible, 1982, Conan the Defender, 1982, Conan the Triumphant, 1983, Conan the Unconquered, 1983, Conan the Destroyer, 1984, Conan the Magnificent, 1984, Conan the Victorious, 1985, The Eye of the World, 1990, The Great Hunt, 1990, The Dragon Reborn, 1991, The Shadow Rising, 1992, The Fires of Heaven, 1993, Lord of Chaos, 1994, A Crown of Swords, 1996, The Path of Daggars, 1998, Winter's Heart, 2000, Crossroads of Twighlight, 2003, New Spring, 2004, Knife of Dreams, 2005. Died Sept. 16, 2007.

RIKHYE, INDAR JIT, retired military officer; b. Lahore, India, July 30, 1920; arrived in U.S., 1960; s. Madan Lal and Raj (Rani) R.; m. Usha Erry, Mar. 5, 1946 (div. Jan. 1974); children: Ravi, Bhalinder; m. Cynthia De Haan, Feb. 13, 1974. Grad., Ind. Mil. Acad., 1939, Indian Def. Svcs. Staff Coll., 1952; LHD (hon.), U. Bridgeport, 1982; LLD (hon.), Carleton U., Ottawa, Ont., Can., 1987. Commd. officer Indian Army, 1939, advanced through grades to maj. gen.; chief staff UN Emergency Force, Gaza, Egypt, 1958-60, comdr. Gaza and Sinai. Egypt, 1966-67; mil. adv. to sec. gen. UN, NYC, 1960-69; ret., 1967; pres. Internat. Peace Acad., NYC, 1970-89, U.S.-India Soc., 1989-90. Disting. fellow U.S. Inst. of Peace, 1991, sr. adv. on UN Affairs; pres. Himtrek Adventures, Inc. Author: The Thin Blue Line, 1974, Sinai Blunder, 1978, Theory and Practice of Peacekeeping, 1984, Military Advisor to Hammerskjold and Thaunt, 1992. Recipient medal of honor Kyung Hee U., Seoul, 1981, prize for peace edn. UNESCO, 1985. Mem. India Internat. Ctr., India Coun. World Affairs, Indian Cavalry Officers Assn. (U.K. and India), Bronxville Field Club, Lake Isle Club (Eastchester, N.Y.), Army and Navy Club (Washington), Cavalry and Guards Club (London), Def. Svcs. Officers Club. Hindu. Home: Charlottesville, Va. Died May 21, 2007.

RIMERMAN, MORTON WALTER, utility executive; b. Wilmington, Del., Aug. 7, 1929; m. Helen Holland, Sept. 1960; 1 dau., Jennifer. BS, LaSalle Coll., 1958; MBA, Drexel U., 1962; postgrad. Exec. Devel. Program, Grad. Sch. Bus. and Pub. Adminstrn., Cornell U., 1973. With Phila. Electric Co., from 1948, asst. treas., 1970-73, treas., 1973-86, v.p. fin. and acctg., 1986-89; v.p. fin., 1989-90; v.p. fin., treas. PECO Energy Co., 1990-94. Trustee Magee Rehab. Hosp. With U.S. Army, 1951-53. Mem. Am. Gas Assn., Fin. Analysts of Phila., Fin. Execs. Inst., Edison Electric Inst. Died Feb. 14, 2006.

RINACA, JAMES M., lawyer; b. Harrisonburg, Va., Dec. 12, 1950; BS in Nuclear Engring. with highest distinction, Univ. Va., 1973, JD, 1976. Bar: Va. 1976. Ptnr., regulated industries, govtl. rels.; co-head, energy, telecom. team Hunton & Williams LLP, Richmond, Va. Mem.: ABA, Va. Engring. Found. (past pres., bd. dir.), Va. State Bar Assn., Richmond Bar Assn., Raven Soc., Omicron Delta Kappa, Tau Beta Pi. Died Dec. 6, 2006.

RINGEL, ROBERT LEWIS, academic administrator; b. NYC, Jan. 27, 1937; s. Benjamin Seymour and Beatrice (Salis) R.; m. Estelle Neuman, Jan. 18, 1959; children— Stuart Alan, Mark Joseph. BA, Bklyn. Coll., 1959; MS, Purdue U., 1960, PhD, 1962. cert. speech pathologist. Rsch. scientist, laryngeal rsch. lab. Ctr. Health Scis., UCLA, 1962-64; asst. prof. communication disorders U. Wis., 1964-66; from mem. faculty to provost Purdue U., 1966—91, provost, 1991—2001, prof. speech, lang. & hearing scis., Donald S. Powers disting. univ. adminstr., from 2001. Vis. prof. Inst. Neurology and Nat. Hosps. Coll. Speech Scis., U. London, 1985; cons. NIH, NEH, Bur. Edn. Handicapped of U.S. Office Edn.; bd. dirs. Indpls. Ctr. for Advanced Rsch., 1988-92; hon. prof. Coll. of Computer Scis. and Mgmt., Rzeszów, Poland, 2000—; bd. dir., faculty adv. Hillel Found. Purdue U., 2000-. Author sci. articles; contbr. to monographs and textbooks; cons. editor Chapman & Hall, London. Bd. dirs. Lafayette Home Hosp., 1978-87, Lafayette Symphony Orch., 1983-85. Recipient Rsch. Career Devel. award Nat. Inst. Dental Rsch., 1967-70, Award for highest merit for sci. article Jour. Speech and Hearing Rsch., 1979, Disting. Alumnus award Bklyn. Coll., 1985; Para-Rabbi fellow Hebrew Union Coll., 2001—; Robert L. Ringel Art Gallery at Purdue U. named in his honor. Fellow Am. Speech and Hearing Assn. (v.p. Found. 1990—, honors 1998); mem. Nat. Assn. State Univs. and Land Grant Colls. (exec. com. 1988-91, rsch. policy and grad. edn., exec. com. coun. on acad. affairs 1991-2001, com. on instnl. coop., exec. com. provosts instn. coop. com. 1991-2001), Sigma Xi (v.p. 1986-90). Home: West Lafayette, Ind. Died May 12, 2006.

RIORDAN, ROBERT EMMET, publisher; b. NYC, Jan. 20, 1930; s. Timothy Joseph and Anna Veronica (Sweeney) R.; m. Mary Anne Pfenninger, Dec. 28, 1957; children: Kathleen, Timothy, Robert. AB, St. Peter's Coll., 1951. Copywriter, mgr. circulation Esquire, Inc., NYC, 1956-60; mgr. subscription sales Conde Nast Pubs., NYC, 1961-65; mgr. circulation to sr. v.p. Newsweek Mag., NYC, 1965-76; chmn. Family Media, Inc., NYC, from 1976. Bd. dirs. Audit Bur. Circulations, Schaumburg, Ill. Served with U.S. Army, 1953-55. Mem.: Sky (N.Y.C.); Turnberry Yacht and Country, Williams Island Country (Miami). Home: Lghthse Point, Fla. Died May 12, 2006.

RISEMAN, EDWARD M., electrical engineering educator; b. Washington, Aug. 15, 1942; s. Harry and Matilda (Sandler) R.; married; children: Sarah, Seth. BSEE, Clarkson Coll. of Tech., 1964; MSEE, Cornell U., 1966, PhD in Elec. Engring., 1969. Asst. prof. computer sci. dept. U. Mass., 1969-73, assoc. prof. computer sci. dept., 1973-78, chmn. computer sci. dept., 1981-85, prof., dir. Computer Vision Lab., from 1978. Observer and cons. SRI, Menlo Park, Calif., 1978. Mem. editl. bd.: Internat. Jour. on Computer Vision, 1987—, Computer Vision, Graphics, and Image Processing, 1989-95; co-author: Computer Vision Systems, 1978; contbg. author books in field; contbr. articles to profl. jours. Rsch. grantee U.S. Army Rsch. Office, 1993-95, Advanced Rsch. Projects Agy., 1982-95, NSF, 1975-95, numerous others. Fellow AAAI. Died Feb. 26, 2007.

RISSER, WILLIAM RICHARD, JR., sales representative; b. Yeadon, Pa., Feb. 24, 1950; s. William Richard and Marion (Weng) R.; m. Barbara Jean Tegge, Mar. 6, 1971 (div. 1973); m. M. Carol Giver, Aug. 16, 1975. Student Drexel U., 1969-73. Salesman H & L Industries, Downingtown, Pa., 1973-78; salesman, sales mgr. Northeastern Wallcovering, Boston, 1978-80; salesman Collins and Aikman, Cleve., 1980—. Mem. Chester County Citizens Concerned About Life, West Chester (Pa.), 1984; treas. House of His Creation Maternity Home, Coatesville, (Pa.), 1985. Mem. Cloud Niner's Soaring Club (pres.). Republican. Presbyterian. Avocations: gliding; skiing; bicyling. Home: Narvon, Pa. Died Aug. 12, 2007.

RIVERS, WILGA MARIE, language educator; b. Melbourne, Australia, Apr. 13, 1919; arrived in U.S., 1970; d. Harry and Nina Diamond (Burston) Rivers. BA, U. Melbourne, 1939, diploma in Edn., 1940, MA, 1948; Licence es L., U. Montpellier, France, 1952; PhD, U. Ill., 1962; MA (hon.), Harvard U., 1974; PhD of Langs. (hon.), Middlebury Coll., 1989. H.S. tchr., Victoria, Australia, 1940-48; asst. in English lang. France, 1949-52; tchr. prep. schs., 1953-58; asst. prof. French No. Ill. U., DeKalb, 1963-64; assoc. prof. Monash U., Australia, 1964-69; vis. prof. Columbia U., 1970-71; prof. French U. Ill., Urbana-Champaign, 1971-74; prof. Romance langs. and lit., coord. lang. instrn. Harvard U., 1974-89, prof. emerita, from 1989. Cons. NEH, Ford Found., Rockefeller Found., others; lectr 44 countries and throughout U.S.; mem. adv. bd. Modern Lang. Ctr., Ont. Inst. for Studies in Edn., Nat. Fgn. Lang. Ctr., Lang. Acquire Rsch. Ctr., San Diego. Author: The Psychologist and the Foreign-Language Teacher, 1964, Teaching Foreign-Language Skills, 1968, 2d edit., 1981, Speaking in Many Tongues, 1972, 3d edit., 1983, A Practical Guide to the Teaching of French, 1975, 2d edit., 1988, 3d edit. (on Web), 2001, Opportunities for Careers in Foreign Languages, 1993; co-author: A Practical Guide to the Teaching of German, 1975, 2d edit., 1988, A Practical Guide to the Teaching of Spanish, 1976, 2d edit., 1988, A Practical Guide to the Teaching of English as a Second or Foreign Language, 1978, Communicating Naturally in a Second Language, 1983, Teaching Hebrew: A Practical Guide, 1989, others; editor, contbr. Interactive Language Teaching, 1978, Teaching Languages in College: Curriculum and Content, 1992, Down Under/Up Top: Creating a Life, 2004; writing translated into 11 langs.; editl. bd. Studies in Second Language Acquisition, Applied Linguistics, Language Learning, Mosaic, System; adv. com. Can. Modern Lang. Rev.; contbr. articles to profl. jours. Decorated chevalier des Palmes Académiques; recipient Disting. Fgn. Lang. Leadership award N.Y. State Assn. Fgn. Lang. Tchrs., 1974, Disting. Alumni award U. Ill., 1999, Dean's Disting. Svc. award Harvard Continuing Edn., 2004. Mem. MLA, Am. Assn. Applied Linguistics (charter pres.), Am. Coun. on Tchg. Fgn. Langs. (Florence Steiner award 1977, Anthony Papalia award 1988), Mass. Fgn. Lang. Assn. (Disting. Svc. award 1983), Tchrs. of English to Spkrs. of other Langs., Am. Assn. Tchrs. French, Linguistic Soc. Am., Am. Assn. Univ. Suprs. and Coords. Fgn. Lang. Programs Northeast Conf. (Nelson Brooks award 1983), Internat. Assn. Applied Psycholinguistics (v.p. 1983-89), Japan Assn. Coll. English Tchrs. (hon.), Am. Assn. Tchrs. German (hon.), Internat. Assn. Lang. Labs. (hon.). Episcopalian. Died June 23, 2007.

RIVOIRE, JOHN, marketing consultant; b. Pawling, NY, Dec. 10, 1921; s. John Louis and Anne Ross (Mackenzie) Rivoire; m. Jeanne Louise Hopson, 1951 (div. 1956); m. Alice Cecilia Sanderson, 1959. BS, Cornell U., Ithaca, NY, 1942, MBA, 1948. Mktg. analyst Pfizer, Inc., NYC, 1952—55; mgr. market rsch. FMC Corp., NYC, 1955—58; mktg. cons. NYC, 1958—69, from 1984; writer, editor Chem. Week Mag., McGraw-Hill, Inc., NYC, 1969—84. First lt. US Army, 1942—46, NATOUSA, ETO. Mem.: Chem. Mgmt. and Resources Assn. Democrat. Avocations: photography, travel. Died Jan. 8, 2007.

RIZLEY, ROBERT SEAL, federal magistrate; b. Guymon, Okla., June 11, 1923; s. Ross and Ruby Elaine (Seal) R.; m. Katherine Louise Kemp, Sept. 5, 1953 (div.); children— Mary Katherine Rizley Davis, Sarah Louise, Robert Kemp, Nancy Carron, Julia Ann Rizley Stewart. B.A., Okla. U., Norman, 1949; LL.B., U. Mich., 1953. Bar: Okla. 1953, U.S. Dist. Ct. (we., ea. and no. dists.) Okla. 1955, U.S. Ct. Appeals (10th cir.) 1955, U.S. Supreme Ct. 1959. With legal dept. Skelly Oil Co., 1953-54; asst. U.S. atty. Dept. Justice, 1954-55; assoc., ptnr. Martin, Logan, Moyers, Martin & Hull, 1955-59; U.S. atty. No. Dist. Okla., 1959-61; ptnr. Crawford & Rizley; ptnr. Rizley, Prichard Norman & Reed, until 1977; magistrate U.S. dist. Ct. (no. dist.) Okla., Tulsa, 1977-85; ptnr. Shallcross & Rizley, 1985—. Bd. dirs. Tulsa Opera Inc., 1955—, pres., 1956-59, 75-77. Served to capt. USMC, 1942-46, 51-52. Mem. ABA, Okla. Bar Assn., Phi Delta Phi. Republican. Methodist. Died Oct. 31, 2006.

RIZZUTO, PHIL (PHILIP FRANCIS RIZZUTO, SCOOTER), sports broadcaster, retired professional baseball player; b. Brooklyn, NY, Sept. 25, 1917; s. Fiore Francesco and Rose Rizzuto. m. Cora Rizzuto; 4 children, 2 grandchildren. Shortstop N.Y. Yankees, NYC, 1941-43, 46-56, radio and TV broadcaster, 1956-96. USN, Pacific theatre, 1943-45. Named to MLB All-Star game, 1942, 1950-1953, named MLB MVP, 1950, World Series MVP, 1951; inducted into the Baseball Hall of Fame, 1994. Achievements include mem. World Series Champion New York Yankees, 1941, 1947, 1949-1953; #10 retired by the New York Yankees, 1985. Died Aug. 14, 2007.

ROACH, MAXWELL LEMUEL, musician; b. Elizabeth City, NC, Jan. 10, 1924; s. Alphonzo and Cressie (Saunders) R.; m. Mildred Wilkinson, Jan. 14, 1949 (div.); children: Daryl, Maxine; m. Abbey Lincoln, Mar. 3, 1962 (div.). Student, Manhattan Sch. Music, NYC; Mus.D. (hon.), New Eng. Conservatory Music, 1982. Prof. music U. Mass., 1973—2007. Adapted use of tympani in jazz; musician specializing percussion instruments; with Charlie Parker, 1946-48, later appeared with Thelonious Monk, Bud Powell, Dizzy Gillespie; co-leader Max Roach-Clifford Brown Quintet; with Sonny Rollins, Harold Land, 1954-56, later with Booker Little, Ray Bryant, Eric Dolphy; appearances at Paris Jazz Festival, 1949, Newport Jazz Festival, 1972; composer: integration of jazz and dance Freedom Now suite; albums include: Percussion Bitter Sweet, It's Time, Drums Unlimited, Speak Brother Speak, The Loadstar, Conversations, Long as You're Living, Survivors, The Long March, Jazz in 3/4 Time, Scott Free, To the Max!, 1991, It's Time, 1996, The New Orchestra of Boston and The So What Brass Quintet, 1996 (with Dizzy Gillespie) Max and Dizzy: Paris 1989; producer, dir. and choreographer. Recipient Best Record of Year award Down Beat mag. 1956; winner Down Beat poll 1955, 57, 58, 59, 60, 84, metronome poll 1951-54. Mem. Jazz Artists Guild Inc. (organizer), Am. Acad. and Inst. of Arts and Letters (Hon.), 1992. Died Aug. 16, 2007.

ROACH, THOMAS J., insurance executive; b. New Rochelle, NY, Oct. 31, 1932; s. John Joseph and Beatrice F. (Carton) R.; m. Rosemary E. McCaffrey. Oct. 31, 1959; children: Debbie, Thomas. BS in Econs., Fordham U., 1954; grad. advanced mgmt. program, Harvard U., 1982. Sr. v.p. ops. and systems Equitable Life Ins. Co., NYC, 1957-85; sr. v.p. telecommunications Mut. of Am., NYC, from 1985. Chmn. ins. div. United Way, Columbus, Ohio, 1980. Served to 1st lt. U.S. Army, 1954-56. Mem. Life Office Mgmt. Assn. (bd. dirs. 1984-88), Harvard Bus. Sch. Club N.Y. Clubs: Larchmont Shore (N.Y.). Roman Catholic. Avocation: baseball card collecting. Home: New Rochelle, NY. Died Feb. 15, 2007.

ROBBINS, HARVEY ARNOLD, textile company executive; b. NYC, Apr. 29, 1922; s. Ira B. and Mildred (Lowy) R.; m. Carolyn Edith Goldsmith, June 8, 1947; children: Margaret Ann (Mrs. Lew Enker), James Andrew. Student, U. Mich., 1940-42, Cornell U., 1943, Columbia U., 1945. V.p. Silberstein-Goldsmith, NYC, 1946-50, North Advt., Chgo., 1950-59, M. Lowenstein & Sons, Inc., NYC, also pres. Wamsutta/Pacific Domestic divsn., 1959-69; pres. Burlington Domestics divsn. Burlington Industries, 1969-73; v.p. United Mchts. & Mfrs., 1973-78, PRF Corp., 1978-80; exec. v.p. Whisper Soft Mills, NYC, 1980-84; dir. product devel. Springs Industries, 1984-85, textile cons., from 1985. Bd. dir. Ednl. Found. for Fashion Industries; corp. mem. Lesley Coll., Cambridge, Mass. With U.S. Army, 1942-45. Decorated Purple Heart, Combat Inf. badge. Mem. Am. Mgmt. Assn., Am. Arbitration Assn., Textile Distbrs. Assn., U. Mich. Alumni Club. Died May 1, 2007.

ROBBINS, JAMES O., retired communications executive; b. Mt. Kisco, NY, July 4, 1942; m. Debby Robbins; children: Jane, Payson, Hilary. BS in Am. Studies, U. Pa.; MBA, Harvard U., 1972. Mng. editor WBZ-TV News, Boston, 1969-72; mgmt. position Continental Cablevision, 1972-79, Montachusett Cable TV, 1972-79; v.p., gen. mgr. Viacom Cablevision, LI, NY, 1979-83; pres., CEO Cox Comm., Inc., 1983—2005. Bd. dirs. NCR Corp., Teleport Communications, Inc., TeleWest., Cox Enterprises, 2006-07 Treas., bd. dirs. Nat. Cable Television Assn., exec. com. Cable Satellite Pub. Affairs Network; v.p. Cable in Classroom; trustee Westminster Sch., Atlanta. Died Oct. 10, 2007.

ROBBINS, KENNETH L., advertising agency executive; b. Berkeley, Calif., Aug. 28, 1935; BA, U. Pa. With J.W. Thompson, 1963-80; Exec. v.p. SSC&B (now Lintas Worldwide), N.Y.C., 1980—; now chmn., CEO Lintas Worldwide; bd. dirs. The Interpublic Group of Cos., Inc. Home: Hastings Hdsn, NY. Died Apr. 11, 2006.

ROBBINS, PAUL HEBERT, civil engineer; b. Syracuse, NY, Feb. 15, 1914; s. James H. and Jessie E. (Lair) R.; m. Hester Becker, Apr. 24, 1937; children: Susan Jane, David Paul. BS, Syracuse Univ., NY, 1935; S.M., MIT, 1936; postgrad., Columbia U., 1938-41; D.Eng., Rose Poly. Inst., 1964, Norwich U., 1979. Registered profl. engr. Draftsman and estimator Pitts. Bridge & Iron Works, 1936-37; mem. civil engring. faculty Cooper Union, 1937-41, U. Maine, summers 1938, 39, 40, NYU, summer 1939; lectr. civil engring. Cooper Union, 1941-46; cons. engring. tng. NYC, 1941-43; expert examiner (engring.), 1938-42; dir. civilian tng. N.Y. Port of Embarkation, 1943-45, dir. tng. and employee relations, 1945-46; exec. dir. Nat. Soc. Profl. Engrs., Washington, 1946-78. Sec. Nat. Soc. Profl. Engrs. Ednl. Found.; Mem. several adv. coms. to Fed. Govt. Author: (with B.B. Talley) Photographic Surveying, 1944, Building for Professional Growth, 1984. Bd. visitors Norwich U. Served as cons. on tng. U.S. Army Transp. Corp, 1944-46. Received War Dept. Commendation for Meritorious Service, 1946 Fellow AAAS; mem. Soc. Am. Mil. Engrs., Nat. Soc. Profl. Engrs. (award for contbns. to engring. profession 1984), Jr. Engring. Tech. Soc. (dir. 1969-79), Am. Soc. Engring. Edn., Tau Beta Pi (dir. fellowships 1947-78, pres. 1982-86), Phi

Kappa Phi, Delta Sigma Rho, Sigma Tau. Clubs: University, Columbia. Lodges: Rotary. Republican. Congregationalist. Home: Silver Spring, Md. Died Dec. 18, 2006.

ROBBINS, SARA ELLEN, law librarian, educator; b. Balt., Mar. 3, 1952; d. Malcolm Lee and Norma Robbins. BA, U. Cin., 1974; MLS, Pratt Inst., 1977; JD, Ohio State U., 1985. Bar: Ohio 1985. Cataloger Bklyn. Law Sch. Libr., 1977-79, assoc. libr., 1984-85, acting dir., 1985-86, dir., from 1986. Head tech. svcs. Cardozo Law Sch. Libr., N.Y.C., 1979-81; rsch. editorial asst. Law Sch. Libr., Yale U., New Haven, 1982-83. Author: Surrogate Parenting: Annotated Review of the Literature, 1984, Baby M Case: The Complete Trial Transcripts, 1988, Law: A Treasury of Art and Literature, 1990; (with others) Library Automation: A Systems and Software Sampler, 1985. Recipient Am. Jurisprudence award Lawyer's Coop. Pub. Co., 1984. Mem. ABA, Ohio Bar Assn., Am. Assn. Law Librs., Law Libr. Assn. Greater N.Y. Home: Brooklyn, NY. Died Dec. 13, 2006.

ROBERTS, JAMES E., civil engineer; b. Jameson, Mo., Nov. 24, 1930; BS, U. Calif. Berkeley, 1953; MS, U. So. Calif., 1966. Registered profl. engr., Calif. Mgr. bridge design sect. Calif. Dept. Transp., 1968-72, chief engr. equipment divsn., 1976—81, from project dir. to chief dep. dir. ops. and engring., 1981—2001; with Imbsen and Assocs., Sacramento, from 2001. Fellow ASCE (Constrn. Mgmt. award 1996); mem. Nat. Acad. Engring., Am. Concrete Inst., Am. Welding Soc., Am. Assn. State Hwy. & Transp. Ofcls. Home: Carmichael, Calif. Died July 5, 2006.

ROBERTS, NEIL FLETCHER, management consulting company executive; b. Salem, Oreg., Feb. 4, 1914; s. Harold D. and Rhoda (Haynes) R.; m. Lee (Roberts) R., June 23, 1937; children— Stephen L., Susan A. (Mrs. J.B. Persson). AB, Dartmouth Coll., 1935; MBA, Harvard U., 1937. With United Bank Denver N.A. (formerly U.S. Nat. Bank, merger with Denver Nat. Bank 1959, became Denver U.S. Nat. Bank), 1937—, v.p., 1948-54, exec. v.p., 1954-62, pres., 1962-69, vice chmn., from 1971, chief exec. officer, 1969-71; v.p. United Banks Colo., Inc. (formerly Denver U.S. Bancorp., Inc.), 1964-70, exec. v.p., 1971-72, pres., 1972-77, chief exec. officer, 1974-79, chmn. bd., 1977-79; chmn. United Mortgage Co., 1971-74, dir., 1968-71, 74-77; chmn. United Banks Service Co., 1971-75, dir., 1975-77. Trustee Mile High United Way, 1971-79, chmn., pres., 1969-71. Served as lt. (j.g.) USNR, 1944-46. Mem. Phi Kappa Sigma. Episcopalian. Home: Englewood, Colo. Died Dec. 11, 2005.

ROBERTSON, GEORGE LEONARD, lawyer; b. Austin, Tex., Aug. 28, 1922; s. George Leonard and Pensive (Cocke) R.; m. Elizabeth Lauretta Reilly, Dec. 28, 1946; children— Nancy, Patricia, George Philip, Carol, David BBA, U. Tex., 1943, LL.B., 1948. Bar: Tex. 1948. Atty. Atlantic Refining Co., Dallas, 1948-52; ptnr. Barrow, Bland, Robertson & Rehmet, Houston, 1952-58, Butler & Binion, Houston, from 1958. Served to lt. USNR, 1943-46 Mem. ABA, State Bar Tex., Houston Bar Assn. Clubs: Petroleum (Houston). Methodist. Home: Houston, Tex. Died Mar. 27, 2007.

ROBINSON, DANIEL THOMAS, brokerage company executive; b. Los Angeles, June 17, 1925; s. George Thomas and Helen Theresa (Walsh) R.; m. Diane W. Robinson; children— Marc David, Matthew Curtis. BS, U. So. Calif., 1948, MBA, 1950. Pres. Horton & Converse Inc., from 1961; v.p. Dart Industries, Inc., Los Angeles, 1962-63; sr. v.p. Bergen Brunswig Corp., Los Angeles, 1972-80; dir. bus. devel. Merrill Lynch, Los Angeles, 1981-82; with Internat. Network Brokerage, from 1983. Bd. dirs. K.D.L. Corp., Home Interstate Bank Fin. Svcs., Healthbank Corp. Author: Medical Marketing of Seventies, 1968, Marketing Challenges of Biomedical Industry, 1969, Biomedical Marketing, 1975, Biomedical Representation, 1976, Real Estate Funding Principles, 1988, Desert Properties for a Future, 1988, Sea and Desert Investments, 1989, Principles of Network Brokerage Marketing, 1991, Medical Products Brokerage Avocation, 1993, Brokerage Marketing Through Network Brokers, 1996. Past pres., bd. dirs. Trojan Club, U. So. Calif.; past pres. Cardinal and Gold; past pres. U. So. Calif., bd. councillors. Mem. Am. Coll. Pharmacists (dir., past pres.), Am., Man. surg. trade assns., Health Industries Assn. Died Apr. 29, 2006.

ROBINSON, EDDIE GAY, retired college football coach; b. Jackson, La., Feb. 13, 1919; s. Frank Robinson & Lillie Stewart; m. Doris Mott Robinson; children: Lillian Rose, Eddie Jr. BA, Leland Coll., 1940; MS, U. Iowa, 1954; LLD (hon.), La. Tech. Head coach Grambling State U. (formerly Louisiana Negro Normal & Industrial Inst.), La., 1941—97; v.p. athletics Grambling State U., La., asst. v.p. univ. rels. La., sr. adv. to pres. for nstnl. advancement La. Head coach East-West Shrine Game, 1977. Co-author (with Richard Lapchick): Never Before, Never Again: The Autobiography of Eddie Robinson, 1999; co-author: (with Aaron S. Lee) Quotable Eddie Robinson: 408 Memorable Quotes about Football, Life, and Success, by and about College Football's All-time Winningest Coach, 2003. Recipient: Whitney M. Young Jr. Meml. award NY Urban League, 1983, Molder of Champion award B'nai B'rith Internat., 1988, Horatio Alger award Nat. Football Found., 1988, Heritage award, 1990, Maxwell award Maxwell Found., 1991, Francis J. Reds Bagnell award, Maxwell Club, 1991, Outstanding Contribution to Amateur Football award, 1992, Bobby Dodd award, 1993; Spl. Commendations from Pres. Ronald Reagan, Nat. Collegiate Athletic Assn., U.S. Congress, State of La., B'nai B'rith; inducted into Coll. Football Hall of Fame, 1997 Mem. Nat. Assn. Sports & Phys. Edn., Nat. Assn. Intercollegiate Athletics, Southwestern Athletic Conf., La. Sports Hall of Fame, Pop Warner, Sugar Bowl, Black Coll. Achievements include winning 10 nat. Black coll. football championships; retired as head coach of Grambling State University with 408 career victories. Died Apr. 3, 2007.

ROBINSON, HUGH R., retired marketing executive; b. Syracuse, NY, Sept. 18, 1922; s. Frank J. and Gladys (Hunt) R.; m. Evelyn De Mattia, Nov. 24, 1949; children: Susan, Hugh R., Patrice. BS, Syracuse U., 1949. Dist. mgr. Syracuse China, 1949-59; with Royal Worcester Porcelain Co., NYC, 1959-77, v.p. sales, 1971-75, pres., 1975-76, Royal Worcester Spode, Inc., 1977, Lance Internat., NYC, 1977-84; v.p., dir. Caithness Glass Inc., NYC, 1980-84; v.p. sales and mktg. Weil Ceramics & Glass Inc., 1985-86, CEO, exec. v.p., 1986-88; CEO LLadro U.S.A. Inc., 1988-91; v.p. Lladro Realty, Inc., 1988-94, Lladro Galleries, Inc., 1988-94; retired, 1994. Advisor Lladro Group, Valencia, Spain, 1991-97; cons. in giftware industry. Served with USAAF, 1942-46. Mem. Alumni Assn. Syracuse U. Home: Bradenton, Fla. Died Mar. 14, 2007.

ROBINSON, JOSEPH ROBERT, pharmacy educator; b. NYC, Feb. 16, 1939; s. Alton Josiah and Eva Marie (Parker) R.; married, Oct. 28, 1958; children: James Colin, Nancy Lynn, Daniel George. BS, Columbia U., 1961, MS, 1963; PhD, U. Wis., 1966; D of Honoris Causa (hon.), Royal Danish Sch. Pharmacy, 1992. From asst. prof. to prof. Sch. Pharmacy U. Wis., Madison, from 1966. V.p. R & D Columbia Labs., Miami, Fla., 1987—; disting. lectr. U. Leiden, Netherlands. Editor: Controlled Drug Delivery, 1978, Ocular Drug Delivery, 1990. Recipient Ebert prize Am. Pharmacy Assn., 1988, Rsch. Achievement award, 1991; Nagai lectureship Japan Pharm. Assn., Tokyo, 1990. Fellow AAAS, Am. Assn. Pharm. Sci. (pres. 1990); mem. Controlled Release Soc. (pres. 1990). Republican. Baptist. Home: Madison, Wis. Died Sept. 4, 2006.

ROBINSON, LILLIAN ARBELL, insurance agency executive; b. Rome, Ga., Aug. 2, 1922; d. Malvin Roeser and Birdie Lee (Draper) Brown; m. Glen G. Robinson, Mar. 3, 1942; children— Glenda Lee Robinson Stanley, Robert Gary. Student Gregg Bus. Coll., Phoenix, 1940-41, Ins. Inst. Am., Phoenix, 1978-83, Soc. Cert. Ins. Counselor, Tempe, Ariz. 1981. Acct. Thunderbird Flight Sch. Glendale, Ariz., 1941-42; co-owner Glenzona Ins., Glendale, 1960-80, office mgr., 1975-80, owner, mgr., 1980—; co-dir., owner H & R Assocs. Investments, Glendale, 1947—; co-owner, bd. dirs. Lake Mary Park Investments, 1960—. Pres. Women's Soc. Bethany Bible, Phoenix, 1960-65; bd. dirs. Camelback Girls Residence Aux., Phoenix, 1970-71. Mem. Kachina West Ins. Women, Nat. Assn. Ins. Women (cert. profl. ins. woman). Republican. Home: Glendale, Ariz. Died Aug. 21, 2006.

ROBINSON, NELL BRYANT, nutrition educator; b. Kopperl, Tex., Oct. 15, 1925; d. Basil Howell and Lelia Abiah (Duke) Bryant; m. Frank Edward Robinson, July 14, 1945 (dec.); 1 child, John Howell. BS, North Tex. State U., 1945; MS, Tex. Woman's U., 1958, PhD, 1967. Registered dietitian, Tex. Tchr. Comanche H.S., Tex., 1945-46, Kopperl H.S., 1946-48; county extensin agt. Agrl. Extension Svc., Tex., 1948-56; prof. nutrition Tex. Christian U., Ft. Worth, 1957—92, chmn. dept. nutrition and dietetics, 1985-91; ret., 1992. Contbr. chpt. to book. Pres., bd. dirs. Sr. Citizens Svcs. Greater Tarrant County, 1990-91. Named Top Prof., Tex. Christian U. Mortar Bd., 1978. Mem. Am. Dietetic Assn. (del. 1983-88, ethics com. 1985-88, coun. edn. 1988-90, chmn. coun. on edn. divsn. edn. accreditation and approval 1989-90, Medallion award 1990), Am. Assn. Family and Consumer Scis., Tex. Dietetic Assn. (pres. 1972-73, Disting. Dietitian awafd 1981), Tex. Assn. Family and Consumer Scis. (pres. 1978-80, Home Economist of Yr. award 1975), Ft. Worth Women's Club, Order Ea. Star. Home: Fort Worth, Tex. Died Aug. 11, 2006.

ROBINSON, SUMNER MARTIN, college administrator; b. Boston, Dec. 7, 1928; s. Eli and Fannie (Solov) R.; m. Leanore Reiss, Dec. 20, 1953; children: Andrew, Eric, Evan. AB, U. Maine, 1949; BS, Mass. Coll. Pharmacy, 1954, MS, 1956, PhD, 1961. Asst. prof. pharmacology Mass. Coll. Pharmacy, Boston, 1961-65; research biologist-pharmacologist U.S. Army Research Inst. Environ. Medicine, Natick, Mass., 1965-76, cons., from 1976; dean Mass. Coll. Pharmacy, Boston, 1976-83; pres. St. Louis Coll. Pharmacy, 1983-93, Mass. Coll. Pharmacy & Applied Health Sci., Boston, from 1993. Recipient Coll. medal Mass. Coll. Pharmacy, 1983 Mem. Am. Assn. Colls. Pharmacy, Am. Pharm. Assn., Nat. Assn. Retail Druggists. Democrat. Home: Sharon, Mass. Died Feb. 25, 2007.

ROBINSON, THOMAS BULLENE, retired civil engineer; b. Kansas City, Mo., Feb. 28, 1917; s. David Beach and Aileen March (Weaver) R.; m. Suzanne Callaway, May 24, 1941; children: Suzanne, Thomas Bullene, Alice Robinson Levy. BS, Kans. U., 1939; MS, Columbia U., 1940. Diplomate: Am. Acad. Environ. Engrs. Asst. engr. Black & Veatch (cons. engr.), Kansas City, 1940-43, prin. asst. engr., prin. engr., 1946-56, partner, 1956-65, asst. mng. partner, 1965-72, mng. partner, 1973-82. Chmn. bd. Black & Veatch Internat., 1973-82; cons., 1982—. Past pres. Heart of Am. United Campaign; trustee Kansas City U., U. Kans. Endowment Assn., Midwest Research Inst. Served to lt. Civil Engr. Corps, USNR, 1943-46. Recipient Honor award for disting. service in engring. U. Mo., 1971; Disting. Service citation U. Kans., 1975; Disting. Engring. Service award U. Kans., 1982 Fellow ASCE (hon. mem.), Am. Cons. Engrs. Council (pres. 1970-71); mem. Nat. Acad. Engring., Nat. Soc. Profl. Engrs., Am. Water Works Assn. (hon.), Sigma Xi, Tau Beta Pi, Sigma Tau, Beta Theta Pi. Clubs: Kansas City Country (Kansas City). Home: Lenexa, Kans. Died Jan. 16, 2006.

ROBINSON, WAYNE E., lawyer; b. Grant, Mich., Mar. 17, 1928; s. Clarence Allen and Gladys (Brown) R.; m. Lillian Fernandez, June 26, 1954; children— Liliana Robinson Graham, Wayne E. B.A. in Econs., Mich. State U., 1949, M.A. in Econs., 1951; J.D., Suffolk U., 1968. Bar: Mass. 1968, Colo. 1978. Commd. 1st lt. U.S. Air Force, 1954, advanced through grades to lt. col., 1971; asst. prof. air sci. U. P.R., 1960-64; adv. to Vietnam Air Force, 1969-70; staff judge adv. Air Force Acctg. and Fin. Ctr., Denver, 1974-78, ret., 1978; sole practice Aurora, Colo., 1978—. Decorated Bronze Star medal, Meritorious Service medal, Legion of Merit; recipient Disting. Fed. Atty. award Denver Fed. Exec. Bd., 1977. Mem. Fed. Bar Assn. (v.p. 1975-76, Earl W. Kintner award 1976), Colo. Bar Assn., Aurora Bar Assn. (pres. 1981-82), ABA, Am. Soc. Mil. Comptrollers, Air Force Assn. Republican. Roman Catholic. Lodge: Rotary. Home: Boulder, Colo. Died Aug. 16, 2007.

ROBINSON, WILLIAM PETERS, JR., state legislator; b. Washington, Oct. 14, 1942; m. Sylvia T. Thompson; children: William P. III, Trevor J., Justin M., Danica A. BA, Morehouse Coll., 1964; LLB, Harvard U., 1967. Mem. Va. State Legis., from 1981, co-chair transp. com., mem. appropriations com., mem. corps. ins. & banking com., mem. militia & police com. Democrat. Episcopalian. Died Dec. 18, 2006.

ROBY, JASPER, bishop; b. Miss., Apr. 19, 1912; m. Malinda Roby; 6 children. Sr. bishop, exec. head Apostolic Overcoming Holy Ch. of God, Inc., Birmingham, Ala. Died Mar. 29, 2006.

ROCA, GASPAR, newspaper publisher; Founder, pub. El Vocero de Puerto Rico, Old San Juan, 1974—2007. Died Apr. 8, 2007.

ROCHE, JOHN JEFFERSON, retired lawyer; b. NYC, Apr. 12, 1934; s. William and Florence E. (Garvey) R.; m. Judith J. Stackpole, Sept. 4, 1980; 1 child from previous marriage, Forrest B. AB, Brown U., 1957; LL.B., Boston U., 1964. Bar: Mass. 1964, U.S. Tax Ct. 1976. Asst. atty. gen. Dept. Atty. Gen., Boston, 1964-67; ptnr. Hale and Dorr, Boston, 1967-90; pvt. practice Cambridge, Mass., 1991-2001; ptnr. Taylor, Ganson & Perrin LLP, Boston, 2001—03; ret., 2004. Trustee The Hotchkiss Sch., 1986-91, Archaeol. Inst. Am., 1998-2004; bd. dirs. Indian Soc. Served with U.S. Army, 1959-62. Fellow Am. Coll. Trusts and Estates, Internat. Acad. Estate and Trust Law; mem. ABA, Mass. Bar Assn., Boston Bar Assn., Masons, Wig and Penn Club (London), Winchester Country Club. Republican. Congregationalist. Home: Cambridge, Mass. Died Jan. 27, 2006.

ROCKSTEIN, MORRIS, science writer, editor, consultant; b. Toronto, Ont., Can., Jan. 8, 1916; came to U.S., 1923; s. David and Mina (Segal) R.; children: Susan M. Bumgarner, Madelaine Jo Sottile. AB magna cum laude, Bklyn. Coll., 1938; MA, Columbia U., 1941; PhD, U. Minn., 1948; cert., Oak Ridge Inst. Nuclear Studies, Tenn., 1950. Research asst. entomology U. Minn., St. Paul, 1941-42; asst. prof., assoc. prof. zoophysiology Wash. State U., Pullman, 1948-53; asst. prof., then assoc. prof. physiology NYU Sch. Medicine, NYC, 1953-61; prof. physiology U. Miami Sch. Medicine, 1961-81, chmn. dept., 1967-71; pres. Cortisol Med. Research, Inc., 1983-85. Chmn. sci. adv. bd. Anorexia Nervosa Inst., Melbourne, Fla., 1983-85, Fla. Med. Ctr., Lauderdale Lakes, 1971-78; cons. entomology APHA, 1961-81; del. White House Conf. on Aging, Washington, 1961, 71; cons. insect physiology Sect. Tropical Medicine and Parasitology NIH, Washington, 1962-66, NASA, 1980-92, BIOS, 1983-85; mem. corp. Marine Biol. Lab., 1961—, trustee, 1961-63, life mem., trustee emeritus, 1993—; vis. lectr. Minority Insts. FASEB MARCPROG, 1983-88. Sr. author: Biology of Human Aging, 1978; editor: (with G.T. Baker) Molecular Genetic Mechanisms in Development and Aging, 1972, Development and Aging in the Nervous System, 1973, Physiology of Insecta, 6 vols., 1973-74, Theoretical Aspects of Aging, 1977; (with R.T. Goldman) Physiology and Pathology of Human Aging, 1978, Biochemistry of Insects, 1978; editor Miscellaneous Publs. and Thos Say Found. Monographs, 1983-92; contbr. articles to profl. jours. Mem. resource and mgmt. com. Area Agy. on Aging, 1988-90. Served with USAAF, 1942-46, lt. comdr., USPHS res., 1951-81. NRC fellow in natural scis. U. Minn., 1946-48; recipient Disting. Alumnus award Bklyn. Coll., 1959, Outstanding Alumnus Achievement award U. Minn., 1977, Post 50th Alumni Lifetime Achievement award Bklyn. Coll. Alumni Assn., 1998, A.C. Hodson Meml. award lectr. U. Minn., 1999; named knight comdr. of merit Knights of Malta, 1982. Fellow AAAS (life, mem. coun. 1962-64), Gerontol. Soc. (pres. 1965-66), Entomol. Soc. Am. (life mem.); mem. Internat. Assn. Gerontology (mem. exec. coun. 1963-66), Internat. Assn. Prolongation of Human Life Span (v.p. 1974-92), Am. Physiol. Soc., Am. Soc. Zoologists, Soc. Gen. Physiologists, Sunflower Soc. Miami (v.p. 1986-88),Elks Lodge 948, Army-Navy Club, Coral Gables Country Club (bd. dirs. Fleet 1994-96, 97-98), Century Club of Coral Gables, Phi Beta Kappa, Sigma Xi. Home: Coral Gables, Fla. Died June 19, 2007.

RODDICK, ANITA, shop owner; b. Littlehampton, Eng., Oct. 23, 1942; m. Gordon Roddick; children: Sam, Justine Founder The Body Shop, Brighton, England, 1976—2007; non-exec. dir. The Body Shop Internat., 2002—07. Trustee Body Shop Found., New Acad. Bus.; mem. Bus. for Social Responsibility, Social Venture Network-Europe, Mother Jones' Mag. Found. for Nat. Progress, USA, 1994-2001, Women Inc., Human rights Watch, 1996-97, The Ruckus Soc., 1999-2007, Nuclear Age Peace Found., 2003-2007; U.S.A. bd. advisors Forum for Future; U.K. coun. mem. Non-Violence Project Found. Recipient awards Veuve Clicquot Bus. Woman Year, 1984, Order of Brit. Empire, 1988, World Vision award, Ctr. World Develop. Educn., 1991, Nat. Audobon Soc. medal, 1993, U. Mich. ann. bus. leadership award, 1st ann. Woman Power award Women's Bus. Devel. Ctr., Hunter Coll. Campus Schs. Am. Dream award, Dame Commander British Empire, 2003; named Philanthropist of Yr., Inst. Charitable Fundraising Mgrs. Died Sept. 10, 2007.

RODMAN, LEROY ELI, lawyer; b. NYC, Feb. 22, 1914; s. Morris and Sadie (Specter) R.; m. Toby Chertcoff, Mar. 14, 1943; children: John Stephen, Lawrence Bernard. AB, CCNY, 1933; JD (James Kent scholar), Columbia, 1936. Bar: NY 1937. Pvt. practice, NYC, 1937—43, from 1946; law sec. to US dist. judge Bklyn., 1936; law asst. Am. Law Inst., NYC, 1937; chief food enforcement unit NY Regional Office, OPA, 1942—43; mem. firm Lawrence R. Condon, NYC, 1937—42; ptnr. Joseph & Rodman, NYC, 1946—53; sr. ptnr. Rodman, Maurer & Dansker, NYC, 1964—73, Carro, Spanbock, Londin, Rodman & Fass, NYC, 1973—78, Rodman & Rodman, NYC, 1978—89, Teitelbaum, Hiller, Rodman, Paden & Hibsher, P.C., NYC, 1990—96; of counsel Morrison, Cohen, Singer & Weinstein LLP, NYC, 1996—2004. Edtl. bd.: Columbia Law Rev., 1934-36; Contbr. articles to legal jours. V.p. Ctrl. Synagogue, pres. brotherhood, 1958—60, hon. trustee; bd. dirs. Manhattan coun. Boy Scouts Am., v.p., 1961—68, pres., 1972—75, exec. bd. Greater NY coun. Capt. JAGD US Army, 1943—46. Recipient Certs. Svc., Silver Beaver award Boy Scouts Am., 1962, Eagle Scout, Ten Mile River Camps Hallop Fame award, 2005. Fellow: Am. Coll. Trust Estate Counsel; mem.: ABA, Judge

Adv. Assn., Assn. Bar City NY, NY County Lawyers Assn., Metropolis Country Club (White Plains, NY) (sec. 1976—77, 1980—82, v.p. 1977—78, bd. govs. 1976—82), Univ. Club (NYC), Phi Beta Kappa. Died Mar. 9, 2007.

RODRÍGUEZ, PLINIO, bank executive; b. Juana Díaz, PR, Feb. 18, 1942; s. Fidel A. and Nelina (Rivera) R.; m. María de los Angeles García, June 2, 1978; Enrique, Clara. BBA, U. P.R., 1963. Cert. protection profl. Commd. lt. U.S. Army, 1967; served with mil. intelligence U.S. and Vietnam; advanced through grades to capt.; resigned, 1975; sr. v.p., dir. of security Banco Popular de P.R., San Juan, from 1976. Chmn. security commn. Bank Adminstrn. Inst., Rolling Meadows, Ill., 1987-88. Decorated Bronze Star; recipient Top Mgmt. award Sales & Mktg. Execs., San Juan, 1982. Mem. Am. Soc. Indsl. Security, Internat. Assn. Chiefs of Police, Internat. Assn. Credit Card Investigators. Lodges: Rotary (pres. Santurce club 1985-86). Roman Catholic. Home: San Juan, PR. Died July 30, 2007.

ROEDDER, EDWIN WOODS, geologist; b. Monsey, NY, July 30, 1919; s. Hans and Edna (Woods) R.; children: Spencer, Lucy; m. Margaret Reinhart, Nov. 3, 1994. BA, Lehigh U., 1941; MA, Columbia U., 1947, PhD, 1950; DSc (hon.), Lehigh U., 1976. Rsch. engr. Bethlehem Steel Corp., Bethlehem, Pa., 1941-46; predoctoral fellow Geophys. Lab., Carnegie Inst., Washington, 1946-47; asst. in geology Columbia U., NYC, 1946-49; asst. prof., assoc. prof. U. Utah, Salt Lake City, 1950-55; chief solid state group U.S. Geol. Survey, Washington, 1955-60, staff geologist, 1960-62, geologist, 1962-73, rsch. geologist, 1974-87; assoc. Harvard U., from 1987; scientist emeritus U.S. Geol. Survey, Washington, from 1987. Mem. or cons. various adv. bds, vis. coms., panels for U.S. govt. and several universities. Author: Composition of Fluid Inclusions, 1972, Fluid Inclusions, 1984; editor: Research on Mineral Forming Solutions, 1965, Fluid Inclusion Research (ann. book), 1968—; patentee in field. Recipient Exceptional Sci. Achievement medal NASA, 1973, Disting. Svc. medal U.S. Dept. Interior, 1978, Abraham Gottlob-Werner medaille Deutschen Min. Gesellschaft, 1985, Cyril Purkyne medal Czech Geol. Survey, 1991, first H.C. Sorby medal, 1993, First N.P. Ermakov prize for disting. svc. to thermobarogeochemical rsch., 1999; grantee NSF, others. Fellow AAAS, Am. Geophys. Union (pres. V.G. and P. sect. 1978-80), Mineral Soc. Am. (v.p. 1981-82, pres. 1982-83, Washington A. Roebling medal 1986); mem. NAS, Geochem. Soc. (sec. 1967-70, v.p. 1975-76, pres. 1976-77), Soc. Econ. Geologists (R.A.F. Penrose medal 1988). Avocations: music, travel, stamp collecting/philately. Home: Gloucester, Mass. Died Aug. 1, 2006.

ROGERS, CHARLES FORD, II, architect; b. Middlebury, Vt., May 22, 1937; s. Benjamin Earle and Elsie (Jenney) R.; m. Marga Rapuano, 1960 (div. 1992); children: Mara, Charles III; m. Alice B. Hyde, Aug. 30, 1992. BArch, Cornell U., 1960, MArch, 1962. Registered architect, 1971. Archtl. designer Freeman, French & Freeman, Burlington, Vt., 1957-58; architect, designer Office Dan Kiley, Charlotte, Vt., 1959-60, Office Werner Seligman, Cortland, N.Y., 1961-62, Aebli & Hoesli, Zurich, Switzerland, 1963-65, Office Karl Fleigh, Zurich, 1963-65, Perry, Dean, Hepburn & Stewart, Boston, 1965-71; prin. Perry, Dean, Ptnrs., Boston, 1971-84; pres. Perry, Dean, Rogers & Ptnrs., Boston, 1984-93, chmn. bd., from 1993. Archtl. draftsperson Cornell-Harvard Archaeol. Expedition, Sardis, Turkey, 1959-60; assoc. prof. coll. architecture Cornell U., Ithaca, N.Y., 1962-63; asst. prof. Swiss Fed. Inst. Tech., Zurich, 1963-65; design critic in architecture Harvard U., 1980. Prin. works include Wellesley Coll. Sci. Ctr., 1976, Hall Mercer Children's Ctr., 1980, Seeley Mudd Chemistry Bldg., 1985, Roe Visual Arts Bldg., 1985, Wesleyan Olin Libr., 1986, Amherst Campus Ctr., 1987, William M. Bristol Jr. Pool, 1988, Catoctin Broodmare Barns, 1989, Kreitzberg Libr. Norwich U., 1992, U.S. Embassy, Amman, Jordan, 1992, Bienecke Student Village Hamilton Coll., 1994, Richard Riley Hall Furman U., 1994. Trustee New Eng. Bapt. Hosp., Boston, 1977-92, William M. Bristol Jr. Swimming Pool, 1988. Biddle Found. scholar, 1959. Mem. AIA. Clubs: Union (Boston). Episcopalian. Died Aug. 13, 2007.

ROGERS, ELDON ALKIRE, retired construction company executive; b. Knowles, Okla., Nov. 15, 1918; s. Charles Lewis and Zella Barthena (Alkire) R.; m. Mary Elizabeth Smith, Oct. 5, 1941; children: Janice L., Ned H. BSC.E., Okla. U., 1940. Registered profl. engr., Okla. Chief engr. Tulsa Rig, Reel Mfg. Co., 1951-66; v.p. Flintco, Inc., Tulsa, 1966-80, pres., 1981-83, dir., 1975-83. Served to lt. col. U.S. Army, 1941-46. Mem.: Tulsa Rotary. Republican. Methodist. Home: Tulsa, Okla. Died Sept. 6, 2006.

ROGERS, EUGENE CHARLES, retired investment firm executive; b. Bklyn., Sept. 29, 1932; s. Eugene Aloysius and Agnes Hilda (Scharbach) R.; m. Anita Therese Tobin, May 13, 1961; 1 son, Eugene Charles. BBA, St. John's U., Bklyn., 1954; MBA, N.Y. U., 1960. C.P.A., N.Y. Staff accountant Haskins & Sells (C.P.A.s), NYC, 1954-60, Bache & Co., NYC, 1960-62; controller, then chief fin. officer Reynolds Securities Inc., NYC, 1962-72, v.p., treas., from 1972; 1st v.p., treas. Dean Witter Reynolds Inc., 1978-81, sr. v.p., treas., from 1981. Guest lectr., panelist in field. Bd. advisors Coll. Bus. Adminstrn., St. John's U. Served with U.S. Army, 1954-56. Mem. N.Y. State Soc. C.P.A.'s, Fin. Execs. Inst., Fin. Club of N.Y. U. Grad. Sch. Bus., Securities Industry Assn. (past pres. fin. mgmt. div.), Sun and Surf Beach Club, Hempstead Golf and Country Club. Roman Catholic. Died Jan. 13, 2007.

ROGERS, ISABEL WOOD, retired theological educator; b. Tallahassee, Aug. 26, 1924; d. William Hudson and Mary Thornton (Wood) R. BA, Fla. State U., 1945; MA, U. Va., 1947; MRE, Presbyn. Sch. Christian Edn., 1949; PhD, Duke U., 1961; DD (hon.), Austin Coll., 1986; LLD (hon.), Westminster Coll., 1988; LHD, Centre Coll., 1989. Campus min. 1st Presbyn. Ch., Milledgeville, Ga., 1949-52; campus chaplain Ga. Coll., Milledgville, 1952-61; prof. applied Christianity Presbyn. Sch. Christian Edn., Richmond, Va., 1961-98; ret., 1998. Elder Ginter Pk. Presbyn. Ch., Richmond, 1976-79, 89—; moderator of Gen. Assembly, Presbyn. Ch. U.S.A., 1987-88; lectr. Presbyn. chs. Author: The Christian and World Affairs, 1965, In Response to God, 1969, Our Shared Earth, 1980, Sing A New Song, 1981, Toward a Liberating Faith: A Primer on Feminist Theology, 1999. Vol. Richmond Community Action Program, 1968-75, YWCA, Women's Advocacy Program, 1982—; bd. dirs. Massanetta Conf. Ctr., Richmond, 1987—. Du Pont fellow U. Va., 1946. 47, Kearns fellow Duke U. Mem. Soc. Christian Ethics, Phi Kappa Phi, Phi Beta Kappa. Democrat. Presbyterian. Avocations: hiking, jogging, tennis, gardening, stamp collecting/philately. Home: Richmond, Va. Died Mar. 18, 2007.

ROGERS, JOHN S., retired union official; b. Scranton, Pa., Nov. 19, 1930; Student, U. Wis., 1959-61, U. Mich., 1963; student spl. studies, Am. U., 1965-66, Harvard U. Bus. Sch., 1967. Internat. rep. United Brotherhood of Carpenters and Joiners of Am., Washington, 1958-65, asst. to gen. pres., 1966-74, dir. edn., 1971-82, mem. gen. exec. bd., 1974-78, gen. sec., 1978-91, ret., 1992. Sec.-treas. Suffolk County (N.Y.) Dist. Coun. Carpenters, 1957-58; v.p. N.Y. State Bldg. and Constrn. Trades Council, 1974-78, N.Y. State Fedn. Labor, 1974-78; pres. N.Y. State Coun. Carpenters, 1974-78; vice chmn. N.Y. State Commn. Jobs and Energy; mem. Suffolk County Pub. Employment Rels.s Bd.; vis. lectr. George Meany Ctr. Labor Studies. Author numerous trade union leadership mans. and instructional materials, 1966-79. Bd. dirs. L.I. action com. Assn. Help for Retarded Children, 1956-60; labor co-chmn United Cerebral Palsy, N.Y.C., 1977-78; v.p. Leukemia Soc. Mem. Harvard Trade Union Alumnae Assn. Home: Boynton Beach, Fla. Died Aug. 12, 2007.

ROGERS, JONATHAN W., mayor, director; b. New Haven, June 5, 1928; s. Maurice and Harriet (Woodruff) R.; m. Patricia Beach Murchison, Sept. 11, 1954; children: Jonathan W., Louise B., Patricia M., Samuel M. BS, Yale U., 1950. Sales engr. Alcoa Co., Los Angeles, 1953-56; sales engr. George S. Thomson Co., El Paso, Tex., 1956-60; stockbroker Quinn & Co., El Paso, 1960-63; pres. Mortgage Investment Co., El Paso, 1963-84; mayor City of El Paso, from 1981. Chmn. Indsl. Devel. Corp., El Paso, 1977-78. Served to 1st lt. U.S. Army, 1950-53 Recipient Outstanding Citizen award El Paso Realtors Assn., 1983, El Paso Mortgage Bankers, 1982, Outstanding Border Mayor award Govt. of Mex., 1983, Disting. Service award Tex. Mortgage Bankers, 1980. Mem. Tex. Mortgage Bankers Assn. (bd. dirs., pres. 1975), Mortgage Bankers Assn. (bd. govs. 1979-86), Tex. Mcpl. League (bd. dirs. 1981—). Clubs: El Paso Country (bd. dirs. 1964-68). Avocation: golf. Home: El Paso, Tex. Died Mar. 10, 2007.

ROGERS, WILLIAM DILL, retired lawyer, former federal agency administrator; b. Wilmington, Del., May 12, 1927; m. Suzanne Rochford, Sept. 7, 1926; children: William Rogers, Daniel. BA, Princeton U., 1948; LL.B., Yale U., 1951. Bar: D.C. 1952, U.S. Supreme Ct. 1954. Law clk. to Hon. Charles E. Clark US Ct. Appeals (2nd Cir.), 1951—52; law clk. to Justice Stanley Reed US Supreme Ct., 1952—53; ptnr. Arnold & Porter LLP, Washington, 1953—62, 1965, 1966—74, 1977—2004; dep. US coord. Alliance for Progress, AID, 1962-65; pres. NY Ctr. Inter.-Am. Rels., 1965-72; asst. sec. of state inter-Am. relations US Dept. State, Washington, 1974-76, under sec. for econ. affairs, 1976-77; mem. law faculty Cambridge U., 1982-83; v.p. Kissinger Associates, 2004—07. Sr. counselor Bipartisan Commn. on Central Am., 1983-84; vice chmn. Kissinger Assocs. Inc. Author: The Twilight Struggle: The Alliance for Progress and U.S.-Latin-American Relations, 1967. Co-chmn. U.S.-Mexico Binat. Commn.; bd. dirs. Coun. Fgn. Rels., 1981-90. Mem. Am. Soc. Internat. Law (pres. 1971-73), ABA. Died Sept. 22, 2007.

ROGLIANO, ALDO THOMAS, publishing executive; b. Tuckahoe, NY, Mar. 7, 1925; s. Alfred and Nancy (Morrone) R.; m. Bettie Eleanor Fehrs, June 13, 1948; children: Susan Rogliano Shortley, Betsy Rogliano Dyer, Guy, Barbara Rogliano Tracy, Robert. Student, Syracuse U., 1946-49. Newsstand promotion mgr. Fawcett Publs. Inc., Greenwich, Conn., 1949-54, promotion mgr., 1957-68, MacFadden Pub. Co., NYC, 1954-57; account exec., promotion mgr. Dell Pub. Co., 1968-71; v.p., dir. pub. relations MacFadden-Bartell Corp., NYC, 1971-74; promotion dir. Internat. Circulation Distbrs., NYC, 1974-77, Kable News Co., 1977-78; v.p., dir. promotion and publicity Publishers Distbg. Corp. (a Filmways co.), NYC, 1978-80; advt. and promotion dir. Flynt Distbg. Co., Los Angeles, 1980-83. Served with USMCR, 1943-45. Decorated Purple Heart; recipient Pub. Relations Gold Key award, 1971 Home: Unionville, Conn. Died July 18, 2007.

ROHRBERGER, MARY HELEN, English language educator; b. New Orleans, Jan. 22, 1929; d. Adolph and Flora (Ketry) R. BA in English with honors, Newcomb Coll., 1950; MA, Tulane U., 1952, PhD, 1961. Tchr. Westwego (La.) Jr. High Sch., 1956-58, Dillard U., New Orleans, 1958-59; part-time instr. Tulane U., New Orleans, 1959-61; asst. prof. Okla. State U., Stillwater, 1961-65, assoc. prof., 1965-71, prof., from 1971, dir. curricular affairs and spl. acad. programs, 1971-90; head dept. English U. No. Iowa, Cedar Falls, from 1990. Author: Hawthorne and the Modern Short Story, 1966, The Art of Katherine Mansfield, 1977, Story to Anti-Story, 1979; contbr. articles to profl. publs. Mem. Phi Beta Kappa, Sigma Tau Delta. Home: New Orleans, La. Died Mar. 7, 2007.

ROLLINS, EDWARD TYLER, JR., retired newspaper executive; b. Durham, NC, May 23, 1922; s. Edward Tyler and Bessie (Steed) R.; m. Frances Louise Page, Oct. 5, 1963; children: Edward Tyler III, William Lawson. AB, U. N.C., 1947. V.p., asst. sec. Durham (N.C.) Herald Co., 1949-69, v.p., sec.-treas., 1969-81, pres., pub., 1982-88, chmn., bd. dirs., 1985—2004; ret., 2004. Pres. Durham Radio Corp. Stas. WDNC-AM, WDCG-FM, 1982-88. Bd. dirs. Chowan Coll. Graphic Arts Found., 1986-95; bd. dirs. Sch. of Journalism Found. of N.C., 1982-88; mem. Friends of Duke Art Mus., mem. adv. bd. N.C. Nat. Bank, 1979-89; mem. Gov.'s Bus. Coun. on Arts and Humanities, 1989-90; mem. Duke Pres.'s Art Mus. com., 1994-2001; trustee Meredith Coll., Raleigh, N.C., 1966-69, Durham Pub. Libr., 1961-81; former bd. dirs. Durham Salvation Army; pres. Durham YMCA, 1952; former bd. dirs. Family Svc. Assn. With U.S. Army, 1943-46. Mem. The English Speaking Union, Durham C. of C. (bd. dirs. 1969), Brummer Soc.-Duke (Nasher) Art Mus., Kiwanis, Hope Valley Country Club, Univ. Club, Carolina Club. Presbyterian. Home: Durham, NC. Died Nov. 5, 2006.

ROMAINE, HENRY SIMMONS, retired investment company executive, consultant; b. NYC, May 30, 1933; s. Theodore Cole and Cornelia (Simmons) R.; m. Susan Donaldson; children: Henry, Hilary, Kathryn. BA, Harvard U., 1954. Asst. security analyst Mutual Life Ins. Co., NYC, 1958-60, investment analyst, 1960-61, investment specialist, 1961-64, asst. dir. investments, 1964, dir. investments, 1964-66, asst. v.p. for securities investment, 1966-68, 2d v.p. for securities investment, 1969-71, v.p. for securities investment, 1971-72, sr. v.p., 1972-78, sr. v.p., chief investment officer, 1976-78, exec. v.p., 1978-81, pres., 1981-86; vice chmn., chief investment officer Am. Gen. Corp., Houston, 1986-93. Dir. MONY Life Ins. Co. of Can.; chmn. bd. MONY Real Estate Investors, 1978-86; mem. adv. bd. Chem. Bank, 1974-93. Served with USN, 1954-57. Mem.: Harvard Club. Home: Sullivans Island, SC. Died Aug. 22, 2007.

ROMANS, ROBERT CHARLES, biological sciences educator; b. Hawthorne, Wis., Oct. 12, 1937; s. James Harlan and Jeannette Caroline (Johnson) R.; m. Jean Marie Law, Jan. 4, 1983; 1 son, Bradley Keith. B.S., U. Wis.-Superior, 1965, M.S.T., 1966; Ph.D., Ariz. State U., 1969. Teaching asst. U. Wis.-Superior, 1965-66; research fellow Ariz. State U., Tempe, 1966-69; asst. prof. biol. sci. Bowling Green State U., Ohio, 1969-75, assoc. prof., 1975—. Editor: Geobotany, 1972; Geobotany II, 1976. Precinct committeeman Republican party, Foxboro, Wis., 1961; deacon Plain Congl. Ch., Bowling Green, Ohio, 1978-82. Recipient Disting. Teaching award Bowling Green State U. Alumni Assn., 1973, Faculty of Yr. award Alpha Lambda Delta, 1977, Faculty Excellence award Bowling Green State U. Student Govt. Assn., 1980. Mem. Internat. Orgn. Paleobotany, Bot. Soc. Am., Ohio Acad. Sci. (sec. 1983-84), Omicron Delta Kappa. Home: Bowling Green, Ohio. Died May 11, 2007.

ROMNEY, CLYDE ANDERSON, lawyer, government relations consultant; b. Altadena, Calif., Apr. 8, 1943; s. Clyde and Almera (Anderson) R.; m. Deborah C. Dedekind, July 11, 1969; children: Christian, Elizabeth, Ann, Miles, David, Maren. BA, Stanford U., 1965; JD, U. Utah, 1970. Bar: Calif. 1971. Assoc. atty. Gray, Cary, Ames & Fre, San Diego, 1970-74; ptnr. Munns, Kofford & Romney, San Diego, 1979-82, Romney & Anderson, San Diego, 1979-82; chief of staff U.S. Congressman Ron Packard's Office, Washington, 1983-86; ptnr. Higgs, Fletcher & Mack, Escondido, Calif., from 1987. Cons. Vista (Calif.) Irrigation Dist. 1986—, San Luis Rey Indian Water Authority, Pala, Calif.; San Luis Rey Indian Water Settlement Task Force, Washington, 1984-86. Trustee Solano Beach Elem. Sch. Dist.; v.p. San Diego County Council Boy Scouts Am., Nuclear Safety Task Force for State Senate, Sacramento, 1987-88, Calif. Rep. Cen. Com. Mem. ABA. Clubs: C.O.G.G. Lodges: Rotary. Avocations: reading, back packing, politics. Home: Escondido, Calif. Died Aug. 26, 2006.

RONDINELLI, DENNIS A(UGUST), business administration educator, researcher; b. Trenton, NJ, Mar. 30, 1943; s. August P. and Vincentia Rondinelli; m. Soonyoung Chang, Dec. 19, 1976; children: Linda, Lisa. BA, Rutgers U., 1965; PhD, Cornell U., 1969. Asst. prof. urban affairs U. Wis., Milw., 1971-73; assoc. prof. grad. sch. of mgmt. Vanderbilt U., Nashville, 1973-76; assoc. prof. planning Maxwell Sch. of Citizenship and Pub. Affairs Syracuse U., NY, 1976-79, prof. social scis. NY, 1979-86; prin. scientist and sr. policy analyst Office for Internat. Programs, Research Triangle Inst., Research Triangle Park, NC, 1986-90; Glaxo Disting. Internat. Prof. Mgmt. emeritus Kenan-Flagler Bus. Sch., from 2005, emeritus, from 2005; sr. rsch. scholar Duke Ctr. Internat. Devel., from 2005; dir. Pacific Basin Rsch. Ctr., Soka U. Am., from 2005. Cons. World Bank, U.S. Dept. State, UN Devel. Program, Govts. of Colombia, South Korea, Can., Indonesia, Philippines, China, India, mem. com. of experts on pub. adminstrn. UN Econ. and Social Coun., 2002—. Author: Decentralization and Development: Policy Implementation in Developing Countries, 1983, Applied Methods of Regional Analysis: The Spatial Dimensions of Development Policy, 1985, Development Administration and U.S. Foreign Aid Policy, 1987, Urban Services in Developing Countries: Public and Private Roles in Urban Development, 1988, Planning Education Reforms in Developing Countries, 1990, Development Projects as Policy Experiments, 1993, Privatization and Economic Reform in Central Europe, 1994, Expanding Sino-American Business and Trade: China's Economic Transition, 1994, Great Policies: Strategic Innovations in Asia and the Pacific, 1995, Policies and Institutions for Managing Privatization, 1996, Market Reform in Vietnam, 1999, Reinventing Government for the 21st Century, 2003, Beyond Reconstruction in Afghanistan, 2004, Globalizataion and Change in Asia, 2007, Decentralizing Governance, 2007; mem. editl. bd. Leadership Rev., Jour. Internat. Bus. Edn., Jour. Internat. Devel. Planning; contbr. articles to profl. jours. Mem. expert com. pub. admin. econ. and social coun. UN, from 2002. Capt. US Army, 1965—72. Decorated Julio Lieras Order of Merit (Colombia), 1988; recipient Rural Devel. medal Republic of Vietnam, 1971, Ethnic Minorities Devel. medal, 1971, W. Bloomberg award for excellence in futures studies, 1997, Weatherspoon Disting. Rsch. award, 1997; East-West Ctr. sr. fellow, 1975-76, Pacific Basin Rsch. Ctr./Soka U. of Am./Harvard U. rsch. fellow, 1991-92. Avocations: gardening, writing nonfiction. Home: Hillsborough, NC. Died Mar. 7, 2007.

RONEY, PAUL HITCH, federal judge; b. Olney, Ill., Sept. 5, 1921; m. Sarah E. Eustis; children: Susan M., Paul Hitch Jr., Timothy Eustis. Student, St. Petersburg Jr. Coll., 1938—40; BS in Econs., U. Pa., 1942; LLB, Harvard U., 1948; LLD, Stetson U., 1977; LLM, U. Va., 1984. Bar: N.Y. 1949, Fla. 1950. Assoc. Root, Ballantine, Harlan, Bushby & Palmer, NYC, 1948—50; ptnr. Mann, Harrison, Roney, Mann & Masterson (and predecessors), St. Petersburg, Fla., 1950—57; pvt. practice, 1957—63; ptnr. Roney & Beach, St. Petersburg, 1963—69, Roney, Ulmer, Woodworth & Jacobs, St. Petersburg, 1969—70;

judge U.S. Ct. Appeals (5th cir.), St. Petersburg, 1970—81, U.S. Ct. Appeals (11th cir.), St. Petersburg, 1981—86, chief judge, 1986—89, sr. cir. judge, 1989—2006. Adv. com. on adminstrv. law judges U.S. CSC, 1976—77; pres. judge U.S. Fgn. Intelligence Surveillance Ct. of Rev., 1994—2001; lectr. Stetson U. Coll. of Law. With US Army, 1942—46. Fellow: Am. Bar Found.; mem.: ABA (chmn. legal adv. com. Fair Trial-Free Press 1973—76, task force on cts. and public 1973—76, jud. adminstrn. divsn., chmn. appellate judges conf. 1978—79, Gavel Awards com. 1980—83), Jud. Conf. U.S. (subcom. on jud. improvements 1978—84, exec. com. 1986—89, com. to review circuit coun. conduct and disability orders 1991—93), Nat. Jud. Coll. (faculty 1974—75), St. Peterburg Bar Assn. (pres. 1964—65), Fla. Bar Assn., Am. Law Inst., Am. Judicature Soc. (bd. dirs. 1972—76). Died Sept. 16, 2006.

ROOSEVELT, OLIVER WOLCOTT, II, classical music critic, arts editor; b. NYC, Mar. 2, 1927; s. Oliver Wolcott and Mary deVerdery (Akin) R.; m. Ann Taylor, Sept. 4, 1948; children: Verdery Anne, Oliver W. III, Laura Gibbs, Mary Nicholas, Carolyn Taylor. BA, Harvard U., 1948. Programmer, writer WQXR, NYC, 1948-50; mgr. Birmingham (Ala.) Symphony Orchestra, 1950-52; editor-in-chief Shades Valley Sun, Birmingham, 1955-60; writer, editor The Birmingham (Ala.) News, from 1960. Music tchr. Univ. Ala., Birmingham, 1976—; coord. Basically Bach Festival of Ala. (340 concerts), 1985, Amadeus Festival of Ala., 1990-91. Founding pres. Shades Cliff Community Pool, Birmingham, 1966. With USN, 1945-46. Recipient Obelisk award, Greater Birmingham Arts Alliance, 1977. Mem. Music Critics Assn. Avocation: gardening. Home: Birmingham, Ala. Died Jan. 9, 2007.

ROOT, ALAN CHARLES, diversified manufacturing company executive; b. Essex, Eng., Apr. 11, 1925; arrived in U.S., 1951, naturalized, 1959; s. Charles Stanley and Lillian (Collins) Root. BA, Oxford U., 1943; MA, Cambridge U., 1951; MBA, Stanford U., 1953. Rsch. analyst Dow Chem. Co., Midland, Mich., 1954—55; mgr. mktg. rsch. GE Co., 1955—61; v.p. bus. planning Mosler Safe Co., Hamilton, Ohio, 1961—70; v.p. corp. planning Am. Standard Inc., NYC, 1970—76, sr. v.p. ops. svcs., 1976—86, sr. v.p., 1986—88, sr. advisor, 1989. Trustee 1995 Trust Fund; sr. advisor Unit Ice, 1995—; bd. dirs. Am.-Standard Energy Inc., Amstan Trucking Inc., 1976-86. Trustee, treas. N.J. Chamber Music Soc., 1988—95; mem. Sheriff's Jury, N.Y. Cty., 1971—79; bd. dirs., chmn. Brit. Schs. and Univs. Found., 1970—2002, hon. dir., from 2002. Capt. Brit. Army, 1944—48. Admission to Order of St. John of Jerusalem sanctioned by Her Majesty Queen Elizabeth II, 1986, comdr., 1994. Mem. AIChE (assoc. producer TV series Midland sect. 1955), Pilgrims U.S., Newcomen Soc. N.Am., Univ. Club (N.Y.C.). Home: Rancho Santa Fe, Calif. Died Feb. 24, 2006.

ROOT, WILLIAM LUCAS, electrical engineering educator; b. Des Moines, Oct. 6, 1919; s. Frank Stephenson and Helen (Lucas) R.; m. Harriett Jean Johnson, Dec. 10, 1918; children: William Lucas Jr., Wendy Elizabeth Root Cate. BEE, Iowa State U., 1940; MEE, MIT, 1943, PhD in Math., 1952. Staff mem. MIT Lincoln Lab., Lexington, Mass., 1952-61, group leader, 1959-61; lectr. Harvard U., Cambridge, Mass., 1958-59; visitor U. Wis., Madison, 1963-64; vis. prof. Mich. State U., East Lansing, 1966, 68, U. Calif., Berkeley, 1966-67; prof. aerospace engring. U. Mich., Ann Arbor, 1961-87, prof. emeritus, from 1988. Visitor U. Cambridge (Eng.), 1970; mem. U.S. Army Sci. Bd., 1979-82. Co-author: Random Signals and Noise, 1958 (Russian and Japanese transls.); assoc. editor: (IEEE) Information Theory Transactions, 1977-79; Soc. Indsl. and Applied Math. Jour. Applied Mathematics, 1962-72; contbr. 65 articles to profl. jours., book chpts. and conf. procs. Served to lt. USMCR, 1943—45. NSF Sr. postdoctoral fellow, 1970, vis. fellow Cambridge Clare Hall, 1970; recipient Claude E. Shannon award IEEE Info. Theory Soc., 1986, Career Achievement award ComCon Conf. Bd., 1987. Life fellow IEEE (vice chmn. adminstrv. com. info. theory group 1965-66); mem. Am. Math. Soc. Home: Ann Arbor, Mich. Died Apr. 22, 2007.

ROQUEMORE, NANCY GWEN, magazine editor; b. Atlanta, Jan. 15, 1949; d. Robert Lee Roquemore and Helen (Davis) Cox. BA in English, Ga. Southwestern Coll., 1973; MLS, Atlanta U., 1978. Tchr., librarian Lee Crest Acad., Fayetteville, Ga., 1973-75; librarian Clayton County, Riverdale, Ga., 1975-80; photo librarian Atlanta Jour.-Constn., 1980-81, typesetter mag., 1981-82, copy editor mag., 1982-84, assoc. editor mag., from 1984. Mem.: Order Eastern Star (worshipful master 1981-82). Avocations: needlecrafts, travel, plants. Home: Atlanta, Ga. Died May 16, 2007.

RORER, WILLIAM HERBERT, III, academic administrator; b. Abington, Pa., June 21, 1936; s. Herbert C. Rorer and Adelaide (Brown) Richards; m. Susan Straus, June 14, 1958; children: William H. IV, Suzanna P., Samantha R. BS, U.S. Naval Acad., 1958. Commd. ensign USN, 1958, advanced through grades to lt., 1960; grad. USN Submarine Sch., New London, Conn.; submarine officer USN, 1960-63, resigned, 1963; dir. prodn. services William H. Rorer, Inc., Ft. Washington, Pa., 1963-66, indsl. rels. mgr., 1966-73, v.p. engring., 1967-77, pres., 1977-85; pres. Rorer subs. cos. Dermik Labs, Inc., Ft. Washington, 1974-76, Barcroft Co., Ft. Washington, 1968-73; sr. v.p. Rorer Group Inc., Ft. Washington, 1986-87, also bd. dirs. Bd. dirs. Immunomedics Inc. Pres. Ft. Washington Indsl. Park Mgmt. Assn., 1970-72; mem. Service Acad. Selection Bd. for 13th Congl. Dist., 1973-74; health industry laison com. Am. Acad. Dermatology, 1975-76; mem. Citizens Crime Commn. Phila., 1978-82, 86—; sr. council Phila. Drug Exchange, 1970—, pres. 1977-78; trustee Phila. Coll. Pharmacy and Sci., 1978-89, U.S. Naval Acad. Found., Annapolis, Md., 1981—; mem. Abington Hosp. Health Care Corp., 1985—; mem. USN Fed. Adv. Com., 1985-87, S.E. Pa. chpt. ARC, 1989—; pres., trustee Del. Valley Coll., Doylestown, 1987—. Mem. Phila. chpt. Navy League U.S. (v.p. 1978-80), Pa. Soc. S.R., Pa. Soc. Clubs: Nantucket (Mass.) Yacht. Republican. Episcopalian. Home: Lumberville, Pa. Died Aug. 24, 2007.

RORTY, RICHARD MCKAY, philosophy educator; b. NYC, Oct. 4, 1931; s. James Hancock and Winifred (Raushenbush) R.; m. Amelie Sarah Oksenberg, June 15, 1954 (div. 1972); 1 son, Jay; m. Mary R. Varney, Nov. 4, 1972; children: Patricia, Kevin. BA, U. Chgo., 1949, MA, 1952; PhD, Yale U., 1956; DHL, Northwestern U., 1992, Fla. Internat. Univ., 1994. Instr. philosophy Yale U., 1955-57; instr. Wellesley Coll., 1958-60, asst. prof., 1960-61; mem. faculty Princeton U., 1961-82, prof. philosophy, 1970-81, Stuart prof. philosophy, 1981-82; Univ. prof. humanities U. Va., 1982—98; prof. comparative lit. Stanford U., 1998—2007. Author: Philosophy and the Mirror of Nature, 1979, Consequences of Pragmatism, 1982, Contingency, Irony and Solidarity, 1989, Objectivity, Relativism and Truth, 1991, Essays on Heidegger and Others, 1991. Served with AUS, 1957-58. Guggenheim fellow, 1973-74; MacArthur fellow, 1981-86. Mem. Am. Philos. Assn. (pres. Eastern div. 1979), Am. Acad. Arts and Scis. Home: Charlottesville, Va. Died June 8, 2007.

ROSA, RICHARD JOHN, mechanical engineer, educator; b. Detroit, Mar. 19, 1927; s. Richard Kellock and Beatrice (Boleau) R.; m. Jane Norton, Sept. 2, 1950 (div. 1970); children: Katrina, Richard Scott, Cynthia; m. Marion Hogarty, Sept. 16, 1978. BEP, Cornell U., 1953, PhD, 1956. Prin. research scientist AVCO Research Lab., Everett, Mass., 1956-75; prof. mech. engring. Mont. State U., Bozeman, from 1975. Cons. in field; vis. scholar U. Sydney, Australia, 1977; vis. prof. Tokyo Inst. Tech., 1981; U.S. coordinator U.S.-Japan Coop. Program in Magnetohydrodynamics, 1982-86. Author: MHD Energy Conversion, 1968, 2d edit., 1987; contbr. articles to profl jours.; patentee in field. Served to lt. (j.g.) USN, 1945-49. NSF grantee, 1982-87, Dept. Edn. grantee, 1988—. Mem. IEEE (sr.), AIAA (sr., com. mem.), ASME, AAAS. Avocations: skiing, sailing, hiking. Home: Polson, Mont. Died Dec. 22, 2006.

ROSE, DAVID, painter-printmaker, artist-reporter, educator; b. Malden, Mass., Mar. 10, 1910; s. Isaac and Dora (Susman) R.; m. Ida Claire Shapiro, July 13, 1945 (dec.); children— Marsha Annette, Lisa Joan. B.S. in Art Edn., Mass. Coll. Art, 1934; student Sch. of Mus. Fine Arts, Boston, 1932, Herman Struck, Haifa, 1933, Chouinard Art Inst., Los Angeles, 1938-40, Art. Ctr. Coll. of Design, 1940-42. Exhibited one-man shows including Magnes Mus., Berkeley, Calif., Klutznick Mus., Washington, Yeshiva U. Mus., New York, Heritage Gallery, L.A., UCLA, U. Ariz.; exhibited group shows Pa. Acad. Fine Arts, Bklyn. Mus., Los Angeles County Mus. Art, Calif. State Mus., Los Angeles; represented in permanent collections including Libr. Congress, U.S. Holocaust Meml. Mus., Royal Danish Libr., Copenhagen, Skirball Mus., Los Angeles, Israel Mus., Jerusalem, Mus. Modern Art, Haifa, USAF Documentary Art Coll., Washington, UCLA Spl. Collections, L.A.; layout artist Walt Disney Studios, 1936-40; art. dir. advt. agys., 1945-60; art dir., illustrator, designer film and TV, Warner Bros., Burbank Universal Pictures, KCET Community TV, NBC Burbank, 1945-60; ind. artist-reporter, court trials and news events for TV, newspapers and mags. including Cable Network News, ABC World News, NBC Nightly News, Newsweek, Time, Los Angeles Herald Examiner, Los Angeles Daily News, Chgo. Tribune, AP, UPI, San Francisco Examiner, Jerusalem Post; mem. faculty continuing edn. dept. Otis Art Inst., Parsons Sch. Design; lectr. various univs. and art socs. Mem. graphic arts council Los Angeles County Mus. Art. Served with Signal Corps, U.S. Army, 1943-45. Recipient award Army Pictorial Service, 1945; 2 medals Art Dirs. Club, Los Angeles; others. Mem. Soc. Illustrators, Los Angeles Printmaking Soc. Home: Los Angeles, Calif. Died Mar. 4, 2006.

ROSE, ERNEST WRIGHT, JR., architect; b. Richmond, Va., Mar. 12, 1939; s. Ernest Wright and Josie (Peebles) R.; m. Diane Hickman, Sept. 7, 1959 (div. 1964); m. Connie Coffman, Apr. 17, 1971; children— David Christopher, Andrew Frederick, Jonathan Wright. B.Arch., Va. Poly Inst., 1963. Registered architect, Va., Ala., Conn., Fla., Ga., Md., Pa., N.C., S.C., Tenn., W.Va., N.Y. Designer, project mgr. Alan McCullough, Richmond, 1963-70; prin. Ernie Rose Architect, Richmond, 1970-75, pres., 1975—; dir. Dragon Chem., Roanoke, Va. Pres. Rock Creek Park Civic Assn., Richmond, 1975-78. Mem. AIA, Constrn. Specifications Inst. (pres. 1981-83). Club: Engineers (pres. 1983-84) (Richmond). Avocations: sailing; antique auto restoration; woodworking. Home: Richmond, Va. Died Aug. 11, 2006.

ROSEN, EDWARD, retired commodity house executive; b. New Orleans, July 10, 1928; s. Louis Leucht and Nita Mildred (Silverstein) R.; m. Carol Elizabeth Heinberg, Sept. 30, 1950; children— Catherine Elizabeth Rosen Hinnant, Geri Anne Rosen Rubin. B.S., Tulane U., 1950. Salesman Leon Israel Bros., New Orleans, 1950-61, v.p., N.Y.C., 1961-70; exec. v.p. Coffee div. ACLI Internat., N.Y.C., 1970-79, pres., 1979-84, ret.; bd. mgrs. N.Y. Coffee, Cocoa, Sugar Exchange, 1982-84; former advisor for coffee to U.S. Trade Rep., Washington. Bd. govs. Tulane U. Hosp. and Clinic, New Orleans, 1985—. Served to lt. U.S. Army, 1951-52, Korea. Mem. Republican. Jewish. Club: Lakewood Country. Avocations: golf; swimming; fishing. Home: New Orleans, La. Died May 1, 2007.

ROSENBAUM, IRVING M., retail store executive; b. Dresden, Germany, Apr. 20, 1921; came to U.S., 1938, naturalized, 1943; s. Max and Clara (Koerner) R.; m. Hanni Schein, Oct. 15, 1953; children: Eli M., Daniel S., Michael J. BA in Econs., New Sch. Social Research, 1953; MA in Econs., NYU, 1956. Stockman, S.E. Nichols Inc., NYC, 1938-40, asst. store mgr., 1940-43, store mgr., 1946-48, buyer, 1949-56, mdse. mgr., 1957-60, pres., 1960-72, chmn. bd., 1972-83, vice-chmn. bd., 1983-85, also bd. dirs.; v.p. Venture Israel Ltd., Balt., from 1985, Israel Pharms., Balt., 1976-83. Chmn. bd. F.R. Schreiber Co., Lititz, Pa., 1975-82; adv. com. mem. AMIFID Ptnrs. L.P., N.Y.C. Bd. dirs., chmn. bd. overseers Solomon Schechter Day Sch., Nassau and Suffolk Counties, 1985-90; bd. dirs. United Jewish Appeal, Fedn. Jewish Philanthropies, Israel Bond Orgn. Greater N.Y.; nat. chmn. Friends of the Open U. Israel, 1989—. With U.S. Army, 1943-45. Recipient Prime Minister's medal Israel, 1976, 88. Mem. Nat. Mass Retailing Inst., U.S. C. of C. (govt. and regulatory affairs com. 1977-79, adminstrv. law coun. 1980-85). Clubs: Lake Mohawk Country (Sparta, N.J.). Home: Great Neck, NY. Died July 21, 2007.

ROSENBERG, ABRAHAM, biochemist, researcher; b. NYC, Aug. 12, 1924; s. Isaac Joseph and Helen (Bohrer) R.; m. Estelle Ruminek, June 20, 1948; children: Ruth Ann, Jonathan. B.Sc., U. Ill., 1947; M.Sc., Poly. Inst. Bklyn., 1952; PhD, Columbia U., 1957. Research assoc. biochemistry Columbia U., NYC, 1957-60; ast. prof. biochemistry Coll. Physicians and Surgeons, 1961-67; assoc. prof. biochemistry M.S. Hershey (Pa.) Med. Ctr., 1968-71, prof., 1971-79; prof., chmn. dept. biochemistry and biophysics Loyola U. Stritch Sch. Medicine, Maywood, Ill., from 1979; mem. mental retardation research com. Nat. Inst. Child Health and Human Devel., Washington, 1974-82; mem. med. adv. bd. Leukemai Research Found., Chgo., 1983-87. Author: Biological Roles of Sialic Acid, 1967; contbr. articles to profl. jours. Served with U.S. Army, 1942-46, ETO. NIH research grantee, 1961—; U. Gothenburg guest prof., 1967; Fulbright fellow U. Strasbourg, 1974; N.Y. Heart Assn. sr. postdoctoral fellow, 1960 Fellow Am. Inst. Chemists; mem. Am. Soc. Biol. Chemists, Sigma Xi Democrat. Jewish. Home: Oak Park, Ill. Died Dec. 23, 2006.

ROSENBERG, STUART, film director; b. Bklyn., Aug. 11, 1927; s. David and Sara (Kaminsky) R.; m. Margot Pohoryles, Aug. 4, 1950; 1 son, Benjamin. BA, NYU, 1949. Dir. (films) Murder, Inc., 1960, Cool Hand Luke, 1967, The April Fools, 1969, Move, 1970, WUSA, 1970, Pocket Money, 1972, The Drowning Pool, 1974, Voyage of the Damned, 1977, The Amityville Horror, 1979, Love and Bullets, 1979, Brubaker, 1980, The Pope of Greenwich Village, 1984, Let's Get Harry, 1986, My Heroes Have Always Been Cowboys, 1991; dir., prodr. (films) The Laughing Policeman, 1973; (TV movies) A Small Rebellion, 1966, Fame Is the Name of the Game, 1966; (TV episodes) Decoy, 1957, Naked City, 1958-59, Alfred Hitchcock Presents, 1959-61 The Barbara Stanwyk Show, 1960, Hong Kong, 1960,The Untouchables, 1960-62 Adventures in Paradise, 1961, Question 7, 1961, Bus Stop, 1961-62, The Nurses, 1962, Ben Casey, 1962, The Twilight Zone, 1960-63, The Richard Boone Show, 1963, Espionage, 1963, Bob Hope Presents the Chrysler Theatre, 1963-66 Calhoun: Countty Agemnt, 1964, The Reporter, 1964, The Defenders, 1962-64, Memorandum for a Spy, 1965, For the People, 1965, Rawhide, 196, The Trials of O'Brien, 1965, A Small Rebellion, 1966; Recipient Emmy award for dramatic directing 1962, Dir.'s Guild award nominee (4). Served with USNR, 1945-47. Died Mar. 15, 2007.

ROSENCRANS, EVAN WILLIAM, retired air force officer; b. Sayre, Pa., May 31, 1926; s. Lloyd Calvin and Martha (Meredith) R.; m. Wilma Ruth Buchholz; children: Karen L., Linda M., Cynthia L., Douglas E. BS, U.S. Mil. Acad., 1948; MBA, George Washington U., 1968. Commd. 2d lt. USAF, 1948, advanced through grades to lt. gen., 1979; pilot 80th Fighter-Bomber Squadron, Korea, 1950-51; flight comdr. RAF, Chivenor, U.K., 1953-55; ops. officer, comdr. 3597th Combat Crew Tng. Squadron, Nellis AFB, Nev., 1955-56; co-comdr. dept. tactics U.S. Mil. Acad., 1957-59; ops. officer, comdr. 531st Tactical Fighter Squadron Misawa AFB, Japan, 1960-63; ops. officer Hdqrs. Pacific Air Forces Hickam AFB, Hawaii, 1963-65; ops. officer, dep. chief staff plans and ops. Hdqrs. USAF, 1965; mem. gen. purposes forces br., chmn. spl. study group Joint Chiefs Staff, 1966-67; asst. dep. comdr. ops. 37th Tactical Fighter Wing Phu Cat AFB, Vietnam, 1968-69; vice comdr. 4531st Tactical Fighter Wing Homestead AFB, Fla., 1969-70; comdr. 354th Tactical Fighter Wing Myrtle Beach AFB, S.C., 1970-71; dir. inspection Air Force Inspection and Safety Center, 1971-73; comdr. 3d Air Force RAF Mildenhall, U.K., 1973-77; vice comdr. Air Tng. Command Randolph AFB, Tex., 1977-79; dep. comdr. in chief UN Command Korea, U.S. Forces Korea; comdr. Air Forces Korea, 1979-81; ret., 1981. Decorated Def. D.S.M., AF D.S.M., Legion of Merit with 2 oak leaf clusters, D.F.C. with 3 oak leaf clusters, Air medal with 16 oak leaf clusters. Mem. Air Force Assn., Order of Daedalians (nat. comdr. 1993). Presbyterian. Home: Hollywood Park, Tex. Died May 8, 2007.

ROSENFELD, NAOMI EVE, corporate communications specialist; b. Jerusalem, Oct. 14, 1944; d. Franz and Marianne Renate (Imberg) Winkler; m. Steven B. Rosenfeld, Aug. 21, 1965; children: Kathryn Anne, Elizabeth Jane. BA, Sarah Lawrence Coll., 1966. V.p. Drexel Burnham Lambert, NYC, 1981-86, first v.p., 1986-90; ptnr., mng. dir. Morgen-Walke Assocs., NYC, from 1990. Mem. Met. Opera Club. Home: New York, NY. Died Apr. 19, 2006.

ROSENFELT, FRANK EDWARD, retired film company executive; b. Peabody, Mass., Nov. 15, 1921; s. Samuel and Ethel (Litvack) R.; m. Judith Roman, Nov. 1, 1943; children: Fred, Peter, Karen. BS, Cornell U., 1948, LL.B., 1950. Bar: N.Y. 1950, Mass. 1950, Calif. 1971. Atty. RKO Radio Pictures, 1950-55; with Metro-Goldwyn-Mayer, Inc., 1955—90, pres., CEO, 1973-90; chmn. bd., CEO Metro-Goldwyn-Mayer Film Co., 1980-83, vice chmn. bd. emeritus in charge European ops. London, 1983-85; vice chmn. bd. in charge European ops. MGM/UA Communications Co. (formerly MGM/UA Entertainment Co.), London, 1985-90; exec. cons. Metro-Goldwyn-Mayer Inc., Culver City, Calif. Bd. editors: Cornell Law Quar, 1948-50. Served with inf. AUS, World War II. Decorated Purple Heart. Mem. Acad. Motion Picture Arts and Scis. (bd. govs. 1977-85), Order of Coif. Died Aug. 2, 2007.

ROSENTHAL, EARL EDGAR, art history educator; b. Milw., Aug. 26, 1921; s. Edgar Ernst and Reneé (Wyler) R. BS, U. Wis. at, Milw., 1943; PhD, NYU, 1953; Doctor honoris causa, U. Granada, 1994. Asst. dir. Milw. Art Inst., also Layton Art Gallery, Milw., 1952-53; vis. lectr., dept. art history U. Chgo., from 1953, prof., 1968-91, prof. emeritus, from 1991. Author: The Cathedral of Granada, 1961; The Palace of Charles V in Granada, 1985, translated to Spanish 1988, Arquitectura imperial, 1988. Contbr. articles to profl. publs. Served to lt. (j.g.) USNR, 1943-46, PTO. Recipient Gold medal in Fine Arts King of Spain, 1989, medal of honor Fundación Rodríguez Acosta (Granada), 1989; Spanish govt. grantee, 1948-49; Fulbright grantee Italy, 1949-50; Fulbright grantee Spain, 1963-64; Guggenheim grantee Italy, 1963-64 Mem. Hispanic Soc. Am., Coll. Art Assn., Soc. Archtl. Historians (dir. 1957-58, 66-69), Academia de San Fernando (Madrid) (corr.), Academia de Bellas Artes (Granada) (corr.). Home: Santa Barbara, Calif. Died Sept. 14, 2007.

ROSENTHAL, HERBERT CARL, graphics design executive; b. Winnipeg, Man., Can., Oct. 4, 1917; came to U.S., 1918; s. Michael Charles and Anna (Frankel) R.; m. Margaret Halmy, Sept. 12, 1940 (div. July 1969); children— Lawrence, Steven, Robert; m. Rhoda Jean Turteltaub, Mar. 2, 1970. B.A., Columbia Coll., 1938. Reader, 20th Century Fox, N.Y.C., 1938; assoc. editor Ice Cream Field Mag., N.Y.C., 1939; asst. to pres., v.p. Pictograph Corp., N.Y.C., 1940-44; graphics editor Newspaper PM, N.Y.C., 1944-45; founder, pres. Graphics Inst., Inc., N.Y.C., 1944-82; mng. dir. Graphics Inst. div. Creamer Dickson Basford, N.Y.C., 1983—; trustee Pub. Ind. Group Ins. Fund, N.Y.C., 1975-83. Co-author: Sex Habits of American Women, 1951; A Visual History of the United States, 1961; The Medigraph Manual, 1973; conbtbr. numerous articles to mags. Mem. Internat. Assn. Bus. Communicators, Phi Beta Kappa. Home: Westport, Conn. Died Jan. 15, 2007.

ROSENTHAL, MITCHELL, healthcare executive; b. Newark, Mar. 13, 1949; s. Morris Robert and Edythe (Kurtz) R.; m. Margaret Fridel, Aug. 18, 1974; children: Michelle Sara, David Joseph. BA in Psychology, Rutgers U., 1970; MA in Psychology, Fairleigh Dickinson U., 1972; PhD in Clin. Psychology, U. Cin., 1975. Staff psychologist Children's Psychiat. Ctr., Cin., 1974-75; dir. rehab. psychology Med. Coll. of Va., Richmond, 1975-79, New Eng. Med. Ctr., Boston, 1979-86; dir. psychol. medicine Marianjoy Rehab. Ctr., Wheaton, Ill., 1986-89; prof., assoc. chmn. of phys. medicine and rehab. Wayne State U., Detroit, from 1990; v.p. rsch. and edn. Rehab. Inst. of Mich., Detroit, from 1990—. Trustee Comm. on Accreditation of Rehab. Facilities, Tuscon, Ariz., 1991—. Editor: (book) Rehabilitation of Adult and Child With Trauma Brain Injury, 1990; editor: Jour. of Head Trauma Rehab., 1985—. Recipient 1st Clin. Svc. award Nat. Head Injury Found., Washington, 1988; long-term tng. grantee in rehab. psychology Rehab. Svcs. Adminstrn., Washington, 1994, grantee Nat. Inst. on Disability and Rehab. Rsch., Washington, 1993. Fellow Am. Psychol. Assn. (pres. divsn. of rehab. psychology 1991-92); mem. Am. Congress of Rehab. Medicine, Internat. Neuropsychol. Soc. Home: Basking Ridge, NJ. Died May 31, 2007.

ROSENZWEIG, DAVID, former newspaper editor; b. Jersey City, Feb. 17, 1940; s. Herbert and Ethel (Hinkes) Rosenzweig; m. Lael Rubin; 2 stepchildren BA in History, Rutgers U., 1961. Reporter Newark Star Ledger, 1962-63, Newark Evening News, 1963-64, AP, 1964-71, L.A. Times, 1971-79, asst. met. editor, 1979-83, met. editor, 1983-89, asst. mng. editor, 1989—93, reporter, 1993—2005. Home: Santa Monica, Calif. Died May 2, 2007.

ROSS, ARTHUR, philanthropist, retired financier; b. NYC, Nov. 25, 1910; s. Adolph and Estelle R.; m. Gloria Frankenthaler (div. 1970); children: Alfred F., Beverly, Clifford Arthur; m. Janet C. Neff, Sept. 17, 1984 Student, Wharton Sch., U. Pa., 1927-30; BS, Columbia U., 1931; degree (hon.), LI U., 1988. With Sutro Bros. & Co. (mems. N.Y. Stock Exchange), 1932-37, Central Nat. Corp., 1938—, v.p., 1945-56, mng. dir., 1956-80, exec. v.p., 1956-74, vice chmn., 1974, Central Nat.-Gottesman Inc.; dir. Dreyfus Cash Mgmt. Group, Lazard Spl. Equities Fund. Mem. U.S. del. 38th, 39th, 52d assemblies Econ. and Social Council of UN; fgn. affairs adviser to U.S. Mission to UN; sr. adviser U.S. del. UNESCO 18th Biennial Conf., Paris, 1974; mem. U.S. del. to 21st Bennial Conf., Belgrade, 1980; sr. adviser U.S. del. to 22d Biennial Conf., Paris, 1983; mem. UNESCO Monitoring Panel, 1984; adviser U.S. del. UN Water Conf., Mar del Plata, Argentina, 1977; past mem. Nat. Export Expansion Council; expert witness Congressional Sub-com. on Econ. Growth, 1974 Mem. editorial bd.: Washington Quar. Bd. dirs. Barnard Coll., N.Y.C., Parks Council, Central Park Community Fund, N.Y. Landmarks Conservancy, Bryant Park Restoration Corp., N.Y.C., Central Park Conservancy, N.Y.; trustee Am. Acad. in Rome, Riverdale Country Sch., Am. Mus. Natural History; trustee, v.p. Spanish Inst.; bd. overseers U. Pa. Grad. Sch. Fine Arts; mem. council Cooper-Hewitt Mus. Served as lt. USNR, 1942-45; lt. comdr. Res. Mem. UN Assn. U.S.A. (dir.), Center for Strategic and Internat. Studies, Fgn. Policy Assn. N.Y. (dir.), Internat. Inst. Strategic Studies (London), Asia Soc. (dir., trustee), Council on Fgn. Relations, AAAS (mem. investment and fin. com.), Beta Gamma Sigma. Clubs: Century Country (White Plains, N.Y.); Century Assn. (N.Y.C.). Home: New York, NY. Died Sept. 10, 2007.

ROSS, DOUGLAS TAYLOR, retired software company executive; b. Canton, Republic of China, Dec. 21, 1929; (parents Am. citizens); s. Robert Malcolm and Margaret (Taylor) R.; m. Patricia Mott, Jan. 24, 1951; children: Jane Louise, Kathryn R. Chow, Margaret R. Thrasher. AB in Math. cum laude, Oberlin Coll., 1951; SM, MIT, 1954, postgrad., 1958; DSc (hon.), Oberlin Coll., 2001. Head computer applications group elec. systems lab. MIT, Cambridge, 1952-69, lectr. dept. elec. engring. and computer sci., 1960-69, 83—, exec. com. MIT Enterprise Forum, 1984-89; founder, pres. SofTech, Inc., Waltham, Mass., 1969-75, chmn. bd., 1975-89, 91-93, chmn. emeritus, 1989-91, 93-94, ret., 1994. Mem. town meeting, Lexington, Mass., 1960-70; trustee, bd. dirs. Charles Babbage Inst., 1984-2001, emeritus trustee, 2002—. Mem. United Ch. of Christ. Home: Lexington, Mass. Died Jan. 31, 2007.

ROSS, JANET, retired English language educator; b. Duluth, Minn., Apr. 19, 1914; d. Guy Whittier Chadbourn and Helen (Mason) Ross. Student, Carleton Coll., 1931-32; BA, U. Minn., 1935, MA, 1940; PhD, U. Iowa, 1960. Asst. prof. English Fla. State U., Tallahassee, 1949-52, Macalester Coll., St. Paul, 1957-60; instr. English U. Iowa, Iowa City, 1952-54, 55-57, U. B.C. (Can.), Vancouver, 1960-62; prof. English, coord. MA teaching English as fgn. lang. Ball State U., Muncie, Ind., 1961-80, prof. emeritus, from 1980. Vis. prof. U. Colo., Boulder, summers 1956-58, 60, 71-72, 83-85, Pontificia U. Rio Grande do Sol, Porto Alegre, Brazil, 1973; guest lectr. Montgomery (Md.) Community Coll., 1977, U. Saga (Japan), 1980, U. Panama, Panama City, 1981. Co-author: Language and Life in the U.S.A., 1961, 4th edit., 1982, To Write English, 1965, 3rd edit., 1984; author: Understanding English, 1982. Fulbright fellow, Netherlands, 1954-55; Danforth Found. grantee U. Mich., 1964; Nat. Assn. Fgn. Student Affairs travel study grantee Yale U., 1962, travel grantee, France, 1966. Mem. Tchrs. English to Speakers Other Langs. (regional sec. 1976-80), Colo. Authors League (sec. 1987—). Home: Boulder, Colo. Died Oct. 7, 2006.

ROSS, WILLIAM WARFIELD, lawyer; b. Washington, Oct. 3, 1926; s. W. Warfield and Vera Elfleda (Payne) R.; m. Jennie Fitch, Jan. 30, 1963; children— James, Mary, Billy; m. Nan Robertson, Sept. 25, 1999. AB, St. John's Coll., Annapolis, Md., 1948; LL.B., Yale U., 1951. Bar: D.C. 1951. Legal asst. Exec. Office Pres. Harry S. Truman, 1952-53, Pres. Dwight D. Eisenhower, 1953; atty. appellate sect. civil div. Dept. Justice, Washington, 1954-57; asst. to solicitor FPC, Washington, 1957-59; ptnr. Wald, Harkrader & Ross, Washington, 1963-87, Pepper, Hamilton & Scheetz, Washington, 1987-91. Adj. prof. Cornell U. Grad. Sch. Bus. and Pub. Adminstrn., 1977-80; chmn. D.C. Council Commn. on Bd. Appeals and Rev. of D.C. Govt., 1972 Chmn. Nat. Capital area ACLU, 1966-68; chmn. audit hearing panel Title I ESEA of 1965, 1976-80. Served with USN, 1945-46 Mem. ABA (chmn. sect. adminstrv. law 1978-79), Bar Assn. D.C. (chmn. adminstrv. law sect. 1968-69, gov. 1969-70), D.C. Bar, Fed. Bar Assn., Fed. Energy Bar Assn. (contbr. articles to jour.). Home: Bethesda, Md. Died July 4, 2006.

ROSSER, RICHARD FRANKLIN, educational association administrator, consultant, retired academic administrator; b. Arcanum, Ohio, July 16, 1929; s. Harold Arm and Margaret (Whitacre) R.; m. Donna Eyssen., Mar. 21, 1951; children— Eric, Carl, Edward. BA, Ohio Wesleyan U., 1951; MPA, Syracuse U., 1952, PhD, 1961. Joined USAF, 1952, advanced through grades to col., 1968; prof. polit. sci. USAF Acad., Colorado Springs, Colo., 1959-73, head dept., 1967-73, ret., 1973; prof. polit. sci., dean Albion (Mich.) Coll., 1973-77; pres. DePauw U., Greencastle, Ind., 1977-86, chancellor, 1986; pres. Nat. Assn. Ind. Colls. and Univs., Washington, 1986-93; cons. in higher edn. pvt. practice, Racine, Wis., 1993—2007. Author: An Introduction to Soviet Foreign Policy, 1969; contbr. articles to profl. jours. Mem. univ. senate United Meth. Ch., 1980-84; mem. spl. commn. of Chief of Staff on Honor Code U.S. Mil. Acad., 1989; bd. visitors Air U., 1991-94; bd. trustees Ohio Wesleyan U.; mem. nat. adv. com. Instnl. Quality and Integrity; co-chair Citizens for Librs., Grand Traverse County, 1995-96. Decorated Legion of Merit with oak leaf cluster. Mem. Phi Beta Kappa, Omicron Delta Kappa. Unitarian. Died Sept. 21, 2007.

ROSSIER, ALAIN BENJAMIN, paraplegist, physician; b. Lausanne, Switzerland, Nov. 29, 1930; came to U.S., 1973, naturalized, 1979; s. Guy Henri and Denise Frances (Cordey) R.; m. Birte Andersen, Mar. 28, 1959. Fed. Diploma, U. Lausanne, 1957, MD, 1958, PhD. Fellow spinal cord injury svc. Cantonal Hosp., Zurich, 1960; intern neurosurg. and surg. svcs. VA Hosp., Long Beach, Calif., 1961-62, Inst. Phys. Med. and Rehab., NYC, 1962, Albert Einstein Coll. Medicine (others); chief spinal cord injury svc. Beau-Sé Jour Hosp.; asst. chief phys. medicine and rehab. svc. Univ. Hosp., Geneva, 1964-73; chief spinal cord injury svc. West Roxbury (Mass.) VA Med. Center, 1973-84; prof. spinal cord rehab. Harvard Med. Sch., 1973-84. Cons. Mass. Rehab. Hosp., Braintree (Mass.) Hosp.; cons. neurosurgery and orthopedic surgery Children's Hosp. Med. Center, Boston; prof. paraplegia, Zurich, 1986-89 Author: (with A.G. Hardy) Spinal Cord Injuries. Orthopedic and Neurological Aspects, 1975; contbr. 140 articles to med. jours. Recipient Premio Missione del Medico Carlo Erba Found. Italy, 1973 Mem. Am. Urol. Assn., Am. Assn. Neurol. Surgeons, Internat. Med. Soc. Paraplegia, Internat. Continence Soc., Am. Assn. Orthopedic Surgeons, Am. Spinal Injury Assn., Am. Congress Rehab. Medicine. Clubs: Rotary. Died May 12, 2006.

ROSTROPOVICH, MSTISLAV LEOPOLDOVICH, conductor, musician, music director; b. Baku, Azerbaijan, Mar. 27, 1927; s. Leopold and Sofia (Fedotova) Rostropovich; m. Galina Pavlovna Vishnevskaya, 1955; children: Olga, Elena. Grad., Moscow Conservatory 1948; Mus D (hon.), Oxford, 1980; numerous hon. doctorate degrees. Faculty mem. Moscow Conservatory, 1953, prof., 1960; head cello and double-bass dept., formerly prof. Leningrad Conservatory; music dir., conductor Nat. Symphony Orch., Washington, 1977-94; hon. prof. Cuban Nat. Conservatory, 1960-78. Pres. Evian Internat. Music Festival. Debut as violoncellist, 1940; performer (world concert tours): Moscow Philharm. Orch.; recordings include with various artists Mstislav Rostropovich Melodiya Recordings, 1949—56, 1948—59, The Young Rostropovich: Rare Recordings, 1950—52, Schnittke's Cello Concerto No. 2, In Memorium, Return to Russia. Decorated Hon. Knight of Brit. Empire, Officer's Cross of Merit Fed. Republic Germany, Comdr. French Legion of Honor, Order of Service to the Fatherland; named Musician of Yr., Music Am., 1987; recipient First prize, All-Union Competition of Musicians, 1945, Internat. Cellist Competitions, Prague, 1947, 1951, Internat. Cellist Competitions, Budapest, 1949, USSR State prize, 1951, Stalin prize, 1951, 1953, Lenin prize, 1963, Gold medal, Royal Philharm. Soc., Siemens prize, Sonning prize, Denmark, Grammy award, 1970, 1977, 1980, 1984, Life in Music prize, 1984, Albert Schweitzer Music award, 1985, Presdl. medal of Freedom, 1987, Ditson Condr.'s award, Columbia U., 1990, Four Freedoms award, Franklin and Eleanor Roosevelt Inst., 1992, Kennedy Ctr. hon., 1992, Imperial award, 1993, Wolf Prize in the Arts, 2004. Mem.: Acad. Arts of French Inst.-Forty Immortals, Union Soviet Composers, Am. Acad. Arts and Scis., Acad. of St. Cecilia, Rome (hon.), Brit. Royal Acad. Music (hon.). Died Apr. 27, 2007.

ROSTVOLD, GERHARD NORMAN, economist, consultant; b. Nashwauk, Minn., Oct. 15, 1919; s. Arndt and Olive Mathilda (Ness) R.; m. Virginia Fay Faubion, Feb. 3, 1945; children— Roger Mark, Laura Ann, Christine Marie, Ellen Alicia. AB in Econs.-Accountancy with great distinction, Stanford, 1948, MA in Econs, 1949, PhD in Econs, 1955. Instr. Stanford U., 1949-51; prof. econs. and acctg. Pomona Coll., Claremont, Calif., 1952-66; cons. Urbanomics Rsch. Assoc., Laguna Hills, Calif., from 1966. Adj. prof. econs. Pepperdine U.; econ. newscaster Sta. KHJ-TV, L.A., 1978-82; econ. cons. to govt., industry; trustee Mortgage & Realty Trust. Author: The Southern California Metropolis— 1980, 1960, Financing California Government, 1967, The Economics of Energy, 1975, Economics and the Environment, 1975, The Economics of the Public Utility Enterprise, 1976, Understanding How the Economic System Works, 1976, Teacher's Instructional Program for Understanding How the Economic System Works, 1976, Charting Your Path to Economic and Financial Survival in the 1980's, 1979, How to Stretch your Dollars to Cope with the Inflation of the 1980's, 1981; co-author: California Local Finance, 1960, Garcia-Rostvold Work Experience Education Series, 1974, (with Thomas J. Dudley) Congressional report, New Perspectives on Grazing Fees and Public Land Management in the 1990s, 1992; social sci. editor: Stone/Leswing Social Sci. Series; editor: Rostvold Econ. Outlook and Personal Money Mgmt. Newsletter; contbr. articles to profl jours. Chmn. nat. adv. bd. Coun. Pub. Lands; mem. Calif. advisory bd., mem. Calif. Coun. Econ. Edn. Served with USAAF, 1942-45. NSF fellow Stanford U., 1965-66; recipient Wig Disting. Professorship award Pomona Coll., 1962; Conservation award Dept. Interior, 1975. Mem. Am. Econ. Assn., Western Econ. Assn. (pres. 1966-67), Nat. Tax Assn. (pres.), Lambda Alpha. Home: Laguna Niguel, Calif. Died Mar. 15, 2007.

ROTHMAN, STEWART NEIL, photographer; b. Rochester, N.Y., Dec. 27, 1930; s. Morris Zeus and Rose Mary (Cotler) R.; student Wayne State U., 1952-54; m. Shirley Mae Derry, Sept. 12, 1957; children— Leslie Paula, Karen Pat. Free-lance photographer, Detroit, 1952-57; photographer NASA, Gilmore Creek, Alaska, 1965-68; writer, photographer Jessen's Daily, Fairbanks, Alaska, 1968-69; propr. The Lens Unlimited, Fairbanks, 1959-—; staff photographer Gen. Mac Arthur's Hdqrs., Tokyo, 1948-50; pres., chmn. bd. Arctic Publs., 1968-72; pres. Public Relations Specialists Co., 1973-—; editor Arctic Oil Jour., 1968-72, This Month in Fairbanks, 1974--85; pub. The Fairbanks Mag., 1985—. Publicity adviser to mayor of Fairbanks; pres. Tanana-Yukon Hist. Soc. Served with U.S. Army, 1948-52, Korea, then USAF, 1957-65. Decorated Purple Heart with oak leaf cluster. Fellow Master Photographers Assn. Gt. Britain; mem. European Council Photographers, Fairbanks C. of C. Club: Farthest North Press. Lodges: Lions (pres.), Elks. Author: Nudes of Sixteen Lands, 1971; Hobo and Dangerous Dan McGrew, 1975; The Lens is My Brush, 1977; China, The Opening Door, 1980; Pope John Paul II's First Visit to Alaska, 1981; Window on Life, 1982; The Pope and the President, 1984, Alaska and the World, 1993. Died Feb. 8, 2007.

ROTHSCHILD, DIANE, advertising agency executive; b. NYC, Apr. 11, 1943; d. Morton Royce and Marjorie Jay (Simon) R.; m. Alan M. Pando, 1998; 1 child, Alexandra Rothschild Spencer. BA, Aldephi U., 1965. Copywriter Doyle Dane Bernbach Advt., Inc., NYC, 1967-73, v.p., 1973-79, sr. v.p., assoc. creative dir., 1979-85, exec. v.p., creative dir., 1985-86; pres. Grace and Rothschild, NYC, 1986—2000. Bd. mem. Lung Cancer Alliance, 2005—07. Recipient maj. advt. awards; inducted into the One Club Creative Hall of Fame, 2005 Mem. YWCA Acad. Women Achievers. Home: New York, NY. Died Mar. 31, 2007.

ROTMAN, ARTHUR, former social welfare administrator; b. Montreal, Que., Can., Nov. 29, 1926; came to U.S., 1968; s. Myer Rotman and Mollie Schachtman; m. Anita Schecter, Sept. 4, 1947; children: Stephen, Laurie, Carol. BA, George Williams Coll., Montreal, 1947; MS, Case Western Res. U., 1949. Various positions YM-YWHA, Montreal, 1949-66, assoc. exec. dir., 1966-68; exec. dir. Jewish Community Ctr., Pitts., 1968-76; exec. v.p. Jewish Community Ctrs. Assn. N.Am., NYC, 1976-94; ret., 1994; lectr. Sch. Social Work, McGill U., Montreal, 1958-68. Contbr. chpts. to books, articles to profl. jours. Mem. Assn. Jewish Ctr. Workers (past v.p.), World Conf. Jewish Communal Service (pres., past treas.). Democrat. Jewish. Home: Arkville, NY. Died May 10, 2007.

ROTMAN, WALTER, electrical engineer; b. St. Louis, Aug. 24, 1922; m. Molly Shapiro; children: Stanley, Ruth. BSEE, MIT, 1947, MSEE, 1948. Br. chief Air Force Cambridge Rsch. Lab. USAF, Bedford, Mass., 1948-65, br. chief Rome Air Devel. Ctr., Lexington, Mass., 1965-80; tech. staff MIT Lincoln Lab., Lexington, from 1980. Fellow IEEE (life mem., Centennial medal 1984). Democrat. Jewish. Home: Brookline, Mass. Died May 19, 2007.

ROTT, NICHOLAS, fluid mechanics educator; b. Budapest, Hungary, Oct. 6, 1917; came to U.S. 1951; s. Alexander and Margaret (Pollak) R.; m. Rosanna Saredi, Sept. 30, 1944; children: Paul, Kathy. Diploma in Mechanical engring., Swiss Fed. Inst. Tech., Zurich, 1940; PhD, ETH, Zurich, 1944. Rsch. asst., pvt. dozent Aerodynamics Inst., Zurich, 1944-51; prof. Grad. Sch. Aeronautical Engring. Cornell U., Ithaca, N.Y., 1951-60; prof. UCLA, 1960-67, ETH, Zurich, 1967-83. Vis. prof. Stanford (Calif.) U., 1983—. Fellow AIAA, Am. Phys. Soc.; mem. NAE, Acoustical Soc. Am. Home: Palo Alto, Calif. Died Aug. 10, 2006.

ROUSE, IRVING, anthropologist, emeritus educator; b. Rochester, NY, Aug. 29, 1913; s. Benjamin Irving and Louise Gillespie (Bohachek) R.; m. Mary Uta Mikami, June 24, 1939; children: Peter, David. BS, Yale U., 1934, PhD, 1938; D in Philosophy and Letters (hon.), Centro de Estudios Avanzados de Puerto Rico y el Caribe, 1990. Asst. anthropology Yale Peabody Mus., 1934-38, asst. curator, 1938-47, assoc. curator, 1947-54, rsch. assoc., 1954-62, curator, 1977-85, emeritus curator, from 1985; instr. anthropology Yale U., 1939-43, asst. prof., 1943-48; assoc. prof. Yale, 1948-54; prof. Yale U., 1954-69, Charles J.

MacCurdy prof. anthropology, 1969-84, prof. emeritus, from 1984. Author monographs on archaeology of Fla., Cuba, Haiti, P.R., Venezuela, Antigua. Recipient Medalla Commemorativa del Vuelo Panamericano pro Faro de Colon Govt. Cuba, 1945, A. Cressy Morrison prize in natural sci. NY Acad. Sci., 1951, Viking fund medal Wenner-Gren Found., 1960, Wilbur Cross medal Yale U., 1992; Guggenheim fellow, 1963-64; fellow Phi Beta Kappa, 1996. Mem. Am. Anthrop. Assn. (pres. 1967-68), Ea. States Archeol. Fedn. (pres. 1946-50), Assn. Field Arch. (pres. 1977-78), Soc. Am. Arch. (editor 1946-50, pres. 1952-53), Nat. Acad. Sci., Am. Acad. Arts and Sci., Arch. Soc. of Conn. (hon. mem.), Fla. Arch. Soc. (hon. mem.), Internat. Assn. Caribbean Arch. (hon. mem.), Soc. Antiquaries (London). Home: North Haven, Conn. Died Feb. 4, 2006.

ROWE, BRIAN H., aeronautical engineer, electrical engineer; b. London, May 6, 1931; BS, Durham U., Eng., 1955. Various engrng. positions Gen. Elec. Co., 1957-68, gen. mgr. CF6 project dept., 1968-72, v.p., gen. mgr. com. engine project divsn., 1972-74, v.p., gen. mgr. airline prog divsn., 1974-76, v.p., gen. mgr. aircraft engrng. divsn., 1976-79, sr. v.p., from 1979, chmn. aircraft engines, from 1993. Recipient R. Tom Sawyer award AIAA, 1994. Fellow Royal Aeron. Soc.; NAE. Died Feb. 22, 2007.

ROWE, JOYCE MORGAN, health care consultant; b. Floral Park, N.Y., June 17, 1937; d. F. Howard and Else Helene (Rietheimer) Morgan; m. Allen Martin Rowe, Dec. 26, 1959; children— Amy, Jeffrey, Jon, Carrie Beth. B.S. in Edn., SUNY-Oneonta, 1959; 5th yr. health info. services cert. U. Seattle, 1978. Accredited record technician, registered record adminstr. Tchr., St. Paul's Sch., Norwich, N.Y., 1967-71; quality assurance coordinator St. Joseph's Hosp. and Health Ctr., Syracuse, N.Y., 1975-78; quality assurance specialist U. Ill. Med. Ctr., Chgo., 1979-82; mgr. med. records South Suburban Hosp., Hazel Crest, Ill., 1982-83; founder, pres. JR Assocs., Oaklawn, Ill., 1983—. Instr., Chgo. State U., 1979-83. Mem. adv. com. Morraine Valley (Ill.) Community Coll., 1982-83. Mem. Am. Med. Record Assn., Ill. Med. Record Assn., Chgo. Vicinity Med. Record Assn. (pub. relations com. 1983), Soc. Computer Sci., Fedn. Internat. Health Instrs., Bus. and Profl. Women (pres. chpt. 1977), Am. Legion Aux. (pres. chpt. 1966-67, treas. chpt. 1966-67), Theta Phi Epsilon. Contbr. articles to profl. jours.; author: Medical Record Maintenance: A Costing and Personnel Assessment. Home: La Grange Park, Ill. Died Feb. 1, 2007.

ROWLAND, HERBERT LESLIE, public relations executive; b. NYC, Dec. 4, 1925; s. I. Martin and Matilda (Appelbaum) R.; m. Joan Feldman, Apr. 9, 1949 (div. 1970); children: Russell Lloyd, Daryl Verne, Julie Anne; m. Patricia Dickson George, Nov. 9, 1985. BS, CCNY, 1948; MA, Columbia U., 1951. Corr. N.Y. Times, 1949-50; editor Where mag., also TV Week mag., 1951-53; gen. mgr. Roger Brown, Inc., NYC, 1954-56; ptnr. Brown & Rowland, NYC, 1957-60; pres. Rowland Co., NYC, 1961-88; chmn., chief exec. officer Rowland Worldwide, Inc., NYC, from 1988. With USAAF, 1944-46. Mem. Pub. Rels. Soc. Am. Home: New York, NY. Died Feb. 8, 2007.

ROWLEY, PETER TEMPLETON, pediatrician, educator; b. Greenville, Pa., Apr. 29, 1929; s. George Hardy and Susan Mossman (Templeton) R.; m. Carol Stone, Mar. 19, 1967; children: Derek Stone, Jason Templeton. AB magna cum laude, Harvard U., 1951; MD, Columbia U., 1955. Diplomate: Am. Bd. Internal Medicine. Intern med. service N.Y. Hosp.-Cornell Med. Center, 1955-56; clin. assoc. Nat. Inst. Neurol. Disease and Blindness, NIH, 1956-58; asst. resident, then resident Harvard Med. Service, Boston City Hosp.; asst. in medicine Harvard U. Med. Sch. and researcher Thorndike Meml. Lab., 1958-60; hon. research asst. dept. eugenics, biometry and genetics Univ. Coll., U. London, 1960-61; postdoctoral fellow dept. microbiology NYU Sch. Medicine, 1961-63; asst. prof. medicine Stanford U., 1963-70; assoc. prof. medicine pediatrics and genetics U. Rochester, 1970-75, prof. medicine, pediatrics, genetics and microbiology, from 1975, prof. oncology, from 1991, chmn. div. genetics, from 1990; physician, pediatrician Strong Meml. Hosp., from 1970. Mem. N.Y. State Exec. and Adv. Coms. on Genetic Disease, 1979—; WHO vis. scholar Inst. Biol. Chemistry, U. Ferrara, Italy, 1970. Editor (with M. Lipkin Jr.): Genetic Responsibility: On Choosing Our Children's Genes, 1974; co-editor: Genetic Testing. With USPHS, 1956-58. Recipient Excellence in Teaching award U. Rochester Class of 1976, 1973; NRC fellow, 1960-63; Buswell research fellow, 1970-71, 71-72 Fellow ACP, Am. Coll. Genetics; mem. Am. Fedn. Clin. Rsch., Am. Soc. Hematology, Am. Soc. Human Genetics (social issues com. 1980-89, program com. 1993-96), N.Y. State Health Rsch. (sci. bd. 1997—). Home: Rochester, NY. Died Mar. 27, 2006.

RUBIN, BERNARD, chemist; b. Boston, July 1, 1922; s. Morris and Anna (Kaplan) R.; m. Selma Lois Wenesky, June 29, 1952; children: Susan M., Eric R., David H. AB, Harvard U., 1944; PhD, Ohio State U., 1951. Rsch. chemist Nat. Bur. Standards, Washington, 1951-54; br. chief Air Force Camb. Res. Labs., Bedford, Mass., 1954-66; research scientist NASA Electronics Rsch. Ctr., Cambridge, 1966-70; program mgr. NASA Hdqrs., Washington, 1970-80; cons. chemist Bethesda, Md., 1980-84, program mgr. Nichols Rsch. Corp., McLean, Va., 1984-87; con. NASA Hdqrs., 1987—. Contbr. articles to profl. jours. Patentee in field. Served to lt. (j.g.), USNR, 1943-46; PTO. Mem. Am. Chem. Soc., Sigma Xi. Avocation: swimming. Home: Bethesda, Md. Died May 24, 2007.

RUBIN, WILLIAM, editor; b. NYC, Jan. 10, 1928; s. Herman and Molly (Goodman) R.; m. Claire Levine, Aug. 30, 1953; children: Deborah E., Joan S., Howard I. BA, Bklyn. Coll., 1953. Tech. editor Drug Trade News, NYC, 1952-63; dir. pub. info. Nat. Vitamin Found., NYC, 1958-61; editorial dir. FDC Reports & Drug Rsch. Reports, Washington, 1963-64; proprietor Sci. Reports and Projects, Bethesda, MD., 1964-67; editor Internat. Med. News Group, Rockville, Md., 1967-91; editorial cons., from 1992. Editor Clin. Psychiatry News, Family Practice News, Internal Medicine News, Ob-Gyn. News, Pediatric News, Skin & Allergy News, Internat. Med. News Group. Bd. dirs. Washington chpt. Am. Found. for Suicide Prevention; chmn. Md. Adv. Coun. on Arthritis and Related Diseases; bd. dirs. Reginald Lourie Ctr. for Infants and Young Children; mem. spkrs' bur. Met. Washington chpt. Arthritis Found.; vice chmn. Montgomery County (Md.) Libr. Bd. With USAAF, 1946-47. Mem. Nat. Assn. Sci. Writers (life), Am. Med. Writers Assn., N.Y. Acad. Scis., Nat. Press Club. Avocations: book accumulating, reading history, woodworking. Home: Chevy Chase, Md. Died May 12, 2007.

RUEGG, DONALD GEORGE, retired rail transportation executive; b. LaJunta, Colo., Sept. 11, 1924; s. George Albert and Cecilia Corrine (Decker) R.; m. Ruth Carson, June 27, 1946 (dec. 1963); m. Mary Ann Eichelberger, June 24, 1964. BA, Dartmouth Coll., 1947; MBA, U. Chgo., 1972. Sec. to trainmaster, trainmaster's clk. Atchison, Topeka & Santa Fe Ry. Co., 1942—50, traveling car agt. Chgo., 1950—51, transp. inspector, 1951—52; safety supr. Atchison Topeka & Santa Fe Ry. Co., Emporia, 1952—53, trainmaster, 1953—68; asst. to v.p. info. sys. Atchison, Topeka & Santa Fe Ry. Co., Topeka, 1968—69, asst. to v.p. operation, 1969—72, gen. mgr. LA, 1972—73, asst. v.p. ops., 1973—78, v.p. ops., 1978—83, exec. v.p., 1983—86; ret., 1986. Home: Durham, NC. Died Oct. 22, 2006.

RUETZ, JULIANNE MARGARET, communications educator, consultant; b. Los Angeles, Apr. 6, 1929; d. Paul and Margaret Emma (Zinke) Brueggemann; m. Edward Joseph Ruetz, Sept. 30, 1950 (div.); children— Jeffrey Edward, Lynn Karen Ruetz Hertwig. M.A., U. Denver, 1969; Ph.B., Marquette U., 1950. Tchr. speech, English, Sch. Dist. 6, Littleton, Colo., 1961-71; instr. Arapahoe Community Coll., Littleton, 1971-74, adminstr., 1974-79; media services dir. corp. pub. relations dept. Mountain Bell Co., Denver, 1979-81; asst. prof. pub. relations dept. tech. journalism Colo. State U., Fort Collins, 1982-85; instr. speech Met. State Coll., Denver, 1985—. Mem. Pub. Relations Soc. Am., Internat. Soc. Bus. Communicators, Assn. Edn. in Journalism and Mass Communication. Democrat. Unitarian. Home: Castle Rock, Colo. Died Mar. 2, 2006.

RUGOFF, MILTON, editor, author; b. NYC, Mar. 6, 1913; s. David and Jennie (Joseph) R.; m. Helen Birkenbaum, Jan. 31, 1937; 1 child, Kathy. BA, Columbia U., 1933, MA, 1934, PhD, 1940. Editor Alfred A. Knopf, Inc., 1943-47, The Magazine, 1947-48, Readers Subscription Book Club, 1953; editor, v.p. Chanticleer Press, NYC, 1948-83. Author: Donne's Imagery, 1940, Penguin Book of World Folk Tales, 1949, The Great Travelers, 1960, Prudery and Passion: Sexuality in Victorian America, 1970, The Beechers: An American Family in the Nineteenth Century, 1981 (Am. Book award nominee), America's Gilded Age: Intimate Portraits from an Era of Extravagance and Change, 1989; editor: Britannica Ency. American Art, 1973, The Wild Places, 1974 Served with AUS, 1943-46. Home: Elmsford, NY. Died Feb. 17, 2007.

RUH, EDWIN, ceramic engineer, consultant, researcher; b. Westfield, NJ, Apr. 22, 1924; s. Harry John and Martha A. (Grasing) R.; m. Elizabeth J. Mundy, June 14, 1952; children: Edwin Jr., Elizabeth Jeanne. BS in Ceramic Engring. with honors, Rutgers U., 1949, MS in Ceramic Engring., 1953, PhD in Ceramics, 1954. Registered profl. engr., Pa. Rsch. engr. Harbison Walker Refractories Co., Pitts., 1954-57, asst dir. rsch., 1957-70; dir. rsch. Harbison Walker Refractories Div. Dresser Ind., Pitts., 1970-73, dir. advanced tech., 1973-74; v.p. rsch. Vesuvius Crucible Co., Pitts., 1974-76; adj. prof. Carnegie Mellon U., Pitts., 1976-84; rsch. prof. Rutgers U., New Brunswick, NJ, 1984—94. Pres. Ruh Internat., Inc., Pitts., 1976-2003. Author: Refractories for the Chemical Process Industries, 1984; editor Metallurgical Transactions, 1979-84; author chpts. to books; contbr. articles to profl. jours. With U.S. Army, 1943-46, ETO. Fellow: Am. Ceramic Soc. (disting. life mem., pres. 1985—86, Founders award Phila. sect. 1989, Bleininger award Pitts. sect. 1990); mem.: AIME, AAAS, Keramos (nat. pres. 1970—72, Greaves-Walker Roll of Honor 1976), Australasian Ceramic Soc., Acad. Ceramics (prof.), Iron and Steel Soc., Minerals, Metals and Materials Soc., Ceramic Assn. NJ (pres. 1991—92, Ann. award 1988), Nat. Inst. Ceramics Engrs. (P.A.C.E. award 1963, Greaves-Walker award 1999). Republican. Presbyterian. Avocations: antiques, antique autos. Home: Pittsburgh, Pa. Died Jan. 28, 2007.

RUND, WILLIAM DRAKE, lawyer; b. St. Louis, Feb. 14, 1927; s. Emmet Henry and Emily Lee (Taylor) R.; m. Lois Ruth Darr, May 20, 1950; children— William Drake, Christine Eldarrat, Mark, Mary Ann, James, Kathryn Becker, Thomas, Margaret, Robert. B.S., St. Louis U., 1948; J.D., Wash. U., 1954. Bar: Mo. 1954, U.S. Dist. Ct. (ea. dist.) Mo. 1955. Law clk. Judge Roy W. Harper, St. Louis, 1954-55; pvt. practice, 1954-57; asst. cir. atty. City of St. Louis, 1957-58; v.p., sec., gen. counsel Gen. Contract Fin. Corp. and Securities Investment Co., St. Louis, 1958-68; ptnr. Fordyce & Mayne, 1968-72; clk. U.S. Dist. Ct. (ea. dist.) Mo., 1972-79, U.S. magistrate, 1972-76, clk. of ct. U.S. Bankruptcy Ct., 1979-89. Served with USAAC, 1945-46. Mem. ABA, Mo. Bar Assn., Met. St. Louis Bar Assn., Nat. Conf. Bankruptcy Clks., Soc. for Preservation and Encouragement of Barber Shop Quartet Singing in Am., Phi Delta Phi. Roman Catholic. Died Jan. 7, 2006.

RUNKE, DARRELL M., food co. exec. b. Mapleton, Minn., July 16, 1919; s. Max E. and Cora (McMahon) R.; m. Phyllis Elsie Wilkens, Mar. 27, 1943; children— Vicky Anne, Kenneth Darrell, Timmy Lee, Sally Jean, Betsy Sue. BS in Chemistry, Mankato State Coll., Minn., 1946. Tchr. Mapleton Pub. Schs., 1946-48; chemist Central Bi-Products Co., Redwood Falls, Minn., 1948-52; dir. animal nutrition Internat. Milling Co., New Ulm, Minn., 1952-53, sales mgr., 1953-56, sales mgr. formula feeds Des Moines, 1956-57, Mpls., 1957-61, gen. mgr. formula feeds, 1961-63, v.p. formula feeds, 1963-66, v.p. overseas div., 1966-69; also dir.; group v.p., dir. Internat. Multifoods Corp., Mpls., 1969-74, pres., chief operating officer, 1974-83, vice chmn., from 1983. Dir. 1st Nat. Bank Mpls. Served to 1st lt. USAAF, 1941-46, PTO. Mem. Am. Feed Mfrs. Assn. (dir. 1965-66, vice chmn. exec. com. sales execs. council 1966), N.W. Feed Mfrs. Assn. (dir. 1962-63) Home: Naples, Fla. Died Mar. 21, 2007.

RUPP, PETER E., truck manufacturing and sales executive; b. Munich, Germany, Apr. 25, 1930; came to U.S., 1980; s. Otto Richard-Karl and Emily Maud (Wilmersdoerfer) R.; m. Christel Ott, Mar. 7, 1964; B.Commerce, Melbourne U., Sidney, Australia, 1956. Vice chmn., pres., chief exec. officer Volkswagen-Australia, 1970-75; resident dir. Daimler-Benz A.G., Tabriz, Iran, 1975-77, dir. spl. projects, Stuttgart, Fed. Republic Germany, 1979-80; mng. dir. Anambra Motor Mfrs., Enugu, Nigeria, 1977-79; pres. Euclid, Inc., Cleve., 1980-82; pres., chief exec. officer Freightliner Corp., Portland, Oreg., 1982—; mem. adv. panel on transp., Australia; dir. Daimler-Benz N.Am. Holding, N.Y.C., Mercedes-Benz N.Am., Montvale, N.J., Mercedes Benz Brasil, Sao Paulo, Western Hwy. Inst. Mem. Nat. Assn. Mfrs. (bd. dirs.), German-Am. C. of C. (bd. dirs.), Greater Cleve. World Trade Assn. (bd. dirs.), Australian Vehicle Assemblers Assn. (chmn.), Fed. Chamber Automotive Industry Australia (exec. mem.). Died Mar. 19, 2006.

RUSSELL, ROBERT ALAN, garden supply company executive; b. N.Y.C., Oct. 16, 1920; s. George Doan and Dorothy (Laws) R.; m. Ann Margaret Horan, Oct. 1, 1966; children— Pamela Ann, Robert A., Elena Maria. Mgr. office N.Y. Worlds Fair, Flushing, 1938-39, Hearst Realties, N.Y.C., 1939-42; with J&L Adikes, Inc., Jamaica, N.Y., 1946-51, pres., 1952—. Introduced first fine leaved perennial ryegrass to home lawn industry, 1959, hybrid Ky. bluegrass to industry, 1971. Scoutmaster Nassau County council Boy Scouts Am., 1960-66; vol. United Fund, 1980-84, Bishops Appeal, 1978-84; master ceremonies Sch. Community Assn., 1962—. Served to capt. U.S. Army Corps Engrs., 1942-46, 51-52. Decorated Bronze Star, Purple Heart. Mem. N.Y. State Turfgrass Assn. (Merit award 1980), Am. Seed Trade Assn. (Merit award 1982), various offices, coms.), Lawn Inst. (sec., treas. 1972-87). Republican. Roman Catholic. Avocations: woodworking; golf. Home: Manhasset, NY. Died Aug. 8, 2007.

RUTELIONIS, ALGIMANTAS JONAS, information technology executive; b. Kaunas, Lithuania, May 19, 1939; came to U.S., Sept. 12, 1949; naturalized, 1956; s. Vytautas and Julika (Malinauskas) R.; m. Lolita Anne Borzello, May 6, 1967 (div. 1979); 1 child, Aras Andrius; m. Sue Ellen Vandenberg, Dec. 8, 1982. A.A., Montgomery Jr. Coll., 1962; B.S., U. Md., 1964. Vice pres. internat. devel. Info. Handling Services Inc., Englewood, Colo., 1975-76, research and devel., 1976-77, internat. planning, 1977-78, internat. sales, mktg., 1978-79, v.p. new product devel., Denver, 1979-81, pres. internat., Englewood, 1983—; pres. Internat. Info. Tech. Group, London, 1981-83. Served to lt. U.S. Army, 1958-60. Mem. Info. Industries Assn., Internat. Micrographics Council, Nat. Micrographics Assn., Standards Engrng. Soc. Republican. Roman Catholic. Home: Littleton, Colo. Died Jan. 12, 2007.

RYAN, PATRICK MICHAEL, lawyer; b. Chgo., May 26, 1944; s. Edward Michael and Kathleen Teresa (Crimmins) R.; m. Holly Ann Daleske, Aug. 31, 1968; children: Rebecca Eileen, Brendan Patrick, Abigail Christine, Lucas Christopher. BA, St. Mary's Coll., Winona, Minn., 1966; JD, Marquette U., 1969. Bar: Wis. 1969. Law clk. Wis. Supreme Ct., Madison, 1969-70; ptnr. Quarles & Brady LLP, Milw., 1970—2001, chmn., mng. ptnr., from 2002. Dir. and officer several pvt. bus. corps. Mem. ABA, Wis. Bar Assn., Milw. Bar Assn. Avocations: reading, sports. Home: Cedarburg, Wis. Died Aug. 22, 2007.

RYAN, WILLIAM R., mechanical engineer; b. NYC, Sept. 19, 1911; s. William Joseph and Lillian Theresa R.; m. Nancy West, June 26, 1937 (dec. 1989); children: Susan, Christine, Richard; m. Joan Sparks, Mar. 10, 1990 ME, Stevens Inst. Tech., 1934. Dir. engring. EDO Corp., College Point, N.Y., 1946-52, v.p., 1952-60, exec. v.p., 1960-62, pres., chief exec. officer, chmn., 1962-83, chmn. bd., from 1983. Cons. in field. Recipient Stevens Honor award Stevens Inst. Tech., 1985. Mem. IEEE, AIAA, ASME, Soc. Automotive Engrs., Soc. Naval Architects and Marine Engrs., Am. Soc. Naval Engrs., N.Y. Athletic Club, N.Y. Yacht Club, Cruising Club of Am., Storm Tyrsail Club, Met. Club. Home: Vero Beach, Fla. Died Apr. 3, 2006.

RYU, JAI HYUN, scientist, educator; b. Ham-nam, Korea, Oct. 27, 1940; s. Chang Yul and Byung Sun (Park) R.; came to U.S., 1960, naturalized, 1973; B.S.E. in Aerospace Engring., U. Mich., 1966, M.S.E. in Bio-Mech. Engring., 1972; Ph.D. in Bio-Systems Engring., U. Iowa, 1979; m. Jacqueline Ellen Brisbin, June 16, 1973; children— Juliette Jaie, Jessica Jaie, Jennifer Jaie. Research asst. dept. otorhinolaryngology U. Mich., 1961-66; asso. research scientist dept. otolaryngology U. Iowa, 1966-74, research scientist, 1974-80, dir. vestibular research labs., 1974-80, assoc. prof., dir. research, 1980-84, prof. surgery (otolaryngology); dir. research Bowman Gray Sch. Medicine, Wake Forest U., 1984—. Mem. Barany Soc., AIAA, Aerospace Med. Assn., Soc. Neurosci., Bioengring. Soc., Am. Acad. Otolaryngology, N.Y. Acad. Sci., Centurion Deafness Research Found., Korean Otolaryngology Soc., Am. Neurotology Soc., Assn. for Research in Otolaryngology, Am. Otologic Soc., N.C. Soc. Otolaryngology, CDRC, NIDCD, HIH, Sigma Xi. Author: The Vestibular System, 1975; Vestibular Physiology in Understanding the Dizzy Patient, 1980; contbr. articles to profl. jours. Home: Dewey, Ariz. Died Oct. 11, 2006.

SABELLA, NORMA A., state legislator; b. Verdun, Que., Can., Feb. 18, 1932; m. Joseph; 3 children., MacDonald Coll., McGill U. State rep. N.H. Ho. Reps. Mem. Munic — county govt. com. Mem. Derry Sch. Bd., N.H., 1978-84, chmn., 1979-80. Mem. Smithsonian Inst., Friends of Iona Abbey (Scotland). Home: Derry, NH. Died Nov. 14, 2006.

SABHARWAL, RANJIT SINGH, mathematician; b. Dhudial, India, Dec. 11, 1925; came to U.S., 1958, naturalized, 1981; s. Krishan Ch and Devti (An) S.; m. Pritam Kaur Chadha, Mar. 5, 1948; children— Rajinderpal, Amarjit, Jasbir. BA with honors, Punjab U., 1944, MA, 1948; MA U. Calif, Berkeley, 1962; PhD, Wash. State U., 1966. Lectr. math. Khalsa Coll., Bombay, India, 1951-58; teaching asst. U. Calif., Berkeley, 1958-62; instr. math. Portland (Oreg.) State U., 1962-63, Wash. State U., 1963-66; asst. prof. Kans. State U., 1966-68; assoc. prof. math. Calif.

State U., Hayward, 1968-74, prof. math., 1974-92, prof. emeritus math., from 1992. Author papers on non-Desarguesian planes. Mem. Am. Math. Soc., Math. Assn. Am., Sigma Xi. Died July 23, 2006.

SACKETT, ROSS DEFOREST, publisher; b. Chgo., Mar. 26, 1930; s. DeForest and Margaret (Ross) S.; m. Marvyda Wild, Sept. 1, 1951; children: David, Scott, Cynthia, Amy, Stuart. BA, Lawrence Coll., 1951. Editor in chief Charles Merrill Books, Inc., Columbus, Ohio, 1959-61; gen. mgr., v.p., exec. v.p., dir. Holt, Rinehart & Winston, NYC, 1961-67, pres., dir., 1967-70, chmn. bd., 1970-72; pres. CBS Edn. Pub. Group, 1970-72, Ency. Brit. Ednl. Corp., 1972-76; chmn. Crescent Park Press, Angeles Toy Corp., Childs/Play, Inc.; chmn. bd. Big Toys Inc.; pres., chmn. bd. Kompan Holdings; dir. Ency. Brit. Corp., Kompan, Inc.; former dir. CBS. Trustee Highscope Ednl. Rsch. Found. Mem. Assn. Am. Pubs. (chmn.), Civil War Round Table, Delta Tau Delta, Eta Sigma Phi. Episcopalian. Died Aug. 16, 2007.

SADEK, GEORGE, graphic designer, educator, former dean; b. Czechoslovakia, Oct. 12, 1928; Student, Hunter Coll., CUNY; BA, M.F.A., Ind. U. From instr. to asst. prof. graphic design Ind. U., Bloomington, 1960-66; prof. graphic design Cooper Union Sch., NYC, 1966—92, chmn. dept. art, 1966-68, dean sch. art, 1968—92, Frank Stanton prof. design, 1981—92, prof. emeritus, 1992—2007. Exhbns. include Type Dirs. Club N.Y., 1969, Am. Inst. Graphic Arts, 1970, Typomondus, Frankfurt, Fed. Republic Germany, 1971; represented in permanent collections Mus. Modern Art, N.Y.C., Library of Congress, Morgan Library Died Feb. 5, 2007.

SADIK-KHAN, ORHAN IDRIS, financial executive; b. Laghman, Afghanistan, July 3, 1929; came to U.S., 1951; s. Alim Jan and Shemsulbenat (Ashrat) Idris; m. Karen Lamond, May 3, 1969; children: Janette, Alim Jan, Karim, Kadria, Altan. BA, Am. U., Cairo, 1951; MBA, Stanford U., Calif., 1953; PhD, Ricker Coll., 1970. Dir. tech. research and services Dean Witter & Co., NYC, 1954-61; instl. research Schirmer Atherton & Co., 1961-62, F. Eberstadt, 1962-63; ptnr. charge research Ira Haupt Co., 1963; dir. research N.Y. Securities Co., NYC, 1964-65; v.p. planning bus. equipment group Litton Industries, Inc., Beverly Hills, Calif., 1965-67; sr. v.p. Norton Simon Inc., NYC, 1967-81; pres. Millicom, Inc., NYC, 1982-84; mng. dir. Paine Webber, Inc., NYC, from 1986-88. Pres. ADI Corp., Old Greenwich, Conn., 1975—. Mem. N.Y. Soc. Security Analysts, Boston Soc. Security Analysts, Econs. Club, Chemists Club (N.Y.C.). Republican. Home: Old Greenwich, Conn. Died Aug. 1, 2007.

SADLER, ROBERT LIVINGSTON, banker; b. Beloit, Kans., Dec. 19, 1935; s. D.M. and Retha (Livingston) S.; m. E. Ellen Lewis, July 14, 1957; children: Diane, Julia. AB, Baker U., 1958; MBA, Ind. U., 1959; student, Rutgers U., 1970. Dir. alumni relations Baker U., Baldwin, Kans., 1957-58; indsl. engr. Colgate-Palmolive Co., NYC, 1958-60, pers. mgr., 1961-64, product mgr., 1964-65; v.p. pers. and adminstrv. svcs. Old Kent Bank & Trust Co., Grand Rapids, Mich., 1965-72, exec. v.p., 1972-86, Old Kent Fin. Corp., Grand Rapids, 1972-89, vice chmn., from 1989; pres. Old Kent Bank, Grand Rapids, 1994-95, pres., CEO, from 1995. Pres. Grand Rapids Jr. Achievement, 1976; pres. United Way Kent County, 1982; chmn. Grand Rapids Found., 1987; Davenport Coll. Bus., Grand Rapids. Mem. Am. Bankers Assn. (chmn. communications council 1980—, dir. 1982-83), Sigma Iota Epsilon, Delta Mu Delta Clubs: Cascade Country (dir. 1978-80); University (Grand Rapids). Republican. Methodist. Home: Montague, Mich. Died June 4, 2007.

SAENGER, EUGENE LANGE, radiology educator, laboratory director; b. Cin., Mar. 5, 1917; s. Eugene and Therese (Lange) S.; m. Sue Reis, June 18, 1941 (dec.); children: Katherine Saenger Soodek (dec.), Eugene Lange. AB, Harvard U., 1938; MD, U. Cin., 1942. Diplomate: Am. Bd. Radiology, Am. Bd. Nuclear Medicine. Intern Cin. Gen. Hosp., 1942-43, resident in radiology, 1943-46; asst. prof., then assoc. prof. radiology U. Cin. Med. Ctr., 1949-62, prof., vice chmn. dept., 1962-87, prof. radiology emeritus, 1987—2007; radiation therapist Children's Hosp., Cin., 1947-87; dir. E.L. Saenger Radioisotope Lab., U. Cin., 1950-87. Cons. AEC and NRC, 1962-88, to med. liaison EPA, 1968-2007; dir. Nat. Coun. Radiation Protection, 1967-2007; mem. Internat. Com. on Radiation Protection, 1977-84. Author: Medical Aspects of Radiation Accidents: A Handbook for Physicians, Health Physicists and Industrial Hygienists, 1963. Trustee Cin. Community Chest and Council, 1964-70. Served to maj. M.C. U.S. Army, 1953-55. Recipient Gold medals Am. Roentgen Soc., 1998, The Radiologic Soc. Am., 1998. Mem. Soc. Med. Decision Making (pres., co-founder 1979-80), Nat. Coun. Radiation Protection (hon. mem.), Queen City Club, Literary Club (Cin.), Cosmos Club (Washington), Optimists Club. Jewish. Home: Key Largo, Fla. Died Sept. 30, 2007.

SAGER, WILLIAM FREDRICK, retired chemistry professor; b. Glencoe, Ill., Jan. 22, 1918; s. Fred Anson and Alta (Stansbury) S.; m. Marilyn Olga Williams, Dec. 26, 1941; children: Karen Louise Sager Dickinson, Judith Lynn Sager Peyton), Kathryn Gwen Sager Potts. BS in Chemistry, George Washington U., 1939, MA in Organic Chemistry, 1941; PhD in Organic Chemistry, Harvard U., 1948. Research chemist The Texas Co., 1941-45; prof. chemistry George Washington U., 1948-65, U. Ill.-Chgo., 1965-86, prof. emeritus, from 1986, chmn., 1965-80. Cons. to govt. and industry, 1952—. Founder, pres. Sager Innovations, Inc. Patentee (U.S. patents on evergy saving devices.). Recipient Disting. Service award U. Ill. Alumni Assn., 1985; Guggenheim fellow, 1954-55. Mem. Am. Chem. Soc., Sigma Xi, Alpha Chi Sigma. Died Dec. 15, 2006.

SAHLBERG, CHARLES VICTOR, manufacturing company executive; b. Oak Park, Ill., July 2, 1935; s. Carl Victor and Lucile Lynette (Dunn) S.; m. Ruth Erma Stenger, June 22, 1957; children: Jeffrey Lee, Cynthia Lynn, Jennifer Ruth. BS, Miami U., Oxford, Ohio, 1957, MBA, 1963. Indsl. engr. Champion Paper Co., Hamilton, Ohio, 1957-61; supr. cen. services Miami U., 1961-64; office supr. Moderncote Co., New Castle, Ind., 1964-69; purchasing mgr. New Castle Products, 1969-79; material mgr. Modernfold, New Castle, 1979-83, v.p. material mgmt. Modernfold, 1983-85; v.p. MATL'S/Services, 1985—. Contbr. articles to bus. jours. Pres. First Nighters, New Castle, 1978, YMCA, New Castle, 1980, trustee, 1993; elder Presbyn. Ch., New Castle, 1984—; mem. New Castle Tourism Commn., 1989—, Henry County Econ. Devel. Corp., 1993. Recipient Best Article award Am. Purchasing Soc., 1973, Good Citizenship award Mut. Trust Ins. Co., 1969; Nat. Assn. of Purchasing Mgmt. Presdl. scholar Indpls., 1979. Mem. Indpls. Purchasing Mgmt. Assn. (sec. 1983-84, treas. 1984, 2d v.p. 1985, 1st v.p. 1986, pres. 1987-88, bd. dirs. 1983-91), New Castle C. of C. (v.p. 1985—, pres. 1986-87), Jaycees (v.p. 1960-61). Republican. Lodge: Rotary (pres. 1980-81). Avocations: racquetball, photography, water skiing, softball, reading. Home: New Castle, Ind. Died Sept. 29, 2006.

SAHNI, ATAM PARKASH, powder coating company executive, researcher; b. Kuffri, India, Aug. 12, 1937; came to U.S., 1961, naturalized, 1965; s. Chanan S. and Lajwanti (Suri) S.; m. Veena K. Suri, Feb. 23, 1966; children— Sanjay, Sangeeta. B.Chem. Engring., U. Delhi, India, 1960; M.S. in Chem. Engring., Okla. State U., 1962; postgrad. in chem. engring., NYU 1962-65. Research scientist NYU, 1962-66; sr. research engr. Monsanto Co., Springfield, Mass., 1966-74; dir. research and devel. Ferro Corp., Cleve., 1974—. Patantee in field (Weaver award 1980). Mem. Am. Inst. Chem. Engrs., Assn. for Finishing Processes. Avocations: photography, tennis, sightseeing. Home: Cleveland, Ohio. Died Aug. 29, 2006.

SAINI, GULSHAN RAI, soil physicist, agricultural hydrologist; b. Oct. 1, 1924; s. Ram Saran and Parmeshri Devi (Bhondi) S.; m. Veena Chaudhri, Jan. 14, 1950; 1 child, Vikas. BSc, Panjab U., 1945, MSc, 1956; PhD, Ohio State U., 1960. soil and water conservation cert. USDA Tng. Ctr., 1959; notary pub. State of Mass., 1989—. Rsch. asst. Govt. Agrl. Coll., Ludhiana, India, 1945-57; rsch. assoc. Ohio State U., Columbus, 1957-60; asst. prof. Punjab Agrl. U., Ludhiana, 1960-61; rsch. scientist Can. Dept. Agriculture, Fredericton, N.B., 1962-84. Adj. prof. Faculty of Forestry, U. N.B., Fredericton, 1968-76; founding bd. dirs. U. Human Rights Group, Inc.; vis. prof. Rutgers U., 1984-85; mem. hydrology subcom. Atlantic Provinces Inter-Univ. Com. on Scis., 1966-76, Atlantic Provinces Soil & Water Engring. Com., 1972-82; mem. Restore Olmsted's Waterway Coalition, 1986-96, treas. 1990-93, chair 1994-96; CSO tech. adv. com. Commonwealth of Mass., 1995-99; founder, trustee Saini Found. Contbr. articles to profl. jours. Bd. dirs. Coalition for a Strong UN, 1994-99; treas. Fredericton br. Can. Inst. Internat. Affairs, 1975-80. Fellow Internat. Inst. Land Reclamation and Improvement; mem. Indian Sci. Congress Assn. (life), Profl. Inst. Pub. Svcs. Can. (nat. v.p. 1980, 81, chmn. Atlantic regional coun. 1978, 79), Union Concerned Scientists, Fredericton Rotary Club (dir. internat. svc. 1967-68), 3d World Scholars Consortium (treas. 1995-2005). Home: Brookline, Mass. Died Feb. 3, 2007.

ST. JOHN, ADRIAN, II, retired military officer; b. Ft. Leavenworth, Kans., Nov. 16, 1921; s. Adrian and Marie (McMahon) St John; m. Petronella Elizabeth Durham, Jan. 19, 1943 (dec. 1982); children: Adrian III (dec.), Brian; m. Florence Tucker Parrish, Jan. 29, 1998. BS, U.S. Mil. Acad., 1943; MA, U. Va., 1951; MPA, Am. U., 1981; postgrad., Army War Coll., 1960, U. Hawaii, 1963, Am. U., 1977-82. Commd. 2d lt. U.S. Army, 1943, advanced through grades to maj. gen., 1969; co. comdg. officer 15th Cav. U.S. Army, Europe, 1943—45; intelligence staff officer U.S. Army, Berlin, 1945—47, China desk officer gen. staff Washington, 1951—53, bn. comdg. officer 3d Bn., 31st Inf. Regt. Korea, 1954, comdr. 73d Tank Bn. Korea, 1955; mem. faculty Command and Gen. Staff Coll., Ft. Leavenworth, 1956—59; faculty adviser Iranian Def. Coll., 1959; S.E. Asia plans officer G3, U.S. Army-Pacific, 1960—64; long range plans br. Strategic Div., Orgn. Joint Chiefs of Staff, Washington, 1964—66; chief Surface P & O Div. J3, USMACV, Vietnam, 1966—67; comdg. officer 14th Armored Cav. Regt., Germany, 1967—69; asst. div. comdr. 4th Armored Div., Europe, 1969-70; chief Strategic Plans and Policy Div. J5, Orgn. Joint Chiefs of Staff, Washington, 1970-71; dir. plans gen. staff U.S. Army, Washington, 1971-72; comdg. gen. 1st Armored Div., Europe, 1972-74; vice dir. joint staff Joint Chiefs of Staff, 1974-76; ret., 1976; mem. adv. council on internat. security affairs Republican Nat. Com., 1977-80; del. Va. State Rep. Conv., 1980, 81; sr. mil. adv. U.S. Negotiating Del. Mut. Balanced Force Reductions, Vienna, 1982—87; Joint Chiefs of Staff rep. U.S. Del. Conventional Stability Talks, Vienna, 1987-88, negotiations on Conventional Armed Forces, Europe, 1989-92. Del., presenter Congress Arms Control Mid. East, Delphi, Greece, 1994; U.S. del. World Helicopter Championships, Moscow, 1994, Oreg., 1996; chmn. operational working group internat. conf. on arms control in Mid. East, Jordan, 1994; mem. advance party OSCE to prepare for elections, Bosnia, 1997; presenter plaques signed by Sec. of Def. to Australian authorities in 6 cities during ceremonies commemorating VJ Day, 1995; supr. parliamentary elections, Bosnia, 1997. Co-chmn. orchestral benefit ball Austrian Embassy, 1993, 1994; supr. Mcpl. Election Commn., Bosnia, 2000; participant in Conf. on Application European Arms Control Negotiations to Pakistan-India Situation, U.K., 2001; election supr. Kosovo, 2001. Decorated D.S.M. with oak leaf cluster, Silver Star, Legion of Merit with 3 oak leaf clusters, Bronze Star with V device, Joint Svc. Commendation medal, Army Commendation medal with oak leaf cluster, Joint Meritorious Unit award, French Croix de Guerre with silver star, Vietnamese Gallantry Cross with palm; recipient European Comdr. in Chief's Individual Project partnership award, 1968, Presdl. award Disting. Citizen, 1993, Dept. State Superior honor award, 1989, 91, Sec. of Def. medal for disting. pub. svc., 1992, medal as disting. grad. U.S. Mil. Acad., 1998. Mem. Am. Security Coun., Am. Fgn. Affairs Coun., Heritage Found., World Affairs Coun., Leadership Inst. Roman Catholic. Died Jan. 6, 2007.

SALISBURY, ALVIN BURTON, JR., physician; b. Rockford, Ill., Mar. 11, 1922; s. Alvin Burton and Mildred Elizabeth (Scott) S.; m. Cecelia Mitchell, Aug. 26, 1944; m. 2d, Jane Jefford, Aug. 26, 1976; children: Jennifer lee, Elizabeth Ann, Robert Alvin. Student, Beloit Coll., 1941-43, Vanderbilt U., 1943-44; MD, Ohio State U., 1949. Intern White Cross Hosp., Columbus, Ohio, 1949-50; practice medicine, Fairborn, Ohio, 1952—, Piqua, Ohio, 1979-80; mem. staff Greene Meml. Hosp., Xenia, Ohio; courtesy staff Piqua Meml. Hosp., Miami Valley, St. Elizabeth's hosps., both Dayton, Ohio; founder, pres. Ankh Labs., Inc., Fairborn, 1955-69. Editor, pub. Adventures of Col. Daniel Boone (John Filson), 1968; patentee med. instruments. Founder Mus. of Old Northwest Frontier, Lockington, 1970. Served to capt. M.C., AUS, 1943-46, 51-52. Mem. AMA, Miami County Med. Soc., Ohio State Med. Assn. Died Oct. 16, 2006.

SALTMAN, ELLEN SHIRLEY, Jewish art history and Judaica educator, writer; b. Schenectady, Aug. 17, 1919; d. William M. and Eva (Mintz) Shirley; m. David Saltman, Dec. 14, 1941; children— William, Paul. B.A., Mt. Holyoke Coll., South Hadley, Mass., 1941; M.A., Smith Coll., Northampton, Mass., 1971. Lectr. Jewish studies courses and program for religious and communal orgns., 1959—; vis. instr. Jewish Art history, Mt. Holyoke Coll., 1976, 83, U. Mass.-Amherst, 1978, 81; guest lectr. Smith Coll., 1973-75; lectr., panel mem. TV Jewish Heritage Program, Springfield Jewish Fedn. (Mass.), 1979, 80, 83; presenter paper 1st Internat. Seminar on Jewish Art, Israel, 1985. Contbr. articles in field to profl. jours. Bd. dirs., sec. Holyoke United Way, 1956-61; bd. dirs., sec. Holyoke Vis. Nurse Assn., 1957-63, v.p., 1962-63. Recipient Woman of the Yr. award Sisterhood of Congregation Sons of Zion, 1968. Mem. Am. Acad. Religion, Archaeol. Inst. Am. Club: Mt. Holyoke. Home: Holyoke, Mass. Died Mar. 30, 2007.

SALTZ, STEPHEN T., lawyer; b. Phila., Nov. 11, 1941; s. Joseph B. and Evelyn (Karmatz) S.; m. Rowena D. Castle, Mar. 29, 1980. BS, U. Miami, 1964; JD, Villanova U., 1967. Bar: Pa. 1968, U.S. Dist. Ct. (ea. dist.) Pa. 1970, U.S. Ct. Appeals (3d cir.) 1976, U.S. Dist. Ct. (mid. dist.) Pa. 1984. Assoc. Law Office of Stanley M. Poplow, Phila., 1967-68; atty. pub. defenders office State of Pa., Phila., 1969-71, atty. city solicitors office, 1972-80; ptnr. Saltz Mongeluzzi Barrett & Bendesky PC, Phila., Daniels, Saltz & Assocs., Ltd., Phila., from 1998, from 1998. Mem. Phila. Bar Assn. (chmn. state civil jud. com. 1986), Phila. Trial Lawyers Assn. (bd. dirs. 1984-88, pres.-elect, 1991-92, pres., 1992-93); Pa Trial Lawyers Assn. (mem. bd. govs. 1992) Home: Philadelphia, Pa. Died Sept. 5, 2006.

SALVATORE, JAMES DANIEL, data processing administrator; b. Columbus, Ohio, Sept. 20, 1947; s. Dante and Lulu Louise (Kinzelman) S.; BS, Ohio State U., 1970; postgrad. Mata Coll., 1970; MBA, Xavier U., 1975. Cert. systems profl. Data processing mgr. Robershaw Controls Co., Columbus, 1971-75, W.A. Butler Co., Columbus, 1975-84; dir. acad. computer ctr. Franklin U., Columbus, 1984—. Chmn., Ohio Spl. Olympics for retarded children and adults. Recipient cert. in data processing Inst. for Certification Computer Profls. Mem. Assn. Masters of Bus. Adminstrn. Execs., Data Processing Mgmt. Assn., Assn. for Systems Mgmt. Republican. Roman Catholic. Clubs: Guild Athletic; Ohio State U. Pres.'s. Home: Columbus, Ohio. Died Mar. 19, 2006.

SALWEN, MICHAEL BRIAN, communication educator; b. Perth Amboy, NJ, Jan. 15, 1954; s. Harry and Zelda Salwen; m. Okhee Lee, Aug. 7, 1959. Ba in English and Psychology, Trenton State U., 1977; MA in Journalism, Pa. State U., 1980; PhD in Comm., Mich. State U., 1985. Journalist The Bucks County Courier Times, Levittown, Pa., 1977-79, The News Tribune, Woodbridge, N.J., 1979-80; prof. comm. U. Miami, Coral Gables, Fla., 1985—2007. Book rev. editor World Comm., Coral Gables, 1993—; assoc. editor Journalism and Mass Comm. Quarterly, Columbia, S.C., 1995—. Author: Latin American Journalism, 1991, Radio and TV in Pre-Castro Cuba, 1994; editor: Integration Theory and Research in Communication, 1996. Democrat. Avocations: bicycling, computers, wines, race car driving. Home: Miami, Fla. Died July 17, 2007.

SAMARA, GEORGE ALBERT, engineer; b. Lebanon, Dec. 5, 1936; BS, U. Okla., 1958; MS, U. Ill., Urbana, 1960, PhD in Chemical Engring., Physics, 1962. Staff mem. physics rsch. Sandia Labs., 1962-63, divsn. supr., High Pressure Physics Divsn., 1967-71, dept. mgr. physics solid rsch., 1971-89, dept. mgr. Condensed Matter & Device Physics, 1979-83, dept. mgr. Condensed Matter & Sci. Rsch., 1983-89, dept. mgr. Condensed Matter Rsch., 1989-93, dept. mgr. Nano Structure & Advanced Mat. Cham., from 1993. With U.S. Army Signal Corps., 1963-65. Recipient Ipatieff prize Nat. Acad. Engring., 1974. Mem. ACIE, AAAS, Nat. Acad. Engring., Am. Phys. Soc., Mats. Rsch. Soc. Died Dec. 30, 2006.

SAMEK, MICHAEL JOHANN, retired manufacturing executive; b. Vienna, Feb. 26, 1920; came to U.S., 1939; s. Berthold and Leontine (Bruell) S.; m. Edith Raymond, Apr. 1948 (div. 1961); m. Stacy Graham, Dec. 20, 1964 (div. 1974). BS, Vienna, 1938; postgrad., Columbia U., 1949-51. Pres. Computech Inc., NYC, 1956-60; v.p. Data Systems ITT, Paramus, N.J., 1961-64; mgr. dir. internat. Auerbach Corp., Europe and U.S., 1964-69; v.p. Celanese Corp., NYC, 1969-83. Pres. Primary Care Software Inc., Riverhead, N.Y., 1987-95; chmn. Am. Mgmt. Assn. Info. Systems and Tech. Council, 1960-83; chmn. adv. com. on data processing City of N.Y., 1963—; vol. cons. Nat. Exec. Svcs. Corps., 1983—. Served to lt. col. USAF, 1941-45, ETO. Mem. AAAS, AIAA, Assn. Computing Machinery, N.Y. Acad. Scis. Home: New York, NY. Died Apr. 21, 2007.

SAMMOND, JOHN STOWELL, lawyer; b. Milw., Dec. 27, 1928; s. C. Frederic and Marie (Freitag) S.; m. Cynthia Miller, Feb. 13, 1951 (dec. Dec. 1992); m. Diana Denholm, July 1995; children: Frederic, Christopher, Nicholas, Timothy. BA, Yale U., 1950; SJD, Harvard U., 1955. Bar: Wis. 1955, Fla. 1969, D.C. 1972, Fla. Supreme Ct. as Cir. Ct. mediator, 1990. Assoc. predecessor firm to Quarles & Brady, Milw., 1955-60; ptnr. Quarles & Brady (and predecessor firms), Milw., from 1961, Quarles & Brady, West Palm Beach, Fla., from 1969. Bd. dirs. Medalist Industries Inc., Milw., Associated Commerce Bank, Milw., Tropical Plant Rentals Inc., Riverwoods, Ill., Kelley Co. Inc., Milw., others. Bd. dirs., officer Univ. Sch., Milw., Lakeside Children's Ctr., Milw., Palm Beach Habilitation Ctr., Lake Worth, Fla.; sr. warden Christ Episcopal Ch., Whitefish Bay, Wis. Maj. USMCR, 1948-63. Mem. ABA, Wis. Bar Assn., Milw. Bar Assn., Fla. Bar Assn., Palm Beach County Bar Assn., D.C.

Bar Assn., Bath and Tennis Club (Palm Beach), Everglades Club (Palm Beach), Milw. Country Club, Milw. Club, Governor's Club (Palm Beach). Republican. Home: West Palm Beach, Fla. Died Jan. 31, 2006.

SAMS, DALLAS C., state legislator; b. Aug. 30, 1952; m. Elaine Sams; 4 children. Student, Brainerd CC, Minn.; BS, U. Minn., 1974. Mem. Minn. Senate from 11th dist., St. Paul, from 1991. Vice-chmn. health care com., mem. agrl. and rural devel. com., mem. govt. ops. and reform com., mem. health care com., family svc. fin. divsn. com., tax com., tax laws com.; farmer; farm bus. mgmt. instr. Home: Staples, Minn. Died Mar. 5, 2007.

SAMSON, ALVIN, former distributing company executive, consultant; b. NYC, May 2, 1917; s. Morris and Jennie (Buitekant) S.; m. Ann Carol Furmansky, Aug. 15, 1942; children: Leslie Joan, Marla Adriane. Br. mgr. U.S. Hardware and Paper Co., 1947-51; mdse. mgr. U.S. Servateria, 1951-57; dir. purchasing U.S. Consumer Products, Los Angeles, 1959-64, v.p. ops., 1964-66, pres., 1966-72, San Diego, Bakersfield, Las Vegas, Phoenix, 1966-72, Zelman Co., Los Angeles, San Francisco and Las Vegas, 1968-72, Triple A Corp., Los Angeles, 1966-72, U.S. Consumer Products-Wesco Mdse., Los Angeles, 1972-74; v.p. APL Corp., NYC, 1967-74; pres. USCP-WESCO, 1974-85; cons. A. Samson Cons., Beverly Hills, 1985-92; retired, 1992. Active USCG Aux., 1981-02, divsn. capt., 1992—. With USAAC, 1942-45. Named Man of Year Housewares Club So. Calif., 1965 Mem. Nat. Assn. Service Merchandisers (dir. 1982-85) Died Nov. 8, 2006.

SANDERS, CARL JULIAN, minister; b. Star, NC, May 18, 1912; s. Hugh T. and Annie Margaret (Crowell) S.; m. Eleanor Louise Lupo, Sept. 28, 1935; children: Lundi (Mrs. John R. Martin), Eleanor (Mrs. Paul E. Kasler). BA, Wofford Coll., 1933, D.D. (hon.), 1973; B.D., Candler Sch. Theology, 1936; D.D. (hon.), Randolph Macon Coll., 1953, Athens Coll., Ala., 1972, Huntingdon Coll., 1975; L.H.D. (hon.), Birmingham-So. Coll., 1977. Ordained to ministry Methodist Ch., 1934; pastor Cheriton, Va., 1936-40, Chase City, Va., 1940-44, Roanoke, Va., 1944-48, Richmond, Va., 1948-55; supt. Petersburg (Va.) Dist., 1955-56, Richmond Dist., 1956-61, Norfolk (Va.) Dist., 1965-71; pastor Richmond, 1961-65, Arlington, Va., 1971-72; bishop Birmingham (Ala.) Area, 1972-80; exec. dir. Ala.-West Fla. United Meth. Found., 1980-85, Found. for Bibl. Studies, from 1980. Pres. com. relief United Meth. Ch., 1972-76, v.p. bd. global ministries, 1972-76; mem. World Meth. Council, 1971-80. Trustee Emory U., 1973—, Carraway Med. Center, Birmingham, 1972-80, Athens Coll., 1972-80, Huntington Coll., Montgomery, Ala., 1972-80, Va. Wesleyan Coll., Norfolk, 1960-72. Recipient Grand Cross Scotish Rite. Mem. Masons (grand chaplain supreme coun. So. Jurisdiction U.S.A.), Omicron Delta Kappa. Home: Birmingham, Ala. Died Mar. 7, 2007.

SANDERS, FREDERICK, meteorologist; b. Detroit, May 17, 1923; s. Frederick William and Dorothy Gail (Martin) S.; m. Nancy Seabury Brown, Nov. 30, 1946; children: Christopher Martin, John Arnold, Frederick Duncan. BA, Amherst Coll., 1944; Sc.D., M.I.T., 1954. Forecaster U.S. Weather Bur., NYC, 1947-49; teaching asst. MIT, 1949-51, instr. meteorology, 1951-56, asst. prof., 1956-59, asso. prof., 1959-69, prof., 1969-84, prof. emeritus, from 1984. Cons. in field. Author: (with H.C. Willett) Descriptive Meteorology, 1955, (with D.M. Houghton) Weather at Sea, 1988; editor Monthly Weather Rev., 1986—; contbr. numerous articles to profl. jours. Served with USAAF, 1942-46. Recipient award for applied research Nat. Weather Assn., 1978; NSF grantee, 1958—; NOAA grantee, 1956-78; Office Naval Research grantee, 1979-92; USAF grantee, 1954-78 Fellow AAAS, Am. Meteorol. Soc.; mem. Royal Meteorol. Soc. (fgn.). Clubs: Eastern Yacht (Marblehead, Mass.). Died Oct. 6, 2006.

SANDERS, ROBERT DONALD, psychologist; b. Headland, Ala., Sept. 26, 1937; s. Chester Lee and Eunice M. S.; m. Nancy Fortune Pruetti, June 4, 1977; 1 son, Robert D. BS in English, Troy State U., 1960; M.Ed., Auburn U., 1968, MS, 1970, PhD, 1972. Tchr. Fla. Sch. Boys, Okeechobee, 1960-62, Sumter (S.C.) City Schs., 1962-63, Ribault Sr. High Sch., Jacksonville, Fla., 1963-64, Parrish High Sch., Selma, Ala., 1964-67; co-dir. edn. E. Ala. Head Start, Auburn, 1969-70; psychol. trainee E. Ala. Comprehensive Mental Health Center, Opelika, 1971-72; dir. field research project UEC, Inc., NYC, 1972; psychologist IV, dir. adolescent and young adult treatment unit Ala. Dept. Mental Health, Mt. Vernon, 1972-74; dir. Eufaula Adolescent Adjustment Center, 1974-75; supt. Partlow State Sch. and Hosp., Tuscaloosa, 1975-80; asso. commr. for mental retardation Ala. Dept. Mental Health, Tuscaloosa, from 1980. Adj. prof. psychology U. Ala., Tuscaloosa, 1980—; mem. Ala. Bd. Examiners in Psychology.; Mem. health professions adv. council Auburn U. Recipient Spl. award for outstanding service in mental health Ala. Assn. Mental Health Center Dirs., 1981 Mem. Ala. Psychol. Assn., So. Psychol. Assn., Nat. Assn. State Mental Retardation Program Dirs., Tuscaloosa Assn. Retarded Citizens, Phi Kappa Phi. Clubs: Kiwanis. Democrat. Baptist. Died Nov. 23, 2005.

SANGMEISTER, GEORGE EDWARD, lawyer, consultant, former congressman; b. Joliet, Ill., Feb. 16, 1931; s. George Conrad and Rose Engaborg (Johnson) S.; m. Doris Marie Hinspeter, Dec. 1, 1951; children: George Kurt, Kimberley Ann. BA, Elmhurst Coll., 1957; LLB, John Marshall Law Sch., 1960, JD, 1970. Bar: Ill. 1960. Ptnr. McKeown, Fitzgerald, Zollner, Buck, Sangmeister & Hutchison, 1969-89; justice of peace, 1961-63; states atty. Will County, 1964-68; mem. Ill. Ho. of Reps., 1972-76, Ill. State Senate, 1977-87, US Congress from 4th (now 11th) Ill. Dist., 1989-95; cons. McKeown, Fitzgerald, Zollner, Buck, Hutchison, Ruttle and Assocs., 1990—2007. Chmn. Frankfort Twp. unit Am. Cancer Soc., Will County Emergency Housing Devel. Corp.; past trustee Will County Family Svc. Agy.; past bd. dirs. Joliet Jr. Coll. Found., Joliet Will County Ctr. for Econ. Devel., Silver Cross Found., Silver Cross Hosp. With inf. AUS, 1951-53. Mem. ABA, Ill. Bar Assn., Assn. Trial Lawyers Am., Am. Legion, Frankfort (past pres.), Frankfort C. of C., Old Timers Baseball Assn., Lions. Achievements include establishing Abraham Lincoln National Cemetery for Veterans in 1992. Home: Mokena, Ill. Died Oct. 7, 2007.

SANKEY, JAMES LEROY, religious studies educator, retired; b. New Castle, Pa., July 16, 1924; s. William Edward and Verna Pearl (McConnell) S.; m. Carra Mae Bartlett, Apr. 14, 1953; children: Bruce Lee, Shawn Thomas. BS in Christian Edn., Bethany Nazarene Coll., 1970; MA in Christian Edn., Scaritt Coll. Christ. Workers, Nashville, 1976. Enlisted USMC, 1942, advanced through grades to 1st sgt.; dir. Christian edn. Bethel Ch. of Nazarene, Nashville, 1965-67, Oklahoma City 1st Ch. of Nazarene, 1967, Trinty Ch. of Nazarene, Oklahoma City, 1967-70; min. Christian edn. First Ch. of Nazarene, Nashville, 1970-79; prof., chmn. dept. Christian edn. Nazarene Bible Coll., Colorado Springs, Colo., 1979-94, adj. prof. Christian edn., 1994-95. Editor, compiler: A Multiple Staff Handbook, 1985; contbr. articles to profl. jours. Sunday sch. clin. dir. Tenn. Dist. Ch. of Nazarene, Nashville, 1966-67, dist. news editor, 1975-77, chmn., supt., 1977-79, freelance cons., seminar leader, 1975-94. Mem. Nazarene Multiple Staff Assn. (v.p. 1977-80, pres. 1980-85). Avocations: hiking, travel, volunteer work. Home: Colorado Springs, Colo. Died Sept. 11, 2006.

SANSBURY, JOHN THADDEUS, lawyer; b. Danville, Ill., Oct. 2, 1929; s. William Joseph and Catherine (Flattery) S.; m. Elizabeth Schmitt, Apr. 23, 1955 (dec. Apr. 1966); children—Stephen, Hugh, Susan, Ellen, Cathleen; m. Peggy Sue McPherson, Dec. 27, 1967; stepchildren— Mark, Scott. B.S., Canisius Coll., 1951; J.D., Fordham U., 1961. Bar: Ohio 1964. Counsel, U.S. Life Co., N.Y.C., 1961-71, atty. Nationwide Ins., Columbus, Ohio, 1961-71; sole practice, Columbus, 1964—. Bd. dirs. Nat. Kidney Found., Columbus, 1967—, pres., 1973; treas. St. Agatha Parish Council, 1974, pres. 1984—. Recipient Service award, Nat. Kidney Found., 1968, 72. Mem. Columbus Bar Assn., Ohio State Bar Assn. Republican. Roman Catholic. Clubs: Swim and Racquet, Racquet. Avocations: gardening; tennis. Home: Boca Raton, Fla. Died Sept. 5, 2006.

SANTORO, ARLENE TREPTOW, librarian; b. Chgo., Mar. 18, 1938; d. Arthur Ruben and Edna Karoline (Scior) T.; m. August John Santoro, June 27, 1959 (div. Feb. 1970); children—John August, Wayne Arthur. B.A., Blackburn Coll., Carlinville, Ill., 1959; M.A., U. Chgo., 1974. Research asst. Am. Meat Inst./U.Chgo., 1959-63; librarian Frankfort Pub. Library (Ill.), 1966-74, adminstrv. librarian, 1974—; dep. registrar Will County (Ill.), 1975—; cons. to various pub. libraries, Ill., 1983—; mem. Ill. adv. com. State Library, 1980-81. Ill. State scholar, 1971. Mem. ALA, Ill. Library Assn., Beta Phi Mu. Unitarian. Home: Chicago, Ill. Died July 25, 2006.

SARABIA, ANTONIO ROSAS, lawyer; b. Chihuahua, Mex., June 29, 1913; s. Rafael Rosas and Maria S.; children— Antonio Rosas II, Sean Rosas. B.S. in Chem. Engring., Ind. Tech. Coll., 1942; J.D., U. Chgo., 1949. Bar: Ill. 1950. Assoc. Baker, McKenzie & Hightower, Chgo., 1949-52, ptnr., 1952-62; sole practice, Chgo., 1962-64; sr. assoc. Lord, Bissell & Brook, Chgo., 1964-65, ptnr., 1966-83; faculty mem. Lawyers Inst. John Marshall Law Sch., Chgo., 1962-73. Mem. legis. com. Chgo. Crime Commn., 1971—; bd. dirs. Geographic Soc. of Chgo., 1970-78, 3d v.p., 1978—. Mem. ABA (internat. law sect. 1970—, council 1971-75, budget officer 1972-78), Inter-Am. (membership com.), Ill. State Bar Assn. (internat. law sect. chmn. 1965-66, council 1974-75), Chgo. Bar Assn. (charter flight com. 1961-82, internat. and fgn. law com. 1982—, internat. human rights 1978—, chmn. 1980—), Am. Fgn. Law Assn. (pres. Chgo. br. 1952-59), Am. Arbitration Assn., Mexican Am. Lawyers Assn. Clubs: Univ., Mid-Am. Contbr. articles to profl. jours. Home: Rch Palos Vrd, Calif. Died Apr. 26, 2006.

SARDI, VINCENT, JR., retired restaurant executive; b. NYC, July 23, 1915; s. Vincent S.; m. Carolyn Euiller, 1939 (div. 1946); m. Adelle Ramsey, 1946 (div.); m. June Keller; children Paul, David, Tabitha, Jennifer (dec.) Pre-med. student, Columbia U.; earned degree, Columbia Bus. Sch., 1937. Learned restaurant bus. for two years Ritz-Carlton; dining room captain Sardi's restaurant, 1939, Owner NYC, 1947—85, 1991—97, Sardi's restaurant (123 East 54th St.), NYC, 1958—68; retired, 1997. Owner 700 Seat Dinner Theater on Franklin Sq., NY, 1974—76. Guest appearance Catch a Falling Star, Now, Where Was I?"; co-author (with Helen Bryson): (cookbook) Curtain Up at Sardi's, 1957. Joined, ran bachelor officers' mess at the Cherry Point Air Station in North Carolina USMC, 1942, sent to Okinawa to supervise a rest camp USMC, 1943, rose to the rank of capt. USMC, 1946. Recipient Spl. Tony award for providing the best transient home and haven for show people League N.Y. Theatres and Producers Died Jan. 4, 2007.

SARIDIS, GEORGE NICHOLAS, engineering educator, researcher; b. Athens, Greece, Nov. 17, 1931; arrived in U.S., 1961, naturalized, 1971; s. Nicholas and Anna (Tsofa) S.; m. Panayota Dimarogona, Apr. 10, 1985. Diploma in Mech. and Elec. Engring., Nat. Tech. U., Athens, 1955; MSEE, Purdue U., 1962, PhD, 1965. Instr. Nat. Tech. U., 1955-63, Purdue U., West Lafayette, Ind., 1963-65, asst. prof., 1965-70, assoc. prof., 1970-75, prof., 1975-81; prof. elec., computer and sys. engring. Rensselaer Poly. Inst., Troy, N.Y., 1981-96, dir. Robotics and Automation Lab., 1982-96, prof. emeritus, from 1997. Dir. NASA Ctr. for Intelligent Robotic Systems for Space Exploration, 1988-92; engring. program dir. NSF, Washington, 1973; hon. prof. Huazhong U., Wuhan, China. Author: Self-Organizing Control of Stochastic Systems, 1977, Stochastic Processes Estimation and Control, 1995, Entropy in Control Engineering, 2001, Hierachically Intelligent Machines, 2002; co-author: Intelligent Robotic Systems: Theory and Applications, 1992, Reliable Plan Selection by Intelligent Machines, 1996, Design of Intelligent Control System Based on Hierarchical Stochastic Automata, 1996; contbr. articles to profl. publs.; co-author: Intelligent Robotic Sys.; co-editor, contbg. author: Fuzzy Automata, 1977, editor, contbg. author: Advances in Automation and Robotics, Vol. 1, 1985, Advances in Automation and Robotics, Vol. 2, 1990. Recipient Ktesibios award, Med. Control Assn., 2003. Fellow IEEE (founding pres. robotics and automation coun. 1981-84, Centennial medal 1984, Third Millennium medal 2000, Disting. Mem. award Control Sys. Soc. 1989) Mediterranean Control Assn. (Ktesibios award 2003); mem. ASME, Soc. Mfg. Engrs./Robotics Internat.-Machine Vision Assn. (sr.), Am. Soc. Engring. Edn., N.Y. Acad. Scis., Acad. Athens (Greece). Home: Loudonville, NY. Died Oct. 29, 2006.

SARKESIAN, BARBARA ANN, freelance writer, historian; b. Providence, Jan. 19, 1933; d. Joseph and Virginia (Bargamian) Casparian; m. Haig Sarkesian, Aug. 11, 1957 (dec. 1984). B.A. cum laude, Brown U., 1954; writing cert. Famous Writers Sch., 1965. Tchr. Cranston Sch. Dist., R.I., 1954-59; free-lance writer, 1970—; tchr. adult edn. Scituate Sch. Dist., R.I., 1981—; editor Scituate Bee, 1982—. Contbr. numerous articles to mags. and newspapers. Pres., edn. chmn. Scituate Preservation Soc., 1981; sec. North Scituate Pub. Library Assn., 1976—. Recipient commendation Town of Scituate, 1981. Mem. Brown U. Alumni Assn., (sec. Class of 1954, Pembroke Coll. 1977—), Pembroke Assocs. Club: Scituate Olde Home Day Com. (chmn.). Avocations: reading; artifact collecting; collecting antiques; historical research. Died Jan. 20, 2007.

SASKI, WITOLD, pharmaceutics educator; b. Brest, Poland, Dec. 4, 1909; s. Jerzy Edmund and Teresa Franciszka (Marszalska) S.; came to U.S., 1951; widowed, July 1980. BA (equivalent), R. Traugutt Gimnasium, Brest, 1927; BSc in Pharmacy, U. Nebr., 1954; M in Pharmacy, Stefan Batory U., Poland, 1933; D Pharmacy, U. Bologna, Italy, 1946; Pharm. Chemist, Brighton Tech. Coll., 1947; diploma in Optometry, Inst. Optical Sci., London, 1950. Registered pharmacist, Eng., Nebr. Profl. pharmacist, Poland, 1933-36; insp. Pharmacy Ministry of Health, Warsaw and Tarnopol, Poland, 1937-39; chief pharmacist Bulstrode Str. Med. Clinic, London, 1947-48; sr. pharmacist Brit. Ministry Health, London, 1948-51; asst. prof. U. Montana, Missoula, 1951-52; asst. prof. to prof. pharmaceutics U. Nebr., Lincoln, 1952-75, prof. emeritus, 1975—. Author Crossing Many Bridges, 1988; co-author: Experimental Pharmaceutics, 1961, 4th edit., 1977; contbr. articles, abstracts to nat. and internat. sci. jours. Mem. editorial bd. Inst. Sci. Info. Current Contents, 1970-86. Participant Mayor's Com. for Internat. Friendship, Lincoln, 1970—. 2d lt. Second Polish Corps in 8th Brit. Army, World War II, Italy. Decorated Polish, Italian and Brit. govts.; recipient Lederle Pharmacy awards, 1962, 64, 66; grantee Fulbright, Italy, 1968, USPHS, 1964, 65, 66; U.S. Acad. Scis. Exchange Scientist, Poland, 1970. Fellow Acad. Pharm. Scis.; mem. Polish Inst. Arts and Scis. Am., Nebr. Pharmacists Assn., Great Navy State Nebr. (Adm. 1970), Nebr. Art Assn., Sigma Xi, Kappa Psi, Rho Chi. Avocations: swimming; bicycling; gardening. Home: Lincoln, Nebr. Died Aug. 4, 2006.

SATA, LINDBERGH SABURO, psychiatrist, educator; b. Portland, Oreg., Jan. 6, 1928; s. Charles Kazuo and Ito (Kojima) S.; m. Yuriko Kodama, Aug. 19, 1956; children: Roberta, Camille, Holly, John. BS, U. Utah, 1951, MD, 1958, MS, 1964. Intern U. Utah Coll. Medicine, Salt Lake Gen. Hosp., 1958-59, resident in psychiatry, 1959-62, chief resident in psychiatry, 1961-62; adminstrv. chief resident neurology U. Utah Coll. Medicine, VA Hosp., Salt Lake City, 1960-61; fellow Inst. for Mental Retardation, Letchworth Village, Thiells, N.Y., 1962; intern Behavioral Sci. Intern Program Nat. Tng. Labs., Bethel, Maine, 1966; instr. U. Utah, 1962-64; asst. prof. The Psychiat. Inst. U. Md., Balt., 1964-67, assoc. prof., 1967-68, U. Wash., Seattle, 1968-77, asst. dean, 1969-70, prof., 1977-78; prof., chmn. St. Louis U. Sch. Medicine, 1978-94, prof. emeritus, chmn. emeritus, from 1994. Fellow Am. Coll. Psychiatrists, Am. Psychiat. Assn., Pacific Rim Coll. Psychiatrists (founding); mem. Am. Assn. for Social Psychiatry. Died Aug. 4, 2006.

SATTER, LARRY DEAN, nutritionist; b. Madelia, Minn., July 30, 1937; m. 1966; 3 children. BS, S.D. State U., 1960; MS, U. Wis., 1962, PhD in Biochemistry and Dairy Sci., 1964. Asst. prof. to assoc. prof. dairy sci. U. Wis., Madison, 1964-73, prof., 1973-81; mem. staff U.S. Dairy Forage Rsch. Ctr., U. Wis., USDA, Madison, 1981-87, dir., 1987-98, rsch. dairy scientist, from 1998. Recipient Am. Feed Mfrs. award, 1977. Mem. Am. Dairy Sci. Assn., Am. Soc. Animal Sci., Am. Inst. Nutrition. Died Aug. 13, 2006.

SATULA, ANTHONY E., JR., lawyer; b. Phila., July 2, 1947; AB, Calvin Coll., 1969; JD, Duke U., 1972. Bar: N.Y. 1973. Ptnr. Fried, Frank, Harris, Shriver & Jacobson, NYC. Mem. Product Liability Adv. Coun., Inc. Editorial bd. Duke Law Jour., 1971-72; bd. editors Leader's Product Liability Law and Strategy. Mem. ABA (environ. litigation com. litigation sect.), N.Y. State Bar Assn., Assn. Bar City of N.Y. (com. product liability 1982-85). Died Apr. 7, 2006.

SATZ, RONALD NORMAN, university dean, American Indian history educator; b. Chgo., Feb. 8, 1944; s. David H. and Gertrude (Smith) S.; m. Christa G. Ilgaudas, July 4, 1969; children: Ani B., Jacob S. BS, Ill. Inst. Tech., 1965; MA, Ill. State U., 1967; PhD, U. Md., 1972. Asst. prof. Am. Indian history U. Tenn., Martin, 1971-75, assoc. prof., 1975-80, prof., 1980-83, dean grad. studies, 1976-83, dean rsch., 1977-83; prof. U. Wis., Eau Claire, from 1983, dean grad. studies and rsch., from 1983, dir. Ctr. Excellence for Faculty and Undergrad. Rsch., from 1988. Cons. Native Am. Rights Fund, Boulder, Colo., 1977-80, other cons. positions. Author: American Indian Policy in the Jacksonian Era, 1975, Tennessee's Indian Peoples, 1979, America: Changing Times, 1979, 80, 82, 84, Chippewa Treaty Rights, 1991, Classroom Activities on Chippewa Treaty Rights, 1991, Classroom Activities on Wisconsin Indians: Treaties and Tribal Sovereignty, 1993; (booklet) Recruitment, Admission and Retention of Black Students, 1982, 2nd edit., 1987; contbr. articles to profl. jours; mem. editorial bd. Am. Indian Quar., 1977-82, U. Tenn. Press, Knoxville, Bd. dirs. U. Tenn. Rsch. Corp., Knoxville, 1981-83, Chippewa Valley Mus., 1992—. Stone scholar Ill. Inst. Tech., 1964, state scholar, 1965; NDEA fellow U. Md., 1970; Ford Found. fellow in ethnic studies, 1971; Younger Humanist Rsch. fellow NEH, 1974; Title III grantee U.S. Office Edn., 1978, 81, 82; grantee U. Wis. System Undergrad. Teaching Improvement Coun., Book award of Merit State Hist. Soc. Wis., 1992. Mem. Midwestern Assn. Grad. Studies (editor 1988-90), Am. Hist. Assn., Orgn. Am. Historians, Western History Assn. (chair student awards 1986),

Nat. Coun. Univ. Rsch. Adminstrs., Phi Kappa Phi (v.p. Eau Claire chpt. 1989-90, pres. Eau Claire chpt. 1990-91). Home: Eau Claire, Wis. Died Mar. 7, 2006.

SAUSEDO, ANN ELIZABETH, newspaper librarian; b. Douglas, Ariz., Nov. 19, 1929; d. Eugene Ephraim and Bertha Evelyn (Kimpton) Bertram; m. Richard Edward Sausedo, July 22, 1952 (div. 1966); 1 dau., Robin Marie. Student Calif. schs. Asst. librarian Stockton Record (Calif.), 1948-51, head librarian, 1955-67; stewardess Calif. Central Airlines, 1951; library dir. Washington Star, 1967-76; free-lance organizer file systems, Palo Alto, Calif., 1976-78; library dir. Los Angeles Herald Examiner, 1978—. Contbr. chpt. to book in field. Mem. Spl. Libraries Assn., Nat. Assn. Female Execs. Home: Morro Bay, Calif. Died July 25, 2007.

SAVAGE, NAOMI, photographer; b. NJ, June 25, 1927; d. Samuel and Elsie (Ray) Siegler; m. David C. Savage, Oct. 11, 1950; children— Michael, Lourie. Student, Bennington Coll., 1945-47; pvt. photography study with, Man Ray, 1948-49. Free lance photographer including portraits, Versailles, tennis, dental and opthal. equipment, trees, flowers, abstract designs, masks, hands; photographer variety of techniques including photo-engraving, photograms, photo-collages, combination negative-positive photos, porcelain photos. Cassandra Found. grantee, 1970; Nat. Endowment for Arts photography fellow, 1971; recipient One-Show-Silver award Art Dirs. Club N.Y., 1976 Mem. Friends Photography, Internat. Center Photography. Home: Warren, Vt. Died Oct. 31, 2005.

SAVELL, EDWARD LUPO, lawyer; b. Atlanta, Apr. 29, 1921; s. Leon M. and Lillian (Lupo) S.; m. Bettie Patterson Hoyt, Oct. 11, 1944; 1 dau., Mary Lillian Savell Clarke. BBA, Emory U., 1947, LL.B., 1949. Bar: Ga. 1948, U.S. Dist. Ct. (mid. and no. dist.) Ga. Assoc. A.C. Latimer, Atlanta, 1948-53; ptnr. Carter, Latimer & Savell, Atlanta, 1953-56, Woodruff, Latimer & Savell (and successor firms), Atlanta, 1956-87; of counsel Savell & Williams LLP, Atlanta, 1987—2007. Instr. John Marshall Law Sch., 1951—55; dir. Legal Aid Soc., 1955—58; investigator Fulton county Judges Grievance Com. Contbr. articles to legal jours. With USAF, 1942-45, CBI. Fellow Internat. Acad. Trial Lawyers (pres. 1978-79, Dean of Acad. 1976); mem. Atlanta Bar Assn. (sec.-treas. 1953-54), ABA, State Bar Ga., Ga. Def. Lawyers Assn. (founder, v.p.), Internat. Assn. Ins. Counsel, Atlanta Claims Assn., Lawyers Club Atlanta, Cherokee Town and Country Club, Commerce Club, Univ. Yacht Club (past commodore), Chi Phi, Phi Delta Phi (past pres.). Presbyterian. Home: Atlanta, Ga. Died June 12, 2006.

SAVILLE, DUDLEY ALBERT, chemical engineering educator; b. Lincoln, Nebr., Feb. 25, 1933; s. George A. and Alta (Goddard) S.; m. Joy Wagner, Mar. 7, 1959; children: Alexander, Andrea. BS, U. Nebr., 1954, MS, 1959; PhD, U. Mich., 1966. Engr. Carbide & Carbon Chem. Co. (Institute), W. Va., 1954-55; research engr. Chevron Research Corp. (Richmond), Calif., 1959-61, Shell Devl. Co., Emeryville, Calif., 1966-68; asst. prof. Princeton U. (N.J.), 1968-71, assoc. prof., 1971-77, prof. dept. chem. engring., 1977, Stephen C. Mocaleer prof. Engring. and Applied Sci., 2001. Assoc. editor Jour. Physico-Chem. Hydrodynamics, 1980-87; mem. adv. bd. Jour. Colloid Interface Sci., 1992-94; contbr. articles to profl. jours. Served to 1st lt. USAF, 1955-58. Recipient Alpha Chi Sigma award for chem. engring. rsch. AIChE, 1997. Mem. NAE, AIChE, Am. Chem. Soc., Am. Phys. Soc. Home: Princeton, NJ. Died Oct. 4, 2006.

SAVLOV, EDWIN DAVID, surgeon, oncologist, educator; b. Carbondale, Pa., July 11, 1924; s. Hyman and Ruth (Stone) S.; m. Peggy Weisberg, 1951 (div. 1962); children: Meg, John; m. Jean Kams; 1 child, Marc. BA, U. Rochester, 1946, MD, 1948. Diplomate Am. Bd. Surgery. Assoc. prof. surgery U. Rochester, 1968-80; prof. surgery Texas Tech, Amarillo, Tex., 1980-88, U. Nevada, Reno, from 1989. Home: Reno, Nev. Died Mar. 21, 2007.

SAWYER, RAYMOND LEE, JR., motel chain executive; b. New Orleans, Oct. 7, 1935; s. Raymond Lee Sawyer and Eloise Falvy (Searcy) Easley; m. Dolores Jean Young, June 11, 1960; children: Lisa Kay, Linda Faye. BA, Northwestern State U., 1959. Art dir., advt. mgr. Natural Food and Farming Mag., Atlanta, Tex., 1959-66, editor, 1963-66; asst. editor, editor Tourist Court Jour./Southwest Water Works Jour., Temple, Tex., 1966-73, editor, 1973-75; founding ptnr., sr. v.p. Budget Host Inns, Ft. Worth, 1975-83, pres., chief exec. officer, from 1983. Named Man of Yr. Motel Brokers Assn. Am., 1974; recipient Bob Gresham Meml. award Nat. Innkeeping Assn., 1975. Mem. Am. Automobile Assn. (mem. lodging adv. panel 1990—). Methodist. Avocations: photography, writing. Home: Arlington, Tex. Died Mar. 1, 2007.

SAXL, JANE WILHELM, state legislator; b. NYC, Aug. 26, 1939; d. Seymour F. and Doris (Fuld) Wilhelm; m. Joseph Saxl, Nov. 17, 1957; children: Susan S., Ruth L., Mary-Anne, Michael V. BA, U. Ill., Springfield, 1973, MA, 1974. City councilor City of Bangor, Maine, 1987-93; mem. Maine Ho. Reps., Augusta, from 1992, chair banking and ins. com. Sec./treas. Penobscot Valley Coun. Govts., 1988-91. Mem. Bangor Sch. Bd., 1984-87, Family Planning Maine, Natural Resources Coun., Penobscot Dem. Com.; bd. dirs. Bangor Beautiful, Bangor Conv. and Visitors Bur.; past chmn. Bangor Recycling. Recipient 1st Maine Waste Mgmt. award, 1995, Toll Fellow Scholarship award, 1996. Mem. LWV (pres. Maine chpt. 1987-93), Nat. League State Legislators, E./W. Hwy Assn., Maine Women's Lobby, Friends of Bangor Pub. Libr., Spruce Run Assocs., Maine Audubon Soc. (award 1999), Tuesday Forum, Maine Women's Legis. Lobby. Democrat. Jewish. Avocations: birdwatching, fly fishing. Home: Bangor, Maine. Died Feb. 14, 2006.

SAYRE, EDWARD VALE, chemist; b. Des Moines, Sept. 8, 1919; s. Edward Agnew and Audrey (Vale) S.; m. Virginia Nelle Rogers, Oct. 20, 1943. BS, Iowa State U., 1941; AM, Columbia U., 1943, PhD, 1949. Mgr. rsch. sect. Manhattan Dist. project Columbia U., 1942-45; rsch. chemist Eastman Kodak Rsch. Labs., Rochester, N.Y., 1949-52; sr. chemist Brookhaven Nat. Lab., Upton, N.Y., 1952-84; rsch. phys. scientist Smithsonian Instn., Washington, from 1984. Dir. rsch. Museum Fine Arts, Boston, 1975-80, sr. scientist, 1980-84; sr. scientist Alexander von Humboldt Found., 1980; vis. lectr. Stevens Inst. Tech., 1955-61; adj. prof. fine arts Inst. Fine Arts, N.Y. U., 1960-74; disting. vis. prof. Am. U. Cairo, 1970; Regents prof. U. Calif., Irvine, 1972; mem. sci. adv. coun. Winterthur Mus. Contbr. numerous rsch. articles to profl. jours.; assoc. editor Archaeometry, 1969-93, Art and Archaeology Tech. Abstracts, 1970-87, Jour. Archaeol. Sci., 1971-77. Guggenheim fellow, 1969; recipient U.S. sr. scientist award Alexander von Humboldt Found., 1980-81, George von Hevesy medal, 1984, Alumni Disting. Achievement citation Iowa State U., 1996, Pomerance award Archaeol. Inst. Am., 1999. Fellow Internat. Inst. for Conservation of Hist. and Artistic Works, Am. Inst. for Conservation of Hist. and Artistic Works; mem. Am. Chem. Soc. Clubs: Cosmos. Home: Washington, DC. Died May 25, 2007.

SBACCHI, ALBERTO, history educator; b. Palermo, Italy, Nov. 25, 1937; came to U.S., 1960; s. Enrico and Franca (Mariano) S.; m. Margareta Karlman, Sept. 11, 1963; children— Ingrid, Paul. B.A., Columbia Union Coll., Takoma Park, Md., 1962; M.A., Pacific Union Coll., Angwin, Calif., 1963; Ph.D., U. Ill.-Chgo., 1975. Missionary, head social sci. dept. Ethiopian Adventist Coll., Addis Ababa, 1963-68; research fellow U. Pavia, Italy, 1970-72; prof. history Atlantic Union Coll., South Lancaster, Mass., 1974—; missionary Atlantic Union of Seventh-Day Adventists, Lancaster, Mass., 1974—. Editor: Italian Colonialism in Ethiopia, 1980; Mussolini's Ethiopia, 2d edit., 1985. Contbr. articles to profl. jours. Fellow U. Ill.-Chgo., 1970; grantee Am.-Italy Soc., 1971, Am. Council Learned Socs., 1977, Am. Philos. Soc., 1980-81; Fulbright-Hays scholar, East Africa and Italy, 1981-82. Mem. Am. Hist. Assn., Assn. Seventh-day Adventist Historians (sec. 1975-77, pres. 1980-81), African Studies Assn., Soc. for Italian Hist. Studies, Assn. Italian Africanists, Afro-Italian Inst., Clinton Hist. Soc. Home: Lancaster, Mass. Died Sept. 14, 2006.

SCHACHTER, MYRON MARVIN, retired research chemist, engineer; b. Bklyn., Nov. 28, 1922; s. Mary (Deutsch) S.; m. Marilyn Bedell, Aug. 12, 1962; 1 child, Alana Diane. BS, CCNY, 1948; MA in Sci., Bklyn. Coll., 1962. Quality controller Kollsman Instrument Co., Elmhurst, N.Y., 1953-61; rsch. chemist FDA, Washington, 1961-83; innovative sci. engring. rschr. Chromalcarb Co., Washington, from 1983, innovative rschr., from 1983; quality auditor Hekimian Labs., Inc., from 1989. Cons. in field. Patentee in field. Mem. AAAS, Am. Chem. Soc. Avocation: electronic instrument design and construction for scientific research. Home: Washington, DC. Died June 10, 2007.

SCHAEDLER, RUSSELL WILLIAM, microbiologist, physician, educator; b. Hatfield, Pa., Dec. 17, 1927; s. Robert and Sophia Louise (Enz) S. BS, Ursinus Coll., 1949; MD, Jefferson Med. Coll., 1953. Intern Jefferson Med. Coll. Hosp., Thomas Jefferson U., Phila., 1953-54, prof., chmn. dept. microbiology, 1968-91, Plimpton-Pugh prof., 1985—2003, prof. emeritus, 2003—07. Asst. Rockefeller Inst. for Med. Research, asst. physician Hosp. of Rockefeller Inst., 1954-57; asst. prof. Rockefeller Inst., resident asso. physician, 1957-62, asso. prof., physician to Hosp., 1962-68; asso. mem. Armed Forces Epidemiology Bd., Enteric Commn., 1967-72; mem. bacteriology and mycology study sect. NIH, 1970-74, chmn., 1973-74; mem. and chmn. NIH bacteriology and mycology AHR study sect., 1978-82 Mem. editorial bd. Jour. Bacteriology, 1965-69, Jour. Infection and Immunity, 1970-72; contbr. articles to sci. jours. Bd. dirs. Cardeza Found. Served with U.S. Army, 1946-47. Mem. Am. Assn. Immunologists, Am. Soc. Microbiology, Am. Gastroent. Assn., Infectious Disease Soc. Am., Coll. Physicians Phila., Harvey Soc., AAAS, J. Aitken Meigs Med. Assn., N.Y. Tb and Health Assn. (bd. dirs. 1965-68), Sigma Xi, Alpha Omega Alpha. Clubs: Vesper, Sydenham Coterie. Research in anaerobes and microecology of the gut. Home: Philadelphia, Pa. Died May 8, 2007.

SCHAFER, JOHN FRANCIS, plant pathologist, researcher; b. Pullman, Wash., Feb. 17, 1921; s. Edwin George and Ella Frances (Miles) S.; m. Joyce A. Marcks, Aug. 16, 1947; children— Patricia, Janice, James BS, Wash. State U., Pullman, 1942; PhD, U. Wis., Madison, 1950. Asst. prof. to prof. plant pathology Purdue U., West Lafayette, Ind., 1949—68; head dept. plant pathology Kans. State U., Manhattan, 1968—72; chmn. dept. plant pathology Wash. State U., Pullman, 1972-80; integrated pest mgmt. coordinator sci. and edn. USDA, Beltsville, Md., 1980—81, acting nat. research program leader plant pathology Agrl. Research Service, 1981—82; dir. cereal rust lab. USDA U. Minn., St. Paul, 1982-87, biol. sci. collaborator, 1987-95; ret., 1995. Vis. rsch. prof. Duquesne U., 1965-66; adj. prof. plant pathology U. Minn., 1982-92. Contbr. chapters to books, articles to profl. jours. With AUS, 1942-46. Phi Sigma scholar, 1942. Fellow AAAS, Ind. Acad. Sci., Am. Phytopathol. Soc. (past pres.); mem. Am. Soc. Agronomy, Crop Sci. Soc. Am., Coun. for Agrl. Sci. and Tech. Achievements include identification of increased resistance to wheat leaf rust by genetic recombination; demonstration of probabilities of virulence to genetic resistance combinations, of tolerance as a mechanism of disease control, and of use of cultivaral diversity for disease protection; bred (with others) over 30 disease resistant cultivars of cereal crops, including Arthur wheat. Home: Santa Rosa, Calif. Died May 5, 2007.

SCHANZER, WOLFGANG, symphony and opera conductor; b. Dortmund, Germany, Nov. 8, 1924; came to U.S., 1939, naturalized, 1944; s. Rudolf and Erna Marie (Priester) S.; m. Fannie Whitfield Lloyd, June 13, 1948; 1 child, David. B.Music, Manhattan Sch. Music, 1947, M.Music, 1948. Chmn. dept. music Marymount Coll., Tarrytown, N.Y., 1951-77; music dir., condr. Chappaqua Orch., N.Y., 1969-82; condr. Chautauqua Opera Co., N.Y., 1969-80; music dir., condr. Bergen Philharm. Orch., Teaneck, N.J., 1973-78; guest condr. throughout U.S.A., 1950-73. Composer string quartet, piano concerto, sonnet for voice and orch., 3 songs for high voice and orch., prelude, chorale and fugue, (opera) The Holy Devil. Recipient 1st prize Pitts. Concert Soc., 1943, N.C. Symphony Competition, 1950; Harold Bauer Meml. award Manhattan Sch. Music, 1948. Republican. Home: Tequesta, Fla. Died Feb. 20, 2006.

SCHAUB, RAYMOND C., food products company executive, lawyer; b. NYC, Aug. 22, 1929; s. William C. and Jane T. (Conroy) S.; m. Mary Ellen Adams, May 22, 1954; children— Faith, Hope, William Raymond, Charles, Mary Ellen, Francis, Christopher BBA, St. John's U., NYC, 1954, LL.B., 1960. Bar: N.Y. 1961. Tax specialist Gen. Foods Corp., White Plains, N.Y., 1949-70, asst. tax dir., 1970-77, tax dir., 1977-82, v.p. tax, from 1982. Served with U.S. Army, 1954-56 Mem. Tax Execs. Inst., Delta Mu Delta Clubs: Rockland Country. Roman Catholic. Avocations: golf; swimming. Home: Vero Beach, Fla. Died Sept. 29, 2006.

SCHAUERMANN, FLOYD L., machinery manufacturing company executive; b. Ft. Morgan, Colo., Oct. 30, 1924; s. Conrad and Margaret (Bott) S.; m. Kathryn Eaton, Sept. 18, 1949; children— Donald Eaton, James Lynn, Ellen Kay. B.S.E.E., Univ. Wyo., 1950. Registered elec. engr. Engr., Gen. Electric Co., Schenectady, N.Y., Shelbyville, Ind., 1950-62; devel. dir. Coleman Instruments, Maywood, Ill., 1962-64; mgr. engring. Selas Corp. Am., Dresher, Pa., 1964-66; dir. engring. FECO, Cleve., 1966-69; pres. Graham Door Co., Cleve., 1969-71; exec. v.p. sales Herr-Voss Corp., Callery, Pa., 1971-80; v.p. machinery sales Mesta Machine Co., Pitts., 1980-85; sales mgr. cold mills and process lines Tippins Inc., Pitts., 1985—. Patentee incineration and metal working fields. Served to tech. sgt. Inf., U.S. Army, 1943-46. Assoc. mem. Am. Iron and Steel Inst.; mem. Sigma Tau. Republican. Home: Gibsonia, Pa. Died Jan. 10, 2006.

SCHEEL, PAUL JOSEPH, insurance company executive; b. Balt., Nov. 15, 1933; s. Joseph A. and Julia S.; m. Beverly Ann Mitchell, June 1, 1957; children: Mary Claire, Paul Joseph. BS in Math., Loyola Coll.-Balt., 1959. With U.S. Fidelity & Guaranty Co., Balt., 1959-90, assoc. actuary, 1971, v.p., sr. actuary, 1971-78, exec. v.p., 1978-82, pres., chief operating officer, 1982-90. Bd. dirs. Fidelity and Guaranty Ins. Co., Thomas Jefferson Life Ins. Co., Fidelity Ins. Co. Can. Spl. asst. to the pres., Loyola Coll., 1990-93. With U.S. Army, 1953-55. Fellow Casualty Actuarial Soc.; mem. Am. Acad. Actuaries. Roman Catholic. Home: Lutherville Timonium, Md. Died Nov. 17, 2005.

SCHEIBNER, RUTH MARTIN (MRS. LAWRENCE F. SCHEIBNER JR.), psychologist, emeritus educator; b. Phila., Aug. 24, 1921; d. James Frederick and Rebecca Bamford (Carmen) Martin; A.B., Temple U., 1960, M.A., 1962, Ph.D., 1969; m. Lawrence Frederick Scheibner, Jr., May 27, 1950; 1 dau., Judith (Mrs. John Joseph Massaro). Psychology intern VA Hosp., Coatesville, Pa., 1961-62, VA Hosp., Phila., 1962-63; instr., counseling psychologist, acad. adviser Temple U., 1963-69; sch. psychologist, Marlton, N.J., 1966-67; lectr. Thomas Jefferson U., 1968-69; asst. prof. Phila. Coll. Pharmacy and Sci., 1968-70, assoc. prof., 1971-75, prof., 1976-85, prof. emeritus, 1986—, chmn. dept. humanities and social scis., 1980-85; individual practice psychotherapy, 1968—; counsellor family relations com. Phila. Soc. Friends, 1969-75. Bd. dirs. Phila. br human engring. lab. Johnson O'Connor Research Found., 1954-56. Recipient award for excellence in psychology Psi Chi, 1962. Mem. Am., Eastern, Pa. psychol. assns., AAUP, AAAS, Phila. Soc. Clin. Psychologists (past chmn. continuing edn. com. Human Services Ctr. 1977-80), Kappa Epsilon. Home: Ambler, Pa. Died Dec. 24, 2006.

SCHEMBECHLER, BO (GLENN EDWARD SCHEMBECHLER), former professional sports team executive, retired college football coach; b. Barberton, Ohio, Apr. 1, 1929; m. Mildred L. (Millie) Schembechler, 1968 (dec. 1992); 1 child, Glenn Edward III; m. Cathy Schembechler, 1993; stepchildren: Geoffrey, Matthew. BS, Miami U., Oxford, Ohio, 1951; MA, Ohio State U., 1952. Asst. coach Presbyn. Coll., 1954, Bowling Green State U. Falcons, 1955, Northwestern U. Wildcats, 1956-57, Ohio State U. Buckeyes, Columbus, 1958-62; head coach Miami U. Redskins, Oxford, Ohio, 1963-69, U. Mich. Wolverines, Ann Arbor, 1969-89, athletic dir., 1987-89; pres. Detroit Tigers, 1990-92; football broadcaster, analyst ABC Sports, 1991—92. Pres. Am. Football Coaches Assn., 1983. Co-author (with Mitch Albom): Bo, 1989; co-author: (with Dan Ewald) Tradition: Bo Schembechler's Michigan Memories, 2003. Served in US Army, 1952—54. Named Mid-Atlantic Conf. Coach of Yr., 1965, Ohio Coach of Yr., 1966, Coach of Yr., Am. Football Coaches Assn., 1969, Regional Coach of Yr (7), Big-Ten Coach of Yr (4); named to State of Mich. Sports Hall of Fame, 1989, Miami U. (Ohio) Hall of Fame, 1972, U. Mich. Hall of Honor, 1992, Rose Bowl Hall of Fame, 1993, Coll. Football Hall of Fame, 1993, Nat. Football Found. Hall of Fame, 1993; recipient Amos Alonzo Stagg award, Am. Football Coaches Assn., 1999. Achievements include being the winningest coach in U. Mich. football history; won 13 Big Ten Championships and appeared in 17 Bowl games as U. Mich head coach; retired with 234 career coaching victories. Died Nov. 17, 2006.

SCHENKEL, JAMES JOSEPH, architect; b. Ft. Wayne, Ind., Mar. 21, 1933; s. William Francis and Georgia Ruth (haaga) S.; m. Janice Mary Hillyard, June 23, 1956; children: Ellen, Scott Linda, Rita, Stewart. BArch, U. Notre Dame, 1956. Architect ptnr. Schenkel & Lawrence, Ft. Wayne, 1959-66; architect, pres Schenkel & Shultz Inc., Ft. Wayne, from 1966. Served to capt U.S. Army, 1957-60. Mem. Ind. Archtl. Found. (bd. dirs 1981—, pres. 1970-71; Edward D. Pierre Meml. medal 1978) No. Ind. Chpt. Ind. Soc. Architects (pres. 1969-70), Ft. Wayne C. of C. Clubs: Ft. Wayne Country. Lodges: Rotary. Republican Roman Catholic. Avocations: golf, fishing, trumpet. Home: Fort Wayne, Ind. Died July 14, 2006.

SCHETLIN, ELEANOR M., retired associate dean; b. NYC, July 15, 1920; d. Henry Frank and Elsie (Chew) Schetlin. BA Hunter Coll., 1940; MA, Tchrs. Coll., Columbia U., 1942, EdD 1967. Playground dir. Dept. Parks, NYC, 1940-42; libr. Met Hosp. Sch. Nursing, NYC, 1943-44, dir. recreation and guidance, 1945-58, historian Alumnae Assn., 2000—06; coord student activities SUNY, Plattsburgh, 1959-63, asst. dean students, 1963-64; asst. prof., coord. student personnel svcs CUNY, Hunter Coll., 1967-68; asst. dir. student personne

Columbia U., Coll. Pharm. Scis., NYC, 1968-69, dir. student personnel, 1969-71; assoc. dean students Health Scis. Ctr. SUNY, Stony Brook, 1971-73, asst. v.p. student svcs., 1973-74, assoc. dean students, dir. student svcs., 1974-85. Founding mem. Sea Cliff unit 300 Nassau County Aux. Police; founding mem. Nassau NOW Women of Color Task Force. Author: Myths of the Student Personnel Point of View, The Peter Principle and Student Personnel Work; contbr. articles to profl. jours. Recipient NOW Alliance PAC award, 1991, 1999, Lifetime Achievement award, Nassau NOW, 1992, Task Force Women of Color award, NOW, 1994. Mem.: So. Poverty Law Ctr., Wellesley Ctrs. Rsch. Women, Nat. Women's History Project, Women's Environment and Devel. Orgn., Nat. Mus. Women in the Arts. Home: East Hampton, NY. Died Feb. 22, 2007.

SCHICK, ROBERT LEROY, fire chief; b. Davenport, Iowa, July 13, 1940; s. Lester Roy Schick and Annabel Marzee (Bonbrake) Kirkman; m. LaVern Florence Rhode, Aug. 9, 1960 (dec. June 1972); children— Sheryl Lee, Lynn Marie; m. Mary Louise Smith, Oct. 2, 1973. Student Palmer Jr. Coll., 1970, Scott Community Coll., 1976, Muscatine Community Coll., 1977. Chief Davenport Fire Dept., 1983—. Bd. dirs. Illowa chpt. ARC, Rock Island, Ill., 1983—. Mem. Internat. Assn. Fire Chiefs, Mo. Valley Fire Chiefs (state v.p. 1984—), Iowa Paid Fire Chiefs Assn., Nat. Fire Prevention Assn., Iowa Soc. Fire Service Instrs. (past bd. dirs.). Lutheran. Lodges: Rotary (com. chmn. 1985), Moose (bldg. chmn. 1965—). Home: Davenport, Iowa. Died Feb. 26, 2006.

SCHILDHAUSE, SOL, lawyer; b. NYC, Sept. 5, 1917; s. Jacob and Fannie (Gerber) S.; m. Phyllis Sydell, May 23, 1943 (divorced); children: Susan Schildhause Tash, Peter, Richard. BS, CUNY, 1937; JD, Harvard U., 1940. Bar: N.Y. 1941, D.C. 1972, U.S. Ct. Claims 1975, U.S. Supreme Ct. 1978. Mng. ptnr. Sta. KOMA-AM, Oklahoma City, 1956-57; adminstrv. law judge FCC, Washington, 1963-66, chief cable TV bur., 1966-73; ptnr. D.C. office Farrow, Schildhause & Wilson, 1973-93; chmn. bd., gen. counsel The Media Inst., Washington. Lectr. Practicing Law Inst., 1985. Mem. ABA (asst. chmn. cable TV com. 1986), FCC Bar Assn. Clubs: Harvard (Washington). Democrat. Jewish. Home: Chevy Chase, Md. Died Sept. 15, 2006.

SCHILLER, ARTHUR A., architect, educator; b. NYC, July 23, 1910; s. Valentine and Rose (Bayer) Schiller; m. Anne O'Donnell, June 12, 1937; children: Valerie Schiller Schaefer, Virginia Schiller Waicul, Eileen Schiller Toomey. BArch, NYU, 1933; diploma, Beaux Arts Inst. Design, NYC, 1935; MArch, MIT, 1939. Registered profl. architect, N.Y. Architect U.S. Govt., Washington, 1936-38, N.Y.C. Dept. Parks, 1938-47; chief architect Bd. Higher Edn., NYC, 1947-51, dir. architecture and engring., 1951-67; coord. campus planning Queens Coll., NYC, 1967-73; adj. prof. N.Y. Inst. Technology, Old Westbury, 1973-91. Cons. Triboro Bridge Authority, N.Y.C., 1946; lectr. CCNY, 1957-67. Mayor Village of Plandome Manor, N.Y., 1965-87, trustee, 1960-65; trustee Sci. Mus. L.I. 1986—; conductor defensive driving courses for older citizens. Named Man of Yr. AARP, 1990, Sr. Citizen of Yr. Nassau County, State of N.Y., 1992. Fellow AIA (pres. Queens chpt. 1957-58); mem. N.Y. State Assn. Architects (dir. 1959-60), Assn. Univ. Architects (emeritus), U.S. Power Squadron (comdr. 1961-62, budget dir. 1988-91), Elks (life). Avocations: boating, gardening. Died May 9, 2007.

SCHILLING, KATHERINE LEE TRACY, retired principal; b. Mitchell, S.D., May 31, 1925; d. Ernest Benjamin and Mary Alice (Courier) Tracy; BA, Dakota Wesleyan U., 1947; MA, U. S.D., 1957; postgrad. U. Wyo., U. Nebr., Kearney State Coll.; m. Clarence R. Schilling, Oct. 14, 1951; 1 child, Keigh Leigh. Tchr. elem. and secondary schs., also colls., S.D. and Nebr. Mem. staff S.D. Girls' State, 1950-51; mem. S.D. Gov.'s Com. on Library, Nebr. Gov.'s Com. on Right to Read; prin. Mitchell (S.D.) Christian Sch., 1987-94; ret., 1994. Recipient Outstanding Tchr. award S.D. High Sch. Speech Tchrs., 1966. Mem. NEA, Nebr., Thurston County (pres.) edn. assns., Winnebago Tchrs. Assn., Delta Kappa Gamma. Clubs: Internat. Toastmistress (internat. dir. 1963-65, Mitchell Toastmistress of Year 1959), Order Eastern Star. Contbr. articles to profl. jours., also poetry. Home: Mitchell, SD. Died May 26, 2006.

SCHIRRA, WALTER MARTY, JR., (WALLY SCHIRRA), business consultant, retired astronaut; b. Hackensack, NJ, Mar. 12, 1923; s. Walter Marty and Florence (Leach) S.; m. Josephine Cook Fraser, Feb. 23, 1946; children: Walter Marty III, Suzanne Karen. Student, Newark Coll. Engring., 1940-42; BS, U.S. Naval Acad., 1945; Safety Officers Sch., U. So. Calif., 1957; US Navy Test Pilot Sch. (N.A.T.C.), 1958, NASA Astronaut Tng. Sch., 1959—69; PhD Astronautical Engring. (hon.), Lafayette Coll., 1969; DSc (hon.), U. So. Calif., 1969; PhD Astronautics (hon.), NJ Inst. Tech., 1969. Commd. ensign US Navy, 1945, advanced through grades to capt., 1965; designated naval aviator, 1948; service aboard battle cruiser Alaska, 1945-46; service with 7th Fleet, 1946; assigned Fighter Squadron 71, 1948-51; exchange pilot 154th USAF Fighter Bomber Squadron, 1951; engaged in devel. Sidewinder missile China Lake, Calif., 1952-54; project pilot F7U-3 Cutlass; also instr. pilot F7U-3 Cutlass and FJ3 Fury, 1954-56; ops. officer Fighter Squadron 124, U.S.S. Lexington, 1956-57; assigned Naval Air Safety Officer Sch., 1957, Naval Air Test Ctr., 1958-59; engaged in suitability devel. work F4H, 1958-59; joined Project Mercury, man-in-space, NASA, 1959; pilot spacecraft in 6 orbital flights Sigma 7, 1962; in charge operations and tng. Astronaut Office, 1964-69; command pilot Gemini 6 which made rendezvous with target, Gemini 7, 1965; comdr. 11 day flight Apollo 7, 1968; ret., 1969; pres. Regency Investors, Inc., Denver, 1969-70; chmn., chief exec. officer ECCO Corp. (Environ. Control Corp.), Englewood, Colo., 1970-73; chmn. Sernco, Inc., 1973-74; with Johns-Manville Corp., Denver, 1974-77; v.p. devel. Goodwin Cos., Inc., Littleton, Colo., 1978-79; pres., ind. cons. Schirra Enterprises, 1979-80. Dir. Imperial Am. (Oil & Gas), 1967, 1968, 1969, J.D. Jewel, 1971, 1972, 1973, First Nat. Bank, Englewood, Colo., 1971-78, Rocky Mountain Airlines, 1973-1984, Carlsberg Oil & Gas, 1974, 1975, Advertising Unlimited, Sleepy Eye, N.Mex., 1978-87, Electromedics, Denver, COlo., 1979-85, Finalco, McLean, Va., 1983-88, Cherokee Data Systems, Boulder, Colo., 1984-86, Net Air Int., Van Nuys, Calif., 1982-89, Kimberly Clark, 1983-91, Zero Plus Telecommunications, Inc, Campbell, Calif.; Belgian Consulate for Colo. and N.Mex., 1971-84. Co-author: We Seven, 1962; co-author: (with Ed Buckbee) The Real Space Cowboys, 1971; co-author: (with Richard Billings) Schirra's Space, 1988. Trustee Colo. Outward Bound Sch., 1970—74, regional trustee; dir. San Diego Aerospace Mus., Scripps Aquarium; mem. adv. bd., coun. US Nat. Parks, 1973—85; dir. Denver Organizing Com. for 1976 Olympics, 1973—75; mem. adv. bd. Internat. "Up With People"; founder, dir. Mercury Seven Found., 1984—2007; mem. adv. com. Oceans Foundations, San Diego, from 1985; advisor, Flight for Life Mercy Hosp., Denver, 1978—86; mem. internat. coun. The Salk Inst., La Jolla, Calif.; bd. dir. Sharps Hosp., San Diego. Decorated DFC (3), Air medal (3), Navy DSM; recipient Distinguished Service medal (2) NASA, Exceptional Service medal, Commdr. Philippines Legion of Honor, Collier Trophy, 1962, Kincheloe award, Soc. Exptl. Test Pilots, 1963, Haley Astronautics award, Am. Inst. Aeronautics and Astronautics, 1963, 1969, Harmon Internat. Trophy, 1965; inducted into Internat. Aviation Hall of Fame, San Diego, Calif., 1970, NJ Aviation Hall of Fame, Teterboro, NJ, Internat. Space Hall of Fame, Alamagordo, N.Mex., 1981, Nat. Aviation Hall of Fame, Dayton, Ohio, 1986, Naval Aviation Hall of Honor, 2000. Fellow Am. Astronautical Soc., Soc. Exptl. Test Pilots, Explorers Club; mem. Makai Country Club, Rancho Santa Fe Tennis Club, San Diego Yacht Club, Charlie Russell Riders (charter mem.), Rancheros Vistadores, Desert Caballeros, Durango Mountain Caballeros, The Golden Eagles (Naval Aviators). Avocations: skiing, hunting, sailing, fishing. Died May 3, 2007.

SCHLEH, EUGENE PAUL ANDERSON, historian, educator; b. NYC, Aug. 7, 1939; s. Eugene B. and Anna H. (Anderson) S.; children: Eugene R.R., Bruce G.W., Kristine A.M. BA, Union Coll., 1961; MA, Yale U., 1962, PhD, 1968. From asst. prof. to prof. U. So. Maine, Gorham, from 1965. Co-editor: Comsumable Goods II, 1988; editor, co-author: Mysteries of Africa, 1991; contbr. articles to profl. jours. John Anson Kittridge Edn. Fund Trust fellow, 1990, Republic of South Africa rsch.-travel fellow, 1980. Republican. Episcopalian. Avocations: stamp collecting/philately, reading. Home: Gorham, Maine. Died June 28, 2007.

SCHLESINGER, ARTHUR, JR., (ARTHUR MEIER SCHLESINGER JR.), writer, educator, historian; b. Columbus, Ohio, Oct. 15, 1917; s. Arthur M. and Elizabeth (Bancroft) S.; m. Marian Cannon, 1940 (div. 1970); children: Stephen Cannon, Katharine Kinderman, Christina, Andrew Bancroft; m. Alexandra Emmet, July 9, 1971; 1 child, Robert Emmet Kennedy, 1 stepchild Peter Allan. AB summa cum laude, Harvard U., 1938; postgrad. (hon.), Cambridge U., 1938—39; degree (hon.), Muhlenberg Coll., 1950, Bethany Coll., 1956, U. NB, 1966, New Sch. Social Rsch., 1966, Tusculum Coll., 1966, RI Coll., 1969, Aquinas Coll., 1971, Western New Eng. Coll., 1974, Ripon Coll., 1976, Iona Coll., 1977, Utah State U., 1978, U. Louisville, 1978, Northeastern U., 1981, Rutgers U., 1982, SUNY, 1984, U. NH, 1985, U. Oxford, 1987, Akron U., 1987, Brandeis U., 1988, U. Mass., Boston, 1990, Hofstra U., 1991, Adelphi U., 1992, Dominican Coll., 1992, Mt. Ida Coll., 1993, Middlebury Coll., 1994, Roosevelt U., 1995, Lynn U., 1996, No. Ill. U., 1996, City U. NY, 1999, Harvard U., 2001, U. SC, 2001, Miami U., 2001, Pa. State U., 2002, Ohio State U., 2003, U. South, 2003, Whitman Coll., 2003. With OWI, 1942-43, OSS, 1943-45; assoc. prof. history Harvard U., 1946-54, prof., 1954-62; vis. fellow Inst. Advanced Study, Princeton, NJ, 1966; Albert Schweitzer prof. humanities CUNY, 1966-95, Albert Schweitzer prof. humanities emeritus, 1995—2007. Cons. Econ. Cooperation Adminstrn., 1948, Mutual Security Adminstrn., 1951-52; spl. asst. to Pres., The White House, 1961-64; mem. jury Cannes Film Festival, 1964; mem. Adlai E. Stevenson campaign staff, 1952, 56; chmn. Franklin Delano Roosevelt Four Freedoms Found., 1983-2007; trustee Robert F. Kennedy Meml., Twentieth Century Fund.; adv. Arthur and Elizabeth Schlesinger Library. Author: Orestes A. Brownson, 1939, The Age of Jackson, 1945 (Pulitzer Prize for History 1946), The Vital Center, 1949, The Age of Roosevelt Vol. I: The Crisis of the Old Order 1919-1933, 1957 (Francis Parkman prize Soc. Am. Historians 1957, Frederic Bancroft prize Columbia U. 1958), The Age of Roosevelt Vol. II: The Coming of the New Deal, 1958, The Age of Roosevelt Vol. III: The Politics of Upheaval, 1960, Kennedy or Nixon: Does It Make Any Difference?, 1960, The Politics of Hope, 1963, A Thousand Days, 1965 (Pulitzer Prize for Biography 1966, Nat. Book award 1966), The Bitter Heritage: Vietnam and American Democracy, 1941-1966, 1967, Violence: America in the Sixties, 1968, The Crisis of Confidence: Ideas, Power, and Violence in America, 1969, The Origins of the Cold War, 1970, The Imperial Presidency, 1973 (Sidney Hillman Found. award 1973), Robert Kennedy and His Times, 1978 (Nat. Book award 1979), Creativity in Statecraft, 1983, The Cycles of American History, 1986, JFK Remembered, 1988, War and the Constitution: Abraham Lincoln and Franklin D. Roosevelt, 1988, Is the Cold War Over?, 1990, The Disuniting of America: Reflections on a Multicultural Society, 1991, A Life in The 20th Century: Innocent Beginnings, 1917-1950, 2000, War and the American Presidency, 2004, Journals: 1952-2000, 2007 (published posthumously); co-author: (with R.H. Rovere) The General and the President, 1951, (with John Blum) The National Experience, 1963; contbr. articles to mags. and newspapers; film reviewer: Show mag, 1962-64, Vogue, 1967-72, Saturday Rev., 1977-80, Am. Heritage, 1981-82; editor: Harvard Guide to American History, 1954, Guide to Politics, 1954, Paths to American Thought, 1963, The Promise of American Life, 1967, The Best and the Last of Edwin O'Connor, 1970, History of American Presidential Elections 1789-1972, 1971, 1972-1984, 1986, The Coming to Power, 1972, The Dynamics of World Power: A Documentary History of United States Foreign Policy 1945-1973, 1973, History of U.S. Political Parties, 1973, Congress Investigates, 1975, Running for President, 1994; screenwriter: (teleplay) The Journey of Robert F. Kennedy; contributing blogger at The Huffington Post, 2005-2007. Served with AUS, 1945. Decorated comdr. Order of Orange-Nassau, The Netherlands, Ordem del Libertador, Venezuela, Order of St. Michael and St George, Gt. Britain; recipient Gold medal in History & Biography, Am. Acad. Arts and Letters, 1967, Award for History, Govt. of Ohio, 1973, Eugene V. Debs Award in Edn., 1974, Fregen Prize for Lit., 1983, Harry S. Truman Good Neighbor award, Harry S. Truman Good Neighbor Award Found., 1992, Award for Internat. Understanding, U. Thant, 1998, Nat. Humanities Medal, 1998, Four Freedoms award, 2003, Paul Peck award, 2006; fellow, Guggenheim, 1946; grantee, Am. Acad. Arts and Letters, 1946. Mem. Am. Hist. Assn., Orgn. Am. Historians, Soc. Am. Historians (pres. 1989-92), Am. Acad. Arts and Letters (pres. 1981-84, chancellor 1984-87), Am. Philos. Soc., Mass. Hist. Soc., Colonial Soc. Mass., Russian Acad. Scis., Franklin and Eleanor Roosevelt Inst. (co-chmn. 1983—), ACLU, Coun. Fgn. Rels., Americans for Dem. Action (nat. chmn. 1952-54), Century Assn., Knickerbocker Club, Phi Beta Kappa. Democrat. Unitarian. Died Feb. 28, 2007.

SCHLOSS, MILTON JOSEPH, former food company executive; b. Louisville, Nov. 15, 1913; s. Milton Joseph and Matilda (Kahn) S.; m. Mary Louise Telker, Mar. 19, 1941; children: Milton Joseph, Bert J., James D. BA, U. Mich., 1934; JD, U. Cin., 1937. With Kahn's and Co., Cin., 1929—, dept. supr., 1937-46, v.p., 1946-48, pres., 1948-78, chmn., from 1978; now ret. Adj. prof. bus. mgmt. U. Cin., 1983—; dir. Ohio Nat. Life Ins. Co. Served to capt. AUS, 1942-46, ETO. Decorated Bronze Star medal. Mem. Am. Meat Inst. (dir.), Order of Coif, Phi Epsilon Pi., B'nai B'rith. Home: Cincinnati, Ohio. Died July 9, 2007.

SCHLUETER, JOHN J., retail company executive; b. Milw., Oct. 9, 1939; s. Clement M. and Gertrude (Bethke) S.; m. Joan Cudihy, July 11, 1964; children: John Jr., Michael E., Edward J. BBA with honors, Boston Coll., 1963; MBA with distinction, Babson Coll., 1964; cert. in advanced mgmt. program, Harvard U., 1985. CPA, Mass. Fin. analyst Ford Motor Co., Dearborn, Mich., 1964-66; acct. Arthur Young & Co., Boston, 1966-70; v.p., chief fin. officer King Size Inc., Brockton, Mass., 1970-73; v.p. fin., chief fin. officer Sam Solomon & Co., Charleston, S.C., 1973-79, McRae's Dept. Stores, Jackson, Miss., 1979-80, Knapp King-Size Corp., Brockton, 1980-85; exec. v.p. Knapp Shoes Inc., Brockton, 1985-86, pres., chief exec. officer, from 1986, also bd. dirs. Author, speaker on point of sales in the Mass. mdse. industry, 1978-80. Mem. Charleston Hist. Soc., 1973-80, Duxbury (Mass.) Hist. Soc., 1980—. Mem. Mass. Soc. CPA's, Fin. Execs. Inst., Harvard Bus. Sch. Soc. Home: Duxbury, Mass. Died Sept. 29, 2006.

SCHMIDT, GARY EMIL, corporate executive manager; b. Toledo, Oct. 30, 1940; s. Emil August and Edna (Mowery) S.; BA, Northwestern U., 1962. Bus. editor Calif. Apparel news, weekly newspaper, L.A., 1968-69; feature editor Men's Stylist mag., monthly, L.A., 1970-71; mng. editor Style for Men, weekly, L.A., 1971-72; pres. Am. Century Mktg., Inc., L.A., 1973-79, also dir; investment adv., Studio City, Calif., 1979-87; pres. New Century Rhinoceros, Inc., Panorama City, Calif., 1987-89, also dir. Served with U.S. Army, 1962-65. Mem. Authors League Am., Authors Guild. Republican. Unitarian. Home: Albuquerque, N.Mex. Died Sept. 19, 2006.

SCHMIDT, WALLACE VERE, speech communication educator; b. Aberdeen, S.D., July 31, 1946; s. Clarence W. and Sylvia (Tarnasky) S.; m. Susan Ruth Osborn, Dec. 21, 1969; 1 child, Matthew Wallace. B.A. cum laude, Midland Coll., Nebr., 1968; M.A., U. Nebr., 1972; Ph.D., NYU, 1979. Tchr., Glenwood High Sch., Iowa, 1968-73; asst. prof. Hofstra U., Hempstead, N.Y., 1973-80, Tex. Tech. U., Lubbock, 1980-83; assoc. prof. speech communication U. Tex.-Tyler, 1983—. Author: (with Jo-Ann Graham) The Public Forum: A Transactional Approach to Public Communication, 1979; Organizational Communication: Principles and Practices, 1988; (with Keith Erickson) Relating, Communicating Interpersonally; also articles. Democratic precinct chair, Tyler, 1984—; bd. dirs. Tyler chpt. Am. Diabetes Assn., 1984—; cert. Better Bus. Bur. arbitrator, 1985—. Mem. Internat. Soc. History of Rhetoric (program planning com. U.S. br. 1983-84), Tex. State Speech Communication Assn. (pres. rhetoric group 1983-84, v.p. group 1982-83), Internat. Communication Assn., Am. Bus. Communication Assn., Rhetoric Soc. Am., Acad. Internat. Bus., others. Lutheran. Avocations: golf; fishing; chess. Home: Orlando, Fla. Died Feb. 25, 2007.

SCHMITT, HANS ADOLF, history educator, writer; b. Frankfurt-am-Main, Hesse, Germany, June 6, 1921; came to U.S., 1938; s. Julius and Elisabeth Dorothea (Hamburger) S.; m. Florence Arlene Brandow, Sept. 8, 1944; children— Anthony Richard, Jennifer Elizabeth Davis, Christopher Rene AB, Washington & Lee U., 1940; MA, U. Chgo., 1943, PhD, 1953. Asst. prof. U. Okla., Norman, 1953-57, assoc. prof., 1957-59, Tulane U., New Orleans, 1959-61, prof., 1961-67, NYU, 1967-71; prof. history U. Va., Charlottesville, from 1971. Author: The Path to European Union, 1962 (Beer prize 1962); Charles Peguy, 1967; European Union From Hitler to De Gaulle, 1969; co-author: The German Democratic Movement, 1976 Vice pres. Jefferson Com. for Better Schs., Jefferson Parish, La., 1963-64; mem. exec. com. Cook County Young Democrats, Chgo., 1952-53, Cleveland County Democrats, Norman, 1955-58 Louis Asher fellow U. Chgo., 1951; Carnegie fellow U. Chgo., 1952; Fulbright fellow, 1956-57 Mem. Am. Hist. Assn. (co-chmn. program com. 1976-77), Societe d'Hist. Moderne, So. Hist. Assn. (mem. exec. council 1974-77, chmn. European sect. 1980-81), German Studies Assn., AAUP, Soc. French Hist. Studies (pres. 1966-67) Home: Charlottesville, Va. Died Feb. 15, 2006.

SCHNAPER, HAROLD WARREN, medical educator; b. Boston, Nov. 11, 1923; s. Julius Hasse and Minnie Ruth (Galler) S.; m. Edna Ruth Stern, Jan. 21, 1951; children— Jonathan Hasse (dec.), Ann Rebecca, Brett Eliot, Michelle Helene, Deborah Lynn. A.B., Harvard U., 1945; M.D., Duke U., 1949. Diplomate Am. Bd. Internal Medicine. Intern, Boston City Hosp., 1949-50; resident Mt. Sinai Hosp., N.Y.C., 1953-54; cardiovascular research fellow Georgetown U. Sch. Medicine, Washington, 1951-52, instr. 1954-56, asst. prof., 1956-67; chief med. research VA Central Office, Washington, 1960-62, assoc. dir., nat. acting dir. research service, 1962-67; assoc. prof. U. Ala., Birmingham, 1967-69, prof., 1969—, co-dir. cardiovascular research and tng. ctr., 1967-73, exec. vice chmn. dept.

medicine, 1967-73, dir. hypertension programs, 1973—, dir. Ctr. for Aging, 1976—, prof., dir. div. gerontology and geriatric medicine. Served to 1st lt. AUS, 1943-46, 51-53; ETO. Mem. ACP, Council on Epidemiology-Am. Heart Assn., Am. Coll. Cardiology, Am. Pub. Health Assn., AAAS, Gerontol. Soc., Am. Geriatric Soc., So. Gerontol. Soc., Ala. Gerontol. Soc., N.Y. Acad. Scis. Clubs: Harvard, Duke Med. Alumni (Birmingham). Contbr. numerous articles to med. jours. Home: Birmingham, Ala. Died June 25, 2007.

SCHNEIDER, WILLIAM GEORGE, retired insurance company executive; b. Shenandoah, Iowa, Jan. 18, 1919; s. Fred M. and Abba F. (Ferguson) S.; m. Phyllis Welch, Mar. 28, 1943; children— Stephen F., Richard W. BA, State U. Iowa, 1940; postgrad., N.Y. U. With Met. Life Ins. Co., 1940-41, 45-46; with Bankers Life Co. (now named Prin. Fin. Group), Des Moines, 1946-84; sr. v.p. Bankers Life Co., 1970-82, exec. v.p., 1982-84, ret., 1984. Served with AUS, 1941-45. Fellow Soc. Actuaries; mem. Am. Acad. Actuaries, Des Moines Golf and Country Club, Phi Beta Kappa. Republican. Home: Urbandale, Iowa. Died Mar. 16, 2006.

SCHOENFELD, ROBERT LOUIS, biomedical engineer; b. NYC, Apr. 1, 1920; s. Bernard and Mae (Kizelstein) S.; m. Helene Martens, Jan. 22, 1944 (div. 1965); children: David, Joseph, Paul; m. Florence Moskowitz, Dec. 11, 1965 (dec. 1989); children: Nedda, Bethany; m. Shulamith Stechel, July 8, 1990. BA, Washington Square Coll., 1942; BSEE, Columbia U., 1944; MEE, Poly. Inst. Bklyn., 1949, DEE, 1956. Rsch. assoc. Columbia U. Med. Sch., NYC, 1947-51; rsch. fellow Sloan Kettering Cancer Rsch. Inst., NYC, 1951-56; assoc. prof. Poly. Inst. Bklyn., 1957—59; biomed. engr. Rockefeller U., NYC, 1957—59, from asst. prof. to assoc. prof., 1957-90, prof. emeritus, from 1990. Contbr. articles to profl. jours. Lt. Signal Corps, U.S. Army, 1944-46, ETO. Fellow IEEE (mem. editl. bd. 1965-75, Centennial medal 1985), Am. Inst. for Med. and Biol. Engring. Democrat. Jewish. Achievements include pioneering application of computer automation to biological laboratory experiments. Died May 22, 2007.

SCHOENHERR, WALTER JOSEPH, bishop; b. Detroit, Feb. 28, 1920; s. Alex M. and Ida (Schmitz) S. Student, Sacred Heart Sem., Detroit, 1935-42, Mt. St. Mary's Sem., Norwood, Ohio, 1942-44, S.S. Cyril and Methodius Sem., Orchard Lake, Mich., 1944-45. Ordained priest Roman Catholic Ch., 1945; asst. pastor Detroit Parishes of St. Davids, St. Leos, St. Roses, Presentation and St. Bedes, Southfield, Mich., 1959-61; pastor St. Aloysius Parish, Detroit, 1961-65, Blessed Sacrament Cathedral, 1965-68; bishop of Detroit, from 1968; appointed to serve South region Archdiocese of Detroit, from 1977. Mem. Permanent Diaconate and Pastoral Ministry to Correctional Instns., Archidocesan Liturgical Commn.; founding chaplain De LaSalle council K.C. Served with Mich. N.G., 1952-67. Died Apr. 27, 2007.

SCHOFIELD, WILLIAM, psychologist, educator; b. Springfield, Mass., Apr. 19, 1921; s. William and Angie Mae (St. John) S.; m. Geraldine Bryan, Jan. 11, 1946; children: Bryan St. John, Gwen Star. BS, Springfield Coll., 1942; MA, U. Minn., 1946, PhD, 1948. Diplomate Am. Bd. Profl. Psychology. Instr. U. Minn., Mpls., 1947-48, asst. prof., 1948-51, assoc. prof., 1951-59, prof. psychology, 1959-88, prof. emeritus, from 1988. Vis. prof. U. Wash., 1960, U. Colo., 1965; Cons. VA Hosp., Mpls.; examiner, instr. USCG Aux., 1968—; mem. adv. council VA, 1970-75; Mem. med. policy adv. com. Dept. Pub. Welfare Minn., 1960-68; mem. mental health services research rev. com. NIMH, 1969-73; bd. dirs. Profl. Exam. Service, 1976-81; mem. editorial bd. Roche Psychiat. Service Inst.; mem. Minn. State Bd. Psychology, 1983-86. Author: Psychotherapy: The Purchase of Friendship, 1964, 2d edit., 1986, Pragmatics of Psychotherapy, 1988; contbr. articles to profl. jours. Served with USAAF, 1943-46. Fellow Am. Psychol. Assn. (com. on health ins. 1968-71, membership com. 1968-71, sec.-treas. clin. div. 1969-72, chmn. task force on health research 1973-75, chmn. sect. health research div. psychologists in pub. service 1977, mem. com. profl. standards 1982-85, chair com. 1984-85); mem. Midwestern Psychol. Assn., Minn. Psychol. Assn. (exec. sec. 1954-59), AAAS, AAUP, Assn. Am. Med. Colls. (chmn. com. on measurement of personality 1970-74), Sigma Xi, Pi Gamma Mu. Home: Minneapolis, Minn. Died Aug. 12, 2006.

SCHOMP, JOY JANETT, investor, lobbyist; b. Taloga, Okla., Sept. 20, 1932; d. Ranza Bennett and Nettie Alice (Pollock) Boggess; m. Dale Loyd Schomp, Mar. 23, 1951; children— Bonnie, DaLynne, Jacqueline. B.S., Okla. State U., 1957, M.S., 1962. Cert. tchr., Okla. Extension home economist Okla. State U., Payne and Custer counties, 1957-69; mgr.-owner Mini Storage Co., Weatherford, 1974—; with Add-vance Co., Weatherford, 1981-82; pvt. investor, Weatherford, 1983—; bd. dirs. Okla. Mineral Owners Assn., Weatherford, 1984—, pres., 1984, sec., 1985—, lobbyist, 1985—. Pres. Weatherford Sch. Bd., 1982, 87, Okla. Vet. Assn. Aux., 1971; chmn. capital campaign com. YMCA, 1987. Recipient Outstanding Service citation Nat. Assn. Royalty Owners, 1985. Mem. Okla. State Sch. Bds. Assn. Democrat. Mem. Disciples of Christ. Avocations: reading, sewing, travel. Home: Weatherford, Okla. Died Oct. 20, 2006.

SCHONEMAN, JOHN ARNOLD, insurance company executive; b. Chgo., July 9, 1928; s. Edwin H. and Florence (Drews) S.; m. Mary Fairhank, Nov. 4, 1950; children— Judy Beirne, Jim Schoneman, Robert Schoneman, Carolyn Schoneman. B.S., Ill. Inst. Tech., 1950; M.B.A., U. Chgo., 1956; postgrad. Advanced Mgmt. Program, Harvard U., 1974. Exec. v.p. Atlantic Mutual Ins. Co., N.Y.C., 1955-75; exec. v.p. Wausau Ins. Cos. (Wis.), 1976-77, pres., chief exec. officer, 1977-81, chmn., chief exec. officer, 1981—; exec. com., dir. Alliance Am. Insurers, Schaumburg, Ill.; dir. Ins. Services Office, N.Y.C., Am. Inst. Property and Liability Underwriters, Malvern, Pa., Mosinee Paper Corp. (Wis.), Central Wis. Bankshares, Wausau, Forward Communications Corp., Wausau. Mem. policy devel. council Marshfield Med. Found. (Wis.); bd. dirs. Wis. Found. Ind. Colls., Milw., Wausau YMCA Found., Wausau Health Found., Inc. Republican. Lutheran. Mem. Wausau Area C. of C. (pres.), Soc. Fire Protection Engrs., Assn. Mfrs. and Commerce Milw. (dir.). Clubs: Pinnacle (N.Y.C.); Chicago; Wausau. Home: Wausau, Wis. Died Nov. 9, 2006.

SCHOOLEY, ELMER WAYNE, artist; b. Lawrence, Kans., Feb. 20, 1916; s. Sparks Sylvester and Nella (Winey) S.; m. Gertrude Lucille Rogers, Sept. 2, 1942; children: David, Edwin, John, Theodore. B.F.A., U. Colo., 1938; MA, State U. Iowa, 1942. Grade sch. tchr., Lafayette, Colo., 1940-41; instr. N.Mex. State Tchrs. Coll., Silver City, 1946-47; prof. dept. arts and crafts N.Mex. Highlands U., Las Vegas, 1947-77. Paintings represented in permanent collections U. Okla. Art Mus., Mus. N.Mex., Roswell (N.Mex.) Mus., Hallmark Collection, Kansas City (Mo.) Mus. Modern Art, Munson Gallery, Santa Fe, Albuquerque N.Mex. Mus., Tucson Ariz. Mus. of Art; prints represented in permanent collections Met. Mus., Bklyn. Art Mus., Library of Congress, Dallas Art Mus., Wichita Art Assn., Mus. N.Mex.; one man show include Tucson Mus. Art, 1991-92, N.Mex. Mus. Art Gallery, Santa Fe, 1992. Served to capt. AUS, 1942-46. Recipient N.Mex. Gov.'s Excellence of Achievement in Visual Arts award, 1986. Democrat. Mem. Soc. Of Friends. Home: Roswell, N.Mex. Died Apr. 25, 2007.

SCHOTTENSTEIN, SAUL M., retired retail company executive; b. Apr. 3, 1922; married. Pres. Schottenstein Stores, Columbus, Ohio, 1972—2007. Died Aug. 11, 2007.

SCHREIBER, MARVIN MANDEL, agronomist, educator; b. Springfield, Mass., Oct. 17, 1925; s. William and Florence Schreiber; m. Phyllis E. Altman, Dec. 18, 1949; 1 child, Michelle. BS, U. Mass., 1950; MS, U. Ariz., 1951; PhD, Cornell U., 1954. Asst. prof. dept. agronomy Cornell U., Ithaca, N.Y., 1954-59; assoc. prof. dept. botany and plant pathology Purdue U., West Lafayette, Ind., from 1959-73, prof., from 1973; rsch. agronomist Agrl. Rsch. Svc. USDA, West Lafayette, from 1959. Fellow AAAS, Am. Soc. Agronomy, Weed Sci. Soc. Am.; mem. Internat. Weed Sci. Soc. (pres. 1979-81), Controlled Release Soc., Coun. Agrl. Sci. and Tech., Sigma Xi. Avocations: golf, gardening. Died Apr. 14, 2006.

SCHREURS, BRIAN FREDERICK, editor, publisher; b. Wakefield, Mass., June 4, 1974; s. Stephen Frederick and Susan Jeanette (Clement) S. BS in Journalism, W.Va. U., 1997. Pres. Coltrane Prodns., Marytown, W.Va., from 1989; tech. editor Silver Chips, Silver Spring, Md., 1990-92; reporter, columnist The Daily Athenaeum, Morgantown, 1993-96; promotion designer WCLG AM/FM, Morgantown, W.Va., 1997; editor-in-chief The Inn Times, Washington, 1997; editor State Tax One Disc, Arlington, Va, 1998-2000; tech. editor Sci. Applications Internat. Corp., Herndon, Va., 2000—02, Performance Results Corp., Morgantown, W.Va., from 2002. Author: S.H.A.L.T.: The Book, 1990, The Hot Rodder's Quck Reference, 1995, Insert Stupid Catchphrase Here, 1997, Hodge Podge, 1997, Loose Ends, 1998, Nine Lives, 2000. Patrolman Morgantown Police Res., 1996. With U.S. Army, 1995-97. Mem. NRA, Soc. Profl. Journalists, Sports Car Club of Am. Avocations: hot rodding, target shooting, amateur racing. Home: Morgantown, W.Va. Died Dec. 8, 2006.

SCHRIEVER, JOHN HENRY, former chemical company executive; b. Clarkstown, NY, Apr. 27, 1922; s. John H. and Edna (Hopf) S.; m. Doris Flavell, Sept. 8, 1945; children: Joanne Marie, Susan Karen. BS in Chemistry, Duke U., 1943. With Am. Cyanamid Co., 1948-83; v.p. mktg. Am. Cyanamid Co. (Lederle div.), 1972-77; pres. Am. Cyanamid Co. (Cyanamid Americas, Far East div.), Wayne, N.J., 1978-83. Officer, dir. fgn. subsidiaries; now ret. Contbr. articles to profl. jours. Pres. congregation Bethlehem Lutheran Ch., Atlanta, 1960-62; bd. dirs. Duke Hosp. Children's Classic, 1974-87. Served to 1st lt., inf. AUS, 1942-45. Decorated Purple Heart, Bronze Star, battle stars (6). Mem. Pharm. Mfrs. Assn., Am. Topical Assn., Mil. Order World Wars, AARP. Clubs: High Mountain Golf, Country of N.C.; Hong Kong. Republican. Died Mar. 19, 2006.

SCHROEDER, ALFRED CHRISTIAN, electronics research engineer; b. West New Brighton, NY, Feb. 28, 1915; s. Alfred and Chryssa (Weishaar) S.; m. Janet Ellis, Sept. 26, 1936 (dec.); 1 child, Carol Ann Schroeder Castle.; m. Dorothy Holloway, Nov. 21, 1981. BS, MS, MIT, 1937. Mem. tech. staff Sarnoff, Inc., Princeton, NJ, 1937-2000; ret. Contbr. articles to profl. jours. Recipient RCA Lab. awards, 1947, 50, 51, 52, 57, 70 Fellow IEEE (Vladimir Zworykin award 1971); mem. AAAS, Optical Soc. Am., Soc. Motion Picture and TV Engrs. (David Sarnoff Gold medal 1965), Soc. Info. Display (Karl Ferdinand Braun prize 1989), Sigma Xi. Mem. Soc. Of Friends. Achievements include 75 patents for color TV products including shadow mask tube. Home: Newtown, Pa. Died Oct. 21, 2006.

SCHROTE, JOHN ELLIS, retired federal agency administrator; b. Findlay, Ohio, May 6, 1936; s. Millard L. and Alberta (Ellis) S.; m. Rachel Daly, Mar. 2, 1957; children: LTC James D., Gretchen, Wade. BS in Agr., The Ohio State U., 1958; MBA, Xavier U., 1964. Buyer-expediter McGraw Constrn. Co., Middletown, Ohio, 1958-59; buyer Armco Corp., Middletown, 1959-66; adminstrv. asst. to Congressman D.E. Lukens US Congress, Washington, 1967-71; prin. asst. to assoc. dir. OEO, Washington, 1971-72; spl. asst. to sec. USDA, Washington, 1972-77, nat. rep. congl. com., 1977-79; adminstrv. asst. to Congressman F.J. Sensenbrenner, Jr. US Congress, Washington, 1979—81, 1984—89; acting asst. sec. USDA, Washington, 1981-82; dep. dir. presdl. pers. office The White House, 1982-83; exec. v.p. Bishop Bryant & Assocs., Washington, 1983-84; asst. to sec. and dir. cong. affairs US Dept. Interior, Washington, 1989, dep. asst. sec. for policy, mgmt. & budget, 1989-91, asst. sec. for policy, mgmt. and budget, 1991-93. Mem. Nat. Policy Forum, The Environ. Policy Coun., 1994-96, NC Seafood Indsl. Park Authority, 1994-97; mem. Currituck County Econ. Devel. Bd., 1994-2007; mem. Currituck County Rep. Exec. Com., 1993, 3d Dist. Rep. Exec. Com., 1994-97, NC State Rep. Exec. Com., 1994-97; Currituck County Ext. Svc. Adv. Leadership Coun., 1994-2000; bd. dir. Currituck County 4-H Found.; mem. Ocean Hills Property Owners Assn., 1994-2007 (treas. 1997-2000, v.p., 1996-97, 2003-04); commr. Northeastern NC Regional Econ. Devel. Commn., 1997-2007. Mem. Reagan-Bush Alumni Assn., Bush-Quayle Alumni Assn. Episcopalian. Home: Corolla, NC. Died Mar. 14, 2007.

SCHRUM, MARION MARGARET, university dean, nursing educator; b. Bryant, Iowa, Feb. 1, 1924; d. William and Agnes (Matthiesen) S. Diploma, Mt. St. Clare Coll., 1942; BS in Nursing Edn, St. Louis U., 1945; MS in Nursing Edn, Cath. U. Am., 1953; Ed.D., Stanford, 1958. Instr. Mercy Hosp. Sch. Nursing, Burlington, Iowa, 1946-49; asst. prof., chmn. founds. nursing dept. Coll. Nursing, State U. Iowa, 1950-56; asst. prof. chmn. gen. nursing program St. Louis U. Sch. Nursing and Health Services, 1958-60; asso. prof., dean Coll. nursing Villanova U., 1960-65; prof., dean Coll. nursing Villanova U. (Coll. Nursing), 1965-68; prof., chmn. dept. nursing San Francisco State U., 1968-73; prof., dean Sch. Nursing, U. Wyo., Laramie, 1973-80, Sch. Nursing, U. Nev., Reno, 1981-87. Mem. exec. bd. Western Council on Higher Edn. for Nursing, chmn. council, 1977-79; bd. dirs., treas. Wyo. Health Services Agy., 1974-80 Recipient Fellowship award Nat. League Nursing, 1957; John Switzer Honors award Stanford, 1957; Disting. Alumni award Mt. St. Clare Coll., 1980 Mem. Am. Nurses Assn., Wyo. Nurses Assn. (bd. dirs.), Nev. Nurses Assn. (v.p. 1982-84), San Francisco Nurses Assn. (dir.) Home: Reno, Nev. Died Feb. 3, 2007.

SCHUERCH, CONRAD, educator, chemist; b. Boston, Aug. 2, 1918; s. Conrad and Emma Melanie (Steinmuller) S.; m. Margaret Childs Pratt, June 26, 1948; children: Barbara Merle, Conrad, William Edward, Peter Henry. BS, MIT, 1940, PhD, 1947. With McGill U., 1947-49; mem. faculty SUNY Coll. Environ. Sci. Forestry, Syracuse, from 1949, prof. chemistry, from 1956, chmn. dept., 1956-72, SUNY disting. prof., 1978-83, disting. prof. emeritus, from 1983. Served to 1st lt. USAAF, 1943-45. Decorated Air medal with 3 oak leaf clusters, D.F.C., Purple Heart; Harold Hibbert Meml. fellow McGill U., 1948-49; Guggenheim fellow, 1959-60 Mem. Am. Chem. Soc. (chmn. Syracuse sect. 1962, chmn. cellulose, paper and textile div. 1977, Anselm Payen award 1972, Syracuse sect. award 1973), TAPPI. Research synthetic and natural polymers, carbohydrate and wood chemistry. Home: Washington, DC. Died July 15, 2007.

SCHULTZ, LESLIE KRENN, petroleum geologist, consultant; b. Visalia, Calif., Jan. 6, 1928; s. Rudolph August Schultz and Berniece Emily (Kalb) Putnam; m. Darlene Betty Jean, Oct. 2, 1950; children— Stephen, Karen, Eric. A.B., U. Calif.-Berkeley, 1952. Geologist Mobil, Houston, 1971-75, mgr. exploration, Denver, 1975-76, Dallas, 1976-81, coordinator new plays fgn., 1981-85; pres. SFC Petroleum Inc., Lake Dallas, Tex., 1985—, PXI Inc., Lake Dallas. Served with USAF, 1946-48, PTO. Mem. Am. Assn. Petroleum Geologists, Houston Geol. Soc. Avocations: travel; photography; fishing. Home: Dallas, Tex. Died June 3, 2006.

SCHUMACHER, EUGENE, college president; b. Tracy, Minn., Dec. 26, 1925; s. Frederick Wilhelm and Dorothea (Kurth) S.; m. Bonnie Scott, Apr. 5, 1950 (dec. Feb. 1989); children: Scott, Kim, Gina; m. Tania Volhontseff, Apr. 26, 1991. AA, Westminster Coll., Salt Lake City, 1947, BA in Math., 1949; MA in Student Pers., Columbia U., 1954; EdD in Ednl. Adminstrn., UCLA, 1971. Tchr. math. Elko County High Sch., Elko, Nev., 1949-56, counselor, 1954-56, vice prin., 1955-56; supt. schs. Eureka County Sch. Dist., Eureka, Nev., 1956-58; asst. dean students Antelope Valley Coll., Lancaster, Calif., 1958-61, dean student pers. svcs., 1961-67, dean instrn., 1967-70; pres., supt. Coll. of Siskiyous, Weed, Calif., from 1970. Bd dirs., chief exec. officer Calif. Community Coll., 1989—. Author: Student Personnel Records, 1971. Named Citizen of Yr. City of Weed, 1973; fellow Ford Found., 1953-54. Mem. Am. Assn. Community and Jr. Colls. (small rural coll. commn.), Assn. Calif. Community Coll. Adminstrs. (adminstrv. rep.), Community and Jr. Coll. Assn. (legis. com.), Calif. Community Colls. Chief Exec. Officers (past pres. no. Calif.), Weed C. of C (bd. dirs. 1989—), Rotary (bd. dirs. Weed 1985—), Lions (bd. dirs. Weed 1975—), Elks, Phi Delta Kappa. Avocations: woodworking, gardening, reading. Home: Weed, Calif. Died Aug. 26, 2007.

SCHUMANN, ADOLPH ALFRED, JR., architect; b. Chgo., Nov. 18, 1925; s. Adolph and Alvina (Hackert) S.; m. Margaret Nancy Kramer, July 15, 1935; children: Paula, Stacy. BArch, Ill. Inst. Tech., 1952. Registered architect, Ill., 1954. Architect Holabird, Root & Burgee, Chgo., 1951-53, Esposito & Co., G.C., Oak Park, Ill., 1953-59; ptnr. Schumann & Straka Architects, Oak Park, 1959-70; prin. A.A. Schumann, Jr., Chgo. 1970-77 and from 95; architect Consoer, Morgan, Ltd., Chgo. 1973-78, Designex, Chgo., 1977-78, Sente & Rubel, Ltd. Northbrook, Ill., 1980-81, 88-95, Facilities Design, Ltd. Hickory Hills, Ill., 1981-88. Dir. Adolph Schumann Ski Sch. various cities, No. Ill., 1961-75. Prin. works include Grove Meml. Funeral Home, Elk Grove Village, Ill. and Buffalo Grove, Ill., Ice Rink at Santa's Village, East Dundee, Ill., bldg. addition at Adventureland, Medinah, Ill., underground parking facility for Svec Funeral Home, Berwyn, Ill., Wastewater Treatment Plant, St. Cloud, Minn., Vernon Hills, Ill., Engring. Ctr. of Morraine Valley C.C., recreational bldg. Joliet (Ill.) Prison numerous bus., med. and apt. bldgs. in Oak Park, also various comml. and indsl. bldgs.; rennovation of Maine North H.S. for Ill. State Police Bldg. Active Sertoma Orgn., Evanston, 1958-59. With USAF, 1945-46. Mem. Oak Park Ski Club (life, co-author club constitution and by-laws 1955-56, trip chmn. 1955-56, ski master 1956-57, pres. 1957-58, New Skis award 1958). Avocations: skiing, sailing, photography, fishing. Died June 20, 2006

SCHUMER, MIRIAM HERNANDEZ, scientific journal editor; b. Aguas Buenas, P.R., Sept. 11, 1925, came to U.S., 1944 d. Ramon and Mary (Melendez) Hernandez; children— Gerard M. Soto, Leonard, Daniel Anthony, Naomi Nilza Jacobson; m William Schumer. Student U. P.R., Rio Piedras, 1942-43 CCNY, 1944-45, Brown's Bus. Coll. and Edison Ediphone Sch. N.Y.C., 1947-48, spl. programs cons. on rehab. tuberculosis and health assn., N.Y.C., 1947, Sacramento Coll., 1965-67. Exec sec. physics Meml. Cancer Ctr. and Sloan-Kettering Inst. N.Y.C., 1952-53, U.S. Vitamin Corp., N.Y.C., 1953-55; con sumer columnist El Diario de Nueva York, N.Y.C., 1955-57; adminstrv. asst. dept. surgery Chgo. Med. Sch., 1960-65, U. Calif.-Davis, 1965-67, U. Ill. and VA West Side Hosp., Chgo., 1967-75; adminstrv. and editorial asst. dept. surgery U. of Health Scis./Chgo. Med. Sch. and VA North Chicago (Ill.) Med. Ctr., 1975-80; asst. editor dept. surgery U. of Health Scis./Chgo. Med. Sch., North Chicago, Ill., 1980—; asst. exec. editor Circulatory Shock jour., N.Y.C., 1979-88, cons. editorial office, N.Y.C., 1988—; counselor equal opportunity employment 1976-79. Founder Beneficent Hispanic Soc. N.Y., 1947; founding mem. Hispanic Theater of N.Y., 1948; mem. Lake County Health Systems Agy., 1980-81. Recipient commendations VA, 1971, 79. Club: Espanol of North Shore. Home: Benicia, Calif. Died Mar. 19, 2006.

SCHUUR, ROBERT GEORGE, lawyer; b. Kalamazoo, Dec. 5, 1931; s. George Garrett and Louise Margaret (DeVries) S.; m. Susan Elizabeth White, Sept. 28, 1968; children— Arah Louise Adele, Jeremiah Donald Garrett. A.B., U. Mich., 1953, LL.B., 1955. Bar: Mich. 1955, N.Y. 1956. Assoc. Reid & Priest, N.Y.C., 1955-65, ptnr., 1966—. Served with USN, 1956-58. Mem. ABA, N.Y. State Bar Assn., Assn. of Bar of City of N.Y., Phi Beta Kappa. Club: University (N.Y.C.). Home: New York, NY. Died Mar. 3, 2007.

SCHUYLER, WILLIAM EARL, JR., lawyer; b. 1914; m. Jean Horton, 1938 (dec. 2005); children: William, Majel, Elizabeth. BEE, Cath. U. Am., 1935; JD, Georgetown U., 1940. Bar: D.C. 1940. Commr. US Patent & Trademark Office, US Dept. Commerce, 1969—71; ptnr. Schuyler, Banner, Birch, McKie and Beckett, 1971—83. Bd. regents Catholic U., 1986—91. Mem. ABA (bd. govs., bd. nat. conf. adminstrv. law judges). Roman Catholic. Died July 25, 2007.

SCHWARTZ, ALLEN, lawyer; b. Cleve., Aug. 2, 1930; s. Albert and Sylvia (Dusek) S.; m. Regina Marie Geissenhainer, Aug. 26, 1958; children: Mary Regina, Allen Christopher. BA, Oberlin Coll., 1952; JD with distinction, U. Mich., 1955. Bar: Mich. 1955, Ohio 1955. Atty. SEC, Washington, 1957-58; assoc. Miller, Canfield, Paddock & Stone, Detroit, 1958-66, ptnr., from 1967. V.p., pres. 1st Eng./Evang. Luth. Ch., Grosse Pointe Woods, Mich., 1983-87. With U.S. Army, 1955-57. Mem. ABA, Mich. Bar Assn. (sec. real property law coun. 1980—, vice chmn. 1981-82, chmn. elect 1982-83, chmn. 1983-84, svc. award 1988), Detroit Bar Assn., Am. Coll. Real Property Lawyers, Gowanie Golf Club (Mt. Clemens, Mich.). Avocations: sports, classical music, reading. Home: Sarasota, Fla. Died Aug. 18, 2006.

SCHWARTZ, IRVING DONN, architect; b. Chgo., June 11, 1927; s. Simon S. and Rose P. S.; children: Charles, Linda. BS, U. Ill., 1949, BS in Architecture, 1965, MS in Architecture, 1972. Registered architect, Ill., Ind., Fla., D.C., Ohio, Ga., Ala., Calif., N.H., Va., Md., Pa, Tenn., La., N.J., Tex., Mo., N.C., S.C., Ark. Chief standard cost and indsl. engring. Lanzit Corrugated Box Co., Chgo., 1950-53; pres. Kaufman, Inc., Champaign, Ill., 1953-60; v.p. Hart Mirror Plate Co., Grand Rapids, Mich., 1953-60; assoc. Richardson, Severns, Scheeler & Assos., Inc., Champaign, Ill., 1960-71; pres. IDS, Inc., Champaign, Ill., 1971-83, ADI, Dallas, 1983-86, IDS/B, Inc., Dallas, 1986—2007. Prof. architecture Grad. Sch. Architecture, U. Ill., 1976-83; assoc. prof. design U. North Tex.; cons. in field. Mem. Champaign County Devel. Council; mem. Model Community Coordinating Council, Champaign; co-chmn. bldg. com. Mercy Hosp.; bd. frat. affairs U. Ill.; bd. dirs. United Fund. Served to 2d lt. U.S. Army, 1945-47. Recipient archtl. design research award, graphic design citation Progressive Architecture mag., 1974, Gold Key Design award Hospitality Mag., 1994, John Robinson award, 2001. Fellow Am. Soc. Interior Designers (treas. 1976, nat. pres. 1978, Louis Tregre award 1992, Nat. design award 1983); mem. AIA (Design award 1983), Nat. Council Archtl. Registration Bds., Nat. Council Interior Design Qualifications (bd. dirs., pres. 1980), Tex. Assn. Interior Design (pres. 1993). Clubs: Standard (Chgo.). Home: Dallas, Tex. Died Feb. 1, 2007.

SCHWARTZKOPF, EDWARD, child care agency director; b. Lincoln, Nebr., Aug. 8, 1919; s. Wilhelm and Kathryn (Sterger) S.; m. Dorothy Frances Filley, June 16, 1946; children: William Clyde, Linda Kay, Steven Edward. BA, U. Nebr., 1948, MA, 1954, postgrad., 1966. Tchr., coach Lincoln Pub. Schs., 1950-56, coord. ind. edn., 1956-65, dir. out of sch. learning, 1956-84; exec. dir., v.p. The Cedars Home for Children Found., Inc., Lincoln, from 1985. Mem. Gov.'s Task Force on Edn., Lincoln, 1972-82. Author: (learning program) U.S. Minute Man Developmental Learning Programs for Schs. and Mil. Components, 1977. Mem. Pres.' Adv. Coun. for Food and Nutrition, Washington, 1971-74; regent U. Nebr., Lincoln, 1967-84; civilian aide Sec. of Army for Nebr., Lincoln, 1974-79; mem. exec. coun. Boy Scouts Am., Lincoln, 1976—; del. Rep. Nat. Conv., 1972, 76; trustee Nebr. Human Resources Found., 1966—. Major U.S. Army, 1941-45. Named to U. Nebr. Football Hall Fame, 1988, Lincoln High Sch. Athletic Hall Fame, 1984, U. Nebr. Agrl. Hall Achievement, 1989. Mem. Am. Hist. Soc. for Germans from Russia (pres. 1978-84), Lincoln C. of C., Lincoln Downtown Sertoma Club (pres. 1964-65, recipient Gold Coat), Lancaster County Human Soc. (pres. 1972-74). Mem. United Ch. Christ. Avocations: theater and the arts, gardening, volunteer work. Home: Lincoln, Nebr. Died June 15, 2006.

SCHWEBEL, BERNICE LOIS, corporate executive, educator; b. Hartford, Conn., Sept. 27, 1916; d. Joseph and Sara (Brewer) Davison; m. Milton Scwebel, Sept. 3, 1939; children: Andrew, Robert BA, Russell Sage Coll., 1938; teaching cert. SUNY, 1949; MA, NYU, 1963. Co-founder, dir. Counseling and Placement Svcs. for Refugees, Jewish Community Ctr., Troy, N.Y., 1936; social case worker Troy Orphan Asylum, 1938-39; cottage mother Pleasantville (N.Y.) Cottage Sch., 1939-40; head tchr. Birnby Nursery Sch., N.Y.C., 1945-46; tchr. kindergarten, primary grades, Valley Stream, N.Y., 1950-67; supr. student tchrs. edn. dept. Douglass Coll., Rutgers U., New Brunswick, N.J., 1973-76; v.p. ednl. programs and materials Univ. Assocs., Columbus, Ohio, 1976—; treas. Continental Land Holding, New Brunswick, 1984—. Author (with others) film scipt Risistance to Learning, 1962, Student Teachers Handbook, 1979, A Guide to a Happier Family, 1989; contbr. articles to various publs. Trustee Rutgers-Livingston Day Care Ctr., 1977-80; chmn. Rutgers-Old Queens Visitation Com., New Brunswick Tercentenary, 1979-80. Mem. NOW, LWV, Authors Guild, Russell Sage Alumnae Assn., NYU Alumni Assn. Died May 12, 2007.

SCORDELIS, ALEXANDER COSTICAS, civil engineering educator; b. San Francisco, Sept. 27, 1923; s. Philip Kostas and Vasilica (Zois) S.; m. Georgia Gumas, May 9, 1948; children: Byron, Karen. BS, U. Calif., Berkeley, 1948; MS, M.I.T., 1949. Registered profl. engr., Calif. Structural designer Pacific Gas & Electric Co., San Francisco, 1948; engr. Bechtel Corp., San Francisco, summer 1951, 52, 53, 54; instr. civil engring. U. Calif., 1949-50, asst. prof., 1951-56, assoc. prof., 1957-61, prof., 1962-89, asst. dean Coll. Engring., 1962-65, vice chmn. div. structural engring, structural mechanics, 1970-73, Nishkian prof. emeritus, 1990—2007. Cons. engring. firms, govt. agys. Contbr. articles on analysis and design of complex structural systems, reinforced and prestressed concrete shell and bridge structures to profl. jours. Served to capt., C.E. U.S. Army, 1943-46, ETO. Decorated Bronze star, Purple Heart; recipient Western Electric award Am. Soc. Engring. Edn., 1978; Axion award Hellenic Am. Profl. Soc., 1979; Best paper award Canadian Soc. Civil Engring., 1982, K.B. Woods award NAS Transp. Rsch. Bd., 1983, Citation U. Calif. Berkeley, 1989, Disting. Engring. Alumnus award Berkeley Engring. ALumni Soc., 1993, Leadership award Am. Segmental Bridge Inst., 1993, Freyssinet medal Internat. Fedn. for Prestressed Concrete, 1994. Fellow ASCE (hon. mem. 1989, Moissieff award 1976, 81, 92, Howard award 1989), Am. Concrete Inst.; mem. Internat. Assn. Shell and Spatial Structures (hon., Torroja medal 1994), Internat. Assn. Bridge and Structural Engring. (Tedesko medal 1998), Structural Engrs. Assn. Calif., Nat. Acad. Engring. Home: El Cerrito, Calif. Died Aug. 27, 2007.

SCOTT, FRANK EDWARD, savings and loan executive; b. Los Angeles, Feb. 24, 1920; s. Walter Benjamin and Katherine Ella (Walters) S.; m. Juanita E. Stephens, Feb. 28, 1937 (div. Jan. 1960); children— Richard W., Elizabeth Scott Foremaster; m. Charlene E. Duff, Dec. 22, 1962; 1 child, Rick L. Ed., high sch., Las Vegas, Nev. Owner, gen. mgr. Roberts Roof & Floor Co., Las Vegas, Nev., 1946-73; owner Dealers Wholesale, Las Vegas, 1952-65; v.p., dir. Stocks Mill & Supply, Las Vegas, 1962-73; chmn. bd., chief exec. officer Scott Corp. dba Union Plaza Hotel, Las Vegas, 1962-87; chmn. bd. First Western Fin., Las Vegas, 1971-88, Dres Media, Inc. (KRLR-TV), Las Vegas, from 1983; dir., v.p. First Western Savs. Assn., Tom Coward Lincoln Mercury, Nev. Power Co., Las Vegas; pres., chief operating officer HSST Nev. Corp., Las Vegas, from 1987. Bd. dirs. Boy Scouts Am., New Horizon Ctr. for Learning; mem. Sheriff's Mounted Posse, 1947—, capt., 1957-59; trustee Nev. Mus. Fine Arts, U. Nev.-Las Vegas Found.; pres. Nev. Devel. Authority, 1974-75; mem. Nev. State Contractors Licensing Bd., 1975-73, Las Vegas Conv. Authority, 1971-73. Served to 2d lt. inf., U.S. Army, 1944-46; PTO Recipient Man of Yr. award Sales Mgmt. Assn., 1982 Mem. Las Vegas C. of C. (pres. 1966-67), Nev. Resort Assn. (pres. 1975-77, dir., mem. exec. com. 1985), Federated Employers Nev. (pres. 1956-57), Rancheros Vistadores Club (pres. bd. dirs.), Bohemian Club, Hualapai Club, Las Vegas Country Club, Masons. Democrat. Avocations: tennis; thoroughbred horses. Home: Las Vegas, Nev. Died Feb. 22, 2006.

SCOTT, GEORGE MATTHEW, state supreme court judge; b. Clark, NJ, Sept. 14, 1922; s. Francis Patrick and Harriet Ann (O'Donnell) S.; m. Joyce E. Hughes, July 26, 1947; children: Dan, Neil, Brian, George Matthew, Sheila. BS, U. Minn.; JD, William Mitchell Coll. Law. Bar: Minn. Practice law, 1951-55; dep. atty. gen. State of Minn., 1955; atty. Hennepin County, Mpls., 1955-73; justice Minn. Supreme Ct., St. Paul, from 1973. Contbr. articles to profl. jours. Trustee William Mitchell Coll., 1960; del. Democratic Nat. Conv.; campaign chmn. Hubert H. Humphrey for Senator, 1960. Served with AUS, 1942-45. Mem. ABA, Minn. Bar Assn., Nat. Dist. Atty's. Assn. (pres. 1964-65), Am. Legion. Clubs: Optimists. Roman Catholic. Died May 25, 2006.

SCOTT, JIMMIE DOW, health facility administrator; b. Milo, Okla., Jan. 1, 1930; s. Preston William and Elnora Mae (Hancock) S.; B. Liberal Studies, U. Okla., 1974, M.P.A., 1976, M.H.R., 1982; m. Wanda Mae Tippit, Oct. 5, 1952; children— Jimmie Dow, Dwain Dawson. Seaman recruit U.S. Navy, 1948, advanced through grades to lt. comdr., 1968; asst. adminstr. patient affairs, security and edn. U.S. Naval Hosp., Pensacola, Fla., 1959-63; asst. adminstr. Yokosuka (Japan) Naval Hosp., 1963-67; chief patient relations br. Bur. Medicine and Surgery, Washington, 1967-71; ret., 1971; exec. asst. for adminstrn. Univ. Hosp. and Clinics, Oklahoma City, 1980-83; adminstrv. asst. for adminstrn., assoc. adminstr. Okla. Meml. Hosp. and Clinics, Oklahoma City, 1983-85; assoc. adminstr. Okla. Teaching Hosps., Oklahoma City, 1985—. Mem. Am. Acad. Med. Adminstrs., Am. Soc. Public Adminstrs., Am. Coll. Hosp. Adminstrs., Acad. Polit. Sci., Am. Acad. Polit. and Social Sci. Republican. Baptist. Home: Moore, Okla. Died June 30, 2006.

SCOTT, JOHN EDWARD SMITH, lawyer; b. St. Louis, Aug. 6, 1936; s. Gordon Hatler and Luella Margarite (Smith) S.; m. Beverly Joan Phillips, Dec. 17, 1960; 1 dau., Pamela Anne. AB, Albion Coll., 1958; JD, Wayne State U., 1961. Bar: Mich. 1961, U.S. Dist. Ct. (ea. dist.) Mich. 1962, U.S. Dist. Ct. (we. dist.) Mich. 1970, U.S. Tax. Ct. 1979, U.S. Ct. Appeals (6th cir.) 1964, U.S. Supreme Ct. 1966. Law clk. Supreme Ct. Mich., Lansing, 1961-62; assoc. Dickinson, Wright, Moon, Van Dusen & Freeman, Detroit, 1962-69, ptnr., 1970—2007. Adj. prof. U. Detroit Law Sch., 1967-71. Supreme Ct. appointee State Bar Rep. Assembly, Detroit, 1972-77; mayor City of Pleasant Ridge, Mich., 1973-81; commr. Mich. Appellate Defender Commn., Detroit, 1979-2007, chmn., 1992-2007; hearing referee Mich. Civil Rights Commn., Detroit, 1974-80; chmn. Detroit Legal Aid & Defender Commn., 1972-77; chmn. case flow mgmt. com. Mich. Supreme Ct., 1989-90. Fellow Am. Coll. Trial Lawyers, Internat. Soc. Barristers, Internat. Acad. Trial Lawyers; mem. ABA (chmn. trial evidence com. sect. litigation 1988-91), Am. Bar Found., Mich. Bar Found., Detroit Golf Club, Order of Coif (hon.). Home: Troy, Mich. Died Oct. 16, 2007.

SCOTT, NATHAN ALEXANDER, JR., minister, literary critic, religious educator; b. Cleve., Apr. 24, 1925; s. Nathan Alexander and Maggie (Martin) S.; m. Charlotte Hanley, Dec. 21, 1946; children: Nathan Alexander III, Leslie K. AB, U. Mich., 1944; BD, Union Theol. Sem., 1946; PhD, Columbia U., 1949; LittD, Ripon Coll., 1965, St. Mary's Coll., Notre Dame, Ind., 1969, Denison U., 1976, Brown U., 1981, Northwestern U., 1982, Elizabethtown Coll., 1989; LHD, Wittenberg U., 1965; DD, Phila. Div. Sch., 1967; STD, Gen. Theol. Sem., 1968; LHD, U. D.C., 1976; DD, The Protestant Episcopal Theological Seminary in Va., 1985; HumD, U. Mich., 1988; LHD, Wesleyan U., 1989, Bates Coll., 1990; STD, Univ of the South, 1992; DD, Kenyon Coll., 1993, Wabash Coll., 1996; Ordained priest Episcopal Ch., 1960; canon theologian Cathedral St. James, Chgo., 1967-76. dean of chapel, Va. Union U., 1946-47; instr. humanities, Howard U., 1948-51, asst. prof., 1951-53, assoc. prof., 1953-55; asst. prof. theology and literature, U. Chgo., 1955-58, assoc. prof., 1958-64, prof., 1964-72, Shailer Mathews prof. of theology and lit., 1972-76, prof. English, 1967-76; Commonwealth prof. religious studies, U. Va., 1976-81, William R. Kenan prof. religious studies, 1981-90, prof. English, 1976-90, prof. emeritus, 1990—. Author: Rehearsals of Discomposure: Alienation and Reconciliation in Modern Literature, 1952, The Tragic Vision and the Christian Faith, 1957, Modern Literature and the Religious Frontier, 1958, Albert Camus, 1962, Reinhold Niebuhr, 1963, The New Orpheus: Essays toward a Christian Poetic, 1964, The Climate of Faith in Modern Literature, 1965, The Broken Center: Studies in the Theological Horizon of Modern Literature, 1966, Ernest Hemingway, 1966, The Modern Vision of Death, 1967, Adversity and Grace: Studies in Recent American Literature, 1968, Negative Capability: Studies in the New Literature and the Religious Situation, 1969, The Unquiet Vision: Mirrors of Man in Existentialism, 1969, The Wild Prayer of Longing: Poetry and the Sacred, 1971, Nathanael West, 1971, Three American Moralists: Mailer, Bellow, Trilling, 1973, The Poetry of Civic Virtue: Eliot, Malraux, Auden, 1976, Mirrors of Man in Existentialism, 1978, The Poetics of Belief: Studies in Coleridge, Arnold, Pater, Santayana, Stevens and Heidegger, 1985, Visions of Presence in Modern American Poetry, 1993; co-editor Jour. Religion, 1963-77, (with Ronald Sharp) Reading George Steiner, 1994; adv. editor Religion and Lit., Literature and Theology, Callaloo. Fellow Am. Acad. of Arts and Scis.; mem. Soc. Arts, Religion and Contemporary Culture, Soc. for Values in Higher Edn. (Kent fellow), MLA., Am. Acad. Religion (pres. 1986), Century Assn. (N.Y.C.), Quadrangle Club, Arts Club (Chgo.), Greencroft Club (Charlottesville, Va.). Home: Charlottesville, Va. Died Dec. 20, 2006.

SCOTT, RUTH HAWLEY, art educator; b. Oneida, NY, Dec. 10, 1920; d. Lynn Arnold and Bertha Doris (Seybold) Sterling; m. Jack H. Hawley, July 22, 1945 (wid. Apr. 1946); m. George Herbert Scott, Jr., Nov. 2, 1962. BS in Art Edn., Buffalo State, 1943. Home: Eden, NC. Died Jan. 12, 2006.

SCOTT, WILLIAM PAUL, lawyer; b. Staples, Minn., Nov. 8, 1928; m. Elsie Elaine Anderson, Feb. 7, 1968; children: Jason Lee, William P., Mark D., Brian D., Scott; stepchildren: Thomas J. (dec.), Terri L. Weeding-Berg. ALA, U. Minn., 1949; BSL, St. Paul Coll. Law, 1952, JD, 1954. Bar: Minn. 1954. Atty., right of way divsn. Minn. Hwy Dept., 1945-52, civil engr., traffic and safety divsn., 1953-55; practice law Arlington, Minn., 1955-61, Gaylord, Minn., 1963-67; sr. ptnr. Scott Law Offices and predecessors, Pipestone, Minn., from 1967. Probate, juvenile judge Sibley County, Minn., 1956-61; Minn. pub. examiner, 1961-63; county atty. Sibley County, 1963-68, city atty., Pipestone, 1979-2002. Sibley County Rep. chmn., 1961. Served with USMCR, 1946-50, from 2d lt. to lt. col. USAF Res., 1950-88, ret. Recipient George Washington Honor medal Freedoms Found., 1970, 72. Mem. MOAA, VFW, DAV, Minn. Bar Assn., Mensa, Am. Legion, Mil. Officers Assn. Am. Home: Pipestone, Minn. Died Aug. 29, 2006.

SCOTTI, MICHAEL JOHN, JR., medical association executive; b. NYC, Oct. 30, 1938; s. Michael John and Florence (Ellis) S.; m. Susan Faye Suit, Aug. 25, 1961; children: Michael John III, Pamela Anne, Jennifer Beth. BS, Fordham Coll., 1960; MD, Georgetown U., 1965; postgrad., Indsl. Coll., Washington, 1982-83. Diplomate Am. Bd. Internal Medicine, Am. Bd. Family Practice; CAQ Geriat. Commd. 2d lt. U.S. Army, 1963, advanced through grades to maj. gen., 1990, ret., 1995; dir. residency program Dept. Family Practice, Ft. Gordon, Ga., 1976-79; family practice cons. Surgeon Gen., Washington, 1979-80; dir. Grad. Med. Edn. U.S. Army, Washington, 1980-82; comdr. army hosp. Ft. Polk, La., 1983-86; dir. quality assurance Army Med. Dept., Washington, 1986-88, dir. profl. svcs., 1988-90; comdg. gen. European 7th Med. Comd, Heidelberg, Fed. Republic Germany, 1990-95. Assoc. prof. Georgetown U. Sch. Medicine, 1986; chmn. Def. Med. Standardization, Ft. Detrick, Md., 1988-90; prof. Uniformed Svcs. U., Bethesda, Md., 1990. Health cons. Nat. PTA, Chgo., 1976-79. Named Person of Yr. Phi Delta Kappa, 1976. Fellow: ACP, Am. Acad. Family Physicians (vice spkr. 1988—90, bd. dirs. 1990—92, apkr.); mem.: AMA (v.p. med. edn. 1995—2000, sr. v.p. profl. stds. 2000—07). Home: Arlington, Va. Died Sept. 12, 2007.

SCRIBNER, BARBARA COLVIN, museum administrator; b. Dec. 18, 1926; d. Howard Morton and May Josephine (Tierney) Colvin; m. Harold B. Scribner, Mar. 10, 1956 (dec. June, 1982); 1 child, Scott Colvin. Student, Pratt Inst., 1945-46. Assoc. editor McCall's Mag., NYC, 1950-59, Am. Home, NYC, 1960-64, contbg. editor, 1964-67; freelance writer, editor NYC, 1968-77; dir. pub. info. Stamford Mus. and Nature Ctr., Conn., from 1978. Curator Going to Blazes exhbn., 1988-89, Music Mania exhbn., 1988-89, Antiuqe Toy Banks exhbn., 1990-91, Antique Bottles exhbn., 1992-93, Toy Bldg. Sets exhbn., 1994—, Bendel Estate Exhibit, 1994—, Puzzling Challenges Exhibit, 1997-98, Perfect Paperweights exhbn., 1999. Cons. Episcopal Ch. Women, Darien, 1970-78, Darien H.S. Parents Assn., 1980-82, Conn.

Humanities Coun., 1997—; exec. bd. Coun. Darien Sch. Parents, Conn., 1974-82, mem. steering com.; mem. attractions com. State of Conn., 1982—; mem. product com. New Eng. U.S.A. Found., 1989-90, Am. Trail, 1990—, Tourism Network Conn., 1992-94; mem. pub. rels. com. Sch. to Career Stamford, 1998. Mem. Southwestern Area Commerce and Industry Assn. (women work initiatives 1998—), Stamford C. of C., Order Ea. Star. Republican. Home: Darien, Conn. Died Sept. 18, 2006.

SCRIBNER, JEAN ELIZABETH, retired vocational counselor, English educator; b. Leroy, Mich., Dec. 18, 1922; d. Cassius Mayne and Bessie Belle (Bowen) Kenney; m. Delbert Paul Scribner, Oct. 8, 1943. BS in Edn., Goshen Coll., 1961; M in Eng., Montclair State Coll., 1969. Cert. Eng. tchr., vocat. counselor. Tchr. Penn-Harris-Madison Schs., Mishawaka, Ind., 1961-66, W. Orange-Maplewood Schs., West Orange, N.J., 1967-69, Graham High Sch., St. Paris, Ohio, 1969-71; vocat. counselor Chgo., Aurora, Ill., 1972-88. Vol. probation officer Elkhart County (Ind.) Cts., 1989—, tax preparer numerous Elkhart County locations, 1989—, Elkhart Coun. on Aging (recipient vol. month award, Feb., 1992); ins. preparer YMCA County Coun. on Aging, Elkhart, 1990—. Mem. LWV (editor, mem. bd. dirs. Elkhart chpt. 1990—), AAUW (treas. Elkhart chpt. 1990—), AFSCME, Women for Meaningful Summits, Learning Soc. of Elkhart. Avocations: writing, baking, travel, photography, crafts. Home: Elkhart, Ind. Died Apr. 12, 2006.

SCRIPPS, CHARLES EDWARD, retired publishing executive; b. San Diego, Jan. 27, 1920; s. Robert Paine and Margaret Lou (Culbertson) S.; m. Louann Copeland, June 28, 1941 (div. 1947); m. Lois Anne MacKay, Oct. 14, 1949 (dec. 1990); children: Charles Edward Jr., Marilyn Joy, Eaton Mackay, Julia Osborne; m. Mary Elizabeth Breslin, Sept. 7, 1993. Student, Coll. William and Mary, 1938-40, Pomona Coll., 1940-41. Reporter Cleve. Press, 1941; successor-trustee Edward W. Scripps Trust, 1945, chmn. bd. trustees, 1948—2003; v.p. E.W. Scripps Co., from 1946, chmn., 1953—94, chmn. exec. com., 1994—2003. Bd. dirs., E.W. Scripps Co., 1953-2003 Mem. nat. adv. bd. Salvation Army; trustee Freedoms Found. Served to lt. (j.g.) USCGR, 1942-45. Mem. CAP, Theta Delta Chi. Home: Cincinnati, Ohio. Died Feb. 3, 2007.

SCRIVEN, L. E(DWARD), engineering educator; b. Battle Creek, Mich., Nov. 4, 1931; s. L. Edward and Esther Mabel (Davis) S.; m. Dorene Bates Hayes, June 19, 1952; children: Ellen Dorene, Teresa Ann, Mark Hayes. BS, U. Calif., Berkeley, 1952; PhD, U. Del., 1956. Rsch. engr. Shell Devel. Co., Emeryville, Calif., 1956-59; asst. prof. chem. engring. and fluid mechanics U. Minn., Mpls., 1959-62, assoc. prof., 1962-66, prof., 1966-89, Regents' prof., from 1989, assoc. dept. head, 1975-78, program dir. Ctr. Interfacial Engring., 1988-90. Cons. in fields; advisor to Humboldt Found., Fed. Republic of Germany; vis. com. to chem. engring. MIT, sci. assoc. Jet Propulsion Lab., 1977, 79; tech. expert UN Indsl. Devel. Orgn., Vienna, Austria, 1979-88; exec. com. on chem. engring. frontiers NRC, 1984-87; mem. NRC Bd. on Chem. Scis. and Tech., 1987-92, chmn., 1992; mem. NRC Commn. on Phys. Scis., Math. and Applications, 1994—; sci. adv. com. Packard Found., 1988—. Editor: Physico-chemical Hydrodynamics (V.G. Levich), 1992; assoc. editor Jour. Fluid Mechanics, 1970-75; adv. editor Jour. Coll. Interfluid Sci., Physics of Fluids, L.Am. Jour. Chem. Engring. and Applied Chemistry, Internat. Jour. Numerical Methods in Fluid Mechanics; contbr. numerous articles to sci. jours.; patentee in field. Recipient chem. engring. award Am. Soc. Engring. Edn., 1968, Minn. Achievement award, 1989, Murphree award Am. Chem. Soc., 1990; named Fairchild disting. scholar Calif. Inst. Tech., 1989; Guggenheim fellow, 1969-70, fellow Minn. Supercomputer Inst., 1984—. Mem. NAE, Am. Inst. Chem. Engrs. (mem. nat. program. com. 1964-69, Colburn award 1960, Walker award 1977, Tallmadge award 1992, Founders award 1997), Am. Phys. Soc., Soc. Petroleum Engrs., Gordon Rsch. Confs., Chem. Soc. (Faraday div.), Soc. Indsl. and Applied Math., Soc. Rheology. Achievements include research in capillarity, fluid mechanics and coating processes, porous media, cold-stage electron microscopy, microstructured fluids and interfaces, origins of pattern and form, supercomputer-aided analysis. Died Aug. 3, 2007.

SCUDDER, HARVEY ISRAEL, microbiologist, medical entomologist, educator, consultant; b. Elmira, NY, Jan. 2, 1919; s. Henry Spaulding and Charlotte Evelyn (Draper) S.; m. Florence Viola Graff, June 16, 1945; children: Paul Harvey, Barbara Carol. BS, Cornell U., 1939, PhD, 1953; postgrad., NYU, 1939-42. Commd. scientist officer USPHS, 1943, advanced through grades to capt., 1963, exec. sec. NIH rsch. grant study sections, 1957-59, chief/founder viruses and cancer program Nat. Cancer Inst. Bethesda, Md., 1959-62, chief/founder health manpower office Bur. State Svcs. Washington, 1965-66, ret., 1966; prof. microbiology, founder Baccalaureate nursing program Calif. State U., Hayward, 1967-80, head div. biol. and health scis., 1967-70, prof. emeritus, from 1980. Malaria cons. AID, Washington, 1979-83, 84-85; coord. Stewart Valley (Nev.) Paleontol. Inventory, U.S. Bur. Land Mgmt., Reno, 1982-86. Contbr. articles on med. entomology and environ. scis. to profl. jours.; pub. numerous reports on pub. health, disease control and natural hist. Mem. air conservation com. Alameda County Lung Assn., Oakland, Calif., 1970-80; mem. Alameda County Comprehensive Health Planning Coun., 1973-76; mem. Alameda County Mosquito Abatement Dist. Bd., 1982—; bd. dirs. Marine Sci. Inst., Redwood City, Calif., 1971—, chmn. bd. dirs., 1974-80, 82—; bd. dirs. St. Rose Hosp., Hayward, Calif., 1969-83, chmn. bd. dirs., 1973-74, mem. instnl. rev. com. Mem. Am. Mosquito Control Assn., AAAS, Am. Pub. Health Assn., Am. Soc. Microbiology, Am. Soc. Tropical Medicine and Hygiene, Western Regional Assn. Advisors for the Health Profession of Am. Assn. Med. Colls., Entomol. Soc. Am., Mosquito and Vector Control Assn. Calif. (trustee corp. bd., sec. 1988, vice-chair 1989, chair 1990, v.p. bd. dirs. 1998), Soc. for Vector Ecology (chmn. adhoc manpower com. 1988-90), Calif. Acad. Scis. (hon. fellow 1987—), Sigma Xi, Phi Kappa Phi. Clubs: Pub. Health Svc. (Bethesda)(pres. 1962). Democrat. Mem. Christian Ch. (Disciples Of Christ). Avocations: stamp collecting/philately, decision processing, natural history, fuzzy logic applications. Home: Dublin, Calif. Died Dec. 19, 2006.

SEABURY, ROBERTA, newspaper music critic, journalist; b. Boise, Idaho, Aug. 18, 1942; d. Robert Louis and Lucy Stephens. AA, Diablo Valley Coll., 1980; BA, Calif. State U., 1983. Violist Diablo Symphony, others, Walnut Court, Calif., 1965-89, publicist, 1976-88; freelance writer arts publs., Walnut Court, 1980-86. Mem. Danville (Calif.) Arts Coun., 1985-87, Diablo (Calif.) Property Owners Bd., 1982-86. Recipient Gen. Excellence award for entertainment coverage Suburban Newspapers Am., 1990. Mem. Music Critics Assn. Home: Diablo, Calif. Died Oct. 10, 2006.

SEARLE, PHILIP FORD, banker; b. Kansas City, Mo., July 23, 1924; s. Albert Addison and Edith (Thompson) S.; m. Jean Adair Hanneman, Nov. 22, 1950 (dec. Nov. 1990); 1 child, Charles Randolph; m. Jean Walker, Oct. 4, 1992 (dec. oct. 1993); m. Elizabeth Gordon, Nov. 4, 1994. AB, Cornell U., 1949; grad. in banking, Rutgers U., 1957-64. With Geneva (Ohio) Savs. & Trust Co., 1949-60, pres., 1959-60; pres., sr. trust officer Northeastern Ohio Nat. Bank, Ashtabula, 1960-69; pres., CEO BancOhio Corp., Columbus, 1969-75; chmn., CEO Flagship Banks, Inc., Miami, 1975-84; chmn. bd. Sun Banks, Inc., Orlando, 1984-85, cons., 1986-94. Faculty Sch. Banking, Ohio U., 1959-70, Nat. Trust Sch., Northwestern U., Evanston, Ill., 1965-68; corp. adv. com. Nat. Assn. Securities Dealers, 1981-83; v.p., fed. adv. coun. to bd. govs. FRS, 1983-85; chmn. Nat. Adv. Bd. to Oversight Bd. for Resolution Trust Corp., 1991-92. Co-author: The Management of a Trust Department, 1967. Past chmn. bd. regents Stonier Grad. Sch. Banking, Rutgers U., 1974-76, past mem. faculty; trustee Fin. Acctg. Found., Norwalk, Conn., 1989-93. Capt. AUS, 1943-46, 51-52, ETO. Decorated Bronze Star; named outstanding citizen in Ashtabula County, 1967. Mem. Am. Bankers Assn. (bd. dirs. 1972-74, governing coun.), Bank Adminstrn. Inst. (nat. chmn. 1987-88, bd. dirs. Chgo. 1985-89), Fla. Bankers Assn. (bd. dirs. 1979-81, coun. 1981), Ohio Bankers Assn. (pres. 1970-71), Assn. Bank Holding Cos. (pres. 1979-81), Fla. C. of C. (bd. dirs. 1978-82), Royal Poinciana Golf Club (Naples, Fla.), Catawba Island Club (Port Clinton, Ohio), Phi Kappa Tau. Home: Naples, Fla. Died June 13, 2007.

SEARS, GORDON MORTIMER, public relations consultant; b. Bristol, Tenn., June 25, 1923; s. Harold Mortimer and Kythe Carlisle (McClellan) S.; m. Mabel Cecilia Waddell, Aug. 28, 1948; children: Kythe Lee, Patricia Gordon, Elizabeth Baker. BA in Journalism, Emory U., 1943. With United Press, 1947-51; account exec. Carl Byoir & Assocs., NYC, 1952-60; pub. rels. dir. Kern County Land Co., San Francisco, 1960-64; v.p. Pacific T.J. Ross and Assocs., San Francisco, 1964-68, exec. v.p. NYC, 1969-71, pres., 1971-78, chmn., CEO, 1978-86; chmn. Douglas G. Hearle & Assoc., NYC, 1987-89; cons. Columbia, S.C., from 1991. Bd. dirs. Roper Ctr. for Pub. Opinion Rsch., Storrs, Conn. Capt. USMC, 1942-52. Mem. Soc. Profl. Journalists, Pub. Rels. Soc. Am., Sertoma Internat., Media Club (Columbia), Kappa Alpha, Omicron Delta Kappa. Republican. Anglican. Avocations: flying, golf, natural history. Home: Columbia, SC. Died Nov. 23, 2006.

SEATON, WILLIAM RUSSELL, oil company executive; b. Ashland, Ky., Jan. 2, 1928; s. Edward William and Virginia (Russell) S.; m. Suzanne Webb, Aug. 9, 1950; children: Katherine Graham Seaton James, Suzanne Elizabeth Seaton Beach, Mildred Webb Seaton Grizzle, Edward William II. BS, Yale U., 1949. Trainee Ashland Oil, Inc., Ky., 1949, trainee personnel dept., 1950, jr. engr. personnel dept., 1950, adminstrv. asst. personnel, 1951-52, asst. ins. mgr., 1953-55, ins. mgr., 1955-60, exec. asst., 1960-67, v.p., 1967, adminstrv. v.p., 1968, dir., 1969-88, sr. v.p., chief adminstrv. officer, 1970-72, vice chmn., 1972-88, vice chmn., chief fin. officer, 1982-88, ret., 1988. Trustee Woodberry Forest Sch., 1976-85; bd. regents Morehead State U., 1986—. Mem. 25-Yr. Club of Petroleum Industry, Chi Psi. Home: Ashland, Ky. Died July 15, 2007.

SEAVER, RICHARD CARLTON, oil field equipment company executive, lawyer; b. Los Angeles, June 10, 1922; s. Byron D. and Mary Louise (Schmidt) Seaver; children: Richard Carlton, Christopher T., Patrick T., Victoria, Martha. BA, Pomona Coll., 1946; JD, U. Calif.-Berkeley, 1949. Bar: Calif. 1950. Assoc. Thelen, Marrin, Johnson & Bridges, Los Angeles, 1950-57; sec., counsel Hydril Co., Los Angeles, 1957-64, pres., 1964-86, chmn., 1986—2007. Dir. DeAnza Land & Leisure Corp. Vice chmn., bd. dirs. Seaver Inst.; trustee Los Angeles County Mus. Natural History, Episcopal Diocesan Investment Trust, Doheny Eye Inst., Pomona Coll., Calif. Inst. Arts; bd. dirs. Hosp. of Good Samaritan; bd. dirs., pres. L.A. Music Ctr. Opera Assn.; bd. overseers Hoover Inst., Palo Alto. Served to capt. inf. AUS, 1942-46, PTO. Decorated Bronze Star with oak leaf cluster Mem. ABA, Calif. Bar Assn., Los Angeles Bar Assn. Clubs: St. Francis Yacht, Los Angeles Country, Los Angeles Yacht, California (Los Angeles); Newport Harbor Yacht (Balboa). Republican. Home: Los Angeles, Calif. Died June 10, 2007.

SEBESTYEN, OUIDA GLENN, author; b. Vernon, Tex., Feb. 13, 1924; d. James Ethridge and Byrd (Lantrip) Dockery; m. Adam Sebestyen, Dec. 21, 1960 (div. 1966); 1 child, Corbin. Student, U. Colo. Speaker, leader workshops at pub. schs. and ednl. orgns. Author: Words by Heart, 1979 (Internat. Reading Assn. award 1979, Am. Book award 1982), Far from Home, 1980 (Silver Pencil award 1984), IOU's, 1982 (Tex. Inst. Letters award 1983), On Fire, 1985, The Girl in the Box, 1988, Out of Nowhere, 1994; author short stories in 3 anthologies. Avocations: gardening, travel, crafts, hiking, western history. Died Apr. 28, 2007.

SEBETIC, EMIL, lawyer; b. Kenosha, Wis., Nov. 21, 1924; s. George and Josephine (Babich) S.; m. Joanne E. Deasy, Feb. 13, 1960; children— Mark, Paul, Stephen. Ph.B., Marquette U., 1949, LL.B., 1951; LL.M. in Taxation, NYU, 1957. Bar: Wis. 1951, U.S. Dist. Ct. (ea. dist.) Wis. 1951, N.Y. State, 1960, U.S. Ct. Appeals (2d cir.) 1962, U.S. Dist. Ct. (so. and ea. dists.) N.Y. 1962. With Whyte, Hirschboeck & Minahan, N.Y.C., 1951-55; trial atty. IRS, N.Y.C., 1955-59; assoc. Kramer, Marx, Greenlee & Backus, N.Y.C., 1959-60; sole practice, N.Y.C., 1960-74; ptnr. firm of Al Bienstock, N.Y.C., 1974-76; sole practice, Manhasset, N.Y., 1977—; adj. assoc. prof. Fordham Law Sch., 1962-72; adj. lectr. C.W. Post Coll., 1977-81. Served as sgt. U.S. Army, 1943-45; ETO. Decorated Purple Heart. Mem. ABA, N.Y. State Bar, N.Y. County Lawyers Assn., Nassau County Bar Assn., Internat. Assn. Fin. Planners. Republican. Roman Catholic. Author: The Marital Deduction Simplified, 1967; Professional Corporation Forms, 1971; Through The Tax Shelter Maze Safely, 1982; Retirement in the Sun, 1982., IRS Practice Guidebook 1984. Died Dec. 28, 2006.

SEDERBAUM, ARTHUR DAVID, lawyer; b. NYC, Sept. 14, 1944; s. William and Harriet (Warschauer) Sederbaum; m. Francine Haba, Dec. 30, 1967 (div. Aug. 1982); children: Rebecca, David; m. Phyllis Padow, Jan. 18, 1988 (div. Aug. 2002); 1 child, Elizabeth. AB cum laude, Columbia U., 1965, JD, 1968; LLM, NYU, 1972. BAr: N.Y. 1968, Fla. 1980, U.S. Dist. Ct. (so. and ea. dists.) N.Y. 1972. Assoc. Zissu Nelper & Martin, NYC, 1968-70, Berlack, Israels & Liberman, NYC, 1970-72, Rubin Baum Levin Constant & Friedman, NYC, 1972-76; ptnr. Certilman, Haft, Balin, Buckley, Kremer & Hyman, NYC, 1976-88, Olshan, Grundman, Frome, Rosenzweig & Orens, NYC, 1988-92, Patterson, Belknap, Webb & Tyler, L.L.P., NYC, from 1992. Mem. adv. bd. Bur. Nat. Affairs Estates, Gifts and Trusts Jour.; mem. adv. bd. NYU Inst. Fed. Taxation, CCH Fin. and Estate Planning. Author: Setting Up and Executing Trusts, 1988; contbr. articles to Tax Mgmt. Estates, Gifts and Trusts Jour. Recipient J.K. Lasser Tax prize NYU Inst. Fed. Taxation, 1968. Fellow Am. Coll. Trusts and Estates Coun.; mem. ABA, N.Y. State Bar Assn. (vice chmn. com. on estate planning trustes and estates law sect.), Assn. Bar City N.Y. (com. surrogates cts.), Practicing Law Inst. (chmn. income taxatin of estates and trusts program). Home: New York, NY. Died Jan. 19, 2007.

SEDERBAUM, WILLIAM, marketing professional; b. NYC, Dec. 22, 1914; s. Harry and Sarah (Steingart) S.; m. Harriet Warschauer, Aug. 29, 1940 (dec. Mar. 1980); children: Arthur David, Caroline Joan; m. Pearl Leibowitz, Jan. 11, 2003. BS, NYU, 1936, MA, 1943, PhD. Assoc. Sigmund Pines Co., Pub. Accts., 1935-38; tchr. N.Y.C. pub. schs., 1935-39; restaurant propr., 1939-41; v.p. Schenley Distillers Co., NYC, 1941-61; pres. Distbrs. New Eng., 1956-61, Melrose Distillers Co., 1959-60, Park & Tilford Distillers Co., 1959-61; exec. v.p. Meade & Co., 1961-62; v.p., mktg. dir. J. T. S. Brown Distillers Co., 1962-65; mktg. cons., 1965-67; exec. v.p., gen. mgr. Fulton Distbg. Co., 1967-77; asst. gen. mgr., dir. spl. projects Am. Distbrs. Fla., from 1977. Instr. acctg. Fla. Jr. Coll., 1984-89 Active Eleanor Roosevelt Cancer Com., U.S. Olympic Games Com.; exec. com. Fedn. Jewish Charities, March of Dimes; bd. dirs. Jacksonville Urban League, 1975-87; mem. Com. of 100; bus. cons. Jr. Achievement Project, Jacksonville; chmn. bd. trustees, pres. men's club Reform Cong. of Merrick, L.I. Recipient Arch award NYU; named Chevalier, Confrerie de la Chaine des Rotisseurs, Bailliage de Jacksonville, Fla. Mem. Jacksonville Wholesale Liquor Assn. (pres. 1970-76), Jacksonville Symphony Assn., Jacksonville Civic Music Assn., Jacksonville C. of C. (econ. edn. com., airline svc. com., hon. adm. of flag ship Am. Airlines), Kappa Phi Kappa. Clubs: River, Carriage (N.Y.C.); NYU, Playboy, Key. Home: Jacksonville, Fla. Died Apr. 5, 2007.

SEELEY, JOHN GEORGE, horticulture educator; b. North Bergen, NJ, Dec. 21, 1915; s. Howard Wilson and Lillian (Fiedler) S.; m. Catherine L. Cook, May 28, 1938 (dec. Feb. 21, 1999); children: Catherine Ann, David John (dec. Dec. 1995), Daniel Henry, George Bingham, Thomas Dyer. BS, Rutgers U., 1937, MS, 1940; PhD, Cornell U., 1948. Research asst. N.J. Agrl. Exptl. Sta., 1937-40, foreman ornamental gardens, 1940-41; instr. floricultural sci. Cornell U., Ithaca, N.Y., 1941-43, 45-48, asst. prof., 1948-49, prof. floricultural sci., 1956-83, prof. emeritus, from 1983, head dept. floriculture, 1956-70; prof. floriculture Pa. State U., 1949-56, 1949—56; D.C. Kiplinger chair floriculture, prof. horticulture Ohio State U., 1984-85. Asst. agronomist Bur. Plant Industry Dept. Agr., 1943-44; chemist Wright Aero. Corp., Paterson, N.J., 1944-45. Trustee Kenneth Post Found., 1956-84, Fred. C. Gloeckner Found., 1970—, pres., 1993-2004. Recipient Best Sr. award in Agriculture, Rutgers U., 1937, S.A.F. Found. for Floriculture Rsch. & Edn. award, 1965, Cornell Edgerton Career Teaching award, 1983. Fellow: AAAS, Am. Soc. Hort. Sci. (pres. 1982—83, chmn. bd. 1983—84, Leonard H. Vaughan rsch. award 1950, Bittner Extension award 1982); mem.: Pa. Flower Growers Assn., N.Y. Flower Growers Assn., Am. Carnation Soc., Ohio Florists' Assn. (hon.), Internat. Soc. Hort. Sci. (hon.), Am. Acad. Floriculture (hon.), Mass. Hort. Soc. (Silver medal 1980), Soc. Am. Florists (Hall of Fame 1979), Am. Hort. Soc. (Liberty Hyde Bailey award 1998), Rotary (dist. gov. 1973—74), Pi Alpha Xi (pres. 1951—53), Phi Kappa Phi, Sigma Xi, Phi Epsilon Phi, Epsilon Sigma Phi, Alpha Zeta (chancellor 1936—37). Presbyterian. Home: Ithaca, NY. Died May 9, 2007.

SEFERIAN, ALBERT, government official; management analyst; b. Boston, Feb. 17, 1943; s. Albert and Rose Sally (Hagopian) S.; m. Marguerite Del Visco, July 8, 1967; children— Leesa, Mark. B.A., Colby Coll., 1965; postgrad. Syracuse U., 1965-68. Research assoc. Eastern Regional Inst. Edn., Syracuse, N.Y., 1968-70; staff assoc. Curriculum Devel. Assocs., Washington, 1970-72; dir. Early Childhood Learning Ctr., Fairfax County Schs., Fairfax, Va., 1972-74; cons. U.S. Dept. Agr. Grad. Sch., Washington, 1974-75; program analyst Office Personnel Mgmt., Washington, 1975-82; mgmt. analyst Office Mgmt. and Budget, Exec. Office of Pres., Washington, 1982—. Author: Encounters in Thinking, 1968. Exec. com. Reston Commuter Bus, Inc., 1976; bd. dirs. Greater Reston Arts Ctr., 1982. Mem. Porsche Club Am. Home: Reston, Va. Died Mar. 18, 2007.

SEIDLER, NORMAN HOWARD, lawyer; b. NYC, July 5, 1919; s. Charles M. Seidler and Malvina Lassell; m. Muriel P. Tolchin, Nov. 24, 1949; children— Terry Lisa, JoLinda LL.B., NYU, 1948. Bar: N.Y. Trial atty. U.S. Dept. Justice, Cleve., 1948-55, chief Great Lakes Office antitrust div., 1955-66, chief N.Y. Office antitrust div. NYC, 1966-74; ptnr. Lord, Day &

Lord, NYC, from 1974. Served to 1st lt. U.S. Army, 1941-46, ETO Mem. ABA (antitrust sect., litigation sect.) Home: Boca Raton, Fla. Died Dec. 17, 2006.

SEITH, ROBERT THEODORE, management consultant; b. Racine, Wis., Aug. 12, 1926; s. Theodore Lewis and Ruth (Cleaver) S.; m. Ruth Marilyn Sievert, Oct. 12, 1946; children: Michael Robert, Deborah Lynn, Elizabeth Jane. BSChemE, Purdue U., 1949; cert. mgmt. cons. Inst. Mgmt. Cons. With Mosinee Paper Mills Co. (Wis.), 1949-69, successively research chemist, dir. product devel., sales mgr., 1957-61, v.p. marketing, 1961-69, exec. v.p. Celluponic System, Inc., 1962-69; v.p. marketing, paper div. Gulf States Paper Corp., 1969-77; mgmt. cons., 1977—; pres. R.M. Assocs. Inc., 1983—, Arma Ltd., 1981—; dir. Bag West Paper Co., 1965-69; dir. Shuld Mfg. Co. Active Children's Service Soc. Wis., Wis. Assn. for Mental Health. Co-chmn. Republican party Marathon County, 1953. Served with AUS, 1944-46. Mem. Def. Supply Assn. (dir., past pres. Midwest), Salesmens Assn. Paper Industry (v.p. Wis. div. 1962-63, nat. pres. 1966—), Am. Paper Inst. (bd. govs.), Am. Legion, Bleached Converting Assn. (dir.), Kraft Paper Assn. (exec. com. 1960, mem. research and devel. com.), Ala. World Trade Assn., Assn. Mgmt. Cons., Am. Legion, Sigma Phi Epsilon. Episcopalian. Mason, Lion (pres. 1953-54). Author various articles profl. jours. Patentee in field. Home: Tuscaloosa, Ala. Died Feb. 23, 2007.

SELANDER, LORRAINE FYDA, university administrator; b. Chgo., July 2, 1927; d. Michael F. and Marie T. (Ziemba) Fyda; m. John Kenneth Robe, Aug. 23, 1947 (div.); m. Richard Brent Selander, Nov. 4, 1960 (dec. Aug. 1992); children: John Michael, Donna Marie, Timothy Charles, Steven Richard. BA, U. Ill., 1967, MS, 1976, MBA, 1983. Asst. to head sociology dept. U. Ill., Urbana, 1975-80; asst. to dir. Coord. Sci. Lab., U. Ill., Urbana, 1980-86, asst. dir., from 1986. U. Ill. scholar, 1980-83; NSF fellow, 1965-67. Mem. Soc. of Rsch. adminstrs. (mem. internat. com. 1986—), Nat. Coun. of Univ. Rsch. Adminstrs. Avocations: travel, art, book collecting, reading. Home: Champaign, Ill. Died May 24, 2006.

SELBERG, ATLE, retired mathematician; b. Langesund, Norway, June 14, 1917; came to U.S., 1947; married, 1947. D, U. Oslo, 1943; postgrad. Inst. Advanced Study, Princeton U., 1947-48, 49. Rsch. fellow U. Oslo, 1942-47; assoc. prof. math. Syracuse U., 1948-49; prof. Inst. Advanced Study, Princeton U., 1949-87, prof. emeritus, 1987—2007. Editor: (with others) Axel Thue's Selected Mathematical Papers, 1977; author: Reflections Around the Ramanujan Centenary, 1989, Number Theory, Trace Formulas & Discrete Groups, 1989, Collected Papers, 1991. Recipient Fields medal Internat. Congress Math., Harvard U., 1950, Wolf prize in math. Wolf Found., Israel, 1986. Mem. Norwegian Acad. Sci., Royal Danish Acad. Scis. and Letters, Am. Acad. Arts and Scis. Achievements include elementary proof of the prime number theorem, with a generalisation to prime numbers in an arbitrary arithmetic progression. Died Aug. 6, 2007.

SELL, EDWARD SCOTT, JR., lawyer; b. Athens, Ga., Mar. 13, 1917; s. Edward Scott and Nettie Ruth (Whatley) S.; m. Mary Deupree Eckford, Sept. 14, 1940; 1 son, Edward Scott. AB, U. Ga., 1937, JD cum laude, 1939. Bar: Ga. bar 1938. Ptnr. firm Lewis & Sell, 1940-55, Lane & Sell, 1955-56, Sell & Comer, Macon, Ga., 1956-69, Sell, Comer & Popper, Macon, 1969-80, Sell & Melton, from 1980. City atty., Macon, 1947-53; atty. Macon-Bibb County Planning & Zoning Commn., 1953-65; county atty. Bibb County, Ga., 1965—; lectr. law Mercer U., 1958-60 Trustee Wesleyan Coll., Macon, 1973-96, emeritus, 1997—. Served with U.S. Army, 1942-46. Decorated Bronze Star, Army Commendation medal. Fellow Am. Bar Found.; mem. State Bar Ga. (bd. govs. 1947-50), Macon Bar Assn. (past pres.), Macon Cir. Bar Assn. (past pres.), City Club of Macon, River North Club, Lions, Shriners, Masons, Phi Beta Kappa, Phi Kappa Phi, Phi Delta Phi. Clubs: City Club of Macon, Lions, Shriners, Masons, River North. Home: Macon, Ga. Died Feb. 2, 2007.

SELONICK, JAMES BENNETT, department store executive; b. NYC, July 6, 1925; s. Stanley E. and Cecile R. (Rosenblum) S.; m. Peggy Frieder, Nov. 19, 1949; children: Ellen, James, William. AB, U. Cin., 1948, LLB, 1949. Bar: Ohio bar 1949, U.S. Dist. Ct. bar 1949. Asso. firm Harmon Colston, Goldsmith & Hoadley, 1949-52; asso. co. counsel, asst. mgr. real estate Federated Dept. Stores, Cin., 1952-61; exec. v.p. Simon Enterprises, Inc., Reston, Va., 1961-64, v.p., 1964-65, exec. v.p., 1965-68; v.p. Mugar Group, Boston, 1968-70; v.p. property devel. Federated Dept. Stores, 1970-73, sr. v.p., 1973-87. Pres. Federated Stores Realty, Inc., 1973-78, chmn. bd., chief exec. officer, 1978-83. Treas. Rockdale Temple, Cin., 1975-79, 1st v.p., 1981, pres., 1985-87; chmn. Cin. Historic Conservation Bd., 1980—. With USNR, 1943-46. Mem. Internat. Coun. Shopping Ctrs. (trustee), Urban Land Inst. (trustee 1983—), Losantiville Country Club. Home: Cincinnati, Ohio. Died May 18, 2007.

SELTZER, LEO, cinematographer, educator; b. Montreal, Que., Can., Mar. 13, 1910; came to U.S., 1916; s. Boris and Atalia (Gerowitz) S.; m. Elaine Basil, Apr. 15, 1941 (div. 1950); children: Janzie, John; m. Dicky Ransohoff, 1951 (div. 1963). BA, U. Mass., 1979. Faculty CCNY, 1949-54, New Sch. Social Rsch., 1949-51; pres. Leo Seltzer Assocs., Inc., NYC, 1950-90; faculty Columbia U., 1954-60, Phila. Coll. Art, 1955-56, NYU, NYC, 1966-67; dir. audio-visual therapy program pediatrics ward Univ. Hosp., NYC, 1970-76; instr. film prodn. workshop Sch. Visual Arts, NYC, 1969-84; adj. prof. performing and creative arts Coll. S.I., NY, 1977-78; prof. film Bklyn. Coll., 1978-83, prof. emeritus film, from 1983. Lectr. in U.S. and abroad, including Mus. Modern Art, N.Y.C., Marymount Coll., Ghent U., Belgium, Libr. Congress, others. Prodr., dir. over 60 social documentaries and TV films in 35 countries, including First Steps, UN Divsn. Social Affairs, 1946 (Acad. award for best documentary 1947), Fate of a Child, UN Divsn. Tech. Assistance, 1949, For the Living, City of N.Y., 1952, (with Walter Cronkite) Conquest of Aging, 1958, All the Years, 1959, Jacqueline Kennedy's Asian Journey, 1962, Progress Through Freedom (pres. Kennedy's visit to Mex.), 1962, (with Edward R. Murrow) The American Commitment, USIA, 1963, Report on Acupuncture, 1977, (with John Huston) Let There Be Light; prodr., dir.: Nat. Film Bd. Can., 1941, films include Air-Sea Rescue Techniques; chief cons. visual aids City of N.Y., 1941-42; prodr.: N.Y.C. Mcpl. Film and TV Unit Sta. WNYC, 1949-50; film biographer to White House for Pres. Kennedy, 1962; exec. prodr. Quadrant Comms., Inc., 1973-75 (7 citations Cannes and Edinburgh Film Festivals 1948-63); films are in U.S. Nat. Archives, Libr. of Congress, in collection and distributed by Mus. Modern Art; photographs are in Houston Mus. Fine Arts collection, Nat. Gallery Can., Visual Studies Workshop, Rochester, N.Y., N.Y.C. 5th Ave. Libr.; reconstructed 6 Am. social documentary films of 1930's in 1978 for Mus. Modern Art Film Archives, 1976-77,; edited and filmed much of original footage; subject of TV program by Bill Moyers, A Walk Through the Twentieth Century, Blackside Prodns., CBC, BBC TV; contbr. film footage to Nat. Geographic, History Channel, others. 1st lt. Signal Corps. U.S. Army; directed tng. and information films for U.S. Army and public; officer in charge of Film and Equipment Depot, ETO, 1947. Recipient Acad. award for best documentary, 1948, Silver medals Venice Film Festival, 1949, Freedom's Found. award, 1953, Golden Reel award Scholastic Mag., 1955, Robert Flaherty award CCNY, 1956, Silver medal Atlanta Internat. Film Festival, 1977; honored in tribute Mus. Modern Art, 1990; oral history N.Y. Fifth Ave. Libr. Archives. Mem. Dirs. Guild Am. (charter). Achievements include research on Early American social documentary films. Died Jan. 27, 2007.

SELZER, MILTON, actor; b. Lowell, Mass., Oct. 25, 1918; s. Abraham and Leah (Mandelkern) S.; m. Alice Hickox, Dec. 24, 1953; 1 son, Ethan. Student, U. N.H., Am. Acad. Dramatic Art, Dramatic Workshop of New Sch. Broadway appearances in Julius Caesar; film appearanges in Blue Collar; TV appearances include Hill St. Blues, Trapper John, Dynasty, Fame, others; TV movies include Why Me?, 1983, The Million Dollar Face, 1981, People vs. Jean Harris, 1981, Adventures of Nellie Bly, 1981. Served with AUS, World War II. Mem. Actors Equity, Screen Actors Guild, AFTRA, Acad. Motion Picture Arts and Scis., Can. Equity. Died Oct. 21, 2006.

SERBEIN, OSCAR NICHOLAS, business educator, consultant; b. Collins, Iowa, Mar. 31, 1919; s. Oscar Nicholas and Clara Matilda (Shearer) S.; m. Alice Marie Bigger, Sept. 16, 1952; children: Mary Llewellyn Serbein Parker, John Gregory. BA with highest distinction, U. Iowa, 1940, MS, 1941; PhD, Columbia U., 1951. Grad. asst. math. U. Iowa, Iowa City, 1940-41; clk. Met. Life Ins. Co., NYC, 1941-42; lectr. U. Calif., Berkeley, summer 1948, 50; lectr., asst. prof., assoc. prof. Columbia U., NYC, 1947-59; prof. ins. Stanford (Calif.) U., 1959-89, dir. doctoral program Grad. Sch. Bus., 1960-64, prof. emeritus ins., 1989—2006. Cons. Ins. Info. Inst., N.Y.C., 1971-78, N.Am. Re-Assurance Life Service Co., Palo Alto, 1973, SRI Internat., Menlo Park, Calif., 1980-81, other bus.; cons., expert witness various law firms. Author: Paying for Medical Care in the U.S., 1953, Educational Activities of Business, 1961; coauthor: Property and Liability Insurance, 4 ed., 1967, Risk Management: Text and Cases, 2 ed., 1983; also articles. Bd. dirs. Sr. Citizens Coord. Coun., Palo Alto, 1986-89, dir. emeritus, 1990-2006. Maj. USAF, WWII. Decorated Bronze Star, 1944. Mem. Am. Risk and Ins. Assn., Western Risk and Ins. Assn., Phi Beta Kappa, Sigma Xi, Beta Gamma Sigma. Clubs: Stanford Faculty. Democrat. Methodist. Avocation: gardening. Home: Fullerton, Calif. Died Jan. 21, 2006.

SERRAL, FREDERICK AMOS, tobacconist; b. Ambler, Pa., Apr. 30, 1922; s. Anthony and Lydia (Saylor) S.; m. Barbara Carrol Elliott, June 28, 1958; children: Amie C., Fred H., Elliott A. Student, Tusculum Coll. Asst. v.p. Austin Co., Inc., Greeneville, Tenn., 1952-56, v.p., 1956-74, sr. v.p., 1974-80, pres., 1980-90, ret., 1990. Pres. U.S. Burley and Dark Leaf Exporters Assn., Lexington, Ky., 1963— Served with USMC, 1940-46. Decorated Silver Star, Bronze Star; recipient Tusculum Coll. Pioneer award, 1966. Mem.: Link Hills Country (pres. 1966-67). Republican. Methodist. Home: Greeneville, Tenn. Died Aug. 19, 2006.

SERVAN-SCHREIBER, JEAN-JACQUES, author; b. Paris, Feb. 13, 1924; s. Emile and Denise (Bresard) Servan-S.; grad. Ecole Polytechnique, Paris, 1947; children: David, Emile, Franklin, Edouard. Sr. writer, fgn. affairs editor Le Monde, Paris, 1948-53; Groupe Expres, mags. L'Express, 1953-73; mem. nat. Parliament from Nancy; pres. Radical Party, 1971-79; dep. for Lorraine region, French Nat. Assembly, 1975-78, min. reforms, 1974; chmn. Groupe de Paris (Europe, Japan, Arabia); chmn. World Center for Informatics and Human Resources, Paris, 1982-85; chmn. internat. com. Carnegie-Mellon U., Pitts., 1985-2006. Served as fighter pilot Free French Forces, World War II. Decorated Cross of Mil. Valor. Author: Lieutenant in Algeria, 1957, The American Challenge, 1967, The Radical Manifesto, 1971, The World Challenge, 1981, The Chosen and the Choice, Passions, 1991, Les Fossoyeurs, 1993. Died Nov. 7, 2006.

SESSIONS, CLIFTON FARR, retired journalist; b. Bolton, Miss., Sept. 26, 1931; s. Valentine Hunter and Daisy Belle (Farr) S.; m. Shirley Ann Edwards, Dec. 31, 1952; children: Carol Renee, Steven Clifton. BS, U. So. Miss., 1955. Announcer, program dir. Sta. WFOR, Hattiesburg, Miss., 1952-57; corr. UPI, Jackson, Miss., 1957-64, Washington, 1964-66; dir. pub. info. U.S. Dept. Justice, Washington, 1966-69; editor Nat. Jour., Washington, 1969-71; exec. dir. communications Am. Bankers Assn., Washington, 1971-78; dep. asst. sec. U.S. Dept. HHS, Washington, 1978-81; mgr. pub. info. Gen. Foods USA, White Plains, NY, 1981—91. With U.S. Army, 1951-52. Democrat. Home: Biloxi, Miss. Died Dec. 24, 2005.

SESSOMS, WALTER WOODROW, telecommunications executive; b. Darlington, SC, Jan. 14, 1934; s. Frank Darlington and Maggie (Garrison) S.; m. HArriet Floyd, June 14, 1957; children: Lee, Kay. BA, Wofford Coll., 1956. Asst. engr. So. Bell, Columbia, S.C., 1956-64, forecast supr. Greenville, S.C., 1964-65, mgr. pub. rels. Spartanburg, S.C., 1965-66, dist. engr. Florence, S.C., 1967-69, gen. mktg. mgr. Charlotte, N.C., 1974-77, v.p. Miami, Fla., 1978-79, Atlanta, 1979-89, sr. v.p., 1989-91; fin. supr. AT&T, NYC, 1969-73; pres. svcs. group BellSouth Telecomm. Inc., Atlanta, from 1991. Practitioner, lectr. U. Ga., Athens, 1984—. Trustee Ga. Bd. Edn., Atlanta, 1989—; chmn. bd. trustees Wofford Coll., Spartanburg, 1990-91; chmn. bd. dirs. Metro Atlanta chpt. Salvation Army, 1990—; chmn. Atlanta Partnership Bus. and Edn., 1990-91; mem. Ga. Edn. 2000, 1991—. 1st lt. U.S. Army, 1957-59. Recipient U.S. Fed. Govt. Pres. Outstanding Svc. award, 1974. Mem. Telephone Pioneers of Am. (sr. vice pres., 1995), Ga. C. of C. (chmn. bd. dirs. 1991-92), Presdl. Exec. Interexch. Assn., Commerce Club, Ashford Club, Rotary. Methodist. Home: Atlanta, Ga. Died July 2, 2006.

SEVERINO, DOMINICK ALEXANDER, emeritus educator; b. Boston, Sept. 14, 1914; s. Nicholas and Amalia (Giordano) S.; m. Fehrn E. Dirkman, Aug. 27, 1940; children: Douglas Alexander, Donald Arthur; m. Jill Daniels, Oct. 8, 2000 (dec. March 23, 2006). BS, Mass. Sch. Art, 1937; Ed.M., Boston U., 1939; Ed.D. (Carnegie fellow A.I.A.), Harvard, 1943. Art instr. R.I. Coll. Edn., 1939-43; asst. dean R.I. Sch. Design, Providence, 1947-48; chmn. art dept. Bradford Durfee Tech. Inst., 1948-52; prof. art U. Wis., 1952-55; dir. Sch. Fine and Applied Arts Ohio State U., Columbus, 1955-57, assoc. dean for acad. affairs Coll. Edn., 1957-75, prof. higher edn., 1975-81, prof. emeritus, from 1981, campus coordinator India Project, Coll. Edn., 1957-69. Cons. continuing med. edn. Vis. summer prof. Harvard, 1942, U. Minn., 1948; Mem. Nat. Com. Art Edn. Contbr. articles on esthetic, environmental issues to profl. jours. Mem. Franklin County Com. on Drug Edn., Columbus; mem. commn. on role professions in soc. Acad. for Contemporary Problems, Columbus. Served with USNR, 1943-46, PTO. Mem. Coll. Art Assn. Am., Nat. Art Edn. Assn., Am. Fedn. Art, Am. Assn. Sch. Adminstrs., N.E.A., Phi Delta Kappa. Presbyterian. Home: Columbus, Ohio. Died Mar. 23, 2006.

SEWARD, WILLIAM W(ARD), JR., writer, educator; b. Surry, Va., Feb. 2, 1913; s. William Ward and Elizabeth (Gwaltney) S.; m. Virginia Leigh Widgeon, Dec. 27, 1941 (dec. Feb. 2005); children: Virginia S. Godwin, Leigh S. Huston. AB, U. Richmond, 1934, MA, 1935. English tchr. pub. schs., 1935-38; instr. U. Richmond, 1939-40, summer 1944; head English dept. Greenbrier Mil. Sch., 1941-42; prof., head English dept. Tift Coll., 1942-45; faculty Old Dominion U., Norfolk, Va., 1945, 47—, prof., 1957-77, prof. emeritus, from 1977, head dept. English, 1947-61. Lectr. U. Va. extension div., 1952-54 Author: The Quarrels of Alexander Pope, 1935; editor: The Longer Thou Livest the More Fool Thou Art (W. Wager), 1939, Literature and War, 1943, Skirts of The Dead Night, 1950, Foreword to Descent of the White Bird (Barbara Whitney), 1955, Contrasts in Modern Writers, 1963, My Friend Ernest Hemingway: An Affectionate Reminiscence, 1969, 2003; contbr. to book: The True Gen: An Intimate Portrait of Hemingway by those Who Knew Him (Denis Brian), 1988, Remembering Ernest Hemingway (interviews by James Plath and Frank Simons), 1999; mem. editl. bd.: Lyric Virginia Today, 1956; contbr. articles to profl. jours. Grad. fellow Duke U., 1938-41; recipient Charles T. Norman medal U. Richmond, 1934 Mem. Poetry Soc. Va. (pres. 1952-55), Hemingway Soc., Internat. Mark Twain Soc. (hon.), Va. Writers Club (emeritus), Virginia Beach Sports Club, Phi Beta Kappa, Kappa Alpha, Pi Delta Epsilon. Methodist. Home: Virginia Beach, Va. Died Nov. 30, 2006.

SHACKELFORD, BARTON WARREN, retired utility executive; b. San Francisco, Oct. 12, 1920; s. Frank Harris and Amelia Louise (Schilling) S.; m. Charlaine Mae Livingston, July 24, 1949; children: Frank, Joan, Linda, Ann. BS in Civil Engring, U. Calif., Berkeley, 1941. Jr. engr. Todd-Calif. Shipbldg. Corp., 1941-44; with Pacific Gas & Electric Co., 1946-85, chief planning engr., 1963—66, chief civil engr., sr. v.p., then exec. v.p. San Francisco, 1976-79, pres., 1979-85. Bd. dirs. Harding Assocs., Inc., CalEnergy Co., Inc. (emeritus). Died July 7, 2007.

SHAFER, RAYMOND PHILIP, lawyer, former governor; b. New Castle, Pa., Mar. 5, 1917; s. David Philip and Mina Belle (Miller) S.; m. Jane Harris Davies, July 5, 1941; children: Diane Elizabeth, Raymond Philip, Jane Ellen. AB cum laude, Allegheny Coll., 1938; LLB, Yale, 1941; LLD, Allegheny Coll., 1963; LLD (hon.). Bar: N.Y., Pa. Assoc. Winthrop, Stimson, Putnam & Roberts, NYC; pvt. practice Meadville, Pa., 1945-63; counsel Shafer, Swick, Bailey, Irwin and Stack; dist. atty. Crawford County, 1948-56; mem. Pa. State Senate from 50th Dist., 1959-63; lt. gov. State of Pa., Harrisburg, 1963-67, gov., 1967-71; vis. prof. U. Pa., Phila., 1973—2006; counselor to v.p. of U.S. The White House, Washington, 1975-77; ptnr., sr. counselor Coopers & Lybrand, 1977-88; pres. Allegheny Coll., 1985—86. Past pres., chmn. bd. trustees Allegheny Coll., Meadville, Pa. Chmn. Nat. Commn. on Marijuana and Drug Abuse; chmn. Nat. Com. U.S.-China Rels., 1982-92; chmn. Nat. Coun. on Pub. Svc.; world bd. govs. USO; mem. adv. bd. Am. Enterprise Inst.; active charitable, cmty. drives; bd. dirs., vice chmn. Atlantic Coun. U.S., Am.-China Soc.; trustee Cleve. Clinic Found., Freedoms Found; vice chmn. Nat. Legal Ctr. Pub. Interest. With USNR, 1942-45, PTO. Recipient Gold medal Soc. Family of Man, 1972, numerous humanitarian and civic awards; named to Acad. Athletic All Am. Hall of Fame, 2002. Mem. ABA, Pa. Bar Assn., Crawford County Bar Assn. (pres. 1961-63), Council Fgn. Relations, Masons (33d degree), Phi Beta Kappa, Phi Kappa Psi. Republican. Died Dec. 12, 2006.

SHAMES, HENRY JOSEPH, lawyer; b. Milw., Jan. 20, 1921; s. Aron and Jennie (Greenberg) S.; m. Beverly Cleveland Van Wert, June 9, 1972; children: Stephen H., Suzanne Shames Sattelmeyer, Sarah Shames Phillips, Diana Shames Strandberg. AB, U. Chgo., 1942; JD, Harvard U., 1948. Bar: Ill. 1949, Calif. 1962. Mem. firm Arvey, Hodes & Mantynband, Chgo., 1949-61; partner Pacht, Ross, Warne, Bernhard & Sears, Los Angeles, 1962-75, Grossman & Shames, Los Angeles, 1975-83, Rosenfeld, Parnell & Shames Inc., Los Angeles, 1984-86; counsel Patterson, Belknap, Webb and Tyler, Los Angeles, 1986-87. Chmn. bd. Switzer Center, Los Angeles, 1966-73 Served with USNR, 1943-46. Mem. Assn. Bus. Trial Lawyers (bd. govs.

1973-76, v.p. 1973-76), Calif. State Bar Assn., So. Calif. Def. Counsel, Los Angeles County Bar Assn., Phi Beta Kappa. Home: Santa Barbara, Calif. Died Mar. 1, 2007.

SHANAHAN, JAMES B., bank holding company executive; b. Buffalo, Dec. 15, 1921; s. Bart J. Shanahan and Florence E. Shanahan Dietrich; m. Therese M. Coonly, June 21, 1952; children— James B. Jr., Michael, Kathleen. BS, Canisius Coll.; postgrad., U. Buffalo. Sales engr. Walker, Wallace, Inc., Buffalo, 1949-54; v.p. sales APV Co., Buffalo, 1954-64, pres., 1964-82; div. chief exec. officer APV Holdings PLC, Buffalo, 1982-84; also dir. Bd. dirs. Nat. Assn. Dairy Equipment Mfrs., Washington, 1970-75, Dairy and Food Industries Assn., Washington, 1980-84 Served to lt., USN, 1943-46, PTO Mem.: Park Country (Williamsville, N.Y.). Avocation: golf. Home: Buffalo, NY. Died Feb. 1, 2007.

SHAPELL, NATHAN, financial and real estate executive; b. Poland, Mar. 6, 1922; s. Benjamin and Hela S. Shapell; m. Lilly Szenes, July 17, 1948 (dec. 1994); children: Vera Shapell Guerin, Benjamin(dec.). Co-founder Shapell Industries, Inc., Beverly Hills, Calif., 1955, chmn. bd., CEO. Mem. adv. bd. Union Bank, Beverly Hills, Calif.; mem. residential bldgs. adv. com. Calif. Energy Resources Conservation and Devel. Commn.; speaker in field. Author: (novels) Witness to the Truth, 1974. Mem. adv. coun. Pres.'s Commn. on the Holocaust, 1979; pres. Am. Acad. Achievement, from 1975; prisoner in Auschwitz, 1943—45; Mem. Calif. Commn. Govt. Reform, 1978; Atty. Gen. Calif. Adv. Coun.; Dist. Atty. Los Angeles County Adv. Coun.; chmn. Calif. Govt. Commn. Orgn. and Economy, 1975—2007; mem. Gov.'s Task Force on Affordable Housing, from 1980; mem. dean's coun. UCLA Sch. Architecture and urban Planning, from 1976; trustee U. Santa Clara, Calif., from 1976; bd. councillors U. So. Calif. Med. Sch., from 1973. Recipient Golden Plate award, Am. Acad. Achievement, 1974, Fin. World award, 1977. Mem.: Hillcrest Country Club (Los Angeles). Jewish. Died Mar. 11, 2007.

SHAPIRO, PHYLLIS (MRS. ABRAHAM SHAPIRO), hotel administrator; b. Montreal, Que., Can., Mar. 12, 1922; d. Isadore and Sadie (Novack) Hochmitz; student Sullivan Bus. Coll., Montreal, 1939-41; m. Abraham Shapiro, Aug. 22, 1961; children— Gerri and Jewel (twins). Asst. mgr. Nat. Food Store Ltd., Montreal, 1942-45; office comptroller Dixon Watch Importing Co., 1945-48, adminstr. Bernard Schaeffer & Sons, importing agy., 1948-51; exec. sec. William Rosenberg, architect, 1951-57; exec. sec. Eugene Meth Assos., financier, 1957-61; adminstr. Twin City Motel, Brewer, Maine, 1968—; pres. The Carriage Inn, Pittsfield, Maine, 1978—. Jewish. Mem. B'nai Brith, Hadassah. Home: Bangor, Maine. Died Mar. 14, 2006.

SHAPIRO, SANDOR SOLOMON, hematologist; b. Bklyn., July 26, 1933; BA, Harvard U., 1954, MD, 1957. Intern Harvard med. svc. Boston City Hosp., 1957-58, asst. resident, 1960-61; asst. surgeon divsn. biol. std. NIH, USPHS, 1958-60; NIH spl. fellow MIT, 1961-64; from instr. to assoc. prof. Cardeza Found. Jefferson Med. Coll., Phila., 1964-72, prof. medicine, 1972—2003, assoc. dir., 1978-85, dir., 1985-2000, prof. biochem. and molecular pharmacology, from 1987, rsch. prof. physiology and biophysics, from 2003. Mem. hematology study sect. NIH, 1972-76, 78-79; mem. med. adv. coun. Nat. Hemophilia Found., 1973-75; chmn. Pa. State Hemophilia Adv. Com., 1974-76. Fellow AAAS; mem. Am. Soc. Clin. Investigation, Am. Soc. Hematology, Am. Assn. Immunologists, Assn. Am. Physicians, Internat. Soc. Thrombosis and Hemostasis. Achievements include research in hemostasis and thrombosis, prothrombin metabolism, hemophilia, lupus anticoagulants, endothelial cells, filamins. Died July 21, 2007.

SHAPIRO, SUMNER, consulting firm executive, retired military officer; b. Nashua, NH, Jan. 13, 1926; s. Maurice David and Hannah (Goodman) S.; m. Eleanor S. Hymen, June 14, 1949; children: Martha, Steven, Susan. BS, U.S. Naval Acad., 1949; MS, George Washington U., 1966; postgrad., Naval War Coll., 1966, U.S. Army Inst. Advanced Soviet and Eastern European Studies, 1961. Commd. ensign U.S. Navy, 1949, advanced through grades to rear adm. Moscow, 1965, ret., 1982; dep. asst. chief of staff for intelligence U.S. Naval Forces Europe, London, 1967-69; comdg. officer Naval Intelligence Processing System Support Activity, Washington, 1969-72; asst. chief staff for intelligence U.S. Atlantic Command and U.S. Atlantic Fleet, Norfolk, Va., 1972-76; dep. dir. naval intelligence, 1976-77; comdr. Naval Intelligence Command, Washington, 1977-78; dir. naval intelligence Washington, 1978-82; v.p. for advanced planning BDM Internat., 1983-89; pres. The Sumner Group Inc., 1989—2006. Pres. Naval Intelligence Found. Decorated D.S.M., Legion of Merit and others., Nat. Intelligence D.S.M., Netherlands Order Orange-Nassau, Brazil Order Naval Merit, French Nat. Order Merit, others Mem. Naval Intelligence Found. (pres.), Naval Intelligence Profls. (bd. dirs.), U.S. Naval Inst., Assn. Former Intelligence Officers, Nat. Mil. Intelligence Assn., Nat. Security Industries Assn., U.S. Naval Acad. Alumni Assn., Naval Submarine League. Home: Mc Lean, Va. Died Nov. 14, 2006.

SHARMA, RAGHU NANDAN, technical corporation executive, electronic design engineer; b. Dist. Montgomery, Pakistan, Mar. 28, 1938; came to U.S., 1963; s. Shambhu Dutt and Ladwati (Devi) S.; m. Kaushalya Devi, Feb. 18, 1963 (div.); m. Patricia Jean Buchholz; children— Janel Kumari, Mathew Raghu, Adrienne Devi. B.S. in Physics with honors, U. Delhi, 1957; D.I.I.Sc., Indian Inst. Sci., Bangalore, 1960, M.Engring., 1962; Ph.D. in Elec. Engring., U. Minn., 1969. Founder, pres. Multi-Tech Systems, Mpls., 1971-74, pres., New Brighton, Minn., 1977—, dir., 1971—; staff engr. Warner Swasey Co., Mpls., 1974-76; with Anderson-Cornelius Co., Eden Prairie, Minn., 1976-77. Designer all modems sold by Multi-Tech Systems. NSF scholar, 1969, postdoctoral fellow, 1970. Hindu. Home: Saint Paul, Minn. Died Apr. 17, 2007.

SHARP, JACK, state legislator; b. Knoxville, Feb. 21, 1936; married; 4 children. Mem. Tenn. State Legis. Republican. Methodist. Home: Chattanooga, Tenn. Died Mar. 12, 2006.

SHARP, WILLIAM WHEELER, geologist; b. Shreveport, La., Oct. 9, 1923; s. William Wheeler and Jennie V. (Benson) S.; m. Rubylin Slaughter, 1958; children: Staci Lynn, Kimberly Cecile; 1 child from previous marriage, John E. BS in Geology, U. Tex., Austin, 1950, MA, 1951. Lic. pvt. pilot. Geol. Socony-Vacuum, Caracas, Venezuela, 1951-53, surface geol. chief Creole, 1953-57; dist. devel. geologist, supr. exploration, devel. unitization of 132 multi-pay oil and gas fields, expert geol. witness, coll. recruiter, rsch. adviso ARCO, 1957—85. Discovered oil and gas at Bayou Boullion, Bayou Sale, Jeanerette, La., Chandeleur Sound and Beauregaurd Parish, La.; petroleum exploration in Alaska, Aus., Can., U.S. and S.A. Contbr. articles to profl. jours.; included in From Acorn to Oakbourne—History of Oakbourne Country Club, 1998.; contbr. artifacts/photos to Nimitz Mus., Fredricksburg, Tex., Nat. Mus. Pacific War, Nat. WWII Meml., Washington, Tex. Meml. Mus., Benson Latin Am. Libr., U. Tex., Austin. Past dir. and chmn. U.S. Tennis Assn. Tournaments; pres. Lafayette Tennis Adv. Com., 1972; pres. Oakbourne Tennis Assn.; past dir. Jr. Achievement and United Fund Programs. With USAF, 1943-46, PTO. Winner and finalist more than 75 amateur tennis tournaments including Confederate Oil Invitational, Gulf Coast Oilmen's Tournament, So. Oilmen's Tournament, Tex.-Ark.-La. Oilmen's Tournament, top La. State Ranking; named Hon. Citizen of New Orleans, 1971, recipient Key to New Orleans; named in Registry of Remembrances Nat. WWII Meml., Washington. Mem. Dallas Geol. Soc., Lafayette Geol. Soc. (bd. dirs. 1973-74), Am. Assn. Petroleum Geologists (emeritus, co-author Best of SEG conv. 1982), Tex. Astron. Soc., VFW, Am. Legion, Lafayette Petroleum Club, Appaloosa Horse Club, Collin County Hist. Soc., Am.'s Nat. World War II Mus. (charter, Brookhaven Country Club (Dallas), Oakbourne Country Club Tennis Assn. (pres. 1976, organizer USTA nat. boys tennis tournament 1976). Republican. Methodist. Achievements include drilling of more than 30 successful wells at Bayou Boullion Field; report/recommendations that resulted in Atlantic Refining Co. office at Anchorage, 1962. Avocations: sports, music, history. Home: Dallas, Tex. Died July 11, 2007.

SHARPE, RICHARD SAMUEL, architectural company executive; b. New Haven, Conn., Aug. 7, 1930; s. Herman and Betty (Silberman) S.; m. Anne Johnson; children: Peter, Andrew, Rebecca. BArch, U. Pa., 1953; postgrad., U. Liverpool, Eng., 1953-54. Registered architect, Conn., N.Y., R.I., Mass. Prin. Richard Sharpe Assocs. P.C., Norwich, Conn., from 1957. V.p. Pan-Am. Fedn. Architects, 1972-78. Bd. dirs. Conn. Humanities council, 1974-78; pres. Conn. Habitat, 1978-79; pres. Thames River Devel. Corp., 1982-83. Recipient Ann. award Producers Council, 1974-78, Ann. Craft award Slater Mus., Norwich, 1986, spl. citation AIA, 1978. Fellow Am. Inst. Archs.; mem. Conn. Soc. Archs. (v.p. 1963, pres. 1966), Hist. Dist. Conn. (com. chmn.), S.E. Conn. Grievence Comm., Rotary. Avocations: wood pottery, photography, pre-columbian art collecting, sailing. Home: Norwich, Conn. Died Jan. 1, 2007.

SHAVELSON, MELVILLE, scriptwriter, theater producer, director; b. NYC, Apr. 1, 1917; s. Joseph and Hilda (Shalson) S.; m. Lucille T. Myers, Nov. 2, 1938; children: Richard, Lynne. AB, Cornell U., 1937. Mem. faculty sch. profl. writing U. So. Calif., 1998—2006. Author: How to Make a Jewish Movie, 1970, Lualda, 1975, The Great Houdinis, 1976, The Eleventh Commandment, 1977, Ike, 1979, Don't Shoot, It's Only Me, 1990, How To Succeed in Hollywood Without Really Trying, P.S. You Can't, 2006; writer Bob Hope Pepsodent Show, NBC radio, 1938-43; screenwriter The Princess and the Pirate, 1944, Wonder Man, 1944, Room for One More, 1951, I'll See You in My Dreams, 1952; screenwriter, dir. The Seven Little Foys, 1954, Beau James, 1956, Houseboat, 1957, The Five Pennies, 1958, It Started in Naples, 1959, On the Double, 1960, Yours, Mine and Ours, 1968, The War Between Men and Women, 1972, The Legend of Valentino, 1975, Deceptions, 1985; screenwriter, dir., producer The Pigeon That Took Rome, 1962, A New Kind of Love, 1963, Cast a Giant Shadow, 1966, Mixed Company, 1974, The Great Houdinis, 1976, Ike, 1979; dir. The Other Woman, 1983; creator TV shows including Danny Thomas Show, ABC-TV, 1953, My World— and Welcome To It, NBC-TV, 1969; author Broadway mus. Jimmy, 1969. Bd. dirs. Motion Picture Fund Found., Studio City, Calif., 2000—07. Recipient Screen Writers Guild award, 1959, Christopher award, 1959, Sylvania TV award, 1953, Acad. Award nominations (screenplay), 1955, 58, Screen Writers Ann. award nominations (screenplay), 1952 (2), 58, 59, 62, 68, 72, 75, Screen Writers award (best written Am. mus.), 1959, Award of Merit United Jewish Appeal, 1966. Mem. Dirs. Guild Am., Writers Guild Am. (exec. bd. dirs 1960-75, 78, pres. screen writers br. 1967, pres. found. 1975-96, pres. emeritus 1997—, v.p. 1996—), Acad. Motion Picture Arts and Scis. (mem. bd. govs.), Writer Guild Am. West (pres. 1969-70, 79-81, 85-87, Valentine Davies award 1979, Laurel award 1984, Morgan Cox award 1998), Writers Guild Found. Shavelson-Webb Libr., Sigma Delta Chi. Died Aug. 8, 2007.

SHAW, CURTIS LEWIS, programmer, analyst; b. Beckley, W.Va., May 22, 1948; s. William S. and Helen S. A.S., Allegheny Community Coll., 1974. Tchr., St. Joseph's Elem. Sch., Pitts., 1971-72; computer operator Blue Cross Western Pa., Pitts., 1972-77; systems engr. NCR Corp., Pitts., 1977-80; programmer Carnegie Mellon U., Pitts., 1980-81; programmer analyst U. Pitts., 1981—; software cons., Pitts., 1988—. Trustee Mt. Ararat Bapt. Ch., sec. credit union. Mem. Soc. Advancement Mgmt., Assn. Systems Mgmt., Nat. Tech. Assn. Club: Racquetball One. Home: Hiller, Pa. Died Feb. 10, 2007.

SHAW, GEORGE ROBERT, manufacturing executive; b. Circleville, Ohio, Apr. 22, 1930; s. Floyd and Bessie Mae (Cutright) S.; m. Norma Jean Barthelmas, July 30, 1949; children: Bruce Robert, Brooks Cameron, Kara Elizabeth. Attended, Lincoln Inst., U. Ga.; BS/BA, U. Md., 1954. Asst. to plant supt. Ralston Purina Co., Circleville, 1949-55; staff advisor Dept. of Army, Columbus, Ohio, 1955-57; mgr. dist. sales Nationwide Mut. Ins. Co., Columbus, 1957-64; pres. Bus. Builders Inc., Dayton, Ohio, 1964-68; dir. field ops. and pub. relations Nat. Mgmt. Assn., Dayton, 1968-75, v.p. mktg., 1975-80; also editor-in-chief Manage mag.; exec. dir. Lockheed Missiles & Space Co., Sunnyvale, Calif., from 1980. Founder, pres. Omnibus 2000; chmn. World Congress Mgmt., Cairo, 1985; profl. speaker Author: What's In It For Me?, 1967, Uncork Your Hidden Talent, Developing Your Competitive Edge, also personal devel. seminar. Pres. Nat. Found., 1957-59. Served with AUS, 1951-54. Named Master Motivator of Year, 1967; hon. State Senator La., 1973 Mem. Assn. U.S. Army, Public Relations Soc., Nat. Mgmt. Assn. (bd. dirs.), Sales Execs. Am., Meeting Planners Internat. Clubs: Masons, Commonwealth of Calif. Home: San Jose, Calif. Died Feb. 27, 2007.

SHAW, MILTON CLAYTON, mechanical engineering educator; b. Phila., May 27, 1915; s. Milton Fredic and Nellie Edith (Clayton) S.; m. Mary Jane Greeninger, Sept. 6, 1939; children: Barbara Jane, Milton Stanley. BSME, Drexel Inst. Tech., 1938; M of Engring. Sci., U. Cin., 1940, ScD, 1942; PhD (hon.), U. Louvain, Belgium, 1970; DEng (hon.), Drexel U., 1996. Rsch. engr. Cin. Milling Machine Co., 1938-42; chief materials br. NACA, 1942-46; with MIT, 1946-61, prof. mech. engring., 1953-61, head materials processing divsn., 1952-61; prof., head dept. mech. engring. Carnegie Inst. Tech., Pitts., 1961-75; univ. prof. (hon.) Carnegie-Mellon U., 1974-77; prof. engring. Ariz. State U., Tempe, 1977-86, emeritus prof. engring., from 1986. Cons., lectr. in field; pres. Shaw Smith & Assos., Inc., Mass., 1951-61; Lucas prof. Birmingham (Eng.) U., 1961; Springer prof. U. Calif., Berkeley, 1972; Distinguished guest prof. Ariz. State U., 1977, mem. Nat. Materials Adv. Bd., 1971-74; v.p. conf. com. Engring. Found., 1976-78. Recipient Outstanding Research award Ariz. State U., 1981, Am. Machinist award, 1972, Schlesinger award German Govt., 1997; P. McKenna award, 1975; Guggenheim fellow, 1956; Fulbright lectr. Aachen T.H., Germany, 1957; OECD fellow to Europe, 1964—. Fellow Am. Acad. Arts and Scis., ASME (Hersey award 1967, Thurston lectr. 1971, Outstanding Engring. award 1975, ann. meeting theme organizer 1977, Gold medal 1985, hon. 1980), Am. Soc. Lubrication Engrs. (hon., nat. award 1964), Am. Soc. Metals (Wilson award 1971, fellow 1981); mem. Internat. Soc. Prodn. Engring. Research (pres. 1960-61, hon. mem. 1975), Am. Soc. for Engring. Edn. (G. Westinghouse award 1956), Soc. Mfg. Engrs. (hon. mem. 1970, Gold medal 1958, Internat. Edn. award 1980, M.C. Shaw award 1999), Nat. Acad. Engring., Polish Acad. Sci., Am. Soc. Precision Engrs. (hon.), Japan Soc. Precision Engrs. (Internat. award 1999), Drexel 100. Home: Tempe, Ariz. Died Sept. 7, 2006.

SHAW, STANFORD J., history educator; b. St. Paul, May 5, 1930; s. Albert G. Shaw and Belle (Paymar) Jaffey; m. Ezel Kural, June 15, 1938; 1 child, Wendy Miriam Kural. BA, MA, Stanford U., 1952; MA, PhD, Princeton U., 1958; MA (hon.), Harvard U., 1966; PhD (hon.), Bosporus U., Istanbul, Turkey, 1986. Asst. prof. Turkish history Harvard U., Cambridge, Mass., 1960-65, assoc. prof. Turkish history, 1965-68; prof. Turkish and Judeo-Turkish history UCLA, from 1968. Vis. prof. U. Bosporus, 1990-91. Author: Between Old and New, 1971, History of the Ottoman Empire and Modern Turkey, 2 vols., 1976-77, Turkey and The Holocaust, 1992, The Jews of the Ottoman Empire and the Turkish Republic, 1992, Between Empire and Republic: The Turkish War of National Liberation, 1918-1923, 1998; editor-in-chief Jour. Mid. East Studies, 1967-80; contbr. articles to profl. jours. Recipient Medal of Honor, Am. Friends of Turkey, 1992, Medal of Honor, Rsch. Ctr. on Islamic History, Art and Culture, Istanbul, 1990, Guggenheim fellowship, 1966-67, NEH fellow, 1972-73, 78-80. Fellow Inst Turkish Studies (sr.); mem. AAUP, Am. Hist. Soc., Turkish Hist Soc. Jewish. Avocations: amateur radio, shortwave listening, photography. Home: Los Angeles, Calif. Died Dec. 15, 2006.

SHEARER, WILLIAM KENNEDY, lawyer, publishing executive; b. Marysville, Calif., Jan. 21, 1931; s. William and Eva (Kennedy) S.; m. Eileen Mary Knowland; Nov. 25, 1956; 1 child, Nancy Lorena; stepchildren: David, Douglas, Dianne. BA San Diego State U., 1955; JD, Western State U., 1975. Bar Calif. 1975, U.S. Dist. Ct. (so. dist.) Calif. 1975, U.S. Ct. Claims 1976, U.S. Supreme Ct. 1982, U.S. Ct. Appeals (fed. cir.) 1982 U.S. Ct. Appeals (9th cir.) 1983. Legis. asst. to Congressman James Utt, 1953, 55-56; exec. dir. San Diego County Rep. Cen Com., 1956-58; pub. Oceanside-Carlsbad Banner, Oceanside Calif., 1958-63; adminstrv. asst. Assemblyman E.R. Barnes Sacramento, Calif., 1963-65; polit. campaign cons. Banner Advt., San Diego, Los Angeles, 1964-75; atty. Duke, Gerstel Shearer LLP, San Diego, from 1975. Pub. (newsletters) Calif Statesman, from 1962, Legis. Survey, from 1963, Fgn. Policy Rev., from 1972, Am. Ind., from 1974. Rep. nominee for State Assembly, San Diego County, 1956, 58; state chmn. Am. Ind Party, Calif., 1967-70, nat. chmn. 1968-71, 73-77; nat. vice chmn. U.S. Taxpayers Party, 1992-96, chmn. 1996-99; Am. Ind nominee for Gov., 1970; adv. com. Elections Com., Calif Legislature, Sacramento, 1971-76; mem. Blue Ribbon Task Force on Calif.'s Home Constrn. Industry, 1996-97; bd. dirs. San Diego Gilbert & Sullivan Co., 1984-90, pres. 1986-88, v.p. 1985-86, 88-90. With U.S. Army, 1953-55. Mem.: San Diego County Bar Assn., Calif. Bar Assn. Avocations: gardening music, history. Home: Lemon Grove, Calif. Died Mar. 3, 2007

SHEEHAN, EDWARD JAMES, retired night vision and electro-optics specialist; b. Johnstown, Pa., Dec. 31, 1935; s. Louis A. and Ethel F. (Schaefer) Sheehan; m. Florence Ann Hartnett, June 17, 1958; children: Edward, James, John, William, Mary. BS in Physics, St. Francis Coll., 1959; MS (Sloan fellow), Mass. Inst. Tech., 1972. Project engr. Electronic Command, Dept. Army, 1959-61, project team leader electro optic equipment for tanks, 1961-63, project team leader electro optic equipment for infantry, 1963-65, tech. area dir. electro optic night vision equipment, 1965-73, asso. lab. dir. for devel engring., 1973-76; lab. dir. Night Vision Lab., Fort Belvoir, Va. 1976-79; founder, pres. Sheehan Assos. Inc., Alexandria, Va 1979-92; founder, CEO, chmn. Stardyne, Inc., Johnstown 1990-96; ret., 1996. Chmn. Nat. and Internat. Symposia for Electro-Optical Tech. and Applications. Named Man of the Yr. Combined Svc. Clubs, 1993; recipient Meritorious Civilian Svc award, Dept. Army, Disting. Alumnus award in Sci., St. Francis Coll., 1989, others. Home: Johnstown, Pa. Died Aug. 8, 2006

SHEEHY, EDWARD JOSEPH, chemical executive; b. Bklyn., Aug. 6, 1923; s. Edward John and Lucille (Florentine) S m. Rosemary Rita Reilly, June 6, 1945; children: Edwar

Michael, Christine, Richard, Dennis, Andrew, Terence, Eileen, Kathleen, Kelly. Student, Rensselaer Poly. Inst., 1941-42; BS, U.S. Naval Acad., 1945; postgrad., MIT, 1952-53; MS, Lehigh U., 1954. Enlisted USN, 1945, advanced through grades to lt. comdr., 1953, resigned, 1960; supt. rocket research Hercules Inc., Cumberland, Md., 1960-62, program mgr. Wilmington, Del., 1962-63, mgr. advt. programs, 1963-65, tech. supt. Kenvil, N.J., 1965-66, dir. devel. Wilmington, Del., 1967-71, dir. environ. program, 1971-75, dir. product mgmt., 1976-78, dir. purchasing, 1980-84, v.p., 1984-87; pres. Hercules Aerospace Co., Wilmington, 1987-90, ret., 1990. Chmn. bd. BAT USA, Inc. Bd. dirs. Del. Lung Assn., Wilmington, 1972—; chmn. adv. council Del. Seagrant Program U. Del., Newark, 1981—. Mem. U.S. Naval Inst. Home: Wilmington, Del. Died Aug. 7, 2007.

SHEETS, HERMAN ERNEST, marine engineer; b. Dresden, Germany, Dec. 24, 1908; s. Arthur Chitz and Gertrude (Stern) S.; m. Norma Sams, Oct. 17, 1942 (dec. Dec. 1970); m. Paulann Hosler, May 29, 1982; children: Lawrence S., Michael R., Arne H., Diana E., Elizabeth J., Karn N. M.E., U. Dresden, 1934; Dr. Tech. Scis. in Applied Mechanics, U. Prague, Czechoslovakia, 1936. Engr. Prvni Brněnska Strojima, Brno, 1936-39; Chief engr. Chamberlin Research Corp., East Moline, Ill., 1939-42; mgr. research St. Paul Engring. & Mfg. Co., 1942- 44; project engr. Elliott Co., Jeannette, Pa., 1944-46; engring. mgr. Goodyear Aircraft Corp., Akron, Ohio, 1946-53; v.p. Electric Boat div. Gen. Dynamics Corp., Groton, Conn., 1953-69; v.p. engring, and research; prof. dept. ocean engring. U. R.I., Kingston, 1969-80, dept. chmn., 1971-79; dir. engring. Analysis and Tech., North Stonington, Conn., 1979-84; cons. engr. Groton, from 1980. Author numerous articles in field. Recipient citation sec. war. Fellow AIAA (asso.), ASME, AAAS; mem. N.Y. Acad. Scis., Nat. Acad. Engring., Soc. Naval Architects and Marine Engrs., Am. Soc. Naval Engrs., Marine Tech. Soc., Pi Tau Sigma. Died Apr. 22, 2006.

SHEETZ, DAVID PATRICK, chemical company executive; b. Colebrook, Pa., Dec. 4, 1926; s. David S. and Ella (Youtz) S.; m. Mary Blumer, Feb. 24, 1946; children: Michael, Matthew, Martha. BS in Chemistry, Lebanon Valley Coll., 1948; MS in Phys. Chemistry, U. Nebr., 1951, PhD in Phys. Chemistry, 1952. In various research and devel. mgmt. positions Dow Chem. Co., Midland, Mich., 1952-67, asst. dir. research and devel. Mich. div., 1967-71, dir. research and devel. Mich. div., 1971-78, v.p., dir. R & D, 1980-85, sr. v.p., chief scientist, from 1985, also bd. dirs.; tech. dir. Dow Chem. U.S.A., Midland, 1978, v.p., dir. R & D, 1978-80. Mem. Chem. Scis. and Tech. Bd. NRC; mem. Matrix Midland Sci. Com., 1978—; adv. bd. Nat. Sci. Resources Ctr., Soc. Chem. Industry; mem. Merrell Dow Bd. Patentee in field. Served with USN, 1945-46. Fellow Am. Inst. Chemists; mem. Am. Chem. Soc., Indsl. Rsch. Inst. (alt. rep.), Coun. for Chem. Rsch. (alt. rep.), Sigma Xi. Died Apr. 13, 2007.

SHELDON, SIDNEY, writer, television director, television producer; b. Chgo., Feb. 11, 1917; s. Otto and Natalie (Marcus) S.; m. Jorja Curtright, Mar. 28, 1951 (dec. 1985); 1 child, Mary; m. Alexandra Kostoff, 1989. Student, Northwestern U. Started as reader, Universal and 20th Century Fox Studios; author: (screenplays) South of Panams, 1941, Gambling Daughters, 1941, Borrowed Hero, 1941, Mr. District Attorney in the Carter Case, 1941, Fly-By-Night, 1942, She's in the Army, 1942, The Bachelor and the Bobby-Soxer (Acad. award for Best Original Screenplay, 1947), 1947, Easter Parade (SAG award for Best Musical, Box Office Blue Ribbon award), 1948, The Barkleys of Broadway, 1949, Nancy Goes to Rio, 1950, Annie Get Your Gun, 1950, Three Guys Named Mike, 1951, No Questions Asked, 1951, Rich, Young and Pretty, 1951, Just This Once, 1952, Remains to Be Seen, 1953, Dream Wife, 1953, You're Never Too Young, 1955, The Birds and the Bees, 1956, Anything Goes, 1956, Pardners, 1956, The Buster Keaton Story, 1957, All in a Night's Work, 1961, Billy Rose's Jumbo, 1962; (novels) The Naked Face (Best First Novel, Edgar Allen Poe award, Mystery Writers Am.) 1970, The Other Side of Midnight, 1973, Sranger in the Mirror, 1976, Bloodline, 1977, Rage of Angels, 1980, Master of the Game, 1982, If Tomorrow Comes, 1985, Windmills of the Gods, 1987, The Sands of Time, 1988, Memories of Midnight, 1990, The Doomsday Conspiracy, 1991, The Stars Shine Down, 1992, Nothing Lasts Forever, 1994, Morning, Noon and Night, 1995, The Best Laid Plans, 1997, Tell Me Your Dreams, 1998, The Sky is Falling, 2001, Are You Afraid of the Dark?, 2004; (non-fiction) The Other Side of Me, 2005; author: (plays) Roman Candle, Jackpot, Dream With Music, Alice in Arms, Redhead (Tony award for Best Musical, 1959); creator, writer, prodr. (TV series) Nancy, 1970, Hart to Hart, 1979-84; writer (TV series) The Patty Duke Show, 1963-66, I Dream of Jeannie, 1965-70; dir. (films) Dream Wife, 1953, The Buster Keaton Story, 1957, Buster and Billie, 1974; exec. prodr. (TV movies) Rage of Angels, 1983, Rage of Angels: The Story Continues, 1986, Memories of Midnight, 1991, The Sands of Time, 1992 Served with USAAF, World War II, 1941 Inducted into the Guinness Book of Records as the Most Translated Author for 1997; recipient Will Rogers Meml. award, 2002. Died Jan. 30, 2007.

SHELDON, THOMAS DONALD, academic administrator; b. Canastota, NY, July 15, 1920; s. Harry Ellsworth and Sadie Joyce (McNulty) S.; m. Helen Elizabeth Kyser, Aug. 29, 1941; children: Thomas, Paul, Edward, Patricia, Curtis, Roberta, Kevin, Kelly. BS, Syracuse U., 1942, MS, 1949, Ed.D., 1958; grad., Air Command and Staff Coll., 1972. Tchr. sci., coach Split Rock (N.Y.) High Sch., 1942-43; tchr. sci., coach, vice prin., prin. Minoa (N.Y.) High Sch., 1946-59; prin., asso. supt. Hempstead (N.Y.) High Sch., 1959-63; supt. Hempstead Pub. Schs., 1963-68, Balt. City Schs., 1968-71; dep. commr. N.Y. State Edn. Dept., Albany, 1971-77; pres. Utica Coll. of Syracuse U., 1977-82; interim pres. Mohawk Valley Community Coll., 1983; then interim pres. Onondaga Community Coll., 1984, now pres. emeritus; prof. ednl. adminstrn. Syracuse U., NY, 1984-85; supt. Sewanhaka Central High Sch. Dist., 1985-86; interim pres. Munson-Williams-Proctor Inst., 1990-91; exec. dir. Syracuse U. Relations, NYC, 1987-93; chmn. Edn. Profls. Internat., 1977-9. Co-author and editor various N.Y. State Regents publs., 1971-76. Served with U.S. Army, 1943-46; served to col. USAF, 1972-77, Berlin; to brig. gen. Air N.G. 1955-77. First recipient Outstanding Grad. award Syracuse U. Sch. Edn., 1977; recipient Outstanding Md. Educator award Md. State Council PTA's, 1969; Disting. Am. Educator award Freedoms Found., 1966; Conspicuous Service medal N.Y. State Gov., 1976; N.Y.C. PSAL medal, 1978; named to Balt. Afro-Am. Honor Roll, 1970 Mem. VFW (life), N.Y. State PTA (hon. life), N.Y. State Coaches Assn. (pres. 1957), Am. Legion, Phi Delta Kappa. Clubs: Lions (hon. life). Home: Liverpool, NY. Died Aug. 14, 2006.

SHELLHORN, RUTH PATRICIA, landscape architect; b. LA, Sept. 21, 1909; d. Arthur Lemon and Lodema (Gould) S.; m. Harry Alexander Kueser, Nov. 21, 1940 (dec. 1991). Student dept. landscape architecture, Oreg. State Coll., 1927—30; BA in Landscape Arch., Cornell U., 2005, BA in Architecture, 2005. Pvt. practice landscape architecture, various cities, Calif., from 1933; exec. cons. landscape arch. Bullocks Stores, Calif., 1945-78, Fashion Sqs. Shopping Ctrs., Calif., 1958-78, Marlborough Sch., LA, 1968-93, El Camino Coll., Torrance, Calif., 1970-78, Harvard Sch., North Hollywood, Calif., 1974-90. Cons. landscape arch., site planner Disneyland, Anaheim, Calif., 1955, U. Calif., Riverside Campus, 1956-64, numerous others, also numerous gardens and estates; landscape arch. Torrance (Calif.) City Goals Com., 1969-70; cons. landscape arch. City of Rolling Hills (Calif.) Cmty. Assn., 1973-93. Contbr. articles to garden and profl. publs.; subject of Oct. 1967 issue Landscape Design & Constrn. mag. Named Woman of Year, L.A. Times, 1955, Woman of Year, South Pasadena-San Marino (Calif.) Bus. Profl. Women, 1955; recipient Charles Goodwin Sands medal, 1930-33, Landscape Architecture award of merit Calif. State Garden Clubs, 1984, 86, Horticulturist of the Yr. award So. Calif. Hort. Inst., numerous nat., state, local awards for excellence. Fellow Am. Soc. Landscape Archs. (past pres. So. Calif. chpt., Lifetime Achievement award, 2005), Phi Kappa Phi, Kappa Kappa Gamma (Alumni Achievement award 1960, 2006), Garden Club Am. (Civic Improvement award 2006). Achievements include oral history and biography published by Pasadena Heritage, 2002. Died Nov. 3, 2006.

SHEMER, MARTHA EVVARD, investment company executive; b. Ames, Iowa, Apr. 19, 1919; d. John Marcus and Martha (Cooper) Evvard; m. Jack Corvin Shemer, June 24, 1937 (dec. 1967); children: Jack Evvard, William Barry Pioneer of properties, Phoenix, Scottsdale, Ariz., LaJolla, Calif. and Del Mar, Calif., 1941-75; pres. Shemer Enterprises, Phoenix, 1975-83, Shemer Investment Co., Phoenix, 1975—. History columnist Paradise Valley Ind. newspaper, 1987. Benefactor Shemer Art Ctr. and Mus. to City of Phoenix, 1984. Martha Evvard Shemer Day proclaimed by City of Phoenix, 1994; recipient Quill and Scroll nat. contest award, 1936, C. of C. Art Advocate of Yr. award, 1995; named Benefactor to City of Phoenix Cmty. Gift of Land, 1996. Republican. Avocations: helping humanity, writing, travel, inventing, needlepoint. Home: Phoenix, Ariz. Died Feb. 17, 2006.

SHEMITZ, SYLVAN ROTTMAN, lighting consultant, designer; b. New Haven, Apr. 18, 1925; m. Paula Shiff, Aug. 27, 1953; children: Julie, Elizabeth, Allison. B.S. in Econs., U. Pa., 1949. Prin. Sylvan R. Shemitz & Assocs., Inc., West Haven, Conn., 1962—2007; pres., founder Elliptipar, Inc., West Haven, 1977—2007; vis. lectr. U. Pa., 1968-74, Princeton U., 1972-79, Yale U. Grad. Sch. Arch., 1973-87. Contbr. articles to profl. jours.; patentee (15). Lighting designer Thomas Jefferson Meml., Washington, U.S. Supreme Ct., Washington, CN Tower, Toronto, Ont., Can., Arco, Phila. Recipient HUD design awards for Mass. Bay Transp. Authority, 1968; Sylvania Lamp div. regional award, 1969; achievement award and citation Fed. Energy Adminstrn. Region III, 1975; CASI award, 1977; AIA honor award, 1979, 80, 83, 84; silver award Inst. Bus. Designers and Contract mag. 1981; commendation for design excellence award US Dept. Transp. and Nat. Endowment for Arts, 1982. Fellow Illuminating Engring. Soc. (applied lighting competition award 1960, 62), Conn. Soc. Architects. Home: Woodbridge, Conn. Died July 5, 2007.

SHEN, PING KANG, chemist; b. Shanghai, China, Oct. 11, 1917; came to U.S., 1958, naturalized, 1964; s. Yih Jung and Mary Shiu-nan (Tai) S.; m. Yar Tsing Chen, May 21, 1944; children— Chyau Nien, Hwa Nien. B.Sc., Soochow U., China, 1934; M.Sc., U. Nanking, China, 1938. Chief engr. Vegetable Oil Refinery, Ministry of War, Chungking, China, 1939-43; mgr. Nanyang Chem. Industries, Ltd., Chungking, 1943-47; head research and devel. dept. Taiwan Fertilizer Co., Hsinchu, 1948-52; mgr. factory 2, Keelung, Taiwan, 1952-54; v.p., chief engr. Formosa Plastics Corp., Taipei, Taiwan, 1954-57; project leader Thermoplastics div. Borden, Inc. Leominster, Mass., 1959-79; head assay br. U.S. Mint, Phila., 1982-84, ret. 1984; commr. Motor Fuel Tech. Commn., Trans. Control Bur., Chungking, 1943. Mem. Chinese Chem. Soc. (bd. dirs. 1954-57, editor-in-chief jour. 1954-56). Died Jan. 2, 2006.

SHEN, SHAN-FU, aeronautical engineering educator, consultant; b. Shanghai, Aug. 31, 1921; came to U.S., 1945; s. Tsu-Wei and Sien-Hwa (New) S.; m. Ming-Ming, Dec. 16, 1950; children: Hsueh-Yung, Hsueh-Lang. BS in Aero. Engring., Nat. Cen. U., Republic of China, 1941; DSc in Aero. Engring., MIT, 1949. Asst. then assoc. rsch. scientist Bur. Aero. Rsch., Chinese Air Force, Republic of China, 1941-45; rsch. assoc. in math. dept. MIT, Cambridge, 1948-50; asst., assoc. then prof. aero. engring. U. Md., College Pk., 1950-61; prof. aerospace engring. Cornell U., Ithaca, N.Y., 1961-78, John Edson Sweet prof. engring., from 1978. Vis. prof. U. Paris, 1964-65, 69-70, Tech. U. Vienna, Austria, 1977, U. Tokyo, 1984-85. Author over 100 tech. jour. articles. Guggenheim fellow, 1957; recipient engring. award Washington Acad. Sci., 1958, Sr. Scientist award Humboldt Found. Republic of West Germany, 1985. Mem. NAE, Internat. Acad. Astronautics (corr.), Academia Sinica of Taiwan. Home: Ithaca, NY. Died Dec. 22, 2006.

SHENEFIELD, JOHN HALE, lawyer; b. Toledo, Jan. 23, 1939; s. Hale Thurel and Norma (Bird) S.; m. Judy Simmons, June 16, 1984; children: Stephen Hale, Christopher Newcomb. AB, Harvard U., 1960, LLB, 1965. Bar: Va. 1966, D.C. 1966. Assoc. to ptnr. Hunton & Williams, Richmond, Va., 1965-71, 71-77; dep. asst. atty. gen. antitrust div. Dept. Justice, Washington, 1977, asst. atty. gen., 1977-79, assoc. atty. gen., 1979-81; ptnr. Milbank, Tweed, Hadley & McCloy, 1981-86, Morgan, Lewis & Bockius, Washington, from 1986, chmn., 1995-98. Assoc. prof. law U. Richmond, 1975; prof. law Georgetown Law Ctr., 1981-83; chmn. Nat. Commn. for Rev. Antitrust Law and Procedures, 1978-79. Co-author The Antitrust Laws - A Primer, 3d edit., 1998; contbr. articles on law to profl. jours. Sec. Va. Dem. Com., 1970-72, treas., 1976-77; chmn. Richmond Dem. Party, 1975-77; bd. govs. St. Albans Sch., 1983-90, 97-2000, chmn. 1988-90; mem. chpt. Washington Cathedral, 1988-98, 2000—; pres. Nat. Cathedral Assn., 1993-96; chmn. Va. Racing Commn., 1989-97. 2d lt. U.S. Army, 1961-62; to capt. Res., 1965. Mem. ABA, Va. Bar Assn. Home: Great Falls, Va. Died Mar. 1, 2007.

SHEPARD, BRUCE M., retired anesthesiologist; b. Leadville, Colo., Nov. 15, 1911; AB, U. Ill., 1932; MD, Harvard U., 1940. Diploamte Am. Bd. Anesthesiology. Commd. 2d lt. USN, 1941, ret., 1961; intern Bellevue Hosp., NYC, 1941-42; resident in anesthesiology Univ. Hosps. Minn., Mpls., 1956-58; pvt. practice; anesthesiologist St. Bernardine Med. Ctr., San Bernardino, Calif.; ret., 1999. Fellow Am. Coll. Chest Physicians; mem. AMA, Am. Soc. Anesthesiologists. Died Nov. 5, 2006.

SHEPHERD, ALICE ALLYNE, research and manufacturing company executive, communications specialist; b. Phoenixville, Pa., Oct. 27, 1931; d. Gustav Adolph and Celeste Lenore (Hoffman) Gertzen; m. Daryl Edwin Shepherd, Mar. 7, 1953 (div.); children— Alda Eugene, Roxanne. Student Met. Jr. Coll. Dist., Kansas City, Mo., 1972-73, Columbia Basin Coll., 1979-80. WAC/WAF recruiter, U.S. Air Force 1950-53; with U.S. Civil Service, U.S. and overseas, 1954-75, mgmt. asst. Hdgrs. Air Force Communications Service, Richards-Gebaur AFB, Mo., 1972-75; documentation auditor Burns & Roe, Richland, Wash, 1976-77; mgr. tech. editing Sigma Research, Inc., Richland, 1977-81, dir. corp. communications, 1981—. Active Nature Conservancy, 1981—. Recipient Zero Defects Program award Air Force Systems Command, Vandenberg, AFB, Calif., 1966-67; Superior Performance award Dept. Air Force 6200 Air Base Wing Clark Air Base, Philippines, 1968-69. Mem. Am. Advt. Fedn., Am. Mgmt. Assn., Nat. Assn. Female Execs., Tri-Cities C. of C., Am. Contract Bridge League (Unit 442). Republican. Author publs. in field. Home: Richland, Wash. Died Sept. 23, 2006.

SHERMAN, JOHN HARVEY, JR., engineering physicist; b. Roanoke, Va., Aug. 12, 1918; s. John Harvey and Mary (Stephens) S.; student Oberlin Coll., 1936-37; A.B., U. Tampa, 1940; M.S., Lehigh U., 1947; postgrad. Cornell U., 1940-41, N.C. State Coll., 1950-51; m. Marie Louise Weill, Mar. 31, 1943; children— Mary Esther (Mrs. Howard J. Ramagli, Jr.), Ida S. Cole. Optician Spencer Lens Co., Buffalo, 1941-42; asst. prof. elec. engring. N.C. State Coll., 1947-50; engr. Gen. Electric Co., Syracuse, N.Y. and Lynchburg, Va., 1951-80, quartz crystal engr., 1953-80, tech. leader quartz crystal design, 1957-80; cons. to quartz crystal industry, 1980—; mem. Electronic Industries Assn. Working Group P5.4, 1960-80, chmn., 1970-79. Founder Lynchburg Fine Arts Symphony Orch. (name now Lynchburg Symphony), 1965; bd. dirs. Lynchburg Community Concert Assn., 1968—, pres., 1970-75. Mem. IEEE (sr. life), Elfun Soc., Sigma Xi, Eta Kappa Nu. Unitarian. Home: Lynchburg, Va. Died Apr. 7, 2006.

SHERWOOD, LOUIS MAIER, endocrinologist, pharmaceutical executive; b. NYC, Mar. 1, 1937; s. Arthur Joseph and Blanche (Burger) S.; m. Judith Brimberg, Mar. 27, 1966; children: Jennifer Beth, Arieh David. AB with honors, Johns Hopkins U., 1957; MD with honors, Columbia U., 1961. Diplomate Am. Bd. Internal Medicine, Subsplty. Bd. in Endocrinology and Metabolism. Intern Presbyn. Hosp., NYC, 1961-62, asst. resident in medicine, 1962-63; clin. assoc. research fellow Nat. Heart Inst., NIH, Bethesda, Md., 1963-66; NIH trainee endocrinology and metabolism Coll. Physicians and Surgeons, Columbia U., NYC, 1966-68; assoc. medicine Beth Israel Hosp. and Harvard Med. Sch., Boston, 1968-69; chief endocrinology Beth Israel Hosp., 1968-72; asst. prof. medicine Harvard U., 1969-71, assoc. prof., 1971-72; physician-in-chief, chmn. dept. medicine Michael Reese Hosp. and Med. Ctr., Chgo., 1972-80; prof. medicine, div. biol. scis. Pritzker Sch. Medicine, U. Chgo., 1972-80; Ted and Florence Baumritter prof. medicine and biochemistry Albert Einstein Coll. Medicine, 1980-88, vis. prof. medicine, 1989—2007, chmn. dept. medicine, 1980-87; physician-in-chief Montefiore Hosp. and Med. Ctr., NYC, 1980-87; adj. prof. medicine U. Pa., 1993—2007. Sr. v.p. med. and sci. affairs Merck, Sharp & Dohme Internat., 1987-89; exec. v.p. worldwide devel. Merck, Sharp & Dohme Rsch. Labs., 1989-92, sr. v.p. U.S. Med. and Sci. Affairs Merck Human Health, 1992-2002; pres. MEDSA, LLC, 2002-07; Josiah Macy Jr. Found. fellow and vis. scientist Weizmann Inst., Israel, 1978-79; assoc. mem. bd. on subcom. endocrinology and metabolism Am. Bd. Internal Medicine, 1977-83; med. adv. bd. HPR, 1996-99; pres., chief med. officer Bone Measurement Inst., 1996-2002; mem. nat. rsch. adv. com. Dept. Vets. Affairs, 2000-07, clin. rsch. roundtable Inst. Medicine, 2000-04. Editor: Beth Israel seminars New Eng. Jour. Medicine, 1968-71; mem. editorial bd. Endocrinology, 1969-73; assoc. editor Metabolism, 1970-85, Gen. Medicine B Study Sect., NIH, 1975-79; mem. editorial bd. Yr. in Endocrinology, 1976-86, Calcified Tissue Internat., 1978-80, Internal Medicine Alert, 1979-89; contbr. numerous articles on endocrinology, protein hormones, calcium metabolism and ectopic proteins to jours. Trustee Michael Reese Med. Ctr., 1974-77; vis. council CUNY Med. Sch., 1986-95; alumni council Columbia Coll. Physicians and Surgeons, 1986-2007; bd. dirs. Jewish Fedn. Phila., 1997-2007, Alliance on Aging Rsch., 1997-2002. Served as surgeon USPHS, 1963-66. Recipient Joseph Mather Smith prize for outstanding alumni rsch. Coll. Physicians and Surgeons, Columbia U., 1972, Sr. Class Tchg. award U. Chgo., 1976, 77, Spl. Achievement award Assn. Profs. Medicine, 2002; grantee USPHS, 1968-88. Master: ACP (Outstanding Contbn. to Internal Medicine award 1987); mem.: AAAS, Acad. Pharm. Physicians and Investigators, Chgo. Soc. Internal Medicine, Assn. Program Dirs. Internal Medicine (coun. 1979—85, pres. 1983—84), Ctrl. Soc. Clin. Rsch., Mass. Med. Soc., Am. Soc. Hypertension (bd. dirs. 1992—97), N.Y. Acad. Medicine (bd. dirs. 1991—95), Am. Acad. Pharm. Physicians (trustee 2000—02, v.p. strategic alliances and planning 2000—03, sec. 2003—04, pres., chmn. bd. 2005—06, Lifetime Achievement award in Pharm. Medicine 2001), Am. Physicians Fellowship for Medicine in Israel (pres. 1993—97, Disting. Med. Svc. award 1998), Endocrine Soc. (bd. dirs. Hormone Found. 2002—05), Assn. Am. Physicians, Am. Soc. Clin. Investigation (pres. 1982—83), Am. Soc. Biol. Chemists, Am. Inst. Chemists, Am. Fedn. Clin. Rsch. (bd. dirs. Found. 1989—92, Spl. Recognition award 1992), Interurban Clin. Club, Alpha Omega Alpha, Phi Beta Kappa. Achievements include research in protein and polypeptide hormones: structure, function and regulation of secretion; molecular studies of hormone biosynthesis; clinical pharmacology, new drug development, outcomes research and disease; quality of care. Home: Delray Beach, Fla. Died Jan. 25, 2007.

SHIELDS, WILLIAM BRYAN, engineering executive; b. Bluefields, Nicaragua, Apr. 22, 1920; s. John and Helen (Rayford) Shields; m. Grace Marie Allsbrook, Apr. 11, 1944; children: G. Megan Shields Duggan, William Bryan. BSEE, Lehigh U., 1948. Registered profl. engr., N.Y., Ill., Pa., Mich. Project elec. engr. Gilbert Assocs., Reading, Pa., 1951—69, chief elec. engr., 1969—72, engring. mgr., 1972—74, also bd. dirs.; v.p., gen. mgr. power and indsl. divsn. Gilbert/Commonwealth, Jackson, Mich., 1974—84, sr. v.p., from 1984. Bd. dirs. Commonwealth Assocs. Served to lt. comdr. USN, 1941—46, PTO. Mem.: IEEE (sr.), Mich. Soc. Profl. Engrs., Instrument Soc. Am., Jackson C. of C. (chmn. 1981), Jackson Country Club. Republican. Achievements include co-inventor 120/240 volt station battery ground detector. Home: Jerome, Mich. Died Apr. 16, 2007.

SHIH, JOAN FAI, artist, educator; b. Guangdong, China, Sept. 4, 1932; came to U.S., 1953; d. Henry Ken-Wai and Laura Suk-Wee (Chen) S. Student, Art Students' League, N.Y.C., 1953; BFA, Kansas City Art Inst., 1956, MFA, 1961; postgrad., Pa. Acad. Fine Arts, 1957-59, 61-63. Instr. art Kansas City (Mo.) Art Inst., 1959-61, Converse Coll., Spartanburg, S.C., 1966-67; lectr. painting Rosemont (Pa.) Coll., 1969-88. One woman shows include Brit. Council, Gloucester Bldg., Hong Kong, 1956, Cedar Crest Coll., Allentown, Pa., 1969, Danville (Va.) Mus. Fine Arts, 1986, Penn Wynne Libr. Wynnewood, Pa., 1991; exhibited in group shows including Nelson and Atkins Mus. Art, Kansas City, Mo., 1954, Pa. Acad. Fine Arts, 1963, 69-70, 72, 74, 76, 81, 83, Phila. Civic Ctr. Mus., 1970, 74, 79-80, 82, Woodmere Art Mus., Phila., 1987, Art Inst. Phila., 1987, 90, 91, John Geiszel All Transparency Watercolor Show., Phila, 1988-91, Plastic Club Ann. Art Exhbn., Phila., 1985, 89-91 (Marion Cohee Meml. award 1989), Phila. Watercolor Club 72d Ann. Exbhn. Chester County Art Assn., 1991, Flum Gallery, Paoli, Pa., 1992; traveling exhbn. Nat. Assn. Women Artists, 1978-80, 80-82, 83-85, 85-87, Huntington Mus., N.Y.C., 1981, Bergen Mus., Paramus, N.J., 1983; represented in permanent collections including D.W. Newcomer's Sons Gallery, Kansas City, Mo. (Ann. Show award 1960), Meth. Hosp., Phila., Arco Chem. Co., Newtown Square, Pa., 1991. Recipient 1st prize Plastic Club All Media Art Exhbn., Phila., 1990; Kansas City Art Inst. scholar, 1953-56; Kansas City Art Inst. grantee, 1959-61. Mem. Nat. Assn. Women Artists (Elizabeth Erlanger Meml. prize 1980), Fellowship of Pa. Acad. Fine Arts, Phila. Watercolor Club, Hong Kong Art Club. Episcopalian. Died Aug. 8, 2007.

SHINE, NEAL JAMES, journalism educator, former newspaper editor, publisher; b. Grosse Pointe Farms, Mich., Sept. 14, 1930; s. Patrick Joseph and Mary Ellen (Conlon) Shine; m. Phyllis Theresa Knowles, Jan. 24, 1953; children: Judith Ann, James Conlon, Susan Brigid, Thomas Patrick, Margaret Mary, Daniel Edward. BS in Journalism, U. Detroit, 1952; PhD (hon.), Cleary Coll., 1989, Siena Heights Coll., 1995, U. Mich., 1995, U. Detroit Mercy, 1966, Ctrl. Mich. U., 1996. Mem. staff Detroit Free Press, 1950—95, asst. city editor, 1963—65, city editor, 1965—71, mng. editor, 1971—82, sr. mng. editor, 1982—89, pub., 1990—95; prof. journalism Oakland U., Rochester, Mich., 1995—2007. Host, moderator Detroit Week in Rev., Sta. WTVS-TV, 1981—89; host Neal Shine's Detroit, 1989—91. Bd. dir. Children's Hosp.; trustee, vice chmn. bd. trustees Youth for Understanding, 1973—75, chmn., 1975—78; mem. bd. for student publs. U. Mich.; bd. dir. Econ. Club Detroit, Detroit Renaissance, New Detroit, Inc., Detroit Symphony Orch., Detroit Inst. Arts, Detroit Hist. Soc., United Way of Southeastern Mich., Met. Detroit Conv. and Visitors Bur., Operation ABLE, Detroit Press Club Found. With US Army, 1953—55. Named to Mich. Journalism Hall of Fame, 1990. Mem.: Soc. of Profl. Journalists, AP Mng. Editors, Mich. Press Assn. (bd. dirs. 1990—95), Am. Newspaper Pub. Assn., Am. Soc. Newspaper Editors, Neal Shine Fund for Ethics in Journalism, Inc. Soc. Irish-Am. Lawyers, Sons of Whiskey Rebellion (comdr.-in-chief 1979), Detroit Press Club (charter, bd. govs. 1966—89, sec. 1957—68, v.p. 1969—71, pres. 1971—73). Died Apr. 3, 2007.

SHIPTON, HAROLD WILLIAM, biomedical engineering educator, researcher; b. Birmingham, Eng., Sept. 29, 1920; came to U.S., 1957; Student, Shrewsbury Tech. Coll., Eng., 1938. Engr. Burden Neurol. Inst., Bristol, Eng., 1946-57; asst. prof. biomed. engring. U. Iowa, Iowa City, 1957-59, prof., 1959-79; prof. biomed. engring. Washington U., St. Louis, 1979-89, prof. emeritus, from 1989, chmn. dept., 1986-89, chmn. pro tem dept. elec. engring., 1986-87. Mem. study sect. NIH, 1965-70. Assoc. editor Jour. EEG and Clin. Neurophysiology; contbr. articles to profl. jours. Served with RAAF, 1940-47. Grantee NIH, 1968-76. Fellow Am. EEG Soc. (hon.); mem. The EEG Soc. U.K. (hon.), Cen. Assn. EEG (pres. 1975). Unitarian Universalist. Avocation: literature; lic. pilot. Home: Saint Louis, Mo. Died Apr. 9, 2007.

SHIRES, GEORGE THOMAS, surgeon, educator; b. Waco, Tex., Nov. 22, 1925; s. George Thomas and Donna Mae (Smith) S.; m. Robbie Jo Martin, Nov. 27, 1948; children: Donna Jacquelyn Blain, George Thomas III, Jo Ellen. MD, U. Tex. Southwestern Med. Sch., Dallas, 1948. Intern Mass. Meml. Hosp., Boston, 1948—49; resident in surgery Parkland Meml. Hosp., Dallas, 1950—53; faculty U. Tex. Southwestern Med. Sch., Dallas, 1953—60, assoc. prof. surgery, acting chmn. dept., 1960—61, prof., chmn. dept., 1961—74; surgeon in chief surg. svcs. Parkland Meml. Hosp., 1960—74; prof., chmn. dept. surgery U. Wash. Sch. Medicine, Seattle, 1974—75; chief of svc. Harborview Med. Ctr., Seattle, Univ. Hosp., Seattle, 1974—75; chmn. dept. surgery N.Y. Hosp.-Cornell U. Med. Coll., 1975—91; dean, provost for med. affairs Cornell U. Med. Coll., 1987—91, prof. emeritus, 1996—2007; prof., chmn. surgery Tex. Tech. U., Lubbock, 1991—95, Canizaro disting. prof. surgery, 1995—97; prof. surgery U. Nev. Sch. Medicine, Las Vegas, 1997—2007; dir., Trauma Inst, U. Nev., Sch. Medicine, Las Vegas, Nev. Cons. Surgeon Gen., U.S. Army, 1965—75, Jamaica Hosp., 1978—91, Inst. Medicine NAS, 1975—2007; metabolism and trauma com. NAS-NRC, 1964—71, com. trauma, 1964—71; rsch. program evaluation com., reviewer clin. investigation applications career devel. program VA, 1972—76; gen. med. rsch. program projects com. NIH NIH, 1965—69; mem. Surgery A study sect., 1970—74, chmn., 1976—78; mem. Nat. Adv. Gen. Med. Scis. Coun., 1980—84; cons. editl. bd. Jour. Trauma, 1968—88. Mem. editl. bd.: Year Book Med. Publs., 1970—92, Annals of Surgery, from 1972, Surg. Techniques Illustrated: An International Comparative Text, 1974—75, Am. Jour. Surgery, from 1968, Contemporary Surgery, 1973—89, assoc. editor-in-chief: Infections in Surgery, 1981, mem. editl. bd.: Jour. Clin. Surgery, 1980—82; editor: Surgery, Gynecology and Obstetrics, 1982—93. Lt. M.C. USNR, 1949—50, Lt. M.C. USNR, 1953—55. Fellow: Coll. Medicine South Africa (hon.); mem.: AMA, ACS (bd. regents 1971—82, chmn. bd. regents 1978—80, pres. 1981—82), James IV Assn. Surgeons (bd. dirs. 1980—81, sec. 1981—87, pres. 1987—91), Allen O. Whipple Surg. Soc., Western Surg. Assn., N.Y. Surg. Soc. (pres. 1981—82), So. Surg. Assn., Soc. Univ. Surgeons (chmn. publs. com. 1969—71), Soc. Surg. Chairmen (pres. 1972—74), Soc. Clin. Surgery, Soc. Surgery Alimentary Tract, Pan Pacific Surg. Assn., Pan-Am. Med. Assn. (surgery coun. 1971), Am. Burn Assn., Internat. Surg. Soc. (sec. 1978—81, v.p. 1982—83, pres. U.S. chpt. 1984—85), Internat. Soc. Burn Injuries, Halsted Soc., Digestive Disease Found. (founding mem.), Am. Surg. Assn. (sec. 1969—74, pres. 1980), Am. Burn Assn., Am. Assn. Surgery Trauma, Dallas Soc. Gen. Surgeons (pres. 1972—74, pres.-elect), Am. Bd. Surgery (dir. 1968—74, chmn. 1972—74, diplomate), Surg. Biology Club (sec. 1968—70), Phi Beta Pi, Alpha Pi Alpha, Alpha Omega Alpha. Home: Henderson, Nev. Died Oct. 18, 2007.

SHIRK, CHARLES ALBERT, retired engineering and construction company executive; b. Gary, Ind., May 15, 1920; s. Joel B. and Mary A. (Pearson) S.; m. Norma Fisher, Oct. 26, 1944; children: Peter J., Wendy C., Jill K. BS in Civil Engring., U. Notre Dame, 1942. Registered profl. engr., 49 states, D.C. Structural engr. Curtiss-Wright Corp., Buffalo, 1942-46, Hazelet & Erdal, Chgo., 1946-48; with Austin Co., Cleve., 1948-85, supr. engring. Chgo., 1948-57, asst. dist. engr., 1957-60, mgr. research and devel. div. Cleve., 1961-62, dist. engr. Chgo., 1962-65, asst. dist. mgr., 1965-70, v.p., process div. mgr., 1970-72, asst. gen. mgr. Cleve., 1972-73, pres., gen. mgr., chief exec. officer, 1973-85, dir., 1971-85, dep. chmn., 1979-85. Bd. dirs. Greater Cleve. Growth Assn.; Mem. gen. bd. Greater Cleve. chpt. ARC; trustee Euclid Gen. Hosp. Assn., Cleve. Health Edn. Mus.; bd. dirs. Bluecoats, Inc., The 50 Club. Fellow ASCE; mem. Nat. Soc. Profl. Engrs., Am. Welding Soc., Am. Concrete Inst., Cleve. Engring. Soc., Newcomen Soc. N.Am. Clubs: Union (Cleve.). Roman Catholic. Home: Bradenton, Fla. Died Apr. 27, 2007.

SHIRK, KENELM LAWRENCE, JR., lawyer; b. Lancaster, Pa., June 26, 1922; s. Kenelm Lawrence and Beatrice Marie (Wertz) Shirk; m. Romaine Sensenig, Nov. 10, 1945; children: Kenelm Lawrence III, Kathie R. Shirk Gonick, Kraig Leofric. BA, Washington and Le eU., 1943; JD, Dickinson Sch. Law, 1948; D of Pub. Svcs. (hon.), Thaddeus Stevens Coll. Tech., 2003. Bar: Pa. 1949, U.S. Supreme Ct. 1954. Sole practice, Lancaster, 1949, 1956—67; ptnr. Shirk and Shirk, Lancaster, 1950—56, Shirk Reist, and predecessors and successors, Lancaster, from 1967. Charter pres. Lancaster Mediation Ctr. Co-chmn. Bi-partisan Com. for study Lancaster County Govt.; chmn. Shade Tree Meml. Com. Ch., Lancaster County, Rep. Com. Lancaster County, 1964—71; res. elder First Presbyn. Ch., Lancaster; bd. dirs. Urban League Lancaster County (Pa.), 1985—91, from 1998, Cmty. Hosp. Lancaster, Spanish-Am. Civic Assn. Devel. Corp.; charter mem. bd. dirs. Jr. Achievement Lancaster County, Inc. Served to capt. USAAF, 1943—45, with USAF, 1951—53. Decorated Air medal, Presdl. citation; named Jaycee of World, Jr. Chamber Internat., 1960, Boss of Yr., Legal Secs. Assn., 1981; recipient Disting. Service award, Lancaster Jr. C. of C., 1954, Good Govt. award, 1970, Humanitarian award, Lancaster City-County Human Relations Commn., 1981, Adult Human Relations award, Lancaster Chpt. NCCJ, 1986, Cmty. Svc. award, Rotary, 1999, Exemplar award, Lancaster C. of C. and Industry, 2001, Svc. to Mankind award, Sertoma, 2001, Appreciation award, Lancaster County Conservancy, 2004. Fellow: Am. Bar Found.; mem.: ABA (chmn. sect. coms.), Am. Coll. Real Estate Lawyers (charter mem.), Am. Coll. Trust and Estate Counsel, World Peace Through Law Ctr. (past chmn. com. resolutions), Lancaster Bar Assn. (pres. 1980), Pa. Bar Assn. (ho. of dels. 1979—88, chmn. sect. mcpl. law 1980—81, chmn. sect. real property, probate and trust law 1981—82, bd. govs. 1985—88, Spl. Achievement award 1979—80), Am. Judicature Soc., Inst. for Land Info. (past pres.), Nat. Sojourners (Lancaster chpt.), Lancaster Rifles (Heroes of '76), Tucquan Club (past sec.), Hamilton Club, Elks (pres. South Cen. dist. Pa. 1956—57, lodge exalted ruler Lancaster chpt. 1952—53, Elk of Yr. 1956). Died Jan. 19, 2006.

SHOESMITH, THOMAS PAUL, former ambassador; b. Palmerton, Pa., Jan. 25, 1922; s. Thomas Shoesmith and Emma Irene (Mitch) S.; m. Martha Flagler Houser, Apr. 28, 1945; children: Thomas Mark, Jo Ann. BA in Edn., U. Pa., 1943; MA in Internat. Affairs, Harvard U., 1951. Various positions US Dept. State, 1951-55, commd. fgn. service officer, 1955, assign, 1956-66; dir. Office Republic of China Affairs, 1966-71; mem. sr. seminar US Dept. State, 1971-72; dep. chief mission Am. Embassy, Tokyo, 1972-77, consul gen. Hong Kong, 1977-81; dep. asst. sec. for East Asian and Pacific Affairs Bur. US Dept. State, Washington, 1981-83, US amb. to Malaysia, 1983-87. Served to 1st lt. U.S. Army, 1943-48. Mem. Am. Fgn. Service Assn. Episcopalian. Died Apr. 26, 2007.

SHOLTESS, CALVIN DORREL, manufacturing and marketing company executive; b. Longdale, Okla., Jan. 10, 1926; s. Verden D. and Harriet Opal S.; m. Frances L. Moreno, Aug. 8, 1947; children— Diana, Janet, Debra, Denise. BSM.E., U. Tex., 1950. With Hughes Tool Co., successively v.p. indsl. products sales Dallas, sr. v.p. Europe, Middle East, Africa ops. London, div. pres., chief exec. officer Hughes Tool div. Houston., corp. exec. v.p., dir. subs. Houston. Served to lt. USNR, 1943-46. Recipient Disting. Grad. award U. Tex., 1984 Mem. Am. Petroleum Inst., Am. Soc. Metals, Ind. Petroleum Assn., Internat. Assn. Drilling Contracts, Houston Engring. and Sci. Soc., Petroleum Equipment Suppliers Assn., Can. Inst. Mining and Metallurgy, NOMADS, Houston C. of C. Clubs: Petroleum, Houston, Warick, Rotary, Brae-Burn; Chaparral (Dallas). Methodist. Home: Conroe, Tex. Died Apr. 21, 2007.

SHORT, HOWARD ELMO, church history educator; b. Salem, Ind., Nov. 27, 1907; s. Walter Hartford and Nettie May (Gilstrap) S.; m. Margaret Duncan, June 29, 1935 (dec. July 2000); children: Charlotte May Drummond, Catherine Jean Clark. AB, Eureka Coll., Ill., 1929; BDiv, Hartford Theol. Sem. 1932; PhD, Hartford Seminary Found., 1942; LLD (hon.) Eureka Coll., 1958; LittD (hon.), Bethany Coll., W.Va., 1973 Min. First Christian Ch., Springfield, Mass., 1934-36, Cuyahoga Falls, Ohio, 1936-41; prof. philosophy Lake Erie (Ohio) Coll. 1942-43; prof. philosophy and religion Hiram (Ohio) Coll. 1942-46; prof. ch. history Lexington (Ky.) Theol. Sem., 1946-58, prof. ch. history emeritus, 1993; editor The Christian 1958-74; disting. editor emeritus Christian Bd. of Publ., St Louis, 1974. Author: Doctrine and Thought of the Disciples of Christ, 1951, Christian Unity is our Business, 1953; contbr. chpts. to 14 books. Trustee Eureka Coll.; program com. Am Soc. of Ch. History; del. observer 2nd Vatican Coun. Mem Disciples of Christ Hist. Soc. (life, bd. trustee 1950—). Republican. Avocations: travel, crossword puzzles, sports. Home Indianapolis, Ind. Died June 8, 2007.

SHORT, IRENE THERESA, office automation consultant; b. St. Louis, Oct. 31, 1936; d. William H. and Anna E. (Weidinger) Volmert; m. James Robert Short, June 11, 1960; children— Douglas James, Brenda Marie. B.A. cum laude, Fontbonne Coll., St. Louis, 1979; A.A.S., Meramec Community Coll. 1977, A.A., 1975. Instr., VA Vocat. Rehab., St. Louis, 1975-77 systems analyst McDonnell Douglas Corp., St. Louis, 1979-81 fin. systems analyst Nat. Marine, St. Louis, 1981-82; cons. Networking Resources, St. Louis, 1982-83; pres. Profl. Office Automation, Inc., St. Louis, 1983—; cons. Jewish Vocat. Employment Service, Metro Tng. Ctr., Occupational Tng. Ctr. (all St. Louis), 1983-84. Mem. Assn. Systems Mgmt. (chmn. publicity com. 1982-84), Assn. Women in Computing (charter; v.p. 1979-80), Phi Theta Kappa, IBM-PC Users Group. Roman Catholic. Avocation: tennis. Home: Saint Louis, Mo. Died Aug 10, 2007.

SHUGART, ALAN FIELD, venture capitalist, retired electronics executive; b. LA, Calif., Sept. 27, 1930; m. Rita Shugart children: Chris, Teri, Jill, Mia, Dana. BS in Engring. and Physics, U. Redlands, 1951. Dir. engring. IBM, San Jose, Calif. 1952—69; v.p. Memorex Corp., Sunnyvale, Calif., 1969—72 pres. Shugart Assocs., 1972—78; co-founder, chmn., pres. CEO, COO Seagate Tech. LLC, Scotts Valley, Calif., 1979—98 pres., chmn., CEO Al Shugart Internat., Calif., 1998—2006 Author: Ernest Goes to Washington (Well, Not Exactly): The True Story About the Dog Who Ran For Congress, 1998 Recipient Rey Johnson award, IEEE, 1997, Fellow award Computer History Mus., 2005. Died Dec. 12, 2006.

SHWEDO, JOHN JOSEPH, marine electronics company executive; b. Tarrytown, N.Y., Apr. 26, 1928; s. John Joseph and Agnes Frances (Kelly) S.; B.A. in bus. admintrn. St. Lawrence U. 1952, B.A. in Psychology, Marymount Coll. 1977; M.Div. Union Theol. Sem. 1980; postgrad. Columbia U. 1980-81 S.T.M., N.Y. Theol. Sem. 1984; children— Robin Jane Shwedo Goff, Amy Anne Shwedo Fernold, Gregory John. Sales trainee IBM 1952; mgr. Shwedo Electronics Co. Inc., White Plains N.Y., 1954-67; sales rep. Broadcast & Communications div. Radio Corp. Am., 1968-69; sr. sales engr. marine products Harris Corp., 1969-70; mfrs. rep. 1971-75; service mgr. Griffith Marine Nav. Inc., New Rochelle, N.Y. 1975-76, sales rep., 1977, sales mgr. 1978-80, sales and mktg. dir., 1981-85; v.p. Nau-Control Halesite, N.Y., 1985-87; sales and mktg. dir. Griffith Marine Nautical Inc., 1988—. Instr., councilor Westchester Council Alcoholism, White Plains, 1976-86; assoc. chaplain Bellevue Hosp. N.Y.C. 1979-80, 88-89; hospice chaplain United Hosp. Port Chester, N.Y., 1989—; hospice chaplain Sullivan County Hospice, Montichello, N.Y., 1990—; lectr. Sch. Religion, Diocese of N.Y., Episcopal Ch.; dep. dir. Civil Def., Westchester County 1964-66; pres. Thompson (Conn.) Village Assn. 1967-68; co-founder Thompson Hist. Assn. 1968; mem. vestry Episcopal Ch. Pomfret, Conn. 1966-67, Southbridge, Mass. 1968-69 Served with U.S. Army 1946-48, 52-53. Mem. Nat. Marine Electronics Assn., Maritime Assn. Port of N.Y., Hellenic-Am. C. of C., English-Speaking Union, Tau Kappa Alpha. Republican. Home: Tarrytown, NY. Died July 1, 2007.

SIBLEY, JACK RAYMOND, philosophy and religious studies educator, researcher; b. Arnett, Okla., June 17, 1930; s. Clifford Raymond and Juanita Faye (Stiles) S.; m. Norma Lee Hanan Jan. 20, 1949; childen: Jackie Ruth Sibley Gunn, James Raymond. BA, Phillips U., 1954; BD, Phillips Grad. Sem., 1957 MA, U. Chgo., 1963, PhD, 1967. Ordained to ministry Christian Ch., 1957. Asst. prof. philosophy and religious studies Bethany (W.Va.) Coll., 1967-70; prof. philosophy and religious studies Tex. Woman's U., Denton, from 1970. Author: Logic for Life 1983, Classical Ethics for Contemporary Times: A Heuristic Approach, 1987. Divsn. chair United Way, Denton, 1986. Mem. Found. Philosophy of Creativity (sec.-treas. 1987-93). Democrat. Avocations: travel, hunting, fishing, bicycling, walking. Home: Denton, Tex. Died June 5, 2007.

SIEGEL, ALBERT, educator; b. NY, Aug. 20, 1924; s. Isaac and Jeanette (Kostinsky)S.; m. Betty Lois Knack, Nov. 17, 1925; children: Laurel Gord, Jacqueline Bartelt, Robin, Timothy. BS, Cornell U., 1947; PhD, Calif. Inst. Tech., 1951. Rsch. botanist UCLA, 1951-59; prof. U. Ariz., Tucson, 1959-72, Wayne State U., Detroit, from 1972. Vis. investigator Virus Rsch. Unit ARC, Cambridge, Eng., 1965-68; program dir. NSF, Washington, 1967-68; vis. prof. U. Mich., 1979-80; bd. dirs. Mich. bd. Myasthenia Gravis Assn. Contbr. articles to profl. jours. With U.S. Army, 1945-46. Fellow AAAS, Am. Phytopathological Soc.; mem. Genetics Soc. Am., Am. Soc. for Virology, Am. Soc. for Cell Biology, Am. Soc. for Microbiology. Avocations: bicycling, gardening. Home: Detroit, Mich. Died Aug. 3, 2007.

SIEGEL, MAYER, lawyer; b. Bklyn., Sept. 29, 1936; s. Israel and Rose (Bernstein) S.; m. Sheila Siegel (div.); children: David, Jonathan; m. Carol Buckmann. BBA, CCNY, 1956; LLB, NYU, 1961, LLM, 1964. From assoc. to ptnr. Fried, Frank, Harris, Shriver & Jacobson, NYC, from 1961. Mem. ABA, N.Y. State Bar Assn., Assn. Bar City N.Y. Jewish. Died Mar. 1, 2007.

SIGBAND, NORMAN BRUCE, communications educator; b. Chgo., June 27, 1920; s. Max and Bessie S.; m. Joan C. Lyons, Aug. 3, 1944; children: Robin, Shelley, Betsy. BA, U. Chgo., 1940, MA, 1941, PhD, 1954; LHD (hon.), DePaul U., 1986. Asst. prof. bus. communication DePaul U., 1946-50, assoc. prof., 1950-54, prof., 1954-65; prof. mgmt. communication U. So. Calif., from 1965, chmn. dept. mktg., 1970-72, assoc. dean Sch. Bus., 1975-80, Disting. prof. emeritus, from 1989. Disting. Centennial lectr. U. Tex., Austin, 1986; cons. to industry; spkr., condr. workshops, seminars in field; scholar-in-residence Va. Commonwealth U., 1987, DePaul U., 1988; Borchard lectr., 2003. Author books including: Practical Communication for Everyday Use, 25th edit., 1954, Effective Report Writing for Business, Industry and Government, 1960, Communication for Management, 1970, Communicacion Para Directivos, 1972, Management Communication for Decision Making, 1972, Communication for Management and Business, 1976, Communication for Managers, 6th edit., 2001, Communicating in Business, 1987, 3d edit., 1989, in Spanish, 1993, in Chinese, 2001, Patient-Pharmacist Consultation: A Communication Skills Approach, 1993, Communication for Pharmacists and Other Health Professionals, 1995, 2d edit., 1996, (with J. Biles) The Status of American Universities: Challenges and Opportunities, 2003; movies include: Communication Barriers and Gateways, 2d edit., 1993, Listening: A Key to Problem Solving (award winner), 2d edit., 1993, The Grapevine, The Power of a Minute, 1992; gen. editor books including: Harcourt Brace Jovanovich Bus. series; contbr. numerous articles to profl. jours., mags. Served to capt. AUS, 1942-46, ETO. Decorated Bronze Star; recipient recognition award City of L.A., 1985, hon. alumnus award U. So. Calif., 1991. Fellow Am. Bus. Communication Assn. (pres. 1964-65); mem. Internat. Communication Assn., Acad. Mgmt., Anti-Defamation League, Hadassah Assocs., Blue Key, Phi Kappa Phi, Alpha Kappa Psi, Beta Gamma Sigma. Democrat. Jewish. Home: Studio City, Calif. Died Jan. 24, 2007.

SILBERMAN, ROSALIE GAULL (RICKY SILBERMAN), former federal official; b. Jackson, Miss., Mar. 31, 1937; d. Samuel and Alice (Berkowitz) Gaull; m. Laurence H. Silberman, Apr. 28, 1957; children: Katherine, Anne, Robert. BA, Smith Coll., 1958. Tchr., 1967-72; bd. dirs. Natl. Adv. Coun. on Edn. of Disadvantaged Children, 1973-75, Widening Horizons, 1973-75; dir. comm., press sec. Sen. Robert Packwood, 1977-79; exec. dir., sec., treas. New Coalition for Econ. and Social Change, 1981-83; dir. pub. rels. San Francisco Conservatory of Music, 1982-83; spl. asst. Commr. Mimi Weyforth Dawson FCC, 1983-84; commr. EEOC, 1984-86, 1994-95, vice chmn., 1986-94; exec. dir. Office of Compliance US Congress, Washington, 1995—2000. Co-founder Ind. Women's Forum, 1991; mem. Adv. Commn. on Status of Women US Dept. Def., 2001. Died Feb. 18, 2007.

SILETS, HARVEY MARVIN, lawyer; b. Chgo., Aug. 25, 1931; s. Joseph Lazarus and Sylvia Silets; m. Elaine L. Gordon, June 25, 1961; children: Hayden Leigh, Jonathan Lazarus (dec.), Alexandra Rose. BS cum laude, DePaul U., 1952; JD (Frederick Leicke scholar), U. Mich., 1955. Bar: Ill. 1955, U.S. Dist. Ct. (no. dist.) Ill. 1955, N.Y. 1956, U.S. Tax Ct. 1957, U.S. Ct. Mil. Appeals 1957, U.S. Ct. Appeals (7th cir.) 1958, U.S. Supreme Ct. 1959, U.S. Ct. Appeals (6th cir.) 1965, U.S. Ct. Appeals (2d cir.) 1971, U.S. Ct. Appeals (5th cir.) 1972, U.S. Ct. Appeals (11th cir.). Assoc. Paul, Weiss, Rifkind, Wharton & Garrison, NYC, 1955—56; asst. atty. U.S. Dist. Ct. (no. dist.) Ill., 1958—60; chief tax atty. Office US Atty. (no. dist.) Ill. US Dept. Justice, Chgo., 1960—62; ptnr. Harris, Burman & Silets, Chgo., 1962—79, Silets & Martin, Ltd., Chgo., 1979—92, Katten Muchin Zavis Rosenman, Chgo., 1992—2007. Asst. advance tng. program IRS, U. Mich., 1952-53; law lectr. advance fed. taxation John Marshall Law Sch., 1962-66; adj. prof. taxation Chgo.-Kent Coll. Law, 1985-2007; gen. counsel Nat. Treasury Employees Union, 1968-92; mem. adv. com. tax litigation U.S. Dept. Justice, 1979-82; mem. Tax Reform Com., State of Ill., 1982-83; mem. Speedy Trial Act Planning Group U.S. Dist. Ct. (no. dist.) Ill., 1976-79; mem. civil justice reform act adv. com. U.S. Dist. Ct. (no. dist.) Ill., 1991-94; lectr. in field. Contbr. articles to profl. jours. Trustee Latin Sch., Chgo., 1970-76; active Chgo. Crime Commn., 1975-93, Govv.'s Commn. Reform Tax Laws, Ill., 1982-83. With AUS, 1956-58. Fellow Am. Coll. Trial Lawyers (chmn. com. on fed. rules of criminal procedure 1982-91, fed. rules of evidence com. 1988-93, jud. com., fed. criminal procedures com., Upstate Ill. com. chmn. 1990-91), Am. Coll. Tax Counsel, Internat. Acad. Trial Lawyers, Soc. Advanced Legal Studies (London); mem. ABA (active various coms.), Bar Assn. 7th Fed. Cir. (chmn. com. criminal law and procedure 1972-82, bd. govs. 1983-86, sec. 1986-88, v.p. 1989-90, pres. 1990-91), NACDL, FBA (bd. dirs. 1971-2007, pres. 1977-78, v.p. 1976-77, sec. 1975-76, treas. 1974-75, active various coms.), Chgo. Bar Assn. (tax com. 1958-66, com. devel. law 1966-72, 78-88, com. fed. taxation 1968-2007, com. evaluation candidates 1978-80, exec. com. tax sect. 1994-2007), Am. Bd. Criminal Def. Lawyers, Decalogue Soc. Lawyers, Bar Assn. N.Y. City, Standard Club, Chgo. Club, Phi Alpha delta, Pi Gamma Mu. Home: Barrington, Ill. Died Jan. 23, 2007.

SILLS, BEVERLY (BELLE SILVERMAN, MRS. PETER B. GREENOUGH), performing company executive, singer; b. Bklyn., May 25, 1929; d. Morris and Sonia (Bahn) Silverman; m. Peter B. Greenough, 1956 (dec. Sept. 7, 2006); children: Meredith Holden, Peter Bulkeley; stepchildren: Lindley Thomassett, Nancy Bliss, Diana Greenough. Studied with Estelle Leibling, studied with Paolo Gallico, studied with Desire Defrere; doctorate (hon.), Harvard U., NYU, New Eng. Conservatory, Temple U.; degree (hon.), Harvard U., NYU, Calif. Inst. Arts. Gen. dir. N.Y.C. Opera, 1979-1989; pres. N.Y.C. Opera Bd., 1989-90; mng. dir. Met. Opera, NYC, 1991-94; chairwoman Lincoln Ctr. for Performing Arts, Inc., NYC, 1994—2002, Met. Opera, NYC, 2002—05. Bd. dirs. Met. Opera, 1991-2005; cons. Nat. Coun. on Arts. Radio debut as Bubbles Silverman on Uncle Bob's Rainbow House, 1932; appeared on Major Bowes Capitol Family Hour, 1934-41, on Our Gal Sunday; toured with Shubert Tours, Charles Wagner Opera Co., 1950, 51; operatic debut Phila. Civic Opera, 1947; debut, N.Y.C. Opera Co. as Rosalinda in Die Fledermaus, 1955; debut San Francisco Opera, 1953; debut La Scala, Milan as Pamira in Siege of Corinth, 1969, Royal Opera, Covent Garden in Lucia di Lammermoor, London, 1973, Met. Opera, N.Y.C., 1975, Vienna State Opera, 1967, Teatro Fenice in La Traviata, Venice; appeared Teatro Colon, Buenos Aires; recital debut Paris, 1971, London Symphony Orch., 1971; appeared throughout U.S., Europe, S. Am. including Boston Symphony, Tanglewood Festival, 1968, 69, Robin Hood Dell, Phila., 1969; title roles in: Don Pasquale, Norma, Ballad of Baby Doe, Thais, La Traviata, Anna Bolena, Maria Stuarda, Lucia de Lammermoor, Barber of Seville, Manon, Louise, Tales of Hoffmann, Daughter of the Regiment, The Magic Flute, Elizabeth in Roberto Devereaux, I Puritana, Julius Caesar, Suor Angelica, Il Tabarro, Gianni Schicchi, Faust, La Loca, Merry Widow, Turk in Italy, Rigoletto, I Capuleti e I Montecchi, Lucrezia Borgia, Ariodante, Le Coq D'Or, others; recordings include The Art of Beverly Sills, Welcome to Vienna, Great Scores (with Placido Domingo); ret. from opera and concert stage, 1980; numerous TV spls; author: Bubbles:A Self-Portrait, 1976, Bubbles: An Encore, Beverly: An Autobiography. Active with March of Dimes, 1971-1994 (Past chmn. bd. trustees, past nat. chmn. Mothers' March on Birth Defects); bd. dirs. Apollo Theatre Found., 1999-2001. Recipient Handel medallion, 1973, Pearl S. Buck Women's award, 1979, Emmy award for Profiles in Music, 1976, Emmy award for Lifestyles with Beverly Sills, 1978, Presdl. Medal of Freedom, 1980, Kennedy Ctr. Honors award, 1980, Heinz award in Arts and Humanities, 1995, Grammy award for Best Classical Vocal Soloist Performance, 1976, Best Opera Recording, 1978, Bess Wallace Truman award, March of Dimes, 1994, Juanita Kreps award, JC Penny Co., 1996, MS Hope award, Nat. Multiple Sclerosis Soc., 1998, Medal of the Order of Arts and Letters, Min. French Culture, 2000. Died July 2, 2007.

SILVER, GEORGE, metal trading and processing company executive; b. Warren, Ohio, Dec. 17, 1918; s. Jacob and Sophie (Bradlyn) S.; m. Irene Miller, Aug. 5, 1945. Student, U. Ala., 1938; BA, Ohio U., 1940; postgrad. law sch., Ohio State U., 1940—41; grad., Adj. Gen. Sch., 1944. Pres. Riverside Indsl. Materials, Bettendorf, Iowa, 1947-70, Metalpel subs. Continental Telephone Co., Bettendorf, Iowa, 1970-71, Riverside Industries Inc., Bettendorf, Iowa, from 1971. Pres. Scott Resources Inc., Davenport, Iowa; v.p. Durbin Midwest, Davenport, 1987—90; mktg. dir. NAMCO Internat., Miami; cons. Waste Mgmt.-Non Ferrous Mktg., from 1990, Snyer Steel Casting, Iowa, Riverside Products, Ill., 1992—93, Tamron Internat. Ltd., Shanghai, 2002; founder Iowa Steel Mills (named changed to North Star Steel), Cargill and Wilton; mktg. dir. NAMCO Environ. Svcs. Corp., Miami, Fla., from 1995; bd. dirs. NAMCO Trading Co., Miami; cons. metal trading Cricket Club, Miami. Contbr. articles to profl. jours. Mem. Nat. UN Day Com., 1975-83. Capt. AC, USAF, 1941-46, 50-51, Korea. Named to Hon. Order Ky. Cols., 1991. Mem. Nat. Assn. Recycling Industries (co-chmn. nat. planning com., bd. dirs.), N.Y. Acad. Scis., Copper Club, Paper Stock Inst. Am. (exec. com.), Bur. Internat. de la Recuperation (chmn. adv. com.), Inter Global Trading Group (chmn. bd. dirs.), Mining Club N.Y.C., Outing Club, Hatchet Men's Chowder and Protective Assn., Copper Club, Jockey Club Miami, Williams Island Club, Rock Island Arsenal Officer's Club, Chemist Club (N.Y.C.), Crow Valley Country Club, Elks, Phi Sigma Delta. Home: New Rochelle, NY. Died Jan. 19, 2006.

SILVERMAN, BELLE See SILLS, BEVERLY

SILVERMAN, FREDERIC NOAH, physician; b. Syracuse, NY, June 6, 1914; s. Max and Sophia S.; m. Carolyn R. Weber, Jan. 14, 1945. AB, Syracuse U., 1935, MD, 1939. Intern Yale U., 1939-40; resident in pediatrics Johns Hopkins U., Balt., 1940-41; fellow in pediatric pathology Columbia U., NYC, 1941-42; in pediatric radiology Babies Hosp., NYC, 1945-47; dir. dept. radiology Children's Hosp., Cin., 1947-75; asst. prof. to prof. radiology and pediatrics U. Cin., 1947-76; prof. clin. radiology and pediatrics Stanford (Calif.) U., 1976-79, emeritus, from 1979. Ad hoc cons. HEW, NAS Chief editor Caffey's Pediatric X-Ray Diagnosis, 1978-96; mem. editl. bd. pediatric and radiol. jours.; contbr. articles to profl. jours. With AUS, 1942-46, South West Pacific area. Decorated Combat Med. Badge; recipient medal Centre Antoine Béclère, Paris, 1981, Gold medal Assn. Univ. Radiologists, 1993, Daniel Drake medal Coll. Medicine, U. Cin., 1998. Mem. Am. Acad. Pediatrics, Am. Pediatric Soc., Soc. Pediatric Research (past v.p.), Soc. for Pediatric Radiology (past pres., Gold medal 1988); hon. mem. Am. Roentgen Ray Soc., European Soc. Pediatric Radiology, Spanish Radiology Soc., El Salvador Pediatrics Soc., Chilean Radiol. Soc., regional radiol. socs. Home: Palo Alto, Calif. Died Mar. 15, 2006.

SIMMONS, EDWIN HOWARD, military officer, historian; b. Paulsboro, NJ, Aug. 25, 1921; s. Edwin Lonsdale and Nettie Emma (Vankirk) S.; m. Frances G. Bliss, Apr. 25, 1962; children: Edwin Howard, Clarke Vankirk, Bliss, Courtney. BA, Lehigh U., 1942; MA, Ohio State U., 1955; postgrad., Amphibious Warfare Sch., 1949—50, Nat. War Coll., 1966—67. Commd. 2d lt. USMC, 1942, advanced through grades to brig. gen., 1967; asst. prof. NROTC, Ohio State U., 1952-55; with Hdqrs. Marine Corps, 1955- 59; naval attache Dominican Republic, 1959-60; with Hdqrs. Marine Corps and Joint Staff, 1962-65, 3d Marine Divsn., 1965-66, 1st Marine Divsn., Vietnam, 1970-71; dep. fiscal dir. Marine Corps, 1967-70; dir. Marine Corps history and museums USMC Hdqrs., Arlington, Va., 1971-95, dir. emeritus, 1996—2007. Pres. Am. Mil. Inst., 1979; v.p. U.S. Commn. Mil. History, 1979-83; exec. v.p. Marine Corps Hist. Found., 1979-96; pres. Coun. Am. Mil. Past, 1991-95. Author: The United States Marines, 1974, 76, 98, 2002, Marines, 1987, Over the Seawall: U.S. Marines at Inchon, 2000, Frozen Chosin: U.S. Marines at the Changjin Reservoir, 2002; editor: The Marines, 1998; (novels) Dog Company Six, 2000; mng. editor: Marine Corps Gazette, 1946-49; sr. editor: Publs. Group, Marine Corps Schs., 1960-61; Contbr. to numerous books, encys., mags., jours. and annuals. Decorated D.S.M., Silver Star, Legion of Merit with two gold stars, Bronze Star with gold star, Meritorious Svc. medal, Navy Commendation medal, Purple Heart; knight Nat. Order of Vietnam, Vietnamese Cross of Gallantry with 2 palms and silver star; recipient Centennial Disting. Grad. medallion Ohio State U., 1970. Fellow Co. Mil. Historians; mem. Am. Soc. Mil. Comptrollers (nat. v.p. 1967-69, pres. 1969-70), Nat. War Coll. Alumni Assn. (v.p. 1969-70, 74-75), Phi Beta Kappa, Omicron Delta Kappa, Phi Sigma Kappa. Home: Alexandria, Va. Died May 5, 2007.

SIMMONS, FREDERIC RUDOLPH, pediatrician; b. Balt., Apr. 19, 1921; s. Frederic Rudolph and Jessie Agnes (Smith) S.; m. Vera Caldwell, June 24, 1950; children— Mary R., Carol E., Frederic Rudolph, James W., Josephe, Michael T. B.S., Loyola Coll., Balt., 1946; M.D., U. Md., 1950. Diplomate Am. Bd. Pediatrics. Rotating intern Walter Reed Army Hosp., Washington, 1950-51; resident pediatrics Johns Hopkins Hosp., Balt., 1951-53; practice medicine specializing in pediatrics, Daytona Beach, Fla., 1956—; mem. med. staff Halifax Hosp. Med. Center, Daytona Beach, 1956—. Served to maj. USAAF, 1942-45, 50-56. Decorated Air medal with 2 oak leaf clusters, Purple Heart. Mem. AMA, Am. Acad. Pediatrics, Fla. Med. Assn., Alpha Omega Alpha. Republican. Roman Catholic. Home: Sun City Center, Fla. Died July 23, 2007.

SIMMONS, HOMER FISCHER, JR., petroleum geologist, consultant; b. Whittier, Calif., Nov. 12, 1923; s. Homer Fischer and Agnes Jane (Smith) S.; m. Betty Jane Porter, July 29, 1943; 1 child, Pamela Sue Blodgett. A.A., Pasadena Jr. Coll., 1947; B.A., Pomona Coll., 1949. Cert. petroleum geologist. Geologist, various managerial positions Shell Oil Co., Midcontinent, Wichita Falls, Tex., 1949-57, Gulf Coast La. and Tex., 1957-77, head office, N.Y.C., 1963-64; geologist N.A.M., Assen, Nederland, 1971-73; practicing cons. Gulf Coast, Slidell, La. and Monteagle, Tenn., 1977—. Served to sgt. U.S. Army, 1943-46, CBI. Mem. Am. Assn. Petroleum Geologists, Soc. Ind. Profl. Earth Scis. Republican. Avocation: genealogy. Died Apr. 4, 2007.

SIMMONS, ROY WILLIAM, banker, director; b. Portland, Oreg., Jan. 24, 1916; s. Henry Clay and Ida (Mudd) S.; m. Elizabeth Ellison, Oct. 28, 1938; children— Julia Simmons Watkins, Matthew R., Laurence E., Elizabeth Jane Simmons Hoke, Harris H., David E. Asst. cashier First Nat. Bank Layton, Utah, 1944-49; Utah bank commr., 1949-51; exec. v.p. Bank of Utah, Ogden, 1951-53; pres. Lockhart Co., Salt Lake City, 1953-64, Zion's First Nat. Bank, Salt Lake City, 1964-81, chmn. bd., 1965-98. Chmn., CEO Zion's Bancorp, 1965-91, chmn. bd., 1991—; chmn. bd. Zion's Savs. & Loan Assn., 1961-69; pres. Lockhart Co., 1964-87; bd. dirs. Ellison Ranching Co. Chmn. Utah Bus. Devel. Corp., 1969-80; Mem. Utah State Bd. Regents, 1969-81. Mem. Salt Lake City C. of C. (treas. 1964-65), Sigma Pi. Republican. Mem. Ch. of Jesus Christ of Latter Day Saints. Home: Kaysville, Utah. Died May 9, 2006.

SIMMONS, SHERWIN PALMER, lawyer; b. Bowling Green, Ky., Jan. 19, 1931; AB, Columbia U., 1952, LLB, 1954, JD, 1969. Bar: Tenn. 1954, Fla. 1957. Assoc. Fowler, White, Collins, Gillen, Humkey & Trenam, Tampa, Fla., 1956-60, ptnr., 1960-70, Trenam, Simmons, Kemker, Scharf & Barkin, Tampa, 1970-77; stockholder, pres. Trenam, Simmons, Kemker, Scharf, Barkin, Frye & O'Neill, PA, Tampa, 1977-94; ptnr., chair tax group Steel Hector & Davis, LLP, Miami, Fla., 1994—2005; shareholder, vice chair tax group, chair tax practice Buchanan Ingersoll PC, Miami, from 2005. Atty. adv. U.S. Tax Ct., Washington, 1954—56, mem. nominating comm., 1978—81; mem. adv. group Commr. of IRS, 1978—79, 1989—90, U.S. Dept. Justice, 1979—80; adj. prof. U. Miami, from 1995. Contbr. articles to profl. jours. Trustee Hillsborough County Soc. Crippled Children & Adults, 1956—85, pres., 1960—61; mem. adv. bd. Salvation Army, 1959—62, 1964—66, sec., 1960—61; treas., chmn. Hillsborough County Pub. Edn. Study Commn., 1965—66; chmn., bd. dirs. Fla. Orch., 1987—89; founding trustee, pres. Am. Tax Policy Inst., 1996—99; trustee Tampa Bay Performing Arts Ctr., Inc., 1984—93, mem. program adv. com., 1985—89, mem. investment com., 1986—91. Fellow: Am. Coll. Tax Counsel (regent 1987—93, vice chmn. 1989—91, chmn. 1991—93), Am. Bar Found. (mem. devel. com. 1992—94), Am. Coll. Trust and Estate Counsel (bd. regents 1982—88); mem.: ABA (vice chmn. adminstrn. taxation sect. 1972—75, chmn. 1975—76, ho. of dels. 1985—90, bd. govs. 1990—93, chmn. bd. govs. fin. com. 1992—93, chmn. commn. multidisciplinary practice 1998—2000), Am. Law Inst. (mem. coun. from 1985, mem. exec. com. 1994—97, from 1999, mem. com. from 1997, chmn. from 1999), Internat. Fiscal Assn., Internat. Acad. Estate and Trust Law, So. Fed. Tax Inst. (trustee, pres. 1974, chmn. 1975, trustee emeritus from 1999), Am. Judicatrue Soc., Fla. Bar Assn. (chmn. taxation sect. 1964—65), Am. Law Network ABA-Am. Law Inst. (mem. com. continuing profl. edn. from 1973), Am. Bar Retirement Assn. (bd. dirs. 1984—90, v.p. 1987—88, pres. 1988—89). Home: Miami, Fla. Died May 24, 2006.

SIMMONS, VIRGINIA LEE COWAN, principal; b. Ft. Wayne, Ind., May 17, 1921; d. James Clarence and Julia (Webster) Cowan; A.B., Ind. U., 1942, Ed.S., 1970; M.S., Butler U., 1957; postgrad. U. Wis., 1964-67; m. Eric L. Simmons, Apr. 25, 1943 (div. 1948); children— Nancy Lee (Mrs. Roy Green), Eric Leslie. Market research analyst McCann-Erickson, Chgo., 1944-48; retail mcht. Aquatic Galleries, Cin., 1949-52; sales, alvt. Empire Tropical Fish Import Co., N.Y.C., 1952-53; Direct Mail Advt., Halvin Products, Bklyn., 1953-55; tchr. Indpls. Sch. 76, 1955-60; asst. prin. Sch. 61, 1960-61, asst. prin. Sch. 101, 1962-63; prin. Lew Wallace Sch. 107, Indpls., 1964-72, Frances Bellamy Sch. 102, Indpls., 1972-74, William H. Evans Sch. 95, Indpls., 1974-80, G.B. Loomis Sch. 85, Indpls., 1980-82; cons. prin., Indpls., 1982-88—; tchr. Palm Beach County, Boca Raton, Fla., 1988—; program supr. audio-visual center Ind. U., Bloomington, 1961-62; lectr. Butler U., summer 1965; cons. Ind. U., summer 1969. Contbg. mem. Childrens Mus.; mem. Indpls. Mus. Art, Indpls. chpt. Project HOPE; sponsoring mem. Met. Indpls. TV Assn., Inc., 1969-73; coordinator Christmas gift and hobby show Indpls. Public Schs., 1969-75. Bd. dirs. Young Audiences of Ind., 1969-80, co-chmn., 1976-78, chmn., 1977-78; bd. dirs. Indpls. chpt. Freedoms Found. at Valley Forge, 1st v.p., 1971-73, 75-77, 83—, pres., 1973-75, v.p., 1977-83, also awards, 1977-83. Recipient Am. Educators medal Freedoms Found., 1972. Mem. NEA (life), Ind. U. Alumni Assn. (life), Indpls. Zool. Soc. (charter), Ind. Tchrs. Assn., Bus. and Profl. Women's Clubs, Inc., Indpls. Council Adminstrv. Women Edn., (dir.), Nat. Soc. Study Edn., Nat. Congress Parents and Tchrs., Butler U. Alumni Assn., Nat. Elem. Prin. Assn., Ind. Edn. Art Assn., Hoosier Salon, Assn. Supervision and Curriculum Devel., Internat. Reading Assn., Indpls. Art League, Brown County Art Gallery Assn., Watercolor Soc. Ind., AAUW, Izaak Walton League Am., DAR, Alpha Chi Omega, Delta Kappa Gamma, Phi Delta Kappa (hon.), Pi Lambda Theta. Methodist. Clubs: Ind. Schoolwomens; Century, Indpls. Propylaeum, Indpls. Athletic, Women's Dept. Author monographs. Compiler, editor: Elementary School Principals Handbook, 1985. Home: Boca Raton, Fla. Died Apr. 21, 2007.

SIMON, BRADLEY ALDEN, librarian; b. Meriden, Conn., Mar. 9, 1929; s. Walter Henry and Rachel (Wetherbee) S.; student Shenandoah Coll., 1947-48; B.S., So. Conn. State Coll., 1951; M.S., Fla. State U., 1955; postgrad. U. Miami (Fla.), 1956-57, Ariz. State U., Tempe, 1965-66. Extension librarian, Ft. Meade, Md., 1955-56; base librarian Homestead AFB, Fla., 1956-57; asst. dir. libraries Pub. Library Charlotte and Mecklenburg County (N.C.), 1957-61; dir. libraries Volusia County Pub. Libraries, Daytona Beach, Fla., 1961-64; library cons. M. Van Buren, Inc., Charlotte, N.C., 1964; head librarian Central Piedmont Community Coll., Charlotte, 1964-65; cons. Colo. State Library, 1965-66; coordinator Ariz. Library Survey, Ariz. State U., 1966; library dir. Scottsdale (Ariz.) Pub. Library, 1966-71; city librarian Pomona (Calif.) Pub. Library, 1971-77, Newport Beach (Calif.) Pub. Library, 1977-78, Chula Vista (Calif.) Public Library, 1978—; exec. dir. Southeastern Pub. Library Sytem Okla.; cons. on bldg. and adminstrn. various libraries, Calif., N.C., Fla., Colo., Ariz.; pres. Pub. Library Film Circuit. Mem. Scottsdale Fine Arts Commn., 1966-71; adminstrv. council Met. Coop. Library System, Los Angeles. Served with Intelligence Service, USAF, 1951-53. Recipient John Cotton Dana Library Pub. Relations award, 1974, 75, 76; Hometown Builder award, 1975. Mem. ALA (bd. dirs. Pub. Library Assn. 1975-79), Ariz. (pres. pub. libraries sect. 1969-70), Calif., Southwestern library assns., Pub. Library Execs. So. Calif. (pres. 1975-76), Library Automation, Research and Cons. Assn. (steering com. 1969-71), Royal Arcanum, Nat. Mgmt. Assn., Pomona Municipal Mgmt. Assn. (dir.), Newport Harbor Art Mus., Newport Harbor C. of C., Pub. Library Dirs. (chmn. council Okla. 1987-88), Pomona Valley Hist. Soc., Kappa Delta Phi. Presbyterian. Club: Rotary. Contbr. articles to profl. jours. Died July 26, 2007.

SIMON, MORDECAI, religious organization administrator, minister; b. St. Louis, July 19, 1925; s. Abraham M. and Rose (Solomon) S.; m. Maxine R. Abrams, July 4, 1954; children: Ora, Eve, Avrom. BA, St. Louis U., 1947; MA, Washington U., St. Louis, 1952; MHL, Rabbi, Jewish Theol. Sem. Am., NYC, 1952, DD (hon.), 1977. Ordained rabbi, 1952. Rabbi in, Mpls., 1952-56, Waterloo, Iowa, 1956-63; exec. dir. Chgo. Bd. Rabbis, 1963-80, exec. v.p., 1980-95, exec. v.p. emeritus, 1995—2007. Nat. chaplain Jewish War Vets., 1977-78. Host: (weekly program) What's Nu?, Sta. WGN-TV, 1973-92. With AUS, 1943-46. Recipient citation Jewish War Vets., 1967, Boy Scouts Am., 1966, 74, 88, Chgo. chpt. Am. Jewish Congress, 1973, Chgo. Conf. Jewish Women's Orgns., 1973, Chgo. Bd. Rabbis, 1973, Rabbinical Svc. award of Appreciation, Jewish Theol. Sem. Am., 1988, Raoul Wallenberg Humanitarian award, 1989, citation and commendation Ill. Ho. Reps., 1995, Order of Merit, The Equestrian Order of the Holy Sepulchre of Jerusalem, 1996; Rabbi Mordecai Simon Day proclaimed by Gov. James Edgar, State of Ill., 1995. Mem. Rabbinical Assembly. Home: Highland Park, Ill. Died May 16, 2007.

SIMON, WILLIAM HENRY, information specialist; b. New Haven, Dec. 26, 1928; s. Henry Charles and Florence (Shaw) S.; A.A., Jr. Coll. Commerce, New Haven, 1948; B.A., U. Bridgeport, 1950; M.S. in L.S., Columbia, 1955; M.B.A., Western New Eng. Coll., 1964; m. Dorothy Elaine Beckett, Oct. 1, 1955; children— Stephen Eric, William Edward. Circulation desk asst. Sterling Meml. Library, Yale U., New Haven, 1951-52; profl. asst. bus. and technology dept. Bridgeport Public Library, Bridgeport, Conn., 1955-56; chief librarian New Haven Research Library Olin-Mathieson Chem. Corp., New Haven, 1956-61; tech. info. supr. Nuclear Power Systems, Combustion Engring., Inc., Windsor, Conn., 1961, mgr. info. and adminstrv. services, 1961-85, library, records mgmt cons., 1985—; research mgr. Miller, Starrett, West and Assos., Inc., mgmt. cons. and research firm, Hartford, 1961-62. Mem. Conn. adv. com. Inter-Library Coop., 1967-68; sub. chmn. adv. com. Conn. Public Library Standards, 1967-68; bd. dirs. Capitol Region Library Council, 1970-73. Chief merit badge counselor, dist. tng. chmn. Metacomet dist. Long Rivers council Boy Scouts Am., asst. dist. commr., vigil honor mem. Order of Arrow, Nat. Eagle Scout Assn. Publicity chmn. Windsor Republican Com., mem. Windsor Town Com.; justice of peace, 1965-73; chmn. bd. dirs. Windsor Public Library, 1969-74; vice-chmn. Windsor Red Cross Drive, 1962. Recipient Gen. Scholar, Sch. Library Sci., Columbia U., 1955; Wood Badge, Boy Scouts Am., 1972, Merit award, 1974. Mem. Nat. Micrographics Assn. (dir. chpt. 1979-80), Assn. Records Mgrs. Adminstrs., Assn. Conn. Library Bds. (chmn. public relations and publicity com., del.), Yale Library Assos., Am. Library Assn., Conn. Library Assn., Nat. Rifle Assn. (instr.), Nuclear Records Mgmt. Assn. (publs. chmn. 1977-79, adv. bd. 1980-84, charter mem.), Alpha Phi Omega, Beta Phi Mu. Episcopalian. Clubs: Masons (32 degree), Elks (chmn. youth activities com.), Green Mountain. Home: Windsor, Conn. Died Jan. 24, 2006.

SIMONS, LEWIS MARTIN, journalist; b. Paterson, NJ, Jan. 9, 1939; s. Abram and Goldie (Fleisher) S.; m. Carol Lenore Seiderman, Feb. 7, 1965; children: Justine, Rebecca, Adam P.D. BA, NYU, 1962; MS, Columbia U., 1964. Corr. AP, Kuala Lumpur, Singapore, Saigon, Denver, 1965-70, Washington Post, Bangkok, New Delhi, Washington, 1971-82; bur. chief Knight-Ridder Newspapers, Tokyo and Beijing, 1982-95; fgn. policy corr. Time mag., 1996-97; freelance writer, from 1997. Author: Worth Dying For, 1987; contbg. author: Crimes of War, 1999, The World of Islam, 2001, Breach of Faith, 2002; contbr. to Nat. Geog. mag., Smithsonian mag., Atlantic Monthly, N.Y. Times, Washington Post. With USMC, 1962-64. Recipient Grand prize and Investigative Reporting award Am. Newspaper Guild, 1981, Citation for Excellence, Overseas Press Club Am., 1983, Jessie Meriton White award Friends World Coll., 1986, Investigative Reporters and Editors award U. Mo., 1986, Award of Excellence, World Affairs Coun., 1984, 86, 89, 92, Pulitzer Prize, 1986, George Polk award, 1985, Malcolm S. Forbes award Overseas Press Club Am., 1986, 92, Gerald Loeb award UCLA, 1993, Alumni award Columbia U. Grad. Sch. Journalism, 2004; Edward R. Murrow fellow Coun. of Fgn. Rels., 1970-71. Mem. Fgn. Corrs. Club Japan (bd. dirs. 1991-92, pres., 1993-94), Washington Inst. Fgn. Affairs. Died June 14, 2006.

SIMONS, MARLENE JUANITA, state legislator, rancher; b. Deadwood, SD, July 1, 1935; d. Royal B. Mills and Elsie M. Snook; m. Frank Simons, Sept. 24, 1951; children: Greg, Linda, Sully. Grad. high sch., Sundance, Wyo. Mem. Wyo. Ho. of Reps., from 1979. Mem. various house coms. including chmn. Agr. com., v.chmn. Appropriations com., others; vice chmn. Pub. Lands Adv. Coun., 1986-90; with Farm Bur., Wyo.; rancher, outfitter; chmn. agr. com. Pres. Wyo. Multiple Use Coalition, Ranch A Restoration Found.; mem. Black Hills Multi-Use Coalition; mem. Madison water steering com. Black Hills Hydrology Study, Farm Bur. Rep. Women; leader 4-H. Republican. Home: Beulah, Wyo. Died Mar. 12, 2006.

SIMONS, SAMUEL STONEY, health consultant, retired bank executive; b. Charleston, SC, May 10, 1920; s. Albert and Harriet Porcher (Stoney) S.; m. Virginia Laurie Cooke, Sept. 9, 1944; children: Samuel Stoney, Richard C., Ellen Daniel, Anne Dixon, Elizabeth Gaillard. AB, Princeton U., 1942, postgrad., 1946. Successively market research analyst, asst. to exec. v.p., head new products dept., asst. mgr. research and devel. Smith Kline & French Labs., Phila., 1946-66; v.p. Western Savs. Bank, Phila., 1966-70, exec. v.p., 1970-77; prin. Third Age Inc., life care and long term care consultants, 1978-83; v.p. Berwind Realty Services, 1983-84. Vice pres. Children's Aid Soc., Children's Services, Inc.; chmn. bd. Chestnut Hill Hosp., 1974-78, Fox Chase Cancer Center; pres. Henrietta Tower Wurtz Meml. Found.; chmn. bd. Council Voluntary Child Care Agys., Phila., 1968-73; bd. chmn. Health and Welfare Council Phila., 1955-61; bd. dirs. Oncological Hosp. Bd. dirs. Tri-County Health and Welfare Council.; treas. Corp. Relief of Widows and Children of Clergymen in the Communion of Protestant Episcopal Ch. in Pa.; chmn. bnd. Springside Sch., 1961-66; chmn. Commn. on Ministry, 1978-84. Served with USNR, 1942-46. Decorated Purple Heart. Republican. Episcopalian (vestryman). Died Oct. 1, 2007.

SIMONSEN, VERNER MARVIN, osteopathic ophthalmologist and otorhinolaryngologist; b. Rome, N.Y., Nov. 3, 1931; s. Verner Marvin and Pauline Ann (Whitmeyer) S.; m. Cleona Eleanor Brooks, June 2, 1959; children— Kristine Pauline Simonsen Monas, Karin Diane. B.S., St. Lawrence U., 1953; D.O., Kirksville Coll. Osteopathy and Surgery, 1959. Intern Greencross Gen. Hosp., Cuyahoga Falls, Ohio, 1959-60; resident in ophthalmology and otorhinolaryngology Detroit Osteo. Hosp., 1962-65; practice osteo. medicine specializing in ophthalmology and otorhinolaryngology, Toledo and Perrysburg (Ohio), 1965—; mem. staff Parkview Hosp., also chmn. dept. ophthalmology and otorhinolaryngology; mem. staff Riverside Hosp., St. Luke's Hosp., Maumee, Ohio; instr. Ohio U. Coll. Osteopathy. Fellow Osteo. Coll. Ophthalmology and Otorhinolaryngology (cert.); mem. Toledo Dist. Osteopathy, Am. Osteo. Assn., Ohio Osteo. Assn., Ohio Med. Assn., Physician for Golden Gloves Boxing of Toledo. Republican. Methodist. Club: Brandywine Country. Lodges: Elks, Masons, Shriners. Home: Cape Coral, Fla. Died Apr. 20, 2007.

SIMPSON, DOROTHY MAE, educational administrator; b. Longview, Tex., Aug. 25, 1932; d. Duff and Eliza (Griffin) Hanson; m. Claude Simpson. B.S., Bishop Coll., 1953; M.Ed., Prairie View A & M U., 1978. Cert. tchr. mid-mgmt., Tex. Tchr., Dallas Ind. Sch. Dist., 1954-73, specialist in community relations, 1974-81, specialist in community affairs, 1982—; dir. NW dist. Bapt. Assn. North Tex., 1961—; dir. community relations Lincoln High Sch., Dallas, 1974-78; cons. Goodstreet Service Ctr., Dallas, 1981—. Author: BM&E Guide for Young People (Plaque 1970), 1969. Named Communicator of Yr., Dallas Ind. Sch. Dist., 1974; recipient Merit award Goodstreet Bapt. Ch., 1975, Merit award Bethel Bapt. Ch., 1981, Merit award R. L. Thornton Sch., 1982. Mem. Delta Sigma Theta. Democrat. Home: Dallas, Tex. Died June 5, 2007.

SIMPSON, JOHN W., lawyer; b. Pitts., Sept. 29, 1922; s. John E. and Gail (White) S.; m. Virginia S. Simpson, June 16, 1951; children— Thomas, William, Cynthia BA, U. Rochester, 1944; LL.B., Harvard U., 1948. Atty. CAB, Washington, 1949-51; atty. Western Air Lines, Los Angeles, 1952-67; assoc. Koteen & Burt, Washington, 1967-81, Kelley, Drye & Warren, Washington, from 1981. Served to 1st lt. U.S.Army, 1943-45, ETO Presbyterian. Home: San Diego, Calif. Died July 20, 2006.

SIMPSON, JOHN WISTAR, retired utilities executive; b. Glenn Springs, SC, Sept. 25, 1914; s. Richard Caspar and Mary (Berkeley) S.; m. Esther Slattery, Jan. 17, 1948 (dec. 2004); children: John Wistar, Carter B., Patricia A., Barbara J. Student, Wofford Coll., 1932-33, DSc, 1972; BS, U.S. Naval Acad., 1937; MS, U. Pitts., 1941; DSc (hon.), Seton Hill Coll., 1970. With Westinghouse Electric Corp., 1937-77; mgr. Navy and Marine switchboard engring., switchgear div., on leave as mgr. nuclear engring. Daniels pile group, Oak Ridge Nat. Lab., successively as Westinghouse Electric Corp. (Bettis Atomic Power div.), 1949-58; v.p. Westinghouse Electric Corp.; gen. mgr. Westinghouse Electric Corp. (Bettis atomic power lab.) 1958-59, v.p., gen. mgr. atomic power divs., 1959-62, v.p. engring. and research, 1962-63, v.p. electric utility group 1963-69, pres. power systems, corp. exec. v.p., dir., 1971-77, chmn. bd. Internat. Energy Assocs. Ltd., 1976-80; pres. Simpson Bus. Services, Inc., 1980-86; v.p. Sea Pines Assocs., Hilton Head Island, SC, 1989-91, also bd. dirs., 1987-91; bd. dirs. Sea Pines Real Estate Cos., Hilton Head Island, SC, 1987-91. Pvt. energy cons.; mem. adv. bd. Lawrence Livermore Nat. Lab. Fusion, 1975-88; mem. Naval Tech. Mission to Japan, 1945; del. 1st Internat. Conf. on Peaceful Uses Atomic Energy, Geneva, Switzerland, 1955, Conf. on Peaceful Uses Atomic Energy (2d Internat. Conf.), 1958; chmn. Atomic Indsl. Forum, 1974-75; mem. energy research adv. bd. Dept. Energy, 1981-83; chmn. com. on outlook for fusion hybrid and tritium breeding fusion reactors NRC; mem. sci. adv. bd. Notre Dame, 1974-86. Author: Nuclear Power from Underseas to Outer Space, 1994. Mem. governing bd. Nat. Coun. Chs., 1979-81; trustee Seton Hall Coll., 1969-76, Point Park Coll., 1973—, Wofford Coll., 1973-87. Recipient Navy cert. of merit for civilian svc. in World War II, 1947, Gold medal for advancement of rsch. Am. Soc. Metals 1973, Disting. Alumnus award U. Pitts., 1975. Fellow IEEE (Edison medal 1971), ASME (hon. mem., George Westinghouse Gold medal 1975), Am. Nuclear Soc. (pres. 1973, Henry Dewolf Smyth Nuclear Statesman award 1997); mem. Nat. Acad. Engring., Franklin Inst. (Newcomen Gold medal), Rolling Rock Club (Ligonier, Pa.), Daufuskie Island Club, Bear Creek Golf Club, Sea Pines Club (Hilton Head, S.C.). Died Jan. 4, 2007.

SIMPSON, RILEY JAMES, lawyer; b. Mobile, Ala., Aug. 27, 1943; s. Vernon Denson and Genoa Marie (Schaubhut) S.; m. Mary Ladshaw, Aug. 21, 1964; children— Andrew, Peter, Bronwyn. B.A., William Carey Coll., 1965; J.D., U. Tex., 1967; postgrad. Mary Hardin Coll., 1968. Bar: Tex. 1967, U.S. Dist. Ct. (we. dist.) Tex. 1969, U.S. Ct. Appeals (5th cir.) 1981. Sole practice, Copperas Cove, Tex., 1969—; city atty., Copperas Cove, 1969—. Del., Tex. State Democratic Conv., 1972, 76, 80. Recipient Meritorious Service award V.F.W., 1973. Mem. Assn. U.S. Army, Tex. City Attys. Assn., Am. Assn. Hosp. Attys., Tex. Bar Assn., Bell Mills Lampasas Bar Assn., Coryell County Bar Assn. (pres. 1972-74), 52d Dist. Bar Assn. (pres. 1974-75). Baptist. Clubs: Exchange, Masons. Contbr. articles to prof. jours. Home: Baytown, Tex. Died June 4, 2007.

SIMS, BENNETT JONES, minister, educator; b. Greenfield, Mass., Aug. 9, 1920; s. Lewis Raymond and Sarah Cosett (Jones) S.; children: Laura (Mrs. John P. Boucher), Grayson, David. AB, Baker U., 1943, LHD (hon.), 1985; postgrad. Princeton Theol. Sem., 1946-47; BD, Va. Theol. Sem., 1949, DD, 1966, U. South, 1972; Merrill fellow, Harvard U., 1964-65; postgrad., Cath. U., 1969-71. Ordained to ministry Episc. Ch. as deacon, 1949, priest, 1950. Rector Ch. of Redeemer, Balt. 1951-64; dir. continuing edn. Va. Theol. Sem., 1966-72; bishop of Atlanta, 1972-83; vis. prof. theology Emory U., Atlanta, 1980-88, founder Inst. for Servant Leadership, from 1988; priest-in-charge St. Alban's Ch., Tokyo, 1962, 69. Author: Invitation to Hope, 1976, Purple Ink, 1982, Servanthood: Leadership for the Third Millennium, 1997, Why Bush Must Go, A Faith Based Challenge, 2004, The Time of My Life, a Autobiography of Hope, 2006. Trustee U. of South. With USNR, 1943-46. Named Young Man of Yr. Balt. C. of C., 1953; Disting. Alumnus of Yr., Baker U., 1972 Episcopalian. Died July 1[illegible] 2006.

SIMSON, THEODORE R., banker; b. N.Y.C., Sept. 17, 191[illegible]; s. Abe and Molly (Polly) S.; m. Bevlyn Thall, Mar. 25, 193[illegible]; children— Sherran Simson Blair, Douglas. B.A., Ohio State U., 1939. C.P.A., Ohio. Chmn. bd. First Community Bank, Columbus, 1984—, pres., 1960-83; chmn. bd. First Investment Co. Columbus, First Real Estate Investment Co. of Ohio, Simson First Found. Recipient Civic award, Columbus Jr. Theatre, 197[illegible]; Disting. Service award Columbus Art League, 1982. Named Man of the Year, Temple Israel, 1978. Mem. Bd. Realtors, Ohio Soc. C.P.A.'s, Ohio Mortgage Bankers Assn. (pres. 1970, trustee 1972-76). Died Jan. 1, 2006.

SINGER, ARMAND EDWARDS, foreign language educator; b. Detroit, Nov. 30, 1914; s. Elvin Satori Singer and Frederick Elizabeth (Edwards) Singer Goetz; m. Mary Rebecca White, Aug. 8, 1940 (dec. Mar. 11, 2004); 1 child, Fredericka Ann Hi[illegible]. AB, Amherst Coll., Mass., 1935; MA, Duke U., Durham, NC, 1939, PhD, 1944; Diplôme, U. Paris, 1939; postgrad., Ind. U., Bloomington, 1964. Teaching fellow in sci. Amherst Coll., Mass., 1935—36; instr. French and Spanish, part-time Duke U., Durham, NC, 1938—40; from teaching fellow Romance lang. to prof. emeritus W.Va. U., Morgantown, 1940—80, prof. emeritus, 1980—2007. Dir. annual colloquium modern lit. and film W.Va. U., 1976—80, 1985—86, 1996—97, 1999—200[illegible], 2005, 07; W.Va. U. rep. Da Ponte Inst. for Librettologie Don Juan Forschung und Sammlungsgsochichte, from 2005. Author: A Bibliography of the Don Juan Theme: Versions and Criticism, 1954, The Don Juan Theme, Versions and Criticism: An Annotated Bibliography, 1965, Paul Bourget, 1975, The Don Juan Theme: A Bibliography of Versions, Analogues, Uses, and Adaptations, 1993, supplement, 2003, The Armand E. Singer Tibet, 1809-1975, 1995, supplement, 1998, The Armand [illegible] Singer Nepal, 1772-1961 and Beyond, 1997, The Officials [illegible] Tibet, 1999, The Chinese Presence in Tibet, 2002, The Essa[illegible] and Proofs of Tibet, 2004, 2d edit., 2006,(with J.F. Stasn[illegible]) Anthology of Readings: Humanities I, 1966, Anthology [illegible] Readings: Humanities II, 1967, (with R.F. Gould) A Grade[illegible] Catalog of Himalayan Mountaineering Correspondence, 200[illegible], 2d edit. rev. and enlarged, 2006; editor: West Virginia Geor[illegible] Sand Conference Papers, 1981, (with Jürgen E. Schlunk) Mart[illegible] Walser: International Perspectives, 1987, Doctor Faustus: A[illegible]chetypal Subtext at the Millennium, 1999; editor W.Va. [illegible] Philol. Papers, 1948-50, 53-55, editor-in-chief, 1951-52, 195[illegible] 2004, co-editor, 2005—; editor: 1001 Horny Limericks by Wa[illegible]

Marden, 1996, 500+ of Marden's Favorite Limericks, 2004; editor, contbr. Essays on the Literature of Mountaineering, 1982; bd. editors, The European Legacy, 2003-; contbr. numerous articles to profl. and philatelic jours. Bd. dirs. Cmty. Concert Assn., Morgantown, 1959—60, Humanities Found. W.Va., 1981—87. Recipient 4th Ann. Humanities award, W.Va. Humanities Coun., 1990, Armand E. and Mary W. Singer Professorship in Humanities named in honor of Armand Singer and wife Mary Singer, 1999. Mem. MLA (internat. bibliography com. 1956-59, nat. del. assembly 1975-78), So. Atlantic MLA (exec. com. 1971-74), Am. Assn. Tchrs. Spanish and Portuguese, Am. Philatelic Soc., Nepal and Tibet Philatelic Study Cir. (pres. 1999-2007), Nepal Philatelic Soc., Collectors Club of N.Y., Phi Beta Kappa. Republican. Home: Morgantown, W.Va. Died July 12, 2007.

SINGER, DAVID HARRIS, lawyer; b. Wilkes-Barre, Pa., Apr. 3, 1947; s. Julian B. and Bernice (Albert) S.; m. Carol S. Seeherman, July 5, 1970; children— Julie Elayne, Shellie Hope. A.B., George Washington U., 1969; J.D., U. Miami, 1972. Bar: Fla. 1972, Pa. 1972, U.S. Dist. Ct. (mid. and so. dists.) Fla., U.S. Ct. Appeals (5th cir.), U.S. Ct. Appeals (11th cir.). Sole practice Law Offices D.H. Singer, Miami, Fla., 1973—. Mem. Fla. Bar, Dade County Trial Lawyers Assn., Acad. Fla. Trial Lawyers, Assn. Trial Lawyers Am. Home: Miami, Fla. Died June 6, 2006.

SIROTKIN, PHILLIP LEONARD, academic administrator; b. Moline, Ill., Aug. 2, 1923; s. Alexander and Molly (Berghaus) S.; m. Cecille Sylvia Gussack, May 1, 1945; children— Steven Marc, Laurie Anne. BA (McGregor Found. scholar), Wayne State U., 1945; MA, U. Chgo., 1947, PhD (Walgreen Found. scholar, Carnegie fellow), 1951. Lectr. U. Chgo., 1949-50; instr. Wellesley Coll., 1950-52, asst. prof. polit. sci., 1953-57; assoc. dir. Western Interstate Commn. Higher Edn., Boulder, Colo., 1957-60; exec. asst. to dir. Calif. Dept. Mental Hygiene, Sacramento, 1960-63; asst. dir. NIMH, 1964-66, asso. dir., 1967-71, cons., 1971-73; exec. v.p., acad. v.p. State U. N.Y. at Albany, 1971-76; exec. dir. Western Interstate Commn. Higher Edn., Boulder, Colo., 1976-90, sr. adviser, from 1990, Midwestern Legis. Higher Edn. Steering Com., Boulder, Colo., 1990-91; sr. cons. Midwestern Higher Edn. Commn., from 1991; mem. oversight com. Hispanic Agenda, Larasa, 1992-98. Cons. Nebr. Post-Secondary Edn. Commn., 1994; nat. adv. com. Soc. Coll. and Univ. Planning, 1976, adv. panel, rev. state system higher edn. in N.D., 1986, gov.'s com. on bi-state med. edn. plan for N.D. and S.D., 1988-90, Edn. Commn. States' Nat. Task Force for Minority Achievement in Higher Edn., 1989-91; cons. Bur. Health Manpower Edn., NIH, 1972-74, Nat. Ctr. Health Svcs. Rsch., 1975-85; spl. cons. AID, 1963-64; case writer Resources for the Future, 1954-55; mem. 1st U.S. Mission on Mental Health to USSR, 1967. Author: The Echo Park Dam Controversy and Upper Colorado River Development, 1959. Bd. dirs. Council Social Work Edn., 1959-60. 1st lt. AUS, 1943-46. Recipient Faculty Rsch. award Wellesley Coll., 1956, Superior Svc. award HEW, 1967, Founder award Midwestern Higher Edn. Commn., 1999. Achievements include had Phil Sirotkin award established by Midwestern Higher Edn. Commn. for role as founding father of the commn., 1999. Home: Boulder, Colo. Died Apr. 4, 2007.

SISSON, GEORGE ALLEN, SR., physician, educator; b. Mpls., May 11, 1920; s. Clark R. and Alberta (Chatfield) S.; m. Mary Alice Reed, Mar. 25, 1944; children: Marjorie Ann Sisson Swelsted, George Allen, Kathryn Alberta. AB, Syracuse U., 1942, MD, 1945. Intern Syracuse Med. Ctr., 1945-46, Bellevue Hosp. NYU Postgrad. Sch., 1948-49; resident Manhattan Eye, Ear and Throat Hosp., NYC, 1949-51, Am. Cancer Soc. head and neck fellow, 1952-53; practice medicine specializing in head and neck surgery Syracuse, 1953-67, Chgo., 1967; prof., chmn. dept. otolaryngology, head and neck surgery Northwestern U. Med. Sch., 1967-89, prof. and chmn. emeritus, from 1989. Prof. otolaryngology, bronchoesophagology Rush Med. Coll., Chgo; sr. attending physian dept. otolaryngology-head and neck surgery Rush-Presbyn.-St. Luke's Med. Ctr., Chgo.; attending physician Holy Family Med. Ctr., Des Plaines, Ill.; chmn., rehab. com. head and neck surgery Northwestern Meml. Hosp., 1967-89; sr. attending physician Cook County Hosp., 1989—; chmn., rehab. com. head and neck surgery Ill. div. Am. Cancer Soc.; adv. com. Nat. Inst. Neurol. Disease, 1975-78 Editorial bd.: Archives of Otolaryngology, Head and Neck Cancer Jour.; contbr. articles to profl. jours. and chpts. to books; producer films illustrating operative techniques for facial plastic and reconstructive surgery. Capt. M.C. U.S. Army, 1946-48. Fellow ACS (gov. 1965, adv. com. 1967-68, cancer comm. 1986—), Am. Acad. Otolaryngology-Head and Neck Surgery (pres. 1983); mem. Am. Laryngeal, Rhinol. and Otol. Soc., Am. Soc. Head and Neck Surgery (pres. 1969-70), Assn. Acad. Depts. Otolaryngology (pres. 1978-79), Soc. Univ. Otolaryngologists (pres. 1971-72), Am. Acad. Facial Plastic and Reconstructive Surgery (v.p. 1972, pres. 1978-79), Soc. Head and Neck Surgeons, Am. Laryngol. Soc., Am. Bd. Otolaryngology (pres. 1979-83). Home: Hinsdale, Ill. Died Aug. 6, 2006.

SIVACEK, EMIL ELMER, engineering and general management executive; b. Chgo., Oct. 29, 1920; s. Michael and Anna (Ribnikar) S.; m. Virginia Louise Milcer, May 15, 1943; children— John Michael, James Elmer BMechE, Tri-State U., Angola, Ind., 1941; postgrad., Harvard U., 1960. With King Seeley Thermos, Ann Arbor, Mich., 1941-68, v.p., 1963-68; gen. plants mgr. Chrysler Corp., Detroit, 1968-80, v.p., 1980-82; pres. Chrysler Def., Inc., Detroit, 1980-82; sr. v.p. Hoover Universal, Inc., Ann Arbor, Mich., from 1982. Dir. Great Lakes Fed., Ann Arbor, Control Gaging, Inc., Patentee in field Bd. dirs. Ocean Trail Condominium, Jupiter, Fla., 1982— Recipient Disting. Service award Tri-State U., 1966 Mem. Tau Beta Pi, Tau Sigma Eta Clubs: Barton Hills Country (pres. 1982-83), Ann Arbor Bus. Men's, Harvard Bus. Sch. (Ann Arbor). Republican. Avocations: gun collection; golf. Home: Ann Arbor, Mich. Died Jan. 22, 2007.

SKEEN, HENRY GENE, army officer; b. Dale County, Ala., May 26, 1933; s. Mark Pomeroy Skeen and Willie Mae (Bass) Brooks; m. Pauline E. Kean BS, U. Omaha, 1964; M.Ed., Boston U., 1969; grad., Army War Coll., 1976, Armed Forces Staff Coll., 1969. Commd. 2d lt. U.S. Army, 1953, advanced through grades to maj. gen., comdr. 88th Supply and Service Bn., Vietnam, 1971-72, comdr. Regional Support Command, 1972, chief functional software div., Computer Systems Command, Ft. Belvoir, Va., 1972-73, chief systems devel. bd., Army Materiel Command Alexandria, Va., 1973-75, comdr. Logistics Evaluation Agy. New Cumberland, Pa., 1976-77, comdr. Burtonwood Army Depot Burtonwood, Eng., 1977-79, dep. comdr. readiness 32d Army Air Def. Command Darmstadt, Fed. Republic Germany, 1979-80; asst. dept. chief staff logistics U.S. Army Europe, Heidelberg, Fed. Republic Germany, 1980-81; comdr. def. property disposal service U.S. Army, Battle Creek, Mich., 1981-83, comdr. Def. Indsl. Supply Ctr. Phila., 1983-84, dir. supply and maintenance, Office Dep. Chief of Staff for Logistics Washington, 1984-86, comdr. Troop Support Command St. Louis, from 1986. Decorated Def. Superior Service medal, Legion of Merit with oak leaf cluster, Bronze Star medal, Meritorious Service medal with 2 oak leaf clusters, Army Commendation medal with oak leaf cluster Baptist. Died Jan. 12, 2006.

SKINNER, CHARLES GORDON, chemistry educator; b. Dallas, Apr. 23, 1923; s. Charles Grady and Benona (Skiles) S.; m. Lilly Ruth Brown, Apr. 15, 1943; children— Robert Gordon, Gary Wayne BS, North Tex. State U., 1944, M.S, 1947; PhD, U. Tex., Austin, 1953. Prof. chemistry U. North Tex., Denton, from 1964, chmn. chemistry dept., 1969-76, chmn. dept. basic health scis., 1970-87; asst. dean basic sci. Tex. Coll. Osteo. Medicine, Fort Worth, 1976-79, coordinator research, 1976-84. Research chemist Celanese Corp., Corpus Christi, Tex., 1949-51; research scientist Clayton Found. Biochemistry, Austin, Tex., 1955-64; postdoctoral fellow U. Tex.-Austin, 1952-55 Contbr. articles to profl. jours.; patentee in field Bd. dirs. Denton Diabetic Assn., Tex., 1979-81 Research grantee NIH, NSF, Welch Found., Austin, Denton, 1957-87. Fellow Am. Inst. Chemistry, Tex. Acad. Sci. (v.p., chmn. 1968); mem. Am. Chem. Soc. (Doherty award 1978, counselor 1975), Am. Soc. Biol. Chemists. Avocation: woodworking. Home: Denton, Tex. Died May 2, 2007.

SKINNER, DOROTHY LAVERNE, chamber of commerce executive; b. Conway, Ark., Aug. 12, 1943; d. William Sykes and Reba Doyce (Mauldin) Mason; m. Allison Hardy Skinner, Dec. 23, 1961; children— Allison H., Christie Danette, Gary Bruce. Student Comml. Coll., 1961, U. Central Ark., 1978-81. Bookkeeper Robert F. Rabb Tax Preparer, Conway, 1970-75, Weinstein Realty Co., Northampton, Pa., 1975-77; sec. U. Central Ark., 1978-81; office mgr. Mason and Co., Kermit, Tex., 1981-82; sec., receptionist Sta. KERB, 1982; exec. dir. Kermit C. of C., 1982—; sec., KISD Vocat. Adv. Council, Kermit, 1982—. Inst. scholar C. of C. Execs. Assn. West Tex., 1984. Mem. Permian Basin C. of C. (sec. 1982-84, pres. 1985), C. of C. Execs. Assn. West Tex. (sec. 1983—, bd. dirs. 1984—) West Tex. C. of C., U.S. C. of C., Tex. C. of C. Execs. Democrat. Baptist. Home: Kermit, Tex. Died June 26, 2006.

SKIPPER, JAMES EVERETT, librarian; b. Bartow, Fla., Dec. 10, 1920; s. Glenn Blount and Nina (Bigham) S.; m. Florene Wilkins, Aug. 9, 1947 (div.); children: Glenn Michael, Nancy Sue; m. Margaret L. Meigs, June 10, 1961; children— William Meigs, Ann Meigs. AB, U. N.C., 1943; BS in L.S, U. Mich., 1948; MS in L.S, 1949, PhD, 1960; postgrad. (Carnegie fellow advanced library adminstrn.), Rutgers U., 1958. Asst. librarian Washington and Jefferson Coll., 1949-50; asst. acquisitions librarian, then acquisitions librarian Ohio State U., 1950-55; instr. library sci. U. Mich., 1954; asst. librarian tech. services Mich. State U., 1956-59; dir. libraries U. Conn., Storrs, 1959-63; exec. sec. Assn. Research Libraries, 1963-67; assoc. librarian Princeton Library, 1967-68; chief U. Calif. at Berkeley Library, 1968-71; exec. v.p. Kraus-Thomson Orgn., 1971-74; dir. Research Libraries Group, 1974-79; exec. dir. Midwest Regional Library Network, 1980-83. Contbr. articles to profl. jours. Served with AUS, 1943-45, ETO. Mem. ALA, Mich. Library Assn. (pres. coll. sect. 1957-58), New Eng. Library Assn., Conn. Library Assn., Franklin County (Ohio) Library Assn. (pres. 1953-54), Mich. Acad. Arts, Letters and Sci., Conn. Acad. Arts and Scis., Phi Eta Sigma, Beta Phi Mu. Clubs: Cosmos, Yale. Home: Tucson, Ariz. Died Nov. 4, 2005.

SKLAR, ALEXANDER, electric company executive; b. NYC, May 18, 1915; s. David and Bessie (Wolf) S.; m. Hilda Rae Gevarter, Oct. 27, 1940; 1 dau., Carolyn Mae (Mrs. Louis M. Taff). Student, Cooper Union, NYC, 1932—35; MBA, Fla. Atlantic U., 1976. Chief engr. Aerovox Corp., New Bedford, Mass., 1933-39; mgr. mfg., engring. Indsl. Condenser Corp., Chgo., 1939-44; owner Capacitron Inc., 1944-48; exec. v.p. Jefferson Electric Co., Bellwood, Ill., 1948-65; v.p., gen. mgr. electro-mechs. divsn. Essex Internat., Detroit, 1965-67. Advisor, bd. dirs. various corps.; vis. prof. mgmt. Fla. Atlantic U., Boca Raton, 1971-92, ret., 1993; lectr. profl. mgmt. UCLA, Harvard U. Grad. Sch. Bus. Adminstrn., U. Ill. Mem. Acad. Internat. Bus., Soc. Automotive Engrs. Died July 22, 2007.

SLACK, NELSON HOSKING, biostatistician; b. Burlington, Vt., Feb. 7, 1935; s. Errol C. and Ivy (Hosking) S.; m. Patricia Jane Billow, Sept. 10, 1960; children— Gregory and Gordon (twins), Brian. B.S., U. Vt., 1957; M.S., Rutgers U., 1963, Ph.D., 1964. Research asst. Rutgers U., New Brunswick, N.J., 1959-64; cancer research scientist Roswell Park Meml. Inst., Buffalo, 1964-66, sr. cancer research scientist, 1966-70, assoc. cancer research scientist, 1970—, head collaborative studies service unit in biostats., 1966-74, program in biometrics and epidemiology, 1974-77, statistician for nat. prostatic cancer program, 1977-84, dept. biomath., 1984—. Contbr. articles to profl. jours., chpts. to books. Served with U.S. Army, 1957-59. Nat. Cancer Inst. grantee, 1966-74. Mem. Am. Assn. Cancer Research, Am. Statis. Assn., AAAS, Sigma Xi. Avocations: hunting; skiing; gardening; raising beef cattle. Home: Waterville, Vt. Died Aug. 15, 2007.

SLAMECKA, VLADIMIR, retired information scientist; b. Brno, Czechoslovakia, May 8, 1928; came to U.S., 1956, naturalized, 1961; s. Alois and Kristina (Vasicek) S.; m. Elba I. Seoane, Oct. 1962; children— John Vladimir, Alois William. MS, Columbia, 1958, D. Libr. Sci., 1962; postgrad., U. Sydney, Australia, 1951-53, U. Munich, Germany, 1954-56. Chem. engr. Brookvale Brewery, New South Wales, 1953-54; head chemistry librarian Columbia, 1958-62; mgr. spl. studies Documentation, Inc., Bethesda, Md., 1963; mgr. cancer chemotherapy Nat. Data Service, Documentation, Inc., 1964; prof. Sch. Info. and Computer Sci., Ga. Inst. Tech., Atlanta, 1964-88, prof. emeritus, from 1988, dir. Sch. Info. and Computer Sci., 1964-78. Vis. prof. Emory U., 1968, clin. prof. Sch. Medicine, 1979—; cons. NAS, NSF, UN, OAS, HEW, USAF, Washington, Computer Scis. Corp., Scott Paper Co., Coca-Cola Co., Aqua-Ion Co. Author: Science in Czechoslovakia, 1963, Science in East Germany, 1963, The Coming Age of Information Technology, 1965, Studies in Technical Data Management, 1967, National Science Information Systems, 1972, all monographs, also articles. Mem. Sigma Xi. Patentee in field. Home: Atlanta, Ga. Died June 17, 2006.

SLAUGHTER, LOGAN ALLEN, lawyer; b. Ft. Benning, Ga., Feb. 11 1942; s. Wilbur Logan and Florence Elizabeth (Ray) S.; m. Barbara Jean Waddell, Nov. 23, 1967; 1 child, Stacy Elizabeth. B.A., U. Miss., 1964; J.D., U. Ark., 1971. Bar: Ark. 1971, Tex. 1973, U.S. Dist. Ct. (ea. dist.) Ark. 1971, U.S. Dist. Ct. (so. dist.) Tex. 1975, U.S. Dist. Ct. (we. dist.) Tex. 1982. Assoc. Rose Law Firm, Little Rock, 1971-73; dist. counsel VA, Houston, Tex., 1973—. Contbr. to legal publs. Served to capt. U.S. Army, 1964-66. Mem. Tex. Bar Assn., Fed. Bar Assn. (bd. dirs.). Baptist. Home: Houston, Tex. Died Jan. 13, 2007.

SLAVENS, WALTER DONALD, manufacturing executive; b. Newport, RI, June 3, 1952; s. Thomas I. and Gloria A. (Wilkins) S.; m. Ruth Ann Cottrell; children: Jennifer, Jeffrey. BBA, Bryant Coll., 1974. Cost acctg. mgr. Pearson Yachts Div. Grumman, Portsmouth, Rhode Island, 1972-75, controller League City, Tex., 1975-77; cost mgr. Schlumberger Ltd., Sugarland, Tex., 1977-78; controller TPI, Warren, Rhode Island, 1978-80; cost acctg. mgr. Hasbro Inc., Pawtucket, Rhode Island, 1980-82, dir. tresury ops., 1982-84, treas., 1984-87, v.p., treas., from 1987. Mem. Fin. execs. Inst., Nat. Assn. Accts. Avocations: racquet ball, sailing, gardening. Home: Ocala, Fla. Died Apr. 14, 2006.

SLIGER, BERNARD FRANCIS, academic administrator, economist, educator; b. Chassell, Mich., Sept. 30, 1924; s. Paul and Hazel (MacLauchlin) S.; m. Greta Taube, Sept. 1, 1945; children: Nan, Paul, Greta Lee, Sten. BA in Econs. with high hons., Mich. State U., 1949, MA, 1950, PhD, 1955; postgrad., U. Minn., 1961-62. Mem. faculty La. State U., 1953-61, prof. econs., 1961, head dept., 1961-65, vice chancellor, dean acad. affairs, 1965-68; sec. adminstrn. State of La., 1968—69; sec.-treas. La. Office Bldg. Corp., 1969-72; organizer, exec. dir. La. Coordinating Council Higher Edn., 1969-72; prof. econs. Fla. State U., Tallahassee, 1973—2003, prof. econ. emeritus, from 2003, exec. v.p. Tallahassee, 1972-76, chief acad. officer, 1973-76, pres., 1977-91, interim pres., 1993, dir. univ.'s London Study Ctr., 1975, pres. emeritus, 1992—2003. Mem. staff sci. and tech. com. Fla. Ho. of Reps., 1979; mem. V.P. Mondale's Select Com. on Sci. and Tech., 1980; mem. bd. dirs. Fed. Res Bank of Atlanta, 1983-88; cons. econ. theory and pub. fin. to pvt. and pub. commns., orgns.; mem., chief cons. Gov. La.'s tax study com., 1968; formerly La. commr. adminstrn. and chief budget officer; mem. NCAA pres.'s commn., 1987-91. Author: (text) Public Finance, 1964, rev. edit., 1970, (with others) Municipal Finance Administration, 1976, rev.; contbr. to profl. publs. Vol. economist Tallahassee C. of C., 1977, Fla. C. of C., 1978; mem. Acad. Task Force for Review of the Ins. and Tort Systems, 1986-88; trustee The Nature Conservancy, 1986-2007; trustee Am. Coll. Testing Corp., 1981-87, chmn. 1985-87; ex-officio mem. Fla. Coun. 100. With C.E., U.S. Army, 1943-46. Named Dir. Practical Politics La. Ho. of Reps., 1969; Bernard F. Sliger Eminent scholar Chair in Econ. Edn. created in his name by Fla. State U., 1987, Bernard F. Sliger Bldg. dedicated at univ.-related rsch. park, Bernard F. Sliger Tower in Univ. Ctr. Bldg. dedicated, 1999. Mem. Kiwanis, Phi Beta Kappa, Omicron Delta Kappa, Phi Kappa Phi, Omicron Delta Epsilon, Alpha Kappa Psi, Beta Gamma Sigma, Phi Eta Sigma. Presbyterian. Home: Tallahassee, Fla. Died Oct. 10, 2007.*

SLOAN, RICHARD, artist; b. Chgo., Dec. 11, 1935; s. Samuel Theodore and Lelia (Beach) S.; m. Arlene Florence Miller, Aug. 11, 1962 (dec. June 1994). Attended, Am. Acad. Art, 1951-53. Advt. illustrator; staff artist Lincoln Park Zoo., Chgo.; master wildlife artist Leigh Yawkey Woodson Art Mus., 1994. One-man shows include N.C. Mus. Natural Scis., 2003, exhibitions include Explorer's Hall Nat. Geographic Soc., Brit. Mus. Natural History, Royal Scottish Acad., Carnegie Mus., Calif. Acad. Scis., Boston Mus. Sci., Am. Mus. Natural History, Nat. Collection Fine Art Smithsonian Inst., Washington, 1979, Leigh Yawkey Woodson Art Mus. (20 exhbns.), from 1979, Beijing Mus. Natural History, 1987, Roger Tory Peterson Inst. Natural History nat. mus. tour, 1993, James Ford Bell Mus. Nat. History, U. Minn., 1994; spl. guest artist 1st Vancouver Internat. Wildlife Art Show, 1994; Represented in permanent collections Smithsonian Inst., Leigh Yawkey Woodson Art Mus., Ill. State Mus., pvt. collections throughout world; contbr. Nat. Wildlife Stamp Program, World Wildlife Fund, internat. stamps; paintings featured in Nat. and Internat. Wildlife Mag., U.S. Art, Wildlife Art News, Ariz. Wildlife Mag., numerous others, artist, illustrator Ency. Brit., 1963, (book) Raptors of Arizona, 1998. Recipient Award of Excellence Cin. Mus. Nat. History, 1984, Award of Merit Anchorage Audubon Soc., 1985, Southwest Book award Border Regional Libr. Assn., 1998, Peoples Choice award Bonnet House, 2002; inducted into Ariz. Outdoor Hall of Fame, 2003. Mem.: Soc. Animal Artists (award of excellence 1990—98, People's Choice award 2002). Home: Palm City, Fla. Died Mar. 25, 2007.

SMALL, ROBERT SCOTT, textile company executive; b. Charleston, S.C., July 18, 1915; s. Robert Scott and Louise (Johnson) S.; m. Sallie Tyler, June 17, 1938; children— Sallie Small Johnson, Robert Scott, Oscar Johnson, Charles Innes, Elizabeth Johnson. B.S., Coll. Charleston, 1936; LL.D., Clemson U., 1964, Furman U., 1968, Coll. Charleston, 1970. Mgr. S.C. Nat. Bank, Pickens, 1936-38, asst. mgr., Greenville, 1938-41, cashier, trust officer, 1941-47, now dir., Charleston; pres., treas. Ottaray Textiles, Inc., Anderson, S.C., Haynsworth Mills, Anderson, 1947-51; v.p., dir. Woodside Mills, Greenville, S.C., 1951-58, pres., 1958-66; chief exec. officer, treas., dir.; pres., chief exec. officer Dan River Mills, Inc., 1966-77, chmn., chief exec. officer, from 1977; dir. So. Bell Tel. & Tel., Liberty Corp., Greenville, Piedmont Natural Gas Co., Charlotte, N.C., Textile Hall Corp., Greenville, Dan River Mills, Inc. Campaign mgr. United Fund, 1957; Trustee, chmn. Greenville Gen. Hosp., 1960-66, Coll. Charleston, 1960-66; trustee J.E. Sirrine Found.; adv. com. Furman U.; fin. com. Episcopal Ch. Home for Children. Mem. Am. Textile Mfrs. Assn. (past pres.), S.C. Textile Mfrs. Assn. (pres. 1963). Clubs: Green Valley Country (pres. 1961), Cotillion (sr. com. 1960-62), Greenville Country, Poinsett (all Greenville); Carolina Yacht (Charleston). Home: Greenville, SC. Died Aug. 24, 2007.

SMALLEY, BARBARA MARTIN, English educator; b. Connersville, Ind., Apr. 20, 1926; d. Floyd Stanley and Esther Anna (Davis) Martin; m. Donald Arthur Smalley, Sept. 8, 1952. B.S., Ind. U., 1954; M.A. in French, U. Ill., 1965, Ph.D. in Comparative Lit., 1968. Asst. prof. comparative lit. and English Lit., U. Ill., Urbana, 1968-75, assoc. prof. English and comparative lit., 1975—. Author: George Eliot and Flaubert: Pioneers of the Modern Novel, 1974; editor: Ranthorpe (G.H. Lewes), 1974; (with others) Third Force: Psychology and the Study of Literature, 1986; contbr. articles to profl. jours. Mem. Am. Comparative Lit. Assn., MLA, AAUP, Can. Comparative Lit. Assn., Internat. Comparative Lit. Assn. Died Aug. 6, 2006.

SMARIGA, LILLIAN ALLEN, accountant; b. Waco, Tex., Sept. 2, 1927; d. Homer Eugene and Lillian Louise (Smith) Allen; student U. Houston, 1964-65; m. Stanley Edward Smariga, Apr. 21, 1950; children— Robert, Melanie, Mary Hope, Russell. Bookkeeper, sec. Houston Carbide Corp., 1951-55; div. sec., bookkeeper, office mgr. Houston Carbide div. Firth Sterling, Inc., 1955-68; asst. to acctg. mgr. F. W. Gartner Co., Houston, 1968-70, asst. to acctg. mgr., office mgr., 1970-75, acctg. mgr., asst. sec.-treas., 1975—, controller, asst. sec.-treas., 1977—. Mem. Nat. Assn. Accts., Am. Soc. Women Accts. Republican. Episopalian. Home: Pasadena, Tex. Died July 25, 2007.

SMART, CHARLES RICH, retired surgeon; b. Ogden, Utah, Nov. 7, 1926; s. Junius Hatch and Avon (Rich) S.; m. Dorothea Jean Cannon Sharp, Dec. 23, 1952; children— Thomas, Edward, Christopher, Angela, Cynthia, David BS with honors, U. Utah, 1945; MD with honors, Temple U., 1955. Intern Los Angeles County Hosp., 1955-56; resident Hosp. U. Pa., Phila., 1956-61; asst. prof. surgery in residence UCLA, 1963-66; assoc. prof. surgery Coll. Medicine, U. Utah, 1966-69, cancer coordinator, 1967-69, clin. assoc. prof. surgery, 1969-75, clin. prof. surgery, 1975-85; mem. staff, chief of surgery Latter-day Saints Hosp., 1974-84; chmn. SEER Group Nat. Cancer Inst., 1976-78, chief community oncology and rehab. br., 1985-86, chief early detection br., 1987-92; ret., 1992. Dir. Rocky Mountain Coop. Tumor Registry, 1969-85; bd. dirs. Am. Cancer Soc., 1976-79 Contbr. research articles to med. jours. Fellow ACS; mem. Utah Med. Assn., AMA, Pan-Pacific Surg. Soc., Bay Surg. Soc., Los Angeles Surg. Soc., Salt Lake Surg. Soc., Internat. Soc. Chemotherapists, Am. Assn. Cancer Edn., Am. Soc. Clin. Oncology, Soc. Head and Neck Surgeons, Am. Soc. Surg. Oncologists, Alpha Omega Alpha Republican. Mem. Lds Ch. Home: Salt Lake City, Utah. Died Jan. 28, 2006.

SMART, DAVID LOUIS, retired finance executive; b. Dallas, Jan. 29, 1941; s. John Paul and Faye (McDonald) S.; m. Janice Bremer, Jan. 26, 1963; children: Robert, Sharon. BBA with honors, N. Tex. State U., 1963. Various positions, C.P.A. firms, 1963-69; mem. corp. staff Tyler Corp., Dallas, 1970-72, asst. treas., 1976-78, treas., 1979-89, v.p., 1985-89. V.p., sec., dir. Smart & Young, Inc., Dallas, 1973-75 Republican. Baptist. Home: Huntsville, Tex. Died Oct. 8, 2006.

SMART, JACOB EDWARD, management consultant, retired military officer; b. Ridgeland, SC, May 31, 1909; s. William Edward and Alma (Nettles) S.; m. Elizabeth Gohmert, Feb. 20, 1932 (div. 1946); children— Joan Elizabeth(dec.), Jacklyn Cabell, William Edward, Rosemary(dec.). Student, Marion Mil. Inst., 1926-27; BS, U.S. Mil. Acad., 1931; student, Nat. War Coll., 1949-50. Commd. lt. USAF, 1931, advanced through grades to gen., 1963, ret., 1966; served various posts U.S. and Europe, 1931-55; asst. vice chief of staff USAF, Washington, 1955-59; comdr. (12th Air Force), Waco, Texas, 1959-60; vice comdr. tactical air command Langley AFB, 1960-61; comdr. 5th Air Force and U.S. Forces in Japan, Japan, 1961-63, Cinc. Pacific Air Forces, 1963-64; dep. comdr. in chief U.S. European Command, 1964-66; ret., 1966; spl. asst. to adminstr. NASA, 1966-67, asst. adminstr. for policy, 1967-68; asst. adminstr. US Dept. Def., 1968-73; v.p. Earth Satellite Corp., Washington, 1973-75; cons., from 1975. Decorated D.S.C., D.S.M. with 4 oak leaf clusters, Legion of Merit, D.F.C., Air medal with 3 oak leaf clusters, Purple Heart, Commendation Ribbon; hon. comdr. Order Brit. Empire; Order of Service Merit 1st class Korea; Medal of Cloud and Banner with Grand Cordon China; comdr. Legion of Honor France; Order of Sacred Treasures Japan). Mem. Assn. Grads. U.S. Mil. Acad., Air Force Assn. Home: Arlington, Va. Died Nov. 12, 2006.

SMEDLEY, ALFRED BROADBELT, public relations executive; b. Media, Pa., June 13, 1927; s. Alfred Broadbelt and Frances Baker (Jones) S.; m. Mary Eleanor Burns, June 9, 1951; children— Lynn Smedley Jennings, Laurie Smedley Slinger, Steven A., Thomas A., Kristina L. B.S., Temple U., Phila., 1952. Reporter/columnist Fairchild Publs., Upper Darby News, Phila., 1952-57; v.p. APCL&K Public Relations, Phila., 1957-61; v.p. Burson-Marsteller, N.Y.C., 1961-65, v.p., asst. gen. mgr., Chgo., 1971-82, sr. v.p., dir. media relations, N.Y.C., 1983—; dir. corp. communications Scott Paper Co., Phila., 1965-71. Served with USN, 1944-47. Mem. Pub. Relations Soc. Am. (Silver Anvil award 1971), Nat. Investor Relations Inst., Soc. Profl. Journalists. Clubs: Glen Oak Country (Glen Ellyn, Ill.); Chgo. Press, Chgo. Athletic; Pickwick (Niles, Mich.). Died Feb. 18, 2006.

SMILEY, CLEERETTA HENDERSON, educator, home economist; b. Whatley, Ala., June 20, 1930; d. Edward and Rebecca Ann (Odom) Henderson; children: Consuela Angelia, Robert Edward, Lisa Kay, Joan Alyssa. BS, Miles Coll., 1954; MS, U. Md., 1971, postgrad., 1972-73, DD Ogun State Coll., Nigeria, 1988; diploma esoteric sci. and psychology Am. U., 1976. Correctional officer Fed. Reformatory for Women, Alderson, W.Va., 1954-55, culinary officer, 1955-56, tchr. home econs., 1956-61, asst. vocat. ednl. dir., 1959-61; tchr. gen. home econs. edn. D.C. Public Schs., 1963-80, asst. supervising dir. home econs., 1980-84, dir. Model HERO Youth Employment Tng. Program, Coolidge Sr. High Sch., 1975-80; state adv. for D.C., Future Homemakers Am./HERO, 1980-84; profl. spiritual counselor, transformation practitioner, 1970—; bd. dirs. Network of Light, Lorton Transformation Project, The Internat. Conf. of Clergy Alumni Assn., The Divine Universal Sisterhood, The Interfaith Conf. of Metro. Washington; condr. fashion shows, model; tchr. coord. Show Prodns. Tng. Program, 1967-80; mem. Home Econs. Adv. Coun., D.C. Pub. Schs. and Logan Community Sch. Adv. Coun.; practitioner esoteric sci. Minority affairs adv. to bd. dirs. Social Svcs. Agy., Eastern region Ch. Jesus Christ of Latter-day Saints, 1979-82, steering com. Genesis group, consulting liasion to pub. communications dir., stake missionary, edn. counselor Relief Soc., ward missionary, gospel essentials tchr., ward activities com.; mem. hosting com. Public Communications Council, Kensington, Md., 1979-81; co-chairperson Health Commn., D.C. PUSH, 1972-75; bd. dirs. Aum Spiritual Sci. Ctr., Washington, 1980-82; mem. First Spiritual Leadership Conf. Network Leaders, McLean, Va., 1981; mem. family and futures bd. dirs. of FHA; mem. Worldwide Peace Found, Washingon Peace Movement, Friends Kennedy Ctr.; mem. adv. coun. World U.; sr. fellow John F. Kennedy Library Found.; founder, dir. Higher Self Collective, 1990, I Am Prosperity Coun., 1990. Named Mrs. D.C., Mrs. America Pageant, 1968, Mrs. D.C. Savs. Bonds, 1968; Harambee Mother of Yr., Sta. WDVM-TV, 1969. Mem. Am. Vocat. Edn. Assn., D.C. Vocat. Edn. Assn., Future Homemakers Am. Home Econs. Related Occupations Youth Orgn., Nat. Assn. Black Am. Vocat. Educators (life), Am. Assn. Retired Persons, Nat. Collaboration of Youth Orgns., Nat. Assn. Female Execs., World Modeling Assn., Coun. Women Ministers of D.C. (life), Afro Am. Jubilee Commn., Am. Meta-Phys. Inst. Network Soc., Nat. Assn. Single Persons, Inst. Noetic Sci., Internat. Platform Assn., Nat. Hist. Preservation Soc., Brigham Young U. Mgmt. Soc., Iota Phi Lambda. Democrat. Club: Circle I Am. Lodges: Order Eastern Star, Majestic Eagles Inc. (internat. program devel.). Home: Silver Spring, Md. Died Aug. 7, 2006.

SMITH, ALBERT ALOYSIUS, JR., electrical engineer, consultant; b. Yonkers, NY, Dec. 2, 1935; s. Albert Aloysius and Jean Mary (Misiewicz) S.; m. Rosemarie Torricelli, Apr. 4, 1964 (dec. 1982); children: Denise, Matthew. BSEE, Milw. Sch. Engring., 1961; MSEE, NYU, 1964. Staff engr. Adler/Westrex, New Rochelle, NY, 1961-64; adv. engr. IBM, Kingston, NY, 1964-78, sr. engr. Poughkeepsie, NY, 1978-85, Kingston, 1985-91; cons., from 1991. Author: Coupling of External Electromagnetic Fields to Transmission Lines, 1977, Measuring the Radio Frequency Environment, 1985, Radio Frequency Principles and Applications, 1998. Com. chmn. Woodstock Boy Scout Troop 34, 1978-79; com. chmn. Woodstock Cub Pack 34, 1976-78. Served with USN, 1953-56. Recipient Outstanding Alumnus award Milw. Sch. Engring., 1981; Invention Achievement awards IBM, 1979, 90, Div. award, 1981. Fellow IEEE (tech. com. on electromagnetic environments, assoc. editor Trans. on EMC); mem. Am. Nat. Standards Com. Roman Catholic. Home: Valatie, NY. Died July 30, 2006.

SMITH, ANNA NICOLE (VICKIE LYNN HOGAN), television personality, model; b. Mexia, Tex., Nov. 28, 1967; d. Donald Eugene and Virgie (Hart) Hogan; m. Billie Smith, Apr. 4, 1985 (div. 1987); 1 child, Daniel (dec.); m. J. Howard Marshall II, June 27, 1994 (dec. Aug. 4, 1995); m. Howard K. Stern, Sept. 28, 2006; 1 child, Dannielynn Hope with Larry Birkhead. Former model for Guess? jeans; weekly gossip columnist Nat. Enquirer, from 2005. Spokesperson Trim Spa X32 (Ephedra Free), 2003—07. Actress: (films) Naked Gun 33 1/3: The Final Insult, 1994, The Hudsucker Proxy, 1994, To the Limit, 1995, Skyscraper, 1997, Illegal Aliens, 2006; (TV series) N.Y.U.K., 2000, The Anna Nicole Smith Show, 2002-04;(TV appearance) MadTV, 1998, Veronica's Closet, 1999, Ally McBeal, 1999; prodr., screenwriter, dir. (video) Anna Nicole Smith: Exposed, 1988 Named Playmate of the Month, Playboy mag., 1992, Playmate of the Yr., 1993. Died Feb. 8, 2007.

SMITH, CHARLES KENT, family medicine educator; b. Des Moines, June 30, 1938; s. Herman Joseph and Elizabeth (Opinham) S.; m. Patricia Hughes Moore, Sept. 1977; children: Laurence, Eleanor, Andrew, Matthew. BA, Northwestern U., 1960, MD, 1963, MS, 1964. Diplomate Am. Bd. Internal Medicine, Am. Bd. Family Practice. Rotating intern U. Mich. Hosp., Ann Arbor, 1963-64, asst. resident medicine, 1967-68; sr. rsch. fellow in medicine (endocrinology) U. Wash. Hosp., Seattle, 1968-70, resident dept. psychiatry, 1970-72, attending staff, 1972-85; instr. dept. internal medicine U. Wash., 1970-71, from instr., asst. prof. to assoc. prof. dept. family medicine, 1971-81, prof., 1981-85, acting chmn. dept., 1976, vice chmn. dept., 1977-85, affiliate Diabetes Rsch. Ctr., 1980-85; prof., chmn. dept. family and community medicine Ea. Va. Med. Sch., Norfolk, 1985-88, mem. dean's coun. chmn. and allied coms., mem. minority affairs coms., 1985-88; prof., chmn. dept. family medicine Case Western Res. U., Cleve., from 1988, Dorothy Jones Weatherhead prof. dept. family medicine, from 1992, acting vice dean Sch. Medicine, 1995-96; mem. com. on med. edn., med. coun. and allied coms. U. Hosps. Cleve., from 1988, chmn. com. med. edn., from 1992, dir. family medicine dept. Gen. practice, locum tenens, Wrangell, Alaska, May.-June, 1970; attending staff Children's Orthopedic Hosp., Seattle, 1972-85, Med. Ctr. Hosps., Norfolk, 1985-88, Children's Hosp. of King's Daughters, Norfolk, 1986-88; cons. family mediation panel Family Ct., Superior Ct. King County, Wash., 1976-80; co-presenter 6th Internat. Workshop/Seminar Life Planning Ctr., Practice and Edn. Primary Care Medicine, Jichi Med. Sch., Japan, 1983; vis. prof. Hunan Med. Sch., Changsha, Peoples Republic China, 1984; grant reviewer HHS, Health Resources Adminstrn., Bur. Health Professions, others. Author numerous abstracts, proc., book revs., articles in profl. jours.; reviewer Jour. Family Pactice, 1977-90, books Jour. AMA, 1977—. Capt. USAF, 1963-65. Royal Soc. Medicine U.K. travelling fellow, 1974; grantee prin. investigator Spl. Project Family Medicine, 78-61, U. Wash., 1981-86, Ea. Va. Med. Sch., 1986-89, 87-90, 88-91, Case Western U., 1988-94. Fellow ACP, Am. Acad. Family Physicians (mem. chpts. in Wash. Va., Ohio, others; mem. Soc. Tchrs. Family Medicine (constn. and by-laws com. 1982-84), Assn. Depts. Family Medicine (treas. 1988—), N.Am. Primary Care Rsch. Group (mem. exec. steering com., sec. 1977-80, co-chmn. 7th ann. meeting 1979), Am. Psychiat. Assn. Home: Cleveland, Ohio. Died Nov. 16, 2005.

SMITH, CHARLES PAUL, newspaper publisher; b. Hartford, Conn., Nov. 1, 1926; s. Thomas S. and Kathryn (Klingler) S.; m. Carolyn Calkins, Feb. 12, 1966; children: Charles, Timothy. BS, U.S. Naval Acad., 1947. Commd. ensign USN, 1947, advanced through grades to lt., line officer, 1947-58, resigned; mgr. Container Corp. Am., Phila., 1958-66, Chattanooga, 1966-68; pub. Daily Intelligencer, Doylestown, Pa., from 1968. Roman Catholic. Died Jan. 7, 2006.

SMITH, DAVID, chemistry educator; b. Fall Rivers, Mass. Nov. 7, 1939; s. Jacob M. and Bertha (Horvitz) S.; m. Renee Gutfreund, Nov. 23, 1968; children: Aliza, Miriam, Shimon, Shmuel, Yanky, Leeba, Aharon, Bryna, Esther. BS, Providence Coll., 1961; PhD, MIT, 1965. Instr. Bklyn. Coll., 1965-68; prof. Pa. State U., Hazleton, from 1969. Contbr. articles to profl. jours. including Jour. of Chem. Physics. Mem. Am. Chem. Soc., Am. Phys. Soc. Jewish. Home: Passaic, NJ. Died Apr. 2, 2007.

SMITH, DEUEL COILY, JR., deacon; b. Muskogee, Okla. Feb. 19, 1943; s. Deuel Coily and Jewell G. (Burkett) S.; m. Sharon Jean Mann, Dec. 3, 1960; 1 child, Rebekah. BA in Sociology, N.E. La. U., 1967, MA in Criminal Justice, 1981, MDiv, Episc. Theol. Sem. S.W., 1988. With Troop F, La. State Police, 1964-66; with Monroe (La.) Police Dept., 1966-69; Gov.'s Commn. on Law Enforcement, 1969-70; spl. agt. FBI, 1970-76; security cons. to bus. and industry, 1976-78; security mgr. Mid-Continent Wood Products Mfg. div. Ga.-Pacific Corp. Crossett, Ark., 1978-85; seminarian Episcopal Theol. Sem. of the S.W., Austin, Tex., 1985-88, deacon Episc. Ch., 1988—; lectr. corporate security mgmt. Ind. U., 1979-82. Vestryman, sr. warden, St. Mark's Episcopal Ch., Crossett, 1979-81. Served as M.P., U.S. Army, 1961-64. Mem. Am. Soc. Indsl. Security (charter mem. Ark.; cert. protection profl.), Republican. Lodges: Masons, Shriners (Monroe, La.). Home: Austin, Tex. Died Apr. 8, 2007.

SMITH, DONALD EUGENE, health facility administrator; b. Mishawaka, Ind., Oct. 15, 1936; s. Ernest Hartmann and Lucile Emma (Krumanaker) S.; m. Nancy Mae Jaffke, Sept. 2, 1961; children: Adam, Reid, Lynn. AB, Wabash Coll., 1959; MBA, U. Chgo., 1963. Adminstrv. resident Ind. U. Med. Ctr., 1960-61; assoc. dir. Ind. U. Hosps., 1966-72; pres. Henderson & Smith Corp., Indpls., 1978. Lectr. in health adminstrn. Ind. U., 1965-66, adj. asst. prof. in health adminstrn., 1966-78; ptnr. Carmel (Ind.) Care Ctr., Countryside Manor, Anderson, Ind., Dearborn Enterprises, Lawrenceburg, Ind., Rawlins House, Pendleton, Ind., Manor House of Carmel, Ind.; chmn. Ind. State Bd. Registration and Edn. Health Facility Adminstrs., 1969-82. Bd. dirs. Ind. U. Med. Ctr. Fed. Credit Union, 1965-68, Ind. Blue Cross, 1966-71; med. ctr. chmn. United Fund Drive, 1962-65; sec. Carmel (Ind.) Classic, 1979, v.p., 1981, pres., 1982-83; bd. trustees Wabash Coll., 1986—, mem. exec. com., 1986—, chmn. capital campaign drive, 1987-91, mem. long range planning com., 1985; active Hamilton County Rep. Fin. Com., 1990—. Fellow ACHS; mem. Am. Health Care Assn., Ind. Health Care Assn., Wabash Coll. Alumni Assn., U. Chgo. Hosp. Adminstrn. Alumni Assn., Woodland Country Club, Vero Beach Country Club. Home: Carmel, Ind. Died Feb. 2007.

SMITH, DOUGLAS LARUE, marketing executive; b. Madison, Minn., July 25, 1917; s. Julius Waldo and Blanche (LaRue) S.; m. Jean Hefty, Feb. 8, 1941 (dec. 1979); children: Pamela Jean (Mrs. Robert Graham), and Gregory Douglas.; m. Annie Kerwin, Mar. 20, 1982. BA, U. Minn., 1948. Employed with U.S. Gypsum Company, Chicago, Ill., 1938-42; account exec. Melamed-Hobbs, Inc. (advt.), Mpls., 1946-49; product mgr. Swift & Co., Chgo., 1949-53; account exec. Batten, Barton, Durstine & Osborn, 1953-55; advt. mgr. Johnson's Wax Co. Racine, Wis., 1955-56, dir. advt. and mktg., 1956-64; sr. v.p. Lennen & Newell, Inc., NYC, 1965-70; also dir., mem. exec. com.; sr. v.p. On-Line Decisions, Inc. (became Planmetrics, Inc. 1975), NYC, from 1970; exec. v.p. Planmetrics, Inc., NYC, 1981-88. Lectr. and author, 1988—; chmn. bd. dirs. Assn. Nat. Advertisers, N.Y.C., 1965; bd. dirs. Advt. Fedn. Am., 1961—, Advt. Assn. West, 1962— Author: Winged Foot Story, 1984, 94; editor Footnotes, Winged Foot's Historian, 1984—. Mem. exec. com. Rep. Party N.Y.C.; founder German-Am. Peace Monument, 1994. Maj., inf. AUS, 1942-46, ETO. Decorated Silver Star and Bronze Star with bronze oak leaf cluster, Combat Infantryman's Badge, Purple Heart. Mem. Am. Assn. Advt. Agys. (gov. Ea. divsn.), Internat. Radio and TV Soc. (dir., treas. Univ. Club (N.Y.C., Chgo.), Mid-Am. Club (Chgo.), Winged Foot Golf Club. Home: Rye Brook, NY. Died June 16, 2007.

SMITH, EDWARD PHILIP, legal association administrator; b. Providence, Dec. 24, 1923; s. Joseph E. and Madge F. (Lynch) S.; m. Barbara Masterson, July 18, 1954; children: Anne Marie, Susan, Edward. BBA, U. R.I., 1948. Sales rep. Burroughs Bus. Machines, Providence and Detroit, 1948-51; alumni sec. U. R.I., Kingston, 1951-54; personnel mgr. Acushnet Process, New Bedford, Mass., 1954-58; exec. dir. R.I. Bar Assn., Providence, 1958-87, exec. dir. emeritus, from 1987. Mem. Nat. Assn. Bar Execs. (pres. 1973-74, treas. 1969-71, Bolton award 1984), New Eng. Bar Assn. (treas./sec. 1978-79, 84-85), Am. Soc. Assn. Execs. (New Eng. bd. dirs. 1979-80, 87-88), U. R.I. Alumni Assn. (pres. 1964). Home: Providence, RI. Died Aug. 2007.

SMITH, ELWIN EARL, mining and oil company executive; b. Ellicottville, NY, Sept. 30, 1922; s. Henry B. and Beatrice M. (Spellman) S.; m. Mary Ellen Kirchmaier, Nov. 4, 194 children: Peter E., Michael E., Timothy E. Student, U. Ala., 1940, NYU, 1954, Harvard Bus. Sch., 1962. Sales engr. Cities Service Oil Co., NYC, 1949-55; gen. sales mgr. Climax Molybdenum Co., NYC, 1955-64; exec. v.p., dir. Lithium Corp. Am., Gastonia, N.C., 1964-69, pres., CEO, 1969-77; v.p. Gulf Resources & Chem. Co., Houston, 1970-77; pres., dir. Asia Lithium Corp., Osaka, Japan, 1970-77; pres. Amax Iron Ore, Greenwich, Conn., 1977-80, corp. v.p., group exec. for indsl. minerals and resources group, 1978-80; exec. v.p. Amax Inc., Greenwich, 1981-82, sr. exec. v.p., 1982-85; prin. Elwin Smith Internat. Sales Engrs., Darien, Conn., from 1986. Bd. dirs. Am. Metal & Coal Co., Greenwich, Conn., Freeport Copper & Gold, Ethanol Corp., Sydney, Australia, First Dynasty Mines, Denver, IMR Industries, Ltd., London; chmn. Seven Seas Cinema, Stamford, Conn., 1985-95. 1st lt. U.S. Army Paratroopers, 1943-48. Decorated Combat Inf. badge, Bronze Star, sr. parachute badge. Mem. AIME, Am. Petroleum Inst., Am. Chem. Soc., Am. Australian Assn., Japan Soc., Asia Soc., Mining and Petroleum Club of Sydney, Copper Club N.Y., Weeburn Country Club, Masons. Republican. Died Apr. 25, 2007.

SMITH, EUGENE VALENTINE, chemical engineer; b. Ossian, Ind., Jan. 7, 1924; s. Keith R. and Clona M. (Valentine) S.; B.S. in Mech. Engring., Purdue U., 1948; s. Maxine Louise Byerly, May 19, 1945; children— Penelope Ann, Rebecca Jo Smith Schinderle. Mech. engr., plant engr. Stanolind Oil and Gas Co., Midwest, Wyo., 1948-54; sr. project engr. Amoco Chems. Corp., Brownsville, Tex., 1954-57, asst. chief plant engr., Texas City, Tex., 1957-61, ops. supr., 1961-65, supt. ops., Joliet, Ill., 1965-71, tech. dir., 1972—. Trustee Jesse Walker United Meth. Ch., 1968—, pres. trustees, 1972-74, v.p. bd., 1978—; mem. Will-Grundy Mfg. Environ. Control Commn., 1965—; dir. Homeowners Assn., 1971-74. Served with USAAF, 1943-45. Mem. ASME (past pres. Texas City chpt.), Am. Inst. Chem. Engrs. (dir. Joliet sect. 1976—), Assn. Energy Engrs., Three Rivers Mfg. Assn., Joliet C. of C., Pi Tau Sigma, Tau Beta Pi. Republican. Died Nov. 22, 2006.

SMITH, EUGENIA SEWELL, funeral home executive; b. Albany, Ky., Oct. 24, 1922; d. Leo Matheny and Marjorie (Warinner) Sewell; m. James Frederick Smith, June 25, 1948; 1 child, Bryson Sewell (dec.). Student Berea Coll., 1937-41, Bowling Green Coll. Commerce, 1944-45. Owner, operator Sewell Funeral Home, Albany, 1977—; bd. dir. Citizens Bank of Albany, Ky., 1989—. Sec. Albany Woman's Club, 1950-54; den mother Cub Scouts, Boy Scouts Am., 1958-62; pres. Clinton County Homemakers, Albany, 1968-70, Modern Homemakers, 1992-98; mission action chmn. Missionary Baptist Ch., 1965-91; v.p. Modern Homemakers Club of Albany, 1990-92, pres., 1994-98. Democrat. Lodge: Demolay Mother's (pres. Albany club 1966-67), Order Eastern Star (former assoc. conductress, former Martha and Esther). Home: Albany, Ky. Died Apr. 17, 2006.

SMITH, GARDNER WATKINS, physician; b. Boston, July 2, 1931; s. George Van Siclen and Olive (Watkins) S.; m. Susan Elizabeth Whiteford, Sept. 6, 1958; children: Elizabeth Whiteford, Rebecca Tremain, George Van Siclen II. Grad., Phillips Acad., 1949; MD, Harvard U., 1956; AB, Princeton U., 1969. Diplomate: Am. Bd. Surgery, Am. Bd. Thoracic Surgery. Intern Johns Hopkins Hosp., Balt., 1956-57, asst. resident, 1958-59, fellow, 1957-58, asst. in surgery, 1957-59, prof. surgery, 1970-96, emeritus prof. surgery, from 1996, dep. dir. dept. surgery, 1978-85. Asst. resident U. Va., Charlottesville, 1959-61, resident, 1961-62, asst. in surgery, 1959-63, cardiovascular resident, 1962-63, instr., 1963-65, asst. prof., 1965-67, assoc. prof., 1967-70, surgeon, 1963-70; chief surgery Balt. City Hosp., 1970-79, vis. surgeon, 1979-85; chmn. sect. surg. scis. Johns Hopkins Bayview Med. Ctr., 1985-96; bd. dirs. Blue Hill Meml. Hosp. Found., 1998-06, chair, 1999-00; bd. dirs. Blue Hill Meml. Hosp., 1998-05, chair, 2000-04; cons. Greater Balt. Med. Ctr., 1970-91, Loch Raven VA Hosp., Balt., 1971-92, Walter Reed Army Med. Ctr., 1976-90, Nat. Naval Med. Ctr., 1984-90; trustee Kneisal Hall, 2005—. Contbr. articles to med. jours. Mem. ACS, Soc. U. Surgeons, Am. Surg. Assn., So. Surg. Assn., Am. Gastroenterol. Assn., Assn. for Acad. Surgery, Balt. City Med. Soc., Halsted Soc., Med. and Chirurgical Faculty of Md., Soc. Surgery Alimentary Tract, Soc. Vascular Surgery, Internat. Cardiovascular Soc., So. Soc. Clin. Surgeons, Southeastern Surg Congress, So. Assn. Vasular Surgery, Va. Surg. Assn., Cum Laude Soc., Alpha Omega Alpha, Nu Sigma Nu. Died Oct. 5, 2006.

SMITH, GEORGE DEE, banker; b. Winston-Salem, NC, Nov. 23, 1929; s. George Franklin and Vera Virginia (Hilton) S.; m. Jeannine Rose Meacham, May 23, 1953; 1 dau., Dee Ann. AB, U. N.C., 1951. With R.J. Reynolds Tobacco Co., 1955-85, comptroller, 1970-72, v.p., chief fin. officer, 1972-73, sr. v.p., 1973-74, chmn. bd. dirs., chief exec. officer Macdonald Tobacco Can. subs., 1974-76; pres., chief oper. officer R.J. Reynolds Tobacco Internat., Inc., 1976-80; exec. v.p. R.J. Reynolds Tobacco Co., 1981-83, exec. v.p., asst. to pres. and chief exec. officer, 1983-85; pres., chief oper. officer 1st Home Fed., Greensboro, N.C., from 1986, also bd. dirs. Bd. dirs. Carolina Medicorp, Inc. Bd. dirs. Med. Park Hosp., Piedmont Entrepreneurs Network; trustee Old Salem, Inc.; trustee, chmn. Forsyth Mem. Hosp./Carolina Medicorp, Inc. Served to Lt. USNR, 1951-55. Mem. Greater Winston-Salem C. of C. (dir., pres. 1985-86). Home: Winston Salem, NC. Died June 15, 2006.

SMITH, HARDING EUGENE, astrophysicist; b. San Jose, Calif., May 10, 1947; s. Harding Eugene and Frances Bernice S.; m. Carol Jean Lonsdale, Aug. 26, 1989. BS, CalTech, 1969; PhD, U. Calif., Berkeley, 1974. Asst. rsch. physicist U. Calif., San Diego, 1974-78, asst. prof. physics, 1978-80, assoc. prof. physics, 1980-86, prof. physics, from 1986; vis. assoc. Calif. Inst. Technology, Pasadena, from 1989. Cons. in field. Author: Understanding Space & Time; contbr. articles to profl. jours. Mem. AAAS, Am. Astron. Soc., Internat. Astron. Union, Astron. Soc. Pacific. Achievements include rsch. in physics of emission regions in active galaxies; rsch. in nature of quasar absorption lines and relation to galaxy formation; chem. and phys. evolution of galaxies. Home: Encinitas, Calif. Died Aug. 16, 2007.

SMITH, HARRIET FULLEN, author, civic worker; b. Vincennes, Ind., Sept. 12, 1906; d. William Martin and Zola (Stewart) Fullen; m. Lewis Elden Smith, Aug. 12, 1934 (dec. 1964); children— Hannah Kully, Lewis, Deborah, Martin. B.A., U. So. Calif., 1926, M.A., 1927, postgrad., 1927-30, postgrad. in counseling, 1977-78; postgrad. Columbia U. Tchrs. Coll., summer 1929; postgrad. in poetry UCLA, 1960-65. Teaching asst., instr. U. So. Calif., Los Angeles, 1926-30; instr. in psychology, dean of women Compton (Calif.) Jr. Coll., 1930-36; textbook author Ginn and Co., Boston, 1943-76; free-lance writer, 1976—. Bd. dirs. Fullen-Smith Found., 1964—, Child Guidance Clinic, Los Angeles, 1964-71, Los Angeles chpt. ARC, 1965-66, Continuing Edn. Women, Claremont Coll., 1966-76, Internat. Assn. Vol. Edn., 1970—, Blaisdell Inst. Claremont Coll., 1971-83, Otis Art Inst., 1979-80; nat. bd. dirs. Exptl. Internat. Living, 1970-79. Recipient Appreciation award Goodwill Industries So. Calif. Mem. Town Hall Los Angeles, World Affairs Council, Women's Council Community TV of Los Angeles (hon. life), Trojan League, U. So. Calif. Assocs., Claremont Grad. Sch. Assocs., The Amazing Blue Ribbon (music ctr.), Phi Beta Kappa, Phi Kappa Phi, Pi Lambda Theta, Alpha Delta Pi. Democrat. Congregationalist. Author: (with Florence Means) Raphael and Consuelo, 1929; My Shadow Self, 1931; Your Life as a Citizen, 1952, rev. edits., 1961, 65, 67, 70, 76. Home: Los Angeles, Calif. Died Mar. 30, 2007.

SMITH, JACK C., supermarket executive; b. Aug. 21, 1925; Ptnr. Smith Realty, Grundy, Va., from 1955; chmn. K-VA-T Food Stores, Abington, Va. Died Mar. 15, 2007.

SMITH, JAMES ALTON, organization administrator; b. Corpus Christi, May 28, 1942; s. Hugh Alton and Alice Marie (Vaughn) S.; m. Sarah Ann Wiatt, Feb. 9, 1974; children: James Wiatt, Susan Marie, Stephen Alton. BA in Psychology, Covenant Coll., 1969; MEd in Counseling, West Ga. Coll., 1972; D.Min. in Family Counseling, Luther Rice Sem., 1984. Lic. profl. counselor, Ga; cert. med. psychotherapist. Counselor, Ga. Dept. Offender Rehab., Valdosta, 1972-74; family counselor, Huntsville, Ala., 1974-78; family seminar dir. Presbyn. Evangelistic Fellowship, Atlanta, 1975-78; area dir. Christian Broadcasting Network 700 Club, Atlanta, 1978-84; founding dir. Inst. Bibl. Therapy, Huntsville, 1984—; asst. prof. Atlanta Sch. Bibl. Studies, 1978-84; dir. counseling Ingleside Presbyn. Ch., Atlanta, 1978-84. Served with USNR, 1960-66. Republican. Pentecostal. Avocations performing with auto-harp. Home: Brownsboro, Ala. Died Jan. 15, 2007.

SMITH, JAMES IGNATIUS, III, bar association executive; b. Grosse Pointe, Mich., May 23, 1931; s. James I. and Jacqueline Mary (Moran) S.; m. Deborah L. Eyler, Mar. 17, 1983. BS, U. Notre Dame, 1953. Sales mgr., gen. mgr. Esmeralda Canning Co., Circleville, Ohio, 1955-57; gen. reporter The Herald, Circleville, 1957-60; asst. exec. sec., dir. pub. rels. Ohio State Bar Assn., Columbus, 1960-62; exec. dir. Allegheny County Bar Assn., Pitts., 1963—; pres. Profl. Seminars and Designs, Pitts., 1972—. Editor: (mng.) Pittsburgh Legal Jour., The Allegheny Lawyer. Chmn. Re-apportionment com., Bethel Park, Pa., 1969-71; dir. Mt. Lebanon Little League, 1989—. Served with U.S. Army, 1953-55. Recipient Journalism award Ohio State Bar Assn., Columbus, 1959; named Man of Yr., Notre Dame Club Pitts., 1972, Man of Yr. State of Israel Bonds Tri-State Area, 1988. Mem. Nat. Assn. Bar Execs. (pres. 1977-78), Legal Svcs. Assn. (bd. dirs., 1st sec. 1966—), Pitts. Soc. Assn. Execs. (pres. 1973-74), Assn. Continuing Legal Edn. Adminstrs., Pitts. C. of C., Pitts. Press Club, Notre Dame Club (pres. 1970-71), Serra Club (dir. 1971-72), Elks. Democrat. Roman Catholic. Home: Pittsburgh, Pa. Died Feb. 10, 2006.

SMITH, JOHN ANTHONY, lawyer; b. Poughkeepsie, NY, Sept. 10, 1942; s. John Charles and Eunice C. (Hatfield) S.; m. Carol A. Bechtel; children: Jessica R., Michael Anthony. BS, Cornell U., 1964, JD, 1971. Bar: Alaska 1971, U.S. Dist. Ct. Alaska 1971, U.S. Cts. Appeals (9th & 11th cirs.) 1971, U.S. Supreme Ct. 1978, DC. Assoc. Kay, Miller, Libbey, Kelly, Christie & Fuld, 1971, ptnr., 1972-73, Gruenberg, Willard & Smith, 1973-74; sole practice Anchorage, 1974-77; ptnr. Smith & Taylor, 1978, Smith, Taylor & Gruening, Anchorage, 1979, sr. ptnr., 1979-84; sr. ptnr. Smith, Robinson & Gruening, 1984-85; sr. ptnr. Smith, Robinson, Gruening & Brecht, 1985-86, Smith, Gruening, Brecht, Evans & Spietzfadden, 1986; commr. Commerce and Econ. Devel., State of Alaska, 1986-88; ptnr. Davis, Wright & Tremaine, 1989-92; of counsel Bliss & Riordan, 1993-94, Baker, Brattain and Huguelet; ptnr. Schmeltger, Aptaker & Shepard, from 1994; sr. coun. Schmeltger, Aptaker & Shepard, PC., Washington. Chmn. State Bond Com., State of Alaska, 1987-88; chmn. Alaska Housing Fin. Corp., 1986-88, Alaska Indsl. Devel. and Export Authority, 1986-88; chmn. Alaska Mcpl. Bond Bank 1989-91; chmn. Alaska Ctr. for Internat. Bus., 1987-91, dir. 1992—; adj. prof. U. Alaska Sch., 1977-79; Criminal Justice; bd. dirs. Alaska Bus. Monthly; bd. dir. Ctr. for Nat. Policy, OAS Young Am. Bus. FUnd; internat. bd. advisors Zamovance, 1996—; mem. working group Devel. of a Strategic Econ. Devel. Plan for Washington, 1997—; atty. Embassy of Honduras, St. Paul Island, Alaska. Columnist Anchorage Times; contbg. editor Alaska Jour. Commerce. Mem. exec. com. House-Senate Dem. Coun.; nominee U.S. Senate 1992, U.S. House, 1994; pres. Alaska Inst. Rsch. and Pub. Svc.; coord. U. Alaska Paralegal Program; chmn. Bus. Justice Com.; chmn. Gov.'s Bodily Injury Reparation Commn., 1979-80; mem. internat. rels. com. Nat. Olympics Com., 1986-93; mem. exec. com. Anchorage Organizing Com. for the Winter Olympics; bd. dirs., counsel Anchorage Olympic Devel. Com.; dir. Glacier Creek Acad. Served to lt. (j.g.) USN, 1964-67. With USN, 1964—67. Named Who's Who in the World, Who's Who in Am., Who in the W., Who's Who in the Law; recipient Dean's Prize, Cornell U., 1971. Mem. Alaska Bar Assn. (chmn. specialization com.), ABA, Am. Judicature Soc., Am. Trial Lawyers Assn. (Admiralty Sect.), Anchorage C. of C., bd. Ctr. Nat. Policy, Trade Policy Grp., Bar Assn DC, Anchorage Bar Assn. Democrat. Mem. Soc. Of Friends. Home: Steamboat Springs, Colo. Died Dec. 8, 2006.

SMITH, JOHN FRANCIS, materials science educator; b. Kansas City, Kans., May 9, 1923; s. Peter Francis and Johanna Teresa (Spandle) S.; m. Evelyn Ann Ross, Sept. 1, 1947 (dec. July 1994); children— Mark Francis, Letitia Ann Smith Harder; m. Eileen R. Ross, Apr. 12, 1997. BA with distinction, U. Mo., Kansas City, 1948; PhD, Iowa State U., Ames, 1953. Grad. asst. Iowa State U., Ames, 1948-53, faculty and rsch. scientist, 1953—88, dept. chmn., div. chief Ames Lab., 1966-70, prof. emeritus, 1988. Cons. Tex. Instruments, Inc., Dallas and Attleboro, Mass., 1958-63, Argonne Nat. Lab., Ill., 1964-70, Iowa Hwy. Commn., Ames, Los Alamos Nat. Lab., N.Mex., 1984-88, bur. standards Nat. Inst. Standards and Tech., Gaithersburg, Md., 1988-91, Sandia Nat. Lab., Albuquerque, N.M., 1991-92, ASM Internat., Cleve., 1992—. Patentee ultrasonic determination of texture in metal sheet and plate, lead-free solder; author: Phase Diagrams of Binary Vanadium Alloys; Hellcats Over the Philippine Deep; co-author: Thorium: Preparation and Properties, 1975; editor: Calculation of Phase Diagrams and Thermochemistry of Alloy Phases, 1978, Jour. Phase Equilibrium and Diffusion, 1988-; contbr. articles to profl. publs. Mem. former comdr. Ames-Boone Squadron CAP, 1970-75. With USN, 1942-46, PTO, comdr. USNR, 1946-64. Decorated Air medal with cluster; recipient Disting. Svc. award CAP, Maxwell AFB, Ala., 1979, faculty citation Iowa State U. Alumni Assn., Ames, 1977. Fellow Am. Inst. Chemists, ASM (chmn. Des Moines chpt. 1966); mem. AIME, Materials Rsch. Soc., Polish Acad. Arts and Scis. (fgn.), Am. Legion, Silent Knights, Inc. (trustee 1980-96), Exptl. Aircraft Assn., Alpha Sigma Mu (trustee 1984-86). Roman Catholic. Avocation: flying. Home: Ames, Iowa. Died July 9, 2006.

SMITH, JOHN JAMES, JR., environmental engineering consultant; b. Franklin, NJ, Dec. 6, 1936; s. John James Smith and Estelle Mary (Gurka) Cook; m. Sondra Lanphear, Dec. 19, 1956; 1 child, James H. BS in Chemistry, U. Fla., 1967. Dir. consulting svcs., v.p. Black, Crow & Eidsness, Gainesville, Fla., 1968-77; divsn. mgr., v.p. water & wastewater CH2M Hill, Gainesville, 1977-78, regional mgr., sr. v.p. water & wastewater, 1978-90, dist. mgr., sr. v.p. Envrinon. Engring. Lab., 1990-93; pres. Quality Analytical Labs. CH2M Hill Ltd., Gainesville, 1994-95; dir., sr. v.p. Gulf Coast Chem. & Petrochem. Program CH2M Hill, Gainesville, from 1996. Bd. dirs. N. Fla. Tech. Innovation Corp., N.E. Fla. Ednl. Delivery Sys.; chmn. U. Fla. Engring. Adv. Coun., 1994-96. Author conf. proc.; contbr. articles to profl. jours. Bd. dirs. Fla. Arts Celebration, Coun. on Econ. Outreach, Ctr. Performing Arts. With USAF. Mem. Am. Chem. Soc., Am. Water Works Assn. (nat. chmn. water quality monitoring com., trustee Fla. sect. 1979-82, chmn. Fla. sect. 1985-86, George Warren Fuller award 1988), Fla. Inst. Cons. Engrs., Fla. Chem. Industry Coun., Internat. Assn. Water Pollution Rsch., Water Pollution Control Fedn., Rotary, Sigma Xi. Achievements include development, design and research in numerous water and wastewater systems and facilities. Home: Alachua, Fla. Died Dec. 21, 2005.

SMITH, JOHN RICHARD, railroad executive; b. Appalachia, Va., Jan. 24, 1927; s. Robert Clarence and Mary Lettitia (Mullins) S.; m. Betty Jane Humbert, Mar. 26, 1947; children— Margaret Lettitia Smith Kibler, John Richard, Mary Jane Smith Wardlow. Student Hiwassie Coll., 1950-52; B.A., Lincoln Meml. U., 1954. Tchr., football/basketball coach Big Stone Gap High Sch. (Va.), 1954-55, St. Paul High Sch. (Va.), 1955-56, Handley High Sch., Winchester, Va., 1957-60; with So. R.R. Co., Appalachia, Va., 1960—, supt. safety, Somerset, Ky., 1972—. Served with USN, 1944-46. Decorated Bronze Stars. Mem. Nat. Safety Council, Ky. Peace Officer Assn. Democrat. Methodist. Club: Optimist. Home: Somerset, Ky. Died May 9, 2006.

SMITH, JOSEPH R., neurosurgeon, educator; b. Seattle, Sept. 20, 1940; m. Peach Smith; 1 child, Jordan. BS in Psychology, U. Wash., 1963, MD, 1967. Diplomate Am. Bd. Neurosurgery. Straight surg. intern Kans. U. Med. Ctr., 1967-68; resident in neurosurgery U. Wash. Med. Sch., Seattle, 1968-73; fellow in physiol. neurosurgery Med. Coll. Ga., Augusta, 1985, instr. neurosurgery, 1985-86, assoc. prof. surgery (neurosurgery), 1986-91; attending neurosurgeon VA Med. Ctr., Augusta, 1986-92, cons. neurosurgeon, from 1992. Presenter in field. Contbr. numerous articles to profl. jours. Fellow ACS; mem. Congress of Neurol. Surgeons, Am. Soc. Stereotaxic Neurosurgery, World Soc. Stereotaxic Neurosurgery, Am. Acad. Clin. Neurophysiology, Internat. Assn. Study of Pain, Am. Assn. Neurol. Surgeons, Am. Epilepsy Soc., Ga. Neurosurg. Soc. Died June 12, 2006.

SMITH, LEO EMMET, lawyer; b. Chgo., Jan 6, 1927; s. Albert J. and Cecilia G. (Dwyer) S.; m. Rita Gleason, Apr. 14, 1956; children: Mary Cecilia, Gerianne, Kathleen, Leo A., Maureen. JD, DePaul U., 1950. Admitted to Ill. bar, 1950; assoc. with law firm also engaged in pvt. industry, 1950-54; asst. states atty. Cook County, Ill., 1954-57; asst. counsel Traffic Inst., Northwestern U., Evanston, Ill., 1957-60; asst. exec. sec. Comml. Law League Am., Chgo., 1960-61, exec. dir., 1961-83, editor Comml. Law Jour., 1961-89, editor emeritus, 1989—; assoc. Howe & Hutton, Ltd., Chgo., 1985—. Fellow Chgo. Bar Found. (life); mem. Chgo. Bar Assn. (chmn. libr. com. 1983, sec. sr. lawyers com. 1994-95), Am. Acad. Matrimonial Lawyers (exec. dir. 1982-84), World Assn. Lawyers (founding mem. 1975), Am. Soc. Assn. Execs., Assn. Forum, Assn. Econs. Coun., Friends of Northwestern Sta. (spokesperson 1984). Contbr. articles to legal jours. Home: Evanston, Ill. Died Feb. 19, 2006.

SMITH, MARILYN VIOLA, metaphysician, minister; b. Astoria, L.I., N.Y., Aug. 25, 1934; d. Bernard P. and DeRetta (Williamson) S.; B.S., U. Tex., 1955; grad. Esoteric Philosophy Center, Houston, 1984. m. Charles Stoneberg, June 28, 1958 (dec. Apr. 1968); m. Jon E. Curtis, Mar. 28, 1969 (div. May 1975); m. Charles Marchand, Aug. 21, 1981 (div. Oct. 1983). Ordained Minister, 1982. Pharmacist, Med. Arts Pharmacy, San Antonio, 1955-56, Northside Drug, San Antonio, 1956-58; pharmacist Jones Apothecary, Houston, 1958-68, 73-83; pharmacist Madings Drugs, 1968-69, Phillips Pharmacy, 1968-70, Gloyer's Pharmacy, 1969-73, Fed-Mart Pharmacy, Pasadena, Tex., 1970-72, Walgreen's, Houston, 1983—; founder Ctr.

Metaphys. Studies, 1983, head creative manifestation of soul power, lectr. Esoteric Philosophy Center; tchr. New Age Chs., other orgns. flight instr. Barstow Aviation, Houston, 1962, free lance, 1962-64, Consol. Aero, Houston, 1967-68; participant Powder Puff Derby, 1960, Internat. Air Race, 1962, All Women's Internat. Air Race, 1964, other races; mem. 1st Women's Nat. Pylon Racing Team, 1967-71. Mem. Tex. Aviation Assn. (sec.-treas. 1962-64), Petticoat Pilots (pres. 1964-65), 99's (pres. Houston 1966-68), Aircraft Owners and Pilots Assn., Nat. Assn. Flight Instrs., Houston Metaphys. Council, Animal Behavior Soc., NOW, Tex. and Harris County Womens Polit. Caucus. Died Mar. 26, 2007.

SMITH, MARY LEVI, academic administrator; b. Jan. 30, 1936; Pres. Ky. State U., Frankfort. Died Apr. 21, 2007.

SMITH, MAURICE EDWARD, lawyer, business consultant; b. Denver, Mar. 30, 1919; s. Edward Daniel and Junie Ardella (Fox) S.; m. Gloria Tanner, June 17, 1944; children: Christine, Kathryn, Carol (dec.), Daniel. Student, Brigham Young U., 1938-40; BS in Commerce, U. Denver, 1942; LLB, Stanford U., 1948. Mem. staff Ralph B. Mayo & Co., Denver, 1949-50; v.p. fin., gen. counsel Husky Oil Co., Cody, Wyo., 1950-61; exec. v.p. Cen. Nat. Ins. Group, Omaha, 1961-65; treas., legal counsel Sunnen Products Co., St. Louis, 1965-69; v.p., treas. Global Marine, Inc., Los Angeles, 1969-78; pvt. bus. cons., from 1978. Mem. Cody City Council, 1955-57. Served with USNR, 1942-45. Mem. Calif. Bar Assn., Kiwanis Club of Provo. Mem. Ch. Jesus Christ of Latter-day Saints. Home: Saint George, Utah. Died Mar. 9, 2007.

SMITH, MICHAEL BRYANT, chemistry educator; b. Detroit, Oct. 17, 1946; s. Charles Marion and Nancy (Bryant) S.; m. Sarah Caterino, Aug. 25, 1947; 1 child, Steven Michael. AA, Ferrum Coll., 1967; BS in Chemistry, Va. Polytech. Inst. & State U., 1969; PhD in Organic Chemistry, Purdue U., 1977. Chemist Newport News (Va.) Shipbuilders, 1969-72; teaching asst. Purdue U., West Lafayette, Ind., 1972-77; rsch. asst. Ariz. State U., Tempe, 1977-78; asst. prof. U. Conn., Storrs, 1979-86, assoc. prof., 1986-94, prof., from 1994. Vis. prof. Cath. U., 1986. Contbr. articles to profl. jours. Mem. Am. Chem. Soc., Am. Assn. Pharm. Scientists, Am. Assn. Pharm., Internat. Soc. Heterocyclic Chemists. Democrat. Home: Willington, Conn. Died July 8, 2007.

SMITH, MICHAEL WILLIAM, safety, personnel executive; b. Clarksville, Tenn., Jan. 27, 1947; s. Burch Lee and Mary Patrice (Kilpatrick) S.; m. Marie-Dominique Beauvalet, Apr. 2, 1970; children— Christopher, Nicholas. B.S., Peabody Coll., 1977, M.S., 1978. Cert. safety exec.; cert. hazard control mgr. Mental therapist DeDe Wallace Community Mental Health, Nashville, 1978-80; loss prevention rep. Liberty Mut. Ins. Co., Memphis, 1980-81; dir. safety, personnel Fischer Steel Corp., Memphis, 1981—. Served with USAF, 1967-74. Grantee NIMH, 1977, Biomed. Research Support, 1978, HEW, 1978. Mem. Am. Soc. Safety Engrs. (v.p. 1984, pres. 1985 W. Tenn. Chpt.), Nat. Fire Prevention Assn. Republican. Presbyterian. Avocations: photography; canoeing; sailing; gardening. Home: Memphis, Tenn. Died May 1, 2006.

SMITH, MILLARD GAMBRELL, JR., educational administrator, cattle rancher; b. Birmingham, Ala., Sept. 14, 1928; s. Millard G. and Cornelia (Matthews) S.; m. Doris Jean Hamby, Feb. 7, 1968; 1 child, Michelle Renae. Student U. Ala., 1946-48; B.B.A. in Pre-Law, Huntingdon Coll., 1951; postgrad. Clemson U., 1971-81, U. S.C., 1982-83. Dir., coordinator Summer Youth Programs Starr, S.C. Sch. Dist. 3, S.C., 1976-82; dir. pre-vocat. edn., 1969-82; exec. sec., supt. schs. Anderson County Bd. Edn., S.C., 1982—. Exec. committeeman Anderson County Democratic Party S.C., 1974—; del. state conv. Dem. Party S.C., Cola, 1982—. Recipient Outstanding Contbn. to Edn. award Anderson County Bd. Edn., 1982; Starr charge, treas., chmn. United Meth. Pastor Parrish Com. Mem. S.C. Edn. Assn. (Starr charge 1987-89), S.C. Vocat. Edn. Assn. (state pres. 1976-81, bd. dirs., v.p.), Anderson County Tchrs. Fed. Credit Union (pres. 1982-85). S.C. Prevocat. Tchrs. Assn. (state pres. 1976-81, life mem., pres. elect 1988-89, Outstanding Leadership award 1982-83, Outstanding Educator of Yr. 1987), Piedmont Credit Union Assn., Santa Gertrudis Breeders Internat., Am. Quarter Horses Assn., Alpha Tau Omega. Methodist. Club: Donalds Grange (S.C.). Lodge: Rotary. Avocations: sports; hunting; fishing; horses. Home: Starr, SC. Died Aug. 26, 2006.

SMITH, NEVILLE VINCENT, physicist; b. Leeds, Eng., Apr. 21, 1942; came to U.S., 1966; s. Horace J.H. and Ethel S.; m. Elizabeth Jane Poulson, 1970; children: Katherine, Elizabeth. BA, Cambridge U., Eng., 1963, MA, PhD, Cambridge U., Eng., 1967. Rsch. assoc. Stanford (Calif.) U., 1966-68; mem. staff AT&T Bell Labs., Murray Hill, N.J., 1969-94, head condensed state physics rsch. dept., 1978-81; scientific program head Advanced Light Source Lawrence Berkeley Nat. Lab., Berkeley, Calif., from 1994. Contbr. articles to jours. in field. Fellow Am. Phys. Soc. (Davisson-Germer prize 1991). Died Aug. 18, 2006.

SMITH, PAUL JAMES, manufacturing executive; b. Trumbull, Tex., July 16, 1932; s. Earl J. and Bessie K. (Pierce) S.; m. Barbara A. McConnell, Aug. 9, 1954; children: Marc, Cynthia. BSEE, U. Tex., 1959; postgrad., So. Meth. U., 1959-60. Mgr. mil. computer bus., consumer calculator bus., div. gen. mgr. digital systems Tex. Instruments, Dallas, 1959-75; dir. comml. electronics Martin Marietta Corp., Orlando, Fla., 1975-79; v.p., gen. mgr. semiconductor digital products div. Harris Corp., Melbourne, Fla., 1979-83; group v.p. line printer, then exec. v.p Dataproducts Corp., Woodland Hills, Calif., 1983-88; sr. v.p. Data Products div. Xidex/Anacomp Corp., Santa Clara, Calif., from 1988. Served with USN, 1953-55. Mem. IEEE, Machinery and Allied Products Inst., Mensa, Tau Beta Pi, Eta Kappa Nu. Died May 24, 2007.

SMITH, RICHARD FREDERICK, chemist, educator; b. Lockport, NY, Jan. 31, 1929; s. Frederick E. and Dorothy (Iles) S.; m. Eleanor Dolores Besemer, Nov. 24, 1951; children— Marilyn Elizabeth, Kenneth Richard, Janet Louise. BS, Allegheny Coll., 1950; PhD, U. Rochester, 1954. Research chemist Monsanto Chem. Co., 1953-55, Sterling Winthrop Research Inst., 1955-57; asso. prof., then prof. State U. N.Y. at Albany, 1957-65; NSF faculty fellow U. Calif. at Los Angeles, 1962-63; prof. chemistry, chmn. dept. State U. Coll. at Geneseo, 1965-68, prof., 1968-74, Univ. Disting. Teaching prof., 1974, vis. scholar, from 1974. Vis. prof. Dartmouth Coll., 1981, 83, 87, Wesleyan U., 1985-86 Contbr. articles to profl. jours. Recipient Miller Music prize Allegheny Coll., 1950, Alumni Gold citation Allegheny Coll., 1987; research grantee Research Found. State U. N.Y., 1958-67; research grantee NSF and Petroleum Research Found. of Am. Chem. Soc., 1963-86. Mem. Am. Chem. Soc., Chem. Soc. London, Sigma Xi. Home: Geneseo, NY. Died June 30, 2006.

SMITH, RICHARD MULDROW, lawyer; b. Jefferson City, Mo., Sept. 2, 1939; s. Elmer Clyde and Mary (Muldrow) S.; children: Stephen, Michael. JD, U. Ark., 1963; postgrad., U. Ill., 1963-64. Bar: Ark. 1963, D.C. 1980, U.S. Ct. Appeals (D.C. cir.) 1980, U.S. Supreme Ct. 1980. Asst. prof. U. N.C., Chapel Hill, 1964-67, assoc. prof., 1967-73, prof., 1973-79; spl. counsel FPC, Washington, 1976-77; mem. White House Energy Policy Staff, Washington, 1978-79; dir. Office of Policy Coordination, Dept. of Energy, Washington, 1978-79; ptnr. Mayer, Brown & Platt, Washington, 1979-91; pres. Little Creek Marina Inc., Norfolk, Va., from 1992. Author: (with others) North Carolina Uniform Commercial Code Forms Annotated, 2 vols., 1967. Mem. ABA (pub. utility law sect., coun. mem. 1985-88, chmn. gas com. 1988-89, chmn. publ. com. 1989-91). Home: Virginia Beach, Va. Died July 14, 2006.

SMITH, ROBERT EARL, dentist; b. Merryville, La., Oct. 30, 1932; s. Matthew Robert and Lottie Viola (Johnson) S.; m. Kathryn Isabel Tilly, June 4, 1953; children— Victoria Lynn Stretch, Robert Brent. B.S., U. Okla., 1954; D.D.S., U. Mo.-Kansas City, 1958. Gen. practice dentistry, Kansas City, 1958—. Mem. ADA, Mo. Dental Assn., Kansas City Dist. Dental Soc. (pres. 1975), Kansas City Dental Abstract Study Club (pres. 1968). Episcopalian. Clubs: Saddle and Sirloin (Leawood, Kans.) (pres. 1980-81); Mission Valley Hunt (Stilwell, Kans.) (v.p.). Avocations: horseback riding; foxhunting. Home: Shawnee Mission, Kans. Died Mar. 16, 2006.

SMITH, ROBERT MCKAIN, international studies educator; b. Detroit, Sept. 12, 1922; s. Robert McKee and Mary (McKain) S.; m. Margaret Jean Bennett, June 14, 1946; children: Susan, Barbara, Ann, Eric. BS in Bus., Babson Coll., Wellesley, Mass., 1956; MA in Asian History, Am. U., 1963, PhD in Internat. Studies, 1971. Commd. 2d lt. U.S. Army, 1943, advanced through grades to col., 1967, served in U.S., Europe, Asia, 1943-71; asst. internat. policy Joint Chiefs of Staff, 1966-69; asst. project mgr. Dept. of Army, Washington, 1969-70; Asia tng. and supply Comdr.-in Chief of Pacific Forces, Honolulu, 1971; ret. U.S. Army, 1971; prof. internat. studies Chaminade U., Honolulu, 1971-93, prof. emeritus, from 1993. Spl. scholar London Sch. Econs. and Polit. Sci., 1981; prof. Fgn. Affairs Coll., Beijing, China, 1989; cons. U.S. Dept. State, 1990—, USIA, 1989—; lectr. in field. Contbr. articles to profl. jours. Decorated Legion of Merit; recipient grants to study and do rsch. in Taiwan, 1975, 80. Fellow Ctr. of Asian Studies in Hong Kong; mem. Law of Sea Inst., UN Assn. (Hawaii bd. dirs.), Pacific and Asian Affairs Coun. Hawaii (bd. dirs.), Hawaii Geog. Soc. (bd. dirs.), Pacific Sci. Assn., Internat. Geog. Union (commn. on environ. problems), Honolulu Rotary Club (scholarship com. 1977—). Avocations: travel, hiking, reading. Home: Anchorage, Alaska. Died Aug. 11, 2006.

SMITH, ROBERT SHERLOCK, state appeals court judge; b. NYC, Aug. 31, 1944; s. Robert and Janet W. (Welt) S.; m. Dian Goldston Smith, Aug. 31, 1969; children: Benjamin Eli, Emlen Matthew, Rosemary Friedman. BA with great distinction, Stanford U., 1965; LLB magna cum laude, Columbia U., 1968. Bar: N.Y. 1968, U.S. Dist. Ct. (so. dist.) N.Y. 1969, U.S. Dist. Ct. (ea. dist.) N.Y. 1977, U.S. Ct. Appeals (2d cir.) 1970, U.S. Ct. Appeals (4th cir.) 1986, U.S. Ct. Appeals (1st cir.) 1988, U.S. Ct. Appeals (7th cir.) 1989, U.S. Ct. Appeals (6th cir.) 1995, U.S. Ct. Appeals (D.C. and 8th cirs.) 1997, U.S. Ct. Appeals (5th cir.) 1999, U.S. Tax Ct. 1974, U.S. Supreme Ct. 1979. Assoc. Paul, Weiss, Rifkind, Wharton & Garrison, NYC, 1968-76, ptnr., 1976—2003; individual practitioner, spl. counsel Kornstein, Veisz, Wexler & Pollard, NYC, 2003—04; assoc. judge NY State Ct. Appeals, NYC, from 2004. Vis. prof. Columbia Law Sch., N.Y.C., 1980-81, lectr. law, 1981-90; adj. Benjamin N. Cardozo Sch. Law, 2006—. Editor-in-chief Columbia Law Review. Mem. ABA, N.Y. State Bar Assn. (vice chair com. ct. adminstrn. 2001-04), Assn. Bar City N.Y. (com. fed. legis. 1981-84, com. on judiciary 1984-87, com. on bicentennial of U.S. Constitution 1988-91), Federalist Soc. N.Y. (pres. lawyers chpt. 1994-2003). Republican. Mem. Reformed Ch. Died Oct. 9, 2006.

SMITH, ROBERT THORNTON, lawyer; b. Englewood, NJ, Aug. 14, 1943; AB, Princeton U., 1965; JD, Harvard U., 1968. Bar: N.J. 1968, N.Y. 1970. Mem. White & Case, NYC. Adj. prof. taxation NYU, 1980—. Mem. ABA, N.Y. State Bar Assn. Died May 20, 2007.

SMITH, RODNEY, retired electronics executive; b. Oldham, England, 1941; m. Mary Smith. BSEE, Southampton Coll. Advanced Tech., Eng. Various positions to v.p., gen. mgr. Fairchild Semiconductor Corp., Mountain View, Calif., 1969-83; pres., CEO Altera Corp., San Jose, Calif., 1983—2000, chmn., 1983—2003, ret., 2003. Died May 25, 2007.

SMITH, WILLIAM GEORGE, sales executive; b. Woodland, Calif., Oct. 14, 1937; s. George William and Olive Vera (Gumz) S.; 1 child, Laura Michelle. A.Arts and Sci., Solano Coll., 1976. Br. officer various banks, 1958-69; v.p. Bank of Fairfield, Calif., 1969-72; asst. v.p. Barclays Bank Calif., San Francisco, 1975-78; gen. mgr. Kalleens, San Rafael, Calif., 1978-81, gen. sales mgr., 1981-83, dir. corp. accounts, 1983—; cons. L.T.J., Inc., 1981—. Com. mem. Solano County Republicans, Fairfield, Calif., 1980, mem. com. to re-elect Neil Crawnford, 1978; mem. com. to elaect County Assessor, 1986. Served with U.S. Army, 1955-58. Mem. Soc. for Preservation and Encouragement of Barber Shop Quartet Singing in Am., Assn. Info. Systems Profls. Republican. Club: Green Tree Golf. Lodges: Kiwanis, Lions, Masons, Order/DeMolay, Elks. Home: Fairfield, Calif. Died Apr. 19, 2007.

SMITH, WILLIAM JAY, author; b. Winnfield, La., Apr. 22, 1918; s. Jay and Georgia (Campster) S.; m. Barbara Howes, Oct. 1, 1947 (div. June 1965); children: David Emerson, Gregory Jay; m. Sonja Haussmann, Sept. 3, 1966. Student, Institut de Touraine, Tours, France, 1938; BA, Washington U., St. Louis, 1939, MA, 1941; postgrad., Columbia U., 1946-47; postgrad. Rhodes scholar, Oxford U., 1947-48; postgrad., U. Florence, Italy 1948-50; Litt.D., New Eng. Coll., 1973. Asst. in French Washington U., 1939-41; instr. English and French Columbia U. 1946-47; lectr. English Williams Coll., 1951, poet in residence lectr. English, 1959-64, 66-67; Ford Found. fellow Arena Stage Washington, 1964-65; writer in residence Hollins Coll., 1965-66, prof. English, 1967, 70-80, prof. emeritus, 1980. Poet laureate Libr. Congress, Washington, 1968-70, hon. cons. in Am letters, 1970-76; vis. prof., acting chmn., writing divsn. Sch Arts, Columbia U., 1973, 74-75; mem. staff Salzburg (Austria) Seminar, 1975; mem. jury Nat. Book award, 1962, 70, 75 Neustadt Internat. prize for lit., 1978, Com. of Pegasus Prize for Lit., 1979-98; poet in residence Cathedral St. John the Divine N.Y., 1985-88. Author: Poems, 1947, Celebration at Dark, 1950 Laughing Time, 1955, Poems, 1947-57, Boy Blue's Book of Beasts, 1957, Puptents and Pebbles: A Nonsense ABC, 1959 Typewriter Town, 1960, The Spectra Hoax, 1961, What Did See, 1962, Ho for a Hat, 1964, (with Louise Bogan) The Golden Journey; Poems for Young People, 1965, The Tin Can and Other Poems, 1966, If I Had a Boat, 1966, Poems from France, 1967 Mr. Smith and Other Nonsense, 1968, New and Selected Poems 1970, The Streaks of the Tulip, selected criticism, 1972, Poem from Italy, 1973, Venice in the Fog, 1975, The Telephone, 1977 Laughing Time, 1980, The Traveler's Tree, New and Selected Poems, 1980, Army Brat, a Memoir, 1980, A Green Place Modern Poems, 1982, Plain Talk: Epigrams, Epitaphs, Satires Nonsense, Occasional Concrete and Quotidian Poems, 1988, Ho for a Hat (rev.), 1989, Collected Poems 1939-1989, 1990 Laughing Time: Collected Nonsense, 1990, Birds and Beasts 1990, Big and Little, 1992 (with Carol Ra) Behind the King' Kitchen: A Roster of Rhyming Riddles, 1992, The Cyclist, 199 (with Carol Ra) The Sun is Up: A Child's Year of Poems, 1996 The World Below the Window: Poems 1937-1997, 1998, Here i My Heart: Love Poems, 1999, The Cherokee Lottery: A Sequence of Poems, 2000, Around My Room, 2000, The Spectr Hoax (paperback reissue), 2000, The Girl in the Glass: Lov Poems, 2002; translator: (with Emanuel Brasil) Brazilian Poetr 1950-80, 1984, (with Ingvar Schousboe) The Pact: My Friendship with Isak Dinesen by Thorkild Bjørnvig, 1983, (with J.S Holmes) Dutch Interior: Post-War Poetry of the Netherlands an Flanders, 1984, Scirocco by Romualdo Romano, 1951; Poem of a Multimillionaire by Valery Larbaud, 1955, Selected Writings of Jules Laforgue, 1956, Children of the Forest by Els Beskow, 1969, Two Plays by Charles Bertin: Christophe Columbus and Don Juan, 1970, The Pirate Book by Lenna Hellsing, 1972, (with Leif Sjöberg) Agadir by Artur Lundkvis 1979, Moral Tales of Jules Laforgue, 1985, Collected Translations: Italian, French, Spanish, Portuguese, 1985, (with Dan Gioia) Poems from Italy, 1985, (with Leif Sjöberg) Wil Bouquet: Nature Poems by Harry Martinson, 1985, (with Son Haussmann Smith) The Madman and the Medusa by Tchicaya Tam'Si, 1989, Songs of Childhood by Federico Garcia Lorca 1994, Berlin: The City and the Court, 1996, (with Leif Sjöberg The Forest of Childhood: Poems from Sweden, 1996, Gyul Illyés: Selected Poems, 1999; editor: Herrick, 1962, Light Vers and Satires by Witter Bynner, 1978, (with F.D. Reeve) An Arro in the Wall: Selected Poetry and Prose by Andrei Voznesensk 1986 (one of 16 Best Books of 1986, N.Y. Times), Lif Sentence: Selected Poems of Nina Cassian, 1990. Mem. Vt. H of Reps., 1960-62. Served to lt. USNR, 1941-45. Recipien Alumni citation Washington U., 1963; prize Poetry mag., 194 64; Henry Bellamann Major award, 1970; Russell Loines awar Nat. Inst. Arts and Letters, 1972; Gold medal Labor Hunga 1978; Golden Rose award New Eng. Poetry Club, 197 médaille de vermeil French Acad., 1991, Pro Cultura Hungaric medal, Hungary, 1993; Nat. Endowment for Arts fellow, 197 95; NEH fellow, 1975, 89; Ingram Merrill fellow, 1982; Camargo Found. fellow, 1986, René Vásquez Díaz prize Swedis Acad., 1997. Mem. Am. Acad. Arts and Letters (v.p. f literature 1986-89), Am. Assn. Rhodes Scholars, Acad. Ar Poets, Authors Guild, P.E.N. Clubs: Century. Home: Cummington, Mass. Died Dec. 28, 2006.

SMITH, WILLIAM MARTIN, sociology educator; b. Flin Mich., Nov. 24, 1911; s. William Martin and Mertie (Holida S.; m. Ruth Elaine Henderson, Sept. 3, 1938; children: Colbo W., Elaine Y., Maureen B., Deborah G. BS, Ohio State U., 193 MS, Cornell U., 1937, PhD, 1942; fellow, Merrill-Palmer Ins 1954-55. Extension asst. Ohio State U., 1934-35; mem. sta Community Inst., 1943-45; extension asst. Cornell U., 1935-3 instr. rural sociology extension, 1937-43; asst. prof. U. Il 1945-47; mem. faculty Pa. State U., University Park, from 194 prof. family relations, from 1950, state 4-H leader, 1959-6 asst. dir. family, youth and community devel. coop. extensio service, 1963-69, prof. rural sociology, 1969-76, prof. emeritu from 1976, chmn. faculty senate, 1971-72. Vis. prof. U. Ark Columbia Tchrs. Coll., Ariz. State Coll., Flagstaff; Fulbrig prof. The Netherlands, 1964-65, research prof., 1973-74 Autho (with Bernard and Buchanan) Dating, Mating and Marriag 1958, (with Raymond Coward) The Family in Rural Societ 1981, Family Services: Issues and Opportunities in Contemporary Rural America, 1983; also research bulls.; Editor: T Family Coordinator, 1968-70. Mem. State Coll. Communi Devel. Council, 1948-50; mem. Gov. Pa. Com. Children a Youth, 1963-70; adv. Nat. Assn. Extension Home Economis 1967-69. Recipient 4-H Alumni award Pa., 1955; fellow Gra Found., 1954-55; hon. mem. Pa. Future Homemakers Ass 1955 Fellow Am. Sociol. Assn.; mem. Nat. Council Fami Relations (pres. 1966-67), Am. Assn. Marriage and Fami Therapists, Am. Edn. Assn., Rural Sociol. Soc., AAUP, P Kappa Phi, Alpha Zeta, Gamma Sigma Delta, Phi Delta Kapp Epsilon Sigma Phi, Pi Gamma Mu, Alpha Kappa Delta. Episcopalian (vestry 1950-51). Home: State College, Pa. Died M 18, 2006.

SMITH, WILLIAM ROBERT, utility company executive; b. Mt. Clemens, Mich., Nov. 11, 1916; s. Robert L. and Elsie (Chamberlain) S.; m. Sandra Martha Philips; children from previous marriage: William R. (dec.), Laura A. (dec.). BS, Detroit Inst. Tech., 1947; postgrad., Detroit Coll. Law, U. Mich. Grad. Sch. Bus. Adminstrn. Registered profl. engr., Mich., Ohio. Indsl. engr. Detroit Edison Co., 1934-60; mgr. econ. devel. East Ohio Gas Co., Cleve., 1960-80; mgr. nat. accounts Consol. Natural Gas Co., Cleve., 1980-85; dir. mktg. Edison Polymer Innovation Corp., 1985-88; exec. dir. Western Res. Econ. Devel. Coun., 1988-97; pres. T.S.T. Corp.; ret. Bd. dirs. Animal Protective League and Humane Soc. Served with USAAF, 1942-45. Fellow Am. Indsl. Devel. Coun.; mem. Indsl. Devel. Rsch. Coun., Assn. Ohio Commodores, Delta Theta Tau. Presbyterian. Home: Painesville, Ohio. Died Mar. 6, 2007.

SMITH, WILLIAM STANLEY, construction company executive; b. Chgo., July 7, 1933; s. Stanley William and Lillie Lou (Peck) S.; m. Susan D. Dixson, Dec. 21, 1957; children— Cynthia Elizabeth, Nancy Anne, Christine Louise. B.A., Beloit Coll., 1955. Indsl. relations mgr. Container Corp. Am., Chgo., 1955-60; v.p. Crampton, Inc., 1960-78, pres., 1978—. Mem. Archtl. Woodworkers Inst., Nat. Club Assn. Republican. Presbyterian. Clubs: Glen Oak Country, Perry Park Country. Home: Glen Ellyn, Ill. Died Jan. 5, 2006.

SMITH, WILMA JANICE, writer, columnist; b. Pryor, Okla., Aug. 15, 1926; d. William Henry and Mary Jo (Buffington) Bell; m. Merle Thomas Smith, Apr. 30, 1948. Student Okla. A&M Coll., 1946, Okla. Sch. Bus., 1947; continuing edn. in law, history and theology. Clk. U.S. Postal Service, Tulsa, 1945; clk.-typist Social Security Office, Tulsa, 1947-50; rec. sec. Acad. Country Music, Hollywood, Calif., 1975-78; contbg. editor Nashville Star Reporter, 1977-78; freelance writer on country music field, 1973-85; publicist U. Ill. Press, Urbana, 1975-76; profl. talent booker, Hollywood, 1975-80; freelance writer on country music for TV and radio, 1985—; record and book reviewer various pubs.; biographer, cons. to Country and Western music performers; pub. rels. worker various artists; photographer for Country and Western publs., frequent TV and Radio guest; contbr. to Am. Poetry Anthology, 1989; country music writer Rag mag.; writer Mo. column Reunion Newspaper, 1995—; columnist Reunion News, 1997. Rep. precinct worker, So. Ill. area, 1960, So. Calif. area, 1964-85; speaker in field. Mem. Acad. Country Music (sec. 1975-77), Calif. Country Music Assn. Mem. Ch. of Nazarene, Smithsonian Instn. (assoc.). Lodge: Rainbow Girls. Avocations: collecting celebrity and presidential autographed photos, raising and showing Boston terriers, Indian affairs, world travel, gardening. Died Feb. 13, 2007.

SMITH, ZACHARY TAYLOR, II, retired tobacco company executive; b. Mt. Airy, NC, June 15, 1923; s. Eugene Gray and Leonita (Yates) S. AB in Econs., U. N.C., 1947; LLD (hon.), Wake Forest U., 1989. With R.J. Reynolds Tobacco Co., 1947-85, treas., dir., 1970-85. Trustee, past pres. Z. Smith Reynolds Found.; life trustee Wake Forest U.; bd. dirs., past pres. Mary Reynolds Babcock Found., past bd. dirs. Arts and Scis. Found., U. NC; past nat. devel. coun. U. NC, Chapel Hill; past bd. dirs. Med. Found. N.C.; past bd. dirs. Leadership Winston-Salem; past mem. adv. coun. The Carolina Challenge; past chmn. bd. visitors U. N.C. Chapel Hill; past Reynolds Scholarship Com., past bd. vis. Wake Forest U.; past bd. visitors Inst. policy studies and pub. affairs Duke U.; past mem. adv. bd. Duke U. Hosp.; past bd. dirs., NC Sch. Arts Found., Devotion Found., NC Outward Bound Sch., Small Bus. Devel. Com., Winston-Salem Symphony, Citizens Planning Coun.; past trustee Forsyth Hosp. Authority; past pres., dir. Child Guidance Clinic Forsyth County, YMCA, Red Shield Boy's Clubs; past chmn. indsl. divsn. Arts Coun. fund drive; past v.p., dir. Arts Coun.; past v.p., dir. Amos Cottage; past bd. visitors Meredith Coll.; past trustee St. Augustine Coll.; past bd. dirs. alumni assn. U. NC; vice chmn., dir. Friends of U. NC-Greensboro Libr. Lt. USNR, 1943—46, PTO. Mem. Old Town Club, Rotary. Democrat. Episcopalian. Home: Winston Salem, NC. Died Jan. 14, 2007.

SMUIN, MICHAEL, choreographer, director, dancer; b. Missoula, Mont., Oct. 13, 1938; m. Paula Tracy, 1961 (div. 2000); 1 child, Shane. Studied with Christensen Bros.; studied, San Francisco Ballet Sch.; DFA, U. Mont., 1984. Dancer U. Utah Ballet, Salt Lake City, 1955-57; dancer, choreographer, dir. San Francisco Ballet, 1957-62, 73-85; dancer Am. Ballet Theatre, N.Y. State Theatre, NYC, 1967; prin. dancer, choreographer Am. Ballet Theatre, 1969-73, resident choreographer NYC, 1992—2007; founder, dir. Smuin Ballets/SF, 1994—2007. Worked as free-lance dancer with wife Paula Tracy, ind. choreographer; co-chmn. dance adv. panel Nat. Endowment for the Arts, Washington; mem. U.S. dance study team, People's Republic of China, 1983. Dir., musical stager, choreographer: with Donald McKayle) Sophisticated Ladies, 1981 (Tony award nomination best direction of musical 1981, Outer Critics Circle award 1981); dir., choreographer: Chaplin, 1983, Shogun, 1990; choreographer: Anything Goes, 1987 (Tony award best choreography 1988, Drama Desk award best choreography 1988), Pulcinella Variations, Private Lives, 1991; staged dance works for Leslie Caron, Mikhail Baryshnikov, Rudolf Nureyev with Am. Ballet Theatre/Paris Opera Ballet, 1986; prodr. for San Francisco Ballet: Cinderella, Romeo and Juliet, The Tempest, A Song for Dead Warriors; dir.: Faustus in Hell, Peter and the Wolf, Very Merrily, Verdi, To The Beatles, Revisited, 2001, Stabat Mater, 2001; choreographer: (films) Rumble Fish, 1983, The Cotton Club, 1984, Fletch Lives, 1989, Bram Stoker's Dracula, 1992, So I Married an Axe Murderer, 1993, Angie, 1994, The Fantasticks, 1995; tech. adviser: (film) The Golden Child, 1986, Star Wars Trilogy, 1997; choreographer: (TV) The Tempest, 1981 (Emmy award nomination outstanding achievement in choreography, 1981), A Song for Dead Warriors, 1984 (Emmy award outstanding achievement in choreography 1984), Cinderella, 1985, Romeo and Juliet; dir. Suites by Smuin, Nutcracker on Ice; (TV spls.) Jinx, 1985, Voice/Dance: Bobby McFerrin and the Tandy Beal Dance Company, 1987; choreographer: (TV episode) Corridos! Tales of Passion and Revolution, 1987; creator: (TV show) The Omo, 1987; dir., choreographer: (TV spl.) Linda Ronstadt's Canciones de Mi Padre, 1989, Aid and Comfort. Recipient Dance Magazine award, 1983. Died Apr. 24, 2007.

SMURL, JAMES FREDERICK, religious studies educator; b. Wilkes-Barre, Pa., Aug. 20, 1934; s. James J. and Rita R. (Gildea) S.; m. Mary Hennigan, Sept. 12, 1967; children: Peter, Linda, Beth, Paul. BA in Philosophy, St. Mary's U., Balt., 1955; STL in Theology, Gregorian U., Rome, 1959; STD in Religious Ethics, Cath. U. Am., 1963. Prof. in moral theology St. Pius X Sem., Scranton, Pa., 1963-67; prof. Okla. State U., 1968-73; prof. religious studies Ind. U., Indpls., from 1973. Author: Religious Ethics, 1972 (award), A Primer in Ethics, 1985, The Burdens of Justice, 1994; contbr. articles to profl. publs. Lilly Endowment fellow, 1981. Mem. Am. Acad. Religion, Soc. Christian Ethics, Am. Acad. Religion. Home: Charlemont, Mass. Died May 26, 2007.

SMYTH, CRAIG HUGH, fine arts educator; b. NYC, July 28, 1915; s. George Hugh and Lucy Salome (Humeston) S.; m. Barbara Linforth, June 24, 1941; children: Alexandra, Edward Linforth (Ned). BA, Princeton U., 1938, MFA, 1941, PhD, 1956; MA (hon.), Harvard U., 1975. Sr. mus. aid, rsch. asst. Nat. Gallery Art, Washington, 1941-42; officer-in-charge, dir. Cen. Art Collecting Point, Munich, 1945-46; lectr. Frick Collection, NYC, 1946-50; asst. prof. Inst. Fine Arts NYU, 1950-53, assoc. prof. Inst. Fine Arts, 1953-57, prof. Inst. Fine Arts, 1957-73, acting dir. Inst. Fine Arts, acting head dept. fine arts Grad. Sch. Arts and Scis., 1951-53, dir. inst., head dept. fine arts Grad. Sch., 1953-73; prof. fine arts Harvard U., 1973-85, prof. emeritus, 1985—2006; Samuel Kress prof. Ctr. for Advanced Study in Visual Arts Nat. Gallery Art, Washington, 1987-88; dir. Villa I Tatti Harvard U. Ctr. Italian Renaissance Studies, Florence, 1973-85. Art historian in residence Am. Acad. in Rome, 1959-60; mem. U.S. Nat. Com. History Art, 1955-85; alt. U.S. mem. Comité Internat. d'Histoire de l'Art, 1970-83, U.S. mem., 1983-85; chmn. adv. com. J. Paul Getty Rsch. Inst. History of Art and Humanities, 1982-99; mem. architect selection com. J. Paul Getty Trust, 1983-84; mem. organizing com., keynote speaker 400th Anniversary of Uffizi Gallery, 1981-82; vis. scholar Inst. Advanced Study, Princeton, N.J., 1971, mem., 1978, visitor, 1983, 85-86; vis. scholar Bibliotheca Hertziana, Max Planck Soc., Rome, 1972, 73; mem. vis. com. dept. art and archaeology Princeton U., 1956-73, 85-89; mem. adv. com. Villa I Tatti, 1985-92; trustee Hyde Collection, Glens Falls, N.Y., 1985-87, The Burlington mag., 1987—; mem. commn. Ednl. & Cultural Exch. between Italy and U.S., 1979-83. Author: Mannerism and Maniera, 1963, rev. edit. with introduction by E. Cropper, 1992, Bronzino as Draughtsman, 1971, Michelangelo Architetto (with H.M. Millon), 1988, English edit., 1988, Repatriation of Art from the Collecting Point in Munich After World War II, 1988; editor: Michelangelo Drawings (Nat. Gallery of Art), 1992; editor (with Peter M. Lukehart), contbr.: The Early Years of Art History in the United States, 1993; founding chmn. (periodical) I Tatti Studies: Essays in the Renaissance, 1984-85; contbr. to profl. jours. Hon. trustee Met. Mus. Art, N.Y.C., 1968—2006; trustee Inst. Fine Arts, NYU, 1973-2006; mem. mayor's com. Piazza Della Signoria, Florence, 1975-78. Lt. USNR, 1942-46. Decorated Chevalier Legion of Honor France, U.S. Army Commendation medal, Netherlands Medal for Svc. to the State; sr. Fulbright Rsch. fellow, 1949-50, honored by establishment of CHS professorship, Inst. of Fine Arts NYU, 1999. Mem. Am. Acad. Arts and Scis., Am. Philos. Soc., Coll. Art Assn. Am. (bd. dirs. 1953-57, sec. 1956), Accademia Fiorentina delle Arti del Disegno (academician, assoc.), Accademia di San Luca (hon. 1995), Harvard Club (N.Y.C.), Century Assn. (N.Y.C.), Phi Beta Kappa. Died Dec. 22, 2006.

SNELL, WILLIAM ROBERT, history educator; b. Birmingham, Ala., Oct. 16, 1930; s. Eugene B. and Cora A. (Hirschy) S.; m. Cora Mae Rickey, Aug. 27, 1956 (div. 1961); children— William R. Jr., Mark E.; m. Janet Elizabeth Warren, Sept. 2, 1963; children— Stephen Michael, Jeffrey Alan. B.S., Samford U., 1952; B.D., So. Sem., 1956, Th.M., 1957; M.A., Samford U., 1967; Ph.D., U. Ala., 1973. Asst. pastor 1st Baptist Ch., Talladege, Ala., 1957-59; pastor Camp Hill Bapt. Ch., 1959-61; tchr. Weogufka (Ala.) High Sch., 1961-62, Mountain Brook Jr. High, Birmingham, 1964-66, Mountain Brook High Sch., 1966-67, Lee Coll., Cleveland, Tenn., 1970—; instr. Samford U., Birmingham, 1962-64. Editor: Hard Times Remembered, 1983. Contbr. articles to hist. jours. City historian City of Cleveland, 1982. R.J. Reynolds Tobacco Co. fellow, 1966. Mem. Orgn. Am. Historians, So. Hist. Assn., East Tenn. Hist. Soc., Bradley County Hist. Soc. (pres. 1978-79), Ala. Hist. Assn. Democrat. Avocation: book collecting. Home: Cleveland, Tenn. Died Jan. 14, 2007.

SNELSON, ROY, prosthetist; b. Oklahoma City, Sept. 4, 1927; s. Albert B. and Mary (Johnson) S.; m. Bernadette Kowske, Nov. 8, 1947 (div. 1974); 1 child, Daniel B.; m. Vivian Conklin, Oct. 9, 1976. Student, UCLA, 1947-49. Clin. instr. prosthetics UCLA Sch. Medicine, 1950-57; chief prosthetic rsch. Rancho Los Amigos Hosp. and UCLA Sch. Medicine, 1957-67, project dir. amputation fracture rsch., from 1967; pres. Orthopaedic Supplies Co. Inc., Downey, Calif., 1957-70, Orthomedics Inc., Downey, 1970-88, Brea, Calif., 1979-88, Wings of Calvary, Brea, from 1988. Clin. instr. prosthetics U. Wash., Seattle, 1976—; mem. com. prosthetic R & D, NAS; mem. exec. com. Med. Engring. Ctr. U. So. Calif., 1971—; sec., dir. Am. Bd. for Cert. in Orthotics and Prosthetics, 1975-77, pres., 1978. With U.S. Army, 1945-47. Recipient Outstanding Contbn. award Soc. Orthotists and Prosthetists, 1957; HEW grantee, 1970-71. Mem. Am. Orthotic and Prosthetic Assn. (pres. 1970-71, Prosthetist of Yr. award 1951). Home: West Covina, Calif. Died Apr. 24, 2006.

SNOW, REUBEN JOSEPH, business executive; b. Cedar City, Utah, Oct. 15, 1937; s. Glenn E. and Laura (Gardner) S.; m. Marilyn Melville, June 20, 1962; children: Gina Lynne, Laura Dawn, Scott Glenn, Sara Noelle. BA, U. Utah, 1962, MA, 1964; MA, Northwestern U., 1965, PhD, 1966; postgrad. Harvard Inst. Ednl. Mgmt., summer 1982. Postdoctoral fellow Ctr. Advanced Study Ednl. Adminstrn. U. Oreg., Eugene, 1966-67; asst. prof. polit. sci. U. Calif.-Santa Barbara, 1967-73, assoc. dir. Study Ctr. U. Bordeaux III, 1971-73; mem. faculty U. Utah, 1973-85, assoc. prof. polit. sci., 1974-85, dir. Hinckley Inst. Politics, 1975-85, v.p. univ. relations, 1975-84, v.p. student and univ. relations, 1984-85; pres. The Jacobsen Co., 1985—. Vice pres., bd. dirs. Utah Symphony, 1979-83; co-chmn. Greater Salt Lake Area United Way, 1982, 83, 85, bd. dirs., 1982—; mem. Com. on Exec. Reorgn. State of Utah, 1978-83; chmn. Sta. KSL-AM-TV Adv. Bd., 1982—; chmn. spl. gifts Utah affiliate Am. Diabetes Assn., 1983-84, bd. dirs., 1984—, chmn. bd., 1985—; mem. gov. bd. Latter-day Saints Hosp., 1984—. Social Sci. Research Council tng. fellow, 1965-66. Mem. Utah Hist. Soc., Nat. Collegiate Athletic Assn. (exec. com. 1984-85), Phi Beta Kappa, Phi Kappa Phi. Democrat. Mem. Ch. Jesus Christ Latter-day Saints. Home: Provo, Utah. Died June 6, 2006.

SNYDER, CLAIR A., state legislator; b. Boston, Oct. 6, 1924; divorced; 2 children. BS, N.H. Coll., Portsmouth, 1978; postgrad., U. N.H., Durham. Formerly acct. and bus. mgr.; now mem. N.H. Ho. of Reps. Bd. dirs. N.H. Sch. Bd. Assn., 1987—; trustee various trust funds; chmn. N.H. Sch. Bd. Ins. Trust, 1993-94. Mem. Bus. and Profl. Women. Home: Somersworth, NH. Died Oct. 12, 2006.

SNYDER, CLIFFORD CHARLES, plastic surgeon, educator; b. Fort Worth, Feb. 16, 1916; s. Charles L. and Olga (Agnas) S.; m. Mary Odessa Morris, Mar. 12, 1939; 1 child, Clifford Charles BS, U. Tenn., 1940, MD, 1944. Diplomate Am. Bd. Surgery, Am. Bd. Plastic Surgery (examiner 1964-70, chmn. resident rev. com. 1970, sr. examiner 1970-86). Intern U.S. Naval Hosp., Mare Island, Calif., 1944-45; resident in gen. surgery Jackson Meml. Hosp., U. Miami Sch. Medicine, Fla., 1946-49; resident in plastic surgery U. Tex. Med. Br., Galveston, 1949-52, instr. surgery, 1952-53, asst. prof., 1953-54; asst. prof. surgery U. Miami Sch. Medicine, 1954-59, assoc. prof., 1959-67; chief plastic surgery Shriners Hosp. Crippled Children, Salt Lake City, 1967-88, pres. staff, 1985; chief surg. service VA Hosp., Salt Lake City, 1967-81; chief plastic surgery Variety Children's Hosp., Miami, 1956-66, pres. staff, 1960-66; attending Doctors Hosp., Coral Gables, Fla., 1955-66, hon. staff, from 1966; assoc. dean. U. Utah Sch. Medicine, Salt Lake City, endowed Clifford C. Snyder chair surgery, prof. emeritus dept. surgery, chmn. honors program adv. com., 1987-89. Sr. plastic surgery cons. VA Hosp., Coral Gables, 1954-66, U.S. Air Force, Fla., 1956-66; mem. adv. bd. Crippled Children's Soc. Fla., 1956-66, Vocat. Rehab. Fla., 1960-66; mem. Fla. Gov.'s Com. Rehab., 1960-66; mem. specialists panel Ethicon, 1965—, chmn., 1970-75; mem. nat. surg. cons. com. VA, 1960-73, chief surgery com., 1974-78; faculty rep. Western Athletic Conf., 1976-80, bd. athletics, 1971-73, 75-81; mem. com. emergency services NRC, 1977; bd. dirs. Far Ea. Meml. Hosp., Taipei, Taiwan, 1985—. Mem. editorial bd. Jour. Plastic and Reconstructive Surgery, 1962-80, assoc. editor, 1957-63, editor internat. abstracts, 1963-69, co-editor, 1973-80, book rev. editor, 1973-80; editorial bd. Jour. Toxicology, 1989—; assoc. editor Small Animal Clinician, 1965-80; spl. editor Vet. Medicine, 1965-80; contbr. over 181 articles to profl. jours. Served to lt. (s.g.) USNR, 1941-45 Deocrated officer Order of St. John; recipient Best Prof. award U. Tex., 1953, U. Utah, 1974, Merit award Miami Dental Soc., 1959, Disting. Svc. award Fla. West Coast Dental Assn., 1960, Sci. Achievement award Fla. Med. Assn., 1961, 63, Commendation VA Hosp., 1972, Ohio State U. Guest of Honor award, Ethicon Plastic Surgery citation; named Disting. Alumnus U. Tenn., 1988, Disting. Honors Prof. U. Utah, 1989. Fellow N.Y. Acad. Scis.; mem. ACS (bd. govs. 1963-64, pres. Greater Miami chpt. 1964-66), Am. Assn. Plastic Surgeons (trustee 1964-76, v.p. 1973-74, pres. 1975-76), Am. Burn Assn., Am. Coll. Vet. Surgeons (1st hon. mem., Mark Allam award), AMA, Am. Soc. Plastic and Reconstructive Surgeons (v.p. 1967-68, treas. Ednl. Found. 1962-67, trustee 1960-71), Am. Soc. Surgery of Hand, Am. Trauma Soc., Am. Assn. Hand Surgeons, Am. Animal Hosp. Assn. (hon.; Disting. Service award 1974), Am. Vet. Neurology Assn., Assn. VA Surgeons, Fla. Acad. Sci., Fla. Cleft Palate Assn. (pres. 1960-63), Fla. Med. Assn. (chmn. archives 1960-67), Fla. Soc. Plastic and Reconstructive Surgeons (pres. 1959-60), Fla. Med. Vet. Assn. (hon.), Internat. Congress Plastic Surgeons, Mexican-Am. Plastic Surgery Soc., Pan Am. Cancer Cytology Soc., Pan-Pacific Surg. Assn. (v.p. 1980-83), Plastic Surgery Research Council, Soc. Plastic and Reconstructive Surgeons Thailand (hon.), Assn. Surgeons of S.E. Asia, Asian Surg. Assn., Salt Lake Surg. Soc., Singleton Surg. Soc., Soc. Head and Neck Surgeons, Southeastern Plastic and Reconstructive Surgery Soc. (pres. 1962-63), So. Med. Assn. (sect. pres. 1964), So. Surg. Assn., Tex. Med. Assn., Am. Soc. Aesthetic Plastic Surgery, Tex. Soc. Plastic Surgery (hon.), Utah State Plastic Surgery Soc. (charter), Salt Lake Surg. Soc., Utah Med. Soc. (del. 1977-81), Utah Hist. Soc. (pres. 1973), U. Utah Alumni Assn. (bd. dirs. 1975-80), Acad. Surg. Research, Plastic Surgery Soc. of the Americas (pres. 1986-87), Phi Kappa Phi, Alpha Delta Sigma, Alpha Epsilon Delta (Outstanding Achievement award 1971). Mem. LDS Church. Invented surg. instruments, bandage, suture, snake bite vaccine, antivenom, force feeding pump. Died June 15, 2007.

SNYDER, GENE (MARION GENE SNYDER), lawyer, retired congressman; b. Louisville, Jan. 26, 1928; s. M. G. and Lois (Berg) S.; 1 son, Mark; m. Patricia C. Robertson, Apr. 10, 1973; 2 step-children. LLB cum laude, Jefferson Sch. Law, Louisville, 1950; JD, U. Louisville, 1969. Bar: Ky. bar 1950, D.C. bar 1970. Practiced law, Louisville, 1950-76; ret.; farmer, 1957-80; city atty. Jeffersontown, 1953-57; magistrate 1st dist. Jefferson County, 1957-61; real estate broker, 1949—89; mem. US Congress from 3d Ky. Dist., 1963-65, US Congress from 4th Ky. Dist., 1967-87; sole practice, 1987-91. V.p. Ky. Magistrates and Commrs., 1958. Vice pres. Jeffersontown Civic Center, 1953-54; pres. Lincoln Republican Club Ky., 1960-61, 1st Magisterial Dist. Rep. Club, 1955-57. Mem. Ky. Bar Assn., Ky. Farm Bur., Optimists (pres. Jeffersontown club 1957-58), Jesters, Shriners, Masons. Died Feb. 16, 2007.

SNYDER, GILES D. H., lawyer; b. Charleston, W.Va., May 28, 1931; s. Harry L. and Cora Ella (Houston) S.; m. Dale S. Davis, May 23, 1975; children— Jesse D. H., Benjamin D. H.; children by previous marriage— Anne H., Giles G., Matthew D. AB, W.Va.U., 1952, LL.B., 1954. Bar: W.Va. Ohio 19, D.C. 19, U.S.

Ct. Appeals 19, U.S. Supreme Ct. Asst. atty. gen. State of W.Va., Charleston, 1956-60; atty. Columbia Gas System, NYC, 1960-68; asst. sec. Columbus Group of Columbia System, Ohio, 1968-73, Columbia Gas Transmission Corp., Charleston, W.Va., 1973-83, sec., gen. counsel, 1983-94; spl. counsel Bowles Rice McDavid Graff and Love, Charleston, from 1994. Mem. ABA, W.Va. Bar Assn., Ohio State Bar Assn., Fed. Energy Bar Assn., Order of Coif, Phi Beta Kappa. Democrat. Episcopalian. Home: Charleston, W.Va. Died Nov. 10, 2006.

SNYDER, LOIS DE ORSEY, public relations executive; b. Whitinsville, Mass., Aug. 12, 1929; d. Francis X. and Germaine Gagnon De Orsey; A.B., Lenoir-Rhyne Coll., 1953; postgrad. Duke U., 1953-56; m. Harry M. Snyder, Jr. (dec. 1974); children: Stephen De Orsey, Melissa Anne. French tchr. Lenoir-Rhyne Coll., 1952-53; tchr. English, speech and drama Hickory (N.C.) High Sch., 1953-54; dir. public relations Hickory Furniture Mart, 1979-81; pvt. practice public relations, Hickory, 1981—. Pres., Hickory Dyslexia Found., Catawba County Arts Council, Hickory Landmarks Soc., ARC, Catawba County Mental Health Assn., N.C. Cerebral Palsy Assn.; lay reader St. Alban's Episc. Ch., Hickory. Recipient Outstanding Service award N.C. Assn. Cerebral Palsy, 1965. Mem. Catawba County Execs. Club, Internat. Platform Assn., Catawba County C. of C. (dir.), Lenoir-Rhyne Coll. Alumni Assn. (past pres., bd. dirs.), Alpha Psi Omega, Iota Epsilon Omega. Republican. Home: Hickory, NC. Died May 29, 2006.

SOIKA, HELMUT EMIL, retirement plan executive; b. NYC, May 22, 1941; s. Hubert E. and Berta Antonia (Metzger) S. BS, Fordham U., 1963, JD, 1968. Asst. trust officer Nat. Bank of N.Am., NYC, 1968-71; trust officer Bank of N.Y., Westchester, 1971-72; atty. O'Neill, DiManno & Kelly, NYC, 1972-76; atty. & div. mgr. Mut. of Am., NYC, 1976-82; v.p., mgr. retirement plans Prudential-Bache Securities, NYC, 1982-86; sr. v.p., dir. retirement plans Gruntal & Co. Inc., NYC, from 1986. Home: New York, NY. Died Sept. 23, 2006.

SOKATCH, JOHN ROBERT, biochemistry educator; b. Joliet, Ill., Dec. 20, 1928; s. John Peter and Christina (Yuratik) S.; m. Carol Koch, June 10, 1957; children: David, Barbara, Karen. BS, U. Mich., 1950; MS in Bacteriology, U. Ill., 1952, PhD, 1956. Research asso. Wash. State U., 1956-58; asst. prof. microbiology U. Okla. Sch. Medicine, 1958-61, asso. prof., 1961-65, prof., from 1967, prof. biochemistry and molecular biology, from 1968, chmn. dept., 1984-91, George Lynn Cross research prof., from 1983, asst. dean Grad. Coll., Med. Center Campus, 1970-71, asso. dean, from 1971, asso. dir. research adminstrn., 1973; interim dean U. Okla. Sch. Medicine (Coll. Pharmacy), from 1976. Mem. microbial physiology study sect. NIH, 1980-84, 89-92, chmn., 1981-83; vis. prof. GBF, Braunschweig, Germany, 1989. Author: Bacterial Physiology and Metabolism, 1969; co-author: Basic Bacteriology and Genetics, 1976; co-editor: The Bacteria, Vols. 6, 7, 8, 9, 10. Recipient Research Career Devel. award NIH, 1962-72; Am. Soc. Microbiology Pres.'s fellow, 1961; Fulbright Sr. Research scholar Sheffield U., Eng., 1963-64; Fogarty sr. internat. fellow Cambridge (Eng.) U. Mem. Am. Soc. Microbiology, Am. Acad. Microbiology, Am. Soc. Biol. Chemists. Research on microbial biochemistry including metabolism of branched chain amino acids by bacteria, regulation of catabolic and biosynthetic pathways. Home: Oklahoma City, Okla. Died Feb. 6, 2006.

SOKOL, SI, insurance company executive, director; b. Columbus, Ohio, Dec. 22, 1927; s. Nathan and Rose (Klyst) S.; m. Barbara Sokol, June 29, 1958; children: John, James, Carla. Student, Ohio State U., 1949—52. Exec. v.p. Beverlee Dr. Ins., Columbus, 1949—62; ptnr. DeWitt, Sokol & Co., Columbus, 1962—70; pres., chmn. Ohio Indemnity Co., Columbus, from 1970. Pres. Comty. Venture, Columbus, 1975—81; dir. Dollar Savs. & Loan, Columbus, 1962—70, Am. Savs. & Loan, Cin.; prin. owner Si Sokol & Assocs.; pres. Westford Group, Inc., from 1980; chmn. Am. Legal Pub. Co., from 1988; mergers and acquisitions cons., Columbus. Pres. Comty. Venture, Columbus, 1975—81. Mem.: Cin. Club, Athletic Club. Home: Columbus, Ohio. Died July 3, 2007.

SOLLEY, THOMAS TREAT, museum director; b. NYC, Sept. 4, 1924; s. John Beach and Katherine (Lilly) S.; children— Evan L., Robert L., Katherine H., Virginia H. BA, Yale U., 1950; MA, Ind. U., 1966, postgrad., 1966-68. Archtl. project engr. Eli Lilly & Co., Indpls., 1951-61; pvt. archtl. practice Indpls., 1961-64; asst. dir. Ind. U. Art Mus., Bloomington, 1968-71, dir., from 1971. Adv. trustee Children's Mus., Indpls.; mem. governing bd. Yale U. Art Gallery Bd. dirs. Ind. U. Art Mus., 1976-86. Served with AUS, 1943-46. Mem. Assn. Art Mus. Dirs. Died Apr. 8, 2006.

SOLOMON, M. MICHAEL, manufacturing executive; b. Phila., Sept. 20, 1924; s. Bernard and May (Klein) Solomon; m. Selma Sion, Dec. 19, 1948; children: Meryl Meg Cooperman, Jodee Royce. BA, Temple U., 1945; MA, Temple U., 1947; PhD, Purdue U., 1951. Scientist Worcester Found., Shrewsbury, Mass., 1950—52; devel. chemist Gen. Electric Co., Waterford, NY, 1952—60, mgr. sci. liaison King of Prussia, Pa., 1960—66, mgr. R & D Phila., 1966—83; pres. Maxicom, Inc., Phila., 1983—85; cons. materials chemistry Dove Assocs., Phila., from 1985. Capt. Brentwood Town Watch, Abington, from 1984. Mem.: Am. Chem. Soc., IEEE (sr.), Masons, B'nai B'rith, Phi Lambda Upsilon, Sigma Xi. Achievements include patents for silicone chemistry, 1955, 56, 57. Avocations: tennis, opera, symphony. Home: Abington, Pa. Died Jan. 4, 2007.

SOLOMON, ROBERT CHARLES, philosopher, educator; b. Detroit, Sept. 14, 1942; s. Charles M. and Vita (Petrosky) S. BA, U. Pa., 1963; MA, U. Mich., 1965, PhD, 1967. Teaching fellow U. Mich., Ann Arbor, 1965-66; lectr. Princeton (N.J.) U., 1966-67, 67-68; asst. prof. U. Pitts., 1969-71, CUNY, 1971-72; assoc. prof. philosophy U. Tex., Austin, 1972-77, prof., 1977—2007, Quincy Lee Centennial prof., 1986-97, disting. tchg. prof., 1997—2007. Vis. prof. U. Pa., UCLA, U. Auckland, N.Z., La Trobe U., Melbourne, Australia, U. B.C.; chmn. Phi Beta Kappa Emerson Award Com.; cons. in field. Author: From Rationalism to Existentialism, 1972, The Passions, 1976, Introducing Philosophy: Problems and Perspectives, 1977, History and Human Nature: A Philosophical Review of European History and Culture, 1750-1850, 1979, Love: Emotion, Myth and Metaphor, 1981, In the Spirit of Hegel, 1983; (with C. Calhoun) What Is an Emotion?, 1984, It's a Good Business, 1985; (with Kristine Hanson) Above the Bottom Line, 1983, From Hegel to Existentialism, 1987, Continental Philosophy After 1750, 1988, About Love, 1988, A Passion for Justice, 1990, Ethics: A Briefer Introduction, 1991, Ethics and Excellence, 1992, Entertaining Ideas, 1992; (with J. Solomon) Up the University, 1993; (with Kathleen Higgins) A Short History of Philosophy, 1996, A Passion for Wisdom, 1997, A Better Way to Think About Business, 1999, The Joy of Philosophy, 1999, What Nietzsche Really Said, 2000; (with Fernando Flores) Building Trust, 2000, Spirituality for the Skeptic, 2002, Not Passions Slave, 2003, Living with Nietzsche, 2003, In defense of Sentimentality, 2004; editor: Phenomenology and Existentialism, 1972, Nietzsche, 1973, Existentialism, 1974; (with Kathleen Higgins) Reading Nietzsche, 1988, From Africa to Zen, 1993, The Age of German Idealism, 1993, (with Mark A. Murphy) What Is Justice?, 1990, Wicked Pleasures: Meditations on the Seven Deadly Sins, 1999, What is an Emotion, 2003, Thinking about Feeling, 2004; contbr. articles to profl. jours. Recipient Outstanding Tchr. award Standard Oil Co., 1973, Pres.' Teaching Excellence award, 1985, 96., Chad Oliver Honors Tchg. award, 1998; named to Acad. Disting. Tchrs., 1997. Mem. Am. Philos. Assn., N.Am. Nietzsche Soc., Internat. Soc. Rsch. on Emotions (pres.), Soc. for Bus. Ethics, Acad. Disting. Tchrs. Home: Austin, Tex. Died Jan. 2, 2007.

SOMBART, PAUL C., former state legislator; b. Boonville, Mo., Dec. 24, 1920; s. Bernice Sombart; children: Lisa, Kevin. Dairy farmer; former cir. clk. and recorder Cooper County, Mo.; rep. Mo. State Ho. Reps. Dist. 117, 1991-97, mem. agr., children, youth and families coms., mem. correctional inst. and fees and salaries Coms. Mem. Boonville and Calif. C. of C., Cooper County Farm Bur. Died Dec. 24, 2005.

SOMMER, FRANK HENRY, III, librarian, archeologist, author, educator; b. Newark, July 30, 1922; s. George R. and Abigail Woodruff (Van Horn) S. BA, Yale U., 1943, PhD, 1950; diploma gen. archeology, Cambridge U., 1948. Keeper folk art Winterthur (Del.) Mus., 1958-63; head of libraries Wintherthur (Del.) Mus., from 1963; mem. faculty U. Del., from 1948, prof. history of art, from 1958. Cons. Nat. Gallery, 1971, Nat. Endowment Humanities, 1978; dir. Furniture Library. Contbr. articles to profl. jours. Henry fellow, 1947-48 Mem. Am. Assn. Archtl. Bibliographers, Soc. Archtl. Historians. Clubs: Grolier (N.Y.C.); Odd Volumes (Boston); Franklin Inn (Phila.); Elizabethan (New Haven). Republican. Roman Catholic. Died Oct. 20, 2006.

SOMMERS, LAWRENCE MELVIN, geographer, educator; b. Clinton, Wis., Apr. 17, 1919; s. Emil L. and Inga (Anderson) S.; m. Marjorie Smith, Apr. 26, 1948; 1 dau., Laurie Kay. BS, U. Wis., 1942, Ph.M., 1946; PhD, Northwestern U., 1950. Prof. geography Mich. State. U., East Lansing, from 1949, successively instr., asst. prof. dept. geography, assoc. prof., 1949-55, prof., 1955-89, prof. emeritus, asst. provost emeritus, from 1989; chmn. dept. geography Mich. State U., East Lansing, 1955-79, mem. Environ. Quality Ctr., 1979-81, asst. provost, 1987-89. Mem. adv. com. geography Office Naval Rsch. and NRC, 1958-61; fellow Am. Scandinavian Found.; bd. dirs. Am. Paytel Corp.; mem. commn. on dynamics of marginal and critical regions Internat. Geog. Union, 1996—. Co-author: Outside Readings in Geography, 1955, Introduction to Geography-Selected Readings, 1967, Cultural Geography-Selected Readings, 1967, Physical Geography-Selected Readings, 1967, Economic Geography-Selected Readings, 1970, World Regional Geography, 1976, Energy and the Adaptation of Human Settlements, 1980, Planning Issues in Marginal Areas, 1991; author: Michigan: A Geography, 1984; editor: Atlas of Michigan, 1977, Fish in Lake Michigan, 1981, Land Use: A Spatial Approach, 1981; contbr. articles on Norwegian, European, Mich., marginal areas, and econ. geography to profl. jours. Served with adj. gen. dept. AUS, 1942-45. Office Naval Rsch. grant for rsch. in Denmark, 1953, Travel grant to Europe, 1960, 82, 86, Social Sci. Rsch. Coun. and Am. Scandinavian Found. grantee for rsch. in Norway, 1948. Mem. AAAS, Nat. Coun. Geog. Edn., Am. Geog. Soc., Assn. Am. Geographers (exec. com. 1967-70, chmn. cons. svc. 1970-77, publ. com. 1968-70), Western Region Sci. Assn., Mich. State U. Acad. Coun. and Grad. Coun. (chmn. steering com. 1981-84), Am. Scandinavian Found., Internat. Region Sci. Assn., Scandinavian Studies Assn., Explorers Club, Sigma Xi (pres. Mich. State U. chpt. 1959-60), Phi Kappa Phi (pres. Mich. State U. chpt. 1980-82, v.p. North Ctrl. region 1986-89, nat. pres.-elect 1989-92, exec. com. 1992—, nat. pres. 1992-95, past pres. 1995—), Retired Geographers Orgn. (bd. dirs. 1998—), Phi Delta Beta. Home: Okemos, Mich. Died Aug. 3, 2007.

SOMMERS, WILLIAM PAUL, management consultant, research and development company executive; b. Detroit, July 22, 1933; s. William August and Mary Elizabeth (Baietto) S.; m. Josephine A. Sommers; children: William F., Clare M., John C. Hughes, Joanna M. Weems, Russell L. Hughes. BSE (scholar), U. Mich., 1955, MSE, 1956, PhD (Riggs fellow, Texaco fellow, Univ. fellow), 1961. Rsch. assoc. U. Mich. Inst. Sci. and Tech., Ann Arbor, 1958-61; chief chem. propulsion space and missile sys. Martin Marietta Corp., Balt., 1956-58, 61-63; v.p. Booz, Allen & Hamilton, Inc., Bethesda, Md., 1963-70, pres. Tech. Mgmt. Group, 1973-79, sr. v.p., 1979-92; exec. v.p. Iameter, Inc., San Mateo, Calif., 1992-94; pres., CEO SRI Internat., Menlo Park, Calif., 1994-98, ret., 1998. Bd. dirs. Gukenheimer Enterprises, H2 Gen. Contbr. articles to profl. jours., also chpt. in book. Pres. Washington chpt. U. Mich. Alumni Club, 1970-71; v.p. Wildwood manor Citizens Assn., 1968-70; chief Adventure Guide program YMCA, 1971-72; bd. visitors Coll. Engring. U. Calif., Davis; mem. nat. adv. bd. Coll. Engring. U. Mich.; mem. conf. bd. Internat. Coun. on Innovation and Tech. Mem.: Wianno Country Club, Nianno Club, Ponte Vedra Lodge and Club, Hyannis Yacht Club, Met. Club (D.C.), Marsh Landing Country Club, Wianno Yacht Club, Ponte Vedra Inn and Club, Pi Tau Sigma, Tau Beta Pi, Sigma Xi. Republican. Roman Catholic. Home: Ponte Vedra Beach, Fla. Died Jan. 7, 2007.

SOMMERVILLE, MARGARET JEAN LOSEKE, physician; b. Columbus, Nebr., Feb. 21, 1925; d. Edward G. an Emma C. (Luers) Loseke; m. James J. Sommerville, Nov. 6 1954; children— Jean, Ann, Peggy. B.A., M.D., U. Iowa Diplomate Am. Acad. Family Practice. Intern, Kings Col Hosp., Bklyn., 1951-53; individual practice, specializing i family medicine, Strawberry Point, Iowa, 1953-55, Des Moines 1955, White Plains and Port Chester, N.Y., 1956-59, Atlanta 1959—; mem. wellness com. Northside Hosp., Atlanta. Mem Nu Sigma Phi. Republican. Lutheran. Died May 2, 2006.

SONNABEND, ILEANA, art dealer; b. Bucharest, Romania Oct. 28, 1914; d. Mihail Schapira; m. Leo Castelli (div. 1959 1 child, Nina; m. Michael Sonnabend (dec. 2001); 1 adopte child, Antonio Homem. Owner Sonnabend Gallery, NYC, Gale rie Ileana Sonnabend, Paris. Died Oct. 21, 2007.*

SONNENBERG, WALTER ADOLF, association executive; b Bklyn., Oct. 28, 1921; s. Adolf and Olga (Bartz) S.; m Marguerite Ehlert, June 6, 1946; 1 child, Scott B. BA, Norwic U., 1949; MBA, Dartmouth Coll., 1953. Asst. to contr. MIT Cambridge, Mass., 1956—64; pvt. practice acctg. Northfiel Vt., 1960—63; dean of adminstrn. New Coll., Sarasota, Fla 1964—65; bus. mgr. Am. Physiol. Soc., Bethesda, Md 1965—88. With USMC, 1942—46, with USMC, 1950—5 with USCG, 1958—62. Decorated Bronze Star. Mem.: AICPA Fla. Soc. CPAs, Vt. Soc. CPAs, Nat. Assn. Accts., Aircra Owners and Pilots Assn., Sigma Phi Epsilon. Republica Lutheran. Home: Bradenton, Fla. Died July 14, 2007.

SONNENBLICK, EDMUND HIRAM, medical educator, cardiologist; b. New Haven, Oct. 7, 1932; s. Ira J. and Rosalin (Helfand) S.; m. Linda Bland, Dec. 21, 1954; children: Emil Sonnenblick Offit, Charlotte Sonnenblick Van Doren, Annie (dec.). BA, Wesleyan U., Middletown, Conn., 1954; MI Harvard U., 1958. Diplomate Am. Bd. Internal Medicin Resident in medicine Presbyn. Hosp., NYC, 1958-60, 62-63; investigator Nat. Heart Inst., Bethesda, Md., 1960-62, 63-6 asst. prof. medicine Harvard Med. Sch., Boston, 1968-70, asso prof., 1970-75; co-dir. cardiology Peter Bent Brigham Hosp Boston, 1968-75, dir. cardiovasc. rsch., 1970-75; Olson pro medicine, chief carddiology Albert Einstein Coll. Medicin Bronx, NY, 1975—96, Edmond J. Safra disting. prof. medicin 1996—2007, chief emeritus cardiology, 1996—2007. Vis pro medicine NY Med. Coll.; assoc. dir. Cardiovasc. Rsch. Ins Valhalla, NY; editor Progress in Cardiovasc. Diseaess; contb over 600 articles to med. jours. Author 15 books and chpts. books. Trustee Wesleyan U., 1994-97. Sr. surgeon USPH 1960-62. Fellow ACP, Am. Coll. Cardiology (Disting. Scienti award 1989), Internat. Soc. for Heart Rsch.; mem. Am. Hea Failure Soc. Am., Am. Hypertension Soc. (co-founder), A Coll. Physicians, Am. Assn. Physicians, Century Assn., A Soc. Clin. Investigation, Am. Physiol. Soc., Interurban Club, N Yacht Club, Noroton Yacht Club, Woods Hole Yacht Cl Avocation: sailing. Home: Darien, Conn. Died Sept. 22, 200

SORKIN, GERALD B., management and marketing executiv b. Bklyn., June 20, 1932; s. Nathan and Dora (Butlin) S. A.I Dartmouth Coll., 1953; m. Eleanor Smith, Sept. 30, 195 children: Andrea Joyce, Lynn Harriet, Jessica Lee. Art di prodn. mgr. Wesley H. Porter, Advt., L.A., 1953-56; advt. m Plastix Footwear Corp., 1956-58; mgr. sales promotion, bra mgr. Hunt Foods & Industries, Inc., Fullerton, Calif., 1958-6 prin. G.B. Sorkin & Co., L.A., 1963-64; pres. Sorkin/Hudsc L.A., 1964-67, 69-72; v.p. West Coast, Adams/Dana/Silverstei L.A., 1967-69; v.p. David W. Evans, Advt., Inc., L.A., 1972-7 pres., 1973-77; ind. mktg. cons., 1977-78; dir. advt. Shap Industries, Inc., Beverly Hills, Calif., 1978-79; dir. sales a mktg. Arvida Southern, Miami, Fla., 1979-82; sr. v.p. Ventu Devel. Corp., Miami, 1982-83; v.p. mktg. ITT Commun Devel. Corp., Palm Coast, Fla., 1983-90; mktg. cons. G. Sorkin & Co., 1990—; v.p., bd. dir. Rinkled Raisin, Inc., L.A Diamond Fork Land Cattle Co., Cedar City, Utah; bd. dir. Dav W. Evans, Inc., Salt Lake City, 1973-77. Trustee, Eddie Can Charitable Found., 1972-79; v.p. Mid-Fla. ARC, 1988-9 commr. Wilshire Blvd. Temple Camps, 1973-79. Mem. As Nat. Advertisers, Am. Resort and Residential Devel. Ass Urban Land Inst., Nat. Assn. Home Builders, B'nai B'rith (S awards 1973, 74, 75, 76). Republican. Jewish. Lodge: Rot (founding pres. Flagler/Palm Coast Sunrise). Author, co-aut TV scripts and movies. Home: Longwood, Fla. Died Aug. 2006.

SOSMAN, MARTHA BROWNING, state supreme court ju tice; b. Boston, Oct. 20, 1950; BA Middlebury Coll, JD U. Mi Assoc. Foley, Hoag & Eliot, Boston, 1979—84; with U Atty.'s Office, Boston, 1984—89; founding ptnr. Kern, Sosm Hagerty, Roach & Carpenter, Boston, 1989—93; judge Ma Superior Ct., 1993—2000; assoc. justice Mass. Supreme J Ct., 2000—07. Mem. bd. directors Planned Parenthood Leag of Mass. Mem.: Mass. Bar Assn., Mass. Women's Bar As Died Mar. 11, 2007.

SOTER, RICHARD P., retired academic administrator; Boston, Oct. 24, 1927; m. Ruth Colby, 1950 (dec. 1963); Margaret Fairbanks, 1965; children: Paul, Bruce, Caroli Anne. BA in European History, Northeastern U.; Ph.D, Harv U. Comml. banker Citibank; Korea expert US Dept. St 1965—66; instr. Queens Coll., SUNY, Oswego, Wilkes C Kendall Coll., Evanston, Ill.; pres. Barat Coll., Lake Forest, 1984—88; aid specialist US Dept. State, 1966—68; exec. Japan Am. Soc., Chgo., 1988—2003. Served in USN. Died M 27, 2007.

SOTT, HERBERT, lawyer; b. Detroit, Jan. 26, 1920; s. Ha and E. Helen (Nalven) S.; m. Elaine D. Davidson, Oct. 14, 19 children by previous marriage; Lesley Sott Geary, Lynne S Jackson. AB, U. Mich., 1940, MBA, 1942, JD with distincti 1943. Bar: Mich. 1946. Since practiced in Detroit; ptnr. Fri man, Meyers & Keys, 1951-68; partner Barris, Sott, Denn Driker, from 1968. Active Founders Soc. Detroit Inst. A Detroit Grand Opera Assn., Detroit Symphony Assn., Det Zool. Assn.; bd. dirs. Detroit Symphony Orch., Mich. He Assn., Mich. Cancer Found., Jewish Home for Aged, Jew

Family and Children's Service, Jewish Vocat. Service. Served as lt. (j.g.) USNR, 1943-46. Mem. Detroit, Mich., Am. bar assns. Clubs: Detroit, Franklin Hills. Died Mar. 16, 2007.

SOUTHWELL, LEONARD J., dairy corporation executive; b. Sioux City, Iowa, Nov. 9, 1924; s. George P. and Nellie (Van Houten) S.; m. Rosemary Kathern Kirsch, June 9, 1951; children: George, Christine, John. BS in Dairy Ind., Iowa State U., 1951. Mgr. Equity Creamery, Pana, Ill., 1951-64; sales mgr. Prairie Farms Dairy, Carlinville, Ill., 1964-72, asst. gen. mgr., 1972-80, chief oper. officer, 1980-88, chief exec. officer, from 1988. Bd. dirs. Milk Industry Found. With USN, 1943-46. Mem. Elks, Masons, Shrine, Consistory. Home: Pana, Ill. Died Aug. 8, 2006.

SPARE, ANTHONY EDWARD, investment company executive; b. Chgo., Oct. 1, 1939; s. Alexander T. and Rita H. S.; m. Eleanor Doyle, July 14, 1962; children— Alexander, Samantha, James. BA, Tufts U., 1961; MBA, Stanford U., 1963. With Bank of Calif., San Francisco, 1963—, analyst, 1965-74, dir. rsch., 1975-86; chief investment officer Merus 1986—. Pres. Hillsborough Schs. Found; active fund-raising various local and univ. groups. Chartered fin. analyst. Mem. Nat. Assn. Bus. Economists, Security Analysts San Francisco (past pres.), Fin. Analyst Fedn. Home: Burlingame, Calif. Died Jan. 16, 2007.

SPARKS, DAVID STANLEY, retired academic administrator; b. Phila., Dec. 8, 1922; s. Richard Frederick and Grace Dorothy (Tuttle) S.; m. Phyllis Ann Bate, June 12, 1949 (dec. 1996); children: Robert F., E. Anne. AB, Grinnell Coll., Iowa, 1944; MA, U. Chgo., 1945, PhD, 1951. Instr., asst. prof., asso. prof. U. Md., College Park, 1947-65, prof. history, 1965—91, assoc. dean grad. studies and research, 1967-70, dean, 1970-77, acting vice chancellor for acad. affairs, 1976-77, acting v.p. grad. studies and research, 1978-79, v.p. grad. studies and research, 1979-87, acting v.p. for acad. affairs, 1982-83, v.p. acad. affairs, grad. studies and research, 1987-88, vice chancellor for acad. affairs, 1988-91, vice chancellor emeritus, 1991—2007. Vis. professorial lectr. dept. history Johns Hopkins, 1965; mem., chair Grad. Record Examinations Bd., 1979-85. Co-editor, author: American Civilization: A History of the United States, 1960, The Making of American Democracy, Readings and Documents, 2 vols, 1962; Editor: Inside Lincoln's Army: The Diary of General Marsena Rudolph Patrick, 1964. Recipient research awards Am. Philos. Soc., 1958, Social Sci. Research Council, 1957 Mem. Am., So. hist. assns., Orgn. Am. Historians, Am. Assn. U. Profs. (pres. U. Md. chpt.), Nat. Acad. Univ. Research Adminstrs., Phi Kappa Phi. Clubs: Cosmos (Washington). Home: Rockville, Md. Died Apr. 17, 2007.

SPARKS, KIMBERLY, German language educator; b. Balt., Oct. 2, 1930; married; 3 children AB, Princeton U., 1956, MA, 1959, PhD in German, 1963. Instr. German Princeton (N.J.) U., 1960-63, asst. prof., 1963-66; assoc. prof. Middlebury (Vt.) Coll., 1966-71, Charles A. Dana prof., from 1971, chmn. com. for langs., from 1973, chmn. dept. German, chmn. div. for lang., 1966-71. Chmn. exam com. German Achievement Test, 1966—; dir. N.E. Conf. Teaching for Lang., 1968—. Co-author: Der Weg zum Lesen, 1967; German in Review, 1967, Modern German, 1971, So ist es, 1971, Thomas Mann's Tonio Kroger als Weg zur Literatur, 1974, The Realization of Space in Kafka from On Kafka, 1977; contbr. chpts. to books and articles to profl. jours. Mem. MLA Died Oct. 30, 2006.

SPARR, DANIEL BEATTIE, retired federal judge; b. Denver, June 8, 1931; s. Daniel John and Mary Isabel (Beattie) S.; m. Virginia Sue Long Sparr, June 28, 1952; children: Stephen Glenwood, Douglas Lloyd, Michael Christopher. BSBA, U. Denver, 1952, JD, 1966. Bar: Colo. U.S. Dist. Ct. Assoc. White & Steele, Denver, 1966-70; atty. Mountain States Telephone & Telegraph Co., Denver, 1970-71; ptnr. White & Steele, Denver, 1971-74; atty. Wesley H. Doan, Lakewood, Colo., 1974-75; prin. Law Offices of Daniel B. Sparr, Denver, 1975-77; judge 2d dist. Colo. Dist. Ct., Denver, 1977-90; judge U.S. Dist. Ct. Colo., Denver, 1990—2001. Mem. Denver Bar Assn. (trustee 1975-78), Denver Paralegal Inst. (bd. advs. 1976-88), William E. Doyle's/Am. Inns of Ct., Am. Bd. Trial Advs., ABA, Colo. Bar Assn. Home: Colorado Spgs, Colo. Died Nov. 9, 2006.

SPEAR, MARSHALL NEWTON, auditor; b. Perham, Maine, July 31, 1922; s. Newton Guy and Helen Edna (Huston) S.; m. Gloria Mercy Gould, Oct. 23, 1948; children: Sandra Leigh, Sonya Fay, Eric Newton. ASA, Bentley Coll., 1962; diploma, Air Command and Staff Coll., 1960; cert., Indsl. Coll. Armed Forces, 1967; student, La Salle Ext. U., 1968. Cert. fed. taxation Accreditation Coun. for Accountancy, lic. enrolled to practice before IRS. Office mgr., acct. Taterstate Products Inc., Washburn, Maine, 1948—53; commd. 2d lt. USAF, 1943, advanced through grades to maj., 1953, ret., 1969; office mgr., tax preparer H & R Block, Austin, Tex., 1970; auditor Tex. Dept. Welfare, Austin, 1970—79, program audit mgr., 1979—86; pvt. practice tax preparer Austin, from 1986. Mem. exch. coun. U.S. Congl. Adv. Bd., Nat. Rep. Presdl. Task Force. With US Army, 1941—45. Decorated Meritorious Svc. medal; recipient Air Force Commendation medal, Presdl. Achievement award, 1982. Mem.: Travis County React Team, Am. Security Coun. (nat. adv. bd.), Ret. Officers Assn., Tex. Assn. Enrolled Agts., Nat. Assn. Enrolled Agts., Shriners, Mason. Methodist. Died June 27, 2007.

SPEARS, JAMES M(IT), lawyer; b. San Benito, Tex., Dec. 1, 1952; BA, Tex. Tech. Univ., 1975; JD, Univ. Tex., 1978. Bar: Tex. 1978, D.C. 1998. Dep. asst. atty. gen. Lands & Natural Resources div., U.S. Dept. Justice, Washington, 1983—84, Civil div., U.S. Dept. Justice, Washington, 1985—88; gen. counsel FTC, Washington, 1993—94; ptnr. litigation dept. & head antitrust & trade litigation practice group Ropes & Gray, Washington. Contbr. articles to profl. jours. Died June 10, 2007.

SPENCER, DEREK WARDLE, oceanographic researcher; b. South Shields, Durham, Eng., May 2, 1934; came to U.S., 1965; s. Samuel Bertie and Mary (Dixon) S.; m. Ann Lowe, Aug. 10, 1957; children— Andrew Maxwell, Caroline Ann, Roger Alexander B.Sc. with 1st class honors, Manchester U., 1954, PhD, 1957. Supr. geochem. research Imperial Oil Ltd., Calgary, Alta., Can., 1957-65; assoc. scientist Woods Hole Oceanographic Inst., Mass., 1965-71, sr. scientist Mass., 1971-74, chmn. dept. chemistry Mass., 1974-78, assoc. dir. research Mass., from 1978. Cons. Societe Nationale du Petrole D'Aquitaine, Pau, France, 1966-69; mem. ocean scis. bd. Nat. Acad. Scis., Washington, 1976-79 Assoc. editor: Geochimica et Cosmochimicalota, 1970-74; contbr. articles to profl. jours. Served as pilot officer RAF 1952-57 Mem. Am. Geophys. Union, AAAS, Univ. Nat. Oceanographic Lab. System (chmn. 1981-83) Clubs: Cosmos. Avocations: computing; reading; travel. Home: Tucson, Ariz. Died Jan. 16, 2006.

SPENCER, LEWIS NEAL, construction company executive; b. Lander, Wyo., May 9, 1923; s. Clyde Hudson and Mary Neal (McCann) S.; m. Mary Lucille Ikard, Nov. 25, 1949; children— Melissa, Mark. BS, Oreg. State Coll., 1947. Engring. aide C.E., U.S. Army, Bonneville (Oreg.) Dam, 1947-48; city engr. Ontario, Oreg., 1948; with Morrison-Knudsen Co., Inc., 1948-84, v.p., 1968-73; mgr. Morrison-Knudsen Co., Inc. (No. Constrn. Co. div.), 1968-71; v.p. charge Morrison-Knudsen Co., Inc. (Canadian and European ops.), 1971-72, v.p. charge internat. ops., 1972-73, exec. v.p. internat. Boise, Idaho, 1973-84, also dir. Served with C.E. U.S. Army, 1943-46, 51-52. Mem. Asso. Gen. Contractors Am., The Beavers. Clubs: Arid (Boise), Hillcrest Country (Boise); Capilano Golf and Country (Vancouver, B.C., Can.); Internat. (Washington); World Trade (San Francisco). Home: Boise, Idaho. Died Dec. 13, 2006.

SPENCER, WARREN FRANK, historian, educator; b. Swan Quarter, N.C., Jan. 27, 1923; s. Carroll Baxter and Lucille Gertrude (Mann) S.; student George Washington U., 1942, U. Fla., 1942-43; B.S.S. cum laude, Georgetown U., 1947; M.A., U. Pa., 1949, Ph.D., 1955; m. Elizabeth Jolanda Toth, Sept. 6, 1947; children— Lucille Mann, Carroll Baxter. Instr. history Salem Coll., Winston-Salem, N.C., 1950-53, asst. prof., 1953-56; asst. prof. Old Dominion U., Norfolk, Va., 1956-57, assoc. prof., 1957-61, prof., 1961-67, chmn. div. social studies and dept. history, 1961-67; prof. history U. Ga., Athens, 1967—, Sandy Beaver teaching prof. history, 1978-82. Served with AUS, 1943-45. Vis. scholar, Duke, 1952; Am. Philos. Soc. fellow, 1958, 70, 75; recipient 1st ann. Faculty award Old Dominion U., 1961-62; Best History Book Published in 1970 award Phi Alpha Theta, 1971; named Outstanding Honors Tchr., U. Ga., Athens, 1977, 85, recipient creative research award, 1984. Mem. Am. Hist. Assn., So. Hist. Assn. (chmn. European History sect. program com. 1970), Ga. Assn. Historians (pres. 1979-80), Soc. French Hist. Studies, Phi Alpha Theta. Democrat. Episcopalian. Co-founder, pres. Norfolk Hist. Soc., 1966-67. Author: (with Lynn M. Case) The United States and France: Civil War Diplomacy, 1970; The Confederate Navy in Europe, 1983, (chpt.) Commanders of the Old Steam Navy, 1985. Contbr. to profl. jours. Home: Charlottesvle, Va. Died Mar. 3, 2007.

SPIEGEL, VIRGINIA ANN, nurse; b. N.Y.C., Oct. 20, 1952; d. Charles Martin and Sophie (Kuzmyn) S.; R.N., Queens Hosp., Jamaica, N.Y., 1974; B.S. in Nursing, Seton Hall U., 1978; M.S.N., Hunter Coll., 1981; doctoral student Tchr.'s Coll., Columbia U., 1982—. Staff nurse Columbia-Presbyterian Hosp., N.Y.C., 1974, Meml. Sloan-Kettering Cancer Center, N.Y.C., 1975; staff nurse Lyons (N.J.) VA Hosp., 1975-77, instr., 1977-79, nursing supr., 1979-80; nurse recruiter Bergen Pines Hosp., Paramus, N.J., 1980-83, assoc. dir. nursing, 1983, asst. exec. dir., dir. nursing, 1983—. Mem. Am. Nurses Assn., N.J. State Nurses Assn., N.J. Soc. Nursing Service Adminstrs., Sigma Theta Tau. Roman Catholic. Home: Burlington, NJ. Died Dec. 7, 2006.

SPIELMAN, ANDREW, entomology educator; b. NYC, Feb. 24, 1930; m. Judith Miller, Dec. 25, 1956; children: David, Debora, Susan. BS in Zoology, Colo. Coll., 1952; ScD in Pathobiology, Johns Hopkins U., 1956; MA, Harvard U., 1989. Entomologist, malariologist Tenn. Valley Authority, Wilson Dam, Ala., 1953-56; from instr. to prof. Harvard Sch. Pub. Health, Boston, 1959—2006. Author, dir. med. film (Freddy award Am. Film Inst., 1992); co-author: (films) Ticks and the Transmission of Lyme, 1991; contbr. more than 260 articles to profl. jours. Lt. comdr. USN, 1956-59, Cuba. Recipient Merit award Nat. Inst. Allergy and Infectious Diseases, 1989; Rozeboom lectr. Johns Hopkins Sch. Hygiene, 1972. Mem. AAAS, Am. Soc. Tropical Medicine and Hygiene, Entomol. Soc. Am., Am. Mosquito Control Assn. (medal of honor 1989), Cambridge Entomol. Soc. Achievements include patent for method and apparatus for administering acaricides and insecticides to ectoparasites of rodents. Home: Needham, Mass. Died Dec. 20, 2006.

SPINNLER, JOSEPH FRANK, retired chemist; b. Greenwood, SC, July 8, 1931; s. Frank Joseph and Sara Rebecca (Lanford) S.; m. Mary Vivian Simmons, Sept. 1, 1962; children: Rebecca Louise, Frank Joseph. BS in Chemistry, Lafayette Coll., 1953; MS, Yale U., 1958, PhD in Phys. Chemistry, 1961. Scientist rschr. Rohm & Haas Co. Redstone Arsenal Rsch. Divsn, Huntsville, Ala., 1960-72, Rohm & Haas Co. Agr. Products, Bristol, Pa., 1972-74, Rohm & Haas Co. Environ. Dept., Spring House, Pa., 1974-80; group leader Rohm & Haas Co. Agtox Analysis Grou, Spring House, 1981-96; cons. Enviro-Bio-Tech, Ltd., Bernville, Pa., 1996-2000. 1st Lt. Army Ordinance Corps, 1955-56, Korea. Avocations: photography, sailing. Home: Travelers Rest, SC. Died Mar. 16, 2006.

SPRAGENS, THOMAS ARTHUR, educational consultant; b. Lebanon, Ky., Apr. 25, 1917; s. William Henry and Lillian (Brewer) S.; m. Catharine Smallwood, May 24, 1941; children: Thomas Arthur, Barbara Allen, David William. AB, U. Ky., 1938, LL.D., 1964; Maxwell fellow pub. adminstrn., Syracuse U., 1939-40; LL.D., Westminster Coll., Fulton, Mo., 1958, Berea Coll., 1982, Centre Coll., 1982; Litt. D., U. Ala., 1967; H.H.D., Ky. State U., 1984. Research asst. Ky. Dept. Revenue, 1938-39, adminstrv. asst. to commr., 1941-42; adminstv. analyst U.S. Bur. Budget, 1940-41, sr. analyst, 1942-45; asst. chief food allocations Fgn. Econ. Adminstrn., 1945; asst. to pres. Stanford U., 1945-51; sec., treas. Fund for Advancement Edn., 1951-52; pres. Stephens Coll., 1952-57, Centre Coll. of Ky., Danville, 1957-81, pres. emeritus, from 1981; pres. Spragens Assocs., Inc. Cons. in institutional devel. Mem. Ohio Valley Regional Coun., 1973-75; pres. So. Coll. Univ. Union, 1970-74, So. Univ. Conf., 1975; trustee Pikeville Coll., 1985-91; bd. dirs. Shakertown at Pleasant Hill, Ky., 1973-91, Leadership Ky., Inc., 1985—; city commr. Danville, Ky., 1990-94; del. Nat. Dem. Conv., 1968. Mem. Am. Council Edn. (dir. 1966-69), Ky. Hist. Soc. (bd. dirs.), Pendennis Club, Filson Club, Rotary, Phi Beta Kappa, Omicron Delta Kappa. Presbyterian (mem. bd. Christian edn. 1968-73). Home: Columbia, SC. Died Feb. 11, 2006.

SPRIGGS, RICHARD MOORE, ceramics engineer, science administrator, researcher; b. Washington, Pa., May 8, 1931; s. Lucian Alexander and Kathryn (Aber) S.; m. Patricia Anne Blaney, Aug. 1, 1953 (dec. 2002); children: Carolyn Elizabeth Spriggs Muchna, Richard Moore, Alan David; m. Brenda L. Ferrier, May 5, 2005. BS in Ceramics, Pa. State U., 1952; MS in Ceramic Engring., U. Ill., 1956, PhD, 1958. Sr. research engr. Ferro Corp., Cleve., 1958-59; sr. staff scientist, group leader, ceramics rsch. AVCO Corp., Wilmington, Mass., 1959-64; assoc. prof. metall. engring. Lehigh U., Bethlehem, Pa., 1964-67, prof. metallurgy and materials sci. and engring., 1967-80, adminstrv. asst. to pres., 1970-71, asst. v.p. for adminstrn., 1971-72, v.p. for adminstrn., 1972-78, dir. phys. ceramics lab., 1964-70, assoc. dir. Materials Research Ctr., 1964-70; vis. sr. staff assoc. Nat. Materials Adv. Bd. NRC, Washington, 1979-80, sr. staff officer, staff scientist, 1980-87, staff dir. bd. on assessment of NBS programs, 1984-87; J.F. McMahon prof. ceramic engring., dir. NYS Ctr. Advanced Ceramic Tech. N.Y. State Coll. Ceramics, Alfred (N.Y.) U., 1987-97, dir. office of sponsored programs, 1988-97, prof. emeritus, from 1997. Affiliate staff scientist Pacific Northwest Lab., 1994—. Contbr. articles to profl. publs. Co-patentee in field Pres., bd. dirs. YMCA, Bethlehem, Pa., 1978-79. Served to lt. USNR, 1952-56 Fellow Armco Steel Corp., 1956-58, Am. Coun. on Edn., 1970-71; Centennial fellow Coll. Earth and Mineral Scis., Pa. State U., 1996, Alumni Achievement award, 1999, 30th Ann. SHS Medal of Honor, 1997, Disting. Engring. Alumnus awrd U. Ill., 1988. Fellow: Brit. Inst. Materials, Ceramic Soc. Japan (Centennial medal 1991), Am. Ceramic Soc. (trustee pension trust fund 1979—84, pres. 1984—85, coord. programs and meetings 1991—92, Ross Coffin Purdy award 1965, Hobard M. Kraner award Lehigh Valley sect. 1980, Orton lectr. 1988, McMahon lectr. 1988, Mueller lectr. 1996, Albert Victor Bleininger award Pitts. sect. 2000, disting. life); mem.: Serbian Acad. Scis. and Arts (fgn.), Ceramic Assn. N.Y. (sec.-treas. 1988—99), Fed. Materials Socs. (trustee 1978—84), Materials Rsch. Soc., Materials Rsch. Soc. Japan (hon.), World Acad. Ceramics (trustee 1988—96, from 2006), Brit. Ceramic Soc., Ceramic Ednl. Coun., Nat. Inst. Ceramic Engrs., Internat. Inst. for Sci. of Sintering, Rotary (dir. 1982—87, pres. 1985—86). Home: Alfred, NY. Died July 21, 2007.

SPRINGER, DAVID EDWARD, lawyer; b. Chgo., Jan. 20, 1952; s. Edward W. and Mildred (Bergmark) S. AB summa cum laude, Yale U., 1974, JD, 1977. Bar: Ill. 1977, US Ct. Appeals (5th cir.) 1978, US Dist. Ct. (no. dist.) Ill. 1978, US Ct. Appeals (7th cir.) 1981, US Supreme Ct. 1981, US Ct. Appeals (4th cir.) 1982, US Ct. Appeals (Fed. cir.) 1983, Wis. 1990, US Dist. Ct. (D.C. cir.) 1991, US Ct. Appeals (8th cir.) 1992. Ptnr. Kirkland & Ellis LLP, Chgo., 1977-86, Skadden, Arps, Slate, Meagher & Flom LLP, Chgo., 1986—2007. Contbr. articles to profl. jours. Mem. Yale Law Sch. Assn. (bd. dirs. 1999-2007), Chgo. Club, City Club Chgo., Phi Beta Kappa, charter mem. Trial Bar US Dist. Ct. (no. dist.) Ill. Republican. Protestant. Died June 19, 2007.

SPRINSON, DAVID BENJAMIN, biochemistry educator; b. Raigorod, Ukraine, Apr. 5, 1910; came to U.S., 1921; s. Moses and Rebecca (Skolnick) S.; m. Helen Evans Yeargain, Oct. 8, 1943; children: Joan, Mary, John. BS, CCNY, 1931; MS, NYU, 1936; PhD, Columbia U., 1946, DSc (honoris causa), 1991. Rsch. assoc. Columbia U., NYC, 1946-51, asst. prof. biochemistry, 1951-54, assoc. prof., 1954-58, prof., 1958-78, prof. biochemistry and molecular biology emeritus, from 1978, St. Luke's/Roosevelt Hosp. Ctr., NYC, 1979-97. Career investigator Am. Heart Assn., 1958-75. Contbr. articles to sci. jours. Grantee NIH, NSF, Am. Heart Assn., Am. Cancer Soc., 1950-91; recipient Disting. Svc. award Coll. Physicians and Surgeons, 1995. Mem. NAS, AAAS, Am. Soc. for Biochemistry and Molecular Biology, Am. Chem. Soc. Home: Leonia, NJ. Died Feb. 28, 2007.

SPROWL, CHARLES RIGGS, lawyer; b. Lansing, Mich., Aug. 22, 1910; s. Charles Orr and Hazel (Allen) S.; m. Virginia Lee Graham, Jan. 15, 1938; children: Charles R., Robert A., Susan G., Sandra D. AB, U. Mich., 1932, JD, 1934. Bar: Ill. 1935. Pvt. practice, from 1934; of counsel Taylor, Miller, Sprowl, Hoffnagle & Merletti, from 1986. Dir. Simmons Engring. Corp., Petersen Aluminum Corp. Mem. Bd. Edn., New Trier Twp. High Sch., 1959-65, pres. 1962-65; mem. Glencoe Zoning Bd. Appeals, 1956-76, chmn., 1966-76; mem Glencoe Plan Commn., 1962-65; bd. dirs. Glencoe Pub. Libr., 1953-65, pres. 1955-56; trustee Highland Park Hosp., 1959-69; bd. dirs. Cradle Soc., 1968-92. Fellow Am. Coll. Trial Lawyers; mem. Chgo. Bar Assn. (bd. mgrs. 1949-51), Ill. Bar Assn., ABA, Juvenile Protective Assn. (dir. 1943-53), Northwestern U. Settlement (pres. 1963-70, dir.), Soc. Trial Lawyers, Law Club (pres. 1969-70), Legal Club (pres. 1953-54), Skokie Country Club, Delta Theta Phi, Alpha Chi Rho. Presbyterian. Home: Winnetka, Ill. Died Aug. 7, 2006.

SPRUCH, LARRY, physicist, researcher; b. Bklyn., Jan. 1, 1923; BA, Bklyn. Coll., 1943; PhD in Physics, U. Pa., 1948. From asst. instr. to instr. physics U. Pa., 1943-48; Atomic Energy Commn. fellow MIT, 1948-50; from asst. prof. to assoc. prof. NYU, NYC, 1950-61, prof. physics, from 1961. Cons. Lawrence Radiation Lab., 1959-66; vis. prof. inst. theoretical physics U. Colo., 1961, 68; mem. Inst. Advanced Study, 1981-82; del. China U.S. Physics Exam and Application, 1985, 86; mem. adv. bd. inst. theoretical atomic and molecular physics Harvard-Smithsonian Ctr. Astrophysics, 1989-91. Corr. Comments Atomic & Molecular Physics, 1972—. Recipient von Humboldt Sr. award, 1985, 88, Alumni award of Merit Bklyn. Coll., 1967; Tyndale fellow U. Pa., 1946-48, NSF sr. fellow U.

London, Oxford U., 1963-64. Fellow Am. Phys. Soc. (Davisson-Germer prize 1992). Achievements include research in Beta decay, nuclear moments, isomeric transitions, internal conversion, atomic and nuclear scattering, variational principles, astrophysics, charge transfer, Thomas-Fermi theory, radiative corrections, atoms in magnetic fields, Levinson's theorem, casimir interactions, semi-classical radiation theory. Died Aug. 10, 2006.

SPURR, GREGORY WATERMAN, JR., banker; b. Rye, NY, Dec. 10, 1923; s. Gregory Waterman and Jean Armour (Dunlop) S.; m. Cynthia J. Holmes, Dec. 12, 1953; children: Gregory W., Jeffrey H., Cynthia D., Pamela P. BA, Yale U., 1948; MBA, Dartmouth Coll., 1950. With Bank of N.Y., from 1950, asst. v.p., 1958-62, v.p., 1962-69, sr. v.p., 1969-76, vice chmn. credit com., exec. v.p., from 1976, sr. loan and loan policy officer, 1979-82, sr. exec. v.p., from 1982. Mem. Robert Morris Assocs., Assn. Res. City Bankers Clubs: Short Hills, Baltusrol Golf. Died Feb. 26, 2007.

STACK, MAURICE DANIEL, retired insurance company executive; b. NYC, Dec. 15, 1917; s. Maurice E. and Margaret (Brooks) S.; m. Catherine T. O'Connor, Nov. 25, 1943; children: Mary Jane, Eileen, Peter, Clare. Student, U. Notre Dame, 1935-36; BBA, Manhattan Coll., 1939; MBA, Harvard, 1941. Investment analyst Carnegie Corp., NYC, 1946-48; adminstrv. asst. Tchrs. Ins. & Annuity Assn., 1948-49; investment analyst First Nat. Bank N.Y., 1949-54; fin. sec. Atlantic Mut. Ins. Co., NYC, 1954-56, v.p., 1957-60, fin. v.p., trustee, 1961-66, chmn. fin. com., 1966-83. Trustee emeritus Atlantic Mutual Ins. Co. Trustee emeritus, adviser St. Vincent's Hosp.; trustee emeritus YWCA. Maj., C.E., AUS, 1941-46. Mem. K.M. Club (N.Y.C.), Harvard Club (N.Y.C.). Home: Point Lookout, NY. Died Nov. 3, 2005.

STADELMANN, EDUARD JOSEPH, retired plant physiologist, educator, researcher; b. Graz, Austria, Sept. 24, 1920; s. Eduard Joseph and Josefa (Eigner) S.; m. Ok Young Lee, Mar. 22, 1975 (dec. 2005) BS, Bundesrealgymnasium, Graz, Austria, 1939; PhD, U. Innsbruck, Austria, 1953; Pvt. Docent, U. Freiburg, Switzerland, 1957; PhD (hon.), Agrl. U. Vienna, 1989. Sr. asst. U. Freiburg, 1962-63; rsch. assoc. U. Minn., Mpls., 1963, asst. prof., 1964-66, assoc. prof., 1966-72, prof. hort. sci., 1972-91, prof. emeritus, from 1991. Muellhaupt Scholar in Biology, Ohio State U., 1958-59; Humboldt Found. awardee, 1974-75; Fulbright award, Coun. Internat. Exchange, 1979-80, 87-88. Mem. Am. Inst. Biology, Am. Soc. Plant Biologists, German Bot. Soc., Swiss Bot. Soc., Sigma Xi. Roman Catholic. Home: Saint Paul, Minn. Died Sept. 14, 2006.

STAFFINS, RALPH CALVIN, JR., iron company executive; b. Atlanta, Dec. 13, 1949; s. Ralph Calvin and Gladys Charlene (Morgan) S.; m. Carolyn Elizabeth Metheny, Oct. 17, 1987; children from previous marriage: Ralph Calvin III, Gary Christopher. Grad. high sch. Clarkston, Ga., 1967. Vice pres. Artistic Ornamental Iron Co., Inc., Atlanta, 1969—. Lt. col. Gov.'s Staff, State of Ga., 1983—; dep. lt. Sheriff Dekalb County, Ga., 1985. Mem. Nat. Ornamental Miscellaneous Metal Assn., Greater Atlanta Ornamental Iron and Miscellaneous Metal Mfrs. Assn. Democrat. Methodist. Avocations: hunting, fishing. Home: Loganville, Ga. Died Aug. 20, 2006.

STAFFORD, ROBERT THEODORE, lawyer, retired senator; b. Rutland, Vt., Aug. 8, 1913; s. Bert L. and Mable R. (Stratton) S.; m. Helen C. Kelley, Oct. 15, 1938; children: Madelyn, Susan, Barbara, Dianne. BS, Middlebury Coll., 1935, LL.D., 1960; postgrad., U. Mich., 1936; LL.B., Boston U., 1938, LL.D., 1959, Norwich U., 1960, St. Michaels Coll., 1967, U. Vt., 1970. Bar: Vt. bar 1938. City prosecutor, Rutland, 1939-42; state's atty. Rutland County, 1947-51; dep. atty. gen. State of Vt., 1953-54, atty. gen., 1954-56, lt. gov., 1957-58, gov., 1959-60; mem.-at-large US Congress from Vt., 1961—71; apptd. US Senate, 1971; US Senator from Vt., 1972-89; chmn. com. on environment and public works, 1981-87; chmn. edn. subcom., 1981-87; ranking mem., 1987-89; ptnr. Stafford, Abiatell & Stafford, 1938-46; sr. ptnr. Stafford & LaBrake, 1946-51. Author: How to End the Draft: The Case for an All-Volunteer Army, 1967. Chmn. UN-U.S.A. Assn. Panel UNESCO, 1989—. Lt. comdr. USNR, 1942-46, 51-52; capt. Res. Named Disting. Scholar U. Vt., 1989, Disting. Prof. Pub. Affairs Castleton State Coll., 1989. Mem. V.F.W., Am. Legion. Clubs: Elk. Died Dec. 23, 2006.

STAINE, ROSS (ROSS DONAN ALLISON JR.), lawyer; b. El Paso, Tex., July 13, 1924; s. Ross Donan Allison and Dennie Joe (Stowe) S.; m. Mary Louise Sibert, Aug. 15, 1947; children: Martha Louise, Julie Ann, Ross. BA, Tex. A&M U., 1947; LL.B., U. Tex., 1950. Bar: Tex. Assoc. Baker Botts, Houston, 1947, ptnr., from 1962. Served to 1st lt. U.S. Army, 1943-46, 1950-52,PTO. Mem. State Bar Tex., Houston Bar Assn., Tex. Law Rev. Assn., Chancellors, Forest Club (Houston), Order of Coif, Phi Delta Phi. Baptist. Home: Houston, Tex. Died Nov. 10, 2006.

STAINTON, BRIAN JAMES, food products co. exec.; b. N.Y.C., June 29, 1942; s. Richard G. and Edna M. (Kane) S.; B.A., U. South Fla., 1966; M.B.A., U. N.C., 1972; m. Josephine Tooker, Dec. 8, 1963. Mgr. acctg. Continental Baking Co., Tampa, Fla., 1967-68; mgr. acctg. ITT, Tampa, 1968-71, comptroller, Raleigh, N.C., 1971-78; v.p. fin. Shrimp Peddler Cos., San Diego, 1978-83; comptroller ITT DiCarlo Baking Co., San Pedro, Calif., 1983—. Mem. Nat. Assn. Accts. Republican. Roman Catholic. Died Mar. 27, 2007.

STAISCH, KLAUS JUERGEN, obstetrician-gynecologist; b. Stettin, Fed. Republic Germany, Aug. 28, 1938; came to U.S., 1968; s. Emil and Dorothea (Reck) S.; m. Christina Maria Rodriguez, Mar. 8, 1982; children: Julia, Lydia. BS, Philips U., Marburg, Germany, 1963; MD, Freie U., Berlin, 1966. Intern U. Berlin Hosp., 1966-67, Passaic (N.J.) Gen. Hosp., 1968-69; resident U. Minn., Mpls., 1969-73; fellow in perinatology U. So. Calif., Los Angeles, 1971-72; assoc. prof. UCLA, 1973-84, U. Minn., Mpls., 1984-87; dir. obstetrics Hennepin County Med. Ctr., Mpls., 1984-87, dir. maternal-fetal medicine, 1984-87; assoc. prof. sch. medicine Washington U., St. Louis, from 1987; obstetrician/gynecologist-in-chief St. Louis Regional Med. Ctr., 1987-96; mem. staff Barnes Jewish Hosp., St. Louis, from 1996. Fellow Am. Coll. Ob-Gyn; mem. Soc. Perinatal Obstetricians, Am. Acad. Pediatrics (Investigator award 1983), St. Louis Ob/Gyn. Soc. Avocations: hunting, photography. Home: Saint Louis, Mo. Died Oct. 26, 2005.

STAMPKE, STUART REH, physicist, researcher; b. Burbank, Calif., Apr. 20, 1950; BS in Physics summa cum laude, Calif. State U., Northridge, 1973; PhD in Physics, Calif. Inst. Tech., Pasadena, 1982. Rsch. fellow in physics Calif. Inst. Tech., Pasadena, 1982; rsch. assoc. Mich. State U., East Lansing, 1982-86; scientist I Superconducting Super Collider Lab., Waxahachie, Tex., 1989-94; sr. scientist Aura Sys., Inc., El Segundo, Calif., 1996—2003. From vis. asst. prof. to vis. assoc. prof. U. Notre Dame, Ind., 1986-88; mem. part-time faculty Calif. State U., Northridge, 1994-96. Contbr. articles to profl. jours. on particle physics, detectors, and accelerator physics. Mem. IEEE, Am. Phys. Soc., Am. Solar Energy Soc. Home: Tucson, Ariz. Died May 21, 2006.

STAMPLEY, NORRIS LOCHLEN, former electric utility executive; b. Bentonia, Miss., Dec. 21, 1920; s. Orville K. and Norma Eloise S.; m. Mary Virginia Russum, May 28, 1942; children: Mary Lynn, Virginia Kaye. Registered profl. engr., Miss. Engr. U.S. Navy Dept., Washington, 1942-45; with Miss. Power & Light Co., Jackson, 1947-84, chief engr., 1968-72, v.p., 1972-80, sr. v.p., 1980-84, now ret. Pres. Met. YMCA, Jackson, 1980, 85; trustee Mcpl. Separate Sch. Dist., 1980-90, Miss. Baptist Found., 1981-85, 87-92; chmn. So. Baptist Conv. Brotherhood Commn., 1985-86. Served with Signal Corps, U.S. Army, 1945-47. Named Alumnus of Yr. Hinds Jr. Coll., 1980 Mem. Nat. Soc. Profl. Engrs., Miss. Engring. Soc. (Engr. of Yr. 1974), IEEE, Am. Nuclear Soc., Jackson C. of C. (dir.), Phi Theta Kappa (Alumnus of Yr. 1977) Clubs: Exchange (pres. 1975). Home: New Bern, NC. Died Jan. 14, 2007.

STANGER, ABRAHAM M., lawyer; b. NYC, Sept. 25, 1921; s. Joseph I. and Tillie (Rothfield) S.; m. Claire Y. Schwebel, Sept. 18, 1948; children: Richard, Jordan, Hope. BA cum laude, CCNY, 1941; LLB, NYU, 1948, LLM, 1952, Dr. Jud. Sci., 1958. Bar: N.Y. 1949, U.S. Tax Ct. 1951, U.S. Dist. Ct. (so. dist.) N.Y. 1951, U.S. Dist. Ct. (ea. dist.) N.Y. 1953, U.S. Supreme Ct. 1958, U.S. Ct. Appeals (2d cir.) 1960, U.S. Ct. Claims 1984; CPA, N.Y. Sr. ptnr. corp. fin. reporting, disclosure issues and tax matters Stanger, Robson & Rothstein, NYC, 1960-72; sr. ptnr. corp. div. fin. reporting, disclosure issues and tax matters Trubin Sillcocks Edelman & Knapp, NYC, 1972-83; sr. ptnr. corp. fin. reporting, disclosure issues and tax matters Seyfarth, Shaw, Fairweather & Geraldson, NYC, from 1983. Adj. prof. law NYU, 1958—; mem. Fin. Acctg. Standards Adv. Council, 1979-83. Contbr. numerous articles on fin. reporting and disclosure to profl. jours; edit. staff NYU Law Rev., 1947-48; columnist Corp. Law Rev., 1978-86. Recipient Scroll Appreciation award, NYU. Fellow Am. Bar Found.; mem. AICPA (futures issues com. 1985-88), ABA (standing com. on audit 1996—, chmn. com. law and acctg. sect. bus. law 1980-85, liaison to FASB, AICPA and chief acct. SEC 1998—, chmn. subcom. lawyers replies to auditors 1985—, chmn. subcom. acctg. methods of com. tax acctg. problems sect. of taxation 1982-86, vice chmn. com. tax acctg. problems 1986-90, mem. nat. conf. of lawyers and CPA's 1988-91), N.Y. State Bar Assn., Assn. of Bar of City of N.Y., N.Y. County Lawyers Assn., Internat. Bar Assn. (rep. on consultative group internat. acctg. stds. com. 1987—, rep. on consultative group internat. auditing practices com. 1995—), Am. Judicature Soc. Home: New York, NY. Died June 1, 2007.

STANGER, DAVID N., newspaper publishing executive; b. Boston, Dec. 5, 1926; s. Michael and Annie (Cohen) S.; m. Ruth Shapiro, June 25, 1950; children: Amy Stanger Furman, Jay. BSBA, Northeastern U., 1950. Various positions in mgmt. Globe Newspaper Co., Boston, from 1942, sr. v.p., gen. mgr., from 1986. Trustee Brookline (Mass.) Hosp., Hebrew Rehab. Ctr., Boston, Beth Isreal Hosp., Boston; bd. dirs. Coolidge Corner Co-op Bank, Brookline. With USN, 1944-46. Mem. New England Newspaper Assn. (bd. dirs. 1986). Clubs: University (Boston) (bd. govs. 1981). Home: Chestnut Hill, Mass. Died Aug. 3, 2007.

STANNARD, DAVID EDWARD, American studies educator, author, consultant; b. Teaneck, NJ, June 11, 1941; s. David L. and Florence E. (Harwood) S.; children: Timothy, Adam. BA, San Francisco State U., 1971; MA, Yale U., 1972, MPhil, 1973, PhD, 1975. Asst. prof., assoc. prof. Yale U., New Haven, 1974-79; assoc. prof. Am. studies U. Hawaii, Honolulu, 1979-81, prof., from 1981. Vis. prof. Conn. Coll., New London, 1974, Stanford (Calif.) U., 1976, 78, U. Colo., Boulder, 1994. Author: The Puritan Way of Death, 1977, Shrinking History, 1980, Before the Horror, 1989, American Holocaust, 1992; editor: Death in America, 1975; contbr. numerous articles to profl. jours. Recipient Excellence in Tchg. award U. Hawaii Bd. Regents, 1987; rsch. fellow Guggenheim Found., 1978-79, Am. Coun. Learned Socs., 1985-86, Rockefeller Found., 1993-94. Home: Kaneohe, Hawaii. Died Mar. 1, 2007.

STANSBURY, PHILIP ROGER, lawyer; b. Milw., May 7, 1931; s. Carroll and Margaret (Manning) S.; m. Daviette Clagett Hill, Dec. 5, 1959; children: Henry Tayloe, Catherine Contee. AB, Haverford Coll., Pa., 1953; JD, Harvard U., 1956. Bar: D.C. 1956, U.S. Ct. Appeals (D.C. crct.) 1956. Assoc. Covington & Burling, Washington, 1958-66, ptnr., from 1966. Contbr. articles to profl. jours. Mem. Southwestern Legal Found. (adv. bd.). Republican. Roman Catholic. Died Jan. 25, 2006.

STANTON, FRANK NICHOLAS, retired broadcast executive; b. Muskegon, Mich., Mar. 20, 1908; s. Frank Cooper and Helen Josephine (Schmidt) S.; m. Ruth Stephenson, 1931 (dec. 1992). BA, Ohio Wesleyan U., 1930; PhD, Ohio State U., 1935. Diplomate Am. Bd. Profl. Psychology. Audience researcher CBS, NYC, 1935-45; pres. CBS Inc., NYC, 1946-71, vice chmn., 1971-73. Chmn. The Rand Corp., 1961-67, Capital Income Builder, Inc., Sony Music Entertainment Inc., Internat. Herald Tribune (Paris), Interpub. Group of Cos., 1976-95; dir. Capital World Growth & Income Fund, London Observer, 1977-85; chmn. U.S. Adv. Commn. Info., Washington, 1964-7 Co-author: The Study of Psychology, 1935, Radio Researc 1941, 42-43; author: International Information, Education ar Cultural Relations: Recommendations for the Future, 197 co-editor Communications Rsch., 1943-49 Bd. overseers Ha vard Coll., 1978-84, chmn. vis. com. Kennedy Sch. Gov 1979-85, chmn. vis. com. Harvard Grad. Sch. Design, 1990-9 founding mem., chmn. Ctr. for Advanced Study in Behavior Scis., Stanford, Calif., 1953-60, trustee, 1953-71; chmn. AR Washington, 1973-79, vice chmn. League of Red Cross Soc Geneva, Switzerland, 1973-80; mem. Pres.'s Com. Arts ar Humanities, Washington, 1983-90, Nat. Portrait Galle Commn., Washington, 1973-92, Bus. Coun., Washington, 195 2006 (hon.); dir., trustee Bryant Park Restorarion Corp., Edr Broadcasting Corp. (hon.), Internat. Design Conf. in Aspe Colo., Lincoln Ctr. Inst., Mus. of TV and Radio, Record Anthology Am. Music; emeritus trustee, dir. Lincoln Ctr. f Performing Arts, Rockefeller Found., Carnegie Instn. Washin ton. Recipient Peabody awards, 1959, 60, 61, 64, 72, Truste award Nat. Acad. TV Arts and Scis., 1959, 72, Paul Whi Meml. award Radio and TV News Dirs. Assn., 1957, 71, Sp Honor award AIA, 1967, Internat. Directorate award Nat. Aca TV Arts and Scis., 1980, Trustees award Calif. Inst. Arts, 199 named to TV Acad. Hall of Fame, 1986, Market Rsch. Coun. N.Y., 1988. Fellow AAAS, Am. Psychol. Assn., Am. Acad. A and Scis., N.Y. Acad. Scis., Century Assn., Harvard Clu Cosmos Club. Home: Boston, Mass. Died Dec. 24, 2006.

STANTON, JOHN WALKER, management educator, to director, poet; b. Casablanca, Morocco, May 2, 1937; s. Willa Quincy and Madeleine Frances (O'Brien) S.; m. Rebec Dearborn, Jan. 3, 1962; children: John Jr., Andrew, Willar Madeleine, Abraham, Tara, Erin, Shannon, John K. BA, Mi So. Coll., 1961; MA, Ctrl. Mo. State U., 1966; JD, U. N.Me 1970; LLM, U. Miami, 1973; MPA, Harvard U., 1981. Lawy various orgns., 1970-85; prof. City Coll. Seattle, 1986-91; pr mgmt. Sch. Extended Studies, Park Coll., Luke AFB, Ariz., fro 1991; prof. mgmt. Park U., Fort Bliss, Tex., from 2004. V prof. La. State U., Shreveport, 1993-95; tour dir., U.S. a overseas. Author: Tomorrow Never Knows, 1995; contbr. ticles to profl. jours. Dem. presdl. campaign advisor, Seatt 1988. mem. dem. leadership coun., Anglican Ch. Am.; wi USMC, 1954-57, USAF, 1963-67, Viet Nam. Decorated Bron Star, USAF, 1967. Poetry selected for Best Poems of 19 Mem. AFGE (AFL-CIO), Air Commando Assn., Marine Cor Assn., Mil. Officers Assn., Ret. Officers Assn., Nat. Geog. So VFW; Sigma Phi Epsilon. Democrat. Anglican. Avocatio bulldogs, oriental rugs, travel. Home: Las Cruces, N.Mex. Di Mar. 17, 2007.

STANTON, THOMAS COUSAR, university president; Dillon County, SC, June 13, 1929; s. Hugh Cousar and K Margaret (Jones) S.; m. Sara Louise Thomas, July 20, 19 children: Sara Kate, Thomas C. Jr. BS, U. Md., 1960; MS in F Mgmt., George Washington U., 1966, Dr. Bus. Adminstr 1974. Commd. 2d lt. U.S. Army, 1952, advanced through grad to lt. col., 1967, ret., 1972; v.p. acad. affairs, prof. b adminstrn. James Madison U., Harrisonburg, Va., 1974-83; pr Francis Marion U., Florence, S.C., from 1983. Assoc. prof. b adminstrn. James Madison U., Harrisonburg, Va., 1974-76, he dept., 1975-76; assoc. prof. Teheran U., Iran, 1968-70; cons. field. Contbr. articles to profl. jours. Pastor Zoar Bapt. C Bristersburg, Va., 1970-79; bd. dirs. Pee Dee Heritage C 1983—. Decorated Purple Heart, Meritorious Service Med others; recipient Ann. Authors award Assn. Govt. Accts., 19 Mem. S.C. Assn. Colls. and Univs. (pres. 1986-87), Rota Home: Florence, SC. Died Oct. 9, 2006.

STANTON, THOMAS MITCHELL, lawyer, educator; Vicksburg, Miss., Sept. 30, 1922; s. John Francis and Ha Florence (Mitchell) S.; m. Jean Aldrich Herron, Oct. 31, 19 children: Lucinda S. Duddy, Amy S. Conklin, Thomas Herr BS, Harvard U., 1943, JD, 1948. Bar: Ohio 1949, Wis. 19 Pvt. practice law, Cin., 1949-56; corp. atty. Kroger Co., Ci 1957-61; with Kimberly-Clark Corp., Neenah, Wis., 1962- v.p., gen. counsel, 1971-84, v.p., internat. counsel, 1985-86, r 1986; pvt. practice law Neenah, from 1987. Trustee Friends Bronze Age Archeology in the Aegean Area. Capt. A 1943-46. Mem. ABA, Wis. Bar Assn., Am. Corp. Counsel As (internat. legal affairs com.), North Shore Golf Club, Univ. Cl Home: Sanibel, Fla. Died May 3, 2006.

STANTON, WILLIAM ALSPAUGH, retired educator; Chgo., Mar. 9, 1924; s. Robert Hart and Sue Margaret (spaugh) S.; m. Mary Claire Bechtold, July 9, 1982; children Susan C., David William, Donald F. B. Vocat. Edn., La. St Coll., 1957; M.A. in Edn., Long Beach State Coll., 1960; Ed. UCLA, 1967. Lic. radio engr., FCC. Dean vocat. tech. edn. C of Redwoods (Calif.), 1966-68; assoc. prof. indsl. edn. Pur U., West Lafayette, Ind., 1968-75; chmn. dept. vocat. edn. Cin., 1975-78, prof. edn., 1978-85, prof. emeritus, 1985—; co desktop computers. Served with USAF, 1942-45, 47-50. Fulbright scholar, Cyprus, 1972-73; Fulbright exchange pr France, 1978. Mem. IEEE, Phi Delta Kappa. Roman Catho Author: Pulse Technology, 1964, Polish transl., 1966. Died M 14, 2007.

STAPLES, EUGENE LEO, hospital administrator; b. Walk Minn., Aug. 26, 1926; s. Frank August and Elizabeth Joseph (Leibl) S.; m. Noreen Janice Henry, June 23, 1951; 1 ch Barbara Elizabeth. BA, U. Minn., 1950, M.H.A., 1952. Adm istrv. asst. U. Minn. Hosps., Mpls., 1952-53, asst. to d 1953-55, asst. dir., 1955-60; dir. W.Va. U. Hosp., Morganto 1960-82; assoc. prof. W.Va. U. Hosp. (Sch. Medicine), 1964- clin. prof., 1975-82; hosp. adminstr., prof. Kans. U. M Center, 1982-84, prof., vice chancellor, 1984-90, ret., 19 cons. to chancellor, from 1990; mem. liaison com. Grad. M Edn., 1974-80. Cons. NIH, 1968, Fla. Dept. Profl. Regulati 1987; mem. grad. med. edn. nat. adv. com. Health Resour Adminstrn., 1977-80, chmn. liaison com. grad. med. edn., 19 dir. Westover Bank, W.Va.; civilian advisor to Surgeon G USAF. Bd. dirs. United Fund, 1966-72, Am. Cancer Soc., 19 Morgantown Hosp. Service, W.Va. Hosp. Service Inc., W. Hosp. Research and Edn. Found., Inc., Kansas City Area H ssn., chmn. coun. Media and Community Rels., 1988-89, ans. Hosp. Assn., chmn. bd. trustees Coun. on Human Resources, 1989—; trustee Vis. Nurse Assn. of Greater Kansas City, 1989—, Family Practice Found., U. Kans., 1990. Served with USNR, 1944-46. Fellow Am. Coll. Hosp. Adminstrs. regent 1972-75); mem. W.Va. Hosp. Assn. (pres. 1969-71), Am. Hosp. Assn. (ho. dels. 1963-66, 72-78, trustee 1979-82), Southastern Hosp. Conf. (dir. 1970-72), Ohio Valley Hosp. Conf. pres. 1965-66, dir. 1960-82), AMA, Am. Assn. Med. Colls. coun. teaching hosps. 1972-73, ACME adv. goup, 1988—), U. Kans. Med. Alumni Assn. (hon). Died Oct. 21, 2006.

STAPLETON, CHRISTOPHER GEORGE, educational administrator; b. Pasadena, Calif., Dec. 23, 1919; s. Christopher Charles and Elizabeth Hannah (Dubberly) S.; B.A. in Psychology, Lewis and Clark Coll., 1949, M.Ed., 1956; Ph.D. in Ednl. Adminstrn., U. Minn., 1981; m. Rosemary Norris, Mar. 15, 1947; children— Linda Elizabeth, Sally Ann Stapleton Clapp, Christopher Joseph. Tchr. Russellville Sch., Portland, 1949-52; rin. Sunnyside Sch., Milwaukee, Oreg., 1952-56; tchr. gen. sci. Oregon City Jr. High Sch., 1956-57; asst. prin. Clackamas Oreg.) Sch., 1957-58; tchr. Portland Schs., 1958-62; asst. editor Am. Printing House for Blind, Louisville, 1962-65; cons. dept. dn. St. Paul, Minn., 1965-66; dir. spl. edn. Rochester (Minn.) chs., 1966-80, asst. for fin. and acctg., 1980-82, asst. dir. spl. dn., 1982-85. Served with USN, 1940-46, USNR, 1962-66. Fellow AAAS; mem. NEA, Phi Delta Kappa. Presbyterian. Club: Rotary, Masons. Home: Navarre, Fla. Died Oct. 30, 2006.

STAPP, WILLIAM EDWARD, lawyer; b. Yoakum, Tex., Aug. 8, 1917; s. William Edward and Lillian (Franks) S.; m. Isabelle Pool, June 30, 1945; children: Barbara, Will. BA, LL.B., U. Tex., Austin. Bar: Tex. 1941. Asst. atty. gen., Tex., 1946-47; ecurities commr. Tex. Sec. State's Office, 1948-49; ptnr. Vinson & Elkins, Houston, from 1965. Mem. Tex. Gov.'s Com. Codification Sch. Laws, 1968-69 Served to lt. USNR, 1942-45, PTO. Decorated Purple Heart Mem. Tex. Assn. Sch. Bds. (council sch. ttys.), Houston Bar Assn. Clubs: Houston. Democrat. Presbyterian. Home: Houston, Tex. Died Sept. 18, 2006.

STARR, CHAUNCEY, research institute executive; b. Newark, Apr. 14, 1912; s. Rubin and Rose (Dropkin) Starr; m. Doris Evelyn Debel, Mar. 20, 1938; children: Ross M., Ariel E. Wooley. EE, Rensselaer Poly. Inst., 1932, PhD in Physics, 1935, DEng (hon.), 1964, Swiss ETH, 1980; DSci (hon.), Tulane U., 1986. Rsch. fellow physics Harvard U., 1935—37; rsch. assoc. MIT, 1938—41; rsch. physicist D.W. Taylor Model Basin, Bur. Ships, 1941—42; staff radiation lab. U. Calif., 1942—43, Tenn. Eastman Corp., Oak Ridge, 1943—46, Tenn. Eastman Corp. Clinton Labs.), 1946; chief spl. rsch. North Am. Aviation, Inc., Downey, Calif., 1946—49, dir. atomic energy rsch. dept., 1949—55, v.p., 1955—66; gen. mgr. North Am. Aviation, Inc. Atomics Internat. divsn.), 1955—60, pres. divsn., 1960—66; ean sch. engring. & applied sci. UCLA, 1966—73; cons. prof. Stanford U., 1974—2007; founding pres. Electric Power Rsch. Inst., 1972—78, vice chmn., 1978—87, pres. emeritus, 1987—2007. Dir. Atomic Indsl. Forum. Contbr. articles to profl. jours. Decorated Legion of Honor France; recipient Henry D. Smyth award, Atomic Indsl. Forum, 1983, Nat. Medal of Tech., 1990. Fellow: AAAS (dir.), Am. Phys. Soc. (Pake prize), Am. Nuc. Soc. (founder, past pres.); mem.: NAE (v.p., Arthur M. Bueche award 2006), AIAA (sr.), Royal Swedish Acad. Engring. Scis., Am. Power Conf., Sigma Xi, Eta Kappa Nu. Died Apr. 17, 2007.

STARR, DAVID, makeup company executive, beauty expert, author; b. LA, Oct. 4, 1950; Student biol. sci. and medicine, Stanford U., 1966; BFA, UCLA, 1972. Owner, makeup artist David Starr Enterpirses, San Francisco and L.A., 1971-80; dir. mktg., makeup artist Chanel Beauty-West Coast, San Francisco, 1980-81; owner, mgr. David Starr Makeup Ctr., San Francisco, from 1984. Cons. Motown Records-Artist Advancement, L.A., 1974, Sta. KGO-TV, 1987-88, Sta. KCRA-TV, Sacramento, 1988; beauty judge Miss Gilroy (Calif.) Pageant, 1986, Miss Oakland (Calif.) Pageant, 1988. One-man photo exhbn. Acad. of Art, San Francisco. Fund-raiser Pacific Presbyn. Hosp., Project Open Hand, San Francisco, 1987—, San Francisco Zool. Soc.; mem. San Francisco Opera Guild, Mus. of Modern Art. Named Best Makeup Artist, Harper's Bazaar, 1986, San Francisco Mag., 1987, 88, Nob, Hill Gazette, 1990; recipient Achievement Award Doer's Scotch, 1988, Cable Car award, 1990; named Most Outstanding AIDS Fundraiser, 1990. Mem. San Francisco C. of C. Avocations: exercising, painting, rowing, collecting art. Home: San Francisco, Calif. Died Feb. 2, 2006.

STAUFFACHER, CHARLES B., newspaper publishing executive; b. Karuizawa, Japan, July 13, 1916; came to U.S., 1916; s. Albert Daniel and Anna Dorothy (Marty) S.; m. Lillian Frances Moss, Dec. 27, 1941; children: Charles D., Lillian S. Mullies. Student, Lingnan U., Canton, China, 1935-36; AB, Pomona Coll., 1937; A.M., Am U., 1938, Harvard, 1940. Research asst. Brookings Instn., 1940-41; with Bur. Budget, Washington, 1941-52, exec. asst. dir. bur., 1950-52; on leave as asst. to Dir. Def. Moblzn., 1951-52; lectr. George Washington U.; control officer Continental Can Co., 1952-54, v.p. finance, 1955-58, exec. v.p. paper products group, 1959-65, exec. v.p. finance and adminstrn., 1966-68, sr. exec. v.p., 1969-71, vice chmn., chief adminstrv. and financial officer, 1971-74; pres., chief exec. officer Field Enterprises, Inc., Chgo., 1974-80. Fin. cons. Universe Tank Ships, 1980-84; bd. dirs. Kubir Nicholson Co., 1st Am. Bank Hon. trustee Pomona Coll.; bd. dirs. Nat. Exec. Service Corps. Served as lt. USNR, 1943-46. Mem. Nat. Acad. Pub. Adminstrn., Phi Beta Kappa. Clubs: Chicago; Greenwich (Conn.) Country; Augusta Nat. Golf, Lost Tree Golf. Home: West Palm Beach, Fla. Died Feb. 11, 2006.

STAUR, MARTIN JOHN, architect; b. Bridgeport, Conn., July 1, 1933; s. John and Julia Anna (Tudos) Staurovsky. Registered architect, Calif., N.Y., Conn., Ariz, Nev. Apprentice architect Anderson & Petrofsky, architects, Bridgeport, 1952-62; project architect A.J. Palmieri Co., Bridgeport, 1974-75, Bennett-Essnick Ptnrship, Westport, Conn. and Boston, 1976-78, Valus & Carpenter, Westport, 1979-80; architect Vineyard Realty Corp., White Plains, N.Y., 1980-83; prin. Martin J. Staur, AIA, Westport, 1983—; cons. architect Gassner Assocs., Westport, 1985—. Mem. AIA, Conn. Soc. Architects, Nat. Council Archl. Registration Bds. Republican. Roman Catholic. Avocations: building models, computers, gardening, sailing, golf. Died July 18, 2007.

STAVIS, BARRIE, playwright, historian; b. NYC, June 16, 1906; s. Abraham Max and Fanny Beatrice (Garfinkle) S.; m. Leona Heyert, 1925 (div. 1939); m. Bernice Sylvia Coe, May 17, 1950; children: Alexander Mark, Jane Devon. Student, Columbia U., 1924-27. Journalist, war corr., NY and Europe, 1937-47; guest spkr. seminars, colls., univs., insts., U.S. and abroad, 1938—; vis. fellow Inst. for the Arts and Humanistic Studies, Pa. State U., 1971; playwright, historian, lyricist; co-founder, mem. bd. New Stages, 1947, 48, U.S. Inst. for Theatre Tech., 1961-64, 69-72. Author: (novels) The Chain of Command, 1945, Home, Sweet Home!, 1949, (biography) John Brown: The Sword and the Word, 1970, (plays) In These Times, 1932, The Sun and I, 1933, Refuge, 1938, Lamp at Midnight, 1948, one-hour abridgment, 1974, The Man Who Never Died, 1958, Harpers Ferry, 1967, Coat of Many Colors, 1968, The Raw Edge of Victory, 1976, The House of Shadows, 1992; contbr. articles to profl. jours.; librettist: opera Joe Hill (Alan Bush), 1970; oratorio Galileo Galilei (Lee Hoiby), 1975; author, co-editor: (with Frank Harmon) The Songs of Joe Hill, 1955. Served with AUS, 1942-45. Yaddo fellow, 1939; Am. Theatre Assn. fellow, 1982 Fellow Coll. Fellows Am. Theatre; mem. PEN, ASCAP, Dramatists Guild, Authors Guild, Nat. Theatre Conf. (award 1948, 49), U.S. Inst. for Theatre-Tech., Internat. Theatre Inst., ANTA. Home: New York, NY. Died Feb. 2, 2007.

STEDMAN, MURRAY SALISBURY, JR., political science educator; b. Pitts., Dec. 2, 1917; s. Murray Salisbury and Viola (Lanich) S.; m. Susan Winter, Jan. 3, 1942 (div. 1970); children: Emily, Nancy; m. Evelyn Dennys, Sept. 29, 1970. BA, Williams Coll., 1939; MA, Columbia U., 1940, PhD, 1947. Asso. prof. polit. sci. Swarthmore (Pa.) Coll., 1950-57; dir. Office Information, U.P. Ch. U.S.A., NYC, 1957-60; gen. dir. pub. interpretation Nat. Council Chs. of Christ U.S.A., NYC, 1961-64; polit. sci. specialist UNESCO, Paris, France, 1953-54; dir. Religion in Am. Life, 1957-60; lectr. social studies Columbia Tchrs. Coll., 1961-64; chmn. dept. govt. Trinity Coll., Hartford, Conn., 1964-69; prof. polit. sci. Temple U., Phila., 1969-84, prof. emeritus, from 1985. Author: Exporting Arms, 1947, (with Susan W. Stedman) Discontent at the Polls, 1950, (with John P. Roche) Dynamics of Democratic Government, 1954, Religion and Politics in America, 1964, (with Eugene J. Meehan, John P. Roche) Dynamics of Modern Government, 1966, Urban Politics, 1972, co-author 3d and 4th rev. edits., 1985-91, State and Local Governments, 1976, 3d edit., 1982; editor: Modernizing American Government, 1968; contbr. articles to profl. jours. Trustee Protestant Radio-TV Center, Atlanta, 1957-60; mem., bd. dirs. Pub. Affairs Com., Inc., N.Y.C., 1961-83. Served to capt. AUS, 1941-45. Mem. Am. Polit. Sci. Assn., Am. Acad. Polit. and Social Sci., ACLU, Nat. Municipal League. Presbyterian. Home: Philadelphia, Pa. Died Jan. 28, 2006.

STEED, ERNEST HORACE JOSEPH, minister; b. Bendigo, Victoria, Australia, Mar. 18, 1925; s. Edward Horace and Violet May (Gadsen) S.; m. Roda Joan Shaw, May 18, 1948; children: Lincoln, Leonie, Martin. Student, Avondale Coll., N.S.W., 1943; diploma in Salesmanship and Sales Mgmt., Internat. Corr. Schs., London, 1952; LLD (hon.), Grant Theol. Sem., 1976; PhD in Behavioral Sci., Pacific Western U., Los Angeles, 1986. Ordained to ministry Seventh-day Adventist Ch., 1960. Pub. sec. West Australia Conf., 1945-47; home missions, pub. relations dir. West Australia Sabbath Sch., 1947-52; youth pub. relations and temperance dir. Australian Div., 1959-66; assoc. dir. temperance dept. Gen. Conf., Washington, 1966-68, dir., 1968-80; spl. asst. to pres. gen. Conf. of Seventh-day Adventists, 1980-88; exec. dir. Real Life Inc., Takoma Park, Md., 1989-95. Author: Impaled, 1970, Answer to Alcoholism, 1972, The Great Alternative, 1976, Two be One, 1978, Winds of Change, 1987; editor Alert mag., 1959-66; exec. dir. Listen mag., 1968-80; editor ICPA Quar., 1966-88. Exec. dir. Internat. Commn. for Prevention Alcoholism, 1966-88, hon. pres., spl. cons. 1988—; exec. dir. Internat Temperance Assn., 1968-80, Am. Temperance Soc., 1968-80; v.p. Am. Council on Alcohol Problems, 1968-95; dir. Inst. Sci. Studies for Prevention Alcoholism, Australia, 1960-66; exec. dir. Narcotics Edn., Inc., 1968-80, Non-Smokers Internat, 1968-80; chmn. Washington Council on Smoking and Health, 1971-72; UN rep. for Internat. Commn. for Prevention Alcoholism as Non Govt. Orgn., 1971-90; v.p. Nat. Temperance Council (U.S.), 1972-74, pres. 1987-89; ofcl corr. Olympic Games, 1956, 64. Recipient St. Ambrose medal City of Milan, 1968, Freedom of City, Medal Sao Paulo, Brazil, 1984. Mem. Pub. Relations Inst. Australia, Pub. Relations Soc. Am., Religious Pub. Relations Council, Internat. Narcotics Law Enforcement Officers Assn., Pub. Health Assn. of Seventh-day Adventist, Christian Writers Assn. N. Am., N.Y. Acad. Scis. Clubs: U.S. Nat. Press. Home: De Bary, Fla. Died July 25, 2006.

STEELE, EVELYN JANE, public relations and advertising executive; b. Berkeley, Calif., Feb. 14, 1911; d. Carlos Louis and Jane Catherine (Jensen) de Clairmont; grad. Munson Bus. Coll., San Francisco, 1929-30; m. Donald Dickinson Steele, May 8, 1932; 1 son, Donald de Clairmont. Pvt. sec., 1930-32; engaged in public relations, publicity and advt., 1940—; v.p., dir. Steele Group, San Francisco, 1977—; sec.-treas. Internat. Pub. Relations Co., Ltd., San Francisco; sec.-treas. Internat. Bus. Interface, Inc., Don Steele Advt. Pres. Ladies Aid Retarded Children, San Francisco, 1977-78, bd. dirs., 1978-88. Mem. Fashion Group (regional dir. 1965-67). Republican. Unitarian. Clubs: Metropolitan (dir. 1961-68), Order Rainbow Girls. Home: Los Angeles, Calif. Died Aug. 24, 2006.

STEELE, THOMAS MCKNIGHT, law educator; b. Bartlesville, Okla., June 4, 1948; s. James Robert and Erma Blanche (McKnight) S.; m. Barbara Van Curen, Mar. 23, 1973 (div. 1985); children: James Robert, Ryan Thomas, David Christopher Joyce, Justin Daniel Joyce; m. Martha Bolling Swann, Apr. 1985 (div. 1990); m. LeAnn P. Joyce, Jan. 1995. BA in History, Okla. State U., 1969; MLS, U. Oreg., 1974; JD, U. Tex., 1977. Adminstrv. asst. Tarlton Law Libr. U. Tex., Austin, 1975-77; acting law librarian Underwood Law Libr. So. Meth. U., Dallas, 1977-78, asst. law librarian, 1978-79; assoc. prof. law, dir. Franklin Pierce Law Ctr., Concord, N.H., 1979-82; asst. prof., dir. U. Miss. Law Libr., University, 1982-85; assoc. prof., dir. Wake Forest U. Sch. Law Libr., Winston-Salem, N.C., 1985-91; dir. Profl. Ctr. Libr. Wake Forest U., Winston-Salem, NC, 1991—99, prof. law, from 1991. Cons. in field; exec. dir. SCRIBES, Am. Soc. Writers on Legal Subjects, 1988—97, bd. dirs., from 2002. Editor (newsletter) Scrivener, 1986-88; mng. editor Scribes Jour. Legal Writing, 1989-91; editor Pub. Librs. and Pub. Laws, 1986-88; compiler bibliography IDEA, 1981-83, Jour. Air Law and Commerce, 1977-81; co-author: A Law Library Move: Planning Preparation and Execution, 1994, Materials and Cases on Law Practice Management: A Learning Tool for Law Students, 2003. With U.S. Army. Mem.: Legal Mkrg. Assn., Assn. Legal Adminstrs. Democrat. Baptist. Died Mar. 27, 2007.

STEELE, WALLACE ANDERSON, chemical company executive; b. Ashville, N.C., Mar. 14, 1927; s. Luell F. and Nell (Allen) S.; m. Barbara Olds, Aug. 27, 1949; children— Randall O., Melinda Steele Switzer. B.S., U. Cin., 1949, M.S. with honors, 1950; grad. advanced mgmt. program Harvard U., 1968. Vice pres., gen. mgr. Inmont Corp., Clifton, N.J., 1967-71; mktg. dir. Lilly Indsl. Coatings, High Point, N.C., 1972-77; gen. mgr. Pratt & Lambert, Buffalo, 1978-81, v.p., 1981-82, pres. indsl. coatings div., 1982—; bd. dirs. Powder Coatings Inst., Washington, 1983—. Patentee method of producing low-flame spread rated plywood. Missions dir. Word of Faith Fellowship, Alden, N.Y. Served with USN, 1944-46. Mem. Am. Chem. Soc., Nat. Paint and Coatings Assn., Soc. Mfg. Engrs., Beta Theta Pi, Phi Lambda Epsilon. Republican. Home: East Aurora, NY. Died June 6, 2007.

STEEN, CARLTON DUANE, private investor, retired food products executive; b. Walnut Grove, Minn., June 12, 1932; s. Conrad Wendell and Hilda (Eng) S.; m. Dorothy Corinne Sorknes, Aug. 16, 1953; children: James, Craig, Jennifer. BA in Econs. cum laude, St. Olaf Coll., 1954; MA in Indsl. Relations, U. Minn., 1957. Job analyst Exxon Corp., Roselle, NJ, 1958-59; personnel adminstr. Kraft Inc., Chgo., 1959-65, compensation mgr., 1965-69, plant mgr. Decatur, Ga., 1969-70, Champaign, Ill., 1971-74, v.p. prodn. Chgo., 1974-76; pres. Indsl. Foods div., Memphis, 1976-82, Indsl. Foods Group, 1982-87. Served to capt. USAF, 1955-57. Republican. Lutheran. Died Oct. 8, 2006.

STEIGER, HOWARD PAUL, dermatologist; b. Williamsport, Pa., Nov. 2, 1915; s. Howard L. and Helen E. (Taylor-Ring) S.; m. Elizabeth Butler, Aug. 17, 1940; children— Helen Steiger Kellicut, Louise Steiger Heizer, Edith Steiger Seaman, Howard Paul Jr. B.S., Duke U., 1937, M.D., 1940. Diplomate Am. Bd. Dermatology. Intern, Ga. Bapt. Hosp., Atlanta, 1940, U.S. Marine Hosp., New Orleans, 1940-41; resident U. Pa. Hosp., Phila., 1941-47; practice medicine specializing in dermatology, Charlotte, N.C., 1947-87; mem. staff Charlotte Meml. Hosp., Presbyn. Hosp., Mercy Hosp. Served with USPHS, 1940-41, 42-47. Mem. AMA, Am. Acad. Dermatology, N.Am. Clin. Dermatol Soc. Republican. Episcopalian. Clubs: Myers Park Country (Charlotte); Litchfield Country (Pawleys Island, S.C.). Lodges: Mason, Shriners. Home: Charlotte, NC. Died June 23, 2007.

STEIN, GEORGE HENRY, history professor, former academic administrator; b. Vienna, May 18, 1934; came to U.S., 1939, naturalized, 1948. m. Dorothy Ann Lahm, Nov. 22, 1963; 1 child, Kenneth. BA with honors (State Regents scholar), Bklyn. Coll., 1959; MA in History (Regents fellow), Columbia U., 1960, PhD in History (Pres.'s fellow), 1964. Lectr. history City Coll., CUNY, 1962-63; instr. dept. history Columbia U., NYC, 1963-65, asst. prof., 1965-66; assoc. prof. dept. history SUNY-Binghamton, 1966-70, prof., 1970-73, disting. teaching prof., 1973-98, prof. emeritus, 1998—2007, vice chmn. grad. affairs, 1974-76, v.p. acad. affairs, 1976-87, provost, 1985-87, acting pres., 1986-87. Manuscript evaluator and cons. to numerous publishers, 1964-2007 Author: The Waffen SS: Hitler's Elite Guard at War, 1939-45, 1966, paperback edit., 1984 (transl. into German, 1967, French, 1967, Spanish, 1973, Portuguese, 1970, Japanese, 2002, Finnish, 2004); contbr. articles on modern European history to scholarly publs.; editor: Hitler, 1968; contbr. book revs. to hist. jours. Served with USAF, 1953-57. NEH fellow, 1970-71 Mem. Am. Hist. Assn. (mem. conf. group on cen. European history, conf. group for use of psychology in history), Acad. Polit. Sci., Assn. of Contemporary Historians, Am. Assn. Higher Edn., Nat. Assn. State Univs. and Land Grant Colls. (mem. council acad. affairs 1976-87), Am. Counc. Edn. (exec. com. nat. coun. chief acad. officers 1983-85), Com. Internat. d'Histoire de la Deuxieme Guerre Mondiale, WWII Studies Assn. Home: Ithaca, NY. Died July 13, 2007.

STEIN, JAY WOBITH, legal research and education consultant, mediator arbitrator; b. Sauk Centre, Minn., June 19, 1920; s. Julius A. and Emaline (Wobith) S.; children: Holly Jayne, Navida Carol, April Jae, Andrew John, John Henry. BA cum laude, U. Minn., 1942; MA, Stanford U., 1949, Syracuse U., 1960; MS, Columbia U., 1950, PhD, 1952. Dir. CIA rsch. team, 1947-49; dir. library, asst. prof. social studies Southwestern U., Memphis, 1954-57; asst. dir. librs., adminstv. assoc. to v.p. Syracuse (N.Y.) U., 1958-61; faculty Maxwell Sch., Syracuse, 1959-61; asst. to pres. Drake U., Des Moines, Iowa, 1961-64; dir. State Higher Edn. Commn., Des Moines, 1964-67; dean Coll. Arts and Scis., prof. polit. sci. Western Ill. U., Macomb, 1967-69, prof. polit. sci. and edn., 1969-87; rsch. libr. John Marshall Law Sch. Libr., Chgo., 1989-94; ind. rsch. cons. law, libr., edn. Columbus, Ohio, from 1995; founder Rsch. & Resolution, Columbus, Ohio, from 1996. Catalogue planner, econs. and govt., N.Y. Pub. Library, 1953; proposal reviewer U.S. Dept. Edn. Fund for the Improvement of Post-secondary Edn., 1982. Author: The Mind and the Sword, 1961, How Society Governs Education, 1975, Mass Media, Education and a Better Society, 1979, Society, Culture and Education, 1984, Advertising in the Legal Profession, 1993, Ten Years or Ten Days-Litigation and Mediation, 1998; editor Scholar and Educator jour., 1977-85; contbr. articles to profl. jours. Mem. Coun. of Faculties of Bd. Govs. State Colls. and Univs., 1980-86, chmn., 1984-85; Family Cultural Ensemble, 1968-71; active with ch. and civic groups. With USN, 1942-46. Coolidge Found. fellow, 1984; grantee Univ. Rsch. Coun., others; recipient various overseas grants, 1970-80, including U. Bonn Acad. Exch., Germany, Internat. Recreation Assn., Switzerland, U.S. Dept. Edn., Europe and Egypt, also Iran, USSR. Mem. ABA (assoc.), ALA (life), ASPA, Am. Arbitration Assn. (panel of arbitrators), Am. Judicature Soc., Columbus Bar Assn. (assoc.), Soc. Educators and Scholars (founder 1976, exec. dir. 1976-82, chmn. bd. 1980-88), Rotary, Phi Beta Kappa, Phi Kappa Phi, Phi Delta Kappa, Alpha Mu Gamma, Pi Sigma Alpha, Lambda Alpha Psi. Avocations: books, swimming, running. Died May 17, 2007.

STEIN, KENNETH BEN, clinical psychologist; b. Detroit, Feb. 21, 1921; s. Nathan and Sylvia (Drecksler) S.; m. Laurel B. Heyman, June 24, 1951; children— Nathan, Cheryl, David. B.A., Wayne U., 1942; Ph.D., Kans. U., 1952. Cert. Am. Bd. Profl. Psychology. Clin. psychologist VA, Seattle, 1952-58, San Francisco, 1958-63; lectr. and research psychologist U. Calif.-Berkeley, 1963-75; practice clin. psychology, Piedmont, Calif., 1975—. Contbr. numerous articles to profl. jours. Served with U.S. Army, 1944-46. Recipient Outstanding Achievement award VA, 1960; NIMH grantee, 1963-70. Mem. Am. Psychol. Assn., Calif. Psychol. Assn., Alameda County Psychol. Assn. Home: Piedmont, Calif. Died Sept. 9, 2006.

STEINBERG, ARTHUR G(ERALD), geneticist; b. Port Chester, NY, Feb. 27, 1912; s. Bernard Aaron and Sarah (Kaplan) S.; m. Edith Wexler, Nov. 22, 1939; children: Arthur E., Jean E. Strimling. BS, CCNY, 1933; MA, Columbia U., 1934, PhD (Univ. fellow), 1941. Mem. genetics dept. McGill U., Montreal, Que., Can., 1940-44; chmn. dept. genetics Fels Research Inst., asso. prof. genetics Antioch Coll., Yellow Springs, Ohio, 1946-48; cons. divsn. biometry and med. stats. Mayo Clinic, Rochester, Minn., 1948-52; geneticist Children's Cancer Research Found. and research asso. Children's Hosp., Boston, 1952-56; prof. biology Case We. Res. U., Cleve., 1956-72, asst. prof. human genetics, dept. preventive medicine, 1956-60, asso. prof., 1960-70, prof. human genetics, dept. reproductive biology, from 1970, Francis Hobart Herrick prof. biology, 1972-82, emeritus and from 1982, prof. human genetics, dept. medicine, 1975-82. Lectr. genetics dept. orthodontics Harvard Sch. Dental Medicine, 1956-58; dir. heredity clinic Lakeside Hosp., Cleve., 1958-76; vis. prof. Albert Einstein Med. Coll., N.Y.C., 1962, 64, 66, Ind. U., Bloomington, 1972, N.Y. U. Sch. Medicine, 1977; XIIth Ann. Raymond Dart lectr. U. Witwatersrand, Johannesburg, S.Africa, 1975; mem. permanent com. to arrange Internat. Congresses Human Genetics; mem. med. adv. bd. Cystic Fibrosis Found. Cleve., 1957-69; mem. sci. adv. bd. Nat. Cystic Fibrosis Research Found., 1961-63; cons. to expert adv. panel on human genetics WHO, 1961, mem. expert adv. panel, 1965-85; mem. research adv. com. United Cerebral Palsy Found., 1962-65; mem. med. adv. bd. Nat. Genetics Found., 1966-68, chmn., 1968-80; dir. WHO Collaborating Centre for Reference and Research on Genetic Factors of Human Immunoglobulins, 1966-78; cons. study of diabetes in Pima Indians NIH, 1970—. Editor: Am. Jour. Human Genetics, 1956-61; sr. editor: Progress in Med. Genetics, 1960-83; mem. internat. bd. editors: Human Genetics Abstracts, 1962—; cons. editor: Transfusion, 1964—; contbg. editor: Vox Sanguinis, 1965-79; contbr. articles to sci. jours. Bd. dirs. Cleve. Zoo; mem. Cleve. Inst. Art, Cleve. Mus. Art, Cleve. Health Mus., Mus. Natural History. Fellow Australian Acad. Sci. (sr.), AAAS; mem. Am. Soc. Human Genetics (pres. 1964, dir. 1954-66), Genetics Soc. Am., Am. Assn. Immunologists, Japanese Soc. Human Genetics (hon.), Societe Francaise d'Anthropologie et d'Ecologie Humaine (fgn. mem. sci. counsel 1972), Sigma Xi. Home: Cleveland, Ohio. Died May 31, 2006.

STEINBERG, BERNARD D., retired engineering educator; b. Bklyn., Oct. 19, 1924; s. Irving L. and Frances (Flax) S.; m. Jacqueline Ruth Feinberg, May 9, 1948 (dec. 2003); children: Geoffrey, Harris, Lowell, Emily; m. Barbara Block, 2005 B.E.E., M.E.E., MIT, 1949; PhD, U. Pa., 1971. Project engr. Philco Corp., Phila., 1949-56; v.p. Gen. Atronics, Phila., 1957-71; prof. engring. U. Pa., Phila., 1971—2000, prof. emeritus, 2000—07. Chmn. Interspec Inc., Ambler, Pa., 1979-89, chmn. emeritus, 1989-2007; cons. Naval Rsch. Lab., Washington, 1972-83; dir. Valley Forge Rsch. Ctr. Author: Principles of Aperture and Array System Design, 1976, Microwave Imaging with Large Arrays: Radio Camera Principles and Techniques, 1983, (with H. Subbaram) Microwave Imaging Techniques, 1991; contbr. articles to profl. jours.; patentee in radar and electronics. Bd. dirs. Jewish Campus Activities Bd., Phila., 1973-78; mem. exec. com. Orgn. Democratic Party, Springfield Twp., Pa., 1965-75. Served with U.S. Army, 1943-46. US Dept. Def. grantee, 1960 Fellow IEEE (vice-chmn. 1960's, Disting. Lectr. Antennas and Propagation Soc. 1988-91); mem. AAAS, Internat. Radio Scientists Union, Engrs. and Scientists, B'nai B'rith, Sigma Xi, Eta Kappa Nu. Home: Philadelphia, Pa. Died Feb. 21, 2007.

STEINFELDT, WILLIAM MARTIN, retired chemical engineer, state legislator; b. Rochester, N.Y., Mar. 22, 1917; s. William George and Anna Martha (Stunz) S.; m. Jeanne Ladue, Oct. 27, 1947; children— Philip, Lois, Emily, Christine. B.S. in Chem. Engring., Purdue U., 1938. Registered profl. engr., N.Y. Engr., Eastman Kodak Co., Rochester, N.Y., 1939-74; supr. Monroe County, Rochester, 1961-66, county legislator, 1978-82; mem. N.Y. State Assembly, 1970-74; mem. N.Y. State Senate, Albany, 1982-85. Served to 1st lt. AUS, 1942-46. Recipient Rudolfs award Fed. Water Pollution Control Assn., 1971. Republican. Baptist. Home: Rochester, NY. Died Sept. 4, 2006.

STEMMER, EDWARD ALAN, surgeon, educator; b. Cin., Jan. 20, 1930; s. Edward Purcell and Helen Marie (Smith) S.; m. Lois Jean Moss, May 1, 1954; children: Susan Helen, Linda Diane, Paul Frederick, Nancy Joan, Carol Jean. BA, U. Chgo., 1949, MD, 1953. Diplomate Am. Bd. Surgery, Am. Bd. Thoracic Surgery. Resident in surgery U. Chgo., 1953-60; chief resident in surgery Stanford U., Palo Alto, Calif., 1960-62, instr. surgery, 1962-64; asst. prof. surgery U. Utah, Salt Lake City, 1964-65; from asst. prof. surgery to prof. surgery U. Calif., Irvine, from 1966. Acting chmn. surgery U. Calif., Irvine, 1978-80; chief surg. svc. VA Hosp., Long Beach, Calif., 1965—. Editor: Vascular Disease in the Elderly, 1997; contbr. articles to profl. jours., chpts. to books. Capt. USAF, 1955-57, maj. USAFR, 1957-72. Grantee NIH, Am. Heart Assn., 1962-72; recipient disting. svc. award Am. Heart Assn., 1971. Mem. Am. Assn. Thoracic Surgery, Assn. VA Surgeons (pres. 1979-80, disting. svc. award 1995), Am. Surg. Assn., Am. Coll. Surgeons (pres. So. Calif. chpt. 1974-75), L.A. Surg. Soc. (pres. 1986-87), Sigma Xi. Avocations: carpentry, gardening, electronics. Home: Seal Beach, Calif. Died July 21, 2007.

STERBENZ, JOANNE RUTH, accountant; b. New Orleans, June 16, 1947; d. Joseph Roch and Merlin (Prieto) S.; B.S., U. Southwestern La., 1969; M.B.A., Tulane U., 1971. With Arthur Young & Co., Los Angeles, 1971-83, mgr., 1976-80, coordinator computer auditing, 1976-79, prin., 1980-83, office dir. edn., 1979; controller Met. Theatres, Los Angeles, 1985—. Assoc. v.p. for ticketing Los Angeles Olympic Organizing Com., 1984. C.P.A., Calif.; Tulane U. fellow, 1969-71. Mem. Am. Inst. C.P.A.s, Nat. Assn. Female Execs., Am. Women's Soc. C.P.A.s, EDP Auditors Assn., NOW, Tulane Assn. Bus. Alumni, Greater Los Angeles Zoo Assn., Smithsonian Assos. Democrat. Roman Catholic. Home: Santa Monica, Calif. Died June 27, 2007.

STERN, DANIEL, writer, language educator; b. NYC, Jan. 18, 1928; s. Morris and Dora (Hochman) S.; m. Gloria Shapiro, Nov. 9, 1963; 1 son, Eric Branfman. Sr. v.p., mng. dir., mem. bd. mgmt. McCann-Erickson Advt., Inc., NYC, 1964-69; v.p. advt. and publicity worldwide, also dir. Warner Bros., 1969-72; v.p., dir. mktg. Longchamps, Inc., NYC, 1972-73; v.p., creative dir. Lubar-Southard, Inc., NYC, 1973; fellow Ctr. for Humanities, Wesleyan U., 1969, vis. prof. letters and English, 1976-79; v.p. promotion East Coast CBS Entertainment, NYC, 1979-86; pres. entertainment divsn. McCaffrey & McCall, Advt., NYC, 1986; prof. English & creative writing U. Houston, 1992—2007, Cullen Disting. prof. English, 1993—2007. Dir. Humanities, 92nd St. YMHA, 1988. Author: Girl with Glass Heart, 1953, The Guests of Fame, 1955, Miss America, 1959, Who Shall Live, Who Shall Die, 1963 (Internat. Remembrance award for fiction Bergen Belsen Assn. 1973), After the War, 1967, The Suicide Academy, 1968, The Rose Rabbi, 1971, Final Cut, 1975, An Urban Affair, 1980, Twice Told Tales: Stories, 1989 (Richard and Hinda Rosenthal Fiction award AAAL 1990), Twice Upon a Time, 1992, One Day's Perfect Weather: More Twice Told Tales, 1999, In the Country of the Young, 2001, A Little Street Music: Novella and Stories, 2004. With U.S. Army, 1946-47. Recipient Internat. Prix du Souvenir, O. Henry award (2), Pushcart prize (2), Brazos prize for best short story Tex. Inst. Letters, 1996, Fiction prize Tex. Rev. Press, 2003. Mem. PEN, Nat. Book Critics Circle, Author's League. Died Jan. 24, 2007.

STERN, MADELEINE BETTINA, rare book dealer, writer; b. NYC, July 1, 1912; d. Moses Roland and Lillie (Mack) S. BA, Barnard Coll., 1932; MA, Columbia U., 1934. Tchr. English N.Y.C. High Schs., 1934-43; ptnr. Leona Rostenberg Rare Books, NYC, 1945—2007, Leona Rostenberg and Madeleine B. Stern Rare Books, NYC, 1980—2007. Lectr. history of book, feminism, pub. history, lt. Author: We Are Taken, 1935, The Life of Margaret Fuller, 1942, Louisa May Alcott, 1950, new edit., 1996, Purple Passage: The Life of Mrs. Frank Leslie, 1953, Imprints on History: Book Publishers and American Frontiers, 1956, We the Women: Career Firsts of Nineteenth Century America, 1962, new edit., 1994, So Much in a Lifetime: The Story of Dr. Isabel Barrows, 1965, Queen of Publishers' Row: Mrs. Frank Leslie, 1966, The Pantarch: A Biography of Stephen Pearl Andrews, 1968, Heads and Headlines: The Phrenological Fowlers, 1971, Books and Book People in 19th-Century America, 1978, Antiquarian Bookselling in the United States: A History from the Origins to the 1940s, 1985, Nicholas Gouin Dufief of Philadelphia Franco-American Bookseller, 1776-1834, 1988, The Life of Margaret Fuller: A Revised Second Edition, 1991, Louisa May Alcott: From Blood & Thunder to Hearth & Home, 1998; (with Leona Rostenberg) Old and Rare: Forty Years in the Book Business, 1974, rev. edit. 1988, Between Boards: New Thoughts on Old Books, 1978, Bookman's Quintet: Five Catalogues about Books, 1980, Quest Book-Guest Book: A Biblio-Folly, 1993, Connections: Our Selves-Our Books, 1994, Old Books in the Old World: Reminiscences of Book Buying Abroad, 1996, Old Books, Rare Friends: Two Literary Sleuths and Their Shared Passion, 1997, New Worlds in Old Books, 1999, Books Have Their Fates, 2001, Bookends: Two Women, One Enduring Friendship, 2001, From Revolution to Revolution: Perspectives on Publishing and Bookselling, 2002; editor: Women on the Move, 4 vols., 1972, Victoria Woodhull Reader, 1974, Louisa's Wonder Book-An Unknown Alcott Juvenile, 1975, Behind a Mask: The Unknown Thrillers of Louisa May Alcott, 1975, new edit., 1995, Plots and Counterplots: More Unknown Thrillers of Louisa May Alcott, 1976, Publishers for Mass Entertainment in 19th-Century America, 1980, A Phrenological Dictionary of 19th-Century Americans, 1982, Critical Essays on Louisa May Alcott, 1984, A Modern Mephistopheles and Taming a Tartar by Louisa May Alcott, 1987, Louisa May Alcott Unmasked: Collected Thrillers, 1995, Modern Magic by Louisa May Alcott, 1995, The Feminist Alcott: Stories of a Woman's Power, 1996, Louisa May Alcott: Signature of Reform, 2002; co-editor: Selected Letters of Louisa May Alcott, 1987, A Double Life: Newly Discovered Thrillers of Louisa May Alcott, 1988, The Journals of Louisa May Alcott, 1989, Louisa May Alcott: Selected Fiction, 1990, (co-editor) Freaks of Genius: Unknown Thrillers of Louisa May Alcott, 1991, From Jo March's Attic: Stories of Intrigue and Suspense, 1993 (Victorian Soc. award), The Lost Stories of Louisa May Alcott, 1995. Recipient Medalie award, Barnard Coll., 1982, Victorian Soc. award, Disting. Alumna award, 1997;, Guggenheim fellow, 1943—45. Mem. Antiquarian Booksellers Assn. Am. (gov. 1966-68, 78-80), Internat. League Antiquarian Booksellers, MLA, Am. Printing History Assn. (co-recipient award 1983), Authors League, Manuscript Soc. (former trustee), Phi Beta Kappa. Jewish. Home: New York, NY. Died Aug. 19, 2007.

STERN, MILTON, chemical company executive; b. Boston, Apr. 20, 1927; s. Morris and Lily (Colton) S.; m. Roberta L. Navisky, July 10, 1949; children— Mark, Lawrence, Brian. BS, Northeastern U., 1949; MS (Alcoa fellow), MIT, 1950, Sc.D. (Alcoa fellow), 1952. Postdoctoral fellow in metallurgy MI 1952-54; with Union Carbide Corp., NYC, 1954-73, v.p. ele tronics div., 1968-69, exec. v.p. mining and metals div., 1969-7 v.p. exploration Kennecott Corp., NYC, 1973-76, sr. v.p 1976-78, exec. v.p., 1978-82, also dir.; sr. exec. v.p. Stauff Chem. Co., Westport, Conn., 1982-84, vice chmn., from 198 also dir. Contbr. numerous articles in electrochemistry an metallurgy to tech. jours.; patentee n field. Mem. vis. cor M.I.T., 1972-75; mem. corp. Northeastern U.; mem. Whi House Task Force on Am. Indian, 1966; bd. dirs. Assn. Ar Indian Affairs. Served with USNR, 1945-46. Recipient Nuode award Northeastern U., 1949; Sears B. Condit award, 19 Mem. AIME, Nat. Assn. corrosion Engrs. (Willis R. Whitne award 1963), Am. Soc. Metals, Electrochem. Soc. (Your Authors award 1955, 58, jour. div. editor 1958-61), PGA Na Club, Sigma Xi, Tau Beta Pi. Home: West Palm Beach, Fl Died May 19, 2006.

STETSON, JOHN CHARLES, corporate executive; b. Chgo Sept. 6, 1920; s. John Charles and Dorothy H. (Eckman) S.; r Gayle McDowell, Jan. 1, 1946; children: Sherry, Robert, Susa BS, Mass. Inst. Tech., 1943; postgrad., Northwestern U. Bu Sch., 1946-48. Partner Booz Allen & Hamilton, Chgo., 1951-6 pres. pub. div. Houston Post Co., Houston, 1963-70; pres. A. Dick Co., Chgo., 1970-77; also dir.; sec. of the Air Forc Washington, 1977-79; nat. chmn. com. for employer support guard and res. Dept. Def., Washington, 1980-81; pres. J. Stetson, Inc., from 1981. Dir. Kemper Corp., NIBCO, In Madison-Kipp Corp., Helene Curtis, Inc., Magna Photo In Chgo. Tube and Iron, In, Laser Tech., Inc. Trustee Chg Symphony Orch., Falcon Found., Kemper Found. With US 1945-46. Recipient Disting. Service award Dept. Def., Distir Service award also USAF. Mem.: Chicago, Knollwood, Taver Home: Lake Forest, Ill. Died Aug. 1, 2007.

STEVENS, ANNETTE MARIE, librarian; b. Dallas, May 1936; d. Alexander C. and Catherine Ann (Redmond) Zeck; Harrell Stevens, June 8, 1957 (div. 1973); children— Catherir Caryn. B.A., North Tex. State U., 1957; M.Ed., East Tex. Sta U., 1976. Cert. tchr., librarian Tex. Librarian, Dallas Ind. Sc Dist., 1958—. Vice pres. PTA, Dallas, 1978, 83; campai worker Dallas Democratic Com., 1982, 84. Mem. Dallas As Sch. Librarians, Classroom Tchrs. Dallas, Tex. Tchrs. Ass NEA, Delta Kappa Gamma (sec. 1980-82), Zeta Tau Alph Roman Catholic. Home: Dallas, Tex. Died Mar. 1, 2007.

STEVENS, GEORGE L., city councilman; b. Junction Ci La., Feb. 6, 1932; m. Brenda Stevens; children: Gary, Er Marc, Michelle. AA, Imperial Valley Coll.; BA, San Diego St U., 1958; postgrad., Calif. C.C., 1970. Assoc. pastor Calva Bapt. Ch., 1958-93; engring. adminstr. Lockheed Aircraft C 1965-66; dir. job devel. San Diego Urban League, 1966-68; recruitment Philco-Ford, 1968-69; job agt. State of Cal 1969-70; instr. black history San Diego State U., 1970-7 affirmative action officer County of San Diego, 1971-72; mktg. Voice and Viewpoint News, 1972-74; assoc. min. Mt. E Bapt. Ch.; chief of staff to San Diego County Supr. Jim Bat 1974-82; spl. asst. to Congressman Jim Bates, 1982-90; c councilman San Diego, from 1991. Bd. dirs. San Diego Stadi Bd. With U.S. Army, 1953-55. Recipient Freedom award Acti Interprises Devel., Inc., 1982, Presdl. award Black Adv. in St Govt., 1991, Adv. of Yr. award Black Contractor's Assn., 19 Unity award Black Police Officers Assn., 1992, Peace Ma award San Diego Mediation Ctr., 1993. Mem. Kappa Alpha P Home: San Diego, Calif. Died Oct. 16, 2006.

STEVENS, JOHN CHRISTOPHER, retired academic adm istrator; b. Richland, Tex., July 15, 1918; s. John Christoph and Ella (Hardin) S.; m. Ruth Rambo, Dec. 16, 1948; children John Clark, Joyce Stevens Cole BA, Abilene Christian U., 19 D.Litt. (hon.), 1985; MA, U. Ark., 1948, PhD, 1954; LL. Pepperdine U., 1980; D.H., Okla. Christian Coll., 1981; DC Amber U., 1986. Ordained minister Church of Christ, 19 Minister Ch. of Christ, Jasper and Beaumont, Tex., 1938- mem. faculty dept. history Abilene Christian U., Te 1948—2007, dean of students Tex., 1950-56, asst. pres. Te 1956-69, pres. Tex., 1969-81, chancellor Tex., 1981-91, ch cellor emeritus Tex., 1991—2007. Mem. Tex. Guaranteed S dent Loan Corp., Austin, 1980-85, chmn., 1982-84 Me Abilene City Council, 1967-70. Served to maj. Chaplain Co U.S. Army, 1943-46, ETO Named Citizen of Yr., Abilene C. C., 1981 Mem. Assn. Tex. Colls. and Univs. (pres. 1974-7 Ind. Colls. and Univs. Tex. (sec. 1971-81). Lodges: Kiwa (pres. Abilene 1954-55). Democrat. Home: Abilene, Tex. D May 1, 2007.

STEVENS, MILTON LEWIS, JR., trombonist; b. Gt. B rington, Mass., Nov. 10, 1942; s. Milton Lewis and Edna La (Coates) S.; m. Elizabeth Mruk Stevens, June 14, 1966 (d June 1984); m. Priscilla Storms, Dec. 28, 1985. Mus.B., Obe Conservatory Music, 1965; Mus.M., U. Ill., 1966; D.M Boston U., 1975. Instr. Oberlin (Ohio) Conservatory Mu 1967-68; asst. prof. Boston U., 1970-73, Ohio State U., Colu bus, 1973-74; prin. trombonist Denver Symphony, 1974-78, N Symphony Orch., Washington, from 1978. Adj. prof. Cath. Am., 1978—; adj. prof. U. Md., College Park, 1987—, ass artist, 1999—; vis. prof. of trombone Oberlin Coll. Conser tory, 1998-99. Condr. Intersvc. Trombone Choir, Washingt 1991—, Washington Symphonic Brass, 1993—. Recipient bert Spaulding award Berkshire Music Center, 1968 Me Internat. Trombone Assn. Home: Falls Church, Va. Died July 2007.

STEVENS, WILLIAM KENNETH, lawyer; b. Chgo., Apr. 1917; s. Ernest James and Elizabeth (Street) S.; m. A Hughes, Jan. 4, 1943; children: Anne Elizabeth Stevens Fi man, William Hughes Stevens, Mary Carol Stevens Willia Martha Street Stevens Gingrich. AB cum laude, U. Ca Berkeley, 1938; MA, U. Chgo., 1940; JD, Harvard U., 19 Bar: Ill. 1948, Fla. 1977. With First Nat. Bank Chgo., 1948- asst. v.p., 1958-61, v.p., 1961-74; ptnr. McDermott, Will Emery, Chgo., 1974-85, Myers Krause & Stevens, Naples, F 1986—2001; of counsel Fowler White Boggs Banker, Nap Fla., 2001—07. Author: Illinois Estate Administration, 19

Chmn. Ill. Inst. Continuing Legal Edn., 1971-72; pres. Hinsdale (Ill.) Pub. Libr., 1977-79. Lt. USNR, 1941-45. Recipient Disting. Svc. award Chgo. Estate Planning Coun., 1981. Fellow Am. Coll. Trust and Estate Counsel; mem. ABA, Am. Law Inst., Chgo. Bar Assn., Ill. Bar Assn., Fla. Bar Assn. (bd. cert. estate planning and probate lawyer), Internat. Acad. Estate and Trust Law. Clubs: Mid-Day, Hinsdale Golf; Chikaming Country (Lakeside, Mich.), The Club at Pelican Bay (Naples). Died Oct. 28, 2007.

STEVENSON, ERNEST VAIL, retired farmer cooperative executive; b. Streator, Ill., Mar. 18, 1922; s. James Vail and Lucile (Needham) S.; m. Inez Ruth Schoellerman, Sept. 18, 1948; children: Karen Brown, Teresa (Mrs. William J. Murphy), Roger, Linda (Mrs. Brian K. Abbott). BS, U. Ill., 1943; postgrad., 1946-47, Advanced Mgmt. Program, Harvard Bus. Sch., 1964. Research asst. U. Ill., 1946-47; with GROWMARK, Inc. (formerly FS Services, Inc.), Bloomington, Ill., 1947-82, sales edn. dir., 1947-49; dist. mgr. Growmark, Inc. (formerly FS Services, Inc.), 1950-51, mgr. feed div., 1952-55, asst. gen. mgr., 1956-67, v.p. ops., 1967-68, exec. v.p., chief exec. officer, 1968-82, Ill. Grain Corp., 1969-80. Chmn. bd. CF Industries Inc., 1967-74, dir., 1957-77; pres. St. Louis Grain Corp., 1969-82; chmn. bd. Agri-Trans. Corp., 1977-82; past dir. Farmers Export Co., Nat. Council Farmer Coops., Internat. Energy Coop., LVO Internat., Nat. Potash Co., Nat. Coop. Refinery, 1st Nitrogen Corp., Central Nitrogen Inc., St. Paul Ammonia Products, Coop. Farm Chems. Past mem. adv. com. Ill. Bd. Higher Edn.; Past bd. dirs. U. Ill. Agrl. Alumni Assn. Served as pilot USNR, 1943-45. Recipient hon. state farmer degree Future Farmers Am., award of merit U. Ill. Agrl. Alumni Assn., 1975, Bronze tablet Phi Eta Sigma Mem. Assn. Commerce, Farmhouse Frat., Phi Kappa Phi, Gamma Sigma Delta, Alpha Zeta, Ma-Wan-Da. Presbyterian. Home: Bloomington, Ill. Died June 7, 2007.

STEVENSON, IAN PRETYMAN, psychiatrist, educator; b. Montreal, Que., Can., Oct. 31, 1918; s. John Alexander and Ruth Cecilia (Preston); m. Octavia Reynolds, Sept. 13, 1947 (dec. Nov. 1983); m. Margaret H. Pertzoff, Nov. 29, 1985. Student, U. St. Andrews, Scotland; BS, McGill U., 1942, MD, CM, 1943. Cert. Am. Bd. Psychiatry, 1952. Asst. prof. psychiatry La. State U., New Orleans, 1949-52, assoc. prof. psychiatry, 1953-57; prof. psychiatry, chmn. U. Va. Sch. Medicine, Charlottesville, 1957-67, Carlson prof. psychiatry, head divsn. personality studies, 1967—2002, rsch. prof. psychiatry, 2001—02; assoc. mem. Darwin Coll., U. Cambridge, 1981-96; ret., 2002. Author: The Diagnostic Interview, 1960, Twenty Cases Suggestive of Reincarnation, 1966, Cases of the Reincarnation Type. Vol. I. Ten Cases in India, 1975, Cases of the Reincarnation Type. Vol. II: Ten Cases in Sri Lanka, 1978, Cases of the Reincarnation Type. Vol. III: Twelve Cases in Lebanon and Turkey, 1980, Cases of the Reincarnation Type. Vol. IV: Twelve Cases in Thailand and Burma, 1983, Unlearned Language: New Studies in Xenoglossy, 1984, Reincarnation and Biology: A Contribution to the Etiology of Birthmarks and Birth Defects, 1997, Where Reincarnation and Biology Intersect, 1997, Children Who Remember Previous Lives: A Question of Reincarnation, 2001, European Cases of the Reincarnation Type, 2003; contbr. 250 articles to profl. jours. Fellow: Am. Psychiat. Assn. (life disting. fellow); mem.: Soc. for Sci. Exploration (founding com.), Am. Soc. for Psychical Rsch., Soc. for Psychical Rsch. London (coun. and pres. 1988—89), Oxford and Cambridge Club, Colonnade Club. Home: Charlottesvle, Va. Died Feb. 8, 2007.

STEVENSON, ROBERT LOUIS, journalism educator; b. Pine River, Wis., Jan. 11, 1941; s. Clifford L. and Leone B. (Cate) S. BA, U. Wis., 1963, MA, 1969; PhD, U. Wash., 1975. Prof. U. N.C., Chapel Hill, from 1975. Author: Communication, Development and the Third World, 1988; editor: Foreign News and the New World Information Order, 1984. Capt. U.S. Army, 1964-68, Vietnam. Fulbright scholar, 1985-86. Home: Chapel Hill, NC. Died Nov. 25, 2006.

STEWART, C(ORNELIUS) VAN LEUVEN, lawyer; b. Balt., Sept. 22, 1936; s. Charles Morton and Lillie Emerson (Van Leuven) S.; m. Clare Wright Horsley, June 18, 1960; children: Clare Winston, Lillie Elliotte, Jenett Ten Eyck (dec.). BA, Yale U., 1958; LLB, U. Va., 1961. Bar: Md. 1962, D.C. Bar 1982. Assoc. in law U. Calif. Law Sch., Berkeley, 1961-62; assoc. Venable, Baetjer & Howard, Balt., 1962-69, ptnr., 1970-91, Stewart, Plant & Blumenthal, LLC, Balt., from 1991. Bd. dirs., past pres. Irvine Natural Sci. Ctr.; past bd. overseers Balt. Sch. for the Arts; past bd. dirs. Pks. and People Found., Balt. Symphony Orch. Assn., Internat. Visitors Coun. of Balt., Roland Park Country Sch., Magic Me.; past pres. Md. Ballet Co., Met. Balt. Mental Health Assn. Mem. ABA, State Bar Assn., Balt. City Bar Assn., D.C. Bar Assn., Am. Coll. Trust and Estate Counsel (Md. chpt., past state chair), Internat. Acad. of Estate and Trust Law, Balt. Estate Planning Coun. (pres. 1987). Republican. Episcopalian. Home: Stevenson, Md. Died Jan. 16, 2007.

STEWART, DWIGHT CALVERT, philosophy educator; b. Ionia, Mich., Oct. 10, 1930; s. Paul Lemuel and Brite Frances (Beal) S.; m. Jane Hale Howerton, Dec. 28, 1951; children—Carol Jane, Joseph Dwight, Paul Robert. B.A., Culver-Stockton Coll., 1952; M.Div., Drake U., 1955; A.M., Harvard U., 1960; Ph.D., Northwestern U., 1973. Asst. prof., then assoc. prof. religion and philosophy Culver-Stockton Coll., Canton, Mo., 1959-65; asst. prof. religion Boston U., 1968-73; assoc. prof. philosophy Union Coll., Barbourville, Ky., 1974-77, prof., 1977-84, dean undergrad. acad. affairs, 1978-79, dean of faculty, 1979-83, v.p. acad. affairs, 1983-84; dean acad. affairs Midway Coll., Ky., 1984-86, pres., Stewart Info. Services, Inc., 1986—. Danforth Found. grantee, 1966. Mem. AAUP, Am. Acad. Religion. Contbg. editor publs. in field. Home: Versailles, Ky. Died Oct. 12, 2006.

STEWART, HOMER JOSEPH, engineering educator; b. Elba, Mich., Aug. 15, 1915; s. Earl Arthur and Alta Fern (Stanley) S.; m. Frieda Klassen, June 15, 1940; children: Robert Joseph, Katherine Stanley, Barbara Ellen. Student, U. Dubuque, 1932—33; B in Aero. Engring., U. Minn., 1936; PhD, Calif. Inst. Tech., 1940. Faculty Jet Propulsion Lab. Calif. Inst. Tech., Pasadena, 1938—2007, prof. aeros., 1949-80, prof. emeritus, 1980—2007, chief rsch. analysis sect., 1945-56, chief Liquid Propulsion Systems divsn., 1956-58, spl. asst. to dir., 1960-62, chief Advanced Studies Office, 1963-67, advanced studies adviser, 1967-76. Dir. Sargent Industries, Inc., 1964-79, Office Program Planning and Evaluation, NASA, 1958-60; mem. tech. adv. bd. Aerojet-Gen. Corp., 1956-58, 61-70; mem. tech. evaluation group guided missile com. R & D. Bd., 1948-50, chmn., 1951; mem. sci. adv. bd. USAF, 1949-56, 1959-64; mem. sci. adv. com. Ballistics Rsch. Lab., 1959-69, 73-77. Author: Kinematics and Dynamics of Fluid Flow, sect. VI Handbook of Meteorology, 1945; contbr. articles to tech. jours. Recipient Outstanding Achievement award U. Minn., 1954, NASA Exceptional Svc. medal, 1970, I.B. Laskowitz award N.Y. Acad. Scis., 1985. Fellow AIAA; mem. Am. Meteorol. Soc., Internat. Acad. Astronautics, Sigma Xi, Tau Beta Pi. Home: Altadena, Calif. Died May 26, 2007.

STEWART, IRIS PARSONS, corporate executive; b. Lakeland, Fla., Aug. 13, 1926; d. Charles Erwin and Nancy Blanche (Baker) Parsons; m. James Randolph Stewart, Sept. 3, 1950 (dec. Jan. 1974); 1 child, James Randolph Jr. BS, Fla. State U., 1948. Sec. to dean. U. Fla., Gainesville, 1948-49, sec., pres.'s office, 1949-52; sec. State Farm Ins. Cos., Daytona Beach, Fla., 1952-53, Burdine's Dept. Store, Ft. Lauderdale, Fla., 1953; fin. sec. Faith Presbyn. Ch., Tallahassee, 1972-73; adminstrv. asst. Foremost Ins. Co., Clearwater, Fla., 1974-80; exec. sec. to chmn. bd. Fortune Savs. Bank, Clearwater, 1980-90; corp. sec. Fortune Fin. Group, Inc., Clearwater, 1984-90, asst. sec.; asst. sec., exec. asst. to exec. v.p. Fortune Bank, from 1990; corp. sec. Fortune Mortgage Corp., Fortune Appraisal Svcs., Inc., from 1990. Mem. Kappa Delta Alumnae Assn. (pres. 1964-66, treas. 1981-88). Presbyterian. Home: Clearwater, Fla. Died Jan. 2, 2006.

STEWART, JOHN LINCOLN, former academic administrator; b. Alton, Ill., Jan. 24, 1917; s. Frederick William and Hilda (Denovan) S.; m. Joan Elsdon Guthridge, Sept. 23 1939 (div. 1964); children: Leslie Cythera Stewart Chalmers, Ann Guthridge Stewart Nutt; m. Ruth Peabody Quinn, July 11, 1964; stepchildren: Geoffrey Cornelius Quinn, Andrew Dean Quinn. AB, Denison U., 1938, ArtsD (hon.), 1964; MA, Ohio State U., 1939, PhD, 1947. From tchg. asst. to instr. Ohio Sate U., Columbus, 1939-47; instr. UCLA, 1947-49; from asst. prof. to prof. English Dartmouth Coll., Hanover, N.H., 1949-64; prof. Lit. U. Calif., San Diego, 1964-87, provost John Muir Coll., 1965-87. Author: Exposition for Science and Technical Students, 1950, The Essay, 1952, John Crowe Ransom, 1962, The Burden of Time, 1965; (with others) Horizons Circled, 1974, Ernst Krenek, 1990; contbr. articles to profl. jours. Assoc. dir. Hopkins Ctr. for Arts, 1961-64; dir. Mandeville Ctr. for Arts, 1974-76; mem. Dartmouth Community Symphony Orch., 1949-58; trustee Kinhaven Music Sch., 1960-64, Fla. West Coast Symphony, 1958, Oakland Cmty. Orch., 1997-2002; bd. dirs. Theater and Arts Found. San Diego County, 1970; pres. La Jolla (Calif.) Friends Sch. Music, 1971-73, Friends of Music, U. Calif., San Diego. Served with Aus, 1942-45. Howard Found. fellow, 1953-54, Dartmouth Coll. fellow, 1962-63. Democrat. Avocation: performer with music ensembles. Home: Oakland, Calif. Died Aug. 31, 2007.

STEWART, MARGARET MCBRIDE, biology professor, researcher; b. Guilford County, NC, Feb. 6, 1927; d. David Henry and Mary Ellen (Morrow) S.; m. Paul C. Lemon, June 1962 (div. 1968); m. George Edward Martin, Dec. 19, 1969. AB, U. N.C.-Greensboro, 1948; MA, U. N.C.-Chapel Hill, 1951; PhD, Cornell U., 1956; DSc (hon.), U. P.R., Mayaquez, 1996. Instr. biology Greensboro Evening Coll. U. N.C., Greensboro, 1950-51; instr. biology Catawba Coll., Salisbury, N.C., 1951-53; extension botanist Cornell U., Ithaca, N.Y., 1954-56; asst. prof. biology SUNY, Albany, 1956-59, assoc. prof., 1959-65, prof. vertebrate biology, 1965-97, disting. tchg. prof., from 1977, disting. tchg. prof. emerita, 1997; dir. Program in Biodiversity Conservation and Policy, 1997-2000. Faculty rsch. participant Oak Ridge Assoc. Univs., 1983. Author: (with A.H. Benton) Keys to the Vertebrates of the Northeastern States, 1964, Amphibians of Malawi, 1967; contbr. numerous articles and revs. to profl. jours. Bd. dirs. E.N. Huyck Nature Preserve, Rensselaerville, N.Y., 1976-86; bd. dirs. Ea. N.Y. chpt. Nature Conservancy, 1983-88, 90-96, 97-2004, N.Y. State chpt., 1987-90; mem. Albany Pine Bush Commn., 1993-2004. Recipient Citizen Laureate award SUNY Found., 1987, Oak Leaf award Nature Conservancy, 1997; Am. Philos. Soc. rsch. grantee, 1975, 81, NSF grantee, 1978-80, Oak Ridge Assocs. Univs. grantee, 1983-97. Fellow Herpetologists' League (bd. dirs. 1978-80); mem. Soc. for Study of Amphibians and Reptiles (pres. 1979), Am. Soc. Ichthyologists and Herpetologists (bd. govs. 1975-80, 87-90, 96—, herpetology editor 1983-85, pres. 1996, historian 1999-2004, Johnson award 2005, Fitch award 2005), Ecol. Soc. Am., Assn. for Tropical Biologists, Soc. Study of Evolution, III World Congress of Herpetology (mem. exec. com. 1995-01), Sigma Xi, Sigma Delta Epsilon, Phi Beta Kappa (emeritus), Phi Kappa Phi. Democrat. Presbyterian. Avocations: photography, gardening, reading, travel. Home: Voorheesville, NY. Died Aug. 2, 2006.

STEWART, WARREN EARL, chemical engineer, educator; b. Whitewater, Wis., July 3, 1924; s. Earl Austin and Avis (Walker) S.; m. Jean Durham Potter, May 24, 1947; children— Marilyn, David, Douglas, Carol, Margaret, Mary Jean. BS in Chem. Engring, U. Wis., 1945, MS in Chem. Engring, 1947; Sc.D. in Chem. Engring, Mass. Inst. Tech., 1951. Project chem. engr. Sinclair Research Labs., Harvey, Ill., 1950-56, cons., 1956-83; from asst. prof. to prof. chem. engring. dept. U. Wis., Madison, 1956—96, chmn. dept., 1973-78, McFarland-Bascom prof., 1983-96, prof. emeritus, from 1997; pres. Stewart & Assoc. Engring. Software, Inc., from 1998. Cons. Engelhard Industries, Inc., Newark, 1956-58; instr. spl. courses transport phenomena Chemstrand Corp., Pensacola, Fla., 1962, Nat. U. La Plata, Argentina, 1962, Esso Rsch. & Engring. Co., 1963, 66, Phillips Petroleum Co., 1963, Am. Inst. Chem. Engrs., 1965, 68-69, Inst. Tec. Celaya (Mex.), 1983, U. Autonoma de Mex., 1985; Reilly lectr. Notre Dame U., 1993. Author: (with R.B. Bird and E.N. Lightfoot) Transport Phenomena, 1960, 2d edit., 2002, Special Topics in Transport Phenomena, 1965, (with R.B. Bird, E.N. Lightfoot and T.W. Chapman) Lectures in Transport Phenomena, 1969; editl. adv. Latin Am. Applied Rsch., Computers and Chem. Engring., 1977—. Recipient Benjamin Smith Reynolds teaching award, 1981, Byron Bird rsch. award, 1991. Fellow Am. Inst. Chem. Engrs. (Computing in Chem. Engring. award 1985); mem. NAE, Am. Chem. Soc. (Murphree award 1989), Am. Soc. for Engring. Edn., (Chem. Engring. Lectureship award 1983), Wis. Acad. Scis., Arts and Letters, Phi Beta Kappa, Sigma Xi, Alpha Chi Sigma (Rsch. award 1981), Phi Eta Sigma, Tau Beta Pi, Phi Lambda Upsilon, Phi Kappa Phi. Conglist. (deacon, moderator). Home: Madison, Wis. Died Mar. 27, 2006.

STICHT, J. PAUL, retired food products and tobacco company executive; b. Clairton, Pa, Oct. 3, 1917; m. Ferne Cozad, 1940; children: David, Mark. BA, Grove City Coll., 1939, LLD (hon.), 1968. With US Steel Corp., 1939-44; pers. dir. Trans World Airlines, 1944-48; v.p. Campbell Soup Co., 1947-57, pres. internat., 1957-60; exec. v.p. Federated Dept. Stores, Inc., 1960—67, pres., 1967—72; chmn. exec. com., COO R.J. Reynolds Industries, Inc., Winston-Salem, NC, 1972-73, pres., CEO, 1978-79, chmn., 1979-85, RJR Nabisco, Inc., Winston-Salem, 1987-89, acting chmn., CEO, 1989; pres. Castle Springs, LLC, Winston-Salem, 1992—2002, chmn., 2002—03. Mem. Bd. Trustees Grove City Coll., 1968-2007, chmn., 1998-2003; mem. bd. visitors Wake Forest U. Med. Sch., former chmn. bd. visitors; mem. bd. visitors Fuqua Sch. Bus. Duke U. Recipient Alumni Achievement award, Grove City Coll., 1967, Disting. Svc. award, 2003. Home: Winston Salem, NC. Died Mar. 27, 2007.

STILWELL, JOHN QUINCY, lawyer; b. Columbia, SC, Sept. 20, 1933; s. James Raymond and Edna (Douglass) S.; m. Regina Besman, Apr. 18, 1965 (div. Mar. 1977); 1 child, Laura Douglass; m. Nancy O'Neil, Mar. 20, 1987; children: William S. Rogers, Richard Blake Rogers, Stephen J. Rogers, Stewart D. Rogers. AB, U. N.C., 1954; LLB, Columbia U., 1961; MA, U. Tex., Dallas, 1988, PhD, 1994. Bar: N.Y. 1962, Tex. 1990. Assoc. atty. Winthrop, Stimson, Putnam & Roberts, NYC, 1961-68; v.p., gen. counsel Total Energy Leasing Corp., NYC, 1968-70, pres., 1970-72; ptnr. Gibbons, Green & Rice, NYC, 1972-74; chmn. Transcable Inc., NYC, 1974-77, John Stilwell Assocs., Inc., Fairfield, Conn., 1977-79; sr. v.p. Kidde, Inc., Saddle Brook, N.J., 1979-85; assoc. gen. counsel Mut. of N.Y. Life, NYC, 1985-87; ptnr. Akin, Gump, Strauss, Hauer & Feld, L.L.P., Dallas, 1987-99. Mediator and arbitrator Am. Arbitration Assn. Panels. Bd. dirs., sec. Shared Housing Ctr., Inc., Dallas, 1993—; bd. dirs. Dallas County Local Workforce Devel. Bd., 1996—, chmn., 1997-99; trustee Consensus Found., Dallas, 1990. Served to lt. USN, 1954-58. Mem. Soc. Profls. in Dispute Resolution (bd. dirs. Dallas chpt. 1998—), Assn. Bar City N.Y., Dallas Bar Assn. Avocation: philosophy and communication theory. Home: Dallas, Tex. Died Feb. 28, 2006.

STILWELL, VICTOR E., lawyer; b. New Brunswick, NJ, Nov. 17, 1939; BArch, Tulane U., 1965; MArch, Princeton U., 1967; JD, Loyola U. of South, 1976. Bar: La. 1976; registered architect, La. Atty. Deutsch, Kerrigan & Stiles, New Orleans. Vis. lectr. Tulane U. Sch. Architecture, 1980—; active Nat. Coun. Archtl. Registtration Bd., 1972—. Mem. ABA, AIA, La. Architects Assn., La. State Bar Assn., Tau Sigma Delta. Died Nov. 24, 2006.

STIVENDER, DONALD LEWIS, mechanical engineering consultant; b. Chgo., May 8, 1932; s. Paul Macon and Grace (Larsen) S.; m. Margaret Ann Lourim, Apr. 14, 1956; children—Anne, Robert, Carole. BS in Engring, U.S. Coast Guard Acad., 1954; MS, U. Mich., 1959. Registered profl. engr., Mich. R & D engr. Rsch. Labs., GM Corp., Warren, Mich., 1959-92, sr. rsch. engr., 1968-92; owner, consulting engr. Stivender Engring. Assos., from 1980. Cons. engine, thermodynamics, emissions and systems engring. disciplines. Contbr. articles tech. jours. on diesel, gas turbine and spark ignition engine combustion, emission, constrn. and electronic control aspects. Engring. officer USCG, 1950-58. Fellow Soc. Automotive Engrs. (Arch T. Colwell award 1968, 69, 79, governing bd. 1971-73); mem. NAS (naval studies bd. 1990-92), ASME, NRC, Combustion Inst., Sigma Xi. Achievements include inventions of internal combustion engines and electronic control systems. Home: Bloomfield Hills, Mich. Died Sept. 28, 2006.

STIVER, INEZETTA OREL ELIASON, accountant; b. Centerville, Ind., Mar. 26, 1916; d. Wood Esta and Pearl Mae (Davis) Eliason; m. Roy Carl Stiver, Nov. 24, 1940. Diploma, Ind. Bus. Coll., 1948. Pvt. practice acctg., Centerville, 1955-87. Instr. acctg. Richmond (Ind.) Bus. Coll., 1945-48. Author: Wilderness Opportunity, 1964; compiler, pub.: Townsend-Elias Family Cookbook, 1991; columnist Centerville Crusader Silhouettes. Clk. Centerville Christian Ch., 1955-84; bd. dirs. Hist. Centerville Inc., 1969-84, 86-91; mem. Centerville Planning Commn., 1975-77, Wayne County (Ind.) Resource Inventory Commn., 1985-88. Recipient civic award Centerville Jaycees, 1971, This Is Your Life award, 1978, Scouters Wife Heart of Gold award, 1979, Outstanding Citizen award Centerville Lions Club, 1986. Mem. Nat. Soc. Pub. Accts., Ind. Soc. Pub. Accts., Soc. Ind. Pioneers, Am. Legion Aux., Centerville Women's Cemetary Assn. (treas. 1980—), Alliance Wayne County Mus. (bd. dirs.), DAR, Colonial Dames 17th Century, Daus. Am. Colonists, Studebaker Family Assn., Ind. Genealogy Soc., Ill. Genealogy Soc., Iowa Genealogy Soc., Ohio Genealogy Soc., Md. Genealogy Soc., Del. Genealogy Soc., Pa. Genealogy Soc., Joshua Eliason Family Descendants (historian). Republican. Died Apr. 14, 2006.

STOCK, GEORGE E., banker; b. Bklyn., Mar. 23, 1921; s. Samuel and Ethel V (Fitzgerald) S.; m. Stephanie Tactikos, Sept. 16, 1951; children: George, Fredric, S., Cynthia E., James G. BS in Econs., Wharton Sch., U. Pa., 1942; postgrad., Rutgers U., 1958. With Chase Manhattan Bank, NYC, 1946-59; with 1st Jersey Nat. Bank, Jersey City, 1959-65; pres., dir. United Bancshares Fla., Inc., Coral Gables, 1965-72; exec. v.p., dir. Norin Corp., North Miami, Fla., 1972-74; dir. Midlantic Banks Inc., Edison, N.J., from 1974, pres., from 1978; pres., dir. Midlantic Nat. Bank/Citizens, Englewood, N.J., from 1974. Bd.

dirs. Commerce and Industry Assn. No. N.J., chmn., 1979; bd. dirs. Bergen County council Girl Scouts U.S.A.; mem. Fla. Council 100, 1968—. Served with U.S. Army, 1942-46. Mem.: Ridgewood Country, Knickerbocker Country, La Gorce Country, Seaview Golf. Republican. Died May 5, 2006.

STOCKANES, HARRIET PRICE, publishing executive, consultant; b. Crawford, Nebr., Oct. 31, 1923; d. Joseph Hartwell and Lyda Marie (Chadderdon) Price; m. Robert Ward O'Brien, Dec. 28, 1946 (div. Aug. 1964); children— Nan O'Brien Beman, Julia O'Brien Domingue, Lewis W.; m. 2d, Anthony Edward Stockanes, Jan. 7, 1966. Student Carleton Coll., 1941-43; A.B., U. Wis., 1945. Sec., Bitker & Marshall, Milw., 1945-46, Hale & Dorr, Boston, 1946-47; underwriter Standard Annuity & Life Ins. Co., Champaign, Ill., 1964-67; sec. U. Ill., Champaign, 1967-75; rights mgr. U. Ill. Press, Champaign, 1975—. Village clk., Park Forest, Ill., 1950-54. Republican. Home: Urbana, Ill. Died Sept. 26, 2006.

STOCKING, CLIFFORD RALPH, emeritus botany educator; b. Riverside, Calif., June 22, 1913; s. Clifford Dodge and Laura (Stephenson) S.; m. Elsie Irene Taylor, Aug. 31, 1937; children— Kathleen Ann (Mrs. Warren Cropper), Margery BS with highest honors in Plant Nutrition, U. Calif., Berkeley, 1937, MS in Plant Physiology, 1939; PhD, U. Calif., Davis, 1943. Asso. botany U. Calif., Davis, 1939-42, asst. prof. botany, asst. botanist, 1946-52, asso. prof., asso. botanist, 1952-55, prof. botany, botanist, 1958-81, prof. emeritus, from 1981, chmn. dept. botany and agrl. botany, 1968-74. Chemist Pucunelli Packing Co., Turlock, Calif., 1942-45 Author: (with A.S. Crafts, H.B. Currier) Water in Physiology of Plants, 1949, (with W. Robbins, T.E. Weier) Botany-An Introduction to Plant Science, 3d edit, 1964, (with T.E. Weier, M.G. Barbour and T. Rost) Botany— An Introduction to Plant Biology, 6th edit, 1981. Merck sr. postdoctoral fellow, 1955-56; NSF fellow London, 1963-64; NSF sr. postdoctoral fellow Kings Coll., London, 1971-72 Fellow A.A.A.S.; mem. Calif. Acad. Scis., Botany Soc. Am., Am. Soc. Plant Physiologists, Phi Beta Kappa. Died May 22, 2006.

STOERMER, PHILLIP H., lawyer; b. LA, July 25, 1940; BA, U. So. Calif., 1961; JD, Southwestern U., 1968. Bar: Calif. 1969. Atty. Tarkington, O'Connor & O'Neill, San Francisco. Instr. Calif. Coll. Law, 1971-72. Mem. ABA (mem. real property, probate and trust law, corporation, banking and bus. law sects.), Internat. Coun. Shopping Ctrs., State Bar Calif., Urban Land Inst. Died July 20, 2006.

STOKER, WARREN CADY, university president; b. Union Springs, NY, Jan. 30, 1912; s. Ray W. and Dora Maude (Cady) S.; m. Ruth Eleanor Gabb, Aug. 30, 1934; children: Robert Warren, W. Lance, Lois Ruth. EE, Rensselaer Poly. Inst., 1933, MEE, 1934, PhD, 1938; D Humanities, Hartford Grad. Ctr., 1994. Instr. to asso. prof. elec. engring. Rensselaer Poly. Inst., 1934-51, prof., from 1951, head computer lab., 1952-55; dir. Hartford Grad. Center, 1955-57; dean Hartford Grad. Center (Grad. Center), 1957-70; asso. dean Rensselaer Poly. Inst. Grad Sch., 1957-69; v.p. Rensselaer Poly. Inst. Conn., 1961-74, pres., 1974-75, also trustee, Hartford Grad. Center (formerly Rensselaer Poly. Inst. Conn.), 1975-76, pres. emeritus, from 1976, trustee, from 1975. Trustee Mechanics Savs. Bank, Hartford, 1969-82, incorporator, 1969— Fellow IEEE; mem. Sci. Rsch. Soc. Am., Newcomen Soc. N.Am., Am. Soc. Engring. Edn., Conn. Acad. Sci. and Engring., Sigma Xi, Tau Beta Pi, Eta Kappa Nu. Clubs: Hartford (Conn.). Home: Manchester, Conn. Died Nov. 16, 2006.

STOLLAR, RICHARD LLOYD, geologist; b. Wheeling, W.Va., May 10, 1951; s. Willis Blaine and Marjorie Jean (Wallace) S.; m. Elaine Jill Huffman, Aug. 23, 1975; children: Sarah Elizabeth, Rachael Lillian. BS in Geology, Mt. Union Coll., 1973; MS in Geology, Kent State U., 1976. Registered profl. geologist, Va. Geologist, Columbia Gas Trans. Corp., Charleston, W.Va., 1977-79, geologist, 1979-82; sr. geologist Columbia Gas Trans. Corp., Charleston, 1982-85; supervisory geologist Columbia Natural Gas Resources, Inc., Charleston, 1985-87, chief geologist, 1987—. Mem. Geol. Soc. Am., Am. Assn. Petroleum Geologists (ho. of dels. 1986-88), Appalachian Geol. Soc. (pres. 1982-83), Am. Soc. Ret. Ged. Ho. Dels. (re-elected 1989—). Republican. Ch. of Christ. Home: Winfield, W.Va. Died Apr. 22, 2006.

STOLLER, MICHAEL JAY, publishing executive; b. NYC, July 4, 1931; s. Alfred and Anne (Etra) S.; m. Regina Roman, Apr. 23, 1963 (div. 1969); 1 child, Joshua Alfred BS, U. Pa., 1953; MBA, NYU, 1956. Buyer Bloomingdale Bros., NYC, 1953-58; advt. sales mgr. Breskin Publ. Co., NYC, 1959-63; dist. mgr. McGraw Hill, NYC, 1963-78, Bus. Week Mag., NYC, 1979-82; pub. Hearst Bus. Communications, NYC, 1982-87; advt. dir. McGraw-Hill, NYC, 1988; pub. Discount Merchandiser McFadden Publs., NYC, from 1989. Served with USAF, 1960-63 Mem. Bus. and Profl. Advt. Assn. Democrat. Jewish. Home: New York, NY. Died May 15, 2007.

STOLNITZ, ARTHUR H., television production executive; b. Rochester, NY, Mar. 13, 1928; s. Jesse and Mary (Aiole) S.; m. Jamie Fein, 1949 (div. 1954); m. Suzanne E. Goodman, Aug. 30, 1964; 1 child, Scott. LLB, U. Tenn., 1952. Exec. v.p. Metromedia Producers Corp., LA, 1970-73, Charles Fries Prodns., Studio City, Calif., 1973-74; sr. v.p. bus. affairs Warner Bros. TV, Burbank, Calif., 1977-90; exec. v.p. bus., fin. affairs Lorimar TV, Burbank, from 1990. Producer TV series Grizzly Adams, 1976; TV pilot Jeremy of Jacobs Neck, 1976; TV movies Secret Night Caller, 1974, Foster & Laurie, 1975; exec. in charge of procdn. TV movie Call of the Wild, 1975. Withe USNAF, 1946-48. Mem. Hollywood Radio and TV Soc. (bd. dirs.), Acad. TV Arts and Scis., Acad. Motion Picture Arts and Scis., Calif. Yacht Club, Navy League, Phi Alpha Delta. Republican. Jewish. Avocation: sailing. Home: Palm Desert, Calif. Died Mar. 22, 2007.

STONE, ALLAN BARRY, art gallery director; b. NYC, Feb. 6, 1932; s. Herbert Daniel and Ruth (Klein) S.; m. Marguerite Cullman, Jan. 6, 1956 (div. 1965); children: Allison M., Jeremy, Claudia, Heather; m. Clare Chester, Sept. 3, 1965; children: Jessie Chester, Posy Merriweather. BA, Phillips Acad., 1950, Harvard U., 1954; LLB, Boston U., 1958. Atty. Legal Aid Soc., Boston, 1956-57; atty. civil frauds US Dept. Justice, Washington, 1958-59; assoc. Wicks, Riddell, Bloomer, Jacoby & McQuire, NYC, 1959-60; pres. Allan Stone Gallery, NYC, 1960—2006. Cons. in field. Pres. Purchase Environ. Protection Assn., N.Y., 1978-85; fellow Woodrow Wilson Found., 1982; mem. Presdl. Fellowship Com., 1980. Avocations: gardening, tennis. Home: Purchase, NY. Died Dec. 15, 2006.

STONEKING, LEWIS WILLIAM, college dean; b. Hannibal, Mo., July 5, 1923; s. Lewis Levi and Arlene (Wolfgram) S.; m. Lena Precup, Nov. 24, 1949; children— Lewis Michael, Leslie Myron, Lisa Arlene, Lori Ann. B.A., Harris Tchrs. Coll., 1950, M.A., Ball State U., 1957, Ed.D., Ind. U., 1960. Cert. supt., curriculum dir., elem. tchr., secondary tchr. Tchr. St. Louis Pub. Schs., 1950-54; tchr. secondary sch. University City Pub. Schs., Mo., 1954-56, Anderson Pub. Schs., Inc., 1956-57; asst. prof. edn. Ball State U., Muncie, Ind., 1956-57; vis. lectr. Ind. U., Bloomington, 1959-60; prof. edn. George Peabody Coll. Tchrs., Nashville, 1960-65; vis. prof. edn. Central Washington State Coll., Ellensburg, 1969, Eastern Washington State Coll., Cheney, 1967; chmn. dept. edn. Parsons Coll., Fairfield, Iowa, 1965-72; dean Coll. Edn., U. Wis.-Whitewater, 1972—. Author: Modern Elementary Mathematics, 1966. Contbr. articles to profl. jours. Served as tech. sgt. USMC, 1943-46. Mem. NEA, Assn. Childhood Edn. Internat. (editorial bd.) Lodge: Rotary. Died Dec. 14, 2006.

STONER, BARTINE ALBERT, JR., advertising executive; b. Trenton, NJ, Apr. 18, 1926; s. Bartine Albert and Estella (Hart) S.; m. Elizabeth Ann Bond, Mar. 18, 1949 (div. 1973); children: Bartine Albert III, Jonathan West; m. Madeleine Ruskin, 1973. BS, Princeton U., 1948. With Westinghouse Electric Corp., Boston, Newark and Phila., 1948-56; account exec. N.W. Ayer & Son, Inc., Phila., 1956-65, v.p., dir. account service, 1965-67, dir., exec. v.p., gen. mgr. Phila. region, 1967-73, dir. internat. ops. NYC, 1974-76, also bd. dirs.; pres. Ayer Baker Advt., Seattle, 1974-75; mng. dir. Ayer Barker Hegemann Internat. B.V., London, 1976-79; pres., chief exec. officer Ayer, Jorgensen, Macdonald, Los Angeles, 1979-80; exec. v.p., dir. N.W. Ayer Inc.; pres. N.W. Ayer Inc. (Western div.), 1981-83, chmn., chief exec. officer, from 1983. Dir., pres. Settembrini and Tecchio ABH Internat., Milan, Italy, 1976-79; Charles Barker, Gmbh, Frankfurt, Fed. Republic of Germany, 1978-79; dir Moussault ABH Internat., Amsterdam, Holland and Antwerp, 1976-79, O'Hara, Hannigan and Reid, ABH Internat., Toronto, 1975-76. Bd. dirs. Greater Phila. Movement, 1973-74, Elwyn Inst.-Hosp., 1967-76; bd. pensions U.P. Ch. U.S.A., 1971-76; pres., trustee Internat. Assn. Shipboard Edn.; mem. Town Hall Calif., Los Angeles, The Founders of Music Ctr., Los Angeles, Museum Contemporary Art, Los Angeles, Los Angeles County Art Mus., Natural History Mus. Los Angeles County. Served to lt. (j.g.) USNR, 1944-46. Mem. Pa. Soc., Princeton Club of So. Calif., Greater Los Angeles C. of C., Los Angeles World Affaris Council, Japan Am. Soc. Presbyterian (elder). Clubs: Phila. Racquet; Hurlingham (London); Princeton (N.Y.C.); Jonathan (Los Angeles), Rotary (Los Angeles), Riviera Tennis (Los Angeles). Home: Yardley, Pa. Died Jan. 13, 2007.

STOPHER, JOSEPH E., lawyer; b. Louisville, May 10, 1914; s. George Edward and Hattie Owen (DeGaris) S.; m. Marie Harmon Estes, Sept. 19, 1942; children— Edward H., Ann Stopher Dalzell, Robert E. JD, U. Louisville Sch. Law, 1938. Bar: Ky. 1937. Assoc. Davis Boehl Viser & Marcus, Louisville, 1938-46, ptnr., 1946-52, Boehl Stopher Graves & Deindoerfer, Louisville, from 1952. Mem. Ky. State Fair Bd., Louisville, 1968— Recipient Outstanding Lawyer award Louisville Bar Assn., 1971 Fellow Am. Coll. Trial Lawyers; mem. ABA (bd. govs. 1984-86), Ky. Bar Assn., Louisville Bar Assn. Clubs: Pendennis. Republican. Baptist. Avocations: breeding saddle horses. Home: Louisville, Ky. Died Apr. 27, 2006.

STORM, DOROTHY DICKINSON, city official; b. Columbus, Nebr., Dec. 28, 1918; d. Oscar Dwight and Ethel Sarah (Myers) Dickinson; m. Roland B. Storm, Dec. 23, 1942; children— Vicki Lynn Storm McDonald, Douglas Dwight. Student Grand Island Bus. Coll., 1938. Cert. mcpl. clk. Dep. clk. dist. ct. Hall County, Grand Island, Nebr., 1938-46; dep. clk. City of Brea, Calif., 1959-68, clk., 1968—. Charter mem. Brea Republican Women. Mem. So. Calif. City Clks. Assn. (dir. 1984—). Home: Carlsbad, Calif. Died Feb. 20, 2006.

STORY, PETER REINALD, state senator, rancher; b. Los Angeles, Dec. 19, 1932; s. Malcolm Chilton and Rose (Ashby) S.; B.S., Colo. U.; m. Eileen Cavanaugh, June 14, 1958; children— Robert, Michael, Nelson, Rose, Tom. Owner, operator Story Ranch, Emigrant, Mont., 1958—; mem. Mont. Senate, 1973—, chmn. state adminstrn. com., vice chmn. fin. and claims com. Served with USNR, 1955-58. Republican. Club: Elks. Home: Carlsbad, Calif. Died July 3, 2006.

STRAIGHT, WILLIAM GILBERT, hospital administrator, consultant; b. St. Petersburg, Fla., Feb. 1, 1931; s. Alfred and Wilma Ruth (Brooks) S.; m. Carol Joyne Goodner, Sept. 15, 1950; children— Joyce Lynette, Toni Marie Straight Davis. B.S. in Bus. Adminstrn., So. Coll., Collegedale, Tenn., 1960; postgrad., Franklin U., 1977, U. Dayton, 1979. Adminstr., Watkins Meml. Hosp., Ellijay, Ga., 1963-68; regional systems mgr. United Med. Labs., Portland, Oreg., 1968-73; assoc. adminstr. Harding Hosp., Worthington, Ohio, 1974-80; adminstr. Windsor Hosp. (Mo.), 1980-81; sr. v.p. Battle Creek Adventist Hosp. (Mich.), 1981—; design cons. to psychiatric hosps., mental health ctrs. Trustee Good Samaritan Hospice, Battle Creek, 1981—, Moberly Regional Med. Ctr. (Mo.), 1980-81; former mem. County Disaster Planning Commn.; bd. dirs. New Day, Inc., Berrian Springs, Mich., 1983—. Served with U.S. Army, 1956-58. Recipient Outstanding Achievement award Harding Hosp., 1977, Top Three award U.S. Army Med. Corps., 1956. Mem. Am. Coll. Hosp. Adminstrs., Epsilon Delta Chi. Lodge: Lions. Home: Battle Creek, Mich. Died July 18, 2006.

STRAITS, BEVERLY JOAN, gynecologist; b. Aurora, Ill Jan. 29, 1939; d. Ernest Joseph and Mildred Betty (Shobe) S children: Kell Donald, Jill Elizabeth. BA, Carleton Coll., 1961 MD, Northwestern U., 1965. Diplomate in gynecology an obstetrics. Intern Passavant Hosp., Chgo., 1965-66; residenc Lutheran Hosp., Milw., 1966-69; pvt. practice Wheat Ridge Colo., from 1969. Fellow Am. Coll. Obstetrics & Gynecology Avocations: skiing, camping. Home: Golden, Colo. Died Ap 26, 2007.

STRASMA, JOHN DRINAN, economist, educator; b. Kanka kee, Ill., Mar. 29, 1932; s. Roy and Charlotte Wilkins (Deselm S.; m. Judith Feaster, Mar. 18, 1956 (div. 1983); children: Anne Patricia, Susan, Kenneth, Mary; m. Anne Corry, July 21, 1984 AB, DePauw U., 1953; AM, Harvard U., 1958, PhD, 1960 Research asst. Fed. Res. Bank of Boston, 1958-59; prof. Econs Inst., U. Chile, Santiago, 1959-72; economist UN Secretaria 1964-65; advisor Ministry of Economy and Fin., Lima, Peru 1970; prof. econs. and agrl. econs. U. Wis., Madison, from 1972 dir. Ctr. for Development Univ. Wis., Madison, 1996-98. Cons in field; v.p., dir. Latin Am. Scholarship Program of Am. Univs 1970-74; chmn. fin. com. Wesley Found. of Wis., 1978-87 public mem. Wis. Legis. Council Com. on Mining, 1975-90 Author: State and Local Taxation of Manufacturing Industry 1969, Agrarian Reform in El Salvador, 1982, Agricultural Lan Taxation in Developing Countries, 1987, Land Tax Reform Alternatives in Zimbabwe, 1990, Options for Redistributin Land in the New South Africa, 1993, Market-Based Lan Redistribution in the New South Africa, 1993, Resolving Lan Conflicts in Nicaragua, 1996, Developing Financial Markets i the Dominican Repubic, 1997, Rebuilding Agriculture After th Hurricane in Central America, 1999. Served with U.S. Army 1954-56. Danforth fellow, 1956-60; Recipient Outstanding Pub lic Service award Wis. Environ. Decade, 1978 Mem. Am. Econ Assn., Am. Agrl. Econs. Assn., Internat. Agrl. Econs. Assn Latin Am. Studies Assn., Soc. Internat. Devel. Methodist. Home Madison, Wis. Died July 13, 2007.

STRAUB, CONRAD PAUL, retired environmental healt educator, consultant; b. Irvington, NJ, June 21, 1916; s. Georg and Bertha (Piekarski) S.; m. Anne Bertha Dyak, Apr. 2, 194 children: Conrad P. Jr., Patricia Anne, Cathleen Mary, Micha Andrew. BSCE, Newark Coll. Engring., 1936, DEng (hon 1967; MCE, Cornell U., 1940; postgrad., Harvard U., 194 PhD, Cornell U., 1943. Insp., screw machine operator Phoeni Brass Fittings Corp., Irvington, N.J., 1936; draftsman, comput U.S. Engrs. Office, Ithaca, N.Y., 1937-39; fellow W.K. Kellog Found., Charlotte, Mich., 1939; sanitary engr. U.S. Pub. Healt Svc., Overseas and Domestic, 1941-66; prof. environ. healt Sch. Pub. Health U. Minn., Mpls., 1966-81. Cons. WHO various locations, 1955-81; USPHS, US EPA, U.S. Arm 1966-81, various mcpl. health depts. and private industrie Author: Low Level Radiological Wastes, 1965 (Russian trans. editor Rev. Jour. on Environ. Control, 1969-93, also 6 hand books on environ. subjects, 1974-91; contbr. chpts. to 5 book on environ. health. Capt. USPHS, 1942-66. Recipient Fuert medal Cornell U., Ithaca, 1954, Outstanding Grad. awar Newark Coll. Engring., 1955. Mem. ASCE (pres. Oak Ridg sect. 1955, life), Am. Water Works Assn. (life), Fedn. of Sewag Works Assn. (life), Am. Pub. Health Assn. (life), Health Physi Soc. (Elda Anderson Meml. award 1955). Avocation: stam collecting/philately. Home: Columbia Hgts, Minn. Died Oct. 1 2006.

STRAUS, STEPHEN EZRA, federal agency administrato biomedical researcher; b. NYC, Nov. 23, 1946; s. Samuel Lie and Dora Beatrice (Drattel) S.; m. Barbara Ellen Portnoy, Ju 24, 1973; children: Kate, Julie, Benjamin. BS, MIT, 1968; MI Columbia U., 1972. Diplomate in internal medicine and infe tious diseases Am. Bd. Internal Medicine. Intern and resident internal medicine Washington U., St. Louis, 1972-73, 75-76; investigator Nat. Inst. Allergy and Infectious Diseases, B thesda, Md., 1979—2006, chief Lab. Clin. Investigatio 1991—2003; dir. Nat. Ctr. Complementary and Alternati Medicine, NIH, Bethesda, Md., 1999—2006. Contbr. over 4 articles to profl. jours. Med. dir. USPHS, 1973-75, 79-200 Recipient 5 medals USPHS, 1983, 87, 90, 98, 2000. Mem. Ass Am. Physicians, Am. Soc. for Clin. Investigation, Infectio Diseases Soc. Am. Achievements include research and fund mental discovery on treatment and pathogenesis of human vir infections and immunological disorders. Home: Potomac, M Died May 14, 2007.

STRAUSS, KARL MARTIN, management consultant; b. Mi den, Germany, Oct. 5, 1912; came to U.S., 1939, naturalize 1944; s. Albrecht and Mathilde (Lilienfeld) S.; m. Irene Vo weiler, Jan. 31, 1939 (dec. Mar. 1978); m. Marjean Schaef May 25, 1980. Grad., Sch. Brewing Tech., Munich Tech. U 1933; student, UCLA, 1955-56. Various positions breweries a malt houses, Germany, to 1939; with Pabst Brewing Co., Milv 1939-83, asst. to gen. supt. Milw. plant, asst. supt. brewing a malting, asst. supt. indsl. products div., Peoria, Ill., 1st asst. su brewing and malting, plant ops. supt. LA, 1948-56, tech. d plant ops. and planning, v.p. prodn. Milw., 1956-80, v.p., asst. chmn., 1980-83; pvt. practice mgmt. cons., since 1983; ex v.p. tech. services Brewing Systems, Inc., St. Petersburg, Fl 1987-91, also bd. dirs. Mem. Master Brewers Assn. Am. (p pres., past dist. pres., hon. pres.), Am. Soc. Brewing Chemis Inst. Mgmt. Cons. (cert.). Clubs: Milw. Athletic. Home: M waukee, Wis. Died Dec. 21, 2006.

STRAW, BARBARA CURTIS, management analyst; b. Phil Nov. 22, 1950; d. James Robert and Marie Lily (Phillips) Curt B.S. with distinction, Pa. State U., 1973; M.S., Drexel U., 197 m. Ronald Charles Straw, June 29, 1974; 1 son, Jonathan Dav Mgmt. analyst mgmt. analysis br. Navy Ships Parts Contr Center, Mechanicsburg, Pa., 1973-78, orgn. and manpow devel. sect., 1978-80, supr. orgn. and position mgmt. sec 1980-82, head orgn. planning br., 1982—; mem. fed. womer program subcom., 1975-79; career counselor, 1979—. Me Federally Employed Women (program chairperson Alme chpt. 1978-79, pres. 1979-81, treas. 1982-83, mem. nat. awar com. 1982-83, chmn. scholarship and tng. com. 1983-84, chm nominating com. 1984-85), Exec. Assn. Central Pa. Nat. Ichthyosis Found., Nat. Assn. Female Execs., Psi Chi. Roman Catholic. Home: Gaithersburg, Md. Died Aug. 14, 2006.

STRAWN, HARRY CULP, former mayor; b. Swissvale, Pa., Aug. 23, 1918; s. Harry Cornelius and Arminta (Brown) S.; m. Marjorie E. Asquith, Oct. 30, 1943; children: Nancy E. Adams, Mark E., Carolyn A. Lollar. Student, Pa. State U., 1936-38; BA, U. Pitts., 1940. Salesman Art Metal Constrn. Co., 1940-41; owner, operator Wholesale Leather Co., Little Rock, 1946-54; mgr. Crystal Springs Fishing Village, Hot Springs, Ark., 1955-60, Indsl. Waste Disposal Co., Springfield, Mo., 1960-78; mem. City Council, Springfield, 1977-81, 85-89; mayor City of Springfield, 1981-83. Mem. Airport Bd., 1965-67; mem. Environ. Bd., 1967-69; bd. dirs. Meth. Ch., 1965-70; mem. Clean Water Commn., Goals for Springfield. With USAF, 1940-46. Decorated Air medal with 3 clusters, D.F.C., Purple Heart. Mem. Kidney Found., Make A Wish Found., ARC, Rotary, Masons, Shriners. Republican. Home: Springfield, Mo. Died Apr. 7, 2006.

STREAM, JAY WILSON, financial consultant; b. Farlan, Iowa, Apr. 17, 1921; s. Adrian M. and Theo (Bennett) S.; m. Dorothy McCullough, May 20, 1960; children: Carol, James, Cindy, Linda. Student, Milw. State Tchrs. Coll., 1943. Casualty ins. underwriter R.A. Napier & Co., Chgo., 1939-41; with Wallace Supply Mfg. Co., Chgo., 1941-42; quality control specialist Am. Torpedo (Amertorp), Franklin Park, Ill., 1945-47; home office rep. John Hancock Life Ins. Co., Chgo., 1946-48; partner ready-mix concrete co. Chgo., 1949-52; owner, operating officer Jay W. Stream Assocs., Midwest Land Corp., Hydrostructures; founder, builder others; founder Village of Carol Stream, Ill., 1952-64; founder, pres., chmn. bd. Hawthorne Bank of Wheaton, Ill., 1961-68, dir., from 1961; cons. San Luis Obispo, Calif., from 1970; founder, chmn. steering com. World Arabian Horse Assn., 1967-72, 1st pres., from 1972. Head career level., Wayne Newton, 1971-80; exec. producer several films and TV prodns. Mem. U.S. Trade Relations-U.S. Dept. Agr. Policy Adv. Com. for Trade. Served to 2d lt. USAAC, 1942-45. Republican. Home: San Luis Obispo, Calif. Died Jan. 26, 2006.

STREB, ALAN JOSEPH, government official, engineer; b. Balt., Mar. 12, 1932; s. H. Albert and Anna Marie (Minderlein) S.; m. Dorothy Anne Forestal, Apr. 14, 1956; children: John A., David A., Mark A., Marla A., Christopher A. BMechE, Johns Hopkins U., 1954; MS, Drexel U., 1961. Engr. Glenn L. Martin, Balt., 1951-60; tech. dir. Martin Marietta, Balt., 1960-63, mgr. adv. programs, 1963-67; v.p. mktg. Dynatherm Corp., Cockeysville, Md., 1967-76; dep. asst. sec. Dept. Energy, Washington, from 1977. Contbr. numerous articles on energy-related subjects to profl. publs.; patentee in field Pres., treas. Homeowner's Assn., Glen Arm, Md., 1967-72; bd. dirs., mem. architecture com. Homeowner's Assn., Bethany Beach, Del., 1979— Named Inventor of Yr., Martin Marietta Corp., 1964 Home: Glen Arm, Md. Died Nov. 1, 2005.

STREIBEL, BRYCE, state senator; b. Fessenden, ND, Nov. 9, 1922; s. Reinhold M. and Frieda I. (Broschat) S.; m. June P. Buckley, Mar. 23, 1947; 1 child, Kent. Attended U. N.D., Grand Forks; BS, San Francisco State Coll., 1947. Engr. U.S. Govt., Napa, Calif., 1943-46; dir. Martin Funeral Home, Stockton, Calif., 1946-55; owner Streibel Twin Oaks Farm, Fessenden, N.D., from 1955; state sen. State of N.D., Bismarck, from 1981, pres. pro tempore, 1995, state rep., 1957-75, majority leader, 1966-74. Author: Pathways Through LIfe, 1983. Chmn. N.D. Legis. Coun., Bismarck, 1969-75; councilman Town of Fessenden, 1976-84; former pres. 20-30 Internat. Group, Sacramento, trustee, 1952-54; dir. World Coun., Sacramento, 1951-53; bd. dirs. U. N.D. Fellows, Grand Forks, 1982-86; pres. Fessenden Airport Authority, 1980—; mem. N.D. Bd. Higher Edn., 1977-81; chmn. N.D. adv. commn. U.S. Commn. on Civil Rights, 1988-93. Recipient Sioux award U. N.D. Alumni Assn., 1976, Benefactor award U. N.D. Found., 1982, William Budge award, 1983, Outstanding Svc. award Jaycees, 1988, Nat. Barn Again Farm Heritage award, 1996; named Outstanding Alumnus Theta Chi, 1987. Mem. N.D. Centennial Farm, Commodore N.D. Mythical Navy, Masons (Master), Elks, Kiwanis, Shriners, Farm Bur. Republican. Baptist. Avocations: golf, stamp collecting/philately. Died Aug. 13, 2006.

STRICKLAND, LEE STEPHEN, educator, consultant; b. Birmingham, Ala., Jan. 4, 1950; s. Warren Candler and Mary Stone Strickland; m. Karen L. Lucas, June 20, 1994. BS, U. Ctrl. Fla., 1970; M in Computer Sci., U. Va., 1971; JD, U. Fla., 1974. Bar: D.C. 1975, Va. 1981. Atty. CIA, Washington, 1975—2003, cons., from 2004. Vis. prof. U. Md., College Park, from 2000. Recipient Intelligence Commendation medal, Dir. Ctrl. Intelligence, 1999. Mem.: ACLU, IEEE, ALA, Soc. Competitive Intelligence Profls., Am. Soc. for Info. Sci. and Tech. Achievements include research in information policy balancing civil liberties and government powers; restructuring national intelligence functions; design of quality methodologies in IT development efforts. Home: Clifton, Va. Died Jan. 23, 2007.

STRIFFLER, FRANK SHERIDAN, funeral and related services company executive; b. McKeesport, Pa., Nov. 19, 1928; s. Edgar Jacob and Hilda (Sheridan) S.; children— Frank C., Edgar P., Sue Ann. A.A., Belmont Abbey Coll., 1948; grad. Pitts. Inst. Mortuary Sci., 1950, Nat. Found. Funeral Service Sch. Mgmt., 1966. Lic. embalmer, funeral dir. Pa.; lic. funeral dir. N.Y. Pres., Striffler Funeral Homes, McKeesport, 1965—, Fieldstone Inc., McKeesport, 1970—, All Aboard Travel Agys., McKeesport, 1977—, Design Monuments Co., 1977—; v.p. Halcyon Hills Meml. Park & Mausoleum, Wheeling, W.Va., 1984—; founder Builder Energies Co., Frast Realty Co.; cons. antique car values. Mem. Downtown McKeesport Bus. Authority, 1983—; mem. adv. bd. White Oak Athletic Assn. Mem. Nat. Selected Morticians, Initial Order of Golden Rule, Am. Cemetery Assn., Allegheny County Funeral Dirs. Assn., Nat. Funeral Dirs. Assns., Greater McKeesport Jaycees (life), Amvets (hon.). Roman Catholic. Lodges: Lions, Elks. Home: Mc Keesport, Pa. Died Mar. 26, 2006.

STRINGER, MARY EVELYN, art historian, educator; b. Huntsville, Mo., July 31, 1921; d. William Madison and Charity (Rogers) S. AB, U. Mo., 1942; AM, U. N.C., Chapel Hill, 1955; PhD (Danforth scholar), Harvard U., 1973. From asst. prof. art to prof. Miss. State Coll. for Women (now Miss. U. for Women), Columbus, 1947-91, prof. emeritus, from 1991. Regional dir. for Miss., Census of Stained Glass Windows in Am., 1840-1940. Bd. dirs. Mississippians for Ednl. Broadcasting; mem. Miss. com. Save Outdoor Sculpture, 1992-93. Recipient Medal of Excellence award Miss. U. Women, 2003; named Honored Artist Miss. Chpt. Nat. Mus. Women in Arts, 2003; scholar Fulbright Found., 1955-56; grantee Harvard U., 1966-67, NEH, 1980. Mem. AAUW (Medal of Excellence award Miss. chpt., 2003), Coll. Art Assn., Southeastern Coll. Art Conf. (dir. 1975-80, 83-89, Disting. Svc. award 1992, Miss. Hist. Soc. (Merit award 1995), Internat. Ctr. Medieval Art, Am. Birding Assn., Aududon Soc., The Nature Conservancy, Sierra Club, Phi Beta Kappa, Phi Kappa Phi. Democrat. Episcopalian. Home: Columbia, Mo. Died Nov. 9, 2005.

STRODE, WILLIAM HALL, III, photojournalist; b. Louisville, Aug. 6, 1937; s. William Hall and Margaret (Diehl) S.; m. Elizabeth Ann Wheeler, Nov. 26, 1960 (div. 1973); children: Alissa Michelle, Erin Hall; m. Hope Powel Alexander, Nov. 12, 1977 (div. 1997); children: Hope Ives, Charlotte Alexander. BS, Western Ky. U., 1959. News photographer Courier Jour. and Louisville Times, 1960-64, asst. dir. photography, 1968-75; photographer Courier Jour. mag., 1964-77; founder William Strode Assocs., photog. and pub. co., Louisville, 1978—2006; formed Harmony House pubs., 1984—2006. Author 24 books; exhbns. include Fine Arts III, 1961, Profile in Poverty, Smithsonian Instn., 1966, Documerica, in Corcoran Gallery, Washington, 1972, 73, Picture of the Year Travelling Exhibits; one man show includes Speed Mus. Active local Boy Scouts Am., Eagle Scout; founder Nat. Press Photographers Found., 1975. Served with AUS, 1959. Recipient Headliners best photojournalism award, 1965; award for excellence for best mag. photog. reporting Overseas Press Club, 1967; co-recipient Pulitzer Prize for pub. service Courier Jour., 1967, for feature photography, 1976; Art Dirs. Gold medal, 1980, World Press Photog. Arts and Scis. award, 1985 Mem. Nat. Press Photographers Assn. (nat. ednl. chmn. 1966-68, v.p. 1973, pres. 1974, Photographer of Yr. 1966, Newspaper Mag. Picture Editor of Yr. 1968), Am. Soc. Mag. Photographers, Soc. Profl. Journalists, Masons (32 deg.), Scottish Rite, Knights Templar, Soc. Colonial Wars, Sigma Chi (Significant Sig award, 2005), Kappa Alpha Mu. Methodist. Died May 15, 2006.

STROHBEHN, JOHN WALTER, retired engineering science educator; b. San Diego, Nov. 21, 1936; s. Walter William and Gertrude (Powell) S.; children from previous marriage: Jo, Kris, Carolyn; m. Barbara Ann Brungard, Aug. 30, 1980 BS, Stanford U., 1958, MS, 1959, PhD in Elec. Engring., 1964. Assoc. prof. engring. sci. Dartmouth Coll., Hanover, N.H., 1968-73, prof., 1973-94, assoc. dean, 1976-81, adj. prof. medicine, 1979-90, Sherman Fairchild prof., 1983-91, acting provost, 1987-89, provost, 1989-93; provost, prof. biomed. engring. Duke U., Durham, N.C., 1994-99. Disting. lectr. IEEE Antennas and Propagation Soc., 1979-82; vis. fellow Princeton (N.J.) U., 1993-94. Editor: Laser Propagation in the Clear Atmosphere, 1978; assoc. editor Trans. Ant and Propagation, 1969-71, Trans. Biomed. Engring., 1981-87; contbr. articles to profl. jours. Scoutmaster Boy Scouts Am., Norwich, Vt., 1971-73; bd. dirs. Norwich Recreation and Conservation Council. Fellow AAAS, IEEE, Optical Soc. Am., Am. Inst. Med. Biol. Engring. (founding); mem. Radiation Rsch. Soc., Bioelectromagnetics Soc. (bd. dirs. 1982-85), N.Am. Hyperthermia Group (pres. 1986). Avocations: jogging, hiking, skiing. Home: Durham, NC. Died Feb. 22, 2007.

STRONG, HENRY, foundation executive; b. Rochester, NY, Oct. 6, 1923; s. L. Corrin and Alice (Trowbridge) S.; m. Malan Swing, June 30, 1951; children: Sigrid Anne, Barbara Kirk, Dana Elizabeth, Henry Lockwood. AB, Williams Coll., 1949; LHD, Mt. Vernon Coll., 1999. Joined Fgn. Service, 1950; with US Dept. State, 1950-51; vice consul The Hague, 1951-54, Washington, 1954-55; 2d sec. US Embassy, Copenhagen, 1955-58, State Dept., 1958-62, Djakarta, Indonesia, 1962-64; resigned, 1968; chmn. bd., pres. Hattie M. Strong Found., 1968—2007. Mem. D.C. Commn. Arts, 1968-75; mem. DC Bd. Higher Edn., 1973-76; vice chmn. bd. trustees J.F. Kennedy Ctr. for Performing Arts, 1975-90, hon. trustee, 1991—; bd. dir. Nat. Symphony Orch., Pomfret Sch., 1967-1990, M.M. Post Found. DC, Community Found. of Greater Washington, 1974-91, Mt. Vernon Coll., 1969-88, 91-98, Nat. Capital chpt. ARC, 1994—. Lt. (j.g.) USNR, 1943-46. Mem.: Chevy Chase; Metropolitan (Washington); Gibson Island (Md.). Republican. Episcopalian. Home: Washington, DC. Died Mar. 22, 2007.

STROSNIDER, JOHN A., dean; b. Owosso, Mich., Oct. 29, 1947; m. Jo Ann Strosnider; children: John Adam, Alisha, Paul. BS Gen. Sci., Northeast Mo. State U., 1971; DO, Kans. City Coll., 1975; rotating intern, Lakeside Osteo. Hosp., 1976; student, Continuing Med. Edn., from 1976. V.p., ptnr. Family Care, Inc., Kansas City, Mo., 1976—91; dir. med. edn., med. dir. Lakeside Osteo. Hosp., Kansas City, Mo., 1978—90; v.p., med. dir. Med. Rev. Cons., Inc., Independence, Mo., 1985—92; assoc. dean acad. affairs/clin. scis. U. Health Scis. Coll. Osteo. Medicine, Kansas City, Mo., 1991—95; dean Pikesville Coll. Sch. Osteo. Medicine, from 1992. Mem. bd. trustees Lakeside Hosp., Inc., 1987—93; mem. bd. dirs. Med. Rev. Cons., 1985—92, v.p., 1985—92; mem. Ctr. Dist. #58 Bd. Edn., 1992—95. Recipient MAOPS Medallion award, outstanding achievement in osteo. med. edn., 1993, Mo. Ho. Reps. Resolution 304, promotion osteo. medicine Mo., 1991, Mo. Senate Resolution 220, leadership in osteo. med. edn. Mo., 1991, MAOPS Ho. Dels. REsolution, outstanding leadership osteo. medicine, 1992. Mem.: Ky. Osteo. Med. Assn. (ad hoc bd. trustees from 1996), Soc. Tchrs. Family Medicine, Nat. Sch. Bds. Assn., Assn. Osteo. Med. Dirs. and Educators, Am. Coll. Osteo. Family Physicians, Jackson County Osteo. Assn. (pres. 1981—82, bd. trustees 1978—84), Mo. Assn. Osteopathy Physicians and Surgeons (pres. 1919—92, bd. trustees 1988—94, chmn. mem. com. 1992—96), Am. Osteo. Assn. (bd. trustees from 1992, chmn. dept. bus. affairs 1994—96, chmn. bur. student affairs 1994—96, exec. com. bd. 1994—97, chmn. dept. ednl. affairs 1996—97, bur. ins. from 1997, vice chair bur. small states' concerns from 1997, vice chair com. on memberships from 1997, com. strat. planning from 1997, task force healthcare facilities accreditation from 1997, adv. task force osteo. medicine accreditation). Avocations: reading, fishing, travel, political debate, golf. Died June 21, 2007.

STROUD, RICHARD HAMILTON, aquatic biologist, scientist, consultant; b. Dedham, Mass., Apr. 24, 1918; s. Percy Valentine and Elizabeth Lillian (Kimpton) S.; m. Genevieve Cecelia DePol, Dec. 20, 1943; children: William DePol, Jennifer Celia Trivett. BS, Bowdoin Coll., 1939; MS, U. N.H., 1942; postgrad., Yale U., 1947-48, Boston U. Sch. Edn., 1948-49. Asst. aquatic biologist N.H. Fish and Game Dept., Concord, 1940-41; jr. aquatic biologist TVA, Norris, Tenn., 1942, asst. aquatic biologist, 1946-47; chief aquatic biologist Mass. Div. Fisheries and Game, Boston, 1948-53; asst. exec. v.p. Sport Fishing Inst., Washington, 1953-55, exec. v.p., 1955-81, editor monthly bull.; sr. scientist Aquatic Ecosystems Analysts, Fayetteville, Ark., 1983-88. Del. Rio Conf. of Plenipotentiaries on Conservation of Tuna and Tuna-Like Fishes, 1966; founder., mng. v.p., trustee Sport Fishery Rsch. Found., Washington, 1967-88; cns. aquatic resources, 1981-89, cons. editor fish sci. publs., 1982-95; rsch. adv. bd. Sport Fishing Inst. Fund, 1988-94; Pentelow lectr. U. Liverpool, England, 1975; mem. Marine Fisheries adv. com. Dept. of Commerce; fishery expert advisor to Senate select com. on govt. ops.; fishery advisor Calif. Fish and Game Dept. 1965-66, Ark. Game and Fish Commn., 1969, Iowa Cons. Commn., 1970-71, Tenn. Valley Authority, 1972; guest lectr. Japan Sport Fishing Found., 1976. Author Fisheries Report for Massachusetts Lakes, Ponds, and Reservoirs, 1955; editor (ann. series) Marine Recreational Fisheries Symposia, 1982-95, Nat. Leaders of American Conservation, 1985, World Angling Resources and Challenges, 1985, Fish Culture in Fisheries Management, 1986, Multi-Jurisdictional Management of Marine Fisheries, 1986, Management of Atlantic Salmon, 1988, Planning the Future of Billfishes, Part 1, 1989, Part 2, 1990, Stemming The Tide of Coastal Fish Habitat Loss, 1991, Fisheries Management and Watershed Development, 1992, Conserving America's Fisheries, 1994; co-editor The Biological Significance of Estuaries, 1971, Black Bass Biology and Management, 1975, Predator Prey Systems in Fisheries Management, 1979, N. Am. Jour. of Fisheries Mgmt., 1980—; contbr. articles to profl. jours. Bd. dirs. Nat. Coalition Marine Conservation, 1977-96; treas. Natural Resources Coun. Am., 1961-68, chmn., 1969-71, hon. mem., 1981—. Served with U.S. Army, 1942-46. Decorated Croix de Guerre with cluster.; recipient Conservation Achievement award Nat. Wildlife Fedn., 1975, 81, SOAR award Boy Scouts Am., 1972; named to Nat. Fishing Hall of Fame, 1984 Fellow Am. Inst. Fishery Research Biologists (emeritus, Outstanding Achievement award 1981), Am. Fisheries Soc. (pres. 1979-80, hon. life, emeritus, Outstanding Achievement award 1990, initiated N. Am. Jour. Fisheries Mgmt.); mem. Internat. Fish and Wildlife Agys., Freshwater Biol. Assn. (U.K.), Fisheries Soc. Brit. Isles. Achievements include being a leading advocate of fisheries research and a nationally recognized exponent of catch-and-release philosophy of recreational fisheries management. Died Sept. 4, 2006.

STRUDLER, ROBERT JACOB, real estate development executive; b. NYC, Sept. 22, 1942; m. Ruth Honigman, Aug. 29, 1965; children: Seth, Keith, Craig. BS in Indsl. and Labor Relations, Cornell U., 1964; LLB, Columbia U., 1967. Bar: N.Y. 1967, Fla. 1973. Assoc. Wickes, Riddell, Bloomer, Jacobi & McGuire, NYC, 1967—69, London, Buttenwieser & Chalif, NYC, 1969—71; v.p., chmn. operating com. U.S. Home Corp., Clearwater, Fla., 1972-76, v.p. legal affairs, 1976-77, v.p. ops., 1977-79, sr. v.p. ops. Houston, 1979-81, sr. v.p. acquisitions, 1981-84, pres., COO, 1984-86, CEO, 1986-2000; vice-chmn. Lennar Corp., Miami, Fla., 2000—04, COO, 2000—04, chmn., 2004—06. Pres., trustee Sch. for Young Children; mem. pres.' adv. coun. U. St. Thomas. Co-recipient Builder of Yr. award Profl. Builder Mag., 1994, Bronze award Wall Street, 1995, Hearthstone Builder Lifetime Pub. Svc. award, 2003, Legend of Residential Mktg. award Nat. Sales and Mktg. Coun., 2004; elected to Nat. Housing Hall of Fame, 2000. Mem. ABA, N.Y. State Bar Assn., Fla. Bar Assn., Cornell Real Estate Coun., Nat. Assn. Homebuilders (chmn. high prodn. coun. 1991-93). Home: Houston, Tex. Died Nov. 7, 2006.

STRUPP, HANS HERMANN, psychologist, educator; b. Frankfurt am Main, Germany, Aug. 25, 1921; came to U.S., 1939, naturalized, 1945; s. Josef and Anna (Metzger) S.; m. Lottie Metzger, Aug. 19, 1951; children: Karen, Barbara, John. AB with distinction, George Washington U., 1945, AM, 1947, PhD, 1954; MD (hon.), U. Ulm, Fed. Republic of Germany, 1986. Diplomate in clin. psychology Am. Bd. Profl. Psychology; lic. clin. psychologist, Tenn. Research psychologist Human Factors Ops. Research Labs., Dept. Air Force, Washington, 1949-54; supervisory research psychologist, personnel research br. Adj. Gen.'s Office, Dept. of Army, Washington, 1954-55; dir. psychotherapy research project Sch. Medicine, George Washington U., Washington, 1955-57; dir. psychol. services, dept. psychiatry U. N.C. Sch. Medicine, Chapel Hill, 1957-64, asso. prof. psychology, 1957-62, prof., 1962-66; prof. dept. psychology Vanderbilt U., Nashville, 1966-76, dir. clin. tng., dept. psychology, 1967-76, disting. prof., 1976-94, Harvie Branscomb disting. prof., 1985-86, disting. prof. emeritus, 1994—2006. Mem. editorial adv. bd. Psychotherapy: Theory, Research and Practice, 1963-97, Jour. Cons. and Clin. Psychology, 1964—2006, Jour. Nervous and Mental Disease, 1965—2006, Jour. Am. Acad. Psychoanalysis, 1972—2006, Jour. Contemporary Psychotherapy, 1972-86, Psychiatry Research, 1979-86, Jour. Profl. Psychology, 1976-89; founding editor Psychotherapy Rsch., 1990-95; others; contbr. chpts. to books, articles and revs. to profl. jours. Recipient Helen Sargent meml. prize Menninger Found., 1963; Alumni Achievement award George Washington U., 1972; Disting. Profl. Achievement award Am. Bd. Profl. Psychology, 1976, Disting. Profl. Contbns. to Knowledge award Am. Psychol. Assn., 1987; others Fellow Am. Psychol. Assn. (mem. exec. council 1964, exec. bd. 1969-72, council of reps. 1970-73, chmn. com. on fellows div. psychotherapy 1970-74, pres. div. clin. psychology 1974-75, recipient Disting. Profl. Psychologist award 1973, Disting. Scientist award 1979), Tenn.

Psychol. Assn., AAAS; mem. Eastern Psychol. Assn., Southeastern Psychol. Assn., Am. Psychopathol. Assn., Am. Psychoanalytic Assn. (hon.), Soc. for Psychotherapy Research (pres. 1972-73, Career Contbr. award 1986), Psychologists Interested in Advancement of Psychoanalysis, Phi Beta Kappa, Sigma Xi. Died Oct. 5, 2006.

STUART, HAROLD CUTLIFF, lawyer, business executive; b. Okla. City, July 4, 1912; s. Royal Cutliff and Alice (Bramlitt) S.; m. Joan Skelly, June 6, 1938 (dec. 1994); children: Randi Stuart Wightman, Jon Rolf; m. Frances Langford, Nov. 18, 1994. JD, U. Va., 1936. Bar: Okla. 1936, DC 1952. Ptnr. Stuart, Biolchini, Turner & Givray, Tulsa; judge Common Pleas Ct., 1941-42; asst. sec. USAF, 1949-51; chmn. bd. 1st Stuart Corp., radio, oil, real estate and investments, Tulsa; dir. Lowrance Electronics, Inc., Tulsa. Spl. cons. to sec. Air Force, 1961-63; mem. Okla. Hwy. Commn., 1959-63; bd. dirs. Great Empire Broadcasting Inc., Wichita, Kans. Trustee emeritus Lovelace Found., Albuquerque; trustee N.Am. Wildlife Fedn; mem. Nat. Eagle Scout Coun. Boy Scouts Am., Disting. Eagle Scout; past pres. Air Force Acad. Found., chmn. bd. Served from 1st lt. to col. USAAF, 1942-46, ETO. Decorated Bronze Star and 6 battle stars; comdr. Order of St. Olav; King Haakon 7th Victory medal; medal of Liberation (Norway); Croix de Guerre (Luxembourg); named to Okla. Aviation and Space Hall of Fame, Okla. Hall of Fame. Mem. ABA, Okla. Bar Assn., DC Bar Assn., Air Force Assn. (dir., nat. pres., chmn. bd. 1951-52), Tulsa C. of C., Tulsa Headliner, Falcon Found. (vice chmn.), Ducks Unltd. (trustee), Southern Hills Country Club, The Boston Club (Tulsa), Burning Tree Club (Washington), Willoughby Golf Club, The Amb. Club (Stuart, Fla.), Delta Kappa Epsilon. Democrat. Died June 25, 2007.

STUART, JOHN MCHUGH, JR., public relations consultant, retired foreign service officer; b. Albany, NY, Apr. 21, 1916; s. John McHugh and Marie (Fitzgerald) S.; m. Ruth Sherman, June 24, 1944 (dec. May 1977). Student, U. Santa Clara, 1934-35; BA, Georgetown U., 1939; MA, George Washington U., 1966; grad., Air War Coll., 1966. Reporter, editor, 1938-44; fgn. service officer Office Mil. Govt. U.S., Germany, 1945-50, USIA, 1954-71; press attache Am. embassy, New Delhi, 1962-65; pub. affairs officer U.S. Mission in Geneva, 1956-61; fgn. corr. Voice of Am., Korea and Germany, 1950-56; press counselor Am. embassy, Saigon, 1966-67; sr. adviser pub. affairs U.S. Mission to UN, NYC, 1967-71; spl. adviser U.S. del. 26th UN Gen. Assembly, 1971; spokesman U.S. del. conf. on human environment, Stockholm, 1972; adviser 31st Gen. Assembly, 1976, 3d UN Law of Sea Conf., N.Y., 1977, VIth and Xth Spl. Gen. Assemblies on Disarmament, 1978, 82; now cons. internat. pub. affairs NYC, also Washington. Adviser European Security Conf., USIA, 1973, Agri-Energy Roundtable, Geneva, 1981. Served with SHAEF, World War II. Mem. Nat. Press Club. Died Mar. 28, 2007.

STURM, FRED GILLETTE, philosopher, educator; b. Batavia, NY, Oct. 15, 1925; s. Fred William and Eleanor Louise (Gillette) S.; m. Margaret Schaeffer (dec. Nov. 1953); children: Margaret Louise Sturm Almony, Fred Schaeffer; m. Hilda Lowd (dec. July 1963); m. Julienne Mullette (div. July 1970); m. Katharine Ehrgood, Oct. 16, 1971. AB, Allegheny Coll., 1946; MDiv, Union Theol. Sem., NYC, 1948; AM, U. Rochester, 1950; PhD, Columbia U., 1961; postgrad., Vanderbilt U., 1949, Tunghai U., Taichung, Rep. of China, 1963, Chinese U., Hong Kong, 1972. Prof. Greek and N.T. Faculdade de Teologia da Igreja Metodista do Brasil, São Paulo, 1950, 51; prof. religion Inst. Pōrto Alegre, Brasil, 1952; prof. philosophy Western Coll., Oxford, Ohio, 1954-74, coord. intercultural emphasis, 1966-70; prof. philosphy U. N.Mex., Albuquerque, from 1975, acting chair dept., 1978-79, chair dept., 1982-90, interim dean Coll. Arts and Scis., 1986-87. Vis. prof. religion Miami U., Oxford, Ohio, 1957-58; vis. prof. philosophy Sem. Teológico da Igreja Episcopal do Brasil, São Paulo, 1965; vis. prof. fgn. langs. and lits. Shaanxi Tchrs. U., Xi'an, People's Republic China, 1982, hon. prof., 1982—; adj. assoc. prof. philosophy, SUNY, Buffalo, 1974-75; dir. Inst. for Pueblo Indian Studies, Indian Pueblo Cultural Ctr., Albuquerque, 1976-88, assoc. dir. for R&D, 1988—. Author: Introduction to Logic, 1961, Existence in Search of Essence: The Philosophy of Spirit of Raimundo de Farias Brito, 1961, Chinese Culture, Non-Western Studies, and the Liberal Arts College, 1962, O Significado Atual do Pensamento Britiano, 1962; translator: Panorama of the History of Philosophy in Brazil, 1962; editor: Fuentes de la Filosofía Latinoamericana, 1967, Brazilian Studies: A Guide to the Humanities Literature, 1986, Pueblo Style and Regional Architecture, 1990; editor in chief Jour. Chinese Studies, 1983—; contbr. book chpts., articles to profl. jours. Fulbright rsch. grantee, Republic of China, 1963, Brasil, 65, 88, Social Sci. Rsch. Coun. grantee, Mexico, 1966, Calouste Gulbenkian Found. rsch., Portugal, 1981. Fellow Soc. Philosophers in Am. (bd. dirs. 1990—), Royal Asiatic Soc. (fgn.), Internat. Ctr. for Asian Studies, Centro de Estudos do Pensamento Luso-Brasileiro; mem. Am. Assn. for Chinese Studies (bd. dirs. 1964-87), Am. Philos. Assn., Am. Soc. for Aesthetics,Inst. Brasileiro de Filosofia (hon.), Academia Brasileira de Filosofia (effective mem. in perpetuity), Internat. Husserl and Phenomemological Soc., Internat. Soc. for Chinese Philosophy (co-dir. rsch. group on Chinese and comparative aesthetics), Latin Am. Indian Lits. Assn., Rsch. Inst. for Global Philosophy (adv. bd. 1967—), Soc. for Iberian and Latin Am. Thought (exec. com. 1976-78, v.p., 1978-80, pres. 1980-82, pres.-elect 1992-94, pres. 1994—), Soc. for Advancement Am. Philosophy, The China Acad. (internat. Sinological rsch. com. 1969—), N.Am. Soc. for Social and Polit. Philosophy (editorial bd. 1987—), Phi Beta Kappa. Socialist. Methodist, United Ch. of Christ. Home: Albuquerque, N.Mex. Died Jan. 21, 2006.

STURM, NICHOLAS, biology professor, writer; b. Meriden, W.Va., Dec. 19, 1931; s. Henry Earl and Beulah Agnes (Coffman) S. BS, W.Va. Wesleyan Coll., 1952; MS, Purdue U., 1955; postgrad., U. Tex., 1956-59. Head sci. dept. S.W. Tex. Jr. Coll., Uvalde, 1959-61; instr. Amarillo Coll., Tex., 1961-64; asst. prof. Youngstown U., Ohio, 1964-67; prof. biol. scis. Youngstown State U., 1967-95, prof. emeritus, from 1995. Cons. on edn. texts various pubs., 1969-90; field editor various pubs., 1972-86; cons. on computer applications S&S Software, Youngstown, 1986-95, Philippi, 1995—. Author: Exploring Life, 1972, 3d edit., 1986, (computer software) Natural Selection, 1992. Mem. Am. Fern. Soc. (life), Brit. Lichen Soc., Antiqus Mysticusque Orda Rosae Cruris. Avocations: photography, local history, computer programming, multimedia design, nature study. Home: Belington, W.Va. Died Nov. 26, 2006.

STURTEVANT, WILLIAM CURTIS, retired anthropologist; b. Morristown, NJ, July 26, 1926; s. Alfred Henry and Phoebe (Reed) S.; m. Theda Maw (div. 1986); children: Kinthi D.M., Reed P.M., Alfred B.M. (dec.); m. Sally McLendon, 1990. BA, U. Calif.-Berkeley, 1949; PhD, Yale U., 1955. Instr. dept. anthropology, asst. curator anthropology Peabody Mus., Yale U., 1954-56; ethnologist, gen. anthropologist Bur. Am. Ethnology Smithsonian Instn., Washington, 1956-65, curator N.Am. ethnology dept. anthropology Nat. Mus. Natural History Smithsonian Instn., from 1965. Fulbright lectr. U. Oxford, 1967-68; Regents lectr. U. Calif., Berkeley, 1981; vis. fellow Worcester Coll., U. Oxford, 1986-87; adj. prof. anthropology Johns Hopkins U., 1974-89; ethnol. fieldwork Seminole, Fla., 1950-67, 85 (18 months), Burma, 1955, 63-64 (12 months), Iroquois, 1952-65 (8 months), others. Author monographs, chpts. in books.; Gen. editor: Handbook of N.Am. Indians; Contbr. articles to profl. jours. Trustee Mus. Am. Indian, Heye Found., N.Y.C., 1976-82, 84-86; bd. dirs. Survival Internat. USA, 1982-88; mem. internat. exec. Survival Internat., 1986-88. Served with USNR, 1945-46. Fellow Royal Anthrop. Inst. Gt. Britain and Ireland, Am. Anthrop. Assn. (book rev. editor 1962-66, exec. bd. 1974-77, pres. 1981), AAAS (del. coun. 1974-77, mem. coun. affairs 1974-75), Soc. des Américanistes, Am. Soc. Ethnohistory (pres. 1965-66), Coun. Mus. Anthropology (pres. 1979-81), Am. Ethnol. Soc. (pres. 1976-77), Soc. Am. Archaeology, Soc. Study Indigenous Langs. Ams., Royal Geog. Soc.; mem. Hakluyt Soc., Champlain Soc., Anthrop. Soc. Washington (pres. 1992-93). Home: Washington, DC. Died Mar. 2, 2007.

STYLES, MARGRETTA MADDEN, nursing educator; b. Mount Union, Pa., Mar. 19, 1930; d. Russell B. and Agnes (Wilson) Madden; m. Douglas F. Styles, Sept. 4, 1954; children: Patrick, Michael, Megan. BS, Juniata Coll., 1950; M. in Nursing, Yale U., 1954; EdD, U. Fla., 1968; doctorate (hon.), Valparaiso U., 1986, U. Athens, Greece, 1991. Staff nurse VA Hosp., West Haven, Conn., 1954-55; instr. Bklyn. Hosp. Sch. Nursing, 1955-58; supr. North Dist. Hosp., Pompano Beach, Fla., 1961-63; dir. nursing edn. Broward Community Coll., Ft. Lauderdale, Fla., 1963-67; assoc. prof. Sch. Nursing Duke U., Durham, N.C., 1967-69, dir. undergrad. studies, 1967-69; prof., dean Sch. Nursing U. Tex., San Antonio, 1969-73; dean, prof. Coll. Nursing Wayne State U., Detroit; prof. nursing U. Calif., San Francisco, from 1977, dean Sch. Nursing, 1977-87; chairperson Com. for Study of Credentializing in Nursing, 1976-79; mem. adv. group div. nursing HEW, 1977. Asst. dir. nursing svcs. U. Calif. Hosps. and Clinics, 1978-87; mem. Nat. Commn. Nursing, 1980—; mem. Calif. Bd. Registered Nursing, 1985—; mem. Sec.'s Commn. on Nursing HHS, 1988—. Author: On Nursing: Toward a New Endowment (Am. Jour. Nursing Book of Yr. award 1982); co-author (with A. Affara) From Principle to Power: A Guidebook to Regulation in Nursing, 1992. Recipient Disting. Alumna award Yale U. Sch. Nursing, 1979; Am. Nurses' Found. 1st disting. scholar, 1983 Fellow Am. Acad. Nursing; mem. Nat. Acad. Scis., Am. Nurses Assn. (pres. 1986-88), Internat. Coun. Nurses (bd. dirs. 1989—), Sigma Theta Tau. Home: Vallejo, Calif. Died Nov. 20, 2005.

STYRON, WILLIAM, writer; b. Newport News, Va., June 11, 1925; s. William Clark and Pauline Margaret (Abraham) S.; m. Rose Burgunder, May 4, 1953; children: Susanna Margaret, Paola Clark, Thomas, Claire Alexandra. Student, Christchurch Sch., Davidson Coll.; Litt.D., Davidson Coll., 1986; AB, Duke U., 1947, Litt.D., 1968. Fellow Am. Acad. Arts and Letters at Am. Acad. in Rome, 1953; fellow Silliman Coll., Yale, 1964-99. Jury pres. Cannes Film Festival, 1983. Author: (novels) Lie Down in Darkness, 1951, The Long March, 1953, Set This House on Fire, 1960, The Confessions of Nat Turner, 1967 (Pulitzer prize 1968, Howells medal Am. Acad. Arts and Letters 1970), Sophie's Choice, 1979 (Am. Book award 1980), In the Clap Shack (play), 1972, This Quiet Dust and Other Writings, 1982, Darkness Visible: A Memoir of Madness, 1990, A Tidewater Morning: 3 Tales from Youth, 1993; also articles, essays, revs.; editor: Best Stories from the Paris Rev., 1959; adv. editor: Paris Rev., 1953—2006; mem. editorial bd. The Am. Scholar, 1970-76. Decorated Commandeur de l'Ordre des Arts et des Lettres, Commandeur Legion d'Honneur (France); recipient Duke U. Disting. Alumni award, 1984, Conn. Arts award, 1984, Prix Mondial del Duca, 1985, Elmer Holmes Bobst award for fiction, 1989, Edward MacDowell medal for excellence in the arts, 1988, Nat. Mag. award, 1990, Nat. medal of Arts, 1993, Medal of Honor, Nat. Arts Club, 1995, Common Wealth award, 1995, F. Scott Fitzgerald award, 1996. Mem. Am. Acad. Arts and Scis., Am. Acad. Arts and Letters, Soc. Am. Historians, Signet Soc., Harvard, Académie Goncourt, Phi Beta Kappa. Democrat. Home: Roxbury, Conn. Died Nov. 1, 2006.

SUBAK, JOHN THOMAS, lawyer; b. Trebic, Czechoslovakia, Apr. 19, 1929; came to U.S., 1941, naturalized, 1946; s. William John and Gerda Maria (Subakova) S.; m. Mary Corcoran, June 4, 1955; children: Jane Kennedy, Kate, Thomas, Michael. BA summa cum laude, Yale U., 1950, LLB, 1956. Bar: Pa. 1956. From assoc. to ptnr. Dechert, Price & Rhoads, Phila., 1956-76, v.p., gen. counsel, dir., 1976-77; group v.p., gen. counsel, dir. Rohm and Haas Co., Phila., 1977-93; counsel Dechert Price & Rhoads, Phila., 1994—2001. Editor: The Bus. Lawyer, 1982-83. Bd. dirs. Am. Cancer Soc., 1982-95; trustee Smith Coll., 1991-2001; pres. Gasparilla Island Conservation and Improvement Assn., 2001-03. Lt. (j.g.) USN, 1950-53. Mem. ABA (chmn. corp. and bus. law sect. 1984-85), Am. Law Inst. (coun. mem.), Defender Assn. of Phila. (v.p., bd. dirs. 1982-95), Merion Cricket Club, Lemon Bay Club. Democrat. Roman Catholic. Died Jan. 28, 2007.

SUGERMAN, ABRAHAM ARTHUR, psychiatrist, educator; b. Dublin, Jan. 20, 1929; came to U.S., 1958, naturalized, 1963; s. Hyman and Anne (Goldstone) S.; m. Ruth Nerissa Alexander, June 5, 1960; children: Jeremy, Michael, Adam, Rebecca. BA Trinity Coll., 1950, MB, BChir, BA in Obstetrics, 1952; DSc SUNY Bklyn., 1962. Diplomate Am. Bd. Psychiatry and Neurology. House officer Meath Hosp., Dublin, 1952—53, St Nicholas Hosp., London, 1953—54; sr. house physician Brool Gen. Hosp., London, 1954; registrar in psychiatry Kingswa Hosp. Derby and Kings Coll. Med. Sch., Newcastle, Englanc 1955—58; clin. psychiatrist Trenton Psychiat. Hosp., NJ 1958—59; rsch. fellow Downstate Med. Ctr., Bklyn., 1959—61 chief investigative psychiatry sect. N.J. Bur. Rsch., Princetor 1961—73; cons. psychiatry, 1964—80; cons. rsch., assoc. psychiatrist Carrier Clinic, Belle Mead, NJ, 1968—72, 1978—9(dir. outpatient svcs., 1972—74, 1977—78, med. dir., 1974—77 dir. rsch. Carrier Found., Belle Mead, 1972—79; med. di addiction recovery svcs. Cmty. Mental Health Ctr. U. Medicin and Dentistry of N.J., Piscataway, 1990—93; cons. psychiatr Med. Ctr., Princeton, 1972—2001, assoc. in psychiatry 2001—03, attending, from 2003, sr. attending, from 2005; clir assoc. prof. psychiatry Rutgers Med. Sch. (now Robert Woo Johnson Med. Sch.), New Brunswick, NJ, 1972—78, clin. prof from 1978. Vis. prof. Rutgers Ctr. for Alcohol Studies, 1977-8: Hahnemann Med. Coll., Phila., 1978-93; contbg. faculty Grac Sch. Applied and Profl. Psychology, Rutgers U., 1974-78 Editor: (with Ralph E. Tarter) Alcoholism: Interdisciplinar Approaches to an Enduring Problem, 1976, Expanding Dimer sions of Consciousness, 1978; contbr. articles to profl. jours. Bc dirs. N.J. Mental Health R & D Fund, Princeton, 1968-74; v.p Jewish Family Svc., Trenton, 1972-78; 1st v.p. Trenton Hebrew Acad., 1972-75. Fellow Am. Psychiat. Assn. (disting. life), Am Coll. Neuropsychopharmacology, Am. Coll. Clin. Pharmaco ogy, Am. Coll. Psychiatrists, Royal Coll. Psychiatrists; mem AMA, Soc. Biol. Psychiatry, Assn. Rsch. Nervous and Menta Diseases. Died Jan. 24, 2007.

SUGG, JOHN LOGAN (JACK SUGG), advertising execu tive; b. Hillsboro, Ill., June 2, 1914; s. Norman J. and Clyther (McDavid) S.; m. Jean Ellen Morrison, Feb. 7, 1942; childrer Michael L., Patrick M., Terry Jean. BA, Lake Forest Coll., 1938 Engaged in newspaper work, 1938-41; with Cole & Weber, Inc from 1946, pres., 1968-72, chmn. bd., 1972-76, chmn. exec com., 1976-80; ret., 1981. Pres. Assoc. Oreg. Industrie 1968-69 Bd. dirs. Emanuel Med. Center Found.; chmn. bd. dir Portland Better Bus. Bur., 1975—. Served to lt. comdr. USN 1941-45. Named Oreg. Advt. Man of Year, 1965 Mem. Portlan C. of C. (dir.), Am. Assn. Advt. Agys. (chmn. Western regio 1970-71) Clubs: Arlington (pres. 1975—), Multnomah Athleti Portland Golf. Home: Portland, Oreg. Died July 29, 2006.

SUGIYAMA, TOKU MARY, retired school administrator; Sacramento, Sept. 6, 1921; d. Sakae and Kuniko (Kosaka) Kod m. George Y. Morishita, Mar. 23, 1942 (dec. Mar. 1949 children: Maeona, Carolyn, George m. Yone J. Sugiyama, Ap 5, 1952 (dec. March, 2006) Jr. cert., U. Calif., Berkeley, 194 BA, Towson State U., 1980, MA, 1984. Tchr. Poston Relocatio Ctr., Ariz., 1941-44; purchasing agt. U.S. Dept. Def., Toky Ordnance Depot, 1952-56; instr. Ikebana Sogetsu Sch., Toky 1956-67; exec. dir. Sogetsu USA, sch. Japanese flower arrange ment, 1967-93; ret., 1993. Author: Sogetsu Ikebana Notes, 199 Recipient Mohan Sho, Sogetsu Sch., 1960, Sofu Sho, 196 Flower Arranger of Yr. award Nat. Coun. State Garden Club 1979, 1st Sofu Teshigahara Meml. award, 1991, Japan's Mini try of Fgn. Affairs award to commemmorate 157th anniversa of U.S. and Japan's relationship, 2004. Mem. Md. Fedn. Garde Clubs, Ikebana Internat. (charter), Balt.-Kawasaki Sister Ci Cultural Com. Home: Baltimore, Md. Died May 14, 2006.

SULLIVAN, JAMES STEPHEN, retired bishop; b. Kalam zoo, July 23, 1929; s. Stephen James and Dorothy Mar (Bernier) S. Student, St. Joseph Sem.; BA, Sacred Heart Sem postgrad., St. John Provincial Sem. Ordained priest, Roma Cath. Ch., 1955, consecrated bishop, 1972. Assoc. pastor S Luke Ch., Flint, Mich., 1955-58, St. Mary Cathedral, Lansin Mich., 1958-60, sec. to bishop, 1960-61; assoc. pastor St. Josep (Mich.) Ch., 1961-65, sec. to bishop, 1965-69; assoc. past Lansing, 1965; vice chancellor, 1969-72; aux. bishop, vicar ge Diocese of Lansing, 1972-85, diocesan consultor, 1971-8 bishop Fargo, ND, 1985—2002; ret., 2002. Pres. World Apo tolate Fatima; episc. liaison Cath. Mktg. Network; nat. episcop liaison to the Cath. Cursillo Movement. Mem. U.S. Conf. Cat Bishops. Roman Catholic. Died June 12, 2006.

SULLIVAN, BROTHER JEREMIAH STEPHEN, form college president; b. Boston, June 25, 1920; s. John Joseph ar Bridget Claire (Quirke) S. BA, Cath. U. Am., 1943, STL, 195 STD, 1959; MA in Classics, Manhattan Coll., 1950; MA Philosophy, Boston Coll., 1955; LLD (hon.), La Salle U., 197 LHD (hon.), Coll. Mt. St. Vincent, 1987. Tchr. St. Peters Hig Sch., SI, N.Y., 1943-48, St. Marys High Sch., Waltham, Mas 1948-53; instr. theology and classics De La Salle Coll., Was ington, 1953-59; asst. prof. theology Manhattan Coll., NY 1959-63, assoc. prof., 1963, acad. v.p., 1963-70, exec. v.p provost, 1970-75, pres., 1975-87; La Salle provincialate, d devel. programs Christian Bros. Acad., Lincroft, N.J., fro 1988. Contbr. articles to profl. jours. Chmn. N.Y.C. com. on In Colls. and Univs., 1978-79; chmn. com. on Sci. and Tech., 198 trustee African Med. Rsch., LaSalle U.; bd. dirs., chmn., FS Found. Mem. Coll. Theology Soc. (dir., nat. treas. 1960-71 Cath. Theol. Soc. Am., Cath. Bibl. Assn., Nat. Cath. Ednl. Ass Nat. Cath. Devel. Coun., AAUP, Phi Beta Kappa, Delta M Delta. Died Jan. 9, 2007.

SULLIVAN, JOANN MARIE, medical technologist; b. Butt Mont., May 31, 1938; d. Joseph D. and Ann E. (Melvin) Bracc m. Thomas Roy Sullivan, Jan. 25, 1964; children: Michelle An Renee Marie. BS, Carroll Coll., 1960; grad., internship f medical tech. Sacred Heart Hosp., Spokane, Wash., 1960. L med. technologist, Calif. Med. technologist, hematology Wash. Hosp., Seattle, 1960-63, Stanford U. Hosp., Palo Al Calif., 1963-64; med. technologist, hematology supr. Gua Meml. Hosp., Tamuning, 1964-65; med. technologist Sevent Day Adventist Clinic, Agana Heights, Guam, 1965-67; c owner, med. technologist, dir. Physicians Diagnostic Lal Tamuning, 1972—; mem. adv. council for med. technolog program U. Guam, 1975; chmn. adv. bd. for med. technologis

Guam Community Coll., 1988—. Bd. dirs. Am. Cancer Soc., 1971-78, P.E.A.C.E. Found., 1975—; mem. Comprehensive Health Planning Bd., 1973-75; pres. Blood Exchange Bd., 1977-79. Mem. Am. Soc. Clin. Pathologists (affiliate; med. technologist), Am. Soc. Med. Technologists, Beta Sigma Phi. Roman Catholic. Home: Agana, Guam. Died Jan. 10, 2006.

SULLIVAN, JOSEPH PATRICK, agricultural product company executive; b. Newton, Mass., Apr. 10, 1933; s. Joseph Patrick and Ruth Ann (Kelter) S.; m. Jeanne Marie Baldi, Oct. 19, 1957; children: Deirdre, Barbara, Mark. BA cum laude, Harvard U., 1954, MBA, 1956. With Swift & Co., Chgo., 1959-73; pres. Swift Chem. Co., 1972-73, Estech Inc., Chgo., 1973-80; pres., chief exec. officer Swift & Co., Chgo., 1980-83; chmn. bd. Vigoro Industries Inc., Fairview Heights, Ill., from 1983, dir.; chmn. exec. com. IMC Global (merged with Vigoro), Chgo., from 1996. Mem. bus. adv. com. Coll. Commerce and Bus. Adminstrn., U. Ill. Bd. dirs. Chgo. Opera Theater, Am. Refugee Com.; trustee Mundelein Coll., Chgo. Acad. Scis.; trustee, mem. fin. com. Farm Found., Oak Brook, Ill.; past pres. trustees Latin Sch., Chgo., 1977—; co-chmn. Emergency Task Force for Indochinese Refugees. Served with AUS, 1956-59. Mem. Presidents Assn. Clubs: Chicago (Chgo.), Economic (Chgo.), Union League (Chgo.), Saddle and Cycle (Chgo.), Harvard (Chgo.); Harvard (Boston). Roman Catholic. Home: Chicago, Ill. Died Sept. 27, 2006.

SULLIVAN, LAWRENCE A., law educator, lawyer; b. 1923; m. Joane Sullivan, children: Larry, Mark, Neil; stepchildren: Eric, Douglas, Jonathan, Emily; BA, UCLA, J.D., Harvard U., 1951, LLD, Southwestern Law Sch., 2002 Bar: Mass. 1952. Law clk. to Hon. Calvert Magruder, US Ct. Appeals (1st cir.), 1951-52; assoc. Foley, Hoag & Eliot, Boston, 1952-54, 56-59, ptnr., 1959-65; vis. assoc. prof. U. Calif. Law Sch. Berkeley, 1954-56, prof., 1966-1991, Earl Warren prof. pub. law, 1979-1991, prof. emeritus, 1991-2007, Irwin R. Buchalter prof. law, Southwestern Law Sch., 1991-2007; mem. Nat. Com. for Revision Antitrust Laws and Procs., 1978-79. Served to sgt. USAAF, 1942-46. Guggenheim fellow, 1978. Author: Handbook on the Law of Antitrust, 1977; former mem. editorial bd. Harvard Law Rev.; named Antitrust Lawyer of Yr., Calif. State Bar Antitrust & Trade Regulation Sect., 1992 Died Oct. 7, 2007.

SULLIVAN, MICHAEL FRANCIS, lawyer; b. Hartford, Conn., Apr. 7, 1942; s. Francis Joseph and Elizabeth Pauline (Collins) S.; m. Jerrie Anne Johnson, Feb. 2, 1963; children: Kirsten Anne, Kathleen Elizabeth, Megan Lea. BA, Yale U., 1964; JD, U. Chgo., 1967. Bar: Ohio, 1967, U.S. Dist. Ct. (so. dist.) Ohio 1968, U.S. Ct. Appeals (6th cir.) 1968. Law clk. Ford Motor Co., Dearborn, Mich., 1966; assoc. Bricker & Eckler, Columbus, Ohio, 1967-71, ptnr., from 1971, mng. ptnr., 1987-89. Mem. ABA, Ethics in Econs., Ohio State Bar Assn. (corp. law com.), Columbus Bar Assn., Univ. Club Columbus. Home: West Worthington, Ohio. Died Jan. 29, 2007.

SULLIVANT, BRYAN STERLING, state legislator; b. Rochester, Minn., June 13, 1955; m. Melissa Sullivant; 1 child. BA, Westminster Coll., 1978; MBA, U. Phoenix. Energy conservation engr. Johnson Controls; mem. Colo. State Ho. of Reps. Dist. 2, Denver, 1995-98, Colo. State Senate, Denver, from 1999, vice chmn. bus. affairs and labor com., mem. local govt. com. Former mem. CAP; former v.p. Plins Met. Dist., Summit Sch. Dist.; pres. Denver Young Reps.; sec. Denver Rep. Com.; mem. Denver Bd. Edn., 1992-94. Mem. Assn. Energy Engrs., Profl. Skl Instr. Am., Lincoln Club Colo. (v.p.), Rotary. Republican. Presbyterian. Home: Breckenridge, Colo. Died Sept. 9, 2006.

SUNDERMANN, JUSTUS DANIEL, college president, educational consultant, real estate investor, mediator; b. Cin., Jan. 2, 1934; s. Louis William and Velma Loretta (Kline) S.; m. Sally Lynette Pounds, Sept.12, 1954; children: Cindy Lynette, Deborah Ruth, Justus F. II, Sarah Loretta. B.Sc., Ohio State U., 1955; M.Ed., U. Cin., 1959, Ed.D., 1965. Asst. to sr. v.p. and dean of univ. adminstrn. U. Cin., 1957-65; charter dean of student services Monroe County Community Coll., 1965-72; pres. Glen Oaks Community Coll., 1972-76, Anne Arundel Community Coll., 1976-79; dean Ohio U., Zanesville, 1979-81; cons. Coll. of Mainland, Texas City, Tex., 1981-83; pres. Eastfield Coll., Mesquite, Tex., from 1986. Mem. adv. bd. dirs. East Park Nat. Bank, Dallas. Past mem. bd. dirs. Bethesda Hosp., Zanesville, Muskingum County Council on Alcoholism, United Way of Muskingum County, Zanesville Improvement Corp.; bd. dirs. Galveston County Family Service; bd. dirs., vice chmn. budget and fin. United Way of Mainland, Tex.; mem. Houston-Galveston Area Council Govts., chmn. health planning council; mem. Area Wide Indigent Health Care Adv. Com., Houston; mem. adv. bd. Dallas Can! Acad.; bd. dirs. Mesquite Symphony Orch; mem. East Dallas Community and Indsl. Devel. Group; bd. dirs. Mesquite Meml. Hosp.; chmn. East Dallas County Consortium for Econ. Expansion. Recipient Spl. Tribute Mich. Legislature, 1976, Congressional award, 1978, award for community service United Way of Central Md., 1978, Disting. service award Anne Arundel Community Coll., 1978, citation of honor Mich. Minuteman, 1971 Mem. Am. Assn. Higher Edn. Am. Assn. Community and Jr. Colls., East Dallas C. of C., Garland C. of C., Mesquite C. of C. (indsl. devel. com., bd. drs.), Garland Corp. Coun., Phi Delta Kappa (Kappa Delta Pi.) Clubs: Episcopalian. Lodges: Rotary (pres. club). Died Dec. 18, 2005.

SUSKIND, SIGMUND RICHARD, microbiology educator; b. NYC, June 19, 1926; s. Seymour and Nina Phillips S.; m. Ann Barker, July 1, 1951; children: Richard, Mark, Steven. AB, NYU, 1948; PhD, Yale U., 1954. Research asst. biology div. Oak Ridge Nat. Lab., 1948-50; USPHS fellow NYU Med. Sch., NYC, 1954-56; mem. faculty Johns Hopkins U., Balt., from 1956, prof. biology, 1965-96, univ. prof., 1983-96, prof. emeritus, 1996—2006, Univ. ombudsman, 1988-91, dean grad. and undergrad. studies, 1971-78, dean Sch. Arts and Scis., 1978-83. Head molecular biology sect. NSF, 1970-71; cons. NIH, 1966-70, Coun. Grad. Schs., Mid States Assn. Colls. and Secondary Schs., NSF, 1986; vis. scientist Weizmann Inst. of Sci., Israel, 1985; trustee Balt. Hebrew U., 1985-93; mem. adv. bd. La. Geriatric Ctr. Author: (with P.E. Hartman) Gene Action, 1964, 69, (with P.E. Hartman and T. Wright) Principles of Genetics Laboratory Manual, 1965; editor: (with P.E. Hartman) Foundations of Modern Genetics series, 1964, 69; mem. sci. editorial bd. Johns Hopkins U. Press, 1973-76, 88-91. With USNR, 1944—46. NIH grantee, 1957-76 Fellow AAAS; mem. Am. Soc. Microbiology, Genetics Soc. Am., Am. Assn. Immunology, Am. Soc. Biol. Chemistry and Molecular Biology, Coun. Grad Schs., Assn. Grad. Schs., Northeastern Assn. Grad. Schs. (exec. com. 1975-76, pres. 1977-78). Avocation: research in microbial biochemical genetics and immunogenetics. Home: Worton, Md. Died Dec. 5, 2006.

SUTTON, JAMES ANDREW, diversified utility company executive; b. Gary, Ind., June 29, 1934; s. Winfield Alexander and Margaret (Aulwurm) S.; m. Beverly Joan McCorkle, Aug. 27, 1955; children— James II, Susan, Stephen, Scot. BSChemE, Purdue U., 1957. V.P., gen. mgr./gas products Linde div. Union Carbide Corp., Danbury, Conn., 1978-82; sr. v.p. compressed gases UGI Corp., Valley Forge, Pa., 1982-84, exec. v.p., COO, 1984-85, pres., COO, 1985-86, pres., CEO, 1986-88, chmn., pres., CEO, 1989-94, chmn., CEO, 1994-95, chmn., 1995-96. Bd. dirs. Gilbert Assocs., Inc., Reading, Pa.; former mem. Mellon PSFS Bd., Phila.; former mem. bd. trustees Thomas Jefferson U. Former mem. bd. trustees Thomas Jefferson U.; chmn. United Way Chester/Montgomery Counties Region, 1991; former mem., bd. dirs., mem. exec. com. Reading is Fundamental, Washington. Lt. U.S. Army, 1958. Mem. Phila. Country Club, Oyster Reef Country Club. Home: Flower Mound, Tex. Died Nov. 1, 2005.

SUTTON, RICHARD DONALD, banker, lawyer; b. Lakewood, NJ, Mar. 12, 1925; s. Frank Waldron and Ruth (Richtmeyer) S.; m. Mary Lou Sawyer, Dec. 26, 1950; children: Susan, Jullie, Nora, Frank Waldron. BA, U. N.C., 1950. Bar: N.J. 1954, U.S. Supreme Ct. 1968. Sr. ptnr. Sutton, Heim & Callahan, Toms River, N.J., from 1956; chmn. bd. First Nat. Bank of Toms River, from 1977, dir.; chmn. bd. Statewide Bancorp, Toms River, from 1982. Bd. dirs. United Way of Ocean County, N.J.; elder Presbyterian Ch., Toms River. Served with USNR, 1943-46. Mem. N.J. Bar Assn. (pres. 1964, sec. ethics com. 1958-63, pres. ethics com. 1963), Ocean County Lawyers Club (pres. 1953), Phi Delta Phi, Phi Gamma Delta Lodges: Rotary (Toms River). Home: Island Heights, NJ. Died Aug. 12, 2006.

SUTTON, WALTER, language educator; b. Milw., Jan. 25, 1916; s. Walter Evender and Maud (Farrington) S.; m. Vivian Irene Ryan, Dec. 22, 1941; 1 dau., Catherine S. Penner. BA, Heidelberg Coll., 1937; MA, Ohio State U., 1938, PhD, 1946. Instr. English U. Rochester, 1946-47; successively asst. prof., asso. prof., prof. English, dir. grad. studies, chmn. dept. English Syracuse (N.Y.) U., from 1948, now distinguished prof. humanities, from 1971. Vis. prof. U. Minn., summer 1960; vis. prof., sr. vis. fellow Council Humanities Princeton, 1960-61; vis. prof. U. Wash., summer 1966, Colgate U., 1967, U. Hawaii, summer 1968; Mem. com. examiners advanced lit. test Grad. Record Exam., 1962-72 Author: The Western Book Trade, 1961, Modern American Criticism, 1963, American Free Verse: The Modern Revolution in Poetry, 1973; Editor: Ezra Pound: A Collection of Critical Essays, 1963, (with Richard Foster) Modern Criticism: Theory and Practice, 1963, (with Vivian Sutton) Plato to Alexander Pope: Backgrounds of Modern Criticism, 1966, (with others) American Literature: Tradition and Innovation, 1969-74, Pound, Thayer, Watson and The Dial: A Story in Letters, 1994; editorial bd.: (with others) Am. Lit., 1973-76. Served with USCGR, 1942-45. Recipient Ohioana Book award, 1963; Howald fellow Ohio State U., 1947-48 Mem. AAUP, Am. Soc. Aesthetics, Am. Studies Assn., Modern Lang. Assn. Am. Died Feb. 23, 2006.

SVEC, HARRY JOHN, chemist, educator; b. Cleve., June 24, 1918; s. Ralph Joseph and Lilian Josephine (Pekarek) S.; m. Edna Mary Bruno, Oct. 27, 1943; children— Mary, Peter, Katherine, Jan, Thomas, Jeanne, Benjamin, Daniel, Lillian. BS, John Carroll U., 1941; PhD in Phys. Chemistry, Iowa State U., 1949. Asst. chemist Iowa State U., 1941-43; rsch. assoc. Inst. Atomic Rsch., 1946-50, asst. prof. chemistry, 1950-55, assoc. prof., 1955-60, prof., 1960-83, emeritus prof. chemistry, from 1983, Disting. prof. in scis. and humanities emeritus, from 1978; assoc. chemist Ames Lab., 1950-55; chemist Ames Lab., Dept. Energy, 1955-60, sr. chemist, 1960-85, program dir., 1974-85, assoc. scientist, from 1983. Jr. chemist Manhattan Project, Iowa State Coll., 1943-46; cons., lectr. in field. Author lab. manual in phys. chemistry; contbr. articles to profl. jours.; founding editor: Internat. Jour. Mass Spectrometry and Ion Processes, 1968-86. NSF grantee, 1972-82; EPA grantee, 1974-81; AEC grantee, 1950-74; ERDA grantee, 1974-77; Dept. Energy grantee, 1977-87; Am. Water Works Assn. grantee, 1977-79 Fellow: AAAS, The Chem. Soc.; mem.: ASTM, Am. Soc. Mass Spectroscopy (charter, v.p. 1972—74, pres. 1974—76), Geochem. Soc., Am. Chem. Soc. (emeritus), Alpha Chi Sigma (cons. from 1985), Phi Lambda Upsilon, Alpha Signa Nu, Sigma Xi. Roman Catholic. Home: Ames, Iowa. Died Nov. 28, 2006.

SVOBODA, RICHARD FRANK, accountant, writer; b. Cleve., June 25, 1926; s. Frank William and Mary Elizabeth Violet Stanczak, June 28, 1947; children— David, Joan, Daniel, Douglas, Wendy. Student, Baldwin-Wallace Coll., 1944-47, Case Western Res. U., 1948. Acct. Restemeir Co., Cleve., 1947-49; salesman Continental Baking Co., Cleve., 1949-51; asst. controller Cleve. Press., 1951-82, Sritek, Inc., Brecksville, Ohio, 1983—; baseball writer U.P.I., Cleve., 1966—; dir. Fourth Estate Credit Union, Cleve., 1970-82. Author: Baseball, Your Father's Favorite Game, 1982. Served with USN, 1944-46. Mem. Baseball Writers Assn. Am. (sec.-treas. 1968—, chmn. 1974), Sports Media Cleve. (treas. 1983—), Basketball Writers Assn. Am., Fedn. Musicians. Republican. Roman Catholic. Avocations: music, sports Died Sept. 25, 2006.

SWAIM, GLENN EUGENE, health care products company executive; b. Detroit, Mar. 20, 1942; s. Charles Miller and Margaret Ann (Swigart) S.; m. Lynn Ann Fortuna, Aug. 26, 1966 (div. Sept. 1976); children— Timothy, Thomas, Christine; m. Diane Phyllis Hayna, Nov. 20, 1976; children— Jeannette, Kathryn. B.S., Pa. State U., 1964; M.B.A., Fairleigh Dickinson U., 1972. Engr. Parke, Davis Co., Detroit, 1965-72; engr., sec. mgr. Ortho Diagnostics Inc., Raritan, N.J., 1972-74; project mgr. Kitchens of Sara Lee, Deerfield, Ill., 1974-78; mgr. mfg. engring. Abbott Labs., North Chicago, Ill., 1978—. Chmn. Bus. and Econ. Devel. Commn., Vernon Hills, Ill., 1980-82; pres. bd. edn. Hawthorn Community Consol. Dist. 73, Vernon Hills, Ill., 1983—. Mem. Am. Inst. Indsl. Engrs. (chpt. v.p. 1972-73), Am. Soc. Mfg. Engrs. (program chmn. 1975). Club: Detroit Yacht (social chmn. 1968-70). Lodge: Lions. Avocations: sailboat racing; skiing. Died Feb. 6, 2006.

SWAN, KENNETH CARL, surgeon; b. Kansas City, Mo., Jan. 1, 1912; s. Carl E. and Blanche (Peters) S.; m. Virginia Grone, Feb. 5, 1938; children: Steven Carl, Kenneth, Susan. AB, U. Oreg., 1933, MD, 1936. Diplomate: Am. Bd. Ophthalmology (chmn. 1960-61). Intern U. Wis., 1936-37; resident in ophthalmology State U. Iowa, 1937-40; practice medicine specializing in ophthalmology Portland, Oreg., from 1945; staff Good Samaritan Hosp.; asst. prof. ophthalmology State U. Iowa, Iowa City, 1941-44; assoc. prof. U. Oreg. Med. Sch., Portland, 1944-45, prof., head dept. ophthalmology, 1945-78, prof. emeritus, 2004—07. Chmn. sensory diseases study sect. NIH; mem. adv. council Nat. Eye Inst.; also adv. council Nat. Inst. Neurol. Diseases and Blindness. Contbr. articles on ophthalmic subjects to med. publs. Recipient Proctor Rsch. medal, 1953, Disting. Svc. award U. Oreg., 1963, Meritorious Achievement award U. Oreg. Med. Sch., 1968, Howe Ophthalmology medal, 1977, Aubrey Watzek Pioneer award Lewis and Clark Coll., 1979, Disting. Alumnus award Oreg. Health Scis. U. Alumni Assn., 1988, Disting. Svc. award, 1988, Mentor award Oreg. Health Scis. Found., 1996; named Oreg. Scientist of Yr. Oreg. Mus. Sci. and Industry, 1959. Mem. Assn. Rsch. in Ophthalmology, Am. Acad. Ophthalmology (v.p. 1978, historian), Soc. Exptl. Biology and Medicine, AAAS, AMA, Am. Ophthal. Soc. (Howe medal for disting. service 1977), Oreg. Med. Soc., Sigma Xi, Sigma Chi (Significant Sig award 1977) Home: Portland, Oreg. Died Feb. 23, 2007.

SWANGER, STERLING ORVILLE, appliance manufacturing company executive; b. Jan. 5, 1922; s. Orville M. and Alma Louise Swanger; m. Maxine O. Hindman, July 2, 1950; 1 child, Eric. BS, Iowa State U., 1947; postgrad., U. Va., 1965. Registered profl. engr., Iowa. Indsl. engr. Maytag Co., Newton, Iowa, 1947—52, methods engr., 1952—54, asst. chief methods engr., 1954—57, chief methods engr., 1957—68, mgr. prodn. engring., 1968—71, mgr. engring., 1971—74, asst. v.p. mfg., 1974—75, v.p. mfg., 1975—86, sr. v.p. and chief mfg. officer, 1986—87, also dir., cons., from 1987. Mem. Newton Pllanning and Zoning Commn., 1966—70; trustee Newton Skiff Hosp., 1970—85, chmn., 1982—85; trustee Progress Industries, 1987—90, chmn., 1991. With AUS, 1943—46. Mem.: NSPE, A. Ordnance Assn., Am. Mgmt. Assn., Nat. Mgmt. Assn., Iowa Engring. Soc., Newton Country Club, Elks. Republican. Presbyterian. Home: Newton, Iowa. Died May 28, 2007.

SWANSON, ROBERT DRAPER, retired academic administrator; b. Sioux City, Iowa, Aug. 6, 1915; s. Alfred and Tida Ruth (Draper) S.; m. Roberta B. Clements, May 5, 1941 (dec. Oct. 1975); children: Sara Louise, Mark Robert; m. Dorothy B. Howe, Aug. 4, 1979. AB, Park Coll., 1937; student, U. Iowa, 1937; B.D., McCormick Theol. Sem., 1941; D.D., James Millikin U., 1950; L.H.D., Tusculum Coll., 1966, Olivet Coll., 1971, Central Mich. U., 1979, Alma Coll., 1981; LL.D., Hillsdale Coll., 1968, Hope Coll., 1981. Dir. athletics, phys. edn. Park Coll., 1937-38; ordained to ministry Presbyn. Ch., 1941; pastor Second Presbyn. Ch., Tulsa, 1941-45; dean of students McCormick Sem., 1946-47, v.p., prof. preaching, 1948-56; pres. Alma Coll., 1956-80, pres. emeritus, 1980—2006. Dir. Gen. Telephone Co. Mich. Served as lt. (j.g.), Chaplain's Corps USNR, 1945-46. Recipient Disting. Alumni award, Pk. Coll., 1971, Disting. Alumnus award, McCormick Theol. Sem., 1981, Higher Edn. Honors award, Presbyn. Ch., 2002. Mem. Phi Beta Kappa. Clubs: Rotary (Alma). Home: Alma, Mich. Died Sept. 15, 2006.

SWEARINGEN, JOHN ELDRED, retired oil industry executive; b. Columbia, SC, Sept. 7, 1918; s. John Eldred and Mary (Hough) S.; m. Bonnie L. Bolding, May 18, 1969; children by previous marriage: Marcia L. Swearingen Pfleeger, Sarah K. Swearingen Origer, Linda S. Swearingen Arnold. BS, U. SC, 1938, LLD (hon.), 1965; MS, Carnegie-Mellon U., 1939, degree (hon.), 1981; degrees (hon.). With Standard Oil Co. (Ind.), 1939-83, v.p. prodn., 1954-56, exec. v.p., 1956-58, pres., 1958-65, CEO, 1960-83, chmn. bd., 1965-83, ret., 1983; chmn., CEO Continental Ill. Corp., Chgo., 1984-87, chmn. exec. com., 1987-88, ret., 1988. Bd. dirs. AON Corp., Gulfstream Aerospace Corp., Organization Resources Counselors, In., Coun. Mgmt. Advisors, Dean Witter Reynolds Inc. Mem. adv. bd. Hoover Instn. on War, Revolution and Peace; trustee Carnegie Mellon U., DePauw U., 1966-81, Chgo. Orchestral Assn., 1973-79; bd. dirs. McGraw Wildlife Found., 1964-75, Automotive Safety Found., 1959-69, chmn., 1962-64, Hwy. Users Fedn. for Safety and Mobility, 1969-75; trustee Northwestern Meml. Hosp. Corp. (life); chmn. Nat. Petroleum Coun., 1974-76, Am. Petroleum Inst., 1978-79; pres. Boys and Girls Clubs, Chgo., 1982-84, chmn. 1984-86. Decorated by govts. of Iran, Italy, Egypt, Philippines; recipient Washington award Western Soc. Engrs., 1981, Gold medal for disting. achievement, Am. Petroleum Inst., 1983; laureate Nat. Bus. Hall of Fame, Jr. Achievement, 1984. Fellow Am. Inst. Chem. Engrs.; mem. Am. Inst. Mining, Metall. and Petroleum Engrs. (Charles F. Rand Meml. gold medal 1980), Am. Chem. Soc., Nat. Acad. Engring., Phi Beta Kappa, Sigma Xi, Omicron Delta Kappa, Tau Beta Pi. Clubs: Mid-Am., Chgo., Racquet (Chgo.); Bohemian (San Francisco); Eldorado Country (Indian Wells, Calif.); Old Elm (Lake Forest, Ill.); Glen View (Golf, Ill.). Home: Chicago, Ill. Died Sept. 14, 2007.

SWEARINGEN, LOUISE ADELINE (LOUISE ADELINE POE), counselor, educator; b. Buhl, Idaho, Mar. 5, 1918; d. George Perry, Sr. and Louise Sophia (Larson) Poe; m. Gordon Clifford Swearingen, Dec. 26, 1939 (div.); children: Dona Louise Swearingen McLean, Ann Marie Swearingen DeFrance, James Gordon, Jean Leinani Swearingen Martin. Teaching cert. Albion (Idaho) State Normal Sch., 1938; BA in Psychology and

Sociology, Adams State Coll., 1967, MA in Guidance and Counseling, 1968; postgrad. U. Iowa, 1974-75, Utah State U., summer 1983—, U. Nev.-Las Vegas, 1982-83, U. Nev.-Reno, 1969-70, Oreg. State U., 1973-74. Elem. tchr., Bliss, Idaho, 1938-40; social worker state depts. welfare Colo. and Mo., 1962-67; high sch. counselor, Ely, Nev., 1968-79, elem. counselor, Ely, 1979-83, jr. and sr. high sch. counselor, 1982—; part-time instr., counselor with parents No. Nev. CC1981-83; condr. community classes in parenting; cons., speaker in field. Cmty. counselor Mental Health Adv. Council Ely, 1975-83; Vocat. and Adult Edn. Adv. Coun. Ely, 1973-83. ESEA Title IV-C grantee, 1979-82. Mem. Am. Vocat. Assn., Nev. Vocat. Assn., Nev. Personnel and Guidance Assn., Sch. Counselors Assn., NEA, Nev. Edn. Assn. Republican. Mormon. Home: Ely, Nev. Died Dec. 25, 2006.

SWEENEY, URBAN JOSEPH, librarian; b. St. John, N.B., Can., Jan. 18, 1922; came to U.S., 1927, naturalized, 1945; s. Urban James and Dorothy E. (Murray) S.; B.S., N.Y. U., 1956; M.S., Pratt Inst., 1957; m. Margaret Stretz, Jan. 12, 1952; children— Dennis, Steven, Edward, Mark, Barbara. Chief librarian Republic Aviation, Farmingdale, N.Y., 1958-66; chief librarian electronics div., Gen. Dynamics, Rochester, N.Y., 1966-71, Convair div., San Diego, 1971-85; project mgr. Integrated Library Systems, US Naval Ocean Systems Ctr., San Diego, 1985-88; vis. instr. Sch. Library Sci., SUNY, Geneseo, N.Y., 1967-70. Served with USAAF, 1941-45; ETO. Mem. Am. Soc. Info. Sci., Spl. Libraries Assn. (chmn. aerospace div. 1978-80, chpt. pres. 1973-74). Contbr. articles to profl. jours. Home: San Diego, Calif. Died Mar. 21, 2006.

SWEET, BERNARD, airline executive; b. Cin., Dec. 6, 1923; s. William B. and Elizabeth (Krent) S.; m. Betty Sweet, May 29, 1946; 1 child, Laurie Narda. BA, U. Wis., 1947. Chief acct. VA Hosp., Madison, Wis., 1948; with North Central Airlines (now Republic Airlines), 1948-84, pres., dir., 1969-80, chief exec. officer, 1976-80, vice chmn. bd., 1980-84. Dir. Republic Energy, Inc., Republic Airlines, Inc. G & K Services, Inc., Rykoff-Sexton, Inc. Served with USAAF, 1943-46. Died July 24, 2006.

SWEET, ORVILLE KENNETH, food products association executive, animal scientist; b. Wichita Falls, Tex., June 21, 1923; s. Forest Albert and Mary B. (Fitts) S.; m. Mary Lewellwyn Gwaltney, May 25, 1946; children— Michael Linn, Cinda Lew, Lisa Sue, Eva Lea BS, Okla. State U., Stillwater, 1948, MS, 1960. Instr. vocat. agr. Ryan High Sch., Okla., 1948-50; instr. vocat. agr. Synder High Sch., Okla., 1950-55; mgr. cattle ranch Windsweep Ranch, Thomaston, Ga., 1955-60; beef cattle specialist U. Ga., Athens, 1960-63; pres. Am. Polled Hereford Assn., Kansas City, Mo., 1963-79; chief exec. officer Nat. Pork Producers Council, Des Moines, from 1979. Dir. Agrl. Hall of Fame, Kansas City, 1969-79; pres. U.S. Beef Breeds Council, Kansas City, 1978, Nat. Soc. Livestock Records, Kansas City, 1976 Author: Birth of a Breed, 1975; other publs. in field Served to ensign USN, 1942-60; PTO Decorated D.F.C., Air medal (4). Mem. Am. Soc. Animal Sci., Am. Soc. Assn. Execs. Republican. Mem. Chs. of Christ. Avocations: golf; water skiing. Home: Panora, Iowa. Died Apr. 19, 2007.

SWENSON, KENNETH BURDETTE, hospital administrator; b. Rockford, Ill., July 13, 1945; s. Gust Harold and Edith Linnea (Kjederquist) S.; m. Kathleen Beth Leeper, June 7, 1970; children: Emily Marie, Eric Leeper. BA, U. Evansville, 1970; MHA, Ga. State U., 1972. Adminstrv. asst. Roanoke (Va.) Meml. Hosp., 1971-72; asst. adminstr. Prince William Hosp., Manassas, Va., 1972-83, sr. v.p., 1983-88, pres., 1988—2000. Bd. dirs. Blue Ridge Speech/Hearing Ctr., Manassas, 1973-78; exec. com. Prince William United Way, Manassas, 1983-2000, chmn., 1991, campaign chmn., 1988; adminstrv. bd. Grace United Meth. Ch., Manassas; dir., treas. Insight, Inc., Manassas, 1973-79. With U.S. Army, 1967-68, Vietnam. Mem. Am. Coll. Healthcare Execs., Va. Hosp. Assn., Md./D.C./Va. Hosp. Assn. (pres. 1982-83, Past Pres. award 1983), Rotary Club. (pres. 1978-79). Republican. Home: Manassas, Va. Died Mar. 29, 2007.

SWENSON, MARVIN OLIVER, college administrator; b. Audubon, Minn., Mar. 26, 1926; s. Oscar Nathaniel and Iva Kathleen (Sando) S.; m. Dorothy Marie Oliver, Aug. 15, 1946 (dec. 1959); children— Marva, Michael, Patrick; m. Chellis Diane Smith, Jan. 30, 1960; children— Paul, James. B.S., Mont. State U., 1950; M.A., U. Minn., 1953; Ed.D., Wash. State U., 1972. Tchr., counselor Forsyth High Sch., Mont., 1950-53; tchr., counselor, coach Red Lodge High Sch., Mont., 1954-56; activities program advisor Wash. State U., Pullman, 1956-62, asst. dir. coll. union, 1962-63, acting dir., 1963-64; gen. mgr. student union U. Alta., Edmonton, 1964-69; dir. coll. union Pacific Luth. U., Tacoma, 1969—; cons. coll. unions Frank Noffke Assn., U. Alta., Guelph, Man., Tacoma Community Coll. Author: Mr. Chairman, a Handbook of Parliamentary Procedure, 1957; Mr. Committee Chairman, a Handbook for Committee Chairmen, 1958; Mr. Faculty Adviser, a Handbook for Faculty Advisers to Student Organizations, 1959; contbr. articles to profl. jours. Bd. dirs. Tacoma Luth. Home, 1982-84; council mem. Trinity Luth. Ch., Tacoma, 1977-80, 83-86; regent Camrose Luth. Coll., Alta., Can., 1966-69; coach Youth Soccer, Baseball, Tacoma, 1975-80. Served with USN, 1943-46; Guam. Mem. Profl. Guidance Assn., Am. Coll. Personnel Assn. (dir. commn. 9, 1976-79), Assn. Coll. Unions (regional dir. 1967-70, chmn. research commn. 1983-86), Nat. Assn. Student Personnel Adminstrs., Nat. Orientation Dirs. Assn., Internat. Assn. Auditorium Mgrs. (10 yr. Service award 1981), others. Democrat. Club: Circle K (adv. 1982, Tacoma). Lodges: Kiwanis (pres. 1983-84), Elks. Home: Tacoma, Wash. Died Mar. 24, 2007.

SWIHART, JOHN MARION, retired aircraft manufacturing company executive; b. New Winchester, Ohio, Dec. 27, 1923; s. Harry Miron and Fay I. (Cress) S.; m. Gail G. Carter, Nov. 8, 1986; children from previous marriages: Vicki Ann, John Richard, Thomas Marion, Mark Andrew, Karen Lee, Laurie Christine, Stacey Anne. BS in Physics, Bowling Green State U., 1947; BS in Aero. Engring., Ga. Inst. Tech., 1949, postgrad., 1951-53, U. Va., 1951-53. Asst. group leader propulsion group NASA, 1956-58, group leader spl. projects, 1958-59, head advanced configurations group aircraft, 1959-62, chief large supersonic tunnels br., 1962; with Boeing Co., 1962-89, dep. dir. internat. sales Renton, Wash., 1974-75, v.p. Japan Boeing Internat. Corp. Tokyo, 1973-74, program mgr. 7X7 Kent, Wash., 1975-76, dir. new airplane product devel., sales, mktg. Seattle, 1976-78, dir. product devel., sales mktg., 1978-79, v.p. U.S., Can. sales, 1979-83, v.p. govt. tech. liaison, 1983-85, corp. v.p. airplane market analysis, 1985, corp. v.p. internat. affairs Seattle, 1985-89; ret., 1989. Contbr. over 100 articles to profl. jours. 1st lt. USAAF, 1943-45. Decorated D.F.C., Air medal with 3 oak leaf clusters; recipient Wright Bros. Meml. Lectureship award, 1987, Maurice Roy medal for internat. cooperation Internat. Coun. Aeronautical Scie., 1992. Fellow AIAA (hon., chmn. airdraft design com. Pacific N.W. sect. 1969-70, gen. chmn. aircraft sys. and design meeting 1977, pres. 1990-91), Royal Aero. Soc., Internat. Soc. for Air-Breating Engines (pres. 1993—); mem. Japan-Am. Soc. (pres. 1978-79), Wash. State China Rels. Coun. (past pres.). Home: Medina, Wash. Died Mar. 24, 2007.

SYMMONDS, DEBRA ELAINE, city government official; b. San Luis Obispo, Calif., Nov. 7, 1952; d. Dean W. Duncan and Joyce M. (Hennager) Kjelland; m. Matthew M. Symmonds, Sept. 5, 1976. B.A., San Diego State U., 1976. Cert. mcpl. clk. Banquet mgr. Far West Services, Inc., San Diego, 1974-79; city clk. City of Mercer Island, Wash., 1980—. Mem. Internat. Inst. Mcpl. Clks., Wash. State Mcpl. Clks. Assn. (bd. dirs.). Home: Mercer Island, Wash. Died May 25, 2007.

SYTSMA, JOHN FREDERICK, union official; b. Paterson, NJ, July 22, 1921; s. Frederick J. and Alice (Hutchinson) S.; m. Phyllis Stingle, Sept. 11, 1942; children: Ruth Ann Sytsma Lubbers, Jacqueline Sytsma Pruitt. Student, Coll. Paterson, NJ, 1939-41. Clk., Am. Surety Co., NYC, 1939-41; locomotive fireman, engr. N.Y.S. & W. R.R., 1941-56; office mgr. Brotherhood Locomotive Engrs., Cleve., 1956-62, gen. sec.-treas., 1962-74, 1st v.p., 1974-76, internat. pres., from 1976. Pres. Locomotive Engrs. Bldg. Assn., Locomotive Engrs. Mut. Life and Accident Ins. Assn. Author: Ahrens-Fox, A Pictorial History of a Great Name in Fire Apparatus, 1971, Ahrens-Fox Album, 1973, 100 Favorite Fire Rigs, 1978, Fire Rigs Fighting Fires, 1982. Mem. Republican Inner Circle, Rep. Congl. Leadership Council. Served with AUS, World War II, PTO. Mem. Fraternal Investment Assn., Internat. Assn. Firefighters Mem. Dutch Reformed Ch. Home: Medina, Ohio. Died May 29, 2007.

SZARKOWSKI, JOHN (THADDEUS JOHN SZARKOWSKI), retired museum administrator; b. Ashland, Wis., Dec. 18, 1925; s. Julius and Rose (Woychik) Szarkowsk; m. Jill Anson, Oct. 14, 1963 (dec. Dec. 31, 2006); children: Nina, Natasha. BS, U. Wis., 1948; BS hon. degrees, Phila. Coll. Art, 1972; BS, Mpls. Coll. Art and Design, 1974. Photographer Walker Art Center, Mpls., 1948-51; instr. in photography U. Minn., 1950, Albright Art Sch., U. Buffalo, 1951-53; dir. dept. photography emeritus Mus. Modern Art, NYC, 1962—2007. Author: The Idea of Louis Sullivan, 1956, The Face of Minn., 1958, The Photographer & the Am. Landscape, 1963, The Photographer's Eye, 1966, Walker Evans, 1971, Looking at Photographs, 1973, Mirrors & Windows: Am. Photography Since 1960, 1978, Irving Penn, 1984, Photography Until Now, 1990, Ansel Adams at 100, 1991, Atget, 2000, Photographs, 2005; co-author (with Alfred Stieglitz): Alfred Stieglitz at Lake George, 1995. With US Army, 1945—46. Fellow John Simon Guggenheim Found., 1954, 1961. Mem.: Century Assn. Home: New York, NY. Died July 7, 2007.

SZOGYI, ALEX, Romance languages educator, author; b. NYC, Jan. 27, 1929; s. Arpad and Vera Irene (Hoffmann) S. BA, Bklyn. Coll., 1950; MA, Yale U., 1954, PhD, 1958. Mem. faculty Yale U., 1952-55, Wesleyan U., 1955-61; mem. faculty Hunter Coll., NYC, from 1961, prof. Romance langs., from 1971, chmn. dept., 1970-77. Translater plays, book reviewer Author: Anthologie d'Humour francais, 1970; translator: Grotowski (Temkine), 1972, Moliere Abstrait, 1985; also all of Chekhov's plays and plays of Gorki, Giraudoux, Anouilh, Beaumarchais, Marivaux, Musset, Marquis de Sade, George Sand, Verga, Strindberg and Feydeau; translator and performer: Marriage of Figaro (Beaumarchais), 1982, Apostrophes, 1985, La Bibliotheque Idéale, 1988, Black Snow (Bulgakov), 1988; editor: Candide (Voltaire), 1962, George Sand Studies, 1980, Vol. II, 1982, Dialectic of the Heart, 1986; monthly columnist: Cook's Books, Bon Appétit mag., 1979-81. Decorated chevalier dans l'Ordre Palmes Académiques, 1974, officier, 1980; recipient Disting. Alumnus award Bklyn. Coll., 1974, award for short story Father: Let me In NEH-PEN Club, 1984; French Govt. fellow, 1950-51; Danforth Found. fellow, summer 1959; Guggenheim Found. fellow, 1962-63. Mem. MLA, Am. Assn. Tchrs. French (pres. Met. chpt. 1978-82), PEN (syndicated fiction award for short story 1983), Am. Comparative Lit. Assn., Soc. des Professeurs de Francais en Amerique, Les Amis de George Sand (editor jour.), Dramatists Guild, Nat. Book Critics Circle, Century Assn., Phi Beta Kappa (pres. Hunter Colll. chpt. 1982—), Pi Delta Phi, Sigma Delta Pi. Home: New York, NY. Died Apr. 23, 2007.

TABENKEN, GERALD MARCUS, beverage distributor; b. Portland, Maine, Oct. 31, 1922; s. Harry and Leah (Marcus) T.; m. Ruth Goldberg, Mar. 28, 1953; children: Matthew, Lee. BA, U. Maine, 1946. Vice pres. H. Tabenken & Co. Inc., Bangor, Maine, 1955-68, exec. v.p., 1968-77, pres. Tabenken Corp., Bangor, 1977—; founding dir. United Bank, Bangor, 1980—. Spl. U.S. ambassador to St. Lucia, B.W.I., 1979; adv. com. John F. Kennedy Ctr. Performing Arts, Washington, 1979-80; mem. White House Commn. Small Bus., 1980, Pres.'s Commn. Exec. Exchange, 1980; trustee Unity Coll., Maine, 1980-83, Maine State Retirement System, 1983—. Recipient Industry Achievement award Pa. Importing Master Distbrs. Assn., 1978; named Man of Yr., Modern Brwery Age Mag., 1978. Mem. Nat. Beer Wholesalers Assn. (pres. 1977-79, dir. emeritus 1981, Man of Yr. 1978), U. Maine Alumni Assn. (ambassador), Maine Wine and Beer Wholesalers Assn. (pres. 1973-74). Democrat. Jewish. Clubs: Commonwealth of Calif.; Penobscot Valley Country. Lodges: Anah Shriners, Masons. Avocations: art disciplines, internat. relations, internat. trade. Died Apr. 13, 2006.

TABER, ROBERT CLINTON, retired army officer; b. Ithac NY, Oct. 11, 1917; s. Laurence Sebring and Ethel (Lanning) T m. Jane Feeter, July 20, 1940 (dec. 1982); 1 child, John Robert m. Lynn Parker, June 12, 1992. BS, Cornell U., 1938; grad Army War Coll., 1958. Commd. 2d lt. U.S. Army, 194(advanced through grades to lt. gen.; comdg. gen. Joint U.S. Mi Adv. Group Cambodia, 1963; asst. div. comdr. 82d Airborn Div., 1964-65; asst. comdt. U.S. Army Command and Gen. Sta Coll. Leavenworth, Kans., 1965-66; chief of staff U.S. Arm Vietnam, 1967-68; dir. doctrine and systems Dept. Army 1968-69; comdg. gen. 3d Inf. Div. Germany, 1970-71; prin. dep asst sec. def. manpower and res. affairs, 1971-74. Decorate DSM with 2 oak leaf clusters, Legion of Merit with 3 oak lea clusters, Soldiers medal, Bronze Star, Purple Heart, Joint Com mendation medal, Army Commendation medal with 2 oak lea clusters, Air medal with 2 oak leaf clusters. Mem. U.S. Nava Acad. Sailing Sqdn. Clubs: Cruising of Am, Ocean Cruising Internat. Aerobatic. Home: Sun City Center, Fla. Died Feb. 2 2007.

TAGGART, GANSON POWERS, management consultant; b Albany, NY, Aug. 16, 1918; s. Ralph Cone and Ruth Harrie (Townsend) T.; m. Paulett Long, June 30, 1945; children: H.Te Paulett Long, Cornelia V.C. BSChE, U. Mich., 1940, MSChE 1941; postgrad., NE Sch. Advanced Mgmt., 1964. Registere engr., Mass. Mng. dir. Badger N.V., The Hague, Netherland 1965—70; v.p. world sales Badger Co., Cambridge, Mass 1970—71; sr. v.p., dir. Badger Co. Inc., Cambridge, 1978—8 mgmt. cons. Devel. Scis. Inc., Sandwich, Mass., 1972—7 chmn. bd. Serapis Energy Inc., Boston, 1982—85, dir.; pre Mgmt. Sys. Inc., from 1984. Chmn. bd. dirs. William K. Stou Pub. Co., 1995—; bd. dirs. E.F. Schumacher Soc. Contb articles to mags. Oil mem. Energy Facilities Siting Coun. Mass Boston, 1979-82; mem. Winchester (Mass.) Planning Bd., 197 77, Winchester Town Meeting, 1960-64; mem. exec. com Internat. Sch. The Hague, 1965-70; trustee Ledges Cond minium Assn., 1992-98, chmn., 1998; trustee USS Constr Mus., 1989-95, treas. 1991-92; moderator Winchester Unitaria Soc., 1983-93; active Mus. Sci., Boston, Found. Global Cmt Lt. (j.g.) USNR, 1944-48. Mem. AIChE (chmn. Boston sec 1955, Order of Xiphias), Soc. Chem. Industry (London), Co servation Law Found., Am. Chem. Soc., World Bus. Acad., In Noetic Scis., Chemists Club (N.Y.C.), Annisquam Yacht Cl (Gloucester, Mass.), Harvard Club (Boston). Home: Bedfor Mass. Died July 17, 2007.

TAISHOFF, LAWRENCE BRUCE, publishing company ex ecutive; b. Washington, Aug. 30, 1933; s. Sol Joseph and Bet (Tash) T.; m. Nancy Lee Stuckey, Sept. 17, 1962 (div. 1979 children: Robert Paul, Randall Lawrence, Jonathan Bradfor AB, Duke U., 1955. Asst. dir. Sta. WTOP-TV, Washingto 1955-56; with Broadcasting Publs., Inc., Washington, 1958—9 pres., pub., 1971-91, chmn., 1991—95; adviser Cahne Consumer/Entertainment Pub. divsn. Cahners Pub. Co., Wash ington, 1991—95; v.p. Jolar Corp., Washington, 1952-72, di 1958-72. Gen. ptnr. Jolar Assocs., Washington, 1972-200 chmn. bd., pres. Graphictype, Inc., 1976-86, also dir.; chmn pres. Solar Corp., 1982-86; chmn. Broadcasting-Taisho Found., 1982-2001; chmn., CEO Chuckie Broadcasting, Ar more, Okla., 1993-2006, Trustco, Washington, 1988-2006; CE Solar Investments, Naples, Fla., 1996-2006. Co-author radio an TV segment Britannica Book of the Yr., 1983-2006. Truste Washington Journalism Ctr., 1982-93, Nat. Press Found., 199 2006, mem. adv. bd., 1993-2006; bd. dirs. Nat. Press Found 1982-2006, mem. exec. com., 1990-94; mem. journalism an comms. exec. com. Capital Campaign for Arts and Scis., Duk U., 1984-2006, mem. athletic adv. bd., 1999-2006; bd. adviso Am. Journalism Ctr., Budapest, 1991-95; mem. White Hous Press Corps, 1983-2006; mem. Met. Washington Bd. Trad 1970-2006; team capt. pubs. divsn. United Givers Fund driv 1965; mem. admissiosn adv. com. Duke Alumni Assn,. 1968-7 mem. U.S. Senate and Ho. of Reps. Periodical Press Galler 1958-95; trustee Broadcast Pioneers Ednl. Fund Inc., 198 judge VFW Voice of Democracy contest, 1978-2006; mem. b judges Peabody awards, 1985-91; mem. Am. U. Sch. Comm Disting. Adv. Commn., 1985-2006; mem. Founders Soc. Duk U., 1985-2006, Duke Athletic Adv. Bd., The Mus. of TV an Radio Roundtable, 1988-89; bd. dirs. Ardissone, Naples, Fla 1994-99; chmn., trustee Taishoff Family Found. With AU 1956-58. Mem. IEEE (sr.), Internat. Radio & TV Soc., Broa cast Pioneers (life, bd. dirs., exec. com. Broadcast Pionee Libr.), Am. Sportscasters Assn. (exec. com. 1990-2006), Whi House Corrs. Assn., Nat. Press Club, Woodmont Country Cl (Rockville, Md.), Cosmos Club (Washington), Sigma Delta Ch Zeta Beta Tau. Jewish. Home: Naples, Fla. Died Nov. 1, 200

TAKAMUNE, ROBERT KATSUTOSHI, life insuran agent; b. Paauilo, Hawaii, Nov. 20, 1929; s. Koichi and Edi Nobue (Nakashima) T.; student Hilo Comml. Coll., 1947-49; r Janet Tsurue Kawahara; children: Audrey, Claire, Daniel, Joyc Bookkeeper, Frank Huff Agy., Hilo, Hawaii, 1949-52, Yama Ins. Agy., Ltd., Honolulu, 1952-63; div. mgr. Investors Equi Life Ins. Co. Hawaii, Ltd., Honolulu, 1963-70; spl. agt. Nort western Mutual Life Ins. Co., Honolulu, 1970—. Treas., L Underwriters Polit. Action Com., 1978-80; treas. Parents Scou ers Guild, 1976-81, pres., 1981-82, committeman, 1981—; pa chmn. bd. trustees Harris United Meth. Ch., Honolulu. Recipie Diamond award Northwestern Mutual Life Ins. Co., 1977. Me Am. Soc. C.L.U.'s (C.L.U. Jour. discussion moderator Haw chpt. 1980-81, dir. Hawaii chpt. 1981-84, treas. 1984-86, se 1986-87, pres. 1988-89), Benefit Engring., Inc. (pres. 1990— Life Underwriting Tng. Coun. (advanced sales course moderat 1980-81), Nat. Assn. Life Underwriters, East Honolulu As Life Underwriters (treas. 1982-84, sec. 1984-85, v.p. 1985-8 pres. 1987-88), Hawaii Estate Planning Council, Million Dol Roundtable (life), Honolulu Assn. Life Underwriters (fin. chm 1980-81). Home: Honolulu, Hawaii. Died July 16, 2006.

TALBERT, PRESTON TIDBALL, chemist, educator; Washington, Feb. 17, 1925; s. James Loraine and Grace An (Johnson) T.; m. Rebecca L. Chandler, Aug. 8, 1956. BS cu laude, Howard U., 1950, MS, 1952; PhD, Washington U., Louis, 1955. Postdoctoral fellow U. Wash., Seattle, j71955-5 asst. prof. Howard U., Washington, 1959-63, asso. prof., 196 70, prof., from 1970, asso. chmn. dept. bio-organic chemist

966-87. Mem. nat. needs postdoctoral fellowships panel NSF, 978-80; mem. postdoctoral fellowships panel for minorities Ford Found., 1983 Contbr. articles to profl. jours. Served with USAF, 1943-46. Nat. Heart Inst. fellow, 1957-59 Mem. Am. Chem. Soc., AAUP, AAAS, N.Y. Acad. Scis., Beta Kappa Chi. Democrat. Methodist. Home: Silver Spring, Md. Died Aug. 22, 2006.

TAMA, PHYLLIS ELAINE, executive search consultant; b. Bklyn., Sept. 23, 1938; d. Louis and Fritzi (Perschetz) T. A.A.S., Bklyn Coll., 1961. Fashion coordinator V.F. Corp., NYC, 1962-73; v.p., dir. corp. exec. placement May Dept. Stores, NYC, 1973-78, Saks Fifth Ave., NYC, 1978-80; div. v.p., exec. placement Associated Merchandising Corp., NYC, 1980-82; exec. search cons. Thorndike Deland Assocs., NYC, 1982—. Mem. The Fashion Group, Nat. Assn. Female Execs., Networks Unlimited, Inc. Contbr. article to profl. jours. Home: New York, NY. Died June 10, 2007.

TAN, JAMES, internist, educator; b. Aug. 3, 1938; married. AA, U. Philippines, 1960, MD, 1965. Diplomate in internal medicine and infectious disease Am. Bd. Internal Medicine; cert. physician, Ohio. Intern Philippine Gen. Hosp., Manila, 1964-65, resident in internal medicine, 1965-67; tng. Bangkok, 1967-68; fellow in infectious diseases U. Cin. Coll. Medicine, 1968-71; mem. staff U. Cinn. Med. Ctr., other Cin. hosps., 1971-74; active staff Summa Health System, from 1975; prof. medicine Northeastern Ohio Univs. Coll. Medicine, Rootstown, from 1979, vice chmn. dept. internal medicine, from 1993, chmn. infectious disease sect., from 1977; chmn. dept. of programs Summa Health Sys., Akron, Ohio, from 1992. Contbr. articles to profl. jours.; reviewer for jours. Fellow Am. Coll. Chest Physicians, Infectious Disease Soc. Am. (sec. Ohio 1994—), ACP-Am. Soc. Internal Medicine (master, gov. Ohio chpt. 1995-99); mem. Am. Soc. for Microbiology, Ohio Med. Soc., Soc. for Hosp. Epidemiologists, Alpha Omega Alpha. Died May 25, 2006.

TANNER, GEORGE WOOLF, librarian; b. Cardston, Alta., Can., Apr. 5, 1919; came to U.S., 1936; s. John Sidney and Orrilla (Woolf) T.; m. Laura Webb, Dec. 12, 1952; children— Craig, Stephen, Jean, Wayne, Kara. B.F.A., U. Iowa, 1948, M.A., 1951; M.L.S., U. Denver, 1963. Instr. in theatre UCLA, 1951-52, Utah State U., Logan, 1952-55; costumer, instr. Brigham Young U., Provo, Utah, 1955-58; lang. specialist Ch. Coll. N.Z., Hamilton, 1958-63; librarian Weber State Coll. Ogden, Utah, 1963-69; librarian, drama dir. Utah Tech. Coll., Provo, 1969—; chmn. Utah Coll. Library Council, Salt Lake City, 1976. Liaison Nat. Council Boy Scouts N.Z., Hamilton, 1958-62; former scoutmaster Boy Scouts Am.; mem. Orem City Library Bd., Utah, 1973-79, pres., 1974. Mem. Utah Library Assn. (pres. 1974), Ednl. Theatre Am. Home: Orem, Utah. Died Mar. 7, 2006.

TAPE, GERALD FREDERICK, retired educational association administrator; b. Ann Arbor, Mich., May 29, 1915; s. Henry A. and Flora (Simmons) T.; m. Josephine Waffen, June 18, 1939; children: Walter Richard, James William, Thomas Gerald. AB, Eastern Mich. U., 1935, Sc.D. (hon.), 1964; MS, U. Mich., 1936, PhD, 1940. Asst. physics Eastern Mich. U., 1933-35, U. Mich., 1936-39; instr. physics Cornell U., 1939-42; staff mem. radiation lab. Mass. Inst. Tech., 1942-46; asst., then assoc. prof. physics U. Ill., 1946-50; asst. to dir., then dep. dir. Brookhaven Nat. Lab., 1950-62; v.p., then pres. Associated Univs., Inc., 1962-63, pres., 1969-80, spl. asst. to pres., 1980-82; commr. AEC, 1963-69; U.S. rep. to IAEA with rank of amb., 1973-77; former pres., cons. Associated Univs., Inc. Dir. Sci. Svc. Inc., 1971—2002, Atomic Indsl. Forum, 1970-73; mem. Pres.'s Sci. Adv. Com., 1969-73, Def. Sci. Bd., 1970-73, chmn., 1970-72; mem. sci. adv. com. IAEA, 1972-73; mem. gen. adv. com. ERDA, 1975-77; mem. adv. council Electric Power Rsch. Inst., 1978-85; mem. U. Chgo. bd. govs. for Argonne Nat. Lab., 1982-85; cons. Def. Nuclear Facilities Safety Bd., 1991-2000. Author: (with L.J. Haworth) Relay Radar Chapter of MIT Radiation Laboratory Technical Series, 1947; also papers, reports. Named Disting. Alumnus, Ea. Mich. U., 2005; recipient Army-Navy Certificate of Appreciation, 1947, Meritorious Civilian Service medal Sec. Def., 1969, Dept. State Tribute Appreciation, 1969, Dept. Def. medal for pub. service, 1973; Henry DeWolf Smyth Nuclear Statesman award Atomic Indsl. Forum/Am. Nuclear Soc., 1978; Disting. Pub. Service award NSF, 1980; Disting. Assoc. award Dept. Energy, 1980; Enrico Fermi award U.S. Energy Dept., 1987; decorated comdr. Order Leopold II, Belgium. Fellow Am. Phys. Soc., Am. Nuclear Soc., AAAS; mem. Nat. Acad. Engring., Am. Astron. Soc., Phi Beta Kappa, Sigma Xi, Phi Kappa Phi, Kappa Delta Pi. Home: Bethesda, Md. Died Nov. 20, 2005.

TAPLETT, LLOYD MELVIN, human resources specialist, consultant; b. Tyndalll, SD, July 25, 1924; s. Herman Leopold and Emiley (Nedvidek) T.; m. Patricia Ann Sweeney, Aug. 21, 1958; children: Virginia Ann, Sharon Lorraine, Carla Jo, Carolyn Patricia, Catherine Marie, Colleen Elizabeth. BA, Augustana Coll., 1949; MA, U. Nebr., 1959; postgrad., S.D. State U., U. S.D., U. Iowa, Colo. State U. Accredited personnel dir.; prof. human resources; life cert. tchr. & counselor. Tchr. Sioux Falls Pub. Schs., SD, 1952—69; with All-Am. Transport Co., Sioux Falls, 1969—78, Am. Freight Sys., Inc., Overland Park, Kans., 1978—79; dir. human resources & pub. rels., corp. affirmative action Chippewa Motor Freight, Inc., Sioux Falls, 1979—80; cons. human resources & mgmt., 1980—81; mgr. Sioux Falls Job Svcs., 1981—85, Pioneer Enterprises, Inc., 1985—86; ops. mgr. ATE Environ., Inc., 1986—88; cons. Royal River Casino, 1988—90; acad. dean Huron U., Sioux Falls, 1990—97; instr. cons. Coll. Bus., 1992—98. Chmn. Chippewa Credit Union; mem. adv. bd. dirs. Nelson Labs., Sioux Falls, 1981-82; evening mgmt. instr. Nat. Coll., Sioux Falls, 1981-90, chmn. adv. com., 1984-90, Huron U., 1990-97, S.F. Washington H.S. Sports Heritage 1889-98; spkr. in field. Author: American Business, 2005; contbr. articles to popular mags. Past bd. dirs. Jr. Achievement, United Way, Sioux Vocat. Sch. Handicapped; past mem. Gov.'s Adv. Bd. Cmty. Adult Manpower Planning; chmn. bus. edn. adv. com. Sioux Falls Pub. Schs., 1982-85; chmn. adv. com. South East Area Vocat. Sch., 1982-85; mem. alumnae bd. Augustana Coll., 1985-88. Capt. USMC, 1943-46, 50-52, WWII, Korea. Recipient USMC Letter of Commendation award, 1944, Liberty Bell award S.D. Bar Assn., 1967, Sch. Bd. award NEA/Thom McAn Shoe Corp., 1966, S.D. Unsung Heroes Edn. Recognition award Sta. KSFV-TV, 1998; named Boss of Yr., Sioux Falls, 1977. Mem. NEA (life, Pacemaker award), Am. Soc. Pers. Adminstrn. (accredited pers. mgr., profl. human resources, life, S.D. dist. dir. 1980-84), Am. Trucking Assn. (pub. rels. coun.), S.D. Edn. Assn. (life), Sioux Falls Pers. Assn. (past pres.), Sales and Mktg. Club Sioux Falls, Sioux Falls Traffic Club, VFW (life, Nat. Polit. Action Recognition award 1990), Am. Legion, Toastmasters (past gov. dist. 41, Disting. Toastmaster award, Outstanding Toastmaster award dist. 41, Hall of Fame 1977), Elks. Republican. Roman Catholic. Died June 25, 2006.

TAPLEY, MERLE PARKER, writer, editor, photographer, printer; b. West Brooksville, Maine, Feb. 10, 1920; s. Jerome Perkins and Ada Littlefield (Mills) T.; m. Dorothy Lina Parker, June 5, 1948. Cert. in journalism U. Chgo., 1944; cert. in photography U. Mich., 1946; A.S., U. Hartford, 1962, B.A. in English, 1966. Tech. writer Hamilton Standard, Windsor Locks, Conn., 1962-68; sr. author, editor, 1968-83; pres. People-to-People Communications, South Windsor, Conn., 1983—; editor Scottish Rite Pubs., Hartford, Conn., 1960—; dir. publs. and pub. relations Conn. state staff Order of DeMolay, 1979—. Editor FAMA, 1984—, Nutmeg Digest, 1980—, Connecticut Square & Compasses, 1988—. Contbr. hist. research articles to various publs. Past chmn. Republican Orgn., South Windsor; past bd. dirs. March of Dimes, South Windsor; past mem. Indsl. Devel. Commn., South Windsor; exec. sec.-treas. Northeast Conf. on Edn. and Libraries, 1975—. Served with U.S. Army, 1943-45. Recipient Pierpont Edwards medal Grand Lodge Conn., Masons, 1964; Christopher Champlin medal Grand Lodge R.I., Masons, 1972; Legion of Honor, Internat. Supreme Council DeMolay, 1983 (actice 1988); named Master of Research, Philosophic Lodge of Research, Hartford, Conn., 1980. Mem. Soc. Tech. Writers and Pubs. (sr.), Conn. Soc. Profl. Communicators, Hamilton Standard Retirees Conn. (v.p. 1985, pres. 1987-88). Congregationalist. Lodge: Masons (master 1955, grand master 1971). Avocations: golf; travel; photography; geneology. Home: South Windsor, Conn. Died June 27, 2006.

TARAS, ARNOLD ELIOT, management consultant; b. N.Y.C., Oct. 5, 1935; s. David William and Lillian M. (Peckett) T.; student Yale U., 1952-53; B.A., U. Vt., 1956, M.S., 1957; M.B.A., NYU, 1958; m. Madeleine J. Baumgarten, June 24, 1958; children— Jeffrey Mark, Debra Joy, Buffy Ann. Vice pres., gen. mgr. Diamond Tool Inc., N.Y.C., 1958-65; v.p. Law Engring. Testing Co., Atlanta, 1965-68; pres., chief exec. officer Piedmont Devel. Co., Atlanta, 1968-71; pres., chief exec. officer Crow, Pope and Land Enterprises, Atlanta, 1971-76; pres. Diversified Investment Assos., Atlanta, 1976-79; mng. partner Barton Sans Internat., Atlanta, 1979-83; pres. Taras Assocs. Inc., Atlanta, 1983—; dir. Piedmont Devel. Co., Law Engring; instr. Ga. State U. Div. pres. United Way, Atlanta, 1974-75. Recipient Service commendation Nat. Assn. Homebuilders, Dept. Def. Mem. Urban Land Inst., Am. Land Devel. Assn., Internat. Council Shopping Centers, Nat. Assn. Homebuilders, Inst. Real Estate Mgmt., Atlanta Apt. Owners Assn. Republican. Clubs: Atlanta City; Lan Mar Yacht; Chatahoochie Plantation; B'nai B'rith. Home: Marietta, Ga. Died June 28, 2006.

TARRANT, ROBERT FRANK, soil science educator, researcher; b. Portland, Oreg., Mar. 11, 1918; s. Frank A. and Vera Leona (Tibbils) T.; m. Jean Inez Horton, Sept. 20, 1941; children: Christopher R., Susan J., Brian H., Stephanie A. Tarrant Martin. BS, Oreg. State U., 1941. Soil scientist USDA Pacific N.W. Forest Research Sta., Portland, 1946-71, asst. dir., 1971-74, dep. dir., 1975, dir., 1975-79; prof. forest scis. Oreg. State U., Corvallis, from 1979. Co-editor: The Biology of Alder, 1968, From the Forest to the Sea, 1988, Biology and Management of Red Alder, 1994; contbr. articles, reports to profl. jours. Bd. dirs. Oreg. Easter Seal Soc., Portland, 1969-75, pres., 1971-73. Served to lt. comdr. USN, 1942-45, ETO, PTO, also 1950-52. Recipient Superior Svc. award USDA, Washington, 1971, Tarrant Rsch. fellowship Oreg. State U., 1993—. Mem. N.W. Sci. Assn. (hon. life), Oreg. Hardwoods Commn., Sigma Xi Rsch. Soc. Episcopalian. Home: Corvallis, Oreg. Died Apr. 6, 2006.

TARRANTS, WILLIAM EUGENE, retired federal official; b. Liberty, Mo., Dec. 9, 1927; s. Joseph Eugene and Mildred Jane (Wright) Tarrants; m. Mary Jo Edman, Jan. 19, 1952 (div. 1981); children: James Timothy, Jennifer Lynn; m. Loma D. Lundberg, Sept. 24, 1988; stepchildren: David Murphy, Christine Walls, Janelle McCrea. B in Indsl. Engring., Ohio State U., 1951; MS in Indsl. Engring., 1959; PhD, NYU, 1963. Instr. indsl. engring. Ohio State U., Columbus, 1958-59; asst. prof., research assoc. N.Y.U., 1959-64; chief accident research div. Bur. Labor Stats., US Dept. Labor, Washington, 1964-67; dir. manpower devel. div. Nat. Hwy. Traffic Safety Adminstrn., Dept. Transp., 1967-80; chief scientist Office of Program and Demonstration Evaluation, 1980-84; program analyst Office of Occupant Protection, 1984-87, program analyst evaluation staff, 1987-90, chmn. sci. and tech. info. adv. bd., 1984-91. Cons. safety program evaluation Indsl. Commn. Ohio, 1959; instr. Johns Hopkins U., 1984—91, U. Md., 1991—92; planning and adminstrn. transp. safety mem. Transp. Rsch. Bd., NAS; mem. exec. com. Related Accreditation Commn., from 1994; accreditation bd. Engring. and Tech., Inc., from 1994. Co-author: A Selected Bibliography of Reference Materials in Safety Engineering and Related Fields, 1967, Selected Readings in Safety, 1973, Readings in Industrial Accident Prevention, 1980, Dictionary of Terms Used in the Safety Profession, 1971, Measurement of Safety Performance, 1980, Handbook of Occupational Safety and Health, 1987; contbr. articles to profl. jours.; mem. editl. bd. Jour. Safety Rsch., Accident Analysis and Prevention; editor-in-chief: Traffic Safety Evaluation Rsch. Rev. Region 8 rep. to bd. trustees E. Coast Conf., 1986—92; trustee, ch. chmn. Evang. Covent Ch., 1976—80, 1984—88. Capt. USAF, 1951—57. Named to Safety and Health Hall of Fame Internat., 1990; recipient Founder's Day award, NYU, 1963, 1st pl., Nat. Tech. Paper Awards, 1961, 1963, 1967, cert. for outstanding performance, Nat. Hwy. Traffic Safety Adminstrn., 1973, 1986, Disting. Svc. to Safety award, Nat. Safety Coun., 1989, Disting. Career Svc. award, U.S. Dept. of Transp., 1990. Fellow: Am. Soc. Safety Engrs. (dir., v.p. rsch. and tech. devel., pres. 1977—78, chmn. acad. accreditation coun. 1978—97, chmn. profl. and ednl. stds. com. from 1997, fellow rev. bd. 1980—88, Pres.'s award 1996); mem.: AAAS, Nat. Safety Coun. (chmn. rsch. proejcts com. 1973—78, mem. exec. com. indsl. conf. 1977—78, Disting. Svc. award 1989), Soc. Risk Analysis, Am. Nat. Stds. Inst. (mem. stds. com.), Vets. Safety, Evaluation Rsch. Soc., Sys. Safety Soc., Human Factors Soc., Am. Inst. Indsl. Engrs., Am. Soc. Safety Rsch. (trsutee), Kappa Delta Pi, Alpha Pi Mu. Home: Crownsville, Md. Died Oct. 13, 2007.

TATE, FREDERICK GEORGE, lawyer; b. Boston, Feb. 9, 1925; s. Wills Hill and Nellie (Mytson) T.; m. Janice O'Brien Shatton, Sept. 23, 1988; 1 child by previous marriage, Thomas. AB magna cum laude, Brown U., 1951; JD, Harvard U., 1954. Bar: N.Y. 1955, U.S. Dist. Ct. (so. and ea. dists) N.Y. 1955, U.S. Ct. Appeals (2d cir.) 1975. Assoc. Rogers & Wells, NYC, 1954-67, ptnr., 1968-92, sr. counsel, from 1993. Employee Marshall Plan, OSR, Paris, 1948-49; Served as sgt. USMC, 1942-46, PTO. Mem. ABA (bus. law sect.), Assn. of Bar of City of N.Y., Am. Arbitration Assn. (com. panel), Phi Beta Kappa. Clubs: Harvard (N.Y.C.). Democrat. Episcopalian. Avocations: art, music, theater, reading, travel. Home: Washington, DC. Died Feb. 27, 2006.

TATUM, GORDON, JR., fine arts editor, critic; b. Mobile, Ala., Aug. 8, 1940; s. Gordon Sr. and Maggie Virginia (Wright) T.; m. Katherine Alexandra Kosko, Aug. 29, 1970; children: Sheldon Parrish, Sterling Andrew. Student, Birmingham So. Coll., 1958-60, U. South Ala., 1969. Editor, reporter, critic Mobile (Ala.) Press Register, from 1961. Regional critic Met. Opera News, N.Y.C., 1987—. Mem. adv. bd. Saenger Theater USA Series, Mobile, 1989—; pres. Oakleigh Garden Dist. Hist. Soc., Mobile, 1973-74; soloist St. Paul's Episcopal Ch., Mobile, 1961-85, Birmingham Symphony Pops Orch., 1960, Mobile Symphony Orch., 1967, Mobile Opera, 1968, St. Paul's Choral Soc., 1965-70; mem. chorus Mobile Opera, 1955, 62, 67, 69; actor Joe Jefferson Players, Mobile, 1958, 61-63, Mobile Theater Guild, 1961-63; bd. dirs. Symphonic Pops Band, Mobile, 1976—, Hist. Mobile Preservation Soc., 1990—, Mobile Mental Health, September Celebration Festival of the Arts, 1989—. Recipient Govs. Arts award Ala. State Arts Coun., 1982. Mem. Ala. Fedn. Music Clubs (bd. dirs.). Avocations: historic preservation, gardening, church work. Home: Mobile, Ala. Died Dec. 2, 2006.

TAUBE, HENRY, chemistry professor; b. Sask., Can., Nov. 30, 1915; arrived in U.S., 1937, naturalized, 1942; s. Samuel and Albertina (Tiledetski) Taube; m. Mary Alice Wesche, Nov. 27, 1952; children: Linda, Marianna, Heinrich, Karl. BS, U. Sask., 1935, MS, 1937, LLD, 1973; PhD, U. Calif., 1940; PhD (hon.), Hebrew U. of Jerusalem, 1979; DSc (hon.), U. Chgo., 1983, Poly. Inst., NYC, 1984, SUNY, 1985, U. Guelph, 1987, Seton Hall U., 1988, Lajos Kossuth U. Debrecen, Hungary, 1988; DSc, Northwestern U., 1990; DSc (hon.), U. Athens, 1993. Instr. U. Calif., Berkeley, 1940—41; instr., asst. prof. Cornell U., 1941—46; faculty U. Chgo., 1946—62, prof., 1952—62, chmn. dept. chemistry, 1955—59; prof. chemistry Stanford U., 1962—86, chmn. dept. chemistry, 1972—74, 1978—79, Marguerite Blake Wilbur prof., 1976; prof. emeritus Stanford U, 1986—2005. Baker lectr. Cornell U., 1965; cons. Catalytica Assocs., Inc., Mountain View, Calif. Contbr. articles to profl. jours. Recipient Chandler medal, Columbia U., 1964, F. P. Dwyer medal, U. NSW, 1973, Nat. medal of sci., 1976—77, Excellence in Grad. Tchg. and Innovative Sci. award, Allied Chem., 1979, Nobel prize in chemistry, 1983, Bailar medal, U. Ill., 1983, award in chemistry, Robert A. Welch Found., 1983, Disting. Achievement award, Internat. Precious Metals Inst., 1986, Merit award, Brazilian Order of Sci., 1994; fellow, Guggenheim, 1949, 1955. Fellow: Royal Soc. Can. (hon.), Indian Chem. Soc. (hon.), Royal Soc. Chemistry (hon.); mem.: NAS (award in chem. scis. 1983), Engring. Acad. Japan (fgn. assoc.), Royal Soc. (fgn. mem.), Royal Danish Acad. Scis. and Letters, Finnish Acad. Sci. and Letters (fgn. mem.), Am. Philos. Soc., Royal Physiographical Soc. of Lund, Am. Chem. Soc. (award for nuclear applications in chemistry 1955, Harrison Howe award, Rochester sect. 1960, John Gamble Kirkwood award, New Haven sect. 1966, Disting. Svc. in Advancement Inorganic Chemistry award 1967, Nichols medal 1971, Willard Gibbs medal, Chgo. sect. 1971, T.W. Richards medal, Northeastern sect. 1980—81, Monsanto Co. award in inorganic chemistry 1981, Linus Pauling award, Puget Sound sect. 1981, Priestley medal 1985, Oesper award, Cinn. sect. 1986, G.M. Kosolapoff award, Auburn sect. 1990), Australian Acad. Scis. (corr.), Brazilian Acad. Scis. (corr.), Am. Acad. Arts and Scis. (PR) (corr.), Chem. Soc. Japan (hon.), Hungarian Acad. Scis. (hon.), Can. Soc. Chemistry (hon.), Coll. Chemists of Catalonia and Beleares (hon.), Sigma Xi, Phi Beta Kappa, Phi Lambda Upsilon (hon.). Died Nov. 16, 2005.

TAUBER, SELMO, mathematics educator, structural engineer; b. Shang-Hai, China, Aug. 24, 1920; came to U.S., 1957; s. Arthur and Dora (Stein) T.; m. Edith Ferrera, Dec. 21, 1950; 1 child, Louis A. Diploma civil engring., Ecole Française, Beyrouth, Lebanon, 1943; Lic. ès-Sci., U. Lyon, France, 1947; Ph.D., U. Vienna, Austria, 1950. Registered profl. engr., Oreg. Educator, 1943-57; instr. math. Kans. U., Lawrence, 1957-58, asst. prof., 1958-59; assoc. prof. Portland State U., 1959-63, prof., 1963—; cons. engring. firms. Author: Introduction Practical Physics, 1951, 2d edit., 1954; Systems Analysis, 1969. Contbr. articles in field to profl. jours. Home: Portland, Oreg. Died Feb. 10, 2007.

TAYLOR, GEORGE FARRELL, bank executive; b. Bridgeport, Conn., July 18, 1932; s. George and Margaret (Farrell) T.; m. Margaret Broderick, June 10, 1967. BS in Econs., U. Bridgeport, 1955; MBA, NYU, 1961. Trust investment officer Citytrust Bancorp, Inc., Bridgeport, 1960-64, treas., 1964-74, exec. v.p., 1974-76, chief fin. officer, vice chmn. bd., 1976-79, pres., chief exec. officer, 1979-80, chmn., chief exec. officer, from 1980. Trustee U. Bridgeport; bd. dirs. St. Vincent's Med. Ctr., Bridgeport. Mem. Nat. Assn. Bus. Economists, Hartford Soc. Fin. Analysts. Roman Catholic. Home: Fairfield, Conn. Died May 24, 2006.

TAYLOR, HELEN JEAN, health service administrator; b. Dixonville, Pa., May 14, 1927; d. Robert Clyde and Helen (Coalmer) Sickenberger, R.N., Jefferson Med. Coll., 1948; BA in Health Edn., Calif. State U., Northridge, 1971, MS in Health Sci., 1976; postgrad. UCLA, 1978 U. So. Calif., 1982—; 1 child, Brian Robert. Staff nurse Santa Monica Hosp., Calif., 1948-51; sch. nurse St. Martin's in the Fields, Canoga Park, Calif., 1963-65; sch. nurse, health educator, tchr., dist. health supr. William S. Hart Union HS Dist., Newhall, Calif., 1971-79; adminstr. Mgmt. Health Services, Glendale Unified Sch. Dist., 1979—, Calif.; cons. AIMS Cahill Films, Bur. Indsl. Edn., Calif. Dept. Edn.; vol. clinic nurse Intensive Vaccination Program, LA County Health Dept., 1961-63; chmn. Maternal, Child, Adolescent Health Coun., North Area, LA County Health Dept., 1983-84. Mem. Glendale Cmty. Coordinating Coun., v.p., 1982-83; active ARC Disaster Nursing; mem. Am. Lung Assn.'s Children Health Com., chmn. substance abuse prevention com., 1983-84; active Tree People (Calif. Conservation project). Mem. Assn. of Calif. Sch. Adminstrs., Calif. Sch. Nurses Orgn., LA County Sch. Nurses Assn., Glendale Mgmt. Assn., Calif. State U., Northridge Alumni Assn., Jefferson Med. Coll. Nurses' Alumni Assn., Delta Kappa Gamma. Died Apr. 22, 2006.

TAYLOR, HENRY FULLER, research laboratory administrator; b. Fort Worth, Sept. 27, 1940; s. Henry Fuller and Delmer Doris (Hunley) T.; m. Clara Melinda Rikard, Aug. 18, 1967; children— Eric, Andrew, Philip BA, Rice U., 1962, MA, 1965, PhD, 1967. Physicist Naval Electronics Lab. Ctr., San Diego, 1967-78; prin. scientist Rockwell Internat., Thousand Oaks, Calif., 1978-80; br. head Naval Research Lab., Washington, from 1980. Recipient ann. sci. achievement award Naval Electronics Lab. Ctr., 1974 Fellow IEEE, Optical Soc. Am.; mem. Am. Soc. Naval Engrs. (Solberg award 1975), Am. Phys. Soc. Died Apr. 24, 2006.

TAYLOR, JAMES MARSHALL, food products executive; b. MorganField, Ky., Dec. 13, 1929; s. James Mansfield and Hester Louise (Marshall) T.; m. Pauline Elizabeth Kasper, Feb. 1, 1959; children: Christopher David, Timothy Michael. BSc, U. Louisville, 1958, MBA, 1963. Asst. treas. Savannah (Ga.) Foods and Indys., 1968-72, asst. v.p. corp. devel., 1972-75, v.p. corp. devel., 1975-88, sr. v.p. adminstrn., from 1988. Served to cpl. U.S. Army, 1951-53. Mem.: Chatham, Marswood. Republican. Avocations: golf, lepidopterist. Home: Savannah, Ga. Died June 1, 2006.

TAYLOR, JOHN FRANK, II, lawyer; b. Fort Worth, May 26, 1939; s. Frank F. and Mildred (Mitchell) T.; m. Diane S. Settle, March 22, 1968; children: John F. III, Alicia L. BA, Texas Christian Univ., 1965; LLB, Baylor Univ., 1968. Bar: Tex., U.S. Dist. Ct. (no. dist.) Tex. 1969, U.S. Ct. Appeals (5th cir.) 1970. Ptnr. Cantey & Hanger, L.L.P., Ft. Worth, from 1968. Bd. dirs. Am. Ice Machines, Inc. Ft. Worth, Texas. Mem. Phi Delta Phi. Died Mar. 30, 2006.

TAYLOR, MARY ALICE, bank executive; b. West Point, Miss., Feb. 11, 1950; d. James and Mary Alice (Talbot) Wooten; m. Robert Glenn Taylor, Apr. 28; children: Mary Carole, Emily Cristen. BA in Bus., Miss. State U., 1971; LHD (hon.), So. Coll. Optometry, 1994. CPA. Sr. acct. Shell Oil Co., New Orleans, 1971-73; contr. Cook Industries, Memphis, Tenn., 1973-77; fin. planning mgr. Northern Telecom., Memphis, 1977-80; sr. mgmt. info. systems Fed. Express Corp., Memphis, 1980-82, mgr. fin., 1982-83, mng. dir. bus. svc. ctr. divsn., 1983-85, v.p. logistics, 1985-88, v.p. so. region ground ops., 1988-91, sr. v.p. ctrl. support svcs., 1991-94, sr. v.p. U.S. and Can., 1994-97; corp. exec. v.p. global ops. and tech. Citibank, NYC, from 1997. Bd. dirs. Perrigo Co., Allegan, Mich., Autodesk, San Rafael, Calif., Allstate Corp., Chgo. Exec. dir. Chikasaw Coun. Boy Scouts Am., Memphis; mem. external rsch. adv. com. Miss. State U., mem. found. bd.; mem. exec. adv. bd. Transp. Studies MIT. Roman Catholic. Home: Fairhope, Ala. Died Nov. 24, 2006.

TAYLOR, THEODORE LANGHANS, retired author; b. Statesville, NC, June 23, 1921; s. Edward Riley and Elnora Alma (Langhans) T.; m. Gweneth Ann Goodwin, Oct. 25, 1946; children: Mark, Wendy, Michael; m. Flora Gray Schoenleber, Apr. 18, 1981. Student, Fork Union Mil. Acad., 1939-40, U.S. Mcht. Marine Acad., 1942-44. Reporter Portsmouth (Va.) Star, 1941-42, Bluefield (W.Va.) News, 1946-47; sportswriter NBC-Radio, NYC, 1942; asst. dir. pub. relations N.Y. U., 1947-48; dir. pub. relations YMCA Schs. and Colls., NYC, 1948-50; publicist Paramount Pictures, Hollywood, Calif., 1955-56; assoc. producer Perlberg-Seaton Prodns., Hollywood, 1956-61; ret., 1961. Free lance writer 1961—; author: The Magnificent Mitscher, 1954, Fire on the Beaches, 1957, People Who Make Movies, 1968, The Cay, 1969 (Jane Addam's Children's Book award 1970), The Children's War, 1971, Air Raid: Pearl Harbor, 1971, The Maldonado Miracle, 1973, Rebellion Town, 1973, Showdown, 1973, Teetoncey, 1974, Teetoncey and Ben O'Neal, 1975, Battle in the Arctic Seas, 1976, The Odyssey of Ben O'Neal, 1977, A Shepherd Watches, A Shepherd Sings, 1977, Jule, 1979, Battle of Midway Island, 1981, The Trouble with Tuck, 1981, Sweet Friday Island, 1981, HMS Hood vs Bismarck, 1982, Battle in the English Channel, 1983, The Cats of Shambala, Rocket Island, 1985, Walking Up a Rainbow, 1986, The Stalker, 1987, The Hostage, 1988, Monocolo, 1989, Sniper, 1989, Tuck Triumphant, 1991, The Wierdo, 1991, Maria, 1992, To Kill the Leopard, 1993, Timothy of the Cay, 1993, The Bomb, 1995, Rogue Wave, 1996, The Flight of Jesse Leroy Brown, 1998, A Sailor Returns, 2000, The Boy Who Could Fly Without A Motor, 2002, Lord of The Kill, 2002, Hello, Artic, 2002, Ice Drift, 2005, Making Love to Typewriters, 2005, Billy the Kid, 2005, The Magnificent Mitscher, 2006. Served with USNR, 1945-46, 50-55. Recipient Lewis Carroll Shelf award, 1970, Silver medal Commonwealth Club, 1970, Best Book award So. Calif. Coun. on Children's Lit., 1970, Best Book award U. Calif. at Irvine, 1970, 74, Best Non-Fiction award Western Writers Am., 1977, Young Reader's Medal Calif. Reading Assn., 1984, 92, Edgar Allan Poe award, 1992, Utah Young Adult Book award, 1993, Md. Children's Book award, 1994, Scott O'Dell Best Hist. Fiction award, 1995, The Kerlan Body of Work award, 1997. Mem. Calif. Writers Guild, Acad. Motion Picture Arts and Scis., Screen Writers Guild. Republican. Lutheran. Died Oct. 26, 2006.

TAYLOR, WAYNE FLETCHER, lawyer; b. Evansville, Ind., Jan. 23, 1943; s. Fletcher S. and Dortha Mae (Schnute) T.; m. Mary Sue Stephens, June 13, 1965; children: Wayne F. Jr., Deborah G. BBA, Vanderbilt U., 1965, JD, 1968. Bar: Tenn. 1968, Ohio 1970. Assoc. Dearborn Berry and Warner, Nashville, 1968-69; asst. corp. counsel The Midland Co., Cin., 1969-74, Emery Industries Inc., Cin., 1974-78; sec., corp. counsel Cin. Milacron Inc., 1978-90, v.p., gen. counsel, sec., from 1990. Republican. Avocations: photography, sports, woodworking, fishing, gardening. Home: Cincinnati, Ohio. Died Aug. 27, 2006.

TAYLOR, WILLIAM AL, church administrator; b. Danville, Va., Sept. 26, 1938; s. Preston Floyd and Helen Elizabeth (Doss) T.; m. Brenda Flo Owen, June 4, 1961 (dec. 1996); children: Fawnia Rae Ricks, Albert Todd, Athena Dawn Jarman; m. Norma S. Pierce, June 28, 1997. AA, Lee Coll., 1957; postgrad., U. Calif., Santa Barbara, 1980. Br. mgr. Ency. Britannica, Greensboro, NC, 1960-62, divsn. trainer Mpls., 1963, dist. mgr. Omaha, 1964-72; adminstrv. asst. Forward in Faith Internat. Broadcast, Cleveland, Tenn., 1972-80; gen. mgr. Sta. WQNE-FM, Cleveland, from 1980; cons. stewardship Ch. of God Internat. Offices, Cleveland, 1980—2004. Pres. Pathway Credit Union, Cleveland, 1985-2005, Vision Found., Cleveland, 1985—, exec. dir., 1979-80; chmn. Internat. Commn. on Prayer, Cleveland, 1986—. Author: Proving God, 1991, Days of Heaven on Earth, 1993, Stewardship Masterplanning, 1993, The Power of Vision, 2003. Pres. Clean Water Soc., Gastonia, N.C., 1974-75; speaker Citizens Against Legalized Liquor, Bradley County, Tenn., 1973, 75; advisor Mothers on March, Cleveland, 1976; active Nat. Conf. on Drug Abuse, Washington, 1978; master of ceremonies Nat. Religious Leaders Conf. on Alcohol and Drug Abuse, Indpls., 1979; pres. Ch. of God Found., 2002. Recipient Mass Communications award Ch. of God Media Ministries, 1980, Stephen award Ch. of God Lay Ministries, 1990. Mem. Nat. Assn. Evangelicals (bd. adminstrs. 1985-98, chmn. stewardship commn. 1985-89), Christian Stewardship Assn. (bd. dirs. 1990-96, nat. prayer com. 1999—, Best of the Best Faculty award 1999, Outstanding Stewardship Profl. award 2000). Mem. Ch. Of God. Avocations: flying, travel, racquetball. Home: Cleveland, Tenn. Died Apr. 29, 2007.

TEAGUE, BARRY ELVIN, lawyer; b. Dayton, Ohio, Mar. 10, 1944; s. Arthur Leo and Mary Catherine (Pendley) T.; m. Dianne Duke, Dec. 30, 1966; children: Matthew Patrick, William Clay. BA, Asbury Coll., 1966; JD, Jones Law Sch., 1971. Bar: Ala. 1972. Tchr., coach Montgomery County (Ala.) Sch. System, 1966-68, tchr., 1968-71; dep. clk. U.S. Dist. Ct., Middle Dist., Ala., 1971-73; asst. atty. gen. Ala., 1973-74; chief dep. dist. atty. 15th Jud. Circuit Ala., 1974-77; U.S. atty. for Middle Dist. Ala., 1977-81; mem. Ala. senate, 1983; spl. asst. atty. gen. State of Ala., 1983-87; pvt. practice Montgomery, Ala., from 1981. Mem. Fed. Bar Assn. Ala. Bar Assn., Montgomery County Bar Assn. (dir. young lawyers sect.), Montgomery Fed. Bar Assn. (pres. 1980-81), Ala. Jr. C. of C. (state govt. affairs chmn.), Montgomery Jr. C. of C. (dir., legal counsel) Presbyterian. Died July 23, 2006.

TEEM, JOHN MCCORKLE, retired association executive; b. Springfield, Mo., July 23, 1925; s. Lon Vester and Judith (McCorkle) T.; m. Sylvia Victoria Konvicka; children— Judith Majka Teem Donald, Paul Norman AB, Harvard U., 1949, MA, 1951, PhD, 1954. Sr. research fellow Calif. Inst. Tech., Pasadena, 1954-60; v.p., chief scientist Electro Optical Systems, Pasadena, 1960-67; dir. tech. staff, research and devel. Xerox Corp., Stamford, Conn., 1967-72; asst. gen. mgr., dir. phys. research AEC, Washington, 1973-75; asst. adminstr. ERDA, Washington, 1975-76; pres. Assn. Univs. for Research in Astronomy, Washington, 1977-86. Served with U.S. Army, 1943-46 Recipient Disting. Service medal AEC, 1975; named Fairchild Disting. scholar Calif. Inst. Tech., 1976-77 Fellow AAAS; mem. Am. Astron. Soc. Democrat. Roman Catholic. Home: Arlington, Va. Died Mar. 5, 2007.

TEETER, KARL VAN DUYN, retired linguistic scientist, educator; b. Berkeley, Calif., Mar. 2, 1929; s. Charles Edwin and Lura May (Shaffner) T.; m. Anita Maria Bonacorsi, Aug. 25, 1951; children— Katharine Emilie, Judith Ann, Teresa Maria, Martha Elisabeth. AB in Oriental Langs. with highest honors, U. Calif., Berkeley, 1959, PhD Linguistics, 1962; AM (hon.), Harvard U., 1966. From instr. to prof. linguistics Harvard U., 1962-89, prof. emeritus, from 1989, chmn. dept. linguistics, 1966-69, 70-71, 77-78. Assoc. Kirkland Ho., Harvard U., 1977-82, fellow, 1983-89, hon. assoc., 1989—; guest rsch. fellow Rsch. Inst. Logopedics and Phoniatrics, Faculty of Medicine, Tokyo U., 1969-70; mem. summer faculty U. Mich., 1962, UCLA, 1966, U. N.C., 1972. Author: The Wiyot Language, 1964, Wiyot Handbook, I and II, 1993; editor: In Memoriam Peter Lewis Paul, 1902-89, 1993. Bd. dirs. Mass. Found. for Humanities and Pub. Policy, 1984-90, exec. com., 1985-89; bd. dirs. New Eng. Found. for Humanities, 1986-93; active New Eng. Native Am. Inst., 1992—. Served with AUS, 1946, 51-54. Fulbright rsch. fellow Japan, 1969-70, Jr. fellow Soc. of Fellows Harvard U., 1959-62; NSF grantee, 1990—. Mem. Linguistic Soc. Am. (life mem., long range planning com. 1969-73, lang. rev. com. 1980-82), Soc. Study Indigenous Langs. of the Ams. (v.p. 1998, pres. 1999), N.Am. Assn. for the Historiography of Linguistics (nominating com. 1998—), Phi Beta Kappa, Sigma Xi. Home: Cambridge, Mass. Died Apr. 20, 2007.

TEEVAN, RICHARD COLLIER, retired psychology professor; b. Shelton, Conn., June 12, 1919; s. Daniel Joseph and Elizabeth (Halliwell) T.; m. Virginia Agnes Stehle, July 28, 1945; children— Jan Elizabeth, Kim Ellen, Clay Collier, Allison Tracy. BA, Wesleyan U., Middletown, Conn., 1951; MA, U. Mich., 1952, PhD, 1955. Rubber buffer Sponge Rubber Product Co., Derby, Conn., 1939-41; with U. Mich., 1951-57, teaching fellow, 1951-53, instr., 1953-57; asst. prof. Smith Coll., 1957 60; assoc. prof. Bucknell U., 1960-64, prof., 1964-69; chmn psychology, prof. to prof. emeritus SUNY-Albany, from 1969 pres. Teevan Assocs., Cons., from 1991. Cons. on coll. teaching 1989—. Author: Reinforcement, 1961, Instinct, 1961, Colo Vision, 1961, Measuring Human Motivation, 1962, Theories o Motivation in Learning, 1964, Theories of Motivation in Per sonality and Social Psychology, 1964, Motivation, 1967, Fear o Failure, 1969, Readings in Elementary Psychology, 1973 contbr. articles to sci. jours. Served to capt. AUS, 1941-47 prisoner of war 1943-45, Ger. Office Naval Research grantee 1958-72; recipient Lindbach award Bucknell U., 1966 Mem AAAS, AAUP, Am. Psychol. Assn. (Disting. visitor 1981-85 Eastern Psychol. Assn., Phi Beta Kappa, Sigma Xi. Died June 2006.

TEITLER, PAUL HUGH, judge; b. NYC, Apr. 30, 1935; s Jules R. and Sarah (Cheson) T.; m. Lenore S. Kirshner, Sept. 29 1972; children: Avery Scott, Brooke Dara. BA, NYU, 1956; JD Bklyn. Law Sch., 1959. Bar: N.Y. 1960, U.S. Dist Ct. (ea. an so. dists.) N.Y. 1971, U.S. Dist. Ct. (no. dist.) Tex. 1979, U.S Supreme Ct. 1979. Ptnr. Teitler & Teitler, Bklyn., 1960-1974 chief judge HHS, Camden, N.J., 1974-85; dist. chief judge Dep Labor, Camden, 1985-87. Adminstrv. law judge, N.Y.C., 1970 74; mem. jud. adminstrn. div. Nat. Conf. Adminstrv. Law Judges, 1987. Mem. prof. ethics com. Bklyn. Bar Assn., 1970 74. Mem. ABA (exec. com. 1982—), Assn. Adminstrv. Law Judges (jud. adminstrn. div., bd. dirs region II 1980-85). Lodges Masons (dist. dep. grand master 1971-72, grand standard beare 1973-74), Assn. Kings (2d dist. pres., charities fund pres. Tuscan #704 (master 1969). Home: Mount Laurel, NJ. Die May 10, 2007.

TELESCA, FRANCIS EUGENE, architect; b. Dunmore, Pa Oct. 22, 1921; s. Joseph J. and Bernetta (Bocchiccio) T children: Celeste Ann Sullivan, Anthony, Francis Eugene (Gino), Tina Lee; m. Alyce G. Wuenstel, July 28, 1992. B.Arch summa cum laude, Catholic U. Am., 1953. Designer-draftsman architect various archtl. and engring. firms, Washington an Miami, Fla., 1951-59; pvt. practice architecture Miami, 1959 63; pres. Greenleaf/Telesca, engrs., planners and architect Miami, 1964-85; exec. v.p. Genesis III, Miami Lakes, Fla 1985-87; chief programming Miami Internat. Airport, fro 1987. Dir. Greenleaf Enterprises, Inc., Bonefish Towers, Inc mem. Nat. Com. Architecture for Commerce and Industr 1965-66, Fla. Planning and Zoning Assn., 1960—, Met. Dad County Uniform Code Enforcement Com., 1963-64; bd. dir South Fla. Inter-Profl. Council, 1965; planning com. U. Mian Inst. Urban Affairs, 1965; adv. com. City Miami Coconut Grov Zoning, 1965; adv. com. dept. architecture and bldg. constr Miami Dade Jr. Coll., 1966. (award of merit Fla. chpt. AIA f Miami Lakes Sr. High Sch., award of excellence for 20th S Transfer Sta., Dade County 1980, Archtl. award of excellenc for Hangar 2, Miami Internat. Airport, Am. Inst. Steel Constr 1974, also Grand Conceptor award Am. Cons. Engrs. Counc 1974, award of excellence for Primera Casa, Fla. Internat. U Fla. Concrete and Products Assn. 1973, award for outstandin concrete structure for Acad. One Bldg., Fla. Internat. U. 1980 Past pres., dir. Coconut Grove Assn. (arts festival), Grove Hous (sch. and marketplace for Fla. craftsmen). Served with AUS 1940-45, 50-51. Decorated Bronze Star; recipient Grand Na award Nat. Community Fallout Shelter competition (shoppin center), 1964 Mem. AIA (pres. Fla. South chpt. 1965, dir. Fl 1966-69), Coconut Grove C. of C. (past pres., dir.), Great Miami C. of C. (mem. aviation com.), Phi Eta Sigma. Roma Catholic. Home: Miami, Fla. Died Dec. 8, 2005.

TELMOSSÉ, ROBERT DENNIS, marketing and advertisin executive; b. Jersey City, July 17, 1941; s. Emile Oliver an Corine (Giampacaro) T.; children: Gina Marie, David Rober Mgr., pres. Furniture Warehouse, Colorado Springs, Colo.; pre Denver Warehouse, from 1968, chmn. bd., 1979-81; pres chmn. bd. Sta. KILO-FM, Colorado Springs, 1977-84. Owne sr. ptnr. Tel-Moore Mktg.; owner Telmossé Properties; ptn Sibling Leasing Co., Lomas & Assocs., Hals & Beinbruch Va Condos and Vail Income Properties; sr. ptnr. Better Livir Shopping Ctr.; lectr. various clubs and colls.; owner, chief exe officer MEGA-Marts Inc., 1989—. Mem. adv. bd. Jr. Achieve ment, Colorado Springs, 1981—; bd. dirs. Goodwill, 1986-8 Spl. Olympics of So. Colo., 1977-80; fund raising chmn. S Colo. Ronald McDonald House; chmn. Penrose Projec founder, developer SafeChild Project; mem. Pikes Peak Poli Action Com., Pikes Peak council Boy Scouts Am.; former ass fund raising chmn. Easter Seals Telethon; former chmn. S Colo. St. Jude's Childrens Hosp.; active Muscular Dystroph Telethon, 1977—, fund raising for Martin Luther Home; orga nizer event to aid the 1984 Olympics, L.A.; former adv. b mem. Domestic Violence Ctr. Work Out Ltd. program, U. Colo Colorado Springs Art Gallery, Colorado Springs Silver Key S Citizens Orgn.; former bd. dirs. La Casa Contenté, USO; b dirs. Penrose-St. Francis Hosp., 1987—. With USAF, 1960-6 Recipient Free Enterprise award Internat. Salesman With Purpose Clubs, Service to Mankind award Sertoma, Citation Merit Muscular Dystrophy Assn., Citation of Merit St. Jude Hosp., Cache award Pikes Peak Community Coll., 1981, Palm award for outstanding contbn. to the City of Colorado Spring 1986; named Advt. Man of Yr. Dist. 12 Am. Advt. Fedn., 198 ann. celebration named for, S.A. Wilson Sch. Mem. Pikes Pe Advt. Fedn. (Silver medal award 1980), Colo. Home Furnis ings Dealers Assn. (past pres.), Nat. Assn. Home Builder Better Bus. Bur. (exec. bd. Colorado Springs), Colorado Sprin C. of C. (past bd. dirs., past vice chmn. retail and small bu councils, moderator check fraud seminars), Pikes Peak Jayce (hon.), Pikes Peak Apt. Assn., Colorado Springs Exec. Clu Pikes Peak Hill Climb Club, Civitan (Pikes Peak club). Repu lican. Roman Catholic. Home: Colorado Springs, Colo. Di May 23, 2006.

TEMPLETON, JOHN YOUNG, III, retired surgeon, educ tor; b. Portsmouth, Va., July 1, 1917; s. John Young Jr. and Ma Etta (Williams) T.; m. Dorothy Ethelreda Fraley, April 30, 19 (dec. 2005); children: Mary Brem, Frances Etheldra, Doroth Alicia, Richard Bruce. BS, Davidson Coll., 1937; MD, Jeffers Med. Coll., 1941; DSc (hon.), Davidson Coll., 1987; LL (hon.), Jefferson Med. Coll., 1987. Diplomate Am. Bd. Surge

Am. Bd. Thoracic Surgery. From instr. to clin. prof. surgery Jefferson Med. Coll., Phila., 1950-64; prof. surgery U. Pa., Phila., 1964-67, U. Pa. Grad. Sch. Medicine, Phila., 1964-67; Samuel D. Grois prof. surgery Jefferson Med. Coll., Phila., 1969-87, prof. surgery, 1969-87, emeritus prof. surgery, 1987—2007. Trustee Thomas Jefferson U., Phila., 1989-2007 Contbr. over 60 articles to profl. jours. Major MC AUS, 1942-46. Recipient Alumni Achievement award Jefferson Alumni Assn., 1983, Strittmatter award Phila. County Med. Soc., 1992; clin. fellow Am. Cancer Soc., 1951, Damon Runyan Jefferson Hosp., 1952. Fellow Am. Surg. Assn., Am. Assn. Thoracic Surgeons, Am. Coll Surgeons (gov. 1969-73); mem. Pa. Med. Soc. (pres. 1983-84), Pa. Soc. Thoracic Surgery (pres. 1979-80), Phila. County Med. Soc. (pres. 1974-75). Avocations: fishing, hunting, canoeing, boat building. Home: Bryn Mawr, Pa. Died Mar. 27, 2007.

TENNENT, DAVID MADDUX, retired pharmaceutical company executive, consultant; b. Bryn Mawr, Pa., Oct. 2, 1914; s. David Hilt and Esther Margaret (Maddux) T.; m. Martha Alice Meloy, Apr. 21, 1945; children— Isabel Blythe, Meredith Meloy, David Lambie, Charles Maddux. A.B., Yale U., 1936, Ph.D., 1940. Research asst. Yale U., New Haven, 1940-42; research assoc. Merck Inst., Rahway, N.J., 1942-60; asst. dir. research Hess & Clark div. Richardson-Merrell, Inc. (became Hess & Clark div. Rhodia Inc. 1971, now Rhone Poulenc Inc.), Ashland, Ohio, 1960-63, dir. research and devel., 1963-69, v.p. research and devel. Hess & Clark div. Rhodia Inc., Ashland, 1969-75, cons. vet. affairs Rhodia, Inc., N.Y.C., 1975-79. Contbr. articles to profl. sci. jours. Patentee (6) in field. Trustee Ashland Pub. Library; mem. Street Tree Commn., Ashland. Fellow AAAS, Am. Heart Assn. Council on Arteriosclerosis (retired); mem. Am. Soc. Biol. Chemists, Soc. for Exptl. Biology and Medicine (emeritus), Am. Chem. Soc. (emeritus). Republican. Avocations: travel, woodworking, Bridge. Home: Ashland, Ohio. Died Nov. 5, 2006.

TENNEY, DANIEL GLEASON, JR., lawyer; b. NYC, Nov. 5, 1913; s. Daniel Gleason and Marguerite Sedgwick (Smith) T.; m. Constance Lippincott Franchot, Sept. 16, 1939; children— Constance Franchot (Mrs. Peter Allan Rafle), Pamela Marguerite (Mrs. Keith E. Simpson), Alexandra Diane (Mrs. Arthur G. Potts, Jr.), Daniel Gleason III. Grad., Choate Sch., 1931; BA, Yale U., 1935, LL.B., 1938. Bar: N.Y. 1938. Assoc. Milbank, Tweed & Hope, NYC, 1938-42; now ptnr. Milbank, Tweed, Hadley & McCloy. Pres. bd. trustees Green Vale Sch., 1958-62; trustee Choate Sch. Found., 1951-76, pres. bd. trustees, 1967-73; trustee, v.p. ICD Internat. Center for Disabled, N.Y.C., 1953-87; trustee, sec. Trudeau Inst. Inc., Saranac Lake, N.Y., 1968-89, St. Timothy's Sch., 1960-70; trustee Russell Sage Found., 1949-67, vice-chmn., 1955-67; hon. trustee Boys' Club. of N.Y. Served to lt. comdr. USNR, 1942-45. Mem. N.Y. State Bar Assn., Assn. Bar City N.Y. Home: Locust Valley, NY. Died Mar. 28, 2006.

TERRAS, VICTOR, literature and language professor; b. Toltsamaa, Estonia, Jan. 21, 1921; arrived in US, 1952, naturalized, 1956; s. Evald and Elena (Rosenberger) T.; m. Rita Schubert, 1951; 1 child, Alexander. MPhil, U. Tartu, Estonia, 1942; PhD, U. Chgo., 1963. Lectr. U. Tartu, 1943-44; instr. to assoc. prof. U. Ill., Urbana, 1959-64, prof. Slavic langs., 1965-66; prof. U. Wis., Madison, 1966-70; prof. Slavic langs. and comparative lit. Brown U., Providence, 1970-88, prof. emeritus, from 1988. Author: The Young Dostoevsky: A Critical Study, 1969, Belinskij and Russian Literary Criticism, 1974, A Karamazov Companion, 1981, 2d edit. 2002, Vladimir Mayakovsky, 1983; editor: Handbook of Russian Literature, 1984, The Idiot: An Interpretation, 1990, A History of Russian Literature, 1991, Russian Poetry of the Silver Age, 1998, Reading Dostoevsky, 1998. Mem. Am. Assn. Advancement Slavic and East European Studies, Am. Assn. Tchrs. Slavic and East European Langs. (pres. 1981-82), Internat. Dostoevsky Soc. (v.p. 1983—). Home: Chevy Chase, Md. Died Dec. 17, 2006.

TERRIE, HENRY LARKIN, JR., retired educator; b. Charleston, W.Va., Jan. 10, 1921; s. Henry Larkin and Mary Gibson (Hunley) T.; m. Jeanne Margaret Cox, June 12, 1948; children: Henry Larkin III, David Leslie. BA, Yale U., 1943; MA, Princeton U., 1952, PhD, 1955. Instr. English, Phillips Andover Acad., 1948; Instr. English U. Minn., 1948-49; instr. English, Dartmouth Coll., Hanover, N.H., 1952-59, prof., 1959-86, chmn. humanities, 1959-63, chmn. dept. English, 1967-72, assoc. dean of faculty for humanities, 1972-76. Prof. Bread Loaf Sch. English, 1958 Editor: (with A.J. Porter) American Literature, 1964, Henry James: Tales of Art and Life, 1984. contbr. articles to profl. jours. Mem. alumni bd. Yale U., 1964-71. Served to lt. USNR, 1943-46. Mem. MLA, Zeta Psi. Home: Charleston, SC. Died Nov. 1, 2006.

TERRY, ROLAND, architect; b. Seattle, June 2, 1917; s. Clyde Cosper and Florence Ester (Beach) T. BArch, U. Wash., 1941. Registered architect, Wash., Oreg. Prin. Tucker, Shields & Terry, Seattle, 1945-51, Terry & Moore, Seattle, 1952-59, Roland Terry Architect & Assoc., Seattle, 1959-78 and from 87, Terry & Egan Architects, Seattle, 1978-87. Contbr. articles to profl. jours.; numerous awards from instns. mags., 1960-75. Mem. adv. commn. Seattle Ctr., 1963-75. Staff sgt. USAAF, 1942-46. Recipient Legion of Honor award Seattle Ctr., 1988. Mem. AIA (Edward Langley Travel scholar S.Am. 1941-42), Tau Sigma Delta. Episcopalian. Avocations: painting, gardening, sailing, hiking. Died June 8, 2006.

TERWILLIGER, JOHN WILLIAM, substance abuse facility administrator, consultant; b. Elwood, Ind., Aug. 2, 1927; s. William Armenius and Bessie Pearl (Moore) T.; m. Gloria Helen Pasquini, Oct. 21, 1950 (div. Aug. 1976); children— Constance Kay, Eric William; m. Yvonne Lilani Shook, Aug. 12, 1976. B.A., Ind. U., 1954; M.S., So. Ill. U., 1975; cert. in occupational program cons. Nat. Occupational Alcoholism Tng. Inst., Washington, 1975. Cert. alcoholism counselor, D.C., Md., Va., employee assistance profl. Commd. 2d lt. U.S. Marine Corps, 1954, advanced through grades to maj., 1966; occupational research analyst U.S. Marine Corps, Washington, 1968-71, ret., 1971; dir. Alcohol Safety Action Project, Balt., 1971-73; assoc. dir. Washington Hosp. Ctr. Counseling Ctr., 1973-75, T.H.E. Counseling Ctrs., Inc., Washington, 1975-84; program dir. New Beginnings at Psychiat. Inst., Washington, 1984-87; exec. dir. New Beginnings at Meadows, 1987—; sr. mgmt. cons. Sci. Mgmt. Corp., Washington, 1974-77; lectr. on alcohol and hwy. safety in pub. and pvt. sectors. Mem. legis com. Area Council on Alcoholism, Balt., 1971-73; bd. dirs. Women's Home, Inc., Arlington, Va., 1969-73. Recipient cert. appreciation AFL-CIO Community Services, 1973. Mem. NOW, Am. Coll. Addiction Treatment Adminstrs., Assn. Labor-Mgmt. Adminstrs. and Cons. on Alcoholism, Assn. Employee Assistance Program Practitioners, Washington Area Council on Alcoholism and Drug Abuse (profl. assoc., sec. exec. bd. 1980-82), Profl. Counselors Assn. on Alcoholism (pres. 1975-76), Va. Assn. Alcoholism and Drug Abuse Counselors (dir. 1982-83). Methodist. Avocations: photography; fishing; egyptology. Home: Stafford, Va. Died Feb. 20, 2007.

TERZIAN, KARNIG YERVANT, retired civil engineer; b. July 4, 1928; arrived in U.S., 1951; s. Yeznig and Marie Terzian; m. Helen S., Dec. 21, 1958. BCE, Am. U. Beirut, Lebanon, 1949; MCE, U. Pa., 1954. Assoc. L. T. Beck & Assocs., 1956-60; prin. Urban Engrs., Inc., Phila., 1960—93, sr. v.p., sec.-treas., 1960-93, co-founder, ptnr., 1993-99; ret., 1999. Cons. major transp. projects in Pa., N.Y., N.J., Nigeria, Zaire; cons., exec. Urban Engrs., 1993—. Bd. dirs. Armenian Sisters Acad., 1970-74. Mem. ASCE (Life Membership award 1993), ASTM, Prestressed Concrete Inst. Armenian Apostolic. Home: Bryn Mawr, Pa. Died May 10, 2007.

TETZELI, FREDERICK EDWARD, banker; b. Chomutove, Czech Rep., Sept. 12, 1930; came to U.S., 1961; s. Louis and Sophie (Deym) T.; m. Margaret Lee Weld, Sept. 6, 1958; chilren: Frederick John, William George, Christopher Weld. BS, Georgetown U., 1952. Assoc. Merrill Lynch, Havana, Cuba, 1952-54; treas. Cuban Trading Co., Havana, 1954-61; exec. adminstr. Waterman S.S. Corp., Mobile, Ala., 1962-64; mng. dir. J.P. Morgan, NYC, from 1964. Bd. dirs., chmn. investment com. Luso Am. Bus. Council. Chmn., mem. exec. com. Am. Portuguese Soc., 1980—, bd. dirs., past chmn. Spain-U.S. C. of C., 1979—, past pres., bd. dirs. Belgian-Am. C. of C., 1973—; councillor French C. of C., 1973—; bd. dirs., past pres. Am.-Italy Soc., 1973—; bd. dirs. U.S.-Netherlands C. of C., 1980—; bd. dirs., mem. exec. com. France Am. Soc. Decorated grand officer Order of Italian Republic, knight Order of Royal House for Civilian Merit, Spain; mem. Legion of Comdrs. (Italy). Mem. U.S.-Italy C. of C. (bd. dirs.), Am. C. of C. Cuba (bd. dirs., vice chmn.), Bankers Assn. for Fgn. Trade (vice chmn. membership com.). Clubs: Downtown Assn., Met. (N.Y.C.); Sloane (London). Republican. Roman Catholic. Home: Brooklyn, NY. Died Nov. 8, 2005.

THAL, LEON JOEL, neuroscientist; b. Bklyn., June 17, 1944; s. Bernard and Esther (Beller) T.; m. Donna Jean Norbo, June 25, 1967. MD, Downstate Med. Ctr., NYC, 1969. Diplomate Am. Bd. Psychiatry and Neurology. Instr., asst. prof., assoc. prof. neurology Albert Einstein Coll. Medicine, Bronx, 1975-85; assoc. prof. neuroscience U. Calif., San Diego, 1985-89, prof., 1898—2007, chmn. dept. neuroscience, 1993—2007. Editor: Cognitive Disorders, 1992; contbr. chpts. in books and articles to profl. jours. Lt. comdr. USPHS, 1970-72. Recipient Potamkin prize for Alzheimer's Rsch., 2004. Home: Cardiff By The Sea, Calif. Died Feb. 3, 2007.

THARRINGTON, ROBERT WILLIAM, aerospace company executive; b. Girard, Kans., Feb. 28, 1919; s. Robert C. and Anne M. (Hamilton) T.; m. Shirley L. McFarland, Sept. 28, 1941; 1 son, William S. BS in Bus. Adminstrn, Kans. State Coll., 1940; grad. exec. devel. program, Cornell U., 1956. With Boeing Co., 1941-44, 48-88, asst. gen. mgr. aerospace div., 1961-62, v.p., from 1962, now sr. v.p.; v.p., gen. mgr. Vertol div. Morton, Pa., 1962-71; v.p., dir. Boeing Can. Ltd., 1962-71; pres., chief exec. officer Boeing Computer Services Co., Morristown, N.J., from 1971; chmn. bd. Boeing Computer Services (Europe) Ltd., from 1980. Mem.: Seattle Golf (Seattle), Rainier Golf and Country (Seattle); Orange Lawn Tennis (South Orange, N.J.). Home: Short Hills, NJ. Died Nov. 15, 2006.

THAYER, GERALD CAMPBELL, beer company executive; b. Rockville Centre, NY, July 19, 1943; s. Gerald Earl and Celia Storrs (Campbell) T.; m. Candace Wheatley, June 29, 1968; children— Jonathan, Matthew. BA, Middlebury Coll., 1965; MBA, Columbia U., 1970. Sr. planning analyst Anheuser-Busch Co., St. Louis, 1970-73, asst. to v.p. fin., 1973-75, asst. treas., 1975-81, treas., 1981-85, v.p., treas., 1985-93, v.p., contr., from 1994. Served to capt. U.S. Army, 1966-68, Vietnam Home: Wolfeboro, NH. Died Aug. 23, 2007.

THAYER, SUSAN BERMAN, cable television executive; b. Bayonne, N.J., July 11, 1941; d. Arthur Milton and Beatrice (Goldklang) Kaufman; m. Jack G. Thayer, Nov. 28, 1978; children— Jennifer, Rachel. B.A., Oberlin Coll., 1962; postgrad. Queens Coll., 1967-68, Baruch Coll., 1975-76. Editor, writer Ms. Mag. Corp., N.Y.C., 1972-77; pres. Susan K. Berman Assocs., N.Y.C., 1977-78; dir. mktg. Met. Transp. Authority, N.Y.C., 1978-81; account exec. Lifetime Network, N.Y.C., 1981—. Author published articles. Bd. dirs. Women's Action Alliance, N.Y.C., 1982-84. Mem. Internat. Radio and TV Soc., Women in Communications, Women in Cable. Jewish. Home: New York, NY. Died Jan. 24, 2006.

THEOBALD, H RUPERT, retired political scientist, legislative staff member; b. Berlin, Mar. 12, 1930; came to U.S., 1950; s. Hans Herman and Marlene (Rackow) T.; m. Elizabeth Joanna Frisella, Nov. 3, 1951 (dec. Mar. 1996); children: H. Michael, Marlies J., Peter J.; m. M. Jean Esch, Apr. 18, 1998. MA, U. Wis., 1960, PhD, 1971. Rschr. Wis. Legis. Reference Bur., Madison, 1957-60, coord., 1960-63, acting chief, 1963-64, chief, 1964-94; ret., 1994. Lay mem. bd. govs. State Bar Wis., 1994-96. Editor: Laws of Wisconsin, 1991-94; contbr. articles to profl. jours. Mem. Coun of State Governments, 1963-94 (Charles McCarthy award 1986), Com. on Suggested State Legis., 1964-94. Home: Madison, Wis. Died Nov. 9, 2005.

THIEL, JOHN MELVIN, physician, b. Cin., Nov. 10, 1912; s. John Nicholas and Mary Ida (Renschen) T.; m. Dorothy Felicie Taggart, June 6, 1942; children— Beverly, Diane, Camille, John Joseph, Louis Joseph. Student Xavier U., 1930-32; B.S., U. Cin., 1934, M.B., 1936, M.D., 1937; Sc.D., St. Edwards U., 1957. Intern Good Samaritan Hosp., Cin., 1936-37, resident, 1937-40; assoc. Venable Clinic, San Antonio, 1940-41; practice medicine specializing in surgery, Galveston, Tex., 1941—; mem. staff John Sealy Hosp., St. Mary's Hosp.; mem. control group 1st State Bank of Hitchcock, Tex., Bank of W. Galveston, Bank of Santa Fe, Tex., Gulf Nat. Bank, Texas City, Gulf Shore Bank, Crystal Beach, Tex.; owner Circle JT Ranches, Atascosa County, Coryell County and Victoria County, Tex.; real estate executive; involved in oil and gas prodn.; horse breeder and racer. Bd. dirs. Galveston County unit Am. Cancer Soc. Served to surgeon USPHS. Fellow ACS; mem. SW Surg. Congress, Tex. Surg. Soc., Singleton Surg. Soc., Tex. Med. Assn., So. Med. Assn., Galveston County Med. Assn., AMA, Nat. Rifle Assn. Am., AAUP. Clubs: Serra of Galveston, Galveston Country, Pelican, Galveston Skeet and Trapshooting Assn., Galveston Rifle and Pistol, Galveston Artillery, Bob Smith Yacht, Sunday Morning Coffee, Port Bay Hunting and Fishing, Quarterdeck, Tandem. Lodge: Rotary. Home: Galveston, Tex. Died Dec. 8, 2005.

THIES, AUSTIN COLE, retired utility company executive; b. Charlotte, NC, July 18, 1921; s. Oscar Julius and Blanche (Austin) T.; m. Marilyn Joy Walker, June 26, 1945 (dec. Dec. 1992); children: Austin Cole, Robert Melvin, Marilyn Leone. BSME, Ga. Inst. Tech., 1943. With Duke Power Co., Charlotte, 1946-86, mgr. steam prodn., 1963-65, asst. v.p., 1965-67, v.p. prodn. and operation, 1967-71, sr. v.p., 1971-82, exec. v.p., 1982-86, also dir. Past chmn. prodn. com., engrng. and operating div. Southeastern Electric Exchange; chmn. tech. advisory com. Carolinas Va. Nuclear Power Assos.; chmn. N.C. Air Control Advisory Council. Mem. nat. adv. bd. Ga. Inst. Tech.; pres. Arts and Scis. Council; chmn. bd. dirs. Mercy Hosp.; trustee Alexander Childrens Center; bd. visitors Boy's Town.; 1st v.p. Sci. Museums of Charlotte; bd. dirs. Sci. Mus. Served with USNR, 1943-46. Decorated Purple Heart; named to Ga. Tech. Hall of Fame, 1994. Mem. Edison Electric Inst. (past chmn. engrng. and oper. divsn. exec. com.), IEEE, Charlotte C. of C., ASME (past chmn. Piedmont Carolina sect.), Am. Nuclear Soc., Air Pollution Control Assn., N.C. Soc. Engrs. (past pres., Engr. of Yr. 1985), Charlotte Engrs. Club (Disting. Service award 1984), Nat. Rifle Assn. (life), Kappa Sigma. Presbyterian (elder). Clubs: Rotary (past pres., dir. N. Charlotte), Cowans Ford Country (bd. dirs.), Quail Hollow Country (bd. dirs.), Charlotte City (bd. dirs.), Charlotte Ga. Inst. Tech. (past pres.), Charlotte Rifle and Pistol (past pres.). Home: Charlotte, NC. Died Jan. 13, 2006.

THOMAS, CARMEN CHRISTINE, retired dermatologist; b. Germany, Apr. 15, 1908; arrived in U.S., 1921; d. Paul Ernest and Huberta (Mohr) Thomas. AB, U. Del., 1929; MD, Woman's Med. Coll. Pa., 1932; DSc, U. Pa., 1940. Diplomate Am. Bd. Dermatology. Asst. chief resident Phila. Gen. Hosp., 1934-35; fellow in dermatology U. Pa., Phila., 1936-39, asst. prof. dermatology, 1940-67; prof. dermatology Woman's Med. Coll. Pa., Phila., 1941-68, dir. dept. oncology, 1952-66, emeritus prof. dermatology, from 1968; chief dermatologist Phila. Gen. Hosp., 1944-77; pvt. practice Phila., 1939-77. Cons. Vets. Hosp., Memor Hosp., Phila., 1950—77, Elwyn Inst., Devereux Sch., 1950—69. Contbr. articles to profl. jours. Fellow: Phila. Coll. Physicians; mem.: Phila. County Med. Soc. (life), Phila. Dermatol. Soc. (life; pres. 1942), Am. Acad. Dermatology (life), Sigma Xi, Alpha Omega Alpha, Phi Beta Kappa. Avocations: travel, photography, music archeology. Home: Philadelphia, Pa. Died Feb. 11, 2006.

THOMAS, CRAIG LYLE, senator; b. Cody, Wyo., Feb. 17, 1933; m. Susan Roberts; children: Peter, Paul, Patrick, Alexis. BA in Agrl., U. Wyo., 1955; LLB, La Salle U., 1963. V.p. Wyo. Farm Bur., Laramie, 1959-66; nat. resource dir. Am. Farm Bur., 1966-75; gen. mgr. Wyo. Rural Elec. Assn., 1975-89; mem. Wyo. Ho. of Reps., 1984—89, US Congress from Wyo., Washington, 1989—95; US Senator from Wyo. Washington, 1995—2007. Mem. energy and natural resources com., environment and pub. works com., fin. com., Indian affairs com. Former chmn. Natrona County (Wyo.) Rep. Com.; state rep. Natrona County Dist.; del. Rep. Nat. Conv., 1980. Served in USMC, 1955—59. Recipient William Penn Mott, Jr. Park Leadership award, Nat. Parks & Conservation Assn., 1999, Frank M. Tejada Leadership award, Marine Corps Res. Offices Assn., 2000, Community Health Superhero award, Nat. Assn. Community Health Centers, 2002, Disting. Alumni award, U. Wyo., 2002, Golden Triangle award, Nat. Farmers Assn., 2003, Legis. Svc. award, Am. Counseling Assn., 2003. Mem. Am. Soc. Trade Execs., Masons, Nat. 4-H Hall of Fame Republican. Methodist. Died June 4, 2007.

THOMAS, SIR DONALD LLEWELLYN, banker; b. Niagara Falls, NY, Mar. 5, 1917; s. Phillip Charles and Dora Ellen (Redpath) T.; m. Lady Barbara Thomas, May 20, 1942; children— Donald Llewellyn, Rhys Evans BBA magna cum laude, Niagara U.; postgrad. Stonier Grad. Sch. Banking, Rutgers U.; DCS (hon.), Niagara U., 1988. Treas. Niagara Falls Savs. Bank, 1945-54; v.p. No. Trust Co., Chgo., 1955-65; chmn., chief exec. officer Anchor Savs. Bank FSB, Hewlett, N.Y., from 1966, Thomas Property Corp., Marietta, Ga., from 1970, Anchor Mortgage Resources, Atlanta, from 1980, Anchor Mortgage Services, Wayne, N.J., from 1983; chmn. bd. Residential Funding Corp., Mpls., from 1988. Mem. faculty Grad. Sch. Savs. Banking, Brown U., Stonier Sch. Banking, Rutgers U.; mem. thrift adv. bd. Fed. Res. Bank N.Y. Co-author: Commercial Bankers Handbook, Savings and Time Deposit Banking Vice chmn. bd. trustees Lutheran Med. Ctr., N.Y.C.; past pres. Council of Chs. City of N.Y.; mem. council bd. guardians Soc. of Family of Man; past chmn. Community Preservation Corp. N.Y.C., bd. dirs., exec. com. Community Preservation Corp; chm. exec. com. Housing Mortgage Ptnrship Corp.; bd. dirs. Bklyn. Sunday Sch. Union, Bklyn. Philharm., N.Y. Gov.'s Com. for Aging Decorated Knight of Malta; recipient Man of Yr. award Council of Chs., Bklyn. div., 1976, Indsl. Home for Blind, 1979, Sword of Hope-Am. Cancer Soc., 1980, Montauk Club, 1978, Citizens Recognition award Bklyn. YMCA, hon. Doctorate in Comml. Sci. Niagara U., 1988. Mem. Nat. Council Savs. Instns. (bd. dirs.), U.S. League Savs. Assns. (legis com.), Savs. Banks Assn. N.Y. State, Bklyn. C. of C. (bd. dirs.), NCCJ, Fed. Nat. Mortgage Assn. (adv. bd.). Clubs: Cherokee Town and Country (Atlanta); Cherry Valley (Garden City, N.Y.); Metropolitan, Marco Polo (N.Y.C.). Republican. Home: Hewlett, NY. Died Dec. 2, 2005.

THOMAS, GARNETT JETT, accountant; b. Farmington, Ky., July 27, 1920; s. Pinkney Madison and Ethel (Drinkard) T.; m. Katherine Gardner, Mary. 26, 1948 (dec. Sept. 1979); m. Nell Penton, May 23, 1981; stepchldren: Vernon Bice, Michael Bice, Gina Black. BS, Lambuth U., 1947; MS, Miss. State U., 1949. Clk., acct. Ill. Cen. R.R., Paducah, Ky., 1941-42; mgr. Coll. Bookstore Lambuth U., Jackson, Tenn., 1946-47; acct. Miss. Agrl. and Forestry Expt. Sta., Mississippi State, 1948-60, chief acct., 1960-75, administrv. officer and chief acct., 1975-85; administrv. officer emeritus, from 1985; pres. PBR Corp., Starksville, Miss., 1974-84. Fin. adminstr. seed tech., rsch. internat. programs Brazil, India, Guatemala, Columbia, Thailand, Kenya, 1958-85; pres. Govt. Employees Credit Union. Mem. adv. bd. Nat. Bank of Commerce of Miss., 1974—; fin. administr. seed tech, research internat. programs Brazil, India, Guatemala, Columbia, Thailand, Kenya, 1958-85; bd. dirs. Govt. Employees Credit Union, 1967-86, pres., 1969-73. With USN, 1942-46. Decorated Bronze Star with oak leaf cluster. Mem. Nat. Assn. Accts., Asn. Govt. Accts., Am. Assn Accts., Acad. Acctg. Historians, So. Assn. Agrl. Scientists, Rotary (pres., 1959-90, dist. 682 gov. 1977-78, adv. com. to pres. 1979-80, dist. chmn. Poloplus, 1987-90). Republican. Methodist. Home: Starkville, Miss. Died Sept. 7, 2006.

THOMAS, JOHN MELVIN, retired surgeon; b. Carmarthen, U.K., Apr. 26, 1933; U.S, 1958; s. Morgan and Margaret (Morgan) T.; m. Betty Ann Mayo, Nov. 3, 1958; children: James, Hugh, Pamela. MB, BChir, U. Coll. Wales, U. Edinburgh, 1958. Intern Robert Packer Hosp., Sayre, Pa., 1958-59, chief surg. resident, 1963, pres. med. staff, 1968; assoc. surgeon Guthrie Clinic Ltd., Sayre, 1963-69, chmn. dept. surgery, 1969-91; vice chmn. Guthrie Healthcare System, 1995—99. Pres. bd. dirs. Guthrie Clinic Ltd., 1972-89; pres. bd. dirs. Donald Guthrie Found., 1983-95; chmn. Chemung Springwater Co.; trustee Robert Packer Hosp.; chmn. exec. com. Guthrie Healthcare Sys., 1990-92, dir., 1994-2001; guest examiner Am. Bd. Surgery, 1979, 81, 85; bd. dirs. Measurement Innovations Corp., Mansfield, Pa., Trianalytics Corp., First Citizens Nat Bank; cons. The Hunter Group, 1993-96; interim pres., Citizen Fin. Bank, 2003—; arbitrator Nat. Assn. Securities Dealers, 2005—. Bd. dirs. Donald Guthrie Found. for Rsch., pres., 1983-94; bd. dirs. Pa. Trauma Sys. Found., 1984-90, pres., 1988, 89; chmn. licensure and accountability Gov.'s Conf., 1974; bd. dirs. Vol. Hosps. Am., 1993-95; trustee Mansfield (Pa.) U. Found., 1991-98; trustee Mansfield Univ. Found., 1991-95. Fellow ACS (gov. 1985-91); mem. AMA, Am. Group Practice Assn., Soc. for Surgery Alimentary Tract, Pa. Med. Soc., Bradford County Med. Soc., Cen. NY Surg. Soc., Internat. Soc. Surgery, Soc. Surgery Alimentary Tract, Ea. Vascular Soc., Ithaca Country Club, Whitchurch Golf Club, Country Club Naples, Tower Club (Ft. Lauderdale). Presbyterian. Home: Naples, Fla. Died Aug. 6, 2007.

THOMAS, ORVILLE C., retired allergist; b. Haynesville, La., Aug. 23, 1915; children— David, Diane, Cody Pre-med. Student, Marian Mil. Inst., 1932-33, Tulane U., 1933, MD, 1939. Diplomate Am. Bd. Pediatrics. Diplomate Am. Bd. Allergy and Immunology. Intern Shreveport Charity Hosp., La., 1939-40; asst. resident in pediatrics Children's Meml. Hosp., Chgo., 1946-47, resident in pediatrics, 1947, chief resident in pediatrics, 1948; sr. staff pediatrics Confederate Meml. Hosp., Shreveport, La., 1948-61; chief pediatrics Schumpert Meml. Hosp., Shreveport, La., 1958-61, chief of staff, 1958; active staff Tex. Children's Hosp., Houston, from 1962, fellow in pediatric allergy, 1963-65, chief allergy sect., 1973-78; fellow in pediatric allergy Baylor Coll. Medicine, Houston, 1963-65; active staff Highland Hosp., Shreveport, La., 1948-61, North La. Hosp., Shreveport, La., 1948-61, Physicians and Surgeons Hosp., Shreveport, La., 1948-61, Ben Taub Gen. Hosp., Houston, from 1962, Hermann Hosp., Houston, 1966-69; hon. staff St. Luke's Hosp., Houston, from 1962; cons. staff Meth. Hosp., Houston, from 1962, St. Joseph Hosp., Houston, from 1966, Bellaire Gen. Hosp., Tex., 1966-86, Rosewood Gen. Hosp., Houston, from 1967, Meml. Bapt. Hosp., Houston, from 1968, Pasadena Bayshore Hosp., Pasadena, Tex., from 1970; instr. pediatrics Northwestern U. Sch. Medicine, Chgo., 1948; assoc. prof. pediatrics La. State U. Postgrad. Sch. Medicine, 1956-61; clin. instr. pediatrics Baylor Coll. Medicine, Houston, 1961-66, asst. clin. prof. pediatrics, 1966-76, assoc. clin. prof. pediatrics, 1977—91; ret., 1991. Assoc. clin. prof. allergy and immunology U. Tex. Grad. Sch. Biomed. Scis., Houston, 1970—. Book reviewer: Venom Diseases; Aspects of Allergy and Applied Immunology. Contbr. articles to profl. jours. Served to maj. USMC AUS, 1942-46. Fellow Am. Coll. Allergy and Immunology (pediatrics com. 1964—, pres. 1978), Am. Acad. Allergy and Immunology, Am. Assn. Cert. Allergists (bd. govs. 1974, pres. 1979); mem. AMA, Am. Acad. Pediatrics, So. Med. Assn. (chmn. allergy sect. 1970-71), Tex. Allergy Research Found. Houston(research and edn. com. 1966-86, chmn. sci. adv. council 1973—), Tex. Pediatric Soc., Harris County Med. Soc., Tex. Med. Assn. (chmn. allergy sect. 1976-77), Am. Assn. for Inhalation Therapy (awards com. 1969-72, spl. edn. com. 1969-72), Greater Houston Allergy Soc. (pres. 1977), Joint Council of Allergy and Immunology, Internat. Assn. of Allergology and Clin. Immunology (U.S. rep. 1981-85). Home: Willis, Tex. Died Apr. 13, 2007.

THOMAS, RUBY BELL, educator; b. Van Buren, Ark., Sept. 2, 1916; d. Oscar Isaac and Ollie Pearl (Flanagan) Gulley; m. Foster Oliver Thomas, July 3, 1943; children— Candetta Kay, Catrena Renee. Student Okla. State U., 1969. Tchr. Ark. Bd. Edn., Van Buren, 1936-41; electric engr. Lockheed Aircraft, Maywood, Calif., 1942-44; owner Lady Kay Beauty Salon, Tulsa, 1951-78; sales and info. specialist Airport Ins., Tulsa, 1979-82; ins. agt., Tulsa, 1983-85; owner Lady Kay Beauty Salon, 1985—. Club: Sweet Adelines. Lodge: Eastern Star. Avocations: fishing; boating; hiking; singing; sewing. Home: Tulsa, Okla. Died Feb. 5, 2006.

THOMAS, WILLIAM GRIFFITH, lawyer; b. Washington, Nov. 1, 1939; s. Henry Phineas and Margaret Wilson (Carr) T.; m. Suzanne Campbell Foster, June 7, 1960. Student, Williams Coll., 1957-59, Richmond Coll., 1960; JD, U. Richmond, 1963. Bar: Va. 1963. With Hazel & Thomas (combined with Reed Smith in 1999), 1973—99; ptnr. Reed Smith LLP, Falls Church, Va., from 1999, mem. exec. com. Dir. Va. Electric and Power Co.; mem. 4th circuit judicial conf. Sec. Va. Dem. Com., 1968-70, chmn., 1970-72. Named Administrative Law Super Lawyer, Va. Super Lawyers Mag., 2006. Mem. ABA, Va. State Bar Assn., Am. Law Inst., Am. Coll. Real Estate Lawyers. Home: Aylett, Va. Died Mar. 30, 2007.

THOMLINSON, RALPH, demographer, educator; b. St. Louis, Feb. 12, 1925; s. Ralph and Ora Lee (Barr) T.; m. Margaret Mary Willits, Dec. 21, 1946; children: Elizabeth Barr, William Lockwood. BA, Oberlin Coll., 1948; postgrad., U. Pitts., 1943-44, Harvard U., 1948; MA, Yale U., 1949; PhD, Columbia U., 1960. Asst. town planner, Montclair, N.J., 1949-50; asst. city planner Paterson, N.J., 1950; research asst. Bur. Applied Social Research, NYC, 1952; med. statistics asst. actuarial dept. Met. Life Ins. Co., NYC, 1952-53; instr. statistics and population U. Wis., 1953-56; instr. sociology and anthropology Denison U., Granville, Ohio, 1956-59; asst. prof. sociology Calif. State U., LA, 1959-62, assoc. prof., 1962-65, prof., 1965-88, prof. emeritus, from 1988, chmn. dept. sociology, 1967-69; vis. prof. sociology U. Alta., Can., 1966; vis. prof. biostatistics U. N.C., Chapel Hill, 1972-73; demographic adviser Inst. Population Studies, Chulalongkorn U., Bangkok, Thailand, 1969-71; cons. Nat. Family Planning Program, Thailand, Census of Thailand, 1970-71, Population/Food Fund, 1977-79, also various research centers abroad, 1969-73. Cons. to fourteen book pubs., 1965—; field assoc. Population Coun., N.Y.C., 1969-71; rsch. adviser Ctr. for Rsch. and Demographic Studies, Rabat, Morocco, 1972-73; acad. visitor Population Investigation Com., London Sch. Econs., 1973; vis. scholar Nat. Inst. Demographic Studies, Paris, 1973-74 Author: A Mathematical Model for Migration, 1960, Population Dynamics, 2d edit, 1976, Sociological Concepts and Research, 1965, Demographic Problems, 2d edit, 1975, Urban Structure, 1969, Thailand's Population, 1971, (with others) The Methodology of the Longitudinal Study of Social, Economic and Demographic Change, 1971; editor: (with Visid Prachuabmoh) The Potharam Study, 1971; adv. editor: Sociol. Abstracts, 1963-67, Sociology Quar, 1978-84; cons. editor: As-Soukan, 1972-73; assoc. editor: Pacific Sociol. Rev, 1976-83; Sociol. Perspective, 1983-85; chmn. editorial bd. Calif. Sociologist, 1981-84; cons.: Dictionary of Modern Sociology, 1969; contbr. to: Dictionary of Demography, 5 vols., 1985-86; books, profl. jours. Served with AUS, 1943-45, ETO. Mem. Population Assn. Am., Internat. Union for Sci. Study Population, Am. Sociol. Assn., Internat. Assn. Survey Statisticians, Assn. Asian Studies. Home: Millbrae, Calif. Died Feb. 8, 2007.

THOMPSON, ANNE MARIE, newspaper publisher; b. Des Moines, Feb. 7, 1920; d. George Horace and Esther Mayer Sheely; m. J. Ross Thompson, July 31, 1949; children: Annette McCracken, James Ross. BA, U. Iowa, 1940; postgrad. U. Colo., 1971. Co-pub. Baca County Banner, Springfield, Colo., 1951-54, Rocky Ford (Colo.) Daily Gazette, 1954-82, pub., 1982—. Editor Toastmasters, 1983-94. Mem. Otero Jr. Coll. Coun., 1987-93, Colo. Ho. of Reps., 1957-61; Colo. presdl. elector, 1972; chmn. Colo. adv. com. SBA, 1979-81. Recipient Community Service award Rocky Ford C. of C., 1975; named Colo. Woman of Achievement in Journalism, 1959, Colo. Bus. Person of Yr., Future Bus. Leaders of Am., 1981; elected to Colo. Community Journalism Hall of Fame, 1981. Mem. Nat. Fedn. Press Women (dir. 1971-81), Nat. Newspaper Assn. (Emma C. McKinney award 1984), Colo. Press Assn. (dir. 1981-83, Golden Make-Up award 1991), Colo. Press Women, PEO, Bus. and Profl. Women's Club. Republican. Methodist. Died Aug. 25, 2006.

THOMPSON, BRUCE ALLAN, oil company executive, consultant; b. Alliance, Ohio, Apr. 24, 1938; s. George Otho and Gwendoline E. (Copeland) T.; m. Geraldine Ann Manley, June 15, 1963; children— Heather, Bruce, Jayson, Winston. B.S., Kent State U., 1960; M.S., Miami U., Oxford, Ohio, 1963. Cert. profl. geologist. Asst. dist. geologist Texaco Inc., Casper, Wyo., Billings, Mont., 1963-68; regional geologist Inexco Oil Co., Denver, Houston, 1968-79; exploration mgr. United Natural Resource, Denver, 1979-82; owner, mgr. Skull Creek Oil Co., Denver, 1982—; dir. Knee Hill Energy Co., Denver; cons. Viersen and Cochran, Denver, 1987—. Author: Stratigraphy of the Dunkard Basin, 1963; exploration guide Hydrocarbon Potential in Wyoming, 1974. Alt. del. Republican Party, Sedalia, Colo., 1984; active Ducks Unlimited, Castle Rock, Colo., 1983-84. Mem. Am. Assn. Petroleum Geologists, Am. Radio Relay League, Wyo. Geol. Assn. Houston Geol. Soc., Rocky Mountain Assn. Petroleum Geologists, Casper Petroleum Club, Denver Petroleum Club, Sigma Gamma Epsilon (Geol. Merit award 1962). Episcopalian. Clubs: Diehl Lake Country (Ohio) (fin. com. 1984—); Brown Palace (Colo.). Died Aug. 18, 2006.

THOMPSON, CAROL LEWIS, editor; b. NYC, Dec. 26, 1918; d. Jasper Robert and Freda (Rafalsky) Lewis; m. Elbert Paul Thompson, July 4, 1942; children: Timothy Lewis, Ellen, John, Abigail. AB, Wellesley Coll., 1940; MA, Mt. Holyoke Coll., 1942. Asst. editor Current History, 1943, asso. editor, 1943-55, editor, 1955-91, editorial cons., 1991—; editor Ency. of Developing Nations; asso. editor Forum mag., 1945-49; contbr. to Ency. Brit., World Book Ency. Mem. Am. Hist. Assn., Nat. Council Social Studies, Phi Beta Kappa. Mem. Soc. Of Friends. Died Jan. 29, 2007.

THOMPSON, HANK (HENRY WILLIAM THOMPSON), musician; b. Waco, Tex., Sept. 3, 1925; m. Dorothy Jean Ray (div.); m. Ann Williams Songs include Whoa Sailor, 1946, Humpty Dumpty Heart, 1948, Today, 1948, Green Light, 1948, The Wild Side of Life, 1952, She's a Whole Lot Like You, 1965, I've Come Awful Close, 1971, Cab Driver, 1972, Who Left the Door to Heaven Open?, (with Junior Brown) Gotta Sell Them Chickens, 1997; (albums) Songs of the Brazos Valley, 1955, North Of The Rio Grande, 1956, New Recordings of Hank Thompson's All Time Hits, 1956, Hank, 1957, Dance Ranch 1958, Favorite Waltzes, 1958, Songs for Rounders, 1959, This Broken Heart of Mine, 1960, Most of All, 1960, An Old Love Affair, 1961, At the Golden Nugget, 1961, #1 Coountry/Western 1962, Cheyenne Frontier Days, 1962, The Best of Hank Thompson, 1963, State Fair of Texas, 1963, Golden Country Hits, 1964 Its Christmas Time With Hank, 1964, Especially For You, 1964 Breakin In Anoither Heart, 1965, Luckiest Heartache in Town 1966, A Six Pack To Go, 1966, Breakin' The Rules, 1966 Where Is The Circus, 1966, The Best of Hank Thompson Vol. 2 1967, Just An Old Flame, 1967, The Countrypolitan Sound of Hank Thompson, 1967, The Gold Standard Collection, 1967 Country Blues, 1968, Hank Thompson Sings the Gold Standards, 1968, On Tap, In the Can, Or In The Bottle, 1968 Smokey the Bar, 1969, Salutes Oklahoma, 1969, The Instrumental Sounds of Hank Thompson, 1970, Next Time I Fall In Love (I Won't), 1971, A Salute to Mills Brothers, 1972, Hank Thompson's Greatest Hits Vol.1, 1972, Kindly Keep It Country 1973, 25th Anniversary Album, 1974, A Six Pack To Go (Twin Set), 1974, Movin' On, 1974, Hits of Nat "King" Cole, 1975 Back in the Swings of Things, 1976, The Thompson Touch 1977, Doin' My Thing, 1977, Country Comes to Carnegie Hall 1977, Brand New Hank, 1978, Take Me Back to Tulsa, 1980 The Best of the Best of Hank Thompson, 1980, 1000 and Other Nighters, 1983, 20 Golden Pieces, 1984, Hank Thompson, 1986 Here's To Country Music, 1988, Hank Thompson's Greatest Hits Vol. I, 1995, Hank Thompson's Greatest Hits Vol. II, 1995 The Best of Hank Thompson 1966-1979, 1995, Hank Thompson and Friends, 1996, Hank World, 1999, Seven Decades, 2000 Hank Thompson On Standard Time, 2004, Hank Thompson Drinkin' Songs, 2004, Hank Thompson and the Brazos Valley Boys-the Instrumentals, 2006, Hank Thompson and the Brazos Valley Boys-My Personal Favorites, 2006 Served in USN Inducted into Country Music Hall of Fame, Country Music Assn., 1989, Nashville Songwriters Hall of Fame, 1997 Died Nov. 6, 2007.*

THOMPSON, JAMES HOWARD, historian, librarian; b. Memphis, Aug. 20, 1934; s. Curtis Barnabas and Clara (Terry) T.; m. Margareta Ortenblad, Nov. 24, 1961; children— Ralph, Anna, Howard. BA in History, Rhodes Coll., Memphis, 1955 MA, U. N.C., Chapel Hill, 1957, PhD in History, 1961; MS in LS, U. Ill., 1963. Teaching fellow U. N.C., Chapel Hill 1955-56, departmental asst., 1956-57, reference asst., 1959-61 dir. undergrad. library, lectr. in history, 1968-70; circulation asst U. Ill., 1961-63; asst. Center for Russian Area and Lang Studies, 1962-63; cataloger Duke U., 1963-65; asst. prof. history U. S.W. La., 1965-66; asst. prof. U. Colo., 1966-68; dir libraries, prof. history U. N.C., Greensboro, 1970-94; ret., 1994 Bd. dirs. Southeastern Library Network, 1979-82, treas. 1981-82 Contbr. articles, revs. to profl. jours. Ford Found research fellow, 1957-58; U. Colo. grantee, 1967; U. N.C. at Greensboro grantee, 1977-78, 89. Mem. Phi Beta Kappa (chpt pres. 1979-80), Beta Phi Mu, Phi Alpha Theta, Chi Beta Phi Episcopalian. Home: Durham, NC. Died Nov. 8, 2006.

THOMPSON, JOHN ARMIN, educator; b. LaCrosse, Wis. Apr. 11, 1928; s. Eric and Esther (Hoklund) T.; m. Dorothy A Greer, Aug. 2, 1950; children: James E., Patricia A. BS, U. Wis. LaCrosse, 1950; MS, U. Wis., Madison, 1965, PhD, 1968. Tchr. adminstr., pub. schs., Wis., 1950-65; asst. to dean U. Wis. Madison, 1966-68; dir. grad. studies U. N.D., Grand Forks 1968-70; assoc. prof. ednl. adminstrn. U. Hawaii, Honolulu 1970-73, prof., 1973—, chmn. dept. ednl. adminstrn., 1974-84 mem. Edn. Commn. of States, Denver, 1983-87, mem. steering com., 1984-87. Co-author: Crime in Hawaii: Perspectives in Early Prevention, 1980; Assessing the Impact of Faculty Collective Bargaining, 1982, Funding and Spending in Paradise 1988, Funding Rural and Isolated Schools in Hawaii, 1990 author monograph: Cost consideration of Reward for Service Plans, 1984, The Second Wave of Education Reform: Implications for School Leadership, Administration and Organization 1986. Mem. Am. Ednl. Research Assn., Am. Sch. Fin. Assn. NEA (bd. dirs. 1977-81, chmn. higher edn. div. 1979-81) Disting. Service award 1977-80), Phi Delta Kappa. Lodge: Elks Home: Grants Pass, Oreg. Died Aug. 12, 2006.

THOMPSON, JOHN BROCKWAY, chemical engineer; b. Lincoln, Nebr., Oct. 1, 1920; s. John Morrison and Ethel (Brockway) T.; m. Lucille Cox, July 26, 1944; children— Jan, Dorothy, Roger Paul. B.Sc. with distinction, U. Nebr., 1947 M.S., 1949, Ph.D., 1951. Research assoc. E.I. DuPont de Nemours & Co., Inc., Wilmington, Del., 1951—. Contbr. articles to profl. jours. Patentee in field. Served with U.S. Army 1940-45, PTO. Dupont Co. research fellow, 1950. Mem. Am. Chem. Soc. Avocation: music (flute, piccolo). Home: Wilmington, Del. Died July 6, 2006.

THOMPSON, JOHN LARKIN, health insurance company executive; b. N.Y.C., Nov. 16, 1930; s. Leslie Eugene and Agnes (McDonough) T.; m. Adrienne Marie Barry, May 6, 1967 children: John Larkin, Jr., Edward Kiley, Sarah Wood. BS Villanova U., 1952; MS, Columbia U., 1955; JD, Boston U. 1963. Bar: Mass. 1963. Salesman Gen. Electric Co., various locations, 1955-60; assoc. Palmer & Dodge, Boston, 1964-69 ptnr., 1969-70; pres. Blue Cross and Blue Shield of Mass., Inc Boston, 1987—; Blue Shield of Mass., Inc., Boston, 1971-87 dir. Bank of New Eng. N.A., EG&G, Inc., Wellesley, Mass. mem. adv. com. health ins. benefits HEW, Washington, 1975-78 Bd. dirs. Boston Pvt. Industry Council, 1980—; chmn. Mass Port Authority, Boston, 1969-72, Boston Opera Assn., 1978— United Way of Mass., Boston, 1986—, New Eng. Aquarium Boston, 1986—; mem. Boston Found., 1983—. Served with USN, 1952-54, comdr. Res. ret. Recipient Disting. Citizen award NCCJ, 1983. Mem. Boston Bar Assn., Boston U. Law Sch. Alumni Assn. (exec. com. 1980—, Disting. Pub. Service award 1983), Greater Boston C. of C. (pres. 1977-79). Republican. Roman Catholic. Avocations: fishing, boating. Home Scituate, Mass. Died Sept. 23, 2006.

HOMPSON, WILLIAM, public relations executive, consultnt; b. Escanaba, Mich., Sept. 16, 1922; s. Waino Alexander and 'iola Ellen (Wood) T.; m. Dorothy Elizabeth Zum Buttel, July 1, 1945; children— Stephanie Jo Thompson Graves, Craig onald, Brian William. Student Wabash Coll., 1944-45; B.S., ieorge Washington U., 1965; grad. Harvard U. Bus. Sch. dvanced Mgmt. Program, 1970. Enlisted U.S. Navy, 1942, ommd. ensign, 1945, advanced through grades to rear adm., 971; spl. asst. for pub. affairs Sec. of Navy, 1964-70; dep. chief f info. Navy Dept., Pentagon, Washington, chief of info., 971-75, ret., 1975; pres. Admiralty Communication, Inc., AcLean, Va., 1978—, U.S. Navy Meml. Found., Washington, 978-93, pres. emeritus, 1993—; dir. Internat. Consortium Rsch. lealth Effects of Radiation; chmn. bd., dir. Admiralty Gen. Corp. (Real Estate Fund), McLean, 1983—; pub. relations cons., 975—. Decorated D.S.M., Legion of Merit. Mem. Pub. Relaons Soc. Am. (Silver Anvil award for best press relations 962), USN Pub. Affairs Alumni Assn. (founder), Sigma Chi. Club: Army Navy Country (Arlington, Va.). Home: Mc Lean, 'a. Died Sept. 15, 2006.

HOMPSON, WILLIAM, JR., engineering educator; b. Hynnis, Mass., Dec. 4, 1936; s. William and Dinella Helen Szeliga) T.; m. Martha Marion Cate, July 4, 1959; children: Aelanie A., Sharon E., Jennifer L., Keith W. SB, MIT, 1958; AS, Northeastern U., 1963; PhD, Pa. State U., 1971. Staff engr. aytheon Co., Wayland, Mass., 1958-60; sr. engr. Cambridge Mass.) Acoustical Assocs., 1960-66; rsch. asst. Applied Rsch. ab., State College, Pa., 1966-72; asst. prof. engring. sci. Pa. itate U., University Park, 1972-78, assoc. prof., 1978-85, prof., 985-2001, prof. emeritus, 2001—07. Head transducer group applied Rsch. Lab., State College, 1971-80; sabbatic leave Naval Rsch. Lab., Orlando, Fla., 1988-89; chairperson IBM Aaster Tchrs. Team, 1997-98. Contbr. articles to profl. jours.; atentee in field. Bd. dirs., treas., past pres. Nittany Mountain hpt. Am. Diabetes Assn., State College, 1979-92; bd. dirs., asst. reas., treas. Mid-Pa. affiliate, Bethlehem, 1980-90; bd. dirs. ight-Loss Support Group of Ctrl. Pa., 1999, treas. 2000-05. Recipient Disting. Svc. citation Mid-Pa. Affiliate Am. Diabetes Assn., 1981, and Affiliate Svc. award, 1988, J.R. Cardenuto ward, Sight-loss Support Group of Ctrl. Pa., 1998. Fellow Acoustical Soc. Am. (patent reviewer of soc. jour. 1990-2007); nem. Soc. Engring. Sci., Lions (pres. State College 1981-82, 9-90, sec.-treas. 1984-88, 90-92, treas. 1992-2005, dist. diabees chmn. 1983-88, 94-2005, chmn. Ctr. Lions Foresight Commn. 1992-2004, Melvin Jones fellow 1991, internat. leadrship award 1998, dist. chmn. Habitat for Humanity Project, 2001-04), Cen. Pa. Ballroom Dancers Assn. (pres.-elect 1997-98, pres. 1998-99). Republican. Avocations: sports, reading, hotography, ballroom dancing. Home: State College, Pa. Died 'eb. 13, 2007.

THOMPSON, WILLIAM WEST, allergist, immunologist, ediatrician; b. Hallsboro, NC, Apr. 6, 1921; MD, Duke U., 947. Diplomate Am. Bd. Allergy and Immunology, Am. Bd. Pediatrics. Intern Mountainside Hosp., Montclair, 1947-48; esident in pediatrics Duke Hosp., Durham, N.C., 1948-49, efferson Davis Hosp., Houston, 1949-50; fellow in allergy Ark. Allergy Clinic, Little Rock, 1956-57; staff mem. Humana Hosp., Fort Walton Beach, Fla.; pvt. practice. Mem. AMA, Am. Acad. Allergy and Immunology, Am. Acad. Pediatrics, Am. Coll. Allergy and Immunology. Died Jan. 2, 2007.

THORBECK, THOMAS GEORGE, lawyer; b. Fremont, Nebr., Dec. 6, 1945; s. George H. and Gay (Porter) T.; m. Mary Anne Romano, Sept. 2, 1967; children: Alexandra, Catherine. BA, DePauw U., 1968; JD cum laude, U. Mich., 1974. BAr: Wash. 1974, U.S. Dist. Ct. (ea. and we. dists.) Wash. 1974. Ptnr. Davis Wright Tremaine (formerly Davis Wright & Jones), Seattle, from 1974. Home: Seattle, Wash. Died July 11, 2006.

THORESEN, ASA CLIFFORD, biology educator; b. Bleneim, New Zealand, Sept. 9, 1930; came to U.S., 1949, aturalized, 1959; s. Francis Olaf and Helen (Hagan) T.; m. Shirley Avona Scarr, Aug. 31, 1952; children: Davona Gae, Aeylan Craig. BA, Andrews U., 1954; MA, Walla Walla Coll., 958; PhD, Oreg. State U., 1960. Asst. prof. biology Andrews J., Berrien Springs, Mich., 1960-63, assoc. prof., 1963-67, prof., 1967-92, chmn. dept. biology, 1963-83; prof. emeritus, rom 1992. Vis. prof. biology Walla Walla Coll. Marine Biol. Sta., summers, 1960, 63, 70, 77, 85 Served with AUS, 1954-56. Aem. Ornithol. Union Am., Cooper, Electron Microscopy Soc. Am. Mem. Seventh-day Adventist Ch. Home: Mcminnville, Oreg. Died May 31, 2006.

THORN, ARLINE ROUSH, English language educator; b. New Haven, Nov. 22, 1946; d. Jack and Joy (Yonker) Roush; m. Eric Paul Thorn, June 10, 1968 (div. 1991); 1 child, Paul Arthur. BA, Marshall U., 1967; MA, U. Ill., 1968, PhD, 1971. Prof. W.Va. State Coll., Institute, from 1971, chair dept. English, 986-94, adj. prof. Coll. Grad. Studies, from 1989. Pub. Trillium Press Appalachian Writers, 1992—; cons. W.Va. Humanities ound., Charleston, 1987—; chair adv. coun. faculty State Coll. ystem, 1992-94, bd. dirs., 1994—. Author: Mining the Seam, 992, Fire and Ice, 1993; editor: Origins: Texts for an Inquiry, 988. Woodrow Wilson Found. fellow, 1970; grantee Fund for mprovement of Postsecondary Edn., 1986-89; named Outstandng Prof., W.Va. State Legis., 1989; Fulbright Seminar, Brazil, 993. Mem. MLA, W.Va. Assn. Coll. English Thrs. (pres. 1988), Audubon Soc. (editor newsletter Huntington tri state chpt. 987-94). Avocations: birding, poetry. Home: Saint Albans, W.Va. Died July 2, 2006.

THORNE, JERROLD L., state legislator; b. Idaho Falls, May , 1929; m. Lois Thorne; children: Mark, Jon. BS in Edn., Brigham Young U., 1951. Mem. Idaho Senate, Dist. 12, Boise, rom 1984. Chair local govt. and tax. com., mem. fin. and transp. oms. With USNR, 1948-55. Recipient Silver Beaver award, Boy Scouts Am. Mem. PTA, C. of C. (past pres.), Rotary (pres. 977-78, Paul Harris fellow). Republican. Home: Nampa, Idaho. Died Jan. 18, 2006.

THORNTON, ROBERT DONALD, emeritus English language educator; b. West Somerville, Mass., Aug. 10, 1917; s. John William and Winifred (Harrington) T.; m. Grace Ellen Baker, May 22, 1943; children— Robert, David. BA with high distinction (Denison fellow, Caleb Winchester fellow), Wesleyan U., Middletown, Conn., 1939; MA in English, Western Res. U., 1940; MA in English (Univ. fellow), Harvard, 1942, PhD (Dexter fellow), 1949. Instr. English Fenn Coll., Cleve., 1939-40, Worcester Acad., Mass., 1940-41; teaching fellow English Harvard U., 1941-42, 46-49; asst. prof. English U. Colo., Boulder, 1949-56; chmn. English St. Stephen's Episcopal Sch., Austin, Tex., 1956-57; assoc. prof. English U. S.C., Columbia, 1957-60; prof. English Kans. State U., Manhattan, 1960-68; prof. English, world lit., chmn. dept. SUNY-New Paltz, 1968-71, faculty research fellow, 1973; univ. exchange scholar SUNY Coll. New Paltz, 1974-82, emeritus prof. English, SUNY exchange scholar, from 1982. Author: A Manual for Reading Improvement, 1953, The Tuneful Flame, 1957, James Curie: The Entire Stranger and Robert Burns, 1963, Selected Poetry and Prose of Robert Burns, 1966, William Maxwell to Robert Burns, 1979, The American Legion in South Carolina, 1989, SNAFU, 1993; contbr. to Ency. World Lit. in Twentieth Century, Ency. Poetry and Poetics; cons. editor: The Robert Burns Song Book, 1996—. Served with USNR, 1942-46, PTO. Grantee Am. Philos. Soc., 1955-56, Am. Council Learned Socs., 1963; Guggenheim fellow, 1958-59 Mem. MLA, Modern Humanities Research Assn., AAUP, Am. Soc. Eighteenth-Century Studies, Internat. Soc. Eighteenth-Century Studies, Chi Psi. Clubs: Folio, S.C. Harvard. Republican. Episcopalian. Home: Cheraw, SC. Died Oct. 24, 2006.

THORSON, NANCY ANN, health care manager, consultant; b. Oak Hill, Ohio, May 11, 1939; d. Clarence and Mary (Harrell) Harless; m. James M. Thorson, Sr.; 1 son, James M. B.F.A., Ohio U., 1961. With Good Samaritan Med. Ctr., Zanesville, Ohio, 1967—, dir. speech pathology/audiology dept., 1967-79, asst. dir. rehab. ctr., 1979-80, dir. community relations, 1980-82, communication/liasion specialist, 1982—. Bd. dirs. Zanesville Civic League; mem. Zanesville City Sch. Bd., Zanesville Vocat. Sch. Bd. Named Outstanding Sch. Bd. Mem. Southeastern Ohio, 1983. Mem. Ohio Soc. Hosp. Pub. Relations, Am. Soc. Hosp. Pub. Relations, Ohio Sch. Bd. Assn., Nat. Sch. Bd. Assn., C. of C. Protestant. Club: Republican of Zanesville. Died Aug. 5, 2007.

THOW, JOHN H., music educator, composer; b. LA, Oct. 6, 1949; s. George H. and Marie (Dykes) T.; m. Margaret Wait, June 24, 1971; children: Diana Corinna, Caroline Miranda. BMus in Composition magna cum laude, U. So. Calif., 1971; MA in Music Composition, Harvard U., 1973, PhD in Music Composition, 1977; diploma d'onore (Composition), Accademia Musicale Chigiana, Siena, Italy, 1974. Asst. prof. music theory and composition Boston U. Sch. for the Arts, 1978-80; asst. prof. in music composition U. Calif., Berkeley, 1981-86, assoc. prof., 1986-90, prof., 1990—2007. Composer: Madrone (Bklyn. Philharm. commn. 1987), Image Double & Envoi, All Hallows, 1982 (NEA rec. grant 1983, Boston Musica Viva/New Eng. Found. for the Arts Commn. 1981), Breath of the Sun, 1993, Seven Charms for a New Day, Canto del Quetzal, Chinese Poems, Divergences, Trombone Concerto, Songs for the Earth, 1994 (Am. Acad. award 1994), Into the Twilight, 1988 (San Francisco Symphony commn. 1988), Trigon, 1974 (Debut Orchesta award 1976), Live Oak (Musical Elements N.Y. commn. 1983), Trilce, 1992, To Invoke the Clouds (award Nat. Flute Assn. 1997), Cantico, 1998; recs. include Neuma, Music and Arts, Cantilena. Guggenheim fellowship Guggenheim Fdn., 1986, Djerassi Fdn. fellowships, 1986, 87, Regents Jr. Faculty fellowship U. Calif., 1983, Goddard Lieberson fellowship Am. Acad. and Inst. of Arts and Letters, 1983, Dorland Mountain Colony fellow, 1981, Yaddo fellowships, 1976, 1980, John Knowles Paine Travelling fellowship (Harvard), 1976-77, Fulbright Grad. fellowship to Italy, 1973-74; Margaret Jory Fairbanks Copying Assistance grants (The Am. Music Ctr.), 1978, 92, Meet the Composer grants, 1980, 82, 86, 87, 92, 95; Acad. award in Music Composition AAAL, 1994, Newly Published Music award Nat. Flute Assn., 1997. Fellow Am. Academy in Rome (Rome Prize fellowship 1977); mem. BMI, Am. Music Ctr., Am. Composers Forum. Home: Albany, Calif. Died Mar. 4, 2007.

THRALL, ROBERT MCDOWELL, mathematician, educator; b. Toledo, Ill., Sept. 23, 1914; s. Charles Haven and Gertrude (Gerking) T.; m. Natalie Hunter, Sept. 3, 1936; children: Charles A., James H., Mary Emily. BA, Ill. Coll., 1935, Sc.D., 1960; MA, U. Ill., 1935, PhD, 1937. Teaching fellow U. Ill., 1935-37; instr. math. U. Mich., 1937-42, asst. prof., 1942-48, assoc. prof., 1948-55, prof., 1955-69, prof. operation analysis, 1956-69; head ops. research dept. U. Mich. Research Inst., 1957-60; prof., chmn. dept. math. scis. Rice U., Houston, 1969-78, Noah Harding prof. math. scis., 1978-84, prof. emeritus, from 1984; prof. Jones Sch. Adminstrn. Adj. prof. biomath. dept. rehab. Baylor Sch. Medicine, 1969—; adj. prof. Computer Sci. Inst., 1971-75, U. Tex. Sch. Pub. Health, 1971—; vis. prof. Sch. Bus., Tex. A&M U.; faculty Stanford Summer Inst., 1957; Faculty Dartmouth Summer Inst., 1953, Inst. Advanced Study, Princeton, 1940-42; cons. RAND Corp., 1951-74, U.S. Army OCRD, 1958-78, Holt, Rinehart & Winston, Inc., 1961-76, Gen. Electric Co., 1963-69, Dow Chem. Co., 1965-69, Comshare Co., 1967-69, Gen. Motors Corp., 1967-69, Nat. Water Commn., 1970-71; pres. R.M. Thrall & Assos., Inc., 1970-81, chmn. bd., 1981—; regional lectr. Math. Assn. Am., 1961; Sigma Xi nat. lectr., 1968-69, SIAM lectr., 1970-72, TIMS-ORSA lectr., 1972-75; mem. NRC div. math. scis., 1967-70; program dir. decision and mgmt. scis. NSF, 1985 Author: (with E.B. Miller) College Algebra, 1950, (with L. Tornheim) Vector Spaces and Matrices, 1957, (with A. Spivey) Linear Optimization, 1970; Editor-in-chief: Mgmt. Sci, 1960-69; mem. editorial bd.: SIAM Rev, 1959-76, Operational Research Quar, 1960-69, Jour. of Conflict Resolution, 1961-71, Behavioral Sci, 1964—, Operations Research, 1965-69, Zeitschrift fur Wahrscheinlichkeitstheorie und verwandte Gebiete, 1962-71; Contbr. articles to profl. jours. Recipient Henry Russell award U. Mich., 1947, Distinguished Faculty award U. Mich., 1965 Mem. AAAS, AAUP, Am. Math. Soc., Econometric Soc., Math. Assn. Am., Nat. Council Tchrs. Math., Inst. Mgmt. Scis. (Disting. Service medal 1985), Ops. Research Soc. Am., Psychometric Soc., Soc. for Indsl. and Applied Math., Consortium for Math. and Its Applications (trustee, treas. 1985—), Phi Beta Kappa, Sigma Xi, Phi Kappa Phi. Home: Philadelphia, Pa. Died Apr. 11, 2006.

THURNER, JOSEPH JOHN, chemist; b. Middletown, N.Y., Oct. 26, 1920; s. Joseph John and Mary Theresa (McHugh) T.; B.S., Hartwick Coll., 1949; M.A., Harvard U., 1951; m. Mary Jean King, Dec. 26, 1948; children— John King, Laura Jean. Instr., Colgate U., 1951-53, asst. prof. chemistry, 1954-60, asso. prof., 1961-68, prof., 1968—, chmn. dept. chemistry, 1967-70, 74-81, dir. sci. div., 1970-73; cons. Indium Corp. Am., 1953-58, 81—. Served with USNR, 1941-45. Mem. Am. Chem. Soc., AAAS, Sigma Xi. Democrat. Research in analytical and synthetic chemistry of indium; expts. in chem. edn. Home: Hamilton, NY. Died Jan. 2, 2006.

TICKNOR, DANIEL HAROLD, academic program director b. Johnson City, N.Y., Mar. 3, 1942; s. Robert Wayne and Gwen Grace (Smith) T. B.A., Marietta Coll., 1963; M.A., U. Okla., 1969. Prof. art SUNY-Oneonta, 1963-73, dir. pub. relations, 1973-84, dir. internships, 1984—; nat. trainer Am. Cancer Soc., chmn. bd. N.Y. State div. Author: Doing it with Style, 1982. Editor: (newsletter) Communique, 1980—. Contbr. drawings to various mags., 1975—. Bd. dirs. Am. Cancer Soc., 1990-91, chmn. nat. soc. tng. com., 1989-91. Mem. Am. Assn. Univ. Adminstrs., Adult Edn. Assn. Home: Otego, NY. Died Dec. 26, 2006.

TIEDEMANN, ARTHUR EVERETT, college dean, historian; b. Bklyn., Mar. 22, 1921; s. William Frederick and Mary Agnes (Hailey) T.; m. Margaret Nicholson, Jan. 22, 1949; children: Karl Christopher, Eric Scott. BSS., CCNY, 1943; MA, Columbia U., 1949, PhD, 1959. Faculty, CCNY, from 1949, prof. history, from 1968, chmn. dept., 1965-69, 75-77, dean social sci., 1977-82, acting pres., 1980-81; adj. prof. modern Japanese history Columbia U., from 1988. Author: Modern Japan: A Brief History, rev. edit, 1962; editor: An Introduction to Japanese Civilization, 1974. Served with AUS, 1942-46. Mem. Am. Hist. Assn., Assn. Asian Studies, Japan Soc. N.Y., Soc. Sr. Scholars Columbia U., Internat. House of Japan, Phi Beta Kappa. Died July 6, 2006.

TIEMANN, JEROME J., physicist; b. Yonkers, NY, Feb. 21, 1932; ScB, MIT, 1953; PhD in Physics, Stanford U., 1960. Asst. Stanford (Calif.) U., 1953-55, 56-57; physicist R&D Ctr. GE, Schenectady, N.Y., from 1957. Cons. radiation lab. U. Calif, Berkeley, 1955-57. Fellow IEEE; mem. Nat. Acad. Engring. Achievements include research contributing to the knowledge of quantum mechanics, electronics and solid state electronic device phenomena; development of electronic circuit and system designs, signal processing circuit and system designs. Home: Schenectady, NY. Died Apr. 25, 2006.

TIENKEN, ARTHUR T., retired foreign service officer; b. Yonkers, NY, Aug. 5, 1922; BA, Princeton U., 1947, MA, 1949. With U.S. Fgn. Svc., 1949-87, dep. chief mission Tunis, Tunisia, 1973-75, Addis Ababa, Ethiopia, 1975-77; Ambassador to Gabonese Republic and Democratic Republic of Sao Tome and Principe, Libreville, Gabon, 1978-81; dir. Fgn. Svc. Assignments and Career devel. Dept. State, 1981-85, sr. insp., 1985-87, ret., 1987. Diplomat-in-residence Marquette U., 1972-73 Served with U.S. Army, 1943-46. Mem. Diplomatic and Consular Officers Ret. (bd. govs. 1999—2005). Home: Arlington, Va. Died May 7, 2006.

TILLER, FRANK MONTEREY, chemical engineering educator; b. Louisville, Ky., Feb. 26, 1917; s. Frank McCorkill and Nellie Barker (Lawson) T.; m. Ann Wesley Quiggins, Dec. 20, 1941 (dec. July 1981); children: Fay Lee Tiller Bryan, Richard Bertrand; m. Martha Rowan Browder (dec. 2004), Apr. 17, 1982. BSChemE, U. Louisville, 1937; MS, U. Cin., 1939, PhD, 1946; D honoris causa, U. Brazil, 1963, State U. Rio de Janeiro, 1967. Lab technician Charles R. Long Co., Paint Mfr., Louisville, 1934-35; chemist Durkee Famous Foods, Louisville, 1936, Colgate Palmolive Peet Co., Jeffersonville, Ind., 1937; civil engr. U.S. Engrs. Flood Control, Louisville, 1939; chem. engr. C.M. Hall Lamp Co., Detroit, 1940; teaching asst., instr. U. Cin., 1937-42; asst./assoc. prof. Vanderbilt U., Nashville, 1942-51; exec. dir. Gupton-Jones Coll. Mortuary Sci., Nashville, 1946-51; dean of engring., chmn. chem. engring., dir. rsch. Lamar U., Beaumont, Tex., 1951-55; dean engring., prof. chem. and electrical engring. U. Houston, 1955-63, dir. internat. affairs Ctr. Study Higher Edn. in Latin Am., 1963-72, M.D. Anderson prof. chem., civil and environ. engring., 1963—2006. Vis. prof. Inst. de Oleos, Conselho Nac. de Petroleo, Rio de Janeiro, 1952, U. Ctrl. del Ecuador, U. de Guayquil, Ecuador, 1958, U. de Brasil, Rio de Janeiro, 1962-63, U. Coll., London, 1970, Rice U., Houston, 1973-74, Loughborough U., Eng., 1976, U. Fed do Rio de Janeiro, U. Fed. de Sergipe, Brazil, 1979, Nat. Taiwan U., Taipei, 1982, Nagoya (Japan) U., 1982-83, 86, CSIRO, Canberra, Australia, 1986. Author: Vector Analysis, 1964; founding editor Fluid/Particle Separation Jour., 1988-93; contbr. articles to profl. jours. Recipient Disting. Alumnus award U. Cin., 1969, Gold medal Filtration Soc. (U.K.), 1978, Dukler Disting. Faculty award U. Houston Engring. Alumni Assn., 1996. Fellow AIChE (Colburn award 1950, Presentation award 1952, 62, Best Paper award Suth Tex. sect. 1959, Founders award 1987); mem. Am. Soc. Engring. Edn., Am. Filtration and Separations Soc., Internat. Assn. Water Quality, Water Environment Fedn. Avocations: gardening, swimming, theater, music. Home: League City, Tex. Died Jan. 3, 2006.

TILLEY, RALPH W., bank executive; b. Madison, Ind., Nov. 5, 1929; s. James Byron and Elizabeth (Campbell) T.; m. Jean Trowbridge, June 17, 1951; children: Steven, Claudia Wendling, Carol. BS, Ind. U., 1951. Salesman Studebaker Corp., South Bend, Ind., 1953—55; trainee Vevay Deposit Bank, Ind., 1955—56, asst. cashier Ind., 1956—62, cashier, exec. v.p. Ind., 1962—71, pres. Ind., from 1971. Chmn. Vevay Switzerland County Found., Inc., from 1980; pres. Vevay Econ. Devel. Commn., from 1982. 1st lt. USAF, 1951—53. Mem.: Ind.

Bankers Assn. Region 5 (pres. 1982—83), Ind. Bankers Assn. Am. (dir. Ind. from 1983), Ind. Bank Assn. (pres. 1973—74), Kiwanis. Republican. Methodist. Home: Vevay, Ind. Died June 28, 2006.

TILLINGHAST, PARDON ELISHA, historian, educator; b. Providence, Apr. 19, 1920; s. Frederick W. and Helen (Darling) T.; children— Margaret, Anne, Elizabeth. Student, Williams Coll., 1938-41; AB, Brown U., 1942; postgrad., U. Okla., 1944-45; MA, Harvard, 1947, PhD, 1952. Instr. Middlebury (Vt.) Coll., 1947-65, prof., 1965-90, prof. emeritus, 1990. Author: Approaches to History, 1963, The Specious Past, 1972. Served with USNR, 1942- 46. Fulbright fellow, 1956-57 Mem. Phi Beta Kappa. Episcopalian. Home: Middlebury, Vt. Died May 13, 2007.

TIMOTHY, RAYMOND JOSEPH, television executive; b. NYC, Mar. 23, 1932; s. Richard and Mary Ann (O'Connor) T.; m. Kathleen Shanahan, May, 1964; children: Matthew, Patrick, Luke. BA in Polit. Sci., Queens Coll., 1954; LLB, Bklyn. Law Sch., 1963. Bar: N.Y. 1964. Various broadcasting positions, 1954—76; v.p., gen. mgr. WNBC-TV, NYC, 1976—77; exec. v.p. affiliate rels. NBC, NYC, 1977—79; exec. v.p. NBC-TV Network, NYC, 1979—81; pres. NBC, NYC, 1981—82, group. exec. v.p., 1982—84; group exec. v.p. NBC Entertainment, 1984—86; with Furman Selz, 1989—97; founder Salem Partners, 1997—2007. Active N.Y.C. affiliate Nat. Coun. on Alcoholism. With US Army, 1956—58. Mem.: Nat. Acad. Arts and Scis. (pres. internat. coun.). Died Sept. 27, 2007.

TINDALL, GEORGE BROWN, retired historian, educator; b. Greenville, SC, Feb. 26, 1921; s. Goin Roscoe and Nellie Evelyn (Brown) Tindall; m. Carliss Blossom McGarrity, June 29, 1946; children: Bruce McGarrity, Blair Alston Mercer. AB, Furman U., 1942, LittD, 1971; MA, U. N.C., 1948, PhD, 1951. Asst. prof. history Ea. Ky. State Coll., 1950—51; asst. prof. U. Miss., 1951—52, U. N.C. Woman's Coll., 1952—53, La. State U., 1953—58; assoc. prof. U. N.C., Chapel Hill, 1958—64, prof., 1964—69, Kenan prof., 1969—90, Kenan prof. emeritus, 1990—2006. Vis. prof. Coll. Charleston, 1951, Kyoto Am. Studies Sem., 1977; Fulbright guest prof. U. Vienna, 1967—68; mem. Inst. Advanced Study, 1963—64, Ctr. Advanced Study Behavioral Scis., 1979—80. Author: South Carolina Negroes, 1877-1900, 1952, The Emergence of the New South, 1913-1945, 1967 (Jules F. Landry award, 1968, Mayflower Cup, 1968, Lillian E. Smith award, 1968, Charles S. Syndor award, 1968), The Disruption of the Solid South, 1972, The Persistent Tradition in New South Politics, 1975, The Ethnic Southerners, 1976, America: A Narrative History, 1984, Natives and Newcomers: Ethnic Southerners and Southern Ethnics, 1995; co-author (with David Shi): America: A Narrative History, 1999; editor: The Pursuit of Southern History, 1964, A Populist Reader, 1966. Fellow Guggenheim, 1957—58, Social Sci. Rsch. Coun., 1959—60, Ctr. Advanced Study Behavioral Scis., 1979—80. Mem.: So. Hist. Assn. (pres. 1973), Orgn. Am. Historians, N.C. Lit. and Hist. Soc., Hist. Soc. N.C. (pres. 1990), Am. Hist. Assn. Home: Chapel Hill, NC. Died Dec. 2, 2006.

TINEN, JOHN VICTOR, concrete additives sales company executive; b. Berwyn, Ill., Jan. 24, 1922; s. John Victor and Jane (Mills) T.; B.B.A., Northwestern U., 1946; m. Lois Jean Heicher, Jan. 23, 1943; children— Susan J., Diane E., Mary E., Brian R. Controller, Howard Foundry Co., 1954-58; regional acctg. dir. U.S. Post Office, 1958-60; exec. v.p., treas. Walter N. Handy Co., Inc., Springfield, Mo., 1960-63, pres., 1963—, also dir.; pres. Handy Splty. Products, 1985—; chmn. bd. Fly Ash Sales Co., 1969—, Ozark Concrete Co., 1969—, Handy Trucking Co., 1973—; dir. Handy Geotech. Instruments Co. Served with USAAF, 1942-46. C.P.A., Ill. Mem. Am. Inst. C.P.A.s, Mo. Soc. C.P.A.s, Beta Alpha Psi, Sigma Nu. Methodist. Club: Hickory Hills. Home: Springfield, Mo. Died June 9, 2007.

TINGHITELLA, STEPHEN, publishing company executive; b. Bklyn., May 21, 1915; s. Michael and Carmela (Cestaro) T.; m. Inez Barbara Albertelli, May 20, 1945; children— Vilma, Stephen, John. Student, Acad. Advanced Traffic, 1946-50. Traffic mgr. John Sexton & Co. (wholesale grocery distbn.), Long Island City, N.Y., 1947-53; v.p. Rupp Trucking Co., NYC, 1953-56; dir. transp. Commerce and Industry Assn. N.Y., NYC, 1956-62; editor-in-chief Traffic Mgmt. mag. Cahners Pub. Co., NYC, from 1962, pub., from 1970, v.p., from 1975. Author: Introduction of Traffic and Transportation, 1986; Sponsoring editor: Red Book on Transportation of Hazardous Materials, 1977. Served to master sgt. AUS, 1942-46. Recipient Spl. citation Pres's. Com. Employment of Handicapped, 1967, Editor's award Cahners Pub. Co., 1968, Editorial Achievement award Am. Bus. Press, 1974, 78 Mem. Delta Nu Alpha (Transp. Man of Year award 1964) Home: Massapequa, NY. Died Dec. 27, 2005.

TINSTMAN, ROBERT MECHLING, utility executive; b. Johnstown, Pa., Apr. 4, 1928; s. Carl C. and Irene (Mechling) T.; m. Lela Jane Akin, Jan. 8, 1977; children by previous marriage: Robert O., Torre R., Tracy D. BS in Archtl. Engring., Pa. State U., 1950; MA in Govtl. Adminstrn, U. Pa., 1955. Asst. city mgr., Kansas City, Mo., 1954-59; mgr. Downtown Com., Kansas City, Mo., 1959-60; city mgr. Abilene, Tex., 1960-63, Oklahoma City, 1963-67, Austin, Tex., 1967-69; v.p., gen. mgr. E.E. Stuessy Co., Inc., Austin, 1969-73, pres., 1973-75; asst. gen. mgr. Lower Colo. River Authority, 1975-81, dir. adminstrn., 1981-87. Trustee Oklahoma City Airport Trust, 1963-67; bd. dirs. Tex. Mcpl. League, 1962-63; bd. dirs. Capitol Area United Way, 1968-76, pres., 1975, chmn. bd. trustees, 1976; bd. govs. Austin Community Found., 1977-81, sec., 1980-81, v.p., 1981-82; pres. Community Council, 1977-78; mem. exec. com. United Way of Tex., 1983—, 1st v.p., 1985-86, pres., 1987-88. Served with AUS, 1951-54. Mem. Internat. City Mgrs. Assn., Austin C. of C. (dir. 1975-77, v.p. 1977), Am. Pub. Works Assn., Tau Beta Pi, Sigma Tau, Alpha Rho Chi, Scarab, Beta Theta Pi. Lodges: Masons. Home: Leander, Tex. Died Nov. 28, 2005.

TITUS, DAVID ANSON, political science educator; b. Cleve., Dec. 2, 1934; s. Jesse Edmund and Anne (Bonnette) T.; m. Kaoru Matsumura, Sept. 3, 1960 (div. 1966); m. Rachel Thankful Roberts, Aug. 3, 1968; children: Jeffrey, Brian. BA, Harvard U., 1956; MA, Columbia U., 1962, PhD, 1970. Instr. Wesleyan U., Middletown, Conn., 1966-70, asst. prof., 1970-73, assoc. prof., 1973-79, prof. govt., from 1979, co-chmn. Coll. Social Studies, 1972-75, 81-84, 93-96, chmn. dept. govt., 1976-78, chmn. East Asian Studies Program, 1976-78, 1979-81, 1988-90. Mem. staff Joint Com. Japanese Studies, N.Y.C., 1968-70; chmn. bd. dirs. Associated Kyoto Program, 1976-77. 79-82, resident dir., 1975-76, 84-85, 96-97. Author: Palace and Politics in Prewar Japan, 1974; translator: Japan's Road to the Pacific War—The Final Confrontation: Japan's Negotiations with the United States, 1941, 1994. Founder Mattabeseck Audubon Soc., Middletown, Conn., 1974. Served to lt. (j.g.) USN, 1956-58. Recipient Ansley award Columbia U. Press, 1970; vis. scholar Corpus Christi Coll., Cambridge, Eng., 1978-79, Doshisha U., Kyoto, Japan, 1987, 93. Mem. Assn. Asian Studies (council confs. 1983-86, chmn. studies program com. 1975). Home: Cromwell, Conn. Died June 13, 2006.

TOBIAN, LOUIS, JR., medical educator; b. Dallas, Jan. 26, 1920; s. Louis and Isabelle (Franklin) T.; m. Frances Williams, Oct. 18, 1951; 1 child, Anne Simpson. BA, U. Tex., 1940; MD, Harvard Med. Sch., 1943. Diplomate Am. Bd. Internal Medicine. Intern Brigham-Womens Hosp., Boston, 1944; resident U. Calif. Hosp., San Francisco, 1944-45, Parkland Hosp., Dallas, 1945-46; fellow in medicine U. Tex. Southwestern Med. Sch., Dallas, 1946-49, rsch. fellow, 1949-51, asst. prof. medicine, 1951, 54; rsch. fellow biol. chemistry Harvard Med. Sch., Boston, 1951-53; assoc. prof. medicine U. Minn. Hosp. and Med. Sch., Mpls., 1954-64, prof. medicine, from 1964. Contbr. over 200 articles to profl. jours. Chmn. NIH Task Force on Hypertension, 1972-73, Coun. for High Blood Pressure Rsch., AHA, 1974-76. Franz Volhard award Internat. Soc. Hypertension, 1988. Mem. Am. Assn. Physicians, Am. Soc. Clin. Investigation, Am. Physiol. Soc. (chmn. circulation group 1977), Am. Soc. Hypertension (pres. 1992-94, Richard Bright award 1992), Am. Soc. Nephrology (John P. Peters award 1990), Coun. for High Blood Pressure Rsch. (chmn. 1974-76). Avocations: gofling, tennis, skiing, theater, symphony. Home: Minneapolis, Minn. Died Sept. 2, 2006.

TOBIAS, RICHARD CLARK, humanities educator; b. Xenia, Ohio, Oct. 10, 1925; s. Raymond L. and Cathryn (Eckerle) T.; m. Barbara N. Tobias, June 18, 1949 (dec. 1993); children: Leslie Tobias Olsen, Alan Clark Tobias, Emily Tobias Profitt. BS, Ohio State U., 1947, MA, 1951, PhD, 1957. Asst. instr. Ohio State U., Columbus, 1951-52, grad. asst., 1955-57; instr. U. Colo., Boulder, 1952-55; from asst. prof. to prof. U. Pitts., from 1957. Author: Art of James Thurber, 1970, Thomas Edward Brown, 1978; editor: Shakespeare's Late Plays, 1974, Bibliogs of Studies in Victorian Literature, 1991. Cpl. U.S. Army, 1944-46, ETO. Mem. MLA (chair Victorian divsn. 1974-76). Home: Pittsburgh, Pa. Died Sept. 12, 2006.

TOBIN, RICHARD J., lawyer; b. Boston, Aug. 1, 1934; s. Richard Charles and Eleanor Marie (Leary) T.; m. Esther Hanley, Oct. 27, 1962; children: Margaret Alicia, Joseph Hanley, Richard Neil, David Lawrence, Mary Courtney. BS, Boston Coll., 1956, LLD, 1962. Bar: Conn., 1967, Mass. 1962, Fla., 1993. Asst. corp. counsel law dept. City of Boston, 1962-65; asst. gen. counsel New Haven Redevel. Agy., 1966-67; ptnr. Cummings and Lockwood, Stamford, Conn., 1967-94; judge Superior Ct. State of Conn., from 1994. Chmn. Stamford Transit Dist., 1970-72; mem. Dem. City Com., Stamford, 1970-76. Capt. USMCR, 1956-60. Mem. Conn. Bar Assn. (exec. com. planning and zoning sect. 1980-94), Mass. Bar Assn., Fla. Bar Assn., Greater Stamford Bar Assn. (pres. 1977-78), Stamford Yacht Club (bd. dirs. 1980-85, 90—). Roman Catholic. Died Sept. 1, 2006.

TODD, JOHN, mathematician, educator; b. Carnacally, Ireland, May 16, 1911; came to U.S., 1947, naturalized, 1953; s. William Robert and Catherine (Stewart) T.; m. Olga Taussky, Sept. 29, 1938 (dec. 1995). BS, Queen's U., Belfast, Ireland, 1931; research student, St. John's Coll., Cambridge U., Eng., 1931-33. Lectr. Queen's U., 1933-37, King's Coll., London, 1937-49; chief computation lab., then chief numerical analysis Nat. Bur. Standards, 1947-57; prof. math. Calif. Inst. Tech., 1957—2007; Fulbright prof. Vienna, 1965. Hon. fellow Barbara Bodichon Found., Girton Coll., Cambridge (Eng.) U., 2005. Author, editor books on numerical analysis and tables; editor in chief: Numerische Mathematik; assoc. editor Aequationes Mathematicae, 1967-85, 89-95, Jour. Approximation Theory, 1967-93. Mem. Am. Math. Soc., Soc. Indsl. and Applied Math., Math. Assn. Am. (gov. 1980-83) Died June 21, 2007.

TODMAN, HOWARD FRANKLIN, television production company executive; b. NYC, Nov. 24, 1920; s. Frederick Simpson and Helena Diana (Orlowitz) T.; m. Constance White, July 15, 1945 (div. 1974); children— Katharine, Leslie; m. 2d, Fern Roberta Weiss; children— Myka, Raleigh BS, Hamilton Coll., 1941. Treas. Goodson-Todman, NYC, 1946-53, dir. bus. affairs, v.p., from 1953. Producer, dir. radio shows: Winner Take All, Beat the Clock, Hit the Jackpot Chmn. radio and TV div. Am. Cancer Soc., N.Y.C., 1958—. Served to 2d lt. U.S. Army, 1941-45 Democrat. Jewish. Avocations: golf; tennis; fishing. Home: New York, NY. Died May 2, 2007.

TOFIAS, ALLAN, retired accountant; b. Boston, Apr. 13, 1930; s. George I. and Anna (Seidel) T.; m. Arlene Shube, Aug. 30, 1981; children: Bradley Neil, Laura Jean Silver. BA, Colgate U., 1951; MBA, Harvard U., 1956. CPA, Mass. Sr. acct. Peat, Marwick, Mitchell & Co., Boston, 1956—60; mng. ptnr. Tofias, Fleishman, Shapiro & Co., P.C., Boston, 1960-96, chmn. bd., 1996-97. Bd. dir. Rowe Cos.; trustee Gannett, Welch & Kotler Mut. Funds, 1996-2002. Mem. Brookline (Mass.) Town Meeting, 1970-77, mem. fin. adv. bd., 1975-81; mem. New Eng. Bapt. Health Care Corp., 1985—, trustee, 1998-, chmn. fin. com., 1998-2002; bd. dir. West Newton YMCA, 1986-89; mem. exec. com. Boston Aid to Blind, bd. dir., 1988-97, pres., 1993-94. Lt. USNR, 1951-54. Mem. AICPA (coun. 1995-99), Mass. Soc. CPA's (pres. 1995-96), Nat. CPA Group (exec. com. 1983-88, vice chmn. 1985-88), BKR Internat. (world bd. dirs. 1988-97, chmn. 1994-96), Wightman Tennis Club (treas. 1974 76), Newton Squash and Tennis Club (bd. dirs. 1966-99) Masons. Home: Wayland, Mass. Died Nov. 1, 2005.

TOFTNER, RICHARD ORVILLE, engineering executive; b Warren, Minn., Mar. 5, 1935; s. Orville Gayhart and Cor Evelyn (Anderson) T.; m. Jeanne Bredine, June 26, 1960 children: Douglas, Scott, Kristine, Kimberly, Brian. BA, U Minn., 1966; MBA, Xavier U., 1970. Registered environ assessor Calif. Sr. economist Federated Dept. Stores, Inc., Cin 1967-68; dep. dir. EPA, Washington and Cin., 1968-73; mgm cons. environ. affairs, products and mktg., 1973-74; prin PEDCo Environ., Cin., 1974-80; trustee PEDCo trusts, 1974-80 pres. ROTA Mgmt., Inc., Cin., 1980-82; gen. mgr. CECOS 1982-85; cons., from 1985; v.p. Smith, Stevens & Young 1985-88; real estate developer, from 1980. Pres., CEO Toxitro Internat., Inc., 1988-89; dir. Environ. Svcs. Belcan Engring Group, Inc., Cin., 1989-92; prin. exec. cons. Resource Mgm Internat., Inc., 1994—; adj. prof. environ. engring. U. Cin. 1975-86; lectr. Grad. fellowship rev. panel Office of Edn. 1978-79; advisor, cabinet-level task force Office of Gov. of P.R. 1973; pvt. investor, 1991—; bd. dirs. EnviroAudit Svcs., Inc. pres., CEO, 1992—; mem. legis. com. Ohio Chem. Coun. 1995—; v.p. environ. engring. CSA Architects & Engrs., 1996 2001; client svc. mgr. Weston Solutions, Inc. Environ. Cons. 2001—; subcom. Nat. Safety Coun., 1972; mem. exec. environ briefing panels Andersen Consulting, 1991-92; nominee comm PUCO, Ohio; chmn. Cin. City Waste Task Force, 1987-88 co-chair Hamilton County Resource Recovery Com., 1989— Contbr. articles on mgmt. planning and environ. to periodicals chpts. to books; inventor, developer Toxitrol Waste Minimiza tion; inventor EnviroAudit. With AUS, 1954-57. Mem. U.S Tennis Assn., Nat. Registry Environ. Profl. Rep., Engring. Soc Cin., Assn. Corp. Environ. Execs., Cin. C. of C., Global Assn Corp. Environ. Execs. (charter). Republican. Lutheran. Home Cincinnati, Ohio. Died Feb. 14, 2006.

TOKAY, RONALD NAYLAND, contract research and devel opment company executive, consultant; b. South Bend, Ind. May 5, 1933; s. Emery A. and Sophie C. (Barna) T.; Marlen Marie Serritella, Jan. 29, 1954; children— Brenda Marie, Mar Nayland, Lori Lizabeth. B.S. in Bus., Miami U., 1955; M.B.A. George Washington U., 1970. Cert. profl. contracts mgr., pur chas mgr. Enlisted U.S. Navy, 1955, advanced through grades t comdr., 1969, ret., 1978; contract specialist Battelle Meml. Inst. Richland, Wash., 1978-85; cons., 1985—; sr. specialist Lo Alamos Nat. Lab., 1987—. Mem. Nat. Contract Mgmt. Assn. Nat. Assn. Purchase Mgmt., Clover Island Yacht Club (bd. dirs 1981-83), Santa Fe Country Club, Delta Sigma Pi. Roma Catholic. Home: Granger, Ind. Died June 12, 2007.

TOLEDANO, RALPH DE, columnist, writer, poet; b. Interna Zone of Tangier, Aug. 17, 1916; m. Nora Romaine, July 6, 193 (div. 1964); children: James, Paul Christopher; m. Eunic Marshall, Apr. 19, 1979 (dec. Aug. 1999). BA, Columbia Coll. 1938; postgrad., Cornell U., 1943. Founder, co-editor Cross Town, 1932-33; Founder, co-editor Jazz Info., 1938-39; assoc editor The New Leader, 1941-43; editor The Standard, 1946 mng. editor Plain Talk, 1946-47; pub. dir. Dress Joint Bd. Internat. Ladies Garment Workers Union, 1947-48; asst. edito Newsweek, 1948, nat. reports editor, 1950-60, asst. chief Wash ington Bur., 1956-60; syndicated columnist King Features 1960-71, Nat. News Research Syndicate, 1971-74, Copley New Service, 1974-89, Heritage Features Syndicate, 1989-91, Cre ators Syndicate, 1991-98, Nat. News Rsch. Syndicate 1998—2007; editor House Republican Leadership report Am Mil. Strength and Strategy, 1960; chief Washington Bur., Taf Broadcasting Co., 1960-61; dir. polit. intelligence Goldwate Presdl. Campaign, 1963-64; contbg. editor Nat. Rev. 1960—2001; pres. Nat. News-Rsch., 1960—2007, Anthen Books, 1960—2007; editor-in-chief Washington World, 1961 62. Vice-chmn. Am. Conserva-Union, 1965-66; mem. 20th Century Fund Task Force on Freedom Press, 1971-72. Author Seeds of Treason, 1950, Spies, Dupes and Diplomats, 1952, Day of Reckoning, 1955, Nixon, 1956, Lament for a Generation 1960, The Greatest Plot in History, 1963, The Winning Side 1963, The Goldwater Story, 1964, RFK: The Man Who Would be President, 1967, America, I-Love-You, 1968, One Man Alone: Richard M. Nixon, 1969, Claude Kirk: Man and Myth 1970, Little Cesar, 1971, J. Edgar Hoover: The Man in His Time 1973, Hit and Run: The Ralph Nader Story, 1975, Let Our Citie Burn, 1975, Poems: You & I, 1978, Devil Take Him, 1979, Th Apocrypha of Limbo (poems), 1994, Notes from the Under ground: The Chambers-Toledano Letters, 1997, Cry Havoc: Th Secret War on America, 2006; editor: Frontiers of Jazz, 1947 Mark Twain on Practically Anything, 2001; co-editor: (wit Melvin Laird) The Conservative Papers, 1962,; editor-in-chief Political Success, 1968-69; mem. editl. bd. Yale Lit. Mag 1981-86; contbg. editor Insight, Washington Times; contbr articles to nat. mags. Bd. dirs. Americans for Constitutiona Action, 1966-67, Constructive Action, 1990-2000 With OSS AUS, 1943-46. Recipient Freedoms Found. award, 1950, 61, 74 Americanism award VFW, 1953; Disting. Journalism fellow Heritage Found. Mem. Internat. Mark Twain Soc., Bibl. Arche ology Soc., Dutch Treat Club (N.Y.), Nat. Press Club, Naval an Mil. Club (London), Am. Legion (comdr. Pershing/NPC post) Sigma Delta Chi. Died Feb. 3, 2007.

TOMLINSON, NORMAN THOMAS, retired governmen official, specialist; b. Alexandria, Va., July 21, 1932; s. Thoma Perry and Beulah Opal (Blackmore) T.; BBA, Ga. Coll. Milledgeville, 1979, postgrad. in bus. adminstrn.; postgrad. Ai Command and Staff Coll., Robins AFB, Ga.; m. Donna Rut Dodds, July 28, 1961; children: Jean Marie, Christine Opal Automotive repair and serviceman, 1955-60; mem. faculty Keesler Air Tng. Ctr., Miss., 1963-64; life ins. agt., 1965-68 trainer U.S. Govt., 1968-74; staff cons. on productivity an quality of worklife Warner Robins AFB, 1974—. Deacon, dir Sunday sch. Baptist Ch. Served with USAF, 1951-55, 60-64 Korea. Mem. Am. Soc. Tng. and Devel., Soc. Logistics Engrs. Air Force Assn., Fed. Mgrs. Assn., Better Mgmt. Assn. Home Perry, Ga. Died Sept. 23, 2006.

TOMPKINS, HAROLD, judge; b. N.Y.C., Dec. 13, 1932; s. Max G. and Elsie (Cohen) T.; m. Frances Fish, June 28, 1959; 1 son, Laurence A. F. B.A., Syracuse U., 1954; J.D., Cornell U., 1957. Bar: N.Y. 1957, U.S. Supreme Ct. 1961. Atty. U.S. Bur. Customs, N.Y.C., 1957-60; sole practice, N.Y.C., 1960-75; asst. atty. gen. State of N.Y., 1975-81; judge Civil Ct. City of N.Y., 1982—. Mem. Assn. Bar City N.Y., N.Y. State Bar Assn., N.Y. County Bar Assn. Home: New York, NY. Died May 2, 2007.

TONG, HING, mathematician, educator; b. Canton, China, Feb. 16, 1922; s. Shen-Beu and Fung-Kam (Cheng) T.; m. Mary Josephine Powderly, Aug. 19, 1956; children— Christopher Hing, Mary Elizabeth, William Joseph, Jane Frances, James John. AB, U. Pa., 1943; PhD, Columbia, 1947; MA (hon.), Wesleyan U., Middletown, Conn., 1961. NRC postdoctoral fellow Inst. Advanced Study, Princeton, 1947-48; lectr. Canton (China) U., 1949; Cutting travelling fellow Inst. Henri Poincare, Paris, 1950-51; asst. prof. Reed Coll., 1952-53; vis. asst. prof. Barnard Coll., 1953-54; mem. faculty Wesleyan U., 1954-67, prof. math., 1960-67, chmn. dept., 1962-64; prof. math. Fordham U., Bronx, NY, 1966-84, chmn. dept., 1967-74. Contbr. profl. jours. Mem. Phi Beta Kappa, Sigma Xi. Home: Oradell, NJ. Died Mar. 4, 2007.

TONGUE, WILLIAM WALTER, economics and business consultant, educator; b. Worcester, Mass., May 24, 1915; s. Walter Ernest and Lena (Brown) T.; m. Beverly Harriet Cohan, Dec. 26, 1936; children— Barbara Tongue Duggan, Kathleen Tongue Alligood. AB, Dartmouth, 1937, M.C.S., 1938; PhD, U. Chgo., 1947. Jr. acct. Price, Waterhouse & Co. (C.P.A.'s), NYC, 1938; instr. Coe Coll., Cedar Rapids, Iowa, 1941-42; spl. cons. OSS, 1942; fin. economist Fed. Res. Bank Chgo., 1942-44; economist Jewel Companies, Inc., Chgo., 1944-64; prof. econs. and finance U. Ill. Chgo., 1965-80. Prof. emeritus, 1980—; econ. cons. LaSalle Nat. Bank, Chgo., 1968-91; mem. com. CNA Fin. Separate Fund B., 1997-2003; dir. St. Joseph Light & Power Co., Mo., 1965-86; trustee Signode Employees' Savs. and Profit Sharing Trust Fund, 1980-89. Author articles; contbr.: to books including How We Can Halt Inflation and Still Keep Our Jobs, 1974. Bd. dirs., v.p. rsch. and stats. Chgo. Assn. Commerce and Industry, 1968-69; bd. dirs. Luther Village Owners Corp., v.p., 2002-05 Mem. Nat. Assn. Bus. Economists (pres. 1962-63), Conf. Bus. Economists, Am. Statis. Assn. (pres. Chgo. chpt. 1951-52), Econ. Club Chgo., Investment Analysts Assn. Chgo., Inst. Chartered Fin. Analysts (chartered fin. analyst 1963), Midwest Fin. Assn. (pres. 1972-73). Died Mar. 7, 2007.

TORNABENE, CHARLES AUGUSTUS, management consultant; b. Pitts., Dec. 22, 1918; s. Carmelo and Ignazia (Teresi) T.; m. Kathryn Moran, Feb. 11, 1942; children: Charles Augustus, Thomas, Rosemary. Grad., Wittenberg U., 1940. Gen. sales mgr. Kellogg Co., Battle Creek, Mich., 1958—60, v.p., gen. sales mgr., 1960—67, dir. sales co., 1966—76, pres. sales co., 1968—76, dir., from 1969, chmn. bd. sales co., 1969—76, vice-chmn. corp., 1976—81, internat., 1977—81, vice-chmn. bd., 1981—83; pres. Tornabene Assocs, Inc., internat. and domestic mgmt. cons., Battle Creek, from 1984. Dir. Wm. R. Biggs/Gilmore Assocs., Inc., Norman Grocery Co.; chmn. suppliers bd. Internat. Chain Stores; past chmn. Cereal Inst. Trustee, mem. exec. com. Mich. Colls. Found.; bd. dirs Calhoun County United Way; founder, chmn. Battle Creek's Keep Am. Beautiful; bd. dirs Catholic Family Svcs. Kalamazoo Diocese, Cmty. Coll. Allegheny County; bd. govs. St. Joseph U. With US Army, 1942—45. Named Man of Yr., Internat. Assn. Chain Stores, 1979; recipient Nat. Mgmt. Assn. award, 1982. Mem.: Conf. Bd. (internat. coun.), Illuminators Club, Asparagus Club. Roman Catholic. Home: Battle Creek, Mich. Died Apr. 6, 2007.

TORRES, FERNANDO, physician, educator; b. Paris, Nov. 29, 1924; s. Calixto and Dona Isabel (Restrepo) Torres-Umana; m. Komtesse Edeltraud Maria Schradin, Nov. 15, 1955. BA, German Coll., Bogota, Colombia, 1941; MD, Nat. U., Bogota, 1948. Diplomate Am. Bd. Clin. Neurophysiology, Am. Bd. Psychiatry and Neurology. Resident physician medicine and surgery Hosp. San Jose, Bogota, 1948-49; asst. in neurosurgery Instituto de Medicine Experimental, Buenos Aires, 1949-50; research fellow Johns Hopkins, Balt., 1950-52; postdoctoral research fellow NIH, Bethesda, Md., 1952-53; asst. resident in neurology Montefiore Hosp., NYC, 1953-54; resident, 1954-55; asst. neurology Columbia, 1954-55; practice medicine specializing in neurology and electroencephalography Bogota, 1955-56; dir. EEG Lab., Hosp. San Juan de Dios, Bogota, 1955-56; faculty U. Minn., Mpls., from 1956, prof. neurology, from 1964, dir. electroencephalography lab., from 1956. Cons. prof. neurology U. P.R. Med. Sch., 1961; spl. fellow Nat. Inst. Neural Diseases and Blindness, NIH, USPHS, Lab. EEG and Applied Neurophysiology, LaSalpetriere Hosp., Paris, 1963-64; consul of Colombia in Mpls., 1960—; staff neurologist S.S. Hope, Cartagena, Colombia, 1967; mem. exec. com. profl. adv. bd. Epilepsy Found. Am., 1970-77, sec. profl. adv. bd., 1975-77; mem. Am. Bd. Qualification in Electroencephalography, 1972-81, sec.-treas., 1974-81 Fellow Am. Acad. Neurology, Am. Electroencephalographic Soc. (pres. 1976-77); mem. Am. Neurol. Assn., Central Assn. Electroencephalographers (pres. 1971-72), AAAS, Soc. Neuroscis., Acad. Medicine Colombia, Nat. Acad. Medicine Buenos Aires, Minn. Consular Assn. (pres. 1989); corr. mem. Venezuelan Neurol. Soc., Peruvian Soc. for Neurology, Psychiatry and Neurosurgery, Chilean Soc. Electroencephalography Clin. Neurophysiology, Peruvian Soc. Electroencephalography, Royal Soc. Medicine, World Fedn. Neurology (mem. exec. com. research group on cerebrovascular disease). Research and publs. in neurology and electroencephalography. Home: Minneapolis, Minn. Died Jan. 21, 2007.

TOSI, GEORGE, lawyer; b. Passaic, N.J., Jan. 27, 1933; s. George Charles and Angelina (Colandro) T.; m. Evelyn Ann Tosi, June 7, 1958; children— David, Lawrence, Eric, Sharon. B.A., Fairleigh Dickinson U., 1957; LL.B., Georgetown U., 1960. Bar: Fla. 1962, N.J. 1969, U.S. Dist. Ct. N.J. 1969, U.S. Ct. Mil. Appeals 1965, U.S. Supreme Ct. 1978. First asst. pub. defender Passaic County, N.J., 1969-75; chief trial counsel Prosecutors Office, Passaic County, 1975-79; sole practice, Totowa, N.J., 1979—; prosecutor, Twp. of Little Falls, N.J., 1975—; atty. Pre Paid Legal Fund, Little Falls, N.J., 1984—; mem. N.J. Supreme Ct. Adv. Com. Mclp. Cts., 1984—. Pres., Jackson Park Civic Assn., Little Falls, 1962, Unico, Little Falls, 1973; mem. Passaic Valley Bd. Edn., Little Falls, 1975. Served with USMC, 1950-54, to capt., 1964-68. Decorated Purple Heart. Recipient Civics award Jaycees, 1973. Mem. Nat. Assn. Dist. Attys., Passaic County Bar Assn., Fla. Bar Assn., Assn. Trial Lawyers of N.J., Am. Legion, D.A.V. Republican. Russian Orthodox. Club: Little Falls Athletic (pres. 1962). Home: Little Falls, NJ. Died Feb. 20, 2006.

TOUSSAINT, WAYNE E., manufacturing executive; b. Princeton, Minn., Jan. 22, 1918; s. Jacob and Lettie (Nichols) T.; m. Frances Cooper, Aug. 14, 1939; children: Jacqueline Carol Toussaint Rapp, Laurel Patrice Toussaint (Bik). BS, Northwestern U., 1939. C.P.A., Ill. With Barrow, Wade, Guthrie & Co., Chgo., 1939-42; pres., chief exec. officer Frederick Post Co. (now Teledyne Post), Chgo., 1942-71, 73-75; chmn., chief exec. officer Vance Industries, Inc., Chgo., from 1971. Served with USNR, 1945-46. Mem. Ill. Soc. C.P.A.'s, Delta Sigma Pi, Beta Gamma Sigma. Clubs: Minocqua Country (Wis.). Lodges: Masons (32 deg.). Died Jan. 14, 2007.

TOWER, DONALD BAYLEY, neuroscientist; b. Orange, N.J., Dec. 11, 1919; s. Walter Sheldon and Edith Florence (Jones) T.; A.B., Harvard U., 1941, M.D., 1944; M.Sc., McGill U., Montreal, 1948, Ph.D., 1951, D.Sc. (hon.), 1984; m. Arline Belle Croft, Aug. 5, 1947; 1 dau., Deborah Alden Tower Fretwell. Intern in surgery U. Minn. Hosp., Mpls., 1944-45; research fellow neurochemistry Montreal Neurol. Inst., 1947-48, 49-51, asst. resident in neurosurgery, 1948-49, asso. neurochemist, 1951-53; instr., then asst. prof. exptl. neurology McGill U. Med. Sch., 1951-53; joined USPHS, 1953, asst. surgeon gen., 1975-81; chief sect. clin. neurochemistry Nat. Inst. Neurol. Diseases and Stroke, NIH, HEW, Bethesda, Md., 1953-61, chief lab. neurochemistry, 1961-74, dir. Nat. Inst. Neurol. and Communicative Disorders and Stroke, 1974-81; clin. asso. prof. neurology Georgetown U. Med. Sch., 1953-81; chmn. U.S. neurochemistry del. to USSR, 1969; temp. adviser neurosci. WHO, 1976-81, neurosciences delegation to Peoples Republic of China, 1979, ret. Recipient Lasker awards Jury 1975-80, Disting. Svc. medal USPHS, 1977, History prize Justus-Liebig U., 1984. John and Mary R. Markle scholar acad. medicine, 1951-53. Mem. AAAS, Am. Acad. Neurology, Am. Neurol. Assn. (hon.), Internat Soc. Neurochemistry, Am. Soc. Neurochemistry (co-founder 1968, historian), Am. Soc. Biol. Chemists, Can. Neurol. Soc., Can. Physiol. Soc., Internat. Brain Research Orgn. (cen. coun. 1973-91), Soc. Neurosci., Washington Acad. Medicine (bd. dirs. 1985-91), Peruvian Soc. Psychiatry, Neurology and Neurosurgery (hon.). Author: Neurochemistry of Epilepsy, 1960; Hensing, 1719: An Account of the First Chemical Examination of the Brain and the Discovery of Phosphorus Therein, 1983; also numerous research papers. Editor: The Nervous System, 3 vols., 1975; chief editor Jour. Neurochemistry, 1968-73. Achievements include research on neurochemistry of epilepsy, amino acids, fluids and electrolytes (cerebral edema), comparative neurochemistry, history of neurochemistry. Died Sept. 29, 2007.

TOWNE, RUTH H., state legislator; b. Manchester, Conn., June 17, 1928; m. Roderick E. Towne (dec.); 2 children. BS, U. Conn., 1949. Dairy farmer, Berlin, Vt.; rep. Dist. 5 State of Vt., from 1977. Breeder Morgan horses; mem. U-32 H.S. Bd. Dirs., chairwoman; treas. Washington Ctrl. Supervisory Union; consumer mem. Bd. Vet. Registration and Exam.; mem. Vt. Ext. Svc., 1949-52; rep. dist. 4-2 Barre City Berlin. Named Woman of Yr. Vt. Farm. Bur., 1989. Mem. DAR Marquis de Lafayette chpt., Vt. Farm Bur., Washington County 4-H Club (agt.), Berlin Hist. Soc. (v.p. 1985-2000). Home: Berlin, Vt. Died May 16, 2007.

TOWNSEND, EARL C., JR., lawyer, writer; b. Indpls., Nov. 9, 1914; s. Earl Cunningham and Besse (Kuhn) T.; m. Emily Macnab, Apr. 3, 1947 (dec. Mar. 1988); children: Starr, Vicki M., Julia E. (Mrs. Edward Goodrich Dunn Jr.), Earl Cunningham III, Clyde G. Student, De Pauw U., 1932-34; AB, U. Mich., 1936, JD, 1939. Bar: Ind. 1939, Mich. 1973, US Supreme Ct. 1973, US Ct. Appeals (4th, 5th, 6th, 7th cirs.), US Dist. Ct. (no. and so. dists.) Ind., US Dist. Ct. (ea. dist.) Va., US Dist. Ct. (ea. dist.) Mich. Sr. ptnr. Townsend & Townsend, Indpls., 1941-64, from 1984, Townsend, Hovde & Townsend, Indpls., 1964-84. Dep. prosecutor, Marion County, Ind., 1942-44; radio-TV announcer WIRE, WFBM, WFBM-TV, Indpls., 1940-53, 1st TV announcer Indpls. 500 mile race, 1949, 50; Big Ten basketball referee, 1940-47; lectr. trial tactics U. Notre Dame, Ind. U., U. Mich., 1968-79; chmn. faculty seminar on personal injury trials Ind. U. Sch. Law, U. Notre Dame Sch. Law, Valparaiso Sch. Law, 1981; mem. Com. to Revise Ind. Supreme Ct. Pattern Jury Instrns., 1975-83; lectr. Trial Lawyers 30 Yrs. Inst., 1986; counsel atty gen., 1988-92. Author: Birdstones of the North American Indian, 1959; editor: Am. Assn. Trial Lawyers Am. Jour., 1964-88; contbr. articles to legal and archeol. jours.; composer (waltz) Moon of Halloween. Trustee Cathedral High Sch., Indpls., Eiteljorg Mus. Am. Indian and Western Art, Cale J. Holder Scholarship Found. Ind. U. Law Sch.; life trustee, bd. dirs., mem. fin. and bldg. coms. Indpls. Mus. Art; life trustee Ind. State Mus.; founder, dir. Meridian St. Found.; mem. dean's coun. Ind. U.; founder, life fellow Roscoe Pound/Am. Trial Lawyers Found., Harvard U.; fellow Meth. Hosp. Found. Recipient Ind. Univ. Writers Conf. award, 1960, Hanson H. Anderson medal of honor Arsenal Tech. Schs., Indpls., 1971, Lifetime Achievement award, 2002; named to Coun. Sagamores of Wabash, 1969; Rector scholar, 1934, Ind. Basketball Hall of Fame, Newcastle, 1981; hon. chief Black River-Swan Creek Saginaw-Chippewa Indian tribe. Fellow: Ind. Bar Found. (life trustee, disting. fellow award), Internat. Soc. Barristers, Internat. Acad. Trial Lawyers; mem.: ATLA (v.p.), ABA (com. on trial techniques 1964—76, aviation and space from 1977), ASCAP, Mich. Trial Lawyers Assn., Bar Assn. 7th Fed. Cir. (bd. govs. 1966—68), 34th Jud. Cir. Bar Assn., Roscommon County Bar Assn., State Bar of Mich. (Champion of Justice award 1989), Am. Judicature Soc., Am. Arbitration Assn. (nat. arbitrators panel), Am. Bd. Trial Advocates (diplomate, pres. Ind. chpt. 1980—86), Ind. Trial Lawyers Assn. (pres. 1965, pres. Coll. Fellows 1984—90), Indpls. Bar Found. (disting. charter 1986), Ind. State Bar Assn. (Golden Career award 1989), Genuine Indian Relic Soc. (founder, pres., chmn. frauds com.), Trowel and Brush Soc. (hon.), Marion County/Indpls. Hist. Soc. (bd. dirs.), Ind. Hist. Soc., Soc. Mayflower Descendants (gov. 1947—49), Columbia Club, U. Mich. Pres. Club, Key Biscayne Yacht Club, The Players Club, U. Mich. Victors Club (founder, charter mem.), Shriners, Masons (33 degree), Scottish Rite, Phi Kappa Phi, Delta Kappa Epsilon. Republican. Methodist. Avocations: art, Indian relics. Home: Indianapolis, Ind. Died Aug. 5, 2007.

TOZAKI, SEIKI, import-export company executive; b. Mar. 18, 1910; m. Misao Tozaki. Grad., Tokyo Coll. Commerce, 1934. With C. Itoh & Co. Ltd., Tokyo, from 1934, pres., from 1970, now chmn.; also chmn. C. Itoh & Co. (Am.) Inc., NYC. Recipient medal of Honor with Blue ribbon, 1972. Died July 3, 2006.

TRACI, DONALD PHILIP, retired lawyer; b. Cleve., Mar. 13, 1927; m. Lillian Traci Calafiore; 11 children. BS cum laude, Coll. of the Holy Cross, Worcester, Mass., 1950; JD magna cum laude, Cleve. State U., 1955; LLD (hon.), U. Urbino, Italy, 1989. Bar: Ohio 1955, U.S. Dist. Ct. (no. and so. dists.) Ohio 1955, U.S. Ct. Appeals (3d, 6th and 7th cirs.), U.S. Dist. Ct. (we. and ea. dists.) Pa., U.S. Supreme Ct. 1965. Ptnr. Spangenberg, Shibley, Traci, Lancione & Liber, Cleve., 1955-94; ret., from 1994. Lectr. York U., Toronto, Ont., Can., Case Western Res. U., Cleve. Marshall Law Sch., U. Mich., Akron U., U. Cin., Ohio No. U., Harvard U. Trustee Cath. Charities Diocese of Cleve., past pres. Bd. Cath. Edn.; former chmn. bd. regents St. Ignatius H.S., Cleve.; mem. pres.'s coun. Coll. of Holy Cross; Eucharist min. St. Rose of Lima Ch. With USN, 1945-46. Fellow Am. Coll. Trial Lawyers, Internat. Acad. Trial Lawyers (past pres.), Am. Bd. Trial Advocacy; mem. ABA, ATLA (trustee Lambert Chair Found., lectr. trial practice), Ohio State Bar Assn. (lectr. trial practice), Ohio Acad. Trial Lawyers (past chmn. rules seminar, lectr. trial practice), Cuyahoga County Bar Assn. (lectr. trial practice), Cleve. Acad. Trial Lawyers (lectr. trial practice), Trial Lawyers for Pub. Justice (sustaining founder), Cleve. Bar Assn. (chmn. Advocacy Inst., trustee, CLE com., jud. selection com., spl. justice ctr. com., fed. ct., common pleas ct. and ct. appeals com., pres. 1986), Jud. Conf. U.S. 6th Cir. Ct. (life), Jud. Conf. 8th Jud. Dist. Ohio life), Knights of Malta, Knights of Holu Sepulchre of Jerusalem, Delta Theta Phi. Home: Lakewood, Ohio. Died Oct. 24, 2006.

TRAINER, ORVEL LEROY, economics educator, novelist; b. Milliken, Colo., Sept. 26, 1925; s. Charles Wesley and Elda May (Easton) T.; m. Joanne Irene Gasser, June 1, 1952; children: Ryan Thomas, Eric John. BA, U. Colo., 1950, MA, 1955, PhD, 1960; diploma, U. Oslo, 1953. Lifetime teaching cert., Colo. Instr. in econs. U. Colo., Boulder, 1959-60; asst. prof. econs. U. No. Colo., Greeley, 1960-65, assoc. prof., 1965-70, prof., from 1970, dean Sch. Ednl. Change and Devel., 1974-75, dean. Coll. Edn., 1981-82. Founding dir. Educators Life Ins. Co., Denver, 1963-68; bd. dirs. Read Constrn. Co., Cheyenne, Wyo., 1968-69, Inst. New World Archaeology, Chgo., 1983— Author: (novels) Wakau, 1970, Ice Harvest, 1971, Ashes, 1972, Death Roads, 1979. Bd. dirs. Urban Renewal Authority, Greeley, 1971-72. Served with USN, 1943-46. Fulbright-Danish Govt. grantee Copenhagen, 1956-57 Fellow Am. Econ. Assn., NEA Republican. Home: Greeley, Colo. Died May 10, 2006.

TRAPP, ALLAN LAVERNE, veterinarian, educator; b. Stockbridge, Mich., July 20, 1932; s. Howard Russel and Ada Evelyn (Corser) T.; m. Joyce Eileen Ellison, Jan. 2, 1955; children: Katherine Anne, John Allan, Caryn Sue, William Laverne. BS, Mich. State U., 1954, DVM, 1956; PhD, Iowa State U., 1960. Veterinarian livestock insp. USDA, Hart, Mich., 1956-57; rsch. assoc. Iowa State U., Ames, 1957-60; asst., assoc. prof. Ohio Agrl. Ctr., Wooster, 1960-66; assoc. prof. Mich. State U., E. Lansing, 1966-69, prof., from 1969. Chmn. necropsy sect. Mich. State Univ., 1980-90. Contbr. articles to profl. jours. Adv. coun. Forestview Citizens, Lansing, Mich., 1967-75. Mem. AVMA, Am. Assn. Vet. Lab. Diagnosticians, Wildlife Disease Assn. Home: Lansing, Mich. Died May 15, 2007.

TRATNIK, FRANCES ELIZABETH, press clipping bureau executive; b. Nashville, Nov. 18, 1924; d. Louis Willson and Ella Lucille (Johnson) Royster; m. Joseph Steven Tratnik, Oct. 3, 1941 (dec. June 1947); children— Joseph Steven, Louis Henry. Supr., Ohio News Bur., Cleve., 1947-79, pres., 1979—. Mem. Fedn. Internat. Press Services, Conf. Press Services (pres. 1958—), Mich. Press Services (pres. 1979—), Fedn. Press Clipping Burs., N. Am. Press Clipping Burs. (pres. 1983—), Mich. Press Club (pres. 1979). Republican. Baptist. Home: Aurora, Ohio. Died Mar. 28, 2006.

TRAVELSTEAD, CHESTER COLEMAN, b. Franklin, Ky., Sept. 25, 1911; s. Conley and Nelle (Gooch) T.; m. Marita Hawley, Aug. 1, 1936; children: Coleman, Jimmie. AB, Western Ky. State Coll., Bowling Green, 1933; M of Music, Northwestern U., 1947; PhD, U. Ky., 1950; HHD, Morehead State U., Ky., 1975; PhD, John F. Kennedy U., Buenos Aires, 1975; LHD, U. N.Mex., 1980. Tchr., prin. rural and consol. schs., Mecklenberg County, Va., 1931-32, 33-35; tchr. gen. sci., math., music Picadome H.S., Lexington, Ky., 1935-37; dir. music Henry Clay H.S., Lexington, 1937-42; personnel supr. Lexington Signal Dept., Dept. War, 1942-43; supr. music Lexington pub. schs., 1945-47; rep. Investors Diversified Services, Inc., 1947-48; coordinator in-service tchr. edn. Ky. Dept. Edn., 1950-51; asst. prof. edn., asst. dean Coll. Edn., U. Ga., Athens, 1951-53; dean Sch. Edn., U. S.C., Columbia, 1953-56; dean Coll. Edn. U. N.Mex., Albuquerque, 1956-68, v.p. acad. affairs, 1968-76, provost, 1976-77. Mem. Nat. Council Accreditation Tchr. Edn., 1960-66, chmn., 1963-65 Author books; contbr. articles in field to profl. jours. Pres. bd. dirs. N.Mex. Symphony Orch., 1977-78, 84-85; mem. N.Mex. Jud. Stds. Commn., 1995-96. With USNR, 1943-45; PTO. Mem. AAUP, NEA, Nat. Assn. Scholars, Soc. Advancement Edn., Phi Kappa Phi, Phi Delta Kappa., Kappa Delta Pi. Home: Albuquerque, N.Mex. Died Dec. 27, 2006.

TRAVIS, MARTIN BICE, retired political scientist, educator; b. Iron Mountain, Mich., Sept. 22, 1917; s. Martin Bice and Helen (Carrett) T.; m. Olivia Brewster Taylor, Nov. 29, 1942; children: Elizabeth Nichols (Mrs. Usama Mugharbil), Helen

Willard. AB, Amherst Coll., 1939; student, Heidelberg U., Germany, 1937; MA, Fletcher Sch. Law and Diplomacy, 1940; PhD, U. Chgo., 1948. Asst. prof. internat. relations Syracuse U., 1948-49; asst. prof. polit. sci. Duke U., 1949-52; asst. prof., then asso. prof. polit. sci. Stanford U., 1953-61; prof. polit. sci. SUNY-Stony Brook, 1961-92; coordinator SUNY Program Am. U., Beirut, 1972-73; chmn. dept., 1961-68; dir. Inst. Am. Studies SUNY-Stony Brook, 1965-93; ret., 1993. Vis. prof. Sch. Internat. Affairs, Columbia, 1956-57; vis. summer prof. U. Guadalajara, Mex., 1959, 62, U. Wash., 1961; Bd. dirs. State U N.Y. Inst. Am. Studies in France, 1966-77; cons. to industry. Author: (with E.E. Robinson) Powers of the President in Foreign Affairs, 1966; Co-editor, contbr.: (with Philip W. Buck) Control of Foreign Relations in Modern Nations, 1957; bd. editors: Western Polit. Quar, 1956-58; adv. bd.: Almanac of Current World Leaders, 1957—; editorial critic for book pubs. Mem. sch. bd., Cold Spring Harbor, N.Y., 1965-71, v.p. 1967-68, pres. 1968-69; trustee Village of Laurel Hollow, 1983-95, police com., 1983-85, mayor, 1985-95; established Martin B. Travis Scholarship fund for pre-law majors at SUNY, Stonybrook, 1995. Grantee Ford Found. 1960-61; recipient Hugh Cleland Meml. Outstanding Prof. award Alumni Assn. SUNY Stony Brook, 2000. Mem. Coun. Fgn. Rels., Phi Delta Theta, Phi Delta Kappa. Home: Syosset, NY. Died Apr. 26, 2006.

TREFONAS, LOUIS MARCO, academic administrator, chemistry educator; b. Chgo., June 21, 1931; s. Peter and Eugenia (Xidis) T.; m. Gail Haley Thames, Nov. 10, 1957; children: Peter, Stephanie, Jennifer, Mark, Paul, Jason. BA, U. Chgo., 1951, MS, 1954; PhD, U. Minn., 1959. Asst. prof. U. New Orleans, 1959-62, asso. prof., 1962-66, asso. prof., chmn. chemistry dept., 1963-66, prof., chmn., 1966-80, program dir., 1979-81; v.p. sponsored rsch. U. Central Fla., Orlando, 1981-85, grad. dean, assoc. v.p. acad. affairs, 1986-92, acting chmn. chem. dept., fall 1987; prof., from 1992. Pres. Fla. Coun. Grad. Schs.; cons. Tex. Sch. Bd., 1989; chmn. bd. U. Cen. Fla. Press, 1983—. Author: Integrated Laboratory Sequence, Vols. I and II, 1967, Vol. III, 1970; editor: Physical Methods, Heterocyclic Chemistry, 1983; contbr. articles to profl. jours. Chmn. bd. U. Cen. Fla., Arboretum, 1985—; dir. East Cen. Fla. Ctr. of Excellence, 1985. Named hon. research asso. Harvard, 1972-73; NIH Spl. fellow, 1972-73 Mem. AAUP, Am. Chem. Soc., Am. Crystallographic Assn., Am. Phys. Soc., Council Grad. Schs. in U.S., Am. Assn. State Colls. and Univs., Conf. So. Grad. Schs., So. Assn. Colls. and Schs., Nat. Assn. Univ. Research Adminstrs., Soc. Research Adminstrs., So. Regional Edn. Bd., Quill (bd. dirs. 1984—), Scroll (bd. dirs. 1986—), Sigma Xi. Greek Orthodox. Avocations: tennis, stamp collecting/philately, dog training, bonsai gardening. Home: Oviedo, Fla. Died Mar. 2, 2006.

TRELLO, FRED A., state legislator; b. Coraopolis, Pa., Nov. 14, 1929; m. Betty Meanor; 3 children. Student, Robert Morris Coll. Mem. Allegheny County Dem. Com.; dem. chmn. Borough of Coraopolis; councilman Coraopolis; chmn. Dem. State Party; Pa. state rep. Dist. 45, from 1974, chmn. pub. safety com.; housing and redevel. com., chmn. house fin. com. Pa. House Rep. Recipient Man of Yr. award West Hills Jaycees, 1978. Mem. VFW, Lions, K.C. Democrat. Home: Coraopolis, Pa. Died Mar. 28, 2006.

TRELOAR, RONALD C., manufacturing executive; b. Petoskey, Mich., June 5, 1933; m. Barbara J. Treloar; children: Mark, Bridget Treloar Raulerson, Tamara J.; m. 2d, Sandra A. Treloar. BS, GM Inst. Engring. and Mgmt., 1956. Successively plant layout engr., methods engr., purchasing engr., sr. project engr., staff engr. Saginaw Steering Gear div. GM, Saginaw, Mich., 1955-70, prodn. mgr., 1970-74, plant mgr., 1974-77, mgr. Ala. ops., 1977-80, gen. dir. mfg. svc., 1980-81, gen. sales mgr., 1981-84, Harrison Radiator div. GM, Lockport, N.Y., 1984-87, gen. dir. heat exchanger bus. unit, from 1987. Former exec. bd. dirs. Tenn. coun. Boy Scouts Am.; past div. co-chmn. United Way Saginaw County; past bd. dirs. United Way Morgan County, Community Rels. Assn., Jr. Achievement of Decatur; pres. Burningtree Country Club, 1978. Mem. Ea. Niagara C. of C., Lockport Town and Country Club, Lyman Spalding Soc. Died Nov. 26, 2006.

TREMAINE, FRANK BENJAMIN, writer; b. Detroit, May 30, 1914; s. Gage Canfield and Kate Amelia (Rutter) T.; m. Katherine McCoy Newland, Sept. 2, 1939; children: Nancy McCoy, Frank Gage. BA, Stanford U., 1936. With United Press Assns. (became United Press Internat., Inc. 1958), 1936-80; successively assigned Salt Lake City, San Diego, San Francisco, NYC, 1936-41; mgr. Honolulu, 1941; war corr. in charge coverage Pacific Ocean areas (including Pearl Harbor attack, Japanese surrender), 1941-45; mgr. Tokyo, 1945, Mexico-Central Am., 1946-49, Los Angeles, 1949-52; temporarily assigned Tokyo to direct Korean War coverage, 1950-51, San Francisco to cover Japanese Peace Conf., 1951; asst. gen. mgr. newspictures dept., 1952-55; gen. mgr., 1955-58; v.p., dir., gen. mgr. newspictures and film UPI, 1958-65, v.p., gen. bus. mgr., 1965-69, v.p., gen. mgr. N.Am., 1969-76, mgr. internat. ops., 1976-80, sr. v.p., 1972-80; dir. UPITN, 1969-80. Cons., freelance writer, 1980-2006; prof. emeritus mass communications Savannah State Coll., 1983-2006; vol. exec. Internat. Exec. Service Corps, 1987. Co-author: (with K. Tremaine) The Attack on Pearl Harbor by Two Who Were There, 1997. Mem. Soc. Profl. Journalists, Phi Kappa Psi. Clubs: Dutch Treat, Savannah Golf, Savannah Yacht. Presbyterian. Home: Savannah, Ga. Died Dec. 7, 2006.

TRENT, RICHARD O(WEN), financial executive; b. Ft. Worth, Nov. 13, 1920; m. Phoebe Ann Clark, 1947. Attended, U. Okla., 1940—47; grad., Inst. Life Ins. Mktg., So. Meth. U., 1948. Agt. Mass. Mut. Life Ins. Co., Okla. City, 1946—55; founder Mid-Am. Life Ins. Co., Okla. City, 1955, pres., chmn. bd., 1955—65; pres. Richard O. Trent and Assocs., Inc., Okla. City, from 1965; chmn. Sales, Mergers and Acquisitions-Worldwide, from 1966. Dir. Okla. Mut. Investors, Inc.; past pres., chmn. bd. Liberty Investment Corp.; v.p., dir. Lee Realty Corp.; past v.p., dir. Cleary Petroleum Corp.; pres. Southwest Mut. Casualty Co. Mem. Okla. City C. of C., YMCA, Okla. Econ. Club. Lt. col. (ret.) USAF, 1942—66, sr. pilot USAF, 1946—53, command pilot USAF, 1953—66. Decorated D.F.C., Purple Heart, Air medal. Mem.: Nat. Assn. Life Underwriters (life mem. Million Dollar Round Table), Assn. Corp. Growth, Okla. City Golf and Country Club, Men's Dinner Club, Jesters, Shriners, Masons, Am. Legion. Died Nov. 14, 2006.

TRIMMER, ROBERT MARELL, finance company executive; b. Waterbury, Conn., Nov. 11, 1950; s. Robert Eugene and Kaye Imogene (Sturges) T.; m. Verdery Cunningham, Sept. 5, 1987; children: Crawford Cummings, Robert Clayton. BA in Italian Lit., SUNY, Binghamton, 1974; MBA, U. Fla., 1976. Securities lic. series 4, 7, 8, 24, 53, 55, 63. First v.p., sr. investment officer S.E. Banking Corp., Miami, Fla., 1976-79; first v.p. Robinson Humphrey Co., Atlanta, 1979-87; sr. v.p., dir. capital markets Rausher, Pierce/IFG, Dallas, 1987-90; sr. v.p., dir. equity trading Tucker Anthony, Boston, 1990; sr. v.p., dir. sales and mktg. Keogler, Morgan & Co., Atlanta, 1991-92; sr. v.p. Josephthal, Lyon & Ross, Atlanta, 1992-93; dir. capital markets Fin. Svc. Corp., Atlanta, 1994-2000; exec. v.p., dir. sales Neovest Inc., Atlanta, from 2000. Editor various articles Jour. Fin., 1974-76. Cycling fundraiser Nat. Multiple Sclerosis Soc., Atlanta, 1996—; coach, fundraiser East Side Baseball, Cobb County, Ga., 1997—. U.S. Naval ROTC scholar USN/Brown U., 1967; Walter S. Bourlier Engring. scholar Syracuse U., 1968. Mem. Securities Industry Assn., Ga. Securities Assn., Dallas Securities Dealers Assn., Phi Kappa Phi. Avocations: flying, scuba, baseball memorabilia, skiing, coaching. Home: Marietta, Ga. Died Apr. 24, 2006.

TRINKL, FRANK HERMAN, economist, educator; b. Cudahy, Wis., July 3, 1928; s. Frank and Celia (Damhazel) T.; m. Barbara Ruth Henry, June 9, 1951; children: Peter, Garth, Alison. MA in Econs., PhD in Econs., U. Mich.; MS in Statistics, Stanford U. Staff scientist Ramo-Wooldridge Corp., LA, 1956-57; staff mem. RAND Corp., Santa Monica, Calif., 1957-61; spl. asst. to asst. sec. def. U.S. DOD, Washington, 1961-65; cons. various orgns., 1966-70, 74-79; sr. lectr. grad. sch. pub. policy U. Calif., Berkeley, 1970-74; pres., dir. for planning and econ. analysis Ctr. for Policy Studies, Inc., Berkeley, 1979-83; prin. cons. Calif. Legislature, Sacramento, 1983-85; dir. pub. law rsch. inst., adj. prof. U. Calif. Hastings Coll. Law, San Francisco, 1986-93, ret. Contbr. articles to profl. jours. Fellow AAAS; mem. Am. Econ. Assn. Home: Berkeley, Calif. Died Jan. 30, 2007.

TROMBOLD, WALTER STEVENSON, supply company executive; b. Chanute, Kans., June 21, 1910; s. George John and Margaret (Stevenson) T.; m. Charlotte Elizabeth Kaufman, Dec. 28, 1941; children: Joan Benjamin, Lynn Oliphant, Walter Steven, David George, Charles Phillip. AA, Iola Jr. Coll., 1930; BS in Bus., U. Kans., 1932; spl. degree Balliol Coll., Oxford U., 1943. Pers. worker with evangelist Billy Sunday, 1928; asst. mgr. S.H. Kress & Co., 1932-38; counsel Penn. Mut. Life Ins. Co., 1938-40; field mgr. Travelers Ins. Co., Kansas City, 1940-41; with Reid Supply Co. Wichita, Kans., Kansas City, Mo., Topeka, 1946-86; pres., chmn. bd. Reid Supply Co., Inc., 1954-86; chmn. bd. Trombold Consultation Svc., from 1986. Bd. dirs., v.p. Nat. Distbrs. Coun.; active amateur photographer, 1924—. Bd. dirs., officer YMCA, 1920—; merit badge councilor Boy Scouts Am.; bd. dirs. Wesley Hosp. Assocs., 1972-82, Camp Fire Girls, Salvation Army, adv. bd., 1988—, Salvation Army Rehab. Ctr., 1988—; life mem. PTA, 1953—, pres., 1952; chmn. pers. adv. bd. City of Wichita, Kans., 1956-86; commr. Gen. Assembly Presbyn. Ch. USA, past deacon, elder, trustee; commr. Synods of Mid-Am., Presbytery of So. Kans.; assoc. chmn. Nat. Laymen's Bible Week, 1972-86; mem. Super Sr. Tennis, 1970-98; area chmn. Neighbor Watch, 1990—; ofcl. photographer U. Kans. Relays. Lt. comdr. USN, 1942-46. Seaman USN World War II 1st Class to lt. comdr; exec. officer, commdg. officer USSLST55; participant in fateful Tiger Exercise and D-Day, 1944; v.p. Civic Progress Inc., Sales Mgmt., Inc. Recipient award Nat. Jr. C. of C., Wichita Jr. C. of C., Laundry and Cleaners Allied Trades, Old Timer Club Nat., Nat. Distributors Coun., Sr. Men's Tennis Assn., U. Kans. Relays, Kans. State H.S. Assn., Wichita Swim Club, Am. Athletic Union, YMCA, Salvation Army, Rotary, Boy Scouts. Am., Camp Fire Girls, Sr. Men's Swimming, City of Wichita, 3 Navy Compaign Ribbons, Silver Star. Mem. Textile Allied Trades Assn. (bd. dirs., dist. chmn. Hon. Man 1976), Kans. LST Assn. (charter pres. 1990), Kans. U. Alumni Assn. (life), Kans. C. of C., Wichita C. of C., Sales and Mktg. Execs. (bd. dirs., v.p.), Old Timer Club (sec., treas. 1964-86, Hon. Man of Yr. 1977), Wichita Racquet Club, Knife and Fork Internat. Club (bd. dirs., v.p.), Univ. Club (chmn. bd. dirs., v.p.), Rotary (bd. dirs., ofcl. photographer, historian, Disting. Svc. award 1989, 96), Masons (32 degree), Alpha Tau Omega. Republican. Presbyterian. Home: Wichita, Kans. Died Aug. 2, 2006.

TROXEL, LARRY LEE, retail building materials and ready-mixed concrete products company executive; b. Battle Creek, Mich., Apr. 18, 1942; s. Emerald V. and Melba Lucille (Church) T.; student Kellogg Community Coll., 1960-62; m. Marilyn Jean Richman, Feb. 2, 1963; children— Jodi Lyn, Karla Sue, Ronna Kay. Mgr., V.E. Troxel & Sons, Inc., Battle Creek, 1960-68, corp. sec., gen. mgr., 1973-81; also dir.; mgr. Lumber div. Wickes Corp., Saginaw, Mich., 1968-73; pres. L-M Troxel Services, Inc., Battle Creek, 1981—; pres. V.E. Troxel & Sons, Inc., Battle Creek, 1982—. Constable, Emmett Twp., 1976-80, trustee, 1984—; mem. Calhoun County Citizens Coalition Against Crime, 1976-79; advisor Jr. Achievement South Central Mich., 1979-80; v.p. West End Devel. Assn. of Battle Creek, 1984—. Recipient Spoke award Battle Creek Jaycees, 1975, Spark Plug award, 1976, 77, 78; named Outstanding Young Man of the Yr., Dale Carnegie, 1977. Mem. Battle Creek Area C. of C. Republican. Baptist. Club: Optimists (pres. 1967-68). Died Mar. 16, 2007.

TRUE, JEAN DURLAND, entrepreneur, oil industry executive, gas industry executive; b. Nov. 27, 1915; d. Clyde Earl and Harriet Louise (Brayton) Durland; m. Henry Alfonso True Jr., Mar. 20, 1938; children: Tamma Jean (Mrs. Donald G. Hatten), Henry Alfonso III, Diemer Durland, David Lanmon. Student, Mont. State U., 1935-36. Ptnr. True Drilling Co., Casper, Wyo., 1951—94, True Oil Co., Casper, 1951-94, Eighty-Eight Oil LLC, 1955-94, True Geothermal Energy Co., 1980—2006, True Ranches, 1981-94. Officer, dir. White Stallion Ranch, Inc. Tucson, Smokey Oil Co., Casper. Mem. steering com. YMCA Casper, 1954-55, bd. dirs., 1956-68; bd. dirs Gottsche Rehab Ctr., Thermopolis, Wyo., 1966-93, mem. exec. bd., 1966-93 v.p., 1983-90; mem. adv. bd. for adult edn. U. Wyo., 1966-68 mem. Ft. Casper Commn., Casper, 1973-79; bd. dirs. Mus. o Rockies, Bozeman, Mont., 1983-87, mem. Nat. Adv. Bd. 1997-2000; bd. dirs. Nicolaysen Art Mus., 1988-93, Nat. Cowboy and We. Heritage Mus., 1997-2002, dir. emeritus, 2002-06 mem. Nat. Fedn. Rep. Women's Clubs; dep. Rep. Nat. Conv. 1972; trustee Trooper Found., 1995-2006. Mem.: Casper Area C of C., Casper Country Club, Petroleum Club, Alpha Gamma Delta. Episcopalian. Home: Casper, Wyo. Died Sept. 15, 2006

TRUSTY, ROY LEE, former oil company executive; b. Paris Ark., Nov. 27, 1924; s. Bennie Otis and Katy Jane (Williamson) T.; m. Caroline Sue Thibaut, Nov. 23, 1950; children: Rebecca Sue, Sara Elizabeth, Jane Ellen, Roy Lee. BS in Chem. Engring La. State U., 1949. Engr. Esso Standard Oil Co., Baton Rouge 1949-61; mgr. Humble Oil and Refining Co., Houston, 1961-64 Standard Oil of N.J., NYC, 1964-68; pres. Lago Oil and Transp Co. Ltd., Aruba, Netherlands Antilles, 1970-73; various exec positions Exxon Co. U.S.A., Houston, 1973-76, sec., 1976-83 trustee, exec. dir. Exec. Service Corps, Houston, 1983-92 Served with U.S. Army, 1943-46, ETO. Republican. Methodist Home: Round Top, Tex. Died Nov. 19, 2006.

TRUTTER, JOHN THOMAS, telecommunications industry executive, educator, writer; b. Springfield, Ill., Apr. 18, 1920; s. Frank Louis and Frances (Mischler) T.; m. Edith English Woods II, June 17, 1950 (dec.); children: Edith English II, Jonathan Woods. BA, U. Ill., 1942; postgrad., Northwestern U., 1947-50 U. Chgo., 1947-50; LHD (hon.), Lincoln Coll., 1986. Various positions Ill. Bell, Chgo., 1946-58, gen. traffic mgr., from asst v.p. pub. rels. to gen. mgr., 1958-69, v.p. pub. rels., 1969-71, v.p operator svcs., 1971-80, v.p. community affairs, 1980-85; mem hdqs. staff AT&T, NYC, 1955-57; pres. John T. Trutter Co., Inc. Chgo., from 1985; pres., CEO Chgo. Conv. and Visitors Bur. 1985-88; pres. Chgo. Tourism Coun., 1988-90; v.p. Profl Impressions Media Group, Inc., 1998-2000, prof. emeritus 2001. Mem. adv. bd. The Alford Group, Chgo., 1984—, Bozell Worldwide, Chgo., 1994-96; chancellor Lincoln Acad. of Ill. 1985-2001. Co-author: Handling Barriers in Communication 1957, The Governor Takes a Bride, 1977 Past chmn., life trustee Jane Addams Hull House Assn.; chmn. United Cerebral Palsy Assn. Greater Chgo., 1967-95, hon. chmn., 1995—, chmn Canal Corridor Assn., 1991-99; bd. dirs. Chgo. Crime Commn., Abraham Lincoln Assn., Lyric Opera Chgo.; v.p. English Speaking Union, 1989-91, bd. govs., 1980—; chmn. bd. City Colls. Chgo. Found., 1987-91; past chmn. Children's Home and Aid Soc. Ill.; v.p. City Club Chgo.; treas. Chgo. United, 1970-85 mem. Ill. Econ. Devel. Commn., 1985; past presiding co-chmn. NCCJ; numerous others; bd. govs. Northwestern U. Libr. Coun. 1984—; trustee Lincoln (Ill.) Coll., 1987-90, Mundelein Coll. 1988-91; mem. sch. problems coun. State Ill. Assembly, 1985-91, spl. commn. on adminstrn. of justice in Cook County 1986-92; founding chmn. adv. coun. Evanston Hist. Soc., 1995-98. Lt. col. U.S. Army, 1945. Decorated Legion of Merit recipient Laureate award State of Ill., 1980, Outstanding Exec Leader award Am. Soc. Fundraisers, Humanitarian of Yr. award, Jane Addams award The Hull House Assn., 1991, Nat. Infinitec award for individual leadership in assistive technology for disabled people, 1997, Jack Brickhouse award for outstanding svcs., 2000. Mem. Pub. Rels. Soc. Am., Sangamon County Hist Soc. (founder, past pres.), Ill. State Hist. Soc. (pres. 1985-87), Coun. on Ill. History (chmn. 1991—), U. Ill. Alumni Assn. (bd. dirs. 1990-94), Tavern Club, Econ. Club, Mid-Am. Club, Alpha Sigma Phi (Nat. Merit Achievement award 1994), Phi Delta Phi. Died Feb. 2, 2007.

TRUXAL, JOHN GROFF, retired electrical engineering educator; b. Lancaster, Pa., Feb. 19, 1924; s. Andrew Gehr and Leah Deldee (Groff) T.; m. Doris Teresa Mastrangelo, June 11, 1949 children— Brian Andrew, Carol Jean. AB, Dartmouth, 1944 BS, Mass. Inst. Tech., 1947, Sc.D., 1950; D.Eng. (hon.), Purdue U., 1964, Ind. Inst. Tech., 1971. Asso. prof. elec. engring Purdue U., 1950-54; asso. prof. elec. engring. Poly. Inst. Bklyn. 1954- 57, prof., head dept., 1957-72, v.p. ednl. devel., 1961-72 dean engring., 1964-66, provost, 1966-68, acad. v.p., 1969-72 dean engring. State U. N.Y., Stony Brook, 1972-76; prof. engring. SUNY, 1976-91, Disting. Teaching prof. emeritus, 1991—1994. Cons. control engring. Author: Automatic Feedback Control System Synthesis, 1955, Introductory System Engineering, 1972, (with W.A. Lynch) Signals and Systems in Electrical Engineering, 1962; co-author: (with W.A. Lynch) The Man Made World, 1969, Man and His Technology, 1973, Technology: Handle With Care, 1975, The Age of Electronic Messages, 1991; editor: Control Engineers' Handbook, 1958. Recipient Rufus Oldenburger medal ASME, 1991. Fellow IEEE, AAAS; mem. NAE, Instrument Soc. Am. (pres. 1965), Am. Soc Engring. Edn., Phi Beta Kappa, Sigma Xi, Tau Beta Pi, Eta Kappa Nu, Phi Kappa Psi. Home: Dix Hills, NY. Died Feb. 16, 2007.

TUCKER, DONALD, assemblyman; b. Mar. 18, 1938; BA in Urban Planning, Goddard Coll. Councilman at large City of Newark, NJ, from 1974; assemblyman N.J. New Gen. Assembly, from 1998; spkr. pro tempore NJ, from 2002. Mem. Passaic Valley Sewerage Commn., from 1985. 2d class airman USAF, 1955—59. Democrat. Died Oct. 17, 2005.

TUFTS, ARTHUR JAMES, former trade association executive; b. Washington, Jan. 29, 1914; s. William O. and Glenn (Spurr) T.; A.B., Oberlin Coll., 1934; m. Gladys L. Cowsill, Oct. 1, 1936; children— Adrienne, Carolyn, Alyson. Mktg. rep. Burroughs Corp., Washington, 1935-43; asst. to comptroller Capital Transit Co., Washington, 1943-47; systems analyst Equitable Life Ins. Co., Washington, 1947-52; v.p. systems and procedure Life Office Mgmt. Assn., N.Y.C., 1952-78; cons. Acctg. & Bookkeeping Services, East Norwich, N.Y.; instr. office mgmt. Bklyn. Coll., Southeastern U., Washington. Pres.

riends of Channel 21 (PBS), 1978-79; mem. Nat. Panel Consumer Arbitrators, Council Better Bus. Burs.; tax aide Am. Assn. Ret. Persons. Club: North Hempstead Country. Died June , 2006.

TUFTS, J. ARTHUR, state legislator; b. Lowell, Mass., Dec. 8, 1921; s. James A. and Hazel (Weinbeck) T.; m. Jean Staples, 950 (dec.); children: James A., Anne E., Peter C., Thomas W. BS, U. N.H., 1948; MEd, Boston U., 1961. Owner Granite State Nurseries, from 1948; rep. N.H. Ho. Reps., 1961-63, 79-92, rep. dist. 20, from 1995. Chmn. edn. com. N.H. Ho. Reps., 1987, chmn. state inst. housing com.; N.H. State Senate, 1963-71, pres. 1969-70; commr., mediator Rock County, N.H., 1970-71; chmn. State-Fed. Rels. and Vets. Affairs Com., 1998-2000; mem. Sci., Tech. and Energy Com. Trustee U. N.H. Sys., 963-67, Nat. Recreation & Parks Assn. Army med. adminstr., 942-46. Recipient nat. 4-H alumni award, svc. award N.H. Recreation Soc. Mem. Nat. Ice Hockey Ofcls. Assn., New Eng. Folk Festival Assn., Sea Coast Mental Health Assn., N.H. Farm Bur., N.H. Summer Soccer Conf., VFW, Rotary. Home: Exeter, NH. Died Mar. 27, 2007.

TULLIS, EDWARD LEWIS, retired bishop; b. Cin., Mar. 9, 917; s. Ashar Spence and Priscilla (Daugherty) T.; m. Mary ane Talley, Sept. 25, 1937; children: Frank Loyd, Jane Allen (Mrs. William Nelson Offutt IV); m. Katharine Crum Irwin, Sept. 4, 1997. AB, Ky. Wesleyan Coll., 1939, LHD, 1975; BD, Louisville Presbyn. Theol. Sem., 1947; DD, Union Coll., Barbourville, Ky., 1954, Wofford Coll., 1976; LHD, Claflin Coll., 976, Lambuth Coll., 1984. Ordained to ministry Methodist Ch., 941; service in chs. Frenchburg, Ky., 1937-39, Lawrenceburg, Ky., 1939-44; asso. pastor 4th Ave. Meth. Ch., Louisville, 944-47, Irvine, Ky., 1947-49; asso. sec. ch. extension sect. Bd. Missions, Meth. Ch., Louisville, 1949-52; pastor First Meth. Ch., Frankfort, Ky., 1952-61, Ashland, Ky., 1961-72; resident bishop United Meth. Ch., Columbia, SC, 1972-80, Nashville area, 1980-84, ret., 1984. Instr. Bible Ky. Wesleyan Coll., 947-48; instr. Louisville Presbyn. Theol. Sem., 1949-52; mem. Meth. Gen. Conf., 1956, 60, 64, 66, 68, 70, 72, Southeastern Jurisdictional Conf., 1952, 56, 60, 64, 68, 72, bd. mgrs. Bd. Missions, 1962-72, mem. bd. discipleship, 1972-80, v.p. Gen. Coun. on Fin. and Adminstrn., 1980-84; Chaplain Ky. Gen. Assembly, 1952-61; chmn. Frankfort Com. Human Rights, 956-61, Mayor's Adv. Com. Human Rels., Ashland, 1968-72. Author: Shaping the Church from the Mind of Christ, 1984, The Birth of the Book: A Study in the Origin and Growth of the Bible, 1998. Contbr. articles to religious jours. Sec., bd. dirs. Magee Christian Edn. Found.; trustee Emory U., 1973-80, Alaska Meth. U., 1965-70, Ky. Wesleyan Coll., Martin Coll., Lambuth Coll., McKendree Manor, Meth. Hosps., Memphis, Lake Junaluska Assembly, 1966-88; chair adv. bd. Found. for Evangelism, United Meth. Ch., 1991—. Recipient Outstanding Citizen award Frankfort VFW, 1961, Mayor's award for outstanding svc. Ashland, 1971, Heroes, Sts. and Legends award, Wesley Meth. Village Ky., 1997, Chief Junaluska award Lake Junaluska Assembly, 1998, Outstanding Alumnus award Ky. Wesleyan Coll., 2000, Disting. Alumnus award Louisville Presbyn. Sem., 2002; named to Ky. Wesleyan Coll. Hall of Fame, 2004. Mem.: Kiwanis. Methodist. Home: Lake Junaluska, NC. Died Oct. 6, 2005.

TUPPER, STANLEY ROGER, lawyer; b. Boston, Jan. 25, 1921; s. Asa D. and Elizabeth M. (Fowles) T.; m. Esther M., June 4, 1941 (div. 1967); 1 child, Stanley R.; m. Jill Kaplan; 1 child, Lara Abigail. Student Middlebury Coll., 1939-40; LL.B., LaSalle U., 1948; LL.D., Ricker Coll., Houlton, Maine, 1966. Bar: Maine 1949, U.S. Dist. Ct. Maine 1950, U.S. Supreme Ct. 1952. Of counsel Tupper & Tupper, Boothbay Harbor, Maine, 1949-53, 57-61, 72—; ptnr. Ruyall, Koegel & Wells, Washington, 1969-72; pres. States Urban Action Ctr., Inc., Washington, 1967-69. Author: One Continent-Two Voices, 1967. Mem. U.S. Ho. of Reps., 1961-67; ambassador Can. Centennial Internat. Exhbn., Montreal, Que., 1967; commn. Internat. Commn. on Northwest Fisheries, 1975-76; commr. Dept. Sea and Shore Fisheries, Augusta, Maine, 1953-57; mem. Maine Ho. of Reps., Augusta, 1953; selectman, chmn. Town of Boothbay Harbor, 1948-50. Mem. Lincoln County Bar Assn. Republican. Methodist. Home: Boothbay Hbr, Maine. Died Jan. 6, 2006.

TURBAYNE, COLIN MURRAY, philosopher; b. Tanny Morel, Queensland, Australia, Feb. 7, 1916; came to U.S., 1947, naturalized, 1957; s. David Livingston and Alice Rene (Lahey) T.; m. Ailsa Margaret Krimmer, June 22, 1940 (dec. Sep. 1991); children: Ronald Murray, John Garvald. BA, U. Queensland, 1940, MA, 1950; PhD, U. Pa., 1950; LHD (hon.), Bowling Green State U., 1990. Instr. in philosophy U. Pa., Phila., 1947-50; asst. prof. philosophy U. Wash., 1950-55; asst. prof. speech U. Calif., Berkeley, 1955-57; asso. prof. philosophy U. Rochester, 1957-62, prof., 1962-81, prof. emeritus, from 1981. Author: The Myth of Metaphor, 1962, 2d, rev. edit., 1970, Spanish edit., 1974, Metaphors for the Mind, 1990, also articles. Served with Australian Mil. Forces Intelligence, 1940-45. Fulbright fellow, 1963; Guggenheim fellow, 1965-66; Nat. Endowment for Humanities sr. fellow, 1974; Am. Council Learned Soc. grantee, 1958-59; Am. Philos. Soc. grantee, 1958-59 Mem. Am. Philos. Assn., AAUP. Home: Rochester, NY. Died May 16, 2006.

TURK, RUDY HENRY, artist, retired museum director; b. Sheboygan, Wis., June 24, 1927; s. Rudolph Anton and Mary Gertrude (Stanisha) T.; m. Wanda Lee Borders, Aug. 4, 1956; children: Tracy Lynn, Maria Teresa, Andrew Borders, Jennifer Wells. BS in Edn., U. Wis., 1949; MA in History, U. Tenn., 1951; postgrad., Ind. U., 1952-56. Instr. art history, gallery dir. U. Mont., Missoula, 1957-60; dir. Richmond (Calif.) Art Ctr., 1960-65; asst. dir. San Diego Mus. Art, 1965-67; dir. Ariz. State U. Art Mus., 1967-92; from assoc. prof. to prof. art Ariz. State U., 1967-77. Painter, paintings exhibited in solo and group exhbns. including Stable of Udinotti Gallery, Scottsdale, 1970—; mus. cons., juror, art cons., art lectr.; author: (with Cross and Lamm) The Search for Personal Freedom, 2 vols., 1972, 76, 80, 85, Merrill Mahaffey: Monumental Landscapes, 1979, (with others) Scholder, 1983, also commentaries and critiques. Bd. dirs. Chandler Arts Com., 1987-89, Friends of Mex. Art, Ariz., 1986-96, pres. 1988-90; mem. Tempe Arts Com., 1987-89, Ariz. Living Treasures Com., 1988-93; bd. dirs. Ariz. Mus. for Youth, 1993—; mem. adv. bd. Tempe Hist. Mus., 1995—. Recipient merit award Calif. Coll. Arts and Crafts, 1965, Senator's Cultural award State of Ariz., 1987, Golden Crate award Western Assn. Art Mus., 1974, Ariz. Gov.'s Art award, 1992; named Hon. Ariz. Designer Craftsman, 1975; named dir. emeritus Ariz. State U. Art Mus., 1992, Rudy Turk Gallery at Ariz. State U. Art Mus. named in his honor, 1992; Fulbright scholar U. Paris, 1956-57; hon. fellow Am. Craft Coun., 1988. Mem. Nat. Coun. Edn. Ceramic Arts (hon. mem. coun. 1991), Phi Alpha Theta, Phi Kappa Phi. Democrat. Home: Tempe, Ariz. Died Aug. 14, 2007.

TURNBULL, DAVID, retired physics professor; b. Elmira, Ill., Feb. 18, 1915; s. David and Luzetta Agnes (Murray) T.; m. Carol May Cornell, Aug. 3, 1946; children: Lowell D., Murray M., Joyce M. BS, Monmouth Coll., Ill., 1936, DSc (hon.), 1958; PhD, U. Ill., 1939; MA (hon.), Harvard U., 1962; DSc (hon.), Case-Western Res. U., 1990, Claude Bernard U., Lyon, France, 1993. Tchr. research Case Sch. Applied Sci., 1939-46; scientist Gen. Electric Co. Research Lab., 1946-62, mgr. chem. metallurgy sect., 1950-58; adj. prof. metallurgy Rennselaer Poly. Inst., 1954-62; Gordon McKay prof. applied physics Harvard U., 1962-85, prof. emeritus, 1985—2007. Chmn. Gordon Conf. Physics and Chemistry Metals, 1952; Internat. Conf. Crystal Growth, 1958; Internat. Conf. Chem. Physics of Non-metallic Crystals, 1961; Office Naval Research panel study growth and morphology crystals, 1959-60 Editor: (with Seitz, Ehrenreich) Solid State Physics, 35 vols., 1955-92, co-founding editor (with Seitz), 1993—; editor: (with Doremus, Roberts) Growth and Perfection of Crystals, 1958; assoc. editor: Jour. Chem. Physics, 1961-63; editorial adv. bd.: Jour. Physics and Chemistry Solids, 1955-93. Chmn. citizens curriculum com. Niskayuna (N.Y.) Sr. High Sch., 1954. Recipient von Hippel award, 1979, Japan Prize in Materials Sci. and Tech., 1986, Franklin medal, 1990. Fellow Am. Phys. Soc. (Internat. prize new materials 1983), N.Y. Acad. Scis., Am. Soc. Metals (chmn. seminar com. 1954), Am. Inst. Mining and Metall. Engrs. (lectr. Inst. Metals div. 1961, Hume-Rothery award 1986, Bruce Chalmers award 1991); mem. Am. Chem. Soc., Nat. Acad. Scis., Am. Acad. Arts and Scis., Am. Ceramic Soc. (hon.). Home: Cambridge, Mass. Died Apr. 28, 2007.

TURNER, DAVID REUBEN, publisher, author; b. NYC, Dec. 9, 1915; s. Charles and Eva (Turner) Moskowitz; m. Ann Louise Perkins, Apr. 29, 1946 (div. 1976); children— Eve (Mrs. William Watters), Ruth. BS, Coll. City N.Y., 1936, MS in Edn, 1937. Co-founder Arco Pub. Co., NYC, 1937, pub., dir., 1937-78; v.p. parent co. Prentice-Hall, Inc., 1979-80; pres. Turner Pub., 1980-92. Pub. cons. under Ford Found. contract Burma Translation Soc., Rangoon, 1955—60. Author: more than 300 books on tests and testing, including High School Equivalency Diploma Tests, 1951, 75, How to Win a Scholarship, 1955, Scoring High On College Entrance Tests, 1969, 71, Food Service Supervisor, 1968, Bank Examiner, 1968, Accountant-Auditor, 1960, 77, Officer Candidate Tests, 1978, Professional-Administrative Career Exams, 1979, English Grammar and Usage for Test-Takers, 1976, College Level Examination Program, 1979. Adviser bd. publs. Union Am. Hebrew Congregations. Died Jan. 6, 2006.

TURNICK, MICHAEL, fire chief, consultant; b. Scalp Level, Pa., Oct. 25, 1925; s. Charles and Anna (Shenigo) T.; m. Alice Elezibeth Kennemer, June 28, 1944 (div. 1965); children: Carol Ann, Michael, Ronald; m. Mary Louise Udey, Aug. 15, 1969; stepchildren: Cynthia Ann, Steven, Neil. Student, Santa Rosa Jr. Coll., U. Calif., Berkeley, U. Calif., LA, U. Calif., Davis. Logger Union Lumber Co., Ft. Bragg, Calif., 1946-51; lumberer Miranda, Calif., 1951-54; fireman Santa Rosa (Calif.) Fire Dept., 1954-57, capt., 1957-59, fire marshal, 1959-70, asst. fire chief, 1970-72, fire chief, 1972-89; interim fire chief Vallejo (Calif.) Fire Dept., from 1992. Bd. dirs. League Calif. Cities, 1982. With USN, 1943-46. Mem. Calif. Fire Chiefs Assn. (pres. 1984), Kiwanis (lt. gov. 1965, pres. 1966). Democrat. Roman Catholic. Avocations: golf, boating. Home: Santa Rosa, Calif. Died Mar. 11, 2007.

TURRELL, RICHARD HORTON, SR., banker; b. Kingston, Pa., Apr. 9, 1925; s. George Henry and Margaret (Clark) T.; m. Sally Wolfe, May 28, 1955; children: Richard H. Jr., David C., Douglas W. (dec.). Student, Cornell U., 1943; BS in Commerce, Washington and Lee U., 1949. Rep. sales Del. Lackawanna and Western Coal Co., Phila., 1949-51; asst. to pres. NYC, 1951-58; broker Auchincloss Parker & Redpath, NYC, 1958-61; mgr. investments Fiduciary Trust Co. Internat., NYC, 1961-94, v.p., 1965-94, sr. v.p., 1968-94, sec., 1971-84. Asst. sec. Blue Coal Corp., N.Y.C., 1953-58; v.p., bd. dirs. Pine Raleigh (N.C.) Corp., 1966-93. Trustee, overseer Simon's Rock of Bard Coll., Gt. Barrington, Mass., 1968-93; trustee Monmouth U., West Long Branch, NJ, 1980-2007, chmn. bd. trustees, 1989-92; chmn. Millburn-Short Hills Rep. Com., NJ, 1973-78; trustee Children's Specialized Hosp. Found., Mountainside, NJ, 1989-95; bd. dirs. ARC Martin County, Fla., 2000. With Signal Corps, U.S. Army, 1943-46, PTO. Named Disting. Alumnus, Washington and Lee U., 1986. Mem. Baltusrol Golf Club (Springfield, N.J., gov. 1977), Capitol Hill Club (Washington), Turtle Creek Club (Tequesta, Fla.), Masons, Irem Temple Aaonms, Phi Beta Kappa, Phi Eta Sigma, Alpha Kappa Psi, Omicron Delta Kappa (hon.), Beta Gamma Sigma, Phi Delta Theta. Presbyterian. Avocations: golf, history, education. Home: Tequesta, Fla. Died Aug. 22, 2007.

TURTON, DOROTHY LOUISE, food service consultant; b. Waterloo, Ill., Feb. 13, 1919; d. Friedrich Wilhelm and Bertha Emilia (Schmitt) Braun; m. Roger Charles Dale, Dec. 8, 1944 (dec. Oct. 11, 1964); children: Barbara, Diane; m. 2d, Robert Allen Turton, Feb. 13, 1970; children by previous marriage: Beth, Andrew, Roberta. BS, Sam Houston State U., 1940. Cert. permanent high sch. tchr., dietary cons., vocat. tchr., Tex. Tchr. homemaking League City High Sch. (Tex.), 1940-43; intern Deaconess Hosp., St. Louis, 1943-44, teaching dietitian, 1943-46; tchr. sci. Belville High Sch. (Tex.), 1946-49; food service dir. Heights Hosp., Houston, 1949-53, San Jacinto Hosp., Baytown, Tex., 1955-59, Spring Br. Hosp., Houston, 1959-64; therapeutic dietitian Meml. Baptist Hosp., Houston, 1953-55, chief dietitian, 1964-71; freelance cons. to several hosps. and nursing homes, Houston, 1971-74; area cons. Cantex Nursing Homes, Houston, 1974-81; dir. Dietitics Belt Way Community Hosp., Pasadena, 1981-88, ret., 1988, free lance cons., 1988—; cons. adv. staff San Jacinto Coll. Mem. Phi Theta Kappa. Republican. Mem. United Ch. Christ. Clubs: C.P.A. Aux., St. Peters Womens Guild (Houston) (pres. 1971-75, 80-83); Spring Woods Townhouse (aux. pres. 1980-81). Home: Georgetown, Tex. Died Oct. 15, 2006.

TUTTLE, ROBERT D., manufacturing and distributing company executive; b. July 16, 1925; married. BS, Northwestern U., 1951; MBA, U. Chgo., 1960. Mktg. mgr. The H.M. Harper Co., Morton Grove, Ill., 1951-60; mgmt. cons. Booz Allen & Hamilton, Chgo., 1960-62; vice chmn. bd., exec. v.p. ops. Ill. Tool Works Inc., 1962-80; pres., chief operating officer SPX Corp., Muskegon, Mich., 1980-84, pres., chief exec. officer, 1984-85, chief exec. officer, 1985-89, chmn., 1985-90. Bd. dirs. CMS Energy Corp., Woodhead Industries, Walbro Corp., Consumers Power Co., Guardsman Products, Inc., FMB Corp., Little Rapids Corp., Batts Corp. Served to 2d lt. USAF, 1943-46. Named Industrialist of Yr. Mich.'s Impression 5 Sci. Mus., Lansing, 1988. Died Feb. 9, 2007.

UBELL, EARL, writer, consultant; b. Bklyn., June 21, 1926; s. Charles and Hilda (Kramer) U.; m. Shirley Leitman, Feb. 12, 1949; children— Lori Ellen, Michael Charles. BS, CCNY, 1948; DSc (hon.), N.Y. Tech., 2001. With N.Y. Herald Tribune, 1943-66, successively messenger, asst. sec. to mng. editor, reporter, 1943-53, sci. editor, 1953-66, syndicated columnist, 1956-66; sci. commentator MBS, 1958-59; spl. sci. editor WNEW, N.Y., 1962; health and sci. editor WCBS-TV, NYC, 1966-72, 78-95; health editor PARADE mag., 1983-97, contbg. editor, 1997—2007. Dir. TV news NBC News, N.Y.C., 1972-76; producer spl. broadcasts TV news, 1976-78; producer documentaries Medicine in America, 1977, Escape from Madness, 1977; author: The World of Push and Pull, 1964, The World of The Living, 1965, The World of Candle and Color, 1969, How to Save Your Life, 1972, (with Carol C. Flax) Mother/Father/You, 1980, (with Randi Londer) Parade Family Health Companion, 1996. Pres. Council Advancement Sci. Writing, Inc., 1960-66, bd. dirs., 1960-96, founder, 1996-2007; chmn. Center Modern Dance Edn., Inc., 1962-82; pres. North Jersey Cultural Coun., 1966-72; bd. dirs. Dance Notation Bur., 1968—2007, chmn. bd., 1975-94; bd. dirs. Sex Info. and Edn. Council U.S., 1967-69, YMHA, Bergen County, 1968-73, Nat. Center Health Edn., 1977. Served as aviation radioman USNR, 1944-46. Recipient Mental Health Bell award N.Y. State Soc. Mental Health, 1957, Albert Lasker med. journalism award, 1958, Nat. Assn. Mental Health award for radio program, 1962, Sci. Writers award Am. Psychol. Found., 1965, Westinghouse award AAAS, 1960, Empire State award, 1963, TV Reporting award N.Y. Assoc. Press, 1969, 71, N.Y. Emmy award, 1971, Samuelson award N.Y. League for Hard of Hearing, Legal-Med. award Milton Helpern Library of Legal Medicine, Spl. Achievement award Deadline Club, 1982, Disting. Contbn. award, 1983, Nat. Media award Am. Diabetes Assn., 1985, N.Y. State Mental Health Council award, 1987, Ann. Svc. award Dance Notation Bur., 1990. Mem. Nat. Assn. Sci. Writers (pres. 1960-61), Nuclear Energy Writers Assn. (pres. 1965-66), Phi Beta Kappa (pres. Gamma chpt. 1976-77). Home: New York, NY. Died May 29, 2007.

UEHLING, THEODORE EDWARD, philosophy educator; b. Scranton, Pa., July 31, 1935; s. Theodore Edward and Ella Cuthbertson (MacMurray) U.; m. Anne Stewart Bevis, Aug. 10, 1957; children: Theodore Edward, Thomas August, Trent Stewart, Robert Carl. Student, Univ. Cin., 1953-54; BA, Ohio State U., 1959, PhD, 1965. Asst. prof. U. Minn., Morris, 1963-68, assoc. prof., 1968-72, asst. dean, 1968-72, prof. philosophy, from 1972. Cons. U.S. Dept. Edn., Washington, 1987—. Author: The Notion of Form in Kant's Critique of Judgment, 1971; articles in field. Cons. NEH, Washington, 1986—. Served as sgt. USAF, 1954-57. Recipient Morse award for Contributions to Edn., U. Minn. Mem. N.Am. Kant Soc. (v.p. 1985—), Am. Philos. Assn., Australasian Assn. for Philosophy, Minn. Philos. Soc. Home: Ely, Minn. Died Mar. 6, 2006.

ULRICH, REINHARD, educator, clergyman; b. Treysa, Germany, July 1, 1929; came to U.S., 1949, naturalized, 1959; s. Karl and Martha (Hubach) U.; m. Helen E. Neuhaus, June 10, 1952; children— Martin K., Joan M., Karl R. B.A., Lakeland Coll., 1951, LL.D. (hon.), 1984; B.D., Mission House Theol. Sem., 1953; S.T.M., Luth. Sch. Theology, 1960, S.T.D., 1963. Ordained minister United Ch. Christ. Instr., Lakeland Coll., Sheboygan, Wis., 1951-53, prof., 1964—, chmn. dept. philosophy and religion, 1964—, chmn. div. humanities, 1973—; pastor Saron United Ch., Sheboygan, 1953-56, Eden United Ch., Chgo., 1953-64; interim pastor United Ch. of Christ; lectr. in field. Author: (with W. Jaberg et al) A History of Mission House/Lakeland, 1962; transl. Church as Dialogue, 1968; Theology of Play, 1972; also articles. Bd. dirs. Howards Grove Bd. Edn., Wis., 1974—, pres., 1979—. Mem. Wis. Assn. Sch. Bds. (bd. dirs. 1982—, v.p. 1983-84, pres. 1985), AAUP, Am. Philos. Assn. Home: Plymouth, Wis. Died Jan. 11, 2007.

UMBREIT, WAYNE WILLIAM, bacteriologist, educator; b. Markesan, Wis., May 1, 1913; s. William Traugott and Augusta (Abendroth) U.; m. Doris McQuade, July 31, 1937; children: Dorayne Loreda, Jay Nicholas, Thomas Hayden. BA, U. Wis., 1934, MS, 1936, PhD, 1939. Instr. soil microbiology Rutgers U., 1937-38; faculty U. Wis., Madison, 1938-44, asst. prof. bacteriology and chemistry, 1941-44; faculty Cornell U., 1944-47, prof. bacteriology, 1946-47; head dept. enzyme chemistry Merck Inst., Rahway, NJ, 1947-58; asso. dir., 1958; chmn. dept. bacteriology Rutgers U., New Brunswick, NJ, 1958-75, prof. microbiology, dir. grad. programs, 1969-83, prof. emeritus microbiology, from 1983; dir. labs. So. Br. Watershed Assn., 1983-89. Author: (with Burris, Stauffer) Manometric Techniques, 1945, 5th edit., 1972, (with Oginsky) An Introduction to Bacterial Physiology, 1954, Metabolic Maps, 1960, Modern Microbiology, 1962, Essentials of Bacterial Physiology, 1976;

Editor: Advances in Applied Microbiology, vols. 1-10, 1959-68; Contbr. articles to profl. jours. Recipient Biochem. Congress Symposium medal Paris, France, 1952 Fellow Am. Acad. Microbiology, NY Acad. Sci., AAAS; mem. Am. Soc. for Microbiology (Eli Lilly award 1947, Carski Found. award 1968), Soc. Biol. Chemists, Am. Chem. Soc., Theobald Smith Soc. (Waksman award 1957, past pres.), AAUP, Sigma Xi. Home: Rockville, Md. Died Aug. 4, 2007.

UNGARO, JOSEPH MICHAEL, newspaper publishing executive, consultant; b. Providence, Nov. 4, 1930; s. Rocco and Lucy (Motta) U.; m. Evelyn Short, Apr. 15, 1961; children: Elizabeth Anne, Joseph Michael, Ellen Lucia. BA, Providence Coll., 1952; MS in Journalism, Columbia, 1953. With Providence Jour.-Bull., 1951-73, mng. editor Evening Bull., 1967-72; mng. editor Eve. Bull., also dir. planning and devel. Providence Jour. and Bull., 1972-73; mng. editor Westchester-Rockland Newspapers, White Plains, NY, 1974-75, v.p., exec. editor, 1975-84, pres., gen. mgr., 1984-86, pres., publisher, 1986-90; pres., CEO Detroit Newspaper Agy., 1990-91; cons., 1991—2006. Mem. Am. Newspaper Pubs. Assn. (past chmn. research inst., conv. program com.), Am. Soc. Newspaper Editors, AP Mng. Editors Assn. (past pres.) Home: Charlestown, RI. Died Nov. 12, 2006.

UNGER, ALBERT HOWARD, allergist, immunologist; b. Chgo., June 24, 1923; MD, Northwestern U., 1947. Diplomate Am. Bd. Allergy and Immunology. Rotating intern Wesley Meml. Hosp., Chgo., 1946-47; resident in Internal Medicine Cook County Hosp., Chgo., 1947-49; with Sierra Med. Ctr., El Paso, Tex.; ret. Fellow AMA, Am. Assn. Allergy and Immunology; mem. Am. Assn. Clin. Immunology and Allergy, Am. Coll. Chest Physicians. Died Apr. 1, 2006.

UNSELL, LLOYD NEAL, energy executive, retired journalist; b. Henryetta, Okla., May 12, 1922; s. John William and Rhoda Elizabeth (Martinez) U.; m. Nettie Marie Rogers, Sept. 24, 1944 (dec. 1990); children: Lloyd Neal, Jonna Kay Unsell Wilhelm, James Allan (dec. 1994). Student, U. Ill., Kalamazoo Coll., 1942-43. Mem. editl. staff Tulsa Daily World, 1947-48; with Ind. Petroleum Assn. Am., 1848—1987, exec. v.p. Washington, 1964—76, pres., CEO, 1976—87. Chmn. selection com. for Milburn Petty award Am. Petroleum Inst.-Assn. Petroleum Writers, 1972-86 Author reports and articles in field. Co-chmn. corp. adv. com. Vietnam Vets. Meml., 1981-82. Served with U.S. Army, 1942-46, ETO, PTO. Recipient Spl. award as outstanding petroleum industry communicator Assn. Petroleum Writers, 1960, Russell B. Brown Meml. award, 1981, Robert J. Enright award Am. Petroleum Inst./Assn. Petroleum Writers, 1986, Disting. Service award Nat. Energy Resources Orgn., 1987, Lloyd N. Unsell award established in his honor Ind. Petroleum Assn. Am., 1993; named Hon. Chief Roughneck U.S. petroleum industry, 1986. Mem. Nat. Press Club, Rocky Mountain Oil and Gas Assn. (hon. life), The Jefferson Energy Found. (co-founder 1987). Republican. Baptist. Home: Coltons Point, Md. Died Apr. 7, 2007.

UPCHURCH, THURMAN HOWELL, pipe products company executive; b. Raleigh, N.C., Nov. 6, 1926; s. Auba Merriman and Mertie Mae (Howell) U.; m. Elizabeth Short Daniels, Aug. 7, 1949; children— William Howell, Thurman, Daniel, Mary Elizabeth. B.S. in Metall. Engring., N.C. State U., 1961; grad. Inst. Mgmt., Lynchburg (Va.) Coll., 1970; grad. Mng. Corp. Resources Program, U. Va., 1970, grad. Indsl. Mgmt. Basic Comuter Systems Program, 1968. Asst. mgr. Sungas of the Carolinas, Inc., Raleigh, 1947-49; mgr. Blue Flame Gas Co., Durham, N.C., 1949-55; research asst. dept. engring. research N.C. State U., 1955-61; dir. engring. and prodn. Hardy & Newsome, Inc., LaGrange, N.C., 1961-65; dir. maintenance Glamorgan Pipe and Foundry Co. (name now Griffin Pipe Products Co.), Lynchburg, 1965-66, plant engr., 1966-67, prodn. mgr., 1967, works mgr., 1967-71, dir. mfg., 1971-73, dir. ops., 1971-73, dir. ops. and central iron research and devel., 1973-78, dir. research, 1978—. Chmn. Old Dominion Com. for Fair Utility Rates; past bd. dirs. Lynchburg Central YWCA; City of Lynchburg rep., chmn. Central Va. Air Pollution Control Com. Served with USN, 1944-46. Mem. Am. Soc. for Metals (past chmn. Central Va. chpt.), Lynchburg Soc. Engring. and Sci. (past chmn.), Am. Foundrymen's Soc. (past dir. Piedmont chpt.), Aircraft Owners and Pilots Assn. Republican. Southern Baptist. Clubs: Boonsboro Country, Peakland Swimming (Lynchburg). Patentee control of centrifugal pipe casting operation. Home: Swansboro, NC. Died Oct. 26, 2006.

UPSHUR, DORIS NASH, interior designer, consultant, researcher; b. Charlotte, NC, Oct. 21, 1921; d. John Clayton and Jessie (Bound) Nash; m. Robert Irving Upshur, May 30, 1918; children: David Nash, John Irving. BA, U. S.C., 1944. Interior designer Dora Gray Studios, Columbia, S.C., 1944-65, Columbia Office Supply Co., 1964-65; owner Doris Upshur Interiors, Columbia, from 1965. Pres. Carolinas chpt. Am. Inst. Decorators, 1950-70, accredited mem., 1970; nat. dir., charter mem. Carolinas chpt. Nat. Home Fashions League, 1967; design coord. Women's Symphony Showhouse, 1980-81, 85-86. Bd. dirs. Columbia Lyric Opera, 1979-89; mem. Trinity Housing Corp., Trinity Environ. Task Force; pres. Episc. Ch. Women, 1971; pres. Opera Guild Greater Columbia, 1990; chmn. Wednesdays at Trinity. Fellow Am. Soc. Interior Designers (life, nat. v.p. southeastern region 1969-71, Dora Gray award Carolinas chpt. 1984); mem. Nat. Trust for Hist. Preservation (bd. mem. 1989-90) Republican. Home: Columbia, SC. Died Feb. 9, 2006.

URBAN, GILBERT WILLIAM, banker; b. Silver Lake, Minn., Oct. 20, 1928; s. William and Alice (Polak) U.; m. Elvera Mattson, Feb. 23, 1954; children: Lisa Alice Marie, Leann Kay. BBA, U. Minn., 1949. Sr. acct. Price Waterhouse and Co., Chgo., 1949-50; chief acct. Calif. Bank, LA, 1950-51; asst. contr. 1st Nat. Bank, Mpls., 1951-63, contr., 1963-69; v.p., cashier La. Nat. Bank, Baton Rouge, 1969-73, v.p. assets and liabilities, 1973-86; sr. v.p. fin. policy Premier Bancorp Inc., Baton Rouge, from 1986. Instr. evening sch. U. Minn., 1956-69, La. State U., 1970—, So. U., Baton Rouge, 1989—; instr. Nat. Assn. Bank Auditors and Contrs. Sch., U. Wis., 1960-63, sect. leader, 1963-69; chmn. dept. controllership Bank Adminstrn. Inst., 1970—; course coord. Banking Sch. of South, 1970, 79—. Mem. Beta Alpha Psi, Alpha Kappa Psi. Lutheran. Home: Baton Rouge, La. Died Jan. 22, 2006.

URBANTKE, HUGH EDMUND, business educator, economist; b. Brenham, Tex., July 31, 1922; s. Hugo E. and Linda K. (Kleb) U.; m. E. Linda Paxson, May 10, 1944; children: Karen Crawford, Hugh Stanley. BBA, U. Houston, 1948; MBA, U Houston, 1957; PhD, U. Houston, 1966. Prof. econs. La. Tech. U., 1966-70; head dept. mktg. U. Ark.-Little Rock, 1970-75; dean sch. bus. Centenary Coll., Shreveport, La., 1975-81; dean sch. mgmt. Oklahoma City U., 1981-82, C.R. Anthony prof. competitive enterprise, 1981-84. Dir. Centenary Coll. Ctr. for Mgmt. Devel., 1975-81, now adj. prof.; adj. prof. La. Tech. U.; bd. dirs., v.p. Support Ctr., Oklahoma City, 1982-83; regional bd. dirs. SBA, Oklahoma City, 1982-84; adj. prof. La. State U., Shreveport, 1987, Centenary Coll., 1988, La. Tech. U., 1989. Author: (with R.M. Davis) 200 Years of Free Enterprise in America, 1976, Free Enterprise Economy and Free Enterprise, 1982; editor: Free Enterprise 5 Years of Free Enterprise, 1980, Procs. Free Enterprise Conf., 1981, Bus. Views columnist Jour. Record, 1981-84 Bd. dirs. Jr. Achievement, Oklahoma City, 1981-84; mem. adv. bd. Leadership, 1982-84; chmn. edn. Ptnrs. of Ams.-Okla., 1983-84. Grantee Internat. Econ. Research Found., 1978-84; recipient disting. service award Sales and Mktg. Execs., Little Rock, 1973, pres.'s award, 1974, Jack Timmons award free enterprise Better Bus. Bur., Shreveport, 1980 Mem. Am. Mgmt. Assn., Am. Econ. Assn., Acad. Mgmt., So. Econ. Assn., Southwestern Mktg. Assn., Am. Soc. Tng. Dirs. Home: Shreveport, La. Died Dec. 8, 2006.

URCIA, JOSE MITSUO, planning consultant; b. Aica, Hawaii, Jan. 18, 1931; s. S.D. and Kimie (Yoshitake) U.; m. Ingeborg Oppel, July 25, 1958; children— Benjamin, Gwendolyn. B.A., U. Hawaii, 1953; M.Urban Planning, U. Wash., 1960. Cert. planner, Am. Int. Cert. Planners. Exec. dir. Whitman County Regional Planning Conf., Colfax, Wash., 1968-72; exec. dir. Spokane Regional Planning Conf., Wash., 1972-78; planning cons. Spokane, 1978-84; planning dir. Spokane Indian Tribe, Wellpinit, Wash., 1984—. Past chmn. Resource Conservation Devel., 1978; assoc. supr. Soil Conservation Dist. Spokane, 1972—. Served to 1st lt. U.S. Army, 1953-55. Mem. Regional Sci. Assn., Western Govt. Research Assn., Soc. Polit. and Social Scis., Am. Planning Assn. Home: Cheney, Wash. Died Mar. 7, 2007.

USHIJIMA, JOHN TAKEJI, state legislator, lawyer; b. Hilo, Hawaii, Mar. 13, 1924; s. Buhachi and Sano (Nitahara) U.; m. Margaret Kunishige, June 6, 1954. BA, Grinnell Coll., 1950; JD, George Washington U., 1952. Bar: Hawaii, 1953. Ptnr. Pence & Ushijima, Hilo, 1953-61, Ushijima & Nakamoto, Hilo, 1961-69; mem. Hawaii Senate, from 1959, pres. pro tem, from 1974. Bd. dirs. Cyanotech Corp., Woodinville, Wash. Bd. dirs. Waiakea Settlement YMCA. With AUS, 1943-46, ETO. Mem. Am. Bar Assn., Phi Delta Phi. Democrat. Home: Hilo, Hawaii. Died Aug. 13, 2006.

VACIK, JAMES PAUL, retired academic administrator; b. North Judson, Ind., Nov. 30, 1931; s. George J. and Elsie E. (Paulsen) V.; m. Dorothy M. Nobles, Dec. 27, 1967; children: Deborah, Pamella, James, Stephen, Joshua, Jonathan. BS in Pharmacy, Purdue U., 1955, MS in Medicinal Chemistry, 1957, PhD in Bionucleonics, 1959. Cert. hazard control mgr.; registered bio-safety profl., registered pharmacist, Ind., N.D., Ala.; registered profl. indsl. hygienist. Asst. prof. bionucleonics dept. Purdue U., Lafayette, Ind., 1959-60; assoc. prof., dept. chmn. pharm. chemistry & bionucleonics N.D. State U., Fargo, 1960-63, prof., dept. chmn. pharm. chemistry & bionucleonics, 1963-76; assoc. prof. pharmacology Univ. S. Ala., Mobile, 1976-82, adj. prof., dir. environ. safety, 1982-98. Pub. Health Svc. grant dir. N.D. State U., Fargo, 1963-71; VA Hosp. cons. VA Hosp. System, Washington, 1966; vis. prof. Nat. Reactor Testing Sta., Idaho Falls, Idaho, 1968; pvt. cons. to various indsl. firms, 1970—. Contbr. articles to profl. Mem., first dir. "Showboat on the Red," Jaycees, Fargo, 1965. With U.S. Army, 1949-52, ETO. Named Outstanding Educator Am., Fuller & Dees, Washington, 1975. Mem. Am. Chem. Soc., Am. Pharm. Assn., Am. Health Physics Soc. (chmn. com.), Am. Biol. Safety Assn. (bd. dirs. 1985-87), Health Physics Soc. (pres., treas., bd. dirs. Ala chpt. 1977—, pres., bd. dirs. N. Ctrl. chpt. 1969—), Masons. Baptist. Avocations: camping, fishing, woodworking. Home: Mobile, Ala. Died Apr. 15, 2006.

VAILE, JEAN ELIZABETH, business owner; b. Cut Bank, Mont., July 18, 1938; d. Leo M. and Evelyn A. (Hensrude) Baker; m. Alvin L. Vaile (div.); children— Arthur Henry, Sheila Jean, Leo Michael. Student Kinman Bus. Sch., 1956-57, Fresno City Coll., 1975-76, U. San Francisco, 1980, State Center Community Coll., Fresno, Calif., 1981-82. Lic. life disability ins. agt., real estate agt., Calif.; notary pub., Calif. Mgr., Glacier Drug, Browning, Mont., 1958-60, Club Cafe, Browning, 1960-67; office mgr. J.C. Penny Co., Mont., 1967-69, Bob Ward & Sons, Inc., Missoula, Mont., 1970-73; acct. Sun Fruit, Ltd., Fresno, 1973-76; bus. adminstr. Assn. for Retarded Citizens, 1976-82; adminstrv. asst. to sr. v.p. Guarantee Savs., Fresno, 1985-90; owner Fin. Mgmt. Svc., bookkeeping and tax svcs., 1990—; owner fin. mgmt. svc., bookkeeping & tax preparation svc. Chmn. supervisory com. Fresno Consumers Credit Union, 1979; voting mem. two social service health orgns., 1979—. Mem. Rep. Presdl. Task Force. Mem. Fresno C. of C., Toastmasters. Lutheran Home: Fresno, Calif. Died July 1, 2007.

VALENTI, JACK JOSEPH, retired motion picture association executive; b. Houston, Sept. 5, 1921; m. Mary Margaret Wiley, June 1, 1962; children: Courtenay Lynda, John Lyndon, Alexandra Alice. BA, U. Houston, 1946; MBA, Harvard U., 1948. Co-founder, formerly exec. v.p. Weekley and Valenti, Inc. (advt.), 1952-63; spl. asst. to Pres. Lyndon Johnson The White House, 1963-66; chmn., CEO Motion Picture Assn. Am., Inc., 1966—2004. Adj. prof. govt. and pub. adminstrn. Am. U., 1977; bd. dirs. Riggs Nat. Corp. Washington. Author: Bitter Taste of Glory, 1971, A Very Human President, 1976, Speak Up With Confidence: How To Prepare, Learn and Deliver an Effective Speech, 1982, Protect and Defend, 1992, Speak Up With Confidence, 2002, This Time, This Place: My Life in War, the White House, and Hollywood, 2007; contbr. articles to mags Trustee, bd. dirs. Am. Film Inst. Served with USAAF, 1942-45 Decorated D.F.C., Air medal with five oak leaf clusters, Disting Unit Citation with cluster, European Theater Ribbon with 4 battle stars, Chevalier de la Legion d'honneur (France). Died Apr. 26, 2007.

VALENTINE, FOY DAN, clergyman; b. Edgewood, Tex., July 3, 1923; s. John Hardy and Josie (Johnson) V.; m. Mary Louise Valentine, May 6, 1947; children: Mary Jean, Carol Elizabeth Susan Foy. BA, Baylor U., 1944, LLD (hon.), 1979; ThM Southwestern Baptist Theol. Sem., 1947, ThD, 1949; DD William Jewell Coll., 1966, Louisiana Coll., 1989. Ordained to ministry Bapt. Ch., 1942. Dir. Bapt. student activities colls. in Houston, 1949-50; pastor First Bapt. Ch., Gonzales, Tex., 1950-53; dir. Christian life commn. Bapt. Gen. Conv. Tex., 1953-60; exec. dir., treas. Christian life commn. So. Bapt. Conv., 1960-87, exec. officer for devel., 1987-88; chmn. So. Bapt inter-agy. council, 1965-67. Willson lectr. applied Christianity Wayland Bapt. Coll., 1963; Christian ethics lectr. Bapt. Theol Sem., Ruschlikon-Zurich, Switzerland, 1966; Layne lectr. New Orleans Bapt. Theol. Sem., 1974; Jones lectr. Union U., 1976; Staley Disting. Christian scholar/lectr. La. Coll., 1981; Simpson lectr. Acadia Divinity Coll., Nova Scotia, 1982; H.I. Hester lectr. on preaching Midwestern Bapt. Theol. Sem., 1984; Belote lectr. Christian ethics Hong Kong Bapt. Theol. Sem., 1990; co-chmn. commn. religious liberty and human rights Bapt. World Alliance, 1966-75, chmn. commn. Christian ethics, 1976-80, mem. gen. coun., 1976-80; mem. Nashville Met. Human Rels. Commn., 1966-78, Pres.'s Commn. for Nat. Agenda for the Eighties, 1980; guest columnist USA Today; lectr. on Christian ethics Bible Inst. for Evangelism and Missions, St. Petersburg, USSR, 1991; co-chmn. Baylor U. Heritage Club, 2000-01. Author: Believe and Behave, 1964, Citizenship for Christians, 1965, The Cross in the Marketplace, 1966, Where the Action Is, 1969, A Historical Study of Southern Baptists and Race Relations 1917-1947, 1980, What Do You Do After You Say Amen?, 1980, Hebrews, James, 1 and 2 Peter: Layman's Bible Book Commentary, 1981, Whatsoever Things Are Lovely, 2004; editor: Christian Faith in Action, 1956, Peace, Peace, 1967, Christian Ethics Today, 1995-2000; contbr. to numerous anthologies, articles to profl. jours. Pres. Ctr. for Christian Ethics, 1990-2000; trustee Interfaith Alliance, 1994—, Ams. United for Separation of Ch. and State, 1960-93, pres., 1989-93; bd. dirs. Bapt. Joint Com. Pub. Affairs, 1960-87, Chs. Ctr. Theology and Pub. Policy, 1976-87, T.B. Maston Found., Texans Against Gambling; mem. bd. fellows Interpreter's House, 1967-78, Ctr. for Dialogue and Devel., 1987-96. Recipient Disting. Alumnus award Southwestern Bapt. Theol. Sem., 1970, Brooks Hays Meml. Christian Citizenship award, 1983, Disting. Alumni award Baylor U., 1987. Mem. Am. Soc. Christian Ethics. Democrat. Died Jan. 7, 2006.

VANCE, CARL BRUCE, retired utility company executive; b. Bagnell, Mo., Apr. 12, 1915; s. Homer Benton and Hattie Fugitt (Hallar) V.; m. Ruth Brenneman, Mar. 11, 1939; children— Janet Vance Smith, Julia Vance Keller, Carl Bruce. BS inMech. Engring, U. Okla., 1936; postgrad., U. Mich., 1960, Columbia U., 1961, Am. Mgmt. Assn. Sr. Mgmt. Program, 1977. Registered profl. engr., Ohio, Ind. Sales-service engr. Bailey Meter Co., Cleve., St. Louis and Kansas City, Mo., 1936-39; test engr. Gen. Electric Co., Schenectady, 1940; sr. engr. prodn. dept. Cleve. Electric Illuminating Co., 1940-42; mech. engr., supt. power and distbn. Mil. Chem. Works, Jayhawk Ordnance Works, Pittsburg, Kans., 1942-45; with Indpls. Power & Light Co., 1945-80, mech. engr., supt. power prodn., 1957-62, asst. v.p. power prodn., 1962, v.p. power prodn., 1963-75, sr. v.p. ops., 1975-78, exec. v.p. ops., 1978-80, ret., 1980, cons. and dir., mem. exec. com., 1980-85. Chmn. City of Indpls. Air Pollution Adv. Com., 1966-67; Chmn. City of Indpls. Air Pollution Control Bd., 1968-70, mem. bd., 1968-76; tech. cons. State of Ind. Air Pollution Control Bd., 1968-70, mem. Bd., 1969-70; mem. Environ. Quality Control Air Com., 1972-80; bd. dirs. Indpls. Sci. and Engring. Found., 1971-74, mem. nominating com., 1973-76; mem. Mayor's Solid Waste Task Force, 1976-80. Fellow ASME (vice chmn. air pollution standards com. 1964-68, chmn. exec. com. air pollution controls div. 1967-68); mem. Ind. Soc. Profl. Engrs., Edison Electric Inst. (chmn. prime movers com. 1963-65, mem. exec. com. engring. and operating div. 1965-70, chmn. air and water problems subcom. 1967-70), Assn. Edison Illuminating Cos. (power generation com. 1965-80), East Central Area Reliability Group (chmn. generation adv. panel 1967-69), Ind. Electric Assn. (chmn. environ. policy com. 1969-72, 76-77), Engrs. Joint Council (commr. Nat. Engrs. Commn. on Air Resources 1970-71), Electric League Ind., Tau Beta Pi. Clubs: Meridian Hills Country. Presbyterian. Died July 2, 2007.

VANCE, ELBRIDGE PUTNAM, mathematics educator; b. Cin., Feb. 7, 1915; s. Selby Frame and Jeannie (Putnam) V.; m. Margaret Gertrude Stoffel, Aug. 5, 1939 (div. 1975); children: Susan (Mrs. Timothy Griffin), Peter Selby, Douglas Putnam, Emily (Mrs. Charles Harold Beynon III); m. Jean Haigh, Jan. 1975. Student, Haverford Coll., 1932-33; AB, Coll. Wooster, 1936; MA, U. Mich., 1937, PhD, 1939. Asst. U. Mich., 1937-39; instr. U. Nev., 1939-41, asst. prof., 1941-43; vis. lectr. Oberlin (Ohio) Coll., 1943-46, asst. prof., 1946-50, asso. prof., 1950-54, prof., 1954-83, prof. emeritus, from 1983, chmn. dept., 1948-77, acting dean Coll. Arts and Scis., 2d semester, 1965-66, 1st semester, 1970-71. Chmn. advanced placement com. Coll. Entrance Exam. Bd., 1961-65, chief reader, 1956-61; chmn. com. examiners math. Comprehensive Coll. Tests, Ednl. Testing Service, 1965-67 Author: Trigonometry, 2d edit, 1969, Unified Algebra and Trigonometry, 1955, Fundamentals of Mathematics, 1960, Modern College Algebra, 3d edit, 1973, Modern Algebra and Trigonometry, 3d edit, 1973, An Introduction to Modern Mathematics, 2d edit, 1968, Mathematics 12, 1968, Solution Manual for Mathematics 12, 1968; Book review editor: Am. Math. Monthly, 1949-57; asso. editor, 1964-67. Mem. Oberlin Sch. Bd., 1952-60, pres., 1957-60. NSF Faculty fellow, 1960-61 Mem. Math. Assn. Am., Nat. Council Tchrs. of Math., Am. Math. Soc., Phi Beta Kappa, Sigma Xi, Phi Kappa Phi. Died Feb. 17, 2007.

ANCE, ROY NEWTON, state supreme court justice; b. aducah, Ky., Nov. 14, 1921; s. Roy Newton and Mary Louise 3ryan) V.; m. Euleen Hamilton, Oct. 20, 1949; children: Linda, eresa, Roy Newton III. LL.B., U. Ky., 1942. Bar: Ky. 1942. ounty atty. McCracken County, (Ky.), 1949-53; commonealth's atty. 2d Jud. Dist. Ky., 1953-57; mem. Vance, Grimes nd Carlick, Paducah, 1957-70; commr. Ct. Appeals of Ky., rankfort, 1970-76, judge, 1976-83; justice Ky. Supreme Ct., om 1983. Served with AUS, 1942-46. Mem. Order of Coif ome: Frankfort, Ky. Died Jan. 17, 2007.

ANDER JAGT, GUY, retired congressman; b. Cadillac, lich., Aug. 26, 1931; s. Harry and Marie (Copier) Vander J.; m. arol Doorn, Apr. 4, 1964; 1 dau., Virginia Marie. AB, Hope oll., 1953; B.D., Yale U., 1957; LL.B., U. Mich., 1960; ostgrad., U. Bonn, Germany, 1955-56. Bar: Mich. 1960. ractice in, Grand Rapids; mem. firm Warner, Norcross & Judd, 960-64; mem. Mich. State Senate, 1964-66, US Congress from th Mich. dist., 1966—93; mem. ways and means com., trade nd select revenue measures subcoms. Nat. Rep. Congl. Com., hnm.; keynote spkr. Rep. Nat. Conv., Detroit, 1980; of counsel aker & Hostetler LLP, 1993—2007. Mem. Joint Com. on axation. Named One of Five Most Outstanding Young Men in lich., Mich. Jr. C. of C., 1956 Mem. Capitol Hill Club, Hope oll. Alumni Assn. Washington (pres.) Republican. Died June 2, 2007.

ANDERLINDE, RAYMOND EDWARD, clinical chemist; b. lewark, NY, Feb. 28, 1924; s. Isaac Edward and Hazel Effie Robinson) V.; m. Ruth Louise Hansen, June 19, 1948; children: usan Kay, Jeanne, William Edward. AB magna cum laude, yracuse U., 1944, MS, 1945, PhD in Med. Biochemistry, 1950. iplomate: Am. Bd. Clin. Chemistry. Asst. prof. biochemistry . Md. Sch. Medicine, 1950-53, assoc. prof., 1953-57; lab. dir., sst. prof. Syracuse Meml. Hosp.-Upstate Med. Center, Syraluse, 1957-62; clin. chemist Meml. Hosp., Cumberland, Md., 962-65; dir. labs. for clin. chemistry N.Y. State Dept. Health, lbany, 1965-76; prof. pathology and lab. medicine Hahnemann ., Phila., 1977-90, prof. emeritus, from 1991. Mem. lab. tech. dv. com. Pa. Dept. Health, 1981-85; mem. Coun. Nat. Refernce Sys. in Clin. Chemistry, 1978—, vice chair holder, 1987, 1-93, chair holder, 1988-90; mem. Commn. on Accreditation in lin. Chemistry, 1980-93; mem. enzyme subcom. Commn. on Vorld Standardization, World Assn. Socs. of Pathology, 1978-0. Editor: Selected Methods of Clinical Chemistry, 1977-83, nnals of Clinical and Laboratory Science, 1981-93, Clinical hemistry, 1983-92. Chmn. council on ministries, lay del. to nnl. conf. Berwyn United Methodist Ch., 1979-82. Nat. Inst. rthritis, Metabolism and Digestive Diseases grantee, 1977-81; IIH Lab. Standardization Panel for Lipids, 1986-90. Fellow m. Assn. for Clin. Chemistry (bd. dirs. 1979-81, Fisher award 985, Rheinhold award 1992); mem. Am. Chem. Soc., Am. Soc. lin. Pathologists (assoc.), Acad. Clin. Lab. Physicians and cientists, Assn. of Clin. Scientists, Soc. Mayflower Descs. of m., Masons, Rotary (past pres. Delmar, N.Y.), Phi Beta Kappa, igma Xi. Democrat. Methodist. Home: Catonsville, Md. Died uly 14, 2007.

ANDERSTAPPEN, HARRIE ALBERT, art educator; b. leesch, The Netherlands, Jan. 21, 1921; arrived in US, 1959; s. ohannes and Johanna (van de Poel) V. Student, Theol. Sch., lelvoirt and Teteringen, The Netherlands, 1939-45, Chinese ang. Sch., Peking, People's Republic of China, 1946-48; PhD n Far Eastern Art, U. Chgo., 1955. Ordained priest Roman Cath. h., 1945. Student lang., also tchr., writer, Tokyo, 1955-57; tchr. lanzan U., Nagoya, Japan, 1957-59; prof. Far Eastern art U. hgo., 1959-92, chmn. dept. art, 1964-69, prof. emeritus dept. rt, 1991—2007. Author: The T.L. Yuan Bibliography of Chiese Art and Archaeology, 1975; author, editor: Ritual and everence, 1989; assoc. editor Monumenta Serica, 1955—2007; ontbr. articles to profl. jours. Recipient Teaching of Art History ward Nat. Coll. Art Assn. Am., 1985; Harrie A. Vanderstappen isting. Chair established at U. Chgo., 1995. Mem. Asia Soc., ssn. Asian Arts Home: Techny, Ill. Died Jan. 25, 2007.

ANDERVOORT, PETER, lawyer; b. Paterson, NJ, Dec. 15, 929; s. Vincent and Jeannette Barbara (Scott) V.; m. Elena rake, June 26, 1971. BA, Williams Coll., 1951; LLB, U. Va., 954. Bar: Va. 1953, N.J. 1958. Assoc. Evans Hand, Paterson, 958-62, ptnr. West Paterson, N.J., 1963-97; of counsel Harvood Lloyd, Hackensack, N.J., from 1997. Asst. sec. Essex hem. Corp., Clifton, N.J., 1963-83, sec., 1983-88. Trustee West ide Presbyn. Ch., Ridgewood, N.J., 1961-67, Family Counseling Service of Ridgewood, 1968-77, Soc. Valley Hosp., Ridgevood, 1976-88; vice chmn. Valley Care Corp., 1988-96; bd. irs. Paterson YMCA, 1959-76, pres. 1967-74, trustee 1978-96, hmn. 1984-88. Fellow Am. Coll. Trust and Estate Counsel; nem. ABA, N.J. Bar Assn., Va. Bar Assn., Ridgewood Country lub, Williams Club (N.Y.C.), Order of Coif, Phi Beta Kappa. ome: Bath, Maine. Died Oct. 11, 2005.

VAN EERDE, KATHERINE S(OMMERLATTE), history ducator and administrator; b. Terre Haute, Ind., June 17, 1920; . Ewald and Flora Lillian (Hoff) Sommerlatte; m. John A. Van erde, July 23, 1946; 1 dau., Elizabeth Marie. B.A., Coll. of Vooster, 1941; M.A., Yale U., 1942, Ph.D., 1945. Instr. Scripps oll., Claremont, Calif., 1944-46, Smith Coll., Northampton, lass., 1946-48, Johns Hopkins U., Balt., 1948-51; reviewing fficer Dept. of State, Intelligence, Washington, 1951-55; asst. rof. U. R.I., 1955-61; assoc. prof., prof. Muhlenberg Coll., llentown, Pa., 1961—, head history dept., 1978-84. Author: ohn Ogilby, 1976; Wenceslaus Hollar, 1970; contbr. articles to ubls. Com. mem. synodical United Ch. of Christ. Guggenheim ellow, 1971; Huntington Library fellow, 1979; grantee Am. hilos. Soc., 1974, Ford Found. (3); recipient Lindback teaching ward, 1968. Mem. Am. Hist. Assn., Renaissance Soc. Am., onf. on Brit. Studies, Lehigh County Hist. Soc., AAUP, Am. rinting History Assn., Phi Beta Kappa. Democrat. Mem. United h. of Christ. Home: Allentown, Pa. Died Aug. 15, 2006.

VAN HAUER, ROBERT, former health care company execuive; b. Chgo., June 9, 1910; s. Francis Anthony and Della Agnes Mulhern) Van H.; m. Elaine Greenwood, July 24, 1944 (dec. Nov. 1961); children: Peter, Jan, Mary, Christopher, Gretchen, Juliana; m. Margaret Ann St. Pierre Viehman, May 4, 1968; stepchildren: Gayle, Edwin, Thomas, John, Michael, Daniel. BA in Econs; BBA in Accounting (Reiman scholar), U. Mont., Missoula, 1938; MA in Econs, U. Minn., Mpls., 1940. Jr. Auditor Peat Marwick Mitchell, C.P.A.'s, Mpls., 1938-40; asst. sales mgr. North Star Woolen Mill, Mpls., 1940-42; dir. contracts Mpls. regional office VA, 1946-51; with Health Central, Inc., Mpls., 1951-78, exec. v.p., 1965, pres., chief exec. officer, 1970-78; exec. dir. Health Found., Mpls., 1979-81. Mem. planning commn. Golden Valley, Minn., 1959-66; past trustee St. Margaret's Acad., Benilde-St. Margaret's High Sch. Served to maj. AUS, 1941-46. Decorated Commendation ribbon; Rieman fellow, 1938-40 Mem. Am. Hosp. Assn., Minn. Hosp. Assn. (trustee, com. chmn. 1974-79), War Meml. Blood Bank (pres., dir. 1967), Physicians Health Plan Mpls. (dir., exec. com.), Am. Legion. Clubs: Mpls. Athletic, Minn. Valley Country, Elks; Union Hills Country (Sun City, Ariz.). Republican. Roman Catholic. Home: New Hope, Minn. Died June 4, 2007.

VAN HENGEL, MAARTEN, banker; b. Amsterdam, Mar. 29, 1927; came to U.S., 1950, naturalized, 1957; s. Adrianus J. and Helena (Gips) van H.; m. Drusilla Drake Riley, Dec. 1, 1951; children: Maarten, Virginia, Hugh, Drusilla. Student, Kennemer Lyceum, Bloemendaal, Holland, 1939-45. With tng. programs of Amsterdamsche Bank, N.V., Amsterdam, Lazard Bros. & Co. Ltd., London and Canadian Bank of Commerce, Montreal, Que., Canada, 1945-49; with Brown Bros. Harriman & Co., from 1950, ptnr., from 1968. Bd. dirs. Netherlands-Am. Found. Served with AUS, 1951-53. Mem.: India House, Netherland (N.Y.C.); Fishers Island Country, Hay Harbor (Fishers Island); Sleepy Hollow Country (Scarborough, N.Y.). Home: Briarcliff Manor, NY. Died Dec. 29, 2006.

VAN SICKLE, BRUCE MARION, retired federal judge; b. Minot, ND, Feb. 13, 1917; s. Guy Robin and Hilda Alice (Rosenquist) Van S.; m. Dorothy Alfreda Hermann, May 26, 1943; children: Susan Van Sickle Cooper, John Allan, Craig Bruce, David Max. BSL, JD, U. Minn., 1941. Bar: Minn. 1941, N.D. 1946. Title atty. Bonneville Power, Portland, Oreg., 1946—47; pvt. practice law Minot, 1947-71; mem. N.D. Ho. of Reps., 1957—59; judge U.S. Dist. Ct. N.D., 1971-85, sr. judge, 1985—2002. Served with USMCR, 1941-46. Mem. ABA, N.D. Bar Assn., N.W. Bar Assn., Ward County Bar Assn., Am. Trial Lawyers Assn., Am. Coll. Probate Counsel, Am. Judicature Soc., Bruce M. Van Sickle Inns of Ct., Masons, Shriners, Elks, Delta Theta Phi. Died Apr. 21, 2007.

VASEEN, VESPER ALBERT, engineering company executive, environmental and sanitary engineer; b. Denver, Sept. 13, 1917; s. Albert and Ruby Cornelia (Weisz) V.; m. June L. Novak, Feb. 2, 1941; children: Gail C. Vaseen Moler, Dale A. MS, Colo. Sch. Mines, 1939; cert., Denver U., 1940; postgrad., U. Mich., 1941, Colo. State U., 1942-86; DSci, U. Del Norte, Coquimbo, Chile, 1981. Registered profl. engr., Colo., Kans., Utah, Pa., Alaska. Pres. Ripple & Howe Inc., Denver, 1946-79; project engr. Stearns Roger Corp., Denver, 1966-79; pres. AVASCO, Wheat Ridge, Colo., from 1979, Technometrics Inc., Wheat Ridge, 1982-87. Cons. Internat. Execs. Service Assn., N.Y.C., 1981. Contbr. articles to profl. jours; inventor, patentee in field. Served to maj. AUS, 1943-49. Recipient cert. of merit various C. of C.'s nationwide, 1952—. Mem. Am. Water Works Assn. (life), Water Pollution Control Fedn. (life), U.S. Dept. Commerce (past mem. exec. res.). Lodges: Kiwanis, Masons, Order Rosicrucians. Republican. Died Mar. 28, 2007.

VEENHUIS, BRIAN CHARLES, lawyer; b. Flint, Mich., Sept. 14, 1944; s. Melvin Leslie and Carolyn Eileen (Burr) V.; m. Jeanette Carol Barajas, Oct. 17, 1975; children— Erik Brian, Ethan Daniel. B.S. in Edn., Central Mich. U., 1968; J.D., Detroit Coll. Law, 1982. Bar: Mich. 1983, U.S. Dist. Ct. (ea. dist.) Mich. 1983. Clk. Fisher Body, Grand Blanc, Mich., 1966; tchr. North Branch Schs., Mich., 1966-67, Flint Pub. Schs., Mich., 1967-83; sole practice, Flint, 1983-85; assoc. O'Rourke, Goldstein, Joseph & Kelly, P.C., 1986—. Mem. staff Reigle for Congress, Flint, 1972, Kildee for Commr., Flint, 1984; dir. Kildee for State Rep., Flint, 1980; student vol. coordinator Carter Townhall Meeting, Flint, 1980; bd. dirs. Social Services for Hearing Impaired, Flint, 1984—. Mem. ABA, State Bar Mich., Mich. Edn. Assn., Genesee County Bar Assn. (com. chair 1983), United Tchrs. Flint (pres. 1973-74). Democrat. Home: Flint, Mich. Died Dec. 2, 2006.

VEENING, HANS, retired chemistry educator; b. Arnhem, The Netherlands, May 7, 1931; came to U.S., 1944; s. John Dirk and Cornelia J. (DeGoede) V.; m. Elizabeth I. Timmerman, Sept. 7, 1957. AB, Hope Coll., 1953; PhD, Purdue U., 1959. Instr. chemistry Bucknell U., Lewisburg, Pa., 1958-60, asst. prof. chemistry, 1960-67, assoc. prof. chemistry, 1967-72, prof. chemistry, 1972-97, chmn. chemistry dept., 1986-97, presdl. prof. chemistry, 1990-97, prof. chemistry emeritus, 1997. Vis. prof. U. Amsterdam, The Netherlands, 1966-67, Oak Ridge (Tenn.) Nat. Lab., 1972-73, Free U., Amsterdam, 1984-85, U. Amsterdam, 1995. Contr. more than 60 articles to profl. jours. NSF fellow, 1966; grantee NSF, NIH, Petroleum Rsch. Fund and Camille and Henry Dreyfus Found., 1966-92. Mem. Am. Chem. Soc. (chmn. 1970), Royal Netherlands Chem. Soc., Phi Beta Kappa (hon.), Sigma Xi. Achievements includes first to report liquid chromatographic separation of metal complexes. Home: Lewisburg, Pa. Died Dec. 27, 2006.

VEGA, BENJAMIN URBIZO, retired judge, television producer; b. La Ceiba, Honduras, Jan. 18, 1916; m. Janie Lou Smith, Oct. 12, 1989. AB, U. So. Calif., 1938, postgrad., 1939—40; LLB, Pacific Coast U. Law, 1941; postgrad., Washington & Lee U., 1943. Bar: Calif. 1947, U.S. Dist. Ct. (so. dist.) Calif. 1947, U.S. Supreme Ct. 1958. Assoc. Anderson, McPharlin & Connors, LA, 1947—48, Newman & Newman, LA, 1948—51; dep. dist. atty. County of L.A., 1951—66; judge L.A. County Mcpl. Ct., East L.A. Jud. Dist., 1966—86; ret., 1986. Leader faculty seminar Calif. Jud. Coll. at Earl Warren Legal Inst., U. Calif.-Berkeley, 1978. Mem. Calif. Gov.'s Adv. Com. on Children and Youth, 1968; del. Commn. of the Califs., 1978; pres. Argentine Cultural Found., 1983; bd. dirs. Los Angeles-Mexico City Sister City Com. Recipient award for outstanding services from Mayor of L.A., 1973, award, City of Commerce, City of Montebello, Calif. Assembly, Southwestern Sch. Law, Disting. Pub. Svc. award, Dist. Atty. L.A. Mem.; Conf. Calif. Judges, Beverly Hills Bar Assn., Mcpl. Ct. Judges' Assn. (award for Outstanding Svcs.), Am. Judicature Soc., Navy League L.A. County, World Affairs Coun., Rotary (hon.), Pi Sigma Alpha. Home: Santa Monica, Calif. Died June 2006.

VELIZ, RUBEN DE JESUS, physician; b. Manzanillo, Oriente, Cuba, Apr. 23, 1941; s. Ruben Nueva and Ismenia Petronila (Oliva) V.; m. Maria Nieves, Nov. 11, 1969; children— Nieves Maria, Ruben Miguel. Student U. Havana (Cuba), 1959-62, U. Miami, 1962-64, UCLA, 1965-66, U. So. Calif., 1965-66; M.D., U. Madrid, Spain, 1970. Intern, U. Madrid Hosps. and Clinics, 1973-74; pvt. practice family medicine Los Angeles, 1970-73, Miami, Fla., 1973-75; resident surgery Coll. Medicine and Dentistry N.J.-Morristown 1975-76; commd. lt. USPHS, 1976, advanced through grades to comdr., 1978; med. resident Columbia U. Coll. Physicians Surgeons/Morristown Meml. Hosp., 1978-81; pvt. practice medicine specializing in internal medicine-critical care medicine Miami, 1981—; mem. staffs Jackson Meml. Hosp./U. Miami Med. Center, Cedar's Med. Center, Miami, Mercy Hosp., Miami, South Miami Hosp., Coral Gables Hosp. (Fla.), Am. Hosp., Miami, Palmetto Gen. Hosp., Hialeah, Hialeah Hosp. (Fla.). Mem. Republican Nat. Com., Washington, 1983, Cuban Am. Nat. Found., Miami and Washington, 1983. Mem. AMA, ACP, Am. Soc. Internal Medicine, Assn. Mil. Surgeons U.S., Soc. Critical Care Medicine, So. Med. Assn., Am. Acad. Family Physicians. Republican. Roman Catholic. Home: Miami, Fla. Died Sept. 2, 2006.

VENGLARCHIK, ANDREW STEFAN, JR., insurance executive; b. Monaca, Pa., Nov. 23, 1922; s. Andrew Stefan and Mary Martha (Stas) V. Student Western Res. U., 1945-50. Clk. typist Comml. Motor Freight Co., Cleve., 1941; jr. buyer S.K. Wellman div. Abex Corp., Bedford, Ohio, 1941-66; pres. Slovak Gymnastic Union Sokol of U.S.A., East Orange, N.J., 1967-83; pres. Sokol Apts., Inc., Astoria, N.Y., 1975-83, Falcon Apts. Inc., 1967-74, 78-83; adminstrv. mgr. research and devel. Mego Corp., 1979-83. Mem. N.J. Ethnic Communities Congress, N.J. Bicentennial Ethnic Council, Nat. Ethnic Racial Alliance of Am. Revolution Bicentennial Commn., AAU, Nat., N.J. (pres. 1976-77), N.Y. fraternal congresses. Roman Catholic. Clubs: Slovak Gymnastic Union Sokol of U.S.A., Nat. Slovak Soc. U.S.A. Home: Arlington Heights, Ill. Died Mar. 2, 2007.

VERITY, C. WILLIAM, JR., (CALVIN WILLIAM VERITY JR.), former secretary of commerce; b. Middletown, Ohio, Jan. 26, 1917; s. Calvin William Verity & Elizabeth O'Brien; m. Margaret Wymond; children: Peggy, Jonathan George, William Wymond BA, Yale U., 1939. Various mgmt. positions, 1940-65; pres., CEO Armco Inc., Middletown, 1965-71, 72-82; co-chmn. U.S.-U.S.S.R. Trade and Econ. Council, 1977-84; chmn. U.S. C. of C., 1980-81, Presdl. Task Force on Pvt. Initiatives, Washington, 1981-83; mem. Presdl. Adv. Council on Pvt. Sector Initiatives, 1983; sec. US Dept. Commerce, Washington, 1987-89. Served with USN, 1942-46. Home: Middletown, Ohio. Died Jan. 3, 2007.

VERNON, ROBERT GERARD, lawyer, consultant; b. N.Y.C., July 9, 1935; s. Weston, Jr., and Adelaide (Neilson) V.; m. Kathryn Barnes, Sept. 16, 1966 (div. Sept. 1986); children: David Cannon, Linda, Richard Daniel. Student Columbia Coll., 1952-54; BA, U. Utah, 1956; postgrad. George Washington U. Law Sch., 1959; JD, Columbia U., 1963. Bar: Utah 1964, U.S. Dist. Ct. Utah 1964. Atty.-landman Skyline Oil Co., Salt Lake City, 1964-79, asst. sec., 1964-72, sec., 1972-77; pvt. practice, Salt Lake City, 1979-83, 88—; oil and gas lease investor and cons., Salt Lake City, 1979-83; v.p., legal counsel Crossroads Oil Co., 1983-88. Chmn. Rep. voting dist. 2644, Salt Lake City, 1970-71. Recipient E.B. Convers Prize, Columbia Law Sch., 1963. Mem. ABA, Utah State Bar (first chmn. oil and gas com. 1978-79), Utah Assn. Petroleum and Mining Landmen (pres. 1971), Am. Assn. Petroleum Landmen (cert. profl. landman). Mormon. Contbr. articles, papers to profl. publs. and confs. Home: Salt Lake City, Utah. Died Jan. 28, 2007.

VERRILLO, RONALD THOMAS, neuroscience educator, researcher; b. Hartford, Conn., July 31, 1927; s. Francesco Paul and Angela (Forte) V.; m. Violet Silverstein, June 3, 1950; children: Erica, Dan, Thomas. BA, Syracuse U., NY, 1952; PhD, U. Rochester, 1958. Asst. prof. Syracuse U., 1957-62, rsch. assoc., 1959-63, rsch. fellow, 1963-67, assoc. prof., 1967-74, prof., 1974-94, prof. emeritus, from 1995, assoc. dir. Inst. Sensory Rsch., 1980-84, dir., 1984-93, dir. grad. neurosci. program, 1984-93. Advisor com. on hearing, bioacoustics and biomechanics NRC. Author: Adjustment to Visual Disability, 1961 (award 1962); contbr. chpts. to books, articles to profl. jours. With USN, 1945-46. Fellow Am. Found. for Blind, 1956, NATO, 1970; grantee NSF, 1969-72, 84-87, NIH, 1972—; recipient Internat. Sensory Aids award, 1998. Fellow Acoustical Soc. Am. (Silver medal 1999); mem. Soc. for Neurosci., N.Y. Acad. Scis., Sigma Xi (Rsch. award 1982). Home: Syracuse, NY. Died Mar. 21, 2007.

VER STEEG, CLARENCE LESTER, historian, educator; b. Orange City, Iowa, Dec. 28, 1922; s. John A. and Annie (Vischer) Ver S.; m. Dorothy Ann De Vries, Dec. 24, 1943; 1 child, John Charles. AB, Morningside Coll., Sioux City, Iowa, 1943; MA, Columbia U., 1946, PhD, 1950; LHD, Morningside Coll., 1988. Lectr., then instr. history Columbia U., NYC, 1946-50; mem. faculty Northwestern U., Evanston, Ill., 1950—2007, prof. history, 1959—2007, dean grad. sch., 1975-86. Vis. lectr. Harvard U., 1959-60; mem. council Inst. Early Am. History and Culture, Williamsburg, Va., 1961-64, 68-72, chmn. exec. com., 1970-72; vis. mem. Inst. Advanced Study, Princeton, NJ, 1967-68; chmn. faculty com. to recommend Master Plan Higher Edn. in Ill., 1962-64; mem. Grad. Record Exam. Bd., 1981-86, chmn., 1984-86; pres. Assn. Grad. Schs., 1984-85; mem. steering com. Grad. Research Project, Consortium on Financing Higher Edn., 1981-85; working group on talent Nat. Acad. Scis., 1984-87; mem. Higher Edn. Policy Adv. Com. to OCLC, Online Computer Libr. Ctr., 1984-87. Author: Robert Morris, Revolutionary Financier, 1954, A True and

Historical Narrative of the Colony of Georgia, 1960, The American People: Their History, 1961, The Formative Years, 1607-1763, 1964 (Brit. edit.), 1965, The Story of Our Country, 1965, (with others) Investigating Man's World, 6 vols., 1970, A People and a Nation, 1971, The Origins of a Southern Mosaic: Studies of Early Carolina and Georgia, 1975, World Cultures, 1977, American Spirit, 1982, rev. edit., 1990; sr. author: Heath Social Studies, 7 Vols., 1991, Planning at Northwestern University in the 1960s, 1993; editor: Great Issues in American History, From Settlement to Revolution 1584-1776, 1969; editl. cons.: Papers of Robert Morris, vols. I-IX, 1973-99; contbr. articles to profl. jours. With USAAF, 1942—45. Decorated Air medal with 3 oak leaf clusters; 5 Battle Stars; Social Sci. Research Council fellow, 1948-49, George A. and Eliza Gardner Howard Found. fellow, 1954-55, Huntington Library research fellow, 1955, Am. Council Learned Socs. sr. fellow, 1958-59, Guggenheim fellow, 1964-65, NEH sr. fellow, 1973; Northwestern U. Clarence L. Ver Steeg Professorship established in his honor, 1997. Mem. AAUP, Am. Hist. Assn. (nominating com. 1965-68, chmn. 1967-68, Albert J. Beveridge prize 1952, hon. mention 1991 Eugene Asher Disting. Teaching award), Orgn. Am. Historians (editorial bd. Jour. Am. History 1968-72), So. Hist. Assn. (nominating com. 1970-72). Presbyterian. Home: Evanston, Ill. Died July 2, 2007.

VESCI, JOSEPH VINCENT, accountant; b. Phila., Dec. 26, 1940; s. Joseph Francis and Susie Ann (Visco) V.; BS, LaSalle Coll., 1965, MBA, 1981; m. Lorraine D'onofrio, Nov. 21, 1970; children: Susan C., Joseph C., Rosemarie, Christopher M. Supr. trainee I-T-E Imperial Corp. (subs. Gould, Inc. 1976), Phila., 1967-68, fin. analyst, 1968-71, supr. budgets and reporting, 1971-74, mgr. gen. acctg., 1974-78; corp. budget and forecasting acctg. systems dir. Extracorporeal Med. Spltys., Inc. subs. Johnson & Johnson, King of Prussia, Pa., 1978-81, mgr. fin. planning, reporting and analysis, 1981-84; corp. contr. Crown Textile Co., Jenkintown, Pa., 1984-87; controller, chief fin. officer Bankcrafters Inc., Phila., 1987-89, Interstate Steel Supply Co., Phil., 1990—. Rep. com. rep., Phila., 1967-71, 60-64; bd. dirs. Upper Darby Forum, Upper Darby Performing Arts Ctr. With USN, 1964-67. Mem. Nat. Assn. Accts., Pa. Assn. Notaries, The Drexelbrook Club. Roman Catholic. Home: Drexel Hill, Pa. Died June 20, 2007.

VICKERY, TRAMMELL EUGENE, lawyer; b. Dalton, Ga., Sept. 6, 1932; s. James Edmond and Eva Mae (Houston) V.; m. Mae Gohley, Feb. 11, 1955; children— Trammell Eugene, David Ray, Alan Scott BA, Emory U., 1953, LL.B., 1956. Bar: Ga. 1955. Assoc. Jones, Bird & Howell, Atlanta, 1955-75; assoc. Hansell & Post, Atlanta, 1975-89; ptnr. Troutman Sanders, Atlanta, from 1989. Chmn. NCBE, Chgo., 1977-78; chmn. State Bd. Bar Examiners Ga., 1971-74; faculty mem. Emory U. Sch. of Law, Atlanta, 1968-70; lectr. Legal Edn. Ga. Contbr. articles to Bus. Law jours., Ency. Ga. Law. Mem. ABA, Atlanta Bar Assn., Am. Coll. Trial Lawyers. Home: Atlanta, Ga. Died Feb. 9, 2007.

VIERTEL, PETER, writer; b. Dresden, Germany, Nov. 16, 1920; s. Berthold Viertel and Sara Salomea Steurmann; m. Virginia Ray (div. 1959); 1 child, Christine; m. Deborah Kerr Trimmer, July 23, 1960 (dec. Oct. 17, 2007). Student, Dartmouth Coll., UCLA. Writer The David O. Selznick Studio, Culver City, Calif., 1939-41. Author: (books) The Canyon, 1940, Line of Departure, 1947, White Hunter Black Heart, 1953, Love Lies Bleeding, 1964, Bicycle on the Beach, 1971, American Skin, 1984, Dangerous Friends: At Large With Huston and Hemingway in the Fifties, 1992, Loser Deals, 1995; (screenplays) Saboteur, 1942, The Hard Way, 1943, We Were Strangers, 1949, Roughshod, 1949, Decision Before Dawn, 1951, The African Queen, 1951, The Sun Also Rises, 1957, Les Bijoutiers du clair de lune, 1958, The Old Man and the Sea, 1958, Le Couteau dans la plaie, 192, White Hunter Black Heart, 1990 Served to 2d lt. USMCR, 1942-45, ETO, PTO. Decorated Bronze Star. Mem. Writers Guild West. Avocations: tennis, golf, skiing. Home: Klosters, Switzerland. Died Nov. 4, 2007.*

VIGILANTE, JOSEPH LOUIS, social worker, social policy educator; b. Phila., June 21, 1925; m. Florence W. Vigilante; children: Amy, Grace, Theodore. AB, Temple U., 1950; MS, Columbia U., 1951, D.S.W., 1968. Cert. social worker, N.Y. Child welfare worker Div. Children and Youth Wis. Dept. Welfare, 1951-53; caseworker, student supr. VA Hosp., Northport, N.Y., 1953-55; part-time caseworker, case supr., chief social worker Mid-Nassau Community Guidance Clinic, Hicksville, N.Y., 1955-60; dir. field work, asst. prof. Sch. Social Work, Adelphi U., Garden City, N.Y., 1955-60, asst. prof., asst. dean, 1960-62, assoc. prof., acting dean, 1962, prof., dean, 1962-87, univ. prof. social policy, from 1987, exec. v.p. Inst. for Child Mental Health, 1976-89. Prof. part-time New Sch. for Social Rsch., N.Y.C., 1972-75, Florence Hollis prof. Social Policy, summer 1988, Smith Coll., Northampton, Mass., 1987—; vis. prof. Rutgers U., 1987, Yeshiva U., 1988; cons. South Oaks Hosp., L.I., 1987-92, ICMH, N.Y., 1989—, cons. to Office Sec. Health, Edn, and Welfare, Washington, 1965; team leader, Social Welfare Mission, Agy. Internat. Devel., Egypt, 1974; rep. Nat Coun. Aging, UN NGO Com. Aging, 1994—; ptnr. Balaban Assocs.; performer, dir. Adelphi Film Co.; speaker in field. Editor: (with others) Social Service Delivery Systems: An International Annual; Sophie Moses Robison; Twentieth Century Women, 1982; editor in chief Ency. of Social Work; mem. editorial bd.: Smith Coll. Studies in Social Work, 1989—; contbr. articles to profl. jours. Bd. dirs. Nassau County Health and Welfare Coun., Huntington Hosp., N.Y., 1982, Cmty. Advs., Great Neck, N.Y., 1975, Cmty. Coun. of Greater N.Y., Young Adult Inst., 1982-95; chair Joint Task Force on Labor Force Needs, NASW/Coun. Social Work Edn. Mem. NASW, AAUP, N.Y. State Assn. Deans of Schs. Social Work (pres. 1975), Acad. Cert. Social Workers, Acad. Polit. Sci., Coun. Social Work Edn., Phi Gamma Mu. Home: New York, NY. Died Dec. 25, 2005.

VILIMAS, JACQUELINE SMITH, counselor, educator; b. Chgo., Jan. 22, 1931; d. James Leo and Catherine Ann (Schaack) Smith; B.A., DePaul U., 1954; M.Ed., Boston Coll., 1972, postgrad., 1972—; m. Joseph Vilimas, Sept. 6, 1952; 1 dau., Joanna Marie. Asst. dir. Office Student Devel., Bentley Coll., Waltham, Mass., 1972-74; treatment/process cons. Community Alcoholism Services, Portland, Maine, 1972-74; program devel. specialist Alcoholism Research and Tng. Center, Framingham, Mass., 1974-77; psychol. asst. Assoc. Psychologists Inc., 1976—, Therapeutic Tutors and Counseling, Westford, Mass., 1982-83; curriculum devel. specialist Boston State Coll., 1977-83, adj. assoc. prof. psychology, 1977-83; adj. lectr. U. Mass., 1983—; clin. dir. Brighton Ct. Alcoholism Program, 1984—; cons. J.F. Kennedy Multi-Service Center, Hope House, Inc., Steppingstone, Inc.; speaker Emmanuel Coll., U. Maine, 1975, Boston Coll., 1976—. Program leader Great Books Program, 1967-70; mem. Watertown (Mass.) Town Meeting, 1965-67. Recipient Disting. Columnist award DePaul U., 1952, 53, 54. Mem. Am. Psychol. Assn., Am. Personnel and Guidance Assn., Assn. for Advancement Behavior Therapy. Home: Newton, Mass. Died Mar. 23, 2007.

VILINSKY, MURIEL, data collection services executive; b. NYC, Aug. 9, 1923; d. Joseph and Rose (Migdal) Putterman; m. Abraham Jack Vilinsky, Jan. 25, 1945; children: Robert Paul, Jeffrey Steven. Student Fairleigh Dickenson U., New Sch. Social Research, 1968—. Sec., bookeeper Stickless Printing Co. and Whitely Tailleurs Corp., NYC, 1940-48, mktg. research interviewer, Fair Lawn, NJ, 1962-63; ptnr., owner No. Jersey Market Surveyors, Fair Lawn, 1963-73; pres. Interviewers for Research Inc., Fair Lawn and Edison, NJ, 1973—. Sec., trustee Sisterhood Congregation B'nai Israel, 1952-65; mem. edn., fin. and budget coms. LWV, 1965-67. Mem. Mktg. Research Assn., Democrat. Avocations: Playwriting; piano; theatre. Home: Fair Lawn, NJ. Died July 11, 2007.

VINCIGUERRA, SALVATORE JOSEPH, scientific instrument company executive; b. Methuen, Mass., Jan. 21, 1938; s. Joseph Frederick and Erminia (Bonnacorsi) V.; m. Grace Stevens, Apr. 20, 1963; children: Elizabeth, Catherine, Joseph, Suzanne. BSE, Princeton U., 1959; MBA, Harvard U., 1968. Systems analyst GE, Phoenix, 1962-63; cons. Arthur D. Little, Inc., Cambridge, Mass., 1964-66; with Instron Corp., from 1968; contr. Canton, Mass., 1968-71; treas., 1971-76; gen. mgr. Asia/Pacific Ops. Toyko, 1976-81; v.p., gen. mgr. Western Hemisphere Ops. Canton, 1981-85; pres., from 1985, Serro Fluidics, Inc., Nashua, N.H., from 1995. Dir. Lytron Inc., Woburn, Mass. Dir. Japan Soc. Boston, 1986—; corp. mem. Children's Mus. Boston, 1984—. Mem. High Tech. Council, Internat. Bus. Ctr. Clubs: Harvard (Boston); Harvard of Japan (Toyko) (treas. 1978-81). Home: Buzzards Bay, Mass. Died June 1, 2006.

VINK, PIETER CAREL, manufacturing executive; b. Eindhoven, Holland, Sept. 18, 1919; s. Hermanus and Catherina (Pellekaan) V.; m. Thea Fluijt, June 7, 1945. Grad., Lorenz Lyceum, Eindhoven, 1937. With N.Am. Philips Corp. (and subs.), 1939—; gen. mgr. Philips South Africa, chmn. mng. dir. ops. Iran, India, Australia, 1948-65; pres. N.Am. Philips Co., 1965-69, N.Am. Philips Corp., NYC, 1969-78, chmn., 1978-84, chief exec. officer, 1978-81, also dir. Dir. PEPI, Inc. Served with Brit. Army, 1944-45. Decorated Order Brit. Empire. Mem. Newcomen Soc. N.Am. Clubs: Stanwich (Greenwich, Conn.), Indian Harbor Yacht (Greenwich, Conn.); Blind Brook (Port Chester, N.Y.); Economic (N.Y.C.), Sky (N.Y.C.). Died Mar. 17, 2006.

VINOCOUR, LEE ANDRE, lawyer; b. Washington, Oct. 30, 1951; s. Seymour Murray Vinocour and Barbara Earle (Mabee) Vinocour deBeauchamp. B.S.F.S., Georgetown U., 1972; M.A., Monterey Inst. Fgn. Studies, 1975; J.D., New Coll., Law, 1981. Bar: Calif. 1981, U.S. Dist. Ct. (no. dist.) Calif. 1981, D.C. 1982. Legis. asst. U.S. Senator Howard Cannon, Washington, 1970-73, 75-77, 80-82; staff atty. Exec. Office Mayor Marion Barry, Office of Documents, Washington, 1982—; intern Internat. Atomic Energy Agy., Vienna, Austria, 1974, U.S. Senator Alan Cranston, San Francisco, 1981-82. Mem. ABA, Am. Trial Lawyers Assn., D.C. Bar Assn. Democrat. Unitarian. Died June 29, 2007.

VINSON, MURRY EDGAR, SR., aviation company executive; b. Aquilla, Tex., Apr. 30, 1926; s. Stanley Livingston and Bertha Texas (Prewitt) V.; m. Mary Evelyn Hayes, Jan. 25, 1952; children: Murry Edgar, Stanley Wayne, Johnny Cay. BBA, U. Houston, 1951, Internat. Acctg. Inst., Dallas, 1955; MBA, Pacific U., 1984, PhD, 1986. Chief fin. officer Saturn Airways, Oakland, Calif., 1972-75; treas. Alaska Internat. Industries, Anchorage, 1975-77; v.p. Evergreen Internat. Aviation, McMinnville, Oreg., 1977-81, pres., 1981-82, vice-chmn. bd., 1983-85; prin. M. Vinson Inc., from 1985; assoc. fin. officer, analyst Interstate Airlines, Inc. Served as officer USN, 1944-46, PTO. Mem. Airlines Traffic Assn. (dir. 1978—) Clubs: Little Rock Tennis. Republican. Home: Sheridan, Oreg. Died Apr. 28, 2007.

VITTORI, RAMON DEL, city official; b. Oakland, Calif., Dec. 6, 1940; s. Peter and Cornelia Ardell (Nagle) V.; m. Jacky Ann Kohlberg, Nov. 9, 1963; children— Peter Dante, Christopher Lee. A.A., Merritt Coll., 1973, Diablo Valley Coll., 1975; B.A., St. Mary's Coll., Moraga, Calif., 1981. Cert. in fire sci.; cert. first aid instr.; cert. tchr., Calif. tool and die maker Fed. Stamping, St. Petersburg, Fla., 1962-63; machinist, Johnson Gear, Berkeley, Calif., 1964-65; from firefighter to fire chief, City of Emeryville, Calif., 1965—. Asst. scoutmaster Oakland Bay Area council Boy Scouts Am., Oakland, Calif., 1968-69. Served with USAF, 1959-62. Mem. Internat. Assn. Fire Chiefs, Nat. Fire Protection Assn., Western Fire Chiefs Assn., Calif. Fire Chiefs Assn., Bay Area Fire Forum, Internat. Assn. Firefighters, Alameda County Fire Chiefs Assn. (sec./treas. 1984, v.p. 1985—), Am. Fedn. Tchrs. Calif. Roman Catholic. Lodge: Lions. Home: El Cerrito, Calif. Died Jan. 30, 2007.

VLADECK, JUDITH POMARLEN, lawyer; b. Norfolk, Va., Aug. 1, 1923; d. Joseph and Ida Pomarlen; m. Stephen Vladeck (dec. 1979). BA, Hunter Coll., 1945; JD, Columbia U., 1947. Bar: NY 1947, US Supreme Ct. 1962. Assoc. Conrad & Smith, NYC, 1947-51; sole practice NYC, 1951-57; mem. Vladeck, Elias, Vladeck & Engelhard P.C., NYC, 1957—2007; sr. ptnr. Vladeck, Waldman, Elias & Englehard, P.C., NYC. Adj. prof. Fordham Law Sch. Mem. adv. bd. Inst. for Edn. and Rsch. on Women and Work, Cornell U.; bd. dirs. N.Y. Civil Libertie Union, 1963-68; bd. dir., counsel Tamiment Inst., Inc.; mem advisory bd. R. Wagner Labor Archives, Tamiment Inst. Libr. bd. dirs. lawyers' coordinating com. AFL-CIO; bd. mem Non-Traditional Employment for Women. Recipient Hunte Coll. Profl. Achievement award, 1992, Edith Spivack award 1998, Women of Power and Influence award NY NOW, 1998 ORT Jurisprudence award, 1996; elected to Hunter Coll. Hall o Fame, 1988; Non-Taditional Employment for Women name building Judith P. Vladeck Ctr. for Women, 1989; Margare Brent Award, ABA 2002; Columbia Law Sch. Assoc. Medal fo Excellence, 2003; NEW 25th Anniv. Equity Leadership Award 2003, 60th Ann. NYS Human Rights Law award for Excellence NYS Divsn. Human Rights, 2005, Peggy Browning Fun Lifetime Achievement award, 2006. Fellow Am. Bar Found. Coll. of Labor and Employment Lawyers; mem. ABA (co-chmn labor law and equal employment coms., N.Y. State Bar Assn (labor law com.), Assn. of Bar of City of N.Y., N.Y. County Lawyers Assn., Fed. Bar Assn., Women's Bar Assn., Am Arbitration Assn. (panel of arbitrators), Columbia Law Sch Alumni Assn. (bd. dir.), Harlem Inst. Fashion (counsel, bd. dir.) Home: New York, NY. Died Jan. 8, 2007.

VOGEL, GEORGE SIGMUND, physician; b. Bklyn., May 22, 1912; s. Sigmund and Bessie (Cohen) V.; B.S., N.Y.U., 1932 M.D., U. Hamburg, 1936; m. Franzi Leopold, June 22, 1938 children— Susan Marcia, Michael Lee. Intern, Lutheran Hosp. Manhattan, N.Y.C., 1937-39; practice medicine, Croton-on Hudson, N.Y., 1943-79; attending physician Phelps Meml Hosp., North Tarrytown, N.Y., pres. med. staff, 1966-67, chmn gen. practice dept., 1969-72; hon. attending staff Peekskil Hosp., N.Y.; surg. N.Y.C. R.R., 1944-79; sch. physician Croton Harmon Sch. System, 1953-79; former police surgeon, Croton on-Hudson; med. dir. Cedar Manor Nursing Home, Ossining N.Y., 1976-87; assoc. med. dir. Brandywine Nursing Home Ossining, 1976—, assoc. med. dir. Briarcrest Nursing Home Ossining, 1987; cons. Health and Welfare Dept. Served to 1st lt M.C., AUS. Named Man of Year, Croton-on-Hudson C. of C. 1976. Diplomate Am. Bd. Family Practice. Mem. Am., N.Y State, Westchester County med. assns., Am. Acad. Family Practice (chpt. sec., chpt. v.p., pres. Westchester chpt. 1973-74) Profl. Standards Rev. Orgn. Jewish. Clubs: Masons, Lions Home: Somers, NY. Died Jan. 26, 2006.

VOGEL, HENRY JAMES, biochemist, educator; b. Berlin June 1, 1920; came to U.S., 1939, naturalized, 1943; s. Pau Theodor and Erna (Italiener) V.; m. Ruth Hermine, May 17 1946; 1 child,Stephen Mark. MS, N.Y. U., 1941, PhD, 1949 Asso. prof. microbial biochemistry Rutgers U., New Brunswick N.J., 1957-60, prof. microbiology, 1960-68, Coll. Physicians and Surgeons, Columbia U., NYC, from 1968, Delafield prof pathology and microbiology, from 1985. Cons. NIH, 1973-76 Joint editor: Informational Macromolecules, 1963, Evolving Genes and Proteins, 1965, Organizational Biosynthesis, 1967 Neuronal Information Transfer, 1978, Cells of Immunoglobulir Synthesis, 1979, Regulatory T Lymphocytes, 1980, Bioregulators of Reproduction, 1981, Pathobiology of the Endothelia Cell, 1982, Genes and Proteins in Oncogenesis, 1983, Transfe and Expression of Eukaryotic Genes, 1984, Cell Biology of the Major Histocompatability Complex, 1985, Biological Organization: Macromolecular Interactions at High Resolution, 1987 Processing and Presentation of Antigens, 1988, Immune Recognition and Evasion: Molecular Aspects of Host-Parasite Interaction, 1990, Molecular Mechanisms in Cellular Growth and Differentiation, 1991, Mechanisms of Eukaryotic DNA Recombination, 1992, Molecular Mechanisms of Immunological Self-Recognition, 1993, Cell-Cell Signaling in Vertebrate Development, 1993; editor: Metabolic Regulation, 1971, Nucleic Acid - Protein Recognition, 1977; series editor: P & S Biomed. Scis Symposia, 1976—; editorial bd.: Jour. Molecular Evolution 1971—. USPHS fellow Cornell U., 1950-52; Damon Runyon Meml. fellow Yale U., 1952-56; recipient Lindback Found award, 1967; Japan Soc. for Promotion of Sci. fellow, 1981 Mem. Am. Soc. Biochemistry and Molecular Biology, Am. Soc Microbiology, Genetics Soc. Am. Died Aug. 19, 2007.

VOHS, THOMAS RAYMOND, advertising executive; b. NYC, Jan. 21, 1920; s. Ernest J. and Gertrude C. (Moore) V.; m Marie C. Tierney, Dec. 13, 1944; children— Thomas J., James R., John L. BA cum laude, Colgate U., 1942. With Chirurg & Cairns, Inc., Advt. (formerly John A. Cairns & Co.), NYC, from 1946, v.p., 1951-55, exec. v.p., 1955-69, pres., also chief exec. officer, from 1969; chmn. bd. Advt. Crafts, Inc., NYC, from 1960. Dir. Am. Assn. Advt. Agys., 1970-71 Served to lt. (s.g.) USNR, World War II. Mem. Delta Upsilon. Clubs: Union League (N.Y.C.); Huntington (N.Y.) Country Club. Home: Montauk, NY. Died Mar. 22, 2006.

VOLMAN, DAVID HERSCHEL, chemistry professor; b. LA, July 10, 1916; s. Carl Herman and Blanche (Taylor) V.; m. Ruth Clare Jackson, Sept. 15, 1944 (dec. Dec. 2001); children: Thomas Peter, Susan Frances, Daniel Henry. BA, UCLA, 1937, MS, 1938; PhD, Stanford U., 1940. Mem. faculty U. Calif.-Davis, 1940—41, from 1946, prof. chemistry, 1956-87, emeritus prof. chemistry, from 1987, chmn. dept., 1974-81, chmn. Acad. Senate, 1971-72; rsch. chemist OSRD, 1941-46; rsch. fellow Harvard U., 1949-50. Vis. prof. U. Wash. 1958. Editor: Advances in Photochemistry, 1983-98; mem. editl. bd. Jour. Photochemistry and Photobiology, 1972-98; contbr. articles to profl. jours. Grantee Rsch. Corp. Am.; grantee NIH; grantee U.S. Army Rsch. Office; grantee NSF;Std. Oil Co. fellow, 1940; Guggenheim fellow, 1949-50. Mem. Am. Chem. Soc., Inter-Am. Photochem. Soc., Sigma Xi. Home: Washington, DC. Died Jan. 8, 2007.

VOLZ, MARLIN MILTON, law educator; b. Cecil, Wis., Sept. 3, 1917; s. Edward A. and Mae C. (Winter) V.; m. Esther R. Krug, Aug. 23, 1941; children: Marlin M., Karen D., Thomas A. BA, U. Wis., 1938, JD, 1940, SJD, 1945; LLD (hon.), San Juan Law Sch., PR, 1957. Bar: Wis. 1940, Mo. 1951, Ky. 1958. Asst. prof. law sch. faculty U. Wis., 1946-50; prof., dean sch. law U. Kansas City (now U. Mo. in Kansas City), 1950-58; dean sch. law U. Louisville, 1958-65, prof. sch. law, 1965-87, ret., 1987; county judge pro tem, probate judge Jefferson County, Ky.,

970-74; chmn. Ky. Pub. Svc. Commn., Frankfort, 1981-82. lem. panel labor arbitrators Fed. Mediation and Conciliation vc., Am. Arbitration Assn.; reporter on legal draftsmanship m. Law Inst.; adviser San Juan (P.R.) Sch. Law; mem. Nat. oun. Legal Clinics, Chgo., 1960-67; mem. Louisville Labor lgmt. Com. Co-author: Drafting Partnership Agreements, 7th dit., 1984, 86, Wisconsin Practice Methods, 1949, Missouri ractice Methods, 1953, Iowa Practice Methods, 1954, Kansas ractice Methods, 1957; co-author, gen. editor rev. edit. West's ederal practice Manual; co-author, gen. editor Kentucky Legal orms, vol. 3 and 4, 1965, co-author, vol. 5 and 6, gen. editor evision, 1985; co-author, gen. editor Caldwell's Kentucky orm Book; editor: Cases and Materials, Civil Procedure, 1975, 3; co-editor Elkouri and Elkouri, How Arbitration Works, 5th dit. Chmn. Ky. Com. Correctonal Rsch., Frankfort, 1962-65, ouisville Human Rels. Commn., 1962-65; candidate for mayor, ouisville, 1965. Sgt. U.S. Army, 1943-46. Recipient Teaching nd Major Svc. awards. Mem. ABA (co-chair arbitration com. 986-89), Fed. Bar Assn., Ky. Bar Assn., Wis. Bar Assn., Am. udicature Soc. (bd. dir. 1976-80), Nat. Orgn. Legal Problems dn. (nat. pres. 1963), Nat. Acad. Arbitrators (com. chmn. 987-88, bd. govs. 1989-92), Rotary. Democrat. Methodist. lome: Davenport, Iowa. Died Nov. 27, 2006.

ON BROCK, A. RAYMOND, architect; b. Greenwich, onn., Mar. 18, 1922; s. Harold Jarvis and Lu (Lown) von. B.; . Norma J. Westra, Dec. 22, 1958; children: Meredith, Alison racey. Registered architect, N.Y., Conn., Va.; cert. Nat. Coun. rchtl. Registration Bds. Architect Neumann & Struppmann, YC, 1946-50, Sherwood, Mills & Smith, Stamford, Conn., 952-58, ptnr., 1958-70; pres., ptnr. SMS Architects, New anaan, Conn., 1970-82; archtl. cons. Bohannon, Va., from 982. 1st lt. U.S. Army, 1943-46, ETO. Recipient Nat. Merit ward Bell System, 1976. Fellow AIA (Merit award for disting. rchtl. achievement 1968, honor award 1971-75); mem. Am. rbitration Assn. Home: Bohannon, Va. Died Mar. 7, 2006.

ON DRAN, RAYMOND, dean, library and information cience educator; AB, Seton Hall U., 1968; MLA, U. Wis., ladison, 1971, MA in History, 1972, PhD in Info. Sci., 1976. sst. prof. Sch. Libr. and Info. Sci., Cath. U. Am., Washington, 976—81, assoc. chair, 1977—81, assoc. dean, 1981—83, dean, ssoc. prof., 1983—87; dean, prof. Sch. Libr. and Info. Scis., U. lorth Tex., Denton, 1987—95, chair Info. Resources Coun., xec. asst. to provost for info. resources, 1990—95; dean, prof. ch. Info. Studies, Syracuse U., NY, from 1995, chair Com. fo. and Comm. Tech. Issues NY, 1996—97. Sr. cons. Network evel. Office Libr. Congress, 1978—82; coord., project mgr. lat. Rehab. Info. Ctr., 1983—87; cons. in field. Contbr. articles o profl. jours. Mem.: ALA, Soc. Info. Mgmt., Educause (mem. onf. Planning Com.), NY Libr. Assn., Decision Scis. Inst., ssn. Info. Sys., Assn. Computing, Assn. Libr. and Info. Sci. dn., Am. Soc. Info. Sci. and Tech., Beta Phi Mu. Home: yracuse, NY. Died July 23, 2007.

ON GIERKE, HENNING EDGAR, biomedical science ducator, former government official, researcher; b. Karlsruhe, ermany, May 22, 1917; arrived in U.S., 1947, naturalized, 977; s. Edgar and Julie (Braun) Von Gierke; married; 2 hildren. Dipl. Ing., Karlsruhe Tech., 1943, Dr. Engr., 1944. sst. in acoustics Karlsruhe Tech., 1944—47, lectr., 1946; cons. erospace Med. Research Labs, Wright-Patterson AFB, Ohio, 947—54, chief bioacoustics br., 1954—63, dir. biodynamics nd bionics div., 1963—88; assoc. prof. Ohio State U., 963—88; clin. prof. Wright State U., from 1980. Mem. com. earing bioacoustics and biomechanics NRC, 1953—93, chmn., 990—93, bio-astronaut com., 1959—61; mem. adv. com., light medicine and biology NASA, 1960—61. Author numerous tech. publs., book chpts.; patentee in field. Fellow: Am. Inst. Med. and Biol. Engring., Coll. Fellows, Aerospace Med. Assn. v.p. 1966—67, E. Liljenkrantz award 1966, A.D. Tuttle award 974, John Paul Stapp award 2004), Inst. Environ. Scis. (hon.), coustical Soc. Am. (pres. 1979—80, Silver medal 1981, Gold edal 1999); mem.: Internat. Acad. Astronautics, Mil. Audiology Assn. (hon.), Biomed. Engring. Soc., Inst. Noise Ctrl. ngring., Internat. Acad. Aviation and Space Medicine, NAE. chievements include research in bioacoustics, acoustics, biomechanics and bioengineering. Home: Yellow Springs, Ohio. Died Mar. 11, 2007.

VON GLAHN, KEITH G., lawyer; b. Passaic, NJ, May 4, 952; BA, St. Peter's Coll., 1974; JD, Vermont Law Sch., 1977. Bar: NJ 1978, US Tax Ct. 1982, US Dist. Ct. NJ, US Supreme Ct. 1983, NY 1988, US Dist. Ct. NY, US Dist Ct. (ea. and so. dists.) NY, 1982, US Ct. Appeals (3rd cir.), 1983. Law clk. to Hon.William Arnold, 1977-78; asst. prosecutor Paterson, NJ, 987-81; spl. dep. atty. gen. Passic County, NJ; ptnr. Wilson, Elser, Moskowitz, Edelman and Dicker LLP, Newark, from 983. Mem. ABA, NJ Bar Assn., Essex County Bar Assn., William Brennan Inn of Ct. (master), Soc. for Health Care Risk Mgmt. of NJ. Died July 23, 2007.

VOSS, JACK DONALD, international business consultant, lawyer; b. Stoughton, Wis., Sept. 24, 1921; s. George C. and Grace (Tusler) V.; m. Mary Josephine Edgarton, May 7, 1955; children: Julia, Jennifer, Andrew, Charles. Ph.B., U. Wis., 1943; JD, Harvard U., 1948. Bar: Ill. 1949, Ohio 1963. From assoc. to ptnr. Sidney & Austin predecessor firm, Chgo., 1948-62; gen. counsel Anchor Hocking Corp., Lancaster, Ohio, 1962-67, v.p., gen. counsel, 1967-72, gen. mgr. internat., 1970-86; pres. Anchor Hocking Internat. Corp., Lancaster, 1972-86; mng. ptnr. Voss Internat., Lancaster, from 1986. Chmn. Internat. Coun. Conf. bd., 1985-87. Mem. Fairfield County Rep. Ctrl. and Exec. Com.; pres. Fairfield Heritage Assn., 1966-69; v.p. Lancaster Community Concert Assn., 1965-73; trustee, chmn. Ohio Info. Com. With USNR, 1943-46, ATO, MTO, PTO. Mem. ABA (internat. law & practice and bus. law sects.), Ohio Bar Assn. (chmn. corp. counsel sect. 1966), Columbus Bar Assn., Chgo. Bar Assn., Fairfield County Bar Assn., Licensing Execs. Soc., Am. Arbitration Assn. (panel mem.), Ctr. for Internat. Comml. Arbitration (panel mem.), Harvard Law Sch. Assn., Ohio Mfrs. Assn. (trustee, v.p. 1970-72), Symposiarch, Alpha Chi Rho. Clubs: Rotary (pres. Lancaster 1968), Racquet (Chgo.); Landsdowne (London). Lutheran. Home: Lancaster, Ohio. Died Mar. 24, 2007.

VOTAW, CHARLES LESLEY, academic dean; b. Chgo., Oct. 11, 1929; m. May Louise Korteling; children: John Ralph, Diana Lynn, Paul Charles. BA, Hope Coll., 1951; MD, U. Mich., 1955, PhD, 1959. Intern St. Joseph Mercy Hosp., Ann Arbor, Mich., 1955-56; instr. in anatomy U. Mich. Med. Sch., Ann Arbor, 1956-60, asst. prof., 1960-64, assoc. prof., 1964-70, prof., 1970-77, asst. dean for curriculum, 1971-75, assoc. dean, 1975-77; prof. James H. Quillen Coll. Medicine, East Tenn. State U., Johnson City, from 1977, assoc. dean clin affairs, 1977-80, assoc. dean acad. affairs, 1980-85, exec. assoc. dean acad. affairs, from 1985. Cons. dept. neurology VA Hosp., Ann Arbor, 1968-76; chmn. accreditation task force James H. Quillen Coll. Medicine, 1992—, accreditation site visitor, 1991, dir. space mgmt. and capital expansion program, 1989—. Author: (with E. W. Lauer) A Laboratory Guide to Neuroanatomy, 1963; contbr. articles to profl. jours. Local chmn. bd., pres. and treas coun. PTO, Ann Arbor; chmn. election proposals com., mem. ad hoc fin. com. Ann Arbor Pub. Schs.; active Family Life Health Edn. Com., Ann Arbor, local Little League orgn.; mem. adv. com. Glaxo Pathway Program, 1986-91. Lederle Found. fellow, 1954, UCLA fellow, 1962-63. Mem. AAAS, Am. Assn. Anatomy, Am. Assn. Med. Colls. (chmn. so. region group on ednl. affairs 1989-91, mem. nat. steering com. group on ednl. affairs 1989-91), Am. Acad. Neurology (assoc.), Am. Soc. Zoologists, Soc. for Neurosci., Blue Key, Cajal Club, Sigma Xi, Phi Kappa Phi, Alpha Omega Alpha, Phi Chi. Presbyterian. Home: Johnson City, Tenn. Died Jan. 5, 2007.

VOVAKIS, LEWIS HARRY, management consultant, lawyer; b. Carlisle, Pa., Jan. 31, 1934; s. Harry D. and Harriett H. (Gasparis) V. AB, U. Pa., 1955; JD, Dickinson Sch. Law, 1963. Bar: US Dist. Ct. DC 1964, US Ct. Appeals (DC cir.) 1964, US Supreme Ct. 1968. Counsel, Am. Maritime Assn., Washington, 1964-66; legal asst. Govt. of DC, 1966-67; ptnr. Rhyne & Rhyne, Washington, 1967-69; v.p. Autocomp, Inc., Washington, 1969-74, Aspen Systems Corp., NYC, 1974-80, Informatics Gen. Corp., Rockville, Md., 1980-83; sr. v.p. Wells Internat., Washington, 1983-84; law firm mgmt. cons., Washington, 1984-86, v.p. Am. Legal Systems, 1986-87, Acumenics Rsch. and Tech., Inc., Washington, 1989-90; legal info. mgmt. cons., 1990—; mem. George Bush Campaign, 1988, presdl. transition office, 1988, 89. Lt. USNR, 1956-59. Mem. ABA, DC Bar Assn., Rep. Nat. Lawyers Assn., Nat. Press Club (Washington). Republican. Greek Orthodox. Died May 20, 2006.

VOWELL, JACK C., former state legislator, investor; b. May 9, 1927; s. Jack C. and Daurice (McDaniel) V.; m. Mary Johnson, Apr. 19, 1957; 1 child, Janice Vowell Alexander. BS in Fgn. Svc., Georgetown U., 1948, MS in Fgn. Svc., 1952; MA in History, Tex. Western Coll., 1952; postgrad., Harvard U., 1953-55. Mem. faculty Sch. Fgn. Svcs. Georgetown U., Washington, 1948-49, U. Tex., El Paso, 1955-60; exec. v.p. Vowell Constrn. Co., El Paso, 1962-69, pres., chmn. bd. dirs., 1969-73; rep. Tex. Ho. of Reps., Austin, 1980-95, mem. numerous coms. 68th to 73rd legis., 1980-95; personal investor, from 1973. Chmn. Tex. sunset commn., 1987-89. Pres. Yucca Coun., Boy Scouts Am., 1972-74, mem. adv. bd., 1987-92, adv. bd. we. region, 1993—; bd. dirs. South Ctrl. region, 1973-86, mem. adv. bd., 1987—, nat. coun., 1971-87; mem. adv. bd. Hotel Dieu Hosp., 1974-87; adv. dir. Tex. Art Alliance, 1981-83; bd. dirs. Goodwill Industries of El Paso, 1973-77, El Paso Indsl. Devel. Corp., 1962-82; pres. El Paso Hist. Soc., 1957-59, assoc. editor Password, 1962-64; chmn. pers. com. El Paso Pub. Libr. Sys., 1969-74, bd. dirs., 1969-74; adminstrv. adv. bd. City of El Paso, 1973-74; coun. state policy and planning agencies, 1989-92; adv. comm., 1985-89; Tex. coun. on disabilities, 1984-85; state coun. on child abuse, 1984-85. With U.S. Army, 1946-47. Recipient City of El Paso Conquistador award, 1967, 73, Goodwill Industries of El Paso Outstanding Svc. award to Handicapped Workers, 1972, Disting. Eagle award Boy Scouts Am., 1972, Silver Beaver award, 1973, Silver Antelope award, 1983, Tex. Assn. for Marriage and Family Therapy Recognition cert., 1982, U. Tex. El Paso Coll of Edn. Clin. Programs Assistance award, 1985, award for Commitment to Reshaping and Improvement of Svcs. MHMR, 1985, Texans for Children Support for Needy Children, 1985, U. Tex. El Paso Spl. Edn. commendation for Spl. Achievement Autism Program, 1985, Coalition of Texas with Disabilities Pub. Servant of Yr. award, 1985, Anti-Defamation League of El Paso Torch of Liberty award, 1985, Tex. Network of Youth Svcs. Outstanding Youth award, 1987, Nat. Coun. of State Human Svcs. Adminstrs. Nat. commendation, 1987, Disting. Svc. Award Tex. Assn. Deaf, 1987, Am. Public Welfare Assn. Nat. Recognition of Statesmanship in Tex. Ho. Reps., 1987, Better Life award Tex. Health Care Assn., 1987, Legis. Excellence award Tex. Health Care Assn., 1987, United Way of El Paso vol. of the year award, 1988, Am. Coll. of Health Care Adminstrs. Tex. chpt. award, 1988, award for contbn. developmentally delayed and at risk infants, 1988, 94, Tex. Head Injury Legislative award, 1991, Legis. award Tex. Rehab. Assn., 1991, Rio Grande Coun. Govt. Legislative Leadership in Human Svcs. award, 1992, Helen Farabee Leadership award Tex. Perinatal Assn., 1992, Friend of Child award Tex. Coalition Juvenile Justice, 1993, Alviane NO-AD, Public Svc. award, 1993, Unite El Paso Appreciation award, 1993, Gran Paseño award U. Tex. El Paso, 1994, Good Hands award Tex. Dept. Transp., 1994. Mem. El Paso C. of C. (bd. dirs. 1962-69), Rotary (bd. dirs. 1967-68, pres. 1968, Disting. Svc. award 1988). Republican. Episcopalian. Home: El Paso, Tex. Died Aug. 29, 2006.

WADSWORTH, HOWARD MARVIN, marketing professional; b. Syracuse, NY, Apr. 20, 1907; s. Marvin Orin and Elizabeth (Aylward) W.; m. Helen Kathrine Matthews, May 28, 1936 (div. Dec. 1965); children: H. Duane, Fay Lydia Whitney; m. June Miller Baker, Sept. 21, 1966 (dec. Dec. 1977); m. Enid Miller Baker, July 14, 1979. Attended, Syracuse U. Extension, 1927. Founder, sr. ptnr. Wadsworth & Lees, Syracuse, 1930—42; owner, gen. mgr. Wadsworth Mfg. Assocss., Liverpool, NY, 1942—60, pres., 1960—68, chmn. bd., from 1968. Mgr. mktg. Warren Components Corp., Pa., 1949—68, chmn., Pa., 1969, pres., CEO, Pa., from 1972; chmn. Osgood-Warren Corp., 1968—69; founder, v.p. mktg. Greenfield Components, Mass., 1959—61; exec. v.p., dir. Allegheny Glasseals, Warren, 1959—61; v.p. mktg., dir. Saegertown Glasseals, San Rafael, Calif., 1961—62; pres. Wadsworth Pacific Mfg. Assocs., Palo Alto, Calif., 1961—71; chmn. Carler Products, Inc., Syracuse, 1963—71; ptnr., gen. mgr. Uni-Tel., Liverpool, 1940—77; chmn. bd. Western Sci., Oakland, Calif., 1968—70; dir., mktg. cons. Aerospace Electronics, Miami Springs; pres. DelMond Mfg. Co., Richmond, B.C., Canada, 1967—68, H.M.W. Midland Corp., Liverpool, from 1972. Mem. Liverpool Vol. Fire Dept., 1935—38. With USCGR, 1940—45. Mem. N.Y. State Soc. Plastic Engrs., Electronic Reps. Assn., Gov.'s Club, Lotos Club (N.Y.C.), Univ. Club, Penn Athletic Club (Phila.), Liederkranz (Syracuse), Capital Hill Club (Wash.), Nautique Club, Jacques Cartier de Gaspe (Gaspe, Que., Can.), Masons, Shriners. Patentee in field. Home: Bernhards Bay, NY. Died Feb. 2, 2006.

WAEHNER, RALPH LIVINGSTON, business forms company executive, consultant; b. Bay City, Mich., Nov. 21, 1935; s. Ralph Otto W.; m. Donna Jean Kennie, Feb. 1, 1958; children: Eric R., Julie K., Jill A. BSME, U. Mich., 1959; MBA, Northwestern U., 1964. Devel. engr. Sikorsky Aircraft, Stratford, Conn., 1959-60, Chgo. Rawhide Mfg. Co., 1960-62; with Moore Bus. Forms & Systems, from 1962, mfg. staff, Park Ridge, Ill., 1962-68, plant supt., Charleston, Ill., 1968-70, plant mgr., Albany, Ga., 1970-76, prodn. mgr., Niagara Falls, N.Y., 1976-78, dir. mfg., Glenview, Ill., 1978-83, v.p. mfg., 1983-88, also bd. dirs.; pres. Moore Bus. Forms & Systems, Ltd., Toronto, Ont., Can., 1988-91; v.p. Moore-N.Am. Procurement, Lake Forest, Ill., from 1991. Chmn. bd. Command Records, Toronto, 1988-91. With Mich. N.G., 1955-58 Mem. Can. U.S. Bus. Assn. (bd. dirs. 1989), Ivanhoe Country Club. Republican. Roman Catholic. Avocation: golf. Died Apr. 19, 2007.

WAGNER, BERNARD RAYMOND, social services consultant; b. Chgo., June 17, 1940; s. Bernard Anthony and Anne (Leemputtee) W.; m. Joyce Stumpf; children— Christine, Amy, Gary. B.A., U. Denver, 1962; M.A., U. Ill., 1965, Ph.D., 1967. Dir. PACE, Decatur, Ill., 1968-73; acting area dir. Devel. Disabilities Area Cen. Ind., 1978-81; supt. New Castle Hosp., Ind., 1973-82, Ga. Retardation Ctr., Atlanta, 1982-87; pres. Wagner Cons. Group, Atlanta, 1987—; mem. adj. faculty Ga. State U., Atlanta, 1985, U. Ill., Urbana, 1969-73; cons. in field. Contbr. articles to profl. jours. Chmn. bd. dirs. Henry County Community Action Program, Ind., 1980, Fontainebleau Community Ctr., Atlanta, 1985. Named Outstanding State Employee Ill., 1971. Fellow Am. Assn. on Mental Deficiency (v.p. 1985—); Nat. Assn. Supts. Pub. Residential Facilities for Mentally Retarded (pres. 1983-84), Nat. Assn. of Devel. Disabilities Mgrs. (pres. 1985—). Club: New Castle Country (Ind.) (bd. dirs. 1981-82). Died July 4, 2006.

WAGNER, FREDERIC EMIL, oil and gas company executive; b. Waco, Tex., Aug. 14, 1920; s. Frederic Emil and Ernestine (Clements) W.; student U. Tex., Arlington, 1940-42, So. Meth. U., 1942-43; B.S., U. Tex., Austin, 1946; m. Ellen Marie Seay, Dec. 15, 1964; children— Jory, Hilda. Founder, Williams & Wagner Constrn. Co., Inc., Dallas, 1946, founder oil div. Eldorado Oil and Gas, Inc., 1950, pres. Williams & Wagner Constrn., Co., Inc. and Eldorado Oil and Gas, Inc., 1946—; U.S. rep. Lifefield N.V. Mem. oil and gas com. Tex. Gov.'s Energy Commn., 1976-77; mem. oil and gas com. Tex. Energy Adv. Council, 1978-79. Recipient Disting. Service award Nat. Exchange Club, 1950. Mem. Council Sci. Socs., Am. Soc. Photogrammetry, Photogrammetry Soc. London, Calif. Racing Hall of Fame, Soc. Petroleum Engrs., Tex. Thoroughbred Breeders Assn., Tex. Thoroughbred Racing Assn., Calif. Thoroughbred Breeders Assn., Horsemen's Benevolent Protective Assn., U.S. Power Squadron, USCG Aux., Dallas Opera Guild, others. Clubs: Brookhaven Country, Cipango, Petroleum, Commerce, Dallas Gun, Pala Mesa Golf, Brook Hollow Golf. Author: Aircraft Lofting Practice, 1943. Home: Dallas, Tex. Died June 16, 2006.

WAGNER, JEAMES ARTHUR, research physiologist, environmental physiology educator; b. New Prague, Minn., Sept. 5, 1944; s. Stanley Francis and Lillian Katherine (Sladek) W.; m. Priscilla Louise Polk, Aug. 7, 1971 (div. 1979); 1 child, Chad Andrew. B.Sc. in Biology, St. John's U., 1966; M.A. in Physiology, U. S.D., 1967; Ph.D. in Physiology, U. Western Ontario, 1970. Vis. asst. prof. physiology Ind. U., Bloomington, 1969-71; asst. research physiologist U. Calif.-Santa Barbara, 1971-80, assoc. research, 1980-84, research physiologist, 1984—; guest lectr. Westmont Coll., Santa Barbara, 1977, U. Calif., 1971—; peer review cons. NIH, 1986—; program chmn. Internat. Symposium Environmental Stress, 1976-77. Co-editor: Environment Stress: Individual Adaptation 1978; editorial referee Jour. Applied Physiology, Jour. Gerontology, Jour. Metabolism; contbr. more than 50 articles to profl. jours. Com. mem. Santa Barbara Lung Assn., 1980; cons. Am. Heart Assn., 1983-86, mem. com. 1980—. Trainee NSF, 1966-67; grantee NIH, 1979-86, Calif. Air Resources Bd., 1983-84, Health Effects Inst., 1984-86. Mem. Am. Physiology Soc., Internat. Union Physiol. Sci., Am. Coll. Sports Medicine, AAAS, Fedn. Am. Scientists. Democrat. Roman Catholic. Home: Santa Barbara, Calif. Died June 7, 2006.

WAGNER, KEITH ANTHONY, association executive, lawyer; b. Pitts., Mar. 15, 1932; s. John Felix and Margaret (Curran) W.; m. Barbara Ann Kandera, Feb. 1, 1958; children— Ann-Margaret, Keith John. BA, Duquesne U., 1954, JD, 1964. Bar: Pa. 1965, D.C. 1965, U.S. Supreme Ct. 1971. Commd. lt. col. U.S. Army, 1970, advanced through grades to col., 1977; asst. comdt. U.S. Army Legal Sch., Charlottesville, Va., 1970-74; staff judge adv. U.S. Army Okinawa, Naha, 1974-75, U.S. Army Japan, Tokyo, 1975-77, U.S. Army Combined Arms Ctr., Fort Leavenworth, Kans., 1977-81; ret., 1981; exec. dir. Am. Philatelic Soc., State College, Pa., from 1981; also adminstr. Am. Philatelic Rsch. Libr., State College, from 1981. Bd. dirs. Patton Twp. Bus. Assn., State College, 1984-90. Decorated Legion of Merit with oak leaf cluster Mem. Pa. Bar Assn., Am. Philatelic

Congress (bd. dirs. 1983—), Coun. Philatelic Orgns. (adminstr. 1984—). Roman Catholic. Avocations: stamp collecting; model railroads. Home: State College, Pa. Died Dec. 6, 2006.

WAGONER, PORTER, country music singer, composer; b. West Plains, Mo., Aug. 12, 1927; s. Charles and Bertha W.; children: Richard, Denise, Debra. Former clerk, butcher. Singer, composer, radio and TV personality, 1950—2007, rec. artist, RCA Record Co., 1952-82, MCA/DOT Records, 1986; Gusto/King Records, 2004, ANTI-Records, 2006-2007; radio and TV appearances include radio, KWPM, West Plains, Mo., 1950, KWTO, Springfield, Mo., 1951, Ozark Jubilee, U.S.A, ABC-TV, 1955, radio, WSM Grand Ole Opry, Nashville, Tenn., 1957—2007, Porter Wagoner TV Show, 1960-81; formed band Wagonmasters, 1957; Albums include (with Gary Walker) Trade Mark, 1953, A Satisfied Mind, 1956, Sing Duets, 1962, Slice of Life-Songs Happy 'N' Sad, 1962, Y'All Come, 1963, Confessions of a Broken Man, 1966, The Grand Ole Gospel, 1966, Green, Green Grass of Home, 1967, More Grand Old Gospel, 1967, Soul of a Convict & Other Great Prison Songs, 1967, The Cold Hard Facts of Life, 1967, In Gospel Country, 1968, Just Between You & Me, 1968, The Bottom of the Bottle, 1968, Always, Always, 1969, Me & My Boys, 1969, The Carroll County Accident, 1969 (Song of Yr., Country Music Assn., 1969), Three Country Gentleman, Heartwarming Songs, Porter Wayne and Dolly Rebecca, 1970, Porter Wagoner & Dolly Parton, 1970, Skidrow Joe-Down in the Alley, 1970, You Got-ta Have a License, 1970, Porter Wagoner Sings His Own, 1971, Simple as I Am, 1971, The Silent Kind, 1971, Porter Wagoner Today, Best of Porter Wagoner, Two of a Kind, 1971, Ballads of Love, 1972, Experience, 1972, The Right Combination, 1972, What Ain't to Be, just Might Happen, 1972, I'll Keep on Loving You, 1973, Love and Music, 1973, The Farmer, 1973, Highway Headin' South, 1974, Porter 'n' Dolly, 1974, Tore Down, 1974, Sing Some Love Songs, Porter Wagoner, 1975, When I Sing for Him, 1979, Porter & Dolly, 1980, A Fool Like Me, 1981, Not a Cloud in the Sky, 1981, A Good Time Was Had By All, 1982, Viva Porter Wagoner, 1982, Down Home Country, 1982, Natural Wonder, 1982, One for the Road, 1982, Love Shine, 1984, Porter Wagoner and the Right Combination, 1984, Porter Wagoner, 1986, Sorrow on the Rocks, 1989, Greatest Songs, 1995, Greatest Hits, 1996, The Best I've Ever Been, 2000, Unplugged, 2002, 22 Grand Old Gospel 2004, 2003, Something to Brag About, 2004, 18 Grand Old Gospel 2005, Misery Loves Company, 2005, 20 All Time Greatest Hits, 2005, Gospel 2006, The Versatile, 2006, Wagonmaster, 2007; composer songs including (with Michael Pearson) Bottom of the Fifth, 1982; songs include Setting the Woods on Fire, 1952, (with Carl Smith) Trademark, 1953, Company's Comin', 1954, Satisfied Mind, 1955, Eat, Drink, and Be Merry (Tomorrow You'll Cry), 1959, Daddy Was an Old Time Preacher Man, Holding On to Nothin' I Thought I Heard You Call My Name, Just Someone I Used to Know, Please Don't Stop Loving Me, Sorrow On the Rocks,Skid Row Joe, Misery Loves Company, Trouble in Amen Corner, Ole Slew Foot, The Cold Hard Facts Of Life, The Last Thing On My Mind, Uncle Pen, We'll Get Ahead Someday, What Would You Do (If Jesus Came to Your House), You Old Love Letters, Sunny Side Of The Mountain, Green Green Grass of Home, (with Pam Gadd) Something To Brag About, 2004,; guest appearance (movie) Honky Tonk Man, 1982. Recipient (with Blackwood Brothers) Grammy award Best Gospel Performance, 1969, (with Dolly Parton) Vocal Group of Yr. award, Vocal Duo of Yr. award Country Music Assn., 1970, 71; named to Country Music Hall of Fame, 2002. Died Oct. 28, 2007.

WAHL, ARTHUR CHARLES, retired chemistry educator; b. Des Moines, Sept. 8, 1917; s. Arthur C. and Mabel (Mussetter) W.; m. Mary Elizabeth McCauley, Dec. 1, 1943; 1 child, Nancy Wahl Miegel. BS, Iowa State Coll., 1939; PhD, U. Calif., Berkeley, 1942. Group leader Los Alamos (N.Mex.) Nat. Lab., 1943-46; assoc. prof. chemistry Washington U., St. Louis, 1946-53, Farr prof. of radiochemistry, 1953-83, prof. emeritus, from 1983. Cons. Los Alamos Nat. Lab., 1950—. Author, editor: Radioactivity Applied to Chemistry, 1951; contbr. articles to profl. jours. NSF fellow, 1967; recipient Sr. Vis. Scientist Humboldt award Humboldt Found., 1977. Mem. Am. Chem. Soc. Home: Los Alamos, N.Mex. Died Mar. 6, 2006.

WAHLEN, EDWIN ALFRED, lawyer; b. Gary, Ind., Mar. 12, 1919; s. Alfred and Ethel (Pearson) W.; m. Alice Elizabeth Condit, Apr. 24, 1943 (div. 1983); children: Edwin Alfred, Virginia Elizabeth, Martha Anne; m. Elizabeth L. Corey, Nov. 23, 1984. Student, U. Ala., 1936-38; AB, U. Chgo., 1942, JD, 1948. Bar: Ill. 1948. Practiced in, Chgo., from 1948; mem. firm Haight, Goldstein & Haight, 1948-55; ptnr. Goldstein & Wahlen, 1956-59, Arvey, Hodes, Costello & Burman (and predecessor), 1959-91, Wildman, Harrold, Allen & Dixon, from 1992. Author: Soldiers and Sailors Wills: A Proposal For Federal Legislation, 1948. Served to 2d lt. AUS, 1942-46. Decorated Silver Star medal, Bronze Star medal. Mem. ABA, Ill. Bar Assn., Chgo. Bar Assn., Order of Coif, Phi Beta Kappa, Phi Alpha Delta. Home: Lake Forest, Ill. Died June 8, 2007.

WAKEMAN, HAROLD MAX, JR., banker; b. Laconia, NH, July 15, 1928; s. Harold Max and Mabel (Hanson) W.; m. Virginia Elinor Reiley, Nov. 11, 1950; children: Beth Ann, Brian Harold. BSBA, Boston U., 1950. Asst. cashier Laconia Peoples Nat. Bank, 1952—65, exec. v.p., 1965—73, pres., 1973—88, sr. account exec., from 1988. Treas. County of Belknap, Laconia, from 1965; pres. Lakes Region United Way, 1968—69, 1986—87; chmn. ARC, Laconia, 1968; mem. C. of C., pres., 1970, dir., 1965—75. Recipient James Irwin Cmty. award, Lakes Region C. of C., 1982. Mem.: Am. Bankers Assn., N.H. Bankers Assn. (pres. 1978—79), Kiwanis, Masons. Republican. Unitarian. Home: Laconia, NH. Died Jan. 26, 2007.

WALDFOGEL, MORTON SUMNER, prefabricated housing/plywood company executive; b. Somerville, Mass., Nov. 5, 1922; s. Benjamin and Gertrude (Levins) W.; m. Lillian Thelma Gouse, June 16, 1949; children: Peter Douglas, Jane Leslie. AB, Harvard U., 1944; MBA, Boston U., 1948. Assoc. prof. math. econs. Boston U., 1947-48; mgr. Roddis Plywood Co., Cambridge, Mass., 1948-51; partner East Coast Mill Sales, from 1951; chmn. bd., chief exec. officer Allied Industries Inc., Charlestown, Mass., 1954-89; chmn., chief exec. officer Gilwal Industries, Charlestown, Mass., from 1982; pres. United Internat. Inc., Boston, from 1990. Served with USNR, 1942-47. Decorated Letter of Commendation. Jewish. Home: Swampscott, Mass. Died Oct. 21, 2005.

WALDHEIM, KURT, former President of Austria, former Secretary General of the United Nations; b. Sankt Andrä-Wördern, Austria-Hungary, Dec. 21, 1918; m. Elizabeth Ritschel, 1944; 3 children. Student, U. Vienna; D Jurisprudence; LL.D. (hon.), Fordham U., 1972, Carleton U., Ottawa, Can., 1972, U. Chile, Santiago, 1972, Rutgers U., 1972, Jawarharlal Nehru U., India, 1973, U. Bucharest, Rumania, 1973, Wagner Coll., 1973, Cath. U. Am., 1974, Wilfrid Laurier U., Canada, 1974, Cath. U. Leuven, Belgium, 1975, Charles U., Czechoslovakia, 1975, Hamilton Coll., 1975, U. Denver, 1976, U. Philippines, 1976, Am. U., 1977, Kent State U., 1977, U. Warsaw, 1977, Moscow State U., 1977, Mongolian State U., 1977, U. Atlanta, Humboldt U. Berlin, U. SC, 1980, U. Notre Dame, South Bend, Ind., 1981. Entered Austrian Fgn. Service, 1945; served Ministry Fgn. Affairs; mem. Austrian del. Negotiations on Austrian State Treaty, Paris, London, Moscow, 1945-47; 1st sec. Austrian Embassy, Paris, 1948-51; head personnel divsn. Ministry Fgn. Affairs Govt. of Austria, Paris, 1951-55, permanent Austrian observer to UN, 1955-56, min. to Can., 1956-58, amb. to Can., 1958-60, dir. gen. for polit. affairs, 1960-64, permanent rep. to UN, 1964-68, 1970-71; chmn. outer space com. UN, 1965-68, 70-71; min. fgn. affairs Govt. of Austria, 1968-70, pres. Vienna, 1986-92; sec.-gen. UN, 1971-82. Guest prof. diplomacy Georgetown U., Washington, 1982-84; chmn. Inter Action Coun. Former Heads of State & Govt., 1982-85 Author: Der Österreichische Weg, 1971, The Austrian Example, 1973, Un Metier Unique au monde, 1977, Der schwierigste Job der Welt, 1978, Challenge of Peace, 1980, Building the Future Order, 1980, Im Glaspalast der Weltpolitik, 1985, Die Antwort Recipient: George Marshall Peace award, 1977, Karl Renner prize, City of Vienna, 1978, Order of Pope Pius IX, 1994 Home: Vienna, Austria. Died June 14, 2007.*

WALKER, BRUCE EDWARD, anatomy educator; b. Montreal, Que., Can., June 17, 1926; s. Robinson Clarence and Dorothea Winston (Brown) W.; m. Lois Catherine McCuaig, June 26, 1948; children: Brian Ross, Dianne Heather, Donald Robert, Susan Lois. BS, McGill U., 1947, MS, 1952, PhD, 1954; MD, U. Tex. at Galveston, 1966. Instr. anatomy McGill U., 1955-57; asst. prof. anatomy U. Tex. Med. Br., 1957-61, assoc. prof. anatomy, 1961-67; prof. Mich. State U., East Lansing, from 1967, chmn. dept., 1967-75. Contbr. articles to profl. jours. Mem. Am. Assn. Anatomists, Teratology Soc., Am. Assn. for Cancer Rsch. Died July 12, 2007.

WALKER, CLINTON W., manufacturing executive; b. Fall River, Mass., Dec. 3, 1917; s. Harry and Effie E. (Mercer) W.; m. Janet E. Harris, Apr. 16, 1966; children: Kristine, Hilary, Marion, Soame. Student, Tufts U. Civilian with Navy Dept., 1937-42; with Howe Scale Co., Rutland, Vt., 1945-47, Ethan Allen Inc., Danbury, Conn., from 1947, formerly pres., formerly vice chmn., cons. Served with USAAF, 1943-45. Mem. Nat. Assn. Furniture Mfrs. (dir.) Died Dec. 29, 2006.

WALKER, DOUGLAS CRAIG, publishing company executive; b. Kansas City, Mo., May 7, 1944; s. Garnet Cleveland Walker and Mary Frances (Schuette) Bivins. BS, U. Mo., 1966, MA, 1968. Editorial mgr. Hallmark Cards, Kansas City, Mo., 1974-81; editorial dir. Hippocrene/Lee Publs. Group, NYC, 1981-82; book club dir. Scholastic Inc., NYC, 1984-91; pub., v.p. Putnam/Grosset & Dunlap, NYC, 1991-94; editl. dir. Scholastic paperbacks Scholastic Inc., NYC, from 1994. Editor, creator children's sci. book series The Magic Schoolbus, 1990— (Boston Globe Hornbook award for nonfiction 1990). With U.S. Army, 1968-70. Democrat. Lutheran. Home: New York, NY. Died July 1, 2007.

WALKER, EDWARD BULLOCK, III, petroleum company executive; b. Norfolk, Va., Jan. 10, 1922; s. Edward Bullock, Jr. and Mary Rennick (Ray) W.; m. Katherine Evelyn Miller, Sept. 5, 1953; children: Edward Bullock, Richard Miller. BS, Mass. Inst. Tech., 1946, MS, 1947. Exploration mgr. Mene Grande Oil Co., Venezuela, 1947-62, v.p., 1967-68; exploration coordinator Gulf Eastern Co., London, Eng., 1962-67; dir. exploration div. Gulf Research & Devel. Co., Harmarville, Pa., 1967; pres. mineral divisional co. Gulf Oil Corp., Denver, 1968-71, pres. exploration and prodn. divisional co. Houston, 1975-78, v.p. Pitts., 1971, exec. v.p., 1971-75, Houston, 1978-81, pres., chief operating officer Pitts., 1981-84, dir., 1974-84; pres., chief exec. officer San Tomé Venture Corp., Houston, from 1984. Dir. Tex. Eastern Corp. Served with AUS, 1943-46. Decorated Bronze Star with oak leaf cluster. Fellow London Geol. Soc.; mem. Am. Assn. Petroleum Geologists, Am. Petroleum Inst., Am. Inst. Profl. Geologists. Clubs: Rolling Rock (Ligonier, Pa.); Cherry Hills (Denver); River Oaks (Houston), Ramada (Houston). Home: Pittsburgh, Pa. Died Apr. 28, 2006.

WALKER, EVAN HARRIS, physicist; b. Birmingham, Ala., Feb. 15, 1935; s. James William and Eva Victoria (Harris) W.; m. Helen Marie Moseley, Sept. 6, 1958. B.S., U. Ala., 1955, M.S., 1956; Ph.D., U. Md., 1964. Assoc. prof. Memphis State U., 1957-58; asst. prof. U. Miami, Coral Gables, Fla., 1964-66; research physicist NASA, Cambridge, Mass., 1967-68; physicist Ballistic Research Lab., Aberdeen, Md., 1968—; guest prof. U. Md., College Park, 1967-68; dir. Walker Cancer Research Inst., Aberdeen, Md., 1980—. Originator observational theory in field of parapsychology, 1972; developer time delay toxin activation chemotherapy in cancer, 1980; inventor antifratricide protection on Abrams tank, 1982. Johns Hopkins U. fellow, 1975-79. Mem. AAAS, Am. Geophys. Union, Parapsychology Assn., Sigma Xi. Baptist. Home: Aberdeen, Md. Died Aug. 17, 2006.

WALKER, FLOYD LEE, lawyer; b. Kiefer, Okla., Mar. 27, 1919; s. Willis and Sarah Josephine (McFarl) W.; children by previous marriage: Mary Lea Walker Byrd, Cheryl Sue Walker Newman, James M.; m. Virginia Gifford Raines, Oct. 8, 1971. LLB, Tulsa U., 1949. Bar: Okla. 1949. Claims atty. Standard Ins. Co., Tulsa, 1949-53; pvt. practice Tulsa, from 1953. 1st lt. USAAF, 1942-45. Decorated DFC, Air medal with 3 oak leaf clusters. Fellow Am. Coll. Trial Lawyers; mem. ABA, ATLA Okla. Bar Assn. (bd. govs. 1979-82), Tulsa County Bar Assn (pres. 1973), Okla. Trial Lawyers Assn. Home: Tulsa, Okla Died Dec. 13, 2006.

WALKER, JAMES KENNETH, judge; b. Decatur, Tex., Jan 10, 1936; s. James Bluford and Elmer Vernice (Clark) W.; m Mary Frank Garrett, July 9, 1960 (dec. Nov. 1976); children—James Garrett, Steven Wade; m. Jo Beth Robertson, July 28 1978; 1 child, Ann Elizabeth. LLB, Baylor U., 1960. Bar: Tex 1960. Practice law, Lubbock, Tex., 1960-63, Morton, Tex. 1963-84; judge 286th Dist. Ct., 1984-91. Cochran County atty. 1965-73, 79-84 Mem. Tex. Bar Assn. Methodist. Home: Levelland, Tex. Died Aug. 22, 2006.

WALKER, RANDY, college football coach; b. May 29, 1954 m. Tamara Weikert; children: Abbey, Jaime. BA in Social Studies, Miami University, Ohio, 1976. Grad. asst. Univ. Miami (Oh.), 1977, head football coach, 1990—99; fullbacks coach UNC, 1978—81, quarterbacks caoch, 1982—87, offensive coord., 1985—87; running backs coach Northwestern U. 1988—89, head coach, 2000—06. Named to Miami Univ. (Oh.) Hall of Fame, 1999. Died June 29, 2006.

WALKER, WILLIAM EARL, pharmacist; b. Frostproof, Fla., July 20, 1929; s. William Pernal and Pearl (Prevatt) W.; m. Barbara Maxine Bell; children: Timothy Earl, Ginger Lynn Walker McIntyre, Diane Elizabeth Walker Shane, Jon Scott. BS in Pharmacy, U. Fla., 1952. Pharmacist Varn's Pharmacy, Inc. Ft. Meade, Fla., 1954-75; pharmacist, owner Walker's Pharmacy, Inc., Ft. Meade, from 1975. Served as 1st lt. U.S. Army 1952-54. Mem. Fla. Pharmacy Assn., Polk County Pharmacy Assn., Nat. Assn. Retail Druggists. Avocations: fishing, hunting woodworking. Home: Fort Meade, Fla. Died Apr. 26, 2007.

WALKER, WILLIE MARK, electronics engineering executive; b. Bessemer, Ala., Aug. 18, 1929; s. Johnnie and Annie Maimie (Thompson) W.; m. Mae Ruth Fulton, Apr. 28, 1952; children: Patricia Ann, Mark William, Karen Marie. BEE Marquette U., 1958; MSEE, U. Wis., 1965. Registered profl. engr., Wis. Devel. technician AC Spark Plug, Milw., 1953-56, project engr., 1956-60, engring. supr., 1960-65; sr. devel. engr. AC Electronics, Milw., 1965-71; sr. prodn. engr. Delco Electronics, Oak Creek, Wis., 1871-94; owner, prin. Walker Engring., from 1994. Author various proprietary reports. Pres. Potawatomi Area coun. Boy Scouts Am., Waukesha, Wis., 1982-84, chief camp insp. area 1, east ctrl. region, 1987, 99, v.p. program area 1, 1988-93, v.p. area 3 ctrl. region, 1993-96, mem. ctrl. region bd., 1994—, commr. east ctrl. region Scout Jamboree, 1989, internat. commr. ctrl. region Scout Jamboree, 1993; loaned exec. United Way Greater Milw., 1983; uhser, min. communion St. Mary Cath. Ch., Menomonee Falls, Wis., 1967—. With USAF, 1949-53. Elected to Black Achievers in Bus. and Industry, Milw. Met. YMCA, 1984; recipient Civic Svc. award Rotary Club, 1983, GM award for Excellence, 1980, St. George award Milw. Archdiocese, 1974; Silver Beaver award Boy Scouts Am., 1973, Silver Antelope award, 1987. Mem. IEEE (computer soc., sr. mem.), Computer Automated Sys. Assn., Soc. Mfg. Engrs., Wis. Soc. Profl. Engrs., Inst. Indsl. Engrs. (sr. mem., cert. sys. integrator), BRA (life), N.Am. Hunting Club (life), Lions (chpt. pres. 1979-80, sec. 1974-75), KC (recorder 1966-67, advocate 1975-76). Home: Germantown, Wis. Died July 15, 2007.

WALL, JOHN DAVID, lawyer; b. Houston, Apr. 6, 1967; s. Jerry Don and Jacquelyn (Finley) W.; m. Kimberly Robyn Weber, Sept. 16, 1995. BSBA in Acctg./Data Procesing, U. Ark., 1989, JD, 1992. Bar: Ark. 1992, Okla. 1993, U.S. Dist. Ct. (ea. and we. dists.) Ark. 1993, Mo. 2003. Atty. Bassett Law Firm, Fayetteville, Ark., from 1992, ptnr., 1999—2006. Pres. Sigma Nu Alumni Housing Bd., Fayetteville, 1994—. Mem. ABA, Ark. Bar Assn., Okla. Bar Asn., Wash. County, Mo. Bar Assn., ArKans. Workers Compensation Commn., Okla. Workers Compensation Ct. Methodist. Avocations: golf, handball, computers, bar-be-que, music. Home: Fayetteville, Ark. Died Jan. 10, 2006.

WALLACE, DONALD QUERK, architect, civil engineer; b. Harlan, Ky., July 29, 1931; s. Harry E. and Nell May (Wilson) W.; m. Geraldine Royse, May 10, 1958; children: Donald Querk Jr., Jon Paul. BSCE, U. Ky., 1959. Registered architect and profl. engr., Ky. Architect Brock & Johnson, Lexington, Ky., 1959-60; architect, owner D.Q. Wallace, Lexington, 1960-62, Affiliated Architects, 1962-63, CMW, Inc., 1963-83, D.Q.W. Inc. & Assocs., Lexington, 1983-92, ARCH II, Inc. & Assoc., Lexington, from 1992. Design critic U. Ky., 1961-72; dir. Ky. Archtl. Registration Bd., 1983-92; vice chmn. Ky. Dept. Housing, Bldg. and Constrn., 1978-85. Bd. dirs. U. Ky. Nat. Alumni Bd., 1980-86; vice chmn. Lexington Econ. Devel. Commn., 1974-86, Lexington Home Builders Scholarship Found., 1979-84; chmn. bd. dirs. Lexington Convention and Visitors Bur., 1986-91. Fellow AIA; mem. Ky. Soc. Architects, Greater Lexington C. of C., Lexington Club (bd. govs. 1982—). Democrat. Baptist. Home: Lexington, Ky. Died Jan. 21, 2007.

WALLACE, FURMAN T., physician; b. Chester, SC, Sept. 25, 1917; MD, Med. Coll., SC, 1941. Diplomate Am. Bd. Surgery. Intern Meth. Hosp., Indpls., 1941-42; resident in surgery Roper Hosp., Charleston, S.C., 1942-45; fellow in tchg. Med. Coll. S.C. Hosp., 1945; mem. staff Spartanburg Gen. Hosp., Mary Black Meml. Hosp.; assoc. clin. prof. surgery Med. U. S.C., emeritus assoc. clin. prof. surgery. Fellow ACS, Internat. Coll. Surgeons; mem. So. Med. Assn., S.E. Surg. Congress. Died Mar. 22, 2006.

WALLACE, HERBERT WILLIAM, physician, surgery educator, researcher; b. Bklyn., Dec. 11, 1930; s. Philip and Jean (Brand) W.; m. Rosalie Sandra Becker, Dec. 18, 1954; children: Ira, Ellen, Lisa. AB, Harvard U., 1952; MD, Tufts U., 1956, MS, 1960; MBA, U. Pa., 1981, MA (hon.), 1973. Diplomate Am. Bd. Surgery, Am. Bd. Thoracic Surgery. Resident in gen. surgery Tufts U.-New Eng. Med. Ctr., Boston, 1956-61; thoracic and cardiovascular surg. resident Mt. Sinai Hosp., NYC, 1963-65; assoc. in surgery and physiology U. Pa., Phila., 1966-70, asst.

prof. surgery, 1970-72, assoc. prof. surgery, physiology and bioengring., 1972-76, prof., 1976-99. Chief div. thoracic and cardiovascular surgery Grad. Hosp. U. Pa., 1976-79; assoc. in univ. seminar on biomaterials Columbia U., N.Y.C., 1972—. Contbr. over 100 articles to profl. jours. Rsch. grantee NIH, 1965—. Fellow Am. Coll. Surgeons, Am. Heart Assn.; mem. Am. Assn. Cancer Rsch., Am. Assn. Thoracic Surgery, Am. Thoracic Soc., Biomedical Engring. Soc., Soc. Thoracic Surgeons, others. Avocations: computers, squash, sailing, skiing. Home: Wynnewood, Pa. Died Oct. 10, 2006.

WALLACE, ROBERT EARL, geologist; b. NYC, July 16, 1916; s. Clarence Earl and Harriet (Wheeler) Wallace; m. Gertrude Kivela, Mar. 19, 1945; 1 child, Alan R. BS, Northwestern U., Evanston, Ill., 1938; MS, Calif. Inst. Tech., Pasadena, 1940, PhD, 1946. Geologist US Geol. Survey, various locations, 1942-98, regional geologist Menlo Park, Calif., 1970-74, chief scientist Office of Earthquakes, Volcanoes and Engring., 1974-87, emeritus, 1987-98; asst. and assoc. prof. Wash. State Coll., Pullman, 1946-51; prof. emeritus U. Nev., Reno, 1998—2003. Adv. panel Nat. Earthquake Prediction Evaluation Coun., 1980-90; adv. com. Stanford U. Sch. Earth Sci., 1972-82; engring. criteria rev. bd. San Francisco Bay Conservation and Devel. Commn., chmn. 1981-92. Contbr. articles to profl. jours. Recipient Alfred E. Alquist award Calif. Earthquake Safety Found., 1995. Fellow AAAS, Geol. Soc. Am. (chmn. cordillidan sect. 1967-68, Career Contbn. award Structural Geology and Tectonics, 2002), Earthquake Engring. Rsch. Inst. (hon. 1999), Calif. Acad. Scis. (hon.); mem. Seismol. Soc. Am. (medalist 1989) Avocations: birdwatching, amateur radio, painting. Home: Reno, Nev. Died Jan. 8, 2007.

WALLACE, ROBERT FERGUS, banker; b. Bklyn., Oct. 5, 1934; s. Fergus F. and Isabelle (Wilson) W.; m. Florence Faminow, Dec. 18, 1959; children: Douglas, Barbara. BA, Colgate U., 1956. Comml. loan officer Chem. Bank, NYC, 1956-68; chmn. First Interstate Bank, Portland, Oreg., 1968-81; pres. Nat. Westminster Bank U.S.A., NYC, from 1982; now chmn. bd. dirs. Nat. Westminster Bancorp, NYC. Bd. dirs. N.Y.C. Opera Co., 1986—. Served to lt. USN, 1957-60. Mem. Assn. Res. City Banks, Downtown-Lower Manhattan Assn. (treas. 1988). Clubs: Econ. of N.Y. Republican. Presbyterian. Home: New York, NY. Died Dec. 22, 2005.

WALLING, CHEVES THOMSON, chemistry professor; b. Evanston, Ill., Feb. 28, 1916; s. Willoughby George and Frederika Christina (Haskell) W.; m. Jane Ann Wilson, Sept. 17, 1940; children: Hazel, Rosalind, Cheves, Janie, Barbara AB, Harvard, 1937; PhD, U. Chgo., 1939. Rsch. chemist E.I. duPont de Nemours, 1939-43, U.S. Rubber Co., 1943-49; tech. aide Office Sci. Research, Washington, 1945; sr. rsch. assoc. Lever Bros. Co., 1949-52; prof. chemistry Columbia U., NYC, 1952-59; Disting. prof. chemistry U. Utah, Salt Lake City, 1970-91, prof. chemistry emeritus, from 1991. Author: Free Radicals in Solution, 1957, Fifty Years of Free Radicals, 1995; also numerous articles. Fellow AAAS; mem. Nat. Acad. Scis., Am. Acad. Arts and Scis., Am. Chem. Soc. (editor jour. 1975-81, James Flack Norris award 1970, Lubrizol award 1984) Home: Jaffrey, NH. Died June 19, 2007.

WALLMAN, LESTER JULIAN, retired medical educator; b. NYC, June 25, 1914; s. Samuel Wallman and Hannah Sarner; m. Elizabeth Rosalie Kaunitz, Dec. 21, 1941; children: Ruth, Julia Wallman Thayer, James. BA, Yale U., 1934, MD, 1938. Diplomate Am. Bd. Neurol. Surgery. Asst. pathology Karolinska Inst., Sweden, 1938; intern in surgery New Haven Hosp., 1939-40; resident in neurology Hartford (Conn.) Hosp., 1940-41; resident in surgery Meml. Hosp., Wilmington, Del., 1941-42, 44-46; from instr. to prof. neurosurgery U. Vt., Burlington, 1948-76, chair divsnd. neurosurgery, 1976-77, emeritus prof., from 1977. Contbr. articles to med. jours. Chair Vt. State Bd. Health, Montpelier, 1962-68; bd. dirs., chair ARC No. Vt. Capt. Med. Corps U.S. Army, 1941-44, ETO. Home: Burlington, Vt. Died July 23, 2006.

WALSER, MACKENZIE, internist, educator; b. NYC, Sept. 19, 1924; s. Kenneth Eastwood and Jean (Mackenzie) W.; m. Elizabeth C. Gearon, Sept. 17, 1988; children from previous marriage: Karen D., Jennifer McK., Cameron M., Eric H. Grad., Phillips Exeter Acad., 1941; AB, Yale, 1944; MD, Columbia, 1948. Diplomate: Am. Bd. Internal Medicine. Intern Mass. Gen. Hosp., Boston, 1948-49, asst. resident in medicine, 1949-50; resident Parkland Hosp., Dallas, 1950-52; staff mem. Johns Hopkins Hosp., Balt., from 1957; instr. U. Tex. at Dallas, 1950-51, asst. prof., 1951-52; investigator Nat. Heart Inst., Bethesda, Md., 1954-57; asst. prof. pharmacology Johns Hopkins Med. Sch., 1957-61, assoc. prof., 1961-70, prof., from 1970, asst. prof. medicine, 1957-64, assoc. prof., 1964-74, prof., from 1974. Med. dir. USPHS, 1970—, pharmacology study sect., 1968-72 Co-author: Mineral Metabolism, 2d edit., 1969, Handbook of Physiology, 1973, The Kidney, 1976, 5th edit., 1996, Coping with Kidney Disease, 2004, also articles; co-editor: Branched-Chain Amino and Ketoacids, 1981, Nutritional Management, 1984. Served with USNR, 1942-45; to lt. M.C. USNR, 1952-54. Recipient Research Career Devel. award USPHS, 1959-69, Lifetime Achievement award Nat. Kidney Found., Md., 2000. Mem. AAAS, AAUP (pres. Johns Hopkins 1970), Am. Soc. Clin. Investigation, Assn. Am. Physicians, Am. Fedn. Clin. Rsch., Am. Physiol. Soc., Biophys. Soc., Am. Soc. Pharmacology and Exptl. Therapeutics (Exptl. Therapeutics award 1975), Am. Soc. Nephrology, Am. Inst. Nutrition, Am. Soc. Clin. Nutrition (Hermann award 1988), Internat. Soc. Nutrition and Metabolism in Renal Disease (Addis award 1994). Home: Timonium, Md. Died Oct. 28, 2006.

WALSH, ANNMARIE HAUCK, research firm executive; b. NYC, May 5, 1938; d. James Smith and Ann-Marie (Kennedy) Hauck; m. John F. Walsh, Jr., Aug. 20, 1960; children: Peter Hauck, John David. BA, Barnard Coll., 1961; MA, Columbia U., 1969, PhD, 1971. Sr. staff mem. Inst. Pub. Adminstrn., NYC, 1961-72, pres., 1982-89, trustee, Gulick scholar, from 1989, dir. programs in Ctrl. Europe and NIS, from 1991; dir. Ctr. for Urban and Policy Studies, CUNY Grad. Ctr., NYC, 1972-79, Govs.' Task Force on Regional Planning, N.Y., Conn., N.J., 1979-81. Disting. vis. prof. Bklyn. Coll., CUNY, 1991-93; adj. prof. Robert Wagner Sch. Pub. Svc., NYU, 1998—; cons. pub. enterprise, civil svc., urban and regional mgmt., tng., pub. fin. adminstrn. reform UN, China, Indonesia, Bangladesh, Czech Republic and Slovakia, Poland, Macedonia, Uzbekistan, Kazakstan, state and local govts., U.S. Postal Svc., U.S. Dept. Transp., Senate com. govt. ops. Author: Urban Government for Zagreb, Yugoslavia, 1968, Urban Government for Lagos, Nigeria, 1968, Urban Government for the Paris Region, 1968, The Urban Challenge to Government: An International Comparisons of Thirteen Cities, 1969, The Public's Business: Politics and Practices of Government Corporations, 1978, 2d edit., 1980, Designing and Managing the Procurement Process, 1989, Privatization-Implications for Public Management, 1996; editor: Agenda for a City, 1970. Project dir. 20th Century Fund, Pub. Enterprise, 1972-76, pub.-pvt. partnerships, 1989-93; bd. dirs. Ralph Bunche Inst., UN, 1978-82, Regional Plan Assn., 1987-91. Herbert Lehmann fellow, 1966-69 Fellow, Nat. Acad. Pub. Adminstrn. (bd. dirs. 1996—); mem. Phi Beta Kappa. Home: New York, NY. Died Jan. 11, 2007.

WALSH, BILL (WILLIAM ERNEST WALSH), retired professional football coach; b. LA, Nov. 30, 1931; m. Geri Walsh; children: Steve(dec.), Craig, Elizabeth. Student, San Mateo Jr. Coll.; BA, San Jose State U., 1954, MA in Edn., 1959. Grad. asst. coach Monterey Peninsula Coll., 1955; asst. coach San Jose State U., 1956; head coach Washington Union High Sch., Fremont, Calif., 1957-59; defensive coord. U. Calif., Berkeley, 1960-62; defensive backs coach Stanford U., 1963-65; offensive backs coach Oakland Raiders, 1966-67; head coach San Jose Apaches, Continental Football League, 1967; offensive coord. Cin. Bengals, 1968-75; asst. coach San Diego Chargers, 1976; head coach Stanford U., 1977-78; head coach, gen. mgr. San Francisco 49ers, 1979-89, exec. v.p., 1989; broadcaster NBC Sports, 1989-91; cons. San Francisco 49ers, 1996-99; head coach Stanford U., 1992-95; v.p., gen. mgr. San Francisco 49ers, 1999—2001. Co-author (with Glenn Dickey): Building a Champion, 1989. Named NFL Coach of Yr., Sporting News, 1981, UPI, 1981, 1984, AP, 1981, Pro Football Weekly, 1981; named to Pro Football Hall of Fame, 1993. Head coach, Superbowl Champion San Francisco 49ers, 1981, 1984, 1988. Died July 30, 2007.

WALSH, JOHN JOSEPH, medical school administrator, physician; b. NYC, July 31, 1924; s. Patrick Joseph and Elizabeth (Lawless) W.; m. Gloria Paolini (dec. 1971); children: Maureen Walsh Garland, John Joseph Jr., Kathleen Walsh Saer; m. Dorothy B. Ray, 1989. Student, Fordham U., 1941-43, Cornell U., 1943-44; MD, L.I. Coll. Medicine, 1948; postdoctoral, Tulane U., 1957-58; ScD (hon.), SUNY, 1989. Diplomate Am. Bd. Internal Medicine. Commd. USPHS, 1948, advanced through grades to rear admiral, 1966; intern USPHS Hosp., Staten Island, N.Y., 1948-49, resident Seattle, 1951-54, asst. chief medicine New Orleans, 1954-56, dep. chief, 1956-57, chief research activites, 1958-64, chief med. service, 1963-64, med. dir., med. officer in charge, 1964-66; asst. surgeon gen., dir. div. direct health services USPHS, 1966-68, ret., 1968; instr. Tulane U. Sch. Medicine, New Orleans, 1957-58, asst. prof., 1958-60, assoc. prof., 1960-67, prof., 1967-89, prof. medicine emeritus, from 1989, dean, 1968-69; dean, coordinator health sci. and programs Tulane U. Med. Ctr., New Orleans, 1968-69, v.p. health affairs, 1969-78, chancellor, 1973-89, chancellor emeritus, from 1989, acting dean sch. pub. health and tropical medicine New Orleans, 1974, Jack R. Aron prof. in adminstrv. medicine, 1978-89; adj. prof. Tulane U. Sch. Pub. Health and Tropical Medicine, 1978-89; pres., CEO Mahorner Clinic, Kenner, La., 1989-92. Cons. VA Hosp., New Orleans, 1969-89, VA Hosp., Alexandria, La., 1969-89, USPHS Hosp., New Orleans, 1968-89; vis. physician Charity Hosp., New Orleans, 1957-66, sr. vis. physician, 1966-89, chief service Tulane div., 1968-69, acting chief service Tulane div., 1972; instr. La. State U. Sch. Medicine, New Orleans, 1956-57; mem. bd. cons. to comdr. Naval Med. Command Dept. Navy, Washington, 1983-86; mem. adv. com. to dir. NIH, 1983-85. Contbr. articles to profl. jours. Mem. planning com. Touro Infirmary, New Orleans; bd. dirs., mem. exec. com. Am. Cancer Soc., Internat. House, 1978-82, 83-84; mem. New Orleans Area Health Planning Council, 1968-70, task force in health manpower; trustee La. Sci. Ctr., 1983-85, La. Regional Med. Programs, 1969; bd. dirs. Friends of Charity Inc., 1986-89, Blue Cross, Washington, 1966-68, New Orleans Area/Bayou-River Health Systems Agy., 1978-82, Tuberculosis Assn. Greater New Orleans, 1968—, Flint-Goodridge Hosp., New Orleans, 1978-82. Fellow Tulane U. Sch. Medicine, 1957-58; recipient Outstanding Alumni award Downstate Med. Ctr., 1973. Fellow ACP, Am. Coll. Cardiology, Am. Coll. Chest Physicians, Am. Coll. Clin. Pharmacology and Chemotherapy; mem. AMA (com. on emergency health service), Am. Thoracic Soc. (councilor), La. Thoracic Soc. (pres. 1964), Nat. Adv. Rsch. Resources Coun. (mem. health care tech. study sect. 1970-74, chmn. 1972-74), Am. Lung Assn. La. (hon. life.), Delta Omega, Kappa Delta Phi, Alpha Epsilon Delta, Omicron Delta Kappa, Alpha Omega Alpha. Roman Catholic. Home: Metairie, La. Died Oct. 2, 2006.

WALSH, RALPH EDWARD, retired captain fire department, state senator; b. Pawtucket, RI, Aug. 12, 1923; s. Joseph Edward and Jane (Pennington) W.; m. Hope F. Walsh; children: Michael Edward, Mary Elaine, Maureen Elizabeth, Thresa Marie, Brian Joseph. AS, R.I. Jr. Coll., 1975; BA, Providence Coll., 1977. Letter carrier U.S. Post Office, Warwick, R.I., 1949-56; capt., fire fighter City of Warwick Fire Dept., 1956-84; ins. inspector Equifax Corp., Warwick, 1979-89; state senator R.I. State Legislature, Providence, from 1988. Pres. Apponaug Area Improvement Assn., Warwick, 1988—. With AUS, 1943-46, ETO. Mem. Exeter Country Club, KC (lectr. 1970). Democrat. Roman Catholic. Avocations: community affairs, golf. Home: Warwick, RI. Died Dec. 22, 2006.

WALSH, THOMMIE, choreographer; b. Auburn, NY, Mar. 15, 1950; s. Thomas Joseph Jr. and Eleanor Louise (Cosentino) W. Student, Boston Conservatory Music, 1968-71. Mem. chorus various Broadway prodns., 1973-77; (films) Jesus Christ Superstar, 1972; originated role of Bobby Mills, III in A Chorus Line, 1975; choreographer Broadway prodns.: The 1940's Radio Hour on Broadway, 1979, (with Tommy Tune): The Best Little Whorehouse in Texas, 1978, A Day in Hollywood/A Night in the Ukraine, 1979 (Tony and Drama Desk awards for Choreography), Nine, 1982, Do Black Patent Leather Shoes Really Reflect Up?, 1982, My One and Only, 1983 (Tony award for Choreography), My Favorite Year, 1993; co-author: (with Baayork Lee & Robert Viagas) On the Line: The Creation of A Chorus Line, 1990 Mem. Dance Masters Am., Profl. Dance Tchrs. Am., Stage Dirs. and Choreographers, Actors Equity Assn., Screen Actors Guild. Died June 16, 2007.

WALSH, WILLIAM RAYMOND, JR., foundation executive; b. Elizabeth, NJ, June 10, 1927; s. William Raymond and Mildred M. (Precheur) W.; m. Helen Torsiello, Aug. 26, 1950; children: Karen, William Raymond III, Colleen. BA, Rutgers U., 1953. Bus. adminstr. Piscataway Twp. (N.J.) Sch. Dist., 1954-66; v.p. fin. and adminstrn. Middlesex County (N.J.) Coll., 1966-72; exec. v.p. Robert Wood Johnson Found., Princeton, N.J., from 1972. Mem. adj. faculty Rutgers U. Grad. Sch., 1969-72; past guest lectr. Columbia U. Grad. Sch. Edn.; bd. dirs. Peoples Nat. Bank of Cen. Jersey. Trustee, chmn. bd. Robert Wood Johnson U. Hosp., New Brunswick, N.J.; trustee Middlesex-Somerset chpt. Nat. Multiple Sclerosis Soc., 1969-82, ARC Endowment fund. Served with USAAF, 1947-49. Mem.: Kiwanis (past chpt. pres.). Roman Catholic. Died Oct. 22, 2006.

WALTER, BRUCE ALEXANDER, physician; b. Seattle, Apr. 15, 1922; s. Ernest R. and Marion (Alexander) W.; BA, U. Wash., 1944, BS, 1948, MD, 1951; MPH, UCLA, 1962; m. Gloria Helen Parry, Feb. 4, 1956; children: Maia Marion, Wendy Diane, Shelley Kathleen, Allison Ann. Cert. Am. Bd. Preventative Medicine. Intern Los Angeles County Gen. Hosp., 1951-52; resident internal medicine Wadsworth Hosp., U. Calif., 1952-54; dir. grad. program hosp., health facilities adminstrn. UCLA, 1965-68; attending staff Salt Lake County Hosp., 1954-55; fellow medicine U. Utah, 1954-55; fellow medicine U. So. Calif., 1955-56, mem. faculty, 1956-65; attending staff Los Angeles County Hosp., 1956-65; physician internal medicine, Palm Springs, Calif., 1956-61; chief staff Desert Hosp., 1960-61; dir. med. care studies Calif. Dept. Pub. Health, Berkeley, 1962-65; dir. Med. Care Services, State of Utah, 1969-71, dep. dir. health, 1971-79, acting dir. health, 1979; cons. Newport Med. Group and Advanced Health Systems, Inc., Newport Beach, Calif., 1979-84; practice medicine specializing in internal medicine, Costa Mesa, Calif., 1984—; asst. prof. community and family medicine U. Utah Sch. Medicine, Salt Lake City, 1969-79; mem. Utah State Bd. Aging; bd. dirs. South Coast Inst. Applied Gerontology, Blue Shield of Utah, Utah Profl. Standards Rev. Orgn. 1st lt. Signal Corps, AUS, 1943-46. Fellow Am. Coll. Preventative Medicine; mem. Am. Coll. Hosp. Health Administrs., Nat. Assn. Health Facility Licensing and Certification Dirs. (pres. 1975-76), Alpha Delta Phi, Alpha Kappa Kappa, Alpha Delta Sigma. Home: Corona Dl Mar, Calif. Died Dec. 7, 2006.

WALTERS, ROBERT, savings and loan association executive; b. Paola, Kans., Nov. 7, 1937; s. James Burton and Helen Lucille (Wiseman) W.; m. Jacqueline June Rowland, June 2, 1958; children: Machelle, Casey, Alecia. BS in Econs., Ctrl. Mo. State U., 1963. Asst. v.p. and comml. mgr. Amortibanc Investment Co., Wichita, Kans.; v.p. Farm & Home Savs. Assn., Nevada, Mo., 1970—75; pres., CEO Home Fed. Savs. & Loan Assn., Greensboro, N.C., 1976—78; sr. v.p. Farm & Home Savs. Assn., Nevada, Mo., 1978—81; pres. Benjamin Franklin Savs. Assn., Houston, 1981—84, Nowlin Savs. Assn., Ft. Worth, from 1984. With USCG, 1957—60. Republican. Methodist. Home: Fort Worth, Tex. Died June 26, 2007.

WALTON, HELEN (HELEN ROBSON WALTON), philanthropist; b. Claremore, Okla., Dec. 3, 1919; d. L.S. and Hazel Carr Robson; m. Samuel (Sam) Moore Walton Feb. 14, 1943 (dec. Apr. 6, 1992, founder of Wal-Mart); c. S. Robson (Rob), John T.(dec. June 27, 2005), Jim, Alice. BA in Fin., U. Okla. Co-owner Arvest Bank; founder (with Sam M. Walton), also pres. Walton Family Found., 1987; contbr. Walton Family Arts Center, Fayetteville. Mem. bd. trustees Univ. Osarks, Clarksville, 1975—2007, chair bd. dirs. Known for philanthropic contributions, specifically to Arkansas, arts, education, families and children; established the Walton Scholars program for children of Wal-Mart employees; along with husband led to the development of a program to bring students from Ctrl. Am. to three private Arkansas colleges to study. Named one of World's Richest People, Forbes, 2001—07, Richest Americans, 2006. Died Apr. 19, 2007.

WANG, CHEH CHENG, mechanical engineer; b. Chuan Chow, Fukien, China, Mar. 3, 1930; came to U.S., 1963, naturalized, 1976; s. Pi-Chen and Ling-Fung (Lee) W.; m. Esther Chun-Mei Chu, Aug. 12, 1967; children— Albert, Edward, Sophia. Diploma Engring., Nanking Inst. Tech., Peoples Republic of China, 1953; M.Sc., U. Calif.-Berkeley, 1965; Ph.D., U. Sheffield, Eng., 1976. Registered mech. engr., Wash. Lectr. Xian Inst. Aero. Engring., Peoples Republic of China, 1953-58; prin. designer V.K. Song & Co., Ltd., Hong Kong, 1959-62; asst. chief engr. Fulton Shipyard, Antioch, Calif., 1963-67; sr. mech. engr. Lockheed Shipbuilding, Seattle, 1967-68; chief mech. engr. Interactive Tech. Inc., Santa Clara, Calif., 1971-72; sr. staff engr. Central Engring. Labs., FMC Corp., Santa Clara, 1972-86; v.p. Pacific Applied Tech. Internat., Fremont, Calif., 1987—; founder 3E Software, 1986—; cons. in field. Contbr. articles to profl. jours. Mem. ASME (sec. Ditto, Santa Clara Valley sect. 1980-81), Am. Acad. Mechs., Soc. Indsl. and Applied Maths. Current work: Gear dynamics, applied numerical methods; computer aided engineering in solid mechanics areas; modeling and simulation of mechanical systems. Subspecialties: Mechanical engineering; Computer-aided design. Home: San Jose, Calif. Died Apr. 5, 2006.

WANG, CHIA PING, physicist, researcher; b. The Philippines; came to U.S., 1963, naturalized; (parents Chinese citizens). s. Guan Can and Tah (Lin) W. BS, U. London, 1950; MS, Brit. U. Malaya in Singapore (now U. Singapore), 1951; PhD in Physics, Brit. U. Malaya (now U. Singapore) and U. Cambridge, 1953; DSc in Physics (hon.), U. Singapore, 1972. Asst. lectr. U.

Malaya, Singapore, 1951—53; mem. faculty Nankai U., Tientsin, China, 1954—58, prof. physics, 1956—58, head electron physics divsn., 1955—58; head electron physics Lanchow (China) Atomic Project, 1958; faculty Hong Kong U., Chinese U., Hong Kong, 1958, prof. physics, 1959—63, acting head physics, math. depts., 1959; rsch. assoc. lab. nuc. studies Cornell U., Ithaca, NY, 1963—64; assoc. prof. space sci. and applied physics Cath. U. Am., Washington, 1964—68; assoc. prof. physics Case Inst. Tech., Case Western Res. U., Cleve., 1966—70; vis. scientist, vis. prof. Cavendish Lab., U. Cambridge (Eng.), Inst. Theoretical Physics, U. Louvain (Belgium), Cosmic Ray Lab., U.S. Naval Rsch. Labs. (concurrently U. Md.) MIT, 1970—75; rsch. physicist radiation lab. U.S. Army Natick (Mass.) R & D Command, 1975—2007. Steering com. sci. and tech. directorate U.S. Army Natick R & D Command, 1993-2007; steering com. nuc. physics divsn. Nankai U., Tientsin, 1956-58; vis. scientist, vis. prof. U. Cambridge (Eng.), U. Leuven, Belgium, U.S. Naval Rsch. Labs., U. Md., MIT, 1970-75. Co-author: Atomic Structure and Interactions of Ionizing Radiations with Matter in Preservation of Food by Ionizing Radiation, 1982; contbr. over 80 articles to profl. jours. Recipient Outstanding Performance award Dept. Army, 1980, Quality Increase award, 1980, Sustained Superior Performance awards, 1990, 96. Mem. AAAS, Am. Nuc. Soc., Am. Phys. Soc., Inst. Physics London (chartered physicist), N.Y. Acad. Scis., Sigma Xi. Achievements include pioneering research in nucleon substructure (now often referred to as parton), established quantum fluctuating 3-quark-many-qq-bar (called Ylon, later known as Valence Quarks, Sea Quarks) nuclear sub-unit structure from MIT/SLAC/CERN deep inelastic electron-neutrino-nucleon scattering experiments; multiparticle production, cosmic radiation, picosecond time to pulse-height conversion, thermal physics, power law of laser steel melting, microwaves absorption and scattering, initiating cosmic-ray extensive air shower research in China; visualizing with Otto Frisch the sinusoidal interference laser light waves in Frisch's laser interferometer. Died Dec. 22, 2006.

WANG, YUNG, real estate development company executive; structural engineer; b. Sczchuan, China, Jan. 6, 1942; came to U.S. 1968, naturalized, 1976; s. Schek-Yai; m. Chuan-Ying H. Wang, Dec. 28, 1969. BS, Chung Hsing U., Taiwan, 1967; MS in Aero. Sciences, U. Calif., Berkeley, 1971, MS in Structural Engring., 1973. Cert. structural engr., Calif. Pres. Struxkon Corp., Walnut Creek, Calif., 1979—. Mem. ASCE, ASME, Bldg. Owners and Mgrs. Assn. Home: Orinda, Calif. Died June 4, 2007.

WAPPNER, REBECCA SUE, pediatrics educator; b. Mansfield, Ohio, Feb. 25, 1944; d. William Henry and Helen Elizabeth (Gilmore) W. BS in Zoology, Ohio U., 1966; MD, Ohio State U., 1970. Cert. Am. Bd. Pediatrics, clin. and clin. biochem. Am. Bd. Med. Genetics. Intern in pediatrics The Children's Hosp., Ohio State U., Columbus, 1970-71, resident in pediatrics, 1971-72, asst. chief resident, 1972-73; fellow in pediatric metabolism and genetics Ind. U. Sch. Medicine, Indpls., 1973-75, asst. prof. dept. pediatrics, 1975-78, assoc. prof. dept. pediatrics, 1978-92, prof. dept. med. & molecular genetics, from 1993, prof. pediats., from 1992. Mem. Am. Acad. Pediatrics, Am. Soc. for Human Genetics, Soc. for Inherited Metabolic Disease, Soc. for the Study of Inborn Errors of Metabolism, Soroptimist Internat., Mortar Bd., Iota Sigma Pi, Sigma Xi, Phi Beta Kappa. Home: Carmel, Ind. Died Sept. 6, 2006.

WARD, JAMES KIRK, manufacturing company executive; b. Winston Salem, N.C., Aug. 23, 1932; s. James Leonard and Evelyn (Edwards Kirk) W.; m. Joe Anne Frier, July 7, 1956; children— Sidney Kirk, Julie Anne. A.A., Mars Hill Coll., 1952; B.F.A., Coll. William and Mary, 1955. Dir. advt. Erwin Lambeth Inc., Thomasville, N.C., 1958-60; v.p. design Heirloom Furniture Inc., High Point, N.C., 1960-78, pres., 1978—, also dir. Rep., Triad Council Govts., Greensboro, 1978; mem. adv. bd. Mars Hill Coll. (N.C.), 1973; pres. Sch. Bd. Thomasville, N.C., 1976; pres. N.C. Bapt. Homes for Aging, Winston Salem, 1983. Named Lion of Yr., 1974. Mem. Am. Soc. Interior Design Industry Found. Democrat. Baptist. Club: Furniture. Lodge: Lions (pres. 1975-76 Thomasville). Home: Dallas, Tex. Died June 30, 2007.

WARK, ROBERT RODGER, retired curator; b. Edmonton, Can., Oct. 7, 1924; came to U.S., 1948, naturalized, 1970; s. Joseph Henry and Louise (Rodger) W. BA, U. Alta., 1944, MA, 1946, LLD (hon.), 1986; AM, Harvard, 1949, PhD, 1952. Instr. art Harvard U., 1952-54; instr. history art Yale U., 1954-56; curator art Henry E. Huntington Library and Art Gallery, San Marino, Calif., 1956-90. Lectr. art Calif. Inst. Tech., 1960-91, UCLA, 1966-80. Author: Sculpture in the Huntington Collection, 1959, French Decorative Art in the Huntington Collection, 1961, Rowlandson's Drawings for a Tour in a Post Chaise, 1963, Rowlandson's Drawings for the English Dance of Death, 1966, Isaac Cruikshank's Drawings for Drolls, 1968, Early British Drawings in the Huntington Collection 1600-1750, 1969, Drawings by John Flaxman, 1970, Ten British Pictures 1740-1840, 1971, Meet the Ladies: Personalities in Huntington Portraits, 1972, Drawings from the Turner Shakespeare, 1973, Drawings by Thomas Rowlandson in the Huntington Collection, 1975, British Silver in the Huntington Collection, 1978; editor: Sir Joshua Reynolds: Discourses on Art, 1959. Served with RCAF, 1944-45; Served with RCNVR, 1945. Mem. Coll. Art Assn. Died June 8, 2007.

WARMAN, C. DALE, retail company executive; b. Springfield, Conn., July 4, 1929; s. William Thomas and Ella (Nagel) W.; m. Marilyn Trudgeon, Feb. 14, 1950; children: Douglas, Sharon, Ronald. Student, Warner Pacific Coll., Portland State U. With Fred Meyer, Inc., Portland, Oreg., 1949-72, 75—, mdse. mgr., supr. mktg., until 1975, exec. v.p. mktg., from 1975, pres. food group; exec. v.p. Allied Supermarkets, Detroit, 1973-75. Trustee Warner Pacific Coll.; chmn. United Way. Republican. Mem. Ch. of God. Club: Toastmasters. Home: Vancouver, Wash. Died Mar. 21, 2007.

WARNER, CECIL FRANCIS, retired mechanical engineering educator; b. Parker, Ind., June 13, 1915; s. Leslie Clyde and Dollie May (Cecil) W.; m. Melda M. Needler, Dec. 27, 1939; children— Robert Earl, James Bruce. BSM.E., Purdue U., 1939, PhD, 1945; MS, Lehigh U., 1941. Registered profl. engr., Ind. Instr. Lehigh U., 1940-42; instr. Purdue U., 1942-45, asst. prof. mech. engring., 1945-50, asso. prof., 1950-55, prof., 1955-86, ret., 1986; engring. specialist Aerojet Gen. Corp., 1953-54, sr. engr., 1963-65. Cons. in field. Author: (with C. W. Messersmith) Mechanical Engineering Laboratory, 1950, (with K. Wark) Air Pollution, Its Origin and Control, 1976, 2 edit., 1981; contbr. articles on rocket jet propulsion to profl. jours. Mem. ASME (pres. local sect. 1955-56), Air Pollution Control Assn., Sigma Xi. Clubs: Kiwanis (pres. Lafayette club 1974-75). Methodist. Home: West Lafayette, Ind. Died Dec. 8, 2005.

WARNER, OSWALD GLADSTONE, surgeon, educator; b. Kingston, Jamaica, West Indies, May 21, 1934; came to U.S., 1956; s. Harold Theodore and Gladys (McCalla) W.; m. Barbara H. Warner, June 29, 1960; children: Oswald Gladstone Jr., Faith Ann Marte, Chris Anthony, Charles Orville. BSc, Howard U., 1960, MD, 1964. Resident surgery Howard U., Washington, 1964-69; resident cardiology Boston City U. Hosp., 1969-71; assoc. surgery Boston U., 1969-71; asst. prof. Howard U., Washington, 1971-77, assoc. prof., from 1977, acting chief cardiology, 1980-83. Fellow ACS, Am. Coll. Cardiology. Democrat. Mem. Ch. of Brethren. Avocations: running, fishing. Home: Potomac, Md. Died Apr. 15, 2006.

WARNER, ROBERT MARK, dean, archivist, historian; b. Montrose, Colo., June 28, 1927; s. Mark Thomas and Bertha Margaret (Rich) W.; m. Eleanor Jane Bullock, Aug. 21, 1954 (dec. Aug. 2006); children: Mark Steven, Jennifer Jane. Student, U. Denver, 1945; BA, Muskingum Coll., 1949, LL.D. (hon.), 1981; MA, U. Mich., 1953, PhD, 1958; H.H.D. (hon.), Westminster Coll., Pa., 1981; L.H.D. (hon.), DePaul U., 1983. Tchr. high sch., Montrose, Colo., 1949-50; lectr. dept. history U. Mich., 1958-66, assoc. prof., 1966-71, prof., 1971-97, prof. emeritus, 1997—2007, prof. Sch. Info., 1974-97, dean Sch. Info. & Library Studies, 1985-92, univ. historian, 1992—2007, interim dir. Univ. Libraries, 1988-90; asst. in rsch. Bentley Hist. Libr., 1953-57, asst. curator, 1957-61, asst. dir., 1961-66, dir., 1966-80; archivist of U.S., 1980-85. Mem. exec. com. Bentley Hist. Libr., 1988-2007; bd. visitors Sch. Libr. Sci., Case Western Res. U., 1976-80, chmn., 1980-84, Maxwell Sch. Govt., Syracuse U., 1982-87; chmn. Gerald R. Ford Presdl. Libr. Bldg. Com., 1977-79; bd. dirs., sec. Gerald R. Ford Found., 1987-2007; trustee Woodrow Wilson Internat. Ctr. for Scholars, 1980-85, chmn. fellowship com., 1983-85; chmn. Nat. Hist. Publs. and Records Commn., 1980-85; mem. exec. com. Internat. Coun. on Archives, 1984-88; pres. 2d European Conf. on Archives, 1989; comptroller gen. U.S. Rsch. and Edn. Adv. Com., 1988-2000; rsch. adv. com. Online Computer Libr. Ctr., 1990-93; bd. govs. Clements Libr., 1988-90, 93-2004, Clark Hist. Libr. Ctrl. Mich. U., 1987—; vis. prof. UCLA, 1993. Author: Chase S. Osborn, 1860-1949, 1960, Profile of a Profession, 1964, (with R. Bordin) The Modern Manuscript Library, 1966, (with C.W. Vanderhill) A Michigan Reader: 1865 to the Present, 1974, (with F. Blouin) Sources for the Study of Migration and Ethnicity, 1979, Diary of a Dream: A History of the National Archives Independence Movement, 1980-1985, 1995. Served with U.S. Army, 1950-52. Recipient Disting. Svc. award Muskingum Coll., 1990, Disting. Svc. award Nat. Hist. Pub. and Records Commn., 1992. Fellow Soc. Am. Archivists; mem. Am. Hist. Assn. (council 1981-85), Orgn. Am. Historians, ALA (council 1986-91), Assn. for Library and Info. Sci. Edn., Presbyn. Hist. Soc. (bd. dirs. 1987-91), Am. Assn. State and Local History, Hist. Soc. Mich. (trustee 1960-66, v.p. 1972-73, pres. 1973-74), Soc. Am. Archivists (mem. council 1967-71, sec., exec. dir. 1971-73, v.p. 1974-75, pres. 1976-77), Am. Antiquarian Soc., Phi Alpha Theta, Beta Phi Mu. Clubs: U. Mich. Research. Lodges: Rotary. Presbyterian. Home: Ann Arbor, Mich. Died Apr. 24, 2007.

WARREN, ALBERT, publishing executive; b. Warren, Ohio, May 18, 1920; s. David and Clara W.; m. Margaret Yeomans, Jan. 9, 1947; children: Ellen, Paul, Claire, Daniel, Thomas, Joan. BA in Journalism, Ohio State U., 1942. Assoc. editor TV Digest, Washington, 1945-50, sr. editor, 1950-58, chief Washington Bur., 1958-61; chmn., editor, pub. Warren Comm. News, Inc., Washington, 1961—2006. Lectr. Columbia Grad Sch Journalism, NYC, 1962—75; mem. alumni adv. coun. Ohio State U., Columbus, 1982—88, mem. adv. coun. Sch. Journalism; pub. 10 comm. periodicals. Contbr. articles to profl jours. With USNR, 1942—45, PTO. Mem.: Soc. Profl. Journalists (Hall of Fame 1991), US Congress Periodical Gallery, Internat. Radio and TV Soc. Pubs., Cable TV Pioneers, Broadcast Pioneers (Annual Recognition Award 1982, Hall of Fame 1995), Newsletter Pub. Assn. (Hall of Fame 1985), Ind. Newsletter Assn. (co-founder 1963, pres 1965—66), Cosmos Club. Home: Washington, DC. Died Nov. 26, 2006.

WARREN, WILLIAM MICHAEL, association executive; b. Bancroft, Mich., July 5, 1917; s. Perrin Charles and Gladys May (Hill) W.; m. Rebecca Carolyn Glass, Dec. 20, 1945; children: William Michael, Jr., Charles, John, James, Joseph, Andrew. BS, Mich. State U.-East Lansing, 1940; MS, Tex. A&M U., 1948; PhD, U. Mo., 1952. Instr. Tex. A&M U., Coll. Sta., 1940-42, asst. prof., 1946-50, assoc. prof., 1952-55; prof. Auburn U., Ala., 1955-57, prof., dept. head, 1957-80, prof. emeritus, 1980—; exec. dir. Santa Gertrudis Breeders Internat., Kingsville, Tex., 1980—. Contbr. articles to scientific jours. Gen. Edn. Bd. scholar, 1950-52. Mem. Am. Soc. of Animal Sci., Southern Sect., Am. Soc. of Animal Sci. Lodge: Kiwanis. Methodist. Home: Kingsville, Tex. Died Mar. 27, 2006.

WASHBURN, BRADFORD (HENRY BRADFORD WASHBURN JR.), museum administrator, cartographer, photographer; b. Cambridge, Mass., June 7, 1910; s. Henry Bradford and Edith (Hall) W.; m. Barbara Teel Polk, Apr. 27, 1940; children: Dorothy Polk, Edward Hall, Elizabeth Bradford. Grad., Groton Sch., 1929; AB, Harvard U., 1933, A.M., 1960, D.H.L. (hon.), 1975; postgrad., Inst. Geog. Exploration, 1934-35; postgrad. hon. degrees; PhD, U. Alaska, 1951; DSc, Tufts U., 1957, Colby Coll., 1957, Northeastern U., 1958; D.Sc., U. Mass., 1972; DSc, Curry Coll., 1982; DFA, Suffolk U., 1965; DHL, Boston Coll., 1974; LLD, Babson Coll., 1980. Instr. Inst. Geog. Exploration, Harvard U., 1935-42; dir. Mus. Sci., Boston, 1939-80, chmn. of the corp., 1980-85, hon. dir., 1985—2007. Dir. Mountaineer in Alps, 1926-31; explorer Alaska Coast Range, 1930-40; served as leader numerous mountain, subarctic area explorations; cons. various govtl. agys. on Alaska and cold climate equipment; leader in spl. expdns. investigating high altitude cosmic rays, Alaska, 1947; rep. Nat. Geog. Soc., 17th Internat. Geog. Congress, 1952; leader Nat. Geog. mapping expdns. to, Grand Canyon, 1971-75; chmn. Mass. Com. Rhodes Scholars, 1959-64; chmn. arts and scis. com. UNESCO conf., Boston, 1961; mem. adv. com. John F. Kennedy Library, 1977; mem. vis. com. Internat. Mus. Photography, 1978; mem. U.S. Nat. Commn. for UNESCO, 1978; lectr. work of Yukon Expdn., Royal Geog. Soc., London, 1936-37, on mapping Grand Canyon, 1976; lectr. Mus. Imaging Tech., Bangkok, 1989, Royal Geog. Soc., London, on mapping Mt. Everst, 1990; lectr. Antarctica, 1994. Contbr. articles, photographs on Alaska, Alps, glaciers, and mountains to mags., books.; editor, pub. 1st large-scale map Mt. McKinley, Am. Acad. Arts and Scis.-Swiss Found. Alpine Rsch., Bern, 1960; mapped Mt. Kennedy for Nat. Geog. Soc., 1965, Grand Canyon, 1971-74, Muldrow Glacier (Mt. McKinley), 1977; editor new chart, Squam Lake, N.H., 1968, new Grand Canyon map for Nat. Geog. Soc., 1978, Bright Angel Trail map, 1981; photo-mapped Mt. Everest for Nat. Geog. Soc., 1984; dir., pub. large-scale map of Mt. Everest for Nat. Geog. Soc., 1984-88; project chief new 1:50,000 map of Mt. Everest for Nat. Geog. Soc. and Boston Sci. Mus., 1988; pub. Tourist Guide to Mt. McKinley, 1971, new map of Presdl. Range, N.H, 1989; completed new large-scale relief model Mt. Everest, 1990; one-man photographic shows Whyte Art Mus., Banff, Can., Internat. Mus. Photography, N.Y.C., Rochester, N.Y. Bd. overseers Harvard, 1955-61; trustee Smith Coll., 1962-68, Richard E. Byrd Found., 1979-84, Mt. Washington Obs., 1979-2007; mem. Task Force on Future Financing of Arts in Mass., 1978; hon. bd. dirs. Swiss Found. Alpine Research, 1984-2007. Recipient Royal Geog. Soc. Cuthbert Peek award for Alaska Exploration and Glacier Studies, 1938, Burr prize Nat. Geog. Soc., 1940, 65, Stratton prize Friends of Switzerland, 1970, Lantern award Rotary Club, Boston, 1978, New Englander of Yr. award New Eng. Coun., 1974, Gold Research medal Royal Scottish Geog. Soc. (with wife), 1979, Alexander Graham Bell award Nat. Geog. Soc., 1980, Disting. Grotonian award Groton Sch., 1979, Explorers medal Explorers Club, 1984, award for lifelong contbns. to cartography and surveying Engring. Socs. New Eng., 1985, King Albert medal of merit, 1994, Commonwealth award State of Mass., 1999; named Bus. Statesman of Yr. Harvard Bus. Sch. Assn., Boston, 1970; named to Acad. Disting. Bostonians Boston C. of C., 1983; one of nine Photographic Masters, Boston U., prize for outstanding contbn. to pub. understanding of geology Am. Geol. inst., 1996, Discovery Lifetime award Royal Geog. Soc., 2000. Fellow Royal Geog. Soc. London (hon., Commonwealth award State of Mass. 1999), Harvard Travelers Club (Gold medal 1959), Nat. Geog. Soc. (with wife, Centennial award 1988), AAAS, Am. Acad. Arts and Scis., Am. Geog. Soc. (hon., major photographic exhibit for ann. conv. 1993-2007), Commercial Club, Harvard Varsity Club, St. Botolph Club (hon. life), Aero Club of New Eng. Club (hon.), Harvard Mountaineering Club (Cambridge, hon., past pres.), Am. Alpine Club (N.Y.C., hon.), Alpine Club (London, hon.), Sierra Club of San Francisco (hon.), Mountaineers Club (Seattle, hon.), Mountaineering of Alaska Club (hon.); hon. mem. several clubs. Achievements include leading 1st ascent Mt. Crillon, Alaska, 1934, Nat. Geog. Soc. Yukon Expdn., 1935; leading 1st aerial photog. exploration Mt. McKinley, 1936, ascending its summit, 1942, 47, 51; leading 1st aerial exploration St. Elias range, 1938; 1st ascents Mount Sanford and Mount Marcus Baker in Alaska, 1938, Mt. Lucania, Yukon, 1937, Mt. Bertha, Alaska, 1940, Mt. Hayes, Alaska, 1941; 1st ascent West side Mt. McKinley 1951; leader Nat. Geog. Soc. Mt. Everest mapping project, 1981-88; expdn. to S.E. Asia, guest Chinese Acad. Scis., met with King of Nepal, 1988; leader expdn. to Nepal, 1992; 1st laser-distance observation to summit of Mt. Everest, 1992; 50th trip to Alaska to open exhibit of own photos Anchorage Art Mus., 1993; 57th Alaska-Yukon trip on occasion of 60th anniversary of Lucania ascent, 1997. Home: Lexington, Mass. Died Jan. 10, 2007.

WATERS, JAMES LIPSCOMB, composer, music educator; b. Kyoto, June 11, 1930; came to U.S., 1932; s. George Lipscomb and Octavia (Clegg) W.; m. Ann Walkowski, Jan. 16, 1964; children: George, Helen, Robert. MusB, Westminster Choir Coll., 1952, MusM, 1953; student, Sorbonne, Paris, 1955-57; PhD, Eastman Sch. Music, 1967. Faculty Westminster Choir Coll., Princeton, N.J., 1957-68; prof. music Kent (Ohio) State U., from 1968. Composer: Goal, 1981, Songs of Life, 1983, Four Visions of War, 1985. Fellow NEA, 1979-80; Ohio Arts Council grantee, 1982-83. Mem. Am. Soc. Univ. Composers (regional chmn. 1982-83). Home: Kent, Ohio. Died July 26, 2006.

WATERS, RUSSEL DEAN, auto parts retail executive; b. Rock Springs, Wyo., Sept. 14, 1939; s. Cecil Bruce and Carmen Marcella (Aurberger) W.; m. Lavanetta Pearl Forbes, Sept. 20, 1960; children— Timothy M., Jackson B., Dale D., Jerry L. Student U.S. Navy Electronic Sch., 1958-59. Counterman Auto Parts Co., 1964-67; parts mgr. Whisler Chevrolet, 1967-69; mgr. Adams' Auto Supply, 1969-80; owner, mgr. Adams Big A Auto Parts, all Rock Springs, Wyo., 1980—; mem. dist. adv. bd. Big A Auto Parts System. Capt. Sweetwater County (Wyo.) Search and Rescue, 1973—; bd. dirs. Little League Baseball and Football, Babe Ruth Baseball, ARC, all Rock Springs. Served with USN, 1957-64; Cuba. Mem. Wyo. Peace Officers Assn. Democrat. Congregationalist. Clubs: Shriners, Masons, Order Eastern Star, Order Demolay (chmn. chpt.), Jobs Daus. (assoc. guardian). Home: Rock Springs, Wyo. Died July 23, 2006.

WATSON, ALONZO WALLACE, JR., lawyer; b. Salt Lake City, May 3, 1922; s. Alonzo Wallace and Lolita Byrd (Osbourn); m. Mary Louise Koch; children: Robert Wallace, Hillary Anne. BA, U. Utah, 1943, JD, 1951; BS in Fgn. Svc., Georgetown U., 1947; LLD (hon.), Westminster Coll., 1982. Bar: Utah 1951, Calif. 1956. Atty. tax div. Dept. Justice, Washington,

1952-55; atty. regional counsel's office IRS, San Francisco, 1955-56; atty. Gray, Cary, Ames & Frye, San Diego, 1956-57, Severson, Davis & Larson, San Francisco, 1957-59, Godfrey & Kahn, Milw., 1959-60; atty., pres. Ray, Quinney & Nebeker, Salt Lake City, from 1961. Corp. counsel, sec. 1st Security Corp., 1979—; sec., dir. Marriner S. Eccles Found., Salt Lake City, 1978—, George S. and Dolores D. Eccles Found., Salt Lake City, 1980—; bd. dirs. Nora Eccles Treadwell Found., Salt Lake City, 1980—. Trustee Westminster Coll., Salt Lake City, 1975—, chmn., 1977-80; bd. dirs., exec. com. Utah Symphony, Salt Lake City, 1979—; mem. nat. adv. com. U. Utah, Salt Lake City, 1985—. Mem. ABA, Utah State Bar Assn., Calif. State Bar Assn., Alta Club, Salt Lake Country Club. Episcopalian. Avocations: skiing, tennis, golf, swimming. Home: Salt Lake City, Utah. Died Oct. 24, 2005.

WATTENBERG, ALBERT, physicist, researcher; b. NYC, Apr. 13, 1917; s. Louis and Bella (Wolff) W.; m. Alice von Neumann, May 23, 1992; children from a previous marriage: Beth, Jill, Nina Diane. BS, Coll. City N.Y., 1938; MA, Columbia, 1939; PhD, U. Chgo., 1947. Spectroscopist Schenley Distilleries, NYC, 1939-42; physicist Manhattan Project, Metall. Lab., Chgo., 1942-46; group leader Argonne Nat. Lab., Chgo., 1946-50; asst. prof. U. Ill., Urbana, 1950-51, prof. physics, from 1958. Research physicist Mass. Inst. Tech., 1951-58 Recipient award for 1st nuclear reactor Am. Nuclear Soc., 1962; Nuclear Pioneer award Soc. Nuclear Medicine, 1977; NSF fellow U. Rome, 1962-63 Achievements include pioneering controlled nuclear reactor. Home: Champaign, Ill. Died June 27, 2007.

WAXMAN, DAVID, internist, consultant, academic administrator; b. Albany, NY, Feb. 7, 1918; s. Meyer and Fannie (Strosberg) W.; m. Jane Zabel; children: Gail, Michael, Dan, Ann, Steve, Abby. BS, Syracuse U., 1942, MD, 1950. Intern Grace Hosp., Detroit, 1950-51; resident in medicine, fellow in cardiology Kans. U. Med. Ctr., Kansas City, 1958-61, instr. internal medicine, 1961-64; asst. prof. internal medicine Kans. City Med. Ctr., 1964-69, assoc. prof., 1969-77, prof., from 1977, dir. dept. medicine outpatient service, 1970-74, asst. dean, 1970-71, assoc. dean for student affairs, 1971-72, dean of students, 1972-74, vice chancellor for students, 1974-76, vice chancellor, 1976-77, exec. vice chancellor, 1977-83, spl. cons. to chancellor for health affairs, 1983-94; ret. Nat. cons. to surgeon gen. USAF. Contbr. articles to med. jours. Mem. Kans. State Bd. Healing Arts, 1984-88. Maj. gen. USAFR ret. Decorated D.S.M., Legion of Merit with one oak leaf cluster. Fellow ACP, Alpha Omega Alpha; mem. Kans. Med. Soc., Soc. Med. Cons. to the Armed Forces. Home: Leawood, Kans. Died May 19, 2007.

WAYLETT, THOMAS ROBERT, management consultant executive; b. Toronto, Ont., Can., Apr. 27, 1941; s. Robert George and Frances Jean (Thomson) W.; m. Nancy Jean Parkinson, May 12, 1961 (div.); children: Cherie Lynne, Mathew; m. Karen P. Pritchard, Jan. 23, 1989. With Nat. Life, Imperial Life, Indsl. Life, Toronto; v.p. William M. Mercer Ltd., Toronto, 1966-75; dir. William M. Mercer, Inc., NYC, 1975-82; mng. dir. Marsh & McLennan Cos., NYC, 1982-91; exec. v.p. William M. Mercer Cos., NYC, from 1991; chmn. Mercer Mgmt. Consulting, Inc., NYC, from 1992. Bd. dirs. Nat. Econ. Rsch. Assocs., White Plains, N.Y., William M. Mercer Cos., Inc., N.Y.C. Home: Kiawah Island, SC. Died May 10, 2007.

WAYMAN, C(LARENCE) MARVIN, materials science and engineering educator, consultant; b. Wheeling, W.Va., Aug. 12, 1930; s. Clarence McColloch and Mary (Leach) W.; m. Patricia Smith, Jan. 28, 1956; children: Karen E., Stephen K. BS, Purdue U., 1952, MS, 1955; PhD, Lehigh U., 1957. 1st lt. USAF Materials Lab., Dayton, Ohio, 1952-54; asst. prof. U. Ill., Urbana, 1957-60, assoc. prof., 1960-64, prof. metallurgy mining engring., from 1964, head dept. metallurgy mining engring., 1986-87. Cons. Memry Corp., Stamford, Conn., 1986—, bd. dirs. 1986—; IBM, Poughkeepsie, N.Y., 1984-86, Eaton Corp., Milw., 1984—. Author: Martensitic Transformations, 1964; contbr. 325 sci. articles to profl. jours. Advisor Boy Scouts Am., 1973, coach Little League Baseball, Urbana, 1971-73. Recipient Eminent Faculty award Coll. Engring., U. Ill., 1991; Guggenheim fellow, 1969, Churchill Coll. fellow, 1969. Fellow Am. Soc. Metals (Zay Jeffries award 1977), AIME (Mathewson Gold medal 1981), Metall. Soc. AIME, Japan Soc. Promotion Sci.; mem. Materials Research Soc., Japan Inst. Metals. Clubs: Young Faculty Mens (Urbana) (pres. 1959-61). Republican. Presbyterian. Avocations: gardening, woodworking. Home: Urbana, Ill. Died July 29, 2007.

WEARN, WILSON CANNON, retired media executive; b. Newberry, SC, Oct. 7, 1919; s. George F. and Mary (Cannon) W.; m. Mildred Colson, Feb. 21, 1948; children: Jean Wearn Held, Joan Wearn Gilbert, Wilson Cannon Jr. B.E.E., Clemson U., 1941. Engr. Westinghouse Electric Corp., Pitts., 1941, FCC, Washington, 1946-48; assoc. cons. electronic engr. firm Weldon & Carr, Washington, 1948-50; ptnr. Vandivere, Cohen & Wearn (cons. engrs.), Washington, 1950-53; with Multimedia Broadcasting Co., Greenville, S.C., 1953-68, organizer of corp., 1953, became corp. officer, 1960, pres., 1966-77, Multimedia, Inc., Greenville, 1977-81, chief exec. officer, 1978-84, chmn. bd., 1981-89, chmn. emeritus Greenville, 1989-95. Instr. electronic engring. Clemson U., 1946. Mem. S.C. Hosp. Adv. Council, 1969-71; bd. dirs. Family and Children Service of Greenville County, 1967-69, pres., 1969; bd. dirs. Newspaper Advt. Bur., 1981-85; trustee Greenville Symphony Assn., 1960-62, 71-77, pres., 1977; trustee Greenville Hosp. System, 1964-70, chmn., 1968-70; trustee Broadcast Rating Council, 1969-73, chmn., 1971-73; trustee Clemson U. Found., 1973-79, pres., 1979; trustee Presbyn. Coll., F.W. Symmes Found. Served to capt. Signal Corps, AUS, 1941-45, PTO. Decorated Bronze Star; recipient Outstanding Alumni award Clemson U., 1972 Mem. Nat. Assn. Broadcasters (chmn. bd. 1975-77), S.C. Broadcasters Assn. (pres. 1967), Greater Greenville C. of C. (pres. 1972), Nat. Assn. Securities Dealers (bd. govs. 1985-88), Kiwanis (Greenville), Poinsett Club (Greenville), Augusta (Ga.) Nat. Golf Club. Presbyterian (elder). Home: Atlanta, Ga. Died May 27, 2007.

WEAVER, BRUCE EVERETT, osteopathic anesthesiologist; b. Amarillo, Tex., Mar. 5, 1935; s. James C. and Mayvi H. (Smith) W.; m. Barbara Ann Gillespie, June 24, 1961; children— James Laurie, Margaret Carey, Alicia Brooke. B.A., Baylor U., 1957; D.O., Kansas City Coll. of Osteo Medicine, 1969. Diplomate Nat. Bd. Examiners for Osteo Physicians and Surgeons; cert. Am. Osteo Bd. of Anesthesiology. Intern, Lakeside Osteo. Hosp., Kansas City, Mo., 1969-70; resident in anesthesiology, 1970-71; resident Kansas City Coll. of Osteo Medicine (Mo.), 1971-72, asst. prof., 1972-73; attending anesthesiologist St. Luke's Hosp., Kansas City, 1973-74, chief of cardiocascular anesthesiology, 1974-78; chief of cardiovascular anesthesia Boone County Hosp., Columbia, Mo., 1978—, vice chmn. dept. of anesthesia, 1981—. Mem. nat. faculty for advanced cardiac life support Am. Heart Assn., 1982—, mem. bd. dirs. Boone div. pres.-elect Kansas City chpt., 1978-79; deacon Baptist Ch., 1980—. Served with U.S. Army, 1957-59. Fellow Am. Osteo Coll. of Anestesiology (gov., v.p. 1982-83); mem. Am. Osteo Assn., Mo. Assn. Osteo. Physicians and Surgeons, Midwest Osteo. Soc. of Anesthesiologists, Am. Soc. Anesthesiologists, MidAm. Regional Council for Emergency Rescue, Republican. Died July 8, 2006.

WEAVER, DAVID, geography educator; b. Eng., Dec. 27, 1942; BA in geography, U. Manchester, UK, 1964; MA in geography, U. Fla., Gainsville, 1967, PhD in geography, 1972; MCP in city planning, Ga. Inst. Tech., Atlanta, 1980. Grad. rsch. asst. Caribbean Studies Program U. Fla., 1964—65, grad. tchg. asst. Dept. Geography, 1965—67, instr., 1969—70; asst. lectr. Dept. Geography U. Manchester, England, 1967—68; lectr. Dept. Geography U. Leicester, England, 1968—69; asst. prof. Dept. Geography West Ga. Coll., 1970—74, assoc. prof., 1974—77; assoc. prof. Dept. Geology and Geography U. Ala., Tuscaloosa, 1977—82, dir. Regional and Urban Planning Program, from 1979, prof. Dept. Geography, from 1982, chair Dept. Geography, 1987—2000. Dir. Map Libr. U. Ala., Tuscaloosa, 1984—87. Recipient Disting. Tchr. Coll/Univ. award Nat. Coun. for Geog. Edn., 1992. Died Apr. 3, 2006.

WEAVER, DAVID LEO, physicist, educator; b. Albany, NY, Apr. 18, 1937; s. Benjamin Patrick and Dorothy Virginia (Waterman) W.; m. Elena Bonelli, July 16, 1966; children: Christopher, Timothy, Ashley. BS in Chemistry, Rensselaer Poly. Inst., 1958; PhD in Chemistry and Physics, Iowa State U., 1963. Research asst. Iowa State U., Ames, 1958-62, research assoc., 1963-64; asst. prof. Tufts U., Medford, Mass., 1964-69, assoc. prof., 1969-77, prof., from 1977. Vis. scientist CERN, Geneva, 1965-66, 67, 69; research assoc. U. Rome, 1968-69; cons. sci. research council Daresbury Nuclear Physics Lab. Univ. Coll., London, 1971; vis. scientist Chemistry Dept. Harvard U., 1972; cons. Lab. Chem. Biology Nat. Inst. Arthritis, Metabolism and Digestive Diseases NIH, Bethesda, Md., 1974; vis. scientist MRC Lab. Molecular Biology, Cambridge, Eng., 1977, Lab. Molecular Biophysics, Oxford, Eng., 1977; sr. research assoc. NRC-NASA Ames Research Ctr., 1981-82; hon. research fellow Lab. Molecular Biophysics Dept. Crystallography Birkbeck Coll., London, 1985-86. Contbr. articles to profl. jours. Fellow Am. Phys. Soc.; mem. AAAS, Molecular Graphics Soc., Sigma Xi, Phi Lambda Upsilon. Died Apr. 4, 2006.

WEBBER, ROBERT EUGENE, theology educator; b. Stouchburg, Pa., Nov. 27, 1933; s. Chester R. and Harriet B. (Russell) W.; m. Dawn McCollum, June 21, 1964 (div. Apr. 1977); children: John, Alexandra, Stephanie; m. Joanne Lindsell, May 4, 1978. BA, Bob Jones U., 1956; BD, Reformed Episcopal Sem., Phila., 1959; ThM, Covenant Theol. Sem., St. Louis, 1960; ThD, Concordia Theol. Sem., St. Louis, 1968. Prof. theology Wheaton (Ill.) Coll., 1968—2000; dir. worship & spirituality program Northern Baptist Theological Seminary, Lombard, 2000—07. Founder, pres. Inst. Worship Studies, 1991-2007, Robert E. Webber Inst. for Worship Studies, Orange Park, Fla., 1998-2007 Author: Common Roots, 1978, The Secular Saint, 1980, The Moral Majority, 1980, Worship Old and New, 1982, The Church in the World, 1985, The Majestic Tapestry, 1985, The Book of Family Prayer, 1985, Celebrating Our Faith, 1986, People of the Truth, 1988, Evangelicals on the Canterbury Trail, 1989, What Christians Believe, 1990, Worship Is a Verb, 1991, Signs of Wonder, 1991. Mem. N.Am. Acad. Liturgy. Episcopalian. Home: Wheaton, Ill. Died Apr. 27, 2007.

WEBBER, ROLLAND LLOYD, state legislator; b. Doylestown, Ohio, Apr. 28, 1932; s. Leland Leon and Stella (Fielder) W.; m. Betty Barbara Ball, 1952; children: Rickey Leon, Jeffrey Allen. Grad., Anderson H.S., 1950. Formerly rep. employee health and safety Delco-Remy divsn. GMC; mem. from 37th dist. Ind. Ho. of Reps., from 1984. Chmn. labor com.; mem. elections and apportionment, ethics, pub. policy, vet. affairs, urban affairs, aged and aging coms. Dem. precinct committeeman, Anderson, Ind., 1974—; ward chmn. Anderson City Dem. Com., 1982-84. Mem. Eagles, Am. Legion, Amvets. Home: Anderson, Ind. Died Nov. 2, 2006.

WEBER, EUGEN, historian, educator, writer; b. Bucharest, Romania, Apr. 24, 1925; arrived in U.S., 1955; s. Emanuel and Sonia (Garrett) Weber; m. Jacqueline Brument-Roth, June 12, 1950. Student, Inst. d'études politiques, Paris, 1948-49, 51-52; BA, Emmanuel Coll., 1950; MA, Emmanuel Coll., Cambridge U., 1954, M.Litt., 1956; D of Humanities, Occidental Coll., LA, 2006. History supr. Emmanuel Coll., 1953—54; lectr. U. Alta., 1954—55; asst. prof. U. Iowa, 1955—56; from asst. prof. history to prof. UCLA, 1956—84, Joan Palevsky prof. modern European history, 1984—2007, chmn. dept., 1965—68; dir. study center U. Calif., France, 1968—70; dean social scis. UCLA, 1976—77, dean Coll. Letters and Scis., 1977—82. Frum Meml. lectr. Toronto U., 1999; Ford faculty lectr. Stanford U., 1965; Patten lectr. Ind. U., 1981; vis. prof. Collège de France, Paris, 1983; dir. d'études Ecole des hautes études, Paris, 1984—85; Christian Gauss lectr. Princeton U., 1990. Author: Nationalist Revival in France, 1959, The Western Tradition, 1959, Paths to the Present, 1960, Action Francaise: Royalism and Reaction in Twentieth-Century France, 1962, Satan Franc-Maçon, 1964, Varieties of Fascism, 1964; author: (with H. Rogger) The European Right, 1965; author: A Modern History of Europe, 1970, Europe Since 1715, 1972, Peasants Into Frenchmen: The Modernization of Rural France, 1880-1914, 1976 (Commonwealth prize Calif., 1977), La Fin des Terroirs, 1983 (Prix de la Société des gens de lettres, 1984), France Fin-de-siècle, 1986 (Commonwealth prize Calif., 1987), The Western Tradition (WGBH/PBS TV Series), 1989, My France, 1990, Movements, Currents, Trends, 1991, The Hollow Years: France in the 1930s, 1994, La France des annèes trente, 1995, Prix M. Baumont, 1995, Prix Etats-Unis/France, 1995, Prix de l'Academie des Jeux Floraux, 1997, Apocalypses, 1999; adv. editor: Jour. Contemporary History, 1966—2005, French History, from 1985, French Cultural Studies, from 1990, Am. Scholar, 1992—98, Nuova Storia Contemporanea, from 1999. Capt. Brit. Army, 1943—47. Decorated Ordre Nat. des Palmes Académiques, France; recipient Luckman Disting. Tchg. award, UCLA Alumnae Assn., 1992; fellow, Fulbright Found., 1952, Rsch. fellow, Am. Philos. Soc., 1959, Am. Coun. Learned Soc., 1962, Guggenheim fellow, 1963—64, sr. fellow, NEH, 1973—74, 1982—83; grantee, Social Sci. Rsch. Coun., 1959—61; Fulbright fellow, 1982—83. Fellow: Am. Philos. Soc., Am. Acad. Arts and Scis., Netherlands Inst. Advanced Studies, Assn. Française de Sci. Politique; mem.: Soc. French Hist. Studies, Soc. d'histoire moderne, Am. Hist. Assn. (scholarly distinction award 1999), Phi Beta Kappa (hon.; senator 1988—2000, Ralph Waldo Emerson prize 1977). Home: Los Angeles, Calif. Died May 17, 2007.

WEBER, JULIAN L., retired lawyer, former publishing and entertainment company executive; b. Des Moines, July 19, 1929; s. Milton and Zelda (Robinson) W.; m. Idelle Feinberg, Apr. 17, 1957; children— Jonathan Todd, Suzanne. BA, UCLA, 1951; JD, Harvard U., 1955. Bar: N.Y. 1956. Partner Botein Hays & Sklar, 1964-79; pres. Nat. Lampoon, Inc., NYC, 1979-84; pvt. practice law NYC, from 1984. Dir. Viaweb, Inc., 1995—. Mem. ABA, Assn. of Bar of City of N.Y. Died Aug. 20, 2006.

WEBER, WALTER JACOB, JR., engineering educator; b. Pitts., June 16, 1934; Sc.B., Brown U., 1956; MSE., Rutgers U., 1959; A.M., Harvard, 1961, PhD, 1962. Registered profl. engr. Diplomate Am. Acad. Environ. Engrs. Engr. Caterpillar Tractor Co., Peoria, Ill., 1956-57; instr. Rutgers U., 1957-59; engr. Soil Conservation Service, New Brunswick, N.J., 1957-59; research, teaching asso. Harvard, 1959-63; faculty U. Mich., Ann Arbor, from 1963, prof., chmn. water resources program, 1968-91, The Earnest Boyce Disting. Prof. of Engring., 1987-94, The Gordon Maskew Fair and Earnest Boyce Disting. U. Prof. Ann Arbor, from 1994; dir. Inst. Environ. Scis., Engring. & Tech. Great Lakes & Mid-Atlantic Hazardous Substance Rsch. Ctr. Internat. cons. to industry, govt. Author: (with K.H. Mancy) Analysis of Industrial Wastewaters, 1971, Physicochemical Processes for Water Quality Control, 1972, (with F.A. DiGiano) Process Dynamics in Environmental Systems, 1996, Environmental Systems and Processes-Principles, Modeling and Design, 2001; editor, author: (with E. Matijevic) Adsorption from Aqueous Solution, 1968; contbr. numerous articles and chpts. to tech. and profl. jours. and books. Recipient Disting. Faculty awards U. Mich., 1967, 78, Rsch. Excellence award, 1980, Stephen S. Attwood award, 1977; Disting. Faculty award Mich. chpt. Assn. Gov. Bds. of State Univs., 1989; Disting. Scientist award U.S. EPA, 1991; Athalie Richardson Irvine Clarke prize Nat. Water Rsch. Inst., 1996. Mem. NAE, Am. Acad. Environ. Engrs. (Diplomate 1975, Gordon Maskew Fair award, 1995), Am. Chem. Soc. (cert. of merit 1962, F.J. Zimmerman award 1982), Am. Inst. Chem. Engrs., ASCE (Rudolph Hering medal 1980, Thomas R. Camp award 1982, Simon W. Freese award 1984, G. Brooks Earnest award 1985), Am. Water Works Assn. (life, Acad. Achievement awards 1981, 89, A.P. Black Rsch. award 1991), Assn. Environ. Engring. Profs. (Disting. Faculty award 1968, NALCO rsch. award 1979, Engring. Sci. rsch. award 1984, Outstanding Publ. award 1989, Disting. Lectr. award 1990), Internat. Assn. for Water Pollution Rsch. and COntrol (Founders Outstanding Publ. award 1987, 92), Water Pollution Control Fedn. (John R. Rumsey Meml. award 1975, Willard F. Shepard award 1980, Thomas R. Camp medal 1988, Gordon Maskew Fair medal 1990), Tau Beta Pi, Sigma Xi, Chi Epsilon, Delta Omega. Home: Ann Arbor, Mich. Died Jan. 13, 2006.

WEBSTER, EDWARD WILLIAM, physicist; b. London, Apr. 12, 1922; came to U.S., 1949, naturalized, 1957; s. Edward and Bertha Louisa (Cornish) W.; m. Irene Ruth Henry, June 4, 1950 (dec. 1958); m. Dorothea Anne Wood, June 24, 1961; children: John, Peter, Anne, Edward, Mark, Susan. BSc in Elec. Engring., U. London, 1943, PhD, 1946; postgrad., MIT, 1949-51, 65-66, Columbia U., 1966; AM (hon.), Harvard U., 1989. Diplomate in radiol. physics Am. Bd. Radiology, examiner 1958-84, chmn. physics com. 1966-76; diplomate Am. Bd. Health Physics. Research engr. English Electric Co., Stafford, Eng., 1945-49; travelling fellow lab. for nuclear sci. MIT, 1949-50, staff scientist, 1950-51; lectr. U. London, 1952-53; physicist Mass. Gen. Hosp., Boston, 1953-2000, chief radiol. scis. div., 1970-2000; prof. radiology Harvard U. Med. Sch., Boston, 1975-92, prof. emeritus, from 1992; prof. radiology div. health scis. and tech. Harvard-MIT, 1978-86. Mem. com. on dose distbns. of high energy radiation beams for cancer therapy Internat. Atomic Energy Agy., Vienna, Austria, 1960-64; mem. com. radiology NAS, 1962-68; mem. com. on planning radiotherapy facilities, WHO, Geneva, Switzerland, 1964, Radiological Health Study section, U.S. Environ. Control Adminstrn., 1969-72, biol. effects of ionizing radiation com. NAS, 1977-80, oversight com. on Radioepidemiologic Tables, NAS, 1983-84; adv. com. on environ. hazards VA, 1985-95, Med. Use of Isotopes, U.S. Nuclear Regulatory Commn., 1971-93; U.S. del. UN Sci. Com. on Effects of Atomic Radiation, 1987-97; sec.-gen. 2d Internat. Conf. Med. Physics, Boston, 1966-69; lectr. Harvard Sch. Pub. Health, 1971-86; Garland lectr. Calif. Radiol. Soc., 1980; cons. Radiation Effects Rsch. Found., Hiroshima, Japan, 1988; Adams lectr. U Okla. Med. Ctr., 1989; Langham lectr. U. Ky. Coll. Medicine, 1989; Taylor lectr. Nat. Coun. on Radiation Protection, 1992, mem., 1965-89, hon. mem., 1989—, cons. Presdl. Adv. Com. on Human Radiation Experiments, 1994-95. Author: A Basic Radioisotopes Course, 1959, Atlas of Radiation Dose Distributions, 1965, Physics in Diagnostic Radiology, 1970; co-author: Instrumentation and Monitoring Methods for Radiation Protection, 1978, Low-level Radiation Effects, 1982; coeditor: Advances in Medical Physics, 1971, Biological Risks of

Medical Irradiations, 1980; inventor composite shields against low energy X-rays, 1970. Robert Blair travelling fellow London County Council, 1949; USPHS fellow, 1965-66; NIH grantee, 1958-80. Fellow Health Physics Soc. (Landauer award 1985, Failla award 1989), Am. Coll. Radiology (commn. mem. 1963-93, Gold medal 1991), Am. Assn. Physicists in Medicine (founding mem., dir. 1958-65, pres. 1963-64, Coolidge medal 1983); mem. Soc. Nuclear Medicine (trustee 1973-77), Radiol. Soc. N.Am. (v.p. 1977-78), New Eng. Roentgen Ray Soc. (hon., exec. com. 1976-77), Radiation Rsch. Soc., Sigma Xi (nat. lectr. 1988-89). Home: Bedford, Mass. Died Dec. 17, 2005.

WEBSTER, EDWIN HENRY, steel company executive; b. Hulmeville, Pa., Feb. 7, 1918; s. Jesse Gilbert and May Flowers (Hibbs) W.; m. Mildred Theresa Matthews, Feb. 16, 1948; children: Marian Webster Olson, Jes Gilbert. BSC.E., U. Pa., 1939. Registered profl. engr., Pa. Engr., draftsman Am. Bridge-Dravo, Trenton, N.J., Pitts., 1939-43; v.p. Luria Engring. Corp., Behelehm, Pa., 1947-56; exec. v.p. Whitehead & Kales Co. (river Rouge), Mich., 1956-74; chmn., chief exec. officer Carolina Steel Corp., Greensboro, N.C., from 1974; pres. W & K Erectors, River Rouge, 1964-74, W & k Engrs., River Rouge, 1964-74. Dir. Greenville Machinery Corp., S.C., 1978-73 Served to lt. USN, 1943-47. Fellow ASCE; mem. Am. Inst. Steel Constrn. (pres. 1970-71), NAM (regional v.p. 1979-82) Clubs: Country (Greenboro, N.C.). Lodges: Masons. Republican. Presbyterian. Home: Winthrop, Wash. Died Apr. 17, 2006.

WECHSLER, EDWARD CHARLES, school administrator; b. N.Y.C., Nov. 4, 1946; s. Morris and Rose (Barbers) W. B.A., Fla. So. Coll., 1968; M.A., U. Fla., 1972. Tchr. Duval Dist. Schs., Jacksonville, Fla., 1968-73, asst. prin., 1973-80, vice prin., 1980-81, prin., 1981—. Contbr. articles to profl. jours. Recipient Asst. Adminstr. of Yr. award Duval County Assn. Secondary Sch. Adminstrs., 1981. Mem. Duval County Assn. Secondary Sch. Adminstrs. (bd. dirs. 1973-74, 84-85), Fla. Assn. Sch. Adminstrs., Nat. Assn. Secondary Sch. Adminstrs., Duval County Jr. High Athletic Assn. (sec. 1981-82, v.p. 1982-83, pres. 1984-85). Home: Jacksonville, Fla. Died Sept. 8, 2006.

WEICHSEL, HANS MILTON, JR., retired helicopter company executive; b. St. Louis, Aug. 25, 1919; s. Hans and Alice (Knapp) W.; m. Gillette Spencer, Oct. 15, 1949; children— Hans Bradley, Alice Linda, Herbert Spencer. BS, U. Mich., 1943. Registered profl. engr., Tex. Flight research engr., pilot Cornell Research Labs., 1943-50; with Bell Helicopter Co., Ft. Worth, from 1950, v.p., 1961-70, v.p. marketing and logistics, 1970-72, sr. v.p., 1972-85. Contbr. articles to profl. jours., also articles on canoeing. Past chmn. bd. trustees, bd. dirs. Selwyn Internat. Coll. Prep. Sch.; bd. dirs. Southwest Outward Bound. Recipient Congl. citation for helicopter contbn. to Vietnam War, 1965 Fellow Am. Helicopter Soc. (hon., past nat. dir., past nat. sec.); asso. fellow Am. Inst. Aeros. and Astronautics; mem. Assn. U.S. Army (pres. Ft. Worth chpt. 1971-72), Soc. Logistics Engrs. (sr. mem.), Quiet Birdmen, Twirlybirds, U. Mich. Alumni Assn., Army Aviation Assn., Am. Whitewater Assn., Alpha Delta Phi. Clubs: Sierra, Ozark Wilderness Waterway; Ridglea Country (Ft. Worth); University (Washington). Home: Fort Worth, Tex. Died Mar. 13, 2007.

WEIDNER, EDWARD WILLIAM, retired academic administrator, political scientist; b. Mpls., July 7, 1921; s. Peter Clifford and Lillian (Halbe) W.; m. Jean Elizabeth Blomquist, Mar. 23, 1944 (dec. Apr., 1997); children: Nancy Louise, Gary Richard (dec.), Karen, William; m. Marjorie M. Fermanich, June 6, 1998. BA magna cum laude, U. Minn., 1942, MA, 1943, PhD, 1946; postgrad., U. Wis., 1943-45; LHD (hon.), No. Mich. U., 1969; PhD (hon.), Linköping U., Sweden, 1975. Staff mem. Nat. Mcpl. League, 1944, research assoc., 1944-45; cons. govts. div. U.S. Bur. Census, 1945, statistician Washington, 1946; lectr. U. Wis., Madison, 1945; instr. U. Minn., Mpls., 1945-47, asst. prof., 1947-49, asst. dir. research in inter-govtl. relations, 1946-53; asst. prof. UCLA, 1949-50; faculty Mich. State U., East Lansing, 1950-62, from assoc. prof., dir. govtl. research bur., to prof. polit. sci., 1952-62, chmn. polit. sci. dept., 1952-57; coordinator, chief adviser Vietnam Project, 1955-57; dir. Inst. Research on Overseas Programs, 1957-61; sr. scholar E.W. Ctr., 1961—62, vice chancellor, 1962—65; prof. polit. sci., dir. ctr. for devel. change U. Ky., Lexington, 1965-67; chancellor U. Wis., Green Bay, 1966-86, prof. polit. sci., 1966-89, chancellor emeritus, prof. emeritus, 1989—2007, dir. Cofrin Arboretum, 1986-89. Planning dir. Weidner Ctr. for the Performing Arts, 1987-93; bd. dirs. Univ. Bank, Green Bay; cons. Fgn. Ops. Adminstrn., Vietnam, 1954-55, Baltimore County (Md.) Reorgn. Commn., 1953-54, Ford Found., Pakistan, 1956, Nat. Assn. Fgn. Student Advisers, 1959-60, Pres.'s Task Force Fgn. Econ. Assistance, 1961, Dept. State, 1962-63, AID, 1964-65, Lees Coll., 1971-72, Green Bay Bot. Garden, 1997-98; mem. Gov. Mich. Commn. Inter-Govtl. Rels., 1954-55. Author: (with William Anderson) American Government, 1951, State and Local Government, 1951, (with others) The International Programs of American Universities, 1958, Intergovernmental Relations as Seen by Public Officials, 1960, (with William Anderson, Clara Penniman) Government for the Fifty States, 1960, The World Role of Universities, 1962, Technical Assistance in Public Administration Overseas, 1964; editor: Development Administration in Asia, 1970. Mem. Wis. Gov.'s Commn. on UN, 1975-81; trustee Prairie Sch., 1969-91, mem. adv. bd., 1991-2006; bd. dirs. Inst. for Shipboard Edn., 1976-89; mem. Lab. Ornithology, Cornell U., bd. dirs. 1989-98; chmn. adv. bd. Lakeland chpt. ARC, 1981-84; mem. N.Am. adv. group UN Environ. Programme, 1983-90; bd. advisers Nature Conservancy Wis., 1984-91; bd. dirs. Heritage Hill Found., 1987-92, 95-97, pres. 1991-92; bd. dirs. Assn. Am. Colls., 1978-80, Brown County, Family Svc. Assn., 1988-93; chmn. Brown County Cultural Coun., 1991-94; mem. nat. coun. ASPA, 1947-50; mem. internat. coun. UN U., 1974-80; bd. dirs. Am. Coun. on Edn., 1971-74, sec. bd., 1971-72; mem. nat. coun. Am. Polit. Assn., 1950-52. Recipient Outstanding Achievement award U. Minn., 1975. Mem. Wis. Soc. Ornithology, Wilderness Soc., World Wildlife Fund, Interfaith Alliance, Common Cause, Nature Conservancy, Audubon Soc., Am. Birding Assn., Green Bay Area C. of C. (bd. dirs. 1970-74), Mcpl. Clks. Edn. Found. (bd. dirs. 1980-97), Phi Beta Kappa, Pi Sigma Alpha. Home: Green Bay, Wis. Died June 6, 2007.

WEIN, JOSEPH ALEXANDER, lawyer; b. Montreal, Que., Can., June 4, 1931; s. Jacob and Eugenia (Szour) W.; m. Libby Wein, June 23, 1957; children— Michele G., Paul F. A.A., UCLA, 1950, B.A., 1952, J.D., 1955. Bar: Calif. 1956. Assoc. Buchalter Nemer Fields Chrystie & Younger, Los Angeles, 1962-68, ptnr., 1968—, also pres., chief fin. officer, mng. ptnr.; chmn. panel prejudgment remedies Western Regional Comml. Law League Am., 1976. Mem. ABA, Internat. Bar Assn., Fin. Lawyers Conf., Nat. Comml. Fin. Conf., Los Angeles County Bar Assn., Comml. Law League Am., UCLA Sch. Law Alumni Assn. (founder 1981). Home: Los Angeles, Calif. Died Jan. 22, 2006.

WEINHAUER, WILLIAM GILLETTE, retired bishop; b. NYC, Dec. 3, 1924; s. Nicholas Alfred and Florence Anastacia (Davis) W.; m. Jean Roberta Shanks, Mar. 20, 1948; children: Roberta Lynn, Cynthia Anne, Doris Jean. BS, Trinity Coll., Hartford, Conn., 1948; MDiv, Gen. Theol. Sem., 1951, STM, 1956, ThD, 1970. Ordained to ministry Episcopal Ch., 1951. Pastor Episcopal parishes Diocese N.Y., 1951-56; prof. N.T. St. Andrews Theol. Sem., Manila, Philippines, 1956-60; asst. prof. N.T. Gen. Theol. Sem., 1961-71; rector Christ Ch., Poughkeepsie, N.Y., 1971-73; bishop Episcopal Diocese of Western N.C., Black Mountain, 1973-90, ret., 1990. Vis. prof. religion Western Carolina U., Cullowhee, N.C., 1991-98; adj. faculty Seabury-Western Theol. Sem., Evanston, Ill., 19991-94. Served with USN, 1943-46. Mem. Soc. Bibl. Lit. Episcopalian. Home: Asheville, NC. Died Jan. 26, 2007.

WEINSTEIN, GEORGE WILLIAM, retired ophthalmology educator; b. East Orange, NJ, Jan. 26, 1935; s. Henry J. and Irma C. (Klein) W.; m. Sheila Valerie Wohlreich, June 20, 1957; children: Bruce David, Elizabeth Joyce, Rachel Andrea. AB, U. Pa., 1955; MD, SUNY, Bklyn., 1959. Diplomate Am. Bd. Ophthalmology (bd. dirs. 1981-89). Intern then resident in ophthalmology Kings County Hosp., Bklyn., 1959-63; asst. prof. ophthalmology Johns Hopkins U., Balt., 1967-70; head ophthalmology dept. U. Tex., San Antonio, 1970-80; prof., Jane McDermott Shott chmn. W.Va. U., Morgantown, 1980-95, ret., 1999. Author: Key Facts in Ophthalmology, 1984; editor: Open Angle Glaucoma, 1986; editor Ophthalmic Surgery jour., 1971-81, Current Opinion in Ophthalmology jour., 1988—; contbr. articles to profl. jours. Served to lt. comdr. USPHS, 1963-65. Sr. Internat. fellow Fogarty Internat. Ctr. NIH, 1987. Mem. ACS (bd. govs. 1983-85, bd. regents 1987-92), Assn. Univ. Profs. Ophthalmology (pres. 1986-87, exec. v.p. 1994), Am. Acad. Ophthalmology (bd. dirs. 1980-92, chmn. long range planning com. 1986-89, pub. and profl. sec. 1983-89, pres.-elect 1990, pres. 1991, Honor award, Sr. Honor award), Alpha Omega Alpha (faculty 1987), Am. Ophthalmology Soc. (coun. 1992-97, chair 1996-97). Jewish. Avocations: jazz, banjo, photography, tennis, reading. Home: New York, NY. Died May 12, 2007.

WEINSTEIN, SIDNEY TOM, retired military officer; b. Camden, NJ, 1934; m. Pauline Weinstein; children: Halee, Mila, Michael. BS in Mil. Engring., U.S. Mil. Acad., 1956; MS in Bus. Adminstrn., U. Rochester, 1970; PhD (hon.), Def. Intelligence Coll. Commd. lt. U.S. Army, 1956, advanced through grades to comdr., 1981, dep. comdr. intelligence & security commd., 1980—81, comdr. intelligence ctr. & sch., 1981—84, dep. chief of staff intelligence, 1984—89, ret., 1989; sr. v.p. Electronic Warfare Assoc., Inc., Herndon, Va., from 1989. Decorated Disting. Svc. medal, Legion of Merit, Meritorious Svc. medal, Air medal; named to Mil. Intelligence Hall of Fame. Died May 24, 2007.

WEISS, ALLAN JOSEPH, transport company executive, lawyer; b. Boston, Nov. 1, 1932; s. Mark and Eve S. (Kane) Weiss; m. Sherrill Roecker, Feb. 18, 1973 (dec. Jan. 2004); children: Stephanie Eve, Mark Allan. BS, U.S. Mcht. Marine Acad., 1955; JD, Cornell U., 1961. Bar: N.Y. 1961, D.C. 1962, Calif. 1965, U.S. Supreme Ct. 1965. Trial atty. admiralty and shipping U.S. Dept. Justice, 1961-67, chief trial atty. admiralty office San Francisco, 1967-74; Pacific counsel Sea-Land Service, Inc., Oakland, Calif., 1974-76, dep. gen. counsel, 1977-78, gen. counsel, 1978-82, sec., 1979-82; assoc. gen. counsel Sea-Land Industries, 1979-82; pres. Freights Unltd., Inc., from 1982; gen. counsel Toledo, Peoria & Western Rwy., 1991-96. Adj. prof. law McGeorge Sch. Law, 1974-76 Served with U.S. Navy, 1956-57. Mem. Fed. Bar Assn., Calif. Bar Assn., D.C. Bar Assn., San Francisco Bar Assn., Maritime Law Assn. U.S., Cornell U. Law Assn., Kings Point Alumni Assn. Home: Martinsville, NJ. Died Sept. 27, 2006.

WEISS, WILLIAM, retired medical educator; b. Phila., July 30, 1919; s. William and Anna (Grossman) Weiss; m. Esther E. Sabul, June 22, 1941 (dec. 1990); children: Winifred A., Seth S., Deborah E. BA, U. Pa., 1940, MD, 1944. Clin. dir. pulmonary disease svc. Phila. Gen. Hosp., 1950—74; chest cons. Norristown State Hosp., Pa., 1951—60; dir. Pulmonary Neoplasm Rsch. Project, Phila., 1957—67; faculty U. Pa. Grad. Sch. Medicine, Phila., 1952—66, Med. Coll. Pa., Phila., 1952—86; from assoc. prof. to prof. medicine Med. Coll. Pa., Hahnemann U., Phila., 1966—84; prof. emeritus Drexel U., Phila., from 1984. Cons. to various indsl. cos. Pa., NJ, 1962—2002. Author: (novel) Khaki in a Long White Coat, 2002; editor: Phila. Medicine, 1976—99; mem. editl. bd.: Arch. Environ. Health, 1968—86; contbr. more than 229 articles to profl. jours., more than 125 editls. to profl. jours., 18 chpts. to books. Bd. dirs. Am. Cancer Soc., Phila., 1980—86; cons. on asbestos Bd. Edn., Phila., 1983; mem. EPA Sci. Rev. Panel for Health Rsch., Washington, 1980—81; mem. toxic/health effects adv. com. Pa. Dept. Health, 1985—87. Capt. USAF, 1953—55. Recipient Ann. Sci. award, Phila. divsn. Am. Cancer Soc., 1979. Fellow: ACP, Am. Coll. Occupl. and Eviron. Medicine (merit in authorship award 1974, 1985), Coll. Physicians Phila.; mem.: AMA, Phila. County Med. Soc. (Strittmatter award 1991, Gold medal), Pa. Med. Soc., Am. Thoracic Soc., Phila. Occupl. Med. Assn. (pres. 1980—81), Laennec Soc. Phila. (pres. 1970). Avocation: classical music. Home: Philadelphia, Pa. Died Mar. 8, 2007.

WEISSBARD, SAMUEL HELD, lawyer; b. NYC, Mar. 3, 1947; children: Andrew Joshua, David S. BA, Case Western Res. U., 1967; JD with highest honors, George Washington U., 1970. Bar: D.C. 1970, U.S. Supreme Ct. 1974, Calif. 1998. Assoc. Fried, Frank, Harris, Shriver & Kampelman, 1970-73, Arent, Fox, Kintner, Plotkin & Kahn, 1973-78; prin. Weissbard & Fields, P.C., 1978-83; shareholder, v.p. Wilkes, Artis, Hedrick & Lane, Washington, 1983-86; ptnr. Foley & Lardner, Washington, 1986-97, LA, 1997-98, co-chair creditors' rights workout and bankruptcy group Washington, 1992-95; sr. counsel Cox, Castle & Nicholson, L.L.P., Newport Beach, Calif., 1998—2001; exec. v.p., gen. counsel Makar Properties, LLC, Newport Beach, from 2001. Editor in chief George Washington U. Law Rev., 1969-70. Bd. dirs. Luther Rice Soc., George Washington U., 1985-87, Atlanta Coll. Art, 1993, Nat. Learning Ctr., 1993-96, Georgetown Arts Commn. and gen. counsel 1995-96; Chmn. steering com. of Lawyer's Alliance for Nat. Learning Ctr. and Capital Children's Mus., 1989-90; mem. steering com. DC/NLC Don't Drop Out Campaign, 1992,93, bd. dirs., 1994-96; devel. com. Shelter for the Homeless, 1998-99. Recipient John Bell Larner medal, 1970. Mem. ABA, D.C. Bar, Calif. Bar Assn., Orange County Bar Assn., Georgetown Bus. and Profl. Assn. (bd. dirs. 1993-96, sec., gen. counsel 1993-96), Orange County Bus. Assn. (legis. com. 1998-99), Order of Coif. Home: Newport Beach, Calif. Died Sept. 2, 2006.

WEISSMAN, JACOB IRA, economics educator; b. Detroit, Dec. 14, 1913; s. Samuel and Ida (Goldberg) W.; m. Shirley Weissman; 1 son from previous marriage, Stephen. AB, U. Mich., 1935, JD, 1936; PhD, U. Calif., Berkeley, 1956. Gen. mgr. N.Y. Bed Spring Co., Detroit, 1937-47; instr. econs. Columbia, 1950-56; research assoc. in law and econs. Law Sch. U. Chgo., 1956-58, assoc. prof. Bus. Sch., 1958-63; prof. econs., chmn. econs. dept. Hofstra U., Hempstead, N.Y., from 1963, dean Sch. Bus., 1982-83. Author: Law in a Business Society, 1964. Bd. dirs. Jewish Community Center, Jewish Social Service Bur. Mem. Am. Econ. Assn., State Bar Mich., Order of Coif, Phi Beta Kappa, Phi Kappa Phi. Died July 11, 2006.

WEISSMAN, SAMUEL ISAAC, chemistry educator; b. South Bend, Ind., June 25, 1912; married 1943; two children. BS, U. Chgo., 1933, PhD in Phys. Chemistry, 1938, U. Siena, 1986, Washington U., 1988. Fellow U. Chgo., 1939-41, NRC, U. Calif., 1941-42; rsch. chemist Manhattan Project, Calif., 1942-43, N.Mex., 1943-46; asst. prof., then assoc. prof. Washington U., St. Louis, 1946-55, prof., 1955-80, emeritus prof. chemistry, 1980—2007. Mem. Am. Chem. Soc. Died June 12, 2007.

WEITZER, BERNARD, telecommunications executive; b. Bronx, NY, Sept. 22, 1929; s. Morris R. and Eva (Kurtz) W.; m. Anne DeHaven Jones, Nov. 5, 1982. BS, CCNY, 1950; MS, NYU, 1951, postgrad., 1951-54. Mgr., asst. v.p. systems engring and analysis Western Union Telegraph Co., Upper Saddle River, N.J., 1966-71, v.p. engring. and computer systems, 1976-85, sr. v.p. ops., 1985-90; cons. pvt. practice, Fort Lee, N.J., from 1990; exec. v.p., gen. mgr. Western Union Teleprocessing Industries, Inc., Mahwah, N.J., 1971-76. Dir. U.S. Telecomm. Tng. Inst.; mem. adv. com. TV comm. U.S. Info. Agy. Pres. Ft. Lee Bd. Edn.; pres., bd. trustees Ft. Lee Pub. Libr. Served to lt. U.S. Army, 1954-57. Mem. Chaines des Rotisseurs, Internat. Wine Food Soc. Home: New York, NY. Died Jan. 4, 2006.

WELCH, WILLIAM HENRY, oil service company executive, consultant; b. Pharr, Tex., Nov. 24, 1929; married. AA, Edinburg Jr. Coll., Tex., 1949; BS, Trinity U., 1951. Sales engr. NL Baroid div. NL Industries, Inc., Liberty, Tex., 1955-58, dist. mgr. Liberty, Alvin (Tex.), New Orleans, Ardmore (Okla.), 1958-65, gen. mgr. Baroid de Venezuela Marcaibo, 1965-69, mgr. Latin Am. ops. Baroid Internat. Houston, 1969-71, mgr. Latin Am. ops., 1971-74, dir. internat. drilling svcs. NL Baroid div., 1974-77, pres. NL Atlas Bradford, 1977-81; sr. v.p. NL Ind., 1981; pres. NL Oilfield Svcs. NL Industries, Inc., 1981-83, pres. NL Baroid, 1983-86, pres., chief operating officer NL Petroeum Svcs., 1986-87, cons., 1987; retired, from 1987; chmn. Valley Shamrock Inc., from 1987. Chmn. bd. dirs. Cottonwood Ctrs., 1993. Bd. dirs. Jr. Achievement Southeast Tex., Houston, 1985-86; fund raiser United Way, Houston, 1985-86. 1st lt. U.S. Army, 1952-55. Mem. Petroleum Equipment Supplies Assn. (1st v.p. 1988-89), Nat. Oilfield Material and Del. Soc. (pres. 1984-85), Am. Petroleum Inst., Soc. Petroleum Engrs., Nat. Oil-Equipment Mfrs. and Dels. Soc., Petroleum Club, Sugar Creek Country Club. Avocations: golf, fishing, travel. Home: Georgetown, Tex. Died Dec. 7, 2006.

WELLER, DAVID LLOYD, botanist, educator; b. Munfordville, Ky., Sept. 28, 1938; married, 1938; 1 child. BS, Rochester Inst. Tech., 1962; PhD in Biochemistry, Iowa State U., 1966. Rsch. fellow molecular biology Children's Cancer Rsch. Found., Boston, 1966-67; asst. prof. agrl. biochemistry U. Vt., 1967-71, chmn. biology sci. program, 1971-75, chmn. cell biology, 1972-75, asst. dean Coll. Agr., assoc. dir. agr. experiment sta., 1975-77, assoc. prof., 1971-77, prof. botany, from 1977. Recipient Ruth Allen award Am. Phytopathol. Soc., 1997. Mem. Am. Chem. Soc., Biophysics Soc., N.Y. Acad. Sci., Am. Inst. Chemistry, Soc. Protozoologists. Achievements include research in isoelectric focusing of proteins; ribosomes and RNAases of entamoeba. Died Dec. 26, 2006.

WELLS, HENRY, retired political scientist; b. Macomb, Ill., Dec. 15, 1914; s. Maurace Henry and Dorcas (Hart) W.; m. Patricia Paul Brown, June 24, 1950; children: Jane Elizabeth Wells Sadtler, Mary Paul, Thomas Gideon, Alexandra, Anthony Morris, Emily Hollingsworth. AB, U. Ill., 1937; MA, La. State U., 1939; PhD, Yale, 1947. Instr. polit. sci. Yale U., 1947-49, asst. prof., 1949-53; assoc. prof., research asso. U. P.R., 1953-56; assoc. prof. polit. sci. U. Pa., 1956-69, prof., 1969-85, prof. emeritus, 1985—2007, chmn. dept., 1980-83, chmn. internat. relations grad. program, 1970-74; dir. U. Pa. Anspach Inst. for Diplomacy and Fgn. Affairs, 1970-74. Mem. OAS electoral missions to Dominican Republic, 1961-62, Honduras, 1963, Costa Rica, 1966, Bolivia, 1966, Nicaragua, 1972; Fulbright prof. Sch. Polit. Sci., U. Costa Rica, 1969-70 Author: The Modernization of Puerto Rico: A Political Study of Changing Values and Institutions, 1969; Contbr. numerous articles to profl. jours. Mem. bd. aldermen, New Haven, 1950-51; mem. City Plan Commn., 1950-51; judge of elections 36th div. 59th Ward, Phila., 1962-64. Served to lt. USNR, 1942-46. Fellow Social ci. Research Council, 1946-47, 60-61; Am. Philos. Soc. re-earch grantee, 1977, 84 Mem. Am. Polit. Sci. Assn., Latin Am. tudies Assn., Caribbean Studies Assn., Phi Beta Kappa. Demo-rat. Episcopalian (vestryman 1965-69, 78-82). Home: Philadel-hia, Pa. Died Oct. 1, 2007.

VELLS, VALDA EVELYN, management consultant; b. I.Y.C., June 23, 1935; d. William Frederick and Valda Elva Baldwin) W.; B.A. in Econs., N.Y. Sch. Social Research, I.Y.C., 1967. With Gen. Electric Co., N.Y.C., 1964-80, cons. nternat. trade policy devel., 1973-75, mgr. internat. research rograms, 1975-80; pres. Wellspring, N.Y.C., 1980—; co-dir. 'W Assocs., 1983—; tchr. profl. communication. Mem. Women Bus. Owners N.Y., Ind. Citizens Research Found, Nat. Assn. emale Execs., Am. Soc. Profl. and Exec. Women, Internat. latform Assn. Democrat. Presbyterian. Died Jan. 15, 2007.

VELLS, VICTOR HUGH, JR., retired advertising agency xecutive; b. Bloomington, Ill., Apr. 19, 1924; s. Victor Hugh nd Wilma Julia (Codlin) W.; m. Jacqueline L. Wade, Nov. 25, 949; children— Victor Hugh, III, Polly Jo, Ken Douglas. BS, radley U., 1948. Copywriter Chgo. Tribune, 1949-54, Earle udgin & Co., Chgo., 1954-58, creative dir., 1959-64; group reative dir. Tatham-Laird, Chgo., 1958-59; founder, creative ir., pres. Rink Wells & Assos. (advt. agy.), Chgo., 1964-72; xec. v.p., dir. creative services N.W. Ayer Inc., Chgo., 1972-84, NYC, 1984-86, also bd. dirs.; cons. N. W. Ayer Inc., NYC, 986-91; ret., 1991. Served to 2d lt. AC U.S. Army, 1943-45. Recipient various advt. creative awards, including Clio, Andy wards. Home: Madison, Wis. Died May 26, 2007.

VELSH, ROBERT FRANCIS, insurance company executive; . Omaha, Aug. 28, 1925; s. Francis Joseph and Katherine 'heresa (Mulvihill), W.; m. Margaret Jean Soat, Feb. 5, 1949; hildren: Susan, Mary, Terence, Patricia, James, Sheila. BS in Commerce, Creighton U., 1949. CLU. Underwriter Mut. of Omaha, Omaha, 1949-51, Prudential Ins. Co., Newark, 1951-53, Mpls., 1953-57, mgr., 1957-63, assoc. gen. mgr., 1963-68, v.p. Boston, 1968-74, Newark, 1974-84, sr. v.p., from 1984. Bd. dirs. r. Achievement, Boston, 1970-73, United Way, Newark, 1974-5. Mem. Life Office Mgmt. Inst. (bd. dirs. 1985—). Clubs: Mendham (N.J.) Country. Republican. Roman Catholic. Avoca-ons: golf, reading. Home: Basking Ridge, NJ. Died June 12, 007.

VENDORF, HULEN DEE, retired law educator, writer; b. Vest, Tex., Oct. 29, 1916; s. Reinhardt and Laura (Blume) W.; n. Mary Jane Pfeffer, June 13, 1939; children: Robert Joseph, Donald Joseph, Florence Ann. BS, U.S. Mil. Acad., 1939; JD, 'ale U., 1951. Bar: Conn. 1951, Tex. 1961, U.S. Ct. Mil. Appeals 1952, U.S. Supreme Ct. 1958, U.S. Dist. Ct. 1960. Commd. 2d lt. U.S. Army, 1939, advanced through grades to ol., ret. as chief of adminstrv. law div. Office Judge Adv. Gen., 959; practice El Paso, Tex., 1959-61; prof. law Baylor U. Law ch., 1961-86, prof. emeritus, from 1986. Former chmn. and ong-time mem. Citizens Adv. Com. to Juvenile Judge; former ir. Heart of Tex. Legal Aid Assn. Author: Texas Law of Evidence Manual, 1983, 5th rev. edit., 1998, also 3 law sch. asebooks; columnist United Retirement Bull.; contbr. various rticles to law revs. Rsch. dir. Texans War on Drugs, 1980-81; hmn. Food Bank, 1981—. Decorated Legion of Merit, Bronze tar, Army Commendation medal Mem. Waco-McLennan County Bar Assn. (former dir., former v.p.), Phi Delta Phi. Home: Birmingham, Ala. Died Sept. 21, 2006.

VENDT, LLOYD, writer; b. Spencer, SD, May 16, 1908; s. Leo L. and Marie (Nylen) W.; m. Helen Sigler, June 16, 1932 dec. Jan. 1980); 1 child, Bette Joan; m. Martha Toale, 1981 tudent, Sioux Falls Coll., 1928-29; S.B., Northwestern U., 931, MS, 1934. Reporter, later columnist, drama reviewer Sioux Falls (S.D.) Press, 1927-28; publicity dir. S.D. Demo-ratic Central Com., 1928; reporter Daily Argus-Leader, 1929, elegraph editor, 1932-33; also tchr. journalism Sioux Falls Coll.; joined staff Chgo. Tribune, 1934; as reporter, becoming pl. feature writer mag. sect., later editor Grafic mag., Sunday ditor, assoc. Sunday editor, assoc. editor, 1975-77; CEO Chgo. Am. newspaper, 1961-69; pub., editor Chgo. Today, 1969-74, res. Freelance writer, 1977-2007; author: (with Herman Kogan) ords of the Levee, 1943, Gunners Get Glory, 1944, Bright 'omorrow, 1945, Bet a Million: the Story of John W. Gates, 948, Give the Lady What She Wants, 1952, Big Bill of Chicago, 1953, Chicago: A Pictorial History, 1958, Chicago 'ribune, the Rise of a Great American Newspaper, 1979, The Vall Street Journal, the Story of Dow Jones and the Nation's Business Newspaper, 1982, Swift Walker, Informal Biography f Gurdon Saltonstall Hubbard, 1986 (non-fiction award Chgo. 'ound. for Lit. 1986), Dogs: A Historical Journey, 1999. Pres. oc. Midland Authors, 1947-50. Served to lt. comdr. USNR, 942-46. Recipient Disting. Svc. award Nat. Soc. Journalists, 980, award of merit Northwestern U. Alumni Assn., 1953. Home: Nokomis, Fla. Died Oct. 21, 2007.

VENTWORTH, JOHN WARREN, electronics engineer, echnical writer, educator; b. Greenville, Maine, Nov. 3, 1925; s. Chauncey Depew and Sara Katherine (Taudvin) W.; m. Annabel Ruth Shields, June 20, 1953 (dec. 1978); children— Sara Louise, Alexander Davey; m. Dorothy Beryl Plasket, Mar. 31, 979 BS in Elec. Engring., U. Maine-Orono, 1949. Lic. profl. ngr., N.J. Design and devel. engr. RCA Broadcast Systems, Camden, N.J., 1949-53, engring. mgr., 1953-59, mgr. broadcast ech. tng., 1973-82; mgr. ednl. electronics RCA Corp., Camden nd Cherry Hill, N.J., 1960-63, mgr. continuing engring. edn. Camden, 1963-67, mgr. edn. devel. engring. NYC and Cherry Hill, 1968-73, mgr. broadcast tech. tng., 1973-83. Author: Color 'elevision Engineering, 1955; author-instr.-producer (TV series) Electronics at Work (Ohio State award 1962), 1962-63; (text vith video tapes) Digital Computer Fundamentals, 1971; contbr. rticles to profl. jours.; patentee in field. Com. mem. Troop 65, Camden County council Boy Scouts Am., 1968-73; bd. dirs. Haddonfield Adult Sch., N.J., 1973-75; active Camden County list. Soc., 1984-85. Served to T-4 U.S. Army, 1944-46, ETO, 'TO. Recipient award of Merit, RCA Victor div., 1953, honor-ble mention award Eta Kappa Nu Recognition of Outstanding 'oung Elec. Engrs., 1959, Disting. Sci. and Engring. award U. Maine, 1981 Fellow Soc. Motion Picture and TV Engrs. (bd. editors 1971-84), IEEE; mem. Sigma Xi, Tau Beta Pi, Phi Kappa Phi Republican. Methodist. Avocations: choral music; theologi-cal studies; gardening; travel. Died Nov. 3, 2006.

WENTZ, SIDNEY FREDERICK, insurance company execu-tive, foundation administrator; b. Dallas, Mar. 27, 1932; s. Howard Beck and Emmy Lou (Cawthon) W.; m. Barbara Strait, Sept. 9, 1961; children: Eric, Jennifer, Robin. AB, Princeton U., 1954; LLB, Harvard U., 1960. Bar: N.Y. 1961. Atty. White & Case, NYC, 1960-65, Western Electric Co., 1965-66, AT&T Corp., 1966-67; with Crum & Forster Inc., Morristown, N.J., from 1967, v.p., gen. counsel, 1967-71, sr. v.p., gen. counsel, 1971-72, exec. v.p., 1972, pres., 1972-87, chmn. bd., 1987-88, chmn. exec. com., 1988-90, also bd. dirs.; chmn. bd. Robert Wood Johnson Found., Princeton, N.J., 1989-99. Trustee Mor-ristown Meml. Hosp., 1974-96, Drew U., 1991—. Served to lt. (j.g.) USNR, 1954-57. Mem. Morris County Golf Club, Sakon-net (R.I.) Golf Club, Baltusrol Golf Club, Jupiter Hills (Fla.) Golf Club, Loblolly Pines (Fla.) Golf Club, Carnegie Abby Golf Club (R.I.). Home: Hobe Sound, Fla. Died July 18, 2007.

WEST, BYRON KENNETH, banker; b. Denver, Sept. 18, 1933; s. Willis Byron and Cecil Bernice (Leathers) W.; m. Barbara Huth, June 25, 1955. AB, U. Ill., 1955; MBA, U. Chgo., 1960. With Harris Bank, Chgo., from 1957, investment analyst, 1957-62, v.p., 1966-76; group exec. Harris Bank Internat. Banking Group, Chgo., 1974-76, head banking dept., exec. v.p., 1976-80, pres., 1980; chmn. bd., chief exec. officer Harris Bankcorp, Inc., Chgo., from 1984, also bd. dirs.; chmn., chief exec. officer Harris Trust and Savs. Bank, Chgo., from 1985. Bd. dirs. Motorola, Inc., Assn. Res. City Bankers. Trustee U. Chgo., Rush-Presbyn.-St. Luke's Med Center; mem. governing bd. Chgo. Orchestral Assn.; bd. dirs. U. Ill. Found. Served with USN, 1955-57. Mem. Res. City Bankers Assn., Christian Lay-men of Chgo., Phi Beta Kappa. Clubs: Skokie Country (Glen-coe, Ill.); Pine Valley (N.J.); Univ., Chgo., Commonwealth, Comml., Econ. (Chgo.). Republican. Home: Winnetka, Ill. Died May 14, 2006.

WEST, GEORGE RAYMOND, insurance company executive; b. Boston, Apr. 11, 1920; m. Marion Huxley. BS in Econs, Harvard U., 1942, MBA, 1947. With Mut. Boiler & Machinery Ins. Co., Waltham, Mass., 1947-68; sr. v.p. adminstrn. Arkwright-Boston Mfrs. Mut. Ins. Co., Waltham, 1968-79; pres., chief exec. officer Allendale Mut. Ins. Co., Johnston, R.I., 1979-80, chmn. bd., pres., from 1980. Dir. First Nat. Bank Boston, Mohawk Data Scis. Co., Eastern Co., Factory Mut. Ltd., London. Served to 1st lt., pilot USAAF, 1942-45. Mem. Inst. Inst. Am. (dir.) Clubs: Hope, Univ, R.I. Country, Harvard. Republican. Home: Waltham, Mass. Died Apr. 4, 2007.

WEST, ROBERT VAN OSDELL, JR., retired petroleum executive; b. Kansas City, Mo., Apr. 29, 1921; s. Robert Van Osdell and Josephine (Quistgaard) W.; divorced; children: Robert Van Osdell III, Kathryn Anne, Suzanne Small, Patricia Lynn; m. Helen L. Boecking, 1978. BS, U. Tex., 1942, MS, 1943, PhD, 1949. Registered profl engr., Tex. Petroleum engr. Slick Urschel Oil Co., 1949-56; pres. Slick Secondary Recovery Corp., 1956-59; v.p. Texstar Corp., 1959; pres. Texstar Petro-leum Co. subs. Texstar Corp., 1959-64; founder Tesoro Petro-leum Corp., San Antonio, 1964, chmn. bd. dirs., CEO, 1971-88, chmn. bd., 1989-92, CEO, 1964-92. Bd. dirs. Frost Nat. Bank. Mem. engring. found. adv. coun. U. Tex., mem. at large and life Centennial Commm.; former bd. visitors McDonald Obs. and Astronomy; mem. devel. bd. U. Tex. San Antonio Health Sci. Ctr.; assoc. mem. bd. visitors U. Tex. M.D. Anderson Cancer Ctr., Houston; Trinity U. Assoc., San Antonio; mem. adv. coun., trustee St. Mary's U. Sch. Bus.; past trustee San Antonio City Public Service Bd.; trustee S.W. Research Inst.; past chmn. San Antonio Econ. Devel. Found.; bd. dirs. World Affairs Council, San Antonio; chmn. St. Luke's Luth. Hosp. Found., San Anto-nio; emeritus chmn. bd. trustees San Antonio Symphony; founder, former chmn. bd. dirs. Tiwanaku Archaeol. Found., Bolivia.; founder, former chmn. exec. com. Caribbean/L.Am. Action, Washington; trustee Ams. Soc. N.Y.; chmn. gen. cam-paign United Way of San Antonio and Bexar County, 1986, vice chmn. bd. trustees; chmn. pub. sector campaign subcom. United Way of Am. Named Disting. Grad., U. Tex. Coll. Engring., 1973; recipient People of Vision award Nat. Soc. Prevention of Blindness, 1982, Internat. Citizens award World Affairs Coun., 1986, Good Scout award Boy Scouts Am., 1987, Alexis de Tocqueville award United Way of San Antonio and Bexar County, 1990. Mem. Ind. Petroleum Assn. Am., Soc. Petroleum Engrs. (past chmn. San Antonio-Austin chpt.), 25 Yr. Club Petroleum Industry, Pvt. Enterprise Edn. (Herman W. Lay Meml. award 1986), Am.'s Soc., All-Am. Wildcatters Club, Sigma Chi (Significant Sig award 1979). Episcopalian. Home: San Antonio, Tex. Died Nov. 16, 2006.

WESTMEYER, PAUL HENRY MARTIN, education educa-tor, researcher; b. Dillsboro, Ind., Dec. 9, 1925; s. Martin Herman John and Emma Matilda (Rump) W.; m. June Kay Van Skyock, Aug. 23, 1947; children: Jean Elizabeth Ann, Paul Joseph, Crystal Sue, Kenneth Martin, Paula Marie, Henry Matthew. BS, Ball State U., 1949, MS, 1953; EdD, U. Ill., 1960. Cert. tchr., Ind. Sci. tchr. North Vernon (Ind.) High Sch., 1949-52, Univ. High Sch., Urbana, Ill., 1953-60; asst. prof. U. Ill., Urbana, 1961-62; assoc. prof. U. Tex., Austin, 1963-66, prof. San Antonio, from 1973; prof., dept. head sci. edn. Fla. State U., Tallahassee, 1966-72. Project mem. Chem. Bond Approach Curriculum Project, Richmond, Ind., 1960-62, Phys. Sci. for Non-Sci. Majors Curriculum Project, Rensselaer Poly Inst., Troy, N.Y., 1965-68; rsch. assoc. Med. Info. Tech. Rsch. Group, Uniformed Svcs. U. of Health Scis. Acad. Health Sci., San Antonio, 1986-89. Author 6 books for profl. educators; contbr. articles to profl. jours. Grantee U. Tex., Austin, 1965-66, Fla. State U., 1967-72. Fellow AAAS, Tex. Acad. Sci., Am. Inst. Chemists; mem. NSTA, Am. Chem. Soc., Assn. for Rsch. in Sci. Tchg., Assn. for Edn. Tchrs. in Sci. (pres. 1971-72), Sigma Xi. Republican. Lutheran. Avocations: round and square dancing, teaching round dancing, wood carving. Home: Pipe Creek, Tex. Died May 28, 2006.

WESTON, ROY FRANCIS, environmental consultant; b. Reedsburg, Wis., June 25, 1911; s. Charles Frederick and Hattie (Jensen) W.; m. Madeleen Elizabeth Kellner, Dec. 31, 1934 (dec. 2002); children: Susan Weston Thompson, Katherine Weston Swoyer Fittipaldi. B.C.E., U. Wis., 1933; M.C.E., NYU, 1939; D.Engring. (hon.), Drexel U., 1981; DSc (hon.), U. Wis. Madison, 1995. Registered profl. engr., 18 states; diplomate Am. Acad. Environ. Engrs. (pres. 1973-74). Jr. hwy. engr. Wis. Hwy. Dept., 1934-36; dist. engr. Wis. Dept. Health, 1936-37; san. engring. research fellow NYU, NYC, 1937-39; san. engr. Atlantic Refining Co., Phila., 1939-55; chmn. bd. Roy F. Weston, Inc., West Chester, Pa., 1955-91, chmn. emeritus, 1991—2007; environ. cons. Contbr. numerous articles on envi-ron. control and sustainable devel. to profl. publs. Vis. com. dept. civil and urban engring. U. Pa., Phila., also Ctr. for Marine and Environ. Studies, Lehigh U.; bd. overseers Sch. Engring., Pa. State U., former mem. indsl. and profl. adv. com. Pa. State U.; past bd. overseers Duke U. Sch. Engring.; past trustee Phila. Coll. Pharmacy and Sci.; former mem. Pa. Gov.'s Energy Coun. Recipient Disting. Svc. citation U. Wis., 1975, George Wash-ington medal Phila. Engrs., 1973, Samual S. Baxter Meml. award Water Resources Assn. of Delaware River Basin, 1994, Nat. Engring. award Am. Assn. Engring. Socs., 1994, Gordon Maskew Fair award Am. Acad. Environ. Engrs., 1977. National Engineering Award, 1994; American Assn of Engineering Soci-eties. Mem. ASCE (Simon W. Freese Environ. Engring. award and lecture 1995, Hon. Mention award 1994), APHA, NSPE (Engr. of Yr. award 1973), NAE, AIChE (environ. divsn. Lawrence K. Cecil award 1993), Am. Assn. Engring. Socs. (nat. engring. award 1994), Am. Chem. Soc., Air Pollution Control Assn., Cons. Engrs. Coun., Water Resources Assn., Pa. Soc. Profl. Engrs. (Engr. of Yr. 1970, 73), Water Pollution Control Fedn. (Arthur Sidney Bedell award 1959, Indsl. Wastes medal 1950, hon.), Delaware River Assn. (pres. 1976-77), Overbrook Golf Club, Phila. Engrs. Club. Died Aug. 18, 2007.

WESTRAN, ROY ALVIN, insurance company executive; b. Taft, Oreg., Apr. 30, 1925; s. Carl A. and Mae E. (Barnhart) W.; m. Dawn M. Oeschger, Oct. 18, 1952; children: Denise, Tho-mas, Michael, Dawna. BBA, Golden Gate Coll., 1955, MBA, 1957. Mem. sales staff C.A. Westran Agy., Taft, 1946-49; underwriter Fireman's Fund Group, San Francisco, 1949-52; ins. mgr. Kaiser Aluminum Chem. Co., Oakland, 1952-66; pres., dir. Citizens Ins. Co., Howell, Mich., from 1967. Chmn. bd. 1st Nat. Bank, Howell; pres. Am. Select Ins. Co., Columbus, Ohio, 1967-85, dir., 1967—; pres. Beacon Ins. Co. Am., Westerville, Ohio, 1967-85, dir., 1967—; pres., dir. Citizens' Man, Inc.; v.p., dir. Hanover Ins. Co., Massachusetts Bay Ins. Co.; bd. dirs. Oakland Kaiser Fed. Credit Union, 1957-60, Calif. Compensa-tion Fire Co. Mem. ins. adv. council Salvation Army, San Francisco, 1957-60; chmn. drive United Way, Livingston County, 1980; bd. dirs., mem. exec. com. Portage Trails council Boy Scouts Am., 1970-72; trustee, mem. exec. com. Child and Family Services Mich., 1972-75; past bd. dirs. McPherson Health Ctr., Howell; bd. dirs. Cleary Coll., 1984-85; mem. adv. council Olivet Coll., 1984—. Served with U.S. Army, 1943-46. Mem. Ins. Inst. Am., Mich. C. of C. (past dir.), Am. Soc. Ins. Mgmt. (past pres.), Soc. CPCU's (nat. pres. 1968-69), Traffic Safety Assn. Detroit (trustee 1967—), Traffic Safety for Mich. Assn. Home: Oldsmar, Fla. Died Sept. 18, 2006.

WETMORE, THOMAS HALL, educator; b. Kempner, Tex., July 30, 1915; s. Thomas Hall and Mary Sue (Whitcomb) W.; m. Rosamond Bayne, July 5, 1941; children: Stephen Bayne, Allyn Christophers. AB, Lincoln Meml. U., Harrogate, Tenn., 1934; MA, Duke, 1940; PhD (Horace Rackham fellow), U. Mich., 1956. Prin. Rehobeth Elementary Sch., Galivants Ferry, S.C., 1934-37; tchr. English James Gray High Sch., Winston-Salem, N.C., 1937-40; prin. Shelby (N.C.) Jr. High Sch., 1940-42, Shelby Sr. High Sch., 1942-44; faculty Ball State U., Muncie, Ind., 1946-69, prof. English, chmn. dept., 1960-69; chmn. dept. English Wright State U., Dayton, O., 1969-71, assoc. dean grad. studies, 1971-73, prof. English, 1973-85, coordinator cert. program in TESOL, 1980-85. Mem. linguistics com. Conf. Coll. Composition and Communication, 1960-63; English lang. instn. Commn. English, Coll. Entrance Exam. Bd., 1961-62; linguis-tics cons. Harper-Row, 1965-66; chief area judge Book of Month Club award for coll. writing, 1967-68, 68-69; edn. cons. Coronet Films. Author: The Low-Central and Low-Back Vowels in the English of the Eastern United States, 1959; chpt. on vowel pronunciation in A Various Language, 1971; co-author: New Dimensions in English, 1966, New Approaches to Language and Composition, 1969; editor: Ball State Forum, 1960-61, Midwest English Rev, 1959-60, Twenty-Two Young Indiana Writers, 1962, Indiana Sesquicentennial Poets, 1967, Twenty Four Young Ohio Writers, 1969; guest editor: English jour, 1963; editor: Linguistics in the Classroom, 1964; English editor: Elementary English, 1960; editor: Pardon's Progeny, 1977—, Robert Frost and Wade Van Dore, 1987. Served to lt. (j.g.) USNR, 1944-46. Mem. MLA (chmn. present day English sect. 1965-66, mem. adv. com. of sect. 1965-69, chmn. 1969), AAUP (pres. Ind. 1959), TESOL, Nat. Council Tchrs. English (dir.-at-large 1960-63, mem. commn. English lang. 1960-63), Linguistic Soc. Am., Internat. Reading Assn., Canadian Linguistics Assn., Ind. Coun-cil Tchrs. English, Am. Dialect Soc., Midwestern English Conf. (dir., exec. com. 1957-60, 75-80), Ind. Tchrs. Assn., NEA, Coll. English Assn. (nat. bd. dirs. 1968-71), Ind. Coll. English Assn. (pres. 1967), Ohio English Assn., Assn. Higher Edn., Speech Assn. Am. Home: Salisbury, NC. Died Dec. 21, 2005.

WETSTONE, HOWARD JEROME, physician, administrator; b. Hartford, Conn., Apr. 27, 1926; s. Murray and Natalie (Tonkonow) W.; m. Roan Joy Horowitz, May 8, 1947; children— Robin Lee Wendehack, Mark Lawrence, Scott Lewis, Jeffrey Bennett. BA, Wesleyan U., 1946; MD, Tufts U., 1951. Intern New Eng. Med. Ctr. Hosp., 1951-52, resident, 1952-53, Hartford Hosp., 1953-55, dir. med. rsch., 1958-65, asst. dir. dept. medicine, 1965-72, dir. ambulatory svcs., 1972-84, v.p. corp. med. affairs, 1984-87; v.p. med. affairs Conn. Health System, Hartford, 1987-92; med. dir. MEDSPAN, 1992-98; ret., 1998. Assoc. prof. U. Conn. Med. Sch., Farmington, 1975—; chmn. Med. Delivery Svcs., Inc., 1985-91; mem. Bloomfield Ethics Commn.; chmn. profl. adv. com. Capitol Area Health Consortium; bd. dirs., Gaylord Hosp., mem. exec. com., 1995—, chmn. joint comf. com., 1994—. Contbr. articles to profl. jours. Mem. Bloomfield Bd. Edn., Conn., 1955-69, chmn., 1961-69; pres. Conn. Assn. Bds. Edn., 1961-63; exec. com. Conn. Pub. TV Corp., Hartford, 1963-87, chmn., 1970-74; pres. Capitol Region Edn. Coun., Hartford, 1965-66; chmn. Govtl. Rels. Com. With USAAF 1946-47. Mem. AMA, Am. Coll. Emergency Physicians, Conn. Hosp. Assn. (hon.), Conn. State Med. Soc. (pres., chmn. legis. com., vice speaker ho. of dels. 1994-95, speaker 1995—), Hartford County Med. Assn. (bd. dirs. 1978-94, pres. 1985-86). Republican. Jewish. Home: Bloomfield, Conn. Died May 24, 2006.

WHEAT, WILLIS JAMES, retired dean, finance educator; b. Oklahoma City, Feb. 28, 1926; s. Willis R. and Aubyn (Roach) W.; m. Julia Francis Maguire, July 4, 1946; children: Willis J., Chatham James. BS, Okla. State U., Stillwater, 1949, MS, 1950; DPA in Pub. Adminstrn., U. Pacific, 1968; LLD, Tex. Wesleyan Coll., 1962; DrCommlSci, Oklahoma City U., 1980. Prof. mgmt., dean Sch. Bus. Oklahoma City U., 1954-64; exec. v.p., dir. mktg. Liberty Nat. Bank & Trust Co., Oklahoma City, 1964-87; mem. faculty Stonier Grad. Sch. Banking, Rutgers U., New Brunswick, N.J., 1975-87; pres. Oklahoma City U., 1979-80, dean Meinders Sch. Bus., 1987-89; mem. faculty Essentials of Banking Sch., Norman, Okla., 1980-82, Grad. Sch. Banking of the South, Baton Rouge, 1981-83. Bd. dirs., chmn. United Bank Okla., 1987-95; bd. dirs. Pace Co., Baldor Electric Co. Contbr. articles to profl. jours. Chmn. Oklahoma City Plan Adv. Com., 1974-81, Okla. Employment Security Commn., Oklahoma City, 1981-89; trustee, mem. exec. com. Oklahoma City U., 1975-87. Served with U.S. Army, World War II. Recipient Disting. Svc. citation U.S. SBA, 1978, Disting. Svc. award Oklahoma City U., 1980, Okla. Coun. Econ. Edn., 1982. Mem. Am. Bankers Assn., Soc. Advancement of Mgmt. (past pres.), Nat. Coun. for Small Bus. Mgmt. Devel., Okla. Polit. Sci. Assn., Okla. Coun. on Econ. Edn., Masons, Shriners, Jesters, Delta Sigma Pi, Beta Gamma Sigma. Methodist. Home: Oklahoma City, Okla. Died June 10, 2006.

WHEELER, CLAYTON EUGENE, JR., dermatologist, educator; b. Viroqua, Wis., June 30, 1917; s. Clayton Eugene and Vista Beulah (Heal) W.; m. Susie Brooks Overton, Oct. 11, 1952; children: Susan Brooks, Margaret Ann, Elizabeth Clayton. BA, U. Wis., 1938, MD, 1941. Diplomate Am. Bd. Internal Medicine, Am. Bd. Dermatology (dir. 1970-79, vice pres. 1977-78, pres. 1978-79). Intern Cin. Gen. Hosp., 1941-42; resident in internal medicine U. Mich. Hosps., 1942-44, research fellow endocrinology and metabolism, 1947-48, resident in dermatology, 1948-51; from asst. prof. to prof. dermatology U. Va. Med. Sch., 1951-62; prof. dermatology U. N.C. Med. Sch., Chapel Hill, from 1962, chmn. div., 1962-72, chmn. dept., 1972-87, chmn., exec. com. Med. Faculty Practice Plan, 1986-90. Cutaneous commn. Armed Forces Epidemiol. Bd., 1961-72; dermatology tng. grants com. NIAMD, 1963-67, residency rev. com. dermatology, 1973-79, chair, 1975-79; chair task force ednl. programs faculty Nat. Program Dermatology, 1969-74; trustee Dermatology Found., 1975-79. Author: Practical Dermatology, 3d edit, 1967, also articles. Served to maj. M.C. AUS, 1944-47. Recipient U. N.C. Med. Alumni Disting. faculty award, 1986, Disting. Svc. award U. N.C. Med. Alumni, 1997; honored with establishment of Clayton E. Wheeler Jr. Professorship of Dermatology position, 1991, recipient David Martin Carter Mentorship Award, 2002. Mem. Soc. Investigative Dermatology (bd. dirs. 1970-73, pres. 1974-75, Rothman award 1979, hon. mem. 1993), Assn. Profs. Dermatology (bd. dirs. 1969-71, 76-79, sec.-treas. 1971-74, pres. 1975-76), Am. Dermatol. Assn. (pres. 1982-83, hon. mem. 1997), Am. Acad. Dermatology (past dir., pres.-elect 1983-84, pres. 1984-85, past pres. 1985-86, hon. mem. 1988, masters in dermatology 1993, Gold medal 1993), Am. Skin Assn. (David Martin Carter award 2002), Phi Beta Kappa, Alpha Omega Alpha. Methodist. Home: Chapel Hill, NC. Died Feb. 4, 2007.

WHITAKER, GILBERT RILEY, JR., economics professor, academic administrator, business economist; b. Oklahoma City, Oct. 8, 1931; s. Gilbert Riley and Melodese (Kilpatrick) W.; m. Ruth Pauline Tonn, Dec. 18, 1953; children: Kathleen, David Edward, Thomas Gilbert. BA, Rice U., 1953; postgrad., So. Methodist U., 1956-57; MS in Econs., U. Wis., Madison, 1958, PhD in Econs. (Ford Found. dissertation fellow), 1961. Instr., Sch. of Bus. Northwestern U., 1960-61, asst. prof. bus. econs., Sch. of Bus., 1961-64, assoc. prof., Sch. of Bus., 1964-66, rsch. assoc. Transp. Center, Sch. of Bus., 1962-66; assoc. prof. Washington U., St. Louis, 1966-67, prof., 1967-76, adj. prof. econs., 1968-76, assoc. dean Sch. Bus. Adminstrn., 1969-76; dean, prof. bus. econs. M.J. Neeley Sch. Bus., Tex. Christian U., 1976-79; dean U. Mich., 1979-90; prof. Sch. Bus. Adminstrn. U. Mich., 1979-97; provost, v.p. acad. affairs U. Mich., Ann Arbor, 1990-93, provost, exec. v.p. acad. affairs, 1993-95; sr. adv. Andrew W. Mellon Found., 1996—2004; dean Jesse Jones Grad. Sch. Mgmt. Rice U., Houston, 1997—2005, prof. bus. econs., 1997—2007. Dir. Am. Assembly of Collegiate Schs. of Bus., 1984-91, v.p., pres.-elect, 1988-89, pres., 1989-90, dir. Washington campus, 1980-89, chmn., 1985-88; bd. dirs. Westlake Chem.Co.; sr. economist banking and currency com. U.S. Ho. of Reps., 1964; mem. Grad. Mgmt. Admissions Coun., 1972-75, chmn., 1974-75; bd. dirs. Washtenaw County United Way, 1990-96. Author: (with Marshall Colberg and Dascomb Forbush) Business Economics, 6th edit., 1981; (with Roger Chisholm) Forecasting Methods, 1971. Bd. trustees, sec.-treas. JSTOR, 1995-2002. With USN, 1953-56. Mem.: Am. Econ. Assn., Ft. Worth Boat Club. Home: Houston, Tex. Died June 21, 2007.

WHITAKER, MEADE, federal judge; b. Washington, Mar. 22, 1919; s. Spier and Haidee (Meade) W.; m. Frances Dunn Baldwin, Feb. 10, 1945; children: Meade, Martin Baldwin (dec.), Frances Dunn Whitaker Schoonover; m. Carol Dekleva, Dec. 26, 1972. BA, Yale U., 1940; LL.B., U. Va., 1948. Bar: Ala. 1948. Ptnr. Cabaniss & Johnston and successor firms, Birmingham, 1948-69, 70-73; tax legis. counsel Treasury Dept., Washington, 1969-70; chief counsel (IRS), Washington, 1973-76; ptnr. Arter & Hadden, Cleve., 1977-78; asst. gen. counsel Ford Motor Co., Dearborn, Mich., 1978-81; judge U.S. Tax Ct., Washington, from 1982. Served as officer USMCR, 1941-46. Mem. ABA, Am. Law Inst., D.C. Bar Assn. Episcopalian. Died Oct. 5, 2005.

WHITE, ALVIN SWAUGER, aerospace scientist, consultant; b. Berkeley, Calif., Dec. 9, 1918; s. Harold Hubbard and Ruth Amelia (Winkleman) W.; m. Betty Tomsett, Apr. 6, 1991; children from previous marriages: Stephen Alan, Cathie Lee, Leslie Ann. Student, U. Calif., Davis, 1936-37, U. Calif., Berkeley, 1937, 39-41, BME, 1947. Engr., test pilot N.Am. Aviation, Inc., LA, 1954-61, chief test pilot L.A. divsn., 1961-66; mgr. flight ops., R & D TWA, NYC, 1967-69; aerospace cons. Tuscon, from 1969. With USAAF, 1941-46; with USAF, 1948-54. Decorated D.F.C., Air medal with 9 oak leaf clusters; recipient Warsaw Uprising Cross, Republic of Poland, 1944, Iven C. Kincheloe award Soc. Exptl. Test Pilots, 1965, Golden Plate award Am. Acad. Achievement, 1966, Harmon Internat. trophy, 1967, Richard Hansford Burroughs Jr. award Flight Safety Found., 1969, Aerospace Walk of Honor, 1994. Fellow AIAA (assoc., Octave Chanute award 1965), Soc. Exptl. Text Pilots (pres. 1960-61): mem. Delta Upsilon. Republican. Episcopalian. Died Apr. 29, 2006.

WHITE, BARRY A., lawyer; b. Chgo., May 26, 1948; BA, U. Wis., 1970; JD cum laude, Northwestern U., 1973. Bar: Ill. 1973. Ptnr. Mayer, Brown & Platt, Chgo. Mem. Phi Eta Sigma, Phi Kappa Phi. Died Sept. 3, 2006.

WHITE, CHARLES ALBERT, JR., medical educator, obstetrician-gynecologist; b. San Diego, Aug. 1, 1922; s. Charles Albert and Helen (Hardy) W.; m. Suzan A. Alikadi, Dec. 6, 1960; children: Craig, Scott, Jennifer. D.V.M., Colo. State U., 1945; MD, U. Utah, 1955. Diplomate: Am. Bd. Ob-Gyn. Intern Salt Lake County Hosp., 1955; resident in ob-gyn U. Iowa, 1959-61, mem. faculty ob-gyn, 1961-74; chmn. dept. ob-gyn W. Va. U., Morgantown, 1974-80; prof., chmn. dept. ob-gyn La. State U. Med. Ctr., New Orleans, 1980-92. Served to lt. comdr. USNR, 1957-59. Fellow ACS, Am. Gyn-Ob Soc.; mem. Am. Coll. Ob-Gyn, Central Assn. Ob-Gyn Died Apr. 27, 2007.

WHITE, DAVID CLEAVELAND, microbial ecologist, toxicologist; b. Moline, Ill., May 18, 1929; s. Frederick Berryhill and Dorothy (Cleaveland) W.; m. Sandra Jean Shoults, July 7, 1957; children: Winifred Shoults, Christopher Cleaveland, Andrew Berryhill. AB magna cum laude, Dartmouth Coll., 1951; MD, Tufts U., 1955; PhD, Rockefeller U., 1962. Rotating intern Hosp. of U. Pa., 1955-56; asst. prof., assoc. prof., then prof. biochemistry U. Ky., Lexington, 1962-72; prof. biol. sci. Fla. State U., Tallahassee, 1972-86; disting. scientist U. Tenn./Oak Ridge Nat. Lab., Knoxville, 1986—2000; prof. microbiology, ecology U. Tenn., Knoxville, from 1986, Disting. prof., from 2000; prin. investigator Oak Ridge (Tenn.) Nat. Lab., from 1988. Mem. adv. com. Ctr. Theol. Inquiry, Princeton (N.J.) U., 1986-91; exec. dir. Ctr. for Environ. Biotech., 1991-2000; dir. Ctr. for Biomarker Analysis, 2001—; founder Inst. Applied Microbiology, Knoxville, 1986-91; mem. sci. adv. panel Mich. State Ctr. Microbial Ecology, Lansing, 1989-92, Mont. State Ctr. for Biofilm Engring., Bozeman, Mont., 1991-95; mem. sci. adv. bd. Nat. Water Rsch. Inst., 1993—; mem. Naval Rsch. Adv. Commn., 1995-96; dir. Microbial Insights, Inc., Knoxville, 1992-95; Wellcome vis. prof. U. Okla., Norman, 1984-85; spkr. profl. confs.; disting. vis. scientist Jet Propulsion Lab., Pasadena, 1998-99. Author: Sex, Drugs and Pollution, 1983, 2d edit., 1985; founding editor-in-chief Jour. Microbiol. Methods, 1985—2000; author numerous refereed sci. publs. Lt. M.C. USN, 1956-58. Recipient P.R. Edwards award S.E. br. Am. Soc. Microbiology, 1981, Procter & Gamble Applied and Environ., Microbiology award Am. Soc. Microbiology, 1993, Applied and Environ. Microbiol. award ASM, 1993, Antarctic Svc. medal USN/NSF, 1984, Sci. and Tech. Achievement award EPA, 1987, Athalie Richardson Clarke prize in water sci. and tech. Nat. Water Rsch. Inst., 1995. Presbyterian. Achievements include discovery of signature biomarker technique for microbial biomass, community structure and nutritional status from environmental samples, microbial ecology of deep subsurface, tropical and antarctic sediments, microbial biofilms in microbial influenced corrosion, biosensors environmental biotechnology, planetary protection in mans sample return missions, analysis of breath aerosols for regulatory lipids as harbingers of pulmonary pathobiology. Home: Knoxville, Tenn. Died Oct. 25, 2006.

WHITE, JEFFREY LOUIS, advertising agency executive; b. Evanston, Ill., Dec. 4, 1945; s. Arnold Vincent and Marion Hattie (Morse) W.; m. Suzanne Lois Loesch, Aug. 3, 1968; 1 child, Bradley Thomas. BS, U. Ill., 1968. From trainee to v.p. acctg. div. J. Walter Thompson, Chgo., 1968-84, sr. v.p., gen. mgr. Washington, 1984-87, exec. v.p., gen. mgr. Atlanta, from 1987. 1st lt. USMC, 1968-71. Home: Atlanta, Ga. Died Nov. 5, 2005.

WHITE, JOE LLOYD, soil scientist, educator; b. Pierce, Okla., Nov. 8, 1921; s. Claud Amos and Alta Maurice (Denney) W.; m. Wanita Irene Robertson, May 29, 1945; children—Lerrill, Darla, Ronna, Bren, Janeil Student, Connors State Agrl. Coll., 1940-42; BS, Okla. State U., 1944, MS, 1945; PhD, U. Wis., 1947. Asst. prof. agronomy Purdue U., West Lafayette, Ind., 1947-51, assoc. prof., 1951-57, prof., 1957-88. Cons. Bancroft Co., William H. Rorer Co., Chattem Chem. Co., Merck Sharp & Dohme Rsch. Lab. Patentee in field Fellow NSF, 1965-66, Guggenheim Found., 1972-73; Fulbright scholar, 1973; recipient Sr. U.S. Scientist award Alexander von Humboldt Found., 1980-81 Fellow AAAS, Am. Soc. Agronomy, Am. Inst. Chemists, Soil Sci. Soc. Am., Mineral Soc. Am., Royal Soc. Chemistry; mem. Am. Chem. Soc., Clay Minerals Soc. (disting.), Am. Pharm. Assn., Coblentz Soc., Geochem. Soc., Internat. Soil Sci. Soc., Internat. Assn. Colloid and Interface Scientists, N.Y. Acad. Sci., Royal Soc. Chemists (chartered chemist), Soc. Petroleum Engrs. of AIME, Internat. Zeolite Assn., Soc. Applied Spectroscopy, Sigma Xi, Phi Kappa Phi, Phi Lambda Upsilon Mem. Ch. of Christ Achievements include patents for use of zeolites in ruminant nutrition, for stable dried aluminum hydroxide gel, for method and composition for treatment of hyperphosphatemia; establishment of the role of carbonate in inhibiting crystallization of aluminum hydroxide; definitive characterization of aluminum-containing adjuvants used in vaccines. Died Oct. 5, 2005.

WHITE, JOHN M., state legislator; b. Manchester, NH, June 1, 1926; m. Joan L.; five children. AB, St. Anselm, 1949; MEd, Boston U., 1952; postgrad., U. N.H., 1970-71. Del. N.H. State Assembly, 1960-70; rep. dist. 46 N.H. Ho. Reps., from 1970. Edn. com. N.H. Ho. Reps.; ret. elem. sch. prin. Mem. Manchester Tchr.'s Guild (exec. bd. 1966-70), N.H. Student-Tchrs. Assn., NEA, N.H. Edn. Assn. Died Nov. 14, 2006.

WHITE, JOHN ROBERT, state legislator; b. New Albany, NY, May 9, 1937; m. Ann Hoover. Student, N.E. Jr. Coll., U. Miss., So. Coll. of Optometry. Senator State of Miss., 1984-97. Chmn. local and pvt., vice chair of oil, gas and other minerals coms.; mem. appropriations, county affairs, fees, salaries and adminstrn., pub. health & welfare and pub. property. Mem. Miss. Optometric Assn., Am. Optometric Assn., Lions Internat. Died July 3, 2007.

WHITE, LELAND I., hospital administrator; b. Bklyn., Aug. 30, 1946; s. Milton Leonard and Jean W.; m. Lene Petersen, Aug. 16, 1969; children: Kevin, Jason, Erik. AB, Rutgers U., 1968; M.P.H., U. Calif., 1970. Adminstrv. asst. Jersey City Med. Ctr., 1971-73, asst. adminstr., 1973-76; assoc. adminstr. Med. Coll. Pa., Phila., 1976-79, hosp. adminstr., 1979-84, exec. dir., 1984-87, asst. prof. dept. community medicine, 1984-87; pres., chmn. bd. dirs. Health Ptnrs. of Phila., 1985-86; pres. Paoli (Pa.) Meml. Hosp., from 1987; v.p. Main Line Health, Inc., from 1987. Chmn., bd. dirs. Health Ptnrs. of Phila., 1985-86; trustee Health Systems Agy. of Southeastern Pa. Served to capt. Med. Service Corps. U.S. Army, 1968-76. Fellow Am. Coll. Healthcare Execs. (mem. policy rev. group 1987—); mem. Am. Coll. Hosp. Adminstrs., Am. Hosp. Assn., Hosp. Assn. Pa. (trustee, chmn. com. on health care delivery systems 1983-86, mem. audit com.), Delaware Valley Hosp. Council (treas. 1981-83, trustee, chmn. com. on quality assurance 1983-86, fin. com. 1987—), Hosp. Purchasing Services Assn. (mktg. com., trustee 1984-87), Old York Rd. Country Club (Spirng House, Pa.) (trustee 1990), Maple Manor Swim Club, Riverside Racquet Club (Bala Cynwd, Pa.). Home: Ambler, Pa. Died Jan. 4, 2006.

WHITE, LOUISE HUMPHRIES, publisher, psychological counselor; b. Grayson, La., Mar. 30, 1926; d. Ernest Christopher and Mary Vina (Elder) Humphries; BA, Centenary Coll. of La., 1962; M.S. in Counseling, Ga. State U., 1971; m. Verlin Ralph White, Mar. 11, 1944 (div. 1986); children: Carol Louise White Kelly, Verlin Ralph, Jr. Employment counselor La. State Employment Service, Shreveport, 1966-68; master counselor Ga. Dept. of Labor, Profl. Office, Job Svc. Ctr., Atlanta, 1968-81; owner Counseling Assos., Atlanta, 1981—; pub., owner Archive Enterprises. Mem. Cathedral of St. Philip, Atlanta, 1968—, Sunday sch. tchr., 1975-78, Daughter of the King, 1973—, Episcopal ch. women, 1973—, Internat. Christian Community Network, 1973-79; Foyer group leader for reconciliation, 1974-84; bd. dirs. Resource Ctr. at Cathedral St. Philip, 1983-84. Recipient Jongleurs award for service to Marjorie Lyons Playhouse, Centenary Coll., 1963; Nat. award for service in resettlement of Indochinese refugees U.S. Catholic Conf. Mem. Am. Personnel and Guidance Assn., Nat. Employment Counselors Assn., Internat. Assn. Personnel in Employment Svc., Atlanta C. of C., Cobb County C. of C. AAUW, LWV, Atlanta Hist. Soc., Ga. Hist. Soc., Kennesaw Hist. Soc. (treas.; editor soc. book on local families 1980—). Episcopalian. Club: Northside Woman's (dir., chmn. arts dept. 1979-80). Died Mar. 7, 2007.

WHITE, SAMUEL AUGUSTUS, JR., security company executive, retired military officer; b. Savannah, Ga., Nov. 16, 1918; s. Samuel Augustus and Henrietta Lynah (Glover) W.; m. Sara Crigler, Sept. 14, 1946 (dec. Nov. 1973); children— Samuel Augustus III, W. Kingman, Catherine R., Sara E. Student Va. Mil. Inst., 1939-41; B.S., Air U., 1956. Commd. 2d lt. U.S. Air Force, 1941, advanced through grades to lt. col., 1955; chief combat ops. div. Air Def. Command, Colorado Springs, Colo., 1951-54; chief air def. div. Hdqrs. U.S. Air Forces in Europe, Wiesbaden, W.Ger., 1954-58; with War Plans Directorate, Hdqrs. U.S. Air Force, Washington; research dir. Aerospace Studies Inst., Maxwell AFB, Ala., 1962-66; dir. ops. JUSMAG, Bangkok, 1966-68; ret., 1969; pres. So. Security Inc., Savannah, 1971-73, Preventor Security Ctr., Inc., Savannah, 1973—; Author analytical studies on mil. pacts. Campaigner Republican Nat. Com., 1980—. Recipient numerous mil. awards and decorations. Mem. Nat. Burglar and Fire Alarm Assn., Air Force Assn., Ret. Officers Assn., Mil. Order World Wars, Soc. of Cincinnati of S.C., Soc. Colonial Wars of Ga., Savannah C. of C. (crime prevention com. 1974-75). Episcopalian. Club: Oglethorpe (Savannah). Lodge: Rotary. Home: Savannah, Ga. Died Nov. 28, 2006.

WHITE, TERRY EDWARD, physician; b. Springfield, Mo., May 30, 1954; s. Roy Edward and Eselean (Moffis) W.; m. Susan Marie Peters, Aug. 16, 1981. BA, Drury Coll., 1976; MD, U. Mo., 1980. Diplomate Am. Bd. Physical Medicine and Rehab. Physician Lakeshore Hosp., Birmingham, Ala., 1983-86; clin. instr. U. Ala., Birmingham, 1984-86; physician Thomas Rehab., Asheville, NC, 1986-97, chief staff, 1994-97, vice-chief staff, 1992-94; physician Rehab. Solutions Western N.C., Asheville, from 1998; attending physician Mission Hosp., from 1986. Alternate Medicare State Carrier adv. com., Greensboro, N.C., 1993; bd. dirs. Nationwide Post Polio Support Group Dallas, N.C., 1992-94; vice chmn. Western N.C. Health Care Provider Coun., 1995-96, chmn., 1996-97; mem. editl. adv. com. Stroke Rehabilitation. Author: A Patient's and Physician Guide to Late Effects of Polio, 1995; mem. editl. staff Stroke Rehabilitation-Patient Education Guide, 1995. Named Rehab Physician Yr., N.C. Med. Soc., 1993. Fellow Am. Acad. Phys. Medicine and Rehab.; mem. N.C. Soc. Phys. Medicine and Rehab. (v.p. 1989-91, pres. 1991-93). Republican. Mem. Christian Ch. Avocations: gardening, woodwork, metal work, reading, music. Home: Asheville, NC. Died Jan. 31, 2007.

WHITTINGTON, MARY JAYNE GARRARD, journalist; b. Monteagle, Tenn., Aug. 13, 1915; d. William Mountjoy and Mabelle Moseley (Smith) Garrard; grad. Nat. Cathedral Sch. 1934; student King-Smith Studio Sch., 1934-35; m. William Madison Whittington, Jr., Dec. 27, 1945; children— Jamie Garrard Whittington Gasner, William Madison, Anna Aven

Contbg. editor Delta Rev., Memphis, 1964-69, Mississippi mag., 1977-82; freelance writer, columnist, Greenwood, Miss., 1956—. Mem. exec. bd. Greenwood Found. Arts, 1962-83; mem. Ctr. Study So. Culture, Oxford, Miss.; bd. govs. Greenwood Little Theatre, 1956-66, 75-82; trustee Ballet Miss.; bd. dirs. Mimi Garrard Dance Co., N.Y.C., Ctr. Study So. Culture, Internat. Ballet Competition IV, Jackson, Miss., Mississippians for Ednl. TV, Friends of Art in Miss., Friends of Art Mus., Naples, Fla. Served to capt. WAC, 1942-45. Mem. Nat. League Am. Pen Women, So. Debutante Assembly, DAR, First Families Va., Delta Cotton Wives, Nat. Soc. Colonial Dames, Order Crown Am. Jr. Aux. (life), Kappa Pi (hon.). Clubs: Arts, Naples, Fla., Greenwood Garden, Greenwood Country. Died Nov. 14, 2006.

WHYTE, JAMES PRIMROSE, JR., former law educator; b. Columbus, Miss., Aug. 25, 1921; s. James P. and Mary (Savage) W.; m. Martha Ann Jones, Sept. 11, 1948; children— James Jones, Stuart Ward, Wilson Scott. AB, Bucknell U., 1943; MA, Syracuse U., 1948; JD, U. Colo., 1951. Bar: Okla. 1951, Mo. 1957, Va. 1961. With firm Gordon & Whyte, McAlester, Okla., 1951-55; county atty. Pittsburg County, Okla., 1955-56; atty. Great Lakes Pipe Line Co., Kansas City, Mo., 1957; prof. law Coll. William and Mary, 1958-82, asst. dean, 1958-68, assoc. dean, 1969-70, dean, 1970-75. A former ad hoc arbitrator Fed. Mediation and Conciliation Svc., Va. Dept. Labor, also industry and govt. panels. Contbr. profl. jours.; Mem. editorial adv. bd.: John Marshall Papers, 1966-77. Mem. Bd. Zoning Appeals, Williamsburg, 1971-77, chmn., 1977; trustee, pres. Williamsburg Regional Libr., 1965; trustee Williamsburg Area Meml. Community Ctr., 1963-68, pres., 1966-67. Served with USNR, 1943-46. Mem. Va. State Bar, Phi Beta Kappa, Tau Kappa Alpha, Sigma Tau Delta. Died Jan. 7, 2007.

WICK, ERIKA ELISABETH, psychologist, educator, researcher; b. Basel, Switzerland, July 31, 1937; came to U.S., 1964; d. Josef and Martha (Gabriel) W. Tchr.'s diploma, Tchr.'s Coll., Basel, 1958; MA, PhD, U. Basel, 1964. Diplomate Am. Bd. Psychol. Hypnosis; lic. psychologist, N.J.; cert. sch. psychologist, N.Y. From asst. to assoc. prof. St. John's U., Queens, N.Y., 1966-75, prof. psychology, from 1975. Author: Zur Psychologie der Reue, 1971. Fellow Soc. Clin. and Exptl. Hypnosis; mem. APA, N.J. Psychol. Assn. Died Nov. 1, 2005.

WICK, HILTON ADDISON, lawyer; b. Mt. Pleasant, Pa., Feb. 11, 1920; m. Barbara G. Shaw; children: James H., William S., B. Jane, Ann W., Julia A. BA, Maryville Coll., 1942; JD, Harvard U., 1948. Bar: Vt. 1948. Practiced in, Burlington; ptnr. Wick, Dinse & Allen, 1949-72; CEO Chittenden Bank, Chittenden Corp., 1969—85; bd. dirs. Sentinel Funds, 1970—76; of counsel Dinse, Allen & Erdmann, Burlington, 1972-80; bd. dirs. Nat. Life Ins. Co., 1976—92; of counsel Wick & Maddocks, Burlington, from 1980; state senator Vt., 1989-91; COO Gifford Med. Ctr., Inc., Randolph, 1993-95. Bd. dirs. Blue Cross/Blue Shield Vt., Beach Properties, Inc., Vt. Pub. Radio, chmn., 1990-96. Trustee Middlebury Coll., 1969-85, Champlain Coll., 1974-94, Maryville Coll., 1981-86, Shelburne Mus., 1985-94, Ethan Allen Homestead, 1989-96, Vt. Assn. for Blind and Visually Impaired, 1992-2001; pres. Coll. St. Congl. Ch., 1996-98; bd. dirs. Vt. divsn. Am. Cancer Soc., 1979-93, Intervale Found.; pres. bd. trustees Vt. Law Sch., 1975-95; chmn. bd. trustees Vt. Cmty. Found., 1985-91; chancellor Vt. State Colls., 1984-85; chmn. bd. dirs. Middlebury Coll., 1981-84. Mem. ABA, Vt. Bar Assn. (pres. 1967-68), Chittenden County Bar Assn. (pres. 1963-64), Internat. Soc. Barristers, Am. Bankers Assn. (bd. dirs. 1975-76), Vt. Bankers Assn. (pres. 1973-74), Ethan Allen Club, Harvard Club (Boston and N.Y.C.), Phi Kappa Delta. Home: Shelburne, Vt. Died Mar. 17, 2006.

WIES, BARBARA, publishing executive, editor; b. Dec. 5, 1939; BA, U. Conn., 1961; student, New Sch. for Social Rsch., 1961-62. Product devel. Fearn Soya, Melrose Park, Ill., 1973-75; product devel. Modern Products, Milw., 1973-75; editor, pub. Bestways Mag., Carson City, Nev., 1977-89; pub. The Healthy Gourmet Newsletter, 1989-91, Fine Wine-Good Food Newsletter, from 1991; publicity dir. Nev. Artists Assn., from 1994; owner Gualala (Calif.) Galleries, 1989-90; assoc. pub., mgr. Edn. Range Mag., 1998—2005. Owner, operator cooking sch. Greensboro N.C. 1969-73; instr. Very Spl. Arts Nev., 1997. Author: Natural Cooking, 1968, Wok and Tempura, 1969, Japanese Home Cooking, 1970, The Wok, 1971, Super Soy, 1973, The Health Gourmet, 1981, International Healthy Gourmet, 1982; editor: Desert News, from 2004; one-woman shows include paintings Dolphin Gallery, Gualala, Calif., 1990, River Gallery, Reno, from 1994, 2-woman shows, 1992, 1994, 1996, Dolphin Gallery, Calif., 1994, solo exhbn., Nev. Artists Assn. Gallery, 1993, 1995, 1996, 1997, featured artist, Nev. State Libr., 1996, Silver State Gallery, Reno, 1998, West Nev. CC, 1996, art show judge, 1997; restaurant critic Reno Gazette Jour., 1995—2001, editor, designer Nev. Episcopal Diocesan newsletter Desert Spirit, from 2004, Bishop's Staff, Episcopal Diocese of Nev., 2005—06, The Vineyard, St. James Episcopal Ch., Wilmington, NC, from 2007. Staff assoc. Wilmington Children's Mus., from 2006; del. Nev. Episcopal Diocese Conv., 2002; vestry St. Peter's Episcopal Ch., from 2003, sr. warden, 2005; performer Nev. Arts sponsored Tumblewords, from 2000. Grantee Nev. Arts Coun., 2002; recipient First Place adult fiction Nev. State Lit. Co., 1995, First Place fiction State Lit. Comp., 1998, 2d Place fiction Writers Block; Nev. Arts Coun. fellow, 1999-2000. Mem. Nat. League Am. Pen Women (chair 1st and 2d ann. lit. competition Reno br., chairperson 1st Nat. Lit. award), Inst. Food Technologists, Pastel Soc. of the West Coast, Inst. Am. Culinary Profls. Home: Wilmington, NC. Died Aug. 10, 2007.

WIGGINS, NORMAN ADRIAN, academic administrator, law educator; b. Burlington, NC, Feb. 6, 1924; s. Walter James and Margaret Ann (Chason) W.; m. Mildred Alice Harmon. AA, Campbell Coll., 1948; BA, Wake Forest Coll., 1950, LLB, 1952; LLM, Columbia U., 1956, JSD, 1964; Exec. Program, U. N.C., 1968-69; LLD, Gardner-Webb Coll., 1972. Deacon Wake Forest Baptist Ch., Winston-Salem, N.C., 1963-66, Buies Creek (N.C.) Bapt. Ch., from 1973; deacon, tchr. Sunday sch., from 1952; lay preacher, 1953—2007; pres. N.C. Found. of Ch.-Related Coll., 1969-70, Campbell U., Buies Creek, 1967—2003, chancellor, 2003—07, prof. law, 1976—2003. Mem. Chief Justice Commn. on Professionalism, from 2004. Author: Wills and Administration of Estates in North Carolina, (with Gilbert T. Stephenson) Estates and Trusts, 1973; Editor: N.C. Will Manual, Trust Functions and Services, 1978; Contbr. articles to legal jours. Chmn. Gov.'s Task Force Com. on Adjudication of the Com. on Law and Order, 1969-71; mem. Com. on Drafting Intestate Succession Act for N.C., 1957-59; mem. Com. for Revision of the Laws Relating to the Adminstrn. of Descs.' Estates, 1959-67, chmn., 1964-67; trustee Sunday Sch. Bd., So. Bapt. Conv., chmn. bd. trustees, nominations com.; pres. Bapt. State Conv. N.C., 1983-85; bd. dirs. N.C. Cititzens for Bus. and Industry. Recipient Outstanding Civilian Svc. award Dept. Army, 1985, Comdr.'s award for Pub. Svc., 1995, Internat. Freedom of Mobility award, 1995, Patriotic Civilian Svc. award U.S. Dept. Army, 1998, award longest tenure as univ. pres. Coalition Christian Colls. and Univs., 1998, The Order of the Long Leaf Pine award, 1998, John J. Parker award, 1999, NC Bapt. Heritage award, 2004, Bapt. State Conv., 2005, The Charles D. Johnson Outstanding Educator award, 2005, James Iredell award, 2006; Campbell Law Sch. renamed in his honor the Norman Adrian Wiggins Sch. of Law, 1989; recognized for outstanding svc. to high edn. and legal edn. Newcomen Soc. U.S., 1993; named to List of 100 Influential Bapt. Leaders in 20th Century, 2000. Mem. ABA, Nat. Assn. Coll. and Univ. Attys. (pres. 1972-73, Disting. Svc. award 1991), Am. Assn. Presidents Ind. Colls. and Univs. (pres. 1981-83), N.C. Assn. Colls. and Univs. (exec. com., pres. 1984-85), N.C. Assn. Ind. Colls. and Univs. (pres. 1970-72, exec. com. 1980-81), N.C. Bar Assn., Harnett County Bar Assn., Nat. Fellowship Baptist Men (pres. 1987-90), Jay Waugh Evang. Assn. (dir./pres. 1970-72), Dunn Area C. of C., Wake Forest Alumni Assn., Rotary (hon. mem. Dunn club), Phi Alpha Delta, Phi Kappa Phi, Omicron Delta Kappa. Died Aug. 1, 2007.

WIGHT, ALBERT BARBER, electronics company executive; b. Quincy, Mass., June 16, 1921; s. Donald and Grace Regina (Ballou) W.; m. Margaret T. McDermott, Dec. 10, 1948; children: Barbara Ann Wight Darby, Donald Paul, Thomas Christopher. AB in Physics, Bates Coll., 1943; BSE.E., Washington U., St. Louis, 1944. Various mgmt. and engring. positions LFE, Inc., 1946-67, v.p. bus. devel. and v.p. ops., 1946-67; v.p. research and engring. Electronics div., 1946-67; with Sanders Assocs., Nashua, N.H., from 1967, v.p. ops., 1977-80, exec. v.p., 1980-82, pres., from 1982; v.p. Lockheed Corp. Trustee N.H. Coll., 1984—. Served with U.S. Army, 1943-46. Mem.: Nashua Country. Home: Nashua, NH. Died Jan. 29, 2006.

WIGHT, DONALD LEO, dentist; b. Beloit, Wis., Aug. 23, 1924; s. Charles Leo and Mary Lucille (Bittner) W.; m. Barbara Lee Cole, June 12, 1946; children— Barbara Ann, Charles Foster. A.B., Transylvania U., 1946; D.D.S., Northwestern U., 1950. Gen. practice dentistry, Marion, Ky., 1950—. Mem. Crittenden County Bd. Edn., Marion; elder Disciples of Christ Ch., Marion. Mem. West Central Dental Soc., Ky. Dental Assn., ADA, Kappa Alpha, Psi Omega. Republican. Lodges: Masons, Shriners. Avocations: hunting; fishing; raising bird dogs; reading. Home: Marion, Ky. Died Apr. 22, 2006.

WILBER, ROBERT EDWIN, import/export company executive; b. Boston, Dec. 15, 1932; s. Charles Edwin and Mary Charles (Gay) Wilber; m. Bonnie Marilyn Jones; children: Debra, Kathleen, Robert Jr., Thomas, Jeffrey, Mark, Matthew. BSBA in Acctg., Bowling Green State U., 1954. CPA, Mass., Tex. Sr. acct. Peat, Marwick, Mitchell and Co., Boston, 1954-58; gen. mgr. Door Controls Inc., Boston, 1958-59; asst. controller MKM Knitting Mills Inc., Manchester, N.H., 1959-63; internal audit supr. Raytheon Co., Lexington, Mass., 1963; asst. treas. Glens Falls (N.Y.) Ins. Co., 1963-66; controller Pnobscott Co., Boston, 1966-67; v.p. fin. and adminstrn. S.S. Pierce Co., Boston, 1967-73; v.p. Samson Ocean Systems Inc., Boston, 1973-78; v.p., chief acctg. officer Enserch Corp., Dallas, 1978-88; pres. Trade U.S.A., from 1990. Mem. AICPAs, Nat. Assn. Trade Exchanges, Mass. Soc. CPAs, Fin. Execs. Inst., BANC, Pres.'s Club (Bowling Green, Ohio). Home: Dallas, Tex. Died July 16, 2007.

WILBUR, BRAYTON, JR., distribution company executive; b. San Francisco, Oct. 2, 1935; s. Brayton and Matilda (Baker) W.; m. Judith Flood, June 29, 1963; children: Jennifer, Edward, Claire, Michael. BA, Yale U., 1957; MBA, Stanford U., 1961. With Arthur Young & Co., San Francisco, 1962-63; v.p. Wilbur-Ellis Co., San Francisco, 1963-74, exec. v.p., 1974-89, also dir.; dir. Chronicle Pub. Co., San Francisco, 1983-89; pres., CEO Wilbur-Ellis Co., San Francisco, 1989-99, chmn., 2000—05. Pres. San Francisco Symphony, 1980-87, San Francisco Opera Assn., 2005—; v.p. Sponsors for Performing Arts Ctr., San Francisco, 1975—; trustee Fine Art Mus. of San Francisco, 1978-81, Asia Found., 1972—, chmn. 1990—. With USAR, 1958—63. Mem.: Council on Fgn. Rels., Burlingame Country Club, Cypress Point Club, Pacific Union Club, Bohemian Club. Republican. Home: Burlingame, Calif. Died Mar. 24, 2006.

WILE, JULIUS, former corporate executive, educator; b. NYC, Apr. 17, 1915; s. Irwin and Harriet (Brussel) W.; m. Ruth Miller, June 26, 1941 (dec. Feb. 3, 1992); children: Barbara Miller Wile Schwarz, Andrew Brussel. BS in Mech. Engring. and Aeronautics, NYU, 1936; DFA (hon.), Culinary Inst. Am., 1994. With Julius Wile Sons & Co. Inc., NYC, 1936-41, 45-76, v.p., 1955-66, sr. v.p., 1967-76; prodn. engr. Brewster Aero. Corp., L.I City, N.Y., 1942-44, Greer Hydraulics Inc., Bklyn., 1944-45; trustee Culinary Inst. Am., Hyde Park, N.Y., 1970-79, 81-90, chmn. bd. trustees, 1981-83, chmn. emeritus, from 1983. Vis. lectr. Sch. Hotel Adminstrn. Cornell U., Ithaca, N.Y., 1953-82; wines and spirits lectr.; v.p. New Eng. Distillers Inc., Teterboro, N.J., 1955-72 Contbr. Brit. Book of Yr, 1957-75; editor: Frank Schoonmaker's Encyclopedia of Wine, 7th edit., 1978. V.p. Spain-U.S. C. of C., N.Y.C., 1972; bd. dirs. Scarsdale Family Counseling Service, N.Y., 1973-79; chmn. ann. drive ARC, Scarsdale, 1976. Decorated Ordre de l'Economie Nationale France, Ordre National du Merite France, Membre d'Honneur Academie du Vin de Bordeaux. Mem. Commanderie de Bordeaux (founding, gov. 1959—, dep. grand maitre 1978-88, grand chancelier 1988-2000), Soc. Wine Educators (bd. dirs. 1980—, treas. 1986-93), Wine and Food Soc. N.Y. (bd. dirs. 1971-73, 77-83), Nat. Assn. Beverage Importers (chmn. table wine com. 1954-60, 65-76), Explorers Club, Quaker Ridge Golf Club (Scarsdale). Democrat. Jewish. Died Dec. 12, 2005.

WILEY, THOMAS GLEN, retired investment company executive; b. Salt Lake City, Feb. 1, 1928; s. Thomas J. and Juanita (Dean) W.; m. Linda A. W.; children: Jana Lynn, Jill, Tina Elizabeth, Tova Suzanne. BBA cum laude, U. Wash., 1951, postgrad., 1954. With Shell Chem. Co., 1954-61, fin. analyst NYC, 1960-63; mgr. fin. analysis and pricing Lear Siegler, Los Angeles, 1963-72; v.p. finance, treas. Electronic Memories & Magnetics Corp., Los Angeles, 1963-72; exec. v.p. Hale Bros. Assocs., San Francisco, 1972-80; pres. Computer Election Systems, Berkeley, Calif., 1980-84, Texport, Inc., Anaheim, Calif., 1988-89; dir. Osmotics, Denver, 1994-97; ret. 1st lt. AUS, 1951-53. Died Apr. 20, 2007.

WILKEN, EARL WESTON, editor, journalist; b. Port Warren, N.J., Jan. 12, 1923; s. Ernest Earl and Blanch Hazel (Smith) W.; student Tufts Coll., 1941-42, Columbia U., 1946-47; m. Nancy Miflin Bradford, Jan. 1, 1965; 1 son, Richard Parker. Salesman, Remington Rand, Los Angeles, 1953-55, Thompson Pub., Los Angeles, 1955-57, N.Y.C., 1960-66; pub. Wilken Pub., Santa Barbara, Calif., 1957-59; sales/editorial, assoc. editor Editor & Publisher mag., N.Y.C., 1966-82; assoc. editor Graphic Arts mag., 1982—; cons., pub. Icarus Pub. Served to capt. USAAF, 1942-46. Episcopalian. Home: New York, NY. Died Jan. 4, 2007.

WILKENING, ROLLAND MELVIN, construction company executive; b. Deshler, Nebr., Mar. 10, 1926; s. William H. and Ida (Struve) W.; m. Virginia Muriel Lockwood, June 23, 1950; children: Nancy, William, Janet. BS in Civil Engring., Purdue U., 1950. Registered profl. engr., Mich. Field project engr. Barton-Malow Co., Detroit, 1950-60, v.p., 1960-64, exec. v.p., dir., 1964-76, pres., dir., 1976-81; vice chmn. bd. Barton-Malow, Detroit, from 1981; exec. v.p. Cloverdale Equipment Co., Oak Park, Mich. Co-author: Construction Management for the General Contractor, 1973; contbr. to: Directions for Managing Construction, 1980. Pres. East Central region Boy Scouts Am.; mem. exec. com., met. bd. dirs. YMCA, Detroit; bd. dirs. Inner-City Bus. Improvement Forum Detroit. Served with USNR, 1944-46, PTO. Named Luth. Layman of Yr. Luth. Luncheon Club, Detroit, 1974; recipient Disting. Engring. Alumnus award Purdue U., 1976, Silver Antelope award Boy Scouts Am., 1980, John W. Armstrong Humanitarian award YMCA, Detroit, 1981 Fellow Engring. Soc. Detroit; mem. Assoc. Gen. Contractors Am. (nat. dir.), Nat. Soc. Profl. Engrs., Mich. Soc. Profl. Engrs. (Engr. of Yr. award 1974), ASCE (Constrn. Mgmt. award 1980), Mich. Soc. Civil Engrs., Constrn. Specifications Inst., Mich. Assn. Profls. Clubs: Detroit Athletic, Renaissance. Lodges: Rotary. Republican. Home: Ann Arbor, Mich. Died Jan. 9, 2007.

WILKINS, JERRY L., lawyer, clergyman; b. Big Spring, Tex., June 1, 1936; s. Claude F. and Grace L. (Jones) W.; children by previous marriage: Gregory, Tammy, Scott, Brett; m. Valerie Ann Nuanez, Aug. 1, 1986. BA, Baylor U., 1958, LLB, 1960. Bar: Tex. 1960, U.S. Dist. Ct. (no. dist.) Tex. 1960, U.S. Ct. Appeals (5th cir.); ordained to ministry, 1977. Pvt. practice, Dallas, 1960—; capt. Air Am., Vietnam, 1967-68, Joint Church Aid, Biafra, 1969-70, TransInternat. Airlines, Oakland, Calif., 1977-79; gen. counsel First Tex. Petroleum, Dallas, 1982; owner Wooltex, Inc., Dallas, 1983—; owner, dir., legal counsel Intermountain Gas Inc., Dallas, 1983-84; legal counsel, dir. USA First (co-founder USA First Panama); co-founder Nederlandse Fin. Panama; founder, dir. Comanche Peak Reclamation Inc.; bd. dirs. Engineered Roof Cons., Continental Tex. Corp., Arlington, Landlord Rsch. Inc., Acklin Pain Rsch. Inst., Inc., Irving, Tex., Silver Leaf Metals Internat. Inc., Silver Leaf Mining Inc., Tex. Recycling Industries, Inc., Minerals Exploration Inc., Land Techs. Inc., Environ. Techs. Inc., Environ. Contractors Inc., Environ. Enterprises Inc., Desert Resources Inc.; founder, chmn. bd. dirs. Tex. Reclamation Industries, Inc.; founder Oxford Securities Funding Inc., Manchester Securieties Funding Inc., Cambridge Securities Funding Inc.; bd. dirs., v.p. for legal affairs, underwriter Lloyds U.S. Inc.; bd. dirs., co-founder R.O.A.S., Inc., Maritime Internat., Inc., Maritime Oil Recovery, Inc., Moriah Oil Recovery Barges, Inc., Megas Homes Internat., Urex Internat., Landlord Rsch. Co., Inc.; mem. legal counsel, bd. dirs. U.S. Fiduciary Co. Inc., U.S. Fiduciary Trust Co. Inc.; bd. dirs., legal counsel Lloyds U.S. Corp., Lloyds Link Inc., Lloyds Am. Inc., Image Security Co., Inc., Manchester Funding, Inc.; founder Kenai Cold Storage Inc., Kenai Pure Water Co., Arctic Pure Water Co., Arctic Cold Storage Inc., Shiloh Inc., Receivers, Inc., Internat. Equity Founding, Inc., C3 Plus Inc., UBO Sonoma Fin., UBO Caribbean Funding, Capstone Corp., Prowler Fouler Inc., Pacific Atlantic Funding Inc., Atlantic Funding, Inc.; bd. dirs., CEO Celex Nev., Inc.; bd. dirs. Minerals Exploration, Inc., Land Tech., Inc., Environ. Techs., Inc., Environ. Enterprises, Inc., Desert Gold Resources, Inc., Environ. Contractors, Inc.; co-founder USA First; cons. in field. Author: Gods Prosperity, 1980; So You Think You Have Prayed, 1980, Gods Hand in my Life, America, The Land of Sheep for Slaughter, I.R.S., America's Gestapo; Editor numerous books; contbr. articles to profl. jours. Bd. dirs., pres. Beasley For Children Found. Inc., Dallas, 1978—; mem. Rep. Presdl. Task Force, Washington, 1984—, Rep. Senatorial Inner Circle; bd. dirs., pilot Wings for Christians, Dallas, 1976—, Wings for Christ, Waco, Tex., 1976—. Recipient Cert. of Appreciation Parachute Club of Am., 1966; cert. of record holder for high altitude sky diving State of Tex., 1966, 67; Cert. of Achievement, Tex. State Guard, 1968. Mem. ABA, Nat. Lawyers Assn., Plaintiff Trial Lawyers Assn., Internat. Platform Assn., Tex. Trial Attys. Assn., Assn. Trial Lawyers Am., Quiet Birdmen, Tex. Outdoor Writers Assn., NRA, Tex. Rifle Assn., Parachute Assn. Am., P51 Mustang Pilots Assn., Phi Alpha Delta, U.S. Parachute Club (Monterey, Calif.). Avocations: shooting, hunting, fishing, flying, sports. Achievements: atty. (2 Tex. landmark cases) securing custody of female child for stepfather against natural parents (set the precedent which is now the standard visitation regarding children in divorce cases in Tex.), securing outside jail work program for convicted man, others. Home: Dallas, Tex. Died July 1, 2006.

WILKINSON, CECILIA ALTA, public relations executive; b. Long Beach, Calif., June 30, 1949; d. Charles Roswell and Amanda (Melendez) W.; children: Mallory Fletcher Winfield. BA, U. So. Calif., 1972, M, 1980. Coord. pub. rels. Long Beach Press-Telegram, 1972-78; corp. communications asst. Dart Industries, LA, 1980-81; assoc. Rifkind Pondel & Parsons, LA, 1981-83, v.p., 1983-87, sr. v.p., from 1987. Co-author: We Are Not A Minority, 1980. Bd. dirs. So. Calif. Entrepreneurship Acad., 1988-91. Mem. Pub. Rels. Soc. Am. (1st v.p., bd. dirs. L.A. chpt. 1986-91), U. So. Calif. Journalism Alumni Assn. (v.p., bd. dirs. 1980-88). Died Sept. 27, 2006.

WILKINSON, DONALD MICHAEL, JR., lawyer; b. Detroit, Apr. 22, 1931; s. Donald Michael and Martha Mary (Dursek) W.; m. Minette Yoshimoto, Oct. 26, 1963; children: Phoebe, Donald, Heidi, Genevieve. BA, U. Mich., 1951, JD, 1954. Bar: Mich. 1954, N.Y. 1957. Assoc. White & Case, NYC, 1957-68, ptnr., from 1968, resident ptnr. London, 1979-83. Editor: Mich. Law Rev., 1954; contbr. articles to legal periodicals. Trustee Village of Laurel Hollow, N.Y., 1969-79, dep. mayor, 1976-79. Served to 1st lt. U.S. Army, 1955-57. Mem. ABA, N.Y. State Bar Assn., Assn. Bar City N.Y., Order of Coif Clubs: Huntington Country (N.Y.); Princeton (N.Y.C.); Wentworth (Virginia Lake, Eng.). Democrat. Roman Catholic. Home: Syosset, NY. Died Aug. 18, 2006.

WILKINSON, DOROTHY COLBY, business educator; b. Chgo., June 10, 1920; d. Merrill Whitney and Harriet Ellen (Shade) Colby; m. Jack Harwood Menning, Mar. 6, 1943 (dec. 1973); children— Whitney Harwood, Colby Harwood; m. Clyde Winfield Wilkinson, Dec. 14, 1974. B.S., U. Ill., 1942, M.A., U. Ala., 1966. Instr. U. Ala., Tuscaloosa, 1948-62, asst. prof., 1976—; instr. City Bd. Edn., Tuscaloosa, 1964-76; cons. in field. Co-author: Communicating Through Writing and Speaking in Business, 1986. Author textbooks in field. Contbr. articles to profl. jours. Pres. Tuscaloosa City Tchrs., 1968; mem. Beautification Com. Womens C. of C. Recipient Disting. Prof. award New Coll., 1987. Fellow Assn. Bus. Communications (com. 1984-86); mem. Commerce Exec. Soc., Alpha Chi Omega. Episcopalian. Clubs: U. Womens, Masquers, Cook Guild, Avant Garde. Avocations: travel; cooking; gardening; photography; swimming. Home: Tuscaloosa, Ala. Died Jan. 22, 2007.

WILL, W. MARVIN, political science educator; b. Peace Valley, Mo., Mar. 25, 1937; m. Doreen Huebner, 1962. B.A., McPherson Coll., 1960; M.A. in Polit. Sci., U. Mo., 1963, Ph.D., 1972. Asst. to dir. Brethren Service Commn., Elgin, Ill., 1958-59; instr. Gasconade R-11 Schs., Owensville, Mo., 1960-62; asst. instr. to instr. U. Mo.-Columbia, 1962-64, 67-69; instr. St. Louis Community Coll., 1964-69; adj. prof. Washington U., St. Louis, 1976-78; dir. Civic Edn. Ctr., St. Louis, 1976-78; asst. prof. to assoc. prof. U. Tulsa, 1969-76, 79—; lectr., cons. in field. Author: Revolution or Order?, 1985. Editor/author: (with R. Millett) Crescents of Conflict, 1986; The Restless Caribbean, 1979. Contbr. articles to profl. jours. Mem. Greater Tulsa Council and Planning Team, 1975-76. Mellon-ILAS fellow, 1984; U. Tulsa fellow, 1982, 84; Hazen Found. grantee, 1977-78, 80, many others. Mem. Midwest Assn. Latin Am. Studies (exec. council, pres. 1985-86), Caribbean Studies Assn. (exec. council), Congress of Americanists, Am. Polit. Sci. Assn. Internat. Studies Assn., Southwestern Social Sci. Assn., So. Polit. Sci. Assn., Pi Sigma Alpha. Ch. of Brethren. Died July 22, 2006.

WILLARD, ROGER LEE, electronics technology educator; b. Kimball, W.Va., Aug. 6, 1940; s. Elmer Slemp and Sylvania (Church) W.; m. Garcia Lou Young, Aug. 22, 1989. BA, Western Ill. U., Macomb, 1992; MS, Thomas Edison State Coll., Trenton, NJ, 1994; MEd, U. Phoenix, 1996. Sr. prof. DeVry Inst. Tech., Phoenix, from 1970. Author: DC Electronics Workbook, 1997. With USN, 1960-64. Mem. IEEE, Am. Soc. Engring. Edn., N.Y. Acad. Sci., Phi Kappa Phi. Republican. Avocations: travel, astronomy, scuba diving, hardware development and industrial micro controller systems. Home: Peoria, Ariz. Died Mar. 13, 2006.

WILLBERN, YORK, retired political science professor; b. Runge, Tex., Dec. 29, 1915; s. David York and Berta (Young) W.; m. Johnne Bryant, Dec. 25, 1937; children: Cynthia, Ann Bryant. AB, Southwest Tex. State Coll., 1934; A.M., U. Tex., 1938; PhD, 1943. Tchr. high schs. of, Tex., 1934-39; asst., tutor, instr. U. Tex., 1939-43; asst. prof. govt. North Tex. State Coll., 1942-43; asst. prof. pub. adminstrn., asst. dir. bur. pub. adminstrn. U. Ala., 1946, assoc. prof., asst. dir., 1947-49, prof., acting dir., 1949-50, prof. polit. sci., head dept. polit. sci., dir. bur. pub. adminstrn., 1950-56; prof., head dept. polit. sci., coodinator Univ. Study and Planning Program, 1956-57; prof. govt., dir. bur. govt. research Ind. U., 1957-63, dir. Inst. Pub. Adminstrn., 1963-66, prof. polit. sci., 1964-81, prof. pub. & environmental affairs, 1972-81, prof. emeritus, 1981—2007; vis. prof. Duke U., 1956, Columbia U., 1957, Syracuse U., 1968, U. Tex., 1971, Lewis and Clark Coll., 1979, Portland State U., 1979; lectr. pub. adminstrn. Victoria U. (N.Z.), 1954; vis. prof. pub. adminstrn. Am. U., Beirut, 1967. Chmn. adminstrv. com. So. Regional Tng. Program Pub. Adminstrn., 1949-57 Author: Cities and Riverfront Lands, 1947, The Withering Away of the City, 1963, Governing Metropolitan Indianapolis, 1985; editor in chief: Public Administration Review, 1956-58; compiler: Technical Assistance to Alabama Governments: A Directory, 1949; contbr. articles to profl. jours. Dir. urban obs. project Nat. League Cities, 1968-74; chmn. Ind. Housing Bd., 1975-77. Served to 1st lt. USAAF, 1943-46. Mem. Am. Polit. Sci. Assn. (council 1956-58, exec. com. 1957-58), Am. Soc. Pub. Adminstrn. (v.p. 1958-59, council 1959-67, pres. 1963-64), AAUP (pres. Ala. conf. 1955-56, council, nat. 2d v.p. 1966-68), Am. Soc. Planning Ofcls. (bd. dirs. 1963-66), Internat. Assn. U. Profs. and Lecturers (exec. com. 1966-68), Nat. Acad. Pub. Adminstrn. (exec. com. 1967-70, trustee 1970-73), So. Polit. Sci. Assn. (past council mem.), Phi Beta Kappa. Clubs: Cosmos (Washington). Home: Bloomington, Ind. Died Apr. 13, 2007.

WILLCOX, BRECKINRIDGE LONG, lawyer, former prosecutor; b. San Diego, Aug. 2, 1944; s. Arnold Augur and Christine Graham (Long) W.; m. Laura Henderson, Nov. 21, 1973 (div.); children: Blair Breckinridge, Christopher Henderson; m. Lynn Braitman, 2002 BA, Yale U., 1966; JD, Duke U., 1969. Bar: Ma. 1969, U.S. Dist. Ct. (D.C. dist.) 1969, Hawaii 1972. Legis. asst. to Sen. Charles McC. Mathias Jr. US Senate, 1973—75; criminal div. staff US Dept. Justice, Washington, 1975-81, sr. litigation counsel, 1981-84, US atty. (Dist. Md.) Balt., 1986—91; ptnr. McKenna, Conner & Cuneo LLP, Washington, 1984-86, Arent Fox LLP, 1986—2002. Served to capt. USMC, 1970-73. Mem. ABA, Md. Bar Assn., D.C. Bar Assn., Hawaii Bar Assn. Died Nov. 16, 2006.

WILLEY, DARRELL S., education educator; b. Farmington, Utah, May 9, 1925; s. R.C. Willey and Helen (Swaner) Barber; m. Velma Roush, June 7, 1947 (dec. May 1971); children: Randie Carol Boldra, Trica L. Hazelton, Jacqui I, Monninger; m. Irene Knox Mayfield, May 30, 1972; 1 foster child, Roger E. Mayfield III. AB, Denver U., 1948; MS, Utah State U., 1949; EdD, U. Utah, 1953; postdoctoral, U. So. Calif., 1957. Cert. sch. mgmt., Utah, Colo., N.Mex. Prin. Wendover (Utah) Sch., 1949-50, West Sch., Littleton, Colo., 1952-53; from asst. prof. to assoc. prof. edn. mgmt. and devel. N.Mex. State U., Las Cruces, 1953-61, prof., 1962-89; prof. emeritus, from 1989; dir. edn. research ctr. N.Mex. State U., Las Cruces, 1969-82, head dept. edn. mgmt. and devel., 1962-70, dir. ERIC-CRESS program, 1966-68, dir. edn. research tng. program, 1966-72. Cons. NIH, NSF, U.S. Dept. Edn., U.S. Civil Rights Commn., 1963—. Author N.Mex. Survey Vocat. Tech. Ednl. Needs, 1963-64, numerous other publications. Senator's del. White House Conf. on Children, 1970. Staff sgt. USAAF, 1943-45, CBI, commd., 1948-68. Mem. AAAS, Am. Assn. Sch. Adminstrs., Am. Edn. Rsch. Assn., Hump Pilots Assn., 7th Bombardment Group Hist. Assn., Phi Delta Kappa. Lodges: Elks. Democrat. Mem. Lds Ch. Avocations: travel, color photography, coins. Home: Mesilla, N.Mex. Died July 11, 2006.

WILLIAMS, CHARLES EDWARD, writer, historian; b. Syracuse, N.Y., Sept. 5, 1946; s. Edward Myron and Mary Agnes (Blank) W. AB in History, Cornell U., 1968; PhD, SUNY-Binghamton, 1980. Instr., Broome Community Coll., Binghamton, N.Y., 1980; writer/editor USDA, Washington, 1980-88, program analyst, 1989—. Author: The French Oratorians and Absolutism 1611-1641, 1980, 89. Served with USN, 1969-73. Decorated Air medal. Recipient cert. of merit USDA, 1982, 86; French Govt. fellow, 1977-78. Mem. Am. Hist. Assn., VFW. Roman Catholic. Home: Arlington, Va. Died Jan. 11, 2007.

WILLIAMS, CHARLES STANLEY, JR., former university official and naval officer; b. San Pedro, Calif., Nov. 18, 1921; s. Charles Stanley and Lillian Mabel (Odell) W.; m. Elizabeth Bleecker Henry, June 10, 1945; children: Elizabeth Seton Williams Garry, Alison Lee Williams Mueller. BS, U.S. Naval Acad., 1945; MA in Edn., Stanford U., 1959. Enlisted USN, 1940, commd. ensign, 1945, designated naval aviator, 1949, advanced through grades to rear adm., 1973; service in China, Japan, Trinidad, Philippines, Italy, Spain; comdr. (Fleet Air Mediterranean), 1974-76, (Task Force 67), 1974-76, Maritime Air Forces, Mediterranean, 1974-76; dir. aviation manpower and tng. (Office Chief Naval Ops.), 1976-78; v.p., chancellor Embry-Riddle Aero. U., Daytona Beach, Fla., 1978-88. Bd. dirs. Pacer Systems, Inc.; nat. dir. Naval League U.S., 1980-81. Chmn. Mediterranean dist. Boy Scouts Am., 1974-76; pres. exec. bd. Naples (Italy) USO, 1974-76. Decorated Legion of Merit, Bronze Star, Meritorious Service medal; named Distinguished Eagle in Europe Boy Scouts Am., 1976 Mem. Daytona Beach C. of C. (bd. govs. 1979-82). Republican. Presbyterian. Home: Ormond Beach, Fla. Died July 8, 2007.

WILLIAMS, CHARLES V., state legislator; b. Memphis, Nov. 28, 1944; Student, N.W. Miss. C.C., U. Miss. State legislator Miss. Ho. of Reps., 1976-97, chmn. ways and means com. Mem. mgmt., oil and gas, exec. contingency fund, investigate state offices coms. Miss. Ho. of Reps.; exec. com. Coun. of State Govts.; former chmn.-elect So. Legis. Conf. Mem. Rotary, C. of C. Republican. Methodist. Home: Senatobia, Miss. Died Jan. 9, 2007.

WILLIAMS, DONALD RAY, operations research educator; b. Ponca City, Okla., June 17, 1937; s. James Lester and Opal Angeline (Taylor) W.; m. Mary Frances Reeg, Mar. 6, 1976; m. Dixie Lee Carroll, Sept. 6, 1957 (div. Dec. 1975); children— Donna, Dee Ann, Donald Ray, Deborah, Doris. A.S., Eastern Okla. A&M Coll., 1957; B.S., Okla. State U., 1959, M.S., 1960, Ph.D., 1963. Sr. computing specialist Aerojet Gen. Corp., Sacramento, 1963-64; sr. research specialist Tex. Instruments Inc., Dallas, 1964-67; asst. prof. mgmt. sci. U. Tex., Arlington, 1967-70; assoc. prof. mgmt. sci. Okla. State U., Stillwater, 1970-74, prof. N. Tex. State U., Denton, 1974—. Cons., 1974—; dir. Citizens Nat. Bank, Denton; pres. Mgmt. Resource Assocs., Denton, 1977—. Co-author: Statistical Analysis for Business, 1970; Mathematical Analysis for Business, 1979, Modern Mathematics with Applications, 1975, Finite Mathematics with Applications, 1975, Applied Calculus with Applications, 1976; contbr articles to profl. jours.; pub. Stockmarket Newsletter The Cycle Technician, 1982-84. Pres., PTA, Stillwater, 1973; coach City League Basketball, 1971-74; bd. dirs. Denton Assn. Retarded Citizens, 1983—. Mem. Am. Inst. Decision Scis. (v.p. student liaison 1973-74, council 1974-79), Southwest Fedn. Adminstrv. Disciplines (v.p. 1974-75, pres. 1975-76), Inst. Mgmt. Sci., Am. Statis. Assn. Mem. Ch. Jesus Christ Latter-day Saints. Avocations: flying; basketball; jogging; stockmarket analysis, skiing. Home: Denton, Tex. Died July 21, 2007.

WILLIAMS, EDWARD ALLEN, religious educator, minister; b. Middlesboro, Ky., Dec. 30, 1948; s. Roy Newton and blanche Marie (Byrd) W.; m. Beverly Claire Jones, May 30, 1969; children: Rebekah C. Olney, Leah M., Mark E. BA, Bapt. Bible Coll., Springfield, Mo., 1982; MDiv, Detroit Bapt. Sem., 1982, ThM, 1989; DMin, Westminister Theol. Sem., Phila., 1993. Ordained to ministry, Bapt. Ch., 1972. Pastor Calvary Bapt. Ch., Quincy, Mich., 1984-92; prof. Bible Northland Bapt. Bible Coll., Dunbar, Wis., 1993-95, Maranatha Bapt. Bible Coll., Watertown, Wis., from 1995. Mem. Hon. Order Ky. Cols. (col. 1992-97). Avocation: reading. Home: Lincoln Park, Mich. Died June 17, 2006.

WILLIAMS, FREDERICK DEFORREST, history educator, b. Braintree, Vt., May 13, 1918; s. Frank Arthur and Florence Gertrude (Bigford) W.; m. Florence McKay Green, Apr. 8, 1944 children: Sandi Suzanne, Craig Allen, Julianne, Kathy Marie. BA, Middlebury Coll., 1947; MA, U. Conn., 1948; PhD, Ind. U. 1953. Instr. history Wayne State U., Detroit, 1950-54; from asst. prof. to prof. history Mich. State U., East Lansing, 1954-89, adj. prof. mil. sci., 1969-89, chmn. dept. history, 1982-89, faculty grievance ofcl., 1980-82, ret., 1988. Speaker various radio stas. Mich., 1960—, Images of Am. program Nat. Edn. TV, Ann Arbor, 1961, various service clubs, schs., orgns. and alumni groups in Midwest, 1954—; mem. U.S. Army Adv. panel on ROTC Affairs, Washington, 1969-75; editorial referee various comml. and univ. presses, NEH, 1960—. Author: Michigan Soldiers in the Civil War, 1960; editor: The Wild Life of the Army: Civil War Letters of James A. Garfield, 1964, The North West Ordinance, 1989; co-editor: The Diary of James A Garfield 4 Vols., 1967-81; contbr. articles to encys., profl. and scholarly jours., revs. to jours.; mem. editorial bd. The Old Northwest, A Journal of Regional Life and Letters, 1981— Mem. Mich. Civil War Centennial Commn., 1960-66. Served to capt. USAAF, 1942-45. Recipient Outstanding Tchr. award Men of Excalibur, Mich. State U., 1962-63, Mich. State U. Disting Faculty award, 1986, Dept. Army Outstanding Civilian Service Medal, 1987, Mich. State U. Sr. Council Outstanding Faculty award, 1987, Spartan Bn. Outstanding Service award, 1987; named Hon. Coach Mich. State U., 1989—; ann. Frederick D Williams award to outstanding grad. history student created in his honor Mich. State U., 1991. Mem. Am. Hist. Assn., Orgn. of Am. Historians, Confederate Meml. Soc. (mem. awards com 1978-81, chmn. 1980-81, Jefferson Davis awards com. 1987-90 chmn. 1989-90), Phi Kappa Phi. Clubs: Mich. State U. Pres.'s (East Lansing); Univ. of Mich. State U. (Lansing) (v.p. 1973-74 pres. 1974-75). Avocations: hunting, fishing, golf, boating Home: East Lansing, Mich. Died May 20, 2007.

WILLIAMS, GEORGE EARNEST, retired engineer, retired corporate financial executive; b. Bartow, Fla., Nov. 27, 1923; s Earnest Roscoe and Ruby Barnett (Mathews) W.; m. Muriel Theodorsen, June 9, 1949. BS in Engring. with honors, USCG Acad., 1944; postgrad., Harvard U., Cambridge, Mass., 1945-46; SM in Mgmt., MIT, Cambridge, 1949. Registered profl engr. 2 states. Project engr., bus. cons. Ebasco, NYC; design engr., prodn. supr. Minute Maid Corp., Orlando, Fla.; asst contr., div. contr., group contr., corp. dir. fin. planning and analysis United Technologies Corp., Hartford, 1957-76, v.p. 1977-82; sr. v.p. fin. Otis Elevator Co., NYC, 1976-77; sr. v.p Kensington Mgmt. Cons., 1982-84; ret., 1984. Exec. com. Conn Commn. Services and Expenditures, 1971, Under then Gov Meskill. Contbr. articles to profl. jours., chapters to books Served with USCG, 1941-47, PTO and Atlantic. Mem. AIAA Fin. Execs. Inst., Army and Navy Club (Washington), Naples Yacht Club, Port Royal Club. Achievements include development of pricing system purchase of Fla. oranges for concentrate mfg. Avocation: yachting. Home: Naples, Fla. Died Feb. 15 2007.

WILLIAMS, HAZEL MAY, real estate executive; b. San Diego, Oct. 21, 1926; d. William and Alice May (Yarno) Roth B.A., San Diego State U., 1946; student West Valley Jr. Coll. 1970-73; grad. Realtors Inst.; m. Shelley S. Willians, Jr., Aug 24, 1947; 1 dau., Christabel May. V.p. Shelley Williams Assos. Inc., Saratoga, Calif., 1968—. Active Los Gatos chpt. ARC Community Hosp. Aux., West Valley Republican Women Named Woman of Yr., Santa Clara chpt. Women's Council Realtors; cert. residential specialist, Realtor and broker; cert real estate brokerage mgr. Mem. Nat. Assn. Realtors (dir 1986—), Calif. Assn. Realtors (dir. 1974-79, 84, regional v.p 1981, dir.-at-large 1983, chmn. policy com. 1985—), Los Gatos-Saratoga Bd. Realtors (ombundsman, pres. 1978, certs. of merit, Realtor of Yr. 1980), San Jose Real Estate Bd., Women's Council Realtors, Calif. Assn. Real Estate Tchrs., DAR (Los Gatos chpt.). Clubs: Saratoga Foothill, San Jose Women's Home: Saratoga, Calif. Died Mar. 21, 2007.

WILLIAMS, MARTHA ETHELYN, information science educator; b. Chgo., Sept. 21, 1934; d. Harold Milton and Alice Rosemond (Fox) Williams. BA, Barat Coll., 1955; MA, Loyola U., 1957. With IIT Rsch. Inst., Chgo., 1957-72, mgr. info. scis. 1962-72, mgr. computer search ctr., 1968-72; adj. assoc. prof sci. info. Ill. Inst. Tech., Chgo., 1965-73, lectr. chemistry dept. 1968-70; rsch. prof. info. sci., coordinated sci. lab. Coll Engring. U. Ill., Urbana, also dir. info. retrieval rsch. lab., from 1972, prof. info. sci. grad. sch. of libr. info. sci., from 1974 affiliate, computer sci. dept., from 1979. Chair large data base conf. Nat. Acad. Sci./NRC, 1974, mem. ad hoc panel on info storage and retrieval, 1977, numerical data adv. bd., 1979-82 computer sci. and tech. bd., nat. rsch. network rev. com. 1987-88, chair utility subcom., 1987-88, subcom. promoting access to sci. and tech. data for pub. interest; task force on sci info. activities NSF, 1977; U.S. rep. review com. for project on broad system of ordering, UNESCO, Hague, Netherlands, 1974 vice-chair Gordon Rshc. Conf. on Sci. Info. Problems in Rsch. 1978, chair, 1980; mem. panel on intellectual property rights in age of electronics and info. U.S. Congress, Office of Tech Assessment; program chmn. Nat. Online Meeting, 1980-2001 founder, pres. Info. Market Indicators, Inc., 1982-; cons. in field invited lectr. Commn. European Communities, Industrial R&D adv. com., Brussels, 1992. Editor-in-chief: Computer-Readable Databases Directory and Data Sourcebook, 1976—89, founding editor:, from 1989; editor: Ann. Rev. Info. Sci. and Tech. 1976—2001, Online Rev., 1979—92, Online and CD-ROM Rev., 1993—2000; mem. editl. adv. bd.: Database, 1978—88 mem. editl. bd.: Info. Processing and Mgmt., 1982—89, The Reference Libr., founding editor: Online Info. Rev., from 2000 contbr. articles to profl. jours. Trustee Engirng. Info., Inc. 1974-87, bd. dirs., 1976-91, chmn. bd. dirs., 1982-91, v.p

1978-79, pres., 1980-81; regent Nat. Libr. Medicine, 1978-82, chmn. bd. regents, 1981; mem. task force on sci. info. activities NSF, 1977-78; mem. nat. adv. com. ACCESS ERIC, 1989-91. Recipient best paper of year award H. W. Wilson Co., 1975; Travel grantee NSF, Luxembourg, 1972, Honolulu, 1973, Tokyo, 1973, Mexico City, 1975, Scotland, 1976 Fellow: AAAS (mem. nominating com. 1983, 1985), Nat. Fedn. Abstracting and Info. Svcs. (hon.), Inst. Info. Scis. (hon.); mem.: NAS (mem. joint com. with NRC on chem. info. 1971—73), Internat. Fedn. for Documentation (U.S. nat. com.), Assn. Sci. Info. Dissemination Ctrs. (v.p. 1971—73, pres. 1975—77), Assn. Computing Machinery (pub. bd. 1972—76), Am. Soc. Info. Sci. (councilor 1971—72, mem. publs. com. from 1974, pres. 1987—88, councilor 1987—89, contbg. editor bull. column 1974—78, Award of Merit 1984, Pioneer Info. Sci. award 1987, Watson Davis award 1995), Am. Chem. Soc. Home: Monticello, Ill. Died July 5, 2007.

WILLIAMS, MELVIN JOHN, sociologist, educator; b. Stovall, NC, Feb. 13, 1915; s. John Presley and Mary Jenera (Wilkerson) W.; m. Frances Clark, Oct. 15, 1936; children—Kay Frances (Mrs. Bradley Yount), Dorothy Virginia (dec.), Melvin John, Deborah Susan (Mrs. Monte F. Little), Steven Clark, Eric Stanton. AB, Duke, 1936, B.D., 1939, PhD, 1941. From instr. to asst. prof. sociology Albion (Mich.) Coll., 1941-44; prof. sociology, head dept. Wesleyan Coll., Macon, Ga., 1944-47; asso. prof. sociology Fla. State U., Tallahassee, 1947-52; prof. sociology, head dept. Stetson U., De Land, Fla., 1952-60, prof. sociology, chmn. social work, 1960-63; prof. sociology. East Carolina U., Greenville, from 1963, chmn. dept. sociology, 1963-71. Vis. prof. summers Mich. State Normal Coll., 1943, Whittier Coll., 1957, U. N.C., 1970; With Duke Found., summer 1936 Author: with others Contemporary Social Theory, 1940, Catholic Social Thought, Its Approach to Contemporary Problems, 1950, Social Norms of Adolescents, A Study in Social Guidance, 1959, Moral and Spiritual Values in Education, 1955; Contbr. articles to profl. publs. Co-dir. Addison project Kresge Found., 1942-44; dir. YWCA Community Survey, Macon, Ga., 1944; dir., family counselor Children's Center, Macon, 1946-47; dir. Adolescent Research project Wesleyan Coll., 1944-46, East Carolina U., 1963; research and sociol. cons., 1946—; dir. NSF Inst. in Sociology, 1967. Fellow Am. Sociol. Assn.; mem. AAAS, AAUP, Am. Acad. Polit. and Social Sci., So. Sociol. Soc. (sec. treas. 1953-55, 1st v.p. 1955-56), Groves Conf., Nat. Council Family Relations, S.A.R., Omicron Delta Kappa, Alpha Kappa Delta, Pi Gamma Mu. Clubs: Lion (pres. DeLand, Fla. 1960). Methodist. Home: Greenville, NC. Died Nov. 1, 2005.

WILLIAMS, MILLER, retired poet, writer, translator; b. Hoxie, Ark., Apr. 8, 1930; s. Ernest Burdette and Ann Jeanette (Miller) W.; m. Lucille Day, Dec. 29, 1951 (div.); m. Rebecca Jordan Hall, Apr. 11, 1969; children: Lucinda, Robert, Karyn. BS, Ark. State Coll., 1951; MS, U. Ark., 1952; postgrad., La. State U., 1951, U. Miss., 1957; HHD (hon.), Lander Coll., 1983; DHL, Hendrix Coll., 1995. Instr. in English La. State U., 1962-63, asst. prof., 1964-66; vis. prof. U. Chile, Santiago, 1963-64; assoc. prof. Loyola U., New Orleans, 1966-70; Fulbright prof. Nat. U. Mex., Mexico City, 1970; co-dir. grad. program in creative writing U. Ark., 1970-84, assoc. prof., 1971-73, prof. English and fgn. langs., dir. program in transl., 1973-87, univ. prof., 1987—2004, dir. poetry-in-the prisons programs div. continuing edn., 1974-79, chmn. program in comparative lit., 1978-80; ret., 2004. Fellow Am. Acad. in Rome, 1976—, mem. adv. coun. Sch. Classical Studies, 1985-91; first U.S. del. Pan Am. Conf. Univ. Artists and Writers, Concepcion, Chile, 1964; invited del. Internat. Assembly Univ. Press Dirs., Guadalajara, Mex., 1991; mem. poetry staff Bread Loaf Writers Conf., 1967-72; founder, exec. dir. Ark. Poetry Cir., 1975; founding dir. U. Ark. Press, 1980-97; participant Assn. Am. Univ. Presses Soviet Mission, 1989. Author: (poems) A Circle of Stone, 1964, Recital, 1965, So Long At the Fair, 1968, The Only World There Is, 1971; (criticism) The Achievement of John Ciardi, 1968, The Poetry of John Crowe Ransom, 1971; (with John Ciardi) (criticism) How Does a Poem Mean?, 1974; (poems) Halfway From Hoxie: New & Selected Poems, 1973, Why God Permits Evil, 1977, Distractions, 1981, The Boys on Their Bony Mules, 1983; translator: (poems) Poems & Antipoems (Nicanor Parra), 1967, Emergency Poems (Nicanor Parra), 1972, Sonnets of Giuseppe Belli, 1981; editor: (poems) 19 Poetas de Hoy en Los Estados Unidos, 1966, (with John William Corrington) Southern Writing in the Sixties: Poetry, 1967, Southern Writing in the Sixties: Fiction, 1966, Chile: An Anthology of New Writing, 1968, Contemporary Poetry in America, 1972, (with James A. McPherson) Railroad: Trains and Train People in American Culture, 1976, A Roman Collection: An Anthology of Writing about Rome and Italy, 1980, Ozark, Ozark: A Hillside Reader, 1981, (criticism) Patterns of Poetry, 1986, (poetry) Imperfect Love, 1986, Living on the Surface: New and Selected Poems, 1989, Adjusting to the Light, 1992, Points of Departure, 1995, The Ways We Touch, 1997, Some Jazz A While: The Collected Poems, 1999, The Lives of Kevin Fletcher: Stories Mostly Short, 2002, Making a Poem: Some Throughts About Poetry and the People Who Write It, 2006; poetry editor La. State U. Press, 1966-68; contbr. articles to profl. publs. Named Bread Loaf fellow in poetry, 1963; recipient Henry Bellaman Poetry award, 1957, award in poetry, Arts Fund, 1973, Prix de Rome, Am. Acad. Arts and Letters, 1976, Nat. Poets prize, 1990, Charity Randall citation, Internat. Poetry Forum, 1993, John William Corrington award for excellence in lit., Centenary Coll., Shreveport, La., 1994, Acad. Lit. award, AAAL, 1995, Presdl. Inaugural Poet, 1997. Mem. MLA, PEN, AAUP, South Ctrl. MLA, Am. Lit. Translators Assn. (v.p. 1978-79, pres. 1979-81), Authors' Guild, Soc. Benemerito dell'Assn. Centro Romanesco Trilussa (Rome). Home: Fayetteville, Ark. Died Oct. 13, 2006.

WILLIAMS, PATRICIA CAROLYN, telecommunications company official; b. Jacksonville, Fla., Feb. 28, 1954; d. Robert Lee Charles Williams and Mary Ella (Bigham) Stallings; B.A., Spelman Coll., 1975; M.A., Northwestern U., 1976. Bus. office supr. So. Bell Tel. & Tel. Co., Columbus, Ga., 1976-78, asst. mgr. tng., Decatur, Ga., 1978-79, assoc. mgr. tng., 1979, mgr. work relationships, Atlanta, 1980-84, mgr. legis. affairs, 1984—; mgmt. skills cons., 1978—. Bd. dirs. Urban League, Columbus, 1976-78; adv. Jr. Achievement, 1976-83; active Future Pioneers Am., 1976-78, Ga. Soc. for Prevention Blindness, 1976-78; chmn. Spelman Coll. Interest Group, 1976-78; Explorer Scouts adv. Boy Scouts Am., 1978-80; solicitor United Negro Coll. Fund, 1978-79, team capt., 1980; fund raiser Am. Cancer Soc., 1978. Nat. Fellowship Found. fellow, 1975-76. Mem. Spelman Coll. Alumni Assn. (Centennial program com. co-chmn. 1981, mem. Alumni Glee Club 1976—), Atlanta U. Cluster Nat. Alliance Businessmen, Am. Bus. Women's Assn. (pres., Woman of Yr. 1984), Nat. Black M.B.A. Assn. (Outstanding Service award 1984), Atlanta Women's Network (mid-career seminar co-chmn. 1981), Am. Soc. Tng. and Devel., World Future Soc., Alpha Kappa Alpha. Democrat. Methodist. Died Feb. 20, 2006.

WILLIAMS, RALPH MAYNARD, oral surgeon; b. Johnson City, Tenn., Sept. 11, 1927; s. Dewey Maynard and Mary Alice (Crumley) W.; m. Ann Marie Ryan, Dec. 29, 1955; children—William Joe, Dewey Maynard, Dana Beth. B.S., Lincoln Meml. U., 1949; D.D.S., U. Tenn. Coll. Dentistry, 1953. Resident in oral surgery U. Okla. Hosps., 1953-54, Scott and White Hosp., Temple, Tex., 1954-55, U. Tenn. Hosps., Knoxville, 1955-56; pvt. practice oral surgery, Bartlesville, Okla., 1956—. Deacon First Bapt. Ch., Bartlesville, 1970—; bd. reps. Fellowship Christian Athletes for Okla., March Dimes, 1984-85; chmn. Washington County Republican Party, 1969-73. Mem. ADA, Okla. Dental Assn., Internat. Soc. Oral and Maxillofacial Surgeons, Am. Soc. Oral and Maxillofacial Surgeons, Southwest Soc. Oral and Maxillofacial Surgeons (pres. 1977), Midwest Soc. Oral and Maxillofacial Surgeons, Okla. Soc. Oral and Maxillofacial Surgeons (pres. 1961-63), Am. Coll. Oral and Maxillofacial Surgeons, Internat. Acad. Dentistry, No. Dist. Dental Assn. (pres. 1965-67), Bartlesville C. of C., Delta Sigma Delta. Club: Sunset Country (Bartlesville). Lodges: Rotary (bd. dirs. Bartlesville), Elks. Home: Bartlesville, Okla. Died Mar. 8, 2007.

WILLIAMS, ROBERT JENE, lawyer, rail car company executive; b. Darby, Pa., Oct. 30, 1931; s. Joslyn Justus and Dolores Marie (Dugan) W.; m. Shirley Geraldine Fiedler, Aug. 8, 1953; children: Robin Jeanne, Sara Ann. BS, Ursinus Coll., 1953; JD, U. Pa., 1956. Bar: N.J. 1957, Pa. 1959, Ill. 1973. Asso. firm Bleakly, Stockwell & Zink, Camden, N.J., 1956-58; atty., asst. gen. atty. Reading Co., Phila., 1958-69; gen. counsel, sec. Trailer Train Co., Phila., 1969-71, Trailer Train Co. (now TTX Co.), Chgo., 1971-94; v.p. Trailer Train Co., 1975-94; ret., 1994. Mem. Ill. Bar Assn. Home: Cape May Court House, NJ. Died Nov. 23, 2006.

WILLIAMS, ROBERT LUTHER, city planning consultant; b. Porterville, Calif., June 24, 1923; s. Luther Esco and Mary (Lyon) W.; children: Jeffrey Robert, Derrick Paul, Gail Diane. Student, Utah State Coll., 1944; AB, U. Calif.-Berkeley, 1949, M.C.P., 1951. Asst. planning dir., Stockton, Calif., 1951-54; planning dir. Alameda, Calif., 1954-57, Alameda County, 1957-63; exec. dir. Am. Inst. Planners, Washington, 1963-69; v.p. Hill Devel. Corp., Middletown, Conn., 1969-71; dir. land mgmt. dept. Gulf Oil Corp., Reston, Va., 1971-74; pres. Coleman-Williams, Inc., Greenbrae, Calif., 1975-78, Robert Williams Assocs., Inc., San Rafael, Calif., 1978-87; mem. community affairs panel KQED-TV, San Francisco, 1991-94. Lectr. U. Calif. at Berkeley extension, 1956-59; tech. adviser regional planning Assn. Bay Area Govts., Calif., 1961-63; vis. prof. U. R.I., 1969-71; pres. G.I.F.T. Inst., Inc., 1991-94. Bd. dirs. Planning Found. Am., 1965-70, Communities Found., Inc., 1973-77. Served to 1st lt. AUS, 1943-46, 52, ETO. Named Young Man of Year Alameda, 1956 Mem. Am. Inst. Cert. Planners (pres. Calif. chpt. 1960), Am. Planning Assn., World Future Soc., Lambda Alpha, Lambda Chi Alpha. Presbyterian. Home: Lincolnville, Maine. Died June 18, 2006.

WILLIAMS, RONALD BETHEL, graphic designer; b. Winston-Salem, N.C., Mar. 31, 1943; s. Kenneth Raynor and Edythe W.; m. Phyllis Jean Johnson, Apr. 24, 1971; children: Melissa Patrice, Darold Scott. Student Morehouse Coll., 1961-63, Studio Sch. Art and Design, Phila., 1963-65. Engring. illustrator underseas div. Westinghouse Electric Co., Balt., 1965-67; editor publs. sect. Def. Pers. Support Center, Phila., 1967-68; art dir., mgr. graphic svcs. div. Fed. Res. Bank of Phila., 1968—; cons. designer, 1989—. V.p. home and sch. assn. C.W. Henry Elem. Sch., Phila., 1977-78, pres., 1978-79; chmn. ednl. communications steering com. Office Multi-Media Edn., Sch. Dist. Phila.; mem. Pa. Humanities Coun., 1983-86, Found. for Architecture, 1983-86. Mem. Artists Guild of Delaware Valley, Art Dirs. Club Phila., Am. Inst. Graphic Arts, Phila. Art Alliance (former dir.). Home: Elkins Park, Pa. Died Mar. 26, 2006.

WILLIAMSON, DORIS, retired business education educator; b. Salt Lake City, July 1, 1937; d. Frank Farrow and Ruby Dean (Andersen) W. A.S., Coll. So. Utah, Cedar City, 1957; B.S. in Bus. Edn., Brigham Young U., 1959; M.S. in Bus. Edn., Utah State U., 1974. Cert. secondary tchr., Utah. Tchr., Salt Lake City Schs., 1959-64; tchr. typewriting Granite Sch. Dist., Salt Lake City, 1964-70; asst. prof. bus. edn. Idaho State U., 1973-76; assoc. prof. So. Utah State Coll., Cedar City, 1976—02, chmn. dept., 1985-2002, ret., 2002; pres. faculty senate, So. Utah State Coll., 1981-82; lectr. workshops in teaching methodology and secretarial sci. Trustee Utah Summer Games, 1985-1995; state advisor, 1985-91. EDPA fellow, 1971-73; recipient Leadership award Delta Pi Epsilon, 1976; Outstanding Tchr.-Bus. Edn. award Utah Bus. Edn. and Utah Vocat. Assns. 1979; Disting. Educator award So. Utah State Coll., 1983; named Advisor of Yr. So. Utah U., 1989, 90. Mem. Utah Bus. Edn. Assn., Utah Vocat. Edn. Assn., Nat. Bus. Edn. Assn., Am. Vocat. Assn., Bus. and Profl. Women Internat. (Woman of Achievement award Cedar City 1983), Utah Shakespeare Guild (pres. 1983-1991), Cedar City C. of C. (bd. dirs. 1981-83, pres. 1982-83, Outstanding Educator award 1985), Western Bus. Edn. Assn., Classroom Edn. of Bus. Assn., Delta Pi Epsilon, Delta Kappa Gamma, Phi Kappa Phi, Phi Beta Lambda (state advisor 1984-90). Mormon. Home: Cedar City, Utah. Died July 28, 2007.

WILLIAMSON, JACK (JOHN STEWART WILLIAMSON), writer; b. Bisbee, Ariz., Apr. 29, 1908; s. Asa Lee and Lucy Betty (Hunt) W.; m. Blanche Slaten Harp, Aug. 15, 1947 (dec. Jan. 1985); stepchildren: Keigh Harp (dec.), Adele Harp Lovorn. BA, MA, Eastern N.Mex. U., 1957, LHD (hon.), 1981; PhD, U. Colo., 1964. Prof. english Ea. N.Mex. U., Portales, 1960-77, prof. emeritus, 1977—2006. Author: (novels) The Legion of Space, 1947, Darker Than You Think, 1948, The Humanoids, 1949, The Green Girl, 1950, The Cometeers, 1950, One Against the Legion, 1950, Seetee Scock, 1950, Seetee Ship, 1950, Dragon's Island, 1951, The Legion of Time, 1952, Undersea Quest, 1954, Undersea Fleet, 1955, Undersea City, 1956, Dome Around America, 1955, The Trial of Terra, 1962, Golden Blood, 1964, The Reefs of Space, 1964, Starchild, 1965, The Reign of Wizardry, 1965, Bright New Universe, 1967, Trapped in Space, 1968, Rogue Star, 1969, The Pandora Effect, 1969, People Machines, 1971, The Moon Children, 1972, H.G. Wells: Critic of Progress, 1973, The Farthest Star, 1975, Teaching SF, 1975, The Early Williamson, 1975, The Power of Blackness, 1976, The Best of Jack Williamson, 1978, Brother to Demons, Brother To Gods, 1979, Teaching Science Fiction: Education for Tomorrow, 1980, The Alien Intelligence, 1980, The Humanoid Touch, 1980, Manseed, 1982, The Queen of a Legion, 1983, Wall Around a Star, 1983, Wonder's Child: My Life in Science Fiction, 1984 (Hugo award 1985), Lifeburst, 1984, Firechild, 1986, Land's End, 1988, Mazeway, 1990, Beachhead, 1992, Demon Moon, 1994, The Black Sun, 1996, The Fortress of Utopia, 1998, The Silicon Dagger, 1999, The Stone from the Green Star, 1999, Terraforming Earth, 2001, The Stonehenge Gate, 2005; co-author: (with Frederik Phhl) Star Bridge, 1955, The Singers Of Time, 1991, (with Miles J. Breuer) The Birth of an New Republic, 1981. Served as staff sgt. USAAF, 1942-45. Mem. Sci. Fiction Writers Am. (pres. 1978-80, Grand Master Nebula award 1976), Sci. Fiction Research Assn. (Pilgrim award 1968), World Sci. Fiction, Planetary Soc. Avocations: travel, astronomy, photography. Home: Portales, N.Mex. Died Nov. 10, 2006.

WILLIS, GEORGE EDWARD, electronics technology educator, land developer; b. Del Rio, Tex., Dec. 24, 1932; s. Robert Dean and Ruthie Lee (Jones) W.; m. Clara Lou Remmert, Dec. 28, 1954; 1 child, Edward Dean. BS, SW Tex. State U., 1958; MEd, Sul Ross State U., 1966; EdD, Tex. A&M U., 1972. Cert. tchr. in postsecondary tech. edn., high sch. sci. tchr. and supr., prin. Tchr. physics and electronics Permian High Sch., Odessa, Tex., 1959-66; chmn. instrumentation and electronic data processing Odessa Coll., 1976-79, instr., chmn. dept, electronics, 1966-72, prof., chmn. dept. electronics, 1972-89, prof. electronics, from 1989. Author: (lab. manual) Microprocessors, 1989. With USAF, 1951-53; Korea. Recipient Community Svc. award Mayor of Odessa, 1978. Mem. IEEE (sr.; chmn. 1977-78), Tex. Jr. Coll. Tchrs. Assn. Republican. Avocations: travel, rodeo. Died Nov. 27, 2006.

WILLIS, ISAAC, dermatologist, educator; b. Albany, Ga., July 13, 1940; s. R.L. and Susie M. (Miller) W.; m. Alliene Horne, June 12, 1965; children: Isaac Horne, Alliric Isaac. BS, Morehouse Coll., 1961, DSc (hon.), 1989; MD, Howard U., 1965. Diplomate Am. Bd. Dermatology. Intern Phila. Gen. Hosp., 1965-66; fellow Howard U., Washington, 1966-67; resident, fellow U. Pa., Phila., 1967-69, assoc. in dermatology, 1969-70; mem. staff Phila. Gen. Hosp., 1969-70; instr. dept. dermatology U. Pa., Phila., 1970-72; mem. staff Moffit Hosp. U. Calif., San Francisco, 1970-72; asst. prof. Johns Hopkins U., Johns Hopkins Hosp., Balt., 1972-73; mem. staff Johns Hopkins Hosp., Balt. City Hosp., Good Samaritan Hosp., Balt., 1972-72; asst. prof. Emory U., Atlanta, 1973-77; mem. staff Crawford W. Long Meml. Hosp., Atlanta, from 1974, West Paces Ferry Hosp., Atlanta, 1974-2000; assoc. prof. Emory U., Atlanta, 1977-82; prof. Morehouse Sch. Medicine, Atlanta, from 1982, chief dermatology, from 1991; mem. staff Piedmont Hosp., Atlanta, from 2000. Dep. commdr. of 3297th USA Hosp. (1000B), 1990-; mem. gen. medicine group IA study sect., NIH, 1985-; mem. grants review panel EPA, 1986—; adv. bd. Arthritis and Musculoskeletal and Skin Diseases, 1991-, U. Pa. Sch. Medicine, 1995-, adv. bd. U. of Calif. Sch. of Engring. LaJolla, 2000-, Emory U., 1994-; chmn. inst. review bd., mem. pharmacy and therapeutic com.; bd. dirs. Comml. Bank Gwinnett, Comml. Bank of Ga., Heritage Bank, Landmark Bank Fla., Learning Framework, West Paces Med. Ctr., Lupus Specialists, Inc., InterVu, Inc., Lupus Erythematrosus Found., Jacquelyn McClure Lupus Erythematrosus Clinic, Skin Cancer Found., World Network Solutions; bd. dirs., chmn. audit com. Comml. Bank of Ga., 2000-, Landmark Bank of Fla., 1999-; mem. med. staff Piedmont Hosp., 2000-; adv. bd. Enable, Inc.; mem. adv. coun. U. Calif. Jacobs Sch. Engring., San Diego, 2001-; vice coun. Internat. Biographical Ctr., 2002; cons. in field. Author: Textbook of Dermatology, 1971; contbr. articles to profl. jours. Trustee Friendship Bapt. Ch., Atlanta, 1980-82; mem. gov.'s commn. on effectiveness and economy in govt. State of Ga. Human Resources Task Force, 1991—, Ga. State Bd. of worker's Compensation Med. subcom., 1997—; mem. nat. alumni coun. U. Pa., 1995—; mem. coun. of advisors U. Calif. San Diego Jacobs Sch. Engring., 2001--. Col. USAR, 1983-95. Recipient Benny Trailblazer award, Morehouse Coll., 2004. Fellow Am. Acad. Dermatology, Am. Dermtol. Assn., Am. Soc. Laser Medicine and Surgery, Inc.; mem. AAAS, AMA, Nat. Cancer Inst., Soc. Investigative Dermatology, Nat. Med. Assn., Internat. Soc. Tropical Dermatology, Pan Am. Med. Assn., Am. Fedn. Clin. Rsch., Am. Soc. Photobiology, U. Pa. Nat. Alumni Adv. Coun., State of Ga. Dermatology Found., Frontiers Internat., Sportsman Internat., Phi Beta Kappa, Omicron Delta Kappa. Achievements include a patent for the development of a shaving composition and method for preventing Pseudofollientitis Barbae, 1999; subspecialties in the areas of dermatology and cancer research (medicine). Home: Atlanta, Ga. Died Aug. 7, 2007.

WILLIS, ROY EDWARD, corporate program manager, consultant; b. Waukesha, Wis., Aug. 28, 1930; s. Orea Willis and Blanche Josephine (Boyle) Wanchura; m. Dorothy Mae Gest, Apr. 28, 1951 (div. 1977); children— Anne, Kathy Boehm, Mary, Pam Drimilla; m. Alice Jane Fairlee, June 23, 1979. B.S., U. Wis.-Platteville, 1952; M.S., U. Wis.-Madison, 1955. Tchr., coach Clifton Jr. High Sch., Ill., 1955-57, Crystal Lake Jr. High

Sch., Ill., 1957-64, McHenry High Sch., Ill., 1964-65; prin. McHenry Jr. High Sch., 1965-66; with IBM, Chgo., 1966-74 Rochester, Minn., 1974-76, Austin, Tex., 1976—, program mgr., Austin, 1982—; cons. ARC, Tex. Legal Services. Recreation dir. Crystal Lake Park Bd., 1959-64. Served to cpl. U.S. Army, 1952-54. Mem. Am. Soc. Tng. and Devel. Republican. Presbyterian. Lodge: Elks. Avocations: Reading; golf; travel; bridge. Home: Austin, Tex. Died May 27, 2007.

WILLS, DUANE ARTHUR, marine officer; b. Independence, Mo., Mar. 10, 1939; s. Vernon Robert and Sonoa Lucielle (Gregory) W.; m. Patty Jean Reslock, June 23, 1961; children: Cynthia Lee, Roamy Jean, Laurie Susan. BA in History, UCLA, 1961; MS in Pers. Mgmt., George Washington U., 1972, AA in Systems Mgmt., 1973; postgrad., Army War Coll., 1980-81. Commd. 2d lt. USMC, 1961, advanced through grades to lt. gen., comdg. officer Marine Fighter Squadron 235 Kaneone, Hawaii, 1981-82, comdr. Marine Aircraft Group 24, 1983-84, comdr. 31st Marine Amphibious Unit Western Pacific, 1984-85, chief of staff Fleet Marine Forces Pacific Honolulu, 1985-87, dir. Plans Div. Washington, 1988-89, comdg. gen. 1st Marine Aircraft Wing Okinawa, Japan, 1989-90, dep. chief of staff aviation Washington, from 1990. Mem. Nat. Aero. Soc., Marine Corps Aviation Assn., Am. NELO Soc. Republican. Presbyterian. Home: Tucson, Ariz. Died May 21, 2007.

WILLYOUNG, DAVID MAC CLEGGAN, engineering executive, consultant; b. Ridgewood, NJ, May 7, 1924; s. Charles Kittenger and Elizabeth Mae (Smith) W.; m. Ernestine Frances Rist (dec. May 1974); children: Karen Frances Willyoung Czerkies, Tim D.; m. Irene C. Hogan. MSME, Union Coll., Schenectady, NY, 1967; BME, Stevens Inst. Tech., 1945. Registered profl. engr., N.Y. Devel. engr., analyst, inventor, design engr. GE (Turbine div.), Schenectady, 1946-72; mgr. tech. resource planning GE, Schenectady, 1972-79, mgr. advanced electric propulsion systems, 1979-81, cons. engr., 1981-87, ret., 1987; pres. MacCleggan Co., Scotia, N.Y., from 1987. Holder 38 patents in large turbine generators/systems and in fluidized bed//cogeneration/combined cycles. With USN, 1944. Fellow IEEE, ASME. Home: Burlington Flats, NY. Died Jan. 28, 2006.

WILSON, AVON W., state representative; b. Wichita Falls, Tex., Sept. 24, 1929; m. Bill Wilson. BA, N. Tex. State U., 1949; MED, Ea. N.Mex. U., 1996. Tchr. Fort Stockton and Big Spring Schs., Tex., 1949—55, Roswell Ind. Sch. Dist., N.Mex., 1955—80; owner Gift Shop, Roswell, 1976—86; ednl. cons. Roswell, from 1986; state rep. dist. 59 N.Mex. State Legis., Santa Fe, from 2001. Mem. energy and natural resources N.Mex. State Legis., Santa Fe, mem. Human Resources/Labor com., mem. interim com. Indian affairs. Mem.: Altrusa Internat. Roswell (v.p./pres. from 1992). Republican. Methodist. Home: Roswell, N.Mex. Died July 10, 2006.

WILSON, CAROL LYNN, high technology company executive; b. San Jose, Calif., Aug. 12, 1935; d. Leonard Joseph and Frances Odessa (Foster) Pritchard; children— Darelyn K. Carpenter Christmon, Kevin G. Carpenter; m. Richard M. Wilson, Dec. 3, 1980. A.A. with high honors, Foothill Coll., 1975; student in journalism and pub. relations San Jose State U., 1976-81. Accredited bus. communicator. Various communications positions Saga Corp., Menlo Park, Calif., 1967-79, dir. corp. communications, 1979-82; v.p. investor services Fox & Carskadon Fin. Corp., San Mateo, Calif., 1982-83; mgr. pub. relations Measurex Corp., Cupertino, Calif., 1983—. Named Disting. Woman, Mid-Peninsula Girls' Club; Mentor, Dept. Journalism and Mass Communications, San Jose State U.; recipient 26 awards for achievements in communications. Mem. Internat. Assn. Bus. Communicators, Calif. Press Women, Nat. Fedn. Press Women, Pub. Relations Soc. Am., Nat. Investor Relations Inst. Club: Los Altos Golf and Country. Home: San Francisco, Calif. Died June 24, 2006.

WILSON, GEORGE PETER, international organization executive; b. Perth, Scotland, July 6, 1935; came to U.S., 1985; s. Alan Johnson and Doris L. (Allan) W.; m. Sandra Graham, Feb. 6, 1960 (div. 1984); 1 child, Iain; m. Robbyn Dee LaCroix, Nov. 17, 1984; 1 stepchild, Orion. Diploma in Hotel Mgmt., Scottish Coll. Commerce, Glasgow, 1954. Chartered acct., 1965, cert. internal auditor, 1985. Hotel mgr., auditor Can. Nat. Rys., Ottawa and Montreal, 1956-65; fin. officer Treasury Bd. Can., asst. sec. to Cabinet, dir. Pub. Service Commn., counsellor external affairs Govt. of Can., Ottawa, Geneva, 1965-78; dir. gen. audit UN, NYC, 1978-80; dep. auditor gen. of Can. Govt. of Can., Ottawa, 1980-85; pres. Inst. Internal Auditors, Orlando, Fla., 1985-92; dir. audit FAO UN, Rome, 1992-97, insp. gen., 1997—2003; pres. The Orion Group, Orlando, Fla., from 2003. Contbr. articles to profl. jours. Mem. Can. Inst. Chartered Accts. (com. mem.), Inst. Internal Auditors (com. mem.), Can. Comprehensive Audit Found. (gov. 1985-88), Internat. Consortium on Govt. Fin. Mgmt. (bd. dirs. 1983-92), Inst. for Fin. Crime Prevention. Home: Celebration, Fla. Died Jan. 30, 2006.

WILSON, JAMES HAMLETT, investment broker, adviser; b. Richmond, Va., July 14, 1954; s. George Price and Louise (Smith) W. BA in Econs., Hampden-Sydney Coll., 1976. Corporate banking officer nat. accounts Bank of Va., Richmond, 1976-79; investment broker Cecil, Waller & Sterling, Richmond, 1980-83; v.p. E.F. Hutton & Co., Richmond, 1983—, asst. br. mgr.; mgr. various investment clubs. Mem. Henrico County Rep. Com., 1985; del. Va. Rep. conv., 1985; bd. dirs. Am. Heart Assn., Richmond, 1982—. Named to Pres.' Club, E.F. Hutton, 1983, Blue Chip Club, 1984, 85, 86, 87. Clubs: Country of Va., Issac Walton (Richmond). Presbyterian. Avocations: car collector, tennis, hunting, martial arts. Home: Richmond, Va. Died July 21, 2006.

WILSON, JOHN HENRY, theatrical manager; b. Concord, NH, Sept. 13, 1922; s. Henry John and Marjorie Grace (Robinson) W. BA, U. N.H., 1951. With Ogunquit (Maine) Playhouse, 1949-54, Hurok Concert, Inc., Seattle, 1957-64, performing arts dept, World's Fair, Seattle, 1962, N.Y.C. World's Fair, 1963-65; gen. mgr. Nat. Ballet of Can., 1965-67; co. mgr. Hurok Concerts, 1967-76; mgrs. Bolshoi Ballet, Royal Ballet, Stuttgart Ballet, others; now presentations mgr. Met. Opera Assn., Lincoln Center, NYC. Lectr. on theatrical mgmt. Served with USN, 1942-46. Decorated Bronze Star medal. Died Mar. 21, 2007.

WILSON, LEONARD GILCHRIST, medical educator; b. Orillia, Ont., Can., June 11, 1928; s. George Edward and Mary Agnes (MacPhee) W.; m. Adelia Katherine Hans, June 7, 1969; 1 child, George Edward Hans. BA, U. Toronto, Can., 1949; M.Sc., U. London, 1955; PhD, U. Wis., Madison, 1958. Lectr. Mount Allison U., Sackville, N.B., Canada, 1950-53; vis. instr. U. Calif., Berkeley, 1958-59; asst. prof. Cornell U., Ithaca, NY, 1959-60, Yale U., New Haven, 1960-65, assoc. prof., 1965-67; prof., head dept. history of medicine U. Minn., Mpls., 1967-98, prof. emeritus, from 1998. Author: Charles Lyell: The Years to 1841: The Revolution in Geology, 1972, Medical Revolution in Minnesota, 1989, Lyell in America: The Trans Atlantic Years, 1841-1853, 1998; editor: Benjamin Silliman and His Circle, 1979, Sir Charles Lyell's Scientific Journals on the Species Question, 1971; editor Jour. History Medicine and Allied Scis., 1973-82; co-editor: Readings in History of Physiology, 1966; mem. bd. mgrs. Jour. Hist. Medicine, 1962—. Fellow AAAS; mem. Am. Assn. History of Medicine, Am. Hist. Assn., History of Sci. Soc., Minn. Acad. Medicine (pres. 1984-85, sec.-treas. 1989-98), Brit. Soc. for the History of Sci., Soc. for the History of natural History. Home: Saint Paul, Minn. Died Nov. 30, 2005.

WILSON, ROBERT ANTON, author; b. Bklyn., Jan. 18, 1932; s. John Joseph and Elizabeth Loretta (Milli) W.; m. Arlen Riley, Jan. 4, 1959 (dec. 1999); children: Christina, Alexandra, Graham. Student, NYU, 1956; PhD, Paideia U., 1979. Assoc. editor Playboy mag., 1965-71; freelance writer, 1971—2007. V.p., Inst. Study Human Future, Berkeley, Calif., 1979. Author: Feminine Forever, 1966, Playboy's Book of Forbidden Words, 1972, Sex and Drugs, 1973, The Book of the Breast, 1974, Gertrude Stein: A Bibliography, 1974, Cosmic Trigger, 1977, The Illuminati Papers, 1980, The Schrodinger's Cat Trilogy, 1979-81, Masks of Illumanti, 1981, Right Where You Are Sitting Now, 1982, The Earth Will Shake, 1982, Prometheus Rising, 1983, The Widow's Son, 1985, The New Inquisition, 1987, Wilhelm Reich in Hell, 1987; co-author: (with Robert J. Shea) The Illuminatus! Triology, 1975, Neuropolitcs, 1977. Libertarian. Died Jan. 11, 2007.

WILSON, WILLIAM STANLEY, oceanographer; b. Alexander City, Ala., June 5, 1938; s. Norman W. and Helen C. (Hackemack) W.; m. Anne M. Stout; children: Lauren, Jonathan (dec.). BS, William & Mary Coll., 1959, MA, 1965; PhD, Johns Hopkins U., 1972. Marine biol. collector Va. Inst. Marine Sci., Gloucester Point, 1959-62, computer systems analyst, 1964-65, Chesapeake Bay Inst., Balt., 1965-66; phys. oceanography program mgr. Office of Naval Rsch., Washington, 1972-78; chief oceanic processes program NASA, Washington, 1979-89, program scientist earth observing sys., 1989-92; asst. adminstr. for ocean svcs. and coastal zone mgmt. NOAA, Washington, 1992-97, dep. chief scientist, 1997—2002; sr. scientist Nat. Environ. Satellite Data and Info. Svc., from 2002. U.S. rep. intergovtl. oceanographic commn. UNESCO, 1993—2003. Recipient Antarctica Svc. medal NSF, 1961, Superior Civilian Svc. award USN, 1979, Exceptional Sci. Achievement medal NASA, 1981, Disting. Achievement award MTS and Compass Publs., 1989, award Remote Sensing Soc., 1992, medal French Space Agy., 1994, Portuguese Naval Cross, 1997, Australian Antarctic Divsn. medal, 1998, Group Achievement award NASA, 2000. Mem. Am. Meteorol. Soc., Am. Geophys. Union (Ocean Scis. award 1984), Oceanography Soc. (com. chmn. 1989-92), Sigma Xi, Omicron Delta Kappa. Avocations: bicycling, scuba diving. Home: Baltimore, Md. Died Mar. 29, 2007.

WINANDY, DONALD HARRY, educational administrator, state official; b. Gary, Ind., June 20, 1934; s. John P. and Marie E. (Gallion) W.; m. Rosemary Borsattino, Aug. 20, 1960; children— Susan M., Angela L. B.S., Marian Coll., 1956; M.S., Ind. U., 1959; Ph.D., Fla. State U., 1967; M.S., Hartford Grad. Ctr., 1981. Dir. admissions and records Lewis U., Lockport, Ill., 1959-65; research assoc. Ill. Bd. Higher Edn., Springfield, Ill., 1967-69; programs adminstr. Va. Council of Higher Edn., Richmond, 1969-75; dir. accreditation Conn. Dept. Higher Edn., Hartford, 1975—; dir. Intensive Edn. Ctr., West Hartford, 1984—; mem. exec. com. Conn. Council on Higher Edn., Hartford, 1977—. Contbr. articles to profl. jours. Served with U.S. Army, 1956-58. Hartford Grad. Ctr. corp. fellow, 1980. Mem. State Lic. and Accrediting Officers, Am. Assn. Higher Edn. Roman Catholic. Avocations: furniture reproductions; rock hunting. Home: West Hartford, Conn. Died June 20, 2006.

WINBURN, GENE MACK, lawyer; b. Hartsville, SC, Feb. 1, 1937; s. William McLendon and Mary Elizabeth (Mullis) W.; m. Beverly Booker, July 18, 1962; children: Whitney, Paige. BBA, U. Ga., 1961. Bar: Ga. 1961, U.S. Dist. Ct. (no. and mid. dists.) Ga. 1961, U.S. Tax Ct. 1962. Conf. coord. Ga. Ctr. Continuing Edn., Athens, 1961-62; ptnr. Fortson, Bentley & Griffin, Athens, 1962-82, Winburn, Lewis & Barrow, Athens, from 1982. Instr. U. Ga., 1962-72, Ga. Inst. Trial Advocates, 1983—, Emory U., 1982—, Cardosa Law Sch., 1988, Hofstra U., 1986—, Del. Law Sch., 1987—. Mem. Ga. Bar Assn. (pres. 1989-90), Ga. Trial Lawyers Assn. (pres. 1987), Phoenix Soc., Internat. Acad. Trial Lawyers, Internat. Soc. Barristers, Am. Bd. Trial Advocates, Atlanta Lawyers Club, Phi Delta Phi, Sigma Alpha Epsilon. Baptist. Home: Athens, Ga. Died Mar. 20, 2006.

WINE, SHERWIN THEODORE, rabbi; b. Detroit, Jan. 25, 1928; s. William Harry and Tillie (Israel) W. BA, U. Mich., 1950, A.M., 1952; B.H.L., Hebrew Union Coll., Cin., M.H.L., rabbi, Hebrew Union Coll., Cin., 1956. Rabbi Temple Beth El, Detroit, 1956-60, Windsor, Ont., Can., 1960-64, Birmingham (Mich.) Temple, 1964—2007. Cons. editor Humanistic Judaism, 1966—2007 Author: A Philosophy of Humanistic Judaism, 1965, Meditation Services for Humanistic Judaism, 1977, Humanistic Judaism-What Is It?, 1977, Humanist Haggadah, 1980, High Holidays for Humanists, 1980, Judaism Beyond God, 1985, Celebration, 1988, Staying Sane in a Crazy World, 1996. Founder Ctr. for New Thinking, Birmingham, 1977-2007; founder Soc. Humanistic Judaism, 1969; pres. N.Am. Com. for Humanism, 1982-93. Chaplain U.S. Army, 1956-58. Mem. Conf. Liberal Religion (chmn. 1985-96), Leadership Conf. Secular and Humanistic Jews (chmn. 1983-93), Internat. Inst. Secular Humanistic Judaism (co-chmn. 1986-2007), Internat. Assn. Humanist Educators, Counselors and Leaders (pres. 1988-93), Internat. Fedn. Secular Humanistic Jews (co-chmn. 1993-2007). Home: Birmingham, Mich. Died July 21, 2007.

WING, THOMAS, micrometrologist, engineer, consultant; b. Shanghai, China, Mar. 12, 1929; came to U.S., 1930, naturalized, 1950; s. Lim and Fong Shee W.; B.S. in Engring. cum laude, Purdue U., 1953, postgrad., 1957-60; postgrad. CCNY, 1953-55; m. Catherine Amajelia Scambia, Nov. 27, 1954; children— Karen Elyse, Thomas Scambia, Robert Frank Joseph, David Anthony. Sr. project mgr. Gulton Industries, Metuchen, N.J., 1960-63; adv. engr. IBM, Lexington, Ky., 1963-65; with guidance and control systems div. Litton Industries, Woodland Hills, Calif., 1966-69, mem. tech. staff, 1976-92; cons. in field, 1992—; staff cons. Devel. Consultants, Cin., 1965-66; image tech. mgr. Fairchild Semiconductor, Mountain View, Calif., 1969-71; gen. mgr. research and devel., v.p., Jade Corp., HLC Mfg. Co., Willow Grove, Pa., 1971-75; pres. Photronic Engring. Labs., Inc., Danbury, Conn., 1975-76; lectr. in micro-photo lithography, Inst. Graphic Communication, Boston; cons. engr. in micro image tech. and metrology; founding mem. Thermo Phys. Properties Research Center, Purdue U.; pres., staff cons. Zantec Inc., North Hollywood, Calif., 1981-86; cons. Kasper Instruments, Sunnyvale, Calif., 1977-79, Quintel Corp., San Jose, Calif., 1979—. Coach, v.p. Roadrunners Hockey Club, 1972-75, founder, 1972, Bristol, Pa.; founder, pres. Eastridge Jr. Hockey Club, San Jose, Calif., 1970-71; coach Belmont (Calif.) Jr. Hockey Club, 1969; v.p. Greater Los Angeles Minor Hockey Assn., 1968-69; v.p., coach West Valley Minor Hockey Club, Tarzana, Calif., 1968-69; coach Topanga Plaza Jr. Hockey Club, 1967. Mem. ASME, ASTM (mem. F-1 com. on microelectronics 1972-75), Soc. Photog. Instrumentation Engrs., Soc. Photog. Scientists and Engrs., Tau Beta Pi, Pi Tau Sigma, Phi Eta Sigma. Organizer first internat. lecture series on micro photo lithography, Boston, 1974; contbr. articles to profl. publs.; patentee currency counter, trimming inductor, damped high frequency accelerometer, three phase dithered pivot, auto focus for step and repeat camera, temperature compensated dither drive for laser gyro, proximity printing mechanism, equilbrator for howitizer. Died Aug. 1, 2007.

WINGATE, MARCEL EDWARD, speech educator; b. New Castle, Pa., Feb. 27, 1923; s. Morton Harvey and Elizabeth (Martin) Wingett; m. Elaine C. Kayser, June 8, 1948 (div. July 1968); children: Nancy, Amy, Jennifer; m. Cicely Anne Johnston, June 7, 1969; children: Marcel Richard, Cicely Anna Marie. BA, Grinnell Coll., Iowa, 1948; MA, U. Wash., 1952, PhD, 1956. Lic. psychologist, Wash., N.Y. Psychologist Childrens Hosp., Seattle, 1953-57, Wash. State C.P. Ctr., Seattle, 1954-57; asst. prof. U. Wash., Seattle, 1957-65, assoc. prof., 1965-68; prof. SUNY, Buffalo, 1968-73, U. Ariz., Tucson, 1973-75; prof. speech, hearing sci. Wash. State U., Pullman, from 1975. Cons. psychologist St. Mary's Hosp., Lewiston, N.Y., 1969-73; internationally recognized expert on stuttering. Author: Stuttering: Theory and Treatment, 1976, Structure of Stuttering, 1988, Stuttering: A Short History of a Curious Disorder, 1997; assoc. editor Jour. Speech/Hearing Disorders, 1966-73; editorial cons. Jour. Speech/Hearing Rsch., 1974-80; editorial bd. Jour. Fluency Disorders, 1974—; contbr. articles to profl. jours., chpts. to books. With U.S. Army, 1942-45, ETO. Fellow Am. Speech and Hearing Assn. Avocations: flying, mountain climbing, sailing, carpentry/cabinetry, astronomy. Home: Pullman, Wash. Died Nov. 29, 2006.

WINJUM, STEPHEN J., medical association administrator; b. Long Beach, Calif., 1963; BSBA cum laude in Acctg., Creighton U., 1985; JD cum laude, U. Notre Dame, 1988. Atty. Latham & Watkins, Katten Muchin Zavis Rosenman; prin., owner Chgo. 1990—94; founder NovaMed Eyecare Inc., Chgo., from 1995, pres., from 1995, CEO, from 1995, chmn. bd. Died Mar. 30, 2005.

WINN, EDWARD BURTON, lawyer; b. Dallas, Sept. 23, 1920; s. Edward Frost and Verdie Catherine (Robbins) W.; m. Conchita Elisa Hassell, June 1, 1945; children— Edward Arthur, David Burton, William Hassell, Richard Wellington, Alan Randolph. BA, U. Tex., 1942; LL.B., Yale, 1948. Bar: Tex. bar 1948. Since practiced in, Dallas; ptnr. Lane, Savage, Counts & Winn, 1958-81, Winn, Beaudry & Virden, 1981-91, Winn, Beaudry & Winn, L.L.P., from 1992. Pres. Dallas Jr. Bar Assn., 1951, Jr. Bar Tex., 1953, Dallas Estate Council, 1954-55; adv. council Dallas Community Chest Trust Fund, 1965-68; mem. staff armed forces preparedness subcom U.S. Senate, 1951; chmn. Inst. on Wills and Probate, Southwestern Legal Found., 1966— Co-author: Texas Estate Administration, How to Live and Die with Texas Probate, 1985; Contbr. articles to profl. jours. Chmn. Dallas County Profl. and Bus. Men for Kennedy-Johnson, 1960; vice chmn. Dallas County Democratic Exec. Com., 1964-66; Bd. dirs Operation LIFT, 1962-82; trustee Nat. Pollution Control Found. Southwestern Legal Found., 1986—. Served to lt. USNR 1942-46, ETO. Decorated with the Admirals' Commendations 1943; recipient William W. Treat award Nat. Coll. Probate Judges, 1985. Fellow Am. Coll. Probate Counsel (pres. 1974-75), Am. Coll. of Trust and Estate Council; mem. ABA (bd govs. 1985-88, council 1955-84, sect. chmn. 1963-64, sect. real property probate and trust law, ho. of dels. 1965-66, 78-84 85-90, conf. of sect. and div. dels. 1982-84), Dallas Bar Assn (dir. 1959-61), Dallas UN Assn. (pres.), UN Assn. of U.S. (gov 1980-84, dir., pres. Tex. div. 1967-71), State Bar Tex. (chmn sect. real estate, probate and trust law 1962-63), Am. Bar Found., Tex. Bar Found., Dallas Council World Affairs (pres young execs. group 1959-60, bd. dirs. 1958-73), Yale Law Sch Alumni Assn. N. Tex. (pres. 1962-66, regional rep. 1966-72), U Tex. Ex-Students Assn. Dallas (pres. 1963-64), Dallas Club Dallas Knife and Fork Club (pres. elect 1994-95, bd. dirs.) Calyx Club, Rotary (Park Cities club, pres. elect 1995—), Ph Kappa Sigma (pres. Sigma chpt. 1941-42), Phi Eta Sigma Home: Dallas, Tex. Died Mar. 11, 2007.

WINNERT, FRANKLIN ROY, consultant, former building materials manufacturing executive; b. Buffalo, Sept. 28, 1932; s. Franklin R. and Verna W.; m. Carol Elaine Cochran, Sept. 10, 1955; children: Laurie Ellen Canning, Deborah Kim Scheiber. B.Sc., Cornell U., 1954, MBA, 1955. Salesman to v.p.-gen. mgr. Owens-Corning Fiberglas, NYC, 1955-69; chief oper. officer, pres., bd. dirs. CertainTeed Corp., Valley Forge, Pa., 1970-80, Safeguard Bus. Systems Inc., Ft. Washington, Pa., 1980-84; sr. v.p. door and speciality prodns. residential Dallas Corp., 1985-89; pres. Winnert Assocs., Dallas, 1989-91; exec. dir. Preservation Soc. Newport County, 1989-91; prin. Winnert Assocs., Jameston, R.I., from 1991. Dir. U.S. Pro Indoor Tennis Corp. Bd. dirs. Phila. Ballet, 1983-85; dir. fund raising Phila. chpt. Heart Fund, 1982-84; pres. Johnson Grad. Sch. Mgmt. Cornell U., Ithaca, N.Y., 1986—; mem. adv. coun. U. Tex.-Dallas Sch. Mgmt., 1987—. Mem. Cornell Alumni Assn. (pres. 1978-80) Republican. Presbyterian. Avocations: tennis, running, savoring fine wines. Home: Lake Kiowa, Tex. Died Dec. 25, 2006.

WINNICK, LOUIS, former foundation executive; b. Bucharest, Rumania, Apr. 1, 1921; came to U.S., 1922, naturalized, 1936; s. David and Ida (Cushing) W.; m. Wilma Artus, Dec. 26, 1948; children— Pamela, Holly. B.A., Bklyn. Coll., 1946; M.A., Columbia U., 1947, Ph.D., 1953. Research dir. N.Y.C. Planning Commn., 1957-59; exec. dir. N.Y. Gov.'s Commn. on N.Y. Economy, N.Y.C., 1959-61; research dir. N.Y.C. Housing and Redevel. Bd., 1961-63; dep. v.p. nat. affairs. divsn. Ford Found., N.Y.C., 1968-86; lectr. grad. sch. bus. Columbia U., N.Y.C., 1960-63; trustee Coop. Assistance Fund, Washington, 1969; Author: American Housing and Its Use, 1957; Housing Choices and Constraints, 1960. Bd. dirs. Citizens Housing and Planning Council, N.Y.C.; mem. citizens adv. com. N.Y.C. Office of Mgmt. and Budget. Served with USN, 1943-45. Mem. Am. Econ. Assn., Am. Statis. Assn. Home: Great Neck, NY. Died July 29, 2006.

WINSTON, WILLIAM LITTLETON, retired judge; b. Richmond, Va., Aug. 7, 1923; s. Joseph Mosby and Mary Lucile (Brauer) W.; m. Mildred Suzanne Ryland, Oct. 1, 1949; children: Joseph, William, Beverly, Ellen. Student, Randolph-Macon Coll., 1941-43; LLB, U. Va., 1948. Bar: Va. 1948, U.S. Dist. Ct. (ea. dist.) Va. 1948. Assoc. Jesse, Phillips, Klinge & Kendrick, Arlington, Va., 1948-53; ptnr. Ryland & Winston, Ryland, Winston & Carpenter and sole practice, Arlington, 1953-66; judge Cir. Ct. of Arlington County, 1966—98, chief judge, 1974—98. Chmn. Jud. Inquiry and Rev. Com., 1978-85; mem. Jud. Council Va., 1985-96. Mem. Va. House of Dels, 1956-66. Served as sgt. AUS, 1943-46. Mem. ABA, Va. Bar Assn., Va. State Bar, Arlington County Bar Assn. (pres. 1963), Army-Navy Country Club. Home: Arlington, Va. Died Nov. 6, 2007.*

WINTERS, ROBERT CHARLES, architect; b. Cleve., July 8, 1946; s. Charles J. Winters and Grace (Campbell) Patchin; m. Janis Jaclyn Robison, Aug. 31, 1968; children: Jason Andrew, Aaron Robert. BArch, Kent State U., 1971. Project architect, designer Forest City-Dillon/Hecky and Yee Architects, Akron, Ohio, 1971-73; assoc., project architect Fletcher Properties Inc., Jacksonville, Fla., 1973-75; designer, architect Richard L. Bowen and Assoc., Cleve., 1975-76; v.p. design Hass and Reed Architects Inc., Jacksonville, 1976-78; archtl. mgr. Structures Med. East Corp., Jacksonville, 1978-81; owner Winterstudio, Jacksonville, from 1980; ptnr., exec. v.p. Manss and Winters Architects and Planners Inc., Jacksonville, 1983-86; pvt. practice architecture Jacksonville, from 1986. Mem. AIA, Constrn. Specification Inst., Nat. Council Archtl. Registration Bds., Jacksonville C. of C. (com. 100 1986—), Epsilon Delta Rho. Avocations: photography, art, music. Home: Jacksonville, Fla. Died Feb. 15, 2007.

WINTHROP, BARBARA SEVERY, chef, food consultant; b. Oceanside, Calif., Oct. 30, 1945; d. George Fairburn and Dorothy Mary (Severy) Winthrop. BA, Hunter Coll., 1969. Chair dept. phys. edn. Packer Collegiate Inst., Bklyn., 1969-75; coach, tchr. Chapin Sch., N.Y.C., 1975-81; mgr. Servomation Corp., Stamford, Conn., 1981-82; chef Alpen Pantry, N.Y.C., 1982-83; head chef Bagels & Caviar, Bklyn., 1983-85, Heights Casino, Bklyn., 1985-87, Christopher's Restaurant, N.Y.C., 1987-88, Portland Yacht Club, Falmouth, Maine, 1988—; mem. Mid. States Evaluation, N.Y.C., 1974. Vol. Dem. Party, 1985. Mem. NOW, Audubon Soc., Ms. Found. for Women, Wilderness Soc., Athletic Assn. Ind. Schs. Home: Cape Eliz, Maine. Died May 7, 2007.

WIRTH, SANDRA LEE, real estate company owner; b. Buffalo, June 8, 1945; d. Dominic A. and Santina (Lopez) Liberatore; 1 child, H. William III. Prin. Metro Sandra Lee Wirth Robshaw Gallery of Homes, Tonawanda, N.Y.; regional mgr. Paul Robshaw Galler of Homes, Tonawanda, N.Y., mgr. the Cheektowaga, N.Y.; broker assoc. B.W. Morris and Son Realtors, Buffalo; owner Metro Sandra Lee Wirth, Real Estate; mem. N.Y. Assembly, Dist. 148, Albany, from 1994. Chmn., past pres. West Seneca Druga Abuse Prevention Coun.; sponsor Call Home Free Program, Nat. Crime Prevention Coun.'s Nat. Night Out. Named Realtor of the Yr., Elma Bus. Person of the Yr. Mem. Nat. Assn. Realtors (cert.), N.Y. Assn. Realtors (state dir.), Greater Buffalo Bd. Realtors (1st v.p. 1988, treas. 1989, pres. elect 1990), Greater Buffalo Assn. Realtors (pres.), Buffalo and West Seneca C. of C. Died Mar. 11, 2006.

WIRTZ, BILL (WILLIAM WADSWORTH WIRTZ), real estate company executive, professional sports team executive; b. Detroit, Oct. 5, 1929; s. Arthur Michael and Virginia (Wadsworth) Wirtz; m. Joan Roney, Dec. 15, 1950 (dec. May 1983); children: William R., Gail W., Karey K., Peter R., Alyson M.; m. Alice Pirie Hargrave, Dec. 1, 1987. AB, Brown U., 1950. Pres. Chgo. Blackhawks, 1966—2007, Chgo. Stadium Corp., 1966—2007, Consol. Enterprises, Inc., Chgo., 1966—2007, Forman Realty Corp., Chgo., 1965—2007, 333 Bldg. Corp., Chgo., 1966—2007, Wirtz Corp., Chgo., 1964—2007. Former chmn. bd. govs. NHL; mem. Winter Olympic Com., 1980, 84. Named to Hockey Hall of Fame, 1976, US Hockey Hall of Fame, 1985; recipient Lester Patrick Trophy, 1978. Mem.: Sunset Ridge Country Club, Fin and Feather Club, Mid-America Club, Racquet Club, Saddle and Cycle Club. Died Sept. 26, 2007.

WISE, MARVIN JAY, retired lawyer; b. San Antonio, Apr. 6, 1926; s. Philip and Anna Edith (Corman) W.; m. Gloria Marian Johnston, Sept. 19, 1954; children: Philip Johnston, Jennifer Lea, Amelia Ann. BA magna cum laude, U. Tex., 1945; LL.B. cum laude, Harvard U., 1949; diploma comparative legal studies, U. Cambridge, Eng., 1950. Bar: Tex. 1949. Assoc. Thompson & Knight, Dallas, 1950-57; ptnr. Wise and Stuhl, Dallas, 1957-88; of counsel Novakov Davis, Dallas, 1988-98 and from 99. Bd. dirs. Dallas Assn. Mental Health, Isthmus Inst., Dallas Home Jewish Aged, Dallas Civic Ballet Soc., Walden Prep. Sch. Served with AUS, 1945-46. Fulbright scholar, 1949-50 Fellow Tex. Bar Found.; mem. ABA, Tex. Bar Assn., Dallas Bar Assn. (chmn. probate, trusts and estates sect. 1981-82), Am. Coll. Trust and Estate Counsel, UN Assn. (dir. Dallas chpt.), Phi Beta Kappa, Alpha Phi Omega, Phi Eta Sigma, Pi Sigma Alpha. Clubs: Crescent. Jewish. Home: Dallas, Tex. Died July 3, 2006.

WISNIEWSKI, JOE, environmental scientist, editor; b. Elizabeth, NJ, Sept. 16, 1950; s. Joseph and Julia (Korona) W.; m. Jan Riche, Oct. 14, 1995. BA in Math., BA in Chemistry, U. Del., 1972; MS in Atmospheric Scis., U. Miami, 1974; PhD in Environ. Scis., U. Va., 1977; MBA in Internat. Fin., George U., Washington, 1983. Postdoctoral fellow U.S. Congress Weather Modification Adv. Bd., Princeton, N.J., 1977-78; group leader environ. scis. The MITRE Corp., McLean, Va., 1978-80; dir. environ. scis. dept. Gen. Rsch. Corp., McLean, Va., 1980-83; pres. Wisniewski & Assocs. Inc., Falls Church, Va., from 1983. Adj. prof. N.C. State U. Coll. Forestry, 1994—. Editor/co-editor chpts. numerous books including Water Air and Soil Pollution, 1988, Environmental Management, 1996, Elsevier Science Book, 1997, Environmental Professional, 1997, Critical Reviews in Environmental Science and Technology, 1997; editor-in-chief Elsevier Sci.'s Jour. Environ. Sci. and Policy, 1998—; contbr. some 30 articles to profl. jours. Roman Catholic. Avocations: running, biking, skiing, travel, wine. Died Aug. 9, 2006.

WITMER, JOHN ALBERT, librarian; b. Lancaster, Pa., Nov. 29, 1920; s. Albert Franklin and Mary Esther (Conrad) W.; m. Doris May Ferry, June 10, 1943; children: Marilyn May Witmer Custis, John Richard, Deborah Witmer Jones. AB, Wheaton Coll., 1942, AM, 1946; ThM, Dallas Theol. Sem., 1946, ThD, 1953; MS in L.S., East Tex. State U., 1969; cert. Archival Adminstrn., U. Tex., Arlington, 1988. Grad. fellow Wheaton Coll., 1942-44; mng. editor Child Evanglism mag., Dallas, 1944-46; instr. Child Evangelism Inst., Dallas and Chgo., 1945-47; instr. systematic theology Dallas Theol. Sem., 1947-54, asst. prof., 1954-86, assoc. prof., 1986-87, assoc. prof. emeritus, from 1987; librarian Mosher Library, 1964-86, archivist, from 1987. Cert. instr. Dale Carnegie Course, 1956-92, instr. emeritus, 1992—. Contbr. articles to profl. jours., essays; editor: The Christian Librarian, 1972-74. Treas. Evang. Communications Research Found., 1970-73; bd. dirs. Dallas Bible Coll., 1972-83, chmn., 1974-77, sec., 1979-82; bd. dirs. Evang. Projects, 1975-92. Mem. Assn. Christian Librs., Evang. Philos. Soc., Evan. Theol. Soc., Soc. Am. Archivists, Soc. Southwest Archivists, Grace Evang. Soc. Died Jan. 5, 2007.

WITTEN, DAVID MELVIN, retired radiology educator; b. Trenton, Mo., Aug. 16, 1926; s. Buford Isom and Mary Louise (Melvin) W.; m. Netta Lee Watkins, Dec. 23, 1950; children— David Melvin, II, Michael Lee. Student, Trenton Jr. Coll., 1943-44, 46-47; AB, Washington U., St. Louis, 1950, MD, 1954; MS in Radiology, U. Minn., 1960. Diplomate: Am. Bd. Radiology. Intern Virginia Mason Hosp., Seattle, 1954-55; practice medicine specializing in family medicine Trenton, Mo., 1955-57; fellow in radiology Mayo Clinic/Mayo Found., Rochester, Minn., 1957-60; cons. in diagnostic roentgenology Mayo Clinic, 1960-70; instr. Mayo Grad. Sch. Medicine, Rochester, 1960-66, asst. prof. radiology, 1966-70; pvt. practice medicine specializing in radiology Aberdeen, Wash., 1970-71; clin. assoc. prof. U. Wash., 1970-71; prof. diagnostic radiology, chmn. dept. diagnostic radiology U. Ala., Birmingham, 1971-82; diagnostic radiologist in chief Univ. Hosp., Birmingham, 1971-82; prof., chmn. dept. radiology U. Mo., Columbia, 1982-87, prof. emeritus, 1987—2007, interim chmn. dept. radiology, 1998-99. Pres. U. Ala. Health Services Found., 1973-75 Author: Atlas of Tumor Radiology-The Breast, 1969, Clinical Urography, 1970, 77; contbr. articles on radiology of breast cancer, urologic and gastrointestinal disease to profl. jours.; mem. editorial bd. Am. Jour. Roentgenology, 1976-87, Applied Radiology, 1978-87, Urologic Radiology, 1979-87, Radiographics, 1983-87. Served with USNR, 1944-46. Fellow Am. Coll. Radiology; mem. AAAS, AMA, Radiol. Soc. N.Am., Am. Roentgen Ray Soc., Soc. Uroradiology (pres. 1981-82, Gold medal 2003), Soc. Uroradiology (gold medal 2003), Assn. Univ. Radiologists, Mo. Radiol. Soc. (pres. 1988-89), Mo. State Med. Assn., Can. Assn. Radiologists (hon.), Audubon Soc. (editor The Bluebird chpt. 1990-98). Home: Columbia, Mo. Died May 12, 2007.

WITTRY, DAVID BERYLE, physicist, researcher; b. Mason City, Iowa, Feb. 7, 1929; s. Herman Joseph and Edna Pearl (Filbey) W.; m. Mildred Elizabeth DuBois, July 1, 1955; children: James David, Robert Andrew, Kristopher Lee, Diane Marie, Linda Beryle. BS, U. Wis., 1951; MS, Calif. Inst. Tech., 1953, PhD, 1957. Research fellow Calif. Inst. Tech., Pasadena, 1957-59; asst. prof. U. So. Calif., Los Angeles, 1959-61, assoc. prof. dept. elec. engring., 1961-69, prof. dept. materials sci. and elec. engring., 1969-98, disting. prof. emeritus, from 1998. Cons. Hughes Semiconductors, 1958-59, Applied Research Labs., Inc., 1958-83, Exptl. Sta., E.I. du Pont de Nemours & Co., 1962-71, Gen. Telephone and Electronics Research Labs., 1966-72, Autonetics div. N. Am. Aviation, 1961-63, Electronics Research div. Rockwell Internat., 1976-81, Atlantic Richfield Co. Corp. Tech. Lab., 1981-87, Jet Propulsion Lab., 1985-88, Hitachi Instruments, 1989-90; vis. scientist Japan Soc. Promotion of Sci., U. Osaka Prefecture, 1974. Editor 3 proceedings of cons. Contbr. articles to profl. jours. Patentee in field. Recipient first award essays on gravity, Gravity Research Found., 1949, Disting. Scientist award phys. scis. Microscopy Soc. Am., 1995, Disting. Svc. citation U. Wis. Coll. Engring., 1996; Guggenheim fellow, 1967-68; Knapp scholar U. Wis., 1949-51. Mem. IEEE, Electron Microscopy Soc. Am. (dir. phys. scis. 1979-81, pres. 1983), Microbeam Analysis Soc. (sec. organizing com. 1966, exec. council 1970-72, pres. 1988, Presdl. award 1980, Birks award 1987, 89, hon. mem.), Am. Phys. Soc., Sigma Xi. Methodist. Home: Pasadena, Calif. Died May 5, 2007.

WITZIG, WARREN FRANK, nuclear engineer, educator; b. Detroit, Mar. 26, 1921; s. Arthur Judson and Mary (Bender) W.; m. Bernadette Sullivan, Mar. 31, 1942; children: Eric, Leah, Marc, Lisa Witzig Davidson. BEE, Rensselaer Poly. Inst., 1942; MS, U. Pitts., 1944, PhD, 1952. Registered profl. engr., Pa., Wash. Rsch. engr. Westinghouse Research, Pitts., 1942-48; mgr. reactor physics, engr. Bettis Atomic, Pitts., 1948-60; co-founder, sr. v.p., dir. NUS Corp., Washington, 1960-67; head dept. nuclear engring. Pa. State U., 1967-87, pres. emeritus, 1987—2007. Cons. nuclear engr. utilities industry; chmn. Pa. Gov.'s Com. on Atomic Energy Devel., 1970-80; mem. Saxton safety com., 1970-72; mem. waste com. Atomic Indsl. Forum, 1971-73; adv. com. Dept. Energy, 1980-82; mem. ops. rev. com. Tex. Utility; nuclear safety and compliance com., bd. dirs. GPU, 1983-92; mem. nuclear oversight com. PSE&G, 1983-91; mem. accrediting bd. Inst. Nuclear Power Ops., 1992-96; safety rev. bd. TVA, 1986-91; chmn. Westinghouse Nuclear Safety and Environ. Commn., 1988-93; chmn. safety audit bd. Centichem., 1989; safeguards com. Pa. State U., 1993—, interim dir. nuclear reactor, 1996-97. Designer S5W submarine reactor, 1956-60. Mem. bd. mgmt. YMCA, 1955-64. Fellow AAAS, Am. Nuc. Soc. (exec. com. edn. divsn., past chmn. nat. com. on public info., chmn. nuc. engring. dept. head com. 1980); mem. Am. Phys. Soc., IEEE (past chmn. nuc. engring. and plasma divsn.), Sigma Xi, Eta Kappa Nu, Pi Kappa Alpha, Sigma Pi Sigma (Power Engring. Educator spl. citation) Presbyterian (elder). Achievements include design of S5W submarine reactor; criticality engineer on Nautilus maiden voyage; developed continuing and long distance education in nuclear engineering. Home: State College, Pa. Died June 14, 2007.

WOHLSCHLAG, DONALD EUGENE, zoologist, marine ecologist, educator emeritus; b. Bucyrus, Ohio, Nov. 6, 1918; s. Herman Albert and Agnes Mae (Canode) W.; m. Elsie Marjorie Baker, June 5, 1943; children: William Eugene, Nancy Sue (dec.), Sarah Ann. BS, Heidelberg Coll., 1940; PhD, Ind. U., 1949. Research assoc. in zoology U. Wis., 1948-49; asst. prof. biol. scis. Stanford U., 1949-56, asso. prof., 1956-64, prof., 1964-65; prof. zoology and marine scis. U. Tex., Port Aransas, 1965-86, prof. emeritus zoology and marine scis., from 1986; dir. Marine Sci. Inst., 1965-70. Mem. U.S. Marine Subcom. for Internat. Biol. Program, 1966-71; mem. com. on ecol. research interocean-canal Nat. Acad. Scis., 1969-70; mem. Tundra Biome Panel, NSF, 1971-74; mem. water ecosystems com. Inst. Ecology, 1974-76 Contbr. numerous articles on arctic, antarctic and Gulf Coast fish ecol. research to profl. publs.; editor: Contbns. in Marine Sci, 1974-88. Served to 1st lt. USAAF, 1942-46. Recipient Antarctic medal NSF, 1965; NSF grantee, 1955-70; NOAA grantee, 1976-79; Office Naval Research grantee, 1952-54; Tex. Dept. Water Resources grantee, 1975-79 Fellow AAAS, Am. Inst. Fisheries Research Biologists, Arctic Inst. N. Am.; mem. Am. Fisheries Soc., Am. Soc. Limnology and Oceanography, Am. Soc. Zoologists, Am. Soc. Ichthyology and Herpetology, Ecol. Soc. Am. (pres. Western sect. 1965), Estuarine Research Fedn. (dir. 1976-78), Gulf Estuarine Research Soc. (pres. 1976-78), Sigma Xi. Home: Port Aransas, Tex. Died May 15, 2007.

WOHLSTETTER, ROBERTA MORGAN, retired military analyst; b. Duluth, Minn., Aug. 22, 1912; d. Edmund Morris and Elsie Morgan; m. Albert Wohlstetter, June 7, 1939; 1 child, Joan. B.A., Vassar Coll., 1933; M.A., Columbia U., 1936. Cons. research Rand Corp., Santa Monica, Calif., 1949-87; cons. Science Applications, Century City, Calif., 1974-79; sr. analyst def. research Research and Devel. Assocs., Marina del Rey, Calif., 1979—. Author: Pearl Harbor: Warning and Decision, 1962. Fellow AAUW, 1940-41. Recipient Bancroft award Columbia U., 1963. Named Los Angeles Times Woman of Year, 1963; recipient Presdl. Medal of Freedom, 1985. Mem. Council Fgn. Relations, Internat. Council Internat. Inst. Strategic Studies (London), Internat. Council, Georgetown U. Csis. Home: Los Angeles, Calif. Died Jan. 6, 2007.

WOLCOTT, ROBERT BOYNTON, JR., public relations executive; b. San Francisco, Sept. 24, 1920; s. Robert Boynton and Carrie (Rommel) W.; m. Ruth Denas, Oct. 8, 1949; children— Robin Laurine Fayette, Denis McKennett, Stephen Randall. BA, UCLA, 1942. Pub. relations rep. Time Inc. So. Calif., 1944-46; asst. to pub. Time mag., 1946-47, Life mag., 1947-48; dir. public relations Calif. Loan and Fin. Assn., 1949-50; founder Robert B. Wolcott Assocs., Inc., Los Angeles, 1950, pres., 1950-67; chmn. Wolcott, Carlson & Co., Inc., 1967-73, Wolcott, Carlson & Co., Inc. (merged with Burson-Marsteller 1973); exec. v.p. (parent co.), 1973-77; prin. Robert B. Wolcott Jr. Inc. (Pub. Relations Cons.), from 1977. Mem. Pub. Rels. Soc. Am. (dir., v.p. 1965-66, pres. 1966, chmn. public service council 1969-72, Presdl. citation for Meritorious Service 1959, 60, 67, 69, 72), Nat. Investor Rels. Inst. (v.p., dir.), Alpha Tau Omega. Clubs: California, Oakmont Country, El Niguel Country. Home: Glendale, Calif. Died June 19, 2007.

WOLF, ALFRED CLARENCE, retired economist; b. Phila., Nov. 5, 1911; s. Louis and Clara (Ost) Wolf; m. Agnes Strauss, June 30, 1945; children: Sally Kathryn, John Alexander, Steven Sidney, Andrew Michael David. AB, Harvard U., 1934, MPA, 1954; postgrad., Grad. Sch. Arts and Scis., 1935—37, Army Indsl. Coll., 1941. Rsch. supr., asst. rsch. economist, assoc. rsch. economist, divsn. rsch. Works Project Adminstrn., Washington, 1938—41; head Navy Indsl. Manpower Program USN, 1941—46; spl. asst. Vet. Emer. Housing Expediter Office of War Mobilization and Reconversion, 1946—47; mem. staff office of sec. of the interior U.S. Dept. Interior, 1947—49, dir., 1949—50, exec. asst. to the sec. for defense prodn. office of the sec. of interior, 1950—53; rsch. dir. Harvard-Pakistan Planning

Bd. project Harvard U., 1953—55; asst. dir. overseas devel. program Ford Found., 1955—57, developed program in Africa, 1957—58, dir. program L.Am. and Caribbean NYC, 1959—61; dir. social devel. divsn. Inter-Am. Devel. Bank, Washington, 1961—64, program advisor to pres., 1964—77, ret., 1977. Cons. Inter-Am. Devel. Bank, Devel. & Resources, Inc., Nat. Acad. Pub. Adminstrn., George Washington U., Carnegie Endowment for Internat. Peace, The Policies Sci. Ctr., Inc., Wilcox an dAssocs., others, from 1977. Comdr. USNR, 1938—68, ret. USNR, 1968. Decorated Legion of Merit; recipient Disting. Svc. awsard, Interior Dept., 1953; fellow Conservation fellow, Harvard U., 1953—54. Mem.: Cosmos Club (Washington), Harvard Club (N.Y.C.). Home: Mc Lean, Va. Died June 9, 2006.

WOLF, FRANK GERALD, magazine publisher; b. Omaha, Nov. 12, 1922; s. Joseph Louis and Anna (Wirthsafter) W.; m. Judith Hermine Cohn, Jan. 8, 1944; children: Jeffrey L., Wendy C. BA, Pomona Coll., 1944. With TV Guide mag., 1954-72, nat. advt. mgr., 1962-72; pub. Good Food mag., 1973-74, Seventeen mag., NYC, 1974-85; group pub. Good Food and Seventeen mags., from 1985. Served with AUS, 1943-46. Decorated Army Commendation ribbon. Home: New York, NY. Died Nov. 9, 2005.

WOLF, JAMES STUART, retired surgeon; b. Chgo., Mar. 1, 1935; s. Carl Walter and Margaret Vera (Goddard) W.; m. Marjorie Ann Voytilla, July 26, 1958; children: James Stuart, Jr., Anne Elizabeth. AB, Grinnell Coll., 1957; MD, U. Ill., Chgo., 1961. Diplomate Am. Bd. Surgery. Resident in surgery Med. Coll. Va., Richmond, 1967, prof. surgery, 1968-76; chief of surgery McGuire VA Hosp., Richmond, 1968-76; prof. surgery Northwestern U., Chgo., 1976-94, assoc. dean med. edn., 1990-94, emeritus prof. surgery, 1994—2007. Chmn. divsn. transplantation Northwestern U., 1976-91; pres. United Network for Organ Sharing, 1990-91, dir. med. affairs, 1994-2000; chmn. Regional Bank of Ill., Chgo., 1988-89; vice chmn. Ill. Network for End Stage Renal Disease, Chgo., 1984-88. Bd. dirs. Nat. Kidney Found., Chgo., 1984-91, Chgo. Episcopal Charities, Chgo., 1990-94. Recipient Gift of Life award Nat. Kidney Found., 1992. Fellow Am. Coll. Surgeons; mem. Ctrl. Surg. Soc., Soc. Univ. Surgeons, Am. Soc. Transplant Surgeons, Transplantation Soc., Focus Club Richmond. Republican. Home: Hilton Head, SC. Died Aug. 6, 2007.

WOLFF, SANFORD IRVING, lawyer; b. Chgo., Apr. 13, 1915; s. Herbert Barron and Libby (Levey) W.; m. Ann Barry, Mar. 21, 1970; children: Paul, David, Laura. BA, Knox Coll., 1936; grad., John Marshall Law Sch., U. Chgo., 1940. Bar: Ill. 1940, N.Y. 1973. Pvt. practice, Chgo. and NYC, from 1945; chief exec. AFTRA, AFL-CIO, NYC, 1968-85; of counsel Becker, London & Kossow, NYC, from 1985; chief exec. and counsel Am. Guild of Musical Artist, AFL-CIO, 1988-93. Trustee Harris Sch., Chgo. Served with AUS, 1940-45. Decorated Combat Inf. badge, Purple Heart, Bronze Star with cluster, Silver Star. Mem. ABA, Chgo. Bar Assn., NY Bar Assn. Home: New Canaan, Conn. Died Apr. 14, 2007.

WOLFSON, ROBERT LOWELL, retired diversified financial services company executive, retired professional sports team executive; b. Velva, ND, Mar. 24, 1918; s. Abraham Samuel and Sarah Ruth (Weisberg) W.; m. Suzanne Feld, June 7, 1947 (div. Jan. 1962); children: Andrew Scott, Anne Feld, Robert Lowell; m. Ethel Coopersmith, Nov. 14, 1963. Student, U. Minn., 1935-37. Chmn. bd. Feld Chevrolet, Inc., St. Louis, Manchester Lease Corp., Brentwood Volvo, Ltd., Progress Mark Twain Bank, St. Louis; organizer Gem Internat. (and predecessor companies), St. Louis, chmn. bd., 1957-65; chmn. exec. com. Parkview-Gem, 1965-67; pres. Dubob Realty, St. Louis; treas., v.p. St. Louis Arena Corp.; treas., v.p., co-owner St. Louis Blues, NHL, 1967-77. Chmn. Mo. Gaming Commn., 1993—98. Chmn. bd. Jewish Community Centers Assn., St. Louis; bd. dirs. Jewish Hosp.; trustee Brandeis U. Served to capt. AUS, 1943-46, CBI. Recipient Nat. Leadership award Boys Town of Italy, 1961 Mem.: Westwood Country; Westview Country (Miami, Fla.). Jewish. Died Feb. 2, 2007.

WOLMER, BRUCE RICHARD, magazine editor; b. NYC, Mar. 9, 1948; s. Simon and Elaine (Richelson) Katz; m. Colleen Babington, Nov. 20, 1995. BA, Wesleyan U., Middletown, Conn., 1968; Licence es Lettres, Paris U., 1971; MPhil, Johns Hopkins U., 1976; postgrad., Ecole du Louvre, Paris, 1969-71. Rschr. dept. prints Met. Mus. Art, NYC, 1972-73; editor Mus. Modern Art, NYC, 1976-80; assoc. editor ARTnews Mag., NYC, 1980-82, exec. editor, 1982-84; editor-in-chief Art and Antiques Mag., NYC, 1984-85; pvt. art dealer London, Paris, 1986-90; exec. editor Art & Auction Mag., NYC, 1990-94, editor-in-chief, 1994—2007. Contbr. book, art revs. to N.Y. Observer, Sunday Times (London), ARTS, Artforum, Forward, others. Mem. Reform Club (London). Jewish. Home: New York, NY. Died Aug. 11, 2007.

WONDER, JOHN PAUL, educator; b. Long Beach, Calif., July 29, 1921; s. John Paul and Etta (Jones) W.; m. Jane Josephine Walder, Dec. 22, 1946; children: John Walder, Peter Charles. AB, Stanford U., 1943, A.M., 1948, PhD, 1952; Exchange scholar, Universidad Central, Madrid, 1950-51. Grad. fellow Stanford, 1946-50; instr., asst. prof. Spanish U. Ariz., 1951-56; dir. Binational Center, Belo Horizonte, Brazil; with USIA, also Rio de Janeiro and Port-au-Prince, Haiti, 1956-62; asst. prof. Los Angeles State Coll., 1962-63; prof. Spanish U. Pacific, Stockton, Calif., 1963-91, chmn. dept. modern langs., 1964-75; dir. Center for Internat. Programs, 1979-82. Author: (with Aurelio M. Espinosa, Jr.) Gramática Analítica, 1976; assoc. editor: (theoretical linguistics) Hispania, 1979-89. Served as 1st lt., arty. M.I. AUS, 1943-46, ETO. Mem. Alpha Tau Omega. Home: Walnut Creek, Calif. Died May 2006.

WONG, KUANG CHUNG, anesthesiology and pharmacology educator; b. Chung King, China, Nov. 12, 1936; m. Janny Wu; children: Jade, Shale, Amber, Kaston. BS in Chemistry, Iowa State U., 1959; MS in Pharmacology, State U. Iowa, 1962; PhD in Pharmacology, U. Nebr., Omaha, 1966, MD, 1968. Diplomate Am. Bd. Anesthesiology (assoc. examiner 1979-83). Instr. then asst. prof. pharmacology U. Nebr., Omaha, 1965-69; intern Bishop Clarkson Hosp., Omaha, 1968, U. Nebr. Coll. Medicine, Omaha, 1968, resident in anesthesia, 1968-69; resident, then fellow U. Wash. Sch. Medicine, Seattle, 1969-70; mem. assoc. grad. faculty U. Nebr., Omaha, 1968-69; asst. to assoc. prof. anesthesiology and pharmacology U. Washington, Seattle, 1970-74; assoc. prof. U. Utah, Salt Lake City, 1974-77, prof., from 1977, chmn. dept., 1976-98. Vis. prof. numerous univs. throughout world, also various hosps.; mem. adv. com. anesthetic and life support drugs FDA, 1982-83; attending anesthesiologist U. Wash. Med. Ctr. and affiliated hosps., Seattle, 1970-74; staff anesthesiologist U. Utah Med. Ctr., Salt Lake City, 1974—; mem. surgery, anesthesia and trauma study sects. NIH, 1982-86. Mem. editorial bd. Anesthesia and Analgesia, 1980-89. Served with U.S. Army, 1955-57. Dr. Ernest Tibbets Manning Meml. scholar, 1965-66, U. Nebr. Upper Regents' scholar, 1966-67; grantee NIH, 1969-72, 80-85, Wash. State Heart Assn., 1972-74, Utah Heart Assn., 1975-76, 78-80, U. Utah, 1975-76, 76-77, Knoll Pharm. Co., 1976-79; Riker Labs., Inc., 1976-78, Smith Kline and French, 1979-89, Glaxo Wellcome, 1995-97. Mem. AMA, Am. Heart Assn., Am. Soc. Anesthesiologists (ad hoc com. self-evaluation 1979), Am. Soc. Clin. Pharmacology and Chemotherapy, Am. Soc. Pharmacology and Exptl. Therapeutics, Assn. Cardiac Anesthesiologists, Assn. Univ. Anesthesiologists, Internat. Anesthesia Rsch. Soc. (trustee 1989—), Salt Lake County Med. Soc., Utah Heart Assn., Utah Med. Soc., Utah Soc. Anesthesiologists, Soc. Acad. Anesthesia Chairmen, Sigma Xi, Alpha Omega Alpha. Home: Salt Lake City, Utah. Died May 18, 2006.

WOOD, RICK DALE, association executive; b. El Paso, Tex., Feb. 4, 1944; s. Robert Samuel and Alma Louise (Dale) Wood; m. Karyn Lee Newby, July 23, 1966; children: Laura Lea Newby, Leah Louise Newby, Lei-Lani Newby, Lisa Lynn Newby. BS, Sul Ross Coll., 1961. Coach Ysleta Sch. Dist., El Paso, 1966—69; dir. Midland YMCA, Tex., 1969—74, El Paso YMCA, 1974—75, San Angelo YMCA, Tex., 1975—78, Hereford YMCA, Tex., 1979; exec. v.p. Ft. Stockton C. of C., Tex., from 1979. Exhibitions include photography This is West Texas, World of Big Bend. Pres. Mgrs. Permian Basin, Ft. Stockton, 1983; bd. dirs. Ft. Stockton Theater, from 1982, Ft. Stockton United Way, from 1984. Mem.: Hwy. 67 Assn. (pres. 1982—83), Chamber Dirs. West Tex. (bd. dirs. from 1983), Lions (bd. dirs. from 1983), Rotary. Methodist. Home: Midland, Tex. Died Nov. 19, 2006.

WOOD, ROBERT WINFIELD, retired science administrator, biophysicist; b. Detroit, Mich., Dec. 31, 1931; BS, U. Detroit, 1953; MA, Vanderbilt U., 1955; PhD Biophysics, Cornell U., 1961. Sci. fellow Nat. Inst. Gen. Medicine, 1961-62; radiation physicist AEC, 1962-73; dir. phys. and tech. rsch. divsn.Office of Health and Environmental Rsch. U.S. Dept. Energy, Washington, 1973-91, dir. med. applications and biophysics dvsn., 1991-94. Recipient Presidential Meritorious Rank award, 1990, Meritorious Svc. award Dept. Energy, 1990. Mem. Health Physics Soc., Radiation Rsch. Soc., Sigma Chi. Died Jan. 5, 2007.

WOODIWISS, KATHLEEN ERIN, author; b. Alexandria, La., June 3, 1939; d. Charles Wingrove, Sr. and Gladys (Coker) Hogg; m. Ross Eugene Woodiwiss, July 20, 1956 (dec. 1996); children: Sean Alan, Dorren James, Heath Alexander. Student pub. schs., La. Author: The Flame and the Flower, 1972, The Wolf and the Dove, 1974, Shanna, 1977, Ashes in the Wind, 1979, A Rose in Winter, 1982, Come Love a Stranger, 1984, So Worthy My Love, 1990, Married at Midnight, 1996, Petals on the River, 1997, The Elusive Flame, 1998, Forever in Your Embrace, 1999, A Season Beyond a Kiss, 2000, The Reluctant Suitor, 2003, Everlasting, 2007 Recipient Lifetime Achievement award, Romance Writers Assn. Am., 1988. Republican. Died July 6, 2007.

WOODRUFF, TRUMAN O(WEN), physicist, emeritus educator; b. Salt Lake City, May 26, 1925; s. Wilford Owen and Evelyn (Ballif) W.; m. Ambrosina Lydia Solaroli, Sept. 14, 1948 (dec. June 1991); m. Patricia O'Keefe Vincent, Sept. 23, 1995. AB, Harvard U., 1947; BA, Oxford U., Eng., 1950; PhD, Calif. Inst. Tech., 1955. Nat. scholar Harvard, 1942-44, 46-47, Sheldon traveling fellow, 1947-48; Rhodes scholar Oxford U., 1948-50; Dow Chem. Co. fellow, Howard Hughes fellow Calif. Inst. Tech., 1950-54; research asso. physics U. Ill., 1954-55; physicist Gen. Elec. Research Lab., 1955-62; prof. physics Mich. State U., 1962-85, prof. emeritus, from 1985, chmn. dept., 1972-75; sr. scientist research labs. Hughes Aircraft Co., Malibu, Calif., 1986-87; cons. in physics Los Angeles, 1987-91. Vis. prof. Scuola Normale Superiore, Pisa, Italy, 1982—. Contbr. articles to sci. jours. Served with USNR, 1944-46. Fulbright fellow U. Pisa, 1968-69 Fellow Am. Phys. Soc.; mem. Assn. Harvard Chemists, Phi Beta Kappa, Sigma Xi. Home: Galt, Calif. Died Apr. 13, 2007.

WOODS, GURDON GRANT, sculptor; b. Savannah, Ga., Apr. 15, 1915; s. Frederick L. and Marion (Skinner) W. Student, Art Student's League N.Y.C., 1936-39, Bklyn. Mus. Sch., 1945-46; PhD (hon.), Coll. San Francisco Art Inst., 1966. Exec. dir. San Francisco Art Inst., 1955-64; dir. Calif. Sch. Fine Arts, 1955-65; prof. Adlai E. Stevenson Coll., U. Calif. at Santa Cruz, 1966-74; dir. Otis Art Inst., Los Angeles, 1974-77; asst. dir. Los Angeles County Mus. Natural History, 1977-80; Sculptor mem. San Francisco Art Commn., 1954-56; mem. Santa Cruz County Art Commn., Regional Arts Council of Bay Area. Exhibited: N.A.D., 1948, 49, San Francisco Art Assn. anns., 1952-54, Denver Mus. Anns., 1952, 53, Whitney Mus. Ann., 1953, Sao Paulo Biennial, 1955, Bolles Gallery San Francisco, 1969, 70, 72, L.A. Mcpl. Gallery, 1977, San Jose Inst. Contemporary Art (Calif.), Washington Project for the Arts retrospective, 1968-85, Washington, 1985, Retrospective Art Mus. Santa Cruz County, Calif., 1987, d.p. Fong Gallery, 1993, 94, Michael Angelo Gallery, Santa Cruz, 1995; commns. include: cast concrete reliefs and steel fountain, IBM Ctr., San Jose, Calif., fountain, Paul Masson Winery, Saratoga, Calif., McGraw Hill Pubs. (now Birkenstock), Novato, Calif.; work in permanent collection Oakland (Calif.) Mus.; papers in Archives of Am. Art, Smithsonian Instn., Washington. Recipient citation N.Y.C., 1948; prize N.A.D., 1949; Chapelbrook Found. research grantee, 1965-66; Sequoia Fund grantee, 1967; Research grantee Creative Arts Inst., U. Calif., 1968; grantee Carnegie Corp., 1968-69 Mem. Artists Equity Assn (pres. No. Calif. chpt. 1950-52, nat. dir. 1952-55) Died July 31, 2007.

WOODS, HARRIETT RUTH, political organization worker, former lieutenant governor; b. Cleve., June 2, 1927; d. Armin and Ruth (Wise) Friedman; m. James B. Woods, Jan. 2, 1953; children: Christopher, Peter, Andrew. Student, U. Chgo., 1945; BA, U. Mich., 1949; LLD (hon.), Webster U., 1988, U. Missouri, 2003. Reporter Chgo. Herald-Am., 1948, St. Louis Globe-Democrat, 1949-51; prodr. Star, KPLR-TV, St. Louis, 1964-74; moderator, writer Sta. KETC-TC, St. Louis, 1962-64; council mem. University City, Mo., 1967-74; mem. Mo. Hwy. Commn., 1974, Mo. Transp. Commn., 1974-76, Mo. State Senate, 1976-84; lt. gov. State of Mo., 1985-89; pres. Inst. for Policy Leadership, U. Mo., St. Louis, 1989-91, lectr., from 1995; commentator KWMU Radio, from 1985. Pres. Nat. Women's Polit. Caucus, 1991-95; fellow inst. politics John F. Kennedy Sch. Govt., Harvard U., 1988; adj. prof. U. Mo., St. Louis, 1995-2007, Hunter Coll., N.Y.C., 2004-07, Pace U., 2006-07 Author: Stepping Up to Power: The Political Journey of American Women, 2000. Bd. dirs. LWV of Mo., 1963, Nat. League of Cities, 1972-74; Dem. nominee for U.S. Senate, 1982, 86; commr. St. Louis Regional Conf. and Sports Complex Authority, 2000-07. Jewish. Home: Saint Louis, Mo. Died Feb. 8, 2007.

WOODWARD, GRETA CHARMAINE, construction company executive, rental and investment property manager; b. Congress, Ohio, Oct. 28, 1930; d. Richard Thomas and Grace Lucetta (Palmer) Duffey; m. John Jay Woodward, Oct. 29, 1949; children: Kirk Jay, Brad Ewing, Clay William. Bookkeeper Kaufman's Texaco, Wooster, Ohio, 1948-49; office mgr. Holland Furnace Co., Wooster, 1948-49; acctg. clk. Columbus and So Ohio Electric, 1949-50; interviewer, clk. State Ohio Bur. Employment Services, Columbus, 1950-51; clk. Def. Constrn Supply Ctr. (U.S. Govt.) (formerly Columbus Gen. Depot) 1951-52; treas. Woodward Co., Inc., Reynoldsburg, Ohio 1963—. Newspaper columnist Briarcliff News, 1960-63. Active Reynoldsburg PTA, 1960-67; Reynoldsburg United Meth. Ch. mem. women's service bd. Grant Hosp. Avocations: bike riding crocheting, writing poetry, water aerobics. Home: Pickerington Ohio. Died Jan. 11, 2006.

WOODWARD, LAWRENCE GODFREY, retired federa[l] agency administrator; b. Arlington, Va., May 14, 1925; s. Ray Lawrence and Amanda Lydia (Beyer) W.; m. Nancy Rika Hanck, Dec. 23, 1947 (dec. 1999); children: Lawrence William Garry Hanck. B.A., George Washington U., 1948, M.A., 1949 Ph.D., Am. U., 1959. Research psychologist USMC, Washington, 1949-52; pers. officer CIA, Washington, 1952-81, dep. dir pers. for recruitment & placement, 1978-81; dir. personnel Sch Advanced Internat. Studies The John Hopkins U., Washington 1982—2007; adj. prof. U. Md., Taipei, Republic of China 1960-63, U. Va., McLean, 1974-75. Served to Aviation Cade USN, 1943-45. Recipient Intelligence Medal of Merit CIA 1981. Mem. Internat. Personnel Mgmt. Assn., Am. Soc. for Pub Adminstrn., Coll. and Univ. Personnel Assn. Home: Arlington Va. Died Apr. 28, 2007.

WOOLFENDEN, GLEN E., ornithologist; b. Elizabeth, NJ Jan. 23, 1930; married 1954; 3 children. BS, Cornell U., 1953 MA, U. Kans., 1956; PhD, U. Fla., 1960. Instr. biol. U. Fla. 1959-60; from instr. to assoc. prof. zool. U. South Fla., Tampa 1960-70, prof. biol., 1970-87, disting. rsch. prof. biology, from 1988. Vis. prof. U. Kans., 1985. Ellow Am. Ornithologists Union (Brewster medal 1985), Animal Behavior Soc., Germa[n] Ornithology Soc. Died June 19, 2007.

WOOTEN, FRANCIS LAKEY, chemical company executive b. East Bend, NC, Jan. 23, 1922; m. Lois Cason, June 17, 1960 1 dau., Ann. BS in Chemistry, N.C. State U., 1947. Gen. sale[s] mgr. Armour Fort Works, Atlanta, 1956-64; v.p. mktg. Kaise[r] Agrl. Chems., Savannah, Ga., 1965-69, v.p., gen. mgr., 1969-76 pres., 1977-84. Gen. campaign chmn. United Way, Savannah 1982, chmn., chief vol. officer, 1985; v.p. fin. Boy Scouts Am. 1982; gen. chmn. capital campaign Wesley Community Ctrs. 1983—; Chatham County commr., 1985—. Served to capt. U.S Army, 1942-46, 51-52, Korea. Named Indsl. Man of Yr. Indsl Mgmt. Club, Savannah, 1979 Mem. Fertilizer Inst. (chmn 1977-78) Methodist. Home: Savannah, Ga. Died Feb. 7, 2007

WOOTEN, OSCAR SMITH, financial company executive; b Camden, SC, Aug. 26, 1923; s. Ernest L. and Carrie (Durrette W.; m. Helen Lawson, Apr. 15, 1950; children: Oscar, Charles Catherine, Richard. BS in Bus. Adminstrn, U. Richmond, 1948 C.P.A., S.C. Acct. firm Derrick, Stubbs & Stith, Columbia, S.C. 1948-51; audit supr. AEC, Aiken, S.C., 1951-54; with S.C Electric & Gas Co., Columbia, 1954-83, v.p., mem. exec. com 1967-68, sr. v.p., 1968-77, exec. v.p. finance, 1977-83, also dir dir., mem. adv. bd. Citizens & So. Nat. Bank, Columbia 1967-72, chmn., 1972-84; pres. The Wooten Co., fin. cons Columbia, from 1983; dir., mem. exec. com. 1st Bankshare Corp.; dir. 1st Nat. Bank S.C.; dir. emeritus S.C. Nat. Corp 1984-87; dir. Comsouth Bankshares, from 1988, Comml. Ban[k] of South, 1988. Bd. dirs., chmn., chief exec. officer Capital Ct[y] Travel, 1989—. Bd. dirs. United Community Services; truste[e] Palmer Coll. Served to 1st lt. USAAF, 1943-46. Mem. S.C Assn. C.P.A.'s, Am. Inst. C.P.A.'s, Southeastern Electric Ex change (chmn. accounting div.), Edison Electric Inst., Columbi[a] C. of C. (dir.), Kappa Alpha. Presbyterian (elder). Clubs Palmetto (Columbia), Forest Lake (Columbia), Capital Cit[y] (dir., treas. 1987—); Rotary. Home: Columbia, SC. Died Jul 27, 2007.

WORK, HENRY HARCUS, psychiatrist, educator; b. Buffal[o] Nov. 11, 1911; s. Henry Harcus and Jeannette (Harcus) W.; m Virginia Codington, Oct. 20, 1945 (dec. Nov. 1991); childre[n] Henry Harcus III, David Codington, William Bruce, Stua[rt] Runyon. AB, Hamilton Coll., Clinton, NY, 1933; MD, Harvar[d] 1937. Intern, resident Boston Children's Hosp., 1937-40, Emm[a] P. Bradley Home Providence, 1940, Buffalo Children's Hosp 1940-42, N.Y. Hosp., 1945-47; psychiat. services adviser, chi[ef] U.S. Children's Bur., Washington, 1948-49; assoc. prof. pedia[t] ics U. Louisville, 1949-55; mem. faculty UCLA, 1955-72, prof. psychiatry and pub. health, 1966-72; chief profl. svcs. Am. Psychiat. Assn., Washington, 1972-83; clin. prof. George Washington U., Georgetown U., Uniformed Svcs. U. of Health Scis., U. Md., 1973—84. Author: A Guide to Preventive Child Psychiatry, 1965, Minimal Brain Dysfunction: A Medical Challenge, 1967, Psychiatric Emergencies in Childhood, 1967, Crisis in Child Psychiatry, 1975, also articles. Served to capt. AUS, 1942-45. Recipient Simon Wile Award, Amer. Acad. of Child and Adolescent Psychiatry, 1994. Mem. So. Calif. Psychiat. Assn. (pres. 1966-67), Am. Orthopsychiat. Assn. (v.p. 1968-69), Am. Coll. Psychiatry (sec.-gen. 1979-93), Group for Advancement of Psychiatry (pres. 1982-85) Home: Bethesda, Md. Died Mar. 21, 2007.

WORLEY, ROBERT WILLIAM, JR., retired lawyer; b. Anderson, Ind., June 13, 1935; s. Robert William and Dorothy Mayhew (Hayler) W.; m. Diana Lynn Matthews, Aug. 22, 1959; children: Nathanael, Hope Hillegas. BS in Chem. Engring., Lehigh U., 1956; LLB, Harvard U., 1960. Bar: Conn. 1960, U.S. Supreme Ct. 1966, Fla. 1977. Assoc. then ptnr. Cummings & Lockwood, Stamford, Conn., 1960-91; gen. counsel Consol. Asset Recover Corp. sub. Chase Manhattan Corp., Bridgeport, Conn., 1991-94; v.p., asst. gen. counsel The Chase Manhattan Bank, NYC, 1994-2001; ret., 2001. Trustees com. on bequests and trusts Lehigh U., 1979—2006; mem. Conn. Legis. Task Force on Probate Court Sys., 1991-93; chmn. Greenwich Arts Coun., 1981-82; v.p., bd. dirs. Greenwich Choral Soc., 1962-77, 80; bd. dirs. Greenwich Ctr. for Chamber Music, 1981-85, Greenwich Symphony, 1986-89; commr. Greenwich Housing Authority, 1972-77; bldg. com. for sr. ctr. Greenwich Bd. Selectman, 1980-81. Capt. JAGC, AUS, 1965. Mem. Conn. Bar Assn. (exec. com. probate sect. 1980), Sippican Choral Soc., Harvard Club Boston. Christian Scientist. Home: Marion, Mass. Died May 26, 2007.

WORTMAN, GLORIA CLARA, food service executive; b. St. Louis, June 22, 1925; d. John Adolph and Mary Louise (Kulage) Pfeiffer; m. James Bernard Wortman, June 14, 1947; children—Mary, Sarah, Susan, Martha. B.S. in Home Econs., Fontbonne Coll., St. Louis, 1947. Cert. home economist. Mgr., Luncheon is Served, St. Louis, 1948-52; owner Glo-Jon Foods, St. Louis, 1971-74; home economist-sales J & R Custom Food, St. Louis, 1974-77, United Instl. Sale, St. Louis, 1977-82, Food Service Enterprises, St. Louis, 1982—. Pres., Ladies of Lourdes, St. Louis, 1969; leader St. Louis council Girl Scouts U.S.A., 1964-69; v.p. Rosati Kain PTA, St. Louis, 1977-79, pres., 1979-80. Mem. Sch. Food Service Assn., Home Economists in Bus. (pres. 1978-79), Am. Home Econs. Assn. Republican. Roman Catholic. Home: Chesterfield, Mo. Died Oct. 25, 2006.

WOSKOW, MARVIN ZANE, chemical company executive; b. Kansas City, Mo., Dec. 11, 1929; s. Joseph Leon Woskow and Esther (Burdman) Seltzer; m. Terry Ann, June 23, 1934; children: Joseph Steven, Nancy Joy, Beth Michelle. BA in Chemistry, Rice U., 1950; MS in Chemistry, La. State U., 1957. Chemist Baylor Coll. Medicine, Houston, 1954-55; research chemist Am. Oil Co., Texas City, Tex., 1957-60, Petro-Tex Chem. Co., Houston, 1960-64, research mgr., 1964-67, tech. services mgr., 1967-71, plant mgr., 1971-75, v.p., 1975-77; exec. v.p. Denka Chem. Corp., Houston, 1977-83, pres., 1983-88, Mobay Synthetics Corp., Houston, from 1988. Numerous patents in catalysis and chem. processing. Served with USN, 1951-55, Korea. Mem. Internat. Inst. Synthetic Rubber Producers (pres. 1984-85), Tex. Chem. Council (bd. dirs. 1986-87), Am. Chem. Soc. (rubber div.), AAAS. Home: Houston, Tex. Died Apr. 28, 2007.

WOTIZ, HERBERT HENRY, biochemist, educator, medical research director; b. Vienna, Oct. 8, 1922; came to U.S., 1938; s. Edward and Irene (Politzer) Wottitz; m. Miriam Selma Rose, June 15, 1947; children: Sue Wotiz Goldstein, Robert P., Richard A. BS, Providence Coll., 1944; PhD, Yale U., 1951. Instr. biochemistry Boston U., 1950-53, asst. prof., 1953-55, assoc. prof., 1955-63, prof., from 1963, rsch. prof. urology, from 1978, dir. Hubert H. Humphrey Cancer Rsch. Ctr., from 1984. Cons. U.S. Army, 1952-54. Co-author: Gas Chromatography of Steroids, 1966; sect. editor Chem. Abstracts; assoc. editor Steroids; contbr. numerous articles to profl. jours., chpts. to books. Bd. dirs. Milton (Mass.) Mus. Found., 1989—; trustee Milton Pub. Libr., 1987—; mem. Milton Sch. com., 1959-68. With U.S. Army, 1944-45. Sr. rsch. fellow NIH, 1960-65, career devel. fellow, 1965-70. Mem. AAAS, Am. Chem. Soc., Am. Assn. Biol. Chemists Inc., Endocrine Soc., Am. Assn. Cancer Rsch., Sigma Xi (lectr. N.E. region 1975-78). Avocation: art collecting and restoration. Home: Milton, Mass. Died Feb. 14, 2007.

WRIGHT, ARTHUR MCINTOSH, lawyer, industrial products consultant; b. El Dorado, Kans., Dec. 9, 1930; s. Ray Arthur and Anna (McIntosh) W.; A.B., Grinnell Coll., 1952; LL.B., Harvard, 1958; m. Mary Alice Smaltz, June 23, 1956; children: David A., Steven E., Carolyn E. Bar: Mo. 1959, Ill. 1964. Assoc. Swanson, Midgley, Jones, Blackmar & Eager, Kansas City, Mo., 1958-64; corp. atty. Baxter Labs., Inc., Morton Grove, Ill., 1964-67; v.p., sec., counsel N.Am. Car Corp., Chgo., 1968-71; sec., corp. counsel Ceco Corp., Chgo., 1971-77; v.p., gen. counsel, sec. Ill. Tool Works Inc., Glenview, 1977-91. Mem. New Trier Twp. High Schs. Bd. Edn., 1977-85, pres., 1983-85; mem. bd. advisors Chgo. Vol. Legal Svcs. Found., 1982-90, chmn., 1984-86; mem. bd. dirs. The Desert Chorale, Santa Fe, N.M., 1992-94, Food For Santa Fe, 1995—. Served with U.S. Army, 1953-55. Mem. Ill. Bar Assn., Am. Judicature Soc., Sigma Delta Chi. Presbyterian. Home: Santa Fe, N.Mex. Died Feb. 27, 2007.

WRIGHT, DOROTHY MARIE, educational administrator; b. Kansas City, Mo., Mar. 9, 1926; s. Everett and Gertrude (Kerr) W. A.A., Kansas City Jr. Coll., 1946; B.S. in Edn., Central Mo. State Coll., Warrensburg, 1948; M.A., U. Iowa, 1951; Pd.D., Iowa U., Fort Lauderdale, Fla., 1976. Cert. tchr., Mo., Kans. Tchr., Lyndon Pub. Sch., Kans., 1948-51, Winfield Pub. Sch., Kans., 1951-55; tchr., counselor Penn Valley Community Coll., Kansas City, Mo., 1955-64, registrar, dir. admissions, 1965-70, dean instrn., 1970-79, 80-84, interim pres., 1979-80, asst. to pres., 1984—, mem. speakers' bur., 1980—; evaluator North Central Assn., Chgo., 1975—; test evaluator Stevens Thorow, Chgo., 1965—. Author: (corres. manual) Guide For Writing, 1970. Contbr. articles, poems to profl. publs. Mem. Women's C. of C., Am. Vocat. Assn., Mo. Vocat. Assn., Am. Assn. Women in Community and Jr. Colls., Nat. Assn. Acad. Deans (pres. 1980), Mo. Assn. Community and Jr. Colls., Nat. Assn. Acad. Deans (pres. 1980), Mo. Assn. Community and Jr. Colls., Nat. Assn. Community Colls, Alpha Delta Kappa, Sweet adelines (sec., vice regent, regent). Republican. Presbyterian. Club: Women's City (Kansas City, Mo.). Avocations: Singing barbershop harmony, teaching knitting, stained glass, reading, writing poetry. Home: Kansas City, Mo. Died May 29, 2007.

WRIGHT, GEORGE WALTER, aeronautical engineer, former state legislator; b. Boston, July 20, 1923; s. George Wright and Ethel Maude (Alward) W.; widowed; 4 children. BA, Boston Coll., 1950; postgrad., Northeastern U., 1952-54; DD (hon.), Cooper State U., 1962. Aircraft mechanic N.E. Airlines, Presque Isle, Maine, 1942-43, airline pilot Boston, 1947-57, Delta Airlines, Boston and Atlanta, 1957-77; antique aircraft restorer Penguin Aeroplane Co., Brookline, N.H., 1977-94; surveyor State of N.H., 1984-91; mem. from Hillsborough County N.H. Ho. of Reps., Concord, 1989-98. Flight instr. Airline Pilots Assn., N.H., 1952—; asst. minister Enoch Ch. Br. Davidian, Idaho and Tex., 1976-81; mechanic for restoration of various vintage cars. Author I Told You I Was Sick, 1960 (Ugliest Book of Yr. 1961) newspaper column Under the Golden Dome, 1960—. Pres. Granite State Bus. Assn., Nashua, N.H., 1981-84; operator N.H. Recycling Orgn., Concord, 1980-81; brother NAACP, New Eng., 1960-63. Lt. (s.g.) USNR, 1943-45. Recipient Gold medal for decathalon Sr. Olympics, 1972; named Businessman of Yr., 1952 Republican. Avocations: skeet shooting, swimming, hockey, billiards, embroidery. Home: Lebanon, Maine. Died June 5, 2006.

WRIGHT, GORDON BROOKS, conductor, educator; b. Bklyn., Dec. 31, 1934; s. Harry Wesley and Helen Philomena (Brooks) W.; m. Inga-Lisa Myrin Wright, June 13, 1958 (div. 1979); children: Karin-Ellen Sturla, Charles-Eric, Daniel Brooks. MusB, Coll. Wooster, 1957; MA, U. Wis., 1961; postgrad., Salzburg Mozarteum, 1972, Loma Linda U., 1979; studied with, René Leibowitz, Carl Melles, Wilfred Pelletier, Herbert Blomstedt, Hans Swarowsky. Founder, music dir. Wis. Chamber Orch., 1960-69; music dir. Fairbanks (Alaska) Symphony Orch., 1969-89; prof. music U. Alaska, Fairbanks, Alaska, 1969-89, prof. emeritus, 1989—2007; founder, music dir. Arctic Chamber Orch., Fairbanks, Alaska, 1970-89; exec. dir. The Reznicek Soc., Indian, Alaska, 1982—2007. Prin. guest condr. Fla. Keys Chambor Orch., from 2003. Guest condr. Philharmonia Hungarica, Philomusica London, Norwegian Radio Orch., Orch. St. Luke's, Anchorage Symphony Orch., Musashino Orch., Tokyo, Tohoku Orch., Sendai, Japan; prin. guest condr. Fla. Keys Chamber Orch., 2003-07; composer: Suite of Netherlands Dances, 1965, Six Alaskan Tone Poems, 1974, Symphony in Ursa Major, 1979 (Legis. award 1979), 1984 Overture, Scott Joplin Suite, 1987, Toccata Festiva, 1992, Meditation for Orchestra, 2000; columnist Alaska Advocate. Founder, bd. dirs. No. Alaska Environ. Ctr., Fairbanks, 1971-78. Served as pvt. AUS, 1957-59. Mem.: Am. Fedn. Musicians, Arturo Toscanini Soc., Condr.'s Guild, Am. Symphony Orch. League, Royal Musical Assn., Am. Musicol. Soc., Ctr. for Alaskan Coastal Studies (bd. dirs. from 1982), Alaska Conservation Soc. (editor Rev. 1971—78), Audubon Soc., Wilderness Soc., Friends of Earth-Alaska (bd. dirs. from 1978), Sierra Club (chmn. Fairbanks Group 1969—71). Avocations: hiking, kayaking, collecting books, photography. Home: Indian, Alaska. Died Feb. 14, 2007.

WRIGHT, GUY DARRELL, newspaper columnist; b. Carmi, Ill., Oct. 12, 1922; s. William Guy and Kathryn Mae (Jones) W.; m. Kevin Marie McTigue, Oct. 31, 1968; children— Pamela Marie, Gregory Drew B. in Journalism, U. Mo., 1949. Columnist San Francisco Examiner, San Francisco, from 1965. Died Jan. 25, 2006.

WRIGHT, HARRY FORREST, JR., retired banker; b. Woodbury, NJ, Nov. 9, 1931; s. Harry Forrest and Bertha (Strumpfer) W.; m. Lorraine Catherine McLaughlin, Oct. 16, 1954; children: Harry Forrest III, Lonni Caryn, Gregory William, Douglas Carl. Student, Temple U., 1949-50, Am. Inst. Banking, 1950-52; accounting certificate, Wharton Sch., U. Pa., 1960, asso. degree, 1962. Clk. First Nat. Bank, Phila., 1951-60; asst. comptroller, then asst. v.p. First Pa. Co., 1960- 64; v.p. Md. Nat. Bank, Balt., 1964-66, v.p., comptroller, 1966-70, sr. v.p., comptroller, 1970-73, exec. v.p., 1973-81, sr. exec. v.p., 1981-89, also bd. dirs., ret., 1989. V.p., treas. Md. Nat. Corp., 1974-77, sr. v.p., 1977-83; exec. v.p., chief fin. officer MNC Fin., Inc., 1983-88, ret., 1989; treas., dir. Md. Nat. Optimation Svcs., Inc., 1969-76, chmn., 1976-79; sec. Md. Switch, Inc., 1976-79; treas., dir. Manab Properties, Inc.; pres., dir. 10 Light St. Corp., 1973-82; affiliate Property Tax Cons., San Diego, 1990—. Treas. Cub Scouts Am., Severna Park, Md., 1965-66, St. Martin's Kindergarten, 1967-72, Bayberry Hill Property Owners Assn., 1985—; bd. dirs. Greater Balt. chpt. Nat. Found. March of Dimes, 1972-89, v.p., 1977-79, pres., 1979-81, chmn., 1981-84; bd. dirs. Nat. Coun. Vols., 1983-85, 89-95, Nat. Fin. Task Force, 1989-95; bd. dirs. Md. Sch. for Blind, 1975—, v.p., 1981-88, pres., 1988-94, chmn. bd., 1994-98, chmn. emeritus, 1998—; chmn. Richard E. Hoover Commn. for Low Vision and Blindness at Greater Balt. Med. Ctr., 1990-92, treas., 1992—. Mem. Bank Adminstrn. Inst. (pres. Balt. 1970-71, state dir. 1971-73, dist. dir. 1977-79), Fin. Execs. Inst. (dir. 1976-78), Sigma Kappa Phi. Clubs: Mchts. (Balt.) (bd. dirs. 1974-87, v.p. 1976-79, pres. 1979-82). Died June 30, 2006.

WRIGHT, JAMES EDWARD, judge; b. Arlington, Tex., Jan. 15, 1921; s. James Robert and Clairette (Smith) W.; m. Eberta Adelaide Slataper, June 25, 1946; 1 child, Patricia Diane Wright Rogers. JD, U. Tex., 1949. Bar: Tex. 1949. Practice in, Ft. Worth, 1949-69; city atty. Arlington, 1951-61; judge 141st Dist. Ct., Ft. Worth, 1970-88, sr. dist. judge, 1988—2006. Served with USAAF, World War II. Paul Harris fellow, 1981; named Disting. Alumnus U. Tex.-Arlington, 1982; named to Mil. Sci. Dept. Hall of Honor, U. Tex.-Arlington, 1985 Fellow Tex. Bar Found. (life); mem. ABA, Ft. Worth-Tarrant County Bar Assn. (pres. 1958-59), Tex. Bar Assn., Sons of the Rep. of Tex., Rotary (pres. Downtown Ft. Worth club 1966-67), Masons (32 degree), Shriners, Jesters (life), Phi Alpha Delta. Methodist. Home: Arlington, Tex. Died 2006.

WRIGHT, MARTIN CLARKE, public relations company executive, consultant; b. Morrisville, Pa., June 21, 1911; s. Martin Van Buren and Sara Mae (Clarke) W.; m. Hettie Scott, Aug. 18, 1935; children— Jane Wright Loeffler, Martin C. B.S. in Econs., Wharton Sch., U. Pa., 1933; M.A., Columbia U., 1937. Editor, treas. Morrisville Herald (Pa.), 1933-35; reporter Bergen Evening Record, Hackensack, N.J., 1935-41; pres. rep. Gen. Electric Co., Schenectady, 1941-43; gen. news editor, personnel adminstrn. officer AP, N.Y.C., 1943-46; pres. Martin Wright and Assocs., Inc., Guilford, Conn., 1946-80; cons. Buth & Wright Assocs., Inc., Guilford, 1980—. Contbg. author: Public Relations Ideas in Action; contbr. articles to profl. jours. Mem. Town of Guilford Bd. Fin. Mem. Pub. Rels. Soc. Am. (charter, cert. pub. rels. counselor), Guilford Preservation Assn. (bd. dirs.), Guilford Land Conservation Trust, Soc. of Silurians Inc. Republican. Episcopalian. Home: Peterborough, NH. Died Apr. 8, 2007.

WRIGHT, RICHARD ALLEN, journalist, educator; b. East Liverpool, Ohio, Oct. 15, 1933; s. Orrin Bennett and Dorothy Louise (Marquette) W.; m. Joan Margaret Puchalski, June 21, 1959 (div. 1981); children: Douglas R., Judith A., Deborah E. BA, Wayne State U., 1959, JD, 1965. Bar: Mich. 1966, U.S. Fed. Bar, 1966. Reporter, copy editor Detroit Free Press, 1956-61, reporter, 1968-69; reporter, editor Automotive News, Detroit, 1961-68, editor, 1970-84; film writer Chrysler Corp., Center Line, Mich., 1969-70; reporter, editor Detroit News, 1984-88; prof. Wayne State U., Detroit, from 1985. Author: Love and Revolution, 1987, Detroit Inc., 1995; editor: Reuther: A Daughter Strikes, 1991. With U.S. Army, 1953-56. Episcopal. Avocation: old cars. Home: Grosse Pointe, Mich. Died Dec. 9, 2006.

WURSTER, DALE ERWIN, pharmacist, educator, retired dean; b. Sparta, Wis., Apr. 10, 1918; s. Edward Emil and Emma Sophia (Steingraeber) W.; m. June Margaret Peterson, June 16, 1944; children: Dale Eric, Susan Gay. BS, U. Wis., 1942, PhD, 1947. U. Wis. Sch. Pharmacy, Madison, 1958-71, mem. faculty, 1947-71; prof., dean N.D. State U. Coll. Pharmacy, 1971-72; prof. Dale E. Wurster Ctr. Pharm. Tech., Iowa City, 2003, dean, 1972-84, dean emeritus, from 1984. George B. Kaufman Meml. lectr. Ohio State U., 1968; Hancher Finkbine Medallion prof. U. Iowa, 1984; Joseph V. Swintosky disting. lectr. U. Ky., 2000; cons. in field; phys. sci. adminstr. USN, 1960-63; sci. advisor U. Wis. Alumni Rsch. Found., 1968-72; mem. revision com. U.S. Pharmacopoeia, 1961-70; mem. pharmacy rev. com. USPHS, 1966-72; mem. tech. adv. com. contraceptive R&D program Ea. Va. Med. Sch., 1987-2002, rsch., U. Wis. Contbr. articles to profl. jours., chpts. to books; patentee in field. With USNR, 1944-46. Recipient Superior Achievement citation Navy Dept., 1964, merit citation U. Wis., 1976, Disting. Alumni award U. Wis. Sch. Pharmacy, 1984, Takeru Higuchi Rsch. award Acad. Pharm. Scis., 2007; Dale E. Wurster Ctr. Pharm. Tech. at U. Iowa named in his honor. Fellow Am. Assn. Pharm. Scientists (founder, sponsor Dale E. Wurster rsch. award 1990—, Disting. Pharm. Scientist award 1991); mem. Am. Assn. Colls. Pharmacy (exec. com. 1964-66, chmn. conf. tchrs. 1960-61, vis. scientist 1963-70, Disting. Educator award 1983), Acad. Pharm. Scis. (exec. com. 1967-70, chmn. basic pharmaceutics sect. 1965-67, pres. 1975, Indsl. Pharm. Tech. award 1980), Am. Pharm. Assn. (chmn. sci. sect. 1964-65, rsch. achievement award 1965, Wis. Disting. Svc. award 1971), Iowa Pharmacists Assn. (Robert G. Gibbs award 1983), Wis. Acad. Scis., Arts and Letters, Soc. Investigative Dermatology, Rumanian Soc. Med. Sci. (hon.), Am. Found. Pharm. Edn. (bd. grants 1987-92), Sigma Xi, Kappa Psi (past officer), Rho Chi, Phi Lambda Upsilon, Phi Sigma. Home: Iowa City, Iowa. Died Apr. 5, 2007.

WURSTER, WILLIAM HORACE, retired international trade company executive; b. Phila., Apr. 24, 1923; s. Horace F. and Ruth Ann (Morris) Wurster; m. Jeanne Cleaver Diesinger, Nov. 10, 1945 (dec. 2006); children: Janine Ann, William Glendon. BSc in Naval sci., Pa. Maritime Acad., 1944; postgrad., U. Pa., 1946—47, postgrad., 1950—51, Harvard U., 1962, Stanford U., 1983. Trader Woodward & Dickerson, Phila., 1949—53, asst. v.p., 1953—55, v.p., dir., 1955—64, pres., 1964—80, chmn. bd. Brym Mawr, Pa., 1980—86. Founder William H. Wurster Ctr. for Internat. Mgmt. Studies, Wurster Family Found. Author: The World Is Our Playground, 2002. Bd. dirs. Greater Phila. Internat. Network, from 1983. Capt. U.S. Mcht. Marines, 1944—46. Mem.: Merion Golf Club, U.S. Export Expansion Coun. (bd. dirs.), Regional Export Coun. (vice chmn.), Ocean Reef Club, Pine Valley Golf Club, Phila. Country Club, Union League. Republican. Home: Haverford, Pa. Died June 18, 2007.

WURTEMBURG, GLADYS VIRGINIA, writer, public relations consultant; b. N.Y.C., Mar. 16, 1925; d. William George and A. Gladys (Cronin) W. BA, Queens Coll., 1947; MA, NYU, 1987. Asst. dir. publicity Internat. Com. YMCAs, N.Y.C., also Toronto, 1957-60; dir. pub. relations Queens Coll. CUNY, 1960-76, pres. G.V. Wurtemburg Assocs. Inc., N.Y.C., 1976-79, 86—; dir. pub. relations CCNY, 1979-86; cons. in field. Author: (with R. Marshak) Memoirs of a City College President, 1982. Producer, dir.: (videotape) Her Story, 1984; (slide show) Swinging on a Star, 1983. Co-editor Kaleioscope, 1984—. Mem. Older Women's League Lobbyist Group, 1983—, Friends N.Y. Library, N.Y. Zool. Assn. Recipient City Woman of Yr. award CCNY, 1984; Alumna of Yr. award Queens Coll., 1976. Mem. N.Y. Press Club, Council for Advancement of Higher Edn., Nat. Writers Union, Mystery Writers Am. Club: L.I. Photography. Avocations: photography; journal and fiction writing. Died May 1, 2006.

WYATT, DAVID KENT, history professor; b. Fitchburg, Mass., Sept. 21, 1937; s. Kenneth Hall and Rebecca Westervelt (Chasteney) W.; m. Alene Frances Wilson, July 15, 1959; children— Douglas Stewart, Andrew Richard, James Wilson AB, Harvard Coll., 1959; AM, Boston U., 1960; PhD, Cornell

U., 1966. Lectr. southeast Asia Sch. of Oriental and African Studies, U. London, England, 1964-68; asst. prof. U. Mich., Ann Arbor, 1968-69; assoc. prof. Cornell U., Ithaca, N.Y., 1969-75, prof. S.E. Asian history, 1975-94, dir. S.E. Asia program, 1976-79, chmn. dept. history, 1983-87, 88-89, John Stambaugh prof. S.E. Asian History, 1994—2006. Author: The Politics of Reform in Thailand, 1969; co-author: In Search of Southeast Asia: A Modern History, 1971, rev., 1987, Hikayat Patani: The Story of Patani, 1970, Thailand: A Short History, 1984, Studies in Thai History, 1994. NEH fellow, 1974-75, Guggenheim fellow, 1984, Fulbright-Hays fellow, 1991. Mem. Assn. for Asian Studies (v.p. 1992-93, pres. 1993-94), The Siam Soc., Royal Asiatic Soc. (Malaysian br.). Home: Ithaca, NY. Died Nov. 14, 2006.

WYMAN, JANE (SARAH JANE FULKS), actress; b. St. Joseph, Mo., Jan. 4, 1914; d. R. D. and Emme (Reise) Fulks; m. Ernest Eugene Wyman, Apr. 8, 1933 (div.); m. Myron Futterman, June 29, 1937 (div. Nov. 1, 1938); m. Ronald Reagan, Jan. 26, 1940 (div. June 28, 1948); children: Maureen Reagan Revell (dec. 2001), Michael; m. Fred Karger, Nov. 1, 1952 (div. Dec. 7, 1954); m. Fred Karger, March 11, 1961 (div. March 9, 1965) Student, U. Mo., 1935. Formerly radio singer, chorus girl in movie musicals; actress. Chorus girl: Gold Diggers of 1937; actress: (films) The Kid from Spain, 1932, Elmer the Great, 1933, All the King's Horses, 1934, College Rhythm, 1934, Rumba, 1935, George White's 1935 Scandals, 1935, Stolen Harmony, 1935, King of Burlesque, 1936, Anything Goes, 1936, Bengal Tiger, 1936, My Man Godfrey, 1936, Stage Struck, 1936, Cain and Mabel, 1936, The Sunday Round-Up, 1936, Polo Joe, 1936, Here Comes Carter, 1936, Gold Diggers of 1937, 1936, Smart Blonde, 1937, Ready, Willing and Able, 1937, The King and the Chorus Girl, 1937, Slim, 1937, Little Pioneer, 1937, The Singing Marine, 1937, Public Wedding, 1937, Mr. Dodd Takes the Air, 1937, Over the Goal, 1937, The Spy Ring, 1938, He Couldn't Say No, 1938, Fools for Scandal, 1938, Wide Open Faces, 1938, The Crowd Roars, 1938, Brother Rat, 1938, Tail Spin, 1939, The Kid from Kokomo, 1939, Torch Blane...Playing with Dynamite, 1939, Kid Nightingale, 1939, Private Detective, 1939, Brother Rat and a Baby, 1940, An Angel from Texas, 1940, Flight Angels, 1940, Gambling on the High Seas, 1940, My Love Came Back, 1940, Tugboat Annie Sails Again, 1940, Alice in Movieland, 1940, Honeymoon for Three, 1941, Bad Men of Missouri, 1941, You're in the Army Now, 1941, The Body Disappears, 1941, Larceny, Inc., 1941, My Favorite Spy, 1942, Footlight Serenade, 1942, Priness O'Rourke, 1943, Make Your Own Bed, 1944, The Doughgirls, 1944, Crime by Night, 1944, The Lost Weekend, 1945, One More Tomorrow, 1946, The Yearling, 1946 (Acad. award nomination), Night and Day, 1946, Cheyenne, 1947, Magic Town, 1947, Johnny Belinda, 1948 (Acad. Award for Best Actress), A Kiss in the Bark, 1949, The Lady Takes a Sailor, 1949, Stage Fright, 1950, The Glass Menagerie, 1950, Three Guys Named Mike, 1951, Here Comes the Groom, 1951, The Blue Veil, 1951, The Story of Will Rogers, 1952, Just for You, 1952, Let's Do It Again, 1953, So Big, 1953, Magnificient Obsession, 1954, Lucy Gallant, 1955, All That Heaven Allows, 1955, Miracle in the Rain, 1956, Holiday for Lovers, 1959, Pollyanna, 1960, Bon Voyage!, 1962, How to Commit Marriage, 1969; (TV movies) The Bamboo Cross, 1955, The Failing of Raymond, 1971, Amanda Fallon, 1973, The Incredible Journey of Doctor Meg Laurel, 1979; (TV series) Fireside Theater, 1955, Jane Wyman Presents The Fireside Theater, 1955-58, Falcon Crest, 1981-90 (recipient Golden Globe award Best Actress in Series-Drama, 1984); (TV appearances) Amelia, 1955, General Electric Theater, 1955, Lux Playhouse, 1959, Westinghouse Desilu Playhouse, 1960, Checkmate, 1960, The Investigators, 1961, Wagon Train, 1962, The Bell Telephone Hour, 1964, Bob Hope Presents the Chrysler Theatre, 1966, Insight, 1967-70, The Sixth Sense, 1972, The Bold Ones: The News Doctors, 1972-73, Owen Marshall: Counselor at Law, 1974, The Love Boat, 1980, Charlie's Angels, 1980, Dr Quinn: Medicine Woman, 1993 Died Sept. 10, 2007.

WYNNE, LYMAN CARROLL, psychiatrist; b. Lake Benton, Minn., Sept. 17, 1923; s. Nels Wind and Ella C. (Pultz) W.; m. Adele Rogerson, Dec. 22, 1947; children: Christine, Randall, Sara, Barry, Jonathan. War certificate, Harvard, 1943, MD, 1947, PhD in Social Psychology, 1958; MD (hon.), Oulu U., Finland, 1989. Med. intern Peter Bent Brigham Hosp., Boston, 1947-48; grad. fellow social relations dept. Harvard U., 1948-49; resident neurology Queen Square Hosp., London, Eng., 1950; resident psychiatry Mass. Gen. Hosp., Boston, St. Elizabeth's Hosp., Washington, also NIMH, 1951-54; psychoanalytic tng. Washington Psychoanalytic Inst., 1954-60, teaching analyst, 1965-72. Cons., investigator WHO, 1965—2007; staff NIMH, 1954-57, chief sect. family studies, 1957-61, chief adult psychiatry br., 1961-72; mem. faculty Washington Sch. Psychiatry, 1956-72; prof. U. Rochester Sch. Medicine and Dentistry, 1971-98, chmn. dept. psychiatry, 1971-77, dir. div. family programs, 1971-83; psychiatrist-in-chief Strong Meml. Hosp., Rochester, N.Y., 1971-77, prof. emeritus psychiatry, 1998-2007; vis. lectr. Am. U., Beirut, Lebanon, 1963-64 Bd. dirs. Family Process, 1969-97; mem. editl. adv. bd. Jour. Nervous and Mental Diseases; sr. editor: The Nature of Schizophrenia, 1978; editor: The State of the Art in Family Therapy Research; co-editor: Psychosocial Intervention in Schizophrenia, 1983, Children at Risk for Schizophrenia, 1984, The Language of Family Therapy, 1985; sr. editor Systems Consultation, 1986 Chmn. AAMFT Rsch. & Edn. Found., 1992-94. Med. dir. USPHS, 1961-72; mem. NRC, 1969-72. Recipient Commendation medal USPHS, 1965; Hofheimer prize Am. Psychiat. Assn., 1966; Frieda Fromm-Reichmann award Am. Acad. Psychoanalysis, 1966; Meritorious Service medal USPHS, 1966; Stanley Dean award Am. Coll. Psychiatrists, 1976; McAlpin Research Achievement award, 1977, Disting. Achievement in Family Therapy Research, Am. Family Therapy Assn., 1981; Disting. Research Achievement award Assn. Marriage and Family Therapy, 1982, Disting. Profl. Contbn. award Am. Assn. for Marriage and Family Therapy, 1985, Disting. Contbn. to Family Therapy award Am. Family Therapy Assn., 1989. Fellow: Am. Acad. Psychoanalysis, Am. Psychiat. Assn. (life); mem.: Soc. for Rsch. in Psychopathology, Nat. Coun. for Family Relations, Assn. for Clin. Psychosocial Rsch. (coun. 1984—91), Am. Psychoanalytic Assn., Am. Assn. for Marriage and Family therapy (bd. dirs. 1992—94), Am. Family Therapy Acad. (pres. 1986—87), Am. Coll. Psychoanalysts, Western N.Y. Psychoanalytic Soc. (pres. 1986—87), Psychiat. Rsch. Soc. Home: Pittsford, NY. Died Jan. 17, 2007.

WYSE, LOIS, advertising executive, writer; b. Cleve., Oct. 30, 1926; d. Roy B. Wohlgemuth and Rose (Schwartz) Weisman; m. Marc Wyse (div. 1980); m. Lee Guber (dec. 1988). Pres. Wyse Advt. Inc., 1951—2007. Author: 60 books; syndicated columnist: Wyse Words; contbg. editor: (mag.) Good Housekeeping, 1983—98. Mem. bd. overseers Beth Israel Med. Ctr. Ctr. for Comms., NYC; trustees East Hampton Hist. Soc. Mem. Woman's Forum, PEN, Author's Guild, League of Profl. Theater Women. Home: East Hampton, NY. Died July 6, 2007.

WYTON, ALEC, composer, organist; b. London, Aug. 3, 1921; came to U.S., 1950, naturalized, 1968; s. Gilbert and Jessie (Burrage) W.; m. Mary Thornton Broman; children: Vaughan, Richard, Patrick, Christopher. BA, Oxford U., 1945, MA, 1949; Mus.D. (hon.), Susquehanna U., Pa., 1970; DHL (hon.), Va. Theol. Sem., 1997. Asst. organist Christ Church Cathedral, Oxford U., 1943-46; organist St. Mathews Ch., Northampton, Eng., 1946-50, Christ Church Cathedral, St. Louis, 1950-54, Cathedral St. John the Divine, NYC, 1954-74, St. James's Ch., NYC, 1974-87, St. Stephen's Ch., Ridgefield, Conn., 1987-96; chair dept. music Manhattan Sch. Music, 1984-93; ret., 1993. Adj. prof. music Union Theol. Sem., N.Y.C., 1960-73; chmn. dept. ch. music Manhattan Sch. Music, 1984-93; coord. standing commn. on ch. music Episcopal Ch., 1974-85. Composer numerous pieces.; Contbr. articles to profl. jours. Served with Brit. Army, 1941-42. Fellow Royal Coll. Organists, Am. Guild Organists (hon. fellow, pres. 1964-69), Royal Canadian coll. Organists, Royal Acad. Music, Royal Sch. Ch. Music. Republican. Episcopalian. Home: Ridgefield, Conn. Died Mar. 18, 2007.

YAGER, JOSEPH ARTHUR, JR., economist, consultant; b. Owensville, Ind., Apr. 14, 1916; s. Joseph Arthur and Edna (Pratt) Y.; m. Virginia Estella Beroset, Sept. 2, 1938; children: Thomas, Martha. AB, U. Mich., 1937, JD, 1939, MA, 1940; grad., Nat. War Coll., 1955. Economist OPA, 1942-44; economist State Dept., 1946-47, chief China research br., 1949-50, chief div. rsch. for Far East, 1952—57; attaché U.S. consulate gen., Canton, China, 1947-48, consul Hong Kong, 1950-51; econ. counselor Taipei, 1957-59; dep. chief of mission, 1959-61; dir. Office Chinese Affairs, 1961, Office East Asian Affairs, 1961-63; mem. Policy Planning Council, 1963-66, vice chmn., 1966-68; dep. dir. internat. and social studies div. Inst. Def. Analyses, 1968-72; sr. fellow Brookings Instn., 1972-83, guest scholar, 1983-86; resident cons. Sci. Applications Internat. Corp., 1986-89, sr. fellow, 1989-96; cons., from 1996. Author: Transforming Agriculture in Taiwan, 1988, Prospects for Nuclear Weapons Proliferation in a Changing Europe, 1992; co-author: Energy and U.S. Foreign Policy, 1974, New Means of Financing International Needs, 1978, Military Equation in Northeast Asia, 1979, Nonproliferation and U.S. Foreign Policy, 1980, International Cooperation in Nuclear Energy, 1981, Energy Balance in Northeast Asia, 1984, Energy Policy Experience of Asian Countries, 1987. Served in AUS, 1944-45. Mem. Phi Delta Phi, Delta Tau Delta. Home: Bowie, Md. Died Apr. 5, 2007.

YANCEY, ROBERT EARL, JR., retired oil industry executive; b. Ashland, Ky., June 16, 1945; s. Robert E. Sr. and Estelline (Tackett) Y.; m. Nina McGee, June 16, 1962; children: Rob, Yvonne, Elizabeth. BS in Chem. Engring., Cornell U., 1969. Sr. v.p., group operating officer; supt. Catlettsburg (Ky.) Refinery, 1976-79; exec. asst. Ashland (Ky.) Petroleum Co., 1979-80, group v.p., 1980-81, sr. v.p., 1981-86, pres., from 1986; sr. v.p., group operating officer Ashland Inc., 1988-97; ret. Republican. Avocations: golf, hunting, fishing. Home: Ashland, Ky. Died Aug. 11, 2006.

YANNOPOULOS, JOHN C., metallurgical consultant; b. Greece, Nov. 16, 1925; s. Constantin J.; m. Ada H.; children: Constantin, Panos. Diploma chem. engr., Tech. U., Athens, 1954; M in Applied Sci., U. Toronto, Ont., Can., 1965; D in metal engring., Tech. U. of Athens, 1978. Rsch. engr. Noranda Rsch, Ctr, Montreal, 1970-79; prof. extractice metal Athens Tech. U., 1979-82; asst. to v.p. metal ops. Newmont Mining, NYC, 1982-83, v.p., 1983-87; cons. Westport, Conn., from 1987. Editor Extractive Metal of Copper, 1976; author: Extractice Metallurgy of Gold, 1991, Metallurgia Extractiva Del Oro, 1994. Home: Westport, Conn Died Apr. 8, 2007.

YARINGTON, CHARLES THOMAS, JR., surgeon, educator, health facility administrator; b. Sayre, Pa., Apr. 26, 1934; s. C.T. and Florence (Hutchinson) Yarington; m. Barbara Taylor Johnson, Sept. 28, 1963; children: Leslie Anne, Jennifer Lynne, Barbara Jane. AB, Princeton U., 1956; MD, Hahnemann Med. Coll., 1960; grad., Army Command and Gen. Staff Coll., 1969, Air War Coll., 1973, Indsl. Coll. Armed Forces, 1974. Intern Rochester Gen. Hosp., NY, 1960-61; resident Dartmouth Hosp., 1961-62, U. Rochester Strong Meml. Hosp., 1962-65; instr. otolaryngology U. Rochester Sch. Medicine, 1962-65; chief ENT US Army Hosp., Ft. Carson, Colo., 1965—67; asst. prof. surgery W.Va. U. Sch. Medicine, 1967-68; assoc. prof., chmn. dept. otorhinolarygology U. Nebr. Med. Ctr., 1968-69, prof., chmn. dept. otorhinolaryngology, 1969-74; clin. prof. otolaryngology U. Wash., Seattle, from 1974; clin. prof. surgery Uniformed Svcs. U. Health Scis., Bethesda, Md., from 1985; chief otolaryngology Virginia Mason Med. Ctr., Seattle, 1978-88, 92-95, chief dept. surgery, 1988-91; surgeon Mason Clinic, Seattle, 1974-97. Cons. Surg. Gen. USAF, Hunter Group Med. Mgmt. Cons., 1996-98, Seattle Multispecialty Panel, 1998—; pres. Virginia Mason Rsch. Ctr., Seattle, 1983-85; trustee Mason Clinic, 1988-91; adv. coun. Nat. Inst. Neurol. Diseases, Communicative Diseases, Stroke of NIH, Bethesda, Md., 1986-90; bd. dirs. Virginia Mason Hosp., Virginia Mason Med. Ctr., bd. govs., 1989-98; bd. regents Uniformed Svcs. U. Health Scis., Bethesda, 2006—. Mem. editl. bd. Aviation, Space, Environ. Med. Jour., Otol. Clinics of N.Am., Mil. Medicine, Otolaryngology-Head and Neck Surgery; contbr. articles to profl. jours. Trustee Seattle Opera Assn., 1983-89. Served to lt. col. USAR, 56-70, to brig. gen. USAF, 1970-86. Decorated D.S.M., Legion of Merit, comdr. Venerable Order St. John (Gt Britain), companion with star Order Orthodox Hospitallers (Republic of Cypress), knight grand cross Mil. and Hospitalle Order of St. Lazarus; recipient Sir Henry Wellcome medal 1984. Fellow ACS, Royal Soc. Medicine, Am. Acad. Otolaryngology (Barraquer Meml. award 1968, mem. standing com., bd govs. 1982-88, Honor award 1974); mem. AMA, Am. Broncho Esophagological Assn. (coun., treas. 1982-86, pres. 1987-88) Am. Laryngol. Assn., Pacific Coast Soc. Ophthalmology and Otolaryngology (coun., pres. 1987-88), Soc. Med. Cons. to Armed Forces, Am. Soc. Head and Neck Surgery, N.W. Acad Head and Neck Surgery (pres. 1984-86), Am. Soc. Otology Rhinology and Laryngology (v.p. 1992-93, coun. 1997-2000) Res. Officers Assn. (past pres. Seattle chpt., nat. officer), Soc Colonial Wars, Sons Revolution (pres. Wash. 1985-87), Internat Power Boat Assn. (comdr. 1999-2000), Seattle Yacht Clu (trustee 2001-05), Princeton Quadrangle Club, Broadmoor Gol Club, RAF Club (London), Sigma Xi. Died May 30, 2007.

YATES, CHARLES RICHARDSON, former arts center executive; b. Atlanta, Sept. 9, 1913; s. Presley Daniel and Juli (Richardson) Y.; m. Dorothy Malone, May 20, 1944; children Dorothy Y. Kirkley, Charles R., Sarah F., J. Comer. BS wit honors, Ga. Inst. Tech., 1935; DLitt (hon.), Emory U., 199 With 1st Nat. Bank Atlanta, 1935-47, asst. v.p., 1940-47; wit Joshua L. Baily & Co., Inc., Atlanta, 1947-60, v.p., 1956-60; v.p finance Atlantic Coast Line R.R. Co. and L. & N. R.R. Co 1960-67; v.p. Seaboard Coast Line R.R. Co., 1967-71, v.p finance, 1971-73, L. & N. R.R. Co., 1967-73; pres. Atlanta Art Alliance, 1973-83. Dir. Technology Park/Atlanta. Trustee Ga Tech. Found., Woodruff Arts Ctr. Served with AUS, 1941-42; l USNR, 1942-46. Mem. Ga. C. of C. (dir., pres. 1965-67), Eas Lake Golf Club (pres. 1995—), Augusta Nat. Club (sec. Atlanta Athletic Club, Peachtree Golf Club, Capital City Clut Royal and Ancient Golf Club. Episcopalian. Home: Atlanta, Ga Died Oct. 17, 2005.

YATES, ELLA GAINES, librarian, consultant; b. Atlanta, Jun 14, 1927; d. Fred Douglas and Laura (Moore) Gaines; m. Josep L. Sydnor (dec.); l child, Jerri Gaines Sydnor Lee; m. Clayton R Yates (dec.). AB, Spelman Coll., Atlanta, 1949; MS in L.S Atlanta U., 1951; JD, Atlanta Law Sch., 1979. 1954Asst. b librarian Bklyn. Pub. Library, 1951; head children's dep Orange (N.J.) Pub. Library, 1956—59; br. librarian East Orang (N.J.) Pub. Library, 1960—69; med. librarian Orange Mem Hosp., 1967—69; asst. dir. Montclair (N.J.) Pub. Librar 1970—72, Atlanta-Fulton Pub. Library, 1972—76, dir 1976—81; dir. learning resource ctr. Seattle Opportunities In dustrialization Ctr., 1982—84; asst. dir. adminstrn. Friendshi Force, Atlanta, 1984—86; state librarian Commonwealth of Va 1986—90; library cons. Price Waterhouse, 1991; adv. bo Library of Congress Center for the Book, 1977—85; interim di Atlanta-Fulton Pub. Libr., 1998—99; cons., dir. Woodruff Libr Atlanta, 2000—02. Cons. in field; vis. lectr. U. Wash., Seattle 1981-83; mem. Va. Records Adv. Bd., 1986-90; mem. Nagar Exec. Bd., 1987-91. Contbr. to profl. jours. Vice chmn. N. Women's Coun. on Human Rels., 1957-59; chmn. Friend Fulton County Jail, 1973-81; bd. dirs. United Cerebral Pals Greater Atlanta, Inc., 1979-81 Coalition Against Censorshi Washington, 1981-84, YMCA Met. Atlanta, 1979-81, Exe Women's Network, 1979-82, Freedom To Read Found., 197 85, Va. Black History Mus., Richmond, 1990-91; sec., exec. di Va. Libr. Found. Bd., 1986-90; founder Coretta Scott King Boo Award, Ala., 1968—. Recipient meritorious svc. award Atlan U., 1977, Phoenix award City of Atlanta, 1980, Serwa awar Nat. Coalition 100 Black Women, 1989, Black Caucus awar 1989, disting. svc. award Clark-Atlanta U., 1991, ednl. suppo svc. award Tuskegee Airmen, 1993, Alumnae Achieveme award Spelman Coll., 1998, Annie McPheters award Atlanta Fulton Pub. Libr., 1998, Disting. Alumnae award Clark Atlan U., 2001; named profl. woman of yr. NAACP N.J., 197 outstanding chum of yr., 1976; named outstanding alum Spelman Coll., 1977, named to alumni hall of fame, 1995. Mer ALA (exec. bd. 1977-83, commn. freedom of access to info founder Coretta Scott King Book Award 1968), NAACP, Sout eastern Libr. Assn., Nat. Assn. Govt. Archives and Recor Adminstrn. (exec. bd. 1987-91), Delta Sigma Theta (Pinnac leadership award 2001). Baptist. Died June 27, 2006.

YEAGER, ANSON ANDERS, writer, retired editor, retir columnist; b. Salt Lake City, June 5, 1919; s. Charles Frankl and Elise Marie (Thingelstad) Yeager; m. Ada May Bidwel Sept. 10, 1944; children: Karen Ann, Anson Anders, Harry H Terry Douglas, Ellen Elise. BS, S.D. State U., Brookings, 194 LLD (hon.), Dakota State Coll., Madison, SD, 1972; DPub.Sv (hon.), S.D. State U., Brookings, 1991. Commd. lt. U.S. Arm 1942, advanced through grades to lt. col., 1961, ret., 197 printer's devil, linotype operator Faith Ind. and Gazette (S.D. 1935-38; printer S.D. State U., 1940-41; staff writer Arg Leader, Sioux Falls, SD, 1947-55, Sunday editor, 1955-60, exe editor, 1961-77, assoc. editor, 1977—84, editor editl. pag 1961-84, columnist, 1984-98, author travel articles and con mentary. Lectr. dept. journalism U. S.D., 1953—55. Contbr. World Book Ency., 1966—84; author: Anson Yeager's Storie 2000. Bd. dirs. Sioux Falls Area C. of C., 1964—70, Sioux Fal Devel. Found., 1967, Boys Club of Sioux Falls, 1966—68, S.I State U. Found., 1987—99, chmn., 1988—89; bd. dirs. Siou Coun., Boy Scouts Am., Sioux Falls, 1967—72, v.p., 1970—7 coun. mem. Ctr. for We. Studies, from 2002. Lt. col. S.D. Arm N.G., 1961—64. Named Newsman of Yr., 1978; named to S. Newspaper Hall of Fame, 1994, S.D. Hall of Fame, 199 recipient S.D. Sigma Delta Chi award, 1956, Editl. Excellen award, William Allen White Found., 1976, Disting. Alum award, S.D. State U., 1980, Friend of Augustana Coll. awar 1980, Ralph D. Casey Minn. award for disting. svc. in journa ism, U. Minn., 1981, Eminent Svc. award, East River Ele Power Coop., 1984, Mass. Comms. award, S.D. State U., 198 Les Helgeland Cmty. Svc. award, S.D. AP Mng. Editors, 198 Disting. Svc. award, S.D. Press Assn., 1988, A.H. Panko award, 1995, Jerome J. Lohr award, S.D. State U. Foun Western Am. award, Ctr. for Western Studies, Augustana Co 2000. Died Sept. 29, 2006.

YEARLEY, DOUGLAS CAIN, mining and manufacturing company executive; b. Oak Park, Ill., Jan. 7, 1936; s. Bernard Cain and Mary Kenny (Howard) Y.; m. Elizabeth Anne Dunbar, Feb. 8, 1958; children: Sandra, Douglas Jr., Peter, Andrew. BMetE, Cornell U., 1958; postgrad., Harvard U., 1968. Engr. welding Gen. Dynamics, Groton, Conn., 1958-60; devel. engr. Phelps Dodge Copper Products, Elizabeth, NJ, 1960-68; mgr. ops. Phelps Dodge Internat. Co., NYC, 1969-71; v.p. ops. Phelps Dodge Tube Co., LA, 1971-73; exec. v.p. Phelps Dodge Cable and Wire Co., Yonkers, N.Y., 1973-75; pres. Phelps Dodge Brass Co., Lyndhurst, N.J., 1975-79, Phelps Dodge Sales Co., NYC, 1979-84, v.p. mktg., 1981-82; sr. v.p. Phelps Dodge Corp., Phoenix, 1982-86, exec. v.p., 1987-89, chmn., CEO, 1989-2000, pres., 1991-97, chmn. emeritus, 2000—07. Bd. dirs. Phelps Dodge Corp., 1986-2001, U.S. Steel Corp., Pitts., Lockheed Martin Corp., Bethesda, Md., Marathon Oil Co., Houston, Heidrick & Struggles Internat., Chgo., 2000-02; chmn. Internat. Coun. on Metals and Mining. Bd. dirs. Am. Grad. Sch. Internat. Mgmt., 1990-92, Phoenix Symphony, 1988-2000; chmn. Arts Coalition, 1989-90; trustee Phoenix Art Mus., 1994-96. Mem. Nat. Elec. Mfrs. Assn. (bd. dirs. 1983-92), Internat. Copper Assn. (bd. dirs. 1987-2000, chmn. 1990-97), Am. Mining Congress (vice chmn.), Nat. Mining Assn. (chmn. 1997-98), Copper Devel. Assn. (chmn. 1989-93, dir. 1989-92), Nat. Assn. Mfrs. (bd. dirs. 1988-94), Bus. Roundtable, Bus. Coun., Sky Club, Echo Lake Country Club, Blind Brook Country Club. Republican. Congregationalist. Avocations: tennis, golf, classical music. Died Oct. 7, 2007.

YELLIN, VICTOR FELL, composer, music educator; b. Boston, Dec. 14, 1924; s. Mendl and Sarah (Fell) Y.; m. Isabel Joseph, May 26, 1948; 1 son, Garo. AB cum laude, Harvard U., 1949, AM, 1952, PhD, 1957. Tchg. fellow Harvard U., Cambridge, Mass., 1952-56; asst. prof. NYU, NYC, 1956-58, assoc. prof., 1961-64, prof., from 1964; asst. prof. Williams Coll., Williamstown, Mass., 1958-60; assoc. prof. Ohio State U., Columbus, 1960-61; coord. NY Metro-Fulbright-Hayes Vis. Scholars, 1978-82. Mem. editl. adv. bd. Am. Music. Composer: (opera) Abaylar, 1974 (song cycle) Dark of the Moon, 1986; condr.: Mrs. H.H.A. Beach's Grand Mass in E-flat, NYC, 1982; author: Chadwick, Yankee Composer, 1990, The Omnibus Idea, 1996, Bye Bye Blues Variations for Violin and Piano, Tully Hall, NYC, 1992, for Cello and Piano, Merkin Hall, NYC, 2002, Retrospective Concert 27th East Anglian Internat. Summer Music Festival, Eng., 2005; contbr. articles in Early Melodrama in Am., The Aethiop, Orchestral Restoration, Am. Music, A Celebration Am. Music, Jour. Musicology, Music in Early Va. Served with US Army, 1943-46, ETO. Recipient grant NEH, 1978. Mem. Am. Musicol. Soc., Sonneck Soc. Died Oct. 24, 2005.

YELTSIN, BORIS NIKOLAYEVICH, former President of Russia; b. Butka, Sverdlovsk, USSR, Feb. 1, 1931; s. Nikolai Ignatycvich and Klavdiya (Vassilyevna) Y.; m. Naina Iosifovna Girina, 1956; children: Yelena, Tatyana. Grad., Urals Poly. Inst., 1955. Mem. Communist Party Soviet Union, 1961-90; foreman, supt., sr. engr., head constrn. bd. Yuzhgorstroi trust, 1955-63; chief engr., head Sverdlovsk House-Bldg. Factory, 1963-68; dep. head, sec. Sverdlovsk Regional Party Com., 1968-76, First sec., 1976—85; mem. Presidium USSR Supreme Soviet, 1976-85; mem. ctrl. com. Communist Party Soviet Union, 1985-87; first dep. chmn. State Constrn. Com., Moscow, 1987-89; pres. Russian Fedn., 1991-99. Author: Against the Grain, 1990, The Struggle for Russia, 1994, Midnight Diaries, 2000. Recipient Order Service to the Fatherland of 1st Degree, Order of Lenin, Order of Red Banner of Labour (2), Badge of Honour, Royal Order of Peace and Justice, UNESCo, Shield of Freedom for Selflessness and Courage, U.S., Order of Grand Cross, Italy, Order of Malta; named Man of Yr., 1996, German Press. Avocations: tennis, volleyball, hunting, the cinema. Died Apr. 23, 2007.

YOCHELSON, ELLIS L(EON), paleontologist; b. Washington, Nov. 14, 1928; s. Morris Wolf and Fannie (Botkin) Y.; m. Sally Witt, June 10, 1950; children: Jeffrey, Abby, Charles. BS, U. Kans., Lawrence, 1949, MS, 1950; PhD, Columbia U., NYC, 1955. Paleontologist U.S. Geol. Survey, 1952-85, scientist emeritus, from 1991; biostratigrapher, specializing in Paleozoic gastropods and minor classes of extinct mollusks; lectr. night sch. George Washington U., 1962-65; lectr. Univ. Coll., U. Md., 1966-74; rsch. assoc. Smithsonian Instn., Washington, from 1967; lectr. U. Del., 1981; vis. prof. U. Md., 1986-87; organizer N.Am. Paleontol. Conv., 1969, 1996, editor proc., 1970-71. Co-editor: Essays in Paleontology and Stratigraphy, 1967; editor: Scientific Ideas of G.K. Gilbert, 1980; editorial bd. Nat. Geog. Rsch. and Exploration; contbr. numerous articles to profl. jours.; sec. Internat. Congress Carb. Stratigraphy, 1979. Author: Charles Doolittle Walcott, Paleontologist, 1998, Smithsonian Institution Secretary Charles Doolittle Walcott, 2001. Fellow AAAS (chmn. sect. E 1971), Geol. Soc. Am. (History Geology Divsn. award 2003); mem. Soc. Systematic Zoology (sec. 1961-66, councilor 1973), Internat. Paleontol. Assn. (treas. 1972-76), Paleontol. Soc. (pres. 1976, Centennial fellow 2006), History of Earth Sci. Soc. (hon. life; sec.-treas. 1982-85, sec. 1986-87, pres. 1989), N.Am. Paleontol. Conv. (hon. life; sec.), Smithsonian Instn. (150th Anniversary com.), Sigma Xi. Home: Washington, DC. Died Aug. 30, 2006.

YOCK, NORMA IRIS, counselor, music educator; b. Pekin, Ill., Apr. 18, 1920; d. John Battista and Pauline (Gianessi) Lami; m. John Matthew Yock, June 1, 1946 (dec. July 1957); 1 child, Julie Ann. B. in Music Edn., Ill. Wesleyan U., 1941; M.A., Bradley U., Peoria, Ill., 1961; specialist cert. Ill. State U., 1961, 63; U. Louisville, 1965, U. Ill., 1975. Cert. sch. counselor. Supr. music, art High Sch., Venice, Ill., 1941-45; dir. vocal music Edison Jr. High Sch., Pekin, 1952-58; supr. music Pekin Pub. Schs., 1958-62; counselor Pekin Community High Sch., 1962-84; sales rep. Sutton Travel Services, 1984-90, ret. 1990. Pres., Pekin Jr. Women's Club, 1948-50; Pekin Civic Chorus, 1959—; bd. dirs. YWCA, Am. Cancer Soc., 1983—, Channel 47, Peoria, Ill., 1983—; pres. United Way, 1988—; mem. Dirksen Ctr. Guild, YWCA Adv. Panel, Cen. Ill. Wesleyan U. Bd. Cited for Outstanding Contbn. to Sch. and Community, Pekin Community High Sch. Bd. of Edn., 1984; chmn. United Way, 1985, pres. Pekin Civic Chours, 1953-2003. Recipient Outstanding Citizen award Pekin C. of C., 1982. Mem. Altrusa Internat., NEA, Ill. Edn. Assn., Tri-County Guidance, Federated Bus. and Profl. Women's Club (pres. 1970-75), Delta Kappa Gamma (pres. 1961-64), Sigma Alpha Iota (pres. 1940-44). Republican. Roman Catholic. Avocations: music; reading; travel. Home: Pekin, Ill. Died June 18, 2007.

YOHE, WILLIAM POE, economics educator; b. Clifton Forge, Va., Feb. 22, 1931; s. William Oldfield and Pearl Winifred (Poe) Y.; m. Virginia Lee Wilson, Sept. 8, 1953 (div. Dec. 1973); children: William W., Mary, Kristine; m. Susan Hoggard, Feb. 15, 1974; children: Chelsea, Peter. AB, Kenyon Coll., 1953; AM, U. Mich., 1954, PhD, 1959. Instr. U. Mich., Ann Arbor, 1956-58; asst. prof. Duke U., Durham, N.C., 1958-61, assoc. prof., 1961-66, prof., from 1966. Vis. prof. Fed. Res. Bank St. Louis, 1969-70. Author: (book and software) Interactive Money and Banking, 1994; co-author: The Analytics and Institutions of Money and Banking, 1966; assoc. editor econ. Social Sci. Computer Rev., Raleigh, N.C., 1985—; contbr. numerous articles to profl. jours. Recipient Disting. Undergrad. Teaching award Duke U. Alumni, Durham, 1972. Mem. Phi Beta Kappa, Phi Kappa Phi. Republican. Episcopalian. Avocations: choral singing, dogs, cats. Home: Durham, NC. Died Apr. 21, 2007.

YORKE, JOHN BUNDY, lawyer; b. Rock Hill, SC, Aug. 5, 1954; s. N. Felix and Lane Knox Yorke; children: H. Spencer, N. Greer. BA, Wofford Coll., 1976; JD, Wake Forest U., 1979. Bar: N.C. 1979, S.C. 1987. Assoc. Wardlow, Knox, Knox, Freeman & Scofield, Charlotte, NC, 1979—87; v.p., gen. counsel World Way Corp., 1987—96; gen. counsel Integon Corp., Winston-Salem, NC, 1996—98; mem. Helms Mulliss & Wicker, PLLC, Charlotte, NC, from 1998. Dir. New South Pizza, Inc, Charlotte, NC. Trustee Thompson Child & Family Focus, Charlotte, NC, 2001. Mem.: Wake Forest Law Alumni Bd., N.C. Bar Assn. (chmn. corp. counsel sect. 1991—92), ABA, Wofford Coll. Nat. Alumni Assn. (pres. 2001), Phi Beta Kappa. Avocation: golf. Died July 17, 2007.

YOSHIDA, AKIRA, biochemist; b. Okayama, Japan, May 10, 1924; arrived in US, 1961; s. Isao and Etsu (Kagawa) Y.; m. Michiko Suzuki, Nov. 10, 1954; 1 child, Emmy. MSc, U. Tokyo, 1947, DSc, 1954. Assoc. prof. U. Tokyo, 1952-60; sr. rsch. fellow U. Pa., Phila., 1960-63; rsch. scientist NIH, Bethesda, Md., 1963-65; rsch. prof. U. Wash., Seattle, 1965-72; dir. dept. biochem. genetics City of Hope Med. Ctr., Duarte, Calif., 1972—98, emeritus prof., from 1998. Contbr. more than 300 articles to profl. jours. Scholar Rockefeller Found., 1955-56; recipient Merit award Japanese Soc. Human Genetics, 1980, Achievement award City of Hope, 1981, Merit Grant award NIH, 1988. Mem. AAAS, Am. Soc. Biol. Chemists, Am. Soc. Human Genetics (assoc. editor), Am. Soc. Hematology, NY Acad. Scis. Home: Altadena, Calif. Died Dec. 24, 2005.

YOUMANS, WILLIAM BARTON, retired physiologist; b. Cin., Feb. 3, 1910; s. Charles Trimble and Lucy May (Gardiner) Y.; m. Cynthia McCreary Holbrook, Nov. 24, 1932; children: William Barton, Carol Anne, Charles Gilbert. Student, Vanderbilt U., 1928—29; BS, Western Ky. State Coll., Bowling Green, 1932; MS, Western Ky. State Coll., 1933; PhD, U. Wis., 1938; MD, U. Oreg., 1944. Intern Henry Ford Hosp., Detroit, 1944-45; instr. biology Western Ky. U., Bowling Green, 1932-35; rsch. asst. physiology U. Wis., Madison, 1935-36, instr. physiology, 1936-38; instr. physiology to assoc. prof. physiology U. Oreg. Med. Sch., Portland, 1938-42, prof. physiology, 1942-46, head physiology dept., 1946-52; prof. and chmn. dept. physiology U. Wis., Madison, 1952-71, prof. physiology, 1971-76, prof. emeritus, from 1976. Mem. physiology study sect. USPHS, 1952-56, mem. tng. grant and fellowship rev. panels, 1956-60, 60-64. Author: Nervous and Neurohumoral Regulation of Intestinal Motility, 1949, Hemodynamics in Failure of the Circulation, 1951, Basic Medical Physiology, 1952, Fundamentals of Human Physiology, 1957, others; contbr. articles to profl. jours. including the Pharos. Recipient Meritorious Achievement award, U. Oreg. Med. Sch. Alumni Assn., 1967, Emeritus Faculty award, U. Wis. Med. Alumni Assn., 1985. Fellow AAAS; mem. Am. Physiol. Soc., Am. Soc. Pharmacology and Exptl. Therapeutics, Am. Heart Assn., Alpha Omega Alpha, Phi Sigma, Gamma Alpha. Avocations: tenor banjo, gardening, camping. Home: Columbia, Mo. Died Nov. 10, 2006.

YOUNG, JAMES WADE, electrical engineering consultant; b. Union, Iowa, Aug. 18, 1925; s. Wesley Haden Tucker and Ina Catherin Drake; m. Irene M. Timmerman, June 28, 1985; children: Terry J., Pamela Jo, Wendy Kay, Samantha L. Degree in elec. engring. U.S. Navy, 1945; grad. in Meter Engring., Ft. Wayne Corr. Sch., 1946. Meterman, Iowa Electric Light and Power Co., Eldora, 1942-43, engr., Cedar Rapids, 1946-52, dist. engr., asst. operating mgr., Iowa Falls, 1952-58, system operator, Cedar Rapids, 1958-64, mgr. electric ops., 1964-72, mgr. purchasing and stores, mgr. electric ops., 1972-75; exec. v.p. Challenge Ministries Inc., Dallas, 1975-76, pres., chief exec. officer, bd. dirs., Dallas, 1976—; pres., treas. CSS, Inc., Dallas, 1979—, also dir.; mng. ptnr. CSS Enterprises, Dallas, 1983—; cons. in elec. engring., bus. adminstrn. Bd. dirs. Evangel Coll., Springfield, Mo., 1960-69 1st Assembly God Ch., Cedar Rapids, 1946-75. Served with USN, 1943-46; PTO. Decorated Purple Heart. Republican. Home: Joplin, Mo. Died Jan. 24, 2007.

YOUNG, JEFFRY, psychologist, gerontologist, educator, statistician; b. Harvey, Ill., Aug. 23, 1952; s. Harold Joyce and Marion June Young. Student, St. Patrick's Coll., Mountain View, Calif., 1971-73; BA in Philosophy & Psychology, San Jose State U., 1977, MA in Gen. Psychology, 1978; PhD in Pub. Affairs, Claremont Grad. U., Calif., 1986. Coord., rsch. assoc. Ctr. for Applied Social Rsch. Claremont Grad. Sch., 1979-86; postdoctoral intern, behavioral scis. svc. sect. L.A. Police Dept., 1986-87; assoc. dir. Ruby Gerontology Ctr. Calif. State U., Fullerton, 1988-91, dir. Gerontology Rsch. Inst., 1989-92, rsch. prof. Sch. Humanities and Social Scis., 1986-93, assoc. dir. Roybal Inst. for Applied Gerontology LA, 1991-94, dir. Gerontology Rsch. Ctr., 1991-94; dir. advocacy and demonstration projects Nat. Asian Pacific Ctr. Aging, Seattle, 1994-97; rsch. dir. Puget Sound Coun. Sr. Citizens, from 1996; gen. mgr. Sound Rsch. Assoc., Rollingbay, Wash., from 1997. Adj. asst. prof. Sch. Gerontology, U. So. Calif., L.A., 1991-94; adj. prof. dept. psychology Calif. State U., L.A., 1991-94; co-prin. investigator Alzheimer's Outreach Project Nat. Inst. on Aging, UCLA, 1992-95; cons. health resources and svcs. adminstrn. Alzheimer's Demonstration project East L.A., Calif., 1992-94; project dir. Alzheimer's Disease Rsch. Ctr., Nat. Inst. on Aging, U. So. Calif. and U. Calif., Irvine, 1991-94; dir. Adminstrn. Aging Project, 1994—; prin. investigator Agy. Health Care Policy and Rsch., 1995; facilitator White House Conf. on Aging, 1995; mem. tech. adv. com. Assn. Asian Pacific Health Care Orgns., 1996. Author abstracts, monographs, and articles. Chair adv. bd. com. Rancho Los Amigos Med. Ctr., Downey, Calif., 1993—; touch judge uni. div. So. Calif. Rugby Football Union, 1988-91; pres. Meals on Wheels of Fullerton, Calif., 1993-94; chmn. instl. rev. bd. Calif. State U., L.A., 1994. Recipient Cert. of Recognition, L.A. Police Dept., 1987, Points of Light award, 1992, others; named to Outstanding Young Men of Am., 1986. Mem. APA, Am. Psychol. Soc., Gerontol. Soc. Am., Am. Evaluation Assn. (charter mem.), Am. Bd. Forensic Examiners, N.Am. Mycological Soc. (life), Cascade Sports Collectors Assn., Phi Beta Delta, Sigma Phi Omega (life). Roman Catholic. Avocations: mycology, rare books, rugby, nordic skiing, microscopy. Home: Bremerton, Wash. Died May 12, 2007.

YOUNG, JOSEPH LOUIS, artist; b. Pitts., Nov. 27, 1919; s. Louis and Jennie (Eger) Y.; m. Millicent Goldstein, June 19, 1949; children: Leslie Sybil, Cecily Julie. Grad., Westminster Coll., New Wilmington, Pa., 1941, D. Litt., 1960; Edwin Austin Abbey mural painting scholar, 1949; grad., Boston Mus. Sch. Fine Arts, 1951; Albert H. Whitin traveling fellow, Am. Acad. in Rome, 1951-52. Newspaperman, Pitts. and NYC, 1941-43; lectr. Tufts Coll., 1949; painting instr. Boston Mus. Sch., 1950; Idylwild Arts Found., 1959; Brandeis Camp Inst., 1962-74; founder, dir. Joseph Young Mosaic Workshop, from 1953; founding chmn. dept. archtl. arts Brooks Santa Barbara (Calif.) Sch. Fine Arts, 1969-75; head mus. exhibits Bowers Mus., Santa Ana, Calif., 1977-78; head visual arts CETA program, City of Los Angeles, 1978-80. Organized internat. sculpture competition for city of Huntington Beach, Calif., 1974; art cons. Allied Arts Commn., City of Huntington Beach, 1973-74; cons. Art in Public Bldgs. Program, Calif. Arts Council, 1976-77; field adminstr. CCA/CETA Program, Los Angeles.; Invited prin. speaker at nat. convs. A.I.A., Am. Craftsmen Council, 4th Congress I.A.P.A., 7th Nat. Sculpture Conf., Council of Am., U. Kans.; lectr. Rome, Venice, Florence (as guest) Italian govt., 1959 Restoration of mosaics from Greek and Roman periods and Della Robbia sculpture, 1972-73; author: A Course in Making Mosaics, 1957, Mosaics, Principles and Practice, 1963, also articles in profl. jours.; pub. mural painting bibliography, 1946; asso. founding editor: Creative Crafts mag, 1960-64; concept and design: ART$MARKET, 1979; work featured 16mm documentary film The World of Mosaic; true fresco, oil and mosiac mural commns. in, Boston, Chgo., Pitts., Los Angeles, survey govt. sponsored mural painting programs, 1951; one man show, Pitts. Arts and Crafts Center, 1950, Falk-Raboff Gallery, Los Angeles, 1953, ten year retrospective exhbn. archtl. art work, Desert Mus., Palm Springs, Calif., 1963, Calif. council A.I.A. Fine Arts Architecture Exhbn., 1964, Nat. Gold Medal Exhbn. of N.Y. Archtl. League, 1951, Platt Gallery, Bel Air, Calif., 1996; work reproduced in numerous books, mags., newspapers throughout the world; invited to submit designs for Nebr. State Capitol murals, paintings and mosiacs in numerous pvt. collections; executed mosiac murals Los Angeles Police Facilities Bldg., 1955, Don Bosco Tech. High Sch., 1956, Temple Emanuel, 1957, Southland Shopping Center, 1958, Our Lady of Lourdes Ch., 1959, Cameo residence, Beverly Hills, Calif., 1961, Santa Barbara Stock Exchange, 1960, St. Martins Ch., La Mesa, Calif., 1966, stained glass windows, liturgical art program, Congregation Beth Sholom, San Francisco, 1966, West Apse of Nat. Shrine of Immaculate Conception, Washington, 1966, mosiac arch, Eden Meml. Park, San Fernando, Calif., 1960; commd. to execute mural, Los Angeles County Hall of Records, Shalom Meml. Park, Chgo., B.V.M. Presentation Ch., Midland, Pa., 1961, Hollenbeck Police Sta., Los Angeles, 1963, Beth Emet Temple, Anaheim, Calif., 1963, Temple Sinai, Glendale, Calif., 1963, Sinai Temple, Los Angeles, 1963, Valley Beth Israel, Sun Valley, Calif., 1964, Beth Tikvah, Westchester, Calif., 1964, Belmont High Sch., Los Angeles, 1972; commd. to design and execute 14 bas-relief concrete-mosaic murals for exterior of, Math. Scis. Bldg. at UCLA, bronze sculpture, La Mirada (Calif.) Civic Theatre, 1979; did liturgical art programs for, Congregation B'nai B'rith, Santa Barbara, Temple Beth Torah, Alhambra, Temple Beth Ami, West Covina, Temple Menorah, Redondo Beach, Temple Solael, Canoga Park, Temple Bamidbar, Lancaster, Temple Beth Jacob, Redwood City (all Calif.), other congregations in Calif., concrete bas reliefs, Southgate County Pub. Library, 1973, mosaics for, St. Mary of Angels, Hollywood, Calif., 1973, Triforium polyphonoptic, kinetic tower, Los Angeles Mall, 1969-75; multimedia presentations for, 400th Anniversary Michelangelo, Italian Trade Commn., Casa de Maria, Santa Barbara, Hancock Coll., Santa Maria, Los Angeles County Mus. Art, U. Calif., Los Angeles and Irvine., designs for Holocaust Monument for Pan-Pacific Park in Los Angeles won national competition and dedicated in 1992; appointed to City of West Hollywood Arts Commn.; chmn. Fine Arts Bd., U. of Judaism, L.A.; completed cycle of Stained Glass windows for Ventura County Jewish Community Ctr. devoted to theme of Seven Days of Creation, 12 tribes stained glass for Temple Beth Israel, West Hollywood, Calif., 1991; work subject of restrospective exhbn. at the Jewish Community Galleries, 1986; commd. projects now represented by Yanov & Gold, Ltd. of Los Angeles, Calif.; chapel design Heritage Pointe, Mission Viejo, Calif. Served with USAAF, 1943-46. Recipient Nat. Army Arts contest award, 1945; Huntington Hartford Found. fellow, 1952-53; named Cavaliere della Republica Italiana, 1975. Fellow Internat. Inst. Arts and Letters (life); mem. Nat. Soc. Mural Painters (nat. v.p.), Artists Equity Assn. (pres. So. Calif. chpt. 1956, nat. v.p 1960), Calif. Confedn. Arts (founding pres. 1976) Home: Los Angeles, Calif. Died Aug. 23, 2007.

YOUNG, ROY ALTON, university administrator, educator; b. McAlister, N.Mex., Mar. 1, 1921; s. John Arthur and Etta Julia (Sprinkle) Y.; m. Marilyn Ruth Sandman, May 22, 1950; children: Janet Elizabeth, Randall Owen. BS, N.Mex. A&M

Coll., 1941; MS, Iowa State U., Ames, 1942, PhD, 1948; LLD (hon.), N.Mex. State U., Las Cruces, 1978. Tchg. fellow Iowa State U., 1941-42, instr., 1946-47, Indsl. fellow, 1947-48; asst. prof. Oreg. State U., 1948-50, assoc. prof., 1950-53, prof., from 1953, head dept. botany and plant pathology, 1958-66, dean rsch., 1966-70, acting pres., 1969-70, v.p. rsch. and grad. studies, 1970-76, dir. Office for Natural Resources Policy, 1986-90; chancellor U. Nebr., Lincoln, 1976-80; mng. dir., pres. Boyce Thompson Inst. Plant Rsch., Cornell U., Ithaca, NY, 1980-86. Mem. Commn. on Undergrad. Edn. in Biol. Scis., 1963-68; mem. Gov.'s Sci. Coun., 1987-90; cons. State Exptl. Stas. divsn. USDA; chmn. subcom. plant pathogens, agriculture bd. NAS-NRC, 1965-68; mem. exec. com. study on problems of pest control, 1972-75; mem. exec. com. Nat. Govs.' Coun. on Sci. and Tech., 1970-74; mem. US com. man and biosphere UNESCO, 1973-82; mem. com. to rev. US component Internat. Biol. Program, NAS, 1974-76; mem. adv. panel on postdoctoral fellowships in environ. sci. Rockefeller Found., 1974-78; bd. dirs. Pacific Power & Light Co., 1974-91, PacifiCorp., 1984-91, Boyce Thompson Inst. for Plant Rsch., 1975-93, Boyce Thompson Southwestern Arboretum, 1981-92, Oreg. Grad. Inst., 1987-94; mem. adv. com. Directorate for Engring. and Applied Sci., NSF, 1977-81; mem. sea grant adv. panel, 1978-80; mem. policy adv. com. Office of Grants, USDA, 1985-86. Trustee Ithaca Coll., 1982-89. Lt. USNR, 1943-46. Recipient Disting. Svc. award Oreg. State U., 1978. Fellow AAAS (exec. com. Pacific div. 1963-67, pres. div. 1971), Am. Phytopathology Soc. (pres. Pacific div. 1957, chmn. spl. com. to develop plans for endowment 1984-86, bd. dirs. 1986-88); mem. Oreg. Acad. Sci., Nat. Assn. State Univs. and Land Grant Colls. (chmn. coun. for rsch. policy and adminstrn. 1970, chmn. standing com. on environment and energy 1974-82, chmn. com. on environment 1984-86), Sigma Xi, Phi Kappa Phi, Phi Sigma, Sigma Alpha Epsilon. Home: Corvallis, Oreg. Died Jan. 24, 2007.

YOUNG, WALTER KWAI WHUN, otolaryngologist; b. Honolulu, Sept. 24, 1934; s. Leong Quan and Mildred (Chang) Y.; m. Joan Audrey Nichols, Mar. 30, 1963; children: Walter Leong, Adriene Lianne, Curt Yen Pui. Student, Gettysburg Coll., 1954-56, BA, 1956; MD, Jefferson Med. Coll., 1960. Diplomate Am. Bd. Otolaryngology. Intern, then resident in gen. surgery St. Luke's Hosp., Bethlehem, Pa., 1960-62; resident in otolaryngology Grad. Hosp., Phila., 1962-63, Upstate Med. Ctr., Syracuse, N.Y., 1963-65; pvt. practice Honolulu, from 1968. Assoc. prof. John A. Burns Sch. Medicine U. Hawaii, past chief of surgery Children's Hosp.; past chief of pediatric surgery Kapiolani Med. Ctr. Women and Children. Bd. dirs. Hawaii Bd. Hearing Aid Dealers and Fitters, 1991-93. Capt. USAF, 1965-67. Fellow Am. Acad. Otolaryngology and Head and Neck Surgery, ACS; mem. AMA, Hawaii Med. Assn., Honolulu County Med. Soc., Am. Coll. Surgeons, Pacific Coast Ophthalmology and Otolaryngology Assn., Pan Pacific Surg. Assn. Presbyterian. Avocation: electronics. Home: Honolulu, Hawaii. Died Feb. 21, 2006.

YOUNG, WILLIAM JOHN, French language educator, retired university president; b. Toronto, Ont., Can., Apr. 24, 1925; came to U.S., 1955; s. George Samuel and Dorothy Helen (Moroney) Y. BA, U. Toronto, 1948, MA, 1952; postgrad., U. Paris, 1955; PhD, U. Laval, Que., Can., 1956. Ordained priest Roman Cath. Ch., 1951. Head modern langs. St. John Fisher Coll., Rochester, N.Y., 1955-58, U. St. Thomas, Houston, 1958-62, v.p., dean, 1962-66, pres., 1966-67, 1979-85, chancellor, 1985-87, pres. emeritus, from 1987; mem. gen. adminstrn. Congregation St. Basil, Toronto, 1967-77. Translator: Basilian History to 1864, 1975. Pres. Houston Coun. Fgn. Lang. Tchrs., 1965-66; mem. equity-quality-audit com. Houston Ind. Sch. Dist., 1985-89; mem. Cert. Adv. Com., Austin, 1984-90. Decorated chevalier Palmes Académiques (France). Mem. Alliance Francaise de Houston (pres. 1964-65), Forum Club of Houston (bd. dirs.1980-86). Home: Houston, Tex. Died Aug. 8, 2006.

YOUNT, ERNEST HARSHAW, JR., retired medical educator; b. Lincolnton, NC, Feb. 23, 1919; s. Ernest H. and Marguerite (Smith) Y.; m. Betty Lindsay Shuford, June 8, 1942; children: Ernest H. III, Peter Shuford, Martha Lindsay. AB, U. N.C., 1940; MD, Vanderbilt U., 1943; postgrad. student, U. Chgo., 1943-48. Instr. medicine Bowman Gray Sch. Medicine, Wake Forest U., 1948-50, asst. prof., 1950-52, assoc. prof., 1952-53, prof. medicine, 1953-85, prof. emeritus medicine, from 1985, chmn. dept., 1952-72. Founder's medalist Vanderbilt U., 1943; Markle scholar med. sci., 1950-55; Distinguished Service award in medicine U. Chgo., 1958 Fellow ACP; mem. Phi Beta Kappa, Sigma Xi, Alpha Omega Alpha. Episcopalian. Home: Winston Salem, NC. Died Mar. 15, 2006.

YOUTCHEFF, JOHN SHELDON, physicist; b. Newark, Apr. 16, 1925; s. Slav Joseph and Florence Catherine (Davidson) Y.; m. Elsie Marianne, June 17, 1950; children: Karen Janette, John Sheldon, Mark Allen, Heidi Mary Anne, Lisa Ellen AB, Columbia U., 1949, BS, 1950; PhD, UCLA, 1953. Registered profl. engr., Calif., DC. Ops. analyst GE Co., Ithaca, NY, 1953—56, cons., engr. missile & space divsn. Phila., 1956—64, mgr. advanced reliability programs, 1964—72; mgr. reliability and maintainability Litton Industries, College Park, Md., 1972—73; program mgr. U.S. Postal Svc. Hdqrs., Washington, from 1973. Instr. U. Pa., 1965-66, Villanova U., 1957— Lt. USAAF, 1943-46; to comdr. USNR, 1946— Fellow AAAS, Br. Interplanetary Soc., AIAA, Explorers Club; mem. IEEE (sr.), Ops. Rsch. Soc., Rsch. Soc. Am., Am. Math. Soc., Am. Physics Soc., Am. Chem. Soc., Am. Astron. Soc., Am. Geol. Soc., NSPE, Engring. and Tech. Socs., Coun. Del. Valley (spkrs. bur.), USCG Aux. (flotilla comdr.), Res. Officers Assn., Am. Legion, Optimists Internat. (pres. Valley Forge chpt. 1970-71) Roman Catholic. Died Feb. 15, 2007.

YUAN, SHAO WEN, aerospace engineer, educator; b. Shanghai, Apr. 16, 1914; came to U.S., 1934, naturalized, 1954; s. Ti An and Chieh-huang (Chien) Y.; m. Hui Chih Hu, Nov. 5, 1950. BS, U. Mich., 1936; ME, Stanford U., 1939; MS, Calif. Inst. Tech., 1937, PhD, 1941. Rsch. engr. Glenn Martin Co., 1942-43; chief of rsch. Helicopter div. McDonnell Aircraft Corp., 1943-45; instr. Washington U., St. Louis, 1944-45; adj. prof. Poly. Inst. Bklyn., 1946-49, assoc. prof., 1949-54, prof., 1954-57; ptnr. von Kármán, Yuan & Arnold Assocs., 1955-63; prof. aerospace engring. U. Tex., 1958-68; prof., chmn. mech. engring. div. George Washington U., 1968-78, chmn. civil, mech. and environ. dept., 1973-78, 80-81, prof. emeritus, 1984; pres. RISE, Inc., 1977-85. Canadair Chair prof. U. Laval, Can., 1957-58; chmn. adv. com. Joint Inst. for Advancement of Flight Sci., 1970-84; hon. prof. Zhejiang U., 1987—; cons. Edo Aircraft Corp., Aerojet Corp., Cornell Aero. Lab., Dept. of Interior, Oak Ridge Nat. Lab., N.Am., Aviation, Inc., Fairchild-Hiller Corp., McDonnell-Douglas Corp., The World Bank; hon. adviser Nat. Center Research of China, Taiwan, 1958-68; chmn., founder 1st U.S.-China Conf. on Energy, Resources, and Environment, 1982; founder Consortium of Univs. for Promoting Grad. Aerospace Studies, 1984; founder Disting. Lecture Series on Founds. of Aerospace Research and Devel., 1986. Author: Foundations of Fluid Mechanics, 1967; Contbr. to: High Speed Aerodynamics and Jet Propulsion series, 1959, Energy, Resources, and Environment: Procs. at 1st U.S.-China Conf., 1982. Founder Yuan Engring. Libr., Zhejiang U., China. Recipient Outstanding Achievements and Contbns. award George Washington U., 1981; named Outstanding Educator of Am., 1970, Outstanding Chinese American, 1983, others; Yuan Engring. Libr. established, 2002. Fellow AAAS, AIAA, Internat. Biog. Assn; mem. ASME (life), Am. Soc. Engring. Edn., Soc. Engring. Sci. (bd. dirs. 1973-78, pres. 1977), Torchbearers Caltech, Founding Grant Soc. of Stanford U. (charter), John Montieth Soc. of U. Mich. (charter), Sigma Xi, Phi Kappa Phi, Phi Tau Phi, Sigma Gamma Tau, Pi Tau Sigma, Tau Beta Pi, Tau Xi Sigma. Achievements include patents in field. Home: San Francisco, Calif. Died Apr. 12, 2006.

YUROW, JOHN JESSE, lawyer; b. Washington, Jan. 30, 1931; s. Louis and Lauretta (Jedeikin) Y.; m. Bette Hilary Troshinsky, Aug. 1, 1953; children— Michael Jay, Gary Alan, Diane Ruth Yurow Beckwith, Lois Anne. AB, George Washington U., 1953, JD, 1958. Bar: D.C. 1958, Mich. 1961. Trial atty. Office Regional Counsel, IRS, Detroit, 1958-62; assoc. Arent, Fox, Kintner, Plotkin & Kahn, Washington, 1962-68, ptnr., from 1969. Professorial lectr. in law George Washington U., Washington, 1974-76 Past mem. editorial bd. George Washington U. Law Rev.; contbr. articles on tax subjects to profl. publs. Served with U.S. Army, 1953-55 Mem. ABA, D.C. Bar Assn. (chmn. taxation div. 1977-78), Fed. Bar Assn. (chmn. taxation com. 1972-73), Order of Coif, B'nai B'rith, Phi Delta Phi Democrat. Avocations: tennis; travel. Home: Westfield, NJ. Died Sept. 27, 2006.

ZACHARIAS, JOHN ELLING, chemical company executive; b. Connellsville, Pa., Sept. 8, 1915; s. Johannes M. and Louise M. (Elling) Z.; m. Muriel C. Eckes, Sept. 21, 1946; children— Jane E., Thomas E. AB, Princeton, 1936; student, Grad. Sch. Bus. Adminstrn., N.Y. U., 1937-38, Law Sch., 1939-40. Estate adminstrn. U.S. Trust Co. of N.Y., 1936-43; prodn. mgr. Whitehall Pharm. Co., 1946-48; dir. operations Jamieson Pharm. Co., 1948-51; with McKesson & Robbins, Inc. (co. name now McKesson, Inc.), NYC, 1952-77, v.p., 1956-77; pres. Cord Assos., Ltd., 1978-83; assoc. Smith, Stanley & Co., Inc., from 1978. Served with USNR, 1943-46. Mem.: Princeton (N.Y.C.); Old Lyme Country; Woodstock Country (Vt.). Home: Essex, Conn. Died June 23, 2006.

ZAWINUL, JOSEF, bandleader, composer, keyboardist, synthesist; b. Vienna, July 7, 1932; came to U.S., 1959; s. Josef and Maria (Hameder) Z.; m. Maxine Byars, Mar. 16, 1964; children— Anthony, Erich, Ivan. Student, Realgymnasium, Vienna, 1945-49, Vienna Conservatory Music, 1942-47; Dr. honoris Causa, 1969. Keyboardist Internet Music Network, Gloucester, Mass. Appeared with Vienna Radio Orch., 1952-58, Maynard Ferguson, 1959; mem. Fatty George Band, 1956-58; accompanist Dinah Washington, 1959-61, Joe Williams, 1961; mem. Cannonball Adderley Quintet, 1961-70; recs. with Miles Davis include BitchesBrew, In a Silent Way; founder own group Weather Report, 1970-85, Zawinul Syndicate, 1985—; recs. include: Weather Report, Vitous, 1971, I Sing the Body Electric, 1972, Tale Spinnin', Black Market, 1974, Heavy Weather, 1977, Mr. Gone, 1978,Mysterious Traveler, Night Passage, Sportin Life, Weather Report with Jaco Pastorius, 1981, This is This, 1986, (with Miles Davis), In a Silent Way, 1969, Bitches Brew, 1970, (with Salifkeita) Amen, 1992, (solo) Dialects, Zawinul, (with Zawinul Syndicate) Immigrants, Black Water, 1989, Lost Tribes. Recipient Jazz Record of Year award 5 of 8 albums, 1973-78; named Best Synthesizer player Downbeat mag., 1984, 85, 89 Died Sept. 11, 2007.

ZEDLER, EMPRESS YOUNG, psychologist; b. Abilene, Tex., Nov. 9, 1908; d. William James and Edith (Deaver) Young; m. Paul Louis Zedler, June 5, 1928. B.A., U. Tex., 1928, M.A., 1948, Ph.D., 1952. Chairperson dept. spl. edn. Southwest Tex. State U., San Marcos, 1960-78, disting. prof. emeritus, 1988—; pvt. practice child psychologist, Luling, Tex., 1978-94; ret. 1994. Fellow Am. Speech Lang. and Hearing Assn., Acad. Cerebral Palsy and Rehabilitative Medicine; mem. Assn. Children's Learning Disabilities (Founders Gold Key award), Am. Psychol. Assn., Tex. Psych. Assn., Tex. Speech Lang. and Hearing Assn. (Internat. award), Acad. Aphasia, Phi Beta Kappa. Episcopalian. Club: Country (Austin). Author: Listening for Speech Sounds, 1955; (with others) Principles of Childhood Learning Disabilities, 1972. Home: Luling, Tex. Died May 30, 2006.

ZENZIE, HENRY, finance company executive; b. Windsor, Conn., Sept. 30, 1929; m. Beatrice Ufford, Oct. 25, 1935; children: Henry Hazard, Beatrice W., Charles U., Elizabeth C. BS in Econs., U. Pa., 1954; MBA, Harvard U., 1956. Gen. ptnr. Sci. Assocs., Princeton, NJ, from 1975; pres. Viskon-Aire Corp., Salisbury, Md., from 1979, Isomet Corp., Springfield, Va., from 1981. Bd. dirs. Gearhart Industries Inc., Ft. Worth. Mem. Pres.'s Export Coun., Washington, from 1982; chmn. adv. com. Reagan-Bush Campaign, 1984. Mem.: Tennis Club, Pretty Brook Club. Home: Princeton, NJ. Died Jan. 5, 2006.

ZGUSTA, LADISLAV, linguist, educator; b. Libochovice, Czechoslovakia, Mar. 20, 1924; came to U.S., 1970, naturalized, 1977; s. Ladislav and Sonya (Bernasova) Z.; m. Olga Janouskova, Apr. 10, 1948; children: Monica, Richard. PhD, Caroline U., Prague, Czechoslovakia, 1949; D.Sc., Czech Acad Scis., 1964. Asst. prof. Caroline U., Prague, Czechoslovakia 1948-52; sr. research mem. Oriental Inst., Prague, 1952-70, heac dept. lexicography, 1958-69; vis. prof. Cornell U., Ithaca, N.Y. 1970; prof. linguistics and classics U. Ill., Urbana, from 1970 dir. Ctr. Advanced Study, permanent mem. Ctr. Advanced Study Head dept. lexicography German Acad. Scis., Berlin, 1960-70 instr. U. Brno, Czechoslovakia, 1965-69; Ford Found. instr. India, 1975, 89, Philippines, 1979; rsch. cons. Linguistics Rsch Ctr., U. Tex., Austin, 1970-72; condr. seminar NEH, 1978; cons NSF. Author: Personennamen griech. Stadte, 1955, Kleinasi atische Personennamen, 1964, Anatol. P.N. Sippen, 1964, Neu Beitrage, 1970, Manual of Lexicography, 1971, Chinese transl. 1984, Kleinasiatische Ortsnamen, 1984, Lexicography Today 1988; contbr. articles to profl. publs. Guggenheim fellow, 1977 84; Am. Council Learned Socs. grantee, 1973, 81, Deutsch Forschungsgemeinschaft grantee, 1971, 72, 73, 74, NEH grantee, 1989-91. Fellow Dictionary Soc. N.Am. (pres. 1983 85); mem. Am. Acad. Arts and Scis., Linguistic Soc. Am., Am Names Soc. (hon.), Indogermanische Gesellschaft (exec. com 1956-64), Austrian Acad. Scis. (corr.) Died Apr. 27, 2007.

ZIELASKO, GUS WILLIAM, judge; b. Canton, Ohio, June 15, 1915; s. Gustav A. and Marie (Gross) Z.; m. Marilyn A Jenkins, Oct. 21, 1956; children— Douglas E., Becky J., Tracy J. B.A., Coll. of Wooster, 1938; M.A., U. Mich., 1939; postgrad Ohio State U., 1939-40; LL.B., William McKinley Sch. of Law 1950. Bar: Ohio 1950. Instr., coach U. N. Mex., Albuquerque 1941-42, 46-47; mem. firm Eberly, Lesh & Miller, Canton 1950-81; judge Canton Mcpl. Ct., 1981-88; ret., 1988—. Bd dirs. N.C. Student Loan Found. Served to 2d lt. U.S. Army 1942-46, ETO. Mem. Stark County Bar Assn. (pres. 1975-76) Ohio State Bar Assn., Ohio Mcpl. Judges Assn. Republican Methodist. Avocations: photography, golf. Home: North Canton Ohio. Died July 2, 2007.

ZIMMER, PAUL HOWARD, housing and transportatio manufacturing company executive; b. Detroit, Apr. 18, 1929; s Donald R. and Ora E. (Howie) Z.; m. Rosina Procopio, Dec 1979; children: Mark Louis, Christina Lee; children by previou marriage: Mallory (Mrs. Carl M. Scholl), Mary J., Robert I Student, Fla. So. Coll., 1949. With Zimmer Boat & Trailer Co Detroit, 1946-50; sec., treas., later pres. Zimmer Industries Elwood, Ind., 1959-61; founder, chmn. bd., pres., chief exec officer Zimmer Corp., from 1961. Died Oct. 11, 2005.

ZIMMER, WILLIAM, art critic; b. Santa Fe, NMex. BA Columbia U.; MA in Art History, U. Tex. With The Soho News 1977; art critic The NY Times, 1981—2004. Lectr. in field juried art exhbns. Died Sept. 28, 2007.

ZIMRING, LOIS EILEEN JACOBS, physical science educator; b. Chgo., Nov. 19, 1923; d. Edward Lawrence and Lon Marie (Bert) Jacobs; m. Fred Martin Zimring, Dec. 17, 194 (div. Dec. 1962); 1 son, Craig Marshall. BS, U. Chgo., 194 MS, 1949, PhD, 1964. Lab research asst. to Prof. Robe Mulliken U. Chgo., 1946-48, lectr., 1959-61, instr., 1961-64 instr. chemistry Morgan Park Jr. Coll., Chgo., 1949-51; ass prof. U. Minn., Morris, 1964-66, Mich. State U., East Lansing 1966-69, asso. prof., 1969-73, prof. dept. natural sci., 1973-89 prof. Ctr. Integrative Studies-Sci., from 1989. Contbr. articles t profl. jours. Edith Barnard fellow, 1955-57; Joseph B. Lo wenthal fellow, 1957-59; Leavell fellow, 1957-58; Charles F Viol fellow, 1957-59; Guastaveous Swift, 1958-59 Mem AAAS, AAUP. Home: East Lansing, Mich. Died Nov. 6, 200

ZIRKIND, RALPH, physicist, educator; b. NYC, Oct. 2 1918; s. Isaac and Zicel (Lifshitz) Z.; m. Ann Goldman, Nov. 2 1940; children: Sheila Zirkind Knopf, Elaine Zirkind Gorman Edward I. BS, CCNY, 1940; MS, Ill. Inst. Tech., 1945; pos grad., George Washington U., 1946-47; PhD, U. Md., 195 D.Sc., U. R.I., 1968. Physicist Dept. Navy, 1945-50, chi physicist, 1951-60; physicist Oak Ridge Nat. Lab., 1950-5 Advanced Research Project Agy., Washington, 1960-63; pro Poly. Inst. Bklyn., 1963-70, U. R.I., Kingston, 1970-72, ad prof., from 1972; physicist Advanced Rsch. Projects Agy Arlington, Va., 1972-74, cons., 1974—2007. Lectr. U. Md 1947-48, 48-50, George Washington U., 1952-53, U. Mich 1964, 66, Haifa Inst. Tech., 1971; cons. ACDA, Jet Propulsio Lab., Calif. Inst. Tech.; cons. to industry, 1974-2007. Contb author: Jet Propulsion Series, 1952, FAR Infrared Properties Materials, 1968, NAS Study Biology and Exploration of Mar 1966; editor: Electromagnetic Sensing of Earth, 1967, Proc SPIE-Developments in Electronic Imaging Techniques, vol. 3 1972; mem. editl. bd. Infrared Physics, 1963-2007; contb articles profl. jours. Recipient Meritorious Civilian Svc. awa US Dept. Navy, 1957; Meritorious Civilian Svc. award US Dep Def., 1970; Outstanding Educator of Am. medal, 1972; Ma Contbn. award BMDO/AIAA, 1994; Spl. Lifetime Achieveme Award for Pioneering Work in Sensors, SPIE, 2002. Mem. Am Phys. Soc., N.Y. Acad. Scis., Sigma Xi, Sigma Pi Sigma (SPI Aerosense Lifetime Achievement award 2002), Eta Kappa N Home: Silver Spring, Md. Died Jan. 21, 2007.

ZOBRIST, BENEDICT KARL, retired library director, histo rian; b. Moline, Ill., Aug. 21, 1921; s. Benedict and Lila Agn (Colson) Z.; m. Donna Mae Anderson, Oct. 23, 1948; childre Benedict Karl II, Markham Lee, Erik Christian. AB, Augustan Coll., Rock Island, Ill., 1946; postgrad., Stanford U., 1946-4 MA, Northwestern U., 1948, PhD, 1953; postgrad., U. Ill., 196 Tunghai U., Taiwan, 1962, Columbia U., 1962-63, Fed. Exe Inst., Charlottesville, Va., 1974, Hebrew U., Israel, 1978; LH Avila Coll., 1995. Manuscript specialist in recent Am. histo Library of Congress, Washington, 1952-53; asst. referen librarian Newberry Library, Chgo., 1953-54; command histori Ordnance Weapons Command, Rock Island Arsenal, 1954-6 prof. history, chmn. dept. Augustana Coll., 1960-69, asst. de faculty, 1964-69, asso. dean, dir. grad. studies, 1969; asst. d Harry S. Truman Libr., Independence, Mo., 1969-71, di 1971-94. Exec. sec. Harry S. Truman Libr. Inst., Independenc 1971-94; mem. steering com. Harry S. Truman Statue Com Independence, 1973-76; dir., regent Harry S. Truman Go Neighbor Award Found., 1974-2007; mem. Independence Tr man Award Commn., 1975-94, Mo. Hist. Records Adv. B

978-2007; adj. prof. history U. Mo.-Kansas City, 1975-94, Ottawa U., Kansas City, 1977-94, U. Mo. St. Louis, 1987-94; chmn. Independence Commn. Bicentennial of U.S. Constitution, 1987, Uptown Independence, Inc., 1989-94; mem. adv. coun. Truman Little White House State Historic Site, Key West, Fla., 1987-94. Contbr. articles, revs. to profl. jours. Trustee Heritage League of Greater Kansas City, 1981-2007, Liberty Meml. Assn., Kansas City, Mo., 1990-2002, Black Archives Mid-Am., Inc., Kansas City, 1992-94; mem. Truman Nat. Centennial Com., 1982-84; Served with AUS, 1942-46. Recipient Outstanding Alumni Achievement award Augustana Coll., 1975, Bronze Good Citizenship medal Kans. SAR, 1986, People's Choice award Independence (Mo.) Neighborhood Councils, 1987, Mid-Am. Regional Council award for contbns. to met. community, 1987, Citizen Achievement award Black Archives of Mid-Am., 1988, Silver Good Citizenship medal Mo. SAR, 1988, Special Recognition award City of Independence, 1988, Outstanding Civic Leader in Independence, 1989, Gold Medal of Honor DAR, 1990, Spl. Commendation award Nat. Park Svc., 1993; named World Citizen of Yr. Kans. City Mayor's UN Day Com., 1994; named to Hall of Honor Moline (Ill.) HS, 2005. Mem. AAUP, Am. Hist. Assn., Jackson County (Mo.) Hist. Soc. (v.p. 1972-82, 93-95), Orgn. Am. Historians, Assn. Asian Studies, Am. Assn. State, Local History, Soc. Am. Archivists, U.S. Power Squadron, Am. Legion, La Societe des 40 Hommes et 8 Chevaux, VFW. Home: Lake Lotawana, Mo. Died Apr. 19, 2007.

ZOOK, DONOVAN QUAY, foreign service officer; b. Akron, Ohio, Oct. 22, 1918; s. David Blough and Lena May (Landis) Z.; m. Theresa Fuetterer, June 21, 1941; children: Theodore Alan, Jacqueline Deborah (Mrs. Campbell Carrington Cochran IV). AB, Ohio U., 1940; adminstrv. intern, Nat. Inst. Pub. Affairs, 1940-41; MA, Am. U., 1946. Budget and planning examiner U.S. Housing Authority, 1940-42; adminstrv. analyst OPA, 1942-43; staff Office Shore Establishments and Indsl. Pers., Navy Dept., 1943-44; div. chief Fgn. Econ. Adminstrn., 1945-46; asst. chief mgmt. office Office Chief of Staff, War Dept., 1946-47; mgmt. cons. Dept. State, 1947-49, exec. officer Office Departmental Adminstrn., 1949-51, spl. asst. to dep. under-sec. of state, 1951-53; exec. sec. Bd. of Fgn. Service, 1951-57; exec. asst. to asst. sec. state, contr. Dept. State, 1953-55, spl. asst. to dep. under-sec. state, 1955-57; chief polit. sect. Am. Embassy, Santiago, Chile, 1957-59, counselor for polit. affairs, 1959-61, dep. chief of mission and counselor of embassy Montevideo, Uruguay, 1961-63; dir. Bd. Examiners for Fgn. Svc. and chief recruitment and exam. div. Dept. State, 1963-65, consul gen., 1965; dir. Office of Atomic Energy Affairs, Bur. Internat. Sci. Affairs, 1965-73. Sr. polit. adviser to U.S. del. to Inter-Am. Nuclear Energy Commn., also mem. U.S. del. Gen. Conf. and bd. govs. IAEA, 1965-72; mem. U.S. del. 4th UN Conf. on Peaceful Uses Atomic Energy; cons. to sec. state's adv. com. on sci. and fgn. affairs, 1973-74, also com. on sci. and tech. cooperation between Japan and U.S., 1975, survey of tech. and fgn. affairs, 1976. Contbr. profl. jours. Recipient Superior Honor award State Dept., 1968 Mem. Diplomatic and Consular Officers, Pa. German Soc., Lancaster Mennonite Hist. Soc., Mennonite Hist. Assocs., Nat. Genealogical Soc., Va. Genealogical Soc., The Nature Conservancy, World Wildlife Found., Sierra Club, Phi Beta Kappa, Tau Kappa Alpha, Phi Eta Sigma. Presbyterian. Home: Alexandria, Va. Died Sept. 18, 2006.

ZOX, LARRY, artist; b. Des Moines, May 31, 1937; s. Oscar and Mildred (Friedman) Z.; m. Jean Marilyn Glover, July 19, 1965; children: Melinda, Alexander Cassidy. Student, Okla. U., 1955-56, Drake U., 1957, Des Moines Art Center, 1955-57. Vis. critic Cornell U., summer 1967; faculty (Sch. Visual Arts), 1967-68, 69-70, 70-76, Yale, summer, 1972, Kent State U., summer 1974 Exhibited one man shows at Am. Gallery, N.Y.C., 1962, Kornblee Gallery, N.Y.C., 1964-66, 68, 69, 70, 71, Andre Emmerich Gallery, 1973, 75, 76, Whitney Mus. Am. Art, 1973, Galerie Rocke, Cologne, Germany, 1968, Janie C. Lee Gallery, Houston, 1974, Hokin Gallery, Bay Harbor Islands, Fla., 1981, Meridith Long & Co., Houston, 1981, Hokin Gallery, Palm Beach, 1981, Salander-O'Reilly Galleries, N.Y., 1982, Rubiner Gallery, West Bloomfield, Mich., 1985, 90, Images Gallery, Toledo, 1986, 90, 91, Percival Gallery, Des Moines, 1987, 89, 91, Marsh Gallery U. Richmond, Va., 1992, Robert Strin-St. Louis, Mo., 1992, C.S. Schulte Gallery, Millburn, N.J., 1993-94, Gallery One Toronto, Can., others; exhibited group shows at Am. Gallery, 1963, Am. Fedn. Art, 1963-65, Mus. Modern Art, N.Y.C., 1964, Albright-Knox Art Gallery, Buffalo, 1964, Washington Gallery Modern Art, 1964, Gallery Modern Art, N.Y.C., 1965, Tibor de Nagy, N.Y.C., 1965, ann., Whitney Mus., N.Y.C., 1965-70, one-man retrospective, 1973, Art Inst. Chgo., 1965, Kornblee Gallery, 1966, Guggenheim Mus., N.Y.C., 1966, Expo Am. Pavilion, 1967, Palm Springs Desert Mus., 1973, Daniel Templon Gallery, Paris, 1975, Andre Emmerich Gallery, 1975, Andre Emmerich Gallery, N.Y., 1975, Edmonton (Alta., Can.) Art Gallery, 1977, Old Vanderbilt Mansion, Old Brookville, N.Y., 1979, Allen Rubiner Gallery, Royal Oak, Mich., 1980, Meredith Long & Co., N.Y., 1980, Md. Inst. Coll. Art, Balt., 1980, Meredith Long & Co., Houston, 1980, Mus. Fine Arts, Boston, 1981, Solomion R. Guggenheim Mus., N.Y., 1981, Salander-O'Reilly Gallery, N.Y., 1981, St. Lawrence U., 1985, Rubiner Gallery, West Bloomfield, 1986, Percival Gallery, Des Moines, 1987, Gallery of Art, 1988, Charles H. MacNider Mus., 1988, Sioux City Art Ctr., 1988, Des Moines Art Ctr., 1988, Blanden Meml. Art Mus., 1988, Muscatine Art Ctr., 1988, C.S. Shulte Gallery, N.Y. and N.J., 1991, others; represented in permanent collections Am. Republic Ins. Corp., Des Moines, J. & L. Hudson Co., Detroit, Joseph H. Hirshhorn Mus., U.S. Steel Corp., Mus. Modern Art, N.Y.C., Philip Johnson Collection, Dallas Mus. Fine Arts, Des Moines Art Center, Met. Mus. Art, N.Y.C., Indpls. Mus., Whitney Mus.; artist in residence, Juniata Coll., Huntingdon, Pa., 1964, U. N.C., 1967, Mitchell Angus Gall., 1999. Recipient Nat. Council Arts award, 1969; Guggenheim fellow, 1967 Home: Colchester, Conn. Died Dec. 16, 2006.

ZUCKER, MARJORIE BASS, medical researcher, hematologist; b. NYC, June 10, 1919; d. Murray H. and Agnes (Naumburg) Bass; m. Howard D. Zucker, June 25, 1938; children: Andrew A., Ellen Zucker Harrison, Joan, Barbara Zucker-Pinchoff. AB, Vassar Coll., 1939; postgrad., Columbia Coll. Medicine, 1943-45; PhD, Columbia U., 1944. Rsch. asst. Coll. Physicians and Surgeons Columbia U., NYC, 1944-49; asst. to assoc. prof. physiology Coll. of Dentistry NYU, 1949-54; assoc. mem. Sloan Kettering Inst., NYC, 1955-63; asst. rsch. dir. ARC Rsch. Lab NYU Med. Ctr., NYC, 1963-70, assoc. prof. pathology, 1963-71, prof. pathology, 1971-92, prof. emeritus, from 1992. Mem. various rev. coms. NIH, Bethesda, Md., 1971-85. Co-author: The Physiology of Blood Platelets, 1965; co-patentee composition containing platelet factor 4, 1988; contbr. numerous articles to prof. jours. Recipient award N.Y. Met. chpt. Am. Women in Sci., 1986. Mem. Internat. Soc. Thrombosis (mem. coun., Marian Barnhart Lecture award 1989), Soc. for Exptl. Biology and Medicine (pres. 1983-85), Choice in Dying (dir., v.p. 1990). Democrat. Avocation: bird-watching. Died Mar. 7, 2006.

ZUCKERMAN, SIDNEY, retired allergist, immunologist; b. NYC, May 2, 1918; s. Max and Rose (Katz) Z.; m. Irene Elinor Cohen, Oct. 27, 1945; children: Elaine, Laurie, Jed, Amy. BA, Columbia Coll., 1939; MD, N.Y. Med. Coll., 1943. Diplomate Am. Bd. Internal Medicine, Am. Bd. Allergy and Immunology. Chief medicine 172 Sta. Hosp. US Army Med. Corps., Sendai, Japan, 1945-47; med. dir. Ford Instrument Co. divsn. Sperry Corp., NYC, 1947-60; pvt. practice NYC, 1947-91; med. dir. Unysis Corp., Great Neck, NY, 1960-90. Capt. U.S. Army Med. Corps., 1945-47, Japan. Fellow ACP, Am. Coll. Allergy, Asthma and Immunology, Am. Acad. Allergy, Asthma and Immunology, Am. Coll. Occupational and Environ. Medicine, Am. Assn. Cert. Allergists; mem. Masons (jr. warden), Soc. Columbia Grads. Avocations: woodworking, golf. Home: Boca Raton, Fla. Died Dec. 14, 2005.